INTRODUCTION

The two volumes of the Art Sales Index contain the price and details of Oil Paintings, Watercolours, Drawings, Miniatures and Sculpture sold at public auction around the world during the twelve month period of the international auction season, August in one year until July in the next. The works of nearly 30,000 Old Master, 19th Century, Modern and Contemporary artists are represented in these volumes. ASI records over 100,000 sale results each season and handles some 1800 sale catalogues from 350 different auctioneers. Items for the different media qualify for entry when they exceed a certain "starting" price. Over the years, starting prices have been raised so as to take inflation into account.The levels for the season are given on the sub-title page of the appropriate section of the book. Artists are shown alphabetically A to K in Volume I and L to Z in Volume II. Sale prices are listed in ascending order. For each artist, Oil Paintings are given first, followed, in *italics,* by Watercolours, Drawings and Miniatures. Details of Sculpture and three dimensional works are shown in a separate section at the end of Volume II.

Sources of information

The index is compiled from catalogues, price lists and other information provided by auctioneers. ASI takes great care in extracting information accurately. However, ASI cannot be held responsible for errors unwittingly made, nor for unknowingly reproducing incorrect information. ASI cannot vouch for the authenticity of pictures recorded. It is the reputation and integrity of the auctioneer which does this.

"Bought-in" pictures

Pictures offered for sale at auction usually have a "reserve" placed on them by the owner in order that they should not be sold at a price which he considers to be below their real value. If the bidding does not reach this reserve, the pictures are deemed to have been unsold. In England, these items are known as "bought-in". ASI DOES NOT RECORD "BOUGHT-IN WORKS". The majority of auctioneer contributors exclude "bought-in" prices from their price lists. However, there might be occasions when a "bought-in" price is inadvertently included. If any price is of particular importance to a subscriber, then he would be advised to check directly with the auctioneers.

Prices, buyer's premium and exchange rates

ASI DOES NOT INCLUDE THE BUYER'S PREMIUM. The price recorded is the "hammer" price, the price which is called out at auction and at which the item is "knocked down" to the bidder. During the course of the auction season, all entries to the ASI Data Bank are made at the EXCHANGE RATE APPLICABLE TO THE DATE OF THE SALE.

Country	Auction season				
Currency code	86/87	87/88	88/89	89/90	90/91
Australia (A.D)	2.22	2.38	2.13	2.04	2.36
Austria (A.S)	21.42	21.31	22.46	20.56	20.67
Belgium (B.FR)	59.63	63.36	66.55	59.85	60.57
Canada (C.D)	1.98	2.23	2.04	1.85	2.13
Denmark (D.KR)	11.11	11.59	12.35	11.08	11.28
Eire (E.P)	1.04	1.14	1.17	1.08	1.10
Finland (F.M)	-	-	7.45	6.61	7.00
France (F.FR)	9.54	10.08	10.71	9.48	9.94
Germany (DM)	2.87	3.03	3.15	2.84	2.94
Hong Kong (HK.D)	-	-	-	12.62	15.20
Italy (I.L)	2007.00	2228.00	2317.00	2071.00	2196.24
Japan (J.Y)	-	-	-	231.00	-
Netherlands (D.FL)	3.25	3.39	3.56	3.15	3.31
Norway (N.KR)	-	-	11.45	10.78	11.45
New Zealand (NZ.D)	-	2.63	2.79	2.65	3.01
Poland (P.Z)	-	-	-	-	18208.00
South Africa (SA.R)	3.58	3.57	4.38	4.15	4.85
Spain (S.P)	193.03	202.32	200.08	180.00	183.74
Sweden (S.KR)	9.91	10.73	10.87	10.12	10.80
Switzerland (S.FR)	2.38	2.50	2.65	2.53	2.49
USA (US.D)	1.45	1.78	1.69	1.60	1.85

Average exchange rates to the £ sterling over the past five seasons

Exchange rates used throughout the year are those **applicable** to the date of the sale.

Presentation of artists' names

The convention adopted by ASI in the presentation of artists' names is to show the surname first, followed by the forenames, followed by the "de", "de la", "van" and "von" etc. Hence, Sir Anthony van Dyck is listed as "DYCK, Sir Anthony van." Le Corbusier is shown as "CORBUSIER, Le". An exception is made where the "de", etc is embedded in the name, for example: Anne Louis Girodet de Roucy Trioson is shown as : "GIRODET DE ROUCY TRIOSON, Anne Louis". Where the qualifications "after", "circle", "attrib", "studio" and "style" are used, they are shown after the name. A picture catalogued as "Style of Abraham Calraet" is shown as : "CALRAET, Abraham (style)". Wherever possible, ASI uses the name given by the auctioneer in the sale catalogue. Obvious spelling mistakes are corrected but other changes are kept to a minimum. However, in some instances, and especially with Old Masters, it is necessary to adopt standardisation (there are 15 ways of spelling Bartholomew in European languages !). Also, the presentation of an artist's name is not uniform throughout the world. But there are certain "conventions" which responsible auctioneers follow.

IRISH
ARTS REVIEW

YEARBOOK 1991-1992

This superb publication can be ordered from the editorial office
of Irish Arts Review, 22 Crofton Road, Dun Laoghaire, Co Dublin. Ireland
Telephone +353-1-2808415. Fax +353-1-2808309
Hardback: Stg£29.00 to Ireland and England, Stg£31.00 to the rest of
Europe, US$53.00 to North America and other continents.
Paperback: Stg£19.00 to Ireland and England, Stg£21.00 to the rest of
Europe, US$37.00 to North America and other continents.

Contents

Introduction in English/French/German/Spanish .... 7 - 26

Auction houses, codes, sale dates and titles .... 31 - 64

Index by artists, A-K of oil paintings, watercolours, drawings
and miniatures sold at auction during the 1990/91 season .... 1 - 1100

Note: Sculpture appears at the end of Volume II

List of Advertisers

Apollo Magazine - UK	Vol 1 rear end papers
Art Newspaper - UK	page 28 & 29
Braswell Galleries - USA	adjacent to DREWES, Werner
Christie's - UK	Vol I front cover
Dobiaschofsky Auktionen - Switzerland	Vol 1 front end papers
Eberhart Auktionen - Switzerland	Vol I spine
Edmund Peel - Spain	Vol I page 22 & Vol II front end papers
Hanzel Galleries - USA	adjacent to NICHOLS, Dale
Hindman - USA	Vol II rear cover
International Directory of Art - Germany	Vol II rear end papers
Irish Arts Review - Ireland	page 6
Leonard Joel - Australia	Vol I rear cover
G A Key - UK	adjacent to BEAVIS, Richard
Kunstpreis Jahrbuch - Germany	page 16
Lawrence - UK	Vol 1 front end papers
Mystic Fine Arts - USA	adjacent to BUTTERSWORTH, James E
Phillips, Leeds - UK	adjacent to KRAMER, Jacob
Skinner, Inc - USA	adjacent to HARTMANN, Ludwig
C G Sloan & Company - USA	adjacent to SOROLLA Y BASTIDA, Joaquin
Tennants Auctioneers - UK	adjacent to GODWARD, John William
Trace Publications Ltd	page 21
Watercolours, Drawings & Prints Magazine - UK	Vol II rear end papers
Weltkunst - Germany	Vol 1 rear end papers
William Doyle Galleries - USA	adjacent to CAMPIGLI, Massimo
Wolf's Auctioneers - USA	Vol II spine & Vol II front end papers
Woolley & Wallis - UK	adjacent to O'CONOR, Roderick
Young Fine Arts Gallery Inc - USA	Vol II Contents page

The
Art Sales Index
1990/91

The
Art Sales Index
1990/91

23rd annual edition

Volume I

Oil Paintings, Watercolours, Drawings and Miniatures
Artists A - K

Edited by
Richard Hislop

Published by

ART SALES INDEX LTD
1 THAMES STREET, WEYBRIDGE, SURREY, ENGLAND

ISBN 0 903872 40 4

Published, computer composition and typeset by
Art Sales Index Ltd
1, Thames Street, Weybridge, Surrey

Printed and bound by
BPCC Wheatons Ltd
Hennock Road, Marsh Barton, Exeter

CARh

These are best illustrated by quoting directly from a Christie's catalogue:
a) a work catalogued with the name(s) or recognised designation of an artist, without qualification, is in our opinion a work by the artist.
b) in other cases, in our opinion, the following expressions, with the following meanings are used:

- *attributed to*	probably a work by the artist in whole or in part (ASI use "attrib");
- *workshop of/ studio of*	a work executed in the studio or workshop possibly under his supervision (ASI use "studio");
- *circle of*	a work of the period of the artist and showing his influence. (ASI use "circle");
- *follower of*	a work executed in the artist's style but not necessarily by a pupil (ASI use "style");
- *manner of*	a work executed in the artist's style but of a later date. (ASI use "style");
- *after*	a copy (of any date) of a work of the artist. (ASI use "after").

Note also the views on signature as recorded in Sotheby's catalogues:
a) references to signature, inscription, dates refer to the present state of the work;
b) the term "bears a signature" and/or "date" and/or "inscription" means that in our opinion the artist's name and/or date and/or inscription have been added by another hand;
c) the term "signed" and/or "dated" and/or "inscribed" means that in our opinion the signature and/or date and/or inscription are from the hand of the artist.

Abbreviations

From January 1991 ASI now record miniatures this is shown as min. in the picture detail.

Abbreviations used in the index include:

3D = three dimensional	d = dated	mono = monogram
attrib = attributed to	f = foundry	pat = patina
bears sig = bears signature	fl = flourished	/R = illustrated in catalogue
C = Century	htd = heightened	rec = rectangular
chk = chalk	i = inscribed	s = signed
chl =- charcoal	ins = inches	snr = senior
cm = centimetres	inits = initials	st = stamped
col = colour	jnr = junior	W/C = watercolour
	min = miniature	(?) = unknown dimensions

Medium and dimensions

All pictures listed are oil on canvas *unless* otherwise stated. Watercolours, Drawings and Miniatures are shown in *italics* and are grouped to follow the Oil Paintings under each artist.   Measurements of pictures are "height by width" and measurements of 3-dimensional pieces are "height by width by depth".

How to read an entry:

FRY Roger, (1866-1943) British
£3600 $5472   (19-2-87   S 39/R)   Vase with tulips (30x52cm-12x20in) s.d.1917

FRY	artist's name
Roger	artist's forename(s)
(1866-1934) British	artist's nationality and dates of birth and death
£3600 $5472	price realised in £ and $
(19-2-87	date of auction
S	auctioneer's reference code - S=Sotheby's, London
398	lot number of picture
/R)	illustrated in the sale catalogue
Vase with Tulips	title of description of picture
(30x52cm-12x20in)	dimensions, height by width in centimetres and inches
s.d.1917	signed and dated 1917

Auctioneer codes

In order to make each entry in the index as complete as possible and to make it easy to understand in many different countries, a code is used to indicate the auctioneer or the sale room where the picture has been sold.   The code is a simple alphabetical code based primarily on the initial letter(s) of the auctioneer's name and, if held outside the UK, on the initial letters of the town where the sale was held.   The codes fall into three main groups:

a) British auctioneers	one, two or three letters without punctuation eg. S=Sotheby's C=Christie's
b) Auctioneers outside Great Britian	the initial letter(s) of their name(s) followed by a full stop and then the initial letter of the town or sometimes the country in which the sale was conducted. eg. EA.Z=Eberhart Aucktions,Zurich F.M=Finarte Milan
c) Sales held by Christie's and Sotheby's outside Great Britian	CH or SY followed by the initial letter(s) of the town or country in which the sale was held. eg. CH.NY=Christie's New York SY.NY=Sotheby's, New York

In all cases, the full name of the auctioneer can be seen, together with the title of the sale, against the appropriate date in the chronological list of sales.

Introduction

Les deux volumes d'Art Sales Index (Répertoire des Ventes d'Oeuvres d'Art) donnent le prix et les détails relatifs à des peintures à l'huile, aquarelles, dessins et sculptures vendus aux enchères dans le monde entier au cours des douze mois écoulés - du mois d'Août au mois de Juillet de l'anné suivante. Nous appelons cette période la "saison de ventes". Dans ces deux volumes figurent quelque 30,000 Maîtres anciens, artistes du 19ème siècle, artistes modernes et contemporains. Chaque saison, L'ASI traite100,000 résultats de ventes et dispose de 1800 catalogues de vente provenant de 350 commissaires-priseurs différents. Les oeuvres en tous genres peuvent être répertoriées lorsque leur prix initial dépasse un certain seuil. Au fil des ans, les prix initiaux ont été relevés pour tenir compte de l'inflation. Les niveaux de prix pour la saison figurent à la page des sous-titres du chapitre approprié. Les artistes sont classés par ordre alphabétique, de A à K dans le volume I, de L à Z dans le volume II. Les prix de vente sont répertoriés par ordre croissant. Pour chaque artiste, les peintures à l'huile figurent en première place, suivies, en italique, des aquarelles, des miniature et des dessins. Le détail des sculptures et des oeuvres tridimentionnelles fait l'objet d'un chapitre spécial à la fin du volume II.

Sources d'Information

Le Répertoire est compilé à partir de catalogues, de listes de prix et autres informations fourniés par les commissaires-priseurs. L'ASI recueille les informations avec le plus grand soin. Toutefois, l'ASI ne peut être tenu responsable recueille des erreurs accidentelles ni de la reproduction involontaire d'informations erronnées. L'ASI ne peut pas garantir l'aunthenticité des tableaux répertoriés. La réputation et l'intégrité du commissaire-priseur sont là pour ça.

Tableaux "rachetés" (ou "Invendus")

Le propriétaire d'un tableau mis aux enchères place généralement une "réserve" sur ce tableau pour éviter qu'il ne soit vendu à un prix qu'il considère inférieur à sa valeur réelle. Si les enchères n'atteignent pas ce niveau, on considère que le tableau n'a pas été vendu. En Angleterre, ces articles sont appelés "Rachetés" (ou "Invendus") L'ASI NE REPERTORIE QUE LES VENTES REELLES: LES PRIX "RACHETES" NE SONT PAS ENREGISTRES. La plupart des grands commissaires-priseurs ne font pas figurer les prix "rachetés" sur leurs listes de prix. Il peut cependant arriver que des commissaires-priseurs de moindre importance fassent figurer ces prix "rachetés" sur leurs listes. L'ASI n'est pas toujours à même de faire la distinction. Lorsqu'un prix spécifique est d'une importance capitale il est conseillé de procéder à une vérification auprès des commissaires-priseurs eux-mêmes.

Prix, taux de change et commission

Le prix indiqué par le ASI est, dans tous les cas, le prix "du marteau" celui qui est atteint lors des enchères et auquel l'oeuvre est adjugée à l'enchérisseur. Dans la plupart des pays, l'acheteur doit s'attendre à payer des frais supplémentaires de 5 à 15%. Au Royaume-Uni, ces frais sont appelés "Buyer's Premium" (Commission). CETTE COMMISSION N'EST PAS COMPRISE DANS LE PRIX INDIQUE. Les afoutés impôts locaux ou nationaux, les commissions ne sont pas non plus ajoutées au prix indiqué. Lorsqu'une "paire" de tableaux a été vendue, le prix s'entend pour la paire, et non pour chacun des tableaux.

11

Presentation du nom des artistes

L'ASI a convenu de présenter le nom des artistes en faisant figurer d'abord le nom de famille, puis les prénoms, puis les particules "de", "de la", "van", "von", etc. Ainsi, Sir Anthony van Dyck figure sous "DYCK, Sir Anthony van". Le Corbusier figure sous "CORBUSIER, Le". Une exception est faite lorsque le "de" etc fait partie intégrante du nom, par exemple: Anne Louis Girodet de Roucy Trioson figure sous "GIROUDET DE ROUCY, Anne Louis" Lorsque les termes "d'apres", "cercle de", "attrib", "atelier de" et "style" sont utilisées, ils viennent après le nom. Un tableau répertorié "Style d'Abraham Calraet" figure sous "CALRAET, Abraham (style)".

Dans touts la mesure du possible, l'ASI utilise le nom donné par le commissaire-priseur dans le catalogue de vente. Les fautes trop évidentes sont rectifées, mais on limite autant que possible les autres modifications. Pourtant, dans certains cas - tout particulièrement avec les maître anciens - il convient d'adopter un nom standard (le nom Bartholemew revêt quinze orthographes différentes dans les langues européenes!) De plus, la présentation du nom d'un artiste n'est pas uniforme dans le monde entier. Mais il existe certaines "conventions" que les commissaires-priseurs sérieux suivant généralement. Le plus simple est de citer directement un catalogue de Christie's:

a) Une oeuvre catalogué avec le(s) nom(s) ou la désignation, reconnue d'un artiste, sans autre qualificatif, est selon nous l'oeuvre de cet artiste.

b) Dans les autre cas, on utilise les expressions suivantes, qui signifient:

- *attribué à*	Selon nous, probablement une oeuvre de l'artiste en totalité ou en partie (l'ASI utilise "attrib")
- *Atelier de*	Selon nous, une oeuvre exécutée dans l'atelier de l'artiste, et peut-être supervisée par lui (l'ASI utilise "studio")
- *Cercle de*	Selon nous, une oeuvre de la période de l'artiste et témoignant de son influence (l'ASI utilise "circle")
- *Dans le style de*	Selon nous, une oeuvre exécutée dans le style de l'artiste, mais pas nécessairement par un élève (l'ASI utilise "style")
- *A la manière de*	Selon nous, une oeuvre exécutée dans le style de l'artiste, mais à une date ultérieure (l'ASI utilise "style")
- *D'après*	Selon nous, une copie (date quelconque) d'une oeuvre de l'artiste (l'ASI utilise "after")

Noter également le point de vue sur la signature tel qu'il figure sur les catalogues de Sotheby's:

a) Les références à la signature, à l'inspection et aux dates visent l'état actuel de l'oeuvre.

b) Le terme PORTE une "signature" et/ou une "date" et/ou une "inscription" signifie que, selon nous, le nom de l'artiste et/ou la date et/ou l'inscription ont étéajoutés par une autre main.

c) Le terms "signé" et/ou "daté" et/ou "inscrit" signifie que, selon nous, la signature et/ou la date et/ou l'inscription sont de la main de l'artiste.

Types d'oeuvres et dimensions

Tous les tableaux listés sont des huiles sur toile, sauf indication contraire. Pour chaque artiste, les aquarelles et les dessins figurent en italique après les peintures à l'huile. Les dimensions des tableaux s'entendent "hauteur x largeur" et les dimensions des pièces tridimentionnelles s'entendent "hauteur x largeur x profondeur".

Abbreviations

Les abbréviations utilisées dans le Répertoire sont:

3D = tridimentionnel	d = daté	mono = monogramme
attrib = attribué à	f = la fonderie	pat = patiné
bears sig = porte signature	fl = fleuri	\R = illustré sur catalogue
C = siècle	htd = rehaussé	rec = rectangulaire
chk = pastel	i = inscrit	s = signé
chl = fusain	ins = les pouces	snr = senior
cm = centemètres	inits = initiales	st = porte un cachet
col = couleur	jnr = junior	W/C = aquarelle
	min = miniature	(?) = pas de dimensions

Codes des commissaires-priseurs

Afin que chaque insertion dans le répertoire soit aussi complète que possible et pour les rendre compréhensibles dans de nombreux pays, un code est utilisé pour indiquer le commissaire-priseur par lequel, ou la salle des ventes dans laquelle le tableau a été vendu.

Le code est un simple code alphabétique basé principalement sur la première lettre du nom du commissaire-priseur, et, au cas où la vente a eu lieu à l'étranger, sur les premières lettres du nom de la ville où la vente a eu lieu. Les codes sont répartis en trois groupes:

a) Commissaires-Priseurs
   Britanniques:

une, deux ou trois lettres sans ponctuation
ex: S=Sotheby's, C=Christie's

b) Commissaires-Priseurs
   hors de Grande-Bretagne

la ou les premières lettres de leur nom suivie (s) d'un point, puis la première lettre
de la ville dans laquelle la vente a eu lieu
ex: EA.Z=-Eberhart Auktionen, Zurich
F.M=Finarte, Milan

c) Ventes organisées par
   Christie's et Sotheby's en
   dehors du Royaume Uni

CH. ou SY. suivies par la première lettre de
la ville et parfois du pays de la vente
ex: CH.NY=Christie's New York
SY.NY=Sotheby's New York

Dans tous les cas, le nom complet du commissaire-priseur est indiqué, avec le titre de la vente, à la date correspondante sur la liste chronologique des ventes.

Comment lire une entrée
FRY, Roger (1866-1934) British
£3600 $5472 (19-2-87 S 398/R) Vase with tulips (30x52cm - 12x20in) s.d.1917

FRY	Nom de l'artiste
Roger	Prénom de l'artiste
(1866-1934) BRITISH	Nationalité de l'artiste: Dates de naissance et décès.
£3600 $5472	Prix obtenu en Livres et en Dollars
(19 - 2 - 87	Date de la vente aux enchères
S	Code de la référence de commissaire-priseur
	(S = Sotheby's Londres)
398	No de lot du tableau
/R)	Illustré dans le catalogue des ventes
Vase with tulips	Titre ou description du tableau
(30x52cm - 12x20in)	Dimensions, hauteur par largeur, en cms et pouces
s.d. 1917	Signé et daté 1917.

THE DECADE PUBLICATIONS
1970 to 1980

Ten year's sales results divided into periods:
Old Masters, 19th Century artists, 20th Century artists
(and Impressionists). 400,000 pictures.
Same content and format as the Art Sales Index.
5 volumes - contains illustrations.

	UK £	Overseas £	DM	US Dollars $	France F.fr	Europe
20th C. & Imp.	60	75	180	130	600	63
19th C.	60	75	180	130	600	63
Old Masters	30	45	90	70	300	33

Art Sales Index Ltd.,1 Thames Street, Weybridge, Surrey KT13 8JG, UK.
tel: (0932) 856426   fax: (0932) 842482

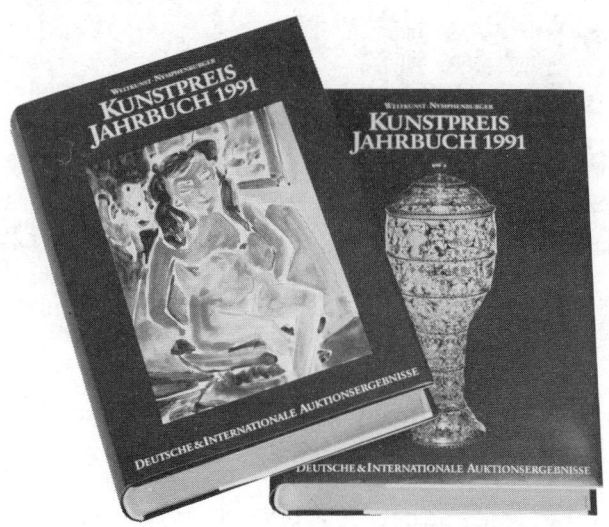

Einleitung

Die beiden Bände des Art Sales Index enthalten die Preise und Angaben über Ölgemälde, Aquarelle, Zeichnungen und Skulpturen, die in einer 12 monatigen Zeitspanne auf öffentlichen Auktionen in der ganzen Welt versteigert wurden, und zwar von August eines Jahres bis zum Juli des nächsten Jahres. Dies wird bei uns als "Auktionsjahr" beschrieben. Werke von circa 30,000 Künstlern, dazu zählen alte Meister und die Künstler des 19. Jahrhundert sowie moderne und zeitgenössische Künstler, sind in beiden Bänden aufgeführt. Im ASI werden in jedem Jahr 100,000 Verkaufsergebnisse bearbeitet aus etwa 1800 Verkaufskatalogen von 350 verschiedenen Auktionatoren. Die Kunstobjekte kommen dann für eine Eintragung in Frage, wenn sie über einem gewissen "Starting"-Pries liegen. Im Laufe der letzten Jahre wurden die Startpries erhöht, um die Inflation mit in Betracht zu ziehen. Die verschiedenen Angaben für das Jahr sind auf den Untertitelseiten des betreffenden Teils des Werkes aufgeführt. Die Namen der Künstler sind im 1. Band in alphabetischer Reihenfolge von A bis K und im 2. Band von L bis Z angegeben. Die Verkaufspreise stehen in aufsteigender Reihenfolge. Bei jedem Künstler werden zuerst die Ölgemälde aufgeführt, dann folgen in Kursivschrift die Aquarelle, Zeichnungen und miniaturen: Angaben über Skulpturen und dreidimensionale Werke sind in einem separaten Abschnitt am Ende des 2 Bandes aufgeführt.

Bezugsquellen für die Information

Das Verzeichnis wurde von Katalogen, Preislisten und anderen Angaben, die von Auktionatoren gestellt wurden, zusammengestellt. Der ASI hat die Information mit grosser Sorgfalt von den Quellen entnommen. Der ASI übernimmt keine Verantwortung weder für unabsichtliche Fehler oder für falsche Informationen, die unbewusst abgedruckt wurden. Der ASI gewährt keine Garantie für die Authentizität der aufgeführten Gemälde. Ruf und Integrität des Auktionators sind hierfür verantwortlich.

"Bought-in" Gemälde

Die Gemälde, die auf einer Auktion zum Verkauf angeboten werden, sind vom Besitzer gewöhnlich mit einem 'Limitpreis' eingereicht worden, damit sie nicht zu einem solchen Preis verkauft werden, der für zu tief unter dem tatsächlichen Wert liegt. Wird dieser Limitpreis beim Bieten nicht erreicht, so werden diese Gemälde als nicht verkauft betrachtet. In England werden solche Gegenstände als 'bought-in' beschrieben. DER ASI VERZEICHNET ABER NUR DIE EIGENTLICHEN VERKÄUFE, 'BOUGHT-IN'-PREISE WERDEN, NICHT AUFGEFÜHRT. Die meisten grösseren Auktionshäuser schliessen die 'bought-in' Preise nicht in ihrer Preisliste ein. Es kommt jedoch vor, dass die 'bought-in' Preise auf den gedruckten Preislisten von kleineren Auktionatoren zu finden sind. Der ASI kann immer nicht den einen von dem anderen unterscheiden. Sollte ein gewisser Preis für einen Abonnenten äusserst wichtig sein, so möchten wir ihm raten, bei den Auktionatoren selbst nachzufragen.

Schreibung der Namen der Künstler

Die Reihenfolge, in welcher der ASI die Namen der Künstler aufführt, ist so angeordnet, dass der Familienname zuerst steht, dann Vorname(n) und dahinter steht "de", "de la", "van" und "von" etc. Somit findet man Sir Anthony van Dyck als "DYCK, Sir Anthony van". Le Corbusier steht als "CORBUSIER, Le". Eine Ausnahme wird gemacht wenn das "de" mitten zwischen den Namen steht, zum Beispiel: Anne Louis Girodet de Roucy Trioson ist dann als "GIRODET DE ROUCY TRIOSON, Anne Louis" aufgeführt. Wenn nähere Bestimmungen angegeben sind, wie "after", "circle", "attrib", "studio" und "style", dann stehen diese hinter dem Namen. Ein Gemälde, das als "Style of Abraham Calraet" katalogisiert ist, findet man dann als "CALRAET, Abraham (style)".

Überall wo möglich, verwendet der ASI der Namen, der vom Auktionator im Verkaufskatalog angegeben ist. Eindeutige Schreibfehler werden berichtigt aber andere werden auf ein Minimum beschränkt. In manchen Fällen, besonders bei alten Meistern, ist es notwendig, eine Standardisierung (in den europäischen Ländern wird Bartholemew auf 15 verschiedene Weisen geschrieben). Hinzu kommt auch, dass Namensschreibung eines Künstlers nicht immer überall in der Welt die gleiche ist. Es bestehen aber gewisse Richtlinien, an die sich verantwortliche Auktionatoren halten. Als bestes Beispiel hierfür geben wir einige Katalogauszüge von Christie an:

a) Ein werk, das mit dem Namen bzw, den Namen oder mit dem Erkennungszeichen eines Künstlers katalogisiert ist aber ohne nähere Bestimmungen, ist unserer Meinung nach ein Werk dieses Künstlers;

b) In anderen Fällen werden folgende Ausdrücke mit den folgenden Bedeutungen verwendet:

- attributed to	Unserer Meinung nach wahrscheinlich ein Werk des Künstlers selbst oder teilweise (ASI verwendet die Bezeichnung "attrib");
- studio of workshop of	Unserer Meinung nach ein Werk, das in dem Studiooder in der Werkstatt unter seiner Aufsicht entstanden ist (ASI verwendet die Bezeichnung "studio")
- circle of	Unserer Meinung nach wahrscheinlich ein Werk ausder Zeit des Künstlers das seinen Einfluss zu erkennen gibt. (ASI verwendet die Bezeichnung "circle")
- follower of	Unserer Meinung nach wahrscheinlich ein Werk, das im stil des Künstlers erstellt wurde aber nicht unbedingt von einem Schüler. (ASI verwendet die Bezeichnung "style")
- manner of	Unserer Meinung nach wahrscheinlich ein Werk im Stil des Künstlers aber zu einer späteren Zeit. (ASI verwendet die Bezeichnung "style")
- after	Unserer Meinung nach eine Reproduktion (beliebiges Datum) eines Werkes des Künstlers (ASI verwendet die Bezeichnung "after")

Bitte nehmen Sie auch die Anmerkungen im Sotheby's Katalog zur Kenntnis:

a) Bemerkungen über die Signatur, Inschrift und Daten beziehen sich auf den augenblicklichen Zustand des Werkes;

b) die Bezeichnung bears (trägt) eine 'signature' (Signatur) bzw 'date' (Datum) oder 'inscription' (Inschrift) bedeutet, dass unserer Meinung nach der name des Künstlers bzw, das Datum bzw, die Inschrift von andere Hand hinzugefügt wurde;

c) die Bezeichnung 'signed' - gezeichnet bzw 'date' (Datum) oder 'inscribed' (Inschrift) bedeutet unserer Meinung nach, dass die Signatur bzw, das Datum oder die Inschrift von Hand des Künstlers sind.

Preise, Wechselkurse und Käuferprämie

Der vom ASI angegebene Preis ist in allen Fällen der Zuschlagpreis, also der Preis, der auf der Auktion ausgerufen wird und zu dem der Gegenstand dem Bieter zugeschlagen wird. In den meisten Ländern muss ein Käufer damit rechnen, dass er noch zwischen 5% und 15% zusätzlich zahlen muss. In Grossbritannien wird dies als "Buyer's Premium" also als eine Käuferprämie bezeichnet. Die aufgeführten Preis des ASI schliessen die Käuferprämie nicht ein, ebenfalls sind zu dem Preis noch keine lokalen oder Staatssteuern oder Provisionen hinzugefügt. Wenn ein Bilderpaar verkauft worden ist, dann bezieht sich der Preis auf das Paar, nicht auf jedes einzelne Bilde.

Medium und Masse

Alle aufgeführten Bilder sind Ölgemälde, es sei dann, dass etwas anderes angegeben ist. Aquarelle und Zeichnungen sind in Kursivschrift aufgeführt und stehen bei jedem Künstler zusammen hinter den Ölgemälden. Die Masse der Bilder sind "Höhe auf Breite" und die Masse von dreidimensionalen Werken sind "Höhe mal Breite mal Tiefe".

Abkürzungen

Zu den in diesem Index verwendeten Abkürzungen gehören:

3D = dreidimensional	d = datiet	mono = Monogramm
attrib = zurückzuführen auf	f = giesserei	pat = patina
bears sig = trägt Signatur	fl = tätig	rec = rechteckig
C = Jahrhundert	htd = erhöht	/R = illustriert
chk = Kreide	i = mit Inschrift	s = signiert
chl = Kohle	inits = Initiale	snr = senior
cm = Zentimeter	ins = Zoll	st = gestempelt
col = Farbe	jnr = junior	W/C = Aquarell
	min = miniaturen	(?) = keine Massangabe

Wie versteht man einen Eintrang
FRY, Roger (1866-1934) British
£3600 $5472 (19-2-87 S 398/R) Vase with Tulips (30x52cm - 12x20ins) s.d.1917

FRY	Name des Künstlers
Roger	Vorname
(1866-1934)	Geburts - und Todesjahr und Nationalität
British	des Künstlers
£3600 $5472	erzielter Preis in £ und $
(19-2-87	Tag der Auktion
S	Nachschlagekode des Auktionators
	(S=Sotheby's London)
398	Katalognummer des Bildes
/R)	im Verkaufskatalog illustriert
Vase with Tulips	Titel oder Beschreibung des Bildes
(30x52cm - 12x20ins)	Grösse, Höhe mal Breite in Zentimetern und Zoll
s.d.1917	1917 gezeichnet und datiert

Auktionatorkode
Um jeden Eintrag im Art Sales Index so vollständig wie möglich zu machen, und damit man ihn in allen Ländern leicht verstehen kann, wird eine Kode für den Auktionator oder die Auktionshalle angegeben, bei dem oder in der das Bild verkauft worden ist. Der Kode ist ein einfacher alphabetischer Kode, der hauptsächlich auf dem Anfangsbuchstaben des Namens des Auktionators und, falls ausserhalb von England, auf den Anfangsbuchstaben der Stadt in der Verkauf stattfand, basiert. Die Kodes fallen in drei Hauptgruppen:

a) Britische Auktionatoren Interpunktion.
= ein, zwei oder drei Buchstaben ohne
z.B: S=Sotheby's   C=Christie's

b) Auktionatoren ausserhalb Grossbritanniens
= der Anfangsbuchstabe des Auktionator Namens, dahinter ein Punkt und dann der Anfangsbuchstabe der Stadt, in welcher der Verkauf stattgefunden hat.
z.B: EZ.A=Eberhart Auktionen,Zurich
F.M=Finarte, Milan

c) Verkäufe, die von Christie und Sotheby's ausserhalb von Grossbritannien abgehalten wurden
= CH. oder SY. dahinter der An fangsbuchstabe der Stadt (oder manchmal des Landes) in welcher/m der Verkauf stattgefunden hat.
z.B: CH.NY=Christie's, New York,
SY.NY=Sotheby's, New York.

In allen Fällen kann man den volständigen Namen des Auktionators, zusammen mit der Objektbezeichnung des Verkaufs neben dem entsprechenden Datum auf der chronologischen Liste der Verkäufe ersehen.

20

Don't be sunk without Trace

FOR nearly three years Trace has been re-uniting victims of burglaries and theft with their valuable works of art and antiques. The theft of the Roelandt Savery work pictured above was notified in Trace. After it became too hot to handle the thieves tried to sell it back through a loss adjuster and were apprehended.

Trace is distributed to every police force in Britain and to major auction houses. Most loss adjusters notify losses in the magazine. Its growing reputation has ensured that law enforcement agencies throughout the world, dealers and art galleries are also subscribers.

Trace is not just a means of recovering valuables. It also prevents dealers and auction houses from unwittingly buying or selling stolen works of art. For instance, an expert on miniatures at a large auction house helped to recover an exquisite gold and enamel snuff box after it was brought in for valuation because she recognised the miniatures on it from a photograph she had seen a few days earlier in Trace.

As with the miniatures expert, it may save you time, or even financial embarrassment, if you remain vigilant with Trace. The old adage about prevention being better than cure was never more apt than in this business. Ring for a free copy and subscription rates on

0752-228727 (24 hours)

INTRODUCCION

Dentro de los dos tomos del Art Sales Index, pueden consultarse los precios y las características de los óleos, obras de los Grandes Maestros, acuarelas, dibujos y esculturas que se han vendido en subasta por todo el mundo durante los doce meses de la temporada internacional de subasta, es decir de agosto de un año a julio del año siguiente. Se incluyen las obras de alrededor de 30.000 artistas - Grandes Maestros, artistas del siglo XIX, modernos y contemporáneos. En el ASI se registran más de 100,000 artículos vendidos durante cada temporada, datos que se recopilan con la ayuda de una base de más de 1.800 catálogos, procedentes de unas 350 salas de subastas. Todo tipo de obra apropiada estará representada, siempre y cuando el precio de adjudicación sobrepase los límites mínimos establecidos, siendo incrementados estos límites según el nivel de inflación vigente en cada año. Las escalas para la temporada en curso están detalladas en la primera pagina de cada sección de los dos tomos. Los nombres de los artistas están clasificados alfabeticamente, desde la A hasta la K en el Tomo I y desde la L hasta la Z en el Tomo II. Los precios de adjudicación se relacionan en orden ascendente. Dentro de la sección pertinente a cada artista, se detallan los óleos, y a continuación las acuarelas y los dibujos, cuyos datos se escriben en letra itálica. Hay un capitulo dedicado a las esculturas y las obras tridimensionales, que está situado al final del Tomo II.

Fuentes de información

El contenido de la guía se basa en los datos facilitados por diversas salas de subastas, proviniéndose de los catálogos, listas de precios y otros fuentes. La firma ASI reproduce la información facilitada con mucho cuidado y consideración a los detalles, no obstante no puede aceptar alguna responsabilidad por los errores o erratas de reproducción, ni de la posible inserción, de forma inconsciente, de cualquier informacion incorrecta. Asimismo, ASI no puede garantizar que las obras sean auténticas, suponiéndose que tanto la buena reputación como la profesionalidad de las salas de subastas, avalan estos datos.

Cuadros "bought-in" (reservas pactadas)

Los cuadros ofrecidos en subasta suelen tener un precio de "reserva", fijado por el propietario, para evitar que estas obras se adquieran por un precio por debajo de su valor real. Si las pujas no alcanzan el precio de "reserva", entonces los cuadros no se consideran vendidos. En Inglaterra dichas obras están conocidas como lotes "bought-in". LAS OBRAS "BOUGHT-IN" NO ESTAN INCLUIDAS EN EL ASI. En la mayoría de los casos, los precios "bought-in" están excluídos de las relaciones de precios facilitadas por las salas de subastas, participantes en esta guia. No obstante, la involuntaria inclusión de una obra de este tipo puede ocurrirse, por lo tanto es recomendable contactar con la sala de subastas correspondiente, en caso de tener un interés especial en el precio de cualquier obra.

23

Precios, comisión al comprador y cambio de divisas

LOS PRECIOS CONTENIDOS EN EL ASI NO INCLUYEN LA COMISION AL COMPRADOR. El precio facilitado corresponde a lo del "martillo", es decir el precio de adjudicacion anunciado a favor del mejor postor. Los precios que componen la base de datos del ASI y cualquier actualización realizada a lo largo de la temporada, están calculados SEGUN EL TIPO DE CAMBIO VIGENTE EN LA FECHA DE VENTA.

Presentación de los nombres de los artistas

El sistema adoptado por el ASI para relacionar los nombres de los artistas es de indicar, en primer lugar, el apellido, seguido por los nombres y a continuación por las palabras "de", "de la", "van", "von", etc. Por lo tanto, es posible encontrar la sección de Sir Anthony van Dyck bajo, "DYCK, Sir Anthony van". Le Corbusier aparece como "CORBUSIER, Le". La excepcion en este caso se produce cuando la palabra "de" y similares, forma parte integra del nombre, por ejemplo, Anne Louis Girodet de Roucy Trioson aparece bajo:"GIRODET DE ROUCY THIOSON, Anne Louis". En el caso do los términos interpretativos, "after", "circle", "attrib", "studio" and "style", - (ver tabla mas abajo) - estos se colocan después del nombre. Un cuadro clasificado "Estilo de Abraham Calraet", figura como: "CALRAET, Abraham (style)".

Los editores del ASI respetan el nombre dado por la sala de subastas, siempre y cuando esto sea posible. Se corrigen las erratas pero se mantienen al mínimo otros cambios. Sin embargo, hay veces, sobre todo en el caso de los Grandes Maestros, cuando es necesario estandardizar la forma de deletrear los nombres (i existen en Europa 15 formas distintas de deletrear el nombre Bartholomew!) Además, aunque no existe uniformidad mundial en la presentación de los nombres de los artistas, hay algunas normas que rigen en las salas de subastas conocidas. Para un mejor entendimiento de estas normas, se puede acudir al catálogo de "Christie's":

a) una obra que aparece en el catálogo con el nombre o la denominación reconocida de un artista, sin ningún término interpretativo, significa que, en nuestra opinión, se trata de una obra auténtica del artista mencionado.

b) para otros casos, se utilizan los siguientes términos:

- (atribuído a)   una obra probable del mencionado
               artista, total o parcialmente (en el ASI = "attrib");
- (taller de)   una obra realizada en el estudio o
               taller del artista, posiblemente
               bajo su propia dirección (en el ASI = "studio");
- (círculo de)   una obra de la época del artista,
               mostrando aparentemente su influencia (en el ASI = "circle");
- (estilo de)   una obra realizada al estilo
               del artista mencionado, aunque el pintor no sea necesariamente su
               discípulo (en el ASI = "style");
- (estilo de...   una obra realizada al estilo del
  posterior)   artista, pero de una época
               posterior a su período activo (en el ASI = "style")
- (copia)   se trata de una copia de una obra
               del artista, realizada durante
               cualquier época (en el ASI = "after").

Las opiniones de Sotheby's con respeto a las firmas de los artistas, son también de interés:

a) cualquier referencia a la firma, inscripción o fecha, se hace con vistas al estado actual de la obra;

b) el término "bears a signature" (con firma) y/o "date" (con fecha) y/o "inscription" (con inscripción), significa que, en nuestra opinión, el nombre del artista y/o la fecha y/o la inscripción han sido realizados por una mano distinta a la del artista.

c) el término "signed" (firmado) y/o "dated" (fechado) y/o "inscribed" (inscrito) significa que, en nuestra opinión, la firma y/o fecha y/o inscripción son de la mano del artista mencionado.

Abreviaturas

Se utilizan las siguientes abreviaturas en el Indice:

3D = tridimensional	d = fechado	mono = monograma
attrib = atríbuido a	f = fundición	pat = pátina
bears sig = con firma	fl = de época	/R = foto en catálogo
c = siglo	htd = retocado	rec = miniatura rectangular
chk = pastel	i = inscrito	s = firmado
chl = al carbón	ins = pulgadas	snr = padre
cm = centímetros	inits = iniciales	st = sellado
col = color	jnr = hijo	w/c = acuarela
	min = miniatura	(?) = dimensiones desconocidas

Tipo de obra y dimensiones

Todos los cuadros son de óleo sobre lienzo, salvo indicación al contrario. Para cada artista, se detallan los óleos, y a continuación los acuarelas y dibujos con letra itálica. Las medidas de los cuadros son "altura por ancho", mientras las medidas de las obras tridimensionales son "altura por ancho por profundidad".

Como interpretar un apunte

FRY, Roger, (1866-1943) British
£3600 $5472 (19-2-87 S 39/R) Vase with tulips (30x52cm-12x20in) s.d.1917

FRY	apellido del artista
Roger	nombre/s del artista
(1866-1934) British	nacionalidad del artista y fechas de nacimiento y fallecimiento
£3600 $5472	precio de adjudicación en £ y $
(19-2-87	fecha de la subasta
S	codigo de referencia de la sala de subastas - S = Sotheby's, Londres
398	número de lote del cuadro
/R)	hay fotografía en el catálogo
Vase with Tulips	título o descripción del cuadro
(30x52cm - 12x20in)	dimensiones, altura por ancho, en centímetros y pulgadas
s.d.1917	firmado y fechado 1917

Codigos de referencia de las salas de subastas

Para asegurar que los apuntes contenidos en el Indice sean lo más completo posible, y para facilitar su entendimiento en diversos países, se utiliza un sistema de codigos para los subastadores y salas de subastas, donde el cuadro fue vendido. Se basa en codigos alfabéticos sencillos, donde el codigo consiste fundamentalmente en la primera letra o letras del nombre de la sala de subastas y, si la subasta se celebró fuera del Reino Unido, en las primeras letras de la ciudad donde se celebró la subasta. Hay tres grupos principales de codigos:

a) Salas de subastas británicas
    -una, dos o tres letras, sin punctuación, p.ej. S=Sotheby's C=Christie's

b) Salas de subastas fuera del Reino Unido
    -la primera letra o letras del nombre o nombres, seguido por un punto y la primera letra de la ciudad o, en algunas casos, el pais en el cual se celebró la subasta, p.ej. EA.Z=Eberhart Aucktions, Zurich F.M.=Finarte Milan

c) Subastas de Christie's y Sotheby's, celebradas fuera del Reino Unido
    -Ch o SY y, a continuación, la primera letra o letras de la ciudad o pais donde se celebró la subasta, p.ej. CH.NY=Christie's, New York.
    SY.NY=Sotheby's, New York.

En todo caso, se puede consultar el nombre completo de la sala de subastas en cuestión, junto con las materias de cada subasta, bajo la fecha correspondiente en la relación cronológica de ventas.

PRICES OF ASI PUBLICATIONS

THE ART SALES INDEX	UK £	DM	French F.fr	US £	Overseas £	Europe £
23rd edition (90/91 season)	90	275	930	180	105	93
22nd edition (89/90 season)	85	270	880	180	100	88
21st edition (88/89 season)	80	250	830	160	95	83
20th edition (87/88 season)	80	250	830	160	95	83

THE DECADE PUBLICATIONS
1970-1980

	UK £	DM	French F.fr	US £	Overseas £	Europe £
DP1 Impressionist/20th C Artists 2 vol	60	180	600	130	75	63
DP2 19th C Artists 2 vol	60	180	600	130	75	63
DP3 Old Masters 1 vol	30	90	300	70	45	33

MICROFICHE (6 issues per season)

	UK £	DM	French F.fr	US £	Overseas £	Europe £
1991/92 season	88	250	880	170	88	-
1990/91 season	88	250	880	170	88	-

AUCTION PRICES OF AMERICAN ARTISTS

	UK £	DM	French F.fr	US £	Overseas £	Europe £
7th edition (88-90)	20	60	200	40	-	-
6th edition (86-88)	20	60	200	40	-	-

some earlier editions available

PICTURE PRICE GUIDE
- UK

	UK £	DM	French F.fr	US £	Overseas £	Europe £
4th edition (1991)	17	50	170	30	20	-

PICTURE PRICE GUIDE
- USA & CANADA

	UK £	DM	French F.fr	US £	Overseas £	Europe £
2nd edition (1991)	10	-	-	20	-	-
1st edition (1990)	10	-	-	20	-	-

ORDER BY
  POST, PHONE or FAX
PAY BY
  CHEQUE OR CREDIT CARD

CHEQUES
Cheques payable to
  Art Sales Index Ltd
Acceptable in:
  Sterling, French Fr., DM
  Eurocheques in £ sterling only

Art Sales Index Ltd.,1 Thames Street, Weybridge, Surrey KT13 8JG, UK.
tel: (0932) 856426   fax: (0932) 842482

ISSN 0960-6556

Complete official list
of German national treasures

Includes the Art Market Section

INTERNATIONAL EDITION

THE ART NEWSPAPER

UMBERTO ALLEMANDI & CO. PUBLISHING, LONDON — EVENTS, POLITICS AND ECONOMICS — FOUNDED 1983, VOL. II, NO. 10, JULY-SEPTEMBER 1991 £ 2.00

The proper business of newspapers

This newspaper has just conducted a survey of the coverage of the arts in the English quality newspapers...

Art market

Brodsky tables bills to trammel N.Y. auction houses

Populist legislation involves no more "chandelier" bids, loans to buyers, or secret reserves

More real than Vermeer

Variations on the Rijksmuseum's "The love letter" (left) and H. Mäkle Queen's "Lady at a spinet" (right): by Teniers? x-rays, happy, seen in Amsterdam (see p.22)

Cultural property

Some Czech citizens will get back their buildings, businesses and works of art

Parliament is privatising property confiscated in 1948

October is the next issue
of The Art Newspaper
after the summer break

In this issue

New 'face' to long the new wing
of the National Gallery p. 4

Pop art at the R.A.
and the Japan Festival p. 5

This year's Carnegie
International p. 6

David Wheler asks about
the Schindel show p. 7

Germany's
cultural treasures pp. 10, 11

The use
of unlisted treasures
by Roger Scruton p. 12

The value of the TV show
'Relative Values'
by Brian Sewell p. 12

1400 Egyptologists
in Turin p. 14

John Richardson
interviewed on Picasso p. 15

ART MARKET

Old Masters sales
dissected p. 15

Sotheby's own record
in Berlin p. 18

The Jobs sales p. 19

Decline and fall
of the Huns p. 20

Forthcoming shows
in the commercial galleries
of London, Switzerland,
Berlin, Paris, Italy,
New York
and Los Angeles p. 21

Madrid

Spanish government retreats over art Wealth Tax

Only works over Ptas 7 million in value need be declared

Warsaw

Buy a Nazi tank and help a Polish museum

For sale: military equipment perfectly preserved in bogs

Plans to re-erect Schinkel's Bauakademie

London

Sixty-three drawings from Holkham for sale

A quarter of the last but one of England's great drawing collections dating from the eighteenth century is being dispersed

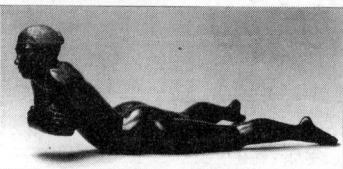

Not another art magazine but the only newspaper
about the art world: politics, economics, law, exhibitions,
personalities, opinions, museums, archaeology,
conservation, dealers and galleries, publications and future events

Auction House, code and sale title

AAA.S Australian Art Auctions, Sydney - Australia
  15 Oct 90 Australian & International Oil Paintings & Watercolours
  15 Apr 91 Oil Paintings & Watercolours
  1 Jul 91 Oil Paintings & Watercolours

AB.L Auktion Burkard, Luzern - Switzerland
  24 Nov 90 20th Century Contemporary Art - Sale No. 30
  25 May 91 20th Century & Contemporary Art - Sale No. 31

AB.S AB Stockholms Auktionsverk, Stockholm - Sweden
  8 Oct 90 Oil Paintings & Watercolours
  13 Nov 90 Oil Paintings, Watercolours & Sculpture - Sale No. 98
  27 Nov 90 Modern Watercolours & Drawings - Sale No. 36
  5 Dec 90 Modern Oil Paintings, Watercolours & Sculpture - Sale No. 99
  11 Mar 91 Watercolours & Drawings
  28 May 91 Oil Paintings, Watercolours & Sculpture

ACA Academy Auctioneers, London - UK
  11 Dec 90 Oil Paintings & Watercolours
  26 Feb 91 Oil Paintings & Watercolours
  30 Apr 91 Oil Paintings & Watercolours
  25 Jun 91 Oil Paintings & Watercolours

AG Anderson & Garland, Newcastle - UK
  4 Dec 90 Oil Paintings & Watercolours
  5 Mar 91 Oil Paintings & Watercolours
  30 Apr 91 Oil Paintings, Watercolours & Sculpture
  25 Jun 91 Oil Paintings & Watercolours

AG.W Agra, Warsaw - Poland
  20 Jan 91 Oil Paintings & Watercolours
  10 Mar 91 Oil Paintings & Watercolours
  23 Mar 91 Oil Paintings & Watercolours
  24 Mar 91 Oil Paintings & Watercolours

AGB.P Artus, Gridel & Boscher, Paris - France
  15 May 91 Russian Art
  10 Jun 91 Oil Paintings & Watercolours

AGS.P Audap Godeau & Solanet, Paris - France
  17 Dec 90 Old Master & Modern Oil Paintings, Watercolours & Sculpture
  24 Jan 91 Old Master Watercolours & Drawings
  12 Apr 91 19th Century & Old Master Oil Paintings, Watercolours & Sculpture
  7 Jun 91 Oil Paintings & Watercolours
  14 Jun 91 Oil Paintings, Watercolours & Sculpture

AH Andrew Hilditch & Son Ltd, Sandbach - UK
  28 Nov 90 Oil Paintings & Watercolours
  19 Jun 91 Oil Paintings & Watercolours

AL.W Altius, Warsaw - Poland
  2 Feb 91 Oil Paintings & Watercolours
  16 Mar 91 Oil Paintings & Watercolours

ANS.M Ansorena, Madrid - Spain
  22 Oct 90 Oil Paintings & Watercolours
  15 Nov 90 Oil Paintings & Watercolours
  19 Dec 90 Oil Paintings & Watercolours
  6 Feb 91 Oil Paintings & Watercolours
  5 Mar 91 Oil Paintings & Watercolours
  3 Apr 91 Oil Paintings & Watercolours
  16 May 91 Oil Paintings & Watercolours
  11 Jun 91 Oil Paintings & Watercolours

APT.P Ader Picard & Tajan, Paris - France
  10 Oct 90 Oil Paintings & Sculpture
  12 Oct 90 19th Century Oil Paintings & Watercolours
  15 Oct 90 Oil Paintings, Watercolours & Sculpture
  26 Oct 90 Modern Oil Paintings, Watercolours & Sculpture
  30 Oct 90 The Art of Henry Moret
  7 Nov 90 Old Master Oil Paintings & Watercolours & Modern Oil Paintings
  20 Nov 90 Oriental Oil Paintings, Watercolours & Sculpture
  24 Nov 90 Important 19/20th Century Paintings
  27 Nov 90 19/20th Century Oil Paintings & Watercolours
  27 Nov 90 Old Master Watercolours & Drawings
  30 Nov 90 Old Master Paintings
  5 Dec 90 Important Old Master Paintings
  12 Dec 90 Modern Oil Paintings, Watercolours & Sculpture
  17 Dec 90 Art Nouveau & Art Deco

31

Auction House, code and sale title

APT.P Ader Picard & Tajan, Paris - France
30 Jan 91   Old Master Paintings
 6 Mar 91   Modern Oil Paintings & Watercolours
16 Mar 91   19th Century Oil Paintings, Watercolours & Sculpture
22 Mar 91   Old Master Watercolours
 9 Apr 91   Art Nouveau
 9 Apr 91   Old Master Oil Paintings
14 Apr 91   Contemporary Oil Paintings, Watercolours & Sculpture
18 Apr 91   Old Master Oil Paintings
27 May 91   Islamic Art
18 Jun 91   Modern Oil Paintings & Watercolours
18 Jun 91   Old Master Drawings & Watercolours
20 Jun 91   Modern Oil Paintings & Watercolours
25 Jun 91   Old Master Paintings
27 Jun 91   Old Master Paintings
 1 Jul 91   The Alain Leseutre Collection
 5 Jul 91   Modern Oil Paintings & Watercolours

ARC.P Arcole, Paris - France
10 Oct 90   Contemporary Oil Paintings & Watercolours
15 Oct 90   19/20th Century Paintings, Watercolours & Sculpture
17 Oct 90   Modern Paintings & Watercolours
13 Nov 90   Oriental & African Art
19 Nov 90   Oil Paintings, Watercolours & Sculpture
27 Nov 90   The Art of Jean Cocteau
30 Nov 90   Oil Paintings & Watercolours
 6 Dec 90   Old Master Watercolours & Drawings
11 Dec 90   Studio of Lucien Coutaud
12 Dec 90   Watercolours & Drawings
12 Dec 90   Oil Paintings & Watercolours
14 Dec 90   19/20th Century Oil Paintings & Watercolours
17 Dec 90   Oriental & African Art
17 Dec 90   Old Master Oil Paintings, Watercolours & Sculpture
18 Feb 91   Russian Art
19 Feb 91   Oil Paintings, Watercolours & Sculpture
 4 Mar 91   Oil Paintings & Watercolours
13 Mar 91   Modern Oil Paintings & Watercolours
18 Mar 91   The School of Kiev
25 Mar 91   The Russian School
 8 Apr 91   Old Master Paintings, Watercolours & Sculpture
12 Apr 91   Art Nouveau
26 Apr 91   Russian Art
26 Apr 91   Oil Paintings & Watercolours
29 May 91   Russian Artists
17 Jun 91   Oil Paintings & Watercolours
19 Jun 91   Art of the Kiev & Odessa Schools
24 Jun 91   Art Nouveau & Art Deco
28 Jun 91   Modern Oil Paintings, Watercolours & Sculpture
 9 Jul 91   Oil Paintings, Watercolours & Sculpture

AW.H Arno Winterberg, Heidelberg - Germany
12 Oct 90   15th-20th Century Oil Paintings & Watercolours - Sale No. 41
12 Apr 91   Oil Paintings & Watercolours - Sale No. 42

B   Bonhams, London - UK
16 Aug 90   Marine Pictures & Related Works Of Art
12 Sep 90   Works from the studio of Jo Jones (Lots Road)
26 Sep 90   19th Century Watercolours
 9 Oct 90   Post War & Contemporary Art
25 Oct 90   Old Master & British Paintings
31 Oct 90   19th Century Watercolours
 1 Nov 90   Modern British & Continental Paintings, Watercolours & Sculpture
21 Nov 90   Fine English Watercolours
29 Nov 90   19th Century English, Continental & Australian Oils & Watercolours
 3 Dec 90   Cats in Art
 6 Dec 90   Paintings from the Studio of Miguel Canals (Chelsea)
 8 Dec 90   Sir William Russell Flint Watercolours & Drawings
13 Dec 90   Old Master & British Paintings & Watercolours
17 Dec 90   Works by Tom Keating
10 Jan 91   Marine Pictures & Related Works of Art
15 Jan 91   Dogs In Art
15 Jan 91   Dogs In Art Part I (Chelsea)
23 Jan 91   19th Century Watercolours
13 Feb 91   Painting Today
20 Feb 91   19th Century Watercolours
21 Feb 91   Modern British & Continental Pictures & Drawings
21 Feb 91   Modern Oil Paintings & Watercolours (Chelsea)
28 Feb 91   Old Master & British Paintings
13 Mar 91   Fine English & Continental Watercolours
14 Mar 91   19th Century English & Continental Pictures
18 Apr 91   English & Continental Watercolours

32

Auction House, code and sale title

B   Bonhams, London - UK
30 Apr 91   Modern British & Continental Pictures & Watercolours
2 May 91   Modern British & Continental Pictures & Drawings
9 May 91   English & Continental Watercolours
18 May 91   Watercolours & Drawings by Sir William Russell Flint
4 Jun 91   Children's Books & Original Illustrations
6 Jun 91   English & Continental Watercolours
19 Jun 91   Fine English & Continental Watercolours
20 Jun 91   Fine 19th Century English & Continental Pictures
4 Jul 91   Old Master & British Paintings & Old Master Drawings
11 Jul 91   English & Continental Watercolours
18 Jul 91   Modern British & Continental Pictures, Watercolours & Sculpture

B.G   Blache, Grenoble - France
15 Oct 90   Oil Paintings, Watercolours & Sculpture

B.O   Blomquist, Oslo - Norway
15 Oct 90   Oil Paintings & Watercolours
10 Dec 90   Jubilee Auction of Paintings, Watercolours & Sculpture
11 Mar 91   Oil Paintings, Watercolours & Sculpture
29 Apr 91   Watercolours & Drawings
3 Jun 91   Oil Paintings, Watercolours & Sculpture

B.P   Barridoff Galleries, Portland - USA
1 Aug 90   American & European Art
7 Feb 91   American & European Art

B.PA   Beaupuis, Pont Audemer - France
25 Nov 90   Old Master & Modern Oil Paintings, Watercolours & Sculpture
27 Jan 91   Oil Paintings & Watercolours
21 Apr 91   Oil Paintings, Watercolours & Sculpture

B.SF   Butterfields, San Francisco - USA
19 Sep 90   Oil Paintings, Watercolours & Sculpture
10 Oct 90   California Paintings - Sale No. 4388P
24 Oct 90   Contemporary Paintings - Sale No. 4385K
7 Nov 90   American Paintings - Sale No. 4409P
7 Nov 90   European Paintings - Sale No. 4404P
13 Feb 91   Oil Paintings & Watercolours
27 Mar 91   European Oil Paintings, Watercolours & Sculpture
24 Apr 91   Contemporary Oil Paintings, Watercolours & Sculpture
1 May 91   American Paintings & Sculpture
19 Jun 91   Modern & European Paintings

BA.S   Beijers Auktioner, Stockholm - Sweden
6 Nov 90   Oil Paintings, Watercolours & Sculpture - Sale No. 43
4 Dec 90   Oil Paintings, Watercolours & Sculpture - Sale No. 44
20 Mar 91   Watercolours & Drawings - Sale No. 46
24 Apr 91   Oil Paintings, Watercolours & Sculpture - Sale No. 47
22 May 91   Oil Paintings, Watercolours & Sculpture - Sale No. 48

BAR.M   Douglas Barrios, Montevideo - Uruguay
1 Nov 90   Oil Paintings & Watercolours

BAV.M   Eugenio Bavastro, Montevideo - Uruguay
1 Aug 90   Oil Paintings & Watercolours

BEL   John Bellman, Billingshurst - UK
21 Feb 91   Oil Paintings & Watercolours
21 Mar 91   Oil Paintings & Watercolours

BG.M   Boos Gallery, Michigan - USA
21 Sep 90   The Estate of Dr Walter N Koelz including Oils, Watercolours & Sculpture
9 Nov 90   Oil Paintings, Watercolours & Sculpture
18 Dec 90   Sale including Oil Paintings & Watercolours
27 Feb 91   Oil Paintings & Watercolours
4 Apr 91   Oil Paintings, Watercolours & Sculpture
21 May 91   Oil Paintings, Watercolours & Sculpture
16 Jul 91   Oil Paintings, Watercolours & Sculpture

BG.P   Binoche et Godeau, Paris - France
27 Oct 90   Modern Oil Paintings, Watercolours & Sculpture
20 Nov 90   Modern Oil Paintings, Watercolours & Sculpture
24 Jan 91   Avant-Garde Art
22 Mar 91   Oil Paintings & Watercolours
9 Apr 91   Oil Paintings, Watercolours & Sculpture - Hoppenot Estate
25 Jun 91   Modern & Contemporary Art

BL.P   Beaussant & Lefevre, Paris - France
27 Sep 90   Old Master Oil Paintings, Watercolours & Sculpture
10 Dec 90   Oil Paintings & Watercolours

Auction House, code and sale title

BL.P Beaussant & Lefevre, Paris - France
3 Apr 91 Sculpture
24 Jun 91 Oil Paintings, Watercolours & Sculpture

BM.B Bolland & Marotz, Bremen - Germany
26 Oct 90 Oil Paintings, Watercolours & Sculpture - Sale No. 64
14 Dec 90 Oil Paintings, Watercolours & Sculpture - Sale No. 65
12 Apr 91 Oil Paintings, Watercolours & Sculpture - Sale No. 66
28 Jun 91 Oil Paintings, Watercolours & Sculpture - Sale No. 67

BOY Boye's, London - UK
23 Apr 91 Sale including Oil Paintings & Watercolours

BR Bracketts, Tunbridge Wells - UK
26 Apr 91 Oil Paintings & Watercolours

BR.M Breraarte, Milan - Italy
22 Oct 90 Contemporary Art (Sale No 97 and 98)
20 Nov 90 Contemporary & Abstract Art

BRA.N Braswell Galleries, Connecticut - USA
20 Oct 90 Oil Paintings, Watercolours & Sculpture

BT Bearnes, Torquay - UK
5 Sep 90 Oil Paintings & Watercolours
19 Sep 90 Oil Paintings
16 Jan 91 Oil Paintings & Watercolours
15 May 91 Oil Paintings & Watercolours

BU.H Bukowskis, Helsinki - Finland
17 Nov 90 Oil Paintings, Watercolours & Sculpture - Sale No. 32
15 Dec 90 Oil Paintings & Watercolours - Sale No. 33
14 Apr 91 Oil Paintings, Watercolours & Sculpture - Sale No. 35

BU.K Bukowskis, Copenhagen - Denmark
18 Sep 90 International Classical Art - Sale No. 1
10 Dec 90 Oil Paintings, Watercolours & Sculpture - Sale No. 2
22 Apr 91 Oil Paintings, Watercolours & Sculpture - Sale No. 3
28 May 91 Modern Art - Sale No. 4

BU.M Bukowskis, Malmo - Sweden
9 Sep 90 Oil Paintings, Watercolours & Sculpture
21 Oct 90 Oil Paintings, Watercolours & Sculpture
10 Feb 91 Oil Paintings & Watercolours - Sale No. 8
17 Mar 91 Oil Paintings & Watercolours
21 Apr 91 Oil Paintings & Watercolours - Sale No. 10

BU.O Bukowskis, Oslo - Norway
11 Oct 90 Oil Paintings & Watercolours
12 Dec 90 Oil Paintings & Watercolours - Sale No. 90/4
13 Dec 90 The Hilmar Reksten Collection
13 Dec 90 Modern Paintings, Watercolours & Drawings
9 Feb 91 Saturday Auction
14 Mar 91 Oil Paintings & Watercolours - Sale No. 91/1
20 Apr 91 Saturday Auction
4 May 91 Saturday Auction
4 Jun 91 Oil Paintings & Watercolours - Sale No. 91/2

BU.S Bukowskis, Stockholm - Sweden
30 Oct 90 Sale including Oil Paintings & Watercolours - Sale No. 475
27 Nov 90 Modern Paintings, Watercolours & Sculpture - Sale No. 476
12 Dec 90 Winter Auction - Sale No. 477
18 Apr 91 Modern Oil Paintings, Watercolours & Sculpture - Sale No. 478
14 May 91 Oil Paintings, Watercolours & Sculpture - Sale No. 479

BUR.F Jeffery Burchard, Florida - USA
10 Dec 90 Oil Paintings & Watercolours

BW Biddle & Webb, Birmingham - UK
5 Oct 90 Oil Paintings & Watercolours
2 Nov 90 Oil Paintings & Watercolours
7 Dec 90 Oil Paintings & Watercolours
4 Jan 91 Oil Paintings & Watercolours
1 Feb 91 Oil Paintings & Watercolours
1 Mar 91 Oil Paintings & Watercolours
5 Apr 91 Oil Paintings & Watercolours
3 May 91 Oil Paintings, Watercolours & Sculpture
7 Jun 91 Oil Paintings & Watercolours
5 Jul 91 Oil Paintings & Watercolours

Auction House, code and sale title

C   Christie's, London - UK
20 Sep 90   British & Irish Traditionalist & Modern Oils, Watercolours & Sculpture
27 Sep 90   The Nineteenth Century
5 Oct 90   19th Century Continental Pictures & Watercolours
10 Oct 90   Imperial & Post-Revolutionary Russian Oils, Watercolours & Sculpture
16 Oct 90   Modern Belgian Oil Paintings & Watercolours
17 Oct 90   Sculpture from 1880 to Present Day
18 Oct 90   Contemporary Oil Paintings, Watercolours & Sculpture
19 Oct 90   Impressionist & Modern Oil Paintings, Watercolours & Sculpture
26 Oct 90   Old Master & British Oil Paintings
1 Nov 90   Victorian Oil Paintings, Watercolours & Sculpture
8 Nov 90   British & Irish Traditionalist & Modernist Paintings & Watercolours
9 Nov 90   Post-War & Contemporary Paintings, Watercolours & 20th Century Sculpture
13 Nov 90   British Drawings & Watercolours
16 Nov 90   Important British Pictures
27 Nov 90   Icons, Russian Pictures & Works of Art
29 Nov 90   Important Scandinavian Pictures, Watercolours & Sculpture
30 Nov 90   19th Century Pictures
3 Dec 90   Impressionist & Modern Paintings & Sculpture - Sale No.4423
4 Dec 90   Impressionist & Modern Watercolours & Drawings - Sale No. 4424
4 Dec 90   Impressionist & Modern Paintings & Sculpture - Sale No. 4425
6 Dec 90   Works from the Rene de Montaigu Collection
11 Dec 90   Important European Sculpture & Works of Art
11 Dec 90   Old Master & Architectural Drawings
18 Dec 90   Fine Portrait Miniatures
15 Jan 91   Man's Best Friends
25 Jan 91   British & Irish Paintings & Watercolours
7 Feb 91   Old Master Pictures
8 Feb 91   Victorian Pictures & Watercolours
14 Feb 91   Nineteenth Century Sculpture
15 Feb 91   19th Century Continental Pictures & Watercolours
19 Feb 91   Watercolours & Pictures of Birds
1 Mar 91   British & Old Master Pictures
7 Mar 91   British & Irish Traditionalist & Modern Paintings & Watercolours
8 Mar 91   Post-War & Contemporary British Paintings, Watercolours & Sculpture
19 Mar 91   Impressionist & Modern Paintings, Drawings & Sculpture
20 Mar 91   Fine Portrait Miniatures
21 Mar 91   Contemporary Art
9 Apr 91   British Drawings & Watercolours
12 Apr 91   British Pictures
16 Apr 91   Important European Sculpture & Works of Art
16 Apr 91   Old Master Drawings
17 Apr 91   Decorative Arts from 1880 to Present Day
18 Apr 91   Old Master Pictures
19 Apr 91   Fine Old Master Pictures
2 May 91   British & Irish Modern Oil Paintings & Watercolours
17 May 91   19th Century Continental & Scandinavian Pictures & Watercolours
23 May 91   The Nineteenth Century
24 May 91   Important Old Master Pictures
30 May 91   Maritime Sale
4 Jun 91   Garden Statuary (Wrotham Park)
6 Jun 91   British & Irish Traditional & Modern Paintings & Watercolours
7 Jun 91   Post-War & Contemporary Paintings, Watercolours & Sculpture
14 Jun 91   Victorian Oil Paintings, Drawings & Watercolours
21 Jun 91   19th Century Continental Pictures & Drawings
24 Jun 91   Impressionist & Modern Paintings & Sculpture - Sale No. 4562
25 Jun 91   Impressionist & Modern Paintings, Sculpture, Watercolours & Drawings
27 Jun 91   Contemporary Art
2 Jul 91   Old Master Drawings from Holkham Hall - Sale No. 4569
2 Jul 91   Old Master Drawings from The Woodner Collection - Sale No. 4595
2 Jul 91   Old Master Drawings
2 Jul 91   Important European Sculpture & Works of Art - Sale No. 4570
4 Jul 91   Old Master Pictures
5 Jul 91   Important Old Master Pictures from F W Field Collection - Sale No. 4575 Part I
5 Jul 91   Important & Fine Old Master Pictures - Sale No. 4575 Part II
9 Jul 91   British Drawings & Watercolours
10 Jul 91   Fine Portrait Miniatures
12 Jul 91   British Pictures
16 Jul 91   Man's Best Friends
17 Jul 91   Decorative Arts from 1880 to the Present Day

C.A   Campo, Antwerp - Belgium
23 Oct 90   Oil Paintings, Watercolours & Sculpture - Sale No. 174
4 Dec 90   Oil Paintings & Watercolours - Sale No. 175
12 Mar 91   Oil Paintings & Watercolours - Sale No. 176
23 Apr 91   Oil Paintings, Watercolours & Sculpture
28 May 91   Oil Paintings, Watercolours & Sculpture - Sale No. 178

C.P   Cheval, Paris - France
21 Nov 90   Contemporary Oil Paintings & Watercolours
16 Jun 91   Russian Art

Auction House, code and sale title

CB.P Claude Boisgirard, Paris - France
18 Oct 90   Contemporary Oil Paintings & Watercolours
25 Oct 90   Modern & Contemporary Oil Paintings & Watercolours
21 Nov 90   Art Nouveau - Art Deco
26 Nov 90   Islamic Oil Paintings & Watercolours
30 Nov 90   Modern & 19th Century Oil Paintings & Watercolours
 6 Dec 90   Marine Oil Paintings & Watercolours
 7 Dec 90   Old Master Oil Paintings & Watercolours
20 Jan 91   19/20th Century Art
 1 Mar 91   Modern Oil Paintings & Watercolours
 4 Apr 91   Lalique Watercolours & Drawings
 6 Apr 91   Parisian Illustrators
10 Apr 91   Old Master Oil Paintings, Watercolours & Sculpture
17 Apr 91   Art Nouveau
19 Apr 91   Oriental Oil Paintings & Watercolours
19 Jun 91   Art Nouveau Art Deco
26 Jun 91   Oil Paintings, Watercolours & Sculpture

CBB Bigwood Ltd, Stratford on Avon - UK
24 Aug 90   Oil Paintings & Watercolours
21 Sep 90   Oil Paintings & Watercolours
19 Oct 90   Oil Paintings & Watercolours
23 Nov 90   Oil Paintings & Watercolours
14 Dec 90   Oil Paintings & Watercolours
18 Jan 91   Oil Paintings & Watercolours
15 Feb 91   Oil Paintings & Watercolours
22 Mar 91   Oil Paintings & Watercolours
19 Apr 91   Oil Paintings & Watercolours
24 May 91   Oil Paintings & Watercolours
21 Jun 91   Oil Paintings & Watercolours
19 Jul 91   Oil Paintings & Watercolours

CBS Chrystals Auctions, Isle of Man - UK
 7 Dec 90   Oil Paintings & Watercolours
10 May 91   Oil Paintings & Watercolours

CC.P Catherine Charbonneaux, Paris - France
 1 Oct 90   Abstract Oil Paintings, Watercolours & Sculpture
26 Oct 90   Modern Oil Paintings, Watercolours & Sculpture
 9 Dec 90   New York 80's Contemporary Art
10 Feb 91   Collection of 20th Century & Lusson Oil Paintings & Watercolours
15 Apr 91   20th C Oil Paintings, Watercolours & Sculpture
16 Jun 91   Modern Oil Paintings, Watercolours & Sculpture

CD Capes Dunn & Co., Manchester - UK
30 Oct 90   Oil Paintings & Watercolours by Adolphe Valette
 6 Nov 90   Oil Paintings & Watercolours
26 Feb 91   Oil Paintings & Watercolours
21 May 91   Oil Paintings & Watercolours
 2 Jul 91   Oil Paintings & Watercolours

CD.P Christian Delorme, Paris - France
12 Dec 90   Old Master & Modern Oil Paintings, Watercolours & Sculpture
14 May 91   The Art of A Reiss
22 May 91   Oil Paintings & Watercolours
 3 Jul 91   Oil Paintings, Watercolours & Sculpture

CE.NY Christie's East, New York - USA
25 Sep 90   19/20th Century American Watercolours
31 Oct 90   19th Century Works of Art
 6 Nov 90   Contemporary Art Part III
13 Nov 90   Modern Paintings, Drawings & Sculpture
 7 May 91   Modern & Contemporary Paintings, Drawings & Sculpture
14 May 91   19th Century Sculpture & Decorative Objects
21 May 91   American & 19th C European Paintings, Watercolours & Sculpture
30 May 91   Old Master Paintings & Drawings

CG Christie's, Glasgow - UK
30 Aug 90   Oil Paintings & Watercolours
17 Sep 90   Floors Castle - Oil Paintings, Watercolours & Sculpture
27 Sep 90   Contemporary & Modern Paintings & Sculpture
11 Oct 90   Oil Paintings & Watercolours
16 Oct 90   Sale including Oil Paintings (Arthurstone, Perthshire)
26 Oct 90   Fine Irish Paintings & Drawings
22 Nov 90   Fine Paintings & Drawings
 6 Dec 90   Four Scottish Colourists
 6 Dec 90   British & Continental Paintings & Watercolours
 5 Feb 91   Oil Paintings & Watercolours
14 Mar 91   Oil Paintings & Watercolours
17 Apr 91   Contemporary & Modern Pictures & Sculpture
 2 May 91   Oil Paintings & Watercolours

Auction House, code and sale title

CG   Christie's, Glasgow - UK
13 May91   Sale including Oil Paintings & Watercolours (Netherbyres, Eyemouth)
13 Jun 91   Oil Paintings & Watercolours
27 Jun 91   British & Continental Paintings & Drawings

CGC   Cheffins Grain & Comins, Cambridge - UK
13 Jun 91   Oil Paintings & Watercolours

CH.AM Christie's, Amsterdam - Netherlands
 1 Sep 90   Oil Paintings & Watercolours
11 Sep 90   Pictures, Watercolours & Drawings
22 Sep 90   Oil Paintings, Watercolours & Sculpture
20 Oct 90   Sale including Oil Paintings & Watercolours
30 Oct 90   19th Century European Watercolours & Drawings - Sale No. 2124
30 Oct 90   19th Century European Pictures - Sale No. 2123
12 Nov 90   Dutch, Flemish & German Drawings
13 Nov 90   Old Master Pictures
12 Dec 90   Impressionist & Modern Art from Bremmer-Hollmann Collection
12 Dec 90   Modern & Contemporary Art
 2 May91   Old Master Pictures - Sale No. 2141
22 May91   Modern & Contemporary Art

CH.BR Christie's, Brussels - Belgium
13 Dec 90   Paintings & Sculpture donated by Benedict Goldschmidt

CH.E Christie's, Dublin - Eire
12 Dec 90   Fine Irish Paintings and Drawings (RHA Gallagher Gallery)

CH.G Christie's, Geneva - Switzerland
13 Nov 90   Sale including Miniatures

CH.HK Christie's, Hong Kong - Hong Kong
 9 Oct 90   Fine China Trade Paintings & Printed Material

CH.ME Christie's, Victoria - Australia
12 Nov 90   Works on Paper
 9 Apr 91   Works on Paper & Australian Paintings

CH.MO Christie's, Monaco - Monaco
 7 Dec 90   Old Master & 19th Century Pictures & Drawings
 7 Dec 90   Collection of Marine Watercolours by Antoine Roux
22 Jun 91   Old Master & 19th Century Oil Paintings & Watercolours

CH.NY Christie's, New York - USA
27 Sep 90   American Watercolours, Paintings & Sculpture of 19/20th Century
 2 Oct 90   Impressionist & Modern Oil Paintings & Watercolours
 5 Oct 90   Contemporary Oil Paintings, Watercolours & Sculpture
10 Oct 90   Old Master Oil Paintings
24 Oct 90   19th Century European Paintings, Watercolours & Sculpture
 7 Nov 90   Contemporary Art
 8 Nov 90   Contemporary Drawings, Watercolours & Collages - Sale No. 7152
 8 Nov 90   Contemporary Art Part II - Sale No. 7154
14 Nov 90   Impressionist & Modern Paintings & Sculpture - Part I
15 Nov 90   Impressionist & Modern Paintings & Sculpture - Part II
15 Nov 90   Impressionist & Modern Drawings & Watercolours
20 Nov 90   Latin American Paintings, Drawings & Sculpture
20 Nov 90   Contemporary Prints & Multiples
30 Nov 90   Important American Paintings, Drawings & Sculpture of 18/20th Century
 9 Jan 91   Property from the Estate of E Maurice Bloch Part II
 9 Jan 91   Old Master Drawings
11 Jan 91   Important Old Master Paintings
11 Jan 91   Important Paintings by Old Masters
26 Jan 91   Important American Folk Art
14 Feb 91   Impressionist & Modern Paintings, Drawings & Sculpture
14 Feb 91   Contemporary Art
28 Feb 91   19th Century European Paintings, & Watercolours
14 Mar91   American Watercolours, Paintings & Sculpture
22 Mar91   The Elizabeth Parke Firestone Collection Part II
 1 May91   Contemporary Art Part I
 2 May91   Contemporary Art Part II
 8 May91   Impressionist & Modern Paintings & Sculpture Part I
 9 May91   Impressionist & Modern Drawings & Watercolours
 9 May91   Impressionist & Modern Paintings & Sculpture Part II
15 May91   Latin American Paintings, Watercolours & Sculpture
22 May91   American Paintings from the Mrs George Arden Collection Part I
22 May91   Important American Paintings, Drawings & Sculpture
23 May91   19th Century European Paintings Watercolours & Sculpture
31 May91   Important Old Master Paintings

CH.R Christie's, Rome - Italy
23 Oct 90   Sale including Oil Paintings & Watercolours - Sale No. 191

38

AUCTION PRICES OF AMERICAN ARTISTS

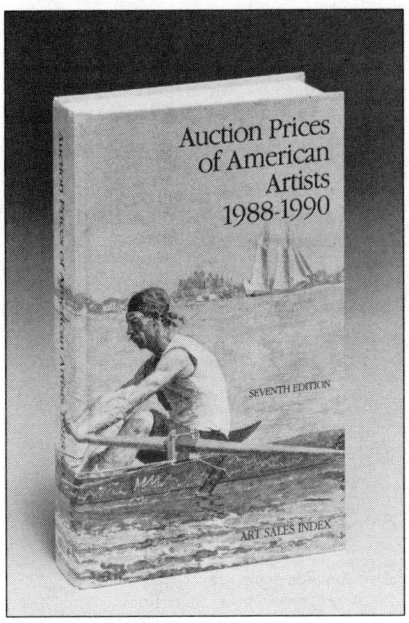

Did you know that: the world turnover in works by
North & South American artists and sculptors was $392 million in 1988/89 and
$495 million in 1989/90 and that 75% of all works by American artists sell
at price below $10,000?

pocket sized - 500 pages   1991 edition - $40.00

example

UFER, Walter (1876-1936) American
£17089	$27000	(24-May-89 SY.NY69/R) Nude in interior (76x76cm-30x30in) s.
£17722	$28000	(24-May-89 SY.NY70/R) Indian family (63x76cm-25x30in) s.
£22436	$35000	(1-Dec-89 CH.NY95/R) Singing Indian (76x64cm-30x25in) s.
£22727	$42500	(1-Dec-88 SY.NY109/R) Indians on horseback (49x59cm-19x23in) s.
£37433	$70000	(1-Dec-88 SY.NY119/R) Indian Scouts (61x75cm-24x30in) s.
£47468	$75000	(24-May-89 SY.NY76/R) Taos Indian (76x63cm-30x25in) s. i.verso
£60897	$95000	(1-Dec-89 CH.NY96/R) Fantasies (107x96cm-42x38in) s.

UHART, Pedro (1938-) Chilean
| £1719 | $2767 | (7-Mar-90 HC.P117) Tropical Band (106x142cm-42x56in) s. acrylic |
| £3008 | $4842 | (7-Mar-90 HC.P116/R) Grace J Sofa (150x188cm-59x74in) s.acrylic |

ULH, S Jerome (1842-1916) American
| £1045 | $1924 | (6 Dec-88 P.Q98) The midget (30x25cm-12x10in) s.i. (C.D 2300) |

ULP, Clifford (1885-1957) American
| £613 | $1000 | (19-Jan-90 LIT.L105) Winter nocturne (23x30cm-9x12in) s. i, verso board |

UNSWORTH, Edna Ganzhorn (1890-?) American
| £1163 | $2000 | (22-Mar-89 B.SF3165/R) He dealt his last hand (58x43cm-23x17in) |

Art Sales Index Ltd.,1 Thames Street, Weybridge, Surrey KT13 8JG, UK.
tel: (0932) 856426   fax: (0932) 842482

Auction House, code and sale title

CH.R Christie's, Rome - Italy
19 Nov 90 Important Old Masters
27 Nov 90 Sale including Sculpture
 3 Dec 90 Modern & Contemporary Art
11 Dec 90 Important 19th Century Oil Paintings & Watercolours
 8 Apr 91 Old Master Paintings
16 Apr 91 19th Century Paintings, Watercolours & Sculpture - Sale No. 205
23 Apr 91 Sale including Sculpture & Miniatures
24 Apr 91 Sale including Sculpture - Sale No. 207
13 May91 Modern & Contemporary Art - Sale No. 208
 4 Jun 91 Old Master Paintings & Sculpture - Sale No. 212 (Bologna)

CH.S Christie's, Sydney - Australia
31 Oct 90 Australian Pictures

CHAP Chapmans, Scarborough - UK
19 Feb 91 Oil Paintings & Watercolours
19 Mar 91 Oil Paintings, Watercolours & Sculpture
16 Apr 91 Oil Paintings & Watercolours
14 May91 Oil Paintings & Watercolours

CJ.N Courchet, Palloc & Japhet, Nice - France
29 Mar 91 Oil Paintings & Watercolours
 6 Jun 91 Oil Paintings, Watercolours & Sculpture

CK.P Cardinet & Kalck, Paris - France
 4 Apr 91 Old Master & Modern Paintings, Watercolours & Sculpture
21 Jun 91 Oil Paintings, Watercolours & Sculpture

CL.E Champin, Lombrail & Gautier, Enghien - France
21 Nov 90 Modern Oil Paintings, Watercolours & Sculpture
16 Dec 90 Modern Oil Paintings, Watercolours & Sculpture
19 Jun 91 Modern Oil Paintings, Watercolours & Sculpture

CN.P Couturier & Nicolay, Paris - France
12 Nov 90 20th Century Decorative Arts - including Sculpture
14 Nov 90 19/20th Century Oil Paintings, Watercolours & Sculpture
 7 Dec 90 Old Master Oil Paintings & Watercolours
27 Mar 91 Oil Paintings, Watercolours & Sculpture
15 May91 Oil Paintings, Watercolours & Sculpture

COB Cobern, Southport - UK
27 Feb 91 Oil Paintings & Watercolours

COL.M Collins, Maine - USA
11 Aug 90 American & European Oil Paintings,& Watercolours

CR.P Claude Robert, Paris - France
11 Mar 91 Oil Paintings & Watercolours of Marcel Belle & Isaac Lisie
11 Mar 91 Oil Paintings & Watercolours of Baroukh
25 Mar 91 Modern Oil Paintings, Watercolours & Sculpture
 8 Apr 91 Modern Oil Paintings, Watercolours & Sculpture

CS.L Chenu & Scrive, Lyon - France
16 Oct 90 Oil Paintings, Watercolours & Sculpture
 3 Dec 90 Oil Paintings, Watercolours & Sculpture

CSC.P Cornette de St.Cyr, Paris - France
28 Sep 90 Old Master Oil Paintings, Watercolours & Sculpture
 3 Oct 90 Religious Oil Paintings, Watercolours & Sculpture
 9 Oct 90 Modern Oil Paintings, Watercolours & Sculpture
15 Oct 90 Contemporary Oil Paintings, Watercolours & Sculpture
23 Oct 90 Contemporary Oil Paintings, Watercolours & Sculpture
29 Oct 90 The Pont-Aven School
12 Nov 90 Old Master Oil Paintings, Watercolours & Sculpture
19 Nov 90 19/20th Century Oil Paintings & Watercolours
28 Nov 90 Modern & Contemporary Art
16 Dec 90 20th Century American Oil Paintings, Watercolours & Sculpture
20 Jan 91 L'Art Et Son Concept
30 Jan 91 Old Master Oil Paintings, Watercolours & Sculpture
 5 Feb 91 Modern Oil Paintings, Watercolours & Sculpture
11 Feb 91 Modern & Old Master Oil Paintings & Watercolours
 8 Apr 91 Contemporary Art
15 Apr 91 Modern Oil Paintings, Watercolours & Sculpture
19 Apr 91 Old Master Oil Paintings, Watercolours & Sculpture
10 Jun 91 Art Nouveau Art Deco
11 Jun 91 Modern & Contemporary Oil Paintings, Watercolours & Sculpture
13 Jun 91 Old Master Paintings
 3 Jul 91 Contemporary Art

40

Auction House, code and sale title

CSK   Christie's Kensington, London - UK
1 Aug 90   English & Continental Oil Paintings,& Watercolours
16 Aug 90   Modern British & Continental Oil Paintings,
22 Aug 90   English & Continental Watercolours
6 Sep 90   English & Continental Paintings
12 Sep 90   English & Continental Watercolours
13 Sep 90   Old Master Oil Paintings
18 Sep 90   Sale Including Oil Paintings, Watercolours & Sculpture (Landue House, Cornwall)
20 Sep 90   Modern British & Continental Paintings, Watercolours & Drawings
24 Sep 90   Sale Including Oil Paintings & Watercolours (Old Lodge, Nutley)
27 Sep 90   English & Victorian Pictures
2 Oct 90   Wrotham Park - Sculpture
4 Oct 90   19/20th Century Continental Oil Paintings
10 Oct 90   English & Continental Watercolours
11 Oct 90   Oil Paintings & Watercolours from Orlando Greenwood's Studio
18 Oct 90   Studio of George Sherwood Hunter
18 Oct 90   Maritime Sale (Christie's King Street)
25 Oct 90   Old Master Pictures
31 Oct 90   English & Continental Pictures
1 Nov 90   Naive, English & Victorian Pictures
1 Nov 90   Sale including Oil Paintings & Watercolours (Pearl Assurance)
8 Nov 90   Modern British & Continental Pictures
14 Nov 90   Pictures & Watercolours of the 19th/20th Century
15 Nov 90   Topographical Pictures
21 Nov 90   European Works of Art & Sculpture
22 Nov 90   Victorian & Continental Paintings & Watercolours
29 Nov 90   Old Master Pictures
6 Dec 90   Impressionist & Modern Australian Paintings & Watercolours
6 Dec 90   Modern British & Continental Paintings, Watercolours & Sculpture
12 Dec 90   Original Book Illustrations
13 Dec 90   English & Continental Pictures
20 Dec 90   English & Continental Pictures
16 Jan 91   English & Continental Watercolours & Pictures
22 Jan 91   Sale including Miniatures
24 Jan 91   Modern British & Continental Oil Paintings & Watercolours
30 Jan 91   English & Continental Pictures & Watercolours
7 Feb 91   Old Master & English Pictures
14 Feb 91   Continental Oil Paintings & Watercolours of the 19/20th Century
19 Feb 91   Sale including Miniatures
20 Feb 91   Continental Watercolours & Pictures
7 Mar 91   Oil Paintings & Watercolours
19 Mar 91   Sale including Miniatures
21 Mar 91   British & Victorian Watercolours & Pictures
28 Mar 91   Modern Oil Paintings & Watercolours
10 Apr 91   Oil Paintings & Watercolours
10 Apr 91   Works of Art & Sculpture
16 Apr 91   Sale including Miniatures
18 Apr 91   Old Master Pictures
24 Apr 91   19/20th Century Paintings & Watercolours
9 May 91   Continental Watercolours & Pictures
16 May 91   English & Continental Pictures
21 May 91   Objects of Vertu & Miniatures
22 May 91   English & Continental Oil Paintings & Watercolours
6 Jun 91   English & Continental Pictures
13 Jun 91   English & Victorian Pictures & Watercolours
18 Jun 91   Objects of Vertu & Miniatures
19 Jun 91   English & Continental Pictures
24 Jun 91   Impressionist & Modern Paintings, Watercolours & Sculpture - Sale No.4318
28 Jun 91   Modern & Contemporary Paintings, Watercolours & Sculpture
3 Jul 91   European Works of Art & Sculpture
4 Jul 91   Old Master Pictures
10 Jul 91   Original Illustrations & Books
11 Jul 91   English & Continental Pictures
18 Jul 91   19/20th Century Continental Pictures & Watercolours
24 Jul 91   English & Continental Pictures & Watercolours
30 Jul 91   Objects of Vertu & Miniatures
1 Aug 91   Modern British & Continental Oils & Watercolours

D   Duke & Son, Dorchester - UK
1 Nov 90   Oil Paintings & Watercolours
7 Mar 91   Oil Paintings & Watercolours
4 Jul 91   Oil Paintings & Watercolours

D.L   Desbuisson, Lille - France
14 Oct 90   19th Century & Modern Oil Paintings & Watercolours
11 Feb 91   Oil Paintings & Sculpture
17 Jun 91   Oil Paintings, Watercolours & Sculpture

D.NY   Doyle, New York - USA
12 Sep 90   Belle Epoque 19th/20th Century Decorative Arts
10 Oct 90   English & Continental Oil Paintings, Watercolours & Sculpture

Auction House, code and sale title

D.NY Doyle, New York - USA
24 Oct 90 Sale including Oil Paintings & Watercolours
7 Nov 90 Sale including Oil Paintings & Watercolours
15 Nov 90 Modern & European Paintings & Sculpture
28 Nov 90 Sale including Oil Paintings & Watercolours
5 Dec 90 American Paintings & Sculpture
13 Dec 90 Sale of Property of Sir Rex Harrison
9 Jan 91 Oil Paintings, Watercolours & Sculpture
23 Jan 91 Sale including Oil Paintings, Watercolours & Sculpture
6 Feb 91 Sale including Oil Paintings & Watercolours
20 Feb 91 Oil Paintings & Watercolours
6 Mar 91 Oil Paintings & Watercolours
27 Mar 91 Oil Paintings & Watercolours
17 Apr 91 American Paintings & Sculpture
1 May 91 English & Continental Oil Paintings & Watercolours
15 May 91 Oil Paintings, Watercolours & Sculpture
22 May 91 Modern & European Paintings & Sculpture
5 Jun 91 19/20th Century Decorative Arts
26 Jun 91 Oil Paintings & Watercolours
10 Jul 91 Oil Paintings & Watercolours
24 Jul 91 Oil Paintings & Watercolours

D.P Dumousset, Paris - France
22 Nov 90 Old Master Oil Paintings, Watercolours & 19th Century Sculpture
12 Dec 90 Modern Oil Paintings & Watercolours
15 Dec 90 Contemporary Oil Paintings, Watercolours & Sculpture
6 Mar 91 Oil Paintings & Watercolours
21 Jun 91 Oil Paintings, Watercolours & Sculpture

D.V Dorotheum, Vienna - Austria
20 Sep 90 Modern Oil Paintings & Watercolours - Sale No. 1593
27 Sep 90 19th Century Oil Paintings & Watercolours - Sale No. 1594
11 Oct 90 Oil Paintings & Watercolours - Sale No. 1596
18 Oct 90 20th Century Art - Sale No. 1597
25 Oct 90 Oil Paintings & Watercolours - Sale No. 1598
8 Nov 90 Sale including Sculpture - Sale No.1599
14 Nov 90 Old Master Paintings - Sale No. 1600
22 Nov 90 Sale including Paintings, Watercolours & Sculpture - Sale No. 1601
29 Nov 90 19th Century Oil Paintings - Sale No. 1602
6 Dec 90 Modern & Contemporary Art - Sale No. 1604
13 Dec 90 Oil Paintings & Watercolours - Sale No. 1605
24 Jan 91 Modern & Contemporary Art - Sale No. 1606
31 Jan 91 Oil Paintings & Watercolours - Sale No. 1607
7 Feb 91 20th Century Art - Sale No. 1608
28 Feb 91 Oil Paintings, Watercolours & Sculpture - Sale No. 1609
7 Mar 91 20th Century Art - Sale No. 1610
14 Mar 91 Old Master Paintings - Sale No. 1611
21 Mar 91 Sale including Sculpture and Oil Painting - Sale No. 1612
11 Apr 91 19th Century Oil Paintings & Watercolours - Sale No. 1613
25 Apr 91 Watercolours,Drawings & Miniatures - Sale No. 1615
8 May 91 Modern & Contemporary Art - Sale No. 1616
16 May 91 19th Century Oil Paintings - Sale No. 1617
23 May 91 Art Deco - Sale No. 1618
6 Jun 91 Old Master Paintings - Sale No. 1620
20 Jun 91 Oil Paintings & Watercolours from Kremlacek - Sale No. 1621
27 Jun 91 Oil Paintings & Watercolours - Sale No. 1622

DA Dee & Atkinson, Driffield - UK
28 Sep 90 Oil Paintings
30 Nov 90 Sale including Oil Paintings & Watercolours
8 Feb 91 Oil Paintings & Watercolours
14 Jun 91 Sale including Oil Paintings

DA.R Dapsens, Reims - France
21 Oct 90 Oil Paintings, Watercolours & Sculpture
16 Dec 90 19/20th Century Oil Paintings, Watercolours & Sculpture
17 Mar 91 Oil Paintings, Watercolours & Sculpture
21 Apr 91 Oil Paintings, Watercolours & Sculpture
9 Jun 91 Oil Paintings, Watercolours & Sculpture

DA.W Daes, Warsaw - Poland
1 Mar 91 Oil Paintings & Watercolours

DAR.P Daussy & Ricqles, Paris - France
21 Dec 90 Oil Paintings & Watercolours
28 Mar 91 Modern Oil Paintings & Watercolours
5 Apr 91 Old Master Paintings, Watercolours & Sculpture
3 Jul 91 Old Master Oil Paintings & Watercolours

DE.B Desa, Wroclaw - Poland
1 Feb 91 Oil Paintings & Watercolours

Auction House, code and sale title

DE.B Desa, Wroclaw - Poland
12 Feb 91   Oil Paintings & Watercolours

DL.P Delavenne & Lafarge, Paris - France
17 Oct 90   Oil Paintings, Watercolours & Sculpture
20 Mar 91   Oil Paintings, Watercolours & Sculpture
24 Jun 91   Oil Paintings, Watercolours & Sculpture

DLY   David Lay, Penzance - UK
8 Nov 90   Oil Paintings & Watercolours
28 Feb 91   Oil Paintings & Watercolours
20 Jun 91   Oil Paintings & Watercolours

DM.D   Du Mouchelle, Detroit - USA
17 Aug 90   Oil Paintings & Watercolours
14 Sep 90   Oil Paintings & Watercolours
19 Oct 90   General Sale including Oil Paintings, Watercolours & Sculpture
16 Nov 90   Oil Paintings, Watercolours & Sculpture
14 Dec 90   Oil Paintings, Watercolours & Sculpture
11 Jan 91   Oil Paintings & Watercolours
15 Feb 91   Oil Paintings, Watercolours & Sculpture
15 Mar 91   Oil Paintings & Watercolours
19 Apr 91   Oil Paintings, Watercolours & Sculpture
17 May 91   Oil Paintings, Watercolours & Sculpture
21 Jun 91   Oil Paintings, Watercolours & Sculpture
19 Jul 91   Oil Paintings, Watercolours & Sculpture

DO.H   Dorling, Hamburg - Germany
5 Dec 90   Oil Paintings & Watercolours - Sale No. 137
5 Jun 91   Oil Paintings, Watercolours & Sculpture - Sale No. 139

DOU.M Douglas, South Deerfield - USA
10 Aug 90   Oil Paintings & Watercolours
19 Oct 90   Oil Paintings & Watercolours
9 Nov 90   Oil Paintings & Watercolours
28 Dec 90   Oil Paintings & Watercolours
22 Mar 91   Oil Paintings & Watercolours
12 Apr 91   Oil Paintings & Watercolours

DR   Dreweatt Neate, Newbury - UK
24 Oct 90   Oil Paintings & Watercolours
6 Mar 91   Oil Paintings & Watercolours

DS.W   Dunbar Sloan, Wellington - New Zealand
7 Nov 90   Oil Paintings & Watercolours
17 Apr 91   Oil Paintings & Watercolours

DU.E   Dunning's, Illinois - USA
7 Oct 90   Oil Paintings & Watercolours
21 Apr 91   Oil Paintings & Watercolours

DUR.M Duran, Madrid - Spain
23 Oct 90   Oil Paintings, Watercolours & Sculpture
20 Nov 90   Oil Paintings
18 Dec 90   Oil Paintings & Watercolours
19 Feb 91   Oil Paintings & Watercolours
20 Mar 91   Oil Paintings
23 Apr 91   Oil Paintings, Watercolours & Sculpture
21 May 91   Oil Paintings, Watercolours & Sculpture
17 Jun 91   Oil Paintings, Watercolours & Sculpture

E.EDM Eldred, Massachusetts - USA
9 Aug 90   Oil Paintings, Watercolours & Sculpture
20 Aug 90   Japanese Art
16 Nov 90   Oil Paintings & Watercolours
29 Mar 91   Oil Paintings, Watercolours & Sculpture
25 Jul 91   Marine Art
26 Jul 91   Oil Paintings & Watercolours

E.LA   Elkaim, L'Isle Adam - France
30 Sep 90   Modern Oil Paintings & Watercolours
2 Dec 90   Modern Oil Paintings, Watercolours & Sculpture
9 Dec 90   Modern Oil Paintings, Watercolours & Sculpture
17 Feb 91   Modern & Contemporary Art
24 Mar 91   The Studios of Lewitska, Piet, Fintz, Weller, Sourdillon & Marchou
21 Apr 91   Oil Paintings, Watercolours & Sculpture
26 May 91   Oil Paintings & Watercolours

EA.M   Empire Auctions, Montreal - Canada
29 Aug 90   Oil Paintings & Watercolours
26 Sep 90   Oil Paintings & Watercolours

Auction House, code and sale title

EA.M Empire Auctions, Montreal - Canada
24 Oct 90   Evening Sale of Oil Paintings & Watercolours
25 Oct 90   Oil Paintings & Watercolours
21 Nov 90   Oil Paintings & Watercolours
12 Dec 90   Oil Paintings & Watercolours
23 Jan 91   Oil Paintings & Watercolours
20 Feb 91   Oil Paintings, Watercolours & Sculpture
20 Mar 91   Oil Paintings & Watercolours
17 Apr 91   Oil Paintings & Watercolours
22 May 91   Oil Paintings, Watercolours & Sculpture
19 Jun 91   Oil Paintings & Watercolours
17 Jul 91   Oil Paintings & Watercolours

EA.Z Eberhart Auktionen, Zurich - Switzerland
15 Nov 90   Oil Paintings & Watercolours - Sale No. 81
16 Nov 90   Oil Paintings & Watercolours - Sale No. 82
22 Mar 91   Modern Oil Paintings & Watercolours
30 May 91   Oil Paintings & Watercolours - Sale No, 86-88

EDD   Eddisons, Huddersfield - UK
20 Mar 91   Oil Paintings & Watercolours

EH   Edgar Horn, Eastbourne - UK
27 Mar 91   Oil Paintings & Watercolours
4 Jun 91   Oil Paintings & Watercolours

EP.M Edmund Peel, Madrid - Spain
30 Oct 90   Old Master & 19th Century Paintings
22 Nov 90   Impressionist & Modern Paintings
13 Dec 90   Contemporary Art
24 Jan 91   Oil Paintings & Watercolours
28 Feb 91   Old Master Paintings
25 Apr 91   Modern & Contemporary Art
21 May 91   Old Master & 19th Century Paintings
18 Jun 91   Modern & Contemporary Art
27 Jun 91   Oil Paintings & Watercolours

F.M   Finarte, Milan - Italy
27 Sep 90   Contemporary Art - Sale No. 748
18 Oct 90   19th Century Oil Paintings
23 Oct 90   20th Century Oil Paintings, Watercolours & Sculpture - Sale No. 753
24 Oct 90   Contemporary Oil Paintings, Watercolours & Sculpture - Sale No. 754
13 Nov 90   Sale including Old Master Paintings - Sale No. 757
14 Nov 90   Neoclassical & Romantic Paintings, Watercolours & Sculpture
21 Nov 90   19th Century Oil Paintings & Watercolours
29 Nov 90   Old Master Paintings
3 Dec 90   Modern Watercolours & Drawings - Sale No. 767
5 Dec 90   19th Century Paintings - Sale No. 770
12 Dec 90   Sale including Oil Paintings, Watercolours & Sculpture - Sale No. 775
12 Dec 90   20th Century Watercolours & Drawings - Sale No. 773
13 Dec 90   Contemporary Art - Sale No. 774
12 Mar 91   19th Century Paintings & Watercolours including Paintings of G Fattori
19 Mar 91   Old Master Watercolours & Drawings - Sale No. 778
26 Mar 91   Contemporary Art - Sale No. 780
8 Apr 91   Old Master Paintings - Sale No. 781
7 May 91   Contemporary Drawings & Watercolours - Sale No. 785
23 May 91   Sale including Old Master Paintings
23 May 91   Sale including Oil Paintings, Watercolours & Sculpture
30 May 91   Old Master Paintings
6 Jun 91   19th Century Paintings, Watercolours & Sculpture - Sale No. 793
19 Jun 91   Existential Realism - Sale No. 796
19 Jun 91   20th Century Drawings & Watercolours - Sale No. 795
20 Jun 91   Contemporary Art - Sale No. 797

F.R   Finarte, Rome - Italy
30 Oct 90   Contemporary Oil Paintings & Watercolours
20 Nov 90   Old Master Paintings
4 Dec 90   19th Century Paintings - Sale No. 763
9 Apr 91   Contemporary Art - Sale No. 783
23 Apr 91   Old Master Paintings & a Collection of Still Lifes
28 May 91   19th Century Oil Paintings & Watercolours - Sale No. 787

FA.PH Freeman Fine Arts, Philadelphia - USA
20 Oct 90   Oil Paintings, Watercolours & Sculpture
6 Dec 90   Oil Paintings, Watercolours & Sculpture
11 Apr 91   Oil Paintings, Watercolours & Sculpture
13 Jun 91   Oil Paintings & Watercolours

FAL.M Falkkloos, Malmo - Sweden
10 Nov 90   Oil Paintings, Watercolours & Sculpture - Sale No. 16
13 Apr 91   Oil Paintings & Watercolours

44

Auction House, code and sale title

FB.M Fraser Auctions, Montreal - Canada
  5 Nov 90 Oil Paintings & Watercolours
  4 Jun 91 Oil Paintings & Watercolours

FB.P Francis Briest, Paris - France
  25 Sep 90 20th Century Watercolours
  29 Oct 90 Contemporary Oil Paintings, Watercolours & Sculpture
  14 Nov 90 19th Century Oil Paintings & Watercolours
  16 Nov 90 Abstract & Contemporary Oil Paintings, Watercolours & Sculpture
  26 Nov 90 The Art of Jean Arp
  6 Feb 91 Modern Paintings & Watercolours
  15 Mar 91 Modern, Abstract & Contemporary Art
  18 Apr 91 The Work of Jean Peyrissac
  24 May 91 19th Century Oil Paintings & Watercolours
  30 May 91 Abstract & Contemporary Art
  14 Jun 91 Modern Art
  15 Jun 91 Impressionist & Modern Oil Paintings, Watercolours & Sculpture
  10 Jul 91 Modern, Abstract & Contemporary Art

FDN.W Fundusz Daru Narodowego, Warsaw - Poland
  10 Feb 91 Oil Paintings & Watercolours

FE.P Feletin, Provins - France
  30 Sep 90 Oil Paintings & Watercolours
  4 Nov 90 Oil Paintings
  2 Dec 90 Oil Paintings & Watercolours
  27 Jan 91 Oil Paintings, Watercolours & Sculpture
  24 Feb 91 Oil Paintings & Watercolours
  31 Mar 91 Oil Paintings & Watercolours
  28 Apr 91 Oil Paintings & Watercolours
  30 Jun 91 Oil Paintings, Watercolours & Sculpture

FEN Fenner & Co, Tavistock - UK
  18 Mar 91 Oil Paintings & Watercolours

FER.M Fernando Duran, Madrid - Spain
  17 Oct 90 Oil Paintings, Watercolours & Sculpture
  11 Dec 90 Oil Paintings, Watercolours & Sculpture
  16 Jan 91 Oil Paintings, Watercolours & Sculpture
  13 Mar 91 Oil Paintings, Watercolours & Sculpture
  8 May 91 Oil Paintings, Watercolours & Sculpture
  25 Jun 91 Oil Paintings, Watercolours & Sculpture

FN.S Fritz Nagel, Stuttgart - Germany
  25 Sep 90 Oil Paintings, Watercolours & Sculpture - Sale No. 332
  4 Dec 90 Oil Paintings, Watercolours & Sculpture - Sale No. 335
  12 Mar 91 Oil Paintings, Watercolours & Sculpture - Sale No. 336
  19 Apr 91 Oil Paintings, Watercolours & Sculpture - Sale No. 337
  8 Jun 91 Oil Paintings, Watercolours & Sculpture (Leipzig)
  18 Jun 91 Oil Paintings, Watercolours & Sculpture - Sale No.338

G.SB Guichard, Saint Brieuc - France
  28 Oct 90 Oil Paintings, Watercolours & Sculpture

G.Z Germann, Zurich - Switzerland
  17 Oct 90 Oil Paintings, Watercolours & Sculpture - Sale No. 9003
  7 Dec 90 Oil Paintings, Watercolours & Sculpture - Sale No. 9004
  24 Apr 91 Modern Oil Paintings, Watercolours & Sculpture - Sale No. 9101
  21 Jun 91 Oil Paintings & Watercolours

GA General Accident, Canterbury - UK
  14 Aug 90 Oil Paintings
  9 Oct 90 Oil Paintings & Watercolours
  29 May 91 Oil Paintings & Watercolours (Worthing)

GAB.G Galerie Pierre-Yves Gabus, Geneva - Switzerland
  2 Dec 90 Oil Paintings, Watercolours & Sculpture
  8 Dec 90 Oil Paintings & Watercolours

GAM Clarke Gammon, Surrey - UK
  23 Oct 90 Oil Paintings & Watercolours
  23 Apr 91 Oil Paintings & Watercolours

GB.B Galerie Bassenge, Berlin - Germany
  7 Dec 90 Oil Paintings, Watercolours & Sculpture - Sale No. 56
  31 May 91 Oil Paintings, Watercolours & Sculpture - Sale No. 57

GC Geering & Colyer, Hawkhurst - UK
  12 Dec 90 Oil Paintings & Watercolours (Nutbourne Manor)
  27 Mar 91 Oil Paintings & Watercolours
  10 Jul 91 Oil Paintings & Watercolours

Auction House, code and sale title

GC.M Gomensoro & Castells, Montevideo - Uruguay
   1 Aug 90 Oil Paintings & Watercolours
   1 Oct 90 Oil Paintings & Watercolours
  15 Oct 90 Oil Paintings & Watercolours
   1 Nov 90 Oil Paintings & Watercolours
  27 May 91 Oil Paintings, Watercolours & Sculpture
   1 Jul 91 Oil Paintings & Watercolours

GD.B Galerie Dobiaschofsky, Berne - Switzerland
  24 Oct 90 Oil Paintings, Watercolours & Sculpture - Sale No. 71
   1 May 91 Oil Paintings & Watercolours

GF.H Peter Gunnemann, Hamburg - Germany
  16 Nov 90 Oil Paintings, Watercolours & Sculpture
  28 Jan 91 Oil Paintings & Watercolours
  16 Feb 91 Oil Paintings, Watercolours & Sculpture

GF.L Galerie Fischer, Lucerne - Switzerland
   6 Nov 90 Oil Paintings, Watercolours & Sculpture - Sale No. 322
  13 Nov 90 Watercolours & Drawings - Sale No. 323
  14 May 91 Oil Paintings, Watercolours & Sculpture - Sale No. 324

GG.TA Gordon Galleries, Tel Aviv - Israel
   1 Jan 91 Oil Paintings, Watercolours & Sculpture - Sale No. 27 Part I & II
   2 Jan 91 Oil Paintings, Watercolours & Sculpture . Sale No. 27 Parts III & IV
  12 Jun 91 Oil Paintings, Watercolours & Sculpture - Sale No. 28

GGL.L Genin, Rambert, Leseuil, Lyon - France
   9 Oct 90 Old Master & Modern Oil Paintings, Watercolours & Sculpture
  18 Mar 91 Oil Paintings, Watercolours & Sculpture

GK.B Galerie Kornfeld, Berne - Switzerland
  19 Jun 91 19/20th Century Oil Paintings & Watercolours -Sale No. 205 & 206 Part II
  21 Jun 91 19/20th Century Oil Paintings & Watercolours - Sale No. 206 Part I

GK.Z Galerie Koller, Zurich - Switzerland
  19 Sep 90 Oil Paintings, Watercolours & Sculpture - Sale No. 76
  16 Nov 90 Oil Paintings, Watercolours & Sculpture - Sale No. 77
  13 Mar 91 Oil Paintings, Watercolours & Sculpture - Sale No. 78
  27 May 91 Oil Paintings, Watercolours & Sculpture - Sale No. 79

GL.P Guy Loudmer, Paris - France
   6 Oct 90 Modern Oil Paintings & Watercolours
  28 Oct 90 Contemporary & Abstract Art
  25 Nov 90 Modern Paintings from the Alain Delon Collection
  26 Nov 90 Important Modern Paintings
   7 Dec 90 Modern Oil Paintings & Watercolours
  14 Dec 90 Sale including Sculpture
  16 Dec 90 Abstract & Contemporary Art
  18 Jan 91 Modern Oil Paintings & Watercolours
  20 Jan 91 Modern Oil Paintings & Watercolours
  14 Feb 91 Abstract & Contemporary Paintings
  11 Mar 91 Modern & Contemporary Art
  17 Mar 91 Modern Oil Paintings, Watercolours & Sculpture
   6 Apr 91 Art Deco - Art Nouveau
  14 Apr 91 Contemporary Jewish Oil Paintings, Watercolours & Sculpture
  25 May 91 Important Modern Paintings
  29 May 91 Modern, Abstract & Contemporary Art
   2 Jun 91 Abstract & Contemporary Art
  16 Jun 91 Modern Oil Paintings, Watercolours & Sculpture
   1 Jul 91 Oil Paintings & Watercolours
   4 Jul 91 Modern, Abstract & Contemporary Art

GM.B Galerie Moderne, Brussels - Belgium
  28 Aug 90 Oil Paintings, Watercolours & Sculpture
  25 Sep 90 Oil Paintings & Watercolours
  24 Oct 90 Oil Paintings, Watercolours & Sculpture
  21 Nov 90 Oil Paintings & Watercolours
  18 Dec 90 Oil Paintings, Watercolours & Sculpture - Evening Sale
  18 Dec 90 Oil Paintings & Watercolours - Sale No. 90-12
  15 Jan 91 Oil Paintings, Watercolours & Sculpture
  12 Feb 91 Oil Paintings, Watercolours & Sculpture - Sale No. 91-02
  12 Mar 91 Oil Paintings, Watercolours & Sculpture
   9 Apr 91 Oil Paintings & Watercolours - Sale No. 91-04
  14 May 91 Oil Paintings, Watercolours & Sculpture - Sale No. 91-05
  11 Jun 91 Oil Paintings & Watercolours - Sale No. 91-06
  12 Jun 91 Evening Sale of Oil Paintings & Watercolours

GO.G Goteborgs Auktionsverk, Goteborg - Sweden
  17 Oct 90 Watercolours
  20 Nov 90 Oil Paintings & Watercolours

Auction House, code and sale title

GO.G Goteborgs Auktionsverk, Goteborg - Sweden
  9 Apr 91 Oil Paintings, Watercolours & Sculpture
14 May91 Oil Paintings & Watercolours

GRA.B Jochen Granier, Bielefeld - Germany
29 Sep 90 Old Master & Modern Oil Paintings & Watercolours - Sale No. 29
22 Mar 91 Oil Paintings & Watercolours - Sale No. 30

GRA.P Granville, Granville - France
28 Oct 90 Modern Oil Paintings & Watercolours

GRO.B Grogan & Company, Massachusetts - USA
25 Oct 90 Oil Paintings, Watercolours & Sculpture
30 Jan 91 Oil Paintings, Watercolours & Sculpture
21 May91 Oil Paintings, Watercolours & Sculpture
 3 Jun 91 Oil Paintings, Watercolours & Sculpture

GS.B Galerie Stuker, Berne - Switzerland
22 May91 Oil Paintings, Watercolours & Sculpture

GSP Graves Son & Pilcher, Hove - UK
24 Aug 90 Oil Paintings & Watercolours
13 Sep 90 Oil Paintings
12 Oct 90 Oil Paintings, Watercolours & Sculpture
 9 Nov 90 Oil Paintings & Watercolours
 7 Dec 90 Oil Paintings & Watercolours
10 Jan 91 Oil Paintings & Watercolours
 7 Feb 91 Oil Paintings & Watercolours
14 Mar91 Oil Paintings & Watercolours
11 Apr 91 Oil Paintings & Watercolours
13 Jun 91 Oil Paintings & Watercolours
11 Jul 91 Oil Paintings & Watercolours

H Holloways, Banbury - UK
25 Sep 90 Oil Paintings & Watercolours
 2 Oct 90 Sculptures
 9 Apr 91 Oil Paintings & Watercolours
17 Apr 91 Oil Paintings & Watercolours
14 May91 Oil Paintings & Watercolours
15 May91 Oil Paintings & Watercolours

H.A Holz, Arles - France
18 Nov 90 Oil Paintings & Watercolours

H.AP Hours, Aix-en-Provence - France
13 Oct 90 Oil Paintings & Watercolours

H.C Hindman Galleries, Chicago - USA
 7 Sep 90 Sale including Oil Paintings & Watercolours
14 Oct 90 Oil Paintings, Watercolours & Sculpture
10 Dec 90 Oil Paintings & Watercolours
10 Mar91 Oil Paintings, Watercolours & Sculpture
12 May91 Oil Paintings, Watercolours & Sculpture
23 Jun 91 Oil Paintings & Watercolours

HAR Andrew Hartley, Ilkley - UK
15 Aug 90 Oil Paintings & Watercolours
16 Oct 90 Sale including Oil Paintings & Watercolours
11 Dec 90 Oil Paintings & Watercolours
20 Feb 91 Oil Paintings & Watercolours
16 Apr 91 Oil Paintings & Watercolours
11 Jun 91 Oil Paintings & Watercolours

HB Heathcote Ball, Leicester - UK
29 Nov 90 Oil Paintings & Watercolours
13 Dec 90 Oil Paintings & Watercolours
 7 Feb 91 Oil Paintings & Watercolours
 2 May91 Oil Paintings, Watercolours & Sculpture

HC Hobbs & Chambers, Cheltenham - UK
12 Oct 90 Oil Paintings & Watercolours
18 Dec 90 Oil Paintings & Watercolours
21 Jun 91 Oil Paintings & Watercolours

HC.P Herve Chayette, Paris - France
13 Nov 90 Hungarian & Russian Art
17 Nov 90 Oil Paintings & Watercolours
 5 Dec 90 Modern Oil Paintings & Watercolours
28 Jan 91 Studio of Pereira Leal
12 Feb 91 Modern Art
 6 Mar91 Oil Paintings & Watercolours

Auction House, code and sale title

HC.P Herve Chayette, Paris - France
5 Jun 91   The Art of Robert Pikelny
14 Jun 91   Art Nouveau & Art Deco

HF.NY Habsburg, New York - USA
10 Apr 91   Old Master & 19th Century Paintings

HG.C Hanzel Galleries, Chicago - USA
21 Oct 90   Oil Paintings, Watercolours & Sculpture
28 Apr 91   American & European Oil Paintings, Watercolours & Sculpture

HN.H Hauswedell & Nolte, Hamburg - Germany
6 Jun 91   Modern Art II - Sale No. 289
7 Jun 91   Modern Art I - Sale No. 289
8 Jun 91   Art After 1945 - Sale No. 290

HO.ED Hodgins, Calgary - Canada
12 Nov 90   Oil Paintings & Watercolours
27 May 91   Oil Paintings, Watercolours & Sculpture

HO.P Horn, Poznan - Poland
23 Mar 91   Oil Paintings & Watercolours

HOR.H Horhammer, Helsinki - Finland
24 Nov 90   Oil Paintings, Watercolours & Sculpture - Sale No. 58
20 Apr 91   Oil Paintings, Watercolours & Sculpture - Sale No. 62
14 May 91   Oil Paintings & Watercolours - Sale No. 63

HR   Chancellors, Kingston upon Thames - UK
21 Feb 91   Oil Paintings & Watercolours - Chancellors (Kingston-upon-Thames)

HS   Henry Spencer, Retford - UK
7 Aug 90   Oil Paintings & Watercolours
13 Aug 90   Watercolours of Donald McGill
18 Sep 90   Oil Paintings & Watercolours
24 Oct 90   Oil Paintings & Watercolours
30 Oct 90   Oil Paintings & Watercolours (Carmarthen)
26 Nov 90   Sale including Oil Paintings, Watercolours & Sculpture
11 Dec 90   Oil Paintings & Watercolours (Carmarthen)
28 Jan 91   Oil Paintings & Watercolours
18 Feb 91   Sale including Sculpture
11 Mar 91   Oil Paintings & Watercolours
12 Mar 91   Sale at Gamston Manor
22 Apr 91   Sculpture
29 Apr 91   Oil Paintings & Watercolours
30 Apr 91   Oil Paintings
11 Jun 91   Oil Paintings & Watercolours (Dyfed)
24 Jun 91   Oil Paintings, Watercolours & Miniatures
23 Jul 91   Oil Paintings & Watercolours (Dyfed)
29 Jul 91   Oil Paintings & Watercolours

HUN   Hunts, Taunton - UK
29 Aug 90   Oil Paintings & Watercolours
26 Sep 90   Oil Paintings & Watercolours
31 Oct 90   Oil Paintings & Watercolours
30 Jan 91   Oil Paintings & Watercolours
27 Mar 91   Oil Paintings & Watercolours
24 Apr 91   Oil Paintings & Watercolours
26 Jun 91   Oil Paintings & Watercolours
31 Jul 91   Oil Paintings & Watercolours

HW.H   Henner Wachholtz KG, Hamburg - Germany
1 Dec 90   Oil Paintings & Watercolours - Sale No. 9
6 Jun 91   Oil Paintings & Watercolours - Sale No. 10

I.N   Ionesco, Neuilly - France
30 Oct 90   19/20th Century Oil Paintings & Watercolours
11 Nov 90   Old Master Oil Paintings, Watercolours & Sculpture
14 Nov 90   Modern Oil Paintings & Watercolours
15 Nov 90   Abstract Oil Paintings, Watercolours & Sculpture
4 Dec 90   Abstract & Contemporary Art
5 Dec 90   Des artistes pour des artistes
3 Feb 91   Modern Oil Paintings & Watercolours
7 Apr 91   Modern Oil Paintings & Watercolours
16 Apr 91   Contemporary Oil Paintings, Watercolours & Sculpture
11 Jun 91   Modern Oil Paintings & Watercolours
30 Jun 91   Abstract & Contemporary Art

IH.NY Illustration House, New York - USA
1 Jun 91   Illustration & Cartoon Art

Auction House, code and sale title

IMC Ibbett Mosely, Sevenoaks - UK
11 Oct 90   Oil Paintings & Watercolours
13 Jun 91   Oil Paintings & Watercolours

J.M Joel, Victoria - Australia
13 Nov 90   Oil Paintings, Watercolours & Sculpture
16 Apr 91   Oil Paintings, Watercolours & Sculpture

JH Jacobs & Hunt, Petersfield - UK
24 May 91   Oil Paintings & Watercolours

JM.P Morelle, Paris - France
14 Dec 90   19/20th Century Watercolours
12 Apr 91   19/20th Century Oil Paintings & Watercolours
19 Jun 91   Oil Paintings & Watercolours

JOY.T Joyner Fine Art, Toronto - Canada
20 Nov 90   Canadian Art
14 May 91   Canadian Art

JPB.P Bondu, Paris - France
12 Feb 91   The Art of Adrienne Jouclard

JRB.C James Bakker, Cambridge - USA
18 Nov 90   Oil Paintings, Watercolours & Sculpture
14 Apr 91   Oil Paintings & Watercolours
25 Jun 91   Oil Paintings, Watercolours & Sculpture

JRL.S James R Lawson, Sydney - Australia
25 Sep 90   Modern Paintings & Watercolours
27 Nov 90   Australian & European Paintings
26 Mar 91   Oil Paintings & Watercolours
21 May 91   Oil Paintings & Watercolours
16 Jul 91   Oil Paintings & Watercolours

JT James Thompson, Kirby Lonsdale - UK
19 Sep 90   Oil Paintings & Watercolours
21 Nov 90   Oil Paintings & Watercolours
23 Jan 91   Oil Paintings & Watercolours
20 Mar 91   Oil Paintings & Watercolours
22 May 91   Oil Paintings & Watercolours
24 Jul 91   Oil Paintings & Watercolours

K Keys, Aylesham - UK
17 Aug 90   English & Continental Oil Paintings & Watercolours
12 Oct 90   English & Continental Oil Paintings & Watercolours
7 Dec 90   Oil Paintings & Watercolours
8 Feb 91   Oil Paintings & Watercolours
19 Apr 91   Oil Paintings & Watercolours
14 Jun 91   Oil Paintings & Watercolours

KF.M Karl & Faber, Munich - Germany
28 Nov 90   Oil Paintings, Watercolours & Sculpture - Sale No. 180
28 May 91   Oil Paintings, Watercolours & Sculpture - Sale No. 181

KH.K Kunsthallen, Copenhagen - Denmark
29 Aug 90   Oil Paintings & Watercolours
19 Sep 90   Oil Paintings, Watercolours & Sculpture - Sale No. 391
31 Oct 90   Modern Oil Paintings, Watercolours & Sculpture - Sale No. 393
14 Nov 90   Modern Oil Paintings, Watercolours & Sculpture - Sale No. 394
5 Dec 90   Oil Paintings & Watercolours - Sale No. 395
13 Feb 91   Modern Oil Paintings & Watercolours - Sale No. 397
1 May 91   Oil Paintings, Watercolours & Sculpture - Sale No. 401
29 May 91   Modern Oil Paintings & Watercolours - Sale No. 402

KING Alder King, Bath - UK
21 Feb 91   Oil Paintings & Watercolours

KM.K Kunsthaus am Museum, Cologne - Germany
26 Oct 90   Oil Paintings, Watercolours & Sculpture - Sale No. 131
24 Nov 90   Modern Oil Paintings, Watercolours & Sculpture - Sale No. 132
20 Mar 91   Oil Paintings, Watercolours & Sculpture - Sale No. 134
26 Apr 91   Modern Art - Sale No. 135
26 Jun 91   Oil Paintings, Watercolours & Sculpture - Sale No. 136

KRA.D Krauth, Dusseldorf - Germany
13 Oct 90   Oil Paintings, Watercolours & Sculpture - Sale No. 75
2 Mar 91   Oil Paintings, Watercolours & Sculptures

KV.L Kunstgalerij de Vuyst, Lokeren - Belgium
6 Oct 90   Old Master & Modern Oil Paintings & Watercolours

Auction House, code and sale title

KV.L Kunstgalerij de Vuyst, Lokeren - Belgium
  8 Dec 90 Oil Paintings, Watercolours & Sculpture - Sale No. 68
 16 Mar 91 Oil Paintings, Watercolours & Sculpture - Sale No. 69
 25 May 91 Oil Paintings, Watercolours & Sculpture - Sale No. 70

L   Lane, Penzance - UK
 27 Sep 90 Oil Paintings & Watercolours
 14 Mar 91 Oil Paintings & Watercolours
 13 Jun 91 Oil Paintings & Watercolours

L.C LeLievre, Chartres - France
 21 Oct 90 Old Master & Modern Oil Paintings, Watercolours & Sculpture
 25 Nov 90 Oil Paintings, Watercolours & Sculpture
 17 Mar 91 Oil Paintings, Watercolours & Sculpture
 12 May 91 Oil Paintings, Watercolours & Sculpture

L.K Lempertz, Cologne - Germany
 20 Nov 90 Oil Paintings, Watercolours & Sculpture - Sale No. 656
 22 Nov 90 Oil Paintings, Watercolours & Sculpture - Sale No. 658
 10 Dec 90 Oil Paintings & Watercolours - Sale No. 660
 27 May 91 Oil Paintings, Watercolours & Sculpture - Sale No. 664
 14 Jun 91 Contemporary Art - Sale No. 667
 15 Jun 91 Modern Art - Sale No. 668

L.V Lunds Auctioneers, Victoria - Canada
 20 Aug 90 Oil Paintings & Watercolours
 10 Dec 90 Oil Paintings & Watercolours
 15 Apr 91 Oil Paintings & Watercolours
 17 Jun 91 Oil Paintings & Watercolours

LAE.L Louisiana Auction Exchange, Louisiana - USA
  1 Sep 90 Oil Paintings & Watercolours
 13 Oct 90 Oil Paintings & Watercolours
  1 Dec 90 American & European Paintings
 12 Jan 91 Oil Paintings & Watercolours
 23 Mar 91 American & European Oil Paintings & Watercolours
  1 Jun 91 Oil Paintings & Watercolours

LC.P Libert, Castor. Paris - France
 17 Oct 90 Oil Paintings & Watercolours
 29 Oct 90 Modern Oil Paintings, Watercolours & Sculpture
 25 Nov 90 20th Century Oil Paintings & Watercolours
 21 Mar 91 Old Master & Modern Oil Paintings, Watercolours & Sculpture
 19 Jun 91 Oil Paintings, Watercolours & Sculpture
 28 Jun 91 Old Master Drawings & Watercolours

LD.P Lenormand, Paris - France
  9 Nov 90 Art Nouveau - Art Deco
  7 Dec 90 The Art of Rene Buthaud
 10 Dec 90 Modern Oil Paintings, Watercolours & Sculpture
 19 Dec 90 Old Master & 19th Century Oil Paintings & Watercolours
  6 Feb 91 Watercolours
 31 May 91 Old Master Paintings
  7 Jun 91 Modern Oil Paintings & Watercolours

LE   Locke & England, Leamington Spa - UK
  6 Sep 90 Oil Paintings & Watercolours
 18 Oct 90 Oil Paintings, Watercolours & Sculpture
  6 Dec 90 Oil Paintings & Watercolours
 28 Feb 91 Oil Paintings & Watercolours
 18 Apr 91 Oil Paintings & Watercolours
 13 Jun 91 Oil Paintings & Watercolours

LEB.P Le Blanc, Paris - France
 14 Dec 90 Old Master & 19th Century Watercolours
  4 Feb 91 Old Master & Modern Oil Paintings & Sculpture
 27 Feb 91 Drawings & Watercolours

LGB.P Laurin Guilloux Buffetaud Tailleur, Paris - France
 16 Nov 90 Oil Paintings & Watercolours
  4 Feb 91 Modern Oil Paintings & Watercolours
  5 Apr 91 Modern Oil Paintings & Watercolours
 17 Apr 91 Modern Oil Paintings & Watercolours
 29 Apr 91 Modern Oil Paintings & Watercolours
 17 May 91 Oil Paintings & Watercolours
  1 Jul 91 Oil Paintings, Watercolours & Sculpture
  3 Jul 91 Modern Oil Paintings & Watercolours

LIT.L Litchfield Auction Gallery, Litchfield - USA
  4 Aug 90 Oil Paintings & Watercolours
 25 Aug 90 Oil Paintings & Watercolours

50

LIT.L Litchfield Auction Gallery, Litchfield - USA
  9 Sep 90 Oil Paintings & Watercolours
23 Sep 90 Sale including Oil Paintings & Watercolours
  7 Oct 90 American & European Oil Paintings & Watercolours
27 Oct 90 Oil Paintings & Watercolours
11 Nov 90 Oil Paintings & Watercolours
16 Dec 90 Oil Paintings & Watercolours
  6 Jan 91 Oil Paintings & Watercolours
27 Jan 91 Oil Paintings & Watercolours
10 Feb 91 Oil Paintings & Watercolours
  3 Mar 91 Oil Paintings & Watercolours
24 Mar 91 Oil Paintings & Watercolours
  7 Apr 91 Oil Paintings & Watercolours
28 Apr 91 American Oil Paintings & Watercolours
19 May 91 Oil Paintings & Watercolours
  9 Jun 91 Oil Paintings, Watercolours & Sculpture
30 Jun 91 Oil Paintings & Watercolours
21 Jul 91 Oil Paintings & Watercolours

LJ   Langlois, Jersey - UK
20 Sep 90 Oil Paintings & Watercolours
12 Dec 90 Oil Paintings & Watercolours
10 Apr 91 Oil Paintings & Watercolours

LR   Lots Road Auction Galleries, London - UK
24 Jun 91 Oil Paintings & Watercolours

LS   Lacy Scott, Bury St.Edmunds - UK
  3 Dec 90 Oil Paintings & Watercolours
24 Jun 91 Oil Paintings & Watercolours

LT.P Lombrail et Teucquam, Paris - France
17 Oct 90 19th Century & Modern Paintings, Watercolours & Sculpture
27 Oct 90 19th Century & Modern Paintings, Watercolours & Sculpture
  8 Dec 90 Modern Oil Paintings, Watercolours & Sculpture
27 Jan 91 Oil Paintings & Watercolours by Roland Hamon
  3 Feb 91 19th Century & Modern Oil Paintings, Watercolours & Sculpture
10 Mar 91 Oil Paintings & Watercolours
  7 Apr 91 Modern Oil Paintings, Watercolours & Sculpture
  5 May 91 Oil Paintings & Watercolours
19 May 91 Modern Oil Paintings & Watercolours
  2 Jun 91 Oil Paintings, Watercolours & Sculpture
16 Jun 91 Contemporary Art
  4 Jul 91 Oil Paintings, Watercolours & Sculpture

LV   Thomas Love & Sons Ltd, Perth - UK
31 Oct 90 Oil Paintings & Watercolours

LW   Lawrences, Bletchingley - UK
12 Sep 90 Oil Paintings & Watercolours
23 Oct 90 Oil Paintings & Watercolours
  3 Dec 90 Oil Paintings & Watercolours
29 Jan 91 Oil Paintings & Watercolours
12 Mar 91 Oil Paintings & Watercolours
11 Jun 91 Oil Paintings & Watercolours
23 Jul 91 Oil Paintings & Watercolours

M   Mallams, Oxford - UK
20 Sep 90 Oil Paintings & Watercolours
25 Oct 90 Oil Paintings & Watercolours
13 Dec 90 Oil Paintings & Watercolours

M.V Martin et Desbenoit, Versailles - France
28 Oct 90 Modern Oil Paintings & Watercolours
11 Nov 90 17/18th Century Oil Paintings & Watercolours
  2 Dec 90 Modern Oil Paintings & Watercolours
16 Dec 90 Old Master Oil Paintings & Watercolours
17 Mar 91 Oil Paintings, Watercolours & Sculpture

MA.V Maynards, Vancouver - Canada
30 Oct 90 Oil Paintings & Watercolours
20 Mar 91 Oil Paintings & Watercolours
22 May 91 Oil Paintings & Watercolours
10 Jul 91 Oil Paintings & Watercolours

MB.P Boscher, Paris - France
19 Oct 90 Oil Paintings & Watercolours
14 Jun 91 Oil Paintings & Watercolours

MCB McCartney Fine Art, Ludlow - UK
19 Nov 90 Oil Paintings & Watercolours

Auction House, code and sale title

ME   Morgan Evans, Anglesey - UK
15 Sep 90   Oil Paintings & Watercolours
17 Jul 91   Oil Paintings & Watercolours

MF.P Ferri, Paris - France
20 Nov 90   Modern Oil Paintings & Watercolours

MFA.C Mystic Fine Arts, Connecticut - USA
30 Aug 90   Oil Paintings & Watercolours
29 Nov 90   Oil Paintings & Watercolours
28 Feb 91   Oil Paintings & Watercolours

MGS.S Mason Gray & Strange, Sydney - Australia
17 Sep 90   Fine Australian & European Paintings
19 Nov 90   Oil Paintings & Watercolours
18 Mar 91   Oil Paintings & Watercolours
17 Jun 91   Oil Paintings & Watercolours

MJ.P Millon Jutheau, Paris - France
8 Oct 90   The Art of Georges Moullade
8 Oct 90   The Art of Jean Corbet
22 Oct 90   The Art of Andre Dignimont
24 Apr 91   Oil Paintings, Watercolours & Sculpture
27 Apr 91   Contemporary Art

MMB   Messenger, May & Baverstock, Godalming - UK
5 Sep 90   Oil Paintings & Watercolours
7 Oct 90   Oil Paintings & Watercolours
12 Dec 90   Oil Paintings & Watercolours
27 Feb 91   Oil Paintings & Watercolours
24 Apr 91   Oil Paintings, Watercolours & Sculpture

MN   Michael Newman, Plymouth - UK
29 Aug 90   Oil Paintings & Watercolours

MO   Morphets, Harrogate - UK
14 Feb 91   Oil Paintings & Watercolours
11 Apr 91   Oil Paintings & Watercolours   .
13 Jun 91   Oil Paintings & Watercolours

MOR.P John Moran, Pasadena - USA
12 Feb 91   Oil Paintings & Watercolours
11 Jun 91   Oil Paintings & Watercolours

N   Neale & Son, Nottingham - UK
15 Feb 91   Oil Paintings & Watercolours
12 Mar 91   Oil Paintings & Watercolours (Derby)

N.M   Neumeister, Munich - Germany
19 Sep 90   Oil Paintings, Watercolours & Sculpture
21 Sep 90   Oil Paintings & Watercolours - Sale No. 57
7 Nov 90   Oil Paintings, Watercolours & Sculpture - Sale No. 58
24 Nov 90   Oil Paintings, Watercolours & Sculpture - Sale No. 8
11 Dec 90   Evening Auction of Sculpture
12 Dec 90   Oil Paintings & Watercolours - Sale No. 259
13 Dec 90   Oil Paintings, Watercolours & Sculpture - Sale No. 59
6 Feb 91   Oil Paintings, Watercolours & Sculpture
13 Mar 91   Oil Paintings, Watercolours & Sculpture - Sale No. 260
14 Mar 91   Oil Paintings & Watercolours - Sale No. 61
24 Apr 91   Oil Paintings & Watercolours - Auction No. 62
25 May 91   Modern Oil Paintings, Watercolours & Sculpture - Sale No. 9
11 Jun 91   Sculpture - Sale No. 261
12 Jun 91   Oil Paintings & Watercolours - Sale No. 262

NA.BA Naon & Cia, Buenos Aries - Argentina
21 Nov 90   Oil Paintings, Watercolours & Sculpture

NM.P Neret-Minet, Paris - France
16 Nov 90   Old Master & Modern Oil Paintings, Watercolours & Sculpture
6 Dec 90   Oil Paintings, Watercolours & Sculpture
12 Dec 90   Modern Oil Paintings, Watercolours & Sculpture
26 Apr 91   Oil Paintings, Watercolours & Sculpture
10 Jun 91   Oil Paintings & Watercolours

OD.P Oger, Dumont, Paris - France
17 Nov 90   Old Master Oil Paintings & Watercolours
27 May 91   Oil Paintings, Watercolours & Sculpture
21 Jun 91   Important Modern Paintings
3 Jul 91   Oil Paintings & Watercolours

OT   Osmond Tricks with Allen & Harris, Bristol - UK
  4 Sep 90 Oil Paintings & Watercolours
27 Nov 90 Oil Paintings & Watercolours
29 Jan 91 Oil Paintings & Watercolours
19 Mar 91 Oil Paintings & Watercolours - Allen & Harris
30 Apr 91 Oil Paintings & Watercolours
18 Jun 91 Oil Paintings & Watercolours

P.Q   Pinneys, Montreal - Canada
  4 Dec 90 Canadian & European Oil Paintings & Watercolours

P.V   Perrin, Versailles - France
30 Sep 90 Oil Paintings & Watercolours
21 Oct 90 Modern Oil Paintings, Watercolours & Sculpture
18 Nov 90 Oil Paintings & Watercolours
25 Nov 90 Old Master & Modern Oil Paintings, Watercolours & Sculpture
16 Dec 90 Modern & Contemporary Art
24 Feb 91 Modern Oil Paintings & Watercolours
21 Apr 91 Abstract & Contemporary Art
16 Jun 91 Oil Paintings, Watercolours & Sculpture
23 Jun 91 Abstract & Contemporary Oil Paintings, Watercolours & Sculpture

PER.M Peron, Melun - France
  1 Dec 90 19th Century French Landscape Masters (Barbizon)

PH   Phillips, London - UK
10 Sep 90 English & European Watercolours
18 Sep 90 19th Century Oil Paintings & Sculpture
18 Sep 90 Modern British & Irish Oil Paintings, Watercolours & Sculpture
  8 Oct 90 English & European Watercolours
15 Oct 90 19/20th Century Continental Oil Paintings, Watercolours & Sculpture
30 Oct 90 Old Master Paintings
  6 Nov 90 British & Irish Oil Paintings, Watercolours & Sculpture
12 Nov 90 Fine English Watercolours & Drawings
13 Nov 90 British & Victorian Paintings
20 Nov 90 British, Victorian & Topographical Paintings & Watercolours
20 Nov 90 Sale including Sculpture
27 Nov 90 19th Century European Paintings & Watercolours
  5 Dec 90 Modern Paintings & Drawings
11 Dec 90 Fine Old Master Paintings
12 Dec 90 Old Master Drawings
12 Dec 90 European Works of Art
17 Dec 90 English & European Drawings & Watercolours
22 Jan 91 British & Victorian Paintings
29 Jan 91 Modern British & Irish Paintings
25 Feb 91 English & European Drawings & Watercolours
26 Feb 91 19th Century Sculpture & Works of Art
  5 Mar 91 Old Master Paintings
  5 Mar 91 Modern & Contemporary Oil Paintings, Watercolours & Sculpture
12 Mar 91 19th Century European Paintings & Watercolours
26 Mar 91 British, Victorian & Animal Pictures
16 Apr 91 Fine Old Master Paintings
17 Apr 91 European Sculpture & Works of Art
22 Apr 91 English Watercolours, Drawings & Miniatures
30 Apr 91 British & Victorian Paintings
30 Apr 91 19th Century Sculpture & Works of Art
  7 May 91 Modern British & Irish Paintings & Sculpture
20 May 91 English & European Drawings & Watercolours
  4 Jun 91 British & Irish Traditional Modern Paintings & Sculpture
11 Jun 91 Oil Paintings & Watercolours from Studio of Sir Ponsonby Staples
18 Jun 91 19th Century European Paintings & Watercolours
25 Jun 91 Sale including Sculpture
  2 Jul 91 Fine Old Master Paintings
  9 Jul 91 British & Victorian Paintings
15 Jul 91 English Watercolours. Drawings & Portrait Miniatures

PH.T Phillips, Toronto - Canada
28 Nov 90 European Oil Paintings & Watercolours

PHB   Phillips, Bath - UK
10 Dec 90 Oil Paintings & Watercolours
  4 Mar 91 Oil Paintings & Watercolours
  3 Jun 91 Oil Paintings & Watercolours

PHC   Phillips, Chester - UK
19 Sep 90 Oil Paintings & Watercolours
26 Feb 91 Oil Paintings & Watercolours
29 May 91 Oil Paintings & Watercolours
16 Jul 91 Golfing Memorabilia

THE POCKET PICTURE PRICE GUIDE
to the U.K art market

Summarised from: over 27,000 sale results exclusively from British auctioneers
for a complete calendar year to show: by medium for each artist/sculptor,
the highest, lowest, median price, the total value and the total number of works sold:
pocket sized - 400 pages   1991 edition - £17.00

Name	No:	Total Sales Value	lowest	-Prices- median	*example:* highest
CONROY, Stephen (1964-) British					
oil	1	40,000		40,000	
wc/d	7	13,500	600	1,500	3,300
CONSTABLE (19/20th C) British					
oil	1	1,050		1,050	
CONSTABLE, James Lawson (1890-?) British					
oil	1	580		580	
CONSTABLE, John (1776-1837) British					
Oil	3	10,220,000	180,000	240,000	9,800,000
wc/d	5	31,300	2,800	3,000	13,000
CONSTABLE, John (after) (1776-1837) British					
oil	1	3,400		3,400	

Art Sales Index Ltd.,1 Thames Street, Weybridge, Surrey KT13 8JG, UK.
tel: (0932) 856426   fax: (0932) 842482

54

Auction House, code and sale title

PHE   Phillips, Edinburgh - UK
  7 Sep 90   Oil Paintings & Watercolours
21 Sep 90   Watercolours
  2 Nov 90   Oil Paintings
23 Nov 90   Watercolours
  5 Dec 90   20th Century Paintings
  1 Feb 91   Oil Paintings & Watercolours
  1 Mar 91   Oil Paintings
22 Mar 91   Watercolours
  5 Apr 91   Oil Paintings & Watercolours
  3 May 91   Fine Paintings & Sculpture
  7 Jun 91   Oil Paintings
  5 Jul 91   Oil Paintings & Watercolours
26 Jul 91   Watercolours & Prints

PHF   Phillips, Folkestone - UK
27 Sep 90   Oil Paintings, Watercolours & Sculpture

PHG   Phillips, Glasgow - UK
  1 Oct 90   Sale of Furniture including Sculpture
10 Oct 90   Scottish Contemporary Art
17 Oct 90   19th Century Oil Paintings & Watercolours
12 Dec 90   Small Contemporary Pictures
  8 Apr 91   Sale including Sculpture
28 May 91   Oil Painting, Watercolours & Sculpture (Savoy Croft, Ayr)
19 Jun 91   Scottish Contemporary Art

PHI   Phillips, Ipswich - UK
  8 Nov 90   Oil Paintings & Watercolours
  4 Jul 91   Oil Paintings & Watercolours

PHK   Phillips, Knowle - UK
  5 Jun 91   Oil Paintings & Watercolours

PHL   Phillips, Leeds - UK
12 Sep 90   Oil Paintings & Watercolours
17 Oct 90   Yorkshire & Sporting Pictures
  5 Dec 90   Oil Paintings & Watercolours
13 Feb 91   Oil Paintings & Watercolours
  1 May 91   Oil Paintings & Watercolours

PHM   Phillips, Marylebone - UK
  3 Aug 90   Oil Paintings & Watercolours
10 Aug 90   Oil Paintings & Watercolours
31 Aug 90   Oil Paintings & Watercolours
  7 Sep 90   Oil Paintings & Watercolours
21 Sep 90   Oil Paintings & Watercolours
12 Oct 90   Oil Paintings & Watercolours
19 Oct 90   Oil Paintings & Watercolours
26 Oct 90   Old Master Paintings
  2 Nov 90   Oil Paintings & Watercolours
23 Nov 90   Oil Paintings & Watercolours
  7 Dec 90   20th Century British Pictures
14 Dec 90   Old Master Paintings

PHP   Phillips, Plymouth - UK
  8 Aug 90   Marine Oil Paintings,& Watercolours

PHS   Phillips, Sevenoaks - UK
20 Sep 90   Oil Paintings & Watercolours
12 Dec 90   Sale including Oil Paintings & Watercolours
27 Mar 91   Sale including Oil Paintings & Watercolours
19 Jun 91   Oil Paintings & Watercolours

PHX   Phillips, Exeter - UK
29 Nov 90   Sale Including Oil Paintings & Watercolours
14 Mar 91   Oil Paintings & Watercolours
18 Jul 91   Oil Paintings & Watercolours

PLF.P Poulain et Le Fur, Paris - France
28 Oct 90   Art Nouveau & Art Deco
16 Nov 90   Old Master Oil Paintings, Watercolours & Sculpture
23 Nov 90   Modern Oil Paintings & Watercolours
  4 Feb 91   Watercolours
25 Mar 91   Oil Paintings, Watercolours & Sculpture
22 May 91   Old Master Watercolours & Drawings
  3 Jul 91   Oil Paintings, Watercolours & Sculpture

PO.BA Posadas Remates S.A., Buenos Aries - Argentina
11 Sep 90   Oil Paintings & Watercolours
27 Nov 90   Oil Paintings & Watercolours

Auction House, code and sale title

PO.BA Posadas Remates S.A., Buenos Aries - Argentina
22 Apr 91   Oil Paintings & Watercolours

PO.M Porton de San Pedro, Montevideo - Uruguay
1 Nov 90   Oil Paintings & Watercolours

PPB.K Palac pod Baranami, Krakow - Poland
3 Mar 91   Oil Paintings & Watercolours

PPB.P Pescheteau, Paris - France
26 Oct 90   Oil Paintings & Watercolours
13 Nov 90   Art Nouveau - Art Deco
20 Nov 90   Old Master & Modern Oil Paintings, Watercolours & Sculpture
28 Jan 91   Modern Oil Paintings, Watercolours & Sculpture
4 Apr 91   Oil Paintings & Watercolours
16 Apr 91   Modern Oil Paintings & Watercolours
13 May91   Modern Oil Paintings & Watercolours

PR.P Renaud, Paris - France
24 Jun 91   Oil Paintings & Watercolours

PSA.W Polswiss Art, Warsaw - Poland
26 Jan 91   Oil Paintings & Watercolours
2 Mar 91   Oil Paintings & Watercolours

QWA.P Quay & Watine-Arnault, Paris - France
3 Oct 90   Soviet Art
11 Oct 90   19th Century & Modern Oil Paintings, Watercolours & Sculpture
28 Oct 90   Animal Paintings, Watercolours & Sculpture
29 Nov 90   Provence Art
13 Dec 90   19/20th Century Oil Paintings, Watercolours & Sculpture
25 Mar 91   Animal Paintings & Sculpture
16 Apr 91   Art Nouveau
5 Jul 91   Art Nouveau & Art Deco

R.P Rogeon, Paris - France
28 Oct 90   Contemporary Oil Paintings, Watercolours & Sculpture
7 Feb 91   L'Or de L'Art
14 Apr 91   Modern Oil Paintings, Watercolours & Sculpture

R.T Ritchie, Toronto - Canada
3 Dec 90   Canadian Art
4 Dec 90   European & American Art
3 Jun 91   Canadian Art
4 Jun 91   European, American & Russian Art

RAS.K Rasmussen, Copenhagen - Denmark
22 Aug 90   Oil Paintings & Watercolours
25 Sep 90   Oil Paintings & Watercolours - Sale No. 544
10 Oct 90   Modern Oil Paintings, Watercolours & Sculpture - Sale No. 545
14 Nov 90   Oil Paintings & Watercolours - Sale No. 548
21 Nov 90   Sale Including Sculpture - Sale No. 548 - Part 2
4 Dec 90   The Art of Knud Muhlhausen
12 Dec 90   Modern Oil Paintings, Watercolours & Sculpture - Sale No.551
6 Feb 91   Oil Paintings & Watercolours - Sale No. 552
5 Mar 91   Modern Art - Sale No. 553
9 Apr 91   Oil Paintings & Watercolours - Sale No.557
23 Apr 91   Oil Paintings & Watercolours - Sale No. 558
29 Apr 91   Sale including Sculpture - Sale No. 558
15 May91   Modern Oil Paintings, Watercolours & Sculpture - Sale No. 559
6 Jun 91   Oil Paintings & Watercolours - Sale No. 560

RAS.V Rasmussen, Vejle - Denmark
10 Aug 90   Oil Paintings, Watercolours & Sculpture - Sale No. 1
14 Sep 90   Oil Paintings,Watercolours & Sculpture - Sale No. 2
19 Oct 90   Oil Paintings, Watercolours & Sculpture - Sale No. 3
22 Nov 90   Sale including Oil Paintings, Watercolours & Sculpture - Sale No. 4
27 Dec 90   Oil Paintings & Watercolours - Sale No. 5
31 Jan 91   Oil Paintings, Watercolours & Sculpture - Sale No.6
14 Mar 91   Oil Paintings, Watercolours & Sculpture
2 May91   Sale including Oil Paintings, Watercolours & Sculpture - Sale No. 8
13 Jun 91   Oil Paintings, Watercolours & Sculpture - Sale No. 9

RB Riddetts, Bournemouth - UK
26 Sep 90   Oil Paintings & Watercolours
20 Nov 90   Oil Paintings & Watercolours
12 Feb 91   Oil Paintings & Watercolours
27 Mar 91   Oil Paintings & Watercolours
16 Jul 91   Oil Paintings & Watercolours

Auction House, code and sale title

RB.HY Richard Bourne, Hyannis - USA
  7 Aug 90   Marine Oil Paintings & Watercolours
 24 Aug 90   American & European Oil Paintings. Watercolours & Sculpture
 24 Nov 90   Oil Paintings & Watercolours
  1 Mar 91   Oil Paintings, Watercolours & Sculpture

RBB Russell, Baldwin & Bright, Leominster - UK
  2 Aug 90   Oil Paintings & Watercolours
  5 Sep 90   Oil Paintings & Watercolours
  4 Oct 90   Oil Paintings & Watercolours
  8 Nov 90   Oil Paintings & Watercolours
 30 Jan 91   Oil Paintings & Watercolours
  6 Mar 91   Oil Paintings & Watercolours
  3 Apr 91   Oil Paintings & Watercolours
  1 May 91   Oil Paintings, Watercolours & Sculpture
  5 Jun 91   Oil Paintings & Watercolours
  3 Jul 91   Oil Paintings & Watercolours

RCJ.P Rabourdin & Choppin de Janvry, Paris - France
 29 May 91   Polish Art

REM.W Rempex, Warsaw - Poland
 25 Jan 91   Oil Paintings & Watercolours
  3 Mar 91   Oil Paintings & Watercolours

RG Rowland Gorringe, Lewes - UK
 11 Sep 90   Oil Paintings & Watercolours
 25 Oct 90   Oil Paintings & Watercolours
  4 Dec 90   Oil Paintings & Watercolours
 29 Jan 91   Oil Paintings & Watercolours
 12 Mar 91   Oil Paintings & Watercolours
 23 Apr 91   Oil Paintings & Watercolours
  4 Jun 91   Oil Paintings & Watercolours
 16 Jul 91   Oil Paintings & Watercolours

RO.BA Roldan & Cia, Buenos Aries - Argentina
 18 Sep 90   Oil Paintings, Watercolours & Sculpture
  8 May 91   Oil Paintings, Watercolours & Sculpture

RS Richardson & Smith, Whitby - UK
  4 Apr 91   Oil Paintings & Watercolours
 27 Jun 91   Oil Paintings & Watercolours

RU.ZU Rudolf Mangisch, Zurich - Switzerland
  8 Dec 90   Contemporary Art

RY.P Ribeyre, Paris - France
 14 Dec 90   Modern Oil Paintings, Watercolours & Sculpture
  3 Jun 91   Old Master Oil Paintings & Watercolours

S Sotheby's, London - UK
 28 Aug 90   Scottish & Sporting Paintings & Watercolours (Gleneagles Hotel)
 26 Sep 90   Victorian Paintings, Drawings & Watercolours
 10 Oct 90   Modern British & Irish Oil Paintings, Watercolours & Sculpture
 17 Oct 90   Impressionist & Modern Paintings, Watercolours & Sculpture
 18 Oct 90   Post War and Contemporary Art
 19 Oct 90   Applied Arts from 1880
 24 Oct 90   Topographical Watercolours & Drawings
 31 Oct 90   Old Master & British Paintings 1500-1850
  1 Nov 90   Portrait Miniatures
  2 Nov 90   19th & 20th Century Furniture & Sculpture
  7 Nov 90   Modern British & Irish Paintings, Watercolours & Sculpture
 14 Nov 90   British Paintings 1500-1850
 15 Nov 90   18/19th Century British Drawings & Watercolours
 23 Nov 90   19/20th Century Sculpture
 28 Nov 90   19th Century European Paintings, Drawings & Watercolours
  4 Dec 90   Impressionist & Modern Paintings & Sculpture Part I
  5 Dec 90   Impressionist & Modern Paintings & Sculpture Part II
  5 Dec 90   Impressionist & Modern Drawings & Watercolours
  6 Dec 90   Post War & Contemporary Art
  6 Dec 90   Illustrated Books & Related Drawings
 12 Dec 90   Old Master Paintings
 13 Dec 90   European Sculpture & Works of Art
 30 Jan 91   Early British & Victorian Drawings & Watercolours
  5 Feb 91   Scottish & Sporting Paintings & Watercolours (Glasgow)
 13 Feb 91   Victorian Paintings
 18 Feb 91   Old Master Drawings
  1 Mar 91   Sculpture
 20 Mar 91   Impressionist & Modern Art
 21 Mar 91   Post War & Contemporary Art
 27 Mar 91   Modern British & Irish Paintings, Watercolours & Sculpture

Auction House, code and sale title

S   Sotheby's, London - UK
10 Apr 91   British Oil Paintings 1500-1850
11 Apr 91   18/19th Century British Watercolours
17 Apr 91   Old Master Paintings
23 Apr 91   Scottish & Sporting Oil Paintings & Watercolours (Hopetoun House)
 1 May 91   Modern British & Irish Paintings & Drawings
 3 May 91   Applied Arts from 1880
22 May 91   Marine Pictures & Works of Art
31 May 91   19/20th Century Furniture & Decorations
 5 Jun 91   Victorian Paintings, Drawings & Watercolours
 7 Jun 91   19/20th Century Furniture & Decorations
19 Jun 91   Nineteenth Century European Paintings, Drawings & Watercolours
25 Jun 91   Impressionist, Modern & Contemporary Art from Chester Beatty Collection
25 Jun 91   Impressionist & Modern Paintings and Sculpture Part I
26 Jun 91   Impressionist & Modern Paintings & Sculpture Part II
26 Jun 91   Impressionist & Modern Drawings & Watercolours
27 Jun 91   Post War & Contemporary Art
 1 Jul 91   Post War & Contemporary British Art & 20th Century Sculpture
 1 Jul 91   Old Master Drawings including British Rail Pension Fund Collection
 3 Jul 91   Old Master Paintings
 4 Jul 91   European Sculpture & Works of Art
10 Jul 91   British Paintings 1500 - 1850
11 Jul 91   Early English Watercolours from Colin Hunter Collection
11 Jul 91   18/19th Century British Watercolours & Miniatures

S.BM Skinner, Bolton, Mass. - USA
18 Aug 90   Sale including Oil Paintings & Watercolours - Sale No. 1338
24 Aug 90   Oil Paintings & Sculpture
14 Sep 90   American & European Oil Paintings & Watercolours
26 Sep 90   English & Continental Sculpture
27 Oct 90   Americana Sale including Oil Paintings, Watercolours & Sculpture
 3 Nov 90   Sale including Oil Paintings & Watercolours
16 Nov 90   American & European Paintings
 8 Mar 91   Oil Paintings & Watercolours - Sale No. 1369
10 May 91   Oil Paintings & Watercolours - Sale No.1381

S.S Siboni, Sceaux - France
18 Nov 90   Oil Paintings, Watercolours & Sculpture

S.SL Selkirks, St. Louis - USA
24 Sep 90   Oil Paintings, Watercolours & Sculpture
26 Nov 90   Sale including Oil Paintings, Watercolours & Sculpture
 4 Feb 91   Oil Paintings & Watercolours
29 Apr 91   Oil Paintings, Watercolours & Sculpture

S.W Sloan, North Bethesda - USA
15 Sep 90   Oil Paintings, Watercolours & Sculpture
26 Oct 90   Sale including Oil Paintings, Watercolours & Sculpture
 7 Dec 90   Oil Paintings & Watercolours - Sale No. 817
 1 Feb 91   Oil Paintings, Watercolours & Sculpture - Sale No. 818
22 Mar 91   Oil Paintings, Watercolours & Sculpture
10 May 91   Oil Paintings, Watercolours & Sculpture - Sale No. 820
 5 Jul 91   Oil Paintings, Watercolours & Sculpture

S.Z Schneider Auktionen, Zurich - Switzerland
28 Sep 90   Graphics and Sculpture - Sale No. 90/4
17 Nov 90   Oil Paintings, Watercolours & Sculpture
15 Dec 90   Watercolours & Drawings - Sale No. 90/7
16 Mar 91   Oil Paintings, Watercolours & Sculpture
10 May 91   Modern Oil Paintings, Watercolours & Sculpture

SA.A Schloss Ahlden, Ahlden - Germany
14 Sep 90   Oil Paintings, Watercolours & Sculpture - Sale No. 67
24 Nov 90   Oil Paintings & Watercolours
 1 Dec 90   Oil Paintings, Watercolours & Sculpture - Sale No. 69
 3 May 91   Oil Paintings, Watercolours & Sculpture - Sale No. 70

SC   Sotheby's, Chester - UK
16 Aug 90   Oil Paintings & Watercolours
 4 Sep 90   Sutton Brailes Manor
20 Sep 90   Oil Paintings & Watercolours
18 Oct 90   Oil Paintings, Watercolours & Sculpture
30 Oct 90   Paintings & Watercolours of Scottish Interest (RSAC Glasgow)
15 Nov 90   Oil Paintings & Watercolours
28 Nov 90   Oil Paintings & Watercolours
 3 Dec 90   Oil Paintings & Watercolours
19 Feb 91   Sale including Sculpture
 6 Mar 91   Oil Paintings & Watercolours

SG.M Schrager Galleries, Milwaukee - USA
12 Nov 90   Oil Paintings & Watercolours

Auction House, code and sale title

SG.M Schrager Galleries, Milwaukee - USA
18 Mar 91   Oil Paintings & Watercolours

SHER Sherwood Fine Arts, Nottingham - UK
19 Mar 91   Oil Paintings & Watercolours

SIM   Simmons and Sons, Henley - UK
14 Jun 91   Oil Paintings & Watercolours

SO.S Soderkopings, Soderkoping - Sweden
27 Apr 91   Oil Paintings, Watercolours & Sculpture

STR   Stride & Son, Chichester - UK
26 Oct 90   Oil Paintings & Watercolours

SWO   G.E. Sworder & Son, Bishop's Stortford - UK
12 Feb 91   Oil Paintings & Watercolours

SWS Sotheby's, Billingshurst - UK
 6 Aug 90   Oil Paintings & Watercolours
 3 Sep 90   Oil Paintings & Watercolours
18 Sep 90   Oil Paintings & Watercolours
25 Sep 90   Garden Statuary & Architectural Items
22 Oct 90   Sale including Oil Paintings & Watercolours
23 Oct 90   Sale including Oil Paintings & Watercolours
24 Oct 90   House Sale including Oil Paintings & Watercolours (Hill House, Glos.)
 6 Nov 90   Sale including Sculpture
13 Nov 90   Selected Watercolours & Paintings by Women Artists
19 Nov 90   Oil Paintings & Watercolours
26 Nov 90   British Oil Paintings & Watercolours
 5 Dec 90   Sale including Oil Paintings & Watercolours
12 Dec 90   Sale including Oil Paintings, Watercolours & Sculpture
 8 Jan 91   Sale including Sculpture
15 Jan 91   Selected Watercolours & Oil Paintings
22 Jan 91   Oil Paintings & Watercolours
19 Feb 91   Oil Paintings & Watercolours
 5 Mar 91   Oil Paintings, Watercolours & Sculpture
23 Apr 91   Oil Paintings & Watercolours
 7 May 91   Sale including Sculpture & Miniatures
14 May 91   Oil Paintings & Watercolours
20 May 91   Oil Paintings & Watercolours
21 May 91   Sale including Sculpture
29 May 91   Garden Statuary
 4 Jun 91   Oil Paintings & Watercolours
18 Jun 91   Sale including Paintings & Sculpture
 2 Jul 91   Sale including Oil Paintings & Watercolours
16 Jul 91   Sale including Sculptures & Miniatures
22 Jul 91   Sale including Oil Paintings & Watercolours
30 Jul 91   Oil Paintings & Watercolours

SY.AM Sotheby's, Amsterdam - Netherlands
11 Sep 90   Sale including Oil Paintings & Watercolours - Sale No. 537
 6 Nov 90   19th Century European Paintings
13 Nov 90   Fine Decorative Arts - Sale No. 540
14 Nov 90   Old Master Paintings - Sale No. 541
27 Nov 90   General Sale
13 Dec 90   Modern & Contemporary Art - Sale No. 544
18 Dec 90   20th Century Decorative Arts
19 Mar 91   Fine Decorative Arts
23 Apr 91   19th Century European Paintings - Sale No. 547
23 May 91   Modern & Contemporary Art - Sale No. 549
18 Jun 91   Fine Decorative Arts

SY.BE Sotheby's, Berlin - Germany
30 May 91   German Art of the 20th Century

SY.F Sotheby's, Firenze - Italy
29 Oct 90   Sale including Old Master Paintings & Watercolours
 3 Dec 90   Old Master Oil Paintings & Watercolours
 3 Dec 90   Sculpture
25 Mar 91   Old Master & 19th Century Oil Paintings, Watercolours & Sculpture

SY.J Sotheby's, Johannesburg - South Africa
27 Aug 90   Decorative & Fine Arts
15 Oct 90   Sale including Oil Paintings & Watercolours
25 Oct 90   Decorative & Fine Arts (Cape Town)
26 Nov 90   Decorative & Fine Arts
11 Feb 91   Decorative & Fine Arts
18 Feb 91   Decorative & Fine Arts (Cape Town)
15 Apr 91   Decorative & Fine Arts
27 May 91   Decorative & Fine Arts

Auction House, code and sale title

SY.J Sotheby's, Johannesburg - South Africa
8 Jul 91 Decorative & Fine Arts

SY.ME Sotheby's, Melbourne - Australia
14 Aug 90 Australian Oil Paintings & Watercolours (Sydney)
27 Aug 90 Warren Thompson Collection
17 Sep 90 Fine Australian & European Paintings
26 Nov 90 Australian & European Oil Paintings & Watercolours
22 Apr 91 Fine Australian Paintings & Decorative Arts
16 Jun 91 100 Works from Museum of Contemporary Art, Brisbane

SY.MI Sotheby's, Milan - Italy
22 Nov 90 19th Century Oil Paintings & Watercolours
27 Nov 90 Modern Oil Paintings, Watercolours & Sculpture
13 Dec 90 20th Century Sculpture
21 May91 Important Old Master Paintings
21 May91 Sale including Sculpture
28 May91 Modern & Contemporary Art

SY.MO Sotheby's, Monaco - Monaco
14 Oct 90 20th Century Decorative Arts
7 Dec 90 Important Old Masters
8 Dec 90 19th Century Paintings & Watercolours
21 Apr 91 20th Century Decorative Art
21 Jun 91 Old Master Paintings from the Peyriague Collection
21 Jun 91 Important Old Master & 19th Century Paintings

SY.MU Sotheby's, Munich - Germany
12 Dec 90 19th Century German Paintings & Watercolours
12 Jun 91 German & Austrian Oil Paintings & Watercolours of the 19th Century

SY.NY Sotheby's, New York - USA
19 Sep 90 19th Century Oil Paintings & Sculpture
26 Sep 90 American Oil Paintings, Watercolours & Sculpture
3 Oct 90 Impressionist & Modern Paintings, Watercolours & Sculpture
4 Oct 90 Contemporary Oil Paintings, Watercolours & Sculpture
10 Oct 90 Modern & Contemporary Paintings, Watercolours & Sculpture (Arcade)
11 Oct 90 Old Master Paintings
23 Oct 90 19/20th Century Scandinavian Paintings & Sculpture
23 Oct 90 19th Century European Paintings, Drawings & Sculpture
26 Oct 90 Property of a European Foundation
6 Nov 90 Contemporary Art Part I
7 Nov 90 Contemporary Art Part II
12 Nov 90 Oil Paintings, Watercolours & Sculpture from Henry Ford II Estate
13 Nov 90 Impressionist & Modern Paintings & Sculpture Part I
13 Nov 90 The Collection of Jerome K Ohrbach
14 Nov 90 Impressionist & Modern Paintings & Sculpture Part II
14 Nov 90 Impressionist & Modern Drawings - Part I
14 Nov 90 Property from the Estate of Ned L Pines
15 Nov 90 The Greta Garbo Collection
19 Nov 90 Latin American Art
29 Nov 90 American Paintings, Drawings & Sculpture
17 Dec 90 American Paintings, Drawings & Sculpture - Sale No. 1343 (Arcade)
8 Jan 91 Old Master Drawings
10 Jan 91 Old Master Paintings
12 Jan 91 European Works of Art
12 Feb 91 Modern & Contemporary Paintings, Watercolours & Sculpture - Sale 1349 (Arcade)
15 Feb 91 Impressionist, Modern & Contemporary Oil Paintings, Watercolours & Sculpture
21 Feb 91 19th Century Decorations & Works of Art
27 Feb 91 19th Century Paintings, Drawings & Sculpture (Arcade)
11 Apr 91 Old Master Paintings
12 Apr 91 American Oil Paintings, Watercolours & Sculpture
30 Apr 91 Contemporary Art Part I
1 May91 Contemporary Art Part II
7 May91 Impressionist & Modern Paintings, Watercolours & Sculpture Part I
8 May91 Impressionist & Modern Paintings Watercolours & Sculpture Part II
15 May91 American Paintings, Drawings & Sculpture (Arcade)
22 May91 19th Century European Paintings, Drawings & Sculpture
23 May91 American Paintings, Drawings & Sculpture
30 May91 Old Master Paintings
1 Jun 91 European Works of Art & Furniture
7 Jun 91 Sporting & Marine Paintings & Sculpture
12 Jun 91 Modern & Contemporary Paintings, Drawings & Sculpture (Arcade)
19 Jun 91 Russian Works of Art and Objects of Vertu
17 Jul 91 Old Master & 19th Century European Paintings & Drawings (Arcade)

SY.T Sotheby's, Toronto - Canada
30 Oct 90 Important Canadian Art
6 May91 Important Canadian Art

THE POCKET PICTURE PRICE GUIDE
to the U.S and Canadian auction market

Summarised from: over 20,000 sale results exclusively from auctions in
Canada and the United States for a complete calendar year to show: by medium
for each artist/sculptor, the highest, lowest, median price,
the total value and the total number of works sold:
pocket sized - 300 pages   1991 edition - $20.00

Name	No	Total Sales US Dollars	lowest	-Prices US Dollars - median	example highest
CORNWELL, Dean (1892-1960) American					
oil	3	28,900	2,400	4,500	22,000
CORONA, Leonardo (attrib) (1561-1605) Italian					
wc/d	1	7,000		7,000	
CORONEL, Pedro (1923-) Mexican					
oil	4	191,000	11,000	50,000	80,000
CORONEL, Rafael (1932-) Mexican					
oil	8	100,600	1,600	11,500	30,000
wc/d	6	31,900	1,400	2,875	19,000
COROT, Jean Baptiste Camille (1796-1875) French					
oil	18	6,810,000	35,000	280,000	1,250,000
wc/d	2	5,200	1,200	2,600	4,000

Art Sales Index Ltd.,1 Thames Street, Weybridge, Surrey KT13 8JG, UK.
tel: (0932) 856426   fax: (0932) 842482

Auction House, code and sale title

SY.Z Sotheby's, Zurich - Switzerland
   21 Nov 90   Swiss Art from 18 - 20th Century
    5 Jun 91   18/19th Century Swiss Art

T   Taylors, Honiton - UK
   17 Aug 90   Oil Paintings & Watercolours
    5 Oct 90   Oil Paintings & Watercolours
   30 Nov 90   Oil Paintings & Watercolours
    8 Feb 91   Oil Paintings & Watercolours
   22 Mar 91   Oil Paintings & Watercolours
    3 May 91   Oil Paintings & Watercolours
   14 Jun 91   Oil Paintings & Watercolours
   26 Jul 91   Oil Paintings & Watercolours

T.B   Thierry, Brest - France
   16 Dec 90   Oil Paintings & Watercolours
   12 May 91   Modern Oil Paintings, Watercolours & Sculpture

TA.B Temple Auctions, Temple, N.Ireland - UK
   17 Nov 90   Oil Paintings & Watercolours
   16 Feb 91   Oil Paintings & Watercolours
   30 Mar 91   Oil Paintings
   20 Apr 91   Oil Paintings & Watercolours
   11 May 91   Oil Paintings & Watercolours

TAY   Louis Taylor, Stoke on Trent - UK
   11 Sep 90   Oil Paintings, Watercolours & Sculpture
    3 Dec 90   Oil Paintings & Watercolours
   10 Jun 91   Oil Paintings & Watercolours

TE   Tennants, Leyburn - UK
    1 Nov 90   Sale including Oil Paintings & Watercolours

TL   Lawrence, Crewkerne - UK
    1 Aug 90   Oil Paintings & Watercolours
    6 Sep 90   English & Continental Paintings
    8 Nov 90   English & Continental Paintings
    6 Dec 90   English & Continental Paintings

UL.T Tore Ulving, Tonsberg - Norway
   11 Sep 90   Oil Paintings & Watercolours
    4 Dec 90   Oil Paintings, Watercolours & Sculpture
   29 Jan 91   Oil Paintings & Watercolours
   19 Mar 91   Oil Paintings & Watercolours

UNI.W Unicum, Warsaw - Poland
   20 Jan 91   Oil Paintings & Watercolours
   17 Mar 91   Oil Paintings & Watercolours

V.BA VerBo, Buenos Aries - Argentina
    5 Sep 90   Oil Paintings & Watercolours
   14 Nov 90   Oil Paintings & Watercolours
    8 May 91   Oil Paintings & Watercolours

VG.B Villa Grisebach, Berlin - Germany
   23 Nov 90   Oil Paintings, Watercolours & Sculpture - Sale No. 15
   24 Nov 90   Oil Paintings, Watercolours & Sculpture - Sale No. 16
   31 May 91   Oil Paintings, Watercolours & Sculpture - Sale No. 18
    1 Jun 91   Oil Paintings, Watercolours & Sculpture - Sale No. 18,19 & 20

VN.R Vendu Notarishaus, Rotterdam - Netherlands
   25 Oct 90   Oil Paintings & Watercolours - Sale No. 179
   26 Feb 91   Oil Paintings & Watercolours - Sale No. 180
   26 Mar 91   Oil Paintings & Watercolours - Sale No. 181
   18 Jun 91   Oil Paintings & Watercolours - Sale No. 182

W.T   Waddington, Toronto - Canada
   12 Nov 90   Sale of Inuit Sculpture
   27 Nov 90   Oil Paintings, Watercolours & Sculpture
   10 Jun 91   Oil Paintings, Watercolours & Sculpture

W.W   Weschler, Washington - USA
   20 Oct 90   American Paintings, Drawings & Sculpture
    8 Dec 90   European Paintings, Watercolours & Sculpture
   16 Feb 91   American Oil Paintings, Watercolours & Sculpture
   16 Mar 91   Oil Paintings, Watercolours & Sculpture
   18 May 91   American & European Paintings, Watercolours & Sculpture
   14 Jun 91   Modern & Contemporary Paintings, Watercolours & Sculpture

WAL   Walter's, Lincoln - UK
   10 Jul 91   Contemporary Works of Art

Auction House, code and sale title

WE.MU Weiner, Munich - Germany
10 Oct 90   Oil Paintings & Watercolours - Sale No. 57
12 Dec 90   Jubilee Auction
17 Apr 91   Oil Paintings & Watercolours - Sale No. 61
3 Jul 91   Oil Paintings & Watercolours - Sale No. 64

WHB   William H Brown, Leicester - UK
17 Sep 90   Oil Paintings & Watercolours
30 Jan 91   Sale including Sculpture (Grantham)
18 Mar 91   Oil Paintings & Watercolours

WI   Wintertons, Lichfield - UK
20 Sep 90   Oil Paintings & Watercolours
15 Nov 90   Oil Paintings & Watercolours
20 Mar 91   Oil Paintings & Watercolours
15 May 91   Oil Paintings & Watercolours
17 Jul 91   Oil Paintings & Watercolours

WIN   Dominic Winter, Swindon - UK
22 May 91   Oil Paintings & Watercolours

WK.M   Galerie Wolfgang Ketterer, Munich - Germany
20 Oct 90   Modern Art - Sale No. 152
26 Nov 90   Modern & Contemporary Art - Sale No. 154
8 Dec 90   Oil Paintings & Watercolours - Sale No. 157
23 Mar 91   Modern Art - Sale No. 158
21 May 91   Modern Art - Sale No. 161
22 Jun 91   Oil Paintings, Watercolours & Sculpture - Sale No. 162

WO.CO Woodwards, Cork - Eire
12 Sep 90   Oil Paintings & Watercolour
10 Oct 90   Oil Paintings & Watercolours
14 Nov 90   Oil Paintings & Watercolours
23 Jan 91   Oil Paintings & Watercolours

WOL.C Wolfs, Cleveland - USA
22 Sep 90   Oil Paintings, Watercolours & Sculpture
19 Oct 90   Oil Paintings, Watercolours & Sculpture
16 Nov 90   Oil Paintings, Watercolours & Sculpture
2 Mar 91   Oil Paintings, Watercolours & Sculpture
20 Apr 91   Oil Paintings, Watercolours & Sculpture
17 May 91   Oil Paintings, Watercolours & Sculpture

WSW   Warner William H.Brown, Harrogate - UK
3 Dec 90   Oil Paintings & Watercolours

WW   Woolley & Wallis, Salisbury - UK
16 Oct 90   Sale at Egbury House including Oils, Watercolours & Sculpture (St. Marybourne)
15 Apr 91   Oil Paintings & Watercolours

YC.P   Yves de Cagny, Paris - France
29 Oct 90   Modern Sculpture
12 Nov 90   Modern & Contemporary Art
29 Nov 90   Traditional Russian Paintings
14 Jan 91   Modern & Contemporary Art
22 Jan 91   Oil Paintings & Watercolours
4 Feb 91   Sculptures
10 Feb 91   19th Century Russian Oil Paintings & Watercolours
5 Jul 91   Oil Paintings & Watercolours & Russian Art

YFA.M Young Fine Arts Gallery, Maine - USA
29 Sep 90   Oil Paintings & Watercolours
24 Nov 90   Oil Paintings & Watercolours
23 Feb 91   Oil Paintings & Watercolours
27 Apr 91   Oil Paintings & Watercolours
13 Jul 91   Oil Paintings & Watercolours

ZEL.L Michael Zeller, Lindau - Germany
10 Oct 90   Oil Paintings & Watercolours - Sale No. 44
6 May 91   Oil Paintings, Watercolours & Sculpture - Sale No. 45

ZOF.Z Auktionshaus Zofingen, Zofingen - Switzerland
14 Sep 90   Sale including Oil Paintings, Watercolours & Sculpture
14 Dec 90   Oil Paintings, Watercolours & Sculpture
7 Jun 91   Oil Paintings, Watercolours & Sculpture - Sale No. 5

ZZ.B Other British Auctioneers, - UK
19 Sep 90   Oil Paintings & Watercolours - Phillips Cornwall
27 Sep 90   Oil Paintings & Watercolours - John Walsh & Co
5 Oct 90   Oil Paintings & Watercolours - Jacobs & Hunt
22 Jan 91   Oil Paintings & Watercolours - Phillips Cornwall

Auction House, code and sale title

ZZ.B Other British Auctioneers, - UK
23 Jan 91   Oil Paintings & Watercolours - Phillips West Two
24 Jan 91   Oil Paintings & Watercolours - John Walsh & Co
6 Feb 91   Oil Paintings & Watercolours - Phillips West Two
20 Feb 91   Oil Paintings & Watercolours - Phillips West Two
6 Mar 91   Oil Paintings & Watercolours - Phillips West Two
14 Mar 91   Oil Paintings & Watercolours - Phillips East Anglia
19 Mar 91   Oil Paintings & Watercolours - Phillips Cornwall
20 Mar 91   Oil Paintings & Watercolours - Phillips West Two
4 Apr 91   Oil Paintings & Watercolours - Phillips West Two
11 Apr 91   Oil Paintings & Watercolours - Ewbank (Guildford)
17 Apr 91   Oil Paintings & Watercolours - Phillips West Two
1 May 91   Oil Paintings & Watercolours - Phillips West Two
8 May 91   Watercolours - Sale held by Nigel Papworth
15 May 91   Oil Paintings & Watercolours - Phillips West Two
29 May 91   Oil Paintings & Watercolours - Phillips West Two
11 Jun 91   Sale at Smithwood House - Phillips Guildford
12 Jun 91   Oil Paintings & Watercolours - Phillips West Two
10 Jul 91   Oil Paintings & Watercolours - Phillips West Two
18 Jul 91   Oil Paintings & Watercolours - Ewbank

ZZ.F Other French Auctioneers, - France
12 Oct 90   Oil Paintings & Watercolours - Boisgirard, Ionesco & Marumo
27 Oct 90   Modern & Contemporary Oil Paintings & Watercolours - Sale held by Tripier
29 Oct 90   Belgian Oil Paintings & Watercolours - Sale held by Tripier
30 Oct 90   Modern Oil Paintings, Watercolours & Sculpture - Morand & Morand
31 Oct 90   Modern & Contemporary Art - Labat & Thierry
11 Nov 90   Oil Paintings & Watercolours - Eric Pillon
15 Nov 90   Sale including Watercolours & Sculpture - Millon & Robert
19 Nov 90   Old Master Oil Paintings & Watercolours - Sale held by Millon/Robert
22 Nov 90   Modern & Contemporary Art - Viviane Jutheau
25 Nov 90   Oil Paintings & Watercolours - Sale held by Lesieur/Le Bars
25 Nov 90   Oil Paintings & Watercolours - Sale held by Mercier
27 Nov 90   The Art of Claude Descomps and Others - Labat & Thierry
29 Nov 90   Modern & Contemporary Art - Labat & Thierry
2 Dec 90   Oil Paintings, Watercolours & Sculpture - Regis & Thiollet
5 Dec 90   Modern & Contemporary Art - Millon & Robert
8 Dec 90   Russian Paintings & Watercolours - Chochon, Chochon-Barre & Allardi
9 Dec 90   Oil Paintings, Watercolours & Sculpture - Labat & Thierry
12 Dec 90   Oil Paintings, Watercolours & Sculpture - Viviane Jutheau
17 Dec 90   Oil Paintings & Watercolours - Sale held by Quay/Cheval/Robert
26 Jan 91   L'Art et le Cheval - Millon & Robert
4 Mar 91   Russian Art - Chochon-Barre & Allardi
14 Apr 91   Contemporary Oil Paintings, Watercolours & Sculpture - Sale held by Morand/Morand
19 May 91   Oil Paintings, Watercolours & Sculpture - Eric Pillon
26 May 91   Oil Paintings & Watercolours - Eric Pillon
3 Jun 91   Sculpture - Millon Robert Hoebank & Couturier
10 Jun 91   Leningrad Figuration - Chocon, Chocon-Barre & Allardi
11 Jun 91   Oil Paintings, Watercolours & Sculpture - Sale held by Chaussin, Guillamot & Bremens (Lyon)
12 Jun 91   Oil Paintings, Watercolours & Sculpture - Millon & Robert
19 Jun 91   Oil Paintings & Watercolours - Viviane Jutheau
28 Jun 91   Oil Paintings, Watercolours & Sculpture - Christian de Quay
1 Jul 91   The Art of Gin Coste-Crasnier - Millon & Robert
5 Jul 91   Oil Paintings, Watercolours & Sculpture - Vincent Wapler
11 Jul 91   Russian Art - Chochon-Barre & Allardi

Number of sales covered in this edition - 1785

Index

Oil paintings, watercolours, drawings and miniatures
sold during the auction season are covered
by this book

Artists A - K

STARTING PRICES

Oil Paintings - £500
Miniatures - £300
Watercolours and drawings - £400
National or regional "schools" - £1000

AACHEN, Hans von (1552-1616) German
£1368 $2448   (14-Mar-91 D.V297/R) Jupiter and Antiope (23x31cm-9x12in) (A.S 28000)

AACHEN, Hans von (after) (1552-1616) German
£1350 $2336   (20-May-91 SWS27) The Martyrdom of Saint Sebastian (46x32cm-18x13in)
               bears init.d.1604 verso panel

AACHEN, Hans von (attrib) (1552-1616) German
£2988 $5139   (14-May-91 GF.L2026/R) Allegory of the three theological virtues
               (75x105cm-30x41in) panel (S.FR 7500)
£517 $925   (12-Apr-91 AW.H187/R) St Hieronymus in the desert (20x15cm-8x6in) i.
               pen wash one of pair (DM 1550)
£517 $925   (12-Apr-91 AW.H186/R) Penitent Magdalen (21x16cm-8x6in) pen wash one of
               pair (DM 1550)

AACHEN, Hans von (circle) (1552-1616) German
£1300 $2535   (25-Oct-90 CSK87) Entombment (28x22cm-11x9in) on copper
£5000 $9750   (26-Oct-90 C62/R) Venus and Adonis (20x17cm-8x7in) copper

AACHEN, Hans von (style) (1552-1616) German
£800 $1384   (20-May-91 SWS124/R) Saint Francis receiving the stigmata
               (54x44cm-21x17in) gisaille oil
£1647 $2783   (2-May-91 CH.AM83) Saint Sebastian assailed by arrows (104x80cm-41x31in)
               (D.FL 5500)
£1835 $3523   (30-Nov-90 APT.P42) La Flagellation du Christ (40x30cm-16x12in) on
               bronze (F.FR 18000)
£1946 $3289   (2-May-91 CH.AM1) The Adoration of the shepherds (51x37cm-20x15in) panel
               (D.FL 6500)
£2732 $5355   (24-Jan-91 EP.M5/R) La adoracion de los Pastores (120x83cm-47x33in)
               panel (S.P 500000)

AAGAARD, C F (1833-1895) Danish
£626 $1240   (31-Jan-91 RAS.V461) River through wood (53x81cm-21x32in) s.d.1877
               (D.KR 7000)
£627 $1254   (6-Feb-91 RAS.K384) Autumn lake landscape with two men fishing from boat
               (47x31cm-19x12in) s.d.1883 (D.KR 7000)
£1526 $3006   (14-Nov-90 RAS.K728/R) Landscape, Mons cliffs (117x186cm-46x73in) s.
               (D.KR 17000)
£2210 $4156   (10-Aug-90 RAS.V423/R) Wooded lake (77x115cm-30x45in) s.d.1882
               (D.KR 25000)

AAGAARD, Carl Frederic (1833-1895) Danish
£6573 $11174   (28-May-91 AB.S4727/R) View from an Italian pergola (68x100cm-27x39in)
               s. (S.KR 70000)

AAGAARD, Martin (1863-1913) Norwegian
£564 $942   (3-Jun-91 B.O169/R) Fjord landscape with sailship and steamship
               (44x60cm-17x24in) s. (N.KR 6500)
£1158 $2234   (10-Dec-90 B.O158/R) Coastal landscape with boat (32x104cm-13x41in) s.
               i.verso (N.KR 13000)

AALTO, Ilmari (1891-1934) Scandinavian
£3281 $6431   (24-Nov-90 HOR.H31/R) Still life on table (46x55cm-18x22in) s.
               (F.M 23000)

AAS, Alf Jorgen (1915-1981) Norwegian
£569 $1019   (11-Mar-91 B.O158/R) Wooded landscape (47x60cm-19x24in) s.d.1941 panel
               (N.KR 6500)
£1394 $2718   (15-Oct-90 B.O144/R) Studio interior (38x46cm-15x18in) s.d.1945 panel
               (N.KR 16000)

AASEN, Astri (1875-1935) Norwegian
£832 $1489   (11-Mar-91 B.O159/R) Interior from Brittany (72x92cm-28x36in) s.d.1912
               (N.KR 9500)

ABADES, E Martinez (19/20th C) Continental
£1734 $3000   (21-May-91 CE.NY51/R) Busy port (39x59cm-15x23in) s.

ABADES, Juan Martinez (1862-1920) Spanish
£6552 $11335   (8-May-91 FER.M133/R) Ninos jugando bajo el monumento de Bilbao
               (45x31cm-18x12in) s. (S.P 1200000)
£10326 $18277   (3-Apr-91 ANS.M89/R) Pescadores al atardecer (54x70cm-21x28in) s.d.1908
               (S.P 1900000)
£16304 $31304   (19-Dec-90 ANS.M26/R) Pescadores al atardecer (54x70cm-21x28in) s.d.1908
               (S.P 3000000)
£492 $949   (11-Dec-90 FER.M131/R) Cordillera del Sueve, Asturias (23x28cm-9x11in)
               s.d.1904 W/C (S.P 90000)
£601 $1160   (11-Dec-90 FER.M132/R) Cordillera del Sueve (37x28cm-15x11in) s.d.1909
               W/C (S.P 110000)

ABADIA, Juan de la (1473-1496) Spanish
£2000 $3400   (30-May-91 CE.NY84) The Madonna (74x35cm-29x14in) panel gold ground
£36000 $60840   (19-Apr-91 C106/R) Saints Michael and Engracia (148x98cm-58x39in) gold
               ground panel
£88235 $150000   (30-May-91 SY.NY20/R) Virgin and child with Saint Anne
               (152x96cm-60x38in) panel

ABATE, Alberto (1946-) Italian
£2542 $4905   (13-Dec-90 F.M327/R) Aurora (75x55cm-30x22in) s.i.d.1986verso
                  (I.L 5500000)

ABATTUCI, Pierre (1871-1942) Belgian
£818 $1391   (28-May-91 C.A1) Park in Westerlo (110x90cm-43x35in) s. (B.FR 50000)

ABBATE, Niccolo dell' (1512-1571) Italian
£14211 $27000   (8-Jan-91 SY.NY145/R) Landscape with Hercules killing the Nemaen lion
                  (23x16cm-9x6in) i. verso ink wash htd.white

ABBATE, Niccolo dell' (attrib) (1512-1571) Italian
£6200 $10106   (1-Jul-91 S161/R) Apollo driving chariot (24x20cm-9x8in) brush wash htd
                  white over black chk irregular

ABBEMA, Louise (1858-1927) French
£1506 $2425   (28-Jun-91 ARC.P47) Portarit de jeune femme a la robe blanche
                  (55x45cm-22x18in) s.i.d.98 panel (F.FR 15000)
£2821 $5500   (26-Oct-90 SY.NY113/R) Japanese flower arrangement (56x46cm-22x18in)
                  s.d.1920

ABBEY, Edwin Austin (1852-1911) American
£20231 $35000   (22-May-91 SY.NY94/R) Flametta's song (132x264cm-52x104in) s.d.1894
£529 $1000   (25-Sep-90 CE.NY273/R) The mad maydes songe (44x28cm-17x11in) s.i.d.July
                  186 gouache en grisaille pen board
£529 $1000   (25-Sep-90 CE.NY272/R) Frolicking virgins (41x27cm-16x11in) s.i.d.1880-1
                  gouache en grisaille pen board
£1005 $1971   (20-Nov-90 GO.G305) Kitchen interior with woman (48x30cm-19x12in) s.
                  gouache (S.KR 11000)

ABBIATI, Julius (19th C) Austrian?
£759 $1359   (11-Apr-91 D.V225/R) Former Schloss Schwarzenberg in Neuwaldegg
                  (56x69cm-22x27in) s. paper on canvas (A.S 16000)

ABBOTT, John White (1763-1851) British
£550 $985   (9-Apr-91 C117/R) Fordland (15x18cm-6x7in) i.d.1827 pen ink wash
£1700 $3332   (21-Nov-90 B21/R) Kenilworth Castle (18x23cm-7x9in) pen W/C
£2800 $4620   (11-Jul-91 S138/R) Greenaway on the Dart, Devon (19x24cm-7x9in) pen ink
                  W/C
£3200 $5280   (11-Jul-91 S137/R) Caldicot Castle, Monmouthshire (16x23cm-6x9in)
                  s.d.1797verso pen ink W/C

ABBOTT, John White (circle) (1763-1851) British
£950 $1568   (9-Jul-91 C17/R) Rocks and fall at Cannon Weir near Exeter
                  (33x41cm-13x16in) i.d.09 pen ink wash

ABBOTT, Lemuel Francis (1760-1803) British
£2000 $3580   (12-Apr-91 C125/R) Portrait of George Forester M.P., hunting whip and
                  cap beside him (75x62cm-30x24in)
£3000 $5910   (31-Oct-90 S279/R) Portrait of officer (75x62cm-30x24in)

ABBOTT, Lemuel Francis (attrib) (1760-1803) British
£640 $1107   (20-May-91 SWS279) Portrait of Robert Collins, wearing a brown coat
                  (68x56cm-27x22in) oval

ABEL, Joseph (circle) (1764-1818) Austrian
£879 $1574   (14-Mar-91 D.V307/R) Portrait of noble lady wearing pearls in hair
                  (98x74cm-39x29in) (A.S 18000)

ABEL-TRUCHET (1857-1918) French
£1992 $3446   (26-May-91 ZZ.F81/R) Grand canal a Venise (54x65cm-21x26in) s.
                  (F.FR 20000)
£2000 $3260   (1-Jul-91 APT.P150/R) Paysage de campagne (65x81cm-26x32in) s.
                  (F.FR 20000)
£4482 $7754   (24-May-91 FB.P77/R) Place de la republique, la marchande de fleurs
                  (40x32cm-16x13in) s. panel (F.FR 45000)

ABELOOS, Victor (1881-1965) Belgian
£1315 $2564   (23-Oct-90 C.A3) Le paravent chinois (85x70cm-33x28in) s.d.1917
                  (B.FR 80000)
£1638 $3096   (25-Sep-90 FN.S2100) Vase with paeonies in sitting room interior
                  (72x58cm-28x23in) s. (DM 4800)

ABELS, Jacobus Theodorus (1803-1866) Dutch
£509 $855   (23-Apr-91 SY.AM191) River landscape by moonlight (23x29cm-9x11in) panel
                  (D.FL 1700)
£2727 $5264   (10-Dec-90 L.K715/R) Moonlit river landscape with church
                  (33x43cm-13x17in) mono. panel (DM 7800)

ABERDAM, Alfred (1894-1963) Polish
£942 $1800   (1-Jan-91 GG.TA204/R) Nymphs (81x65cm-32x26in) s. s.d.1962verso
£982 $1600   (12-Jun-91 GG.TA227/R) Nymphs (80x40cm-31x16in) s.
£989 $1771   (14-Apr-91 GL.P38) Groupe de femmes (55x44cm-22x17in) s. (F.FR 10000)
£1118 $2236   (6-Feb-91 FB.P1) Nymphe (125x52cm-49x20in) s. (F.FR 11000)
£2176 $3895   (14-Apr-91 GL.P177) Le repas dans l'atelier (73x92cm-29x36in) s. i.
                  verso (F.FR 22000)

ABERDAM, Alfred (1894-1963) Polish-cont.
£2473 $4426   (14-Apr-91 GL.P35/R) Composition (97x161cm-38x63in) s.d.1055
                    (F.FR 25000)

ABERG, Emil (1864-1940) Swedish
£1097 $2150   (20-Nov-90 GO.G297) Lake idyll with women fishing (102x67cm-40x26in) s.
                    (S.KR 12000)

ABERG, Pelle (1909-1964) Swedish
£1112 $2158   (4-Dec-90 BA.S626/R) Musicians in the restaurant (27x22cm-11x9in) s.
                    cardboard (S.KR 12000)
£1981 $3427   (22-May-91 BA.S279/R) Clown wearing hat (26x21cm-10x8in) s. panel
                    (S.KR 21000)
£2410 $4675   (4-Dec-90 BA.S623/R) The aperitif (65x54cm-26x21in) s. panel
                    (S.KR 26000)
£2502 $4854   (4-Dec-90 BA.S624/R) Girl wearing hat with flowers (46x38cm-18x15in) s.
                    (S.KR 27000)
£2583 $4959   (27-Nov-90 BU.S363/R) The green hat (46x38cm-18x15in) s. panel
                    (S.KR 28000)
£2966 $5753   (4-Dec-90 BA.S620/R) By the Djurgard's ferry (49x61cm-19x24in) s. panel
                    (S.KR 32000)
£3522 $6832   (4-Dec-90 BA.S621/R) Clown (54x46cm-21x18in) s. panel (S.KR 38000)
£6181 $11867   (27-Nov-90 BU.S361/R) Girl in Paris (99x62cm-39x24in) s. (S.KR 67000)

ABERLI, Johann Ludwig (1723-1786) Swiss
£2381 $4119   (22-May-91 GS.B2001/R) Portrait of preacher Daniel Hunziker. Portrait of
                    Josina Hunziker (42x43cm-17x17in) pair (S.FR 6000)
£643   *$1259*   *(21-Nov-90 SY.Z6/R) Country house by Lake Biel (8x13cm-3x5in) W/C
                    (S.FR 1600)*

ABERLI, Johann Ludwig (attrib) (1723-1786) Swiss
£873 $1510   (22-May-91 GS.B2002/R) Portrait of Fraulein von Sturler on balcony with
                    view of landscape (39x32cm-15x13in) (S.FR 2200)
£2143 $3707   (22-May-91 GS.B2003/R) Portrait of Fraulein von Sturler as huntress with
                    dog (38x32cm-15x13in) (S.FR 5400)

ABGRALL, Monique (?) ?
£816 $1412   (12-May-91 T.B69/R) Composition au vase de fleurs et au plan d'eau
                    (80x65cm-31x26in) s. (F.FR 8200)

ABILDGAARD, N A (1743-1809) Danish
£54577 $91690   (23-Apr-91 RAS.K2/R) The philosopher - allegorical female figure
                    (72x56cm-28x22in) s.d.1800 (D.KR 620000)
£886   *$1497*   *(1-May-91 KH.K210/R) Lioness with young (14x23cm-6x9in) pen Indian ink
                    (D.KR 10000)*
£1240   *$2096*   *(1-May-91 KH.K211/R) Fortune and Mercur's ssesaw (14x22cm-6x9in) pen
                    pencil (D.KR 14000)*
£1949   *$3293*   *(1-May-91 KH.K209/R) Zeus reclining with eagle and thunder wedge
                    (13x21cm-5x8in) pen Indian ink wash (D.KR 22000)*

ABLETT, William Albert (1877-1937) French
£2055 $3988   (9-Dec-90 ZZ.F17) L'elegante (92x65cm-36x26in) s.d.05 (F.FR 20000)

ABNER (20th C) ?
£3009 $5868   (10-Oct-90 ARC.P127/R) Les signaux (92x73cm-36x29in) s.d.54 (F.FR 30000)

ABRAHAMS, Anna Adelaide (1849-1930) Dutch
£1703   *$3286*   *(12-Dec-90 CH.AM102/R) Still life of flowers in glass vases
                    (70x53cm-28x21in) s. W/C (D.FL 5500)*

ABRAHAMSEN, Emil (1875-1964) Norwegian?
£2352 $4586   (15-Oct-90 B.O1/R) Summer garden (76x100cm-30x39in) s. (N.KR 27000)

ABRAHAMSON, Ola (1883-?) Norwegian
£1338 $2596   (4-Dec-90 UL.T180/R) Coastal landscape 1937 (115x125cm-45x49in)
                    (N.KR 15000)

ABRAHAMSSON, Anette (20th C) Danish
£792 $1363   (15-May-91 RAS.K33) Composition with three figures (280x150cm-110x59in)
                    s.d.1984verso (D.KR 9000)

ABRAM, Charles Frederic (fl.1879-1888) French
£2426 $4585   (27-Sep-90 D.V78/R) Painters in landscape (43x55cm-17x22in) s.
                    (A.S 50000)

ABRAMS, Lucien (1870-1941) American
£930 $1600   (15-May-91 SY.NY124/R) Montagne Rouge (58x71cm-23x28in) indist.s.

ABRIL Y BLASCO, Salvador (1862-1924) Spanish
£4319 $7428   (16-May-91 D.V65/R) Ship Capeando in heavy seas (114x183cm-45x72in)
                    s.i.d.1901 (A.S 90000)

ABRY, Leon Eugene (1857-1905) Belgian
£671 $1288   (27-Nov-90 SY.AM3555/R) Soldiers on battlefield (46x76cm-18x30in) s.
                    (D.FL 2200)

ABSOLON, John (1815-1895) British
£460	$796	(20-May-91 PH100) Telling time (9x18cm-4x7in) init. W/C htd white
£520	$853	(19-Jun-91 B91) Fisherfolk in coastal village (19x35cm-7x14in) s. W/C bodycol
£650	$1092	(23-Apr-91 SWS455/R) A rest from work (29x57cm-11x22in) s.
£1500	$2880	(26-Nov-90 SWS98/R) Near Hastings (31x74cm-12x29in) W/C gouache
£1600	$2688	(22-Apr-91 PH298/R) The letter (26x21cm-10x8in) s. W/C bodycol.
£1818	$3600	(1-Feb-91 S.W2534/R) Twickenham meadows (30x58cm-12x23in) s. W/C
£2000	$3780	(26-Sep-90 RB668/R) Continental lake scene with woman playing mandolin and a man in a boat (51x71cm-20x28in) s. W/C htd. white

ABSOLON, Kurt (1925-1958) Austrian
£584	$1145	(24-Jan-91 D.V269/R) Landscape (33x47cm-13x19in) s.d.1956 pen indian ink (A.S 12000)
£1491	$2893	(6-Dec-90 D.V177/R) Nude facing back (31x48cm-12x19in) s.d.1954 pen brush indian ink W/C (A.S 30000)
£1552	$2918	(20-Sep-90 D.V229/R) Landscape (32x48cm-13x19in) s.d.1956 pen (A.S 32000)
£1697	$3191	(20-Sep-90 D.V232/R) Mother and child (32x48cm-13x19in) s.d.1957 pen (A.S 35000)
£2425	$4559	(20-Sep-90 D.V228/R) Avenue (34x51cm-13x20in) s.d.1958 pen W/C (A.S 50000)
£2734	$5303	(6-Dec-90 D.V183/R) Sumpftiere (34x48cm-13x19in) s.d.1954 pen indian ink W/C (A.S 55000)
£2982	$5785	(6-Dec-90 D.V184/R) The Crucifixion (32x47cm-13x19in) s.i.d.1957 pen indian ink wash (A.S 60000)

ABSOLON, L (19th C) British
| £480 | $802 | (7-Jun-91 BW27) The reaper (36x25cm-14x10in) s. i.verso W/C |

ABT, Otto (1903-) Swiss
| £711 | $1209 | (27-May-91 GK.Z5500) Bouquet of flowers (33x22cm-13x9in) s. gouache (S.FR 1800) |

ABULARACH, Rodolfo (20th C) Mexican
| £3061 | $6000 | (20-Nov-90 CH.NY285/R) Espacial No. 23 Marte (203x203cm-80x80in) s.d.76 s.i.d.verso |

ACCARD, Eugene (1824-1888) French
| £578 | $1121 | (4-Dec-90 P.Q57 a) The recital (31x20cm-12x8in) s. (C.D 1300) |

ACCARDI, Carla (1924-) Italian
£2050	$3486	(28-May-91 SY.MI108/R) Concentrico (54x60cm-21x24in) s.d.58 tempera caseine paper (I.L 4500000)
£2977	$5716	(27-Nov-90 SY.MI197/R) Integrazione (63x63cm-25x25in) s.d.1958 tempera paper (I.L 6500000)
£5776	$11148	(13-Dec-90 F.M437/R) Rossoblu 264 (59x70cm-23x28in) s.d.61 (I.L 12500000)
£6871	$13192	(27-Nov-90 SY.MI215/R) Grande rettangolo (108x133cm-43x52in) s.d.60 tempera caseine (I.L 15000000)
£7269	$14321	(30-Oct-90 F.R243/R) Composizione (50x70cm-20x28in) s.d.56 (I.L 16000000)
£7654	$14926	(22-Oct-90 BR.M76/R) Minimo il cielo (100x130cm-39x51in) s.d.1989 acrylic (I.L 17000000)
£7746	$13168	(28-May-91 SY.MI140/R) Rettangolo blu (73x116cm-29x46in) s.d.60 d.1960verso tempera caseine (I.L 17000000)
£9113	$15492	(28-May-91 SY.MI192/R) Forme sospese (70x130cm-28x51in) s.d.60 s.d.1960verso tempera caseine (I.L 20000000)
£9568	$16266	(28-May-91 SY.MI163/R) Due cerchi (91x141cm-36x56in) s.d.1960 tempera caseine (I.L 21000000)
£20612	$39575	(27-Nov-90 SY.MI232/R) Integrazione (145x145cm-57x57in) s.d.57 tempera caseine canvas (I.L 45000000)

ACCARISI, L (19th C) Italian
| £4100 | $7626 | (3-Sep-90 SWS1215/R) Peasants in Roman campagna (68x49cm-27x19in) s.i.d. painted ovals pair |

ACEVES, Gustavo (1931-) Mexican
| £1327 | $2600 | (20-Nov-90 CH.NY288/R) Desnudos (125x93cm-49x37in) chl paste white chk pencil |

ACHEN, Georg (1860-1912) Danish
| £1345 | $2583 | (27-Dec-90 RAS.V3/R) Sunny interior with painting by Jens Juel on wall (70x57cm-28x22in) s.d.1901 (D.KR 15000) |
| £3693 | $6205 | (24-Apr-91 BA.S1/R) Middle-class interior (68x57cm-27x22in) s.d.1901 (S.KR 39000) |

ACHENBACH, A (1815-1910) German
| £699 | $1350 | (13-Dec-90 N.M2635/R) Sailing ship in choppy sea (23x29cm-9x11in) panel (DM 2000) |

ACHENBACH, Andreas (1815-1910) German
| £946 | $1845 | (26-Oct-90 KM.K1079) Figures in rowing boat fighting rough sea (16x19cm-6x7in) s. (DM 2800) |
| £1174 | $2290 | (13-Oct-90 KRA.D168/R) Seascape off Isle of Wight (28x39cm-11x15in) mono.i.d.1838 panel (DM 3500) |

ACHENBACH, Andreas (1815-1910) German-cont.
£2055	$3678	(13-Mar-91 N.M445/R) Stormy sea and fishermen on jetty (16x24cm-6x9in) s.d.1898 panel (DM 6000)
£14094	$27483	(13-Oct-90 KRA.D167/R) Coastal landscape near Scheveningen (107x137cm-42x54in) s.d.1857 and 1858 (DM 42000)
£19257	$32736	(27-May-91 L.K237/R) At the beach near Scheveningen (100x127cm-39x50in) s.d.1862 (DM 57000)
£476	$843	(22-Mar-91 GRA.B2576/R) Wooded landscape with mountain stream (6x8cm-2x3in) s.d.1843 W/C bodycol board (DM 1400)
£776	$1474	(3-Mar-91 REM.W1) By the river (45x52cm-18x20in) s.d.37 chk (P.Z 14000000)

ACHENBACH, Andreas (attrib) (1815-1910) German
£1610	$2881	(13-Mar-91 N.M446/R) Fishing boats offshore and beached (24x38cm-9x15in) mono. panel (DM 4700)

ACHENBACH, Oswald (1827-1905) German
£1500	$2595	(9-May-91 CSK187/R) Moonlit view of Bay of Naples from Posillipo (24x38cm-9x15in) s. panel
£2517	$4908	(13-Oct-90 KRA.D170/R) Italianate coastal landscape (25x34cm-10x13in) s.i.d.82 board (DM 7500)
£2872	$4853	(3-May-91 SA.A1714/R) Scene on the Tiber in Rome (44x63cm-17x25in) i.d.1884 board (DM 8500)
£2972	$5736	(12-Dec-90 SY.MU19/R) In the gardens of the Villa Borghese (59x83cm-23x33in) s. canvas on panel (DM 8500)
£3425	$5582	(12-Jun-91 SY.MU128/R) Venice (25x33cm-10x13in) s. paper (DM 10000)
£6000	$10320	(17-May-91 C215/R) Aragonese Castel, Ischia (77x100cm-30x39in) s.
£15734	$30367	(12-Dec-90 WE.MU51/R) Bay of Naples with fisher folk (80x116cm-31x46in) s.d.1887 (DM 45000)
£21959	$41723	(14-Sep-90 SA.A1239/R) Landscape with pilgrims, Sabine mountains (111x160cm-44x63in) s. i.verso (DM 65000)
£34965	$67483	(12-Dec-90 SY.MU20/R) Pilgrims in Roman landscape near Sabine Mountains (100x158cm-39x62in) s. i.verso (DM 100000)
£50336	$98154	(13-Oct-90 KRA.D169/R) Kirmes am Niederrhein (56x70cm-22x28in) s.d.1858 (DM 150000)

ACHILLES, August (19th C) ?
£606	$1175	(22-Aug-90 RAS.K127) Mountainous landscape with lake (82x110cm-32x43in) s.d.1886 (D.KR 7000)

ACHINI, Angelo (1850-1930) Italian
£459	$749	(10-Jun-91 W.T1280) Three sisters (39x62cm-15x24in) s. W/C (C.D 850)
£2273	$4455	(21-Nov-90 F.M157) Volto di bimba con cappello. Volto di bimba col nastro azzurro (38x29cm-15x11in) s. W/C pair (I.L 5000000)

ACHT, Rene-Charles (1920-) Swiss
£556	$928	(7-Jun-91 ZOF.Z1257) Sahara vision I (27x41cm-11x16in) d.57 s.i.verso (S.FR 1400)
£1746	$3021	(25-May-91 AB.L99/R) Cool figure (140x105cm-55x41in) s.d.1956 s.i.d.verso (S.FR 4400)

ACHTSCHELLINCK, Lucas (1626-1699) Flemish
£12146	$23806	(22-Nov-90 D.P5/R) Paysage forestier avec cavaliers et promeneurs (51x73cm-20x29in) panel (F.FR 120000)

ACHTSCHELLINCK, Lucas (style) (1626-1699) Flemish
£1743	$3434	(13-Nov-90 AB.S846/R) Landscape with buildings and figures (20x26cm-8x10in) panel (S.KR 19000)

ACKE, Johan Axel Gustaf (1859-1924) Swedish
£917	$1807	(13-Nov-90 AB.S332/R) The Prodigal Son (154x111cm-61x44in) s.d.1882 (S.KR 10000)

ACKEIN, Marcelle (1882-1952) French
£8621	$16552	(17-Dec-90 ARC.P106/R) Le marche de poterie africain (54x65cm-21x26in) s. i. verso (F.FR 85000)

ACKER, Flori-Marie van (1858-1940) Belgian
£1349	$2617	(4-Dec-90 C.A371) Farmer in the fields (88x200cm-35x79in) s. (B.FR 80000)

ACKERMAN (?) ?
£2243	$4328	(16-Dec-90 GL.P185) Le couple (146x114cm-57x45in) s. (F.FR 22000)
£2568	$4598	(14-Mar-91 N.M2625/R) Female nude from behind (100x151cm-39x59in) s.i. (DM 7500)

ACKERMAN, Paul (1908-1981) French
£593	$1062	(8-Apr-91 CR.P84/R) Conversation (54x65cm-21x26in) studio st. (F.FR 6000)
£829	$1617	(15-Oct-90 CSC.P8) Sans titre (60x42cm-24x17in) s. hardboard (F.FR 8200)
£930	$1814	(15-Oct-90 CSC.P7) Sans titre (68x43cm-27x17in) s. acrylic (F.FR 9200)
£1039	$1859	(8-Apr-91 CR.P85/R) La visite de Dame Aglae (45x65cm-18x26in) studio st. (F.FR 10500)
£1385	$2479	(8-Apr-91 CR.P86) Une facon de sublimer le desir (134x125cm-53x49in) studio st. (F.FR 14000)
£1517	$2958	(15-Oct-90 CSC.P9/R) Sans titre (81x100cm-32x39in) (F.FR 15000)

ACKERMAN, Paul (1908-1981) French-cont.
£3557 $7114   (6-Feb-91 FB.P3) Composition (64x81cm-25x32in) s. (F.FR 35000)

ACKERMANN, Gerald (1876-1960) British
£1400	$2352	(15-Jul-91 PH177) Whitby (24x35cm-9x14in) s.d.1909
£900	$1611	(14-Mar-91 ZZ.B60) Priory Mill, Blakeney (24x36cm-9x14in) s. W/C
£1500	$2820	(20-Sep-90 CSK82/R) Lincoln (23x35cm-9x14in) s. W/C pencil
£1900	$3800	(8-Feb-91 K450/R) August Blue, Blakeney (25x36cm-10x14in) s. W/C
£1900	$3211	(19-Apr-91 K527/R) Autumn (23x36cm-9x14in) s.i.d.1910 W/C
£2800	$4676	(3-Jun-91 PHB24) Gloucester from meadows (24x35cm-9x14in) s. i.verso pencil W/C
£2800	$5432	(7-Dec-90 K507/R) North Norfolk coastal scene with sailing boats (23x33cm-9x13in) s. W/C

ACKERMANN, Max (1887-1973) German
£1096	$1786	(15-Jun-91 L.K3/R) Scene with figures (22x21cm-9x8in) s.verso panel (DM 3200)
£1164	$1898	(15-Jun-91 L.K2/R) Two ladies in park (29x21cm-11x8in) s.indis.d.1947verso panel (DM 3400)
£1644	$2679	(15-Jun-91 L.K1/R) Female nude seated seen from behind (30x19cm-12x7in) s.d.1942 panel (DM 4800)
£1689	$3294	(20-Oct-90 WK.M1/R) Composition (37x31cm-15x12in) s.d.1970 s.d.verso board (DM 5000)
£1689	$3294	(20-Oct-90 WK.M2/R) Composition (34x24cm-13x9in) s.d.1970 oil over ball point board on panel (DM 5000)
£2378	$4613	(5-Dec-90 DO.H2420/R) Composition (16x13cm-6x5in) s.d.1949 tempera oil board (DM 6800)
£3793	$7283	(26-Nov-90 WK.M100/R) Composition (30x48cm-12x19in) s.d.1962 board (DM 11000)
£3885	$6605	(28-May-91 KF.M409/R) Jubilieren I (24x19cm-9x7in) s.i.d.1957 panel (DM 11500)
£5517	$10593	(28-Nov-90 KF.M503/R) Untitled (65x40cm-26x16in) s.d.1960 (DM 16000)
£13492	$22127	(21-Jun-91 G.Z86/R) Hymne II (117x57cm-46x22in) s. i.verso (S.FR 34000)
£16064	$26988	(24-Apr-91 G.Z62/R) An die Freude III (120x50cm-47x20in) s.d.1958 (S.FR 40000)
£17065	$33447	(24-Nov-90 N.M2/R) Composition (119x60cm-47x24in) s.c.1957 (DM 50000)
£610	$1019	(6-Jun-91 HN.H103/R) Composition (30x17cm-12x7in) s.d.1944 chk. (DM 1800)
£736	$1243	(19-Apr-91 FN.S1480/R) Man smoking (18x20cm-7x8in) s.i. pencil col.chk (DM 2200)
£1365	$2676	(22-Nov-90 L.K801) Colour composition and lines (10x13cm-4x5in) mono.d.1924 col.chk pencil (DM 4000)
£1365	$2676	(22-Nov-90 L.K802/R) Composition (25x17cm-10x7in) s.d.1938 col.chk (DM 4000)
£1486	$2527	(28-May-91 KF.M407/R) Untitled (12x16cm-5x6in) s. pastel (DM 4400)
£1638	$3211	(22-Nov-90 L.K800/R) Composition (13x16cm-5x6in) mono.d.1923 col.chk pencil (DM 4800)
£2055	$3349	(15-Jun-91 L.K5/R) Rome (50x35cm-20x14in) s.i.d.1964 pastel (DM 6000)
£2218	$4348	(24-Nov-90 KM.K391/R) Composition in blue (50x35cm-20x14in) s.62 pastel (DM 6500)
£2230	$3791	(28-May-91 KF.M406/R) Composition (31x12cm-12x5in) s.d.1954 mixed media chl (DM 6600)
£2345	$4502	(28-Nov-90 KF.M507/R) Untitled (49x31cm-19x12in) s.i.d.1972 pastel (DM 6800)
£2414	$4634	(28-Nov-90 KF.M505/R) An die Freude (48x31cm-19x12in) s.d.1958 pastel (DM 7000)
£2703	$5270	(20-Oct-90 WK.M4/R) Composition (50x33cm-20x13in) s.d.1973 pastel (DM 8000)
£3041	$5929	(20-Oct-90 WK.M3/R) Composition (46x38cm-18x15in) s.d.1972 pastel (DM 9000)
£3547	$6030	(28-May-91 KF.M404/R) Woman bathing (25x16cm-10x6in) s.d.1940 pastel (DM 10500)
£3547	$6030	(28-May-91 KF.M405/R) Woman bathing (16x25cm-6x10in) s.d.1940 pastel (DM 10500)
£3885	$6605	(28-May-91 KF.M408/R) Jubilieren (65x40cm-26x16in) s.i.d.1955 mixed media hessian (DM 11500)
£4483	$8607	(28-Nov-90 KF.M504/R) Evening music (33x24cm-13x9in) d.1955 i.verso mixed media board (DM 13000)

ACS, Agostos (1889-1947) Hungarian
£727 $1170   (27-Jun-91 D.V36) Sunday idyll (60x80cm-24x31in) s. (A.S 15000)

ACS, Joe (1936-) Canadian
£655 $1290   (12-Nov-90 HO.ED294) Town of Munson, Alberta (122x153cm-48x60in) s.i. acrylic (C.D 1500)

ADAM (jnr) (19th C) ?
£2151 $4301   (6-Feb-91 RAS.K27) Ships portrait 'Thor' of Marstal (62x92cm-24x36in) s.d.1899 (D.KR 24000)

ADAM, Albrecht (1786-1862) German
£3041 $5169   (27-May-91 L.K238/R) Cavallery at manoeuvre (55x74cm-22x29in) (DM 9000)
£9699 $16391   (19-Apr-91 FN.S1661/R) Battle scene of Napoleonic Wars (60x72cm-24x28in) s.d.1843 (DM 29000)

ADAM, Benno (1812-1892) German
£5090 $8500   (7-Jun-91 SY.NY81/R) In the barn (57x78cm-22x31in) s.d.1857

ADAM, Benno (attrib) (1812-1892) German
£1570 $3077   (24-Nov-90 SA.A636/R) The restive horse (32x26cm-13x10in)
            i.d.1867stretcher canvas laid down (DM 4600)

ADAM, E (19th C) German
£1850 $3589   (6-Dec-90 CB.P69/R) Le vapeur mixte (62x92cm-24x36in) s. (F.FR 18000)

ADAM, Edouard (19/20th C) German
£1064 $2000   (7-Aug-90 RB.HY299/R) British steamer 1896 (56x76cm-22x30in) s.d.96
£2834 $5555   (25-Nov-90 ZZ.F1/R) Retour des pecheurs (60x92cm-24x36in) s.d.1915
            (F.FR 28000)

ADAM, Emil (1843-1924) German
£9000 $17280   (28-Nov-90 S210/R) Missouri with jockey E.Pretzner up (72x92cm-28x36in)
            s.i.d.1917
*£3420 $6497   (28-Feb-91 D.V77/R) After the stag hunt (24x39cm-9x15in) s.i.d.1885 W/C
            bodycol (A.S 70000)*

ADAM, Emile (1839-1937) French
£1103 $2151   (12-Oct-90 ZZ.F54) Paysage au bord de mer s. (F.FR 11000)

ADAM, Eugen (1817-1880) German
£853 $1672   (24-Nov-90 SA.A781/R) Ambush (29x45cm-11x18in) s.d.1862 indis.i.d.verso
            paper on canvas (DM 2500)
£3082 $5517   (13-Mar-91 N.M447/R) Horses in puszta landscape (51x68cm-20x27in)
            rem.sig. (DM 9000)

ADAM, Heinrich (1787-1862) German
£6507 $11647   (13-Mar-91 N.M448 a/R) Farmhouse in mountain valley with peasant family
            on path by stream (36x50cm-14x20in) s.d.1832 one of pair (DM 19000)
£8904 $15938   (13-Mar-91 N.M448 b/R) Mill in mountain valley with shepherd and cattle
            on path (36x50cm-14x20in) s.d.1832 one of pair (DM 26000)
*£1500 $2940   (14-Feb-91 CSK14/R) A village on an Alpine Lake (20x30cm-8x12in)
            init.i.d.1831 pencil W/C*

ADAM, J D (1842-1896) British
£1050 $1754   (5-Jun-91 S120/R) Wild roses (30x25cm-12x10in) s.d.1861 s.i.d.stretcher

ADAM, Joseph Denovan (1842-1896) British
£1300 $2119   (13-Jun-91 CSK263/R) Highland cattle (127x102cm-50x40in) s.
£2200 $3718   (3-May-91 PHE155/R) In the byre (75x75cm-20x30in) s.
£2400 $4176   (26-Mar-91 PH115) Herding cattle on a wooded path (101x66cm-40x26in)
            s.d.1878
£2911 $5502   (27-Sep-90 D.V21/R) Sheep in flowering coastal landscape
            (70x122cm-28x48in) s. (A.S 60000)
£3000 $5160   (14-May-91 SWS267/R) Still life study of mixed fruit, butterfly and bee
            (65x58cm-26x23in) s.d.1860

ADAM, Joseph and ADAM, Joseph Denovan (19th C) British
£1400 $2730   (24-Oct-90 SWS343/R) Sheep beneath tree (25x33cm-10x13in) s.
£1500 $2820   (10-Aug-90 PHM253) Driving in the hills (77x127cm-30x50in) s.
£1800 $3366   (28-Aug-90 S763/R) Highland cattle (76x127cm-30x50in) s.d.1865
£3800 $7448   (13-Feb-91 S52/R) Droving in hills (78x127cm-31x50in) init.

ADAM, Julius (1826-1874) German
£3000 $5040   (16-Jul-91 C161/R) Best friends (14x20cm-6x8in) s. panel
£6894 $13030   (25-Sep-90 FN.S2101/R) Cat with kittens in interior (16x20cm-6x8in)
            s.d.1887 panel (DM 20200)
£10274 $16747   (12-Jun-91 N.M360/R) Two kittens at feeding bowl and butterfly in wine
            leaves on house wall (54x38cm-21x15in) s. (DM 30000)
£14211 $27000   (28-Feb-91 CH.NY67/R) Any room in the basket (14x20cm-6x8in) s. panel

ADAM, Julius II (1852-1913) German
£9797 $16655   (28-May-91 KF.M134/R) Kitten lying (15x19cm-6x7in) s.i.d.1888 panel
            (DM 29000)
*£1448 $2781   (28-Nov-90 KF.M314/R) Kittens playing with box of matches
            (30x45cm-12x18in) s.d.1896 chl htd.white (DM 4200)*

ADAM, Patrick William (1854-1929) British
£880 $1505   (30-Jul-91 SWS194) Les fleurs d'ete (49x39cm-19x15in) s.i. verso
£900 $1683   (28-Aug-90 S968/R) Pont d'Austerlitz (22x29cm-9x11in) s.i. panel
£920 $1730   (18-Sep-90 PH29/R) Autumn landscape (28x18cm-11x7in) board
£1300 $2600   (5-Feb-91 S93/R) St Giles cathedral, Edinburgh (109x61cm-43x24in)
            s.d.1924 s.i.stretcher
£1600 $3152   (31-Oct-90 LV169/R) Anemones (51x41cm-20x16in) s.d.1927
£1650 $3251   (31-Oct-90 LV170) Anemones touched with light (48x38cm-19x15in) s.
£1900 $3705   (17-Oct-90 PHG60/R) Contemplation (98x81cm-39x32in) s.d.1883
£2200 $3696   (23-Apr-91 S114/R) Sunlit garden (27x40cm-11x16in) bears sig.verso
            canvas on board
£3000 $5880   (22-Nov-90 CG611/R) The Ponte Vecchio, Florence (68x97cm-27x38in)
            s.i.d.1888
£3500 $5915   (3-May-91 PHE166/R) Interior, Signet Library (104x57cm-41x22in) s.d.1917

ADAM, Patrick William (1854-1929) British-cont.
£7000 $11830   (2-May-91 CG478/R) Venice, Piazetta (53x102cm-21x40in) s.i.d.1890 i.verso
£18000 $34920   (5-Dec-90 PHE111/R) 10 Kensington Park Gardens (90x104cm-35x41in) s.d.1912
£2300 $4301   (28-Aug-90 S1061/R) Interior with a looking glass (54x36cm-21x14in) s.d.1922 gouache

ADAM, Richard Benno (1873-1937) German
£2007 $3391   (17-Apr-91 WE.MU247/R) Portrait of lady with greyhound (43x32cm-17x13in) s.i.d.1898 panel (DM 6000)

ADAM, Victor (attrib) (1801-1866) French
£2055 $3988   (8-Dec-90 SY.MO359/R) Le depart des courses (31x40cm-12x16in) (F.FR 20000)

ADAM, William (1846-?) American
£1300 $2184   (23-Apr-91 S38/R) Fishing boats off shore (61x91cm-24x36in) s.d.90

ADAMI, Valerio (1935-) Italian
£6030 $9889   (19-Jun-91 CL.E38/R) Lo Speechio (73x60cm-29x24in) s.d.1965 (F.FR 60000)
£7035 $11538   (19-Jun-91 CL.E37/R) Il sofa (81x100cm-32x39in) s.d.29-7-65/8-8-65 (F.FR 70000)
£7603 $12393   (11-Jun-91 CSC.P39/R) Portrait d'homme (91x79cm-36x31in) s. verso (F.FR 75500)
£8405 $16558   (30-Oct-90 F.R237/R) Il bacio (55x38cm-22x15in) s.d.1986verso acrylic (I.L 18500000)
£8657 $14717   (28-May-91 SY.MI182/R) Composizione (72x90cm-28x35in) s.d.4.64 (I.L 19000000)
£10628 $20513   (13-Dec-90 F.M418/R) Arena (62x82cm-24x32in) s.d.1963verso (I.L 23000000)
£11089 $21623   (28-Oct-90 GL.P99/R) Paesaggio di rovine (75x100cm-30x39in) init. i. verso (F.FR 110000)
£11706 $22828   (23-Oct-90 F.M73/R) Note alla casa di Faulkner (100x81cm-39x32in) i.d.1966verso (I.L 26000000)
£13000 $20930   (27-Jun-91 C40/R) La Vetrina (80x99cm-31x39in) s.i.verso
£15712 $30323   (13-Dec-90 F.M426/R) Studio per disegno di un paesaggio (92x73cm-36x29in) s.d.1974verso (I.L 34000000)
£16310 $31478   (16-Dec-90 P.V94/R) Il sofa (81x100cm-32x39in) s.i.d.26/7/65-15/8/65 verso (F.FR 160000)
£19255 $31578   (20-Jun-91 F.M445/R) Ex libris, disegno di rovine (96x130cm-38x51in) s.i.verso acrylic (I.L 42000000)
£20233 $39453   (21-Oct-90 P.V78/R) O Bella Bionda (130x97cm-51x38in) i. s.i.d.1987 verso acrylic (F.FR 200100)
£20812 $40376   (3-Dec-90 CH.R171/R) L'alpinista (96x73cm-38x29in) s.i.verso acrylic (I.L 45000000)
£22000 $38940   (21-Mar-91 S62/R) Capriccio Americano (130x97cm-51x38in) s.d.30.3.78-1.12.78 verso
£26000 $50700   (18-Oct-90 C457/R) La palestra (100x81cm-39x32in) s.i.d.68verso acrylic
£26114 $50923   (22-Oct-90 BR.M59/R) La vasca ed altri racconti (116x89cm-46x35in) s.d.1965-66 verso (I.L 58000000)
£27888 $47410   (30-May-91 FB.P87/R) J. Ruskin-Chiron teaching Achilles to play the lyre (197x148cm-78x58in) s.i.d.4.1.79/3.3.79 acrylic (F.FR 280000)
£30000 $53100   (21-Mar-91 C270/R) Corsa a ostacoli a Ascot (129x162cm-51x64in) s.i. verso acrylic
£33797 $57117   (21-Apr-91 P.V57/R) Prometeo (198x147cm-78x58in) s.i.d.2.1.79/12.3.79 verso (F.FR 340000)
£38306 $74698   (28-Oct-90 GL.P92/R) L'Angelus, il n'y a pas de guerre juste (147x198cm-58x78in) s.i.d.28.5.78-28.9.78 verso acrylic (F.FR 380000)
£44807 $88269   (29-Oct-90 FB.P54/R) Cartolina di un amico dai Caraibi (130x97cm-51x38in) s.i.d.16.8.74 d.23.10.84 verso acrylic (F.FR 440000)
£1024 $2007   (24-Nov-90 VG.B402/R) Private life (48x36cm-19x14in) s.i.d.1970 graphite board (DM 3000)
£1136 $1965   (7-May-91 F.M296/R) Il quadrato (44x32cm-17x13in) s.i.d.1966 pencil (I.L 2500000)
£1953 $3788   (4-Dec-90 I.N3/R) Valencia (47x35cm-19x14in) s.i.d.1982 lead pencil (F.FR 19000)
£2081 $4038   (3-Dec-90 CH.R43/R) Spettacolo (48x66cm-19x26in) s.i.d.1962verso pencil (I.L 4500000)
£2172 $4192   (12-Dec-90 F.M97/R) Studio per combattimento della Bicocca (49x66cm-19x26in) s.d.1962 pencil (I.L 4700000)
£3409 $6683   (20-Nov-90 BR.M16/R) Brodway (36x48cm-14x19in) s.i.d.1972 pencil (I.L 7500000)
£8000 $15600   (18-Oct-90 C440/R) La casa sul lago (55x75cm-22x30in) s.i. W/C ink

ADAMO, Max (1837-1901) German
£2622 $5087   (4-Dec-90 FN.S1730/R) Old man in Spanish costume with girl in landscape with castle ruin (72x55cm-28x22in) s.d.1879 canvas laid down (DM 7500)

ADAMOWICZ, Ewa (20th C) ?
£791 $1416   (14-Apr-91 R.P199/R) Papillon de nuit (65x92cm-26x36in) s. mixed media canvas (F.FR 8000)
£813 $1626   (7-Feb-91 R.P84/R) Sans isu (89x116cm-35x46in) s. mixed media canvas (F.FR 8000)

ADAMOWICZ, Ewa (20th C) ?-cont.
£857 $1671   *(28-Oct-90 R.P94/R) Trace perdue (89x116cm-35x46in) s. mixed media canvas (F.FR 8500)*
£915 $1829   *(7-Feb-91 R.P158/R) Morceau de bonheur (89x116cm-35x46in) s. mixed media canvas (F.FR 9000)*
£940 $1682   *(14-Apr-91 R.P75) Eclosion crepusculaire (81x100cm-32x39in) s. mixed media canvas (F.FR 9500)*
£940 $1682   *(14-Apr-91 R.P130/R) Erois dame blanche (83x116cm-33x46in) s. mixed media canvas (F.FR 9500)*
£1270 $2541   *(7-Feb-91 R.P215) Aile froissee (89x116cm-35x46in) s. mixed media canvas (F.FR 12500)*

ADAMS, Alfred (?) British
£600 $1062   *(20-Mar-91 WI1181) Farm at Llwynguril, Wales (36x51cm-14x20in) s. W/C*

ADAMS, Charles James (1857-1931) British
£300 $531   *(21-Mar-91 CSK87) The road across the moors (38x53cm-15x21in) s. W/C*
£430 $735   *(29-Jul-91 HS190/R) Rural landscape with cattle beside pool in foreground (19x27cm-7x11in) s. W/C*
£550 $897   *(14-Jun-91 C157 a) Woodland road near Farnham, Surrey (28x39cm-11x15in) s. i.verso pencil W/C*
£820 $1402   *(29-Jul-91 HS145/R) Extensive landscape with sheep grazing beneath trees, figure on path (36x54cm-14x21in) s. W/C*
£820 $1517   *(5-Mar-91 AG88) Duck pond (31x23cm-12x9in) s. W/C*
£1200 $2004   *(22-Jul-91 SWS811/R) Travellers on a moorland road. Sheep grazing by a river s. two*
£1300 $2574   *(30-Jan-91 S259) Surrey lane (38x56cm-15x22in) s. W/C*
£8000 $15120   *(26-Sep-90 S321/R) Watering work horses (51x76cm-20x30in) s. W/C*

ADAMS, Charles Partridge (1858-1942) American
£957 $1800   *(19-Sep-90 B.SF2803/R) Morning haze (25x38cm-10x15in) s.d.'98*
£1515 $2500   *(13-Jul-91 YFA.M21/R) Rocky mountain landscape (36x51cm-14x20in) s.*
£2312 $4000   *(12-May-91 H.C119/R) Last gleaming (61x91cm-24x36in) s.*
£3352 $6000   *(11-Apr-91 FA.PH791) Autumn landscape (58x76cm-23x30in) s.*
£928 $1550   *(9-Jun-91 LIT.L361) Pike's Peak (18x23cm-7x9in) s. W/C*

ADAMS, Douglas (19th C) British
£1200 $2016   *(18-Jul-91 PHX311/R) Pheasant shooting (61x76cm-24x30in)*

ADAMS, J Seymour (19th C) British
£950 $1872   *(13-Nov-90 SWS231/R) The young anglers (29x39cm-11x15in) s.*

ADAMS, John Clayton (1840-1906) British
£680 $1170   *(14-May-91 SWS233) River scene with punt (30x45cm-12x18in) s.d.1895*
£2041 $4000   *(7-Nov-90 B.SF1174/R) Young fisherman (30x25cm-12x10in) s.d.1868*
£2237 $4250   *(27-Feb-91 SY.NY249/R) Summer landscape with cattle ggrazing along river (51x76cm-20x30in) s.d.1904*
£2400 $4728   *(1-Nov-90 D174/R) Spring time with blossoming tree on downland and weald beyond (51x76cm-20x30in) s.*
£2973 $4846   *(10-Jun-91 W.T1343/R) Harvesting (61x122cm-24x48in) s. (C.D 5500)*
£3600 $7056   *(13-Feb-91 S53/R) Ewhurst Hill, near Guildford (56x97cm-22x38in) s.d.1885 s.i.stretcher*
£4400 $8668   *(1-Nov-90 D175/R) Harvesting on downs with weald beyond (51x76cm-20x30in) s.d.1877*
£9966 $18935   *(2-Mar-91 KRA.D272/R) Weedy corner, landscape with harvest scene (106x152cm-42x60in) s.d.1886 (DM 29000)*

ADAMS, John Ottis (1851-1927) American
£9249 $16000   *(22-May-91 CH.NY250/R) Spring along the creek (56x81cm-22x32in) s.d.1897*

ADAMS, Wayman (1883-1959) American
£1444 $2700   *(1-Aug-90 B.P35/R) Mother and baby (20x25cm-8x10in) s.*
£1497 $2800   *(1-Aug-90 B.P36/R) Mother and two children (20x25cm-8x10in) s.*

ADAMS, Willis Seaver (1842-1921) American
£1515 $3000   *(1-Feb-91 S.W2563/R) Trompe l'oeil still life - roses and butterflies (107x51cm-42x20in) panel*

ADAMSKI, Hans Peter (20th C) ?
£898 $1769   *(17-Nov-90 S.Z3) Boy with tulip (59x47cm-23x19in) s.d.1986verso gouache (S.FR 2200)*
£12245 $24122   *(17-Nov-90 S.Z4/R) The birth of science (150x220cm-59x87in) d.1981 s.i.verso dispersion cotton (S.FR 30000)*

ADAMSON, Dorothy (?-1934) British
£1796 $3000   *(7-Jun-91 SY.NY115/R) Study of a hare (34x44cm-13x17in) chl.pastel*

ADAMSON, H (?) ?
£620 $1011   *(5-Jul-91 BW408) Young lady amidst roses (61x51cm-24x20in) s.*

ADAMSON, Harry Curieux (20th C) American
£1406 $2700   *(17-Dec-90 SY.NY279 a/R) Secluded waters, hooded Mergansers (61x76cm-24x30in) s.*

ADAMSSON, Bo Ake (1941-) Swedish
£802 $1387   *(22-May-91 BA.S301/R) My pink horse (81x100cm-32x39in) s. (S.KR 8500)*

ADAMUS, John Quincy (1874-1933) Austrian
£1196 $2069   (8-May-91 D.V68/R) Female nude in landscape (70x47cm-28x19in) s. board
                      (A.S 25000)

ADDAMS, Charles (20th C) American
£941 $1600   (1-Jun-91 IH.NY110/R) She shows up every Halloween, gag cartoon with
                      witch stirring pot (28x33cm-11x13in) s. brush ink

ADDERTON, Charles William (1866-?) British
£480 $850   (22-Mar-91 T168) Lake scene with figures on a jetty (33x48cm-13x19in) s.

ADEMOLLO, Luigi (1764-1849) Italian
£9500 $16055   (19-Apr-91 C31/R) Edward and Eleonora (124x155cm-49x61in)
£3800 $6194   (2-Jul-91 C298/R) Edward and Eleonora (16x24cm-6x9in) black chk W/C
                      bodycol

ADGAMOV, Roman (1951-) Russian
£553 $907   (19-Jun-91 ARC.P188/R) Lilas (100x67cm-39x26in) s.d.88 (F.FR 5500)

ADIE, Edith Helena (fl.1892-1930) British
£400 $716   (13-Mar-91 B134) A view of Lake Annecy from a terraced garden
                      (36x53cm-14x21in) s. W/C
£400 $760   (25-Feb-91 PH60) Swan River, Perth, Australia (11x26cm-4x10in) s. W/C
£1700 $3213   (26-Sep-90 S275/R) Garden in Taormina (19x28cm-7x11in) s. W/C

ADLER, Edmund (1871-1957) German
£2517 $4908   (10-Oct-90 WE.MU237/R) The precious treasure (68x55cm-27x22in) s.
                      (DM 7500)
£5000 $9600   (28-Nov-90 S214/R) Preparing to go tobogganning (55x67cm-22x26in) s.
£5895 $9962   (15-Apr-91 SY.J410/R) Birdsong (53x101cm-21x40in) s. (SA.R 28000)
£5944 $11472   (12-Dec-90 WE.MU107/R) The mail has arrived (56x69cm-22x27in) s.
                      (DM 17000)

ADLER, Jankel (1895-1949) Polish
£2069 $3972   (26-Nov-90 WK.M105/R) Anchor (39x64cm-15x25in) s. (DM 6000)
£2712 $4420   (3-Jul-91 WE.MU233/R) Rabbi Balshem in Constantinople (108x48cm-43x19in)
                      (DM 8000)
£5242 $9384   (14-Apr-91 GL.P285/R) Composition (46x51cm-18x20in) s. hardboard
                      (F.FR 53000)
£9424 $18000   (1-Jan-91 GG.TA208/R) Two dogs (81x100cm-32x39in) d.1938
£445 $726   (15-Jun-91 L.K8) Female nude seated (63x48cm-25x19in) indian ink brush
                      (DM 1300)
£548 $893   (15-Jun-91 L.K7) Elderly woman seated (64x50cm-25x20in) indian ink brush
                      (DM 1600)
£681 $1300   (1-Jan-91 GG.TA209/R) Nacht (20x25cm-8x10in) s. mixed media
£681 $1300   (1-Jan-91 GG.TA210/R) Composition (18x22cm-7x9in) s. gouache W/C
£1096 $1786   (15-Jun-91 L.K6/R) Couple standing (47x31cm-19x12in) s. ochre
                      (DM 3200)
£2086 $3400   (12-Jun-91 GG.TA229/R) Figures (16x22cm-6x9in) s. W/C

ADLER, Jules (1865-1952) French
£6030 $10794   (11-Mar-91 GL.P30/R) Le pecheur (54x65cm-21x26in) s. (F.FR 60000)

ADNET, Francoise (1924-) French
£553 $989   (11-Mar-91 GL.P31) Les poupees et la lampe a petrole (73x50cm-29x20in)
                      s. (F.FR 5500)
£1006 $1700   (1-May-91 D.NY1) Nature morte aux poires (64x91cm-25x36in) s. s.i.verso
£1417 $2777   (19-Nov-90 CSC.P2/R) Portrait de jeune fille (100x81cm-39x32in) s.
                      (F.FR 14000)

ADOLFS, Gerard Pieter (1897-1968) Dutch
£1808 $3525   (23-Oct-90 C.A5/R) A small village on Java (50x65cm-20x26in) s.
                      (B.FR 110000)

ADRIAENSSEN, Alexander (1587-1661) Flemish
£3436 $6735   (16-Feb-91 GF.H1/R) Still life of fishes and mussels with carp in brass
                      basin (39x69cm-15x27in) s.d.1642 (DM 10000)
£10703 $21086   (14-Nov-90 SY.AM100/R) Still life of hunting trophy (43x57cm-17x22in)
                      panel (D.FL 35000)
£56000 $91280   (3-Jul-91 S28/R) Still life of mixed flowers in glass vase, on marble
                      ledge (80x45cm-31x18in) panel

ADRIAN, M (19th C) German
£650 $1300   (6-Feb-91 D.NY1) Harbour scene with figures (30x51cm-12x20in) s.

ADRIAN-NILSSON, Gosta (1884-1965) Swedish
£9651 $18915   (10-Nov-90 FAL.M2/R) Kungsgat's viaduct, Kungsholmen in background
                      (58x49cm-23x19in) mono. panel (S.KR 105000)
£14981 $25768   (14-May-91 BU.S85/R) Composition (178x204cm-70x80in) s. (S.KR 160000)
£23063 $44280   (27-Nov-90 BU.S6/R) Harbour scene (103x75cm-41x30in) init. (S.KR 250000)
£538 $1043   (4-Dec-90 BA.S155/R) Factory (32x17cm-13x7in) init. Indian ink
                      (S.KR 5800)
£1174 $1995   (28-May-91 AB.S5160/R) 'Eldeling' - costume sketch for Moses Pergament's
                      ballet (31x24cm-12x9in) s. W/C pencil (S.KR 12500)
£1297 $2517   (5-Dec-90 AB.S7003/R) Grey head (20x15cm-8x6in) s.d.54 W/C (S.KR 14000)

ADRIAN-NILSSON, Gosta (1884-1965) Swedish-cont.
£1668 $3236   *(4-Dec-90 BA.S154/R) Medieval virgin (34x22cm-13x9in) init. W/C (S.KR 18000)*
£2170 $3754   *(22-May-91 BA.S55/R) Youth on beach at sunset (23x35cm-9x14in) s. gouache (S.KR 23000)*
£2317 $4495   *(4-Dec-90 BA.S152/R) Grynmalargatan in Lund, street scene (30x30cm-12x12in) s.verso mixed media (S.KR 25000)*
£2317 $4495   *(4-Dec-90 BA.S150/R) Barge by quay (31x40cm-12x16in) init. gouache (S.KR 25000)*
£2317 $4495   *(4-Dec-90 BA.S151/R) Indian (31x47cm-12x19in) init. gouache (S.KR 25000)*

ADRION, Lucien (1889-1953) French
£508 $1000   *(13-Nov-90 CE.NY138/R) A la plage (24x33cm-9x13in) s. panel*
£800 $1560   *(15-Oct-90 PH3) Maison de Banlieu (39x55cm-15x22in) s.*
£1104 $1800   *(12-Jun-91 SY.NY41/R) La Grand Rue St. Malo (82x60cm-32x24in) s.d.37 s.verso*
£1351 $2297   *(1-Jun-91 VG.B402/R) Corpus Christi Procession in French town (60x73cm-24x29in) s. (DM 4000)*
£1419 $2412   *(1-Jun-91 VG.B401/R) Town in river valley (60x72cm-24x28in) s. (DM 4200)*
£1618 $2800   *(7-May-91 CE.NY51/R) Bievres en automne (53x74cm-21x29in) s.d.38 s.i.verso*
£1626 $3252   *(6-Feb-91 FB.P4/R) Le senat (38x46cm-15x18in) s. (F.FR 16000)*
£1929 $3800   *(13-Nov-90 CE.NY129/R) Le Pont de Bir Hakeim (65x81cm-26x32in) s.*
£1953 $3788   *(8-Dec-90 LT.P23/R) L'apres-midi en bord de mer (15x19cm-6x7in) s. panel (F.FR 19000)*
£2000 $3440   *(14-May-91 SWS363/R) Winter (37x52cm-15x20in) s.*
£2437 $4800   *(13-Nov-90 CE.NY111/R) Le Touquet (46x55cm-18x22in) s. s.i.verso*
£2640 $5200   *(13-Nov-90 CE.NY89/R) Place de la Concorde (63x91cm-25x36in) s. s.i.verso*
£2700 $5265   *(15-Oct-90 PH2/R) Le jardin des tuileries (42x53cm-17x21in) s. canvasboard*
£2854 $5509   *(12-Dec-90 APT.P57) Paris, le pont du Carrousel (65x81cm-26x32in) s. (F.FR 28000)*
£2877 $4948   *(19-May-91 ZZ.F116/R) Les bords de la Canche au Touquet (46x55cm-18x22in) s. (F.FR 29000)*
£3452 $6800   *(13-Nov-90 CE.NY90/R) Concorde et Tuilleries (51x61cm-20x24in) s. s.i.verso*
£3468 $6000   *(7-May-91 CE.NY57/R) Les falaises (59x79cm-23x31in) s.d.36 s.i.verso*
£3553 $7000   *(13-Nov-90 CE.NY51/R) Le boulevard Saint Martin (65x73cm-26x29in) s.*
£3670 $7083   *(12-Dec-90 APT.P60) Paris, les Champs Elysees au 14 Juillet (54x65cm-21x26in) s. (F.FR 36000)*
£3754 $7358   *(24-Nov-90 N.M5/R) Rue Royale with view of Madeleine (54x64cm-21x25in) s. (DM 11000)*
£4032 $7863   *(28-Oct-90 M.V116/R) Le pantheon (60x81cm-24x32in) s. (F.FR 40000)*
£5155 $9794   *(2-Mar-91 KRA.D443/R) Cannebiere in Marseille (73x101cm-29x40in) s. (DM 15000)*
£6294 $12147   *(12-Dec-90 WE.MU198/R) Park landscape with cars and figures (60x92cm-24x36in) s. (DM 18000)*

ADUATZ, Fritz (1907-) Polish
£1435 $2483   *(8-May-91 D.V108/R) Women at fountain (72x85cm-28x33in) s.i.verso (A.S 30000)*

ADVOCAAT, Gunnvor (1912-) Scandinavian
£1432 $2793   *(11-Oct-90 BU.O1/R) Composition in black and green (65x100cm-26x39in) s. (N.KR 16500)*
£1432 $2793   *(11-Oct-90 BU.O2/R) Composition (61x76cm-24x30in) s. (N.KR 16500)*

AEGERTER, Karl (1888-1969) Swiss
£598 $1165   *(24-Oct-90 GD.B8/R) Winterwald (82x110cm-32x43in) board (S.FR 1500)*
£1160 $2274   *(24-Nov-90 N.M6/R) Winter in Bunden (100x80cm-39x31in) mono. board (DM 3400)*
£1182 $2046   *(25-May-91 N.M2/R) Grimmialp in winter (79x114cm-31x45in) s. board (DM 3500)*
£1807 $3542   *(21-Nov-90 SY.Z108/R) Viamala (130x160cm-51x63in) s. (S.FR 4500)*

AEL, Jules van (20th C) Belgian?
£722 $1250   *(25-May-91 KV.L290) Children's joy (95x112cm-37x44in) s.d.1968 W/C (B.FR 44000)*

AELST, Pieter Coecke van (attrib) (1502-1550) Flemish
£7059 $12000   *(31-May-91 CH.NY73/R) Vanitas (52x43cm-20x17in) panel*

AELST, Pieter Coecke van (circle) (1502-1550) Flemish
£4000 $8000   *(7-Feb-91 CSK32/R) Judgement of Soloman (67x53cm-26x21in) d.1576 panel*
£4359 $8500   *(10-Oct-90 CH.NY109/R) The Conversion of St Paul (34x37cm-13x15in) panel*

AELST, Pieter Coecke van (school) (1502-1550) Flemish
£4872 $9500   *(10-Oct-90 CH.NY82/R) St Catherine of Alexandria (132x43cm-52x17in) panel wing of triptych*
£5128 $10000   *(10-Oct-90 CH.NY136/R) Madonna and Child (48x33cm-19x13in) panel arched top*

AELST, Pieter Coecke van (studio) (1502-1550) Flemish
£10398 $20483   (14-Nov-90 SY.AM84/R) Adoration of the Magi (85x61cm-33x24in) panel
                        (D.FL 34000)
£16820 $33135   (13-Nov-90 CH.AM183/R) Adoration of Magi, Adoration of Shepherds and
                        Circumcision (88x101cm-35x40in) panel shaped top triptych (D.FL 55000)
£33639 $66269   (13-Nov-90 CH.AM140/R) Adoration of Kings (69x89cm-27x35in) panel shaped
                        top triptych (D.FL 110000)

AELST, Pieter Coecke van (style) (1502-1550) Flemish
£850 $1386   (4-Jul-91 CSK2) Holy Family (28x23cm-11x9in) panel
£980 $1597   (4-Jul-91 CSK46/R) Saint Jerome (30x22cm-12x9in) panel
£4748 $8499   (8-Apr-91 ARC.P5/R) Vierge a l'enfant avec Saint Antoine
                     (77x62cm-30x24in) panel (F.FR 48000)
£6116 $12049   (13-Nov-90 CH.AM190/R) Christ among doctors. Christ on way to Calvary
                       (10cm-4ins circular) panel pair (D.FL 20000)

AELST, Willem van (1626-1683) Dutch
£8537 $14000   (19-Jun-91 B.SF1667/R) Game with implements of the chase on ledge
                       (91x71cm-36x28in)
£64220 $126514   (14-Nov-90 SY.AM36/R) Still life of flowers in vase on marble ledge
                       (42x33cm-17x13in) s.d.1682 canvas on panel (D.FL 210000)

AELST, Willem van (attrib) (1626-1683) Dutch
£29052 $57232   (14-Nov-90 SY.AM42/R) Still life of glass beaker, salt and oysters on
                       draped marble ledge (46x33cm-18x13in) indis.s.1659 panel (D.FL 95000)

AELST, Willem van (circle) (1626-1683) Dutch
£12500 $21125   (17-Apr-91 S139/R) Swag of flowers (88x116cm-35x46in) canvas on panel
£19500 $31785   (3-Jul-91 S105/R) Still life of flowers in glass vase with butterfly on
                     partly draped ledge (49x41cm-19x16in) bears sig.

AERDE, J P van (18th C) Dutch
£750 $1500   (7-Feb-91 CSK126 a) Seamstress (67x51cm-26x20in) s.

AERENS, Robert (20th C) Belgian
£900 $1512   (23-Apr-91 C.A270) Landscape (50x75cm-20x30in) s.d.1923 (B.FR 55000)

AERT, Berthe (19th C) Belgian
£616 $1103   (12-Mar-91 FN.S2263) Roses and forget-me-not on ground with beetles and
                     butterflies (29x35cm-11x14in) mono. board on canvas (DM 1800)

AERTSEN, Pieter (1507-1575) Dutch
£3590 $7000   (10-Oct-90 CH.NY91 a/R) Head of woman (30x20cm-12x8in) panel
£7000 $13650   (26-Oct-90 C73/R) Elders gesticulating (70x77cm-28x30in) panel

AERTSEN, Pieter (circle) (1507-1575) Dutch
£7000 $11410   (2-Jul-91 PH209/R) The Nativity (58x39cm-23x15in) panel

AERTSEN, Pieter (school) (1507-1575) Dutch
£941 $1600   (30-May-91 CE.NY83) Christ at the Supper in the House of Simon the
                     Pharisee (81x67cm-32x26in) panel

AESCHER, Heinrich (19th C) German
£2857   *$5543*   *(8-Dec-90 GAB.G2083/R) Interieur mauresque (65x46cm-26x18in) s. W/C*
                     (S.FR 7000)

AFFANDI (20th C) Indonesian
£1800 $3042   (1-May-91 GD.B3/R) Sunflowers (98x128cm-39x50in) s.d.1974 (S.FR 4500)

AFFLECK, William (1869-?) British
£700   *$1372*   *(19-Nov-90 SWS715/R) Cottage garden (31x42cm-12x17in) s. W/C*
£880   *$1716*   *(15-Jan-91 SWS75/R) By the cottage gate (42x28cm-17x11in) s. W/C*
                     htd.bodycol
£1071   *$2057*   *(27-Nov-90 W.T1317/R) Cottage in Gloucestershire (29x41cm-11x16in) W/C*
                     (C.D 2400)
£1300   *$2535*   *(15-Jan-91 SWS76/R) By the stream (41x28cm-16x11in) s. W/C htd.bodycol*
£1300   *$2457*   *(26-Sep-90 S283/R) Shepherd passing thatched cottages (28x38cm-11x15in)*
                     s. W/C
£2100   *$4032*   *(17-Dec-90 PH25/R) Summer flowers (41x29cm-16x11in) s. W/C*
£2800   *$5488*   *(22-Nov-90 CSK80) Picking summer flowers (30x42cm-12x17in) s. pencil W/C*
£2966   *$5724*   *(12-Dec-90 BU.S1/R) Her morning visitors (42x31cm-17x12in) s. W/C*
                     (S.KR 32000)
£3500   *$6860*   *(22-Nov-90 CSK79/R) Elegant young lady in country garden*
                     (29x41cm-11x16in) s. pencil W/C

AFRICANO, Nicholas (20th C) American?
£2792   *$5500*   *(4-Oct-90 SY.NY262/R) Study for grandmother (51x82cm-20x32in) s.d.1984*
                     verso acrylic oil magna linen 2 panels
£7107   *$14000*   *(4-Oct-90 SY.NY242/R) Evelina (218x168cm-86x66in) s.d.1984 verso acrylic*
                     oil magna linen 2 panels

AFRO (1912-1976) Italian
£6244 $12113   (3-Dec-90 CH.R117/R) Donna seduta (100x65cm-39x26in) s. (I.L 13500000)
£10086 $16541   (20-Jun-91 F.M428/R) Natura morta (37x57cm-15x22in) s.d.39 panel
                     (I.L 22000000)

AFRO (1912-1976) Italian-cont.

£29773	$57164	(27-Nov-90 SY.MI173/R) La lampada azzurra (63x53cm-25x21in) s.d.48 (I.L 65000000)
£71429	$140000	(7-Nov-90 SY.NY146/R) Anticipation of a voyager (160x208cm-63x82in) s.d.56
£107640	$206669	(27-Nov-90 SY.MI247/R) La Persiana (78x117cm-31x46in) s.d.54 (I.L 235000000)
£12729	$24948	(20-Nov-90 BR.M82/R) Composizione (33x48cm-13x19in) s.d.1948 mixed media (I.L 28000000)
£31714	$55183	(26-Mar-91 F.M136/R) La Forcola (80x100cm-31x39in) s.d.71 mixed media canvas (I.L 70000000)
£43553	$71427	(20-Jun-91 F.M449/R) Giallo, rosso e nero (70x100cm-28x39in) s.d.64 s.i.d.verso mixed media paper on canvas (I.L 95000000)

AFRO, Basaldella (1912-1976) Italian

£3077	$6000	(24-Oct-90 B.SF1562/R) untitled (48x33cm-19x13in) s.num.9491 W/C pastel board
£7614	$15000	(4-Oct-90 SY.NY8/R) Composition (26x22cm-10x9in) s.d.51 W/C chl crayon
£7614	$15000	(4-Oct-90 SY.NY7/R) Composition (22x30cm-9x12in) s.d.51 W/C chl crayon
£14877	$26629	(9-Apr-91 F.R108/R) Untitled (35x50cm-14x20in) s.d.61 mixed media paper laid down on canvas (I.L 33000000)

AGABITI, Pietro Paolo (fl.1511-1540) Italian

£25000	$48250	(12-Dec-90 S16/R) Madonna and Child, with infant St.John and St.Catherine of Alexandria (192x149cm-76x59in) bears sig.d.1522 tempera panel

AGAM, Yaacov (1928-) Israeli

£5607	$10821	(16-Dec-90 GL.P179/R) Du soir a la nuit (35x35cm-14x14in) s.i. verso aluminium (F.FR 55000)
£13198	$26000	(4-Oct-90 SY.NY123/R) Model Leverkusen (57x76cm-22x30in) s.verso corrugated aluminium
£26650	$52500	(14-Nov-90 SY.NY322/R) Appearances (116x157cm-46x62in) s.d.1972-77 acrylic lacquer on aluminium

AGAR, Eileen (1904-) British

£950	$1786	(18-Sep-90 PH202/R) Autumn leaves (76x56cm-30x22in) s.
£1100	$2156	(6-Nov-90 PH156/R) Jug of verse (76x63cm-30x25in) s. s.d.1949verso
£1300	$2249	(7-May-91 PH111) The football (61x51cm-24x20in) s. s.i.d.1966verso
£1450	$2726	(18-Sep-90 PH203/R) Football (61x51cm-24x20in) s. s.d.1966 verso
£1500	$2940	(6-Nov-90 PH157) Pigeon post (51x91cm-20x36in) s. s.d.1969verso
£1600	$2672	(7-Jun-91 C332/R) Morse code (76x95cm-30x37in) s. s.i.d.1963verso acrylic
£2200	$4136	(20-Sep-90 C113/R) Fruit and jug (39x59cm-15x23in) s. s.i.d.1967 stretcher
£2200	$4290	(9-Oct-90 B31/R) Untitled (106x185cm-42x73in) acrylic canvas
£3000	$5550	(8-Mar-91 C132/R) Landscape of a dream (61x76cm-24x30in) s. s.i.d.1984verso
£5000	$9250	(8-Mar-91 C111/R) Jug of Verse (76x63cm-30x25in) s.i.d.1949 s.i.verso
£6500	$10985	(1-May-91 S40/R) Ancient memory (51x61cm-20x24in) s. s.d.1941 s.i.d.stretcher
£914	$1800	(15-Nov-90 D.NY75 a) Birth of minotaur (74x54cm-29x21in) s. d.1947 verso gouache

AGARD, Charles (1866-?) French

£1000	$1880	(20-Sep-90 M11) Village rooftops (25x46cm-10x18in) s.
£1500	$2820	(20-Sep-90 M12) Seated nude with mirror (46x56cm-18x22in)
£1550	$2914	(20-Sep-90 M10) Puy casquier (30x38cm-12x15in) s. board
£1600	$3008	(20-Sep-90 M9) The mirror (30x51cm-12x20in) s.

AGASSE, Jacques Laurent (style) (1767-1849) Swiss

£2800	$4872	(26-Mar-91 PH53/R) Mastiffs harassing a caged leopard (131x180cm-52x71in)

AGAZZI, Ermenegildo (1866-1945) Italian

£727	$1426	(22-Nov-90 SY.MI32/R) Corpus Domini (25x36cm-10x14in) s. panel (I.L 1600000)

AGAZZI, Rinaldo (1857-1939) Italian

£2182	$4277	(22-Nov-90 SY.MI8/R) Madonna con le rose (109x75cm-43x30in) s. (I.L 4800000)

AGGER, Knud (20th C) Scandinavian

£710	$1400	(31-Oct-90 KH.K1) Landscape with houses, Thy (90x100cm-35x39in) s. (D.KR 8000)

AGLIETTI, G (?) Australian?

£1800	$2934	(4-Jul-91 C511) Madonna dell'Impannata (139x104cm-55x41in) after Raphael
£1900	$3097	(4-Jul-91 C509/R) Madonna and child with Saint Elizabeth and infant Saint John the Baptist (139x103cm-55x41in) after Andrea del Sarto

AGLIO, Agostino (1777-1857) Italian

£8500	$15215	(10-Apr-91 S22/R) Italianate landscape with rustics and animals by classical ruins (97x138cm-38x54in) s.

14

AGNEESENS, Edouard (1842-1885) Belgian
£675 $1309   (4-Dec-90 C.A2) Woman with an orange (50x40cm-20x16in) s. (B.FR 40000)
£2308 $4524   (21-Nov-90 GM.B903/R) Les enfants colard (45x55cm-18x22in) s.
                (B.FR 140000)

AGNELL, Olle (1923-) Swedish
£649 $1259   (5-Dec-90 AB.S7004) Coastal landscape, Halland (66x92cm-26x36in) s.
                (S.KR 7000)

AGOSTA, Giovanni di Cristoforo (17th C) Italian
£917 $1761   (27-Nov-90 APT.P25) David le prophete (28x20cm-11x8in) pierre noire
                sanguinne (F.FR 9000)

AGOSTINI, G (19th C) Italian
£1450 $2451   (16-Apr-91 CH.R58) Paesaggio (38x45cm-15x18in) s.d.1872 board
                (I.L 3200000)

AGOSTINI, Guido (19th C) Italian
£1300 $2132   (18-Jun-91 PH178/R) Figure on hilltop, Florence beyond (23x27cm-9x11in)
                s.d.1877 board oval
£1443 $2800   (8-Dec-90 W.W77/R) The Matterhorn (43x33cm-17x13in) s. i.stretcher
£1500 $2925   (16-Oct-90 CG246/R) View of Florence (18x23cm-7x9in) s.d.1879 board
                painted oval

AGOSTINI, Max (1914-?) Italian
£1508 $2472   (18-Jun-91 APT.P165) Jardin fleuri (46x65cm-18x26in) s. (F.FR 15000)
£1608 $2878   (11-Mar-91 GL.P32) Paysage de Provence (33x55cm-13x22in) s. (F.FR 16000)
£2161 $3544   (18-Jun-91 APT.P163/R) Coquelicots (54x73cm-21x29in) s. i. verso
                (F.FR 21500)
£4824 $8635   (11-Mar-91 GL.P33) Champ de coquelicots (60x92cm-24x36in) s.
                (F.FR 48000)
£6524 $12526 (30-Nov-90 ARC.P150/R) Le jardin des Tuileries (73x115cm-29x45in) s.
                (F.FR 64000)

AGOSTINI, Tony (1916-?) Italian
£597 $1039   (28-Mar-91 DAR.P38) Bouquet de fleurs (67x49cm-26x19in) s. paper
                (F.FR 6000)
£663 $1307   (18-Nov-90 S.S1) Vase fleuri (46x38cm-18x15in) (F.FR 6500)
£846 $1472   (28-Mar-91 DAR.P52/R) Port de Marseille (65x80cm-26x31in) s. (F.FR 8500)
£965 $1931   (6-Feb-91 FB.P5) Interieur de cuisine (81x60cm-32x24in) s. (F.FR 9500)

AGRASOT Y JUAN, Joaquim (1837-1919) Spanish
£2632 $5000   (27-Feb-91 SY.NY364/R) Sultan and harem (32x53cm-13x21in) s.

AGREN, Olof (1874-1962) Swedish
£760 $1474   (4-Dec-90 BA.S627/R) Scene from Menton (60x80cm-24x31in) s.d.1932
                (S.KR 8200)
£6181 $11867 (27-Nov-90 BU.S3643/R) Hill planted with vines (175x220cm-69x87in)
                s.d.1927 (S.KR 67000)

AGRESTI, Livio (1508-1580) Italian
£3500 $5705   (1-Jul-91 S177/R) Design for spandrel - Roman martyr and two putti
                (24x26cm-9x10in) pen wash htd white

AGRICOLA, Carl Joseph (1779-1852) German
£534 $1009   (27-Sep-90 D.V229/R) Two sisters in hunting outfit with dog
                (33x26cm-13x10in) s.d.1829 W/C (A.S 11000)
£800 $1352   (16-Apr-91 CSK6/R) Portrait of lady in lace trimmed dress with white
                sash (6x?cm-2x?in) min. s.octagonal

AGRICOLA, Christoph Ludwig (1667-1719) German
£850 $1632   (18-Feb-91 S284/R) Bird on flowering branch (29x21cm-11x8in) gouache
                vellum
£2200 $3586   (2-Jul-91 C376/R) River landscape with fortified bridge. River landscape
                with travellers (17x22cm-7x9in) black chk bodycol vellum pair
£2500 $4425   (22-Mar-91 APT.P1/R) Oiseaux perches sur les branches d'un arbre
                (28x25cm-11x10in) gouaches pair (F.FR 25000)

AGRICOLA, Christoph Ludwig (attrib) (1667-1719) German
£612 $1205   (12-Nov-90 CH.AM227/R) Overgrown ruins in hilly landscape with traveller
                resting near urn (18x22cm-7x9in) bodycol vellum (D.FL 2000)

AGRICOLA, Christoph Ludwig (circle) (1667-1719) German
£733 $1312   (14-Mar-91 D.V316/R) River landscape with shepherd and herd
                (69x90cm-27x35in) (A.S 15000)

AGRISTI, Luigi (19th C) ?
£1200 $2364   (4-Oct-90 CSK207/R) In the tavern (30x41cm-12x16in) s.

AGUAYO, Fermin (20th C) ?
£1711 $3370   (15-Nov-90 ANS.M38/R) Mujeres desnudas (46x55cm-18x22in) s.d.74
                (S.P 315000)

AGUELI, Ivan (1869-1917) Swedish
£4717 $8160   (22-May-91 BA.S532/R) Landscape (21x25cm-8x10in) unfinnished painting
                verso (S.KR 50000)

AGUELI, Ivan (1869-1917) Swedish-cont.
£6887 $11914   (22-May-91 BA.S531/R) Egyptian girl (28x32cm-11x13in) (S.KR 73000)
£7229 $14024   (5-Dec-90 AB.S7005/R) Southern landscape with trees by water
(32x45cm-13x18in) (S.KR 78000)
£8824 $17294   (6-Nov-90 BA.S3/R) Outskirts of town (27x40cm-11x16in) (S.KR 96000)

AGUIAR, Jose (1895-?) Spanish
£1100 $1968   (13-Mar-91 FER.M210/R) Unamuno (63x51cm-25x20in) s. (S.P 200000)
£2474 $4428   (13-Mar-91 FER.M245/R) El tren atraviesa los campos de Soria
(85x110cm-33x43in) s. (S.P 450000)

AGUIARI, Tito (1834-1908) Italian
£3560 $6372   (11-Apr-91 D.V57/R) Leda with swan (158x73cm-62x29in) s. (A.S 75000)

AGUILA, J P del (?) ?
£439   *$847*   *(13-Dec-90 CH.BR68) Seduction (40x30cm-16x12in) s. ink wash (B.FR 26000)*
£473   *$912*   *(13-Dec-90 CH.BR50/R) Chrysalides (41x31cm-16x12in) s. ink wash*
(B.FR 28000)

AGUILAR MORE, Ramon (1924-) Spanish
£1243 $2424   (22-Oct-90 ANS.M108/R) Bulevar parisino (36x47cm-14x19in) s. panel
(S.P 230000)

AHLBERG, Arvid Magnus (1851-1932) Swedish
£514 $921   (17-Mar-91 BU.M184) Seascape at night (38x65cm-15x26in) s.d.83
(S.KR 5500)

AHLBORN, August (1796-1857) German
£12969 $24382   (19-Sep-90 N.M411/R) Bay of Naples at sunset (24x81cm-9x32in) s.d.1832
(DM 38000)

AHLERS-HESTERMANN, Friedrich (1883-1973) German?
£608   *$1034*   *(28-May-91 KF.M417) Landscape with riverside houses, possibly Bad*
Oldesloe (42x59cm-17x23in) s.d.1945 pastel (DM 1800)

AHLGREN, Lauri (1929-) Finnish
£642   *$1258*   *(24-Nov-90 HOR.H33/R) Blue (64x48cm-25x19in) s.d.1971 gouache*
(F.M 4500)

AHLSTEDT, Fredrik (1839-1901) Finnish
£2557 $4577   (14-Apr-91 BU.H9/R) Lake landscape (27x34cm-11x13in) s. (F.M 18000)

AHRENDTS, Carl Eduard (1828-1898) Dutch
£1273 $2393   (22-Sep-90 CH.AM103) Skaters on frozen river by ruin. Shepherdess and
flock in hilly landscape (11x18cm-4x7in) s. panel pair (D.FL 4200)

AHTOLA, Taisto (1917-) Finnish
£863 $1666   (15-Dec-90 BU.H9) Self portrait wearing harlequin costume
(27x22cm-11x9in) s.d.85 panel (F.M 6000)

AIGNER, Eduard (1903-1978) German
£542 $884   (3-Jul-91 WE.MU64/R) Umbrian landscape (50x65cm-20x26in) s. i.verso
(DM 1600)
£576 $939   (3-Jul-91 WE.MU35/R) Tricesimo (80x61cm-31x24in) s.i.d.62 (DM 1700)
£600 $1074   (12-Apr-91 AW.H1028/R) Female nude in studio (49x43cm-19x17in) board
(DM 1800)
£811 $1403   (25-May-91 N.M4) Autumn landscape at the Danube (60x76cm-24x30in)
s.d.1951 i.stretcher (DM 2400)
£845 $1461   (25-May-91 N.M5/R) Altmuhltal (80x100cm-31x39in) mono.d.1965 (DM 2500)

AIKMAN, William (1682-1731) British
£1800 $2970   (12-Jul-91 C156/R) Portrait of John, 2nd Duke of Argyll, wearing Star of
Order of Garter (122x106cm-48x42in) i.

AIKMAN, William (attrib) (1682-1731) British
£950 $1530   (27-Jun-91 CG59/R) Portrait of Lady Aylesford (127x102cm-50x40in)

AILLAUD, Gilles (19th C?) French
£859 $1683   (12-Feb-91 HC.P13) Nomades au bord du ravin (41x51cm-16x20in) s. board
(F.FR 8500)
£822   *$1595*   *(9-Dec-90 CC.P70/R) Terrier (65x50cm-26x20in) s.d.1974 W/C (F.FR 8000)*

AIMETTI, Carlo (1901-) Italian
£612 $1200   (6-Nov-90 GF.L2525/R) Macugnaga, Valle Anzasca (60x45cm-24x18in) s.d.49
s.i.verso panel (S.FR 1500)

AINMULLER, Max Emanuel (1807-1870) German
£621   *$1192*   *(28-Nov-90 KF.M315) Design for gothic church window depicting St Peter*
(70x14cm-28x6in) s.d.1849 W/C indian ink (DM 1800)

AIRENS, H (19th C) American
£1277 $2400   (22-Sep-90 WOL.C81) Court scene (109x132cm-43x52in) s.

AISTROP, E (19/20th C) British
£550 $919   (4-Jun-91 SWS1834) Study of head of King Charles spaniel (22x17cm-9x7in)
indist.s. board

AITCHISON, Craigie (1926-) British
£1500 $2955   (1-Nov-90 B130/R) Freesias in pot (35x33cm-14x13in)
£8200 $14514   (21-Mar-91 S63/R) Crucifixion (46x36cm-18x14in) d.1984 verso

AITKEN, James A (1846-1897) British
£487 $950   (13-Oct-90 LAE.L92/R) Sunset on Norfolk Broads (36x51cm-14x20in) s. W/C
£850 $1471   (10-May-91 CBS211/R) Port St. Mary (25x36cm-10x14in) s. W/C

AITKEN, John Ernest (1881-1957) British
£350 $620   (21-Mar-91 CSK78) Ebb tide at Crail (30x48cm-12x19in) s.i. verso W/C
£420 $727   (10-May-91 CBS253) Continental harbour scene (28x36cm-11x14in) s. W/C
£580 $1114   (27-Nov-90 W.T1278/R) Scarborough Harbour (35x50cm-14x20in) s. W/C
    (C.D 1300)
£600 $1170   (18-Oct-90 CSK52/R) The Morning Catch (33x49cm-13x19in) s.
    indist.i.verso pencil W/C
£900 $1593   (21-Mar-91 CSK46/R) The busy market place (36x51cm-14x20in) s. pencil
    W/C
£1200 $2328   (7-Dec-90 CBS216) The morning catch - Port St.Mary (33x48cm-13x19in) s.
    W/C
£1250 $2150   (14-May-91 SWS29/R) Scarborough Harbour (35x50cm-14x20in) s. W/C
£1600 $2752   (14-May-91 SWS33/R) Waterway in S'Hertogenbosch, Holland
    (49x75cm-19x30in) s. i.verso W/C
£1650 $2838   (14-May-91 SWS34/R) Crabbers (69x104cm-27x41in) s. i.verso W/C
£2100 $3633   (10-May-91 CBS260/R) Boats and figures by slipway (36x43cm-14x17in) s.
    W/C
£2300 $4531   (13-Nov-90 SWS37/R) The glow of the morning (70x105cm-28x41in) s. i.
    label

AIVAZOFFSKI, Ivan (1817-1900) Russian
£4281 $8263   (12-Dec-90 ZZ.F15/R) L'entree du voilier au port (22x27cm-9x11in) s.
    (F.FR 42000)
£4500 $8640   (27-Nov-90 C45/R) Summer calm off the Crimea (23x30cm-9x12in) s.d.1886
£5974 $11710   (6-Nov-90 BA.S5/R) Life saving in rough seas (31x27cm-12x11in) s.
    (S.KR 65000)
£6500 $10660   (18-Jun-91 PH95/R) Figures beneath coastal watchtower by moonlight,
    sailing vessel offshore (77x59cm-30x23in) s.d.1863
£12821 $25000   (23-Oct-90 SY.NY28/R) The rescue (61x92cm-24x36in) s.d.1849
£13000 $24960   (27-Nov-90 PH102/R) Vessel off coast by moonlight (61x91cm-24x36in)
    s.d.1859
£20000 $39000   (10-Oct-90 C208/R) Coastal shipping on Black Sea (36x59cm-14x23in) s.
    s.d.1895 verso
£23000 $44160   (28-Nov-90 S202/R) Fishermen on beach at sunset (41x51cm-16x20in)
    s.d.1866
£1838 $3603   (6-Nov-90 BA.S352/R) Harbour in early morning (19x29cm-7x11in) s. W/C
    htd white (S.KR 20000)

AIVAZOFFSKI, Ivan (attrib) (1817-1900) Russian
£1056 $1775   (23-Apr-91 RAS.K206/R) Moonlit landscape with sailship at anchor
    (24x36cm-9x14in) (D.KR 12000)
£1232 $2070   (23-Apr-91 RAS.K205) Moonlit landscape with men having campfire on town
    beach (42x58cm-17x23in) (D.KR 14000)
£2154 $4244   (14-Nov-90 RAS.K191/R) Fishingboats off the coast by large castle
    (32x52cm-13x20in) i. (D.KR 24000)
£13652 $26758   (24-Nov-90 SA.A635/R) Oriental coastal landscape with figures, evening
    (62x96cm-24x38in) canvas laid down (DM 40000)

AIZPIRI, Paul (1919-) French
£4563 $7895   (25-May-91 AB.L46/R) Still life (55x45cm-22x18in) s. (S.FR 11500)
£7653 $15000   (12-Feb-91 SY.NY165/R) Nature morte (28x41cm-11x16in) s. s.i.verso
£10660 $21000   (13-Nov-90 CE.NY107/R) Nature morte aux fruits (35x26cm-14x10in) s.
£17857 $35000   (12-Feb-91 SY.NY177/R) Tete du clown (56x46cm-22x18in) s.
£18090 $32382   (16-Mar-91 APT.P55/R) Le Brusc (73x92cm-29x36in) s. i. verso
    (F.FR 180000)
£19231 $37500   (10-Oct-90 SY.NY302/R) Still life with flowers and bird
    (41x33cm-16x13in) s. i.verso
£20408 $40204   (16-Nov-90 FB.P103/R) Bouquet de fleurs (60x30cm-24x12in) s.
    (F.FR 200000)
£22959 $45000   (12-Feb-91 SY.NY176/R) Still life with pitcher and flowers
    (66x53cm-26x21in) s.
£22959 $45000   (12-Feb-91 SY.NY144/R) Bateaux aux voiles dans un port (64x53cm-25x21in)
    s. board
£23077 $45000   (10-Oct-90 SY.NY239/R) Le petit clown (61x51cm-24x20in) s.
£23121 $40000   (7-May-91 CE.NY134/R) Le clown (65x54cm-26x21in) s.
£25381 $50000   (13-Nov-90 CE.NY212/R) Jeune homme (66x55cm-26x22in) s.
£25510 $50255   (16-Nov-90 FB.P101/R) Le clown (55x39cm-22x15in) s. (F.FR 250000)
£25641 $50000   (10-Oct-90 SY.NY285/R) Model and artist (64x53cm-25x21in) s. i.verso
£26531 $52265   (16-Nov-90 FB.P100/R) Bouquet de fleurs (42x33cm-17x13in) s.
    (F.FR 260000)
£27523 $52844   (30-Nov-90 CB.P118/R) Collioure (73x91cm-29x36in) s. (F.FR 270000)
£28061 $55000   (12-Feb-91 SY.NY143/R) Venetian canal (99x135cm-39x53in) s.
£32051 $62500   (10-Oct-90 SY.NY227/R) Le port, St Tropez (53x64cm-21x25in) s.
    i.stretcher
£39744 $77500   (10-Oct-90 SY.NY271/R) Still life with flowers (74x58cm-29x23in) s.
£40816 $80408   (16-Nov-90 FB.P99/R) La bougie tricolore (114x162cm-45x64in) s.
    (F.FR 400000)

AIZPIRI, Paul (1919-) French-cont.
£45918 $90459   (16-Nov-90 FB.P98/R) Saint-Tropez (78x97cm-31x38in) s. hardboard
                  (F.FR 450000)
£60914 $120000 (13-Nov-90 CE.NY116/R) Portrait de femme (114x90cm-45x35in) s.
£3400 $6630   (15-Oct-90 PH1 a) Bouquet de fleurs (83x44cm-33x17in) s. gouache
*£3680 $7250   (15-Nov-90 D.NY73/R) Three figures and horse (41x56cm-16x22in) s. W/C
                  ink*
*£5076 $10000 (13-Nov-90 CE.NY196/R) Clown (49x39cm-19x15in) s. W/C gouache pen ink
                  paper on board*
£12821 $25000 (10-Oct-90 SY.NY229/R) Quai a St Tropez (51x53cm-20x21in) s. oil black
                  marker canvas
£15369 $29970 (17-Oct-90 LT.P129/R) Fleurs dans un vase (63x48cm-25x19in) s. gouache
                  (F.FR 152000)
£15385 $30000 (10-Oct-90 SY.NY291/R) Loiseau bleu (76x56cm-30x22in) s. gouache

AJDUKIEWICZ, Sigismund (1861-1917) Polish
£1550 $2666   (14-May-91 SWS350/R) Centaurs playing by shepherd (33x57cm-13x22in) s.
                  panel
£1946 $3600   (10-Mar-91 H.C2/R) Man on horseback (30x20cm-12x8in) s. cradled panel

AJMONE, Giuseppe (1923-) Italian
£1261 $2458   (22-Oct-90 BR.M340/R) Nudino (33x55cm-13x22in) s.d.1969 (I.L 2800000)
£3189 $5422   (28-May-91 SY.MI134/R) Composizione (70x58cm-28x23in) s.d.55
                  (I.L 7000000)
*£916 $1759   (27-Nov-90 SY.MI16/R) Figura di donna (49x32cm-19x13in) s.d.84
                  col.pastels (I.L 2000000)*

AKEN, Francois van (attrib) (17th C) Dutch
£2400 $4632   (11-Dec-90 PH263/R) Brawl in tavern (56x66cm-22x26in)

AKEN, Leo van (1856-1904) Belgian
£4564 $8170   (9-Apr-91 GM.B552/R) Mater Dolorosa (84x100cm-33x39in) s. (B.FR 280000)

AKERBLADH, Alexander (?) Swedish
£1387 $2400   (8-May-91 RO.BA16) Apres la fenetre (39x50cm-15x20in) s.d.

AKERS, Vivian Milner (1886-?) American
£590 $950   (25-Jun-91 JRB.C68/R) Landscape with house and pond (61x51cm-24x20in)
                  s.d.21 canvasboard

AKERSTROM, Jonas (1759-1795) Swedish
*£551 $1081   (6-Nov-90 BA.S428/R) Battle at Lutzen (37x53cm-15x21in) mixed media
                  (S.KR 6000)*

AKIMOW, Ivan Akimowitsch (1753-1814) Russian
£1100 $1793   (3-Jul-91 PLF.P40) Le Christ et la Samaritaine (42x48cm-17x19in) s.
                  (F.FR 11000)

AKKERINGA, Johannes Evert (1894-?) Dutch
£1497 $2844   (11-Sep-90 CH.AM220) Woman seated outside a house peeling potatoes
                  (55x45cm-22x18in) s. (D.FL 5000)
£2287 $4482   (6-Nov-90 SY.AM140/R) Still life with flowers (36x36cm-14x14in) s.
                  (D.FL 7500)
£2424 $4776   (30-Oct-90 CH.AM56/R) Stable friends (24x32cm-9x13in) s. panel
                  (D.FL 8000)
£2591 $5079   (6-Nov-90 SY.AM5) Children with sledge (15x31cm-6x12in) s. panel
                  (D.FL 8500)
£2727 $5373   (30-Oct-90 CH.AM300/R) Primroses in ginger jar and freesias in
                  apothecary jar on table (42x34cm-17x13in) s. board (D.FL 9000)
£5455 $10745 (30-Oct-90 CH.AM240/R) Women reading in dunes (40x57cm-16x22in) s.
                  (D.FL 18000)
£9581 $16096 (23-Apr-91 SY.AM84/R) Children playing on beach (33x46cm-13x18in) s.
                  (D.FL 32000)
£12195 $23902 (6-Nov-90 SY.AM199/R) Children on Scheveningen beach (26x33cm-10x13in)
                  s. panel (D.FL 40000)
£449 $754   (23-Apr-91 SY.AM25) Hay-wagon (18x35cm-7x14in) s. W/C (D.FL 1500)

AKKERSDIJK, Jacob (1815-1862) Dutch
£1842 $3500   (27-Feb-91 SY.NY37/R) Wedding dance (69x52cm-27x20in) s.indist.d. panel
£2312 $4000   (23-May-91 CH.NY186/R) The new doll (36x49cm-14x19in) s.d.1850 panel
£3010 $5087   (17-Apr-91 WE.MU234/R) Peasant wedding (68x52cm-27x20in) s.d.1843 panel
                  (DM 9000)

AKNIN, Anne (1924-) Russian?
£895 $1512   (16-Apr-91 PPB.P167) Le Sacre Coeur (65x50cm-26x20in) s. (F.FR 9000)

ALANDI (19th C) Spanish
£2220 $3730   (22-Apr-91 PO.BA7) Bebedores y majas en la taberna (152x107cm-60x42in)
                  s.

ALANKO, Uuno (1878-1964) Finnish
£791 $1527   (15-Dec-90 BU.H12) Still life of flowers (55x65cm-22x26in) s.d.1953
                  (F.M 5500)
*£1165 $2005   (14-May-91 HOR.H9) Model with dark hair (33x25cm-13x10in) s.d.1951 dr
                  (F.M 8100)*

ALARCON, Jose (19th C) Spanish
£1355 $2643   (17-Oct-90 FER.M81/R) Torero y maja (48x36cm-19x14in) s. panel
                   (S.P 250000)

ALARCON-SUAREZ, Jose (19th C) Spanish
£750 $1478   (4-Oct-90 CSK164/R) A spanish beauty (100x75cm-39x30in) s.
£900 $1512   (18-Jul-91 CSK133) Portrait of Spanish lady, seated on sofa, in
                   mantilla, holding fan (99x75cm-39x30in) s.

ALAUX, Gustave (1887-1965) French
£1500 $2955   (15-Nov-90 CSK11/R) Promenade Sentimentale (38x46cm-15x18in) s.
                   s.i.stretcher

ALAUX, Jean Pierre (1783-1858) French
£583 $950   (12-Jun-91 SY.NY124/R) Beauty and Beast (65x81cm-26x32in) s.

ALBANI, Francesco (1578-1660) Italian
£40000 $65200   (3-Jul-91 S61/R) Holy Family (33x25cm-13x10in) copper
£1510 $2975   (13-Nov-90 GF.L5001/R) Annunciation (42x28cm-17x11in) sepia W/C
                 (S.FR 3700)
£13000 $21190   (2-Jul-91 C19/R) Head of woman turned to left (32x23cm-13x9in) chk

ALBANI, Francesco (after) (1578-1660) Italian
£1188 $2103   (4-Apr-91 CK.P27) Les amours desarmes (72x91cm-28x36in) (F.FR 12000)

ALBANI, Francesco (circle) (1578-1660) Italian
£3200 $6240   (16-Oct-90 CG244/R) The Flight into Egypt (76x69cm-30x27in)

ALBANI, Francesco (style) (1578-1660) Italian
£746 $1260   (18-Apr-91 APT.P2) Le Christ sur le Mont des Oliviers (26x26cm-10x10in)
                 copper octagonal (F.FR 7500)
£1014 $2008   (30-Jan-91 APT.P30/R) La derniere communion de Sainte Marie Madeleine
                 (58x44cm-23x17in) (F.FR 10000)
£1500 $2445   (4-Jul-91 CSK122/R) Diana with nymphs at chase (57x42cm-22x17in) panel
£1946 $3289   (2-May-91 CH.AM118/R) Bacchus and Ariadne (87x114cm-34x45in) (D.FL 6500)
£2600 $4394   (18-Apr-91 C137) Diana bathing after the chase (23x34cm-9x13in)
£3378 $5743   (27-May-91 L.K2/R) Apollo and Daphne (76cm-30ins circular) (DM 10000)
£3571 $6000   (17-Jul-91 SY.NY91/R) The judgement of Paris (85x102cm-33x40in)
£1063 $2083   (22-Nov-90 D.P6) Leda et ses fils (76x59cm-30x23in) pastel (F.FR 10500)

ALBAREDE, Andre Rene (20th C) French
£763 $1412   (4-Mar-91 ARC.P79/R) Charlotte at 9 ans (46x38cm-18x15in) s.d.1891
                 (F.FR 7600)

ALBERICI, Augusto (1846-?) Italian
£1094 $1859   (28-May-91 F.R94) Deserto (23x54cm-9x21in) s. (I.L 2400000)
£3409 $6683   (22-Nov-90 SY.MI33/R) Bottino di guerra (80x162cm-31x64in)
                 (I.L 7500000)

ALBEROLA, Jean Michel (c.1953-) French
£2193 $3619   (10-Jul-91 FB.P112/R) Sans titre (73x73cm-29x29in) i.d.1988 mixed media
                 (F.FR 22000)
£5139 $9969   (9-Dec-90 CC.P46/R) Theme VIII (130x150cm-51x59in) s.i.d.1984 pastel
                 (F.FR 50000)

ALBERS, Josef (1888-1976) American
£8876 $15000   (2-May-91 CH.NY103/R) Study for homage to square (31x33cm-12x13in) paper
£17857 $35000   (7-Nov-90 SY.NY218/R) Study for homage to the square - dimmed look
                 (41x41cm-16x16in) init.d.66 i. verso masonite
£20305 $40000   (4-Oct-90 SY.NY68/R) Homage to square - grey turns violet
                 (50x50cm-20x20in) init.d.56 s.d.1956 verso board
£20408 $40000   (8-Nov-90 CH.NY309/R) Study for homage to the square - Entrada
                 (62x62cm-24x24in) s.i.d.1962 verso masonite
£20710 $35000   (1-May-91 SY.NY200/R) Study for homage to square - reddish orange with
                 grey (40x40cm-16x16in) init.d.59 s.i.d.1959 verso masonite
£21000 $33810   (27-Jun-91 C30/R) Towards Fall I (61x61cm-24x24in) mono.d.58 s.i.d.1958
                 verso masonite
£21574 $42500   (4-Oct-90 SY.NY28/R) Construction - on yellow (57x64cm-22x25in)
                 init.d.38 s.d.38 verso masonite
£22843 $45000   (4-Oct-90 SY.NY37/R) Homage to square - from yellow to brown
                 (46x46cm-18x18in) s.d.1957 acrylic masonite
£22843 $45000   (4-Oct-90 SY.NY113/R) Study for homage to square - secco
                 (46x46cm-18x18in) init.d.69 s.d.1969 verso masonite
£22959 $45000   (7-Nov-90 SY.NY214/R) Homage to the square - engaged (76x76cm-30x30in)
                 init.d.58 i.verso masonite
£23673 $46637   (17-Nov-90 S.Z6) Expanded, study for Homage to the Square
                 (61x61cm-24x24in) s.d.1967 oil board (S.FR 58000)
£25000 $44250   (21-Mar-91 S67/R) Hommage to square - green grey shield A
                 (61x61cm-24x24in) init.d.62 s.i.d.1962 verso masonite
£26000 $41860   (27-Jun-91 S7/R) Study to homage to the square, floating
                 (61x61cm-24x24in) mono.d.58 s.i.d.verso board
£27000 $43470   (27-Jun-91 S8/R) Study to homage to the square, sedate (76x76cm-30x30in)
                 mono.d.57 s.i.d.verso board
£29586 $50000   (1-May-91 CH.NY1/R) Study to In and Out, early (61x61cm-24x24in)
                 mono.d.58 s.d.1958 verso masonite

ALBERS, Josef (1888-1976) American-cont.
£30769 $52000   (1-May-91 CH.NY2/R) Homage to square - light reveille (61x61cm-24x24in)
          mono.d.64 s.d.1964 verso masonite
£38000 $73720   (6-Dec-90 S51/R) Hommage to the Square (75x75cm-30x30in) init.d.64
          i.verso masonite
£38462 $65000   (1-May-91 SY.NY246/R) Study for homage to square - wide sight
          (76x76cm-30x30in) init.d.63 s.i.d.1963 verso masonite
£39941 $67500   (1-May-91 SY.NY212/R) Study to homage to square - there and back
          (81x81cm-32x32in) s.d.1961 verso masonite
£42000 $81480   (6-Dec-90 S52/R) Study for Hommage to the Square - Confirmed
          (61x61cm-24x24in) init.d.54 s.i.verso masonite
£43147 $85000   (5-Oct-90 CH.NY14/R) Homage to the square - surprise (102x102cm-40x40in)
          s.d.63 panel
£132653 $260000   (6-Nov-90 SY.NY1/R) Study for homage to the square - starblue
          (122x122cm-48x48in) init.d.58 i. verso masonite
£4847 $9500   (7-Nov-90 SY.NY111/R) Study for Gaebundeit (33x44cm-13x17in) s.d.1925
          W/C
£12000 $23400   (18-Oct-90 C385/R) Untitled (20x28cm-8x11in) s.d.53/54verso paper
          collage cardboard

ALBERT, Adolphe (19/20th C) French
£3161 $5500   (27-Mar-91 B.SF4094/R) Pont sur la Seine (46x55cm-18x22in) s.d.1899

ALBERT, Ernest (1857-1946) American
£788 $1300   (13-Jul-91 YFA.M24/R) Seascape (61x76cm-24x30in) s.
£893 $1500   (28-Apr-91 HG.C30) The plum jar (51x61cm-20x24in) s.d.1934
£1105 $2100   (28-Feb-91 MFA.C80) Rocky coastal scene (58x64cm-23x25in) s.
£1250 $2100   (28-Apr-91 HG.C16) Middle pasture (58x64cm-23x25in) s. board
£1488 $2500   (28-Apr-91 HG.C21) After the rain (64x76cm-25x30in) s.
£1734 $3000   (21-May-91 CE.NY552/R) Garden pond (25x20cm-10x8in) s. board
£2262 $3800   (28-Apr-91 LIT.L105) Spring landscape (51x61cm-20x24in) s.
£7821 $14000   (14-Mar-91 CH.NY112/R) Frozen landscape (103x127cm-41x50in) s.

ALBERT, Gustaf (1866-1905) Swedish
£568 $955   (24-Apr-91 BA.S3/R) Sailingboats at sea (16x30cm-6x12in) init.d.86
          (S.KR 6000)
£3933 $6764   (14-May-91 BU.S1/R) Summer landscape with watercourse and lock, South of
          France (66x55cm-26x22in) s. (S.KR 42000)

ALBERT, Jos (1886-?) Belgian
£900 $1512   (23-Apr-91 C.A272) Town scene (23x30cm-9x12in) s. panel (B.FR 55000)
£985 $1704   (25-May-91 KV.L5) The crab (24x30cm-9x12in) s. (B.FR 60000)
£2492 $4061   (12-Jun-91 GM.B4132) Ferme ardennaise (41x52cm-16x20in) s. wood
          (B.FR 150000)
£3987 $6498   (12-Jun-91 GM.B4111) Les tournesols (70x80cm-28x31in) s. (B.FR 240000)
£5648 $9206   (12-Jun-91 GM.B4127) Paysage enneige (80x100cm-31x39in) s. (B.FR 340000)

ALBERTI (?) ?
£750 $1470   (14-Feb-91 CSK87) Beagles in a landscape (25x20cm-10x8in) s. panel

ALBERTI, Cherubino (1553-1615) Italian
£714 $1200   (17-Jul-91 SY.NY14/R) Figure study of a man pulling to the left
          (22x16cm-9x6in) blk.chk. paper laid down on board
£2736 $4843   (19-Mar-91 F.M249/R) Studio di tre figure femminili (27x20cm-11x8in) ink
          over pencil (I.L 6000000)
£3000 $5790   (12-Dec-90 PH312/R) Study of room and gallery with putti and musicians
          above (24x39cm-9x15in) pen ink wash
£3100 $5053   (1-Jul-91 S131/R) Study of male nude with right arm raised and sketch of
          same (26x17cm-10x7in) num.20 black chk

ALBERTI, Giovanni (1558-1601) Italian
£2508 $4439   (19-Mar-91 F.M297/R) Angeli musicanti (11x18cm-4x7in) ink over pencil
          two (I.L 5500000)

ALBERTI, Giuseppe Vizzotto (19th C) Italian
£9000 $19000   (18-Oct-90 F.M5/R) Incontro galante in piazza San Marco, Venezia
          (47x34cm-19x13in) s. panel (I.L 21000000)

ALBERTI, Piotr (1913-) Russian
£595 $1024   (15-May-91 AGB.P121/R) Le bain de soleil (23x35cm-9x14in) s. hardboard
          (F.FR 6000)
£595 $1024   (15-May-91 AGB.P120/R) Rocking-chair (17x28cm-7x11in) s. (F.FR 6000)
£610 $1220   (10-Feb-91 YC.P12) Paysanne dans sa cuisine (42x34cm-17x13in) s.d.1950
          verso (F.FR 6000)
£754 $1297   (15-May-91 AGB.P124/R) Fillette au foulard brode (32x22cm-13x9in) s.
          board (F.FR 7600)
£1042 $1792   (15-May-91 AGB.P119/R) Les ecolieres (33x46cm-13x18in) s. board
          (F.FR 10500)

ALBERTINELLI, Mariotto (1474-1515) Italian
£600 $1170   (16-Jan-91 CSK267) The Visitation (213x135cm-84x53in) s. after Raphael

ALBERTINELLI, Mariotto (after) (1474-1515) Italian
£950 $1644   (20-May-91 SWS82/R) The Visitation (155x105cm-61x41in) c.1700 indist.i.
          verso

ALBERTINI, Oreste (1887-1953) Italian
£1182 $2317   (21-Nov-90 F.M70) Ponte Tresa (24x29cm-9x11in) s.d.1922 panel
     (I.L 2600000)

ALBERTIS, Sebastiano de (1828-1897) Italian
£591 $1158   (21-Nov-90 F.M144) Soldato con cavallo (12x8cm-5x3in) s. W/C
     (I.L 1300000)
£1824 $3046   (6-Jun-91 F.M225) Dopo la battaglia (6x15cm-2x6in) s. W/C (I.L 4000000)

ALBONI, Paolo Antonio (?-c.1760) Italian
£570 $1112   (12-Oct-90 AW.H1171) Study of tree (29x20cm-11x8in) indian ink
     (DM 1700)

ALBOTTI, Francesco (1721-1753) Italian
£12632 $24000   (11-Jan-91 CH.NY10/R) Figures before a town on a hill in a mountainous
     landscape (73x97cm-29x38in)
£20000 $38000   (11-Jan-91 CH.NY23/R) Figures in a capriccio of stairs and monuments in
     an extensive landscape (72x93cm-28x37in)
£88000 $143440   (3-Jul-91 S79/R) Venice, Grand Canal looking towards Scalzi. Venice,
     Piazza San Marco (62x98cm-24x39in) pair

ALBRACHT, Willem (1861-?) Belgian
£915 $1500   (19-Jun-91 B.SF1901/R) Interieur (57x47cm-22x19in) s. s.stretcher

ALBRICI, Enrico (1714-1775) Italian
£10535 $20227   (29-Nov-90 F.M107/R) La tazza di cioccolata (53x72cm-21x28in)
     (I.L 23000000)
£18186 $31462   (21-May-91 SY.MI1064/R) Nani che prendono vino (37x47cm-15x19in)
     (I.L 40000000)

ALBRIGHT, Adam Emory (1862-1957) American
£867 $1500   (12-May-91 H.C155/R) Two girls at water's edge (51x41cm-20x16in) s.
£1949 $3800   (14-Oct-90 H.C394/R) Two boys at shore (46x61cm-18x24in) s.
£2793 $5000   (14-Mar-91 CH.NY127/R) Berry pickers (66x51cm-26x20in) s.d.1916

ALBRIGHT, Henry James (19/20th C) American
£1304 $2100   (25-Jun-91 JRB.C52/R) Nasturtiums (61x71cm-24x28in) s.

ALBRIGHT, Ivan le Lorraine (1897-1983) American
£592 $1000   (21-Apr-91 DU.E172/R) Hopi indians (30x36cm-12x14in) s.d. board

ALCAIN, Alfredo (1936-) Spanish
£867 $1692   (17-Oct-90 FER.M121/R) La casa amarillo limon (80x105cm-31x41in) s.
     (S.P 160000)

ALCAYAR (19th C) ?
£9016 $16139   (8-Apr-91 CH.R118/R) Veduta laterale del Monastero di San Lorenzo
     all'Escorial. Paesaggio con complesso architettonico (8x11cm-3x4in)
     s.d.1826 silvered metal pair (I.L 20000000)

ALCIATI, Ambrogio (1878-1929) Italian
£3000 $6000   (18-Oct-90 F.M9/R) Ritratto femminile (80x59cm-31x23in) s.
     (I.L 6500000)
£4091 $8019   (22-Nov-90 SY.MI69/R) Ritratto maschile (113x89cm-44x35in) s.i.
     (I.L 9000000)

ALCIBAR, Jose de (1751-1803) Mexican
£601 $1160   (11-Dec-90 FER.M76/R) San Antonio (19x14cm-7x6in) s.verso copper
     (S.P 110000)
£14286 $28000   (19-Nov-90 SY.NY2/R) San Jose con el Nino (105x67cm-41x26in)

ALDE, Yvette (1911-) French
£508 $1000   (13-Nov-90 CE.NY140/R) Les roses et les cerises (61x38cm-24x15in) s.d.62
     s.i.d.verso
£655 $1067   (14-Jun-91 FB.P3) Coupe de fruits (38x61cm-15x24in) s. i.d.1955 verso
     (F.FR 6500)

ALDERSON, E M (20th C) British
£2000 $3940   (1-Nov-90 TE584/R) Loading the cart (25x41cm-10x16in) s.d.1927 W/C

ALDIN, Cecil (1870-1935) British
£400 $672   (16-Jul-91 C116/R) Scraps (31x24cm-12x9in) s.d.1902 chk htd.white
£450 $797   (21-Mar-91 CSK99/R) Olive trees at the foothills of a mountain
     (33x51cm-13x20in) s. pencil col.chks.htd.white ivorine
£580 $1102   (28-Feb-91 DLY147/R) West Highland terrier (13x18cm-5x7in) s. ink
     ivorine
£660 $1102   (22-Jul-91 SWS853/R) Juggler (27x36cm-11x14in) s.i.
     col.chks.htd.bodycol.
£1100 $1837   (3-Jun-91 PHB9/R) Outside Heinemann's library (19x21cm-7x8in) s. pen W/C
£1150 $2208   (17-Aug-90 K489/R) Shire horse and foal (48x69cm-19x27in) s. pastel dr
£1250 $2088   (22-Jul-91 SWS851/R) A West Highland terrier (14x20cm-6x8in) s.
     blk.crayon htd.white
£2000 $3360   (15-Jul-91 PH162/R) Resting scottie (24x32cm-9x13in) s. pencil on
     ivorine
£2168 $3750   (10-May-91 S.W2486/R) What's become of the plum pudding
     (30x48cm-12x19in) s. W/C

ALDIN, Cecil (1870-1935) British-cont.
£2200 $4290   (15-Jan-91 SWS101/R) Ploughing (37x47cm-15x19in) s. i.verso col.chk
£2700 $4509   (22-Jul-91 SWS868/R) Horse and cart (20x30cm-8x12in) s. col.chks.htd.bodycol. with three others
£3200 $6240   (15-Jan-91 B334/R) Rosemary (34x27cm-13x11in) s.i. col.chk bodycol
£5000 $9450   (26-Sep-90 S362/R) Coach has arrived (49x71cm-19x28in) s. W/C gouache over black chk

ALDINE, Marc (1917-) Italian
£2228 $3943   (7-Apr-91 LT.P89) Vue de Venise (24x19cm-9x7in) s. (F.FR 22500)
£2312 $4000   (8-May-91 RO.BA201/R) Canal in Venice (65x50cm-26x20in) s.
£2789 $4825   (24-May-91 FB.P133/R) Vue d'un canal a Venise (55x38cm-22x15in) s. (F.FR 28000)
£5810 $11214   (16-Dec-90 DA.R1/R) Vues de Venise (55x38cm-22x15in) both s. two (F.FR 57000)

ALDINI, Casimiro see TOMBA, Casimiro

ALDIS, Paul Owen (?) Australian?
£1131 $1912   (16-Apr-91 J.M308) Grazing sheep, Flinders Ranges (89x135cm-35x53in) s.d. '85 (A.D 2500)

ALDOR, Janos Laszlo (1895-?) Polish?
£943 $1631   (6-May-91 ZEL.L1572/R) Portrait of young woman wearing fur coat (84x66cm-33x26in) s.d.1926 board (DM 2800)

ALDRICH, George Ames (1872-1941) American
£829 $1600   (10-Dec-90 H.C1055) Landscape with river and village (64x76cm-25x30in) s.
£872 $1700   (14-Oct-90 H.C387/R) Winter landscape (41x51cm-16x20in) s. board
£898 $1500   (5-Jun-91 D.NY2) Snowy embankment (58x74cm-23x29in) s. board
£973 $1800   (10-Mar-91 H.C155/R) Snowy river scene with houses (64x76cm-25x30in) s.
£1557 $2600   (5-Jun-91 D.NY1) Mill beside stream (64x76cm-25x30in) s.
£1622 $3000   (10-Mar-91 H.C156/R) Mill (76x89cm-30x35in) s.
£2560 $4300   (28-Apr-91 HG.C33) Mending nets (94x94cm-37x37in) s.
£3121 $5400   (12-May-91 H.C118 a/R) Winter landscape with creek (64x76cm-25x30in) s.

ALDRIDGE, Frederick James (1850-1933) British
£550 $1018   (7-Mar-91 CSK77) Fishing smacks off coastline (61x91cm-24x36in) s.
£950 $1568   (9-Jul-91 PH205) Getting side lights on 'Er (81x101cm-32x40in) mono.d.1923 i.verso
£1300 $2470   (10-Jan-91 B112/R) Sailing vessels off coastline (51x76cm-20x30in) s.
£340 $629   (5-Mar-91 SWS1641) Venice (18x13cm-7x5in) s.i. W/C
£500 $835   (22-Jul-91 SWS845/R) Pont Flaman, Bruges (25x37cm-10x15in) s.i.d.1914
£520 $879   (15-Apr-91 WW181) Sailing vessels off Venice (25x18cm-10x7in) s. W/C
£560 $935   (22-Jul-91 SWS834/R) Coming in, Shoreham (25x37cm-10x15in) s.
£600 $1152   (16-Aug-90 B218) Giardino Publico (26x37cm-10x15in) s.i. W/C
£633 $1071   (16-Apr-91 J.M602) Off to the fishing grounds (27x38cm-11x15in) s. W/C (A.D 1400)
£640 $1216   (27-Feb-91 MMB145) Venice and Dort - coastal views (15x10cm-6x4in) both s. pair
£650 $1203   (7-Mar-91 D25/R) Clipper in choppy seas with other shipping beyond (25x36cm-10x14in) s. W/C htd.white
£720 $1210   (22-Apr-91 PH285) On the Thames (37x52cm-15x20in) s.i. W/C
£780 $1271   (13-Jun-91 CSK126) Paddle tug towing schooner in heavy seas (35x53cm-14x21in) s.d.1902 pencil W/C
£800 $1560   (18-Oct-90 CSK55/R) Strong breeze (51x76cm-20x30in) s.i.d.91 W/C
£880 $1514   (15-May-91 BT162 b) Bosham running for harbour (13x20cm-5x8in) s.i. W/C pair
£900 $1548   (15-May-91 BT162 a) Shipping in a swell (25x36cm-10x14in) s.d.19 W/C
£950 $1615   (30-May-91 C22/R) Proceeding up River at Tilbury (51x76cm-20x30in) s. pencil W/C htd white
£950 $1872   (5-Oct-90 T208) Off coast of Devon (36x53cm-14x21in) s. W/C
£1000 $1730   (22-May-91 S42/R) Going out (24x37cm-9x15in) s. W/C
£1000 $1980   (29-Jan-91 RG1993) Coastal scene (36x53cm-14x21in) s.d. W/C drawing
£1000 $1790   (12-Mar-91 RG2680) Sailing vessels in a choppy sea (46x70cm-18x28in) s. W/C
£1000 $1900   (25-Feb-91 PH78) Off to fishing grounds (35x52cm-14x20in) s. W/C htd white
£1100 $1870   (30-May-91 C24/R) Shipping at anchor, thought to be off Tilbury (50x75cm-20x30in) s. pencil W/C
£1100 $1870   (30-May-91 C23/R) Barges in East Anglian estuary (46x72cm-18x28in) s. pencil W/C
£2000 $3340   (22-Jul-91 SWS835/R) Fishing boats at sea (28x43cm-11x17in) both s. pair

ALDRIDGE, John Arthur Malcolm (1905-1983) British
£800 $1416   (20-Mar-91 ZZ.B178) The Place House, Great Bardfield (61x76cm-24x30in) s.d.'72
£1500 $2925   (10-Oct-90 S93/R) Still life with tulips and books (91x76cm-36x30in) s.d.1959

ALECHINSKY, Pierre (1927-) Belgian
£12613 $21820   (22-May-91 CH.AM630/R) La regne vegetale (62x55cm-24x22in) s. acrylic paper on canvas (D.FL 42000)
£13000 $23010   (21-Mar-91 S64/R) Le Zele en personne (45x36cm-18x14in) s. s.d.1978

ALECHINSKY, Pierre (1927-) Belgian-cont.

£14861	$28681	(13-Dec-90 SY.AM264/R) Nu tete (66x52cm-26x20in) s. acrylic paper on canvas (D.FL 48000)
£20000	$35400	(21-Mar-91 C200/R) Solitaire a Plusieurs (65x54cm-26x21in) s. s.i.d.1964 verso
£21930	$37281	(29-May-91 KH.K33./R) Composition (90x70cm-35x28in) s.d.49 (D.KR 250000)
£29293	$57414	(14-Feb-91 GL.P68/R) Sans miroir (53x96cm-21x38in) s.d.1960 (F.FR 290000)
£30612	$60000	(7-Nov-90 SY.NY192/R) Oxydation des souvenirs (99x152cm-39x60in) s.i.d.1972 verso acrylic paper laid on canvas
£33163	$65000	(7-Nov-90 SY.NY191/R) Tirage au sort (100x155cm-39x61in) s.i.d.1976 verso acrylic paper laid on canvas
£35714	$70000	(8-Nov-90 CH.NY327/R) Sous le Bithume (187x95cm-74x37in) s.d.1987 i. verso acrylic paper mounted canvas
£38265	$75000	(7-Nov-90 SY.NY199/R) Lecture entre les lignes (114x152cm-45x60in) s.i.d.1970 verso acrylic paper laid on canvas
£42000	$81480	(6-Dec-90 S45/R) Massacre du Printemps (119x152cm-47x60in) s. s.i.d.1967 verso acrylic paper on canvas
£68548	$133669	(28-Oct-90 GL.P62/R) C'est jusque La (116x89cm-46x35in) s.i.d. verso (F.FR 680000)
£71429	$140000	(7-Nov-90 SY.NY145/R) Les enfants sages (114x145cm-45x57in) s.d.1961 i. stretcher
£129648	$212623	(19-Jun-91 CL.E21/R) La responsabilitie VIII (205x200cm-81x79in) s.d.VIII 1960 - VI 1961 verso (F.FR 1290000)
£939	*$1860*	*(31-Jan-91 RAS.V544/R) Composition (21x28cm-8x11in) s. Indian ink (D.KR 10500)*
£1359	*$2622*	*(12-Dec-90 RAS.K139/R) Composition (21x28cm-8x11in) s.d.62 Indian ink (D.KR 15000)*
£1390	*$2697*	*(5-Dec-90 AB.S7006/R) Composition (65x54cm-26x21in) s. Indian ink ricepaper (S.KR 15000)*
£2312	*$4138*	*(15-Mar-91 FB.P28/R) Composition (31x44cm-12x17in) s.d.69 ink wash (F.FR 23000)*
£3084	*$6013*	*(24-Oct-90 EA.M539/R) Hors rang (97x59cm-38x23in) s.d.1976 W/C (C.D 7000)*
£3100	*$5053*	*(3-Jul-91 CSC.P95/R) Composition (42x28cm-17x11in) s.d.VII 1971 W/C (F.FR 31000)*
£4260	*$7200*	*(2-May-91 CH.NY107/R) Untitled (44x27cm-17x11in) s.d.1960 gouache W/C*
£4926	*$8522*	*(25-May-91 KV.L426/R) Monkey business (38x58cm-15x23in) s.d.1975-88 brush ink (B.FR 300000)*
£5071	*$9534*	*(19-Sep-90 KH.K36/R) Composition (27x44cm-11x17in) s.d.1963 i.verso W/C crayon Indian ink (D.KR 57000)*
£7335	*$12030*	*(20-Jun-91 F.M461/R) Composizione e figure (94x185cm-37x73in) s.d.1970 ink W/C (I.L 16000000)*
£8122	*$16000*	*(4-Oct-90 SY.NY47/R) Untitled (26x44cm-10x17in) s.d.61 W/C*
£19298	*$32807*	*(29-May-91 KH.K80/R) Irriguee par le bleu (95x65cm-37x26in) s.d.1979 acrylic W/C Japan paper on canvas (D.KR 220000)*

ALEGIANI, Francesco (19/20th C?) Italian?

£2273	$4500	(1-Feb-91 S.W2535/R) Trompe l'oeil still life (99x74cm-39x29in) s.d.
£3428	$6753	(14-Nov-90 F.M11/R) Trompe l'oeil con la Beatrice Cenci di Guido Geni e paesaggio (55x30cm-22x12in) s. (I.L 7500000)

ALENZA Y NIETO, Leonardo (1807-1845) Spanish

£49060	$84873	(21-May-91 EP.M14/R) La muerte de Daoiz en el Parque de Artilleria de Monteleon (105x203cm-41x80in) (S.P 9000000)

ALESSANDRO, Victoria (18th C) French

£854	*$1401*	*(21-Jun-91 CK.P9) Etude d'homme assis, de trois-quarts, tourne vers la droite (43x28cm-17x11in) sanguinne htd.white (F.FR 8500)*

ALEXANDER, Douglas (?) British

£541	*$1054*	*(10-Oct-90 WO.CO3) The Blue Hills near Recess, Connemara (25x36cm-10x14in) s. W/C (E.P 600)*
£631	*$1230*	*(10-Oct-90 WO.CO2) Gathering turf, Maam Cross, Connemara (25x36cm-10x14in) s. W/C (E.P 700)*
£648	*$1277*	*(14-Nov-90 WO.CO1) Near Louisburgh, Connemara (25x36cm-10x14in) s. W/C (E.P 700)*
£676	*$1318*	*(10-Oct-90 WO.CO1) Russet and gold (23x36cm-9x14in) s. W/C (E.P 750)*

ALEXANDER, Edwin (1870-1926) British

£4100	*$8036*	*(8-Nov-90 TL55) Ducks (20x34cm-8x13in) s.*
£550	*$1056*	*(26-Nov-90 SWS115/R) Knarled age (53x36cm-21x14in) init.d.1904 i.verso W/C*
£680	*$1326*	*(17-Oct-90 PHG76/R) Restharrow (36x17cm-14x7in) mono. W/C*
£900	*$1728*	*(19-Feb-91 C35/R) Blue tit on twig (25x33cm-10x13in) init. W/C*
£1800	*$3348*	*(5-Sep-90 BT58/R) Hen with chicks (18x25cm-7x10in) init. W/C*

ALEXANDER, Keith (20th C) South African

£970	$1601	(8-Jul-91 SY.J329/R) The terrace (73x39cm-29x15in) s.d.'90 (SA.R 4600)

ALEXANDER, Lena (?) ?

£680	*$1136*	*(26-Jul-91 PHE42) Still life of pink and yellow roses (37x47cm-15x19in) s.d.1946 pastel*
£700	*$1169*	*(26-Jul-91 PHE135) Gondola on Venetian canal (34x49cm-13x19in) s. pastel*
£700	*$1358*	*(5-Dec-90 PHE56) Still life of roses (38x48cm-15x19in) s.d.1946 pastel*
£850	*$1598*	*(21-Sep-90 PHE1) Still life of roses (53x60cm-21x24in) s. pastel*

ALEXANDER, Lena (?) ?-cont.
£950 $1786   *(21-Sep-90 PHE87) White Fresias (50x57cm-20x22in) s. pastel*

ALEXANDER, Peter (20th C) American
£615 $1200   *(24-Oct-90 B.SF1593) Chico (46x61cm-18x24in) init.d.3/16/88 W/C pastel*

ALEXANDER, Robert (1896-1940) British
£780 $1513   (5-Dec-90 PHE6) Study of a bay horse in a stable (45x60cm-18x24in) s.

ALEXANDER, Robert L (1840-1923) British
£8000 $13440   (16-Jul-91 C145/R) The evening meal (104x137cm-41x54in) s.d.1884

ALEXANDRE, N (?) ?
£625 $1050   (27-Apr-91 SO.S262/R) Cattle and figures by well (36x48cm-14x19in) s.
                              panel (S.KR 6600)

ALEXANDROVNA, Grand Duchess Olga (1882-1960) Russian
£683 $1338   (24-Nov-90 SA.A722/R) Park landscape with country estate, afternoon
                              (50x60cm-20x24in) s.d.1945 board (DM 2000)

ALFELT, Else (1910-1975) Danish
£877 $1491   (29-May-91 KH.K44/R) Mountains (29x46cm-11x18in) s.d.41 (D.KR 10000)
£4093 $7694   (19-Sep-90 KH.K68/R) Composition (70x70cm-28x28in) (D.KR 46000)
£8497 $16655   (13-Feb-91 KH.K1/R) Mars Mountain, Lapland, Sweden (80x136cm-31x54in)
                              s.d.46 (D.KR 95000)
£660 $1287   *(10-Oct-90 RAS.K33) Composition (24x30cm-9x12in) s.d.1971 W/C*
                              (D.KR 7500)
£987 $1945   *(14-Nov-90 KH.K2/R) Mountains, Sweden, 1946 (22x30cm-9x12in) s.d.46*
                              crayon (D.KR 11000)
£1114 $1994   *(14-Mar-91 RAS.V750/R) Wood (49x31cm-19x12in) s. W/C (D.KR 12500)*
£1320 $2575   *(10-Oct-90 RAS.K32) Clouds before the moon (31x48cm-12x19in) s.d.49 W/C*
                              (D.KR 15000)
£1521 $2980   *(13-Feb-91 KH.K2/R) Giri Lake, Sweden (38x45cm-15x18in) s.d.46 W/C*
                              (D.KR 17000)
£2817 $5493   *(10-Oct-90 RAS.K31/R) Fire in the mountains (31x48cm-12x19in) s.i.d.51*
                              W/C (D.KR 32000)

ALFIERI, G (1864-1931) Italian
£2053 $3900   (14-Sep-90 S.BM295/R) Parisian scene (89x130cm-35x51in) s.

ALFONS, Sven (1918-) Swedish
£1604 $2775   (22-May-91 BA.S303/R) Youthful memories (81x61cm-32x24in) s.d.56 panel
                              (S.KR 17000)

ALFRED, Henry Jervis (2nd half 19th c) British
£1400 $2366   (1-May-91 GD.B5/R) Still life of Thames fish (61x92cm-24x36in) s.d.1855
                              (S.FR 3500)

ALGARDI, Alessandro (1602-1654) Italian
£1600   *$3088*   *(12-Dec-90 PH311/R) Design for doorway. Study of caryatid form below*
                              cornice with ballustrade (27x20cm-11x8in) pen ink over chk
                              double-sided
£8000   *$15440*   *(12-Dec-90 PH282/R) Study for arched window with putti and vases*
                              (22x14cm-9x6in) pen ink over chk
£14000   *$22820*   *(2-Jul-91 C37/R) Two putti supporting cardinal's hat and escutcheon with*
                              arms (18x12cm-7x5in) i. chk pen ink wash
£45000   *$73350*   *(2-Jul-91 C36/R) Design for the prow of the galley of Pope Urban VIII*
                              (22x4cm-9x2in) lead pen ink

ALIMANDI, Enrico (20th C) Italian
£1367 $2324   (28-May-91 SY.MI69/R) Composizione (46x54cm-18x21in) s. (I.L 3000000)

ALINARI, Luca (20th C) Italian?
£693 $1338   (13-Dec-90 F.M394/R) Untitled (39cm-15ins circular) s. panel
                              (I.L 1500000)
£910 $1720   (27-Sep-90 F.M27/R) Paesaggio e albero (50x70cm-20x28in) s.
                              (I.L 2000000)
£1092 $2064   (27-Sep-90 F.M111/R) Fiori nel paesaggio (70x70cm-28x28in) s.
                              (I.L 2400000)
£1812 $3153   (26-Mar-91 F.M13) Montagne (68x68cm-27x27in) s. panel (I.L 4000000)
£3664 $7036   (27-Nov-90 SY.MI37/R) Paesaggio (71x169cm-28x67in) s. panel
                              (I.L 8000000)
£3928 $7581   (13-Dec-90 F.M325/R) Composizione (108x166cm-43x65in) s. s.verso canvas
                              on panel oval (I.L 8500000)
£675 $1317   *(23-Oct-90 F.M76) Paesaggio (40cm-16ins circular) s.verso oil mixed*
                              media panel (I.L 1500000)
£855 $1668   *(22-Oct-90 BR.M179/R) Pellicola in se (70x100cm-28x39in) s.d.1974 oil*
                              pastel canvas (I.L 1900000)
£911 $1549   *(28-May-91 SY.MI46/R) Via della mura (100x50cm-39x20in) s. mixed media*
                              canvas (I.L 2000000)
£991 $1932   *(23-Oct-90 F.M1) Una chiesa dietro l'altra (49x70cm-19x28in) s. mixed*
                              media canvas (I.L 2200000)
£1146 $1880   *(20-Jun-91 F.M331/R) Paesaggio orizzonte (33x70cm-13x28in) s. i.verso*
                              mixed media canvas on panel (I.L 2500000)
£1531 $2985   *(22-Oct-90 BR.M100/R) Paesaggio (130x84cm-51x33in) s. mixed media canvas*
                              (I.L 3400000)

ALIX, Yves (1890-1969) French
£905 $1619   (11-Mar-91 GL.P34) Elegante au chapeau noir (51x38cm-20x15in) s.
                                     (F.FR 9000)
£2286 $3864   (15-Apr-91 CC.P93/R) Les joueurs de cartes (55x46cm-22x18in) studio st.
                                     verso (F.FR 23000)

ALKEMA, F W (20th C) ?
£667 $1300   (15-Jan-91 GM.B702) Paysage en hiver (70x83cm-28x33in) s. wood
                                     (B.FR 40000)

ALKEN, Henry (jnr) (1810-1894) British
£2000 $3940   (31-Oct-90 S398/R) Over the brook. Full cry. The death (18x28cm-7x11in)
                                     s. panel set of three
£7186 $12000   (7-Jun-91 SY.NY106/R) In Tandem (30x44cm-12x17in) s. panel
£10778 $18000   (7-Jun-91 SY.NY91/R) The fall (37x62cm-15x24in) s.
£10778 $18000   (7-Jun-91 SY.NY131/R) The Royal Mail arriving at a farriers by night.
                                     The Royal Mail outsidea coach house in winter (30x41cm-12x16in) each
                                     s. panel pair
£23353 $39000   (7-Jun-91 SY.NY107/R) The meet (45x76cm-18x30in) s. panel
*£1300 $2145   (11-Jul-91 S146) Preparing for the hunt (26x36cm-10x14in) s. W/C over
                                     pencil bodycol*

ALKEN, Henry (jnr-circle) (1810-1894) British
£1437 $2400   (7-Jun-91 SY.NY48/R) The home stretch (17x48cm-7x19in) panel
£2400 $3936   (20-Jun-91 B31/R) Horse and hounds at trough (17x23cm-7x9in) panel

ALKEN, Henry (snr) (1785-1851) British
£2994 $5000   (7-Jun-91 SY.NY128/R) End of the day (30x40cm-12x16in) s. panel
£3593 $6000   (7-Jun-91 SY.NY70/R) Taking a fence (37x46cm-15x18in) s.d.1816 panel
£11976 $20000   (7-Jun-91 SY.NY66/R) Full cry. The kill (45x61cm-18x24in) both s. pair
£38000 $74860   (14-Nov-90 S80/R) The meet. Jumping the fence. Full cry. The death
                                     (24x34cm-9x13in) s. set of four
£70000 $115500   (12-Jul-91 C99/R) Oakley Hunt (102x162cm-40x64in)
*£1034 $1800   (27-Mar-91 B.SF4240/R) Gentleman riding to hounds (26x36cm-10x14in) W/C
                                     paper laid down*

ALKEN, Henry (snr-circle) (1785-1851) British
£3000 $5850   (26-Oct-90 C306/R) Over the fence (44x60cm-17x24in) s.

ALKEN, Samuel (18/19th C) British
£4200 $7308   (26-Mar-91 PH80/R) Hare coursing (41x63cm-16x25in) s.
£15000 $29550   (16-Nov-90 C97/R) Coursing, setting out. Returning (29x41cm-11x16in)
                                     pair

ALKEN, Samuel (snr) (1756-1815) British
£5000 $8250   (12-Jul-91 C96/R) Drawing cover - huntsmen and hounds in extensive
                                     wooded landscape (61x79cm-24x31in) s.d.1807

ALKEN, Samuel Henry see   ALKEN, Henry (jnr)

ALKHOVSKY, Alexander (1912-1978) Russian
£600 $1008   (26-Apr-91 ARC.P168/R) Nature morte a la pasteque (89x79cm-35x31in) s.
                                     verso (F.FR 6000)

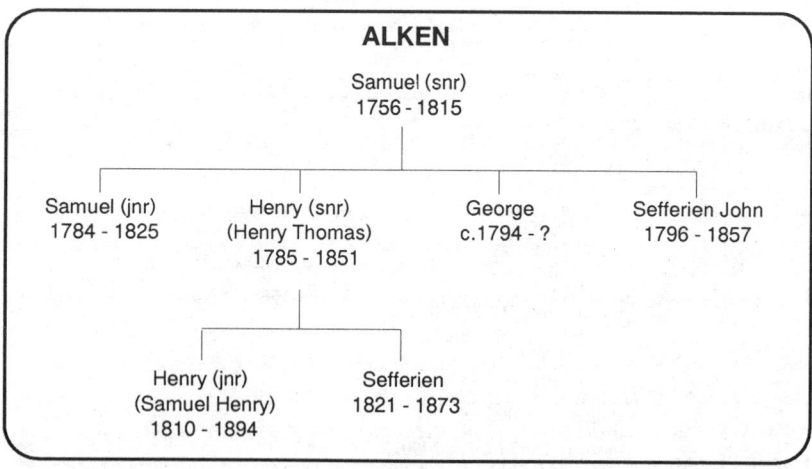

ALLAN, Archibald Russell Watson (1878-1959) British
£520 $868   (7-Jun-91 PHE11) A wooded river landscape (58x81cm-23x32in) s.

ALLAN, David (1744-1796) British
£941 $1600   (30-May-91 CE.NY85) Portrait of Nicolas Vleughels at easel
                 (61x50cm-24x20in)
£6000 $10740   (10-Apr-91 S55/R) Neapolitan musical party (96x75cm-38x30in)
*£2000 $3940   (13-Nov-90 C21/R) Roman amusement. Neapolitan amusement
                 (36x46cm-14x18in) i. pencil chk. incised two*

ALLAN, R W (1852-1942) British
£1158 $2200   (27-Feb-91 SY.NY294/R) Lace parasol (56x67cm-22x26in) s.

ALLAN, Robert Weir (1852-1942) British
£850 $1649   (6-Dec-90 CG39/R) Schooners moored off Venice (46x61cm-18x24in) s.
£1200 $2244   (28-Aug-90 S951/R) Arrival of the fishing fleet (35x51cm-14x20in) s.
                 panel
£1302 $2200   (20-Apr-91 WOL.C191/R) Net tenders (38x51cm-15x20in) s. panel
£23560 $39346   (4-Jun-91 R.T167/R) Tate-Yama, Japan (76x152cm-30x60in) s.d.1908
                 s.stretcher (C.D 45000)
£650 $1092   (23-Apr-91 S116) Market day (28x35cm-11x14in) s. W/C
£720 $1181   (19-Jun-91 B94) Continental street scene (51x36cm-20x14in) s. W/C
*£750 $1223   (14-Jun-91 C154/R) Cairo, looking towards the Citadel (50x75cm-20x30in)
                 s.i. pencil W/C*
*£820 $1369   (22-Jul-91 SWS839/R) Home from herring fishing (51x74cm-20x29in) s. W/C
                 pencil*
*£2000 $3260   (14-Jun-91 C159/R) Fishing boats in a harbour (28x53cm-11x21in) s.
                 pencil W/C*

ALLAN, Sir William (circle) (1782-1850) British
£950 $1758   (5-Mar-91 SWS1434) John Knox preaching to Mary Queen of Scots
                 (100x150cm-39x59in)

ALLARD, R (?) ?
*£340 $575   (16-Apr-91 CSK20) Portrait of lady standing full-length by urn
                 (11x?cm-4x?in) min. oval*

ALLBON, Charles Frederick (19th C) British
£560 $935   (4-Jun-91 SWS2031/R) Scheveningen, Holland (40x67cm-16x26in) mono.i.d.92

ALLCOT, John (1888-1973) Australian
£556 $933   (16-Jul-91 JRL.S94) Mountain landscape (46x62cm-18x24in) s. canvas board
                 (A.D 1200)
£814 $1376   (16-Apr-91 J.M266 a) The R.M.S. Matiades (45x61cm-18x24in) s.i. board
                 (A.D 1800)
£905 $1529   (16-Apr-91 J.M208) Mount Cook (49x61cm-19x24in) s. canvas on board
                 (A.D 2000)
£1044 $2005   (26-Nov-90 SY.ME155/R) Clipper Mersey (22x29cm-9x11in) s.i.d.1914 board
                 (A.D 2600)
£1786 $3107   (26-Mar-91 JRL.S144/R) Hesperus (49x59cm-19x23in) s. canvas board
                 (A.D 4000)
*£463 $778   (16-Jul-91 JRL.S44) The James Wallace (23x31cm-9x12in) s. gouache
                 (A.D 1000)*
£620 $1147   (6-Mar-91 DR2) Battleship in Sydney harbour (27x37cm-11x15in) s. gouache
£1081 $2130   (13-Nov-90 J.M320 a) In the storm (25x37cm-10x15in) s. W/C (A.D 2800)
*£1351 $2662   (13-Nov-90 J.M160 a) Joseph Conrad (26x37cm-10x15in) s.d.36 W/C
                 (A.D 3500)*

ALLEBE, Augustus (1838-1927) Dutch
*£2322 $4481   (12-Dec-90 CH.AM111/R) Peasant woman entering farmhouse (29x23cm-11x9in)
                 init.d.68 s.verso pen htd white W/C (D.FL 7500)*

ALLECCY, V (20th C) French
£804 $1560   (4-Dec-90 FN.S1735) Angler by stream in wooded landscape and
                 thunderstorm rising (50x75cm-20x30in) s. panel (DM 2300)

ALLEGRAIN (studio) (17/18th C) French
£3300 $5841   (20-Mar-91 DL.P108/R) Paysage classique (54x38cm-21x15in) (F.FR 33000)

ALLEGRAIN, Etienne (attrib) (1653-1736) French
£5025 $8241   (21-Jun-91 SY.MO196/R) Paysge Romain (68x56cm-27x22in) (F.FR 50000)

ALLEGRAIN, Etienne (style) (1653-1736) French
£1300 $2197   (18-Apr-91 C42/R) Nymphs by a woodland pool (35x26cm-14x10in)

ALLEGRE, Raymond (1857-?) French
£2000 $3580   (12-Mar-91 PH76/R) Lady alighting from gondola (120x91cm-47x36in) s.

ALLEGRI, Antonio (after) (16th C) Italian
£1710 $3061   (14-Mar-91 D.V157/R) Jupiter and Jo (164x74cm-65x29in) (A.S 35000)
£1710 $3061   (14-Mar-91 D.V184/R) The Mystic Marriage of St Catherine
                 (29x23cm-11x9in) (A.S 35000)
£3428 $6753   (14-Nov-90 D.V222/R) Amor sharpening arrow (54x61cm-21x24in)
                 (A.S 70000)

ALLEGRI, Antonio (school) (1587-1663) Italian
£1546 $3029   (20-Nov-90 F.R101/R) Pieta (44x36cm-17x14in) panel (I.L 3400000)

ALLEGRI, Giovanni (18/19th C) Italian
£617 $1196   (7-Dec-90 CN.P15/R) Etude pour un Arc de Triomphe (42x30cm-17x12in)
                    s.d.1808 pen wash (F.FR 6000)

ALLEGRI, Pomponio (attrib) (1521-1593) Italian
£7500 $12225   (5-Jul-91 C237/R) Madonna and Child with Saint Sebastian
                    (76x56cm-30x22in) marouflaged panel

ALLEGRINI, Flaminio (17th C) Italian
£25083 $41888   (4-Jun-91 CH.R507/R) Episodio delle imprese di Ercole (66x139cm-26x55in)
                    panel (I.L 55000000)
£636 $1247   (19-Nov-90 CH.R149/R) Progetto per una porta a tre archi e colonne
                    (30x23cm-12x9in) i. pencil pen ink W/C (I.L 1400000)

ALLEGRINI, Francesco (1587-1663) Italian
£900 $1593   (22-Mar-91 APT.P2) Deploration du Christ (9x11cm-4x4in) pen wash
                    sanguinne two (F.FR 9000)
£1003 $1776   (19-Mar-91 F.BM197/R) La chiamata di Pietro. Barca con due figure. Cristo
                    in gloria (9x13cm-4x5in) i. pen bistre ink one double-sided two
                    (I.L 2200000)
£1094 $1937   (19-Mar-91 F.M274/R) Foglio di studi con scena di caccia e angolo di
                    porto (9x13cm-4x5in) bistre ink (I.L 2400000)
£1186 $2098   (19-Mar-91 F.M215/R) Gruppo di cavalieri e figura femminile
                    (9x13cm-4x5in) pen bistre W/C ink (I.L 2600000)
£1596 $2825   (19-Mar-91 F.M195/R) Aristotele e Campaspe (17x12cm-7x5in) ink
                    (I.L 3500000)
£3000 $5790   (12-Dec-90 PH353/R) Study of wall decoration with putti seated on
                    scrolling forms and horses (16x15cm-6x6in) pen ink shaped corners sold
                    with anon scrolling
£26000 $42380   (2-Jul-91 C55/R) Pegasus mastered by Perseus with Jupiter and Diana
                    (36x38cm-14x15in) i. chk brush pen ink wash

ALLEGRINI, Francesco (attrib) (1587-1663) Italian
£952 $1600   (17-Jul-91 SY.NY11/R) Saint interceding with Christ surrounded by angels
                    (37x49cm-15x19in) red chk. paper backed with linen

ALLEN, Charles Curtis (1886-1950) American
£660 $1300   (16-Nov-90 S.BM137/R) On Mount Monadnock (76x91cm-30x36in) s.d.1921
£774 $1300   (27-Apr-91 YFA.M31/R) Mt. Monadnock in winter (46x61cm-18x24in) s. board
£1282 $2500   (25-Oct-90 GRO.B144/R) Two children by the fireplace (102x127cm-40x50in)
                    s.indis.d.1918

ALLEN, Davida (1951-) Australian
£2791 $4688   (22-Apr-91 SY.ME378/R) Rosie's bedroom scene no.2 (84x100cm-33x39in)
                    s.i.d.1986 verso (A.D 6000)
£3271 $5332   (16-Jun-91 SY.ME33/R) Josephine on bed (119x100cm-47x39in) s.d.1984
                    verso (A.D 7000)
£6075 $9902   (16-Jun-91 SY.ME54/R) Sam....on stage, off stage (190x197cm-75x78in)
                    s.d.1986 verso (A.D 13000)

ALLEN, Douglas (20th C) American
£599 $1000   (26-Jul-91 E.EDM48/R) Stone sheep (58x43cm-23x17in) s. board

ALLEN, Greta (1881-?) American
£2959 $5000   (1-May-91 B.SF5081/R) Girl with apple (81x54cm-32x21in) s.d.1926

ALLEN, Harry Epworth (1894-1958) British
£2800 $5460   (17-Oct-90 PHL83/R) Harlech castle (34x49cm-13x19in) s. tempera
£3600 $7020   (17-Oct-90 PHL147/R) The fallen tree (47x59cm-19x23in) s. tempera
£7400 $14430   (17-Oct-90 PHL66/R) Turf cutting near Galway (39x49cm-15x19in) s.
                    tempera
£7800 $13182   (1-May-91 PHL71/R) Road through hills (48x59cm-19x23in) s. tempera
£700 $1358   (5-Dec-90 PHL31) Smoke rising from an Irish village (34x38cm-13x15in) s.
                    pastel
£720 $1397   (5-Dec-90 PHL34) Figures and donkeys working in the fields in Irish
                    landscape (27x37cm-11x15in) s. pastel
£1000 $1950   (17-Oct-90 PHL43) Stalactites (36x50cm-14x20in) s. pastel
£1050 $2048   (17-Oct-90 PHL161) Off Arran - Scotland (36x51cm-14x20in) s. gouache
£1200 $2340   (17-Oct-90 PHL170/R) The Irish ballerina (31x33cm-12x13in) s. pastel

ALLEN, J W (1803-1852) British
£1500 $2655   (21-Mar-91 CSK156) The farm on the hillside (53x79cm-21x31in) s.d.1845

ALLEN, Joseph (1770-1839) British
£9000 $14850   (10-Jul-91 S48/R) Portrait of Mary Evans Mrs. Fryer Todd wearing furs in
                    winter landscape (73x61cm-29x24in) i.verso

ALLEN, Joseph William (1803-1852) British
£2400 $4056   (1-May-91 PHL116/R) Vale of Clwyd (54x99cm-21x39in) s.d.1847

ALLEN, Joseph William (attrib) (1803-1852) British
£582 $1165   (6-Feb-91 RAS.K30) English landscape with sheep and rider
                    (28x46cm-11x18in) s. (D.KR 6500)

ALLEN, Margaret (fl.1853-1894) British
£1000 $1930   (12-Dec-90 MMB343) Portrait of artisan smoking pipe (76x64cm-30x25in)
                       s.d.1863 s.i.indist.verso

ALLEYN, Edmund (1931-) Canadian
£614 $1204   (20-Nov-90 JOY.T304) Germination (57x27cm-22x11in) s.d.61 (C.D 1400)

ALLEYNE, Francis (attrib) (18/19th C) British
£1700 $3145   (4-Mar-91 PHB68/R) Portrait of Frances Molesworth, on terrace. Portrait
                       of Matthew Hill (27x22cm-11x9in) panel oval pair

ALLIEVI, Fernando (1954-) Argentinian
£1786 $3500   (12-Feb-91 SY.NY296/R) Antiquarium (180x122cm-71x48in) s.i. mixed media

ALLINGHAM, Helen (1848-1926) British
£700 $1176   (22-Apr-91 PH264) Mother and children in hayfield (22x35cm-9x14in)
                       s.i.verso W/C
£1300 $2496   (26-Nov-90 SWS88/R) Studies of Canterbury bells and forget-me-nots
                       (11x9cm-4x4in) one i. pencil pair framed as one
£1600 $3168   (30-Jan-91 S266/R) Figure at cottage gate (25x18cm-10x7in) W/C htd
                       scratching out
£1900 $3648   (26-Nov-90 SWS105/R) Marigolds (12x18cm-5x7in) d.96 one s. W/C two
                       framed as one
£2800 $5516   (1-Nov-90 C142/R) The old fruit seller (33x28cm-13x11in) s. pencil W/C
£4000 $6680   (3-Jun-91 PHB26/R) Coming through (21x16cm-8x6in) s. W/C
£4200 $7014   (5-Jun-91 S302/R) Girl with bough of blossom (14x11cm-6x4in) init. W/C
                       htd bodycol
£4400 $8624   (22-Nov-90 CSK39/R) In Pinner garden (24x18cm-9x7in) s. i.verso pencil
                       W/C
£4500 $8865   (12-Nov-90 PH69/R) At Hambledon, Surrey (20x23cm-8x9in) s. W/C
                       scratching out
£4800 $9072   (26-Sep-90 S303/R) Dairy door, Farringford, Lord Tennyson's home
                       (28x20cm-11x8in) s. W/C htd bodycol
£5000 $8350   (5-Jun-91 S235/R) Wiltshire cottage (15x23cm-6x9in) s. s.i.verso W/C
£6200 $11718   (26-Sep-90 S304/R) Contemplation (20x15cm-8x6in) init. W/C
£6400 $12608   (1-Nov-90 C141/R) Fruit stall at base of campanile, San Giovanni
                       Elemosinario, Venice (38x28cm-15x11in) s. i.verso W/C
£6800 $11084   (14-Jun-91 C86/R) Thatched cottage near Peaslake, Surrey (23x24cm-9x9in)
                       s. W/C scratching out
£17000 $30430   (13-Mar-91 B136/R) A Surrey cottage (25x34cm-10x13in) s. W/C scratching
                       out
£19000 $37620   (30-Jan-91 S245/R) Kentish garden (27x23cm-11x9in) s. s.i.verso W/C htd
                       scratching out
£20000 $37800   (26-Sep-90 S302/R) Old cottage at Freshwater, Isle of Wight
                       (27x18cm-11x7in) s. W/C

ALLINSON, Adrian (1890-1959) British
£700 $1316   (20-Sep-90 CSK67) Mountainous estuary (56x68cm-22x27in) s. panel
£1500 $2535   (2-May-91 B67/R) Dahlias (61x51cm-24x20in) s.

ALLONGE, Auguste (1833-1898) French
£603 $1079   (17-Mar-91 L.C2) Peniches et drague (37x64cm-15x25in) s.d.1882 W/C
                       (F.FR 6000)
£815 $1605   (30-Oct-90 I.N188) Le Ruisseau (41x60cm-16x24in) s. W/C (F.FR 8000)
£1314 $2563   (21-Oct-90 DA.R1/R) Bouquet de fleurs colorees dans une corbeille
                       (77x55cm-30x22in) s. W/C (F.FR 13000)
£2854 $5480   (1-Dec-90 PER.M23/R) La mare aux fees (33x51cm-13x20in) s. W/C
                       (F.FR 28000)
£3568 $6850   (1-Dec-90 PER.M57/R) Rochers dans la foret de Fontainebleau
                       (53x73cm-21x29in) s. W/C (F.FR 35000)

ALLORI, Alessandro (1535-1607) Italian
£6000 $9780   (3-Jul-91 S128/R) Portrait of noblewoman (85x68cm-33x27in) panel
£36368 $71281   (19-Nov-90 CH.R171/R) La Sacra Famiglia (142x106cm-56x42in) panel
                       (I.L 80000000)

ALLORI, Alessandro (attrib) (1535-1607) Italian
£1900 $3097   (2-Jul-91 C245/R) Ignudo (40x30cm-16x12in) with i. black chk after
                       Michelangelo

ALLORI, Alessandro (style) (1535-1607) Italian
£6500 $10595   (3-Jul-91 S160/R) Portrait of gentleman, said to be composer Vincenzo
                       Galilei (110x79cm-43x31in) i. panel
£7000 $11830   (19-Apr-91 C128/R) Portrait of a lady, bust length wearing a purple
                       dress (40x31cm-16x12in)

ALLORI, Cristofano (1577-1621) Italian
£10056 $18000   (11-Apr-91 SY.NY73/R) Portrait of Knight of the Order of Santo Stefano
                       (61x47cm-24x19in)

ALLORI, Cristofano (after) (1577-1621) Italian
£900 $1467   (4-Jul-91 C514) Judith with head of Holofernes (149x115cm-59x45in)

ALLOU, Gilles (1670-1751) French
£7136 $13700   (30-Nov-90 APT.P165/R) Portrait de famille (113x147cm-44x58in) s.d.
                       (F.FR 70000)

ALLPORT, Henry Curzon (19th C) British
£4651 $7814   (22-Apr-91 SY.ME286/R) Port Jackson from Point Piper (17x24cm-7x9in) s.
                        W/C (A.D 10000)

ALLPORT, Henry Curzon (attrib) (19th C) British
£717 $1377   (14-Aug-90 SY.ME37) A distant view of Sydney from Rose Bay
                        (12x13cm-5x5in) W/C over pencil (A.D 1700)

ALMA-TADEMA (style) (19th C) British
£1371 $2303   (23-Apr-91 DUR.M13/R) Joven (80x45cm-31x18in) panel (S.P 250000)

ALMA-TADEMA, Anna (1865-1943) British
£11000 $18370   (5-Jun-91 S341/R) Gold room (33x45cm-13x18in) s.d.19/11/84 W/C over pen

ALMA-TADEMA, Lady Laura (1852-1909) British
£5800 $11426   (1-Nov-90 C294/R) A carol (38x23cm-15x9in) s.i. panel
£2273 $4500   (1-Feb-91 S.W2574/R) Flower seller and young couple on building steps in
                        Rome (36x28cm-14x11in) s.i. W/C

ALMA-TADEMA, Sir Lawrence (1836-1912) British
£1531 $3000   (7-Nov-90 B.SF1158/R) Roman maiden crowned by ivy and carrying oil lamp
                        (53x27cm-21x11in) s. panel
£2591 $5079   (6-Nov-90 SY.AM138/R) Portrait of negro-boy (41x34cm-16x13in) panel
                        (D.FL 8500)
£4335 $7500   (10-May-91 S.BM59/R) Stonehenge (23x36cm-9x14in) mono.s.i. i.verso
£68000 $130560   (28-Nov-90 S26/R) The death (200x290cm-79x114in)

ALMOND, William Douglas (1866-1916) British
£480 $830   (20-May-91 PH6) Knitting (25x20cm-10x8in) s. W/C htd white

ALMQVIST, Ester (1869-1934) Swedish
£651 $1164   (9-Apr-91 GO.G1) Factory parts (65x100cm-26x39in) s.d.1916 (S.KR 7000)

ALOCCO, Marcel (1937-) French
£3427 $6683   (26-Oct-90 CC.P48/R) Rubans Serges no 16 17 18 (73x180cm-29x71in) each
                        piece s.i. triptych (F.FR 34000)

ALONSO, Carlos (1929-) Argentinian
£699 $1300   (5-Sep-90 V.BA2) Rincon del pintor (30x30cm-12x12in)
£1218 $2400   (14-Nov-90 V.BA5) Mujer sentada (58x33cm-23x13in)
£4082 $8000   (19-Nov-90 SY.NY247/R) La lenera (100x100cm-39x39in) s.d.84 acrylic

ALONSO-PEREZ (19/20th C) Spanish
£4020 $6593   (18-Jun-91 APT.P168) La loge (40x32cm-16x13in) s. panel (F.FR 40000)

ALOTT, Robert (19th C) Austrian
£1700 $2788   (18-Jun-91 PH104) Drying the nets, Bay of Naples (42x68cm-17x27in)
                        s.d.1881

ALPERIZ, Nicolas (1869-?) Spanish
£870 $1539   (3-Apr-91 ANS.M164/R) Bodegon de lavandera (54x44cm-21x17in) s. tablex
                        (S.P 160000)

ALPINE SCHOOL, 15th C Swiss
£1884 $3070   (12-Jun-91 N.M291/R) Interment of Christ (98x95cm-39x37in) panel
                        (DM 5500)

ALQUIER, Alain (20th C) French
£585 $1140   (28-Oct-90 R.P14/R) Sans titre (89x116cm-35x46in) s.d.89n verso mixed
                        media (F.FR 5800)

ALS, Peder (attrib) (1725-1776) Danish
£2993 $5028   (22-Apr-91 BU.K68/R) Portrait of Princess Sofie Magdalene 1746-1813
                        (79x62cm-31x24in) (D.KR 34000)

ALSINA, Ramon Marti (19th C) Spanish?
£1512 $2706   (13-Mar-91 FER.M131/R) La samaritana (20x31cm-8x12in) s. (S.P 275000)

ALSLOOT, Denis van (style) (c.1570-1628) Dutch
£10256 $20000   (11-Oct-90 SY.NY91/R) Carnival in town square (103x145cm-41x57in)

ALSTON, Abbey (19th C) British
£1321 $2153   (1-Jul-91 AAA.S59) The beauty (66x47cm-26x19in) s. pastel (A.D 2800)

ALT, Franz (1821-1914) Austrian
£525 $883   (25-Apr-91 D.V117/R) The letter, portrait of Grafin Lang (17x24cm-7x9in)
                        s.i.d.1866 W/C possibly pencil (A.S 11000)
£812 $1364   (25-Apr-91 D.V157/R) View of Russian church (17x12cm-7x5in) s.d.1854 W/C
                        (A.S 17000)
£897 $1750   (26-Oct-90 SY.NY37/R) Tomb of Kaiser Frederich III in the Apostle's
                        Choir of Stefansdom, Vienna (20x32cm-8x13in) s. pencil
£1433 $2407   (25-Apr-91 D.V158/R) Moskau theatre after the fire (17x25cm-7x10in)
                        s.d.1854 W/C (A.S 30000)
£2625 $5119   (11-Oct-90 D.V133/R) Interior of Kapuzinerkirche, Vienna
                        (28x37cm-11x15in) s.d.1872 W/C (A.S 55000)

ALT, Franz (1821-1914) Austrian-cont.
£9744 $19000   (26-Oct-90 SY.NY123/R) Viennese drawing room (23x32cm-9x13in) s.d.1872
W/C htd.gouache

ALT, Jacob (1789-1872) German
£716 $1203   (25-Apr-91 D.V184/R) Portrait eines Burgergardisten während Revolution
von 1848 (28x16cm-11x6in) s. W/C paper on board (A.S 15000)
£2149 $3610   (25-Apr-91 D.V160/R) Hilly landscape with cattle (17x25cm-7x10in)
s.d.1853 W/C (A.S 45000)
£2865 $4814   (25-Apr-91 D.V159/R) View of Franciscan monastery Paludi near Spalato
(18x28cm-7x11in) s.d.1840 W/C (A.S 60000)

ALT, Otmar (20th C) German
£1706 $3345   (20-Nov-90 L.K6/R) The Sunday animals (44x38cm-17x15in) s.d.1971
(DM 5000)
£1858 $3215   (21-May-91 WK.M512/R) The green goat and the beautiful dog
(52x43cm-20x17in) s.i.d.1967 s.i.d.verso acrylic board (DM 5500)
£3425 $5582   (14-Jun-91 L.K710/R) Der Elefant aus dem Glockenblumenland
(80x60cm-31x24in) s.d.68 s.i.stretcher (DM 10000)

ALT, Rudolf von (1812-1905) Austrian
£1486 $2824   (14-Sep-90 SA.A1217/R) View of Austrian country estate (39x33cm-15x13in)
s. (DM 4400)
£573 $963   (25-Apr-91 D.V59/R) Dobrotanerin s.i. pencil W/C (A.S 12000)
£2653 $5227   (13-Nov-90 GF.L5004) Innsbruck, Tyrol (18x23cm-7x9in) s.i.d.1828 W/C
over pencil fragment (S.FR 6500)
£2865 $4814   (25-Apr-91 D.V44/R) Wien Neubau, Neugebauers birth place
(27x29cm-11x11in) s.i. i.verso W/C pencil (A.S 60000)
£35971 $69784   (7-Dec-90 CN.P85/R) Vue de la place du Pantheon a Rome (41x56cm-16x22in)
s.d.1875 W/C (F.FR 350000)

ALTAMIRANO, Arturo Pacheco (19/20th C) Chilean
£575 $1000   (27-Mar-91 B.SF4273/R) Fishing boats at dock (44x55cm-17x22in) s.
£632 $1100   (27-Mar-91 B.SF4274/R) Fishing boats moored (50x60cm-20x24in) s. board
£1183 $2000   (20-Apr-91 WOL.C275/R) Shipyard scene (58x74cm-23x29in) s.
£1429 $2800   (20-Nov-90 CH.NY247/R) Marina (60x73cm-24x29in) s.

ALTAMURA (?) ?
£1023 $1995   (10-Oct-90 ARC.P49/R) Venise, place Saint Marc (50x45cm-20x18in) s.
(F.FR 10200)

ALTAMURA, Saverio (1826-1897) Italian
£924 $1784   (11-Dec-90 CH.R46) Ragazza pensosa (30x23cm-12x9in) s. (I.L 2000000)

ALTDORFER, Albrecht (studio) (1480-1538) German
£31832 $62708   (14-Nov-90 D.V28/R) The Adoration of the Magi (106x75cm-42x30in) panel
(A.S 650000)

ALTDORFER, Albrecht (style) (1480-1538) German
£10000 $16300   (5-Jul-91 C250/R) Martyrdom of Saint Florian (34x35cm-13x14in) panel

ALTENBOURG, Gerhard (1926-) German
£612 $1084   (22-Mar-91 GRA.B2770/R) Composition (30x21cm-12x8in) s.d.1987 pencil
col.pencil (DM 1800)
£2116 $4147   (20-Nov-90 L.K7/R) Dieses (33x19cm-13x7in) mono.i.d.1956 W/C pencil
(DM 6200)
£5068 $8767   (21-May-91 WK.M517/R) Berggange (50x64cm-20x25in) s.d.1964
mono.i.d.verso mixed media (DM 15000)

ALTENKIRCH, Otto (1875-?) German
£676 $1318   (26-Oct-90 BM.B736/R) Pond in woods (97x123cm-38x48in) s. i.verso
(DM 2000)

ALTENKOPF, Joseph (attrib) (1818-?) Austrian
£728 $1376   (27-Sep-90 D.V107/R) Lake landscape with house, Salzkammergut
(31x40cm-12x16in) (A.S 15000)

ALTHAUS, F (fl.1881-1914) British
£600 $966   (24-Jun-91 HS76/R) In Christow, Devon - village scene with figures
beside thatched cottages (26x38cm-10x15in) s. W/C

ALTHAUS, Fritz (fl.1881-1914) British
£620 $1221   (1-Nov-90 C28) Near Brampfield Speke near Exeter (28x38cm-11x15in) s.
i.verso W/C htd.white

ALTINK, Jan (1885-?) Dutch
£1377 $2396   (26-Mar-91 VN.R1/R) Farm in a country lane (60x80cm-24x31in) s.
(D.FL 4600)
£1652 $2857   (22-May-91 CH.AM318) Blauwborgje (60x72cm-24x28in) s.d.33 (D.FL 5500)
£511 $883   (22-May-91 CH.AM316) Country road (30x46cm-12x18in) s.d.51 black crayon
W/C (D.FL 1700)

ALTMANN, Alexandre (1885-1932) Russian
£559 $1118   (6-Feb-91 FB.P6) Paysage au pont (53x64cm-21x25in) s. (F.FR 5500)
£593 $1062   (14-Apr-91 GL.P42/R) Pont sur la riviere (73x60cm-29x24in) s.
(F.FR 6000)

ALTMANN, Alexandre (1885-1932) Russian-cont.
£602	$1114	(4-Mar-91 ARC.P81) Le petit bois (50x65cm-20x26in) s. (F.FR 6000)
£751	$1299	(23-May-91 SY.AM10/R) Une pensee pour la terre sainte (73x60cm-29x24in) s. i.verso (D.FL 2500)
£900	$1503	(22-Jul-91 SWS1115/R) The path by the canal (64x80cm-25x31in) s.
£954	$1765	(4-Mar-91 ARC.P80/R) Paysage (79x60cm-31x24in) s. (F.FR 9500)
£967	$1906	(29-Oct-90 ZZ.F23/R) Vue de Paris - le boulevard des Invalides (48x63cm-19x25in) s.d.1909 (F.FR 9500)
£1015	$2000	(13-Nov-90 CE.NY21/R) Paysage avec riviere (54x65cm-21x26in) s.i.d.1916
£1117	$2200	(13-Nov-90 CE.NY24/R) Arbres au bord du lac (50x65cm-20x26in) s.
£1333	$2600	(10-Oct-90 SY.NY23/R) Rocky coast (99x147cm-39x58in) s.d.1913
£1361	$2654	(28-Oct-90 M.V107) Bord de riviere (61x46cm-24x18in) s. (F.FR 13500)
£1531	$3000	(12-Feb-91 SY.NY24/R) Landscape with tree (51x64cm-20x25in) s.
£1531	$3000	(12-Feb-91 SY.NY96/R) Grove of mango trees (58x74cm-23x29in) s.
£1563	$3047	(28-Oct-90 M.V106) La mer (81x60cm-32x24in) s. (F.FR 15500)
£2141	$4131	(14-Dec-90 ARC.P94) Bouquet de fleurs (75x60cm-30x24in) s. (F.FR 21000)
£2231	$4284	(17-Dec-90 AGS.P12/R) Riviere sous la neige (81x100cm-32x39in) s. (F.FR 22000)
£2400	$4008	(22-Jul-91 SWS1106/R) The lily pool (62x76cm-24x30in) s.

ALTOMONTE, Bartholomaus (attrib) (1702-1799) Austrian
| £5387 | $10612 | (14-Nov-90 D.V355/R) Susanna and the Elders (97x117cm-38x46in) (A.S 110000) |

ALTOMONTE, Martino (1657-1745) Italian
| £1714 | $3377 | (14-Nov-90 D.V315/R) Madonna with Child (53x42cm-21x17in) (A.S 35000) |

ALTOMONTE, Martino (style) (1657-1745) Italian
| £1861 | $3666 | (14-Nov-90 D.V327/R) The death of St Joseph (97x69cm-38x27in) (A.S 38000) |

ALTOON, John (1925-?) American
| *£974* | *$1900* | *(24-Oct-90 B.SF1490/R) Untitled (76x102cm-30x40in) s.d.66 W/C pen* |

ALTRUI, E (19th C) ?
| £2000 | $3900 | (16-Oct-90 CG245/R) Sorrento (18x20cm-7x8in) s. panel oval |

ALTSON, Abbey (fl.1894-1917) British
| £3500 | $6720 | (26-Nov-90 HS125/R) Yvette, portrait of young dark haired girl with sunset beyond (58x48cm-23x19in) s. i.verso |
| £4800 | $9408 | (8-Nov-90 PHI209/R) The rose maiden (47x56cm-19x22in) s. |

ALVAREZ (?) ?
| £11500 | $21850 | (1-Mar-91 C138/R) View of Posillipo with peasants merrymaking and Vesuvius erupting beyond (63x76cm-25x30in) |

ALVAREZ CATALA, Luis (1836-1901) Spanish
| £950 | $1900 | (7-Feb-91 B.P93/R) Gondola ride (46x79cm-18x31in) s. board |

ALVAREZ DE SOTOMAYOR, Fernando (1883-1960) Spanish
£2336	$4182	(13-Mar-91 FER.M185/R) Retrato de D.Angel de Echenique (45x36cm-18x14in) s. tablex (S.P 425000)
£3298	$6331	(19-Feb-91 DUR.M32) Retrato (46x38cm-18x15in) canvas laid down on board (S.P 600000)
£6009	$11598	(11-Dec-90 FER.M212/R) Joven gallega (42x33cm-17x13in) s. (S.P 1100000)
£7648	$14761	(11-Dec-90 FER.M214/R) Magnifico estudio de caballo para el cuadro del General Franco (80x100cm-31x39in) s. (S.P 1400000)
£20331	$39645	(17-Oct-90 FER.M211/R) Aldeanas (71x61cm-28x24in) s. (S.P 3750000)

ALVAREZ Y FERNANDEZ, F (?) Spanish
| £500 | $845 | (1-May-91 PHL148) Spanish courtyard (41x74cm-16x29in) s. |

ALVAREZ, Luis (19th C) Spanish
£1200	$2364	(4-Oct-90 CSK166/R) A young spanish beauty (35x26cm-14x10in) s.
£8671	$15000	(23-May-91 CH.NY142/R) Venetian outing (45x80cm-18x31in) s.i. panel
£23121	$40000	(22-May-91 SY.NY282/R) Royal supper (69x100cm-27x39in) s.d.1883

ALVAREZ, Mabel (1891-1985) American
£561	$1100	(12-Feb-91 MOR.P94) Figures under tree (18x23cm-7x9in) estate st. board
£1403	$2750	(12-Feb-91 MOR.P64) Seated figure (30x41cm-12x16in) estate st. canvas on board
£2041	$4000	(13-Feb-91 B.SF2167/R) Portrait of Armen (51x41cm-20x16in) estate st.
£2051	$4000	(10-Oct-90 B.SF645/R) Sunday afternoon (46x51cm-18x20in) estate st.
£2806	$5500	(12-Feb-91 MOR.P53) Nude in interior (51x41cm-20x16in) s. canvas on board

ALVAREZ-SALA, Ventura (1871-?) Spanish
| £1491 | $2907 | (17-Oct-90 FER.M185/R) Lavanderas (46x47cm-18x19in) s.d.1904 (S.P 275000) |

ALVEY, William Charles (fl.1800-1818) British
| *£420* | *$727* | *(7-May-91 SWS1889) Frances Douglas with curled black hair min. gilt frame rectangular* |

ALVIANI, Getulio (1939-) Italian
£1711 $3336   (24-Oct-90 F.M180) Superficie a testura vibratile, Studio
                          (36x42cm-14x17in) s.d.1973 aluminium (I.L 3800000)
£2050 $3486   (28-May-91 SY.MI75/R) Superficie a testura vibratile 71018
                          (84x84cm-33x33in) s.verso aluminium panel (I.L 4500000)
£3602 $7024   (22-Oct-90 BR.M17/R) Superficie a testura vibratile (36x126cm-14x50in)
                          s.st.d.1972 verso aluminium (I.L 8000000)

ALYANAK, Hrand J (20th C) Armenian
£1325 $2558   (12-Dec-90 ZZ.F19/R) Plage d'Etretat (42x72cm-17x28in) s. (F.FR 13000)

AMALER-RAVIV, Arlene (1953-) South African?
£1169 $2280   (15-Oct-90 SY.J188/R) Michele II (90x80cm-35x31in) s.d.'89 (SA.R 5800)

AMAN-JEAN (1860-1935) French
£747 $1270   (27-May-91 OD.P101) Deux femmes agenouillees (45x29cm-18x11in) s.
                          sanguinne htd.white (F.FR 7500)

AMAN-JEAN, Edmond Francois (1860-1935) French
£2368 $4500   (27-Feb-91 SY.NY53/R) Portrait of young woman (73x61cm-29x24in) s.
£5097 $9786   (27-Nov-90 ZZ.F82) Jeune femme au chapeau (54x38cm-21x15in) s. panel
                          (F.FR 50000)
£105000 $185850   (19-Mar-91 C20/R) Dame pensive, assise (55x44cm-22x17in) s.

AMAR, Joseph (1954-) American
£1503 $2600   (7-May-91 CE.NY264/R) Untitled (61x49cm-24x19in) s.d.1986 verso wax lead
                          graphite wood

AMAURY-DUVAL, Eugene Emmanuel (1808-1885) French
£6989 $13558   (9-Dec-90 ZZ.F19/R) Portrait de femme (100x80cm-39x31in) s.d.1862
                          (F.FR 68000)

AMBERES SCHOOL, 17th C ?
£3279 $6426   (24-Jan-91 EP.M25/R) Diana y Actaeon (103x130cm-41x51in) copper
                          (S.P 600000)

AMBERG, Wilhelm (1822-1899) German
£676 $1149   (31-May-91 GB.B5693/R) Misdroy, old farmhouse with treetrunk and goat
                          (33x44cm-13x17in) s.i.d.1868 board (DM 2000)
£1027 $1839   (12-Mar-91 FN.S2266/R) Elegy, portrait of pensive girl seated on rock in
                          mountain landscape (90x53cm-35x21in) s. i.verso (DM 3000)
£2041 $3286   (26-Jun-91 KM.K1378/R) The love letter (61x50cm-24x20in) s. (DM 6000)

AMBERGER, Gustav (1831-1896) German
£3270 $6343   (5-Dec-90 KH.K1/R) Italian landscape with women by well, view towards
                          Rome (40x57cm-16x22in) s. (D.KR 36000)

AMBILLE, Paul (1930-) French
£702 $1369   (10-Oct-90 ARC.P107/R) Fenetre a Clermont (92x65cm-36x26in) s.
                          (F.FR 7000)
£1733 $3327   (2-Dec-90 FE.P53) Quatre chevaux (61x46cm-24x18in) s. F.FR 17000)
£2976 $5119   (19-May-91 ZZ.F176/R) Le depart de la course (73x100cm-29x39in) s.
                          (F.FR 30000)

AMBLER, C (fl.1912-1914) British
£500 $975   (15-Jan-91 C85) Dandie Dinmont (33x33cm-13x13in) s. pencil W/C htd.white

AMBROGIANI, P (1907-1985) French
£3364 $6459   (30-Nov-90 ARC.P135) Femme au divan (53x65cm-21x26in) s. panel
                          (F.FR 33000)

AMBROGIANI, Pierre (1907-1985) French
£653 $1267   (8-Dec-90 GAB.G2321/R) Nature morte aux fleurs (25x33cm-10x13in) s.
                          paper (S.FR 1600)
£2446 $4697   (29-Nov-90 QWA.P209/R) Paysage a Aurel (32x42cm-13x17in) s. (F.FR 24000)
£2900 $4727   (5-Jul-91 APT.P85) La montage de Montbrun, Drome (50x73cm-20x29in) s. i.
                          verso (F.FR 29000)
£3038 $5255   (26-May-91 ZZ.F128/R) Nu debout (99x73cm-39x29in) s. (F.FR 30500)
£3467 $5686   (19-Jun-91 JM.P111) Fleurs (55x46cm-22x18in) s. i. verso (F.FR 34500)
£3815 $7058   (6-Mar-91 APT.P64) Sur la plage (54x73cm-21x29in) s. (F.FR 38000)
£3920 $6428   (18-Jun-91 APT.P166/R) Bateaux a qual (60x81cm-24x32in) s. (F.FR 39000)
£5673 $10494   (6-Mar-91 APT.P63) Les Gondes (60x81cm-24x32in) s. (F.FR 56500)
£403 $786   (20-Jan-91 GL.P1) Femmes au marche (48x63cm-19x25in) s. felt-pen drawing
                          (F.FR 4000)
£403 $657   (10-Jun-91 NM.P3/R) Quartier reserve (48x64cm-19x25in) s. (F.FR 4000)
£410 $803   (11-Nov-90 ZZ.F233/R) Nu allonge (45x60cm-18x24in) s. chl. (F.FR 4000)
£416 $736   (7-Apr-91 LT.P92) Le mas a Aurel (10x16cm-4x6in) s. pastel (F.FR 4200)
£495 $876   (7-Apr-91 I.N13) Pablo Casals (18x16cm-7x6in) s. pastel (F.FR 5000)
£545 $964   (7-Apr-91 I.N7) Personnages (48x63cm-19x25in) s. pen (F.FR 5500)
£545 $964   (7-Apr-91 I.N9) Femme assise (63x44cm-25x17in) s. ink wash (F.FR 5500)
£554 $903   (11-Jun-91 I.N144) Le mas (31x41cm-12x16in) s. chl.ink (F.FR 5500)
£673 $1192   (7-Apr-91 I.N10) Personnages (41x54cm-16x21in) s. W/C (F.FR 6800)
£673 $1192   (7-Apr-91 I.N11) Tete d'enfant (40x31cm-16x12in) s. goauche (F.FR 6800)
£693 $1331   (29-Nov-90 QWA.P58) Port de Plaisance (38x53cm-15x21in) st.sig. felt-pen
                          (F.FR 6800)
£693 $1227   (7-Apr-91 I.N12) Retour de peche (48x64cm-19x25in) s. ink (F.FR 7000)

AMBROGIANI, Pierre (1907-1985) French-cont.
£693 $1227   (7-Apr-91 LT.P141) Les Arlesiennes (64x48cm-25x19in) s. felt pen
                (F.FR 7000)
£693 $1227   (7-Apr-91 LT.P148) Nu allonge (64x48cm-25x19in) s. ink (F.FR 7000)
£703 $1132   (28-Jun-91 ZZ.F16) Les Pheniciens (38x55cm-15x22in) gouache laid down on
                canvas (F.FR 7000)
£803 $1293   (28-Jun-91 ZZ.F156) Personnages (38x55cm-15x22in) s. gouache paper laid
                down on canvas (F.FR 8000)
£1683 $2979   (7-Apr-91 I.N8) Bord de mer (53x73cm-21x29in) s. gouache (F.FR 17000)

AMBROISE, Jules-Francois-Achille (19/20th C) French
£1111 $2156   (4-Dec-90 P.Q81) Summer afternoon's ride (59x79cm-23x31in) s.d.1895
                (C.D 2500)

AMBROSE, C (fl.1824-1848) ?
£2000 $3300   (12-Jul-91 C166/R) Portrait of officer of 12th Royal Lancers, in
                landscape (92x72cm-36x28in) s.d.1837 verso

AMEDEE, Jean Louis (19th C) French
£3591 $7074   (14-Nov-90 RAS.K29/R) Henri II and Diane de Poitiers on palace steps
                (160x115cm-63x45in) s.d.1839 (D.KR 40000)

AMEGLIO, Mario (1897-1970) French
£976 $1894   (5-Dec-90 ZZ.F12/R) La cathedrale de Reims (41x33cm-16x13in) s.
                (F.FR 9500)
£1131 $2193   (5-Dec-90 ZZ.F185/R) Le Pont des Soupirs (37x56cm-15x22in) s.
                (F.FR 11000)
£1594 $2757   (26-May-91 ZZ.F84/R) La place Pigalle a Paris (46x56cm-18x22in) s.
                (F.FR 16000)
£1606 $2972   (10-Mar-91 LT.P65 b/R) Promenade sur le Parvis de Notre-Dame
                (41x33cm-16x13in) s. (F.FR 16000)
£1714 $3342   (28-Oct-90 GRA.P1/R) Rue de l'epicerie a Rouen (46x33cm-18x13in) s.
                (F.FR 17000)
£1734 $3000   (7-May-91 CE.NY41/R) Madeleine (46x55cm-18x22in) s. s.d.58 verso
£1813 $2955   (11-Jun-91 I.N5) Cannes (22x26cm-9x10in) s. hardboard (F.FR 18000)
£2132 $4200   (13-Nov-90 CE.NY66/R) Sur la plage (33x56cm-13x22in) s.
£2254 $4418   (11-Nov-90 ZZ.F76/R) La croisette a Cannes (22x27cm-9x11in) s. panel
                (F.FR 22000)
£2679 $4607   (19-May-91 ZZ.F137/R) Vue de Saint-Tropez (50x60cm-20x24in) s.
                (F.FR 27000)
£4044 $7887   (17-Oct-90 LT.P11/R) Paris Notre Dame (54x81cm-21x32in) s. i.d.57 verso
                (F.FR 40000)
£4044 $7887   (17-Oct-90 LT.P25/R) La Place de la Concorde (46x55cm-18x22in) s.
                (F.FR 40000)

AMELIN, Albin (1902-1975) Swedish
£2452 $4389   (11-Mar-91 B.O1/R) Woman sleeping (60x72cm-24x28in) s.d.29 (N.KR 28000)
£4634 $8990   (4-Dec-90 BA.S6/R) Still life of flowers (81x65cm-32x26in) s.
                (S.KR 50000)
£4889 $9387   (27-Nov-90 BU.S13/R) Still life of flowers (92x73cm-36x29in) s.
                (S.KR 53000)
£5948 $10647   (9-Apr-91 GO.G2/R) Portrait of factory worker outside factory
                (82x66cm-32x26in) s.d.51 (S.KR 64000)
£6554 $11273   (14-May-91 BU.S86/R) Still life of flowers (93x73cm-37x29in) s.
                (S.KR 70000)
£1358 $2350   (22-May-91 BA.S1/R) The accident (72x59cm-28x23in) s.d.1933 gouache
                (S.KR 14400)
£2966 $5753   (5-Dec-90 AB.S7007/R) Still life of cut flowers in jug (99x68cm-39x27in)
                s.d.46 gouache (S.KR 32000)
£5839 $11327   (4-Dec-90 BA.S9/R) Still life of flowers (94x69cm-37x27in) s.d.50
                gouache (S.KR 63000)

AMENOFF, Gregory (20th C) American
£3061 $6000   (6-Nov-90 CE.NY185 b/R) Falling in memory (241x241cm-95x95in) s.i.d.2/85
                verso
£5102 $10000   (15-Feb-91 SY.NY195/R) Lost in the flood (254x208cm-100x82in)

AMERICAN SCHOOL (?) American
£6349 $12000   (27-Sep-90 CH.NY81/R) The banjo player (71x99cm-28x39in)
£8462 $16500   (21-Oct-90 HG.C57) Two women beside river (79x79cm-31x31in) s.
£1190 $2000   (28-Apr-91 LIT.L37) Portrait of woman with bonnet and brooch
                (58x48cm-23x19in) W/C

AMERICAN SCHOOL, 18th C American
£2665 $5250   (16-Nov-90 WOL.C414/R) Bust of Liberty, bordered by wreath
                (23x18cm-9x7in) i. W/C

AMERICAN SCHOOL, 19th C American
£1053 $2000   (1-Mar-91 RB.HY88/R) View of Hudson River with figures working field
                (56x91cm-22x36in)
£1173 $2300   (16-Feb-91 W.W23/R) Portrait of the Flying Cloud (48x74cm-19x29in)
£1212 $2000   (13-Jul-91 YFA.M8/R) A fishing party (76x112cm-30x44in)
£1227 $2000   (5-Jul-91 S.W2626/R) Family portrait - Mother and child daughters
                (41x33cm-16x13in) canvas laid on board oval
£1472 $2400   (5-Jul-91 S.W3058/R) Harper's Ferry landscape (51x61cm-20x24in)
£1479 $2500   (20-Apr-91 WOL.C70/R) Quaker village, Springfield, MA (36x58cm-14x23in)

AMERICAN SCHOOL, 19th C American-cont.

£1622	$3000	(8-Mar-91 S.BM164/R) Opulent still life with fruit and flowers (107x91cm-42x36in) s.
£1786	$3500	(26-Jan-91 CH.NY183/R) View of New York City from New Jersey (63x86cm-25x34in)
£1850	$3200	(21-May-91 CE.NY365/R) George Washington (74x61cm-29x24in)
£1850	$3200	(12-May-91 H.C103/R) Floral still life (76x102cm-30x40in) oval board
£1955	$3500	(14-Mar-91 CH.NY61/R) Boy fishing (39x49cm-15x19in) canvas on masonite
£2119	$3750	(22-Mar-91 S.W2881/R) Daybreak in foothills (30x48cm-12x19in)
£2180	$3750	(15-May-91 SY.NY83/R) Still life with roses and fruits (81x65cm-32x26in)
£2300	$4370	(28-Feb-91 B46/R) Family group seated around supper table (57x67cm-22x26in)
£2398	$4700	(16-Feb-91 W.W19/R) Harbour scene with American frigate and French side-steamer Le Francais (51x71cm-20x28in)
£2428	$4200	(21-May-91 CE.NY368/R) Boy on horse (51x40cm-20x16in)
£2514	$4500	(12-Apr-91 SY.NY27/R) Haywagon (56x96cm-22x38in)
£2604	$5000	(17-Dec-90 SY.NY126 a/R) Bird's nest (74x61cm-29x24in)
£2646	$5000	(27-Sep-90 CH.NY119/R) The long awaited letter (76x101cm-30x40in) indist.s.i.d.1890
£2659	$4600	(12-May-91 H.C99/R) Portrait of Catherine Tingler (56x41cm-22x16in) i.d.1812 panel
£2660	$5000	(19-Sep-90 B.SF2841/R) Indian hunter (21x16cm-8x6in) indist.init.
£2865	$5500	(28-Nov-90 D.NY10/R) Young boy in landscape (102x74cm-40x29in)
£2941	$5500	(4-Aug-90 LIT.L160 a) Portrait of young boy with yo-yo (107x61cm-42x24in)
£3179	$5500	(21-May-91 CE.NY380/R) Lake George (30x51cm-12x20in)
£3316	$6500	(26-Jan-91 CH.NY167/R) American farm - fall view from East (103x132cm-41x52in)
£4337	$8500	(26-Jan-91 CH.NY200/R) Portrait of little girl (76x62cm-30x24in)
£4592	$9000	(24-Nov-90 RB.HY61/R) Docks at Hobobken, N.J. with three large vessels and other shipping (38x64cm-15x25in) indis.s.d.1866 l.verso
£8000	$15600	(24-Oct-90 S9/R) A slave auction (30x50cm-12x20in) arched
£9375	$18000	(28-Nov-90 D.NY12) Indian hunting party resting beside waterfall (86x71cm-34x28in)
£964	*$1900*	*(16-Nov-90 WOL.C855 b/R) Rhoda Steddom, bust length profile portrait, with sitter seated (10x8cm-4x3in) s. W/C*
£1066	*$2100*	*(16-Nov-90 WOL.C855 a/R) Marcus Mote in 21st year (10x8cm-4x3in) i. W/C*
£1250	*$2500*	*(7-Feb-91 B.P140/R) View of Middle Street, Portland - before Great Fire of 1866 (33x43cm-13x17in) W/C pencil*
£1437	*$2400*	*(25-Jul-91 E.EDM325/R) Explosion of American steamship Anglo Norman, in December 1850 (46x66cm-18x26in) W/C tempera*

AMERICAN SCHOOL, 19th/20th C American

£1163	$2000	(18-May-91 W.W116/R) Rapallo across the water (41x51cm-16x20in) i.d.March '93
£6977	$12000	(15-May-91 SY.NY91/R) Summer landscape (91x122cm-36x48in)

AMERICAN SCHOOL, 20th C American

£1050	$2100	(7-Feb-91 B.P19/R) Morning, Monhegan (64x97cm-25x38in)
£1387	$2400	(10-May-91 S.BM88/R) Through the trees to distant meadows (76x76cm-30x30in)
£4335	$7500	(10-May-91 S.BM96/R) Danse de maske (79x91cm-31x36in) indis.s. i.verso
£1117	*$2000*	*(14-Mar-91 CH.NY202/R) Two hundred miles to Philadelphia (51x61cm-20x24in) W/C gouache board*
£2340	*$4400*	*(22-Sep-90 WOL.C256/R) Portrait of young woman by window (36x23cm-14x9in) bears sig. W/C artist board*

AMERLING, Friedrich von (1803-1887) German

£3359	$5777	(16-May-91 D.V62/R) Portrait of Franz Liszt (48x38cm-19x15in) i. (A.S 70000)
£3925	$7537	(29-Nov-90 D.V121/R) Portrait of Italian lady (63x50cm-25x20in) c.1845/50 (A.S 80000)
£9814	$18842	(29-Nov-90 D.V81/R) Portrait of Turk (63x52cm-25x20in) (A.S 200000)
£28902	$50000	(22-May-91 SY.NY38/R) Die schlafenden kinder im walde, vom treuen hunde bewacht (96x136cm-38x54in)

AMERLING, Friedrich von (attrib) (1803-1887) German

£882	$1746	(31-Jan-91 D.V123/R) Portrait study of Kaiser Ferdinand (36x29cm-14x11in) paper on board (A.S 18000)

AMESEDER, Eduard (1856-1938) Austrian

£622	$1076	(8-May-91 D.V74/R) Landscape with cows (33x29cm-13x11in) s. canvas on board (A.S 13000)
£630	$1185	(20-Sep-90 D.V67/R) Canal in Chioggia (41x53cm-16x21in) board (A.S 13000)
£1843	$3465	(20-Sep-90 D.V68/R) Italian harbour (62x76cm-24x30in) s. (A.S 38000)

AMEZAGA, Eduardo (1911-) South American

£649	$1214	(1-Aug-90 GC.M1) Maternidad (83x93cm-33x37in)
£914	$1800	(1-Oct-90 GC.M2) Santo Domingo de Soriano (47x53cm-19x21in)
£1218	$2400	(1-Nov-90 GC.M1) Joven, Casona y Parvas (42x46cm-17x18in) fibre
£1320	$2600	(1-Oct-90 GC.M1) Casonas (83x91cm-33x36in)

AMIDANO, Giulio Cesare (circle) (1566-1630) Italian

£2500	$4225	(19-Apr-91 C145/R) The Madonna and child (80x66cm-31x26in)

34

AMIET, Cuno (1868-1961) Swiss
£2540	$4165	(19-Jun-91 GK.B163) The card player d.1958verso board (S.FR 6400)
£3254	$5337	(19-Jun-91 GK.B161) Sunlit Alpine landscape (30x25cm-12x10in) s.d.1938verso board (S.FR 8200)
£3968	$6865	(22-May-91 GS.B2007/R) Portrait of Anna Amiet wearing necklace (46x38cm-18x15in) mono.d.41 hessian (S.FR 10000)
£3968	$6865	(22-May-91 GS.B2009/R) Wooded lake landscape (24x29cm-9x11in) mono.d.22 paper on board (S.FR 10000)
£5952	$10298	(22-May-91 GS.B2006/R) Female nude seated (26x28cm-10x11in) mono.d.18 board (S.FR 15000)
£7347	$14473	(16-Nov-90 GK.Z5303/R) The hurdy-gurdy player (72x58cm-28x23in) mono.d.1915 s.i.verso (S.FR 18000)
£9921	$16567	(5-Jun-91 SY.Z131/R) In the park (33x41cm-13x16in) mono.d.35 s.i.d.verso (S.FR 25000)
£10442	$17542	(24-Apr-91 G.Z43/R) The painter Johann Peter Fluck (55x46cm-22x18in) mono.d.1946 board (S.FR 26000)
£10939	$21549	(16-Nov-90 GK.Z5302/R) Nature morte au fruit (33x41cm-13x16in) s.d.1935 panel (S.FR 26800)
£11905	$19881	(5-Jun-91 SY.Z147/R) Garden landscape (46x55cm-18x22in) mono.d.52 pavatex (S.FR 30000)
£12048	$23614	(21-Nov-90 SY.Z61/R) Portrait of Hans Adam Flury (46x38cm-18x15in) mono.d.15 i.verso (S.FR 30000)
£13878	$27339	(16-Nov-90 GK.Z5304/R) Winter landscape with construction site (38x45cm-15x18in) mono. (S.FR 34000)
£16000	$31200	(17-Oct-90 G.Z49/R) House and garden in Oschwand (38x46cm-15x18in) mono.d.1945 board (S.FR 40000)
£18474	$36209	(21-Nov-90 SY.Z69/R) Emmental (37x46cm-15x18in) mono.d.25 (S.FR 46000)
£24096	$47229	(21-Nov-90 SY.Z45/R) In the garden (40x53cm-16x21in) mono. (S.FR 60000)
£27778	$45556	(21-Jun-91 GK.B1/R) Farmsteads of Spych near Oschwand (54x64cm-21x25in) mono.d.1901 i.verso (S.FR 70000)
£43651	$71587	(21-Jun-91 GK.B2/R) Garden with trees (73x59cm-29x23in) mono.d.18 canvas on board (S.FR 110000)
£64257	$125944	(21-Nov-90 SY.Z65/R) View of Oschwand (58x72cm-23x28in) mono.d.13 (S.FR 160000)
£595	*$1030*	*(22-May-91 GS.B2010) Woman reading (22x27cm-9x11in) mono.d.52 pencil (S.FR 1500)*
£650	*$1255*	*(14-Dec-90 ZOF.Z1120) Death (14x9cm-6x4in) s.i. indian ink pen drawing (S.FR 1600)*
£723	*$1417*	*(21-Nov-90 SY.Z57/R) Portrait of Madame Pageoni (23x18cm-9x7in) mono. W/C (S.FR 1800)*
£992	*$1627*	*(19-Jun-91 GK.B156) Study for Beggar Boy (35x25cm-14x10in) chl (S.FR 2500)*
£1032	*$1692*	*(19-Jun-91 GK.B155) Study for Adoration (10x10cm-4x4in) col.pencil over indian ink pen (S.FR 2600)*
£1310	*$2148*	*(19-Jun-91 GK.B157) Shepherd girl (29x24cm-11x9in) chl (S.FR 3300)*
£1508	*$2473*	*(19-Jun-91 GK.B158) Study of figure group (20x23cm-8x9in) col.chk over pencil (S.FR 3800)*
£1587	*$2651*	*(5-Jun-91 SY.Z56/R) Study for Truth (69x51cm-27x20in) mono.d.13 chl (S.FR 4000)*
£3175	*$5492*	*(22-May-91 GS.B2008/R) Emmental landscape (19x26cm-7x10in) i.d.1923verso gouache pencil double-sided (S.FR 8000)*
£7347	*$13959*	*(14-Sep-90 ZOF.Z1029/R) Tree in landscape (29x24cm-11x9in) mono. W/C (S.FR 18000)*

AMIGONI, Jacopo (1675-1752) Italian
£2051	$4000	(10-Oct-90 CH.NY212/R) Portrait of gentleman wearing jacket and hat with fur (76x63cm-30x25in)
£10166	$19621	(12-Dec-90 F.M314/R) Ritratto di gentiluomo (88x70cm-35x28in) (I.L 22000000)
£15778	$28243	(8-Apr-91 CH.R220/R) La Madonna della pappa (49x40cm-19x16in) (I.L 35000000)
£22000	$39380	(10-Apr-91 S77/R) Portrait of young girl, holding dog on lap (59x45cm-23x18in)
£32888	$63803	(5-Dec-90 APT.P19/R) La rencontre d'Antoine et de Cleopatre (83x65cm-33x26in) (F.FR 320000)
£37000	$60310	(3-Jul-91 S40/R) Mars and Venus surprised by Vulcan (102x127cm-40x50in)
£50000	$81500	(5-Jul-91 C8/R) Conversion of Saul (122x154cm-48x61in)
£160526	$305000	(11-Jan-91 CH.NY19/R) Mythological subject, possibly Bacchus and Ariadne (75x63cm-30x25in)
£163655	$320764	(20-Nov-90 F.R204/R) Callisto e Giove in sembianze di Diana. Zefiro e Flora (25x35cm-10x14in) copper pair (I.L 360000000)
£289474	$550000	(11-Jan-91 CH.NY54/R) Venus and Adonis (216x150cm-85x59in)
£909	*$1782*	*(19-Nov-90 CH.R232/R) Figura femminile seduta (23x28cm-9x11in) pen ink W/C htd.white (I.L 2000000)*

AMIGONI, Jacopo (after) (1675-1752) Italian
£2718	$4730	(25-Mar-91 SY.F568) Diana e Atteone (28x42cm-11x17in) (I.L 6000000)

AMIGONI, Jacopo (attrib) (1675-1752) Italian
£8824	$15000	(30-May-91 SY.NY50/R) Elegant young girl seated at organ (63x52cm-25x20in)
£15510	$30400	(6-Nov-90 GF.L2031/R) Amor and Psyche (156x109cm-61x43in) (S.FR 38000)
£2095	*$3561*	*(27-May-91 L.K181/R) Drunken Noah with his sons (29x31cm-11x12in) ochre (DM 6200)*

AMIGONI, Jacopo (circle) (1675-1752) Italian
£1830 $3055 (6-Jun-91 D.V145/R) Rebecca and Elieser by fountain (72x95cm-28x37in)
          (A.S 38000)
£4167 $7000 (17-Jul-91 SY.NY178/R) Allegory of autumn (102x127cm-40x50in)

AMIGONI, Jacopo (style) (1675-1752) Italian
£1300 $2119 (4-Jul-91 C502) Group portrait of two girls and boy, with cat
          (81x68cm-32x27in)
£1600 $3072 (29-Nov-90 CSK206) Lot and his Daughters (132x96cm-52x38in) fragment
£2000 $3840 (29-Nov-90 CSK271/R) Infant bacchus (117x147cm-46x58in)
£3800 $7296 (29-Nov-90 CSK197/R) Elijah at the well (100x146cm-39x57in)

AMMANN, Eugen (1882-?) Swiss
£744 $1450 (26-Oct-90 S.W2161/R) Smoking guitarist (69x58cm-27x23in) s.d.1910
          cardboard
£1195 $2056 (14-May-91 GF.L2641/R) Self portrait (69x58cm-27x23in) s.d.1910 board
          (S.FR 3000)

AMMIRATO, Domenico (1833-?) Italian
£2034 $3315 (3-Jul-91 WE.MU40/R) Capri fishermen (34x55cm-13x22in) s. (DM 6000)

AMMIRATO, Domenico (attrib) (1833-?) Italian
£750 $1298 (9-May-91 CSK185) Naples (25x37cm-10x15in) s.d.1887

AMON, Carl (1798-1843) Austrian
£3175 $5684 (14-Mar-91 D.V300/R) Antiochus, Seleukos and Stratonike
          (114x146cm-45x57in) s. (A.S 65000)

AMOR, Rick (1948-) Australian
£543 $918 (16-Apr-91 J.M94 a) Portrait of Peter Dennison (111x83cm-44x33in)
          s.d.'81 (A.D 1200)

AMOROSI, Antonio (1660-1736) Italian
£1818 $3564 (19-Nov-90 CH.R19/R) Ritratto di bambina che disseta un uccellino
          (40x33cm-16x13in) (I.L 4000000)
£4523 $7417 (21-Jun-91 SY.MO199/R) L'enfant aux oiseaux (92x70cm-36x28in)
          (F.FR 45000)
£11820 $23166 (19-Nov-90 CH.R67/R) Giovane suonatore di mandola (96x73cm-38x29in)
          (I.L 26000000)

AMOROSI, Antonio (attrib) (1660-1736) Italian
£1273 $2495 (20-Nov-90 F.R50) La filatrice (40x31cm-16x12in) (I.L 2800000)
£2705 $4842 (8-Apr-91 CH.R211/R) Soccorrere i bisognosi (95x72cm-37x28in) i.
          (I.L 6000000)
£8325 $16150 (3-Dec-90 SY.F1032/R) Ritratti di fanciulli (36x24cm-14x9in) set of four
          (I.L 18000000)

AMOROSI, Antonio (circle) (1660-1736) Italian
£2462 $4800 (10-Oct-90 CH.NY11/R) Summer, lady holding garland of flowers. Autumn,
          lady with tub of grapes (98x75cm-39x30in) pair
£2854 $5480 (30-Nov-90 APT.P18/R) L'ange gardien (196x119cm-77x47in) (F.FR 28000)

AMORSOLO, Fernando (20th C) Philippino
£2155 $3750 (27-Mar-91 B.SF4267/R) Returning from the fields (61x86cm-24x34in)
          s.d.1938 board
£3191 $6000 (19-Sep-90 B.SF2659/R) Bogobo chieftain (63x49cm-25x19in) s.d.1937 board
£3448 $6000 (27-Mar-91 B.SF4269/R) The midday meal (35x45cm-14x18in) s.d.1932 board
£5747 $10000 (27-Mar-91 B.SF4270/R) The washerwomen (61x86cm-24x34in) s.d.1961

AMSTEL, Gretha Leyden van (1903-) Dutch
£574 $993 (8-May-91 D.V180/R) Abstract composition (76x48cm-30x19in) s.d.1972 W/C
          gouache (A.S 12000)

AMTSBUHLER, Reinhard (20th C) German?
£1119 $2159 (13-Dec-90 N.M2638/R) Reaper (64x82cm-25x32in) s.d.1921 (DM 3200)

ANASTASI, Auguste (1820-1889) French
£765 $1468 (1-Dec-90 PER.M55/R) La maison au bord de l'eau (14x26cm-6x10in) studio
          st. d.1856 W/C crayon (F.FR 7500)

ANCELET, Gabriel Auguste (19th C) French
£1410 $2750 (26-Oct-90 SY.NY40/R) Romanesque church in Italy (27x37cm-11x15in)
          s.d.1854 W/C
£1538 $3000 (26-Oct-90 SY.NY163/R) Venise, facade de l'Hopital (32x32cm-13x13in) i.
          W/C

ANCELLET, Emile (19/20th C) French
£1506 $2786 (4-Mar-91 ARC.P82/R) La vieille ferme (32x41cm-13x16in) s.d.1921
          (F.FR 15000)

ANCHER, Anna (1859-?) Danish
£1178 $2273 (10-Dec-90 BU.K9/R) Mrs Brondum (24x19cm-9x7in) s. (D.KR 13000)
£2310 $4458 (10-Dec-90 BU.K35/R) At the blacksmith's (32x24cm-13x9in) panel
          (D.KR 25500)
£2819 $5272 (29-Aug-90 KH.K2/R) Moonlit evening, Skagen lighthouse (21x27cm-8x11in)
          init.d.1904 (D.KR 32000)

ANCHER, Anna (1859-?) Danish-cont.

£3081	$5176	(23-Apr-91 RAS.K124/R) Woman in sunlit kitchen (29x23cm-11x9in) s. (D.KR 35000)
£3961	$6655	(23-Apr-91 RAS.K125/R) Interior with the artist's daughter surrounded by toys (34x27cm-13x11in) (D.KR 45000)
£4363	$8552	(22-Nov-90 RAS.V683) Portrait of my mother (78x66cm-31x26in) s.d.1908 (D.KR 49000)
£4754	$7986	(22-Apr-91 BU.K18/R) Mrs Brondum reading in the blue sittingroom (37x56cm-15x22in) s.d.1909 (D.KR 54000)
£4933	$9471	(27-Dec-90 RAS.V4/R) Small girls playing 'Sleeping Beauty', Osterby road, Skagen (33x39cm-13x15in) s.d.1910 (D.KR 55000)
£5314	$8981	(1-May-91 KH.K4/R) Old woman reading (47x42cm-19x17in) s.d.1882 (D.KR 60000)
£10000	$17200	(17-May-91 C189/R) Girls playing Sleeping Beauty (32x38cm-13x15in) s.d.1910
£10676	$20071	(18-Sep-90 BU.K65/R) Harvesters on way to work (43x56cm-17x22in) s.d.1905 (D.KR 120000)

ANCHER, Michael (1849-1927) Danish

£528	$887	(23-Apr-91 RAS.K365) Artist in his studio (23x28cm-9x11in) (D.KR 6000)
£679	$1311	(10-Dec-90 BU.K8/R) Study of man wearing black hat (20x16cm-8x6in) init. (D.KR 7500)
£884	$1662	(10-Aug-90 RAS.V428/R) Portrait of old Mrs Brondum (27x20cm-11x8in) (D.KR 10000)
£887	$1445	(13-Jun-91 RAS.V505/R) Portrait of Miss Blutner (31x24cm-12x9in) s.i. (D.KR 10000)
£890	$1673	(18-Sep-90 BU.K23/R) Portrait of Lars Gajhede (15x13cm-6x5in) s. cardboard on panel (D.KR 10000)
£906	$1748	(10-Dec-90 BU.K6/R) Small boy asleep (22x24cm-9x9in) init. (D.KR 10000)
£951	$1836	(10-Dec-90 BU.K32/R) Sunset over Skagen North Beach (25x29cm-10x11in) init. (D.KR 10500)
£1064	$1734	(13-Jun-91 RAS.V503/R) Portrait of fisherman with beard (24x24cm-9x9in) init. (D.KR 12000)
£1090	$2114	(5-Dec-90 KH.K4/R) Head of old man (37x27cm-15x11in) init. (D.KR 12000)
£1125	$2182	(22-Aug-90 RAS.K124) Fisherman on beach in sunshine (35x28cm-14x11in) init. (D.KR 13000)
£1125	$2182	(22-Aug-90 RAS.K125/R) Young girl with long blond hair (29x22cm-11x9in) init. (D.KR 13000)
£1178	$2273	(10-Dec-90 BU.K7/R) Madam Bentsen's house, Skagen (21x31cm-8x12in) (D.KR 13000)
£1178	$2273	(10-Dec-90 BU.K30/R) Coastal landscape with view of Frederikshavn church (37x51cm-15x20in) init. (D.KR 13000)
£1211	$2349	(22-Aug-90 RAS.K122/R) Fisherman smoking pipe (36x28cm-14x11in) init. (D.KR 14000)
£1232	$2070	(22-Apr-91 BU.K24/R) Portrait of fisherman wearing sou'wester (46x37cm-18x15in) init.d.17 panel (D.KR 14000)
£1312	$2349	(9-Apr-91 RAS.K2003/R) Fisherman wearing southwester and smoking pipe (37x27cm-15x11in) init.d.06 (D.KR 15000)
£1346	$2653	(14-Nov-90 RAS.K259) Fisherman wearing southwester and smoking pipe (30x25cm-12x10in) init.d.11 (D.KR 15000)
£1404	$2710	(10-Dec-90 BU.K33/R) Coastal landscape with ship on the horizon (42x62cm-17x24in) init. (D.KR 15500)
£1434	$2867	(6-Feb-91 RAS.K250/R) Fishwife from Skagen (46x40cm-18x16in) init.d.15 (D.KR 16000)
£1435	$2755	(27-Dec-90 RAS.V5/R) Sunny landscape with houses, Skagen (44x38cm-17x15in) init.d.06 (D.KR 16000)
£1461	$2470	(2-May-91 RAS.V2/R) Seascape with fisherman in rowingboat at sunrise (41x52cm-16x20in) init. (D.KR 16500)
£1730	$3356	(22-Aug-90 RAS.K123/R) Fisherman wearing black hat and smoking (35x24cm-14x9in) init. (D.KR 20000)
£1812	$3496	(10-Dec-90 BU.K31/R) Coastal landscape with rocks at sunrise (34x50cm-13x20in) init. (D.KR 20000)
£1849	$3106	(23-Apr-91 RAS.K364/R) The fisherman Ole Marstrom (37x29cm-15x11in) init.d.11 (D.KR 21000)
£1975	$3890	(14-Nov-90 RAS.K258/R) Summer landscape with small girl crossing field (42x53cm-17x21in) init. (D.KR 22000)
£2163	$4196	(22-Aug-90 RAS.K108/R) Skagen fisherman Ole Svendsen (31x41cm-12x16in) init. sketch (D.KR 25000)
£2214	$3742	(1-May-91 KH.K5/R) Young girl wearing flowery headscarf (36x28cm-14x11in) init. (D.KR 25000)
£2289	$3845	(22-Apr-91 BU.K19/R) Woman and two small girls in artist's garden (40x32cm-16x13in) init. (D.KR 26000)
£2289	$3845	(23-Apr-91 RAS.K127/R) Fisherman wearing Sunday best and smoking pipe (40x32cm-16x13in) init.d.04 (D.KR 26000)
£2594	$5136	(31-Jan-91 RAS.V463/R) Fishermen and two children (56x38cm-22x15in) s.d.1884 (D.KR 29000)
£2653	$4987	(10-Aug-90 RAS.V427/R) Kitchen interior with young girl (57x57cm-22x22in) init. (D.KR 30000)
£3261	$6293	(10-Dec-90 BU.K84/R) Two fishermen (31x40cm-12x16in) init.d.22 (D.KR 36000)
£3676	$7206	(6-Nov-90 BA.S6/R) Still life of roses in glass vase (41x31cm-16x12in) s.d.99 panel (S.KR 40000)
£3815	$7401	(5-Dec-90 KH.K2/R) Interior with young girl reading by window (40x32cm-16x13in) init.d.1900 panel (D.KR 42000)
£4270	$8028	(18-Sep-90 BU.K71/R) Interior with Holger Drachmann at his writing desk (38x48cm-15x19in) init.d.06 (D.KR 48000)

ANCHER, Michael (1849-1927) Danish-cont.

£4500	$7740	(17-May-91 C190/R) Portrait of Anna Ancher, artist's wife (35x27cm-14x11in) init. board
£4577	$7690	(23-Apr-91 RAS.K81/R) The spinner (53x41cm-21x16in) init.d.14 (D.KR 52000)
£5386	$10610	(14-Nov-90 RAS.K36/R) Waiting for father (72x58cm-28x23in) init.d.15 (D.KR 60000)
£6488	$12587	(22-Aug-90 RAS.K79/R) Interior with two fishermen talking (40x56cm-16x22in) init.d.06 panel (D.KR 75000)
£6732	$13263	(14-Nov-90 RAS.K44/R) Fishermen drying nets (47x63cm-19x25in) init.d.12 (D.KR 75000)
£7623	$14637	(27-Dec-90 RAS.V6/R) Fishermen on Skagen beach in sunshine (44x60cm-17x24in) init.d.12 (D.KR 85000)
£9195	$17287	(10-Aug-90 RAS.V426/R) Three fishermen by boat, Skagens Strand (44x64cm-17x25in) s. (D.KR 104000)
£12567	$24758	(14-Nov-90 RAS.K62/R) Small girl with her teddy (48x40cm-19x16in) init.d.07 (D.KR 140000)
£13465	$26526	(14-Nov-90 RAS.K46/R) Fishermen returning home from Nordstranden, evening sunshine (50x54cm-20x21in) (D.KR 150000)
£16014	$30107	(18-Sep-90 BU.K67/R) Three fishermen in evening sunshine (96x182cm-38x72in) s.d.1901 (D.KR 180000)
£23000	$37720	(19-Jun-91 S298/R) Preparing lunch (66x86cm-26x34in) init.
£25135	$49515	(14-Nov-90 RAS.K43/R) 'The birthday' - interior with girls at piano (64x82cm-25x32in) s.d.01 (D.KR 280000)
£62837	$123788	(14-Nov-90 RAS.K45/R) Will he manage the point - fishermen at Skagen (110x142cm-43x56in) s.d.1885 (D.KR 700000)
£887	*$1445*	*(13-Jun-91 RAS.V504/R) Portrait of fisherman wearing south-wester (30x23cm-12x9in) init.d.91 W/C (D.KR 10000)*

ANDALUCIAN SCHOOL (?) Spanish

£2180	$3772	(21-May-91 DUR.M17/R) El triunfo de la Inmaculada Concepcion (162x212cm-64x83in) (S.P 400000)

ANDERLECHT, Engelbert van (1918-1961) Belgian

£7595	$14658	(13-Dec-90 CH.BR143/R) Composition (122x112cm-48x44in) s.d.1958 num.736 verso (B.FR 450000)
£732	*$1309*	*(16-Mar-91 KV.L281) Composition 338 (29x41cm-11x16in) st.sig.verso W/C (B.FR 44000)*
£1081	*$1934*	*(16-Mar-91 KV.L280/R) Composition No. 28 (65x50cm-26x20in) st.sig.verso pastel (B.FR 65000)*

ANDERMATT, L (20th C) Swiss

£1320	$2231	(1-May-91 GD.B12) Still life of flowers in interior (31x24cm-12x9in) mono. board (S.FR 3300)

ANDERS, Ernst (1845-1911) German

£5200	$8528	(18-Jun-91 PH130/R) Elegant lady reading in interior (83x54cm-33x21in) s.d.88

ANDERSEN, Alfred Emil (1860-1935) Norwegian

£4987	$9624	(12-Dec-90 BU.O1/R) View from Kristiansand (39x58cm-15x23in) init.d.90 (N.KR 56000)

ANDERSEN, Carl Christian (1849-1906) Danish

£9683	$16268	(23-Apr-91 RAS.K53/R) The painting collection at Christiansborg Palace (54x81cm-21x32in) s.d.1882 (D.KR 110000)

ANDERSEN, Cilius (1865-1913) Danish

£797	$1347	(1-May-91 KH.K9/R) Young girl at her morning toilet (39x29cm-15x11in) s.d.1905 (D.KR 9000)

ANDERSEN, F (?) ?

£583	$1149	(14-Nov-90 RAS.K470/R) Trees by lake (88x110cm-35x43in) s. (D.KR 6500)

ANDERSEN, Mogens (20th C) Danish

£884	$1662	(10-Aug-90 RAS.V572/R) 'Standing man' - artist's brother in garden (188x155cm-74x61in) i. (D.KR 10000)
£893	$1652	(5-Mar-91 RAS.K17) Green fantasy (40x55cm-16x22in) init.d.1977 (D.KR 10000)
£893	$1652	(5-Mar-91 RAS.K18) Composition (73x60cm-29x24in) init.d.57 (D.KR 10000)
£1009	$1715	(29-May-91 KH.K201/R) Composition (92x73cm-36x29in) s. (D.KR 11500)
£1140	$1939	(29-May-91 KH.K200/R) Composition (81x65cm-32x26in) s.d.66 (D.KR 13000)
£1188	$2044	(15-May-91 RAS.K1/R) Composition (92x73cm-36x29in) s.d.1965verso (D.KR 13500)
£1297	$2542	(13-Feb-91 KH.K3/R) Composition (91x73cm-36x29in) init. (D.KR 14500)

ANDERSEN, Nils (1897-1972) Norwegian/South African

£769	$1477	(18-Feb-91 SY.J328/R) Cape farmhouse and oak trees (60x90cm-24x35in) s. board (SA.R 3800)

ANDERSEN, Robin Christian (1890-1969) Austrian

£1217	$2384	(24-Jan-91 D.V188/R) Landscape with house behind garden wall (55x69cm-22x27in) (A.S 25000)
£1688	$3292	(18-Oct-90 D.V143/R) Village street (50x61cm-20x24in) s. (A.S 35000)
£2433	$4769	(24-Jan-91 D.V146/R) Still life of jug with flowers, lemons, apples and white cloth (53x62cm-21x24in) s. (A.S 50000)

ANDERSEN, Robin Christian (1890-1969) Austrian-cont.

£2910	$5470	(20-Sep-90 D.V196/R) Flower garden (87x115cm-34x45in) s. (A.S 60000)
£2920	$5723	(24-Jan-91 D.V212/R) Foliate plant (85x110cm-33x43in) mono. panel (A.S 60000)
£3479	$6750	(6-Dec-90 D.V105/R) Still life with fruit and flowers (87x115cm-34x45in) s. (A.S 70000)
£3976	$7714	(6-Dec-90 D.V106/R) View of village (87x115cm-34x45in) s. (A.S 80000)

ANDERSEN, Wilhelm (1867-1945) Danish

£661	$1236	(29-Aug-90 KH.K3) Still life of peonies in vase (80x65cm-31x26in) s. (D.KR 7500)
£1298	$2517	(22-Aug-90 RAS.K128/R) Still life of jug, glass, lemon and teapot (57x63cm-22x25in) s. (D.KR 15000)

ANDERSEN-LUNDBY, A (1841-1923) Danish

£616	$1035	(23-Apr-91 RAS.K286) Coastal landscape with fishermen on beach (55x72cm-22x28in) s. (D.KR 7000)
£718	$1415	(14-Nov-90 RAS.K263) Coastal landscape with fishermen on beach (55x72cm-22x28in) s. (D.KR 8000)
£735	$1426	(22-Aug-90 RAS.K129) Winter landscape at sunset (33x53cm-13x21in) s.d.82 (D.KR 8500)
£6162	$10352	(23-Apr-91 RAS.K120/R) Mountain landscape with snow and sun (120x95cm-47x37in) s.d.1887 (D.KR 70000)

ANDERSEN-LUNDBY, Anders (1841-1923) Danish

£1706	$3345	(24-Nov-90 SA.A772/R) Wooded landscape with faggott gatherer (29x37cm-11x15in) s.d.1886 (DM 5000)
£2498	$4846	(4-Dec-90 UL.T252) On the fjord (60x80cm-24x31in) i.d.1886 (N.KR 28000)
£12969	$24382	(19-Sep-90 N.M412/R) View of Auer Muehlbach in winter at sunset, Munich (108x178cm-43x70in) s.i.d.1884 (DM 38000)

ANDERSON, Abraham Archibald (1847-1940) American

£588	$1100	(30-Aug-90 MFA.C93) Flowers in oriental vase (61x51cm-24x20in) s.

ANDERSON, Doug (1954-) American

£1631	*$3148*	*(16-Dec-90 CSC.P29/R) Superficial mixed media canvas (F.FR 16000)*

ANDERSON, Frederic A (19/20th C) American

£1500	$2940	(20-Nov-90 PH273/R) The rancher's daughter (89x80cm-35x31in) s.

ANDERSON, J B (1886-1938) British

£900	$1755	(17-Oct-90 PHG22) Still life of fruit and objects on a table top (50x60cm-20x24in) s.

ANDERSON, James Bell (1886-1938) British

£1200	$2400	(5-Feb-91 S199/R) Still life with tomatoes, vase, wine and china dalmatian (51x61cm-20x24in) s.
£2500	$4675	(28-Aug-90 S1013/R) Cattle grazing by river (51x64cm-20x25in) s.d.99

ANDERSON, Jeremy (20th C) American

£615	*$1200*	*(24-Oct-90 B.SF1594/R) Untitled (66x51cm-26x20in) i. W/C*

ANDERSON, Robert (1842-85) British

£1892	$3084	(10-Jun-91 W.T1315/R) Boys and donkey cart on a beach (43x69cm-17x27in) s.d.1880 (C.D 3500)
£660	*$1267*	*(29-Nov-90 PHX369/R) Quayside in Brittany (23x36cm-9x14in) s.d.1885 W/C*

ANDERSON, Ronald Lee (1886-1926) American

£865	*$1600*	*(8-Mar-91 S.BM251/R) The blue butterfly (74x56cm-29x22in) s. pastel*

ANDERSON, Sophie (1823-1903) British

£1400	$2296	(20-Jun-91 B91 I) Plaiting hair (30x26cm-12x10in) init.
£10000	$19700	(1-Nov-90 D176/R) Din...ner (91x71cm-36x28in) s.i.stretcher

ANDERSON, Stanley (1884-?) British

£1100	*$2178*	*(29-Jan-91 PH23) Off to market (21x29cm-8x11in) s. W/C*

ANDERSON, Victor C (1882-1937) American

£1775	$3000	(1-May-91 B.SF5277/R) Entering white horses (25x35cm-10x14in) s. i.verso board
£2059	$3500	(1-Jun-91 IH.NY54/R) Young girl at mirror (71x53cm-28x21in) s.d.1919
£3971	$6750	(1-Jun-91 IH.NY88/R) Boy sitting on the moon (56x41cm-22x16in) s.d.1908 board

ANDERSON, W (?) British

£561	$1100	(7-Nov-90 D.NY3) Newsboys, New York (58x43cm-23x17in) s.i.d.05

ANDERSON, Will (fl.1880-1895) British

£340	*$646*	*(25-Feb-91 PH69) Path through hayfield (16x24cm-6x9in) s. W/C htd white*

ANDERSON, William (1757-1837) British

£1100	$2079	(24-Sep-90 CSK245/R) Fishermen in boat, shipping in calm (20x23cm-8x9in) init.
£1900	$3401	(10-Apr-91 S170/R) Fisherfolk selling catch by shore (14x16cm-6x6in) s.indist.d. panel

ANDERSON, William (1757-1837) British-cont.
£2200	$4312	(20-Nov-90 PH15/R) Figures in a fishing smack with other sailing vessels off a Dutchcoastline (23x31cm-9x12in) s.d.1804 panel
£4500	$8775	(18-Oct-90 CSK86/R) Dutch fishing vessels in calm waters with figures on foreshore (38x51cm-15x20in) panel
£4500	$7605	(30-Apr-91 PH2/R) Figures and sailing vessels off coastline (35x48cm-14x19in) s.d.1806 board
£15569	$26000	(7-Jun-91 SY.NY148/R) The battle of the Nile (79x131cm-31x52in) s.d.1801
£800	*$1432*	*(9-Apr-91 C144) Shipping in estuary with sailors loading provisions (18x24cm-7x9in) init.d.1801 pencil wash*

ANDERSON, William (attrib) (1757-1837) British
£1100	$1892	(13-May-91 CG204/R) A frigate and other shipping with a sailing barge in the foreground (23x32cm-9x13in) panel
£1900	$3705	(18-Oct-90 CSK87/R) Sailor's farewell (15x23cm-6x9in) panel
£2800	$5320	(1-Mar-91 C90/R) Gypsy encampment on wooded path in landscape (60x74cm-24x29in) indis.i.verso

ANDERSSON, Karl (1899-) Swedish
£802	$1387	(22-May-91 BA.S533/R) Flowers in blue and white jug (30x30cm-12x12in) s.d.36 (S.KR 8500)

ANDERSSON, Marten (1934-) Swedish
£1673	$2994	(9-Apr-91 GO.G4) Winter landscape with horse and sleigh by house (30x55cm-12x22in) s.d.1964 panel (S.KR 18000)
£7358	$12730	(22-May-91 BA.S3/R) Bridal procession (81x213cm-32x84in) s.d.1963 (S.KR 78000)
£8804	$17081	(4-Dec-90 BA.S13/R) The pretty girl's house (168x122cm-66x48in) s.d.1961 (S.KR 95000)
£1106	*$2168*	*(20-Nov-90 GO.G306) Story illustration with woman bathing (49x26cm-19x10in) s.d.1956 W/C (S.KR 12100)*

ANDERTON, J (?) ?
£730	$1307	(11-Mar-91 HS230) Ford on the Brent with cattle and thatched cottages beyond (50x75cm-20x30in) s. i.verso

ANDERTON, Tom (fl.1921-1928) British
£600	*$1182*	*(30-Oct-90 HS54) Feeding ducks (38x53cm-15x21in) init. W/C*

ANDOE, Joe (1955-) American
£1503	$2600	(7-May-91 CE.NY267/R) Untitled - wheatstalks and flower (102x122cm-40x48in) s.
£2041	$4000	(14-Feb-91 CH.NY82/R) Holly branch (51x61cm-20x24in) s.
£4142	$7000	(2-May-91 CH.NY299/R) Untitled - oak leaf (51x61cm-20x24in) s.
£4142	$7000	(2-May-91 CH.NY265/R) Untitled (102x122cm-40x48in) s.
£5076	$10000	(5-Oct-90 CH.NY135/R) Untitled (51x61cm-20x24in) s.

ANDRE, Albert (1869-1954) French
£1417	$2777	(23-Nov-90 PLF.P29/R) Rue d'un village de Provence (54x65cm-21x26in) s. (F.FR 14000)
£1952	$3377	(22-May-91 CH.AM504) Melon vert et tomates (29x46cm-11x18in) s.d.1911 i.stretcher (D.FL 6500)
£2227	$4364	(23-Nov-90 PLF.P28/R) Vue de Laudum, village (38x58cm-15x23in) s. paper (F.FR 22000)
£5102	$10000	(12-Feb-91 SY.NY27/R) La mer Rue d'Endoume (38x69cm-15x27in) s.
£6116	$11743	(27-Nov-90 APT.P21/R) Glaieuls (72x59cm-28x23in) s. (F.FR 60000)
£6166	$11963	(5-Dec-90 ZZ.F27/R) Vase de fleurs a l'atelier (65x54cm-26x21in) s. (F.FR 60000)
£7500	$14550	(5-Dec-90 S100/R) Pommes et verveines (32x44cm-13x17in) s.
£9246	$16551	(16-Mar-91 APT.P32/R) La terrasse (46x55cm-18x22in) s. (F.FR 92000)
£16444	$31901	(5-Dec-90 ZZ.F24 b/R) Le Sacre-Coeur (65x57cm-26x22in) (F.FR 160000)
£17766	$35000	(3-Oct-90 SY.NY52/R) Femme mangeant des raisins (74x100cm-29x39in) s.
£86294	$170000	(15-Nov-90 SY.NY27/R) Dame en blanc, assise (48x49cm-19x19in) s.
£615	*$1200*	*(10-Oct-90 SY.NY13/R) Seated woman (20x15cm-8x6in) s. W/C pencil*

ANDRE, Carl (1935-) American
£6888	*$13500*	*(8-Nov-90 CH.NY162/R) Untitled (8x14cm-3x6in) paper collage on 124 U.S. postcards*

ANDRE, Charles Hippolyte (1850-?) French
£6154	$12000	(23-Oct-90 SY.NY269/R) Vue du petit bras de Seine a Maisons-Laffitte (113x144cm-44x57in) s.d.1893

ANDRE, Jules (1807-1869) French
£845	$1605	(14-Sep-90 SA.A1260/R) Landscape with hay harvest near farm houses (26x33cm-10x13in) mono. (DM 2500)

ANDREA, Pat (1942-) Dutch
£2786	$5378	(13-Dec-90 SY.AM391) De vreemdeling 2 (122x150cm-48x59in) s.d.1978/81 d.verso oil tempera casein panel (D.FL 9000)
£1176	*$2271*	*(13-Dec-90 SY.AM385/R) Domingo por la manana en Buenos Aires (100x120cm-39x47in) s.d.1976 gouache W/C pencil (D.FL 3800)*

ANDREANI (20th C) ?
£1756	$3389	(12-Dec-90 F.M95) La cuoca (90x112cm-35x44in) s.d.1929 (I.L 3800000)

ANDREASI, Ippolito (c.1548-1608) Italian
£730 $1291   *(19-Mar-91 F.M273/R) Studio di decorazione con due schiavi incatenati (14x24cm-6x9in) pen bistre ink shaped paper (I.L 1600000)*
£4474 $8500   *(8-Jan-91 SY.NY153/R) The Assumption (21x17cm-8x7in) ink wash htd.white traces blk.chk.*

ANDREASSON, Folke (1902-1948) Swedish
£743 $1331   (9-Apr-91 GO.G6) Landscape (62x54cm-24x21in) s. (S.KR 8000)
£1162 $2079   (9-Apr-91 GO.G5) Coastal landscape from Bohuslan (43x48cm-17x19in) init. panel (S.KR 12500)
£1371 $2687   (20-Nov-90 GO.G4/R) Still life of flowers in vase and blue jug (46x65cm-18x26in) s. (S.KR 15000)
£3137 $6022   (27-Nov-90 BU.S15/R) Still life of flowers (78x65cm-31x26in) s.d.1937 (S.KR 34000)

ANDREENKO, Mikhail (1895-?) Russian
£1238 $2390   (12-Dec-90 CH.AM545/R) Geometric figure (54x46cm-21x18in) s. (D.FL 4000)
£661 $1321   *(6-Feb-91 FB.P8) Matiere en mouvement (58x91cm-23x36in) s. oil material canvas (F.FR 6500)*
£1388 $2692   *(8-Dec-90 GAB.G2325/R) Composition (38x45cm-15x18in) s. oil collage (S.FR 3400)*

ANDREEV, Ivan (1907-) Russian
£999 $1918   (29-Nov-90 YC.P132/R) La fille qui peint (59x50cm-23x20in) s.d.69 (F.FR 9800)

ANDREIS, Alex de (19th C) Belgian
£893 $1714   (27-Nov-90 W.T1088/R) Cavalier in gold tunic (80x65cm-31x26in) s. (C.D 2000)
£1000 $1970   (4-Oct-90 CSK203/R) A cavaliers with a lace collar and blue sash holding a book (81x66cm-32x26in) s.
£1200 $2340   (15-Jan-91 SWS169/R) The love song (64x80cm-25x31in) s.
£1421 $2700   (27-Feb-91 SY.NY8 a/R) Amateur d´armes (66x81cm-26x32in) s.

ANDREONI, Cesare (1903-1961) Italian
£2734 $4647   (28-May-91 SY.MI74/R) Dalla finestra (39x49cm-15x19in) s.d.1932 board (I.L 6000000)

ANDREOTTI, Federico (1847-1930) Italian
£2197 $3800   (21-May-91 CE.NY166/R) Woman with kitten (46x35cm-18x14in) s.
£4211 $8000   (28-Feb-91 CH.NY114/R) Peasant girl with basket of flowers (61x49cm-24x19in) s.
£12105 $23000   (28-Feb-91 CH.NY116/R) Young beauty with apron filled with flowers (39x30cm-15x12in) s.
£22000 $35420   (27-Jun-91 CG24/R) Flitation (66x49cm-26x19in) s.
£550 $902   *(18-Jun-91 PH229) Courtship (29x23cm-11x9in) s. W/C*
£789 $1500   *(15-Sep-90 S.W2792/R) Cavaliers revelling with a maid (36x53cm-14x21in) s. W/C*

ANDREOTTI, Federico (style) (1847-1930) Italian
£900 $1764   (22-Nov-90 CSK205) Plucking turkey (63x52cm-25x20in) with sig. d.1878 panel

ANDREU, Mariano (1901-) Spanish
£3279 $6426   (24-Jan-91 EP.M64/R) Familia en el campo (96x77cm-38x30in) s.d.18 (S.P 600000)

ANDREW, Richard (1869-1934) American
£694 $1200   (21-May-91 GRO.B145) Portrait of Harry Dutton (206x157cm-81x62in) s.d.1923

ANDREWS, George H (1816-1898) British
£1468 $2466   (27-Apr-91 SO.S264/R) Women by fountain (34x44cm-13x17in) s. (S.KR 15500)

ANDREWS, Henry (1816-1898) British
£919 $1700   (8-Mar-91 S.BM120/R) The Tryst - A garden scene (51x51cm-20x20in) s.d.1849
£973 $1800   (8-Mar-91 S.BM122/R) The lovers - A garden scene (53x43cm-21x17in) s.
£1243 $2300   (8-Mar-91 S.BM124/R) The courtier (76x64cm-30x25in) s.
£1618 $2800   (21-May-91 CE.NY46/R) Fete champetre (55x44cm-22x17in) s.
£4211 $8000   (28-Feb-91 CH.NY162/R) The bathers (71x91cm-28x36in) s.d.64

ANDREWS, John (19th C) British
£3200 $5408   (30-Apr-91 PH85/R) Old oak (63x76cm-25x30in) s.d.1857

ANDREWS, Michael (1928-) British
£4000 $7400   (8-Mar-91 C160/R) Girl on bed (25x35cm-10x14in) canvasboard
£10500 $20580   (9-Nov-90 C290/R) Head of man (19x21cm-7x8in) board
£12000 $23520   (9-Nov-90 C289/R) Head of man (19x21cm-7x8in) board

ANDREWS, Samuel (c.1757-1807) British
£700 $1176   *(16-Jul-91 SWS1882/R) Gentleman, with powdered grey hair, in green jacket and fur cravat (6x?cm-2x?in) min. init.d. gilt-bronze frame oval*

ANDRI, Ferdinand (1871-1956) Austrian
£895 $1736   (6-Dec-90 D.V39/R) Design for wall painting. Sketches (30x42cm-12x17in)
                 st.sig.verso col.chk double-sided (A.S 18000)

ANDRIESSEN, Juriaan (1742-1819) Dutch
£15000 $28950   (12-Dec-90 S139/R) Classical landscape with figures on road by steps of
                    villa (189x216cm-74x85in) s.d.1787
£2200 $4224   (18-Feb-91 S90/R) Peasants in wooded landscape (35x27cm-14x11in) bears
                  i.verso W/C

ANDRIEU, Pierre (1821-1892) French
£482 $776   (28-Jun-91 LC.P52) Etudes de sculpures avec chevaux (24x37cm-9x15in)
                blk.crayon pen (F.FR 4800)

ANDRIEUX, Clement-Auguste (1829-?) French
£1941 $3668   (27-Sep-90 D.V122/R) Skirmish (60x110cm-24x43in) s.d.1850 (A.S 40000)

ANDROUTZOS, Nicolas (?) ?
£850 $1658   (24-Oct-90 S228/R) A Cairo street (61x36cm-24x14in) s. W/C

ANDRUS, Vera (1896-1979) American
£578 $1000   (21-May-91 GRO.B169/R) Gloucester harbour (61x81cm-24x32in) s.d.37

ANESI, Carlos (1965-) Argentinian
£10465 $18000   (15-May-91 CH.NY195/R) Cavalho (90x130cm-35x51in) init.

ANESI, Paolo (1700-1761) Italian
£4800 $8112   (16-Apr-91 PH9/R) Figures observing fishermen on river before castle
                  keep (42x26cm-17x10in) panel
£55000 $92950   (16-Apr-91 PH52/R) Fishermen bringing in nets on banks of Tiber.
                    Fisherfolk on banks of Tiber before Ponte Rotto (45x97cm-18x38in) pair

ANESI, Paolo (attrib) (1700-1761) Italian
£923 $1800   (24-Oct-90 D.NY50/R) The Magdalen in the wilderness (58x76cm-23x30in)
                 oval
£2235 $4000   (10-Apr-91 HF.NY24/R) Classical landscape with figures (49x65cm-19x26in)

ANESI, Paolo (circle) (1700-1761) Italian
£1800 $3042   (18-Apr-91 C162) Peasants crossing a torrent and shepherd and flock in
                  landscape beyond (65x40cm-26x16in)
£56410 $110000   (10-Oct-90 CH.NY193/R) View of Rome with Colosseum and Arch of
                     Constantine with figures (119x171cm-47x67in)

ANGELI, Eduard (1942-) Austrian
£439 $813   (7-Mar-91 D.V285/R) Vogelflug (36x47cm-14x19in) s.d.78 pastel
                (A.S 9000)
£596 $1157   (6-Dec-90 D.V173/R) Untitled (69x100cm-27x39in) s.d.69 mixed media
                 collage (A.S 12000)
£878 $1625   (7-Mar-91 D.V247/R) Untitled (69x99cm-27x39in) s.d.68 mixed media
                 (A.S 18000)

ANGELI, Filippo (1600-1640) Italian
£30000 $48900   (5-Jul-91 C94/R) Adoration of magi (84x146cm-33x57in)

ANGELI, Filippo (style) (1600-1640) Italian
£2443 $4372   (14-Mar-91 D.V160/R) Still life of fruit (39x57cm-15x22in) one of pair
                  (A.S 50000)
£2931 $5247   (14-Mar-91 D.V159/R) Still life of fruit (39x57cm-15x22in) one of pair
                  (A.S 60000)

ANGELI, Franco (1935-1988) Italian
£916 $1759   (27-Nov-90 SY.MI36/R) Half dollar (69x70cm-27x28in) acrylic
                 (I.L 2000000)
£1001 $1892   (27-Sep-90 F.M31) Composizione (100x100cm-39x39in) s. (I.L 2200000)
£1172 $2098   (9-Apr-91 F.R151) Half dollar (80x100cm-31x39in) s.verso acrylic
                  (I.L 2600000)
£1443 $2582   (9-Apr-91 F.R133/R) Burattini (100x100cm-39x39in) s.verso (I.L 3200000)
£1486 $2897   (24-Oct-90 F.M118/R) Paesaggio (100x70cm-39x28in) s.verso (I.L 3300000)
£1801 $3512   (22-Oct-90 BR.M52/R) Composizione (80x120cm-31x47in) s.verso acrylic
                  (I.L 4000000)
£1801 $3512   (22-Oct-90 BR.M153/R) Cimitero partigiano (70x70cm-28x28in) s.d.1963/69
                  acrylic canvas veil (I.L 4000000)
£1981 $3863   (22-Oct-90 BR.M104/R) Half Dollar (50x70cm-20x28in) s.verso acrylic
                  silver canvas veil (I.L 4400000)
£2045 $4028   (30-Oct-90 F.R90/R) Pali neri (80x80cm-31x31in) s.verso acrylic
                  (I.L 4500000)
£1008 $1935   (27-Nov-90 SY.MI97/R) Composizione (35x33cm-14x13in) s.d.1964 mixed
                  media (I.L 2200000)
£1228 $2322   (27-Sep-90 F.M45/R) A Dino Campana (100x70cm-39x28in) s. mixed media
                  (I.L 2700000)
£1501 $2838   (27-Sep-90 F.M82/R) Simboli (140x100cm-55x39in) s.d.1969 verso spray
                  paint canvas (I.L 3300000)
£1815 $3121   (13-May-91 CH.R60/R) Paesaggio proiettato (200x200cm-79x79in)
                  s.i.d.1980verso enamel acrylic canvas (I.L 4500000)
£3606 $6456   (9-Apr-91 F.R162/R) Inverno a villa Poniathowski (100x150cm-39x59in)
                  s.d.1986 enamel acrylic canvas (I.L 8000000)

ANGELI, Franco (1935-1988) Italian-cont.
£4728 $9219   (22-Oct-90 BR.M90/R) Piramide e guglia sottomarina (130x160cm-51x63in)
                    s.verso enamel canvas (I.L 10500000)
£8104 $15804   (22-Oct-90 BR.M33/R) Paesaggio in Maremma (180x130cm-71x51in) s.d.1987
                    enamel canvas (I.L 18000000)

ANGELI, Guerino (20th C) Italian
£1684 $3200   (3-Mar-91 LIT.L18) Still life with book and fruit (38x48cm-15x19in) s.

ANGELL, Helen Cordelia (1847-1884) British
£450 $752   (5-Jun-91 PHK54) Still life of grapes and an apple (12x16cm-5x6in) s.
               W/C

ANGERER, Tony (1884-1950) Austrian
£394 $788   (7-Feb-91 D.V4/R) In the mountains (36x36cm-14x14in) s.d.1921 gouache
               board (A.S 8000)
£535 $1049   (24-Jan-91 D.V98/R) Alpine landscape in winter (36x36cm-14x14in)
               s.d.1921 gouache board (A.S 11000)

ANGERMAYER, Johann Adalbert (attrib) (1674-c.1740) German
£6728 $13254   (14-Nov-90 SY.AM109/R) Still life of plants and insects with skull
               (62x50cm-24x20in) paper on canvas (D.FL 22000)

ANGILLIS, Pieter (attrib) (1685-1734) Flemish
£562 $1080   (27-Nov-90 JRL.S265) Vegetable seller (30x25cm-12x10in) panel
               (A.D 1400)
£1926 $3216   (6-Jun-91 D.V272/R) Riverside fish and vegetable market
               (30x38cm-12x15in) (A.S 40000)
£1100 $2112   (18-Feb-91 S258/R) Large merry company outside inn (28x42cm-11x17in) pen
               ink wash over chk

ANGILLIS, Pieter (style) (1685-1734) Flemish
£986 $1676   (28-May-91 AB.S4729/R) The sculptor at work in his studio
               (41x33cm-16x13in) (S.KR 10500)

ANGLADE (19/20th C) French
£655 $1245   (1-Mar-91 CB.P198) Bruyere pres du lac (60x73cm-24x29in) s. (F.FR 6500)

ANGLADE, Gaston (1854-?) French
£655 $1278   (28-Oct-90 M.V112/R) Paysage du soir (19x29cm-7x11in) s. (F.FR 6500)
£719 $1396   (3-Dec-90 CS.L15/R) Bord de riviere (50x99cm-20x39in) s. (F.FR 7000)
£806 $1573   (27-Oct-90 LT.P10/R) Paysage aux Bruyeres (54x65cm-21x26in) s.
               (F.FR 8000)

ANGLO-CHINESE SCHOOL, 19th C British/Chinese
£1350 $2268   (22-Apr-91 PH340) Panoramic view of Hong Kong from East Point to
               Victoria (16x23cm-6x9in) W/C bodycol.

ANGLO-DUTCH SCHOOL British/Dutch
£1050 $1817   (20-May-91 SWS89) A winter scene with skaters near classical ruins
               (219x143cm-86x56in) c.1900

ANGLO-DUTCH SCHOOL, 17th C British/Dutch
£4400 $7612   (20-May-91 SWS253) Portrait of a young girl, standing wearing a red
               dress with a white apron (94x59cm-37x23in)
£7179 $14000   (11-Oct-90 SY.NY113/R) Portrait of girl in grey silk (101x122cm-40x48in)

ANGLO-FLEMISH SCHOOL, 18th C British/Flemish
£8800 $14872   (17-Apr-91 S152/R) River landscape with travellers on path
               (95x118cm-37x46in) canvas on panel

ANGLO-FRENCH SCHOOL, 18th C British/French
£1600 $2704   (30-Apr-91 PH64/R) Portrait of young fruit seller, wearing straw bonnet,
               holding basket (91x71cm-36x28in)

ANGO (18th C) French
£1121 $2164   (14-Dec-90 LEB.P46) Iesse - David - Salomon (35x54cm-14x21in) d.1768
               sanguinne semi-circle (F.FR 11000)

ANGO, Robert (18th C) French
£500 $815   (1-Jul-91 S181/R) Allegorical figure in spandrel (18x21cm-7x8in) red chk
£815 $1566   (27-Nov-90 APT.P99/R) Une allegorie (25x45cm-10x18in) sanguinne
               (F.FR 8000)
£1005 $1648   (21-Jun-91 CK.P11/R) Iris et Morphee (30x54cm-12x21in) sanguinne
               (F.FR 10000)
£1711 $3250   (8-Jan-91 SY.NY196/R) Michelangelo's Isaiah from the Sistine ceiling
               (38x31cm-15x12in) chk.

ANGOLO DEL MORO, Battista (1514-1575) Italian
£15789 $30000   (11-Jan-91 CH.NY78/R) Holy Family (99x123cm-39x48in)
£105000 $171150   (3-Jul-91 S3/R) Reclining female nude (120x171cm-47x67in)

ANGRAND, Charles (1854-1926) French
£1937 $3738   (14-Dec-90 JM.P8/R) La jeune servante attisant le feu. Etude d'enfant
               (46x60cm-18x24in) st.mono. chl double-sided (F.FR 19000)

ANGRAND, Charles (1854-1926) French-cont.
£3021 $4924   *(11-Jun-91 I.N145/R) Maternite (63x47cm-25x19in) st.sig. chl.paper laid down on canvas (F.FR 30000)*

ANGUIANO, Raul (1915-) Mexican
£7653 $15000   (20-Nov-90 CH.NY122/R) Malabaristas (58x86cm-23x34in) s.d.1941

ANGUS, Rita (?) Australian
£2167 $4248   (7-Nov-90 DS.W23/R) Portrait of friend (48x36cm-19x14in) s.d.64 (NZ.D 7000)
£950 $1853   *(24-Oct-90 S110/R) Still life with a potted plant (24x18cm-9x7in) s. gouache W/C*

ANGUS, William Louis (1823-?) Belgian
£7086 $12259   (21-May-91 DUR.M29/R) La cena del violinista (52x65cm-20x26in) panel (S.P 1300000)

ANIVITTI, F (1876-?) Italian
£1000 $1680   (18-Jul-91 CSK200/R) Sante Maria della Salute, Venice (49x40cm-19x16in) s.
£1026 $2000   (19-Oct-90 DM.D2138/R) Italian street scene, depicting Spanish Steps, Rome (41x46cm-16x18in) s.

ANIVITTI, Filippo (1876-?) Italian
£1178 $1991   (16-Apr-91 CH.R76) Campagna romana con contadina (38x50cm-15x20in) s. (I.L 2600000)
£7200 $11808   (19-Jun-91 S424/R) Flower vendors on Spanish steps, Rome (39x44cm-15x17in) s.
£647 $1256   *(4-Dec-90 F.R65) Campagna romana (17x23cm-7x9in) s. mixed media panel (I.L 1400000)*
£1200 $2064   *(17-May-91 C210/R) Fiumicino, Rome (33x65cm-13x26in) s.i. pencil W/C paper on card*

ANKAOUA, Christine (20th C) ?
£404 $792   *(12-Feb-91 HC.P16) Sans titre (107x73cm-42x29in) s.d.1987 mixed media (F.FR 4000)*

ANKARCRONA, Alexis (1825-1901) Swedish
£1184 $1989   (27-Apr-91 SO.S265/R) Battle in the desert (29x60cm-11x24in) s. (S.KR 12500)

ANKARCRONA, Henrik (1839-1919) Swedish
£1136 $1909   (24-Apr-91 BA.S4/R) Bedouin and camels (41x56cm-16x22in) s.d.1875 panel (S.KR 12000)

ANKER, Albert (1831-1910) Swiss
£4365 $7552   (22-May-91 GS.B2014) Farmhouse interior (19x31cm-7x12in) s. board (S.FR 11000)
£71429 $119286   (5-Jun-91 SY.Z42/R) Sick girl (42x32cm-17x13in) s.d.1871 sheet metal (S.FR 180000)
£100402 $196787   (21-Nov-90 SY.Z41/R) Girl eating soup (28x34cm-11x13in) s. (S.FR 250000)
£127490 $219283   (14-May-91 GF.L2165/R) Portrait of girl with red necklace (41x33cm-16x13in) s. (S.FR 320000)
£154762 $253810   (21-Jun-91 GK.B5/R) Le chaperon rouge (85x61cm-33x24in) s. (S.FR 390000)
£635 $1041   *(21-Jun-91 G.Z17) Head of woman (27x17cm-11x7in) indian ink pen study after sculpture (S.FR 1600)*
£1200 $2028   *(1-May-91 GD.B1031/R) Hunigerhaus, interior of carpenter's workshop (13x21cm-5x8in) pencil (S.FR 3000)*
£1714 $3257   *(14-Sep-90 ZOF.Z1034) Wooded landscape with figures (10x16cm-4x6in) pencil from sketch book Album de papier d'Amour (S.FR 4200)*
£2008 $3936   *(21-Nov-90 SY.Z31/R) Leander (57x44cm-22x17in) chl htd.white board (S.FR 5000)*
£2191 $4273   *(24-Oct-90 GD.B1029/R) Mother with children in peasant interior (19x11cm-7x4in) pencil (S.FR 5500)*
£3187 $6215   *(24-Oct-90 GD.B1032/R) Grandmother seated knitting (36x28cm-14x11in) st.studio chl (S.FR 8000)*
£3673 $7237   *(16-Nov-90 GK.Z5312/R) Farmhouse in Emmenthal, illustration for Der Besenbinder von Rychismwil (20x28cm-8x11in) indian ink pen (S.FR 9000)*
£3770 $6296   *(5-Jun-91 SY.Z40/R) Peasant smoking pipe (33x23cm-13x9in) chl (S.FR 9500)*
£3770 $6296   *(5-Jun-91 SY.Z64/R) Peasant interior with chair and door open. Garden table laid (20x16cm-8x6in) W/C double-sided (S.FR 9500)*
£5221 $10233   *(21-Nov-90 SY.Z30/R) Musketeer with rapier. Musketeer with dagger and rapier (25x14cm-10x6in) s. W/C two (S.FR 13000)*
£5306 $10453   *(16-Nov-90 GK.Z5313/R) Girl seated on chair writing and boy standing (30x22cm-12x9in) s. indian ink pen (S.FR 13000)*
£6122 $12061   *(16-Nov-90 GK.Z5311/R) Easter celebrations in Kirchberg, illustration for Michels Brautschau (21x28cm-8x11in) s. i.verso indian ink pen (S.FR 15000)*
£6349 $10603   *(5-Jun-91 SY.Z66/R) Girl reading with apple (34x23cm-13x9in) s.d.1902 chl (S.FR 16000)*
£6531 $12865   *(16-Nov-90 GK.Z5308/R) Girl doing house work (20x15cm-8x6in) W/C over pencil (S.FR 16000)*
£8800 $14872   *(1-May-91 GD.B14/R) Young woman standing at table working (20x15cm-8x6in) W/C over pencil study (S.FR 22000)*

ANKER, Albert (1831-1910) Swiss-cont.
£18254	$29937	(21-Jun-91 GK.B4/R) Young girl seated in armchair with knitting in lap and reading book (35x25cm-14x10in) s.d.1909 (S.FR 46000)
£19841	$33135	(5-Jun-91 SY.Z55/R) Girl reading (35x25cm-14x10in) s.d.1909 W/C (S.FR 50000)
£23016	$38437	(5-Jun-91 SY.Z52/R) Peasant woman peeling apples (35x25cm-14x10in) s.d.1902 W/C (S.FR 58000)
£23016	$38437	(5-Jun-91 SY.Z65/R) Girl reading with apple (35x26cm-14x10in) s.d.1902 W/C (S.FR 58000)
£28226	$54194	(2-Dec-90 GAB.G1504/R) Le magister ecrivant (24x35cm-9x14in) s.d.1909 W/C (S.FR 70000)
£32129	$62972	(21-Nov-90 SY.Z36/R) Girl peeling potatoes. Portrait of peasant and study for girl (35x25cm-14x10in) W/C double-sided (S.FR 80000)

ANKER, Herman Wedel (1845-1895) Norwegian
£1148	$2297	(9-Feb-91 BU.O184) Landscape (31x22cm-12x9in) s. (N.KR 13000)
£1476	$2878	(11-Oct-90 BU.O3/R) Landscape with birch trees (45x58cm-18x23in) s.d.78 (N.KR 17000)
£3212	$5364	(4-Jun-91 BU.O11/R) Landscape from Hammeren in Maridalen near Christiania (46x39cm-18x15in) s. s.i.verso (N.KR 37000)
£4192	$7965	(11-Sep-90 UL.T163/R) Autumn landscape (75x100cm-30x39in) s. (N.KR 48000)

ANNA, Alessandro de (18th C) Italian
£13065	$21427	(21-Jun-91 SY.MO228/R) Danse villageoise (50x80cm-20x31in) gouache (F.FR 130000)

ANNENKOFF, Yuri (1889-1974) Russian
£2030	$4000	(13-Nov-90 CE.NY125/R) Portrait de l'artiste (64x49cm-25x19in) s. W/C col.chk ink wash pencil
£8000	$15600	(10-Oct-90 C395/R) Cathedral Arches (133x97cm-52x38in) s. oil enduit canvas

ANNES, M Kainerlingh (19th C) ?
£1900	$3553	(30-Aug-90 CG11) Still life with roses and honesty (36x43cm-14x17in) s.d.1889 W/C htd bodycol.

ANQUETIN, Louis (1861-1932) French
£4615	$9000	(10-Oct-90 SY.NY38/R) Les courses a auteuil (48x61cm-19x24in) s.d.92 paper on paper
£815	$1574	(14-Dec-90 ARC.P99/R) Etude de nu feminin (55x35cm-22x14in) s. pastel chl (F.FR 8000)

ANRROY, Anton van (1870-1949) Dutch
£1500	$2955	(13-Nov-90 SWS428/R) Interior (71x91cm-28x36in) s.

ANSCHUTZ, Hermann (1802-1880) German
£1331	$2183	(18-Jun-91 FN.S1741 a/R) Figures on path before watermill in wooded landscape (63x55cm-25x22in) s.d.1853 (DM 3900)

ANSDELL, Richard (1815-1885) British
£800	$1536	(29-Nov-90 B31/R) The lost sheep (24x47cm-9x19in) board
£4624	$8000	(23-May-91 CH.NY206/R) Goatherds, Bay of Gibraltar (69x122cm-27x48in) s.d.1874
£6000	$9780	(14-Jun-91 C213/R) Going to market, Spain (61x105cm-24x41in) s.d.1858
£6701	$12932	(11-Dec-90 CH.R152/R) Che spavento (125x230cm-49x91in) s.d.1869 (I.L 14500000)
£10778	$18000	(7-Jun-91 SY.NY72/R) After a day's sport (72x92cm-28x36in) s.
£24000	$44880	(28-Aug-90 S760/R) Deer forest (165x76cm-65x30in) s.indist.d.187. s.i.on stretcher
£113772	$190000	(7-Jun-91 SY.NY129/R) Coursing (86x117cm-34x46in) s.d.1845

ANSDELL, Richard (attrib) (1815-1885) British
£800	$1576	(31-Oct-90 S293) Portrait of gentleman standing in landscape (75x49cm-30x19in) arched top

ANSDELL, Richard (circle) (1815-1885) British
£1250	$2438	(15-Jan-91 SWS112/R) Hunter with dog in landscape (54x44cm-21x17in)

ANSDELL, Richard and PHILLIP, John (attrib) (19th C) British
£5000	$9850	(13-Nov-90 PH70/R) Good companions (71x91cm-28x36in)

ANSDELL, Richard and SIDLEY, Samuel (19th C) British
£11000	$17930	(14-Jun-91 C240/R) Annie and Ernest, the children of Angus Holden (163x122cm-64x48in) s.d.1877

ANSELMI, Michelangelo (attrib) (1491-1554) Italian
£4595	$7489	(10-Jun-91 W.T1494) Virgin, Child and Saints (46x41cm-18x16in) (C.D 8500)

ANSHUTZ, Thomas Pollock (1851-1912) American
£8333	$16000	(29-Nov-90 SY.NY79/R) A passing glance (107x76cm-42x30in) s. pastel canvas

ANSINGH, Lizzy (1875-) Dutch
£2252 $4392   (20-Oct-90 CH.AM136/R) Puppets in rose garden (75x61cm-30x24in) s.
                canvas on panel (D.FL 7500)

ANTCHER, Isaac (1899-) Rumanian
£814 $1538   (30-Sep-90 E.LA181) Nature morte aux poivrons (27x41cm-11x16in) s.
                (F.FR 8000)
£904 $1672   (6-Mar-91 APT.P67) Theiere et bouquet (73x54cm-29x21in) s. (F.FR 9000)
£1017 $1923   (30-Sep-90 E.LA185) Nature morte aux bouteilles (38x46cm-15x18in) s.
                (F.FR 10000)
£1424 $2692   (30-Sep-90 E.LA165) Nature morte a la cafetiere (50x61cm-20x24in) s.
                (F.FR 14000)
£1780 $3187   (14-Apr-91 GL.P39) Square Montmartrois (65x81cm-26x32in) s. (F.FR 18000)
£2055 $3988   (9-Dec-90 E.LA36/R) Montsouris (50x61cm-20x24in) s. (F.FR 20000)

ANTES, Horst (1936-) German
£6419 $10912   (1-Jun-91 VG.B376/R) Still life with cube, pipe and ball
                (30x39cm-12x15in) s.i.d.1971verso i.stretcher acrylic (DM 19000)
£7808 $13508   (22-May-91 CH.AM656/R) Kopf (40x32cm-16x13in) (D.FL 26000)
£65000 $104650   (27-Jun-91 S49/R) Blue figure, Franz von Assisi (100x80cm-39x31in)
                s.d.1961-64verso
£75085 $147167   (23-Nov-90 VG.B94/R) June bride (100x90cm-39x35in) oil tempera
                (DM 220000)
£714   *$1279*   *(16-Mar-91 S.Z13/R) Man with letter (50x38cm-20x15in) s. pencil chl W/C*
                (S.FR 1800)
£1365   *$2676*   *(24-Nov-90 N.M15/R) Female figure turning round (33x20cm-13x8in)*
                s.d.1965 W/C collage (DM 4000)
£1695   *$2831*   *(8-Jun-91 HN.H12/R) Figure with dove (35x25cm-14x10in) s. pencil*
                (DM 5000)
£3596   *$5861*   *(14-Jun-91 L.K722/R) Untitled (50x67cm-20x26in) s. W/C col.chk*
                (DM 10500)
£5159   *$8925*   *(25-May-91 AB.L62/R) Untitled (66x48cm-26x19in) s. mixed media*
                (S.FR 13000)
£5405   *$9351*   *(22-May-91 CH.AM657/R) Untitled (66x99cm-26x39in) s. gouache*
                (D.FL 18000)
£5695   *$9511*   *(8-Jun-91 HN.H10) Yellow head (67x51cm-26x20in) s. gouache oil*
                (DM 16800)
£6122   *$12000*   *(15-Feb-91 SY.NY157/R) Male figure with black hat on ochre*
                (54x42cm-21x17in) s. gouache
£6600   *$11418*   *(10-May-91 S.Z1/R) White profile with long yellow arms (97x69cm-38x27in)*
                s. aquatec (S.FR 16500)
£7095   *$12061*   *(1-Jun-91 VG.B377/R) The letter (50x60cm-20x24in) s. pastel (DM 21000)*
£9898   *$19399*   *(24-Nov-90 VG.B375/R) Masked figure (38x29cm-15x11in) s.d.1965/68*
                collage oil chl board (DM 29000)
£12162   *$20676*   *(31-May-91 VG.B67/R) Blue figure in room (50x63cm-20x25in) s. pastel*
                (DM 36000)
£16356   *$32222*   *(30-Oct-90 F.R273/R) Kopf ocker - ocker (120x100cm-47x39in)*
                s.d.1973verso oil mixed media canvas (I.L 36000000)

ANTHONISSEN, Arnoldus van (?-1632) Dutch
£12000 $19560   (3-Jul-91 S228/R) Shipping in choppy sea (39x58cm-15x23in) init. panel

ANTHONISSEN, Hendrick van (1606-?) Dutch
£19553 $35000   (11-Apr-91 SY.NY143/R) Dutch shipping in choppy sea (28x37cm-11x15in) s.
                panel

ANTHONISZ, Aert (attrib) (1580-1620) Flemish
£14371 $24287   (2-May-91 CH.AM69/R) Dutch men of war engaging Turkish ships
                (26x33cm-10x13in) copper oval (D.FL 48000)

ANTHONY, Henry Mark (1817-1886) British
£500 $950   (1-Mar-91 C76/R) View of the Royal Hospital Greenwich from the park
                (46x62cm-18x24in)
£920 $1803   (22-Jan-91 PH112/R) The harvest moon (68x58cm-27x23in) s. s.i.verso

ANTIGNA, Alexandre (1817-1878) French
£1594 $3108   (24-Oct-90 GD.B90/R) The soup eaters, interior with family seated
                (46x38cm-18x15in) s. (S.FR 4000)

ANTIPOVA, Eugenia (1917-) Russian
£500 $840   (26-Apr-91 ARC.P53/R) Les deux bouquets champetres (84x99cm-33x39in)
                s.d.60 (F.FR 5000)
£546 $938   (15-May-91 AGB.P150/R) Fillette en robe jaune (101x106cm-40x42in) s.
                (F.FR 5500)
£602 $1114   (4-Mar-91 ZZ.F2) La lecture (74x56cm-29x22in) s. (F.FR 6000)
£603 $1158   (18-Feb-91 ARC.P162/R) Nature morte aux pommes (94x119cm-37x47in) s.d.64
                (F.FR 6000)
£617 $1073   (25-Mar-91 ARC.P103/R) Premieres gammes (35x26cm-14x10in) s. (F.FR 6200)
£876 $1524   (25-Mar-91 ARC.P100/R) La petite fille aux nattes (34x26cm-13x10in) s.
                (F.FR 8800)
£945 $1645   (25-Mar-91 ARC.P101/R) Soleil du midi (53x85cm-21x33in) s. (F.FR 9500)
£992 $1706   (15-May-91 AGB.P151/R) Nature morte aux fruits (92x102cm-36x40in) s.
                (F.FR 10000)
£995 $1731   (25-Mar-91 ARC.P102/R) Sur la Neva (44x95cm-17x37in) s. (F.FR 10000)
£1493 $2597   (25-Mar-91 ARC.P97/R) Le palais des pionniers (64x78cm-25x31in) s.
                (F.FR 15000)

ANTIPOVA, Eugenia (1917-) Russian-cont.
£1931 $3862   (10-Feb-91 YC.P16/R) La lecon de musique (62x78cm-24x31in) s.d.1950
                              (F.FR 19000)
£3582 $6233   (25-Mar-91 ARC.P99/R) La lecon de musique (19x24cm-7x9in) s.
                              (F.FR 36000)

ANTOINE, Marguerite (20th C) ?
£1274 $2446   (2-Dec-90 M.V29/R) Jeune fille a la rose rouge (80x75cm-31x30in) s.
                              (F.FR 12500)

ANTOINE, Otto (1865-?) German
£699 $1357   (4-Dec-90 FN.S1736) Sail maker on fishing boat (24x31cm-9x12in) s. board
                              (DM 2000)
£699 $1357   (4-Dec-90 FN.S1737) Two old man seated on beach watching fishing boats
                              (24x31cm-9x12in) board after Carlos Grethe (DM 2000)
£1195 $2341   (24-Nov-90 VG.B408/R) Still life of flowers (66x51cm-26x20in) s.
                              (DM 3500)
£2041 $3286   (28-Jun-91 BM.B765/R) Halensee landscape with hammock fixed between two
                              trees (60x80cm-24x31in) s.d.1938 i.verso (DM 6000)
£5802 $11372   (24-Nov-90 VG.B229/R) Schlossbrucke, Berlin with view of cathedral
                              (72x95cm-28x37in) s.d.17 (DM 17000)
£6485 $12710   (24-Nov-90 VG.B228/R) Friedrichsbrucke, Berlin, with view of stock
                              exchange (72x93cm-28x37in) s. (DM 19000)

ANTOLINEZ, Jose (1635-1675) Spanish
£41356 $78577   (28-Feb-91 EP.M7/R) La Inmaculada Concepcion (202x116cm-80x46in)
                              s.d.1663 (S.P 7500000)

ANTONELLO DA MESSINA (after) (15th C) Italian
£1361 $2300   (1-May-91 D.NY59) Portrait of young scholar (36x28cm-14x11in) board

ANTONIO DA VITERBO (school) (15th C) Italian
£7046 $13811   (20-Nov-90 F.R112/R) Madonna col Bambino (34x25cm-13x10in) panel
                              (I.L 15500000)

ANTONIUCCI, Pierre (20th C) ?
£800 $1304   (3-Jul-91 CSC.P170) Le voyage (194x194cm-76x76in) s.i.d.oct.83 verso
                              acrylic (F.FR 8000)

ANTOYAN, Aris (20th C) ?
£1844 $3043   (10-Jul-91 FB.P120/R) Miss midnight (146x89cm-57x35in) s.d.sept 90 i.
                              verso acrylic (F.FR 18500)
£3134 $6112   (15-Oct-90 CSC.P11/R) Septembre (130x97cm-51x38in) s.d.89 i. verso
                              (F.FR 31000)

ANTRAL, Louis Robert (1895-1940) French
£545 $964   (7-Apr-91 I.N15) Le port (28x45cm-11x18in) s. W/C (F.FR 5500)

ANTWERP SCHOOL (?) Flemish
£1000 $1630   (4-Jul-91 C704/R) Good Samaritan (83x112cm-33x44in) c.1700
£1700 $2771   (4-Jul-91 C655/R) River landscape with courting couple and cattle by
                              river, village beyond (64x90cm-25x35in) c.1770
£6000 $9780   (4-Jul-91 C567/R) River landscapes with village, windmills and dancing
                              peasants (13x28cm-5x11in) panel pair c.1630
£24000 $39120   (5-Jul-91 C340/R) Four seasons (28x35cm-11x14in) on copper four c.1700

ANTWERP SCHOOL, 16th C Flemish
£14656 $26234   (14-Mar-91 D.V64/R) Resurrection of Christ. Riders. Christ before
                              Pilate. The Prodigal Son (104x58cm-41x23in) altar panels pair
                              double-sided shaped top (A.S 300000)
£21959 $37331   (27-May-91 L.K4/R) Adoration of the Magi. Adoration of the Shepherds.
                              Presentation of Christ (89x140cm-35x55in) panel triptychon
                              (DM 65000)

ANTWERP SCHOOL, 17th C Flemish
£1200 $2400   (7-Feb-91 C124/R) The Sacrifice of Isaac (81x85cm-32x33in) s.d.1616
£1290 $2218   (19-May-91 ZZ.F79/R) Descente de croix (73x52cm-29x20in) (F.FR 13000)
£3000 $5910   (31-Oct-90 S204) Figures in wooded landscape (9x22cm-4x9in) panel
£3000 $4890   (4-Jul-91 C736/R) Expulsion from Garden of Eden (69x87cm-27x34in) copper
                              on panel
£4000 $7600   (1-Mar-91 C104/R) Woodland clearing with peasants. Wooded path with
                              village beyond (17x22cm-7x9in) c.1630 copper pair
£10000 $19300   (12-Dec-90 S145/R) Diana and her nymphs surprised by Acteon
                              (55x76cm-22x30in) panel

ANUSZKIEWICZ, Richard (1930-) American
£1479 $2500   (20-Apr-91 WOL.C446/R) Untitled (61x46cm-24x18in) s.d.1971 verso acrylic
                              board

ANZINGER, Siegfried (1952-) Austrian
£741 $1438   (5-Dec-90 AB.S7013/R) Taucher (55x42cm-22x17in) s.d.1982 acrylic paper
                              (S.KR 8000)
£1004 $1968   (24-Nov-90 AB.L27/R) Donald Duck (55x42cm-22x17in) s.d.82 s.verso
                              acrylic paper (S.FR 2500)
£1884 $3070   (14-Jun-91 L.K726/R) Muskelmaler (40x60cm-16x24in) d.1985 (DM 5500)
£2397 $3908   (14-Jun-91 L.K727/R) Aeroplane (60x70cm-24x28in) d.1987 (DM 7000)

ANZINGER, Siegfried (1952-) Austrian-cont.
£3828 $6622   (8-May-91 D.V205/R) The murderer 1977 (90x75cm-35x30in) s.i.
                  (A.S 80000)
£488 $903   (7-Mar-91 D.V241/R) Fix Stun (30x42cm-12x17in) s.i. W/C (A.S 10000)
£535 $1049   (24-Jan-91 D.V293/R) Erotic scene. Study (43x30cm-17x12in) s. pencil W/C
                  gouache double-sided (A.S 11000)
£596 $1157   (6-Dec-90 D.V242/R) Three figures (30x40cm-12x16in) mono.s.d.78 pencil
                  W/C (A.S 12000)
£646 $1253   (6-Dec-90 D.V229/R) Man with monster (30x43cm-12x17in) s.i.d.1978 mixed
                  media (A.S 13000)
£683 $1264   (7-Mar-91 D.V296/R) The rivals (39x29cm-15x11in) s.i.d.1978 pencil W/C
                  (A.S 14000)
£957 $1656   (8-May-91 D.V207/R) Jungle (44x57cm-17x22in) mixed media (A.S 20000)
£976 $1806   (7-Mar-91 D.V242/R) Evening (44x65cm-17x26in) gouache (A.S 20000)
£1212 $2279   (20-Sep-90 D.V278) Untitled (59x41cm-23x16in) s. mixed media
                  (A.S 25000)
£1675 $2897   (8-May-91 D.V206/R) Two heads (63x47cm-25x19in) acrylic dispersion
                  (A.S 35000)
£1740 $3375   (6-Dec-90 D.V228/R) Owl (31x47cm-12x19in) s.d.78 mixed media
                  (A.S 35000)
£1740 $3375   (6-Dec-90 D.V172/R) Untitled (58x41cm-23x16in) s.d.84 mixed media
                  (A.S 35000)
£2153 $3725   (8-May-91 D.V208/R) Untitled (60x84cm-24x33in) s.d.1980 mixed media
                  (A.S 45000)
£3110 $5380   (8-May-91 D.V209/R) Untitled (58x83cm-23x33in) d.1980 mixed media
                  (A.S 65000)

AOYAMA, Yoshio (1894-?) Japanese?
£3179 $5500   (7-May-91 CE.NY54/R) La plage (60x73cm-24x29in) s. s.num.VI verso

APOL, Armand-Adrien-Marie (1879-1950) Belgian
£609 $1201   (6-Oct-90 KV.L9) Brabant village in the snow (45x55cm-18x22in) s. panel
                  (B.FR 38000)
£758 $1487   (21-Nov-90 GM.B918) Chenal (47x57cm-19x22in) s. (B.FR 46000)
£900 $1548   (14-May-91 GM.B645/R) Magasins le long du port (54x65cm-21x26in) s.
                  (B.FR 55000)
£910 $1720   (25-Sep-90 GM.B1077/R) Entree du Chenal (47x57cm-19x22in) s.
                  (B.FR 55000)
£1469 $2851   (8-Dec-90 GAB.G2332/R) Ville sous la neige (42x50cm-17x20in) s.d.1910
                  (S.FR 3600)
£1637 $2750   (23-Apr-91 C.A61/R) Rupelmonde Harbour (100x20cm-39x8in) s.
                  (B.FR 100000)

APOL, Louis (1850-1936) Dutch
£664 $1189   (11-Apr-91 D.V223/R) Winter in the Vorstadt (56x72cm-22x28in) s.
                  (A.S 14000)
£703 $1378   (11-Feb-91 SY.J442/R) Winter landscape (32x21cm-13x8in) s. panel
                  (SA.R 3500)
£785 $1484   (25-Sep-90 FN.S2106) Peasant with horse drawn cart fetching wood in
                  winter landscape (46x38cm-18x15in) s. panel (DM 2300)
£1212 $2388   (30-Oct-90 CH.AM246) Washerwoman by stream bordered with trees, in
                  summer (28x34cm-11x13in) s. canvas on panel (D.FL 4000)
£2395 $4168   (26-Mar-91 VN.R3/R) Farm burning in winter landscape (28x38cm-11x15in)
                  s. (D.FL 8000)
£4042 $7033   (26-Mar-91 VN.R2/R) Farmstead by a frozen river (43x58cm-17x23in) s.
                  (D.FL 13500)
£7273 $14327   (30-Oct-90 CH.AM157/R) View in forest in winter, with torrent
                  (55x76cm-22x30in) s. (D.FL 24000)
£427 $811   (26-Feb-91 VN.R5) River landscape with snowy banks (44x52cm-17x20in)
                  (D.FL 1400)
£778 $1479   (11-Sep-90 SY.AM5/R) Harbour in winter (16x20cm-6x8in) s. gouache
                  (D.FL 2600)
£1152 $2268   (30-Oct-90 CH.AM426/R) Peasant and horse by windmill, in winter
                  (17x13cm-7x5in) s. gouache (D.FL 3800)
£1293 $2250   (27-Mar-91 B.SF4252/R) Winter landscape with farmhouse by the Vecht
                  (37x53cm-15x21in) s. W/C gouache board

APOLLINAIRE, Guillaume (20th C) French
£1006 $1972   (24-Jan-91 BG.P28/R) Calligrammes (23x15cm-9x6in) poems (F.FR 10000)

APPEL, Charles P (1857-) American
£595 $1000   (19-Jul-91 DM.D2000/R) Landscape with figures in rowboat
                  (36x51cm-14x20in) s.

APPEL, Karel (1921-) Dutch
£781 $1351   (22-May-91 CH.AM691) Pollard-willows along ditch, farm beyond
                  (45x55cm-18x22in) s.d.1940 (D.FL 2600)
£1652 $2857   (23-May-91 SY.AM24/R) View of Prinseneiland in winter (50x60cm-20x24in)
                  s.d.1941 (D.FL 5500)
£2356 $3982   (18-Apr-91 BU.S1/R) Composition with two figures (28x33cm-11x13in) s.
                  (S.KR 25000)
£2427 $4732   (15-Oct-90 CSC.P2/R) Composition a la tete (76x56cm-30x22in) s. acrylic
                  paper (F.FR 24000)
£2800 $4564   (3-Jul-91 CSC.P94/R) Personnage (76x56cm-30x22in) s. acrylic lithograph
                  sheet laid down on canvas (F.FR 28000)

APPEL, Karel (1921-) Dutch-cont.

£4082	$8000	(12-Feb-91 SY.NY348/R) Cat (56x74cm-22x29in) s.d.69 acrylic paper on canvas
£4082	$8000	(12-Feb-91 SY.NY349/R) Untitled (56x76cm-22x30in) s.d.63 acrylic paper on canvas
£4532	$7387	(11-Jun-91 CSC.P40/R) Personnages (53x78cm-21x31in) s.d.75 acrylic (F.FR 45000)
£4587	$8853	(16-Dec-90 GL.P4/R) Personnage (63x47cm-25x19in) s.d.72 acrylic paper (F.FR 45000)
£5405	$9351	(22-May-91 CH.AM607/R) Figure (24x19cm-9x7in) s. (D.FL 18000)
£5561	$10844	(21-Oct-90 P.V60/R) Sans titre (76x56cm-30x22in) s. acrylic paper laid down on canvas (F.FR 55000)
£6574	$12818	(23-Oct-90 C.A303/R) Composition (76x56cm-30x22in) s. acrylic (B.FR 400000)
£6607	$11429	(23-May-91 SY.AM324/R) Untitled (60x73cm-24x29in) s.d.73 acrylic (D.FL 22000)
£6607	$11429	(22-May-91 CH.AM601 a/R) Two figures (50x64cm-20x25in) s.d.68 acrylic paper on board (D.FL 22000)
£7143	$14000	(14-Feb-91 CH.NY52/R) Small acrylic no 7 (50x63cm-20x25in) s. acrylic paper on board
£7653	$15000	(14-Feb-91 CH.NY17/R) Untitled (66x50cm-26x20in) s.d.69 acrylic paper on canvas
£7740	$14938	(13-Dec-90 SY.AM363/R) Untitled (48x76cm-19x30in) s.d.74 paper (D.FL 25000)
£7808	$13508	(22-May-91 CH.AM601 c/R) Two children (50x64cm-20x25in) s.d.68 acrylic paper on board (D.FL 26000)
£8500	$15045	(21-Mar-91 S31/R) Untitled (46x33cm-18x13in) s.d.1962 verso
£9692	$18899	(24-Oct-90 EA.M509/R) Boy with arms like wings (51x40cm-20x16in) s. (C.D 22000)
£9692	$19189	(29-Jan-91 UL.T145) Figure composition (56x76cm-22x30in) (N.KR 110000)
£10836	$20913	(13-Dec-90 SY.AM260/R) Untitled (109x74cm-43x29in) s. paper on canvas (D.FL 35000)
£10836	$20913	(12-Dec-90 CH.AM417/R) Figure (66x50cm-26x20in) s.d.69 acrylic cardboard on board (D.FL 35000)
£11146	$21511	(13-Dec-90 SY.AM262/R) Tete de chien (65x54cm-26x21in) s. acrylic canvas (D.FL 36000)
£11585	$22475	(4-Dec-90 BA.S15/R) Face (55x45cm-22x18in) s. paper on canvas (S.KR 125000)
£11842	$20132	(29-May-91 KH.K71/R) Trois tetes (59x90cm-23x35in) s. acrylic paper on canvas (D.KR 135000)
£11864	$19814	(8-Jun-91 HN.H18/R) Composition (64x82cm-25x32in) s. acrylic (DM 35000)
£12351	$20996	(2-Jun-91 GL.P168/R) Tete (90x61cm-35x24in) s. acrylic paper laid down on canvas (F.FR 124000)
£12384	$23901	(12-Dec-90 CH.AM429/R) In name of wilderness (74x101cm-29x40in) s.d.75 acrylic paper on canvas (D.FL 40000)
£12601	$24572	(28-Oct-90 M.V63/R) Springtime head (106x75cm-42x30in) s.d.75 paper sheet of metal (F.FR 125000)
£12607	$24584	(22-Oct-90 BR.M7/R) Personaggio (16x22cm-6x9in) s. s.d.1959 verso (I.L 28000000)
£13204	$25748	(10-Oct-90 RAS.K16/R) Composition (46x55cm-18x22in) s. (D.KR 150000)
£14138	$23893	(18-Apr-91 BU.S18/R) Composition with figures (74x108cm-29x43in) s. (S.KR 150000)
£14676	$28765	(24-Nov-90 APT.P106/R) Personnage (61x89cm-24x35in) s.d.69 board (F.FR 145000)
£15228	$30000	(4-Oct-90 SY.NY148/R) Promenade II (152x122cm-60x48in) s. d.1983 stretcher
£15416	$29908	(9-Dec-90 CC.P59/R) Le petit garcon (81x65cm-32x26in) s.d.1969 (F.FR 150000)
£15480	$29876	(13-Dec-90 SY.AM265/R) Two sunny children (51x61cm-20x24in) s.d.74 (D.FL 50000)
£16000	$31200	(18-Oct-90 C345/R) Untitled (76x50cm-30x20in) s. acrylic paper on canvas
£16209	$31607	(22-Oct-90 BR.M99/R) Personaggio (60x50cm-24x20in) s. (I.L 36000000)
£16216	$27568	(31-May-91 GB.B6111/R) Composition (64x49cm-25x19in) s. board (DM 48000)
£17028	$32864	(12-Dec-90 CH.AM411/R) Landscape with clouds (77x168cm-30x66in) s. acrylic oilstick paper on cardboard (D.FL 55000)
£17560	$34241	(22-Oct-90 BR.M48/R) Personaggi (61x50cm-24x20in) s.d.1974 (I.L 39000000)
£17857	$35000	(7-Nov-90 SY.NY173/R) Loving hear dog (91x74cm-36x29in) s.d.71
£18000	$31860	(21-Mar-91 S30/R) Looking around (80x65cm-31x26in) s.
£18576	$35851	(12-Dec-90 CH.AM425/R) Waiting in night (61x76cm-24x30in) s.d.74 (D.FL 60000)
£18576	$35851	(13-Dec-90 SY.AM256/R) Flying big as world (81x100cm-32x39in) s. s.d.1971 verso (D.FL 60000)
£18576	$35851	(13-Dec-90 SY.AM364/R) Figures (83x143cm-33x56in) s. paper on canvas (D.FL 60000)
£18919	$32162	(31-May-91 VG.B68/R) Les siens (46x33cm-18x13in) s.d.1973 s.verso acrylic (DM 56000)
£19289	$38000	(5-Oct-90 CH.NY35/R) Untitled (50x65cm-20x26in) s.d.68 paper on canvas
£19678	$38569	(13-Feb-91 KH.K4/R) Personnage, 1988 (116x81cm-46x32in) s. (D.KR 220000)
£20246	$39481	(10-Oct-90 RAS.K28/R) Yellow composition (80x98cm-31x39in) s. acrylic paper on canvas (D.KR 230000)
£20305	$40000	(5-Oct-90 CH.NY96/R) Fille aux fleurs (162x122cm-64x48in) s.d.69 acrylic col oilstick paper on canvas
£20408	$40000	(14-Feb-91 CH.NY3/R) Tete (74x49cm-29x19in) s.d.56

APPEL, Karel (1921-) Dutch-cont.

£21320	$42000	(5-Oct-90 CH.NY77/R) Flowers as a still life (128x117cm-50x46in) s.
£23789	$46388	(24-Oct-90 EA.M530/R) Abstract composition (90x70cm-35x28in) s. (C.D 54000)
£24313	$47411	(22-Oct-90 BR.M170/R) Personaggi (92x73cm-36x29in) s. (I.L 54000000)
£25000	$48750	(18-Oct-90 S127/R) Untitled (50x65cm-20x26in) s.d.69 acrylic board
£25381	$50000	(14-Nov-90 SY.NY309/R) Tete Problematique (71x55cm-28x22in) s.
£25381	$50000	(5-Oct-90 CH.NY7/R) Tete Atomique (100x82cm-39x32in) s.d.63
£26316	$50789	(13-Dec-90 SY.AM365/R) Personnage (92x72cm-36x28in) s. (D.FL 85000)
£30960	$59752	(13-Dec-90 SY.AM229/R) Vechtende vogels (100x81cm-39x32in) s. (D.FL 100000)
£34056	$65728	(12-Dec-90 CH.AM396/R) Flying birds (70x90cm-28x35in) s.d.56 (D.FL 110000)
£42000	$81480	(6-Dec-90 S25/R) Deux Animaux (89x117cm-35x46in) s.d.59
£50000	$97500	(18-Oct-90 S122/R) L'herbe de la vie (100x81cm-39x32in) s.
£50761	$100000	(4-Oct-90 SY.NY79/R) Les tetes comme les arbres (116x89cm-46x35in) s.
£51778	$100968	(22-Oct-90 BR.M127/R) Personaggio (150x80cm-59x31in) s. (I.L 115000000)
£55000	$107250	(18-Oct-90 S116/R) De grote H (114x87cm-45x34in) s.d.57
£57276	$110542	(13-Dec-90 SY.AM236/R) Untitled (120x82cm-47x32in) s.d.57 (D.FL 185000)
£78000	$130260	(6-Jun-91 CJ.N8/R) Witnessing the dawn (295x295cm-116x116in) (F.FR 780000)
£80000	$128800	(27-Jun-91 S22/R) Composition with animal figures (67x142cm-26x56in) s.d.51 s.i.d.1951stretcher
£110000	$194700	(21-Mar-91 S29/R) Landscape (114x195cm-45x77in) s.d.1959 s.i.d.1959 stretcher
£140000	$225400	(27-Jun-91 S25/R) Kinderenmeisje (130x115cm-51x45in) s.d.50
£420	$727	(22-May-91 CH.AM798) Child and animals (20x26cm-8x10in) s.d.50 W/C on printed base (D.FL 1400)
£541	$935	(22-May-91 CH.AM781) Child and animals (26x20cm-10x8in) s. W/C over printed base (D.FL 1800)
£541	$935	(22-May-91 CH.AM720) Animals (26x20cm-10x8in) s. W/C over printed base (D.FL 1800)
£751	$1299	(22-May-91 CH.AM772) Bird (26x20cm-10x8in) s. W/C over printed base (D.FL 2500)
£806	$1573	(14-Jan-91 YC.P133) Trois personnages et un chien (221x33cm-87x13in) s.d.49 Indian ink col.crayons (F.FR 8000)
£1019	$1967	(16-Dec-90 GL.P1) Personnages et chat (25x17cm-10x7in) s.d.1950 Indian ink (F.FR 10000)
£1019	$1967	(16-Dec-90 GL.P2) Personne (19x13cm-7x5in) s.d.1951 Indian ink pastel (F.FR 10000)
£1106	$1813	(21-Jun-91 CK.P52) Composition (32x49cm-13x19in) s.d.50 ink drawing (F.FR 11000)
£1300	$2510	(13-Dec-90 SY.AM540/R) Untitled (14x20cm-6x8in) s. col.chk (D.FL 4200)
£1331	$2595	(14-Jan-91 YC.P134) Deux personnages et un chien (18x13cm-7x5in) s.d.48 Indian ink col.crayons (F.FR 13200)
£1457	$2390	(21-Jun-91 CK.P52) Personnages (19x13cm-7x5in) s.d.50 ink htd.col.crayons (F.FR 14500)
£1506	$2425	(28-Jun-91 ARC.P45/R) Personnages (25x17cm-10x7in) s. indian ink col.crayons (F.FR 15000)
£1786	$3000	(28-Apr-91 HG.C486) Albieno Neujdier met jong (36x58cm-14x23in) s.d.1949 s.d.verso oil mixed media
£2179	$4250	(10-Oct-90 SY.NY353/R) Girl with spoon (30x23cm-12x9in) s.i.d.1964 mixed media
£2232	$4286	(27-Nov-90 W.T1326) Untitled (49x40cm-19x16in) s. gouache (C.D 5000)
£2613	$4677	(11-Mar-91 GL.P182) L'oiseau (59x59cm-23x23in) s.d.1978 W/C (F.FR 26000)
£3715	$5981	(26-Jun-91 CB.P4/R) Composition (54x41cm-21x16in) s.d.75 gouache (F.FR 37000)
£4000	$6520	(4-Jul-91 GL.P201/R) Tete (37x54cm-15x21in) s.d.1976 gouache (F.FR 40000)
£4082	$8000	(7-Nov-90 B.SF1098/R) Man and woman (43x35cm-17x14in) s. pastel
£5025	$8995	(15-Mar-91 FB.P58/R) Personnage (76x57cm-30x22in) s.d.59 mixed media board (F.FR 50000)
£5535	$10627	(27-Nov-90 BU.S20/R) Composition (68x83cm-27x33in) s.d.1974 mixed media gouache W/C chk (S.KR 60000)
£6192	$11950	(12-Dec-90 CH.AM419/R) Sculpter (84x69cm-33x27in) s.d.81 W/C col.chk (D.FL 20000)
£6441	$10756	(8-Jun-91 HN.H19/R) Bird (24x30cm-9x12in) s.d.1951 gouache (DM 19000)
£6500	$11505	(21-Mar-91 S54/R) Untitled (56x75cm-22x30in) s.d.60 gouache wax crayon
£7000	$13650	(18-Oct-90 C336/R) Dog and cat (49x64cm-19x25in) s. paper collage gouache
£7347	$14253	(7-Dec-90 G.Z103/R) Personnage (63x47cm-25x19in) s.d.1964 col.grease chk (S.FR 18000)
£8163	$16000	(15-Feb-91 SY.NY145/R) Untitled (50x64cm-20x25in) s.d.56 gouache
£8500	$16575	(18-Oct-90 S120/R) Untitled (65x82cm-26x32in) s.d.74 gouache crayon
£9184	$18000	(7-Nov-90 SY.NY151/R) Composition (56x76cm-22x30in) s.d.59 gouache
£9907	$19121	(12-Dec-90 CH.AM393/R) Animal (24x30cm-9x12in) s.d.50 W/C (D.FL 32000)
£10000	$19500	(18-Oct-90 S118/R) Untitled (50x65cm-20x26in) s.d.58 gouache crayon
£10000	$19500	(18-Oct-90 C338/R) Untitled (45x54cm-18x21in) s. W/C gouache paper on canvas
£10660	$21000	(14-Nov-90 SY.NY308/R) Personnages (66x50cm-26x20in) s.d.56 gouache collage
£11100	$21534	(3-Dec-90 CH.R195/R) Portrait dansant (65x50cm-26x20in) s. acrylic paper collage (I.L 24000000)
£11531	$22140	(27-Nov-90 BU.S19/R) Composition (76x58cm-30x23in) s. mixed media paper on canvas (S.KR 125000)

APPEL, Karel (1921-) Dutch-cont.
£12948	$22012	(30-May-91 FB.P22 a/R) Personnages (61x89cm-24x35in) s.d.69 mixed media board (F.FR 130000)
£14213	$28000	(5-Oct-90 CH.NY36/R) Figure with animal (49x63cm-19x25in) s.d.57 gouache
£15015	$25976	(22-May-91 CH.AM602/R) Composition (98x151cm-39x59in) s.d.61 gouache col.crayons (D.FL 50000)
£18018	$31171	(23-May-91 SY.AM256 d/R) The cockrel (40x54cm-16x21in) s.d.53 chk gouache (D.FL 60000)
£19763	$33597	(30-May-91 EA.Z269/R) Personnage et Oiseax II (120x160cm-47x63in) s.d.1970 mixed media (S.FR 50000)
£28084	$54764	(9-Oct-90 CSC.P72/R) Les canards (61x122cm-24x48in) s.d.70 acrylic collage paper laid down on canvas (F.FR 280000)

APPELMAN, Barend (1640-1686) Dutch
£2783	$4704	(18-Apr-91 APT.P62/R) Paysage italianisant aux grands arbres (56x47cm-22x19in) s. (F.FR 28000)

APPERLEY, George Owen Wynne (1884-1960) British
£600	$1170	(25-Oct-90 M2) Still life with shawl, mandolin, flowers and old master painting (53x38cm-21x15in) s.d.1915 W/C gouache
£601	$1039	(23-May-91 SY.AM64/R) View of Granada, Sierra Nevada (12x17cm-5x7in) s.d.1926 W/C (D.FL 2000)
£620	$1190	(21-Feb-91 B180/R) Moroccan street scene (25x34cm-10x13in) s.d.1935 W/C
£680	$1278	(18-Sep-90 PH63) Canal scene, Venice (17x25cm-7x10in) s.d.06 W/C bodycol over pencil
£850	$1641	(12-Dec-90 SWS2376) Spanish memories (55x39cm-22x15in) s.d.1915 W/C gouache

APPERT, George (20th C) French
£518	$1000	(14-Dec-90 DM.D2271/R) Cock fight (51x61cm-20x24in) s. canvas on board

APPIAN, Adolphe (1818-1898) French
£969	$1910	(14-Nov-90 CN.P108) Barque sur la riviere (27x35cm-11x14in) s. (F.FR 9500)
£2449	$4800	(6-Nov-90 GF.L2163/R) Marine (41x69cm-16x27in) s. (S.FR 6000)
£2590	$5050	(24-Oct-90 GD.B95/R) Mill in landscape (37x68cm-15x27in) s. (S.FR 6500)
£3109	$6063	(12-Oct-90 APT.P59/R) Gondole sur la lagune (26x45cm-10x18in) s. paper laid down on canvas (F.FR 31000)
£3262	$6296	(12-Dec-90 D.P133/R) L'embarcadere (26x42cm-10x17in) s. panel (F.FR 32000)
£3337	$6507	(16-Oct-90 CS.L38/R) Bord de riviere avec troupeau et personnages (31x56cm-12x22in) s. (F.FR 33000)
£4032	$7863	(26-Oct-90 APT.P82) Avant la pluie dans les marais de Virieu (101x106cm-40x42in) s. (F.FR 40000)
£4400	$7436	(1-May-91 GD.B24/R) River landscape with shepherd, cattle and washerwomen (47x85cm-19x33in) s. (S.FR 11000)

APPIAN, Louis (1862-1896) French
£1336	$2592	(3-Dec-90 CS.L44/R) Bouquet de fleurs (92x72cm-36x28in) s. (F.FR 13000)

APPIANI, Andrea (18/19th C) Italian
£14625	$28812	(14-Nov-90 F.M49/R) Apollo che canta i trionfi di Giove (97x142cm-38x56in) d.1809 (I.L 32000000)
£821	$1453	(19-Mar-91 F.M261) Scena di conversazione (19x27cm-7x11in) ink (I.L 1800000)
£1824	$3228	(19-Mar-91 F.M186/R) Psiche davanti a Venere (22x33cm-9x13in) i. ink W/C bistre (I.L 4000000)
£2052	$3632	(19-Mar-91 F.M342/R) Madonna col Bambino (15x11cm-6x4in) s. ink W/C bistre (I.L 4500000)
£3420	$6053	(19-Mar-91 F.M188/R) Psiche davanti a Proserpina (22x33cm-9x13in) i. bistre ink W/C (I.L 7500000)
£8684	$17107	(14-Nov-90 F.M43/R) Vulcano e Minerva mostrano a Clio lo scudo istoriato con le imprese diNapoleone (275x295cm-108x116in) pencil (I.L 19000000)

APPLEYARD, Frederick (1874-1963) British
£3200	$5952	(5-Sep-90 BT219/R) Spring (48x41cm-19x16in) s.d.1905 s.i.stretcher
£1600	$3136	(6-Nov-90 PH3/R) Tree sprite (41x38cm-16x15in) s. s.i.verso W/C

APSHOVEN, Thomas van (attrib) (1622-1664) Flemish
£1370	$2452	(12-Mar-91 FN.S2270/R) Peasants in river landscape at the end of day (24x33cm-9x13in) panel (DM 4000)
£2389	$3918	(18-Jun-91 FN.S1743) Figures before thatched farmhouse at the end of day (24x33cm-9x13in) panel (DM 7000)

APT, Ulrich (attrib) (?-1532) German
£19231	$37115	(12-Dec-90 N.M353/R) Portrait of the merchant Anton Rehm from Lindau (48x33cm-19x13in) d.1522 panel (DM 55000)

AQUINO, Luis (1895-1968) Argentinian
£1579	$3000	(11-Sep-90 PO.BA1) Barcos (52x62cm-20x24in) s.

ARAGONESE SCHOOL, 13th C Spanish
£46221	$91055	(30-Oct-90 EP.M2/R) El asesinato del Emperador Domiciano - Franco-Gothic School (98x78cm-39x31in) i. fresco transferred to canvas (S.P 8500000)

ARAKAWA, Shusaku (1936-) Japanese
£10714 $21000   (15-Feb-91 SY.NY182/R) This canvas is perfect rectangle
                              (115x76cm-45x30in) s.i.d.1966 s.d.stretcher
£22843 $45000   (5-Oct-90 CH.NY78/R) 1. Morning picture. 2. Portrait of civilization
                              (122x183cm-48x72in) s.i.d.1969
£25000 $40250   (27-Jun-91 C47/R) Landscape (122x183cm-48x72in) s.i.d.1969 s.i.stretcher
£36000 $70200   (18-Oct-90 S129/R) From Webster's dictionary, no 2 (123x183cm-48x72in)
                              s.d.1965/71 acrylic canvas
£1786   *$3500*   *(12-Feb-91 SY.NY325 a/R) You (76x56cm-30x22in) s.d.1965 graphite*
                              col.pencil gouache
£5867   *$11500*   *(14-Feb-91 CH.NY34/R) Still life (61x84cm-24x33in) s.i.d.1967*
                              s.i.d.verso oil black ink canvas
£32544   *$55000*   *(2-May-91 CH.NY184/R) That in which (168x304cm-66x120in) s.d.1977-78*
                              s.i.d. verso graphite acrylic

ARANA, Alfonso (1927-) Puerto Rican
£3316   *$6500*   *(19-Nov-90 SY.NY246/R) Arpege I (65x50cm-26x20in) s. chl white chk*
                              pastel

ARANDA, Jose Jimenez (1837-1903) Spanish
£12369 $22141   (13-Mar-91 FER.M174/R) El violinista (33x23cm-13x9in) s. panel
                              (S.P 2250000)
£462   *$743*   *(25-Jun-91 FER.M79) Don Quijote se subio sobre una punta de una alta*
                              pena... (18x27cm-7x11in) s. gouache (S.P 85000)
£462   *$743*   *(25-Jun-91 FER.M80) ...se llego a el, y con breves aunque muy discretas*
                              razones... (18x26cm-7x10in) s. gouache (S.P 85000)
£462   *$743*   *(25-Jun-91 FER.M85) 'Que gigantes' dijo Sancho Panza (18x26cm-7x10in) s.*
                              gouache (S.P 85000)
£462   *$743*   *(25-Jun-91 FER.M83) ...Sancho Panza, que tambien tuvo a milagro la*
                              mejoria de su amo... (18x25cm-7x10in) s. gouache (S.P 85000)
£462   *$743*   *(25-Jun-91 FER.M78/R) Sancho se levanto quedandose agobiado en la mitad*
                              del camino... (18x25cm-7x10in) s. gouache (S.P 85000)
£462   *$743*   *(25-Jun-91 FER.M82/R) ...y la asturiana Maritornes curo a Sancho que no*
                              menos lo habia menester (17x24cm-7x9in) s. gouache (S.P 85000)
£462   *$743*   *(25-Jun-91 FER.M81/R) Cerraron la sepultura con una gruesa pena...*
                              (16x25cm-6x10in) s. gouache (S.P 85000)
£462   *$743*   *(25-Jun-91 FER.M84/R) ...iba saltando un hombre de risco en risco y de*
                              mata en mata... (19x27cm-7x11in) s. gouache (S.P 85000)
£491   *$805*   *(17-Jun-91 DUR.M596) Boceto y estudio para el Capitan Montoya*
                              (18x24cm-7x9in) double-sided dr (S.P 90000)
£516   *$831*   *(25-Jun-91 FER.M8/R) Morisco leyendo (28x21cm-11x8in) s. ink dr*
                              (S.P 95000)
£1495   *$2870*   *(18-Dec-90 DUR.M18) El picador (22x14cm-9x6in) W/C (S.P 275000)*

ARAPOV, Vassilii (1934-) Russian
£595 $1024   (15-May-91 AGB.P26) Nu (113x64cm-44x25in) s. (F.FR 6000)
£595 $1024   (15-May-91 AGB.P24/R) Pavots et pivoines (94x75cm-37x30in) s. hardboard
                              (F.FR 6000)

ARATYM, Hubert (1936-?) German?
£389   *$763*   *(24-Jan-91 D.V274/R) Untitled (30x30cm-12x12in) mixed media (A.S 8000)*

ARAUJO Y RUANO, Joaquin (19th C) Spanish
£1639 $3213   (24-Jan-91 EP.M37/R) Galanteo en un jardin (21x27cm-8x11in)
                              (S.P 300000)

ARBO, Peter Nicolai (1831-1892) Norwegian
£3152 $5643   (14-Mar-91 BU.O2/R) Landscape with hunting party (25x35cm-10x14in)
                              init.d.1881 panel (N.KR 36000)

ARBORELIUS, Olof (1842-1915) Swedish
£1576 $3041   (12-Dec-90 BU.S3/R) Wooded landscape with man and horse
                              (105x145cm-41x57in) (S.KR 17000)
£2936 $4932   (24-Apr-91 BA.S5/R) Picnic at the grazing pastures (60x80cm-24x31in) s.
                              (S.KR 31000)
£11405 $22468   (30-Oct-90 BU.S2/R) By Rattviks church (99x148cm-39x58in) s.d.1882
                              (S.KR 125000)
£15055 $29658   (30-Oct-90 BU.S1/R) On the way to wedding, Dalarna (89x134cm-35x53in)
                              s.d.1892 (S.KR 165000)

ARCANGELO (20th C) Italian?
£2927   *$5707*   *(22-Oct-90 BR.M60/R) Notte di teste (112x119cm-44x47in) s.d.1987 carbon*
                              oil canvas (I.L 6500000)

ARCHDUCHESS MARIE-THERESE (1855-?) German
£1470 $2910   (31-Jan-91 D.V117/R) Landscape with mountain stream (21x16cm-8x6in)
                              mono.d.1887 panel (A.S 30000)

ARCHIGUILLE, Francois (c.1923-) French
£2033 $4065   (7-Feb-91 R.P119/R) Composition (97x150cm-38x59in) s. acrylic
                              (F.FR 20000)
£9891 $17705   (14-Apr-91 R.P165 b/R) Transfiguration periode blanche
                              (195x130cm-77x51in) s. acrylic (F.FR 100000)
£1626   *$3252*   *(7-Feb-91 R.P197/R) Composition (97x130cm-38x51in) s. mixed media canvas*
                              (F.FR 16000)

ARCHIGUILLE, Francois (c.1923-) French-cont.
£10500 $17115   (3-Jul-91 CSC.P14/R) Turbulences (203x132cm-80x52in) s.d.71 mixed media
                canvas (F.FR 105000)

ARCHIPENKO, Alexander (1887-1964) Russian
£3637 $7128   (20-Nov-90 BR.M142/R) Nudo disteso (56x36cm-22x14in) s. ink W/C
                (I.L 8000000)
£4061 $8000   (2-Oct-90 CH.NY86/R) Nature morte (31x40cm-12x16in) s. gouache over
                pencil
£4315 $8500   (3-Oct-90 SY.NY102/R) Femme asisse (50x32cm-20x13in) s. col.chk
£8673 $17000   (15-Feb-91 SY.NY43/R) Femme assise (76x50cm-30x20in) s. gouache ink wash
                over crayon paper on board

ARCIMBOLDO, Giuseppe (after) (1527-1593) Italian
£9800 $19110   (26-Oct-90 PHM35/R) The four seasons. Rudolfo II (67x50cm-26x20in) five

ARCIMBOLDO, Giuseppe (style) (1527-1593) Italian
£3041 $5169   (31-May-91 GB.B5006/R) Winter, portrait of old man assembled from roots
                and branches (69x49cm-27x19in) (DM 9000)
£3322 $6444   (7-Dec-90 GB.B5006/R) Autumn, bust of bearded man assembled with fruit
                and vegetables (70x50cm-28x20in) canvas laid down (DM 9500)
£7816 $13991   (14-Mar-91 D.V58/R) Allegory of autumn, portrait of man put together of
                fruit (70x50cm-28x20in) (A.S 160000)

ARCT, Eugeniusz (1899-1974) Polish
£1343 $2378   (23-Mar-91 AG.W1) View from the mountain (67x63cm-26x25in) s.d.1937
                (P.Z 23000000)

ARDEN, Edward see TUCKER, Edward

ARDEN, H (19th C) Belgian
£561 $1099   (21-Nov-90 GM.B1066) Village au bord de la riviere (24x40cm-9x16in) wood
                (B.FR 34000)

ARDEN, Henri (19th C) Belgian
£2085 $4107   (6-Oct-90 KV.L10/R) Departing fishing boats (70x100cm-28x39in) s.
                (B.FR 130000)

ARDISSONE, Yolande (20th C) ?
£684 $1300   (14-Sep-90 DM.D2261) Jardin des Tuileries (66x91cm-26x36in) s.

ARDIZZONE, Edward (1900-1978) British
£3600 $6264   (27-Mar-91 S135/R) In the bar (36x44cm-14x17in)
£300 $522   (28-Mar-91 CSK12/R) Standing female nude (19x11cm-7x4in) init. pen
£400 $740   (4-Mar-91 PHB14) Promenade, reading room, beach and cricket match
                (38x27cm-15x11in) pen wash four sketches one sheet
£450 $833   (4-Mar-91 PHB16) Jellied eels (26x17cm-10x7in) pen W/C
£450 $783   (28-Mar-91 CSK14) Female nude with arms raised (17x11cm-7x4in) init.
                pencil
£500 $925   (4-Mar-91 PHB15) Lavender sellers (20x18cm-8x7in) i. pencil W/C
£600 $1014   (2-May-91 C20/R) Figures in pub garden (19x23cm-7x9in) pencil W/C pen
                wash
£800 $1480   (4-Mar-91 PHB11/R) Fairground scene (23x29cm-9x11in) init. pencil W/C
£900 $1521   (2-May-91 C21/R) Street corner conversation (13x15cm-5x6in) pencil pen
                W/C
£900 $1782   (29-Jan-91 PH56/R) At the local (15x24cm-6x9in) init. W/C over pen
£1000 $1740   (27-Mar-91 S136/R) The antique shop (35x50cm-14x20in) init. ink wash W/C
£1700 $2873   (2-May-91 C22/R) Boys, Blackheath (18x32cm-7x13in) init. pen brush W/C
£2500 $4225   (2-May-91 C23/R) Barristers in court (16x27cm-6x11in) init. pencil brush
                ink W/C

ARDON, Mordechai (1896-?) Israeli
£16582 $32500   (15-Feb-91 SY.NY128/R) Flight at dawn (65x93cm-26x37in) s.i.d.63
£46012 $75000   (12-Jun-91 GG.TA391/R) Talisman for vanishing hours (73x92cm-29x36in)
                s.d.1984 s.verso
£46012 $75000   (12-Jun-91 GG.TA393/R) Nocturne (81x65cm-32x26in) s.
£1840 $3000   (12-Jun-91 GG.TA394/R) Seated girl (25x12cm-10x5in) s. pen

ARELLANO, Juan de (1614-1676) Spanish
£152630 $264050   (21-May-91 EP.M7/R) Florero (66x51cm-26x20in) s. (S.P 28000000)
£413565 $785773   (28-Feb-91 EP.M5/R) Naturaleza muerta con flores y frutas
                (98x63cm-39x25in) s. (S.P 75000000)

ARELLANO, Juan de (circle) (1614-1676) Spanish
£1800 $3348   (4-Sep-90 OT360/R) Mixed flowers in delft vase on shelf
                (44x34cm-17x13in)
£5500 $9295   (18-Apr-91 CSK155/R) Mixed flowers in glass vae on ledge
                (76x104cm-30x41in) bears sig.

ARELLANO, Juan de (style) (1614-1676) Spanish
£2600 $4394   (18-Apr-91 CSK164/R) Still life of mixed flowers in glass vase with
                finch and funghi on ledge (39x29cm-15x11in)
£2800 $4564   (4-Jul-91 CSK160/R) Mixed flowers in basket with fungi (66x88cm-26x35in)
£3210 $6259   (10-Oct-90 APT.P455) Bouquet de fleurs (47x60cm-19x24in) (F.FR 32000)
£3500 $6825   (26-Oct-90 C46/R) Mixed flowers in a glass vase on a ledge
                (47x34cm-19x13in) canvas laid down on panel

AREN, Olof (1918-) Swedish
£1483 $2877   (4-Dec-90 BA.S14/R) View towards the old town (72x116cm-28x46in) s.
         (S.KR 16000)

ARENDS, Jan (1738-1805) Dutch
£1607 $2700   (17-Jul-91 SY.NY94 a/R) Figures by an ornamental pond with manor house
         beyond (33x44cm-13x17in) s.d.1769
£2956   *$5676*   *(27-Nov-90 APT.P197/R) Personnages dans un parc (16x29cm-6x11in)*
         s.d.1771 pen wash (F.FR 29000)

ARENDSEN, Arentina Hendrica (1836-1915) Dutch
£1198 $2084   (26-Mar-91 VN.R4) Still life of fruit on marble table (43x38cm-17x15in)
         s. (D.FL 4000)

ARENZ, Max (19/20th C) German
£1531 $2464   (26-Jun-91 KM.K1380/R) Young woman playing with three children by fire
         place (27x32cm-11x13in) s. panel (DM 4500)

ARESSY, P (19th C) French
£637 $1243   (24-Oct-90 GD.B96/R) Village stream with mill (33x24cm-13x9in) s.d.91
         panel (S.FR 1600)

ARETUSI, Pellegrino (studio) (c.1460-1523) Italian
£15778 $28243   (8-Apr-91 CH.R179/R) Annunciazione. Visitazione. Adorazione del Bimbo.
         Circoncisione. Disputanel tempio (57x153cm-22x60in) panel
         (I.L 35000000)

ARGENT, J F (fl.1885) British
£2600 $4888   (8-Aug-90 PHP119/R) Racing yachts off the Needles, Isle of Wight
         (31x47cm-12x19in) s.d.1882 board pair

ARGILES, Ramon (20th C) Spanish
£1100   *$2200*   *(6-Feb-91 ANS.M171/R) Las tres gracias (31x21cm-12x8in) s. ink W/C dr*
         (S.P 200000)

ARIAS, Francisco (1912-1977) Spanish
£1358 $2186   (27-Jun-91 EP.M79/R) Paisaje castellano con pueblo (46x65cm-18x26in) s.
         (S.P 250000)

ARICO, Rodolfo (1930-) Italian
£1742 $2857   (19-Jun-91 F.M220/R) Composizione (130x130cm-51x51in) s.d.1960
         (I.L 3800000)

ARIKHA, Avigdor (1929-) ?
£9948 $19000   (1-Jan-91 GG.TA230/R) David playing the harp before Saul
         (92x73cm-36x29in) s.d.1955/56
£524   *$1000*   *(1-Jan-91 GG.TA233/R) Portrait (16x23cm-6x9in) s.d.1966 ink*
£995   *$1900*   *(1-Jan-91 GG.TA232/R) Jerusalem (15x22cm-6x9in) s.d.1967 ink*
£1152   *$2200*   *(1-Jan-91 GG.TA231/R) Untitled (24x18cm-9x7in) s.i.d.1964 gouache*

ARIOLA, Fortunato (1827-1872) American?
£1744 $3000   (15-May-91 SY.NY6/R) Shipwreck in Artic (30x51cm-12x20in) s.d.1862

ARIS, Fred (20th C) British
£800 $1504   (20-Sep-90 CSK188/R) Boy and black horse (56x39cm-22x15in) s.
         st.d.1975verso masonite
£1000 $1880   (20-Sep-90 CSK187/R) Allegory of youth (53x41cm-21x16in) s.
         st.d.1976verso masonite

ARIZZI (20th C) ?
£1159   *$2261*   *(28-Oct-90 R.P105/R) Le virgil de la nuit (97x130cm-38x51in) s. mixed*
         media canvas (F.FR 11500)

ARK (19th C) ?
£3963 $7768   (6-Nov-90 SY.AM201/R) Celebrating vintage (62x80cm-24x31in) s.i.
         (D.FL 13000)

ARKHIPOV, Sergei (1897-?) Russian
£630 $1260   (10-Feb-91 YC.P17) Une gitane (87x61cm-34x24in) (F.FR 6200)

ARKLEY, Howard (20th C) Australian?
£841 $1371   (16-Jun-91 SY.ME88) Bodgie (204x79cm-80x31in) s.d.79 verso acrylic
         canvas (A.D 1800)
£841 $1371   (16-Jun-91 SY.ME72) Printout II (90x122cm-35x48in) s.d.1980 verso
         acrylic canvas (A.D 1800)
£935 $1523   (16-Jun-91 SY.ME47) Arabesque (204x79cm-80x31in) s.d.79 verso acrylic
         canvas (A.D 2000)
£1357 $2294   (16-Apr-91 J.M180/R) Abstract (180x162cm-71x64in) s.d.'76 verso
         (A.D 3000)
£3037 $4951   (16-Jun-91 SY.ME5/R) Bungalow home (160x200cm-63x79in) s.d.87 verso
         acrylic canvas (A.D 6500)

ARKWRIGHT, Edith (fl.1884) British
£5000 $9750   (15-Jan-91 C67/R) Little girl with black labrador, toy terrier, bichon
         frise and puppy (128x88cm-50x35in) init.

54

ARLAUD, J A (1668-1746) Swiss
£1100 $1947   *(19-Mar-91 CSK63/R) Portrait of gentleman in embroidered cloak (7x?cm-3x?in) min. vellum on copper chased floral frame oval*

ARLAUD, Jacques Antoine (1668-1746) Swiss
£600 $990   *(10-Jul-91 C190) Prince Charles Edward Stuart (5x?cm-2x?in) min. vellum gilt mount fishskin case oval*
£1200 $1980   *(10-Jul-91 C186) Prince James Francis Edward Stuart (3x?cm-1x?in) min. vellum gold frame spiral cresting oval*

ARLAUD-JURINE, Louis Ami (1751-1829) Swiss
£2400 $3960   *(11-Jul-91 S289/R) Portrait of young girl clutching doll in arms that rest on table (8x?cm-3x?in) min.s. gilt wood composition frame oval*

ARLINGSSON, Erling (1904-1982) Swedish
£743 $1331   *(9-Apr-91 GO.G161) Nude bather and flamingoes (41x70cm-16x28in) init. (S.KR 8000)*
£1226 $2122   *(22-May-91 BA.S288/R) Sailingboats near the quay (46x55cm-18x22in) init. (S.KR 13000)*
£1321 $2285   *(22-May-91 BA.S287/R) Boats near fishing village (55x62cm-22x24in) init. (S.KR 14000)*
£1509 $2611   *(22-May-91 BA.S286/R) Steamboats in harbour (46x61cm-18x24in) init. panel (S.KR 16000)*
£1737 $2953   *(28-May-91 AB.S5319/R) Cargo ship in the strait (49x60cm-19x24in) s. i.d.1978verso (S.KR 18500)*
£2045 $3660   *(9-Apr-91 GO.G163/R) Landscape from Mangskog (60x70cm-24x28in) init. (S.KR 22000)*
£2285 $4479   *(20-Nov-90 GO.G303) Still life of flowers in jug (66x54cm-26x21in) init. panel (S.KR 25000)*
£2453 $4243   *(22-May-91 BA.S285/R) View of Gothenburg's harbour (50x70cm-20x28in) init. panel (S.KR 26000)*
£455 $815   *(9-Apr-91 GO.G243) Lomans Per - landscape with musician (62x50cm-24x20in) init. gouache (S.KR 4900)*
£472 $816   *(22-May-91 BA.S290/R) Walking in the park (23x30cm-9x12in) s. W/C (S.KR 5000)*
£802 $1387   *(22-May-91 BA.S289/R) 'Lomjansgutten' (50x45cm-20x18in) init. gouache (S.KR 8500)*

ARMAN (1928-) Spanish
£1104 $1778   *(24-Jun-91 BL.P41) Sans titre (108x75cm-43x30in) s.d.1959 paper laid down on canvas (F.FR 11000)*
£1850 $3200   *(7-May-91 CE.NY301/R) Untitled (35x33cm-14x13in) s.verso acrylic silkscreened canvas*
£5418 $10457   *(13-Dec-90 SY.AM120/R) Brushes (128x95cm-50x37in) s.overlap oil foam canvas (D.FL 17500)*
£40000 $66800   *(6-Jun-91 CJ.N7/R) Brosses et peinture (200x270cm-79x106in) (F.FR 400000)*
£560 $969   *(10-May-91 S.Z2/R) La lune au rodage (27x21cm-11x8in) s.d.1959 gouache paper on canvas (S.FR 1400)*
£1224 $2400   *(6-Nov-90 CE.NY31/R) Untitled (32x224cm-13x88in) s.i.d.1963 paper collage*
£2806 $5500   *(12-Feb-91 SY.NY433) Untitled (107x74cm-42x29in) s.d.60 W/C oil*
£6932 $13378   *(16-Dec-90 GL.P131/R) Accumulation de tubes de peinture dans une plaque de plexiglas (100x100cm-39x39in) s. (F.FR 68000)*
£12000 $23400   *(18-Oct-90 C428/R) Untitled (136x90cm-54x35in) s. paint brushes oil canvas on board*
£44000 $85360   *(6-Dec-90 C532/R) Gipsy variation (77x64cm-30x25in) s.d.1962 smashed violin with bow painted board*

ARMAN, Fernandez (1928-) Spanish
£2953 $5818   *(31-Oct-90 ZZ.F44/R) Composition abstraite (35x22cm-14x9in) s. hardboard panel (F.FR 29000)*
£3707 $7192   *(4-Dec-90 BA.S21/R) Pistols (107x72cm-42x28in) s. paper on canvas (S.KR 40000)*
£1645 $2714   *(10-Jul-91 FB.P131/R) Colere de lunettes (34x24cm-13x9in) s. broken glasses oil wood (F.FR 16500)*
£1912 $3289   *(14-May-91 GF.L2224/R) Angels (75x108cm-30x43in) s.i. bronze oil panel (S.FR 4800)*
£8163 $16082   *(15-Nov-90 I.N116/R) Rythmes et couleurs (126x96cm-50x38in) gouache paste paper material (F.FR 80000)*

ARMAND-DUMARESQ, Edouard Charles (1826-1895) French
£2000 $3440   *(17-May-91 C17 g/R) Tricky manoeuvre (66x54cm-26x21in) s. oval*
£2500 $4300   *(17-May-91 C17 f/R) Uninvited guests (66x54cm-26x21in) s. oval*

ARMANDO (?) ?
£3003 $5195   *(22-May-91 CH.AM639/R) Waldrand (50x39cm-20x15in) dyptich (D.FL 10000)*
£5263 $10158   *(12-Dec-90 CH.AM355/R) Innenstadt (100x80cm-39x31in) s.d.1983 verso s.i.d.stretcher (D.FL 17000)*
£601 $1039   *(22-May-91 CH.AM739) Three lines (71x99cm-28x39in) s.d.71 pencil (D.FL 2000)*
£1441 $2494   *(23-May-91 SY.AM286/R) Untitled (48x63cm-19x25in) s.d.53 gouache ink (D.FL 4800)*

ARMANET, Francois (20th C) French
£1535 $2716   *(7-Apr-91 I.N16/R) La terrasse (54x81cm-21x32in) s. (F.FR 15500)*

ARMANI, Ernesto Giuliano (1898-) Italian
£466 $833   (12-Mar-91 C.A7) St Peter's in Rome (56x65cm-22x26in) s. W/C
                    (B.FR 28000)

ARMENISE, Raffaello (1852-1925) Italian
£6000 $11520   (27-Nov-90 PH205/R) Musical entertainment (69x101cm-27x40in) s.
£8943 $16008   (12-Mar-91 F.M64/R) Buontemponi all'osteria (69x100cm-27x39in) s.
                    (I.L 19500000)

ARMESTO, Alvarez Primitivo (19th C) Spanish
£700 $1372   (19-Nov-90 SWS477) Outside the harbour (61x81cm-24x32in) s.

ARMFIELD, Diana (1920-) British
£1900 $3306   (27-Mar-91 S105/R) Roses, La Reine Victoria (28x20cm-11x8in) init.
                    s.i.verso board

ARMFIELD, Edward (?) British
£502 $929   (6-Mar-91 APT.P69) Chiens devant l'atre (70x90cm-28x35in) s. (F.FR 5000)
£600 $1170   (15-Jan-91 B152/R) Terriers ratting in barn (41x61cm-16x24in) s.
£700 $1365   (15-Jan-91 C116/R) Spaniels in game larder (61x51cm-24x20in) s.
£800 $1560   (15-Jan-91 B383) Terriers ratting in barn (60cm-24ins circular)
£880 $1654   (10-Aug-90 PHM92) Terriers ratting in stable, horse looking on
                    (51x61cm-20x24in)
£900 $1755   (15-Jan-91 C113/R) English setter and gordon setter with retriever
                    (23x30cm-9x12in) s.
£1004 $1968   (11-Feb-91 SY.J365/R) After the hunt (90x70cm-35x28in) s. (SA.R 5000)
£1500 $2820   (18-Sep-90 SWS657) Terriers by a rabbit hole (24x34cm-9x13in) s. pair
£1800 $3510   (15-Jan-91 B380) Terriers ratting in interior (43x53cm-17x21in) s. pair

ARMFIELD, Edward (attrib) (?) British
£600 $1014   (3-May-91 PHE63) Terriers ratting (50cm-20ins circular)

ARMFIELD, Edwin (?) British?
£1047 $1800   (18-May-91 W.W68/R) Fox and quail (61x94cm-24x37in) s.

ARMFIELD, G (fl.1840-1875) British
£740 $1436   (3-Dec-90 TAY594) Portrait of springer spaniel with pheasant by his side
                    (25x33cm-10x13in) d.1861
£833 $1642   (30-Oct-90 MA.V562) Terriers rounding on possum (30x51cm-12x20in) s.
                    (C.D 1900)

ARMFIELD, George (fl.1840-1875) British
£751 $1300   (21-May-91 CE.NY156/R) Hunting dogs in landscape (30x41cm-12x16in)
                    s.d.1863
£780 $1381   (21-Mar-91 CSK214/R) A terrier at a rabbit hole (25x30cm-10x12in) s.
£860 $1720   (8-Feb-91 T70/R) Spaniels and terriers (41x61cm-16x24in) s. pair
£888 $1500   (20-Apr-91 WOL.C75/R) Three dogs ratting (23x30cm-9x12in) s.
£1000 $1890   (26-Sep-90 S102/R) Danger approaches (46x61cm-18x24in) s.
£1000 $1720   (15-May-91 ZZ.B150 a) Caught (43x53cm-17x21in) s.
£1017 $1800   (24-Mar-91 LIT.L50) Three dogs in a room with fire place
                    (18x25cm-7x10in) s.
£1100 $2123   (12-Dec-90 SWS2120) Spaniels putting up mallard in landscape
                    (24x29cm-9x11in)
£1150 $2220   (12-Dec-90 SWS2186/R) Having feast (69x89cm-27x35in) s.
£1316 $2500   (27-Feb-91 SY.NY252/R) Two spaniels flushing out duck (25x36cm-10x14in)
                    s.d.
£1418 $2312   (13-Jun-91 RAS.V508/R) Wooded landscape with dog chasing pheasant
                    (46x62cm-18x24in) s. (D.KR 16000)
£1500 $2445   (4-Jul-91 PHI194/R) Guarding the bag (76x127cm-30x50in) s.
£2200 $4158   (26-Sep-90 S109/R) Otter hunt - at fault (76x127cm-30x50in) s. i.verso
£2700 $5319   (13-Nov-90 SWS266/R) Rabbiting. Ratting (29cm-11ins circular) both bears
                    sig. pair round
£4000 $7800   (15-Jan-91 C76/R) Blenheim Cavalier King Charles spaniel and terrier in
                    barn (46x61cm-18x24in) s.d.1885

ARMFIELD, George (after) (fl.1840-1875) British
£1050 $1775   (29-Apr-91 HS281/R) Woodland landscape with spaniels and dead game
                    (70x90cm-28x35in)

ARMFIELD, George (attrib) (fl.1840-1875) British
£550 $946   (15-May-91 BT196) Spaniels putting up duck (18x23cm-7x9in) copper
£1127 $1915   (28-May-91 AB.S4730/R) Terriers hunting rabbit (32x33cm-13x13in) s.
                    painted circle (S.KR 12000)

ARMIN, Emil (1883-1971) American
£459 $900   (16-Feb-91 W.W119/R) Houses and street (36x46cm-14x18in) s.d.1934 W/C

ARMINGTON, Frank Milton (1876-1941) Canadian
£1778 $3449   (3-Dec-90 R.T362/R) Rue du Foin, Bruges (33x52cm-13x20in) s.d.1908
                    millboard (C.D 4000)

ARMITAGE, Alfred (19th C) British
£2000 $3780   (27-Sep-90 L101 c) The country gossip (76x61cm-30x24in) s.

ARMITAGE, David (20th C) ?
£619 $1045   (17-Apr-91 DS.W96) Study for Weddes Voyage (178x240cm-70x94in) s.d.1971
                   acrylic (NZ.D 1800)

ARMITAGE, Thomas Liddall (attrib) (fl.1885-1891) British
£1800 $3402   (26-Sep-90 S124/R) Children catching sticklebacks (55x76cm-22x30in)
                   mono.d.89

ARMLEDER, John M (20th C) Swiss
*£2114 $4080   (15-Dec-90 S.Z8) Untitled (90x62cm-35x24in) s.d.1988 indian ink
                   (S.FR 5200)*

ARMOUR, George Denholm (1864-1949) British
£950 $1606   (2-May-91 CG487/R) Monkeys and flowers (30x27cm-12x11in) s.
                   indist.s.i.verso canvas on board
£6200 $10788   (26-Mar-91 PH45/R) Study of a lion and lioness (61x105cm-24x41in) s.
£1600 $3024   (25-Sep-90 H476/R) Safety first - fox breaking cover (30x41cm-12x16in)
                   s. W/C cloth
£2800 $5516   (1-Nov-90 B116/R) The hunt (43x33cm-17x13in) s. W/C linen
£3800 $7030   (7-Mar-91 C18/R) Saving a goal (26x34cm-10x13in) s. W/C bodycol linen

ARMOUR, Mary (1902-) British
£650 $1099   (3-May-91 PHE84) Still life of basket of fruit (30x50cm-12x20in) s.d.73
£2300 $4462   (5-Dec-90 PHE49/R) Flowers with iris (30x25cm-12x10in) s.d.'88 board
£3800 $7106   (28-Aug-90 S1077/R) Pear on plate (30x25cm-12x10in) s.d.1983 board
£4000 $7480   (28-Aug-90 S1096/R) Spring flowers with crocus (23x32cm-9x13in) s.d.1954
                   board
£5000 $9700   (5-Dec-90 PHE83/R) Autumn flowers (92x73cm-36x29in) s.d.1944
£5500 $9295   (3-May-91 PHE121/R) Still life of peonies (53x43cm-21x17in) s.d.64
£9249 $16000   (7-May-91 CE.NY63/R) Autumn flowers (43x56cm-17x22in) s.d.1944
£9300 $18321   (1-Nov-90 B124/R) Bouquet (58x70cm-23x28in) s.d.60 board
£10500 $19635   (28-Aug-90 S1070/R) Flowers with yellow lily (51x61cm-20x24in) s.d.1987
£22000 $44000   (5-Feb-91 S203/R) Bouquet (59x70cm-23x28in) s.d.60 board
£33000 $61710   (28-Aug-90 S1083/R) Blue still life with anemones (74x59cm-29x23in)
                   s.d.1979
*£1050 $1775   (17-Apr-91 CG1/R) Olive groves in Italy (25x28cm-10x11in) s.d.62 pastel
£1900 $3363   (22-Mar-91 PHE77) Flowers with petunas (45x59cm-18x23in) s.d.69 W/C*

ARMOUR, William (1903-1979) British
£800 $1344   (23-Apr-91 S225/R) Glen Lonan, Oban (49x61cm-19x24in) s. W/C bodycol

ARMSTEAD, Henry Hugh (1828-1905) British
£4000 $7680   (29-Nov-90 B74/R) The racehorses Charles XII and Euclid with jockeys up
                   (33x43cm-13x17in) s.

ARMSTRONG, Arthur (?) British
£787 $1519   (12-Dec-90 CH.E179) Twin beaches, evening (61x76cm-24x30in) s. i.verso
                   board (E.P 850)
£1200 $2340   (26-Oct-90 CG83) Field patterns (76x91cm-30x36in) s. board

ARMSTRONG, Geoffrey (20th C) South African?
£670 $1139   (27-May-91 HO.ED29/R) Up to the glacier, Auyuittuq National Park, Baffin
                   Island (91x122cm-36x48in) s. s.i.d.verso acrylic (C.D 1300)

ARMSTRONG, Ian (1923-) Australian
£618 $1217   (13-Nov-90 J.M876) Picnic races at Hanging Rock (75x90cm-30x35in) s.d.70
                   (A.D 1600)

ARMSTRONG, John (1893-1973) British
£1300 $2132   (20-Jun-91 DLY633/R) Universe (18x58cm-7x23in) tempera board
£2200 $4070   (8-Mar-91 C127/R) Composition with classical ewer (49x59cm-19x23in)
                   s.d.55
£2900 $5684   (8-Nov-90 DLY639/R) Thorn and feed (33x46cm-13x18in) s.d.58 board
£3000 $5070   (2-May-91 C152/R) Figure and wild plants on hillside (63x50cm-25x20in)
                   init. board
£3100 $5084   (20-Jun-91 DLY646/R) Classical nude (51x74cm-20x29in) init.
£3800 $6232   (20-Jun-91 DLY634/R) Mother and child afloat (61x61cm-24x24in) init.
£6500 $11310   (27-Mar-91 S143/R) Surreal landscape (56x74cm-22x29in) init.d.48 tempera
                   board
£6800 $12580   (8-Mar-91 C131/R) Harlequin (37x19cm-15x7in) init.d.49 tempera panel
£7400 $12136   (20-Jun-91 DLY645/R) Surreal landscape (76x64cm-30x25in) init.
£11000 $20350   (8-Mar-91 C129/R) The battle of nothing (37x57cm-15x22in) init.d.49
                   tempera board

ARMSTRONG, William (19th C?) ?
*£455 $782   (14-May-91 JOY.T93/R) Red Rock, Nipigon (19x31cm-7x12in) s.d.'04 W/C
                   (C.D 900)
£556 $956   (14-May-91 JOY.T2/R) Dog train, White Horse Plains, Red river
                   (20x31cm-8x12in) s.d.1902 W/C (C.D 1100)
£859 $1485   (6-May-91 SY.T170/R) Indian guides and travellers canoeing in river
                   gorge (10x20cm-4x8in) d.c.1880 verso W/C (C.D 1700)
£1136 $1966   (6-May-91 SY.T15) Storm off Toronto Bay, Lake Ontario (24x37cm-9x15in)
                   s.d.70 W/C (C.D 2250)
£2632 $5158   (20-Nov-90 JOY.T95/R) Sailboats on lake near settlement
                   (30x81cm-12x32in) s.d.72 W/C (C.D 6000)*

ARNAL, Andre Pierre (1938-) French
£2823 $5504 (26-Oct-90 CC.P47/R) Toile libre (214x216cm-84x85in) s.d.1973 verso
water paint glycerol canvas (F.FR 28000)

ARNAL, Francois (1924-) French
£503 $899 (11-Mar-91 GL.P226) Composition a fond bleu (60x74cm-24x29in) s.
(F.FR 5000)
£1690 $2856 (15-Apr-91 CC.P133) La pancarte rouge indien (60x60cm-24x24in) s.d.1984
i. verso acrylic (F.FR 17000)
£1994 $3290 (10-Jul-91 FB.P65/R) Se fair du bien (81x100cm-32x39in) s. i.d.11/60
verso (F.FR 20000)
£3021 $4924 (16-Jun-91 CC.P34/R) Target XIII (107x121cm-42x48in) s.d.1962 i. verso
(F.FR 30000)
£3021 $4924 (16-Jun-91 CC.P47/R) L'injustice de Chine (131x196cm-52x77in) s.d.1985
i. verso acrylic (F.FR 30000)
£3041 $5017 (10-Jul-91 FB.P85/R) Moby Dick 2 (46x55cm-18x22in) s.d.56 i. verso
(F.FR 30500)
£4637 $9042 (28-Oct-90 M.V110/R) Un jardin noir dans lile (73x60cm-29x24in) s.
(F.FR 46000)
£5528 $9894 (15-Mar-91 FB.P42/R) Composition (65x65cm-26x26in) s.d.48 (F.FR 55000)
£18145 $35383 (28-Oct-90 GL.P72/R) Analogie IV et V (161x260cm-63x102in) s. d.1964
verso (F.FR 180000)

ARNAUD, Marcel (?) French
£2574 $4556 (7-Apr-91 I.N17/R) La montagne Saint-Victoire (23x35cm-9x14in) studio
st. verso panel (F.FR 26000)

ARNAUTOFF, Victor Mikhail (1896-1979) American
£8205 $16000 (10-Oct-90 B.SF652/R) Fisherman (86x63cm-34x25in) s. board

ARNAVIELLE, Jean (1881-1961) French
£594 $1051 (7-Apr-91 LT.P177) Vue des hauteurs de Rouen (50x108cm-20x43in) s.
(F.FR 6000)

ARNDT, Franz Gustav (1842-1905) German
£1300 $2548 (14-Feb-91 CSK81/R) A rest on the hillside (71x89cm-28x35in) s.
£2007 $3391 (17-Apr-91 WE.MU107/R) Summer day near Thuringia town (72x91cm-28x36in)
s. (DM 6000)

ARNEGGER, A (1883-1916) German
£751 $1412 (21-Sep-90 N.M3134/R) Winter landscape with Alpine glow
(70x100cm-28x39in) s.i. (DM 2200)
£890 $1594 (14-Mar-91 N.M2629/R) Winter landscape at sunset with view of Jungfrau
mountains (60x80cm-24x31in) s. (DM 2600)
£1365 $2567 (21-Sep-90 N.M3135/R) View of Kitzbuhel covered in snow with Alpine glow
(70x100cm-28x39in) s. (DM 4000)

ARNEGGER, Alois (1879-1967) Austrian
£500 $1000 (6-Feb-91 D.NY7) Sun setting over an Alpine village (69x99cm-27x39in) s.
£510 $821 (28-Jun-91 BM.B766/R) Snow covered wooded landscape in high mountains
(60x80cm-24x31in) s. (DM 1500)
£532 $1000 (22-Sep-90 WOL.C416/R) Mediterranean coastal scene (61x91cm-24x36in) s.
panel
£600 $1074 (12-Mar-91 PH15/R) The Hochkonig mountain bathed in winter sunshine and
chalet below (51x76cm-20x30in) s. i.verso
£650 $1274 (8-Nov-90 PHI200) Evening in the Austrian Alps (57x88cm-22x35in) s.
£689 $1157 (23-Apr-91 SY.AM16/R) Village in mountains in winter (57x89cm-22x35in)
s. (D.FL 2300)
£854 $1529 (11-Apr-91 D.V228/R) Moonlit wooded river landscape with bathers
(75x100cm-30x39in) s.d.1924 (A.S 18000)
£956 $1873 (24-Nov-90 SA.A623/R) View of Capri (46x101cm-18x40in) s. (DM 2800)
£960 $1651 (16-May-91 D.V9/R) Woman collecting faggot in autumnal woods
(74x100cm-29x39in) s. (A.S 20000)
£970 $1823 (20-Sep-90 D.V160/R) Autumnal wood (70x100cm-28x39in) s. (A.S 20000)
£1000 $1720 (14-May-91 SWS438/R) Winter evening (58x78cm-23x31in) s.
£1143 $2251 (16-Nov-90 EA.Z242) Lake Como (90x128cm-35x50in) s. (S.FR 2800)
£1193 $2350 (13-Nov-90 AB.S847/R) Summer landscape with field of flowers
(74x108cm-29x43in) s. (S.KR 13000)
£1300 $2184 (18-Jul-91 CSK197/R) View of Capri with Marina Piccola (59x78cm-23x31in)
s.
£2433 $4769 (24-Jan-91 D.V124/R) Wood clearing (74x100cm-29x39in) s. (A.S 50000)
£2485 $4821 (6-Dec-90 D.V96/R) View of Kitzbuhel (80x115cm-31x45in) s. (A.S 50000)
£3154 $5961 (27-Sep-90 D.V146/R) Southern coastal town (56x76cm-22x30in) s.
(A.S 65000)

ARNEGGER, Alwin (1883-1916) German
£2140 $4194 (24-Nov-90 HOR.H1/R) Autumn day by the brook (74x100cm-29x39in) s.
(F.M 15000)
£3231 $5202 (28-Jun-91 BM.B767/R) View of Capri (60x80cm-24x31in) s. (DM 9500)

ARNEGGER, Gottfried (1905-) Austrian
£711 $1380 (4-Dec-90 R.T173/R) Mediterranean village on coast (60x79cm-24x31in) s.
(C.D 1600)
£4392 $8564 (26-Oct-90 BM.B948/R) Coastal view of Sorrent (69x101cm-27x40in) s.
(DM 13000)

ARNESEN, Vilhelm (1865-1948) Danish
£511	$853	(6-Jun-91 RAS.K6) Copenhagen harbour (28x45cm-11x18in) s.d.1904 (D.KR 5800)
£546	$917	(23-Apr-91 RAS.K256) Fishingvessel and steamship in Kattegat (53x75cm-21x30in) s.d.1920 (D.KR 6200)
£718	$1415	(14-Nov-90 RAS.K265) Yacht racing at Oresund (66x95cm-26x37in) i.verso (D.KR 8000)
£808	$1592	(14-Nov-90 RAS.K264) Seascape with sailship in rough seas (67x99cm-26x39in) s.d.1908 (D.KR 9000)
£865	$1678	(22-Aug-90 RAS.K132/R) Sailing dinghy off Copenhagen harbour (78x51cm-31x20in) s.d.87 (D.KR 10000)
£1674	$3130	(29-Aug-90 KH.K7/R) Nyhavn seen from Gronlands Handelsplads, Copenhagen (47x76cm-19x30in) s.d.1918 (D.KR 19000)
£2289	$3845	(23-Apr-91 RAS.K324/R) Niels Juel's victory of Sweden, battle at sea 1676 (51x76cm-20x30in) s.d.1903 (D.KR 26000)
£6000	$11700	(18-Oct-90 CSK97/R) Danish barque 'Peter Tordenskjold' unloading cargo in Aberdeen Harbour (44x68cm-17x27in) s.d.86
£15000	$25500	(30-May-91 C158/R) Farewell to king - King Haakon VII going to assume Throne of Norway (42x68cm-17x27in) s.d.1905 indist.i.stretcher

ARNHARD-DEININGER, Gabriele (1855-?) German
£685	$1226	(12-Mar-91 FN.S2271/R) Mountain landscape with figures before hut, evening (50x89cm-20x35in) s.d.1891 (DM 2000)

ARNO, Peter (1904-1968) American
£1176	$2000	(1-Jun-91 IH.NY112/R) Well, if you ever need us again, just give a ring, firemen leaving (38x28cm-15x11in) s. brush ink

ARNOLD (?) ?
£38000	$64220	(18-Apr-91 C170/R) Still life of viol, lute, violin, recorder, harpischord and other objects (109x183cm-43x72in) s.i.

ARNOLD, Carl Johann (1829-1916) German
£6316	$12000	(28-Feb-91 CH.NY83/R) Best friends (107x79cm-42x31in) s.

ARNOLD, Christian (1889-?) German
£546	$1070	(24-Nov-90 KM.K400/R) Female nude reclining on divan (33x52cm-13x20in) mono. W/C (DM 1600)
£608	$1186	(26-Oct-90 BM.B608/R) Houses on the dyke (40x59cm-16x23in) mono. mixed media (DM 1800)
£625	$1219	(26-Oct-90 BM.B609/R) Spring (41x29cm-16x11in) mono.i.d.1926/27 chl (DM 1850)
£822	$1340	(15-Jun-91 L.K16/R) Dusk, Odenwald (39x54cm-15x21in) mono.d.1946 W/C (DM 2400)
£959	$1563	(15-Jun-91 L.K15/R) Town with church tower. North German wooded landscape (49x34cm-19x13in) W/C tempera double-sided (DM 2800)
£1027	$1675	(15-Jun-91 L.K14/R) Vor der Schranke (49x40cm-19x16in) mono. W/C (DM 3000)

ARNOLD, H (?) ?
£520	$853	(20-Jun-91 B2) Alchemist (56x70cm-22x28in) s.

ARNOLD, Josef (elder) (1788-1879) Austrian
£1346	$2625	(25-Oct-90 D.V143/R) Young woman with child by rock (23x31cm-9x12in) i.d.1837verso (A.S 28000)

ARNOLD, Reginald Ernest (1853-1938) British
£1397	$2500	(16-Mar-91 W.W55/R) Skating along a canal (48x74cm-19x29in) s.

ARNOLDI, Per (1941-) Danish
£716	$1403	(13-Feb-91 KH.K7) Composition with black background (150x180cm-59x71in) (D.KR 8000)
£716	$1403	(13-Feb-91 KH.K6) Composition with blue background (150x180cm-59x71in) (D.KR 8000)

ARNOTT, James George McLellan (fl.1880-1902) British
£950	$1568	(11-Jul-91 CSK100) Woodland fairy surrounded by goldfinches (165x114cm-65x45in) s.d.1899

ARNOUX, Michel (1833-1877) French
£714	$1400	(7-Nov-90 D.NY4) Family gathered around the table (46x36cm-18x14in) s. panel

ARNSBURG-RAIN, Sofie Maria (1853-1940) Austrian
£525	$1024	(11-Oct-90 D.V166/R) View of Hofgastein (22x30cm-9x12in) s. i.d.1918verso W/C (A.S 11000)

ARNTZENIUS, Floris (1864-1925) Dutch
£1818	$3582	(30-Oct-90 CH.AM302) White roses and wilted leaves in dark glass vase (58x40cm-23x16in) s. (D.FL 6000)
£610	$1171	(27-Nov-90 SY.AM3561/R) Figures in street (15x12cm-6x5in) pastel chk (D.FL 2000)
£3333	$6567	(30-Oct-90 CH.AM518/R) Figures in crowded, rainy street (14x20cm-6x8in) s. black chk W/C bodycol (D.FL 11000)

59

ARNTZENIUS, P (1883-1965) Dutch
£579 $1101 (26-Feb-91 VN.R7) On the canal (33x48cm-13x19in) panel (D.FL 1900)

AROCH, Arieh (?) Israeli
£3988 $6500 (12-Jun-91 GG.TA395/R) Figure (15x41cm-6x16in) s. panda pencil
£5236 $10000 (1-Jan-91 GG.TA229/R) Painting (24x31cm-9x12in) init. panda pencil mixed media

AROE, J A (1803-1870) Danish
£1038 $2014 (22-Aug-90 RAS.K577 a/R) Godthaab colony, Greenland (22x33cm-9x13in) s. W/C (D.KR 12000)

AROSENIUS, Ivar (1878-1919) Swedish
£535 $910 (28-May-91 AB.S4600/R) The Godlen Calf (13x20cm-5x8in) s.d.06 pencil htd white (S.KR 5700)
£686 $1338 (21-Oct-90 BU.M659) See how they love me (16x17cm-6x7in) s.d.07 Indian ink htd white (S.KR 7500)
£790 $1414 (9-Apr-91 GO.G197) Mouring is better that laughing, sorrow improves the soul (14x14cm-6x6in) init.199 (S.KR 8500)
£1116 $2076 (9-Sep-90 BU.M582) From the Garden of Eden (17x21cm-7x8in) mono.d.06 Indian ink htd white (S.KR 12000)
£4401 $7569 (14-May-91 BU.S2/R) Brothel (15x20cm-6x8in) s.d.1905 W/C htd white (S.KR 47000)

ARP, Carl (1867-?) German
£1356 $2264 (5-Jun-91 DO.H2481/R) Schonberger Strand, Baltic Sea (49x76cm-19x30in) s.d.1910 (DM 4000)

ARP, Jean (1887-1966) French
£13761 $26422 (26-Nov-90 FB.P68/R) Mirage d'une voix (34x29cm-13x11in) s. verso wood (F.FR 135000)
£18349 $35229 (26-Nov-90 FB.P66/R) Sans titre (36x45cm-14x18in) s. verso board wood double-sided (F.FR 180000)
£23220 $44814 (12-Dec-90 CH.AM353/R) Presque vase et fleur (66x59cm-26x23in) s.verso on pavatex (D.FL 75000)
£27919 $55000 (3-Oct-90 SY.NY148/R) Interregne (71x53cm-28x21in) s.verso board
£30120 $50602 (24-Apr-91 G.Z41) Composition in yellow and blue (49x52cm-19x20in) s.verso board (S.FR 75000)
£55000 $106700 (5-Dec-90 S181/R) Untitled - three navel man (89x72cm-35x28in) s.verso cut-out board
£60000 $117000 (17-Oct-90 G.Z18/R) Ronde vegetale (65x65cm-26x26in) s.i.d.1946verso (S.FR 150000)
£719 $1396 (7-Dec-90 GL.P207/R) Composition (25x18cm-10x7in) s. verso crayon (F.FR 7000)
£1848 $3567 (12-Dec-90 F.M54/R) Le forme (16x16cm-6x6in) d.1964 W/C (I.L 4000000)
£2518 $4104 (16-Jan-91 CC.P15) Sans titre (34x31cm-13x12in) bears i. verso W/C (F.FR 25000)
£2564 $5000 (10-Oct-90 SY.NY186/R) Untitled (28x20cm-11x8in) s. W/C pencil ink
£2619 $4295 (19-Jun-91 GK.B169) Shapes (29x21cm-11x8in) s. indian ink brush (S.FR 6600)
£2792 $5500 (3-Oct-90 SY.NY150/R) Collage 3 (50x70cm-20x28in) s. collage pen pencil
£2878 $5583 (7-Dec-90 GL.P202/R) Composition (22x17cm-9x7in) s. W/C collage crayon (F.FR 28000)
£3046 $6000 (3-Oct-90 SY.NY149/R) Le soleil recercle (38x37cm-15x15in) st.sig.verso collage on paperboard
£3767 $6140 (15-Jun-91 L.K17/R) Poupee (18x12cm-7x5in) s. collage paper on board (DM 11000)
£3953 $6838 (21-May-91 WK.M549/R) Composition (25x18cm-10x7in) s.verso pencil (DM 11700)
£4000 $7080 (20-Mar-91 S73/R) Projets de vitrail (28x24cm-11x9in) pencil gouache pair
£5556 $9111 (21-Jun-91 G.Z49/R) Composition (29x23cm-11x9in) s. mixed media collage (S.FR 14000)
£5653 $10966 (7-Dec-90 GL.P109/R) Composition (33x21cm-13x8in) s. i. verso lead pencil (F.FR 55000)
£6024 $10120 (24-Apr-91 G.Z77/R) Poupee (49x21cm-19x8in) s. W/C over chl paper collage (S.FR 15000)
£6500 $10465 (25-Jun-91 C257/R) Project pur une tour (66x49cm-26x19in) s.verso paper collage
£7712 $13265 (13-May-91 CH.R84/R) Papiers dechires (33x43cm-13x17in) s. W/C collage board (I.L 17000000)
£10194 $19572 (26-Nov-90 FB.P57/R) Le Siege de l'air (20x39cm-8x15in) s. verso engraved wood relief (F.FR 100000)
£11213 $21529 (26-Nov-90 FB.P70/R) Figure, fleur chute (27x21cm-11x8in) s. verso printing block (F.FR 110000)
£13252 $25443 (26-Nov-90 FB.P58/R) Selon les lois du hasrd (29x43cm-11x17in) s. verso relief natural wood (F.FR 130000)
£13252 $25443 (26-Nov-90 FB.P60/R) Geometrie de serpent (20x45cm-8x18in) s. verso relief natural wood (F.FR 130000)
£14271 $27401 (26-Nov-90 FB.P74/R) Tete a ligne sismique (34x29cm-13x11in) s. verso painted relief (F.FR 140000)
£14271 $27401 (26-Nov-90 FB.P72/R) Tension silencieuse (23x22cm-9x9in) s. verso printing block (F.FR 140000)
£14271 $27401 (26-Nov-90 FB.P62/R) Figure, fleur chute (26x21cm-10x8in) s. verso relief natural wood (F.FR 140000)

ARP, Jean (1887-1966) French-cont.

£15800	$30336	(26-Nov-90 FB.P61/R) Fragment d'une plate-bande (27x41cm-11x16in) s. verso relief natural wood (F.FR 155000)
£16310	$31315	(26-Nov-90 FB.P59/R) Configuration oppression (40x32cm-16x13in) s. verso relief natural wood (F.FR 160000)
£16310	$31315	(26-Nov-90 FB.P71/R) Configuration oppression (30x20cm-12x8in) s. verso printing block (F.FR 160000)
£16820	$32294	(26-Nov-90 FB.P67/R) Oben/Unten (17x24cm-7x9in) s. verso relief (F.FR 165000)
£18349	$35229	(26-Nov-90 FB.P73/R) Geometrie de serpent (27x44cm-11x17in) s. verso printing block (F.FR 180000)
£19878	$38165	(26-Nov-90 FB.P64/R) Constellatin geigy (50x38cm-20x15in) s. verso painted relief (F.FR 195000)
£20387	$39144	(26-Nov-90 FB.P77/R) Soleil recercle, bleu gris, 1966 (21x19cm-8x7in) s. verso printing block (F.FR 200000)
£20387	$39144	(26-Nov-90 FB.P78/R) Squelette d'ombre et fronde, 1958 (33x20cm-13x8in) s. verso printing block (F.FR 200000)
£20387	$39144	(26-Nov-90 FB.P76/R) Soleil recercle, 1966 (19x14cm-7x6in) s. verso printing block (F.FR 200000)
£20387	$39144	(26-Nov-90 FB.P69/R) Place selon les lois du Hasard (27x44cm-11x17in) s. verso printing block (F.FR 200000)
£20387	$39144	(26-Nov-90 FB.P63/R) Fleurs, nuages dans un cercle (18x18cm-7x7in) s. verso painted relief (F.FR 200000)
£23955	$45994	(26-Nov-90 FB.P65/R) Constellation fribourg (46x35cm-18x14in) s. verso painted relief (F.FR 235000)
£28542	$54801	(26-Nov-90 FB.P75/R) Cueillette, 1965 (35x25cm-14x10in) printing block (F.FR 280000)

ARPA Y PEREA, Jose (1862-1903) Spanish

£1086	$1749	(25-Jun-91 FER.M89) Selvatico jardin (26x35cm-10x14in) s. panel (S.P 200000)

ARPAD, Romek (1883-) Hungarian

£707	$1357	(18-Dec-90 DUR.M4) Bodegon trompe l'oeil (54x66cm-21x26in) (S.P 130000)

ARPS, Bernardus (1865-1938) Dutch

£788	$1552	(30-Oct-90 CH.AM192) Still life with pewter dish, flasco, lemons and chestnuts on plate (39x62cm-15x24in) s. (D.FL 2600)

ARREGUI, Romana (1875-1932) French

£1304	$2309	(3-Apr-91 ANS.M135/R) Las hermanas (34x46cm-13x18in) s. (S.P 240000)
£1630	$2624	(25-Jun-91 FER.M125/R) Tres ancianos (37x60cm-15x24in) s. (S.P 300000)

ARRIETA, Pedro de (17/18th C) Mexican

£15116	$26000	(15-May-91 CH.NY60/R) Virgen de Guadalupe (84x56cm-33x22in) s. oil gold paint

ARROYO Y LORENZO, Manuel (1854-1902) Spanish

£978	$1732	(3-Apr-91 ANS.M141/R) Ruinas de portada (46x22cm-18x9in) s. (S.P 180000)

ARROYO, Edouard (1937-) Spanish

£10628	$20830	(20-Nov-90 BG.P7/R) La Mujer del Minero (92x73cm-36x29in) s.d.1968 verso (F.FR 105000)
£25000	$40250	(27-Jun-91 S62/R) Parmi les peintres (116x89cm-46x35in) acrylic
£1508	$2698	(15-Mar-91 FB.P72 a/R) Tanger (40x51cm-16x20in) s.i.d.1985 mixed media collage (F.FR 15000)
£4286	$8443	(16-Nov-90 FB.P84/R) Brelan (33x27cm-13x11in) s.d.1984 W/C (F.FR 42000)
£5544	$10811	(27-Oct-90 BG.P3/R) La femme du mineur (58x79cm-23x31in) s.d.1970 oil crayon (F.FR 55000)
£6606	$13211	(5-Feb-91 CSC.P28/R) Les pyramides (74x116cm-29x46in) s.d.1974 gouache paper laid down on canvas (F.FR 65000)
£7724	$15447	(5-Feb-91 CSC.P29/R) Paysage d'Egypte (74x122cm-29x48in) s.d.1974 gouache paper laid down on canvas (F.FR 76000)

ARSENIUS, John (1818-1903) Swedish

£1379	$2702	(6-Nov-90 BA.S8/R) Horses grazing (20x32cm-8x13in) s. (S.KR 15000)

ARSON, Olimpe (1814-1870) French

£9548	$17090	(17-Mar-91 M.V135/R) Vase de fleurs pose sur un entablement (64x50cm-25x20in) s.i. W/C vellum (F.FR 95000)
£12060	$21588	(17-Mar-91 M.V134/R) Etude de cactee en fleurs (34x26cm-13x10in) s. W/C gouache vellum (F.FR 120000)

ARSTE, Karl (1899-1942) German

£709	$1383	(26-Oct-90 BM.B610/R) By the Wumme (47x64cm-19x25in) s.d.25 panel (DM 2100)

ARTAN, Louis (1837-1890) Belgian

£2629	$5127	(23-Oct-90 C.A16/R) Marine - Dunkirk (46x80cm-18x31in) s. (B.FR 160000)

ARTEMOFF, Georges (20th C) Russian

£1529	$2951	(15-Dec-90 D.P1/R) Jeune femme (56x44cm-22x17in) s. ink sanguine (F.FR 15000)
£1580	$3049	(15-Dec-90 D.P2/R) Jeune homme (56x34cm-22x13in) s. ink stomping (F.FR 15500)

ARTHURS, Stanley Massey (1877-1950) American
£3254 $5500   (20-Apr-91 WOL.C324/R) On road to Boston (71x81cm-28x32in) s.

ARTIAS (1912-) French
£714 $1370   (24-Feb-91 P.V143) Sur un theme revolutionnaire-la marche vers
l'echafaud (53x73cm-21x29in) s.d.JV 1987 i. verso gouache W/C
(F.FR 7100)

ARTIAS, Philippe (1912-) French
£2548 $4893   (2-Dec-90 M.V112/R) Promenade en ville I (100x81cm-39x32in) (F.FR 25000)
£968 $1859   (2-Dec-90 M.V113/R) Dans la ville (50x64cm-20x25in) s.d.70 gouache
(F.FR 9500)

ARTS, Alexis (?) ?
£556 $956   (14-May-91 JOY.T215) Juillet, Lac des Deux Montagnes (50x70cm-20x28in)
s. (C.D 1100)

ARTS, Dorus (1901-1961) Dutch
£622 $1207   (4-Dec-90 R.T203/R) Winter (41x61cm-16x24in) s. (C.D 1400)

ARTSCHWAGER, Richard (1924-) American
£23669 $40000   (1-May-91 SY.NY124/R) Bushes II (61x73cm-24x29in) s.d.70 verso acrylic
celotex
£31065 $52500   (1-May-91 SY.NY138/R) Rug and window (131x132cm-52x52in) s.d.83 verso
acrylic celotex
£2168 $4250   (12-Feb-91 SY.NY327/R) Door window table basket mirror rug no 25
(61x91cm-24x36in) s.i.d.74 ink
£4734 $8000   (2-May-91 CH.NY226/R) Untitled (48x64cm-19x25in) s.d.87 chl
£20710 $35000   (2-May-91 CH.NY229/R) Dinner - A (156x120cm-61x47in) acrylic formica
celotex
£58673 $115000   (6-Nov-90 SY.NY31/R) Office scene (96x96cm-38x38in) s.d.66 verso acrylic
celotex

ARTVELT, Andries van see EERTVELT, Andries van

ARTZ, Constant (1870-1951) Dutch
£599 $1006   (23-Apr-91 SY.AM1) Duck with ducklings on waterfront (17x23cm-7x9in) s.
(D.FL 2000)
£781 $1523   (20-Oct-90 CH.AM137/R) Family reunion (18x24cm-7x9in) s. board
(D.FL 2600)
£794 $1421   (13-Mar-91 GK.Z1) Family of ducks at pond s. (S.FR 2000)
£923 $1800   (21-Oct-90 HG.C30) Seated Dutch girl with flowers and ducks s. cradled
panel
£1003 $1696   (17-Apr-91 WE.MU182/R) Pond landscape with ducks (20x30cm-8x12in) s.
(DM 3000)
£1203 $2370   (6-Oct-90 KV.L12/R) Washerwoman by a windmill (24x18cm-9x7in) s. panel
(B.FR 75000)
£1220 $2390   (6-Nov-90 SY.AM165) Duck with ducklings on waterfront (18x24cm-7x9in) s.
panel (D.FL 4000)
£1257 $2351   (1-Sep-90 CH.AM120) Duck and ducklings going for a swim (24x30cm-9x12in)
s. panel (D.FL 4200)
£1284 $2439   (14-Sep-90 SA.A1198/R) Ducks on bank of pond (18x24cm-7x9in) s. panel
(DM 3800)
£1361 $2190   (26-Jun-91 KM.K1382/R) Ducks by stream (18x24cm-7x9in) s. panel
(DM 4000)
£1365 $2239   (18-Jun-91 FN.S1744/R) Wooded pond landscape with ducks and ducklings
(18x24cm-7x9in) s. panel (DM 4000)
£1437 $2501   (26-Mar-91 VN.R6/R) Peasant couple on a path near windmill
(111x83cm-44x33in) s. (D.FL 4800)
£1488 $2500   (17-Jul-91 SY.NY275/R) Mother duck and her ducklings (24x43cm-9x17in) s.
£1497 $2844   (11-Sep-90 CH.AM57/R) White duck and ducklings in a meadow
(18x24cm-7x9in) s. panel (D.FL 5000)
£1617 $2813   (26-Mar-91 VN.R5/R) Family of ducks by the waterside (38x48cm-15x19in)
s. (D.FL 5400)
£1899 $3133   (8-Jul-91 SY.J183/R) Ducks and ducklings on a river bank
(49x39cm-19x15in) s. (SA.R 9000)
£2695 $5254   (25-Oct-90 VN.R5/R) Duck family by a stream (49x39cm-19x15in) s. panel
(D.FL 9000)
£3000 $5160   (17-May-91 C65/R) Ducks and ducklings on river bank (18x25cm-7x10in) s.
panel pair
£3041 $5929   (26-Oct-90 KM.K1087/R) River landscape with ducks, spring
(40x50cm-16x20in) s. (DM 9000)
£848 $1672   (30-Oct-90 CH.AM493) Wooded river landscape with houses and farmer in
praam (37x53cm-15x21in) s. W/C bodycol (D.FL 2800)

ARTZ, David Adolf Constant (1837-1890) Dutch
£1250 $2450   (22-Jan-91 SWS1005/R) A mother with her sleeping baby (76x53cm-30x21in)
s.
£5455 $10745   (30-Oct-90 CH.AM340 a/R) Fisherman's family seated at table in cottage
(90x130cm-35x51in) s. (D.FL 18000)

ASAM, Cosmas Damian (1686-1739) German
£673 $1165   (6-May-91 ZEL.L1427/R) Guardian angel and archangel Michael
(11x9cm-4x4in) c.1732 pen wash (DM 2000)

ASARTA, Inocencio (19th C) Spanish
£6506 $12686   (17-Oct-90 FER.M223/R) Las lecheras en el Paseo de los Canos de Bilbao
                 (45x60cm-18x24in) s. (S.P 1200000)

ASCENZI, E (?) Italian
£856 $1600   (30-Aug-90 MFA.C145/R) Gypsy caravan (38x56cm-15x22in) s.

ASCH, Pieter Jansz van (1603-1678) Dutch
£1900 $3610   (13-Sep-90 CSK22/R) Wooded landscape with gentleman and page on track
                 passing peasant womanon mule (33x43cm-13x17in) mono. panel
£4444 $7689   (6-May-91 ZEL.L1581/R) Wooded landscape with figures and animals
                 (33x43cm-13x17in) mono. panel (DM 13200)
£7339 $14459   (13-Nov-90 CH.AM113/R) Travellers on country roads in wooded landscapes
                 (24x34cm-9x13in) panel oval pair (D.FL 24000)

ASCH, Pieter Jansz van (style) (1603-1678) Dutch
£1800 $3420   (13-Sep-90 CSK323/R) Abraham and three angels (49x58cm-19x23in) panel

ASCHENBACH, Ernst (1872-1954) Norwegian
£655 $1245   (11-Sep-90 UL.T165) Sawmill by waterfall (60x50cm-24x20in) (N.KR 7500)

ASCHENBRENNER, Lennart (20th C) Swedish
£643 $1261   (10-Nov-90 FAL.M10/R) Putty knife (35x30cm-14x12in) s.d.80 (S.KR 7000)
£1415 $2448   (22-May-91 BA.S312/R) Sycamore key (66x81cm-26x32in) s.d.88 (S.KR 15000)
£7414 $14384   (4-Dec-90 BA.S29/R) From Oslo (143x189cm-56x74in) s.d.1979verso
                 (S.KR 80000)
*£671 $1315   (10-Nov-90 FAL.M9/R) Composition (57x76cm-22x30in) s.d.86 W/C
                 (S.KR 7300)*
*£1408 $2394   (28-May-91 AB.S5161/R) Abstract composition (120x80cm-47x31in) s.d.1984
                 W/C pastel (S.KR 15000)*

ASCHHEIM, Isidor (20th C) Israeli
£1227 $2000   (12-Jun-91 GG.TA396/R) Nude (75x59cm-30x23in) s.d.1945

ASCIONE, Aniello (17/18th C) Italian
£9131 $15341   (23-Apr-91 F.R118/R) Natura morta di uva e pesche. Natura morta di uva e
                 fichi (37x13cm-15x5in) pair (I.L 20000000)

ASCIONE, Aniello (attrib) (17/18th C) Italian
£8205 $16000   (11-Oct-90 SY.NY190/R) Still life of fruit (46x58cm-18x23in)

ASCOL, R (?) ?
£1157 $1944   (16-Jul-91 JRL.S184) Seascape (50x82cm-20x32in) s. (A.D 2500)

ASDRUBALI, Gianni (1955-) Italian
£2927 $5707   (22-Oct-90 BR.M112/R) Astrazione gesto (144x170cm-57x67in) s.d.verso
                 (I.L 6500000)

ASHBURNER, William F (fl.1900-1932) British
£1900 $3743   (12-Nov-90 PH76/R) The bloom of life (51x71cm-20x28in) s. W/C

ASHFORD, E (?) British
£976 $1649   (20-Apr-91 HOR.H1/R) Sailingboats in a calm (24x56cm-9x22in) s.
                 (F.M 6800)

ASHFORD, William (1746-1824) British
£100000 $165000   (12-Jul-91 C68/R) Figures by weir on River Clodiagh at Charleville
                 Forest, Co. Offaly (100x126cm-39x50in) s.d.1801
£120000 $198000   (12-Jul-91 C67/R) Punt on River Clodiagh at Charleville Forest, Co.
                 Offaly, farm and dairy in distance (100x126cm-39x50in) s.d.1801

ASHFORD, William (circle) (1746-1824) British
£2100 $4116   (22-Jan-91 PH25/R) Wooded river landscape with young girl on terrace
                 before waterfall (45x56cm-18x22in) copper
£17000 $33490   (14-Nov-90 S102/R) View of country house on estuary, morning. View from
                 other side, dusk (86x129cm-34x51in) pair

ASHLEY, Clifford Warren (1881-1947) American
£638 $1250   (24-Nov-90 RB.HY194/R) Naushon, small sloop at anchor by point with
                 house (23x28cm-9x11in) i.d.1913 board

ASHTON, Federico (1836-?) Italian
£794 $1373   (22-May-91 GS.B2319) Lago Maggiore with figures and view of Baveno
                 (32x59cm-13x23in) s. i.verso panel (S.FR 2000)

ASHTON, Julian Rossi (1851-1942) British
£2300 $3841   (5-Jun-91 S179/R) By fireside (22x17cm-9x7in) s.d.1876 board
*£995 $1682   (16-Apr-91 J.M4/R) Sydney Harbour (13x33cm-5x13in) s.d.'19 W/C
                 (A.D 2200)*
*£1267 $2141   (16-Apr-91 J.M70/R) Picking Native flowers (21x26cm-8x10in) s.d.1888 W/C
                 (A.D 2800)*

ASHTON, Sir John William (1881-1963) British/Australian
£600 $1170   (15-Oct-90 AAA.S184) Canal scene (23x29cm-9x11in) s. board (A.D 1500)
£683 $1311   (27-Nov-90 JRL.S154) Morning light, Chinaman's Beach (35x43cm-14x17in)
                 s.d.1930 canvasboard (A.D 1700)

ASHTON, Sir John William (1881-1963) British/Australian-cont.

£723	$1388	(26-Nov-90 SY.ME106/R) Canal scene (26x23cm-10x9in) s. board (A.D 1800)
£1175	$2080	(18-Mar-91 MGS.S239/R) Windsor pastoral (36x44cm-14x17in) s. canvas on board (A.D 2750)
£1310	$2345	(9-Apr-91 CH.ME319) Morning light, Chinamans Beach, Middle harbour (35x43cm-14x17in) s.d.1930 i.d.1960 verso canvas on board (A.D 3000)
£1526	$2930	(26-Nov-90 SY.ME259/R) Across Seine (34x43cm-13x17in) s. (A.D 3800)
£1606	$3084	(27-Nov-90 JRL.S165/R) On way to citadel, Cairo s. cardboard (A.D 4000)
£1810	$3059	(16-Apr-91 J.M318/R) Sailing off the headland (44x60cm-17x24in) s. (A.D 4000)
£2317	$4564	(13-Nov-90 J.M280/R) Hazelwood Park (72x58cm-28x23in) s. (A.D 6000)
£2546	$4278	(16-Jul-91 JRL.S249/R) Cattle in meadow, Holland (37x47cm-15x19in) s. board (A.D 5500)
£2594	$4229	(1-Jul-91 AAA.S90 e) The bathers (77x103cm-30x41in) bears sig. (A.D 5500)
£2703	$5324	(13-Nov-90 J.M71) La Vaisseau Vert, Marseilles Harbour, France (35x42cm-14x17in) s. canvas on board (A.D 7000)
£2715	$4588	(16-Apr-91 J.M262) The bathers (74x101cm-29x40in) s. (A.D 6000)
£3167	$5353	(16-Apr-91 J.M10/R) The Harbour Marseilles (37x45cm-15x18in) s. canvas on board (A.D 7000)
£3756	$6160	(17-Jun-91 MGS.S296) Pont Saint Benezet (50x60cm-20x24in) s. (A.D 8000)

ASKENAZY, Maurice (1888-1961) American

£920	$1500	(11-Jun-91 MOR.P95 a) Mother and child (51x41cm-20x16in) estate st. s.verso
£1380	$2250	(11-Jun-91 MOR.P81) Girl in green (58x46cm-23x18in) s. estate st.verso board

ASKEVOLD, Anders Monsen (1834-1900) Swedish

£1481	$2888	(15-Oct-90 B.O2/R) On the road to the outfarm (34x47cm-13x19in) s. (N.KR 17000)
£1982	$3884	(6-Nov-90 SY.AM162/R) View of fjord (34x48cm-13x19in) s.d.88 (D.FL 6500)
£2582	$4984	(10-Dec-90 B.O1/R) Cowgirl and cattle (46x36cm-18x14in) s.d.1884 (N.KR 29000)
£3038	$5074	(3-Jun-91 B.O1/R) Fjord landscape (61x39cm-24x15in) s.i.d.1885 panel (N.KR 35000)
£3125	$5219	(4-Jun-91 BU.O3/R) Cows and children (47x63cm-19x25in) s.i.d.1861 (N.KR 36000)
£4895	$9448	(14-Dec-90 BM.B592/R) Fjord landscape with shipping and village with figures (60x90cm-24x35in) s. (DM 14000)
£5035	$9818	(11-Oct-90 BU.O5/R) Milkmaids, shepherdboy and cattle (40x53cm-16x21in) s.d.1865 (N.KR 58000)
£5743	$10912	(14-Sep-90 SA.A1164/R) Norwegian fjord landscape, morning (61x91cm-24x36in) s.i.d.1895 (DM 17000)
£7315	$14191	(4-Dec-90 UL.T181) At the ferry-step (51x83cm-20x33in) (N.KR 82000)
£7480	$14436	(10-Dec-90 B.O2/R) Landscape from Hjorundfjord (56x90cm-22x35in) s. (N.KR 84000)
£8000	$15360	(28-Nov-90 S90/R) Village by fjord (54x83cm-21x33in) s.d.1889
£8333	$16250	(11-Oct-90 BU.O6/R) Landscape from Dyrdal, Naerofjord (60x90cm-24x35in) s.i.d.1895 (N.KR 96000)
£8406	$15047	(11-Mar-91 B.O2/R) Fjord landscape (55x90cm-22x35in) s.d.1891 (N.KR 96000)
£8844	$14238	(26-Jun-91 KM.K1383/R) Norwegian fjord landscape with shipping (76x121cm-30x48in) s.d.1889 (DM 26000)
£11151	$21632	(4-Dec-90 UL.T182/R) At the outfarm 1968 (77x100cm-30x39in) (N.KR 125000)

ASLUND, Acke (1881-1958) Swedish

£731	$1433	(20-Nov-90 GO.G298) Mountain landscape (49x60cm-19x24in) (S.KR 8000)
£2462	$4136	(27-Apr-91 SO.S642/R) Horses by the sea (47x64cm-19x25in) mono.d.1942 (S.KR 26000)
£3800	$7372	(4-Dec-90 BA.S628/R) Young horses in fieldlandscape, autumn (68x88cm-27x35in) init.d.42 (S.KR 41000)
£492	*$827*	*(27-Apr-91 SO.S643/R) Trotting (23x30cm-9x12in) mono. col.chk (S.KR 5200)*
£521	*$875*	*(27-Apr-91 SO.S645/R) Horses (23x30cm-9x12in) mono. red chk pencil (S.KR 5500)*
£708	*$1224*	*(22-May-91 BA.S283/R) Arriving at church (24x31cm-9x12in) s.d.09 Indian ink wash (S.KR 7500)*
£755	*$1306*	*(22-May-91 BA.S282/R) Horse and foal grazing (30x46cm-12x18in) init.d.42 chk (S.KR 8000)*
£1321	*$2285*	*(22-May-91 BA.S281/R) Horse and foal (48x59cm-19x23in) init.i.d.1946 chk (S.KR 14000)*

ASNAR, Jean Michel (1959-) French

£600	$978	(5-Jul-91 YC.P62) L'heure de fermeture (49x64cm-19x25in) s. (F.FR 6000)

ASOMA, Tadashi (20th C) Japanese

£1037	$1700	(19-Jun-91 B.SF1790/R) Pine tree (127x127cm-50x50in) s.d.72

ASPDEN, David (1935-) Australian

£964	$1851	(26-Nov-90 SY.ME21) Garden II (131x97cm-52x38in) mono. i.d.88 verso acrylic paper (A.D 2400)

ASPERTINI, Amico (attrib) (1474-1552) Italian
£18256 $36146 (30-Jan-91 APT.P1/R) Le mariage de la Vierge (29x60cm-11x24in) panel
(F.FR 180000)

ASPINWALL, Reginald (1858-1921) British
£700 $1316 (19-Sep-90 JT100) Morecambe fishing boats returning s.
£860 $1488 (22-May-91 JT2) Moorland path s.d.1908
£1100 $2156 (21-Nov-90 JT9) Quiet stretch of river (30x46cm-12x18in) s.d.1904 board
£620 $1166 (19-Sep-90 JT201) Bend in the river (33x58cm-13x23in) s.d.1884 W/C
£800 $1504 (19-Sep-90 JT200) River landscape with cattle watering (38x53cm-15x21in)
s.d.1906 W/C
£1000 $1670 (24-Jul-91 JT2) Autumn pastoral caton (25x33cm-10x13in) s.d.1902 W/C

ASPLUND, Tore (?) ?
£532 $925 (29-Mar-91 E.EDM550) Third Avenue L (30x41cm-12x16in) s. board
£4651 $8000 (15-May-91 SY.NY175/R) Brooklyn Dodgers under lights at Ebbets Field
(48x99cm-19x39in) s. canvas on masonite

ASSAR, Nasser (1928-) Iranian
£789 $1554 (1-Oct-90 CC.P139) S.M.Stella (100x72cm-39x28in) s.d.1961 (F.FR 8000)
£1381 $2720 (1-Oct-90 CC.P138) Stella (146x114cm-57x45in) s.d.1961 (F.FR 14000)

ASSE, Geneviève (1923-) French
£690 $1360 (1-Oct-90 CC.P143) L'oeuf (18x14cm-7x6in) s.verso (F.FR 7000)
£2268 $4468 (1-Oct-90 CC.P142/R) Nature morte aux bouteilles (33x45cm-13x18in) s.
(F.FR 23000)
£2888 $4910 (2-Jun-91 GL.P218/R) Composition (130x96cm-51x38in) s. i.d.1958 verso
(F.FR 29000)
£3083 $5982 (9-Dec-90 CC.P77/R) Sans titre (54x81cm-21x32in) s. d.66 verso
(F.FR 30000)
£3589 $5922 (10-Jul-91 FB.P68/R) Carre Orange (43x55cm-17x22in) s. i.d.58 verso
(F.FR 36000)

ASSELIN, Maurice (1882-1947) French
£623 $1196 (24-Feb-91 P.V77) Femme lisant (21x33cm-8x13in) s. W/C (F.FR 6200)
£922 $1807 (11-Nov-90 ZZ.F22/R) Jeune femme a sa lecture (21x33cm-8x13in) s. W/C
(F.FR 9000)

ASSELYN, Jan (1610-1652) Dutch
£4518 $7274 (27-Jun-91 APT.P107/R) Barque accostee au bord de ruines
(52x67cm-20x26in) trace sig. (F.FR 45000)
£4523 $7417 (21-Jun-91 SY.MO259/R) Vue du Lac de Nemi (18x20cm-7x8in) mono. panel
(F.FR 45000)
£7534 $12281 (12-Jun-91 N.M293/R) Shepherds and animals before ruin in landscape
(67x52cm-26x20in) mono.d.1647 panel (DM 22000)

ASSELYN, Jan (attrib) (1610-1652) Dutch
£1149 $2000 (27-Mar-91 B.SF4029/R) Roman capriccio (71x58cm-28x23in)
£1955 $3500 (11-Apr-91 SY.NY170/R) Cavallers at rest (53x61cm-21x24in)
£2294 $4518 (13-Nov-90 AB.S848/R) Figures resting by ruins (70x56cm-28x22in) mono.
(S.KR 25000)
£3400 $6528 (18-Feb-91 S65/R) View of the Arch of Constantine, Rome (24x35cm-9x14in)
pen ink wash over chk

ASSELYN, Jan (circle) (1610-1652) Dutch
£1600 $2960 (5-Mar-91 PH115/R) Herdsman with cattle and sheep beneath rocky bluff
(35x40cm-14x16in) panel
£2701 $5268 (23-Oct-90 CH.R331) Paesaggio fluviale con cavalieri (47x63cm-19x25in)
(I.L 6000000)

ASSELYN, Jan (style) (1610-1652) Dutch
£1150 $2243 (22-Oct-90 SWS1436) Rocky landscape with figures and horse in foreground
(31x22cm-12x9in)
£1223 $2410 (13-Nov-90 CH.AM87) Italianate landscape with travellers by farm,
village beyond (65x78cm-26x31in) with sig. (D.FL 4000)
£3000 $5700 (13-Sep-90 CSK135/R) Peasants, merchants and porters at village jetty
(69x88cm-27x35in)

ASSENDELFT, Cornelis van (1870-1945) German
£449 $876 (25-Oct-90 VN.R352/R) Sowers (69x83cm-27x33in) s. pastel (D.FL 1500)

ASSERETI, G (18th C) Italian?
£4749 $8500 (11-Apr-91 SY.NY29/R) Orientals standing in classical ruins, dome of
St.Peter's beyond (40x26cm-16x10in) s.

ASSERETO, Giovacchino (1600-1649) Italian
£3893 $7475 (29-Nov-90 F.M59/R) Crocefissione (73x57cm-29x22in) (I.L 8500000)

ASSETTO, Franco (20th C) ?
£916 $1759 (27-Nov-90 SY.MI124/R) Rosso XXX 32 (71x100cm-28x39in) s.d.59
(I.L 2000000)
£456 $775 (28-May-91 SY.MI124/R) Composizione (19x24cm-7x9in) s.d.59 oil mixed
media canvas laid down on panel (I.L 1000000)

ASSMUS, Robert (1837-?) German
£683 $1119 (18-Jun-91 FN.S1746) Portrait of elegant young lady wearing plumed hat and fur trimmed dress (38x30cm-15x12in) panel (DM 2000)

ASSUS, Armand Jacques (1892-1977) French
£1837 $3618 (13-Nov-90 ARC.P198/R) Le Port Messagerie Maritime, Alger (42x28cm-17x11in) s. (F.FR 18000)

AST, Balthasar van der (1590-1656) Dutch
£34211 $65000 (11-Jan-91 CH.NY40/R) Basket with mixed fruit, surrounded by more mixed fruit, shells, bees and dragonfly on ledge (29x47cm-11x19in) s.d.1647 panel
£44118 $75000 (31-May-91 CH.NY10/R) Tulip, columbine, grasshopper, dragonfly, shell and insects on ledge (8x17cm-3x7in) s. panel
£180000 $293400 (3-Jul-91 S26/R) Still life of flowers in basket with fruit and shells lying on stone ledge (33x64cm-13x25in) s. panel

AST, Balthasar van der (style) (1590-1656) Dutch
£750 $1268 (18-Apr-91 CSK159/R) Carnations, shell, insects and snail on ledge (12x18cm-5x7in) on copper
£2200 $4180 (13-Sep-90 CSK214/R) Tulip, caterpillar, bee, dragonfly and fly on stone ledge (12x16cm-5x6in) with sig. panel

ASTHER, Nils (20th C) Swedish
£4315 $8500 (15-Nov-90 SY.NY60/R) Platonic love (22x26cm-9x10in) s. masonite

ASTI, Angelo (1847-1903) French
£526 $1037 (30-Oct-90 MA.V554) Wistful young woman (20x25cm-8x10in) s. (C.D 1200)

ASTIER, Paul (19th C) French
£2548 $4893 (1-Dec-90 PER.M75) La ramasseuse de fagot (64x92cm-25x36in) s.d.92 (F.FR 25000)

ASTOIN, Marie (20th C) French
£588 $1165 (3-Feb-91 LT.P145) Pecheurs sur le port (73x54cm-29x21in) s. (F.FR 5800)
£594 $1051 (7-Apr-91 I.N21) Paysage anime (65x54cm-26x21in) s. (F.FR 6000)
£602 $1114 (10-Mar-91 LT.P190) Femmes au cafe (54x65cm-21x26in) s. (F.FR 6000)
£822 $1595 (8-Dec-90 LT.P148) La reception (60x81cm-24x32in) s. (F.FR 8000)
£2041 $4020 (14-Nov-90 I.N117/R) Nu allonge (73x92cm-29x36in) s. (F.FR 20000)

ASTROM, Werner (?) Scandinavian
£999 $1957 (24-Nov-90 HOR.H324/R) Sunny landscape (41x33cm-16x13in) s.d.1919 (F.M 7000)
£1491 $2670 (14-Apr-91 BU.H98/R) Cottages with red roof (55x65cm-22x26in) s.d.56 (F.M 10500)
£1650 $2788 (20-Apr-91 HOR.H245/R) Back of the house (54x47cm-21x19in) s.d.1917 (F.M 11500)

ASTRUP, Nikolai (1880-1928) Norwegian
£668 $1289 (12-Dec-90 BU.O4/R) Foxgloves (40x25cm-16x10in) s. Indian ink wash (N.KR 7500)

ATAMIAN, Charles Garabed (20th C) Turkish
£5789 $11000 (28-Feb-91 CH.NY36/R) La plage (53x65cm-21x26in) s.

ATAR, Chaim (1902-1953) Israeli
£552 $900 (12-Jun-91 GG.TA25/R) Head of bearded man (41x33cm-16x13in) s.
£681 $1300 (1-Jan-91 GG.TA237/R) Head of boy (37x23cm-15x9in) c.1946 s.verso
£736 $1200 (12-Jun-91 GG.TA232/R) Girl (61x38cm-24x15in) s.

ATHERTON, John (?) British
£559 $950 (1-Jun-91 IH.NY13/R) Dogwoods at Monticello, Dixie Bell Gin (43x46cm-17x18in) s.

ATILA (?) ?
£3120 $5397 (25-May-91 KV.L12/R) L'Oiseau - temps (195x130cm-77x51in) s. (B.FR 190000)
£762 $1524 (7-Feb-91 R.P102 b/R) Composition (90x63cm-35x25in) s. W/C (F.FR 7500)
£935 $1870 (7-Feb-91 R.P157 b/R) Composition (51x69cm-20x27in) s. htd.pastel paper laid down on canvas (F.FR 9200)
£1081 $1934 (16-Mar-91 KV.L15/R) Head (60x91cm-24x36in) s. W/C ink (B.FR 65000)

ATILA, Ede Kardy (1931-) French
£3287 $6409 (23-Oct-90 C.A305/R) On peut voir tres loin (165x130cm-65x51in) s.d.1972 (B.FR 200000)
£3287 $6409 (23-Oct-90 C.A306/R) Facettes (165x130cm-65x51in) s.d.1973 (B.FR 200000)

ATKINS, Samuel (fl.1787-1808) British
£720 $1354 (8-Aug-90 PHP17/R) Boat in rough seas (18x26cm-7x10in) W/C
£3500 $6265 (9-Apr-91 C143/R) Dover Harbour (28x39cm-11x15in) s. pencil pen ink W/C

ATKINS, W E (1842-1910) British
£1200 $2076 (22-May-91 S90/R) Royal yacht Victoria and Albert II, Portsmouth (25x43cm-10x17in) s. W/C

ATKINS, William Edward (1842-1910) British
£3000 $5850   (18-Oct-90 CSK34/R) The Victory firing the salute February 19th 1898, Portsmouth (19x28cm-7x11in) s. pencil pen W/C

ATKINSON, J G (19th C) British
£600 $1110   (7-Mar-91 CSK104) Skiddaw from Lowdore, Cumberland (41x66cm-16x26in) s. i.verso

ATKINSON, Jacob (1864-1938) American
£10405 $18000   (22-May-91 CH.NY177/R) A soldier's letter and money - A Trompe l'Oeil (21x30cm-8x12in) s.d. '91

ATKINSON, James (?) British
£840 $1630   (5-Dec-90 PHL146/R) Cavalry skirmish in wooded hilly landscape (59x49cm-23x19in) s.

ATKINSON, John (1863-1924) British
£900 $1521   (30-Apr-91 AG306/R) Mabel - bay hunter in stable (45x65cm-18x26in) s.i.
£600 $1110   (5-Mar-91 AG203/R) Loading bracken (37x54cm-15x21in) s. W/C
£600 $1014   (30-Apr-91 AG193) Sheep in winter farmyard (37x26cm-15x10in) s.d.1901 W/C
£660 $1221   (5-Mar-91 AG204) Cart in cornfield (23x33cm-9x13in) s. W/C
£900 $1467   (14-Jun-91 C65/R) A Dumfrieshire village (28x40cm-11x16in) s.i. pencil W/C htd.white
£950 $1606   (30-Apr-91 AG196) Harvesting (23x30cm-9x12in) s. W/C
£1000 $1690   (30-Apr-91 AG194/R) Donkey and poultry by upturned cart (27x38cm-11x15in) s. W/C
£1350 $2619   (4-Dec-90 AG227) After the fair at Brough (34x53cm-13x21in) s.i.verso W/C
£2050 $3465   (30-Apr-91 AG195/R) Hinderwell foal show (22x30cm-9x12in) s.i.d.1905 W/C
£2200 $4268   (4-Dec-90 AG226/R) Kirkby Stephen Horse Fair (31x37cm-12x15in) s.i. W/C
£3400 $5474   (25-Jun-91 AG359) Gypsy encampment (48x63cm-19x25in) s. gouache
£4000 $7400   (5-Mar-91 AG205/R) Brough Hill (45x59cm-18x23in) s.i. W/C

ATKINSON, John Gunson (circle) (19th C) British
£840 $1436   (30-Jul-91 SWS280) Country folk by a culvert (56x86cm-22x34in) bears sig.d.

ATKINSON, Laurence (?) British
£13000 $25480   (7-Nov-90 S36/R) Vital, study for sculpture (62x46cm-24x18in) W/C over pencil

ATKINSON, Maud Tindal (20th C) British
£1200 $2016   (15-Jul-91 PH115) Red shoes (54x42cm-21x17in) s. W/C

ATL, Dr (1875-1964) Mexican
£13265 $26000   (20-Nov-90 CH.NY87/R) Amanecer (40x61cm-16x24in) s. burlap
£20231 $35000   (8-May-91 SY.NY126/R) Untitled (45x86cm-18x34in) s. Atl colours pastel
£29592 $58000   (20-Nov-90 CH.NY17/R) Bosque con volcanes (87x155cm-34x61in) s. cloth
£37791 $65000   (15-May-91 CH.NY3/R) Paisaje de Popocatepetl (46x70cm-18x28in) init. verso
£5814 $10000   (15-May-91 CH.NY155/R) Paricutin (24x28cm-9x11in) s. chl.

ATLAN, Jean (1913-1960) French
£15000 $26550   (21-Mar-91 C207/R) Composition (72x46cm-28x18in) s.d.59
£17085 $30583   (15-Mar-91 FB.P51/R) Les jardins de carthage (46x38cm-18x15in) s.d.54 i. verso panel (F.FR 170000)
£21608 $35437   (23-Jun-91 P.V19) Composition (55x46cm-22x18in) s.d.1954 (F.FR 215000)
£30000 $53100   (21-Mar-91 S19/R) Composition (81x54cm-32x21in) s.
£50797 $86355   (2-Jun-91 GL.P159/R) Composition (92x60cm-36x24in) s.d.1959 (F.FR 510000)
£91093 $178543   (25-Nov-90 GL.P80/R) Samba zapotheque (116x73cm-46x29in) s.d.57 i. stretcher (F.FR 900000)
£1835 $3541   (16-Dec-90 GL.P172) Compositin (63x50cm-25x20in) sig.apocryphe pastel board (F.FR 18000)
£3670 $7083   (16-Dec-90 GL.P34/R) Composition (37x27cm-15x11in) s.d.1952 pastel (F.FR 36000)
£4625 $8972   (9-Dec-90 CC.P10/R) Composition (33x25cm-13x10in) s.d.1954 pastel (F.FR 45000)
£5612 $11056   (16-Nov-90 FB.P331/R) Composition (50x33cm-20x13in) s.d.49 col.chl. (F.FR 55000)
£8040 $13186   (20-Jun-91 APT.P67/R) Sans titre (31x24cm-12x9in) s.d.59 (F.FR 80000)
£8155 $15739   (16-Dec-90 GL.P40) Composition (33x26cm-13x10in) s.d.1953 pastel (F.FR 80000)
£8534 $13740   (30-Jun-91 I.N116/R) Composition (32x25cm-13x10in) s.d.1954 oil pastel (F.FR 85000)
£8543 $14010   (23-Jun-91 P.V20/R) Composition (24x31cm-9x12in) s.d.1955 pastel (F.FR 85000)
£12456 $23416   (19-Sep-90 KH.K11/R) Composition (57x44cm-22x17in) s.d.49 pastel (D.KR 140000)
£14000 $27300   (18-Oct-90 S37/R) Flamenco IV (54x45cm-21x18in) s.d.59 pastel
£14156 $27604   (21-Oct-90 P.V45/R) Composition (24x32cm-9x13in) s.d.1959 pastel (F.FR 140000)
£16129 $31452   (28-Oct-90 GL.P12/R) Negro Spiritual (32x25cm-13x10in) s.d.58 i. verso pastel htd.oil (F.FR 160000)

ATTARDI, Ugo (1923-) Italian
£2722 $4682   (13-May-91 CH.R142/R) La confessione (100x125cm-39x49in) s.d.1962
                          (I.L 6000000)
£3176 $5462   (13-May-91 CH.R49/R) Nudo (100x80cm-39x31in) s.d.1962 (I.L 7000000)
£5452 $10741   (30-Oct-90 F.R207/R) Tramonto su Tevere (71x125cm-28x49in) s.d.61
                          (I.L 12000000)
£5860 $10490   (9-Apr-91 F.R145) Fanciulla sullo sfondo del Tevere (100x75cm-39x30in)
                          s.d.967 (I.L 13000000)
£6086 $10894   (9-Apr-91 F.R136/R) Lungotevere (75x100cm-30x39in) s. s.d.966verso
                          (I.L 13500000)
£909 $1782   (20-Nov-90 BR.M214/R) Figure sdraiate (70x50cm-28x20in) s.d.1963 gouache
                          paper on canvas (I.L 2000000)

ATTERSEE, Christian Ludwig (1940-) German
£1024 $2007   (20-Nov-90 L.K29/R) Gischttor (31x22cm-12x9in) s.i.d.1989 board
                          (DM 3000)
£2485 $4821   (6-Dec-90 D.V212/R) Hornzungenblut (44x31cm-17x12in) s.i.d.74 s.i.verso
                          acrylic W/C casein pencil (A.S 50000)
£13917 $26998   (6-Dec-90 D.V231/R) Braut-Stuck (121x96cm-48x38in) s.d.1982 acrylic
                          varnish (A.S 280000)
£1220 $2257   (7-May-91 D.V294/R) Dir Durstlosche (24x17cm-9x7in) s.i.d.77 mixed media
                          (A.S 25000)
£1340 $2318   (8-May-91 D.V188/R) Dotterlicht (44x31cm-17x12in) s.i.d.74 s.i.d.verso
                          W/C col.pencil board (A.S 28000)
£1455 $2735   (20-Sep-90 D.V280/R) 'Gelogenes Obst' (30x21cm-12x8in) s.d.87 mixed
                          media (A.S 30000)
£2153 $3725   (8-May-91 D.V157/R) Hemdteufel (44x30cm-17x12in) s.i.d.76 mixed media
                          (A.S 45000)
£2684 $4966   (7-Mar-91 D.V295/R) Knospende Butter (43x30cm-17x12in) s.i.d.87 mixed
                          media oil varnish (A.S 55000)
£7177 $12416   (8-May-91 D.V223/R) Mond zu Dir (71x94cm-28x37in) s.i.d.84verso acrylic
                          varnish canvas (A.S 150000)
£8874 $17392   (24-Nov-90 N.M21/R) Wasseralm (105x105cm-41x41in) s.d.1985 acrylic
                          varnish canvas (DM 26000)

ATTESLANDER, Sofie-Zo (1874-?) Polish
£2400 $4704   (15-Feb-91 C40/R) La Belle Epoque (65x50cm-26x20in) s.d.1900 pastel
                          col.chk

ATWELL, Mabel Lucie (20th C) British
£1000 $1710   (29-Jul-91 HS161/R) Fair haired rosy cheeked girk holding straw hat
                          (27x19cm-11x7in) s. gouache
£1200 $2052   (29-Jul-91 HS162/R) Little child's grace - two rosy cheeked children at
                          tea table (22x35cm-9x14in) s. gouache

ATWOOD, C (20th C) American
£2595 $4800   (10-Mar-91 H.C165/R) Cows by stream (112x160cm-44x63in)

ATWOOD, Clare (1866-1962) British
£600 $984   (20-Jun-91 DLY347/R) Turnip cutters (46x58cm-18x23in) i.verso
£1900 $3211   (2-May-91 C116/R) Billingsgate fish market (61x51cm-24x20in) s.d.1904

ATYEO, Sam (1911-) Australian
£568 $1016   (9-Apr-91 CH.ME51) Scribe (65x47cm-26x19in) s. W/C (A.D 1300)

AUBERJONOIS, Rene (1872-1957) Swiss
£13655 $26763   (21-Nov-90 SY.Z80/R) Femme assise (57x41cm-22x16in) mono. (S.FR 34000)
£14458 $28337   (21-Nov-90 SY.Z77/R) Pecheur au bord du lac (36x46cm-14x18in) s.
                          (S.FR 36000)
£711 $1209   (27-May-91 GK.Z5512) Femme assise (30x26cm-12x10in) s.d.1937 pencil
                          paper on board (S.FR 1800)
£1320 $2231   (1-May-91 GD.B1299) Female nude reclining. Seated woman peeling apple
                          pencil two in one frame (S.FR 3300)
£1508 $2518   (7-Jun-91 ZOF.Z1264/R) Petit gardien de moutons valaisan (18x13cm-7x5in)
                          mono. pencil (S.FR 3800)

AUBERT, Georges (1886-?) Swiss
£816 $1584   (8-Dec-90 GAB.G2345) Poissons II (60x92cm-24x36in) s. (S.FR 2000)
£980 $1900   (8-Dec-90 GAB.G2344/R) Composition a la forme de poisson
                          (53x105cm-21x41in) s.d.57 hardboard panel (S.FR 2400)
£952 $1648   (25-May-91 AB.L43/R) Composition cubiste (50x35cm-20x14in) s. oil mixed
                          media (S.FR 2400)

AUBERT, Jean (?) French
£1508 $2472   (21-Jun-91 CK.P97 a) Le peintre (24x17cm-9x7in) init. lead pencil
                          stumping (F.FR 15000)

AUBERT, Michel (1930-) French
£604 $985   (16-Jun-91 CC.P33) L'immigre (125x86cm-49x34in) s.i.d.20/VIII/85
                          (F.FR 6000)

AUBERTIN, Bernard (20th C) ?
£663 $1279   (16-Dec-90 GL.P121) Rouge rouge rouge (41x24cm-16x9in) s.i.d.1988 verso
                          (F.FR 6500)
£917 $1771   (16-Dec-90 GL.P123) Structure horzontale et verticale (60x60cm-24x24in)
                          s.i.d.1975-78 verso iron filings oil panel (F.FR 9000)

AUBERTIN, Bernard (20th C) ?-cont.

£1835 $3541   (16-Dec-90 GL.P136) Perles de lumiere (100x100cm-39x39in) s.d.1988 l. verso acrylic (F.FR 18000)

£758 $1485   (12-Feb-91 HC.P17) Les allumettes (88x64cm-35x25in) s. verso mixed media aluminium (F.FR 7500)

£1837 $3618   (16-Nov-90 FB.P395/R) Allumettes rouges (59x42cm-23x17in) s.d.1970 burnt matches (F.FR 18000)

£3664 $7036   (27-Nov-90 SY.MI107/R) Combustione di fiammiferi (105x70cm-41x28in) mixed media panel (I.L 8000000)

£4502 $8780   (22-Oct-90 BR.M132/R) Alveoles (38x204cm-15x80in) s.d.1990 painted pressed cardboard (I.L 10000000)

AUBLET, Albert (1851-1938) ?

£3680 $7250   (15-Nov-90 D.NY53/R) End of day (35x28cm-14x11in) s. panel

AUBREY, Christopher (19th C) New Zealander

£1084 $2124   (7-Nov-90 DS.W15) Mountain and river landscape (45x36cm-18x14in) s.d.1888 W/C (NZ.D 3500)

AUBREY, Christopher (attrib) (19th C) New Zealander

£447 $755   (17-Apr-91 DS.W73) South Island and mountain scene (34x51cm-13x20in) W/C (NZ.D 1300)

AUBRY, Etienne (1745-1781) French

£1236 $2213   (10-Apr-91 CB.P25) Portrait de jeune femme (60x50cm-24x20in) oval (F.FR 12500)

£1724 $3414   (30-Jan-91 APT.P115/R) Portrait d'un homme en habit (93x62cm-37x24in) s.d.1772 verso (F.FR 17000)

AUBRY, Etienne (attrib) (1745-1781) French

£841 $1505   (10-Apr-91 CB.P35/R) Portrait de jeune femme (60x49cm-24x19in) oval (F.FR 8500)

£2446 $4697   (30-Nov-90 APT.P110/R) Portrait anciennement dit de Barnave (46x38cm-18x15in) (F.FR 24000)

AUBRY, Louis Francois (1767-1851) French

£750 $1478   (1-Nov-90 S7/R) Portrait of Mlle.Allan (11cm-4ins circular) min. gilt-metal frame

£1020 $2010   (13-Nov-90 CH.G264) Portrait of Jean Jacques Chardon (11x?cm-4x?in) min.s.d.1829 gilt-metal mount oval (S.FR 2500)

£1600 $3072   (18-Dec-90 C49) Portrait of gentleman in black coat, white waistcoat and cravat (5x?cm-2x?in) min.s.chased ormolu mount oval

AUBRY, Louis Francois (attrib) (1767-1851) French

£900 $1485   (10-Jul-91 C57) Monsieur Rivio, a baritone at the Paris opera (14x?cm-6x?in) min.gilt-metal frame oval

AUBRY, Yves (20th C) French

£1223 $2361   (16-Dec-90 CL.E53) Paysage anadalou (92x73cm-36x29in) (F.FR 12000)

AUDIBERT, Ernest (20th C) French

£941 $1665   (7-Apr-91 I.N24) Village de Segreste (65x50cm-26x20in) s. (F.FR 9500)

£1018 $2006   (30-Oct-90 I.N162) Sur la route d'Eygaliere (50x65cm-20x26in) s. (F.FR 10000)

AUDIBERT, Louis (1881-?) French

£406 $803   (3-Feb-91 I.N11/R) Village Provencal (28x38cm-11x15in) s. W/C (F.FR 4000)

AUDY, Jonny (19th C) French

£1761 $3451   (26-Jan-91 ZZ.F59) Jokey (30x49cm-12x19in) both s.d.70 W/C two (F.FR 17500)

AUER, Grigor (1882-1967) Finnish

£633 $1222   (15-Dec-90 BU.H18) Beach landscape (46x59cm-18x23in) s.d.1936 (F.M 4400)

£642 $1258   (24-Nov-90 HOR.H40/R) Stones on beach (46x60cm-18x24in) s.d.1959 (F.M 4500)

£647 $1250   (15-Dec-90 BU.H17) Flower pot (42x52cm-17x20in) s.d.1932 (F.M 4500)

£1220 $2061   (20-Apr-91 HOR.H31/R) Summer's day (41x51cm-16x20in) s.d.1930 (F.M 8500)

£1355 $2656   (24-Nov-90 HOR.H39/R) Arrival of spring (46x60cm-18x24in) s.d.1935 (F.M 9500)

AUERBACH, Arnold (1898-1978) British

£1600 $2784   (27-Mar-91 S68) Conversation (25x36cm-10x14in) s.d.30 pen ink W/C over pencil htd.white

AUERBACH, Frank (1931-) British

£18000 $28980   (27-Jun-91 C38/R) Portrait of E. O. W. III (36x30cm-14x12in) board

£36000 $69840   (6-Dec-90 S53/R) Head of Jym III (50x56cm-20x22in) board

£44000 $70840   (27-Jun-91 S45/R) E.O.W lying on her bed II (51x76cm-20x30in)

£44379 $75000   (1-May-91 CH.NY29/R) Head of Gerda Boehm (61x71cm-24x28in) board

£85000 $150450   (21-Mar-91 S78/R) Mornington crescent - night (122x91cm-48x36in) d.1971 verso board

£850 $1658   (18-Oct-90 S200/R) To the studio (25x31cm-10x12in) wax crayons

AUERBACH, Frank (1931-) British-cont.

£1700	$2839	(6-Jun-91 C264/R) Study for Primrose Hill (20x28cm-8x11in) s.i.d.1978verso pen ink felt tip pen
£2400	$4512	(20-Sep-90 CSK151/R) Still life with kettle, jug and mug on table (33x25cm-13x10in) s.d.48 W/C bodycol pen two
£2400	$4176	(28-Mar-91 CSK212/R) Still life with kettle, jug and book on table (33x25cm-13x10in) s.d.48 W/C bodycol pen pair
£22189	$37500	(30-Apr-91 SY.NY1/R) Head of Gerda Boehm (82x59cm-32x23in) s.d.1964-65 v.oil wax crayon chl paper on board

AUERBACH, Johann Gottfried (1697-1753) German

£3918	$7718	(14-Nov-90 D.V2/R) Empress Elisabeth Christine, mother of Maria Theresia (148x112cm-58x44in) (A.S 80000)

AUERBACH, Johann Gottfried (attrib) (1697-1753) German

£2167	$3618	(6-Jun-91 D.V225/R) Kaiser Franz I Stephan pointing to German Crown (128x95cm-50x37in) (A.S 45000)

AUERBACH, Johann Gottfried (circle) (1697-1753) German

£7328	$13117	(14-Mar-91 D.V76/R) Portrait of Kaiser Karl IV, father of Maria Theresia (240x200cm-94x79in) (A.S 150000)

AUERBACH-LEVY, William (1889-1964) Polish

£550	$1100	(6-Feb-91 D.NY8) The swimmers (61x51cm-24x20in) s.i. studio st. verso board
£1198	$2000	(5-Jun-91 D.NY9) Under the weeping cherry (30x46cm-12x18in) s. st.studio verso board

AUFDENBLATTER, E (20th C) Swiss

£6000	$10140	(1-May-91 GD.B26/R) Rocky Alpine landscape with lakeside chapel (59x43cm-23x17in) s.d.1941 panel (S.FR 15000)

AUFRAY, Joseph (1836-?) French

£1103	$2151	(12-Oct-90 APT.P116) Petite filla la poupee (24x18cm-9x7in) s. panel (F.FR 11000)

AUGE, Philippe (1935-) French

£520	$900	(22-May-91 D.NY105) La fille de Neptune (100x102cm-39x40in) s.
£554	$903	(14-Jun-91 FB.P6) Au-Dela des desirs (89x116cm-35x46in) s. (F.FR 5500)
£694	$1200	(22-May-91 D.NY106) Le parfum de Desir (81x66cm-32x26in) s.
£1503	$2600	(22-May-91 D.NY108/R) Telle qu'en elle-meme, le desire enfin la change (101x104cm-40x41in) s.
£1676	$2900	(22-May-91 D.NY104/R) Voyage vers l'inconnu (131x196cm-52x77in) s.

AUGER, Jacques (1951-) French?

£661	$1321	(6-Feb-91 FB.P19/R) Les corps saints (65x81cm-26x32in) s. (F.FR 6500)
£663	$1272	(29-Nov-90 QWA.P253) Terrasse ensoleillee (82x54cm-32x21in) s. (F.FR 6500)
£711	$1423	(6-Feb-91 FB.P18) Conversation au jardin (73x54cm-29x21in) s. (F.FR 7000)

AUGSBURG SCHOOL, 17th C German

£1954	$3498	(14-Mar-91 D.V291/R) The schoolmaster of Falerii (144x197cm-57x78in) (A.S 40000)

AUGUSTIN (attrib) (?) ?

£2398	$4724	(14-Nov-90 FB.P30/R) Le jeune homme (85x62cm-33x24in) chl. htd.white chk. paper laid down on canvas (F.FR 23500)

AUGUSTIN, Jean Baptiste Jacques (1759-1832) French

£19000	$30970	(2-Jul-91 C342/R) Woman drawing self-portrait (30x24cm-12x9in) black lead black white chk

AUGUSTIN, Pauline (1781-1865) French

£400	$660	(10-Jul-91 C50) A gentleman in black overcoat (11x?cm-4x?in) min.s. gilt-wood frame rec.
£500	$960	(18-Dec-90 C68/R) Portrait of boy embracing chicken (13x?cm-5x?in) min.black chk paper gilt wood frame rec.
£3000	$5310	(20-Mar-91 C60/R) Portrait of lady in white dress with black muslin tunic (8cm-3ins circular) min. gilt-metal mount

AUGUSTSON, Goran (1936-) Finnish?

£1295	$2227	(14-May-91 HOR.H13) Composition (85x100cm-33x39in) s. gouache (F.M 9000)
£1576	$3105	(17-Nov-90 BU.H181/R) Tree of life (47x49cm-19x19in) s.d.74 gouache (F.M 11000)
£1854	$3635	(24-Nov-90 HOR.H43/R) Wind in the sails (48x65cm-19x26in) s.d.1976 gouache (F.M 13000)

AUJAME, Jean (1905-1965) French

£838	$1651	(6-Oct-90 GL.P6) Deux femmes a la toilette (73x35cm-29x14in) s.d.59 (F.FR 8500)
£1631	$3131	(2-Dec-90 M.V74) Femme assise pres de la riviere (33x41cm-13x16in) s. board (F.FR 16000)
£2170	$4274	(6-Oct-90 GL.P7) Bords de l'Allier au printemps (65x81cm-26x32in) s.d. l. verso (F.FR 22000)

AUJAME, Jean (1905-1965) French-cont.
£2959 $5828   (6-Oct-90 GL.P8/R) Nature morte aux fruits (72x92cm-28x36in) s.
               (F.FR 30000)

AULD, James Muir (1879-1942) Australian
£996 $1962   (31-Oct-90 CH.S50/R) The Domain, Sydney (38x45cm-15x18in) s.c.1930 board
               (A.D 2500)
£618 $1217   (13-Nov-90 J.M130 a) Backyard (24x28cm-9x11in) s. W/C (A.D 1600)

AULIE, Reidar (1904-1977) Norwegian
£825 $1608   (11-Oct-90 BU.O10/R) Salvation army officer (40x33cm-16x13in) s.d.31
               panel (N.KR 9500)
£1138 $2038   (11-Mar-91 B.O6/R) Archipelago (31x40cm-12x16in) s. panel (N.KR 13000)
£1307 $2548   (15-Oct-90 B.O5/R) Summer camp (30x41cm-12x16in) s.s.i.verso panel
               (N.KR 15000)
£1313 $2351   (11-Mar-91 B.O5/R) Portor in south west breeze (50x60cm-20x24in) s.d.51
               panel (N.KR 15000)
£1397 $2655   (11-Sep-90 UL.T169/R) Light in the sittingroom (30x40cm-12x16in)
               (N.KR 16000)
£1514 $2922   (10-Dec-90 B.O8/R) Scene from Mexico (32x40cm-13x16in) s. i.d.39verso
               (N.KR 17000)
£2364 $4232   (11-Mar-91 B.O4/R) Houses with flats (46x55cm-18x22in) s. panel
               (N.KR 27000)
£4185 $8077   (10-Dec-90 B.O5/R) Cafe interior (54x81cm-21x32in) s.d.28 (N.KR 47000)
£4452 $8593   (10-Dec-90 B.O6/R) Returning home from work (56x100cm-22x39in) s.d.35
               (N.KR 50000)
£4541 $8765   (10-Dec-90 B.O7/R) Chauffeur waiting (60x73cm-24x29in) s.d.55
               (N.KR 51000)
£13802 $26638   (13-Dec-90 BU.O4/R) The merry funeral 1935 (65x125cm-26x49in) s.d.35
               i.verso (N.KR 155000)

AULT, George C (1891-1948) American
£37989 $68000   (14-Mar-91 CH.NY213/R) Daylight at Russell's Corner (45x71cm-18x28in)
               s.d.44

AUMONIER, J (1832-1911) British
£1000 $1910   (4-Jan-91 BW423 a) Landscape (51x76cm-20x30in) s. W/C

AUMONIER, James (1832-1911) British
£500 $870   (28-Mar-91 CSK64) Old chalk pit at Houghton (30x41cm-12x16in) s.
               s.i.verso
£900 $1773   (1-Nov-90 CSK122) Evening sunlight, Ambershaw Common (61x90cm-24x35in)
               s.i.
£1502 $2553   (27-May-91 GK.Z5002/R) Scottish moor landscape with overcast sky
               (37x46cm-15x18in) s. (S.FR 3800)
£1272 $2200   (21-May-91 CE.NY241/R) Coombe Lane, Lancing, Sussex (61x90cm-24x35in) s.
               i.verso W/C over pencil board
£1400 $2758   (1-Nov-90 C109/R) Sand barges, Shoreham, Sussex (36x53cm-14x21in) s.
               i.verso pencil W/C

AUMONT, Louis (1805-1879) Danish
£4049 $6803   (23-Apr-91 RAS.K21/R) Portrait of the brothers Theodor and Torvald
               Damborg (65x55cm-26x22in) s. (D.KR 46000)

AURELI, Giuseppe (1858-1929) Italian
£1300 $2405   (5-Mar-91 AG220/R) Lady and gentleman taking coffee and liqueurs at
               pavement cafe (59x40cm-23x16in) s.i. W/C

AURIAC, Jacques (20th C) French?
£671 $1341   (7-Feb-91 R.P81/R) Mediterranee (89x116cm-35x46in) s. mixed media canvas
               (F.FR 6600)

AURRENS, Henri (1873-?) French
£2006 $3912   (12-Oct-90 APT.P63/R) Coucher de soleil (65x54cm-26x21in) s.
               (F.FR 20000)

AUSLEGER, Rudolf (1897-) German
£909 $1573   (6-May-91 ZEL.L1582/R) Still life with musical instrument
               (69x50cm-27x20in) s.d.1928 pastel board (DM 2700)

AUSTEN, A (19/20th C) British
£800 $1544   (12-Dec-90 LJ241) Pickwick and friends in courtyard of inn
               (38x58cm-15x23in) s.

AUSTEN, Alexander (19/20th C) British
£750 $1343   (10-Apr-91 CSK202/R) Huntsmen's tales (41x61cm-16x24in) s. pair

AUSTEN, Winifred (1876-1964) British
£650 $1248   (19-Feb-91 C58 a) The white feather (18x20cm-7x8in) s.mono. pencil W/C
               htd.white
£660 $1274   (10-Dec-90 PHB10) Mandarin ducks (26x23cm-10x9in) mono. pencil W/C
£1400 $2688   (19-Feb-91 C18/R) Turtle doves (25x25cm-10x10in) mono. i.verso pencil
               W/C htd.white board
£1500 $2880   (19-Feb-91 C19/R) Making off - bittern (30x43cm-12x17in) mono. pencil
               W/C htd.white

AUSTIN, Charles Percy (1883-1948) American
£745　　$1400　　(19-Sep-90 B.SF2857/R) Painted desert (76x91cm-30x36in) s.

AUSTRALIAN COLONIAL SCHOOL, 19th C Australian
£6751　　$12962　　(14-Aug-90 SY.ME205/R) Grantham at Potts point (42x60cm-17x24in) W/C
over pencil (A.D 16000)

AUSTRALIAN SCHOOL, 19th C Australian
£2500　　$4850　　(6-Dec-90 TL148) Cattle branding (17x24cm-7x9in) init.i. W/C

AUSTRIAN SCHOOL (?) Austrian
£4885　　$8745　　(14-Mar-91 D.V205/R) Still lifes of flowers (26x16cm-10x6in) c.1800
　　　　　　　　indis.s.d. i.verso panel pair (A.S 100000)
£5754　　$9954　　(22-May-91 GS.B2454/R) Shepherds merrymaking in landscape
　　　　　　　　(57x80cm-22x31in) c.1800 mono.verso (S.FR 14500)
£7328　　$13117　　(14-Mar-91 D.V72/R) Portrait of Imperial Ambassador Joachim von
　　　　　　　　Sintzendorff (232x116cm-91x46in) i.d.1600 i.verso (A.S 150000)

AUSTRIAN SCHOOL, 16th C Austrian
£2500　　$4875　　(26-Oct-90 C63/R) Saint Anthony Abbot and Saint Joseph protecting
　　　　　　　　kneeling donors, fatherand son (77x60cm-30x24in) panel
£4057　　$8032　　(30-Jan-91 APT.P85/R) Portrait de l'empereur Maximilien avec l'ordre de
　　　　　　　　la Toison d'Or (42x33cm-17x13in) panel (F.FR 40000)
£7432　　$14493　　(26-Oct-90 KM.K1048/R) Portrait of Freifrau von Alt, aged 30
　　　　　　　　(121x91cm-48x36in) d.1589 (DM 22000)

AUSTRIAN SCHOOL, 17th C Austrian
£1100　　$1793　　(3-Jul-91 S166) Portrait of Archduke Albert of Austria, wearing insignia
　　　　　　　　(74x58cm-29x23in) bears i.verso
£4111　　$7975　　(7-Dec-90 SY.MO133/R) Saint Matthieu (166x71cm-65x28in) (F.FR 40000)
£19541　　$34978　　(14-Mar-91 D.V331/R) Skirmish (168x244cm-66x96in) (A.S 400000)

AUSTRIAN SCHOOL, 18th C Austrian
£963　　$1608　　(6-Jun-91 D.V240/R) Adoration of the Shepherds (33x24cm-13x9in)
　　　　　　　　mono.d.1778 metal (A.S 20000)
£1032　　$1847　　(13-Mar-91 GK.Z70/R) Portrait of female singer holding sheet of music
　　　　　　　　(39x29cm-15x11in) panel (S.FR 2600)
£1130　　$2023　　(13-Mar-91 N.M429 a) Rider and traveller by waterfall in mountain
　　　　　　　　landscape (24x34cm-9x13in) (DM 3300)
£1145　　$1947　　(31-May-91 LD.P20/R) Enfant a la corbeille de fleurs (41x29cm-16x11in)
　　　　　　　　panel (F.FR 11500)
£1466　　$2623　　(14-Mar-91 D.V341/R) Young man with dead hare (63x43cm-25x17in)
　　　　　　　　(A.S 30000)
£2648　　$4422　　(6-Jun-91 D.V229/R) Portrait of noble lady as huntress. Nobleman with
　　　　　　　　glass of wine (41x33cm-16x13in) pair (A.S 55000)
£4795　　$7815　　(12-Jun-91 N.M337/R) Austrian cavalry in hilly landscape near rocks and
　　　　　　　　village beyond (78x110cm-31x43in) (DM 14000)
£8446　　$14358　　(27-May-91 L.K93) The Finding of Moses (130x96cm-51x38in) (DM 25000)
£11821　　$20450　　(21-May-91 SY.MI1042/R) Paesaggi con contadini e signori a cavallo
　　　　　　　　(50x63cm-20x25in) pair (I.L 26000000)
£17647　　$30000　　(30-May-91 SY.NY24/R) Portrait of twins in country dress holding hands,
　　　　　　　　one holding lemon (92x113cm-36x44in)
£1306　　$2573　　(13-Nov-90 CH.G208/R) Portrait of Empress Maria Theresia of Habsburg
wearing widow's weeds (3x?cm-1x?in) min. enamel gilt-metal mount oval
(S.FR 3200)

AUSTRIAN SCHOOL, 19th C Austrian
£1470　　$2910　　(31-Jan-91 D.V99/R) Young monk in his study (26x34cm-10x13in) indis.s.
　　　　　　　　board (A.S 30000)
£1540　　$2680　　(25-Mar-91 SY.F683/R) Paesaggio con pastore (49x64cm-19x25in)
　　　　　　　　(I.L 3400000)
£1711　　$3250　　(27-Feb-91 SY.NY158/R) Praying at Western Wall (46x80cm-18x31in) panel
£1960　　$3880　　(31-Jan-91 D.V59/R) Young girl with rabbit (87x72cm-34x28in) c.1846
　　　　　　　　(A.S 40000)
£2180　　$3510　　(27-Jun-91 D.V115) Wein, Weib und Gesang (92x79cm-36x31in) oval
　　　　　　　　(A.S 45000)
£2205　　$4366　　(31-Jan-91 D.V87/R) Salzkammergut (52x69cm-20x27in) c.1840 (A.S 45000)
£2600　　$4264　　(18-Jun-91 PH96/R) Figures before waterfall in landscape
　　　　　　　　(84x72cm-33x28in) indis.s.d.1869
£4196　　$8098　　(12-Dec-90 N.M659/R) Mountainous lake landscape with farmhouse, possibly
　　　　　　　　Salzkammergut (67x84cm-26x33in) i. i.verso (DM 12000)
£1028　　$1994　　(8-Dec-90 SY.MO419/R) Ananas (42x32cm-17x13in) W/C (F.FR 10000)
£2865　　$4814　　(25-Apr-91 D.V182/R) Views of Vienna (49x26cm-19x10in) min.i.gouache on
paper 8 in folding frame (A.S 60000)
£5253　　$8825　　(25-Apr-91 D.V257/R) View of Venice from San Giorgio Maggiore
(28x42cm-11x17in) i. W/C (A.S 110000)

AUSTRIAN SCHOOL, 20th C Austrian
£2400　　$4704　　(14-Feb-91 CSK92) A horse and cart in front of an onion domed church
　　　　　　　　(23x28cm-9x11in) indist.s.d. board

AUSTRIAN, Ben (1870-1921) American
£1282　　$2500　　(20-Oct-90 FA.PH890) Late summer (41x51cm-16x20in) s. i.verso
£7143　　$12000　　(21-Jul-91 LIT.L229) The chase for the caterpillar (38x51cm-15x20in)
　　　　　　　　s.d.1912
£7216　　$14000　　(7-Dec-90 S.W2663/R) Hen and chicks (38x51cm-15x20in) s.d.1906

72

AUTARD, Georges (20th C) French?
£5040 $9829   (23-Oct-90 CSC.P79/R) Sans titre (210x300cm-83x118in) s.d.septembre 85
                      verso acrylic diptych (F.FR 50000)

AUTISSIER, Louis Marie (1772-1830) French
£1224 $2412   (13-Nov-90 CH.G266) Portrait of young lady wearing gold tiara and
                      blue-grey silk dress (9x6cm-4x2in) min.s.d.1814 gilt-metal mount
                      (S.FR 3000)

AUTRAN, Henri (1926-) French
£545 $964   (7-Apr-91 I.N25) Le village (44x51cm-17x20in) s. panel (F.FR 5500)
£655 $1067   (11-Jun-91 I.N153) Paysage au chemin (61x46cm-24x18in) s. hardboard
                      (F.FR 6500)

AUTREAU, Jacques (1657-1745) French
£28141 $46151   (21-Jun-91 SY.MO14/R) Madame de Tencin servant le chocolat a Bernard le
                      Bovier, Antoine Houdaret Saurin (72x90cm-28x35in) (F.FR 280000)

AVANESSIAN, Alfonso (20th C) ?
£1531 $2985   (22-Oct-90 BR.M251/R) Mare in Puglia (80x60cm-31x24in) s. (I.L 3400000)

AVANZI, Vittorio (1850-1910) Italian
£6533 $10714   (21-Jun-91 SY.MO323/R) Paysage de printemps (64x106cm-25x42in) s.
                      (F.FR 65000)

AVENAL, Vidal G (19/20th C) Spanish
£3289 $6250   (27-Feb-91 SY.NY363/R) Flamenco dance in Seville (53x90cm-21x35in)
                      s.d.1904

AVENALI, Marcello (1912-) Italian
£1531 $2985   (22-Oct-90 BR.M300/R) Figure n.2 (47x42cm-19x17in) s. tempera panel
                      (I.L 3400000)
£955 $1871   (20-Nov-90 BR.M24/R) Figura (46x65cm-18x26in) s.d.1961 ink
                      (I.L 2100000)
£1091 $2138   (20-Nov-90 BR.M180/R) Palazzo del Senato (31x44cm-12x17in) s.d.1961 ink
                      (I.L 2400000)
£2029 $3631   (9-Apr-91 F.R48) Composizione (104x38cm-41x15in) s. mixed media collage
                      paper laid down on panel (I.L 4500000)

AVENDANO, Serafin de (1838-1916) Spanish
£1638 $2834   (8-May-91 FER.M131/R) Apunte de mi pobre rincon (21x16cm-8x6in) s. paper
                      (S.P 300000)
£7025 $13699   (22-Oct-90 ANS.M32/R) Marina (78x122cm-31x48in) s. (S.P 1300000)
£7644 $13224   (8-May-91 FER.M132/R) Aldeana en el camino (35x45cm-14x18in) s.d.94
                      (S.P 1400000)
£601 $1039   (8-May-91 FER.M10/R) Tipos del mercado de Chapela, Vigo
                      (40x25cm-16x10in) s. chl dr (S.P 110000)
£710 $1371   (11-Dec-90 FER.M128/R) El abrevadero (14x21cm-6x8in) s. W/C
                      (S.P 130000)
£715 $1279   (13-Mar-91 FER.M64/R) Vereda del rio. Cipreses frente a la casa. Recodo
                      del rio Mino. Arboleda junto al rio Mino (12x16cm-5x6in) s. chl dr
                      four in one frame (S.P 130000)
£759 $1480   (17-Oct-90 FER.M22/R) Pueblos gallegos (11x15cm-4x6in) s. pencil dr four
                      in one frame (S.P 140000)
£874 $1687   (11-Dec-90 FER.M13/R) Paisajes y casas asturianas y gallegas
                      (16x11cm-6x4in) s. chl dr four in one frame (S.P 160000)
£874 $1687   (11-Dec-90 FER.M16/R) Vistas de Galicia y Asturias (11x16cm-4x6in) s.
                      chl dr four in one frame (S.P 160000)

AVERCAMP, Barent (17th C) Dutch
£57895 $110000   (11-Jan-91 CH.NY91/R) A frozen river with skaters, Kolf players, hunters
                      and figures in a sled (30x54cm-12x21in) s. panel

AVERCAMP, Hendrick (1585-1663) Dutch
£1658 $3250   (7-Nov-90 B.SF1003/R) Winter scene (12x13cm-5x5in) i. indist.st. W/C pen

AVERY, Milton (1893-1965) American
£4233 $8000   (27-Sep-90 CH.NY321/R) Girl with scarf (42x30cm-17x12in) s.d.1955 i.
                      verso board
£4233 $8000   (27-Sep-90 CH.NY320/R) Turbaned girl (25x20cm-10x8in) s.d.1961 i. verso
                      board
£6145 $11000   (14-Mar-91 CH.NY235/R) Fisherman (26x31cm-10x12in) s. board
£6358 $11000   (22-May-91 CH.NY316/R) Feeding the baby (76x57cm-30x22in) s. W/C
                      chl.paper laid down on board
£7407 $14000   (26-Sep-90 SY.NY221/R) Fishing (46x60cm-18x24in) s. canvasboard
£8466 $16000   (26-Sep-90 SY.NY220/R) Ploughed landscape (46x61cm-18x24in) s. i.verso
                      canvasboard
£8671 $15000   (23-May-91 SY.NY94/R) Seated woman sketching (61x46cm-24x18in) s.
                      canvasboard
£9497 $17000   (14-Mar-91 CH.NY214/R) Mug with flowers (51x41cm-20x16in) s.d.1948 board
£10417 $20000   (29-Nov-90 SY.NY113/R) Dancing trees (58x89cm-23x35in) s.d.1960 i.verso
                      paper
£21164 $40000   (26-Sep-90 SY.NY222/R) Orange shade (49x64cm-19x25in) s.d.1949
                      canvasboard
£466 $900   (16-Dec-90 LIT.L38/R) Seated nude (28x20cm-11x8in) s. crayon ink

AVERY, Milton (1893-1965) American-cont.
£529	$1000	(25-Sep-90 CE.NY123/R) Peasant woman (42x36cm-17x14in) s. brush sepia ink
£1387	$2400	(7-May-91 CE.NY152/R) Seated nude (28x21cm-11x8in) s. col.crayons ball-point pen
£1974	$3750	(14-Sep-90 S.BM306/R) Life drawing class (41x33cm-16x13in) s.d.1956 marker
£2083	$4000	(17-Dec-90 SY.NY425/R) Leaning nude (43x33cm-17x13in) s. flobrush
£2083	$4000	(17-Dec-90 SY.NY427/R) Nude with table (41x33cm-16x13in) s. graphite
£3646	$7000	(30-Nov-90 CH.NY210/R) Red landscape, blue trees (43x56cm-17x22in) s.d.1955 oil crayon ink wash
£3776	$7250	(17-Dec-90 SY.NY388/R) Rolling hills (43x58cm-17x23in) s.i.verso gouache W/C
£6145	$11000	(12-Apr-91 SY.NY105/R) Saratoga landscape (46x60cm-18x24in) s.d.1955 pastel

AVERY, Sally Michel (20th C) American
£691	$1300	(11-Aug-90 COL.M71/R) The letter (61x46cm-24x18in) s.d.1969 board

AVISSAR, Simon (1938-) Israeli
£1484	$2656	(14-Apr-91 GL.P41/R) Paysage rouge (73x60cm-29x24in) s. i. verso (F.FR 15000)
£2912	$5387	(6-Mar-91 D.P29/R) Paysage (81x65cm-32x26in) s. (F.FR 29000)

AVNER (?) ?
£1205	$2229	(10-Mar-91 LT.P135) Peintre sur le pont de Paris (46x65cm-18x26in) s. pastel (F.FR 12000)
£1223	$2349	(2-Dec-90 M.V87/R) Les pecheurs (48x62cm-19x24in) s. pastel (F.FR 12000)
£1423	$2462	(12-May-91 T.B50/R) Voiliers dans la Tempete (49x63cm-19x25in) s. pastel (F.FR 14300)
£1631	$3148	(16-Dec-90 T.B232/R) Marche en Bretagne (50x65cm-20x26in) s. pastel (F.FR 16000)
£1940	$3357	(12-May-91 T.B215/R) Scene de moisson (48x63cm-19x25in) s. pastel (F.FR 19500)
£3364	$6492	(16-Dec-90 T.B47/R) Les lavandieres a Trevignon (73x100cm-29x39in) s. pastel (F.FR 33000)

AVNI, Aaron (1906-1951) Israeli
£1885	$3600	(1-Jan-91 GG.TA202/R) Violinist and pianist, artist's daughter (73x62cm-29x24in) s.

AVNI, Shimon (1932-) Israeli
£1099	$2100	(1-Jan-91 GG.TA203/R) Looking for shelter (121x80cm-48x31in) s.d.1987
£1840	$3000	(12-Jun-91 GG.TA226/R) Intimacy (149x120cm-59x47in) s.

AVONT, Pieter van (attrib) (1600-1632) Flemish
£3479	$5880	(18-Apr-91 APT.P34/R) La Sainte Famille. Le Martyre de Saint Etienne (16x21cm-6x8in) copper oval pair (F.FR 35000)
£5245	$10122	(10-Dec-90 L.K3/R) Flight to Egypt with Holy Family and infant St John resting in landscape (34x49cm-13x19in) (DM 15000)

AVONT, Pieter van (circle) (1600-1632) Flemish
£2410	$4651	(12-Dec-90 BU.S116/R) Resting on The Flight to Egypt (90x72cm-35x28in) (S.KR 26000)

AVONT, Pieter van (style) (1600-1632) Flemish
£4200	$6846	(4-Jul-91 C726/R) Rest on Return from Egypt (42x31cm-17x12in) copper

AVRAMIDIS, Joannis (20th C) ?
£680	$1115	(20-Jun-91 D.V140/R) Two nudes (38x27cm-15x11in) s.d.1960 pencil (A.S 14000)
£971	$1592	(20-Jun-91 D.V139/R) Nude (36x25cm-14x10in) d.1960 s.d.verso pencil (A.S 20000)

AVY, Joseph (1871-?) French
£1494	$2585	(24-May-91 FB.P157) Elegante au theatre (54x45cm-21x18in) s. pastel (F.FR 15000)

AXENTOWICZ, Theodor (1859-1938) Polish
£840	$1554	(10-Mar-91 AG.W1) Dziewczynka (49x34cm-19x13in) s. pastel (P.Z 15000000)
£3217	$6305	(26-Jan-91 PSA.W2) Self-portrait with grand-daughter (48x67cm-19x26in) s. pastel (P.Z 60000000)
£3485	$6830	(26-Jan-91 PSA.W1) Self-portrait with young woman (71x50cm-28x20in) s. pastel gouache (P.Z 65000000)

AXER, Otto (1909-1983) Polish ?
£2143	$4243	(1-Feb-91 DE.B1) Figures in landscape (62x57cm-24x22in) s.d.1928 board (P.Z 40000000)

AYALA, Josefa de (style) (c.1630-1684) Spanish
£4200	$7098	(19-Apr-91 C111) Apples in a porcelain bowl with radishes on a ledge (49x49cm-19x19in)
£6800	$11492	(19-Apr-91 C110/R) Apples in a basket with pears and figs in porcelain bowl and other fruit (83x111cm-33x44in)

AYERSTINGRAM, W (?) ?
£550 $1029   (1-Aug-90 CSK87) Moored alongside in river estuary (36x74cm-14x29in) s.
                    W/C

AYLING, Albert W (?-1905) British
£600 $1182   (14-Nov-90 CSK52) Tired out (51x76cm-20x30in) s. i.verso pencil W/C

AYLING, George (20th C) British
£1800 $3114   (22-May-91 S168/R) Moonrise, mist and merchandise on London river
                    (55x75cm-22x30ir.) s. s.i.verso canvas on board
£2400 $4680   (18-Oct-90 CSK73) Barges on Thames at Waterloo Bridge, Shell House
                    beyond (40x56cm-16x22in) s. board

AYLWARD, J D (19/20th C) British
£1050 $1806   (14-May-91 SWS248/R) The latest scandal (21x29cm-8x11in) s. panel

AYLWARD, James D (19/20th C) British
£1800 $3528   (20-Nov-90 PH92/R) Hard times (23x31cm-9x12in) s. panel

AYOTTE, Leo (1909-1976) Canadian
£538 $1039   (12-Dec-90 EA.M621/R) Landscape (20x25cm-8x10in) s. board (C.D 1200)
£758 $1311   (6-May-91 SY.T199 a) Sailboat in harbour (45x36cm-18x14in) s.d.42 panel
                    (C.D 1500)
£1010 $1747   (6-May-91 SY.T165/R) Rural house (37x45cm-15x18in) s. board (C.D 2000)
£1147 $2167   (26-Sep-90 EA.M648/R) Paysage de Laurentides (40x51cm-16x20in) s.d.73
                    (C.D 2500)
£1316 $2579   (21-Nov-90 EA.M687/R) Chemin ombrage par des erables (51x61cm-20x24in)
                    s. (C.D 3000)
£1659 $3252   (5-Nov-90 FB.M177) Village - Chateau-Richer (51x61cm-20x24in) s.d.1967
                    (C.D 3800)
£1674 $3264   (24-Oct-90 EA.M478/R) House in summer landscape (61x76cm-24x30in) s.d.69
                    (C.D 3800)
£1835 $3468   (26-Sep-90 EA.M626/R) Lorsque le Ruisseau devient etang
                    (61x76cm-24x30in) s.d.75 (C.D 4000)

AYRES, Gillian (1930-) British
£2500 $4075   (1-Jul-91 S19/R) Untitled (61x92cm-24x36in) s.d.86
£8000 $15600   (9-Oct-90 B186/R) Lucas (244cm-96ins circular) s. s.i.d.1985 verso tondo
£8000 $15600   (9-Oct-90 B183/R) Sappho (91cm-36ins circular) s.d.88 s.i.d.verso tondo
£8000 $15600   (18-Oct-90 S182/R) Captain Digorie Piper's Galliard (152x152cm-60x60in)
£13500 $24975   (8-Mar-91 C208/R) Abstract composition (213x244cm-84x96in) s.d.87
                    i.verso
£700 $1169   (7-Jun-91 C323/R) Abstract (66x51cm-26x20in) s.d.63 oil gouache collage

AYRTON, Michael (1921-1975) British
£3800 $6346   (6-Jun-91 C216/R) Winter (51x61cm-20x24in) s.d.50 s.i.verso
£7500 $14700   (7-Nov-90 S143/R) Night fall (69x51cm-27x20in) s.d.49 board
£620 $1042   (24-Apr-91 CSK180) Ierapetra II (37x55cm-15x22in) s.i.d.16.4.61 ink wash
£900 $1755   (9-Oct-90 B4/R) La Source (28x43cm-11x17in) pen wash
£1500 $2535   (2-May-91 C113/R) Minotaur (49x36cm-19x14in) s.d.25.10.70 pen
£2500 $4350   (27-Mar-91 S153/R) Apple trees by moonlight (54x40cm-21x16in) s.d.45 pen
                    ink wash over pencil htd.white
£2900 $5626   (7-Dec-90 K649) Tuscan vine workers, 1950 (33x20cm-13x8in) gouache

AZPIROZ, Manuel de (?) ?
£594 $1159   (23-Oct-90 DUR.M62) Mujer con cesto de frutas (25x19cm-10x7in) board
                    (S.P 110000)
£703 $1370   (23-Oct-90 DUR.M31) Pescadora (92x73cm-36x29in) panel (S.P 130000)

AZUZ, David (1942-) Israeli
£663 $1307   (16-Nov-90 LGB.P88) Scene de cafe (37x32cm-15x13in) s. gouache
                    (F.FR 6500)
£940 $1682   (14-Apr-91 GL.P43) Femmes au marche (50x65cm-20x26in) s. oil pastel
                    paper laid down on canvas (F.FR 9500)

B M (?) ?
£994 $1858   (27-Aug-90 SY.J160/R) In the kitchen (42x32cm-17x13in) init.d.1864 panel
                    (SA.R 4800)

BAADE, Knud Andreassen (1808-1879) Norwegian
£574 $1148   (9-Feb-91 BU.O13) Trees (42x29cm-17x11in) s. panel (N.KR 6500)
£1839 $3292   (11-Mar-91 B.O15/R) Alpine mountain landscape (26x42cm-10x17in)
                    mono.d.54 panel (N.KR 21000)
£3659 $7134   (15-Oct-90 B.O10/R) Shipwreck on beach (40x59cm-16x23in) s.d.1874
                    (N.KR 42000)

BAADER, L (19th C) French
£838 $1500   (16-Mar-91 W.W51/R) Nuns and bluebirds (66x86cm-26x34in) s.d.1890 canvas
                    mounted on masonite

BAADER, Louis Marie (1828-1919) French
£4266 $7337   (19-May-91 ZZ.F53/R) La visite impromptue (81x102cm-32x40in) s.
                       (F.FR 43000)

BAADSGAARD, Alfrida (1839-1912) Danish
£718 $1415   (14-Nov-90 RAS.K172) Still life of nuts and fruit on table
                       (32x48cm-13x19in) s. (D.KR 8000)
£814 $1612   (31-Jan-91 RAS.V465/R) Still life of nuts and fruit on table
                       (32x48cm-13x19in) s. (D.KR 9100)
£1182 $2306   (26-Oct-90 KM.K1090) Still life of Christmas roses and other flowers
                       (57x45cm-22x18in) s.d.1896 panel (DM 3500)

BAAGOE, Carl (1829-1902) Danish
£583 $1149   (14-Nov-90 RAS.K278) Seascape with sailship (30x41cm-12x16in) s.d.86
                       (D.KR 6500)
£815 $1573   (10-Dec-90 BU.K55/R) Seascape with sailship, sun breaking through after
                       storm (24x34cm-9x13in) s. (D.KR 9000)
£890 $1745   (22-Nov-90 RAS.V698/R) Seascape with sailship (33x51cm-13x20in) s.d.1871
                       (D.KR 10000)
£1335 $2509   (18-Sep-90 BU.K20/R) Seascape with sailship off Iceland
                       (32x45cm-13x18in) s.d.1857 (D.KR 15000)
£1761 $2958   (23-Apr-91 RAS.K406/R) Seascape with the schooner 'Karrebaek'
                       (49x71cm-19x28in) s.d.1879 (D.KR 20000)
£2083 $4021   (10-Dec-90 BU.K56/R) Sailship in rough seas (24x34cm-9x13in) s.d.84 pair
                       (D.KR 23000)
£430   *$860*   *(6-Feb-91 RAS.K520) The frigate 'Jylland' passing Kronborg*
                       (18x25cm-7x10in) s.d.1897 pencil silver (D.KR 4800)

BAAIJENS, Frans (1896-?) Dutch
£509 $993   (25-Oct-90 VN.R6) Wooded river landscape near Groesbeek
                       (50x70cm-20x28in) s. (D.FL 1700)

BAAR-PLOMMER, Anna (1836-1890) Austrian
£1187 $2124   (11-Apr-91 D.V79/R) Lake landscape with view of town (33x53cm-13x21in)
                       s.d.89 (A.S 25000)

BABKOV, Serguei (1920-) Russian
£697 $1212   (25-Mar-91 ARC.P37/R) Dans l'atelier du peintre (30x36cm-12x14in) s.
                       board (F.FR 7000)
£746 $1299   (25-Mar-91 ARC.P41) La ballerine (35x50cm-14x20in) s. board (F.FR 7500)
£796 $1385   (25-Mar-91 ARC.P40/R) Sur le lac (77x63cm-30x25in) s. (F.FR 8000)
£896 $1558   (25-Mar-91 ARC.P39) Le premier rendez-vous (61x50cm-24x20in) s.
                       (F.FR 9000)
£1144 $1991   (25-Mar-91 ARC.P34/R) L'ecoliere (48x33cm-19x13in) s. board (F.FR 11500)
£1156 $2219   (18-Feb-91 ARC.P196/R) Jeune femme a la robe rouge (109x70cm-43x28in)
                       s.d.74 (F.FR 11500)
£1393 $2424   (25-Mar-91 ARC.P38/R) Les poemes (102x74cm-40x29in) s. (F.FR 14000)
£3483 $6060   (25-Mar-91 ARC.P35/R) La femme en rouge (68x26cm-27x10in) s. board
                       (F.FR 35000)

BABOULENE, Eugene (1905-) French
£2574 $4556   (7-Apr-91 I.N26 b) Les Iles (24x33cm-9x13in) s. (F.FR 26000)
£3244 $6293   (5-Dec-90 AB.S7016/R) Laj chaise bleue (50x65cm-20x26in) s. d.1954verso
                       (S.KR 35000)
£3568 $6850   (30-Nov-90 ARC.P138/R) Bouquet champetre (55x37cm-22x15in) s.
                       (F.FR 35000)
£3586 $6096   (29-May-91 GL.P191) Village de Pissy (50x73cm-20x29in) s. d.1958 verso
                       (F.FR 36000)
£4684 $9228   (30-Oct-90 I.N133/R) Les fleurs (46x33cm-18x13in) s. (F.FR 46000)
£5306 $10453   (18-Nov-90 H.A71) Hameau de Dardennes (38x55cm-15x22in) s.i.
                       (F.FR 52000)
£5754 $9897   (19-May-91 ZZ.F169/R) Le Saint Pierre (60x120cm-24x47in) s. d.1964 verso
                       (F.FR 58000)
£11782 $20854   (7-Apr-91 I.N26/R) Marine (60x92cm-24x36in) s.i.d.1961 (F.FR 119000)
£2535   *$5020*   *(3-Feb-91 I.N13/R) Interieur (41x54cm-16x21in) s. gouache laid down on*
                       canvas (F.FR 25000)

BABUREN, Dirck van (style) (17th C) Dutch
£1710 $3061   (14-Mar-91 D.V286/R) Pipe smoker (73x61cm-29x24in) (A.S 35000)

BACARISAS, Gustavo (19/20th C) Spanish
£1645 $2764   (23-Apr-91 DUR.M9/R) La Feria antigua de Sevilla (80x92cm-31x36in)
                       (S.P 300000)

BACCANI, Attilio (19th C) Italian
£1600 $3120   (18-Oct-90 SC3147/R) Portrait of a lady (140x101cm-55x40in) s.d.1894
£3000 $5910   (4-Oct-90 CSK186/R) Othello a fete champetre (82x128cm-32x50in) s.d.1875

BACCI, Baccio Maria (1888-?) Italian
£8000 $16000   (18-Oct-90 F.M26/R) I vagabondi (129x128cm-51x50in) s.d.1921 i.verso
                       (I.L 18000000)

BACCI, Edmondo (1913-) Italian
£2296 $4500   (6-Nov-90 CE.NY62/R) Avvenimento No.381 (80x110cm-31x43in) s. oil sand

BACCIGALUPPO, Giuseppe (1744-1821) Italian
£110553 $181307 (21-Jun-91 SY.MO129/R) Vue de Port de Genes (85x115cm-33x45in)
s.d.ANMDCCCVIII (F.FR 1100000)

BACH, Alois (1809-1893) German
£5822 $9490 (12-Jun-91 SY.MU40/R) Before the ride (45x60cm-18x24in) s. panel
(DM 17000)

BACH, Andreas (1886-?) German
£671 $1309 (10-Oct-90 WE.MU208/R) View of Nurnberg Altstadt (31x26cm-12x10in) panel
(DM 2000)
£805 $1570 (10-Oct-90 WE.MU209/R) Street in Nurnberg Altstadt (31x26cm-12x10in)
s.d.1920 panel (DM 2400)

BACH, Carl Daniel (1756-1829) German
£5119 $9676 (25-Sep-90 FN.S2107/R) Conquest of Greek town by Roman legions
(117x175cm-46x69in) s. (DM 15000)

BACH, Elvira (1951-) ?
£5236 $8902 (1-Jun-91 VG.B391/R) Morgens mittags abends ... und das Herz von Volker
(190x230cm-75x91in) s.i.d.1981 (DM 15500)

BACH, Guido (1828-1905) German
£1000 $1960 (22-Nov-90 CSK211) Young water carrier (76x60cm-30x24in) s.d.1865
*£900 $1701 (26-Sep-90 S338/R) Negro girl wearing red and purple headscarf
(42x31cm-17x12in) s.d.1877 W/C*

BACH, Max (1841-1914) German
£3754 $7096 (25-Sep-90 FN.S2108/R) View of Rottenburg on the Neckar
(41x59cm-16x23in) s. (DM 11000)

BACHE, Otto (1839-1927) Danish
£717 $1434 (6-Feb-91 RAS.K487/R) Two horses in field (50x65cm-20x26in) s.
(D.KR 8000)
£770 $1486 (10-Dec-90 BU.K12/R) At the helm (24x18cm-9x7in) init. panel (D.KR 8500)
£801 $1571 (22-Nov-90 RAS.V688/R) Four pointers s. (D.KR 9000)
£906 $1748 (10-Dec-90 BU.K51/R) Portrait of a white dog (72x77cm-28x30in) s.d.1913
(D.KR 10000)
£1125 $2182 (22-Aug-90 RAS.K134/R) Two men conversing by horse and cart
(33x42cm-13x17in) s.d.1876 (D.KR 13000)
£1298 $2517 (22-Aug-90 RAS.K87/R) Returning from a day's work (67x90cm-26x35in)
s.d.1922 (D.KR 15000)
£1300 $2535 (15-Jan-91 C128/R) Four fox hounds (20x43cm-8x17in) s.
£1410 $2354 (6-Jun-91 RAS.K189/R) Thorough-bred horse with jockey Warne up
(79x79cm-31x31in) 193 (D.KR 16000)
£1498 $2801 (29-Aug-90 KH.K10/R) Horses grazing (52x79cm-20x31in) s. (D.KR 17000)
£1800 $3096 (17-May-91 C159/R) At races (30x43cm-12x17in) s.d.1877
£2580 $5031 (19-Oct-90 RAS.V456/R) Horses grazing (52x79cm-20x31in) s. (D.KR 29000)
£5824 $11649 (6-Feb-91 RAS.K44/R) Dachshund and puppies (50x67cm-20x26in) s.d.1866
(D.KR 65000)

BACHELIER, Jean Jacques (circle) (1724-1806) French
£2800 $4732 (18-Apr-91 C4/R) A cat taking a rock dove (67x89cm-26x35in)

BACHELIN, Auguste (1830-1890) Swiss
£816 $1584 (8-Dec-90 GAB.G2106/R) Jeune femme au bord de l'eau (25x34cm-10x13in)
mono. wood (S.FR 2000)

BACHMANN (?) ?
£1938 $3276 (19-Apr-91 CB.P126/R) Vue du Bosphore et de Aghia Sofia (24x33cm-9x13in)
s. panel (F.FR 19500)

BACHMANN, Adolphe (19/20th C) Swiss
£2513 $4121 (21-Jun-91 D.P81/R) Venise, embarcadere place Saint Marc
(38x55cm-15x22in) s. (F.FR 25000)

BACHMANN, Alfred (1863-?) German
£996 $1723 (24-May-91 FB.P170) Paysage (33x46cm-13x18in) s.i. (F.FR 10000)
£1156 $2000 (8-May-91 RO.BA17) Paysage anime (31x26cm-12x10in) s. panel
£1156 $2000 (8-May-91 RO.BA18) Paysage anime (31x26cm-12x10in) s. panel
£2191 $3725 (27-May-91 APT.P246/R) Le Bosphore (23x33cm-9x13in) s. panel
(F.FR 22000)
£2879 $4952 (16-May-91 D.V19/R) View of Istanbul (65x81cm-26x32in) s. (A.S 60000)

BACHMANN, Hans (1852-?) Swiss
£1837 $3490 (14-Sep-90 ZOF.Z1037/R) Peasant boy from Luzern (36x28cm-14x11in) s.
(S.FR 4500)
£4762 $7952 (7-Jun-91 ZOF.Z1267) Aargau farmhouse (51x71cm-20x28in) s.d.1908
(S.FR 12000)
£12245 $24000 (6-Nov-90 GF.L2217/R) At grandfather's (91x61cm-36x24in) s. (S.FR 30000)
*£476 $824 (22-May-91 GS.B2026) Children giving presents to couple in interior
(18x24cm-7x9in) indian ink (S.FR 1200)*

BACHMANN, J (19/20th C) ?
£854 $1401 (19-Jun-91 JM.P117) Devant le Palais des Doges (54x73cm-21x29in) s.
(F.FR 8500)

BACHMANN, Otto (1915-) Swiss
£637 $1096   (14-May-91 GF.L2638/R) Playing solitaire (35x27cm-14x11in) mono. canvas
                   on board (S.FR 1600)
£714 $1400   (12-Feb-91 SY.NY216/R) Josette (99x46cm-39x18in) s.d.1958 s.i.verso
                   masonite
£2372 $4032   (27-May-91 GK.Z5302/R) Josette with the blue eyes (100x45cm-39x18in)
                   s.d.1958 s.i.verso (S.FR 6000)
£816 $1584   (7-Dec-90 G.Z290) Outside the cafe (41x47cm-16x19in) s.d.1941 mixed
                   media (S.FR 2000)
£3571 $6179   (25-May-91 AB.L85/R) Untitled (70x50cm-28x20in) s.d.1985 oil mixed media
                   (S.FR 9000)

BACHUR, Anthony (20th C) French
£593 $1062   (14-Apr-91 R.P141/R) Composition (100x81cm-39x32in) s. acrylic
                   (F.FR 6000)
£958 $1867   (28-Oct-90 R.P249) Composition abstraite (130x95cm-51x37in) s. acrylic
                   (F.FR 9500)
£692 $1239   (14-Apr-91 R.P200/R) Composition (130x97cm-51x38in) s. mixed media
                   canvas (F.FR 7000)
£726 $1415   (28-Oct-90 R.P118) Super Nova (130x95cm-51x37in) s. mixed media panel
                   (F.FR 7200)
£762 $1524   (7-Feb-91 R.P202 b) Sans titre (130x87cm-51x34in) s. surpique canvas
                   (F.FR 7500)
£1728 $3455   (7-Feb-91 R.P108) Composition (130x89cm-51x35in) s. verso mixed media
                   canvas (F.FR 17000)

BACICCIA see GAULLI, Giovanni Battista

BACK, Admiral Sir George (1796-1878) British?
£750 $1478   (15-Nov-90 CSK57/R) S.W.view of Great Slave Lake near Fort Providence,
                   Latitude 62.77.24N (17x27cm-7x11in) s.i.d.1823 varnished W/C

BACK, Yngve (1904-) Finnish
£2853 $5592   (24-Nov-90 HOR.H55/R) View from Villa Lante's window (70x65cm-28x26in)
                   s.d.1969 (F.M 20000)

BACKER, Jacob Adriaensz (1608-1651) Dutch
£4000 $6520   (2-Jul-91 C214/R) Young man, wearing plumed hat, leaning on parapet
                   (28x18cm-11x7in) num.6 verso black white chk

BACKER, Jacob Adriaensz (circle) (1608-1651) Dutch
£1162 $2289   (13-Nov-90 CH.AM96) Entombment (71x107cm-28x42in) panel (D.FL 3800)

BACKER, Jacob de (1560-c.1590) Flemish
£16201 $29000   (11-Apr-91 SY.NY163/R) Last Judgment (66x47cm-26x19in) panel

BACKER, Jacob de (after) (1560-c.1590) Flemish
£1500 $2955   (31-Oct-90 S137/R) Portrait of elderly lady (105x88cm-41x35in) panel

BACKER, Jacob de (attrib) (1560-c.1590) Flemish
£6311 $11297   (8-Apr-91 CH.R200/R) Concertino di dama alla spinetta e gentiluomo con
                   liuto (67x52cm-26x20in) panel (I.L 14000000)

BACKER, Jacob de (circle) (1560-c.1590) Flemish
£746 $1260   (18-Apr-91 APT.P42) Le Christ Redempteur (26x18cm-10x7in) l. panel
                   (F.FR 7500)

BACKMANSSON, Hugo (1860-1953) Finnish
£710 $1271   (14-Apr-91 BU.H11/R) Southern beach landscape (27x35cm-11x14in) s.i.
                   (F.M 5000)
£863 $1666   (15-Dec-90 BU.H21) Bazaar scene (40x50cm-16x20in) s.i. (F.M 6000)
£994 $1780   (14-Apr-91 BU.H10/R) A Maroccan (57x43cm-22x17in) s.i.d.1919 panel
                   (F.M 7000)
£1007 $1944   (15-Dec-90 BU.H20) View of street (38x27cm-15x11in) s.i. (F.M 7000)
£1712 $3355   (24-Nov-90 HOR.H45/R) By the well (46x65cm-18x26in) s.d.1920
                   (F.M 12000)
£345 $666   (15-Dec-90 BU.H208) Telephone conversation (22x30cm-9x12in) s.d.1900 W/C
                   (F.M 2400)
£374 $722   (15-Dec-90 BU.H209) Soldier (49x33cm-19x13in) s. gouache (F.M 2600)
£2006 $3951   (17-Nov-90 BU.H182/R) Landscape from the skerries (32x48cm-13x19in)
                   s.id.1937 gouache (F.M 14000)

BACKSTROM, Barbro (1939-1990) Swedish
£1127 $1915   (28-May-91 AB.S5177/R) Untitled (70x100cm-28x39in) s.d.1976 Indian ink
                   (S.KR 12000)

BACKVIS, Francois (1857-1926) Belgian
£2156 $3751   (26-Mar-91 VN.R7/R) Russian horse drawn wagon chased by wolves
                   (79x129cm-31x51in) s. (D.FL 7200)
£2397 $3908   (12-Jun-91 N.M364/R) Flock of sheep and shepherd attacked by wolves
                   (100x170cm-39x67in) s.d.1886 (DM 7000)

BACLER D'ALBE, Baron Louis (1761-1824) French
£15075 $24724   (21-Jun-91 SY.MO300/R) Portrait equestre de Monsieur Berger de Renens
                   (46x67cm-18x26in) s.d.1789 (F.FR 150000)

BACON, Francis (1909-?) British
£330000 $531300 (27-Jun-91 S40/R) Study for self portrait (35x30cm-14x12in)
£460000 $740600 (27-Jun-91 S42/R) Study for nude, 1951 (198x137cm-78x54in)
£1785714 $3500000 (7-Nov-90 CH.NY28 a/R) Portrait of George Dyer staring into mirror
(198x147cm-78x58in) i.d.1967verso

BACON, Henry (1839-1912) American
£1316 $2500 (15-Sep-90 S.W2758/R) Farm girl with scythe, Etretat (23x30cm-9x12in)
s.d.1882 canvas on board
£1445 $2500 (21-May-91 CE.NY602/R) Her first earrings (62x75cm-24x30in) s.d.1886

BACON, I Lewis (1853-1910) American
£809 $1400 (10-May-91 S.BM51/R) Still life with roses and vases (69x91cm-27x36in)
s.d.1872

BACON, John Henry Frederick (1868-1914) British
£700 $1379 (1-Nov-90 C4) Old Danish custom, hanging up cornsheaf on Christmas Eve
(53x36cm-21x14in) s.i.d.95 pencil W/C bound in presentation folder
£700 $1323 (26-Sep-90 S340/R) Tales of new god (47x34cm-19x13in) s.d.07 W/C bodycol

BACON, Peggy (1895-1987) American
£698 $1200 (15-May-91 SY.NY158/R) Driftwood (23x30cm-9x12in) s.d.1969 masonite

BADALOCCHIO, Sisto (attrib) (1581-1647) Italian
£4800 $8112 (16-Apr-91 PH47/R) Rest on flight into Egypt (73x93cm-29x37in)

BADAROCCO, Giovanni Raffaelo (1648-1726) Italian
£2705 $4842 (8-Apr-91 CH.R103/R) La decollazione del Battista (50x38cm-20x15in)
(I.L 6000000)

BADE, A (19th C) European
£880 $1575 (12-Mar-91 PH40) Still life of lilac in vase, silver teapot, decanter
and glasses on table (62x80cm-24x31in) s.

BADEN, Hans Jurriaens van (attrib) (1604-1663) Dutch
£2265 $3942 (25-Mar-91 SY.F734) Cristo scaccia i mercanti dal tempio
(69x48cm-27x19in) panel oval (I.L 5000000)

BADGER, S F M (19/20th C) American
£5851 $11000 (7-Aug-90 RB.HY100/R) Schooner 'Addie Morrill' off Highland Light, Cape
Cod (56x91cm-22x36in) s.d.01

BADGER, Samuel Finley Morse (19/20th C) American
£2811 $4750 (17-Apr-91 D.NY44/R) George V Jordon (56x91cm-22x36in) s.d.50

BADHAM, Herbert Edward (1899-1961) Australian
£1158 $2282 (13-Nov-90 J.M19) Study for the expulsion (39x28cm-15x11in) s.d.56 board
(A.D 3000)
£1205 $2313 (27-Nov-90 JRL.S180/R) Gap, Watson's Bay (24x30cm-9x12in) s.d.35 plywood
(A.D 3000)
£14884 $25005 (22-Apr-91 SY.ME294/R) Oxford Street interior (40x44cm-16x17in) s.d.42
board (A.D 32000)
£24096 $46265 (26-Nov-90 SY.ME196/R) Hotel scene - figures in bar (102x81cm-40x32in)
s.d.40 (A.D 60000)

BADI, Aquiles (1894-1976) Argentinian
£1842 $3500 (11-Sep-90 PO.BA2) Villa en Calabria (45x60cm-18x24in) s.
£636 $1100 (8-May-91 V.BA6) Paisaje (28x39cm-11x15in) W/C

BADIA (20th C) ?
£1187 $2125 (14-Apr-91 R.P185 b/R) La solitude de cette heure de mort
(195x97cm-77x38in) s. (F.FR 12000)
£1210 $2359 (28-Oct-90 R.P244) La femme du marin (126x72cm-50x28in) s. mixed media
wood (F.FR 12000)
£1411 $2752 (28-Oct-90 R.P130/R) L'anonyme paillasse (130x97cm-51x38in) s. mixed
media canvas (F.FR 14000)

BADIALI, Giuseppe (18/19th C) Italian
£866 $1534 (19-Mar-91 F.M49/R) Progetto per la decorazione del soffitto del teatro
comunale di Bologna (47x37cm-19x15in) ink W/C gilding (I.L 1900000)

BADMIN, Stanley Roy (1906-) British
£1050 $2048 (16-Oct-90 WW360) The Dower House, Lavington (23x61cm-9x24in) s.d.1946
i. backboard W/C ink htd.bodycol.
£2200 $3718 (15-Apr-91 WW158) Pick-it-yourself fruit farm, Bury, Sussex
(12x21cm-5x8in) s.d.1976 W/C
£2700 $5292 (25-Jan-91 C1/R) Village street with figures and church tower beyond
(18x30cm-7x12in) init.d.1941 pen ink W/C bodycol
£2700 $4995 (7-Mar-91 C17/R) Harvest (30x44cm-12x17in) s.i. pencil pen ink W/C

BADOWSKI, Zygmunt (1881-1951) Polish
£693 $1316 (3-Mar-91 REM.W2) Wearing a green scarf (76x41cm-30x16in) s.d.1926
canvas on board (P.Z 12500000)

BADY, Yves (1912-) French
£4073 $8024 (4-Nov-90 FE.P81) Sous bois (100x81cm-39x32in) s. (F.FR 40000)

BAECHLER, Christian (20th C) ?
£525 $929   (7-Apr-91 LT.P219) Coucher de soleil a Trouville (27x35cm-11x14in) s.
          (F.FR 5300)
£1316 $2579   (25-Nov-90 ZZ.F4/R) Les volles de la Liberte au soleil couchant
          (90x115cm-35x45in) s. (F.FR 13000)

BAECHLER, Donald (1956-) American
£3571 $7000   (14-Feb-91 CH.NY91/R) Black painting no 5 (91x91cm-36x36in) acrylic
          muslin on canvas
£4142 $7000   (2-May-91 CH.NY266/R) Untitled (152x153cm-60x60in) s.d.1983 verso
          acrylic canvas
£5076 $10000   (4-Oct-90 SY.NY248/R) Double portrait of George Condo (90x91cm-35x36in)
          acrylic paper
£6122 $12000   (8-Nov-90 CH.NY415/R) Untitled (183x183cm-72x72in) s. verso acrylic
£10152 $20000   (5-Oct-90 CH.NY107/R) Untitled - juggling girl (106x106cm-42x42in)
          s.i.d.1985verso acrylic canvas collage

BAECHLER, Donald and others (20th C) American
£76142 $150000   (4-Oct-90 SY.NY238/R) Hommage a Picasso - by eight artists
          (183x198cm-72x78in) mixed media 8 oils 8 drawings

BAELLIEUR, Cornelis de (elder) (1607-1671) Flemish
£1199 $2146   (13-Mar-91 N.M392/R) Entkleidung Christi. Christus an der Geisselsaule
          (22x16cm-9x6in) copper pair (DM 3500)

BAELLIEUR, Cornelis de (elder-attrib) (1607-1671) Flemish
£4000 $7720   (11-Dec-90 PH169/R) Adoration of the Magi (24x21cm-9x8in) quartz

BAEN, Jan de (1633-1702) Dutch
£2545 $4301   (2-May-91 CH.AM63/R) Portrait of an elegant lady, her pet dog by her
          side, landscape beyond (121x100cm-48x39in) s.d.1681 shaped top
          (D.FL 8500)
£2821 $5500   (10-Oct-90 CH.NY115/R) Portrait of lady and gentleman as Atalanta and
          Meleagar (129x130cm-51x51in) s.d.1680

BAENDER, J de (?) ?
£835 $1637   (12-Feb-91 GM.B624) Vue de port anime (49x69cm-19x27in) s. (B.FR 50000)
£917 $1760   (18-Dec-90 GM.B845) Promenade dans la neige (50x70cm-20x28in) s. board
          (B.FR 55000)
£986 $1923   (24-Oct-90 GM.B1166) Paysage hivernal anime (50x70cm-20x28in) s. wood
          (B.FR 60000)
£1083 $2080   (18-Dec-90 GM.B808) Pecheurs sur leurs barques (50x70cm-20x28in) s.
          board (B.FR 65000)

BAENE, Emilie de (19th C) Belgian
£1014 $1976   (26-Oct-90 BM.B740/R) Still life of flowers with hyacinths and pansies
          (53x37cm-21x15in) s. panel (DM 3000)

BAER, Fritz (1850-1919) German
£2448 $4724   (12-Dec-90 N.M437/R) Fields with trees by water (38x46cm-15x18in)
          l.stretcher (DM 7000)

BAER, Jo (1929-) ?
£7143 $14000   (14-Feb-91 CH.NY58/R) Untitled (153x122cm-60x48in) s.d.64-70verso
£9694 $19000   (14-Feb-91 CH.NY32/R) Untitled (183x183cm-72x72in) s.d.72verso
£11834 $20000   (2-May-91 CH.NY172/R) Untitled (265x183cm-104x72in) s.d.68 verso diptych

BAERTLING, Olle (1911-1981) Swedish
£5938 $10035   (18-Apr-91 BU.S24/R) 'Goth' (105x55cm-41x22in) s.s.d.1950verso
          (S.KR 63000)
£40036 $75267   (19-Sep-90 KH.K55/R) IRUI - Composition (92x180cm-36x71in) s.d.1958verso
          (D.KR 450000)
£41470 $70085   (18-Apr-91 BU.S75/R) Xre - composition (195x97cm-77x38in)
          s.i.d.1973verso (S.KR 440000)

BAERTS, Marc (attrib) (?) ?
£1000 $1630   (4-Jul-91 CSK123/R) Peasants on track in extensive landscape
          (26x34cm-10x13in) panel

BAERWIND, Rudi (1910-1982) German
£405 $701   (21-May-91 WK.M564/R) Composition (65x50cm-26x20in) s.d.1962 mixed media
          board (DM 1200)
£405 $701   (21-May-91 WK.M563/R) Composition in red (44x32cm-17x13in) s.d.1960 s.i.
          gouache (DM 1200)
£604 $1178   (12-Oct-90 AW.H1894/R) Flipper (100x35cm-39x14in) s. mixed media canvas
          (DM 1800)
£608 $1052   (21-May-91 WK.M562/R) Composition (53x57cm-21x22in) s.d.1956 pastel
          board (DM 1800)
£608 $1052   (21-May-91 WK.M561/R) Composition (49x62cm-19x24in) s.d.1956 pastel
          (DM 1800)

BAES, Emile (1879-1953) Belgian
£687 $1155   (23-Apr-91 C.A280) Seated figure (61x51cm-24x20in) s. panel (B.FR 42000)
£900 $1755   (15-Oct-90 PH9) Nu debout (85x46cm-33x18in) s.d.1916
£1153 $2249   (9-Oct-90 GGL.L6/R) Nu voile au brasero (89x115cm-35x45in) s.
          (F.FR 11500)

80

BAES, Emile (1879-1953) Belgian-cont.
£1220 $2390   (6-Nov-90 SY.AM181/R) Reclining nude on sofa (70x147cm-28x58in) s.
                  (D.FL 4000)
£2287 $4482   (6-Nov-90 SY.AM117/R) Female nude (73x54cm-29x21in) s. (D.FL 7500)
£2577 $4613   (16-Mar-91 KV.L424/R) Standing nude (130x90cm-51x35in) s. (B.FR 155000)
£2988 $5139   (14-May-91 GF.L2216/R) Female nude standing (146x114cm-57x45in) s.d.1943
                  (S.FR 7500)
£4046 $7000   (23-May-91 CH.NY197/R) Nu de dos (131x91cm-52x36in) s.

BAES, Lionel (1839-1913) Belgian
£569 $956   (23-Apr-91 SY.AM90) Red dress (52x34cm-20x13in) s. (D.FL 1900)

BAES, Rachel (20th C) French
£549 $982   (16-Mar-91 KV.L16) Composition with woman (79x59cm-31x23in) s. canvas on
                  board (B.FR 33000)
£742 $1439   (8-Dec-90 KV.L24) La Guerre en Dentelles (54x65cm-21x26in) s.d.1955
                  (B.FR 44000)

BAETS, Marc (18th C) Flemish
£2041 $4000   (7-Nov-90 B.SF1005/R) River landscapes with figures (11x13cm-4x5in)
                  panel pair

BAETS, Marc (attrib) (18th C) Flemish
£5500 $9295   (18-Apr-91 C94/R) River landscape with a castle above a village and a
                  traveller on a path (91x114cm-36x45in)

BAETS, Marc (circle) (18th C) Flemish
£2800 $4732   (18-Apr-91 C100/R) A village by a river with gentry by a landing stage
                  (65x97cm-26x38in)
£8000 $15600   (26-Oct-90 C116/R) An extensive landscape with cattle herded on a path,
                  a manor house beyond (97x126cm-38x50in)

BAEZA, Manuel (1915-) Spanish
£1237 $2214   (13-Mar-91 FER.M243/R) Tejados con antenas (82x100cm-32x39in) s.
                  (S.P 225000)
*£715 $1279   (13-Mar-91 FER.M242/R) Los barcos fantasma (64x86cm-25x34in) s. mixed
                  media wax W/C (S.P 130000)*

BAGER, Johann Daniel (1734-1815) German
£17460 $31254   (13-Mar-91 GK.Z4/R) Still life of fruit and flowers with jug,
                  butterflies and dragonfly (54x44cm-21x17in) s.d.1785 copper
                  (S.FR 44000)

BAGGE, Eva (1871-1964) Swedish
£1471 $2882   (6-Nov-90 BA.S9/R) Tea time (47x35cm-19x14in) s.d.1951 panel
                  (S.KR 16000)
£1483 $2862   (12-Dec-90 BU.S5/R) Sunny interior (40x32cm-16x13in) panel (S.KR 16000)

BAGGE, Magnus-Thulstrupp (1825-1890) Norwegian
£963 $1850   (19-Dec-90 LD.P136) Vue d'un lac au pied d'une chaine de montagne
                  enneigee (24x35cm-9x14in) s.d.1860 (F.FR 9500)

BAGIENSKI, Stanislaw (1876-1948) Polish
£643 $1273   (1-Feb-91 DE.B2) Soldier and the girl (33x53cm-13x21in) s. board
                  (P.Z 12000000)

BAGLIONE, Cavaliere Giovanni (1571-1644) Italian
*£4200 $6846   (2-Jul-91 C102/R) Father Time unveiling Truth to Peace with Envy and
                  Discord in background (16x25cm-6x10in) red black chk pen wash*

BAGLIONE, Cavaliere Giovanni (attrib) (1571-1644) Italian
£8815 $17365   (14-Nov-90 D.V44/R) Amor sleeping (153x108cm-60x43in) (A.S 180000)

BAGUERO, J (19th C) Spanish
*£1608 $2637   (21-Jun-91 SY.MO352/R) Trompe l'oeil aux coeurs de Jesus Christ et Marie
                  (39x54cm-15x21in) s. pen W/C (F.FR 16000)*

BAHIEU, Jules-G (19th C) Belgian
£1082 $2100   (8-Dec-90 W.W32/R) Farmyard scene (66x53cm-26x21in) s.
£1510 $2945   (10-Oct-90 WE.MU194/R) Chicken yard (49x65cm-19x26in) s. (DM 4500)

BAIER, Jean (1932-) ?
*£437 $716   (21-Jun-91 G.Z26) Composition (61x92cm-24x36in) s.d.1962/65 spray
                  technique steel (S.FR 1100)*
*£873 $1432   (21-Jun-91 G.Z25) Abstract composition (40x120cm-16x47in) s.d.1957 spray
                  technique pavatex (S.FR 2200)*

BAIERL, Theodor (1881-1932) German
£1421 $2700   (12-Sep-90 D.NY1) Burlesque show (53x46cm-21x18in) s.i. board
£1573 $3052   (4-Dec-90 FN.S1553/R) Three nude bacchantes dancing beneath starry sky
                  (54x46cm-21x18in) s. panel (DM 4500)
£1748 $3374   (12-Dec-90 WE.MU183/R) The kiss (40x38cm-16x15in) s. panel (DM 5000)
£1748 $3374   (12-Dec-90 WE.MU182/R) Mild summer evening (44x38cm-17x15in) s. panel
                  (DM 5000)

BAIKOV, Leonid (1919-) Russian
£647 $1125   (25-Mar-91 ARC.P14) Au bord de la riviere (68x117cm-27x46in) s.
     (F.FR 6500)
£945 $1645   (25-Mar-91 ARC.P13/R) Travaux de Printemps a la campagne
     (74x119cm-29x47in) s. (F.FR 9500)

BAIL, Franck Antoine (1858-1924) French
£10256 $20000   (24-Oct-90 CH.NY74/R) Two milkmaids (114x147cm-45x58in) s.d.06

BAIL, Joseph (1862-1921) French
£3075 $5290   (19-May-91 ZZ.F14/R) Jeune femme assise dans son interieur
     (14x10cm-6x4in) s. panel (F.FR 31000)
£3400 $5848   (17-May-91 C28/R) Blowing bubbles (74x98cm-29x39in) s.
£5000 $8950   (12-Mar-91 PH108/R) Maids seated in interior (55x46cm-22x18in) s.
£6358 $11000   (22-May-91 SY.NY193/R) Conversation (65x54cm-26x21in) s.
£6474 $11200   (24-May-91 FB.P84/R) Scene d'interieur (73x60cm-29x24in) s. (F.FR 65000)
£6667 $11600   (25-Mar-91 QWA.P115) Petit chat etmirliton (58x37cm-23x15in) s.
     (F.FR 67000)
£8000 $13120   (19-Jun-91 S161/R) Young cook (120x65cm-47x26in) s.
£11561 $20000   (22-May-91 SY.NY195/R) Little chef (79x58cm-31x23in) s.
£13446 $23262   (24-May-91 FB.P87/R) La jeune fille et les chatons (121x65cm-48x26in) s.
     (F.FR 135000)

BAIL, Louis le (1866-1929) French
£735 $1447   (16-Nov-90 EA.Z256/R) Seine landscape (54x65cm-21x26in) s. (S.FR 1800)
£816 $1608   (16-Nov-90 EA.Z274/R) River landscape (54x65cm-21x26in) s. (S.FR 2000)

BAILEY, Celia (1907-) British
£1000 $1960   (13-Feb-91 B158/R) Song of myself (208x208cm-82x82in) s.i.d.1990 verso

BAILEY, Frederick Victor (20th C) British
£1300 $2496   (29-Nov-90 B44/R) Still life of flowers in a basket with insects
     (52x35cm-20x14in) s.d.1990 board pair
£5200 $8372   (27-Jun-91 CG126/R) Still life with mixed flowers in a glass vase with a
     bee and butterfly (92x74cm-36x29in) s.d.1991 panel
£8163 $16000   (7-Nov-90 B.SF1216/R) Floral still lifes (91x76cm-36x30in) panel pair

BAILEY, Henry (fl.1879-1907) British
£460 $823   (13-May-91 B138) Fly-fishing (28x48cm-11x19in) s.d.'80 W/C

BAILEY, Walter Alexander (1894-?) American
£798 $1500   (22-Sep-90 WOL.C354/R) California landscape (28x38cm-11x15in) s.
     canvasboard

BAILEY, William (1930-) American
£5917 $10000   (2-May-91 CH.NY149/R) Untitled (48x34cm-19x13in) s. graphite three

BAILLY, Alice (1872-1938) Swiss
£1815 $3538   (18-Jan-91 GL.P11) Arlequin et jeune femme nue (91x72cm-36x28in) s.
     (F.FR 18000)
£2800 $4732   (1-May-91 GD.B27/R) Female nude seated with roses (80x100cm-31x39in)
     s.d.1929 (S.FR 7000)
*£952 $1562   (19-Jun-91 GK.B178) Study for Madonna (30x24cm-12x9in) s. pencil
     (S.FR 2400)*

BAIN, Donald (1904-) British
£1200 $1968   (19-Jun-91 PHG49) Still life of flowers (60x50cm-24x20in) s.
£1600 $3024   (27-Sep-90 CG55 b) Bay, Loch Lomond (28x35cm-11x14in) s.s.i.d.1949verso
     board

BAIN, Marcel Adolphe (1878) French
£1474 $2800   (27-Feb-91 SY.NY64/R) Curve in river (61x74cm-24x29in) s.

BAINES, Thomas (1822-1875) British
£833 $1417   (27-May-91 SY.J308) Portrait of gentleman (43x27cm-17x11in)
     i.d.1846verso (SA.R 4000)
£45833 $77917   (27-May-91 SY.J608/R) Fort Beaufort from the west (46x65cm-18x26in)
     s.d.1848 i.verso paper on canvas (SA.R 220000)
£46371 $90423   (15-Oct-90 SY.J77/R) Klaas Smit's river - waggon broken down, crossing
     the drift (45x65cm-18x26in) s.d.Oct. 17th 1848 i. labels stretcher
     (SA.R 230000)
£58333 $99167   (27-May-91 SY.J609/R) The new village of Burgher's Dorp on the Storm
     Berg Spruits River (46x65cm-18x26in) s.d.1848 i.verso paper on canvas
     (SA.R 280000)
*£6000 $11700   (24-Oct-90 S7/R) Eildon, near Grahamstown (20x28cm-8x11in) s.i.d.1849
     oil W/C htd.bodycol.pencil*

BAIRD, Nathaniel Hughes (1865-c.1930) British
£1300 $2431   (29-Aug-90 MN78/R) Fugatives (56x76cm-22x30in) mono.
£500 $865   (20-May-91 PH25) Hay cart (17x26cm-7x10in) mono. W/C htd white
*£667 $1293   (4-Dec-90 R.T121/R) Farmer and team, breezy day (38x27cm-15x11in) mono.
     W/C (C.D 1500)*
*£1300 $2600   (8-Feb-91 C42/R) A waggon team in a snow storm (36x53cm-14x21in) mono.
     pencil W/C htd.white*

BAIRD, William Baptiste (1847-?) American

£1495	$2541	(27-May-91 HO.ED146/R) Une bergerie, interior with sheep (23x35cm-9x14in) s. s.i. panel (C.D 2900)
£1500	$2505	(5-Jun-91 S91/R) Poultry on step (23x33cm-9x13in) s. one s.i.verso board pair
£1837	$3618	(14-Nov-90 FB.P290/R) Le moulin a eau (33x46cm-13x18in) s. (F.FR 18000)

BAISCH, Hermann (1846-1894) German

£751	$1419	(25-Sep-90 FN.S2110/R) Wooded river landscape with farmstead (25x33cm-10x13in) board st.sig.verso (DM 2200)
£2027	$3446	(27-May-91 L.K241) View of town from the Middle Ages (27x21cm-11x8in) s. panel (DM 6000)
£769	$1492	(4-Dec-90 FN.S1741) Peasant watering animals at village well, evening (30x41cm-12x16in) s. d.1895verso W/C (DM 2200)

BAISCH, Hermann (attrib) (1846-1894) German

| £4013 | $6783 | (19-Apr-91 FN.S1663/R) Landscape with shepherd and animals, Camargue (93x138cm-37x54in) bears sig.d.1896 (DM 12000) |

BAITLER, Zoma (20th C) South American

£1878	$3700	(1-Nov-90 GC.M2) Estacion Central (58x78cm-23x31in)
£2193	$4100	(1-Aug-90 BAV.M2) Juan Lacaze (77x62cm-30x24in)
£6845	$12800	(1-Aug-90 BAV.M1) Bahia de Montevideo (220x135cm-87x53in)

BAIXERAS Y VERDAGUER, Dionisio (1862-1943) Spanish

| £13295 | $23000 | (22-May-91 SY.NY297/R) Iglesias y Playa de Sitges, Cataluna (61x100cm-24x39in) s. |

BAJ, Enrico (1924-) Italian

£8115	$14525	(9-Apr-91 F.R122/R) Donna urlante e cinghiale (100x150cm-39x59in) s.d.54 (I.L 18000000)
£8115	$14525	(9-Apr-91 F.R121/R) L'atelier (100x201cm-39x79in) s.d.46 tempera faesite (I.L 18000000)
£8780	$16945	(13-Dec-90 F.M462/R) Donna urlante (100x150cm-39x59in) s.d.54 s.i.d.verso (I.L 19000000)
£12690	$25000	(4-Oct-90 SY.NY19/R) Testa solare (80x58cm-31x23in) s.d.56 s.verso on fabric
£408	$792	(8-Dec-90 GAB.G2356) Le general (52x39cm-20x15in) s. gouache collage tissue (S.FR 1000)
£490	$950	(8-Dec-90 GAB.G2351/R) La fille de joie (52x39cm-20x15in) s. gouache collage tissue (S.FR 1200)
£531	$1029	(8-Dec-90 GAB.G2353/R) Le general (52x39cm-20x15in) s. gouache collage tissue (S.FR 1300)
£531	$1029	(8-Dec-90 GAB.G2352/R) Le soldat a l'uniforme vert (52x39cm-20x15in) s. gouache collage tissue (S.FR 1300)
£531	$1029	(8-Dec-90 GAB.G2354) La fille de joie (52x39cm-20x15in) s. gouache collage tissue (S.FR 1300)
£556	$935	(23-Apr-91 C.A282) Lady Jane Grey (50x40cm-20x16in) s. mixed media (B.FR 34000)
£647	$1256	(3-Dec-90 F.M147) Landscape (43x34cm-17x13in) s.d.1952 ink W/C (I.L 1400000)
£1090	$1886	(7-May-91 F.M164/R) Composizione nucleare (50x35cm-20x14in) s. pastel ink W/C (I.L 2400000)
£1201	$2319	(13-Dec-90 F.M312/R) Ancogo bung (41x32cm-16x13in) s.d.1968 plastic collage (I.L 2600000)
£1779	$2900	(12-Jun-91 SY.NY231/R) Personnage in thought (70x50cm-28x20in) s. conte crayon collage paper
£1779	$2900	(12-Jun-91 SY.NY230/R) Modest personnage (81x62cm-32x24in) s. conte crayon collage paper
£3152	$6146	(22-Oct-90 BR.M177/R) L'amica di Picasso (29x36cm-11x14in) s. acrylic mixed media paper on canvas (I.L 7000000)
£3209	$5263	(20-Jun-91 F.M397/R) Portrait de Sarenco (25x24cm-10x9in) s.i.d.1981verso polimaterico fabric (I.L 7000000)
£4040	$7919	(14-Feb-91 GL.P40/R) L'ora tarda (52x56cm-20x22in) s. i. verso collage mixed media tissue on panel (F.FR 40000)
£7069	$11946	(18-Apr-91 BU.S69/R) Personaggio decorato (55x46cm-22x18in) s. i.verso mixed media (S.KR 75000)
£7213	$12911	(9-Apr-91 F.R222/R) Statale (66x53cm-26x21in) s. acrylic decorations collage cloth (I.L 16000000)
£7380	$14170	(27-Nov-90 BU.S24/R) 'Volti provvisori' (60x50cm-24x20in) mixed media oil collage panel (S.KR 80000)
£7740	$14938	(12-Dec-90 CH.AM398/R) Untitled - painted with Gianni Bertini and Asger Jorn (85x84cm-33x33in) s.d.58 oil fabric collage canvas double-sided (D.FL 25000)
£8104	$15804	(24-Oct-90 F.M222/R) Dipinto nucleare (60x100cm-24x39in) s.d.1952verso enamel canvas (I.L 18000000)
£8201	$13942	(28-May-91 SY.M181/R) Samuel Jordan Kirkwood of Iowa (45x54cm-18x21in) s. i.d.1965verso acrylic wadding braid material (I.L 18000000)
£9184	$18000	(12-Feb-91 SY.NY420/R) Louis Charles Philippe d'Orleans, Duc de Nemours (97x81cm-38x32in) collage upholstery fabric
£9250	$17945	(3-Dec-90 CH.R99/R) Gruppo (50x60cm-20x24in) s.d.1981 oil collage panel (I.L 20000000)
£10077	$19348	(27-Nov-90 SY.MI164/R) Femme en vert (73x60cm-29x24in) s. acrylic collage braid plastic material (I.L 22000000)
£12000	$21240	(21-Mar-91 C250/R) Le Chevalier de Quincy (100x81cm-39x32in) s. i.d.65 stretcher gouache collage canvas

BAJ, Enrico (1924-) Italian-cont.
£12015	$23189	(13-Dec-90 F.M483/R) I danzatori (98x119cm-39x47in) s.d.1955 oil enamel masonite (I.L 26000000)
£12245	$24000	(15-Feb-91 SY.NY156/R) Situations (70x60cm-28x24in) s. i.stretcher oil collage fabric
£19482	$33898	(26-Mar-91 F.M145/R) Marziano (98x115cm-39x45in) s. polimaterico cloth (I.L 43000000)
£21000	$37170	(21-Mar-91 S61/R) Femme assise (146x112cm-57x44in) s. d.1969 stretcher mixed media collage canvas
£23360	$44852	(27-Nov-90 SY.MI151/R) Henry de Lorraine Comte d'Harcourt avec deux soldats de son armee (146x114cm-57x45in) s. acrylic collage wadding braid material (I.L 51000000)

BAJALSKA, Wesna (20th C) ?
£841	$1505	(14-Apr-91 R.P94) Ascension (130x97cm-51x38in) s. (F.FR 8500)
£940	$1682	(14-Apr-91 R.P21) Nocturne abstraite (130x97cm-51x38in) s. (F.FR 9500)

BAK, Samuel (1933-) Israeli
£2304	$4400	(2-Jan-91 GG.TA529/R) Pawn in landscape (27x19cm-11x7in) s.c.1970
£3190	$5200	(12-Jun-91 GG.TA241/R) Imaginary landscape (20x32cm-8x13in) s.
£3665	$7000	(1-Jan-91 GG.TA259/R) Pear (41x33cm-16x13in) s.
£3681	$6000	(12-Jun-91 GG.TA240/R) Imaginary landscape with pears (41x48cm-16x19in) s.
£3717	$7100	(1-Jan-91 GG.TA257/R) The expectation (38x48cm-15x19in) s.c.1970
£552	$900	(12-Jun-91 GG.TA36/R) Landscape with still life (29x21cm-11x8in) s. pen
£859	$1400	(12-Jun-91 GG.TA242/R) Still life (42x22cm-17x9in) s. pastel

BAKALOWICZ (?) ?
£7322	$14278	(12-Oct-90 ZZ.F77/R) Diner galant s. (F.FR 73000)

BAKALOWICZ, Ladislaus (1833-1904) Polish
£1500	$2955	(4-Oct-90 CSK189/R) A bride at her devotions (28x23cm-11x9in) s. i. verso panel
£1500	$2955	(4-Oct-90 CSK187/R) Reading aloud (27x21cm-11x8in) s.i. verso panel

BAKALOWICZ, Stephan Wladislawowitsch (1857-?) Russian
£1735	$3417	(14-Nov-90 FB.P280/R) Jeune femme se levant (28x16cm-11x6in) s. panel (F.FR 17000)

BAKER OF LEAMINGTON, Thomas (1809-1869) British
£1275	$2487	(10-Oct-90 ZEL.L1390/R) Sheep grazing (15x20cm-6x8in) mono. board (DM 3800)
£1700	$2839	(5-Jun-91 S75/R) Cubbington Church near Leamington (54x40cm-21x16in) s.d.1854
£1800	$3420	(28-Feb-91 LE322) Wooded river landscape, evening (51x76cm-20x30in) s.d.1847
£2400	$4296	(14-Mar-91 B47/R) Cattle grazing in parkland (33x48cm-13x19in) s.d.1857
£2500	$4900	(13-Feb-91 S54/R) Warwick Castle (41x56cm-16x22in) s.d.1859
£770	$1509	(15-Feb-91 CBB221) Chesford Bridge (25x36cm-10x14in) s.i.d.1858 W/C

BAKER, Alan Douglas (1914-1987) Australian
£562	$1080	(27-Nov-90 JRL.S240 a) White camellias (31x38cm-12x15in) s. composition board (A.D 1400)
£568	$982	(21-May-91 JRL.S218) Summer landscape (38x59cm-15x23in) s. board (A.D 1300)
£800	$1504	(17-Sep-90 SY.ME43/R) Aboriginal (64x84cm-25x33in) s.d.66 board (A.D 1800)
£995	$1682	(16-Apr-91 J.M277/R) Sunshine and shadow, Lakesland (59x90cm-23x35in) s. board (A.D 2200)
£1205	$2313	(27-Nov-90 JRL.S357/R) White daisies (36x44cm-14x17in) s. composition board (A.D 3000)
£2390	$4709	(31-Oct-90 CH.S7/R) White roses (56x46cm-22x18in) s. board (A.D 6000)

BAKER, Arthur (19th C) British
£1000	$1670	(5-Jun-91 RBB977/R) Landscape with horse-drawn cart and sheep in country lane (53x74cm-21x29in) s.d.1865

BAKER, Blanche (1844-1929) British
£920	$1803	(21-Nov-90 B82) Forester's garden (22x16cm-9x6in) init. W/C

BAKER, Elisha Taylor (attrib) (1827-1890) American
£5389	$9000	(25-Jul-91 E.EDM356/R) American schooner with shoreline behind (66x104cm-26x41in)

BAKER, Ernest (19th C) American
£1138	$1900	(9-Jun-91 LIT.L382) Moonlit harbour scene (33x58cm-13x23in) s.

BAKER, Samuel Henry (1824-1909) British
£3800	$6726	(21-Mar-91 CSK153) The Town Mill, Ludlow (71x107cm-28x42in) s. i. verso
£600	$1116	(5-Sep-90 BT69/R) Cattle in landscape (58x99cm-23x39in) s. W/C
£800	$1376	(14-May-91 SWS36) River scene with figures outside cottage (36x57cm-14x22in) s.d.1867 W/C
£950	$1758	(6-Mar-91 SC4194/R) Borrowdale, Cumberland (43x76cm-17x30in) s. s.i.verso W/C
£1200	$2220	(6-Mar-91 SC4200/R) The Conway near Llandudno Junction (46x76cm-18x30in) s. s.i.verso W/C

BAKER, Samuel Henry (1824-1909) British-cont.
£1200 $2004   (5-Jun-91 S240/R) Cattle in meadows (59x100cm-23x39in) s. W/C htd
                  scratching out

BAKER, William George (19th C) Australian
£687 $1162   (17-Apr-91 DS.W89) Upper Waikanae River (87x50cm-34x20in) s. (NZ.D 2000)
£805 $1578   (7-Nov-90 DS.W104) Kenepuru Sound (45x67cm-18x26in) s. (NZ.D 2600)
£1084 $2124   (7-Nov-90 DS.W84) Hinemoa's Bath, Mokoia Island (46x69cm-18x27in)
                  (NZ.D 3500)
£1375 $2323   (17-Apr-91 DS.W83) Dusky sound (135x89cm-53x35in) s. (NZ.D 4000)

BAKHTIAROVA, Sania (1949-) Russian
£603 $1158   (18-Feb-91 ARC.P122/R) Le premier velo (71x54cm-28x21in) s. (F.FR 6000)

BAKHUYZEN (style) (?) Dutch
£769 $1500   (21-Oct-90 HG.C31) Rough seas (48x61cm-19x24in) panel

BAKHUYZEN, Alexandre H (1826-1878) Dutch
£727 $1433   (30-Oct-90 CH.AM60) Polder landscape with traveller on sandy track, cows
                  in meadow beyond (29x39cm-11x15in) s.d.1877 panel (D.FL 2400)
£1600 $3072   (29-Nov-90 B83/R) Canal scene (12x16cm-5x6in) s. panel pair

BAKHUYZEN, Gerardina Jacoba van de Sande (1826-1895) Dutch
£3673 $6980   (14-Sep-90 ZOF.Z831/R) Bouquet of flowers with wild roses
                  (47x59cm-19x23in) s. (S.FR 9000)
£8289 $15500   (1-Aug-90 B.P57/R) Still life (33x46cm-13x18in) s.
£1667 $3283   (30-Oct-90 CH.AM524/R) Chrysanthemums in vase (52x37cm-20x15in) s. W/C
                  htd white (D.FL 5500)
£1970 $3880   (30-Oct-90 CH.AM528/R) White peony-roses in stoneware jug
                  (68x55cm-27x22in) s. W/C (D.FL 6500)
£2036 $3420   (23-Apr-91 SY.AM293/R) Still life with white roses in basket
                  (27x35cm-11x14in) s. W/C (D.FL 6800)

BAKHUYZEN, Hendrick van de Sande (1795-1860) Dutch
£2317 $3800   (23-Jun-91 H.C1003/R) Cowherd with cattle and goats at rest
                  (56x69cm-22x27in) s. panel
£9091 $17909   (30-Oct-90 CH.AM73/R) Wooded summer landscape with peasants milking and
                  haywagon (54x67cm-21x26in) s.d.1851 panel (D.FL 30000)
£778 $1479   (11-Sep-90 CH.AM375) Travellers on path in hilly landscape
                  (38x53cm-15x21in) s. pencil pen wash W/C (D.FL 2600)

BAKHUYZEN, Julius Jacobus van de Sande (1835-1925) Dutch
£599 $1006   (23-Apr-91 SY.AM66) Shepherd on heath (40x57cm-16x22in) s. panel
                  (D.FL 2000)
£2600 $4836   (5-Sep-90 BT184/R) Minding the flock (64x102cm-25x40in) s.d.01
£3500 $6895   (4-Oct-90 CSK43/R) Figures in a frozen river landscape (38x46cm-15x18in)
                  s. panel
£1212 $2388   (30-Oct-90 CH.AM452) Sunset in woods (55x37cm-22x15in) s. W/C bodycol
                  (D.FL 4000)

BAKHUYZEN, Ludolf (1631-1708) Dutch
£9580 $18873   (30-Oct-90 BU.S225/R) Seascape with vessel flying Swedish flag
                  (49x58cm-19x23in) (S.KR 105000)
£11000 $20900   (1-Mar-91 C113/R) Fishermen in pink in stiff breeze and other shipping
                  (46x61cm-18x24in)
£17500 $28525   (1-Jul-91 S34/R) Shipping in Amsterdam harbour, with figures on jetty
                  preparing to embark (15x21cm-6x8in) init. wash vellum

BAKHUYZEN, Ludolf (attrib) (1631-1708) Dutch
£8000 $13040   (5-Jul-91 C312/R) Buss close-hauled in stiff breeze with pink mooring
                  and other shipping (66x79cm-26x31in)

BAKHUYZEN, Ludolf (school) (1631-1708) Dutch
£2824 $4800   (30-May-91 CE.NY57) Man-o-war and other shipping in choppy sea
                  (86x128cm-34x50in)

BAKHUYZEN, Ludolf (style) (1631-1708) Dutch
£3200 $5216   (4-Jul-91 C525/R) Merchantman clawing off rocky shore in stiff breeze
                  (41x61cm-16x24in) panel
£4500 $7335   (5-Jul-91 C311/R) Dutch merchantman running gale offshore, port beneath
                  mountain beyond (84x107cm-33x42in)
£4500 $8775   (26-Oct-90 C127/R) A three-masted Dutch large flute, a boeir yacht and
                  other ships in achoppy sea (76x105cm-30x41in) indist.s.

BAKKER, Jop Augustus (1796-1876) Dutch
£1946 $3698   (11-Sep-90 CH.AM125/R) Woman driving cattle in summer landscape.
                  Traveller by meadow with cattle (43x55cm-17x22in) one mono.indis.d.
                  panel pair (D.FL 6500)

BAKOF, Julius (1819-1857) German
£2988 $5139   (14-May-91 GF.L2194/R) Urnersee with Urirotstock (45x60cm-18x24in) s.
                  (S.FR 7500)

BAKOS, Jozef G (1891-?) American
£1596 $3000   (19-Sep-90 B.SF2855/R) Adobe in Chimayo, New Mexico (37x51cm-15x20in)
                  s.i.d.'36 W/C

BAKSCHEJEFF, Wassily N see BAKSHEEV, Vasily

BAKSHEEV, Vasily (1862-?) Russian
| £946 | $1845 | (26-Oct-90 BM.B741/R) Still life of flowers (62x50cm-24x20in) s. (DM 2800) |

BAKST, Leon (1866-1924) Russian
£513	$1000	(10-Oct-90 SY.NY139/R) Fabric design for the evergreen house (48x58cm-19x23in) s.i. gouache pencil gold paint
£1026	$2000	(10-Oct-90 SY.NY128/R) Portrait of woman (28x30cm-11x12in) s. chl
£2000	$3220	(24-Jun-91 CSK194/R) Costume design for Aladdin (26x13cm-10x5in) s. W/C pencil paper on card
£3800	$7410	(10-Oct-90 C372/R) Costume design for 'Oedipus at Colonnus' - the Stranger (29x21cm-11x8in) s.i. pencil W/C htd silver paint
£4000	$6520	(1-Jul-91 APT.P18/R) Le Dieu vert (28x12cm-11x5in) s. lead pencil W/C gold (F.FR 40000)
£5200	$10140	(10-Oct-90 C376/R) Costume design for the production Moskwa (49x33cm-19x13in) s.d.1922 pencil gouache silver paint
£6200	$12090	(10-Oct-90 C373/R) Costume design for 'Oedipus at Colonnus' - Antigone (29x21cm-11x8in) s.i. pencil ink W/C htd white
£16000	$31200	(10-Oct-90 C375/R) Costume design for Cleopatra - a dancer (35x25cm-14x10in) s.d.1910 pencil gouache gold paint

BAKSTEEN, Dirk (1886-1971) Dutch
| £1479 | $2884 | (23-Oct-90 C.A26/R) Windmill in landscape (60x62cm-24x24in) pastel (B.FR 90000) |

BALAGUER, Jimenez (20th C) French
| £559 | $945 | (29-Apr-91 LGB.P80) Composition (114x146cm-45x57in) s. mixed media (F.FR 5600) |

BALANDE, Gaston (1880-1970) French
£816	$1584	(8-Dec-90 GAB.G2357) Lauziere (38x46cm-15x18in) s.i.d.48 (S.FR 2000)
£845	$1428	(21-Apr-91 E.LA197 b) Jardin fleuri (33x24cm-13x9in) s. panel (F.FR 8500)
£1469	$2851	(8-Dec-90 GAB.G2360/R) L'arrivee des cyclistes (65x50cm-26x20in) s. (S.FR 3600)
£1500	$2880	(26-Nov-90 SWS146/R) Port de la Rochelle (53x63cm-21x25in) s.d.19 i.stretcher
£1518	$2976	(25-Nov-90 ZZ.F207/R) Pecheurs a Port-Vendres (18x27cm-7x11in) s. panel (F.FR 15000)
£1531	$3000	(12-Feb-91 SY.NY203/R) Townscape (53x66cm-21x26in) s.
£1611	$2626	(11-Jun-91 I.N10) Le jardin public (24x34cm-9x13in) s. panel (F.FR 16000)
£1626	$3252	(6-Feb-91 FB.P23) Venise (46x55cm-18x22in) s. (F.FR 16000)
£1633	$3167	(8-Dec-90 GAB.G2359/R) Le port d'Ouchy (38x46cm-15x18in) s.i.d.43 (S.FR 4000)
£1667	$3250	(19-Oct-90 DM.D2008/R) French landscape scene with river and bridge in foreground (53x71cm-21x28in) s.
£1795	$2961	(10-Jul-91 FB.P1/R) Le Pont d'Avignon (53x73cm-21x29in) s. paper laid down on canvas (F.FR 18000)
£2510	$4041	(24-Jun-91 PR.P91/R) Paysage au pont (38x46cm-15x18in) s. (F.FR 25000)
£2650	$5089	(2-Dec-90 M.V152) Bord de riviere (54x73cm-21x29in) s. (F.FR 26000)
£2956	$5676	(2-Dec-90 M.V151/R) Barque sur la riviere (54x73cm-21x29in) s. (F.FR 29000)
£2970	$5257	(7-Apr-91 I.N29) Enfants jouant a la Luge (45x55cm-18x22in) s. panel (F.FR 30000)
£3287	$5588	(29-May-91 GL.P88/R) Le Port de la Rochelle (54x65cm-21x26in) s.d.1919 (F.FR 33000)
£3486	$5926	(29-May-91 GL.P90/R) Paysage fluvial (54x73cm-21x29in) s.d.1927 paper laid down on canvas (F.FR 35000)
£4061	$8000	(13-Nov-90 CE.NY206/R) Voiliers au port (60x74cm-24x29in) s. s.verso paper on canvas
£5337	$8700	(11-Jun-91 I.N154) Paysage de Charente - Vue de Balzac (54x73cm-21x29in) s.d.1952 (F.FR 53000)
£5408	$10654	(16-Nov-90 FB.P107/R) Le port (50x65cm-20x26in) s. (F.FR 53000)
£5446	$9639	(7-Apr-91 I.N28/R) Seance de peinture au bord de l'eau (54x73cm-21x29in) s. i. verso (F.FR 55000)

BALBI, Angelo (1872-1939) Italian
| £1269 | $2145 | (16-Apr-91 CH.R126) Costa ligure (30x40cm-12x16in) s. panel (I.L 2800000) |

BALDERO, Luigi G (?) ?
| £1500 | $2955 | (4-Oct-90 CSK202/R) Cavaliers in a tavern (48x81cm-19x32in) s. |

BALDESSARI, John (20th C) ?
£54734	$92500	(1-May-91 SY.NY80/R) What this painting aims to do (172x144cm-68x57in) acrylic oil canvas
£11834	$20000	(2-May-91 CH.NY271/R) Blue Hope (19x124cm-7x49in) s.d.85 gouache gelatin silver print on paper
£12690	$25000	(5-Oct-90 CH.NY121/R) Aerial view (203x241cm-80x95in) black white photographs acrylic oil
£15385	$26000	(1-May-91 SY.NY152/R) House - 3 stories (183x99cm-72x39in) black wht photos vinyl paint paperboard 2 parts

BALDESSARI, Roberto Iras (1894-) Italian
£508 $849   (5-Jun-91 DO.H2484/R) Alley way in Malcesine, Lake Garda
                         (69x50cm-27x20in) s.i. canvas on board (DM 1500)

BALDI, Lazzaro (1624-1703) Italian
£4359 $8500   (10-Oct-90 CH.NY98/R) The Delphic oracle (48x66cm-19x26in)

BALDI, Lazzaro (circle) (1624-1703) Italian
£3500 $5915   (19-Apr-91 C15/R) A personification of justice (282x213cm-111x84in) oval

BALDINA, Irina (1921-) Russian
£663 $1272   (29-Nov-90 YC.P142/R) La peche (62x98cm-24x39in) s.d.1957 verso
                         (F.FR 6500)

BALDO (19th C) Italian
£867 $1500   (10-May-91 S.W2509/R) The Doge's Palace (36x51cm-14x20in) s. W/C

BALDOCK, J H (19th C) ?
£650 $1222   (18-Sep-90 CSK143) Country village (23x33cm-9x13in) s.d.1864 W/C htd
*   white*

BALDOCK, James Walsham (19th C) British
£900 $1593   (21-Mar-91 CSK203/R) A saddled bay hunter in a loose box
                         (66x91cm-26x36in) s.i.d.1857
£1500 $2940   (15-Feb-91 N360/R) Donkeys and geese in landscape (28x43cm-11x17in)
                         s.d.1892
£600 $1170   (18-Oct-90 SC3047/R) Deer grazing in parkland (41x63cm-16x25in) s.d.1866
£720 $1188   (11-Jul-91 B153/R) Sheep resting in shady Buckinghamshire Wood
*   (25x18cm-10x7in) s.d.1888 W/C htd bodycol*

BALDRY, Gilbert (fl.1880-1910) British?
£950 $1701   (10-Apr-91 CSK265/R) Village gossips (76x102cm-30x40in) s.d.1907

BALDUCCI, Giovanni (?-1603) Italian
£2500 $4075   (1-Jul-91 S187/R) Procession of soldiers marching and on horseback
*   (26x39cm-10x15in) pen wash over black chk*

BALDUNG GRIEN, Hans (circle) (1484-1545) German
£2473 $4426   (10-Apr-91 CB.P44/R) Portrait de femme (24x19cm-9x7in) panel
                         (F.FR 25000)

BALDUNG GRIEN, Hans (studio) (1484-1545) German
£11000 $17930   (5-Jul-91 C254/R) Christ and twelve apostles (35x176cm-14x69in) gold
                         ground panel

BALDWYN, Charles H C (19th C) British
£1000 $1920   (19-Feb-91 C124/R) Owls in wood (13x20cm-5x8in) s. i.verso pencil W/C
*   htd.white*

BALE, Alice Marion Ellen (20th C) Australian
£763 $1465   (26-Nov-90 SY.ME105) Still life with wattle (51x40cm-20x16in) s.d.1912
                         board (A.D 1900)
£962 $1702   (18-Mar-91 MGS.S242) Children resting (63x48cm-25x19in) s. canvas on
                         board (A.D 2250)

BALE, Charles Thomas (19th C) British
£589 $1136   (10-Dec-90 BU.K64/R) Still life of fruit and stoneware jug
                         (46x35cm-18x14in) mono. (D.KR 6500)
£714 $1200   (19-Jul-91 DM.D2085/R) Still life of fruit (38x48cm-15x19in) s.
£742 $1455   (5-Nov-90 FB.M408) Still life (51x61cm-20x24in) mono.d.1875 (C.D 1700)
£750 $1470   (19-Nov-90 SWS509) Still life study of mixed flowers (44x34cm-17x13in)
                         s.
£780 $1443   (6-Mar-91 SC4252) Still life of fruit and dead game (48x58cm-19x23in)
                         mono.d.1884
£825 $1600   (8-Dec-90 W.W202/R) Still life with game, fruit and blue jug
                         (46x36cm-18x14in) s.mono.
£880 $1470   (5-Jun-91 S123) Still life with mixed fruit (46x36cm-18x14in) s.
£960 $1651   (16-May-91 D.V148/R) The lesson (14x11cm-6x4in) mono.indis.d. board
                         (A.S 20000)
£960 $1651   (16-May-91 D.V149/R) The broken pitcher (11x14cm-4x6in) mono.d.1869
                         board (A.S 20000)
£1050 $1953   (3-Sep-90 SWS1315) Still life with mixed fruit and basket and jugs on
                         table (59x49cm-23x19in) mono.
£1100 $2156   (19-Nov-90 SWS564/R) Still life of mixed fruit and wicker basket
                         (44x34cm-17x13in) s.
£1400 $2338   (5-Jun-91 S126/R) Still life of fruit (51x76cm-20x30in) s.
£1466 $2785   (28-Feb-91 D.V15/R) Still life of fruit (35x46cm-14x18in) mono.
                         (A.S 30000)
£1650 $3086   (1-Aug-90 TL1824/R) Still life with jug, fruit and game on table tops
                         (76x51cm-30x20in) s. pair
£1700 $2771   (13-Jun-91 CSK296/R) Still lifes of mixed fruit on mossy banks
                         (35x46cm-14x18in) s. pair
£1700 $3332   (20-Nov-90 PH178/R) Still life of grapes and other fruit with a bird's
                         nest on a table (61x51cm-24x20in) mono.d.1880
£1800 $3384   (18-Sep-90 SWS662/R) Still life studies of fruit and drinking vessels
                         (61x50cm-24x20in) s. pair

BALE, Charles Thomas (19th C) British-cont.

£1800	$3384	(18-Sep-90 SWS663/R) Still life studies of fruit, basket and jug (61x40cm-24x16in) s. pair
£2100	$3570	(29-May-91 PHC169/R) Still life compositions with mixed fruit on ledges (51x76cm-20x30in) s. pair
£2200	$3894	(21-Mar-91 CSK185/R) Still life of fruit and game birds on a ledge (64x76cm-25x30in) mono.d.1886
£2600	$4238	(14-Jun-91 C197/R) Mallard and woodpigeon with apples and grapes on a ledge (51x61cm-20x24in) mono.d.1884
£2800	$5516	(1-Nov-90 C299/R) Grapes, melon and other fruit on silver gilt salver on draped table (71x91cm-28x36in) s.d.1887
£3200	$5408	(30-Apr-91 PH120/R) Still lives of mixed fruit on mossy banks (61x51cm-24x20in) s. pair
£3947	$7500	(27-Feb-91 SY.NY224/R) Still life with fruit, mallards and jugs (71x92cm-28x36in) mono.

BALE, T (19th C) British

£720	$1418	(13-Nov-90 SWS230/R) The farmyard (23x39cm-9x15in) s.d.1892/3

BALE, Thomas C (fl.1868-1873) British

£1500	$2445	(14-Jun-91 C301/R) A Fete Champetre (32x56cm-13x22in) mono.d.1871 board

BALEN, Hendrik van (1575-1632) Flemish

£4057	$7262	(8-Apr-91 CH.R75/R) Madonna col Bambino e San Giovannino (43x33cm-17x13in) panel (I.L 9000000)
£15036	$25561	(30-May-91 F.M17/R) Diana e le ninfe sorprese dai satiri (112x142cm-44x56in) (I.L 33000000)

BALEN, Hendrik van (attrib) (1575-1632) Flemish

£1835	$3615	(13-Nov-90 CH.AM177) Contest between Apollo and Marsyas (38x57cm-15x22in) panel (D.FL 6000)

BALEN, Hendrik van (style) (1575-1632) Flemish

£800	$1600	(7-Feb-91 C10/R) The Madonna annunciate (25x33cm-10x13in) copper

BALEN, Hendrik van and BRUEGHEL, Jan (elder-style) (16/17th C) Flemish

£5500	$10615	(12-Dec-90 S154/R) Feast of the gods (52x76cm-20x30in) panel

BALEN, Hendrik van and BRUEGHEL, Jan (younger) (16/17th C) Flemish

£52000	$89960	(24-May-91 C11/R) A Feast of the Gods (29x41cm-11x16in) s. by Van Balen copper

BALEN, Hendrik van and BRUEGHEL, Jan (younger-attrib) (17th C) Dutch

£17365	$29347	(2-May-91 CH.AM123/R) The Feast of the Gods (47x67cm-19x26in) panel (D.FL 58000)

BALEN, Hendrik van and BRUEGHEL, Jan (younger-studio) (17th C) Flemish

£3267	$5783	(4-Apr-91 CK.P20/R) Vertumne et Pomone dans un jardin fleuri (40x53cm-16x21in) i. verso (F.FR 33000)

BALEN, Hendrik van and BRUEGHEL, Jan (younger-style) (17th C) Flemish

£898	$1518	(2-May-91 CH.AM9) The Penitent Magdalen (49x64cm-19x25in) panel (D.FL 3000)
£1946	$3289	(2-May-91 CH.AM34/R) The Creation of Eve (62x99cm-24x39in) panel (D.FL 6500)

BALEN, Hendrik van and KESSEL, Jan van (style) (16/17th C) Flemish

£6288	$12073	(17-Dec-90 ARC.P15) Allegorie de l'abondance (37x45cm-15x18in) (F.FR 62000)

BALEN, Jan van (1611-1654) Flemish

£609	$1205	(30-Jan-91 APT.P68) Le Christ et Saint Jean Baptiste (17x24cm-7x9in) panel (F.FR 6000)

BALEN, Jan van (attrib) (1611-1654) Flemish

£1900	$3667	(11-Dec-90 PH188/R) Virgin and Child seated at window before tree in blossom (39x34cm-15x13in) panel

BALEN, Matthys (1684-1766) Flemish

£820	$1419	(20-May-91 SWS158/R) Figures in an extensive river landscape (24x31cm-9x12in) panel
£1096	$2126	(4-Dec-90 C.A13) The promenade (35x44cm-14x17in) (B.FR 65000)
£1518	$2944	(4-Dec-90 C.A14) Rural scene (24x32cm-9x13in) panel (B.FR 90000)

BALEN, van (attrib) (?) Flemish

£2243	$4328	(12-Dec-90 CD.P17/R) Bacchus enfant entoure de six amours (20x24cm-8x9in) panel (F.FR 22000)

BALESTRA, Antonio (1666-1740) Italian

£13966	$25000	(11-Apr-91 SY.NY51/R) Juno bribing Aeolus (213x143cm-84x56in)
£71942	$139568	(5-Dec-90 APT.P16/R) Hercule et Omphale (141x208cm-56x82in) (F.FR 700000)

BALESTRA, Antonio (studio) (1666-1740) Italian

£2800	$4564	(2-Jul-91 PH178/R) Virgin and Child holding apple (91x70cm-36x28in)

BALESTRA, Antonio (style) (1666-1740) Italian
£3400 $6698   (31-Oct-90 S146/R) The Adoration of the Shepherds (73x92cm-29x36in)

BALESTRIERI, Lionello (1872-1958) Italian
£2719 $4596   (16-Apr-91 CH.R95) Lungo la senna (29x39cm-11x15in) s. canvas on board (I.L 6000000)
£911 $1549   (28-May-91 F.R23/R) Natura morta di libri con pipa (32x53cm-13x21in) s. W/C (I.L 2000000)

BALFOUR, J Lawson (1870-?) Australian
£1860 $3126   (22-Apr-91 SY.ME197) Figures on hill (25x35cm-10x14in) s. canvas on board (A.D 4000)
£2674 $4493   (22-Apr-91 SY.ME190/R) Beach scene (21x25cm-8x10in) s. canvas on board (A.D 5750)

BALFOUR-BROWNE, Vincent (1880-1963) British
£550 $902   (19-Jun-91 B137/R) Infernal feminine (9x13cm-4x5in) init. W/C
£650 $1066   (19-Jun-91 B136) Stags on hillside at dusk (9x13cm-4x5in) init.d.1948 W/C
£700 $1344   (19-Feb-91 C127/R) Sparrow hawk on rocky outcrop (36x46cm-14x18in) init.d.1906 i.verso pencil W/C htd.white
£950 $1853   (24-Oct-90 SWS328/R) Stags (11cm-4ins circular). init. W/C
£1750 $2870   (19-Jun-91 B135/R) Stags grazing - spyglass study (11cm-4ins circular) init.d.1948 W/C pair
£2500 $5000   (5-Feb-91 S17/R) Pony path in winter (24x31cm-9x12in) init.d.1907 i.d.verso W/C htd white
£2600 $5200   (5-Feb-91 S16/R) Big six pointer on Loch Ba flats (22x33cm-9x13in) init.d.1912 d.1912 verso W/C
£4200 $7854   (28-Aug-90 S743/R) Driven out (30x46cm-12x18in) init.d.1914 W/C pen htd white
£4800 $8016   (26-Jul-91 PHE88/R) They'll break out soon now (30x46cm-12x18in) init.d.1948 W/C

BALIERI, Carl Banerle (19th C) ?
£13000 $25350   (16-Oct-90 CG257/R) Plenty (64x94cm-25x37in) s. s.i.verso

BALIKOV, Y (20th C) Russian
£402 $659   (19-Jun-91 ARC.P60) Irene (95x72cm-37x28in) s. pastel (F.FR 4000)

BALINER, W (19/20th C) ?
£1500 $2415   (24-Jun-91 CSK41/R) Portrait of young lady wearing flower brimmed hat (49x39cm-19x15in) s.

BALINK, Hendricus (1882-1963) American
£856 $1600   (30-Aug-90 MFA.C70) Flowers in blue vase (51x61cm-20x24in) s.

BALKE, Peder (1804-1887) Norwegian
£1489 $2665   (11-Mar-91 B.O8/R) Cape Horn (10x12cm-4x5in) s. panel on paper (N.KR 17000)
£1870 $3609   (10-Dec-90 B.O11 b/R) Fjord landscape (12x8cm-5x3in) panel (N.KR 21000)
£2760 $5328   (10-Dec-90 B.O11 d/R) Sailing vessel in rough seas (8x11cm-3x4in) s. panel (N.KR 31000)
£3117 $6015   (10-Dec-90 B.O11 c/R) 'Hornelen' (18x34cm-7x13in) panel (N.KR 35000)
£4809 $9280   (12-Dec-90 BU.O6/R) Landscape (30x42cm-12x17in) s.d.1848 panel (N.KR 54000)
£8103 $15639   (10-Dec-90 B.O11 a/R) North Cape (21x26cm-8x10in) (N.KR 91000)
£9083 $17530   (10-Dec-90 B.O10/R) Mountains and moor (35x26cm-14x10in) s.d.1865 panel (N.KR 102000)

BALL, Wilfred Williams (1853-1917) British
£444 $862   (4-Dec-90 R.T115/R) Sunny afternoon, Bosham, Sussex (18x30cm-7x12in) s.d.1910 W/C (C.D 1000)
£460 $800   (27-Mar-91 RB633) Coastal landscape with windmill and fishing boats (23x38cm-9x15in) s.d.1910 W/C
£490 $823   (18-Jul-91 PHX237) Bosham, Sussex (20x38cm-8x15in) s.d.1888 W/C
£600 $1200   (8-Feb-91 C75) The Bridge at Wareham (18x28cm-7x11in) s.d.1912 i. verso W/C
£620 $1017   (20-Jun-91 DLY214/R) Walhampton, farmstead in summer (25x36cm-10x14in) s.d.1911 W/C
£650 $1092   (18-Jul-91 ZZ.B684/R) Landscape with Wells Cathedral in distance (15x23cm-6x9in) W/C
£900 $1755   (16-Jan-91 CSK30/R) Beached fishing vessels at low tide (38x56cm-15x22in) s.d.1900 W/C
£1800 $2934   (14-Jun-91 C52/R) Old Shoreham. Arundel Castle (18x29cm-7x11in) s.i. W/C pair

BALLA, Giacomo (1871-1958) Italian
£5087 $9870   (3-Dec-90 F.M334/R) Motivo floreale per ricamo (14x20cm-6x8in) s.c.1919 tempera (I.L 11000000)
£13156 $22629   (13-May-91 CH.R117/R) Forme e rumore (22x36cm-9x14in) s.i.d.1915verso tempera board (I.L 29000000)
£16365 $32076   (20-Nov-90 BR.M30/R) Motivo floreale (31x43cm-12x17in) s. tempera paper (I.L 36000000)
£23125 $44862   (3-Dec-90 CH.R69/R) Contrasti (57x34cm-22x13in) s. panel (I.L 50000000)
£42000 $67620   (25-Jun-91 C109/R) Bambino (61x50cm-24x20in) s.

BALLA, Giacomo (1871-1958) Italian-cont.
£50874	$98696	(3-Dec-90 CH.R174/R) Ritratto della signora (59x45cm-23x18in) s.d.1904 (I.L 110000000)
£190000	$368600	(3-Dec-90 C26/R) Ritratto della Signora Adelaide Cottreau (100x100cm-39x39in) s.
£225124	$438991	(22-Oct-90 BR.M222/R) Sorge l'idea (29x36cm-11x14in) s. panel (I.L 500000000)
£3209	*$5263*	*(19-Jun-91 F.M42/R) Testina futurista (10x8cm-4x3in) s. pencil (I.L 7000000)*
£3832	*$6859*	*(9-Apr-91 F.R103/R) Figura femminile. Ritratto di Elica (30x21cm-12x8in) pencil paper laid down on board double-sided (I.L 8500000)*
£13863	*$26756*	*(12-Dec-90 F.M48/R) Veduta cittadina (23x31cm-9x12in) s. i.verso pastel (I.L 30000000)*

BALLABENE, Rudolf Raimund (1890-1968) Austrian
£732	$1354	(7-Mar-91 D.V179/R) Seascape with two horses (90x101cm-35x40in) s.d.1949 (A.S 15000)

BALLANTINE, Mary (fl.1920-1939) British
£650	$1300	(5-Feb-91 S161/R) Feeding goldfish (91x69cm-36x27in) bears sig.stretcher
£700	$1176	(23-Apr-91 S153/R) Still life of flowers in vase (91x71cm-36x28in) s.d.47
£700	$1176	(23-Apr-91 S156/R) Still life of vegetables in trug (56x76cm-22x30in) s.indist.d. s.verso
£800	$1600	(5-Feb-91 S198/R) Still life with goldfish and butterfly (71x91cm-28x36in) s.
£3500	$6545	(28-Aug-90 S937/R) Spring flowers (61x91cm-24x36in) s.d.1944

BALLARD, Brian (20th C) British
£602	$1162	(12-Dec-90 CH.E51) Girl against yellow (38x39cm-15x15in) s.d.83 panel (E.P 650)

BALLAVOINE, Jules Frederic (1855-1901) French
£1257	$2098	(4-Jun-91 FB.M174/R) Jeune fille aux fleurs (22x15cm-9x6in) s. board (C.D 2400)
£2254	$3831	(28-May-91 AB.S4732/R) Women on at outing (50x61cm-20x24in) s. (S.KR 24000)
£2500	$4075	(5-Jul-91 APT.P87/R) Lavandiere (33x46cm-13x18in) s. (F.FR 25000)
£3077	$6000	(24-Oct-90 CH.NY51/R) Washerwoman by stream with bridge beyond (46x56cm-18x22in) s.
£6154	$12000	(23-Oct-90 SY.NY289/R) Apollo and Daphne (97x131cm-38x52in) s.

BALLE, Mogens (20th C) Scandinavian
£536	$991	(5-Mar-91 RAS.K113/R) Still life of jug and fruit (109x100cm-43x39in) init. (D.KR 6000)
£543	$1049	(12-Dec-90 RAS.K60) Composition with figures (15x45cm-6x18in) init. (D.KR 6000)
£704	$1373	(10-Oct-90 RAS.K41) Composition (35x27cm-14x11in) init. (D.KR 8000)
£712	$1338	(19-Sep-90 KH.K19) Composition (31x50cm-12x20in) s. paper (D.KR 8000)
£725	$1399	(12-Dec-90 RAS.K59) Composition with figures (24x33cm-9x13in) init. (D.KR 8000)
£760	$1490	(13-Feb-91 KH.K10) Landscape gliding past (21x35cm-8x14in) init. (D.KR 8500)
£792	$1545	(10-Oct-90 RAS.K38) Composition (33x22cm-13x9in) init. (D.KR 9000)
£792	$1545	(10-Oct-90 RAS.K40) Composition with figures (24x33cm-9x13in) init. (D.KR 9000)
£801	$1505	(19-Sep-90 KH.K1) Composition (29x45cm-11x18in) s. paper (D.KR 9000)
£804	$1487	(5-Mar-91 RAS.K112/R) Compositon with figures (35x68cm-14x27in) init. (D.KR 9000)
£880	$1717	(10-Oct-90 RAS.K8) Composition with figures (24x33cm-9x13in) init. (D.KR 10000)
£880	$1717	(10-Oct-90 RAS.K112/R) Moon over town (34x29cm-13x11in) init. (D.KR 10000)
£880	$1717	(10-Oct-90 RAS.K70/R) The golden hare (28x36cm-11x14in) init. gold ground (D.KR 10000)
£893	$1652	(5-Mar-91 RAS.K111) Composition (38x46cm-15x18in) init. (D.KR 10000)
£924	$1802	(10-Oct-90 RAS.K175) Composition with figures (35x27cm-14x11in) init. (D.KR 10500)
£968	$1888	(10-Oct-90 RAS.K7) Composition (46x38cm-18x15in) init. (D.KR 11000)
£1056	$2060	(10-Oct-90 RAS.K36/R) Elegy (33x37cm-13x15in) init. (D.KR 12000)
£1056	$1817	(15-May-91 RAS.K70/R) Composition (50x40cm-20x16in) init. (D.KR 12000)
£1063	$1796	(2-May-91 RAS.V169) Before night (54x65cm-21x26in) init.d.74 (D.KR 12000)
£1107	$1871	(2-May-91 RAS.V168/R) Composition in colour (38x46cm-15x18in) init. (D.KR 12500)
£1163	$2279	(13-Feb-91 KH.K9/R) Composition (24x33cm-9x13in) init. (D.KR 13000)
£1228	$2088	(29-May-91 KH.K111/R) Composition (46x38cm-18x15in) init. (D.KR 14000)
£1257	$2476	(14-Nov-90 KH.K9/R) Composition (24x33cm-9x13in) init. (D.KR 14000)
£1257	$2476	(14-Nov-90 KH.K10/R) Composition (29x34cm-11x13in) init. (D.KR 14000)
£1320	$2575	(10-Oct-90 RAS.K111/R) After the rain 1954 (50x40cm-20x16in) init. (D.KR 15000)
£1337	$2393	(14-Mar-91 RAS.V753/R) Composition with figures (69x43cm-27x17in) s. (D.KR 15000)
£1408	$2746	(10-Oct-90 RAS.K2) Composition (46x38cm-18x15in) init. (D.KR 16000)
£1418	$2312	(13-Jun-91 RAS.V637/R) Composition (71x95cm-28x37in) s. acrylic paper on canvas (D.KR 16000)

BALLE, Mogens (20th C) Scandinavian-cont.

£1491	$2535	(29-May-91 KH.K117/R) Composition (46x55cm-18x22in) init. (D.KR 17000)
£1496	$2918	(10-Oct-90 RAS.K110/R) Composition (46x38cm-18x15in) init. (D.KR 17000)
£1506	$2861	(14-Sep-90 RAS.V713/R) Figure composition (38x46cm-15x18in) init. (D.KR 17000)
£1512	$2843	(19-Sep-90 KH.K2) Dramatic garden (50x35cm-20x14in) init. masonite (D.KR 17000)
£1535	$2610	(29-May-91 KH.K115/R) Composition (38x46cm-15x18in) init. (D.KR 17500)
£1630	$3147	(12-Dec-90 RAS.K20/R) Dying day (58x51cm-23x20in) s. (D.KR 18000)
£1754	$2982	(29-May-91 KH.K40/R) Composition (24x33cm-9x13in) init. (D.KR 20000)
£1761	$3433	(10-Oct-90 RAS.K104/R) Composition (38x46cm-15x18in) init. (D.KR 20000)
£1802	$3117	(23-May-91 SY.AM228/R) Hag (46x55cm-18x22in) init. s.i.d.72verso (D.FL 6000)
£1812	$3496	(12-Dec-90 RAS.K58/R) 'Semafor' - night 1955 (40x50cm-16x20in) init. (D.KR 20000)
£1858	$3585	(13-Dec-90 SY.AM325/R) Untitled (46x38cm-18x15in) init. (D.FL 6000)
£1868	$3512	(19-Sep-90 KH.K108/R) Composition with figure (46x38cm-18x15in) init. (D.KR 21000)
£1993	$3846	(12-Dec-90 RAS.K98/R) Composition (97x67cm-38x26in) (D.KR 22000)
£2113	$4120	(10-Oct-90 RAS.K113/R) Composition (61x50cm-24x20in) init. (D.KR 24000)
£2113	$4120	(10-Oct-90 RAS.K37) Composition (51x50cm-20x20in) init. (D.KR 24000)
£2154	$4244	(14-Nov-90 KH.K7/R) Composition (33x55cm-13x22in) s.d.1979verso (D.KR 24000)
£2201	$4291	(10-Oct-90 RAS.K174/R) Composition (55x37cm-22x15in) init. panel (D.KR 25000)
£2224	$4181	(19-Sep-90 KH.K69/R) 'Et oyebliks spellen' (38x46cm-15x18in) init. (D.KR 25000)
£2224	$4181	(19-Sep-90 KH.K99/R) Composition (38x46cm-15x18in) init. (D.KR 25000)
£2281	$3877	(29-May-91 KH.K52/R) Composition (58x66cm-23x26in) init. (D.KR 26000)
£2289	$4509	(14-Nov-90 KH.K6/R) Composition (38x46cm-15x18in) init. (D.KR 25500)
£2313	$4349	(19-Sep-90 KH.K52/R) Composition (55x46cm-22x18in) init. (D.KR 26000)
£2377	$4635	(10-Oct-90 RAS.K153/R) Under the open sky (38x46cm-15x18in) init. d.61verso (D.KR 27000)
£2500	$4625	(5-Mar-91 RAS.K110/R) Composition (46x55cm-18x22in) init. (D.KR 28000)
£2513	$4952	(14-Nov-90 KH.K8/R) Composition (38x46cm-15x18in) init. (D.KR 28000)
£2632	$4474	(29-May-91 KH.K96/R) Between road and wall (54x65cm-21x26in) init. (D.KR 30000)
£3114	$5854	(19-Sep-90 KH.K87/R) Red composition (50x61cm-20x24in) init. (D.KR 35000)
£3345	$6523	(10-Oct-90 RAS.K109/R) Composition (50x61cm-20x24in) init. (D.KR 38000)
£3578	$7013	(13-Feb-91 KH.K8/R) Composition (81x100cm-32x39in) init. (D.KR 40000)
£3715	$7170	(13-Dec-90 SY.AM237/R) Untitled (100x81cm-39x32in) init.d.65 (D.FL 12000)
£3737	$7025	(19-Sep-90 KH.K13/R) Observation of the dream (65x54cm-26x21in) init. (D.KR 42000)
£4129	$8135	(14-Nov-90 KH.K5 a/R) Shadows (89x116cm-35x46in) init. (D.KR 46000)
£4225	$8239	(10-Oct-90 RAS.K101/R) The family (46x65cm-18x26in) init. (D.KR 48000)
£4401	$7570	(15-May-91 RAS.K68/R) Autumnal portrait (81x100cm-32x39in) init. (D.KR 50000)
£4930	$9613	(10-Oct-90 RAS.K39/R) Compsosition with figures among houses (75x98cm-30x39in) init. (D.KR 56000)
£10231	$19235	(19-Sep-90 KH.K10/R) Composition (132x92cm-52x36in) init. i.d.1949-50 (D.KR 115000)
£716	$1403	(13-Feb-91 KH.K11) Composition (39x40cm-15x16in) s. gouache collage (D.KR 8000)
£751	$1299	(22-May-91 CH.AM779) Abstract composition (31x45cm-12x18in) s.d.85 pencil W/C (D.FL 2500)

BALLE, Mogens and DOTREMONT, Christian (20th C) Scandinavian/Belgian

£965	$1640	(29-May-91 KH.K2) Et si le brouillard c'etais l'entente (53x76cm-21x30in) s.d.69 W/C gouache (D.KR 11000)

BALLESIO, Federico (19th C) Italian

£1060	$1825	(18-May-91 W.W12/R) Woman at the well (51x36cm-20x14in) mono.i. W/C
£1775	$3000	(20-Apr-91 WOL.C110/R) Playing with baby (56x38cm-22x15in) s. W/C
£9605	$17000	(22-Mar-91 S.W2803/R) Celebration Day (69x104cm-27x41in) s. W/C

BALLESIO, G (19th C) Italian

£1302	$2500	(17-Aug-90 DM.D2001/R) Arab figure and oriental rugs (53x46cm-21x18in) s.

BALLESIO, Giuseppe (?) Italian

£450	$752	(22-Jul-91 SWS893/R) The Cardinals' plans (55x37cm-22x15in) s.i. W/C pencil

BALLIN, Hugo (1879-?) American

£888	$1500	(21-Apr-91 DU.E224) Wedding breakfast (76x102cm-30x40in) s.

BALLINGALL, Alexander (19th C) British

£550	$924	(23-Apr-91 S113/R) On shore, Holy Island (32x50cm-13x20in) s.i.d.1900 W/C

BALLION, Michele (20th C) French?

£508	$1016	(7-Feb-91 R.P242/R) Au dela du gris (140x150cm-55x59in) s. acrylic (F.FR 5000)

BALLION, Michele (20th C) French?-cont.
£559 $1118   (7-Feb-91 R.P122) La femme de terre (130x130cm-51x51in) s. acrylic
       (F.FR 5500)

BALLOT, George Henri (1866-?) French
£783 $1449   (4-Mar-91 ARC.P84/R) L'amateur de dessins (130x98cm-51x39in) s.
       (F.FR 7800)

BALMER, George (1806-1846) British
£2700 $5238   (4-Dec-90 AG353/R) Benwell Stalthes by moonlight (39x59cm-15x23in)
£5600 $10864   (4-Dec-90 AG352/R) Old Lighthouse, Sunderland (30x23cm-12x9in)

BALMFORD, Hurst (1871-?) British
£650 $1222   (20-Sep-90 CSK78/R) Boats in harbour (37x49cm-15x19in) s. canvas-board

BALSLOW, A S (19th C) Danish
£1601 $3123   (19-Oct-90 RAS.V459/R) Still life of pink roses and butterflies
       (22x29cm-9x11in) s. (D.KR 18000)
£1690 $3296   (19-Oct-90 RAS.V458/R) Still life of white roses (22x30cm-9x12in) s.
       (D.KR 19000)

BALSON, Ralph (1890-1964) Australian
£4673 $7617   (16-Jun-91 SY.ME44/R) Painting no.8, 1960 (64x59cm-25x23in) s. synthetic
       enamel board (A.D 10000)

BALTEN, Pieter (1552-1598) Flemish
£60000 $115800   (12-Dec-90 S80/R) Village feast (69x129cm-27x51in) panel

BALTHUS (1908-) French
£5584 $11000   (3-Oct-90 SY.NY129/R) Still life (25x19cm-10x7in) board
£86705 $150000   (8-May-91 CH.NY30/R) Lelia Caetani (116x88cm-46x35in) s.d.1935
£159363 $275697   (25-May-91 GL.P39/R) Roger et son fils (130x89cm-51x35in) wood
       (F.FR 1600000)
£1020 $2000   (12-Feb-91 SY.NY55/R) Femme nude assise (41x30cm-16x12in) pencil
       double-sided
£1028 $1994   (7-Dec-90 GL.P126) Personnage accoude sur un banc (22x17cm-9x7in) ink
       (F.FR 10000)
£1028 $1994   (7-Dec-90 GL.P127) Deux personnages (22x17cm-9x7in) ink (F.FR 10000)
£2030 $4000   (3-Oct-90 SY.NY113 a/R) Study for figure of Evangelist Luke. Sketch for
       Beatenberg Church (30x20cm-12x8in) W/C pencil double-sided
£9174 $17615   (26-Nov-90 GL.P1/R) Le sommeil (24x31cm-9x12in) s.d.1949 sanguinne
       col.crayons double-sided (F.FR 90000)

BALUSCHEK, Hans (1870-1935) German
£3413 $6689   (24-Nov-90 VG.B125/R) Sunday walk (98x49cm-39x19in) s.c.1902
       (DM 10000)
£5119 $10034   (22-Nov-90 L.K807/R) Teachers' choir concert (37x59cm-15x23in) s.
       i.verso grease chk board (DM 15000)

BALWE, Arnold (1898-?) German
£1520 $2630   (25-May-91 N.M13/R) Grosshesseloher Brucke (67x97cm-26x38in) (DM 4500)
£1520 $2630   (25-May-91 N.M12/R) The ice cream cart (83x63cm-33x25in) s.i.d.verso
       (DM 4500)
£2730 $5352   (24-Nov-90 N.M26/R) Bunch of flowers in vase on stool (82x59cm-32x23in)
       (DM 8000)
£3754 $7358   (24-Nov-90 N.M27/R) Lake Starnberg in winter (66x84cm-26x33in) s.d.1928
       s.i.d.verso (DM 11000)
£4068 $6631   (3-Jul-91 WE.MU231/R) Landing stage, Chiemsee (60x100cm-24x39in) s.
       (DM 12000)
£4392 $7598   (25-May-91 N.M16/R) Spanish coastal landscape (66x85cm-26x33in) s.
       s.i.verso (DM 13000)
£5119 $9676   (25-Sep-90 FN.S1912/R) Fishing boats returning (50x71cm-20x28in)
       s.i.d.1927 (DM 15000)
£5405 $9351   (25-May-91 N.M14/R) Harbour entrance, Venice (85x110cm-33x43in) s.
       s.i.verso (DM 16000)
£6419 $11105   (25-May-91 N.M15/R) Amsterdam, evening (81x100cm-32x39in) s.i.verso
       (DM 19000)
£7023 $11870   (17-Apr-91 WE.MU306/R) Flowers in vase (83x59cm-33x23in) (DM 21000)
£10239 $19352   (25-Sep-90 FN.S1913/R) Bunch of autumn flowers in jug (86x60cm-34x24in)
       s. s.i.d.1944verso (DM 30000)

BALWE-STAIMMER, Elisabeth (1896-?) ?
£1024 $2007   (24-Nov-90 N.M29) Women on bridge (56x77cm-22x30in) s.c.1968/69 W/C
       (DM 3000)
£1791 $3098   (21-May-91 WK.M568/R) Spanish village (56x77cm-22x30in) s. W/C htd.white
       (DM 5300)
£2196 $3799   (25-May-91 N.M17/R) Southern harbour with boats (55x80cm-22x31in) s. W/C
       (DM 6500)

BALZAC, Alain (1957-) French
£495 $885   (14-Apr-91 APT.P62/R) Drapeau rouge vert blanc (57x75cm-22x30in) mixed
       media canvas (F.FR 5000)

BAMA, James E (1926-) American
£2326 $4000   (15-May-91 SY.NY173/R) Shopping day. Lieutenant (46x75cm-18x30in) s. one
       masonite one board pair

BAMA, James E (1926-) American-cont.
£5820 $11000   (26-Sep-90 SY.NY230/R) How to reduce (71x63cm-28x25in) s. board

BAMBER, Bessie (19/20th C) British
£1000 $1940   (3-Dec-90 B69) Kittens (26x56cm-10x22in) s.with init. panel
£1000 $1940   (3-Dec-90 B80/R) Fluffy friends (32x57cm-13x22in) init.d.09 panel framed
                            in oval mount

BAMBERGER, Fritz (1814-1873) German
£1600 $2624   (20-Jun-91 B11/R) Extensive landscape (30x51cm-12x20in) s.

BAMFYLDE, Coplestone Warre (1719-1791) British
£1845 $3100   (17-Jul-91 SY.NY93/R) A storm (84x112cm-33x44in)
£650 $1092   (22-Apr-91 PH214) Pavilion and Lake at Stourhead, Wiltshire
                            (24x35cm-9x14in) s. ink W/C

BANCHI, Giorgio (1789-1853) Italian
£1154 $2250   (26-Oct-90 SY.NY20/R) Portrait of Vincenzo Bellini (6x4cm-2x2in) s.
                            gouache oval

BANCHIERI, Giuseppe (1927-) Italian
£1001 $1892   (27-Sep-90 F.M104/R) Paesaggio (100x80cm-39x31in) s.d.60 (I.L 2200000)
£1172 $2098   (9-Apr-91 F.R152) Ambiente e finestra (50x70cm-20x28in) s.d.65
                            (I.L 2600000)
£2701 $5268   (22-Oct-90 BR.M268/R) Marina n.14, Ronchi Poveromo (30x30cm-12x12in)
                            s.d.1988 panel (I.L 6000000)
£3438 $5639   (19-Jun-91 F.M217/R) Interno - esterno (80x100cm-31x39in) s.d.1964
                            (I.L 7500000)
£4126 $6767   (19-Jun-91 F.M231/R) Periferia (70x90cm-28x35in) s.d.1959 (I.L 9000000)

BANCROFT, Elias (?-1924) British
£3500 $5775   (9-Jul-91 PH176/R) Minnow catchers. Yorkshire Beck (71x127cm-28x50in)
                            one s. s.i.verso one s.d.1901 s.i.d.verso pair

BANCROFT, Milton Herbert (1867-1947) American
£667 $1300   (20-Oct-90 W.W99/R) Portrait of Mary Evelyn Beatrice Longman
                            (198x102cm-78x40in) s.d.1912

BAND, Max (1900-1974) Israeli?
£785 $1500   (1-Jan-91 GG.TA239/R) Portrait of woman (73x54cm-29x21in) s.
£791 $1416   (14-Apr-91 GL.P54) Les vaches au pre (60x73cm-24x29in) s. (F.FR 8000)
£1043 $1700   (12-Jun-91 GG.TA233/R) Procession (39x46cm-15x18in) s.
£1571 $3000   (1-Jan-91 GG.TA240/R) View of the town's square (60x73cm-24x29in) s.

BANDEIRA, Antonio (1922-1967) Brazilian
£1100 $1771   (28-Jun-91 CSK74) Yellow country (20x30cm-8x12in) s.d.55 s.i.d.verso

BANDINELLI, Baccio (1493-1560) Italian
£4000 $6520   (1-Jul-91 S17/R) Two seated female figures and one crouching
                            (39x26cm-15x10in) pen
£24000 $39120   (2-Jul-91 C3/R) Bearded man seated at table. Standing nude holding
                            studio block (31x21cm-12x8in) chk pen ink double-sided
£38000 $61940   (4-Jul-91 B61/R) Two women, one carrying a child passing through a
                            doorway (20x11cm-8x4in) bears i. pen
£78000 $150540   (13-Dec-90 B52/R) Study of head and shoulders of two youths and two
                            other heads (24x25cm-9x10in) pen

BANDINELLI, Baccio (attrib) (1493-1560) Italian
£1198 $2000   (23-Jan-91 D.NY1) Study of male nude (36x23cm-14x9in) i.verso ink

BANDO (?) ?
£1563 $3047   (27-Oct-90 ZZ.F9) Les Harengs (23x33cm-9x13in) s. (F.FR 15500)

BANDO, Toshio (1890-) Japanese
£1195 $2068   (26-May-91 ZZ.F9/R) Les chardons en fleurs (33x24cm-13x9in) s.
                            (F.FR 12000)
£1953 $3788   (5-Dec-90 ZZ.F186/R) Poissons rouges (22x27cm-9x11in) sig. ideogramme
                            (F.FR 19000)
£2209 $4086   (4-Mar-91 ARC.P85/R) Bouquet champetre (21x27cm-8x11in) s. (F.FR 22000)
£2218 $4258   (2-Dec-90 GAB.G1505/R) L'Eglise du village (24x19cm-9x7in) s.
                            (S.FR 5500)
£2823 $5419   (2-Dec-90 GAB.G1506/R) La petite poupee abondonnee (27x22cm-11x9in) s.
                            (S.FR 7000)
£604 $1183   (22-Jan-91 YC.P13) Lapin albinos (31x47cm-12x19in) s. pastel (F.FR 6000)
£604 $1183   (22-Jan-91 YC.P11) Boquet de fleurs (47x31cm-19x12in) s. pastel
                            (F.FR 6000)

BANDZELADZE, Alexandre (1927-) Russian
£809 $1570   (8-Dec-90 KV.L27) Composition (58x82cm-23x32in) s.d.1987 gouache
                            (B.FR 48000)

BANFI, Gioachino (1851-1885) Italian
£693 $1338   (12-Dec-90 F.M169) Ritratto di gentiluomo (62x48cm-24x19in) s.d.1870
                            (I.L 1500000)

BANG, Peter Marius (1829-?) Danish
£5338 $10036   (18-Sep-90 BU.K113/R) Still life of fruit and flowers on table (87x63cm-34x25in) init.d.75 (D.KR 60000)

BANKS, John (1883-1945) Australian
£1310 $2266   (21-May-91 JRL.S106) Study for a picture (24x29cm-9x11in) s. (A.D 3000)
£1395 $2344   (22-Apr-91 SY.ME189) Hong Kong (39x49cm-15x19in) s. s.l.d.1935 verso canvas on board (A.D 3000)

BANKS, Lesley (20th C) British
£1350 $2282   (17-Apr-91 CG145) Safe inside (61x66cm-24x26in) s.d.90 l. verso

BANKS, Thomas J (19th C) British
£5822 $11004   (27-Sep-90 D.V22/R) Wooded coastal landscape, autumn (183x122cm-72x48in) mono.d.86 (A.S 120000)

BANLIEUE BANLIEUE (20th C) French?
£554 $1081   (28-Oct-90 R.P132) Sans titre (70x100cm-28x39in) s.d.87 mixed media (F.FR 5500)

BANNATYNE, John James (1835-1911) British
£500 $895   (14-Mar-91 CG137) On the Ayrshire coast (46x61cm-18x24in) s.
£1000 $1880   (19-Sep-90 PHC177/R) Anglers in rocky coastal landscape, Scotland (71x92cm-28x36in) s.
£3000 $5610   (28-Aug-90 S802/R) Skipness Castle (71x92cm-28x36in) s.l.
£3200 $5984   (28-Aug-90 S831/R) Bay on the west coast of Scotland (61x92cm-24x36in) s.

BANNISTER, Edward M (1833-1901) American
£923 $1550   (28-Apr-91 LIT.L318) Landscape with building (15x23cm-6x9in) s. board
£1070 $2000   (30-Aug-90 MFA.C42) Figure in landscape (18x15cm-7x6in) s. board

BANNISTER, Thaddeus (1915-1983) ?
£900 $1530   (30-May-91 C111/R) Topsail schooner John W Smart in full sail off coast (52x75cm-20x30in) s.
£1900 $3230   (30-May-91 C110/R) Schooner Yale (61x91cm-24x36in) s.
£1900 $3230   (30-May-91 C109/R) Barque Anglo-Norman approaching south coast of England (61x91cm-24x36in) s.
£2200 $3740   (30-May-91 C113/R) Barquentine Arlington in full sail (51x76cm-20x30in) s.
£2400 $4080   (30-May-91 C112/R) Schooner Aetna off coast (76x102cm-30x40in) s.l.
£2600 $5070   (18-Oct-90 CSK106/R) The American schooner 'John D.Griffin' (61x107cm-24x42in) s.

BANTING, John (1902-1970) British
£2000 $3480   (27-Mar-91 S106/R) Self portrait (38x35cm-15x14in)

BANTING, Sir Frederick Grant (1891-1941) Canadian
£1818 $3127   (14-May-91 JOY.T12/R) Grace Lake (26x34cm-10x13in) s. panel (C.D 3600)
£2000 $3880   (3-Dec-90 R.T368/R) St. Tite des Cap, Quebec (22x27cm-9x11in) s. s.d.1937 verso panel (C.D 4500)
£2222 $4311   (3-Dec-90 R.T369/R) St. Tite des Cap (21x27cm-8x11in) s. s.d.1937 verso panel (C.D 5000)
£8081 $13980   (6-May-91 SY.T11 a/R) Winter in Ste. Irenee, 1931 (53x66cm-21x26in) (C.D 16000)

BAPTISTA, Marciano Antonio (1826-1896) Portuguese
£4967 $9685   (9-Oct-90 CH.HK1341/R) Views of Victoria, Hong Kong (58x80cm-23x31in) pencil pen W/C pair (HK.D 75000)
£7285 $14205   (9-Oct-90 CH.HK1340/R) View of waterfront, Central District, Hong Kong (35x61cm-14x24in) pencil W/C (HK.D 110000)

BAR, Alexandre de (1821-1901) French
£1836 $3250   (22-May-91 S.W2871/R) Shepherdess and sheep in Arcadian landscape (30x46cm-12x18in) s.d.1858
£316 $600   (27-Feb-91 SY.NY74/R) Souvenir des Alpes (36x25cm-14x10in) s. pastel

BAR, Bonaventure de (attrib) (1700-1729) French
£7800 $15210   (25-Oct-90 CSK108/R) Les Plaisirs du Bal. Blindman's Buff (25x35cm-10x14in) panel pair
£16423 $32354   (30-Oct-90 BU.S226/R) Fete champetre (36x52cm-14x20in) (S.KR 180000)

BAR, Bonaventure de (circle) (1700-1729) French
£2941 $5000   (31-May-91 CH.NY248/R) Elegant figures playing cards in interior (25x20cm-10x8in) copper

BAR, Clementine de (1807-1856) French
£2610 $5116   (11-Feb-91 SY.J366/R) Vidas de los santos (128x96cm-50x38in) s.d.1847 (SA.R 13000)

BARABINI, Gaetano (19th C) Italian
£11426 $22509   (14-Nov-91 F.M40/R) Lot e le figlie (150x107cm-59x42in) s. (I.L 25000000)

BARABINO, Angelo (?) Italian
£16650 $32300   (5-Dec-90 F.M112/R) Pieta (98x118cm-39x46in) s. l.verso (I.L 36000000)

BARABINO, Angelo (?) Italian-cont.
£30000 $58000   (18-Oct-90 F.M64/R) Monte Rosa dalla Val d'Ayas (60x66cm-24x26in) s.
                   (I.L 66000000)

BARADUC, Jeanne (20th C) French
£632 $1200   (9-Jan-91 D.NY5) Floral still life (51x38cm-20x15in) s.i. panel

BARATELLA, Paolo (1935-) Italian
£366   *$704*   *(27-Nov-90 SY.MI11) Come se tutto fosse giusto (62x63cm-24x25in)*
                 s.d.72verso mixed media paper on canvas (I.L 800000)

BARATTI, Filippo (19/20th C) Italian
£3243 $6000   (8-Mar-91 S.BM184/R) Place de la Concorde, Sunset (38x46cm-15x18in)
                 s.i.d.1904
£52789 $89741   (27-May-91 APT.P247/R) Captives et butin (90x66cm-35x26in) s.d.1883
                 (F.FR 530000)

BARAU, Emile (1851-1930) French
£1445 $2500   (10-May-91 S.W2502/R) Morning, off shore (74x99cm-29x39in) s.

BARBARIGO, Ida (1923-) Italian
£9712 $18842   (3-Dec-90 CH.R73/R) Realta sconcertante (162x114cm-64x45in) d.1961
                 s.verso (I.L 21000000)

BARBARINI, Emil (1855-1930) Austrian
£735 $1455   (31-Jan-91 D.V126/R) Landscape in thunderstorm (41x42cm-16x17in)
                 (A.S 15000)
£1483 $2862   (12-Dec-90 BU.S6/R) Brussel fishmarket (21x31cm-8x12in) s. panel
                 (S.KR 16000)
£1610 $2705   (24-Apr-91 BA.S8/R) On the way to market (32x63cm-13x25in) s.
                 (S.KR 17000)
£1900 $3097   (2-Jul-91 SWS302/R) In rose garden (56x78cm-22x31in) s.
£2055 $3349   (12-Jun-91 N.M366/R) Fish market by harbour, possibly Brussels
                 (20x30cm-8x12in) s. i.verso panel (DM 6000)
£2453 $4711   (29-Nov-90 D.V44/R) Am Naschmarkt (21x31cm-8x12in) s. panel (A.S 50000)
£2457 $4816   (24-Nov-90 SA.A698/R) Village street scene in rain (62x63cm-24x25in) s.
                 (DM 7200)
£2944 $5653   (29-Nov-90 D.V43/R) Christmas (21x31cm-8x12in) s. panel (A.S 60000)
£3770 $6295   (4-Jun-91 R.T215/R) Flower market (21x32cm-8x13in) s.panel (C.D 7200)
£3797 $6796   (11-Apr-91 D.V129/R) View of Pfunds, Oberinntal (68x105cm-27x41in) s.
                 (A.S 80000)

BARBARINI, Ernst (19th C) Austrian
£3077 $5200   (20-Apr-91 WOL.C108/R) Street scene (64x48cm-25x19in) s.

BARBARINI, Franz (1804-1873) Austrian
£1941 $3668   (27-Sep-90 D.V60/R) Old mill near Bozen (68x105cm-27x41in) i.verso
                 (A.S 40000)
£2385 $4699   (13-Nov-90 AB.S850/R) Alpine landscape with buildings and figures,
                 Partenkirchen (47x69cm-19x27in) s. (S.KR 26000)
£2872 $5600   (26-Oct-90 KM.K1092/R) Village street with peasant couple and
                 horse-drawn cart returning (68x105cm-27x41in) s. (DM 8500)
£5337 $10087   (27-Sep-90 D.V67/R) The Danube valley near Schwechat (34x43cm-13x17in)
                 mono.d.49 (A.S 110000)
£1528   *$2567*   *(25-Apr-91 D.V141/R) View of St Wolfgang (22x32cm-9x13in) s.d.1852*
                 pencil W/C htd.white (A.S 32000)

BARBARINI, Gustav (1840-1909) Austrian
£1466 $2785   (28-Feb-91 D.V20/R) Mountainous landscape (54x68cm-21x27in) mono.
                 (A.S 30000)
£1698 $3210   (27-Sep-90 D.V156/R) Bechtesgaden landscape (21x28cm-8x11in) mono.
                 i.verso board (A.S 35000)
£1748 $3374   (12-Dec-90 N.M439/R) Wooded landscape with cows by stream and peasants
                 before chapel (48x68cm-19x27in) s. (DM 5000)
£1923 $3712   (12-Dec-90 N.M440) View of Heinburg, Upper Austria (50x81cm-20x32in)
                 i.stretcher one of pair (DM 5500)
£1923 $3712   (12-Dec-90 N.M441) Waldsee, Steiermark (50x81cm-20x32in) i.stretcher one
                 of pair (DM 5500)
£2879 $4952   (16-May-91 D.V133/R) Alpine landscape with riverside mill
                 (84x68cm-33x27in) s.d.869 (A.S 60000)
£5888 $11305   (29-Nov-90 D.V3/R) Flupmes, Stubaital, Tyrol (74x100cm-29x39in) mono.
                 i.verso (A.S 120000)
£2450   *$4851*   *(31-Jan-91 D.V170/R) View of Vienna with Burgtheater and Stefansdom*
                 (25x37cm-10x15in) s.i.d.1890 W/C (A.S 50000)

BARBARO, Giovanni (?) Italian?
£340   *$629*   *(5-Mar-91 SWS1626) Picking oranges (128x95cm-50x37in) s.i. W/C*

BARBASAN, Mariano (1864-1924) Spanish
£2726 $4715   (21-May-91 DUR.M49/R) Mosquetero (34x22cm-13x9in) panel (S.P 500000)
£9000 $14760   (19-Jun-91 S396/R) Peasant women in mountain landscape (20x36cm-8x14in)
                 s.d.1910
£31000 $50840   (19-Jun-91 S412/R) Game of boule (25x56cm-10x22in) s.d.1902
£929   *$1792*   *(11-Dec-90 FER.M136/R) Dama con sombrero y toquilla (35x19cm-14x7in)*
                 s.d.1881 W/C (S.P 170000)

BARBATELLI, Bernardino see POCCETTI, Bernardino

BARBEAU, Marcel (1925-) Canadian
£588	$1041	(20-Mar-91 EA.M497) Lac de la Courbe (51x61cm-20x24in) s.d.89 acrylic canvas (C.D 1200)
£1065	$1991	(29-Aug-90 EA.M631) Le soleil se leve (76x91cm-30x36in) s.d.80 (C.D 2300)
£2632	$5184	(30-Oct-90 SY.T101/R) Farouche Crespee (74x91cm-29x36in) s.i.d.72verso acrylic (C.D 6000)

BARBER, Alfred R (19th C) British
| £1900 | $3173 | (5-Jun-91 S88/R) Rabbits (46x35cm-18x14in) s. |
| £2844 | $4750 | (7-Jun-91 SY.NY117/R) Little rabbits (21x26cm-8x10in) s. |

BARBER, Charles Burton (1845-1894) British
| £18000 | $36000 | (8-Feb-91 C195/R) A girl's best friend (71x91cm-28x36in) s.d.1882 |
| £30769 | $60000 | (24-Oct-90 CH.NY332/R) Little girl and her Sheltie (92x72cm-36x28in) s.d.1892 |

BARBER, Frederick Hugh (1847-1919) South African?
| £703 | $1378 | (11-Feb-91 SY.J460/R) Drakensberg, South Africa (61x91cm-24x36in) s. (SA.R 3500) |
| £803 | $1574 | (11-Feb-91 SY.J4612/R) Farmhouse in an extensive landscape O.F.S. (53x91cm-21x36in) (SA.R 4000) |

BARBER, J S (19th C) British
| £804 | $1543 | (28-Nov-90 PH.T54/R) Landscape with figures on road (72x113cm-28x44in) s. (C.D 1800) |

BARBER, Reginald (fl.1882-1908) British
£650	$1300	(8-Feb-91 K577) Portrait of young lady in white dress with flaxon hair (76x48cm-30x19in) mono.
£620	$1011	(13-Jun-91 CSK160/R) Sweet as spring-time flowers (66x49cm-26x19in) mono.d.1886 s.i.verso pencil W/C htd white
£800	$1416	(5-Apr-91 BW395) Head and shoulder portrait study of pretty young lady (69x43cm-27x17in) mono.d. W/C

BARBER, Thomas (1768-1843) British
| £780 | $1451 | (5-Sep-90 MMB291) A long eared doe rabbit, with her young (33x43cm-13x17in) board |
| £8000 | $13200 | (12-Jul-91 C32/R) Group portrait of Elizabeth, Humphrey and Catherine Senhouse with pet greyhound (102x127cm-40x50in) |

BARBEY, Etienne (19th C) French
| £771 | $1495 | (7-Dec-90 CN.P44) Etude pour une maison a St Germain plan et elevation (44x56cm-17x22in) pen W/C (F.FR 7500) |

BARBIE, Simone (fl.1938-1939) French
| £962 | $1885 | (19-Nov-90 CSC.P5) Parc Montsouris (23x33cm-9x13in) s. canvas laid down on board (F.FR 9500) |

BARBIER, Andre (c.1880-c.1970) French
£1721	$3372	(25-Nov-90 ZZ.F7/R) Etretat (24x33cm-9x13in) bears studio st. paper laid down (F.FR 17000)
£2381	$4095	(15-May-91 CN.P62/R) Bord de Seine vers les Andelys (54x65cm-21x26in) s.d.09 (F.FR 24000)
£4694	$9247	(14-Nov-90 I.N83/R) Cannes, l'ancien casino (50x61cm-20x24in) studio st. verso (F.FR 46000)
£1217	$2410	(3-Feb-91 I.N15) Vue de Notre-Dame (35x50cm-14x20in) s. W/C (F.FR 12000)

BARBIER, G P (18th C) French
£2600	$4290	(12-Jul-91 C24/R) Portrait of Henry Rice, in coat and top hat, leaning on armchair (76x63cm-30x25in) s.d.1792 oval
£2800	$4620	(12-Jul-91 C25/R) Portrait of John Rice, seated, in coat and waistcoat (76x63cm-30x25in) oval
£4800	$7920	(12-Jul-91 C23/R) Portrait of Mrs. Henry Rice, seated in dress and bonnet (76x63cm-30x25in) s.d.1792

BARBIER, Georges (1882-1932) French
| £500 | $845 | (17-Apr-91 H357/R) Woman in classical dress with a black panther (20x15cm-8x6in) bodycol. |

BARBIER, Jean Jacques le (1738-1826) French
| £754 | $1236 | (21-Jun-91 CK.P26/R) Thrusis et le chevrier (18x13cm-7x5in) graphite ink wash (F.FR 7500) |

BARBIER, Jean Jacques le (attrib) (1738-1826) French
| £402 | $659 | (18-Jun-91 APT.P91) Un mexicain dans son habit de guerre (33x22cm-13x9in) i. pen W/C (F.FR 4000) |
| £412 | $676 | (21-Jun-91 CK.P27) Les jardins d'une villa a Rome (28x21cm-11x8in) s.d.1768 pen wash pasted on board (F.FR 4100) |

BARBIERI, Contardo (1900-1960) Italian
| £2341 | $4566 | (22-Oct-90 BR.M217/R) Alpi Apuane (90x70cm-35x28in) s. (I.L 5200000) |
| £7204 | $14048 | (22-Oct-90 BR.M275/R) La modella (75x86cm-30x34in) s. s.d.1946verso (I.L 16000000) |

BARBIERI, Giovanni Francesco see GUERCINO, Giovanni Francesco

BARBIERI, Pietro (18th C) Italian
£836 $1613   (14-Dec-90 LEB.P125) Portrait d'homme (35x25cm-14x10in) sanguinne
                     (F.FR 8200)

BARBIERS, Pieter (18/19th C) Dutch
£3673 $7236   (14-Nov-90 D.V214/R) Wooded landscape with farmhouses and bathers in
                     pond (55x82cm-22x32in) panel (A.S 75000)
£880 $1575   (13-Mar-91 B27/R) An artist sketching by a stream with a woman nearby
                     (34x43cm-13x17in) ink W/C

BARBIZON SCHOOL (?) French
£2041 $3959   (8-Dec-90 GAB.G2091/R) Paysage champetre (74x51cm-29x20in) (S.FR 5000)
£2946 $4978   (16-Apr-91 CH.R97) Pastore col gregge (46x72cm-18x28in) (I.L 6500000)

BARBIZON SCHOOL, 19th C French
£992 $1716   (22-May-91 GS.B2320) Wooded landscape with woman carrying heavy load
                     after thunderstorm (54x65cm-21x26in) (S.FR 2500)

BARBLAN, Oscar (1909-1987) Swiss
£776 $1520   (6-Nov-90 GF.L2531/R) Bagnanti (81x60cm-32x24in) s.d.68 s.i.d.verso
                     (S.FR 1900)

BARBOT, E (19th C) French
£1800 $3456   (28-Nov-90 S264/R) View of Palmyra (34x72cm-13x28in) s. W/C

BARBUDO, Salvador Sanchez (1858-1919) Spanish
£1898 $3700   (17-Oct-90 FER.M167/R) Paisaje (8x13cm-3x5in) s. panel (S.P 350000)
£4211 $8000   (27-Feb-91 SY.NY338/R) Christening (25x40cm-10x16in) s.d.1907 panel
£7514 $13000   (22-May-91 SY.NY281/R) Caballero Espanol (39x23cm-15x9in) s.d.1899 panel
£7692 $15000   (24-Oct-90 CH.NY243/R) Engaging conversation (36x25cm-14x10in) s.i.
                     panel
£8092 $14000   (8-May-91 RO.BA1) Contrabandista (65x50cm-26x20in) s.

BARBUT-DAVRAY, Luc (1863-?) French
£925 $1600   (21-May-91 CE.NY333/R) Entering room (58x39cm-23x15in) s.

BARCELO, Miguel (1957-) Spanish
£136575 $263589   (13-Dec-90 EP.M26/R) Cuisine avec assiettes (200x300cm-79x118in)
                     s.d.XII-85verso oil acrylic (S.P 25000000)
£1611 $2626   (16-Jun-91 CC.P67/R) Sans titre (30x42cm-12x17in) s.d.17-11-1988 W/C
                     (F.FR 16000)
£3005 $5799   (13-Dec-90 EP.M30/R) Untitled (50x35cm-20x14in) s. ink W/C (S.P 550000)
£14829 $28767   (5-Dec-90 AB.S7020/R) Pesce in due parti (55x75cm-22x30in) s.
                     i.d.83verso acrylic collage (S.KR 160000)

BARCHUS, Eliza R (fl.1857-1859) American
£549 $950   (10-May-91 S.BM30/R) Mt Hood, Oregon (25x30cm-10x12in) s. i.verso board

BARCLAY, J (?) British
£800 $1344   (16-Jul-91 PHC783/R) John Ball of Hoylake at the end of a full drive
                     (55x40cm-22x16in) pencil drawing

BARCLAY, McClelland (1891-?) American
£781 $1500   (17-Dec-90 SY.NY250/R) Playing fetch (76x66cm-30x26in) s.
£1117 $2200   (16-Nov-90 DM.D2005/R) Portrait of Art Deco Period woman
                     (56x41cm-22x16in) s. i.verso

BARCLAY, William (jnr) (1797-1859) British
£450 $743   (10-Jul-91 C62/R) Lady in a red chair in white dress (11x?cm-4x?in)
                     min.velvet mount gilt-wood frame rec.

BARD, James (1815-1897) American
£35503 $60000   (17-Apr-91 D.NY47/R) Side wheeler Chrystenah on Hudson (58x99cm-23x39in)
                     s.i.d.1870 W/C cardboard

BARDASANO BAOS, Jose (1910-1979) Spanish
£1362 $2342   (16-May-91 ANS.M105/R) Catedral de Oviedo (22x16cm-9x6in) s.
                     s.d.1968verso tablex (S.P 250000)
£2015 $3466   (16-May-91 ANS.M106/R) Mercado al aire libre (27x22cm-11x9in) s.
                     s.d.1968verso tablex (S.P 370000)
£3141 $6063   (11-Dec-90 FER.M226/R) Interior en una casa holandesa del sig.XVII
                     (34x26cm-13x10in) s. panel (S.P 575000)
£5221 $10025   (19-Feb-91 DUR.M1) Praga (59x49cm-23x19in) (S.P 950000)
£7694 $14773   (19-Feb-91 DUR.M2) Notre Dame (80x70cm-31x28in) (S.P 1400000)
£9343 $17939   (19-Feb-91 DUR.M31) Goyesca (116x89cm-46x35in) (S.P 1700000)

BARDELLINI, Pietro (1728-1806) Italian
£1954 $3498   (14-Mar-91 D.V29/R) Death of noble hero (136x100cm-54x39in) (A.S 40000)

BARDI, Alberto (1918-1984) Italian
£900 $1756   (22-Oct-90 BR.M193/R) Composizione (70x100cm-28x39in) s.d.1969 tempera
                     (I.L 2000000)
£410 $697   (28-May-91 SY.MI50/R) Senza titolo (68x68cm-27x27in) s.d.75verso pastel
                     tempera canvas (I.L 900000)

BARDI, Alberto (1918-1984) Italian-cont.
£818 $1611   (30-Oct-90 F.R67) Verde 89/R (50x60cm-20x24in) s.d.76verso wax crayon
                    tempera canvas (I.L 1800000)
£916 $1759   (27-Nov-90 SY.MI2) Sul rosso (82x93cm-32x37in) s.d.1974 pastel tempera
                    canvas (I.L 2000000)

BARDILL, Ralph William (1876-1935) British
£500 $925   (6-Mar-91 SC4224) The mill pool Houghton (38x58cm-15x23in) s.d.1905
                    i.verso W/C pencil
£550 $1084   (15-Nov-90 SC4007) Aber Glaslyn (58x48cm-23x19in) s. W/C
£580 $1143   (15-Nov-90 SC4005) Cemaes village, Anglesey (28x48cm-11x19in) s. i.verso
                    W/C
£900 $1503   (5-Jun-91 S287/R) Mill pool, Houghton (38x59cm-15x23in) s.d.1905 W/C
£1250 $2463   (15-Nov-90 SC4004/R) Pentre Felin village, Glan Conway, North Wales
                    (41x64cm-16x25in) s. i.verso W/C

BARDIN, Jean (1732-1809) French
£1892 $3274   (22-May-91 PLF.P3/R) Scene d'offrande (31x23cm-12x9in) s.d.1778 pen
                    brush wash sketch blk.crayon (F.FR 19000)

BARDONE, Guy (1927-) French
£1793 $3048   (29-May-91 GL.P146/R) Nature morte a la lanterne magique
                    (80x80cm-31x31in) s.i.d.1960-61 (F.FR 18000)
£1815 $3538   (26-Oct-90 APT.P84) Avant l'orage, Ibiza (54x81cm-21x32in) s. d.59 verso
                    (F.FR 18000)
£2022 $3943   (17-Oct-90 ARC.P60) Le pigeonnier a Ibiza (55x33cm-22x13in) s. d. verso
                    (F.FR 20000)
£2637 $5063   (17-Dec-90 AGS.P15/R) Sous-bois a flims (56x46cm-22x18in) s.
                    (F.FR 26000)
£3033 $5915   (17-Oct-90 ARC.P59/R) Noel mexicain Taxco (92x60cm-36x24in) s. d.1966
                    verso (F.FR 30000)
£3265 $6433   (16-Nov-90 FB.P108/R) Arbres au printemps (55x38cm-22x15in) s. i.d.1958
                    verso (F.FR 32000)
£3659 $6000   (19-Jun-91 B.SF1949/R) Nature morte au panier (81x100cm-32x39in) s.

BARDWELL, Thomas (1704-1767) British
£1200 $2280   (1-Mar-91 C8/R) Portrait of Reverend Francis Barton in clerical dress
                    (76x63cm-30x25in) s.d.1765 painted with studio
£1800 $2970   (10-Jul-91 S126/R) Portrait of lady wearing velvet dress with fur and
                    pearls holding rose (99x82cm-39x32in)
£16000 $31520   (14-Nov-90 S33/R) Portrait of Anne Countess of Strafford wearing
                    peeress's robes (234x141cm-92x56in)

BARDWELL, Thomas (circle) (1704-1767) British
£1682 $3313   (13-Nov-90 CH.AM29/R) Portrait of girl, wearing dress and ermine lined
                    velvet cape, flowers in hair (43x33cm-17x13in) i.verso (D.FL 5500)

BARENGER, James (attrib) (1745-1813) British
£2400 $4728   (31-Oct-90 S397/R) Pointer in landscape (71x91cm-28x36in) bears
                    sig.d.1797

BARENGER, James II (1780-1831) British
£4000 $7880   (13-Nov-90 PH126/R) Portrait of Irish wolfhound with catch
                    (71x91cm-28x36in) s.d.1819

BARENTSZ, Dirck (circle) (1534-1592) Dutch
£5882 $11294   (17-Dec-90 ARC.P14/R) Le jugement dernier (47x32cm-19x13in) en grisaille
                    (F.FR 58000)

BAREUTHER, Liesl (1899-1970) ?
£1074 $1986   (7-Mar-91 D.V192/R) Geraniums in courtyard of Vienna suburb
                    (30x20cm-12x8in) s. board (A.S 22000)

BARFUSS, Ina (1949-) German
£743 $1264   (1-Jun-91 VG.B415/R) Zwei strahlende Mumien (75x106cm-30x42in)
                    s.d.82verso gouache board (DM 2200)
£853 $1672   (24-Nov-90 VG.B410/R) Schopfungsakt (65x48cm-26x19in) s.d.1986 gouache
                    W/C (DM 2500)

BARFUSS, Ina and WACHWEGER, Thomas (20th C) German
£1205 $2024   (24-Apr-91 G.Z60/R) Couple (54x74cm-21x29in) s.d.1987 mixed media
                    (S.FR 3000)

BARGHEER, Eduard (1901-1979) German
£4623 $7536   (15-Jun-91 L.K20/R) Fellachen-Dorf (24x33cm-9x13in) s.d.62 i.verso board
                    (DM 13500)
£5085 $8492   (6-Jun-91 HN.H111/R) The Elbe in high summer (74x95cm-29x37in) s.
                    (DM 15000)
£651 $1061   (15-Jun-91 L.K26) Camels (22x31cm-9x12in) s.d.69 W/C (DM 1900)
£676 $1318   (20-Oct-90 WK.M25/R) Dunes in rain (32x43cm-13x17in) s.d.1967 W/C
                    (DM 2000)
£680 $1095   (28-Jun-91 BM.B875/R) Southern town (21x27cm-8x11in) s.d.1946 indian ink
                    (DM 2000)
£878 $1493   (1-Jun-91 VG.B416/R) Dessert (39x53cm-15x21in) s.d.1973 i.verso W/C
                    (DM 2600)

BARGHEER, Eduard (1901-1979) German-cont.

£878	$1493	(28-May-91 KF.M445/R) Barocke Dunen 2 (21x31cm-8x12in) s.d.1966 W/C (DM 2600)
£887	$1739	(24-Nov-90 N.M33/R) Young donkey by wall (21x27cm-8x11in) s.d.1961 W/C over pencil (DM 2600)
£959	$1563	(15-Jun-91 L.K25) Houses in southern landscape (22x31cm-9x12in) s.d.60 W/C (DM 2800)
£959	$1563	(15-Jun-91 L.K27) Abstract composition (33x43cm-13x17in) s.d.61 W/C (DM 2800)
£1017	$1698	(6-Jun-91 HN.H113) Four stables in the desert (31x49cm-12x19in) s.d.1960 W/C (DM 3000)
£1020	$1806	(23-Mar-91 WK.M23/R) Beduin huts 4 (32x42cm-13x17in) s.d.1969 i.verso W/C (DM 3000)
£1233	$2010	(15-Jun-91 L.K29) Houses and gardens (22x32cm-9x13in) s.d.64 W/C (DM 3600)
£1301	$2121	(15-Jun-91 L.K23/R) Southern town. Arabic village (22x32cm-9x13in) s.d.60 W/C double-sided (DM 3800)
£1307	$2262	(21-May-91 WK.M570/R) Women in Ischia (32x43cm-13x17in) s.d.1960 W/C (DM 3870)
£1438	$2345	(15-Jun-91 L.K24/R) Rooftops of southern town (26x39cm-10x15in) s.d.60 W/C (DM 4200)
£1438	$2345	(15-Jun-91 L.K30/R) Southern town (32x44cm-13x17in) s.d.65 s.i.d.verso W/C (DM 4200)
£1622	$2805	(21-May-91 WK.M571/R) Procession (32x45cm-13x18in) s.d.1960 i.d.verso W/C over pencil (DM 4800)
£1644	$2679	(15-Jun-91 L.K28/R) Southern town by the sea (21x31cm-8x12in) s.d.62 W/C (DM 4800)
£1655	$3178	(1-Dec-90 SA.A2466/R) Portrait of southern boy (50x30cm-20x12in) s.d.52 gouache (DM 4800)
£1757	$3426	(20-Oct-90 WK.M26/R) Southern town (53x69cm-21x27in) s.d.1972 W/C over pencil (DM 4800)
£1877	$3679	(24-Nov-90 VG.B411/R) Workmen on beach. Sketch (32x43cm-13x17in) s.d. i.verso W/C double-sided (DM 5500)
£1966	$3774	(28-Nov-90 KF.M537/R) Landscape, evening (32x43cm-13x17in) s.d.1964 W/C (DM 5700)
£2027	$3507	(25-May-91 N.M18/R) Southern town (24x30cm-9x12in) s.d.1967 W/C (DM 6000)
£2123	$3461	(15-Jun-91 L.K21/R) Houses and gardens by the sea (31x43cm-12x17in) s.d.50 W/C over pencil (DM 6200)
£2189	$3677	(26-Apr-91 KM.K206/R) Adoration of the Magi (43x55cm-17x22in) s.indis.d. W/C pencil (DM 6500)
£2304	$3986	(21-May-91 WK.M569/R) Sea spa in winter, child with mask (45x59cm-18x23in) s.d.1936 i.verso W/C htd.white over pencil (DM 6820)
£2321	$4549	(22-Nov-90 L.K809/R) Beach scene (21x27cm-8x11in) s.d.47 W/C over pencil (DM 6800)
£2389	$4683	(24-Nov-90 N.M32/R) Sullberg near Blankenese (27x22cm-11x9in) s.d.1955 W/C (DM 7000)
£2603	$4242	(15-Jun-91 L.K22/R) Ischia (43x61cm-17x24in) s.d.52 pencil W/C (DM 7600)
£3793	$7283	(28-Nov-90 KF.M536/R) San Vito (47x60cm-19x24in) s.d.1942 W/C (DM 11000)

BARGUE, Charles (1826-1883) French

£30769	$60000	(24-Oct-90 CH.NY93/R) La sentinelle (28x21cm-11x8in) s.d.76 panel
£20513	$40000	(23-Oct-90 SY.NY39/R) Eastern coffeehouse (30x22cm-12x9in) s.d.77 W/C

BARILLOT, Leon (1844-1929) French

£765	$1500	(21-Nov-90 NA.BA32) Vaches au paturage (38x55cm-15x22in) s.
£1582	$2800	(22-Mar-91 S.W2859/R) Cows in pasture at dawn (38x56cm-15x22in) s.

BARISON, Giuseppe (1853-1930) Italian

£1017	$1962	(11-Dec-90 CH.R193) Giovane popolana con ventaglio (39x24cm-15x9in) s. panel (I.L 2200000)

BARITEAU, Alcide (?) ?

£1318	$2531	(17-Dec-90 ARC.P72/R) A la fontaine (81x60cm-32x24in) s. (F.FR 13000)

BARKER OF BATH, Benjamin (1776-1838) British

£750	$1478	(1-Nov-90 CSK69/R) Mountainous coastal inlet with drover and cattle on track (47x60cm-19x24in) s.indist.d.18 canvas on board
£1700	$3349	(13-Nov-90 SWS221/R) A wooded river landscape with figures (58x73cm-23x29in) s.
£1800	$2970	(10-Jul-91 S138/R) Landscape with figures by pool and cattle watering (29x39cm-11x15in) i.indis.d. panel
£2011	$3500	(27-Mar-91 B.SF4067/R) Wooded landscape near Bath with peasants and cart on road (36x45cm-14x18in)

BARKER OF BATH, John-Joseph (19th C) British

£700	$1169	(23-Jul-91 LW1864/R) Two boys seated eating apples beside a moorland pool (46x61cm-18x24in) s.

BARKER OF BATH, Thomas (1769-1847) British

£1000	$1960	(8-Nov-90 TL36/R) Wooded river landscape (91x136cm-36x54in)
£1300	$2535	(26-Oct-90 C298/R) A wooded landscape with children, donkeys and a cart outside a cottage (63x78cm-25x31in)

BARKER OF BATH, Thomas (1769-1847) British-cont.
£1500 $2475   (10-Jul-91 S161/R) Wooded landscape with country waggon, milkmaid and
                       drover (127x101cm-50x40in) after Thomas Gainsborough
£1600 $3152   (31-Oct-90 S356/R) Evening river landscape with cattle watering
                       (37x52cm-15x20in) paper on canvas

BARKER, J (19th C) British
£520 $931   (12-Mar-91 RG2695) Snow covered landscape with a figure driving sheep
                       (46x61cm-18x24in) s.
£650 $1086   (4-Jun-91 SWS1807) Sheep resting (62x75cm-24x30in) s.
£700 $1141   (11-Jun-91 HAR464/R) Injured traveller and dog (69x89cm-27x35in)
                       s.d.1877
£700 $1344   (26-Nov-90 HS131/R) The fortune teller, interior scene with figures and
                       dog (62x51cm-24x20in)

BARKER, John (19th C) British
£1800 $3384   (20-Sep-90 CSK147/R) Bird and boat, Chichester harbour (40x58cm-16x23in)
                       s.d.52 s.l.verso
£11282 $22000   (24-Oct-90 CH.NY303/R) Guarding his flock (127x102cm-50x40in) s.

BARKER, John Edward (1889-1953) British
£800 $1552   (6-Dec-90 CSK209/R) Fish shop (61x91cm-24x36in) s.d.49

BARKER, T (?) British
£710 $1200   (21-Apr-91 DU.E168) Morning view (56x69cm-22x27in) s.

BARKER, Thomas Jones (1815-1882) British
£1250 $2400   (28-Nov-90 PH.T58/R) Fast asleep (40x29cm-16x11in) s. l.verso panel
                       (C.D 2800)

BARKER, Wright (19th C) British
£638 $1200   (22-Sep-90 WOL.C196/R) Highland sheep (84x112cm-33x44in) s.
£804 $1319   (19-Jun-91 ZZ.F66) Cheval au pre (61x76cm-24x30in) s. (F.FR 8000)
£5500 $10835   (1-Nov-90 C257 a/R) Mare and foal at ford (71x91cm-28x36in) s.l.verso

BARLACH, Ernst (1870-?) German
£3413 $6689   (24-Nov-90 VG.B133/R) Reclining figure (24x32cm-9x13in) s.d.1909 pen
                       over pencil (DM 10000)
£7770 $13209   (1-Jun-91 VG.B178/R) Old man seated with hands resting on his knees
                       (34x26cm-13x10in) s. chl board (DM 23000)
£8191 $16055   (24-Nov-90 VG.B134/R) Female faggott gatherer (26x34cm-10x13in) s. chl
                       (DM 24000)
£16949 $28305   (7-Jun-91 HN.H2/R) The thirsty one (57x30cm-22x12in) s.d.27 chl
                       (DM 50000)
£30405 $51689   (30-May-91 SY.BE14/R) Russian peasants (44x63cm-17x25in) s. pencil
                       (DM 90000)

BARLAG, Philip (1840-1913) Norwegian
£530 $1060   (9-Feb-91 BU.O15) Landscape from Boverdalen (29x22cm-11x9in) s. panel
                       (N.KR 6000)
£608 $1015   (3-Jun-91 B.O2/R) Landscape with lake (27x20cm-11x8in) s. (N.KR 7000)
£694 $1160   (3-Jun-91 B.O4/R) Landscape (20x30cm-8x12in) s.d.67 (N.KR 8000)
£694 $1160   (3-Jun-91 B.O3/R) Fjord landscape (24x36cm-9x14in) s. (N.KR 8000)
£868 $1450   (4-Jun-91 BU.O65/R) Mountain landscapej with outfarm (34x50cm-13x20in)
                       s. (N.KR 10000)
£1167 $2299   (14-Nov-90 RAS.K193) Fjord landscape. Traveller in mountains
                       (32x25cm-13x10in) s. pair (D.KR 13000)

BARLAND, Adam (19th C) British
£750 $1440   (20-Feb-91 CSK232) River landscape with cattle watering and anglers in
                       punt (50x79cm-20x31in) init.d.67
£1200 $2352   (22-Nov-90 CSK176/R) Drover watering cattle in extensive landscape
                       (46x81cm-18x32in) s.d.1883

BARLOW, Francis (1626-1704) British
£19000 $31350   (12-Jul-91 C62/R) Assembly of birds, in landscape (167x89cm-66x35in)
£35000 $68950   (16-Nov-90 C71/R) Pair of geese with young frightened by springer
                       spaniel in landscape (91x120cm-36x47in)
£4000 $6600   (11-Jul-91 S26/R) Lion attacked by hounds (15x21cm-6x8in) s.d.1694 pen
                       ink wash

BARLOW, Francis (style) (1626-1704) British
£1150 $2001   (26-Mar-91 PH136/R) Two dogs in a landscape (47x79cm-19x31in)

BARLOW, Myron (1873-1937) American
£503 $900   (15-Mar-91 DM.D2126/R) Portrait of man (81x66cm-32x26in) s.
£723 $1250   (21-May-91 BG.M867/R) Portrait of lady with shawl (61x51cm-24x20in) s.
£1982 $3250   (21-Jun-91 DM.D2051/R) Julie in Barlow's garden in Etaples, France
                       (74x74cm-29x29in) s.
£3553 $7000   (16-Nov-90 DM.D2000/R) Young girl standing near table (89x89cm-35x35in)
                       s.
£4734 $8000   (1-May-91 B.SF5069/R) Two women reading (77x77cm-30x30in) s.
£5641 $11000   (19-Oct-90 DM.D2004/R) Woman in landscape (102x102cm-40x40in) s.

BARLYKIO, Mieczyslaw (1923-) Polish
£508 $864   (29-May-91 RCJ.P148/R) Autoportrait (92x65cm-36x26in) s.d.1983
                     (F.FR 5100)

BARNABE, Duilio (1914-1961) Italian
£1844 $3043   (10-Jul-91 FB.P26/R) Le Cardinal (65x46cm-26x18in) s. (F.FR 18500)
£2518 $4104   (11-Jun-91 I.N155/R) Nature morte (24x33cm-9x13in) s. (F.FR 25000)
£3468 $6000   (7-May-91 CE.NY112/R) Natura morta con Anguria (73x105cm-29x41in)
                     s.d.1959
£3571 $7036   (16-Nov-90 FB.P109) Vase de fleurs (65x54cm-26x21in) s. (F.FR 35000)
£3757 $6500   (7-May-91 CE.NY96/R) Paesaggio (65x92cm-26x36in) s.
£5584 $11000   (13-Nov-90 CE.NY179/R) Femme assise avec fleurs (125x100cm-49x39in) s.
£6139 $10865   (7-Apr-91 I.N34/R) Fleur cubiste (55x39cm-22x15in) s. (F.FR 62000)
£8376 $16500   (13-Nov-90 CE.NY180/R) Femme assise (131x99cm-52x39in) s.

BARNARD, Mary B (1870-1946) British
£850 $1590   (28-Aug-90 S1065) Washerwomen (48x64cm-19x25in) s. canvas on board

BARNAY, Marcel (20th C) French
£3055 $6018   (30-Oct-90 ZZ.F71/R) Hommage a Van Gogh (81x60cm-32x24in) s.d.90
                     (F.FR 30000)

BARNES, Archibald George (1887-?) British
£3333 $6500   (23-Oct-90 SY.NY391/R) Secret thoughts (77x72cm-30x28in) s.
£780 $1521   (15-Jan-91 SWS79/R) Nude study with peacocks (50x50cm-20x20in) W/C

BARNES, E R (19th C) British
£700 $1141   (13-Jun-91 CSK201/R) Returning from day's falconing (63x91cm-25x36in)
                     s.d.1858 after Sir Edwin Landseer

BARNES, Edward Charles (19th C) British
£800 $1536   (29-Nov-90 B120/R) A bride (40x30cm-16x12in) mono.
£850 $1658   (16-Jan-91 CSK246) The love letter (76x56cm-30x22in) mono. panel
£1400 $2730   (15-Jan-91 C89) Well deserved treat (49x60cm-19x24in) s.
£3000 $5910   (1-Nov-90 C328/R) The new breeches (71x92cm-28x36in) s.
£6800 $12852   (26-Sep-90 S138/R) Artist's studio (76x107cm-30x42in) mono.d.1855

BARNES, G J (19th C) British
£550 $974   (21-Mar-91 CSK236) Watching over the baby (51x76cm-20x30in) s.

BARNES, James (19/20th C) British
£3600 $7056   (13-Feb-91 S144/R) Sisters (76x55cm-30x22in) s.indist.d. indist.i.verso
*£500 $835   (5-Jun-91 S241) Solitary nook in woods (67x50cm-26x20in) s.i.verso W/C
                     htd bodycol*
£800 $1568   (21-Nov-90 B113) Solitary nook in woods (68x51cm-27x20in) s.i. W/C

BARNES, Robert (1840-1895) British
£6000 $10020   (5-Jun-91 S318/R) Winter sport (32x57cm-13x22in) s.d.1889 W/C

BARNES, S J (19th C) British
£700 $1379   (2-Nov-90 BW396) Stormy mountainous river scene with cattle grazing
                     (117x89cm-46x35in) s.

BARNI, Roberto (1939-) Italian
£1139 $1936   (28-May-91 SY.MI23/R) Cantar Maggio (45x71cm-18x28in) s.verso
                     (I.L 2500000)
£2521 $4135   (20-Jun-91 F.M395/R) Veduta (100x69cm-39x27in) s.i.d.1980verso
                     (I.L 5500000)
£2842 $4662   (20-Jun-91 F.M360/R) Natura morta (100x85cm-39x33in) s. s.i.d.1981verso
                     (I.L 6200000)
£6303 $12292   (22-Oct-90 BR.M135/R) Paternita (110x130cm-43x51in) s.d.1982
                     (I.L 14000000)

BARNOIN, H A (1882-1935) French
£4582 $9027   (30-Oct-90 I.N36/R) Le marche de Quimperle (38x46cm-15x18in) s.
                     (F.FR 45000)

BARNOIN, Henri Alphonse (1882-1935) French
£1226 $1999   (1-Jul-91 AAA.S112) Pecheuse, Concarneau (36x44cm-14x17in) s.
                     (A.D 2600)
£2282 $3925   (15-May-91 CN.P65) Bretagne, la place de l'eglise (33x41cm-13x16in) s.
                     board (F.FR 23000)
£2345 $4525   (16-Dec-90 T.B86) Sur le chemin de halage (38x46cm-15x18in) s.
                     (F.FR 23000)
£2994 $5030   (23-Apr-91 SY.AM4/R) Sailing vessels in French harbour (45x55cm-18x22in)
                     s. (D.FL 10000)
£6626 $12788   (16-Dec-90 T.B85/R) La place du marche a Hennebont (60x73cm-24x29in) s.
                     (F.FR 65000)
£7164 $12394   (12-May-91 T.B70/R) La Place du Marche a Pont Aven (60x73cm-24x29in) s.
                     (F.FR 72000)
*£1631 $3148   (16-Dec-90 T.B23/R) Marche en Bretagne (37x45cm-15x18in) s. W/C
                     (F.FR 16000)*

BARNS-GRAHAM, Wilhelmina (1912-) British
£1200 $1956   (1-Jul-91 S11/R) Tumble (57x90cm-22x35in) s.d.1964 paper
£5500 $8965   (1-Jul-91 S7/R) Snow on Porthmeor (38x46cm-15x18in) s.d.1947 board

BARNS-GRAHAM, Wilhelmina (1912-) British-cont.
£950 $1587   (7-Jun-91 C304/R) Canyon (38x56cm-15x22in) s.d.1955 pencil W/C
£1000 $1880   (20-Sep-90 C132/R) Underwater III (38x49cm-15x19in) s.d.1958 s.i.d.1958
                verso gouache
£1000 $1880   (20-Sep-90 C122/R) Variation on theme, Spanish island (49x38cm-19x15in)
                s.d.1961 s.i.d.1961 verso gouache

BARNUTZ, Friedrich (1791-1867) ?
£769 $1492   (5-Dec-90 DO.H2132) Three Jews conversing (42x35cm-17x14in) s.d.1841
                board (DM 2200)

BAROCCI, Federico (after) (1526-1612) Italian
£1695 $3000   (22-Mar-91 CH.NY637) The infant Christ blessing (24x16cm-9x6in) i.
                blk.red chk.pastel htd.white

BAROCCI, Federico (attrib) (1526-1612) Italian
£1500 $2445   (2-Jul-91 C93/R) Head of old woman, eyes closed (32x22cm-13x9in) red
                black white chk

BAROCCI, Federico (circle) (1526-1612) Italian
£1000 $1630   (2-Jul-91 C247/R) Study of hands praying (18x16cm-7x6in) with i. black
                chk htd white squared

BAROJA, Ricardo (1871-1953) Spanish
£18873 $36991   (20-Nov-90 DUR.M2) Cancion de Sirga (71x102cm-28x40in) board
                (S.P 3500000)

BARON, Henri (1816-1885) French
£1700 $3264   (20-Dec-90 CSK7/R) The garden party (50x88cm-20x35in) s.

BARON, Stephanie (1830-C.1921) French
£2551 $5000   (21-Nov-90 NA.BA19/R) Diane soumise (150x100cm-59x39in) s.

BAROUKH, Ezekiel (1909-1984) Egyptian
£513 $917   (11-Mar-91 CR.P82) Gestuelle couleur no.10 (100x81cm-39x32in) st. verso
                (F.FR 5100)
£553 $989   (11-Mar-91 CR.P88) Gestuelle couleur no 16 (146x114cm-57x45in) s.
                (F.FR 5500)
£593 $1061   (11-Mar-91 CR.P22/R) Graphique no.8 (130x97cm-51x38in) s. (F.FR 5900)
£603 $1079   (11-Mar-91 CR.P124/R) Table bouteille, fond noir et gris
                (92x73cm-36x29in) s. (F.FR 6000)

BARR, William (1867-?) American
£1000 $2000   (5-Feb-91 S186/R) Smithie (32x41cm-13x16in) s.
£3200 $5408   (2-May-91 CG498/R) Recherche (63x76cm-25x30in) s.

BARRABAND, Jacques (1767-1809) French
£25126 $44975   (17-Mar-91 M.V141/R) Composition florale et nid, sur un entablement
                (45x36cm-18x14in) s.i.d.1797 (F.FR 250000)

BARRABLE, George H (19th C) British
£1200 $1956   (11-Jun-91 PH87/R) T.W. Garrett saving ball (62x46cm-24x18in) init.

BARRADA, H (19th C) ?
£500 $980   (14-Feb-91 CSK164) Arab guards in a mosque (64x41cm-25x16in) s.

BARRADAS, Rafael (1890-1919) South American
£2538 $5000   (1-Oct-90 GC.M3) Naturaleza Mta (40x45cm-16x18in) board

BARRATT OF STOCKBRIDGE, Thomas (fl.1852-1893) British
£5200 $8944   (14-May-91 SWS268/R) Farmyard in Hampshire (80x119cm-31x47in) s.
                i.stretcher

BARRAU, Laureano (1864-1957) Spanish
£3947 $7500   (11-Sep-90 PO.BA20) Campesino comiendo manzanas (88x70cm-35x28in) s.
£5263 $10000   (27-Feb-91 SY.NY369/R) Woman with parasol (90x66cm-35x26in)

BARRAUD, Aime (1902-1954) Swiss
£939 $1849   (16-Nov-90 GK.Z5319) Silberdisteln (27x22cm-11x9in) s.i. cotton
                (S.FR 2300)

BARRAUD, Aurele (1903-1969) Swiss
£757 $1476   (24-Oct-90 GD.B113/R) Artist with model in studio (27x22cm-11x9in)
                s.d.43 board (S.FR 1900)
£797 $1554   (24-Oct-90 GD.B110) Still life with willow catkin (92x73cm-36x29in)
                s.d.42 (S.FR 2000)

BARRAUD, Charles (1883-1968) Swiss
£653 $1267   (8-Dec-90 GAB.G2364/R) Sous-bois (35x33cm-14x13in) s. (S.FR 1600)

BARRAUD, Francis (1856-1924) British
£1800 $3024   (23-Apr-91 SWS323) The bachelor (40x57cm-16x22in) s.

BARRAUD, Francois (1899-?) Swiss
£1044 $2047   (21-Nov-90 SY.Z92/R) Still life with pansies (22x22cm-9x9in) s. board
                (S.FR 2600)

BARRAUD, Francois (1899-?) Swiss-cont.
£3373 $5835 (22-May-91 GS.B2030/R) Still life of delphinum in vase and book of poems with table bell (34x31cm-13x12in) s.d.1926 (S.FR 8500)
£913 $1579 (22-May-91 GS.B2031) View of farmhouse with barn and stable beyond (32x37cm-13x15in) s.d.1930 pen (S.FR 2300)

BARRAUD, Gustave Francois (1883-1964) Swiss
£996 $1942 (24-Oct-90 GD.B357/R) La baigneuse (54x65cm-21x26in) s. (S.FR 2500)
£478 $822 (14-May-91 GF.L2697/R) Treelined street (21x23cm-8x9in) s. pastel (S.FR 1200)

BARRAUD, Henry (1811-1874) British
£600 $1110 (7-Mar-91 CSK151/R) Ariadne (51x41cm-20x16in) s. oval
£2000 $3940 (1-Nov-90 CSK12/R) Highland cattle in landscape (66x102cm-26x40in) s.
£3608 $7000 (8-Dec-90 W.W35/R) Mr.Thomas Parr's bay colt, 'Fisherman' by 'Heron' out of 'Main Brace' (71x91cm-28x36in) s.i.d.1860

BARRAUD, Maurice (1889-1954) Swiss
£3968 $6865 (22-May-91 GS.B2034/R) Japanese woman sleeping on blanket (33x41cm-13x16in) st.studio i.verso pavatex (S.FR 10000)
£6375 $10964 (14-May-91 GF.L2240/R) Jeune fille (57x46cm-22x18in) s. (S.FR 16000)
£12851 $25189 (21-Nov-90 SY.Z103/R) L'arlequin au domino (81x65cm-32x26in) s. st.studio verso (S.FR 32000)
£14056 $27550 (21-Nov-90 SY.Z59/R) Petite figure au jardin (33x43cm-13x17in) s. i.verso (S.FR 35000)
£15020 $25534 (30-May-91 EA.Z180) Petite Fille en Claire (69x55cm-27x22in) s. (S.FR 38000)
£16064 $31486 (21-Nov-90 SY.Z96/R) L'arlequin (81x65cm-32x26in) s. st.studio verso canvas on pavatex (S.FR 40000)
£21825 $35794 (21-Jun-91 G.Z90/R) Nu (65x81cm-26x32in) s.d.1945 (S.FR 55000)
£560 $946 (1-May-91 GD.B1319/R) In the citadel (18x24cm-7x9in) s. pencil (S.FR 1400)
£653 $1267 (8-Dec-90 GAB.G2368/R) Jeune fille au chapeau (45x30cm-18x12in) s. pen wash (S.FR 1600)
£913 $1524 (7-Jun-91 ZOF.Z1274/R) Acrobats (16x13cm-6x5in) s. indian ink pen wash (S.FR 2300)
£3213 $6297 (21-Nov-90 SY.Z64/R) Femme sous un parasol (24x42cm-9x17in) s. pencil W/C (S.FR 8000)

BARRAUD, William (1810-1850) British
£5500 $9845 (10-Apr-91 S36/R) Saddled bay hunter in stable (69x89cm-27x35in) s.d.1847
£17365 $29000 (7-Jun-91 SY.NY32/R) A grey and a chestnut outside a barn (63x76cm-25x30in) s.
£35928 $60000 (7-Jun-91 SY.NY33/R) A chestnut hunter with the Badminton hounds (94x122cm-37x48in) s.

BARRAUD, William (circle) (1810-1850) British
£850 $1598 (17-Sep-90 CG258/R) Two Shetland ponies in a barn (51x76cm-20x30in)

BARRAUD-PELLET, Jeanne see JANEBE

BARRE, Martin (1924-) French
£3252 $6504 (10-Feb-91 CC.P3) Sans titre (59x52cm-23x20in) s.d.1958 (F.FR 32000)
£5338 $10036 (19-Sep-90 KH.K38/R) Composition (100x80cm-39x31in) s.d.58 i.verso (D.KR 60000)

BARREIRA, V (20th C) Spanish
£1748 $3374 (12-Dec-90 N.M442/R) Female Spanish guitar player (90x68cm-35x27in) s.i. (DM 5000)

BARRERA, Antonio (1948-) Colombian
£2806 $5500 (20-Nov-90 CH.NY183/R) Palma real (100x80cm-39x31in) s.d.87

BARRET, George (jnr) (1767-1842) British
£420 $777 (4-Mar-91 PHB10) Classical landscape with figures (38x52cm-15x20in) W/C
£543 $1043 (18-Dec-90 DUR.M28) Escena idilica (31x46cm-12x18in) W/C (S.P 100000)
£650 $1281 (13-Nov-90 C55/R) Landscape with shepherd and flock on hillside above river gorge (15x48cm-6x19in) s.d.1834 W/C
£900 $1485 (11-Jul-91 S182) Figures at spring in Italianate landscape (39x52cm-15x20in) W/C over pencil scratching out

BARRET, George (snr) (1728-1784) British
£2600 $4290 (12-Jul-91 C114/R) Extensive mountainous landscape with figures by waterfall (63x77cm-25x30in)
£5500 $9295 (30-Apr-91 PH9/R) Figures in extensive Italianate landscape (90x116cm-35x46in)
£20513 $40000 (10-Oct-90 CH.NY184/R) Mountainous river landscape with fishermen on shore and castle beyond (102x128cm-40x50in)
£4000 $7160 (9-Apr-91 C98/R) Hauling timber through wood (47x63cm-19x25in) W/C bodycol

BARRET, George and GILPIN, Sawrey (19th C) British
£3316 $6500 (21-Nov-90 NA.BA13/R) Landscape with cattle and sheep (63x76cm-25x30in) s.

BARRET, Marius-Antoine (1865-1929) French
£7471 $13000   (27-Mar-91 B.SF4079/R) La fumeuse (129x97cm-51x38in) s.d.98

BARRETT, J (19th C) British
£1618 $2800   (21-May-91 CE.NY152/R) Rocky coast (71x117cm-28x46in) s.d.1871

BARRETT, James (?) British
£10000 $17900   (12-Apr-91 C62/R) View of Belvedere, with shipping on estuary and shepherd in foreground (112x165cm-44x65in)

BARRETT, John (19th C) British
£650   *$1164*   *(13-Mar-91 B147) An autumn evening on the river Teign, Dartmoor (27x44cm-11x17in) s. W/C bodycol. another W/C two*

BARRETT, William S (1854-1927) American
£1015 $2000   (16-Nov-90 E.EDM745/R) Fisherman in storm off the coast of Maine (46x61cm-18x24in) s.c.1900

BARRIAS, Felix (1822-1907) French
£3571 $7036   (14-Nov-90 FB.P218/R) L'obsession (94x76cm-37x30in) s.d.1850 oval (F.FR 35000)

BARRIBAL, William (fl.1919-1938) British
£900   *$1746*   *(6-Dec-90 CSK109) Portrait of artist's wife (49x39cm-19x15in) s.d.1919 W/C bodycol chl*
£900   *$1746*   *(6-Dec-90 CSK108/R) Portrait of artist's wife (49x38cm-19x15in) s.d.1910 W/C bodycol chl*

BARRIE, Mardi (?) British?
£700 $1379   (30-Oct-90 SC259) Promise of winter (84x110cm-33x43in) i.frame
£760 $1497   (30-Oct-90 SC231/R) Town bridge (49x67cm-19x26in) i. board
£800 $1344   (23-Apr-91 S250/R) Summer evening (67x79cm-26x31in) s. board

BARRIERE, Firmin (19th C) French
£1937 $3738   (16-Dec-90 M.V151/R) Scene animee s.d.88 (F.FR 19000)

BARRIOS, Manuel (?) Spanish?
£1621 $3161   (23-Oct-90 DUR.M57) Brindando (50x35cm-20x14in) (S.P 300000)
£1621 $3161   (23-Oct-90 DUR.M25) Guitarrista (50x38cm-20x15in) (S.P 300000)

BARRON, Hugh (1745-1791) British
£1488 $2500   (17-Jul-91 SY.NY181/R) Portrait of Elizabeth Davidson and her son Alexander Hector (74x62cm-29x24in)

BARROW, Joseph Charles (18/19th C) British
£1150   *$1932*   *(22-Apr-91 PH215/R) Country farm (27x40cm-11x16in) s. W/C*
£1500   *$2685*   *(9-Apr-91 C105/R) Figures and soldiers at the edge of village (20x28cm-8x11in) s.d.1795 pencil W/C*

BARRY, Claude-Francis (attrib) (1883-1970) British
£1300 $2197   (2-May-91 B106/R) The Houses of Parliament (71x91cm-28x36in)

BARRY, Frederick (19th C) British
£420   *$689*   *(21-Jun-91 HC2) Haymaking scene with figures and cart (33x56cm-13x22in) W/C*

BARRY, James (1741-1806) British
£5500 $10725   (26-Oct-90 CG165/R) Drawing nets by waterfall in classical Italianate landscape (36x51cm-14x20in) init.d.77 panel oval
£600   *$1074*   *(9-Apr-91 C6/R) Ecce Homo. Classical figures (30x20cm-12x8in) s.i. pen ink wash double-sided*

BARRY, James (fl.1813-1831) British
£1500 $2925   (16-Jan-91 CSK168) Fox (71x91cm-28x36in) s.

BARRY, John (fl.1784-1827) British
£850   *$1505*   *(20-Mar-91 C142/R) Portrait of lady in lace-bordered white dress and bonnet (5x?cm-2x?in) min. oval in rec.papier-mache frame*

BARSOTTI, Hercules (1914-) Brazilian
£3571 $7000   (20-Nov-90 CH.NY282/R) Multileituras Opcionais I (80x80cm-31x31in) s.i.d.1974 verso acrylic canvas

BARTCHENKOV, Nicolas (1918-) Russian
£1259 $2052   (16-Jun-91 C.P6) Le tracteur a Zagorsk (95x133cm-37x52in) s. (F.FR 12500)

BARTELS, Hans von (1856-1913) German
£838 $1500   (16-Mar-91 W.W73/R) Ship at sunset (71x104cm-28x41in) s.
£1031 $1959   (2-Mar-91 KRA.D274/R) Idyllic village scene, spring (31x56cm-12x22in) s.d.1879 board (DM 3000)

BARTH, C W (1847-1919) Norwegian
£548 $1095   (9-Feb-91 BU.O17) Sailingboats at sea (46x55cm-18x22in) s. (N.KR 6200)
£608 $1028   (4-May-91 BU.O8) Bay of Naples (27x36cm-11x14in) s. panel (N.KR 7000)

BARTH, C W (1847-1919) Norwegian-cont.
£629 $1195   (11-Sep-90 UL.T174) Midnight sun at Fugloy, Nordland 1888
                 (20x42cm-8x17in) s. (N.KR 7200)

BARTH, Carl (1896-?) German
£2911 $4745   (15-Jun-91 L.K36/R) Playland (77x59cm-30x23in) s. (DM 8500)

BARTH, Carl Wilhelm (1847-1919) Norwegian
£825 $1377   (4-Jun-91 BU.O9/R) Gondola in Venice (29x22cm-11x9in) init. panel
                 (N.KR 9500)

BARTH, Ferdinand (1842-1892) German
£1793 $3443   (28-Nov-90 KF.M255/R) Snow ball fight (53x42cm-21x17in) s. (DM 5200)

BARTH, Paul Basilius (1881-1955) Swiss
£960 $1622   (1-May-91 GD.B35/R) Houses on hill (64x80cm-25x31in) s.verso (S.FR 2400)
£4781 $8223   (14-May-91 GF.L2241/R) View of Riva (60x73cm-24x29in) s.d.1943
                 (S.FR 12000)

BARTH, Theodor (1875-1949) Swiss
£3968 $6627   (5-Jun-91 SY.Z100/R) Church choir (43x68cm-17x27in) s. panel sold with
                 W/C of same subject (S.FR 10000)

BARTH, Thom (1951-) German
*£980 $1900   (7-Dec-90 G.Z316) Composition 07 (170x139cm-67x55in) d.87 mixed media
                 board (S.FR 2400)*

BARTH, Wolf (1926-) Swiss
£556 $983   (22-Mar-91 EA.Z352) Untitled (93x87cm-37x34in) s.d.88verso acrylic
                 (S.FR 1400)
£2289 $4487   (24-Nov-90 AB.L157/R) Untitled (130x97cm-51x38in) d.1958 acrylic
                 (S.FR 5700)

BARTHE, Gerard de la (attrib) (18/19th C) French
*£900 $1755   (10-Oct-90 C178/R) View of the Stroganov Country House across the Neva
                 (10x24cm-4x9in) W/C gouache htd white paper laid on card*

BARTHELEMY (?) French
£2481 $4690   (25-Sep-90 GM.B1027) Pont sous la neige (81x65cm-32x26in) s.
                 (B.FR 150000)

BARTHELEMY, Camille (1890-1961) Belgian
£1064 $1787   (23-Apr-91 C.A284) Ardenne landscape (64x86cm-25x34in) s.d.1935
                 (B.FR 65000)

BARTHELEMY, Gerard (20th C) French?
£663 $1272   (2-Dec-90 M.V175) Le remorqueur (65x50cm-26x20in) s. (F.FR 6500)

BARTLET, H R (19th C) British?
£1200 $2340   (18-Oct-90 CSK105/R) The schooner 'Red Coat' with paddle steamer on
                 horizon beyond (51x76cm-20x30in) s.d.1869

BARTLETT, Dana (1878-1957) American
£918 $1800   (13-Feb-91 B.SF2098/R) Valley landscape (41x51cm-16x20in) s.
£3681 $6000   (11-Jun-91 MOR.P76) Boat landing (51x61cm-20x24in) s.

BARTLETT, Gray (1885-1951) American
£2041 $4000   (7-Nov-90 B.SF3804/R) Cowboy at mailbox (61x76cm-24x30in) s.
£2551 $5000   (7-Nov-90 B.SF3805/R) Novajo with horse (76x102cm-30x40in) s.

BARTLETT, Jennifer (1941-) American
£38462 $65000   (1-May-91 CH.NY39/R) In garden 118 (213x366cm-84x144in) diptych
£3254 $5500   (2-May-91 CH.NY148/R) In garden no.124 (66x49cm-26x19in) num.124 pen
*£53254 $90000   (30-Apr-91 SY.NY55/R) 17 White Street (295x295cm-116x116in) baked enamel
                 silkscreen grid on 81 enamel plate*
*£94675 $160000 (30-Apr-91 SY.NY62/R) At lake (196x477cm-77x188in) s.d.1978 verso enamel
                 silkscreen steel canvas*

BARTLETT, William Henry (1809-1854) British
£600 $1074   (11-Mar-91 HS213) On the lagoons, Venice - figures unloading hay barge
                 (31x49cm-12x19in) s.d.1883
£1700 $3264   (29-Nov-90 B33/R) Gathering turnips (19x40cm-7x16in) s.d.92 board
£1800 $3114   (22-May-91 S135/R) On lagoons, Venice (31x48cm-12x19in) s.d.1883

BARTLETT, William Henry (attrib) (1809-1854) British
£4847 $9500   (16-Feb-91 W.W18/R) View of the Capitol at Washington (56x71cm-22x28in)

BARTOLENA, Giovanni (1866-1942) Italian
£2046 $4010   (21-Nov-90 F.M134/R) Marina livornese (15x29cm-6x11in) s. board
                 (I.L 4500000)
£4000 $8000   (18-Oct-90 F.M15/R) Natura morta con funghi (30x47cm-12x19in) s. i.verso
                 panel (I.L 9500000)
£6613 $11043   (6-Jun-91 F.M236/R) Vaso verde con garofani (59x27cm-23x11in) s. panel
                 (I.L 14500000)
£8665 $14470   (6-Jun-91 F.M272/R) Pere, mele, fichi e castagne (33x59cm-13x23in) s.
                 panel (I.L 19000000)

BARTOLENA, Giovanni (1866-1942) Italian-cont.
£14000 $28000   (18-Oct-90 F.M17/R) Cavalli a riposo (51x77cm-20x30in) s. panel
                                    (I.L 32000000)

BARTOLI, Jacques (20th C) French
£1173 $2300   (7-Nov-90 D.NY7) Plage a Toulon (33x41cm-13x16in) s.i. verso

BARTOLINI, Frederico (19/20th C) Italian
£2400 $4680   (24-Oct-90 S221/R) The carpet seller (52x36cm-20x14in) s. W/C over
                                    traces pencil
£2700 $5265   (24-Oct-90 S223/R) Outside the mosque (52x35cm-20x14in) s. W/C over
                                    traces pencil

BARTOLINI, Luciano (20th C) Italian
£770 $1340   (26-Mar-91 F.M12/R) Untitled (44x54cm-17x21in) s.d.1979verso collage
                                    pastel (I.L 1700000)
£1818 $3564   (20-Nov-90 BR.M87/R) Composizione (23x154cm-9x61in) s.d.1988verso mixed
                                    media collage (I.L 4000000)
£2251 $4390   (22-Oct-90 BR.M66/R) Composizione (76x99cm-30x39in) s.d.1989 verso
                                    collage mixed media (I.L 5000000)
£2542 $4905   (13-Dec-90 F.M388/R) Untitled (52x75cm-20x30in) s.d.1886verso collage
                                    paint (I.L 5500000)

BARTOLINI, Luigi (1892-1963) Italian
£1262 $2259   (9-Apr-91 F.R53) Le amiche (27x38cm-11x15in) s. mixed media
                                    (I.L 2800000)

BARTOLO, Taddeo di (1363-1422) Italian
£28000 $54040   (12-Dec-90 S14/R) The Baptism of Christ (31x33cm-12x13in) tempera panel
                                    gold ground

BARTOLO, Taddeo di (circle) (1363-1422) Italian
£20286 $36312   (8-Apr-91 CH.R181/R) La Madonna col Bambino (80x37cm-31x15in) gold
                                    ground panel pointed top (I.L 45000000)

BARTOLOMMEO (Veneto-style) (1502-1555) Italian
£2923 $5700   (21-Oct-90 HG.C15) Lucrezia Borgia (84x66cm-33x26in)

BARTOLOMMEO, Fra (1472-1517) Italian
£7368 $14000   (8-Jan-91 SY.NY15/R) The Holy Family with St.John the Baptist and a
                                    kneeling angel (14x12cm-6x5in) blk.chk.htd.white chk.

BARTOLOMMEO, Fra (attrib) (1472-1517) Italian
£8500 $13855   (4-Jul-91 B102/R) The Madonna and Child with St. John the Baptist
                                    (102x78cm-40x31in)

BARTOLOZZI, Francesco (1727-1815) Italian
£1474 $2800   (8-Jan-91 SY.NY74/R) Two young girls and a child with a pet bird
                                    (26x322cm-10x127in) chk. oval
£1505 $2663   (19-Mar-91 F.M192/R) Il sacrificio di Noe (40x49cm-16x19in) mono. ink
                                    (I.L 3300000)

BARTOLUZZI, Millo (20th C) Italian
£2081 $3600   (21-May-91 CE.NY95/R) Grand, Canal, Venice (41x81cm-16x32in) s.
£600 $1140   (12-Sep-90 CSK215/R) Fishing craft and gondolas in St. Mark's Basin,
                                    Venice (28x43cm-11x17in) s. pencil W/C htd white

BARTON, Rose Maynard (1856-1929) British
£1523 $3000   (7-Oct-90 DU.E259/R) Ploughing team in Devon (33x23cm-13x9in) s.d.1889
                                    W/C
£1950 $3822   (12-Feb-91 RB742/R) Young child standing in doorway and writing on wall
                                    (36x25cm-14x10in) s.d.1918 W/C

BARTSCH, Carl-Frederick (1829-1908) Danish
£1014 $1926   (14-Sep-90 SA.A1197/R) Horse and foal in landscape with storm rising
                                    (25x33cm-10x13in) s. panel (DM 3000)

BARTSCH, Friedrich (1843-1900) Austrian?
£962 $1875   (25-Oct-90 D.V8/R) Marswiese im Dornbacher Park, XVII. Bezirk
                                    (17x35cm-7x14in) s. (A.S 20000)

BARTSCH, Philipp Anton (1742-1788) German
£2095 $3561   (27-May-91 L.K183/R) Landscapes with classical ruins and figures
                                    (31x42cm-12x17in) s.d.1778 gouache pair (DM 6200)

BARUCCI, Pietro (1845-1917) Italian
£2500 $4925   (5-Oct-90 C157/R) Collecting reeds (99x75cm-39x30in) s.i.
£2542 $4905   (11-Dec-90 CH.R94) Campagna romana (29x45cm-11x18in) s. panel
                                    (I.L 5500000)
£4335 $7500   (21-May-91 CE.NY274/R) Gypsies returning home (84x146cm-33x57in)
£4546 $8910   (22-Nov-90 SY.MI3/R) Campagna romana (50x105cm-20x41in) s.
                                    (I.L 10000000)
£5682 $11138   (22-Nov-90 SY.MI2) Campagna romana (50x105cm-20x41in) s. (I.L 12500000)
£6100 $10492   (14-May-91 SWS310/R) Fishermen at sea (59x107cm-23x42in) s.i.
£7179 $14000   (24-Oct-90 CH.NY233/R) Crossing the marsh (41x92cm-16x36in) s.i.
£14125 $24012   (28-May-91 F.R128/R) Il guado (60x92cm-24x36in) s. (I.L 31000000)

BARUCCI, Pietro (1845-1917) Italian-cont.
£16000 $26240   (21-Jun-91 C89/R) Gregge al Tramonto (100x200cm-39x79in) s.i.
£1823   *$3098*   *(28-May-91 F.R109/R) Rovine nella campagna romana (43x73cm-17x29in) s.*
        W/C (I.L 4000000)

BARUCHELLO, Gianfranco (1924-) Italian
£681   *$1179*   *(7-May-91 F.M154) De la pictura liniale (50x50cm-20x20in)*
        s.i.d.1973verso alluminium (I.L 1500000)
£1541   *$2604*   *(15-Apr-91 CC.P139) Intano a Tebe, il sacro Battaglione*
        (70x70cm-28x28in) collage paint metal (F.FR 15500)
£1903   *$3311*   *(26-Mar-91 F.M10/R) Di Primavalle si muore (100x100cm-39x39in) s.d.1972*
        aluminium (I.L 4200000)
£3377   *$6585*   *(22-Oct-90 BR.M58/R) Se fossero cicale sulla luna (50x50cm-20x20in)*
        s.d.1987 verso mixed media canvas (I.L 7500000)

BARWELL, Frederick Bacon (?-1897) British
£1200 $2364   (1-Nov-90 C276/R) Portrait of William Bell Scott (51x41cm-20x16in)
        s.i.d.1877verso

BARWOLF, Georges (1872-1935) Belgian
£2874 $5000   (27-Mar-91 B.SF4292/R) Place du Delta, Paris (99x135cm-39x53in) s.d.1910

BARYE, Antoine-Louis (1796-1875) French
£1829 $3585   (6-Nov-90 SY.AM47) Forest of Fontainebleau (18x29cm-7x11in) s.
        (D.FL 6000)
£16583   *$27196*   *(20-Jun-91 APT.P8/R) Tigre devorant un homme (12x23cm-5x9in) bears*
        studio st. W/C (F.FR 165000)

BARZ, Matthias (1895-1972) German
£3691 $7198   (13-Oct-90 KRA.D343/R) Accordion player in pub (180x159cm-71x63in)
        s.d.33 (DM 11000)

BARZAGHI-CATTANEO, Antonio (1837-?) Swiss
£1587 $2651   (7-Jun-91 ZOF.Z1277) Portrait of girl (37x30cm-15x12in) s. (S.FR 4000)

BAS, Edward le (1904-1966) British
£800 $1584   (29-Jan-91 PH9/R) Institute, Paris (25x18cm-10x7in) artist's board
£1350 $2498   (5-Mar-91 PH18) Still life with vase of flowers and bowl of apples
        (41x41cm-16x16in) s. canvas on board
£1600 $2784   (27-Mar-91 S34/R) Whitby harbour (25x46cm-10x18in) panel
£2400 $4680   (10-Oct-90 S32/R) Hauling in the nets (102x127cm-40x50in)
£4000 $7400   (7-Mar-91 C79/R) Poppies in earthenware jug (61x51cm-24x20in) s.

BASALDUA, Hector (1895-1976) Argentinian
£6091 $12000   (14-Nov-90 V.BA7/R) Calle en Suipacha (72x99cm-28x39in)

BASCH, Edith (1895-?) Hungarian
£3349 $5794   (8-May-91 D.V98/R) Female nude before mirror (100x84cm-39x33in) s.d.1934
        (A.S 70000)

BASCHENIS, Evaristo (circle) (1617-1677) Italian
£1891 $3688   (23-Oct-90 CH.R346/R) Natura morta con pesci, frutta e lumache
        (60x140cm-24x55in) (I.L 4200000)

BASCHNY, Emanuel (1876-1932) Austrian
£5758 $9904   (16-May-91 D.V81/R) View of Grinzing in early spring (43x64cm-17x25in)
        s.d.1923 panel (A.S 120000)

BASCOM, Ruth Henshaw (1772-1848) American
£2083   *$4000*   *(18-Aug-90 S.BM149 a/R) Portraits of young gentleman and lady*
        (51x38cm-20x15in) pastel graphite pair
£7179   *$14000*   *(27-Oct-90 S.BM128/R) Profile portrait of Maria D Lincoln*
        (48x36cm-19x14in) i. pastel graphite

BASELITZ, Georg (1938-) ?
£2500 $4875   (18-Oct-90 C414/R) Adler (50x35cm-20x14in) init.d.74 paper
£2853 $4935   (22-May-91 CH.AM666) Untitled (59x42cm-23x17in) s.d.1980 acrylic paper
        (D.FL 9500)
£124260 $210000   (30-Apr-91 SY.NY26/R) Die kuh (162x129cm-64x51in) s.d.68 s.d.1968 verso
£141892 $241216   (31-May-91 VG.B82/R) Head, Elke profile (200x161cm-79x63in) s.d.1977
        s.i.d.verso (DM 420000)
£163265 $320000   (7-Nov-90 CH.NY54/R) Strandbild 5, Maria in Knokke (250x199cm-98x78in)
        s.d.80
£236686 $400000   (30-Apr-91 SY.NY23/R) Akt und flasche (250x340cm-98x134in) s.i.d.77
        verso panel four parts
£2000   *$3900*   *(18-Oct-90 C417/R) Adler (29x21cm-11x8in) s.d.74 pencil*
£2500   *$4875*   *(18-Oct-90 C415/R) Untitled (43x30cm-17x12in) s.indis.i. ink W/C on*
        printed paper
£2786   *$5378*   *(13-Dec-90 SY.AM291/R) Flasche (70x50cm-28x20in) s. gouache pastel*
        crayon (D.FL 9000)
£2800   *$5460*   *(18-Oct-90 C413/R) Adler (42x29cm-17x11in) s.d.1974 ink pencil*
£3000   *$5850*   *(18-Oct-90 C409/R) Adler (34x25cm-13x10in) init.d.74 ink W/C*
£3096   *$5975*   *(13-Dec-90 SY.AM293/R) Flasche (61x43cm-24x17in) s.d.78 12 gouache*
        (D.FL 10000)
£3425   *$5582*   *(14-Jun-91 L.K734/R) Nude bending down (60x43cm-24x17in) s.d.78 W/C chk*
        (DM 10000)

BASELITZ, Georg (1938-) ?-cont.

£3500	$6825	*(18-Oct-90 C410/R) Falke (58x43cm-23x17in) init.i.d.72 ink W/C on printed paper*
£4200	$8190	*(18-Oct-90 C412/R) Adler (43x37cm-17x15in) s.d.74 W/C feltmarker ink*
£7192	$11723	*(14-Jun-91 L.K733/R) Eagle (43x36cm-17x14in) s.d.74 W/C felt tip pen (DM 21000)*
£8562	$13955	*(14-Jun-91 L.K736/R) Untitled (60x43cm-24x17in) d.1983 W/C (DM 25000)*
£9000	$17550	*(18-Oct-90 S158/R) Untitled (66x47cm-26x19in) s.d.85 gouache pencil*
£17857	$35000	*(7-Nov-90 SY.NY335/R) Untitled (48x33cm-19x13in) init. ink W/C pencil*

BASHKIRTSEFF, Maria (1860-1884) Russian

£3000	$5850	*(10-Oct-90 C192/R) Girl reading by waterfall (30x21cm-12x8in) s. pencil W/C*

BASILETTI, Luigi (1780-1860) Italian

£13000	$21320	*(21-Jun-91 C76 a/R) Italianate capriccio landscape with Falls at Tivoli (109x174cm-43x69in) mono.d.1839*

BASILIDES, Barna (20th C) Hungarian

£1419	$2398	*(3-May-91 SA.A785/R) Evening in the village (81x100cm-32x39in) s.d.1941 (DM 4200)*

BASING, Charles (1865-?) American

£2000	$3700	*(8-Mar-91 S.BM220/R) Winter landscape with stone bridge (51x61cm-20x24in) s.*

BASKAKOV, Nicolai (1918-) Russian

£500	$840	*(26-Apr-91 ARC.P195) Sourires ecomplices (50x79cm-20x31in) s. board (F.FR 5000)*
£500	$840	*(26-Apr-91 ARC.P205/R) Paysanne aux champs (115x70cm-45x28in) s. (F.FR 5000)*
£503	$965	*(18-Feb-91 ARC.P205/R) Portrait de Natacha (80x40cm-31x16in) s.d.73 (F.FR 5000)*
£550	$924	*(26-Apr-91 ARC.P199) Le vase bleu (89x75cm-35x30in) s. (F.FR 5500)*
£595	$1024	*(15-May-91 AGB.P59/R) La jeune femme au bouquet de roses (64x78cm-25x31in) s. (F.FR 6000)*
£694	$1194	*(15-May-91 AGB.P60/R) Eclat de rire (35x63cm-14x25in) s. board (F.FR 7000)*
£703	$1300	*(4-Mar-91 ZZ.F6/R) Les enfants (43x53cm-17x21in) s.*
£764	$1314	*(15-May-91 AGB.P62/R) Les amis (70x58cm-28x23in) s. (F.FR 7700)*
£790	$1327	*(26-Apr-91 ARC.P201/R) Petite fille a la poupee (70x60cm-28x24in) s. (F.FR 7900)*
£804	$1544	*(18-Feb-91 ARC.P206/R) Les ballerines (78x70cm-31x28in) s. (F.FR 8000)*
£893	$1536	*(15-May-91 AGB.P58/R) La lac des cygnes (75x53cm-30x21in) s. (F.FR 9000)*
£896	$1558	*(25-Mar-91 ARC.P146/R) Le revell (77x55cm-30x22in) s. (F.FR 9000)*
£945	$1645	*(25-Mar-91 ARC.P148/R) Les glaieuls (98x82cm-39x32in) s. (F.FR 9500)*
£995	$1731	*(25-Mar-91 ARC.P143/R) La procession (49x95cm-19x37in) s. (F.FR 10000)*
£1294	$2251	*(25-Mar-91 ARC.P145/R) La proposition (97x67cm-38x26in) s. (F.FR 13000)*
£1393	$2424	*(25-Mar-91 ARC.P144/R) Les amies (69x59cm-27x23in) s. (F.FR 14000)*
£1493	$2597	*(25-Mar-91 ARC.P150/R) A cote du samovar (73x92cm-29x36in) s. (F.FR 15000)*
£1558	$2991	*(18-Feb-91 ARC.P212/R) Le depart sur le quai (60x100cm-24x39in) s. (F.FR 15500)*
£1891	$3290	*(25-Mar-91 ARC.P147/R) La nappe bleue (69x85cm-27x33in) s. (F.FR 19000)*
£2111	$4052	*(18-Feb-91 ARC.P208/R) Matine de reverie (100x85cm-39x33in) s. (F.FR 21000)*
£2563	$4921	*(18-Feb-91 ARC.P209/R) La course d'attelages (73x100cm-29x39in) s.d.72 (F.FR 25000)*
£3015	$5789	*(18-Feb-91 ARC.P210/R) Derriere la barriere (107x95cm-42x37in) s.d.87 (F.FR 30000)*
£3600	$6048	*(26-Apr-91 ARC.P206/R) Rive de la Neva en ete (96x118cm-38x46in) s.d.60 (F.FR 36000)*

BASKIN, Leonard (1922-) American

£521	$1000	*(17-Dec-90 SY.NY428/R) Bacchi Herm - front view (99x66cm-39x26in) s.d.1966 ink wash*
£582	$1100	*(25-Sep-90 CE.NY229/R) Seated man with bird (100x70cm-39x28in) s.d.1971 i. verso pen brush ink*
£872	$1500	*(15-May-91 SY.NY271/R) Orinoco (76x56cm-30x22in) s.d.1984 W/C*

BASOLI, Antonio (1774-1848) Italian

£388	$686	*(19-Mar-91 F.M2/R) Studio de oreficerie (38x23cm-15x9in) pen W/C ink over pencil (I.L 850000)*
£456	$807	*(19-Mar-91 F.M15/R) Due studi di ventaglio (19x38cm-7x15in) i. ink W/C pencil (I.L 1000000)*
£684	$1211	*(19-Mar-91 F.M11/R) Progetto per decorazione di soffitto (27x40cm-11x16in) i. W/C (I.L 1500000)*

BASQUIAT, Jean Michel (1960-1988) American

£5076	$10000	*(4-Oct-90 SY.NY226/R) Untitled (28x44cm-11x17in) oilstick paper*
£8122	$16000	*(5-Oct-90 CH.NY142/R) Untitled (56x76cm-22x30in) s.d.1981verso col oilstick*
£29880	$50797	*(2-Jun-91 GL.P186/R) Desmond (218x173cm-86x68in) s.i.d.1984 verso acrylic (F.FR 300000)*
£45819	$86139	*(19-Sep-90 KH.K31/R) Ace for hire, New York 1985 (122x91cm-48x36in) s.d.85 acrylic (D.KR 515000)*

BASQUIAT, Jean Michel (1960-1988) American-cont.
£48469 $95000 (7-Nov-90 SY.NY387/R) Untitled (228x117cm-90x46in) acrylic oilstick plywood
£1531 $3000 (12-Feb-91 SY.NY453/R) Face (76x56cm-30x22in) oilstick
£2196 $3799 (21-May-91 WK.M576/R) Famous negro athletes (27x17cm-11x7in) c.1981 col.chk (DM 6500)
£2216 $3611 (11-Jun-91 CSC.P43/R) Homme debout (76x57cm-30x22in) col.crayons (F.FR 22000)
£3061 $6000 (8-Nov-90 CH.NY217/R) Untitled (60x46cm-24x18in) col.crayons
£3590 $7000 (10-Oct-90 SY.NY464/R) Two ply. Triple A (61x46cm-24x18in) s.verso crayon pair
£4032 $7863 (26-Oct-90 CC.P119/R) Tete rouge (46x38cm-18x15in) pastel (F.FR 40000)
£7553 $12311 (16-Jun-91 CC.P80 b/R) Sans titre (76x56cm-30x22in) oil pastel (F.FR 75000)
£8092 $14000 (7-May-91 CE.NY299/R) Untitled (100x70cm-39x28in) s.i.d.83 col.crayons acrylic gouache paper
£8876 $15000 (2-May-91 CH.NY269/R) Untitled (107x67cm-42x26in) col.oilsticks felt-tip pen oil paper
£10405 $18000 (7-May-91 CE.NY296/R) Boone (104x30cm-41x12in) s. collage felt-tip oilsticks masonite on panel
£16582 $32500 (7-Nov-90 SY.NY379/R) Untitled (91x91cm-36x36in) oil crayon paper mounted to canvas
£20710 $35000 (2-May-91 CH.NY307/R) Per Capita (122x76cm-48x30in) s.verso oil graphite felt-tips collage panel
£33163 $65000 (15-Feb-91 SY.NY197/R) Hohner (218x173cm-86x68in) s.i.d.85verso acrylic oil stick col.xerox canvas
£48469 $95000 (7-Nov-90 SY.NY375/R) Ellington (180x80cm-71x31in) s.i.d.85 verso oilstick acrylic collage xerox
£60484 $117944 (26-Oct-90 CC.P127/R) Multiflavors (154x155cm-61x61in) s.i.d.1982 verso acrylic wood string canvas (F.FR 600000)

BASSANI (style) (?) Italian
£1000 $2000 (7-Feb-91 CSK41/R) Adoration of Shepherds (39x48cm-15x19in) panel
£1600 $2704 (18-Apr-91 CSK4/R) Adoration of Shepherds (81x102cm-32x40in)
£2600 $5070 (25-Oct-90 B1/R) The wheat harvest (67x165cm-26x65in)

BASSANO (after) (16/17th C) Italian
£3144 $6225 (30-Jan-91 APT.P192/R) Le retour de la chasse ou l'automne (21x30cm-8x12in) copper (F.FR 31000)

BASSANO (studio) (16/17th C) Italian
£1592 $3088 (8-Dec-90 GAB.G2047/R) La fuite en Egypte - le passage d'une riviere (49x83cm-19x33in) (S.FR 3900)
£4077 $7870 (10-Dec-90 BL.P13/R) Le Christ descendu de la croix (65x79cm-26x31in) (F.FR 40000)
£11857 $19802 (4-Jun-91 CH.R123/R) Allegoria dell'Autunno (131x218cm-52x86in) (I.L 26000000)

BASSANO (style) (16/17th C) Italian
£5500 $9295 (19-Apr-91 C124/R) Summer, peasants harvesting (112x146cm-44x57in)

BASSANO, Francesco (15/16th C) Italian
£30000 $48900 (3-Jul-91 S69/R) Noah and family after flood (125x176cm-49x69in)

BASSANO, Francesco (circle) (15/16th C) Italian
£3182 $6237 (19-Nov-90 CH.R68/R) Cristo in casa di Marta e Maddalena (51x73cm-20x29in) (I.L 7000000)
£3645 $6197 (30-May-91 F.M10) Adorazione dei pastori (91x120cm-36x47in) (I.L 8000000)

BASSANO, Francesco (studio) (15/16th C) Italian
£5455 $10692 (19-Nov-90 CH.R22/R) Convoglio con figure, animali e natura morta (48x69cm-19x27in) (I.L 12000000)

BASSANO, Francesco (style) (15/16th C) Italian
£12170 $23367 (17-Dec-90 ARC.P20/R) L'hiver. L'automne. Le printemps (20x29cm-8x11in) copper three (F.FR 120000)

BASSANO, Francesco (younger) (1549-1592) Italian
£13000 $25090 (12-Dec-90 S167/R) The adoration of the shepherds (81x115cm-32x45in)
£27000 $52110 (12-Dec-90 S24/R) The Birth of the Virgin (44x34cm-17x13in) copper
£70352 $115377 (21-Jun-91 SY.MO106/R) Les Pelerins d'Emmaus. Le Christ dans la maison de Marthe et Marie (77x115cm-30x45in) bears trace sig. pair (F.FR 700000)

BASSANO, Francesco (younger-attrib) (1549-1592) Italian
£13000 $21970 (19-Apr-91 C7/R) Christ in the house of Simon the Pharisee (198x292cm-78x115in)

BASSANO, Francesco (younger-school) (1549-1592) Italian
£3175 $5683 (13-Mar-91 GK.Z5/R) Peasants harvesting wheat, shearing sheep and resting in hilly landscape (81x105cm-32x41in) (S.FR 8000)

BASSANO, Gerolamo (1566-1621) Italian
£11365 $22275 (20-Nov-90 F.R115/R) La primavera (111x148cm-44x58in) (I.L 25000000)

BASSANO, Jacobo (1515-1592) Italian
£73529 $125000   (30-May-91 SY.NY9/R) Madonna and child with infatn Saint John the
       Baptist in landscape (51x41cm-20x16in)

BASSANO, Jacobo (attrib) (1515-1592) Italian
£2000 $3260   (2-Jul-91 C88/R) Head of bearded man (42x29cm-17x11in) col.chk

BASSANO, Jacobo (circle) (1515-1592) Italian
£2010 $3296   (21-Jun-91 SY.MO187/R) Annonce aux bergers (45x38cm-18x15in) canvas laid
       down on panel (F.FR 20000)

BASSANO, Jacobo (school) (1515-1592) Italian
£4885 $8745   (14-Mar-91 D.V194/R) The Adoration of the Shepherds (96x120cm-38x47in)
       (A.S 100000)

BASSANO, Jacobo (studio) (1515-1592) Italian
£2797 $5399   (12-Dec-90 N.M354/R) Annunciation to the Shepherds (81x103cm-32x41in)
       (DM 8000)
£8815 $17365   (14-Nov-90 D.V236/R) Venetian terra ferma inn with Christ and the
       Apostles in landscape (116x149cm-46x59in) (A.S 180000)

BASSANO, Jacobo (style) (1515-1592) Italian
£2800 $4732   (16-Apr-91 PH93/R) Farmer shearing sheep while family picnic in
       extensive rural landscape (81x111cm-32x44in)
£8500 $14365   (17-Apr-91 S127/R) The Good Samaritan (116x86cm-46x34in)

BASSANO, Leandro (1557-1622) Italian
£4412 $7500   (31-May-91 CH.NY221/R) The Mocking of Christ (49x51cm-19x20in)
£6500 $10595   (5-Jul-91 C221/R) Monk in study (63x40cm-25x16in)
£10800 $17604   (2-Jul-91 PH35/R) Portrait of lady with dog (119x96cm-47x38in)
£18421 $35000   (11-Jan-91 CH.NY18/R) The Entombment (52x33cm-20x13in) canvas laid
       on panel

BASSANO, Leandro (attrib) (1557-1622) Italian
£6839 $12242   (14-Mar-91 D.V142/R) Portrait of Nacopo Negretti, known as Palma il
       Giovane (114x93cm-45x37in) (A.S 140000)
£9712 $18842   (3-Dec-90 SY.F1053/R) La pieta (142x216cm-56x85in) panel (I.L 21000000)
£33500 $61975   (6-Mar-91 DR161/R) Animals entering ark (19x24cm-7x9in) on copper

BASSANO, Leandro (style) (1557-1622) Italian
£2010 $3296   (21-Jun-91 SY.MO208/R) Interieur de cuisine (56x72cm-22x28in)
       (F.FR 20000)
£3600 $6084   (17-Apr-91 S5/R) The Supper at Emmaus (84x118cm-33x46in)

BASSEN, Bartholomeus van (1590-1652) Dutch
£10000 $16900   (17-Apr-91 S96/R) Church interior (62x81cm-24x32in) panel
£38235 $65000   (31-May-91 CH.NY52/R) Imaginary church interior with figures
       (66x78cm-26x31in) bears sig. panel

BASSEN, Bartholomeus van (attrib) (1590-1652) Dutch
£676 $1142   (3-May-91 SA.A1609/R) Figures in a palace courtyard (38x33cm-15x13in)
       (DM 2000)

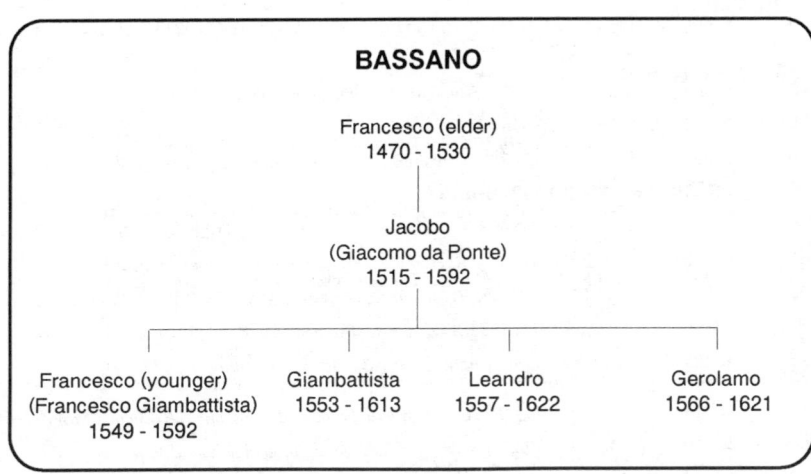

BASSANO

Francesco (elder)
1470 - 1530

Jacobo
(Giacomo da Ponte)
1515 - 1592

Francesco (younger)	Giambattista	Leandro	Gerolamo
(Francesco Giambattista)	1553 - 1613	1557 - 1622	1566 - 1621
1549 - 1592			

BASSETTI, Marcantonio (1588-1630) Italian
£1003 $1776   *(19-Mar-91 F.M179) Il pianto di Giacobbe (14x19cm-6x7in) pen W/C ink over pencil (I.L 2200000)*

BASTERT, Nicolaas (1854-1939) Dutch
£599 $1138   (11-Sep-90 CH.AM5) Houses along the Vecht in winter (35x51cm-14x20in) s. (D.FL 2000)
£898 $1751   (25-Oct-90 VN.R7) Polder landscape (45x34cm-18x13in) panel (D.FL 3000)
£1152 $2268   (30-Oct-90 CH.AM343/R) Sailing boat on river in polder landscape in summer (36x54cm-14x21in) s. (D.FL 3800)
£1524 $2988   (6-Nov-90 SY.AM258/R) Farmyard with children under blossoming tree (34x60cm-13x24in) s. (D.FL 5000)
£727 $1433   *(30-Oct-90 CH.AM451/R) Ducks in meadow with pollard willows (33x55cm-13x22in) s. W/C bodycol (D.FL 2400)*

BASTET, Jean-Celestin (1858-?) French
£10458 $18093   (24-May-91 FB.P142/R) La procession a Benares (81x117cm-32x46in) s. (F.FR 105000)

BASTIANI, Lazzaro (1425-1512) Italian
£66067 $112313   (30-May-91 F.M127/R) L'incontro di Gesu con le pie donne e Ascensione (30x25cm-12x10in) tempera panel (I.L 145000000)

BASTIANI, Lazzaro (circle) (1425-1512) Italian
£4800 $7824   (2-Jul-91 PH40/R) Group of Elders pleading for life of boys burning in tower (42x162cm-17x64in) panel

BASTIDA, Jose Marie de la (18th C) ?
£3824 $6500   (31-May-91 CH.NY249/R) Galatea (24x37cm-9x15in) s.i.d.1783 copper

BASTIEN LEPAGE, Jules (1848-1884) French
£697 $1185   (29-May-91 GL.P20/R) Paysage au clocher (22x28cm-9x11in) s. panel (F.FR 7000)
£17928 $31016   (24-May-91 FB.P165/R) Les foins (40x50cm-16x20in) s.i.d.78 (F.FR 180000)

BASTIEN, Alfred (1873-1955) Belgian
£742 $1439   (8-Dec-90 KV.L28) On the river bank (50x59cm-20x23in) s. panel (B.FR 44000)
£9231 $18000   (24-Oct-90 CH.NY263/R) Floral still life with sculpture (93x133cm-37x52in) s.d.24

BASTIEN, H (17th C) ?
£3200 $6080   (13-Sep-90 CSK58/R) Madonna Annunciate (63x51cm-25x20in) s.d.1622

BASTIN, Henri (1896-1979) Australian
£465 $781   *(22-Apr-91 SY.ME110) Broken Hill (36x49cm-14x19in) s.d.1959 gouache W/C pencil (A.D 1000)*
£637 $1256   *(31-Oct-90 CH.S92/R) Green spotted gums (29x39cm-11x15in) s.d.1973 enamel board (A.D 1600)*
£661 $1249   *(25-Sep-90 JRL.S103/R) The McDonnel Ranges (41x47cm-16x19in) s.d.1959 gouache cardboard on board (A.D 1500)*
£1488 $2500   *(22-Apr-91 SY.ME24) Forest (50x63cm-20x25in) s.d.1960 gouache paper on board (A.D 3200)*

BASTOW (20th C) ?
£1333 $2600   *(15-Jan-91 GM.B533/R) Femme assise (108x55cm-43x22in) s. chl.pastel (B.FR 80000)*

BATAILLE, Noel (19th C) ?
£4000 $7880   (5-Oct-90 C52/R) Washing day (125x90cm-49x35in) s.

BATCHELDER, S (1849-1932) British
£600 $1164   (6-Dec-90 LE290) Mill near Tunstal Dyke (30x61cm-12x24in) W/C
£650 $1086   (3-Jun-91 PHB23) Wherry on Broads (14x23cm-6x9in) s.i.verso W/C

BATCHELDER, Stephen (1849-1932) British
£500 $815   (14-Jun-91 K444/R) Scratby beach and tower (15x23cm-6x9in) s. W/C
£780 $1357   (27-Mar-91 PHS898/R) Bit of blue, Somerton Broad (20x30cm-8x12in) s.i.num.2573 verso W/C
£880 $1690   (19-Feb-91 SWS303/R) Horning ferry (30x60cm-12x24in) init.i. W/C
£950 $1549   (4-Jul-91 PHI115) Mill near Tunstall Dyke (30x60cm-12x24in) s.i. W/C
£950 $1853   (22-Oct-90 SWS255/R) Mill opposite Lipton Dyke (28x59cm-11x23in) s.i. W/C
£1250 $2350   (20-Sep-90 PHS668/R) Evening on Bu, near Wroxham (23x33cm-9x13in) s.i.verso W/C
£1250 $2425   (7-Dec-90 K505) Ellingham Loch (33x48cm-13x19in) s.d.1907 W/C
£1250 $2425   (7-Dec-90 K501/R) Wherries and barges, Braydon Water (20x48cm-8x19in) s. W/C
£1400 $2716   (7-Dec-90 K503/R) Two wherries in broadland landscape (28x20cm-11x8in) s. W/C
£1500 $2910   (7-Dec-90 K502/R) Sailing yachts beyond Potter Heigham Bridge (20x48cm-8x19in) s. W/C
£1500 $2535   (19-Apr-91 K522/R) Wherry at Whitlingham, distant view of Norwich (28x51cm-11x20in) s. W/C
£1800 $3528   (8-Nov-90 PHI86/R) Waiting wind and tide at Norton Staiths on river Yare (30x25cm-12x10in) s. W/C oval pair

BATCHELDER, Stephen (1849-1932) British-cont.
£2000 $3260   (14-Jun-91 K438) Sailing yachts, entrance to Wroxham Broad
                              (20x38cm-8x15in) s. W/C
£2400 $3912   (4-Jul-91 PHI114/R) Salhouse broad (29x50cm-11x20in) s. W/C
£4200 $7098   (19-Apr-91 K521/R) Wherries on river Bure, passing Coltishall Hall
                              (51x71cm-20x28in) s. W/C

BATCHELOR, Arthur (fl.1909-1910) British
£600 $1116   (5-Sep-90 BT111) Horning ferry, Norfolk Broads (30x61cm-12x24in) init.
                              W/C

BATEMAN, H M (1887-1970) British
£1600 $3104   (6-Dec-90 S328/R) Domestic disaster - 'Cook doesn't feel like it'
                              (30x40cm-12x16in) s. ink W/C dr

BATEMAN, Henry Mayo (1887-1970) British
£2000 $3840   (26-Nov-90 SWS77/R) The funny record which all the family knows by heart
                              ... (33x22cm-13x9in) s.d.1910 W/C over pen ink

BATEMAN, James (1815-1849) British
£514 $837   (12-Jun-91 N.M369/R) After the fox hunt (25x19cm-10x7in) s. panel
                           (DM 1500)

BATES, David (c.1841-1921) British
£800 $1512   (27-Sep-90 CSK83) Wooded landscape with young girl by a gate
                              (43x33cm-17x13in) s.
£820 $1607   (19-Nov-90 SWS451/R) Above Betws-y-Coed (22x16cm-9x6in) s.d.1888
                              s.i.d.1888 verso
£850 $1658   (16-Jan-91 CSK236) Arab hoak near Della (76x117cm-30x46in) s.d.1893
                              bears sig.i.verso
£900 $1467   (13-Jun-91 CSK268) In Lledr Valley (37x47cm-15x19in) s.d.1876 s.i.verso
                              board
£920 $1711   (5-Sep-90 BT171/R) English riverside (28x43cm-11x17in) s.d.1877
                              s.i.d.1877 verso
£1000 $1950   (15-Jan-91 SWS140/R) Angler by rocky stream (28x43cm-11x17in) s.d.1879
£1020 $1805   (5-Apr-91 BW406) Rural scene with two girls and dog near Bettws-y-Coed,
                              North Wales (33x51cm-13x20in) s. board
£1100 $2035   (7-Mar-91 CSK101/R) Sheep on common at sunrise (46x61cm-18x24in)
                              s.d.1909
£1300 $2509   (13-Dec-90 CSK61/R) Lumberjacks on edge of lake (61x46cm-24x18in)
                              s.d.1891
£1350 $2200   (5-Jul-91 S.W3065/R) A pathway through the wood, Capel Corig
                              (36x46cm-14x18in) s.d.1885 i. verso
£1350 $2579   (4-Jan-91 BW426) On the Llugwy (25x33cm-10x13in) s.i.verso
£1400 $2590   (7-Mar-91 D130/R) Children beside river with half-timbered cottage
                              beyond (33x43cm-13x17in) s.d.1883
£1600 $3136   (13-Feb-91 S137/R) On Rea, Warwickshire (46x61cm-18x24in) s.d.1899
                              s.i.verso
£1650 $2789   (3-May-91 T79) Cottages, stream and figures at Towyn (41x51cm-16x20in)
                              s.d.1883
£2000 $3540   (21-Mar-91 CSK148) The timber wagon (51x76cm-20x30in) s.d.1908
£2000 $3260   (14-Jun-91 T40/R) Summer evening (41x61cm-16x24in) s.d.1880
£2000 $3540   (18-Mar-91 FEN96) Figures outside cottages at Towyn, Wales
                              (41x48cm-16x19in) s.d.1883
£2000 $3300   (9-Jul-91 PH174/R) Pencraig Moor, Bettws-y-Coed (51x76cm-20x30in)
                              s.d.1901 s.i.d.verso
£2400 $4056   (30-Apr-91 PH89/R) In forest (36x46cm-14x18in) s.d.1886 s.i.d.verso
£2600 $4342   (5-Jun-91 S24/R) Pont-y-Pant (73x52cm-29x20in) s.d.1897
£2600 $5122   (1-Nov-90 CSK88/R) Llugwy near Capel Curig (41x61cm-16x24in) s.d.1878
                              s.i.d.1878 verso
£2600 $4394   (1-May-91 RBB646/R) Evening, Stratford - landscape with figures on river
                              bank (36x53cm-14x21in) s.d.
£2800 $5320   (1-Mar-91 C75/R) Wooded river landscape by chapel of Malvern Abbey and
                              ladies feeding swan (35x53cm-14x21in) s.d.1872
£3000 $5910   (13-Nov-90 PH54/R) Figures in landscape (41x61cm-16x24in) s.d.1898
                              i.verso
£3200 $5664   (20-Mar-91 WI1193/R) Westmorland hayfield - oaks and figures resting
                              middle distance (41x61cm-16x24in) s.d.1906
£3500 $5845   (5-Jun-91 S5/R) By edge of Lake (60x90cm-24x35in) s.d.1873
£3600 $6660   (6-Mar-91 SC4356/R) On the way to the pyramids from Cairo
                              (28x43cm-11x17in) s.d.1892 s.i.d.stretcher
£4200 $8232   (22-Jan-91 PH44/R) Near Bredon, Worcestershire (41x61cm-16x24in)
                              s.d.1894 s.i.verso
£4600 $8970   (18-Oct-90 SC3144/R) Lane near Leicester (59x90cm-23x35in) s.d.1898 i.
                              verso
£5000 $8850   (20-Mar-91 WI1194/R) View near Norton, Worcestershire - brook and
                              figures foreground (41x61cm-16x24in) s.d.1907
£6500 $10595   (14-Jun-91 C194/R) A Warwickshire streamlet (61x91cm-24x36in) s.d.1896
£7101 $12000   (2-May-91 CH.NY315/R) Rodeo (244x199cm-96x78in) s. s.d.86 overlap
£12755 $25000   (7-Nov-90 SY.NY382/R) A warm day in a cool month (153x122cm-60x48in)
                              s.i.d.87 overlap
£440 $814   (6-Mar-91 SC4147) Figure with dog on moorland path (25x36cm-10x14in)
                              s.d.1902 W/C pencil scratching out
£500 $815   (14-Jun-91 K353) Landscape with figures in lane and on stone brige,
                              village beyond (25x33cm-10x13in) s. W/C
£600 $1038   (22-May-91 JT5) Langdale (36x51cm-14x20in) s.d. W/C

BATES, David (c.1841-1921) British-cont.

£600	$1182	(13-Nov-90 SWS31/R) Arthogy moss (25x35cm-10x14in) s.i.d.04 W/C over pencil
£680	$1217	(13-Mar-91 B105) Through the beech woods, Malvern (36x25cm-14x10in) s.
£700	$1365	(18-Oct-90 SC3058) Moorland path at the foot of Siabod (21x33cm-8x13in) s. i. label
£1000	$1640	(19-Jun-91 B69/R) Figures in cart and cattle on heath track with Evesham beyond (36x50cm-14x20in) s.d.1905 W/C
£1100	$1969	(13-Mar-91 B81/R) A Leicestershire Lane (36x52cm-14x20in) s.i.d.1904 W/C
£1100	$1969	(13-Mar-91 B117) Close of the day, a farmstead, Malvern (25x36cm-10x14in) s.d.1905 W/C
£1350	$2268	(22-Apr-91 PH272/R) Harvest of the moor (35x51cm-14x20in) s.d.1904 W/C bodycol.scratching out
£1400	$2282	(14-Jun-91 C96 a/R) In the Vale of the Conway (35x51cm-14x20in) s.d.1905 pencil W/C
£1450	$2799	(13-Dec-90 M1) On the edge of the Malverns. Sheep grazing at sunset (33x48cm-13x19in) s. W/C pair
£1900	$3268	(13-May-91 CG187/R) The timber wagon, West Malvern. Returning from ploughing (36x53cm-14x21in) both s. W/C pair
£2000	$3900	(24-Oct-90 DR55/R) Farmstead, West Malvern, close of day. Beside William Common near Malvern (25x36cm-10x14in) s.d.1905 W/C pair
£3000	$5040	(17-Jul-91 WI1150/R) Returning from ploughing. Timber wagon, West Malvern (36x51cm-14x20in) s. W/C pair

BATES, Dewey (1851-1899) British

£820	$1468	(14-Mar-91 B98/R) A double portrait of Gracy Emily Blundell and Winifred Mary Blundell (76x63cm-30x25in) s.d.1884 indist.i. verso

BATES, Maxwell (20th C) Canadian

£1111	$1911	(14-May-91 JOY.T241/R) Still life with green jug (49x39cm-19x15in) s.d.1972 board (C.D 2200)
£1340	$2278	(27-May-91 HO.ED111/R) Party (41x30cm-16x12in) s.d.1976 i.verso canvas board (C.D 2600)
£3030	$5212	(14-May-91 JOY.T28/R) Circus people (75x90cm-30x35in) s.d.1972 (C.D 6000)

BATET, Francois (1923-) Spanish/French

£712	$1346	(30-Sep-90 E.LA98) Au bord de la mer (27x22cm-11x9in) s. (F.FR 7000)
£763	$1442	(30-Sep-90 E.LA94) Le Gant noir (35x27cm-14x11in) s. (F.FR 7500)
£814	$1538	(30-Sep-90 E.LA96) Dans le parc (35x27cm-14x11in) s. (F.FR 8000)
£1231	$2326	(30-Sep-90 E.LA93) Au paddock (41x33cm-16x13in) s. (F.FR 12100)
£1272	$2403	(30-Sep-90 E.LA95) Reveuse (55x46cm-22x18in) s. (F.FR 12500)

BATON, Claude (20th C) French

£1197	$2250	(19-Sep-90 B.SF2749/R) Bay City omnibus (61x91cm-24x36in) s.

BATONI, Pompeo (1708-1787) Italian

£19076	$30713	(25-Jun-91 APT.P56/R) Portrait d'une jeune femme avec une rose dans les cheveux (60x49cm-24x19in) oval (F.FR 190000)
£220000	$363000	(10-Jul-91 S40/R) Portrait of James Stewart wearing uniform standing by bust on pedestal (137x99cm-54x39in) l.
£1500	$2445	(1-Jul-91 S129/R) Child holding dish, and studies of arm and hands (19x14cm-7x6in) bears sig. black chk
£2000	$3840	(18-Feb-91 S155/R) Studies of two naked figures, possibly Cupid and Psyche, and furniture (22x15cm-9x6in) red chk wash htd.white squared

BATONI, Pompeo (after) (1708-1787) Italian

£2154	$4200	(10-Oct-90 CH.NY113/R) The choice of Hercules (74x97cm-29x38in)
£4412	$7500	(31-May-91 CH.NY229/R) St Mary Magdalene (118x184cm-46x72in)

BATONI, Pompeo (attrib) (1708-1787) Italian

£2300	$4416	(18-Feb-91 S219/R) Angel of the Annunciation. Female figure holding staff (17x14cm-7x6in) chk htd.white squared pair

BATONI, Pompeo (circle) (1708-1787) Italian

£2365	$4020	(28-May-91 KF.M136/R) Allegory of painting, sculpture and architecture (125x94cm-49x37in) (DM 7000)
£5000	$8150	(2-Jul-91 PH301/R) Cleopatra before Augustus (116x138cm-46x54in)

BATONI, Pompeo (style) (1708-1787) Italian

£963	$1608	(6-Jun-91 D.V165/R) Reclining woman reading as Mary Magdalen (28x40cm-11x16in) panel (A.S 20000)
£1138	$1900	(23-Jan-91 D.NY21) Madonna and Child with St. John the Baptist (20x28cm-8x11in) oval
£1667	$3250	(24-Oct-90 D.NY48) Madonna and Child with female saint (66x48cm-26x19in)
£1800	$3474	(13-Dec-90 CSK325/R) Portrait of gentleman, seated on terrace, holding pinch of snuff (106x82cm-42x32in)
£2500	$4075	(3-Jul-91 S174/R) Portrait of gentleman (46x35cm-18x14in)
£2600	$4394	(18-Apr-91 CSK43) Madonna and Child (36cm-14ins circular)

BATTAGLIA, Alessandro (1870-1940) Italian

£7117	$13381	(18-Sep-90 BU.K118/R) Two girl in shadow of tree (65x87cm-26x34in) s. (D.KR 80000)
£9000	$17280	(28-Nov-90 S162/R) Conversation in village square (64x86cm-25x34in) s.

BATTAGLIA, Carlo (1933-) Italian
£910 $1720   (27-Sep-90 F.M44) Garanza (80x200cm-31x79in) s.d.1975 tempera oil
                            (I.L 2000000)

BATTAGLIA, G Pompiani (19th C) Italian
£909 $1800   (1-Feb-91 S.W2590/R) Young love (48x36cm-19x14in) s. W/C

BATTAINI, Rino Gaspare (1892-) Italian
£717 $1398   (24-Oct-90 GD.B117/R) Still life with duck and jug (27x31cm-11x12in)
                            s.d.1931 i.verso panel (S.FR 1800)

BATTARBEE, Rex E (1893-?) Australian
£402 $771   (26-Nov-90 SY.ME110) Landscape, Central Australia (27x31cm-11x12in)
                            s.d.1939 W/C (A.D 1000)

BATTISS, Walter (1906-1982) South African
£864 $1659   (26-Nov-90 SY.J353/R) Huts and palm trees (29x40cm-11x16in) s.
                            (SA.R 4200)
£1579 $2668   (15-Apr-91 SY.J472/R) Nude figures at table (44x63cm-17x25in) s. board
                            (SA.R 7500)
£2218 $4325   (15-Oct-90 SY.J142/R) Figures and calabashes (46x55cm-18x22in) s.
                            (SA.R 11000)
£2222 $4333   (25-Oct-90 SY.J412/R) Fete champetre (121x182cm-48x72in) s.d.27.5.77
                            (SA.R 11000)
£422 $827   (11-Feb-91 SY.J548) Vision beyond the Ninevah and Ur (45x63cm-18x25in)
                            s.d.1969 i. verso pen (SA.R 2100)
£842 $1423   (15-Apr-91 SY.J478/R) Nude figures with hen and chicks. Nude figures in
                            landscape (34x49cm-13x19in) s. ink double-sided (SA.R 4000)

BATTISTA, Giovanni (1858-1925) Italian
£320 $557   (27-Mar-91 PHS900) Naples, general view from Virgils Tomb
                            (33x51cm-13x20in) s. gouache

BATTISTUZZI, A (19th C) Italian
£3167 $5668   (12-Apr-91 BM.B555/R) View of Santa Maria della Salute, Venice
                            (62x47cm-24x19in) s. (DM 9500)

BATTUT, Michele (1946-) French
£1018 $2006   (30-Oct-90 ZZ.F10) Fruits rouges (46x55cm-18x22in) s.d.90 (F.FR 10000)

BAUCHANT, A (?) ?
£750 $1268   (30-Apr-91 B32) Village landscape with two horses (34x43cm-13x17in) s.
                            board

BAUCHANT, Andre (1873-1958) French
£2000 $3220   (24-Jun-91 CSK51/R) Bouquet de fleurs (19x37cm-7x15in) s.d.1944 panel
£5500 $10725   (17-Oct-90 S198/R) L'oiseau au bec long (20x27cm-8x11in) s.d.1927
£5622 $10402   (6-Mar-91 APT.P72/R) Corbeille de fleurs (27x35cm-11x14in) s.d.1944
                            (F.FR 56000)
£5823 $9376   (28-Jun-91 ARC.P70/R) Massif de fleurs (24x35cm-9x14in) s. (F.FR 58000)
£6024 $11145   (6-Mar-91 APT.P73) Le bouquet (27x35cm-11x14in) s.d.1944 (F.FR 60000)
£6481 $10693   (10-Jul-91 FB.P23/R) Chevrefeuille (48x36cm-19x14in) s.d.1941 canvas
                            laid down on hardboard (F.FR 65000)
£7000 $12390   (20-Mar-91 S78/R) Oiseaux dans un paysage (54x73cm-21x29in) s.d.1930
£8205 $16000   (10-Oct-90 SY.NY176/R) Personnages (25x33cm-10x13in) s.d.1937 panel
£10152 $20000   (2-Oct-90 CH.NY108/R) La cruche aux marguerites (73x48cm-29x19in)
                            s.d.1930
£10651 $20982   (6-Oct-90 GL.P9/R) Les roches noires (46x61cm-18x24in) s.d.1929 i. verso
                            (F.FR 108000)
£10854 $17801   (20-Jun-91 APT.P44/R) Village au bord de la riviere (38x46cm-15x18in)
                            s.d.1954 (F.FR 108000)
£11000 $19470   (19-Mar-91 C123/R) Paysage de Savoie (46x63cm-18x25in) s.d.1941
£14368 $25000   (27-Mar-91 B.SF4126/R) Les habitants de ma touraine native
                            (41x53cm-16x21in) s.d.1946 panel
£14500 $25665   (20-Mar-91 S75/R) Deux oiseaux sur une branche (27x35cm-11x14in)
                            s.d.1943
£16650 $32300   (5-Dec-90 ZZ.F165/R) Les jardins suspendus de Babylone
                            (64x100cm-25x39in) s.d.1920 (F.FR 162000)
£62000 $109740   (20-Mar-91 S77/R) Fleurs dans un paysage (145x135cm-57x53in) s.d.1930

BAUDESSON, Nicolas (1611-1680) French
£11055 $18131   (21-Jun-91 SY.MO275/R) Panier de fleurs (33x41cm-13x16in) (F.FR 110000)
£18934 $33892   (8-Apr-91 CH.R36/R) Cesti di fiori (33x41cm-13x16in) pair
                            (I.L 42000000)

BAUDESSON, Nicolas (attrib) (1611-1680) French
£2100 $3885   (5-Mar-91 PH107/R) Still lifes of assorted flowers in porcelain bowl
                            (30x43cm-12x17in) pair panel on panel octagonal
£3484 $6828   (11-Nov-90 M.V40/R) Bouquet de fleurs (37x27cm-15x11in) panel octagonal
                            (F.FR 34000)

BAUDIT, Amedee (1825-1890) Swiss
£1230 $2300   (30-Aug-90 MFA.C131/R) Busy street scene (66x53cm-26x21in) s.
£2457 $4792   (12-Oct-90 ZZ.F66/R) Etang aux canards (80x150cm-31x59in) s.d.1864
                            (F.FR 24500)

BAUDOUIN, Pierre-Antoine (1723-1769) French
£2465 $4141   (23-Apr-91 RAS.K113/R) Courteous scene (35x27cm-14x11in) s.d.1767 panel
           (D.KR 28000)
£23000   *$37490*   *(1-Jul-91 S40/R) La toilette (26x21cm-10x8in) gouache*
£30000   *$48900*   *(1-Jul-91 S41/R) Le lever (24x19cm-9x7in) gouache*

BAUDOUX, H (?) ?
£495   *$969*   *(21-Nov-90 GM.B1256) Jardin en fleurs s. W/C (B.FR 30000)*

BAUDREXEL, Eduard (1890-?) German
£800 $1536   (27-Nov-90 PH140) Portrait of woman before landscape (110x89cm-43x35in)
           s.i.d.1922

BAUER, Carl Franz (1879-1954) Austrian
£1196 $2069   (8-May-91 D.V62/R) Dora, Guerrier-Fleurette (50x61cm-20x24in) s.i. board
           (A.S 25000)
£382   *$642*   *(25-Apr-91 D.V272/R) Jockey seated on Patent Horse (31x42cm-12x17in) s.*
           grisaille (A.S 8000)
£716   *$1396*   *(11-Oct-90 D.V225/R) Horse with jockey up (23x29cm-9x11in) s. pastel*
           (A.S 15000)
£1898   *$3398*   *(11-Apr-91 D.V334/R) Driving team of four horses (23x33cm-9x13in) s. W/C*
           htd.white (A.S 40000)

BAUER, Emil (1891-?) Swiss
£518 $891   (14-May-91 GF.L2570) Wooded mountain valley (75x75cm-30x30in) s.d.1919
           (S.FR 1300)

BAUER, Gerard (20th C) ?
£2581 $5059   (25-Nov-90 ZZ.F8/R) Baserati (65x81cm-26x32in) s. (F.FR 25500)

BAUER, Gustav (1874-1933) Austrian
£1455 $2735   (20-Sep-90 D.V54/R) Little girl seated in a chair in landscape
           (110x90cm-43x35in) s.d.1917 (A.S 30000)
£1889 $3664   (6-Dec-90 D.V51/R) Grinzing in winter (92x61cm-36x24in) s.i.d.1907
           (A.S 38000)

BAUER, Johann Balthazar (1811-1883) German
£3158 $6000   (15-Sep-90 S.W2771/R) The connoisseur. The enthusiast (23x18cm-9x7in)
           s.d.1865 pair

BAUER, John (1882-1918) Swedish
£1930   *$3783*   *(6-Nov-90 BA.S357/R) Knight and virgin (21x15cm-8x6in) mixed media*
           (S.KR 21000)
£7229   *$13952*   *(12-Dec-90 BU.S7/R) The Princess and the Troll (30x31cm-12x12in) s. W/C*
           htd white (S.KR 78000)

BAUER, Marius Alexander Jacques (1867-1932) Dutch
£1081 $2000   (8-Mar-91 S.BM179/R) Early morning at the Nile (58x76cm-23x30in) s.
£1576   *$3104*   *(30-Oct-90 CH.AM494) Figures under arch in oriental city*
           (71x54cm-28x21in) s. W/C (D.FL 5200)
£2096   *$3982*   *(11-Sep-90 CH.AM219) Balinese women on the steps of a temple*
           (74x52cm-29x20in) s. W/C (D.FL 7000)
£2879   *$5671*   *(30-Oct-90 CH.AM495 a/R) Horsemen under portico in oriental town*
           (50x76cm-20x30in) s. W/C bodycol htd white (D.FL 9500)

BAUER, Rudolf (20th C) German
£11168 $22000   (2-Oct-90 CH.NY83/R) White accent (76x115cm-30x45in) s. st.verso board
£12183 $24000   (2-Oct-90 CH.NY82/R) Allegretto IX (61x86cm-24x34in) s. board
£20946 $35608   (31-May-91 GB.B6129/R) Circles and triangles (130x130cm-51x51in) s.
           s.verso (DM 62000)
£21965 $38000   (9-May-91 CH.NY248/R) Intermezzo (131x131cm-52x52in) s.
£23121 $40000   (9-May-91 CH.NY249/R) Gelb and Schwarz (131x131cm-52x52in) s.
£25381 $50000   (3-Oct-90 SY.NY100/R) Composition 28 (111x110cm-44x43in) s. l.stretcher
£28112 $47229   (24-Apr-91 G.Z17/R) Trombino (62x88cm-24x35in) d.1918/20 s.i.verso
           (S.FR 70000)
£1160   *$2274*   *(24-Nov-90 VG.B426/R) Butzenbuck (30x22cm-12x9in) s. W/C indian ink*
           brush gouache htd.white (DM 3400)
£1433   *$2810*   *(24-Nov-90 VG.B425/R) Ich kusse nicht Ihre Hand, Madame (33x24cm-13x9in)*
           s. chl (DM 4200)
£1523   *$3000*   *(13-Nov-90 CE.NY288/R) Komposition abstrakt (33x20cm-13x8in) s. i.verso*
           pen ink crayon
£1795   *$3500*   *(10-Oct-90 SY.NY190/R) Seated cubist woman. Cubist couple dancing.*
           Cubist construction (251x251cm-99x99in) one init. st.studio verso
           pencil set of three
£1929   *$3800*   *(13-Nov-90 CE.NY220/R) Das Paar (41x31cm-16x12in) s. brush pen ink*
           gouache col.chk
£7755   *$15278*   *(16-Nov-90 EA.Z344/R) Curioso (50x36cm-20x14in) s. mixed media collage*
           (S.FR 19000)

BAUERLE, Carl Wilhelm Friedrich (1831-1912) German
£1701 $3010   (22-Mar-91 GRA.B2581/R) Young girl with poppies in cornfield
           (43x53cm-17x21in) s. (DM 5000)
£2594   *$4229*   *(1-Jul-91 AAA.S111) Springtime, Europa and a bull (80x100cm-31x39in)*
           s.d.'81 (A.D 5500)
£47688 $82500   (22-May-91 SY.NY87/R) Cecile and Adela, children of George Drummond, Esq
           (126x103cm-50x41in) s.d.84 i.stretcher

BAUERMEISTER, Mary (1934-) German
£2179 $4250   (10-Oct-90 SY.NY492/R) *Introverted tools (38x38cm-15x15in) s.i.d.verso mixed media assemblage*

BAUERNFEIND, Gustav (1848-1904) Austrian
£15000 $24600   (21-Jun-91 C101/R) Back street, Jaffa (29x45cm-11x18in) s.d.82 panel

BAUGIN, Lubin (school) (1610-1663) French
£2008 $3233   (27-Jun-91 APT.P172/R) Vierge a l'Enfant (22x16cm-9x6in) panel (F.FR 20000)

BAUGNIET, Charles (1814-1886) Flemish
£5128 $10000   (24-Oct-90 CH.NY264/R) Memories (72x60cm-28x24in) s. panel

BAUGNIET, Marcel Louis (1896-?) Belgian
£900   *$1512*   *(23-Apr-91 C.A294) Composition (15x30cm-6x12in) s.d.1930 W/C (B.FR 55000)*

BAUM, Carl (1812-1877) American
£3046 $6000   (16-Nov-90 S.BM61/R) Formal still life with fruits and bird's nest (74x61cm-29x24in) mono. oval
£3352 $6000   (14-Mar-91 CH.NY20/R) Still life with nest and eggs (74x61cm-29x24in) init.
£3352 $6000   (14-Mar-91 CH.NY19/R) Fruits of earth (102x76cm-40x30in) s.

BAUM, Paul (1859-1932) German
£22843 $45000   (2-Oct-90 CH.NY75/R) Landschaft (51x62cm-20x24in) s.
£29371 $56685   (12-Dec-90 WE.MU199/R) Landscape, early spring (50x62cm-20x24in) s. (DM 84000)
£1164   *$1898*   *(15-Jun-91 L.K37/R) Tree on hill by path to sea shore (18x26cm-7x10in) s.d.1910 indian ink pen (DM 3400)*

BAUM, Paul (attrib) (1859-1932) German
£845 $1605   (14-Sep-90 SA.A1410/R) Painter in wooded landscape (28x19cm-11x7in) canvas on panel (DM 2500)

BAUM, Walter Emerson (1884-1956) American
£1638 $2900   (22-Mar-91 S.W2877/R) Fishing in mountain stream s.d.1941
£1734 $3000   (21-May-91 CE.NY591/R) Autumn in Pennsylvania (41x51cm-16x20in) s. canvasboard
£2123 $3800   (14-Mar-91 CH.NY102/R) Winter scene. Lessig's school (28x35cm-11x14in) s. one masonite one board pair
£6704 $12000   (14-Mar-91 CH.NY89 a/R) Lafayette Hill (34x41cm-13x16in) s. board
£621   *$1100*   *(22-Mar-91 S.W2487/R) Winter landscape with stream (36x56cm-14x22in) s. W/C gouache*

BAUMANN, Elisabeth Jerichau see JERICHAU-BAUMANN, Elisabeth

BAUMEISTER, Johann Wilhelm (1804-1846) German
£6020 $10174   (19-Apr-91 FN.S1665/R) Horses gallopping in hilly landscape (40x49cm-16x19in) mono. i.verso (DM 18000)
£6643 $12888   (4-Dec-90 FN.S1748/R) Horses gallopping on road in landscape (40x49cm-16x19in) mono. i.verso (DM 19000)

BAUMEISTER, Willi (1889-1955) German
£4576 $7642   (6-Jun-91 HN.H126/R) Landscape and figure (34x25cm-13x10in) s.d.1912 verso (DM 13500)
£23649 $40203   (30-May-91 SY.BE41/R) Bather in front of red surface (37x51cm-15x20in) s.i.d.1930verso (DM 70000)
£29831 $49817   (7-Jun-91 HN.H5/R) Orbis pictus (64x61cm-25x24in) s.d.1949 board (DM 88000)
£40541 $68919   (31-May-91 VG.B54/R) Belebte Halde (27x45cm-11x18in) s.i.d.1945 board (DM 120000)
£47458 $79254   (7-Jun-91 HN.H3/R) Grey figure on wine red (53x64cm-21x25in) s.d.1947 board (DM 140000)
£47782 $93652   (23-Nov-90 VG.B69/R) African spirits with blue (30x40cm-12x16in) c.1947 board (DM 140000)
£51195 $100341   (23-Nov-90 VG.B70/R) Safer 6, with figure (35x25cm-14x10in) s.d.1954 oil sand board (DM 150000)
£61433 $120410   (23-Nov-90 VG.B68/R) Tableau chaud (35x43cm-14x17in) s.d.1949 s.st.studio i.d.verso (DM 180000)
£64189 $109122   (31-May-91 VG.B56/R) Rendez-vous on pink (45x53cm-18x21in) s.d.1948 i.d.verso panel (DM 190000)
£87838 $149324   (31-May-91 VG.B55 a/R) Sabiha (36x50cm-14x20in) s.i.d.1951 board (DM 260000)
£94595 $160811   (31-May-91 VG.B50/R) Laufer mit stehender Figur (54x65cm-21x26in) s.verso s.i.d.1934stretcher oil sand (DM 280000)
£139932 $274266   (23-Nov-90 VG.B71/R) Ours noir (65x54cm-26x21in) s.d.52/53 i.d.verso panel (DM 410000)
£209459 $356081   (31-May-91 VG.B55/R) Montaru, Amorph (65x81cm-26x32in) s.d.53 s.i.d.verso oil casein panel (DM 620000)
£1297   *$2542*   *(24-Nov-90 VG.B427/R) Female head. Reclining nude (20x20cm-8x8in) mono.d.1923/24 pencil chl double-sided (DM 3800)*
£1587   *$2603*   *(19-Jun-91 GK.B182) Shapes (14x29cm-6x11in) s.d.1943 frottage (S.FR 4000)*

BAUMEISTER, Willi (1889-1955) German-cont.

£2397	$3908	(15-Jun-91 L.K41/R) Composition with lines (33x51cm-13x20in) chl col.chk (DM 7000)
£3220	$5378	(6-Jun-91 HN.H127/R) Memories of Susa (23x34cm-9x13in) mono.d.1946 chl. (DM 9500)
£3378	$5743	(1-Jun-91 VG.B329/R) Dance of Salome (33x48cm-13x19in) s. chl grease chk (DM 10000)
£5000	$8850	(21-Mar-91 S101/R) Linienfiguren im dialog (31x43cm-12x17in) s.d.46 chl
£5000	$8650	(10-May-91 S.Z4/R) Composition (16x24cm-6x9in) s.d.1945 chl (S.FR 12500)
£6081	$10338	(1-Jun-91 VG.B432/R) Untitled (24x30cm-9x12in) s.d.1950 W/C over pencil (DM 18000)
£6897	$13241	(26-Nov-90 WK.M110) Storm XLI (22x33cm-9x13in) i.d.1943 chl (DM 20000)
£7509	$14717	(24-Nov-90 VG.B362/R) Game of skittles and swing (26x49cm-10x19in) s. graphite chk (DM 22000)
£8784	$14932	(1-Jun-91 VG.B331/R) Urzeitgestalten. Parallele Streifen und Kreissegmente (25x36cm-10x14in) s.d.47 s.d.44verso chl ink board double-sided (DM 26000)
£9556	$18730	(24-Nov-90 VG.B361/R) Relief mit schwebender Form (48x31cm-19x12in) s.d.48 chl (DM 28000)
£11034	$21186	(28-Nov-90 KF.M544 a/R) Figures s.d.1944 grease chk pastel (DM 32000)
£17808	$29027	(15-Jun-91 L.K38/R) Aus Esther (28x48cm-11x19in) s.d.46 gouache chl (DM 52000)

BAUMER, Eduard (1892-1977) German

£1093	$2121	(6-Dec-90 D.V69/R) Bunch of flowers with marguerites and lilies (61x43cm-24x17in) s.d.1936 chl W/C (A.S 22000)

BAUMGARTNER, A (19/20th C) ?

£2000	$3940	(4-Oct-90 CSK181/R) The chariot race (70x105cm-28x41in) s.

BAUMGARTNER, H (19th C) German

£867	$1500	(21-May-91 CE.NY189/R) House in mountains (41x57cm-16x22in) s.d.1859
£2341	$3957	(17-Apr-91 WE.MU110/R) Figures resting by banks of river (95x68cm-37x27in) s.d.1849 (DM 7000)

BAUMGARTNER, Johann Wolfgang (1712-1761) German

£676	$1149	(31-May-91 GB.B5426/R) Crucifixion (13x9cm-5x4in) pen wash (DM 2000)

BAUMGARTNER, Johann Wolfgang (attrib) (1712-1761) Austrian

£1748	$3374	(12-Dec-90 WE.MU27/R) Choosing the Diciples (32x22cm-13x9in) canvas on board (DM 5000)
£1748	$3374	(12-Dec-90 WE.MU26/R) Walking over the Water (31x22cm-12x9in) canvas on board (DM 5000)

BAUMGARTNER, Karl (1898-1981) Swiss

£1224	$2400	(6-Nov-90 GF.L2523/R) Landscape near Lungern (32x46cm-13x18in) s.i.d.1940verso (S.FR 3000)

BAUMGARTNER, Peter (1834-1911) German

£10000	$16400	(21-Jun-91 C63/R) St. Martin's goose (76x93cm-30x37in) s.d.1869
£13546	$23299	(14-May-91 GF.L2098/R) Married couple preparing haircut (26x22cm-10x9in) s.d.1872 panel (S.FR 34000)
£15385	$30000	(23-Oct-90 SY.NY33/R) Der erhorte Bittgang, eine Prozession vom Regen uberrascht (142x127cm-56x50in) s.
£25418	$42957	(17-Apr-91 WE.MU241/R) The fulfilled pilgrimage (143x122cm-56x48in) s. (DM 76000)

BAUMGARTNER, Thomas (1892-1962) German

£727	$1193	(18-Jun-91 VN.R16) Two Orientals (110x96cm-43x38in) s.d.1917 (D.FL 2400)
£2560	$5017	(24-Nov-90 N.M43/R) Portrait of young peasant girl (27x26cm-11x10in) s.d.1919 panel (DM 7500)

BAUMONT, Pierre (attrib) (1719-1774) French

£1500	$2535	(18-Apr-91 C158) A cavalryman by an encampment with landscape and town beyond (48x65cm-19x26in)

BAUQUIER, Georges (1910-) French

£1069	$1893	(4-Apr-91 CK.P29) Nature morte aux fruits, couteau, verre et bouteille de vin (51x65cm-20x26in) s.d. (F.FR 10800)

BAUR, Johann Wilhelm (1607-c.1640) Austrian

£653	$1071	(18-Jun-91 APT.P9) Scene de bataille (10x15cm-4x6in) i. pen wash (F.FR 6500)
£12847	$24923	(7-Dec-90 SY.MO137/R) Scenes de batailles (10x17cm-4x7in) gouache pen pair (F.FR 125000)
£28000	$45640	(1-Jul-91 S25/R) Capriccio quayside scenes - conducting business on wharves. Unloading ships (13x21cm-5x8in) s.d.1641 gouache over pen vellum on panel pair

BAUR, Johann Wilhelm (attrib) (1607-c.1640) Austrian

£1397	$2500	(10-Apr-91 HF.NY28/R) View of Italian square (6x9cm-2x4in) gouache

BAUR, Johannes Antonius (18th C) Dutch

£765	$1476	(10-Dec-90 BL.P1) La degustation d'huitres (26x21cm-10x8in) W/C vellum (F.FR 7500)

BAWDEN, Edward (1903-1989) British
£1500 $2820   (18-Sep-90 PH187/R) Coronation (44x29cm-17x11in) s.d.1953 num.3 pen W/C
                              gouache over pencil
£2500 $4350   (27-Mar-91 S142/R) Westleton quarry (44x55cm-17x22in) s.d.1948 W/C
                              gouache over pen ink
£4800 $9360   (10-Oct-90 S139/R) Brick house (44x56cm-17x22in) s.d.1955 gouache pen
                              ink
£5000 $8350   (6-Jun-91 C232 a/R) Thatching (44x56cm-17x22in) s.d.1955 s.i.verso W/C
                              pen ink col.crayon

BAXTER, Charles (1809-1879) British
£1100 $1793   (13-Jun-91 CSK310) Peggy and Jenny (18x19cm-7x7in) indist.s.i.d.1851
                              verso board
£2100 $3759   (10-Apr-91 CSK251/R) Country beauty (76x64cm-30x25in)

BAY SALA (?) Spanish
£2033 $3964   (17-Oct-90 FER.M226/R) El puente nuevo de Paris (48x56cm-19x22in) s.
                              (S.P 375000)

BAYARD, Emile Antoine (1837-1891) French
£2245 $4422   (14-Nov-90 FB.P103/R) Scene galante (46x38cm-18x15in) s.d.1883
                              (F.FR 22000)
£2245 $4422   (14-Nov-90 FB.P49/R) Modele pour la couverture du journal de Nadar,
                              Paris Photographie (22x15cm-9x6in) s. mixed media (F.FR 22000)

BAYER, Anton (19th C) Austrian
£1941 $3668   (27-Sep-90 D.V73/R) Pond landscape with hunter (63x94cm-25x37in)
                              s.d.1858 (A.S 40000)

BAYER, Herbert (1900-) German
£1000 $1610   (24-Jun-91 CSK207/R) Surrealist composition (21x29cm-8x11in) s.d.39 W/C
                              pencil

BAYER, Hermann (1829-1893) German
£1190 $2107   (20-Mar-91 KM.K1093) Sleeping peasant woman seated before house and
                              birds pinching food (66x54cm-26x21in) mono.d.63 (DM 3500)

BAYERLEIN, Fritz (1872-?) German
£1400 $2506   (12-Apr-91 BM.B556/R) Nymphenburger Park (65x50cm-26x20in) s. i.verso
                              board (DM 4200)

BAYES, Alfred Walter (19th C) British
£808 $1358   (23-Apr-91 SY.AM296/R) Market day (70x90cm-28x35in) s. (D.FL 2700)

BAYES, Walter (19/20th C) British
£1350 $2295   (29-May-91 ZZ.B161) Boulogne street scene (44x53cm-17x21in) init.

BAYEU Y SUBIAS, Francisco (attrib) (1734-1795) Spanish
£7059 $12000   (30-May-91 SY.NY70/R) Immaculate conception (17x13cm-7x5in) on copper
                              oval

BAYLISS, Sir Wyke (1835-1906) British
£850 $1666   (20-Nov-90 PH197/R) Light in the West Lyons Cathedral (97x123cm-38x48in)
                              s. i. label verso
£2800 $5600   (8-Feb-91 C82/R) Milan cathedral (46x69cm-18x27in) s.i. pencil W/C gum
                              arabic

BAYNES, Frederick Thomas (19th C) British
£410 $693   (30-Apr-91 AG110) Still life study of grapes and pineapple
                              (25x21cm-10x8in) s. W/C
£480 $826   (14-May-91 SWS86) Spring bank (23x17cm-9x7in) s. W/C gouache
£540 $929   (14-May-91 SWS87/R) Still life study of grapes and other fruit in basket
                              (27x27cm-11x11in) s. W/C gouache
£1050 $1806   (14-May-91 SWS85/R) Still life with primroses and bird's nest
                              (18x27cm-7x11in) s. bodycol

BAYNES, James (1766-1837) British
£1100 $2156   (15-Feb-91 CBB256) Llangynned Lake, North Wales (43x61cm-17x24in) s. W/C

BAYROS, Franz von (1866-1924) Austrian
£845 $1436   (28-May-91 KF.M137/R) Erotic scene (43x38cm-17x15in) s. W/C chk
                              (DM 2500)
£1800 $3456   (28-Nov-90 S229/R) Design for bookplate for Vera Katherine Henriette von
                              Rosenberg (45x39cm-18x15in) s. pencil
£2440 $4514   (7-Mar-91 D.V102/R) Faun laughing (32x28cm-13x11in) s. pen indian ink
                              W/C htd.white (A.S 50000)

BAYROS, Franz von (attrib) (1866-1924) Austrian
£405 $689   (28-May-91 KF.M138) Erotic scene (23x21cm-9x8in) pencil board
                              (DM 1200)

BAZAINE, Jean (1904-?) French
£10000 $17700   (21-Mar-91 C205/R) Neige (15x30cm-6x12in) s.d.64 i. verso
£13814 $23898   (23-May-91 SY.AM263/R) La biche au bois (55x32cm-22x13in) s.d.50
                              (D.FL 46000)

BAZAINE, Jean (1904-?) French-cont.
| £556 | $935 | (23-Apr-91 C.A295) Grimpeur de corde (32x18cm-13x7in) s. ink dr. (B.FR 34000) |

£556 $935   (23-Apr-91 C.A295) Grimpeur de corde (32x18cm-13x7in) s. ink dr.
(B.FR 34000)
£789 $1554   (1-Oct-90 CC.P4) Arbres (17x21cm-7x8in) s.d.1945 pen Indian ink
(F.FR 8000)
£4184 $8242   (16-Nov-90 FB.P23/R) Arbres et buissons (34x52cm-13x20in) s.d.44 W/C
(F.FR 41000)
£4778 $9365   (24-Nov-90 VG.B331/R) Untitled (24x11cm-9x4in) s.d.1952 gouache
(DM 14000)

BAZILE, Castera (1932-1965) Haitian
£7653 $15000   (19-Nov-90 SY.NY308/R) Judgement day (61x51cm-24x20in) s.d.16-11-50
masonite

BAZIOTES, William (1912-1963) American
£7738 $13000   (24-Apr-91 B.SF4626/R) Phantom (28x36cm-11x14in) s. acrylic board
£1077 $2100   (10-Oct-90 SY.NY554/R) Untitled (15x23cm-6x9in) s. gouache
£8122 $16000   (4-Oct-90 SY.NY2/R) Figure in net (46x30cm-18x12in) s. s.d.1947 verso
W/C ink pastel
£16272 $27500   (1-May-91 SY.NY180/R) Night forms (50x37cm-20x15in) s. W/C pencil

BAZZANI, Giuseppe (circle) (1690-1769) Italian
£2564 $5000   (10-Oct-90 CH.NY46/R) The Raising of Lazarus (150x131cm-59x52in)
£3700 $7178   (7-Dec-90 SY.MO120/R) Le Christ se rendant a Emmaus (59x62cm-23x24in)
(F.FR 36000)

BAZZANI, Luigi (1836-1927) Italian
£1698 $3210   (27-Sep-90 D.V188/R) Canal scene, Venice (69x45cm-27x18in) s.
(A.S 35000)
£501 $852   (28-May-91 F.R63) Cortile romano (24x14cm-9x6in) s.d.1873 W/C
(I.L 1100000)
£1458 $2479   (28-May-91 F.R92/R) Veduta di Anticoli Corrado (20x34cm-8x13in) s. W/C
(I.L 3200000)

BAZZANTI, L (19/20th C) Italian
£1011 $1900   (18-Sep-90 RO.BA384) Cesta con flores (60x85cm-24x33in) s.

BAZZARO, Leonardo (1853-1937) Italian
£2736 $4570   (6-Jun-91 F.M227) Figure sul prato (35x50cm-14x20in) s. panel
(I.L 6000000)
£3192 $5331   (6-Jun-91 F.M276/R) Acquaiola (49x33cm-19x13in) s. panel (I.L 7000000)
£3235 $6243   (11-Dec-90 CH.R189/R) Paesaggio montano con contadina (30x43cm-12x17in)
i. s.verso board (I.L 7000000)
£3420 $5712   (6-Jun-91 F.M277/R) Vecchia chioggia (34x55cm-13x22in) s. panel
(I.L 7500000)
£3716 $6280   (3-May-91 SA.A802/R) Mother and children in a fishing harbour
(41x66cm-16x26in) s. (DM 11000)
£5910 $11583   (22-Nov-90 SY.MI76/R) Chioggia (34x50cm-13x20in) s. panel
(I.L 13000000)
£6000 $11000   (18-Oct-90 F.M29/R) Rattoppi alla vela, Chioggia (39x59cm-15x23in) s.
s.i.verso panel (I.L 13000000)

BAZZI, Giovanni Antonio (circle) (1477-1549) Italian
£14359 $28000   (11-Oct-90 SY.NY19/R) Holy family with St John the Baptist
(69cm-27ins circular) panel

BAZZICALUVA, Ercole (17th C) Italian
£1400 $2702   (11-Dec-90 C32/R) The prodigal son feeding the swine (25x38cm-10x15in)
i. ink

BEACH, Thomas (1738-1806) British
£1400 $2310   (10-Jul-91 S130/R) Portrait of George John Audley, merchant of
Liverpool, standing (124x99cm-49x39in) s.d.1793
£1900 $3743   (31-Oct-90 S302/R) Portraits of two officers of the Grimston Yeomanry
Cavalry (99x99cm-39x39in) s.d.1789 painted ovals pair
£3500 $6895   (16-Nov-90 C28/R) Portrait of Reginald Pearch in green jacket with white
stock (76x63cm-30x25in) s.d.1788 painted oval
£7800 $14820   (1-Mar-91 C13/R) Portrait of young girl standing holding basket of roses
in landscape (98x75cm-39x30in)
£400 $708   (20-Mar-91 C113) Portrait of Roger Kemble (5x?cm-2x?in) min. gold frame
oval

BEACH, Thomas (attrib) (1738-1806) British
£1400 $2590   (7-Mar-91 D98/R) Portrait of gentleman wearing naval uniform, possibly
of Gould family (74x61cm-29x24in)

BEACH, Warren (1914-) American
£660 $1300   (18-Nov-90 JRB.C161/R) Hitchhiker (109x58cm-43x23in) init.d.38

BEADLE, James Princep (1863-1947) British
£950 $1862   (13-Feb-91 S7/R) Fishing boats, Scheveningen Beach (42x58cm-17x23in) s.

BEAL, Reynolds (1867-1951) American
£6358 $11000   (22-May-91 CH.NY270/R) Boats in harbour (61x76cm-24x30in) s.d.1939
stretcher

BEAL, Reynolds (1867-1951) American-cont.
£11111 $21000   (26-Sep-90 SY.NY160/R) Provincetown Harbour (56x76cm-22x30in) s.d.1916
     i.verso board
£12426 $21000   (1-May-91 B.SF5111/R) Afternoon in seaside village (74x91cm-29x36in)
     s.d.1922
£750 $1500   *(7-Feb-91 B.P45/R) Circus scene (20x25cm-8x10in) s.d.1922 W/C*
£867 $1500   *(10-May-91 S.BM111/R) Gorman Brothers Circus (28x43cm-11x17in)*
     s.i.d.1936 W/C graphite
£1105 $1900   *(19-May-91 LIT.L82) Great circus scene with early touring car and*
     American flags (28x33cm-11x13in) s. crayon W/C
£1156 $2000   *(21-May-91 GRO.B172/R) Sells Floto circus, Salem (33x51cm-13x20in)*
     s.d.1929 col.pencil
£1162 $2300   *(30-Jan-91 GRO.B93/R) The circus (38x48cm-15x19in) s.i.d.1936*
     col.crayons
£1163 $2000   *(15-May-91 SY.NY221/R) Circus (29x38cm-11x15in) s.d.1915 chl pastel W/C*
£1230 $2300   *(1-Aug-90 B.P32/R) Gorham Brothers Circus (36x46cm-14x18in) s.d.1936 W/C*
     pencil
£1350 $2700   *(7-Feb-91 B.P40/R) Sparks Circus, Gloucester, Massachussetts*
     (36x46cm-14x18in) s.d.1930 crayon
£2246 $4200   *(1-Aug-90 B.P33/R) Downey Brothers Circus (36x48cm-14x19in) s.d.1934 W/C*

BEALE, Charles (1660-?) British
£600 $990   *(11-Jul-91 S42/R) Portrait study of man's face (13x12cm-5x5in) W/C*
     htd.white
£4400 $7260   *(11-Jul-91 S25/R) Portrait of boy (16x12cm-6x5in) chk ink vellum*

BEALE, Mary (1632-1697) British
£1333 $2600   (10-Oct-90 CH.NY204/R) Portrait of gentleman wearing jacket with lace
     cravat (76x63cm-30x25in) painted cartouche
£2000 $3300   (10-Jul-91 S106/R) Portrait of Anne Hyde Duchess of York wearing dress
     decorated with pearls (74x60cm-29x24in) bears i.stretcher oval
£950 $1682   *(19-Mar-91 CSK55/R) Portrait of lady wearing white dress with frilled*
     trim (8x?cm-3x?in) min. shaped tortoiseshell frame oval

BEALE, Mary (attrib) (1632-1697) British
£1100 $2145   (22-Oct-90 SWS1326) Portrait of lady wearing dress and pearls
     (74x61cm-29x24in) painted cartouche

BEAMAN, Waldo Gamaliel (1852-1937) American
£1297 $2400   (8-Mar-91 S.BM150) River view (61x91cm-24x36in) s.d.'80

BEAR, George Telfer (1874-?) British
£550 $924   (23-Apr-91 S159) Still life of flowers in glass vase (61x51cm-24x20in)
     s.
£800 $1600   (5-Feb-91 S200/R) Summer flowers (76x64cm-30x25in) s. s.i.stretcher

BEARD, William Holbrook (1824-1900) American
£1596 $3000   (22-Sep-90 WOL.C153/R) Round and round they went (61x46cm-24x18in)
     s.d.1892

BEARDEN, Romare (1914-) American
£7614 $15000   (15-Nov-90 D.NY13/R) Down home back porch trio (74x101cm-29x40in) s.
     paper
£6122   *$12000*   *(7-Nov-90 SY.NY226/R) The tidings (18x23cm-7x9in) s. paper collage board*
£7653 $15000   *(8-Nov-90 CH.NY143/R) Storyville (39x51cm-15x20in) s. acrylic lacquer*
     collage panel
£11168 $22000   *(5-Oct-90 CH.NY63/R) Constellation of the archer (91x103cm-36x41in) i.*
     oil paper collage masonite

BEARDSLEY, Aubrey (1872-1898) British
£8097 $15870   *(21-Nov-90 CB.P24/R) Au bout de l'Abine (30x21cm-12x8in) s. Indian ink*
     (F.FR 80000)

BEARE, George (attrib) (18th C) British
£4000 $7160   *(10-Apr-91 S105/R) Portrait of girl, in blue dress and cap*
     (44x32cm-17x13in)

BEATON, Sir Cecil (1904-1980) British
£780   *$1498*   *(21-Feb-91 B248/R) First Shoot (47x31cm-19x12in) s. W/C pen htd white*
£800   *$1288*   *(28-Jun-91 CSK125/R) Costume design for Les Illuminations*
     (25x20cm-10x8in) s.i. pen W/C
£1500   *$2955*   *(1-Nov-90 TE589/R) Ascot costumes VIII (46x30cm-18x12in) s. pencil W/C*
     htd white
£3400   *$5916*   *(27-Mar-91 S137/R) Between watches (24x38cm-9x15in) s. pen ink wash*

BEATTIE, A (19th C) British
£1000 $1900   (28-Feb-91 B93) View of Northwick Park, Worcestershire
     (107x154cm-42x61in) s.i.d.1852 verso

BEATTY, John William (1869-1941) American?
£808 $1398   (6-May-91 SY.T138/R) Willows, Port Hope (22x26cm-9x10in) s. board
     (C.D 1600)
£811 $1322   (10-Jun-91 W.T1053 a) Cattle on a farm (28x35cm-11x14in) s.d.06
     (C.D 1500)
£859 $1477   (14-May-91 JOY.T150/R) Small village in countryside (16x24cm-6x9in) s.
     panel (C.D 1700)

BEATTY, John William (1869-1941) American?-cont.
£909 $1564   (14-May-91 JOY.T127/R) Farm buildings overlooking a lake
                   (26x33cm-10x13in) s. panel (C.D 1800)
£1010 $1747   (6-May-91 SY.T1) Early spring (21x27cm-8x11in) s. i.verso panel
                   (C.D 2000)
£1136 $1966   (6-May-91 SY.T177/R) Landscape with bridge (25x30cm-10x12in) s.
                   (C.D 2250)
£1946 $3172   (10-Jun-91 W.T1093) Toronto Harbour (38x56cm-15x22in) s.d. board
                   (C.D 3600)

BEAU, Alcide le (1872-1943) French
£4842 $9345   (16-Dec-90 T.B153/R) Bord de mer en Bretagne (30x41cm-12x16in) s.
                   (F.FR 47500)

BEAUBRUN (studio) (16/17th C) French
£3651 $7010   (21-Dec-90 DAR.P57/R) Portrit d'une dame de qualite tenant un petit
                   chien (74x61cm-29x24in) oval (F.FR 36000)

BEAUBRUN (style) (16/17th C) French
£1014 $2008   (30-Jan-91 APT.P132/R) Portrait de femme au collier (85x54cm-33x21in)
                   oval (F.FR 10000)

BEAUBRUN, Charles (attrib) (1604-1692) French
£6000 $11820   (31-Oct-90 S158/R) Portrait of King Louis XIV and the Duc D'Orleans
                   (133x98cm-52x39in)

BEAUBRUN, Charles and Henri (studio) (17th C) French
£3300 $5379   (3-Jul-91 PLF.P44/R) Portrait de la Grande Mademoiselle, assise, enrobe
                   grise (115x92cm-45x36in) (F.FR 33000)

BEAUCLERK, Lady Diana (1734-1808) British
£1600 $3088   (12-Dec-90 GC251/R) Sarah King, wife of Bishop Walker King of Rochester,
                   landscape beyond (91x71cm-36x28in)

BEAUDIN, Andre (1895-1979) French
£2224 $4338   (17-Oct-90 ARC.P61/R) Flkeurs sauvages (46x33cm-18x13in) s.d.1973
                   (F.FR 22000)
£2399 $4605   (27-Nov-90 BU.S27/R) La nuit (35x27cm-14x11in) s.d.1936 (S.KR 26000)
£3200 $5152   (24-Jun-91 CSK169/R) Deux personnages (38x46cm-15x18in) s.d.1936
£3815 $6143   (24-Jun-91 ARC.P34/R) La bayadere (55x33cm-22x13in) s.d.1926
                   (F.FR 38000)
£4020 $6593   (20-Jun-91 APT.P52/R) Le fumeur (46x38cm-18x15in) s.d.1929 (F.FR 40000)
£7455 $12599   (17-Apr-91 CB.P44/R) L'homme au poisson (100x65cm-39x26in) s.d.1925
                   (F.FR 75000)
£9045 $16191   (17-Mar-91 GL.P39/R) Le regard (81x100cm-32x39in) s.d.1947 (F.FR 90000)
£11055 $18131   (20-Jun-91 APT.P45/R) Apres le dejeuner (100x65cm-39x26in) s.d.1925
                   (F.FR 110000)
£811 $1606   (3-Feb-91 I.N16) Composition (23x27cm-9x11in) W/C (F.FR 8000)

BEAUDUIN, Jean (1851-1916) Belgian
£750 $1478   (4-Oct-90 CSK143/R) A young woman tending her garden (26x34cm-10x13in)
                   s.
£1842 $3500   (27-Feb-91 SY.NY9/R) Peasant girl seated in garden (60x72cm-24x28in) s.
£2105 $4000   (14-Sep-90 DM.D2014/R) Young girl sitting on bundle of wheat in setting
                   overlooking farmland (36x46cm-14x18in) s. panel
£2296 $4500   (12-Feb-91 SY.NY35 a/R) Un coin de mon jardin au soleil
                   (58x74cm-23x29in) s. s.i.d.1901stretcher

BEAUFEU, Pierre A (19/20th C) French
£898 $1742   (8-Dec-90 GAB.G2108/R) L'arlequin au baton (81x66cm-32x26in) s.
                   (S.FR 2200)

BEAUFRERE, Adolphe (1876-1960) French
£1935 $3812   (29-Oct-90 CSC.P57/R) Petite bretonne gardant les vaches (13x12cm-5x5in)
                   st.init. board laid down on canvas (F.FR 19000)
£3262 $6296   (16-Dec-90 T.B265/R) L'Adieu du marin (42x36cm-17x14in) init. board
                   (F.FR 32000)
£3870 $7623   (29-Oct-90 CSC.P114/R) Le port de Cassis (12x17cm-5x7in) st.sig.
                   peinture a l'essence paper laid canvas (F.FR 38000)
£4279 $7402   (12-May-91 T.B72/R) Le Passeur (24x22cm-9x9in) s. panel (F.FR 43000)
£5097 $9837   (16-Dec-90 T.B88/R) La Laita a maree basse (29x28cm-11x11in) s. panel
                   (F.FR 50000)
£6006 $10390   (23-May-91 SY.AM41/R) Les Jardins du Luxembourg (45x62cm-18x24in)
                   (D.FL 20000)
£6524 $12591   (16-Dec-90 T.B87/R) Paysage a la maison et au cheval (37x39cm-15x15in)
                   studio st. paper laid down (F.FR 64000)
£495 $876   (7-Apr-91 I.N37) Calanque en Bretagne (10x10cm-4x4in) s. pen (F.FR 5000)
£663 $1279   (16-Dec-90 T.B66) Lamor plage (13x16cm-5x6in) studio st. crayon drawing
*   (F.FR 6500)*
£815 $1605   (29-Oct-90 CSC.P66) Le port et le phare de Cassis (11x9cm-4x4in)
*   st.init. htd.drawing (F.FR 8000)*

BEAULIEU, Georges (?) French
£1003 $1956   (12-Oct-90 ZZ.F21) La chasse aux canards (45x63cm-18x25in) s.
                   (F.FR 10000)

BEAULIEU, Paul Vanier (1910-) Canadian
£2020 $3495   (6-May-91 SY.T30/R) Still life with pear and plums (26x34cm-10x13in) s.d.55 (C.D 4000)
£2412 $4752   (30-Oct-90 SY.T138/R) Afternoon (59x72cm-23x28in) s.d.49 s.verso (C.D 5500)
£4293 $7427   (6-May-91 SY.T144/R) Still life with fruit (63x79cm-25x31in) s.d.57 (C.D 8500)
£7018 $13825   (30-Oct-90 SY.T32/R) Harlequin playing chess (100x72cm-39x28in) s.d.54 (C.D 16000)
£490 $868   (20-Mar-91 EA.M487) Autumn landscape (48x62cm-19x24in) s.d.71 W/C (C.D 1000)
£568 $1113   (5-Nov-90 FB.M40) Tete de Harlequin (36x25cm-14x10in) s.d.1954 mixed media (C.D 1300)
£882 $1562   (20-Mar-91 EA.M480 a) Chateaux (50x65cm-20x26in) s.d.69 W/C (C.D 1800)

BEAUMONT, Arthur J (1877-1956) American
£670 $1300   (24-Aug-90 RB.HY252/R) Gloucester Harbor (30x41cm-12x16in) s.
£798 $1500   (11-Aug-91 COL.M184/R) Pigeon Cove, Cape Ann (25x25cm-10x10in) s. board

BEAUMONT, Auguste Bouthillier de (1842-1899) German
£1224 $2376   (8-Dec-90 GAB.G2109/R) Sous-bois de la campagne genevoise (56x46cm-22x18in) s.d.1878 canvas laid down on panel (S.FR 3000)
£2390 $4112   (14-May-91 GF.L2094/R) North Italian river landscape (41x72cm-16x28in) s.d.1882 (S.FR 6000)

BEAUMONT, Claudio Francesco (1694-1766) Italian
£1003 $1776   (19-Mar-91 F.M285/R) Studio di figura maschile (34x22cm-13x9in) black and white chk (I.L 2200000)

BEAUMONT, Claudio Francesco (circle) (1694-1766) Italian
£4800 $9264   (11-Dec-90 PH201/R) Venus and Cupid (75x101cm-30x40in)
£11401 $19040   (4-Jun-91 CH.R331/R) Giove e Venere. Marte e Venere (99x104cm-39x41in) pair (I.L 25000000)

BEAUMONT, George Howland (1753-1827) British
£600 $990   (11-Jul-91 S86/R) Lovers surprised by old woman (23x19cm-9x7in) init.d.1798 pen ink wash

BEAUMONT, George Howland (attrib) (1753-1827) British
£970 $1834   (27-Sep-90 D.V142/R) Rocky river landscape (25x39cm-10x15in) (A.S 20000)

BEAUMONT, John Thomas Barber (1774-1841) British
£1000 $1650   (10-Jul-91 C127/R) Mr Howing (7x?cm-3x?in) min.init. gold frame lock of hair verso oval
£2400 $4248   (20-Mar-91 C108/R) Portrait of lady in grey dress. Portrait of man in black coat (8x?cm-3x?in) min.init. gold frame double-sided oval
£4800 $7920   (11-Jul-91 S252/R) Portrait of young negro (6x?cm-2x?in) min.init. gilt metal frame oval

BEAUMONT, R de (?) ?
£4418 $8173   (4-Mar-91 ARC.P86/R) Perroquets et coqs (46x60cm-18x24in) s. (F.FR 44000)

BEAUQUESNE, Wilfrid Constant (1847-1913) French
£2980 $5782   (9-Dec-90 ZZ.F10/R) Le debarquement (65x81cm-26x32in) s. (F.FR 29000)

BEAUVAIS, Armand (1840-1911) French
£7179 $14000   (23-Oct-90 SY.NY253/R) Les glaneuses dans les Chaumes-Berry (79x130cm-31x51in) s.d.75

BEAUVAIS, Walter (20th C) French?
£1000 $1940   (6-Dec-90 CSK95) Trouville (33x51cm-13x20in) board
£1200 $2328   (6-Dec-90 CSK96) Cote d'Azur (37x51cm-15x20in) s. canvas on board

BEAUVERIE, Charles Joseph (1839-1924) French
£668 $1296   (3-Dec-90 CS.L49) Mare a Poirein (46x36cm-18x14in) s. (F.FR 6500)
£1490 $2891   (3-Dec-90 CS.L48/R) Champ de ble (20x40cm-8x16in) s. panel (F.FR 14500)
£1521 $2921   (17-Dec-90 AGS.P16) Diligence sous la neige (81x65cm-32x26in) s.d.1869 (F.FR 15000)

BEAUX, Cecilia (1863-1942) American
£33854 $65000   (30-Nov-90 CH.NY127/R) Dressing dolls (90x74cm-35x29in) s.

BEAVIS, Richard (1824-1896) British
£1868 $3250   (27-Mar-91 B.SF4226/R) Ships off Belem, Lisbon, Portugal (32x36cm-13x14in) s. i.verso
£5200 $10400   (8-Feb-91 K505/R) Thames below Gravesend (53x86cm-21x34in) s.d.1859
£450 $756   (22-Apr-91 PH255) Cow and sheep (16x25cm-6x10in) s.d.63 W/C over pencil

BECCAFUMI, Domenico (1486-1551) Italian
£18000 $30420   (16-Apr-91 C110/R) The head of a bearded man looking to the left (21x17cm-8x7in) watermark red chk.
£32000 $54080   (16-Apr-91 C109/R) The head of a bearded man and a subsidiary study of a man in profile (20x17cm-8x7in) red chk.ink double-sided

BECCAFUMI, Domenico (circle) (1486-1551) Italian
£1000 $1930   *(11-Dec-90 C264) Studies of legs, Angel and a seated woman. Three nudes and two beardedmen (21x14cm-8x6in) blk.chk.ink wash double-sided*

BECCAFUMI, Domenico (style) (1486-1551) Italian
£15000 $28950   (13-Dec-90 B66/R) Holy Family with St. John (67x58cm-26x23in) panel

BECCARIA, Angelo (1820-1897) Italian
£2424 $4776   (30-Oct-90 CH.AM305/R) Shepherds and flock in mountainous Italian landscape. Italian lake with fishermen on bank (30x45cm-12x18in) s.d.1855 board pair (D.FL 8000)

BECH, Poul Anker (20th C) Danish
£704 $1373   (10-Oct-90 RAS.K21) Evening on the beach (105x130cm-41x51in) s.i.verso (D.KR 8000)

BECHI, Luigi (1830-1919) Italian
£3697 $7135   (11-Dec-90 CH.R185/R) Paesaggio toscano (33x41cm-13x16in) s. s.verso board (I.L 8000000)
£12382 $22165   (12-Mar-91 F.M68/R) Pastorella con pecore (50x63cm-20x25in) s. (I.L 27000000)
£16733 $32629   (24-Oct-90 GD.B131/R) The doves, studio interior with little girl in Toscan costume (41x51cm-16x20in) s. (S.FR 42000)

BECHLER, Gustave (1870-?) German
£1138 $2230   (7-Nov-90 N.M833/R) Achensee landscape (56x61cm-22x24in) s.i.d.28 i.verso panel (DM 3300)

BECHSTEIN, Lothar (1884-1936) German
£875 $1514   (6-May-91 ZEL.L1598/R) Landscape with figures, Graubunden (68x93cm-27x37in) s. (DM 2600)

BECHTOLD, J C (18th C) ?
£778 $1316   (2-May-91 CH.AM21) The Madonna and Child enthroned, adored by the infant Saint John the Baptist and other saints (114x76cm-45x30in) s.d.1780 (D.FL 2600)

BECK, Cornelius (19th C) German
£845 $1647   *(26-Oct-90 KM.K1820) Rhine landscape with Rolandsbogen and figures waiting for steam ship (25x44cm-10x17in) s.d.68 W/C (DM 2500)*

BECK, Dunbar D (1902-1986) American
£13873 $24000   *(22-May-91 CH.NY299/R) Lunch break (60x51cm-24x20in) s.d.36 tempera pencil masonite*

BECK, Jacob Samuel (1715-1778) German
£2895 $5500   (11-Jan-91 CH.NY25/R) Melons on ledge (33x39cm-13x15in) s.

BECK, Julia (1853-1935) Swedish
£2688 $5187   (12-Dec-90 BU.S8/R) Landscape from Grez (23x32cm-9x13in) s.i. panel (S.KR 29000)

BECK, Tom (1960-) British
£650 $1274   (13-Feb-91 B161/R) Serenade (101x81cm-40x32in) init.d.89

BECK, Wilhelm (19th C) German
£1347 $2330   (6-May-91 ZEL.L1599/R) Street battle, possible Lothringen, German-French
       War 1870/71 (101x154cm-40x61in) s.i. board (DM 4000)

BECKER, Adolf von (1831-?) Finnish
£4850 $9506   (24-Nov-90 HOR.H46/R) Pears on table (27x35cm-11x14in) s.d.1901
       (F.M 34000)
£106169 $179426   (20-Apr-91 HOR.H38/R) Playing with soap-bubbles (129x90cm-51x35in)
       s.d.1881 (F.M 740000)

BECKER, Albert (1830-1896) German
£946 $1845   (26-Oct-90 KM.K1095) River landscape with farmstead and figures
       (70x81cm-28x32in) s. (DM 2800)
£1149 $2182   (14-Sep-90 SA.A1213/R) Wooded landscape with figures meeting
       (27x36cm-11x14in) mono. (DM 3400)

BECKER, Carl (1862-?) German
£748 $1324   (20-Mar-91 KM.K1096) Fishing boat in choppy sea (80x110cm-31x43in) s.
       (DM 2200)
£1053 $2000   (27-Feb-91 SY.NY170/R) Venetian girl (73x62cm-29x24in) s.d.1879 oval
£8000 $15760   (4-Oct-90 CSK136/R) The lute player (79x112cm-31x44in) s.

BECKER, Curt Georg (1904-1972) German
*£614 $1204   (24-Nov-90 VG.B430/R) Figures in room (48x63cm-19x25in) s.d.1948
       i.d.verso W/C bodycol over chk (DM 1800)*
*£616 $1005   (15-Jun-91 L.K48) Southern landscape (50x63cm-20x25in) s.d.30 W/C over
       pencil board (DM 1800)*

BECKER, Karl (1862-1926) German
£569 $950   (5-Jun-91 D.NY13) Rowing to shore (41x43cm-16x17in) s.i.

BECKER, Michel (20th C) French
£3789 $6251   (10-Jul-91 FB.P121/R) L'orage (73x92cm-29x36in) s. acrylic (F.FR 38000)
£3789 $6251   (10-Jul-91 FB.P122/R) La belle t la bete (65x81cm-26x32in) s.d.88
       acrylic (F.FR 38000)

BECKER-GUNDAHL, Carl Johann (1856-?) German
£4319 $7428   (16-May-91 D.V61/R) Peasant interior with figures (54x72cm-21x28in)
       s.d.92 panel (A.S 90000)

BECKER-TEMPELBURG, Franz (1876-?) German
*£690 $1324   (1-Dec-90 SA.A2410/R) Female nudes in spring landscape (31x47cm-12x19in)
       W/C bodycol (DM 2000)*

BECKETT, Clarice (1887-1935) Australian
£717 $1413   (31-Oct-90 CH.S4) Still life (44x26cm-17x10in) s. (A.D 1800)
£1816 $3215   (18-Mar-91 MGS.S230/R) Still life (44x26cm-17x10in) s. (A.D 4250)
£1931 $3803   (13-Nov-90 J.M155) Port Phillip Mist (32x37cm-13x15in) s. canvas on
       board (A.D 5000)
£2183 $3908   (9-Apr-91 CH.ME177/R) Beach scene (33x43cm-13x17in) s. (A.D 5000)
£2209 $4241   (26-Nov-90 SY.ME182/R) Zinnias (40x49cm-16x19in) s. board (A.D 5500)

BECKMANN, Johann Hans (1809-1882) German
£1061 $2089   (30-Oct-90 CH.AM196) Threatening weather over alpine river valley
       (65x80cm-26x31in) (D.FL 3500)

BECKMANN, Max (1884-1950) German
£200000 $388000   (3-Dec-90 C39 a/R) Heuernte (95x55cm-37x22in) s.d.41
£219595 $373311   (31-May-91 VG.B48/R) Orchestra (89x138cm-35x54in) s.i.d.1932
       (DM 650000)
£307167 $602048   (23-Nov-90 VG.B40/R) Clown (60x40cm-24x16in) s.d.46 (DM 900000)
*£1336 $2177   (15-Jun-91 L.K49/R) Threatening lion (11x19cm-4x7in) s.d.13 chl
       (DM 3900)*
*£1370 $2233   (15-Jun-91 L.K50/R) Zoo visitors before lion cage (14x19cm-6x7in) chl
       (DM 4000)*
*£84746 $141525   (7-Jun-91 HN.H6/R) Reclining figure (54x56cm-21x22in) s.d.1938 W/C over
       chk. (DM 250000)*

BECKWITH, James Carroll (1852-1917) American
£726 $1300   (14-Apr-91 JRB.C97/R) Female nude (23x18cm-9x7in) s.
£1053 $2000   (12-Sep-90 D.NY2) Portrait of woman in purple (61x51cm-24x20in) s.
£3550 $6000   (17-Apr-91 D.NY85) Spanish dancer's glance (36x25cm-14x10in) s.d.1911
£6704 $12000   (14-Mar-91 CH.NY77/R) In yellow light (25x19cm-10x7in) s. panel
£6878 $13000   (27-Sep-90 CH.NY188/R) New Hamburg Gardens (38x45cm-15x18in)

BECQUER, Joaquin (1805-1841) Spanish
*£1600 $2832   (22-Mar-91 PHE28) Portrait of Spanish lady in mantilla (28x19cm-11x7in)
       s.i.d.1833 W/C set of four*
*£2300 $4071   (22-Mar-91 PHE55) Dancing Spanish lady with castenets. Spanish gentlemen
       (28x19cm-11x7in) one s.i.d.1884 W/C set of four*

BECQUER, Valeriano (1834-1870) Spanish
*£437 $843   (11-Dec-90 FER.M17/R) Tipos sorianos (15x20cm-6x8in) s. pencil dr
       (S.P 80000)*

BEDA, Giulio (1879-1954) Italian
£1074 $2094   (10-Oct-90 WE.MU279/R) The actor (16x12cm-6x5in) s. panel (DM 3200)

BEDIKIAN, Krikor (20th C) Libyan
£2834 $5555   (20-Nov-90 APT.P247/R) Enfant a la pasteque (65x54cm-26x21in) s.d.1957
                (F.FR 28000)

BEDINI, Paolo (17th C) Italian
£2400 $4608   (27-Nov-90 PH179/R) The rejected suitor (37x52cm-15x20in) s.d.1887

BEDNAR, Janos (20th C) Hungarian
£6500 $10660   (19-Jun-91 S115/R) Two ladies on beach (114x127cm-45x50in) s.d.1908

BEDOLI, Girolamo Francesco see MAZZOLA, Girolamo Bedoli

BEECHEY, Captain Richard Brydges (1808-1895) British
£3030 $5970   (30-Oct-90 CH.AM96/R) Raft in heavy seas (92x137cm-36x54in) s.d.1860
                (D.FL 10000)

BEECHEY, George (attrib) (1798-1852) British
£1100 $2167   (31-Oct-90 S301/R) Portrait of young boy standing by chair holding white
                hat (72x59cm-28x23in)

BEECHEY, Sir William (1753-1839) British
£2000 $3300   (10-Jul-91 S127/R) Portrait of Mr R Thornton (74x61cm-29x24in)
                mono.d.1797
£2703 $5000   (10-Mar-91 H.C74/R) Portrait of Lady Trafford, in dress and veil
                (91x71cm-36x28in)
£4600 $7498   (11-Jun-91 HAR471/R) Portrait of Earl of Mexborough as child paddling in
                stream (102x124cm-40x49in)
£8854 $17000   (27-Nov-90 PO.BA4) La buena noticia (86x70cm-34x28in) s.
£41176 $70000   (31-May-91 CH.NY199/R) Three children in landscape (162x152cm-64x60in)
£71053 $135000   (10-Jan-91 SY.NY101 a/R) Portrait of Sir Francis Ford's children giving
                coin to beggar boy (180x150cm-71x59in)

BEECHEY, Sir William (attrib) (1753-1839) British
£1294 $2200   (31-May-91 CH.NY94/R) Portrait of gentleman wearing costume with jabot,
                Windsor Castle beyond (77x64cm-30x25in)
£3284 $5713   (25-Mar-91 PLF.P95/R) Portrait presume de Joshua Grigby
                (127x101cm-50x40in) (F.FR 33000)
£9744 $19000   (10-Oct-90 CH.NY22/R) Three children with dog in landscape
                (187x136cm-74x54in)

BEECHEY, Sir William (circle) (1753-1839) British
£2600 $5122   (31-Oct-90 S288/R) Portrait of young boy standing in landscape
                (58x46cm-23x18in)
£4800 $9120   (1-Mar-91 C25/R) Portrait of young boy in midshipman's uniform seated on
                rock beneath tree (201x138cm-79x54in)

BEECHEY, Sir William (school) (1753-1839) British
£1500 $2910   (3-Dec-90 WSW134/R) Portrait of Mrs. Mortimer (76x64cm-30x25in)

BEECHEY, Sir William (studio) (1753-1839) British
£900 $1557   (20-May-91 SWS271) Portrait of a gentleman, wearing a brown coat
                (74x61cm-29x24in)
£1443 $2800   (8-Dec-90 W.W179/R) Portrait of Miss Elizabeth Peacock (79x66cm-31x26in)

BEECHEY, Sir William (style) (1753-1839) British
£720 $1246   (20-May-91 SWS281/R) Portrait of Thomas Duncombe Eden of Beamish Park,
                County Durham (73x62cm-29x24in)
£850 $1403   (9-Jul-91 PH24/R) Portrait of gentleman, thought to be Captain Hare,
                seated (76x63cm-30x25in)
£1500 $2595   (20-May-91 SWS278/R) Portrait of a young girl, in a landscape wearing a
                brown dress (88x67cm-35x26in)
£2300 $4416   (26-Nov-90 SWS137/R) Portrait of officer wearing uniform. Portrait of
                lady wearing white dress (74x61cm-29x24in) pair

BEEK, Andre van (?) ?
£1122 $2211   (18-Nov-90 S.S108/R) La chaumiere fleurie (61x50cm-24x20in) s.
                (F.FR 11000)

BEEK, Jurrien (1879-1965) Dutch
£695 $1369   (13-Nov-90 J.M279) Lago Maggiore (58x78cm-23x31in) s. (A.D 1800)

BEEKMAN, Christiaan (1887-1964) Dutch
£929 $1793   (13-Dec-90 SY.AM9/R) Composition (30x35cm-12x14in) s. cgl col.pencil
                (D.FL 3000)
£1238 $2390   (13-Dec-90 SY.AM15/R) Composition (46x35cm-18x14in) s. col.pencil
                (D.FL 4000)
£1703 $3286   (12-Dec-90 CH.AM58) Abstract composition (20x18cm-8x7in) st.sig. W/C
                (D.FL 5500)

BEELDEMAKER, Adriaen Cornelisz (1625-1701) Dutch
£2211 $3626   (21-Jun-91 SY.MO274/R) Chiens de chasse dans un paysage
                (41x53cm-16x21in) s.d.1690 (F.FR 22000)

BEELDEMAKER, Adriaen Cornelisz (1625-1701) Dutch-cont.
£2500 $4750   (13-Sep-90 CSK52/R) Hounds and spaniels in Italianate landscape with classical ruins beyond (45x53cm-18x21in) s.d.
£3500 $6895   (31-Oct-90 S95/R) Landscapes with dogs (42x56cm-17x22in) one s.d.1695 one s.d.1697 pair
£7600 $12844   (19-Apr-91 C91/R) A hunter and a youth with four munsterlanders at the edge of a wood (46x61cm-18x24in) s.d.1695

BEELDEMAKER, Adriaen Cornelisz (attrib) (1625-1701) Dutch
£800 $1600   (7-Feb-91 C97/R) Dogs cornering a fox (48x65cm-19x26in) indist.sig.
£3279 $6426   (11-Nov-90 I.N3/R) Couples de chiens (16x23cm-6x9in) panel pair (F.FR 32000)

BEELT, Cornelis (1660-1702) Dutch
£13712 $27013   (14-Nov-90 D.V99/R) Market scene with figures (57x60cm-22x24in) (A.S 280000)
£18000 $30420   (16-Apr-91 PH53/R) Elegant figures walking on beach at Scheveningen beside fisherfolk displaying catch (106x150cm-42x59in)

BEER, Franz (1929-) ?
£4573 $9146   (6-Feb-91 FB.P28) Composition (100x65cm-39x26in) s.d.60 mixed media canvas (F.FR 45000)

BEER, Wilhelm Amandus (1837-1907) German
£4842 $8134   (23-Apr-91 RAS.K141/R) Winter landscape with fluteplayer, bear tamer and dancing bear (17x23cm-7x9in) s.d.1886 (D.KR 55000)

BEERBOHM, Sir Max (1872-1956) British
£2500 $4700   (18-Sep-90 PH54) Flask of Bombarolina (31x30cm-12x12in) s.i.d.1923
£700 $1155   (10-Jul-91 CSK94/R) Portrait of Charles Mitchell (25x10cm-10x4in) s.i. pencil pen wash
£750 $1448   (12-Dec-90 CSK20) Self-portrait (15x13cm-6x5in) s.i.d.1946 s.i.verso pencil
£800 $1504   (18-Sep-90 PH55/R) Lord Weardale (26x17cm-10x7in) s.i. pencil W/C
£1000 $1960   (6-Nov-90 PH14/R) Sir George Lewis, Bt (22x16cm-9x6in) s.i.d.1906 W/C pencil
£1400 $2702   (12-Dec-90 CSK19/R) Portrait of Mr. Robert Hichens (30x18cm-12x7in) s.i. pencil pen wash
£2600 $5044   (6-Dec-90 S338/R) William Archer (36x22cm-14x9in) s. pencil W/C
£4500 $7515   (6-Jun-91 C85/R) Chelsea and Mr Steer by moonlight (32x28cm-13x11in) s.i.d.07 pencil pen ink W/C

BEERNAERT, Euphrosine (1831-1901) Flemish
£1473 $2504   (28-May-91 C.A11) Castle in landscape (55x90cm-22x35in) s.d.1863 (B.FR 90000)

BEERS, Jan van (1852-1927) Belgian
£1300 $2236   (17-May-91 C73/R) Young beauty (33x24cm-13x9in) s. panel
£1800 $3474   (13-Dec-90 CSK164/R) Gathering crabs (30x25cm-12x10in) s. board
£2200 $4070   (4-Mar-91 PHB65/R) Le Prie Dieu Improvise (30x20cm-12x8in) s. panel
£2455 $4173   (28-May-91 C.A305/R) Woman with basket of grapes (46x37cm-18x15in) s. panel (B.FR 150000)
£3416 $6388   (27-Aug-90 SY.J192/R) Une vague surprise (32x23cm-13x9in) s. panel (SA.R 16500)

BEERSTRATEN, Anthonie (17th C) Dutch
£4054 $7905   (26-Oct-90 KM.K1000/R) Winter landscape with ice skaters on frozen canal near a village (36x65cm-14x26in) s.d.1661 panel (DM 12000)

BEERSTRATEN, Anthonie (attrib) (17th C) Dutch
£1916 $3200   (23-Jan-91 D.NY71) Frozen winter landscape with skaters (25x38cm-10x15in) panel
£5245 $10122   (10-Dec-90 L.K4) Harbour scene with shipping and figure (60x57cm-24x22in) panel (DM 15000)

BEERSTRATEN, Jan Abrahamsz (1622-1666) Dutch
£23684 $45000   (10-Jan-91 SY.NY39/R) Imaginary Mediterranean harbour scene with village and figures (89x122cm-35x48in) s.d.1650 panel
£93522 $184238   (30-Oct-90 BU.S227/R) Winter scene from Amsterdam with skaters (96x130cm-38x51in) s.d.1666 (S.KR 1025000)

BEERSTRATEN, Jan Abrahamsz (attrib) (1622-1666) Dutch
£12333 $23926   (5-Dec-90 APT.P60/R) Les joies de l'hiver (52x81cm-20x32in) (F.FR 120000)

BEERT, Osias I (c.1570-1624) Flemish
£46000 $79580   (24-May-91 C29/R) Artichoke and shrimps on pewter plates, a Roemer and other objects (50x66cm-20x26in) panel

BEERT, Osias I (studio) (c.1570-1624) Flemish
£6137 $12029   (19-Nov-90 CH.R165/R) Nature morte - ostriche, olive, vasellame, e uva, mele, ciliege e pane (14x20cm-6x8in) panel pair (I.L 13500000)

BEEST, Sybrand van (attrib) (1610-1674) Dutch
£6500 $10985   (17-Apr-91 S108/R) Interior with woman beside vanitas still life (42x70cm-17x28in) indis.i. panel

BEEST, Sybrand van (style) (1610-1674) Dutch
£1600 $3040   (13-Sep-90 CSK213) Lady at vegetable stall (48x39cm-19x15in) panel

BEETHAM, William (attrib) (fl.1834-1853) British
£895 $1700   (27-Feb-91 SY.NY200/R) Lower Dolvan Falls (91x71cm-36x28in)

BEFANIO, Gennaro (1866-?) French
£2282 $3925   (15-May-91 CN.P66/R) Fillette sur un banc (27x35cm-11x14in) s. board
    (F.FR 23000)

BEGA, Cornelis Pietersz (1620-1664) Dutch
£3976 $7832   (12-Nov-90 CH.AM123/R) Woman standing by chair, facing right
*   (27x16cm-11x6in) black white chk ink (D.FL 13000)*

BEGA, Cornelis Pietersz (after) (1620-1664) Dutch
£1386 $2453   (5-Apr-91 DAR.P65/R) Les Caresses refusees (36x28cm-14x11in)
    (F.FR 14000)

BEGA, Cornelis Pietersz (circle) (1620-1664) Dutch
£1000 $1630   (2-Jul-91 PH249) Interior with woman singing to accompaniment of man
    playing violin (41x35cm-16x14in) bears indis.sig.

BEGARAT, Eugene (20th C) French
£600 $1008   (28-Apr-91 FE.P64) Venise (46x38cm-18x15in) s. (F.FR 6000)
£1223 $2349   (2-Dec-90 FE.P66) Le retour des pecheurs a Concarneau (60x73cm-24x29in)
    s. (F.FR 12000)
£1224 $2412   (18-Nov-90 S.S8 b/R) Retour de peche (60x73cm-24x29in) s. (F.FR 12000)
£1343 $2337   (31-Mar-91 FE.P73) Bord de riviere un dimanche s.verso (F.FR 13500)
£2037 $4012   (4-Nov-90 FE.P83) La maison de vacances (73x60cm-29x24in) s.
    (F.FR 20000)

BEGAS, Oskar (1828-1883) German
£2365 $4611   (26-Oct-90 KM.K1096/R) Portrait of young woman seated holding fan
    (88x70cm-35x28in) s. (DM 7000)
£2500 $4800   (27-Nov-90 PH127/R) Villa overlooking the sea (33x41cm-13x16in)
    mono.l.d.1853

BEGAUD, Pierre Albert (20th C) French
£4473 $7560   (21-Apr-91 SY.MO331/R) Diane au paradis (190x92cm-75x36in) s.
    (F.FR 45000)

BEGEYN, Abraham (1637-1697) Dutch
£1600 $2704   (18-Apr-91 CSK108) Two goats grazing in wood (48x34cm-19x13in)
£2407 $4020   (6-Jun-91 D.V266/R) Two goats by edge of wood with view of river
    landscape and arched bridge (39x48cm-15x19in) (A.S 50000)
£2676 $4522   (19-Apr-91 FN.S1666) Arcadian landscape with shepherds and animals
    (34x41cm-13x16in) s. panel (DM 8000)
£3000 $5790   (11-Dec-90 PH162/R) Goats browsing by path overlooking river valley
    (51x44cm-20x17in)
£3242 $6323   (23-Oct-90 DUR.M35) Paisaje mediterraneo (92x114cm-36x45in)
    (S.P 600000)
£9486 $16126   (27-May-91 GK.Z5006/R) Wooded landscape with lizzard, birds, butterflies
    and frog (66x57cm-26x22in) s. (S.FR 24000)

BEGEYN, Abraham (attrib) (1637-1697) Dutch
£3333 $6500   (11-Oct-90 SY.NY5/R) Mountainous landscape with herdsmen and animals
    (81x61cm-32x24in)

BEGEYN, Abraham (style) (1637-1697) Dutch
£1800 $3456   (29-Nov-90 CSK117/R) Italianate landscape with herdsman seated by
    classical fountain (61x54cm-24x21in) bears sig.

BEGGROF, Alexandre (1841-1914) Russian
£1149 $2252   (6-Nov-90 BA.S14/R) By the landing-stage (15x23cm-6x9in) s.d.1891 panel
    (S.KR 12500)

BEGGROW-HARTMANN, Olga (1862-?) German
£1678 $3272   (12-Oct-90 AW.H1355/R) Little girl leaning over balustrade of verandah
    and baby in cart (61x81cm-24x32in) s.l. (DM 5000)

BEHM, Vilhelm (1859-1934) Swedish
£640 $1249   (21-Oct-90 BU.M395) Winter landscape with house and woman walking
    (74x92cm-29x36in) s.d.1901 (S.KR 7000)
£2294 $4518   (13-Nov-90 AB.S340/R) Sunlit pine forest interior (140x110cm-55x43in)
    s.d.1895 (S.KR 25000)

BEHNISCH, Caroline Auguste Hedwig (1873-1963) Dutch
£589 $1002   (28-May-91 C.A174/R) Mother and child (60x48cm-24x19in) s. (B.FR 36000)

BEHR, Carel Jacobus (1812-1895) Dutch
£1198 $2012   (23-Apr-91 SY.AM220/R) View of town-hall, Naarden (31x24cm-12x9in) s.
    panel (D.FL 4000)
£1667 $3133   (22-Sep-90 CH.AM106) View of the Buitenhof with the Hofvijver, The Hague
    (57x73cm-22x29in) s.d.1864 (D.FL 5500)

BEHRENDSEN, August (1819-1886) German
£1748 $3374   (12-Dec-90 WE.MU71/R) Steinbachtal, Harz (33x46cm-13x18in) mono.d.1842
                i.verso (DM 5000)

BEHRENS-HANGELER, Herbert (1898-1981) German
£3147 $6105   (7-Dec-90 GB.B6331) Inferno, abstract figures (90x95cm-35x37in) mono.
                s.i.d.1927verso (DM 9000)

BEICH, Joachim Franz (1665-1748) German
£3497 $6748   (12-Dec-90 WE.MU25/R) Ideal landscape (38x63cm-15x25in) s. (DM 10000)

BEICH, Joachim Franz (attrib) (1665-1748) German
£1107 $2159   (10-Oct-90 ZEL.L1393/R) Southern coastal landscape with figures on beach
                (31cm-12ins circular) panel (DM 3300)
£5853 $11414   (23-Oct-90 CH.R392/R) La battaglia di Sennacherib (74x110cm-29x43in)
                (I.L 13000000)

BEICHLING, Karl Heinrich (1803-1876) German
£757 $1476   (24-Oct-90 GD.B133/R) View of Prague with Karlsbrucke and dome of St
                Niklaus (69x53cm-27x21in) s.d.1864 i.verso (S.FR 1900)

BEILBY, Thomas (18/19th C) British
£1200   *$1980*   *(9-Jul-91 C34 a/R) Prospect of Wheatley, Yorkshire (27x37cm-11x15in)*
                s.i. pencil W/C

BEILBY, William (1740-c.1819) British
£1100   *$1815*   *(9-Jul-91 C34/R) Prospect of Blyth Hall, Nottinghamshire*
                (25x38cm-10x15in) s.d.1778 pencil W/C

BEINASCHI, Giovan Battista (1636-1688) Italian
£4800 $8112   (17-Apr-91 S167/R) Male saint (123x90cm-48x35in)
£8040 $13186   (22-Jun-91 CH.MO117/R) Saint Pierre (133x96cm-52x38in) bers num.641B
                verso (F.FR 80000)
£18000 $30420   (17-Apr-91 S169/R) The Vestal Virgin Tuccia (119x171cm-47x67in)
£717   *$1406*   *(11-Nov-90 M.V9/R) Le martyre de Saint-Laurent (31x42cm-12x17in) sepia*
                wash (F.FR 7000)
£800   *$1536*   *(18-Feb-91 S81) Seated male nudes (49x36cm-19x14in) chk htd.white wash*
                over contours two
£846   *$1633*   *(16-Dec-90 M.V135) La martyre de Saint-Laurent sepia wash (F.FR 8300)*
£1579   *$3000*   *(8-Jan-91 SY.NY18) Study of a standing Bishop holding a book*
                (54x34cm-21x13in) blk.chk.htd.white chk.
£2280   *$4036*   *(19-Mar-91 F.M286/R) La caduta della manna (34x53cm-13x21in) pen brush*
                W/C ink (I.L 5000000)
£2600   *$4992*   *(18-Feb-91 S222/R) Three angels (44x39cm-17x15in) chk wash htd.white*
£2895   *$5500*   *(8-Jan-91 SY.NY1/R) Peasants with their animals (35x51cm-14x20in) bears*
                sig. chk.wash htd.white
£4474   *$8500*   *(8-Jan-91 SY.NY43/R) The abduction of Helen (42x57cm-17x22in) blk.chk.*
                ink wash htd.white

BEINASCHI, Giovan Battista (attrib) (1636-1688) Italian
£3189 $5422   (30-May-91 F.M45/R) Susanna e i vecchioni (100x130cm-39x51in)
                (I.L 7000000)

BEINKE, Fritz (1842-1907) German
£1375 $2612   (2-Mar-91 KRA.D276/R) Ganseliesel (36x27cm-14x11in) s. (DM 4000)
£1877 $3679   (24-Nov-90 SA.A710/R) Feeding the geese (44x31cm-17x12in) s. panel
                (DM 5500)

BEJARANO, Manuel Cabral (19/20th C) Spanish
£1800 $3456   (27-Nov-90 PH210/R) Appreciative audience (30x49cm-12x19in) s.i.d.1882
£2000 $3580   (12-Mar-91 PH54/R) Inriguing visitor (30x42cm-12x17in) s.i.d.1881

BEJOT, Eugene (1867-1931) French
£398   *$689*   *(22-May-91 PLF.P5) Vue de la Seine, le quai d'Anjou (21x24cm-8x9in) s.*
                blk.crayon stumping wash (F.FR 4000)

BEKEN, Ignace van der (1689-1774) Flemish
£2568 $4598   (12-Mar-91 FN.S2276/R) Elegant party merrymaking in interior
                (67x84cm-26x33in) (DM 7500)

BELANGER, Louis (1736-1816) French
£1692   *$2943*   *(27-Mar-91 CN.P26/R) Pecheurs et lavandiere au bord d'une riviere*
                (24x35cm-9x14in) s.d.1787 pen W/C htd ink wash (F.FR 17000)
£7194   *$13957*   *(7-Dec-90 CH.MO233/R) Un paysage (275x443cm-108x174in) s.d.1781*
                blk.chk.pen wash W/C (F.FR 70000)

BELAY, Pierre de (1890-1947) French
£1121 $2164   (16-Dec-90 T.B269/R) Nu au bain (28x22cm-11x9in) s.d.1926 board
                (F.FR 11000)
£1595 $2632   (10-Jul-91 FB.P27/R) La Charrette - Concarneau (23x19cm-9x7in) s. panel
                (F.FR 16000)
£2178 $3659   (27-Apr-91 SO.S270/R) Sailors by the quay (59x72cm-23x28in) s.d.39
                (S.KR 23000)
£3514 $6501   (6-Mar-91 APT.P74) Le ramassage des pommes (50x61cm-20x24in) board laid
                down on canvas (F.FR 35000)

BELAY, Pierre de (1890-1947) French-cont.

£3518	$6754	(24-Feb-91 P.V87/R) Espalion (37x50cm-15x20in) s. peinture a l'essence paper laid down canvas (F.FR 35000)
£3700	$6179	(5-Jun-91 HC.P328) Le marche en Bretagne (46x55cm-18x22in) s. (F.FR 37000)
£4876	$8435	(12-May-91 T.B76/R) Bigoudenne au parapluie (38x46cm-15x18in) s. (F.FR 49000)
£4876	$8435	(12-May-91 T.B74) Le Retour du Marche (30x40cm-12x16in) s. board (F.FR 49000)
£4898	$9649	(16-Nov-90 FB.P115/R) Le peintre a Montmartre (50x61cm-20x24in) s.d.24 board (F.FR 48000)
£6269	$12224	(17-Oct-90 ARC.P64/R) Pecheurs sur la jetee (50x65cm-20x26in) s. board (F.FR 62000)
£6368	$11017	(12-May-91 T.B75/R) Pecheurs sur les quais (50x62cm-20x24in) s. (F.FR 64000)
£7164	$12394	(12-May-91 T.B79) Marche breton (33x41cm-13x16in) s. (F.FR 72000)
£7940	$14212	(15-Mar-91 FB.P27/R) La caleche (81x65cm-32x26in) s.d.1944 l. verso (F.FR 79000)
£8155	$15739	(16-Dec-90 T.B90/R) La partie de cartes (54x64cm-21x25in) s. (F.FR 80000)
£8856	$15320	(12-May-91 T.B78/R) Le Port d'Audierne (38x48cm-15x19in) s. (F.FR 89000)
£418	$723	(12-May-91 T.B37) Plaidoirie au Proces Stavinsky (31x24cm-12x9in) s.d.1936 wash (F.FR 4200)
£452	$742	(18-Jun-91 APT.P7) Collioures (11x26cm-4x10in) s.d.1940 W/C (F.FR 4500)
£498	$861	(12-May-91 T.B217) Les toits rouges (21x29cm-8x11in) s. gouache (F.FR 5000)
£642	$1239	(16-Dec-90 T.B210) Helene au bouquet (14x19cm-6x7in) s.d.1936 W/C gouache (F.FR 6300)
£647	$1119	(12-May-91 T.B36) A la Coupole (32x23cm-13x9in) s.d.1935 wash (F.FR 6500)
£653	$1071	(18-Jun-91 APT.P6) Les confidences (23x27cm-9x11in) s.d.1928 W/C (F.FR 6500)
£704	$1154	(18-Jun-91 APT.P4) Saint-Tropez (22x31cm-9x12in) s.d.mai 40 W/C (F.FR 7000)
£836	$1613	(16-Dec-90 T.B69) Jeune femme de face (33x26cm-13x10in) s.d.1926 oil crayon (F.FR 8200)
£854	$1401	(18-Jun-91 APT.P3) Saint-Tropez, le port (22x31cm-9x12in) s.d.1940 ink htd.W/C varnished (F.FR 8500)
£854	$1401	(18-Jun-91 APT.P5) Paris, les bouquinistes (15x23cm-6x9in) s.d.1932 W/C (F.FR 8500)
£866	$1672	(16-Dec-90 T.B51) Le couple (28x22cm-11x9in) s. gouache (F.FR 8500)
£897	$1731	(16-Dec-90 T.B52) L'elegante (28x22cm-11x9in) s. gouache (F.FR 8800)
£1493	$2582	(12-May-91 T.B52/R) La Lecture (27x33cm-11x13in) s.d.1946 gouache (F.FR 15000)
£2037	$4012	(29-Oct-90 CSC.P52/R) Jeune bretonne au tablier bleu (31x22cm-12x9in) s.i.d.1940 gouache (F.FR 20000)
£2039	$3935	(16-Dec-90 T.B233/R) Elegante au chapeau rose (31x41cm-12x16in) s.d.26 gouache (F.FR 20000)
£3670	$7083	(16-Dec-90 T.B49/R) Pique-nique en Bretagne (47x35cm-19x14in) s.d.1933 gouache (F.FR 36000)
£3781	$6541	(12-May-91 T.B51) La Bourse - La Corbeille s.d.1935 gouache (F.FR 38000)
£4680	$8844	(30-Sep-90 E.LA175/R) Barques sur la plage de Banyuls (38x49cm-15x19in) s.d.1940 gouache (F.FR 46000)

BELGIAN SCHOOL (?) Belgian

£26000	$42380	(5-Jul-91 C60/R) Portrait of gentleman of Wouters Family, aged 70, wearing fur-lined coat (21x16cm-8x6in) l. panel arched top c.1490

BELGIAN SCHOOL, 19th C Belgian

£1173	$2100	(11-Apr-91 FA.PH719/R) Sheep and poultry in landscape (56x71cm-22x28in) cradled panel
£1400	$2352	(18-Jul-91 CSK71/R) In barn (54x66cm-21x26in) bears indist.sig.
£1800	$3097	(14-May-91 GM.B507/R) Retour de l'Ecolier (38x30cm-15x12in) (B.FR 110000)
£4046	$7000	(21-May-91 CE.NY90/R) Elegant woman reading in interior (79x63cm-31x25in) indist.s.

BELIN, Jean see FONTENAY, Jean Baptiste Belin de

BELISARIO, Isaac Mendez (fl.1815-1838) ?

£5000	$9750	(24-Oct-90 S130/R) In the garden of a house in the West Indies (31x42cm-12x17in) s.d.1844 W/C over pencil scratching out

BELKNAP, Zedekiah (1781-1858) American

£888	$1500	(20-Apr-91 WOL.C16/R) Portrait of Richard Lamb (38x33cm-15x13in) s.d.1839

BELKNAP, Zedekiah (attrib) (1781-1858) American

£4592	$9000	(26-Jan-91 CH.NY155/R) Portrait of young boy (48x38cm-19x15in) board c.1830

BELL, A D (20th C) British

£520	$1014	(15-Jan-91 SWS70/R) Happy days (39x61cm-15x24in) s.d.1935 W/C

BELL, Arthur George (1849-1916) British
£680 $1340   (13-Nov-90 SWS308/R) Winter feed (59x44cm-23x17in) s.
£800 $1576   (13-Nov-90 SWS309/R) Moonrise over the snow (44x89cm-17x35in) s. l.
                  label verso panel
£450 $779   (20-May-91 PH62) Haycart crossing bridge (35x52cm-14x20in) s. W/C htd
*   white*

BELL, C Stuart (?) ?
£660 $1221   (7-Mar-91 CSK90/R) River landscape with boys on bank and windmill on
                  hilltop beyond (61x51cm-24x20in) s. indis.i.verso

BELL, Cecil (1906-) American
£2093 $3600   (19-May-91 LIT.L53) Auction a Vermont, household treasures
                  (43x79cm-17x31in) s. board
£2197 $3800   (12-May-91 H.C198) Near the Brooklyn Bridge (71x61cm-28x24in) s.
                  s.i.verso board

BELL, Edward August (1862-?) American
£1250 $2400   (17-Dec-90 SY.NY126/R) Rose (41x30cm-16x12in) s. panel

BELL, George Henry Frederick (1878-1966) Australian
£1397 $2501   (9-Apr-91 CH.ME196/R) Vase of flowers (60x50cm-24x20in) s. (A.D 3200)
£1488 $2500   (22-Apr-91 SY.ME177/R) Nude study (49x38cm-19x15in) s. s.i.verso
                  cardboard (A.D 3200)

BELL, John (19th C) British
£625 $1200   (27-Nov-90 W.T1014) Waiting for the fleet (26x42cm-10x17in) s.
                  (C.D 1400)
£5000 $9350   (28-Aug-90 S828/R) St Andrews (91x142cm-36x56in) s.d.1880

BELL, Mona H (fl.1903-1920) British
£700 $1176   (23-Apr-91 RG2116) Portrait of Arab Atallah Bordcosh (91x71cm-36x28in)
                  s.i.verso

BELL, Robert Anning (1863-1933) British
£600 $1176   (13-Feb-91 PHL119/R) From balcony (25x40cm-10x16in) d.1906 stretcher
                  tempera oil
£1400 $2646   (26-Sep-90 S201/R) Crystal-gazer (47x31cm-19x12in) s. tempera panel

BELL, Trevor (1930-) British
£820 $1369   (4-Jun-91 PH84/R) Swinging forms (54x26cm-21x10in) s.d.58 stretcher
                  s.verso
£1500 $2505   (7-Jun-91 C354/R) Cliff fields (120x30cm-47x12in) s.d.56 board
£1600 $3120   (9-Oct-90 B72/R) On summer's day (76x63cm-30x25in) s. board
£5000 $9250   (8-Mar-91 C174/R) Movement of black, night voyage (122x150cm-48x59in)
                  s.d.1958 i.d.verso board
£700 $1169   (7-Jun-91 C353/R) Strange one (58x38cm-23x15in) s.d.61 gouache oil paper
*   on canvas*

BELL, Vanessa (1879-1961) British
£800 $1336   (6-Jun-91 C96/R) Still life with ripe fruits and flowers in jar
                  (37x45cm-15x18in)
£1050 $1775   (2-May-91 C31 a/R) Seated model at Charleston (72x53cm-28x21in)
£1800 $3042   (2-May-91 C31/R) Still life with glass jar and open book
                  (53x37cm-21x15in) init.
£2600 $4888   (20-Sep-90 C30/R) Tilton House from Charleston (54x39cm-21x15in) init.
                  board
£3000 $5070   (1-May-91 S30/R) Oranges on table-top (46x38cm-18x15in) s.d.1959
£3500 $5915   (1-May-91 S29/R) The apple tree (38x46cm-15x18in) init.i.verso
£3800 $7144   (20-Sep-90 C105/R) Summer flowers in glass bowl (59x44cm-23x17in)
                  init.d.1952 board
£4800 $8880   (7-Mar-91 C64/R) Tilton House (56x40cm-22x16in) init. board
£5000 $9800   (7-Nov-90 S61/R) Dieppe fishmarket (102x99cm-40x39in) init.d.1954
£5600 $9464   (1-May-91 S19/R) Bouquet (56x41cm-22x16in) s. board

BELL, William Charles (1830-1904) British
£460 $773   (22-Apr-91 PH41/R) Portrait of Queen Victoria (3x?cm-1x?in)
*   min.s.i.d.1855verso enamel gold frame oval*

BELL-SMITH, F M (1846-1923) Canadian/British
£814 $1580   (20-Aug-90 L.V4) Woman sitting on beach in front of cabin
                  (23x30cm-9x12in) panel (C.D 1800)
£2149 $4170   (20-Aug-90 L.V3) Trafalgar Square, 1910 (41x61cm-16x24in) W/C
*   (C.D 4750)*

BELL-SMITH, Frederick Marlett (1846-1923) Canadian/British
£628 $1049   (3-Jun-91 R.T96/R) Lake Louise (16x23cm-6x9in) s. board (C.D 1200)
£702 $1375   (20-Nov-90 JOY.T424) Lake Louise (16x24cm-6x9in) s. board (C.D 1600)
£746 $1461   (20-Nov-90 JOY.T317) On Fraser River (14x22cm-6x9in) s. board
                  (C.D 1700)
£804 $1543   (27-Nov-90 W.T885/R) Great glacier of Selkirks, British Columbia
                  (23x20cm-9x8in) s. i.verso board (C.D 1800)
£1818 $3127   (14-May-91 JOY.T25/R) Boats moored on the Thames, St. Pauls in the
                  distance (27x50cm-11x20in) s. (C.D 3600)
£10526 $20632   (20-Nov-90 JOY.T17/R) Regent Street (85x126cm-33x50in) s.d.1910
                  (C.D 24000)

BELL-SMITH, Frederick Marlett (1846-1923) Canadian/British-cont.

£482	$946	(20-Nov-90 JOY.T415/R) Lake in Rockies (27x46cm-11x18in) s. W/C (C.D 1100)
£486	$793	(10-Jun-91 W.T1092) A monarch of the rockies (22x15cm-9x6in) s. i. verso W/C (C.D 900)
£526	$1037	(30-Oct-90 MA.V121) Rocky Mountain scene (23x30cm-9x12in) s. W/C (C.D 1200)
£606	$1048	(6-May-91 SY.T194 a) Coastal seascape (23x48cm-9x19in) s. W/C (C.D 1200)
£703	$1145	(10-Jun-91 W.T1044 g) Near Yale, Fraser river (46x32cm-18x13in) s.i. W/C (C.D 1300)
£800	$1552	(3-Dec-90 R.T275/R) Lake in Rockies (51x34cm-20x13in) s.d.1889 W/C htd white board (C.D 1800)
£877	$1719	(20-Nov-90 JOY.T234/R) River in Rockies (37x53cm-15x21in) s. W/C (C.D 2000)
£960	$1651	(14-May-91 JOY.T89/R) Rail line along the Fraser river (31x22cm-12x9in) s. W/C (C.D 1900)
£1053	$2063	(20-Nov-90 JOY.T299/R) Lake Louise, Alta (27x34cm-11x13in) s. W/C (C.D 2400)
£1053	$2063	(20-Nov-90 JOY.T16/R) Snow-capped mountains in Rockies (33x49cm-13x19in) s.d.04 W/C (C.D 2400)
£1092	$2151	(12-Nov-90 HO.ED71/R) Rocky mountain stream (37x27cm-15x11in) s. W/C (C.D 2500)
£1136	$1966	(6-May-91 SY.T11) River Thames at Westminster (37x23cm-15x9in) s. (C.D 2250)
£1140	$2235	(20-Nov-90 JOY.T260/R) Piccasdilly, looking eastward (26x35cm-10x14in) s. W/C (C.D 2600)
£1768	$3058	(6-May-91 SY.T160/R) London street scene (25x36cm-10x14in) s. W/C (C.D 3500)
£3788	$6553	(6-May-91 SY.T10/R) Pool of London (35x53cm-14x21in) s.d.1892 W/C (C.D 7500)

BELLA, Stefano Della (1610-1664) Italian

£650	$1060	(2-Jul-91 C269/R) Two seated peasants seen from back. Studies after Parmigianino (10x14cm-4x6in) one num.73 one with i. pen two one mount
£909	$1782	(19-Nov-90 CH.R131/R) Studi di figure maschili. Figura maschile con mantello (10x7cm-4x3in) pencil pen ink cardboard (I.L 2000000)
£1550	$2744	(19-Mar-91 F.M224/R) Studio di fantasia orientale con moro, cavallo bardato e cavaliere (15x10cm-6x4in) i.mount bistre ink (I.L 3400000)
£1900	$3648	(18-Feb-91 S231/R) Figures on horseback pen ink over chk pair

BELLA, Stefano Della (attrib) (1610-1664) Italian

£805	$1400	(27-Mar-91 B.SF4001/R) Bacchanal with bacchantes, satyrs and snake (13x21cm-5x8in) pen ink wash
£1325	$2544	(27-Nov-90 APT.P19/R) Projets de char romain (12x16cm-5x6in) pen two same mount (F.FR 13000)

BELLA, Vincenzo la (1872-?) Italian

£634	$1104	(25-Mar-91 SY.F666/R) Nudo femminile seduto (98x108cm-39x43in) s. (I.L 1400000)

BELLACCI, Pier Luigi (1948-) Italian

£940	$1682	(14-Apr-91 APT.P60/R) Ray Man (55x46cm-22x18in) s.i.d.29/1/91 verso (F.FR 9500)
£396	$708	(14-Apr-91 APT.P59) Sans titre (38x20cm-15x8in) s.d.5 Apr.88 mixed media (F.FR 4000)

BELLAGUET, Andree (20th C) ?

£940	$1682	(14-Apr-91 R.P17) Sans titre (82x65cm-32x26in) s. acrylic (F.FR 9500)

BELLANGE, Hippolyte (1800-1866) French

£4269	$7386	(25-May-91 KV.L368/R) Chez le barbier (33x41cm-13x16in) s.d.1836 panel (B.FR 260000)

BELLANGE, Jacques (attrib) (17th C) Italian

£7638	$12527	(18-Jun-91 APT.P3/R) Cavalier vu de dos (43x17cm-17x7in) pen blk.crayon (F.FR 76000)

BELLANGE, Thierry (1594-1638) French

£3200	$5216	(2-Jul-91 C136/R) King Francois I. Louis de Bourbon. King Joan III. Antoine de Leve. Giovanni de Medici (13x11cm-5x4in) i.two s.col.chk htd gold vellum five

BELLANGER, Camille (1853-1923) French

£5789	$11000	(27-Feb-91 SY.NY95/R) La fermiere (135x96cm-53x38in) s.d.1905

BELLANY, John (1942-) British

£650	$1066	(19-Jun-91 PHG122) Relaxation (91x122cm-36x48in) board
£1700	$2856	(23-Apr-91 S220/R) From port Seton to Fife (61x91cm-24x36in) s.i.verso
£5200	$10140	(9-Oct-90 B184/R) Celtic lovers (92x76cm-36x30in) s.

BELLE, Alexis Simon (1674-1734) French

£5500	$10725	(26-Oct-90 C54/R) Portrait of a lady, half length, wearing a red decollete dress (75x61cm-30x24in) oval

BELLE, Alexis Simon (attrib) (1674-1734) French
£10398 $19963   (30-Nov-90 APT.P150/R) Jeune enfant et son chien favori
                         (47x56cm-19x22in) (F.FR 102000)

BELLE, Alexis Simon (circle) (1674-1734) French
£3000 $4890   (3-Jul-91 PLF.P45/R) Portrait d'un jeune homme tenant un gant
                         (79x64cm-31x25in) (F.FR 30000)

BELLE, Karel van (1884-1959) Belgian
£1578 $3109   (29-Oct-90 ZZ.F45/R) Le bal (133x62cm-52x24in) s. panel (F.FR 15500)

BELLE, Marcel (1871-1948) French
£503 $899   (11-Mar-91 CR.P46/R) Les voiles jaunes (59x73cm-23x29in) st.sig.
                         (F.FR 5000)
£523 $935   (11-Mar-91 CR.P9) Barques et bateau lavoir (27x35cm-11x14in) st.sig.
                         paper (F.FR 5200)
£553 $989   (11-Mar-91 CR.P81/R) Voiles brunes a Treboul (33x41cm-13x16in) s. board
                         (F.FR 5500)
£553 $989   (11-Mar-91 CR.P45) Usines sur la Seine (24x33cm-9x13in) s.d.1910
                         (F.FR 5500)
£553 $989   (11-Mar-91 CR.P33) Port du Midi (27x35cm-11x14in) s. board (F.FR 5500)
£553 $989   (11-Mar-91 CR.P78/R) Les quais devant la Tour Eiffel (33x41cm-13x16in)
                         st.sig. (F.FR 5500)
£583 $1043   (11-Mar-91 CR.P54/R) Le chemin de halage, la Seine (33x41cm-13x16in) s.
                         (F.FR 5800)
£603 $1079   (11-Mar-91 CR.P20) Rivage aux voiliers (22x27cm-9x11in) st.sig.
                         (F.FR 6000)
£653 $1169   (11-Mar-91 CR.P26/R) Canal de Bourgogne sous la neige (38x46cm-15x18in)
                         s. board (F.FR 6500)
£683 $1223   (11-Mar-91 CR.P10/R) Paysage de Paris, Ile de la Grande Jatte
                         (38x46cm-15x18in) s. (F.FR 6800)
£704 $1259   (11-Mar-91 CR.P2/R) Peniches a quai (33x41cm-13x16in) s. (F.FR 7000)
£804 $1439   (11-Mar-91 CR.P32/R) La baie de Saint-Tropez (38x46cm-15x18in) s.
                         (F.FR 8000)
£854 $1529   (11-Mar-91 CR.P52/R) Le port de Saint-Tropez (38x46cm-15x18in) s.
                         (F.FR 8500)
£1106 $1979   (11-Mar-91 CR.P64/R) Remorqueurs a quai, Saint-Jean-de-Luz
                         (60x73cm-24x29in) s. board (F.FR 11000)

BELLEFLEUR, Leon (1910-) Canadian
£1316 $2579   (20-Nov-90 JOY.T273) L'ile de juin (50x60cm-20x24in) s.d.70 (C.D 3000)
£1515 $2606   (14-May-91 JOY.T131/R) Petite Huronne (35x26cm-14x10in) s.d.'69
                         (C.D 3000)

BELLEGARDE, Claude (1927-) French
£2590 $4402   (29-May-91 GL.P190) Sans titre (60x100cm-24x39in) s. (F.FR 26000)
£697   *$1185*   *(29-May-91 GL.P193) Composition (76x55cm-30x22in) s. gouache W/C*
                         (F.FR 7000)
£4133   *$8059*   *(26-Oct-90 CC.P9/R) Achrome 89/Temps F (47x63cm-19x25in) s.d.1957*
                         gouache collage (F.FR 41000)

BELLEI, Gaetano (1857-1922) Italian
£1200 $1968   (20-Jun-91 B25/R) Who's fairest of them all (23x30cm-9x12in) s.
£23000 $44000   (18-Oct-90 F.M37/R) Colpo di vento (129x85cm-51x33in) s. i.d.1920verso
                         (I.L 50000000)
£33333 $65000   (24-Oct-90 CH.NY223/R) The card game (67x107cm-26x42in) s. pair

BELLEL, Jean-Joseph (1816-1898) French
£996 $1723   (24-May-91 FB.P37) Route dans la campagne (31x26cm-12x10in) s. paper
                         laid down on canvas (F.FR 10000)
£4564 $9037   (30-Jan-91 APT.P302/R) Chartres, Constantine et Passy s. three panels
                         in same mount (F.FR 45000)
£10256 $20000   (24-Oct-90 CH.NY88/R) Street in Cairo (61x81cm-24x32in) s.d.1857
£1005   *$1648*   *(21-Jun-91 SY.MO319/R) La Place St.Pierre a Rome (320x420cm-126x165in)*
                         mono.d.85 W/C gouache (F.FR 10000)

BELLENGE, Michel Bruno (1726-1793) French
£5097 $9786   (30-Nov-90 APT.P131/R) Vase fleuri entoure de chevrefeuille
                         (80x65cm-31x26in) (F.FR 50000)

BELLERMANN, Ferdinand (1814-1889) German
£21812 $42534   (13-Oct-90 KRA.D174/R) Sunrise at the Orinoko in Venezuela
                         (108x185cm-43x73in) s.d.1869 (DM 65000)

BELLEROCHE, Albert de (19/20th C) French
£850   *$1683*   *(29-Jan-91 PH38) Study of female nude (41x26cm-16x10in) init.d.91 black*
                         chk pair

BELLET DU POISAT, Jean Pierre Joseph Alfred (1823-1883) French
£1285 $2492   (3-Dec-90 CS.L50/R) Autoportrait du peintre (46x39cm-18x15in) s.d.1877
                         pastel (F.FR 12500)

BELLET, Auguste Emile (?-1911) French
£9246 $15164   (20-Jun-91 APT.P18/R) Ce fichu temps (158x116cm-62x46in) s.d.1884
                         (F.FR 92000)

BELLETTE, Jean Mary (1919-) Australian
£769	$1362	(18-Mar-91 MGS.S176/R) Female nude s. card (A.D 1800)
£889	$1671	(17-Sep-90 MGS.S182/R) Polynesian study (36x55cm-14x22in) s. board (A.D 2000)
£1023	$1719	(22-Apr-91 SY.ME170/R) First landing (19x29cm-7x11in) s. paper on cardboard (A.D 2200)
£1860	$3126	(22-Apr-91 SY.ME182/R) Two girls (50x36cm-20x14in) init. i.verso board (A.D 4000)
£2124	$4183	(13-Nov-90 J.M50/R) Nude (39x49cm-15x19in) s.d.56 board (A.D 5500)
£2532	$4861	(14-Aug-90 SY.ME190/R) Allegorical landscape (31x38cm-12x15in) init. paper and board (A.D 6000)

BELLEVOIS, Jacob Adriaensz (style) (1621-1675) Dutch
£820	$1386	(1-May-91 PHL156) Dutch men-of-war and coastal craft offshore (45x60cm-18x24in) panel

BELLI, A (?) ?
£2692	$5250	(10-Oct-90 SY.NY153/R) Moulin de la Galette (61x122cm-24x48in) s.

BELLI, Domenico (1909-1983) Italian
£1330	$2180	(20-Jun-91 F.M365/R) Desiderio dello Zenit (44x31cm-17x12in) s.d.32 s.i.verso oil panel (I.L 2900000)

BELLINGHAM-SMITH, Elinor (1906-) British
£1500	$2775	(7-Mar-91 C61/R) Country down (32x39cm-13x15in)

BELLINGHAM-SMITH, Hugh (19/20th C) British
£2400	$4176	(27-Mar-91 S20/R) On the beach, Swanage (25x36cm-10x14in) panel

BELLINI, Emmanuel (20th C) French
£2049	$4016	(11-Nov-90 ZZ.F169/R) Le Campement des Gitans aux Saintes (37x46cm-15x18in) s.d.1952 panel (F.FR 20000)

BELLINI, Gentile (1429-1507) Italian
£25000	$40750	(3-Jul-91 S20/R) Virgin and Child with Saint Peter and female martyred saint (119x210cm-47x83in) s.d.MCCCCLXXXXI oil tempera silk canvas panel

BELLINI, Giovanni (after) (1430-1516) Italian
£2036	$3441	(2-May-91 CH.AM92/R) The Madonna and Child (76x56cm-30x22in) i. panel (D.FL 6800)

BELLINI, Giovanni (studio) (1430-1516) Italian
£84211	$160000	(11-Jan-91 CH.NY2/R) The Madonna and Child before a ledge in a landscape (75x57cm-30x22in) bears sig.Joannes.Bellinvs.P panel

BELLINI, Giovanni (style) (1430-1516) Italian
£2443	$4372	(14-Mar-91 D.V180/R) Madonna with Child and two saints (44x52cm-17x20in) panel (A.S 50000)

BELLION, Gabriel Joseph (19th C) French
£637	$1096	(14-May-91 GF.L2354) Forest interior with peasant woman and donkey on path (24x19cm-9x7in) s. (S.FR 1600)

BELLIS, Hubert (1831-1902) Belgian
£788	$1552	(30-Oct-90 CH.AM24) Grapes and chrysanthemums in basket (35x50cm-14x20in) s. (D.FL 2600)
£800	$1432	(12-Mar-91 PH6) Still life of flowers in vase (56x40cm-22x16in) s.
£903	$1562	(25-May-91 KV.L15) Still life of flowers (54x46cm-21x18in) s. (B.FR 55000)
£976	$1912	(6-Nov-90 SY.AM18) Still life with oysters and lobster (57x78cm-22x31in) s. (D.FL 3200)
£1007	$1963	(10-Oct-90 WE.MU307/R) Still life with cherries (37x54cm-15x21in) s. panel (DM 3000)
£1220	$2390	(6-Nov-90 SY.AM168) Still life with oysters, mussels and lobster (52x63cm-20x25in) s. (D.FL 4000)
£1356	$2400	(22-Mar-91 S.W2810/R) Cherries and baskets (38x53cm-15x21in) s. panel
£1500	$2880	(18-Dec-90 GM.B4039) Nature morte aux prunes et aux groseilles (59x80cm-23x31in) s. (B.FR 90000)

BELLMAN, J J (?) British?
£2200	$4136	(20-Sep-90 M5) Edwardian teaparty (30x43cm-12x17in) s.

BELLMER, Hans (1902-1975) French
£925	$1794	(4-Dec-90 I.N12/R) Sans titre (18x11cm-7x4in) studio st. lead pencil (F.FR 9000)
£935	$1870	(6-Feb-91 FB.P29/R) Composition aux coeurs (21x19cm-8x7in) s. gouache collage (F.FR 9200)
£950	$1549	(3-Jul-91 CSC.P10) Sans titre (17x7cm-7x3in) s. crayon (F.FR 9500)
£950	$1549	(3-Jul-91 CSC.P8/R) Sans titre (16x19cm-6x7in) s. crayon (F.FR 9500)
£1724	$2965	(13-May-91 CH.R2/R) Composizione (21x16cm-8x6in) s. pencil (I.L 3800000)
£2365	$4020	(1-Jun-91 VG.B358/R) St Cyr (22x14cm-9x6in) s.i.d.1965 pencil paper on board (DM 7000)
£6042	$9849	(16-Jun-91 CC.P45/R) Sans titre (56x47cm-22x19in) s.d.1964 double-sided (F.FR 60000)

BELLON, Jean (1944-) French
£1098 $1900   (22-May-91 D.NY94/R) St. Tropez (66x74cm-26x29in) s.
£1218 $2400   (15-Nov-90 D.NY111/R) St. Tropez (66x74cm-26x29in) s.

BELLONI, Giorgio (1861-1944) Italian
£2819 $5524   (21-Nov-90 F.M167) Barche da pesca a Noli (20x40cm-8x16in) s. panel
     (I.L 6200000)

BELLONI, Serge (1925-) ?
£803 $1293   (28-Jun-91 ARC.P88) Paris - le pont Louis-Philippe et St Gervais
     (26x22cm-10x9in) s. board (F.FR 8000)
£904 $1455   (28-Jun-91 ARC.P89) Les bords de Marne (22x27cm-9x11in) s.d.54 board
     sketch verso (F.FR 9000)

BELLOTTO DI CANALETI, Pietro (18th C) Italian
£18000 $35100   (25-Oct-90 CSK109/R) Entrance to Cannaregio with Church of S. Geremia
     and Palazzo Labia with barges and gondolas (40x52cm-16x20in)

BELLOTTO, Bernardo (1721-1780) Italian
£1165829 $1911960   (22-Jun-91 CH.MO140/R) Vue de la Place Navone a Rome (88x149cm-35x59in)
     (F.FR 11600000)

BELLOTTO, Bernardo (after) (1721-1780) Italian
£2218 $3638   (22-Jun-91 WK.M1339/R) Canale Grande seen from Campo di San Vio towards
     Bacino di San Marco (41x60cm-16x24in) one of pair (DM 6500)
£2218 $3638   (22-Jun-91 WK.M1340/R) Canale Grande with San Geremia and mouth of Cnale
     di Cannaregio one of pair (DM 6500)

BELLOTTO, Bernardo (style) (1721-1780) Italian
£14070 $23075   (21-Jun-91 SY.MO213/R) Vue de la Place Saint Marc (53x70cm-21x28in)
     (F.FR 140000)
£27000 $52650   (26-Oct-90 C25/R) The Arch of Titus (50x38cm-20x15in)

BELLOWS, Albert F (1829-1883) American
£1734 $3000   (21-May-91 CE.NY422/R) Women in farmyard (52x42cm-20x17in) s.

BELLOWS, George (1882-1925) American
£17553 $33000   (22-Sep-90 WOL.C300/R) Bleak Hills (41x61cm-16x24in) l.verso
£34682 $60000   (22-May-91 CH.NY264/R) Headland in fog (38x49cm-15x19in) s. l. verso
     panel
£98266 $170000   (23-May-91 SY.NY69/R) Three children (76x112cm-30x44in) l. sold with chl
     study l.verso

BELLUCCI, Antonio (1654-1726) Italian
£1816 $3250   (11-Apr-91 SY.NY32/R) Venus presenting the Golden Apples to Hippomenes
     (99x128cm-39x50in)
£15294 $26000   (31-May-91 CH.NY37/R) Diana and Endymion (145x150cm-57x59in)

BELLUCCI, Antonio (attrib) (1654-1726) Italian
£3000 $5910   (30-Oct-90 PH6/R) The four elements, sketch for ceiling design
     (47x61cm-19x24in)

BELLY, L (1827-1877) French
£800 $1576   (4-Oct-90 CSK47/R) Autumn on the river (40x50cm-16x20in) s.d.1872

BELLY, Leon Adolphe Auguste (1827-1877) French
£46559 $91255   (20-Nov-90 APT.P251/R) La Caravane a l'oasis (53x77cm-21x30in) s.d.1863
     (F.FR 460000)
£55668 $109109   (20-Nov-90 APT.P252/R) La chasse a la gazelle (74x146cm-29x57in)
     s.d.1857 (F.FR 550000)

BELMONDO, Paul (1898-1982) French?
£1050 $1712   *(5-Jul-91 APT.P5) Modele allonge (25x45cm-10x18in) s. pen wash*
     (F.FR 10500)
£2551 $5026   *(15-Oct-90 ARC.P21/R) Modele assis vu de dos (47x31cm-19x12in) s.i. pen*
     wash Indian ink (F.FR 25000)

BELOFF, Angelina (1905-) Russian
£9884 $17000   *(15-May-91 CH.NY69/R) Mascaras y Munecos (61x70cm-24x28in) s.d.55*
£3316 $6500   *(19-Nov-90 SY.NY149/R) Cuernavaca (29x36cm-11x14in) s.d.1940 W/C ink*

BELOKOUROV, Konstantin (1907-1983) Russian
£647 $1125   (25-Mar-91 ARC.P208) Sur la plage (50x70cm-20x28in) s. (F.FR 6500)
£2985 $5194   (25-Mar-91 ARC.P207/R) Les jouets (64x80cm-25x31in) s. (F.FR 30000)

BELOOUSSOV, Piotr (1912-1989) Russian
£843 $1450   (15-May-91 AGB.P88/R) Les pecheurs au repos (70x90cm-28x35in) s.
     (F.FR 8500)

BELOUSOV, Jkov Andreevich (1838-?) Russian
£2121 $4179   *(30-Oct-90 CH.AM439/R) View of sphinxes and St. Isaac's Cathedral, St.*
     Petersburg, across Neva (23x89cm-9x35in) s. pencil W/C htd white
     (D.FL 7000)

BELTRAN-MASSES, Frederico (1885-1949) Spanish
£1634 $2810   (16-May-91 ANS.M112/R) Figuras y paisaje (23x27cm-9x11in) s. board
     (S.P 300000)
£2457 $4250   (22-May-91 D.NY54/R) La Playa de Valencia (60x72cm-24x28in) s.i. board
£23205 $40145   (8-May-91 FER.M167/R) Bodegon de desnudos, uvas y manzanas
     (99x100cm-39x39in) s. (S.P 4250000)
£24570 $42506   (8-May-91 FER.M166/R) Alegoria de la noche (100x98cm-39x39in) s.
     (S.P 4500000)

BELUKINE, Dimitri (1962-) Russian
£3160 $6067   (29-Nov-90 YC.P60/R) Le lac de Valdai (60x132cm-24x52in) s.d.verso
     (F.FR 31000)

BEMELMANS, Ludwig (1898-1963) American
£510 $1000   (7-Nov-90 D.NY8) The Convent outing (74x53cm-29x21in) s. W/C ink pencil
£824 $1400   (1-Jun-91 IH.NY97/R) Riding lesson (23x30cm-9x12in) s. W/C ink
£828 $1400   (1-May-91 D.NY9) Fishing boats in port (43x64cm-17x25in) s. pastel
*   gouache*
£1693 $3250   (17-Dec-90 SY.NY228/R) Joyeux Noel (46x53cm-18x21in) s. W/C

BEMMEL, Georg Christoph Gottlieb II (1765-1811) German
£395 $672   (30-May-91 EA.Z319/R) Farmstead in landscape (18x23cm-7x9in) s. gouache
*   W/C (S.FR 1000)*
£1130 $2023   (13-Mar-91 N.M286/R) Rider, travellers and shepherd with flock in river
*   landscape (19x26cm-7x10in) s. gouache (DM 3300)*

BEMMEL, Jacob van (fl.1617-1635) Dutch
£3600 $6840   (1-Mar-91 C136 a/R) Italiante rocky landscape with peasants and
     livestock by fountain (52x79cm-20x31in) s. panel

BEMMEL, Johann Christoph (?-1776) German
£890 $1451   (12-Jun-91 N.M294/R) Thunderstorm over mountain landscape with ruins,
     monastery and castle (28x38cm-11x15in) s. metal (DM 2600)

BEMMEL, Karl Sebastian von (1743-1796) German
£2098 $4070   (7-Dec-90 GB.B5424/R) Mountainous river landscape with traveller at
*   sunset (18x23cm-7x9in) bodycol (DM 6000)*

BEMMEL, Peter von (attrib) (1685-1745) German
£1370 $2452   (13-Mar-91 N.M392 b/R) Wooded river landscape with mill and cattle
     (64x86cm-25x34in) (DM 4000)

BEMMEL, Wilhelm von (1630-1708) Dutch
£1107 $1881   (27-May-91 GK.Z5007/R) Traveller with two peasants in rocky landscape
     with torrent (24x28cm-9x11in) mono. (S.FR 2800)
£5000 $9850   (31-Oct-90 S156/R) Hunting party in river landscape (73x92cm-29x36in)
£2200 $3586   (1-Jul-91 S142) Winter scene - figures skating on river running through
*   village (17x22cm-7x9in) mono.gouache vellum*

BEN (1935-) Swiss
£904 $1455   (25-Jun-91 BG.P2) La verite changera l'art (25x20cm-10x8in) s. school
     slate (F.FR 9000)
£1363 $2685   (30-Oct-90 F.R195/R) Jesus Christ etait artiste (24x33cm-9x13in)
     s.d.1971verso acrylic (I.L 3000000)
£1541 $2512   (14-Jun-91 L.K1315/R) Jetzt zugreifen (60x73cm-24x29in) s. acrylic
     (DM 4500)
£1541 $2512   (14-Jun-91 L.K1312/R) Kunst. Die letzten Tage (46x55cm-18x22in) s.
     acrylic (DM 4500)
£1618 $3155   (15-Oct-90 CSC.P22/R) En promotion (38x61cm-15x24in) s. acrylic
     (F.FR 16000)
£1643 $3205   (23-Oct-90 C.A307/R) Autoportrait (40x40cm-16x16in) s. acrylic
     (B.FR 100000)
£2000 $3540   (21-Mar-91 C246/R) Je me suis regarde dans ce miroir plus de 2 heures
     (25x30cm-10x12in) s.i. acrylic mirror
£2022 $3943   (15-Oct-90 CSC.P24/R) Qualite superieure (60x73cm-24x29in) s. acrylic
     (F.FR 20000)
£2022 $3943   (15-Oct-90 CSC.P25) Tout doit disparaitre (60x73cm-24x29in) s. acrylic
     (F.FR 20000)
£2073 $4042   (15-Oct-90 CSC.P23/R) Affaire du jour (65x81cm-26x32in) s. acrylic
     (F.FR 20500)
£2174 $4239   (15-Oct-90 CSC.P21) Occasion a saisir (65x81cm-26x32in) s. acrylic
     (F.FR 21500)
£2224 $4338   (15-Oct-90 CSC.P18/R) Meme ceci (23x46cm-9x18in) s.d.85 verso panel
     (F.FR 22000)
£2341 $4566   (22-Oct-90 BR.M16/R) 'Je suis plus important que picasso et duchamp
     parceque...' i. panel (I.L 5200000)
£2427 $4732   (15-Oct-90 CSC.P17/R) Quick man, quick (30x40cm-12x16in) s. d.79 verso
     panel (F.FR 24000)
£2730 $5324   (15-Oct-90 CSC.P16/R) On est en guerre (65x45cm-26x18in) s.d.86 verso
     panel cut (F.FR 27000)
£2831 $5521   (15-Oct-90 CSC.P19) Ych nag die Deutschen (45x60cm-18x24in) s.d.1987
     verso panel (F.FR 28000)
£3511 $6846   (9-Oct-90 CSC.P71/R) Indifferent (61x74cm-24x29in) s.i. d.1974 verso
     acrylic (F.FR 35000)
£4032 $7863   (26-Oct-90 CC.P74/R) J'ai honte (60x60cm-24x24in) s.d.1970 acrylic panel
     (F.FR 40000)

BEN (1935-) Swiss-cont.
£5359 $10450   (15-Oct-90 CSC.P15/R) C'est le courage qui compte (78x111cm-31x44in)
        s.d.87 verso panel (F.FR 53000)
£659 $1292   (20-Nov-90 BR.M207/R) In that direction at this precise moment someone
        is dying (37x47cm-15x19in) i. ink (I.L 1450000)
£727 $1426   (20-Nov-90 BR.M109/R) Regardez Ben va faire un geste (21x19cm-8x7in)
        d.1962 ink (I.L 1600000)
£2010 $3296   (23-Jun-91 P.V64/R) L'art est pretention (69x69cm-27x27in) s. ink board
        (F.FR 20000)
£2326 $4535   (15-Oct-90 CSC.P20/R) Swedish suicide (28x45cm-11x18in) s. d.79 verso
        oil collage panel (F.FR 23000)
£2435 $4116   (15-Apr-91 CC.P131/R) La couleur est rouge mais passe vite au brun puis
        au noire (35x44cm-14x17in) s.d.1978 acrylic mousetraps panel
        (F.FR 24500)
£2520 $4914   (26-Oct-90 CC.P94/R) Coupe Gloria in excelsis des (50x50cm-20x20in)
        s.i.d.1986 chalise painted wood panel (F.FR 25000)
£3528 $6880   (26-Oct-90 CC.P73/R) Geste - penser l'histoire de l'art
        (75x75cm-30x30in) i.d. acrylic photographs panel (F.FR 35000)

BEN-SHAUL, Dedi (1930-) Israeli
£1227 $2000   (12-Jun-91 GG.TA239/R) Jerusalem Hills (95x94cm-37x37in) s. oil tempera
        board

BENARD, Jean Baptiste (?-1789) French
£2051 $4000   (11-Oct-90 SY.NY39/R) Shepherd seated by well (39x30cm-15x12in)
£5020 $8082   (27-Jun-91 APT.P183/R) La jeune fileuse. Le petit berger
        (32x40cm-13x16in) pair (F.FR 50000)

BENASCHI, Giovan Battista see BEINASCHI, Giovan Battista

BENASSIT, Louis Emile (1833-1902) French
£1071 $1800   (19-Jul-91 DM.D2061/R) Cavalrymen on a beach (33x23cm-13x9in) s.

BENCOVICH, Federico (1675-1753) Dalmatian
£4092 $7079   (21-May-91 SY.MI1039/R) Pieta (50x37cm-20x15in) copper oval
        (I.L 9000000)
£5001 $9801   (19-Nov-90 CH.R82/R) La Madonna col Bambino dormiente (63x49cm-25x19in)
        (I.L 11000000)

BENDA, Wladyslav T (1873-1948) American
£1118 $1900   (1-Jun-91 IH.NY210/R) Smiling woman picking daisies (43x36cm-17x14in) s.
*   chl pastel W/C*

BENDEMANN, Eduard Julius Friedrich (1811-1889) German
£372 $632   (27-May-91 L.K184/R) Allegorical figures seated on stone resting foot on
*   scull (25x13cm-10x5in) mono.d.49 pencil W/C board (DM 1100)*

BENDINI, Vasco (1922-) Italian
£2047 $3869   (27-Sep-90 F.M102) Immagine (100x80cm-39x31in) s.d.1959 verso
        (I.L 4500000)
£3827 $7463   (22-Oct-90 BR.M23/R) Untitled (73x60cm-29x24in) s.d.1960 verso
        (I.L 8500000)
£14408 $28095   (22-Oct-90 BR.M191/R) Composizione (130x200cm-51x79in) s.d.1960verso
        (I.L 32000000)

BENDIX, Leopold (19th C) German
£676 $1318   (26-Oct-90 KM.K1102) Genre scene with mother feeding child in interior
        (39x32cm-15x13in) s. (DM 2000)

BENDIXEN, Arne (?) Scandinavian
£792 $1331   (23-Apr-91 RAS.K273/R) Interior with young lady wearing riding costume
        (124x94cm-49x37in) s.d.95 (D.KR 9000)

BENDIXEN, Siegfried Detlev (1786-1864) German
£2000 $3940   (14-Nov-90 S55/R) Portrait of lady seated by table holding handkerchief
        with view of church (71x58cm-28x23in) s.d.1833

BENDTSEN, Folmer (1907-) Swedish
£725 $1399   (12-Dec-90 RAS.K195) Autumn day, Alexandra Road (38x55cm-15x22in) s.d.68
        (D.KR 8000)
£741 $1438   (5-Dec-90 AB.S7021/R) Street scene, Norrebro (60x70cm-24x28in) s.d.46
        (S.KR 8000)
£762 $1447   (14-Sep-90 RAS.V714/R) Street scene with figures, Alexandra vej
        (60x82cm-24x32in) s. (D.KR 8600)
£897 $1722   (27-Dec-90 RAS.V124/R) Street scene, winter, Alexandravej
        (60x82cm-24x32in) s. (D.KR 10000)
£1155 $2274   (31-Oct-90 KH.K7/R) Two fishermen chatting at the harbour
        (82x125cm-32x49in) s.d.53 (D.KR 13000)

BENDZ, Vilhelm (1804-1832) Danish
£1077 $2122   (14-Nov-90 RAS.K210/R) Portrait of lady wearing pale blue dress
        (67x55cm-26x22in) init.d.1823 (D.KR 12000)

BENEDITO-VIVES, Manuel (1875-1963) Spanish
£5703 $9183   (27-Jun-91 EP.M42/R) Pareja de campesinos (66x48cm-26x19in) s.
        (S.P 1050000)

BENEFIAL, Marco (attrib) (1684-1764) Italian
£1641 $3200   (10-Oct-90 CH.NY211/R) Portrait of lady wearing coat with fur trim and muff leaning on ledge (44x49cm-17x19in)

BENGER, Berenger (1868-1935) British
£500   *$825*   *(11-Jul-91 B167/R) Figure on country track with plough team beyond (28x44cm-11x17in) s.d.1899 W/C*

BENGSTON, Billy Al (1934-) American
£769   *$1500*   *(24-Oct-90 B.SF1572/R) Ka'ao (152x105cm-60x41in) init.d.1984 W/C paper collage*
£1410   *$2750*   *(24-Oct-90 B.SF1571/R) Ka'ao (151x99cm-59x39in) init.d.1984 W/C paper collage*

BENGTS, Carl (1876-1934) Finnish
£604 $1039   (14-May-91 HOR.H20) Stormy weather (35x31cm-14x12in) s.d.1918 (F.M 4200)
£1578 $2667   (20-Apr-91 HOR.H39/R) Reading at the table (26x33cm-10x13in) s.d.1926 (F.M 11000)

BENGTSSON, Dick (1936-1989) Swedish
£1205   *$2337*   *(5-Dec-90 AB.S7022/R) Composition (19x29cm-7x11in) s. W/C collage (S.KR 13000)*
£1549   *$2634*   *(28-May-91 AB.S5162/R) Composition (73x121cm-29x48in) s. collage oil (S.KR 16500)*

BENINI, Luigi (1767-1804) Italian
£10001 $19602   (20-Nov-90 F.R170/R) Pirro rapisce Astianatte alla madre (251x200cm-99x79in) s.d.1798 (I.L 22000000)

BENJUMEA, Rafael (19th C) Spanish
£9500 $17860   (6-Aug-90 SWS160/R) Spanish dancer (46x64cm-18x25in) s.d.1850

BENKER, A (19th C) German
£781 $1500   (17-Aug-90 DM.D2103/R) The card game (58x79cm-23x31in) s. canvas laid down on board

BENLLIURE Y GIL, Jose (1855-1919) Spanish
£1483 $2906   (20-Nov-90 DUR.M5) Gallinas picoteando (11x17cm-4x7in) panel (S.P 275000)
£8691 $13992   (27-Jun-91 EP.M25/R) Soldados en la calle (14x9cm-6x4in) panel (S.P 1600000)
£10526 $20000   (28-Feb-91 CH.NY105/R) Maria (88x59cm-35x23in) s.
£18000 $29520   (21-Jun-91 C99/R) Spaniards drinking in courtyard (13x20cm-5x8in) s. panel
£25641 $50000   (23-Oct-90 SY.NY104/R) Posada del sol (20x33cm-8x13in) s.i. panel

BENLLIURE Y GIL, Juan Antonio (19th C) Spanish
£819 $1582   (11-Dec-90 FER.M86/R) Retrato de nina en blanco y rosa (59x47cm-23x19in) s. (S.P 150000)
£7000 $11480   (19-Jun-91 S376/R) Tea time (93x69cm-37x27in) s.
£811   *$1581*   *(23-Oct-90 DUR.M61) Gitana (43x31cm-17x12in) W/C (S.P 150000)*

BENLLIURE Y GIL, Mariano (1862-?) Spanish
£542   *$1057*   *(17-Oct-90 FER.M41/R) Boceto para el monumento de Barbara de Braganza (29x22cm-11x9in) s. pencil dr (S.P 100000)*
£648   *$1265*   *(22-Oct-90 ANS.M142/R) Toro agonizante (23x31cm-9x12in) s.d.1921 ink (S.P 120000)*
£759   *$1480*   *(17-Oct-90 FER.M42/R) Dos bocetos de la estatua de Emilio Castelar (42x32cm-17x13in) s. pencil dr two in one frame (S.P 140000)*

BENN, Ben (1884-1983) American
£694 $1200   (21-May-91 CE.NY683/R) Cubist still life (51x41cm-20x16in) s.d.17
£1633 $3200   (7-Nov-90 D.NY9) Mountainous landscape (76x94cm-30x37in) s.d.32

BENN, Benejou (1905-) Polish
£750 $1260   (24-Apr-91 MJ.P102/R) Fleurs et livres sur une table (73x60cm-29x24in) s. (F.FR 7500)
£806 $1573   (14-Jan-91 YC.P137/R) Nature morte a la corbeille de fruits, pommes et raisin (46x55cm-18x22in) s. board (F.FR 8000)

BENNEDSEN, Jens Christian (1893-) Danish
£510 $903   (20-Mar-91 KM.K1103) Wooded winter landscape, Smaland (70x100cm-28x39in) s. (DM 1500)

BENNER, Gerrit (1897-1981) Dutch
£8050 $15536   (12-Dec-90 CH.AM378/R) Four horses by moonlight (75x57cm-30x22in) s. board (D.FL 26000)
£8108 $14027   (22-May-91 CH.AM636/R) Landschap met rode wolk (61x61cm-24x24in) init.verso board (D.FL 27000)
£9009 $15586   (23-May-91 SY.AM282/R) Fries landschap (100x80cm-39x31in) s. i.verso (D.FL 30000)
£10526 $20316   (12-Dec-90 CH.AM378 a/R) Landscape at summer, Friesland (73x58cm-29x23in) init.d.verso 69 board (D.FL 34000)
£11146 $21511   (13-Dec-90 SY.AM271/R) Autumn (100x80cm-39x31in) s.verso (D.FL 36000)

BENNER, Gerrit (1897-1981) Dutch-cont.
£12384 $23901   (12-Dec-90 CH.AM386/R) Landscape (80x100cm-31x39in) init.verso
                    (D.FL 40000)
£13003 $25096   (12-Dec-90 CH.AM387/R) Cows in landscape (60x75cm-24x30in) (D.FL 42000)
£13213 $22859   (23-May-91 SY.AM281/R) Landscape (100x80cm-39x31in) s.d.68verso
                    (D.FL 44000)
£18576 $35851   (13-Dec-90 SY.AM274/R) Cows (100x80cm-39x31in) (D.FL 60000)
£1981 $3824   (13-Dec-90 SY.AM405/R) Untitled (24x36cm-9x14in) gouache (D.FL 6400)

BENNER, Johan Philip Christiaan (1876-1956) Dutch
£405 $689   (28-May-91 KF.M468) Eksters (52x77cm-20x30in) mono.d.1927 mixed media
                    (DM 1200)

BENNETT, Alfred (19th C) British
£750 $1470   (21-Nov-90 B65) Arundel Castle, Sussex (34x54cm-13x21in) s.i.d.79 W/C
                    bodycol

BENNETT, Frank Moss (1874-1953) British
£880 $1716   (15-Jan-91 SWS199/R) Weighing the trout (34x25cm-13x10in) s.i.
£900 $1737   (13-Dec-90 CSK185/R) Three philosophers (51x36cm-20x14in) s.d.1928
£900 $1737   (13-Dec-90 CSK184) Three sportsmen (51x36cm-20x14in) s.d.1928
£1500 $3000   (8-Feb-91 C158/R) The novice (51x41cm-20x16in) s.d.1937 i. verso
£2600 $4238   (14-Jun-91 C263/R) The price of a song (91x127cm-36x50in) s.d.1903
£2700 $4509   (5-Jun-91 S171/R) Soldier watering horse (24x34cm-9x13in) s.d.1913
                    i.verso panel
£8800 $17600   (8-Feb-91 C167/R) The game of chess (51x41cm-20x16in) s.
£9800 $16366   (5-Jun-91 S174/R) Great pastry (61x91cm-24x36in) s.
£10000 $18600   (4-Sep-90 SC10/R) Bishop's move (48x38cm-19x15in) s.d.1925
£14000 $26040   (4-Sep-90 SC8/R) Merchant adventure (58x74cm-23x29in) s.d.1935
£15000 $27900   (4-Sep-90 SC11/R) Leisure hour (64x84cm-25x33in) s.
£16500 $30690   (4-Sep-90 SC9/R) Return of privateers (58x76cm-23x30in) s.d.1916

BENNETT, Frank Moss (attrib) (1874-1953) British
£1606 $3149   (11-Feb-91 SY.J380/R) The card players (35x50cm-14x20in) bears sig.
                    (SA.R 8000)
£1606 $3149   (11-Feb-91 SY.J381/R) Earth stopper (35x50cm-14x20in) bears sig.
                    (SA.R 8000)

BENNETT, Gordon (20th C) Australian
£1682 $2742   (16-Jun-91 SY.ME52/R) Man in dark sedan, 1987 (183x351cm-72x138in)
                    s.verso acrylic canvas gold paper curtains (A.D 3600)
£1682 $2742   (16-Jun-91 SY.ME34) Diptych, 1987 (251x358cm-99x141in) acrylic mixed
                    media canvas (A.D 3600)

BENNETT, William (1811-1871) British
£600 $1008   (22-Apr-91 PH248) Deer in hilly glade (27x48cm-11x19in) s. W/C
                    scratching out
£600 $1020   (29-May-91 PHC39) View of Harlech Castle (50x69cm-20x27in) s. W/C
£780 $1396   (14-Mar-91 PHX277/R) An extensive woodland landscape with Bolton Abbey
                    and figures resting (56x91cm-22x36in) s.d.185. W/C

BENNETT, William Rubery (1893-1987) Australian
£1931 $3803   (13-Nov-90 J.M84/R) Quiet waters (24x29cm-9x11in) s. board (A.D 5000)
£2124 $4183   (13-Nov-90 J.M324/R) Sunlit rock face, Central Australia
                    (24x29cm-9x11in) s. board (A.D 5500)
£2160 $3542   (17-Jun-91 MGS.S79) Approaching storm (24x29cm-9x11in) s. canvasboard
                    (A.D 4600)
£2390 $4709   (31-Oct-90 CH.S58) Kanderstag, Bernese Oberland, Switzerland
                    (38x46cm-15x18in) s. (A.D 6000)
£2723 $4466   (17-Jun-91 MGS.S78) Morning light (24x29cm-9x11in) s. board (A.D 5800)
£2723 $4466   (17-Jun-91 MGS.S80) Sunny corner (24x29cm-9x11in) s. canvasboard
                    (A.D 5800)
£2817 $4620   (17-Jun-91 MGS.S81) Road to farms, Murwillumbah (28x36cm-11x14in) s.
                    (A.D 6000)
£3165 $6076   (14-Aug-90 SY.ME298/R) The sunlit sea (29x37cm-11x15in) s. i. verso
                    (A.D 7500)
£3475 $6846   (13-Nov-90 J.M144/R) Reflections (27x28cm-11x11in) s.d.40 board
                    (A.D 9000)
£3475 $6846   (13-Nov-90 J.M4/R) Storm clouds, Silverdale NSW (37x45cm-15x18in) s.
                    (A.D 9000)
£3988 $7817   (19-Nov-90 MGS.S192/R) Burrangorang (34x45cm-13x18in) s. canvas on board
                    (A.D 10250)
£4633 $9127   (13-Nov-90 J.M138/R) Light play, Robertson (36x44cm-14x17in) s. canvas
                    on board (A.D 12000)
£6426 $12337   (26-Nov-90 SY.ME219/R) James Range near Hermansberg (49x59cm-19x23in) s.
                    i.verso (A.D 16000)
£6751 $12962   (14-Aug-90 SY.ME199/R) Afternoon glow (37x45cm-15x18in) s. (A.D 16000)
£8565 $14389   (16-Jul-91 JRL.S269/R) Barrogorang landscape (40x45cm-16x18in) s.
                    (A.D 18500)

BENNETTER, J (19th C) Norwegian
£3057 $5808   (11-Sep-90 UL.T175) Harbour scene from Vestlandet 1891 (30x49cm-12x19in)
                    (N.KR 35000)

BENNETTER, Johan Jacob (1822-1904) Norwegian
£955 $1595   (3-Jun-91 B.O6/R) Seascape (34x50cm-13x20in) s.d.1888 (N.KR 11000)

138

BENOIS, Alexander (1870-1960) Russian
£420 $806   *(27-Nov-90 C43/R) Costume design for The Idiot, Ferdystchenko*
               (49x32cm-19x13in) s.i.d.1924 i.verso pencil pen ink W/C htd.white
£550 $1073   *(10-Oct-90 C191/R) The Bobrinskoi Palace, St.Petersburg (16x22cm-6x9in)*
               i. pencil ink W/C
£600 $1170   *(15-Oct-90 PH13) Le temple d'amour (18x27cm-7x11in) s.d.1935 W/C pen*
               indian ink
£900 $1755   *(19-Oct-90 C183/R) Le lever du soleil (28x46cm-11x18in) s.i.d.1945*
               i.verso W/C pencil pen ink
£1020 $2000   *(12-Feb-91 SY.NY136 a/R) Jardin du Marie Rodin (30x46cm-12x18in)*
               s.i.d.1929 W/C
£1020 $2000   *(12-Feb-91 SY.NY53 a/R) Pont Marie (25x41cm-10x16in) s.i.d.1942 W/C*

BENOIT, Camille (1820-1882) French
£1138 $1980   *(26-Mar-91 VN.R8/R) Dog pulling a cart of vegetables (30x39cm-12x15in)*
               s. panel (D.FL 3800)

BENOIT, Ted (20th C) ?
£396 $701   *(6-Apr-91 CB.P64/R) Le cafe est servi (32x50cm-13x20in) Indian ink*
               (F.FR 4000)

BENRATH, Frederic (1930-) French
£2000 $3360   *(24-Apr-91 MJ.P123/R) L'errance et le retour (189x97cm-74x38in) s.d.1971*
               i. verso (F.FR 20000)

BENSA, Alexander von (1820-1902) Austrian
£1399 $2713   *(4-Dec-90 FN.S1754/R) Hunting party returning to country estate*
               (16x32cm-6x13in) s. panel (DM 4000)
£1399 $2713   *(4-Dec-90 FN.S1755/R) Setting out for the hunt in park landscape with*
               castle (16x31cm-6x12in) s. panel (DM 4000)
£2332 $4548   *(13-Oct-90 KRA.D175/R) Hungarian peasants at work (46x74cm-18x29in) s.*
               panel (DM 6950)
£2400 $4152   *(9-May-91 CSK95/R) Hunting party at rest (37x61cm-15x24in) s. panel*
£2542 $4144   *(3-Jul-91 WE.MU8/R) Kaisertreffen im Manover (25x40cm-10x16in) s. panel*
               (DM 7500)
£3154 $5961   *(27-Sep-90 D.V85/R) Riding out (16x26cm-6x10in) s. panel (A.S 65000)*
£3154 $5961   *(27-Sep-90 D.V86/R) Coach trip (16x26cm-6x10in) s. panel (A.S 65000)*
£4367 $8253   *(27-Sep-90 D.V74/R) Starting the hunt (26x40cm-10x16in) s. panel*
               (A.S 90000)
£7360 $14132 *(29-Nov-90 D.V21/R) Entry into the town (34x57cm-13x22in) s. panel*
               (A.S 150000)
£9597 $16507 *(16-May-91 D.V120/R) The billeting (36x58cm-14x23in) s. panel*
               (A.S 200000)

BENSA, Ernesto (19th C) Italian
£1087 $2087   *(18-Dec-90 DUR.M29/R) Loggia del Vasari (67x39cm-26x15in) W/C*
               (S.P 200000)

BENSA, Francesco (1830-?) Italian
£1350 $2255   *(22-Jul-91 SWS1091/R) Cowherds in a summer landscape (89x140cm-35x55in)*
               s.

BENSON, Ambrosius (after) (?-1550) Flemish
£2500 $4225   *(19-Apr-91 C36/R) Saint Mary Magdalen (185x157cm-73x62in)*

BENSON, Ambrosius (attrib) (?-1550) Flemish
£2874 $5000   *(27-Mar-91 B.SF4009/R) Portrait of young man wearing embroidered coat*
               (31x26cm-12x10in) panel
£18184 $35640 *(19-Nov-90 CH.R170/R) Trittico con la Deposizione di Cristo*
               (105x168cm-41x66in) shaped panel (I.L 40000000)

BENSON, Frank W (1862-1951) American
£1123 $2100   *(1-Aug-90 B.P30/R) Portrait of Alexander Pope (58x51cm-23x20in)*
               s.i.d.1892
£1198 $2000   *(26-Jul-91 E.EDM93/R) Tern alighting on eggs (23x30cm-9x12in) s..d.35*
               inkwash
£2000 $3800   *(18-Sep-90 S.W2729/R) Seascape (38x48cm-15x19in) s.d. W/C*
£2995 $5750   *(17-Dec-90 SY.NY222 a/R) Catching fish (69x51cm-27x20in) s. ink wash*
               over pencil paper on board
£5202 $9000   *(10-May-91 S.BM129/R) Pair of bluebills (41x53cm-16x21in)*
               s.indis.d.verso W/C htd.white graphite
£7813 $15000 *(30-Nov-90 CH.NY140/R) The leaning tree (38x51cm-15x20in) s.d.22 W/C*
               pencil board

BENSON, John P (1865-1947) American
£990 $1900   *(20-Feb-91 D.NY6) Clipper ship at full sail on high seas*
               (81x127cm-32x50in) s.d.1923

BENT, Jan van der (attrib) (1650-1690) Dutch
£4546 $8910   *(19-Nov-90 CH.R17/R) Paesaggio fluviale con rovine e pastori*
               (48x66cm-19x26in) (I.L 10000000)
£4800 $9456   *(30-Oct-90 PH25/R) Herdsmen and livestock resting by classical ruins*
               watching hawking party (77x94cm-30x37in) indis.s.

BENTELI, Wilhelm Bernhard (1839-1924) Swiss
£397 $663   (7-Jun-91 ZOF.Z1280) Winter landscape (32x22cm-13x9in) s. W/C
     (S.FR 1000)

BENTLEY, Charles (1806-1854) British
£8000 $15760   (1-Nov-90 C225/R) Donegal Bay, mist clearing off from Killybeg
     Mountains, Ireland (69x145cm-27x57in) s.d.1854 l.verso
£500 $975   (15-Jan-91 SWS49/R) Sailing barge and other shipping in rough weather
     (28x33cm-11x13in) s. W/C scratching out
£820 $1345   (18-Jun-91 OT415) St Michael's Mount, Cornwall (24x35cm-9x14in) W/C
£900 $1800   (8-Feb-91 C37/R) Fishermen on a river (28x43cm-11x17in) s. W/C gum
     arabic
£1450 $2813   (5-Dec-90 PHL44/R) Landing the catch (25x35cm-10x14in) s. col. washes
£1800 $2970   (11-Jul-91 S201/R) Fishing boats running into harbour and storm rising
     (49x74cm-19x29in) s.d.1848 W/C over pencil htd.bodycol
£2600 $4992   (26-Nov-90 SWS68/R) Bringing in the nets (62x87cm-24x34in) s.d.1845 W/C
     htd.bodycol.scratching out

BENTLEY, Claude (20th C) American
£2564 $5000   (24-Oct-90 B.SF1575/R) Walk on hillside (127x152cm-50x60in) s.d.88
     acrylic canvas

BENTLEY, Edward (19th C) British
£450 $752   (22-Jul-91 SWS879/R) Summer bouquet (40x32cm-16x13in) s. gouache

BENTLEY, John W (1880-?) American
£974 $1850   (14-Sep-90 S.BM232/R) Meandering stream, winter (64x76cm-25x30in) s.

BENTLEY, Joseph Clayton (1809-1851) British
£950 $1682   (21-Mar-91 CSK117/R) A logcart crossing a ford with children on a wooden
     bridge (46x61cm-18x24in) s.d.1847 l. verso

BENTON, Thomas Hart (1889-1975) American
£14451 $25000   (10-May-91 S.BM138/R) Study for Butterfly Chaser (20x15cm-8x6in) s.
     board
£15625 $30000   (30-Nov-90 CH.NY197/R) Watering the horse (8x11cm-3x4in) tin
£145833 $280000   (30-Nov-90 CH.NY197 a/R) The chute, Buffalo River (51x61cm-20x24in)
     s.d.70 egg tempera board
£592 $1000   (21-Apr-91 DU.E209) Island Hay (25x33cm-10x13in) s. W/C
£680 $1150   (21-Apr-91 DU.E210) Boy (23x36cm-9x14in) s. W/C
£1094 $2100   (17-Dec-90 SY.NY352/R) Study for pioneer woman - French (33x20cm-13x8in)
     i. pencil
£1323 $2500   (25-Sep-90 CE.NY92/R) Salvation Army (33x25cm-13x10in) s.d.28-22 ink
     pencil vellum laid down on board
£5263 $10000   (14-Sep-90 S.BM253/R) Landscape with two steer and windmill
     (38x56cm-15x22in) s. W/C ink
£9497 $17000   (12-Apr-91 SY.NY80/R) Two steer and windmill (39x56cm-15x22in) s.i. W/C
£13408 $24000   (14-Mar-91 CH.NY208/R) Bathers (38x33cm-15x13in) s. W/C pastel pencil
£27344 $52500   (29-Nov-90 SY.NY105/R) T.P. and Jake at the hillside (40x53cm-16x21in)
     s.d.40 W/C gouache

BENTZEN, Axel (1893-1952) Danish
£572 $1116   (10-Oct-90 RAS.K266) Evening landscape (97x115cm-38x45in) init.
     (D.KR 6500)
£1246 $2429   (19-Oct-90 RAS.V610/R) Young woman standing (120x90cm-47x35in) init.
     (D.KR 14000)

BENTZEN-BILKVIST, J (1865-1934) ?
£585 $988   (2-May-91 RAS.V302) Man by lake in beechwood, summer (92x74cm-36x29in)
     s.d.87 (D.KR 6600)

BENUZZI, E (?) Italian
£950 $1596   (18-Jul-91 CSK25/R) Fishing craft on Venetian lagoon at sunset
     (72x127cm-28x50in) s.pencil W/C

BENVENISTI, L (19th C) Italian
£1706 $3345   (24-Nov-90 SA.A634/R) Coastal landscape with figures in boat
     (56x90cm-22x35in) s. (DM 5000)

BENVENUTI, E (19/20th C) Italian
£400 $740   (6-Mar-91 SC4173) Waterway in Venice (38x23cm-15x9in) s. W/C
£680 $1136   (4-Jun-91 SWS748/R) Venice (40x68cm-16x27in) s. W/C

BENVENUTO DA GAROFALO see TISIO, Benvenuto da Garofalo

BEOTHY, Etienne (1876-1961) Hungarian
£1104 $1778   (25-Jun-91 BG.P3/R) Composition s.d.1937 gouache pasted board
     (F.FR 11000)

BEOTHY-STEINER, Anne (20th C) ?
£956 $1645   (14-May-91 GF.L2667/R) Composition (40x35cm-16x14in) mono.d.1929 gouache
     (S.FR 2400)

BERAIN, Jean I (1640-1711) French
£900 $1467   (1-Jul-91 S155/R) Costume design (34x23cm-13x9in) bears i.verso pen wash

BERANGER, Jean Baptiste Antoine Emile (1814-1883) French
£1622 $3000   (8-Mar-91 S.BM124 a) The letter (20x15cm-8x6in) s.d.1865 panel
£1900 $3116   (19-Jun-91 S168/R) Waiting for coach (21x16cm-8x6in) s.d.1841 panel
£4800 $7872   (19-Jun-91 S167/R) Young woman sewing (34x27cm-13x11in) s.d.1846 panel

BERARD (?) French
£1720 $2804   (5-Jul-91 QWA.P9/R) Les creations Jose Pasquier (54x37cm-21x15in)
     s.d.1946 wash indian ink W/C (F.FR 17200)

BERARD, Christian (1902-1949) French
£2500 $4200   (26-Apr-91 NM.P11) Le chemin de la vie (45x55cm-18x22in) s. (F.FR 25000)
£905 $1576   (28-Mar-91 DAR.P18) La Bonne Vie - L'Acrobate (20x12cm-8x5in) s. ink
     gouache (F.FR 9100)
£1592 $2770   (28-Mar-91 DAR.P17/R) Personnage aux rideaux (62x47cm-24x19in) W/C
     (F.FR 16000)
£5584 $11000   (15-Nov-90 SY.NY52/R) Portrait of Cecil Beaton (39x28cm-15x11in) s. ink
     W/C htd white
£5584 $11000   (15-Nov-90 SY.NY53/R) Peasant family by the sea (73x102cm-29x40in)
     s.d.1933 W/C ink

BERAUD (?) French
£2214 $3742   (2-May-91 RAS.V11) Anglais au St Remo (52x80cm-20x31in) (D.KR 25000)

BERAUD, Jean (1849-1936) French
£4555 $8927   (19-Nov-90 ARC.P33/R) Les cochers (39x28cm-15x11in) init. panel
     (F.FR 45000)
£6301 $12602   (4-Feb-91 LGB.P152/R) Jeune femme au bouquet de fleurs (35x25cm-14x10in)
     s.i. (F.FR 62000)
£9231 $18000   (23-Oct-90 SY.NY302/R) Portrait d'un homme elegant (38x24cm-15x9in) s.
     panel
£9474 $18000   (28-Feb-91 CH.NY18/R) Escrimeuse (34x15cm-13x6in) s. panel
£12000 $19680   (19-Jun-91 S225/R) Femme dans une barque (57x71cm-22x28in) s.
£15957 $30000   (22-Sep-90 WOL.C228/R) Femme en Priere (53x33cm-21x13in) s. panel
£69364 $120000   (22-May-91 SY.NY76/R) Theatre des Varietes, le Boulevard Montmartre,
     Paris (23x33cm-9x13in) s. panel
£80000 $131200   (19-Jun-91 S208/R) La maison Doree, Paris (40x31cm-16x12in) s.
£408 $792   (8-Dec-90 GAB.G2376/R) Couple etendu (17x22cm-7x9in) mono. W/C
     htd.crayon (S.FR 1000)
£1025 $2008   (7-Nov-90 APT.P452) Au spectacle (23x19cm-9x7in) s. pastel chk.
     (F.FR 10000)
£2561 $5020   (11-Nov-90 ZZ.F21/R) La Parisienne (41x26cm-16x10in) s. Indian ink W/C
     gouache (F.FR 25000)

BERAUD, Jean (after) (1849-1936) French
£1158 $2200   (15-Sep-90 S.W2789/R) Monte Carlo (102x127cm-40x50in) s.d.1886

BERAUD, Jean (attrib) (1849-1936) French
£791 $1400   (18-Mar-91 SG.M1275) Arriving via Hansom cab (64x46cm-25x18in) s.

BERBE, Guy (1937-) ?
£918 $1809   (12-Nov-90 YC.P61/R) Parapluies et bouilloires (119x91cm-47x36in) s.d.77
     acrylic varnish (F.FR 9000)
£986 $1923   (23-Oct-90 C.A308/R) Boites d'allumettes et cintres (80x60cm-31x24in) s.
     (B.FR 60000)

BERCHEM (after) (1620-1683) Dutch
£1653 $3257   (16-Nov-90 NM.P80) Scene campagnarde (121x139cm-48x55in) (F.FR 16200)

BERCHEM (school) (17th C) Dutch
£872 $1700   (24-Oct-90 D.NY24) Shepherds with flock in landscape (33x43cm-13x17in)

BERCHEM, N and POTTER, P (17th C) Dutch
£1050 $2048   (26-Oct-90 PHM2) A seated peasant drinking from a flagon his herd
     gathered around (36x45cm-14x18in) bears sigs.

BERCHEM, Nicolaes (1620-1683) Dutch
£3650 $7190   (30-Oct-90 BU.S228/R) Bird hunting with falcon and hounds
     (30x43cm-12x17in) s. panel (S.KR 40000)
£6145 $11000   (11-Apr-91 SY.NY178/R) Herdsman and washerwoman conversing by stream
     (38x46cm-15x18in) s.indist. panel
£7179 $14000   (11-Oct-90 SY.NY119 a/R) Southern landscape with peasants and animals
     (41x56cm-16x22in) canvas on panel
£11857 $19802   (4-Jun-91 CH.R245/R) Paesaggio con figura a cavallo e armenti
     (78x64cm-31x25in) s. (I.L 26000000)
£1706 $3225   (29-Sep-90 GRA.B2080/R) Shepherd playing a flute with cattle, sheep and
     his dog (19x30cm-7x12in) ochre dr. (DM 5000)

BERCHEM, Nicolaes (after) (1620-1683) Dutch
£1014 $1713   (3-May-91 SA.A1612/R) Pastoral scene (25x30cm-10x12in) metal (DM 3000)
£1115 $1884   (3-May-91 SA.A1614/R) Homeward bound (24x30cm-9x12in) metal (DM 3300)

BERCHEM, Nicolaes (circle) (1620-1683) Dutch
£1372 $2250   (19-Jun-91 B.SF1661/R) Landscape with figures and loaded mules
     (13x18cm-5x7in) panel
£2039 $3547   (25-Mar-91 SY.F577) Scena mitologica (52x68cm-20x27in) (I.L 4500000)

BERCHEM, Nicolaes (circle) (1620-1683) Dutch-cont.
£2041 $3612   (20-Mar-91 KM.K1033/R) Southern mountain landscape with shepherds and
            animals by river (49x68cm-19x27in) panel (DM 6000)
£2390 $4112   (14-May-91 GF.L2265/R) Annunciation to the Shepherds (70x59cm-28x23in)
            panel (S.FR 6000)

BERCHEM, Nicolaes (school) (1620-1683) Dutch
£1198 $2000   (23-Jan-91 D.NY54) Landscape with shepherdesses tending flock
            (64x58cm-25x23in)
£1350 $2200   (5-Jul-91 S.W3043/R) Along the trail (58x81cm-23x32in) indist.sig.
£2938 $5788   (14-Nov-90 D.V109/R) Shepherd scene with classical ruins
            (63x75cm-25x30in) i.d.1674 (A.S 60000)
£6284 $12379   (14-Nov-90 RAS.K9/R) Romantic landscape with shepherd and flock by
            castle (107x137cm-42x54in) (D.KR 70000)

BERCHEM, Nicolaes (style) (1620-1683) Dutch
£2167 $3618   (6-Jun-91 D.V262/R) Shepherd scene (28x41cm-11x16in) panel (A.S 45000)
£2600 $5200   (7-Feb-91 C95) Peasants watering their cattle at a pond
            (46x62cm-18x24in) s.d.1673
£3119 $6145   (13-Nov-90 AB.S851/R) Landscape with ruins, cattle and figures
            (67x83cm-26x33in) (S.KR 34000)
£3285 $6471   (30-Oct-90 BU.S229/R) Italian landscape with figures (82x112cm-32x44in)
            (S.KR 36000)
£3293 $5566   (2-May-91 CH.AM115/R) An Italianate landscape with shepherds, cattle and
            a flock of sheep by a river (47x61cm-19x24in) s. (D.FL 11000)
£4600 $8832   (29-Nov-90 CSK105/R) Levantine scene with traveller by quay and
            man-of-war beyond (69x80cm-27x31in)

BERCHER, Henri Edouard (1877-?) Swiss
£898 $1742   (8-Dec-90 GAB.G2377) Vue de St-Saphorin (61x81cm-24x32in) s. (S.FR 2200)

BERCHERE, Narcisse (1819-1891) French
£917 $1761   (26-Nov-90 CB.P97) La caravane au crepuscule (35x49cm-14x19in) s.
            (F.FR 9000)
£1015 $2000   (16-Nov-90 S.BM82/R) Arabian caravan (36x61cm-14x24in) s. panel
£1538 $3000   (26-Oct-90 SY.NY110/R) Nature morte au fromage (18x34cm-7x13in) init.
            board
£1693 $2878   (27-May-91 APT.P248/R) Dans le desert brulant (37x50cm-15x20in) s.
            (F.FR 17000)
£1942 $3302   (27-May-91 APT.P252/R) Nomades pres du Marabout (35x26cm-14x10in) s.
            panel (F.FR 19500)
£2194 $4322   (18-Nov-90 P.V11) Paysage africain s. (F.FR 21500)

BERCKHEYDE (after) (17th C) Dutch
£1200 $2304   (29-Nov-90 CSK111/R) View of the Grote Kerk, Haarlem (50x61cm-20x24in)
            bears sig.d.1667 canvas on panel

BERCKHEYDE, Gerrit Adriaensz (1638-1698) Dutch
£15541 $26419   (27-May-91 L.K11/R) Departure for the hunt (46x57cm-18x22in) s.
            (DM 46000)

BERCKHEYDE, Gerrit Adriaensz (attrib) (1638-1698) Dutch
£5877 $11577   (14-Nov-90 D.V201/R) Binnenhof in Den Haag (121x150cm-48x59in)
            (A.S 120000)

BERCKHEYDE, Gerrit Adriaensz (circle) (1638-1698) Dutch
£2000 $3800   (28-Feb-91 B62) Elegant couple on horseback taking refreshment
            (50x58cm-20x23in) mono. bears d.1657

BERCKHEYDE, Job Adriaensz (1630-1693) Dutch
£8500 $16575   (26-Oct-90 C148/R) An elegant Company at cards in an interior
            (50x41cm-20x16in)

BERDIA, Norberto (20th C) South American
£690 $1324   (28-Nov-90 KF.M560) Paisaje (53x41cm-21x16in) s. panel (DM 2000)

BEREA, Demetre de (1908-1975) Rumanian
£914 $1800   (13-Nov-90 CE.NY183/R) Balcon a Cannes (60x73cm-24x29in) s.d.49
£914 $1800   (13-Nov-90 CE.NY182/R) Nu sur un canape (73x60cm-29x24in) s.d.56
£1777 $3500   (13-Nov-90 CE.NY208/R) Les chaises rouges (74x91cm-29x36in) s.d.71
£1777 $3500   (13-Nov-90 CE.NY102/R) Jardin fleuri (74x91cm-29x36in) s.d.70
£4913 $8500   (7-May-91 CE.NY10/R) Vase de fleurs (65x46cm-26x18in) s.indist.i.d.50
£7362 $12000   (12-Jun-91 SY.NY139/R) Port at Cannes (73x92cm-29x36in) s.i.
            indist.i.stretcher

BEREAIS (?) ?
£1489 $2814   (25-Sep-90 GM.B966) Dame a sa toilette (70x50cm-28x20in) s. panel
            (B.FR 90000)

BEREND-CORINTH, Charlotte (1880-1967) German
£1092 $2141   (22-Nov-90 L.K833/R) Vase of flowers with autumn leaves
            (50x36cm-20x14in) s.d.1926 W/C (DM 3200)

BERENITTI, A C (19th C) ?
£1400 $2660   (28-Feb-91 B44/R) Figures standing beside Moorish gate in Seville
            (65x85cm-26x33in) init.i. i.verso

BERENNING, K (19/20th C) Russian
£1017 $1658   (3-Jul-91 WE.MU93/R) Horse-drawn sledge with figures (50x60cm-20x24in)
                 s. (DM 3000)

BERENTZ, Christian (1658-1722) German
£7523 $14669   (10-Oct-90 APT.P463/R) Flore pres d'un bouquet (88x118cm-35x46in)
                 (F.FR 75000)

BERESFORD, Cecilia Melanie (fl.1865-1885) British
£500   *$845*   *(1-May-91 ZZ.B180) Children playing beneath arch in backstreet*
                 (35x29cm-14x11in) s. W/C bodycol over pencil

BERG, Adolf Julius (1820-1873) Scandinavian
£852 $1432   (27-Apr-91 SO.S271/R) Landscape with two cows (23x32cm-9x13in) s.d.1871
                 (S.KR 9000)
£1799 $3023   (24-Apr-91 BA.S10 a/R) Calm summer evening (70x97cm-28x38in) s.d.1851
                 (S.KR 19000)

BERG, Albert (1825-1884) German
£1585 $2662   (23-Apr-91 RAS.K128/R) Harbour entrance at sunset (32x47cm-13x19in)
                 s.d.60 (D.KR 18000)
£1761 $2958   (23-Apr-91 RAS.K129/R) Fishing village, Bay of Napoli, evening
                 (31x45cm-12x18in) s.d.1862 (D.KR 20000)

BERG, Andries van den (1817-1880) Dutch
£2424 $4776   (30-Oct-90 CH.AM358/R) Peasant couple drinking coffee in interior
                 (44x57cm-17x22in) s. (D.FL 8000)

BERG, Anna (1875-1950) Swedish
£947 $1591   (24-Apr-91 BA.S11/R) Cala lilie (34x27cm-13x11in) s. (S.KR 10000)

BERG, Else (1877-1942) Dutch
£1548 $2988   (13-Dec-90 SY.AM94/R) Pottenbakker (90x60cm-35x24in) s. (D.FL 5000)
£6192 $11950   (13-Dec-90 SY.AM21/R) Adam en Eva (58x48cm-23x19in) s. (D.FL 20000)

BERG, Frans (1892-1949) Swedish
£1390 $2697   (5-Dec-90 AB.S7023/R) Still life of cut flowers (73x61cm-29x24in) s.
                 (S.KR 15000)

BERG, George Louis (1870-1941) American
£521 $1000   (17-Dec-90 SY.NY263/R) Islands (61x76cm-24x30in) s. d.1923 verso
£1150 $2150   (30-Aug-90 MFA.C141/R) Beyond the island (51x61cm-20x24in) s.d.1928
                 board

BERG, Gunnar (1864-1894) Norwegian
£1215 $2030   (3-Jun-91 B.O7/R) Winter landscape from North of Norway
                 (40x26cm-16x10in) s. canvas on panel (N.KR 14000)
£1226 $2194   (14-Mar-91 BU.O6/R) Svolvaer seen from Svolvaergeita (25x39cm-10x15in)
                 s. paper on canvas (N.KR 14000)
£3310 $6455   (15-Oct-90 B.O7/R) Winter landscape with graveyard (33x47cm-13x19in)
                 s.d.89 (N.KR 38000)

BERG, Simon van den (1812-1891) Dutch
£599 $1168   (25-Oct-90 VN.R8/R) Boy with cattle in landscape (33x42cm-13x17in) s.
                 (D.FL 2000)

BERG, Svante (1885-1946) Swedish
£1057 $2072   (10-Nov-90 FAL.M22/R) Summer (65x55cm-26x22in) s. (S.KR 11500)
£1250 $2450   (10-Nov-90 FAL.M20/R) Artist's wife wearing hat (101x74cm-40x29in) s.
                 (S.KR 13600)

BERG, Werner (1904-1981) Austrian
£6461 $12535   (6-Dec-90 D.V113/R) Tulips (75x40cm-30x16in) mono. (A.S 130000)

BERG, Willem van den (1886-1970) Dutch
£674 $1300   (10-Dec-90 H.C1183) Fishermen and wives (89x66cm-35x26in) s. board
£788 $1552   (30-Oct-90 CH.AM121) Visschers (18x13cm-7x5in) s.l.verso (D.FL 2600)
£800 $1560   (15-Oct-90 PH14) The vulture (105x64cm-41x25in) s. board
£970 $1910   (30-Oct-90 CH.AM119/R) Cattle market, Briancon (18x17cm-7x7in) s.d.1940
                 panel (D.FL 3200)
£3030 $5970   (30-Oct-90 CH.AM122/R) Net-menders (60x44cm-24x17in) s. panel
                 (D.FL 10000)

BERGAMESE SCHOOL, 16th C Italian
£22088 $35562   (27-Jun-91 APT.P31/R) Portrait d'un religieux (110x90cm-43x35in)
                 (F.FR 220000)

BERGAMESE SCHOOL, 17th C Italian
£10050 $16482   (22-Jun-91 CH.MO133/R) Portrait d'un jeune homme, habille de rouge
                 (170x110cm-67x43in) (F.FR 100000)

BERGAMINI, Francesco (1815-1883) Italian
£1300 $2548   (15-Feb-91 C75/R) Young accordian player (24x16cm-9x6in) s.l.
£2800 $5376   (27-Nov-90 PH183/R) Mischievous games (67x44cm-26x17in) s.l.
£3200 $6304   (5-Oct-90 C158/R) Monk's visit (45x67cm-18x26in) s.
£8671 $15000   (22-May-91 SY.NY301/R) School room (51x81cm-20x32in) s.l.

BERGEN, Carl von (1853-1933) German
£2590 $4454   (14-May-91 GF.L2383/R) Returning home from the field (87x68cm-34x27in)
        s.i. (S.FR 6500)

BERGEN, Claus (1885-1964) German
£936 $1583   (17-Apr-91 WE.MU225/R) Fishing boats in harbour (18x24cm-7x9in) s. panel
        (DM 2800)
£1182 $2306   (26-Oct-90 BM.B744/R) Lake landscape (75x121cm-30x48in) s.i. (DM 3500)
£1250 $2100   (17-Jul-91 SY.NY294/R) Returning to port (33x48cm-13x19in) s.d.13
£3041 $5139   (3-May-91 SA.A1740/R) The fleet returning home (58x67cm-23x26in) s.
        (DM 9000)

BERGEN, Dirck van (1645-1690) Dutch
£2079 $4117   (30-Jan-91 APT.P77/R) Le Repos des bergers pres de la fontaine
        (55x65cm-22x26in) s. (F.FR 20500)
£2191 $3769   (14-May-91 GF.L2274/R) Southern landscape with cattle (52x65cm-20x26in)
        (S.FR 5500)

BERGEN, Eugene (19th C) ?
£850 $1675   (4-Oct-90 CSK139/R) The piano lesson (34x24cm-13x9in) s. board

BERGENSTRAHLE, Marie Louise de Geer (1944-) Swedish
£2502 $4854   *(5-Dec-90 AB.S7057/R) Town scene II (61x74cm-24x29in) s.d.1976 W/C*
        (S.KR 27000)
£2873 $5574   *(5-Dec-90 AB.S7058/R) Lady crying (23x17cm-9x7in) s.d.1976 W/C*
        (S.KR 31000)

BERGER (?) ?
£1563 $3000   (18-Dec-90 BG.M1000/R) Armed figures on shore with life boat and
        floundering ship in distance (74x104cm-29x41in) s.

BERGER, Einar (1893-) Norwegian
£742 $1410   (11-Sep-90 UL.T176 a/R) From North of Norway (40x60cm-16x24in)
        (N.KR 8500)
£1223 $2323   (11-Sep-90 UL.T176/R) Fishing fleet going out (90x105cm-35x41in)
        (N.KR 14000)

BERGER, Ernst (1857-1919) Austrian
£3566 $6990   (24-Nov-90 HOR.H3/R) A game of chess (75x91cm-30x36in) s. (F.M 25000)

BERGER, Hans (1882-1977) Swiss
£874 $1687   (14-Dec-90 BM.B715/R) Snowy wooded landscape with frozen pond
        (80x120cm-31x47in) s. (DM 2500)
£2008 $3936   (21-Nov-90 SY.Z87/R) Still life of fruit (34x46cm-13x18in) s.
        (S.FR 5000)
£3953 $6719   (27-May-91 GK.Z5305) Matin d'ete (60x73cm-24x29in) s. (S.FR 10000)
£522 $1023   *(21-Nov-90 SY.Z68/R) Coastal landscape (36x49cm-14x19in) s. W/C*
        (S.FR 1300)
£531 $1029   *(8-Dec-90 GAB.G2378/R) La lecture (24x32cm-9x13in) s. W/C blk.oil crayon*
        (S.FR 1300)
£683 $1338   *(21-Nov-90 SY.Z89/R) Still life of fruit (24x33cm-9x13in) s. W/C*
        (S.FR 1700)

BERGER, Johan Christian (1803-1871) Swedish
£576 $939   (13-Jun-91 RAS.V514/R) Coastal landscape with sailship and full moon
        (25x28cm-10x11in) s. (D.KR 6500)

BERGER, Julius Victor (1850-1902) Austrian
£26392 $45393   (16-May-91 D.V107/R) Young lady at Naschmarkt with Sezession beyond
        (84x68cm-33x27in) s.d.901 (A.S 550000)

BERGERAT, Philippe (1926-) French
£500 $840   (28-Apr-91 FE.P66) La rue commercante (46x55cm-18x22in) s. (F.FR 5000)
£594 $1051   (7-Apr-91 I.N40) La Seine (38x46cm-15x18in) s. (F.FR 6000)

BERGERET (?) French
£2041 $4020   (14-Nov-90 FB.P101/R) La lecon de lecture (41x33cm-16x13in) s.
        (F.FR 20000)

BERGERET, Denis Pierre (1846-1910) French
£1892 $3274   (24-May-91 FB.P117) Scene d'interieur (46x38cm-18x15in) s. (F.FR 19000)
£2100 $3444   (18-Jun-91 PH41/R) Still life with lobster, oysters and other shellfish
        on stone ledge (57x77cm-22x30in) s.i.d.1887

BERGES, Werner (1941-) ?
£629 $1221   (7-Dec-90 GB.B6339) Two young women (60x90cm-24x35in) s.i.d.1977verso
        tempera paper on canvas (DM 1800)

BERGEVIN, Edouard de (1861-1925) French
£2684 $4536   (21-Apr-91 B.PA44) Bord de Seine (38x61cm-15x24in) s.d.1920 (F.FR 27000)

BERGH, Edvard (1828-1880) Swedish
£3030 $5091   (24-Apr-91 BA.S10/R) Figures by the camp-fire (126x168cm-50x66in)
        s.d.1861 (S.KR 32000)

BERGH, Rickard (1858-1919) Swedish

£640	$1254	(20-Nov-90 GO.G11/R) Harbour pier (32x40cm-13x16in) init.d.85 panel (S.KR 7000)
£1610	$2705	(24-Apr-91 BA.S12/R) Coastal field, Halland (26x35cm-10x14in) mono.verso panel (S.KR 17000)
£1705	$2864	(24-Apr-91 BA.S13/R) Lake landscape, Kalvfjarden, Tyreso (74x50cm-29x20in) (S.KR 18000)
£2500	$4925	(5-Oct-90 C118 c/R) Garjekarlen - ferryman (94x110cm-37x43in) st.init. verso

BERGHE, Augustin van den (1756-1836) Flemish

£1276	$2513	(14-Nov-90 FB.P269/R) Autoportrait (27x21cm-11x8in) s.d.1831 (F.FR 12500)
£31000	$50530	(5-Jul-91 C282/R) Portrait of Comte Louis Rene and Comtesse Genevieve Josephine Emilie des Courtils (163x136cm-64x54in) s.d.1808

BERGHE, Christoffel van den (1617-1642) German

£12333	$23926	(7-Dec-90 SY.MO135/R) Paysage d'hiver avec patineurs (13x17cm-5x7in) on bronze (F.FR 120000)
£26000	$50180	(12-Dec-90 S7 a) Still life of flowers copper oval

BERGHE, Frits van den (1883-1939) Belgian

£1473	$2475	(23-Apr-91 C.A232/R) Reclining nude man (30x60cm-12x24in) (B.FR 90000)
£30000	$58500	(17-Oct-90 S68/R) De laatste kanoner (63x46cm-25x18in) s. paper on panel
£42000	$81900	(16-Oct-90 C40/R) Masques (52x35cm-20x14in) s. paper laid down on panel
£108108	$187027	(23-May-91 SY.AM35/R) Fleurs sur la ville I (116x88cm-46x35in) s. (D.FL 360000)
£867	*$1673*	*(13-Dec-90 SY.AM63/R) Untitled (14x11cm-6x4in) mono. ink (D.FL 2800)*
£2024	*$3926*	*(8-Dec-90 KV.L283/R) Seated woman (28x19cm-11x7in) mono.d.1921 W/C (B.FR 120000)*

BERGMAN, Anna-Eva (1909-1987) Swedish/French

£615	$1200	(10-Oct-90 SY.NY328/R) Composition (38x46cm-15x18in) s.d.1961 oil silver paint
£750	$1208	(28-Jun-91 CSK46/R) Petit montagne de Norwege, No. 2, 1965 (33x46cm-13x18in) i.stretcher oil gold silver paint board
£1106	$1979	(11-Mar-91 GL.P229) Composition (38x45cm-15x18in) init.d.1961 oil silver sheet (F.FR 11000)
£1800	$2898	(28-Jun-91 CSK13/R) No. 10, 1964 (100x81cm-39x32in) init.d.1964 i.d.stretcher oil gold paint

BERGMAN, Karl (1891-1965) Swedish

£660	$1109	(23-Apr-91 RAS.K207) Archipelago (30x40cm-12x16in) s. (D.KR 7500)
£671	$1315	(10-Nov-90 FAL.M27/R) Coastal landscape with red cottage (43x55cm-17x22in) s. panel (S.KR 7300)
£791	$1471	(9-Sep-90 BU.M436) Coastal landscape at sunset (32x40cm-13x16in) s. (S.KR 8500)
£919	$1801	(10-Nov-90 FAL.M28/R) Coastal landscape, Blekinge (38x46cm-15x18in) s. (S.KR 10000)
£1103	$2162	(10-Nov-90 FAL.M26/R) Archipelago (49x75cm-19x30in) s. (S.KR 12000)
£1208	$2163	(13-Apr-91 FAL.M23/R) Sunny winter landscape with red cottages (46x58cm-18x23in) s. (S.KR 13000)
£1461	$2864	(10-Nov-90 FAL.M25/R) Sunshine on water, skerries (49x76cm-19x30in) s. (S.KR 15900)

BERGMAN, Oskar (1879-1963) Swedish

£976	$1747	(9-Apr-91 GO.G8) Timber yard (37x40cm-15x16in) s. (S.KR 10500)
£15539	$30457	(20-Nov-90 GO.G13/R) Foreland at Ljustero (100x145cm-39x57in) init.d.1910-1934 (S.KR 170000)
£558	*$998*	*(9-Apr-91 GO.G199) Winter landscape with church (24x33cm-9x13in) s.d.1958 W/C htd white (S.KR 6000)*
£627	*$1223*	*(8-Oct-90 AB.S1012) Bad weather in summer (32x40cm-13x16in) s. W/C (S.KR 6900)*
£994	*$1670*	*(24-Apr-91 BA.S265/R) Wood anemones in birchwood (14x9cm-6x4in) s. W/C (S.KR 10500)*
£1103	*$2162*	*(6-Nov-90 BA.S361/R) Moonlit wood (34x49cm-13x19in) s.d.1924 W/C (S.KR 12000)*
£1509	*$2611*	*(22-May-91 BA.S536/R) Silver birches in spring. Junipers (5x4cm-2x2in) s. W/C pair (S.KR 16000)*
£1549	*$2634*	*(28-May-91 AB.S4602/R) Spring landscapes with trees and houses (6x4cm-2x2in) s. W/C pair (S.KR 16500)*
£1604	*$2775*	*(22-May-91 BA.S535/R) Clouds over Uppland (37x55cm-15x22in) s.d.1937 W/C (S.KR 17000)*
£1989	*$3341*	*(24-Apr-91 BA.S264/R) Dogroses in landscape (20x26cm-8x10in) s. W/C (S.KR 21000)*
£2298	*$4504*	*(6-Nov-90 BA.S359/R) Jetty by Sandhamn (37x55cm-15x22in) s.d.1960 W/C (S.KR 25000)*
£3125	*$6125*	*(6-Nov-90 BA.S358/R) Still life of flowers (31x42cm-12x17in) s.d.1948 W/C (S.KR 34000)*
£3309	*$6485*	*(6-Nov-90 BA.S360/R) Birches in spring (32x32cm-13x13in) s.d.1916 W/C (S.KR 36000)*

BERGMANN, Julius Hugo (1861-1940) German

£30000	$49200	(21-Jun-91 C73/R) Lowen auf dem Raubzuge (137x221cm-54x87in) s.d.90 i.verso

BERGMANN, Max (1884-1955) German

£1351	$2635	(26-Oct-90 BM.B745/R) Cows grazing (54x73cm-21x29in) s. (DM 4000)
£2218	$4193	(25-Sep-90 FN.S2114/R) Two cows in wooded lake landscape (45x60cm-18x24in) (DM 6500)
£2448	$4724	(12-Dec-90 WE.MU156/R) Peasant woman with cows (40x60cm-16x24in) s. board (DM 7000)
£3020	$5889	(10-Oct-90 WE.MU176/R) Girl guarding cows by fence (41x60cm-16x24in) s. panel (DM 9000)
£3147	$6105	(4-Dec-90 FN.S1759/R) Cattle in Worther Auen (69x100cm-27x39in) s. (DM 9000)
£4348	$7348	(19-Apr-91 FN.S1668/R) Cattle by gate in wooded landscape (61x75cm-24x30in) s.d.1906 (DM 13000)
£5802	$10966	(25-Sep-90 FN.S2113/R) Wooded landscape with girl driving cattle (40x60cm-16x24in) s. panel (DM 17000)

BERGMANN-MICHEL, Ella (1896-?) German

| *£2305* | *$3849* | *(6-Jun-91 HN.H162/R) Composition s.d.1928 collage (DM 6800)* |

BERGMANS, Jacques (20th C) Belgian?

| £1096 | $2126 | (8-Dec-90 KV.L36) A street in Ghent (50x60cm-20x24in) s.d.1945 (B.FR 65000) |

BERGMULLER, Johan Georg (attrib) (1688-1762) German

| *£1174* | *$2290* | *(12-Oct-90 AW.H1174/R) Godfather enthroned on clouds surrounded with symbols and angels (36x25cm-14x10in) c.1730 pencil wash (DM 3500)* |

BERGNER, Yosl (1920-) Israeli

£1176	$1988	(16-Apr-91 J.M18/R) Village musicians (50x37cm-20x15in) s. (A.D 2600)
£1963	$3200	(12-Jun-91 GG.TA243/R) Girl (35x27cm-14x11in) s.
£2199	$4200	(1-Jan-91 GG.TA263/R) Saucepans (50x73cm-20x29in) s.c.1971
£2489	$4206	(16-Apr-91 J.M6/R) The wedding (40x50cm-16x20in) s. (A.D 5500)
£2811	$5398	(26-Nov-90 SY.ME297/R) Painting to Franz Kafka's The Trial (48x59cm-19x23in) s.d.87 s.i.verso (A.D 7000)
£2827	$5400	(1-Jan-91 GG.TA264/R) Angels (130x81cm-51x32in) s.d.1960
£3376	$6481	(14-Aug-90 SY.ME265/R) The peacemakers (61x49cm-24x19in) s. i.d.1979 verso (A.D 8000)
£3620	$6118	(16-Apr-91 J.M230 a/R) The predators (81x100cm-32x39in) s. (A.D 8000)
£3721	$6251	(22-Apr-91 SY.ME336/R) Franz Kafka, trial - you are accused man (116x72cm-46x28in) s.i.d.88 s.i.verso (A.D 8000)
£4188	$8000	(1-Jan-91 GG.TA262/R) Two orange growers (50x61cm-20x24in) s. s.i.d.1979
£5581	$9377	(22-Apr-91 SY.ME326/R) Botanist (117x96cm-46x38in) s.d.79 s.i.verso (A.D 12000)
£5882	$9941	(16-Apr-91 J.M142/R) Childhhod memories (100x81cm-39x32in) s. (A.D 13000)
£9424	$18000	(1-Jan-91 GG.TA261/R) Icarus in the sea of tears (100x100cm-39x39in) s.d.1968 s.i.verso
£491	*$800*	*(12-Jun-91 GG.TA40/R) Saucepans - the 60's (34x50cm-13x20in) s. pastel*
£491	*$800*	*(12-Jun-91 GG.TA39/R) Figures - the 50's (61x49cm-24x19in) s. pen*
£541	*$1065*	*(13-Nov-90 J.M261) Acrobats (39x28cm-15x11in) s.d.54 mixed media (A.D 1400)*
£618	*$1217*	*(13-Nov-90 J.M181) Puppets (19x27cm-7x11in) s.d.56 W/C ink (A.D 1600)*
£633	*$1071*	*(16-Apr-91 J.M506) Apples on a table (30x44cm-12x17in) s.d.'56 W/C (A.D 1400)*
£695	*$1369*	*(13-Nov-90 J.M168/R) The clown (48x33cm-19x13in) s.d.58 W/C pencil (A.D 1800)*
£838	*$1600*	*(1-Jan-91 GG.TA265/R) Angels (69x48cm-27x19in) s.i.d.1960 W/C*

BERGOLLI, Aldo (1916-1972) Italian

£683	$1162	(28-May-91 SY.MI53/R) Composizione (69x99cm-27x39in) s.d.56 (I.L 1500000)
£991	$1932	(24-Oct-90 F.M121/R) Figura (70x100cm-28x39in) (I.L 2200000)
£1145	$2199	(27-Nov-90 SY.MI51/R) Composizione (69x69cm-27x27in) s.d.57 (I.L 2500000)
£1374	$2638	(27-Nov-90 SY.MI126/R) Composizione (68x100cm-27x39in) s.d.55 (I.L 3000000)

BERGSLIEN, Nils (1853-1928) Norwegian

£1823	$3555	(11-Oct-90 BU.O14/R) Visiting a sick friend (36x27cm-14x11in) s. (N.KR 21000)
£2493	$4812	(13-Dec-90 BU.O8/R) Waterfall (182x73cm-72x29in) s. (N.KR 28000)
£3740	$7218	(13-Dec-90 BU.O6/R) Cheese-farm girl (183x135cm-72x53in) s. (N.KR 42000)
£6130	$10972	(14-Mar-91 BU.O7/R) Harald Harfagre proposing to Gyda (95x75cm-37x30in) s. (N.KR 70000)
£8014	$15467	(13-Dec-90 BU.O7/R) Boy with flute (183x133cm-72x52in) s. (N.KR 90000)
£10686	$20623	(13-Dec-90 BU.O5/R) High mountains (182x339cm-72x133in) s. (N.KR 120000)

BERGSTROM, Alfred (1869-1930) Swedish

| £900 | $1511 | (24-Apr-91 BA.S16/R) Sunset over the sea (94x139cm-37x55in) s. (S.KR 9500) |
| £1799 | $3023 | (24-Apr-91 BA.S15/R) Wooded landscape with brook (82x100cm-32x39in) s.d.1918 (S.KR 19000) |

BERGUE, Tony Francis de (1820-?) French

| £845 | $1436 | (27-May-91 L.K244) Fishing town, Normandy (25x41cm-10x16in) s. panel (DM 2500) |
| £4615 | $9000 | (23-Oct-90 SY.NY299/R) Vue de Lisbonne (49x80cm-19x31in) s. |

BERJON, Antoine (1754-1843) French
£2373 $4200   (22-Mar-91 CH.NY627/R) A leafy branch with apples. A leafy branch with apricots (47x29cm-19x11in) i. col.chks. pair

BERJON, Antoine (circle) (1754-1843) French
£3000 $5790   (12-Dec-90 PH16/R) Still life of flowers in basket on ledge with view of formal garden (66x50cm-26x20in) gouache

BERJON, Antoine (studio) (1754-1843) French
£11000 $18370   (3-Jun-91 RY.P22/R) Vase fleuri et fruits sur un entablement. Vase fleuri sur un entablement (46x38cm-18x15in) bears sig.d.1813 pair (F.FR 110000)
£2209 $3556   (27-Jun-91 APT.P248/R) Corbeille de fleurs et prunes posees sur un entablement de marbre (67x56cm-26x22in) bears sig.d.1812 gouache (F.FR 22000)

BERKE, Hubert (20th C) German?
£3729 $6227   (8-Jun-91 HN.H31/R) Composition (40x55cm-16x22in) s.d.1955 (DM 11000)
£1027 $1675   (14-Jun-91 L.K746) Untitled (62x48cm-24x19in) s.i.d.1962 indian ink wash W/C htd.white (DM 3000)
£2911 $4745   (14-Jun-91 L.K745/R) Untitled (35x73cm-14x29in) s.d.57 oil plaster board on panel (DM 8500)

BERKELEY, Stanley (?-1909) British
£2308 $4500   (24-Oct-90 CH.NY323/R) Full cry (50x81cm-20x32in) s.

BERKEMEIER, Ludolph (1864-1931) Dutch
£629 $1195   (11-Sep-90 SY.AM17) Langs den plas (129x82cm-51x32in) (D.FL 2100)

BERKES (?) ?
£1327 $2613   (13-Nov-90 HC.P209) Scene de rue (80x118cm-31x46in) (F.FR 13000)

BERKES, Antal (1874-?) Hungarian
£907 $1769   (28-Oct-90 M.V162) Notre Dame (60x81cm-24x32in) s. (F.FR 9000)
£1040 $1800   (21-May-91 CE.NY341/R) Parisian street scene (20x33cm-8x13in) s. panel
£1618 $2750   (1-Jun-91 LAE.L7/R) Winter street scene (53x66cm-21x26in) s.
£2425 $4559   (20-Sep-90 D.V25/R) Evening (92x121cm-36x48in) s. panel (A.S 50000)
£2838 $4626   (10-Jun-91 W.T1412/R) Summer sunlight on a broad boulevard (63x94cm-25x37in) s. (C.D 5250)

BERLEPSCH-VALENDAS, Hans Eduard von (1849-1921) Swiss
£1199 $1954   (12-Jun-91 N.M371/R) Girl picking flowers in field (47x71cm-19x28in) s.i. (DM 3500)

BERLIN, Sven Paul (1911-) British
£1200 $2088   (27-Mar-91 S195/R) Gypsies in the New Forest (25x35cm-10x14in) s.d.1955
£750 $1208   (28-Jun-91 CSK187/R) Cattle resting (14x32cm-6x13in) s.d.48 pen wash

BERLY, Madeleine (1896-1953) French
£968 $1859   (2-Dec-90 M.V155) Jeune fille au collier vert (49x31cm-19x12in) s. gouache (F.FR 9500)
£1061 $2059   (8-Dec-90 GAB.G2379/R) Deux soeurs (64x50cm-25x20in) s. (S.FR 2600)

BERMAN, Eugene (1899-1972) Russian
£510 $1000   (12-Feb-91 SY.NY88/R) Bacchanale (10x15cm-4x6in) s.d.1964 s.i.d.verso W/C gouache pencil pen ink
£798 $1500   (19-Sep-90 B.SF2713/R) Porte du soleil (22x17cm-9x7in) init. i.d.1936 verso ink wash
£1905 $3600   (25-Sep-90 CE.NY152/R) Concerto Barocco stage set. Pillar of Fire. Prato della Valle, Padua s.i.d.1941 s.d.1943 s.d.1932 2 W/C 1 pen three

BERMAN, Leonid (1898-) Russian
£1058 $2000   (27-Sep-90 CH.NY260/R) Japanese fishermen (86x127cm-34x50in) init.d.56 i. verso
£2243 $4328   (16-Dec-90 CL.E17) Le port (60x92cm-24x36in) s.d.avril 27 (F.FR 22000)

BERMUDEZ, Cundo (1914-) Cuban
£6633 $13000   (20-Nov-90 CH.NY221/R) Cena en al puerto (61x79cm-24x31in) s.d.54
£751 $1300   (22-May-91 D.NY128) Woman with fan (93x71cm-37x28in) s. gouache

BERMUTH, Ernst von (1883-1923) German
£1486 $2899   (26-Oct-90 KM.K1104) Wooded landscape with peasant girl carrying basket and rake (90x72cm-35x28in) s. (DM 4400)

BERNALDO, Allan T (1900-1988) Australian
£382 $733   (26-Nov-90 SY.ME149) Lockhard Gorge, Port Campbell (29x41cm-11x16in) s. i.verso W/C paper on board (A.D 950)
£386 $761   (13-Nov-90 J.M925) Old country bridge (34x26cm-13x10in) s. W/C (A.D 1000)
£463 $913   (13-Nov-90 J.M950) Mountain vista (36x45cm-14x18in) s. W/C (A.D 1200)
£683 $1311   (26-Nov-90 SY.ME128) Warburton mountains, western aspect (39x53cm-15x21in) s. i.verso W/C paper on board (A.D 1700)
£1333 $2507   (17-Sep-90 MGS.S232/R) Phlox (39x54cm-15x21in) s. W/C (A.D 3000)
£1810 $3059   (16-Apr-91 J.M8/R) The polo players (33x44cm-13x17in) s. W/C (A.D 4000)
£1860 $3126   (22-Apr-91 SY.ME95/R) Returning home (31x42cm-12x17in) s. W/C (A.D 4000)

BERNALDO, Allan T (1900-1988) Australian-cont.
£3167 $5353   *(16-Apr-91 J.M250 a) Still life, flowers in a vase (65x75cm-26x30in) s. W/C (A.D 7000)*

BERNARD, Emile (1868-1941) French
£1205	$2337	(5-Dec-90 AB.S7028/R) Portrait of lady (64x53cm-25x21in) s.d.40 panel (S.KR 13000)
£1393	$2410	(12-May-91 T.B234) La mise au tombeau (48x40cm-19x16in) s. (F.FR 14000)
£2000	$3540	(22-Mar-91 BG.P80) Maison bretonne (27x35cm-11x14in) s. panel (F.FR 20000)
£2100	$3528	(28-Apr-91 FE.P68) Nature morte aux harengs (65x50cm-26x20in) s. board (F.FR 21000)
£2548	$4918	(16-Dec-90 T.B97/R) Sous bois (100x74cm-39x29in) s. (F.FR 25000)
£2569	$4985	(7-Dec-90 GL.P141) Double portrait (55x71cm-22x28in) board (F.FR 25000)
£4651	$9070	(17-Oct-90 LT.P6/R) Concert dans un parc (24x33cm-9x13in) s.d.1903 (F.FR 46000)
£5747	$10000	(27-Mar-91 B.SF4118/R) Ma chambre a Tonnerre (66x84cm-26x33in) s.d.1920 l.verso
£6042	$9849	(14-Jun-91 MB.P19/R) Le port de Marseille (77x104cm-30x41in) s.d. board (F.FR 60000)
£6626	$12722	(27-Nov-90 APT.P7/R) Les bords du Nil (59x40cm-23x16in) s. (F.FR 65000)
£6633	$13000	(14-Feb-91 CH.NY36/R) Nu couche au bracelet (76x106cm-30x42in) s. board on panel
£7923	$13310	(23-Apr-91 RAS.K57/R) Artist's selfportrait (79x64cm-31x25in) s.d.1912 (D.KR 90000)
£15306	$30153	(16-Nov-90 FB.P119/R) Le soleil (88x77cm-35x30in) bears studio st. (F.FR 150000)
£24490	$48245	(16-Nov-90 FB.P118/R) Jeune homme se reposant (90x84cm-35x33in) s.d.98 (F.FR 240000)
£26839	$45358	(17-Apr-91 LGB.P49/R) Les porteuses d'eau (42x66cm-17x26in) s.d.94 (F.FR 270000)
£37849	$65478	(25-May-91 GL.P48/R) Nature morte aux fleurs, cerise, peches et citrons (62x75cm-24x30in) s. (F.FR 380000)
£40486	$79352	(25-Nov-90 GL.P10/R) Le champ rouge, Pont-Aven (29x37cm-11x15in) s. paper laid down on canvas (F.FR 400000)
£398	$693	*(25-Mar-91 CR.P23/R) Groupe de mendiants Napolitains (27x21cm-11x8in) i.d.1893 ink wash Indian ink (F.FR 4000)*
£500	$835	*(5-Jun-91 HC.P325) Le cloitre des d'Oria a Genes (36x26cm-14x10in) s. sepia wash (F.FR 5000)*
£597	$1039	*(25-Mar-91 CR.P27) Le prisonnier (34x23cm-13x9in) ink wash Indian ink (F.FR 6000)*
£605	$1179	*(28-Oct-90 M.V184) Etude de coiffe bretonne (25x19cm-10x7in) s. chl.double-sided (F.FR 6000)*
£653	$1207	*(6-Mar-91 HC.P10/R) Eglise a Rome (34x24cm-13x9in) s. ink wash (F.FR 6500)*
£693	$1331	*(2-Dec-90 M.V47) Etude coiffes bretonnes (25x19cm-10x7in) s. chl. double-sided (F.FR 6800)*
£929	$1793	*(12-Dec-90 CH.AM70) Paysage (39x33cm-15x13in) s. pen brush (D.FL 3000)*
£1491	$2520	*(17-Apr-91 LGB.P3/R) Prtrait de femme (21x28cm-8x11in) s.d.1893 oil crayon (F.FR 15000)*

BERNARD, Joseph (1864-1933) French
£3000	$4920	(18-Jun-91 PH60/R) In the boudoir (46x22cm-18x9in) s. panel pair
£850	$1386	*(1-Jul-91 APT.P279/R) Danse champetre (24x39cm-9x15in) s. W/C (F.FR 8500)*

BERNARD, Louis Michel (1885-c.1960) French
£1089	$1928	(7-Apr-91 I.N42) Paysage Provencal (38x54cm-15x21in) s. board (F.FR 11000)
£1116	$2209	(3-Feb-91 I.N21) Village mediterraneen (73x92cm-29x36in) s. (F.FR 11000)
£1521	$3012	(3-Feb-91 I.N20/R) Paysage de Provence (73x92cm-29x36in) s. (F.FR 15000)

BERNARD, M (18th C) German
£1800 $3546   (30-Oct-90 PH93/R) Israelites crossing the Red Sea (37x48cm-15x19in) s. panel

BERNARD, Margaret (fl.1883-1924) British
£480 $850   *(18-Mar-91 FEN68) Mayflower steps Plymouth (25x41cm-10x16in) s.d.November 1910 W/C*

BERNASCONI, Ugo (1874-) Italian
£2945 $5124   (26-Mar-91 F.M58/R) Testa al sole (47x38cm-19x15in) mono. s.verso board (I.L 6500000)

BERNATH, Sandor (?) ?
£508 $900   *(24-Mar-91 LIT.L100) Maine dock scene (30x43cm-12x17in) s.d.33*

BERNDTSON, Birger (1890-1940) Swedish
£2468	$4837	(20-Nov-90 GO.G14/R) Washerwomen by waterfall (65x82cm-26x32in) s. (S.KR 27000)
£880	$1708	*(5-Dec-90 AB.S7029/R) Storm and sun - landscape with trees, horse and carriage (26x40cm-10x16in) st.sig. W/C (S.KR 9500)*

BERNDTSON, Gunnar Fredrik (1854-1895) Finnish
£9231 $18000   (24-Oct-90 CH.NY215/R) Lady in black with pink roses (35x27cm-14x11in) s.d.1879 panel

BERNDTSSON, Card (1902-) Swedish
£640 $1254   (20-Nov-90 GO.G15) Landscape from Skane (38x52cm-15x20in) s. (S.KR 7000)

BERNE-BELLECOUR, Etienne Prosper (1838-1910) French
£1302 $2500   (18-Dec-90 BG.M934/R) Standing French military officer lighting cigar
                           (38x28cm-15x11in) s. cradled panel
£1500 $2880   (27-Nov-90 PH46/R) The breach (12x21cm-5x8in) s.d.1874 panel

BERNERS, Lord (20th C) ?
£620 $998   (28-Jun-91 CSK117) Roman bridge at Narni (28x41cm-11x16in) s.d.1930
                      s.i.verso board

BERNI, Antonio (1905-1981) Argentinian
£2632 $5000   (11-Sep-90 PO.BA3) La mendiga (100x73cm-39x29in) s.
£4082 $8000   (20-Nov-90 CH.NY173/R) One more butt (200x200cm-79x79in) s.d.1976 verso
£1675   *$3300*   *(14-Nov-90 V.BA11) El flautista (100x70cm-39x28in) pastel*
£1774   *$3300*   *(5-Sep-90 V.BA10/R) Figura (62x47cm-24x19in) pastel*
£5612   *$11000*   *(19-Nov-90 SY.NY197/R) Juanito Laguna goes to the factory*
                      (183x123cm-72x48in) s.d.77 collage panel

BERNIER, Georges (1862-1918) Belgian
£524 $880   (23-Apr-91 C.A65/R) Dunes in Westende (34x54cm-13x21in) s. (B.FR 32000)
£1510 $2537   (26-Apr-91 ARC.P50/R) Bergere et troupeau (37x53cm-15x21in) s. panel
                      (F.FR 15100)

BERNINGER, Edmund (1843-?) German
£909 $1700   (30-Aug-90 MFA.C187/R) View of Malta (53x81cm-21x32in) s.
£1913 $3750   (24-Nov-90 RB.HY129/R) Coastal landscape, Amalfi (99x150cm-39x59in) s.
£2674 $5000   (30-Aug-90 MFA.C143/R) Monaco (69x114cm-27x45in) indis.s. s.verso
£3421 $6500   (28-Feb-91 CH.NY89/R) View of the Bay of Naples with Vesuvius
                      (54x82cm-21x32in) s.
£4046 $7000   (23-May-91 CH.NY123/R) Monaco (68x116cm-27x46in) s.i.verso

BERNINGHAUS, Oscar E (1874-1952) American
£1479 $2500   (1-May-91 B.SF5181/R) Canyon walls (18x11cm-7x4in) s. panel
£28107 $47500   (1-May-91 B.SF5183/R) Stopped wagon with indians and settlers
                      (76x63cm-30x25in) s.
£94675 $160000   (29-Apr-91 S.SL312/R) Indians hunting in Aspen forest (89x102cm-35x40in)
                      s.

BERNINI, Giovanni Lorenzo (circle) (1598-1680) Italian
£1100   *$2123*   *(12-Dec-90 PH272/R) Designs based on the Triton Fountain, Rome and*
                      another fountain (26x20cm-10x8in) pen ink wash over chk sold with dr
£5500   *$8965*   *(2-Jul-91 C35/R) Design for fountain with conches and tritons, basin*
                      supported by dolphins (34x21cm-13x8in) pen ink wash htd.white

BERNINI, Giovanni Lorenzo (studio) (1598-1680) Italian
£2200   *$4246*   *(12-Dec-90 PH335/R) Design and ground plan for Antonine Column*
                      (38x21cm-15x8in) i.d. pen ink wash over chk

BERNSTEIN, Gerry (20th C) ?
£2860 $5491   (27-Nov-90 BU.S28/R) Window of vulnerability (153x91cm-60x36in)
                      s.i.d.1983verso (S.KR 31000)

BERNSTEIN, Martha (1874-?) German
£2622 $5061   (12-Dec-90 N.M445/R) Beer garden in woods (71x67cm-28x26in) s.
                      (DM 7500)

BERNSTEIN, Theresa F (1895-?) American
£521 $1000   (17-Dec-90 SY.NY198/R) Daniel Garber's studio (20x20cm-8x8in) s.d.14
                      board
£781 $1500   (17-Dec-90 SY.NY329/R) Young artist (51x41cm-20x16in) s.
£851 $1600   (22-Sep-90 WOL.C417/R) View of Paris (41x33cm-16x13in) s. panel
£1250 $2400   (17-Dec-90 SY.NY378/R) Figures on beach (41x51cm-16x20in) s. oil sand
                      paper on board
£1453 $2500   (15-May-91 SY.NY181/R) Beach scene (38x51cm-15x20in) s. paper on board
£1711 $3250   (3-Mar-91 LIT.L200) Young woman knitting (94x69cm-37x27in) s.

BERNT, Rudolf (1844-?) Austrian
£430   *$722*   *(25-Apr-91 D.V261/R) Jugendstil interior (33x61cm-13x24in) s.d.1905 W/C*
                      (A.S 9000)

BERNUTH, Ernst von (1833-?) German
£3839 $6603   (16-May-91 D.V145/R) At the edge of the wood (90x72cm-35x28in) s.d.1881
                      (A.S 80000)

BERNY D'OUVILLE, Claude Charles Antoine (1775-1842) French
£700   *$1344*   *(18-Dec-90 C53/R) Portrait of lady in low-cut white dress (8x?cm-3x?in)*
                      min.s. gilt-metal mount oval
£776   *$1528*   *(13-Nov-90 CH.G267) Portrait of General Dupont (5x?cm-2x?in)*
                      min.s.gilt-metal mount oval in rec.frame (S.FR 1900)

BERONNEAU, Andre (20th C) French
£700 $1400   (6-Feb-91 D.NY11) Port of San Tropez (33x41cm-13x16in) s. panel

BEROUD, Louis (1852-?) French
£14000 $27580   (5-Oct-90 C80 a/R) Sainte Clotilde Square, Paris (55x46cm-22x18in)
           s.d.1896 i.verso
£28902 $50000   (22-May-91 SY.NY78/R) Symphonie en rouge et or (113x146cm-44x57in)
           s.d.1895

BERQUE, Jean (20th C) French
£550 $897   (5-Jul-91 APT.P89) Modele endormi (61x50cm-24x20in) s.d.25 (F.FR 5500)

BERRE, Jean Baptiste (1777-1838) Belgian
£1672 $2826   (17-Apr-91 WE.MU190/R) Shepherdess with cattle and dog in field
           (27x30cm-11x12in) s.d.1838 panel (DM 5000)
£1835 $3523   (1-Dec-90 PER.M108/R) Vaches au paturage (38x46cm-15x18in) s. panel
           (F.FR 18000)

BERRETTINI, Pietro da see CORTONA, Pietro da

BERRETTONI, Nicolo (1637-1682) Italian
£8184 $14158   (21-May-91 SY.MI1008/R) Sacra Famiglia (133x97cm-52x38in)
           (I.L 18000000)
£774 $1300   (17-Jul-91 SY.NY4/R) Bound figure study (37x27cm-15x11in) i. red
           chk.gouache
£26000 $42380   (2-Jul-91 C56/R) Head of child looking down (28x22cm-11x9in) chk

BERRETTONI, Nicolo (attrib) (1637-1682) Italian
£6667 $13000   (10-Oct-90 CH.NY215/R) The Judgement of Midas (74x98cm-29x39in) bears
           Boucher sig.

BERROETA, Pierre de (20th C) French
£781 $1500   (27-Nov-90 PO.BA6) En la playa (58x90cm-23x35in) s.
£1094 $2100   (27-Nov-90 PO.BA5) Place de la Concorde (66x93cm-26x37in) s.
£711 $1423   (6-Feb-91 FB.P34) Composition (38x55cm-15x22in) s. oil mixed media
           canvas (F.FR 7000)

BERRY, Nathaniel L (1859-) American
£707 $1400   (30-Jan-91 GRO.B52/R) Low tide, Ringe beach, Swampscott
           (51x76cm-20x30in) s. i. label stretcher

BERSANI, Stefano (1872-1914) Italian
£1818 $3564   (21-Nov-90 F.M101) Montagne della Val Malenco, Veltellina
           (24x40cm-9x16in) s. panel (I.L 4000000)

BERSCH, Fritz (?) ?
£671 $1309   (10-Oct-90 WE.MU187/R) Coach trip, Meller Hohe (20x25cm-8x10in) s. board
           (DM 2000)

BERT, Emile (1814-1847) Belgian
£805 $1400   (27-Mar-91 B.SF4289/R) Woman drawing water near cottage
           (44x56cm-17x22in) s.d.1845 panel

BERTALAN, Albert (20th C) Hungarian
£802 $1387   (22-May-91 BA.S5/R) Woman dressed in red playing patience
           (100x70cm-39x28in) s.d.1928 (S.KR 8500)
£1182 $1998   (3-May-91 SA.A766/R) Tulips by a window (73x60cm-29x24in) s. (DM 3500)

BERTAULD, P (19th C) French
£872 $1700   (26-Oct-90 SY.NY136/R) Portrait of Philippe Bin (22x16cm-9x6in) s.d.96

BERTELSEN, Albert (1926-) Danish
£668 $1197   (14-Mar-91 RAS.V755/R) Evening, Faroe Islands (61x65cm-24x26in) s.
           i.d.1980verso (D.KR 7500)
£725 $1363   (10-Aug-90 RAS.V574/R) 'Fronnet trae' (160x70cm-63x28in) s. (D.KR 8200)
£797 $1347   (2-May-91 RAS.V171/R) Man resting (48x100cm-19x39in) s.d.1975verso
           (D.KR 9000)
£890 $1745   (22-Nov-90 RAS.V810/R) Lady with large hat (90x105cm-35x41in) s.
           i.d.1977verso (D.KR 10000)

BERTHELEMY, Jean Simon (1743-1811) French
£34619 $61968   (9-Apr-91 APT.P41/R) Jupiter et Antiope (78x96cm-31x38in) s.d.1778
           (F.FR 350000)

BERTHELEMY, Jean Simon (attrib) (1743-1811) French
£1800 $3474   (11-Dec-90 PH261/R) Allegory of National Triumph, modello for ceiling
           decoration (39cm-15ins circular)
£6000 $9780   (2-Jul-91 C340/R) Path between walls of Roman villa (38x51cm-15x20in)
           red chk in cartouche

BERTHELON, Eugene (1829-c.1914) French
£723 $1229   (28-May-91 AB.S4734/R) Summer landscape with figures by lake
           (35x26cm-14x10in) s. panel (S.KR 7700)

BERTHELSEN, Christian (1839-1909) Scandinavian
£717 $1284   (9-Apr-91 RAS.K2013) Wooded landscape (95x125cm-37x49in) (D.KR 8200)

BERTHELSEN, Johann (1883-1969) American

£508	$1000	(16-Nov-90 S.BM206/R) Winter in Central Park (30x23cm-12x9in) s. canvasboard
£558	$1100	(16-Nov-90 S.BM201/R) Times Square in winter (30x23cm-12x9in) s. canvasboard
£609	$1200	(7-Oct-90 DU.E136./R) Washington Square Memorial (30x23cm-12x9in) s. board
£609	$1200	(16-Nov-90 S.BM204/R) Narrow Street, winter (20x15cm-8x6in) s. num.11869 verso canvasboard
£718	$1400	(21-Oct-90 HG.C54) Winter in New York (41x30cm-16x12in) s.
£833	$1600	(17-Dec-90 SY.NY233/R) Fifth Avenue in snow (41x30cm-16x12in) s. canvasboard
£957	$1800	(19-Sep-90 B.SF2834/R) The Lagoon, night, Central Park, New York City (61x91cm-24x36in) s.i.d.1936
£1012	$1700	(28-Apr-91 HG.C31) Times Square, New York (61x51cm-24x20in) s. s.verso
£1066	$2100	(18-Nov-90 JRB.C186/R) The UN Building (41x51cm-16x20in) s.
£1077	$2100	(20-Oct-90 FA.PH789) Winter in Washington Square Park. Fifth Avenue looking south in winter (15x20cm-6x8in) s. canvas board pair
£1618	$2800	(21-May-91 CE.NY619/R) Passing by church in winter, New York City (41x49cm-16x19in) s. canvasboard
£2119	$3750	(22-Mar-91 S.W2840/R) St. Patrick's Cathedral (30x23cm-12x9in) s. canvasboard
£2367	$4000	(1-May-91 B.SF5127/R) Winter, Washington Square Park (61x76cm-24x30in) s.
£4586	$7750	(17-Apr-91 D.NY74/R) Washington Square Park in snow (64x74cm-25x29in) s. canvasboard

BERTHOLLE, Jean (1909-) French

£1019	$1967	(16-Dec-90 GL.P19) Paysage (20x45cm-8x18in) s.d.1964 panel (F.FR 10000)
£2857	$5629	(16-Nov-90 EA.Z329/R) Untitled (82x130cm-32x51in) s.d.1951 (S.FR 7000)
£4893	$9443	(12-Dec-90 APT.P68/R) Composition (60x81cm-24x32in) s.d.57 (F.FR 48000)
£612	*$1188*	*(8-Dec-90 GAB.G2381) Composition (64x15cm-25x6in) s.d.1960 oil chks. paper laid down on paper (S.FR 1500)*

BERTHOME-SAINT-ANDRE (1905-1977) French

£1705	$3325	(10-Oct-90 ARC.P66) Riviere dans la foret (74x94cm-29x37in) s. (F.FR 17000)
£2023	$3500	(22-May-91 D.NY113/R) Reverie (65x81cm-26x32in) s. s.i.verso

BERTHOME-SAINT-ANDRE, Louis (1905-1977) French

£1310	$2555	(28-Oct-90 M.V73/R) La Seugne a Paris (92x73cm-36x29in) s. (F.FR 13000)
£1712	$2791	(11-Jun-91 I.N15) Ludi a contre-jour (47x39cm-19x15in) s. (F.FR 17000)
£1712	$2791	(11-Jun-91 I.N14) Contre-jour a l'eventail (46x38cm-18x15in) s. (F.FR 17000)
£1780	$3187	(12-Apr-91 JM.P38/R) La danseuse (55x33cm-22x13in) s. (F.FR 18000)
£1796	$3036	(5-May-91 LT.P28/R) L'etang de la Roche Bernard (61x50cm-24x20in) s. (F.FR 18000)
£2429	$4761	(25-Nov-90 ZZ.F9) Les boucles brunes (92x73cm-36x29in) s. (F.FR 24000)
£2510	$4644	(10-Mar-91 LT.P43/R) Les jarretieres roses (65x54cm-26x21in) s. i.d.47 verso (F.FR 25000)
£2543	$4807	(30-Sep-90 E.LA66) Les roses (55x46cm-22x18in) s. d.1961 verso (F.FR 25000)
£2883	$4872	(21-Apr-91 E.LA127) La toilette (73x60cm-29x24in) s. (F.FR 29000)
£4629	$8748	(30-Sep-90 E.LA65/R) Reflets (81x65cm-32x26in) s. (F.FR 45500)
£24415	$46144	(30-Sep-90 E.LA64/R) Le Moulin Rouge (162x130cm-64x51in) s. (F.FR 240000)
£301	*$557*	*(10-Mar-91 LT.P14) La belle Espagnole (24x18cm-9x7in) s. Indian ink drawing (F.FR 3000)*
£341	*$632*	*(10-Mar-91 LT.P12) Modele au pied du lit (32x27cm-13x11in) s. ink wash (F.FR 3400)*
£910	*$1529*	*(28-Apr-91 FE.P12) Personnages (49x33cm-19x13in) s. W/C (F.FR 9100)*
£2634	*$4452*	*(21-Apr-91 E.LA130) Jeune brune pensive (45x35cm-18x14in) s. W/C (F.FR 26500)*

BERTHON, Lucienne (20th C) French

£841	$1505	(14-Apr-91 APT.P13) Les fantomes du marais (54x65cm-21x26in) s.d.1988 hardboard (F.FR 8500)
£890	$1593	(14-Apr-91 APT.P12) Le moulin Fou (54x65cm-21x26in) s.d.1990 hardboard (F.FR 9000)

BERTHOUD, Auguste Henri (1829-1887) Swiss

£776	$1504	(8-Dec-90 GAB.G2114/R) Bord de la Sarine (63x109cm-25x43in) s. (S.FR 1900)
£876	$1709	(24-Oct-90 GD.B144/R) The mountain peak with thick clouds (68x100cm-27x39in) s. (S.FR 2200)

BERTHOUD, Leon (1822-1892) Swiss

£1458	*$2479*	*(28-May-91 F.R96/R) Veduta di Capri da Marina Grande (25x44cm-10x17in) i. W/C (I.L 3200000)*

BERTI, T (?) Italian

£620	$1048	(1-May-91 KH.K15/R) Young girl with blue turban (53x43cm-21x17in) s.verso (D.KR 7000)

BERTIN, Emile (1878-1957) French
£5461 $10703   (22-Nov-90 L.K835/R) Beach scene with bathers (56x75cm-22x30in) s.
(DM 16000)

BERTIN, Jean-Victor (1775-1842) French
£1378 $2714   (15-Oct-90 ARC.P61/R) Maison au bord d'un chemin (25x31cm-10x12in)
(F.FR 13500)

BERTIN, Jean-Victor (attrib) (1775-1842) French
£653 $1051   (27-Jun-91 APT.P194/R) Paysage avec un temple grec (21x27cm-8x11in)
(F.FR 6500)

BERTIN, Jean-Victor (style) (1775-1842) French
£880 $1575   (10-Apr-91 CSK271) Woman seated beneath tree and drover with sheep
beyond (46x33cm-18x13in)

BERTIN, Nicolas (1668-1736) French
£11869 $21246   (9-Apr-91 APT.P29/R) Le Christ et la Samaritaine (68x57cm-27x22in)
(F.FR 120000)

BERTIN, Roger (20th C) French
£1205 $1940   (30-Jun-91 FE.P75) Autoportrait au Chevalet (92x65cm-36x26in) s.l.
(F.FR 12000)
£4213 $8215   (11-Oct-90 QWA.P63/R) Rue Maurice Utrillo (65x54cm-26x21in) s.
(F.FR 42000)
£4213 $8215   (11-Oct-90 QWA.P64/R) Faubourg Montmartre (65x81cm-26x32in) s.
(F.FR 42000)
£5714 $11257   (17-Nov-90 HC.P57/R) Gare du Nord (65x81cm-26x32in) s. (F.FR 56000)

BERTINI, Gianni (1922-) Italian
£873 $1510   (25-May-91 AB.L15/R) Untitled (38x46cm-15x18in) s.d.1965 (S.FR 2200)
£1506 $2425   (25-Jun-91 BG.P5/R) Le bonheur de Gordios (70x48cm-28x19in) s.d.1957 l.
verso paper laid down on wood (F.FR 15000)
£1631 $3148   (16-Dec-90 GL.P139) Bruit d'Eros (55x46cm-22x18in) s. l.d.1960 verso
(F.FR 16000)
£2243 $4328   (16-Dec-90 GL.P122) Hector au Congo (73x92cm-29x36in) s. l. verso
acrylic (F.FR 22000)
£3058 $5902   (16-Dec-90 GL.P115) Desiderio di cerere (100x81cm-39x32in) s. l.d.VII
1959 verso acrylic (F.FR 30000)
£3152 $6146   (22-Oct-90 BR.M123/R) Starter (30x40cm-12x16in) s.d.1977 acrylic
(I.L 7000000)
£3571 $7036   (16-Nov-90 FB.P12/R) La legende d'oreade (91x72cm-36x28in) s. l.d.1956
verso (F.FR 35000)
£3602 $7024   (22-Oct-90 BR.M163/R) Donna con maschera (55x80cm-22x31in) s. s.d.1983
verso (I.L 8000000)
£3602 $7024   (22-Oct-90 BR.M93/R) Composizione (61x50cm-24x20in) s. s.d.1953 verso
(I.L 8000000)
£4122 $7915   (27-Nov-90 SY.MI194/R) Venere nera (49x44cm-19x17in) s.d.61
(I.L 9000000)
£4286 $8443   (16-Nov-90 FB.P312/R) Desir d'amalthee (116x81cm-46x32in) s.d.56 l.
verso (F.FR 42000)
£5628 $10975   (22-Oct-90 BR.M43/R) Figura di donna (116x88cm-46x35in) s.d.1976 oil
emulsion (I.L 12500000)
*£2811 $4526   (25-Jun-91 BG.P4/R) La tete de Jeanne (150x97cm-59x38in) s.d.1960 l.
verso mixed media (F.FR 28000)*
*£3262 $6296   (16-Dec-90 GL.P116/R) Le due amiche (70x50cm-28x20in) s. l.d.1976 verso
ink serigraph oil canvas (F.FR 32000)*
*£4179 $8066   (16-Dec-90 GL.P128/R) Le Aiche (115x88cm-45x35in) s.d.1973 l. verso ink
serigraph acrylic canvas (F.FR 41000)*
*£4281 $8263   (16-Dec-90 GL.P112) Partie de campagne (116x81cm-46x32in) s.d.1966 l.
verso ink serigraph canvas (F.FR 42000)*
*£7740 $14938   (12-Dec-90 CH.AM398/R) Untitled- painted with Enrico Baj and Asger Jorn
(85x84cm-33x33in) s.d.58 oil fabric collage canvas double-sided
(D.FL 25000)*

BERTINI, Giuseppe (1825-1898) Italian
£1600 $2864   (14-Mar-91 B63/R) A pretty girl in a landscape (74x51cm-29x20in) s.l.
canvas laid on board
£2544 $4935   (5-Dec-90 F.M11/R) Paesaggio con edifici e figure (21x32cm-8x13in) init.
(I.L 5500000)
£2775 $5383   (5-Dec-90 F.M12/R) Squero di San Trovaso a Venezia (22x32cm-9x13in)
init. (I.L 6000000)

BERTOLETTI, Nino (1890-?) Italian
£2135 $4207   (30-Oct-90 F.R100/R) Natura morta (64x50cm-25x20in) s.d.40
(I.L 4700000)

BERTOLOTTI, Cesare (1855-?) Italian
£15050 $25133   (6-Jun-91 F.M268/R) Tramonto romano (100x100cm-39x39in) s.d.909-907
(I.L 33000000)

BERTOLOTTO, Gianni Lorenzo (1640-1721) Italian
£5853 $11414   (23-Oct-90 CH.R40) Scena di storia antica con due guerrieri che
sorprendono un Re dormiente (193x304cm-76x120in) (I.L 13000000)

BERTON, L (?) ?
£616 $1034   (27-Apr-91 SO.S277/R) Sheep and chickens in barn (56x77cm-22x30in) s. (S.KR 6500)

BERTON, Paul Emile (?-1909) French
£657 $1282   (17-Oct-90 DL.P23/R) Cannes, le suquet (24x35cm-9x14in) s.d.88 panel (F.FR 6500)

BERTRAM, Abel (1871-1954) French
£2083 $4167   (4-Feb-91 LEB.P1/R) Port de peche (38x55cm-15x22in) s. (F.FR 20500)
£2719 $4432   (14-Jun-91 MB.P20) Rue de village animee (65x81cm-26x32in) s. (F.FR 27000)
£3106 $6119   (30-Oct-90 I.N209) Le port (33x41cm-13x16in) s. (F.FR 30500)
£3998 $7836   (25-Nov-90 ZZ.F10/R) Fillettes au pays Bigouden (65x92cm-26x36in) s. (F.FR 39500)
£708 $1380   (17-Oct-90 ARC.P7) Voiliers (25x28cm-10x11in) s. W/C (F.FR 7000)
£1200 $2016   (26-Apr-91 ARC.P26/R) Le modele etendu (32x59cm-13x23in) s. wash Indian ink (F.FR 12000)
£1223 $2361   (14-Dec-90 JM.P26/R) La toilette (49x28cm-19x11in) s. W/C (F.FR 12000)

BERTRAM, Paul (19/20th C) ?
£520 $1019   (15-Feb-91 N288) Bluebell time in the birch wood (51x74cm-20x29in) s.d.98 pencil W/C htd.white

BERTRAND, Fred (?) French
£448 $775   (12-May-91 T.B54) Honfleur - le Port (46x55cm-18x22in) s. gouache board (F.FR 4500)

BERTRAND, Gaston (20th C) Belgian
£4726 $9121   (13-Dec-90 CH.BR158/R) Trois cercles (24x14cm-9x6in) mono. s.i.d.1967 verso panel (B.FR 280000)
£5059 $9815   (8-Dec-90 KV.L386/R) Grande Figure Debout (200x100cm-79x39in) s.d.44-47 (B.FR 300000)
£5401 $10424   (13-Dec-90 CH.BR130/R) Forme II (33x45cm-13x18in) s.d.54 s.i.d.verso (B.FR 320000)
£8101 $15635   (13-Dec-90 CH.BR157/R) Sur frond rouge (27x35cm-11x14in) s. s.i.d.1960 verso panel (B.FR 480000)
£12658 $24430   (13-Dec-90 CH.BR131/R) Composition au triangle jaune (65x81cm-26x32in) s.d.51 s.i.d.verso (B.FR 750000)
£439 $847   (13-Dec-90 CH.BR60) Untitled (30x50cm-12x20in) s.d.63 XVIII pen silk (B.FR 26000)
£810 $1564   (13-Dec-90 CH.BR69) Abstract composition (37x27cm-15x11in) s.d.53 col.crayons pencil (B.FR 48000)
£1603 $3095   (13-Dec-90 CH.BR46/R) Montmajour (52x40cm-20x16in) s.d.59 W/C pen (B.FR 95000)
£1688 $3257   (13-Dec-90 CH.BR48/R) Direction nation (39x28cm-15x11in) s.d.59 W/C pen (B.FR 100000)
£1808 $3525   (23-Oct-90 C.A36/R) Composition (49x39cm-19x15in) s.d.1949 W/C (B.FR 110000)
£1857 $3583   (13-Dec-90 CH.BR21/R) Direction etoile (58x40cm-23x16in) s.d.59 W/C ink (B.FR 110000)
£2194 $4235   (13-Dec-90 CH.BR54/R) Sala Comacina, Italia (38x28cm-15x11in) s.d.61 i.verso W/C pen (B.FR 130000)
£2194 $4235   (13-Dec-90 CH.BR51/R) Montmajour XIV (45x31cm-18x12in) s.d.60 i.verso W/C pen (B.FR 130000)
£2363 $4560   (13-Dec-90 CH.BR52/R) Via Sarpini Giacomo, Sala Comacina, Italia (38x28cm-15x11in) s.d.61 i.verso W/C pen (B.FR 140000)

BERTRAND, Huguette Aimee (1922-) French
£4752 $9267   (21-Oct-90 P.V27/R) Composition (99x50cm-39x20in) s. (F.FR 47000)

BERTRAND, Jean Claude (1928-) French
£598 $1034   (26-May-91 ZZ.F157) Arbres rouges (54x64cm-21x25in) s. i. verso (F.FR 6000)
£598 $1034   (26-May-91 ZZ.F153/R) Verdure (48x65cm-19x26in) s. (F.FR 6000)
£663 $1279   (14-Dec-90 ARC.P5) Le torrent (65x92cm-26x36in) s. (F.FR 6500)

BERTRAND, Paulin Andre (1852-1940) French
£3265 $6400   (6-Nov-90 GF.L2177/R) Calanque provencale (50x73cm-20x29in) s. i.verso (S.FR 8000)

BERTRAND, Philippe (1949-) French
£574 $1016   (6-Apr-91 CB.P236) Jeune femme a la fenetre (15x10cm-6x4in) W/C gouache W/C (F.FR 5800)

BERTRAND, Pierre-Philippe (1884-1975) French
£1320 $2600   (15-Nov-90 D.NY64/R) Fleurs et fruits au balcon, Cannes (61x50cm-24x20in) s. s.i.verso
£1777 $3500   (15-Nov-90 D.NY88/R) Jour de Regates a Cannes (51x61cm-20x24in) s. i.stretcher

BERTRAND, Vincent (18th C) French
£1357 $2225   (19-Jun-91 LC.P10/R) Portrait du jeune Comte Foucher (10x8cm-4x3in) min.s. wood gilt frame oval (F.FR 13500)

BERTUCHI, Mariano (1885-1920) Italian
£815 $1443 (3-Apr-91 ANS.M126/R) Paisaje (20x26cm-8x10in) s. board (S.P 150000)
£870 $1539 (3-Apr-91 ANS.M124/R) Paisaje agostado (20x26cm-8x10in) s. board
(S.P 160000)
£870 $1539 (3-Apr-91 ANS.M125/R) Paisaje (20x26cm-8x10in) s. board (S.P 160000)
£870 $1539 (3-Apr-91 ANS.M123/R) Paisaje con colinas y arboles (20x26cm-8x10in) s.
board (S.P 160000)
£2174 $3848 (3-Apr-91 ANS.M107/R) Procesion en Tetuan (53x40cm-21x16in) s.
(S.P 400000)

BERTUZZI, Nicola (circle) (1710-1777) Italian
£1172 $2098 (8-Apr-91 CH.R227) Armida tenta di uccidere Rinaldo adormentato
(51x54cm-20x21in) panel (I.L 2600000)

BERVOETS, Freddy (1941-) Belgian
£589 $990 (23-Apr-91 C.A303) Little Hitler (76x57cm-30x22in) mono. paper
(B.FR 36000)
£2128 $3574 (23-Apr-91 C.A302/R) Zondagsdroom (108x148cm-43x58in) mono. paper on
canvas (B.FR 130000)
£1233 $2403 (23-Oct-90 C.A40) Love (79x103cm-31x41in) s.d.1989 mixed media
(B.FR 75000)

BERVOETS, Leo (1892-1978) Belgian?
£1796 $3466 (13-Dec-90 SY.AM60/R) Figures in street (36x41cm-14x16in) s. canvas on
panel (D.FL 5800)
£3287 $6409 (23-Oct-90 C.A309/R) The Grote Market in Antwerp (132x100cm-52x39in) s.
(B.FR 200000)

BESCHEY, Balthasar (1708-1776) Flemish
£1200 $2076 (20-May-91 SWS30) The rest on the flight into Egypt (30x25cm-12x10in)
panel
£3000 $5070 (16-Apr-91 PH114/R) Adoration of shepherds (36x29cm-14x11in) on copper
£3637 $7128 (19-Nov-90 CH.R133/R) La veste di Giuseppe mostrata a Giacobbe
(35x27cm-14x11in) panel (I.L 8000000)
£4523 $7417 (21-Jun-91 SY.MO271/R) Adoration des bergers (35x47cm-14x19in) panel
(F.FR 45000)
£6351 $11368 (14-Mar-91 D.V217/R) Flemish river landscape with village and figures
(21x29cm-8x11in) panel (A.S 130000)
£7911 $15663 (30-Jan-91 APT.P251/R) La chasse au lion (58x78cm-23x31in) s.d.1759
panel (F.FR 78000)

BESCHEY, Balthasar (attrib) (1708-1776) Flemish
£1284 $2530 (13-Nov-90 CH.AM82) Holy Family in landscape (18x20cm-7x8in) panel
(D.FL 4200)
£1300 $2249 (20-May-91 SWS145) Franciscan hermits in landscapes (43x32cm-17x13in)
panel pair
£4000 $8000 (7-Feb-91 C30/R) The Madonna and Child with St Elisabeth and infant St
John the Baptist (43x39cm-17x15in) panel after Sir Peter Paul Rubens

BESCHEY, Balthasar (circle) (1708-1776) Flemish
£2400 $4056 (18-Apr-91 C139/R) The rest on the flight into Egypt (26x28cm-10x11in)
panel

BESKOW, Bo (1906-1989) Swedish
£1112 $2158 (4-Dec-90 BA.S46/R) Landscape from Smogen (38x46cm-15x18in) s.d.35 panel
(S.KR 12000)
£1216 $2177 (17-Mar-91 BU.M463) Moroccan market (104x115cm-41x45in) s. (S.KR 13000)
£1668 $3236 (5-Dec-90 AB.S7030/R) Woman seated by table with fruit, bottle and
flowers (98x68cm-39x27in) s.i.d.29 (S.KR 18000)
£2502 $4854 (5-Dec-90 AB.S7031/R) Music at sea (116x104cm-46x41in) s. (S.KR 27000)

BESNARD, Albert (1849-1934) French
£1126 $2208 (24-Nov-90 N.M52/R) Arabic women (64x47cm-25x19in) s.d.1899 (DM 3300)
£2808 $5476 (12-Oct-90 APT.P107/R) Jeune femme pensive (49x61cm-19x24in) s. panel
(F.FR 28000)
£842 $1600 (27-Jun-91 SY.NY55/R) Study of woman in profile (49x36cm-19x14in) s. W/C
gouache
£1026 $2000 (26-Oct-90 SY.NY152/R) Portrait of lady in straw boater (30x23cm-12x9in)
s. pastel
£10246 $20082 (7-Nov-90 APT.P451/R) La nuque rousse (46x37cm-18x15in) s.d.91 pastel
(F.FR 100000)

BESNARD, Charlotte Gabrielle see DUBRAY, Charlotte Gabrielle

BESPALOV, Ivan Nicolayevich (1908-) Russian
£653 $1071 (19-Jun-91 ARC.P158/R) Liuda avec un chaton (60x45cm-24x18in) s.
(F.FR 6500)

BESPERSTOV, Iakov (1938-) Russian
£503 $965 (18-Feb-91 ARC.P28/R) Baignade en foret (63x93cm-25x37in) s. (F.FR 5000)
£804 $1544 (18-Feb-91 ARC.P32/R) L'embarcadere du lac (70x79cm-28x31in) s.
(F.FR 8000)

BESS, Forrest (1911-) American
£9694 $19000 (8-Nov-90 CH.NY314/R) Untitled (28x31cm-11x12in) s.

BESSA, Pancrace (1772-c.1835) French
£769	$1500	(26-Oct-90 SY.NY61/R) Botanical study (18x11cm-7x4in) s. W/C vellum
£2203	$4251	(10-Dec-90 L.K208) South American bird perched on branch (50x38cm-20x15in) s. W/C (DM 6300)
£2814	$4615	(18-Jun-91 APT.P109/R) Oiseau Motmot du Bresil (49x37cm-19x15in) s. W/C gouache vellum (F.FR 28000)
£5000	$8850	(22-Mar-91 APT.P151/R) Un strombe (31x40cm-12x16in) s. W/C gouache (F.FR 50000)
£8000	$14160	(22-Mar-91 APT.P152/R) Cacatoes elegants (56x46cm-22x18in) s.i. W/C vellum (F.FR 80000)

BESSE, Raymond (1899-1969) French
| £1040 | $1800 | (7-May-91 CE.NY39/R) Eglise St. Severin, vieux Paris (73x92cm-29x36in) s. |

BESSERVE, Rene (1883-1959) French
| £1501 | $2972 | (3-Feb-91 I.N22/R) Pomone (98x86cm-39x34in) s. (F.FR 14800) |
| £1558 | $2555 | (21-Jun-91 CK.P100) Leda et le cygne (100x81cm-39x32in) s.d.32 (F.FR 15500) |

BESSIRE, Dale Phillip (1893-1974) American
| £559 | $1000 | (15-Mar-91 DM.D1372/R) Bear Wallow hills (61x76cm-24x30in) |
| £867 | $1500 | (12-May-91 H.C137/R) Late shadows (76x91cm-30x36in) s. |

BESSON, Faustin (1821-1882) French
| £750 | $1425 | (12-Sep-90 CSK165/R) Artist, Lancret, sketching landlord of Gonjoys (41x66cm-16x26in) s.i.verso pencil W/C oval |

BESSONNAT, Jean Claude (20th C) French
| £815 | $1574 | (12-Dec-90 D.P146/R) Les splendeurs de la vallee d'Ys (55x46cm-22x18in) s. (F.FR 8000) |
| £1019 | $1967 | (12-Dec-90 D.P147/R) Les rochers qui parlent (92x73cm-36x29in) s. (F.FR 10000) |

BEST, Hans (1874-1942) German
£962	$1828	(2-Mar-91 KRA.D279) Portrait of peasant (33x24cm-13x9in) s. panel (DM 2800)
£1049	$2024	(12-Dec-90 WE.MU128/R) The gossip (9x9cm-4x4in) s. panel (DM 3000)
£1174	$2290	(10-Oct-90 WE.MU282/R) Portrait of hunter (57x42cm-22x17in) s. (DM 3500)
£2789	$4797	(14-May-91 GF.L2590/R) Young woman wearing riding outfit (140x112cm-55x44in) s. octagonal (S.FR 7000)

BEST, Harry Cassie (1863-1936) American
| £1190 | $2250 | (29-Sep-90 YFA.M7/R) Riders in Yosemite (61x76cm-24x30in) s. |

BESTERS, Albertus Johannes (1747-1819) Dutch
| £1757 | $2986 | (27-May-91 L.K12/R) Dutch landscape with peasant woman and cattle watering (37x48cm-15x19in) s. panel (DM 5200) |

BESTLAND, Charles (18th C) British
| £700 | $1372 | (22-Jan-91 CSK16/R) Portrait of gentleman (7x?cm-3x?in) min.init.d.93 gold case frame, lock of hair oval |

BETHKE, Hermann (1825-1895) German
| £5822 | $10421 | (13-Mar-91 N.M451/R) Grandmother seated in armchair by window and little girl threading needle (77x62cm-30x24in) (DM 17000) |

BETSELLERE, Emile (1847-1880) Dutch
| £8500 | $16320 | (28-Nov-90 S60/R) Scene from the French Revolution (130x194cm-51x76in) s. |

BETTENCOURT, Pierre (20th C) French
| £803 | $1293 | (25-Jun-91 BG.P6/R) Le guide des nations seduit par l'apparition d'une danseuse Tcherkesse (23x30cm-9x12in) mono.i. verso collage paper pasted wood (F.FR 8000) |

BETTERA, Bartolomeo (1639-?) Italian
| £27363 | $45696 | (4-Jun-91 CH.R496/R) Strumenti musicali (81x119cm-32x47in) (I.L 60000000) |

BETTERA, Bartolomeo (circle) (1639-?) Italian
| £15642 | $28000 | (11-Apr-91 SY.NY85/R) Still life of celestial globe, archlute, violin, music sheets and pocket watch (85x120cm-33x47in) |

BETTES, John (younger-attrib) (16th C) British
| £28000 | $46200 | (12-Jul-91 C5/R) Portrait of gentleman, thought to be Edmund, 1st Lord Sheffield, holding book (96x73cm-38x29in) i. panel |

BETTINELLI, Mario (1880-1953) Italian
| £866 | $1447 | (6-Jun-91 F.M107) Figura di donna in riposo (38x55cm-15x22in) s. board pencil study verso (I.L 1900000) |

BETTINI, Domenico (attrib) (1644-1705) Italian
| £5455 | $10692 | (19-Nov-90 CH.R138/R) Boccia di fiori all'aperto con uccelli (52x61cm-20x24in) (I.L 12000000) |

BETTINI, Domenico (circle) (1644-1705) Italian
£5000 $9500   (1-Mar-91 C169/R) Carnations, tulips and other flowers with peach and
           fig on stone ledge (45x35cm-18x14in)

BEUL, Frans de (1849-1919) Belgian
£900 $1764   (22-Nov-90 CSK169/R) Herding flock (38x46cm-15x18in) s.
£1027 $1900   (10-Mar-91 H.C4) Shepherdess knitting (81x66cm-32x26in) s.
£1600 $2688   (18-Jul-91 CSK88/R) Sheep and cattle grazing in pasture
           (110x80cm-43x31in) s.d.1874

BEUL, Henri de (19th C) Belgian
£1250 $2150   (14-May-91 SWS306/R) Poultry in yard (32x43cm-13x17in) s.d.1865
           indis.i.stretcher
£2200 $4334   (5-Oct-90 C5/R) Sheep in meadow (60x80cm-24x31in) s.d.1895

BEUL, Henri de (jnr) (19/20th C) Belgian
£1250 $2150   (14-May-91 SWS305/R) Poultry in farmyard (28x38cm-11x15in) s.d.1863
           panel

BEULAS, Jose (20th C) Spanish?
£1471 $2529   (16-May-91 ANS.M107/R) Paisaje, Huesca (33x46cm-13x18in) s.
           (S.P 270000)
£4616 $9093   (15-Nov-90 ANS.M8/R) Arboles azules (91x71cm-36x28in) s. (S.P 850000)
£652   *$1252*   *(18-Dec-90 DUR.M36) Tierras (33x44cm-13x17in) W/C (S.P 120000)*

BEULLENS, Andre (20th C) Belgian?
£599 $1071   (16-Mar-91 KV.L26) Black sun (60x50cm-24x20in) s.d.62 (B.FR 36000)

BEURDEN, Alfons van (1878-1962) Flemish
£843 $1636   (4-Dec-90 C.A376/R) Boats on a canal (53x67cm-21x26in) s. (B.FR 50000)

BEURMANN, Emil (1862-1951) Swiss
£1036   *$1782*   *(14-May-91 GF.L2606/R) Female nude reclining (24x34cm-9x13in) s. W/C*
           (S.FR 2600)

BEUYS, Joseph (1921-1986) German
£694   *$1346*   *(3-Dec-90 F.M169) Senza titolo (30x21cm-12x8in) s. pencil (I.L 1500000)*
£1536   *$3010*   *(24-Nov-90 N.M53/R) Hat (22x22cm-9x9in) s.d.1981 pencil dr. (DM 4500)*
£2449   *$4751*   *(8-Dec-90 RU.ZU115/R) Conversation (34x26cm-13x10in) s. pencil*
           (S.FR 6000)
£21843   *$42812*   *(20-Nov-90 L.K39/R) Amazone (16x13cm-6x5in) s.i.d.1953 s.i.d.verso*
           gouache pencil (DM 64000)

BEVAN, Robert (1865-1925) British
£4000   *$7400*   (7-Mar-91 C49/R) Study for Sussex farm horse (27x36cm-11x14in)
£900   *$1665*   *(7-Mar-91 C46/R) Grazing by the shore (25x34cm-10x13in) st.mono.i.d.1891*
           black crayon
£1300   *$2262*   *(27-Mar-91 S50/R) Exmoor ponies in the snow. The threshing floor chk*
           two
£1800   *$3510*   *(10-Oct-90 S1/R) Shoeing, Brittany (20x30cm-8x12in) st.studio col.chk*
£2800   *$5180*   *(7-Mar-91 C44/R) Three farm horses, Sussex (28x34cm-11x13in) black*
           crayon
£3800   *$7030*   *(7-Mar-91 C43/R) The harrow, Poland (23x32cm-9x13in) mono.s.i. crayon*
           W/C bodycol
£4200   *$8232*   *(7-Nov-90 S34/R) Polish cottages (23x33cm-9x13in) s. chk W/C*

BEVEREN, Charles van (1809-1850) Belgian
£970 $1910   (30-Oct-90 CH.AM31/R) Young girl at piano (37x28cm-15x11in) mono. panel
           (D.FL 3200)

BEVERLEY, William Roxby (c.1814-1889) British
£520   *$931*   *(11-Mar-91 HS108) Walking up grouse on the Yorkshire Moors*
           (22x32cm-9x13in) i.erso W/C
£1400   *$2758*   *(15-Nov-90 S125/R) Beached fishing boats. Boats offshore*
           (17x30cm-7x12in) W/C over pencil htd.bodycol pair
£2600   *$4654*   *(9-Apr-91 C151/R) Fisherfolk unloading catch at low tide, Hastings*
           (67x93cm-26x37in) htd.bodycol

BEVERLOO, Cornelis Guillaume see CORNEILLE

BEWICK, Pauline (20th C) British?
£400   *$644*   *(28-Jun-91 CSK185) Drunk man, Upper Mount Street, Dublin, 1964*
           (41x29cm-16x11in) s. W/C over artist's proof

BEWLEY, Murray Percival (1884-1964) American
£3307 $6250   (26-Sep-90 SY.NY164/R) Young girl with apple (77x63cm-30x25in) s.

BEY, Barbara le (1939-) American
£691 $1300   (11-Aug-90 COL.M65/R) Garden path (28x36cm-11x14in) s. board

BEYER, Jan de (attrib) (1703-1780) Swiss
£342   *$650*   *(9-Jan-91 CH.NY24/R) Outskirts of village with bridge and windmill*
           beyond (30x26cm-12x10in) bears i. ink wash

BEYER, M O (?) ?
£958 $1820   (11-Sep-90 CH.AM315/R) Still life of poppies in a vase, fruit, bottle of wine and punch bowl (66x110cm-26x43in) s. (D.FL 3200)

BEYER, Otto (20th C) German?
£3072 $6020   (24-Nov-90 VG.B196/R) Female nude. Female nude standing (75x62cm-30x24in) c.1913 (DM 9000)
£3413 $6689   (24-Nov-90 VG.B197/R) Autumn landscape, outskirts of town (62x77cm-24x30in) s.d.1913 (DM 10000)
£405   *$701   (25-May-91 N.M30/R) Female nude amongst trees (35x28cm-14x11in) s. W/C (DM 1200)*

BEYEREN, Abraham van (1620-1675) Dutch
£20000 $34000   (30-May-91 SY.NY29/R) Shipping on choppy sea, city in far distance (51x83cm-20x33in) init. panel
£20000 $38000   (11-Jan-91 CH.NY30/R) Shipping in choppy sea (48x73cm-19x29in) mono. panel
£80838 $136617   (2-May-91 CH.AM114/R) Grapes and peaches on a silva tazza a wine glass and other objectson a marble ledge (74x61cm-29x24in) s. (D.FL 270000)

BEYEREN, Abraham van (circle) (1620-1675) Dutch
£5387 $10612   (14-Nov-90 D.V174/R) Still life with fruit and wine glasses (71x57cm-28x22in) i. canvas on panel (A.S 110000)

BEYEREN, Abraham van (school) (1620-1675) Dutch
£3077 $6000   (10-Nov-90 CH.NY114/R) Fruit in bowl, wineglass, roemer and other things on draped table (64x57cm-25x22in) panel

BEYEREN, Jozef V (?) ?
£917 $1788   (15-Jan-91 GM.B647) Nature morte au chandelier (40x50cm-16x20in) s. wood (B.FR 55000)
£919 $1801   (12-Feb-91 GM.B339) Nature morte au Hanap (40x50cm-16x20in) s. (B.FR 55000)
£993 $1876   (25-Sep-90 GM.B999) Nature morte a la chandelle (40x50cm-16x20in) s. panel (B.FR 60000)
£1003 $1965   (12-Feb-91 GM.B410) Nature morte a la Bougie (39x49cm-15x19in) s. wood (B.FR 60000)

BEYEREN, V (?) ?
£1068 $2083   (24-Oct-90 GM.B1183) Nature morte a la pinte (40x50cm-16x20in) s. (B.FR 65000)

BEZAAN, Johan (1894-?) ?
£1190 $1917   (28-Jun-91 BM.B878/R) Still life with cactus (80x58cm-31x23in) s.indis.d.22 (DM 3500)

BEZARD, H M (20th C) Dutch?
£991 $1912   (12-Dec-90 CH.AM538) Composition (92x65cm-36x26in) s.d.46 init.d.46 verso (D.FL 3200)

BEZEM, Naphtali (1924-) Israeli
£733 $1400   (1-Jan-91 GG.TA252/R) Man and little woman (33x24cm-13x9in) s.
£838 $1600   (2-Jan-91 GG.TA526/R) Woman with candlesticks (46x38cm-18x15in) s.
£995 $1900   (1-Jan-91 GG.TA248/R) Fish and head of boy (46x61cm-18x24in) s.
£2094 $4000   (1-Jan-91 GG.TA247/R) Figure, fish and flower (81x65cm-32x26in) s. s.d.1967verso
£2577 $4200 .   (12-Jun-91 GG.TA234/R) Stroll in mountains (65x50cm-26x20in) s.
£552   *$900   (12-Jun-91 GG.TA34/R) Figures and houses (41x54cm-16x21in) s. W/C pastel*
£613   *$1000   (12-Jun-91 GG.TA235/R) Couple and stork (20x22cm-8x9in) s. mixed media*
£785   *$1500   (1-Jan-91 GG.TA250/R) Triptych (28x60cm-11x24in) s.c.1979 gouache*
£838   *$1600   (1-Jan-91 GG.TA249/R) Man lying between hills (45x64cm-18x25in) s. gouache W/C*
£1466   *$2800   (1-Jan-91 GG.TA251/R) Immigrants on hill (65x100cm-26x39in) s.c.1960 oil mixed media canvas*

BEZOMBES, Roger (1913-) ?
£1077 $2100   (10-Oct-90 D.NY14) Ballet dancer holding bouquet (71x33cm-28x13in) s. s.i.verso board
£1521 $3012   (3-Feb-91 I.N23) L'Auvergne (82x60cm-32x24in) s. panel (F.FR 15000)
£1795 $3500   (10-Oct-90 SY.NY237/R) Odalisque (51x61cm-20x24in) s. s.i.verso panel

BEZZI, Bartolomeo (1851-1925) Italian
£9231 $18000   (24-Oct-90 CH.NY230/R) Harbour scene with view of Venice (65x55cm-26x22in) s.

BEZZI, Giovanni Francesco (?-1571) Italian
£210000 $342300   (3-Jul-91 S89/R) Thyestes and Aerope (200x142cm-79x56in)

BEZZUOLI, Giuseppe (1784-1855) Italian
£1700 $3332   (14-Feb-91 CSK163) A French king entering a town with his troops (112x157cm-44x62in) indist.s.i. stretcher verso

BIAGI, L (?) Italian?
£2055 $3678   (14-Mar-91 N.M2633/R) Madonna with Christ child standing (155x106cm-61x42in) s. after B E Murillo (DM 6000)

BIAGIO DI ANTONIO (attrib) (15th C) Italian
£38000 $74860   (31-Oct-90 S98/R) The Holy Family with Infant St John
        (60cm-24ins circular) panel

BIAGIO, Vincenzo see CATENA, Vincenzo

BIANCA, Angelo dell'Oca see DALL'OCA BIANCA, Angelo

BIANCHI, Domenico (1955-) Italian
£1297 $2517   (5-Dec-90 AB.S7032/R) Untitled - 1984 (32x23cm-13x9in) W/C (S.KR 14000)

BIANCHI, Mose (1840-1904) Italian
£6157 $10282   (6-Jun-91 F.M230/R) Ritratto di fanciulla (50x35cm-20x14in) mono. board
        (I.L 13500000)
£34000 $66000   (18-Oct-90 F.M36/R) Campagna lombarda con contadina e bambino
        (28x38cm-11x15in) s.i.d.1876 (I.L 75000000)
£4621   *$8919*   *(12-Dec-90 F.M166/R) Campagna veronese (65x91cm-26x36in) mono.verso*
        pastel chl. (I.L 10000000)

BIANCHI-FERRARI, Francesco (circle) (1457-1510) Italian
£13524 $24208   (8-Apr-91 CH.R222/R) La Madonna col Bambino fra I Santi Giovanni
        Evangelista e Francesco (157x122cm-62x48in) panel (I.L 30000000)

BIANCHINI, Antonio (19/20th C) Italian
£983   *$1700*   *(21-May-91 CE.NY257/R) Religious procession (43x66cm-17x26in) s. W/C*
        gouache over pencil

BIANCHINI, Arthur (1869-1955) Swedish
£566 $979   (22-May-91 BA.S7/R) Beach at Sandhamn (35x45cm-14x18in) s. (S.KR 6000)
£708 $1224   (22-May-91 BA.S6/R) Landscape, Sandhamn (67x84cm-26x33in) s. (S.KR 7500)
£845 $1437   (28-May-91 AB.S4603/R) Katarina church in Moonlit winter landscape
        (32x46cm-13x18in) s. (S.KR 9000)

BIANCHINI, Charles (1860-1905) French
£888 $1500   (21-Apr-91 DU.E154/R) Portrait of young woman (51x41cm-20x16in) s. panel

BIANCHINI, E (?) Italian
£751 $1300   (8-May-91 RO.BA353) Fiori (100x73cm-39x29in) s.

BIANCL, R (19th C) Italian
£1371 $2701   (14-Nov-90 F.M3/R) Trompe l'oeil con stella de sceriffo, pistola e
        manette (40x30cm-16x12in) s.d.1865 (I.L 3000000)

BIANCO, Pieretto (1875-1937) Italian
£598 $1028   (14-May-91 GF.L2553/R) Midday peace in Italian village (32x45cm-13x18in)
        s. board (S.FR 1500)

BIARD, Francois Auguste (1799-1882) French
£20408 $40000   (7-Nov-90 B.SF1196/R) Piratskeppet - pirate ship (158x216cm-62x85in)
        s.d.1856

BIAUSSAT, Raymond (20th C) French
£615 $1205   (11-Nov-90 ZZ.F248/R) A cache amour (50x64cm-20x25in) s. panel
        (F.FR 6000)
£717 $1406   (11-Nov-90 ZZ.F245/R) Au bord des ombres (50x65cm-20x26in) s. panel
        (F.FR 7000)

BIBIENA (circle) (17/18th C) Italian
£567   *$1014*   *(12-Apr-91 AW.H414/R) Interior with columns (16x19cm-6x7in) pen wash*
        (DM 1700)

BIBIENA, Ferdinando Galli (1657-1743) Italian
£1818   *$3564*   *(19-Nov-90 CH.R246/R) Interno di edificio a pianta centrale a tre ordini*
        con cupola (13x16cm-5x6in) pencil ink W/C sold with sketch
        (I.L 4000000)

BIBIENA, Giuseppe Galli (1696-1756) Italian
£1642   *$2906*   *(19-Mar-91 F.M266/R) Studio di loggiati per scenografia (31x23cm-12x9in)*
        pen W/C ink (I.L 3600000)

BIBIENA, Giuseppe Galli (attrib) (1696-1756) Italian
£1400   *$2688*   *(18-Feb-91 S298/R) Interior of church of S. Maria d'Aracoelli*
        (45x58cm-18x23in) bears i. pen ink wash

BICCHI, Silvio (1874-1948) Italian
£800 $1320   (10-Jul-91 S125/R) Portrait of Colonel James Murray-Baillie standing on
        steps holding shako (241x155cm-95x61in) s.d.1906

BICCI DI LORENZO (1373-1452) Italian
£15000 $25350   (19-Apr-91 C154/R) A Pope Saint blessing a young woman (28x28cm-11x11in)
        panel
£100000 $173000   (24-May-91 C34/R) The Madonna and Child in a Mandorla with Saints John
        the Baptist andFrancis (66x42cm-26x17in) i. tempera gold panel pointed
        top

BICCI, Neri di (1419-1491) Italian
£210526 $400000   (11-Jan-91 CH.NY26/R) The Madonna and Child enthroned with Saints Michael, Bartholomew, Agnes and Catherine (184x108cm-72x43in) tempera panel arched

BICKNELL, Albion Harris (1837-1915) American
£1744 $3000   (15-May-91 SY.NY89/R) October on Lieutenant River (30x41cm-12x16in) s. board

BICKNELL, Frank Alfred (1866-1943) American
£1823 $3500   (29-Nov-90 MFA.C111) River at old Lyme (30x15cm-12x6in) s. board

BIDDLE, George (1885-?) American
£989 $1850   (30-Aug-90 MFA.C62/R) Nudes by lake (48x61cm-19x24in) s.d.1926

BIDDLE, M M (?) ?
£850 $1658   (24-Oct-90 DR129) The race (48x68cm-19x27in) s. panel

BIDEAUX, Gaston (fl.1904-1936) ?
£1007 $1963   (10-Oct-90 WE.MU211/R) French town (60x37cm-24x15in) s.i. pastel canvas (DM 3000)

BIDLO, Mike (20th C) American?
£1020 $2000   (6-Nov-90 CE.NY274/R) Campbell's clam chowder soup (53x41cm-21x16in) acrylic
£4569 $9000   (4-Oct-90 SY.NY247/R) Jackson Pollock No. 10, 1949 (71x325cm-28x128in) s.d.1983 verso
£618 $1187   (27-Nov-90 AB.S4006) Yves Klein performance, 1986 (92x54cm-36x21in) W/C (S.KR 6700)

BIE, Cornelis de (1621-1664) Dutch
£2235 $4000   (11-Apr-91 SY.NY104/R) Dune landscape with figures and village in distance (26x42cm-10x17in) panel

BIECKE, H (19/20th C) Austrian
£2500 $4100   (19-Jun-91 S114/R) Portrait of lady (149x89cm-59x35in) s.

BIEDERMANN, Edward (1864-?) German
£1323 $2500   (25-Sep-90 CE.NY295/R) The Grand Canal at the St. Louis Exposition, 1904 St. Louis World'sFair (55x68cm-22x27in) init.i. W/C gouache pencil

BIEDERMANN, Johann Jakob (1763-1830) Swiss
£13889 $23194   (5-Jun-91 SY.Z21/R) Haute-Savoie (32x44cm-13x17in) mono. (S.FR 35000)

BIEGAS, Boleslas (1877-1954) Polish
£655 $1278   (26-Oct-90 APT.P49/R) Le chateau du passe (52x42cm-20x17in) s. board (F.FR 6500)
£655 $1278   (26-Oct-90 APT.P75/R) Cycles spheriques, personnages (42x37cm-17x15in) s. board (F.FR 6500)
£655 $1278   (26-Oct-90 APT.P50/R) Dans de l'ouragan (54x44cm-21x17in) s. panel (F.FR 6500)
£706 $1376   (26-Oct-90 APT.P79/R) Danse seduisante (57x73cm-22x29in) s. panel (F.FR 7000)
£706 $1376   (26-Oct-90 APT.P77/R) Portrait de femme (146x89cm-57x35in) s. (F.FR 7000)
£706 $1376   (26-Oct-90 APT.P61/R) Temple du mystere de la grotte (62x49cm-24x19in) s. panel (F.FR 7000)
£753 $1393   (6-Mar-91 APT.P76) Cygne d'amour (105x74cm-41x29in) s. panel (F.FR 7500)
£756 $1474   (26-Oct-90 APT.P48/R) Trone de la reine des Tresors Marins (50x61cm-20x24in) s. panel (F.FR 7500)
£857 $1671   (26-Oct-90 APT.P72) Monument de l'infini (48x37cm-19x15in) s. board (F.FR 8500)
£1109 $2162   (26-Oct-90 APT.P54/R) Danse de l'ouragan (60x75cm-24x30in) s. panel (F.FR 11000)
£1200 $1956   (1-Jul-91 APT.P300/R) Personnage chromatique (74x57cm-29x22in) s. panel (F.FR 12000)
£1210 $2359   (26-Oct-90 APT.P44/R) Le trone du tresor (50x61cm-20x24in) s. panel (F.FR 12000)
£1411 $2752   (26-Oct-90 APT.P64/R) La lune (39x24cm-15x9in) s. board (F.FR 14000)
£1613 $3145   (26-Oct-90 APT.P57/R) Temple de l'esperance (81x60cm-32x24in) s. panel (F.FR 16000)
£1714 $3342   (26-Oct-90 APT.P52/R) Cycle spherique - pas d'ame (73x53cm-29x21in) s. (F.FR 17000)
£2016 $3931   (26-Oct-90 APT.P59/R) Ballerines (81x54cm-32x21in) s. (F.FR 20000)
£2016 $3931   (26-Oct-90 APT.P47/R) Lumiere du temple (70x78cm-28x31in) s. panel (F.FR 20000)
£2218 $4325   (26-Oct-90 APT.P46/R) Les couleurs des fleurs (62x41cm-24x16in) s. board (F.FR 22000)
£2218 $4325   (26-Oct-90 APT.P48/R) Enigme (55x42cm-22x17in) s. board (F.FR 22000)
£2621 $5111   (26-Oct-90 APT.P45/R) Danseuse orientale (74x49cm-29x19in) s. paper laid down on board (F.FR 26000)
£2923 $5701   (26-Oct-90 APT.P53/R) Egyptienne (73x60cm-29x24in) s. (F.FR 29000)
£3730 $7273   (26-Oct-90 APT.P60/R) Printemps (130x98cm-51x39in) s. (F.FR 37000)
£3831 $7470   (26-Oct-90 APT.P63/R) Nostalgie (65x49cm-26x19in) s. board (F.FR 38000)
£8065 $15726   (26-Oct-90 APT.P66/R) Danse de la lumiere de vie (200x100cm-79x39in) s. (F.FR 80000)

BIEGAS, Boleslas (1877-1954) Polish-cont.
£1018 $1985   (26-Oct-90 APT.P71/R) Adam (76x49cm-30x19in) s. pastel (F.FR 10100)

BIEGEL, Peter (1913-1988) British
£2300 $4324   (20-Sep-90 C29/R) Hunting on hills (49x59cm-19x23in) s.
£550 $1040   (26-Sep-90 HUN2) The Rut, Exmoor (23x25cm-9x10in) W/C
£900 $1566   (27-Mar-91 HUN2) Dachshund (30x30cm-12x12in) W/C
£3593 $6000   (7-Jun-91 SY.NY225/R) Fairfield Country Hunt (41x56cm-16x22in) s.d. '57
i. W/C gouache pencil

BIEHLE, August (1885-?) American
£710 $1200   (20-Apr-91 WOL.C321) Haystacks (33x48cm-13x19in) s. W/C

BIEHN, Joshua (fl.1891-1899) Canadian
£657 $1136   (6-May-91 SY.T182) Toronto Street vendor (25x18cm-10x7in) s.d.1896 board
(C.D 1300)

BIELCHOWSKI, Karl August (1826-1883) German
£1198 $2275   (11-Sep-90 CH.AM272/R) Fisher girls from Naples (66x51cm-26x20in)
s.d.1852 (D.FL 4000)
£1919 $3301   (16-May-91 D.V121/R) Two Neapolitan fisher girls (66x51cm-26x20in)
s.i.d.1859 (A.S 40000)

BIELER, Andre Charles (1896-) Canadian
£606 $1042   (14-May-91 JOY.T19) Les moutons (30x36cm-12x14in) s. (C.D 1200)
£867 $1466   (17-Apr-91 EA.M470 a) Easter market (30x40cm-12x16in) s.d.76 d.1976
verso (C.D 1700)
£1010 $1737   (14-May-91 JOY.T153) Moisson (35x51cm-14x20in) s. board (C.D 2000)
£1768 $3058   (6-May-91 SY.T78/R) Selling farm (25x33cm-10x13in) s. d.c.1926 verso
board (C.D 3500)
£556 $956   (14-May-91 JOY.T177) La decente (40x54cm-16x21in) s.d. '40 W/C
(C.D 1100)
£614 $1204   (20-Nov-90 JOY.T363/R) Waterton Park, Rocky Mountains (21x29cm-8x11in)
s. W/C (C.D 1400)
£3057 $6022   (12-Nov-90 HO.ED315/R) Blackfoot encampment (56x76cm-22x30in) s.d. mixed
media (C.D 7000)

BIELER, Ernest (1863-1948) Swiss
£3061 $6031   (16-Nov-90 GK.Z5323/R) Study for ceiling decoration In Bern theatre
(35x52cm-14x20in) st.studio board (S.FR 7500)
£10277 $17470   (27-May-91 GK.Z5307/R) Leman et massif de Savole (50x108cm-20x43in)
st.sig. tempera over pencil board (S.FR 26000)
£88710 $170323   (2-Dec-90 GAB.G1507/R) La distribution du pain et du vin apres la messe
a Drone (100x200cm-39x79in) i. tempera paper laid down on canvas
(S.FR 220000)
£408 $792   (8-Dec-90 GAB.G2384/R) Fete des Vignerons - costumes de Berne et de
Oberhadt (17x10cm-7x4in) W/C (S.FR 1000)
£2449 $4751   (8-Dec-90 GAB.G2385/R) Maison Baumann, Loeche (62x45cm-24x18in) s.i.
gouache chk. (S.FR 6000)
£3673 $7237   (16-Nov-90 GK.Z5322/R) Crete de Thyon (35x52cm-14x20in) mono. pastel chl
board (S.FR 9000)
£4082 $7918   (8-Dec-90 GAB.G2386/R) Vue de Salquenen (73x51cm-29x20in) s.i. gouache
(S.FR 10000)

BIELING, Hermann Friedrich (1887-1964) Dutch
£539 $1051   (25-Oct-90 VN.R353/R) Landscape In Brittany (41x49cm-16x19in) s.d.35
(D.FL 1800)
£579 $1101   (26-Feb-91 VN.R21) Winter near Plaswijk In Rotterdam (56x77cm-22x30in)
s.d.36 (D.FL 1900)
£854 $1622   (26-Feb-91 VN.R23) African picture (63x42cm-25x17in) s.d.23 (D.FL 2800)
£1037 $1970   (26-Feb-91 VN.R22/R) Carnival (57x78cm-22x31in) s.d.31 (D.FL 3400)

BIENNOURY, Victor (1823-1893) French
£403 $766   (27-Feb-91 LEB.P88) Etude pour Heudes de Montreuil chl.htd.white
(F.FR 4000)
£1923 $3750   (26-Oct-90 SY.NY71/R) Soldier holding Christ's crown of thorns
(31x22cm-12x9in) s.i. col.chk squared
£3024 $5746   (27-Feb-91 LEB.P87/R) Soldat romain s. blk.crayon htd.white chk.
(F.FR 30000)

BIER, Wolfgang (1943-) German
£1297 $2542   (24-Nov-90 VG.B447/R) Mann mit Schnabelvisier. Sold with dr. of male
nude by Erich Smodics (64x49cm-25x19in) s.i.d.1976 steel leather
collage (DM 3800)

BIERENBROODSPOT, Gerti (1940-) Dutch
£9288 $17926   (13-Dec-90 SY.AM377) Rode wand met zuilen, Pompeii (130x200cm-51x79in)
s.d.1985 tempera canvas (D.FL 30000)

BIERGE, Roland (1922-) French
£665 $1190   (16-Mar-91 KV.L27) La Presq'ile de Glens (55x46cm-22x18in) s. s.d.68
verso (B.FR 40000)

BIERKOWSKA, Leona (1855-1910) Polish
£1340 $2627   (26-Jan-91 PSA.W3) In the farmyard (75x124cm-30x49in) s. (P.Z 25000000)

BIERMANN, Edouard (1803-1892) German
£2797 $5427   *(7-Dec-90 GB.B5746/R) View of Paulskirche and Paulsplatz, Frankfurt (23x34cm-9x13in) s.d.1853 pen over pencil (DM 8000)*

BIERSTADT, Albert (1830-1902) American/German
£1563 $3000   (17-Dec-90 SY.NY148/R) On top of White Mountain (36x46cm-14x18in) paper on canvas
£2312 $4000   (21-May-91 GRO.B59/R) American marine scene sunset over lake (8x8cm-3x3in) init. paper
£2646 $5000   (27-Sep-90 CH.NY9/R) Mountain house (34x50cm-13x20in) init. paper laid down on canvas
£3488 $6000   (15-May-91 SY.NY74/R) Mountain landscape (45x35cm-18x14in) paper on board
£3669 $6200   (20-Apr-91 WOL.C56/R) Precipice (33x25cm-13x10in) s. panel
£4497 $8500   (27-Sep-90 CH.NY47/R) Yosemite Valley (36x48cm-14x19in) bears init. paper laid down on canvas
£4497 $8500   (26-Sep-90 SY.NY48/R) Landscape with distant mountains (35x48cm-14x19in) s.mono. paper mounted on board
£4734 $8000   (20-Apr-91 WOL.C55/R) Salem (48x33cm-19x13in) s.i. cardboard on panel
£5028 $9000   (12-Apr-91 SY.NY10/R) Mountain landscape (35x49cm-14x19in) paper on board
£5028 $9000   (12-Apr-91 SY.NY35/R) Pine forest (48x34cm-19x13in) paper on board
£5233 $9000   (15-May-91 SY.NY25/R) Tropical landscape (35x49cm-14x19in) paper on board
£5820 $11000   (26-Sep-90 SY.NY21/R) Lake in the Rockies (35x47cm-14x19in) paper mounted on board
£6349 $12000   (26-Sep-90 SY.NY49/R) Mountain valley (34x47cm-13x19in) s.mono. paper mounted on board
£7263 $13000   (14-Mar-91 CH.NY59/R) Butterfly (14x21cm-6x8in) s.d.87 paper on board
£7937 $15000   (26-Sep-90 SY.NY63/R) Mountain landscape (50x35cm-20x14in) s.mono. paper mounted on canvas
£10056 $18000   (12-Apr-91 SY.NY22/R) Hatch-Hatchy Valley, California (41x53cm-16x21in) mono. paper on board
£11340 $22000   (5-Dec-90 D.NY65/R) Indians spear fishing (43x66cm-17x26in) init.d.1862
£12139 $21000   (23-May-91 SY.NY18/R) Rainy day in autumn (76x112cm-30x44in) mono.
£12698 $24000   (27-Sep-90 CH.NY32/R) Sunset (17x29cm-7x11in) paper
£16495 $32000   (5-Dec-90 D.NY66/R) The Matterhorn at sunset (147x107cm-58x42in) init.
£20635 $39000   (26-Sep-90 SY.NY36/R) Autumn landscape, the Catskills (75x110cm-30x43in) s.mono.
£23669 $40000   (1-May-91 B.SF5173/R) Wetterhorn, Switzerland (74x51cm-29x20in) s.
£26042 $50000   (29-Nov-90 SY.NY15/R) Sunset on the mountain (36x48cm-14x19in) s.mono. paper mounted on canvas
£248555 $430000   (22-May-91 CH.NY160/R) A lake in the Sierra Nevada (55x76cm-22x30in) init.d.67
£2835 $5500   *(24-Aug-90 RB.HY179/R) Butterfly (10x18cm-4x7in) s.d.April 16/96 W/C gouache ink*
£3093 $6000   *(24-Aug-90 RB.HY180/R) Butterfly (10x18cm-4x7in) s.d.April 16/96 W/C gouache ink*
£7937 $15000   *(26-Sep-90 SY.NY18/R) Butterfly (11x18cm-4x7in) s.d.Jan.20/93 oil pencil*

BIERSTADT, Albert (attrib) (1830-1902) American/German
£867 $1500   (10-May-91 S.W2161/R) Figure standing by rustic cottage in forest (25x36cm-10x14in) paper

BIESE, Helmi (1867-1933) Finnish
£3424 $6710   (24-Nov-90 HOR.H52/R) Drying nets (25x73cm-10x29in) s. (F.M 24000)
£6705 $13141   (24-Nov-90 HOR.H51/R) Sailing in the bay (40x70cm-16x28in) s. (F.M 47000)
£374 $722   *(15-Dec-90 BU.H212) Still life of flowers (37x29cm-15x11in) s.d.1916 W/C (F.M 2600)*

BIESEBROECK, Jules van (1873-1965) Belgian
£1363 $2686   (6-Oct-90 KV.L267/R) Mauresques dans leur interieur (101x76cm-40x30in) s. panel (B.FR 85000)

BIESSY, Marie Gabriel (1854-1935) French
£2023 $3500   (22-May-91 SY.NY185/R) In studio (89x113cm-35x44in) s.

BIESTER, Anthony (1837-C.1917) German
£655 $1100   (28-Apr-91 LIT.L219) Landscape with horses pulling cut logs across brook (56x91cm-22x36in) s.

BIEVRE, Marie de (1865-?) Belgian
£6154 $12000   (24-Oct-90 CH.NY261/R) Interior (46x64cm-18x25in) s.

BIGAND, Auguste (1803-?) French
£4500 $8820   (22-Nov-90 CSK289/R) Les derniers instants de Neron (118x170cm-46x67in) s.indist.d.

BIGARI, Vittori (1692-1776) Italian
£8183 $16038   (20-Nov-90 F.R133/R) Prospettiva architettonica con figure (124x92cm-49x36in) oval (I.L 18000000)
£3420 $6053   *(19-Mar-91 F.M267/R) Scena di trionfo romano (31x24cm-12x9in) pen W/C ink (I.L 7500000)*

BIGARI, Vittori (attrib) (1692-1776) Italian
£427 $700   (23-Jun-91 H.C1078) View of Juvarran church through archway
                    (30x38cm-12x15in) pen wash

BIGAUD, Wilson (1931-) Haitian
£661 $1321   (6-Feb-91 FB.P38) Ceremonie vaudou (60x76cm-24x30in) s. hardboard
                    (F.FR 6500)
£2806 $5500   (19-Nov-90 SY.NY302/R) A table (60x76cm-24x30in) s. board

BIGAUX, Louis Felix (1850-?) French
£819 $1596   (19-Oct-90 RAS.V461/R) Still life of books and candles on table
                    (72x94cm-28x37in) s.d.1882 (D.KR 9200)

BIGGI, Felice Fortunato (17th C) Italian
£11365 $22275   (20-Nov-90 F.R128/R) Vasi di fiori (68x48cm-27x19in) pair
                    (I.L 25000000)

BIGGI, Felice Fortunato (style) (17th C) Italian
£3000 $5190   (20-May-91 SWS8/R) Still life of flowers in an urn with a bird on a
                    garden ledge (96x66cm-38x26in) bears mono.

BIGGS, W (20th C) American
£3457 $6500   (10-Aug-90 DOU.M1) Untitled (84x114cm-33x45in)

BIGGS, Walter (1886-?) American
£1471 $2500   (1-Jun-91 IH.NY162/R) Young woman seated with two men, story
                    illustration (66x86cm-26x34in) s. en grisaille

BIGNON, A (19th C) French
£9045 $14834   (20-Jun-91 APT.P18 b/R) Nature morte aux fleurs et aux oranges
                    (146x115cm-57x45in) s.d.1882 (F.FR 90000)

BIGOT (?) French?
£5120 $9473   (4-Mar-91 ARC.P89) Rue Orientale (38x27cm-15x11in) s. (F.FR 51000)

BIGOT and LABADIE (20th C?) French?
£1143 $1932   (17-Apr-91 CB.P13/R) Projet d'une fontaine (84x122cm-33x48in) s. both
                    artists gouache Indian ink (F.FR 11500)

BIGOT, Georges Ferdinand (19/20th C) French
£20916 $36185   (24-May-91 FB.P34/R) Pecheurs Japonais a Atami (73x162cm-29x64in) s.
                    (F.FR 210000)

BIGOT, Trophime (after) (fl.1620-1635) French
£3984 $6853   (14-May-91 GF.L2267/R) Figures playing with dices (95x137cm-37x54in)
                    (S.FR 10000)

BIHAN, Alexandre le (1839-?) French
£6500 $12480   (27-Nov-90 PH74/R) Embroiderers at work (95x141cm-37x56in) s.

BIHAN, D L (19th C) British
£950 $1568   (9-Jul-91 PH33/R) View of Popes Villa, Twickenham, with figures and
                    boats in foreground (37x78cm-15x31in) s. i.verso

BILBAO Y MARTINEZ, Gonzalo (1860-?) Spanish
£3299 $5904   (13-Mar-91 FER.M191/R) Iglesia de Lasarte, Navarra (42x34cm-17x13in) s.
                    board (S.P 600000)

BILDERS, Johannes Wernardus (1811-1890) Dutch
£781 $1523   (20-Oct-90 CH.AM140/R) Wooded landscape with traveller on sandy track by
                    farm (51x76cm-20x30in) (D.FL 2600)

BILFELDT, Jean Joseph (1792-1849) French
£508 $864   (31-May-91 LD.P56/R) Portrait d'homme, le buste de trois-quart
                    (14x10cm-6x4in) min.s.d.1824 oval (F.FR 5100)

BILIBIN, Ivan (1876-1942) Russian
£1502 $2614   (28-Mar-91 DAR.P29/R) Portrait en pied du Khan Kontchack dans le Prince
                    Igor (43x24cm-17x9in) s. W/C (F.FR 15100)
£1705 $3051   (14-Apr-91 BU.H117/R) Youth (48x30cm-19x12in) s. W/C (F.M 12000)

BILINSKY, Boris (1901-1948) Russian
£1100 $2145   (10-Oct-90 C394/R) Warrior (32x25cm-13x10in) init. pencil W/C
£1200 $2340   (10-Oct-90 C389/R) Bottle (23x19cm-9x7in) init.d.8-21 W/C gouache
£1400 $2730   (10-Oct-90 C393/R) Lightning (33x37cm-13x15in) s. gouache
£1500 $2925   (10-Oct-90 C391/R) Enigma (20x24cm-8x9in) init.d.21-III W/C gouache
                    indian ink
£1500 $2925   (10-Oct-90 C392/R) Abstract hopes (19x25cm-7x10in) gouache
£1600 $3120   (10-Oct-90 C390/R) Study of a head (20x27cm-8x11in) init.d.17-12-22 W/C
                    pencil

BILIVERTI, Giovanni (1576-1666) Italian
£1094 $1937   (19-Mar-91 F.M350/R) Allegoria della virtu (23x16cm-9x6in) ink over
                    pencil squared (I.L 2400000)
£1800 $3042   (16-Apr-91 C156) A soldier in profile to the right (24x12cm-9x5in) red
                    chk.

BILIVERTI, Giovanni (studio) (1576-1666) Italian
£16227 $32130   (30-Jan-91 APT.P4/R) La mort de Cleopatre (247x174cm-97x69in)
                (F.FR 160000)

BILL, Jakob (1942-) Swiss
£816 $1608   (17-Nov-90 S.Z10) No 21 (50x50cm-20x20in) s.d.1973 acrylic (S.FR 2000)

BILL, Max (1908-) Swiss
£7654 $14926   (24-Oct-90 F.M204/R) Helles zentrum (33x33cm-13x13in) s.d.1970verso
                acrylic (I.L 17000000)
£8711 $14285   (20-Jun-91 F.M470/R) Nucleus vert (47x47cm-19x19in) s.l.d.1959/69
                (I.L 19000000)
£8711 $14285   (20-Jun-91 F.M433/R) Senza titolo (40x40cm-16x16in) s.d.1969/73
                (I.L 19000000)
£22843 $45000   (14-Nov-90 SY.NY320/R) White square completed with elementary colours
                (113x113cm-44x44in) s.d.62 verso diagonal
£29716 $57947   (22-Oct-90 BR.M138/R) Composizione (60x60cm-24x24in) (I.L 66000000)

BILLE, Carl (1815-1898) Danish
£643 $1261   (10-Nov-90 FAL.M30/R) Sailship in storm (23x32cm-9x13in) s.d.82
                (S.KR 7000)
£656 $1175   (9-Apr-91 RAS.K2014) Seascape with sailingvessel (35x54cm-14x21in) s.
                (D.KR 7500)
£826 $1627   (13-Nov-90 AB.S856/R) Seascape with sailing vessel, sunset
                (17x26cm-7x10in) s. (S.KR 9000)
£1144 $1923   (22-Apr-91 BU.K42/R) Seascape with sailship, one with American flag
                (47x71cm-19x28in) s.d.1857 (D.KR 13000)
£1161 $2194   (25-Sep-90 RAS.K21/R) Coastal landscape, Bornholm (30x42cm-12x17in)
                s.d.58 (D.KR 13000)
£1429 $2700   (25-Sep-90 RAS.K20) Seascape with sailship in moonlight
                (100x138cm-39x54in) s. (D.KR 16000)
£1690 $2873   (28-May-91 AB.S4736/R) Coastal landscape with sailing vessels in rough
                seas, twilight (63x95cm-25x37in) s.d.1871 (S.KR 18000)
£1690 $2873   (28-May-91 AB.S4738/R) Seascape with sailingvessel in moonlight
                (22x18cm-9x7in) s. (S.KR 18000)
£3756 $6385   (28-May-91 AB.S4735/R) Seascape with sailingvessel (40x62cm-16x24in)
                s.d.87 (S.KR 40000)
£5722 $9613   (23-Apr-91 RAS.K23/R) Seascape with sailing ships off Copenhagen harbour
                (63x92cm-25x36in) s.d.1855 (D.KR 65000)
£10231 $19235   (18-Sep-90 BU.K19/R) Seascape with sailship off Copenhagen
                (60x89cm-24x35in) s.d.1857 (D.KR 115000)

BILLE, Edmond (1878-?) Swiss
£1315   *$2564*   *(24-Oct-90 GD.B125 a) La plaine de Rhone a Sierre (34x51cm-13x20in)*
                s.d.1926 W/C (S.FR 3300)

BILLE, Ejler (20th C) Danish
£10526 $17895   (29-May-91 KH.K70/R) Figurative composition (61x45cm-24x18in)
                s.d.86verso (D.KR 120000)
£14912 $25351   (29-May-91 KH.K38/R) Composition (80x75cm-31x30in) double sided
                (D.KR 170000)
£1436   *$2829*   *(14-Nov-90 KH.K12/R) Composition (27x19cm-11x7in) s.d.1947 W/C Indian*
                ink (D.KR 16000)
£4386   *$7456*   *(29-May-91 KH.K102/R) Composition (60x43cm-24x17in) s.d.49 W/C gouache*
                newspaper (D.KR 50000)

BILLE, S (19th C) Danish
£994 $1780   (14-Apr-91 BU.H118/R) Seascape with sailingboats (56x90cm-22x35in) s.
                (F.M 7000)

BILLE, Vilhelm (1864-1908) Danish
£538 $1075   (6-Feb-91 RAS.K42) Seascape with the frigate Jylland and smaller
                sailship (68x49cm-27x19in) s. (D.KR 6000)
£1056 $1775   (23-Apr-91 RAS.K323/R) Seascape with the frigate 'Jylland' in rough
                seas (90x116cm-35x46in) s. (D.KR 12000)
£1056 $1775   (23-Apr-91 RAS.K287) Battle at sea (63x97cm-25x38in) s.d.85 (D.KR 12000)
£1081 $2098   (22-Aug-90 RAS.K144/R) Seascape with the frigatte 'Jylland' in bresh
                breeze (90x116cm-35x46in) s. (D.KR 12500)
£1346 $2653   (14-Nov-90 RAS.K455/R) Seascape with sailship (100x180cm-39x71in) s.d.93
                (D.KR 15000)
£2379 $3973   (6-Jun-91 RAS.K83/R) Seascape with French ship in battle
                (63x93cm-25x37in) s. (D.KR 27000)

BILLET, Etienne (1821-?) French
£4049 $7935   (20-Nov-90 APT.P249/R) Autour de la fontaine (48x65cm-19x26in) s. panel
                (F.FR 40000)

BILLGREN, Ernst (1957-) Swedish
£2547 $4407   (22-May-91 BA.S317/R) Deer by watercourse (135x220cm-53x87in) init.
                s.verso panel (S.KR 27000)

BILLGREN, Ola (1940-) Swedish
£1661 $3188   (27-Nov-90 BU.S30/R) House and road in the mist (32x47cm-13x19in)
                s.d.1960 (S.KR 18000)
£3707 $7192   (4-Dec-90 BA.S49/R) Arabesque (88x99cm-35x39in) s.d.84verso (S.KR 40000)

BILLGREN, Ola (1940-) Swedish-cont.

£4871 $9548   (10-Nov-90 FAL.M32/R) Stool and table (54x44cm-21x17in) s.d.64
(S.KR 53000)

£5535 $10627   (27-Nov-90 BU.S29/R) Interior (72x57cm-28x22in) s.d.1964 (S.KR 60000)

£1390 $2697   (4-Dec-90 BA.S50/R) In the door opening (30x23cm-12x9in) s.d.1960 W/C
(S.KR 15000)

BILLING, Anna (1849-1927) Swedish

£576 $1129   (20-Nov-90 GO.G310) Lake landscape with boy on pier (36x56cm-14x22in) s.
W/C (S.KR 6300)

BILLING, Teodor (1817-1892) Swedish

£1038 $1795   (22-May-91 BA.S537/R) Coastal landscape with boats (46x64cm-18x25in)
s.d.1885 (S.KR 11000)

£1471 $2882   (6-Nov-90 BA.S17/R) Alpine landscape with figures merrymaking
(92x124cm-36x49in) s.d.1856 (S.KR 16000)

£2451 $4141   (21-Apr-91 BU.M56/R) Mountainous landscape with watermill
(88x132cm-35x52in) s.d.74 (S.KR 26000)

£2557 $4295   (24-Apr-91 BA.S18/R) Lake landscape with cattle (62x94cm-24x37in) s.d.76
(S.KR 27000)

BILLON, Charles (19/20th C) Swiss

£2632 $5000   (27-Feb-91 SY.NY186/R) Le Roi de Cinemas - le Parisiana sur les Grands
Boulevards (65x46cm-26x18in) s.d.1924

BILLOTTE, Rene (1846-1915) French

£1135 $2100   (8-Mar-91 S.BM196/R) Landscape scene (61x74cm-24x29in) s.

BILLOU, Paul (1821-?) French

£2105 $4000   (9-Jan-91 D.NY7/R) Embarking boating party (61x48cm-24x19in) s. canvas
on board

BILQUIN, Jean (1938-) Belgian

£1211 $2035   (23-Apr-91 C.A311/R) The gymnasts (92x62cm-36x24in) s.d.1969 panel
(B.FR 74000)

BILTIOUKOV, Boris (1926-) Russian

£517 $900   (25-Mar-91 ARC.P28) L'automne s. (F.FR 5200)

£547 $952   (25-Mar-91 ARC.P26) Deux a la palge (46x45cm-18x18in) s. (F.FR 5500)

£597 $1039   (25-Mar-91 ARC.P27/R) Sur le chantier (54x35cm-21x14in) s. (F.FR 6000)

£896 $1558   (25-Mar-91 ARC.P23/R) L'ebauche (35x25cm-14x10in) s. board (F.FR 9000)

BILTIUS, Cornelis (17th C) Dutch

£11155 $21753   (24-Oct-90 GD.B150/R) Trompe l'oeil hunting still life with dead game,
gun and other items (68x51cm-27x20in) s. (S.FR 28000)

BILTIUS, Jacobus (1633-1681) Dutch

£5931 $11683   (30-Oct-90 BU.S230/R) Still life of dead game (115x91cm-45x36in) s.
(S.KR 65000)

£6728 $13254   (13-Nov-90 CH.AM141/R) Hunting still life with dead curlew, grebe on
rope, songbirds and cage on marble ledge (101x87cm-40x34in) s.d.1678
(D.FL 22000)

£14691 $28942   (14-Nov-90 D.V134/R) Still life with vegetables, fruit and dead game
(96x91cm-38x36in) s. one of pair (A.S 300000)

£14691 $28942   (14-Nov-90 D.V135/R) Still life with vegetables and dead game
(96x91cm-38x36in) s. (A.S 300000)

BIMBI, Bartolomeo (1648-1725) Italian

£5000 $8150   (2-Jul-91 PH37/R) Great cormorant standing in Oriental landscape
(76x60cm-30x24in)

BIMBI, Bartolomeo (style) (1648-1725) Italian

£6000 $11520   (29-Nov-90 CSK71/R) Upturned basket of cherries (94x130cm-37x51in)

BIMMERMANN, Caesar (19th C) German

£2397 $4291   (12-Mar-91 FN.S2285) Wood transport in forest, winter (77x126cm-30x50in)
(DM 7000)

£5442 $8762   (26-Jun-91 KM.K1396/R) Wooded river landscape with skaters and fortified
castle beyond (58x81cm-23x32in) s. (DM 16000)

£6186 $11753   (2-Mar-91 KRA.D280/R) Fun on the ice at sunset (78x126cm-31x50in)
s.l.d.1882 (DM 18000)

BINARO, H (?) ?

£2455 $4223   (14-May-91 GM.B458/R) Peniches sur le canal (90x120cm-35x47in) s.
(B.FR 150000)

BINDER, Alois (19th C) German

£733 $1392   (28-Feb-91 D.V48/R) Portrait of forest warden's daughter
(27x22cm-11x9in) s. (A.S 15000)

BINDER, H (20th C) ?

£502 $848   (19-Apr-91 FN.S1669) Portrait of Kaiser Franz Josef I of Austria
(59x49cm-23x19in) (DM 1500)

BINDER, Jacob (19/20th C) German

£1607 $2700   (17-Jul-91 SY.NY303/R) The Talmudist (53x51cm-21x20in) s.

164

BINDER, Joseph (1805-1863) Austrian
£721 $1406   (25-Oct-90 D.V72/R) The guardian angel (90x110cm-35x43in) s.d.1848
                 (A.S 15000)

BINDER, Tony (20th C) ?
£960 $1622   (1-May-91 GD.B62/R) Sunset on the Nile with Arab driving camel
                 (14x24cm-6x9in) s.d.1910 panel (S.FR 2400)
£1254 $2044   (3-Jul-91 WE.MU103/R) Orientals bargaining (30x20cm-12x8in) panel
                 (DM 3700)
£1288 $2100   (3-Jul-91 WE.MU102/R) Bazaar scene (29x21cm-11x8in) panel (DM 3800)
£1399 $2699   (12-Dec-90 WE.MU186/R) Altstadtgasse (60x45cm-24x18in) s.d.1923
                 (DM 4000)
£1748 $3374   (12-Dec-90 WE.MU164/R) The nosy geese (41x63cm-16x25in) s.d.1906
                 (DM 5000)
£1748 $3374   (12-Dec-90 WE.MU187/R) The gossip (68x51cm-27x20in) s.d.1923 (DM 5000)
£373 $608   (3-Jul-91 WE.MU111/R) Street scene, Rothenburg ob der Tauber
                 (32x22cm-13x9in) s.i. pen wash W/C (DM 1100)
£746 $1216   (3-Jul-91 WE.MU214/R) Cairo bazaar scene (31x28cm-12x11in) s.i. pen wash
                 W/C (DM 2200)

BINET, Adolphe Gustave (1854-1897) French
£1427 $2740   (2-Dec-90 M.V146/R) La ferme de Valaine (F.FR 14000)
£1445 $2500   (21-May-91 CE.NY149/R) Cows watering (56x81cm-22x32in) s.
£34000 $65280   (27-Nov-90 PH57/R) The coach (162x202cm-64x80in) s.d.81

BINET, George (1865-1949) French
£1164 $2281   (25-Nov-90 ZZ.F15) Roses (24x73cm-9x29in) s. (F.FR 11500)
£5769 $11308   (25-Nov-90 ZZ.F12/R) Les floralies au Havre (25x36cm-10x14in) s. board
                 (F.FR 57000)
£10500 $17220   (19-Jun-91 S159/R) Pots of azaleas by wheelbarrow (124x170cm-49x67in) s.

BINET, Victor Jean Baptiste Barthelemy (1849-1924) French
£4290 $7250   (21-Apr-91 DU.E175/R) Expansive landscape with shepherd and flock
                 (74x117cm-29x46in) s.d.1888

BINETRUY (?) French
£896 $1558   (31-Mar-91 FE.P88) La porte de Moret sur Loing (55x44cm-22x17in) s.
                 (F.FR 9000)

BINETRUY, Claude (?) French
£980 $1646   (28-Apr-91 FE.P70) Le pont neuf (55x44cm-22x17in) s. (F.FR 9800)

BINFORD, Julien (1908-) American
£3261 $5250   (25-Jun-91 JRB.C60/R) Scenic overlook, Golden Gate Bridge
                 (56x64cm-22x25in) s.

BINGHAM, George Caleb (1811-1879) American
£2235 $4000   (14-Mar-91 CH.NY29/R) Caleb Smith Stone (72x61cm-28x24in)

BINGLEY, James George (c.1841-1920) British
£1200 $2268   (27-Sep-90 PHF254/R) Crypt Farm, Cocking, Midhurst (33x45cm-13x18in)
                 mono.
£850 $1428   (23-Apr-91 RG2250) Summer and winter landscapes - Dedham, Essex and
                 Sussex (25x36cm-10x14in) mono. W/C pair

BINKS, Reuben Ward (20th C) British
£1500 $2955   (12-Nov-90 PH89/R) Flat coat Retriever. Type of Whitmore
                 (31x25cm-12x10in) both s.i.d.1921 W/C bodycol.over pencil pair
£2400 $4752   (30-Jan-91 S271/R) Three Pekingese, Tu, Mary and Dusky (64x85cm-25x33in)
                 s.i.d.1913 pastel

BINOIT, Peter (style) (17th C) German
£9629 $16081   (6-Jun-91 D.V78/R) Still life of fruit on stone table in park landscape
                 (96x86cm-38x34in) (A.S 200000)

BINYON, Edward (1830-1876) British
£850 $1462   (16-May-91 CSK107) Figures on steps (51x30cm-20x12in) s.d.1877
£1000 $1720   (16-May-91 CSK41/R) Ray of sunshine in Capri street (32x22cm-13x9in)
                 s.d.1873 s.i.verso

BINZER, William (19/20th C) German/Australian
£1548 $3034   (7-Nov-90 DS.W93) Bluff, New Zealand (70x87cm-28x34in) init. (NZ.D 5000)

BION, Marie Louise (1858-?) Swiss
£1905 $3181   (7-Jun-91 ZOF.Z1282) The singing lesson (133x69cm-52x27in) s.d.99
                 (S.FR 4800)

BIONDA, Mario (1913-) Italian
£728 $1376   (27-Sep-90 F.M41) Figura (70x50cm-28x20in) s.d.76 mixed media
                 (I.L 1600000)

BIOULES, Vincent (1938-) French?
£6552 $12777   (26-Oct-90 CC.P61/R) Apres-midi (130x162cm-51x64in) s. i.d.1978-1979
                 verso (F.FR 65000)

BIRCH, David (c.1895-?) British
£1250 $2038   (11-Jun-91 LW1087) Harvesting on the South Downs overlooking the sea (74x61cm-29x24in) s. board

BIRCH, M E (?) ?
£400 $708   (22-Mar-91 APT.P9) Poeme de Lamartine (43x26cm-17x10in) s. W/C gouache (F.FR 4000)

BIRCH, Reginald Bathurst (1856-1943) American
£2840 $5623   (3-Feb-91 I.N25/R) Nature morte aux fruits et au homard (50x90cm-20x35in) s.d.1905 (F.FR 28000)

BIRCH, Samuel John Lamorna (1869-1955) British
£500 $870   (27-Mar-91 PHS877) Wooded river landscape (36x51cm-14x20in) s.
£500 $960   (19-Feb-91 SWS8/R) Lamorna cove (24x34cm-9x13in) s. board
£540 $880   (2-Jul-91 SWS396) Newlyn harbour, bright sunshine. Farm buildings in autumn landscape (32x39cm-13x15in) s.i.d.1927 verso board double-sided
£580 $1102   (28-Feb-91 DLY123) Incoming tide, Pedn Vounder (23x33cm-9x13in) s. l. verso panel
£650 $1203   (6-Mar-91 DR102/R) Country road with figures and cottages (16x24cm-6x9in) s.d.1898 board
£800 $1520   (28-Feb-91 DLY96) Lamorna stream in spring sunlight (33x48cm-13x19in) traces label verso
£1000 $1680   (23-Apr-91 S127/R) Breezy day, River Garry (43x51cm-17x20in) s.d.1949
£1200 $2088   (28-Mar-91 CSK211) Marshland landscape (26x35cm-10x14in) s.d.95 panel
£1750 $3133   (14-Mar-91 L141) Lamorna Cove (23x36cm-9x14in) s. board
£2500 $4625   (7-Mar-91 C4/R) Clearing after storm (62x75cm-24x30in) s. s.i.verso
£3200 $6240   (10-Oct-90 S8/R) The River Almond, Glen Almond (61x51cm-24x20in) s.
£3200 $6080   (28-Feb-91 DLY378/R) Here dwells peace, Lamorna's stream by Hosking's Mill (76x61cm-30x24in) s.d.1940
£4000 $7600   (28-Feb-91 DLY377/R) My garden, Lamorna (51x61cm-20x24in) s.d.1940 label verso
£4000 $6680   (6-Jun-91 C7/R) Junction Pool where the Taw and Mole meet, grey morning, Lamorna (51x63cm-20x25in) s.d.1946 s.i.d.1947verso l.stretcher
£4000 $6680   (6-Jun-91 C9/R) The river Almond, Perthshire (59x49cm-23x19in) s. s.i.stretcher
£4000 $7680   (26-Nov-90 SWS161/R) Summer by the loch (75x105cm-30x41in) s.d.1936
£4000 $7800   (10-Oct-90 S2/R) The mouth of the Frome at Wareham, Dorset (51x61cm-20x24in) s.d.1942
£5000 $8150   (13-Jun-91 L295/R) Summer by the Loch (74x104cm-29x41in) s.d.1936
£5200 $9776   (18-Sep-90 PH23/R) Old Brig-O-Dee with dark Loch Nagar (51x76cm-20x30in) s.d.1938
£430 $718   (4-Jun-91 SWS2131) Winter (31x23cm-12x9in) s.d.1905 black chk gouache htd bodycol
£440 $744   (3-May-91 T320/R) Souvenir of Sweden (25x36cm-10x14in) s. W/C
£450 $752   (3-Jun-91 PHB10) Cornish river landscape (26x36cm-10x14in) s. W/C
£500 $885   (18-Mar-91 FEN26) The cove of Lamorna (23x33cm-9x13in) s. W/C
£520 $920   (18-Mar-91 FEN41/R) On the banks of lake Como (23x28cm-9x11in) s.i. W/C
£550 $974   (21-Mar-91 CSK75) Looking down the quay, Lamorna, Cornwall (25x36cm-10x14in) s.d.1943 pencil pen W/C
£580 $1125   (5-Dec-90 PHE81) The ale water (32x50cm-13x20in) s.i.d.1926 W/C
£580 $1073   (6-Mar-91 SC4145) Fisherman on the Black Pool at Basle near Dulverton (25x36cm-10x14in) s. W/C pencil
£580 $951   (20-Jun-91 DLY484/R) By mill (36x51cm-14x20in) s. W/C
£600 $1134   (27-Sep-90 L142) Tree lined lake (25x36cm-10x14in) s. W/C
£850 $1615   (28-Feb-91 DLY362) Fishing from a punt on a still river (25x46cm-10x18in) s.d.'45 W/C
£950 $1606   (1-May-91 PHL57/R) River landscape (29x44cm-11x17in) s. col.wash
£1050 $2069   (13-Nov-90 SWS97/R) Over snowy roads (34x53cm-13x21in) s. i. label verso
£1300 $2184   (23-Apr-91 S120/R) Tarbert. Inner Loch Crinan (24x34cm-9x13in) s.i.d.1936 W/C pen pair
£1300 $2561   (13-Nov-90 SWS98/R) Salmon fishing (39x49cm-15x19in) s.d.1952 W/C bodycol.over traces pencil
£1350 $2592   (17-Aug-90 T200/R) Near Okehampton (25x36cm-10x14in) s. W/C

BIRCH, Thomas (1779-1851) American
£1128 $2200   (26-Oct-90 S.W2205/R) Taking a pilot, Delaware Break (23x33cm-9x13in) s.i.d.1837 verso cardboard
£798 $1500   (23-Sep-90 LIT.L235) Shipwreck off rocky coast (18x28cm-7x11in) s.d.1824 W/C

BIRCH, Thomas (after) (1779-1851) American
£3179 $5500   (21-May-91 CE.NY375/R) Sleigh ride (46x69cm-18x27in) bears sig.

BIRCHALL, William Minshall (1884-?) British
£380 $722   (25-Feb-91 PH22/R) Up channel (29x35cm-11x14in) s.i.d.33 W/C bodycol
£380 $703   (6-Mar-91 DR13) Our ships in British waters, 6th Battle Squadron of Allied fleets (23x33cm-9x13in) s.i.d.1919 W/C
£391 $700   (16-Mar-91 W.W78/R) A ship of yesterday (23x33cm-9x13in) s.i. W/C gouache
£421 $800   (3-Mar-91 LIT.L201) Rounding the horn (25x36cm-10x14in) s. gouache
£680 $1292   (10-Jan-91 B78/R) Blackwall Reach (23x52cm-9x20in) s.i.d. W/C bodycol
£760 $1520   (8-Feb-91 T190/R) Off Blackwall (18x28cm-7x11in) s.i. W/C

BIRCK, A (19th C) French
£2126 $4166   *(20-Nov-90 APT.P221/R) Jeune fille aux boucles d'oreilles (32x24cm-13x9in) s.i. W/C (F.FR 21000)*

BIRD, Edward (1772-1819) British
£500 $865   (22-May-91 CSK166) Figures in tavern interior (34x30cm-13x12in) s.d.1810 panel

BIRD, Edward (attrib) (1772-1819) British
£1116 $1919   (14-May-91 GF.L2473/R) Family gathered around kitchen table (25x32cm-10x13in) (S.FR 2800)

BIRD, Harrington (1846-?) British
£600 $1014   *(18-Apr-91 B250/R) Chilly morn in his stable (32x47cm-13x19in) W/C*
£2900 $5742   *(29-Jan-91 OT474/R) An arab mare with foal in desert landscape (26x36cm-10x14in) s.d.1906 W/C*
£4400 $8580   *(24-Oct-90 S222/R) In flower of youth and beauty's pride (35x51cm-14x20in) s.d.1906 W/C over pencil*
£11500 $19320   *(15-Jul-91 PH140/R) Favoured one (45x68cm-18x27in) s.d.1909 W/C over pencil*

BIRD, Mary Holden (fl.1923-1936) British
£500 $885   *(22-Mar-91 PHE52) The sleeping sea (35x50cm-14x20in) mono.W/C*

BIRD, S (19th C) British
£600 $978   (13-Jun-91 CSK283) Rocky coastline with girl on beach (61x91cm-24x36in) s.

BIRD, Samuel C (19th C) British
£13500 $26595   (1-Nov-90 C337/R) Snooding hooks (142x112cm-56x44in) s.d.1877 i.verso

BIRGER, Hugo (1854-1887) Swedish
£3193 $6291   (30-Oct-90 BU.S9/R) Marockans by open fire (46x58cm-18x23in) s.i.d.1884 (S.KR 35000)
£3650 $7190   (30-Oct-90 BU.S10/R) Woman sewing by park steps (46x32cm-18x13in) (S.KR 40000)
£4682 $8052   (14-May-91 BU.S3/R) Young girl daydreaming by open fire (42x35cm-17x14in) s.d.1875 (S.KR 50000)
£11861 $23367   (30-Oct-90 BU.S8/R) Woman at the well (60x73cm-24x29in) s.i.d.1877 (S.KR 130000)
£18248 $35949   (30-Oct-90 BU.S7/R) By the farmhouse (80x65cm-31x26in) s.i.d.1877 (S.KR 200000)
£22810 $44936   (30-Oct-90 BU.S6/R) 'Ekebacken' (110x150cm-43x59in) s.i.d.1886 (S.KR 250000)

BIRGER-ERICSON, Birger (1904-) Swedish
£1033 $1756   (28-May-91 AB.S5163/R) Morning - composition with nude in fantasy landscape (121x121cm-48x48in) s. d.1979verso panel (S.KR 11000)
£1344 $2607   (5-Dec-90 AB.S7034/R) Slaughtering the geese (121x121cm-48x48in) s. d.1981verso panel (S.KR 14500)

BIRKEMOSE, Jens (20th C) Scandinavian
£815 $1573   (12-Dec-90 RAS.K64) Composition (123x72cm-48x28in) init.d.82 s.d.82verso (D.KR 9000)
£1112 $2169   (19-Oct-90 RAS.V615/R) Composition (72x51cm-28x20in) s.i.d.1984 (D.KR 12500)
£1246 $2429   (19-Oct-90 RAS.V614/R) Composition (72x51cm-28x20in) s.d.1984 (D.KR 14000)
£2321 $4295   (5-Mar-91 RAS.K62/R) Composition (132x95cm-52x37in) s.d.1984-86verso (D.KR 26000)
£2729 $5321   (10-Oct-90 RAS.K19/R) Composition (115x89cm-45x35in) s.d.79verso (D.KR 31000)

BIRKHAMMER, A (19/20th C) Danish
£737 $1400   (27-Feb-91 SY.NY319/R) Summer landscape with river beyond (71x100cm-28x39in) s.

BIRKLE, Albert (1900-1986) Austrian
£4850 $9117   (20-Sep-90 D.V205/R) View from Gersbergweg of the Hohensalzburg Fortress (35x49cm-14x19in) s. board (A.S 100000)
£1562 $2889   *(7-Mar-91 D.V129/R) Lady with cigarette (44x28cm-17x11in) mono. chl chk (A.S 32000)*

BIRLEY, Sir Oswald (1880-1952) New Zealander
£1200 $2352   (24-Jan-91 CSK174) Portrait of lady with dog (147x91cm-58x36in) s.

BIRMANN, Peter (1758-1844) Swiss
£342 $650   *(27-Feb-91 SY.NY190/R) Bridge in mountainous landscape (81x63cm-32x25in) s.i.d.1814 pencil W/C*

BIRMANN, Samuel (attrib) (1793-1847) Swiss
£984 $1820   *(6-Mar-91 HC.P12) Fontaine de Cyane a Syracuse (22x29cm-9x11in) W/C (F.FR 9800)*

BIRNEY, William Vierplanck (1858-1909) American
£957 $1800   (22-Sep-90 WOL.C165/R) Reading fortune (46x61cm-18x24in) s.

BIRNEY, William Vierplanck (1858-1909) American-cont.
£2367	$4000	(20-Apr-91 WOL.C129/R) Conversation (46x61cm-18x24in) s.
£3866	$7500	(5-Dec-90 D.NY14/R) A good smoke (25x36cm-10x14in) s.

BIROL (?) ?
£543	$1049	(12-Dec-90 RAS.K109) Woman at table (130x150cm-51x59in) s. (D.KR 6000)

BIROLLI, Renato (1906-1959) Italian
£832	$1615	(3-Dec-90 F.M251) Dormienti (19x24cm-7x9in) d.1935 tempera paper (I.L 1800000)
£14212	$23308	(20-Jun-91 F.M508/R) Canto popolare, Anversa (96x129cm-38x51in) s.d.1957 (I.L 31000000)
£18123	$31533	(26-Mar-91 F.M75/R) Rovi e strada (88x66cm-35x26in) s.d.953 (I.L 40000000)
£23125	$44862	(3-Dec-90 CH.R108/R) Tavola con cactus (81x64cm-32x25in) s. (I.L 50000000)
£999	*$1729*	*(7-May-91 F.M159/R) Figure (36x26cm-14x10in) s.i.d.1949 chl (I.L 2200000)*

BIRR, Jacques (1920-) French
£822	$1577	(17-Dec-90 ZZ.F130/R) Calao d'extreme orient (71x55cm-28x22in) s.d.Septembre 90 (F.FR 8100)
£1210	$2359	(28-Oct-90 QWA.P68) Harpye d'Amerique du sud (74x53cm-29x21in) s.d.24/02/89 paper (F.FR 12000)
£2117	$4128	(28-Oct-90 QWA.P69/R) Autruche male (146x114cm-57x45in) s.d.21/10/89 hardboard (F.FR 21000)

BIRREN, Joseph P (1864-?) American
£854	$1400	(21-Jun-91 DM.D2032/R) Baker's cart (41x30cm-16x12in) s.

BIRSTEIN, Max (1914-) Russian
£601	$1039	(8-May-91 FER.M225/R) Primavera en el lago (73x89cm-29x35in) s.d.75 (S.P 110000)
£765	$1468	(29-Nov-90 YC.P148/R) L'ete (127x70cm-50x28in) s. (F.FR 7500)

BIRTLES, Harry (fl.1880-1905) British
£900	$1692	(18-Sep-90 SWS614/R) Cows by a Loch (40x60cm-16x24in) s.d.1853
£540	*$902*	*(4-Jun-91 SWS2132) Brecon Beacons mist clearing off (30x46cm-12x18in) s.d.73 W/C over pencil*
£560	*$1053*	*(20-Sep-90 SC4105/R) Changing pastures (23x33cm-9x13in) s.d.98 W/C pencil*

BIRTWHISTLE, Cecil H (1910-) British
£750	$1440	(21-Feb-91 B39) Shepherd market (61x51cm-24x20in) s.

BIRZER, Eugen (1847-1905) German
£602	$1017	(19-Apr-91 FN.S1670) Hungarian landscape near Erdo with peasant couple on path (28x38cm-11x15in) s. (DM 1800)

BISBING, Henry Singlewood (1849-1919) American
£1923	$3250	(17-Apr-91 D.NY14/R) Happy family (51x74cm-20x29in) s.

BISCAINO, Bartolomeo (1632-1657) Italian
£16760	$30000	(11-Apr-91 SY.NY146/R) The death of Lucretia (150x195cm-59x77in)
£1800	*$3042*	*(16-Apr-91 C145/R) A rocky landscape with a man reclining by a river (35x27cm-14x11in) red chk.htd.white*

BISCHOFF, Elmer Nelson (1916-) American
£11834	$20000	(1-May-91 SY.NY235/R) No.65 (213x203cm-84x80in) s.d.1982 verso acrylic canvas
£19345	$32500	(24-Apr-91 B.SF4631/R) Landscape (76x81cm-30x32in) s.l.d.1965 verso
£718	*$1400*	*(24-Oct-90 B.SF1604) Untitled - girl leaning on elbow (28x20cm-11x8in) init. indian ink wash*
£1795	*$3500*	*(24-Oct-90 B.SF1515/R) Girl with fur coat (32x35cm-13x14in) s.d.69 pen wash*
£2179	*$4250*	*(24-Oct-90 B.SF1514/R) Seated model (43x35cm-17x14in) init.d.66 chl*

BISCHOFF, Franz A (1864-1929) American
£1148	$2250	(12-Feb-91 MOR.P100 a) Big Pine Canyon (30x41cm-12x16in) s. canvas on board
£1410	$2750	(10-Oct-90 B.SF585/R) Southern California coastline (32x48cm-13x19in) s. board
£1795	$3500	(10-Oct-90 B.SF544/R) Purple cliffs (48x48cm-19x19in) s. board
£1923	$3750	(10-Oct-90 B.SF538/R) The Wash (33x48cm-13x19in) s. board
£1923	$3750	(10-Oct-90 B.SF624/R) Desert foothills (33x44cm-13x17in) s. board
£2308	$4500	(10-Oct-90 B.SF593/R) Arroyo seco (32x40cm-13x16in) s.
£2821	$5500	(10-Oct-90 B.SF516/R) California landscape (33x48cm-13x19in) s. board
£20231	$35000	(22-May-91 CH.NY276/R) Cift Born trees, Point Lobos (102x127cm-40x50in) s. l. verso

BISCHOFF, Friedrich (1819-1873) German
£16185	$28000	(22-May-91 SY.NY35/R) Die gratulanten (107x140cm-42x55in) s.d.1861

BISCHOFFSHAUSEN, Hans (1927-) Austrian
£2392	*$4139*	*(8-May-91 D.V153/R) Untitled (62x53cm-24x21in) s.i.d.1962verso PVC canvas on panel (A.S 50000)*

BISCHOFFSHAUSEN, Hans (1927-) Austrian-cont.
£2485 $4821   *(6-Dec-90 D.V215/R) Prayer panel for dead landscape (50x50cm-20x20in) s.i.d.72 cellulose cement oil nails panel (A.S 50000)*

BISET, Charles-Emmanuel (attrib) (1633-c.1710) Flemish
£4000 $7800   (26-Oct-90 C88/R) A courtesan reclining on a bed (55x49cm-22x19in)

BISHOP, Richard (1887-1975) American
£842 $1600   (14-Sep-90 S.BM257/R) Wild turkeys in flight (61x69cm-24x27in) s.

BISI, Luigi (1814-1886) Italian
£2311 $4459   (11-Dec-90 CH.R196/R) Fedeli nel Duomo di Milano (23x19cm-9x7in) s. board (I.L 5000000)

BISON, Giuseppe Bernardino (1762-1844) Italian
£2564 $5000   (10-Oct-90 CH.NY50/R) Shipping in storm near castle on cliff (47x61cm-19x24in) canvas on aluminum
£2653 $5200   (6-Nov-90 GF.L2066/R) Foundry at night (36x51cm-14x20in) paper on canvas (S.FR 6500)
£3409 $6683   (19-Nov-90 CH.R121/R) Paesaggio lacustre con pescatori (36x44cm-14x17in) tempera paper (I.L 7500000)
£5240 $8908   (30-May-91 F.M123/R) La tentazioni di Sant'Antonio abate (33x28cm-13x11in) paper on canvas (I.L 11500000)
£75000 $129750   (24-May-91 C76/R) Venice, the entrance to the Grand Canal. The Grand Canal with the RialtoBridge seen from the south (37x57cm-15x22in) pair
£1000 $1630   *(1-Jul-91 S205/R) Figure of putto holding wreath (24x17cm-9x7in) s. pen wash over black chk*
£1094 $1937   *(19-Mar-91 F.M103/R) Suonatore di liuto (26x19cm-10x7in) s. ink over pencil (I.L 2400000)*
£1150 $2208   *(18-Feb-91 S138/R) Monk adoring statue of Madonna and Child (29x18cm-11x7in) s. pen ink wash over chk*
£1408 $2761   *(24-Jan-91 AGS.P13/R) Saint Jean-Baptiste prechant (17x23cm-7x9in) s. pen wash pierre noire (F.FR 14000)*
£1913 $3750   *(7-Nov-90 B.SF1022/R) Portrait of venetian dwarf (18x12cm-7x5in) st. pen wash*
£2033 $4065   *(4-Feb-91 PLF.P23/R) Deux portraits d'homme (18x25cm-7x10in) s.i.d.1832 pen W/C (F.FR 20000)*
£2508 $4439   *(19-Mar-91 F.M185/R) Crocefissione (26x18cm-10x7in) s. pen W/C ink over pencil (I.L 5500000)*
£10592 $17689   *(6-Jun-91 D.V28/R) Italian harbour town (30x40cm-12x16in) s. gouache tempera canvas (A.S 220000)*
£26000 $42380   *(2-Jul-91 C296 a/R) Highwaymen robbing coaches in wood (67x90cm-26x35in) bodycol*

BISON, Giuseppe Bernardino (attrib) (1762-1844) Italian
£5028 $9000   (11-Apr-91 SY.NY7/R) Figures on path in southern Italian landscape (50x62cm-20x24in)

BISON, Giuseppe Bernardino (school) (1762-1844) Italian
£3881 $6520   (23-Apr-91 F.R18/R) Architettura fantastica con figure (22x28cm-9x11in) tempera paper three (I.L 8500000)

BISSCHOP, Jan de (1628-1671) Dutch
£1059 $2054   *(7-Dec-90 P.70/R) Vue du temple de Vesta a Rome (12x21cm-5x8in) pen wash (F.FR 10300)*
£2400 $3912   *(2-Jul-91 C218/R) Ruins of circular Roman building and portico (10x16cm-4x6in) black chk pen wash*
£4200 $6846   *(2-Jul-91 C219/R) Roman cavalier on rearing horse (19x19cm-7x7in) black chk pen wash*

BISSCHOP, Suze see ROBERTSON, Suze

BISSI, Cirno Sergio (1902-) Italian
£663 $1300   (7-Nov-90 D.NY11) Sunday in the park (64x56cm-25x22in) s. d.1958 verso

BISSIER, Jules (1893-1965) French
£7107 $14000   (5-Oct-90 CH.NY4/R) 14.X.60 (19x21cm-7x8in) s.i.d.60 oil tempera
£7107 $14000   (4-Oct-90 SY.NY24/R) 12 Feb 61Q (10x20cm-4x8in) s.d.61Q oil tempera linen
£8376 $16500   (4-Oct-90 SY.NY41/R) H 4 Marz 64 (16x21cm-6x8in) s.d.64 oil tempera linen
£8500 $15045   (21-Mar-91 C224/R) Untitled (19x22cm-7x9in) s.d.28.7.58 egg tempera linen
£10059 $17000   (2-May-91 CH.NY112/R) 11 Janvier 61 (23x27cm-9x11in) s.d.61 tempera linen
£11675 $23000   (14-Nov-90 SY.NY312/R) Untitled (19x21cm-7x8in) s.d.64 oil tempera
£14865 $25270   (31-May-91 VG.B63/R) 5 Dez. 59 Mo (16x22cm-6x9in) s.i.d.1959 egg tempera canvas on board (DM 44000)
£15228 $30000   (5-Oct-90 CH.NY37/R) 29.August 59 (23x24cm-9x9in) s.i.d.59 oil tempera
£1587 $2603   *(19-Jun-91 GK.B203) Basel 7.12.56 (24x31cm-9x12in) indian ink brush (S.FR 4000)*
£1757 $2986   *(28-May-91 KF.M476/R) Entwined lines (18x21cm-7x8in) s.d.1955 indian ink pen (DM 5200)*
£2540 $4165   *(19-Jun-91 GK.B204/R) Basel 8.12.56 (24x31cm-9x12in) s.d.1956 indian ink brush (S.FR 6400)*

BISSIER, Jules (1893-1965) French-cont.

£3016	$5398	(16-Mar-91 S.Z46/R) Untitled (16x25cm-6x10in) mono.d.64 indian ink (S.FR 7600)
£3072	$6020	(22-Nov-90 L.K836/R) Composition (36x19cm-14x7in) s.d.1956 indian ink wash (DM 9000)
£3373	$5532	(19-Jun-91 GK.B206) Basel 8.12.56 (24x31cm-9x12in) s.d.1956 indian ink brush (S.FR 8500)
£3571	$6393	(16-Mar-91 S.Z47/R) Untitled (15x24cm-6x9in) s.d.63 indian ink (S.FR 9000)
£3571	$5857	(19-Jun-91 GK.B207/R) 25.1.63 (39x52cm-15x20in) mono.s.i.d.1963 indian ink brush (S.FR 9000)
£4167	$6833	(19-Jun-91 GK.B205) Basel 8.12.56 (24x31cm-9x12in) s.i.d.1956 indian ink brush (S.FR 10500)
£4847	$9500	(14-Feb-91 CH.NY1/R) 29.Jan.59 (39x52cm-15x20in) s.d.59 s.i.d.61 brush ink gouache
£4990	$8583	(13-May-91 CH.R85/R) Sans titre (18x18cm-7x7in) s.d.1959 W/C (I.L 11000000)
£5102	$10000	(14-Feb-91 CH.NY2/R) 5.8.62 (48x65cm-19x26in) s.d.62 s.i.d. brush ink gouache
£5128	$10000	(10-Oct-90 SY.NY474/R) Composition (25x30cm-10x12in) s.d.62 s.d.verso W/C ink
£6102	$10190	(6-Jun-91 HN.H163/R) Composition (49x60cm-19x24in) s.d.1953 ink brush (DM 18000)
£7143	$14000	(7-Nov-90 SY.NY150/R) A15 JULI 62 (13x24cm-5x9in) s.i.d.Juli 62 W/C
£7692	$13000	(2-May-91 CH.NY108/R) J. Lef (24x31cm-9x12in) s.d.64 brush ink gouache
£8122	$16000	(5-Oct-90 CH.NY31/R) 21.3.61 (15x24cm-6x9in) s.d.61 W/C
£10847	$18115	(7-Jun-91 HN.H10/R) Composition (13x24cm-5x9in) s.d.1962 W/C (DM 32000)

BISSIERE, Roger (1884-1964) French

£2811	$5537	(6-Oct-90 GL.P10/R) Nature morte a la table et au vase de fleurs (63x34cm-25x13in) s.d.1923 (F.FR 28500)
£3216	$5757	(15-Mar-91 FB.P12/R) La jeune fille (40x26cm-16x10in) s. panel (F.FR 32000)
£3976	$6720	(16-Apr-91 QWA.P8/R) La dame aux raisins (81x60cm-32x24in) s.i. verso (F.FR 40000)
£6000	$11700	(18-Oct-90 S8/R) Untitled (55x46cm-22x18in) s.d.32
£8000	$14160	(21-Mar-91 C204/R) Journal 14 Janvier (38x19cm-15x7in) s.d.14 Janvier board
£10000	$19500	(18-Oct-90 S32/R) Composition (32x40cm-13x16in) s.d.55
£13000	$23010	(21-Mar-91 S7/R) Quatre saisons No.XXXVI (31x39cm-12x15in) s.d.58 paper on board
£15408	$26039	(16-Apr-91 QWA.P9/R) Trois Harris (100x81cm-39x32in) s.d.1920 (F.FR 155000)
£16327	$32163	(14-Nov-90 I.N29/R) Le concert champetre (146x114cm-57x45in) s. (F.FR 160000)
£26621	$52177	(24-Nov-90 VG.B323/R) Untitled (59x89cm-23x35in) s.d.1955 linen (DM 78000)
£40036	$75267	(19-Sep-90 KH.K41/R) Paysage 1946 (65x100cm-26x39in) s. paper (D.KR 450000)
£52525	$102950	(14-Feb-91 GL.P22/R) Composition rouge (59x89cm-23x35in) s.d.1955 (F.FR 520000)
£1982	$3250	(19-Jun-91 B.SF1776/R) Composition (44x32cm-17x13in) s.d.53 ink
£4158	$7360	(7-Apr-91 I.N43/R) Nature morte aux cerises (48x55cm-19x22in) s. mixed media panel (F.FR 42000)

BISSOLO, Pier Francesco (c.1470-1554) Italian

| £3352 | $6000 | (11-Apr-91 SY.NY5/R) Madonna adoring the sleeping Christ Child (68x53cm-27x21in) canvas transferred from panel |
| £3586 | $6167 | (14-May-91 GF.L2007/R) Holy Family (98x132cm-39x52in) panel (S.FR 9000) |

BISSON (?) ?

| £1104 | $1800 | (5-Jul-91 S.W3049/R) Lady holding a rose (76x64cm-30x25in) s.d.1728 |

BISSON, Edouard (1856-?) French

| £1842 | $3500 | (9-Jan-91 D.NY9/R) Nymphs in clearing (74x56cm-29x22in) s.d.1901 |
| £2890 | $5000 | (21-May-91 CE.NY88/R) Nymphs and putti in landscape (72x56cm-28x22in) s.d.1901 |

BISSON, Lucienne (20th C) French

| £976 | $1894 | (3-Dec-90 CS.L15 b/R) Terrasse fleuri (49x60cm-19x24in) s. (F.FR 9500) |

BISTAGNE, Paul (1850-1886) French

| £941 | $1665 | (7-Apr-91 I.N44/R) Marine (10x20cm-4x8in) s. panel (F.FR 9500) |
| £1020 | $2010 | (13-Nov-90 ARC.P189/R) Voiliers sur le Bosphore (56x91cm-22x36in) s.d.79 (F.FR 10000) |

BISTTRAM, Emil (1895-1976) American

£740	$1450	(27-Jan-91 LIT.L72) Abstraction of fighting cocks (122x81cm-48x32in) s.
£2775	$4800	(12-May-91 H.C185/R) Spring winds. Spiral (69x91cm-27x36in) s.d.58 s.i.verso double-sided
£2890	$5000	(22-May-91 CH.NY308/R) Omnis (56x49cm-22x19in) s.d.52 masonite
£3367	$6600	(7-Nov-90 B.SF3862/R) Space angel (122x91cm-48x36in) s.d.64
£4082	$8000	(7-Nov-90 B.SF3860/R) Towards heavens (100x68cm-39x27in) s.d.59 masonite
£4233	$8000	(26-Sep-90 SY.NY225/R) Abstract composition (63x85cm-25x33in) s.d.64 panel

BISTTRAM, Emil (1895-1976) American-cont.
£10204 $20000   (7-Nov-90 B.SF3812/R) Sangro de Christo mountains (64x76cm-25x30in) s.
£2011 $3800   (25-Sep-90 CE.NY259/R) Abstract (30x22cm-12x9in) s.d.41 W/C gouache
£4190 $7500   (14-Mar-91 CH.NY223/R) Shalako Rain Gods (48x61cm-19x24in) s.d.36 W/C pencil

BITRAN, Albert (1929-) French
£1885 $3714   (14-Nov-90 KH.K13/R) Interieur-Exterieur, Paris 1976 (100x81cm-39x32in) s. (D.KR 21000)

BITTAR, Antoine (?) ?
£606 $1042   (14-May-91 JOY.T51/R) Facade lights (45x60cm-18x24in) s. board (C.D 1200)

BITTIO, Antonio de (1722-1797) Italian
£1000 $1630   (2-Jul-91 C132/R) Alexander and Diogenes (25x39cm-10x15in) black chk pen wash

BIVA, Henri (1848-1928) French
£3947 $7500   (28-Feb-91 CH.NY34/R) Picnic along the river (47x56cm-19x22in) s.
£4872 $9500   (24-Oct-90 CH.NY68/R) Still waters (65x81cm-26x32in) s.
£6154 $12000   (24-Oct-90 CH.NY67/R) The lily pond (74x91cm-29x36in) s.
£6936 $12000   (23-May-91 CH.NY249/R) Summer reflections (60x73cm-24x29in) s.

BIVEL, Fernand Achille Lucien (1888-1950) French
£6500 $12480   (28-Nov-90 S287/R) Summertime (241x300cm-95x118in) s.d.1928

BIXBEE, William Johnson (1850-1921) American
£1429 $2800   (16-Feb-91 W.W64/R) Winter landscape by the water (66x86cm-26x34in) s.

BJARNASON, Ingibjoerg (20th C) Icelandic
£2579 $4462   (25-May-91 AB.L34/R) Composition (61x50cm-24x20in) s. (S.FR 6500)

BJERKE-PETERSEN, Vilhelm (1909-1957) Danish
£649 $1259   (4-Dec-90 BA.S52/R) Geometric composition (27x22cm-11x9in) init.d.55 panel (S.KR 7000)
£849 $1469   (22-May-91 BA.S10/R) Surrealistic landscape (46x54cm-18x21in) init.d.45 panel (S.KR 9000)
£1066 $2068   (4-Dec-90 BA.S51/R) Woman and bird (46x55cm-18x22in) init. panel (S.KR 11500)
£1795 $3537   (14-Nov-90 KH.K15/R) Composition (34x42cm-13x17in) init.d.47 (D.KR 20000)
£1873 $3221   (14-May-91 BU.S87/R) Composition (80x98cm-31x39in) s.d.1947 (S.KR 20000)
£2264 $4370   (12-Dec-90 RAS.K125/R) Sunrise (61x50cm-24x20in) init.d.44 masonite (D.KR 25000)
£2424 $4775   (14-Nov-90 KH.K16/R) Square contact (55x65cm-22x26in) init.d.55 (D.KR 27000)
£3333 $5667   (29-May-91 KH.K203/R) Summer's night (120x60cm-47x24in) init.d.43 (D.KR 38000)
£4448 $8363   (19-Sep-90 KH.K125/R) Eruption, winter 1941 (116x70cm-46x28in) (D.KR 50000)
£313 $614   (13-Feb-91 KH.K27) Composition (28x36cm-11x14in) init. crayon (D.KR 3500)
£313 $614   (13-Feb-91 KH.K26) Composition (31x40cm-12x16in) init.d.48 Indian ink (D.KR 3500)
£313 $614   (13-Feb-91 KH.K38) Composition (24x20cm-9x8in) init.d.51 crayon (D.KR 3500)
£313 $614   (13-Feb-91 KH.K14) Colour movements in snow (42x51cm-17x20in) mono.d.33 W/C (D.KR 3500)
£358 $701   (13-Feb-91 KH.K20) Surrealistic composition (42x51cm-17x20in) init.d.34 Indian ink wash (D.KR 4000)
£358 $701   (13-Feb-91 KH.K28) Composition (47x62cm-19x24in) finit.d.50 chl (D.KR 4000)
£358 $701   (13-Feb-91 KH.K15) Surrealistic composition (42x51cm-17x20in) init.d.34 W/C Indian ink (D.KR 4000)
£358 $701   (13-Feb-91 KH.K25) Composition (40x30cm-16x12in) i.d.51 pencil crayon (D.KR 4000)
£403 $789   (13-Feb-91 KH.K18) Surrealistic composition (41x51cm-16x20in) init.d.34 W/C Indian ink (D.KR 4500)
£403 $789   (13-Feb-91 KH.K29) Concrete composition (47x62cm-19x24in) s.d.50 crayon (D.KR 4500)
£403 $789   (13-Feb-91 KH.K16/R) Surrealistic composition (41x51cm-16x20in) init.d.34 Indian ink (D.KR 4500)
£403 $789   (13-Feb-91 KH.K19/R) Surrealistic composition (41x51cm-16x20in) init.d.34 Indian ink wash (D.KR 4500)
£447 $877   (13-Feb-91 KH.K22) Surrealistic landscape (42x50cm-17x20in) init.d.34 Indian ink wash (D.KR 5000)
£447 $877   (13-Feb-91 KH.K21) Surrealistic composition (42x51cm-17x20in) init.d.34 Indian ink wash (D.KR 5000)
£492 $964   (13-Feb-91 KH.K33) Composition (47x62cm-19x24in) init.d.50 crayon (D.KR 5500)
£581 $1140   (13-Feb-91 KH.K24) Surrealistic landscape (56x33cm-22x13in) init.d.37 W/C chl Indian ink (D.KR 6500)
£581 $1140   (13-Feb-91 KH.K34) Composition (62x47cm-24x19in) s.d.50 crayon (D.KR 6500)

BJERKE-PETERSEN, Vilhelm (1909-1957) Danish-cont.
£581 $1140   (13-Feb-91 KH.K17/R) Surrealistic composition (47x59cm-19x23in)
                 init.d.34 W/C Indian ink wash (D.KR 6500)
£805 $1578   (13-Feb-91 KH.K13/R) 'Distanceret rodt' (48x60cm-19x24in) mono.d.32 W/C
                 (D.KR 9000)

BJORCK, Oscar (1860-1929) Swedish
£1231 $2068   (24-Apr-91 BA.S19/R) Siesta in the harbour (29x46cm-11x18in) s. panel
                 (S.KR 13000)
£4596 $9007   (6-Nov-90 BA.S20/R) Fishermen on beach (47x37cm-19x15in) s. (S.KR 50000)

BJORK, Jakob (1726-1793) Swedish
£1721 $3201   (9-Sep-90 BU.M167) Portrait of Carl Gustaf Lowenhielm (66x59cm-26x23in)
                 after Gustaf Lundberg (S.KR 18500)
£6618 $12971   (6-Nov-90 BA.S22/R) Gustaf III wearing Swedish attire (75x56cm-30x22in)
                 (S.KR 72000)

BJORK, Jakob (attrib) (1726-1793) Swedish
£2936 $4932   (24-Apr-91 BA.S18 a/R) Portrait of Sophia Albertina (63x52cm-25x20in)
                 oval (S.KR 31000)

BJORNBERG, Evald (1895-1971) Swedish
£521 $875   (27-Apr-91 SO.S284/R) Still life of flowers (90x73cm-35x29in) s.d.1935
                 (S.KR 5500)

BJULF, S C (1890-1958) Danish
£538 $1075   (6-Feb-91 RAS.K47) Fish wives selling fish at Gammel Strand
                 (75x94cm-30x37in) s. (D.KR 6000)
£714 $1350   (25-Sep-90 RAS.K24) Postman and the fisherwomen at Gammel Strand
                 (57x47cm-22x19in) s. (D.KR 8000)
£735 $1412   (27-Dec-90 RAS.V14/R) The fisherwomen at Gammel Strand (70x91cm-28x36in)
                 s. (D.KR 8200)
£804 $1519   (25-Sep-90 RAS.K23) Fisherwomen at Gammel Strand (70x100cm-28x39in) s.
                 (D.KR 9000)
£1050 $1879   (9-Apr-91 RAS.K2017) The fisherwomen at Gammel Strand (67x90cm-26x35in)
                 s. (D.KR 12000)
£1057 $1766   (6-Jun-91 RAS.K8) The fisherwomen at Hojbro Square with Absalon statue
                 (90x90cm-35x35in) s. (D.KR 12000)
£1246 $2429   (19-Oct-90 RAS.V462/R) Copenhagen street scene with flower sellers
                 (75x90cm-30x35in) s. (D.KR 14000)
£1384 $2616   (25-Sep-90 RAS.K22) Buying fish at Gammel Strand (70x100cm-28x39in) s.
                 (D.KR 15500)

BJULF, Soren Christian (1890-1958) Danish
£643 $1261   (10-Nov-90 FAL.M36/R) Selling fish (56x47cm-22x19in) s. (S.KR 7000)
£850 $1666   (22-Nov-90 CSK154/R) Fishmarket (70x90cm-28x35in) s.
£915 $1793   (6-Nov-90 SY.AM309/R) Gossip at Copenhagen quay (61x54cm-24x21in) s.
                 (D.FL 3000)
£1122 $1987   (20-Mar-91 KM.K1108/R) Fish market, Copenhagen (65x88cm-26x35in)
                 i.d.1932verso (DM 3300)
£1241 $2432   (10-Nov-90 FAL.M35/R) Fishermen by harbour (90x70cm-35x28in) s.
                 (S.KR 13500)
£1273 $2279   (13-Apr-91 FAL.M30/R) Market day (69x100cm-27x39in) s. (S.KR 13700)

BJURSTROM, Tor (1888-1966) Swedish
£543 $971   (17-Mar-91 BU.M471) Landscape in the skerries, grey day
                 (42x45cm-17x18in) s. (S.KR 5800)
£607 $1213   (10-Feb-91 BU.M147) Coastal landscape (37x47cm-15x19in) s. (S.KR 6600)
£1011 $2022   (10-Feb-91 BU.M241) Landscape (62x70cm-24x28in) s. (S.KR 11000)
£1195 $2390   (10-Feb-91 BU.M255) West coast landscape with boat house
                 (54x65cm-21x26in) s. (S.KR 13000)
£1297 $2517   (4-Dec-90 BA.S57/R) Mountains at Tjorn (62x72cm-24x28in) s. (S.KR 14000)
£1338 $2568   (27-Nov-90 BU.S34/R) Still life (62x73cm-24x29in) st.sig. (S.KR 14500)
£1483 $2877   (4-Dec-90 BA.S54/R) Mountain and water, Bleket, Tjorn (54x65cm-21x26in)
                 s. (S.KR 16000)
£1668 $3236   (5-Dec-90 AB.S7036/R) Landscape with trees (46x68cm-18x27in) s.
                 (S.KR 18000)
£1745 $3019   (22-May-91 BA.S11/R) Still life of bowl of fruit (46x65cm-18x26in) s.
                 panel (S.KR 18500)
£1784 $3033   (28-May-91 AB.S5166/R) The pink house in Bohuslan (74x92cm-29x36in) s.
                 (S.KR 19000)
£1845 $3542   (27-Nov-90 BU.S32/R) The pink house in Bohuslan (74x92cm-29x36in) s.
                 (S.KR 20000)
£2066 $3512   (28-May-91 AB.S5165/R) Just an ordinary day (53x64cm-21x25in) s. panel
                 (S.KR 22000)
£2416 $4325   (9-Apr-91 GO.G11) Reclining woman (50x67cm-20x26in) s. (S.KR 26000)
£2422 $4748   (20-Nov-90 GO.G17/R) Harbour scene, Gothenburg (65x82cm-26x32in) s.
                 (S.KR 26500)
£2602 $4658   (9-Apr-91 GO.G10/R) Harbour scene, Gothenburg (81x65cm-32x26in) s.
                 (S.KR 28000)

BLAAS, Eugen von (1843-1932) Austrian
£3590 $7000   (23-Oct-90 SY.NY355/R) Venetian beauty (58x45cm-23x18in) s.
£4359 $8500   (23-Oct-90 SY.NY356/R) Venetian girl (27x22cm-11x9in) s.d.1882 panel
£6294 $12210   (7-Dec-90 GB.B5747/R) Portrait of young Italian woman (28x21cm-11x8in)
                 s.d.1882 panel (DM 18000)

BLAAS, Eugen von (1843-1932) Austrian-cont.

£10884	$17524	(26-Jun-91 KM.K1398/R) Portrait of girl (44x32cm-17x13in) s.d.1891 panel (DM 32000)
£15805	$27500	(27-Mar-91 B.SF4101/R) Jeune fille aux violets de parme (53x35cm-21x14in) s. panel
£20000	$38400	(28-Nov-90 S206/R) Young woman with basket of fruit (80x39cm-31x15in) s.d.1897 panel
£28000	$45920	(21-Jun-91 C78/R) Water carrier (63x98cm-25x39in) s.d.1880
£31792	$55000	(22-May-91 SY.NY60/R) Grape seller (79x42cm-31x17in) s.d.1904 panel
£3582	*$6017*	*(25-Apr-91 D.V192/R) Peasant interior with figures (50x67cm-20x26in) s. W/C (A.S 75000)*

BLAAS, Eugen von (attrib) (1843-1942) Austrian

| £1372 | $2716 | (31-Jan-91 D.V58/R) Portrait of woman (40x34cm-16x13in) panel (A.S 28000) |

BLAAS, Julius von (1845-1922) Austrian

£949	$1699	(11-Apr-91 D.V98/R) Horses bolting (33x44cm-13x17in) s. panel (A.S 20000)
£1058	$2063	(25-Oct-90 D.V29/R) Cow standing (22x31cm-9x12in) s. (A.S 22000)
£1300	$2496	(27-Nov-90 PH175/R) Portrait of countryman (29x15cm-11x6in) s. panel
£2136	$3823	(11-Apr-91 D.V96/R) Coach trip (33x44cm-13x17in) s. panel (A.S 45000)
£3797	$6796	(11-Apr-91 D.V288/R) The checkpoint (74x100cm-29x39in) s.d.1900 (A.S 80000)
£11500	$22080	(28-Nov-90 S209/R) Emperor Franz Joseph of Austria (121x88cm-48x35in) s.d.1890
£12000	$23040	(30-Nov-90 C46/R) The circus (83x143cm-33x56in) s.d.1896

BLAAS, Karl von (1815-1894) Austrian

| £2500 | $4750 | (27-Feb-91 SY.NY156/R) Proud cavaliers (65x48cm-26x19in) s.d.1864 |
| £3185 | $6306 | (31-Jan-91 D.V71/R) Nymph and faun (85x69cm-33x27in) s.indis.d.1843 (A.S 65000) |

BLACHE, Chr (1838-1920) Danish

£668	$1309	(22-Nov-90 RAS.V692/R) Coastal landscape with sailship, Faborg (39x63cm-15x25in) s.d.95 (D.KR 7500)
£673	$1279	(14-Sep-90 RAS.V552/R) View from Raa fishing village (45x73cm-18x29in) s.d.1885 (D.KR 7600)
£676	$1149	(28-May-91 AB.S4740/R) Seascape with boats and breakers (16x30cm-6x12in) s.d.1910 (S.KR 7200)
£880	$1479	(23-Apr-91 RAS.K274) View of Copenhagen harbour from Amalienborg (25x36cm-10x14in) s.i. (D.KR 10000)
£898	$1768	(14-Nov-90 RAS.K187/R) Sailship off Trekroner (42x70cm-17x28in) s.d.89 (D.KR 10000)
£919	$1801	(10-Nov-90 FAL.M40/R) Harbour scene near Raa (46x74cm-18x29in) s.d.1885 (S.KR 10000)
£1068	$2007	(18-Sep-90 BU.K78/R) The frigatte 'Jylland' (53x75cm-21x30in) s. (D.KR 12000)
£1322	$2207	(6-Jun-91 RAS.K81/R) Summer's day by the coast, women washing clothes and boy with horses (58x94cm-23x37in) s.d.84 (D.KR 15000)

BLACK, Andrew (1850-1916) British

£500	$990	(1-Feb-91 PHE20) Strong breeze (39x59cm-15x23in) s.
£769	$1500	(19-Oct-90 DM.D2144/R) Harvest of sea (76x127cm-30x50in) s.d.1885
£1000	$1870	(28-Aug-90 S950/R) East coast fishing village (40x61cm-16x24in) s.

BLACK, Dorrit (1891-1951) Australian

| £1488 | $2500 | (22-Apr-91 SY.ME26/R) Macquarie Street at midday (26x23cm-10x9in) s. i.verso (A.D 3200) |

BLACK, Olive Parker (1868-1948) American

£761	$1500	(18-Nov-90 JRB.C91) Spring landscape (46x61cm-18x24in) s.
£928	$1800	(7-Dec-90 S.W2725/R) Cows by stream, springtime (41x61cm-16x24in) s.
£938	$1800	(17-Dec-90 SY.NY104/R) Spring landscape (41x61cm-16x24in) s.
£1392	$2700	(24-Aug-90 RB.HY145/R) Early spring (41x61cm-16x24in) s.
£2083	$4000	(29-Nov-90 MFA.C73/R) Autumn river scene (41x61cm-16x24in) s.
£2116	$4000	(27-Sep-90 CH.NY193/R) River reflections (41x61cm-16x24in) s.
£2663	$4500	(17-Apr-91 D.NY20/R) Berkshire brook (51x76cm-20x30in) s. i.verso
£2775	$4800	(21-May-91 CE.NY660/R) Sunny landscape (51x76cm-20x30in) s.

BLACKADDER, Elizabeth (1931-) British

£400	*$692*	*(24-May-91 CBB375) Bathing party s. gouache*
£600	*$1044*	*(28-Mar-91 CSK202) Passion flower (47x59cm-19x23in) s.d.1976 pencil W/C*
£2600	*$5070*	*(9-Oct-90 B112/R) Still life with fish (77x56cm-30x22in) s.d.1972 W/C*

BLACKBURN, Joseph (attrib) (1700-?) American

| £1020 | $2000 | (26-Jan-91 CH.NY232/R) Portrait of gentleman (76x63cm-30x25in) c.1755 |

BLACKLOCK, Thomas Bromley (1863-1903) British

| £6500 | $10985 | (2-May-91 CG482/R) Spring woodland (41x51cm-16x20in) s.d.1900 |

BLACKLOCK, William Kay (1872-?) British

£675	$1141	(16-Apr-91 HAR349/R) Haytime (20x25cm-8x10in) s.d.1917 board
£850	$1437	(16-Apr-91 HAR376/R) Portrait of boy (74x43cm-29x17in) s.d.1918
£950	$1777	(28-Aug-90 S972/R) Southwold from Walberswick (25x35cm-10x14in) s.d.21 artist's board

BLACKLOCK, William Kay (1872-?) British-cont.

£2000	$3380	(16-Apr-91 HAR404) Vegetable market, Bruges
£3200	$6304	(1-Nov-90 C336/R) Picking may blossom (40x32cm-16x13in) s. canvas on panel
£4500	$8505	(26-Sep-90 S78/R) In before storm (56x76cm-22x30in) s.d.1916
£5000	$8450	(1-May-91 S3/R) Rest at noon (55x75cm-22x30in)
£6600	$10758	(13-Jun-91 L300/R) The shepherdess (51x76cm-20x30in)
£580	$1102	(28-Feb-91 DLY190) Evening Dortdrecht (18x25cm-7x10in) s. W/C
£700	$1330	(27-Feb-91 MMB165) Street scene,Richmond (30x18cm-12x7in) s.d.1897 bears i. verso
£800	$1536	(15-Aug-90 HAR260/R) Bay near Looe, Cornwall (25x36cm-10x14in) s. W/C
£910	$1529	(18-Jul-91 PHX247/R) Fishermen preparing to set sail (51x74cm-20x29in) s.d.1915 W/C
£1400	$2366	(1-May-91 PHL25/R) Reading at window (29x21cm-11x8in) s. wash
£2000	$3840	(15-Aug-90 HAR265/R) Sunny corner (28x20cm-11x8in) s. W/C
£2300	$4531	(31-Oct-90 HUN1) Mothers and babies in Victorian kitchens (28x23cm-11x9in) W/C pair
£2700	$5319	(13-Nov-90 SWS115/R) Helping mother - a Dutch interior (30x23cm-12x9in) s. i. verso W/C gouache
£5400	$10152	(19-Sep-90 PHC58/R) Mother's little helper (73x53cm-29x21in) s. W/C

BLACKMAN, Charles (1928-) Australian

£545	$1068	(19-Nov-90 MGS.S183) The breeze (50x70cm-20x28in) s. board (A.D 1400)
£679	$1147	(16-Apr-91 J.M877) Silhouete figures (40x50cm-16x20in) (A.D 1500)
£905	$1529	(16-Apr-91 J.M1112) Sleeping girl (29x37cm-11x15in) s. glass (A.D 2000)
£1081	$2130	(13-Nov-90 J.M20/R) Playing in the park (35x55cm-14x22in) s. board (A.D 2800)
£1120	$2184	(15-Oct-90 AAA.S128/R) Girl dreaming (48x73cm-19x29in) s. paper (A.D 2800)
£1132	$1845	(1-Jul-91 AAA.S160 h) The mystery (47x72cm-19x28in) s. (A.D 2400)
£1267	$2141	(15-Apr-91 AAA.S131) Mystery (72x47cm-28x19in) s. (A.D 2800)
£1321	$2153	(1-Jul-91 AAA.S127) The mango tree (74x48cm-29x19in) s. paper (A.D 2800)
£1351	$2662	(13-Nov-90 J.M162) Remembrances (46x72cm-18x28in) s. (A.D 3500)
£1620	$2722	(16-Jul-91 JRL.S318) Angel by the window (85x104cm-33x41in) s. paper (A.D 3500)
£1709	$3026	(18-Mar-91 MGS.S303) Barbara, artist's wife (76x63cm-30x25in) s.d.1963 board (A.D 4000)
£1719	$2906	(15-Apr-91 AAA.S159) Star garden (47x72cm-19x28in) s. (A.D 3800)
£1784	$2926	(17-Jun-91 MGS.S209) Woman with flower (47x72cm-19x28in) s. (A.D 3800)
£1931	$3803	(13-Nov-90 J.M148) The yacht race (47x73cm-19x29in) s. board (A.D 5000)
£2008	$3855	(27-Nov-90 JRL.S197/R) Young girl, seated (170x142cm-67x56in) s. oil acrylic canvas (A.D 5000)
£4618	$8867	(26-Nov-90 SY.ME310/R) Two schoolgirls. Yellow portrait (38x31cm-15x12in) init.d.53 board double-sided (A.D 11500)
£4651	$7814	(22-Apr-91 SY.ME381/R) Children on mountain (100x134cm-39x53in) s.d.1955 paper on board (A.D 10000)
£5019	$9888	(13-Nov-90 J.M145/R) Fire at Picnic Creek (48x73cm-19x29in) s. board (A.D 13000)
£5019	$9888	(13-Nov-90 J.M106 a/R) Girl with book (73x96cm-29x38in) s. paper on board (A.D 13000)
£9302	$15628	(22-Apr-91 SY.ME344/R) Jumping girl (95x127cm-37x50in) s. board (A.D 20000)
£425	$837	(13-Nov-90 J.M904) Regents Park (37x51cm-15x20in) s.i.d.1965 ink (A.D 1100)
£437	$782	(9-Apr-91 CH.ME293/R) Portrait of girl (100x87cm-39x34in) s.d.62 crayon wash (A.D 1000)
£502	$989	(13-Nov-90 J.M820) Ghosts of the air (76x101cm-30x40in) s. chl (A.D 1300)
£675	$1296	(14-Aug-90 SY.ME122/R) Dream figures (37x50cm-15x20in) s.d.'62 (A.D 1600)
£723	$1388	(27-Nov-90 JRL.S163/R) Child with cat (97x89cm-38x35in) s.d.1962 chl (A.D 1800)
£791	$1328	(22-Apr-91 SY.ME23) Cerise girl (72x51cm-28x20in) s.d.71 i.verso ink W/C wash (A.D 1700)
£837	$1407	(22-Apr-91 SY.ME160) Bending figure in street with terraces (66x85cm-26x33in) s. chl (A.D 1800)
£995	$1682	(16-Apr-91 J.M39) Head of a girl (50x40cm-20x16in) s.i.d.1966 mixed media (A.D 2200)
£1044	$2005	(26-Nov-90 SY.ME47) Boy and girl running (52x69cm-20x27in) s. ink gouache (A.D 2600)
£1121	$1828	(16-Jun-91 SY.ME4) Schoolgirl upside down (60x52cm-24x20in) init.d.52 pencil (A.D 2400)
£1158	$2282	(13-Nov-90 J.M296/R) Butterfly (68x68cm-27x27in) s. mixed media (A.D 3000)
£1267	$2141	(16-Apr-91 J.M193) On rading a Gothic novel (51x45cm-20x18in) s.i.d.1966 mixed media (A.D 2800)
£1395	$2344	(22-Apr-91 SY.ME148/R) School girl in alley (51x59cm-20x23in) s. chl (A.D 3000)
£1689	$3175	(17-Sep-90 SY.ME32/R) Portrait of girl (77x56cm-30x22in) s. W/C (A.D 3800)
£2036	$3441	(16-Apr-91 J.M96 a) Bird (68x89cm-27x35in) s. monotype (A.D 4500)
£3241	$5444	(16-Jul-91 JRL.S280/R) Venus with mirror (119x178cm-47x70in) s. pastel (A.D 7000)

BLACKMAN, Walter (1847-1928) American
£4569 $9000   (7-Oct-90 DU.E139/R) Harbour view with fisherman (74x147cm-29x58in) s.

BLACKSHAW, Basil (20th C) British?
£650 $1268   (26-Oct-90 CG92) Head portrait of young girl (31x28cm-12x11in) s.verso
      panel
£2400 $4680   (26-Oct-90 CG85) Morning exercise (41x61cm-16x24in) s.

BLACKSTADIUS, Johan Z (1816-1898) Swedish
£3013 $5092   (20-Apr-91 HOR.H40/R) Breakfast in the park (34x50cm-13x20in) s.d.1873
      (F.M 21000)
£739   *$1322*   *(14-Apr-91 BU.H100/R) Lute player (32x23cm-13x9in) s.i.d.1853 W/C*
      (F.M 5200)

BLACKWOOD, David L (1941-) Canadian
£438   *$745*   *(27-May-91 HO.ED286/R) Study for Mr Coaker (50x80cm-20x31in) s.d.1984*
      pencil (C.D 850)

BLAIR, John (19th C) British
£700   *$1316*   *(21-Sep-90 PHE60) Largo after stormy night (50x72cm-20x28in) s.i. W/C*

BLAIS, Jean Charles (1956-) French
£3500 $6195   (21-Mar-91 C252/R) Untitled (64x80cm-25x31in) s.d.16.2.85 paper
£8946 $15119   (15-Apr-91 CC.P57/R) Ma plantation (94x120cm-37x47in) s.i.d.16 janvier
      83 verso torn posters (F.FR 90000)
£10718 $20900   (21-Oct-90 P.V138/R) Sans titre (79x175cm-31x69in) s.d.1985 torn posters
      (F.FR 106000)
£11213 $21641   (16-Dec-90 P.V114) Sans titre (70x145cm-28x57in) s.d. acrylic posters
      (F.FR 110000)
£13000 $20930   (27-Jun-91 C56/R) Untitled (90x135cm-35x53in) s.d.86 oil on torn posters
£20875 $35278   (15-Apr-91 CC.P58/R) Baiser vole (245x230cm-96x91in) s.i.d.juin 82 verso
      torn posters (F.FR 210000)
£27638 $45327   (19-Jun-91 CL.E32/R) Retour vers l'enfer (265x265cm-104x104in) s.d.1984
      verso torn posters (F.FR 275000)
£27638 $45327   (23-Jun-91 P.V79/R) Une idee dans l'air (240x210cm-94x83in) s.d.1984
      verso posters (F.FR 275000)
£1360   *$2216*   *(16-Jun-91 CC.P65) Sans titre (22x17cm-9x7in) d.25-10-1986 s. verso oil*
      pastel collage (F.FR 13500)
£1561   *$2544*   *(16-Jun-91 CC.P66) Sans titre (22x17cm-9x7in) d.25-10-1986 s. verso oil*
      pastel collage (F.FR 15500)
£2033   *$4065*   *(10-Feb-91 CC.P6) Amour triste (37x26cm-15x10in) i. s. verso collage*
      paint W/C oil crayon (F.FR 20000)
£2510   *$4041*   *(25-Jun-91 BG.P8/R) Malancolie (37x25cm-15x10in) oil crayon (F.FR 25000)*
£2811   *$4526*   *(25-Jun-91 BG.P7) Une idee sombre (42x29cm-17x11in) s. verso oil crayons*
      (F.FR 28000)
£2811   *$4526*   *(25-Jun-91 BG.P9/R) Tout seul (48x38cm-19x15in) s.i.d.1983 verso oil*
      crayon blotting paper (F.FR 28000)
£2988   *$5080*   *(30-May-91 FB.P107/R) Sans titre (58x49cm-23x19in) s. mixed media*
      (F.FR 30000)
£3058   *$5902*   *(16-Dec-90 GL.P134/R) Homme au chapeau (100x70cm-39x28in) s. ink collage*
      (F.FR 30000)
£3905   *$7577*   *(5-Dec-90 ZZ.F107/R) Thuff Thuff (39x30cm-15x12in) d.82/84 mixed media*
      (F.FR 38000)
£3984   *$6773*   *(30-May-91 FB.P108/R) Sans titre (92x73cm-36x29in) mixed media collage*
      (F.FR 40000)
£5478   *$9313*   *(2-Jun-91 GL.P187/R) Corps d'homme (64x96cm-25x38in) s.d.1985 ink*
      gouache collage (F.FR 55000)
£6116   *$11804*   *(16-Dec-90 P.V112/R) As de pique (38x40cm-15x16in) s.d.1,84 verso*
      gouache chk.pastel (F.FR 60000)
£13238   *$26079*   *(29-Oct-90 FB.P92/R) Sans titre (130x100cm-51x39in) s.d.III 84 gouache*
      pieces of paper pinned (F.FR 130000)
£13265   *$26000*   *(8-Nov-90 CH.NY212/R) Untitled (221x136cm-87x54in) gouache collage*
      straight pins

BLAIZE, Candide (1795-1855) French
£1026   *$2000*   *(26-Oct-90 SY.NY15/R) Portraits of young girls (10x8cm-4x3in) one*
      s.d.1824 pencil pair

BLAKE, Benjamin (1757-1830) British
£1000 $1650   (12-Jul-91 C141) Still lives of dead game on stone ledges
      (25x30cm-10x12in) pair

BLAKE, Leo (1887-1976) American
£642 $1200   (30-Aug-90 MFA.C198/R) Gloucester harbour (41x46cm-16x18in) s. board

BLAKE, Peter (1932-) British
£1200 $2076   (7-May-91 PH106/R) Postcard 2 (32x40cm-13x16in) s.i.d.1968 board
£918   *$1800*   *(12-Feb-91 SY.NY451/R) Props from Cleopatra (30x25cm-12x10in) s.i.d.1963*
      col.pencil crayon pencil
£1600 $3136   (24-Jan-91 CSK50) Waterfront, Gravesend, Kent (15x19cm-6x7in) s. pen W/C
£5000 $8150   (1-Jul-91 S49/R) Snap 1 (74x61cm-29x24in) s.d.1961 stretcher card
      collage enamel board

BLAKE, William (1757-1827) British
£1500   *$2475*   *(9-Jul-91 C86/R) The bed of death (15x14cm-6x6in) pen wash*
£2200   *$3630*   *(9-Jul-91 C85/R) Jonathan (25x18cm-10x7in) i. pencil*

BLAKE, William (1757-1827) British-cont.
£38000 $74860   (13-Nov-90 C92/R) Sketch for Hecate (23x28cm-9x11in) i. pencil

BLAKE, William (attrib) (1757-1827) British
£3800 $7486   (15-Nov-90 S26/R) The Last Judgement (47x35cm-19x14in) pencil

BLAKELOCK, Ralph Albert (1847-1919) American
£802 $1500   (30-Aug-90 MFA.C175) Green pastures (20x36cm-8x14in) s. panel
£1618 $2800   (22-May-91 CH.NY87/R) Autumn landscape (20x14cm-8x6in) s. panel
£1852 $3500   (27-Sep-90 CH.NY48/R) A woodland stream (20x14cm-8x6in) s. panel
£2312 $4000   (22-May-91 CH.NY88/R) Indian woman by stream (41x61cm-16x24in) s. panel
£2381 $4500   (27-Sep-90 CH.NY88/R) Twilight mood (41x61cm-16x24in) s. panel
£2515 $4250   (1-May-91 B.SF5057/R) Meadow, Middleton, New York (13x25cm-5x10in) s. panel
£4046 $7000   (22-May-91 CH.NY91/R) Middletown landscape (14x22cm-6x9in) s.

BLAKELOCK, Ralph Albert (attrib) (1847-1919) American
£847 $1500   (18-Mar-91 SG.M1191) Moonlit landscape (51x66cm-20x26in) s.

BLAKISTON, The Rev Douglas Yeoman (19th C) British
£1700 $3162   (4-Sep-90 OT385/R) Commander Peyton Blakiston, wearing uniform, telescope under arm (125x96cm-49x38in)

BLAMPIED, Edmund (1886-1966) British
£1400 $2702   (12-Dec-90 LJ225) Grey farm horse eating from hedge (36x44cm-14x17in) s. board
£3000 $5070   (2-May-91 CG420/R) Surf riding (20x29cm-8x11in) s. s.l.verso board
£4200 $7098   (2-May-91 CG419/R) Four friends (19x27cm-7x11in) s. s.l.verso card
£7500 $12675   (2-May-91 CG421/R) Joy rider (20x29cm-8x11in) s.d.1947 card
£1150 $1944   (2-May-91 B30/R) Midday rest (21x16cm-8x6in) s. pastel W/C
£1200 $2364   (13-Nov-90 SWS96/R) At the ball (32x21cm-13x8in) s. W/C bodycol.over pen pencil
£1500 $2535   (2-May-91 C88/R) Horse and cart on beach (30x44cm-12x17in) s.d.1962 W/C
£1550 $2945   (27-Feb-91 MMB55/R) A lady resting in an armchair (41x28cm-16x11in) s. pen
£3100 $5983   (12-Dec-90 LJ252) La Rocque slip with horses, cart and figures (39x52cm-15x20in) s.i.d.1937 W/C
£4500 $8730   (5-Dec-90 PHE71/R) A Jersey lane (38x55cm-15x22in) s.d.1931 W/C
£8500 $16320   (26-Nov-90 SWS129/R) St Helen inner harbour (66x48cm-26x19in) s.d.1929 pen ink W/C

BLANCHARD, Antoine (?-1988) French
£782 $1400   (15-Mar-91 DM.D2009/R) Place Vendome (33x46cm-13x18in) s.
£990 $1900   (20-Feb-91 D.NY9) Parisian boulevard (38x76cm-15x30in) s.
£1080 $1825   (1-May-91 GD.B66/R) Busy street scene, Paris (32x45cm-13x18in) s. s.l.verso (S.FR 2700)
£1368 $2600   (28-Feb-91 MFA.C105) Paris street scene (61x76cm-24x30in) s.
£1406 $2700   (18-Dec-90 BG.M1012/R) Paris street scene (33x46cm-13x18in) s.
£1500 $2955   (4-Oct-90 CSK225/R) Place de la Concorde, Paris (33x46cm-13x18in) s.
£1546 $3000   (8-Dec-90 W.W159 a/R) Paris street scene (61x91cm-24x36in) s.
£1732 $3100   (11-Apr-91 FA.PH997) Parisian street scene (30x41cm-12x16in) s.
£1750 $2940   (18-Jul-91 B149/R) Arc de Triomphe (35x48cm-14x19in) s.
£1800 $3006   (22-Jul-91 SWS1117/R) A Parisian square (32x43cm-13x17in) s.
£1800 $3042   (29-Apr-91 HS327/R) Il est tombe de la neige (45x53cm-18x21in) s.
£2000 $3380   (30-Apr-91 B125/R) Boulevard Hausmann, Paris (33x46cm-13x18in) s.
£2054 $3800   (10-Mar-91 H.C57/R) Boulevard de le Madeleine (33x46cm-13x18in) s.
£2284 $4500   (13-Nov-90 CE.NY22/R) Le Quais du Louvre (33x46cm-13x18in) s. s.l.verso
£2287 $3750   (19-Jun-91 B.SF1765/R) Quai du Louvre en hiver (33x46cm-13x18in) s. s.verso
£2402 $4300   (11-Apr-91 FA.PH1002) Parisian street scene (30x41cm-12x16in) s.
£2538 $5000   (15-Nov-90 D.NY93 a/R) Arc de Triomphe a la Brune (33x46cm-13x18in) s.
£2600 $4394   (2-May-91 B52/R) Paris street scene (47x31cm-19x12in) s. i. verso
£2700 $4563   (2-May-91 B53/R) Arc de Triomphe (46x55cm-18x22in) s.
£2800 $4732   (30-Apr-91 B124/R) Cafe de la Paix, Paris (33x46cm-13x18in) s.
£4200 $8274   (5-Oct-90 C72/R) L'Opera, Paris. Porte St. Denis, Grands Boulevards, Paris (45x46cm-18x18in) s. one i.verso pair
£6000 $10140   (29-Apr-91 HS326/R) Paris - Les Champs Elysees (58x90cm-23x35in) s.
£8883 $17500   (13-Nov-90 CE.NY186/R) Paris, Boulevard Madeleine (60x91cm-24x36in) s. s.i.verso

BLANCHARD, Jacques (attrib) (1600-1638) French
£612 $1180   (14-Dec-90 LEB.P19) Vulcain forge les armes d'Achille sur l'ordre de Thetis (28x20cm-11x8in) sanguinne htd.white (F.FR 6000)

BLANCHARD, Maria (1881-1932) Spanish
£64707 $126827   (22-Nov-90 EP.M18/R) Juguetes (92x65cm-36x26in) s. (S.P 12000000)
£7035 $11538   (20-Jun-91 APT.P42/R) Fillette a la poupee (48x31cm-19x12in) bears sig. pastel gouache (F.FR 70000)

BLANCHARD, Maria (attrib) (1881-1932) Spanish
£1097 $2117   (13-Dec-90 CH.BR115/R) Nature morte aux raisins (27x35cm-11x14in) (B.FR 65000)

BLANCHARD, Pascal (19th C) French
£1975 $3890   (14-Nov-90 RAS.K543/R) Man and boy in carpenter's workshop (48x53cm-19x21in) s. (D.KR 22000)

BLANCHARD, Remy (1958-) ?

£1426	$2780	(21-Oct-90 P.V149/R) Sans titre (110x75cm-43x30in) s.d.V/1985 acrylic (F.FR 14100)
£2569	$4985	(5-Dec-90 ZZ.F123) Sans titre (130x160cm-51x63in) s.d.83 acrylic (F.FR 25000)
£3597	$6978	(5-Dec-90 ZZ.F105) Le rond jaune (130x160cm-51x63in) s.d.83 verso acrylic (F.FR 35000)
£5097	$9837	(16-Dec-90 GL.P145/R) La licorne bleue (184x184cm-72x72in) s.d.1988 l. verso (F.FR 50000)

BLANCHE, Jacques Emile (1861-1942) French

£1700	$2737	(28-Jun-91 CSK273/R) Royal Crescent, Bath (26x26cm-10x10in) s. board
£2100	$4095	(16-Oct-90 WW342) Steeplechasing (46x61cm-18x24in) s.d.'25 l. label stretcher
£3571	$7036	(14-Nov-90 FB.P225/R) Bouquet de roses (38x46cm-15x18in) s. canvas laid down on board (F.FR 35000)
£3800	$6232	(18-Jun-91 PH65/R) Portrait of young woman (46x38cm-18x15in) s.l.
£4795	$7815	(15-Jun-91 L.K67/R) Girl before mirror (87x65cm-34x26in) s. (DM 14000)
£35714	$70357	(14-Nov-90 FB.P85/R) Bouquet de fleurs au vase bleu (92x73cm-36x29in) s.d.29 (F.FR 350000)

BLANCHET, Alexandre (1882-1961) Swiss

£988	$1680	(27-May-91 GK.Z5306) Bouquet of flowers (46x38cm-18x15in) s. (S.FR 2500)
£992	$1657	(5-Jun-91 SY.Z96/R) Nature morte avec une pipe (33x41cm-13x16in) mono. (S.FR 2500)
£996	$1942	(24-Oct-90 GD.B155/R) Still life with violin (54x87cm-21x34in) s. (S.FR 2500)
£1984	$3313	(5-Jun-91 SY.Z150/R) Nature morte aux fruits (38x61cm-15x24in) s.d.43 (S.FR 5000)
£4762	$8238	(22-May-91 GS.B2041/R) Les baigneuses (126x38cm-50x15in) s.d.49 l.verso board (S.FR 12000)

BLANCHET, Thomas (1614-1689) French

| £3262 | $6263 | (30-Nov-90 APT.P93/R) Vue du chateau Saint-Ange avec une scene de pillage dans l'Antiquite (44x61cm-17x24in) (F.FR 32000) |
| *£9000* | *$14670* | *(2-Jul-91 C144/R) Saint Mary Magdalene (19x11cm-7x4in) black red chk pen wash squared* |

BLAND, Emily Beatrice (1864-1951) British

£600	$1002	(4-Jun-91 SWS1949) Dahlias in Italian jug (60x50cm-24x20in) s.
£2500	$4800	(26-Nov-90 SWS163/R) Still life study of flowers with view of Cheyne Walk and Thames beyond (59x49cm-23x19in) s. board
£2600	$4992	(21-Feb-91 B62/R) Spring flowers (40x51cm-16x20in) s. board

BLAND, John F (fl.1860-1872) British

| *£500* | *$885* | *(21-Mar-91 CSK70/R) A boating party at Chertsey lock (28x46cm-11x18in) s. pencil W/C htd.white* |

BLANES VIALE, Pedro (20th C) ?

£2824	$4800	(27-May-91 GC.M379/R) Paisaje nocturno de Salto (55x66cm-22x26in)
£2941	$5000	(27-May-91 GC.M378/R) Fuente y figura de Mujer (69x59cm-27x23in) s.
£17949	$35000	(15-Oct-90 GC.M1) Palma de Mallorca (73x95cm-29x37in)

BLANES, Juan Manuel (1830-1901) Uruguayan

| £42781 | $80000 | (1-Aug-90 BAV.M3) Asi Muere un Oriental (101x81cm-40x32in) |

BLANKE, Wilhelm (1873-?) German

£673	$1165	(6-May-91 ZEL.L1610/R) Still life of flowers in vase (70x60cm-28x24in) s. board (DM 2000)
£1196	$2069	(8-May-91 D.V45/R) Amaryllis (100x80cm-39x31in) s. (A.S 25000)
£1329	$2578	(4-Dec-90 FN.S1559/R) Still life with asters in vase (100x89cm-39x35in) s. (DM 3800)

BLANKEN, H (19th C) ?

| *£727* | *$1433* | *(30-Oct-90 CH.AM502) Skaters on frozen waterway by drawbridge leading to village gate (48x59cm-19x23in) s.d.1829 pen W/C bodycol (D.FL 2400)* |

BLANKERHOFF, Jan Teunisz (attrib) (1628-1669) Dutch

| £1422 | $2801 | (13-Nov-90 AB.S859/R) Seascape with sailingvessels, bad weather (45x63cm-18x25in) indist.s. (S.KR 15500) |

BLANKERT, Barend (20th C) Dutch

| £541 | $935 | (23-May-91 SY.AM360/R) Het Sluiswachterhuis in de Lemmer, het Geboortehuis van de Schilder (60x90cm-24x35in) s. panel (D.FL 1800) |

BLARENBERGHE, Jacques Willem van (1669-1742) Dutch

| £5347 | $9250 | (21-May-91 GRO.B16/R) Fruit market (13x15cm-5x6in) s. panel |

BLARENBERGHE, Jacques Willem van (style) (1669-1742) Dutch

| £1800 | $3042 | (18-Apr-91 C48/R) A capriccio of a ruined temple with fishermen in the foreground (43cm-17ins circular) panel round |

BLARENBERGHE, Louis Nicholas van and Henri Joseph van (18th C) French

| *£28249* | *$50000* | *(22-Mar-91 CH.NY615/R) Men o'War at anchor in a harbour before a fort with soldiers. A royalprocession (7x16cm-3x6in) bodycolour pair* |

BLARENBERGHE, Louis Nicholas van and Henri Joseph van (18th C) French-cont.
£39548 $70000   (22-Mar-91 CH.NY614/R) A view of Brest with the Batterie Royale and Men
                                o' War in the bay (38x65cm-15x26in) s.d.1776 bodycolour vellum

BLARENBERGHE, Louis Nicolas van (1716-1794) French
£2740 $4904   (12-Mar-91 FN.S2287/R) So treiben es die feinen Leute (24x30cm-9x12in)
                                s.d.1775 W/C (DM 8000)
£3015 $4945   (18-Jun-91 APT.P17/R) Adoration des rois mages (30x56cm-12x22in)
                                grisaille gouache pen wash parchment (F.FR 30000)
£5403 $10427   (12-Dec-90 ARC.P21/R) Depart d'une mongolfiere dans les jardins de Marly
                                (11x10cm-4x4in) s.d.1792 gouache (F.FR 53000)

BLARENBERGHE, Louis Nicolas van (style) (1716-1794) French
£750 $1223   (4-Jul-91 CSK163) Mediterranian coastal landscape with visitors by ruin
                                (12x18cm-5x7in) panel

BLARENBERGHE, van (attrib) (17/18th C) French
£531 $1045   (13-Nov-90 CH.G247) Mountainous landscape with three peasants, and
                                gentleman on horseback (6x8cm-2x3in) min. vellum gilt-metal mount
                                (S.FR 1300)

BLASHFIELD, Edwin Howland (1848-1936) American
£2249 $4250   (26-Sep-90 SY.NY101/R) Roman flower girl (47x39cm-19x15in) s.i. canvas
                                laid down on board
£3784 $7000   (10-Mar-91 H.C78/R) Sarah Bernhardt in role of Catherine the Great of
                                Russia (36x28cm-14x11in) s.d.76
£8092 $14000   (22-May-91 CH.NY92/R) Waterloo, Total Defeat (46x38cm-18x15in) s.

BLATAS, Arbit (1909-) Baltic
£1286 $2302   (14-Apr-91 GL.P50) Interieur (50x65cm-20x26in) s. (F.FR 13000)

BLATTER, Bruno (19th C) German
£1468 $2466   (27-Apr-91 SO.S293/R) Interior with elegant dancers (58x78cm-23x31in) s.
                                (S.KR 15500)

BLATTERBAUER (19th C) ?
£1536 $2903   (25-Sep-90 FN.S2118/R) Wooded hilly landscape with figures and view of
                                shepherd with flock (42x57cm-17x22in) s.d.1860 (DM 4500)

BLAU, Tina (1845-1916) Austrian
£1823 $3136   (16-May-91 D.V88/R) Study of trees (57x43cm-22x17in) s. board
                                (A.S 38000)
£8874 $16683   (19-Sep-90 N.M430/R) Market day in Szolnok with peasants selling
                                products (22x30cm-9x12in) s.d.75 (DM 26000)
£17065 $32082   (19-Sep-90 N.M429/R) View of alley way with figures (40x20cm-16x8in) s.
                                i.verso panel (DM 50000)
£51370 $83733   (12-Jun-91 SY.MU117/R) Spring bouquet (101x142cm-40x56in) s.
                                (DM 150000)
£473 $818   (25-May-91 N.M375) View of town (14x20cm-6x8in) s.d.1904 ochre sepia
                                wash (DM 1400)
£882 $1746   (31-Jan-91 D.V186/R) Country estate Marsa near Tunis i. W/C sepia set
                                of three (A.S 18000)

BLAUENSTEINER, Leopold (1880-1947) Austrian
£3479 $6750   (6-Dec-90 D.V93/R) Selfportrait (85x74cm-33x29in) s.d.44 i.d.verso board
                                (A.S 70000)

BLAUVELT, Charles F (1824-1900) American
£3352 $6000   (14-Mar-91 CH.NY10/R) Waiting for stage (53x44cm-21x17in) s.d.57

BLECHEN, Karl (1798-1840) German
£9215 $17324   (19-Sep-90 N.M431/R) Landscape with ruin and travellers (27x20cm-11x8in)
                                i.verso canvas on board (DM 27000)
£2448 $4748   (7-Dec-90 GB.B5748/R) Italian woman playing guitar with Vesuvio beyond.
                                Fragment of landscape (14x13cm-6x5in) c.1828/29 pencil wash
                                double-sided (DM 7000)

BLECKNER, Ross (1949-) American?
£6633 $13000   (14-Feb-91 CH.NY81/R) Untitled (66x66cm-26x26in) s.i.d.1986verso
£18499 $35889   (9-Dec-90 CC.P51/R) Companion (213x152cm-84x60in) s. verso (F.FR 180000)
£35503 $60000   (1-May-91 SY.NY147/R) Infatuation (244x508cm-96x200in) s.d.1986-1987
                                verso
£1786 $3500   (6-Nov-90 CE.NY158/R) Untitled (100x71cm-39x28in) s.d.1978 oil col.chks.

BLEECK, Richard van (attrib) (1670-1733) Dutch
£950 $1568   (9-Jul-91 PH47) Portrait of bewigged gentleman, standing before desk
                                with various items (127x101cm-50x40in)
£2200 $4180   (28-Feb-91 B73/R) Portrait of girl, seated with cat on lap
                                (76x63cm-30x25in)

BLEGER, Paul-Leon (1889-?) French
£1116 $1919   (14-May-91 GF.L2621/R) Young woman seated on mule (73x61cm-29x24in) s.
                                (S.FR 2800)
£1596 $3000   (19-Sep-90 B.SF2656/R) Flower market (41x33cm-16x13in) board

BLEIJS, Adrianus (1877-1964) Dutch
£350 $627   (14-Mar-91 B112/R) The old fisherman (58x47cm-23x19in) s. pastel

BLEK (1951-) French
£815 $1605   (31-Oct-90 ZZ.F102/R) La statue de la Liberte (145x89cm-57x35in) s.d.90
                 acrylic (F.FR 8000)

BLEKEN, Hakon (1929-) Norwegian
£1182 $2116   (14-Mar-91 BU.O8/R) Spring thaw 1962 (34x92cm-13x36in) s.d.62 i.verso
                  (N.KR 13500)
£2778 $4639   (4-Jun-91 BU.O40/R) Icehockey player and Spring 1991 (105x109cm-41x43in)
                  s.d.91 (N.KR 32000)

BLENNER, Carle J (1864-1952) American
£2062 $4000   (5-Dec-90 D.NY68/R) French begonias (51x51cm-20x20in) s. i.on stretcher
£2367 $4000   (17-Apr-91 D.NY93) Dogwood in vase (91x76cm-36x30in) s. i.stretcher

BLERMONT, T (19th C) British?
£520 $920   (3-Apr-91 RBB920/R) Two children at cottage door (41x30cm-16x12in) s.
                panel

BLES, David Joseph (1821-1899) Dutch
£2183 $4127   (27-Sep-90 D.V81/R) The music lesson (23x32cm-9x13in) mono. paper on
                  panel (A.S 45000)
£1455 $2865   (30-Oct-90 CH.AM510 a) Sweet dreams (20x26cm-8x10in) s.d.70 pen W/C
                  (D.FL 4800)

BLES, Herri met de (1480-1550) Flemish
£2049 $3852   (19-Sep-90 GK.Z803/R) Ecce Homo in hilly landscape (29x35cm-11x14in)
                  panel painted with studio (S.FR 5000)

BLES, Joseph (1825-1875) Dutch
£751 $1419   (25-Sep-90 FN.S2119) Dutch town scene with figures (23x18cm-9x7in) s.
                 panel (DM 2200)
£2695 $4527   (23-Apr-91 SY.AM31/R) Sunday afternoon by river (54x40cm-21x16in) s.
                  panel (D.FL 9000)

BLESER, August (jnr) (20th C) American?
£1706 $2900   (1-Jun-91 IH.NY35/R) Tennis-playing couple kissing (104x89cm-41x35in) s.

BLEULER, Johann Ludwig (1792-1850) Swiss
£1905 $3124   (19-Jun-91 GK.B92/R) La Chapelle de Guillaume Tell (44x59cm-17x23in) i.
                  gouache (S.FR 4800)
£2183 $3579   (19-Jun-91 GK.B93/R) Vue du Rigi, vers Schwyz (44x59cm-17x23in) i.
                  gouache (S.FR 5500)
£2579 $4230   (19-Jun-91 GK.B94) Le Pont du Diable au St Gotthard (44x59cm-17x23in) i.
                  gouache (S.FR 6500)
£2857 $4686   (19-Jun-91 GK.B90) Lausanne (44x59cm-17x23in) i. gouache (S.FR 7200)
£3770 $6183   (19-Jun-91 GK.B91/R) Vevay et ses environs (44x59cm-17x23in) i. gouache
                  (S.FR 9500)
£3968 $6508   (19-Jun-91 GK.B89/R) Vue generale de Fribourg (44x59cm-17x23in) i.
                  gouache (S.FR 10000)
£4054 $6851   (3-May-91 SA.A1694/R) View of Castle Razuns and the Galanda Mountains
                  (32x48cm-13x19in) i.verso gouache (DM 12000)
£4054 $6851   (3-May-91 SA.A1696/R) The course of the River Rhine with the upper end
                  of Bodensee (33x48cm-13x19in) gouache (DM 12000)

BLEULER, Louis (19th C) Swiss
£6000 $11520   (28-Nov-90 S207/R) View of the Jungfrau and the Staubbachfall, near
                   Lauterbrunnen (48x71cm-19x28in) s.i. pencil bodycol.

BLIECK, Daniel de (17th C) Dutch
£1150 $2208   (18-Feb-91 S10) Architectural view (15x21cm-6x8in) i.d.1665 brush ink
                  over chk

BLIECK, Maurice (1876-?) Belgian
£1149 $1989   (25-May-91 KV.L22) Le borinage (64x76cm-25x30in) s. (B.FR 70000)
£1643 $3205   (23-Oct-90 C.A47) View of London (50x40cm-20x16in) s. panel
                  (B.FR 100000)
£2494 $4464   (16-Mar-91 KV.L29/R) Le Borinage (90x110cm-35x43in) s. (B.FR 150000)
£3200 $6144   (29-Nov-90 B64/R) On the beach (54x87cm-21x34in) s.
£6500 $10660   (19-Jun-91 S41/R) On beach (53x85cm-21x33in) s.

BLIEK, Pieter (1812-1853) Dutch
£1138 $2162   (11-Sep-90 CH.AM344) The doctor's visit (56x49cm-22x19in) s.d.1846 panel
                  (D.FL 3800)
£1152 $2268   (30-Oct-90 CH.AM337 a/R) Contract (35x46cm-14x18in) s. panel (D.FL 3800)

BLINKS, Thomas (19th C) British
£3333 $6500   (24-Oct-90 CH.NY324/R) Two pointers in landscape (35x45cm-14x18in) s.
£7000 $13650   (15-Jan-91 C129/R) Hounds in full cry (81x27cm-32x11in) s.d.89
£16168 $27000   (7-Jun-91 SY.NY98/R) Full cry (77x127cm-30x50in) s.d.1884

BLIOK, Andrei (1946-) Russian
£584 $952   (10-Jun-91 ZZ.F136/R) Macha a la fenetre (84x66cm-33x26in) s.
                (F.FR 5800)

BLISH, Carolyn (20th C) American
£670 $1300   (24-Aug-90 RB.HY21/R) Green dunes (61x91cm-24x36in) s.

BLISS, Lucia Smith Carpenter (1828-1912) American
£435 $700   (25-Jun-91 JRB.C244) Apple Blossoms (61x46cm-24x18in) s. W/C

BLOCH, Carl (1834-1890) Danish
£2467 $4613   (29-Aug-90 KH.K16/R) The patient (58x45cm-23x18in) s.d.1884 panel
                   (D.KR 28000)
£12456 $23416   (18-Sep-90 BU.K16/R) Monk with toothace (37x27cm-15x11in) s. panel
                   (D.KR 140000)

BLOCH, Julius Thiengen (1888-1966) American
£513 $1000   (20-Oct-90 FA.PH863/R) The tired hitchhiker (48x33cm-19x13in)

BLOCK, Eugene Francois de (1812-1893) Belgian
£589 $1002   (28-May-91 C.A51) Tavern scene (22x27cm-9x11in) s. panel (B.FR 36000)

BLOCKLANDT, Anthonie van (1552-1583) Dutch
£5183 $8500   (19-Jun-91 B.SF1657/R) Adoration of the Shepherds (94x121cm-37x48in)

BLOEM, Wolf (1896-1971) German
£514 $837   (15-Jun-91 L.K68) Santa Maria della Salute (40x60cm-16x24in) s. panel
                   (DM 1500)

BLOEMAERT, Abraham (1564-1651) Dutch
£26000 $43940   (17-Apr-91 S180/R) St John the Baptist preaching to the multitude
                   (94x128cm-37x50in)
£188235 $320000   (31-May-91 CH.NY51/R) The Four Evangelists writing the Gospels
                   (178x222cm-70x87in) s.
£734 $1446   (12-Nov-90 L.AM55/R) Studies of three Putti (9x13cm-4x5in) red chk pen
                   htd white (D.FL 2400)
£1774 $3494   (12-Nov-90 CH.AM56/R) Peasants asleep along path (12x21cm-5x8in) num.2
                   verso black chk pen wash htd white (D.FL 5800)
£4211 $8000   (8-Jan-91 SY.NY35/R) A dilapidated stable (120x194cm-47x76in) wash over
                   blk.chk.
£8684 $16500   (9-Jan-91 CH.NY14/R) Man seen from behind, harvesting (12x10cm-5x4in)
                   i.verso black chk ink wash htd white

BLOEMAERT, Abraham (attrib) (1564-1651) Dutch
£405 $689   (31-May-91 GB.B5039) Rest on the Flight to Egypt (26x19cm-10x7in) pen
                   wash (DM 1200)
£900 $1611   (12-Apr-91 AW.H203/R) Assumption of the Virgin Mary with angels crowning
                   her (37x30cm-15x12in) pen brush over pencil (DM 2700)
£1019 $1967   (14-Dec-90 LEB.P81) Mort de Pyrame et de Thisbe (34x30cm-13x12in) pierre
                   noire wash traces htd.white chamois paper (F.FR 10000)

BLOEMAERT, Abraham (circle) (1564-1651) Dutch
£612 $1205   (12-Nov-90 CH.AM59/R) Mother and child (12x15cm-5x6in) black white chk ink
                   (D.FL 2000)

BLOEMAERT, Abraham (style) (1564-1651) Dutch
£838 $1417   (2-May-91 CH.AM27/R) Saint Simeon holding the Infant Christ
                   (78x56cm-31x22in) s. (D.FL 2800)
£1200 $1956   (4-Jul-91 C672/R) Milkmaid seated in landscape, pointing to left
                   (95x117cm-37x46in)
£1573 $3037   (10-Dec-90 L.K9) Adoration of the Shepherds (29x23cm-11x9in) (DM 4500)
£3761 $7410   (13-Nov-90 AB.S860/R) The four evangelists (83x113cm-33x44in) panel
                   (S.KR 41000)
£1189 $2294   (10-Dec-90 L.K210/R) Adam naming the animals (36x24cm-14x9in) pen sepia
                   wash paper laid down (DM 3400)

BLOEMAERT, Adriaen (1610-1666) Dutch
£2800 $5404   (11-Dec-90 PH149/R) Washerwoman and other figures by stream in wooded
                   landscape (62x47cm-24x19in) s. panel

BLOEMAERT, Adriaen (style) (1610-1666) Dutch
£1100 $1859   (18-Apr-91 CSK109) Extensive rocky landscape with peasants on track by
                   waterfall (60x84cm-24x33in) panel

BLOEMAERT, Hendrick (circle) (1601-1672) Dutch
£1200 $2028   (18-Apr-91 CSK68/R) Feast of Herod (98x128cm-39x50in)

BLOEMAERT, Hendrick (style) (1601-1672) Dutch
£3000 $4890   (4-Jul-91 C735/R) Moses striking rock (99x124cm-39x49in) panel

BLOEMEN, Jan Frans van (1662-1749) Flemish
£3767 $6140   (12-Jun-91 N.M295/R) Landscapes with peasant couple resting by river.
                   Shepherds and animals (35x45cm-14x18in) pair (DM 11000)
£8183 $16038   (19-Nov-90 CH.R46/R) Paesaggio fluviale con figure (74x97cm-29x38in)
                   (I.L 18000000)
£10001 $19602   (20-Nov-90 F.R156/R) Paesaggio con cascata e figure (47x63cm-19x25in)
                   (I.L 22000000)
£31822 $62371   (19-Nov-90 CH.R189/R) Paesaggio fluviale con figure (98x73cm-39x29in)
                   (I.L 70000000)

BLOEMEN, Jan Frans van (attrib) (1662-1749) Flemish
£1746 $3021   (22-May-91 GS.B2329) Wooded landscape with figures and thunderstorm rising (71x96cm-28x38in) (S.FR 4400)
£4283 $7666   (8-Apr-91 CH.R144/R) Paesaggio laziale con figure (68x57cm-27x22in) (I.L 9500000)
£6667 $13000   (10-Oct-90 CH.NY16/R) Italianate landscapes with classical figures. Herders beside fountain (73x61cm-29x24in) pair
£8163 $16082   (15-Nov-90 EA.Z207/R) Italianate landscape (99x113cm-39x44in) (S.FR 20000)
£47297 $80405   (27-May-91 L.K13/R) Southern landscape with classical monuments, ruins and figures set of six panel (DM 140000)

BLOEMEN, Jan Frans van (circle) (1662-1749) Flemish
£1300 $2509   (11-Dec-90 PH214) Mountainous landscape with classical figures beneath pine tree (65x48cm-26x19in)

BLOEMEN, Jan Frans van (school) (1662-1749) Flemish
£2028 $4016   (30-Jan-91 APT.P58/R) Paysage anime avec cavaliers (67x97cm-26x38in) (F.FR 20000)

BLOEMEN, Jan Frans van (studio) (1662-1749) Flemish
£18000 $34740   (11-Dec-90 PH12/R) Classical landscape depicting Colosseum and Arch of Constantine, Rome (48x63cm-19x25in)

BLOEMEN, Jan Frans van (style) (1662-1749) Flemish
£900 $1557   (20-May-91 SWS24/R) Landscape with the Baptism of Christ (34x31cm-13x12in) canvas laid down on panel
£917 $1807   (13-Nov-90 CH.AM136 a) Christ on road to Emmaus (67x113cm-26x44in) (D.FL 3000)
£1100 $1859   (18-Apr-91 CSK116) Classical Italiante landscape with figures on river bank, ruins beyond (50x72cm-20x28in)
£1223 $2410   (13-Nov-90 CH.AM138) Italianate landscape with travellers on path, classical ruins beyond (58x51cm-23x20in) (D.FL 4000)
£1257 $2125   (2-May-91 CH.AM65) An Italianate landscape with a peasant couple near classical ruins (18x26cm-7x10in) copper (D.FL 4200)
£1600 $3072   (29-Nov-90 CSK110/R) Arcadian landscape with shepherds on path (76x102cm-30x40in)
£2200 $4180   (13-Sep-90 CSK178/R) Arcadian landscape (73x95cm-29x37in)
£2400 $4800   (7-Feb-91 CSK119/R) Extensive Italiante landscape with washerwoman (71x96cm-28x38in)
£2835 $5074   (13-Apr-91 FAL.M34/R) Landscape with riders resting (75x100cm-30x39in) (S.KR 30500)
£4500 $7785   (20-May-91 SWS55/R) A classical landscape (63x85cm-25x33in)
£5000 $8450   (17-Apr-91 S66/R) Figures in Italianate landscape (50x43cm-20x17in)
£18500 $31265   (17-Apr-91 S99/R) Landscape with soldiers and other figures beside classical ruins (98x72cm-39x28in)

BLOEMEN, Norbert van (1670-1746) Flemish
£800 $1480   (5-Mar-91 PH3) Cattle and sheep resting before town walls (35x41cm-14x16in)
£8725 $17013   (13-Oct-90 KRA.D153/R) Peasants merrymaking (52x63cm-20x25in) mono. (DM 26000)

BLOEMEN, Pieter van (1657-1720) Flemish
£3754 $7358   (24-Nov-90 SA.A583/R) Travellers resting in landscape (25x30cm-10x12in) mono. panel (DM 11000)
£4500 $7335   (4-Jul-91 C528/R) Shepherd boy and muleteer with pack of animals in Italianate landscape (38x49cm-15x19in)
£5474 $10785   (30-Oct-90 BU.S231/R) Cavalry skirmish (80x63cm-31x25in) init.d.1710 (S.KR 60000)
£6085 $12049   (30-Jan-91 APT.P74/R) Cavaliers sous une statue (44x54cm-17x21in) (F.FR 60000)
£7200 $14184   (30-Oct-90 PH31/R) Ambush (83x105cm-33x41in)
£15500 $29915   (11-Dec-90 PH211/R) Soldiers and peasants on outskirts of village, cannon to right (75x98cm-30x39in) init.
£1376 $2711   (12-Nov-90 CH.AM112/R) Mausoleum with later accretions and mask fountain (27x41cm-11x16in) num.12371 verso black chk wash ink (D.FL 4500)

BLOEMEN, Pieter van (attrib) (1657-1720) Flemish
£2080 $4097   (14-Nov-90 SY.AM138/R) Landscapes with cow grazing at foot of tree (16x22cm-6x9in) init. panel pair (D.FL 6800)

BLOEMEN, Pieter van (circle) (1657-1720) Flemish
£1529 $2600   (30-May-91 CE.NY14) Travellers with horses stopped under archway (37x48cm-15x19in)
£2400 $4608   (29-Nov-90 CSK130/R) Courtyard of Italianate inn with women preparing apples (74x103cm-29x41in)

BLOEMEN, Pieter van (style) (1657-1720) Flemish
£3200 $6080   (13-Sep-90 CSK93/R) Peasants and livestock outside barn, farmstead beyond (61x85cm-24x33in)

BLOEMERS, Arnoldus (c.1786-1844) Dutch
£24235 $47500   (7-Nov-90 B.SF1035/R) Still life with mixed flowers in sculpted vase on stone ledge (47x41cm-19x16in) init.

BLOIS, Andre (?) French?
£1224 $2412   (16-Nov-90 LGB.P162/R) Fleurs blanches (100x73cm-39x29in) s.
                                   (F.FR 12000)

BLOM, Jan (1622-1685) Dutch
£2600 $5200   (7-Feb-91 C86./R) A terraced garden with sheep, peacocks and poultry in
                                   the foreground (100x79cm-39x31in) init.

BLOM, Jan (circle) (1622-1685) Dutch
£3293 $5566   (2-May-91 CH.AM55/R) A noble woman seated in the garden of a palace
                                   watching an eagle taking the dove of peace (88x94cm-35x37in)
                                   (D.FL 11000)

BLOMFIELD, Charles (1848-1926) New Zealander
£1036 $2041   (31-Oct-90 CH.S15/R) Rangatoto Channel from the north shore
                                   (14x39cm-6x15in) s.d.1889 board (A.D 2600)

BLOMMAERT, Maximilian (17/18th C) Flemish
£2108 $3395   (27-Jun-91 APT.P106/R) Paysage de riviere (18x22cm-7x9in) panel
                                   (F.FR 21000)
£3976 $7832   (14-Nov-90 SY.AM97/R) Figures outside hut in river landscape
                                   (20x24cm-8x9in) init. pair (D.FL 13000)

BLOMMAERT, Maximilian (attrib) (17/18th C) Flemish
£1800 $3042   (18-Apr-91 CSK146/R) Family in interior (27x38cm-11x15in) init.

BLOMME, Alphonse-Joseph (1889-1979) Belgian
£1096 $2126   (8-Dec-90 KV.L42) Idylle (90x90cm-35x35in) s. panel (B.FR 65000)

BLOMMERS, Bernardus Johannes (1845-1914) Dutch
£2890 $5000   (12-May-91 H.C14/R) Interior with woman and cat (71x53cm-28x21in) s.
£6061 $11939   (30-Oct-90 CH.AM359/R) Replacing mother (25x30cm-10x12in) s.
                                   (D.FL 20000)
£6122 $12000   (7-Nov-90 B.SF1166/R) Mother and children on beach (36x50cm-14x20in) s.
£9827 $17000   (10-May-91 S.BM62/R) Fond farewell, mother and children on beach
                                   (64x48cm-25x19in) s.
£10355 $17500   (29-Apr-91 S.SL314/R) Children with horse drawn cart gathering shellfish
                                   on beach (99x168cm-39x66in) s.
£650   *$1151*   *(22-Mar-91 PHE34) Waiting for the sleet (33x22cm-13x9in) s.*
£1400   *$2758*   *(13-Nov-90 SWS13/R) Watching the fleet (28x39cm-11x15in) s. W/C gouache*
£1667   *$3283*   *(30-Oct-90 CH.AM514 a/R) Little girls reading (25x32cm-10x13in) s.*
                                   pencil W/C bodycol htd white (D.FL 5500)
£5090   *$8551*   *(23-Apr-91 SY.AM195/R) Looking out to sea (28x39cm-11x15in) s. W/C*
                                   (D.FL 17000)

BLOMSTEDT, Juhana (1937-) Finnish
£1223 $2361   (16-Dec-90 GL.P103) Sans titre (146x114cm-57x45in) s.d.1977 verso
                                   (F.FR 12000)

BLOMSTEDT, Vaino (1871-?) Finnish
£5158 $10160   (17-Nov-90 BU.H17/R) Breakwater in the Mediterranean (80x100cm-31x39in)
                                   s.d.1911 (F.M 36000)

BLOND, Maurice (1899-1974) French
£719 $1396   (7-Dec-90 GL.P59) Portrait de jeune garcon (72x60cm-28x24in) s. board
                                   (F.FR 7000)
£754 $1349   (11-Mar-91 GL.P38) Nature morte aux deux pichets (38x46cm-15x18in)
                                   s.d.1965 (F.FR 7500)
£756 $1474   (18-Jan-91 GL.P23) Jeune fille en jaune sur fond d'usine
                                   (60x73cm-24x29in) s.d.61 (F.FR 7500)
£904 $1755   (7-Dec-90 GL.P60) Cheval sur fond jaune (73x91cm-29x36in) s. (F.FR 8800)
£1937 $3719   (2-Dec-90 M.V85/R) Bouquet de fleurs (81x60cm-32x24in) s. (F.FR 19000)

BLONDAL, Gunnlaugur (1893-1962) Icelandic
£2500 $4625   (5-Mar-91 RAS.K125) Fishing vessels by jetty (79x106cm-31x42in) s.
                                   (D.KR 28000)
£3623 $6993   (12-Dec-90 RAS.K186/R) Icelandic landscape (81x100cm-32x39in) s.
                                   (D.KR 40000)
£4577 $7873   (15-May-91 RAS.K92/R) Female model (65x54cm-26x21in) s.d.36 (D.KR 52000)
£4982 $9615   (12-Dec-90 RAS.K190/R) Fishing vessels by bridge (79x106cm-31x42in) s.
                                   (D.KR 55000)
£5986 $11673   (10-Oct-90 RAS.K255/R) Female model (65x54cm-26x21in) s.i.d.36
                                   (D.KR 68000)
£2046   *$3847*   *(19-Sep-90 KH.K105/R) Young girl looking in mirror (58x44cm-23x17in)*
                                   pastel (D.KR 23000)

BLONDEAU, Francoise (20th C) French?
£798 $1316   (10-Jul-91 FB.P135/R) Le grand bleu (165x200cm-65x79in) s. l. verso
                                   (F.FR 8000)

BLONDEAU, Paul (attrib) (19/20th C) French
£1065 $1800   (29-Apr-91 S.SL308/R) Young man in 17th century attire (46x28cm-18x11in)
                                   s.

BLONDEEL, Lancelot (attrib) (16th C) Flemish
£5000 $9500   (11-Jan-91 CH.NY6/R) Madonna and Child under canopy with Saints Damian
                                  and Cosmos (96x77cm-38x30in) panel

BLONDEL, Emile (1893-1970) French
£680 $1108   (5-Jul-91 APT.P94) Au bord du lac (33x41cm-13x16in) s.d.1963 (F.FR 6800)
£1596 $3000   (11-Aug-90 COL.M220/R) Bookstalls along the Seine (46x56cm-18x22in)
                                  s.d.53

BLONDEL, Merry Joseph (1781-1853) French
£3777 $6384   (18-Apr-91 APT.P152/R) Etude pour les Trois Glorieuses (46x38cm-18x15in)
                                  (F.FR 38000)

BLOOMFIELD, Harry (1870-) British
£1518 $2976   (25-Nov-90 ZZ.F16) Ballerine (87x142cm-34x56in) s.d.1917 (F.FR 15000)
£6122 $12000   (12-Feb-91 SY.NY65/R) Woman in garden (246x150cm-97x59in) s.d.1908

BLOOS, Richard (1878-1956) German
£2891 $5117   (20-Mar-91 KM.K1110/R) Market scene, Kevelaer (50x74cm-20x29in) s.d.1920
                                  panel (DM 8500)

BLOOT, Pieter de (1602-1658) Dutch
£5139 $9969   (7-Dec-90 SY.MO158/R) Les jeunes villageois (20x26cm-8x10in) panel
                                  (F.FR 50000)

BLOOT, Pieter de (style) (1602-1658) Dutch
£1350 $2633   (22-Oct-90 SWS1374/R) Peasants playing game outside house
                                  (28x35cm-11x14in) panel

BLOW, Sandra (1925-) British
*£500 $870   (28-Mar-91 CSK223) Blue Brick Black Abstract (91x122cm-36x48in) collage
                                  gouache masonite*
£1500 $2925   (9-Oct-90 B182) Untitled (121x121cm-48x48in) s.d.83 verso mixed media
*£2700 $4995   (5-Mar-91 PH56/R) Abstract composition (139x107cm-55x42in) s. s.d.1956
                                  verso mixed media board*
£3200 $5216   (1-Jul-91 S54/R) Tat'E (91x122cm-36x48in) mixed media collage board

BLUHM, Norman (1920-) American
£2890 $5000   (7-May-91 CE.NY196/R) Untitled (96x122cm-38x48in) s.
*£3590 $7000   (10-Oct-90 SY.NY535/R) Untitled (76x56cm-30x22in) s.d.59 gouache india
                                  ink panel triptych*

BLUM, Jerome S (1884-1956) American
£10059 $17000   (1-May-91 B.SF5101/R) Marseilles (65x77cm-26x30in) s.d.1918

BLUM, Ludwig (1891-1975) Israeli
£2209 $3600   (12-Jun-91 GG.TA237/R) Vase and flowers (41x32cm-16x13in) s.d.1943
£2618 $5000   (1-Jan-91 GG.TA255/R) The market in Mahaneh Yehudah (50x61cm-20x24in)
                                  s.d.1963
£2822 $4600   (12-Jun-91 GG.TA400/R) Jerusalem, old city (29x20cm-11x8in) s.i.d.1925
                                  canvas on board
£3374 $5500   (12-Jun-91 GG.TA399/R) Interior of synagogue (74x60cm-29x24in)
                                  s.i.d.1947
£3927 $7500   (1-Jan-91 GG.TA253/R) Jerusalem, the old city (60x81cm-24x32in) s.d.1947
£7500 $14625   (24-Oct-90 S208/R) The dome of the rock, Jerusalem (70x112cm-28x44in)
                                  s.i.d.1932

BLUM, Robert F (1857-1903) American
£1693 $3250   (17-Dec-90 SY.NY186/R) Bridal maidens (18x18cm-7x7in) s. W/C
£10615 $19000   (14-Mar-91 CH.NY72/R) Venice (25x32cm-10x13in) s.d.85 pastel

BLUMANN, Elise (20th C) ?
£1778 $3342   (17-Sep-90 SY.ME143/R) After the fire (37x50cm-15x20in) s.d.47 paper on
                                  board (A.D 4000)

BLUME-SIEBERT, Ludwig (1853-?) German
£2167 $3878   (12-Apr-91 BM.B563/R) Shoemaker's workshop with young mother and child
                                  (27x21cm-11x8in) s. panel (DM 6500)

BLUMENSCHEIN, Ernest L (1874-1960) American
£751 $1300   (21-May-91 GRO.B140/R) Portrait of boy (74x43cm-29x17in) s.i.d.
                                  i.stretcher

BLUNDEN, Anna (1829-?) British
£400 $760   (1-Mar-91 BW429) On lago di Guarda (41x71cm-16x28in) s.d.1907 W/C

BLYHOOFT, Jacques Zacharias (17th C) Dutch
*£2490 $4308   (22-May-91 PLF.P9) Scene de foire (15x20cm-6x8in) s.d.1671 pen wash
                                  (F.FR 25000)*

BLYK, Frans Jacobus van den (1806-1876) Dutch
£3144 $5281   (23-Jul-91 SY.AM206/R) Sailing vessels near Dordrecht (44x57cm-17x22in)
                                  s. panel (D.FL 10500)

BLYTH, Robert Henderson (1919-1970) British
£1650 $3218   (10-Oct-90 PHG40/R) Summerfield (121x103cm-48x41in) s. board

BLYTH, Robert Henderson (1919-1970) British-cont.
£1800 $3384   (18-Sep-90 PH175) Song Thrush (101x127cm-40x50in) s.d.39

BLYTHE, David Gilmour (1815-1865) American
£20231 $35000   (22-May-91 CH.NY29/R) School master (74x65cm-29x26in) s.

BO, Giacinto (?-1912) Italian
£1505 $2513   (6-Jun-91 F.M21/R) Cacciatore nel bosco (99x60cm-39x24in) s.d.1889
                        (I.L 3300000)
£2280 $3808   (6-Jun-91 F.M65/R) Paesaggio alpino (66x129cm-26x51in) s. (I.L 5000000)
£3469 $6729   (5-Dec-90 F.M58/R) Riviera di Ponente, Liguria (100x140cm-39x55in) s.
                        i.verso (I.L 7500000)

BOBAK, Bruno (1923-) Canadian
£965 $1891   (20-Nov-90 JOY.T418) Acadian village (60x90cm-24x35in) s. (C.D 2200)
£1111 $1911   (14-May-91 JOY.T82/R) Winter in Fredericton (60x90cm-24x35in) s.
                        (C.D 2200)

BOBAK, Molly Lamb (1922-) Canadian
£1010 $1737   (14-May-91 JOY.T83/R) Harness racing (75x100cm-30x39in) s. board
                        (C.D 2000)

BOBERG, Jorgen (1940-) Swedish
£3578 $7013   (13-Feb-91 KH.K39/R) 'Udnaevnerens ankomst' (90x76cm-35x30in) panel
                        (D.KR 40000)

BOBROV, Viktor Alexejewitsch (1842-?) Russian
£2846 $5691   (4-Feb-91 PLF.P24/R) Jeune femme lisant dans un interieur
                        (33x48cm-13x19in) s.d.1894 W/C gouache (F.FR 28000)

BOCARIC, Spiro (1878-1941) Austrian
£1000 $1640   (19-Jun-91 S94/R) Young girl threading necklace (57x42cm-22x17in) s.

BOCCACCINI, Giovanni Francesco (?) Italian
£6834 $11619   (30-May-91 F.M59/R) Veduta del porto di Messina (49x77cm-19x30in) s.d.
                        tempera paper (I.L 15000000)

BOCCACCINO, Boccaccio (c.1467-c.1524) Italian
£22000 $36740   (3-Jun-91 RY.P23/R) Sainte tenant une crix et un livre (40x31cm-16x12in)
                        panel (F.FR 220000)

BOCCACCINO, Boccaccio (circle) (c.1467-c.1524) Italian
£1204 $2347   (10-Oct-90 APT.P464) L'Adoration des bergers (78x52cm-31x20in) panel
                        (F.FR 12000)

BOCCHERINI (20th C) American
£904 $1700   (19-Sep-90 B.SF2750/R) The immigrants' Christmas (61x91cm-24x36in) s.

BOCCIARDO, Clemente (attrib) (1620-1658) Italian
£2600 $4498   (20-May-91 SWS72) A mythological subject (121x177cm-48x70in)

BOCCIARDO, Domenico (attrib) (1686-1746) Italian
£17000 $28730   (19-Apr-91 C115/R) Portrait of two girls with a dog in a palatial
                        interior (156x121cm-61x48in)

BOCCIONI, Umberto (1882-1916) Italian
£60124 $116640   (3-Dec-90 CH.R114/R) Ritratto di gentiluomo (50x72cm-20x28in)
                        (I.L 130000000)
£93899 $180286   (27-Nov-90 SY.MI231/R) Paesaggio (37x35cm-15x14in) s. canvas laid down
                        on masonite (I.L 205000000)
£30000 $58200   (5-Dec-90 S337/R) Testa and Luce (19x20cm-7x8in) s. pen
£78680 $155000   (14-Nov-90 SY.NY115/R) Donna Che Legge (42x30cm-17x12in) s.d.1909 pastel
                        paper on board

BOCH, Anna (1848-1933) Belgian
£3003 $5195   (22-May-91 CH.AM503/R) Still life with onions, cabbage and bread on
                        table with magpie on chair (86x135cm-34x53in) s. (D.FL 10000)

BOCHMANN, Gregor von (1850-1930) German
£4027 $7852   (13-Oct-90 KRA.D176/R) Potatoe harvest, Estland (13x18cm-5x7in) s. panel
                        (DM 12000)

BOCHNER, Mel (1940-) American
£1786 $3500   (6-Nov-90 CE.NY185/R) Vinalhaven (110x111cm-43x44in) s.d.1984-85 oil
                        enamel three sheets paper
£2071 $3500   (2-May-91 CH.NY236/R) Untitled (31x28cm-12x11in) s.d.1973 felt-tip pen
                        col.crayons
£3846 $6500   (1-May-91 SY.NY90/R) Third range (96x127cm-38x50in) s.d.1973 col.ink
                        pencil
£8284 $14000   (1-May-91 SY.NY82/R) Triangular and square - numbers or points
                        (96x127cm-38x50in) s.d.1973 chl gouache

BOCION, Francois (1828-1890) Swiss
£2209 $4329   (21-Nov-90 SY.Z17/R) Coastal landscape, Liguria (21x33cm-8x13in) panel
                        (S.FR 5500)

184

BOCION, Francois (1828-1890) Swiss-cont.
£3200	$5408	(1-May-91 GD.B69/R) Lake Geneva landscape near Rivaz (21x32cm-8x13in) mono.i.d.83 (S.FR 8000)
£7661	$14710	(2-Dec-90 GAB.G1508/R) L'entree dans le port (26x38cm-10x15in) init. paper laid down on board (S.FR 19000)
£15261	$29912	(21-Nov-90 SY.Z24/R) En curtinaux pres de Lutry, avec le chateau de montagny (35x54cm-14x21in) s. (S.FR 38000)
£3815	*$7478*	*(21-Nov-90 SY.Z23/R) Fete de la nautique (18x35cm-7x14in) mono. pencil sepia (S.FR 9500)*

BOCION, Francois (school) (1828-1890) Swiss
£598	$1028	(14-May-91 GF.L2432/R) Lake landscape, evening (24x40cm-9x16in) (S.FR 1500)

BOCK, Adolf (1890-1968) Finnish
£5022	$8486	(20-Apr-91 HOR.H42/R) Sailship at sea (50x70cm-20x28in) s. (F.M 35000)
£402	*$720*	*(11-Mar-91 AB.S1009) The vessel 'The Good Hope' (26x18cm-10x7in) s.i.d.1957 W/C (S.KR 4300)*
£432	*$833*	*(15-Dec-90 BU.H213) Towing vessel (27x18cm-11x7in) s.i. gouache (F.M 3000)*
£2726	$4607	(20-Apr-91 HOR.H43/R) The vessel 'Elakoon' (39x56cm-15x22in) s.d.1919 W/C (F.M 19000)

BOCK, Adolf Georg Friedrich (1854-1917) German
£2196	$4282	(26-Oct-90 BM.B746/R) Sailing ships in early morning mist (62x50cm-24x20in) s.d.1905 (DM 6500)

BOCK, Ludwig (1886-1955) German
£909	$1755	(13-Dec-90 N.M2651) Still life with apples and bananas (36x50cm-14x20in) s.d.52 board (DM 2600)

BOCK, Theophile Emile Achille de (1851-1904) Dutch
£550	$946	(14-May-91 SWS298/R) Landscape with trees (60x37cm-24x15in) s. canvas on panel
£648	$1271	(24-Nov-90 SA.A718/R) Wooded landscape after rain, evening (35x25cm-14x10in) s. (DM 1900)
£659	$1146	(26-Mar-91 VN.R9/R) Figures in a birch wood (18x11cm-7x4in) s. panel (D.FL 2200)
£793	$1522	(27-Nov-90 SY.AM3574) Farm on waterfront (35x50cm-14x20in) s. canvas on panel (D.FL 2600)
£983	$1700	(21-May-91 CE.NY155/R) City gates (28x24cm-11x9in) s. panel
£1061	$2089	(30-Oct-90 CH.AM247/R) Figure on wooded path in forest (24x19cm-9x7in) s. panel (D.FL 3500)
£1497	$2515	(23-Apr-91 SY.AM331) Moored vessel near village (38x58cm-15x23in) s. (D.FL 5000)
£1818	$3582	(30-Oct-90 CH.AM67) Cowhand driving cattle on sandy path along river, at sunset (40x62cm-16x24in) s. (D.FL 6000)
£1858	$3585	(12-Dec-90 CH.AM105) Winter landscape with hunter on road (53x84cm-21x33in) s. (D.FL 6000)
£2232	$4286	(27-Nov-90 W.T1166/R) Coastal cottages and figures (41x53cm-16x21in) s. panel (C.D 5000)
£2439	$4780	(6-Nov-90 SY.AM44/R) Peasant in boat (32x49cm-13x19in) s. panel (D.FL 8000)

BOCKLIN, Carlo (1870-?) Swiss
£1837	$3618	(16-Nov-90 GK.Z5325) Centaur standing on hill looking over mountain landscape (17x23cm-7x9in) panel (S.FR 4500)

BOCKMAN, Bengt (20th C) Scandinavian?
£744	$1384	(9-Sep-90 BU.M385) Satellite (46x45cm-18x18in) s.d.65 acrylic (S.KR 8000)
£908	$1762	(5-Dec-90 AB.S7048/R) Figure in landscape - composition (70x70cm-28x28in) s.d.70 (S.KR 9800)

BOCKSTIEGEL, Peter August (1889-1951) German
£1748	$3392	(7-Dec-90 GB.B6356) Still life with apples (22x30cm-9x12in) s. board (DM 5000)
£24407	$40759	(6-Jun-91 HN.H166/R) Path in a park in winter (77x77cm-30x30in) mono.d.1912 (DM 72000)
£4021	*$7801*	*(7-Dec-90 GB.B6355/R) Landscape with barn (62x86cm-24x34in) s.i.d.1940 pastel (DM 11500)*
£6803	*$12041*	*(22-Mar-91 GRA.B2786/R) Corn stooks in field before farmstead near Werther (47x62cm-19x24in) s.d.1941 pastel (DM 20000)*

BODAMER, Heinz (20th C) German?
£512	$840	(18-Jun-91 FN.S1537/R) Still life with green jug (58x48cm-23x19in) s.d.1962 (DM 1500)

BODDINGTON, E H (19th C) British
£680	$1258	(7-Mar-91 CSK184/R) Figures by still pond, windmill beyond (45x91cm-18x36in) s.d.77

BODDINGTON, Edwin H (1836-1905) British
£650	$1073	(11-Jul-91 CSK97/R) Anglers on riverbank in summer landscape (35x46cm-14x18in) s.d.1853

BODDINGTON, Edwin H (1836-1905) British-cont.
£1500	$2940	(22-Jan-91 PH48/R) Morning on the Dee nr Corwen, N.Wales. Evening on the Wye nr Monmouth (26x46cm-10x18in) one s. one s.d.1867 s.i.d.stretcher pair
£1800	$3528	(22-Jan-91 PH41/R) Angler fishing from punt (20x36cm-8x14in) s. pair

BODDINGTON, Henry John (1811-1865) British
£1579	$3000	(15-Sep-90 S.W2412/R) Shepherd and flock (36x53cm-14x21in) s.i.d.1851
£2455	$4714	(27-Nov-90 W.T1030/R) River landscape with angler and other figures (48x58cm-19x23in) s.d.1840 (C.D 5500)
£2895	$5500	(27-Feb-91 SY.NY240/R) Children in woodland clearing (61x51cm-24x20in) s.d.1844
£3000	$5010	(5-Jun-91 S9/R) Passing storm (30x41cm-12x16in) indist.s.verso panel
£3807	$7500	(15-Nov-90 D.NY18/R) Summer river landscape with cattle watering (77x125cm-30x49in) s.d.1860

BODDINGTON, Henry John (attrib) (1811-1865) British
£785	$1312	(4-Jun-91 R.T159/R) Country lass and dog crossing river (63x51cm-25x20in) (C.D 1500)
£3500	$5705	(14-Jun-91 C250/R) View of Windsor Castle from the thames (71x91cm-28x36in)

BODE, Johan F (1870-1960) Dutch
£1775	$2911	(18-Jun-91 FN.S1760) Fun on the ice with figures in snowy Dutch river landscape (30x45cm-12x18in) s. panel (DM 5200)

BODEMAN, Willem (1806-1880) Dutch
£1364	$2686	(30-Oct-90 CH.AM178) Travellers on clearing in wooded landscape, by stream (12x14cm-5x6in) s. panel (D.FL 4500)
£2098	$4070	(4-Dec-90 FN.S1765/R) Wooded river landscape with figures on path, evening (55x70cm-22x28in) s.d.1861 (DM 6000)
£7692	$15000	(24-Oct-90 CH.NY288/R) Travellers in landscape with town beyond (69x88cm-27x35in) s.d.1841 panel
£9091	$17909	(30-Oct-90 CH.AM256/R) Winter landscape with wood-gatherer on frozen ditch and peasants on snowy path (90x125cm-35x49in) indist.s. bears sig. (D.FL 30000)

BODIFEE, Paul (1866-1938) Dutch
£818	$1612	(30-Oct-90 CH.AM449/R) Farmhouses along canal, in winter (46x65cm-18x26in) s. W/C bodycol (D.FL 2700)

BODLEY, Josselin (1893-1974) British
£1508	$2894	(24-Feb-91 P.V25/R) Venise (46x38cm-18x15in) s.d.1928 (F.FR 15000)

BODMER, Karl (1809-1893) Swiss
£1032	$1785	(22-May-91 GS.B2044) Woodlands with deer (73x59cm-29x23in) s. (S.FR 2600)
£826	$1585	(1-Dec-90 PER.M29/R) La riviere dans la foret (47x28cm-19x11in) s. W/C gouache (F.FR 8100)
£1594	$2757	(24-May-91 FB.P110/R) La foret de Fontainebleau (20x30cm-8x12in) s. W/C (F.FR 16000)

BODMER, Karl (attrib) (1809-1893) Swiss
£754	$1259	(7-Jun-91 ZOF.Z1284) Wood pecker and stag beetle (37x28cm-15x11in) d.1952 panel (S.FR 1900)

BODMER, Paul (1886-1983) Swiss
£677	$1165	(14-May-91 GF.L2565) Portrait of boy (16x14cm-6x6in) s. canvas on board (S.FR 1700)
£757	$1476	(24-Oct-90 GD.B165/R) Das Waldfest (37x27cm-15x11in) s. board (S.FR 1900)
£797	$1554	(24-Oct-90 GD.B162/R) Nun and two women. Landscape with scaffolding (27x40cm-11x16in) s. board double-sided (S.FR 2000)
£833	$1367	(19-Jun-91 GK.B211) Self portrait (28x20cm-11x8in) s. board (S.FR 2100)
£952	$1562	(19-Jun-91 GK.B208) Woman playing violin seated at table with other figures (29x30cm-11x12in) s. board (S.FR 2400)
£1285	$2159	(24-Apr-91 G.Z8/R) Group of girls (53x67cm-21x26in) s. board (S.FR 3200)

BODMER, Walter (1903-1973) Swiss
£3373	$5633	(5-Jun-91 SY.Z181/R) Composition (40x54cm-16x21in) s.d.1960 board (S.FR 8500)
£635	$1060	(5-Jun-91 SY.Z173/R) Composition (26x36cm-10x14in) s.d.59 indian ink W/C (S.FR 1600)

BODOM, Erik (1829-1879) Norwegian
£900	$1611	(12-Apr-91 BM.B565/R) Coastal landscape with lighthouse on island (16x27cm-6x11in) s.d.69 i.verso panel (DM 2700)
£952	$1686	(20-Mar-91 KM.K1111) View of Norwegian highlands with river (27x37cm-11x15in) s.d.1873 (DM 2800)
£4141	$8199	(29-Jan-91 UL.T149/R) Evening landscape (80x110cm-31x43in) (N.KR 47000)
£5800	$9512	(21-Jun-91 C35/R) Waterfall in Norway (98x83cm-39x33in) s.d.1853

BOE, Franz Didrik (1820-1891) Norwegian
£911	$1777	(11-Oct-90 BU.O16/R) Fish (62x54cm-24x21in) s.d.1865 (N.KR 10500)
£1167	$2299	(14-Nov-90 RAS.K197/R) Seascape with vessel at sunset (27x39cm-11x15in) s.d.1855 (D.KR 13000`

BOE, Franz Didrik (1820-1891) Norwegian-cont.
£1226	$2194	(11-Mar-91 B.O14/R) Still life of dead game (32x40cm-13x16in) s.d.1857 (N.KR 14000)
£1519	$2537	(3-Jun-91 B.O14/R) Still life of roses (27x35cm-11x14in) s.d.1881 (N.KR 17500)
£1781	$3437	(10-Dec-90 B.O15/R) Roses (27x34cm-11x13in) s.d.1890 (N.KR 20000)
£5556	$10833	(11-Oct-90 BU.O15/R) Still life of flowers and bird (31x36cm-12x14in) s.d.1852 panel (N.KR 64000)
£10686	$20623	(12-Dec-90 BU.O7/R) Cacti and roses (47x40cm-19x16in) s.i.d.1868 (N.KR 120000)
£11285	$18845	(3-Jun-91 B.O13/R) Still life of flowers (54x48cm-21x19in) s.d.1877 (N.KR 130000)

BOECK, Felix de (1898-) Belgian
£655	$1100	(23-Apr-91 C.A372) Nachtlichten (19x26cm-7x10in) s. panel (B.FR 40000)
£675	$1309	(8-Dec-90 KV.L77) Infinity (40x18cm-16x7in) s.d.1989 verso panel (B.FR 40000)
£1309	$2200	(23-Apr-91 C.A371/R) Abstract landscape with sun (21x60cm-8x24in) mono. panel (B.FR 80000)
£1479	$2884	(23-Oct-90 C.A129) Christ on the Cross (22x35cm-9x14in) s.d.1932 verso panel (B.FR 90000)
£1604	$3160	(6-Oct-90 KV.L62) Self-portrait (28x22cm-11x9in) s.d.1975 verso panel (B.FR 100000)
£2673	$5240	(12-Feb-91 GM.B389/R) Composition avec train, maison et voiture (27x27cm-11x11in) s. wood (B.FR 160000)
£7315	$13094	(16-Mar-91 KV.L395/R) Zelfgave (80x60cm-31x24in) s. s.d.1980 verso panel (B.FR 440000)

BOECKHORST, Jan (1605-1668) German
£80000	$138400	(24-May-91 C17/R) Bellerophon, assisted by Mercury, taming Pegasus with a golden bridle (145x209cm-57x82in)

BOECKHORST, Jan (circle) (1605-1668) German
£15000	$24450	(5-Jul-91 C300/R) Man carrying great bustard (180x105cm-71x41in)

BOECKL, Herbert (1894-1966) Austrian
£40000	$77600	(5-Dec-90 S149/R) Portrat eines jungen mannes mit katze (105x74cm-41x29in) s.d.1928
£2670	$4379	(20-Jun-91 D.V59/R) Children doing homework at table (46x61cm-18x24in) s.d.1931 chk (A.S 55000)
£3231	$6267	(6-Dec-90 D.V117/R) Landscape with trees and houses (33x48cm-13x19in) s.i. chk (A.S 65000)
£3398	$5573	(20-Jun-91 D.V58/R) Portrait of Oskar Boeckl, artist's son (53x40cm-21x16in) s.d.1940 chl (A.S 70000)
£8738	$14330	(20-Jun-91 D.V24/R) Two apples on cloth (37x42cm-15x17in) i.d.verso chl (A.S 180000)

BOEGELT, H (17th C) ?
£2695	$4554	(2-May-91 CH.AM48/R) A view in a Gothic cathedral, looking east towards the choir (59x74cm-23x29in) s.d.1665 panel (D.FL 9000)

BOEHM, E (19th C) ?
£3684	$7000	(27-Feb-91 SY.NY181/R) Rural folk in alpine landscape. Bear hunt. Deer in landscape. Hay gatherers (37x63cm-15x25in) s. four

BOEHM, Eduard (1830-?) German
£627	$1254	(6-Feb-91 RAS.K171/R) Mountainous landscape near Salzburg (60x85cm-24x33in) s. (D.KR 7000)
£685	$1116	(12-Jun-91 N.M372/R) Mountain valley with stream and peasant woman on path (55x69cm-22x27in) s. (DM 2000)
£699	$1350	(12-Dec-90 N.M446/R) Mountain valley with farmstead by stream and snowy peaks beyond (75x100cm-30x39in) i. (DM 2000)
£753	$1228	(12-Jun-91 N.M373/R) Mountain valley with woodland pond and peasant with cart on path (41x65cm-16x26in) s. (DM 2200)
£753	$1228	(12-Jun-91 N.M374) Woodland stream with fisherman in boat (68x55cm-27x22in) s. (DM 2200)
£1102	$2160	(6-Nov-90 GF.L2405/R) Mountainous river landscape with angler (69x56cm-27x22in) s. (S.FR 2700)
£1257	$2389	(11-Sep-90 CH.AM325) A couple with cows in a meadow in alpine landscape (69x106cm-27x42in) s. (D.FL 4200)
£1336	$2391	(12-Mar-91 FN.S2290/R) Mountain lake landscape with figures (32x39cm-13x15in) s. (DM 3900)

BOEHM, Eduard (style) (1830-?) German
£1020	$1643	(26-Jun-91 KM.K1578) Alpine landscape with watermill and figures (130x106cm-51x42in) (DM 3000)

BOEHM, Tuomas von (1916-) Finnish
£1295	$2499	(15-Dec-90 BU.H23) Still life (46x38cm-18x15in) s. (F.M 9000)
£1997	$3914	(24-Nov-90 HOR.H49/R) White houses (54x64cm-21x25in) s. (F.M 14000)
£2710	$5312	(24-Nov-90 HOR.H48/R) Still life with crayfish (50x61cm-20x24in) s.d.1967 (F.M 19000)
£2722	$5362	(17-Nov-90 BU.H141/R) Still life of olives (46x38cm-18x15in) s. panel (F.M 19000)

BOEHME, Karl Theodor (1866-1939) German
£1800 $2952   (18-Jun-91 PH116/R) Coastal landscape (106x156cm-42x61in) s.

BOEL, Maurice (1913-) ?
£540 $1042   (13-Dec-90 CH.BR20/R) Composition (97x40cm-38x16in) s. gouache W/C pen
                    paper on board (B.FR 32000)

BOEL, Pieter (c.1622-1674) Flemish
£8432 $16358   (4-Dec-90 C.A35/R) Hunting scene (125x200cm-49x79in) (B.FR 500000)
£25373 $44149   (25-Mar-91 PLF.P91/R) Le repose du chasseur (100x125cm-39x49in)
                    (F.FR 255000)
£2800 $4564   (2-Jul-91 C353/R) Head of stag and porcupine (31x51cm-12x20in) col.chk

BOELS, Frans (attrib) (?-1594) Dutch
£3364 $6627   (12-Nov-90 CH.AM73/R) Wooded river landscape with travellers by cross on
                    path (8x11cm-3x4in) bodycol on vellum (D.FL 11000)

BOEMM, Ritta (1868-?) Hungarian
£1037 $1990   (27-Nov-90 SY.AM3576) In the garden (99x74cm-39x29in) s. (D.FL 3400)

BOENKER, B (19th C) ?
£1610 $2705   (24-Apr-91 BA.S21/R) Departing Roman soldiers (29x41cm-11x16in) s.d.1819
                    (S.KR 17000)

BOEREWAARD, Door (1893-1972) Belgian
£914 $1637   (16-Mar-91 KV.L33) Farm by moonlight (40x50cm-16x20in) s. (B.FR 55000)
£2727 $5371   (6-Oct-90 KV.L27/R) Marine with threatening clouds (128x148cm-50x58in)
                    s. (B.FR 170000)

BOERO, Renata (20th C) Italian
£2161 $4214   (22-Oct-90 BR.M61/R) Enigma n.1 (130x120cm-51x47in) s.d.1989 vegetable
                    colouring mixed media canvas (I.L 4800000)

BOERS, Sebastian Theodorus Voorn (1828-1893) Dutch
£1445 $2500   (21-May-91 CE.NY327/R) Still life with peonies on table
                    (37x49cm-15x19in) s.

BOESCHLIN, Pierre (20th C) ?
£663 $1279   (12-Dec-90 ZZ.F26/R) Allee de jardin en fleurs (32x41cm-13x16in) panel
                    (F.FR 6500)

BOESEN, Johannes (1847-1916) Danish
£808 $1592   (14-Nov-90 RAS.K437) View from Capri towards Vesuvius (24x62cm-9x24in)
                    s. (D.KR 9000)
£3435 $6595   (29-Nov-90 D.V69/R) Path through wooded landscape (80x90cm-31x35in)
                    s.d.1879 (A.S 70000)

BOETTCHER, Christian Eduard (1818-1889) German
£2365 $4493   (14-Sep-90 SA.A1273/R) Portrait of lady in park landscape, evening
                    (18x90cm-7x35in) (DM 7000)
£1469 $2834   (10-Dec-90 L.K211/R) Rhine landscape with figures outside tavern and
                    ruin beyond (50x74cm-20x29in) s.d.55 (DM 4200)

BOETTI, Alighiero (1940-) Italian
£1818 $3564   (20-Nov-90 BR.M6/R) 1000novecentoottantasette (70x50cm-28x20in) s.d.1987
                    mixed media paper on canvas (I.L 4000000)
£3209 $5263   (20-Jun-91 F.M302) Mimetico (21x29cm-8x11in) s.d.1968 canvas on
                    paniforte (I.L 7000000)
£3571 $7000   (6-Nov-90 CE.NY255/R) Traseese III (151x100cm-59x39in) W/C graphite
                    paper mounted on canvas
£7249 $12613   (26-Mar-91 F.M52/R) Niente da vedere niente da nascondere
                    (99x150cm-39x59in) s.d.1981-82 collage mixed media paper on canvas
                    (I.L 16000000)
£13306 $25948   (26-Oct-90 CC.P95/R) Sans titre (110x110cm-43x43in) s.d.1988 embroidery
                    canvas mounted on panel (F.FR 132000)
£14000 $22540   (27-Jun-91 C42/R) La mappa del mondo (115x178cm-45x70in) s.overlap
                    embroidered fabric on board

BOETTINGER, Hugo (1880-1934) Czechoslovakian
£900 $1728   (27-Nov-90 PH228/R) Boys bathing by stream surrounded by geese
                    (78x103cm-31x41in) pastel

BOEUFF, Pierre le (19th C) French
£1061 $2100   (1-Feb-91 S.W2570/R) Belgian city views (51x76cm-20x30in) s.i.verso pair
£1700 $2924   (17-May-91 C5/R) Bernay, Normandy. Bruges with cathedral belfry
                    (51x76cm-20x30in) s.i.verso pair

BOEVER, Jean Francois de (1872-1949) Belgian
£1150 $2243   (23-Oct-90 C.A130) Le galant (50x60cm-20x24in) s. panel (B.FR 70000)

BOGAERT, Bram (1921-) Dutch
£541 $935   (22-May-91 CH.AM695) Still life with orange flowers in vase
                    (40x50cm-16x20in) s. board (D.FL 1800)
£1502 $2598   (23-May-91 SY.AM297/R) Untitled (67x97cm-26x38in) s.d.1966verso paper
                    (D.FL 5000)

BOGAERT, Bram (1921-) Dutch-cont.

£4263	$8271	(4-Dec-90 BA.S59/R) 'Roedingroen' (39x43cm-15x17in) s.d.67 panel (S.KR 46000)
£18003	$30246	(23-Apr-91 C.A67/R) Panorama de Merida (130x96cm-51x38in) s.d.1956 (B.FR 1100000)
£649	$1259	(5-Dec-90 AB.S7038/R) Brown-black-blue (58x92cm-23x36in) s.d.69 gouache (S.KR 7000)
£713	$1404	(31-Oct-90 ZZ.F3) Composition (20x26cm-8x10in) s.d.57 Indian ink wash (F.FR 7000)
£741	$1438	(5-Dec-90 AB.S7039/R) Orange-blue-black (71x58cm-28x23in) s.d.69 gouache (S.KR 8000)
£929	$1793	(13-Dec-90 SY.AM301/R) Untitled (49x64cm-19x25in) s.d.69 gouache (D.FL 3000)
£929	$1793	(13-Dec-90 SY.AM319/R) Untitled (48x64cm-19x25in) s.d.59 gouache (D.FL 3000)
£1964	$3300	(23-Apr-91 C.A71) Composition (34x42cm-13x17in) s.d.1949 gouache (B.FR 120000)
£2410	$4675	(5-Dec-90 AB.S7037/R) 'Kleinwit' (51x57cm-20x22in) s.d.1964 mixed media (S.KR 26000)
£2922	$4938	(18-Apr-91 BU.S33/R) 'Degelengroen' (52x54cm-20x21in) s.d.1968 mixed media (S.KR 31000)
£2946	$4949	(23-Apr-91 C.A70) White (40x50cm-16x20in) s.d.1972 mixed media (B.FR 180000)
£3287	$6409	(23-Oct-90 C.A312/R) Donker (45x50cm-18x20in) s.d.1974 mixed media (B.FR 200000)
£3864	$6531	(18-Apr-91 BU.S31/R) 'Jaunegeel' (65x75cm-26x30in) s.d.1973 mixed media (S.KR 41000)
£3875	$7439	(27-Nov-90 BU.S38/R) 'Quatorze Jaune' (40x44cm-16x17in) s.d.1971 mixed media (S.KR 42000)
£4204	$7273	(23-May-91 SY.AM303/R) Quatorze jaune (40x45cm-16x18in) s.d.71 i.d.verso mixed media board (D.FL 14000)
£4204	$7273	(23-May-91 SY.AM302/R) Kruis-wit (90x68cm-35x27in) s.d.71 s.i.d.verso mixed media board (D.FL 14000)
£4336	$8325	(27-Nov-90 BU.S37/R) 'Witzwart' (50x53cm-20x21in) s.d.1969 s.i.d.verso mixed media (S.KR 47000)
£4452	$7257	(14-Jun-91 L.K781/R) Moon (55x55cm-22x22in) s.i.d.1964verso (DM 13000)
£4910	$8249	(23-Apr-91 C.A69/R) Blue blue (55x60cm-22x24in) s.d.1971 mixed media (B.FR 300000)
£5565	$9349	(23-Apr-91 C.A68/R) Speelvlak (102x42cm-40x17in) plaster (B.FR 340000)
£5996	$11513	(27-Nov-90 BU.S36/R) 'Kruiswit' (85x68cm-33x27in) s.d.1971 mixed media (S.KR 65000)
£6500	$11505	(21-Mar-91 C212) White wit (78x56cm-31x22in) s.d.75 i. verso pigment board
£7712	$13265	(13-May-91 CH.R103/R) Geelio Baulw (62x48cm-24x19in) i.d.1972verso pigment mixed media canvas (I.L 17000000)
£8050	$15536	(12-Dec-90 CH.AM371/R) Oiseau marchant (57x92cm-22x36in) s.d.55 s.i.d.num.51 mixed media canvas on board (D.FL 26000)
£8669	$16731	(12-Dec-90 CH.AM372/R) Sphere chinois (60x73cm-24x29in) s.d.56 s.i.d.num.36 verso mixed media canvas (D.FL 28000)
£11070	$21255	(27-Nov-90 BU.S35/R) 'Blauwraam' (123x102cm-48x40in) s.i.d.1965verso mixed media (S.KR 120000)
£13000	$23010	(21-Mar-91 C263/R) Bleublack (95x102cm-37x40in) s.i.d.Febr. 1975 verso pigment composition board
£13300	$23807	(16-Mar-91 KV.L404/R) Roorood (100x123cm-39x48in) s.d.65 material picture (B.FR 800000)
£21364	$41660	(23-Oct-90 C.A311/R) Witdoorzwart (160x150cm-63x59in) s.d.1971 verso mixed media (B.FR 1300000)
£58000	$113100	(18-Oct-90 S108/R) Bloemenland (122x153cm-48x60in) s.i.d.1964verso mixed media hessian on board
£65000	$104650	(27-Jun-91 C6/R) Aux fetes rouges (161x213cm-63x84in) s.d.60 s.i.d.verso pigment composition canvas

BOGAERT, Gaston (c.1918-) Belgian

£882	$1738	(6-Oct-90 KV.L29) Neige (33x41cm-13x16in) s. panel (B.FR 55000)
£1349	$2617	(8-Dec-90 KV.L45) Voyage au long cours (61x50cm-24x20in) s.d.1983 panel (B.FR 80000)
£1808	$3525	(23-Oct-90 C.A53/R) On the seashore (50x60cm-20x24in) s. panel (B.FR 110000)

BOGAERT, Hans (17th C) Flemish

£2703	$4595	(27-May-91 L.K14) Peasants eating before fire place. Woman crying in solitor's office (34x25cm-13x10in) s. pair (DM 8000)

BOGAERTS, Jan (?-1656) Dutch

£4633	$8941	(10-Dec-90 L.K11/R) Party merrymaking in pub (46x62cm-18x24in) s. panel (DM 13250)

BOGAIEVSKAIA, Olga (1916-) Russian

£524	$854	(10-Jun-91 ZZ.F29/R) Sur la terrasse (49x40cm-19x16in) s. (F.FR 5200)
£694	$1194	(15-May-91 AGB.P143/R) Fillette au bandeau bleu (47x38cm-19x15in) s. (F.FR 7000)
£803	$1486	(4-Mar-91 ZZ.F87) Les fillettes (44x33cm-17x13in) s. (F.FR 8000)
£823	$1523	(4-Mar-91 ZZ.F88) La couture (47x38cm-19x15in) s. (F.FR 8200)
£992	$1706	(15-May-91 AGB.P146/R) Nature morte au citron (55x66cm-22x26in) s. (F.FR 10000)
£1024	$1895	(4-Mar-91 ZZ.F89) Retour de promenade (77x61cm-30x24in) s. (F.FR 10200)

BOGAIEVSKAIA, Olga (1916-) Russian-cont.
£1190	$2048	(15-May-91 AGB.P145/R) L'ecoliere (28x48cm-11x19in) s. (F.FR 12000)
£1290	$2218	(15-May-91 AGB.P148/R) Interieur (48x43cm-19x17in) s. (F.FR 13000)
£1526	$2823	(4-Mar-91 ZZ.F86/R) Au jardin (52x69cm-20x27in) s. (F.FR 15200)
£1642	$2857	(25-Mar-91 ARC.P126/R) Le petit dejeuner (59x70cm-23x28in) s. (F.FR 16500)
£1692	$2943	(25-Mar-91 ARC.P124/R) Nature morte a la theiere (49x65cm-19x26in) s. board (F.FR 17000)
£2239	$3896	(25-Mar-91 ARC.P123) La premiere bicyclette (53x47cm-21x19in) s. (F.FR 22500)
£2736	$4761	(25-Mar-91 ARC.P121/R) La jeune lectrice (45x49cm-18x19in) s. (F.FR 27500)
£2786	$4848	(25-Mar-91 ARC.P127/R) Nature-morte a la campagne (80x60cm-31x24in) s. (F.FR 28000)
£3274	$5631	(15-May-91 AGB.P142/R) Les jouets (73x88cm-29x35in) s. (F.FR 33000)
£4975	$8657	(25-Mar-91 ARC.P122/R) Le dimanche (74x92cm-29x36in) s. (F.FR 50000)

BOGARD, Francoise (20th C) French
£559	$1118	(7-Feb-91 R.P222) Quand le rabin chante (97x130cm-38x51in) s. acrylic mixed canvas (F.FR 5500)
£495	*$885*	*(14-Apr-91 R.P179 b) Dans la foret du Baal Chem Tov (89x116cm-35x46in) s. mixed media canvas (F.FR 5000)*
£508	*$1016*	*(7-Feb-91 R.P149/R) Quand le rabin pleure (89x116cm-35x46in) s. mixed media canvas (F.FR 5000)*

BOGDANI, Jakob (1660-1724) Hungarian
£7653	$15000	(7-Nov-90 B.SF1040/R) Still life with mixed fruit and two exotic birds (91x122cm-36x48in)
£11952	$20558	(14-May-91 GF.L2032/R) Still life with flowers, fruit and parrot (73x119cm-29x47in) (S.FR 30000)
£13000	$23270	(12-Apr-91 C40/R) Still life with parakeet and mixed fruit on ledge (40x47cm-16x19in)
£13333	$26000	(11-Oct-90 SY.NY170/R) Still life of standing cup with flowers, silver platter and peaches (127x101cm-50x40in)
£18000	$29700	(12-Jul-91 C61/R) Concert of birds (152x183cm-60x72in) s.

BOGDANI, Jakob (attrib) (1660-1724) Hungarian
| £1854 | $3577 | (12-Dec-90 BU.S120/R) Still life of marrow, apples and pears (29x36cm-11x14in) (S.KR 20000) |
| £4800 | $9456 | (31-Oct-90 S113/R) Still life of fruit on stone ledge (46x39cm-18x15in) |

BOGDANI, Jakob (circle) (1660-1724) Hungarian
£4895	$9448	(12-Dec-90 N.M355/R) Parrot, cacadu, pheasants, doves and rabbits in hilly wooded landscape (166x115cm-65x45in) (DM 14000)
£5500	$10450	(28-Feb-91 B41/R) Study of spaniel standing amid mixed fruit (54x63cm-21x25in)
£9500	$18525	(25-Oct-90 CSK105/R) Exotic birds, ducks and fowl by fountain in ornamental park (152x183cm-60x72in)

BOGDANI, Jakob (style) (1660-1724) Hungarian
£1198	$2240	(1-Sep-90 CH.AM123) Summer flowers around an urn and fruit with landscape beyond (78x150cm-31x59in) a dessus-de-porte (D.FL 4000)
£2800	$5460	(22-Oct-90 SWS1512) Ducks and birds in landscape setting (71x58cm-28x23in)
£5500	$9075	(10-Jul-91 S56/R) Silver pheasant, ducks and ibis in landscape (135x95cm-53x37in)
£6000	$11700	(26-Oct-90 C97/R) Mixed flowers in a basket with a parrot and fruit by a broken plinth (73x119cm-29x47in)
£7200	$14184	(14-Nov-90 S65/R) Scarlet macaw, ducks and green-backed gallinule in landscape (135x95cm-53x37in)

BOGDANI, Jakob and JERVAS, Charles (attrib) (18th C) Hungarian/British
| £2287 | $3750 | (19-Jun-91 B.SF1709/R) Young girl seated in park holding bunch of grapes and feeding cockatoo (107x102cm-42x40in) |

BOGDANOFF-BJELSKI, Nikolai (1868-1945) Russian
| £15854 | $31073 | (6-Nov-90 SY.AM82/R) Ukrainian girls (134x104cm-53x41in) s.d.19 (D.FL 52000) |

BOGDANOVE, Abraham J (1888-1946) American
| £2197 | $3800 | (21-May-91 CE.NY652) Lowtide surf (76x91cm-30x36in) s. masonite |
| £3006 | $5200 | (21-May-91 CE.NY658) Locomotive rock (91x76cm-36x30in) s.d. masonite |

BOGERT, George H (1864-1944) American
| £1027 | $1900 | (8-Mar-91 S.BM147/R) Golden twilight (71x102cm-28x40in) s. |
| £1077 | $2100 | (20-Oct-90 W.W50/R) Early morning, low tide (41x61cm-16x24in) s.d.1887 |

BOGGIO, Emile (1857-1920) French/Venezuelan
| £8140 | $14000 | (15-May-91 CH.NY65/R) Vent sur le Strand Nervi (46x37cm-18x15in) s.d.1908 panel |
| *£1046* | *$1778* | *(29-May-91 GL.P176) Venise, Ponte Guerria Degli Arditi (23x31cm-9x12in) i. W/C (F.FR 10500)* |

BOGGS, Frank Myers see FRANK-BOGGS

BOGH, Carl Henrik (1827-1893) Danish
£580	$951	(20-Jun-91 B5/R) Stag with does in mountainous lake landscape (17x22cm-7x9in) s.d.1876
£952	$1846	(22-Aug-90 RAS.K167/R) Landscape with piglets enjoying sunshine (42x62cm-17x24in) s. (D.KR 11000)
£1792	$3584	(6-Feb-91 RAS.K149/R) The Prodigal son (29x40cm-11x16in) s. (D.KR 20000)
£3142	$6189	(14-Nov-90 RAS.K488/R) From farmyard where girl watches rabbits and goat from steps (56x61cm-22x24in) s.d.1863 (D.KR 35000)
£3380	$5746	(28-May-91 AB.S4747/R) Pigs in farmyard (31x40cm-12x16in) s. (S.KR 36000)
£7186	$12000	(7-Jun-91 SY.NY116/R) Three pigs in a summer landscape (41x62cm-16x24in) s.

BOGLE, John (c.1746-1803) British
£5000	*$8250*	*(11-Jul-91 S256/R) Portrait of architect seated resting upon lectern (6x?cm-2x?in) min.s.d.1785 gold frame glazed hair oval*

BOGLER, Karl (1837-1866) German
£839	$1636	(12-Oct-90 AW.H1365/R) Idyllic village scene with children playing outside timber framed houses (19x23cm-7x9in) s.i.verso (DM 2500)

BOGMAN, Hermanus Adrianus Charles (jnr) (1890-?) Dutch
£1078	$1875	(26-Mar-91 VN.R10/R) Houseboats on the Moerweg in The Hague (34x44cm-13x17in) s. panel (D.FL 3600)

BOGMAN, Hermanus Charles Christiaan (1861-1921) Dutch
£515	$845	(18-Jun-91 VN.R32) Cows by a farm in polder landscape (26x40cm-10x16in) s. panel (D.FL 1700)

BOGUET, Didier (1755-1839) French
£4286	$8443	(16-Nov-90 PLF.P24/R) Vue d'un jardin (27x35cm-11x14in) s. (F.FR 42000)

BOHATSCH, Erwin (20th C) ?
£1280	$2214	(10-May-91 S.Z6) Town II (100x90cm-39x35in) s.i.d.1984verso (S.FR 3200)

BOHEMEN, Kees van (1928-1986) Dutch
£3604	$6234	(22-May-91 CH.AM648/R) Abstract composition (49x64cm-19x25in) s. (D.FL 12000)
£3604	$6234	(22-May-91 CH.AM653/R) Abstract composition (60x92cm-24x36in) s.d.1959 verso (D.FL 12000)
£13622	$26291	(13-Dec-90 SY.AM369/R) Untitled (140x140cm-55x55in) s.d.77 (D.FL 44000)
£18576	$35851	(12-Dec-90 CH.AM435/R) Figures in landscape (140x200cm-55x79in) s.d.77 (D.FL 60000)
£901	*$1559*	*(22-May-91 CH.AM742) Abstract composition (40x58cm-16x23in) s.d.59 brush ink W/C (D.FL 3000)*
£1502	*$2598*	*(22-May-91 CH.AM741/R) Nudes in interior (53x73cm-21x29in) s.d.23-1-81 black chk pastel (D.FL 5000)*
£1548	*$2988*	*(12-Dec-90 CH.AM484/R) Liggende ontmoeting (48x62cm-19x24in) s.d.75 mixed media (D.FL 5000)*
£1858	*$3585*	*(13-Dec-90 SY.AM397/R) Untitled (54x74cm-21x29in) s.d.26-1-81 pastel crayon (D.FL 6000)*
£1920	*$3705*	*(13-Dec-90 SY.AM376/R) Untitled (74x98cm-29x39in) s.d.83 W/C pastel crayon pencil (D.FL 6200)*
£2477	*$4780*	*(13-Dec-90 SY.AM378/R) Untitled (72x96cm-28x38in) s.d.21-6-84 gouache W/C pastel crayon (D.FL 8000)*

BOHEMIAN SCHOOL (?) Bohemian
£4000	$6520	(4-Jul-91 C595/R) Portrait of queen, seated, wearing embroidered dress, with sceptre and putto (127x84cm-50x33in) c.1700

BOHEMIAN SCHOOL, 15th C Bohemian
£2622	$5061	(10-Dec-90 L.K10) Pentecost (94x105cm-37x41in) panel (DM 7500)
£9231	$18000	(10-Oct-90 CH.NY41/R) St Francis receiving the stigmata in fantastical rocky landscape (44x32cm-17x13in) l. gold ground panel

BOHEMIAN SCHOOL, 17th C Bohemian
£1700	$2941	(20-May-91 SWS172/R) Portrait of a man (76x63cm-30x25in)

BOHEMIAN SCHOOL, 18th C Bohemian
£1714	$3377	(14-Nov-90 D.V316/R) Portrait of Kreiskommissar Anton Stephan Biener of Bienenberg, Leitmeritz (88x72cm-35x28in) l.verso (A.S 35000)
£2400	$4152	(20-May-91 SWS45) A spaniel disturbing a hen and her chicks (84x120cm-33x47in)

BOHM, Eduard (1830-?) Austrian
£1365	$2676	(24-Nov-90 SA.A688/R) Mountainous river valley (50x39cm-20x15in) s. (DM 4000)
£1470	$2910	(31-Jan-91 D.V94/R) Hunting scene in the Praterauen (42x52cm-17x20in) s. (A.S 30000)
£1710	$3249	(28-Feb-91 D.V5/R) Mountainous river landscape (74x100cm-29x39in) s. (A.S 35000)

BOHM, Max (1868-1923) American
£1534	$2500	(5-Jul-91 S.W3013/R) Reveries (117x89cm-46x35in) s.d.1890

BOHM, Pal (1839-1905) Hungarian
£1014 $1723   (28-May-91 KF.M139/R) Gypsy family resting (34x42cm-13x17in) s.d.1868 (DM 3000)
£1199 $2146   (13-Mar-91 N.M453/R) Children in puszta landscape with windmill and farmhouses beyond (54x45cm-21x18in) s.l. (DM 3500)
£3125 $5250   (17-Jul-91 SY.NY312/R) Venus with putti, flowers and doves (55x121cm-22x48in) s.l.
£3353 $5800   (21-May-91 CE.NY107/R) Gypsy encampment (68x104cm-27x41in) s.l.
£3729 $6078   (3-Jul-91 WE.MU17/R) At the campfire (65x101cm-26x40in) s.l. (DM 11000)

BOHM, Pal (attrib) (1839-1905) Hungarian
£750 $1260   (28-Apr-91 FE.P72) Enfants Tziganes (73x60cm-29x24in) i. verso (F.FR 7500)

BOHMER, Heinrich (1852-?) German
£1284 $2503   (26-Oct-90 KM.K1111) Wooded landscape with deer by stream (70x105cm-28x41in) s. i.verso (DM 3800)

BOHN, German von (1812-1899) German
£3438 $6704   (21-Oct-90 L.C53/R) La charite chretienne s.d.1876 panel triptych (F.FR 34000)

BOHRDT, Hans (1857-?) German
£800 $1312   (18-Jun-91 PH118/R) View of Funchal, Madeira, at sunset (81x120cm-32x47in) s. s.l.verso
£517 $925   (12-Apr-91 BM.B566) SS Oregon offshore (52x34cm-20x13in) s.i.indis.d.89 (DM 1550)

BOHROD, Aaron (1907-) American
£1599 $2750   (15-May-91 SY.NY263 a/R) Off Wylie Street, Pittsburgh (46x61cm-18x24in) s. masonite
£1734 $3000   (10-May-91 S.BM158/R) Gingerbread boy (20x15cm-8x6in) s. i.verso panel
£1164 $2200   (27-Sep-90 CH.NY258/R) Abondonment (37x49cm-15x19in) s. casein paper

BOICHARD, Georges Lucien (19th C) French
£1711 $3250   (27-Feb-91 SY.NY54/R) L'elegante (35x26cm-14x10in) s.d.83 panel

BOIKO, Serguei (1946-) Russian
£603 $989   (19-Jun-91 ARC.P242/R) Nature morte aux trois roubles (50x60cm-20x24in) mono.d.1991 canvas pasted on hardboard (F.FR 6000)

BOILEAU, J J (19th C) ?
£700 $1379   (15-Nov-90 S31) Design for the carpet in the Great Drawing Room, Windsor Castle (33x44cm-13x17in) i. gouache over pencil irregular

BOILLE, Luigi (1926-) ?
£682 $1290   (27-Sep-90 F.M103) Hyperbaroque IV (116x89cm-46x35in) s.d.1961 verso (I.L 1500000)
£4490 $8845   (16-Nov-90 EA.Z333/R) No 4 (130x81cm-51x32in) s.d.1955 (S.FR 11000)

BOILLY (?) French
£3410 $6650   (14-Oct-90 D.L84 a) Portrait du Baron Dubois (22x16cm-9x6in) (F.FR 34000)

BOILLY (style) (18/19th C) French
£1733 $3327   (30-Nov-90 APT.P153/R) Le billet doux (54x45cm-21x18in) (F.FR 17000)

BOILLY, Louis Leopold (1761-1845) French
£550 $1100   (7-Feb-91 C47) Portrait of a lady, bust length, wearing a brown dress (22x16cm-9x6in)
£1006 $1932   (27-Nov-90 SY.AM3579/R) Portrait of man, possibly self portrait (15x12cm-6x5in) panel (D.FL 3300)
£2500 $4325   (22-May-91 GS.B2330) Elegant figures courting in interior (45x38cm-18x15in) (S.FR 6300)
£2564 $5000   (26-Oct-90 SY.NY23/R) Portrait of gentleman (22x16cm-9x6in) i.d.1807stretcher
£2775 $5383   (7-Dec-90 CN.P156/R) Portrait d'homme (22x17cm-9x7in) (F.FR 27000)
£2811 $4526   (27-Jun-91 APT.P230/R) Portrait d'une jeune femme au collier de perles (24x19cm-9x7in) (F.FR 28000)
£3535 $6929   (11-Feb-91 D.L1/R) Portrait d'homme au col de fourrure (22x16cm-9x6in) (F.FR 35000)
£3590 $7000   (26-Oct-90 SY.NY22/R) Portrait of lady in petal hat (22x17cm-9x7in)
£4103 $8000   (26-Oct-90 SY.NY21/R) Portrait of gentleman wearing the Legion d'Honneur (22x17cm-9x7in) i.verso
£1172 $2262   (12-Dec-90 CD.P1) Homme vu de dos assis a terre (25x22cm-10x9in) black chk sanguine (F.FR 11500)
£1200 $2124   (22-Mar-91 BG.P10/R) Portrait de femme (21x17cm-8x7in) pierre noire white chk. (F.FR 12000)

BOILLY, Louis Leopold (attrib) (1761-1845) French
£1355 $2330   (14-May-91 GF.L2356/R) Portrait of gentleman holding scroll (81x64cm-32x25in) i.d.1810 (S.FR 3400)

BOILLY, Louis Leopold (circle) (1761-1845) French
£2994 $5000 (23-Jan-91 D.NY24) Portrait of lady with red embroidered shawl
     (91x71cm-36x28in)
£4523 $7417 (21-Jun-91 SY.MO309/R) Femme, enfant et chien dans un encadrement ovale
     (45x36cm-18x14in) (F.FR 45000)

BOILLY, Louis Leopold (style) (1761-1845) French
£1456 $2344 (27-Jun-91 APT.P222/R) Portrait d'une famille dans un parc
     (54x45cm-21x18in) (F.FR 14500)

BOISECQ, Salomon Alfred (1911-) French
£603 $1158 (24-Feb-91 FE.P55) Le Zuin (38x46cm-15x18in) s. (F.FR 6000)

BOISROND, Francois (20th C) ?
£1511 $2462 (16-Jun-91 CC.P84 b/R) Sans titre (151x64cm-59x25in) paper (F.FR 15000)
£1786 $3500 (6-Nov-90 CE.NY180/R) Untitled (213x151cm-84x59in) s.d.84 verso acrylic
     cotton
£3015 $4945 (23-Jun-91 P.V90/R) Sans titre (120x152cm-47x60in) acrylic paper
     (F.FR 30000)
£4077 $7870 (16-Dec-90 GL.P142/R) Sans titre (100x70cm-39x28in) mono. s.d.88 verso
     acrylic paper (F.FR 40000)
£4133 $8059 (23-Oct-90 CSC.P89/R) Sans titre (210x129cm-83x51in) s.d.83 verso
     acrylic lacquer (F.FR 41000)
£4221 $6923 (23-Jun-91 P.V89/R) Sans titre (130x186cm-51x73in) s.d.1983 verso
     acrylic (F.FR 42000)
£4623 $7582 (23-Jun-91 P.V88/R) Sans titre (154x185cm-61x73in) s.d.1983 verso
     acrylic (F.FR 46000)

BOISSEAU, Alfred (1823-1903) American
£5263 $10316 (20-Nov-90 JOY.T159/R) Artist and models (92x132cm-36x52in) s.d.1895
     (C.D 12000)

BOISSELIER, Antoine (1790-1857) French
£2446 $4697 (30-Nov-90 APT.P162/R) Pecheurs au pied d'une cascade (41x32cm-16x13in)
     num 135 verso (F.FR 24000)

BOISSELIER, Felix (elder) (1776-1811) French
£20513 $40000 (23-Oct-90 SY.NY2/R) Le berger (197x146cm-78x57in) s.i.d.1808

BOISSET, Jean Baptiste (18th C) French
£17085 $28020 (21-Jun-91 SY.MO255/R) Trompe l'oeil a la gravure et aux cartes a jouer
     (49x59cm-19x23in) (F.FR 170000)

BOISSEVAIN, William (1927-) Australian
£930 $1563 (22-Apr-91 SY.ME46) Burning off (83x68cm-33x27in) s.d.79 board
     (A.D 2000)
£1581 $2657 (22-Apr-91 SY.ME5/R) Mixed flowers (90x120cm-35x47in) s.d.88 board
     (A.D 3400)
£1594 $3139 (31-Oct-90 CH.S89) Group of Aboriginals (90x121cm-35x48in) s.d.86
     acrylic board (A.D 4000)
£1600 $3008 (17-Sep-90 SY.ME147/R) Still life (89x120cm-35x47in) s.d.78 acrylic
     board (A.D 3600)
£1600 $2736 (30-Jul-91 SWS65/R) White flowers in a vase (90x101cm-35x40in) s.d.'76
     board
£1867 $3509 (17-Sep-90 SY.ME96/R) Landscape (90x121cm-35x48in) s.d.78 board
     (A.D 4200)
£2000 $3760 (17-Sep-90 SY.ME12/R) Landscape (90x120cm-35x47in) s.d.78 board
     (A.D 4500)
£756 $1420 *(17-Sep-90 SY.ME20/R) Belmont area, Western Australia (31x48cm-12x19in)*
     s. W/C (A.D 1700)

BOISSIEU, Jean Jacques de (1736-1810) French
£612 *$1188* *(8-Dec-90 GAB.G2007) Foret (33x22cm-13x9in) mono.s.d.89 pen wash*
     (S.FR 1500)
£1358 *$2662* *(24-Jan-91 AGS.P39/R) Vue d'un village avec un chateau fort sur une*
     colline (5x23cm-2x9in) wash traces crayon (F.FR 13500)
£2028 *$3914* *(10-Dec-90 L.K212/R) La fontaine de Lorsiere pres de Dargoire*
     (31x43cm-12x17in) mono.d.1790 indian ink brush W/C (DM 5800)
£4500 *$7605* *(16-Apr-91 C210/R) A clump of trees (17x21cm-7x8in) s. blk.chk.ink wash*

BOISSIEU, Jean Jacques de (attrib) (1736-1810) French
£734 *$1417* *(14-Dec-90 LEB.P47) Vue d'une ferme et de ses dependances*
     (16x21cm-6x8in) i. verso blk.crayon pen Indian ink wash (F.FR 7200)
£738 *$1440* *(12-Oct-90 AW.H1177/R) Old man with stick standing and four women in*
     different positions (15x21cm-6x8in) indian ink brush pen over pencil
     (DM 2200)

BOIT, Charles (1662-1727) Swedish
£1800 *$3456* *(18-Dec-90 C30/R) Portrait of James Fitz-James, Duke of Berwick*
     (3x?cm-1x?in) min.s.verso enamel gilt-metal frame oval

BOIT, Edward Darley (1840-1915) American
£642 $1200 (30-Aug-90 MFA.C168/R) Landscape with figure (56x66cm-22x26in) s.d.1911

BOITARD, Francois (c.1670-c.1715) French
£579 $1100   (9-Jan-91 CH.NY26/R) Judgement of Solomon (23x27cm-9x11in) i. ink wash
                     vellum

BOITEL, Maurice (1919-) French
£1109 $2162   (27-Oct-90 LT.P97) Le Jardin a Ambazac (50x61cm-20x24in) s.d.61
                     (F.FR 11000)

BOIVIN, Emile (1846-?) French
£602 $1174   (12-Oct-90 ZZ.F5) Plage en Tunisie (40x61cm-16x24in) s. (F.FR 6000)
£717 $1406   (11-Nov-90 ZZ.F10/R) Interieur de Palais Oriental (46x33cm-18x13in) s.
                     (F.FR 7000)

BOIZOT, Antoine (1752-1817) French
£1947 $3816   (11-Nov-90 M.V47/R) Philosophe se dirigeant vers son ermitage
                     (25x32cm-10x13in) s.d.1816 panel (F.FR 19000)

BOKATSIAMTRES, B (?) Greek
£1200 $2280   (26-Feb-91 ACA739) Greek village street scene (28x41cm-11x16in) s.
                     canvas on board

BOKLEN, Hilde (1897-1987) German
£751 $1419   (25-Sep-90 FN.S2121/R) Two parrots seated on bar (60x44cm-24x17in)
                     s.d.1922 board (DM 2200)

BOL, Ferdinand (1616-1680) Dutch
£4124 $8082   (16-Feb-91 GF.H5/R) Portrait of man before landscape (69x60cm-27x24in)
                     s. (DM 12000)
£4211 $8000   (8-Jan-91 SY.NY28/R) Study of a sleeping figure (42x63cm-17x25in) pen
                     over blk.chk.

BOL, Ferdinand (style) (1616-1680) Dutch
£1000 $1950   (22-Oct-90 SWS1417) Nathan chastising David (99x124cm-39x49in)

BOL, Hans (1534-1593) Dutch
£1937 $3738   (14-Dec-90 LEB.P82/R) Allegorie (15x18cm-6x7in) pen Indian ink wash
                     htd.white traces sanguinne (F.FR 19000)

BOLDINI (?) Italian
£1100 $2134   (3-Dec-90 LS865) Still life of roses (46x41cm-18x16in) W/C

BOLDINI, Giovanni (1842-1931) Italian
£7591 $14879   (20-Nov-90 BG.P12/R) La femme a l'eventail (40x31cm-16x12in) s.
                     (F.FR 75000)
£124513 $242800   (23-Oct-90 SY.NY97/R) Portrait of Mrs Ruth Frost, nee Sterling
                     (201x102cm-79x40in) s.d.1892
£173410 $300000   (22-May-91 SY.NY64/R) In garden (41x29cm-16x11in) s.d.74 cradled panel
£208092 $360000   (22-May-91 SY.NY83/R) Portrait of Pedro and Luis Subercaseaux
                     (135x126cm-53x50in) s.d.1887
£219653 $380000   (23-May-91 CH.NY171/R) Portrait of Josefina Errazuriz holding cat
                     (188x105cm-74x41in) s.d.1910
£429 $849   (1-Feb-91 DE.B3) Portrait of a young woman (15x11cm-6x4in) s. chk
                     (P.Z 8000000)
£7046 $13811   (21-Nov-90 F.M163/R) Nudo di giovane donna (35x22cm-14x9in)
                     i.d.1931verso pencil double-sided (I.L 15500000)
£7645 $14679   (2-Dec-90 M.V70/R) Comtesse de Rasty. Femme a la toilette crayon
                     double-sided (F.FR 75000)
£11820 $23166   (22-Nov-90 SY.MI80/R) Figura femminile e vari schizzi (57x37cm-22x15in)
                     chl chk (I.L 26000000)
£18484 $35675   (11-Dec-90 CH.R221/R) Studio di scultura equestre (44x29cm-17x11in) W/C
                     cardboard (I.L 40000000)
£21000 $41000   (18-Oct-90 F.M76/R) Cheveaux de relais (54x69cm-21x27in) s. ink
                     (I.L 47000000)
£22985 $39994   (25-Mar-91 PLF.P23/R) Portrait de Madame Emme Bardac, devenue madame
                     Debussy en 1908 (49x34cm-19x13in) s.d.1905 W/C (F.FR 231000)

BOLDUC, David (1945-) Canadian
£2525 $4369   (6-May-91 SY.T200/R) Buoys and beacons (178x203cm-70x80in) d.1980 verso
                     acrylic canvas (C.D 5000)

BOLE, Jeanne (fl.1870-1883) French
£1282 $2500   (26-Oct-90 SY.NY149/R) Portrait of young boy in boater (33x25cm-13x10in)
                     s.

BOLENS, Ernest (1881-1959) Swiss
£1526 $2991   (21-Nov-90 SY.Z88/R) Still life of flowers (57x47cm-22x19in) s.d.11
                     (S.FR 3800)
£2579 $4308   (5-Jun-91 SY.Z93/R) Bunch of flowers in vase (61x50cm-24x20in) s.d.10
                     (S.FR 6500)

BOLIN, Gustave (1920-?) Swedish
£1462 $2530   (22-May-91 BA.S326/R) Model resting (100x100cm-39x39in) s. (S.KR 15500)
£1835 $3541   (16-Dec-90 GL.P194) Paysage ensoleille (38x46cm-15x18in) s.d.55
                     (F.FR 18000)
£1988 $3360   (16-Apr-91 I.N13) Bord de plage (50x61cm-20x24in) s.d.1956 (F.FR 20000)
£2191 $3725   (29-May-91 GL.P84/R) Paris (120x120cm-47x47in) s. (F.FR 22000)

194

BOLIN, Gustave (1920-?) Swedish-cont.
£2191 $3725   (29-May-91 GL.P8282/R) Les marronniers (120x120cm-47x47in) s.
                (F.FR 22000)

BOLINBROKE, Minna (fl.1888-1926) British
£620 $1215   (21-Nov-90 B78) Poultry yard (21x25cm-8x10in) s.d.1905 W/C

BOLLIGER, Rodolphe (19th C) Swiss
£898 $1760   (6-Nov-90 GF.L2528/R) Woman in costume with bunch of flowers
                (73x54cm-29x21in) s.d.1910 (S.FR 2200)

BOLLONGIER, Hans (1600-1644) Dutch
£33000 $53790   (5-Jul-91 C352/R) Mixed fruit, peas in pods with fly on ledge
                  (27x34cm-11x13in) mono.d.1650 panel

BOLLONGIER, Hans (style) (1600-1644) Dutch
£2200 $3586   (2-Jul-91 PH349) Four tulips in glass vase (40x30cm-16x12in) panel

BOLOGNESE SCHOOL Italian
£1988 $3360   (18-Apr-91 APT.P6) Le Christ et la Samaritaine (87x110cm-34x43in) panel
                 (F.FR 20000)
£3352 $6000   (11-Apr-91 SY.NY97/R) Nymphs and putti in landscape making offerings to
                 statue of goddess (96x132cm-38x52in) c.1700
£3874 $7437   (30-Nov-90 APT.P12/R) Venus enchainant un satyre (50x65cm-20x26in) oval
                 (F.FR 38000)
£7692 $15000 (11-Oct-90 SY.NY106/R) Head of boy (25x18cm-10x7in) c.1600 canvas on
                 panel
*£2600 $4238   (2-Jul-91 C67/R) Confirmation of Rule of Carmelites by Patriarch of
                  Jerusalem (10x20cm-4x8in) bodycol gold vellum c.1300*
*£3000 $4890   (2-Jul-91 C121/R) Studies of angels, putti and cherubim. Kneeling friar
                  (41x26cm-16x10in) d.1693 verso black red chk double-sided*

BOLOGNESE SCHOOL, 14th C Italian
£5800 $9802   (17-Apr-91 S146/R) Christ on the Cross (42x25cm-17x10in) tempera panel

BOLOGNESE SCHOOL, 15th C Italian
£3077 $6000   (10-Oct-90 CH.NY129/R) Madonna and Child enthroned with female martyr
                 saint (51x37cm-20x15in) gold ground panel
£14118 $24000 (31-May-91 CH.NY22/R) St Nicholas (41x22cm-16x9in) i. tempera gold
                 ground panel

BOLOGNESE SCHOOL, 16/17th C Italian
£2234 $4244   (2-Mar-91 KRA.D248/R) Christ child sleeping on cross in landscape
                 (31x41cm-12x16in) i. panel (DM 6500)

BOLOGNESE SCHOOL, 16th C Italian
*£2000 $3860   (11-Dec-90 C25/R) Saint Helena curing a sick man with the true cross
                  (21x17cm-8x7in) blk.chk.ink wash htd.white*
*£11000 $17930   (1-Jul-91 S37/R) Death of Sons of Niobe (20x26cm-8x10in) pen wash over
                  red chk htd white*

BOLOGNESE SCHOOL, 17th C Italian
£1491 $2520   (18-Apr-91 APT.P14/R) La Nativite (63x48cm-25x19in) (F.FR 15000)
£1506 $2425   (27-Jun-91 APT.P45/R) Etude pour un jeune garcon (36cm-14ins circular)
                 panel round (F.FR 15000)
£1594 $2741   (14-May-91 GF.L2022/R) Mary Magdalen (61x48cm-24x19in) (S.FR 4000)
£1607 $2700   (17-Jul-91 SY.NY101/R) Portrait of a Saint (48x37cm-19x15in) panel
£1868 $3250   (27-Mar-91 B.SF4025) The cardsharp (75x96cm-30x38in)
£1903 $3311   (25-Mar-91 SY.F595) Apollo e Venere in un paesaggio (81x107cm-32x42in)
                 (I.L 4200000)
£2041 $3959   (8-Dec-90 GAB.G2021/R) Scene mythologique - Narcisse (83x65cm-33x26in)
                 (S.FR 5000)
£2492 $4336   (25-Mar-91 SY.F704/R) Ulisse e Circe (57x53cm-22x21in) (I.L 5500000)
£2564 $5000   (11-Oct-90 SY.NY66/R) St Apollonia (71x59cm-28x23in)
£3077 $6000   (11-Oct-90 SY.NY133/R) Portrait of architect (114x86cm-45x34in) i.d.1625
£3180 $6265   (29-Oct-90 SY.F626) Paesaggio con tempesta (126x188cm-50x74in)
                 (I.L 7000000)
£3408 $6713   (29-Oct-90 SY.F610/R) Madonna in preghiera (45x50cm-18x20in)
                 (I.L 7500000)
£3423 $5750   (17-Jul-91 SY.NY49/R) Hercules and Anteus (69x53cm-27x21in)
£3911 $7000   (11-Apr-91 SY.NY94 a/R) Saint Sebastian (132x91cm-52x36in)
£4091 $8019   (20-Nov-90 F.R141) San Giovanni Battista (212x100cm-83x39in)
                 (I.L 9000000)
£5701 $9520   (4-Jun-91 CH.R480/R) Venere con amorino (175x113cm-69x44in)
                 (I.L 12500000)
£6000 $10140 (17-Apr-91 S135/R) The Flight into Egypt (76x68cm-30x27in)
£7362 $12000 (5-Jul-91 S.W3014/R) St. John the Baptist (99x74cm-39x29in)
£8222 $15951 (7-Dec-90 SY.MO76/R) Marie Madeleine (95x79cm-37x31in) (F.FR 80000)
£10030 $19559 (9-Oct-90 GGL.L8/R) Scene allegorique (154x154cm-61x61in) (F.FR 100000)
*£955 $1566   (18-Jun-91 APT.P36/R) Repos pendant la fuite en Egypte (26x19cm-10x7in)
                  pen wash htd.white (F.FR 9500)*
*£1050 $1712   (1-Jul-91 S162) Shepherd (21x17cm-8x7in) red chk htd white over black
                  chk*
*£2105 $4000   (8-Jan-91 SY.NY177) The head of a bearded man looking down
                  (22x18cm-9x7in) chk.*

BOLOGNESE SCHOOL, 17th C Italian-cont.
£2600 $4238 (2-Jul-91 C277/R) Reclining nude, seen from behind and study of man in pain (32x22cm-13x9in) red white chk

BOLOGNESE SCHOOL, 18th C Italian
£2471 $4200 (31-May-91 CH.NY177/R) Roman charity (85x67cm-33x26in)
£2569 $4985 (7-Dec-90 SY.MO128/R) La naissance de Venus (43x32cm-17x13in) (F.FR 25000)
£4103 $8000 (11-Oct-90 SY.NY86/R) The Rest on the Flight into Egypt (54x42cm-21x17in) oval
£4422 $7252 (21-Jun-91 SY.MO198/R) Le Christ et les Apotres (29x16cm-11x6in) (F.FR 44000)
£9092 $17820 (20-Nov-90 F.R107/R) Danae (130x170cm-51x67in) (I.L 20000000)
£14800 $28711 (3-Dec-90 SY.F1026/R) Adorazione dei pastori (150x112cm-59x44in) (I.L 32000000)
£2052 $3632 (19-Mar-91 F.M357/R) Martirio di Sant'Erasmo (38x45cm-15x18in) pen W/C ink over sanguine (I.L 4500000)
£2200 $3586 (4-Jul-91 B60) A classical landscape with sportsmen and their dogs in the foreground (49x65cm-19x26in) gouache
£3874 $7437 (27-Nov-90 APT.P43/R) Projet de decor de theatre avec interieur d'une cour de palais de ruines (42x73cm-17x29in) pen wash (F.FR 38000)

BOLOGNESE SCHOOL, 19th C Italian
£1352 $2421 (8-Apr-91 CH.R116) Ritratto di Luigi Galvani in atto di sperimentare l'elettricita animale (42x30cm-17x12in) bears sig.d.1867 (I.L 3000000)
£997 $1734 (25-Mar-91 SY.F581/R) Fantasia architettonica (78x68cm-31x27in) gouache canvas oval (I.L 2200000)

BOLOMEY, Benjamin Samuel (1739-1819) Swiss
£2072 $3563 (14-May-91 GF.L2317/R) Portrait of man with young boy (65x60cm-26x24in) (S.FR 5200)

BOLOTOWSKY, Ilya (1907-?) Russian
£1888 $3700 (12-Feb-91 SY.NY383/R) Untitled (30cm-12ins circular) s.d.72
£4082 $8000 (6-Nov-90 CE.NY90/R) Yellow tondo (100cm-39ins circular) s.d.71 acrylic

BOLT, Niels Peter (1886-) Danish
£1074 $2094 (13-Oct-90 KRA.D350) Interior with woman seated (94x70cm-37x28in) s.d.1916 panel (DM 3200)

BOLT, Ron (1938-) Canadian
£987 $1944 (30-Oct-90 SY.T126) Vial of Wrath (122x137cm-48x54in) s.i.d.79verso (C.D 2250)

BOLTANSKI, Christian (1944-) French
£7645 $14755 (16-Dec-90 GL.P146/R) Rire aux larmes (98x74cm-39x29in) s.i. gouache pastel photograph (F.FR 75000)
£7769 $13207 (2-Jun-91 GL.P189/R) Les malheurs de bebe (98x74cm-39x29in) s.d.1974 verso gouache pastel photograph (F.FR 78000)
£15152 $29697 (14-Feb-91 GL.P53/R) Sans titre (60x110cm-24x43in) s. mixed media (F.FR 150000)

BOLTON, T (18/19th C) ?
£800 $1552 (6-Dec-90 TL156/R) North West view of Ravensfield House and Park, Yorkshire (38x57cm-15x22in) s.i.d.1800 W/C htd gouache

BOLTON-JONES, Hugh see JONES, Hugh Bolton

BOLTRAFFIO, Giovanni Antonio (attrib) (1467-1516) Italian
£10000 $19000 (11-Jan-91 CH.NY64/R) The Madonna and child (43x31cm-17x12in) panel

BOLTRAFFIO, Giuseppe (circle) (?) ?
£17051 $33250 (10-Oct-90 APT.P467/R) L'Adoration des Mages (98x140cm-39x55in) panel (F.FR 170000)

BOMAN, Lars Henning (attrib) (1730-1799) Swedish
£1112 $2146 (12-Dec-90 BU.S10/R) Diversion from everyday life (27x20cm-11x8in) panel (S.KR 12000)

BOMBELLI, Sebastiano (1635-1719) Italian
£5251 $8821 (23-Apr-91 F.R40/R) Ritratto di magistrato della Serenissima (198x125cm-78x49in) (I.L 11500000)

BOMBERG, David (1890-1957) British
£5200 $9776 (20-Sep-90 C91/R) Miners (30x40cm-12x16in) s. paper
£7500 $14700 (8-Nov-90 C95/R) Self-portrait (60x49cm-24x19in) s.d.'31 board
£18000 $35280 (7-Nov-90 S101/R) The trees, Pitlochry towards Glencoe (40x52cm-16x20in) s.d.32
£18000 $35280 (8-Nov-90 C92/R) San Miguel, Toledo (21x32cm-8x13in) s.d.'29 i. label
£1050 $1712 (4-Jul-91 PHI82/R) Bargees (26x20cm-10x8in) s.i.d./19 ink wash over pencil double-sided
£1400 $2436 (27-Mar-91 S74/R) Vorticist study (32x26cm-13x10in) chk
£1500 $2940 (7-Nov-90 S32/R) Study for reading from the Torah (38x28cm-15x11in) pencil W/C

BOMBERG, David (1890-1957) British-cont.
£1900	$3705	(10-Oct-90 S79/R) Players resting, Ghetto Theatre (20x27cm-8x11in) ink wash over pencil
£2000	$3480	(27-Mar-91 S82/R) Study for dark street, Ronda (61x65cm-24x26in) chk sold with fragment of oil study
£2000	$3760	(20-Sep-90 C120/R) Design for New Art Salon poster, 1914-1918 (50x39cm-20x15in) pastel bodycol
£2300	$4531	(1-Nov-90 B19 a/R) The Cindad de Ronda, Andalusia (48x62cm-19x24in) s.d.56 chl
£3600	$7056	(25-Jan-91 C49/R) Theatre players (48x54cm-19x21in) chl W/C bodycol

BOMBLED, Louis Charles (1862-1927) French
£525	$1050	(6-Feb-91 D.NY12) Soldiers on horseback target shooting (33x41cm-13x16in) s.indist.d. board
£1000	$1640	(18-Jun-91 PH52) At the races (19x24cm-7x9in) s.

BOMBOIS, Camille (1883-?) French
£828	$1400	(1-May-91 D.NY13) Anglers in river landscape (5x8cm-2x3in) s.d.84 panel
£3173	$6250	(15-Nov-90 D.NY58/R) Roses in yellow vase (25x20cm-10x8in) s.
£3571	$7000	(12-Feb-91 SY.NY133/R) Landscape with figures by stream (15x23cm-6x9in) s.
£4615	$9000	(10-Oct-90 SY.NY92/R) Le Cure a Arcolay (15x20cm-6x8in) s.
£5440	$9738	(9-Apr-91 BG.P28/R) Etang avec nenuphars (16x23cm-6x9in) s. board (F.FR 55000)
£5500	$8855	(24-Jun-91 CSK202/R) Groc (27x22cm-11x9in) s.
£5780	$10000	(7-May-91 CE.NY44/R) Paysage pres de Tours (19x27cm-7x11in) s.
£6122	$12000	(14-Feb-91 CH.NY59/R) Le clown Baby (41x33cm-16x13in) s.
£7107	$14000	(13-Nov-90 CE.NY117/R) Vase de roses (24x32cm-9x13in) s. panel
£7614	$15000	(13-Nov-90 CE.NY59/R) Le pont du village (14x22cm-6x9in) s.
£8629	$17000	(2-Oct-90 CH.NY218/R) Paysage avec moutons (22x33cm-9x13in) s.
£8629	$17000	(13-Nov-90 CE.NY54/R) Vase de roses (99x99cm-39x39in) s. pair
£13848	$24787	(9-Apr-91 BG.P17/R) Paysage (58x72cm-23x28in) s.d.1931 (F.FR 140000)
£15029	$26000	(9-May-91 CH.NY238/R) Une petite denicheuse de nid (81x65cm-32x26in) s. i. stretcher
£16751	$33000	(3-Oct-90 SY.NY203/R) Apres l'ecole (53x74cm-21x29in) s.
£18367	$36000	(14-Feb-91 CH.NY88/R) La lettre de deuil (55x47cm-22x19in) s.

BOMMELS, Peter (1951-) German
£1164	$1898	(14-Jun-91 L.K777/R) Butterfly (100x60cm-39x24in) s.i.d.87 acrylic cotton (DM 3400)
£4110	$6699	(14-Jun-91 L.K776/R) Composition with darts (180x220cm-71x87in) s.d.85 acrylic (DM 12000)
£4437	$8696	(20-Nov-90 L.K145/R) Die Seefahrt und der Tod. Tauchen und Siegen. Jonas, leckender Fisch (104x84cm-41x33in) s.d.1981 dispersion set of three (DM 13000)

BOMPARD (19/20th C) ?
£2608	$5085	(12-Oct-90 ZZ.F72/R) Nature morte aux vase de fleurs (82x100cm-32x39in) both s. pair (F.FR 26000)

BOMPARD, Maurice (1857-1936) French
£1223	$2361	(12-Dec-90 ZZ.F27/R) Reines-marguerites dans un vase bleu (65x46cm-26x18in) s. (F.FR 12000)
£1468	$2892	(13-Nov-90 AB.S861/R) Venetian canal scene with gondola (81x65cm-32x26in) s.d.1894 (S.KR 16000)
£1584	$2804	(7-Apr-91 I.N46/R) Venise (26x33cm-10x13in) s. panel (F.FR 16000)
£1619	$3174	(20-Nov-90 APT.P253/R) Algerienne au voile vert (46x38cm-18x15in) s. (F.FR 16000)
£2273	$4068	(14-Apr-91 BU.H119/R) From North Africa (30x23cm-12x9in) s. panel (F.M 16000)
£2551	$4515	(20-Mar-91 KM.K1112/R) Canal scene with gondola and figures on bridge, Venice (81x65cm-32x26in) s.i.d.1894verso (DM 7500)
£8000	$13120	(21-Jun-91 C104/R) Waiting Odalsiques in interior (53x65cm-21x26in) s. panel

BOMPIANI, Augusto (1851-?) Italian
£1272	$2200	(10-May-91 S.W2121/R) Mishap at the well (53x33cm-21x13in) s. W/C

BOMPIANI, Roberto (1821-1908) Italian
£10405	$18000	(22-May-91 SY.NY273/R) Diana and maidens (167x129cm-66x51in)

BOMPIANI-BATTAGLIA, Clelia (1847-1927) Italian
£780	$1303	(5-Jun-91 PHK49/R) Pretty peasant woman off to market (53x37cm-21x15in) s.i. W/C
£1600	$3072	(29-Nov-90 B29 a) At the well (73x51cm-29x20in) s. W/C

BON, Angelo Del (1898-1952) Italian
£694	$1346	(3-Dec-90 F.M210) Leda e il cigno (18x28cm-7x11in) s. tempera paper (I.L 1500000)
£3209	$5263	(20-Jun-91 F.M348/R) Paesaggio montano (50x61cm-20x24in) s. (I.L 7000000)
£3377	$6585	(22-Oct-90 BR.M240/R) Natura morta (46x38cm-18x15in) s. (I.L 7500000)
£4159	$8027	(13-Dec-90 F.M384/R) Campagna milanese (66x96cm-26x38in) s.d.1937 (I.L 9000000)
£879	$1705	(3-Dec-90 F.M11) Vaso di fiori (38x32cm-15x13in) s. pastel W/C (I.L 1900000)

BONALUMI, Agostino (1935-) Italian
£2544	$4935	(3-Dec-90 CH.R42/R) Superficie rossa (40x40cm-16x16in) s.d.1965 oil canvas estroflessa (I.L 5500000)
£5319	$10318	(3-Dec-90 CH.R157/R) Superficie rossa (70x60cm-28x24in) s.d.1973 acrylic canvas estroflessa (I.L 11500000)
£6303	$12292	(22-Oct-90 BR.M97/R) Untitled (100x100cm-39x39in) s.d.1984 verso estroflessa canvas (I.L 14000000)
£7497	$14768	(30-Oct-90 F.R239/R) Untitled (130x140cm-51x55in) canvas estroflessa (I.L 16500000)
£18010	$35119	(22-Oct-90 BR.M44/R) Composizione (240x240cm-94x94in) s.d.1975 verso estroflessa canvas (I.L 40000000)
£1619	$3140	(3-Dec-90 CH.R41/R) Progretto (49x71cm-19x28in) s.d.1971 canvas collage ink paper on masonite (I.L 3500000)
£1666	$3249	(23-Oct-90 F.M6) Black (30x30cm-12x12in) s.d.1980verso canvas estroflessa (I.L 3700000)
£2840	$5453	(27-Nov-90 SY.M100/R) Composizione (47x67cm-19x26in) s.d.MI-71 mixed media estroflessa canvas board (I.L 6200000)
£3209	$5263	(20-Jun-91 F.M311/R) Senza titolo (100x81cm-39x32in) s.d.1966verso canvas estroflessa (I.L 7000000)
£3435	$6596	(27-Nov-90 SY.MI76/R) Rosso (60x70cm-24x28in) s.d.68verso estroflessa canvas (I.L 7500000)
£4531	$7883	(26-Mar-91 F.M82/R) Progetto superficie rossa (100x145cm-39x57in) s.d.72 collage mixed media board four panels (I.L 10000000)

BONAMICI, Louis (19/20th C) ?
£594	$1051	(7-Apr-91 I.N48) La baie des anges (32x41cm-13x16in) s. panel (F.FR 6000)
£842	$1490	(7-Apr-91 I.N47) Bord de mer (33x54cm-13x21in) s. panel (F.FR 8500)
£1217	$2410	(3-Feb-91 I.N28/R) Bord de mer (61x50cm-24x20in) s. (F.FR 12000)

BONAS, Jordi (1937-) French
£553	$989	(11-Mar-91 GL.P39) L'effort final (54x65cm-21x26in) s. (F.FR 5500)
£761	$1506	(28-Jan-91 PPB.P16) Composition aux chevaux (56x76cm-22x30in) s. (F.FR 7500)
£893	$1536	(19-May-91 ZZ.F179/R) Les chevaux a l'arrivee (50x61cm-20x24in) s. (F.FR 9000)
£1019	$1967	(12-Dec-90 APT.P70) Trot attele (73x92cm-29x36in) s. (F.FR 10000)
£419	$699	(4-Jun-91 R.T241/R) Steeple chase (56x75cm-22x30in) s. s.d.74 verso gouache W/C (C.D 800)

BONAVIA, Carlo (18th C) Italian
| £4221 | $6923 | (21-Jun-91 SY.MO216/R) Personnages pres d'une fontaine (63x50cm-25x20in) (F.FR 42000) |

BONAVIA, Carlo (circle) (18th C) Italian
| £1713 | $3066 | (8-Apr-91 CH.R58) Marina all'alba con pescatori (37x95cm-15x37in) (I.L 3800000) |

BONCI, Elia (1866-?) ?
| £1500 | $2580 | (17-May-91 C230/R) Flower seller (91x70cm-36x28in) s. |

BOND, R H (19th C) British
| £990 | $1900 | (20-Feb-91 D.NY11) Watermill at Hartford (58x114cm-23x45in) s. |

BOND, Richard Sebastian (circle) (1808-1886) British
| £750 | $1223 | (4-Jul-91 B9) Seaweed gatherers resting on a beach (28x41cm-11x16in) |

BOND, W J J C (1833-1926) British
| £400 | $676 | (19-Apr-91 K311) Seascape with fishing boats (10x18cm-4x7in) s. W/C |

BOND, William Joseph J C (1833-1926) British
£620	$1110	(14-Mar-91 B120) Green corn (29x44cm-11x17in) s.mono. i. verso board
£700	$1176	(18-Jul-91 ZZ.B707) Fishing boat at sea, stormy sky (28x23cm-11x9in) panel
£731	$1433	(20-Nov-90 GO.G397) Near the port (76x63cm-30x25in) s. (S.KR 8000)
£900	$1764	(20-Nov-90 PH1/R) Unloading the ships (29x21cm-11x8in) s.d.'89 paper
£650	$1235	(10-Jan-91 B89) The morning catch (22x34cm-9x13in) s. W/C scratching out

BONDT, Jan de (17th C) Dutch
| £5800 | $9802 | (17-Apr-91 S17/R) Elderly woman beside table laden with fish (103x128cm-41x50in) |

BONE, Charles Richard (1809-c.1880) British
| £300 | $531 | (20-Mar-91 C32) Portrait of Caroline Vansittart Neale (10x?cm-4x?in) min.s.d.1831 shaped octagonal |

BONE, Henry (1755-1834) British
£600	$990	(10-Jul-91 C131) The Most Rev. Charles Manners-Sutton, Lord Archibishop of Canterbury (8x?cm-3x?in) min.s.i.d.1829 enamel fitted leather case oval
£1000	$1650	(11-Jul-91 S293) Portrait of Lady Anne Fitzpatrick (21x?cm-8x?in) min.enamel gilt wood frame rec.aft.Reynolds
£1100	$1947	(20-Mar-91 C28/R) Portrait of Caroline and Henry Vansittart (13x?cm-5x?in) min.s.i. enamel gilt-metal frame rec.
£1150	$1898	(10-Jul-91 C128/R) Miss H Oakley (8x?cm-3x?in) min.s.d.June 1799 verso enamel gildt frame oval

BONE, Henry (1755-1834) British-cont.
£1300	$2145	(10-Jul-91 C129) Charles Grey, M.P. (9x?cm-4x?in) min.s.d.September 1794 enamel gilt frame oval
£2000	$3300	(11-Jul-91 S280/R) Jupiter and Io embraced (30x?cm-12x?in) min.s.i.d.1813 giltwood frame rec.aft.Correggio
£2800	$4620	(11-Jul-91 S282/R) The Madonna of the Rocks with Christ Child and John the Baptist (37x?cm-15x?in) min.s.i.d.1808 wood frame arched after da Vinci
£3800	$6270	(11-Jul-91 S285/R) Portrait of Lady Emilia Lennox seated reading book (18x?cm-7x?in) min.s.i.d.1819 lacquer frame rec.after Ramsay
£6500	$10725	(11-Jul-91 S284/R) Equestrian portrait of George III (32x?cm-13x?in) min.s.d.1817 enamel giltwood frame rec.

BONE, Henry (school) (1755-1834) British
£450	$779	(21-May-91 CSK169/R) Gentleman in green coat and yellow waistcoat (6x?cm-2x?in) min. enamel oval

BONE, Henry Pierce (1779-1855) British
£1200	$1980	(11-Jul-91 S269/R) Portrait of Mary Queen of Scots (9x?cm-4x?in) min.s.i.d.1851 enamel gilt frame oval
£2000	$3300	(11-Jul-91 S268/R) Portrait of Lady Jane Seymour (11x?cm-4x?in) min.s.i.d.1849 enamel gilt frame oval
£3600	$5940	(11-Jul-91 S281/R) Portrait of George Digby and William, 5th Earl of Bedford (35x?cm-14x?in) min.s.i.d.1836 enamel wood frame after van Dyck

BONE, Sir Muirhead (1876-1953) British
£300	$555	(5-Mar-91 SWS1653) Winchester (16x19cm-6x7in) s.indis.d. i.verso pencil wash
£1300	$2249	(22-May-91 S185/R) Preparing for launch of Queen Elizabeth, Clydebank (81x35cm-32x14in) s.d.1938 col.chk

BONE, Stephen (1904-1958) British
£850	$1658	(16-Oct-90 WW361) The Tin Chapel (46x61cm-18x24in) s.i. verso

BONEH, Schmuel (20th C) Israeli
£552	$900	(12-Jun-91 GG.TA31/R) Seated king (47x38cm-19x15in) s.d.1974

BONEVARDI, Marcelo (1929-) Argentinian
£3061	$6000	(20-Nov-90 CH.NY132/R) Nocturlabio II (70x61cm-28x24in) s.i.d.1978 verso mixed media burlap wood
£7143	$14000	(20-Nov-90 CH.NY36/R) Wall with objects (203x92cm-80x36in) s.i.d.68 verso mixed media on wood construction

BONFANTI, Arturo (1905-) Italian
£5853	$11414	(24-Oct-90 F.M203/R) Composizione A.39 (46x55cm-18x22in) s.d.1961verso panel (I.L 13000000)

BONFIGLI, Benedetto (1420-1496) Italian
£36842	$70000	(11-Jan-91 CH.NY3/R) The Miracle of Saint Peter Martyr (23x53cm-9x21in) tempera panel

BONFILS, Gaston (19th C) French
£1842	$3500	(27-Feb-91 SY.NY38/R) Antique shop (66x81cm-26x32in) s.
£2143	$3600	(17-Jul-91 SY.NY243/R) The antique shop (66x81cm-26x32in) s.

BONGART, Sergei R (1918-1985) American/Russian
£2821	$5500	(10-Oct-90 B.SF502/R) Still life on table top (84x135cm-33x53in) s. acrylic masonite
£3571	$7000	(13-Feb-91 B.SF2142/R) Artist's studio (91x107cm-36x42in) s.d.1973

BONHEUR (?) ?
£1850	$3589	(6-Dec-90 CB.P51/R) Entree au Havre (65x54cm-26x21in) s. (F.FR 18000)

BONHEUR, Auguste (1824-1884) French
£4103	$8000	(24-Oct-90 CH.NY72/R) Shepherd and flock (71x101cm-28x40in) s.

BONHEUR, Ferdinand (19th C) ?
£647	$1120	(26-May-91 ZZ.F67/R) Vapeur et barque devant le port (22x41cm-9x16in) s. panel (F.FR 6500)
£973	$1908	(11-Nov-90 ZZ.F17/R) Moutons au bord de la riviere (24x40cm-9x16in) s. panel (F.FR 9500)
£1243	$2100	(19-Apr-91 CB.P127/R) Les rives du bosphore (21x41cm-8x16in) s. panel (F.FR 12500)
£1243	$2100	(19-Apr-91 CB.P129) Promenade sur le Bosphore (21x41cm-8x16in) s. panel (F.FR 12500)

BONHEUR, Juliette Peyrol (attrib) (1830-1891) French
£620	$1166	(21-Sep-90 PHM69) A shepherd with his flock at sunset (25x44cm-10x17in) panel

BONHEUR, Rosa (1822-1899) French
£600	$984	(18-Jun-91 PH66) Deer in landscape (18x16cm-7x6in) s.st.sig.d.1900stretcher
£712	$1275	(12-May-91 AGS.P25) Etude de chevres (19x16cm-7x6in) s. (F.FR 7200)
£792	$1402	(4-Apr-91 CK.P30) Taurillon (27x35cm-11x14in) studio st. sketch (F.FR 8000)

BONHEUR, Rosa (1822-1899) French-cont.
£983	$1700	(21-May-91 CE.NY38/R) Stag in forest clearing (27x22cm-11x9in) s.
£1538	$2600	(20-Apr-91 WOL.C93/R) Cows in field (36x51cm-14x20in) s.
£2083	$3500	(24-Apr-91 BA.S22/R) Italian landscape with travellers resting (54x76cm-21x30in) s.d.1874 (S.KR 22000)
£2395	$4000	(7-Jun-91 SY.NY21/R) A bay horse in landscape (26x36cm-10x14in) s.
£2600	$4264	(19-Jun-91 S134/R) Sheep and turkeys in meadow (44x58cm-17x23in) s.d.1873
£3024	$5897	(28-Oct-90 QWA.P75/R) Le marche aux chevaux (52x102cm-20x40in) (F.FR 30000)
£5789	$11000	(27-Feb-91 SY.NY251/R) Deer drinking from stream at twilight (75x119cm-30x47in) s.d.1867 chl
£43931	$76000	(23-May-91 CH.NY43/R) Pyrenees farmers market bound (63x101cm-25x40in) s.d.1884
£351	*$650*	*(4-Mar-91 ARC.P72) Etude d'arbres (35x17cm-14x7in) s. W/C (F.FR 3500)*
£495	*$876*	*(5-Apr-91 LGB.P79) Moutons au paturage (28x39cm-11x15in) s. Indian ink wash htd.gouache (F.FR 5000)*
£653	*$1207*	*(6-Mar-91 HC.P11) Arbres en hiver (25x31cm-10x12in) bears st. W/C (F.FR 6500)*
£1937	*$3719*	*(1-Dec-90 PER.M16/R) Taureaux de Camargue (27x49cm-11x19in) s.d.1855 lead pencil htd.chk. (F.FR 19000)*
£2381	*$4000*	*(17-Jul-91 SY.NY218/R) Moonlight battle (58x81cm-23x32in) s.d.1868 pastel*
£8000	*$13120*	*(21-Jun-91 C6/R) Studies for horse fair (32x30cm-13x12in) two i. pencil two htd white three*

BONHEUR, Rosa (after) (1822-1899) French
£1600	$3136	(8-Nov-90 PHI170) The horse fair (120x247cm-47x97in) bears i.

BONHOMME, Leon (1870-1924) French
£3466	*$6654*	*(2-Dec-90 M.V154) Buste de femme (56x40cm-22x16in) s.d.1923 (F.FR 34000)*
£607	*$1183*	*(16-Oct-90 CS.L18) Au cafe (16x20cm-6x8in) s.d.1920 W/C col.chk. (F.FR 6000)*
£700	*$1365*	*(19-Oct-90 C236/R) Bonfemme (43x30cm-17x12in) s.d.1920 gouache pastel*
£1220	*$2159*	*(21-Mar-91 LC.P202/R) Nu au bas bleus (28x22cm-11x9in) s. verso W/C (F.FR 12200)*

BONI, L (19/20th C) Italian
£1277	$2400	(18-Sep-90 RO.BA385) Incantation (100x81cm-39x32in) s.

BONICHI, Claudio (20th C) Italian
£8104	$15804	(22-Oct-90 BR.M328/R) Ragazza che scherza con la luna (90x100cm-35x39in) s. (I.L 18000000)
£1546	*$3029*	*(20-Nov-90 BR.M19/R) La luna (85x70cm-33x28in) s.i.d.1983 pastel (I.L 3400000)*

BONIFAZI, A (19th C) Italian
£28000	$45920	(21-Jun-91 C79/R) Captivated audience (60x106cm-24x42in) s.i.d.1876

BONIFAZI, Anton Angelo (1615-c.1682) Italian
£3187	$5482	(14-May-91 GF.L2010/R) The Martyrdom of St Stephanus (142x83cm-56x33in) (S.FR 8000)

BONIFAZIO DI PITATI (1487-1553) Italian
£38235	$65000	(30-May-91 SY.NY7/R) Pope Urban V bestowing cloak on two beati of Order of Gesuati (249x211cm-98x83in)

BONIFAZIO DI PITATI (attrib) (1487-1553) Italian
£26000	$50180	(12-Dec-90 S149/R) Holy Family with St. Catherine and St.Francis (95x113cm-37x44in)

BONIFAZIO DI PITATI (school) (1487-1553) Italian
£5641	$11000	(10-Oct-90 CH.NY192/R) St Lucy and Infant St John the Baptist in landscape (93x41cm-37x16in)

BONIFAZIO DI PITATI (style) (1487-1553) Italian
£9412	$16000	(31-May-91 CH.NY245/R) Holy Family with Infant St John the Baptist and two other saints (64x86cm-25x34in)

BONIN, Claude (20th C) French
£1578	$3108	(1-Oct-90 CC.P146/R) Le sentier rose dans les Guillons (60x81cm-24x32in) s.d.1988 (F.FR 16000)

BONINGTON, Richard Parkes (1801-1828) British
£62437	$101772	(14-Jun-91 AGS.P17/R) La plage (16x28cm-6x11in) i. board (F.FR 620000)
£850	*$1522*	*(11-Apr-91 S18/R) Figures by river boat beyond (10x12cm-4x5in) pencil*
£900	*$1611*	*(11-Apr-91 S17/R) Haverland Manor, Norfolk (20x23cm-8x9in) i. pencil*
£1500	*$2475*	*(11-Jul-91 S170/R) The pinnacled roofs of chateau (16x11cm-6x4in) i. pencil sold with another drawing*
£9500	*$17005*	*(11-Apr-91 S21/R) Figures and boats on shore in Normandy, France (13x21cm-5x8in) pen wash over pencil*
£15000	*$26850*	*(11-Apr-91 S79/R) Fisherfolk on French coast (14x21cm-6x8in) W/C over pencil*

BONINGTON, Richard Parkes (style) (1801-1828) British
£750	$1223	(3-Jul-91 PLF.P47) Barques et personnages au bord de mer (20x10cm-8x4in) sig. panel (F.FR 7500)
£5000	$8950	(10-Apr-91 S27/R) Chateau of Duchesse de Berry at Rosny, Seine-Et-Oise (35x51cm-14x20in)

BONINO, G (19th C) Italian
£2742	$5402	*(14-Nov-90 F.M16/R) Trompe l'oeil con pagine di libri e incisioni. Carta dell'Africa (36x46cm-14x18in) W/C pair (I.L 6000000)*

BONITO, Giuseppe (1705-1789) Italian
£357895	$680000	(11-Jan-91 CH.NY67/R) Musical party. Poet (101x154cm-40x61in) pair

BONIVENTO, E (1880-1956) Italian
£700	$1372	*(14-Feb-91 CSK21) The Grand Palace. The Grand Canal,Venice (25x38cm-10x15in) both indist.s. pencil W/C two*

BONIVENTO, Eugenio (1880-1956) Italian
£456	$762	*(6-Jun-91 F.M123) Venezia (16x32cm-6x13in) s. W/C (I.L 1000000)*

BONNAR, James King (1885-1961) American
£684	$1300	(14-Sep-90 S.BM279/R) Pigeon Cove (41x51cm-16x20in) s. canvasboard
£722	$1350	(30-Aug-90 MFA.C190/R) Horse and sleigh in snow (51x41cm-20x16in) s. board
£957	$1800	(11-Aug-90 COL.M252/R) Netting a trout (36x28cm-14x11in) s. board
£1734	$3000	(10-May-91 S.BM126/R) View to the harbour, Rockport (51x61cm-20x24in) s.

BONNARD, Pierre (1867-1947) French
£22312	$42840	(17-Dec-90 AGS.P17) Portrait de Mademoiselle A.B (30x24cm-12x9in) s. (F.FR 220000)
£60914	$120000	(13-Nov-90 SY.NY15/R) Coin de table - Tasse a cafe, pain et fleurs (35x26cm-14x10in) s. panel
£115000	$185150	(24-Jun-91 C8/R) Chez la Brodeuse, femmes a la fenetre (34x41cm-13x16in) s. s.verso panel
£131579	$257895	(25-Nov-90 GL.P62/R) La Seine a Vernonnet (45x45cm-18x18in) s. (F.FR 1300000)
£146939	$289469	(16-Nov-90 GK.Z5186/R) Trois femmes dans un paysage (36x57cm-14x22in) s.d.1925 (S.FR 360000)
£150289	$260000	(8-May-91 CH.NY16/R) Se refletant dans un miroir (54x65cm-21x26in) s.
£172065	$337247	(24-Nov-90 APT.P70/R) Jardin a Vernon ou paysage au bord de la Seine (56x72cm-22x28in) s. (F.FR 1700000)
£200000	$322000	(25-Jun-91 S27/R) Jardin meridional au Cannet ou le jardin vu de la terrasse (56x62cm-22x24in) s.
£230000	$446200	(3-Dec-90 C29/R) Femme au peignoir rouge (50x34cm-20x13in) studio st.
£300000	$483000	(24-Jun-91 C12/R) Jeune femme se chaussant (53x63cm-21x25in) st.studio
£364372	$714170	(25-Nov-90 GL.P25/R) Femme au bouquet de violettes (46x38cm-18x15in) s. panel (F.FR 3600000)
£394737	$773684	(24-Nov-90 APT.P75/R) Le compotier (47x31cm-19x12in) s. (F.FR 3900000)
£400000	$776000	(3-Dec-90 C25/R) Femme se deshabillant (56x66cm-22x26in) s.
£455466	$892713	(25-Nov-90 GL.P33/R) Nu dans un interieur (75x63cm-30x25in) s. (F.FR 4500000)
£583756	$1150000	(13-Nov-90 SY.NY11/R) Le Vestibule (99x59cm-39x23in) s.
£736041	$1450000	(12-Nov-90 SY.NY15/R) Femme nue (73x45cm-29x18in) s
£1472081	$2900000	(13-Nov-90 SY.NY27/R) Les coquelicots (70x58cm-28x23in) s.
£561	$1082	*(10-Dec-90 LD.P6/R) Ferme dans les environs d'Uriage (9x14cm-4x6in) blk.crayon (F.FR 5500)*
£612	$1180	*(10-Dec-90 LD.P4/R) Femmes dans le jardin (9x14cm-4x6in) s. blk.crayon (F.FR 6000)*
£653	$1071	*(18-Jun-91 APT.P8) Bords de la Seine, pres de Vernon (11x14cm-4x6in) lead pencil drawing (F.FR 6500)*
£693	$1338	*(10-Dec-90 LD.P5/R) Etude de nu et portrait d'homme au chat (21x17cm-8x7in) blk.crayon double-sided (F.FR 6800)*
£771	$1495	*(5-Dec-90 ZZ.F6/R) Nu feminin debout (28x23cm-11x9in) st.mono blk.crayon (F.FR 7500)*
£918	$1800	*(12-Feb-91 SY.NY11/R) Head of woman (15x10cm-6x4in) st.init. pencil*
£1300	$2535	*(19-Oct-90 C156 a/R) Paysage. Paysage (11x17cm-4x7in) chl htd.white double-sided*
£1531	$3000	*(12-Feb-91 SY.NY6/R) The bather (15x10cm-6x4in) indis.st.init. pencil*
£2035	$3845	*(25-Sep-90 FB.P237/R) Petit solefege illustre (19x26cm-7x10in) W/C drawing (F.FR 20000)*
£3299	$6500	*(3-Oct-90 SY.NY27/R) Etude pour le grand tub (33x25cm-13x10in) chl*
£3500	$5635	*(24-Jun-91 CSK38/R) Paysage du Midi, Antibes (12x15cm-5x6in) st.init. pencil*
£4656	$9126	*(22-Nov-90 ZZ.F15/R) Nature morte aux cerises (11x15cm-4x6in) mono. crayon (F.FR 46000)*
£7645	$14679	*(27-Nov-90 APT.P45/R) Sous la pluie (29x19cm-11x7in) init. Indian ink (F.FR 75000)*
£13873	$24000	*(9-May-91 CH.NY111/R) Portrait de Madame Carlos Maria de Alvear (63x48cm-25x19in) s. pastel paper mounted on board*
£15075	$26985	*(16-Mar-91 APT.P43/R) Sur la plage (29x21cm-11x8in) s. W/C gouache (F.FR 150000)*
£17500	$33950	*(5-Dec-90 S329/R) Croquis pour D'Un Pays Plus Beau Le Voyeur (14x14cm-6x6in) crayon*

BONNAT, Leon (1834-1922) French
£1521	$2921	(17-Dec-90 AGS.P18) Portrait du Docteur Alvarez (27x18cm-11x7in) s.d.1871 panel (F.FR 15000)
£3590	$7000	(14-Oct-90 H.C448/R) Bust of Moroccan (69x56cm-27x22in) s.
£7500	$12225	(3-Jul-91 PLF.P49/R) La jeune italienne (60x48cm-24x19in) s. (F.FR 75000)
£592	*$1148*	*(8-Dec-90 GAB.G2121) Etude pour un projet de plafond (19cm-7ins circular) i. wash photograph round (S.FR 1450)*

BONNECHOSE, R (19/20th C) European
£559	$1000	(11-Apr-91 FA.PH650) Classical Greek female figure in garden (38x53cm-15x21in) s.

BONNEFOIT, Alain (1939-) French
£503	$986	(27-Jan-91 FE.P73) Nue aux cheveux longs (50x65cm-20x26in) s.d.88 peinture essence board (F.FR 5000)
£763	$1442	(30-Sep-90 FE.P78/R) Nue allongee (48x63cm-19x25in) studio st. board (F.FR 7500)
£1978	$3541	(8-Apr-91 CSC.P28/R) Nu (48x80cm-19x31in) s. panel (F.FR 20000)
£9684	$18690	(13-Dec-90 QWA.P18/R) Le sommeil (50x100cm-20x39in) s. (F.FR 95000)
£1020	*$2010*	*(17-Nov-90 HC.P90) Nu de femme (61x89cm-24x35in) s. W/C (F.FR 10000)*

BONNEFOND, Claude (1796-1860) French
£1416	$2760	(16-Oct-90 CS.L39) Fete italienne (65x85cm-26x33in) s. (F.FR 14000)

BONNEFONT (20th C) French?
£1780	$3187	(14-Apr-91 ZZ.F100) Veuve d'Amour (89x116cm-35x46in) s. (F.FR 18000)

BONNEFOY, Henri-Arthur (1839-1917) French
£500	$895	(12-Mar-91 PH101/R) Orchard fence (130x91cm-51x36in) s.

BONNEMAISON, Georges (?-1885) French
£917	$1761	(1-Dec-90 PER.M85/R) La prairie a la lisiere d'un bois (24x35cm-9x14in) s.d.75 (F.FR 9000)

BONNEROT, Pierre (19/20th C) French
£822	$1471	(12-Mar-91 FN.S2292) Moor landscape with avenue, autumn (38x55cm-15x22in) s. (DM 2400)

BONNET, Anne (1885-) Belgian
£986	$1923	(23-Oct-90 C.A57) Summer flowers (47x38cm-19x15in) s.d.1937 panel (B.FR 60000)
£2024	$3926	(8-Dec-90 KV.L392/R) Composition (26x50cm-10x20in) s. canvas on board (B.FR 120000)
£1233	*$2403*	*(23-Oct-90 C.A58) Back street (26x36cm-10x14in) gouache (B.FR 75000)*

BONNET, Felix Alfred (1847-?) French
£2312	$4486	(4-Dec-90 F.R137) Interno di chiesa (97x82cm-38x32in) s. (I.L 5000000)

BONNET, Marc (1958-) French
£708	$1380	(18-Oct-90 CB.P65/R) Chant 1 (F.FR 7000)

BONNIER, Eva (1857-1909) Swedish
£568	$955	(24-Apr-91 BA.S24/R) Panorama view at dusk (14x24cm-6x9in) panel (S.KR 6000)
£1231	$2068	(24-Apr-91 BA.S23/R) Fruit tree in blossom (24x19cm-9x7in) panel (S.KR 13000)

BONNIER, Olle (1925-) Scandinavian
£1576	$3057	(4-Dec-90 BA.S61/R) Untitled (15x33cm-6x13in) cardboard (S.KR 17000)
£6038	$10445	(22-May-91 BA.S321/R) Boogie-Woogie (82x82cm-32x32in) s.i.verso (S.KR 64000)
£13838	$26568	(27-Nov-90 BU.S39/R) The poultry house (73x83cm-29x33in) init. (S.KR 150000)
£425	*$734*	*(22-May-91 BA.S325/R) Nebulosa (30x19cm-12x7in) s.d.89 mixed media (S.KR 4500)*
£610	*$1038*	*(28-May-91 AB.S5174/R) Mexican theme (22x30cm-9x12in) s.d.78 gouache on black background (S.KR 6500)*
£754	*$1274*	*(18-Apr-91 BU.S32/R) Composition (67x49cm-26x19in) s.d.1974 Indian ink wash (S.KR 8000)*
£755	*$1306*	*(22-May-91 BA.S324/R) Geometric composition (39x29cm-15x11in) s.d.1957 W/C (S.KR 8000)*
£806	*$1564*	*(5-Dec-90 AB.S7040/R) Cosmic composition in red and purple (26x36cm-10x14in) s.d.88 pastel (S.KR 8700)*
£830	*$1594*	*(27-Nov-90 BU.S45/R) Baile Mexicano (22x30cm-9x12in) s.d.1978 W/C gouache pencil (S.KR 9000)*
£834	*$1618*	*(4-Dec-90 BA.S63/R) Colour explosion (24x30cm-9x12in) s.d.63 gouache (S.KR 9000)*
£927	*$1798*	*(4-Dec-90 BA.S62/R) Plingeling (20x32cm-8x13in) s. W/C (S.KR 10000)*
£1015	*$1948*	*(27-Nov-90 BU.S43/R) Geometrical composition (30x27cm-12x11in) s.d.1952 gouache (S.KR 11000)*
£1107	*$2125*	*(27-Nov-90 BU.S44/R) Abstract composition (29x38cm-11x15in) s.d.1957 gouache (S.KR 12000)*
£1502	*$2554*	*(28-May-91 AB.S5170/R) Constructive composition (32x33cm-13x13in) s.d.50 W/C (S.KR 16000)*

BONNIER, Olle (1925-) Scandinavian-cont.
£1845	$3542	(27-Nov-90 BU.S40/R) Painting mobile II (67x112cm-26x44in) s.d.1984 mixed media W/C gouache chk (S.KR 20000)
£2254	$3831	(28-May-91 AB.S5168/R) Composition in red and blue (104x74cm-41x29in) s.d.89 pastel (S.KR 24000)
£2356	$3982	(18-Apr-91 BU.S48/R) Blue composition (67x96cm-26x38in) s.d.1958 mixed media paper on panel (S.KR 25000)

BONO, Dorothy E (20th C) British
| £1020 | $2000 | (12-Feb-91 SY.NY76/R) Still life with flowers (51x79cm-20x31in) s. |

BONONI, Carlo (circle) (1569-1632) Italian
| £1695 | $3000 | (22-Mar-91 S.W2863/R) Rest on flight into Egypt (94x69cm-37x27in) |

BONVICINO, Alessandro (1498-1554) Italian
| £1706 | $2952 | (22-May-91 GS.B2331) Madonna with Child (33x26cm-13x10in) panel (S.FR 4300) |
| £2041 | $4000 | (7-Nov-90 B.SF1039/R) Portrait of patrician with dog (108x91cm-43x36in) |

BONVIN, Francois (1817-1887) French
£950	$1853	(12-Oct-90 PHM61) A kitchen maid cleaning glasses (53x38cm-21x15in)
£1210	$2359	(14-Jan-91 YC.P142/R) Femme assise tenant un cuivre (33x24cm-13x9in) s.d.1883 panel (F.FR 12000)
£1429	$2814	(14-Nov-90 CN.P62/R) La sortie de la messe (37x26cm-15x10in) s.d.1864 panel (F.FR 14000)
£4000	$6560	(19-Jun-91 S162/R) Maid cleaning glasses (52x37cm-20x15in)
£4500	$8820	(15-Feb-91 C17/R) Platter of oysters, sliced lemons and glass of red wine on draped table (38x46cm-15x18in) s.
£704	$1217	(22-May-91 EA.M446/R) Figures in street before gothic cathedral (56x76cm-22x30in) s. W/C (C.D 1400)

BONVIN, Francois (attrib) (1817-1887) French
| £1829 | $3000 | (19-Jun-91 B.SF1900/R) Preparing the midday meal (46x34cm-18x13in) s. panel |

BONY, Jean Francois (c.1760-c.1825) French
| £5561 | $10844 | (16-Oct-90 CS.L40/R) Perroquet et corbeille de fleurs (80x62cm-31x24in) i. verso gouache laid down (F.FR 55000) |

BOOG, Carle Michel (1877-?) American
| £1480 | $2900 | (11-Nov-90 LIT.L6) Young girl sewing (51x41cm-20x16in) s. canvas on masonite |

BOOGAARD, W J (1842-1887) Dutch
| £1163 | $1895 | (12-Jun-91 GM.B4060) Le charretier (77x66cm-30x26in) s. (B.FR 70000) |

BOOGAARD, Willem Jacobus (1842-1887) Dutch
| £1190 | $2000 | (17-Jul-91 SY.NY276/R) The haycart (13x20cm-5x8in) s. panel |
| £2619 | $4452 | (28-May-91 C.A22/R) Horses by a river (45x76cm-18x30in) s. (B.FR 160000) |

BOOK, Max Mikael (1953-) Swedish
£2595	$5034	(5-Dec-90 AB.S7045/R) The Channels (60x71cm-24x28in) s.d.1984verso mixed media (S.KR 28000)
£3299	$5575	(18-Apr-91 BU.S21/R) Untitled (150x218cm-59x86in) s.d.1986 mixed media (S.KR 35000)
£3985	$7731	(5-Dec-90 AB.S7044/R) 'Bron Over' (78x102cm-31x40in) s.d.1987verso mixed media (S.KR 43000)

BOONE, Daniel (1630-1700) Flemish
| £2500 | $4875 | (26-Oct-90 C138/R) A servant offering chicken (74x60cm-29x24in) s. |

BOONEN, Arnold (1669-1729) Dutch
£699	$1350	(12-Dec-90 N.M356/R) Portrait of gentleman by window with view of landscape (42x34cm-17x13in) s.d.1694 one of pair (DM 2000)
£874	$1687	(12-Dec-90 N.M357/R) Portrait of lady by window with view of landscape (42x34cm-17x13in) s. one of pair (DM 2500)
£2793	$5000	(10-Apr-91 HF.NY7/R) Four children resting on ledge (49x40cm-19x16in) indist.s.

BOONEN, Arnold (circle) (1669-1729) Dutch
| £2500 | $5000 | (7-Feb-91 CSK91/R) Portrait of lady, seated in landscape holding rosebud (66x56cm-26x22in) |

BOONZAIER, Gregoire (1909-) South African
£844	$1392	(8-Jul-91 SY.J306/R) Trees and houses, Mowbray, Cape (14x18cm-6x7in) s.d.1948 panel (SA.R 4000)
£1113	$2138	(18-Feb-91 SY.J338/R) District six (22x46cm-9x18in) s.d.1951 board (SA.R 5500)
£1474	$2491	(15-Apr-91 SY.J465/R) Fir trees (26x36cm-10x14in) s.d.1938 board (SA.R 7000)
£1553	$2904	(27-Aug-90 SY.J264/R) Farmhouse and trees (29x41cm-11x16in) s.d.1948 board (SA.R 7500)
£1646	$2715	(8-Jul-91 SY.J309/R) Winter landscape (23x32cm-9x13in) s.d.44 (SA.R 7800)
£1684	$2846	(15-Apr-91 SY.J468/R) View to houses through woods (30x34cm-12x13in) s.d.1924 (SA.R 8000)

BOONZAIER, Gregoire (1909-) South African-cont.

£1815	$3538	(15-Oct-90 SY.J148/R) Still life with jug of spring flowers, fruit and objects on a table (55x41cm-22x16in) s.d.1941 board (SA.R 9000)
£1895	$3202	(15-Apr-91 SY.J463/R) Green fields (30x40cm-12x16in) s.d.1938 (SA.R 9000)
£2899	$5420	(27-Aug-90 SY.J268/R) District Six (19x40cm-7x16in) s.d.1949 board (SA.R 14000)
£2917	$4958	(27-May-91 SY.J342/R) Cottage among oaks (25x30cm-10x12in) s.d.1932 (SA.R 14000)
£3165	$5222	(8-Jul-91 SY.J311/R) Still life with pear, mangoes and avocado (40x50cm-16x20in) s.d.1947 (SA.R 15000)
£3229	$5490	(27-May-91 SY.J338/R) Still life with teacup and fruit bowl (28x34cm-11x13in) s.d.1950 board (SA.R 15500)
£3376	$5570	(8-Jul-91 SY.J310/R) Approaching rain, Kenilworth (31x39cm-12x15in) s.d.1972 i. verso board (SA.R 16000)
£3934	$7356	(27-Aug-90 SY.J263/R) District six (50x40cm-20x16in) s.d.1965 (SA.R 19000)
£4211	$7116	(15-Apr-91 SY.J467/R) Seaside cottage, Kommetjie (30x34cm-12x13in) s.d.1925 (SA.R 20000)
£5063	$8354	(8-Jul-91 SY.J308/R) Die Geel Huis, Distrik Ses, Kaapstad (39x60cm-15x24in) s.d.1951 (SA.R 24000)
£6329	$10443	(8-Jul-91 SY.J307/R) District siz (40x49cm-16x19in) s.d.1956 (SA.R 30000)
£7819	$15012	(26-Nov-90 SY.J298 a/R) Grey day, Upper Caledon Street, District Six, Cape Town (65x86cm-26x34in) s.d.1970 s.i.verso (SA.R 38000)
£580	*$1084*	*(27-Aug-90 SY.J97/R) Rooikransboom, Onrus (49x32cm-19x13in) s.d.1987 chl crayon wash (SA.R 2800)*
£605	*$1179*	*(15-Oct-90 SY.J146/R) Street scene, District six (44x32cm-17x13in) s.d.1971 W/C (SA.R 3000)*
£792	*$1346*	*(27-May-91 SY.J343/R) Old oaks and ruins (26x35cm-10x14in) s.d.1952 ink wash (SA.R 3800)*
£870	*$1626*	*(27-Aug-90 SY.J269) Caledon Street, District Six (42x56cm-17x22in) s.d.1963 s.i.verso pastel (SA.R 4200)*
£932	*$1742*	*(27-Aug-90 SY.J265/R) Weatherbeaten oak (55x76cm-22x30in) s.d.1953 pastel W/C (SA.R 4500)*

BOOTH, J W (1867-1953) British

| *£650* | *$1060* | *(13-Jun-91 IMC1/R) Hamlet scene with stream and horses (56x38cm-22x15in) s. W/C* |
| *£750* | *$1223* | *(13-Jun-91 IMC2/R) Haymaking (56x25cm-22x10in) s. W/C* |

BOOTH, James W (1867-1953) British

| £6000 | $11700 | (17-Oct-90 PHL313/R) Expectancy (59x90cm-23x35in) s.d.1897 |

BOOTH, Peter (1940-) Australian

£579	$1141	(13-Nov-90 J.M309) Seated nude (90x75cm-35x30in) d.1963 (A.D 1500)
£28037	$45701	(16-Jun-91 SY.ME37/R) Untitled - purple-black bar, 1973-74 (213x198cm-84x78in) acrylic canvas (A.D 60000)
£1055	*$2025*	*(14-Aug-90 SY.ME67/R) Untitled (45x61cm-18x24in) pastel (A.D 2500)*

BOOTY, Frederick William (19/20th C) British?

| *£480* | *$821* | *(29-Jul-91 HS144/R) North Yorkshire fishing village with fishermen and other figures (73x60cm-29x24in) s.d.1907 W/C* |
| *£900* | *$1593* | *(19-Mar-91 CHAP327/R) Runswick Bay (48x71cm-19x28in) s.d.1909 W/C* |

BOQUET, Jules Charles (1840-1926) French

| £1000 | $1970 | (13-Nov-90 SWS341/R) Sewing (98x70cm-39x28in) s. |

BORCHARDT, Hans (1865-?) German

| £1053 | $1821 | (8-May-91 D.V13/R) Lady seated on couch (60x50cm-24x20in) s.i.d.11 (A.S 22000) |

BORCHGREVINK, Ridley (1898-1981) ?

| £2257 | $3769 | (3-Jun-91 B.O10/R) Still life of potted plants (96x105cm-38x41in) s.d.1940 (N.KR 26000) |
| £2715 | $4859 | (11-Mar-91 B.O10/R) The flight (95x133cm-37x52in) s.d.23 (N.KR 31000) |

BORDES, Leonard (1898-1969) French

| £2584 | $4368 | (21-Apr-91 B.PA43 a) Neige au Mont Gargan (50x61cm-20x24in) s. (F.FR 26000) |
| £2915 | $5713 | (25-Nov-90 B.PA44 d/R) Voiliers dans le port de Rouen (37x45cm-15x18in) s. panel (F.FR 28800) |

BORDONE, Paris (1500-1571) Italian

| £150000 | $244500 | (5-Jul-91 C2/R) Rape of Proserpine (137x124cm-54x49in) s. |

BORDONE, Paris (attrib) (1500-1571) Italian

| *£3500* | *$5705* | *(1-Jul-91 S10/R) Study of doge (31x21cm-12x8in) black chk htd white* |

BORDONE, Paris (style) (1500-1571) Italian

| £2200 | $3586 | (4-Jul-91 B106) The Holy family with St. John the Baptist (37x48cm-15x19in) panel |
| £5500 | $10725 | (26-Oct-90 C7/R) Ecce Homo (83x66cm-33x26in) |

BORDUAS, Paul Emile (1905-1960) Canadian
£11894 $23194   (24-Oct-90 EA.M456/R) Abstract composition (23x32cm-9x13in) s.d.56 (C.D 27000)

BOREIN, Edward (1873-1943) American
£888   *$1500*   *(1-May-91 B.SF5286/R) Pack of horses (19x28cm-7x11in) pen*
£1453   *$2500*   *(15-May-91 SY.NY118/R) Six bucking broncos. Lone rider (22x30cm-9x12in) indian ink pair*
£2806   *$5500*   *(7-Nov-90 B.SF3783/R) Rodeo scenes pen five*
£5307 $9500   (12-Apr-91 SY.NY43/R) Cattle roundup (37x48cm-15x19in) s. W/C gouache paperboard
£11243 $19000   (1-May-91 B.SF5162/R) Roping steer (20x37cm-8x15in) s. W/C
£28107 $47500   (1-May-91 B.SF5158/R) Riding herd (38x49cm-15x19in) s. W/C

BORENSTEIN, Samuel (1908-1969) Canadian
£1101 $2148   (24-Oct-90 EA.M451/R) Lac Paquin - farmhouse (65x90cm-26x35in) s. tempera paper (C.D 2500)
£1744 $2929   (17-Jul-91 EA.M661/R) Montreal, December 1966 (30x40cm-12x16in) s.d.1966 verso masonite (C.D 3400)

BORES, Francisco (1898-1972) Spanish
£3200 $5216   (4-Jul-91 GL.P239/R) Composition bleue (40x50cm-16x20in) s.d.1959 paper laid down on canvas (F.FR 32000)
£5535 $10627   (27-Nov-90 BU.S49/R) Vase et compotier (27x35cm-11x14in) s.d.1951 (S.KR 60000)
£5783 $10872   (19-Sep-90 KH.K28/R) Le port (33x41cm-13x16in) s.d.47 (D.KR 65000)
£7538 $13492   (11-Mar-91 GL.P94/R) Nature morte au citron (50x61cm-20x24in) s.d.1955 (F.FR 75000)
£7562 $14217   (19-Sep-90 KH.K40/R) Nus (38x46cm-15x18in) s.d.48 (D.KR 85000)
£8197 $16066   (24-Jan-91 EP.M69/R) Bodegon (46x55cm-18x22in) s.d.40 (S.P 1500000)
£9225 $17712   (27-Nov-90 BU.S48/R) Enfant assis (47x39cm-19x15in) s.d.1941 (S.KR 100000)
£9363 $16105   (14-May-91 BU.S88/R) Composition Espagnole (54x65cm-21x26in) s.d.1950 (S.KR 100000)
£9400 $15698   (5-Jun-91 HC.P330/R) Nature morte bleue (60x72cm-24x28in) s.d.61 (F.FR 94000)
£10141 $17239   (28-May-91 AB.S5176/R) Nature morte a la leguille (54x65cm-21x26in) s.d.47 (S.KR 108000)
£10366 $17000   (19-Jun-91 B.SF1758 a/R) Mujer en un interior (60x74cm-24x29in) s.d.47
£10609 $20369   (27-Nov-90 BU.S47/R) Enfant et fleurs (38x45cm-15x18in) s.d.1938 (S.KR 115000)
£12454 $23911   (27-Nov-90 BU.S46/R) Bouteille d'Anisette (46x55cm-18x22in) s.d.1943 (S.KR 135000)
£13252 $25576   (12-Dec-90 APT.P73/R) Femme en rose (72x60cm-28x24in) s.d.46 (F.FR 130000)
£13500 $26325   (17-Oct-90 S72/R) Le repas (45x54cm-18x21in) s.d.34
£13744 $24601   (13-Mar-91 FER.M201/R) Bodegon con botella (41x49cm-16x19in) s.d.45 (S.P 2500000)
£13744 $24601   (13-Mar-91 FER.M200/R) Bodegon en azul y amarillo (52x64cm-20x25in) s.d.51 (S.P 2500000)
£17986 $34892   (7-Dec-90 GL.P177/R) Poissons (65x81cm-26x32in) s.d.49 (F.FR 175000)
£18000 $28980   (25-Jun-91 C137/R) Le marin musicien (130x97cm-51x38in) s.d.37
£19153 $37349   (26-Oct-90 CC.P29/R) Nature morte (65x81cm-26x32in) s.d.1961 (F.FR 190000)
£19388 $38194   (16-Nov-90 FB.P129/R) Nature morte au piment (50x61cm-20x24in) s.d.51 (F.FR 190000)
£21804 $35759   (18-Jun-91 EP.M5/R) Pomme rouge et raisin bleu (73x91cm-29x36in) s.d.57 (S.P 4000000)
£24129 $40537   (25-Apr-91 EP.M1/R) Bodegon (81x65cm-32x26in) s.d.52 (S.P 4400000)
£40883 $67048   (18-Jun-91 EP.M3/R) Jeune fille en blanc (162x130cm-64x51in) s.d.58 (S.P 7500000)
£758   *$1479*   *(17-Oct-90 ARC.P9) Nu assis (31x24cm-12x9in) s.d.1958 Indian ink (F.FR 7500)*
£2016   *$3931*   *(26-Oct-90 APT.P1/R) Le jardin public (24x32cm-9x13in) s.d.42 pastel (F.FR 20000)*
£2158   *$4187*   *(5-Dec-90 ZZ.F22/R) Interieur lecon de piano (25x32cm-10x13in) s.d.1942 gouache (F.FR 21000)*
£2716   *$4373*   *(25-Jun-91 FER.M267/R) Nature morte au bougeoir (22x29cm-9x11in) s. gouache (S.P 500000)*
£2932   *$5718*   *(17-Oct-90 ARC.P10/R) Composition (29x39cm-11x15in) s.d.1969 gouache (F.FR 29000)*
£3472   *$5972*   *(19-May-91 ZZ.F157/R) Nature morte au pot et aux raisins (24x32cm-9x13in) s.d.1958 W/C (F.FR 35000)*
£4587   *$8853*   *(10-Dec-90 LD.P18/R) Charlie Chaplin (32x34cm-13x13in) s. gouache (F.FR 45000)*
£13043   *$25043*   *(19-Dec-90 ANS.M75/R) Bodegon (49x64cm-19x25in) s.d.1970 gouache (S.P 2400000)*

BORG, Augusta (19th C) Danish
£1456 $2751   (27-Sep-90 D.V161/R) Walking on the frozen river (67x94cm-26x37in) s.d.1875 (A.S 30000)

BORG, Axel (1847-1916) Swedish
£1255 $2246   (9-Apr-91 GO.G14/R) French street scene (22x29cm-9x11in) s.d.77 (S.KR 13500)

BORG, Axel (1847-1916) Swedish-cont.
£1420 $2386 (24-Apr-91 BA.S26/R) Woman in rowingboat (27x41cm-11x16in) s.d.1909
        panel (S.KR 15000)
£2745 $5352 (21-Oct-90 BU.M577) Winter wood with elk (65x90cm-26x35in) s.
        (S.KR 30000)
£5576 $9981 (9-Apr-91 GO.G15/R) Wooded winter landscape with elk (65x92cm-26x36in)
        s. (S.KR 60000)

BORG, Carl Oscar (1879-1947) American
£798   *$1500* (19-Sep-90 B.SF2852/R) Adobes (24x34cm-9x13in) s. gouache
£930   *$1600* (15-May-91 SY.NY117/R) Western landscape (30x40cm-12x16in) s. W/C
        graphite board
£1587 *$3000* (25-Sep-90 SY.NY268/R) Horseback riding in the valley (27x25cm-11x10in)
        s. W/C gouache
£2734 *$5250* (17-Dec-90 SY.NY162/R) Grand Canyon (41x33cm-16x13in) s.d.1919 gouache

BORGEAUD, Marius (1861-1924) Swiss
£2041 $4000 (6-Nov-90 GF.L2191/R) Coastal landscape, Brittany (32x41cm-13x16in) s.
        panel (S.FR 5000)
£7035 $11538 (19-Jun-91 JM.P120/R) La chambre rouge (60x73cm-24x29in) s.d.1910
        (F.FR 70000)
£7937 $13016 (19-Jun-91 GK.B214/R) Jeune dame assise dans sa chambre a coucher
        (46x55cm-18x22in) s. (S.FR 20000)

BORGEN, Hans Fredrik (1852-1907) Norwegian
£701 $1254 (11-Mar-91 B.O12/R) Working in the field (53x46cm-21x18in) s.d.90
        (N.KR 8000)
£1345 $2247 (3-Jun-91 B.O12/R) Landscape from Ringebu (45x66cm-18x26in) s.
        (N.KR 15500)
£1568 $3057 (15-Oct-91 B.O8/R) Landscape from Mjosa (60x96cm-24x38in) s.
        (N.KR 18000)
£1606 $2682 (3-Jun-91 B.O11/R) Mountain farm and millhouse (84x132cm-33x52in)
        s.d.1879 (N.KR 18500)
£1823 $3044 (4-Jun-91 BU.O47/R) Fjord landscape (32x51cm-13x20in) s. (N.KR 21000)
£2014 $3605 (11-Mar-91 B.O11/R) Evening sunshine (60x75cm-24x30in) s. (N.KR 23000)

BORGES, Jacobo (1931-) Venezuelan
£9184 $18000 (19-Nov-90 SY.NY206/R) Espantapajaro de Chuloma (94x131cm-37x52in)
        s.d.60
£11735 $23000 (19-Nov-90 SY.NY223/R) Who are we (195x120cm-77x47in) s.d.1982

BORGESE, Leonardo (1904-) Italian
£786 $1516 (13-Dec-90 F.M377/R) Fiori (60x50cm-24x20in) s. (I.L 1700000)

BORGET, Auguste (style) (1809-1877) French
£795 $1550 (9-Oct-90 CH.HK1274/R) Junks moored by pagoda on Canton River with
        archers in foreground (53x40cm-21x16in) (HK.D 12000)

BORGHESE, Franz (1941-) Italian
£811 $1452 (9-Apr-91 F.R125) Tre personaggi con cane (30x40cm-12x16in) s.
        (I.L 1800000)
£2063 $3383 (20-Jun-91 F.M343) Pugilatori (55x45cm-22x18in) s. (I.L 4500000)
£2265 $3942 (26-Mar-91 F.M30/R) L'automobile (40x55cm-16x22in) s. (I.L 5000000)
£2290 $4397 (27-Nov-90 SY.MI12/R) Personaggi (60x80cm-24x31in) s. (I.L 5000000)
£2734 $4647 (28-May-91 SY.MI39/R) Personaggi (50x70cm-20x28in) s. (I.L 6000000)

BORGIA, Giancarlo (20th C) Italian
£1441 $2810 (22-Oct-90 BR.M238/R) Giardino di sera (80x100cm-31x39in) s.d.1990verso
        (I.L 3200000)

BORGOGNONE (style) (15/16th C) Italian
£1700 $3162 (5-Sep-90 BT221) Skirmish (38x74cm-15x29in)

BORHDT, J (19th C) ?
£1300 $2535 (18-Oct-90 CSK112/R) Three-decker leaving Portsmouth Harbour,
        H.M.S.Victory beyond (76x127cm-30x50in) s.

BORIONE, Bernard Louis (1865-) French
£2197 $3800 (21-May-91 CE.NY165/R) Cardinal playing lute (41x34cm-16x13in) s.i.
£6696 $12857 (27-Nov-90 W.T1130/R) Les convives musicals du cardinal
        (71x95cm-28x37in) s.i. canvas laid down (C.D 15000)
£351 *$650* (6-Mar-91 APT.P2) Scene de genre (47x38cm-19x15in) s. W/C (F.FR 3500)

BORJE, Gideon (1891-1969) Swedish
£1887 $3264 (22-May-91 BA.S17/R) Landscape, Malaren (51x61cm-20x24in) s.
        (S.KR 20000)
£2453 $4243 (22-May-91 BA.S15/R) Sunflowers (93x61cm-37x24in) s.d.1937 (S.KR 26000)
£3058 $5933 (4-Dec-90 BA.S67/R) Still life of chrysanthemum (65x81cm-26x32in) s.
        (S.KR 33000)
£20389 $39555 (4-Dec-90 BA.S66/R) View of Kastellholmen (59x79cm-23x31in) s.
        (S.KR 220000)

BORKOWSKI, C (19th C) German
£979 *$1890* (10-Dec-90 L.K214) Ensemble of Kolner Stadttheater on stage
        (54x88cm-21x35in) s.d.1868 pencil wash (DM 2800)

BORLASE, Nancy (?) ?
£573 $1082   *(25-Sep-90 JRL.S103/R) Mosman Bay (97x122cm-38x48in) init. mixed media board (A.D 1300)*

BORMAN, Johannes (17th C) Dutch
£20408 $40204   (15-Nov-90 EA.Z228.'R) Still life with peeled lemon on plate, fruit and glass (39x46cm-15x18in) (S.FR 50000)

BORMAN, Johannes (circle) (17th C) Dutch
£2300 $3749   (2-Jul-91 PH199/R) Still life of fruit with filled wine glasses and shell on draped table (46x56cm-18x22in) panel

BORNEMANN, Anna (1874-1956) German
£709 $1156   (13-Jun-91 RAS.V638/R) Flowers s.d.21 (D.KR 8000)
£2617 $5104   (12-Oct-90 AW.H2007/R) Palm tree flowering in conservatory (103x90cm-41x35in) s.d.1922 i.stretcher (DM 7800)

BORNWATER, Jacob Gerritz (attrib) (fl.1574-1588) Dutch
£2000 $3940   (31-Oct-90 S190) St Jerome in his study (80x58cm-31x23in) panel

BOROFSKY, Jonathan (20th C) ?
£38462 $65000   (30-Apr-91 SY.NY58/R) Running man at 2,500,116 (227x280cm-89x110in) i.verso acrylic plywood
£14793 $25000   (1-May-91 SY.NY134/R) Tilted painting no.7 (124x142cm-49x56in) i.overlap chl canvas

BORONKINE, Pavel (1911-1985) Russian
£1121 $2153   (29-Nov-90 YC.P65/R) Les roses sauvages (82x111cm-32x44in) s.verso (F.FR 11000)

BOROWIKOFFSKI, Wladimir Lukitsch (after) (1757-1825) Russian
£2400 $4680   (10-Oct-90 C196/R) Portrait of Ekaterina Aleksandrovna Novosil'tseva (69x55cm-27x22in)

BORRA, Pompeo (1898-1973) Italian
£1001 $1892   (27-Sep-90 F.M34) Bagnanti (70x50cm-28x20in) s. (I.L 2200000)
£1126 $2195   (24-Oct-90 F.M138/R) Due donne (60x50cm-24x20in) s. (I.L 2500000)
£1127 $2017   (9-Apr-91 F.R129) Busto femminile (79x60cm-31x24in) s. (I.L 2500000)
£4078 $7095   (26-Mar-91 F.M19/R) Paesaggio (57x71cm-22x28in) s. (I.L 9000000)

BORRACK, John Leo (1933-) Australian
£797 $1570   *(31-Oct-90 CH.S157) Lake Glenmaggie (59x85cm-23x33in) s. W/C (A.D 2000)*

BORRANI, Odoardo (1834-1905) Italian
£36969 $71349   (11-Dec-90 CH.R202/R) Porta a San Frediano (39x31cm-15x12in) (I.L 80000000)

BORRASSA, Luis (style) (c.1360-1424) Spanish
£11475 $22492   (24-Jan-91 EP.M10/R) San Pedro, San Pablo y los cuatro Evangelistas (56x203cm-22x80in) tempera gold ground panel altarpiece (S.P 2100000)

BORREL, Ramon (?) Spanish
£1902 $3652   (18-Dec-90 DUR.M26) Abrevadero (29x44cm-11x17in) panel (S.P 350000)

BORREMANS, Guglielmo (17/18th C) Flemish
£2955 $5792   (19-Nov-90 CH.R77/R) S.Giorgio libera la principessa (102x102cm-40x40in) (I.L 6500000)

BORRIS (18th C) Danish
£2847 $5352   (18-Sep-90 BU.K45/R) Figures among ruins (94x70cm-37x28in) s. (D.KR 32000)

BORRMEISTER, R (20th C) ?
£1340 $2318   (8-May-91 D.V77/R) Beauty and the beast (40x36cm-16x14in) s.d.1920 (A.S 28000)

BORRONI, Giovanni Angelo (1684-1772) Italian
£3381 $6052   (8-Apr-91 CH.R163/R) Visione di S.Maria Maddalena (60x45cm-24x18in) (I.L 7500000)
£912 $1614   (19-Mar-91 F.M217/R) Diana e Atteone (12x11cm-5x4in) pen bistre W/C ink over sanguine (I.L 2000000)

BORROW, William H (19th C) British
£900 $1665   (7-Mar-91 CSK76/R) Sussex coast between Hastings and Fairlight (27x41cm-11x16in) init.d.1880

BORSA, Emilio (1857-1931) Italian
£4091 $8019   (22-Nov-90 SY.MI64/R) Pascolo (92x71cm-36x28in) s. (I.L 9000000)

BORSA, Roberto (1880-1965) Italian
£638 $1066   (6-Jun-91 F.M91) Veduta montana di Chiareggio (30x40cm-12x16in) s. i.verso board (I.L 1400000)
£684 $1142   (6-Jun-91 F.M90) Paesaggio montano con contadina (30x40cm-12x16in) s. i.verso board (I.L 1500000)

BORSELEN, Jan Willem van (1825-1892) Dutch
£4848 $9552   (30-Oct-90 CH.AM137/R) Anglers by pond in wooded landscape, farmhouse
                         beyond (20x30cm-8x12in) s. panel (D.FL 16000)

BORSOS, Jozsef (1821-1883) Hungarian
£4545 $8909   (11-Feb-91 CSC.P14/R) Portrait d'homme avec son chien. Portrait de dame
                         de qualite (76x62cm-30x24in) pair (F.FR 45000)

BORSSOM, Anthonie van (attrib) (1630-1677) Dutch
£1300 $2600   (7-Feb-91 C93) An italianate landscape with a herdsman by a ruined arch,
                         by a pond (36x48cm-14x19in) indist.sig.

BORSTEL, R A (19/20th C) British?
£950 $1853   (18-Oct-90 CSK104/R) Full-rigged ship 'Ditton' (46x61cm-18x24in) i.
                         board

BORTIGNONI, Giuseppe (19/20th C) Italian
£789 $1500   (27-Feb-91 SY.NY340/R) Well told tale (37x53cm-15x21in) s.d.1891
£1000 $1680   (18-Jul-91 CSK161/R) He loves me, he loves me not (41x30cm-16x12in)
                         s.d.1900
£2600 $4472   (14-May-91 SWS313/R) Testing the vintage (41x32cm-16x13in) s.d.1886

BORTNYIK, Sandor (1893-1976) Hungarian
£1182 $2010   (1-Jun-91 VG.B452/R) Two women seated (36x47cm-14x19in) s.d.1928 gouache
                         (DM 3500)

BORTOLUZZI, Bianco Pietro see BIANCO, Pieretto

BORTOLUZZI, Millo (1868-1933) Italian
£832 $1605   (11-Dec-90 CH.R162 a) Barche in laguna (14x29cm-6x11in) s. W/C
                         (I.L 1800000)

BORVINE-FRENKEL, Boris (20th C) ?
£593 $1062   (14-Apr-91 GL.P79) L'allumage des bougies (35x24cm-14x9in) s. board
                         (F.FR 6000)

BOS, Henk (1901-) Dutch
£508 $1000   (7-Oct-90 DU.E239/R) Roses (51x46cm-20x18in) s.

BOSA, Louis (1905-) American
£729 $1400   (29-Nov-90 MFA.C202/R) Clown (36x61cm-14x24in) s. board

BOSANQUET, John E (attrib) (fl.1854-1861) Irish
£1852 $3574   (12-Dec-90 CH.E5/R) Lough Mahon with Blackrock Castle. Glenbrook and the
                         Turkish Baths (63x94cm-25x37in) W/C gum arabic (E.P 2000)

BOSBOOM, J (1817-1891) Dutch
£1323 $2501   (25-Sep-90 GM.B1109) Interieur d'eglise (33x26cm-13x10in) s. panel
                         (B.FR 80000)

BOSBOOM, Johannes (1817-1891) Dutch
£1198 $2012   (23-Apr-91 SY.AM289/R) Nun playing organ (76x60cm-30x24in) s.d.57
                         (D.FL 4000)
£2121 $4179   (30-Oct-90 CH.AM334/R) Figures in church interior (20x15cm-8x6in) s.
                         panel (D.FL 7000)
£3636 $7164   (30-Oct-90 CH.AM330/R) Interior of Laurenskerk, Alkmaar (19x15cm-7x6in)
                         s. panel (D.FL 12000)
£6098 $11951   (6-Nov-90 SY.AM235/R) Figures in church interior (25x19cm-10x7in) s.
                         panel (D.FL 20000)
£550 $1056   (27-Nov-90 PH220/R) Church organist and bell ringer (27x18cm-11x7in) s.
                         W/C
£670 $1286   (27-Nov-90 W.T1318/R) Interior of the town hall at Hattum
                         (14x21cm-6x8in) s.i. W/C (C.D 1500)
£1515 $2985   (30-Oct-90 CH.AM503/R) Figures in church interior (35x25cm-14x10in) s.
                         W/C bodycol (D.FL 5000)
£2395 $4024   (23-Apr-91 SY.AM112/R) In refectory (25x19cm-10x7in) W/C (D.FL 8000)

BOSC, Antonia (19th C) Italian
£1044 $1806   (6-May-91 ZEL.L1615/R) Landscape with figures and farmstead amongst
                         trees beyond (49x65cm-19x26in) s. (DM 3100)

BOSCARI, F (19th C) ?
£1400 $2758   (4-Oct-90 CSK248/R) On the Venetian lagoon (51x82cm-20x32in) s.

BOSCH, Ernst (1834-?) German
£26351 $51385   (26-Oct-90 KM.K1117/R) Peasant chopping wood before stable
                         (64x50cm-25x20in) s.d.99 (DM 78000)

BOSCH, Hieronymus (style) (1450-1516) Dutch
£17737 $34942   (14-Nov-90 SY.AM133/R) The Last Judgement. Expulsion from Paradise.
                         Damned. Portraits of donors (99x99cm-39x39in) triptych with folding
                         wings (D.FL 58000)

BOSCH, J H van den (18th C) Dutch
£1529 $2951   (12-Dec-90 CD.P22) Paysan et troupeau (30x34cm-12x13in) s.d.1795 panel
                         (F.FR 15000)

BOSCHI, Fabrizio (attrib) (?1570-1642) Italian
£1800 $2934 (1-Jul-91 S182/R) Design for cassone with two choices of decoration
     (21x35cm-8x14in) pen wash htd white over black chk

BOSCO, Nathalie (20th C) ?
£305 $610 (7-Feb-91 R.P52/R) Composition (61x64cm-24x25in) s. mixed media board
     (F.FR 3000)
£356 $711 (7-Feb-91 R.P94) Composition (76x125cm-30x49in) s. mixed media canvas
     (F.FR 3500)

BOSCOLI, Andrea (16th C) Italian
£750 $1268 (16-Apr-91 C125) A seated man asleep at a table (25x20cm-10x8in) i.
     labels red chk. double-sided
£1350 $2201 (1-Jul-91 S227) Military gathering (25x19cm-10x7in) bears num.4 pen wash
£1824 $3228 (19-Mar-91 F.M257/R) Studio di due profeti (26x23cm-10x9in) pen W/C ink
     over sanguine joined paper on board (I.L 4000000)
£1900 $3211 (16-Apr-91 C93/R) A youth sleeping wrapped in his cloak (6x12cm-2x5in)
     blk.chk.ink wash
£13000 $21190 (2-Jul-91 C100/R) Standing youth, partly dressed, wearing doublet,
     pulling up stockings (38x18cm-15x7in) red chk

BOSELLI, Felice (1650-1732) Italian
£7274 $14256 (19-Nov-90 CH.R140/R) Copia dalla Madonna del collo lungo del
     Parmigianino (209x163cm-82x64in) (I.L 16000000)
£9000 $15210 (19-Apr-91 C130/R) A still life of fish on a river bank with an owl
     perched on a tub (112x133cm-44x52in)

BOSELLI, Felice (circle) (1650-1732) Italian
£1600 $3200 (7-Feb-91 C99/R) An oxen's giblet with children and a dog
     (66x94cm-26x37in)

BOSELLI, Felice (style) (1650-1732) Italian
£3000 $5700 (13-Sep-90 CSK83/R) Hens, chicks and cockerel by plinth
     (75x60cm-30x24in)

BOSER, Friedrich (1809-1881) German
£9333 $16707 (12-Apr-91 BM.B567/R) Two little girls selling flowers (71x56cm-28x22in)
     s.d.1850 (DM 28000)

BOSHIER, Derek (1937-) British
£1276 $2500 (6-Nov-90 CE.NY264/R) Fashion victim, snow (221x152cm-87x60in)
     s.i.d.1985 verso

BOSIO, Jean Francois (1764-1827) French
£8000 $13040 (2-Jul-91 C164/R) Musical party (21x30cm-8x12in) black chk pen wash

BOSKEN, Lorenz (1891-1967) German
£612 $986 (26-Jun-91 KM.K1400/R) Lake landscape, summer evening (60x90cm-24x35in)
     s. (DM 1800)
£4530 $8834 (13-Oct-90 KRA.D355/R) Kampfesglut (110x160cm-43x63in) s. (DM 13500)

BOSKERCK, Robert Ward van (1855-?) American
£536 $900 (28-Apr-91 HG.C9) Birches along the river (61x86cm-24x34in) s.
£592 $1000 (1-May-91 B.SF5225/R) Pine trees in valley (62x93cm-24x37in) s.
£787 $1550 (7-Oct-90 DU.E171/R) Canal scene (58x81cm-23x32in) s.
£912 $1550 (1-Jun-91 LAE.L12/R) Tranquil river (61x81cm-24x32in) s.
£1094 $2100 (17-Dec-90 SY.NY67/R) Summer day (51x76cm-20x30in) s.
£2890 $5000 (21-May-91 BG.M985/R) Midsummer, Wakefield Road (41x61cm-16x24in) s.

BOSMAN, Richard (20th C) American
£1667 $3250 (10-Oct-90 SY.NY563/R) Man shaving (137x107cm-54x42in) s.verso

BOSS, Eduard (1873-?) Swiss
£520 $879 (1-May-91 GD.B83/R) Still life of fruit and book (42x53cm-17x21in)
     s.d.21 (S.FR 1300)
£637 $1243 (24-Oct-90 GD.B172/R) Corn harvest (66x91cm-26x36in) s.d.36 (S.FR 1600)
£640 $1082 (1-May-91 GD.B82/R) View of town, winter (38x52cm-15x20in) s.d.20 board
     (S.FR 1600)
£880 $1487 (1-May-91 GD.B85/R) View of Bern with gasworks (80x63cm-31x25in) s.d.20
     (S.FR 2200)
£1120 $1893 (1-May-91 GD.B84/R) Farmhouses in landscape with wooded hills beyond
     (64x100cm-25x39in) s.d.1900 (S.FR 2800)

BOSSCHAERT, Ambrosius (elder) (1573-1621) Flemish
£195000 $317850 (4-Jul-91 B189/R) Still life of a rose, tulip, crocus, a fritillary and
     other flowers ina Wan Li bottle jar (24x18cm-9x7in) st. copper
£400000 $652000 (5-Jul-91 C36/R) Mixed flowers in glass jar with Red Admiral, Chalk Blue
     and flies on stone ledge (23x16cm-9x6in) mono. copper

BOSSCHAERT, Ambrosius (younger) (1609-1645) Dutch
£43967 $78701 (14-Mar-91 D.V82/R) Bunch of tulips, rose and other spring flowers
     (37x49cm-15x19in) panel (A.S 900000)

BOSSCHAERT, Jean Baptiste (1667-1746) Flemish
£11581 $18877 (14-Jun-91 AGS.P38/R) Vases de fleurs sur des entablements
     (43x34cm-17x13in) both s.d. pair (F.FR 115000)

BOSSCHAERT, Jean Baptiste (1667-1746) Flemish-cont.
£12333 $23926   (5-Dec-90 APT.P34/R) Bouquet de fleurs dans une urne sur un entablement
           (85x69cm-33x27in) s. (F.FR 120000)
£13000 $25090   (11-Dec-90 PH221/R) Still life of flowers including roses, peonies,
           convolvulus and tulips (64x76cm-25x30in) s.

BOSSCHAERT, Jean Baptiste (studio) (1667-1746) Flemish
£3550 $7028   (30-Jan-91 APT.P42/R) Bouquets de fleurs dans une urne (40x32cm-16x13in)
           pair (F.FR 35000)

BOSSCHAERT, Thomas see WILLEBOIRTS, Thomas

BOSSCHE, Balthasar van den (1681-1715) Flemish
£27000 $52110   (12-Dec-90 S170/R) Interior of painter's studio. Interior of sculptor's
           studio (68x83cm-27x33in) s. pair

BOSSCHE, Balthasar van den (attrib) (1681-1715) Flemish
£5607 $10765   (30-Nov-90 APT.P87/R) Le tribut du fermier (103x116cm-41x46in)
           (F.FR 55000)

BOSSCHE, Philipp van den (17th C) Dutch
£2141 $4217   *(12-Nov-90 CH.AM63/R) Travellers on road in rocky wooded river
           landscape, town beyond (10x12cm-4x5in) i. pen (D.FL 7000)*

BOSSHARD, Rodolphe-Theophile (1889-1959) Swiss
£2041 $3959   (8-Dec-90 GAB.G2403) Mer avec voilier (23x31cm-9x12in) s.d.30 oil
           pavatex panel (S.FR 5000)
£2800 $4732   (1-May-91 GD.B88/R) Vineyards at Lake Geneva (31x39cm-12x15in)
           (S.FR 7000)
£3586 $6167   (14-May-91 GF.L2204/R) Houses of Paris (30x40cm-12x16in) s.d.1937 panel
           (S.FR 9000)
£4032 $7742   (2-Dec-90 GAB.G1518/R) Les peupliers de Grandvaux (30x45cm-12x18in) i.
           verso panel (S.FR 10000)
£4819 $9446   (21-Nov-90 GAB.G1515/R) Fleurs (46x33cm-18x13in) s.d.45 panel (S.FR 12000)
£5306 $10294   (8-Dec-90 GAB.G2408/R) Nature mrote aux raisins et coings
           (24x35cm-9x14in) s. (S.FR 13000)
£6048 $11613   (2-Dec-90 GAB.G1515/R) Sous-bois et cabane (55x46cm-22x18in) s.
           (S.FR 15000)
£6452 $12387   (2-Dec-90 GAB.G1517/R) Nature morte au pain et au vin (46x38cm-18x15in)
           s.d.39 board (S.FR 16000)
£8032 $15743   (21-Nov-90 SY.Z90/R) Theiere bleue (50x61cm-20x24in) s.d.42 (S.FR 20000)
£10484 $20129   (2-Dec-90 GAB.G1512/R) Nu au viaduc (37x50cm-15x20in) s.d.23 panel
           (S.FR 26000)
£11437 $22417   (25-Nov-90 LC.P123/R) Le repos des modeles (38x55cm-15x22in) s.d.23
           (F.FR 113000)
£12097 $23226   (2-Dec-90 GAB.G1513/R) Le volcan de Santorin (36x49cm-14x19in) s. i.
           verso panel (S.FR 30000)
£16935 $32516   (2-Dec-90 GAB.G1514/R) La mouette blessee (61x73cm-24x29in) s.
           (S.FR 42000)
£30242 $58065   (2-Dec-90 GAB.G1516/R) Nu aux oiseaux (73x92cm-29x36in) s.d.46
           (S.FR 75000)
£571   *$1109*   *(8-Dec-90 GAB.G2402) Nu accoude (31x23cm-12x9in) s.d.49 lead pencil
           (S.FR 1400)*
£816   *$1584*   *(8-Dec-90 GAB.G2409/R) Tete de jeune femme endormie (40x50cm-16x20in)
           mono.i.d.27 sept. 47 crayon htd.ball pen (S.FR 2000)*
£898   *$1742*   *(8-Dec-90 GAB.G2410) Portrait cubiste de femme (42x24cm-17x9in)
           mono.d.1922 chl. (S.FR 2200)*
£968   *$1858*   *(2-Dec-90 GAB.G1519/R) Femme nue allongee (22x31cm-9x12in) s.d.33 Indian
           ink (S.FR 2400)*
£1306   *$2534*   *(8-Dec-90 GAB.G2405/R) Nu etendu (24x41cm-9x16in) s. chl. (S.FR 3200)*
£3360   *$5711*   *(27-May-91 GK.Z5310/R) Nature morte au fruits (23x39cm-9x15in) s. pastel
           (S.FR 8500)*

BOSSI, Domenico (c.1765-?) Italian
£1633   *$3216*   *(13-Nov-90 CH.G276/R) Portrait of young lady wearing black dress with
           white lace ruff (6x5cm-2x2in) min.s.d.1812 gilt-metal frame ribbon-tie
           (S.FR 4000)*

BOSSI, Giuseppe (19th C) Italian
£319   *$565*   *(19-Mar-91 F.M294/R) Scena di storia antica (7x10cm-3x4in) W/C ink
           (I.L 700000)*
£912   *$1614*   *(19-Mar-91 F.M101/R) Studio per figure decorative (24x35cm-9x14in) ink
           (I.L 2000000)*
£1596   *$2825*   *(19-Mar-91 F.M268/R) Studio per l'apoteosi di Bodoni (21x15cm-8x6in) ink
           (I.L 3500000)*
£3420   *$6053*   *(19-Mar-91 F.M231/R) Studio per un ritratto di dama in bianco
           (37x24cm-15x9in) pencil chk (I.L 7500000)*

BOSSI, Giuseppe (attrib) (19th C) Italian
£902 $1614   (8-Apr-91 CH.R47) Supposto ritratto di Eugenio Beauharnais
           (57x46cm-22x18in) (I.L 2000000)

BOSSOLI, Carlo (1815-1884) Italian
£15000 $30000   (18-Oct-90 F.M28/R) La Giralda a Siviglia, Spagna (42x67cm-17x26in)
           s.d.1872 board (I.L 34000)

BOSSOLI, Carlo (1815-1884) Italian-cont.
£18000	$29520	(19-Jun-91 S355/R) Falls of Terni. Monte Viso, Northern Italy (247x132cm-97x52in) s.d.1856 pair
£1407	$2308	(21-Jun-91 SY.MO357/R) La Italien (19x28cm-7x11in) bears sig. gouache (F.FR 14000)
£1500	$2460	(19-Jun-91 B64/R) Lochranza Castle, Arran (27x44cm-11x17in) s. gouache
£12000	$23040	(28-Nov-90 S6/R) View of the Plaza Mayor, Madrid (25x44cm-10x17in) s. W/C gouache
£13000	$24960	(28-Nov-90 S5/R) View of Royal Palace Berlin, looking west towards Unter Den Linden (26x41cm-10x16in) s. W/C gouache

BOSSOLI, Carlo (style) (1815-1884) Italian
£780	$1529	(14-Feb-91 CSK13/R) The city of Pest on the Danube, Hungary (74x58cm-29x23in) bodycol.

BOSSON, Netton (1882-1951) Swiss
£598	$1165	(24-Oct-90 GD.B173/R) Vorstadtleben (29x20cm-11x8in) s.d.50 W/C over pencil (S.FR 1500)

BOSSUET, Francois Antoine (1798-1889) Belgian
£1701	$3010	(20-Mar-91 KM.K1115) Ruin of oriental tower near St Rocque with figures and Gibraltar beyond (58x48cm-23x19in) s.d.51 (DM 5000)
£3000	$5910	(5-Oct-90 C21/R) Boats moored by riverside town, possibly Seville (30x45cm-12x18in) s. panel
£10256	$20000	(23-Oct-90 SY.NY331/R) Tour de L'Or, Seville (50x71cm-20x28in) s.d.1878

BOST, Melanie (19th C) French
£653	$1287	(13-Nov-90 CH.G277) Portrait of young girl wearing white dress and jewelled pendant (5x?cm-2x?in) min.s.gold brooch frame mother-of-pearl oval (S.FR 1600)

BOSTON, Paul (20th C) Australian
£3505	$5713	(16-Jun-91 SY.ME29/R) Untitled (203x136cm-80x54in) s.d.1989 verso (A.D 7500)
£1682	$2742	(16-Jun-91 SY.ME18/R) Untitled - head (106x73cm-42x29in) mixed media Dessin Ja paper (A.D 3600)
£1776	$2894	(16-Jun-91 SY.ME1) Untitled (54x75cm-21x30in) pastel (A.D 3800)

BOTELLO, Angel (1913-1986) Spanish
£5612	$11000	(20-Nov-90 CH.NY304/R) Retrato de Haitiana (51x43cm-20x17in) s. masonite
£6000	$9660	(24-Jun-91 CSK188/R) Las muchachas (76x61cm-30x24in) s. panel
£6500	$10465	(24-Jun-91 CSK190/R) La chica (122x91cm-48x36in) s. panel
£6633	$13000	(20-Nov-90 CH.NY301/R) Hermanas (46x37cm-18x15in) s. num 707 verso panel
£6977	$12000	(15-May-91 CH.NY204/R) Nina con Peine (61x46cm-24x18in) s. panel
£7908	$15500	(19-Nov-90 SY.NY200/R) Ninos (80x65cm-31x26in) s. panel
£8140	$14000	(15-May-91 CH.NY205/R) Musicos (85x71cm-33x28in) s. panel

BOTERO, Fernando (1932-) Colombian
£11735	$23000	(19-Nov-90 SY.NY163/R) Manzana (28x23cm-11x9in) s.d.58 board
£25510	$50000	(20-Nov-90 CH.NY164/R) Gato (51x61cm-20x24in) s.d.65 s.l.d.64 verso
£26163	$45000	(15-May-91 CH.NY77/R) La Pera (48x45cm-19x18in) s.
£76768	$150465	(14-Feb-91 GL.P14/R) La chambre (176x111cm-69x44in) s.d.1982 (F.FR 760000)
£91837	$180000	(20-Nov-90 CH.NY72/R) Juan XXIII de nino (89x82cm-35x32in) s.d.65
£102041	$200000	(20-Nov-90 CH.NY20/R) Santa Isabel de Hungria (124x94cm-49x37in) s.d.70 s.i.d.verso
£112245	$220000	(19-Nov-90 SY.NY75/R) The boss (91x86cm-36x34in) s.d.1963
£151163	$260000	(15-May-91 CH.NY39/R) Autorretrao el Dia de mi Primera Comunion (109x94cm-43x37in) s.d.1970 l. verso
£153061	$300000	(20-Nov-90 CH.NY63/R) Mujer de pie (153x90cm-60x35in) s.d.82
£255102	$500000	(20-Nov-90 CH.NY25/R) La Colombiana (144x199cm-57x78in) s.
£265306	$520000	(19-Nov-90 SY.NY67/R) Three musicians (164x123cm-65x48in) s.d.83
£3486	$5926	(2-Jun-91 GL.P147) Femme au velo (37x31cm-15x12in) s. lead pencil (F.FR 35000)
£3984	$6773	(2-Jun-91 GL.P150/R) Le grand boss (43x55cm-17x22in) s.d.1963 lead pencil Indian ink (F.FR 40000)
£5172	$9931	(26-Nov-90 WK.M7/R) Female nude (56x28cm-22x11in) s.d.1954 pencil dr. (DM 15000)
£5612	$11000	(19-Nov-90 SY.NY164/R) Man on horseback (40x33cm-16x13in) s. pencil
£11735	$23000	(19-Nov-90 SY.NY242/R) Woman - la vie en pierre noir (44x34cm-17x13in) s.d.86 ink chl pencil
£13953	$24000	(15-May-91 CH.NY159/R) El Presidente (43x35cm-17x14in) s.i.d.71 pencil
£14201	$24000	(1-May-91 SY.NY228/R) Still life (69x69cm-27x27in) s. W/C pastel
£15306	$30000	(20-Nov-90 CH.NY204/R) French poodle (71x65cm-28x26in) s.d.67 pastel
£16216	$27568	(1-Jun-91 VG.B361/R) Standing woman drinking (44x35cm-17x14in) s.d.1986 pencil paper on board (DM 48000)
£30612	$60000	(20-Nov-90 CH.NY253/R) Madre Superiora en la Ventana (75x75cm-30x30in) s.d.68 pastel board
£31757	$53986	(31-May-91 VG.B84/R) Dancing couple (51x36cm-20x14in) s.d.1987 chk pencil W/C (DM 94000)
£73964	$125000	(30-Apr-91 SY.NY24/R) Nino de Vallecas (174x126cm-69x50in) s.d.71 pastel toned paper
£163265	$320000	(20-Nov-90 CH.NY50/R) Exhibition (52x196cm-20x77in) s.d.75 collage oil canvas

BOTH, Andries (1608-1650) Dutch
£157895 $300000 (11-Jan-91 CH.NY34/R) Christ crowned with thorns (157x224cm-62x88in)
£4587 $9037 *(12-Nov-90 CH.AM79/R) Dunes on outskirts of Scheveningen with two men and dogs (13x20cm-5x8in) s. pen (D.FL 15000)*

BOTH, Andries (school) (1608-1650) Dutch
£2273 $4455 (20-Nov-90 F.R19/R) Scena di osteria (53x41cm-21x16in) (I.L 5000000)

BOTH, Jan (1618-1652) Dutch
£16000 $30880 (11-Dec-90 PH163/R) Travellers crossing bridge over gorge (102x87cm-40x34in) s.
£18089 $34007 (19-Sep-90 N.M349/R) Wooded landscape with travellers near bridge across stream (82x116cm-32x46in) s. (DM 53000)

BOTH, Jan (after) (1618-1652) Dutch
£883 $1767 (9-Feb-91 BU.O168) The Holy Family in landscape (105x88cm-41x35in) indist.s. (N.KR 10000)
£1000 $1900 (12-Sep-90 LW1765) Extensive landscape with figures, cattle and horses on foreground track (66x81cm-26x32in)
£1926 $3216 (6-Jun-91 D.V301/R) Southern landscape at sunset (56x45cm-22x18in) (A.S 40000)

BOTH, Jan (attrib) (1618-1652) Dutch
£2789 $4797 (14-May-91 GF.L2275/R) River landscape with ruin of aquaduct (45x55cm-18x22in) (S.FR 7000)
£7059 $12000 (31-May-91 CH.NY149/R) Encampment under stone archway with peasants rosting chestnuts (59x48cm-23x19in)

BOTH, Jan (circle) (1618-1652) Dutch
£979 $1928 *(12-Nov-90 CH.AM104/R) Temple of Vesta, Rome (24x35cm-9x14in) with i. verso black lead wash ink (D.FL 3200)*

BOTH, Jan (school) (1618-1652) Dutch
£1786 $3071 (19-May-91 ZZ.F82/R) La halte (40x49cm-16x19in) panel (F.FR 18000)

BOTH, Jan (style) (1618-1652) Dutch
£900 $1800 (7-Feb-91 C88) A extensive landscape with shepherds resting under a tree (25x33cm-10x13in) i.
£1224 $2412 (14-Nov-90 D.V203/R) Mountainous river landscape with travellers (96x79cm-38x31in) (A.S 25000)
£1368 $2285 (4-Jun-91 CH.R19) Paesaggio con viandante (66x82cm-26x32in) (I.L 3000000)
£1500 $2880 (29-Nov-90 CSK112/R) Wooded landscape with peasants and cattle by stream (77x92cm-30x36in)
£1700 $2873 (18-Apr-91 CSK103/R) Extensive Italianate landscape with shepherds on path by river (80x91cm-31x36in)
£1800 $3420 (13-Sep-90 CSK332/R) Shepherds by mill, ruined temple beyond (43x53cm-17x21in) panel
£2200 $3586 (4-Jul-91 C501/R) Extensive Italianate landscape with travellers on path by waterfall (76x109cm-30x43in)
£3800 $7486 (1-Nov-90 CSK58/R) North Italian classical river landscape at sunset with figures by villa (119x164cm-47x65in)
£11000 $18590 (18-Apr-91 C95/R) A mountainous Italianate landscape with a horseman and peasants (82x112cm-32x44in)

BOTHAMS, Walter (?-c.1914) British
£489 $948 *(4-Dec-90 R.T114/R) Sheep in pasture at dawn (8x13cm-3x5in) s. W/C (C.D 1100)*

BOTHE, C (19th C) ?
£1193 $2350 (13-Nov-90 AB.S862/R) Still life of grapes, peaches and raspberries (26x31cm-10x12in) s.d.1835 (S.KR 13000)

BOTHNER, Einar (1886-1955) Norwegian
£1045 $2038 (15-Oct-90 B.O9/R) Street scene (54x65cm-21x26in) s.d.1943 (N.KR 12000)
£1425 $2750 (10-Dec-90 B.O13/R) Garden and shed, 1908 (64x57cm-25x22in) s.d.08 (N.KR 16000)
£1489 $2665 (14-Mar-91 BU.O9/R) Spring flood, Nidelven (68x68cm-27x27in) s.indist.d.42 i.verso (N.KR 17000)

BOTKE, Jessie Arms (1883-?) American
£1354 $2600 (1-Dec-90 LAE.L8/R) Cockatoos in foliage (28x38cm-11x15in) s. gold leaf board
£2168 $4250 (12-Feb-91 MOR.P38) Cranes and water lilies (23x23cm-9x9in) s. gold leaf board
£2564 $5000 (10-Oct-90 B.SF503/R) White peacocks (61x51cm-24x20in) s.
£3571 $7000 (13-Feb-91 B.SF2164/R) Glorious peacock (63x76cm-25x30in) s.d.1926 board

BOTKIN, Henry Albert (1896-1983) American
£316 $600 *(12-Jan-91 LAE.L14/R) Abstract reclining figure (15x20cm-6x8in) s. mixed media board*

BOTT, Francis (1904-?) German
£2200 $3674 (5-Jun-91 HC.P332) Composition sur fond brun (59x72cm-23x28in) s.d.62 (F.FR 22000)

BOTT, Francis (1904-?) German-cont.
£3175 $5492   (25-May-91 AB.L44/R) Cathedral (30x34cm-12x13in) s.d.1975 panel
                        (S.FR 8000)
£4016 $7871   (24-Nov-90 AB.L69/R) Eclat (40x48cm-16x19in) s.d.59 canvas on board
                        (S.FR 10000)
£400 $668   *(5-Jun-91 HC.P331) Composition a la tache jaune (13x18cm-5x7in) s.d.61*
                        mixed media (F.FR 4000)
£3378 $5845   *(25-May-91 N.M31/R) Composition (50x65cm-20x26in) s. pastel col.chk*
                        (DM 10000)
£3800 $7410   *(17-Oct-90 G.Z74/R) Composition (25x20cm-10x8in) s.d.1966 mixed media*
                        relief collage (S.FR 9500)
£5221 $10233   *(24-Nov-90 AB.L70/R) Composition (59x41cm-23x16in) s.d.65 oil mixed*
                        media board (S.FR 13000)
£5556 $9111   *(21-Jun-91 G.Z61) Instant spatial (66x98cm-26x39in) s.d.1956 mixed media*
                        board (S.FR 14000)

BOTTCHER, Hans (1897-1986) German
£507 $877   (21-May-91 WK.M629/R) Untitled picture 14 (80x105cm-31x41in) mono.d.1976
                        s.i.d.verso (DM 1500)
£1689 $2922   (21-May-91 WK.M628/R) Composition (100x200cm-39x79in) mono.d.1964
                        (DM 5000)

BOTTGER, Herbert (1898-1954) German
£1858 $3623   (26-Oct-90 KM.K1114/R) Still life of lady's slipper in vase
                        (35x27cm-14x11in) mono. (DM 5500)

BOTTGER, S (19th C) ?
£1498 $2501   (6-Jun-91 RAS.K243/R) The brig 'St.Thomas' - 1st May 1847
                        (51x72cm-20x28in) s. pen W/C (D.KR 17000)

BOTTI, Italo (1889-1974) Argentinian
£1561 $2700   (8-May-91 RO.BA225) Camino de los cocos (63x80cm-25x31in) s.d.1943
£1579 $3000   (11-Sep-90 PO.BA22) Naturaleza muerta (49x69cm-19x27in) s.
£2632 $5000   (11-Sep-90 PO.BA21) Paisaje serrano (98x122cm-39x48in) s.

BOTTICELLI (circle) (15/16th C) Italian
£26316 $50000   (11-Jan-91 CH.NY25/R) The Virgin and young Saint John the Baptist
                        worshipping the Child (51cm-20ins circular) tempera panel round

BOTTICELLI (style) (15/16th C) Italian
£5378 $9250   (15-May-91 D.NY77) Madonna and child in landscape (84cm-33ins circular)
                        panel

BOTTICELLI, Sandro (after) (1440-1510) Italian
£1118 $1900   (30-May-91 CE.NY36) Madonna and Child with angels (68cm-27ins circular)
                        panel

BOTTICELLI, Sandro (school) (1440-1510) Italian
£7625 $14716   (12-Dec-90 F.M85/R) Sposalizio di S. Caterina (69x52cm-27x20in)
                        (I.L 16500000)

BOTTICELLI, Sandro (studio) (1440-1510) Italian
£45000 $73350   (5-Jul-91 C71/R) Madonna and Child with San Giovanni Gualberto
                        (70x48cm-28x19in) tempera panel
£110526 $210000   (11-Jan-91 CH.NY4/R) The Madonna and Child (35x26cm-14x10in) tempera
                        panel

BOTTICHER, Walter (19/20th C) German
£1356 $2264   (6-Jun-91 HN.H167) Portrait of an old man (56x46cm-22x18in) (DM 4000)

BOTTICINI, Francesco (attrib) (1446-1497) Italian
£15882 $27000   (30-May-91 SY.NY30/R) Virgin and Saitn John the Baptist adoring Infant
                        Christ (62x42cm-24x17in) tempera gold ground panel rounded top

BOTTICINI, Giovanni Domenico (attrib) (15th C) Italian
£57895 $110000   (10-Jan-91 SY.NY2/R) Virgin and Child with four angels
                        (147x72cm-58x28in) tempera panel

BOTTICINI, Raffaello (1477-?) Italian
£28000 $47320   (17-Apr-91 S138/R) Madonna and Child with infant St John
                        (79cm-31ins circular) panel

BOTTIGLIERI, G (19th C) Italian
£683 $1162   (28-May-91 F.R48) Paesaggio (28x42cm-11x17in) faesite (I.L 1500000)

BOTTINI, Georges (1873-1906) French
£1282 $2526   (6-Oct-90 GL.P11) Le reve de la jeune femme (19x33cm-7x13in) s.d.98 W/C
                        wash (F.FR 13000)
£7426 $13144   (5-Apr-91 LGB.P80/R) Scene de bar (21x40cm-8x16in) s. W/C (F.FR 75000)

BOTTOMLEY, Fred (1883-?) British
£675 $1330   (31-Oct-90 HUN3) Boulevard, Southport (61x74cm-24x29in)

BOTTON, Jean Isy de (1898-1978) French
£769 $1500   (10-Oct-90 D.NY17) Tiger lillies (74x61cm-29x24in) s.

BOUCHARD, Lorne Holland (1913-1978) Canadian
£873 $1712   (5-Nov-90 FB.M192 b) Beach at St.George's, Gaspe (31x46cm-12x18in)
     s.verso board (C.D 2000)
£933 $1811   (4-Dec-90 P.Q40) Early May, Petit Lac Ha Ha, Parc des Laurentides
     (35x76cm-14x30in) s. board (C.D 2100)
£1471 $2603   (20-Mar-91 EA.M509) Fishing cove - Gaspe coast (45x76cm-18x30in) s.
     d.1967 verso masonite (C.D 3000)

BOUCHARDON, Edme (1698-1762) French
£1550 $2527   (1-Jul-91 S153/R) Head of Hercules in profile (24x18cm-9x7in) red chk
£4200 $8106   (11-Dec-90 C79/R) Putti and nymph playing with a boar (22x41cm-9x16in)
     i. red chk.
£9000 $17370   (11-Dec-90 C78/R) The Massacre of the innocents (30x45cm-12x18in) s.i.
     red chk.

BOUCHE, Francois (1924-) French
£600 $1038   (10-May-91 S.Z7/R) Les coquilles d'or (50x66cm-20x26in) s. col.pencil
     (S.FR 1500)

BOUCHE, Georges (1874-1941) French
£2008 $3233   (24-Jun-91 DL.P28/R) Femme assise (65x54cm-26x21in) s. (F.FR 20000)

BOUCHE, Louis Alexandre (1838-1911) French
£1829 $3000   (19-Jun-91 B.SF1741/R) Une fleuve dans la Dordogne (46x61cm-18x24in)
     s.d.1906

BOUCHENE, Dimitri (20th C) French
£407 $813   (6-Feb-91 FB.P48) Les jardins du Luxembourg (56x68cm-22x27in) s. pastel
     (F.FR 4000)
£407 $813   (6-Feb-91 FB.P45) Le ballet romantique (67x52cm-26x20in) s. i. verso
     gouache pastel (F.FR 4000)
£453 $739   (14-Jun-91 FB.P26) Hommage a guardi (45x65cm-18x26in) s.i. gouache
     (F.FR 4500)
£508 $1016   (6-Feb-91 FB.P49) Jongleur au cirque (63x48cm-25x19in) s. pastel
     (F.FR 5000)
£558 $1100   (15-Nov-90 SY.NY57) Costume design for an old man (23x15cm-9x6in) s.
     gouache
£1396 $2750   (15-Nov-90 SY.NY55/R) Two decor designs (33x51cm-13x20in) s. gouache
     pair
£1650 $3250   (15-Nov-90 SY.NY56/R) Costume design for carnival character
     (23x15cm-9x6in) s. gouache
£1777 $3500   (15-Nov-90 SY.NY54/R) A new year's greeting (18x25cm-7x10in) s.i.
     gouache foil collage
£3553 $7000   (15-Nov-90 SY.NY56 a) Costume design for a masked lady (23x15cm-9x6in)
     s. gouache

BOUCHER (18th C) French
£867 $1457   (23-Apr-91 CH.R109) Scene galanti (10cm-4ins circular) min. tempera
     gilded wood frame pair (I.L 1900000)

BOUCHER (school) (18th C) French
£797 $1378   (22-May-91 PLF.P14) Femme nue assise (29x21cm-11x8in) crayon sanguinne
     htd.white (F.FR 8000)

BOUCHER (style) (18th C) French
£3974 $7750   (24-Oct-91 D.NY33) Putti angling. Marine putti (53x64cm-21x25in) oval
     pair

BOUCHER, Francois (1703-1770) French
£157895 $300000   (11-Jan-91 CH.NY82/R) Muse Erato (93x132cm-37x52in) and studio
£200000 $380000   (11-Jan-91 CH.NY74/R) The Apotheosis of Aenaes (92x125cm-36x49in)
     s.d.1747
£1800 $3186   (22-May-91 APT.P74/R) Apparition de la Vierge, l'enfant Jesus a un saint
     (34x23cm-13x9in) i. sanguinne (F.FR 18000)
£2381 $4119   (22-May-91 GS.B2332) Portrait of young woman with bird perched on left
     hand (39x32cm-15x13in) pastel (S.FR 6000)
£3500 $5705   (2-Jul-91 C161/R) Pastoral lovers (23x18cm-9x7in) brown black chk
£3500 $6195   (22-Mar-91 APT.P73/R) Soldats au repos (22x30cm-9x12in) pen wash
     sanguine (F.FR 35000)
£4082 $8000   (6-Nov-90 GF.L2060/R) Two Chinese boys playing (20x15cm-8x6in) s. pencil
     (S.FR 10000)
£4300 $7611   (22-Mar-91 APT.P71/R) Le feu (33x23cm-13x9in) i. blk.crayon stumping
     sanguinne htd.cols. (F.FR 43000)
£4520 $8000   (22-Mar-91 CH.NY607/R) La Bohemienne (22x16cm-9x6in) i. blk.chk.
£5000 $8850   (22-Mar-91 APT.P70/R) Tete de femme, vue de profil a droite
     (21x15cm-8x6in) s. pierre noire sanguinne htd.white and cols.
     (F.FR 50000)
£5105 $8525   (4-Jun-91 R.T251/R) Studies of two soldier's heads (33x42cm-13x17in)
     black white chk (C.D 9750)
£6215 $11000   (22-Mar-91 CH.NY608/R) A shepherdess standing in a landscape holding a
     basket under her arm (19x14cm-7x6in) blk.chk.
£7000 $11410   (2-Jul-91 C331/R) Female nude, seen from back (26x39cm-10x15in) with i.
     red white chk
£7500 $14475   (11-Dec-90 C87/R) Study of a child (27x22cm-11x9in) chk.
£9474 $18000   (9-Jan-91 CH.NY52/R) Shepherd and shepherdess with bird trap
     (17x23cm-7x9in) red chk ovcl

BOUCHER, Francois (1703-1770) French-cont.

£10526	$20000	(8-Jan-91 SY.NY170/R) Study of a man raising a hammer (31x19cm-12x7in) chk.
£14070	$23075	(18-Jun-91 APT.P59/R) Berger pres d'une bergere endormie (23x28cm-9x11in) s. sanguinne (F.FR 140000)
£15291	$29511	(12-Dec-90 ARC.P51/R) La passerelle (31x23cm-12x9in) pierre noire stumping (F.FR 150000)
£15789	$30000	(9-Jan-91 CH.NY58/R) Venus presenting arms to Aeneas (24x30cm-9x12in) pen wash htd white
£24000	$39120	(2-Jul-91 C330/R) Head of young girl, looking down to right (23x19cm-9x7in) col.chk
£30000	$48900	(2-Jul-91 C329/R) Mother and child and other figures seen from below (30x41cm-12x16in) with i. black white chk
£33898	$60000	(22-Mar-91 CH.NY606/R) A study of the head of Ariadne, looking up to the left (26x20cm-10x8in) i. blk.red chk. pastel htd.white stumped
£42373	$75000	(22-Mar-91 CH.NY605/R) Head of a woman, bust length, with flowers in her hair (30x23cm-12x9in) blk.white chk.

BOUCHER, Francois (after) (18th C) French

£1582	$3116	(16-Nov-90 PLF.P12/R) La surprise (69x63cm-27x25in) s. (F.FR 15500)
£2000	$3380	(1-May-91 B89/R) Le feu, allegory of fire (77x105cm-30x41in) canvas on board after Duflos (S.FR 5000)
£2200	$4400	(7-Feb-91 C87) The birth and triumph of Venus (66x56cm-26x22in) s.d.1767
£2261	$4386	(7-Dec-90 CN.P145/R) Tete de jeune femme (41x32cm-16x13in) (F.FR 22000)
£4200	$6846	(4-Jul-91 C781/R) Portrait of Madame de Pompadour, seated, in bower (74x58cm-29x23in) with sig.d.1758
£12272	$24298	(30-Jan-91 CSC.P2/R) Diane et Callisto. L'oiseau cheri. Pastorale. L'amour conduisant sesfleches four (F.FR 121000)
£1977	$3500	(22-Mar-91 CH.NY610/R) The head of a woman, in profile, looking down to the right (26x22cm-10x9in) blk.white chk.stumped

BOUCHER, Francois (attrib) (18th C) French

£797	$1378	(22-May-91 PLF.P12/R) Femme assise entouree de ses enfants (16x14cm-6x6in) pen (F.FR 8000)
£1100	$1947	(22-Mar-91 APT.P10) Jeune paysanne au marche (14x10cm-6x4in) pen sepia wash (F.FR 11000)
£1325	$2544	(27-Nov-90 APT.P153/R) Le cireur de chaussure ou le decrotteur (23x16cm-9x6in) wash sketch pierre noire (F.FR 13000)
£1429	$2814	(13-Nov-90 GF.L5022) Head of young woman (20x16cm-8x6in) ochre htd.white (S.FR 3500)
£2111	$3461	(21-Jun-91 CK.P17/R) Villageoise portant un panier et ses trois enfants (27x18cm-11x7in) i. pierre noire htd.white (F.FR 21000)
£3568	$6886	(12-Dec-90 ARC.P50/R) Etude de jeune enfant tenant un bras de femme (24x24cm-9x9in) pierre noire sanguinne htd.white (F.FR 35000)
£4802	$8500	(22-Mar-91 CH.NY609/R) A shepherd and shepherdess in a landscape (27x21cm-11x8in) i. blk.chk.

BOUCHER, Francois (circle) (18th C) French

£2982	$5040	(18-Apr-91 APT.P130/R) Allegorie de la Justice (157x104cm-62x41in) (F.FR 30000)
£3000	$5790	(11-Dec-90 PH133/R) Young woman asleep on chaise longue (30x28cm-12x11in)
£3000	$4890	(5-Jul-91 C268/R) Elisha raising Shunammite's son (36x45cm-14x18in) en grisaille
£1000	$1690	(16-Apr-91 C6/R) A classical sacrifice (15x18cm-6x7in) watermark shield blk.chk.pen wash
£1195	$2068	(22-May-91 CD.P7) Jeune fille a la colombe (44x35cm-17x14in) pastel oval (F.FR 12000)

BOUCHER, Francois (school) (18th C) French

£2783	$4704	(18-Apr-91 APT.P131/R) Le berger couronne (37x27cm-15x11in) (F.FR 28000)

BOUCHER, Francois (studio) (18th C) French

£1005	$1648	(21-Jun-91 SY.MO288/R) Scene galante (58x74cm-23x29in) (F.FR 10000)
£1406	$2263	(27-Jun-91 APT.P203/R) Chinoiserie - le marchand de fleurs (39x55cm-15x22in) (F.FR 14000)
£2915	$4780	(17-Jun-91 ARC.P20/R) Scene pastorale (69x89cm-27x35in) bears sig. (F.FR 29000)
£3083	$5982	(7-Dec-90 SY.MO196/R) Allegorie de la peinture (58x72cm-23x28in) (F.FR 30000)
£7201	$14258	(30-Jan-91 APT.P254/R) Bergere et son troupeau (84x68cm-33x27in) (F.FR 71000)
£1250	$2400	(18-Feb-91 S290/R) Putto (26x19cm-10x7in) chk

BOUCHER, Francois (style) (18th C) French

£1178	$2309	(11-Nov-90 I.N19) Les jeunes amoureux (60x70cm-24x28in) (F.FR 11500)
£1450	$2509	(20-May-91 SWS65) Three cherubs, a landscape beyond (95x133cm-37x52in)
£2200	$4400	(7-Feb-91 C121/R) La Petite Beurriere (61x51cm-24x20in) panel oval
£4000	$6760	(17-Apr-91 S159/R) Putti playing in landscapes (53x64cm-21x25in) pair oval
£6704	$12000	(11-Apr-91 SY.NY57/R) Infant Jesus blessing the Infant Saint John (52x45cm-20x18in) bears sig.d.1758
£8000	$13840	(20-May-91 SWS70/R) Lover disarmed (118x130cm-46x51in)
£18000	$34200	(13-Sep-90 CSK78/R) Extensive landscape with sunset with shepherdess on path by river, millbeyond (127x196cm-50x77in)

BOUCHER, Francois (style) (18th C) French-cont.
£1582 $2800   (22-Mar-91 CH.NY611/R) A landscape with farm buildings (21x33cm-8x13in)
                      i. blk.white chk.stumped
£3107 $5500   (22-Mar-91 CH.NY651) The head of a woman. L'amusements de l'Enfance.
                      Cupid with putti blk.chk.thd.white pastel three
£3672 $6500   (22-Mar-91 CH.NY650) A mill and a boy holding a net in a boat. Diana and
                      her nymphs. Femalenude (16x25cm-6x10in) blk.white chk. three

BOUCHER, Jean (1568-1633) French
£2055 $3988   (7-Dec-90 CH.MO215/R) Le torse du Belvedere (269x205cm-106x81in)
                      s.d.1625 mono. red chk. (F.FR 20000)

BOUCHER, Jean (circle) (1568-1633) French
£4057 $7789   (17-Dec-90 ARC.P25/R) Vierge et donateurs (115x165cm-45x65in)
                      (F.FR 40000)

BOUCHET, Jules Frederic (1799-1860) French
£2179 $4250   (26-Oct-90 SY.NY2/R) Frontispiece for Original de la Maison du Poete
                      Tragique a Pompei 1828 (30x20cm-12x8in) i. W/C gouache

BOUCHOR, Joseph Felix (1853-1937) French
£821 $1600   (25-Oct-90 GRO.B87/R) 4 juillet 1918, Independence Day (25x33cm-10x13in)
                      s.i. panel
£822 $1602   (23-Oct-90 C.A63) Orange market in Venice (38x47cm-15x19in) s.
                      (B.FR 50000)

BOUCHOT, Francois (1800-1842) French
£8205 $16000   (26-Oct-90 SY.NY49/R) Portrait of two brothers (37x29cm-15x11in) s.verso
                      chk htd.white

BOUCHOT, Francois (attrib) (1800-1842) French
£700 $1141   (3-Jul-91 PLF.P50) Napoleon signe son abdication a Fontainebleau
                      (16x19cm-6x7in) (F.FR 7000)

BOUCKHORST, Jan Philipsz (c.1588-1631) Dutch
£450 $864   (18-Feb-91 S185/R) Angel appearing to Manoah and his wife
                      (23x35cm-9x14in) pen ink wash
£5000 $8150   (2-Jul-91 C207/R) Minerva (20x14cm-8x6in) s.d.1619 pen wash htd white
£5263 $10000   (9-Jan-91 CH.NY89/R) Heads of two men and boy (20x16cm-8x6in) s.d.1629
                      pen wash htd white

BOUCLE, Pierre (1610-1673) Flemish
£5882 $11647   (30-Jan-91 APT.P247/R) Un chien devant une table de cuisine
                      (64x81cm-25x32in) mono.d.1630 (F.FR 58000)
£6827 $10992   (27-Jun-91 APT.P134/R) Nature morte aux fruits sur un entablement
                      (43x54cm-17x21in) (F.FR 68000)

BOUDET, Pierre (1925-) French
£1093 $1848   (21-Apr-91 E.LA72) Honfleur - la lieutenance (27x35cm-11x14in) s.
                      hardboard (F.FR 11000)
£1190 $2060   (22-May-91 GS.B2333/R) Honfleur harbour with shipping (27x34cm-11x13in)
                      s. s.i.d.66verso pavatex (S.FR 3000)
£1974 $3750   (15-Sep-90 S.W2682/R) Plage de Deauville (30x38cm-12x15in) s. board
£2308 $4500   (10-Oct-90 SY.NY201/R) Venise (61x61cm-24x24in) s.i.d.60 s.i.d.61verso
                      masonite
£2368 $4500   (15-Sep-90 S.W2680/R) Afternoon along the Seine (46x61cm-18x24in) s.
£3582 $6233   (31-Mar-91 FE.P94) Honfleur (50x61cm-20x24in) s. (F.FR 36000)
£3967 $7498   (30-Sep-90 FE.P81) Les Martigues (50x61cm-20x24in) s. (F.FR 39000)
£5030 $9859   (27-Jan-91 FE.P76) Les bouquinistes auQuai st Michel et Notre Dame
                      (50x61cm-20x24in) s. (F.FR 50000)

BOUDEWYNS (style) (17/18th C) Flemish
£4893 $9639   (14-Nov-90 SY.AM76/R) Peasants in landscape (41x58cm-16x23in)
                      (D.FL 16000)

BOUDEWYNS, Adriaen Frans (1644-1711) Flemish
£2728 $5346   (19-Nov-90 CH.R57/R) Paesaggio fluviale con figure (19x23cm-7x9in) panel
                      (I.L 6000000)
£20286 $36312   (8-Apr-91 CH.R61/R) Fiera di popolani presso dei ruderi. Popolani che
                      assistono ad una recita (40cm-16ins circular) pair (I.L 45000000)

BOUDEWYNS, Adriaen Frans (attrib) (1644-1711) Flemish
£9184 $18000   (7-Nov-90 B.SF1017/R) Figures in forest clearing (71x112cm-28x44in)
                      cradled panel

BOUDEWYNS, Adriaen Frans (style) (1644-1711) Flemish
£1000 $1690   (18-Apr-91 C132) An Italianate landscape with peasants by classical
                      ruins (23x34cm-9x13in) panel

BOUDEWYNS, Adriaen Frans and BOUT, Pieter (17/18th C) Flemish
£5000 $8150   (3-Jul-91 S110/R) Wooded river landscape with many figures
                      (30x43cm-12x17in) panel
£5400 $8802   (3-Jul-91 S249/R) Italiante river landscape with waggons and ferry
                      (24x32cm-9x13in) panel
£11000 $21450   (26-Oct-90 C149/R) Peasants and fisherfolk outside chateau gates with
                      fishermen bringing in their catch (28x44cm-11x17in) panel

BOUDEWYNS, Adriaen Frans and BOUT, Pieter (17/18th C) Flemish-cont.
£12000 $19560   (3-Jul-91 S239/R) Wooded Italinate landscapes with figures
                (27x36cm-11x14in) panel pair

BOUDEWYNS, Adriaen Frans and BOUT, Pieter (style) (17/18th C) Flemish
£2635 $4453   (2-May-91 CH.AM31/R) Travellers and peasants on a country road
                (37x44cm-15x17in) (D.FL 8800)
£6500 $12480   (29-Nov-90 CSK144/R) Capriccio harbour scenes (41x57cm-16x22in) pair

BOUDEWYNS, Nicolas (1660-1700) Flemish
£21739 $36957   (27-May-91 GK.Z5009/R) Southern harbour scene with figures. Coastal
                landscape with figures (27x40cm-11x16in) pair (S.FR 55000)

BOUDIN, Eugene (1824-1898) French
£3543 $6943   (22-Nov-90 F.F23 b) Deux vaches (19x24cm-7x9in) bears st.init. panel
                (F.FR 35000)
£4970 $8400   (21-Apr-91 E.LA71) Vaches au pre (27x35cm-11x14in) s. (F.FR 50000)
£5263 $10000   (28-Feb-91 CH.NY60/R) Vaches dans la prairie (15x24cm-6x9in) s. panel
£6116 $11743   (27-Nov-90 APT.P2/R) Vaches dans un pre (32x46cm-13x18in) bears trace
                sig.d.Sept.79 (F.FR 60000)
£9000 $14490   (25-Jun-91 C102/R) La paturage (33x41cm-13x16in) init.
£14925 $25970   (25-Mar-91 QWA.P138/R) Moutons dans un champs (21x33cm-8x13in) s.
                (F.FR 150000)
£15228 $30000   (2-Oct-90 CH.NY18/R) Trois-mats dans le port (16x24cm-6x9in) s. panel
£16700 $32733   (23-Nov-90 PLF.P100/R) Marche au village (24x33cm-9x13in) s. panel
                (F.FR 165000)
£17341 $30000   (12-May-91 H.C26/R) Le port (28x23cm-11x9in) s. panel
£20398 $35493   (28-Mar-91 DAR.P46/R) Paysage normand (26x44cm-10x17in) s.d.1886 panel
                (F.FR 205000)
£28061 $55000   (14-Feb-91 CH.NY19/R) Pont sur la Touques aux environs de Trouville
                (23x32cm-9x13in) s. panel
£29000 $46690   (26-Jun-91 S112/R) Deauville, voiliers a l'ancre (23x33cm-9x13in) s.
                panel
£30612 $60306   (14-Nov-90 CN.P123/R) Le Havre, le port (25x33cm-10x13in) s. panel
                (F.FR 300000)
£31156 $55769   (16-Mar-91 APT.P8/R) Etretat, la falaise d'aval au soleil couchant
                (46x65cm-18x26in) s.d.90 (F.FR 310000)
£32000 $62080   (4-Dec-90 C267/R) La vallee de la Touques (41x55cm-16x22in) s.
£37000 $59570   (26-Jun-91 S104/R) Dordrecht - vue du port (32x40cm-13x16in) s.d.84
                panel
£37572 $65000   (8-May-91 SY.NY106/R) L'entree du port de Trouville (41x32cm-16x13in)
                s.i.d.94 panel
£40609 $80000   (15-Nov-90 CH.NY201/R) Scene de port (25x36cm-10x14in) s. panel
£45872 $88073   (26-Nov-90 GL.P46/R) Les lavandieres (15x24cm-6x9in) s. panel
                (F.FR 450000)
£53586 $91096   (2-Jun-91 LT.P59/R) Pecheurs et attelages aupres des bateaux echoues a
                Berck (46x65cm-18x26in) s.d.1880 (F.FR 538000)
£60914 $120000   (13-Nov-90 SY.NY4/R) Trouville, marche aux poissons (36x45cm-14x18in)
                s.i. panel
£63584 $110000   (8-May-91 SY.NY107/R) Trouville, vue prise des hauteurs
                (50x74cm-20x29in) s.d.97
£64171 $120000   (1-Aug-90 B.P28/R) Fecamps, 1891 (36x46cm-14x18in) s. cradled panel
£70000 $135800   (4-Dec-90 C260/R) Trouville, les jetees, maree haute (27x35cm-11x14in)
                s.d.94 panel
£72000 $139680   (4-Dec-90 C261/R) Antibes, les Rochers de l'Ilette (41x55cm-16x22in)
                s.i.d.93
£75911 $148785   (24-Nov-90 APT.P46/R) Bordeaux, le port vue de Bacalan (40x66cm-16x26in)
                s. (F.FR 750000)
£90000 $174600   (3-Dec-90 C5/R) Bordeaux, Bacalan.- vue prise du quai (40x65cm-16x26in)
                s.i.d.74
£101523 $200000   (15-Nov-90 CH.NY204/R) Trouville, scene de plage (15x27cm-6x11in)
                s.i.d.81 panel
£102041 $201020   (16-Nov-90 GK.Z5155/R) Berck le depart des barques (65x91cm-26x36in)
                s.d.1879 (S.FR 250000)
£106599 $210000   (12-Nov-90 SY.NY3/R) Scene de plage, le parasol jaune (14x25cm-6x10in)
                s.i.d.87 panel
£121827 $240000   (13-Nov-90 SY.NY8/R) Juan-Les-Pins, La Baie et le Rivage
                (55x90cm-22x35in) s.i.d.93
£1800   *$2898*   *(24-Jun-91 CSK1/R) Pecheurs dechargeant les bateaux (15x25cm-6x10in)*
                pencil
£1913   *$3750*   *(12-Feb-91 SY.NY5/R) Study of cows by the sea (18x25cm-7x10in) st.init.*
                W/C over chk
£2227   *$4364*   *(22-Nov-90 ZZ.F14/R) Barques de pecheurs a quai (21x14cm-8x6in) crayon*
                (F.FR 22000)
£3083   *$5982*   *(7-Dec-90 GL.P100) Village et moulin au bord d'une riviere*
                (27x44cm-11x17in) s.d.1849 lead pencil (F.FR 30000)
£3500   *$6720*   *(29-Nov-90 B13/R) Seated woman holding a parasol (12x9cm-5x4in) pencil*
                W/C
£3976   *$7673*   *(12-Dec-90 APT.P3/R) Sur la plage (13x19cm-5x7in) bears studio st. W/C*
                (F.FR 39000)
£4000   *$6440*   *(24-Jun-91 CSK7/R) Barques sur la plage. Etude marine (14x19cm-6x7in)*
                st.studio wash pencil double-sided
£4020   *$6593*   *(20-Jun-91 APT.P2/R) Pardona Plougastel (26x21cm-10x8in) bears*
                st.init.i.d.71 W/C (F.FR 40000)
£4200   *$7434*   *(19-Mar-91 C1/R) Barques sur la plage (9x12cm-4x5in) init. pastel paper*
                on card

BOUDIN, Eugene (1824-1898) French-cont.
£6218 $12001   (10-Dec-90 BL.P26/R) Les crinolines (8x14cm-3x6in) d.66 W/C (F.FR 61000)
£8258 $13460   (14-Jun-91 AGS.P1/R) Etude de ciel avec collines (15x20cm-6x8in) init.
                   pastel (F.FR 82000)
£12183 $24000   (15-Nov-90 CH.NY101/R) Sur la plage (12x19cm-5x7in) init. W/C over
                   pencil board
£13265 $26133   (14-Nov-90 CN.P47/R) Crinolines et cabine sur la plage (11x22cm-4x9in)
                   s.d.1865 W/C (F.FR 130000)
£13469 $26535   (14-Nov-90 CN.P48/R) Les crinolines (11x22cm-4x9in) s.d.1865 W/C
                   (F.FR 132000)
£13889 $22778   (19-Jun-91 GK.B215/R) Fishing boats, fishermen and bathers on beach
                   (22x29cm-9x11in) i. W/C over pencil (S.FR 35000)
£17000 $27370   (26-Jun-90 S200/R) Personnages sur la plage a Trouville (9x14cm-4x6in)
                   init.d.68 W/C pencil paper on card
£21000 $40740   (4-Dec-90 C100/R) Personnages sur la plage a Trouville (13x26cm-5x10in)
                   studio st.d.1869 W/C pencil

BOUDIN, Eugene (attrib) (1824-1898) French
£1868 $3250   (27-Mar-91 B.SF4309/R) Honfleur (30x41cm-12x16in) bears sig.

BOUDON, Patrick (20th C) ?
£815 $1605   (4-Nov-90 FE.P92) Abstraction (46x60cm-18x24in) s.d.63 panel (F.FR 8000)

BOUDRY, Alois (19th C) Belgian
£578 $1000   (10-May-91 S.BM63/R) The fish monger, peasant woman at fishing dock
                   (64x56cm-25x22in) s.

BOUEL, Louis Francois Numance (19th C) French
£1935 $3250   (17-Jul-91 SY.NY258/R) Chemin dans la foret de Senart (50x61cm-20x24in)
                   s.
£4103 $8000   (23-Oct-90 SY.NY254/R) Paysage de campagne (79x139cm-31x55in) s.

BOUGH, Sam (1822-1878) British
£950 $1530   (27-Jun-91 CG28) The Houses of Parliament from the Thames
                   (23x38cm-9x15in) s. card
£1800 $3546   (1-Nov-90 C235/R) Maryport, Cumberland (61x35cm-24x14in) i.verso panel
£1900 $3724   (20-Nov-90 PH36/R) The otter hunt (92x130cm-36x51in) s.d.1845
£2200 $3696   (23-Apr-91 S9/R) Crossing plain (61x91cm-24x36in) s.d.1860
£3800 $7106   (28-Aug-90 S747/R) Otter hunt (61x46cm-24x18in) s.d.1886
£15000 $28050   (28-Aug-90 S796/R) Peel harbour, Isle of Man (78x122cm-31x48in) s.d.1875
£300 $600   (5-Feb-91 CG23) Herding cattle before castle (36x51cm-14x20in) s. W/C
                   htd bodycol
£380 $760   (5-Feb-91 CG22) Sportsmen before Windsor Castle (38x53cm-15x21in)
                   s.d.1874 W/C htd bodycol
£700 $1309   (30-Aug-90 CG76) Fishermen by Tweed with Neipath Castle in distance
                   (36x53cm-14x21in) s.d.1878 W/C htd white
£1500 $2955   (1-Nov-90 C175/R) The meet (38x53cm-15x21in) s.indis.d. pencil W/C
                   htd.white

BOUGHTON, George Henry (1833-1905) American
£2219 $3750   (1-May-91 B.SF5082/R) Fair daughter of Holland (46x32cm-18x13in) init.
                   board
£2600 $5096   (20-Nov-90 PH90) Idle gossip (41x66cm-16x26in) s.d.'73
£620 $1166   (6-Aug-90 SWS218) Portrait of lady, head and shoulders (43x34cm-17x13in)
                   init. pastel
£925 $1600   (22-May-91 CH.NY112/R) Return of Rip van Winkle (36x27cm-14x11in) init.
                   W/C pencil board

BOUGHTON, H (fl.1827-1872) British
£800 $1576   (1-Nov-90 CSK27/R) Bay stallion in extensive landscape (47x61cm-19x24in)
                   s. indist.i.

BOUGUEREAU, Elizabeth Gardner (1851-1922) French
£1437 $2400   (5-Jun-91 D.NY18) At the wall (122x79cm-48x31in)

BOUGUEREAU, William Adolphe (1825-1905) French
£1805 $3521   (12-Oct-90 APT.P98/R) Etude pour l'amour a la fontaine (22x15cm-9x6in)
                   (F.FR 18000)
£5128 $10000   (24-Oct-90 CH.NY110 a/R) Portrait of Miss Addison Head of San Francisco
                   (65x55cm-26x22in) s.d.1874
£11561 $20000   (22-May-91 SY.NY54/R) La charite (56x46cm-22x18in) s.
£46243 $80000   (22-May-91 SY.NY56/R) Le travail interrompu (100x61cm-39x24in) s.
£57803 $100000   (22-May-91 SY.NY57/R) Yvonne (88x55cm-35x22in) s.d.1896
£75145 $130000   (22-May-91 SY.NY59/R) Avant le bain (137x87cm-54x34in) s.d.1891
£83815 $145000   (22-May-91 SY.NY53/R) La petite tricoteuse (114x81cm-45x32in) s.d.1875
£104046 $180000   (23-May-91 CH.NY0/R) L'amour vainqueur (164x123cm-65x48in) s.d.1886
£138462 $270000   (23-Oct-90 SY.NY63/R) Le crepuscule (127x66cm-50x26in) s.

BOUILLIER, Amable (1867-?) French
£1445 $2500   (22-May-91 D.NY30/R) La bergere tricoteuse (142x99cm-56x39in) s.
                   canvasboard

BOUILLON, H (19th C) French
£3428 $6753   (14-Nov-90 F.M9/R) Trompe l'oeil con parete lignea, flauto, disegni e
                   manoscritti (41x25cm-16x10in) s. panel (I.L 7500000)

BOULANGER, Francois Jean Louis (1819-1873) French
£10000　$16400　(18-Jun-91 PH43/R) View of Ghent (96x120cm-38x47in) s.i.

BOULANGER, Graciela Rodo (1935-) Bolivian
£3316　$6500　(12-Feb-91 SY.NY292/R) Girl with cat (56x46cm-22x18in) s.d.1971 i.verso
£3468　$6000　(12-May-91 H.C215/R) Bouquet de fleurs (58x51cm-23x20in) s.
£4082　$8000　(19-Nov-90 SY.NY198/R) La mere et l'enfant (73x60cm-29x24in) s.d.68

BOULANGER, Gustave Clarence Rodolphe (1824-1888) French
£11282　$22000　(23-Oct-90 SY.NY290/R) La danse amoureuse (141x84cm-56x33in) s.

BOULANGER, L (19th C) French
£2500　$4100　(18-Jun-91 PH77) Still life with mixed flowers and bird's nest
　　　　　　　　(91x65cm-36x26in) s.

BOULANGER, Louis Vercelli (1806-1867) French
£4057　$8032　(30-Jan-91 APT.P152/R) La ronde du Sabbat (152x121cm-60x48in) s.
　　　　　　　　(F.FR 40000)
£4100　$7093　(20-May-91 SWS152/R) Landscape with nymphs frolicking by a column
　　　　　　　　(79x63cm-31x25in) s.

BOULARD, Auguste (1825-1897) French
£579　$1100　(27-Feb-91 SY.NY69) Thatched cottages with figures (41x32cm-16x13in)
　　　　　　　　i.verso panel
£771　$1379　(12-Mar-91 FN.S2294) French farmhouse near Veules le Roses
　　　　　　　　(37x46cm-15x18in) s. panel (DM 2250)
£1204　$2347　(12-Oct-90 APT.P110) L'heure de la priere (40x32cm-16x13in) init.
　　　　　　　　(F.FR 12000)

BOULARD, Emile (1861-1943) French
£1435　$2754　(14-Aug-90 SY.ME166/R) House in Provence (43x53cm-17x21in) indist.sig.
　　　　　　　　(A.D 3400)

BOULARD, Theodore (20th C) French
£1768　$3500　(30-Jan-91 GRO.B96/R) Procession (130x196cm-51x77in) s.

BOULCH, Jean Pierre le (1940-) French
£1205　$1940　(30-Jun-91 I.N96) Dany et 6/24 de seconde du film Aurore Clement
　　　　　　　　(97x146cm-38x57in) s.d.1975 i. verso (F.FR 12000)

BOULENGER, Hippolyte (1837-1874) Belgian
£629　$1056　(23-Apr-91 SY.AM122) Farmyard on sunny day (40x50cm-16x20in) s.
　　　　　　　　(D.FL 2100)
£740　$1442　(23-Oct-90 C.A66) The meadow (11x38cm-4x15in) panel (B.FR 45000)
£740　$1442　(23-Oct-90 C.A65) Landscape in Brabant (14x22cm-6x9in) panel
　　　　　　　　(B.FR 45000)
£3333　$6400　(18-Dec-90 GM.B4073) Paysage marecageux (105x90cm-41x35in) panel
　　　　　　　　(B.FR 200000)

BOULET, Cyprien-Eugene (1877-1927) French
£2000　$3360　(26-Apr-91 ARC.P60/R) Joueuse de tambourin (65x54cm-26x21in)
　　　　　　　　(F.FR 20000)
£2646　$5213　(6-Oct-90 KV.L31/R) After the ball (90x60cm-35x24in) s. (B.FR 165000)
£510　$1000　(21-Nov-90 NA.BA73) Portrait de femme (102x82cm-40x32in) s.d. pastel
　　　　　　　　oval

BOULEZ, Jules (1889-1960) Belgian
£882　$1738　(6-Oct-90 KV.L32) Mare and foal (45x55cm-18x22in) s. (B.FR 55000)
£903　$1562　(25-May-91 KV.L29) Seated girl (60x50cm-24x20in) s. panel (B.FR 55000)
£962　$1896　(6-Oct-90 KV.L33) Still life (46x56cm-18x22in) s. (B.FR 60000)

BOULIER, L (1903-) French
£1184　$2250　(14-Sep-90 DM.D2224/R) Dolls of all Nations (48x56cm-19x22in) s.

BOULIER, Lucien (1890-1964) French
£1091　$1877　(19-May-91 LT.P4/R) Jeune femme accoudee (46x55cm-18x22in) s. board
　　　　　　　　(F.FR 11000)
£1212　$1987　(18-Jun-91 FN.S1541) Portrait of young girl laughing (45x35cm-18x14in)
　　　　　　　　s. board (DM 3550)
£1759　$3377　(24-Feb-91 FE.P58) Nu de dos (101x54cm-40x21in) s. panel (F.FR 17500)
£4925　$8076　(20-Jun-91 APT.P17/R) Le miroir (105x145cm-41x57in) s. oval (F.FR 49000)

BOULIER, Pierre (20th C) French?
£1224　$2412　(18-Nov-90 S.S14/R) Portrait de jeune femme (36x27cm-14x11in) s. board
　　　　　　　　(F.FR 12000)

BOULIER, Raymond (?) ?
£607　$1190　(25-Nov-90 P.V69) Jeune fille (24x20cm-9x8in) s. pastel (F.FR 6000)

BOULLOGNE, Bon de (circle) (17/18th C) French
£2471　$4200　(31-May-91 CH.NY121/R) Leda and the swan (76x65cm-30x26in)

BOULLOGNE, Bon de (elder-attrib) (1649-1717) French
£659　$1266　(21-Dec-90 DAR.P41/R) Mars et Venus (34x47cm-13x19in) i. pen wash
　　　　　　　　htd.white (F.FR 6500)

BOULLOGNE, Louis de (18th C) French
£850 $1437   (16-Apr-91 C200/R) A nude holding a staff (36x29cm-14x11in) blk.white
       chk.

BOULLOGNE, Louis de (younger) (1654-1733) French
£15000 $25350   (17-Apr-91 S54/R) Rinaldo and Armida (84x138cm-33x54in)
£29800 $48574   (3-Jul-91 PLF.P51/R) Le retour de la chasse. Les enfants s'amusant au
       bord d'un etang (74x93cm-29x37in) pair (F.FR 298000)

BOULLOGNE, Louis de (younger-attrib) (1654-1733) French
£8500 $14365   (16-Apr-91 PH19/R) Male nude holding staff in landscape
       (60x74cm-24x29in)

BOULOGNE, Valentin de (after) (1591-1634) French
£6000 $9780   (5-Jul-91 C270/R) Tribute money (28x36cm-11x14in) panel

BOULOGNE, Valentin de (circle) (1591-1634) French
£27632 $52500   (10-Jan-91 SY.NY51/R) Concert with four players and drinking soldier
       (100x145cm-39x57in)
£44000 $71720   (2-Jul-91 PH336/R) The tax collector (129x147cm-51x58in)

BOULTBEE, John (18th C) British
£8000 $13200   (12-Jul-91 C97/R) Saddled grey hunter tethered to tree by stable in
       wooded landscape (72x92cm-28x36in) s.d.1793

BOUMAN, Hans (20th C) ?
£1512 $2949   (26-Oct-90 CC.P111/R) Tete (160x130cm-63x51in) s. verso oil collage
       canvas (F.FR 15000)

BOUMEESTER, Christine (1904-1971) Dutch
£335 $671   (6-Feb-91 FB.P51) Composition (24x35cm-9x14in) s.d.66 W/C (F.FR 3300)
£477 $806   (15-Apr-91 CC.P27/R) Composition (24x33cm-9x13in) s.d.1964 W/C
       (F.FR 4800)
£845 $1428   (15-Apr-91 CC.P33/R) Composition (27x41cm-11x16in) s.d.1939 pastel
       (F.FR 8500)

BOURCE, H (19th C) Flemish
£917 $1760   (18-Dec-90 GM.B877) Lecon de piano (60x80cm-24x31in) s. board
       (B.FR 55000)

BOURDON, Sebastien (1616-1671) French
£22155 $36113   (14-Jun-91 AGS.P36/R) La Sainte Famille au desert (90x195cm-35x77in)
       (F.FR 220000)
£118421 $225000   (10-Jan-91 SY.NY34/R) Bacchus comforting abandoned Ariadne
       (80x111cm-31x44in)

BOURDON, Sebastien (attrib) (1616-1671) French
£1500 $2655   (22-Mar-91 APT.P14) La recolte de la Manne (24x34cm-9x13in) pen wash
       htd.white (F.FR 15000)

BOURDON, Sebastien (style) (1616-1671) French
£1000 $1630   (4-Jul-91 CSK107) Adoration of Golden Calf (65x53cm-26x21in)
£1000 $2000   (7-Feb-91 C138/R) Abraham presented by his sons with Joseph's
       bloodstained coat (43x54cm-17x21in) canvas laid down on panel
£4500 $9000   (7-Feb-91 C123/R) An Arcadian scene (91x145cm-36x57in)

BOURGEOIS, Charles Guillaume Alexandre (1759-1832) French
£704 $1154   (19-Jun-91 LC.P36/R) Charles Marie Timoleon de Cosse-Brissac, Comte de
       Cosse (6cm-2ins circular) min. ebony bronze gilt frame (F.FR 7000)
£735 $1447   (13-Nov-90 CH.G252) Portrait of young lady with multi-coloured cashmere
       shawl (6cm-2ins circular) min.indist.s. gilt-metal mount (S.FR 1800)
£784 $1286   (19-Jun-91 LC.P28/R) Anne du Cluzel, Comtesse de Cosse
       (7cm-3ins circular) min.s. (F.FR 7800)
£854 $1401   (19-Jun-91 LC.P26/R) Charles de Cosse-Brissac, Comte de Cosse
       (7cm-3ins circular) min.s. round shell box encircled gold (F.FR 8500)
£905 $1483   (19-Jun-91 LC.P35/R) Anne du Cluzel, Comtesse de Cosse
       (7cm-3ins circular) min. ebony bronze gilt frame (F.FR 9000)

BOURGEOIS, Eugene (1855-1909) French
£547 $952   (25-Mar-91 CR.P64) Bord de Seine (33x46cm-13x18in) s. (F.FR 5500)

BOURGEOIS, Louis (1873-?) French
£607 $1190   (25-Nov-90 LC.P174) La couture (61x48cm-24x19in) s.d.99 col.chk.
       (F.FR 6000)

BOURGEOIS, Louise (20th C) French
£3846 $7500   (10-Oct-90 SY.NY541/R) Untitled (51x33cm-20x13in) s. ink
£7692 $13000   (2-May-91 CH.NY116/R) Untitled (49x32cm-19x13in) ink

BOURGEOIS, Sir Peter Francis (style) (1756-1811) British
£750 $1425   (28-Feb-91 B92) Extensive landscape with mother and children, dog,
       cattle and lake (76x102cm-30x40in)

BOURGOGNE, Pierre (1838-1904) French
£1084 $2006   (6-Mar-91 APT.P80) Jete de roses au tambourin (35x55cm-14x22in) s.d.1888
       (F.FR 10800)

BOURGOGNE, Pierre (1838-1904) French-cont.

| £2105 | $4000 | (27-Feb-91 SY.NY41/R) Still life with roses, grapes and peaches (33x46cm-13x18in) s.d.1902 |
| £17919 | $31000 | (22-May-91 SY.NY167/R) Fleurs et fruits d'ete (106x140cm-42x55in) s.d.1895 |

BOURHILL, J E (19th C) British

| £550 | $957 | (26-Mar-91 PH22) A rhinoceros charging (58x80cm-23x31in) s.d.1886 |

BOURNE, Jean Baptiste C (19th C) French

| £1020 | $2000 | (7-Nov-90 B.SF1167/R) Winter landscape (55x74cm-22x29in) s.d.1844 |

BOUROV, Vladimir (1939-) Russian

| £854 | $1640 | (18-Feb-91 ARC.P197/R) Sur le balcon (100x49cm-39x19in) s. (F.FR 8500) |

BOURTYOFF, Sophie de (19th C) ?

| £762 | $1494 | (6-Nov-90 SY.AM42/R) Still life with flowers (38x45cm-15x18in) indist.s. d.1899 (D.FL 2500) |

BOUSQUET, Georges (19/20th C) French

| £4587 | $8853 | (16-Dec-90 T.B101/R) Bords de Seine a St Mammes (79x82cm-31x32in) s. i.d.1972 verso (F.FR 45000) |

BOUT, Pieter (1658-1702) Flemish

| £4196 | $8098 | (10-Dec-90 L.K13/R) Figures and animals outside tavern (36x49cm-14x19in) panel (DM 12000) |
| £14796 | $29148 | (12-Nov-90 CSC.P10/R) Scenes de port (43x61cm-17x24in) pair (F.FR 145000) |

BOUT, Pieter (style) (1658-1702) Flemish

£1221	$2186	(14-Mar-91 D.V258/R) Wooded landscape with gateway through rock and figures (23x28cm-9x11in) (A.S 25000)
£2294	$4518	(14-Nov-90 SY.AM77/R) Shepherd and peasant women meeting on country road with village beyond (42x59cm-17x23in) (D.FL 7500)
£3000	$6000	(7-Feb-91 CSK115/R) Landscape with herdsman and cattle and horse-drawn cart on path (41x56cm-16x22in)

BOUT, Pieter and BOUDEWYNS, Adriaen Frans (17/18th C) Flemish

£5000	$8150	(3-Jul-91 S110/R) Wooded river landscape with many figures (30x43cm-12x17in) panel
£5400	$8802	(3-Jul-91 S249/R) Italiante river landscape with waggons and ferry (24x32cm-9x13in) panel
£11000	$21450	(26-Oct-90 C149/R) Peasants and fisherfolk outside chateau gates with fishermen bringing in their catch (28x44cm-11x17in) panel
£12000	$19560	(3-Jul-91 S239/R) Wooded Italianate landscapes with figures (27x36cm-11x14in) panel pair

BOUT, Pieter and BOUDEWYNS, Adriaen Frans (style) (17/18th C) Flemish

| £2635 | $4453 | (2-May-91 CH.AM31/R) Travellers and peasants on a country road (37x44cm-15x17in) (D.FL 8800) |
| £6500 | $12480 | (29-Nov-90 CSK144/R) Capriccio harbour scenes (41x57cm-16x22in) pair |

BOUTCHKINE, Dimitri (1927-) Russian

£704	$1351	(18-Feb-91 ARC.P35/R) La recolte (37x58cm-15x23in) s.d.51 canvas laid down on board (F.FR 7000)
£1508	$2894	(18-Feb-91 ARC.P34/R) La lecture (59x79cm-23x31in) (F.FR 15000)
£2010	$3859	(18-Feb-91 ARC.P36/R) Travaux des champs (20x54cm-8x21in) s.d.50 (F.FR 20000)

BOUTCHKINE, Piotr (1886-1965) Russian

£995	$1731	(25-Mar-91 ARC.P84/R) La petite fille en robe blanche (39x28cm-15x11in) s. (F.FR 10000)
£1005	$1930	(18-Feb-91 ARC.P43/R) Le quai (16x27cm-6x11in) s.d.52 verso board (F.FR 10000)
£1206	$2316	(18-Feb-91 ARC.P40/R) Dans le bois de bouleaux (48x50cm-19x20in) s.d.22 panel (F.FR 12000)
£1711	*$2978*	*(25-Mar-91 ARC.P89/R) Travaux sur la riviere (42x31cm-17x12in) s. W/C (F.FR 17200)*

BOUTELLE, De Witt Clinton (1817-1884) American

| £938 | $1800 | (17-Dec-90 SY.NY118/R) Hudson river landscape (66x91cm-26x36in) s.d.1845 |

BOUTEN, Armand (20th C) ?

£601	$1039	(23-May-91 SY.AM363/R) Untitled (84x66cm-33x26in) s. board (D.FL 2000)
£1201	$2078	(22-May-91 CH.AM336) Cyclops (46x48cm-18x19in) s. (D.FL 4000)
£574	*$1120*	*(26-Oct-90 BM.B952) Harbour scene with prostitutes (24x30cm-9x12in) s.d.1923 gouache (DM 1700)*

BOUTER, Cornelis (1888-1966) Dutch

£1397	$2500	(15-Mar-91 DM.D2001/R) Interior genre scene with mother serving, children gathered round table (51x61cm-20x24in)
£1466	$2448	(4-Jun-91 FB.M86) Morning sunshine (51x61cm-20x24in) s. (C.D 2800)
£1500	$2940	(22-Nov-90 CSK201/R) Fedding baby (24x29cm-9x11in) s.
£1617	$3072	(11-Sep-90 CH.AM208/R) At the farrier's (50x70cm-20x28in) s. (D.FL 5400)
£2083	$3500	(19-Jul-91 DM.D2006/R) Kitchen chores (61x76cm-24x30in) s.
£2197	$3800	(21-May-91 CE.NY216/R) Amusing baby (46x56cm-18x22in) s.

BOUTER, Cornelis (1888-1966) Dutch-cont.
£2232 $3750   (17-Jul-91 SY.NY284/R) Noon day meal (63x76cm-25x30in) s.
£2652 $5250   (1-Feb-91 S.W2547/R) Dutch family scene (76x102cm-30x40in) s.

BOUTER, Pieter (1887-1968) Dutch
£793 $1506   (26-Feb-91 VN.R33/R) Flock of sheep (60x100cm-24x39in) s. (D.FL 2600)

BOUTET de MONVEL, Bernard (1884-1949) French
£2000 $3260   (1-Jul-91 APT.P326/R) Le dandy, place de la concorde (77x73cm-30x29in)
     s. (F.FR 20000)
£3036 $5951   (21-Nov-90 CB.P41/R) La marquise (120x90cm-47x35in) s.d.1912
     (F.FR 30000)
£5071 $9736   (17-Dec-90 ARC.P115/R) Le porteur d'eau (55x43cm-22x17in) s.
     (F.FR 50000)

BOUTIBONNE, Charles-Edouard (1816-1897) Hungarian
£15854 $26000   (19-Jun-91 B.SF1736/R) A toast to be betrothed (53x65cm-21x26in)
     s.d.1893 panel

BOUTIGNY, Paul Emile (1854-1929) French
£2708 $5281   (12-Oct-90 APT.P78/R) Relais a l'auberge (61x81cm-24x32in) s.d.1925
     (F.FR 27000)

BOUTIN, Christophe (20th C) French
£910 $1775   (21-Oct-90 P.V150/R) Sans titre (70x100cm-28x39in) mono.d.28/3/86 pastel
*   (F.FR 9000)*

BOUTS, Albrecht (circle) (1454-1549) Dutch
£33000 $53790   (3-Jul-91 S24/R) Allegoriacl figure of wisdom. Virgin annunciate.
     Allegoriacl figure of Charity. Annunciating angel (57x25cm-22x10in)
     panel double-sided pair

BOUTS, Dirk (studio) (1400-1475) Dutch
£6024 $9699   (27-Jun-91 APT.P85/R) Vierge de douleurs (39x31cm-15x12in) panel
     (F.FR 60000)

BOUTTATS, Frederik (circle) (17th C) Flemish
£5000 $8700   (26-Mar-91 PH49/R) The golden age (98x125cm-39x49in)

BOUTTATS, Frederik (elder) (?-1661) Flemish
£6526 $10507   (27-Jun-91 APT.P89/R) Orphee charmant les animaux (27x37cm-11x15in)
     panel (F.FR 65000)

BOUTTATS, Frederik (style) (17th C) Flemish
£1500 $2445   (4-Jul-91 C619) Expulsion of Adam and Eve (84x81cm-33x32in) panel

BOUVARD (19/20th C) French
£1547 $2614   (5-May-91 LT.P31) Gondole sur le canal a Venise (38x46cm-15x18in) s.
     (F.FR 15500)

BOUVARD, A (19/20th C) French
£1308 $2563   (27-Jan-91 B.PA3) Canal a Venise (46x61cm-18x24in) s. (F.FR 13000)

BOUVARD, Antoine (?-1956) French
£780 $1529   (22-Nov-90 CSK282/R) Sunset on Venetian canal (26x35cm-10x14in) s.
£1300 $2236   (17-May-91 C17 a/R) Canal scene, Venice (26x35cm-10x14in) s.
£1600 $2704   (2-May-91 CG426) Off Grand Canal, Venice (24x34cm-9x13in) s.
£1737 $2900   (26-Jul-91 E.EDM150/R) Venetian canal (25x33cm-10x13in) s.
£1750 $3378   (12-Dec-90 MMB363/R) Venetian canal scene with gondola (46x61cm-18x24in)
     s.
£1754 $3456   (30-Oct-90 MA.V550) Venetian canal scene (23x33cm-9x13in) s. (C.D 4000)
£1800 $3456   (29-Nov-90 B51/R) The Quayside, Venice (50x66cm-20x26in) s.
£1930 $3802   (30-Oct-90 MA.V551) Venetian canal scene (23x33cm-9x13in) s. (C.D 4400)
£2036 $3420   (23-Apr-91 SY.AM143/R) Gondola on Venetian canal (63x48cm-25x19in) s.
     (D.FL 6800)
£2400 $4680   (15-Jan-91 SWS218/R) Venice (49x64cm-19x25in) s.
£2423 $4750   (7-Nov-90 B.SF1062/R) Canal off Giudecca in Venice with gondolier
     (38x55cm-15x22in) s.
£2600 $4472   (17-May-91 C4/R) Venetian backwater (24x33cm-9x13in) s.
£2600 $4342   (22-Jul-91 SWS1116/R) The Grand Canal, Venice (49x64cm-19x25in) s.
£2988 $5169   (24-May-91 FB.P132/R) Gondoles a Venise (51x65cm-20x26in) s.
     (F.FR 30000)
£3468 $6000   (21-May-91 CE.NY247/R) Venetian canal (51x65cm-20x26in) s.
£3659 $6000   (21-Jun-91 DM.D2062/R) Venetian canal (51x64cm-20x25in) s.
£3927 $6558   (4-Jun-91 R.T250/R) Venice (53x80cm-21x31in) s. (C.D 7500)
£4000 $6760   (2-May-91 CG425/R) Grand Canal and Doge's Palace, Venice
     (25x34cm-10x13in) s.
£4100 $7052   (14-May-91 SWS445/R) Evening light, Venice (48x63cm-19x25in) s.
£4200 $8274   (5-Oct-90 C47/R) Grand Canal, Venice (50x65cm-20x26in) s.
£4762 $8000   (17-Jul-91 SY.NY259/R) Venetian canal. Santa Maria Della Maggiore
     (25x33cm-10x13in) both s. pair
£4800 $8256   (17-May-91 C2/R) Canale della Giudecca con San Giorgio Maggiore, Venice
     (49x64cm-19x25in) s.
£5000 $9750   (15-Jan-91 SWS217/R) Sunlit canals in Venice (64x49cm-25x19in) s. pair
£5800 $9512   (20-Jun-91 B91 j) Venice (60x81cm-24x32in) s.
£6000 $11760   (15-Feb-91 C6/R) Bacino of St. Mark's, Venice (51x65cm-20x26in) s.

BOUVARD, Antoine (?-1956) French-cont.

£7800	$15366	(13-Nov-90 SWS375/R) The Doges palace (48x64cm-19x25in) s.
£8000	$15680	(15-Feb-91 C13/R) Gondolas on Grand Canal with La Salute and Punta della Dogana, Venice (50x66cm-20x26in) s.
£9756	$16000	(19-Jun-91 B.SF1745/R) Canal Grande, Venise (65x92cm-26x36in) s.
£11500	$20585	(14-Mar-91 B22/R) A Venetian Canal scene (60x81cm-24x32in) s.
£12874	$21629	(23-Apr-91 SY.AM99/R) View of Dogue Palace, Venice (62x90cm-24x35in) s. (D.FL 43000)
£17000	$30430	(14-Mar-91 B23/R) A Venetian Canal with the Church of S.S.Giovanni e Paolo (65x91cm-26x36in) s.

BOUVARD, Georges Noel (?) French

| £1850 | $3090 | (22-Jul-91 SWS1118/R) Sunlit venetian views (25x33cm-10x13in) s. pair |

BOUVARD, Joseph Antoine (1840-1920) French

| £1372 | $2716 | (31-Jan-91 D.V29/R) View of Venice (38x55cm-15x22in) s. (A.S 28000) |
| £1923 | $3750 | (25-Oct-90 D.V129/R) Canal in Venice (50x64cm-20x25in) s. (A.S 40000) |

BOUVARD, Noel (1912-1975) French

| £2711 | $5015 | (10-Mar-91 LT.P37/R) Au bord de la Lagune (50x65cm-20x26in) s. (F.FR 27000) |

BOUVIER, Agnes Rose see NICHOLL, Agnes Rose

BOUVIER, Armand (1913-) French

£503	$986	(27-Jan-91 FE.P80) Promeneurs au bord du lac (50x61cm-20x24in) s. (F.FR 5000)
£553	$1061	(24-Feb-91 FE.P60) Le chemin de la plage (50x61cm-20x24in) s. (F.FR 5500)
£559	$1118	(6-Feb-91 FB.P53) Le vieux bassin a Honfleur (50x61cm-20x24in) s. l. verso (F.FR 5500)
£713	$1148	(30-Jun-91 FE.P88) Honfleur (54x65cm-21x26in) s. (F.FR 7100)
£846	$1472	(31-Mar-91 FE.P99) Le grand voilier (50x61cm-20x24in) s. (F.FR 8500)

BOUVIER, Auguste (19th C) French

| *£1000* | *$1920* | *(17-Dec-90 PH61) Grecian dancer (55x34cm-22x13in) s. W/C over pencil* |

BOUVIER, Augustus Jules (c.1827-1881) British

| *£1500* | *$2880* | *(17-Dec-90 PH130/R) Youth, the spring of life - spring the youth of the year (53x72cm-21x28in) s. W/C htd.bodycol scratching out* |
| *£2000* | *$3780* | *(26-Sep-90 S322/R) Mother and child (66x49cm-26x19in) s. W/C htd bodycol gum arabic* |

BOUVIER, Jules (1800-1867) British

| *£540* | *$1054* | *(23-Oct-90 DUR.M51) Campesinos de la alta Bohemia (60x50cm-24x20in) W/C (S.P 100000)* |
| *£1000* | *$1890* | *(26-Sep-90 S311/R) Woman in clearing (53x39cm-21x15in) s.d.1860 W/C htd bodycol* |

BOUVIER, Paul (1857-1940) Swiss

| *£735* | *$1425* | *(8-Dec-90 GAB.G2414/R) Bord du lac a Colombier (37x51cm-15x20in) s.d.1933 W/C (S.FR 1800)* |

BOUY, Gaston (1866-?) French

| *£3600* | *$6192* | *(17-May-91 C35/R) La modele (51x30cm-20x12in) s. col.chk* |

BOUYSSOU, Jacques (1926-) French

£860	$1686	(25-Nov-90 ZZ.F214/R) La falaise a Etretat s. (F.FR 8500)
£1012	$1984	(25-Nov-90 ZZ.F23) Plage de Trouville (22x27cm-9x11in) s. (F.FR 10000)
£1014	$1976	(26-Oct-90 KM.K1119/R) Trafic sur le canal, Amsterdam (73x92cm-29x36in) s. l.verso (DM 3000)
£1022	$2004	(25-Nov-90 LC.P151) Scene de plage (22x27cm-9x11in) s. (F.FR 10100)
£1554	$3030	(26-Oct-90 KM.K1120/R) River landscape with shipping, possibly near Conflans (64x81cm-25x32in) s.d.1960 (DM 4600)
£1667	$3250	(10-Oct-90 SY.NY87/R) Venise sur le canal (74x91cm-29x36in) s.
£1856	$3600	(8-Dec-90 W.W161/R) L'escalier (81x99cm-32x39in) s. l.verso
£2016	$3931	(18-Jan-91 GL.P37) Paris, les quais (73x92cm-29x36in) s. (F.FR 20000)
£2308	$4500	(10-Oct-90 SY.NY266/R) Paris Rue Dussoubi (81x99cm-32x39in) s. l.verso
£2347	$4623	(18-Nov-90 H.A91) Deauville, la plage (33x41cm-13x16in) s. (F.FR 23000)
£2407	$4694	(10-Oct-90 ARC.P69/R) Le phare, entree du port de Douelan s. (F.FR 24000)
£2429	$4761	(25-Nov-90 ZZ.F22) La Seine a Conflans (46x55cm-18x22in) s. (F.FR 24000)
£2775	$4800	(7-May-91 CE.NY40/R) Rue de Paris (91x73cm-36x29in) s. l.verso
£2834	$5555	(25-Nov-90 ZZ.F215/R) Le canal de La Villette a Paris, 1969 s. (F.FR 28000)
£2834	$5555	(25-Nov-90 ZZ.F24) Saint-Malo (27x36cm-11x14in) s.d.1963 (F.FR 28000)
£3262	$6296	(10-Dec-90 LD.P64/R) Le terrain vague (81x100cm-32x39in) s. (F.FR 32000)
£3636	$7127	(12-Feb-91 HC.P30/R) La rue Calvin a Paris (81x100cm-32x39in) s. (F.FR 36000)
£3833	$7397	(12-Dec-90 D.P149/R) Le Perreux (60x73cm-24x29in) d.1961 stretcher (F.FR 37600)
£4453	$8729	(25-Nov-90 ZZ.F21/R) Les boulistes (81x100cm-32x39in) s. (F.FR 44000)

BOVIE, E (?) ?

| £702 | $1375 | (12-Feb-91 GM.B589) Enfants assis pres de la riviere (76x96cm-30x38in) s. (B.FR 42000) |

BOVIE, Felix (1812-1880) Belgian
£2100 $3444   (20-Jun-91 B91) Figures crossing stream in extensive wooded landscape (77x101cm-30x40in) s.

BOVIN, Karl (1907-1985) Danish
£624 $1117   (14-Mar-91 RAS.V760/R) Rocky coastal landscape (53x67cm-21x26in) s.d.53 (D.KR 7000)
£801 $1571   (22-Nov-90 RAS.V812/R) Summer landscape (85x100cm-33x39in) s. (D.KR 9000)

BOWEN, Owen (1873-1967) British
£650 $1248   (28-Nov-90 SC4164/R) Cattle watering at shady pool on summer day (33x51cm-13x20in) indist.s.
£750 $1223   (11-Jun-91 HAR478) Summer pastures (23x38cm-9x15in) s. board
£775 $1263   (11-Jun-91 HAR444/R) Dove cote (28x41cm-11x16in) s. board
£775 $1263   (14-Jun-91 T31) Still life of bowl of roses (51x66cm-20x26in) s.
£775 $1511   (16-Oct-90 HAR335) Summer lake side (28x38cm-11x15in) s. board
£850 $1666   (24-Jan-91 CSK175) Walking through water meadow (90x152cm-35x60in) s.d.1891
£1600 $2688   (23-Apr-91 S139/R) Corstorphine Hill, Edinburgh (46x61cm-18x24in) s.d.1924
£1900 $3268   (14-May-91 SWS372/R) A wayside chat (51x76cm-20x30in) s.d.1918 i.stretcher
£4000 $6760   (1-May-91 PHL118/R) Summer morning (77x115cm-30x45in) s.d.1919
£6500 $10595   (14-Jun-91 C316/R) Where the world comes not (101x152cm-40x60in) s.d.1898 pair

BOWERS, George Newell (19th C) American
£990 $1900   (17-Dec-90 SY.NY79/R) Summer landscape (51x76cm-20x30in) s.d.1896 num.14 stretcher

BOWETT, Druie (1924-) British
£550 $1045   (12-Sep-90 PHL124) Percussion (93x123cm-37x48in) s.d.62 s.i.verso board

BOWKETT, Jane Maria (19th C) British
£1200 $1956   (14-Jun-91 C231/R) Pushing off (61x45cm-24x18in) mono.

BOWLER, Thomas W (?-1869) British
£1516 $2562   (15-Apr-91 SY.J442/R) Baakens River (22x32cm-9x13in) s.d.1861 W/C (SA.R 7200)
£5350 $10272   (26-Nov-90 SY.J294 a) Table Mountain from beach (17x26cm-7x10in) s.i.d.1849 W/C (SA.R 26000)
£6584 $12642   (26-Nov-90 SY.J294 b) Shipping in Table Bay (24x34cm-9x13in) s.d.1859 W/C (SA.R 32000)

BOWLEY, Edward O (19th C) British
£640 $1249   (21-Oct-90 BU.M173) Thunderstorm over hills in Surrey (55x122cm-22x48in) s.verso (S.KR 7000)

BOWRING, Joseph (c.1760-1817) British
£540 $907   (22-Apr-91 PH86) Portrait of Naval Officer (7x?cm-3x?in) min.mono.gilt metal frame oval

BOWYER, William (1926-) British
£1350 $2349   (27-Mar-91 S120/R) Chiswick Mall (101x122cm-40x48in) s.d.83
£1700 $3315   (10-Oct-90 S217/R) The Terrace, Richmond (56x84cm-22x33in) s.d.85 board
£1900 $3211   (2-May-91 C139/R) Tower Bridge, London (73x99cm-29x39in) s.

BOX, Henry (19th C) British?
£513 $1000   (26-Oct-90 SY.NY27/R) Portrait of young boy (29x22cm-11x9in) s.d.1839 W/C

BOXALL, Arthur D'Auvergne (1895-1943) Australian
£1606 $3084   (26-Nov-90 SY.ME220/R) Building of Sydney harbour bridge (37x43cm-15x17in) s.d.1930 W/C htd bodycol (A.D 4000)

BOXER, Stanley (1926-) American
£1380 $2250   (12-Jun-91 SY.NY212/R) Plumerose of thunder (203x86cm-80x34in) s.d.3/5 verso
£1538 $3000   (24-Oct-90 B.SF1552/R) V.A.H. Stygiandawn - green dawn, 1971 (183x183cm-72x72in)
£1026 $2000   (24-Oct-90 B.SF1549/R) Summer red bloom (239x51cm-94x20in) d.5/70 verso oil material canvas
£1026 $2000   (24-Oct-90 B.SF1550/R) Dusk window with pink (106x216cm-42x85in) oil material canvas

BOYCE, George Price (1826-1897) British
£2800 $5600   (8-Feb-91 C130/R) Head Study of Ellen Smith (18x15cm-7x6in) panel
£1600 $2704   (15-Apr-91 WW94) Autumn study on Welsh hills (26x38cm-10x15in) mono. s.verso W/C over pencil
£2300 $4600   (8-Feb-91 C7/R) A view from the Riva degli Schiavoni (18x25cm-7x10in) mono.d.54 pencil W/C
£3800 $7524   (30-Jan-91 S287/R) Banks of Thames near Streatley, Berkshire - evening in November (6x27cm-2x11in) s.d.1859 s.i.d.verso W/C
£4000 $7880   (1-Nov-90 C162/R) Great Sphinx at Gizeh (23x28cm-9x11in) s.d.1862 i.d.verso W/C

BOYCE, William Thomas Nicholas (1858-1911) British

| £400 | $760 | (25-Feb-91 PH72) Fishing boats entering port (18x54cm-7x21in) s.d.1908 W/C htd white |
| £950 | $1824 | (16-Aug-90 B348/R) Clipper and steam ships passing sloops returning to harbour (37x53cm-15x21in) s.d.1910 W/C htd white |

BOYD, Arthur Merric (snr) (1862-1940) Australian

| £643 | $1234 | (27-Nov-90 JRL.S114/R) Cows in copse (49x29cm-19x11in) s.d.1903 W/C (A.D 1600) |

BOYD, Arthur Merric Bloomfield (1920-) Australian

£1923	$3250	(15-Apr-91 AAA.S121/R) Pink sky at Bundanon (30x22cm-12x9in) s. board (A.D 4250)
£2510	$4944	(13-Nov-90 J.M156/R) Nebuchadnezzar engulfed by sea (119x90cm-47x35in) s. (A.D 6500)
£2620	$4690	(9-Apr-91 CH.ME329/R) Landscape with cockatoos (30x22cm-12x9in) s. board (A.D 6000)
£2620	$4690	(9-Apr-91 CH.ME335/R) Black swan and hillside (30x22cm-12x9in) s. board (A.D 6000)
£2954	$5671	(14-Aug-90 SY.ME223/R) Shoalhaven landscape (30x20cm-12x8in) s. board (A.D 7000)
£3089	$6085	(13-Nov-90 J.M8/R) Eucalypt Forest (120x90cm-47x35in) s. board (A.D 8000)
£3213	$6169	(26-Nov-90 SY.ME192/R) Nebuchadnezzar running in forest with lion and blackbirds (20x24cm-8x9in) s. i.verso board (A.D 8000)
£3386	$6671	(31-Oct-90 CH.S80/R) Bride over the pool (43x55cm-17x22in) s. board (A.D 8500)
£3846	$6500	(16-Apr-91 J.M12/R) The Potter (75x60cm-30x24in) s. (A.D 8500)
£4633	$9127	(13-Nov-90 J.M32/R) Potter in field (62x76cm-24x30in) s. (A.D 12000)
£5116	$8595	(22-Apr-91 SY.ME302/R) Red lovers in boat (61x74cm-24x29in) s.d.60 linen on board (A.D 11000)
£5792	$11409	(13-Nov-90 J.M92/R) Horse and jinker by the mountain (90x121cm-35x48in) s. board (A.D 15000)
£5823	$11181	(26-Nov-90 SY.ME240) Waterfall - Shoalhaven River (121x90cm-48x35in) s. board (A.D 14500)
£6109	$10324	(16-Apr-91 J.M152/R) Hampstead Heath under snow (108x113cm-43x44in) s. (A.D 13500)
£6226	$12202	(19-Nov-90 MGS.S264 a) Wimmera landscape with sheep and blackbirds (90x121cm-35x48in) s. board (A.D 16000)
£6512	$10940	(22-Apr-91 SY.ME335/R) Landscape with beast (43x107cm-17x42in) s. board (A.D 14000)
£6696	$11652	(26-Mar-91 JRL.S131/R) Hillside with rocks, Shoalhaven Series (90x58cm-35x23in) s. board (A.D 15000)
£6950	$13691	(13-Nov-90 J.M70 a/R) Gathering sea shells near Ricketts Point (32x47cm-13x19in) s. canvas on board (A.D 18000)
£7143	$14071	(13-Nov-90 J.M240/R) Shoalhaven River (120x150cm-47x59in) s. (A.D 18500)
£7407	$12444	(16-Jul-91 JRL.S320) Wimmera landscape with heron and water pump (121x88cm-48x35in) s. board (A.D 16000)
£8491	$13840	(1-Jul-91 AAA.S135) Moon over the Wimmera (91x121cm-36x48in) s. board (A.D 18000)
£8765	$17267	(31-Oct-90 CH.S74/R) Riverbank, Black Swan (121x90cm-48x35in) s. board (A.D 22000)
£8765	$17267	(31-Oct-90 CH.S47/R) Landscape with hay bales and figure (121x151cm-48x59in) s. (A.D 22000)
£8889	$16711	(17-Sep-90 SY.ME101/R) Shoalhaven (60x44cm-24x17in) s. board (A.D 20000)
£8920	$14629	(17-Jun-91 MGS.S102) Fishing at dusk at Shoalhaven (119x98cm-47x39in) s. (A.D 19000)
£9050	$15294	(16-Apr-91 J.M74/R) Shoalhaven River (151x121cm-59x48in) s. (A.D 20000)
£9955	$16824	(16-Apr-91 J.M129) Bride in a Wimmera Landscape (88x121cm-35x48in) s. board (A.D 22000)
£10359	$20406	(31-Oct-90 CH.S124/R) Wimmera landscape (90x121cm-35x48in) s. board (A.D 26000)
£11163	$18753	(22-Apr-91 SY.ME325/R) Sunset - Shoalhaven Riverbank (90x120cm-35x47in) s. board (A.D 24000)
£11814	$22684	(14-Aug-90 SY.ME212/R) Wimmera landscape with grazing sheep, ploughed field figure and birds (18x27cm-7x11in) s. board (A.D 28000)
£13333	$25067	(17-Sep-90 MGS.S223/R) Wimmera (121x151cm-48x59in) s. (A.D 30000)
£13502	$25924	(14-Aug-90 SY.ME264/R) Wimmera landscape (90x120cm-35x47in) s. (A.D 32000)
£13944	$27470	(31-Oct-90 CH.S149/R) Black Swan on Shoalhaven river (123x153cm-48x60in) s. (A.D 35000)
£16026	$28365	(18-Mar-91 MGS.S184/R) Black swan on Shoalhaven River (123x153cm-48x60in) s. (A.D 37500)
£18474	$35470	(26-Nov-90 SY.ME258/R) Shoalhaven River with rose, burning book and aeroplane (158x122cm-62x48in) s. (A.D 46000)
£21395	$35944	(22-Apr-91 SY.ME390/R) Nebuchadnezzar eating grass (176x183cm-69x72in) s. (A.D 46000)
£59072	$113418	(14-Aug-90 SY.ME253/R) The wood gatherers (823x122cm-324x48in) s. board (A.D 140000)
£452	$765	(16-Apr-91 J.M930) The embrace (63x50cm-25x20in) s. W/C (A.D 1000)
£506	$972	(14-Aug-90 SY.ME71) Woman and dog (50x63cm-20x25in) s. ink (A.D 1200)
£935	$1523	(16-Jun-91 SY.ME99) Head with beast in coffin above prostrate beast (51x63cm-20x25in) s. ink (A.D 2000)

BOYD, Arthur Merric Bloomfield (1920-) Australian-cont.

£1275	$2512	(31-Oct-90 CH.S71/R) The lovers (47x61cm-19x24in) s.c.1965 pastel card (A.D 3200)
£2243	$3656	(16-Jun-91 SY.ME28) Girl in bath (47x63cm-19x25in) s. pastel (A.D 4800)
£2489	$4206	(16-Apr-91 J.M321/R) The lovers (47x62cm-19x24in) s. pastel (A.D 5500)

BOYD, David (1924-) Australian

£563	$924	(17-Jun-91 MGS.S116) Swimming in lake (21x29cm-8x11in) s. (A.D 1200)
£563	$924	(17-Jun-91 MGS.S115) Looking for berries (21x29cm-8x11in) s. (A.D 1200)
£584	$1144	(19-Nov-90 MGS.S287) Picking pear blossom (34x39cm-13x15in) s. (A.D 1500)
£618	$1217	(13-Nov-90 J.M15) The beach party (35x45cm-14x18in) s. (A.D 1600)
£640	$1248	(15-Oct-90 AAA.S132) Angel of spring (51x41cm-20x16in) s. (A.D 1600)
£640	$1248	(15-Oct-90 AAA.S151) Picking wildflowers (35x40cm-14x16in) s. board (A.D 1600)
£684	$1210	(18-Mar-91 MGS.S234) Hiking (36x46cm-14x18in) s. (A.D 1600)
£699	$1251	(9-Apr-91 CH.ME314) Feeding bird (34x44cm-13x17in) s. (A.D 1600)
£708	$1153	(1-Jul-91 AAA.S53) In the orchard (38x46cm-15x18in) s. board (A.D 1500)
£723	$1388	(27-Nov-90 JRL.S119) Wading below rapids (40x50cm-16x20in) s. (A.D 1800)
£742	$1284	(21-May-91 JRL.S85) Beach party (49x44cm-19x17in) s. masonite (A.D 1700)
£760	$1482	(15-Oct-90 AAA.S58) The ships sail by (35x45cm-14x18in) s. (A.D 1900)
£760	$1482	(15-Oct-90 AAA.S76) Spring picnic (45x51cm-18x20in) s. board (A.D 1900)
£763	$1465	(27-Nov-90 JRL.S127) Picnic at beach (35x45cm-14x18in) s. (A.D 1900)
£769	$1362	(18-Mar-91 MGS.S136) Day at the beach (34x45cm-13x18in) s. (A.D 1800)
£772	$1521	(13-Nov-90 J.M99) Fossicking in the field (50x60cm-20x24in) s. (A.D 2000)
£778	$1525	(19-Nov-90 MGS.S272) Playing in The Wattle Tree (44x60cm-17x24in) s. (A.D 2000)
£791	$1328	(22-Apr-91 SY.ME74) Children by stream (34x45cm-13x18in) s. (A.D 1700)
£797	$1570	(31-Oct-90 CH.S161) Leaning on blossom tree (35x46cm-14x18in) s. (A.D 2000)
£849	$1384	(1-Jul-91 AAA.S168) Picking wildflowers (34x45cm-13x18in) s. (A.D 1800)
£849	$1384	(1-Jul-91 AAA.S81) Fallen angel (51x41cm-20x16in) s. (A.D 1800)
£881	$1665	(25-Sep-90 JRL.S124) Picnic time (40x50cm-16x20in) s. (A.D 2000)
£893	$1554	(26-Mar-91 JRL.S199) Playing in the apple orchard (44x60cm-17x24in) s. (A.D 2000)
£905	$1529	(15-Apr-91 AAA.S90) Sunflower children (35x47cm-14x19in) s. (A.D 2000)
£930	$1563	(22-Apr-91 SY.ME52) Sunny day in foothills (49x74cm-19x29in) s. l.verso (A.D 2000)
£964	$1851	(26-Nov-90 SY.ME69) Children and birds by pool (50x60cm-20x24in) s. (A.D 2400)
£991	$1873	(25-Sep-90 JRL.S98) Wading in the river (39x50cm-15x20in) s. (A.D 2250)
£995	$1682	(16-Apr-91 J.M112) A summer day (34x44cm-13x17in) s. (A.D 2200)
£995	$1682	(16-Apr-91 J.M221) The picnic (35x40cm-14x16in) s. board (A.D 2200)
£995	$1682	(16-Apr-91 J.M226) Berry pickers by Wattle Tree (40x49cm-16x19in) s. (A.D 2200)
£1000	$1650	(10-Jul-91 WAL226/R) Tom Thumb (72x91cm-28x36in) s.d.1974
£1019	$1711	(16-Jul-91 JRL.S303) Watching the birds in the apple tree (49x60cm-19x24in) s. (A.D 2200)
£1057	$1998	(25-Sep-90 JRL.S84/R) Flight (76x56cm-30x22in) s.d.66 board (A.D 2400)
£1065	$1789	(16-Jul-91 JRL.S281) Picnic under the blossom tree (44x60cm-17x24in) s. (A.D 2300)
£1080	$1771	(17-Jun-91 MGS.S163) Resting under Wattle tree (45x60cm-18x24in) s. (A.D 2300)
£1086	$1835	(15-Apr-91 AAA.S143) Children in blossom tree (36x46cm-14x18in) s. (A.D 2400)
£1111	$1867	(16-Jul-91 JRL.S245) The view of the sailing ship (40x50cm-16x20in) s. (A.D 2400)
£1111	$1967	(18-Mar-91 MGS.S142) Reading under the blossom tree (49x60cm-19x24in) s. (A.D 2600)
£1132	$1845	(1-Jul-91 AAA.S139) Dancing under the flame tree (51x61cm-20x24in) s. (A.D 2400)
£1156	$2172	(17-Sep-90 SY.ME109/R) Swan and seven children (67x90cm-26x35in) s.d.68 (A.D 2600)
£1181	$2268	(14-Aug-90 SY.ME55) The arrival (61x71cm-24x28in) s.d.1976 (A.D 2800)
£1221	$2002	(17-Jun-91 MGS.S164) Playing by waters edge (40x50cm-16x20in) s. (A.D 2600)
£1222	$2065	(16-Apr-91 J.M41) Dancing in the orchard (45x50cm-18x20in) s. board (A.D 2700)
£1266	$2430	(14-Aug-90 SY.ME110) The Patron Saint of Wattle with tall ship approaching (44x60cm-17x24in) s. l. verso (A.D 3000)
£1266	$2430	(14-Aug-90 SY.ME130) After the swim (50x60cm-20x24in) s. (A.D 3000)
£1275	$2512	(31-Oct-90 CH.S77) Wading through the shallows (50x61cm-20x24in) s. (A.D 3200)
£1333	$2507	(17-Sep-90 SY.ME113/R) The intruder (59x69cm-23x27in) s.d.69 (A.D 3000)
£1357	$2294	(15-Apr-91 AAA.S82) Yacht's farewell (61x71cm-24x28in) s. board (A.D 3200)
£1422	$2674	(17-Sep-90 MGS.S194) Girl under blossom tree (50x60cm-20x24in) s. board (A.D 3200)
£1422	$2674	(17-Sep-90 SY.ME112/R) Picnic by the bay (45x55cm-18x22in) s. (A.D 3200)
£1511	$2841	(17-Sep-90 MGS.S230) Wading in the inlet (50x60cm-20x24in) s. (A.D 3400)
£1538	$2600	(15-Apr-91 AAA.S123) Angel of fruit (51x61cm-20x24in) s. (A.D 3400)

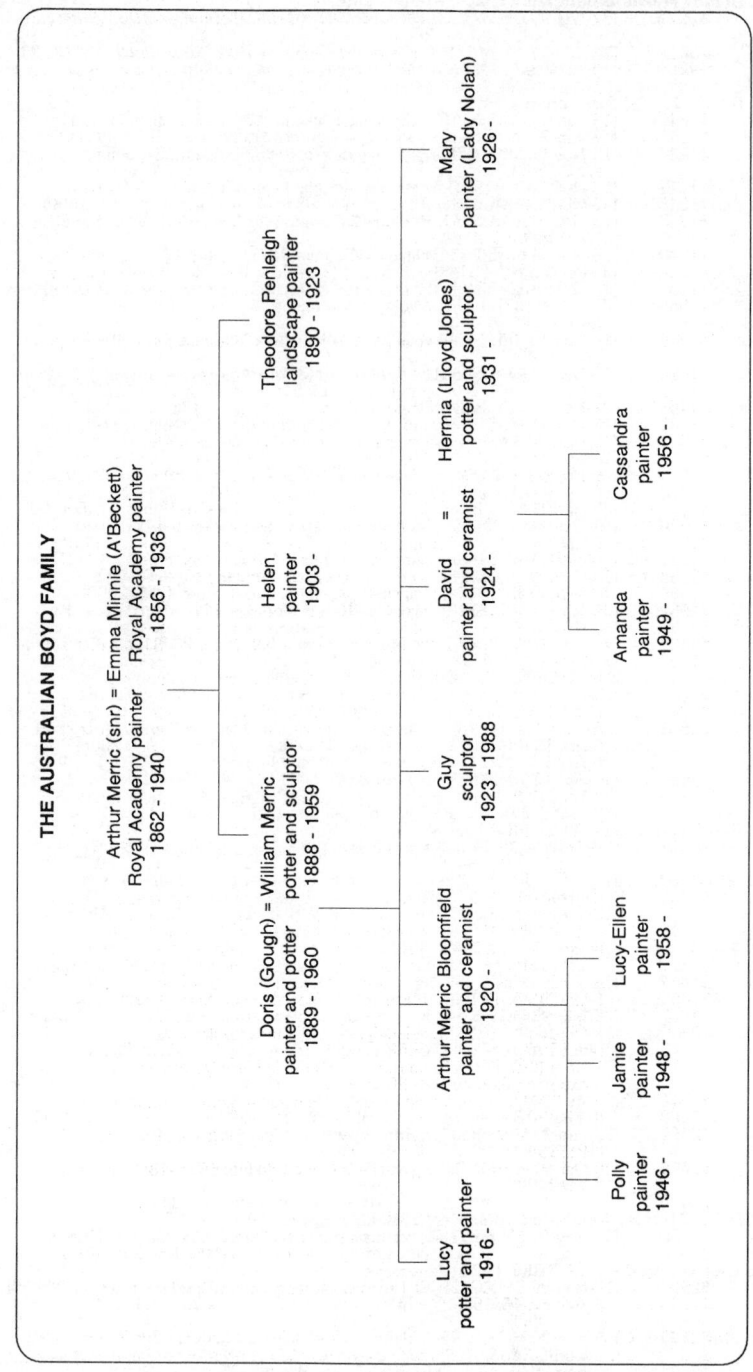

THE AUSTRALIAN BOYD FAMILY

Arthur Merric (snr) = Emma Minnie (A'Beckett)
Royal Academy painter   Royal Academy painter
1862 - 1940   1856 - 1936

Theodore Penleigh
landscape painter
1890 - 1923

Helen
painter
1903 -

Doris (Gough) = William Merric
painter and potter   potter and sculptor
1889 - 1960   1888 - 1959

Guy
sculptor
1923 - 1988

David = Hermia (Lloyd Jones)
painter and ceramist   potter and sculptor
1924 -   1931 -

Mary
painter (Lady Nolan)
1926 -

Arthur Merric Bloomfield
painter and ceramist
1920 -

Lucy
potter and painter
1916 -

Amanda
painter
1949 -

Cassandra
painter
1956 -

Polly
painter
1946 -

Jamie
painter
1948 -

Lucy-Ellen
painter
1958 -

BOYD, David (1924-) Australian-cont.
£1674 $2813   (22-Apr-91 SY.ME109) David and Saul (95x85cm-37x33in) s. s.i.d.1967
                      verso (A.D 3600)
£1810 $3059   (16-Apr-91 J.M98 a) Boy chasing the elusive white cockatoo
                      (82x74cm-32x29in) s. (A.D 4000)
£2390 $4709   (31-Oct-90 CH.S156/R) Burning bush (121x150cm-48x59in) s.d.69
                      (A.D 6000)
£2400 $4680   (15-Oct-90 AAA.S70) Sunflower in the orchid (76x91cm-30x36in) s.
                      (A.D 6000)
£849   *$1384*   *(1-Jul-91 AAA.S128) Spring's bounty (50x46cm-20x18in) s. mixed media*
                      (A.D 1800)

BOYD, Emma Minnie (1856-1936) Australian
£591   *$1134*   *(14-Aug-90 SY.ME82/R) Gums by a stream (37x26cm-15x10in) s.d.1912*
                      (A.D 1400)
£679   *$1147*   *(16-Apr-91 J.M22/R) Near Sandringham (38x24cm-15x9in) s.d.1921 W/C*
                      (A.D 1500)
£884   *$1696*   *(26-Nov-90 SY.ME67/R) Dandenongs (23x34cm-9x13in) s. W/C (A.D 2200)*

BOYD, Jamie (1948-) Australian
£814 $1376   (16-Apr-91 J.M119) Hut by the river (61x71cm-24x28in) s. board
                      (A.D 1800)
£939 $1540   (17-Jun-91 MGS.S165) Hut by river (61x71cm-24x28in) s. board (A.D 2000)

BOYD, Theodore Penleigh (1890-1923) Australian
£543 $918   (16-Apr-91 J.M1167) Landscape (17x23cm-7x9in) indist.s. board
                      (A.D 1200)
£814 $1376   (16-Apr-91 J.M327) Landscape - Blue gum (27x20cm-11x8in) board
                      (A.D 1800)
£1131 $1912   (16-Apr-91 J.M64/R) Autumn on the Yarra (29x21cm-11x8in) s. board
                      (A.D 2500)
£1538 $2600   (15-Apr-91 AAA.S102) Summer haze (16x21cm-6x8in) s. board (A.D 3400)
£3167 $5353   (16-Apr-91 J.M139) Summer morning, Warrandyte (31x44cm-12x17in) s. board
                      (A.D 7000)
£4819 $9253   (26-Nov-90 SY.ME298/R) Peaceful day, Nyora, Healesville
                      (49x74cm-19x29in) s. (A.D 12000)
£6200 $12028   (6-Dec-90 CSK5/R) Bushland (76x92cm-30x36in) s.
£11245 $21590   (26-Nov-90 SY.ME224/R) Kangaroo ground (60x90cm-24x35in) s. (A.D 28000)
£33755 $64810   (14-Aug-90 SY.ME277/R) Sydney harbour (69x79cm-27x31in) s.d.'23
                      (A.D 80000)
£442   *$848*   *(26-Nov-90 SY.ME104) River landscape (26x37cm-10x15in) s.d.1914 W/C*
                      (A.D 1100)
£849   *$1384*   *(1-Jul-91 AAA.S145) The punt (38x49cm-15x19in) s.d.1913 W/C (A.D 1800)*
£1448   *$2852*   *(13-Nov-91 J.M161) Thames mists (36x51cm-14x20in) s.d.1912 W/C*
                      (A.D 3750)

BOYDEN, Dwight Frederick (1860-1933) American
£1676 $2900   (10-May-91 S.BM136/R) June day (81x112cm-32x44in) s.indis.i.d.1908

BOYE, Abel Dominique (1864-1934) French
£3715 $6872   (4-Mar-91 ARC.P92/R) Apres le bain (82x65cm-32x26in) s. (F.FR 37000)

BOYER (?) French
£894 $1735   (8-Dec-90 LT.P153) Place du chatelet en soiree (46x55cm-18x22in) s.
                      (F.FR 8700)
£1028 $1994   (8-Dec-90 LT.P152/R) Animation en soiree sur les Champ-Elysees
                      (46x55cm-18x22in) s. (F.FR 10000)
£1172 $2251   (2-Dec-90 M.V116) La Madeleine, les Grands Boulevards (46x55cm-18x22in)
                      s. (F.FR 11500)
£1195 $2068   (26-May-91 ZZ.F110/R) Place de la Concorde (46x55cm-18x22in) s.
                      (F.FR 12000)
£1210 $2359   (28-Oct-90 M.V51/R) Le Madeleine, les Grands Boulevards
                      (46x55cm-18x22in) s. (F.FR 12000)
£1230 $2410   (11-Nov-90 ZZ.F266/R) La rue de la Paix et la Place Vendome
                      (46x55cm-18x22in) s. (F.FR 12000)
£1325 $2544   (2-Dec-90 M.V66/R) Vu de Paris sous le neige (46x55cm-18x22in) s.
                      (F.FR 13000)
£1411 $2752   (28-Oct-90 M.V150) L'opera, le cafe de la paix sous la neige
                      (46x55cm-18x22in) s. (F.FR 14000)
£1411 $2752   (28-Oct-90 M.V60/R) La place de la Concorde (46x55cm-18x22in) s.
                      (F.FR 14000)

BOYER-BRETON, Marthe Marie Louise (19/20th C) French
£27457 $47500   (22-May-91 SY.NY91/R) Off to school (174x100cm-69x39in) s.d.1906

BOYLE, Charles Wellington (1860-1925) American
£872 $1500   (17-May-91 DM.D2120/R) Landscape scene with rowboat on river
                      (38x48cm-15x19in) s.

BOYLE, Mark (20th C) ?
£3200   *$6272*   *(9-Nov-90 C288/R) Study for sea grass (107x107cm-42x42in) mixed media*
                      construction
£8000   *$15600*   *(18-Oct-90 S175/R) Study from the rock series with rock and sand*
                      (136x136cm-54x54in) sand mixed media fiberglass

BOYS, George (1930-) South African
£562 $1102 (11-Feb-91 SY.J577) Cosmos in an extensive landscape (90x122cm-35x48in)
s. acrylic board (SA.R 2800)
£576 $1106 (26-Nov-90 SY.J373/R) Altar (110x122cm-43x48in) board (SA.R 2800)
£758 $1281 (15-Apr-91 SY.J497) Abstract (97x119cm-38x47in) s. board (SA.R 3600)

BOYS, Thomas Shotter (1803-1874) British
£448 $762 *(27-May-91 OD.P81) Rue Saint Germain l'Auxerrois (17x22cm-7x9in) i.*
blk.crayon (F.FR 4500)
£518 $880 *(27-May-91 OD.P80) rue Bailleul (26x16cm-10x6in) i. blk.crayon*
(F.FR 5200)
£2400 $4032 *(22-Apr-91 PH236/R) Rue de la Licorne, Paris (37x19cm-15x7in) s. W/C*

BOYS, Thomas Shotter (attrib) (1803-1874) British
£1100 $1815 *(9-Jul-91 C82/R) St Paul's Cathedral from Greenwich Park*
(23x32cm-9x13in) pencil W/C scratching out

BOZE, Honore (1830-1908) British
£996 $1693 (27-May-91 APT.P253/R) Marabout et fontaine sur le bord de mer
(30x45cm-12x18in) s. panel (F.FR 10000)

BOZE, Joseph (1744-1826) French
£774 $1300 (17-Jul-91 SY.NY114/R) Portrait of a gentleman (39x33cm-15x13in)
£37186 $60985 (21-Jun-91 SY.MO155/R) Portrait presume de l'artiste (67x82cm-26x32in)
(F.FR 370000)
£40000 $77200 (12-Dec-90 S32/R) Portraits of Louis-Stanislas-Xavier later Louis XVIII,
and of Louise-Marie-Josephine de Savoie (194x138cm-76x54in) s. pair
£3564 $6309 *(5-Apr-91 DAR.P45/R) Portrait de Louis XVI (73x59cm-29x23in) s.d.1784*
pastel oval (F.FR 36000)

BOZNANSKA, Olga (1865-1945) Polish
£1823 $3573 (26-Jan-91 PSA.W4) Study of a woman (35x26cm-14x10in) s. board
(P.Z 34000000)

BOZZANI, Lucien (19th C) Italian
£434 $750 *(10-May-91 S.W2554/R) Players (36x46cm-14x18in) s.i. W/C*

BOZZARICH, Spiro (1878-1941) Yugoslavian
£1003 $1696 (17-Apr-91 WE.MU12) Serbian children by fountain (63x80cm-25x31in) s.
(DM 3000)

BOZZOLINI (?) Italian
£1205 $2229 (6-Mar-91 APT.P82) Composition (55x46cm-22x18in) s.d.56 (F.FR 12000)

BOZZOLINI, Silvano (1911-) Italian
£813 $1626 (10-Feb-91 CC.P8) Chocs no.2 (65x50cm-26x20in) s.d.1960 (F.FR 8000)
£565 $1097 *(9-Dec-90 CC.P96) Composition (42x34cm-17x13in) s.d.1959 gouache*
(F.FR 5500)

BRABAZON, Hercules Brabazon (1821-1906) British
£420 $710 *(18-Apr-91 B228) A view of Lucerne (13x22cm-5x9in) pencil gouache*
£440 $814 *(5-Mar-91 SWS1652) Continental town (30x22cm-12x9in) init. chk gouache*
£480 $802 *(5-Jun-91 PHK63) Capri (24x32cm-9x13in) init. W/C bodycol. over pencil*
£500 $990 *(30-Jan-91 S163) Doge's Palace, Venice (10x13cm-4x5in) indist.s. pencil*
with W/C col.chk
£550 $1089 *(30-Jan-91 S164) Italian tyrol (16x19cm-6x7in) W/C over pencil*
£550 $946 *(14-May-91 SWS66/R) Feluccas on the Nile (10x18cm-4x7in) init. W/C over*
pencil htd.white
£550 $1062 *(10-Dec-90 PHB22/R) Casablanca (17x24cm-7x9in) mono. i.verso pencil*
£560 $1098 *(13-Feb-91 PHL111) Grand Canal, Venice (22x30cm-9x12in) init. col.wash*
£650 $1060 *(14-Jun-91 C150) Figures beside a ruined archway, Casablanca*
(22x28cm-9x11in) init. pencil W/C htd white
£650 $1287 *(30-Jan-91 S158) Lake Maggiore (16x24cm-6x9in) init. col.chk W/C*
£800 $1568 *(21-Nov-90 B115/R) Locarno (16x25cm-6x10in) s. W/C bodycol*
£800 $1584 *(30-Jan-91 S160/R) Street in Sudan (20x14cm-8x6in) W/C over pencil with*
bodycol gum arabic
£850 $1675 *(1-Nov-90 TE566/R) The Piazzetta, Venice, with the Doge's Palace*
(13x20cm-5x8in) pencil W/C htd white
£920 $1546 *(22-Apr-91 PH253) Venice (17x24cm-7x9in) pastel*
£1300 $2548 *(21-Nov-90 B108/R) Aden (20x23cm-8x9in) init. pencil W/C bodycol*
£1400 $2744 *(21-Nov-90 B109/R) Bazaar in Cairo (16x18cm-6x7in) init. pencil W/C*
£5200 $8476 *(14-Jun-91 C157/R) The Piazzetta from the Canal (25x35cm-10x14in) init.*
pencil W/C bodycol.

BRACCHI, Luigi (1892-?) Italian
£739 $1427 (12-Dec-90 F.M180) Natura morta con funghi (50x60cm-20x24in) s. board
(I.L 1600000)

BRACCI, Michele (18th C) Italian
£3656 $7203 *(14-Nov-90 F.M12/R) Trompe l'oeil di paesaggio e libro di legge.*
Paesaggio e una pagina (99x99cm-39x39in) pen ink W/C pair
(I.L 8000000)

BRACHETTI, Paul (1895-?) German
£1014 $1753 (25-May-91 N.M32/R) Still life of flowers in glass vase and pears
(86x68cm-34x27in) s. board (DM 3000)

BRACHO Y MURILLO, Jose Maria (19th C) Spanish
£2143 $3600   (17-Jul-91 SY.NY388/R) Roses. Lilacs (20x25cm-8x10in) both s. panel pair
£7609 $13467   (3-Apr-91 ANS.M84/R) Bodegon de melocotones (82x114cm-32x45in) s.
                (S.P 1400000)
£7609 $13467   (3-Apr-91 ANS.M83/R) Bodegon de uvas, sandia, melon...
                (82x114cm-32x45in) s. (S.P 1400000)

BRACHT, Eugen (1842-1921) Swiss
£656 $1233   (19-Sep-90 GK.Z807) Wooded river landscape, autumn (42x54cm-17x21in) s.
                canvas on board (S.FR 1600)
£1463 $2868   (6-Nov-90 SY.AM14) Deer by Swiss lake (43x68cm-17x27in) s. (D.FL 4800)
£1611 $3141   (13-Oct-90 KRA.D181) Coastal landscape, Insel Rugen (49x38cm-19x15in)
                s.i.d.1877 (DM 4800)
£2098 $4049   (14-Dec-90 BM.B595/R) Landscape with gravel pit (88x103cm-35x41in) s.
                (DM 6000)
£2703 $5270   (26-Oct-90 BM.B749/R) Wooded landscape with cattle (69x87cm-27x34in) s.
                i.verso (DM 8000)
£3147 $6105   (7-Dec-90 GB.B5751/R) View of Schloss Tarasp, Lower Engadin with two
                riders (86x62cm-34x24in) s.d.1913 i.d.verso (DM 9000)
£5420 $10460   (14-Dec-90 BM.B594/R) Coastal landscape with goats grazing, Rugen
                (58x65cm-23x26in) s.d.1911 i.d.verso (DM 15500)
£6375 $10964   (14-May-91 GF.L2142/R) Heath landscape with horse-drawn cart
                (65x125cm-26x49in) s.d.1879 (S.FR 16000)
£7000 $12530   (12-Apr-91 BM.B568/R) Shepherds and flock in wooded landscape, evening
                (90x151cm-35x59in) s. (DM 21000)

BRACK, Cecil John (1920-) Australian
£28037 $45701   (16-Jun-91 SY.ME50/R) Tower (146x114cm-57x45in) s.d.1978 (A.D 60000)
£2150 $3504   *(16-Jun-91 SY.ME68/R) Study for Bacon Cutter Shop no. 1*
                (32x41cm-13x16in) s.d.55 ink (A.D 4600)
£2715 $4588   *(16-Apr-91 J.M151/R) Woman cleaning her teeth (30x46cm-12x18in) s.d.'60*
                W/C (A.D 6000)
£3861 $7606   *(13-Nov-90 J.M98 a) Gymnasts (48x64cm-19x25in) s.d.71 pencil*
                (A.D 10000)

BRACK, Emil (1860-1905) German
£24211 $46000   (28-Feb-91 CH.NY78/R) The reception (84x119cm-33x47in) s.

BRACK, Max Eugen (1878-1950) Swiss
£558 $959   (14-May-91 GF.L2567/R) Lake Thun with Eiger, Monch and Jungfrau
                (80x100cm-31x39in) s. (S.FR 1400)

BRACKETT, Sidney Lawrence (19th C) American
£536 $900   (21-Jul-91 LIT.L133) New England hounds (25x30cm-10x12in) s.

BRACKLE, Jakob (1897-1987) German
£1049 $2035   (4-Dec-90 FN.S1561/R) Road winding through wooded landscape
                (10x12cm-4x5in) s. d.1948verso board (DM 3000)
£1468 $2407   (18-Jun-91 FN.S1544/R) Woodland path (10x12cm-4x5in) s. d.1948verso
                board (DM 4300)
£1644 $2942   (12-Mar-91 FN.S1927/R) Still life with gerbera (34x26cm-13x10in) s.
                (DM 4800)
£1712 $3065   (12-Mar-91 FN.S1926/R) The red wall (60x36cm-24x14in) bears sig.i.verso
                panel (DM 5000)
£1839 $3109   (19-Apr-91 FN.S1491/R) Farmhouse in snowy winter landscape
                (16x20cm-6x8in) s.d.28 board (DM 5500)
£1911 $3134   (18-Jun-91 FN.S1543/R) Lilac bush (20x18cm-8x7in) s.d.1934 d.verso board
                (DM 5600)
£2048 $3358   (18-Jun-91 FN.S545) Spring landscape (12x18cm-5x7in) s.d.1980 panel
                (DM 6000)
£2107 $3561   (19-Apr-91 FN.S1494/R) Wooded landscape in fog (41x31cm-16x12in)
                s.d.1966 panel (DM 6300)
£2341 $3957   (19-Apr-91 FN.S1490/R) Frost in Winterreutte (30x22cm-12x9in) s.d.1932
                board (DM 7000)
£2797 $5427   (4-Dec-90 FN.S1560/R) Landscape with peasants ploughing (20x26cm-8x10in)
                s.d.1943 s.i.verso board (DM 8000)
£3242 $5317   (18-Jun-91 FN.S1542/R) House in winterlandscape, artist's first studio
                (15x11cm-6x4in) s.d.1931 panel (DM 9500)
£4110 $7356   (12-Mar-91 FN.S1925/R) The rodent (64x45cm-25x18in) s.d.1954 panel
                (DM 12000)

BRACKMAN, David (19th C) ?
£780 $1482   *(10-Jan-91 B88) Dropping the tow (43x65cm-17x26in) s.d.87 gouache*
£2800 $4844   *(22-May-91 S213/R) Prince de Neufchatel (44x67cm-17x26in) s.d.88 gouache*
£3000 $5190   *(22-May-91 S193/R) Meteor IV in Heligoland Race (45x68cm-18x27in)*
                s.i.d.89 gouache

BRACKMAN, Robert (1898-1980) American
£1124 $1900   (17-Apr-91 D.NY76/R) Still life of mixed fruit (41x51cm-16x20in) s.
                i.verso
£1337 $2300   (15-May-91 SY.NY217/R) Seated nude (30x51cm-12x20in) s. s.i.d.43 verso
£1406 $2700   (17-Dec-90 SY.NY342/R) Boy from Main Street (81x66cm-32x26in) s.
                s.i.verso
£1842 $3500   (14-Sep-90 S.BM307/R) The bathers (41x51cm-16x20in) s.i.verso
£1933 $3750   (5-Dec-90 D.NY107/R) Standing women (76x61cm-30x24in) s.
£13873 $24000   (22-May-91 CH.NY324/R) Autumn light (200x153cm-79x60in) s.

BRACKMAN, Robert (1898-1980) American-cont.
| £710 | $1200 | (1-May-91 B.SF5146/R) Nude study (38x30cm-15x12in) s. pastel |
| £1094 | $2100 | (17-Dec-90 SY.NY351/R) Study of female nude (61x46cm-24x18in) s. pastel |

BRADBERRY, Georges (1878-1959) French
| £557 | $1091 | (25-Nov-90 ZZ.F216/R) Paysage vallonne (18x26cm-7x10in) s. pastel |
| | | (F.FR 5500) |

BRADBROOK, Jane (1967-) British
£600	$1176	(13-Feb-91 B166) Acacia Avenue II (212x151cm-83x59in)
£650	$1274	(13-Feb-91 B167) William Morris says (152x122cm-60x48in)
£680	$1333	(13-Feb-91 B165/R) Acacia Avenue I (212x151cm-83x59in)

BRADBURY, Arthur Royce (1892-) British
| £11000 | $20350 | (5-Mar-91 PH16/R) Marigold No.1 (76x91cm-30x36in) s.d.1935 |

BRADFIELD, Virginia Palmer (?) American?
| £462 | $800 | (21-May-91 BG.M989) Female nude (25x46cm-10x18in) pastel |

BRADFORD, William (1827-1892) American
£1221	$2100	(15-May-91 SY.NY5/R) Schooner off Labrador Coast (51x76cm-20x30in) s.
£9249	$16000	(22-May-91 CH.NY63/R) Outward bound whaler (51x76cm-20x30in) s.i.
£10582	$20000	(26-Sep-90 SY.NY7/R) The Straits of Belle Isle (30x51cm-12x20in) s.
		i.verso board
£1729	$3250	(7-Aug-90 RB.HY87/R) Whalers in ice (71x104cm-28x41in) s. chl

BRADLEY, Basil (1842-1904) British
£550	$919	(22-Jul-91 SWS1056/R) Calves in a field (22x33cm-9x13in) panel
£720	$1346	(28-Aug-90 S812/R) View of the Nine Pins Mountains, Connemara, Ireland
		(25x36cm-10x14in) s.d.1873 i.d.verso board
£700	$1379	(30-Oct-90 SC39/R) Deer in the highlands (28x97cm-11x38in) s. W/C pencil
£1500	$2520	(16-Jul-91 C123/R) English and gordon setter. Irish setter and pointer
		in landscape (27x19cm-11x7in) s. s.i.verso pencil W/C htd.white pair
£1900	$3097	(11-Jun-91 HS41) Spring in Highlands (53x79cm-21x31in) i.verso W/C
£3000	$5010	(5-Jun-91 RBB972) Partridge season and grouse season, groups of
		retriever dogs (25x18cm-10x7in) s. W/C pair

BRADLEY, Cuthbert (20th C) British
| £1500 | $2925 | (26-Oct-90 C302/R) The Duke of Rutland's hound, Dexter (61x51cm-24x20in) |
| | | s.i.d.1895 coat of arms |

BRADLEY, Edward (fl.1824-1867) British
| £700 | $1155 | (9-Jul-91 PH230) Still life of trout and fishing tackle on river bank |
| | | (40x60cm-16x24in) s.d.1825 panel |

BRADLEY, Helen (1900-1979) British
£2600	$4888	(19-Sep-90 PHC209/R) 'I'm afraid Barney is lost...' (41x31cm-16x12in)
		i.label verso board
£10200	$17034	(22-Jul-91 SWS1129/R) Bell Horse day in Lees (51x77cm-20x30in)
		s.i.d.1967 verso board
£16000	$31360	(7-Nov-90 S159/R) The Whitsun Walk through Lees (66x114cm-26x45in) s.
		s.i.d. d.1968verso board
£5500	$10780	(8-Nov-90 C40/R) The new car (37x57cm-15x22in) s. W/C bodycol.

BRADLEY, Martin (1931-) British
£602	$970	(24-Jun-91 ARC.P14/R) Composition (103x74cm-41x29in) s. (F.FR 6000)
£1300	$2535	(9-Oct-90 B181) Untitled (99x99cm-39x39in) s. s.d.1966 verso
£1321	$2286	(23-May-91 SY.AM349/R) Hidden pearl (119x119cm-47x47in) s.d.1986
		(D.FL 4400)
£1900	$3173	(6-Jun-91 C228/R) Composition (87x162cm-34x64in) s.d.57
£452	$836	(6-Mar-91 HC.P23) Fete enfantine (61x85cm-24x33in) s.i.d.1962 W/C crayon
		(F.FR 4500)
£508	$1016	(10-Feb-91 CC.P9) Composition aux signes (46x38cm-18x15in) s.d.1955
		mixed media gouache (F.FR 5000)

BRADLEY, William (1801-1857) British
£10000	$19000	(10-Jan-91 SY.NY89/R) Portrait of lady (74x61cm-29x24in)
£1400	$2758	(1-Nov-90 C71) Windsor from the Thames on summer morning
		(43x71cm-17x28in) s.d.1880 pencil W/C htd.white

BRAEKELEER, Adrien de (1818-1904) Belgian
£876	$1709	(24-Oct-90 GD.B175/R) Mother and child in interior (23x18cm-9x7in) mono.
		panel (S.FR 2200)
£10983	$19000	(22-May-91 SY.NY211/R) Tavern scene (56x71cm-22x28in) s.d.1852 panel

BRAEKELEER, Ferdinand de (1792-1883) Belgian
£958	$1610	(23-Apr-91 SY.AM275) Severe master (41x54cm-16x21in) s.i. canvas on
		panel (D.FL 3200)
£1500	$2445	(3-Jul-91 PLF.P54) La benediction paternelle (33x127cm-13x50in) s. panel
		(F.FR 15000)
£3373	$6543	(4-Dec-90 C.A79/R) Father's helping hand (27x23cm-11x9in) s. panel
		(B.FR 200000)
£5200	$8684	(3-Jun-91 PHB59/R) Cavalier offering wine to lady (55x46cm-22x18in)
		s.d.1828 panel
£15000	$28800	(28-Nov-90 S49/R) Catching the bat (65x85cm-26x33in) s.d.1858

BRAEKELEER, Ferdinand de (1792-1883) Belgian-cont.
£18003 $30606   (28-May-91 C.A54/R) The admirer (68x56cm-27x22in) s.d.1857 panel
                              (B.FR 1100000)

BRAEKELEER, Henri de (1840-1888) Belgian
£736 $1252   (28-May-91 C.A56) The old tavern (36x28cm-14x11in) s. (B.FR 45000)
£5460 $9500   (27-Mar-91 B.SF4082/R) Young couple making music in window
                              (38x33cm-15x13in) s.d.1854 panel

BRAGAGLIA, Alberto (?) Italian
£1908 $3759   *(30-Oct-90 F.R65) Studio all'aperto (47x65cm-19x26in) s.d.1916 pastel*
                                (I.L 4200000)
£2363 $4654   *(30-Oct-90 F.R151) Motivo prismatico. Albero (64x47cm-25x19in) s.d.1915*
                                mixed media double-sided (I.L 5200000)

BRAHNEWAY, G A (19th C) ?
£769 $1500   (25-Oct-90 D.V33/R) The riding accident (25x36cm-10x14in) s.c.1870 panel
                                (A.S 16000)

BRAITH, Anton (1836-1905) German
£2730 $5160   (25-Sep-90 FN.S2123/R) Cattle in field (34x52cm-13x20in) board
                                (DM 8000)
£8042 $15521   (12-Dec-90 N.M449/R) Calves in sunlit field (25x36cm-10x14in) s.d.1882
                                panel (DM 23000)
£8741 $16958   (4-Dec-90 FN.S1771/R) Lake landscape with sheep and calves watering,
                                evening (29x45cm-11x18in) s.i.d.1894 (DM 25000)
£8741 $16958   (4-Dec-90 FN.S1770/R) Landscape with sheep and shepherd girl, spring
                                (36x48cm-14x19in) s.i.d.1893 (DM 25000)
£9790 $18895   (12-Dec-90 N.M448/R) Cows watering in lake landscape (50x76cm-20x30in)
                                s.i.d.1889 (DM 28000)
£13369 $25000   (1-Aug-90 B.P63/R) Bringing home herd (51x71cm-20x28in) s.
£17123 $27911   (12-Jun-91 SY.MU63/R) Bullocks cavorting (71x115cm-28x45in) s.i.
                                (DM 50000)
£22260 $39846   (13-Mar-91 N.M455/R) Shepherd watering flock in stream and farmhouse
                                amongst trees beyond (75x115cm-30x45in) s. (DM 65000)
£404 $699   *(6-May-91 ZEL.L1440/R) Shepherdess with calves and sheep (11x20cm-4x8in)*
                                s. chl (DM 1200)

BRAITOU-SALA, Albert (1885-?) French
£5139 $9969   *(5-Dec-90 ZZ.F173/R) Jeune femme au boa et au chapeau cloche*
                                (50x46cm-20x18in) s. gouache (F.FR 50000)

BRAKENBURGH, Richard (1650-1702) Dutch
£3800 $6194   (4-Jul-91 C570/R) Peasants drinking and merrymaking in interior
                                (56x67cm-22x26in)
£7703 $12865   (6-Jun-91 D.V86/R) Travelling actors giving performance in Dutch village
                                (40x53cm-16x21in) (A.S 160000)

BRAKENBURGH, Richard (attrib) (1650-1702) Dutch
£719 $1200   (23-Jan-91 D.NY90) Merry gathering in interior (41x48cm-16x19in) bears
                                sig.

BRAKENBURGH, Richard (circle) (1650-1702) Dutch
£1436 $2800   (10-Oct-90 CH.NY131/R) The Seven Acts of Mercy (55x69cm-22x27in) bears
                                init.
£1563 $2798   (14-Mar-91 D.V240/R) La main chaude (30x41cm-12x16in) (A.S 32000)

BRAKENBURGH, Richard (style) (1650-1702) Dutch
£1497 $2530   (2-May-91 CH.AM116/R) A merry company in a brothel, disturbed by the
                              entrance of a gentleman (58x78cm-23x31in) init. (D.FL 5000)

BRAKSPEARE, William Hayward (1819-1898) British
£550 $985   *(11-Apr-91 S105) Model of design for chicken house, Bow Manor, Sale,*
                              Cheshire (24x48cm-9x19in) wood cardboard sand
£700 $1253   *(11-Apr-91 S104) Perspective view of design for St Mary's church,*
                              Bowdon, Cheshire (45x59cm-18x23in) W/C over pen

BRAMBILLA, Ferdinando (1838-1921) Italian
£3669 $6567   (12-Mar-91 F.M25) Chiesa di montagna con fedeli. Battitura del grano
                              (53x37cm-21x15in) one s.d.1881 two (I.L 8000000)

BRAMER, Leonard (attrib) (1596-1674) Dutch
£1300 $2197   (18-Apr-91 CSK40) Deposition with Madonna swooning at foot of cross
                              (69x55cm-27x22in) panel
£531 $1029   *(7-Dec-90 G.Z213/R) Christ Crowned with Thorns (21x16cm-8x6in) indian*
                              ink dr. (S.FR 1300)

BRAMER, Leonard (school) (1596-1674) Dutch
£1567 $3087   (14-Nov-90 D.V189/R) Pyramus and Thisbe (40x53cm-16x21in) panel
                                (A.S 32000)

BRAMLEIGH, Rex (1923-) Australian
£423 $693   *(17-Jun-91 MGS.S155) Little Creek Wamuran (47x36cm-19x14in) s. pastel*
                              (A.D 900)

BRAMTOT, Alfred Henri (1852-1894) French
£5780 $10000   (22-May-91 SY.NY180/R) Tall story (39x60cm-15x24in) s.d.

BRANCACCIO, Carlo (1861-1920) Italian
£1992 $3426   (14-May-91 GF.L2088/R) Rocky coastal landscape (30x40cm-12x16in) s.
      (S.FR 5000)
£5833 $9800   (22-Apr-91 PO.BA8) Boulevard con flacres (50x105cm-20x41in) s.
£7525 $12566   (6-Jun-91 F.M205/R) Boulevard a Parigi (13x20cm-5x8in) s.
      (I.L 16500000)
£9000 $17000   (18-Oct-90 F.M94/R) Vele nella Laguna (46x56cm-18x22in) s. board
      (I.L 19000000)
£12025 $23328   (5-Dec-90 F.M66/R) Veduta di paese con figure (31x22cm-12x9in) s. board
      (I.L 26000000)
£13000 $24960   (27-Nov-90 PH191/R) Bringing in the nets, Bay of Naples
      (61x81cm-24x32in) s.
£21387 $37000   (22-May-91 SY.NY299/R) Paris street scene (51x65cm-20x26in) s.i.
£24425 $42500   (27-Mar-91 B.SF4090/R) View of the Amalfi coast with Naples and Catania
      (75x131cm-30x52in) s.i.
£44369 $86962   (24-Nov-90 SA.A628/R) View of Naples harbour (98x148cm-39x58in) s.i.
      canvas laid down (DM 130000)
£1053   *$2000*   *(11-Sep-90 PO.BA39) Paisaje invernal con personajes en el camino*
      (30x46cm-12x18in) s. W/C board

BRAND, Christian Hilfgott (attrib) (1695-1756) Austrian
£1884 $3372   (13-Mar-91 N.M393/R) Wooded landscape with riders near fountain
      (62x49cm-24x19in) i.verso panel (DM 5500)

BRAND, Erland (1922-) Swedish
£3113 $5386   (22-May-91 BA.S327/R) Composition (218x137cm-86x54in) s. (S.KR 33000)

BRAND, Johann Christian (1722-1795) Austrian
£3918 $7718   (14-Nov-90 D.V290/R) Wooded river landscape with peasant
      (48x37cm-19x15in) one of pair (A.S 80000)
£3918 $7718   (14-Nov-90 D.V289/R) Wooded river landscape with stone bridge and
      anglers (48x36cm-19x14in) one of pair (A.S 80000)

BRAND, Johann Christian (attrib) (1722-1795) Austrian
£3420 $6121   (14-Mar-91 D.V308/R) River landscape with ruins and travellers
      (52x67cm-20x26in) (A.S 70000)

BRAND, Johann Christian (circle) (18th C) Austrian
£1466 $2623   (14-Mar-91 D.V309/R) River landscape with bridge and figures
      (61x113cm-24x44in) (A.S 30000)

BRAND, Johann Christian (style) (1722-1795) Austrian
£1926 $3216   (6-Jun-91 D.V200/R) River landscape with sailing boat (38x52cm-15x20in)
      (A.S 40000)
£4397 $7870   (14-Mar-91 D.V312/R) River landscape. Village street with riders
      (16x21cm-6x8in) copper pair (A.S 90000)

BRANDEIS, Antonietta (1849-?) Bohemian
£1000 $1790   (14-Mar-91 B10/R) A Venetian canal (22x12cm-9x5in) s. board
£1156 $2000   (21-May-91 CE.NY276/R) View of Piazza della Signoria (25x16cm-10x6in)
      init. panel
£1400 $2296   (18-Jun-91 PH88/R) Figures on walkway beside Venetian canal
      (16x26cm-6x10in) mono. i.verso panel
£1445 $2500   (21-May-91 CE.NY252/R) Albergo dei Cappucieri Amalfi (25x15cm-10x6in)
      init. board
£1667 $2800   (17-Jul-91 SY.NY323/R) Ponte Alle Grazie,Firenze (16x23cm-6x9in) s.
      board
£1800 $3510   (15-Jan-91 SWS174/R) The Porta della Carta, the Ducal Palace
      (24x14cm-9x6in) s. board
£1800 $3528   (15-Feb-91 C69/R) Figures by Loggia del Bigallo, Florence
      (22x13cm-9x5in) s. panel
£2183 $4127   (27-Sep-90 D.V90/R) Yard of the Palazzo Vecchio, Florence
      (23x16cm-9x6in) s. panel (A.S 45000)
£4000 $7840   (15-Feb-91 C71/R) Neapolitan street scene (24x15cm-9x6in) s. panel
£4000 $6650   (19-Jun-91 S381/R) In Boboli gardens, Florence (24x14cm-9x6in) s. board
£4200 $8274   (13-Nov-90 SWS369/R) Ducal Palace, Venice. River Schiavoni, Venice
      (16x22cm-6x9in) both s. board
£4800 $8064   (18-Jul-91 CSK201/R) Grand Canal, Venice (22x31cm-9x12in) init. panel
£4800 $9456   (4-Oct-90 CSK241/R) The courtyard of the Palazzo Ducale, Venice
      (24x36cm-9x14in) s.
£10000 $16400   (19-Jun-91 S357/R) Bridge of Sighs. Santa Maria della Salute and Dogana,
      Venice (15x23cm-6x9in) s. pair

BRANDEL, Fritz (1869-?) German
£1224 $2374   (4-Dec-90 FN.S1769/R) Dachauer Moos landscape, spring (75x64cm-30x25in)
      s.i. (DM 3500)

BRANDELIUS, Gustaf (1833-1884) Swedish
£4054 $7703   (14-Sep-90 SA.A1161/R) Horse-drawn sledge with wood on path in winter
      landscape (73x59cm-29x23in) s.d.1869 (DM 12000)

BRANDEN, A R (?) ?
£780 $1466   (8-Aug-90 PHP148) Steam ship 'Campanil' off coastline (55x70cm-22x28in)
                   s.

BRANDENBERG, Wilhelm L (1889-) German
£683 $1119   (22-Jun-91 WK.M1344) Female nude (71x51cm-28x20in) s.d.1924 (DM 2000)

BRANDENBURG, Paul (1866-?) German
£952 $1686   (20-Mar-91 KM.K1117) View of Burg Eltz, autumn (80x50cm-31x20in) s.
                   (DM 2800)
£1020 $1806   (20-Mar-91 KM.K1116) View of Schloss Burresheim in the Eifel
                   (80x60cm-31x24in) s.i. (DM 3000)

BRANDENBURG, Wilhelm (1824-1901) German
£651 $1061   (12-Jun-91 N.M377/R) Mountain lake landscape with boat and traveller on
                   path (63x98cm-25x39in) i.stretcher (DM 1900)

BRANDER, Fredrik (1705-1779) Swedish
£2281 $4494   (30-Oct-90 BU.S11/R) Portrait of Carl Adlerfelt (71x56cm-28x22in)
                   (S.KR 25000)

BRANDES, Peter (20th C) Scandinavian
£623 $1171   (19-Sep-90 KH.K130) Vincent, Colombes 1984 (41x33cm-16x13in) s.d.84
                   acrylic paper on canvas (D.KR 7000)
£1257 $2476   (14-Nov-90 KH.K18/R) Listesko, Colombes 1983 (112x75cm-44x30in) s.d.83
                   paper on canvas (D.KR 14000)
£1316 $2237   (29-May-91 KH.K206) Utopi (70x95cm-28x37in) s.d.82 acrylic paper on
                   canvas (D.KR 15000)
£1585 $3090   (10-Oct-90 RAS.K171/R) Untitled (145x115cm-57x45in) s.d.1983-84verso
                   (D.KR 18000)
£1957 $3680   (19-Sep-90 KH.K129/R) Stabert mates, Colombes 1983 (112x75cm-44x30in)
                   s.d.83 paper on canvas (D.KR 22000)

BRANDI, Domenico (1683-1736) Italian
£1727 $3386   (20-Nov-90 F.R88) Pastore con armenti (74x99cm-29x39in) (I.L 3800000)
£11857 $19802   (4-Jun-91 CH.R465/R) Armenti in un paesaggio. Armenti in un paesaggio
                   con ponte (68x124cm-27x49in) pair (I.L 26000000)
£19425 $37684   (3-Dec-90 SY.F1072/R) Festa paesana (153x230cm-60x91in) s.d.1736
                   (I.L 42000000)

BRANDI, Domenico (attrib) (1683-1736) Italian
£4118 $7000   (31-May-91 CH.NY236/R) Travellers on path approaching stream in
                   mountainous landscape (48x74cm-19x29in)

BRANDI, Domenico (circle) (1683-1736) Italian
£1204 $2010   (6-Jun-91 D.V164/R) Shepherd and flock in landscape (38x64cm-15x25in) i.
                   (A.S 25000)
£1800 $3042   (19-Apr-91 C22/R) A herdsman and a peasant woman in mountainous
                   landscapes (76x104cm-30x41in)

BRANDI, Giacinto (1623-1691) Italian
£5028 $9000   (11-Apr-91 SY.NY108/R) Madonna and Child (73x73cm-29x29in)
£14594 $24371   (4-Jun-91 CH.R534/R) Giacobbe e gli angeli (212x255cm-83x100in)
                   (I.L 32000000)

BRANDI, Giacinto (attrib) (1623-1691) Italian
£1801 $3512   (23-Oct-90 CH.R63) S.Giovanni Battista giovane (73x61cm-29x24in)
                   (I.L 4000000)

BRANDIS, August (1862-1947) German
£2177 $3853   (20-Mar-91 KM.K1119) Rococo interior with set table and view to the
                   garden through door (88x72cm-35x28in) s. canvas on panel (DM 6400)

BRANDNER, Karl (1898-?) American
£1105 $1900   (18-May-91 W.W193/R) Spring (81x91cm-32x36in) s.d.'34

BRANDON, David (?) British
£3500 $6265   (11-Apr-91 S102) Perspective view of design for Colesborne House,
                   Gloucestershire (62x98cm-24x39in) W/C over pencil htd bodycol

BRANDRIFF, George Kennedy (1890-1936) American
£6667 $13000   (10-Oct-90 B.SF539/R) December, San Jancinto Valley (61x71cm-24x28in) s.

BRANDS, Eugene (1913-) Dutch
£619 $1195   (13-Dec-90 SY.AM328 a) White table (49x35cm-19x14in) init. paper
                   (D.FL 2000)
£743 $1434   (12-Dec-90 CH.AM503) Kind II (45x42cm-18x17in) s.d.3.59 s.i.d.1959
                   num.verso paper (D.FL 2400)
£991 $1912   (12-Dec-90 CH.AM562) Portret van een vrouw (33x30cm-13x12in) s.d.10.59
                   paper (D.FL 3200)
£1051 $1818   (22-May-91 CH.AM700) Buddha (47x50cm-19x20in) s. s.i.d.1958 num.1932
                   verso paper on board (D.FL 3500)
£1051 $1818   (23-May-91 SY.AM234/R) Meisje in 't veld (28x31cm-11x12in)
                   s.i.d.1955verso paper (D.FL 3500)
£1084 $2091   (12-Dec-90 CH.AM481) Vrouw met vreemde hoofdtooi (48x50cm-19x20in)
                   s.d.4.58 s.i.d.verso paper (D.FL 3500)

234

BRANDS, Eugene (1913-) Dutch-cont.

£1176	$2271	(12-Dec-90 CH.AM529) Day and night (15x34cm-6x13in) s.d.66 paper (D.FL 3800)
£1351	$2338	(23-May-91 SY.AM231/R) Untitled (45x50cm-18x20in) s.d.53 paper (D.FL 4500)
£1441	$2494	(22-May-91 CH.AM702/R) Composition (28x17cm-11x7in) s.d.8-51-4 paper (D.FL 4800)
£1486	$2868	(12-Dec-90 CH.AM466) Girl (27x26cm-11x10in) s.d.66 paper (D.FL 4800)
£1548	$2988	(12-Dec-90 CH.AM472) Peacock (49x54cm-19x21in) s.d.61 board (D.FL 5000)
£1548	$2988	(12-Dec-90 CH.AM561) Tauruskop (50x50cm-20x20in) s.d.11.59 paper (D.FL 5000)
£1802	$3117	(22-May-91 CH.AM600) Lonesome man in house (29x27cm-11x11in) s.d.4.1960 s.i.d.verso paper (D.FL 6000)
£1952	$3377	(22-May-91 CH.AM696/R) Dans le cirque (49x35cm-19x14in) s.d.1954 paper (D.FL 6500)
£2322	$4481	(13-Dec-90 SY.AM370/R) Vrij, geometrisch - IV (70x80cm-28x31in) s.d.1978 verso (D.FL 7500)
£2786	$5378	(12-Dec-90 CH.AM536 a/R) Woman (49x48cm-19x19in) s.d.59 s.i.d.verso paper (D.FL 9000)
£2853	$4935	(23-May-91 SY.AM239/R) Bloemen in witte vaas II (75x95cm-30x37in) s.i.d.1978verso (D.FL 9500)
£2941	$5676	(12-Dec-90 CH.AM410/R) landschap bij avond (48x54cm-19x21in) s. s.i.d.1974-2 verso paper (D.FL 9500)
£3096	$5975	(12-Dec-90 CH.AM534/R) Portret van mijn vrouw en dochters (46x50cm-18x20in) s.d.8.14.58 i.verso paper on board (D.FL 10000)
£3578	$7013	(13-Feb-91 KH.K42/R) Man with rising moon (70x55cm-28x22in) s. (D.KR 40000)
£4334	$8365	(12-Dec-90 CH.AM390/R) Dream (50x40cm-20x16in) s.d.8-2-52-2 s.i.d.num.152 verso paper (D.FL 14000)
£4954	$9560	(13-Dec-90 SY.AM269/R) Child (70x65cm-28x26in) s. s.d.1966 stretcher (D.FL 16000)
£9288	$17926	(12-Dec-90 CH.AM391/R) Portrait of girl (86x70cm-34x28in) s.d.5.52 s.i.d.verso (D.FL 30000)
£661	$1143	(22-May-91 CH.AM683) Composition (32x41cm-13x16in) s.d.66 s.d. num.2873 verso gouache (D.FL 2200)
£681	$1315	(13-Dec-90 SY.AM330) Desolaat landschap (35x36cm-14x14in) s. oil gouache paper (D.FL 2200)
£805	$1554	(12-Dec-90 CH.AM495) Huis van de Schilder (32x40cm-13x16in) init. s.i.d.IX 79 verso gouache with catalogue (D.FL 2600)
£805	$1554	(12-Dec-90 CH.AM494) Kompositie op oranje fond (48x54cm-19x21in) init. gouache (D.FL 2600)
£805	$1554	(13-Dec-90 SY.AM341) Landschap - een kompositie (68x54cm-27x21in) s. s.d.174-3 verso gouache (D.FL 2600)
£841	$1455	(23-May-91 SY.AM328/R) Composite op Olijfgroen (40x51cm-16x20in) init. s.i.d.1980-1verso gouache (D.FL 2800)
£915	$1756	(27-Nov-90 SY.AM3801/R) Mystery (36x48cm-14x19in) init. gouache (D.FL 3000)
£915	$1756	(27-Nov-90 SY.AM3800) Primaire compositie (48x56cm-19x22in) init.d.1980 gouache (D.FL 3000)
£961	$1662	(22-May-91 CH.AM7787) Colourfull figures (34x46cm-13x18in) s.d.71 gouache (D.FL 3200)
£991	$1912	(12-Dec-90 CH.AM497) Polder II (21x28cm-8x11in) s. s.i.d.1974 num.5786 verso gouache (D.FL 3200)
£1051	$1818	(22-May-91 CH.AM694/R) Figures near oil lamp (47x50cm-19x20in) s.d.5.57 gouache (D.FL 3500)
£1084	$2091	(12-Dec-90 CH.AM485) Compositie op orange fond (48x53cm-19x21in) init. s.d.1989 num.727 verso gouache (D.FL 3500)
£1201	$2078	(22-May-91 CH.AM757) Nightmare (34x45cm-13x18in) s.d.64 s.i.d.10-5-64 num.3321 verso card (D.FL 4000)
£1228	$2088	(29-May-91 KH.K60/R) Composition (35x64cm-14x25in) s.d.63 gouache (D.KR 14000)
£1238	$2390	(13-Dec-90 SY.AM327 a) Sunset (42x54cm-17x21in) s. s.d.1974-1 verso gouache (D.FL 4000)
£1238	$2390	(13-Dec-90 SY.AM346) Red landscape (56x66cm-22x26in) s.d.70 s.d.24.X.1970-3 verso gouache (D.FL 4000)
£1335	$2509	(19-Sep-90 KH.K89/R) Composition (24x20cm-9x8in) s.d.52 Indian ink newspaper (D.KR 15000)
£1351	$2338	(22-May-91 CH.AM758) Huis in de Zon (36x31cm-14x12in) s. s.i.d.25.I.1986 num.4768 verso gouache (D.FL 4500)
£1351	$2338	(22-May-91 CH.AM724) Nachtelijk (34x46cm-13x18in) s.gouache (D.FL 4500)
£1351	$2338	(23-May-91 SY.AM317/R) Dalende zon (55x43cm-22x17in) init. s.i.d.1983-5verso gouache (D.FL 4500)
£1351	$2338	(23-May-91 SY.AM238/R) Blue cano, fancy painting (55x69cm-22x27in) init. s.i.d.1982-1verso gouache (D.FL 4500)
£1512	$2843	(19-Sep-90 KH.K50/R) Composition (50x55cm-20x22in) s.d.65 gouache (D.KR 17000)
£1548	$2988	(12-Dec-90 CH.AM458) Dalende Zon (75x70cm-30x28in) init. s.i.d.1981 num.3 verso chk W/C oil canvas (D.FL 5000)
£1802	$3117	(22-May-91 CH.AM754) Composition with red square (34x42cm-13x17in) s.d.67 gouache (D.FL 6000)
£1802	$3117	(22-May-91 CH.AM721/R) Exotische vogel (50x65cm-20x26in) s.d.6.59 s.i.d num.2187 verso gouache (D.FL 6000)
£1868	$3512	(19-Sep-90 KH.K111/R) Red cockerel (46x50cm-18x20in) s.d.63 acrylic gouache (D.KR 21000)
£1957	$3680	(19-Sep-90 KH.K91/R) Black background (33x41cm-13x16in) s.d.66 gouache (D.KR 22000)

BRANDS, Eugene (1913-) Dutch-cont.
£2012	$3884	(12-Dec-90 CH.AM535/R) Birds (91x37cm-36x15in) gouache three in one frame (D.FL 6500)
£2167	$4183	(13-Dec-90 SY.AM241/R) Tuin in de vroege morgen (53x54cm-21x21in) s.d.62 s.d.2.IX 62-2 verso gouache (D.FL 7000)
£2224	$4181	(19-Sep-90 KH.K88/R) 'Man in Kamer' (51x57cm-20x22in) s.d.60 gouache (D.KR 25000)

BRANDT (?) ?
| £1000 | $1790 | (12-Mar-91 PH43/R) Portrait of woman seated in landscape (63x50cm-25x20in) s.d.1817 |

BRANDT, Carl (?-1930) Swedish
£909	$1527	(27-Apr-91 SO.S290/R) Autumn landscape (55x72cm-22x28in) s. (S.KR 9600)
£1455	$2474	(28-May-91 AB.S4604/R) Northern winter landscape with elk by watercourse (138x160cm-54x63in) s. (S.KR 15500)
£1515	$2545	(27-Apr-91 SO.S289/R) Coastal landscape with boats (71x90cm-28x35in) s. (S.KR 16000)
£1878	$3192	(28-May-91 AB.S4605/R) Northern river landscape with farm in summer (90x128cm-35x50in) s. (S.KR 20000)
£1920	$3762	(20-Nov-90 GO.G22) Northern winter landscape with river (90x125cm-35x49in) s. (S.KR 21000)
£1927	$3795	(13-Nov-90 AB.S347/R) Northern winter landscape with elk by watercourse (138x160cm-54x63in) s. (S.KR 21000)
£2075	$3591	(22-May-91 BA.S538/R) Evening by the lake (65x82cm-26x32in) s.d.1899 (S.KR 22000)
£2083	$3500	(24-Apr-91 BA.S29/R) Fishingvessels in a calm (71x98cm-28x39in) s.d.1900 (S.KR 22000)
£2196	$4282	(21-Oct-90 BU.M414) Northern winter landscape (90x125cm-35x49in) s.d.1922 (S.KR 24000)
£2367	$3977	(24-Apr-91 BA.S28/R) Northern farm in evening light, winter (70x90cm-28x35in) s.d.1917 (S.KR 25000)
£3253	$5822	(9-Apr-91 GO.G16) Water mill in snow (90x124cm-35x49in) s. (S.KR 35000)

BRANDT, Heinrich Carl (attrib) (1724-1787) Austrian
| £2911 | $4745 | (12-Jun-91 N.M297/R) Maria Anna Josepha Charlotte von Pfalz-Sulzbach, Herzogin von Bayern aswidow (86x69cm-34x27in) (DM 8500) |

BRANDT, I H (1850-1926) Danish
| £986 | $1971 | (6-Feb-91 RAS.K63) Breakers and coastal cliffs, Bornholm (66x110cm-26x43in) s.d.1891 (D.KR 11000) |

BRANDT, J (19th C) ?
| £1712 | $3065 | (13-Mar-91 N.M456/R) River landscape with rowing boats (69x106cm-27x42in) s. (DM 5000) |

BRANDT, Johannes Herman (1850-?) Danish
| £1579 | $3000 | (11-Sep-90 PO.BA23) Paisaje costero (90x140cm-35x55in) s.d.1918 |

BRANDT, Josef von (1841-1928) Polish
| £7950 | $14708 | (10-Mar-91 AG.W2) Cossack on patrol (40x53cm-16x21in) s. (P.Z 142000000) |
| £10000 | $19200 | (28-Nov-90 S203/R) Equestrian feats (89x152cm-35x60in) s. |

BRANDT, Marie Louise (1864-?) Swiss
| £1355 | $2330 | (14-May-91 GF.L2431/R) Wooded Alpine landscape (38x46cm-15x18in) mono. (S.FR 3400) |

BRANDT, Otto (1828-1892) German
| £582 | $1042 | (13-Mar-91 N.M457/R) Italian women quarreling at windows (17x22cm-7x9in) s. (DM 1700) |

BRANDTNER, F (1896-1969) Canadian
| £714 | $1179 | (10-Jul-91 MA.V219) The Little Paradise (64x53cm-25x21in) s. (C.D 1350) |

BRANDTNER, Fritz (1896-1969) Canadian
£793	$1546	(25-Oct-90 EA.M611) Driftwood (61x76cm-24x30in) s.i. s.verso panel (C.D 1800)
£1244	$2414	(4-Dec-90 P.Q88) The storm (35x40cm-14x16in) s. board (C.D 2800)
£1307	$2260	(22-May-91 EA.M429) Driftwood (61x76cm-24x30in) s. panel (C.D 2600)
£1322	$2577	(24-Oct-90 EA.M410/R) Landscape (49x38cm-19x15in) s. board (C.D 3000)
£699	$1369	(5-Nov-90 FB.M38) Abstraction (26x36cm-10x14in) s. W/C (C.D 1600)
£965	$1891	(20-Nov-90 JOY.T342/R) Laurentian village (37x50cm-15x20in) s. col.crayons W/C (C.D 2200)
£1263	$2184	(6-May-91 SY.T58/R) Islands in Georgian Bay during rainstorm (41x52cm-16x20in) s.d.1946 W/C (C.D 2500)
£1768	$3058	(6-May-91 SY.T48/R) Abstract composition (27x39cm-11x15in) s.d.34 gouache (C.D 3500)

BRANEGAN, John F (19th C) British
| £300 | $588 | (23-Jan-91 B124) On Medway (23x49cm-9x19in) bears sig.d.1880 i. W/C |

BRANGWYN, Sir Frank (1867-1956) British
| £600 | $1014 | (1-May-91 PHL201) Man and child in cottage interior (23x18cm-9x7in) init.panel |
| £900 | $1728 | (16-Aug-90 B344) Tug boat and other shipping (51x76cm-20x30in) s. |

BRANGWYN, Sir Frank (1867-1956) British-cont.

£1071	$1800	(28-Apr-91 LIT.L199) Man on dock waving to departing sailboat (28x43cm-11x17in) init.d.93 board
£1300	$2496	(20-Feb-91 HAR495) African landscape with figures (28x86cm-11x34in) init. demi lune board
£1300	$2444	(20-Sep-90 CSK99/R) Preaching from the pulpit (36x18cm-14x7in) init. s.verso canvas on panel
£1350	$2646	(25-Jan-91 C25/R) Gypsy caravan (46x54cm-18x21in) board
£2051	$4000	(23-Oct-90 SY.NY400/R) Boat building at harbour or landing the catch (122x126cm-48x50in) init.d.1914
£2763	$5250	(27-Feb-91 SY.NY268/R) Rest (127x102cm-50x40in) init.d.94
£3125	$5250	(17-Jul-91 SY.NY354/R) Queen Elizabeth boarding the Golden Hind (76x61cm-30x24in) mono.
£3600	$5868	(11-Jun-91 ZZ.B417/R) In a peach orchard, South Africa (41x31cm-16x12in) init.d.'91 panel
£3600	$5868	(11-Jun-91 ZZ.B418/R) A Creek, Ida's Valley, South Africa (42x31cm-17x12in) init.d.'91 panel
£8000	$15680	(6-Nov-90 PH76/R) The fruit carrier. The flower girl (39x22cm-15x9in) thinned oil over pencil pair squared
£12105	$23000	(27-Feb-91 SY.NY269/R) Swineherd (140x178cm-55x70in) s.i.verso
£13873	$24000	(22-May-91 SY.NY270/R) Suzannah and elders (120x158cm-47x62in)
£22000	$36740	(6-Jun-91 C12/R) Return of Columbus (86x112cm-34x44in) init. panel
£400	*$668*	*(6-Jun-91 B137/R) Two shepherds and flock (36x44cm-14x17in) s. W/C over chl*
£550	*$930*	*(2-May-91 B1/R) Kneeling figure (46x37cm-18x15in) chl.*
£550	*$1034*	*(18-Sep-90 PH53) Two figures (32x35cm-13x14in) init. red chk*
£620	*$1166*	*(18-Sep-90 PH50) Study for Last Supper (32x51cm-13x20in) init.i. red chk htd white*
£750	*$1388*	*(5-Mar-91 SWS1615/R) Aqueduct at Algeciras (34x47cm-13x19in) s. W/C gouache over pencil*
£880	*$1470*	*(4-Jun-91 SWS1984) Outside Turks Head (32x40cm-13x16in) s.*
£900	*$1692*	*(20-Sep-90 CSK52/R) Outside an inn (20x20cm-8x8in) mono. W/C bodycol chl pencil*
£1100	*$2035*	*(6-Mar-91 DR47/R) Breaking up the Hannibal (57x77cm-22x30in) s.i. W/C*
£2600	*$4654*	*(14-Mar-91 ZZ.B73/R) Puerta De Los Passajes (75x49cm-30x19in) s.d.'92 W/C over pencil*

BRANT, Albert (20th C) ?

| £500 | $835 | (7-Jun-91 LD.P25) La coiffure (73x60cm-29x24in) s. (F.FR 5000) |

BRANTZ, A de (19th C) ?

| £6215 | $11000 | (22-Mar-91 CH.NY664/R) River landscapes (11x16cm-4x6in) both s. panel pair |

BRANWHITE, Charles Brooke (1851-?) British

£850	$1522	(14-Mar-91 B34/R) On the coast of Jersey (55x91cm-22x36in) s. i. verso
£540	*$967*	*(14-Mar-91 PHX252/R) Beached boats at Clovelly, North Devon (36x56cm-14x22in) s.i. verso W/C*
£600	*$1140*	*(11-Sep-90 RG2834) Extensive landscape on Dartmoor, with stream in foreground (41x69cm-16x27in) s. W/C*
£700	*$1253*	*(14-Mar-91 L130) Fishing boats beached at low tide (41x58cm-16x23in) s. W/C*
£750	*$1425*	*(12-Sep-90 CSK187/R) Figures in extensive coastal landscape (36x61cm-14x24in) init.d.1887 pencil W/C htd white*
£780	*$1310*	*(15-Jul-91 PH136/R) Beached boats at sunset (31x46cm-12x18in) s.d.1887 W/C bodycol*
£1050	*$1764*	*(15-Jul-91 PH120/R) Winter scene near Clevedon (35x61cm-14x24in) s. W/C bodycol*

BRAQUAVAL, Louis (1856-1919) French

| £1220 | $2439 | (6-Feb-91 FB.P55/R) La place des martigues (38x45cm-15x18in) s. board (F.FR 12000) |
| *£783* | *$1449* | *(4-Mar-91 ARC.P27/R) Voiliers au crepuscule (29x36cm-11x14in) s.d.1912 gouache (F.FR 7800)* |

BRAQUE, Georges (1882-1963) French

£11723	$22508	(27-Nov-90 APT.P48/R) Compositon geometrique (142x61cm-56x24in) tempera (F.FR 115000)
£50761	$100000	(12-Nov-90 SY.NY29/R) Huitre et Citron sur une Nappe a Carreaux (19x23cm-7x9in) s.
£60000	$96600	(25-Jun-91 C127/R) Vanitas (49x65cm-19x26in) s.d.38 i.verso
£137056	$270000	(15-Nov-90 CH.NY245/R) Verre, pipe et poires (19x32cm-7x13in) s.d.20verso
£152284	$300000	(14-Nov-90 SY.NY446/R) La Theiere - dans un encadrement oval (49x65cm-19x26in) s. d.1952 verso
£489614	$876410	(9-Apr-91 BG.P1/R) Nature morte a la table verte (54x73cm-21x29in) s. (F.FR 4950000)
£1012146	$1983806	(21-Nov-90 CL.E10/R) Nature morte aux cerises (39x46cm-15x18in) s. mono. verso (F.FR 10000000)
£7500	*$14550*	*(5-Dec-90 S376/R) L'Oiseau Bleu (9x15cm-4x6in) s.i.d.1959 pen W/C*
£7508	*$12988*	*(22-May-91 CH.AM533/R) Still life of apples on dish on ledge (13x29cm-5x11in) s. brown crayon (D.FL 25000)*
£13741	*$26383*	*(27-Nov-90 SY.M1222/R) Le soleil (26x39cm-10x15in) W/C pencil paper laid down on canvas (I.L 30000000)*
£14000	*$27160*	*(4-Dec-90 C139/R) Portrait de femme (10x8cm-4x3in) pastel chl*

BRAQUE, Georges (1882-1963) French-cont.

£18000	$28980	(26-Jun-91 S73/R) Les oiseaux (38x29cm-15x11in) s. s.i.d.1960verso gouache card
£36000	$57960	(26-Jun-91 S272/R) Etudes pour Le Plafond au Musee du Louvre (30x18cm-12x7in) s.i.d.1952/53 gouache pencil pen three
£800000	$1552000	(4-Dec-90 S25/R) Le comptier (48x32cm-19x13in) s.verso chl. collage

BRASCASSAT, Jacques Raymond (1804-1867) French

£2600	$4992	(20-Dec-90 CSK95) An unwelcome intrusion (94x127cm-37x50in) indis.s.
£8543	$14010	(21-Jun-91 SY.MO171/R) Boeufs et moutons au paturage (138x192cm-54x76in) s.d.1855 (F.FR 85000)
£13065	$21427	(21-Jun-91 SY.MO170/R) Combat de taureaux (145x192cm-57x76in) s.d.1855 (F.FR 130000)

BRASCH, Morten (17th C) Danish

£4587	$8807	(30-Nov-90 APT.P60/R) Scenes d'interieur a la lueur d'une bougie (23x17cm-9x7in) canvas on panel pair (F.FR 45000)

BRASEN, Hans (1849-1930) Danish

£538	$1075	(6-Feb-91 RAS.K266) Young couple conversing by waterpump (40x42cm-16x17in) s.d.1915 (D.KR 6000)
£590	$1145	(5-Dec-90 KH.K12) Watering cattle (48x73cm-19x29in) mono. (D.KR 6500)
£709	$1198	(1-May-91 KH.K18/R) By the fisherman's cottage (59x69cm-23x27in) s.d.1924 (D.KR 8000)
£789	$1500	(27-Feb-91 SY.NY318/R) Bringing in flock (85x123cm-33x48in) s.d.1907
£1057	$1766	(6-Jun-91 RAS.K162/R) Girl knitting in boat at sunset, Esrum (60x80cm-24x31in) s.d.1926 (D.KR 12000)
£2465	$4141	(23-Apr-91 RAS.K100/R) Young family enjoying sunset and fishermen's return (90x125cm-35x49in) s.d.99 (D.KR 28000)
£3201	$6209	(22-Aug-90 RAS.K38/R) Summer evening (88x120cm-35x47in) s.d.1912 (D.KR 37000)
£4488	$8842	(14-Nov-90 RAS.K47/R) Sunday evening - two girls and man in boat (84x133cm-33x52in) s.d.1902 (D.KR 50000)
£4951	$9309	(10-Aug-90 RAS.V432/R) Coastal landscape with girls and cows (80x110cm-31x43in) s.d.1918 (D.KR 56000)

BRASILIER, Andre (20th C?) French?

£9249	$16000	(7-May-91 CE.NY150/R) Bateaux sur la plage (59x72cm-23x28in) s.
£11561	$20000	(7-May-91 CE.NY133/R) Violon devant la fenetre a Loupeigne (55x46cm-22x18in) s. d.1963 verso
£23121	$40000	(7-May-91 CE.NY52/R) Le lavoir de Mouliherne Anjou (60x73cm-24x29in) s. init.verso
£26012	$45000	(8-May-91 SY.NY232/R) Concours hippique (73x92cm-29x36in) s.i.d.1960 verso
£27749	$53834	(5-Dec-90 ZZ.F65/R) Molyvos, Ile de Lesbos, Grece (60x73cm-24x29in) s. i. stretcher (F.FR 270000)
£32226	$52528	(16-Jun-91 GL.P68/R) Le grand bouquet (115x89cm-45x35in) s. i.d.1972 verso (F.FR 320000)
£38071	$75000	(13-Nov-90 CE.NY247/R) Paysage (81x102cm-32x40in) s.
£38265	$75000	(15-Feb-91 SY.NY53/R) Femme lisant devant la mer (115x89cm-45x35in) s.init.d.1961 i.verso
£50761	$100000	(13-Nov-90 CE.NY270/R) Paysage de l'Ile de France (97x130cm-38x51in) s.
£55838	$110000	(13-Nov-90 CE.NY293/R) Cavalcade dans les flots (81x99cm-32x39in) s. s.i.d.1976verso
£91093	$178543	(25-Nov-90 GL.P85/R) Chevaux en Ile de France (73x92cm-29x36in) s. (F.FR 900000)
£146761	$287652	(25-Nov-90 GL.P84/R) Reprise des Ecuyers (163x130cm-64x51in) s. i.d.1964 verso (F.FR 1450000)
£1745	$2879	(10-Jul-91 FB.P14/R) Jeune femme au jardin (32x24cm-13x9in) s. W/C (F.FR 17500)

BRASSAUW, Melchior (circle) (1709-1757) Flemish

£2000	$3860	(11-Dec-90 PH192/R) Anchovy vendor at arched window with jar and barrel on ledge (27x21cm-11x8in) i. panel

BRATBY, John (1928-) British

£540	$902	(22-Jul-91 SWS1150/R) Striker at Greenhithe (50x61cm-20x24in) s.i.d.'63
£600	$1002	(4-Jun-91 PH50/R) Flowers from Donald Pleasance (68x51cm-27x20in) i.d.1968 stretcher
£700	$1218	(28-Mar-91 CSK42) Large vertical of inverted girl (189x66cm-74x26in) s.
£800	$1568	(25-Jan-91 C122/R) Grasses and two pear trees (122x122cm-48x48in) s.
£900	$1611	(14-Mar-91 L449/R) Woman seated in armchair (58x46cm-23x18in) s. board
£1000	$1930	(12-Dec-90 MMB341/R) Sarah with sunflowers (152x114cm-60x45in) s.i.
£1100	$2145	(10-Oct-90 S221/R) Sunflowers (91x71cm-36x28in) s.
£1450	$2422	(22-Jul-91 SWS1151/R) Mist at Hastings (90x136cm-35x54in) s.i.d.'63
£1500	$2970	(29-Jan-91 PH152/R) On canal, Venice (122x91cm-48x36in) s.
£1800	$3384	(20-Sep-90 C42/R) Expressionistic tiger (110x85cm-43x33in) s.d.11.61
£2500	$4900	(22-Jan-91 SWS934/R) YG490 at Blackheath (101x145cm-40x57in) s. board
£620	$1166	(18-Sep-90 PH156) Self-portrait (126x55cm-50x22in) pencil col.crayons

BRATKOWSKI, Roman (1869-1954) Polish

£643	$1261	(25-Jan-91 REM.W1) Winter landscape (78x100cm-31x39in) s.d.1910 (P.Z 12000000)

BRAUER, Arik (20th C) ?

£1270	$2273	(16-Mar-91 S.Z51) Dance in the forest (38x32cm-15x13in) s.d.1986 gouache tempera (S.FR 3200)
£1284	$2182	(1-Jun-91 VG.B455/R) Der Kipflesser (37x32cm-15x13in) s.d.1962 gouache board (DM 3800)
£2655	$5098	(28-Nov-90 KF.M571/R) Strumpfmadchen (47x35cm-19x14in) s.d.1987 tempera W/C (DM 7700)

BRAUER, Erich (1929-) Austrian

£3041	$5169	(1-Jun-91 VG.B364/R) A hard bed (29x53cm-11x21in) s. panel (DM 9000)

BRAUER, Friedrich (18th C) ?

£904	$1709	(25-Sep-90 FN.S2125 a) Christ as chemist in interior (42x34cm-17x13in) i.d.1737verso (DM 2650)

BRAUN, Adam (1748-1827) Austrian

£1710	$3061	(14-Mar-91 D.V356/R) The interment of Christ (27x33cm-11x13in) s.d.1777 copper (A.S 35000)

BRAUN, Ludwig (1836-1916) German

£769	$1492	(5-Dec-90 DO.H2148) Corpus Christi Procession, Traunstein (41x34cm-16x13in) s. board on panel (DM 2200)
£7432	$14122	(14-Sep-90 SA.A1173/R) Wedding dance before Upper Bavarian farmhouse (33x52cm-13x20in) s. (DM 22000)
£769	$1492	(4-Dec-90 FN.S1466/R) Farmyard scene with two horses (16x20cm-6x8in) W/C (DM 2200)
£1154	$2238	(4-Dec-90 FN.S1775/R) Auf dem Barner im Gosstenhof, Nurnberg (25x32cm-10x13in) s.d.1865 W/C linen (DM 3300)
£1224	$2167	(20-Mar-91 KM.K1121/R) Circus scene, Barner in Grosstenhof, Nuremberg (25x32cm-10x13in) s.d.1865 W/C linen (DM 3600)

BRAUN, Maurice (1877-1941) American

£561	$1100	(12-Feb-91 MOR.P50) Marigolds (61x51cm-24x20in) s.
£974	$1900	(10-Oct-90 B.SF582/R) Marine scene (41x51cm-16x20in) s.
£3175	$6000	(26-Sep-90 SY.NY96/R) California landscape (35x51cm-14x20in) s.
£4082	$8000	(13-Feb-91 B.SF2132/R) Mountain valley (46x62cm-18x24in) s.
£4082	$8000	(13-Feb-91 B.SF2125/R) Brook (61x51cm-24x20in)
£5026	$9500	(26-Sep-90 SY.NY89/R) California landscape (50x61cm-20x24in) s.
£5128	$10000	(10-Oct-90 B.SF608/R) River landing, San Diego (41x51cm-16x20in) s.
£5641	$11000	(10-Oct-90 B.SF540/R) Summer colours (63x76cm-25x30in) s.
£28902	$50000	(23-May-91 SY.NY74/R) Eucalyptus trees overlooking Los Angeles (102x66cm-40x26in) s.d.1911

BRAUND, Dorothy Mary (1926-) Australian

£598	$1177	(31-Oct-90 CH.S189) Shopping (50x39cm-20x15in) s.d.78 W/C gouache (A.D 1500)
£1048	$1876	(9-Apr-91 CH.ME275/R) Bathers (39x49cm-15x19in) W/C gouache (A.D 2400)
£1514	$2982	(31-Oct-90 CH.S70/R) Beach figures (39x49cm-15x19in) s.d.79 gouache (A.D 3800)

BRAUNER, Victor (1903-1966) French

£7107	$14000	(3-Oct-90 SY.NY127/R) Paysage (19x24cm-7x9in) init.d.1953
£8000	$15600	(19-Oct-90 C150/R) Jeune fille en chemise (38x27cm-15x11in) init. board
£85547	$166817	(22-Oct-90 BR.M264/R) Untitled (92x73cm-36x29in) s.d.1956 (I.L 190000000)
£130572	$254615	(24-Oct-90 F.M238/R) Oppression de l'objet (90x116cm-35x46in) s.d.1951 (I.L 290000000)
£765	$1500	(12-Feb-91 SY.NY120/R) Fish (13x20cm-5x8in) i. W/C
£1488	$2560	(17-May-91 LGB.P114/R) La femme au chien (32x25cm-13x10in) init.d.17.X.1953 Indian ink wash pen (F.FR 15000)
£1923	$3769	(25-Nov-90 ZZ.F25/R) Le tigre (11x12cm-4x5in) s.d.55 W/C (F.FR 19000)
£2030	$4000	(13-Nov-90 CE.NY306/R) Narcisse et Orphee dans le meme personnage (33x25cm-13x10in) i.d.1944 pencil
£2199	$4221	(27-Nov-90 SY.MI42/R) Composizione (22x13cm-9x5in) W/C board (I.L 4800000)
£2199	$4221	(27-Nov-90 SY.MI41/R) Composizione (23x13cm-9x5in) W/C board (I.L 4800000)
£3800	$6726	(19-Mar-91 C101/R) Personnage (30x21cm-12x8in) s.i.d.27.1.1961 pen
£7853	$13271	(21-Apr-91 P.V42/R) Sans titre (33x24cm-13x9in) d.27 VI 62 W/C (F.FR 79000)
£17766	$35000	(3-Oct-90 SY.NY123/R) Petites annonces (65x50cm-26x20in) s.d.1959 wax collage masonite
£19036	$37500	(3-Oct-90 SY.NY128/R) Poisson et chat (38x47cm-15x19in) s.d.1953 wax W/C ink pencil paper on masonite
£162437	$320000	(13-Nov-90 SY.NY56/R) Miroir de l'incree (77x56cm-30x22in) s. init.d.15.9.1945 wax W/C ink paper on canvas

BRAUNTUCH, Troy (1954-) American

£1893	$3200	(2-May-91 CH.NY228/R) Untitled (207x71cm-81x28in) s.d.1981 white pencil

BRAUSEWETTER, Otto (1835-1904) German

£3846	$7423	(12-Dec-90 N.M450/R) The wedding picture (82x107cm-32x42in) mono. (DM 11000)

BRAVO, Claudio (1936-) Chilean

£11628	$20000	(15-May-91 CH.NY106/R) Naturaleza Muerta con Flores (22x28cm-9x11in) s.d.MCMLXIV panel
£56122	$110000	(20-Nov-90 CH.NY15/R) Bodegon con vela y vasos (79x100cm-31x39in) s.d.MCMLXXXIII
£94675	$160000	(30-Apr-91 SY.NY9/R) Before game (199x239cm-78x94in) s.d.MCMLXXXIII
£603	$1013	(23-Apr-91 DUR.M22/R) Cabeza de nina (28x22cm-11x9in) dr (S.P 110000)
£2551	$5000	(20-Nov-90 CH.NY196/R) Hombre comiendo una manzana (22x15cm-9x6in) s.d.1955 black chk
£3061	$6000	(19-Nov-90 SY.NY193/R) Sapo (21x17cm-8x7in) s.d.MCMLXV pencil pastel
£17442	$30000	(15-May-91 CH.NY41/R) Dama de Blanco (100x70cm-39x28in) s.d.MCMLXVII pastel pencil paper laid down panel
£22189	$37500	(1-May-91 SY.NY219/R) Enigma (75x110cm-30x43in) s.d.MCMLXVI pastel pencil paper on panel

BRAY, Jan de (1627-1697) Dutch

| £5534 | $9407 | (27-May-91 GK.Z5011/R) Two girls with bird's nest (73x60cm-29x24in) panel (S.FR 14000) |
| £275229 | $542202 | (14-Nov-90 SY.AM69/R) Portrait of boy holding basket of fruit (67x55cm-26x22in) s.d.1658 panel (D.FL 900000) |

BRAY, Jan de (attrib) (1627-1697) Dutch

| £4532 | $7387 | (14-Jun-91 MB.P3/R) Portrait d'homme (73x63cm-29x25in) (F.FR 45000) |

BRAY, Jan de (circle) (1627-1697) Dutch

| £3058 | $6024 | (13-Nov-90 CH.AM168/R) Old woman holding sack (58x47cm-23x19in) panel (D.FL 10000) |

BRAY, Salomon de (circle) (1597-1664) Dutch

| £4200 | $7098 | (18-Apr-91 C161/R) A mother and child (69x54cm-27x21in) sig.d.1657 |

BRAY, Salomon de (style) (1597-1664) Dutch

| £3500 | $7000 | (7-Feb-91 C34/R) Portrait of a girl, bust length (37x30cm-15x12in) panel |

BRAYER, Y (1907-1990) French

| £3009 | $5868 | (13-Oct-90 H.AP2/R) Le marche nicois (45x33cm-18x13in) W/C (F.FR 30000) |

BRAYER, Yves (1907-1990) French

£2823	$5419	(2-Dec-90 GAB.G1525/R) Nu a la chaise rose (46x38cm-18x15in) s.i. (S.FR 7000)
£3614	$5819	(24-Jun-91 ARC.P22/R) Paysage des Baux (38x55cm-15x22in) s. (F.FR 36000)
£6114	$12045	(6-Oct-90 GL.P96) Paysage des Cevennes (54x65cm-21x26in) s. i. verso (F.FR 62000)
£7129	$13188	(6-Mar-91 APT.P81/R) Les Baux, le village (55x65cm-22x26in) s. (F.FR 71000)
£7500	$12225	(3-Jul-91 PLF.P16/R) 14 juillet au Grau-du-Roi (50x65cm-20x26in) s. i. verso (F.FR 75000)
£7811	$15153	(7-Dec-90 GL.P191/R) Chapelle dans le montagnette (38x55cm-15x22in) s. (F.FR 76000)
£7861	$13678	(25-Mar-91 PLF.P24/R) Chevaux en Camargue (53x64cm-21x25in) s. d.1957 verso (F.FR 79000)
£8671	$15000	(7-May-91 CE.NY45/R) Oliviers a Fontvieille (50x65cm-20x26in) s.
£9016	$17672	(11-Nov-90 ZZ.F128/R) Paysage des Cevennes (53x65cm-21x26in) s. (F.FR 88000)
£13664	$26781	(19-Nov-90 ARC.P59/R) Palais de Monaco (59x79cm-23x31in) s.d.1946 (F.FR 135000)
£15045	$29338	(11-Oct-90 QWA.P57/R) Paysage de Camargue (50x65cm-20x26in) s. (F.FR 150000)
£20555	$39877	(9-Dec-90 E.LA87/R) Paysage aux oliviers (73x92cm-29x36in) s. (F.FR 200000)
£21739	$42391	(21-Oct-90 DA.R2/R) Mas de provence (81x100cm-32x39in) s.d.1959 (F.FR 215000)
£23069	$44985	(11-Oct-90 QWA.P41/R) Paysge de Provence (73x92cm-29x36in) s. (F.FR 230000)
£594	$1051	(7-Apr-91 I.N50) Cavalier (20x24cm-8x9in) s.i.d.sept.81 felt pen (F.FR 6000)
£610	$1220	(6-Feb-91 FB.P58) Paysage de Provence (35x26cm-14x10in) s. felt-pen (F.FR 6000)
£814	$1538	(25-Sep-90 FB.P243/R) Entre deux poses (29x18cm-11x7in) s.i.d.5 mai 1932 Indian ink W/C (F.FR 8000)
£1014	$2008	(3-Feb-91 LT.P20) Scene champetre (24x17cm-9x7in) s. W/C (F.FR 10000)
£1143	$2217	(8-Dec-90 GAB.G2800) Rue de New-York (15x23cm-6x9in) s. W/C (S.FR 2800)
£1282	$2526	(6-Oct-90 GL.P97) La famille de gitans (33x25cm-13x10in) s. ink gouache (F.FR 13000)
£1508	$2472	(18-Jun-91 APT.P9) Port mediterraneen (33x51cm-13x20in) s. wash (F.FR 15000)
£1844	$3615	(11-Nov-90 ZZ.F127/R) Cavaliers (27x21cm-11x8in) s. W/C (F.FR 18000)
£2513	$4497	(15-Mar-91 FB.P7/R) Chevaux de Camargue (40x55cm-16x22in) s. W/C (F.FR 25000)
£2749	$5416	(30-Oct-90 I.N155/R) Suzy au bar (28x22cm-11x9in) s.i.d. W/C htd.gouache (F.FR 27000)
£3216	$5274	(19-Jun-91 JM.P74/R) La place de Sauvagnat,Auvergne (48x63cm-19x25in) s. W/C (F.FR 32000)
£3543	$6943	(25-Nov-90 LC.P82/R) Vue du village de Cordes (32x40cm-13x16in) s.d.1940 gouache (F.FR 35000)

240

BRAYER, Yves (1907-1990) French-cont.
£4073 $8024   (30-Oct-90 ZZ.F126 b) Paysage de Provence (40x52cm-16x20in) s. W/C
                       (F.FR 40000)
£5306 $10453   (16-Nov-90 FB.P133/R) Partie de polo a Deauville (48x63cm-19x25in)
                       s.i.d.1972 W/C (F.FR 52000)

BRAZDA, W (?) ?
£600 $1038   (22-May-91 CSK216) Horse-drawn sleigh on winter track (48x79cm-19x31in)
                       s.

BRAZILIAN SCHOOL, 19th C Brazilian
£3500 $6895   (15-Nov-90 CSK22/R) The Harbour of Rio de Janeiro (45x61cm-18x24in)
£20000 $39400   (15-Nov-90 CSK19/R) House of Conde Sebastiao do Pinho at Laranjeiras,
                       Rio de Janeiro (59x106cm-23x42in)

BREA, Ludovico (circle) (15/16th C) French
£39474 $75000   (11-Jan-91 CH.NY53/R) The Assumption and Coronation of the Virgin
                       (88x50cm-35x20in) tempera panel

BREACH, E R (19th C) British
£1250 $2450   (13-Feb-91 S96/R) Land storm (101x127cm-40x50in) s.d.1873 s.i.frame

BREAKSPEARE, William A (1855-1914) British
£3378 $5507   (10-Jun-91 W.T1329) The broken cord (41x61cm-16x24in) s. (C.D 6250)

BREANSKI, A de (snr) (1852-1928) British
£1091 $2073   (12-Sep-90 WO.CO2) Highland landscape with lake and mountains
                       (46x61cm-18x24in) (E.P 1200)

BREANSKI, Alfred Fontville de (1877-1945) British
£600 $1170   (16-Jan-91 CSK284/R) Summer (191x119cm-75x47in) s.d.1904 s.i.d.verso
£600 $1032   (16-May-91 CSK68) Sunrise (36x25cm-14x10in) init.i.d.1937
£658 $1296   (30-Oct-90 MA.V565) Spring on the Wiltshire Downs (41x61cm-16x24in) s.
                       (C.D 1500)
£800 $1568   (20-Nov-90 PH18/R) A breezy morning (50x76cm-20x30in) s.
£800 $1504   (18-Sep-90 SWS606/R) Evening in Perthshire (50x76cm-20x30in) s.i.verso
£816 $1314   (26-Jun-91 KM.K1419) Peasant girl with cattle in river landscape near
                       Taynuilt, evening (41x61cm-16x24in) s. (DM 2400)
£830 $1626   (5-Nov-90 FB.M320/R) Near Aberfoyle (41x61cm-16x24in) s.verso
                       (C.D 1900)
£873 $1712   (5-Nov-90 FB.M402) On the Tary, Dartmoor (41x61cm-16x24in) s.verso
                       (C.D 2000)
£1000 $1950   (11-Oct-90 CG195/R) Early morning, Ville d'Array, near Paris
                       (61x46cm-24x18in) s.d.1903 s.i.d.verso
£1000 $1790   (10-Apr-91 CSK188/R) Llyn Ewynant, North Wales (51x76cm-20x30in) s.
                       i.verso
£1064 $2000   (22-Sep-90 WOL.C216/R) Twilight, Loch Tulla N.B (56x76cm-22x30in) s.
£1131 $1900   (17-Jul-91 SY.NY328/R) Moonlight - the church on the hill
                       (61x41cm-24x16in) s. i. verso
£1220 $2061   (20-Apr-91 HOR.H3/R) Lake and mountain landscape, Scotland
                       (31x62cm-12x24in) s. (F.M 8500)
£1250 $2463   (13-Nov-90 SWS299/R) Sunrise over a loch (50x75cm-20x30in) s. i. verso
£1495 $2646   (20-Mar-91 MA.V432) Evening in Glen Finlas (51x76cm-20x30in) (C.D 3050)
£1500 $2835   (27-Sep-90 L1/R) A highland loch - evening with cattle before a mountain
                       lake (51x76cm-20x30in) s.
£1500 $2835   (27-Sep-90 L2/R) Between the showers - cattle by a mountain lake
                       (51x76cm-20x30in) s.
£1563 $3000   (27-Nov-90 W.T1046) The shores of Loch Long (61x91cm-24x36in) s.
                       s.i.verso (C.D 3500)
£1800 $3402   (27-Sep-90 CSK86) Early morning, Ben Venue. Evening on a Highland loch
                       (76x50cm-30x20in) s. s.i.verso pair
£1842 $3500   (27-Feb-91 SY.NY231/R) Westminster - Houses of Parliament
                       (46x61cm-18x24in) s.
£1900 $3743   (1-Nov-90 TE616/R) The mill pool, evening (51x76cm-20x30in) s. s.i.verso
£2000 $3920   (22-Nov-90 CSK133/R) Abingdon on Thames. Temple Lock on Thames
                       (30x42cm-12x18in) s. i.verso pair
£2200 $4158   (27-Sep-90 CSK78/R) Ullswater from Pooley (61x92cm-24x36in) s. s.i.verso
£2300 $4485   (18-Oct-90 SC3087/R) In the Shakespeare country - Mary Ardens cottage,
                       Wilmcote (39x59cm-15x23in) s. i. verso
£2500 $4900   (13-Feb-91 S48/R) Sunset (61x107cm-24x42in) s.
£3300 $6270   (12-Sep-90 PHL169/R) Evening near Callander, Perthshire
                       (60x39cm-24x15in) s. pair
£4000 $6600   (9-Jul-91 PH145/R) Evening on Highland Loch. On Loch Etive
                       (51x76cm-20x30in) s. s.i.verso pair
£350 $648   (5-Mar-91 AG117) Gaggle of geese at village pond (27x37cm-11x15in) s.
                       W/C
£360 $706   (23-Jan-91 B102) Country church and farm buildings with sheep and pond
                       in foreground (24x34cm-9x13in) s. W/C htd white

BREANSKI, Alfred de (attrib) (19/20th C) British
£502 $984   (11-Nov-90 SY.J394/R) Shepherd and his flock in the mountains
                       (45x61cm-18x24in) bears sig. (SA.R 2500)

BREANSKI, Alfred de (snr) (1852-1928) British
£797 $1371   (14-May-91 GF.L2425/R) On a country road (23x30cm-9x12in) s. board
                       (S.FR 2000)

BREANSKI, Alfred de (snr) (1852-1928) British-cont.

£850	$1420	(5-Jun-91 S12/R) Llyn Gwernan, at foot of Cader Idris, Dolgelly, North Wales (30x48cm-12x19in) s. s.i.d.1875-6 verso board
£1508	$2609	(22-May-91 GS.B2335/R) Mountainous Scottish lake landscape with cattle watering (30x51cm-12x20in) s. s.i.verso (S.FR 3800)
£1550	$2992	(12-Dec-90 PHS762/R) Chislehurst church, Kent (48x74cm-19x29in) s.d.1882 i.stretcher
£1750	$3238	(6-Mar-91 SC4283) Cornfield at Bourne End (30x46cm-12x18in) s. s.i.verso
£2000	$3960	(28-Jan-91 HS280/R) Derwent - Keswick, landscape at sunset with cattle and figure crossing bridge (40x55cm-16x22in) s. i.verso
£2000	$3280	(20-Jun-91 B72) Waterhen's haunts (61x91cm-24x36in) s. s.i.verso
£2610	$5116	(11-Feb-91 SY.J393/R) At Gwyant, North Wales, Moel Siabod, North Wales (50x75cm-20x30in) s. i. verso pair (SA.R 13000)
£2680	$4557	(27-May-91 HO.ED63/R) River Dee and Balmoral Hills (51x76cm-20x30in) s. s.i.verso (C.D 5200)
£2800	$5516	(13-Nov-90 PH52/R) Bealach-Nam-Bow, Lock Katrine (61x92cm-24x36in) s.
£2900	$5713	(13-Nov-90 SWS252/R) The waters of Taing at Arrochar (39x59cm-15x23in) s. i. verso
£3000	$5910	(13-Nov-90 PH51/R) Dunaraggan near the Trossachs (40x61cm-16x24in) s. s.i.verso
£3400	$5848	(16-May-91 CSK103/R) Vale of Langollen, North Wales (41x56cm-16x22in) s. s.i.verso
£3500	$6895	(13-Nov-90 PH39/R) Berkshire homestead (61x102cm-24x40in) s. s.i.verso
£3500	$6790	(5-Dec-90 PHE3/R) Langdale Pikes, sunset (51x76cm-20x30in) s. i. verso
£3500	$5845	(5-Jun-91 S41/R) Thames near Quarry woods, Great Marlow (62x102cm-24x40in) s. s.i.verso
£3800	$7106	(28-Aug-90 S818/R) Ben Ledi from the Pass of Leney (41x62cm-16x24in) s.s.i.verso
£3800	$7182	(27-Sep-90 CSK69/R) Coniston Lake and Old Man (40x55cm-16x22in) s.i.
£4000	$7080	(21-Mar-91 CSK111/R) A spring evening, Burnham Beeches (61x91cm-24x36in) s.i.
£4100	$7257	(3-Apr-91 RBB935/R) Landscape view of the Dee with figures beside waterfall (38x58cm-15x23in) s.d.1898 i.verso
£4200	$6846	(14-Jun-91 C237/R) Sheep grazing by a lake at sunset (76x127cm-30x50in) s.
£4400	$8668	(13-Nov-90 SWS253/R) The valley of the Dee (49x75cm-19x30in) s.d.1886 i. verso
£4800	$8976	(28-Aug-90 S869/R) An autumn evening, the river Teith (53x36cm-21x14in) s.s.i.verso
£5060	$8500	(28-Apr-91 HG.C63) Near Inversnaid (61x91cm-24x36in) s.
£5500	$8965	(14-Jun-91 C269/R) The River Tay (50x76cm-20x30in) s. s.i.verso
£5500	$11000	(5-Feb-91 S45 a/R) Entrance to Glencoe. Heart of Selkirk (41x61cm-16x24in) one s. one bears sig. pair
£5500	$10285	(28-Aug-90 S778/R) Evening in Inversnaid (46x72cm-18x28in) s.s.i.verso
£5800	$11368	(13-Feb-91 S38/R) Wallingford-on-Thames (61x101cm-24x40in) s. s.i.verso
£6200	$12152	(13-Feb-91 S39/R) Llyn Serionedd (40x58cm-16x23in) s.i. verso
£6500	$13000	(5-Feb-91 S28/R) Pass to Loch Awe (51x76cm-20x30in) s. s.i.verso
£7500	$14175	(26-Sep-90 S35/R) Durham Cathedral from Prebends Bridge (61x91cm-24x36in) s. s.i.verso
£8200	$15498	(26-Sep-90 S36/R) Rosy morning, Shabed from Llugwy trout stream, North Wales (51x76cm-20x30in) s. s.i.verso
£9000	$18000	(5-Feb-91 S40/R) Vale of Shiel (61x91cm-24x36in) s.
£9500	$17765	(28-Aug-90 S806/R) Invergarry Loch (51x76cm-20x30in) s.
£10000	$16300	(14-Jun-91 C285/R) Dhu Loch, near Balmoral (61x91cm-24x36in) s.
£10270	$16741	(10-Jun-91 W.T1306/R) In Glen Finlas at sunset (61x91cm-24x36in) s. (C.D 19000)
£10500	$20685	(1-Nov-90 C214/R) Haunt of the Wildfowl, Llyn Crafnaut (61x91cm-24x36in) s. i.verso
£11000	$22000	(5-Feb-91 S29/R) Bealach-Nam-Bo, Loch Katrine (61x91cm-24x36in) s.
£12000	$21480	(11-Mar-91 HS287/R) The evening glow, Inverloch with cattle watering (60x90cm-24x35in) s.
£12500	$21500	(15-May-91 BT251/R) The Borders of Ayr (58x89cm-23x35in) s. i. verso
£12821	$25000	(23-Oct-90 SY.NY379/R) Highland cattle in landscape (76x112cm-30x44in) s.
£15000	$29550	(13-Nov-90 PH49/R) Loch Katrine (76x127cm-30x50in) s. s.i.verso
£16000	$29920	(28-Aug-90 S820/R) Glen Nevis. Loch Awe (31x51cm-12x20in) s.s.i.verso pair
£17919	$31000	(22-May-91 SY.NY249/R) Golden Valley (76x127cm-30x50in) s.
£24000	$47280	(1-Nov-90 C285/R) Windsor Castle, evening (101x178cm-40x70in) s.d.1897 s.i.d.verso

BREANSKI, Alfred de (jnr) see BREANSKI, Alfred Fontville de

BREANSKI, Gustave de (19th C) British

£602	$1181	(11-Feb-91 SY.J357/R) Fishing boats at the harbour entrance (40x70cm-16x28in) s. (SA.R 3000)
£650	$1287	(30-Jan-91 CSK246) Off the coast at Dover (51x76cm-20x30in) s.
£800	$1560	(18-Oct-90 CSK153/R) Off Hastings (30x51cm-12x20in) s. s.indist.i.label verso
£1000	$1960	(13-Feb-91 S8/R) Approaching storm (60x90cm-24x35in) s.
£1081	$2000	(10-Mar-91 H.C81/R) Seascapes (46x81cm-18x32in) pair
£1800	$3474	(13-Dec-90 CSK311/R) Fishing boat in swell off harbour wall (61x102cm-24x40in) s.d.1886
£2000	$3400	(30-May-91 C153/R) Castletown, Isle of Man (79x127cm-31x50in) s.
£2800	$5292	(26-Sep-90 S21/R) Low tide, Dover (61x91cm-24x36in) s.

BREARD, Henri Georges (19th C) French
£576 $973   (1-May-91 KH.K19/R) Auction inspection (85x70cm-33x28in) s. (D.KR 6500)

BREAUTE, Albert (1853-?) French
£3961 $6655   (23-Apr-91 RAS.K136/R) Young girl in her bedroom (74x50cm-29x20in) s.
                          (D.KR 45000)

BRECHET, Andre (20th C) French
£1224 $2376   (8-Dec-90 GAB.G2418/R) Composition rouge et noire (66x207cm-26x81in) s.
                          (S.FR 3000)

BRECK, John Leslie (1861-1899) American
£59896 $115000   (29-Nov-90 SY.NY56/R) Morning fog and sun (81x117cm-32x46in) s.d.1892

BRECKENRIDGE, Hugh Henry (1870-1937) American
£37572 $65000   (22-May-91 CH.NY294/R) A corner of the studio (76x101cm-30x40in) s.
£513 $1000   (20-Oct-90 FA.PH889) Early morning in Manayunk (18x23cm-7x9in) s. pastel
*£698 $1200   (15-May-91 SY.NY140/R) Landscape - April 17, 1905 (43x53cm-17x21in) s.
                          pastel sandpaper on canvas*

BREDA, Carl Fredrik von (1759-1818) Swedish
£7299 $14380   (30-Oct-90 BU.S12/R) Portrait of Margaretha Ulrika Lagerbring
                          (76x63cm-30x25in) s.d.1798 (S.KR 80000)

BREDAEL, Alexandre van (1663-1720) Flemish
£1800 $3510   (26-Oct-90 PHM39) Figures gathered at military encampment
                          (40x54cm-16x21in)

BREDAEL, Alexandre van (style) (1663-1720) Flemish
£2100 $4095   (22-Oct-90 SWS1369/R) Peasants merrymaking outside inn by river
                          (45x68cm-18x27in)

BREDAEL, Jan Frans van (18th C) Flemish
£3000 $5910   (31-Oct-90 S184/R) Soldiers fighting peasants outside house
                          (42x55cm-17x22in)

BREDAEL, Jan Frans van (elder) (1686-1750) Flemish
£1198 $2024   (2-May-91 CH.AM136) A cavalry skirmish near a city (19x27cm-7x11in)
                          panel (D.FL 4000)

BREDAEL, Jan Peter van (17/18th C) Flemish
£5387 $10612   (14-Nov-90 D.V113/R) After the battle (20x27cm-8x11in) panel
                          (A.S 110000)

BREDAEL, Jan Peter van (younger) (1683-1735) Flemish
£23904 $41116   (14-May-91 GF.L2051/R) Skirmishes (43x66cm-17x26in) panel pair
                          (S.FR 60000)

BREDAEL, Jan Peter van (younger-circle) (1683-1735) Flemish
£10000 $20000   (7-Feb-91 C175/R) An extensive landscape with travellers on a wooded
                          track, town witha chateau on a lake beyond (39x49cm-15x19in) copper

BREDAEL, Joseph van (1688-1739) Flemish
£28947 $55000   (11-Jan-91 CH.NY22/R) Village street with figures before inn and
                          travellers resting on path (18x26cm-7x10in) on copper

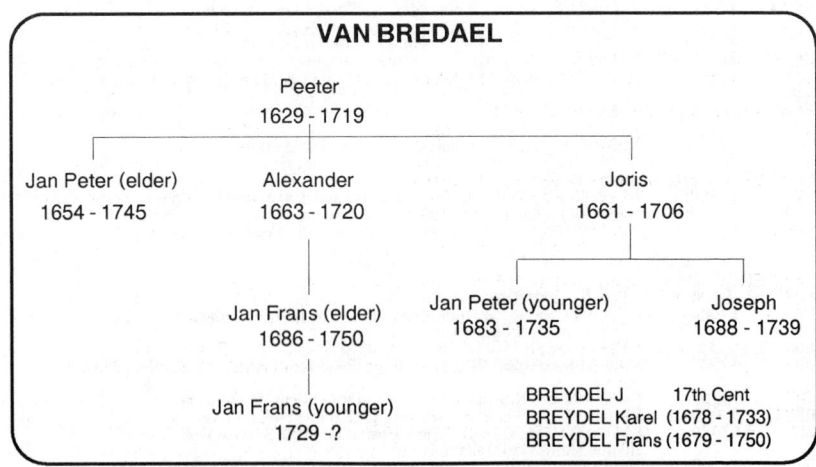

VAN BREDAEL

Peeter
1629 - 1719

Jan Peter (elder)   Alexander   Joris
1654 - 1745   1663 - 1720   1661 - 1706

Jan Frans (elder)   Jan Peter (younger)   Joseph
1686 - 1750   1683 - 1735   1688 - 1739

Jan Frans (younger)   BREYDEL J   17th Cent
1729 -?   BREYDEL Karel (1678 - 1733)
        BREYDEL Frans (1679 - 1750)

BREDAEL, Joseph van (1688-1739) Flemish-cont.
£107034 $210856   (14-Nov-90 SY.AM115/R) The Tower of Babel (51x66cm-20x26in) panel
(D.FL 350000)

BREDAEL, Peeter van (1629-1719) Flemish
£2700 $4401   (4-Jul-91 B128/R) A coastal landscape wiht fishing boats and cattle
watering (53x110cm-21x43in)
£3182 $6237   (19-Nov-90 CH.R37/R) Pastori e popolani fra rovine (77x102cm-30x40in)
(I.L 7000000)
£6633 $13066   (12-Nov-90 CSC.P4/R) La halte devant le port. Paysage anime
(29x39cm-11x15in) pair (F.FR 65000)
£7692 $15000   (11-Oct-90 SY.NY164/R) Landscape with peasants resting by fountain with
ruins of fortifications (94x128cm-37x50in) s.
£8000 $15440   (11-Dec-90 PH220/R) Italian landscape with peasants and livestock
outside walls of city (68x85cm-27x33in) s.
£9443 $15959   (18-Apr-91 APT.P74/R) Paysage de riviere dans les environs de Rome
(70x95cm-28x37in) (F.FR 95000)
£13361 $25920   (5-Dec-90 APT.P61/R) Scene de marche dans un port mediterraneen
(60x84cm-24x33in) (F.FR 130000)
£29311 $52467   (14-Mar-91 D.V50/R) Cattle market before town walls of Rome
(95x128cm-37x50in) s. (A.S 600000)

BREDAEL, Peeter van (attrib) (1629-1719) Flemish
£1520 $2889   (14-Sep-90 SA.A1098/R) Southern coastal harbour with market scene
(40x57cm-16x22in) (DM 4500)

BREDAEL, Peeter van (circle) (1629-1719) Flemish
£1217 $2410   (30-Jan-91 APT.P233/R) Scene de marche (33x42cm-13x17in) (F.FR 12000)
£5000 $9600   (29-Nov-90 CSK119/R) Village kermesse (55x73cm-22x29in)

BREDAEL, Peeter van (style) (1629-1719) Flemish
£2500 $4800   (29-Nov-90 CSK307/R) Winter landscape with sledges and skaters near
castle (58x65cm-23x26in) init.

BREDAL, Niels (19th C) Danish
£1366 $2281   (6-Jun-91 RAS.K34/R) Obelisque at Trinita dei Monti (48x33cm-19x13in) s.
(D.KR 15500)

BREDIN, Ray Sloan (1881-1933) American
£2514 $4500   (14-Mar-91 CH.NY104/R) Along canal (30x35cm-12x14in) s.

BREDOW (19/20th C) German?
£1293 $2288   (20-Mar-91 KM.K1123) Dutch winter landscape with frozen river and
farmhouse, evening (64x98cm-25x39in) s.indis.d.1871 (DM 3800)

BREDSDORFF, Axel (1883-1947) Danish
£683 $1119   (22-Jun-91 WK.M1345/R) Justizpalast, Munich (56x65cm-22x26in) s.i.d.1907
(DM 2000)

BREDT, Ferdinand Max (1860-?) German
£531 $950   (14-Apr-91 JRB.C95/R) Nude reading (36x43cm-14x17in) s. panel
£1900 $3268   (14-May-91 SWS319/R) Arab girl (89x68cm-35x27in) s.

BREE, Anthony de (19th C) Dutch
£800 $1512   (26-Sep-90 S118/R) Black horse by lake (51x69cm-20x27in) s.d.1888

BREE, Jos van (17th C?) Dutch?
£2100 $3612   (14-May-91 SWS300/R) The pet parrot (78x93cm-31x37in) s.

BREE, M I van (1773-1839) Flemish
£831 $1354   (12-Jun-91 GM.B4012) Scene allegorique (74x60cm-29x24in) s. (B.FR 50000)

BREEN, Adam van (17th C) Dutch
£11869 $21246   (9-Apr-91 APT.P24/R) Promenade en barque pres d'un parc
(33x69cm-13x27in) traces sig. panel (F.FR 120000)

BREENBERG, Bartholomaus (1599-1659) Dutch
£28777 $55827   (7-Dec-90 SY.MO23/R) Personnages dans des ruines (48x39cm-19x15in) bears
sig.d.1632 panel (F.FR 280000)
*£10000 $16300   (2-Jul-91 C209/R) Cliff seen from below with Walls of Villa on edge
(25x32cm-10x13in) black chk pen wash*

BREENBERG, Bartholomaus (style) (1599-1659) Dutch
£2500 $5000   (7-Feb-91 C90) Saint Jerome in the wilderness (38x31cm-15x12in) copper
£3500 $7000   (7-Feb-91 CSK16/R) Adoration of Magi (76x98cm-30x39in)

BREHAM, Paul (1850-1933) French
£1350 $2200   (5-Jul-91 S.W3028/R) Serenade outside the cathedral (130x102cm-51x40in)
s.

BREHM, E (19/20th C) ?
£612 $1200   (6-Nov-90 GF.L2518/R) Bernina (60x80cm-24x31in) s. i.stretcher
(S.FR 1500)

BREHM, Worth (1883-1928) American
£1158 $2200   *(9-Jan-91 CH.NY195/R) Jim. Sold with two works by Michel Angelo Wolf (66x49cm-26x19in) init.i. chl board three*

BREITBACH, Carl (1833-1904) German
£578 $1000   (21-May-91 CE.NY159/R) Still life with dead fowl (70x99cm-28x39in) s.

BREITENSTEIN, Ernst (1857-1920) ?
£6866 $11535   (23-Apr-91 RAS.K55/R) Swiss peasant family on the way to a christening (127x97cm-50x38in) s.d.84 (D.KR 78000)

BREITNER, Georg Hendrik (1857-1923) Dutch
£1829 $3585   (6-Nov-90 SY.AM46) Farmyard in snow at sunset (38x61cm-15x24in) s. (D.FL 6000)
£3743 $6287   (23-Apr-91 SY.AM138) View of Rokin, Amsterdam (61x74cm-24x29in) s. board (D.FL 12500)
£4954 $9560   (12-Dec-90 CH.AM139/R) Elegant lady sitting at table (37x27cm-15x11in) s. board (D.FL 16000)
£10606 $20894   (30-Oct-90 CH.AM127/R) View in Belgian town with workhorses drawing cart (38x15cm-15x6in) s. panel (D.FL 35000)
£32012 $62744   (6-Nov-90 SY.AM27/R) View of Eenhoornsluis in Amsterdam (58x98cm-23x39in) s. (D.FL 105000)
£2096 $3521   *(23-Apr-91 SY.AM35/R) Women on bridge in Amsterdam (36x38cm-14x15in) init. black chk (D.FL 7000)*
£2786 $5378   *(12-Dec-90 CH.AM112/R) Maid. Sketch of nude by mirror (42x28cm-17x11in) s. chl pastel double-sided (D.FL 9000)*

BREKELENKAM, Quiryn Gerritsz van (1620-1668) Dutch
£2000 $4000   (7-Feb-91 C44/R) Portrait of a lady, bust length in a black dress and lace collar (67x54cm-26x21in) panel
£3000 $6000   (7-Feb-91 CSK76/R) Mistress paying kitchen maid in interior (46x33cm-18x13in) s. panel
£8939 $16000   (11-Apr-91 SY.NY59/R) Notary in window holding a book (40x32cm-16x13in) i. panel

BREKELENKAM, Quiryn Gerritsz van (style) (1620-1668) Dutch
£1265 $2150   (27-May-91 GK.Z5051/R) Woman selling fish (19x13cm-7x5in) panel (S.FR 3200)
£2200 $3718   (18-Apr-91 C121) A maid buying a chicken at a stall (43x35cm-17x14in) panel

BRELING, Heinrich (1849-?) German
£500 $1000   (5-Feb-91 CG90/R) Thirsty horse (13x8cm-5x3in) s. panel
£1250 $2113   (3-May-91 PHE59/R) New provisions (14x22cm-6x9in) s.d.1886 panel
£2013 $3926   (10-Oct-90 WE.MU185/R) Soldiers resting (21x27cm-8x11in) s.d.1878 panel (DM 6000)
£2226 $3628   (12-Jun-91 N.M378/R) Mountain valley with King Ludwig II in coach (20x27cm-8x11in) s.d.1886 panel (DM 6500)

BRELINGARD, Berthe (1942-) French
£400 $672   *(27-Apr-91 MJ.P102/R) L'ete (61x50cm-24x20in) mono. mixed media canvas (F.FR 4000)*
£550 $924   *(27-Apr-91 MJ.P101/R) Projection d'ete (116x81cm-46x32in) mixed media paper laid down on canvas (F.FR 5500)*
£560 $941   *(27-Apr-91 MJ.P104/R) Projection urbaine (73x99cm-29x39in) mixed media canvas (F.FR 5600)*

BREMEN, Meyer von (1813-1886) German
£2774 $4965   (13-Mar-91 N.M585/R) Girl reading seated at table with lamp (44x33cm-17x13in) (DM 8100)
£3000 $5160   (14-May-91 SWS295/R) The butterfly (13x11cm-5x4in) s.d.1878 panel
£7254 $14000   (14-Dec-90 DM.D2019/R) Children in landscape (33x28cm-13x11in) s.i.
£11480 $22500   (7-Nov-90 B.SF1142/R) Surprise visitor (60x44cm-24x17in) s.d.1885
£11585 $19000   (19-Jun-91 B.SF1717/R) The surprise visitor (60x44cm-24x17in) s.i.d.1885
£23077 $45000   (23-Oct-90 SY.NY350/R) Das Ohrgehange (39x29cm-15x11in) s.i.d.1875
£28902 $50000   (22-May-91 D.NY14/R) Strickendes madchen (53x40cm-21x16in) s.d.1864
£50000 $82000   (21-Jun-91 C59/R) Die uberschwemmten - flood (128x168cm-50x66in) s.d.1846 with i.verso
£1119 $2159   *(10-Dec-90 L.K301/R) The unfaithful lover (23x20cm-9x8in) mono.d.1842 pen wash over pencil (DM 3200)*

BREMEN, Meyer von (attrib) (1813-1886) German
£2181 $4253   (13-Oct-90 KRA.D260/R) Girl with cat (43x33cm-17x13in) (DM 6500)

BREMENTIER, H (?) ?
£536 $1029   (28-Nov-90 PH.T30/R) Claire de lune (63x80cm-25x31in) s. (C.D 1200)

BREMMER, Hendricus Petrus (1871-1956) Dutch
£2167 $4183   (12-Dec-90 CH.AM268/R) Still life of pewter jar, book and pipe on ledge (21x16cm-8x6in) mono.d.1902 (D.FL 7000)
£3715 $7170   (12-Dec-90 CH.AM225/R) Still life of pancakepan, copper kettles and cup on ledge (37x69cm-15x27in) (D.FL 12000)
£5573 $10755   (12-Dec-90 CH.AM265/R) Farm with haystacks, pond in foreground (45x120cm-18x47in) (D.FL 18000)
£7430 $14341   (12-Dec-90 CH.AM218/R) Still life of books and chinese vase on table (55x65cm-22x26in) d.95 (D.FL 24000)

BREMMER, Hendricus Petrus (1871-1956) Dutch-cont.

£7508	$12988	(22-May-91 CH.AM483/R) Still life with copper kettles, stoneware jugs and lantern on table (80x94cm-31x37in) mono. (D.FL 25000)
£8669	$16731	(12-Dec-90 CH.AM219/R) View of farmhouse (45x58cm-18x23in) (D.FL 28000)
£9288	$17926	(12-Dec-90 CH.AM264/R) Still life of lantern, pancakepan and pottery on draped table (83x96cm-33x38in) mono.d.7.1.1895 (D.FL 30000)
£21672	$41827	(12-Dec-90 CH.AM263/R) Still life of oillamp, gingerjar and books on draped ledge (55x65cm-22x26in) mono.d.1894 (D.FL 70000)
£588	*$1135*	*(12-Dec-90 CH.AM216/R) Twig of holly in Mendes da Costa vase. Sketch of farmhouse (30x18cm-12x7in) mono.d.1913 pen painted oval double-sided (D.FL 1900)*
£805	*$1554*	*(12-Dec-90 CH.AM214/R) Trees near Wapenveld (31x47cm-12x19in) s.i.d.1917 pencil pen (D.FL 2600)*

BREMMER, Rudolf (1900-) Dutch

| £2012 | $3884 | (12-Dec-90 CH.AM210/R) View of glasshouses, Loosduinen, church in distance (28x39cm-11x15in) init.d.35 board (D.FL 6500) |

BREMOND (19/20th C) French

| £1102 | $2171 | (16-Nov-90 LGB.P167) Jeune femme arrangeant une guirlande de fleurs (86x70cm-34x28in) s.d.1909 (F.FR 10800) |

BREMONTIER, H (19th C) French

| £785 | $1312 | (4-Jun-91 FB.M185) Canal en hiver (46x54cm-18x21in) s. (C.D 1500) |

BREMY, J R (19th C) ?

| £900 | $1755 | (26-Oct-90 C315/R) A gentleman standing by his saddled hunter in a landscape (51x60cm-20x24in) s.d.1807 |

BREN, Jeffrey (1944-) Australian

| £1448 | $2852 | (13-Nov-90 J.M326) Waiting for dawn (111x83cm-44x33in) s.d.86 (A.D 3750) |

BRENDEKILDE, H A (1857-1942) Danish

£673	$1291	(27-Dec-90 RAS.V17/R) Stork in field by Odense river (40x61cm-16x24in) s. (D.KR 7500)
£700	$1253	(9-Apr-91 RAS.K2031) On the way to church, moonlight (20x29cm-8x11in) init. (D.KR 8000)
£753	$1272	(1-May-91 KH.K20) Summer's day by farmhouse (26x31cm-10x12in) init.d.26 (D.KR 8500)
£757	$1484	(22-Nov-90 RAS.V694/R) Lake in wood, autumn (70x55cm-28x22in) init. (D.KR 8500)
£822	$1594	(22-Aug-90 RAS.K162) Sunset at Gauno (28x40cm-11x16in) s. (D.KR 9500)
£880	$1479	(23-Apr-91 RAS.K291) Wooded landscape (70x55cm-28x22in) init. (D.KR 10000)
£1228	$2383	(22-Aug-90 RAS.K161/R) Small girl by thatched house in winter (29x38cm-11x15in) init. (D.KR 14200)
£1436	$2829	(14-Nov-90 RAS.K176) Italian mountainous landscape with rosebush by cliffs (105x78cm-41x31in) s. (D.KR 16000)
£1868	$3512	(18-Sep-90 BU.K93/R) Stormy clouds over yellow fields (47x59cm-19x23in) s. (D.KR 21000)
£2089	$4053	(5-Dec-90 KH.K13/R) Old woman outside thatched farmhouse, clear winter's day (40x58cm-16x23in) s. (D.KR 23000)
£2151	$4301	(6-Feb-91 RAS.K489/R) Landscape from Jyllinge, Old Lars with his pipe (38x48cm-15x19in) init. (D.KR 24000)
£2941	$5706	(22-Aug-90 RAS.K54/R) Winter landscape, bringing home Christmas trees (53x69cm-21x27in) s.d.86 (D.KR 34000)
£3100	$5239	(2-May-91 RAS.V22/R) Boy with owl and boy with goat meeting on wooded path (48x63cm-19x25in) s.d.84 (D.KR 35000)
£3770	$7427	(14-Nov-90 RAS.K84 a) Sunny winter's day in the country (90x105cm-35x41in) s.d.95 (D.KR 42000)
£3804	$7342	(10-Dec-90 BU.K36/R) Reading Sydsjaelland's newspaper at the coffee table (62x76cm-24x30in) s.d.1909 (D.KR 42000)
£4509	$8477	(10-Aug-90 RAS.V437/R) Woman and two children picking flowers by farmhouse (37x48cm-15x19in) s.d.23 (D.KR 51000)
£5172	$9724	(10-Aug-90 RAS.V436 a/R) Two children talking to old woman by farmhouse (48x52cm-19x20in) init. (D.KR 58500)
£5286	$9885	(29-Aug-90 KH.K21/R) Children playing by farmhouse (48x63cm-19x25in) s. (D.KR 60000)
£5357	$10125	(25-Sep-90 RAS.K38/R) Young girl having picked flowers in garden (50x57cm-20x22in) s.d.28 (D.KR 60000)
£5722	$9613	(23-Apr-91 RAS.K108/R) Winter's day in the village (48x68cm-19x27in) s. (D.KR 65000)
£5788	$11345	(22-Nov-90 RAS.V695/R) Spring wooded landscape with wood anemones (116x148cm-46x58in) init. (D.KR 65000)
£6720	$13441	(6-Feb-91 RAS.K379/R) From a park, small girl near lady on seat (53x79cm-21x31in) s.d.04 (D.KR 75000)
£7785	$15104	(22-Aug-90 RAS.K88/R) Girls' talk in the village street, summer (50x66cm-20x26in) s.d.1921 (D.KR 90000)
£9683	$16268	(23-Apr-91 RAS.K98/R) Young girl and dog in autumn wood (88x79cm-35x31in) s.d.1910 (D.KR 110000)
£12456	$23416	(18-Sep-90 BU.K83/R) Spring wood with beeches and wood-anemones (85x63cm-33x25in) s.d.96 (D.KR 140000)
£26817	$52024	(22-Aug-90 RAS.K43/R) Autumn in the wood, two ladies walking a dog (73x102cm-29x40in) s.d.84 (D.KR 310000)

BRENDEKILDE, Hans Andersen (1857-1942) Danish
£780 $1536   (13-Nov-90 AB.S865/R) Bonaventura monastery, Rome (48x74cm-19x29in)
                          s.d.1908 (S.KR 8500)
£12224 $23960   (10-Nov-90 FAL.M46/R) Two children and woman by flowering shrubs
                          (48x52cm-19x20in) mono. (S.KR 133000)
£14706 $28824   (6-Nov-90 BA.S28/R) Children playing with kitten and dog
                          (48x62cm-19x24in) s. (S.KR 160000)

BRENDSTRUP, Th (1812-1883) Danish
£2303 $3892   (1-May-91 KH.K21/R) Summer landscape with fisherman by river's edge
                          (26x34cm-10x13in) mono.d.43 (D.KR 26000)

BRENDSTRUP, Thorald (1812-1883) Danish
£749 $1251   (6-Jun-91 RAS.K26) View towards Oresund seen from Ermelunden
                          (80x100cm-31x39in) init.d.56 (D.KR 8500)

BRENET, Albert (1903-) French
£1990 $3443   (12-May-91 T.B81/R) Le Port de St-Guenole (43x70cm-17x28in) s. board
                          (F.FR 20000)
*£668 $1296   (6-Dec-90 CB.P79) Long-courrier (25x41cm-10x16in) s. blk.crayon
                          (F.FR 6500)*
*£2929 $5682   (6-Dec-90 CB.P80/R) Escale d'une fregate francaise (31x77cm-12x30in) s.
                          gouache (F.FR 28500)*
*£3700 $7178   (6-Dec-90 CB.P81/R) Le yacht royal anglais (56x76cm-22x30in) gouache
                          (F.FR 36000)*
*£5653 $10966   (6-Dec-90 CB.P82/R) Long-courrier norvegien (41x78cm-16x31in) s. gouache
                          (F.FR 55000)*
*£8736 $16948   (6-Dec-90 CB.P83/R) Terra-neuva au mouillage sur les grands bancs de
                          Terre-Neuve (53x76cm-21x30in) s. gouache (F.FR 85000)*

BRENHAUS, F (?) ?
£993 $1876   (25-Sep-90 GM.B1032) Carrioles sur le canal gele (105x128cm-41x50in) s.
                          panel (B.FR 60000)

BRENNER, Adam (1800-1891) Austrian
£2448 $4724   (12-Dec-90 N.M452/R) Young Italian woman with child seated on beach
                          (118x102cm-46x40in) s.d.1843 (DM 7000)
*£860 $1444   (25-Apr-91 D.V118/R) View of Mariazell (20x25cm-8x10in) s.i. pencil
                          (A.S 18000)*

BRENNER, Carl Christian (1838-1888) American
£745 $1400   (22-Sep-90 WOL.C138/R) Path through forest (51x36cm-20x14in) s.d.1887
£888 $1500   (19-Apr-91 DM.D2006/R) Spring landscape with waterfall (36x20cm-14x8in)
                          s.d.1885
£947 $1600   (19-Apr-91 DM.D2005/R) Fall landscape with stream (36x20cm-14x8in)
                          s.d.1883
£1479 $2500   (19-Apr-91 DM.D2007/R) Landscape with stream (38x48cm-15x19in) s.d.1879
£2367 $4000   (19-Apr-91 DM.D2008/R) Waterfall (76x64cm-30x25in) s.d.1884
£2367 $4000   (19-Apr-91 DM.D2009/R) Kissing rock (46x76cm-18x30in) s.d.1878

BRENNERSTEIN-WICHERA, Raimund Ritter von see WICHERA, Raimund von

BRENNIR, Carl (1850-1920) British
£536 $1029   (28-Nov-90 PH.T90) Sunset on the Avon (34x52cm-13x20in) s.d.1910
                          (C.D 1200)
£848 $1629   (28-Nov-90 PH.T63/R) Cooper Hill (40x60cm-16x24in) s. (C.D 1900)

BRENTANO, Al (?) ?
£1200 $2364   (4-Oct-90 CSK165/R) A girl with a mandolin (104x66cm-41x26in) s.
£1368 $2600   (12-Sep-90 D.NY7/R) Cherry picker (104x71cm-41x28in) s.

BRENTANO, Clemens (1778-1842) German
*£9091 $17636   (7-Dec-90 GB.B5753/R) Schelmuffsky von Christian Reuter als Gansespiel
                          (60x48cm-24x19in) W/C pen 63 small and 6 larger scenes (DM 26000)*

BRENTEL, Friedrich (1580-1651) German
*£1337 $2246   (25-Apr-91 D.V128/R) Birth of Christ with shepherd and angels in stable
                          at Bethlehem (2x16cm-1x6in) s.d.1637 gouache paper on panel
                          (A.S 28000)*
*£3670 $7229   (12-Nov-90 CH.AM224/R) Christ preaching to apostles (7x9cm-3x4in)
                          s.d.1638 bodycol gold vellum (D.FL 12000)*
*£5200 $9984   (18-Feb-91 S286/R) The Last Judgement (20x25cm-8x10in) s.d.1633 gouache
                          htd.gold*

BRESCIAN SCHOOL, 16th C Italian
£1600 $2768   (20-May-91 SWS192/R) Christ crowned with thorns (61x50cm-24x20in)
£13000 $21190   (3-Jul-91 S210/R) Portrait of gentleman (137x117cm-54x46in)

BRESCIAN SCHOOL, 18th C Italian
£3187 $5482   (14-May-91 GF.L2308/R) Elderly woman wearing apron with distaff
                          (128x92cm-50x36in) (S.FR 8000)

BRESCIANINO, Andrea del (studio) (1485-1525) Italian
£10000 $19700   (30-Oct-90 PH79/R) Madonna and Child with St John (88x68cm-35x27in)
                          panel

BRESSLERN-ROTH, Norbertine (1891-1978) Austrian
£3859 $7525   (18-Oct-90 D.V159/R) Zum Wasser (100x100cm-39x39in) s. i.verso hessian
                          (A.S 80000)

BREST, Fabius (1823-1900) French
£2758 $5379   (12-Oct-90 ZZ.F41) Scene de rue (27x34cm-11x13in) s. (F.FR 27500)
£2758 $5379   (12-Oct-90 ZZ.F40/R) A l'ombre du serail (27x34cm-11x13in) s.
                          (F.FR 27500)

BRET, Paul (1902-1956) French
£1058 $2064   (27-Oct-90 ZZ.F27) Madame Gustave Bret a Sainte Croix (61x51cm-24x20in)
                          s.d.52 (F.FR 10500)

BRETLAND, Thomas (1802-1874) British
£1796 $3000   (7-Jun-91 SY.NY90/R) A grey hunter in a landscape, Snenton Village
                          beyond (61x76cm-24x30in)
£2600 $5096   (15-Feb-91 N371/R) Portrait of Welsh horse in Vale of Belvoir with
                          distant castle (61x74cm-24x29in) s.i.d.1856

BRETON, Emile Adelard (1831-1902) French
£1394 $2412   (24-May-91 FB.P123) Paysage (26x29cm-10x11in) s. (F.FR 14000)
£1494 $2585   (24-May-91 FB.P122/R) Paysage (22x31cm-9x12in) s. (F.FR 15000)

BRETON, Emile Adelard (attrib) (1831-1902) French
£628 $1212   (12-Dec-90 EA.M712) Shepherdess and flock in wooded landscape
                          (C.D 1400)

BRETON, Jules Adolphe (1827-1906) French
£1824 $3466   (14-Sep-90 SA.A1302/R) Coastal landscape with figures cutting peat
                          (26x47cm-10x19in) mono panel (DM 5400)
£2976 $5000   (17-Jul-91 SY.NY239/R) Washerwomen at a woodland pond (60x75cm-24x30in)
                          s.d.'73
£5946 $11000   (8-Mar-91 S.BM189/R) Poling the boat (28x43cm-11x17in) s.d.1867 panel
£13873 $24000   (22-May-91 SY.NY16/R) Young woman in field (61x40cm-24x16in)
                          s.indist.i.indist.d.1889
£31792 $55000   (23-May-91 CH.NY256/R) The young gleaner from Courrieres
                          (48x34cm-19x13in) s.d.82
£51282 $100000 (23-Oct-90 SY.NY18/R) L'arc-en-ciel (110x156cm-43x61in) s.d.1883
£4482   *$7754*   *(24-May-91 FB.P166/R) Etude pour la fete du Grand-Pere (40x58cm-16x23in)*
                          s.i. pierre noire oil (F.FR 45000)

BRETON, Jules Adolphe (attrib) (1827-1906) French
£1429 $2400   (17-Jul-91 SY.NY233/R) A young girl (27x22cm-11x9in)

BRETT, Harold M (1880-1955) American
£895 $1700   (14-Sep-90 S.BM249/R) Landscape with passing storm (64x76cm-25x30in) s.
                          board

BRETT, John Edward (19th C) British
£14500 *$23635* *(14-Jun-91 C18/R) Val d'Aosta (24x19cm-9x7in) i.verso pencil W/C gum*
                          arabic htd white

BRETZ, Julius (1870-1953) German
£612 $1084   (20-Mar-91 KM.K1124) Orchard and snow covered mountain peaks beyond,
                          spring (50x61cm-20x24in) s. (DM 1800)
£743 $1449   (26-Oct-90 KM.K1121/R) Dusseldorf zoo (50x63cm-20x25in) s.d.1916
                          (DM 2200)

BREU, Jorg (elder) (1475-1537) German
£30000 $57900   (11-Dec-90 PH116/R) Portrait of man before landscape (53x43cm-21x17in)
                          panel

BREUL, Hugo (1854-1910) American
£434   *$750*   *(10-May-91 S.BM73 a/R) View of the Chicago exposition (25x36cm-10x14in)*
                          s. W/C

BREUN, John Ernest (1862-1921) British
£500   *$885*   *(21-Mar-91 CSK4) Romeo (30x25cm-12x10in) s.i. label pencil W/C*

BREVEGLIERI, Cesare (20th C) Italian
£8549 $16500   (13-Dec-90 F.M452/R) Trattoria (60x70cm-24x28in) s. panel
                          (I.L 18500000)

BREVOORT, James Renwick (1832-1918) American
£2806 $5500   (7-Nov-90 B.SF3721/R) Lake Como (62x89cm-24x35in) s.d.1883
£4913 $8500   (22-May-91 CH.NY71/R) Kennebunkport, Maine (31x57cm-12x22in)

BREWER, Henry Charles (1866-?) British
£680   *$1326*   *(16-Jan-91 CSK47/R) St Paul's Cathedral during the war (28x41cm-11x16in)*
                          s. s.i.verso pencil W/C htd.white
£950   *$1596*   *(22-Apr-91 PH319/R) The High, Oxford (28x42cm-11x17in) s. W/C over*
                          pencil htd white

BREWER, Nicholas R (1857-1949) American
£1396 $2750   (16-Nov-90 S.BM52/R) Chicago river (76x91cm-30x36in) s. i.verso
£2235 $4000   (14-Mar-91 CH.NY194/R) Chicago river (76x91cm-30x36in) s.

BREWSTER, Anna Richards (1870-?) American
£769 $1300   (1-May-91 B.SF5243/R) Italian marketplace, 1902 (25x35cm-10x14in)

BREWSTER, John (jnr-attrib) (1766-1854) American
£3816 $7250   (15-Sep-90 S.W2717/R) Little girl in white dress (71x58cm-28x23in)

BREYDEL, Karel (1678-1733) Flemish
£7923 $13310   (23-Apr-91 RAS.K17/R) Dutch landscape with cavalry in battle (56x75cm-22x30in) s. (D.KR 90000)
£7968 $13546   (31-May-91 LD.P42/R) Le coup de pistolet. Le combat au sabre (16x21cm-6x8in) s. panel pair (F.FR 80000)
£23684 $45000   (11-Jan-91 CH.NY64/R) Cavalry battle between turks and moors (162x204cm-64x80in) indist.s.

BREYDEL, Karel (attrib) Flemish
£1992 $3426   (14-May-91 GF.L2322/R) Battle scene (31x43cm-12x17in) (S.FR 5000)
£3650 $7190   (30-Oct-90 BU.S234/R) Cavalry skirmish (24x30cm-9x12in) panel pair (S.KR 40000)

BREYDEL, Karel (style) (1678-1733) Flemish
£1500 $2850   (13-Sep-90 CSK254/R) Soldiers in camp (23x34cm-9x13in) panel

BREYER, Robert (1866-1941) German
£2797 $5427   (4-Dec-90 FN.S1561 a) Dune landscape (41x55cm-16x22in) s.i. board (DM 8000)
£6643 $12888   (4-Dec-90 FN.S1562/R) Kliffhotel, dune landscape with thatched house and lighthouse (43x62cm-17x24in) mono. i.verso (DM 19000)

BREZE, Louis de (?) ?
£1500 $2820   (18-Sep-90 PH7/R) Preparing fishing fleet (51x76cm-20x30in) s.

BRIANCHON, Maurice (1899-1979) French
£7975 $13000   (12-Jun-91 SY.NY81/R) Le mur de Pelotte Basque (37x45cm-15x18in) s. board
£8871 $17032   (2-Dec-90 GAB.G1527/R) La Serre nantaise au port de la Ramee (60x73cm-24x29in) s. i. verso (S.FR 22000)
£13873 $24000   (8-May-91 SY.NY242/R) Roses elegantines (60x37cm-24x15in) s.
£20000 $39000   (19-Oct-90 C194/R) Nature morte aux cerises et citron (73x60cm-29x24in) s.
£23121 $40000   (8-May-91 SY.NY245/R) Nature morte aux poires (79x98cm-31x39in) s. i.d.1960 verso
£23699 $41000   (8-May-91 SY.NY243/R) Nature morte au lierre (72x58cm-28x23in) s.
£35533 $70000   (3-Oct-90 SY.NY204/R) Jardin du Perigord (65x92cm-26x36in) s.i.d.1961verso
£5847 $11401   (26-Oct-90 APT.P3) Odalisque (25x34cm-10x13in) s. W/C gouache htd.pastel (F.FR 58000)
£7661 $14710   (2-Dec-90 GAB.G1529/R) Carnaval (22x23cm-9x9in) s. gouache panel (S.FR 19000)
£21574 $42500   (3-Oct-90 SY.NY174/R) Nature morte aux poires (37x53cm-15x21in) s. gouache paper on board

BRIAND, C (?) ?
£2264 $4301   (14-Sep-90 SA.A1278/R) Amor with noble lady in park landscape (82x47cm-32x19in) s. (DM 6700)
£2534 $4282   (3-May-91 SA.A1885/R) Amour and a lady from a castle in a park (82x47cm-32x19in) s. (DM 7500)

BRIANSKY, Rita (1925-) Canadian
£529 $1031   (24-Oct-90 EA.M500/R) Sunbathers (40x50cm-16x20in) s.d. (C.D 1200)

BRIANTE, Ezelino (1901-1970) Italian
£729 $1239   (28-May-91 F.R41) Porto (38x49cm-15x19in) s. board (I.L 1600000)
£854 $1400   (21-Jun-91 DM.D2313/R) Boat repairs on beach (41x51cm-16x20in) s. board
£1202 $2333   (4-Dec-90 F.R59) Paesaggio autunnale (67x80cm-26x31in) s. (I.L 2600000)

BRIAUDEAU, Paul Charles Jean (1869-?) French
£615 $1100   (14-Apr-91 JRB.C80/R) Floral still life (74x53cm-29x21in) s.

BRICARD, G (19/20th C) French
£690 $1200   (27-Mar-91 B.SF4324/R) Near Evans, France (46x55cm-18x22in) s.

BRICE, William (1921-) American
£552 $900   (12-Jun-91 SY.NY166/R) Two figures and sea (48x64cm-19x25in) s.d.62 chl

BRICHER, Alfred Thompson (1837-1908) American
£1523 $3000   (18-Nov-90 JRB.C62/R) Coastal pool and rocks (23x46cm-9x18in) s.
£2012 $3400   (20-Apr-91 WOL.C54/R) Landscape (25x20cm-10x8in) s.
£2116 $4000   (27-Sep-90 CH.NY41/R) Rocky shore (19x14cm-7x6in) s. board
£2235 $4000   (14-Mar-91 CH.NY71/R) Coastal inlet (223x46cm-88x18in) s.
£2460 $4600   (30-Aug-90 MFA.C230/R) Houses by lake (23x43cm-9x17in) s.
£4046 $7000   (21-May-91 GRO.B55/R) Lake George, New York (25x20cm-10x8in) s.d.1865
£5587 $10000   (14-Mar-91 CH.NY84/R) Breaking waves (31x41cm-12x16in) s.
£5729 $11000   (30-Nov-90 CH.NY22/R) Mt Desert coastline (23x45cm-9x18in) paper on canvas
£5747 $10000   (29-Mar-91 E.EDM867/R) Shore scene near Manchester, MA (23x46cm-9x18in) s.

BRICHER, Alfred Thompson (1837-1908) American-cont.

£6500	$13000	(7-Feb-91 B.P120/R) Haying season (25x46cm-10x18in) s.d.1869 board
£7542	$13500	(12-Apr-91 SY.NY24/R) Coastal landscape (39x81cm-15x32in) mono.
£8721	$15000	(15-May-91 SY.NY9/R) Sailboats along coast (44x74cm-17x29in) mono.d.1881
£10405	$18000	(22-May-91 CH.NY5/R) Lake George from Bolton (23x45cm-9x18in) s. board
£11168	$22000	(16-Nov-90 E.EDM693/R) Seal Cove, Grand Manan (38x84cm-15x33in) s.
£18519	$35000	(26-Sep-90 SY.NY68/R) Portland Head (66x122cm-26x48in) s.mono.
£20231	$35000	(23-May-91 SY.NY19/R) On Long Island sound (46x86cm-18x34in) s.
£20670	$37000	(12-Apr-91 SY.NY23/R) Afternoon by shore (46x92cm-18x36in) mono.d.1880
£23121	$40000	(22-May-91 CH.NY176/R) Sunrise at Grand Manan (63x127cm-25x50in) mono.
£447	$800	(11-Apr-91 FA.PH899) Near Seal Cove, Maine (8x18cm-3x7in) init. W/C gouache
£462	$800	(21-May-91 CE.NY454/R) Crashing on rocks (11x18cm-4x7in) mono. brush ink
£520	$900	(21-May-91 CE.NY433/R) Breaking waves (8x19cm-3x7in) mono. brush ink
£573	$1100	(17-Dec-90 SY.NY23/R) Coastal scene (33x66cm-13x26in) mono.num.21 W/C paper on board
£1042	$2000	(18-Dec-90 BG.M943/R) Rocky seacoast (33x66cm-13x26in) s. W/C
£1117	$2000	(14-Mar-91 CH.NY69/R) Rocky coast (25x61cm-10x24in) s. W/C pencil
£1302	$2500	(18-Dec-90 BG.M947/R) Boats off mountainous seacoast (38x53cm-15x21in) s. W/C
£1546	$3000	(5-Dec-90 D.NY30/R) Coastal view, Maine (25x53cm-10x21in) init. W/C
£1546	$3000	(5-Dec-90 D.NY32/R) Rocky beach (23x51cm-9x20in) init. W/C
£1587	$3000	(27-Sep-90 CH.NY87/R) Along the shore (23x29cm-9x11in) mono. W/C paper laid down on board
£1804	$3500	(5-Dec-90 D.NY31/R) Rocks and waves (23x51cm-9x20in) init. W/C
£1955	$3500	(14-Mar-91 CH.NY65/R) On a clear day (30x67cm-12x26in) mono. W/C pencil board
£1977	$3500	(22-Mar-91 S.W2831/R) Coastal landscape with lighthouse (25x64cm-10x25in) s.i. W/C
£6349	$12000	(27-Sep-90 CH.NY85/R) Afternoon gusts (50x89cm-20x35in) init. gouache paper laid down on canvas
£16185	$28000	(22-May-91 CH.NY53/R) Indian Rocks, Narragansett Bay (35x56cm-14x22in) init. gouache paper on board

BRICKDALE, Eleanor Fortesque (1871-1945) British

£620	$1042	(15-Jul-91 PH148) Conscience (45x27cm-18x11in) mono.d.1901 W/C
£650	$1229	(26-Sep-90 S334/R) Untied unto world by care - of public fame or private breath (37x26cm-15x10in) mono. i.verso W/C
£2700	$5346	(30-Jan-91 S243/R) Challenge (67x138cm-26x54in) s. i.verso W/C htd bodycol
£3200	$6336	(30-Jan-91 S297/R) Natural magic (54x35cm-21x14in) mono. bears i.verso W/C over pencil
£4624	$8000	(22-May-91 SY.NY257/R) Scenes from literature (38x29cm-15x11in) four init. W/C artistboard five

BRIDGEHOUSE, Robert (19th C) British

£615	$1211	(13-Nov-90 AB.S866/R) Coastal landscape with boats and figures (59x77cm-23x30in) s.d.1842 (S.KR 6700)

BRIDGES, Fidelia (1835-1924) American

£2081	$3600	(21-May-91 CE.NY398/R) Bouncing betts (52x27cm-20x11in) s.d.1889 W/C board

BRIDGMAN, F A (1847-1928) American

£978	$1750	(15-Mar-91 DM.D2128/R) Arab street scene (30x41cm-12x16in) s.

BRIDGMAN, Frederick Arthur (1847-1928) American

£500	$1000	(7-Feb-91 B.P72/R) Mediterranean coast (41x36cm-16x14in) s.
£1369	$2300	(17-Jul-91 SY.NY371/R) Bab el Oued (49x70cm-19x28in) s.
£1420	$2315	(12-Jun-91 ZZ.F22) Coucher de soleil (21x29cm-8x11in) s. (F.FR 14100)
£1775	$3000	(17-Apr-91 D.NY87) Arab horsemen watering horses s.
£2540	$4800	(27-Sep-90 CH.NY111/R) On the terrace (48x65cm-19x26in) s.d.Feb 1886
£2762	$4750	(15-May-91 SY.NY75 a/R) Figures along beach (21x30cm-8x12in) s. panel
£4046	$7000	(21-May-91 CE.NY195/R) Crossing river (41x30cm-16x12in) s.i.d.1872
£4200	$7518	(12-Mar-91 PH46/R) Arab horsemen on the Algerian coast (62x92cm-24x36in) s. s.i.verso
£4656	$9126	(20-Nov-90 APT.P256/R) Le bazar (65x58cm-26x23in) s. (F.FR 46000)
£5780	$10000	(22-May-91 SY.NY144/R) Afternoon haircut (46x55cm-18x22in) s.
£6923	$13500	(23-Oct-90 SY.NY53/R) The return (62x47cm-24x19in) s.d.1892
£7514	$13000	(22-May-91 SY.NY139/R) Terrace in Algiers (48x80cm-19x31in) s.i.
£8671	$15000	(22-May-91 SY.NY140/R) Palace Constantine (51x66cm-20x26in) s.
£21387	$37000	(22-May-91 SY.NY51/R) Scenes prises au Maroc (63x84cm-25x33in) s.d.1885
£30347	$52500	(22-May-91 SY.NY52/R) Retour de chasse (73x96cm-29x38in) s.
£58974	$115000	(23-Oct-90 SY.NY40/R) Funerailles d'une momie (113x232cm-44x91in) s.d.1876-7
£94737	$180000	(28-Feb-91 CH.NY65/R) In village at El Biar, Algiers (91x132cm-36x52in) s.d.1889
£1837	$3618	(14-Nov-90 FB.P291/R) Jeune femme orientale (90x60cm-35x24in) s. pastel canvas (F.FR 18000)

BRIDT, Bernaert de (1688-1722) Flemish

£898	$1768	(14-Nov-90 RAS.K424/R) Still life with cat watching dead game (60x52cm-24x20in) s. (D.KR 10000)

BRIERLY, Sir Oswald Walter (1817-1894) British
£560 $1064   (25-Feb-91 PH118) Study of beach and rock at Port Madoc, N.W.
                 (32x49cm-13x19in) s. i.verso W/C bodycol
£600 $1038   (22-May-91 S138) Moonlight (24x33cm-9x13in) s.d.1873 W/C
£4008 $7696   (14-Aug-90 SY.ME229/R) Study for going to sea - departing Sydney Cove
                 (63x91cm-25x36in) W/C pencil htd.body col. (A.D 9500)
£9200 $18124   (13-Nov-90 SWS118/R) H.M.S. Racoon, Lerwick Harbour, Shetland
                 (57x77cm-22x30in) s. W/C overpencil htd.bodycol.

BRIET, Arthur (1867-1939) Dutch
£509 $886   (26-Mar-91 VN.R13/R) Dutch interior with woman by a fireplace
                 (20x30cm-8x12in) s. (D.FL 1700)

BRIGANTI, N (1895-?) American
£538 $1050   (26-Oct-90 S.W2158) Venice (61x91cm-24x36in) s.

BRIGANTI, Nicholas (1895-?) American
£588 $1100   (30-Aug-90 MFA.C161/R) Venetian scene (61x91cm-24x36in) s.
£638 $1200   (22-Sep-90 WOL.C239/R) Market day (61x91cm-24x36in) s.
£851 $1600   (22-Sep-90 WOL.C252/R) Venetian moonlit scene (51x71cm-20x28in) s.
£1436 $2700   (22-Sep-90 WOL.C358/R) View of Venice (74x102cm-29x40in) s.
£920 $1500   (11-Jun-91 MOR.P118) Still life - autumn harvest (36x53cm-14x21in) s.
                 d.1938 W/C

BRIGDEN, Frederick Henry (1871-1956) Canadian
£446 $857   (27-Nov-90 W.T901) Autumn landscape (25x35cm-10x14in) st.studio W/C
                 (C.D 1000)
£536 $1029   (27-Nov-90 W.T895) Mountain landscape (25x35cm-10x14in) s. st.studio W/C
                 (C.D 1200)
£655 $1290   (12-Nov-90 HO.ED87/R) Through the woods (26x34cm-10x13in) s.i. W/C
                 (C.D 1500)

BRIGGS, Ernest (1866-1913) British
£1200 $2076   (20-May-91 PH83) Falls of Lochay, in flood (77x100cm-30x39in) s. i.verso
                 W/C bodycol
£4200 $7266   (20-May-91 PH84/R) Good catch (50x72cm-20x28in) s. W/C

BRIGHT, Harry (fl.1867-1892) British
£2039 $3935   (14-Dec-90 ARC.P102/R) Le faucon (60x45cm-24x18in) (F.FR 20000)
£584 $1150   (7-Oct-90 DU.E268/R) Friends in Adversity (20x15cm-8x6in) s.d.1876 W/C
£900 $1728   (19-Feb-91 C17/R) Heron at water's edge (41x28cm-16x11in) s.d.1876
                 pencil W/C htd.white

BRIGHT, Henry (1814-1873) British
£632 $1100   (27-Mar-91 D.NY24) Cottage in mountainous landscape (23x36cm-9x14in)
                 bears sig.d.1848
£1100 $2156   (13-Feb-91 S152/R) Rocky coastline (30x48cm-12x19in) s.d.1849
£1600 $2608   (14-Jun-91 K491/R) Castle on cliff top with female shrimper by the sea
                 (28x51cm-11x20in) s.d.1869
£3421 $6500   (27-Feb-91 SY.NY223/R) Evening on Broads (61x109cm-24x43in) s.
£3800 $7486   (1-Nov-90 C229/R) Cottage by river (29x42cm-11x17in) s.indis.d.1845
£580 $1148   (30-Jan-91 S114) Views on Rhine (25x30cm-10x12in) one bears sig. W/C
                 col.chk bodycol pair
£580 $945   (4-Jul-91 PHI107) A view of Norwich from near Telegraph Hill
                 (41x68cm-16x27in) W/C
£650 $1281   (1-Nov-90 D165/R) Norwich (23x33cm-9x13in) s. pastel over pencil
                 vignette

BRIGHT, Henry (attrib) (1814-1873) British
£1056 $1700   (26-Jun-91 D.NY15) Sun setting over river valley with goats and cows
                 grazing on hillside (89x127cm-35x50in) bears sig.d.1867

BRIGHT, Henry (circle) (1814-1873) British
£1200 $2088   (26-Mar-91 PH125) Sheep resting, and figure on a path to a windmill
                 (67x107cm-26x42in)

BRIGNONI, Aranis (1908-) Chilean
£1195 $2331   (24-Oct-90 GD.B182) L'invitation (36x52cm-14x20in) s.d.41 board
                 (S.FR 3000)

BRIGNONI, Sergio (1903-) Swiss
£3213 $6297   (24-Nov-90 AB.L138/R) Masculin - feminin (63x81cm-25x32in) s.d.71
                 acrylic (S.FR 8000)
£3213 $6297   (24-Nov-90 AB.L141/R) Anatomy (82x61cm-32x24in) s.d.1985 acrylic
                 (S.FR 8000)
£3414 $6691   (24-Nov-90 AB.L143/R) Untitled (60x73cm-24x29in) s.d.1962 pavatex
                 (S.FR 8500)
£9524 $15619   (19-Jun-91 GK.B240) Church of Monte Carasso (65x52cm-26x20in) s.d.1929
                 (S.FR 24000)
£653 $1267   (7-Dec-90 G.Z359) Composition (41x55cm-16x22in) s.d.1973 collage mixed
                 media (S.FR 1600)
£735 $1425   (7-Dec-90 G.Z104) Composition (35x35cm-14x14in) s.d.1974 pastel
                 (S.FR 1800)
£1469 $2851   (7-Dec-90 G.Z105/R) Plants by the water (30x42cm-12x17in) s.i.d.1952 W/C
                 (S.FR 3600)

BRIL, Cyriacus (attrib) (17th C) Flemish
£1825 $3595   (30-Oct-90 BU.S297/R) Hunting wild pigs in landscape (20x25cm-8x10in)
                  mono. panel octagonal (S.KR 20000)

BRIL, Mattheus (younger-attrib) (c.1550-1584) Flemish
£1633 $3200   (6-Nov-90 GF.L2017/R) St Hubertus in forest (60x75cm-24x30in)
                  (S.FR 4000)

BRIL, Paul (1554-1626) Flemish
£1486 $2824   (14-Sep-90 SA.A1122/R) Wooded landscape with shepherd couple on river
                  bank (39x76cm-15x30in) s.indis.d. panel (DM 4400)
£2492 $4061   (12-Jun-91 GM.B4084) Paysage arbore avec Sainte Madeleine
                  (16x12cm-6x5in) (B.FR 150000)
£5199 $10242   (12-Nov-90 CH.AM49/R) Landscape with deer hunt (19x28cm-7x11in) with i.
                  black chk pen wash (D.FL 17000)

BRIL, Paul (attrib) (1554-1626) Flemish
£20588 $35000   (31-May-91 CH.NY68/R) Scenes from the life of William Tell
                    (116x158cm-46x62in)
£867 $1647   (27-Feb-91 LEB.P9/R) Etude d'arbre pen wash (F.FR 8600)
£2905 $5723   (12-Nov-90 CH.AM4/R) View on River Tiber near Ponte Molle
                  (13x37cm-5x15in) with i. black chk pen two sheets (D.FL 9500)
£15000 $24450   (2-Jul-91 C63/R) Tree with two birds perching on branch
                    (38x26cm-15x10in) chk bodycol

BRIL, Paul (circle) (1554-1626) Flemish
£898 $1518   (2-May-91 CH.AM11) The Penitent Magdalen (14x11cm-6x4in) i. copper
                  (D.FL 3000)
£1538 $3000   (10-Oct-90 CH.NY81/R) St John the Baptist in the wilderness
                  (27x21cm-11x8in) copper
£2400 $3912   (2-Jul-91 C205/R) Wooded rocky landscape with hermit in grotto
                  (22x31cm-9x12in) with i. black chk pen W/C

BRIL, Paul (studio) (1554-1626) Flemish
£3606 $6456   (8-Apr-91 CH.R104/R) Paesaggio con pastori e mercante (47x53cm-19x21in)
                  (I.L 8000000)
£3864 $7574   (19-Nov-90 CH.R120/R) San Girolamo in un paesaggio (102x134cm-40x53in)
                  (I.L 8500000)
£7937 $13651   (19-May-91 ZZ.F81/R) Paysage anime (16x23cm-6x9in) copper (F.FR 80000)

BRIL, Paul (style) (1554-1626) Flemish
£880 $1487   (1-May-91 GD.B98) Italian coastal landscape with storm clouds over
                  seaside town (38x50cm-15x20in) panel (S.FR 2200)
£5138 $10121   (13-Nov-90 AB.S867/R) Landscape with Tobias and the angel
                    (73x126cm-29x50in) panel (S.KR 56000)

BRILLOUIN, Louis Georges (1817-1893) French
£4200 $6888   (18-Jun-91 PH48/R) Visitor for the patient (66x106cm-26x42in) s.d.1878

BRINCKMANN, Philip Hieronymus (1709-1761) German
£3500 $5705   (5-Jul-91 C339/R) Diana and nymphs in wood (44x35cm-17x14in) canvas on
                  panel

BRINDEAU DE JARNY, Louis Edouard (1943-) French
£996 $1693   (27-May-91 APT.P251) Le repas familial (46x55cm-18x22in) s. (F.FR 10000)

BRINDISI, Remo (1918-) Italian
£637 $1204   (27-Sep-90 F.M49/R) Due figure (50x40cm-20x16in) s. (I.L 1400000)
£1001 $1892   (27-Sep-90 F.M108) Pastorale (40x30cm-16x12in) s. (I.L 2200000)
£1094 $1859   (28-May-91 SY.MI20/R) Pastore (40x30cm-16x12in) s. (I.L 2400000)
£1192 $1955   (20-Jun-91 F.M347) Amanti (73x60cm-29x24in) s. (I.L 2600000)
£2927 $5707   (22-Oct-90 BR.M260/R) La chiesa della Salute (50x60cm-20x24in) s.
                  (I.L 6500000)

BRION, Michel (1927-) French
£500 $840   (28-Apr-91 FE.P81) Bateau a Honfleur (65x50cm-26x20in) s. (F.FR 5000)

BRISCOE, Arthur (1873-1943) British
£2000 $3840   (26-Nov-90 SWS147/R) The storm (42x75cm-17x30in) s.d.37 canvas on board
£3800 $7372   (5-Dec-90 PHE109/R) Getting the anchor over the side (67x102cm-26x40in)
                  s.d.'29
£1150 $1990   (22-May-91 S211) Yachting (25x35cm-10x14in) s.d.1910 W/C

BRISCOE, F D (1844-1903) American
£1479 $2500   (19-Apr-91 DM.D1042/R) Sailing scene depicting fishermen with nets
                  (48x36cm-19x14in) s.d.97

BRISCOE, Franklin D (1844-1903) American
£847 $1500   (22-Mar-91 S.W2485/R) Approaching storm (56x56cm-22x22in) s.d.1902 board
£1436 $2800   (20-Oct-90 FA.PH927/R) Beached vessel (51x51cm-20x20in) s.

BRISPOT, Henri (1846-1928) French
£1103 $2151   (12-Oct-90 ZZ.F3/R) Le petit dejeuner (49x36cm-19x14in) s. (F.FR 11000)
£2613 $4285   (21-Jun-91 CK.P101) Le Cardinal et l'Officier (56x73cm-22x29in) s.d.1908
                  (F.FR 26000)

BRISS, Sami (20th C) ?
£719 $1396   (5-Dec-90 I.N27/R) L'oiseau a l'abri (23x33cm-9x13in) s. acrylic laid down on canvas (F.FR 7000)

BRISSAUD, Jacques (1880-1960) French
£402   *$743*   *(4-Mar-91 ARC.P28) Femma a sa toilette (35x25cm-14x10in) mono. pastel (F.FR 4000)*

BRISSAUD, Pierre (1885-?) French
£504   *$821*   (12-Jun-91 ZZ.F107) Place Vendome (14x17cm-6x7in) s.d.1921 indian ink wash (F.FR 5000)
£554 $903   (12-Jun-91 ZZ.F106) Les retardataires (16x13cm-6x5in) s.d.1920 W/C (F.FR 5500)

BRISSE, Joel (20th C) French
£3262 $6296   (16-Dec-90 P.V110/R) Sans titre (165x160cm-65x63in) s.d.1990 wax zinc (F.FR 32000)

BRISSON, Pierre Marie (1955-) French
£689 $1351   (10-Nov-90 FAL.M47/R) Composition (59x58cm-23x23in) s. paper (S.KR 7500)
£717 $1405   (10-Nov-90 FAL.M48/R) Composition (58x45cm-23x18in) s. paper (S.KR 7800)
£836 $1497   (13-Apr-91 FAL.M38/R) Composition (63x91cm-25x36in) s. paper (S.KR 9000)

BRISSOT de WARVILLE, Felix-Saturnin (1818-1892) French
£1579 $3000   (27-Feb-91 SY.NY132/R) Returning with flock (37x45cm-15x18in) s. panel
£1711 $3250   (27-Feb-91 SY.NY87/R) Troupeau de moutons (46x56cm-18x22in) s.
£2261 $4048   (17-Mar-91 L.C85/R) Berger et ses moutons (33x44cm-13x17in) s. (F.FR 22500)
£1130   *$2000*   *(22-Mar-91 S.W2836/R) Sheep feeding in farmyard (23x33cm-9x13in) s. W/C*
£1149   *$2000*   *(27-Mar-91 B.SF4203/R) Girl feeding sheep (24x35cm-9x14in) s. W/C*
£1223   *$2349*   *(1-Dec-90 PER.M22/R) Le berger et son troupeau (31x53cm-12x21in) s.d.1870 pen (F.FR 12000)*

BRISTOL, John Bunyan (1826-1909) American
£609 $1200   (16-Nov-90 S.BM44/R) By lake's edge (25x38cm-10x15in) s.
£651 $1250   (29-Nov-90 MFA.C167) Floral (30x41cm-12x16in) s.
£963 $1800   (30-Aug-90 MFA.C78/R) Church by the river (36x56cm-14x22in) s.
£1453 $2500   (18-May-91 W.W97/R) Woman strolling by a mountain lake (46x76cm-18x30in) s.
£1546 $3000   (5-Dec-90 D.NY49/R) Lake Dunmore, Vermont (36x58cm-14x23in) s.
£1777 $3500   (7-Oct-90 LIT.L341) Connecticut River landscape, possibly view of Mt. Ascutney (43x74cm-17x29in) s.

BRISTOL, John Bunyan (attrib) (1826-1909) American
£1279 $2200   (15-May-91 SY.NY23/R) Summer landscape with river (46x76cm-18x30in) bears sig.

BRISTOW, Edmund (1787-1876) British
£780 $1521   (16-Jan-91 CSK241) Caning the chair (97x71cm-38x28in) s.d.1824 panel
£820 $1615   (13-Nov-90 SWS230 a) A young shepherd and a horse (34x29cm-13x11in) panel
£1500 $2955   (16-Nov-90 C109/R) Nine pins (11x16cm-4x6in) s. panel
£4200 $8232   (8-Nov-90 TL40/R) Outside the Guard House at Windsor (39x75cm-15x30in) init.
£4500 $8865   (16-Nov-90 C108/R) Mr Ramsbottom's pony (54x73cm-21x29in) s.i.d.1820
£5000 $9850   (16-Nov-90 C86/R) Two saddled bay hunters held by groom in landscape with hunt beyond (56x76cm-22x30in) indis.s.d.1847
£6500 $12805   (14-Nov-90 S122/R) Children fishing on Thames near Windsor with distant view of Bray (45x61cm-18x24in) s. panel

BRITISH SCHOOL (?) British
£1390 $2738   (13-Nov-90 J.M984) Putting the shot (24x37cm-9x15in) (A.D 3600)
£3500 $6195   (20-Mar-91 EDD338) Portrait of two girls with a kitten and embroidery (76x58cm-30x23in)
£4525 $7647   (16-Apr-91 J.M772) Lakescene (54x89cm-21x35in) (A.D 10000)

BRITISH SCHOOL, 18th C British
£1149 $2000   (27-Mar-91 B.SF4044/R) Daniel in the lion's den (104x148cm-41x58in)
£1333 $2600   (14-Oct-90 H.C422/R) Pastoral landscape (259x188cm-102x74in)
£6091 $12000   (15-Nov-90 SY.NY5/R) Ducks in a marsh (31x37cm-12x15in)

BRITISH SCHOOL, 19th C British
£1053 $2000   (27-Feb-91 SY.NY247/R) Grey mare in stable (51x61cm-20x24in)
£1156 $2000   (21-May-91 GRO.B40/R) Brigantina Oporto leaving Belfast (51x61cm-20x24in) i.d.1860
£1711 $3250   (27-Feb-91 SY.NY250/R) Horse and jockey (62x75cm-24x30in) bears sig.d.
£2319 $4521   (15-Oct-90 SY.J5/R) The scribe (76x62cm-30x24in) (SA.R 11500)
£2874 $5000   (27-Mar-91 B.SF4230/R) Ferdinand meets Prospero and Miranda (132x98cm-52x39in)
£3000 $4890   (14-Jun-91 C242/R) Portrait of John Leon Francis Paul with a St Bernard (80x63cm-31x25in) mono.d.1850 i.verso
£3161 $5500   (27-Mar-91 B.SF4045/R) Portrait of earl (127x100cm-50x39in)
£3200 $6048   (27-Sep-90 CSK138/R) The pink rose (60x50cm-24x20in)
£3200 $6048   (27-Sep-90 CSK145/R) Playing the pipes (119x99cm-47x39in)
£4598 $8000   (27-Mar-91 B.SF4254/R) Satyr discovering wood nymph (93x107cm-37x42in) mono.

BRITTAN, Charles Edward (19/20th C) British
£650 $1248   *(20-Feb-91 B21/R) On Dartmoor, sunset (58x90cm-23x35in) s. W/C bodycol.*
£1600 $3072   *(19-Feb-91 C32/R) Prize pigeons (36x46cm-14x18in) s.d.1874 pencil W/C*
                                htd.white

BRITTAN, Charles Edward (jnr) (1870-?) British
£426 $800   *(22-Sep-90 WOL.C250) Loch Rannoch, Scotland (36x53cm-14x21in) s. W/C*

BRITTAN, Charles Edward (snr) (1837-1888) British
£1600 $3152   *(1-Nov-90 TE548/R) Portraits of prize pigeons (33x46cm-13x18in) s.d.1874*
                                W/C htd white pair

BRITTEN, William Edward Frank (19th C) British
£400 $708   *(21-Mar-91 CSK5) Children playing with a frog in a barrel*
                                (61x91cm-24x36in) s.d.1915 pastel paper laid down on board

BRITTEN, van (?) ?
£818 $1341   (17-Jun-91 DUR.M26/R) Bodegon con plato de frutas y tarro de miel
                                (34x46cm-13x18in) panel (S.P 150000)
£818 $1341   (17-Jun-91 DUR.M25/R) Bodegon con ciruelas, panes y jamon
                                (34x46cm-13x18in) s. panel (S.P 150000)

BRITTON, Harry (1878-1958) Canadian
£526 $1032   (20-Nov-90 JOY.T411/R) Boats at low tide (18x22cm-7x9in) s. board
                                (C.D 1200)

BRIZE, Cornelis and GREBBER, Fransz Pieter (17th C) Dutch
£2262 $3823   (21-Apr-91 BU.M313) Allegory of Peace (105x88cm-41x35in) s.d.1654
                                (S.KR 24000)

BROADHEAD, W Smithson (fl.1923-1940) British
£8718 $17000   (24-Oct-90 CH.NY333/R) Lost, lame and winded (51x61cm-20x24in) s. board

BROCA, Alex de (19/20th C) French
£550 $924   (26-Apr-91 ARC.P52) Paysage de la vallee du Drah (89x116cm-35x46in)
                                s.d.1930 (F.FR 5500)

BROCAS, Samuel Frederick (1792-1847) Irish
£2600 $5122   *(13-Nov-90 C125/R) View of post office and Nelson Pillar, Sackville*
                                Street, Dublin (36x56cm-14x22in) s.i.d.1818 pencil W/C

BROCH, A (?) ?
£872 $1500   (17-May-91 WOL.C452/R) Italian peasant girl (61x48cm-24x19in) s.

BROCHART, Constant Joseph (1816-1899) French
£1087 $2098   *(10-Dec-90 BU.K54/R) Young girl wearing pink dress making lace*
                                (73x59cm-29x23in) s. pastel oval (D.KR 12000)

BROCK, Edmund (20th C) British
£2800 $5488   (15-Feb-91 N387/R) Portrait of Nancy Brett (94x112cm-37x44in) s.d.1924

BROCK, William (1874-?) British
£880 $1575   (10-Apr-91 CSK186) The woodland pool (239x297cm-94x117in)

BROCKEN, E (?) German
£909 $1755   (13-Dec-90 N.M2658/R) Shepherd with flock in moor landscape
                                (50x90cm-20x35in) s.i. (DM 2600)

BROCKENBERG (18th C) ?
£4000 $7880   (31-Oct-90 S143/R) Cavalry melee outside besieged town (44x56cm-17x22in)
                                i.d.1708verso

BROCKER, Ernst (1893-1963) German
£1017 $1658   (3-Jul-91 WE.MU41/R) Rowing boat in lake landscape (30x40cm-12x16in)
                                s.i. (DM 3000)

BROCKHURST, Gerald Leslie (1890-1978) British
£2411 $4750   *(15-Nov-90 D.NY47/R) Portrait of artist's wife, Anais (24x20cm-9x8in) s.*
                                pencil

BROCKHUSEN, Theo von (1882-) German
£3000 $5910   (1-Nov-90 B41/R) Sailing boats moored in harbour (81x96cm-32x38in)
                                s.d.09

BROCKTORFF, Charles (19th C) German?
£3000 $5850   *(24-Oct-90 S203/R) View of the Palace with the maypole, Valletta, Malta*
                                (39x54cm-15x21in) i. label verso

BROCQ, Pierre-Jules (1811-) French
£909 $1573   (6-May-91 ZEL.L1620) Still life with asters and dahlias in basket
                                (65x81cm-26x32in) s.d.1891 (DM 2700)

BROCQUY, Louis le (1916-) British
£3000 $4890   (1-Jul-91 S93/R) Lemon (46x38cm-18x15in) s.d.72 verso
£3468 $6000   (22-May-91 D.NY116/R) Ancestral head, no. 149 (69x57cm-27x22in) i.d.1964
                                stretcher

BROCQUY, Louis le (1916-) British-cont.
£5000	$9800	(9-Nov-90 C235/R) Child (30x25cm-12x10in) s.d.54
£6000	$9780	(1-Jul-91 S32/R) Head of a man (91x61cm-36x24in) s.d.68
£6091	$12000	(4-Oct-90 SY.NY23/R) Ancestral head - Opus 210 (73x73cm-29x29in) s.d.68 s.d.1968 stretcher
£650	$1099	(2-May-91 C143) Farmyard in Co. Offaly (12x17cm-5x7in) init.d.45 W/C bodycol pen
£900	$1755	(26-Apr-91 C21/R) Study for child dreaming (12x18cm-5x7in) s.d.48 s.i.d.verso pencil W/C
£1500	$2925	(10-Oct-90 S181/R) Dove (18x25cm-7x10in) s. s.i.d.1956stretcher oil mixed media canvas
£2400	$3912	(1-Jul-91 S14/R) Man with a towell (109x68cm-43x27in) s.d.51 blk.chk. gouache wax crayon
£2500	$4625	(5-Mar-91 PH1/R) Tinker women (30x24cm-12x9in) s.d.46 pen wash

BRODERICK, William (?) British
| £850 | $1479 | (26-Mar-91 PH34) An arctic eagle (107x76cm-42x30in) init. |

BRODIE, J (19th C) ?
| £500 | $865 | (22-May-91 S29/R) View of schooner Udny of Newburgh, David Burgess commander, March 1849 (55x85cm-22x33in) s.i. W/C ink |

BRODOWSKI, Jozef (1828-1900) Polish
| £751 | $1471 | (26-Jan-91 PSA.W5) Self-portrait (24x30cm-9x12in) s.d.1855 canvas on board (P.Z 14000000) |

BRODSKY, Isaac Israelevitch (1883-1939) Russian
| £523 | $857 | (19-Jun-91 ARC.P191) Village ukrainien (30x24cm-12x9in) s.d.1905 (F.FR 5200) |
| £1809 | $2967 | (19-Jun-91 ARC.P192/R) Lenine lisant le 1er numero de la Pravda (63x98cm-25x39in) s. (F.FR 18000) |

BROE, Vern (20th C) American
£536	$1050	(24-Nov-90 RB.HY162/R) Catboats on Sunday sail (41x51cm-16x20in) s. board
£561	$1100	(24-Nov-90 RB.HY137/R) Catboats racing (41x51cm-16x20in) s. board
£609	$1200	(18-Nov-90 JRB.C131/R) Children on the beach (30x41cm-12x16in) s. board
£691	$1300	(7-Aug-90 RB.HY260/R) A Sunday sail (51x76cm-20x30in) s. beaverboard
£722	$1400	(24-Aug-90 RB.HY26/R) Children by the sea (28x36cm-11x14in) s. board

BROECK, Clemence van den (1843-?) Belgian
| £1773 | $2890 | (13-Jun-91 RAS.V518/R) Young lady sitting on terrace (40x33cm-16x13in) s. (D.KR 20000) |

BROECK, Elias van den (1650-1708) Dutch
| £12000 | $20280 | (16-Apr-91 PH51/R) Still life with snake approaching toad at base of thistle, with butterflies hovering around (29x21cm-11x8in) with sig. panel |
| £42000 | $72660 | (24-May-91 C31/R) Poppies, roses, lilies and other flowers in a glass bowl on a ledge witha cabbage white above (69x57cm-27x22in) s. |

BROECK, Elias van den (style) (1650-1708) Dutch
£2000	$3380	(18-Apr-91 C14/R) A forest floor still life of wild roses, butterfly, caterpillarsflies and vines and toadstools (31x23cm-12x9in)
£3200	$5408	(17-Apr-91 S42/R) Still life of flowers in glass vase on stone ledge (45x38cm-18x15in)
£7000	$11830	(19-Apr-91 C79/R) Mixed flowers and blackberries in a glass vase with three butterflies (76x64cm-30x25in)

BROECKAERDT, Herman (1878-1930) Belgian
| £732 | $1309 | (12-Mar-91 C.A30) Trees in landscape (73x100cm-29x39in) s. (B.FR 44000) |

BROGAIRALLES, V (?) ?
| £520 | $900 | (9-May-91 CSK59) Extensive Dutch canal landscape at sunset (61x81cm-24x32in) s. |

BROGE, Alfred (1870-?) Danish
| £2000 | $3440 | (17-May-91 C128/R) At window (53x45cm-21x18in) s. |

BROILUS, Federico (16th C) ?
| £2200 | $3718 | (16-Apr-91 C127/R) The Deposition (27x20cm-11x8in) s. bodycol.htd.gold linen laid on metal plate |

BROMLEY, W (19th C) British
| £720 | $1159 | (25-Jun-91 ACA742/R) 19th Century interior family scene (33x38cm-13x15in) panel |

BROMLEY, William (19th C) British
£660	$1115	(15-Apr-91 WW37) Piggyback (35x25cm-14x10in) s.
£720	$1332	(4-Mar-91 PHB61) On way to market (31x25cm-12x10in) s.
£1064	$2000	(19-Sep-90 B.SF2637/R) Playtime (21x26cm-8x10in) s.
£1500	$2445	(14-Jun-91 C332/R) The contract (23x33cm-9x13in) s.
£1900	$3211	(15-Apr-91 WW38) Gathering flowers (30x25cm-12x10in) s.d.1886
£2400	$3912	(14-Jun-91 C331/R) A rest by the gate (30x25cm-12x10in) s.d.1866

BROMLEY, William (attrib) (19th C) British
£750 $1463   (18-Oct-90 SC3154/R) Children in a garden (23x41cm-9x16in)

BROMLEY, William (circle) (19th C) British
£1100 $2079   (27-Sep-90 CSK131/R) The bird's nest (44x34cm-17x13in)

BROMPTON, Richard (1734-1782) British
£5800 $11426   (16-Nov-90 C18/R) Portrait of Elizabeth Tobin wearing dress with gold
     embroidery and turban (80x67cm-31x26in) l.verso panel

BRONCHORST, Jan Jansz van (1627-1656) Dutch
£49401 $83488   (2-May-91 CH.AM42/R) A young woman seated at a table playing a lute
     (102x81cm-40x32in) with sig.d.1650 (D.FL 165000)

BRONCKHORST, Jan Gerritsz van (style) (1603-1677) Dutch
£735 $1471   (10-Feb-91 BU.M242) Luke the Evangelist being inspired by angel
     (96x76cm-38x30in) (S.KR 8000)

BRONDY, Matteo (19th C) French
£1316 $2579   (20-Nov-90 APT.P257/R) La grande rue de Moulay Idriss (45x37cm-18x15in)
     s. board (F.FR 13000)

BRONZINO, Angelo (after) (1503-1572) Italian
£1204 $2010   (6-Jun-91 D.V190/R) Madonna (48x40cm-19x16in) panel (A.S 25000)

BRONZINO, Angelo (circle) (1503-1572) Italian
£1959 $3840   (6-Nov-90 GF.L2024/R) Portrait of cardinal Giovanni Battista Datis
     (63x50cm-25x20in) panel (S.FR 4800)
£2191 $3769   (14-May-91 GF.L2249/R) Portrait of cardinal Giovanni Battista Datis
     (63x50cm-25x20in) panel (S.FR 5500)
£3500 $6755   (11-Dec-90 PH237/R) Portrait of young man by writing table
     (23x18cm-9x7in) bears d.1560 panel
£7000 $13300   (1-Mar-91 C149/R) Portrait of lady (53x38cm-21x15in) panel

BRONZINO, Angelo (style) (1503-1572) Italian
£2827 $4750   (17-Jul-91 SY.NY132/R) Portrait of Francesco I Grand Duke of Tuscany
     (58x43cm-23x17in) panel
£3200 $5216   (3-Jul-91 S165) Portrait of Francesco de Medici (54x44cm-21x17in) bears
     i. panel
£3590 $7000   (11-Oct-90 SY.NY179/R) Portrait of noble infant holding apple
     (39x30cm-15x12in) panel

BROOK, Alexander (20th C) American
£529 $1000   (25-Sep-90 CE.NY143/R) Self portrait (25x20cm-10x8in) init. brush ink

BROOKE, E Adveno (fl.1844-1864) ?
£1050 $2069   (13-Nov-90 PH57/R) Returning home (61x50cm-24x20in) s.d.1865 panel
£2423 $4750   (7-Nov-90 B.SF1190/R) Haytime in Wye valley (77x108cm-30x43in) s.d.1866

BROOKER, Bertram (1888-1955) Canadian
£703 $1145   (10-Jun-91 W.T110 a) Still life (28x36cm-11x14in) s. board (C.D 1300)
£746 $1461   (20-Nov-90 JOY.T250/R) Paper reflections (28x36cm-11x14in) canvas on
     board (C.D 1700)

BROOKER, Harry (fl.1876-1908) British
£4737 $9000   (27-Feb-91 SY.NY257/R) Young shopkeeper (71x91cm-28x36in) s.d.1897
£6500 $12805   (1-Nov-90 C308/R) Playing school (71x91cm-28x36in) s.d.1893

BROOKER, William (1918-) British
£4500 $8775   (9-Oct-90 B11/R) Studio interior (71x46cm-28x18in) s.d.54 board

BROOKING, Charles (1723-1759) British
£5964 $10080   (18-Apr-91 APT.P65/R) Vaisseaux sur une mer agitee (38x59cm-15x23in)
     (F.FR 60000)
£11000 $19690   (12-Apr-91 C69/R) English merchant-brig and coastal craft becalmed by
     moonlight (38x58cm-15x23in)

BROOKS, Frank Leonard (1911-) Canadian
*£439 $864   (30-Oct-91 SY.T141) Canal, Venice (61x79cm-24x31in) s. i.verso mixed
     media canvas (C.D 1000)*

BROOKS, James (1938-) American
£2308 $4500   (10-Oct-90 SY.NY389/R) Untitled (30x41cm-12x16in) s. board
£14793 $25000   (1-May-91 SY.NY195/R) Berl (157x168cm-62x66in) s. d.1956 verso
£4592 $9000   (7-Nov-90 SY.NY119/R) no. 13 (56x76cm-22x30in) s.d.51 gouache paperboard
£4615 $9000   (10-Oct-90 SY.NY382/R) Untitled (71x56cm-28x22in) s. gouache

BROOKS, Kim (20th C) British?
£508 $1000   (7-Oct-90 DU.E265/R) 'Jaguar' (36x53cm-14x21in) s. W/C gouache

BROOKS, Nicholas Alden (19/20th C) American
£3352 $6000   (14-Mar-91 CH.NY43/R) Ten dollar bill (17x25cm-7x10in) s. canvasboard
£5820 $11000   (27-Sep-90 CH.NY58/R) The ten dollar bill (17x23cm-7x9in) s. panel
£10615 $19000   (14-Mar-91 CH.NY31/R) Reading table (23x28cm-9x11in) s.i.

BROOKS, Robin (?) British
£620 $1209   (16-Jan-91 BT102/R) Fleeing the revenue cutter (48x74cm-19x29in) s.
£820 $1599   (16-Jan-91 BT108/R) Guerriere and Constitution (58x89cm-23x35in) s.
£4200 $7140   (30-May-91 C154/R) Reluctant admiration - 14th December 1772
    (51x101cm-20x40in) s. s.l.verso

BROOKS, S (19th C) British
£1081 $1762   (10-Jun-91 W.T1455) River scene with children bathing (70x96cm-28x38in)
    s. (C.D 2000)

BROOKS, Thomas (1818-1892) British
£929 $1664   (13-Apr-91 FAL.M39/R) Fishwives waiting for husbands to return
    (76x64cm-30x25in) s. (S.KR 10000)
£1600 $2640   (9-Jul-91 PH68) Father's welcome (54x87cm-21x34in) s.d.1871
£1900 $3743   (31-Oct-90 S287/R) The village student (76x63cm-30x25in)
£5200 $8684   (5-Jun-91 S162/R) Pets of our river (81x122cm-32x48in) s.d.1882
    s.l.verso

BROOM, Marion L (fl.1925-1939) British
£1400 $2702   (11-Dec-90 HAR282) Still life with bowl of flowers (66x102cm-26x40in) s.
*   W/C*

BROOME, G J (?) ?
£3000 $5190   (22-May-91 S60/R) To rescue (76x127cm-30x50in) s.d.1881

BROOME, William (1838-1892) British
£806 $1500   (9-Sep-90 LIT.L290) Rescue - depicting rescue of crew of passengers of
    Indian Chief (51x76cm-20x30in) s.
£900 $1530   (30-May-91 C152/R) Fishing smacks preparing for sea (41x61cm-16x24in)
    s.indist.l.verso indist.l.stretcher

BROOMHEAD, Thomas (19th C) British
£5900 $9853   (5-Jun-91 PHK105/R) Cattle and sheep in wooded landscapes
    (72x107cm-28x42in) s.l.verso pair

BROOS, Jean-Jacques (19th C) Flemish
£2700 $5319   (13-Nov-90 SWS365/R) A festival in a Flemish village (31x39cm-12x15in)
    s. panel

BROSE, Emil (1901-1962) German
£680 $1095   (28-Jun-91 BM.B557/R) The new church of Emden in winter
    (46x61cm-18x24in) s. board (DM 2000)

BROTAT, Joan (20th C) Spanish
£1223 $2348   (18-Dec-90 DUR.M33) Mujer con cestas (55x46cm-22x18in) (S.P 225000)
£1511 $2674   (20-Mar-91 DUR.M8) El cazador (55x46cm-22x18in) (S.P 275000)
£2180 $3772   (21-May-91 DUR.M16/R) Hombre con gorro (65x54cm-26x21in) (S.P 400000)

BROTO, Jose Manuel (20th C) ?
£21936 $36852   (25-Apr-91 EP.M32/R) Stereo (190x250cm-75x98in) s.l.d.1981-82
    (S.P 4000000)
£15355 $25797   (25-Apr-91 EP.M34/R) Las cifras ocho (260x200cm-102x79in)
*   s.i.d.1988verso acrylic collage canvas (S.P 2800000)*

BROUILLARD, Eugene (1870-?) French
£1182 $2293   (3-Dec-90 CS.L53) Iles du Roquet a Trevoux (57x88cm-22x35in) s. verso
    board (F.FR 11500)

BROUWER (style) (?) ?
£2650 $5089   (30-Nov-90 APT.P67/R) Musiciens dans une taverne (23x33cm-9x13in) panel
    (F.FR 26000)

BROUWER, Adriaen (1606-1638) Flemish
£11149 $21740   (26-Oct-90 KM.K1003/R) Peasants conversing by fence before house
    (23x27cm-9x11in) mono. panel (DM 33000)

BROUWER, Adriaen (circle) (1606-1638) Flemish
£750 $1223   (4-Jul-91 CSK207) Boor singing (14x11cm-6x4in) on copper shaped top

BROUWER, Adriaen (school) (1606-1638) Flemish
£6351 $11368   (14-Mar-91 D.V254/R) Peasants in pub interior (24x20cm-9x8in) panel
    (A.S 130000)

BROUWER, Adriaen (style) (1606-1638) Flemish
£1100 $1793   (4-Jul-91 C503) Boors fighting over cards outside inn (31x38cm-12x15in)
    panel
£1200 $2400   (7-Feb-91 CSK73/R) Boors in tavern interior (18x23cm-7x9in) with init.
    on copper oval
£3000 $5070   (18-Apr-91 C67/R) Boors making music in an inn (23x19cm-9x7in) panel

BROUWERS, Julius (1869-1955) Dutch
£1497 $2919   (25-Oct-90 VN.R15/R) Fishing boats at sea with coast on the horizon
    (60x80cm-24x31in) s. board (D.FL 5000)

BROWN OF COVENTRY, Edward (attrib) (19th C) British
£3800 $6270   (12-Jul-91 C101/R) Portrait of gentleman, leading saddled chestnut
                    hunter, in landscape (91x137cm-36x54in)

BROWN OF COVENTRY, Edward (circle) (19th C) British
£2600 $4654   (12-Apr-91 C112/R) Farmer, dog and pony in extensive wooded landscape
                    (56x76cm-22x30in)

BROWN, Alexander Kellock (1849-1922) British
£800 $1288   (27-Jun-91 CG97) Winter sunset (87x112cm-34x44in) init. l. verso

BROWN, Byron (1907-1961) American
£615 $1200   (20-Oct-90 FA.PH869) Abstraction with flowers (41x36cm-16x14in) s.

BROWN, Carlyle (?) ?
£576 $962   (4-Jun-91 R.T193/R) Bouquet of carnations (75x50cm-30x20in) s.d.55
                    s.d.1955 verso (C.D 1100)
£769 $1500   (20-Oct-90 W.W272/R) Red cabinet still life (51x58cm-20x23in) s.d.57
                    s.l.d.verso

BROWN, Cecil (19/20th C) British
£800 $1336   (22-Jul-91 SWS1036/R) Over the fence (44x79cm-17x31in) indist.s.

BROWN, Christy (1932-1981) Irish
£926 $1787   (12-Dec-90 CH.E85/R) Three sailing boats (50x81cm-20x32in) board
                    (E.P 1000)
£1111 $2144   (12-Dec-90 CH.E90/R) Portrait head of a girl (91x55cm-36x22in) board
                    (E.P 1200)
£1204 $2323   (12-Dec-90 CH.E89/R) Portrait of an Arab (96x76cm-38x30in) s.d.68 board
                    (E.P 1300)
£1389 $2681   (12-Dec-90 CH.E86/R) Portrait of a black man (76x61cm-30x24in) s.d.69
                    board (E.P 1500)
£1389 $2681   (12-Dec-90 CH.E87/R) Homage to Matisse - Head of a woman
                    (64x61cm-25x24in) s.verso board (E.P 1500)
£1852 $3574   (12-Dec-90 CH.E82/R) Blue evening, Dublin (61x76cm-24x30in) s.d.68 board
                    (E.P 2000)
£2778 $5361   (12-Dec-90 CH.E79/R) Portrait of father (76x73cm-30x29in) board
                    (E.P 3000)
£3889 $7506   (12-Dec-90 CH.E81/R) A self-portrait (67x60cm-26x24in) s.verso board
                    (E.P 4200)

BROWN, David (19th C) British
£650 $1086   (22-Jul-91 SWS963/R) A cornfield, Plaistow, Kent (49x67cm-19x26in)
                    s.d.1889 l. verso

BROWN, Ford Madox (1821-1893) British
£5000 $9600   (29-Nov-90 B115/R) Italian fisherboy (18x16cm-7x6in) s.l.verso paper
                    laid on panel

BROWN, Fred C (19th C) American
£1598 $2700   (17-Apr-91 D.NY4/R) Apples and port (30x41cm-12x16in) s.

BROWN, Frederick (1851-?) British
£4500 $8865   (13-Nov-90 SWS443/R) Peasant fare (51x61cm-20x24in) s.d.1882 l. verso

BROWN, Geo A (19th C) British
£7800 $12792   (19-Jun-91 S354/R) View of Capri with Vesuvius in background
                    (84x150cm-33x59in) s.d.1869

BROWN, George Loring (1814-1889) American
£660 $1300   (7-Oct-90 DU.E41/R) Owl's Head, Maine (25x36cm-10x14in) s.d.1863 l.
£1850 $3700   (7-Feb-91 B.P107/R) Old Bridge and Mill at Compton Village, New
                    Hampshire (25x36cm-10x14in) s.d.1875
£2214 $4250   (17-Dec-90 SY.NY133/R) Palantine Hill (38x56cm-15x22in) s.d.1854
£5202 $9000   (22-May-91 CH.NY156/R) Oysterman's hut (51x76cm-20x30in) s.d.1863 l.
                    verso
£6358 $11000   (22-May-91 CH.NY25/R) Paradise Rock, Newport (45x61cm-18x24in) s.d.1862
*£1842 $3500   (9-Jan-91 CH.NY102/R) Along the shore (15x23cm-6x9in) s.l.d.1834 W/C
                    sold w.works by Greenough,Johnson*

BROWN, Harrison B (1831-1915) American
£1330 $2500   (11-Aug-90 COL.M235/R) Mill pond (30x25cm-12x10in) s. board
£4011 $7500   (1-Aug-90 B.P69/R) Pemaguasset Wilderness, New Hampshire I
                    (33x58cm-13x23in) s.
£4278 $8000   (1-Aug-90 B.P70/R) Pemaguasset Wilderness, New Hampshire II
                    (33x58cm-13x23in) s.

BROWN, Hugh Boycott (1909-) British
£550 $957   (28-Mar-91 CSK66) Yachts in harbour (38x49cm-15x19in) s. board
£600 $1032   (14-May-91 SWS378/R) Stormy day, Pin Mill, Suffolk (39x50cm-15x20in) s.
                    i.stretcher
£600 $1014   (30-Apr-91 B221/R) Barges at sea (46x62cm-18x24in) init. board
£700 $1316   (20-Sep-90 C157/R) Whitstable oyster dredgers, yawls (51x61cm-20x24in)
                    s. i.d.1976 overlap
£775 $1310   (19-Apr-91 K585/R) River scene, Woodbridge with Thames barges
                    (36x48cm-14x19in) s.

BROWN, Hugh Boycott (1909-) British-cont.
£1500 $2820   (20-Sep-90 C176/R) Fishing boats in estuary (58x74cm-23x29in) s. board

BROWN, J Appleton (1844-1902) American
£1006 $1700   (20-Apr-91 WOL.C42/R) Landscape (46x61cm-18x24in) s.

BROWN, J G (19th C) British
£1850 $3700   (10-Feb-91 LIT.L34) Men in boat s.d.1879 en grisaille
£1888 $3700   (27-Jan-91 LIT.L8a) Men in boat (76x51cm-30x20in) s.d.1879 en grisaille

BROWN, James (1951-) American
£8163 $16000   (14-Feb-91 CH.NY100/R) Stabat Mater V (130x90cm-51x35in)
    s.i.d.1988-9verso acrylic lead on board
£14000 $24780   (21-Mar-91 C248/R) Vienna Head II (127x123cm-50x48in) s.i.d.1986-1987
    verso
£16244 $32000   (5-Oct-90 CH.NY143/R) Untitled (165x151cm-65x59in) s.d.1982verso tempera
    board
£16244 $32000   (5-Oct-90 CH.NY150/R) Untitled (165x151cm-65x59in) s.d.1982verso tempera
    board
£26734 $43843   (23-Jun-91 P.V80/R) Black and white nash (183x122cm-72x48in)
    (F.FR 266000)
£27219 $46000   (2-May-91 CH.NY308/R) Cosmos and Damon rewarded (173x146cm-68x57in)
    s.d.1983 overlap
£2600   *$5044*   *(5-Dec-90 PH111/R) Composition in blue (39x27cm-15x11in) W/C*
£2806   *$5500*   *(6-Nov-90 CE.NY306/R) Stabert Mater no.3 (102x66cm-40x26in)*
    init.d.VIIIVIII graphite
£3400   *$6596*   *(5-Dec-90 PH112/R) Giallo di Napoli (52x39cm-20x15in) i.d.87verso*
    gouache
£4569   *$9000*   *(4-Oct-90 SY.NY277/R) Untitled (96x127cm-38x50in) s.d.1983 verso pencil*
£5025   *$8241*   *(23-Jun-91 P.V76/R) Sans titre (101x114cm-40x45in) mono.d.1984 W/C*
    crayons (F.FR 50000)
£8122   *$16000*   *(4-Oct-90 SY.NY271/R) Untitled (97x126cm-38x50in) s.d.1983 verso*
    graphite paper
£8163   *$16000*   *(7-Nov-90 SY.NY339/R) Untitled (101x66cm-40x26in) tempera graphite*
£24490   *$48000*   *(8-Nov-90 CH.NY420/R) Stella Mares IX (198x168cm-78x66in) s.i.d.1985*
    verso enamel stain canvas
£29880   *$50797*   *(30-May-91 FB.P88/R) Sans titre (143x128cm-56x50in) s.d.1963 verso*
    enamel pastel oil canvas (F.FR 300000)
£33797   *$57117*   *(21-Apr-91 P.V107/R) Large wooded head (153x243cm-60x96in) s.d.1983 oil*
    enamel crayon (F.FR 340000)

BROWN, Joan (1938-) American
£1538 $3000   (24-Oct-90 B.SF1519/R) Mary Julia no.30 (91x61cm-36x24in) s.d.8/1/76
    paper
£6122   *$12000*   *(6-Nov-90 CE.NY126/R) The lovers no. 1 (216x188cm-85x74in) s.i.d. verso*
    enamel canvas

BROWN, John Appleton (1844-1902) American
£1777 $3500   (16-Nov-90 S.BM94/R) Poling boat ashore, summer landscape with river
    (51x66cm-20x26in) s.
£5820 $11000   (26-Sep-90 SY.NY69/R) Spring landscape (71x94cm-28x37in) s.

BROWN, John Arnesby (1866-?) British
£600 $966   (28-Jun-91 CSK122) Pasture land with trees (51x61cm-20x24in) s.
£650 $1222   (20-Sep-90 CSK70) Sketch for 'The big river' (16x22cm-6x9in) init.
    s.i.verso panel
£1550 $3038   (6-Nov-90 PH42) Late afternoon, Norfolk Broads (41x51cm-16x20in) s.
£3000 $5640   (20-Sep-90 C156/R) Summer haze (41x51cm-16x20in) s.

BROWN, John George (1831-1913) American
£2706 $5250   (5-Dec-90 D.NY2/R) Young girl with straw basket (25x20cm-10x8in)
    s.d.1860 arched top
£4124 $8000   (5-Dec-90 D.NY10/R) The shoe shine boy (46x30cm-18x12in) s.d.1884
£4330 $7750   (12-Apr-91 SY.NY31/R) Early on stump (29x22cm-11x9in) s.d.1869
£5917 $10000   (1-May-91 B.SF5084/R) Girl on seesaw (61x44cm-24x17in) s.
£8092 $14000   (23-May-91 SY.NY15/R) Bootblack (62x41cm-24x16in) s.i.
£8671 $15000   (23-May-91 SY.NY21/R) Street musician (76x51cm-30x20in) s.i.d.1879
£9012 $15500   (15-May-91 SY.NY66/R) Sorry he spoke (36x32cm-14x13in) s.d.1863
£9249 $16000   (22-May-91 CH.NY83/R) Shoe shine boy (65x52cm-26x20in) s.i.
£9524 $18000   (26-Sep-90 SY.NY15/R) Shoeshine boy with his dog (61x46cm-24x18in) s.
    i.indist.
£10056 $18000   (12-Apr-91 SY.NY29/R) Shoeshine boy with dog (61x43cm-24x17in) s.d.1906
£10405 $18000   (23-May-91 SY.NY22/R) Friends (61x41cm-24x16in) s.i.
£11173 $20000   (12-Apr-91 SY.NY3/R) Paddy's Valentine (61x41cm-24x16in) s.d.1885
£14583 $28000   (30-Nov-90 CH.NY11/R) That's me pumpkin (46x30cm-18x12in) s.d.1879
£16185 $28000   (23-May-91 SY.NY16/R) Bluffing (63x51cm-25x20in) s.d.1885
£16931 $32000   (27-Sep-90 SY.NY76/R) Shoeshine boy (66x46cm-26x18in) s.
£140625 $270000   (30-Nov-90 CH.NY30/R) Watching the train (71x112cm-28x44in) s.d.1881

BROWN, John Lewis (1829-1890) British
£816 $1608   (14-Nov-90 CN.P78/R) Elegante dans un parc (15x9cm-6x4in) init. panel
    (F.FR 8000)
£2071 $3500   (1-May-91 D.NY16) Arab horseman (36x25cm-14x10in) s. board
£2333 $4177   (12-Apr-91 BM.B570/R) Quartering of French soldiers in Alsace town
    (77x70cm-30x28in) s. (DM 7000)

BROWN, John Lewis (1829-1890) British-cont.
£7143 $14071   (14-Nov-90 FB.P181/R) Le renseignement (72x59cm-28x23in) s. panel
                              (F.FR 70000)

BROWN, Marshall (?) ?
£3500 $6790   (5-Dec-90 PHE47/R) Landing the fish, Cockenzie (14x23cm-6x9in) s.
£3800 $6422   (3-May-91 PHE137/R) Wading (25x20cm-10x8in) s.
£5200 $10088   (5-Dec-90 PHE15/R) May blossoms (17x25cm-7x10in) s.d.1906
£7800 $15132   (5-Dec-90 PHE76/R) The look-outs (25x35cm-10x14in) s.

BROWN, Mather (1761-1831) American/British
£1734 $3000   (21-May-91 CE.NY371/R) Miss Blackwood and Major D'Arcy (89x71cm-35x28in)
£2000   *$3800*   (9-Jan-91 CH.NY115/R) Sailor on shore-leave. Sold with works by
                              G.Harding, R.C.Woodville Jnr and E.Ardizzone s.ink wash htd white
                              four

BROWN, Michael (20th C) British
£2400 $4488   (28-Aug-90 S899/R) Two boys watching breakers (41x61cm-16x24in) s.

BROWN, Paul (19/20th C) American
£814   *$1400*   (15-May-91 SY.NY222/R) Picking up scent. Cat and dog (20x37cm-8x15in)
                              one s.i.d.38 one s.i.d.39 W/C pair

BROWN, Robert (18/19th C) British
£500 $860   (16-May-91 CSK67) Portrait of lady, in dress and necklace
                              (46x35cm-18x14in) s.d.1818

BROWN, Roger (20th C) American
£4913 $8500   (7-May-91 CE.NY281/R) Tourist vista (152x244cm-60x96in) l.overlap

BROWN, Roy (1879-1956) American
£3175 $6000   (27-Sep-90 CH.NY230/R) Maine ledges (102x127cm-40x50in) s. oil chl.

BROWN, Samuel John Milton (1873-?) British
£1000   *$1920*   (16-Aug-90 B351/R) Under full sail (33x46cm-13x18in) s. W/C

BROWN, T Bryant (19/20th C) British
£7800 $13494   (22-May-91 S147/R) In south-east trades (129x114cm-51x45in) s.
                              s.l.stretcher

BROWN, Vincent (1901-) Australian
£633 $1071   (16-Apr-91 J.M408) The workers (31x37cm-12x15in) s.d.'40 board
                              (A.D 1400)
£655 $1172   (9-Apr-91 CH.ME152) Puppet murder (36x46cm-14x18in) s. board (A.D 1500)
£930 $1563   (22-Apr-91 SY.ME107) Early morning harvest, Coomera (30x30cm-12x12in)
                              s.d.35 canvas on board (A.D 2000)
£1176 $1988   (15-Apr-91 AAA.S100) Afternoon, Coomera (43x56cm-17x22in) s. board
                              (A.D 2600)
£350   *$686*   (19-Nov-90 MGS.S262) Steamboat on Brisbane River (27x36cm-11x14in)
                              s.d.1927 W/C (A.D 900)
£480   *$831*   (21-May-91 JRL.S158) Steam boat on Brisbane river (27x35cm-11x14in) W/C
                              (A.D 1100)

BROWN, W H (19th C) American
£1117   *$2200*   (16-Nov-90 WOL.C856/R) Portrait of Hon. Cassius M. Clay, soldier, writer
                              and statesman (20x18cm-8x7in) s.d.1845 W/C

BROWN, William Beattie (1831-1909) British
£1000 $2000   (5-Feb-91 S68/R) Near Callander (30x46cm-12x18in) s.

BROWN, William Fulton (1873-1905) British
£1000   *$1870*   (28-Aug-90 S1005/R) Autumn shelter (71x61cm-28x24in) s. W/C htd bodycol

BROWN, William Marshall (1863-1936) British
£1587 $3000   (29-Sep-90 YFA.M11/R) Potatoe harvest (25x36cm-10x14in) s.d.1888
£1750 $2923   (22-Jul-91 SWS1144/R) Return of the boats (19x24cm-7x9in) s.
£3700 $6919   (28-Aug-90 S885/R) Boating (21x25cm-8x10in) s.d.1902 board
£6000 $11220   (28-Aug-90 S883/R) Crab teasing (40x61cm-16x24in) s.
£7400 $14356   (6-Dec-90 CG43/R) By the sea (19x27cm-7x11in) s. board
£11000 $21560   (22-Nov-90 CG573/R) Gathering whelks (41x46cm-16x18in) s.
£15000 $28050   (28-Aug-90 S845/R) Playing in the dunes (35x46cm-14x18in) s.

BROWN, William Mason (1828-1898) American
£1064 $2000   (22-Sep-90 WOL.C161/R) Marshy landscape (33x41cm-13x16in) s.
£1512 $2600   (15-May-91 SY.NY77 b/R) Early snow (20x30cm-8x12in) mono. s.verso board
£1804 $3500   (7-Dec-90 S.W2678/R) Still life with peaches and grapes
                              (38x51cm-15x20in) s.
£3125 $6000   (30-Nov-90 CH.NY25/R) Still life with peaches and melon
                              (51x41cm-20x16in) s.
£5291 $10000   (26-Sep-90 SY.NY1/R) Still life with melon, berries and grapes
                              (51x41cm-20x16in) s.mono.
£8995 $17000   (27-Sep-90 CH.NY12/R) Fruits of autumn (40x51cm-16x20in) s.init.

BROWN, William Theo (1919-) American
£2564 $5000   (24-Oct-90 B.SF1520/R) Still life with toaster (30x41cm-12x16in) s.d.77
                              verso

BROWN, William Theo (1919-) American-cont.
£3590 $7000   (24-Oct-90 B.SF1526/R) Girl on porch (102x135cm-40x53in) s.d.66 verso
                acrylic canvas
£1026   *$2000*   *(24-Oct-90 B.SF1521/R) Untitled (28x33cm-11x13in) s.d.80 gouache*

BROWNE, Belmore (1880-1954) Canadian
£4585 $9033   (12-Nov-90 HO.ED122/R) Sawback range, Canadian rockies
                (76x102cm-30x40in) s. (C.D 10500)

BROWNE, Byron (1907-1961) American
£1546 $3000   (5-Dec-90 D.NY109/R) Aphrodite (74x58cm-29x23in) s.d.1948
£2180 $3750   (15-May-91 SY.NY274/R) Clown (66x51cm-26x20in) s.d.1958 s.i.d.verso
£2610 $5116   (24-Nov-90 AB.L77/R) Vortex (18x14cm-7x6in) s. s.i.d.1955verso
                (S.FR 6500)
£7407 $14000   (27-Sep-90 CH.NY303/R) Cataclysm (76x97cm-30x38in) s. d.1949 i. verso
£476   *$900*   *(25-Sep-90 CE.NY110/R) Lady centaur artist at her easel*
                (51x66cm-20x26in) s.d.July 17 1957 pen brush ink
£833   *$1400*   *(28-Apr-91 HG.C415) Bouquet in vase (71x51cm-28x20in) s. gouache*
£833   *$1600*   *(17-Dec-90 SY.NY432/R) Call it a clown (66x51cm-26x20in) s.d.1949 casein*
                collage
£952   *$1800*   *(25-Sep-90 CE.NY100/R) Row boats, docked (51x66cm-20x26in) s.d.1954*
                gouache ink

BROWNE, Charles Francis (1859-1921) American
£565 $1000   (22-Mar-91 S.W1609) Yellow field (61x76cm-24x30in) s. s.d.1918 verso

BROWNE, George Elmer (1871-1946) American
£1337 $2500   (30-Aug-90 MFA.C134/R) Paris street scene (64x76cm-25x30in) s.d.1902

BROWNE, Richard (1776-1824) ?
£3376   *$6481*   *(14-Aug-90 SY.ME309/R) Burgun (30x22cm-12x9in) i. W/C body col.*
                (A.D 8000)
£3800   *$7410*   *(24-Oct-90 S80/R) The emu (30x23cm-12x9in) s.d.1820 W/C over traces*
                pencil

BROWNE, Samuel (attrib) (?) ?
£860 $1488   (20-May-91 SWS262/R) Portrait of a lady, wearing a brown dress and a
                brocade cloak, a spaneilon her lap (50x44cm-20x17in)

BROWNELL, Peleg Franklin (1857-1946) Canadian
£965 $1891   (20-Nov-90 JOY.T297/R) Lily pads on pond (45x60cm-18x24in) s.
                (C.D 2200)
£1641 $2840   (6-May-91 SY.T205/R) Portrait of woman (61x49cm-24x19in) s.d.85
                (C.D 3250)

BROWNSCOMBE, Jenny (1851-1936) American
£833 $1600   (29-Nov-90 MFA.C203/R) Woman under trellis (25x18cm-10x7in) s. board
£457   *$900*   *(16-Nov-90 DM.D2024/R) Portrait of lady with feathered bonnet*
                (36x25cm-14x10in) s.

BROZIK, Wenceslas (1851-1901) Bohemian
£1695 $3000   (22-Mar-91 S.W2860/R) Peeling radishes (99x79cm-39x31in) s.
£2797 $5399   (12-Dec-90 WE.MU166/R) Man resting in landscape (33x46cm-13x18in) s.
                (DM 8000)

BRUANDET, Lazare (attrib) (1755-1804) French
£1550 $2589   (7-Jun-91 AGS.P51) Dessus de portes (100x130cm-39x51in) pair
                (F.FR 15500)
£1600 $2672   (7-Jun-91 AGS.P50) Paysans sur des chemins boises panel pair
                (F.FR 16000)

BRUCE, Edward (1879-1943) American
£1387 $2400   (21-May-91 CE.NY540/R) Landscape of Provence (54x81cm-21x32in) s. canvas
                on masonite

BRUCE, Patrick Henry (1880-1937) American
£14286 $27000   (26-Sep-90 SY.NY219/R) Bowl of fruit (38x46cm-15x18in) s.

BRUCHL, J (19th C) German
£5000 $9600   (27-Nov-90 PH128/R) Charity (126x149cm-50x59in) s.i.

BRUCK, Hermann (1873-?) German
£1010 $1747   (6-May-91 ZEL.L1624/R) Dutch river landscape with cattle watering
                (70x90cm-28x35in) s. (DM 3000)

BRUCKL, J (19th C) German
£1100 $1903   (9-May-91 CSK119) Judith holding head of Holofernes (93x68cm-37x27in)
                s.d.1866

BRUCKMAN, Lodewijk (1903-) Dutch
£914 $1800   (18-Nov-90 JRB.C157/R) The shirt, portrait of James Simpson
                (94x69cm-37x27in) s.d.54-55

BRUEGHEL, Abraham (1631-1690) Flemish
£42004 $70567   (23-Apr-91 F.R131/R) Natura morta di frutta e ortaggi con rose e
                bassorilievo (96x131cm-38x52in) (I.L 92000000)

BRUEGHEL, Abraham (attrib) (1631-1690) Flemish
£21053 $40000   (10-Jan-91 SY.NY65/R) Still life of fruit with parrot in landscape
                                (66x81cm-26x32in)

BRUEGHEL, Abraham (style) (1631-1690) Flemish
£3000 $4890   (4-Jul-91 B100 l) Still life of flowers in a vase (64x47cm-25x19in)
£4000 $6520   (4-Jul-91 C548/R) Mixed fruit and acorns in dish (61x85cm-24x33in)
                                indist.s.

BRUEGHEL, Ambrosius (1617-1675) Flemish
£56526 $109661   (5-Dec-90 APT.P35/R) Bouquet de fleurs sur un entablement
                                (57x44cm-22x17in) (F.FR 550000)

BRUEGHEL, Jan (attrib) (16/17th C) Flemish
£3058 $5872   (27-Nov-90 APT.P58/R) Rue villageoise avec canal (12x49cm-5x19in) pen
                                (F.FR 30000)

BRUEGHEL, Jan (elder) (1568-1625) Flemish
£106145 $190000   (10-Apr-91 HF.NY16/R) Temptation of St. Anthony (42x58cm-17x23in) on
                                copper
£247280 $442631   (9-Apr-91 APT.P20/R) Le depart vers le marche. Le retour du marche
                                (18x26cm-7x10in) copper pair (F.FR 2500000)

BRUEGHEL, Jan (elder) and BALEN, Hendrik van (style) (16/17th C) Flemish
£5500 $10615   (12-Dec-90 S154/R) Feast of the gods (52x76cm-20x30in) panel

BRUEGHEL, Jan (elder) and RUBENS, Sir Peter Paul (style) (16/17th C) Flemish
£11000 $18590   (19-Apr-91 C93/R) The penitent Magdalen (54x74cm-21x29in) panel

BRUEGHEL, Jan (elder-attrib) (1568-1625) Flemish
£70000 $135100   (12-Dec-90 S21/R) Monks in landscape (54x88cm-21x35in) i. panel
£5505 $10844   (12-Nov-90 CH.AM61/R) Study of windmill (15x16cm-6x6in) black lead pen
                                (D.FL 18000)

BRUEGHEL, Jan (elder-circle) (1568-1625) Flemish
£3058 $6024   (12-Nov-90 CH.AM62/R) Village with fashionable company, woman driving
                              cattle and peasant couple in cart (19x30cm-7x12in) pen W/C
                              (D.FL 10000)

BRUEGHEL, Jan (elder-school) (1568-1625) Flemish
£11414 $19176   (23-Apr-91 F.R80/R) Paesaggio con ninfe e satiri (62x57cm-24x22in) panel
                                (I.L 25000000)

BRUEGHEL, Jan (elder-style) (1568-1625) Flemish
£2600 $5122   (31-Oct-90 S119/R) Cavalier with peasant and dogs in landscape
                                (21x26cm-8x10in) panel
£4893 $9639   (13-Nov-90 CH.AM55) Villahe by river with ferry and moored vessels by
                                quay (22x29cm-9x11in) on copper (D.FL 16000)
£7000 $11830   (17-Apr-91 S79/R) Still life of garland of flowers on gilt tazza and
                                other things on table (25x39cm-10x15in) panel
£9390 $15962   (28-May-91 AB.S4743/R) Still life of tulips and carnations in a tazza
                                (42x30cm-17x12in) panel (S.KR 100000)
£9500 $16055   (18-Apr-91 C165/R) Travellers in a cart near a cottage by a lake,
                                landscape beyond (63x102cm-25x40in)

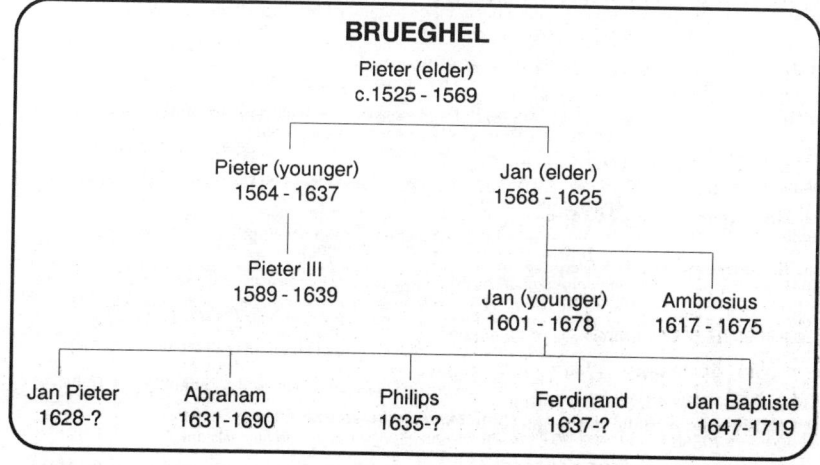

BRUEGHEL

Pieter (elder)
c.1525 - 1569

Pieter (younger)
1564 - 1637

Jan (elder)
1568 - 1625

Pieter III
1589 - 1639

Jan (younger)
1601 - 1678

Ambrosius
1617 - 1675

Jan Pieter
1628-?

Abraham
1631-1690

Philips
1635-?

Ferdinand
1637-?

Jan Baptiste
1647-1719

BRUEGHEL, Jan (elder-style) (1568-1625) Flemish-cont.

£10000	$16900	(17-Apr-91 S156/R) Landscape with travellers on outskirts of riverside village (43x56cm-17x22in)
£11000	$17930	(3-Jul-91 S115/R) Madonna and Child within garland of flowers (104x73cm-41x29in) panel
£16820	$33135	(13-Nov-90 CH.AM154/R) Extensive landscape with peasants resting on way to market (28x40cm-11x16in) copper (D.FL 55000)
£22000	$35860	(3-Jul-91 S109/R) Village beside estuary (27x38cm-11x15in) bears indist.mono.d.1659 copper

BRUEGHEL, Jan (younger) (1601-1678) Flemish

£27523	$54220	(14-Nov-90 SY.AM83/R) Studies of dogs (22x28cm-9x11in) paper on canvas (D.FL 90000)
£32000	$61760	(12-Dec-90 S122/R) Landscape with figures and waggons on outskirts of village (27x36cm-11x14in) bears sig. copper
£234266	$452133	(10-Dec-90 L.K17/R) Figures and animals on road through wooded landscape (48x84cm-19x33in) mono. panel (DM 670000)
£270000	$467100	(24-May-91 C12/R) Archduke Albrecht VII of Austria and Archduchess Isabella Clara Eugenia (47x72cm-19x28in) s.d.1621 panel
£328110	$646376	(14-Nov-90 D.V128/R) Still life of spring flowers in vase on floor and stag-beetle (124x94cm-49x37in) panel (A.S 6700000)
£526316	$1000000	(10-Jan-91 SY.NY102/R) Still life of flowers in blue and white porcelain vase (48x35cm-19x14in) panel

BRUEGHEL, Jan (younger) and BALEN, Hendrik van (17th C) Flemish

£52000	$89960	(24-May-91 C11/R) The Feast of the Gods (29x41cm-11x16in) s. by Van Balen copper

BRUEGHEL, Jan (younger) and BALEN, Hendrik van (attrib) (17th C) Flemish

£17365	$29347	(2-May-91 CH.AM123/R) The Feast of the the Gods (47x67cm-19x26in) panel (D.FL 58000)

BRUEGHEL, Jan (younger) and BALEN, Hendrik van (studio) (17th C) Flemish

£3267	$5783	(4-Apr-91 CK.P20/R) Vertumne et Pomone dans un jardin fleuri (40x53cm-16x21in) i. verso (F.FR 33000)

BRUEGHEL, Jan (younger) and BALEN, Hendrik van (style) (17th C) Flemish

£898	$1518	(2-May-91 CH.AM9) The Penitent Magdalen (49x64cm-19x25in) panel (D.FL 3000)
£1946	$3289	(2-May-91 CH.AM34/R) The Creation of Eve (62x99cm-24x39in) panel (D.FL 6500)

BRUEGHEL, Jan (younger-attrib) (1601-1678) Flemish

£9629	$16081	(6-Jun-91 D.V40/R) Hunters in landscape (21x26cm-8x10in) panel (A.S 200000)

BRUEGHEL, Jan (younger-circle) (1601-1678) Flemish

£21053	$40000	(11-Jan-91 CH.NY77/R) An allegory of Earth (41x71cm-16x28in) bears sig. panel
£24121	$39558	(21-Jun-91 SY.MO235/R) Bouquet de fleurs (21x19cm-8x7in) copper (F.FR 240000)

BRUEGHEL, Jan (younger-school) (1601-1678) Flemish

£977	$1700	(27-Mar-91 B.SF4056/R) Rest on the Flight into Egypt (26x32cm-10x13in)

BRUEGHEL, Jan (younger-studio) (1601-1678) Flemish

£4057	$8032	(30-Jan-91 APT.P48/R) La Circoncision entouree d'une guirlande de fleurs (25x20cm-10x8in) copper (F.FR 40000)

BRUEGHEL, Jan (younger-style) (1601-1678) Flemish

£4532	$7387	(16-Jun-91 P.V37/R) Le retour de chasse (55x89cm-22x35in) panel (F.FR 45000)
£5479	$8932	(12-Jun-91 N.M298/R) Landscape with windmills and figures resting at roadside (39x31cm-15x12in) copper (DM 16000)
£5528	$9065	(21-Jun-91 SY.MO260/R) Allegorie du printemps (55x72cm-22x28in) copper (F.FR 55000)
£9548	$15658	(21-Jun-91 SY.MO257/R) Venus dans la forge de Vulcain (39x49cm-15x19in) copper (F.FR 95000)
£15000	$29550	(31-Oct-90 S84/R) Village by river (20x24cm-8x9in) copper
£18499	$35889	(7-Dec-90 SY.MO139/R) Nymphes endormies surprises par des satyres (64x108cm-25x43in) panel (F.FR 180000)
£21000	$41370	(31-Oct-90 S85/R) Travellers and other figures on woodland road near village (22x28cm-9x11in) copper
£21106	$34613	(22-Jun-91 CH.MO103/R) Vierge a l'enfant avec Saint Jean-Baptiste enfant, entouree d'une couronne de fleurs et fruits (74x60cm-29x24in) on bronze (F.FR 210000)

BRUEGHEL, Jan Baptiste (1647-1719) Flemish

£3075	$5290	(19-May-91 ZZ.F70/R) Jete de fleurs (14x11cm-6x4in) panel (F.FR 31000)

BRUEGHEL, Pieter (elder-circle) (c.1525-1569) Flemish

£16000	*$30880*	*(11-Dec-90 C106/R) A portrait of an artist and his assistant (29x22cm-11x9in) i.d.1537 ink*

BRUEGHEL, Pieter (elder-school) (c.1525-1569) Flemish

£2296	$4500	(7-Nov-90 B.SF1037/R) Flemish proverb (25x25cm-10x10in) panel circle

BRUEGHEL, Pieter (style) (16/17th C) Flemish
£2232 $3750 (17-Jul-91 SY.NY199/R) Two men outside a tavern (24cm-9ins circular) panel round

BRUEGHEL, Pieter (younger) (1564-1637) Flemish
£100000 $169000 (16-Apr-91 PH44/R) Bird trap (38x55cm-15x22in) panel
£157895 $300000 (11-Jan-91 CH.NY74/R) Winter landscape with adoration of magi (36x57cm-14x22in) panel
£289474 $550000 (10-Jan-91 SY.NY42/R) Village Kermesse (55x66cm-22x26in) s.d.1624 panel
£500000 $950000 (11-Jan-91 CH.NY33/R) Wedding dance (40x56cm-16x22in) s.d.1621 panel

BRUEGHEL, Pieter (younger-after) (1564-1637) Flemish
£1000 $1630 (4-Jul-91 B103/R) The Adoration of the Magi (44x59cm-17x23in) panel

BRUEGHEL, Pieter (younger-attrib) (1564-1637) Flemish
£21666 $36182 (6-Jun-91 D.V66/R) The Witsun Wedding with children's procession in village (40x67cm-16x26in) panel (A.S 450000)

BRUEGHEL, Pieter (younger-circle) (1564-1637) Flemish
£45000 $86850 (12-Dec-90 S82/R) The Adoration of the Magi (124x168cm-49x66in) panel

BRUEGHEL, Pieter (younger-school) (1564-1637) Flemish
£17857 $35000 (7-Nov-90 B.SF1041/R) Winterland scene with castle and frozen moat with figures (51x61cm-20x24in) cradled panel

BRUEGHEL, Pieter (younger-studio) (1564-1637) Flemish
£34149 $65566 (30-Nov-90 APT.P47/R) Le repas des noces. La danse. Le coucher de la mariee (26x37cm-10x15in) panel three (F.FR 335000)

BRUEGHEL, Pieter (younger-style) (1564-1637) Flemish
£12000 $23160 (11-Dec-90 PH224/R) Wedding dance in interior (58x83cm-23x33in) panel
£24000 $39120 (3-Jul-91 S134/R) Blind leading blind (23cm-9ins circular) panel

BRUESTLE, George M (1872-1939) American
£564 $1100 (25-Oct-90 GRO.B132/R) New England wayside (30x41cm-12x16in) s. panel
£1198 $2300 (29-Nov-90 MFA.C71/R) Landscape (56x76cm-22x30in) s.
£1302 $2500 (17-Dec-90 SY.NY353/R) Sunlight and shadows (64x76cm-25x30in) s.
£1964 $3300 (21-Jul-91 LIT.L76) Rocky Connecticut Valley (64x76cm-25x30in) s.
£2440 $4100 (21-Jul-91 LIT.L73) Summer landscape (64x76cm-25x30in) s.
£7784 $13000 (26-Jul-91 E.EDM136 m/R) Landscape with barn (30x41cm-12x16in) s.

BRUGAIROLLES, Victor (1869-1936) French
£697 $1212 (25-Mar-91 CR.P67/R) Fin de journee sur le village (133x203cm-52x80in) s. (F.FR 7000)
£1480 $2915 (16-Nov-90 LGB.P170/R) La Seine a Vetheuil (65x92cm-26x36in) s. (F.FR 14500)

BRUGES SCHOOL, 15th C Belgian
£34965 $67483 (10-Dec-90 L.K18/R) Mary with Child and saints. St Jacobus. Adam triptych panel (DM 100000)

BRUGES SCHOOL, 16th C Belgian
£3529 $6000 (31-May-91 CH.NY173/R) Three donors at prayer with warrior (62x40cm-24x16in) l. coat of arms panel wing of triptych

BRUGNER, Colestin (19th C) German
£1100 $1969 (14-Mar-91 B58) A winter landscape with figures (13x20cm-5x8in) s. board pair
£1399 $2699 (10-Dec-90 L.K396) Snowy winter landscape with country estate (15x25cm-6x10in) s. (DM 4000)
£1515 $2985 (30-Oct-90 CH.AM205/R) Winter landscape, peasants conversing on frozen river, skaters beyond (62x89cm-24x35in) s. (D.FL 5000)
£1923 $3712 (10-Dec-90 L.K394) Watermill by mountain river (43x58cm-17x23in) s.d.79 (DM 5500)

BRUGNOLI, Emanuele (1859-1944) Italian
£632 $1200 (9-Jan-91 D.NY10/R) Figures outside entrance of Doge's Palace, Venice (46x36cm-18x14in) s. W/C

BRUGNOT, Henri (1874-1940) French
£911 $1785 (19-Nov-90 CSC.P36 b) Les arbres rouges (49x64cm-19x25in) s. (F.FR 9000)

BRUIN, J R de (?) ?
£635 $1244 (12-Feb-91 GM.B378) Riviere enneigee (50x60cm-20x24in) s. wood (B.FR 38000)

BRULAND, Arne (1920-1980) Norwegian
£1562 $2609 (4-Jun-91 BU.O37/R) Dance (99x81cm-39x32in) s.d.49 s.i.d.48verso (N.KR 18000)
£1870 $3609 (10-Dec-90 B.O14/R) Protest, 1950 (130x100cm-51x39in) s.d.50 (N.KR 21000)

BRUN, Guillaume Charles (1825-1908) French
£3333 $6567 (30-Oct-90 CH.AM168/R) Little flower-seller (80x46cm-31x18in) s.d.1873 (D.FL 11000)

BRUN, Guillaume Charles (1825-1908) French-cont.
£5128 $10000   (23-Oct-90 SY.NY283/R) Le berceuse, souvenir de Constantine, Algerie
                  (90x69cm-35x27in) s.d.1880
£10256 $20000   (24-Oct-90 CH.NY214/R) Basket of ribbons (45x32cm-18x13in) s.d.1869
                  panel

BRUN-BUISSON, G (19/20th C) French
£789   *$1500*   *(9-Jan-91 D.NY11/R) Rosier dans le jardin de la Cure St. Aupre, Loire*
                  (64x48cm-25x19in) s. i.verso W/C

BRUNBERG, Hakan (1905-1978) Finnish?
£3295 $6491   (17-Nov-90 BU.H142/R) In the skerries (46x55cm-18x22in) s. (F.M 23000)
£4708 $9227   (24-Nov-90 HOR.H53/R) From Brunnspark (55x46cm-22x18in) s.d.1960
                  (F.M 33000)

BRUNEL DE NEUVILLE (19/20th C) French
£592 $1000   (20-Apr-91 WOL.C198/R) Cats (36x46cm-14x18in) s.
£1833 $3152   (14-May-91 GF.L2134/R) Still life with peaches and grapes
                  (38x46cm-15x18in) s. (S.FR 4600)
£3410 $6650   (13-Oct-90 H.AP4/R) Les trois chatons et la pelote de laine
                  (46x55cm-18x22in) s. (F.FR 34000)

BRUNEL DE NEUVILLE, Alfred Arthur (1852-1941) French
£711 $1400   (16-Nov-90 S.BM65/R) Kittens with canary (20x28cm-8x11in) s. panel
£766 $1494   (27-Oct-90 LT.P14/R) Nature morte au homard et au cuivre
                  (84x65cm-33x26in) s. (F.FR 7600)
£1053 $2000   (9-Jan-91 D.NY12) Roses and lilacs in golden bowl (53x64cm-21x25in) s.
£1100 $1914   (26-Mar-91 PH52/R) Curiosity (46x39cm-18x15in) s.
£1500 $2520   (16-Jul-91 C75/R) The ball of red wool (50x65cm-20x26in) s.
£1503 $2600   (21-May-91 CE.NY230/R) Lilac and roses in brass bowl (54x65cm-21x26in)
                  s.
£1534 $2500   (5-Jul-91 S.W3037/R) Tabletop still life (53x64cm-21x25in) s.
£1546 $3000   (7-Dec-90 S.W2726/R) Still life of grapes and peaches (46x56cm-18x22in)
                  s.
£1731 $3098   (12-Apr-91 JM.P37) Pichet a vin (54x38cm-18x15in) s. (F.FR 17500)
£1764 $3440   (26-Oct-90 PPB.P83) Nature morte aux groseilles (53x65cm-21x26in) s.
                  (F.FR 17500)
£1800 $3024   (16-Jul-91 C76/R) The paper mouse (55x66cm-22x26in) s.
£2000 $3360   (16-Jul-91 C77/R) The stolen basket (55x65cm-22x26in) s.
£2000 $3360   (16-Jul-91 C71/R) Kittens playing with ball of wool (38x46cm-15x18in) s.
£2218 $4325   (28-Oct-90 M.V158) Nature morte aux coquillages (54x64cm-21x25in) s.
                  (F.FR 22000)
£2319 $4521   (26-Oct-90 PPB.P84) Nature morte aux fruits de mer (54x65cm-21x26in) s.
                  (F.FR 23000)
£2548 $4918   (16-Dec-90 DA.R2/R) Nature morte a la langouste, au bassin de cuivre et
                  a la carafe (54x64cm-21x25in) s. (F.FR 25000)
£3033 $5915   (21-Oct-90 DA.R3/R) Nature morte au chaudron, aux huitres et a la
                  langouste (82x73cm-32x29in) s. (F.FR 30000)
£3205 $6250   (20-Oct-90 FA.PH914/R) Mischievous kittens and inkwell (64x53cm-25x21in)
                  s.
£3590 $7000   (24-Oct-90 CH.NY101/R) Kittens playing on desk (55x65cm-22x26in) s.
£4046 $7000   (21-May-91 CE.NY134/R) Playful kittens (55x66cm-22x26in) s.
£4096 $8027   (24-Nov-90 SA.A655/R) The naughty cats (24x33cm-9x13in) s. canvas laid
                  down (DM 12000)

BRUNEL, Jean Baptiste (1844-1929) French
£2711 $4364   (28-Jun-91 ZZ.F86/R) Les Baux de Provence (160x250cm-63x98in) s.
                  (F.FR 27000)

BRUNELLESCHI, Umberto (1879-) Italian
£712   *$1346*   *(25-Sep-90 FB.P247) Trivellino (46x29cm-18x11in) s. lead pencil*
                  htd.gouache W/C (F.FR 7000)
£712   *$1346*   *(25-Sep-90 FB.P246/R) Demoiselle de compagnie (46x29cm-18x11in) s. lead*
                  pencil htd.gouache W/C (F.FR 7000)
£712   *$1346*   *(25-Sep-90 FB.P245/R) Arlequin (46x30cm-18x12in) s.i.d.6.12.37 crayon*
                  gouache (F.FR 7000)

BRUNERY, Francois (19th C) Italian
£1800 $3024   (18-Jul-91 CSK129) Portrait of elegant lady, standing in white dress, in
                  interior (210x107cm-83x42in) s.d.89
£2800 $4844   (9-May-91 CSK165 a/R) Dancing class (32x23cm-13x9in) s. panel
£3000 $5910   (5-Oct-90 C50/R) Love's duty (32x24cm-13x9in) s.d.77 panel
£3700 $6364   (14-May-91 SWS333/R) He loves me, he loves me not. The lute player
                  (36x25cm-14x10in) s. pair
£10769 $21000   (24-Oct-90 CH.NY224/R) Scheming cavaliers (103x76cm-41x30in) s.
£12000 $23400   (18-Oct-90 SC3080/R) A game of forfeits - Le pont d'amour
                  (54x88cm-21x35in) s.i.d.1888

BRUNERY, Marcel (20th C) French
£5263 $10000   (27-Feb-91 SY.NY106/R) Un baiser qui s'envole (66x54cm-26x21in) s. panel
£7000 $11480   (20-Jun-91 B93/R) Shared joke (61x50cm-24x20in) s.
£8718 $17000   (23-Oct-90 SY.NY319/R) Le mauvais cigare (74x61cm-29x24in) s.
£23684 $45000   (28-Feb-91 CH.NY14/R) The eminent duet (65x81cm-26x32in) s.

BRUNET, G (19th C) British
£2254 $3900   (8-May-91 RO.BA208) Scene de jardin avec personnages (60x73cm-24x29in) s.

BRUNI, Bruno (1935-) Italian
£1085 $1812   (8-Jun-91 HN.H47) Reclining nude (59x75cm-23x30in) s.d.1969 colour pencil (DM 3200)

BRUNIN, Leon (1861-1949) Belgian
£1485 $2821   (11-Sep-90 UL.T179/R) Writing letters (50x70cm-20x28in) (N.KR 17000)
£3325 $5952   (12-Mar-91 C.A33/R) At the art dealers (65x77cm-26x30in) s. (B.FR 200000)
£3333 $6567   (30-Oct-90 CH.AM26/R) Still life with herrings on plate, jug, salt cellar, onions, glass, on draped table (58x77cm-23x30in) s.i. panel (D.FL 11000)

BRUNING, Peter (1929-1970) German
£10169 $16983   (8-Jun-91 HN.H48/R) Composition (80x95cm-31x37in) s.d.1956 board (DM 30000)
£22603 $36842   (14-Jun-91 L.K788/R) Number 30 (60x80cm-24x31in) s.d.60 (DM 66000)
£27586 $52966   (26-Nov-90 WK.M8/R) Composition (150x125cm-59x49in) c.1962 (DM 80000)
£751 $1472   (24-Nov-90 VG.B454/R) Untitled (36x48cm-14x19in) c.1966 pen col.chk felt tip pen (DM 2200)
£1164 $1898   (14-Jun-91 L.K789/R) Untitled (26x37cm-10x15in) s.d.1966 indian ink pen brush (DM 3400)
£2218 $4348   (24-Nov-90 N.M76) Composition (17x29cm-7x11in) s.d.1959 W/C (DM 6500)
£3390 $5661   (8-Jun-91 HN.H49) Composition (36x47cm-14x19in) s.d.1961 pen (DM 10000)
£3413 $6689   (20-Nov-90 L.K159/R) Untitled (44x33cm-17x13in) mixed media (DM 10000)
£4778 $9365   (20-Nov-90 L.K157/R) Composition (19x32cm-7x13in) s.d.1959 W/C indian ink pen (DM 14000)
£4778 $9365   (20-Nov-90 L.K156/R) Untitled (61x86cm-24x34in) d.1957 gouache (DM 14000)
£42000 $67620   (27-Jun-91 C11/R) Untitled - nr. 133 (88x114cm-35x45in) s.d.62 num.133 verso oil col.crayons canvas

BRUNNER, F Sands (1886-1954) American
£4706 $8000   (1-Jun-91 IH.NY190/R) Girl in waves taking off swimsuit (91x66cm-36x26in) init.

BRUNNER, Ferdinand (1870-1945) Austrian
£2153 $3725   (8-May-91 D.V17/R) Country road (25x36cm-10x14in) s.i.d.1908 board (A.S 45000)
£6419 $12517   (26-Oct-90 KM.K1124/R) View of Vigaun near Salzburg with peasant (44x35cm-17x14in) s.d.1900 (DM 19000)

BRUNNER, Hans (1813-1888) German
£1070 $1809   (17-Apr-91 WE.MU294/R) Portrait of Sissi (54x40cm-21x16in) s. panel (DM 3200)

BRUNNER, Hattie K (?) American
£558 $1100   (16-Nov-90 WOL.C101 a) Winter sleigh ride (25x36cm-10x14in) s.d. W/C
£787 $1550   (16-Nov-90 WOL.C101) Amish village (25x36cm-10x14in) s.d.67 W/C

BRUNNER, Josef (1826-1893) German
£1262 $2384   (27-Sep-90 D.V4/R) Mountain landscape with cattle (27x21cm-11x8in) s. panel (A.S 26000)

BRUNNER, Julienne (?) ?
£1831 $3461   (28-Sep-90 CSC.P2/R) Nature morte aux gibiers et aux fruits s. (F.FR 18000)

BRUNNICHE, Andreas (1704-1769) Danish
£1320 $2218   (23-Apr-91 RAS.K176/R) Portrait of Amalie Charisius (76x59cm-30x23in) (D.KR 15000)
£1425 $2793   (22-Nov-90 RAS.V696/R) Portrait of Ingeborg Christiana de Theilmann (78x62cm-31x24in) s.d.1765verso (D.KR 16000)
£1436 $2829   (14-Nov-90 RAS.K170/R) Portrait of de Malville wearing red coat (36x29cm-14x11in) s.d.1762 (D.KR 16000)

BRUNORI, Enzo (1924-) Italian
£911 $1549   (28-May-91 SY.MI55/R) Composizione (50x20cm-20x8in) (I.L 2000000)
£1731 $2943   (28-May-91 SY.MI128/R) Composizione (54x80cm-21x31in) s.d.56 (I.L 3800000)

BRUS, Gunter (1938-) Austrian
£438 $858   (24-Jan-91 D.V287/R) Zur 17. Nachtwache (23x14cm-9x6in) s.i. pencil col.pencil (A.S 9000)
£976 $1806   (7-Mar-91 D.V291/R) Beweis Hase - Beweis Wolf (29x21cm-11x8in) mono.i.d.75 pencil col.pencil (A.S 20000)
£994 $1928   (6-Dec-90 D.V225/R) Die Republik und Sterbmund (29x21cm-11x8in) i.d.75 pencil (A.S 20000)
£1053 $1821   (8-May-91 D.V182/R) Untitled (30x21cm-12x8in) s.d.70 pencil (A.S 22000)
£1914 $3311   (8-May-91 D.V187/R) Gedenken an Elisabeth (37x28cm-15x11in) s.d.1984 pencil col.pencil (A.S 40000)

BRUS, Gunter (1938-) Austrian-cont.
£9940 $19284   (6-Dec-90 D.V197/R) Phantasies and variations to Winterreise by Franz
                   Schubert (30x21cm-12x8in) d.1978 mixed media set of nine (A.S 200000)

BRUSAFERRO, Girolamo (attrib) (1700-1760) Italian
£6316 $12000   (11-Jan-91 CH.NY63/R) The Head of a Cyrus before Queen Tomyris
                   (63x108cm-25x43in)

BRUSASORCI, Felice (school) (1542-1605) Italian
£503 $824   (21-Jun-91 CK.P15) Saint Marc, Sebastien et Roch avec la Vierge et
                   l'enfant Jesus .... pierre noire wash htd.white (F.FR 5000)

BRUSENBAUCH, Arthur (1881-1957) German
£439 $813   (7-Mar-91 D.V214/R) Salzkammergut landscape (36x46cm-14x18in) s. W/C
                   gouache (A.S 9000)

BRUSH, George de Forest (1855-1941) American
£529 $1000   (25-Sep-90 CE.NY90/R) Portrait of the artist's wife (41x36cm-16x14in)
                   s.d.1892 pastel

BRUSSELMANS, Jean (1884-1953) Belgian
£8183 $13748   (23-Apr-91 C.A73/R) Zeebruggen Harbour (67x90cm-26x35in) s.d.1932
                   (B.FR 500000)
£16367 $27496   (23-Apr-91 C.A72/R) A farm in Groot Bijgaarden (69x69cm-27x27in)
                   s.d.1935 (B.FR 1000000)
£29581 $57683   (23-Oct-90 C.A315/R) In Zeebrugge Harbour (77x97cm-30x38in) s.
                   (B.FR 1800000)
£740 $1442   (23-Oct-90 C.A316) Woman with a cigarette (72x45cm-28x18in) s.d.1947
                   mixed media (B.FR 45000)
£14730 $24746   (23-Apr-91 C.A74/R) The sea (74x69cm-29x27in) s.d.1919 W/C (B.FR 900000)

BRUTT, Ferdinand (1849-1936) German
£541 $919   (28-May-91 KF.M142) Brickworks in Holstein (32x41cm-13x16in) mono.d.1894
                   (DM 1600)

BRUXELLES, Dumont (1650-1719) Flemish
£4853 $9464   (21-Oct-90 L.C40) L'Avare surpris par la mort (68x85cm-27x33in) s.
                   (F.FR 48000)

BRUYN, Barthel (elder) (1493-1555) German
£18564 $33229   (14-Mar-91 D.V69/R) Portrait of lady with hands folded. Portrait of
                   gentleman wearing baret (92x70cm-36x28in) panel pair (A.S 380000)
£41971 $82682   (30-Oct-90 BU.S235/R) Portrait of Ludwig Falckenberg (33x24cm-13x9in)
                   d.1530 panel (S.KR 460000)

BRUYN, Barthel (style) (1493-1555) German
£3500 $6895   (31-Oct-90 S21/R) The Crucifixion. Male donor with saint, possibly St
                   Jude. Donor and saint (99x99cm-39x39in) panel triptych

BRUYN, Barthel (younger) (1530-1607) German
£5333 $10240   (18-Dec-90 GM.B4061/R) Portrait d'homme a la collerette, la main gauche
                   posee sur un crane (37x26cm-15x10in) panel (B.FR 320000)

BRUYN, Barthel (younger-style) (1530-1607) German
£3058 $6024   (14-Nov-90 SY.AM27/R) Portrait of nobleman (31x24cm-12x9in) panel
                   (D.FL 10000)

BRUYN, Cornelis Johannes de (c.1800-1844) Dutch
£2600 $4992   (27-Nov-90 PH25/R) Still life of fruit on table (47x36cm-19x14in) init.

BRUYN, Cornelis Johannes de (attrib) (c.1800-1844) Dutch
£3500 $6825   (25-Oct-90 CSK101/R) Mixed fruit and flowers on marble ledge, woodland
                   beyond (21x16cm-8x6in) with sig. panel

BRUYN, Theodore de (circle) (fl.1760-1804) Flemish
£5600 $11032   (1-Nov-90 CSK80/R) Anglers by lock near farmstead (122x76cm-48x30in)

BRUYNE, Dees de (20th C) Belgian
£2291 $3849   (23-Apr-91 C.A377) Morto jiglio era un Rollingstone (125x165cm-49x65in)
                   s. (B.FR 140000)

BRUYNE, Gustaaf de (1914-1981) Belgian
£3941 $6818   (25-May-91 KV.L464/R) Girl in a blue dress (59x54cm-23x21in) s. d.48
                   verso (B.FR 240000)
£665 $1190   (12-Mar-91 C.A48) Fish (23x15cm-9x6in) drawing (B.FR 40000)

BRUZZI, Stefano (1835-1911) Italian
£34000 $66000   (18-Oct-90 F.M74/R) Ritorno dal mercato (91x52cm-36x20in) s.
                   (I.L 75000000)
£66127 $110432   (6-Jun-91 F.M282/R) Ritorno dall'ovile (65x101cm-26x40in) s.
                   (I.L 145000000)
£75000 $144000   (30-Nov-90 C47/R) The road home (71x127cm-28x50in) s.

BRYANS, Lina (1909-) Australian
£1651 $2691   (1-Jul-91 AAA.S105) Autumn Street scene (46x43cm-18x17in) s. (A.D 3500)
£2262 $3824   (16-Apr-91 J.M311/R) The red boat shed (42x49cm-17x19in) s. (A.D 5000)

BRYANS, Lina (1909-) Australian-cont.
£2715 $4588   (16-Apr-91 J.M66/R) Puce landscape (50x61cm-20x24in) s. i. verso board
                     (A.D 6000)

BRYANT, Charles (1883-1937) Australian
£618 $1217   (13-Nov-90 J.M242) Harbour landing (19x23cm-7x9in) s. board (A.D 1600)
£756 $1420   (17-Sep-90 MGS.S211/R) Old Thames Inn (22x31cm-9x12in) s. (A.D 1700)
£1606 $3084   (26-Nov-90 SY.ME143/R) Return of fishing fleet (27x38cm-11x15in) s.
                     board (A.D 4000)
£2232 $3884   (26-Mar-91 JRL.S130/R) Rabaul (90x51cm-35x20in) s. (A.D 5000)

BRYANT, H C (1812-1881) American
£1700 $3332   (22-Jan-91 PH111/R) Market corner (47x55cm-19x22in) s.d.1885
£2100 $3612   (14-May-91 SWS230/R) The farmyard (50x60cm-20x24in) s.
£750 $1268   (29-Apr-91 HS203) Rural landscape with turkey and guinea-fowl in
*   foreground, cattle beyond (20x15cm-8x6in) s. W/C board*

BRYANT, Henry C (19th C) British
£1300 $2548   (20-Nov-90 PH95) Feeding time (51x76cm-20x30in) s.

BRYEN, Camille (1907-1977) French
£5700 $9291   (4-Jul-91 GL.P179/R) Composition abstraite (61x50cm-24x20in) s. d.1961
                     verso (F.FR 57000)
£9045 $14834   (23-Jun-91 P.V14/R) Composition (81x65cm-32x26in) s. (F.FR 90000)
£17893 $30239   (21-Apr-91 P.V34/R) Eclactique continue (100x81cm-39x32in) s.
                     d.1954-1957 verso (F.FR 180000)
£673 $1192   (4-Apr-91 PPB.P40) Composition (27x21cm-11x8in) s. Indian ink gouache
*   (F.FR 6800)*
£755 $1231   (16-Jun-91 CC.P43) Sans titre (43x28cm-17x11in) s. indian ink
*   (F.FR 7500)*
£1250 $2163   (21-May-91 WK.M657/R) Composition (33x25cm-13x10in) s.d.1960 W/C
*   (DM 3700)*
£2480 $4860   (22-Nov-90 ZZ.F18 a) Composition (48x33cm-19x13in) mono. ink gouache
*   (F.FR 24500)*
£2772 $4907   (4-Apr-91 PPB.P39/R) Composition (34x25cm-13x10in) s.d.61 gouache W/C
*   (F.FR 28000)*
£4388 $8644   (15-Nov-90 I.N36/R) Composition (30x25cm-12x10in) s. d.1962 verso
*   (F.FR 43000)*

BRZEZOWSKY, Grete (fl.1910-1920) Austrian
£1056 $1816   (16-May-91 D.V122/R) The flower girl (83x96cm-33x38in) s.d.99
                     (A.S 22000)

BUBA, Adrien (c.1953-) ?
£758 $1479   (15-Oct-90 CSC.P49/R) Guerriers (80x80cm-31x31in) s.d.90 acrylic
                     (F.FR 7500)

BUCCI, Anselmo (1887-1955) Italian
£5178 $10097   (22-Oct-90 BR.M262/R) Alma Nutrix (52x72cm-20x28in) s.d.1932
                     (I.L 11500000)

BUCCIARELLI, Daniele (19th C) Italian
£600 $1074   (12-Mar-91 PH130/R) Street in Lubiaco (50x23cm-20x9in) s. W/C

BUCHANAN, George F (19th C) British
£500 $1000   (7-Feb-91 B.P84/R) Autumn landscape (41x58cm-16x23in) s.

BUCHE, Josef (1848-1917) Austrian
£800 $1352   (1-May-91 GD.B106/R) The letter (38x31cm-15x12in) s. board (S.FR 2000)
£1027 $1675   (12-Jun-91 N.M379/R) Portrait of peasant boy filling his first pipe with
                     tobacco in landscape (63x50cm-25x20in) s. (DM 3000)

BUCHET, Clementin Martin (19th C) French
£900 $1593   (22-Mar-91 APT.P17) Bouquets de fleurs W/C vellum (F.FR 9000)

BUCHET, Gustave (1888-1963) Swiss
£4435 $8516   (2-Dec-90 GAB.G1539/R) Ciel embrase (21x27cm-8x11in) s.d.1949 panel
                     (S.FR 11000)
£10484 $20129   (2-Dec-90 GAB.G1535/R) Pont Neuf, Paris (46x38cm-18x15in) s.d.1940
                     pavatex (S.FR 26000)
£11905 $19881   (5-Dec-90 SY.Z119/R) Composition (42x29cm-17x11in) s.d.1925 panel
                     (S.FR 30000)
£16129 $30968   (2-Dec-90 GAB.G1536/R) Composition (61x49cm-24x19in) s.d.1926
                     (S.FR 40000)
£35714 $59643   (5-Jun-91 SY.Z120/R) Composition aux pinceaux et bouteille
                     (55x46cm-22x18in) s.d.1926 (S.FR 90000)
£40476 $67595   (5-Jun-91 SY.Z81/R) Composition (92x73cm-36x29in) s. (S.FR 102000)
£1200 $2028   (1-May-91 GD.B1330) Portrait of the poet Georges Hofmann
*   (50x38cm-20x15in) s. chl (S.FR 3000)*
£1270 $2197   (22-May-91 GS.B2051) Houses (28x22cm-11x9in) s. i.verso W/C (S.FR 3200)
£2367 $4664   (16-Nov-90 GK.Z5331) Nu allonge (25x36cm-10x14in) s. black pencil dr.
*   (S.FR 5800)*
£2778 $4639   (5-Jun-91 SY.Z116/R) Escale (25x19cm-10x7in) s. st.studio verso W/C
*   (S.FR 7000)*
£3061 $6000   (6-Nov-90 GF.L2269/R) Farmhouse (45x29cm-18x11in) s. W/C (S.FR 7500)

BUCHET, Gustave (1888-1963) Swiss-cont.

£5138	$8735	(30-May-91 EA.Z175/R) House in landscape (56x37cm-22x15in) s. W/C (S.FR 13000)
£6426	$12594	(21-Nov-90 SY.Z78/R) Composition (52x37cm-20x15in) s. gouache (S.FR 16000)
£6855	$13161	(2-Dec-90 GAB.G1533/R) Composition aux formes feminines (37x24cm-15x9in) s.i.d.1927 gouache (S.FR 17000)

BUCHHEISTER, Carl (1890-1964) German

£678	$1132	(6-Jun-91 HN.H182/R) Black square (19x14cm-7x6in) mono.d.1928 pencil (DM 2000)
£1027	$1839	(12-Mar-91 FN.S1932) Composition no 19 (61x42cm-24x17in) i.verso col.chk (DM 3000)
£1424	$2378	(6-Jun-91 HN.H183/R) Composition (42x29cm-17x11in) s.d.1951 verso pencil chk tempera (DM 4200)
£2821	$5500	(10-Oct-90 SY.NY538/R) Untitled (41x25cm-16x10in) init.d.50 mixed media
£4392	$7466	(28-May-91 KF.M494/R) Central Komposition mit plastischen Gallert Formen (33x23cm-13x9in) s.i.d.1951 verso mixed media (DM 13000)
£4773	$9356	(20-Nov-90 BR.M157/R) Composizione (28x40cm-11x16in) c.1953 gouache tempera (I.L 10500000)

BUCHHOLZ, Erich (1891-1972) German

| £2034 | $3397 | (6-Jun-91 HN.H185/R) Composition (25x18cm-10x7in) mono.d.1921 W/C brush ink (DM 6000) |

BUCHHOLZ, Karl (1849-1889) German

| £6238 | $10729 | (16-May-91 D.V164/R) Landscape with figures (30x24cm-12x9in) s.d.81 panel (A.S 130000) |

BUCHNER, Carl (1821-?) German

| £709 | $1206 | (28-May-91 KF.M143) Portrait of girl wearing red dress (21x16cm-8x6in) s. panel (DM 2100) |

BUCHNER, Georg (1858-1914) German

| £518 | $1000 | (10-Dec-90 H.C1161) Bust of young girl (20x15cm-8x6in) s. panel |
| £655 | $1100 | (28-Apr-91 HG.C371) Portrait of young girl (23x15cm-9x6in) s. panel |

BUCHS, Raymond (?) Swiss?

£1224	$2376	(8-Dec-90 GAB.G2425/R) A la pisciculture le soir (44x57cm-17x22in) s. i. verso (S.FR 3000)
£1400	$2366	(1-May-91 GD.B104/R) River Saane landscape with lake near Fribourg (54x59cm-21x23in) s.d.18 i.verso (S.FR 3500)
£2200	$3718	(1-May-91 GD.B103/R) Mountain landscape with view of Hochmatt (62x73cm-24x29in) s.d.17 i.verso (S.FR 5500)

BUCHSER, Frank (1828-1890) Swiss

| £7631 | $14956 | (21-Nov-90 SY.Z33/R) Coastal landscape, Scarborough (20x30cm-8x12in) mono. (S.FR 19000) |
| £16327 | $32163 | (16-Nov-90 GK.Z5332/R) El novelero Andaluz (69x54cm-27x21in) s.d.1858 (S.FR 40000) |

BUCHSER, Frank (attrib) (1828-1890) Swiss

| £717 | $1398 | (24-Oct-90 GD.B189) Lake landscape with party in rowing boat (24x46cm-9x18in) indis.mono. board (S.FR 1800) |
| £2390 | $4112 | (14-May-91 GF.L2477/R) Guitar player (56x46cm-22x18in) rem.sig. (S.FR 6000) |

BUCHTA, Karl (1861-1928) Austrian

| £1697 | $3191 | (20-Sep-90 D.V32/R) The Sunday outing (72x112cm-28x44in) s.d.1914 (A.S 35000) |

BUCHTGER, Robert (1862-1951) German

| £1267 | $2065 | (12-Jun-91 N.M380/R) Peasant with ox-drawn cart in river landscape (135x101cm-53x40in) i.stretcher (DM 3700) |

BUCK, Adam (1759-1833) British

£340	$571	(16-Jul-91 SWS1910) Gentleman, with short cropped grey hair and wearing brown jacket (12x?cm-5x?in) min. s.d.1822 gilt frame on card rectangular
£500	$990	(30-Jan-91 S54) Portrait of young lady (13x11cm-5x4in) s. W/C over pencil
£980	$1735	(21-Mar-91 CSK2) Portrait of three ladies, the younger seated at the keyboards (38x41cm-15x16in) s. pencil col.chks W/C htd.white

BUCK, Adam (style) (1759-1833) British

| £3000 | $4950 | (11-Jul-91 CSK51/R) Portrait of two young ladies, in interior, one by harp, other seated at harpsicord (56x46cm-22x18in) |

BUCK, Evariste de (1892-1974) Belgian

£1146	$1948	(28-May-91 C.A57/R) Country house by a river (110x160cm-43x63in) s. (B.FR 70000)
£3096	$5975	(13-Dec-90 SY.AM46/R) Allegorie du printemps (300x200cm-118x79in) s.d.1920 (D.FL 10000)
£8050	$15536	(13-Dec-90 SY.AM45/R) Landscape with farmhouse (91x117cm-36x46in) s.d.1920 (D.FL 26000)

BUCK, Frederick (1771-1840) Irish
£300	$519	(21-May-91 CSK151) Portrait of Jane Oliver (7x?cm-3x?in) min. oval
£360	$605	(16-Jul-91 SWS1928/R) Officer, with black hair, in uniform, with badge 16th Bengal Infantry (7x?cm-3x?in) min. gilt frame oval
£480	$792	(10-Jul-91 C149) An officer in scarlet uniform (6x?cm-2x?in) min. gold frame plaited hair verso oval
£580	$957	(10-Jul-91 C154/R) An officer, possibly James Davidson (6x?cm-2x?in) min. gold frame mono on plaited hair verso oval

BUCK, Rafael de (1902-1986) ?
£788	$1364	(25-May-91 KV.L76) Young woman (50x40cm-20x16in) s. (B.FR 48000)
£1232	$2131	(25-May-91 KV.L74/R) Three women (90x70cm-35x28in) s. (B.FR 75000)

BUCKEN, Peter (1831-?) German
£1020	$1643	(26-Jun-91 KM.K1403/R) Wood clearing with shepherd girl, sheep and goats (29x35cm-11x14in) s. (DM 3000)
£1259	$2429	(10-Dec-90 L.K398) Eifel landscape with farmhouses and flock of sheep (68x58cm-27x23in) s. (DM 3600)

BUCKLAND, Arthur H (1870-?) British
£14070	$23075	(20-Jun-91 APT.P12/R) Le printemps (183x107cm-72x42in) s.d.1896 (F.FR 140000)

BUCKLER, John Chessel (1793-1894) British
£460	$823	(13-Mar-91 B41) Rievaulx Abbey, Yorkshire (12x20cm-5x8in) s.d.1812 wash
£4000	$6600	(9-Jul-91 C42/R) Ilam Hall, Staffordshire (46x70cm-18x28in) bears sig. pencil W/C

BUCKLEY, Charles F (fl.1841-1869) British
£2800	$5236	(28-Aug-90 S766/R) Scenes on Loch Lomond. Lake Windermere (53x72cm-21x28in) s.d.1866 i.verso W/C htd bodycol three

BUCKLEY, J E (19th C) British
£650	$1203	(7-Mar-91 CSK181) Cattle in wooded river landscape (70x90cm-28x35in) s.d.1848
£432	$705	(10-Jun-91 W.T1245) Rural figures outside a tudor cottage (32x62cm-13x24in) s.d.1875 W/C (C.D 800)
£600	$1176	(19-Nov-90 SWS663) Emilla and Desdemona, scene from Othello (47x37cm-19x15in) s.i.d.1867 W/C over pencil htd bodycol
£600	$1152	(26-Nov-90 SWS8/R) Figures strolling in park (29x47cm-11x19in) s.d.1862 W/C htd.bodycol.

BUCKLEY, John E (19th C) British
£650	$1060	(14-Jun-91 C120/R) Figures in Jacobean costume outside a Lancashire Hall (45x67cm-18x26in) s.d.1872 pencil W/C

BUCKLEY, Stephen (20th C) ?
£1500	$2445	(1-Jul-91 S56/R) Splash (182x205cm-72x81in) s.i.d.1975 verso wood canvas stitched with sisal
£867	$1500	(7-May-91 CE.NY216/R) Drowing (91x129cm-36x51in) s.d.1975 verso oil wood canvas two panels

BUCKMAN, Edwin (1841-?) British
£650	$1060	(4-Jul-91 PHI54) Spanish maiden (24x19cm-9x7in) s.i. W/C htd.bodycol.

BUCKMASTER, Ernest (1897-1968) Australian
£545	$1068	(19-Nov-90 MGS.S221) Cattle grazing (50x60cm-20x24in) s. board (A.D 1400)
£860	$1453	(15-Apr-91 AAA.S101) Feeding time for horses (38x46cm-15x18in) s. (A.D 1900)
£1285	$2467	(26-Nov-90 SY.ME266) Thornton pastoral (59x79cm-23x31in) s. i.strecther (A.D 3200)
£1448	$2447	(16-Apr-91 J.M619) Still life (39x49cm-15x19in) s.d.1933 (A.D 3200)
£1471	$2485	(16-Apr-91 J.M251 a) Early morning reflections (34x44cm-13x17in) s. canvas on board (A.D 3250)
£1471	$2485	(16-Apr-91 J.M297/R) Still life (75x49cm-30x19in) s. (A.D 3250)
£1538	$2600	(16-Apr-91 J.M861) Goulburn Valley (52x70cm-20x28in) s. (A.D 3400)
£1931	$3803	(13-Nov-90 J.M35) Near Silvan (57x85cm-22x33in) s. (A.D 5000)
£2124	$4183	(13-Nov-90 J.M285) Autumn landscape (63x90cm-25x35in) s. canvas on board (A.D 5500)
£2262	$3824	(16-Apr-91 J.M134/R) Billabong, Thornton, Victoria (58x69cm-23x27in) s. (A.D 5000)
£2317	$4564	(13-Nov-90 J.M12/R) Church Street Bridge, Richmond (41x52cm-16x20in) s. board (A.D 6000)
£2489	$4206	(16-Apr-91 J.M254) Spring reflections (66x85cm-26x33in) s. canvas on board (A.D 5500)
£2489	$4206	(16-Apr-91 J.M316/R) Grey winter New Year (67x85cm-26x33in) s.d.'40 canvas on board (A.D 5500)
£2489	$4206	(16-Apr-91 J.M312/R) Still morning, Mornington (39x49cm-15x19in) s. board (A.D 5500)
£2941	$4971	(16-Apr-91 J.M219/R) Goulburn River, morning near Trawool (68x81cm-27x32in) s.d.1940 (A.D 6500)
£3054	$5162	(16-Apr-91 J.M138/R) The bush clearing (74x94cm-29x37in) s. (A.D 6750)
£3089	$6085	(13-Nov-90 J.M166) Yarra glen landscape (70x90cm-28x35in) s. canvas on board (A.D 8000)

BUCKMASTER, Ernest (1897-1968) Australian-cont.
£3167 $5353   (16-Apr-91 J.M20/R) Still life (60x51cm-24x20in) s. canvas on board
       (A.D 7000)
£3167 $5353   (16-Apr-91 J.M309/R) The Venetian vase (68x91cm-27x36in) s. (A.D 7000)
£3394 $5735   (16-Apr-91 J.M166/R) Quiet pool, Yarra at Warburton (62x72cm-24x28in) s.
       (A.D 7500)
£4299 $7265   (16-Apr-91 J.M128/R) Flower piece - delphiniums (67x57cm-26x22in)
       s.d.1941 (A.D 9500)
£6178 $12170   (13-Nov-90 J.M28/R) Rhododendrons (108x77cm-43x30in) s. (A.D 16000)

BUCKNER, Richard (1812-1883) British
£2300 $3956   (14-May-91 SWS239/R) Portrait of lady said to be Lady Rebecca Frankland
       standing (118x95cm-46x37in) s.
£2817 $4789   (28-May-91 AB.S4745/R) Spanish lady holding fan (127x89cm-50x35in) s.
       (S.KR 30000)
£7500 $12375   (12-Jul-91 C175/R) Portrait of Mrs. Holloway and son, by spinet
       (234x149cm-92x59in) s.

BUCKNER, Richard (attrib) (1812-1883) British
£1000 $1650   (10-Jul-91 S115/R) Portrait of lady wearing flowers in hair
       (74x61cm-29x24in) canvas on board oval

BUCQUOIT, Myriam (20th C) French
£930 $1814   (15-Oct-90 CSC.P51/R) Composition (90x90cm-35x35in) s. d.1989 verso
       (F.FR 9200)
£961 $1873   (15-Oct-90 CSC.P50/R) Cathedre II (100x91cm-39x36in) s. d.1989 verso
       (F.FR 9500)

BUDDENBERG, Wilhelm (1890-) German
£940 $1832   (10-Oct-90 WE.MU336) Boars in the snow (60x80cm-24x31in) s. panel
       (DM 2800)
£1119 $2159   (10-Dec-90 L.K397) Capercaillie in heath landscape (27x37cm-11x15in) s.
       (DM 3200)
£1203 $2285   (2-Mar-91 KRA.D290/R) Wild sows in snowy landscape (60x80cm-24x31in) s.
       panel (DM 3500)
£1342 $2617   (13-Oct-90 KRA.D182 a) Two deers running (70x100cm-28x39in) s.
       (DM 4000)

BUDELOT, Philippe (circle) (18/19th C) French
£2041 $4020   (14-Nov-90 FB.P161) La calcehe le soir, promenade le matin
       (33x41cm-13x16in) pair (F.FR 20000)

BUDELOT, Philippe (school) (18/19th C) French
£1304 $2543   (12-Oct-90 ZZ.F18/R) La chasse au cerf (37x45cm-15x18in) panel
       (F.FR 13000)
£1304 $2543   (12-Oct-90 ZZ.F19) Le dejeuner a la campagne (37x45cm-15x18in) panel
       (F.FR 13000)

BUDKO, Joseph (20th C) Israeli
£2094 $4000   (1-Jan-91 GG.TA241/R) Village alley, figure of woman (48x39cm-19x15in)
       s.d.1931 s.d.verso

BUDTZ-MOLLER, Carl (1882-1953) Danish
£976 $1806   (7-Mar-91 D.V40/R) Rainy day (85x109cm-33x43in) s.d.1906 (A.S 20000)
£1000 $1960   (23-Nov-90 PHM121) Prayers at the Lady Chapel (78x102cm-31x40in)
       s.d.1920 i. verso
£1211 $2349   (22-Aug-90 RAS.K24/R) Figures by Sabiner mountain (108x140cm-43x55in) s.
       (D.KR 14000)
£3770 $7427   (14-Nov-90 RAS.K86/R) Cat resting on a piano (75x105cm-30x41in) s.d.1931
       (D.KR 42000)

BUECKELAER, Joachim (after) (1530-1573) Flemish
£4800 $8112   (18-Apr-91 CSK135/R) Lecherous fisherman (104x155cm-41x61in)

BUEHR, Karl Albert (1866-1952) American
£518 $1000   (10-Dec-90 H.C1053) Spring landscape (61x76cm-24x30in) s.
£1463 $2400   (23-Jun-91 H.C996) Spring landscape (64x79cm-25x31in) s. board

BUELL, Alfred (1910-) American
£1471 $2500   (1-Jun-91 IH.NY92/R) The Long Vacation, man having breakfast with his
       family (51x99cm-20x39in) s.

BUENDIA, Pablo (19/20th C) Spanish
£3648 $7113   (22-Oct-90 ANS.M29/R) Bosque (38x61cm-15x24in) s. (S.P 675000)

BUENO FERRER, Pascual (1930-) Spanish
£1366 $2636   (11-Dec-90 FER.M144/R) Puerto con barca en verde (64x80cm-25x31in) s.
       (S.P 250000)

BUENO, Antonio (1918-1984) Italian
£2701 $5268   (24-Oct-90 F.M106/R) Ritratto di bambina (24x17cm-9x7in) s. masonite
       (I.L 6000000)
£3928 $7581   (13-Dec-90 F.M488/R) Bambina (30x40cm-12x16in) s. s.verso masonite
       (I.L 8500000)
£4095 $7739   (27-Sep-90 F.M64/R) Ritratto di ragazza (39x29cm-15x11in) s. masonite
       (I.L 9000000)

BUENO, Antonio (1918-1984) Italian-cont.
£4502	$8780	(24-Oct-90 F.M189/R) Ragazza con cappello (35x25cm-14x10in) s. canvas on masonite (I.L 10000000)
£4543	$8950	(30-Oct-90 F.R221/R) L'amazzone (30x20cm-12x8in) s. faesite (I.L 10000000)
£5403	$10536	(24-Oct-90 F.M124/R) Ragazza con cappello con fascia verde (40x30cm-16x12in) s. masonite (I.L 12000000)
£6754	$13170	(24-Oct-90 F.M152/R) Ritratto femminile (49x40cm-19x16in) s. masonite (I.L 15000000)
£682	*$1290*	*(27-Sep-90 F.M42) Impronta (40x50cm-16x20in) s. mixed media masonite (I.L 1500000)*

BUENO, Pedro (20th C) Spanish
| £715 | $1279 | (13-Mar-91 FER.M248/R) La madre de mi madre (27x19cm-11x7in) s. W/C (S.P 130000) |

BUENO, Xavier (1915-) Spanish
| £4580 | $8794 | (27-Nov-90 SY.MI46/R) Ragazza in blu (101x82cm-40x32in) s. s.d.1964verso (I.L 10000000) |

BUESEM, Jan Jansz (after) (1600-c.1649) Dutch
| £1204 | $2010 | (6-Jun-91 D.V361/R) Peasants in interior (29x36cm-11x14in) i. (A.S 25000) |

BUFF, Conrad (20th C) American
£1276	$2500	(13-Feb-91 B.SF2144/R) Desert landscapes (30x46cm-12x18in) s. board pair
£1786	$3500	(12-Feb-91 MOR.P105) Desert hills (66x97cm-26x38in) s. board
£5128	$10000	(10-Oct-90 B.SF622/R) Purple mountians (122x244cm-48x96in) masonite

BUFFET, Bernard (1928-) French
£8929	$15000	(28-Apr-91 HG.C85) Still life of fish and lemons (76x61cm-30x24in) s.d.57
£20305	$40000	(3-Oct-90 SY.NY188/R) Perroquet (65x46cm-26x18in) s.d.58
£26531	$52000	(14-Feb-91 CH.NY87/R) Tete de femme (65x43cm-26x17in) s.d.53
£28424	$46615	(20-Jun-91 F.M498/R) Paysage au cafe (54x65cm-21x26in) s.d.55 (I.L 62000000)
£28902	$50000	(10-May-91 S.BM148/R) Vase de fleurs (117x74cm-46x29in) s.d.62
£29648	$48623	(21-Jun-91 OD.P8/R) Dans l'atelier (50x61cm-20x24in) s.d.1953 (F.FR 295000)
£34000	$66300	(17-Oct-90 S95/R) Nature morte au poisson et aux citrons (50x65cm-20x26in) s.d.53
£35533	$70000	(3-Oct-90 SY.NY187/R) Nature morte aux verre et fruits (27x41cm-11x16in) s.d.52
£36154	$70501	(23-Oct-90 C.A317/R) Le Guildo - Cote du Nord (89x130cm-35x51in) s.d.1973 (B.FR 2200000)
£38265	$75000	(15-Feb-91 SY.NY118/R) Fleurs dans un vase gris (65x50cm-26x20in) s.d.54
£39196	$64281	(20-Jun-91 APT.P38/R) Vase de roses (65x54cm-26x21in) s.d.63 (F.FR 390000)
£40000	$70800	(19-Mar-91 C131/R) Maison au bord de l'Etang (89x130cm-35x51in) s.d.1975 i.verso
£40609	$80000	(2-Oct-90 CH.NY224/R) L'atelier (61x38cm-24x15in) s.d.53
£42000	$81900	(17-Oct-90 S94/R) Service a cafe (33x41cm-13x16in) s.s. board
£43353	$75000	(9-May-91 CH.NY280/R) Trois iris (65x54cm-26x21in) s.d.61
£45918	$90000	(14-Feb-91 CH.NY99/R) Deux bretonnes (114x146cm-45x57in) s.d.56
£46000	$74060	(26-Jun-91 S174/R) Le legue a Maree Basse (90x130cm-35x51in) s.d.1973 i.verso
£46243	$80000	(8-May-91 SY.NY246/R) Nature morte aux roses (63x53cm-25x21in) s.d.63
£48583	$95223	(24-Nov-90 APT.P96/R) Fleurs rouges dans un pot (73x50cm-29x20in) s.d.1981 (F.FR 480000)
£54781	$94771	(25-May-91 GL.P9/R) Course d'aviron sur la Marne (90x131cm-35x52in) s.d.61 (F.FR 550000)
£54913	$95000	(9-May-91 CH.NY267/R) Nature morte aux fleurs (81x54cm-32x21in) s.d.56
£55838	$110000	(2-Oct-90 CH.NY223/R) La mairie (52x79cm-20x31in) s.d.70 masonite
£56122	$110000	(15-Feb-91 SY.NY123/R) Bouquet de fleurs (81x65cm-32x26in) s.d.1982
£58673	$115000	(7-Nov-90 B.SF1109/R) Les lys (65x51cm-26x20in) s.d.59
£60694	$105000	(8-May-91 SY.NY244/R) Nature morte au table (80x99cm-31x39in) s.d.60
£60804	$108839	(16-Mar-91 APT.P65/R) Loguivy, panorama de la baie en hiver (89x130cm-35x51in) s.d.1975 (F.FR 605000)
£60914	$120000	(2-Oct-90 CH.NY195/R) Nature morte au comptoier (54x65cm-21x26in) s.d.69 masonite
£62000	$120900	(19-Oct-90 C211/R) Fleurs dans un vase bleu (65x51cm-26x20in) s.d.61
£62000	$99820	(26-Jun-91 S150/R) La nappe a carreaux (60x92cm-24x36in) s.d.57
£63452	$125000	(2-Oct-90 CH.NY192/R) Le coq rouge (116x89cm-46x35in) s.d.59
£65990	$130000	(2-Oct-90 CH.NY206/R) Les peupliers (89x132cm-35x52in) s.d.67
£68528	$135000	(3-Oct-90 SY.NY206/R) Dahlias (81x75cm-32x30in) s.d.1971
£70352	$115377	(20-Jun-91 APT.P37/R) Nature morte aux fruits (152x197cm-60x78in) s.d.52 (F.FR 700000)
£71066	$140000	(2-Oct-90 CH.NY205/R) Vase de fleurs (63x48cm-25x19in) s.d.68
£75911	$148785	(24-Nov-90 APT.P95/R) Vase aux dahlias (73x54cm-29x21in) s.d.1971 (F.FR 750000)
£81218	$160000	(14-Nov-90 SY.NY460/R) Tulipes jaune (100x65cm-39x26in) s.d.1958
£86735	$170000	(15-Feb-91 SY.NY115/R) Vase de calalilies (92x73cm-36x29in) s.d.56
£88710	$170323	(2-Dec-90 GAB.G1541/R) Les begonias (65x50cm-26x20in) s.d.1978 (S.FR 220000)
£88832	$175000	(2-Oct-90 CH.NY212/R) Pichet de fleurs (92x65cm-36x26in) s.d.56
£91371	$180000	(3-Oct-90 SY.NY196/R) Maisons au bord de l'eau (79x127cm-31x50in) s.d.64

BUFFET, Bernard (1928-) French-cont.

£91371	$180000	(3-Oct-90 SY.NY197/R) Le jeu (81x60cm-32x24in) s.d.59
£96447	$190000	(3-Oct-90 SY.NY181/R) Vase de chardon (100x65cm-39x26in) s.d.61
£96939	$190000	(14-Feb-91 CH.NY94/R) Ile de Brehat (90x131cm-35x52in) s.d.1973
		l.d.8/7/73 verso
£101523	$200000	(3-Oct-90 SY.NY183/R) Nature morte aux fruits (54x65cm-21x26in) s.d.57
£104046	$180000	(9-May-91 CH.NY263/R) Femme assise (218x194cm-86x76in) s.d.53
£106599	$210000	(3-Oct-90 SY.NY205/R) Peniche sur la canal (89x129cm-35x51in) s.d.1971
£111336	$218219	(24-Nov-90 APT.P93/R) Les volliers bretons (89x130cm-35x51in) s.d.64
		(F.FR 1100000)
£111675	$220000	(15-Nov-90 CH.NY294/R) Vase de fleurs (73x60cm-29x24in) s.d.69
£111675	$220000	(15-Nov-90 CH.NY300/R) Bouquet aux dahlias rouges (100x65cm-39x26in)
		s.d.67
£122449	$240000	(15-Feb-91 SY.NY122/R) Nature morte (81x61cm-32x24in) s.d.64
£127168	$220000	(9-May-91 CH.NY270/R) Nature morte (81x102cm-32x40in) s.d.62
£162437	$320000	(3-Oct-90 SY.NY184/R) Bouquet jaune et bleu (93x73cm-37x29in) s.d.65
£208122	$410000	(15-Nov-90 CH.NY293/R) Dahlias (147x98cm-58x39in) s.d.1964
£253807	$500000	(15-Nov-90 CH.NY285/R) Ombelles et delphiniums (97x161cm-38x63in) s.d.65
		l.verso
£864	$1417	(19-Jun-91 JM.P75) La femme du boucher (22x27cm-9x11in) s. lead pencil
		(F.FR 8600)
£1309	$2500	(1-Jan-91 GG.TA244/R) Nude (16x19cm-6x7in) s.
£2008	$3233	(25-Jun-91 BG.P10/R) Arbre dans la plaine (37x24cm-15x9in) s.d.53 crayon
		(F.FR 20000)
£2126	$4166	(19-Nov-90 ARC.P13/R) Profil (30x23cm-12x9in) s. pen (F.FR 21000)
£2679	$5250	(12-Feb-91 SY.NY118/R) Portrait of M Blot (71x53cm-28x21in) s.i. chl
£2820	$4596	(16-Jun-91 GL.P4/R) Autoportrait dans l'atelier (32x24cm-13x9in)
		s.d.1950 Indian ink lead pencil (F.FR 28000)
£3049	$5000	(19-Jun-91 B.SF1819/R) La femme nue (13x18cm-5x7in) s. pencil
£3303	$5715	(22-May-91 CH.AM532/R) Rose (49x31cm-19x12in) s. pen (D.FL 11000)
£4355	$7143	(19-Jun-91 F.M64/R) Torero (65x50cm-26x20in) s. mixed media paper on
		cardboard (I.L 9500000)
£5594	$10853	(7-Dec-90 GB.B6391/R) Esquisse pour la Passion (36x75cm-14x30in)
		s.i.d.1953 pencil dr (DM 16000)
£6042	$9849	(15-Jun-91 FB.P64/R) Elephant (65x100cm-26x39in) s.d.53 Indian ink
		(F.FR 60000)
£8122	$16000	(2-Oct-90 CH.NY154/R) Rue du village (50x64cm-20x25in) s.d.52 Indian ink
£9137	$18000	(2-Oct-90 CH.NY155/R) Le chemin de fer (50x64cm-20x25in) s.d.53 pencil
£15000	$29100	(4-Dec-90 C223/R) Vase de fleurs (49x64cm-19x25in) s.d.61 col.crayon
		pastel oil ink
£16497	$32500	(3-Oct-90 SY.NY190/R) Girafe (98x64cm-39x25in) s.d.53 india ink
£17500	$30975	(20-Mar-91 S64/R) Les bateaux sur la Seine (47x61cm-19x24in) s.d.69
		gouache W/C crayon indian ink pencil
£17857	$30000	(28-Apr-91 LIT.L155) Harbour scene with lighthouse (48x64cm-19x25in)
		s.d.61 gouache masonite with letter
£19000	$37050	(19-Oct-90 C213/R) La rue abandonnee (50x65cm-20x26in) s.d.53 pen ink
		pencil
£19368	$32733	(15-Apr-91 SY.J415/R) Hotel de la mer (48x63cm-19x25in) s.d.68 W/C ink
		pencil (SA.R 92000)
£19898	$39000	(14-Feb-91 CH.NY104/R) Barques a maree basse (49x65cm-19x26in) s.d.70
		W/C col.crayons indian ink over pencil
£20231	$35000	(9-May-91 CH.NY175/R) Nature mrote aux oursins (48x62cm-19x24in) s.d.49
		ink gouache over pencil paper on board
£21000	$37170	(20-Mar-91 S88/R) Clown (62x47cm-24x19in) s.d.68 gouache W/C col.chk
		indian ink pencil
£22959	$45000	(15-Feb-91 SY.NY114/R) Boite a Sel (50x65cm-20x26in) s.d.50 ink pencil
		paper on canvas on masonite
£24490	$48000	(14-Feb-91 CH.NY71/R) Vase de fleurs (65x51cm-26x20in) s.d.59 W/C crayon
		indian ink paper on masonite
£27919	$55000	(2-Oct-90 CH.NY199/R) Nature morte a l'oeuf sur le plat et bouteille
		(50x65cm-20x26in) s.d.55 W/C Indian ink brush
£30090	$58676	(9-Oct-90 CSC.P82/R) Lampe a petrole, oursins et oignon
		(50x64cm-20x25in) s.d.49 pen htd. (F.FR 300000)
£31472	$62000	(15-Nov-90 CH.NY194/R) Margoulies (65x51cm-26x20in) s.d.63 W/C col.wax
		crayon pencil paper on canvas
£31472	$62000	(2-Oct-90 CH.NY200/R) Bouquet dans le cafetiere (65x50cm-26x20in) s.d.66
		gouache crayons India ink pencil masonite

BUFFET, Maurice (17th C) French

£504	$821	(10-Jun-91 NM.P54) Le mas perche (46x55cm-18x22in) s. (F.FR 5000)

BUFFET, Paul (1864-?) French

£612	$1200	(6-Nov-90 GF.L2390/R) Landscape (50x73cm-20x29in) s. (S.FR 1500)

BUGATTI, Ettore (1881-1947) Italian

£1058	$2064	(28-Oct-90 PLF.P163/R) Etude de carrosserie (12x20cm-5x8in) s.d.1946
		crayon (F.FR 10500)

BUGATTI, Ettore and Rembrandt (20th C) Italian

£1230	$2398	(28-Oct-90 PLF.P164/R) La fusee (22x19cm-9x7in) bears sigs. pen
		double-sided (F.FR 12200)

BUGATTI, Rembrandt (1885-1916) French?

£547	$952	(25-Mar-91 QWA.P139) Ours dansant (24x31cm-9x12in) st.sig. oil crayons
		(F.FR 5500)

BUGATTI, Rembrandt (1885-1916) French?-cont.
£2300 $3749   *(1-Jul-91 APT.P398/R) Lionne couchee (32x64cm-13x25in) st.sig.*
                chl.htd.W/C (F.FR 23000)
£3600 $5868   *(1-Jul-91 APT.P370) Autoportrait (22x20cm-9x8in) st.sig. lead pencil*
                drawing (F.FR 36000)

BUGIARDINI, Giulio (1475-1554) Italian
£19137 $32532   (30-May-91 F.M65/R) San Sebastiano (130x45cm-51x18in) panel
                 (I.L 42000000)
£223529 $380000   (30-May-91 SY.NY16/R) Virgin and child, castle on hilltop beyond
                 (87x65cm-34x26in) touches gilt panel

BUGNON, Roland (1939-) Swiss
£717 $1233   (14-May-91 GF.L2702/R) Composition (60x50cm-24x20in) s.d.1968
                (S.FR 1800)
£562 $1102   *(24-Nov-90 AB.L253/R) Surreal composition (45x56cm-18x22in) s.i.d.1972*
                indian ink bodycol (S.FR 1400)

BUHLER, Robert (1916-1989) British
£550 $897   (12-Jun-91 ZZ.B71) Snow, Bordenwood (40x46cm-16x18in) s. d.1945 verso
                canvasboard
£1200 $2340   (9-Oct-90 B13/R) Woman in striped jumper (46x30cm-18x12in) s. board

BUHLMANN, Johann Rudolf (1802-1890) Swiss
£4898 $9600   (6-Nov-90 GF.L2223/R) View of Basilica, Poseidon and Athene Temples, Bay
                of Salerno (38x88cm-15x35in) s.d.43 (S.FR 12000)
£8201 $13942   (28-May-91 F.R133/R) I templi di Paestum (38x88cm-15x35in) s.d.38
                (I.L 18000000)
£873 $1563   *(13-Mar-91 GK.Z8) Vierwaldstattersee with fishermen and view of*
                Urirotstock (56x76cm-22x30in) s.d. pastel (S.FR 2200)

BUHOT, Felix (1847-1898) French
£1158 $2200   *(9-Jan-91 CH.NY60/R) Chevalier destouches (32x20cm-13x8in) s. pastel W/C*

BUILLY, C (19/20th C) French?
£1131 $2193   *(6-Dec-90 CB.P84) Long-courrier en panne, par grand calme, attendant son*
                canot (29x45cm-11x18in) s. W/C gouache (F.FR 11000)

BUISSERET, Louis (20th C) Belgian
£2958 $5768   (23-Oct-90 C.A318/R) Still life (34x49cm-13x19in) s.d.1941 panel
                (B.FR 180000)

BUIZARD, A (19th C) ?
£2308 $4500   *(26-Oct-90 SY.NY75/R) Study of archer (39x29cm-15x11in) s.d.1820 W/C*

BUKOVAC, Vlacho (1855-1923) Yugoslavian
£1500 $2505   (4-Jun-91 SWS1678/R) Deposition of Christ (100x161cm-39x63in) s.i.d.1905

BULKLEY, C (19th C) British
£467 $935   *(4-Feb-91 PLF.P26) Le musicien nocturne (19x25cm-7x10in) s.i.d.1834 W/C*
                (F.FR 4600)

BULL, Charles Livingston (1874-1932) American
£706 $1200   *(1-Jun-91 IH.NY26/R) Fox family (30x46cm-12x18in) s. chl ink*

BULL, Knud Geelmuyden (1811-1889) Norwegian
£17361 $28993   (4-Jun-91 BU.O70/R) Landscape from Fortundalen (98x122cm-39x48in)
                s.d.1836 (N.KR 200000)
£16988 $33467   *(13-Nov-90 J.M146 a/R) City of Hobart Town (35x59cm-14x23in) W/C*
                (A.D 44000)

BULLEID, George Lawrence (1858-1933) British
£2300 $4531   *(13-Nov-90 SWS88/R) A classical maiden (52x39cm-20x15in) s.d.MDCCCC W/C*
                over traces pencil
£2400 $4728   *(13-Nov-90 SWS87/R) A Roman beauty (53x40cm-21x16in) s.d.MDCCCC W/C over*
                traces pencil
£2800 $5292   *(26-Sep-90 S345/R) Maiden of baths (46x31cm-18x12in) s.d.MCMXXIII W/C*

BULLEY, Ashburnham H (19th C) British
£2200 $4092   (5-Sep-90 BT227/R) Study of two King Charles Spaniels (28x38cm-11x15in)
                s.d.1861 board

BULLINGER, Johann-Balthazar (elder) (1713-1793) Swiss
£1154 $2227   (13-Dec-90 N.M2662/R) Portrait of gentleman (82x65cm-32x26in)
                s.indis.d.1736 (DM 3300)

BULMER, Lionel (20th C) British
£1269 $2500   (15-Nov-90 SY.NY66) Shell and window, second study (15x22cm-6x9in) init.
                masonite

BUMMERSTEDT, Heinrich (1883-?) German
£600 $1074   (12-Apr-91 BM.B447) Allegory of Caritas with woman seated and two
                infants in landscape (120x90cm-47x35in) s. (DM 1800)

BUNBURY, Henry William (1750-1811) British
£550 $924   *(22-Apr-91 PH208/R) The gaming table (30x40cm-12x16in) ink W/C*

274

BUNCE, William Gedney (1840-1916) British
£947   *$1600*   *(17-Apr-91 D.NY61) Venice (30x51cm-12x20in) s.i. i.d.94 verso pastel*

BUNDEL, Willem van den (1575-?) Dutch
£21084 $33946   (25-Jun-91 APT.P13/R) Paysge de foret avec des chasseurs
                     (29x43cm-11x17in) panel (F.FR 210000)

BUNDY, Edgar (1862-1922) British
£1050 $2058   (13-Feb-91 S158/R) Conversation piece (30x30cm-12x12in) s.
£1800 $3006   (24-Jul-91 CSK49) The agreement (130x193cm-51x76in) s.
£2800 $5292   (27-Sep-90 CSK108/R) Visiting the Physician (101x137cm-40x54in) s.
£3800 $6536   (16-May-91 CSK54/R) Visit to physician (102x137cm-40x54in) s.
£3800 $6726   (21-Mar-91 CSK235/R) The agreement (51x76cm-20x30in) s.
£1500   *$2520*   *(15-Jul-91 PH116/R) When rogues are out (50x66cm-20x26in) s. i.verso W/C*
                     htd white
£1600   *$3200*   *(8-Feb-91 C58/R) Gossips, Huntsmen in the interior on an Inn flirting*
                     with a barmaid (36x53cm-14x21in) s. i. verso pencil W/C htd.white

BUNDY, Elizabeth E (fl.1851-1858) British
£2183 $4127   (27-Sep-90 D.V44/R) Girl reading seated at table with with books and
                     bunch of flowers (62x50cm-24x20in) s.d.1866 (A.S 45000)

BUNEL, Francois (younger-style) (16th C) French
£753 $1212   (27-Jun-91 APT.P152/R) Portrait de Henri IV (61x50cm-24x20in)
                     (F.FR 7500)

BUNKE, Franz (1857-?) German
£1200 $2148   (12-Apr-91 BM.B572/R) Woods in autumn (150x110cm-59x43in) s. (DM 3600)

BUNKELL, M A (?) ?
£1200 $2376   (30-Jan-91 CSK332) Cupids with flowers. Cupids with grapes
                     (56x46cm-22x18in) one i. verso after J H Fragonard ovals two

BUNN, Fanny (fl.1896-1921) British
£420   *$701*   *(5-Jun-91 PHK96) La Belle Dame Sans Merci (16x17cm-6x7in) s.i. W/C*
                     bodycol.
£540   *$902*   *(5-Jun-91 PHK99) The victor (22x13cm-9x5in) s.i. W/C bodycol.*

BUNNY, Rupert Charles Wulsten (1864-1947) Australian
£522 $1002   (26-Nov-90 SY.ME146/R) Provencal landscape (20x21cm-8x8in) board
                     (A.D 1300)
£605 $1016   (22-Apr-91 SY.ME157) French Provincial landscape (14x23cm-6x9in) card
                     (A.D 1300)
£698 $1172   (22-Apr-91 SY.ME176) French landscape study (14x23cm-6x9in) paper on
                     board (A.D 1500)
£1023 $1719   (22-Apr-91 SY.ME187) Landscape with mountain (14x23cm-6x9in) paper on
                     board (A.D 2200)
£1688 $2988   (18-Mar-91 MGS.S308) Bathers (15x14cm-6x6in) cardboard (A.D 3950)
£2326 $3907   (22-Apr-91 SY.ME228/R) Poplar wood, 1920's (37x44cm-15x17in) mono.
                     i.verso (A.D 5000)
£2326 $3907   (22-Apr-91 SY.ME227/R) Madame Lul Gardo in peasant costume
                     (57x42cm-22x17in) canvas on board (A.D 5000)
£3256 $5470   (22-Apr-91 SY.ME365/R) Profile of lady in pink (39x31cm-15x12in)
                     (A.D 7000)
£3721 $6251   (22-Apr-91 SY.ME280/R) Yellow scarf - portrait of Henry Handel
                     Richardson (44x36cm-17x14in) mono. i.verso (A.D 8000)
£5581 $9377   (22-Apr-91 SY.ME362/R) Overlooking gorge (53x64cm-21x25in) mono. i.verso
                     (A.D 12000)
£6944 $11944   (15-May-91 CN.P96/R) Autoportrait (81x54cm-32x21in) s.i.d.1911
                     (F.FR 70000)
£7442 $12502   (22-Apr-91 SY.ME321/R) Self-portrait (103x65cm-41x26in) (A.D 16000)
£11163 $18753   (22-Apr-91 SY.ME308/R) Enemy listens (54x65cm-21x26in) i.stretcher
                     (A.D 24000)
£13023 $21879   (22-Apr-91 SY.ME291/R) Two nude women on beach (73x60cm-29x24in)
                     (A.D 28000)
£28000 $54320   (6-Dec-90 CSK21/R) Hay boats, Brittany (51x81cm-20x32in) s. i.stretcher
£50696 $85676   (21-Apr-91 DA.R1/R) Deux femmes dans un jardin (81x54cm-32x21in) s.
                     (F.FR 510000)
£490   *$823*   *(18-Jul-91 PHX264) Elegant lady seated in interior (30x25cm-12x10in)*
                     s.i. monowash

BUNTZEN, Heinrich (1802-1892) Danish
£538 $1075   (6-Feb-91 RAS.K70) View of Sorrento Bay (25x37cm-10x15in) mono.d.1825
                     (D.KR 6000)
£1553 $2934   (27-Sep-90 D.V12/R) Dutch harbour scene with view of town
                     (18x24cm-7x9in) s. panel (A.S 32000)
£2183 $4127   (27-Sep-90 D.V13/R) Dutch harbour scene with view of town
                     (18x24cm-7x9in) s. panel (A.S 45000)
£2238 $4319   (14-Dec-90 BM.B596/R) Ruin of Italian house with dog by painting
                     utensils, snowy peaks beyond (64x79cm-25x31in) s.d.1840 i.verso
                     (DM 6400)
£2729 $4585   (22-Apr-91 BU.K1/R) Rafael's studio in Tivoli off Rome (36x46cm-14x18in)
                     s.d.1859 (D.KR 31000)

BUNZI, Biddy (20th C) British
£750 $1298   (7-May-91 PH90/R) Vase, view through (179x119cm-70x47in)

BUONACCORSI, Pietro (1500-c.1546) Italian
£1842 $3500   (8-Jan-91 SY.NY58) Sheet of studies of figures in classical dress
                      (22x19cm-9x7in) ink
£1900 $3667   (12-Dec-90 PH291/R) Designs for sarcophagus perhaps for Frederico
                      Gonzaga III (27x22cm-11x9in) i. pen ink
£2736 $4843   (19-Mar-91 F.M302/R) Studio di figura inginocchiata (17x12cm-7x5in)
                      bears i. sanguine (I.L 6000000)
£4600 $8878   (12-Dec-90 PH288/R) Design for ceiling decoration (18x29cm-7x11in) pen
                      ink
£5016 $8878   (19-Mar-91 F.M301/R) Foglio di studi con combattimento di cavalli e
                      gambe maschili (12x19cm-5x7in) i. bistre ink (I.L 11000000)
£7500 $14475   (12-Dec-90 PH294/R) Studies of eagle, candelabra and capitol. Endymion
                      sarcophagus, palazzoand winged monster (24x40cm-9x16in) indis.i. ink
                      double-sided
£50000 $95000   (8-Jan-91 SY.NY50/R) Design for a wall decoration with the adoration of
                      the Magi and scenes from the passion of Christ (41x27cm-16x11in) bears
                      i. ink wash

BUONACCORSI, Pietro (attrib) (1500-c.1546) Italian
£2237 $4250   (8-Jan-91 SY.NY56/R) The Madonna and child (25x19cm-10x7in) ink wash
                      over blk.chk.

BUONO, Leon Giuseppe (1888-?) Italian
£636 $1247   (21-Nov-90 F.M172) Dall'alto, Pozzuoli (50x40cm-20x16in) s. s.i.verso
                      masonite (I.L 1400000)
£988 $1700   (18-May-91 W.W46/R) Coastal scene with fishermen (51x71cm-20x28in) s.

BURBANK, Elbridge Ayer (1858-1949) American
£1523 $3000   (16-Nov-90 E.EDM712/R) Portrait of Chief Geronimo Apache
                      (36x28cm-14x11in) s.d.1898 board
£1890 $3250   (15-May-91 SY.NY121/R) Chief Geronimo, Apache. Chief Pretty Eagle,
                      Apache (33x23cm-13x9in) one s.i. one s. pair

BURCH, Henry Jacob (1763-?) British
£1100 $1815   (10-Jul-91 C90/R) Mrs Henry Rice (6x?cm-2x?in) min. maple wood frame
                      oval

BURCH, Henry Jacob (attrib) (1763-?) British
£500 $820   (18-Jun-91 CSK27/R) Gentleman facing left in coat shirt and cravat with
                      powdered hair (7x?cm-3x?in) min. mono.verso coronet on guilloche foil
                      oval

BURCHARTZ, Max (?) German?
£956 $1873   (22-Nov-90 L.K856) Figures with toys (38x51cm-15x20in) s.d.1921 indian
                      ink pen (DM 2800)

BURCHFIELD, Charles (1893-1967) American
£615 $1200   (20-Oct-90 BRA.N41) Untitled mono.d.1917 chl
£1156 $2000   (21-May-91 CE.NY679/R) Tree that reached sky (56x34cm-22x13in) artist
                      st. num.8 chl
£2035 $3500   (15-May-91 SY.NY219 a/R) House by shore (23x30cm-9x12in) d.6-16-1916
                      verso W/C pencil
£2629 $5100   (5-Dec-90 D.NY43/R) Road in the rain, East of Varysburg, New York
                      (53x76cm-21x30in) mono.d.1936 W/C
£3468 $6000   (23-May-91 SY.NY82/R) Old farmhouse (37x53cm-15x21in) init.d.1931 W/C
£6704 $12000   (14-Mar-91 CH.NY201/R) Alley in Salem, Ohio (40x53cm-16x21in)
                      init.d.1917 i.d.1917 verso W/C paper on board
£8671 $15000   (23-May-91 SY.NY75/R) Winter sunshine (71x58cm-28x23in) init.d.1938
                      d.1938 verso W/C
£10983 $19000   (23-May-91 SY.NY83/R) Bridge in rain, Buffalo Harbour (61x75cm-24x30in)
                      init.d.1938 W/C
£14583 $28000   (30-Nov-90 CH.NY196/R) Maytime (45x55cm-18x22in) s.d.1917 W/ pencil
                      paper on board
£40462 $70000   (22-May-91 CH.NY313/R) Lynx woods (83x100cm-33x39in) bears st. W/C
                      pencil chk.paper laid down board
£49133 $85000   (23-May-91 SY.NY76/R) Late winter dawn (126x83cm-50x33in) init.d.1956-65
                      W/C paperboard

BURDIN (?) French?
£1190 $2048   (19-May-91 ZZ.F42/R) Trois mats a quai (41x65cm-16x26in) s. (F.FR 12000)

BUREN, Daniel (1938-) French
£10651 $18000   (2-May-91 CH.NY218/R) Blanc et orange (100x134cm-39x53in) acrylic
                      printed fabric

BURESCH, Anton (1876-1960) Austrian
£8000 $13120   (19-Jun-91 S89/R) Widowhood (157x199cm-62x78in) s.d.1907

BURFIELD, James M (19th C) British?
£3142 $6189   (14-Nov-90 RAS.K148/R) Lover's tiff (77x105cm-30x41in) s.d.82
                      (D.KR 35000)

BURGARITSKI, Joseph (1836-1890) Austrian
£1399 $2699   (14-Dec-90 BM.B597/R) Post station in Garmisch with horses and coach and
                      travellers by well (69x107cm-27x42in) s. i.verso (DM 4000)

BURGARITSKI, Joseph (1836-1890) Austrian-cont.
£2055 $3349   (12-Jun-91 N.M385/R) Horse drawn coach before farmhouse near Garmisch
                             (69x106cm-27x42in) s. (DM 6000)

BURGARITSKI, Joseph (attrib) (1836-1890) Austrian
£1067 $2017   (27-Sep-90 D.V49/R) View of Alpine lake (74x100cm-29x39in) bears sig.
                             (A.S 22000)

BURGDORFF, Ferdinand (1881-?) American
£918 $1800   (13-Feb-91 B.SF2161/R) Forty centuries (60x122cm-24x48in) s.d.1948 board

BURGE, Maude (20th C) New Zealander
£774 $1517   (7-Nov-90 DS.W57) Arched Spanish courtyard (35x44cm-14x17in) (NZ.D 2500)
£1237 $2091   (17-Apr-91 DS.W16) Dans le jardin, Chateaux des Deux Rives
                             (46x57cm-18x22in) s.verso (NZ.D 3600)
*£412 $697   (17-Apr-91 DS.W29) Still life of lillies and fruit (39x45cm-15x18in) W/C
                             (NZ.D 1200)*
£433 $850   (7-Nov-90 DS.W111/R) Portrait (40x30cm-16x12in) W/C (NZ.D 1400)
£452 $765   (16-Apr-91 J.M335) On the beach (27x36cm-11x14in) s. W/C (A.D 1000)
*£464 $910   (7-Nov-90 DS.W108) Village duck pond (33x40cm-13x16in) gouache
                             (NZ.D 1500)*
*£464 $910   (7-Nov-90 DS.W13/R) Beach scene with figures and tent (33x38cm-13x15in)
                             W/C (NZ.D 1500)*
£526 $1032   (7-Nov-90 DS.W22/R) Floral still life (35x40cm-14x16in) W/C (NZ.D 1700)
*£526 $1032   (7-Nov-90 DS.W44) Cafe scene with figures (33x38cm-13x15in) W/C
                             (NZ.D 1700)*
*£588 $1153   (7-Nov-90 DS.W5) Dock scene with sailboats (34x40cm-13x16in) W/C
                             (NZ.D 1900)*
*£650 $1274   (7-Nov-90 DS.W6) Riverside house and path (40x32cm-16x13in) W/C
                             (NZ.D 2100)*
£687 $1162   (17-Apr-91 DS.W82) Still life W/C (NZ.D 2000)
£756 $1278   (17-Apr-91 DS.W49) Rural homestead (32x40cm-13x16in) W/C (NZ.D 2200)
*£929 $1820   (7-Nov-90 DS.W89) Sail boats on lake (27x34cm-11x13in) s. W/C
                             (NZ.D 3000)*
*£1393 $2731   (7-Nov-90 DS.W3/R) Mediterranean village and sail boats
                             (39x45cm-15x18in) s. W/C (NZ.D 4500)*

BURGER, Josef (1887-) German
£1433 $2709   (25-Sep-90 FN.S2128) Still life of flowers on draped table with view of
                             river landscape (62x77cm-24x30in) s.i. (DM 4200)
£2600 $5096   (22-Nov-90 CSK89/R) Still life of mixed flowers beside window, extensive
                             landscape beyond (74x63cm-29x25in) s.i.

BURGER-MUHLFELD, Fritz (1882-?) German
£811 $1581   (20-Oct-90 WK.M71/R) Composition (60x80cm-24x31in) s. (DM 2400)
£1024 $2007   (22-Nov-90 L.K857/R) Composition (33x32cm-13x13in) s.d.1957 board
                             (DM 3000)

BURGER-WILLING, Hans Willi (1882-1969) German
£544 $876   (26-Jun-91 KM.K1407) Eifel landscape with shepherd and flock
                             (60x80cm-24x31in) s. (DM 1600)
£612 $1084   (20-Mar-91 KM.K1130) Peasant with horses in Eifel landscape
                             (90x104cm-35x41in) s. (DM 1800)
£680 $1095   (26-Jun-91 KM.K1406) Peasant woman with cattle grazing before wood
                             (38x52cm-15x20in) s. panel (DM 2000)
£680 $1204   (20-Mar-91 KM.K1129) Peasant woman and three goats in Eifel landscape
                             (90x120cm-35x47in) s. (DM 2000)

BURGERS, Felix (1870-?) German
£1438 $2575   (13-Mar-91 N.M459/R) Lake Barmsee with view of Zugspitz mountain
                             (51x64cm-20x25in) s. (DM 4200)
£2028 $3914   (12-Dec-90 WE.MU170/R) Twilight (66x88cm-26x35in) s. s.i.verso
                             (DM 5800)

BURGERS, Hendricus Jacobus (1834-1899) Dutch
£3625 $5909   (10-Jun-91 NM.P4/R) La jeune fille sur l'echelle (65x45cm-26x18in)
                             (F.FR 36000)

BURGESS OF DOVER, William (1805-1861) British
£980 $1617   (9-Jul-91 PH146/R) Boats on estuary with figures beyond
                             (25x61cm-10x24in) s.
*£950 $1596   (22-Apr-91 PH230) Soldiers on guard at Dover Castle. Baggage train near
                             Canterbury (27x42cm-11x17in) init. W/C bodycol.over pencil pair*

BURGESS, Arthur James Wetherall (1879-1956) Australian
£549 $1053   (14-Aug-90 SY.ME121/R) Baron Inverclyde (49x75cm-19x30in) s. canvas on
                             board (A.D 1300)
£650 $1105   (30-May-91 C179/R) Paddle steamer William Fawcett (33x43cm-13x17in) s.
                             board
£1200 $2040   (30-May-91 C182/R) Under tow (46x61cm-18x24in) s.
£1500 $2550   (30-May-91 C181/R) Off Scillies (46x61cm-18x24in) s. i.verso
£1995 $3750   (19-Sep-90 B.SF2690/R) Australian landscape in the moonlight
                             (91x76cm-36x30in) s.d.1917
£2000 $3720   (5-Sep-90 BT235/R) In tow on flowing tide (74x99cm-29x39in) s.
£2400 $4152   (22-May-91 S169/R) In tow (73x91cm-29x36in) s.

BURGESS, Arthur James Wetherall (1879-1956) Australian-cont.
£6500	$12675	(10-Oct-90 S34/R) The Royal Yacht Victoria and Albert at Cowes (46x56cm-18x22in) s.i.d.05 board
£506	$972	(14-Aug-90 SY.ME43/R) Steamship of the coast (56x78cm-22x31in) s. W/C (A.D 1200)
£900	$1557	(21-May-91 CD58/R) On Thames, tugs manoeuvering steamship, sailing barge in background (36x51cm-14x20in) s. W/C

BURGESS, Eliza Mary (1873-?) British
£580	$1114	(19-Feb-91 SWS326) Autumnal berries (52x36cm-20x14in) s.d.1929 i.verso W/C

BURGESS, Frederick (fl.1882-1892) British
£1448	$2852	(13-Nov-90 J.M338) A view of Repulse Bay, Queensland (34x50cm-13x20in) s. s.i.d.87verso (A.D 3750)

BURGESS, John (1814-1874) British
£800	$1304	(14-Jun-91 C139/R) The Chateau at Dieppe (35x59cm-14x23in) pencil W/C htd.white

BURGESS, John Bagnold (1830-1897) British
£3600	$6012	(5-Jun-91 S200/R) Offering (66x48cm-26x19in) s.
£4000	$7840	(13-Feb-91 S143/R) Spanish gypsy girl (101x74cm-40x29in) s.

BURGH, Pieter Daniel van der (1805-1879) Dutch
£1351	$2297	(31-May-91 GB.B5717/R) View of Dutch town by canal (26x36cm-10x14in) s. panel (DM 4000)

BURGMEIER, Max (1881-1947) Swiss
£600	$1014	(1-May-91 GD.B114/R) Coastal landscape, South of France (60x77cm-24x30in) st.studio verso (S.FR 1500)
£600	$1014	(1-May-91 GD.B116/R) Snowy river landscape, Bundner Land (83x73cm-33x29in) mono.d.16 (S.FR 1500)

BURI, Max (1868-1915) Swiss
£6426	$12594	(21-Nov-90 SY.Z53/R) Portrait of artist's wife (44x44cm-17x17in) s.d.1914 (S.FR 16000)
£14741	$28745	(24-Oct-90 GD.B197/R) Brienzersee lake landscape with view of village (57x72cm-22x28in) s. (S.FR 37000)

BURI, Samuel (20th C) ?
£1587	$2603	(19-Jun-91 GK.B244) Will the sun come out, souvenir du Guggershornli (74x163cm-29x64in) s. i.d.1958 (S.FR 4000)
£898	$1706	(14-Sep-90 ZOF.Z1044/R) Composition in grey and white (30x20cm-12x8in) s. mixed media (S.FR 2200)
£1143	$2171	(14-Sep-90 ZOF.Z1045/R) Printemps (23x15cm-9x6in) s. mixed media (S.FR 2800)
£1984	$3433	(25-May-91 AB.L68/R) America (65x50cm-26x20in) s. oil mixed media (S.FR 5000)
£3469	$6800	(6-Nov-90 GF.L2585/R) Chalet complique (97x130cm-38x51in) s.i.d.1967verso mixed media (S.FR 8500)
£3673	$7237	(16-Nov-90 EA.Z340/R) Les choux (73x102cm-29x40in) s.d.1975 mixed media (S.FR 9000)

BURINI, Antonio (1656-1727) Italian
£600	$978	(1-Jul-91 S154/R) Caricature of cleric (25x18cm-10x7in) bears i. pen wash over red chk

BURINI, Antonio (style) (1656-1727) Italian
£6200	$12090	(22-Oct-90 SWS1403/R) Joseph interpreting Pharaoh's dream (21x32cm-8x13in) paper on board

BURKE, Augustus (19th C) British
£900	$1701	(26-Sep-90 S188/R) Bretons by door (81x65cm-32x26in) s.

BURKEL, Heinrich (1802-1869) German
£1333	$2600	(27-Oct-90 LIT.L101) Peasants in Vosges mountains (36x25cm-14x10in) s.
£5137	$8373	(12-Jun-91 N.M382/R) Horses grazing and shepherd by gate in Alpine landscape (34x48cm-13x19in) mono. (DM 15000)
£6507	$10606	(12-Jun-91 N.M383/R) Peasants and cows on path in Alpine landscape after thunderstorm (32x42cm-13x17in) paper on canvas (DM 19000)
£10490	$20245	(12-Dec-90 N.M455/R) Winter landscape with washerwomen by frozen river and farmhouses nearby (24x33cm-9x13in) s. canvas on panel (DM 30000)
£14384	$23445	(12-Jun-91 SY.MU56/R) The approaching storm (35x52cm-14x20in) s. panel (DM 42000)
£22260	$36284	(12-Jun-91 N.M381/R) Mountain landscape with figures, carts and animals before tavern (42x57cm-17x22in) (DM 65000)
£25685	$45976	(13-Mar-91 N.M460/R) Smugglers resting on path by wayside memorial in rocky mountain landscape (37x32cm-15x13in) s.d.1835 panel (DM 75000)
£26012	$45000	(22-May-91 SY.NY34/R) Mountain well (27x39cm-11x15in) s.d.1845 paper on board
£31469	$60734	(12-Dec-90 SY.MU31/R) Haycart on mountain road (35x42cm-14x17in) s.d.1829 panel (DM 90000)
£49133	$85000	(23-May-91 CH.NY116/R) Uberfall auf eine Reisekutsche (41x53cm-16x21in) s.

BURKEL, Heinrich (1802-1869) German-cont.
£612 $1206   *(13-Nov-90 GF.L5030) Study of two peasants seated and standing (16x21cm-6x8in) W/C over pencil (S.FR 1500)*

BURKEL, Heinrich (attrib) (1802-1869) German
£1027 $1675   (12-Jun-91 N.M384/R) Peasant woman with cattle at Alpine summer farm and view into valley (22x34cm-9x13in) paper on board (DM 3000)

BURKHARD, Ernst (19/20th C) Swiss
£600 $1014   (1-May-91 GD.B119/R) Alpine lake landscape (60x85cm-24x33in) s.d.1925 (S.FR 1500)

BURKHARDT, Emerson C (1905-1969) American
£1031 $2000   (24-Aug-90 RB.HY154/R) Fantasy (64x76cm-25x30in) s. masonite
£1031 $2000   (24-Aug-90 RB.HY198/R) Summer street scene in Provincetown (51x61cm-20x24in) s.
£3968 $7500   (27-Sep-90 CH.NY266/R) Fragmentary history of the iron age (77x99cm-30x39in)

BURKHARDT, Hans Gustav (1904-) American
£769 $1500   *(24-Oct-90 B.SF1487/R) Figure study (62x48cm-24x19in) s.d.1941 pastel*

BURLEIGH, Averil (20th C) British
£2700 $5292   (6-Nov-90 PH75/R) Rest by the way (40x43cm-16x17in) s. tempera over pencil panel

BURLEIGH, C H H (1875-1956) British
£1700 $3315   (10-Oct-90 S37/R) Spanish church (41x51cm-16x20in) s.
£2000 $3900   (10-Oct-90 S66/R) The town square (61x51cm-24x20in) s.

BURLEIGH, Veronica (20th C) British
£700 $1379   (1-Nov-90 B52) At the kitchen sink (102x76cm-40x30in) s.

BURLINGAME, Dennis Meighan (20th C) American
£2601 $4500   (21-May-91 CE.NY520/R) Side show, Ballyhoo (61x76cm-24x30in) s.

BURLISON, Clement (19th C) British
£6000 $10140   (30-Apr-91 PH110/R) Cupid and Psyche (61x50cm-24x20in) init.d.1856

BURLIUK, David (1882-1967) Russian/American
£610 $1000   (19-Jun-91 B.SF1875/R) Italian coastal scene (40x35cm-16x14in) s.i.d.1954 canvas board
£610 $1000   (19-Jun-91 B.SF1874/R) Monarch Park, Colorado (30x55cm-12x22in) s.i.verso panel
£690 $1324   (26-Nov-90 WK.M133/R) Girl and horse (13x17cm-5x7in) s. panel (DM 2000)
£781 $1500   (17-Dec-90 SY.NY369/R) Fish pier (25x36cm-10x14in) s.d.1951 board
£833 $1600   (20-Feb-91 D.NY16) Dinner time (30x41cm-12x16in) s.d.1946 canvasboard
£847 $1600   (29-Sep-90 YFA.M14/R) Flowers in vase (61x81cm-24x32in) s. board
£885 $1700   (17-Dec-90 SY.NY368/R) Winter sleigh rides (28x36cm-11x14in) s.
£930 $1600   (15-May-91 SY.NY183/R) Picnic at beach (33x46cm-13x18in) s.d.1946 burlap
£958 $1600   (26-Jul-91 E.EDM131/R) Woman peasant ploughing fields with mule (30x41cm-12x16in) s.
£988 $1700   (15-May-91 SY.NY252/R) Still life with vase of flowers on beach (51x41cm-20x16in) s.i. burlap
£1146 $2200   (17-Dec-90 SY.NY398/R) Les fleurs du mal (51x41cm-20x16in) s.d.1953
£1173 $2100   (11-Apr-91 FA.PH927/R) Wild flowers (51x41cm-20x16in) s.d.1930
£1354 $2600   (17-Dec-90 SY.NY364/R) Don Quixote (33x46cm-13x18in) s.indist.d. burlap
£1379 $2648   (26-Nov-90 WK.M132/R) Green horse (29x35cm-11x14in) s.d.1949 canvas on board (DM 4000)
£1524 $2500   (19-Jun-91 B.SF1876/R) Farmhouse in Russia (30x41cm-12x16in) s. s.stretcher
£1563 $3000   (17-Dec-90 SY.NY397/R) Positano (51x41cm-20x16in) s.
£1744 $3000   (15-May-91 SY.NY191/R) Landscape with farmhouse (43x56cm-17x22in) s.
£1953 $3750   (17-Dec-90 SY.NY366/R) Teatime (38x46cm-15x18in) s.d.1946 and 1947
£2035 $3500   (15-May-91 SY.NY182/R) On Florida coast (51x76cm-20x30in) s.d.1951
£2762 $4750   (15-May-91 SY.NY197/R) Cup of tea (23x31cm-9x12in) s.d.1945 canvasboard
£10204 $20000   (12-Feb-91 SY.NY36/R) Woman reading in the garden (76x86cm-30x34in)
£487 $925   *(15-Sep-90 S.W2112) Savilla seascape (20x28cm-8x11in) s.d.1938 W/C crayon*
£582 $1100   *(25-Sep-90 CE.NY188/R) Peasant (29x39cm-11x15in) s. WC pencil pen*
£2822 $4600   *(12-Jun-91 GG.TA397/R) Figures in landscape (38x56cm-15x22in) s.d.1941-2 W/C*

BURMANN, Fritz (20th C) German
£6081 $10338   (30-May-91 SY.BE29/R) Woman seated at table (88x50cm-35x20in) s.d.26 s.i.verso panel (DM 18000)

BURMEISTER, Paul (1847-?) German
£2448 $4748   (4-Dec-90 FN.S1780/R) Hunting party resting by farmhouse (30x22cm-12x9in) s. panel (DM 7000)

BURMESTER, Georg (1864-?) German
£4138 $7945   (1-Dec-90 SA.A2398/R) Sailing ships, evening (65x81cm-26x32in) s.d.1919 (DM 12000)

BURNAND, David (19/20th C) Swiss
£853   \$1374   (28-Jun-91 ARC.P69) Baigneuse (97x130cm-38x51in) s.d.24 (F.FR 8500)

BURNAND, Eugene (1850-1921) Swiss
£568   *\$1090*   (17-Dec-90 ARC.P29) *Portrit d'arabe (22x18cm-9x7in) s. chl.sanguinne oil crayon (F.FR 5600)*

BURNAT-PROVINS, Marguerite (1872-C.1950) French
£816   \$1584   (8-Dec-90 GAB.G2428/R) L'homme-fleu (38x53cm-15x21in) s. tempera board (S.FR 2000)

BURNE-JONES, Sir Edward Coley (1833-1898) British
£550   \$930   (30-Apr-91 PH95) Figure with musical instrument (35x25cm-14x10in) panel
£520   \$962   (6-Mar-91 DR68) *Study for Mirror of Venus (20x10cm-8x4in) pencil*
£550   \$924   (15-Jul-91 PH144) *Patrician (33x19cm-13x7in) pencil sanguine*
£650   \$1287   (30-Jan-91 S300/R) *Study for Romaunt of rose (20x28cm-8x11in) pencil*
£700   \$1400   (8-Feb-91 C9/R) *Study for a figure of 'Oblivion' (18x13cm-7x5in) pencil*
£2800   \$5376   (28-Nov-90 S39/R) *Despair (49x56cm-19x22in) i. W/C htd white*
£3590   \$7000   (23-Oct-90 SY.NY397/R) *Study for Knights of the Round Table summoned to Quest by Strange Damsel (51x105cm-20x41in) pencil W/C htd.white*
£4200   \$8274   (1-Nov-90 C169/R) *Portrait of Edward Horner for The Prioress's Tale (23x18cm-9x7in) init.i.d.1898 pencil*
£5000   \$9450   (26-Sep-90 S381/R) *Head of girl (21x14cm-8x6in) init.d.1879 pencil*
£8000   \$15760   (1-Nov-90 C170/R) *Virgil and the Muse of Poetry (36x18cm-14x7in) W/C bodycol.htd.gold*
£36000   \$59040   (19-Jun-91 S233/R) *Cupid's forge (32x50cm-13x20in) init.i.d.1861 W/C bodycol gum arabic on canvas*

BURNEY, Edward Francis (1760-1848) British
£800   \$1576   (15-Nov-90 S66) *Frieze of dancing figurs bringing in harvest (10x63cm-4x25in) pen ink wash*

BURNIER, Richard (1826-1884) Dutch
£719   \$1365   (11-Sep-90 CH.AM227) Huntsmen in landscape (20x31cm-8x12in) init. panel (D.FL 2400)
£1771   \$2994   (2-May-91 RAS.V23/R) Landscape with cow and milkmaid knitting (138x154cm-54x61in) s. (D.KR 20000)

BURNITZ, Karl-Peter (1824-1886) German
£1203   \$2285   (2-Mar-91 KRA.D292/R) Moroccan town view (23x36cm-9x14in) (DM 3500)
£2305   \$3757   (13-Jun-91 RAS.V522/R) Landscape with geese (90x58cm-35x23in) s.d.1882 (D.KR 26000)

BURNS, William (1921-1972) British
£1200   \$2268   (27-Sep-90 CG86) Seahouse 6 (76x102cm-30x40in) board

BURR, George Brainerd (1876-1950) American
£1279   \$2200   (15-May-91 SY.NY142/R) Tooker's farm near Damon Hill (51x63cm-20x25in) estate st.

BURR, George Elbert (1859-1939) American
£580   *\$1137*   (21-Nov-90 B45) *Buen Aventura, Santa Barbara (38x27cm-15x11in) s.d.4.19.07 W/C*
£811   \$1500   (10-Mar-91 H.C116/R) *Lake Lucerne (25x36cm-10x14in) s. W/C*

BURR, John (1831-1893) British
£1050   \$2037   (7-Dec-90 CBS322) The crossing sweeper (18x15cm-7x6in) s.d.1866 panel

BURR, John (circle) (1831-1893) British
£1100   \$1892   (16-May-91 CSK101) Preparing meal (46x76cm-18x30in) with i.

BURRA, Edward (1905-1976) British
£800   \$1560   (10-Oct-90 S59/R) *The magician (25x18cm-10x7in) init.i. pen ink wash*
£3000   \$5880   (7-Nov-90 S44/R) *Backstage (42x37cm-17x15in) s. pen indian ink*
£5600   \$10976   (7-Nov-90 S131/R) *The Gorbals Boys, costume designs for Miracle in the Gorbals (38x51cm-15x20in) i. W/C over pencil*
£20000   \$33400   (6-Jun-91 C234/R) *Wild flowers (68x103cm-27x41in) W/C bodycol pen brush ink*
£30000   \$58800   (7-Nov-90 S128/R) *Figure in the cafe (132x46cm-52x18in) s.d.36 W/C*
£50000   \$98000   (8-Nov-90 C116/R) *Birdman and pots in a landscape (56x78cm-22x31in) W/C bodycol.*

BURRAS OF LEEDS, Thomas (?) British
£2000   \$3300   (12-Jul-91 C132/R) Two spaniels in landscape, with day's bag (60x50cm-24x20in) s.d.1891

BURRI, Alberto (1915-) Italian
£2728   \$5346   (20-Nov-90 BR.M163/R) *Cretto n.8 (96x67cm-38x26in) s.i.d.1981verso mixed media board on panel (I.L 6000000)*
£9704   \$18729   (12-Dec-90 F.M94/R) *Combustione (32x20cm-13x8in) s. paper combustion laid down (I.L 21000000)*
£18638   \$36531   (20-Nov-90 BR.M67/R) *Combustione (28x31cm-11x12in) s.i.d.1965 plastic combustion (I.L 41000000)*
£35836   \$70239   (24-Nov-90 VG.B369/R) *Untitled (62x56cm-24x22in) s.d.1960verso mixed media collage (DM 105000)*

BURRI, Alberto (1915-) Italian-cont.
£67537 $131697   *(22-Oct-90 BR.M151/R) Combustione L9 (32x40cm-13x16in) s.d.1957 combustion board (I.L 150000000)*

BURROUGHS, A Leicester (19th C) British
£892 $1516   (28-May-91 AB.S4746/R) Women resting by lake (96x71cm-38x28in) s. (S.KR 9500)

BURROUGHS, Robert (19th C) British
£1800 $3546   (13-Nov-90 SWS260) Driving cattle (50x75cm-20x30in) s.d.1882

BURROWS, Robert (19th C) British
£750 $1388   (7-Mar-91 D168/R) Coming from market (18x25cm-7x10in) s.
£850 $1666   (13-Feb-91 S80/R) Harvesters (25x36cm-10x14in) s.d.1873

BURSSENS, Jan (1925-) Belgian
£1350 $2606   (13-Dec-90 CH.BR132/R) Lady Godiva (59x52cm-23x20in) s. board (B.FR 80000)
£1855 $3599   (8-Dec-90 KV.L393/R) Composition (63x101cm-25x40in) s.d.1952 (B.FR 110000)

BURT, C T (1823-1902) British
£680 $1122   (11-Jul-91 GSP597) Landscape with stream, ruins in the distance (43x66cm-17x26in) s.

BURT, Charles Thomas (1823-1902) British
£1900 $3173   (22-Jul-91 SWS1033/R) Hunters on a moor (59x97cm-23x38in) s.d.1893

BURTON, Arthur Gibbes (1883-) American
£711 $1400   (16-Nov-90 S.BM135/R) Winter hills - Vermont landscape (76x102cm-30x40in) s.

BURTON, Nancy Jane (fl.1920-1950) British
£650 $1261   (3-Dec-90 SC4267) The best of friends (33x43cm-13x17in) s.d.1928 canvas laid on board
£900 $1512   (23-Apr-91 S87/R) Chihuahua and tabby cat (33x43cm-13x17in) s.d.1928 canvasboard

BURTON, William Henry (19/20th C) British
£400 $676   *(3-May-91 T217) Fishing boats off Filey (20x61cm-8x24in) s.i.d.1900 W/C*

BURTON, William Paton (1828-1883) British
£600 $1062   *(21-Mar-91 CSK62/R) Haymaking outside the barn (25x18cm-10x7in) s.d.1867 pencil W/C htd.white*

BURWOOD, G Vemply (19/20th C) British?
£1300 $2327   (14-Mar-91 ZZ.B124/R) The Gipsey Caravan (35x51cm-14x20in) s. pair

BURZI, Ettore (1872-1937) Italian
£612 $1163   (14-Sep-90 ZOF.Z1046/R) Il lago di Lugano, vista del Bre (99x99cm-39x39in) s. i.verso panel (S.FR 1500)

BUSCAGLIONE, Giuseppe (1868-?) Italian
£727 $1426   (21-Nov-90 F.M148/R) Andando a Messa (29x43cm-11x17in) s. i.verso panel (I.L 1600000)
£1195 $2056   (14-May-91 GF.L519/R) Woodclearing with pond and cattle grazing in high mountains (42x57cm-17x22in) s. panel (S.FR 3000)

BUSCH, Peter Johan Valdemar (1861-1942) Danish
£727 $1368   (20-Sep-90 D.V100/R) Small lake in mountain landscape (41x57cm-16x22in) s. (A.S 15000)

BUSCH, Wilhelm (1832-1908) German
£2838 $5534   (26-Oct-90 BM.B751/R) Peasant man with barrel in interior (14x8cm-6x3in) board (DM 8400)
£3684 $7000   (27-Feb-91 SY.NY165/R) Two peasants with jugs (16x13cm-6x5in) board
£3684 $7000   (27-Feb-91 SY.NY164/R) Peasant carrying large pot (14x9cm-6x4in) board
£1241 $2383   *(28-Nov-90 KF.M322) Travellers watching sunrise (26x37cm-10x15in) s.i.d.1858 pencil (DM 3600)*
£1678 $3272   *(12-Oct-90 AW.H1381/R) Initial D, dem das (11x9cm-4x4in) indian ink pen over col.pencil (DM 5000)*

BUSCIOLANO, Vincenzo (1851-?) Italian
£600 $1014   (1-May-91 GD.B120) A thirsty monk (25x19cm-10x7in) s.d.1918 (S.FR 1500)

BUSH, Harry (1883-1957) British
£600 $1074   (11-Apr-91 GSP503) Wimbledon Common (56x76cm-22x30in) s.i.

BUSH, Jack (1909-1977) Canadian
£7018 $13754   (20-Nov-90 JOY.T137/R) Leap on blue (66x94cm-26x37in) acrylic canvas (C.D 16000)
£13158 $25789   (20-Nov-90 JOY.T23/R) Mar blue (87x146cm-34x57in) acrylic canvas (C.D 30000)
£13158 $25921   (30-Oct-90 SY.T73/R) Low blue (170x86cm-67x34in) s.i.d.1971verso acrylic (C.D 30000)

BUSH, Jack (1909-1977) Canadian-cont.
£13959 $27500   (4-Oct-90 SY.NY106/R) Jan 5 (198x322cm-78x127in) s.d.1972 verso acrylic
                       canvas
£2632   *$5158*   *(20-Nov-90 JOY.T306/R) Untitled (57x89cm-22x35in) init.d.62 gouache*
                       (C.D 6000)

BUSH, Norton (1834-?) American
£703 $1350   (1-Dec-90 LAE.L17/R) Panama no 203 (48x33cm-19x13in) s.verso board
£1020 $2000   (13-Feb-91 B.SF2003/R) Lagoon scene (51x76cm-20x30in)
£1337 $2300   (15-May-91 SY.NY24/R) Tropical landscape (20x30cm-8x12in) s.d.72

BUSI, Luigi (1838-1884) Italian
£38523 $65103   (16-Apr-91 CH.R221) Gioie materne (70x97cm-28x38in) s. (I.L 85000000)

BUSIERI, Giovanni Battista (1698-1757) Italian
£15778 $28243   (8-Apr-91 CH.R67/R) Paesaggio boschivo con lavandaie. Paesaggio boschivo
                       con due figure (75x60cm-30x24in) pair (I.L 35000000)

BUSSCHE, Joseph Emanuel van den (1837-1908) Belgian
£831 $1488   (12-Mar-91 C.A266) The meeting of Charles V and the Yuste monks
                       (130x185cm-51x73in) s. (B.FR 50000)
£2994 $5030   (23-Apr-91 SY.AM56/R) Venetian beauty with pigeons by well
                       (212x109cm-83x43in) s. (D.FL 10000)

BUSSE, Georg Heinrich (1810-1868) German
£2098 $4049   (10-Dec-90 L.K399/R) Monks conversing by river with monastery beyond
                       (55x46cm-22x18in) s. (DM 6000)

BUSSE, Hans (1867-?) German
£650 $1209   (6-Sep-90 CSK191) Moonlit coastal path, village beyond (51x38cm-20x15in)
                       s.d.1904
£1182 $2306   (26-Oct-90 BM.B752/R) Church destroyed by earthquake, Ischia
                       (86x130cm-34x51in) s.d.1905 i.verso (DM 3500)

BUSSET (19th C) French
£735   *$1447*   *(13-Nov-90 CH.G268) Portrait of Louis Benard (13x12cm-5x5in) min.s.*
                       gilt-metal mount fruitwood frame (S.FR 1800)

BUSSIERE, Gaston (1862-1929) French
£1633 $3167   (8-Dec-90 GAB.G2430/R) Jeune baigneuse (46x62cm-18x24in) s. (S.FR 4000)

BUSSON, Charles (1822-1908) French
£2526 $4900   (8-Dec-90 W.W97/R) Landes (61x74cm-24x29in) s.d.1892

BUSSON, Georges (1859-1933) French
£708 $1380   (19-Oct-90 MB.P39) Scene de chasse a courre vraisemblablement le debuche
                       (49x33cm-19x13in) s.d.1917 (F.FR 7000)
£2985 $5194   (27-Mar-91 CN.P80/R) Attelage (50x61cm-20x24in) s.d.1886 (F.FR 30000)
£3781 $6579   (27-Mar-91 CN.P79/R) Rendez-vous de chasse (50x61cm-20x24in) s.d.1887
                       (F.FR 38000)
£3644   *$7142*   *(25-Nov-90 P.V19/R) Le relais de poste (51x67cm-20x26in) s. W/C*
                       (F.FR 36000)

BUSTARD, William (1894-) British/Australian
£633 $1071   (16-Apr-91 J.M802) Farmyard (39x50cm-15x20in) s. canvas on board
                       (A.D 1400)
£679 $1147   (16-Apr-91 J.M49) Beach scene (14x22cm-6x9in) s.d.1923 board (A.D 1500)
£513   *$893*   *(26-Mar-91 JRL.S40) Afternoon light on the Blackall Ranges*
                       (46x35cm-18x14in) s.d.1945 W/C (A.D 1150)

BUSTOS, Hermenegildo (1832-1907) Mexican
£4592 $9000   (19-Nov-90 SY.NY105/R) Senor de la colomna (24x16cm-9x6in) i. tin
£10204 $20000   (19-Nov-90 SY.NY104/R) Four ex Votos tin set of four

BUTHAUD, Rene (1866-?) French
£565   *$1097*   *(7-Dec-90 LD.P9) Leda et le cygne (39x44cm-15x17in) mono. blk.crayon*
                       (F.FR 5500)
£596   *$1156*   *(7-Dec-90 LD.P4) Femme a l'eventail (44x30cm-17x12in) mono. blk.crayon*
                       (F.FR 5800)
£822   *$1595*   *(7-Dec-90 LD.P8) Buste nu au chapeau et a l'eventail (52x41cm-20x16in)*
                       s. blk.crayon (F.FR 8000)
£3762   *$6659*   *(6-Apr-91 GL.P33/R) Trois graces (115x80cm-45x31in) s. gouache paper*
                       laid down on canvas (F.FR 38000)
£6783   *$13159*   *(7-Dec-90 LD.P18/R) Odalisques (75x106cm-30x42in) s. col.crayons*
                       double-sided (F.FR 66000)
£7400   *$14356*   *(7-Dec-90 LD.P21/R) La coiffure de Venus (41x52cm-16x20in) s. W/C*
                       gouache (F.FR 72000)

BUTHE, Michael (1944-) German
£6167 $11038   (12-Apr-91 BM.B956/R) Mythological scene from Terra Humos
                       (128x160cm-50x63in) s.i.d.1977verso wax acrylic gold ground
                       (DM 18500)
£411   *$670*   *(14-Jun-91 L.K794) Various objects for floor of room (59x83cm-23x33in)*
                       s.d.70 mixed media (DM 1200)
£533   *$955*   *(12-Apr-91 BM.B958/R) Man in landscape (29x39cm-11x15in) s.d.1971 mixed*
                       media (DM 1600)

BUTHE, Michael (1944-) German-cont.
£1959 $3860   *(17-Nov-90 S.Z15/R) 1001 nights (39x30cm-15x12in) s.d.1956-79verso mixed media collage canvas (S.FR 4800)*
£2761 $4500   *(12-Jun-91 SY.NY189/R) Untitled (122x102cm-48x40in) acrylic paper wax canvas*
£10239 $20068   *(20-Nov-90 L.K169/R) Untitled (220x340cm-87x134in) s. oil mixed media collage newspaper on canvas (DM 30000)*

BUTI, Ludovico (attrib) (1550-1611) Italian
£400 $768   *(18-Feb-91 S107/R) Heavily draped figure reclining with eyes closed (16x24cm-6x9in) bears i. chk*

BUTINONE, Bernardino (circle) (c.1436-1507) Italian
£10000 $16300   *(5-Jul-91 C231/R) Marriage of Virgin (20x30cm-8x12in) panel*

BUTLER, Elizabeth (1846-1933) British
£18000 $35460   *(13-Nov-90 PH128/R) On the morning of Waterloo the curassiers' last reveille (109x155cm-43x61in) mono.d.1914*

BUTLER, Fray Guillermo (1880-1961) Argentinian
£677 $1300   *(27-Nov-90 PO.BA25) Paisaje serrano (26x37cm-10x15in) tempera*
£983 $1700   *(8-May-91 RO.BA218) Paisaje de Calamuchita (23x30cm-9x12in) s.d.1949 panel*
£983 $1700   *(8-May-91 RO.BA497) Otono (25x35cm-10x14in) s.d.1951 panel*
£1574 $3100   *(14-Nov-90 V.BA13) Paisaje (25x37cm-10x15in)*
£2023 $3500   *(8-May-91 RO.BA22/R) Atardecer (50x70cm-20x28in) s.d.1942*
£2312 $4000   *(8-May-91 RO.BA21/R) Paisaje Serrano (52x56cm-20x22in) s.d.1946 panel*
£2366 $4400   *(5-Sep-90 V.BA13/R) Calle de Paris (37x54cm-15x21in)*

BUTLER, Grace (?) New Zealander?
£756 $1278   *(17-Apr-91 DS.W39/R) Still llife, dahlias (56x67cm-22x26in) s. (NZ.D 2200)*

BUTLER, Herbert E (19th C) British
£870 $1557   *(14-Mar-91 L355/R) Panoramic view of fishing fleet Polperro harbour, Cornwall (28x46cm-11x18in) s.d.1916 W/C*

BUTLER, Horacio (1897-1983) Argentinian
£1218 $2400   *(14-Nov-90 V.BA14) Vendedoras (16x18cm-6x7in) tempera*

BUTLER, Howard Russell (1856-1934) American
£505 $1000   *(1-Feb-91 S.W2897/R) Falls of Yellowstone River, Yosemite Park, WY (51x36cm-20x14in) s. artist's board*
£866 $1550   *(11-Apr-91 FA.PH945/R) Waves exploding on rocks (64x86cm-25x34in) s.*

BUTLER, Joseph Nikolaus (1822-1885) Swiss
£1000 $2000   *(7-Feb-91 B.P81/R) Alpine lake scene (58x89cm-23x35in) s.d.1864*
£3586 $6167   *(14-May-91 GF.L2188/R) Sawmill beside torrent in mountain landscape (83x125cm-33x49in) s.d.1891 (S.FR 9000)*
£3984 $6853   *(14-May-91 GF.L2187/R) Vierwaldstattersee near Neuhbsburg with view of Pilatus (94x139cm-37x55in) s.i.indis.d.18.. (S.FR 10000)*
£4382 $7538   *(14-May-91 GF.L2490/R) View of the Wetterhorn (73x112cm-29x44in) s.i.d.1880 (S.FR 11000)*

BUTLER, Mary (1865-1946) American
£513 $1000   *(20-Oct-90 W.W156/R) Tidelands (61x81cm-24x32in) s.indis.d.*

BUTLER, Mildred Anne (1858-1941) British
£1200 $2340   *(18-Oct-90 SC3034/R) Two peacocks in a garden (13x17cm-5x7in) s.*
£1400 $2800   *(8-Feb-91 C108/R) A bed of roses (25x38cm-10x15in) s. i.d.1929 verso W/C htd.white*
£2100 $3507   *(5-Jun-91 S253/R) Kenmare (29x24cm-11x9in) s.i.d.1892 W/C*
£2200 $4290   *(26-Oct-90 CG16/R) Herbaceous garden with sundial (16x21cm-6x8in) s. W/C htd.white*
£3200 $6048   *(26-Sep-90 S282/R) Flower border (35x25cm-14x10in) s. indist.i.verso W/C*
£7500 $14175   *(26-Sep-90 S361/R) End of day (36x26cm-14x10in) s. indist.i. W/C htd white*

BUTLER, Reg (1913-) British
£800 $1392   *(27-Mar-91 S174/R) Reclining nudes init.i.d.69 pencil two*

BUTLER, Rozel Oertle (20th C) American
£1064 $2000   *(19-Sep-90 B.SF2843/R) Hopi girl in Pueblo (67x46cm-26x18in) s. linen*
£1197 $2250   *(19-Sep-90 B.SF2853/R) Pueblo at night (56x77cm-22x30in)*

BUTLER, Theodore E (1876-1937) American
£8333 $16000   *(30-Nov-90 CH.NY124/R) The Lieutenance, Honfleur (65x81cm-26x32in) s.*
£12139 $21000   *(23-May-91 SY.NY48/R) Steamboats by city (80x80cm-31x31in) s.d.15*
£20118 $34000   *(20-Apr-91 WOL.C177/R) Times Square, Armistice Day (104x89cm-41x35in) s.d.1918*

BUTLER, Thomas (18th C) British
£11000 $19690   *(10-Apr-91 S149/R) Starling, racehorse - Bajazet, bay racehorse - Carlisle, racehorse -Moorcock, racehorse all with joc (30x28cm-12x11in) i. paper on canvas four*

BUTTERSACK, Bernhard (1858-1909) German

£1138	$2197	(14-Dec-90 ZOF.Z929/R) Farmstead (76x55cm-30x22in) s.d.1901 i.verso (S.FR 2800)
£1672	$2826	(19-Apr-91 FN.S1679/R) Wooded landscape, evening (51x71cm-20x28in) s.d.1898 (DM 5000)
£1994	$3250	(12-Jun-91 SY.NY38/R) Springtime on farm (67x80cm-26x31in) s.d.1924
£2560	$4198	(18-Jun-91 FN.S1776/R) Wooded lake landscape with thunderstorm rising (26x35cm-10x14in) s.d.1889 board (DM 7500)

BUTTERSWORTH, James E (1817-1894) American

£4913	$8500	(22-May-91 CH.NY20/R) Dover coming into port (18x26cm-7x10in) s. board
£5521	$9000	(5-Jul-91 S.W3006/R) The yacht race (30x46cm-12x18in)
£7813	$15000	(29-Nov-90 MFA.C252/R) Off Battery (25x30cm-10x12in) s. panel
£8466	$16000	(27-Sep-90 CH.NY42/R) New York Bay (15x25cm-6x10in) s. board
£9091	$18000	(30-Jan-91 GRO.B30/R) Yacht race (23x51cm-9x20in) s.
£10056	$18000	(14-Mar-91 CH.NY24/R) Racing (20x31cm-8x12in) s. board
£12760	$24500	(29-Nov-90 MFA.C253/R) Off City of Albany (36x51cm-14x20in) s.

BUTTERSWORTH, James E (attrib) (1817-1894) American

| £2400 | $3960 | (9-Jul-91 PH4/R) Racing sloop and other shipping off south coast (44x54cm-17x21in) |

BUTTERSWORTH, James E (style) (1817-1894) American

| £3125 | $6000 | (28-Nov-90 D.NY31) Three masted schooner in New York Bay (36x56cm-14x22in) |

BUTTERSWORTH, Thomas (1768-1842) British

£1500	$2940	(15-Feb-91 N377) Shipping off the coast (18x23cm-7x9in) pair
£1600	$2720	(30-May-91 C86/R) Navy to rescue - pirates in retreat (46x61cm-18x24in) s.
£3200	$6272	(15-Feb-91 N378/R) Shipping in the English Channel with storm approaching (41x51cm-16x20in)
£3736	$6500	(29-Mar-91 E.EDM309/R) Eighteen-gun brig sloop off English coast (38x25cm-15x10in) s. panel
£4000	$6800	(30-May-91 C87/R) English packet and Royal Navy sloop off Dover (42x53cm-17x21in) s.
£4500	$8865	(14-Nov-90 S5/R) The Battle of Navarino (34x44cm-13x17in) s.
£5000	$8500	(30-May-91 C85/R) Fishing boat and mail packet sailing off rocky coastaline. Pirate ship escaping frigate at dusk (31x42cm-12x17in) s. one i.stretcher pair
£5000	$8650	(22-May-91 S4/R) Britsih frigate in pursuit of French cutter during Napoleonic wars (53x76cm-21x30in) s.
£5623	$10908	(22-Aug-90 RAS.K35/R) Seascape with vessel in distress, rough seas (72x113cm-28x44in) s.d.1808 (D.KR 65000)
£5800	$11020	(1-Mar-91 C94/R) Dutch galjot, cutter yacht, frigate and other shipping off Kent coast (63x76cm-25x30in)
£8000	$13600	(30-May-91 C88/R) Square-sail schooner, thought to be carrying opium, evading boarding party off South China (41x61cm-16x24in) s.
£8333	$14000	(16-Jul-91 BG.M871/R) English Men-of-War forming up in straights of Dover (43x51cm-17x20in)
£8982	$15000	(7-Jun-91 SY.NY140/R) The capture of the french corvette Bacchante (37x48cm-15x19in) s.
£1300	*$2145*	*(11-Jul-91 S135/R) The Inshore Blocking Squadron off Cadiz, 1797 (42x66cm-17x26in) s.d.1803 pen ink W/C over pencil*

BUTTERSWORTH, Thomas (circle) (1768-1842) British
£14000 $23380 (3-Jun-91 PHB75) Engagement between American and English warships (40x55cm-16x22in)

BUTTERSWORTH, Thomas (jnr) (early 19th C) British
£2400 $4728 (31-Oct-90 S369/R) Engagement between two frigates off the coast (8x24cm-3x9in) s. panel
£2600 $5070 (18-Oct-90 CSK93/R) 'Endeavour' off Dover (30x40cm-12x16in) s.
£4000 $7800 (18-Oct-90 CSK94/R) Frigate on port reach (43x53cm-17x21in) s.

BUTTERSWORTH, Thomas (style) (1768-1842) British
£750 $1290 (15-May-91 BT255/R) The wreck of the Bellissima, off the coast of Cornwall (53x76cm-21x30in)
£780 $1303 (4-Jun-91 SWS1885) Shipping in channel (30x40cm-12x16in)

BUTTERY, Edwin (19th C) British
£1150 $1852 (24-Jun-91 HS237/R) River landscape with figure crossing bridge, haymaking scene. Three children beside stile with cattl (29x44cm-11x17in) s. pair

BUTTNER, Erich (1889-1936) German
£874 $1696 (7-Dec-90 GB.B6379) Beach scene with sailing ships and bathers (48x67cm-19x26in) s.d.1926 (DM 2500)
£699 *$1357* *(7-Dec-90 GB.B6384/R) High jump competition, Berlin (48x63cm-19x25in) s.d.1913-29 pastel (DM 2000)*

BUTTNER, Werner (1954-) American
£3757 $6500 (7-May-91 CE.NY230/R) Working in Abu Dhabi (190x150cm-75x59in) s.d.83

BUVELOT, Abram Louis (1814-1888) Australian
£14000 . $27300 (24-Oct-90 S121/R) Bahia (38x49cm-15x19in) l. lining
£425 *$837* *(13-Nov-90 J.M1023) Yarra Flat (25x36cm-10x14in) i.d.1872 pencil (A.D 1100)*
£579 *$1141* *(13-Nov-90 J.M862) Macedon (31x50cm-12x20in) s.i.d.1872 pencil (A.D 1500)*
£1923 *$3250* *(16-Apr-91 J.M225) At Coleraine (29x48cm-11x19in) s.d.1881 W/C (A.D 4250)*
£3797 *$7291* *(14-Aug-90 SY.ME234/R) Pigeon loft (20x28cm-8x11in) s.d.1870 W/C (A.D 9000)*
£5581 *$9377* *(22-Apr-91 SY.ME313/R) Two riders on bush track (24x33cm-9x13in) s.d.1873 W/C (A.D 12000)*

BUXTON, A (?) British
£1500 $2460 (18-Jun-91 OT435/R) Portrait group of three young ladies in garden (93x127cm-37x50in) s.

BUXTON, Robert Hugh (1871-?) British
£405 *$700* *(8-May-91 RO.BA209) Hunt (37x55cm-15x22in) s. W/C*

BUYCK, Harry (1928-) Belgian
£1227 $2062 (23-Apr-91 C.A324) The admirers (105x75cm-41x30in) s. panel (B.FR 75000)

BUYLE, Robert (1895-) Belgian
£770 $1517 (6-Oct-90 KV.L40) Ball game (54x65cm-21x26in) s. (B.FR 48000)

BUYS, Geertruida Maria (1814-1886) Dutch
£576 $962 (4-Jun-91 R.T261/R) Church interior with villagers (41x33cm-16x13in) s. (C.D 1100)

BUYSSE, Georges (1864-1916) Belgian
£1265 $2454 (8-Dec-90 KV.L51/R) Dawn over the canal (30x38cm-12x15in) mono. canvas on panel (B.FR 75000)

BUZZI, A (19th C) Italian
£960 *$1900* *(1-Feb-91 S.W2576/R) Oriental beggar (46x30cm-18x12in) s. W/C*

BYATT, Edwin (1888-1948) British
£1600 $3072 (26-Nov-90 SWS162/R) Farm at Ockley, Surrey (69x90cm-27x35in) s.

BYLANDT, Alfred Edouard van (1829-1890) Dutch
£915 $1793 (6-Nov-90 SY.AM253) Incoming vessels at sunset (19x25cm-7x10in) s. panel (D.FL 3000)

BYLERT, Jan van (1603-1673) Dutch
£57895 $110000 (11-Jan-91 CH.NY75/R) A cello player (101x84cm-40x33in) s.

BYLERT, Jan van (attrib) (1603-1673) Dutch
£4201 $8234 (11-Nov-90 M.V28/R) La charite (110x90cm-43x35in) (F.FR 41000)

BYLERT, Jan van (circle) (1603-1673) Dutch
£1605 $3129 (10-Oct-90 APT.P468) Le couple illegal (62x52cm-24x20in) panel (F.FR 16000)
£7500 $12675 (16-Apr-91 PH92/R) Young woman seated at table counting money with young man and old woman (79x111cm-31x44in)

BYLERT, Jan van (style) (1603-1673) Dutch
£3000 $5550   (5-Mar-91 PH23/R) Young woman holding clay pipe (54x44cm-21x17in) init. panel

BYNG, Robert (style) (18th C) British
£2500 $4325   (20-May-91 SWS259/R) Portrait of a boy, half-length, wearing a red jacket and blue drape (69x58cm-27x23in)

BYRNE, John (1786-1847) British
£850 $1394   (19-Jun-91 PHG50) Cream Tuesday (118x118cm-46x46in) s. i. verso board
£2000 $3280   (19-Jun-91 PHG116/R) Boy in a red suit (91x91cm-36x36in) s. another painting by different hand verso
£400   *$672*   *(23-Apr-91 S252/R) Susanna, Act I, Outfit (25x18cm-10x7in) i. gouache*

BYRNE, Samuel (1883-1978) Australian
£611 $1094   (9-Apr-91 CH.ME287/R) Slippery dip glacier and Milford sound tunnell (52x46cm-20x18in) s.i. board (A.D 1400)
£1688 $3241   (14-Aug-90 SY.ME316) Duststorm (59x90cm-23x35in) s.i. board (A.D 4000)
£1800 $3510   (24-Oct-90 S101/R) Battling against the storm (60x74cm-24x29in) s.i. board

BYSS, Johann Rudolf (attrib) (1660-1738) Swiss
£4000 $6520   (2-Jul-91 PH32/R) Still life of sculpted urn of summer flowers on stone ledge (71x61cm-28x24in)

BYSTROM, Erik (1902-) Swedish
£943 $1632   (22-May-91 BA.S14/R) Shadows from trees (60x76cm-24x30in) s. (S.KR 10000)
£976 $1747   (9-Apr-91 GO.G19) View from window towards house (60x73cm-24x29in) s.d.39 (S.KR 10500)

BYZANTINE SCHOOL, 18th C Turkish
£2775 $5383   (3-Dec-90 SY.F1022/R) Madonna con Bambino (42x31cm-17x12in) tempera panel (I.L 6000000)

C K (?) ?
£1850 $3645   (13-Nov-90 SWS287/R) By the stream. Still life of chrysanthemum (58x84cm-23x33in) init. double-sided

C L (?) ?
£1800 $3600   (7-Feb-91 C41/R) A portrait of a gentleman, aged 73, wearing a black cloak by a window (91x76cm-36x30in) init.i.d.1698

C M (?) ?
£5199 $10242   (13-Nov-90 CH.AM202/R) Still life with asparagus in basket, strawberries on plate, mixed vegetables and berries on ledge (57x84cm-22x33in) init. (D.FL 17000)

CABAILLOT, Camille Leopold (1839-?) French
£1081 $1762   (10-Jun-91 W.T1383/R) Tea time (45x37cm-18x15in) s. panel (C.D 2000)

CABAILLOT, Louis Simon (1810-?) French
£1150 $2243   (15-Jan-91 SWS157/R) French street scene with figures, cattle and goats (43x54cm-17x21in) s. panel
£1300 $2600   (8-Feb-91 K493/R) Children stealing apples from tree, owner in pursuit (43x28cm-17x11in) s.
£1350 $2322   (14-May-91 SWS337/R) At the village pump (34x25cm-13x10in) s.d.71 i.d.verso panel
£1800 $3528   (14-Feb-91 CSK85/R) Fagot gatherers on a winter track (46x36cm-18x14in) s. panel
£2390 $4661   (24-Oct-90 GD.B200/R) Girl with jug, boy and dog by village well (33x24cm-13x9in) s. panel (S.FR 6000)
£628   *$1049*   *(4-Jun-91 R.T245/R) Back from school (25x21cm-10x8in) s. gouache oil paper (C.D 1200)*

CABALLERO, Jose Luis (20th C) Spanish
£5975 $9620   (25-Jun-91 FER.M248/R) Figura de mujer con luna negra (100x73cm-39x29in) s. (S.P 1100000)
£7061 $11369   (25-Jun-91 FER.M249/R) Figura, luna, pozo y noche (100x73cm-39x29in) s. (S.P 1300000)
£1355   *$2643*   *(17-Oct-90 FER.M237/R) Dama con jarron (76x55cm-30x22in) s. W/C ink (S.P 250000)*
£1762   *$3436*   *(17-Oct-90 FER.M238/R) Dama con guitarra (76x54cm-30x21in) s. W/C ink (S.P 325000)*
£1787   *$3198*   *(13-Mar-91 FER.M249/R) Bodegon de copas y sandias (70x49cm-28x19in) s.d.1953 W/C (S.P 325000)*

CABALLERO, Luis (1943-) Colombian
£10465 $18000   (15-May-91 CH.NY115/R) Untitled (195x130cm-77x51in) s.
£596   *$1008*   *(15-Apr-91 CC.P41) Sans titre (57x76cm-22x30in) oil pastel (F.FR 6000)*
£925   *$1794*   *(9-Dec-90 CC.P88/R) Sans titre (74x103cm-29x41in) s.d.1972 pastel htd.col.crayons (F.FR 9000)*

CABALLERO, Luis (1943-) Colombian-cont.
£1633 $3200   *(20-Nov-90 CH.NY232/R) Untitled (57x77cm-22x30in) s.d.84 mixed media paper on board*

CABALLERO, Maximo (1867-1951) Spanish
£7500 $12900   (17-May-91 C241/R) Young grape-picker (120x80cm-47x31in) s.i.
£21804 $37721   (21-May-91 DUR.M5/R) Una modelo encantadora (66x81cm-26x32in) (S.P 4000000)

CABANEL, Alexandre (attrib) (1824-1889) French
£1796 $3000   (23-Jan-91 D.NY23) Tribute to Desdemona (64x61cm-25x24in)

CABANES, Max (1947-) ?
£644 $1139   *(6-Apr-91 CB.P201/R) La maison (35x47cm-14x19in) col.oil pastel (F.FR 6500)*
£990 $1752   *(6-Apr-91 CB.P200/R) La rue (35x57cm-14x22in) col.oil pastel (F.FR 10000)*

CABAT, Louis (1812-1893) French
£422 $679   *(28-Jun-91 LC.P60) Vue d'un etang a la lisiere d'un bois (30x40cm-12x16in) s.i. pen wash indian ink (F.FR 4200)*

CABAUD, Paul (19th C) French
£5020 $8082   (24-Jun-91 BL.P21/R) Le Lac d'Annecy depuis les hauteurs de Talloires (54x81cm-21x32in) s.d.1870 (F.FR 50000)

CABEL, Adrian van der (c.1631-1705) Dutch
£3000 $5760   (18-Dec-90 GM.B4035/R) Paysage avec pecheurs (32x46cm-13x18in) panel (B.FR 180000)
£40000 $77200   (12-Dec-90 S90/R) Dutch river landscape with bastion (97x133cm-38x52in) s.mono.d.1648

CABEL, Adrian van der (attrib) (c.1631-1705) Dutch
£5000 $8150   (4-Jul-91 C526/R) Mediterranean coastal views at dusk and dawn with merchants, fishermen (36x48cm-14x19in) pair
£6762 $12104   (8-Apr-91 CH.R57/R) Porto di mare con faro e figure (47x73cm-19x29in) (I.L 15000000)

CABEL, Adrian van der (circle) (c.1631-1705) Dutch
£3200 $6080   (13-Sep-90 CSK9/R) Coastal view with English two-decker entering harbour past frigate and galley, men, town beyond (90x141cm-35x56in)
£4200 $8190   (25-Oct-90 CSK11/R) Rocky Mediterranean coastline with Dutch shipping and landing party on shore (43x62cm-17x24in)

CABEL, Adrian van der (style) (c.1631-1705) Dutch
£6200 $10478   (18-Apr-91 C21/R) Capriccios of Mediterranean inlets (18x27cm-7x11in) copper pair

CABELLERO, Luis (20th C) Latin American
£904 $1455   *(25-Jun-91 BG.P11) Nu allonge (70x106cm-28x42in) s. pastel crayon (F.FR 9000)*

CABIANCA, Vincenzo (1827-1902) Italian
£2293 $4105   *(12-Mar-91 F.M17/R) Figure fiorentine in costume del quattrocento (26x24cm-10x9in) s.d.1868 W/C tempera (I.L 5000000)*

CABIE, Louis Alexandre (1853-1939) French
£700 $1141   (5-Jul-91 APT.P98) Cour de ferme (40x32cm-16x13in) s.d.1915 panel (F.FR 7000)
£996 $1723   (26-May-91 ZZ.F70/R) Vue du village de St-Prive dans la Nievre (57x72cm-22x30in) s. (F.FR 10000)
£1439 $2791   (8-Dec-90 SY.MO342/R) Paysage de riviere (55x42cm-22x17in) s.d.1910 (F.FR 14000)
£1953 $3788   (8-Dec-90 SY.MO389/R) Le pont brise (45x56cm-18x22in) s.d.1906 (F.FR 19000)
£2196 $3711   (3-May-91 SA.A1715/R) Sunny woodland glade (92x73cm-36x29in) s. (DM 6500)
£461 $904   *(11-Nov-90 ZZ.F9/R) Paysage Vallonne (37x31cm-15x12in) s.d.1917 gouache (F.FR 4500)*

CABRERA, Miguel (1695-1768) Mexican
£9184 $18000   (19-Nov-90 SY.NY3/R) La Virgen del Carmen (54x39cm-21x15in) s.d.indist.

CABUZEL, Auguste Maurice (1878-) French
£922 $1807   (11-Nov-90 ZZ.F37/R) Portrait d'oriental (24x19cm-9x7in) s. panel (F.FR 9000)

CACCIA, Guglielmo (1568-1625) Italian
£18072 $29096   (25-Jun-91 APT.P7/R) Judith tenant la tete d'Holpherne (114x170cm-45x67in) (F.FR 180000)
£1500 $2535   *(16-Apr-91 C131/R) The Madonna and child flanked by putti (20x19cm-8x7in) blk.chk.ink wash*
£1500 $2445   *(2-Jul-91 C259/R) Woman addressing beggar (18x23cm-7x9in) with i. num.18 black chk pen*
£2280 $4036   *(19-Mar-91 F.M325/R) Sacra conversazione (30x22cm-12x9in) ink white paint (I.L 5000000)*

CACCIA, Guglielmo (1568-1625) Italian-cont.
£5800	$9802	(16-Apr-91 C130/R) The return from the flight to Egypt (18x26cm-7x10in) blk.chk.ink wash
£10000	$16300	(2-Jul-91 C101/R) Studies of putti with musical instruments on clouds (22x15cm-9x6in) num.19 black chk pen wash

CACCIA, Ursola Maddalena (c.1596-1666) Italian
£2272	$4475	(29-Oct-90 SY.F612/R) S. Agnese (84x61cm-33x24in) (I.L 5000000)

CACCIOLA, Enzo (20th C) Italian
£805	$1578	(13-Feb-91 KH.K44) Composition (180x120cm-71x47in) s.d.74verso mixed media (D.KR 9000)

CACHOUD, Francois-Charles (1866-1943) French
£1506	$2425	(28-Jun-91 ARC.P51) Coucher de soleil (49x65cm-19x26in) s. (F.FR 15000)

CADDY, John Herbert (19th C) Canadian
£657	$1136	(6-May-91 SY.T139) Niagara in winter (23x30cm-9x12in) s.i.verso W/C (C.D 1300)

CADELL, Agnes (19th C) British
£1900	$3553	(28-Aug-91 S1058/R) White flowers of a blameless life (145x66cm-57x26in) s.i.d.1955on stretcher

CADELL, Florence St John (fl.1900-1940) British
£600	$1200	(5-Feb-91 S143/R) On terrace. Sketch of tree (32x39cm-13x15in) s. board double-sided
£850	$1590	(28-Aug-90 S1056) A villa (34x27cm-13x11in) s.verso board

CADELL, Francis Campbell Boileau (1883-?) British
£3000	$5070	(2-May-91 CG531) Iona (37x45cm-15x18in) s. panel
£3800	$7106	(28-Aug-90 S1032/R) Mull from Iona (35x45cm-14x18in) s. i.verso canvas on board
£3800	$6422	(2-May-91 CG530/R) Tiree Coal Gabbert (38x46cm-15x18in) s. canvasboard
£4505	$8505	(27-Sep-90 CG115/R) Rhum from Iona (16x22cm-6x9in) s. panel
£5000	$9700	(6-Dec-90 CG259/R) Low tide, Iona, looking towards the Dutchman's Cap. On the Machair (37x44cm-15x17in) s. panel double-sided
£5000	$9450	(27-Sep-90 CG82/R) Cytherea (56x46cm-22x18in) panel
£6000	$11640	(6-Dec-90 CG260/R) Mull from Iona, the red sail (37x44cm-15x17in) s. s.i.verso panel
£7000	$13580	(6-Dec-90 CG258/R) Wet sand, Iona (37x45cm-15x18in) s. i.verso panel
£7500	$14550	(6-Dec-90 CG248/R) Cottage on the shores of Loch Long (45x37cm-18x15in) s. panel
£8000	$15520	(6-Dec-90 CG256/R) Ben Cruachan from Achnacraig, Mull (37x45cm-15x18in) s. init.i.verso panel
£8000	$15520	(6-Dec-90 CG254/R) Cathedral Rock, Iona (37x44cm-15x17in) s. i.verso panel
£10000	$16900	(2-May-91 CG519/R) Calva, Iona (37x45cm-15x18in) s. init.i.verso panel
£10000	$19400	(6-Dec-90 CG251/R) The White Sands, Iona (38x46cm-15x18in) s. board
£10000	$19400	(6-Dec-90 CG255/R) The house by the sea, Iona (37x44cm-15x17in) s. canvas on board
£11000	$21340	(6-Dec-90 CG253/R) Port Bhan, Iona (63x76cm-25x30in) s.
£12000	$23280	(6-Dec-90 CG252/R) The Sound of Mull from Iona (37x45cm-15x18in) s. board
£12000	$20280	(2-May-91 CG518/R) Ben More (37x45cm-15x18in) s. s.i.verso panel
£13000	$24310	(28-Aug-90 S1016/R) Iona (38x46cm-15x18in) s. board
£13000	$25220	(6-Dec-90 CG247/R) Barcaldine Castle, Argyll (63x76cm-25x30in) s. i.verso
£16000	$27040	(2-May-91 CG528/R) Black cockerel (37x45cm-15x18in) s. canvas on board
£16000	$30240	(27-Sep-90 CG79/R) Cottages, Iona (37x45cm-15x18in) s. board
£17500	$33950	(6-Dec-90 CG257/R) Iona (37x45cm-15x18in) s. s.i.verso panel
£25000	$47250	(27-Sep-90 CG80/R) Portrait of Geroge W Service, Esq (104x88cm-41x35in) s.s.i.d.1933verso
£30000	$56100	(28-Aug-90 S1017/R) Family in Iona (37x45cm-15x18in) s. board
£30000	$58200	(6-Dec-90 CG239) Iona (63x76cm-25x30in) s.
£30000	$58200	(6-Dec-90 CG249/R) The famille rose coffee pot (56x46cm-22x18in) s.d.10
£35000	$67900	(6-Dec-90 CG246/R) Iona Sound and Ben More (51x76cm-20x30in) s. i.stretcher
£35000	$67900	(6-Dec-90 CG250/R) Pink roses in glass vase. Girl in white dress and floral hat (72x51cm-28x20in) s.d.11 board double-sided
£94388	$185000	(7-Nov-90 B.SF1065/R) Summer bride (102x79cm-40x31in) s. i.verso
£1300	$2197	(2-May-91 CG433) Red sail, Sound of Iona (13x25cm-5x10in) s. W/C
£1600	$2704	(2-May-91 CG432/R) White sands, Iona (18x25cm-7x10in) s. W/C
£2000	$3920	(22-Nov-90 CG543/R) The orange cloak (38x25cm-15x10in) s. pastel
£3400	$6596	(5-Dec-90 PHE108 a) Mull and Ben More (17x25cm-7x10in) s. W/C
£4000	$6440	(27-Jun-91 CG13/R) Sketching on the sands, Iona (18x25cm-7x10in) s. W/C
£4400	$7392	(23-Apr-91 S180/R) Family outing (33x25cm-13x10in) init.d.15 brush ink wash
£7500	$14025	(28-Aug-90 S1031/R) Gentleman sketching (17x24cm-7x9in) s. i.verso W/C over pencil

CADENASSO, Giuseppe (1858-1918) American
£765	$1500	(13-Feb-91 B.SF2012/R) Clearing in woods (30x41cm-12x16in) s. board
£3077	$6000	(10-Oct-90 B.SF471/R) Eucalyptus in marin landscape (102x76cm-40x30in) s.
£1276	$2500	(13-Feb-91 B.SF2013/R) Twilight on marshes (35x56cm-14x22in) s. pastel

CADES, Giuseppe (1750-1799) Italian
£35000	$59150	(19-Apr-91 C28/R) The Madonna and child with two angels (104x137cm-41x54in)
£80000	$130400	(3-Jul-91 S67/R) Exterior of palace with elegant figures playing chess on balcony (102x103cm-40x41in)
£2368	$4500	(9-Jan-91 CH.NY32/R) Orpheus charming animals (14x41cm-6x16in) black chk pen W/C
£3876	$6860	(19-Mar-91 F.M303/R) Vergine annunciata. Angelo annunciante (25x13cm-10x5in) ink W/C (I.L 8500000)
£3876	$6860	(19-Mar-91 F.M247/R) La fuga in Egitto (26x18cm-10x7in) s. pen W/C ink bistre (I.L 8500000)

CADMUS, Paul (1904-) American
£974	$1900	(14-Oct-90 H.C405/R) Reclining nude (43x36cm-17x14in) s. i.verso conte crayon htd white rose green
£1965	$3400	(21-May-91 CE.NY671/R) Male studies (28x24cm-11x9in) s. pencil pair

CADORET, Michel (1912-1985) French
£917	$1771	(15-Dec-90 D.P24/R) Composition abstraite (40x52cm-16x20in) s. (F.FR 9000)
£1028	$1994	(5-Dec-90 ZZ.F70/R) Space 1 (61x51cm-24x20in) s.d.58 (F.FR 10000)
£2041	$4020	(16-Nov-90 EA.Z309) Untitled (61x50cm-24x20in) st.studio verso (S.FR 5000)
£2224	$4338	(21-Oct-90 P.V13/R) East end (75x50cm-30x20in) s. i.d. stretcher (F.FR 22000)
£2823	$5504	(28-Oct-90 M.V117/R) Oural (50x76cm-20x30in) s. studio st. verso (F.FR 28000)
£612	$1180	(15-Dec-90 D.P25) Abstraction (49x63cm-19x25in) s.d.71 gouache (F.FR 6000)

CADY, Henry (1849-?) American
£1026	$2000	(25-Oct-90 GRO.B57/R) Hastening shoreward (56x91cm-22x36in) s.

CAFFE, Nino (1909-1975) Spanish
£773	$1462	(27-Sep-90 F.M63/R) Pretino e diavoletto (14x19cm-6x7in) s. panel (I.L 1700000)
£1403	$2750	(12-Feb-91 SY.NY106/R) Repertorio (23x28cm-9x11in) s. panel
£1588	$2731	(13-May-91 CH.R47/R) Coretto (30x21cm-12x8in) s. panel (I.L 3500000)
£2128	$4000	(19-Sep-90 B.SF2650/R) Gran Bachetto (25x35cm-10x14in) s. panel
£2821	$5500	(10-Oct-90 SY.NY286/R) Santanelli dal cielo (23x58cm-9x23in) s. s.verso panel
£2890	$5000	(7-May-91 CE.NY98/R) Priests in garden (39x69cm-15x27in) s. panel
£3061	$6000	(7-Nov-90 B.SF1075/R) Suspenseful audience (41x70cm-16x28in) s.
£3179	$5500	(22-May-91 D.NY77/R) Capello in Cielo (35x60cm-14x24in) s. board
£3635	$7160	(30-Oct-90 F.R126/R) In carrozza (28x40cm-11x16in) s. (I.L 8000000)
£4180	$8234	(30-Oct-90 F.R101/R) Moscacieca (33x55cm-13x22in) s. (I.L 9200000)
£4872	$9500	(10-Oct-90 SY.NY288/R) Pandemonio in rosso (56x79cm-22x31in) s. panel

CAFFI, Ippolito (1809-1866) Italian
£24581	$44000	(10-Apr-91 HF.NY62/R) Moccoli evening, Rome (38x47cm-15x19in) s.indist.d.1836
£52000	$85280	(21-Jun-91 C86/R) Piazza di San Pietro, Rome (44x69cm-17x27in) s.d.1843

CAFFI, Ippolito (attrib) (1809-1866) Italian
£1205	$1940	(27-Jun-91 APT.P73/R) Notre Dame de Naples (28x20cm-11x8in) (F.FR 12000)

CAFFI, Ippolito (style) (1809-1866) Italian
£1600	$3136	(14-Feb-91 CSK195) The Forum with the Colosium beyond (36x46cm-14x18in) i.d.1847

CAFFI, Margherita (18th C) Italian
£16444	$31901	(7-Dec-90 CH.MO324/R) Natures mortes aux fleurs sur un entablement (65x54cm-26x21in) pair (F.FR 160000)
£20101	$32965	(22-Jun-91 CH.MO136/R) Une nature morte aux guirlandes de fleurs (189x289cm-74x114in) (F.FR 200000)
£22610	$43864	(7-Dec-90 SY.MO89/R) Natures mortes aux fleurs (61x75cm-24x30in) pair (F.FR 220000)
£25694	$49846	(7-Dec-90 SY.MO20/R) Bouquets de fleurs (63x76cm-25x30in) pair (F.FR 250000)

CAFFI, Margherita (attrib) (18th C) Italian
£32835	$54835	(4-Jun-91 CH.R244/R) Natura morta con vaso di fiori. Natura morta con fiori e fragole (80x104cm-31x41in) pair (I.L 72000000)

CAFFI, Margherita (circle) (18th C) Italian
£11000	$17930	(4-Jul-91 B183/R) Still life of mixed flowers in a bronze vase (84x66cm-33x26in)

CAFFI, Margherita (school) (18th C) Italian
£2443	$4250	(27-Mar-91 B.SF4034/R) Still life with flowers, grapes and parrot in niche (77x64cm-30x25in)

CAFFIERI, Hector (1847-1932) British
£1800	$3402	(26-Sep-90 S337/R) Poppy field (35x25cm-14x10in) s. W/C htd bodycol
£1800	$3528	(21-Nov-90 B59/R) Mother and child looking out to sea (33x50cm-13x20in) s. W/C

CAFFIERI, Hector (1847-1932) British-cont.
£1900 $3648   (26-Nov-90 SWS133/R) Fishergirl and dog on seashore (36x52cm-14x20in) s. W/C
£2000 $3900   (16-Jan-91 BT26/R) Children in courtyard (36x25cm-14x10in) s. W/C htd.bodycol.
£2100 $4032   (26-Nov-90 SWS132/R) Knitting on the shore (36x52cm-14x20in) s. W/C
£2400 $4608   (17-Dec-90 PH27/R) Lady and dog in punt (35x25cm-14x10in) s. W/C htd.bodycol.
£2800 $4676   (5-Jun-91 S328/R) Playing on beach (33x22cm-13x9in) s. W/C
£2900 $4843   (5-Jun-91 S327/R) Fishergirls on beach (34x23cm-13x9in) s. W/C
£3400 $6664   (21-Nov-90 B49/R) In walled garden (25x36cm-10x14in) s. W/C bodycol
£3500 $6895   (1-Nov-90 C155/R) Early morning, possibly Equihen (36x51cm-14x20in) s. W/C htd.white board
£3800 $6346   (5-Jun-91 S326/R) On quayside (40x35cm-16x14in) s. W/C htd white
£9955 $16824   (16-Apr-91 J.M76/R) A quiet afternoon, Poole Harbour (64x105cm-25x41in) s. W/C (A.D 22000)

CAFFYN, Walter Wallor (?-1898) British
£915 $1500   (19-Jun-91 B.SF1916/R) Lane near Tring (18x25cm-7x10in) s.
£1272 $2200   (12-May-91 H.C11/R) Old Mill Maple, Durham on Thames. On the Thames near Caversham, Reading (30x51cm-12x20in) s.d.1887 l.verso pair
£3000 $4890   (14-Jun-91 C219/R) Carting hay near Brockham, Surrey (61x91cm-24x36in) s.l.d.1887
£3500 $6860   (13-Feb-91 S72/R) Summer on river Mole, near Dorking (61x102cm-24x40in) s.d.1892

CAFFYN, Walter Wallor and HERRING, John Frederick (Jnr) (19th C) British
£9100 $17199   (26-Sep-90 RB643/R) River scene with reed cutters and horses watering s.d.1879

CAFISSA, Nicolo see CASISSA, Nicola

CAGLI, Corrado (1910-) Italian
£2962 $5035   (28-May-91 SY.MI6/R) L'Ile de la Cite (52x61cm-20x24in) s. s.d.51verso (I.L 6500000)
£5043 $8270   (20-Jun-91 F.M431/R) Composizione (32x45cm-13x18in) s.d.47 panel (I.L 11000000)
£546 $1032   (27-Sep-90 F.M129) Figura (37x26cm-15x10in) s. mixed media (I.L 1200000)
£1185 $2014   (28-May-91 SY.MI10/R) Silvestro (74x57cm-29x22in) s.d.58 mixed media paper laid down on canvas (I.L 2600000)

CAGNACCI, Guido (1601-1681) Italian
£105882 $180000   (31-May-91 CH.NY47/R) Allegory of human life (48x84cm-19x33in) s.

CAGNACCI, Guido (after) (1601-1681) Italian
£2736 $4570   (4-Jun-91 CH.R247) Figura allegorica (89x85cm-35x33in) (I.L 6000000)

CAGNACCI, Guido (style) (1601-1681) Italian
£8000 $15200   (1-Mar-91 C160/R) Madonna, Magdalen and angel mourning the dead Christ (30x41cm-12x16in) copper

CAGNACCIO DI SAN PIETRO (1879-1946) Italian
£2047 $3869   (27-Sep-90 F.M106) Figura femminile con bambino (55x41cm-22x16in) s. masonite (I.L 4500000)

CAGNIART, Emile (1851-1911) French
£1121 $2164   (12-Dec-90 ZZ.F31/R) Le Moulin de Batz sur Mer (37x45cm-15x18in) s. panel (F.FR 11000)

CAGNONE, Angelo (1941-) Italian
£1137 $2150   (27-Sep-90 F.M69) Objet Cache n.3 (90x70cm-35x28in) s.d.1970 verso acrylic (I.L 2500000)
£1617 $3122   (13-Dec-90 F.M349) Di fronte (89x116cm-35x46in) s.l.d.1972verso acrylic oil (I.L 3500000)
£6078 $11853   (22-Oct-90 BR.M46/R) Le donne vanno e vengono per le stanze parlando di Michelangelo (150x150cm-59x59in) s.d.1954 verso (I.L 13500000)
£2734 $4647   (28-May-91 SY.MI107/R) Dei pronomi (116x89cm-46x35in) s.d.1976verso oil mixed media canvas (I.L 6000000)
£5038 $9674   (27-Nov-90 SY.MI148/R) Icaro (146x81cm-57x32in) s.verso oil mixed media canvas (I.L 11000000)

CAGNONI, Amerino (1853-1923) Italian
£4103 $8000   (23-Oct-90 SY.NY431/R) Keeping abreast of the news (42x32cm-17x13in) s.

CAHN, Marcelle (1895-1981) French
£555 $1077   (7-Dec-90 GL.P6) Sans titre (19x22cm-7x9in) s. col.crayons ink collage (F.FR 5400)

CAHOON, Charles D (1861-1951) American
£612 $1150   (22-Sep-90 WOL.C316/R) Sand dune, Cape Cod (33x51cm-13x20in) s. cardboard
£773 $1500   (24-Aug-90 RB.HY22/R) The Chatham Windmill (25x33cm-10x13in) s.
£838 $1400   (25-Jul-91 E.EDM362/R) Two-masted schooner (28x28cm-11x11in) s. board
£842 $1600   (14-Sep-90 S.BM266/R) Cape Cod dunes scene (30x46cm-12x18in) s.
£902 $1750   (24-Aug-90 RB.HY94/R) Autumn at the beach (23x30cm-9x12in) board

CAHOON, Charles D (1861-1951) American-cont.
£1579 $3000   (1-Mar-91 RB.HY31/R) Cape Cod marshes at dusk (64x76cm-25x30in) s.
£1582 $3100   (24-Nov-90 RB.HY127/R) Cape cod landscape with vine covered cottage and
       barn shaded by trees (30x46cm-12x18in) s.

CAHOON, Martha (20th C) American
£925 $1600   (21-May-91 GRO.B173 a/R) Children playing (46x56cm-18x22in) s.d.82
       masonite

CAHOON, Ralph (20th C) American
£579 $1100   (1-Mar-91 RB.HY25/R) Ship under sail with distant lighthouse
       (25cm-10ins circular) s. masonite
£1015 $2000   (16-Nov-90 E.EDM750/R) Sailor and mermaid on shore (53x66cm-21x26in) s.
       panel
£1053 $2000   (1-Mar-91 RB.HY39/R) Needlepoint at the shore (25x36cm-10x14in) s.
       masonite
£1354 $2600   (28-Nov-90 D.NY34) Mermaids building bridge (28x36cm-11x14in) s.
       masonite
£1418 $2750   (24-Aug-90 RB.HY47/R) A fine day's catch (33x46cm-13x18in) s. masonite
£1667 $3200   (28-Nov-90 D.NY33) Weighing-in (36x46cm-14x18in) s. masonite
£3351 $6500   (24-Aug-90 RB.HY46/R) Quilters, whimsical view of three mermaids
       (53x66cm-21x26in) s.d.1966 masonite
£5263 $10000   (1-Mar-91 RB.HY24/R) Cape Cod Hospital outpatient clinic
       (36x53cm-14x21in) s.i. masonite
£8505 $16500   (24-Aug-90 RB.HY25/R) Mermaids blowing bubbles (41x51cm-16x20in) s.
       masonite

CAILLARD, Christian (1899-1985) French
£2518 $4104   (11-Jun-91 I.N157/R) La plage (65x81cm-26x32in) s. hardboard
       (F.FR 25000)
£2854 $5509   (14-Dec-90 ARC.P11) Paysage (65x80cm-26x31in) s. on isorel (F.FR 28000)

CAILLE, Leon Emile (1836-1907) French
£549 $900   (21-Jun-91 DM.D2040/R) Mother and child in front of fireplace, 1873
       (15x10cm-6x4in) s. panel
£1295 $2500   (10-Dec-90 H.C1171) Wash day (89x58cm-35x23in) s.d.1883
£2400 $4608   (28-Nov-90 S266/R) Rocking the cradle (27x22cm-11x9in) s.d.1891 panel
£2632 $5000   (27-Feb-91 SY.NY98/R) La blanchisseuse (65x82cm-26x32in) s.d.1895
£4615 $9000   (23-Oct-90 SY.NY275/R) Mother and child (93x66cm-37x26in) s.d.1888

CAILLE, Pierre (1912-) Belgian
£788 $1364   (25-May-91 KV.L33) Five figures (98x136cm-39x54in) s.d.1972 panel
       (B.FR 48000)

CAILLEBOTTE, Gustave (1840-1894) French
£52367 $85358   (11-Jun-91 I.N158/R) Coin de Village a Yerres (23x33cm-9x13in) i. verso
       panel (F.FR 520000)
£170000 $273700   (25-Jun-91 S15/R) Maisons au bord de l'eau (65x54cm-26x21in) s.d.1882
£250000 $485000   (4-Dec-90 S9/R) Le Petit Bras de la Seine en Automne (65x54cm-26x21in)
       s.
£379592 $747796   (16-Nov-90 GK.Z5182/R) Paysage en Normandie (63x73cm-25x29in) s.d.1884
       (S.FR 930000)
£20809 $36000   (12-May-91 H.C27/R) Canotiers ramenant sur L'Yerres (18x25cm-7x10in) s.
       black crayon

CAIREY, Jacques (attrib) (1646-1726) French?
£714 $1377   (14-Dec-90 LEB.P21) Soldat romain arrete un cheval fougueux sur un vaste
       piedestal (48x30cm-19x12in) i.d.1715 pen wash Indian ink (F.FR 7000)

CAIRO, Francesco del (1607-1665) Italian
£5862 $10493   (14-Mar-91 D.V18/R) The martyrdom of St Bartholomy (57x40cm-22x16in)
       panel (A.S 120000)
£7035 $11538   (21-Jun-91 SY.MO177/R) Vierge a l'enfant (49x37cm-19x15in) (F.FR 70000)
£11000 $21230   (12-Dec-90 S64/R) The rest on the flight into Egypt (48x38cm-19x15in)
       panel

CAIRO, Francesco del (after) (1607-1665) Italian
£1500 $3000   (7-Feb-91 C27/R) A Sybil, head and shoulders (74x58cm-29x23in)

CAIRO, Francesco del (attrib) (1607-1665) Italian
£2821 $5500   (11-Oct-90 SY.NY80/R) Sleeping Magdalen (49x130cm-19x51in)

CAIRO, Francesco del (style) (1607-1665) Italian
£1200 $2304   (29-Nov-90 CSK174/R) The Mater Dolorosa (75x62cm-30x24in)

CAIRONI, Luigi (19th C) Italian
£1316 $2500   (15-Sep-90 S.W2411/R) The chaperon (163x64cm-64x25in) s.d.1891

CALABRIA, Ennio (1937-) Italian
£4771 $9398   (30-Oct-90 F.R125/R) Donna con ventaglio (130x164cm-51x65in) s.d.1966
       (I.L 10500000)
£1017 $1974   (3-Dec-90 F.M44/R) Danza sulla spiaggia (67x88cm-26x35in) s.d.1966
       gouache (I.L 2200000)
£1262 $2259   (9-Apr-91 F.R51) Corteo (56x50cm-22x20in) s.d.74 mixed media
       (I.L 2800000)

CALAME, Alexandre (1810-1864) Swiss

£1624	$3200	(15-Nov-90 D.NY15/R) Hilly river landscape (58x77cm-23x30in) s.
£2381	$3976	(5-Jun-91 SY.Z34/R) Mountain landscape (19x28cm-7x11in) board on canvas (S.FR 6000)
£2601	$4500	(21-May-91 CE.NY116/R) Classical ruins in landscape (42x57cm-17x22in) s.d.
£4300	$8256	(27-Nov-90 PH111/R) Mountain stream (72x94cm-28x37in) s.d.1846
£4400	$7436	(1-May-91 GD.B125/R) Falaises et rochers au bord d'un lac (35x52cm-14x20in) (S.FR 11000)
£6500	$11505	(21-Mar-91 LC.P58) Paysage de montagne (31x41cm-12x16in) board (F.FR 65000)
£8730	$14579	(5-Jun-91 SY.Z30/R) Le Chateau de Chillon (48x41cm-19x16in) paper on board (S.FR 22000)
£12200	$21594	(21-Mar-91 LC.P57/R) Les coniferes (68x51cm-27x20in) board (F.FR 122000)
£19200	$32448	(1-May-91 GD.B124/R) Torrent de montagne par orage (87x116cm-34x46in) s. (S.FR 48000)
£19355	$37161	(2-Dec-90 GAB.G1550/R) Le Wetterhorn (81x65cm-32x26in) panel (S.FR 48000)
£608	*$1034*	*(27-May-91 L.K187) River landscape with cattle watering (18x26cm-7x10in) s. W/C (DM 1800)*
£898	*$1742*	*(8-Dec-90 GAB.G2148) Buisson d'arbres (36x30cm-14x12in) lead pencil (S.FR 2200)*
£1429	*$2814*	*(16-Nov-90 GK.Z5334/R) Black forest landscape with Wellhorn and Wetterhorn (27x33cm-11x13in) s.d.1854 brush dr. wash bister (S.FR 3500)*

CALAME, Alexandre (attrib) (1810-1864) Swiss

£717	$1398	(24-Oct-90 GD.B203/R) View of Eiger (41x54cm-16x21in) (S.FR 1800)

CALAME, Alexandre (school) (1810-1864) Swiss

£876	$1508	(14-May-91 GF.L2488/R) Landscape with torrent (39x57cm-15x22in) (S.FR 2200)

CALAME, Alexandre and JAECKEL, Henry (19th C) Swiss/German

£3500	$6720	(27-Nov-90 PH121/R) Alpine landscape (42x59cm-17x23in) s. canvas on panel

CALAME, Arthur (1843-1919) Swiss

£1475	$2774	(19-Sep-90 GK.Z810) Summer landscape with figure resting (26x40cm-10x16in) mono. (S.FR 3600)

CALAME, Jean Baptiste Arthur (1843-1919) Swiss

£2653	$5147	(8-Dec-90 GAB.G2161/R) Vue de Pestum (160x140cm-63x55in) s.d.l mai 1865 stretcher (S.FR 6500)
£1796	*$3520*	*(6-Nov-90 GF.L2483/R) Sailing boats offshore (100x80cm-39x31in) pencil indian ink canvas (S.FR 4400)*

CALANDRUCCI, Giacinto (1646-1707) Italian

£765	*$1476*	*(12-Dec-90 CD.P3) Repos de Diane (18x25cm-7x10in) black crayon pen (F.FR 7500)*

CALBET, Antoine (1860-1944) French

£502	$808	(28-Jun-91 ARC.P49) Modele nu accroupi (27x22cm-11x9in) s. (F.FR 5000)
£2004	$3888	(7-Dec-90 GL.P136) Couple dans la clairiere (29x51cm-11x20in) s. (F.FR 19500)
£602	*$1114*	*(4-Mar-91 ARC.P29/R) Nu de dos (32x48cm-13x19in) pastel (F.FR 6000)*
£612	*$1206*	*(14-Nov-90 FB.P200/R) La musicienne (26x18cm-10x7in) ink wash (F.FR 6000)*
£612	*$1206*	*(14-Nov-90 FB.P204/R) La supplication (26x18cm-10x7in) ink wash (F.FR 6000)*
£617	*$1196*	*(7-Dec-90 GL.P133) Orgie romaine (21x15cm-8x6in) s. W/C htd.gouache (F.FR 6000)*
£663	*$1307*	*(14-Nov-90 FB.P194/R) La danse du feu (27x18cm-11x7in) ink wash (F.FR 6500)*
£963	*$1908*	*(3-Feb-91 I.N32) Nymphe et satyre (25x33cm-10x13in) s. W/C lead pencil (F.FR 9500)*
£1012	*$1984*	*(19-Nov-90 ARC.P21) Reverie (33x24cm-13x9in) s. W/C (F.FR 10000)*
£1500	*$2445*	*(1-Jul-91 APT.P45/R) La peche (62x47cm-24x19in) s. pastel (F.FR 15000)*

CALDARA, Polidoro see POLIDORO DA CARAVAGGIO

CALDER, Alexander (1898-1976) American

£7231	$14100	(23-Oct-90 C.A319/R) Composition (74x108cm-29x43in) s.d.1970 acrylic (B.FR 440000)
£7500	$13275	(21-Mar-91 S85/R) Woman and pirate (10x45cm-4x18in) canvas on panel
£1224	$2400	(6-Nov-90 CE.NY8/R) Plants and sun (25x30cm-10x12in) s.d.30 ink
£1429	$2800	(6-Nov-90 CE.NY3/R) Acrobat riding elephant (25x30cm-10x12in) s.d.30 pen
£1429	$2800	(6-Nov-90 CE.NY1/R) Performing elephant (25x30cm-10x12in) s.d.30 pen
£1491	$2520	(15-Apr-91 CC.P51/R) Composition sur fond bleu (37x27cm-15x11in) s. gouache (F.FR 15000)
£1580	$2750	(27-Mar-91 B.SF4164/R) Au cirque, l'homme et la femme aux spirales (27x33cm-11x13in) s.i.d.49 ink
£1633	$3200	(6-Nov-90 CE.NY5/R) Plants and face (25x30cm-10x12in) s.d.30 ink
£1792	$3101	(22-May-91 BA.S328/R) Composition (56x72cm-22x28in) s.d.65 gouache (S.KR 19000)
£1840	$3000	(12-Jun-91 SY.NY168/R) Study of chicken (34x27cm-13x11in) s. ink

CALDER, Alexander (1898-1976) American-cont.

£2388	$4776	(5-Feb-91 CSC.P49/R) Six satellites (76x107cm-30x42in) s.d.65 gouache board (F.FR 23500)
£2551	$5000	(6-Nov-90 CE.NY6/R) Composition and red circle (78x58cm-31x23in) s.d.66 W/C ink
£2761	$4500	(12-Jun-91 SY.NY182/R) Untitled (78x58cm-31x23in) s.d.74 i.num.14558 verso gouache
£2792	$5500	(4-Oct-90 SY.NY115/R) Untitled (39x34cm-15x13in) init. gouache
£3067	$5000	(12-Jun-91 SY.NY179/R) Untitled (75x54cm-30x21in) s.d.65 i.num.405 verso gouache
£3316	$6500	(12-Feb-91 SY.NY378/R) Night sky (46x36cm-18x14in) init.d.63 gouache
£3333	$6500	(10-Oct-90 SY.NY486 a/R) Untitled (64x102cm-25x40in) s.d.74 gouache
£3525	$5745	(16-Jun-91 CC.P17/R) Composition (79x58cm-31x23in) s.d.1973 W/C (F.FR 35000)
£3571	$7000	(6-Nov-90 CE.NY4/R) Spiral and red circle (58x79cm-23x31in) s.d.47 W/C ink
£3571	$6000	(24-Apr-91 B.SF4577/R) Sun and moon (64x94cm-25x37in) s.d.74 gouache
£3590	$7000	(10-Oct-90 SY.NY409/R) The red dome (58x76cm-23x30in) s.d.66 gouache
£3681	$6000	(12-Jun-91 SY.NY180/R) Phrygian cup and orange star (74x109cm-29x43in) s.d.69 gouache indian ink
£3699	$7250	(12-Feb-91 SY.NY376/R) The songbird (74x109cm-29x43in) s.d.72 gouache
£3846	$7500	(10-Oct-90 SY.NY373/R) Airplane (74x104cm-29x41in) init.d.75 gouache
£4046	$7000	(7-May-91 CE.NY160/R) Boomerang and clouded yellow orbs (58x78cm-23x31in) s.d.67 gouache ink
£4082	$8000	(6-Nov-90 CE.NY175/R) Four pyramids, two moons (37x110cm-15x43in) s.d.75 gouache ink
£4103	$8000	(10-Oct-90 SY.NY454/R) Untitled (74x107cm-29x42in) s.d.66 gouache
£4103	$8000	(10-Oct-90 SY.NY376/R) Untitled (74x109cm-29x43in) s.d.71 gouache
£4294	$7000	(12-Jun-91 SY.NY178/R) Untitled (74x109cm-29x43in) s.d.71 gouache
£4310	$7500	(27-Mar-91 B.SF4169/R) Tourbillons (68x102cm-27x40in) s.i.d.62 W/C gouache
£4315	$8500	(3-Oct-90 SY.NY111/R) Billy Sunday, study for the opening curtain (27x28cm-11x11in) s. W/C pencil collage
£4335	$8453	(25-Oct-90 CB.P67) Composition (76x107cm-30x42in) gouache (F.FR 43000)
£4337	$8500	(6-Nov-90 CE.NY76/R) Red nose (74x109cm-29x43in) s.d.69 gouache
£4337	$8500	(6-Nov-90 CE.NY68/R) Untitled (75x109cm-30x43in) s.d.70 gouache
£4337	$8500	(12-Feb-91 SY.NY377/R) Blue and purple discs (74x107cm-29x42in) s.d.64 gouache
£4500	$7965	(21-Mar-91 C231/R) Untitled (110x74cm-43x29in) s.d.72 gouache
£4592	$9000	(6-Nov-90 CE.NY93/R) Watery garden (74x109cm-29x43in) s.d.70 gouache
£4592	$9000	(15-Feb-91 SY.NY152/R) Blue flower and seedling (109x73cm-43x29in) s.d.70 india ink gouache
£4592	$9000	(6-Nov-90 CE.NY91/R) Circles (75x110cm-30x43in) s.d.71 gouache
£4615	$9000	(24-Oct-90 B.SF1480/R) Jongleurs (37x48cm-15x19in) s.d.50 ink W/C
£4771	$8064	(15-Apr-91 CC.P53/R) Composition (77x57cm-30x22in) s.d.1970 gouache (F.FR 48000)
£4872	$9500	(10-Oct-90 SY.NY408/R) Untitled (74x109cm-29x43in) s.d.1974 gouache
£5102	$10000	(6-Nov-90 CE.NY96/R) Composition (110x74cm-43x29in) s.d.70 gouache
£5184	$8761	(17-Apr-91 WE.MU316/R) Composition (59x78cm-23x31in) s.d.1947 W/C ink (DM 15500)
£5202	$9000	(7-May-91 CE.NY207/R) Tancarville (74x110cm-29x43in) s.d.74 gouache
£5478	$9313	(2-Jun-91 GL.P210/R) Tourbillons (68x102cm-27x40in) s.i. gouache W/C (F.FR 55000)
£5607	$10821	(16-Dec-90 P.V63/R) Sans titre (75x108cm-30x43in) s.d.1965 gouache (F.FR 55000)
£5612	$11000	(8-Nov-90 CH.NY101/R) The boss talks (75x108cm-30x43in) s.d.66 i. verso gouache
£5867	$11500	(6-Nov-90 CE.NY172/R) Sun, moon and snake (110x31cm-43x12in) init.d.75 gouache ink
£6020	$10174	(17-Apr-91 WE.MU315/R) Composition (74x100cm-29x39in) s.d.1970 gouache (DM 15000)
£6154	$12000	(10-Oct-90 SY.NY375/R) The blue corner (74x109cm-29x43in) s.d.69 gouache
£6240	$10795	(25-May-91 KV.L418/R) Piramides et soleil (74x55cm-29x22in) s.d.74 gouache (B.FR 380000)
£7000	$13650	(18-Oct-90 S59/R) Untitled (74x109cm-29x43in) s.d.70 gouache
£7143	$14000	(6-Nov-90 CE.NY777/R) Mountain range (75x108cm-30x43in) s.d.65 goauche
£7570	$13020	(14-May-91 GF.L2225/R) Composition (61x60cm-24x24in) s.d.1966 W/C (S.FR 19000)
£7614	$15000	(3-Oct-90 SY.NY110 a/R) Tightrope artist hanging by hands (56x75cm-22x30in) s.d.1932 india ink
£7887	$15379	(17-Oct-90 DL.P14/R) Composition (71x108cm-28x43in) s.d.67 Indian ink W/C gouache (F.FR 78000)
£8000	$15600	(18-Oct-90 C424/R) Untitled (74x104cm-29x41in) s.d.62 gouache
£8586	$16828	(14-Feb-91 GL.P9/R) La fete (110x74cm-43x29in) s.d.1974 gouache (F.FR 85000)
£9005	$17560	(22-Oct-90 BR.M73/R) Composizione (110x75cm-43x30in) s.d.1972 gouache (I.L 20000000)
£9184	$18000	(7-Nov-90 SY.NY210/R) Head (61x107cm-24x42in) s.d.65 gouache
£9500	$16815	(21-Mar-91 C228/R) Untitled (74x110cm-29x43in) s.d.70 gouache
£9645	$19000	(5-Oct-90 CH.NY64/R) Trainer and equestrian (61x44cm-24x17in) init.d.76 gouache
£11000	$19470	(21-Mar-91 S87/R) Untitled (75x110cm-30x43in) s.d.67 gouache
£13361	$25920	(5-Dec-90 ZZ.F94/R) C OO s.d.1966 gouache (F.FR 130000)

CALDERARA, Antonio (1903-) Italian
£1650	$2707	(20-Jun-91 F.M345/R) Ritratto femminile (20x14cm-8x6in) mono. board (I.L 3600000)
£2292	$3759	(20-Jun-91 F.M346/R) Verso sera (16x13cm-6x5in) s. panel (I.L 5000000)
£2734	$4647	(28-May-91 SY.MI7/R) Spazio Luce (38x46cm-15x18in) s.d.1962verso panel (I.L 6000000)
£2800	$4844	(10-May-91 S.Z15) Autoritratto (18x12cm-7x5in) s.d.1951verso board (S.FR 7000)
£2842	$4662	(20-Jun-91 F.M381) Figura (14x11cm-6x4in) s.i.d.1958verso panel (I.L 6200000)
£2960	$5121	(10-May-91 S.Z16) Picolo Porto, Lake Garda (9x41cm-4x16in) s.i.d.1956verso board (S.FR 7400)
£3625	$6307	(26-Mar-91 F.M16/R) Lago d'Orta (18x24cm-7x9in) s. panel (I.L 8000000)
£3700	$6401	(10-May-91 S.Z17/R) Il lago d'Osta (12x22cm-5x9in) s.i.d.1950verso board (S.FR 9250)
£4068	$6793	(8-Jun-91 HN.H58/R) Pittura (21x27cm-8x11in) panel (DM 12000)
£636	*$1100*	*(7-May-91 F.M66) Presenza orizzontale (16x15cm-6x6in) s.d.1967 W/C (I.L 1400000)*
£640	*$1107*	*(10-May-91 S.Z14) Untitled (12x16cm-5x6in) mono.d.1962 W/C over pencil (S.FR 1600)*
£911	*$1549*	*(28-May-91 SY.MI77/R) Composizione (16x15cm-6x6in) mono.d.1974 W/C (I.L 2000000)*
£1139	*$1936*	*(28-May-91 SY.MI93/R) Composizione (16x15cm-6x6in) mono.d.1974 W/C (I.L 2500000)*
£1406	*$2361*	*(24-Apr-91 G.Z5/R) Composition (16x15cm-6x6in) mono.d.1974 W/C (S.FR 3500)*

CALDERINI, Marco (1850-) Italian
| £39306 | $68000 | (22-May-91 SY.NY291/R) Children at play (35x55cm-14x22in) s.d.1887 board |

CALDERON, Charles-Clement (19/20th C) French
£1387	$2400	(8-May-91 RO.BA359) Vue de Venise (46x65cm-18x26in) s.
£2513	$4497	(17-Mar-91 L.C86/R) La place des Doges vue de la Lagune (63x45cm-25x18in) s. (F.FR 25000)
£4764	$9290	(12-Oct-90 APT.P458/R) Venise - trois-mats devant le Palais des Doges (46x65cm-18x26in) st.sig. studio st. verso (F.FR 47500)
£5829	$9560	(18-Jun-91 APT.P174/R) Gondoles sur la lagune (55x81cm-22x32in) bears studio st. (F.FR 58000)

CALDERON, Philip Hermogenes (1833-1898) Spanish
| £1000 | $1740 | (26-Mar-91 PH88/R) Portrait of a lady seated, an azalea behind (61x51cm-24x20in) s.d.1869 |
| £1400 | $2744 | (22-Jan-91 PH104/R) Family affairs (23x46cm-9x18in) s.d.1855 |

CALDWELL, Edmund (1852-1930) British
| £3892 | $6500 | (7-Jun-91 SY.NY158/R) A hound with puppies (30x38cm-12x15in) s.d.1885 |

CALDWELL, John (?) ?
| *£402* | *$699* | *(26-Mar-91 JRL.S205) Mountain landscape (62x98cm-24x39in) s. W/C (A.D 900)* |

CALES, Abbe Pierre (1870-1961) French
| £714 | $1377 | (14-Dec-90 ARC.P92) Les bords de l'Isere (23x67cm-9x26in) s.d.1919 board (F.FR 7000) |
| £1577 | $3076 | (15-Oct-90 B.G25/R) Paysage du Trieves (24x106cm-9x42in) (F.FR 15600) |

CALETTI, Giuseppe (1600-1660) Italian
| £5910 | $11583 | (20-Nov-90 F.R137/R) Salome con la testa del Battista (113x89cm-44x35in) (I.L 13000000) |
| *£1003* | *$1776* | *(19-Mar-91 F.M287/R) Ritratto di gentiluomo con spada (18x13cm-7x5in) ink (I.L 2200000)* |

CALIARI, Benedetto (attrib) (1538-1598) Italian
| *£550* | *$974* | *(22-Mar-91 APT.P18) Saint Gregoire et Saint Jean l'Evangeliste (42x28cm-17x11in) wash htd.white (F.FR 5500)* |

CALIARI, Gabriele (1568-1631) Italian
| *£2200* | *$3586* | *(2-Jul-91 C94/R) Head of young girl, looking down to left (29x20cm-11x8in) pastel* |

CALIARI, Paolo see VERONESE, Paolo

CALIFANO, John (1862-1946) Italian/American
£632	$1200	(14-Sep-90 DM.D2354/R) La Toilette (61x86cm-24x34in) s.
£684	$1300	(15-Sep-90 S.W2108/R) Along the canal (127x76cm-50x30in) s.
£1006	$1700	(20-Apr-91 WOL.C172/R) Still life of fruit (41x51cm-16x20in) s.
£1071	$1800	(19-Jul-91 DM.D2087/R) California coast (76x127cm-30x50in) s.
£1297	$2400	(10-Mar-91 H.C118/R) Lake of Bardonecchia (74x132cm-29x52in) s.
£1302	$2200	(17-Apr-91 D.NY12) Coming in from fields (76x112cm-30x44in) s.
£2261	$4250	(19-Sep-90 B.SF2772/R) Girl and lamb (48x105cm-19x41in) s.

CALL, Jan van (elder) (1656-1703) Dutch
| *£7895* | *$15000* | *(8-Jan-91 SY.NY115/R) A view of Nijmegen from the south. View with Emmerich in the background (16x26cm-6x10in) W/C over pen blk.chk. pair* |

CALLCOTT, Sir Augustus Wall (1799-1844) British
£1200	$1980	(12-Jul-91 C124/R) Extensive Italianate coastal landscape with figure resting on path (24x19cm-9x7in) paper on board
£2789	$5438	(24-Oct-90 GD.B204/R) Evening vessels waiting for the tide off Guernsey (62x118cm-24x46in) s.d.1817 s.i.d.verso (S.FR 7000)
£11000	$18150	(12-Jul-91 C79/R) Entrance to Pisa from Leghorn, with figures on quayside. Italianate river scene (15x23cm-6x9in) pair

CALLET, Antoine Francois (1741-1823) French
| £4077 | $7829 | (30-Nov-90 APT.P108/R) Portrait de Louis XVI en costume de sacre (59x49cm-23x19in) (F.FR 40000) |

CALLET, Antoine Francois (attrib) (1741-1823) French
| £655 | $1245 | *(27-Feb-91 LEB.P56/R) Tete de jeune femme, le profil tourne vers la gauche chl.wash white chk.sanguinne (F.FR 6500)* |

CALLOT, Jacques (1592-1635) French
£600	$1014	*(16-Apr-91 C104) The raising of Lazarus (6x5cm-2x2in) blk.chk. oval*
£3800	$6194	*(2-Jul-91 C140/R) Christ among doctors. Martyrdom of Saint Lawrence (6x5cm-2x2in) black chk oval pair*
£5500	$9295	*(16-Apr-91 C103/R) Studies of friars, a seated woman, a pilgrim and a man lying on sacks red blk.chk. seven another drawing by Luyken*

CALLOT, Jacques (style) (1592-1635) French
| £1600 | $3200 | (7-Feb-91 CSK141) Shipwrights on seashore. Fisherfolk mending nets (16x22cm-6x9in) with sig.verso board pair |

CALLOW, George D (19th C) British
| £550 | $941 | (30-Jul-91 SWS21) Unloading the catch (29x55cm-11x22in) s.d.1858 |

CALLOW, George D (circle) (19th C) British
| £1600 | $2752 | (14-May-91 SWS195/R) Fisherfolk and moored vessels on the shore at evening (68x106cm-27x42in) |

CALLOW, James W (fl.1860-1882) British
| £1955 | $3500 | (10-Apr-91 HF.NY80/R) Coastal landscape with fishermen (53x74cm-21x29in) s. |

CALLOW, John (1822-1878) British
£800	$1504	(8-Aug-90 PHP116) Fisherfolk unloading the catch (43x74cm-17x29in) indist.s.d.1887
£4977	$8412	(16-Apr-91 J.M132/R) A fresh breeze off the South Pier, Sunderland (79x182cm-31x72in) s.i. (A.D 11000)
£600	$1170	*(18-Oct-90 CSK65 a) Collision course (40x59cm-16x23in) s.d.1848 indist. pencil W/C*
£880	$1707	*(3-Dec-90 SC4177/R) Sailing vessels off Hastings (15x25cm-6x10in) init. W/C scratching out*
£920	$1592	*(20-May-91 SWS364/R) A two-master in rough seas (42x65cm-17x26in) s.indist.d. W/C ink scratching out*
£1300	$2249	*(22-May-91 S41/R) Busy shipping lanes (26x42cm-10x17in) s.d.1861 W/C*
£2300	$4255	*(6-Mar-91 DR46/R) Hulks and shipping (30x44cm-12x17in) s.d.1851 W/C pair*

CALLOW, William (1812-1908) British
£717	$1175	(18-Jun-91 FN.S1781) Old mills of Bruges (19x30cm-7x12in) s. i.verso panel (DM 2100)
£717	$1175	(18-Jun-91 FN.S1780) Moonrise on the Modway (19x30cm-7x12in) s. i.verso panel (DM 2100)
£850	$1658	(17-Oct-90 PHG80) A busy shipping scene (60x105cm-24x41in) s.d.'68
£1800	$3060	(30-May-91 C149/R) Cutter running past Steepholm in Bristol Channel (30x46cm-12x18in)
£600	$1140	*(12-Sep-90 CSK184/R) Travellers resting, tower beyond (23x18cm-9x7in) s. pencil W/C*
£720	$1368	*(12-Sep-90 PHL70) Figures in punt before town in wooded river landscape (16x24cm-6x9in) s. col.washes*
£851	$1600	*(22-Sep-90 WOL.C211/R) Oxen and haycart by barn (15x25cm-6x10in) W/C*
£1500	$2475	*(11-Jul-91 S187/R) Travellers on the South Downs (19x30cm-7x12in) s. W/C over pencil*
£1600	$2640	*(11-Jul-91 S205/R) Town by river with stone bridge (16x25cm-6x10in) s. W/C over pencil htd.bodycol*
£1600	$3168	*(30-Jan-91 S146/R) Le Treport, Northern France (37x54cm-15x21in) s.d.1890 W/C over pencil htd bodycol*
£2000	$3580	*(9-Apr-91 C153/R) Old houses at Berne, Switzerland (25x36cm-10x14in) s.i. pencil W/C*
£2400	$4296	*(11-Apr-91 S62/R) Beached fishing boats off Flint Castle (25x50cm-10x20in) s.d.1869 W/C over pencil*
£2600	$5096	*(21-Nov-90 B30/R) View, possibly on Seine, at evening (19x27cm-7x11in) s. W/C*
£2800	$5516	*(12-Nov-90 PH39/R) Bruges (26x35cm-10x14in) s.d.1853 W/C*
£2900	$5655	*(16-Jan-91 BT40/R) Guilleboeuf (28x43cm-11x17in) s.d.1840 W/C stopping out*
£3800	$6270	*(11-Jul-91 S186/R) Water mill on river (18x35cm-7x14in) s. W/C over pencil scratching out*
£4000	$7160	*(11-Apr-91 S90/R) Menaggio, Lake Como, Italy (24x35cm-9x14in) s.d.1865 W/C over pencil*
£4600	$7590	*(11-Jul-91 S128/R) On the Garonne near Bordeaux, France (18x24cm-7x9in) i.verso W/C over pencil scratching out*

CALLOW, William (1812-1908) British-cont.
£9500 $15675   (11-Jul-91 S132/R) The Seine from St Germain (13x32cm-5x13in)
                   i.d.1833verso W/C over pencil

CALLOWHILL, James (19th C) British
£620 $1178   (28-Feb-91 DLY347/R) Near Salwarp,Worcester (30x46cm-12x18in) s.d.1879
                   i. verso

CALLOWHILL, Scott (fl.1880-1890) British
£580 $1148   (1-Feb-91 PHE60) On Lenny (34x51cm-13x20in) s. s.i.d.1881 verso

CALMETTES, Jean-Marie (1918-) French
£978 $1653   (29-Apr-91 LGB.P85/R) Nature morte (100x65cm-39x26in) s.d.1948
                   (F.FR 9800)
£1518 $2976   (25-Nov-90 ZZ.F27/R) Nature morte au pot blanc (73x92cm-29x36in) s.d.53
                   panel (F.FR 15000)
£1578 $3109   (29-Oct-90 LC.P3/R) Composition a la bouteille (81x116cm-32x46in) s.
                   d.1959 verso (F.FR 15500)

CALMEYER, Jacob Mathias (1802-1883) Danish
£712 $1375   (10-Dec-90 B.O16/R) Wooded landscape with brook (31x44cm-12x17in) s.
                   panel (N.KR 8000)

CALMEYER, Jacob Mathias (attrib) (1802-1883) Danish
£574 $1148   (9-Feb-91 BU.O30) Landscape from Holmestrand (33x48cm-13x19in) panel
                   (N.KR 6500)

CALOGERO, Jean (1922-) Italian
£578 $1000   (12-May-91 H.C63) L'idolo (56x46cm-22x18in) s. s.i.verso
£1322 $2499   (30-Sep-90 E.LA58) Gondoles a Venise (46x55cm-18x22in) s. (F.FR 13000)
£1424 $2692   (30-Sep-90 E.LA182) Personnages a Venise (46x55cm-18x22in) s.
                   (F.FR 14000)
£2982 $5040   (21-Apr-91 E.LA205) Danseuses a l'opera (27x22cm-11x9in) s. (F.FR 30000)

CALRAET, Abraham van (1642-1722) Dutch
£9000 $14670   (5-Jul-91 C321/R) Extensive river landscape with drover and other
                   peasants on wooded road (43x56cm-17x22in) panel

CALRAET, Abraham van (attrib) (1642-1722) Dutch
£2000 $3260   (4-Jul-91 D126/R) Still life of fruit in basket and flowers on stone
                   ledge (28x33cm-11x13in)

CALRAET, Barend van (style) (1649-1737) Dutch
£952 $1686   (20-Mar-91 KM.K1027) Soldier and horse before barn and tents beyond
                   (39x58cm-15x23in) (DM 2800)

CALS, Adolphe Felix (1810-1880) French
£941 $1665   (5-Apr-91 LGB.P162) Ferme a Honfleur (21x26cm-8x10in) s.d.1876
                   (F.FR 9500)
£3200 $5664   (22-Mar-91 APT.P19) Les deux amis autour d'une table (31x41cm-12x16in)
                   s.d.1864 chl. stumping htd.white oval (F.FR 32000)

CALVAERT, Dionisio (1540-1619) Flemish
£5929 $9901   (4-Jun-91 CH.R430/R) S.Francesco che cede le stigmate
                   (114x162cm-45x64in) (I.L 13000000)

CALVAERT, Dionisio (attrib) (1540-1619) Flemish
£6500 $10985   (17-Apr-91 S118/R) The Mystic Marriage of St Catherine (46x36cm-18x14in)
                   copper

CALVAERT, Dionisio (circle) (1540-1619) Flemish
£3448 $6621   (17-Dec-90 ARC.P21) Le mariage mystique de Sainte Catherine
                   (43x33cm-17x13in) copper (F.FR 34000)

CALVAERT, Dionisio (style) (1540-1619) Flemish
£1000 $1630   (4-Jul-91 C715) Madonna and child with female saint (104x88cm-41x35in)

CALVERT, Frederick (19th C) British
£515 $1000   (8-Dec-90 W.W182/R) Ships at sea (30x43cm-12x17in) s.d.1830
£800 $1576   (31-Oct-90 S363/R) Figures on the coast with fishermen unloading catch
                   (24x34cm-9x13in) bears sig.
£1050 $1974   (8-Aug-90 PHP163) Off Ramsgate (26x35cm-10x14in) indist.init.
                   i.stretcher verso
£2200 $4180   (10-Jan-91 B118/R) Fishing boats (46x61cm-18x24in) pair
£2500 $4325   (22-May-91 S63/R) Scarborough. Fleet at anchor (25x35cm-10x14in) s. one
                   i.stretcher pair
£3600 $6228   (22-May-91 S69/R) Carnaervon Castle. Unloading catch (46x61cm-18x24in)
                   pair

CALVERT, Henry (1798-?) British
£1344 $2285   (27-May-91 GK.Z5012/R) Portrait of white horse (57x44cm-22x17in)
                   s.d.1852 (S.FR 3400)

CALVES, Marie (1883-?) French
£865 $1410   (10-Jun-91 W.T1370/R) La rentree a la Bergerie (48x63cm-19x25in) s.
                   (C.D 1600)

CALVES, Marie (1883-?) French-cont.
£3811 $7432   (12-Oct-90 APT.P100) Soir de mattue (115x146cm-45x57in) s. (F.FR 38000)

CALVI, Ercole (1824-1900) Italian
£3144 $6100   (8-Dec-90 W.W87/R) Scene of Venice (66x51cm-26x20in) s.d.1880
£6421 $11493   (12-Mar-91 F.M7/R) Paese sul lago di Como (29x38cm-11x15in) s.d.1897
                  paper laid down on panel (I.L 14000000)
£6879 $12314   (12-Mar-91 F.M5/R) Scorcio del lago di Como (29x39cm-11x15in) s.d.1859
                  paper laid down on panel (I.L 15000000)
£20408 $40000   (6-Nov-90 GF.L2073/R) Veduta della Riva del Carbone in Venezia
                  (81x121cm-32x48in) s.d.1859 i.stretcher (S.FR 50000)

CALVI, Jacopo Alessandro (1740-1815) Italian
*£638 $1130   (19-Mar-91 F.M235/R) Studio di composizione con santi martiri e angeli
                  pen W/C ink over pencil (I.L 1400000)*

CALZA, Antonio (attrib) (1653-1725) Italian
£5410 $9683   (8-Apr-91 CH.R226/R) Manovra di soldati a cavallo presso una citta
                  (34x64cm-13x25in) (I.L 12000000)
£6533 $12543   (19-Feb-91 ARC.P20/R) Scene de combat de cavalerie contre les turcs
                  (54x86cm-21x34in) (F.FR 65000)
£19000 $36670   (11-Dec-90 PH65/R) Cavalry skirmish on broad plain at foot of mountain
                  range (97x134cm-38x53in)

CALZA, Antonio (style) (1653-1725) Italian
£1100 $1903   (20-May-91 SWS61/R) A battle between Turks and Austrians
                  (29x39cm-11x15in)

CALZADA, Carl de (19th C?) French
£870 $1478   (27-May-91 GK.Z5013) Maternite (68x55cm-27x22in) s.d.1867 (S.FR 2200)

CALZOLARI, Pier Paolo (1943-) Italian
*£864 $1634   (27-Sep-90 F.M90) Ricostruito (48x68cm-19x27in) s.d.2-75 ink board
                  (I.L 1900000)*
*£3637 $7128   (20-Nov-90 BR.M15/R) Senza titolo (70x50cm-28x20in) s.d.1968 pencil
                  cardboard (I.L 8000000)*

CAMACHO, Jorge (1934-) Cuban
£2251 $4390   (24-Oct-90 F.M158/R) L'oison qui sait approfondir (116x81cm-46x32in)
                  s.d.1965verso (I.L 5000000)
£2854 $5509   (15-Dec-90 D.P27/R) Un personaje se escapa (116x89cm-46x35in) s.d.1960
                  II verso (F.FR 28000)
£4592 $9046   (16-Nov-90 FB.P377/R) La danse de la mort, Opus 1 (116x89cm-46x35in)
                  s.i.d.72 verso (F.FR 45000)
£5025 $8995   (11-Mar-91 GL.P231/R) L'oison qui sait approfondir (116x81cm-46x32in)
                  s.i.d.1965 verso (F.FR 50000)
£5912 $11411   (16-Dec-90 GL.P68/R) Miroir a alouette no.2 (89x146cm-35x57in) s.i.
                  verso acrylic (F.FR 58000)
£8065 $15726   (26-Oct-90 CC.P25/R) Agony of a citizen (114x152cm-45x60in) s.d.1957
                  (F.FR 80000)

CAMACHO, Pedro (attrib) (17th C) Spanish
£3279 $6426   (24-Jan-91 EP.M3/R) La educacion de la Virgen (117x95cm-46x37in)
                  rem.sig. (S.P 600000)

CAMARERA, J L (?) ?
£750 $1260   (18-Jul-91 CSK167/R) Spanish fiesta (46x41cm-18x16in) s.

CAMARLENCH, Ignacio Pinazo (1849-1916) Spanish
£9167 $17967   (22-Nov-90 EP.M2/R) Figuras en la Playa (9x19cm-4x7in) s.d.1881 panel
                  (S.P 1700000)

CAMARO, Alexander (1901-) German
£2534 $4307   (1-Jun-91 VG.B335/R) Fish trap (50x70cm-20x28in) s. i.verso board
                  (DM 7500)
£6143 $12041   (24-Nov-90 VG.B360/R) Harlekin auf weisser Flache (66x54cm-26x21in) s.
                  i.d.1950verso (DM 18000)

CAMBELLE, M (20th C) Belgian?
£818 $1408   (14-May-91 GM.B448) Chez le Marechal-Ferrant (102x140cm-40x55in) s.
                  (B.FR 50000)

CAMBIASO, Luca (1527-1585) Italian
£547 $969   (19-Mar-91 F.M333) Sacra Famiglia (27x21cm-11x8in) ink (I.L 1200000)
*£1049 $2024   (10-Dec-90 L.K220/R) Holy Family with infant St John before column
                  (35x25cm-14x10in) pen sepia wash (DM 3000)*
*£1119 $2159   (10-Dec-90 L.K225/R) The triumph of Amphitrite (31x23cm-12x9in) pen dr.
                  (DM 3200)*
*£1189 $2294   (10-Dec-90 L.K223/R) Study of male figure standing holding scroll
                  (23x12cm-9x5in) i. pen sepia wash (DM 3400)*
*£1259 $2429   (10-Dec-90 L.K226/R) St Francis receiving stigma (28x21cm-11x8in) pen
                  sepia wash dr. (DM 3600)*
*£1277 $2260   (19-Mar-91 F.M334/R) Cristo e la samaritana (41x27cm-16x11in) pen W/C
                  ink (I.L 2800000)*
*£1336 $2592   (6-Dec-90 ARC.P26) La Sainte famille avec Saint Jean Baptiste
                  (25x20cm-10x8in) i. pen (F.FR 13000)*

CAMBIASO, Luca (1527-1585) Italian-cont.
£2600	$4394	(16-Apr-91 C135/R) Study of a man seen from below (37x18cm-15x7in) watermark ink wash horizontal lines red chk.
£2736	$4843	(19-Mar-91 F.M355/R) Episodio di storia antica (20x25cm-8x10in) pen W/C ink squared (I.L 6000000)
£5000	$8150	(2-Jul-91 C9/R) Amazons with horse in procession (29x37cm-11x15in) pen ink wash
£6384	$11300	(19-Mar-91 F.M238/R) Conversione di San Paolo (24x34cm-9x13in) pen bistre W/C ink paper on album leaf (I.L 14000000)
£6384	$11300	(19-Mar-91 F.M343/R) Nesso e Dejanira (32x24cm-13x9in) bears i. ink paper laid down on album leaf (I.L 14000000)
£11856	$20985	(19-Mar-91 F.M209/R) Conversione di San Paolo (28x41cm-11x16in) pen W/C ink (I.L 26000000)
£13000	$21190	(2-Jul-91 C86/R) Holy Family with infant Baptist in carpenter's shop (27x21cm-11x8in) with i. black chk pen

CAMBIASO, Luca (attrib) (1527-1585) Italian
£8835	$14225	(25-Jun-91 APT.P8/R) Psyche et l'amour (120x92cm-47x36in) (F.FR 88000)
£730	$1291	(19-Mar-91 F.M182/R) Madonna col Bambino e due angeli. Studi anatomici (35x25cm-14x10in) ink double-sided (I.L 1600000)
£821	$1453	(19-Mar-91 F.M190/R) Sacra Famiglia con San Giovannino (25x37cm-10x15in) i.verso pen W/C ink over pencil (I.L 1800000)
£1100	$1793	(4-Jul-91 B62/R) The holy family with St. John the Baptist (27x22cm-11x9in) watermark pen wash
£2446	$4697	(27-Nov-90 APT.P9/R) Combat des dieux de la mer (18x41cm-7x16in) pen wash sepia (F.FR 24000)

CAMBIASO, Luca (style) (1527-1585) Italian
£3500	$6720	(29-Nov-90 CSK15/R) Venus and Cupid (152x109cm-60x43in)

CAMBIER, Guy (20th C) French
£808	$1600	(1-Feb-91 S.W2394/R) Three Graces (91x74cm-36x29in) s.
£2591	$4250	(19-Jun-91 B.SF1953/R) The story book (81x65cm-32x26in) s.

CAMBIER, Nestor (19/20th C) Belgian
£633	$1216	(18-Dec-90 GM.B769) Hall de l'Ambassade de Belgique a Londres (54x62cm-21x24in) s. board (B.FR 38000)

CAMENZIND, Balz (1907-) ?
£1714	$3360	(6-Nov-90 GF.L2282/R) Gnarled tree (85x77cm-33x30in) s.d.85 (S.FR 4200)

CAMERINO, Girolamo di Giovanni da (circle) (15th C) Italian
£2800	$4564	(5-Jul-91 C239/R) Saint John the Baptist (116x48cm-46x19in) oil tempera feigned painted arch

CAMERON, Douglas (?) British
£500	$825	(11-Jul-91 CSK149) Highland cattle watering from mountain stream (61x107cm-24x42in) s.
£1000	$1970	(30-Oct-90 SC128/R) Highland rovers (62x75cm-24x30in) s.
£1400	$2352	(23-Apr-91 S73/R) Highland cattle (102x76cm-40x30in) s.

CAMERON, Duncan (19th C) British
£550	$1029	(28-Aug-90 S960/R) On the Esk at Musselburgh (30x45cm-12x18in) s.s.i.verso board
£620	$1097	(5-Apr-91 PHE94) Morning breeze on coast, Berwick (51x76cm-20x30in) s.
£670	$1286	(28-Nov-90 PH.T103/R) Low tide (49x75cm-19x30in) s. (C.D 1500)
£880	$1716	(24-Oct-90 DR175) By the river Clyde (51x76cm-20x30in) s.
£1100	$1859	(2-May-91 CG483) Harvest time on banks of river, possibly at Lanrich, Perthshire (51x76cm-20x30in) s.
£1100	$2200	(5-Feb-91 S77/R) Sunrise (35x53cm-14x21in) s.
£1500	$2955	(30-Oct-90 SC210/R) View of Edinburgh from the river (39x59cm-15x23in) s.
£2200	$3542	(27-Jun-91 CG87) Early autumn, Aberdour, Fife (61x96cm-24x38in) s.
£2400	$4728	(30-Oct-90 SC227/R) St Andrews, looking west from East Sands (76x127cm-30x50in) s.d.76 s.i.verso

CAMERON, Hugh (1835-?) British
£650	$1092	(23-Apr-91 S135/R) Young love (25x15cm-10x6in) s. panel
£1500	$2535	(2-May-91 CG513) Paddling (57x89cm-22x35in) s.d.1901

CAMERON, Katherine (1874-1965) British
£600	$1176	(23-Nov-90 PHE29/R) Bees and clarkia (35x54cm-14x21in) s.
£640	$1261	(30-Oct-90 SC6/R) Lady on staircase (54x40cm-21x16in) s. W/C pencil
£700	$1239	(22-Mar-91 PHE45) Basket of pink and crimson roses (61x75cm-24x30in) init.
£1750	$2940	(23-Apr-91 GAM72/R) Gossips (42x17cm-17x7in) s. pen W/C
£2200	$4114	(28-Aug-90 S1000) Honeysuckle and tortoiseshell butterfly (39x27cm-15x11in) s.i. W/C

CAMERON, Mary (?-1921) British
£12500	$23375	(28-Aug-90 S892/R) Hurst Park races (69x82cm-27x32in) s.

CAMERON, Sir David Young (1865-1945) British
£900	$1800	(5-Feb-91 S156/R) Far Duart (19x27cm-7x11in) s. panel
£1000	$1870	(28-Aug-90 S857/R) The rocky shores of Moray (31x38cm-12x15in) s.
£1200	$2016	(23-Apr-91 S140/R) Boddin cottage (16x24cm-6x9in) init. board

CAMERON, Sir David Young (1865-1945) British-cont.

£2600	$5096	(22-Nov-90 CG619/R) The peaks (61x91cm-24x36in) s.
£2800	$4732	(2-May-91 CG509/R) Durham cathedral (43x57cm-17x22in) s.
£4000	$6760	(3-May-91 PHE83/R) Entrance to the fort (45x50cm-18x20in) init.
£6200	$11594	(28-Aug-90 S939/R) Western Isles (43x63cm-17x25in) s.s.i.verso
£6500	$10985	(3-May-91 PHE108/R) Ben Lomond (70x90cm-28x35in) s.
£6800	$11492	(3-May-91 PHE139/R) Courtyard, Villefranche (62x41cm-24x16in) s.
£7000	$13720	(22-Nov-90 CG618/R) Berwick Old Bridge (69x97cm-27x38in) s. i.verso
£550	*$1073*	*(17-Oct-90 PHG52) Loch Leven (28x47cm-11x19in) s. W/C*
£600	*$1122*	*(28-Aug-90 S887) The Tay (17x34cm-7x13in) s.i. W/C over pencil*

CAMM, Robert (1847-) Australian

£656	$1293	(13-Nov-90 J.M894) Droving the sheep (49x75cm-19x30in) s. (A.D 1700)

CAMMARANO, Michele (1849-1920) Italian

£1848	$3567	(11-Dec-90 CH.R110) Vicolo (64x32cm-25x13in) s. (I.L 4000000)
£38000	$62320	(19-Jun-91 S422/R) Broken fruit dish (204x148cm-80x58in) s.d.1874

CAMMILLIE, Nicolas (fl.1810-1817) ?

£6166	*$11963*	*(7-Dec-90 CH.MO105/R) Un bateau commande par le Capitaine Portal en 1809 (29x39cm-11x15in) s.i.d.1811 lead pencil pen wash W/C (F.FR 60000)*

CAMMILLIERI, Nicolas S (19th C) Canadian?

£2200	*$3806*	*(22-May-91 S31/R) Transport negotiator - Robert Eilley Commander, entering Malta Harbour, April 26th 1855 (41x57cm-16x22in) s.i. W/C*
£2600	*$5070*	*(18-Oct-90 CSK37/R) H.M.S. Caledonia entering Malta Harbour, 16th October 1836 (46x57cm-18x22in) s.i.d. pencil W/C*

CAMOIN, C (1879-1965) French

£2968	$5817	(27-Jan-91 B.PA6/R) Les Santons (26x34cm-10x13in) s. board (F.FR 29500)

CAMOIN, Charles (1879-1965) French

£3050	$5124	(28-Apr-91 FE.P86) Bouquet de tulipes (46x55cm-18x22in) s. (F.FR 30500)
£3300	$5544	(24-Apr-91 MJ.P104/R) Verre et coupe bleue avec fruits (14x22cm-6x9in) canvas pasted on panel (F.FR 33000)
£3424	$5581	(16-Jun-91 GL.P23/R) Brune allongee (27x35cm-11x14in) s. board (F.FR 34000)
£3452	$6800	(13-Nov-90 CE.NY75/R) Saint Tropez, les arbres (25x32cm-10x13in) s. paper
£3800	$7372	(6-Dec-90 CSK141/R) Nature morte aux peches (54x65cm-21x26in) s.
£4000	$6440	(24-Jun-91 CSK142/R) Le compotier bleu (26x34cm-10x13in) s. board
£5200	$10140	(19-Oct-90 C139/R) Fleurs de champs (22x27cm-9x11in) s. paper on canvas
£5344	$10368	(7-Dec-90 GL.P156) Le trou d'eau dans les rochers (65x81cm-26x32in) s. (F.FR 52000)
£6048	$11613	(2-Dec-90 GAB.G1552/R) Nu au bouquet de fleurs (41x27cm-16x11in) s. panel (S.FR 15000)
£6135	$10000	(12-Jun-91 SY.NY28/R) Anemones au fond bleu (35x27cm-14x11in) s.
£6143	$10013	(16-Jun-91 GL.P35/R) Les barques tirees au sec (24x34cm-9x13in) s. panel (F.FR 61000)
£6187	$11878	(17-Dec-90 AGS.P21/R) Portrait d'une indochinoise (65x54cm-26x21in) (F.FR 61000)
£6748	$11000	(12-Jun-91 SY.NY27/R) Narcisses (46x38cm-18x15in) s. panel
£7157	$12095	(21-Apr-91 E.LA102 b) Nature morte au pichet (28x32cm-11x13in) s. (F.FR 72000)
£9184	$18000	(14-Feb-91 CH.NY38/R) Germaine et Lola (46x55cm-18x22in) s.
£10000	$17700	(19-Mar-91 C43/R) Le jardin du Pigonnet, Aix-en-Provence (54x65cm-21x26in) s.
£10072	$19540	(7-Dec-90 GL.P155/R) Le clocher de Saint-Tropez vu de la citadelle (38x46cm-15x18in) s. (F.FR 98000)
£10142	$20081	(3-Feb-91 I.N34/R) Paysage (54x65cm-21x26in) s. (F.FR 100000)
£11168	$22000	(2-Oct-90 CH.NY94/R) Fleurs au pot de cuivre (65x53cm-26x21in) s.
£12000	$23400	(19-Oct-90 C138/R) Fleurs au vase bleu (49x39cm-19x15in) s.
£12755	$25000	(15-Feb-91 SY.NY35/R) Ramatuelle entre les pins, no 3 (65x81cm-26x32in) s.
£14000	$27300	(17-Oct-90 S45/R) La croisette a Cannes (46x38cm-18x15in) s.
£15000	$26550	(20-Mar-91 S76/R) Les tartanes a quai (54x73cm-21x29in) s.
£17329	$33272	(26-Nov-90 GL.P58/R) Port de Saint-Tropez (33x41cm-13x16in) s. board (F.FR 170000)
£18090	$32382	(16-Mar-91 APT.P24 b/R) Aix-en-Provence, le jardin du Pigonnet (65x81cm-26x32in) s. (F.FR 180000)
£20000	$32200	(25-Jun-91 C138/R) L'ecuyere (80x53cm-31x21in) st.studio verso
£20387	$39144	(27-Nov-90 APT.P38/R) Nature morte a la soupiere (65x81cm-26x32in) s. (F.FR 200000)
£20387	$39144	(27-Nov-90 APT.P34/R) Voiliers au port (54x65cm-21x26in) s. (F.FR 200000)
£23350	$46000	(2-Oct-90 CH.NY91/R) Nu de face couche (46x65cm-18x26in) s.
£25862	$49655	(17-Dec-90 AGS.P22/R) Le vieux port a Marseille (65x81cm-26x32in) s. (F.FR 255000)
£32000	$62400	(17-Oct-90 S47 a/R) Le canal (61x81cm-24x32in) s.
£40000	$77600	(5-Dec-90 S109/R) La fille au chat (65x54cm-26x21in) s.
£886	*$1497*	*(1-May-91 KH.K215/R) Portrait of young girl (44x30cm-17x12in) pastel (D.KR 10000)*
£2530	*$4960*	*(23-Nov-90 PLF.P42/R) La lecon de danse (32x50cm-13x20in) s. pastel chl. (F.FR 25000)*
£3511	*$6846*	*(11-Oct-90 QWA.P42/R) Portrait de jeune fille (45x28cm-18x11in) s. chl.col.crayons (F.FR 35000)*

CAMPAGNOLA, Domenico (1484-1550) Italian
£684 $1300 *(8-Jan-91 SY.NY97) Study of a bearded man in profile (94x59cm-37x23in) ink oval*
£1642 $2906 *(19-Mar-91 F.M348/R) Paesaggio fantastico con edifici antichi e il sogno di Giacobbe (11x14cm-4x6in) pen bistre ink (I.L 3600000)*
£3200 $5216 *(1-Jul-91 S120/R) Portrait of Ariosto (24x17cm-9x7in) bears i. num.130 verso pen*
£3500 $5915 *(16-Apr-91 C111/R) A servant helping an aged king to mount a horse, with two women (15x15cm-6x6in) blk.chk.ink*
£4500 $7335 *(2-Jul-91 C75/R) Saint Jerome outside town (25x19cm-10x7in) black chk pen*
£24000 $39120 *(2-Jul-91 C2/R) Montainous wooded landscape with Roman ruins and outskirts of city beyond (19x28cm-7x11in) chk pen ink*

CAMPAGNOLA, Domenico (circle) (1484-1550) Italian
£1400 $2702 *(12-Dec-90 PH347/R) Figures conversing amongst Roman ruins (11x17cm-4x7in) pen ink*

CAMPAGNOLA, Domenico (school) (1484-1550) Italian
£2773 $5351 *(12-Dec-90 F.M316) Madonna con Bambino (47x42cm-19x17in) panel (I.L 6000000)*

CAMPANELLA, Vito (1932-) Argentinian
£645 $1200 *(5-Sep-90 V.BA21) Paisaje (38x48cm-15x19in)*

CAMPBELL, George (1917-1979) British
£722 $1400 *(8-Dec-90 W.W224/R) Spanish treasure fleet (53x64cm-21x25in) s. board*
£926 $1787 *(12-Dec-90 CH.E77) Spanish town, winter (45x33cm-18x13in) s. board (E.P 1000)*
£1852 $3574 *(12-Dec-90 CH.E76/R) Bycycles - Bicicletas (50x76cm-20x30in) s. i.verso board (E.P 2000)*
£600 $1170 *(26-Oct-90 CG20/R) Hombre (30x23cm-12x9in) s. W/C*
£700 $1204 *(14-May-91 SWS159/R) Hauling in the nets (28x36cm-11x14in) init. gouache*

CAMPBELL, James (?-1903) British
£614 $1166 *(12-Sep-90 WO.CO1) Portrait of young match seller (51x46cm-20x18in) s.d. (E.P 675)*

CAMPBELL, John Henry (1755-1828) British
£3600 $6444 *(10-Apr-91 S184/R) Shooting by lake. Huntsmen resting by waterfall (22x33cm-9x13in) panel pair*

CAMPBELL, John Hodgson (1855-1927) British
£300 $555 *(5-Mar-91 SWS1631) The ferryman's bairn, Houghton Castle ferry, North Tyne (34x51cm-13x20in) s.d.85 i.d.verso W/C over pencil htd.bodycol*

CAMPBELL, Nora Molly (fl.1915-1950) British
£600 $1152 *(26-Nov-90 SWS83/R) The boarding house (7x12cm-3x5in) s.i.verso set of three framed as one*
£1300 $2496 *(26-Nov-90 SWS84/R) Varnishing day (29x48cm-11x19in) i.verso W/C*

CAMPBELL, Robert Richmond (1902-1972) Australian
£679 $1147 *(16-Apr-91 J.M131) On the beach (19x29cm-7x11in) s. board (A.D 1500)*
£3023 $5079 *(22-Apr-91 SY.ME53/R) Sydney harbour (19x28cm-7x11in) s. board (A.D 6500)*
£3376 $6481 *(14-Aug-90 SY.ME236/R) Collaroy (40x49cm-16x19in) s. board (A.D 8000)*
£889 $1671 *(17-Sep-90 SY.ME59/R) James Street, Fremantle (28x39cm-11x15in) c.1948 W/C (A.D 2000)*

CAMPBELL, Steven (20th C) American
£4569 $9000 *(5-Oct-90 CH.NY116/R) Reading Wodehouse in a treehouse (287x277cm-113x109in)*
£10500 $20580 *(9-Nov-90 C293/R) Two men with carriage Royale to catch queen bee (284x274cm-112x108in)*
£5000 $9750 *(10-Oct-90 PHG42/R) The acrobat (236x201cm-93x79in) i. mixed media brocade material diptych*
£6000 $11700 *(10-Oct-90 PHG106/R) Falling man (50x40cm-20x16in) s.d.85 gouache*

CAMPBELL, Tom (fl.1901-1940) British
£2400 $4488 *(28-Aug-90 S839/R) Gleam before the gloaming, Glen (102x127cm-40x50in) s.*

CAMPENDONK, Heinrich (1889-1957) German
£15102 $29751 *(16-Nov-90 GK.Z5166/R) Still life with kettle (52x58cm-20x23in) mono.d. canvas on panel (S.FR 37000)*
£25000 $40250 *(25-Jun-91 C157/R) Figuren mit Tieren und Wecker (70x81cm-28x32in) s.verso*
£2703 $4676 *(22-May-91 CH.AM546/R) Kirche in der Bretagne (25x21cm-10x8in) pencil W/C paper on board (D.FL 9000)*
£5405 $9351 *(22-May-91 CH.AM544/R) Der fischerquai (43x48cm-17x19in) init.d.35 pencil col.crayon (D.FL 18000)*
£5405 $9351 *(22-May-91 CH.AM545/R) Kirche in Oostende (42x48cm-17x19in) init.d.35 pencil (D.FL 18000)*
£16949 $28305 *(7-Jun-91 HN.H14/R) Female nude with tree trunk. Cat (54x43cm-21x17in) ink brush double-sided (DM 50000)*

CAMPENDONK, Heinrich (1889-1957) German-cont.

£18000	$34920	(5-Dec-90 S322/R) Frau mit schildkrote (45x39cm-18x15in) s.d.1912 pen brush ink W/C over pencil
£20408	$40204	(16-Nov-90 GK.Z5167/R) The policeman's child (35x29cm-14x11in) oil tempera pastel paper on board (S.FR 50000)
£50676	$86149	(30-May-91 SY.BE9/R) Artist's selfportrait (53x43cm-21x17in) i. W/C gouache over pencil paper on board (DM 150000)
£120000	$232800	(4-Dec-90 C160/R) Die barbarazeche - Penzberg (37x31cm-15x12in) s.d.1919 W/C pencil

CAMPHAUSEN, Wilhelm (1818-1885) German

£4348	$7391	(27-May-91 GK.Z5014/R) Royal hunting party riding horses and view of Dusseldorf with Rhine (107x84cm-42x33in) s.i.d.1881 (S.FR 11000)
£5594	$10797	(10-Dec-90 L.K400/R) Battle scene with Kaiser Wilhelm I in 1870/71 war (53x66cm-21x26in) s.d.84 canvas laid down (DM 16000)
£12308	$24000	(24-Oct-90 CH.NY194/R) The cavalry retreat (129x147cm-51x58in) s.d.1850
£1351	$2297	(27-May-91 L.K188/R) Konig Wilhelm I von Preussen seated on horse with attendants (59x46cm-23x18in) mono.d.61 chk W/C (DM 4000)

CAMPHUYSEN, Govert Dircksz (1624-1672) Dutch

| £21000 | $40530 | (12-Dec-90 S40/R) Sleeping shepherd with two sheep (114x84cm-45x33in) s. panel |

CAMPHUYSEN, Govert Dircksz (circle) (1624-1672) Dutch

| £4000 | $6760 | (18-Apr-91 C102/R) A wooded landscape with a shepherd and shepherdess making music (81x110cm-32x43in) panel |

CAMPHUYSEN, Joachim Govertsz (1602-1659) Dutch

| £6500 | $10985 | (17-Apr-91 S65/R) Landscape with huntsmen on path overlooking river valley (53x40cm-21x16in) mono. panel |

CAMPHUYSEN, Raphael Govertsz (1598-1657) Dutch

| £2600 | $4394 | (17-Apr-91 S153/R) River landscape (23x34cm-9x13in) panel |

CAMPI, Bernardino (1522-1592) Italian

| £917 | $1771 | (14-Dec-90 LEB.P90) Le lavement des pieds (17x12cm-7x5in) pen wash htd.white traces pierre noire (F.FR 9000) |

CAMPI, Bernardino (style) (1522-1592) Italian

| £1647 | $2783 | (2-May-91 CH.AM6) The Adoration of the shepherds (107x78cm-42x31in) (D.FL 5500) |

CAMPI, Giulio (1502-1572) Italian

| £2000 | $3260 | (1-Jul-91 S134/R) Male nude - study for pendentive (18x20cm-7x8in) bears mono. black chk |
| £10000 | $16300 | (2-Jul-91 C80/R) Saint George and dragon (29x20cm-11x8in) i.verso pen |

CAMPI, Giulio (attrib) (1502-1572) Italian

| £13158 | $25000 | (11-Jan-91 CH.NY69/R) Artemisia, fragment (94x99cm-37x39in) |

CAMPI, J (18th C) Italian

| £532 | $867 | (13-Jun-91 RAS.V751) Sewing lesson (45x55cm-18x22in) s. (D.KR 6000) |

CAMPIDOGLIO, Michele di (attrib) (1610-1670) Italian

| £17928 | $30478 | (31-May-91 LD.P44/R) Nature morte aux pasteques, pommes et fleurs sous un vasque devant un tapis... (99x142cm-39x56in) (F.FR 180000) |

CAMPIDOGLIO, Michele di (style) (1610-1670) Italian

| £4000 | $8000 | (7-Feb-91 CSK145) Flowers in vase and fruit on ledge with parrot on upturned basket (67x100cm-26x39in) |

CAMPIGLI, Massimo (1895-1971) Italian

£9547	$18711	(20-Nov-90 BR.M134/R) Teatrino (40x33cm-16x13in) cardboard (I.L 21000000)
£19388	$38000	(14-Feb-91 CH.NY75/R) Tre donne (28x40cm-11x16in) s.d.48 oil transfer paper on masonite
£23442	$41961	(9-Apr-91 F.R228/R) Ritratto femminile con cappellino (32x30cm-13x12in) s.d.71 (I.L 52000000)
£27136	$44503	(20-Jun-91 APT.P49/R) Femmes aux colliers bleus (38x46cm-15x18in) s.d.64 (F.FR 270000)
£32418	$63215	(24-Oct-90 F.M226/R) Cariatide (54x44cm-21x17in) s.d.65 paper (I.L 72000000)
£38000	$73720	(4-Dec-90 C381/R) Quattro teste (39x55cm-15x22in) s.
£38071	$75000	(2-Oct-90 CH.NY146/R) Testa di donna (46x38cm-18x15in) s.d.50
£42000	$81480	(4-Dec-90 C382/R) La Tessitrice (41x24cm-16x9in) s.d.49
£45287	$87403	(13-Dec-90 F.M451/R) Figura (70x45cm-28x18in) s.d.61 s.i.d.verso (I.L 98000000)
£65990	$130000	(2-Oct-90 CH.NY142/R) Busto (60x40cm-24x16in) s.d.50
£66327	$130000	(14-Feb-91 CH.NY72/R) Donne a passeggio (45x65cm-18x26in) s.d.57
£69028	$117348	(28-May-91 SY.MI165/R) Amiche (75x68cm-30x27in) s.d.58 (I.L 151500000)
£69364	$120000	(9-May-91 CH.NY261/R) Donna (81x65cm-32x26in) s.d.61
£100860	$165410	(20-Jun-91 F.M488/R) Due donne (57x22cm-22x9in) s.d.1947verso (I.L 220000000)
£108686	$210850	(3-Dec-90 CH.R138/R) Donna (80x50cm-31x20in) s.d.1948 (I.L 235000000)

CAMPIGLI, Massimo (1895-1971) Italian-cont.
£115607 $200000   (22-May-91 D.NY55/R) Due donne con ventagli (52x67cm-20x26in) s. panel
£125962 $241847   (27-Nov-90 SY.MI228/R) Due donne al pianoforte (60x66cm-24x26in) s.d.48
                            (I.L 275000000)
£126904 $250000   (3-Oct-90 SY.NY130/R) Donne con uccello (73x100cm-29x39in) s.d.49
                            d.verso
£202312 $350000   (8-May-91 CH.NY39/R) Piscina (195x129cm-77x51in) s.d.54
£1617   *$3122*   *(12-Dec-90 F.M2) Studio di figure (26x18cm-10x7in) s.d.1968 ink canvas*
                           (I.L 3500000)
£2806   *$5500*   *(12-Feb-91 SY.NY115/R) Two figures (30x23cm-12x9in) s.d.44 chk*
£6351   *$10924*   *(13-May-91 CH.R33/R) I minareti (29x23cm-11x9in) s.d.1942 sanguine*
                           (I.L 14000000)

CAMPIN, Robert (circle) (1376-1444) Flemish
£26316 $50000   (10-Jan-91 SY.NY12/R) Mass of Pope Gregory (83x70cm-33x28in) indist.i.d.
                           panel

CAMPION, George Bryant (1796-1870) British
£620   *$1035*   *(22-Jul-91 SWS804/R) Denis O'Hagarty, School-Master, with his class*
                           (32x43cm-13x17in) s. W/C pencil scratching out
£650   *$1287*   *(30-Jan-91 S120) Cone signals in Crimea (36x53cm-14x21in) i. pencil W/C*
                           bodycol gum arabic

CAMPO, Federico del (19th C) Peruvian
£15000 $24600   (19-Jun-91 S380/R) Palazzo Vendramini, Venice (41x59cm-16x23in) s.d.1891
£24277 $42000   (23-May-91 CH.NY145/R) Venetian backwater (38x65cm-15x26in) s.
£35838 $62000   (23-May-91 CH.NY144/R) Venetian canal scene with elegant figures in
                           gondola (38x65cm-15x26in) s.
£1000   *$1960*   *(23-Nov-90 PHE108/R) Venetian canal scene (25x18cm-10x7in) s. W/C*

CAMPO, Luigi (?) ?
£1800 $3510   (22-Oct-90 SWS156/R) Siege during risorgimento in Italian courtyard
                           (111x144cm-44x57in) s.

CAMPOREALE, Sergio (1937-) Argentinian
£5523   *$9500*   *(15-May-91 CH.NY133/R) Retrato de Familia (80x120cm-31x47in) s. st.d.4*
                           Dic 1988 W/C pencil

CAMPOS, Florencio Molina (20th C) South American
£4082 $8000   (20-Nov-90 CH.NY306/R) La trinchera No. 3 (40x51cm-16x20in) s.d.944
                           i.verso canvasboard
£2551   *$5000*   *(20-Nov-90 CH.NY305/R) Domando el caballo - Gee Whiz (30x44cm-12x17in)*
                           s.d.947 s.i.d.7.947 verso gouache board

CAMPOS, Manuel de Maria (19th C) Spanish
£5422 $10572   (17-Oct-90 FER.M178/R) Inauguracion del transbordador de Sevilla
                           (73x60cm-29x24in) s.d.1849 (S.P 1000000)

CAMPOVECCHIO, Giovanni (circle) (?) Italian
£1000 $1960   (19-Nov-90 CH.R1/R) Paesaggio con cacciatore (35x45cm-14x18in)
                           (I.L 2200000)

CAMPRIANI, Alceste (1848-1933) Italian
£1400 $2758   (4-Oct-90 CSK91 a) Sheep in a wood (29x44cm-11x17in) s.
£4532 $7659   (16-Apr-91 CH.R41) Golfo di Napoli (54x73cm-21x29in) s. (I.L 10000000)

CAMPRIANI, Alceste (1848-1933) Italian-cont.
£6500 $10660   (18-Jun-91 PH152/R) Fishermen in the Bay of Naples (41x62cm-16x24in)
                   s.i.d.1881 canvas on board
£9146 $17927   (6-Nov-90 SY.AM106/R) Angler by bay (31x48cm-12x19in) s. (D.FL 30000)
£23125 $44862   (5-Dec-90 F.M113/R) Campagna al tramonto con tacchini (62x107cm-24x42in)
                   s. (I.L 50000000)

CAMPROBIN, Pedro de (17th C) Spanish
£108755 $214247   (30-Oct-90 EP.M7/R) Floreros (77x58cm-30x23in) pair (S.P 20000000)

CAMPROBIN, Pedro de (circle) (17th C) Spanish
£1318 $2611   (30-Jan-91 APT.P21/R) Vase de fleurs sur un entablement (23x26cm-9x10in)
                 (F.FR 13000)

CAMRADT, J L (1779-1849) Danish
£5282 $8873   (23-Apr-91 RAS.K20/R) Still life of roses and other summer flowers in
                 glass vase (47x38cm-19x15in) s.d.1834 (D.KR 60000)

CAMUCCINI, Vincenzo (1773-1844) Italian
£1140 $2018   (19-Mar-91 F.M200/R) Scena di storia antica (22x33cm-9x13in) pen W/C ink
*   htd white (I.L 2500000)*

CAMUS, Blanche (19/20th C) French
£3500 $5635   (24-Jun-91 CSK58/R) La fenetre ouverte (81x65cm-32x26in) s.
£7000 $11270   (24-Jun-91 CSK57/R) Matin brumeux a St Tropez (60x73cm-24x29in) s.verso

CAMUS, Georges (19/20th C) French
£893 $1500   (17-Jul-91 SY.NY222/R) Still life with vegetables and poultry
                (59x81cm-23x32in) s.d.Dec.93 canvas laid down on panel

CAMUS, Gustave (1914-1984) Belgian
£1012 $1963   (8-Dec-90 KV.L53) Heure Calme (49x100cm-19x39in) s. (B.FR 60000)

CANAL, Antonio see CANALETTO

CANAL, Francoise (20th C) French
£688 $1341   (15-Oct-90 CSC.P26/R) Les grands nocturnes hypergraphiques
                (146x114cm-57x45in) s. (F.FR 6800)

CANAL, Gilbert von (1849-1927) German
£520 $879   (1-May-91 GD.B132/R) Wooded landscape (31x39cm-12x15in) s.d.1887 board
                (S.FR 1300)

CANAL, von (?) ?
£1845 $3100   (17-Jul-91 SY.NY268/R) View across a river (66x110cm-26x43in) s.

CANALETTO (1697-1768) Italian
£2569 $4985   (7-Dec-90 SY.MO101/R) Vue de Venise (45x57cm-18x22in) (F.FR 25000)
£8736 $16948   (7-Dec-90 SY.MO100/R) Vues du Pont du Rialto et l'eglise de la Carita
                sur le Grand Canal (45x32cm-18x13in) pair (F.FR 85000)
£70000 $121100   (24-May-91 C70/R) The Piazza San Marco, Venice, looking west with the
                base of the Campanile (76x119cm-30x47in)
£70588 $120000   (30-May-91 SY.NY60/R) Entrance to Grand Canal looking east. Grand Canal
                looking west (56x73cm-22x29in) pair
£200000 $346000   (24-May-91 C72/R) The Grand Canal,Venice with the churches of S.Croce,
                Corpus Domini,S. Lucia and the Scalzi (49x79cm-19x31in) or studio
£250000 $432500   (24-May-91 C71/R) The Cannaregio, Venice with Palazzo Testa, Palazzo
                Surian-Bellottoand the Ponte dei Tre Archi (48x77cm-19x30in) or studio
£360000 $694800   (12-Dec-90 S36/R) Dolo on the Brenta, with Church of S.Rocco and Villa
                Zanon-Bon (30x44cm-12x17in)
£529412 $900000   (30-May-91 SY.NY61/R) Grand Canal, Venice from Santa Maria della Carita
                to Bacino di San Marco (46x63cm-18x25in)
£4000 $6520   (2-Jul-91 C123/R) View of Padua - Brenta Canal and Porta Portello
*   (34x66cm-13x26in) black chk pen wash*
£42105 $80000   (8-Jan-91 SY.NY14/R) A Capriccio with a domed church, houses and men at
*   work on scaffolding (13x24cm-5x9in) pen*

CANALETTO (after) (1697-1768) Italian
£9283 $17823   (14-Aug-90 SY.ME179/R) Canal scenes (53x90cm-21x35in) pair (A.D 22000)

CANALETTO (circle) (1697-1768) Italian
£14118 $24000   (31-May-91 CH.NY102/R) Piazza San Marco, Venice, with figures
                (39x52cm-15x20in)
£63158 $120000   (11-Jan-91 CH.NY44 a/R) The Bacino di San Marco, Venice, with the island
                of San Giorgio (62x98cm-24x39in)
£73684 $140000   (11-Jan-91 CH.NY68/R) The Molo,Venice, from the Bacino di San Marco
                (61x97cm-24x38in)
£84211 $160000   (11-Jan-91 CH.NY38/R) The Bacino di San Marco, Venice (43x73cm-17x29in)
£131579 $250000   (11-Jan-91 CH.NY70/R) The Prato della Valle, Padua seen from the North
                East (32x85cm-13x33in)

CANALETTO (school) (1697-1768) Italian
£2030 $4000   (16-Nov-90 S.BM4/R) Piazza Navora. Pantheon (25x36cm-10x14in)
                indist.i.verso panel pair
£3659 $6000   (19-Jun-91 B.SF1682/R) View of Ria del Schiavone from Bacino with goats
                and gondolas (60x94cm-24x37in) s.

CANALETTO (school) (1697-1768) Italian-cont.

£6667	$13000	(10-Oct-90 CH.NY134 a/R) View of the Piazzetta. View of Santa Maria Maggiore, Venice (35x50cm-14x20in) pair
£14706	$25000	(31-May-91 CH.NY153/R) Piazza San Marco, Venice, looking west (53x71cm-21x28in)
£16080	$26372	(22-Jun-91 CH.MO138/R) Vue du Grand Canal, La Pointe des Douanes et Santa Maria della Salute (54x99cm-21x39in) (F.FR 160000)

CANALETTO (studio) (1697-1768) Italian

£5500	$8965	(2-Jul-91 PH15/R) View of the Piazza San Marco looking east (49x84cm-19x33in)
£44737	$85000	(11-Jan-91 CH.NY22/R) A capriccio of a colonnade opening on to the courtyard of a palace (129x94cm-51x37in)
£44737	$85000	(11-Jan-91 CH.NY27/R) The Grand Canal, Venice looking south-west towards the Rialto Bridge and the Palazzo Foscari (63x98cm-25x39in)
£60526	$115000	(11-Jan-91 CH.NY28/R) The Bacino diSan Marco, Venice, from the Piazzetta (62x98cm-24x39in)

CANALETTO (style) (1697-1768) Italian

£750	$1343	(14-Mar-91 B14) The Grand Canal, Venice (46x66cm-18x26in)
£1280	$2163	(1-May-91 GD.B133/R) St Christoforo di Murano, Venice (29x40cm-11x16in) (S.FR 3200)
£1500	$2445	(4-Jul-91 CSK170/R) Caprice of Grand Canal, Venice with Ca' Grande (44x65cm-17x26in)
£1700	$2771	(4-Jul-91 C524/R) Rialto Bridge, Venice (25x42cm-10x17in) panel
£3718	$7250	(24-Oct-90 D.NY77) St Mark's Square, Venice (38x56cm-15x22in) parchment on canvas
£4162	$8075	(3-Dec-90 SY.F1047/R) Capriccio con rovine e ricordi di Padova (62x75cm-24x30in) (I.L 9000000)
£7770	$13209	(27-May-91 L.K21/R) Piazza San Marco, Venice (63x97cm-25x38in) (DM 23000)
£8383	$14000	(23-Jan-91 D.NY92/R) Merchant boats on Grand Canal (58x94cm-23x37in)
£8500	$13855	(4-Jul-91 C721/R) Campo di Santa Maria Formosa, Venice. Santa Maria Gloriosa dei Frari (53x39cm-21x15in) pair
£9459	$16081	(27-May-91 L.K20/R) View of Canale Grande and Rialto Bridge (63x97cm-25x38in) (DM 28000)
£9459	$16081	(27-May-91 L.K23/R) View of Doge's Palace and Piazetta with Santa Maria della Salute beyond (61x96cm-24x38in) (DM 28000)
£9797	$16655	(27-May-91 L.K22/R) View of Canale Grande with palaces (61x96cm-24x38in) (DM 29000)
£10200	$19890	(22-Oct-90 SWS1502/R) Rialto Bridge. Venetian canal (57x100cm-22x39in) pair
£12308	$24000	(11-Oct-90 SY.NY83/R) Grand Canal looking North-East from the Palazzo Balbi to Rialto Bridge (45x73cm-18x29in)
£15000	$29250	(25-Oct-90 CSK106/R) Piazzetta, Venice, looking west with Ducal Palace and Santa Maria della Salute beyond (56x82cm-22x32in)
£16000	$31200	(26-Oct-90 C29/R) The Piazza San Marco, Venice, from the north end of the Piazzetta (61x91cm-24x36in)
£18000	$29340	(4-Jul-91 C720/R) Bacino di San Marco, Venice - Piazzetta and Doge's Palace beyond (53x91cm-21x36in)
£18000	$36000	(7-Feb-91 C191/R) The entrance of the Grand Canal, Venice. The Bacino di San Marco seen from the Grand Canal (55x91cm-22x36in) two
£20000	$33800	(16-Apr-91 PH25/R) Figures gathered in St. Mark's Square, Venice, facade of San Marco to left (79x114cm-31x45in)
£22000	$35860	(3-Jul-91 S185/R) Venice, Molo looking west (77x127cm-30x50in)
£23000	$45310	(31-Oct-90 S6/R) Rialto Bridge from the North. Entrance to the Grand Canal, Venice (65x83cm-26x33in) pair
£25000	$42250	(19-Apr-91 C135/R) The Cannaregio, Venice (69x110cm-27x43in)
£25140	$45000	(11-Apr-91 SY.NY80/R) View of Northumberland House (58x94cm-23x37in)
£40503	$72500	(11-Apr-91 SY.NY81/R) The Horse Guards Parade, Westminster (58x95cm-23x37in)
£44221	$72523	(21-Jun-91 SY.MO212/R) Vue de la Salute (101x127cm-40x50in) (F.FR 440000)

CANALS Y LLAMBI, Ricardo (1876-?) Spanish

| £50000 | $96000 | (28-Nov-90 S177/R) Cigarretas de Sevilla (60x70cm-24x28in) s. |

CANALS, Miguel (studio) (1925-) Spanish

£750	$1455	(6-Dec-90 B76) The beloved (78x82cm-31x32in) after Dante Gabriel Rossetti
£750	$1455	(6-Dec-90 B109/R) Portrait of a warrior (33x38cm-13x15in) after Jean Leon Gerome
£750	$1455	(6-Dec-90 B55) The Grand Canal, Venice (60x120cm-24x47in) after J.M.W.Turner
£750	$1455	(6-Dec-90 B4) A portrait of a young woman in profile (38x57cm-15x22in) after George Frederick Watts
£800	$1552	(6-Dec-90 B27) Madonna at prayer (46x38cm-18x15in) after Lorenzo Veneziano
£800	$1552	(6-Dec-90 B145) Three sisters (100x110cm-39x43in) after Curran
£800	$1552	(6-Dec-90 B144) Family in an interior (127x146cm-50x57in) after Sargent
£800	$1552	(6-Dec-90 B284/R) A young lady strolling against the wind (140x80cm-55x31in) after Sorolla
£800	$1552	(6-Dec-90 B223/R) Ovana Maria (130x100cm-51x39in) after Paul Gauguin
£800	$1552	(6-Dec-90 B8) Harbour scene with barges (60x90cm-24x35in) after J.M.W.Turner

CANALS, Miguel (studio) (1925-) Spanish-cont.

£800	$1552	(6-Dec-90 B263/R) A view of the regatta (40x60cm-16x24in) after Eugene Boudin
£842	$1600	(3-Mar-91 LIT.L1) Parisian street scene (81x99cm-32x39in) bears sig. i.verso after Renoir
£850	$1649	(6-Dec-90 B274) At Trouville (12x19cm-5x7in) panel after Eugene Boudin
£850	$1649	(6-Dec-90 B195/R) A portrait of a lady in a poppy field (120x90cm-47x35in) after Francisco Miralles
£850	$1649	(6-Dec-90 B19) Madonna and child (60x80cm-24x31in) panel after Lucas Cranach
£850	$1649	(6-Dec-90 B256) Picnic on the coast (90x130cm-35x51in) after Benson
£850	$1649	(6-Dec-90 B273) At Trouville (12x25cm-5x10in) panel after Eugene Boudin
£900	$1746	(6-Dec-90 B33) Portrait of a pretty young girl (73x92cm-29x36in) after John Everett Millais
£900	$1746	(6-Dec-90 B246) Watching the sea (47x28cm-19x11in) after Eugene Boudin
£900	$1746	(6-Dec-90 B2) Tropical birds in a landscape (110x100cm-43x39in) after Jacob Bogdani
£900	$1746	(6-Dec-90 B117/R) Half length portrait of a pretty young girl (60x80cm-24x31in) panel after Gomez
£900	$1746	(6-Dec-90 B81/R) A portrait of a gentleman with his dog (100x170cm-39x67in) after Sir Thomas Gainsborough
£900	$1746	(6-Dec-90 B234/R) Sunflowers (93x72cm-37x28in) after Vincent Van Gogh
£900	$1746	(6-Dec-90 B272) The gathering on the beach (30x46cm-12x18in) panel after Eugene Boudin
£900	$1746	(6-Dec-90 B247) Watching the sea (28x32cm-11x13in) after Eugene Boudin
£950	$1843	(6-Dec-90 B199/R) Young ladies on a hillside (130x140cm-51x55in) after Benson
£1000	$1940	(6-Dec-90 B37) Full length portrait of a young gentleman (120x200cm-47x79in) after Francois Gautier
£1000	$1940	(6-Dec-90 B115/R) Arab horsemen in a landscape (81x60cm-32x24in) after Adolf Shreyer
£1000	$1940	(6-Dec-90 B74/R) Proserpine (60x120cm-24x47in) after Dante Gabriel Rossetti
£1100	$2134	(6-Dec-90 B46) Portrait of young lady seated in a rowing boat (120x100cm-47x39in) after J.J.J.Tissot
£1100	$2134	(6-Dec-90 B290) Two young ladies looking out to sea (110x100cm-43x39in) after Benson
£1100	$2134	(6-Dec-90 B17) Full length portrait of a gentleman (95x160cm-37x63in) after Mytens
£1100	$2134	(6-Dec-90 B126/R) Portrait of Giovanna Tornabuani (46x82cm-18x32in) panel after Domenico Ghirlandaio
£1200	$2328	(6-Dec-90 B245) Watching the sea at Trouville (26x13cm-10x5in) after Eugene Boudin
£1200	$2328	(6-Dec-90 B147/R) A portrait of a lady wearing a feather hat (92x73cm-36x29in) after Giovanni Boldini
£1200	$2328	(6-Dec-90 B179/R) The angler (51x61cm-20x24in) after Pierre Auguste Renoir
£1300	$2522	(6-Dec-90 B9) A full length portrait of a bearded gentleman wearing a cloak (120x200cm-47x79in) after the English School
£1300	$2522	(6-Dec-90 B101) Full length portrait of young man (100x120cm-39x47in) after Jan Mytens
£1300	$2522	(6-Dec-90 B105) A gentleman, his horse and dog (130x140cm-51x55in) after James Seymour
£1300	$2522	(6-Dec-90 B40/R) The James' family (100x130cm-39x51in) after Arthur Devis
£1400	$2716	(6-Dec-90 B42) Figures in an ornamental landscape (100x120cm-39x47in) after Giovanni Paolo Panini
£1400	$2716	(6-Dec-90 B97) Full length portrait of a Knight in his armour (170x100cm-67x39in) after the English School
£1400	$2716	(6-Dec-90 B15/R) Still life with a lobster and fruits (90x120cm-35x47in) after de Heem
£1474	$2800	(3-Mar-91 LIT.L3) Aresrea (79x97cm-31x38in) bears sig. i.verso after Gauguin
£1500	$2910	(6-Dec-90 B84) A still life with fruit (100x80cm-39x31in) after the Spanish School
£1500	$2910	(6-Dec-90 B92/R) Soldiers of the 10th Light Dragoons (150x110cm-59x43in) after George Stubbs
£1500	$2910	(6-Dec-90 B236) The family (175x134cm-69x53in) after Giovanni Boldini
£1600	$3104	(6-Dec-90 B1/R) A young lady reclining on a chair (100x130cm-39x51in) after Frank Dicksee
£1700	$3298	(6-Dec-90 B91) Full length portrait of a lady resting her arm against a settle (60x170cm-24x67in) after the English School
£1800	$3492	(6-Dec-90 B104/R) Music party, Petworth (100x130cm-39x51in) after J.M.W.Turner
£1800	$3492	(6-Dec-90 B129/R) Portrait of a gentleman with his horse (170x100cm-67x39in) after Sir Henry Raeburn
£1900	$3686	(6-Dec-90 B59/R) Portrait, Richard Sackville, third Earl of Dorset (170x100cm-67x39in) after William Larkin
£2200	$4268	(6-Dec-90 B112/R) Bridge of Sighs, Ducal Palace and Custom-House, Venice (80x130cm-31x51in) after J.M.W.Turner
£2400	$4656	(6-Dec-90 B28/R) Full length portrait of a gentleman (200x120cm-79x47in) after the English School
£3200	$6208	(6-Dec-90 B131/R) Moulin de la Galette (75x125cm-30x49in) after Pierre Auguste Renoir
£3400	$6596	(6-Dec-90 B293/R) Portrait of a young girl from behind (72x50cm-28x20in) after Anders Zorn

CANALS, Miguel (studio) (1925-) Spanish-cont.

£800	$1552	(6-Dec-90 B164) Two young girls reading (75x86cm-30x34in) pastel dr after Pierre Auguste Renoir
£800	$1552	(6-Dec-90 B209) Woman drying her neck (55x70cm-22x28in) pastel dr after Edgar Degas
£800	$1552	(6-Dec-90 B286) Adjusting her hat (84x75cm-33x30in) pastel dr after Benson
£950	$1843	(6-Dec-90 B66) Portrait of a young woman (50x49cm-20x19in) pastel dr after Dante Gabriel Rossetti
£1400	$2716	(6-Dec-90 B240/R) A portrait of a young girl (100x75cm-39x30in) pastel dr after Pierre Auguste Renoir
£1600	$3104	(6-Dec-90 B248) Horses on the course at Longchamp (63x49cm-25x19in) pastel dr after Edgar Degas
£2200	$4268	(6-Dec-90 B296/R) Mounted jockeys (48x66cm-19x26in) pastel dr after Edgar Degas

CANAS, Benjamin (1937-) Chilean

| £918 | $1800 | (12-Feb-91 SY.NY287/R) Untitled (76x107cm-30x42in) s.d.80 mixed media |

CANDELLE, L (19th C) ?

| £789 | $1500 | (15-Sep-90 S.W2788/R) Sheep herding in winter (56x38cm-22x15in) s. W/C gouache |

CANDIA, Domingo (1896-1976) Argentinian

| £780 | $1350 | (8-May-91 V.BA14) Interior (30x25cm-12x10in) W/C |

CANDID, Peter (1548-1628) Flemish

| £9619 | $18468 | (29-Nov-90 F.M27/R) Annunciazione (22x17cm-9x7in) copper (I.L 21000000) |

CANE, Ella du (?) ?

£700	$1148	(21-Jun-91 CBB169) Le Bardo Algiers - white-washed and tiled courtyard with fountain (43x28cm-17x11in) s. W/C
£720	$1174	(14-Jun-91 T203) Roses on continental terrace (43x30cm-17x12in) s. W/C
£800	$1576	(1-Nov-90 C137/R) The Kobai plum blossom (41x25cm-16x10in) s. pencil W/C
£1100	$2145	(15-Jan-91 SWS89/R) Japanese children waving flags. Playing with tops (17x25cm-7x10in) s. W/C pair

CANE, Louis (1943-) French

£1728	$3455	(10-Feb-91 CC.P15) Trois femmes debout (65x55cm-26x22in) s.d.1984 paper (F.FR 17000)
£3237	$6281	(5-Dec-90 ZZ.F115/R) Deux personnages a table (81x65cm-32x26in) s.d.1989 (F.FR 31500)
£4520	$8679	(27-Nov-90 BU.S54/R) Deux femmes (73x60cm-29x24in) s.d.1984 s.l.d.verso (S.KR 49000)
£5640	$11280	(5-Feb-91 CSC.P31/R) 76-BA-2 (214x160cm-84x63in) s.d.1976 verso (F.FR 55500)
£7207	$12468	(22-May-91 CH.AM589/R) View of mediterranean village near to sea (162x130cm-64x51in) s.d.8/87 (D.FL 24000)
£11952	$20319	(30-May-91 FB.P90/R) Sei Pazzo, e tal morrai (187x142cm-74x56in) s.i.d.mai 1979 (F.FR 120000)
£14617	$28503	(26-Oct-90 CC.P45/R) Sol/mur - bleu (F.FR 145000)
£901	$1559	(22-May-91 CH.AM590) Palmtrees in valley in south of France (73x56cm-29x22in) s.d.23-5-86 W/C oil (D.FL 3000)
£915	$1829	(10-Feb-91 CC.P14) La fenetre (38x32cm-15x13in) s.d.1977 gouache (F.FR 9000)
£1008	$1966	(26-Oct-90 CC.P49/R) Hors cadre no 1 XXIII (60x60cm-24x24in) s.i.d. janvier/fevrier 1975 verso gouache crayon (F.FR 10000)

CANE, Ottaviano (1495-1570) Italian

| £41224 | $79150 | (29-Nov-90 F.M149/R) Madonna in trono con Bambino e angeli (145x63cm-57x25in) panel (I.L 90000000) |

CANELLA, Giuseppe (1788-1847) Italian

| £17112 | $33198 | (5-Dec-90 F.M74/R) Serata parigina (25x33cm-10x13in) s.d.1831verso panel (I.L 37000000) |
| £5929 | $9901 | (6-Jun-91 F.M10/R) Paesaggi della Lombardia, Toscana, Lazio, Trieste e del Lago di Garda pencil set of ten (I.L 13000000) |

CANETTI, Christine (1959-) French?

| £791 | $1416 | (14-Apr-91 APT.P23/R) Sans titre (102x152cm-40x60in) s.d.1988 mixed media (F.FR 8000) |

CANEVARI, Giovanni Battista (1789-1876) Italian

| £450 | $761 | (16-Apr-91 CSK17/R) Portrait of gentleman in fur-bordered coat (9x?cm-4x?in) min. s.rec.gilt mount velvet frame oval |

CANGIULLO, Francesco (20th C) Italian

| £1272 | $2506 | (30-Oct-90 F.R60) Canzone a mare (20x26cm-8x10in) s.i. W/C (I.L 2800000) |

CANINI, Giovanni Angelo (attrib) (1617-1666) Italian

| £450 | $761 | (16-Apr-91 C174) Scenes of suffering (19x14cm-7x6in) blk.chk.wash htd.white |

CANINO, V (20th C) ?
£850 $1666   (8-Nov-90 TL86/R) Street scene with figures near church
                       (28x39cm-11x15in) s. panel

CANINO, Vincenzo (?) Italian
£1000 $1960   (21-Nov-90 F.M10/R) La vecchia Napoli (30x20cm-12x8in) s. panel
                       (I.L 2200000)

CANLASSI, Guido see   CAGNACCI, Guido

CANNATA, Antonio (1895-1960) Italian
£1088 $1838   (16-Apr-91 CH.R130) Barche in secca sullo stretto (60x40cm-24x16in) s.
                       panel (I.L 2400000)

CANNELLA, Pizzi (1955-) American?
£1156   *$2000*   *(7-May-91 CE.NY224/R) Riposti con Cura (75x56cm-30x22in) s.d.1985 verso*
                       col.oilsticks

CANNICCI, Nicolo (1846-1906) Italian
£4625 $8972   (5-Dec-90 F.M27/R) Profilo di ragazza (46x36cm-18x14in) s.
                       (I.L 10000000)
£29643 $49504   (6-Jun-91 F.M284/R) Sotto la neve (75x40cm-30x16in) s.d.1888
                       (I.L 65000000)
£35116 $58643   (6-Jun-91 F.M273/R) Ritorno dalla fonte (75x39cm-30x15in) s.d.1882
                       (I.L 77000000)
£70000 $137000   (18-Oct-90 F.M60/R) Bimbi che bruciano le pigne (117x209cm-46x82in)
                       s.d.1893 (I.L 155000000)

CANO DE LA PENA, Eduardo (1823-1897) Spanish
£1400   *$2688*   *(18-Dec-90 C69/R) Portrait of gentleman, possibly diplomat (8x?cm-3x?in)*
                       min.s.chiselled ormolu mount rec.

CANO, Alonso (1601-1667) Spanish
£6557 $12852   (24-Jan-91 EP.M23/R) La Vision de San Antonio de Padua
                       (125x97cm-49x38in) painted with studio (S.P 1200000)

CANO, Alonso (attrib) (1601-1667) Spanish
£2510 $4041   (27-Jun-91 APT.P21/R) Vanite - Jesus enfant endormi sur un carne
                       (104x125cm-41x49in) (F.FR 25000)

CANO, Alonso (circle) (1601-1667) Spanish
£5000 $9650   (12-Dec-90 S166/R) St.Joseph with the infant Christ (167x119cm-66x47in)

CANO, Louise (20th C) French
£2041 $4020   (14-Nov-90 I.N39/R) La conversation (73x93cm-29x37in) s. panel
                       (F.FR 20000)

CANOGAR, Rafael (1934-) Spanish
£1743 $2998   (16-May-91 ANS.M92/R) Cabeza n.6 (35x27cm-14x11in) s.d.90 (S.P 320000)
£4348 $8348   (19-Dec-90 ANS.M83/R) Cabeza multicolor N.I-90 (73x60cm-29x24in) s.d.90
                       (S.P 800000)
£5522 $10216   (6-Mar-91 APT.P84/R) Cabeza multicolor no 4.89 (73x60cm-29x24in) s.d.89
                       I. verso (F.FR 55000)
£33000 $64350   (18-Oct-90 S88/R) Pintura no. 48 (200x149cm-79x59in) s.d.59
£35000 $68250   (18-Oct-90 S110/R) Untitled (162x130cm-64x51in) s.d.59
£38000 $74100   (18-Oct-90 S77/R) Untitled (199x150cm-78x59in) s.d.59
£1494   *$2405*   *(25-Jun-91 FER.M266/R) Hombre de espalda (70x51cm-28x20in) s.d.73 mixed*
                       media (S.P 275000)
£1630   *$2624*   *(25-Jun-91 FER.M265/R) Detenida (63x42cm-25x17in) s.d.1972 mixed media*
                       (S.P 300000)
£1649   *$2952*   *(13-Mar-91 FER.M216/R) Dos hombres y un muerto (67x42cm-26x17in) s.*
                       mixed media (S.P 300000)
£3000   *$5310*   *(21-Mar-91 C253/R) The Casualty (100x80cm-39x31in) s.d.74 chl.dispersion*
                       wire canvas

CANON, Hans (1829-1885) Austrian
£1434 $2767   (10-Dec-90 L.K401) Reading of the will (56x79cm-22x31in) s.d.853 metal
                       after Joseph Danhauser (DM 4100)

CANOVA, Antonio (1757-1822) Italian
£4560   *$8071*   *(19-Mar-91 F.M171/R) Foglio di studi (20x10cm-8x4in) pencil*
                       (I.L 10000000)
£5941   *$11705*   *(14-Nov-90 F.M35/R) Studio di teste e autoritratto (224x165cm-88x65in)*
                       i.d.verso pencil (I.L 13000000)

CANOVA, Giacomo (1851-1894) Italian
£1974 $3750   (27-Feb-91 SY.NY325/R) Audience with priest (38x30cm-15x12in) s.
                       s.i.verso

CANT, James Montgomery (1911-) Australian
£667 $1253   (17-Sep-90 MGS.S142 b) Factory (30x20cm-12x8in) s.d.1939 (A.D 1500)
£708 $1153   (1-Jul-91 AAA.S154) Bush scene (60x90cm-24x35in) s. board (A.D 1500)
£1209 $2032   (22-Apr-91 SY.ME43/R) Surrealist street scene (30x20cm-12x8in) s.d.1939
                       (A.D 2600)

CANTA, Johannes Antonius (1816-1888) Dutch
£599 $1006   (23-Apr-91 SY.AM50) On road to school (30x23cm-12x9in) s. panel
                  (D.FL 2000)

CANTAGALLINA, Remigio (1582-C1630) Italian
£2964 $5246   (19-Mar-91 F.M328/R) Veduta di Pisa dall'Arno (25x43cm-10x17in) ink
                  (I.L 6500000)
£3158 $6000   (9-Jan-91 CH.NY11/R) Man standing in profile - two seated men and one
                  standing and man from behind (13x25cm-5x10in) with i. black chk pen
                  wash three joined

CANTAGALLINA, Remigio (attrib) (1582-C1630) Italian
£1579 $3000   (9-Jan-91 CH.NY5/R) Wooded landscape with reeds, town beyond
                  (21x33cm-8x13in) i.mount ink

CANTARINI, Simone (1612-1648) Italian
£1200 $2304   (18-Feb-91 S221/R) Jupiter and Ganymede (18x17cm-7x7in) bears i. chk
£1300 $2509   (12-Dec-90 PH123/R) Apollo before nymph (24x19cm-9x7in) black chk
£1494 $2585   (22-May-91 PLF.P17/R) La naissance de la vierge (25x20cm-10x8in)
                  sanguinne (F.FR 15000)
£1824 $3228   (19-Mar-91 F.M312/R) Foglio di studi, Madonna con Bambino, angelo, putti
                  (16x19cm-6x7in) ink (I.L 4000000)

CANTARINI, Simone (circle) (1612-1648) Italian
£5017 $8378   (4-Jun-91 CH.R341/R) La Sacra Famiglia (111x115cm-44x45in)
                  (I.L 11000000)

CANTATORE, Domenico (1906-) Italian
£2521 $4135   (20-Jun-91 F.M321) Paesaggio (40x50cm-16x20in) s. (I.L 5500000)
£4310 $7413   (13-May-91 CH.R173/R) Due figure femminili (30x40cm-12x16in)
                  s.d.1940verso panel (I.L 9500000)
£5437 $9460   (26-Mar-91 F.M98/R) Uomo seduto (80x50cm-31x20in) s. masonite
                  (I.L 12000000)
£5853 $11414   (22-Oct-90 BR.M220/R) Da Lancret 'Figure danzanti' (45x35cm-18x14in) s.
                  acrylic (I.L 13000000)
£947 $1695   (9-Apr-91 F.R56) Paesaggio (30x40cm-12x16in) s.d.64 W/C (I.L 2100000)
£2521 $4917   (22-Oct-90 BR.M283/R) Donna del Sud (25x35cm-10x14in) s. gouache
                  col.crayon paper on canvas (I.L 5600000)
£3000 $5881   (20-Nov-90 BR.M186/R) Cavaliere (39x30cm-15x12in) s. W/C enamel paper on
                  canvas (I.L 6600000)
£4718 $9058   (27-Nov-90 SY.MI81/R) Donna in un interno (50x40cm-20x16in) s. mixed
                  media canvas (I.L 10300000)

CANTI, Giovanni (1653-1716) Italian
£30590 $51391   (23-Apr-91 F.R69/R) Battaglia classica. Lo scoppio della polveriera
                  (73x156cm-29x61in) pair (I.L 67000000)

CANTIN, Roger (1930-) Canadian
£448 $865   (12-Dec-90 EA.M722 a) Fishing dory on strand (46x61cm-18x24in) s. W/C
                  (C.D 1000)

CANTONESE SCHOOL, 19th C Oriental
£3900 $6903   (20-Mar-91 WI1190/R) River landscape with boats, junks beside country
                  house garden (43x58cm-17x23in)

CANU (?) French
£1107 $2169   (27-Jan-91 FE.P86) Bord de mer (50x60cm-20x24in) s. (F.FR 11000)

CANU, Yvonne (1921-) French
£893 $1750   (12-Feb-91 SY.NY237/R) La lecture (25x20cm-10x8in) s. i.verso
£1020 $2000   (12-Feb-91 SY.NY234/R) Chitenay (28x36cm-11x14in) s. i.verso
£1445 $2500   (22-May-91 D.NY90/R) St. Florent. Harbour scene (24x19cm-9x7in) one
                  i.verso s. pair
£1554 $3000   (14-Dec-90 DM.D2165/R) Two ladies in tulip field (23x30cm-9x12in) s.
                  panel
£1793 $3048   (29-May-91 GL.P157/R) Apres les regates (38x46cm-15x18in) s. i. verso
                  (F.FR 18000)
£1833 $3611   (4-Nov-90 FE.P101) Saint Tropez (41x33cm-16x13in) s. (F.FR 18000)
£2105 $4000   (14-Sep-90 DM.D2013/R) Two ladies in tulip field (23x30cm-9x12in) s.
                  panel
£2196 $3711   (5-May-91 LT.P62/R) Saint-Tropez (38x46cm-15x18in) s. (F.FR 22000)
£2284 $4500   (13-Nov-90 CE.NY185/R) St Tropez Rose Bravade (43x60cm-17x24in) s.
                  s.i.verso
£2284 $4500   (15-Nov-90 D.NY107/R) Docked rowboats (38x56cm-15x22in) s. masonite
£3392 $6580   (8-Dec-90 LT.P76/R) Regates a Saint-Tropez (50x65cm-20x26in) s.
                  (F.FR 33000)
£3571 $6143   (19-May-91 ZZ.F100/R) Printemps a Aix-en-Provence (54x73cm-21x29in) s.
                  (F.FR 36000)
£4061 $8000   (13-Nov-90 CE.NY55/R) St Tropez et les pins (60x81cm-24x32in) s.
                  s.i.verso
£5330 $10500   (13-Nov-90 CE.NY56/R) St Florent Comse (65x81cm-26x32in) s. s.i.verso
£323 $613   (1-Mar-91 CB.P27/R) Le port de Honfleur (32x21cm-13x8in) s. W/C
                  (F.FR 3200)
£612 $1188   (8-Dec-90 GAB.G2433/R) Vase de fleurs (32x41cm-13x16in) s. W/C
                  (S.FR 1500)
£638 $1200   (22-Sep-90 WOL.C360/R) Beachscape (38x46cm-15x18in) s. paper collage

CANUTI, Domenico Maria (1620-1684) Italian
£5410 $9683   (8-Apr-91 CH.R85/R) Lo sposalizio mistico di S.Caterina d'Alessandria
     (111x95cm-44x37in) (I.L 12000000)
£1200 $2028   (16-Apr-91 C160/R) Saint Jerome in penitence (25x18cm-10x7in) i.
     watermark pen wash
£1800 $2934   (2-Jul-91 C271/R) River god (15x21cm-6x8in) with i. black chk pen wash
£4500 $7605   (16-Apr-91 C143/R) Daedalus ataching wings to Icarus (20x29cm-8x11in)
     blk.chk.ink wash htd.white
£9000 $14670   (1-Jul-91 S52/R) Hercules received into Olympus (33x28cm-13x11in) pen
     wash over black chk oval

CANUTI, Domenico Maria (circle) (1620-1684) Italian
£850 $1641   (11-Dec-90 C293/R) Juno and Aeolus (38x20cm-15x8in) blk.chk.htd.white

CAPARNE, W J (?) ?
£850 $1437   (18-Apr-91 B271/R) Christ on a hillside (70x97cm-28x38in) s. W/C

CAPELAIN, J le (19/20th C) ?
£520 $931   (10-Apr-91 LJ191) Horse and cart in wooded landscape (41x61cm-16x24in)
     s. W/C

CAPELAIN, John le (19/20th C) ?
£2300 $4324   (20-Sep-90 LJ350) Vraic gatherers with rocks and boat (29x40cm-11x16in)
     s. W/C

CAPELLA, Cheli (19th C) Italian
£642 $1220   (14-Sep-90 SA.A1106/R) Wooded lake landscape, evening (54x61cm-21x24in)
     s. i.verso after Ruisdael (DM 1900)

CAPELLA, Francesco see DAGIU, Francesco

CAPET, Marie Gabrielle (1761-1818) French
£150754 $247236   (17-Jun-91 ARC.P31/R) Madame Labille-Guiard executant du peintre vien,
     Senateur et Comte de L'Empire (68x83cm-27x33in) (F.FR 1500000)

CAPET, Marie Gabrielle (attrib) (1761-1818) French
£791 $1566   (30-Jan-91 CSC.P6/R) Portrait d'enfant en buste (44x36cm-17x14in) oval
     (F.FR 7800)

CAPOGROSSI, Giuseppe (1900-1972) Italian
£3998 $7876   (30-Oct-90 F.R159/R) Superficie (31x19cm-12x7in) s.d.62 tempera board
     (I.L 8800000)
£4083 $7023   (13-May-91 CH.R86/R) Superficie CP 905 (25x34cm-10x13in) s.d.66 tempera
     paper (I.L 9000000)
£6364 $12474   (20-Nov-90 BR.M39/R) Composizione (22x28cm-9x11in) d.1960 tempera paper
     (I.L 14000000)
£12686 $22073   (26-Mar-91 F.M102/R) Superficie 243 (46x32cm-18x13in) s. (I.L 28000000)
£26114 $50923   (24-Oct-90 F.M279/R) Superficie 596 (50x70cm-20x28in) s.d.1950verso
     tempera paper (I.L 58000000)
£37604 $65431   (26-Mar-91 F.M123/R) Superficie (73x60cm-29x24in) s.d.53 (I.L 83000000)
£54368 $94599   (26-Mar-91 F.M134/R) Superficie 223 (100x130cm-39x51in) s.d.57
     (I.L 120000000)
£1781 $2903   (14-Jun-91 L.K799/R) Untitled (38x26cm-15x10in) s.d.51 gouache
     (DM 5200)

CAPON, Georges Emile (1890-) French
£1172 $2297   (12-Feb-91 HC.P43) Bouquet rouge (81x65cm-32x26in) s. (F.FR 11600)
£1717 $3366   (12-Feb-91 HC.P45) Nu au chale vert s.d.52 verso (F.FR 17000)
£3134 $6112   (17-Oct-90 ARC.P66/R) L'anglaise (65x55cm-26x22in) s. (F.FR 31000)

CAPON, William (1757-1827) British
£650 $1255   (11-Dec-90 C217/R) The entrance to Astleys circus (14x19cm-6x7in)
     i.d.1777 pencil ink W/C

CAPONE, Gaetano (1845-1920) Italian
£1458 $2479   (28-May-91 F.R72) La spiaggia di Maiori (17x36cm-7x14in) s. panel
     (I.L 3200000)

CAPOZZELLA, Mario (20th C) ?
£655 $1278   (28-Oct-90 M.V153) La Vendetta (100x100cm-39x39in) s. (F.FR 6500)

CAPPELLA, Francesco (attrib) (1714-1784) Italian
£1317 $2200   (23-Jan-91 D.NY89) St. Joseph and Infant Child (122x97cm-48x38in)

CAPPELLO, Carmelo (1912-) Italian
£740 $1436   (3-Dec-90 F.M262/R) Nudo (40x75cm-16x30in) s.d.1954 mixed media
     (I.L 1600000)

CAPPIELLO, Leonetto (1875-1942) French
£1095 $1904   (25-Mar-91 PLF.P26/R) Madame Suzanne Cappiello (53x42cm-21x17in) s.
     chl.pastel board (F.FR 11000)

CAPRILE, Vincenzo (1856-1936) Italian
£2493 $4213   (16-Apr-91 CH.R56) La donna del pescatore (27x13cm-11x5in) s. panel
     (I.L 5500000)
£2789 $4797   (14-May-91 GF.L2114/R) Portrait of girl (51x41cm-20x16in) s. (S.FR 7000)

CAPRILE, Vincenzo (1856-1936) Italian-cont.
£3500	$5740	(19-Jun-91 S415/R) Plucking chicken (55x44cm-22x17in) s.
£27000	$53000	(18-Oct-90 F.M89/R) Veduta di Cava dei Tirreni (46x67cm-18x26in) s.d.85 (I.L 60000000)
£13863	*$26756*	*(11-Dec-90 CH.R105/R) Testa di bambina (60x45cm-24x18in) s. pastel (I.L 30000000)*

CAPUANO, Francesco (1854-?) Italian
| £1300 | $2548 | (14-Feb-91 CSK49/R) A wooded river landscape with a faggot gatherer (64x74cm-25x29in) s. |

CAPULETTI, Jose Manuel (1925-) Spanish
| £2551 | $5000 | (12-Feb-91 SY.NY262/R) Nude in surreal landscape (64x46cm-25x18in) s.d.1952-53 |

CAPUTO, Ulisse (1872-1948) Italian
£1017	$1962	(11-Dec-90 CH.R99) Donna allo specchio (45x55cm-18x22in) s. (I.L 2200000)
£4211	$8000	(28-Feb-91 CH.NY128/R) Woman reading in garden (36x27cm-14x11in) s. board
£4211	$8000	(28-Feb-91 CH.NY129/R) Les Tuileries (24x33cm-9x13in) s. canvasboard
£5000	$9800	(15-Feb-91 C85/R) La liseuse (37x44cm-15x17in) s. l.verso board
£6007	$11594	(11-Dec-90 CH.R72/R) Figura di donna in un interno (75x92cm-30x36in) s.d.1907 (I.L 13000000)

CARA COSTEA, Philippe (1925-) ?
| £554 | $903 | (14-Jun-91 FB.P30/R) Le port (55x73cm-22x29in) s.d.62 (F.FR 5500) |
| £813 | $1626 | (6-Feb-91 FB.P68) Le port (55x73cm-22x29in) s.d.62 (F.FR 8000) |

CARABAIN, J (1834-1892) Belgian
| *£1333* | *$2560* | *(18-Dec-90 GM.B4004/R) Le petit marche (51x35cm-20x14in) s. W/C (B.FR 80000)* |

CARABAIN, Jacques (1834-1892) Belgian
£1827	$2978	(12-Jun-91 GM.B4067/R) Ruelle animee en Italie (59x30cm-23x12in) s. (B.FR 110000)
£3984	$6853	(14-May-91 GF.L2132/R) Still life with glasses, bottles and pots (38x34cm-15x13in) s.d.1872 panel (S.FR 10000)
£3984	$6853	(14-May-91 GF.L2133/R) Still life with fishes, bread and wine (40x30cm-16x12in) s. panel (S.FR 10000)
£6231	$11154	(13-Mar-91 ARC.P33/R) Vue de la grande place a Capri (76x56cm-30x22in) s. (F.FR 62000)
£7538	$13492	(13-Mar-91 ARC.P31/R) Vue de la grande place de San Remo (60x46cm-24x18in) s.d.1879 (F.FR 75000)
£8241	$14752	(13-Mar-91 ARC.P32/R) Paysage de bord de lac (58x49cm-23x19in) s. (F.FR 82000)
£10000	$19000	(27-Feb-91 SY.NY27/R) Rhenish landscape (53x42cm-21x17in) s. canvas on board
£10000	$16400	(21-Jun-91 C67/R) St. Goar on Rhine, with St. Goarshausen and Katz Castle beyond (58x48cm-23x19in) s. s.indist.l.verso
£15306	$30000	(21-Nov-90 NA.BA10/R) Vue de l'eglise St.Pierre a Bacharach (77x62cm-30x24in) s.d.1865
£15385	$30000	(24-Oct-90 CH.NY283/R) The Weight House, Alkmaar (77x63cm-30x25in) s.
£16174	$31215	(11-Dec-90 CH.R211/R) Sulla spiaggia a Vietri (65x105cm-26x41in) s. (I.L 35000000)
£1479	*$2854*	*(11-Dec-90 CH.R151) Veduta di paese (42x68cm-17x27in) s. W/C (I.L 3200000)*

CARACCIO, Francesco (1950-) Italian
| *£1818* | *$3564* | *(20-Nov-90 BR.M177/R) Le petit jardin (50x70cm-20x28in) s.d.1989 mixed media (I.L 4000000)* |

CARACCIOLO, Giovanni Battista (after) (1570-1637) Italian
| £4508 | $8069 | (8-Apr-91 CH.R70/R) Cupido dormiente (90x145cm-35x57in) (I.L 10000000) |

CARAUD, Joseph (1821-1905) French
| £8205 | $16000 | (24-Oct-90 CH.NY130/R) Marie Antoinette and Louis XVI in garden of Tuileries with Mdme Lambale (89x117cm-35x46in) s.d.1857 |
| £12000 | $23040 | (30-Nov-90 C30/R) Feeding the pigeons (99x67cm-39x26in) s. |

CARAVAGGIO (after) (1573-1610) Italian
| £7200 | $11736 | (2-Jul-91 PH82/R) The Incredulity of St Thomas (110x141cm-43x56in) |
| £9000 | $15210 | (18-Apr-91 C60/R) The cardsharps (99x130cm-39x51in) |

CARAVAGGIO (style) (1573-1610) Italian
£5221	$8406	(27-Jun-91 APT.P29/R) Saint Jean l'Evangeliste et Saint Thomas (94x132cm-37x52in) (F.FR 52000)
£13000	$21190	(4-Jul-91 C633/R) Denial of Saint Peter (95x128cm-37x50in)
£42000	$81060	(12-Dec-90 S1/R) David with the head of Goliath (99x135cm-39x53in)
£51659	$101767	(30-Oct-90 EP.M12/R) La Magdalena en oracion (114x78cm-45x31in) (S.P 9500000)

CARAVAGGIO, Cecco del (attrib) (17th C) Italian
| £39177 | $77179 | (14-Nov-90 D.V54/R) Still life of fishes, wine bottle, bread and utensils (80x95cm-31x37in) (A.S 800000) |

CARBONERO, Jose Moreno (1860-?) Spanish
£2083 $4000   (27-Nov-90 PO.BA13) La Catedral de Burgos (23x33cm-9x13in) s.
£973 $1897   *(23-Oct-90 DUR.M60) Carreta de bueyes (30x39cm-12x15in) W/C*
           (S.P 180000)

CARBONI, Giovanni Bernardo (1616-1683) Italian
£12000   *$19560*   *(2-Jul-91 C54/R) Adoration of the Shepherds (42x31cm-17x12in) i. chk oil*
           colour

CARBONI, Giovanni Bernardo (attrib) (1616-1683) Italian
£4625 $8972   (3-Dec-90 SY.F1062/R) Ritratto di gentiluomo (200x112cm-79x44in)
           (I.L 10000000)
£7000 $13650   (26-Oct-90 C27/R) Portrait of a lady holding a fan with a servant on a
           terrace behind (216x151cm-85x59in)

CARCANO, F (?) Italian
£637 $1101   (23-May-91 F.M270) La Scartocciatura del granoturco (46x63cm-18x25in) s.
           chl (I.L 1400000)

CARCANO, Filippo (1840-1910) Italian
£1834 $3284   (12-Mar-91 F.M40) Veduta dei giardini pubblici di Milano
           (19x25cm-7x10in) board (I.L 4000000)
£11053 $21000   (27-Feb-91 SY.NY347/R) La piccola fioraia (135x99cm-53x39in) s.
£2522   *$4515*   *(12-Mar-91 F.M107/R) Paesaggio (38x50cm-15x20in) s. pastel card laid*
           down on board (I.L 5500000)

CARDELLA, Tony (20th C) ?
£1208 $1970   (11-Jun-91 I.N162) Le Port de Saint-Raphael (73x92cm-29x36in) s.
           (F.FR 12000)

CARDENAS, Augustin (1927-) Cuban
£1011   *$1972*   *(17-Oct-90 LT.P134/R) Composition (48x63cm-19x25in) s.d.80 mixed media*
           (F.FR 10000)

CARDENAS, Santiago (1937-) Colombian
£4070   *$7000*   *(15-May-91 CH.NY135/R) Pizzarron Rojo con Cuerda y Gancho*
           (70x100cm-28x39in) oil pastel

CARDI, Lodovico (1559-1613) Italian
£1171 $2283   (23-Oct-90 CH.R132) Autoritratto (23x16cm-9x6in) panel (I.L 2600000)
£800 $1536   (18-Feb-91 S94/R) The Mocking of Christ (24x18cm-9x7in) bears i.verso
           pen ink wash over chk squared
£2200 $3586   (2-Jul-91 C256/R) Standing man, in profile to left (39x26cm-15x10in)
           with i. num.13 red chk
£30526   *$58000*   *(8-Jan-91 SY.NY16/R) Pope Sixtus V at his desk, inspired by angels*
           (27x22cm-11x9in) ink W/C traces blk.chk.htd.white

CARDI, Lodovico (circle) (1559-1613) Italian
£804 $1319   (19-Jun-91 LC.P40/R) La flagellation du Christ (40x29cm-16x11in) copper
           (F.FR 8000)

CARDI, Lodovico (studio) (1559-1613) Italian
£5410 $9683   (8-Apr-91 CH.R55/R) La pieta (39x30cm-15x12in) copper (I.L 12000000)
£7263 $13000   (11-Apr-91 SY.NY37/R) Virgin and Child, holding flowers in his hand
           (28x21cm-11x8in) panel

CARDI, Lodovico (style) (1559-1613) Italian
£1368 $2448   (14-Mar-91 D.V187/R) St Francis praying (44x35cm-17x14in) copper
           (A.S 28000)

CARDINAL, Emile Valentin (19/20th C) French
£3200 $5248   (19-Jun-91 S175/R) Cat and kittens (37x52cm-15x20in) s. panel

CARDON, Claude (fl.1892-1915) British
£800 $1304   (13-Jun-91 CSK193) Harnessing horses in farmyard (30x43cm-12x17in)
           s.d.07
£1200 $1956   (14-Jun-91 C321/R) In the pigsty (43x47cm-17x19in) s.d.1920
£1800 $3546   (1-Nov-90 CSK94/R) Harnessing horses in farm yard (30x43cm-12x17in)
           s.d.07

CARDONA TORRANDELL, Armando (1928-) Spanish
£907   *$1815*   *(6-Feb-91 ANS.M57/R) Figuras (50x67cm-20x26in) s.d.66 mixed media tablex*
           (S.P 165000)

CARDONA Y TIO, Juan (19/20th C) Spanish
£378   *$738*   *(22-Oct-90 ANS.M168/R) Fiesta en el jardin (33x34cm-13x13in) s.d.907*
           gouache (S.P 70000)

CARDONA, Juan (1877-c.1957) Spanish
£1829 $3659   (6-Feb-91 LD.P19/R) Le leche vitrine (60x47cm-24x19in) s. col.crayons
           htd.white chk. (F.FR 18000)
£1982 $3963   (6-Feb-91 LD.P18/R) Elegante au pardesus (47x34cm-19x13in) s.d.1900
           col.crayons htd.white chk. (F.FR 19500)
£2632 $5158   (20-Nov-90 MF.P8/R) Elegante au renard (53x26cm-21x10in) s.d.900 pastel
           (F.FR 26000)

CARDUCHO, Vicente (style) (1578-1638) Italian
£1800 $3456   (29-Nov-90 CSK305 a/R) Christ on the road to Calvary (132x171cm-52x67in)

CARELLI, Conrad (1869-) British
£1178 $1991   (16-Apr-91 CH.R2) Al Pincio (12x17cm-5x7in) s. W/C (I.L 2600000)

CARELLI, Consalve (1818-1900) Italian
£3469 $6729   (4-Dec-90 F.R162/R) Asinello (20x25cm-8x10in) s. panel (I.L 7500000)
£3571 $7000   (7-Nov-90 B.SF1172/R) Wayward travellers (48x78cm-19x31in) s.d.1854
£4000 $8000   (7-Feb-91 B.P91/R) View of Naples (23x41cm-9x16in) s. board
£4159 $8027   (11-Dec-90 CH.R77/R) Pescatori nel golfo di Napoli (18x30cm-7x12in) s.
         panel (I.L 9000000)
£15725 $30506   (4-Dec-90 F.R157/R) Veduta del Castello di Lettere a Gragnano
         (78x64cm-31x25in) s. (I.L 34000000)
£16187 $31403   (4-Dec-90 F.R158/R) Veduta di Capo Santoro (78x64cm-31x25in) s.
         (I.L 35000000)
£16500 $27060   (19-Jun-91 S359/R) Figures with goats near Baia, Naples
         (30x50cm-12x20in) s. panel
£18000 $30960   (14-May-91 SWS309/R) View across the Bay of Naples (49x73cm-19x29in)
         s.i.
£19000 $31160   (19-Jun-91 S358/R) Busy harbour scene, Naples (30x50cm-12x20in) s.i.
         panel
£1110 $2153   (4-Dec-90 F.R50/R) Paesaggio campano (34x28cm-13x11in) s. W/C
         (I.L 2400000)
£2000 $3940   (5-Oct-90 C143/R) River crossing near Naples (25x35cm-10x14in) s.d.1839
         pencil ink W/C
£2130 $3600   (20-Apr-91 WOL.C102/R) Shepherd and dog (36x48cm-14x19in) s. W/C
£2899 $4900   (20-Apr-91 WOL.C101) Vietri (36x51cm-14x20in) s. W/C
£3597 $6978   (7-Dec-90 CN.P86/R) Vue de clocher de la cathedrale de Gaeta
         (43x29cm-17x11in) s. W/C (F.FR 35000)

CARELLI, D (19th C?) ?
£7000 $13300   (1-Mar-91 C140/R) Ali Pasha being rowed across Lake Butrinto whilst out
         shooting (48x71cm-19x28in) s. panel

CARELLI, Gabrielli (1820-1880) Italian
£2542 $4905   (11-Dec-90 CH.R60/R) Il pasto dei pescatori (26x36cm-10x14in) s.
         (I.L 5500000)
£400 $656   (19-Jun-91 B21) Amalfi (24x16cm-9x6in) s.i.d.1879 W/C
£520 $931   (13-Mar-91 B25) Ischia, looking towards the Castello Aragonese
         (17x27cm-7x11in) s.i. W/C
£1100 $2090   (12-Sep-90 CSK221/R) Rialto Bridge, Venice (33x53cm-13x21in) s.d.1878
         pencil W/C
£1900 $3401   (13-Mar-91 B39 a) Figures in a town square. Fishing port (11x18cm-4x7in)
         W/C two
£3000 $5160   (17-May-91 C207/R) View of Palermo. Santa Croce, Florence
         (25x35cm-10x14in) one d.1872 one s.i. pencil W/C pair
£3172 $5361   (16-Apr-91 CH.R7/R) Alhambra, Granada (37x54cm-15x21in) s. W/C
         (I.L 7000000)

CARELLI, Giuseppe (1858-1921) Italian
£1400 $2338   (22-Jul-91 SWS1098/R) In the Bay, Naples (23x33cm-9x13in) s.i. panel
£1500 $2940   (14-Feb-91 CSK199/R) Fishermen off Capri (13x30cm-5x12in) s. panel
£2800 $4816   (14-May-91 SWS324/R) The Bay of Naples (19x39cm-7x15in) s. panel
£3000 $5760   (27-Nov-90 PH214/R) Bay of Naples (26x47cm-10x19in) s.i.
£3400 $6528   (27-Nov-90 PH182/R) Fishing vessels entering harbour (19x36cm-7x14in) s.
         panel
£4600 $9016   (15-Feb-91 C91/R) Near Naples (25x46cm-10x18in) s. panel
£5400 $10044   (5-Sep-90 BT183/R) Fishing boats in bay (36x64cm-14x25in) s.
£6000 $10320   (17-May-91 C246/R) Bay of Naples (33x51cm-13x20in) s.i. board
£17000 $27880   (21-Jun-91 C88/R) Bay of Naples (62x105cm-24x41in) s.i.
£610 $1220   (4-Feb-91 PLF.P27/R) Vue de ville (17x12cm-7x5in) s.d.1830 W/C traces
         crayon (F.FR 6000)

CARENA, Felice (1880-?) Italian
£4585 $7519   (20-Jun-91 F.M455/R) Marina con cavalli (39x60cm-15x24in) s.d.1939 panel
         (I.L 10000000)
£6701 $12932   (13-Dec-90 F.M385/R) Vaso di fiori (50x35cm-20x14in) s. (I.L 14500000)

CARESME, Jacques Philippe (1734-1796) French
£1217 $2410   (30-Jan-91 APT.P249/R) Une academie d'homme devant une bacchanale
         (78x64cm-31x25in) (F.FR 12000)
£1300 $2509   (11-Dec-90 C80/R) A Satyr and Nymph embracing under a tree with a
         Bacchanal of Putti (20x49cm-8x19in) i. blk.chk.ink wash htd.white
£2010 $3296   (18-Jun-91 APT.P57/R) Tete de femme (24x18cm-9x7in) s.d.1780 col.crayons
         pierre noire chk.sanguinne (F.FR 20000)
£8970 $17313   (12-Dec-90 ARC.P53/R) Nymphes et Satyres (25x29cm-10x11in) both s.
         gouache W/C pair (F.FR 88000)

CARESME, Jacques Philippe (attrib) (1734-1796) French
£850 $1641   (11-Dec-90 C81/R) The Triumph of Bacchus (20x33cm-8x13in) ink wash
         htd.white bodycol.

CAREY, J W (20th C) British
£450 $779   (11-May-91 TA.B535) Near Annalong, Co. Down (28x46cm-11x18in) s. W/C
£850 $1666   (16-Feb-91 TA.B360) Fair Head, Co. Antrim (28x46cm-11x18in) W/C

CAREY, Joseph William (fl.1890-1935) British
£900 $1764   (22-Nov-90 CSK21/R) Walking geese at Port Ballintrae (32x50cm-13x20in)
                s.i.d.96 pencil W/C htd white

CARGALEIRO, Manuel (1927-) Portuguese
£3175 $5460   (19-May-91 ZZ.F203/R) Lumiere de printemps (61x50cm-24x20in) s. i.d.1988
                verso (F.FR 32000)
£4127 $7634   (10-Mar-91 LT.P118/R) Jour et nuit (61x50cm-24x20in) s.d.89 (F.FR 41100)
£4752 $9267   (17-Oct-90 LT.P58/R) La musique a Lucerne (73x60cm-29x24in) s. i. verso
                (F.FR 47000)
£5823 $10773   (10-Mar-91 LT.P111) City interieure, Paris (73x92cm-29x36in) s.d.89
                (F.FR 58000)
£1947 $3816   (11-Nov-90 ZZ.F200/R) Composition (32x32cm-13x13in) s. gouache
                (F.FR 19000)

CARGNEL, Vittore Antonio (1872-1931) Italian
£2273 $4455   (21-Nov-90 F.M26) Casolare con figure (70x89cm-28x35in) s.d.1917 board
                (I.L 5000000)
£3422 $6640   (5-Dec-90 F.M38/R) Terzo sul Dese (34x48cm-13x19in) s. i.d.1921verso
                canvas on board (I.L 7400000)

CARIGIET, Alois (1902-1985) Swiss
£12698 $21206   (5-Jun-91 SY.Z154/R) Two woodcutters (73x60cm-29x24in) mono.d.48
                (S.FR 32000)
£19277 $37783   (21-Nov-90 SY.Z99/R) Resting on mountain peak (88x116cm-35x46in)
                mono.d.54 (S.FR 48000)
£1032 $1785   (22-May-91 GS.B2057) Female gleaner (31x26cm-12x10in) mono.d.42 indian
                ink pen (S.FR 2600)
£1200 $2340   (17-Oct-90 G.Z122/R) Garden with bird cage and dachshound
                (23x30cm-9x12in) s.d.1955 W/C pencil (S.FR 3000)
£1446 $2834   (24-Nov-90 AB.L180/R) Tineli (20x28cm-8x11in) s.d.57 W/C pencil dr.
                (S.FR 3600)
£1918 $3779   (13-Nov-90 GF.L5267/R) Tineli (31x23cm-12x9in) s.i.d.1958 W/C pencil
                (S.FR 4700)
£2410 $4048   (24-Apr-91 G.Z65/R) Sion (25x44cm-10x17in) s.i.d.1943 indian ink
                (S.FR 6000)
£2857 $5629   (17-Nov-90 S.Z18/R) Girl with cross (34x45cm-13x18in) c.1955 i.verso
                indian ink pen (S.FR 7000)
£3061 $6031   (16-Nov-90 GK.Z5339/R) Zottel, Zick und Zwerg (24x32cm-9x13in)
                s.i.d.1965-66 W/C over pencil dr. (S.FR 7500)
£3061 $6031   (16-Nov-90 GK.Z5338/R) Zottel, Zick und Zwerg (24x32cm-9x13in)
                s.i.d.1965-66 W/C over pencil (S.FR 7500)
£3213 $6297   (21-Nov-90 SY.Z102/R) Greek impressions (40x50cm-16x20in) mono.i.d.56
                pencil pastel gouache (S.FR 8000)
£3265 $6335   (7-Dec-90 G.Z148/R) Rider (20x28cm-8x11in) s. W/C over pencil
                (S.FR 8000)
£5714 $11257   (16-Nov-90 GK.Z5336/R) Peasant women, Mykonos (54x65cm-21x26in) s.d.1956
                pastel htd.white (S.FR 14000)
£6939 $13669   (16-Nov-90 GK.Z5335/R) Windmills, Mykonos (54x65cm-21x26in) s.i.d.1956
                tempera over oil chk (S.FR 17000)
£7377 $13943   (28-Sep-90 S.Z75/R) Portrait of daughter (25x50cm-10x20in) mono.d.1942
                gouache (S.FR 18000)
£8163 $16082   (16-Nov-90 EA.Z348/R) Spring landscape with view of Zurich
                (27x20cm-11x8in) W/C gouache over pencil (S.FR 20000)

CARILLI, G (19th C) Italian
£3390 $6000   (22-Mar-91 S.W3105) Coastal views (20x36cm-8x14in) s. pair

CARL, Adolf (attrib) (1814-1845) German
£3082 $5517   (13-Mar-91 N.M463/R) Italian coastal landscape with classical ruins,
                possibly Taormina (54x74cm-21x29in) (DM 9000)

CARL-ROSA, Mario (1855-1913) French
£734 $1446   (13-Nov-90 AB.S870/R) French river landscape (32x55cm-13x22in) s. panel
                (S.KR 8000)

CARLANDI, Onorato (1848-1939) Italian
£1231 $2056   (6-Jun-91 F.M27/R) Fin d'autunno (35x28cm-14x11in) s.d.95 panel
                (I.L 2700000)
£1600 $3168   (30-Jan-91 CSK315/R) A landscape - Tivoli (61x61cm-24x24in) s.i.
£4394 $8524   (4-Dec-90 F.R126/R) Paesaggio con veduta di Tivoli (40x70cm-16x28in) s.
                (I.L 9500000)
£5240 $8908   (28-May-91 F.R140/R) Il Foro Romano (96x59cm-38x23in) s. (I.L 11500000)
£500 $980   (14-Feb-91 CSK19) The forest pool (28x43cm-11x17in) s. pencil W/C
£1110 $2153   (4-Dec-90 F.R77/R) Cipressi a Tivoli (54x37cm-21x15in) s. W/C
                (I.L 2400000)
£1233 $2393   (8-Dec-90 SY.MO434/R) Jeune femme a la fontaine (68x39cm-27x15in) s. W/C
                (F.FR 12000)
£1500 $2850   (12-Sep-90 CSK210) On the Forum (36x53cm-14x21in) s.i. pencil W/C
£1600 $3072   (27-Nov-90 PH260) Figure by ruin in landscape (22x50cm-9x20in) s. W/C
                over pencil
£2773 $5351   (11-Dec-90 CH.R82/R) Campagna romana (25x75cm-10x30in) s.i. W/C tempera
                (I.L 6000000)

CARLBERG, Hugo (1880-1943) Swedish
£597 $1171   (10-Nov-90 FAL.M51/R) The beach, Torekov (64x69cm-25x27in) s.
                 d.1941verso (S.KR 6500)
£744 $1384   (9-Sep-90 BU.M771) Ice-floe on river, Smaland (60x64cm-24x25in) s.
                 (S.KR 8000)
£961 $1873   (21-Oct-90 BU.M391) Spring (66x64cm-26x25in) s.d.34 (S.KR 10500)

CARLEBUR, Francois (18/19th C) Dutch
£727 $1433   (30-Oct-90 CH.AM284) Sailing vessels on Merwede by Dordrecht
                 (30x48cm-12x19in) s.d. (D.FL 2400)
£1216 $2068   (27-May-91 L.K253) Village pond with farmhouses (39x59cm-15x23in) s.
                 (DM 3600)

CARLES, Arthur B (1882-1952) American
£559 $1000   (11-Apr-91 FA.PH788) Landscape with house (18x30cm-7x12in) board
£2718 $5300   (20-Oct-90 FA.PH922/R) Reclining nude, portrait of artist's wife
                 (23x33cm-9x13in) s. board
£3966 $7100   (11-Apr-91 FA.PH959/R) Floral still life (48x58cm-19x23in)
£9497 $17000   (11-Apr-91 FA.PH962/R) Abstract floral arrangement (61x51cm-24x20in)
£741 $1400   (25-Sep-90 CE.NY230/R) Nude (60x48cm-24x19in) pastel pencil

CARLEVARIS, Luca (1665-1731) Italian
£28947 $55000   (11-Jan-91 CH.NY8/R) The Piazza San Marco, Venice looking toward the
                 Procuraturate, with figures (61x57cm-24x22in)
£135242 $242083   (8-Apr-91 CH.R228/R) Porto di mare con figure (95x142cm-37x56in)
                 (I.L 300000000)
£205000 $334150   (5-Jul-91 C106/R) River landscape with capriccio view of Ponte Rotto by
                 castle, various figures and horse-drawn carria (104x176cm-41x69in)
                 init.
£210000 $342300   (3-Jul-91 S87/R) View of Palazzo Ducale, Venice, Church of Santa Maria
                 Salute in distance (51x108cm-20x43in) s.
£410000 $709300   (24-May-91 C73/R) The Piazzetta, Venice looking north-west, with the
                 Libreria, the Campanile ..... (123x162cm-48x64in)
£410000 $709300   (24-May-91 C74/R) The Piazzetta, Venice, looking south from in front of
                 the facade of San Marco ..... (122x161cm-48x63in)
£600000 $1038000   (24-May-91 C75/R) The Piazzetta and the Piazza San Marco, Venice, from
                 the Porta dellaCarta .... (70x119cm-28x47in)
£2599 $4601   (19-Mar-91 F.M218/R) Studio di figure orientali per una scena di mercato
                 (21x15cm-8x6in) ink W/C (I.L 5700000)

CARLEVARIS, Luca (attrib) (1665-1731) Italian
£50000 $84500   (19-Apr-91 C136/R) The Piazzetta,Venice and the Corner of the Doge's
                 Palace (103x126cm-41x50in)

CARLEVARIS, Luca (style) (1665-1731) Italian
£5500 $10450   (13-Sep-90 CSK68/R) Capriccio of Mediterranean seaport with travellers
                 and dockhands on quay (63x98cm-25x39in)
£28000 $45640   (5-Jul-91 C201/R) Piazzetta, Venice. Piazza San Marco (55x80cm-22x31in)
                 pair

CARLIER, M (19/20th C) French
£501 $982   (12-Feb-91 GM.B400) Panier de fleurs (40x60cm-16x24in) s. (B.FR 30000)
£720 $1239   (14-May-91 GM.B665) Gerbe de roses (40x60cm-16x24in) s. (B.FR 44000)
£1180 $2290   (4-Dec-90 C.A52) Still life (80x106cm-31x42in) s. (B.FR 70000)

CARLIER, Marie (1920-1986) Belgian
£422 $814   (13-Dec-90 CH.BR119/R) Nu feminin (33x24cm-13x9in) s. ink pencil
                 (B.FR 25000)

CARLIER, Maurice (1894-1976) Belgian
£602 $1179   (12-Feb-91 GM.B431) Roses (40x560cm-16x220in) (B.FR 36000)
£1686 $3272   (4-Dec-90 C.A53/R) Still life of fruit and flowers (80x120cm-31x47in) s.
                 (B.FR 100000)

CARLIER, Modeste (1820-1878) Belgian
£1096 $2126   (8-Dec-90 KV.L56/R) Flowers in a vase (55x35cm-22x14in) s. (B.FR 65000)
£1146 $1948   (28-May-91 C.A29/R) Bouquet of roses (60x40cm-24x16in) s. (B.FR 70000)
£1227 $2087   (28-May-91 C.A30) Profusion of flowers (91x60cm-36x24in) s. (B.FR 75000)
£2399 $4127   (16-May-91 D.V104/R) Still life of flowers with fruit (80x106cm-31x42in)
                 s. (A.S 50000)
£11282 $22000   (24-Oct-90 CH.NY260/R) Still life with assorted flowers in brass vase
                 (91x61cm-36x24in) s.init. i.d.49-8verso

CARLIERI, Alberto (1672-1720) Italian
£4570 $9004   (13-Nov-90 F.M121/R) Architettura con scena dall'Antico Testamento
                 (73x56cm-29x22in) (I.L 10000000)
£11820 $23166   (19-Nov-90 CH.R142/R) Rovine romane con fontana. Rovine romane con
                 figure (141x118cm-56x46in) pair (I.L 26000000)

CARLIERI, Alberto (attrib) (1672-1720) Italian
£3000 $5850   (26-Oct-90 C23/R) A gentleman with his page at a Roman ruin, Vesuvius
                 beyond (48x38cm-19x15in)

CARLIERI, Alberto (style) (1672-1720) Italian
£4000 $6760   (17-Apr-91 S97/R) Figures beside classical ruins (59x70cm-23x28in)

CARLIN, John (1813-1878) American
£526 $1000   (28-Feb-91 MFA.C207) Young girl in pink (43x30cm-17x12in) s. oval

CARLIN, Michel (1935-) French?
£504 $821   (16-Jun-91 LT.P191) Suzanne au carreau (106x106cm-42x42in) s.d.89 i.
                verso hardboard (F.FR 5000)
£604 $985   (16-Jun-91 LT.P181) Les Suzannes roses (100x130cm-39x51in) s.d.90 i.
                verso (F.FR 6000)

CARLISLE, John (fl.1866-1893) British
*£4200 $8190   (24-Oct-90 S3/R) View of Mauritius (45x132cm-18x52in) s. W/C over pencil
                bodycol.arabic gum scratching*

CARLONE, Carlo (1686-1776) Italian
£1506 $2425   (27-Jun-91 APT.P53/R) Scene allegorique (43x35cm-17x14in) paper pasted
                on canvas oval (F.FR 15000)

CARLONE, Diego (1670-1750) Italian
*£319 $565   (19-Mar-91 F.M164) Foglio di studi con due fregi per scene di baccanale
                (8x44cm-3x17in) i. ink over pencil (I.L 700000)*

CARLOS, Ernest Stafford (1883-1917) British
£517 $900   (27-Mar-91 B.SF4354/R) Guarding the coast (127x140cm-50x55in) s.d.1915
£1000 $1940   (6-Dec-90 CSK86/R) Young boys on cliffside, midsummer (30x40cm-12x16in)
£2900 $5626   (6-Dec-90 CSK80/R) Thirst for knowledge (54x43cm-21x17in) s.

CARLSEN, Carl (1855-1917) Danish
£820 $1468   (14-Mar-91 RAS.V642/R) Still life of fruit and flowers (95x64cm-37x25in)
                s.d.1910 (D.KR 9200)
£1795 $3537   (14-Nov-90 RAS.K619/R) Two art critics (50x39cm-20x15in) s.d.89
                (D.KR 20000)
£2289 $3845   (23-Apr-91 RAS.K354/R) Field landscape with two girls from Brittany
                (45x65cm-18x26in) s.d.82 (D.KR 26000)
£6104 $12025   (14-Nov-90 RAS.K160/R) After the ball (100x125cm-39x49in) s.d.1891
                (D.KR 68000)
£8079 $15916   (14-Nov-90 RAS.K66/R) Gustav Wied reading to a group of artist's in The
                Small Gardens (125x180cm-49x71in) s.d.1894 (D.KR 90000)

CARLSEN, Emil (1853-1932) American/Danish
£851 $1600   (22-Sep-90 WOL.C103/R) Fisherman and boy (30x25cm-12x10in) s.d.76
£2139 $4000   (30-Aug-90 MFA.C234) Autumn landscape (51x41cm-20x16in) s.
£6878 $13000   (26-Sep-90 SY.NY169/R) Still life, brass bowl, copper coffee pot, and
                pigeons (56x84cm-22x33in) s.
£9184 $18000   (7-Nov-90 B.SF3758/R) Woods (85x69cm-33x27in) s.d.1902
£24277 $42000   (22-May-91 CH.NY189/R) Asters in a Canton Vase (89x63cm-35x25in) s.d.93
£28902 $50000   (22-May-91 CH.NY190/R) Coast of Maine (102x127cm-40x50in) s.d.1914
*£867 $1500   (21-May-91 BG.M982/R) View of house by Seine with garden and boat
                (46x25cm-18x10in) s. i.verso W/C*

CARLSEN, Emil Soren (1848-1932) American
£1227 $2000   (5-Jul-91 S.W3088/R) After the hunt still life (30x56cm-12x22in)
                s.d.1897

CARLSON, John F (1875-1945) American
£508 $1000   (18-Nov-90 JRB.C143/R) Across the valley (20x25cm-8x10in) s. s.i.verso
                board
£581 $1000   (19-May-91 LIT.L178) Midsummer (20x25cm-8x10in) s. board
£1016 $1950   (1-Dec-90 LAE.L19/R) Figure among boats and houses (56x43cm-22x17in) s.
£1596 $3000   (19-Sep-90 B.SF2789/R) Quiet woodland (30x42cm-12x17in) s.
£5587 $10000   (14-Mar-91 CH.NY80/R) Afternoon glow (64x77cm-25x30in) s. s.i.stretcher
£10582 $20000   (26-Sep-90 SY.NY155/R) Winter landscape (102x132cm-40x52in) s.
*£781 $1500   (17-Dec-90 SY.NY222/R) Winter landscape with snow (33x41cm-13x16in) s.
                W/C*
£3351 $6500   (24-Aug-90 RB.HY128/R) Rustic byways (64x76cm-25x30in) s. W/C board

CARLSSON, Einer R (20th C) Scandinavian
£906 $1748   (10-Dec-90 BU.K80/R) Interior from a farm cottage (53x41cm-21x16in)
                s.d.1918 (D.KR 10000)

CARLSTEDT, B J (1907-1975) Finnish
£1569 $3076   (24-Nov-90 HOR.H56/R) Anemones (39x46cm-15x18in) s.d.1942 (F.M 11000)

CARLSTEDT, Birger (1907-1975) Finnish
£7386 $13222   (14-Apr-91 BU.H15/R) Still life with gramophone (73x59cm-29x23in) s.d.43
                (F.M 52000)

CARLSTEDT, Mikko (1892-1964) Finnish
£1307 $2339   (14-Apr-91 BU.H19/R) River landscape (46x75cm-18x30in) s.indist.d.14
                (F.M 9200)
£1563 $2797   (14-Apr-91 BU.H20/R) Flowers in jug (65x54cm-26x21in) s.d.52
                (F.M 11000)
£1871 $3610   (15-Dec-90 BU.H31) Still life of vegetables and jug (55x65cm-22x26in)
                s.d.29 (F.M 13000)
£2006 $3951   (17-Nov-90 BU.H18/R) Landscape with waterfall (46x55cm-18x22in) s.d.51
                (F.M 14000)

CARLSTEDT, Mikko (1892-1964) Finnish-cont.
£2152	$3637	(20-Apr-91 HOR.H47/R) Cottage among trees (60x73cm-24x29in) s.d.1947 (F.M 15000)
£4304	$7274	(20-Apr-91 HOR.H45/R) Summer landscape (55x66cm-22x26in) s.d.1937 (F.M 30000)
£4993	$9786	(24-Nov-90 HOR.H57/R) Grey day (66x82cm-26x32in) s.d.1920 (F.M 35000)

CARLSTROM, Gustaf (1896-1964) Swedish
£651	$1164	(9-Apr-91 GO.G25) Landscape view from Sando (61x81cm-24x32in) s. (S.KR 7000)
£1463	$2867	(20-Nov-90 GO.G28) Girl by marsh (60x73cm-24x29in) s. (S.KR 16000)
£1828	$3583	(20-Nov-90 GO.G30) '.. har jag inte bottna' (68x82cm-27x32in) s. panel (S.KR 20000)
£1859	$3327	(9-Apr-91 GO.G27) Flowering school attendance (65x80cm-26x31in) s. panel (S.KR 20000)
£2285	$4479	(20-Nov-90 GO.G27/R) Girl at edge of water (81x65cm-32x26in) s. (S.KR 25000)
£2377	$4658	(20-Nov-90 GO.G32) Girl by watercourse (73x60cm-29x24in) s. (S.KR 26000)
£2416	$4325	(9-Apr-91 GO.G26) Girl by watercourse (46x55cm-18x22in) s. (S.KR 26000)
£2834	$5554	(20-Nov-90 GO.G29) Girls on jetty (60x73cm-24x29in) s. (S.KR 31000)
£3108	$6091	(20-Nov-90 GO.G31/R) Girls picking flowers by stonewall (60x73cm-24x29in) s. (S.KR 34000)

CARLSUND, Otto (1897-1948) Swedish
£1127	*$1915*	*(28-May-91 AB.S5179/R) Illustration to Harald Forss' 'Demaskering' (25x18cm-10x7in) s.d.47 W/C Indian ink (S.KR 12000)*

CARMASSI, Arturo (1925-) Italian
£1171	$2283	(22-Oct-90 BR.M203/R) Repertorio n.1 (46x55cm-18x22in) mono. s.d.1937verso acrylic (I.L 2600000)
£1261	$2458	(24-Oct-90 F.M170/R) Composizione (100x70cm-39x28in) s.d.1957/58verso panel (I.L 2800000)
£2384	$3910	(19-Jun-91 F.M223/R) Senza titolo (100x130cm-39x51in) s.d.1957-58 (I.L 5200000)
£3635	$7160	(30-Oct-90 F.R258/R) I fiori (75x60cm-30x24in) s. s.d.1954/1955verso (I.L 8000000)
£1501	*$2838*	*(27-Sep-90 F.M133) Composizione (150x109cm-59x43in) s. mixed media (I.L 3300000)*

CARMELO DE ARZADUN (1888-1968) Uruguayan
£4302	$8475	(1-Nov-90 BAR.M1) Ciudad de Treinta y Tres (115x95cm-45x37in)
£5348	$10000	(1-Aug-90 BAV.M6) Banistas y Jinetes (270x220cm-106x87in)

CARMI, Eugenio (1920-) Italian
£1374	$2638	(27-Nov-90 SY.MI1) Cerchio instabile (50x50cm-20x20in) s.d.76 acrylic (I.L 3000000)

CARMICHAEL, Franklin (1890-1945) Canadian
£20175	$39544	(20-Nov-90 JOY.T75/R) Upper Ottawa, near Mattawa (25x30cm-10x12in) panel (C.D 46000)
£144737	$283684	(20-Nov-90 JOY.T29/R) Cranberry Lake (75x90cm-30x35in) s.d.1931 (C.D 330000)
£9730	*$15859*	*(10-Jun-91 W.T1076) Northern Lake (25x30cm-10x12in) s.d.1926 W/C (C.D 18000)*

CARMICHAEL, J W (1800-1868) British
£800	$1352	(15-Apr-91 SY.J396/R) Rescue, shipwreck (51x65cm-20x26in) (SA.R 3800)

CARMICHAEL, John Wilson (1800-1868) British
£650	$1261	(22-Aug-90 CSK285) French fishing boat sailing in choppy seas off coastline (15x30cm-6x12in) s. board
£900	$1746	(4-Dec-90 AG396/R) Gentleman on pier watching departing hoy boat (16x13cm-6x5in) s.d.1850 board
£1400	$2254	(25-Jun-91 AG403/R) Old windmill by moonlight (14x15cm-6x6in) s.d.1837
£2400	$4680	(16-Oct-90 CG215/R) St Pierre with peasants and goats (46x76cm-18x30in) s.d.1866 s.i.verso
£3191	$6000	(7-Aug-90 RB.HY186/R) 'Brig Memnon' (46x66cm-18x26in) s.init.d.1826
£4000	$7400	(5-Mar-91 AG297/R) Lifeboat taking off survivors of shipwreck (59x90cm-23x35in) s.d.1863
£4000	$6920	(22-May-91 S15/R) Becalmed (50x78cm-20x31in) init.d.1854
£4200	$8190	(18-Oct-90 CSK120/R) Stiff breeze off south coast (84x122cm-33x48in) s. d.indist.1839
£4790	$8000	(7-Jun-91 SY.NY147/R) Off the needles, Isle of Wight (56x79cm-22x31in) init.d.1848
£5000	$9250	(6-Mar-91 DR115/R) Shipping in storm. Shipping in calm (30x46cm-12x18in) s. pair
£5400	$10206	(26-Sep-90 S17/R) Becalmed (50x78cm-20x31in) init.d.1854
£5500	$10780	(13-Feb-91 S4/R) St Pierre near Aosta (46x76cm-18x30in) s.d.1866 s.i.d.stretcher
£6000	$9660	(25-Jun-91 AG400/R) Dunstanburgh Castle at sunrise (59x108cm-23x43in) s.d.1859
£7000	$12040	(13-May-91 CG208/R) Fishing boats and other vessels making for a harbour (50x74cm-20x29in) s.
£8500	$16660	(15-Feb-91 N388/R) Bamburgh Castle on coast of Northumberland (99x163cm-39x64in) s.

CARMICHAEL, John Wilson (1800-1868) British-cont.

£9000	$16110	(12-Apr-91 C68/R) Indiaman and other shipping at entrance to Thames (79x126cm-31x50in)
£47000	$84130	(10-Apr-91 S10/R) On Thames at Woolwich, with Buckinghamshire, Indiaman, going down river (72x109cm-28x43in) s. indist.i.stretcher
£400	$656	(19-Jun-91 PHS645/R) Flamborough Head (23x33cm-9x13in) s.i. W/C htd white
£400	$784	(23-Jan-91 B41/R) Abruggi possibly in Alto Adige (38x56cm-15x22in) s.i.d.1857 W/C
£620	$1228	(30-Jan-91 S132) Horse and pigs by tent, Cowhill, Lancashire (15x21cm-6x8in) s. W/C over pencil
£900	$1485	(9-Jul-91 C43/R) Benton Park, Newcastle upon Tyne (20x31cm-8x12in) s.d.1837 pencil W/C
£900	$1557	(20-May-91 SWS360/R) A shipwreck (24x35cm-9x14in) s.d.1838 W/C htd.white
£960	$1776	(5-Mar-91 AG145/R) The Abbot's House, Fountain's Abbey, Yorkshire (29x45cm-11x18in) s.i. W/C sketch
£1600	$3152	(15-Nov-90 S95/R) The Hotel at Saltburn, Yorkshire (35x53cm-14x21in) s.i.d.1862 W/C over pencil
£1850	$3423	(5-Mar-91 AG150/R) Women resting at bridge near ruined castle (37x55cm-15x22in) s.d.1857 W/C

CARMICHAEL, John Wilson (after) (1800-1868) British

£650	$1222	(8-Aug-90 PHP114) War ships in stiff breeze (38x56cm-15x22in) i.verso

CARMICHAEL, John Wilson (attrib) (1800-1868) British

£3000	$5370	(10-Apr-91 S194/R) Off Whitby (33x44cm-13x17in) indist.s.d.
£1800	$3222	(13-Mar-91 B57/R) Folkestone Harbour (50x80cm-20x31in) pencil W/C htd.white

CARMICHAEL, Stewart (1867-?) British

£1305	$2558	(11-Feb-91 SY.J435/R) Homage to Scotland (95x122cm-37x48in) s.i.d.1935/6 (SA.R 6500)

CARMIENCKE, J H (1810-1867) Danish/American

£1845	$3100	(28-Apr-91 LIT.L141) Hyde Park, New York (18x25cm-7x10in) s.

CARMIENCKE, Johan-Herman (1810-1867) Danish/American

£1487	$2900	(26-Oct-90 S.W2207/R) The Blue grotto (102x127cm-40x50in) s.i.d.1851
£2226	$3628	(12-Jun-91 N.M387/R) Berchtesgaden with view of Watzmann (32x44cm-13x17in) mono. (DM 6500)
£4000	$6560	(19-Jun-91 S353/R) In blue grotto (100x127cm-39x50in) s.d.51

CARMIGNANI, Guido (1838-1909) Italian

£5800	$11368	(22-Nov-90 CSK175/R) Rocky landscape with drover and cattle (41x62cm-16x24in) s.d.1860

CARMONTELLE, Louis Carrogis (1717-1806) French

£26504	$51152	(12-Dec-90 ARC.P56/R) La Comtesse de Blot et la Marquise de Barbantane (33x23cm-13x9in) pierre noire sanguine W/C (F.FR 260000)

CARMONTELLE, Louis Carrogis (attrib) (1717-1806) French

£915	$1500	(19-Jun-91 B.SF1696/R) Portrait of woman in profile (23x16cm-9x6in) chl sanguine

CARNACINI, Ceferino (1888-1964) Argentinian

£665	$1150	(8-May-91 V.BA15) Paisaje (28x38cm-11x15in)
£1618	$2800	(8-May-91 RO.BA495/R) Ranchos bajo los Ombues (57x102cm-22x40in) s.d.1929
£2344	$4500	(27-Nov-90 PO.BA2) Paisaje (85x121cm-33x48in) s.
£4211	$8000	(11-Sep-90 PO.BA5) Puerto con embarcaciones (68x110cm-27x43in) s. panel

CARNEO, Antonio (17th C) Italian

£15000	$25350	(17-Apr-91 S25/R) Jephthah sacrificing his daughter. Judith returning with head of Holofernes. Joseph interpreting dre set of three

CARNIER, H (?) ?

£750	$1298	(9-May-91 CSK192/R) Bacino di San Marco, Venice (18x30cm-7x12in) s. panel
£1100	$1969	(12-Apr-91 BM.B716/R) Harbour view with fishing boats returning (26x21cm-10x8in) s. panel (DM 3300)

CARO BAROJA, Julio (20th C) Spanish

£1037	$1795	(8-May-91 FER.M160/R) Los puritanos (34x50cm-13x20in) init. rotulador (S.P 190000)

CARO, Baldassare de (18th C) Italian

£1954	$3498	(14-Mar-91 D.V165/R) Mountain landscape with cows and dog (63x49cm-25x19in) mono. (A.S 40000)
£2737	$5392	(30-Oct-90 BU.S236/R) Still life of dead birds in landscape (77x102cm-30x40in) s. (S.KR 30000)
£3800	$7334	(11-Dec-90 PH217/R) Dead birds on bank with frog by thistle (65x77cm-26x30in) s.
£8903	$14957	(23-Apr-91 F.R23/R) Cane da caccia su sfondo di paesaggio (25x31cm-10x12in) pair (I.L 19500000)
£22395	$44118	(13-Nov-90 F.M124/R) Nature morte con fagiani e cani, e con cane e lepre (75x100cm-30x39in) (I.L 49000000)

CARO, Baldassare de (attrib) (18th C) Italian
£1486 $2899   (26-Oct-90 KM.K1005/R) Rocky river landscape with cows and dog
     (63x49cm-25x19in) mono. canvas laid down (DM 4400)

CARO, Baldassare de (circle) (18th C) Italian
£1116 $2209   (30-Jan-91 APT.P16/R) Oiseaux sous une fontaine (87x120cm-34x47in)
     (F.FR 11000)
£1351 $2634   (23-Oct-90 CH.R191) Natura morta di cacciagione (27x40cm-11x16in) canvas
     on board (I.L 3000000)

CAROLUS, Jean (19th C) Belgian
£1982 $3884   (6-Nov-90 SY.AM293) Mother and child in interior (70x58cm-28x23in) s.i.
     (D.FL 6500)
£3468 $6000   (22-May-91 SY.NY213/R) Letter (65x55cm-26x22in) s.
£6200 $11904   (27-Nov-90 PH12/R) The conversation (66x51cm-26x20in) s.i.d.1860

CAROLUS, Jean (circle) (19th C) Belgian
£1800 $3006   (3-Jun-91 PHB41/R) Finishing touch (49x38cm-19x15in) i.verso panel

CAROLUS-DURAN (1838-1917) French
£2165 $3529   (14-Jun-91 MB.P21) Portrait de femme de profil (46x33cm-18x13in) s.d.69
     (F.FR 21500)
£3772 $7242   (30-Nov-90 CB.P69/R) Portrait de Manet (64x50cm-25x20in) s.d.1874
     (F.FR 37000)

CAROLUS-DURAN, Emile Auguste (1838-1917) French
£5025 $8241   (20-Jun-91 APT.P4/R) Portrait de fillette (64x55cm-25x22in) s.d.1911
     oval (F.FR 50000)
£9250 $17945   (8-Dec-90 SY.MO331/R) Portrait de la Marquise de Vaucouleurs de Lonjamet
     (130x90cm-51x35in) s.d.1875 (F.FR 90000)
*£513 $1000   (26-Oct-90 SY.NY13/R) Study of young girl in mob cap (28x20cm-11x8in) s.
     pencil*

CARON (?) French
£1480 $2915   (16-Nov-90 LGB.P175) Nature morte au gibier (59x72cm-23x28in) s.
     (F.FR 14500)

CARON, Jules (19th C) French
£589 $1013   (14-May-91 GM.B485/R) Bords de l'Escaut (50x60cm-20x24in) s.
     (B.FR 36000)

CARON, Paul Archibald (1874-1941) Canadian
£758 $1303   (14-May-91 JOY.T29/R) A winter scene (13x17cm-5x7in) panel (C.D 1500)
£1140 $2235   (20-Nov-90 JOY.T379/R) Steamer approaching Cape Trinity on Saguenay
     (27x22cm-11x9in) s. (C.D 2600)
£1152 $1924   (4-Jun-91 FB.M33) Camp in Laurentians (13x18cm-5x7in) s.i. verso board
     (C.D 2200)
£2402 $4707   (5-Nov-90 FB.M82 b) The last load, Baie St.Paul (51x61cm-20x24in) s.
     (C.D 5500)
*£800 $1552   (3-Dec-90 R.T269/R) Collins' Inn (25x33cm-10x13in) s. i.verso W/C
     (C.D 1800)*
*£1600 $3104   (3-Dec-90 R.T268/R) Family gathering for Christmas (28x39cm-11x15in) s.
     s.d.32/10 verso W/C (C.D 3600)*
*£1641 $2840   (6-May-91 SY.T130/R) Views of American inns and taverns (24x33cm-9x13in)
     s. i.verso W/C three (C.D 3250)*
*£1832 $3060   (4-Jun-91 FB.M53/R) Sainte-Adele, Quebec (37x46cm-15x18in) s.d.'40 W/C
     (C.D 3500)*
*£2273 $3932   (6-May-91 SY.T129/R) Stage coaches at inn, winter. Christmas Eve
     (25x33cm-10x13in) one s. W/C pair (C.D 4500)*
*£3030 $5212   (14-May-91 JOY.T58/R) Laurentian winter landscape (29x39cm-11x15in) s.
     W/C (C.D 6000)*

CAROSELLI, Angelo (1585-1652) Italian
£10000 $17000   (31-May-91 CH.NY72/R) Allegory of luxury (46x37cm-18x15in)
£12500 $21125   (19-Apr-91 C118/R) The Madonna and child (59x47cm-23x19in) canvas
     transferred from panel

CAROSELLI, Angelo (attrib) (1585-1652) Italian
£2535 $5020   (30-Jan-91 APT.P165/R) Allegorie du Vin (68x50cm-27x20in) oval
     (F.FR 25000)

CAROTO, Giovanni Francesco (circle) (1480-1555) Italian
£4310 $7500   (27-Mar-91 B.SF4012/R) Madonna and Child (61x45cm-24x18in) panel

CARPEAUX, Jean Baptiste (1827-1875) French
*£2869 $5623   (7-Nov-90 APT.P453/R) Portrait de la Baronne Aymart (19x14cm-7x6in) s.
     crayon (F.FR 28000)*
*£3968 $6508   (19-Jun-91 GK.B248) Study of architecture with figures (32x24cm-13x9in)
     st.studio indis.d. chl (S.FR 10000)*

CARPENTER, Margaret (1793-1872) British
£5500 $10835   (14-Nov-90 S54/R) Portrait of two children seated in landscape sketching
     dog (108x83cm-43x33in) s.d.1829
£12000 $21480   (10-Apr-91 S102/R) Children of David Baillie (142x109cm-56x43in)
     s.d.1842 i.verso

CARPENTER, Margaret (1793-1872) British-cont.
£3500 $5915 *(3-May-91 T180/R) Portrait of Richard Parkes Bonington (23x18cm-9x7in)*
     i.verso W/C

CARPENTER, Margaret (attrib) (1793-1872) British
£3000 $4950 (10-Jul-91 S114/R) Portrait of lady wearing dress and shawl
     (74x62cm-29x24in)

CARPENTER, Margaret (circle) (1793-1872) British
£1300 $2145 (11-Jul-91 CSK132) Portrait of young boy, in jacket and bow, in
     landscape (76x63cm-30x25in)
£1800 $3222 (12-Apr-91 C144/R) Portrait of lady, seated wearing fur-lined dress,
     shawl. Portrait lady (77x64cm-30x25in) pair

CARPENTERO, Henri Joseph Gommarus (1820-1874) Belgian
£2287 $4482 (6-Nov-90 SY.AM113/R) Musicians in inn (33x41cm-13x16in) s.d.1852 panel
     (D.FL 7500)
£3636 $7164 (30-Oct-90 CH.AM167/R) Peasants merrymaking in inn (41x48cm-16x19in)
     s.d.1850 panel (D.FL 12000)

CARPENTERO, Henri Joseph Gommarus (attrib) (1820-1874) Belgian
£748 $1324 (20-Mar-91 KM.K1133) The last snow, view over hilly landscape
     (36x46cm-14x18in) s. (DM 2200)

CARPENTIER, Charles-Louis-Francois le (1744-1822) French
£2840 $5623 (30-Jan-91 APT.P306/R) Saint Michel terrassant le dragon
     (44x24cm-17x9in) s.d.1782 verso (F.FR 28000)

CARPENTIER, Evariste (1845-1922) Belgian
£693 $1227 (7-Apr-91 I.N60) Nature morte (33x41cm-13x16in) s. (F.FR 7000)
£2000 $3440 (17-May-91 C64/R) Good recovery (47x64cm-19x25in) s.

CARPENTIERS, Adrien (circle) (1739-1778) British
£1900 $3211 (30-Apr-91 PH47/R) Portrait of Neil Segrave, standing wearing
     embroidered coat by table, landscape beyond (127x101cm-50x40in)

CARPI, Aldo (1886-1973) Italian
£6754 $13170 (22-Oct-90 BR.M247/R) Fanciulla e carabiniere (55x43cm-22x17in) s.d.1925
     board (I.L 15000000)

CARPI, Girolamo da (1501-1556) Italian
£1700 $2771 *(2-Jul-91 C240/R) Draped female figure (18x11cm-7x4in) with i. pen*

CARPIONI, Giulio (1611-1674) Italian
£6366 $12542 (14-Nov-90 D.V260/R) Death of Orion (48x55cm-19x22in) (A.S 130000)
£6500 $12545 (11-Dec-90 PH45/R) Head of woman wearing elaborate turban headdress
     (50x39cm-20x15in)

CARPIONI, Giulio (after) (1611-1674) Italian
£2726 $5370 (29-Oct-90 SY.F629/R) Scena con putti che giocano (110x119cm-43x47in)
     (I.L 6000000)

CARPIONI, Giulio (circle) (1611-1674) Italian
£900 $1467 *(2-Jul-91 C314/R) Crucifixion (35x24cm-14x9in) with i. red chk*

CARR, Emily M (1871-1945) Canadian
£5051 $8737 (6-May-91 SY.T59/R) Study of forest interior (38x27cm-15x11in) estate
     st. paper (C.D 10000)
£7071 $12232 (6-May-91 SY.T67/R) Swirling sky, British Columbia Coast
     (54x82cm-21x32in) s. i.verso paper (C.D 14000)
£10101 $17475 (6-May-91 SY.T102/R) Sea and sky (59x63cm-23x25in) s. paper (C.D 20000)
£10811 $17622 (10-Jun-91 W.T1068/R) June (86x58cm-34x23in) s. i. verso paper
     (C.D 20000)
£11404 $22465 (30-Oct-90 SY.T57/R) Sky (57x62cm-22x24in) s.s. i.verso paper
     (C.D 26000)
£46053 $90263 (20-Nov-90 JOY.T22/R) Summer, Mount Douglas, no.12 (90x60cm-35x24in)
     s.d.1942 paper on panel (C.D 105000)
£3728 $7307 *(20-Nov-90 JOY.T167/R) Seated Indian wrapped in blanket (25x20cm-10x8in)*
     s. W/C (C.D 8500)

CARR, Henry (1894-1970) British
£541 $1000 (10-Mar-91 H.C94/R) Two spaniels in landscape (18x25cm-7x10in) s. panel
£1500 $2910 (7-Dec-90 PHM114) Strolling in the park (50x60cm-20x24in) s.

CARR, M (?) Canadian
£3587 $6924 (10-Dec-90 L.V3) European village scene (25x36cm-10x14in) board
     (C.D 8000)

CARR, Samuel S (1837-1908) American
£532 $1000 (22-Sep-90 WOL.C188/R) Mother and child (30x41cm-12x16in) s.
£789 $1500 (15-Sep-90 S.W2755/R) Sheep in a meadow (23x36cm-9x14in) s.
£918 $1800 (12-Feb-91 MOR.P33) Grazing sheep in landscape (36x51cm-14x20in) s.
£1368 $2600 (28-Feb-91 MFA.C169/R) Several children and goat carts playing
     (33x58cm-13x23in) s.
£1800 $3042 (3-May-91 PHE144/R) The young shepherdess (31x41cm-12x16in) s.

CARRA, Carlo (1881-1966) Italian

£35759	$58645	(20-Jun-91 F.M469/R) La piazza di Assisi (38x43cm-15x17in) s.d.1940 i.verso board (I.L 78000000)
£42774	$83408	(22-Oct-90 BR.M209/R) Marina (50x35cm-20x14in) s.d.1943 board (I.L 95000000)
£54521	$107406	(30-Oct-90 F.R233/R) Marina (50x60cm-20x24in) s.d.952 (I.L 120000000)
£106470	$185257	(26-Mar-91 F.M117/R) Monti di Valsesia (36x51cm-14x20in) s. (I.L 235000000)
£5001	$9801	(20-Nov-90 BR.M133/R) Suonatore di cetra (30x40cm-12x16in) d.1945 ink (I.L 11000000)
£10077	$19348	(27-Nov-90 SY.MI139/R) Composizione metafisica (33x24cm-13x9in) s.d.919 pencil (I.L 22000000)
£12367	$23745	(27-Nov-90 SY.MI223/R) Composizione (16x19cm-6x7in) s.d.1914 pencil (I.L 27000000)
£13198	$26000	(14-Nov-90 SY.NY116/R) Volontario garibaldino pancia a terra - sparando (27x38cm-11x15in) s.i.d.1941 pen chl paper on board
£23121	$40000	(8-May-91 SY.NY165/R) Complementarismo-forme-nudo (29x21cm-11x8in) s.i.d.912 brush ink paper laid down on board
£34264	$67500	(14-Nov-90 SY.NY117/R) Donna Sulla Spiaggia (33x24cm-13x9in) s.i.d.912 ink wash pen paper on board

CARRACCI (style) (16/17th C) Italian

£1124	$2011	(14-Mar-91 D.V185/R) Christ and the Woman of Samaria (65x82cm-26x32in) (A.S 23000)

CARRACCI, Agostino (1557-1602) Italian

£5500	$9295	(16-Apr-91 C139/R) Design for an auricular Cartouche of a Cardinal's Coat of Arms (20x17cm-8x7in) i. blk.chk. ink wash
£7000	$11410	(2-Jul-91 C108/R) Christ commanding Saint Peter to walk on water (11x15cm-4x6in) with init. pen
£7000	$11410	(2-Jul-91 C264/R) Wooded river landscape with nymph reclining under tree and hunter (21x29cm-8x11in) pen double-sided
£7500	$12225	(1-Jul-91 S28/R) Studies of St. Jerome and lion (35x23cm-14x9in) bears i.verso pen

CARRACCI, Agostino (after) (1557-1602) Italian

£1600	$2704	(16-Apr-91 PH194/R) Last Supper (99x136cm-39x54in)

CARRACCI, Agostino (attrib) (1557-1602) Italian

£2400	$4608	(18-Feb-91 S188/R) Portrait of cardinal (14x11cm-6x4in) pen ink over chk
£7000	$11410	(2-Jul-91 C96/R) God the Father (32x27cm-13x11in) with i. black chk htd white oval

CARRACCI, Agostino (circle) (1557-1602) Italian

£800	$1304	(2-Jul-91 PH130/R) Satyr whipping nymph (21cm-8ins circular) panel
£2679	$4500	(17-Jul-91 SY.NY48/R) Hades and Cerberus (117x135cm-46x53in)

CARRACCI, Annibale (1560-1609) Italian

£13000	$21190	(2-Jul-91 C107/R) Penitent Magdalen (28x20cm-11x8in) red black chk pen wash htd white
£16000	$26080	(2-Jul-91 C106/R) Classical landscape with groups of figures on road near castle (20x21cm-8x8in) black chk pen
£26504	$51152	(12-Dec-90 ARC.P29/R) Groupe de trois personnages (19x16cm-7x6in) i. pen (F.FR 260000)
£36480	$64569	(19-Mar-91 F.M327/R) Giudizio di Paride. Studio di Dio Padre per una lunetta (20x27cm-8x11in) sanguine brush ink double-sided (I.L 80000000)

CARRACCI, Annibale (after) (1560-1609) Italian

£2028	$4016	(30-Jan-91 APT.P101/R) Le Christ et la Cananeene (92x73cm-36x29in) (F.FR 20000)
£3000	$5850	(26-Oct-90 C2/R) The Lamentation (65x52cm-26x20in) copper
£14359	$28000	(10-Oct-90 CH.NY111/R) Venus, satyr and two amorini (108x140cm-43x55in)

CARRACCI, Annibale (attrib) (1560-1609) Italian

£7500	$12225	(2-Jul-91 C105/R) Boy looking over shoulder (24x33cm-9x13in) with i. red chk

CARRACCI, Annibale (circle) (1560-1609) Italian

£10000	$19500	(26-Oct-90 C6/R) The Adoration of the Shepherds (101x87cm-40x34in)

CARRACCI, Annibale (style) (1560-1609) Italian

£850	$1386	(4-Jul-91 B100 j) Head study of a boy in profile (48x63cm-19x25in)
£879	$1574	(14-Mar-91 D.V176/R) Women caring for three injured men (54x60cm-21x24in) (A.S 18000)
£900	$1467	(4-Jul-91 C732/R) Angel in adoration (31x25cm-12x10in) fragment
£1567	$3087	(14-Nov-90 D.V227/R) Christ lying in the Tomb (19x31cm-7x12in) (A.S 32000)
£1590	$2688	(18-Apr-91 APT.P10/R) La Sainte Famille avec le petit Saint Jean Baptiste (80x57cm-31x22in) (F.FR 16000)

CARRACCI, Lodovico (1555-1619) Italian

£13529	$23000	(31-May-91 CH.NY178/R) Head of youth (42x32cm-17x13in) octagonal
£3200	$5408	(16-Apr-91 C138/R) A nude woman, her arms above her head (25x14cm-10x6in) i. watermark blk.white chk.

CARRACCI, Lodovico (1555-1619) Italian-cont.
| £5500 | $8965 | (2-Jul-91 C265/R) Venus and Cupid (17x10cm-7x4in) with i. black red chk pen wash double-sided |
| £13000 | $21190 | (2-Jul-91 C15/R) Infant Christ, Virgin and St Joseph seated at table attended by angel (13x11cm-5x4in) i. chk pen ink vellum |

CARRACCI, Lodovico (after) (1555-1619) Italian
| £1400 | $2422 | (20-May-91 SWS146/R) The dream of St.Catherine of Alexandria (30x25cm-12x10in) copper |

CARRACCI, Lodovico (style) (1555-1619) Italian
| £900 | $1467 | (4-Jul-91 C753) Madonna and child with Saint Elizabeth and Infant Saint John the Baptist (68x58cm-27x23in) |

CARRADE, Michel (1923-) French
| £1100 | $1771 | (28-Jun-91 CSK77/R) Composition (51x131cm-20x52in) s. s.d.1955 verso |

CARRAND, Louis (1821-1899) French
| £1104 | $2043 | (6-Mar-91 APT.P85/R) Paysage, temps orageux (26x35cm-10x14in) s. board (F.FR 11000) |

CARRASCO (1919-) ?
| £925 | $1794 | (5-Dec-90 ZZ.F23/R) Femme assise (89x61cm-35x24in) s.d.55 oil collage canvas (F.FR 9000) |

CARRE, Leon (19/20th C) French
| £28777 | $55827 | (5-Dec-90 ZZ.F190/R) Apres-midi a Nogent (68x56cm-27x22in) (F.FR 280000) |
| £797 | $1355 | (27-May-91 APT.P227/R) La grande courtisane (28x22cm-11x9in) s.d.1912 gouache (F.FR 8000) |

CARREE, Johannes (1698-1772) Dutch
| £2100 | $3633 | (20-May-91 SWS63/R) A herdsman with cattle in a river landscape with a town in the distance (34x44cm-13x17in) s. |

CARREE, Michiel (style) (1657-1747) Dutch
| £3400 | $5746 | (18-Apr-91 CSK111/R) Itallante landscape with peasants, goats and cow on track (66x61cm-26x24in) |

CARRENO, Mario (1913-) Cuban
£2551	$5000	(20-Nov-90 CH.NY214/R) Paisaje surrealista (64x79cm-25x31in) s.d.70
£13873	$24000	(8-May-91 SY.NY187/R) Dos figuras (76x61cm-30x24in) s.d.45
£15306	$30000	(19-Nov-90 SY.NY42/R) Estudio para fresco (45x52cm-18x20in) s.d.39 tempera
£40698	$70000	(15-May-91 CH.NY5/R) Desnudos (83x60cm-33x24in)

CARRETERO, Francisco (20th C) Spanish
| £1924 | $3444 | (13-Mar-91 FER.M257/R) El saloncito verde con centro de flores (100x80cm-39x31in) s.d.1949 panel (S.P 350000) |

CARRIAT-ROLLANT, G (20th C) French?
| £6030 | $9889 | (19-Jun-91 ZZ.F107 b) Deux pantheres s'abreuvant dans une vegetalton exotique (109x250cm-43x98in) s.d.1931 (F.FR 60000) |

CARRICK, J M (19th C) British
| £700 | $1141 | (13-Jun-91 L270/R) View of Newlyn (18x28cm-7x11in) s.d.1881 |

CARRICK, John Mulcaster (19th C) British
£650	$1274	(20-Nov-90 PH7) A coastal view (31x46cm-12x18in) s.d.1876
£1100	$2156	(20-Nov-90 PH191/R) Street in Dinan - Brittany (26x21cm-10x8in) s.d.1881 i. verso board
£1700	$3349	(13-Nov-90 SWS323/R) The Brentford ferry (35x60cm-14x24in) s.d.1886

CARRICK, Robert (19th C) British
| £400 | $716 | (14-Mar-91 CG57) The skylark (38x48cm-15x19in) s.d.1876 W/C htd.white |

CARRICK, William (1879-?) British
| £580 | $969 | (22-Jul-91 SWS1136/R) Summer (60x90cm-24x35in) s. |

CARRIER-BELLEUSE, Albert (1824-1887) French
| £4615 | $9000 | (26-Oct-90 SY.NY6/R) The three graces (46x36cm-18x14in) s. pencil chk htd.white |

CARRIER-BELLEUSE, Pierre (1851-1932) French
£954	$1765	(6-Mar-91 APT.P85 b) Femme dans un jardin (41x32cm-16x13in) s. (F.FR 9500)
£14359	$28000	(24-Oct-90 CH.NY102/R) The ballet lesson (117x89cm-46x35in) s.d.1914
£18145	$35019	(10-Dec-90 LD.P85/R) Danseurs de Flamenco (24x64cm-9x25in) s.d.1904 pair (F.FR 178000)
£2500	$4925	(5-Oct-90 C80/R) Devant la Vague (114x146cm-45x57in) s.d.1910 pastel canvas
£4000	$7840	(15-Feb-91 C10/R) Pierrot (105x50cm-41x20in) s. pastel
£4000	$7840	(15-Feb-91 C9/R) Columbine (105x50cm-41x20in) s. pastel
£4103	$8000	(24-Oct-90 CH.NY100/R) Young ballerina holding black cat (100x65cm-39x26in) s.d.1895 pastel
£6000	$9780	(3-Jul-91 CD.P22/R) Danseuse de l'Opera appuyee a une barre (200x120cm-79x47in) s.d.1897 pastel canvas (F.FR 60000)

CARRIER-BELLEUSE, Pierre (1851-1932) French-cont.
£6200 $12214   (5-Oct-90 C78/R) Les danseuses (117x75cm-46x30in) s.d.1928 pastel canvas

CARRIERA, Rosalba (1675-1757) Italian
£4800 $7824   (2-Jul-91 C295 a/R) Portrait of young woman, in ermine-trimmed decollete
                   dress and robe (45x35cm-18x14in) pastel
£7194 $13957   (7-Dec-90 CN.P116/R) Portrait d'homme a la veste rouge (48x38cm-19x15in)
                   pastel (F.FR 70000)
£19000 $36670   (11-Dec-90 C47 a/R) Portrait of a gentleman half length, his hat beneth
                   his arm (59x47cm-23x19in) pastel
£20000 $32600   (2-Jul-91 C295/R) Portrait of lady, in ermine-trimmed robe with
                   fleur-de-lys, diamond clasp and earrings (59x46cm-23x18in) pastel

CARRIERA, Rosalba (after) (1675-1757) Italian
£5200 $8788   (18-Apr-91 C74) The four seasons (66x53cm-26x21in) four
£3058 $5872   (30-Nov-90 APT.P28/R) Flore (56x46cm-22x18in) pastel (F.FR 30000)

CARRIERA, Rosalba (attrib) (1675-1757) Italian
£4562 $8987   (30-Oct-90 BU.S179/R) Portrait of young lady (44x36cm-17x14in) pastel
                   (S.KR 50000)
£10703 $20550   (30-Nov-90 APT.P25/R) L'automne (26x23cm-10x9in) pastel (F.FR 105000)

CARRIERA, Rosalba (circle) (1675-1757) Italian
£1000 $1770   (22-Mar-91 APT.P25) Portrait de femme (45x35cm-18x14in) pastel
                   (F.FR 10000)
£11579 $22000   (11-Jan-91 CH.NY20/R) Portrait of a lady, bust length, with flowers in
                   her hair (56x46cm-22x18in) pastel oval

CARRIERA, Rosalba (style) (1675-1757) Italian
£979 $1840   (18-Sep-90 BU.K145/R) Young girl with bouquet of flowers
                   (54x42cm-21x17in) pastel (D.KR 11000)

CARRIERE, Eugene (1849-1906) French
£1061 $2059   (8-Dec-90 GAB.G2165) Bouquet de fleurs (41x33cm-16x13in) panel
                   (S.FR 2600)
£1098 $1900   (21-May-91 CE.NY18/R) Self portrait (25x19cm-10x7in)
£1224 $2412   (14-Nov-90 FB.P138/R) Maternite (46x38cm-18x15in) s. (F.FR 12000)
£2042 $3430   (22-Apr-91 PO.BA10) Enfant a la cacerole (26x36cm-10x14in) s.
£2051 $4000   (26-Oct-90 SY.NY169/R) Portrait of young girl (32x24cm-13x9in) s.
£2449 $4751   (8-Dec-90 GAB.G2166/R) Portrait de femme (54x46cm-21x18in) s.
                   (S.FR 6000)
£2786 $4848   (25-Mar-91 CR.P69) Portrait de femme (41x32cm-16x13in) s. (F.FR 28000)
£3468 $6000   (23-May-91 CH.NY15/R) Landscape (44x34cm-17x13in) s.
£3776 $7438   (14-Nov-90 FB.P139/R) Fillette souriant (29x23cm-11x9in) (F.FR 37000)
£4500 $7380   (19-Jun-91 S196/R) Mother and child and onlooker (32x40cm-13x16in) s.
£4624 $8000   (22-May-91 SY.NY189/R) Reclining nude (30x40cm-12x16in) s.
£4898 $9502   (8-Dec-90 GAB.G2167) Maternite (50x61cm-20x24in) s. (S.FR 12000)
£5202 $9000   (22-May-91 SY.NY187/R) Head of Madame Carriere (46x38cm-18x15in) s.
£6000 $9840   (21-Jun-91 C18/R) Portrait de femme en manteau rouge (27x19cm-11x7in)
                   panel
£6154 $12000   (26-Oct-90 SY.NY168/R) Tete de femme (55x46cm-22x18in)
£6316 $12000   (28-Feb-91 CH.NY26/R) Female head study (41x33cm-16x13in) s.
£6766 $11773   (25-Mar-91 CR.P70/R) La lecon (25x33cm-10x13in) s. (F.FR 68000)
£7085 $13887   (20-Nov-90 BG.P17/R) Visage d'homme (43x33cm-17x13in) s. (F.FR 70000)
£7692 $15000   (23-Oct-90 SY.NY327/R) Portrait of artist's wife (41x33cm-16x13in) s.
£7692 $15000   (23-Oct-90 SY.NY326/R) Portrait d'enfant (41x31cm-16x12in) s.
£8421 $16000   (28-Feb-91 CH.NY27/R) The conversation (41x33cm-16x13in) st.vente seal
                   verso
£8671 $15000   (22-May-91 SY.NY188/R) Portrait de fille d'artiste (41x33cm-16x13in) s.
£10040 $16165   (25-Jun-91 BG.P12/R) Le sculpteur et son modele (65x54cm-26x21in) s. l.
                   verso (F.FR 100000)
£10887 $21230   (27-Oct-90 BG.P12/R) L'attente mystique (38x46cm-15x18in) s.
                   (F.FR 108000)
£14872 $29000   (26-Oct-90 SY.NY167/R) Interior with woman sewing (32x34cm-13x13in) s.
                   board
£40385 $79154   (20-Nov-90 BG.P18/R) Les ages de la vie (250x75cm-98x30in) s.
                   (F.FR 399000)

CARRILLO, G (20th C) ?
£918 $1809   (16-Nov-90 LGB.P192) Les fileuses (94x124cm-37x49in) s.d.1921 after
                   Velasquez (F.FR 9000)

CARRINGTON, Dora (1893-1932) British
£23000 $42550   (7-Mar-91 C59/R) Tulips in Staffordshire jug (71x66cm-28x26in)

CARRINGTON, Leonora (1917-) British
£13953 $24000   (15-May-91 CH.NY160/R) Figuras Miticas, Bailarin I. Bailarin II
                   (12x9cm-5x4in) s.d.Feb.1954 oil gold leaf masonite pair
£19388 $38000   (20-Nov-90 CH.NY38/R) Brindle dog - Well the Wathcers (60x81cm-24x32in)
                   s.d.1967
£58140 $100000 (15-May-91 CH.NY13/R) The hour of the angelus (61x92cm-24x36in) s.
                   tempera panel
£3189 $6250   (19-Nov-90 SY.NY176/R) The joker (30x23cm-12x9in) s.d.1969 W/C ink
£4082 $8000   (20-Nov-90 CH.NY195/R) El toro (34x70cm-13x28in) s.d.1969 pastel gouache
                   chl

CARRUCCI, Jacopo (1493-1558) Italian
£12755 $25000   (7-Nov-90 B.SF1051/R) Portrait of woman (55x44cm-22x17in) cradled panel

CARRUCCI, Jacopo (circle) (1493-1558) Italian
£22368 $42500   (10-Jan-91 SY.NY13/R) Madonna and Child with Saint Joseph, young Saint
                     John the Baptist and others beyond (122x103cm-48x41in) panel

CARSE, Alexander (19th C) British
£1000 $1680   (23-Apr-91 S56/R) Revellers (63x89cm-25x35in)

CARSE, James Howe (19th C) British
£543 $918   (15-Apr-91 AAA.S104) Lansdown Bridge (25x35cm-10x14in) s. panel
                    (A.D 1200)
£930 $1563   (22-Apr-91 SY.ME64/R) Waterfall with kangaroos (29x24cm-11x9in) s.d.1875
                    (A.D 2000)

CARSE, James Howe (attrib) (19th C) British
£1923 $3250   (16-Apr-91 J.M694) River scenes (27x15cm-11x6in) both init. panel pair
                    (A.D 4250)

CARSON, Frank (1881-c.1962) American
£505 $1000   (30-Jan-91 GRO.B91/R) Norumbega park, Newton, Massachusetts
                    (56x61cm-22x24in) s.d.09

CARSON, Robert Taylor (1919-) British
£900 $1755   (26-Oct-90 CG71) Circus in Connemara (61x51cm-24x20in) s. s.i.d.51verso

CARSTENS, Asmus Jacob (attrib) (1754-1798) Danish
£2648 $4422   (6-Jun-91 D.V212/R) Theseus killing centaur (103x94cm-41x37in)
                    i.d.1778verso (A.S 55000)

CARTE, Antoine (1886-1954) Belgian
£4000 $7800   (19-Oct-90 C95/R) Jeune fille a la robe bleue (73x42cm-29x17in) s.d.1932
£20000 $39000   (10-Oct-90 SY.NY169/R) Madonna (104x97cm-41x38in) s.d.1927
£25000 $48750   (16-Oct-90 C51/R) Saint Christophe (120x100cm-47x39in) s.

CARTER, Frank Thomas (1853-1934) British
£733 $1392   (28-Feb-91 D.V44/R) River landscape (36x47cm-14x19in) s. (A.S 15000)

CARTER, Henry Barlow (1803-1867) British
*£580 $980   (16-Apr-91 CHAP236) Fishing boats entering Scarborough harbour in stormy
                    seas (30x43cm-12x17in) W/C*
*£600 $1116   (5-Sep-90 RBB645) Shore scene with figures attending beached fishing
                    boat, castle beyond (25x36cm-10x14in) s.d.1845 W/C*
*£700 $1253   (9-Apr-91 C148) Durham Castle and cathedral from river Wear
                    (18x28cm-7x11in) s. pencil W/C scratching out*
£800 $1568   (14-Feb-91 MO1) Seascape of Scarborough harbour W/C
*£1020 $1989   (17-Oct-90 PHL46/R) A fishing vessel in heavy seas, off Scarborough
                    (22x30cm-9x12in) col.washes scratching out*
*£1400 $2478   (19-Mar-91 CHAP336) Ship entering Scarborough harbour in stormy seas
                    (15x23cm-6x9in) W/C*
*£1750 $3098   (19-Mar-91 CHAP342) Sailing vessel at mouth of Scarborough Harbour in
                    choppy seas (28x43cm-11x17in) s.d.1847 W/C*

CARTER, Henry W (19th C) British
£3800 $6384   (16-Jul-91 C80/R) Staffordshire bull terrier with tabby cat
                    (25x31cm-10x12in) s.d.1890

CARTER, John (1748-1817) British
*£550 $908   (9-Jul-91 C14) Study of canopy from Choir Stall, St George's Chapel,
                    Windsor (50x20cm-20x8in) i.verso pencil wash*

CARTER, Joseph N (1835-1871) British
£2000 $3920   (13-Feb-91 S95/R) Near Torbay. Woodland cottage (30x46cm-12x18in) one
                    s.d.69 one bears sig.d.1969 verso pair

CARTER, Pruett A (1891-1955) American
£2296 $4500   (7-Nov-90 B.SF3848/R) Quest for honour (99x89cm-39x35in) s.d.27

CARTER, Richard Harry (1839-1911) British
*£660 $1076   (13-Jun-91 L185/R) Bringing in the catch (41x71cm-16x28in) s. W/C
                    htd.bodycol.*

CARTER, Samuel (attrib) (19th C) British
£520 $879   (3-May-91 PHE85) The foxhole (50x37cm-20x15in)

CARTER, Samuel John (1835-1892) British
£1150 $1978   (14-May-91 SWS198/R) Study of bay and grey cob in grounds of Nutfield
                    Priory (35x51cm-14x20in) s.d.1862
£10000 $19700   (16-Nov-90 C73/R) Heron feeding their young in nest in pine tree
                    (146x178cm-57x70in) s.d.1889

CARTER, Sydney (19/20th C) British
£617 $1185   (26-Nov-90 SY.J321/R) Cape Homestead (63x76cm-25x30in) s. (SA.R 3000)
£763 $1496   (11-Feb-91 SY.J482/R) Figures beside Cape cottages (60x62cm-24x24in) s.
                    canvas laid down on board (SA.R 3800)

CARTER, Sydney (19/20th C) British-cont.
£1210 $2359   (15-Oct-90 SY.J95/R) African village below the mountains
                  (67x90cm-26x35in) s. (SA.R 6000)

CARTER, William (19th C) British
£2800 $5516   (1-Nov-90 TE606/R) View of Richmond Castle across the Swale
                  (84x117cm-33x46in) bears i.d.1847 verso

CARTON, Charles (1816-1853) Belgian
£1270 $2197   (22-May-91 GS.B2340/R) The singing lesson (60x50cm-24x20in) s.d.1849
                  (S.FR 3200)

CARTWRIGHT, Isabel Branson (1885-?) American
£895 $1700   (15-Sep-90 S.W2750/R) Fishing boats off rocky coast (64x76cm-25x30in) s.

CARTWRIGHT, Reg (1938-) British
*£500 $970   (6-Dec-90 S340/R) Chaucer's 'Canterbury Tales' - heron chased by falcon
                  above three men (68x55cm-27x22in) s.d.88 gouache*

CARUELLE D'ALIGNY, Theodore (1798-1871) French
*£2650 $5115   (14-Dec-90 LEB.P62/R) Rochers dans la foret de Fontainebleau
                  (24x36cm-9x14in) mono.d.1829 Indian ink (F.FR 26000)*

CARUS, Carl Gustav (1789-1869) German
*£1208 $2356   (12-Oct-90 AW.H1388) Fir tree with soldier pulling cart beyond
                  (28x20cm-11x8in) d.13 indis.s.verso W/C pencil (DM 3600)*

CARUSON, Carlo (fl.1876) Italian?
£1300 $2496   (18-Dec-90 C67/R) Portrait of Elisabeth Vigee Lebrun (17x?cm-7x?in)
                  min.s.i.d.1876 carved black wood frame rec.

CARVER, Richard (attrib) (?) ?
£8000 $14320   (10-Apr-91 S164/R) Cephalus and Procris (70x89cm-28x35in)

CARWITHAM, Thomas (fl.1713) British
*£850 $1522   (9-Apr-91 C13/R) Diana's nymphs discovering Callisto's misfortune. Tobit
                  and the angel pen ink wash htd.white two*

CARZOU, Jean (1907-?) French
£1500 $2445   (5-Jul-91 ZZ.F3) Paysage Bourguignon (20x30cm-8x12in) s.d.43
                  (F.FR 15000)
£4400 $7172   (5-Jul-91 ZZ.F4/R) Paysage a la Moissonneuse (37x58cm-15x23in) s.d.43
                  (F.FR 44000)
£6200 $10354   (7-Jun-91 LD.P54/R) Bouquet de fleurs des champs (65x50cm-26x20in)
                  s.d.54 (F.FR 62000)
£7661 $14710   (2-Dec-90 GAB.G1553/R) Rue de village (50x64cm-20x25in) s.d.1957
                  (S.FR 19000)
£15182 $29757   (22-Nov-90 ZZ.F27/R) Cour de ferme (53x64cm-21x25in) s.d.43
                  (F.FR 150000)
*£976 $1894   (8-Dec-90 LT.P128/R) Paysage (32x40cm-13x16in) s.d.1972 col.crayons ink
                  (F.FR 9500)*
*£1122 $2211   (14-Nov-90 CN.P35/R) Ville fantastique (28x37cm-11x15in) s.d.54 ink wash
                  (F.FR 11000)*
*£1200 $2340   (19-Oct-90 C203/R) La route au foret (45x55cm-18x22in) s.d.50 gouache
                  W/C brush ink*
*£2012 $3400   (20-Apr-91 WOL.C426/R) Harlequin dansant (43x30cm-17x12in) s.d.61 W/C
                  acrylic*
£2026 $3951   (25-Oct-90 CB.P53) Paysage (48x56cm-19x22in) s.d.1956 W/C (F.FR 20100)
£2376 $4206   (7-Apr-91 I.N64/R) Paysage (43x54cm-17x21in) s.d.58 W/C (F.FR 24000)
*£2869 $5623   (11-Nov-90 ZZ.F247/R) Arlequin au violon et a la fleur (28x22cm-11x9in)
                  s.d.1983 col.crayons Indian ink (F.FR 28000)*
£4000 $7800   (19-Oct-90 C199/R) Venice (50x65cm-20x26in) s. W/C brush ink

CASA, Giacomo (1835-1887) Italian
£2400 $4728   (5-Oct-90 C145/R) Tis true ther's magic in Web of It-Othello, Act IV,
                  scene i. After Battle of Cyprus-Othello, Act II (35x54cm-14x21in) s.
                  pair

CASALI, Andrea (1720-18??) Italian
£9744 $19000   (11-Oct-90 SY.NY84/R) The family of Darius before Alexander
                  (47x64cm-19x25in) s.d.1737
£14359 $28000   (11-Oct-90 SY.NY49/R) Lot and his Daughters (125x99cm-49x39in) s.

CASAMADA, Alberto Rafols (1923-) Spanish
£2726 $4470   (17-Jun-91 DUR.M40/R) Jardin (72x83cm-28x33in) s. s.i.d.73verso
                  (S.P 500000)
£3824 $7380   (13-Dec-90 EP.M6/R) Espai rosa (73x92cm-29x36in) s.d.79 acrylic
                  (S.P 700000)

CASANOVA, Francesco Giuseppe (1729-1802) Italian
£3918 $7718   (14-Nov-90 D.V62/R) Landscape with figures and animals watering
                  (134x94cm-53x37in) (A.S 80000)
£4192 $7084   (2-May-91 CH.AM33/R) An officer on horseback challenging a foot soldier
                  (38x46cm-15x18in) s.d.1771 (D.FL 14000)
£18499 $35889   (7-Dec-90 SY.MO108/R) La halte devant une auberge (78x141cm-31x56in)
                  (F.FR 180000)

324

CASANOVA, Francesco Giuseppe (1729-1802) Italian-cont.
£553	$907	(21-Jun-91 CK.P16/R) Paysan cheminant avec ses betes (38x19cm-15x7in) s. pierre noire wash (F.FR 5500)
£2000	$3540	(22-Mar-91 APT.P21/R) Convo de militaire et de paysans. La fenaison s. drawing wash (F.FR 20000)
£2672	$5184	(7-Dec-90 CN.P66/R) Scene de bataille (41x54cm-16x21in) wash gouache htd.white (F.FR 26000)

CASANOVA, Francisco Tover (19th C) ?
£1374	$2460	(13-Mar-91 FER.M139/R) Retrato de goyesca con guitarra (43x28cm-17x11in) s. panel (S.P 250000)
£3600	$7020	(18-Oct-90 SC3139/R) Indiscreet intentions (64x82cm-25x32in) s.d.1877

CASANOVAS, Enrique (19th C) Spanish
£3158	$6000	(28-Feb-91 CH.NY102/R) Lumber cart on path in landscape (81x130cm-32x51in) s.

CASARIN, M (1949-) Italian
£952	$1562	(21-Jun-91 G.Z55/R) Solo e senza amore (112x153cm-44x60in) s.d.1987 mixed media canvas (S.FR 2400)

CASATI, Alexandre (19th C) Italian
£800	$1384	(9-May-91 CSK182/R) Wayside shrine (43x66cm-17x26in) s.

CASCELLA, Michele (1892-?) Italian
£1571	$3032	(13-Dec-90 F.M347/R) Paesaggio (18x24cm-7x9in) s. (I.L 3400000)
£2613	$4286	(20-Jun-91 F.M316/R) Campo di papaveri (20x30cm-8x12in) s. (I.L 5700000)
£4502	$8780	(24-Oct-90 F.M111/R) San Fruttuoso (51x62cm-20x24in) s. (I.L 10000000)
£4598	$8000	(27-Mar-91 B.SF4315/R) Bouquet of flowers (91x61cm-36x24in) s. canvasbaord
£6098	$10000	(19-Jun-91 B.SF1748/R) Portofino (76x99cm-30x39in) s.
£6322	$11000	(27-Mar-91 B.SF4314/R) Street in Portofino (89x63cm-35x25in) s.i.d.1960
£6877	$11278	(20-Jun-91 F.M352/R) Paesaggio abruzzese (50x70cm-20x28in) s. (I.L 15000000)
£7290	$12393	(28-May-91 SY.MI130/R) Mazzo di fiori (91x61cm-36x24in) s. (I.L 16000000)
£7290	$12393	(28-May-91 SY.MI116/R) Paesaggio di Ginestre (50x70cm-20x28in) s. (I.L 16000000)
£7654	$14926	(24-Oct-90 F.M219/R) Ricordo di Amalfi (70x50cm-28x20in) s. (I.L 17000000)
£7746	$13168	(28-May-91 SY.MI171/R) Strada di paese (66x101cm-26x40in) s. (I.L 17000000)
£9113	$15492	(28-May-91 SY.MI161/R) Paesaggio (61x91cm-24x36in) s. (I.L 20000000)
£10806	$21072	(22-Oct-90 BR.M205/R) Portofino (75x98cm-30x39in) s.d.1960 (I.L 24000000)
£11706	$22828	(24-Oct-90 F.M261/R) Capri (72x100cm-28x39in) s.d.35 tempera board (I.L 26000000)
£13401	$25864	(13-Dec-90 F.M391/R) Campo di papaveri (70x100cm-28x39in) s. (I.L 29000000)
£2079	$4013	(12-Dec-90 F.M16) Portofino (36x53cm-14x21in) s.d.1952 W/C cardboard (I.L 4500000)
£3377	$6585	(22-Oct-90 BR.M241/R) Casa fra gli alberi (55x39cm-22x15in) s. pastel (I.L 7500000)
£3602	$7024	(22-Oct-90 BR.M277/R) Alberi e ruscello (54x45cm-21x18in) s.d.1919 pastel (I.L 8000000)
£4771	$9398	(30-Oct-90 F.R167/R) Ravello, villa Rufolo (93x100cm-37x39in) s. s.d.1935verso mixed media board (I.L 10500000)
£11846	$20139	(28-May-91 SY.MI122/R) Piazza Cairoli (61x89cm-24x35in) s. pastel (I.L 26000000)

CASCIARO, Giuseppe (1861-1943) Italian
£818	$1375	(22-Apr-91 PO.BA9) Paisaje (41x62cm-16x24in) s.
£1992	$3446	(24-May-91 FB.P176 a) Vue d'un lac (24x37cm-9x15in) s.d.19 Giugni 91 (F.FR 20000)
£2035	$3948	(4-Dec-90 F.R87/R) Paesaggio vesuviano (29x41cm-11x16in) s. tempera (I.L 4400000)
£482	$864	(13-Mar-91 ARC.P3) Personnages dans la campagne (15x26cm-6x10in) s. pastel (F.FR 4800)
£727	$1426	(21-Nov-90 F.M173) Veduta di un golfo (25x47cm-10x19in) s.d.25 pastel (I.L 160000)
£775	$1317	(28-May-91 F.R57) Paesaggio invernale (18x25cm-7x10in) s.d.12 pastel board (I.L 1700000)
£909	$1782	(21-Nov-90 F.M29/R) Paesaggio con figure (23x34cm-9x13in) s.d.1913 pastel (I.L 2000000)
£1364	$2673	(21-Nov-90 F.M105) Costiera napoletana (21x40cm-8x16in) s.d.1900 pastel board (I.L 3000000)

CASE, Edmund E (1840-1919) American
£1031	$2000	(24-Aug-90 RB.HY227/R) The forest interior (46x76cm-18x30in) s.d.80

CASELLI, Cristoforo (1460-1521) Italian
£45460	$89101	(19-Nov-90 CH.R184/R) San Lodovico da Tolosa (126x59cm-50x23in) i. panel (I.L 100000000)

CASENELLI, Victor (20th C) American
£1197 $2250   (19-Sep-90 B.SF2842/R) Indian encampement (21x41cm-8x16in) s. W/C
                     gouache

CASILE, Alfred (1847-1909) French
£5952 $10238   (15-May-91 CN.P75) Marine (32x45cm-13x18in) both s. pair (F.FR 60000)

CASILEAR, John W (1811-1893) American
£925 $1600   (22-May-91 CH.NY44/R) New Hampshire Vista (11x18cm-4x7in) paper on board
£1551 $2900   (30-Aug-90 MFA.C228/R) Forest stream (30x25cm-12x10in) init.d.1876 and
                     1877
£2900 $5800   (7-Feb-91 B.P102/R) Hudson river landscape (23x30cm-9x12in) s.verso
                     board
£12717 $22000   (22-May-91 CH.NY27/R) Moment of solitude (49x76cm-19x30in) init.d.62

CASINI, Giovanni (attrib) (18th C) Italian
£8000 $13040   (3-Jul-91 S246/R) Lamentation (174x123cm-69x48in)

CASISSA, Nicola (?-1730) Italian
£27750 $53834   (3-Dec-90 SY.F1075/R) Nature morte con putti, vasi di fiori e cagnolini
                     (102x76cm-40x30in) pair (I.L 60000000)
£31825 $55058   (21-May-91 SY.MI1071/R) Nature morte con putti e fiori
                     (110x100cm-43x39in) one mono. pair (I.L 70000000)

CASISSA, Nicola (attrib) (?-1730) Italian
£10774 $21224   (14-Nov-90 D.V56/R) Bunch of flowers and vases in landscape with ruins
                     (78x95cm-31x37in) (A.S 220000)

CASISSA, Nicola (circle) (?-1730) Italian
£6000 $11700   (26-Oct-91 C39/R) A rabbit, parrot and a bird with mixed flowers in an
                     urn by a stream (92x134cm-36x53in)

CASISSA, Nicola (style) (?-1730) Italian
£2800 $4564   (4-Jul-91 C543/R) Ducks at fountains (42x32cm-17x13in) pair

CASNELLI, Victor (19th C) American
£1524 $2500   (21-Jun-91 DM.D2014/R) In Sioux country (51x33cm-20x13in) s. W/C

CASOLANI, Alessandro (attrib) (1552-1606) Italian
£2105 $4000   (8-Jan-91 SY.NY25/R) The Virgin of the immaculate conception, with devil
                     and Adam and Eve (37x23cm-15x9in) pen wash htd.white over blk.chk.

CASOLANI, Alessandro (circle) (1552-1606) Italian
£1104 $1778   (27-Jun-91 APT.P23) Sainte Claire (78x58cm-31x23in) (F.FR 11000)

CASORATI, Felice (1886-1963) Italian
£10904 $21481   (30-Oct-90 F.R176/R) Nudo femminile in un interno (48x35cm-19x14in) s.
                     thinned oil paper (I.L 24000000)
£12703 $21849   (13-May-91 CH.R141/R) Nudo (50x38cm-20x15in) s. tempera paper on canvas
                     (I.L 28000000)
£31517 $61459   (22-Oct-90 BR.M255/R) Figure di donna (50x70cm-20x28in) s. tempera board
                     on canvas (I.L 70000000)
£98644 $167696   (28-May-91 SY.MI175/R) Ragazza che legge (66x51cm-26x20in) s.
                     (I.L 216500000)
£101431 $181562   (9-Apr-91 F.R237/R) Interno con bimba allo specchio - Studio per
                     'Beethoven' (41x36cm-16x14in) s. panel (I.L 225000000)
£112562 $219496   (22-Oct-90 BR.M278/R) Natura morta con la montagna (100x65cm-39x26in) s.
                     (I.L 250000000)
£139577 $272175   (24-Oct-90 F.M255/R) Ragazza di Pavarolo (140x55cm-55x22in) s.
                     (I.L 310000000)
£8637 $16929   (20-Nov-90 BR.M26/R) Nudo (36x29cm-14x11in) s.d.c.1946 ink cardboard
                     (I.L 19000000)

CASPAR, Karl (1879-1956) German
£22727 $44091   (4-Dec-90 FN.S1563/R) St Hubertus in wood clearing, autumn
                     (81x118cm-32x46in) mono. (DM 65000)

CASPAR-FILSER, Maria (1878-1968) German
£3846 $7462   (4-Dec-90 FN.S1565/R) Summer flowers in jug (29x21cm-11x8in) mono.d.1906
                     panel (DM 11000)
£5461 $10703   (24-Nov-90 N.M84/R) Winter landscape in pale sunlight, Inn valley
                     (72x96cm-28x38in) mono.d.1937 (DM 16000)
£6826 $13379   (24-Nov-90 N.M83/R) Farmhouses in Switzerland or Wurttemberg, early
                     spring (43x57cm-17x22in) mono.c.1908 (DM 20000)

CASSAB, Judy (1920-) Australian
£749 $1415   (25-Sep-90 JRL.S80) Legend II (91x122cm-36x48in) s.d.1962 board
                     (A.D 1700)
£817 $1602   (19-Nov-90 MGS.S216/R) Paddington (57x78cm-22x31in) s. board (A.D 2100)
£1322 $2498   (25-Sep-90 JRL.S121) Untitled no. 18 (88x100cm-35x39in) s.d.1964
                     (A.D 3000)
£679 $1147   (15-Apr-91 AAA.S85) Self portrait with model (37x51cm-15x20in) s. W/C
                     (A.D 1500)

CASSAIGNE (20th C) ?
£1008 $1966   (28-Oct-90 M.V51 b/R) Fruits exotiques (106x132cm-42x52in) s.d.89
       (F.FR 10000)

CASSAN, Jean Francois Leon (1822-1874) French
£449 $871   (8-Dec-90 GAB.G2168) *Paysage au temple romain (26x33cm-10x13in) s.*
       drawing htd.white gouache (S.FR 1100)

CASSANA, Giovanni Agostino (1658-1720) Italian
£1400 $2366   (16-Apr-91 PH75/R) White hen covering chicks with wings
       (59x72cm-23x28in)
£10774 $21224   (14-Nov-90 D.V55/R) Peasant girl with domestic animals in barn interior
       (91x117cm-36x46in) (A.S 220000)
£13679 $24485   (14-Mar-91 D.V31/R) Birds in landscape (166x115cm-65x45in) (A.S 280000)

CASSANA, Giovanni Agostino (circle) (1658-1720) Italian
£8000 $15600   (26-Oct-90 C38/R) Rabbit eating cabbage with chickens, pigeons,
       ducklings in a basketa mallard and a guinea pig (68x94cm-27x37in) Icke

CASSANA, Giovanni Agostino (studio) (1658-1720) Italian
£4057 $7262   (8-Apr-91 CH.R22/R) *La volpe nel pollaio (104x130cm-41x51in)*
       (I.L 9000000)

CASSANA, Giovanni Agostino (style) (1658-1720) Italian
£3058 $6024   (13-Nov-90 CH.AM36/R) Poultry in farmyard (51x64cm-20x25in) s.
       (D.FL 10000)

CASSANDRE, Adolphe (1901-1968) French
£3000 $4890   (1-Jul-91 APT.P20/R) *Harper's bazsaar - maquette originale*
       (48x36cm-19x14in) s. gouache (F.FR 30000)
£3000 $4890   (1-Jul-91 APT.P21/R) *Harper's bazar - maquette originale*
       (32x24cm-13x9in) s.d.37 gouache (F.FR 30000)
£3800 $6194   (1-Jul-91 APT.P53/R) *With you... everywhere (43x34cm-17x13in) s.i.d.37*
       gouache (F.FR 38000)

CASSAS, Louis-Francois (1756-1827) French
£2548 $4918   (10-Dec-90 BL.P3/R) *Vue de Sidon (22x36cm-9x14in)* pen W/C (F.FR 25000)
£8222 $15951   (7-Dec-90 CN.P87/R) *Paysage avec personnages turques (55x81cm-22x32in)*
       s.d.1822 crayon pen W/C (F.FR 80000)

CASSATT, Mary (1845-1926) American
£24291 $47611   (20-Nov-90 BG.P19/R) *Femme au perroquet (61x46cm-24x18in)* (F.FR 240000)
£2191 $4250   (7-Dec-90 S.W2707) *Figure studies of women (15x10cm-6x4in)* bears estate
       st. pencil three
£3631 $6500   (14-Mar-91 CH.NY70/R) *Chapeau (15x23cm-6x9in)* bears st. pencil
£85000 $136850   (25-Jun-91 S2/R) *Simone in plumed hat (61x50cm-24x20in)* pastel over
       counterproof
£115607 $200000   (7-May-91 SY.NY12/R) *Sketch of Sara in green bonnet (63x33cm-25x13in)* s.
       pastel linen on board
£121387 $210000   (23-May-91 SY.NY68/R) *Mere embrassant son enfant (60x49cm-24x19in)*
       pastel

CASSIDY, Ira Diamond Gerald (1879-1934) American
£7396 $12500   (21-Apr-91 DU.E155/R) Refuge, La Puebla, New Mexico (43x48cm-17x19in) s.
£7692 $13000   (21-Apr-91 DU.E156/R) Travellers (33x48cm-13x19in) s. s.d.1922 verso
£395 $750   (28-Feb-91 MFA.C239) Mountain formations (23x33cm-9x13in) s. W/C
£888 $1500   (1-May-91 B.SF5198/R) Southwest canyon (23x35cm-9x14in) s. W/C

CASSIE, James (1819-1879) British
£2500 $4675   (28-Aug-90 S867/R) Grandmother's darling (82x61cm-32x24in) s.d.1865

CASSIERS, H (1858-1944) Belgian
£1000 $1920   (18-Dec-90 GM.B4007) *Moulin a vent (34x42cm-13x17in)* s. board
       (B.FR 60000)

CASSIERS, Henry (1858-1944) Belgian
£719 $1207   (23-Apr-91 SY.AM15/R) Milking time (30x50cm-12x20in) s. gouache W/C
       (D.FL 2400)
£1972 $3846   (23-Oct-90 C.A323/R) The blue bridge (46x54cm-18x21in) s. gouache
       (B.FR 120000)
£2136 $4166   (23-Oct-90 C.A322/R) Harbour scene (59x47cm-23x19in) s. gouache
       (B.FR 130000)

CASSIERS, Henry (attrib) (1858-1944) Belgian
£761 $1500   (12-Nov-90 SG.M609) Marine landscape with boats and windmill
       (38x30cm-15x12in) s. board

CASSIGNEUL, Jean Pierre (20th C) French?
£4337 $8500   (12-Feb-91 SY.NY151/R) Sur la plage (25x23cm-10x9in) s.
£8603 $16862   (19-Nov-90 ARC.P76/R) Elegante au chapeau blanc (34x27cm-13x11in) init.
       board (F.FR 85000)
£9615 $18846   (19-Nov-90 ARC.P77/R) Elegantes au bord de mer (27x22cm-11x9in) s.i.d.66
       verso board (F.FR 95000)
£11656 $19000   (12-Jun-91 SY.NY111/R) Arbres en fleur (46x38cm-18x15in) s.
£14573 $26085   (16-Mar-91 APT.P64/R) L'heure du the (100x65cm-39x26in) s. (F.FR 145000)
£16244 $32000   (13-Nov-90 CE.NY273/R) La coquette (92x64cm-36x25in) s.d.60

CASSIGNEUL, Jean Pierre (20th C) French?-cont.
£25510	$50000	(12-Feb-91 SY.NY154/R) Le courses (99x74cm-39x29in) s.
£28197	$45962	(16-Jun-91 GL.P67/R) Femme aux poissons rouge (93x73cm-37x29in) s. (F.FR 280000)
£30612	$60000	(12-Feb-91 SY.NY152/R) Pensive (91x66cm-36x26in) s. i.stretcher
£32620	$62630	(27-Nov-90 APT.P119/R) Les planches a Deauville (81x60cm-32x24in) s.i. (F.FR 320000)
£65990	$130000	(13-Nov-90 CE.NY213/R) Les arbres rouges (131x89cm-52x35in) s. s.i.verso
£5521	*$9000*	*(12-Jun-91 SY.NY120/R) Apres le bain (119x80cm-47x31in) s.d.74 i.verso chl pastel board*
£5521	*$9000*	*(12-Jun-91 SY.NY119/R) Nu au feuillage (119x80cm-47x31in) s. pastel*

CASSINARI, Bruno (1912-) Italian
£5497	$10553	(27-Nov-90 SY.MI5/R) Paesaggio (50x70cm-20x28in) s.d.43 (I.L 12000000)
£5550	$10767	(3-Dec-90 CH.R55/R) Natura morta (46x55cm-18x22in) s. (I.L 12000000)
£10024	$17041	(28-May-91 SY.MI160/R) Natura morta (55x70cm-22x28in) s. s.d.49verso (I.L 22000000)
£10806	$21072	(22-Oct-90 BR.M214/R) Figure e cavalli (110x120cm-43x47in) s.d.1968 acrylic tempera (I.L 24000000)
£18780	$36057	(27-Nov-90 SY.MI210/R) Paesaggio (90x90cm-35x35in) s. (I.L 41000000)
£1046	*$2049*	*(20-Nov-90 BR.M189/R) Nudi (42x56cm-17x22in) s.d.1960 W/C (I.L 2300000)*
£1546	*$3029*	*(20-Nov-90 BR.M59/R) Nativita (56x37cm-22x15in) s.d.1950 mixed media (I.L 3400000)*
£2312	*$4486*	*(3-Dec-90 F.M66/R) Nudo femminile (70x49cm-28x19in) s.d.1971 W/C (I.L 5000000)*

CASSIOLI, Amos (1832-1891) Italian
£2985	$5194	(25-Mar-91 CR.P72/R) Le jugement (75x100cm-30x39in) s.d.1874 (F.FR 30000)

CASSON, A J (1898-) Canadian
£3889	$6417	(10-Jul-91 MA.V201) Backwater, La Cloche Island (30x38cm-12x15in) (C.D 7350)

CASSON, Alfred Joseph (1898-) Canadian
£3070	$6018	(20-Nov-90 JOY.T8/R) October showers, Lake Kaminiskeg (30x37cm-12x15in) s. board (C.D 7000)
£3535	$6116	(6-May-91 SY.T38/R) Afternoon sky, Oxtongue Lake (30x37cm-12x15in) s. s.d.1970 verso board (C.D 7000)
£3947	$7776	(30-Oct-90 SY.T54/R) Afternoon haze, Madawaska Valley (30x38cm-12x15in) s. s.i.d.1957verso board (C.D 9000)
£3947	$7737	(20-Nov-90 JOY.T110/R) House at Masham Mills, Quebec, 1951 (24x28cm-9x11in) s. board (C.D 9000)
£4167	$7208	(6-May-91 SY.T36/R) Haliburton, Lake Kashagawigamog (23x28cm-9x11in) s. s.d.1923 verso board (C.D 8250)
£4798	$8301	(6-May-91 SY.T37/R) Summer morning, York river at Bancroft (23x29cm-9x11in) s. board (C.D 9500)
£5263	$10368	(30-Oct-90 SY.T79/R) Morning mist, September (30x36cm-12x14in) s. s.i.verso board (C.D 12000)
£5263	$10368	(30-Oct-90 SY.T65/R) Otter lake (23x29cm-9x11in) s. s.i.d.41 i.verso board (C.D 12000)
£6061	$10424	(14-May-91 JOY.T20/R) A Haliburton road near Redstone Lake (24x28cm-9x11in) s. baord (C.D 12000)
£6140	$12096	(30-Oct-90 SY.T27/R) Old Hotel, Elora (24x28cm-9x11in) s. s.i.d.1929verso board (C.D 14000)
£10965	$21601	(30-Oct-90 SY.T65 a) Island on the Madawaska (74x9cm-29x4in) s. s.i.d.1969stretcher (C.D 25000)
£16447	$32401	(30-Oct-90 SY.T48/R) Summer day (49x59cm-19x23in) s. s.i.verso canvas on panel (C.D 37500)
£22613	$39121	(22-May-91 EA.M414 a/R) Village house, St. George (61x76cm-24x30in) s. d.1975 stretcher (C.D 45000)
£56281	$97367	(22-May-91 EA.M451/R) Windswept pine on rocky coast (61x76cm-24x30in) s. (C.D 112000)

CASTAGNINO, Juan Carlos (1908-1972) Argentinian
£2601	$4500	(8-May-91 V.BA17/R) Maternidad (80x50cm-31x20in)

CASTAIGNE, Andre (19th C) French
£1400	$2688	(27-Nov-90 PH31/R) The menu (55x63cm-22x25in) s.d.99

CASTAN, Gustave-Eugene (1823-1892) Swiss
£776	$1504	(8-Dec-90 GAB.G2169/R) Eiger et Moinola (39x60cm-15x24in) (S.FR 1900)
£920	$1555	(1-May-91 GD.B142/R) Wallis mountain landscape near Arolla (38x57cm-15x22in) s. (S.FR 2300)
£992	$1776	(13-Mar-91 GK.Z10 c) Reichenbach with view of Rosenlaui (43x65cm-17x26in) s. (S.FR 2500)
£1469	$2880	(6-Nov-90 GF.L2227/R) Rhone, Oberwallis (40x59cm-16x23in) s. board (S.FR 3600)
£1639	$3082	(19-Sep-90 GK.Z811/R) Young woman reading in woods (39x58cm-15x23in) s. board (S.FR 4000)
£1796	$3520	(6-Nov-90 GF.L2221/R) View of Maderanertal and Hufigletscher, Kanton Uri (39x60cm-15x24in) s. (S.FR 4400)
£1825	$3267	(13-Mar-91 GK.Z10 b) Landscape with stream in rain (51x71cm-20x28in) s. (S.FR 4600)
£1959	$3860	(15-Nov-90 EA.Z182) A Onans, Doubs (37x52cm-15x20in) s. board (S.FR 4800)

CASTAN, Gustave-Eugene (1823-1892) Swiss-cont.

£2390	$4112	(14-May-91 GF.L2178/R) Stormy Brittany coastal landscape with surf (38x54cm-15x21in) s. s.l.verso panel (S.FR 6000)
£3878	$7639	(15-Nov-90 EA.Z208/R) Resting in wood clearing near St Maurice-sur-Loire (66x99cm-26x39in) s. (S.FR 9500)
£8980	$17420	(7-Dec-90 G.Z96/R) Geneve, Soleil hivernal au quai du Montblanc (33x46cm-13x18in) s. panel (S.FR 22000)

CASTANEDA, Alfredo (1938-) Mexican

£1173	$2300	(19-Nov-90 SY.NY260/R) A veces con mi brazo baldado (41x67cm-16x26in) s.d.72 oil pencil paper
£3316	*$6500*	*(20-Nov-90 CH.NY228/R) Entre muros (38x38cm-15x15in) s.d.72 acrylic gouache collage pencil*
£11735	*$23000*	*(20-Nov-90 CH.NY129/R) En donde se dan los abrazos (100x100cm-39x39in) s.d.72 oil photo-collage panel*

CASTEELS, Alexander (17th C) Flemish

£2600	$5200	(7-Feb-91 C104) A cavalry engagement between Christians and Turks (61x91cm-24x36in) s.

CASTEELS, Peter (after) (17/18th C) Flemish

£3370	$5628	(6-Jun-91 D.V287/R) Stone vase with flowers in park of palace (90x69cm-35x27in) (A.S 70000)

CASTEELS, Peter (attrib) (17/18th C) Flemish

£2039	$3935	(12-Dec-90 ARC.P88/R) Fleurs disposees autour d'un vase (35x30cm-14x12in) canvas laid down on panel oval (F.FR 20000)

CASTEELS, Peter (circle) (17/18th C) Flemish

£2600	$5122	(31-Oct-90 S313/R) Peacocks with rabbit, hens and chicks in ornamental landscape (78x124cm-31x49in)
£9000	$14850	(12-Jul-91 C62 a/R) Various birds in extensive wooded landscape (94x133cm-37x52in) indist.s.

CASTEELS, Peter (style) (17/18th C) Flemish

£1524	$2927	(27-Nov-90 SY.AM3442/R) Still life of flowers in vase (73x59cm-29x23in) canvas on panel (D.FL 5000)
£1800	$3042	(18-Apr-91 CSK154/R) Chinese pheasant and hawk in wooded landscape, cottage beyond (107x84cm-42x33in)
£4500	$7335	(4-Jul-91 C783) Still life of mixed flowers (96x136cm-38x54in)
£10000	$16300	(4-Jul-91 C778/R) Mixed flowers in basket on stone ledge (63x76cm-25x30in)

CASTEELS, Peter III (1684-1749) Flemish

£5641	$11000	(11-Oct-90 SY.NY65/R) Still life of roses, tulips and other flowers in metal vase on ledge (89x68cm-35x27in)
£6300	$10269	(5-Jul-91 C295/R) Sculpted terracotta urn adorned with garland of mixed flowers (73x63cm-29x25in) s.
£7500	$14625	(26-Oct-90 C98/R) Still life of roses, narcissi, peonies and blossom in a basket (48x58cm-19x23in)
£12000	$23400	(25-Oct-90 CSK104/R) Mixed flowers in sculpted urn on pedestal (111x81cm-44x32in) s.
£12243	$24119	(14-Nov-90 D.V132/R) Bunch of flowers in glass vase (48x37cm-19x15in) s. (A.S 250000)
£17000	$30430	(12-Apr-91 C77/R) Poultry in garden of mansion (68x94cm-27x37in) s.
£22353	$38000	(31-May-91 CH.NY4/R) Flowers in basket on ledge (63x112cm-25x44in) s.d.1734
£25000	$44750	(12-Apr-91 C80/R) Cockerel, hens and chicks with pheasant and turkey in ornamental garden (106x128cm-42x50in) s.d.1715
£44000	$72600	(10-Jul-91 S57/R) Still life of vase of flowers on stone ledge (123x122cm-48x48in) s.

CASTEELS, Peter III (attrib) (1684-1749) Flemish

£6000	$9780	(4-Jul-91 C682/R) Mixed flowers in sculpted urn on draped pedestal (105x87cm-41x34in) s.d.
£7500	$13425	(10-Apr-91 S48/R) Still life of ornamental fowl in landscape (95x120cm-37x47in)

CASTEELS, Peter III (style) (1684-1749) Flemish

£2000	$3260	(5-Jul-91 C296) Mixed flowers in sculpted urn on marble ledge (104x81cm-41x32in)
£4800	$9600	(7-Feb-91 C167) Fruit and flowers in a basket on a ledge with a bird's nest (53x60cm-21x24in)
£5000	$9750	(26-Oct-90 C99/R) Mixed flowers in an urn with a parrot on a pedestal (72x90cm-28x35in)

CASTEL, Moshe (1909-) Israeli

£1466	$2800	(2-Jan-91 GG.TA463/R) Safed, feast at Mount Meron (54x46cm-21x18in) s. s.l.d.1959verso
£3141	$6000	(2-Jan-91 GG.TA462/R) Psalms 18 (65x54cm-26x21in) s. s.l.d.1958verso
£3403	$6500	(2-Jan-91 GG.TA457/R) Figures (50x65cm-20x26in) s.d.1939 paper
£3403	$6500	(2-Jan-91 GG.TA456) Safed, landscape and figures (50x35cm-20x14in) s. paper
£4601	$7500	(12-Jun-91 GG.TA346/R) Still life with vase and flowers (62x46cm-24x18in) s. paper

CASTEL, Moshe (1909-) Israeli-cont.
£2513	$4800	(2-Jan-91 GG.TA458/R) Figures in alleys of Safed (55x28cm-22x11in) s.c.1947 gouache
£3681	$6000	(12-Jun-91 GG.TA347/R) Man and woman (46x39cm-18x15in) s. mixed media canvas
£4712	$9000	(2-Jan-91 GG.TA460/R) Psalms 10 (74x54cm-29x21in) s.d.1958 s.i.d.verso oil mixed media canvas
£7362	$12000	(12-Jun-91 GG.TA432/R) Shrine (131x97cm-52x38in) s. s.d.1963 verso basalt mixed media canvas

CASTELL, Anton (1810-1867) German
£1500	$2520	(18-Jul-91 CSK194/R) Lago di Como (56x80cm-22x31in) s.i.d.1841
£3436	$6529	(2-Mar-91 KRA.D294/R) Mountain lake landscape, evening (52x73cm-20x29in) s.d.1842 (DM 10000)
£3679	$6217	(19-Apr-91 FN.S1680/R) Grape harvest in arcadian river landscape, evening (90x114cm-35x45in) (DM 11000)

CASTELLANI, Enrico (1930-) Italian
£11358	$22376	(30-Oct-90 F.R244/R) Polittico (60x60cm-24x24in) s.d.1975verso vinyl estroflessa canvas (I.L 25000000)
£16046	$26315	(20-Jun-91 F.M483/R) Superficie gialla (118x100cm-46x39in) s.i.d.1989verso canvas estroflessa yellow (I.L 35000000)
£18322	$35178	(27-Nov-90 SY.MI198/R) Superficie (100x100cm-39x39in) estroflessa canvas (I.L 40000000)
£20711	$40387	(23-Oct-90 F.M53/R) Superficie bianca (120x90cm-47x35in) s.i.d.1974 canvas estroflessa (I.L 46000000)

CASTELLANO, Carmelo (20th C) ?
£643	$1151	(14-Apr-91 R.P154) Legende d'hiver (130x97cm-51x38in) s. acrylic (F.FR 6500)
£857	$1671	(28-Oct-90 R.P87/R) Cache-cache automnal (116x89cm-46x35in) s.d.90 acrylic (F.FR 8500)
£1109	$2162	(28-Oct-90 R.P246/R) Les grands d'Espagne (78x114cm-31x45in) s. (F.FR 11000)

CASTELLANOS, Carlos Alberto (?) South American
| £1053 | $2000 | (11-Sep-90 PO.BA4) Baile de Dona Sirena (82x90cm-32x35in) |

CASTELLI, Alessandro (1809-1902) Italian
| £6463 | $10405 | (28-Jun-91 BM.B646/R) North Italian lake landscape with shepherds and cattle at dusk (77x108cm-30x43in) s.d.1844 (DM 19000) |

CASTELLI, Arturo (1870-?) Italian
| £1071 | $1864 | (26-Mar-91 JRL.S110) Elegant recital (44x59cm-17x23in) s. (A.D 2400) |

CASTELLI, Filippo (?) Italian
| £320 | $592 | (7-Mar-91 CSK47) By the fire (100x72cm-39x28in) s. pastel |

CASTELLI, Giovanni Paolo see SPADINO, Giovanni Paolo

CASTELLI, Luciano (1951-) Swiss
£1410	$2750	(10-Oct-90 SY.NY362/R) Female nude (79x58cm-31x23in) s.d.82overlap
£4592	$9000	(6-Nov-90 CE.NY282/R) Eunuch I (204x165cm-80x65in) s.i.d.1987 verso acrylic
£6122	$12000	(6-Nov-90 CE.NY284/R) Luciano mit Schwan I (160x200cm-63x79in) s.d.82 verso l. overlap acrylic linen
£6827	$13382	(24-Nov-90 AB.L65/R) Two women (197x138cm-78x54in) s.d.86 acrylic paper (S.FR 17000)
£10194	$19572	(29-Nov-90 ZZ.F53/R) Two Japanese bitch (210x200cm-83x79in) s.d.1980 l. verso acrylic (F.FR 100000)
£11078	$18056	(16-Jun-91 CC.P61/R) Dschungel Love II (200x180cm-79x71in) s.i.d.1983 acrylic (F.FR 110000)
£2022	$3943	(15-Oct-90 CSC.P53) Nu (65x50cm-26x20in) s.d.85 gouache (F.FR 20000)
£2776	$5468	(17-Nov-90 S.Z21) Portrait of B (70x100cm-28x39in) s.i.d.1978verso mixed media chk cotton (S.FR 6800)
£4898	$9649	(17-Nov-90 S.Z22) Devo (100x70cm-39x28in) d.1979 s.verso chk gouache three parts (S.FR 12000)
£5865	$11436	(15-Oct-90 CSC.P54/R) Femme (140x102cm-55x40in) s.d.86 oil gouache (F.FR 58000)

CASTELLO, Jacopo da (1637-1712) Flemish/Italian
| £12000 | $23160 | (12-Dec-90 S191/R) Chickens, ducks and hedgehog around jewel (98x114cm-39x45in) oval |

CASTELLO, Jacopo da (circle) (1637-1712) Flemish/Italian
| £4800 | $8112 | (18-Apr-91 C5/R) A cabbage, onion, grapes and basket on a stone ledge with a hanging flask (76x93cm-30x37in) |

CASTELLO, Valerio (1625-1659) Italian
£1915	$3390	(19-Mar-91 F.M282/R) Cristo e la samaritana (17x15cm-7x6in) ink paper laid down on album leaf (I.L 4200000)
£3000	$5760	(18-Feb-91 S220/R) The Judgement of Solomon (24x21cm-9x8in) ink wash
£36000	$58680	(2-Jul-91 C53/R) The Agony in the Garden (13x16cm-5x6in) i. chk pen ink wash htd.white

CASTELLO, Valerio (circle) (1625-1659) Italian
£7000 $13650   (26-Oct-90 C15/R) Christ and the woman taken in adultery
                                          (74x122cm-29x48in)
£9744 $19000   (11-Oct-90 SY.NY25/R) Lot and his Daughters. The Finding of Moses
                                          (72x109cm-28x43in) pair

CASTELLON, Federico (1914-) American
£4379 $7400   (20-Apr-91 WOL.C418/R) Foundling (56x61cm-22x24in) s.

CASTELUCHO, Claudio (1870-1927) Spanish
£4624 $8000   (23-May-91 CH.NY160/R) En ecoutant la musique (100x72cm-39x28in)
                                        s.indis.i.verso

CASTEX, Simone (20th C) French
£759 $1488   (25-Nov-90 ZZ.F54) La gard de l'Est (59x64cm-23x25in) s. panel
                                         (F.FR 7500)

CASTEX-DEGRANGE, Adolphe Louis (1840-?) French
£5086 $9867   (5-Dec-90 KH.K16/R) Still life of flowers in copper bowl
                                         (98x130cm-39x51in) s.d.1874 (D.KR 56000)
£6842 $13000   (27-Feb-91 SY.NY52 a) Vase of lilacs (130x88cm-51x35in) s.
£9249 $16000   (23-May-91 CH.NY3/R) Floral still life (99x130cm-39x51in) s.d.1874

CASTIGLIONE, Giovanni Benedetto (1616-1670) Italian
£8824 $15000   (31-May-91 CH.NY35/R) The Three Marys at the Tomb (54x38cm-21x15in)
                                         paper on canvas
£20048 $34081   (30-May-91 F.M71/R) Ritratto di gentiluomo in armatura
                                         (154x105cm-61x41in) (I.L 44000000)
£8500   *$16405*   *(11-Dec-90 C37/R) Shepherds and cattle at a ford (19x30cm-7x12in) washes*
£180000   *$293400*   *(2-Jul-91 C52/R) The head of Oriental in profile (19x15cm-7x6in)*
                                         monotype printed in black ink wash

CASTIGLIONE, Giovanni Benedetto (attrib) (1616-1670) Italian
£1000   *$1630*   *(1-Jul-91 S86/R) Two goats (19x28cm-7x11in) oil paper over pen*

CASTIGLIONE, Giovanni Benedetto (style) (1616-1670) Italian
£11009 $21688   (13-Nov-90 AB.S871/R) Rebecca at the well (115x160cm-45x63in)
                                         (S.KR 120000)

CASTIGLIONE, Giuseppe (1829-1908) Italian
£3626 $6127   (16-Apr-91 CH.R88/R) Pescatorelli (50x40cm-20x16in) s. (I.L 8000000)
£5789 $11000   (27-Feb-91 SY.NY366/R) On river at dusk (65x101cm-26x40in) s.

CASTILIAN SCHOOL, 16th C Spanish
£12500 $21125   (17-Apr-91 S133/R) Female saint before king (122x78cm-48x31in) panel
£17000 $28730   (17-Apr-91 S132/R) Adoration of the Magi (126x95cm-50x37in) panel
£26000 $43940   (17-Apr-91 S134/R) St James the Greater (142x100cm-56x39in) panel

CASTILLO Y SAAVEDRA, Antonio del (c.1603-1667) Spanish
£800   *$1304*   *(1-Jul-91 S151) Crucifixion of St. Philip apostle (24x35cm-9x14in) bears*
                                         i. pen
£1176   *$2000*   *(30-May-91 CE.NY4) Studies of heads of old women (28x21cm-11x8in) s. pen*
                                         ink

CASTILLO, Antonio del (attrib) (1565-1626) Spanish
£2653 $5200   (6-Nov-90 GF.L2297/R) The martyrdom of St Paul (149x149cm-59x59in)
                                         (S.FR 6500)

CASTILLO, Jorge (1933-) Spanish
£1348 $2642   (20-Nov-90 DUR.M4) Campesina (15x12cm-6x5in) board (S.P 250000)
£2987 $5884   (15-Nov-90 ANS.M10/R) Desnudo verde (60x86cm-24x34in) s.d.1962 panel
                                         (S.P 550000)
£3000 $5850   (18-Oct-90 S164/R) Hombre pistola (63x81cm-25x32in) i.verso
£5020 $8082   (25-Jun-91 BG.P14/R) Madre (150x100cm-59x39in) s. i.d.74 verso
                                         (F.FR 50000)
£7048 $13744   (17-Oct-90 FER.M250/R) Payaso (87x63cm-34x25in) s.d.62 tablex
                                         (S.P 1300000)
£9556 $18730   (24-Nov-90 VG.B377/R) Figure in green (184x104cm-72x41in) s.d.1963
                                         (DM 28000)
£14617 $28503   (26-Oct-90 CC.P23/R) Petite fille sur un tabouret (149x100cm-59x39in)
                                         s.d.1961 verso (F.FR 145000)
£16452 $27639   (25-Apr-91 EP.M30/R) Naturaleza muerta (100x122cm-39x48in) s. board
                                         (S.P 3000000)
£412   *$738*   *(13-Mar-91 FER.M78/R) Mujer recostada (45x32cm-18x13in) s. col.pencil dr*
                                         (S.P 75000)
£546   *$1070*   *(24-Nov-90 VG.B485/R) Phantastic composition (20x28cm-8x11in) s.d.1970*
                                         pencil (DM 1600)
£685   *$1116*   *(14-Jun-91 L.K803) Comico en el campo (40x32cm-16x13in) W/C indian ink*
                                         (DM 2000)
£685   *$1116*   *(14-Jun-91 L.K800) Figures (39x57cm-15x22in) s.d.72 indian ink pen W/C*
                                         pencil (DM 2000)
£800   *$1560*   *(18-Oct-90 C322) Untitled (69x103cm-27x41in) s. W/C ink*
£850   *$1658*   *(18-Oct-90 C362) Untitled (69x103cm-27x41in) s. W/C ink*
£937   *$1846*   *(1-Oct-90 CC.P8) Personnage (26x17cm-10x7in) s.d.1966 W/C Indian ink*
                                         (F.FR 9500)
£1100   *$2145*   *(18-Oct-90 C360) Untitled (100x70cm-39x28in) s.d.66 W/C ink*

CASTILLO, Jorge (1933-) Spanish-cont.
£1370 $2233   *(14-Jun-91 L.K801) La dama (56x78cm-22x31in) s.d.73 indian ink W/C (DM 4000)*
£1979 $3661   *(5-Mar-91 ANS.M384/R) Celestina (39x28cm-15x11in) s.d.10-9-73 Indian ink W/C (S.P 360000)*
£4365 $7552   *(25-May-91 AB.L5/R) Still life with fish (69x100cm-27x39in) s.d.62 W/C indian ink (S.FR 11000)*
£8446 $14358   *(1-Jun-91 VG.B394/R) Cesto de fruta (100x80cm-39x31in) s.d.1973 mixed media canvas (DM 25000)*

CASTILLO, Jose (18th C) Spanish
£1037 $1795   *(8-May-91 FER.M61/R) Alegoria neoclasica (53x21cm-21x8in) s.d.1780 W/C (S.P 190000)*

CASTOR, Christian (1953-) French
£655 $1278   *(28-Oct-90 R.P19) Bord de Mer (80x120cm-31x47in) s. acrylic (F.FR 6500)*
£958 $1867   *(28-Oct-90 R.P60) Le matin aerien (140x160cm-55x63in) s. acrylic (F.FR 9500)*

CASTRES, E (?) Swiss
£937 $1846   *(30-Oct-90 I.N189) Jeune fille a la harpe (46x38cm-18x15in) mono.d.66 (F.FR 9200)*

CASTRES, Edouard (1838-1902) Swiss
£1224 $2376   *(8-Dec-90 GAB.G2170/R) La campagne militaire (38x55cm-15x22in) s. (S.FR 3000)*
£1310 $2265   *(22-May-91 GS.B2058) Egyptian landscape with pyramids and sphinx of Giseh (24x37cm-9x15in) mono. canvas on board (S.FR 3300)*
£2449 $4800   *(6-Nov-90 GF.L2225/R) Soldiers in mountain village (37x55cm-15x22in) s. (S.FR 6000)*
£6375 $10964   *(14-May-91 GF.L2168/R) Military convoy resting (38x55cm-15x22in) s. (S.FR 16000)*

CASTRO Y VELASCO, Antonio Palomino de (1653-1726) Spanish
£8205 $16000   *(10-Oct-90 CH.NY221/R) St Francis Borgia kneeling before body of Queen Isabella of Spain (107x125cm-42x49in) s.i.*

CASTRO, Laureys A (17th C) French
£25000 $42250   *(19-Apr-91 C137/R) A mediterranean harbour at sunset with a galley and fishing boats (96x175cm-38x69in)*

CASTRO, Laureys A (circle) (17th C) French
£9000 $14670   *(4-Jul-91 C537/R) Mediterranean inlet with galley at anchor and party disembarking shore (62x125cm-24x49in)*

CASTRO, Laureys A (style) (17th C) French
£3500 $5705   *(4-Jul-91 C662/R) Capriccio of Levantine harbour at dusk (63x81cm-25x32in)*

CATALA, Luis Alvarez (19th C) Spanish
£14444 $28022   *(4-Dec-90 R.T280/R) Tea time (39x51cm-15x20in) s.i. (C.D 32500)*

CATALA, Luis Alvarez see ALVAREZ CATALA, Luis

CATALAN SCHOOL, 14th C Spanish
£23743 $42500   *(11-Apr-91 SY.NY159/R) Combat of knights, with one sainted knight leading troop guarding cave (112x70cm-44x28in) tempera oil gold ground panel*

CATALAN SCHOOL, 15th C Spanish
£10000 $16300   *(5-Jul-91 C244/R) Madonna and Child in Glory (123x66cm-48x26in) i. gold ground panels part altarpiece*

CATANO, F (19th C) Italian
£350 $648   *(7-Mar-91 CSK44) Street market in Cairo (65x42cm-26x17in) s. pencil W/C htd.white*

CATARSINI, A (20th C) Italian
£685 $1226   *(12-Mar-91 FN.S1937/R) Untitled (50x70cm-20x28in) s. (DM 2000)*

CATENA, Vincenzo (c.1470-1531) Italian
£18184 $35640   *(20-Nov-90 F.R189/R) Madonna con Bambino (75x60cm-30x24in) panel (I.L 40000000)*

CATERINA, Dario (1955-) Belgian
£1500 $2925   *(15-Jan-91 GM.B545/R) Homme assis et mannequin (168x124cm-66x49in) s. mixed media (B.FR 90000)*

CATHELIN, Bernard (20th C) French
£9744 $19000   *(10-Oct-90 SY.NY332/R) Bonifacio (97x127cm-38x50in) s.*
£11628 $22674   *(17-Oct-90 ARC.P68) Paseo (33x55cm-13x22in) s.d.64 (F.FR 115000)*

CATLIN, George (1794-1872) American
£694 $1200   *(10-May-91 S.W2464/R) Portrait of Charles L White (18x15cm-7x6in) i.verso pencil htd.W/C gouache*

CATS, Jacob (1741-1799) Dutch
£1040 $2048   (12-Nov-90 CH.AM198/R) Windmill by frozen canal with skaters
                                (12x18cm-5x7in) black chk pen wash (D.FL 3400)
£3058 $6024   (12-Nov-90 CH.AM197/R) December - winter landscape with skaters and
                                sledges on frozen river by village (21x28cm-8x11in) s.d.1795 verso
                                black chk pen wash (D.FL 10000)
£9174 $18073   (12-Nov-90 CH.AM196/R) Winter landscape with men chopping ice, with
                                huntsmen and skaters near castle (26x36cm-10x14in) s.d.1791verso black
                                chk pen wash (D.FL 30000)

CATTANEO, Achille (1872-1931) Italian
£1818 $3564   (21-Nov-90 F.M152/R) Naviglio innevato (51x61cm-20x24in) s. panel
                                (I.L 4000000)
£2046 $4010   (21-Nov-90 F.M166) Natura morta con fiori e libro (77x91cm-30x36in)
                                s.d.922 (I.L 4500000)

CATTERMOLE, Charles (1832-1900) British
£450 $756   (22-Apr-91 DNP251) Making an escape (51x73cm-20x29in) s. W/C htd white
£600 $1140   (12-Sep-90 CSK161) Rallying call (30x61cm-12x24in) s.d.75 pencil W/C
£759 $1321   (26-Mar-91 JRL.S95) Don Quixote (27x40cm-11x16in) s. W/C (A.D 1700)

CATTERMOLE, George (1800-1868) British
£600 $990   (9-Jul-91 C125/R) Lady with maid in interior (30x41cm-12x16in) pencil
                                W/C htd.white

CATTI, Aurelio (19th C) Italian
£1192 $2134   (12-Mar-91 F.M6) Autunno a Parigi (50x35cm-20x14in) s. W/C
                                (I.L 2600000)
£1192 $2134   (12-Mar-91 F.M8) Giorno di pioggia (50x35cm-20x14in) s. W/C
                                (I.L 2600000)

CATTORI, Edgardo (1942-) Swiss
£816 $1600   (6-Nov-90 GF.L2639/R) Portrait of young man (74x47cm-29x19in) s.
                                (S.FR 2000)

CAUBERE, Genevieve Jean (1903-1988) French
£1112 $2169   (17-Oct-90 DL.P58/R) St Jean de Luz - Thoniers dans le port
                                (92x60cm-36x24in) s.d.56 studio st. verso (F.FR 11000)

CAUCHOIS, E H (1850-1911) French
£3340 $6547   (25-Nov-90 B.PA47) Bouquet de fleurs (65x54cm-26x21in) s. (F.FR 33000)

CAUCHOIS, Eugene-Henri (1850-1911) French
£500 $835   (5-Jun-91 HC.P334) Le train a vapeur (32x53cm-13x21in) s. (F.FR 5000)
£1220 $2390   (6-Nov-90 SY.AM51) Still life with flowers (54x42cm-21x17in) s.
                                (D.FL 4000)
£1427 $2740   (2-Dec-90 M.V75) La locomotive a Osny (33x55cm-13x22in) s. (F.FR 14000)
£1596 $2601   (13-Jun-91 RAS.V524/R) Flowers in vase on stone ledge (92x73cm-36x29in)
                                s. (D.KR 18000)
£1660 $3254   (22-Jan-91 YC.P39) Fleurs dans un vase (61x50cm-24x20in) s. (F.FR 16500)
£1721 $3372   (25-Nov-90 ZZ.F29/R) Boquet champetre (61x50cm-24x20in) s. (F.FR 17000)
£1846 $3599   (10-Oct-90 WE.MU304/R) Flowering branches in vase (55x33cm-22x13in) s.
                                panel (DM 5500)
£2224 $4338   (21-Oct-90 DA.R4/R) Ruelle animee sous le soleil avec verdure
                                (33x46cm-13x18in) s. (F.FR 22000)
£2390 $4684   (6-Nov-90 BA.S28 a/R) Still life of flowers (64x53cm-25x21in) s.
                                (S.KR 26000)
£2528 $4929   (17-Oct-90 DL.P25/R) Fleurs dans un vase (46x33cm-18x13in) s.
                                (F.FR 25000)
£2890 $5000   (22-May-91 SY.NY194/R) Still life with dahlias and roses
                                (46x38cm-18x15in) s.
£3009 $5868   (9-Oct-90 GGL.L14/R) La jardiniere de fleurs d'ete (46x55cm-18x22in) s.
                                (F.FR 30000)
£3259 $6420   (29-Oct-90 LC.P96/R) Nature morte au bouquet de fleurs (65x80cm-26x31in)
                                s. (F.FR 32000)
£3423 $5750   (17-Jul-91 SY.NY220/R) Still life with daisies, poppies and cornflowers
                                (66x54cm-26x21in) s.
£3571 $6857   (27-Nov-90 W.T1117/R) Still life of roses and wild flowers on ledge with
                                fan (63x53cm-25x21in) s. (C.D 8000)
£3912 $7628   (12-Oct-90 ZZ.F23) Corbeille de fleurs (54x65cm-21x26in) s. (F.FR 39000)
£4000 $6880   (17-May-91 C36/R) Chrysanthemums in walled garden (113x72cm-44x28in)
                                s.d.1906
£4911 $8250   (17-Jul-91 SY.NY221/R) Still life with pansies and geraniums
                                (65x55cm-26x22in) s.
£7800 $15366   (5-Oct-90 C63/R) Roses (50x61cm-20x24in) s.
£13333 $26000   (24-Oct-90 CH.NY6/R) Summer bouquet (70x107cm-28x42in) s.
£15029 $26000   (23-May-91 CH.NY6/R) Still life with flowers and fruit on table
                                (100x81cm-39x32in) s.
£16185 $28000   (23-May-91 CH.NY4/R) Still life with mixed flowers, fruit and objects
                                d'arts on table (101x130cm-40x51in) s.

CAUCHOIS, Eugene-Henri (attrib) (1850-1911) French
£529 $868   (18-Jun-91 FN.S1783/R) Bunch of field flowers in whicker basket
                                (20x25cm-8x10in) s. (DM 1550)

CAULA, Sigismondo (1637-1713) Italian
*£2368 $4500   (9-Jan-91 CH.NY12/R) Finding of Moses (25x34cm-10x13in) red black chk
pen wash htd white*

CAULFIELD, Patrick (1936-) British
£4500 $7515   (6-Jun-91 C262/R) Green drink (76x112cm-30x44in) s.d.1984 acrylic
£1700 $2839   (6-Jun-91 C263/R) Pipe (85x65cm-33x26in) d.1972 poster emulsion paint
                   board
£1750 $3238   (8-Mar-91 C213/R) Composition (84x63cm-33x25in) gouache

CAULLERY, Louis de (16/17th C) French/Flemish
£2600 $4394   (16-Apr-91 PH159) Allegory of love, Venus and Cupid with elegant couples
                   (42x27cm-17x11in) on metal
£6061 $11879   (11-Feb-91 CSC.P15/R) Allegorie de la vue. Allegorie de l'ouie
                   (29x16cm-11x6in) copper pair (F.FR 60000)
£6500 $12545   (11-Dec-90 PH28/R) Elegant couple on hill above encampment. Elegant
                   figures on hill above town panel pair
£11821 $20450   (21-May-91 SY.MI1017/R) Cerere - Allegoria dell'Estate (23x18cm-9x7in)
                   copper (I.L 26000000)
£17794 $33452   (18-Sep-90 BU.K109/R) Saint Mark's Square, Venice (49x74cm-19x29in)
                   panel (D.KR 200000)
£26869 $48095   (14-Mar-91 D.V45/R) Roman capriccio wit view of St Peter's and Vatican
                   (48x723cm-19x285in) (A.S 550000)
£31579 $60000   (10-Jan-91 SY.NY97/R) Horsemen on bluff with view of Escorial beyond
                   (81x110cm-32x43in)
£39755 $78318   (13-Nov-90 CH.AM114/R) Carnival revellers in Piazza San Marco, Venice
                   (50x69cm-20x27in) panel (D.FL 130000)

CAULLERY, Louis de (attrib) (16/17th C) French/Flemish
£3336 $6439   (12-Dec-90 BU.S121/R) Town scene with jesters (49x66cm-19x26in) panel
                   (S.KR 36000)
£3800 $6422   (18-Apr-91 C154/R) The worship of Bacchus (23x19cm-9x7in) copper
£7035 $11538   (21-Jun-91 SY.MO1/R) Scene de la Commedia Dell'arte (24x36cm-9x14in)
                   panel (F.FR 70000)

CAULLERY, Louis de (circle) (16/17th C) French/Flemish
£7059 $12000   (31-May-91 CH.NY118/R) King Nimrod before the Tower of Babel
                   (70x112cm-28x44in) bears mono.d.1631

CAULLERY, Louis de (style) (16/17th C) French/Flemish
£3800 $6422   (17-Apr-91 S83/R) Figures beside ruins (51x45cm-20x18in) panel

CAULLET, Albert (?) ?
£985 $1704   (25-May-91 KV.L37) Cows on a riverbank (70x100cm-28x39in) s.
                   (B.FR 60000)

CAUSSIN, A (19th C) French
£1542 $2991   (6-Dec-90 CB.P84 b/R) Le Cocyte (40x65cm-16x26in) s. (F.FR 15000)

CAUTY, H H (1846-1909) British
£6000 $10140   (3-May-91 BW400/R) Study of family at harvest time (97x183cm-38x72in)
                   s.d.1876

CAUVY, Leon (1874-1933) French
£761 $1460   (17-Dec-90 ARC.P116/R) Algeroises devant le portail du cimetiere d'El
                   Kettar (38x46cm-15x18in) s. board (F.FR 7500)
£1826 $3505   (17-Dec-90 ARC.P110/R) Cafe tunisien (48x54cm-19x21in) s.d.1928 board
                   (F.FR 18000)
£5882 $11294   (17-Dec-90 ARC.P92/R) La Mosquee de la Pecherie, Alger
                   (101x141cm-40x56in) s. (F.FR 58000)
*£3144 $6037   (17-Dec-90 ARC.P32/R) Marche algerois (32x41cm-13x16in) s.d.24 W/C
                   gouache Indian ink (F.FR 31000)*

CAUWER, Emile Pierre Joseph de (1828-1873) Belgian
£1600 $2624   (18-Jun-91 PH32/R) Figures in church interior (20x16cm-8x6in) s.d.1855
                   panel sold with another painting pair

CAVAEL, Rolf (1898-1979) German
£1284 $2221   (21-May-91 WK.M672/R) Composition 190 (13x21cm-5x8in) s.i.d.1950 board
                   (DM 3800)
£1897 $3641   (26-Nov-90 WK.M564/R) Composition (22x33cm-9x13in) mono.s.i.d.1954 board
                   (DM 5500)
£2466 $4267   (21-May-91 WK.M673/R) Composition (25x44cm-10x17in) mono. board
                   (DM 7300)
£3072 $6020   (20-Nov-90 L.K178) 55/D3 (35x50cm-14x20in) mono. s.i.d.74verso
                   (DM 9000)
£3425 $5582   (14-Jun-91 L.K804/R) Composition (50x60cm-20x24in) mono. (DM 10000)
£3584 $7024   (20-Nov-90 L.K177/R) 70 D20 (35x45cm-14x18in) mono.d.1957 s.i.verso
                   (DM 10500)
£5651 $9211   (14-Jun-91 L.K805/R) N 4 (70x80cm-28x31in) mono. s.i.d.1974verso
                   (DM 16500)
*£514 $837   (14-Jun-91 L.K808) Composition (31x24cm-12x9in) mono. i.d.verso graphite
                   (DM 1500)*
*£541 $935   (21-May-91 WK.M676/R) Composition (26x22cm-10x9in) mono. mixed media
                   board (DM 1600)*

CAVAEL, Rolf (1898-1979) German-cont.
£709	$1227	(21-May-91 WK.M675/R) Composition (44x31cm-17x12in) mono.s.i.d.1959 mixed media over monotype (DM 2100)
£759	$1457	(28-Nov-90 KF.M596) Composition (39x28cm-15x11in) mono. col.chk W/C (DM 2200)
£897	$1721	(26-Nov-90 WK.M567/R) Composition (25x36cm-10x14in) mono. felt tip dr. over W/C (DM 2600)
£1199	$1954	(14-Jun-91 L.K807) Untitled (19x23cm-7x9in) mono. col.chk (DM 3500)
£2027	$3446	(28-May-91 KF.M511) Composition with brown and green shapes (22x30cm-9x12in) s.d.1950 mixed media board (DM 6000)
£2027	$3507	(21-May-91 WK.M678/R) Composition (13x22cm-5x9in) mono.s.indis.d. mixed media (DM 6000)

CAVAILLES, Jules (1901-1977) French
£2381	$4095	(19-May-91 ZZ.F128/R) Nature morte a l'ananas (38x55cm-15x22in) s. (F.FR 24000)
£3061	$6000	(12-Feb-91 SY.NY168/R) Still life with flowers and fruit (79x64cm-31x25in)
£3169	$6180	(10-Oct-90 RAS.K275/R) Still life with mandolin (38x46cm-15x18in) s.d.65 (D.KR 36000)
£3444	$6750	(12-Feb-91 SY.NY180/R) Venise (81x53cm-32x21in) s. s.l.verso
£3568	$6886	(14-Dec-90 ARC.P14/R) Le bocal aux poissons rouges (81x54cm-32x21in) s.d.49 (F.FR 35000)
£3680	$7250	(15-Nov-90 D.NY87/R) Les cerises (81x60cm-32x24in) s. s.l.verso
£4221	$6923	(20-Jun-91 APT.P40/R) Nature morte au homard (65x81cm-26x32in) s. (F.FR 42000)
£5076	$10000	(15-Nov-90 D.NY89/R) Parc Tremaux, Tipasa (81x53cm-32x21in) s. s.l.verso
£5584	$11000	(15-Nov-90 D.NY91/R) Le vase d'or (81x51cm-32x20in) s. s.l.verso
£5641	$11000	(10-Oct-90 SY.NY164/R) La nappe rouge (74x91cm-29x36in) s. l.verso
£5828	$9500	(12-Jun-91 SY.NY143/R) Le vase noir (81x65cm-32x26in) s.
£5912	$11352	(27-Nov-90 APT.P107/R) Le vase en Venise (80x58cm-31x23in) s. l. verso (F.FR 58000)
£6091	$12000	(15-Nov-90 D.NY90/R) Fenetre, Cannes (80x65cm-31x26in) s. s.l.verso
£6135	$10000	(12-Jun-91 SY.NY142/R) Bouquet a l'oiseau noir (91x63cm-36x25in) s.
£7949	$15500	(10-Oct-90 SY.NY185 a/R) Bouquet devant le parc (81x66cm-32x26in) s.
£8155	$15657	(27-Nov-90 APT.P111/R) Bouquet devant la fenetre, Paris (92x73cm-36x29in) s. (F.FR 80000)
£8163	$16000	(12-Feb-91 SY.NY167/R) La fenetre sur le port de Cannes (79x54cm-31x26in) s. s.l.verso
£8543	$16402	(24-Feb-91 P.V130/R) Fenetre a Cannes (81x65cm-32x26in) s. (F.FR 85000)
£8563	$16440	(27-Nov-90 APT.P106/R) La fenetre a Cannes (81x60cm-32x24in) s.i.d.1963 (F.FR 84000)
£9231	$18000	(10-Oct-90 SY.NY162/R) Floral still life by open window (91x64cm-36x25in) s.
£9500	$18525	(19-Oct-90 C193/R) Automne a Cannes (81x65cm-32x26in) s. s.l.verso
£10000	$19700	(14-Nov-90 I.N89/R) Nu dans l'atelier (65x54cm-26x21in) s. (F.FR 98000)
£11000	$21450	(19-Oct-90 C172/R) Matinee a Cannes (93x74cm-37x29in) s. s.l.verso

CAVALCANTI, Emiliano di (1897-1976) Brazilian
£8163	$16000	(20-Nov-90 CH.NY102/R) Lupanar (21x26cm-8x10in) s.d.29-30 verso oil pen canvas on board
£23256	$40000	(15-May-91 CH.NY53/R) Carnaval (55x46cm-22x18in) s. d.46 verso
£24419	$42000	(15-May-91 CH.NY17/R) Morro (46x38cm-18x15in) s.d.1926 verso
£27326	$47000	(15-May-91 CH.NY57/R) Maternidad (75x60cm-30x24in) s.
£35714	$70000	(20-Nov-90 CH.NY68/R) Carnaval (59x83cm-23x33in) s.d.46
£13776	$27000	(19-Nov-90 SY.NY10/R) Untitled (55x41cm-22x16in) s. gouache ink

CAVALERI, Ludovico (1867-1942) Italian
£4127	$7388	(12-Mar-91 F.M23) Paesaggio al tramonto con pecore all'abbeverata (93x113cm-37x44in) s. panel (I.L 9000000)

CAVALIERI, Luigi (19th C) Italian
£850	$1632	(27-Nov-90 PH251) Tuning his violin (34x43cm-13x17in) s.i. W/C over pencil

CAVALLERI, Ferdinando (1794-1865) Italian
£2600	$4394	(1-May-91 PHL186/R) Portrait of gentleman, wearing fur-trimmed cloak on terrace (128x97cm-50x38in) s.i.d.1827

CAVALLERI, Vittorio (1860-?) Italian
£1823	$3098	(28-May-91 F.R115) Il campo di fieno (30x39cm-12x15in) s.d.94 panel (I.L 4000000)
£3006	$5832	(5-Dec-90 F.M104/R) Nave scuola per mozzi Garavantini Redenzione, Portofino (34x45cm-13x18in) s. panel (I.L 6500000)

CAVALLI, Emanuele (1904-) Italian
£3544	$6981	(30-Oct-90 F.R122/R) Veduta di Avignone (34x42cm-13x17in) s. panel (I.L 7800000)
£8711	$14285	(20-Jun-91 F.M475/R) Bagnanti (62x76cm-24x30in) s.d.1932 (I.L 19000000)

CAVALLINO, Bernardo (1622-1654) Italian
£2029	$3631	(8-Apr-91 CH.R86/R) Testa di vecchio (43x34cm-17x13in) fragment (I.L 4500000)

CAVALLINO, Bernardo (circle) (1622-1654) Italian
£1542	$2991	(7-Dec-90 SY.MO131/R) Scene religieuse (68x51cm-27x20in) (F.FR 15000)

CAVALLINO, Bernardo (studio) (1622-1654) Italian
£6000 $10140   (16-Apr-91 PH81/R) Allegory of music with young man seated writing, holding trumpet (89x73cm-35x29in)

CAVALLINO, Bernardo (style) (1622-1654) Italian
£900 $1800   (7-Feb-91 C25/R) Venus and Adonis (38cm-15ins circular) round
£7000 $11830   (19-Apr-91 C146/R) Moses striking the rock (99x133cm-39x52in)

CAVALLON, Giorgio (1906-) American
£36735 $72000   (7-Nov-90 SY.NY136/R) Untitled (193x183cm-76x72in) s.d.58

CAVE, Peter le (18th C) British
£440 $739   (15-Jul-91 PH61) Herdsman's family with donkeys and sheep (13x20cm-5x8in) s. W/C ink

CAVE, Peter le (attrib) (18th C) British
£1400 $2366   (16-Apr-91 PH123/R) Shepherds and livestock approaching ruins on hillside (24x34cm-9x13in) panel

CAVEDONE, Giacomo (1577-1660) Italian
£19000 $30970   (2-Jul-91 C18/R) Christ blessing the little children (37x24cm-15x9in) chk pen ink wash htd.white oil varnished

CAVEDONE, Giacomo (attrib) (1577-1660) Italian
£6024 $9699   (27-Jun-91 APT.P20/R) La Sainte famille avec Sainte Anne (73x57cm-29x22in) (F.FR 60000)

CAWEN, Alvar (1886-1935) Finnish
£7450 $14676   (17-Nov-90 BU.H21/R) Landscape from Kokar (60x50cm-24x20in) s. (F.M 52000)
£11412 $22368   (24-Nov-90 HOR.H58/R) Fishing (50x44cm-20x17in) s. (F.M 80000)

CAWRY, F (?) ?
£1850 $3534   (4-Jan-91 BW419/R) Coastal scenes with fishing boats and other vessels (28x38cm-11x15in) s. pair

CAWTHORNE, Neil (?) ?
£800 $1336   (22-Jul-91 SWS1030/R) Neck and neck (45x60cm-18x24in) s.
£898 $1500   (7-Jun-91 SY.NY209/R) Warming up, Newmarket (50x76cm-20x30in) s.d.'84

CAYLEY, Neville (19/20th C) Australian
£440 $739   (16-Jul-91 JRL.S79) Kookaburra and dove (54x42cm-21x17in) s.d.1899 W/C oval (A.D 950)
£491 $854   (26-Mar-91 JRL.S90) Two kookaburras (60x48cm-24x19in) s.d.1897 W/C (A.D 1100)
£700 $1365   (24-Oct-90 S95) Common bronzewings nesting (47x34cm-19x13in) s. W/C over traces pencil

CAYRON, Jules (1868-1940) French
£1020 $2010   (14-Nov-90 FB.P185/R) L'elegante au collier de perles (90x71cm-35x28in) s.d.1922 (F.FR 10000)

CAZABON, Michel J (1814-?) French
£4200 $8274   (12-Nov-90 PH22) A Trinidadian woman in local costume (24x16cm-9x6in) s. W/C bodycol.over pencil
£5000 $9750   (24-Oct-90 S126/R) Two West Indian natives on a path (27x21cm-11x8in) s. W/C htd.bodycol.
£5400 $10638   (12-Nov-90 PH20/R) The Governor's house, Tinidad (30x42cm-12x17in) s. W/C htd.white scratching out
£5600 $11032   (12-Nov-90 PH21/R) An extensive view of Tinidad (21x30cm-8x12in) s. W/C
£8500 $16745   (15-Nov-90 CSK7/R) La Brea from Pitch Point (19x36cm-7x14in) s. i.verso W/C

CAZES, Romain (1810-C.1881) French
£26923 $52500   (26-Oct-90 SY.NY171/R) Studies of muses, spandrel studies for public bath house (43x81cm-17x32in) red chk htd.white semicircular set of four

CAZIN, Jean Charles (1841-1901) French
£1622 $2643   (10-Jun-91 W.T1371/R) Normandy farm in moonlight (32x40cm-13x16in) s. panel (C.D 3000)
£1807 $3343   (4-Mar-91 ARC.P99) Paysge d'Italie (55x73cm-22x29in) s. (F.FR 18000)
£1879 $3250   (21-May-91 GRO.B65 a/R) Haystacks at twilight (53x66cm-21x26in) s.
£1900 $3211   (3-May-91 PHE142/R) Landscape near Fontainebleau (60x72cm-24x28in) s.
£2564 $5000   (25-Oct-90 GRO.B97/R) Thatched cottages (30x41cm-12x16in) s. panel
£4624 $8000   (23-May-91 CH.NY243/R) Bathers in river landscape (60x73cm-24x29in) s.
£15029 $26000   (23-May-91 CH.NY244/R) L'arc en ciel (131x145cm-52x57in) s.d.1888

CAZZANIGA, Giancarlo (1930-) Italian
£682 $1290   (27-Sep-90 F.M132) Interno al Conero (64x80cm-25x31in) s. s.d.1977 verso (I.L 1500000)
£1145 $2199   (27-Nov-90 SY.MI56/R) Jazz Man (81x100cm-32x39in) s. s.d.1963-64verso (I.L 2500000)
£1374 $2638   (27-Nov-90 SY.MI26/R) Per un paesaggio (100x80cm-39x31in) s. s.d.1982verso (I.L 3000000)

CECCHI, Sergio (1921-1986) Italian
£3386 $6604   (24-Oct-90 GD.B587/R) Lake Geneva landscape with view of Quai du Mont
                        Blanc (60x73cm-24x29in) s.d.50 (S.FR 8500)

CECCO BRAVO see MONTELATICI, Francesco

CECCOBELLI, Bruno (20th C) ?
£1220 $2439   (5-Feb-91 CSC.P6/R) Pieta (196x88cm-77x35in) s.i.d.1983 verso
                        (F.FR 12000)
£1351 $2634   (22-Oct-90 BR.M12/R) Vergine della chiave (38x59cm-15x23in) paper
                        (I.L 3000000)
£1601 $3011   (19-Sep-90 KH.K113/R) Trovatore (45x65cm-18x26in) s.d.1986verso oval
                        (D.KR 18000)
£820   *$1394*   *(28-May-91 SY.MI79) Senza titolo (39x25cm-15x10in) mixed media collage
                        board (I.L 1800000)*
£991   *$1932*   *(23-Oct-90 F.M17) Sera di terra (59x76cm-23x30in) s.i.d.1987verso oil
                        mixed media (I.L 2200000)*
£1600 $2608   (3-Jul-91 CSC.P171/R) In virtu sin golare (31x37cm-12x15in) mono. verso
                        mixed media panel (F.FR 16000)
£1823   *$3098*   *(28-May-91 SY.MI103/R) L'uova pesa (40x29cm-16x11in) mono.d.1989verso
                        oil collage wood (I.L 4000000)*
£3640 $7098   (15-Oct-90 CSC.P55/R) Dente usato (322x234cm-127x92in) s.i.d.1984 verso
                        chl.oil (F.FR 36000)
£4852 $9365   (13-Dec-90 F.M382/R) Monafasi (60x97cm-24x38in) s.i.d.1989verso relief
                        tempera wax panel (I.L 10500000)

CECCONI, Alberto (1897-) Italian
£638 $1084   (28-May-91 F.R62) Canale a Burano (41x50cm-16x20in) s. (I.L 1400000)
£683 $1162   (28-May-91 F.R68) Campagna toscana (40x50cm-16x20in) s. (I.L 1500000)
£997 $1685   (16-Apr-91 CH.R62) Paesaggio con buoi (50x35cm-20x14in) s. panel
                        (I.L 2200000)
£1100 $2167   (4-Oct-90 CSK178/R) Children in a spring meadow (50x70cm-20x28in) s.

CECCONI, Eugenio (1842-1903) Italian
£10000 $20000   (18-Oct-90 F.M81/R) Spiaggia della Meremma (19x32cm-7x13in) s. panel
                        (I.L 23000000)
£17576 $34624   (30-Oct-90 CH.AM306/R) Leading the dogs (45x70cm-18x28in) s.
                        (D.FL 58000)

CEDERGREN, Per Vilhelm (1823-1896) Swedish
£939 $1596   (28-May-91 AB.S4608/R) Stockholms Strom in winter (21x30cm-8x12in) s.
                        panel (S.KR 10000)
£947 $1591   (24-Apr-91 BA.S38/R) Hazy view of ship at anchor (63x86cm-25x34in)
                        s.d.64 (S.KR 10000)

CEDERSTROM, Eva (1909-) Finnish?
£1712 $3355   (24-Nov-90 HOR.H62/R) Cubist still life (23x25cm-9x10in) s.d.1971
                        (F.M 12000)
£511   *$915*   *(14-Apr-91 BU.H101/R) Park landscape (28x40cm-11x16in) s.d.1976 pastel
                        (F.M 3600)*

CEDERSTROM, Gustaf (1845-1933) Swedish
£1103 $2162   (6-Nov-90 BA.S31/R) Carolean soldier (21x30cm-8x12in) s.d.02 panel
                        (S.KR 12000)
£6387 $12582   (30-Oct-90 BU.S13/R) Erik Dahlberg showing the way to Karl X
                        (147x89cm-58x35in) s.indist.d.1911-12 (S.KR 70000)

CEI, Cipriano (1867-?) Italian
£2280 $3808   (6-Jun-91 F.M75/R) L'asino (51x39cm-20x15in) s. (I.L 5000000)

CELADA DA VIRGILIO, Ugo (1895-?) Italian
£1500 $2940   (21-Nov-90 F.M178) Natura morta con vasi, libro, lente e strumento
                        musicale (65x90cm-26x35in) s. panel (I.L 3300000)
£1637 $3208   (21-Nov-90 F.M177) Natura morta con libro e vasi (65x85cm-26x33in) s.
                        panel (I.L 3600000)
£2728 $5346   (21-Nov-90 F.M159) La studiosa (65x50cm-26x20in) s. panel (I.L 6000000)
£2955 $5792   (21-Nov-90 F.M162) Natura morta con bicchieri, vasi ed uva
                        (50x65cm-20x26in) s. panel (I.L 6500000)

CELESTI, Andrea (attrib) (1637-1706) Italian
£4560 $7616   (4-Jun-91 CH.R1/R) Bethsabea al bagno (104x134cm-41x53in)
                        (I.L 10000000)
£12871 $22782   (5-Apr-91 DAR.P69/R) L'outrage d'Amnon a sa soeur Tamar. Absalon fait
                        assassiner Amnon (18x24cm-7x9in) copper pair (F.FR 130000)

CELIBERTI, Giorgio (20th C?) Italian
£636 $1253   (30-Oct-90 F.R130) Il gatto (90x63cm-35x25in) s.d.25.V.959verso
                        (I.L 1400000)

CELICE, Pierre (1932-) French?
£3666 $7222   (31-Oct-90 ZZ.F123/R) Composition (76x102cm-30x40in) s.d.janvier 90
                        verso acrylic (F.FR 36000)

CELIE, Pieter (?) Belgian?
£3990 $7142   (16-Mar-91 KV.L435/R) Farmstead in the sun (80x92cm-31x36in) s.d.1921
                        (B.FR 240000)

CELIS, Perez see PEREZ CELIS

CELLINI, Benvenuto (1500-1571) Italian
£28777 $55827   (7-Dec-90 CH.MO202 a/R) Apollon (284x200cm-112x79in) pen wash
                    (F.FR 280000)

CELLINI, G (?) Italian
£1359 $2365   (25-Mar-91 SY.F746) Ventaglio (18x58cm-7x23in) s. gouache (I.L 3000000)

CELOMME, Raffaello (19/20th C) Italian
£1868 $3250   (27-Mar-91 B.SF4199/R) Family playing in the surf (56x86cm-22x34in) s.
£2632 $5000   (27-Feb-91 SY.NY374/R) Young boys on beach (55x87cm-22x34in) s.

CELOMMI, Raffaello (19/20th C) Italian
£698 $1200   (17-May-91 DM.D2231/R) Beached boats (46x66cm-18x26in) s.

CELONI, A (19th C) ?
£1618 $2800   (21-May-91 CE.NY206/R) Afternoon of tea (56x80cm-22x31in) s.i.

CELOS, Julien (1884-) Belgian
£1012 $1963   (4-Dec-90 C.A55/R) Begijnhof (70x90cm-28x35in) s. (B.FR 60000)
£1964 $3339   (28-May-91 C.A34/R) Town scene (100x90cm-39x35in) s. (B.FR 120000)
£655 $1100   (23-Apr-91 C.A329) Beguinage (54x47cm-21x19in) s. mixed media
                (B.FR 40000)

CELS, Cornelius (1778-1859) Belgian
£5274 $10126   (17-Dec-90 ARC.P56/R) Portrait de jeune enfant (83x62cm-33x24in)
                    s.d.1817 (F.FR 52000)

CEMERSKI, Gligor (1940-) Yugoslavian
£2275 $4072   (14-Apr-91 R.P161/R) La nuit du cameleon (66x99cm-26x39in) s. oil
                acrylic canvas (F.FR 23000)
£2374 $4249   (14-Apr-91 R.P46/R) Eldorado (100x70cm-39x28in) s. oil acrylic
                (F.FR 24000)

CENTENTA, Guandallini (19th C) Italian?
£2000 $3960   (28-Jan-91 HS251/R) Dance of Cupid - Venus and Cupid in clouds, Rape of
                Prosperin, temple (61cm-24ins circular) s.d.1838

CENTRAL EUROPEAN SCHOOL (?) European
£1319 $2585   (21-Nov-90 GM.B1060) Mane Thecel Phares (50x70cm-20x28in) wood
                (B.FR 80000)
£1635 $2682   (17-Jun-91 DUR.M7) Batalla naval (130x215cm-51x85in) (S.P 300000)

CENTRAL EUROPEAN SCHOOL, 17th C European
£12333 $23926   (7-Dec-90 SY.MO161/R) Monument allegorique a la glorie des apotres
                    (89x60cm-35x24in) gouache vellum (F.FR 120000)

CENTRAL ITALIAN SCHOOL, 16th C Italian
£1845 $3100   (17-Jul-91 SY.NY10/R) Mary Magdalene washing Christ's feet
                (26x40cm-10x16in) ink gouache drawing verso

CENTRAL ITALIAN SCHOOL, 18th C Italian
£2479 $4438   (8-Apr-91 CH.R76) Paesaggio con capre e viandanti (65x79cm-26x31in)
                c.1700 (I.L 5500000)
£3156 $5649   (8-Apr-91 CH.R100/R) Paesaggio con ruderi classici e cascatella
                (74x102cm-29x40in) (I.L 7000000)

CENTRAL ITALIAN SCHOOL, 18th/19th C Italian
£4283 $7666   (8-Apr-91 CH.R117/R) Paesaggio fluviale con edifici classici. Paesaggio
                rupestre con laghetto (25x34cm-10x13in) panel pair (I.L 9500000)

CENTRAL ITALIAN SCHOOL, 19th C Italian
£992 $1775   (8-Apr-91 CH.R48) Paesaggio con rudere di torre e cascinale
                (34x44cm-13x17in) (I.L 2200000)

CERAMANO, Charles Ferdinand (1829-1909) Belgian
£888 $1500   (20-Apr-91 WOL.C120/R) Summer landscape (71x102cm-28x40in) s.
£1272 $2200   (21-May-91 CE.NY32/R) To open pasture (39x56cm-15x22in) s.
£3187 $5514   (24-May-91 FB.P125/R) Scene pastorale (64x93cm-25x37in) s. (F.FR 32000)

CERCONE, Ettore (1850-1896) Italian
£1903 $3217   (16-Apr-91 CH.R158) Ritratto di fanciulla (33x24cm-13x9in) s.
                (I.L 4200000)

CERDA Y BISBAL, Lorenzo (19/20th C) Spanish
£3000 $5160   (17-May-91 C245/R) At lakeside (59x138cm-23x54in) s.d.89

CERESA, Carlo (attrib) (1609-1679) Italian
£1363 $2685   (29-Oct-90 SY.F647 a) Ritratto di dama (64x47cm-25x19in) (I.L 3000000)
£3352 $6000   (11-Apr-91 SY.NY87/R) Girl holding flowers (69x56cm-27x22in)

CERESA, Carlo (style) (1609-1679) Italian
£7200 $14400   (7-Feb-91 C19/R) Portrait of a young girl in a red dress with white
                    collar holding a book (101x78cm-40x31in)

CERETTI, Mino (1930-) Italian
£2063 $3383   (19-Jun-91 F.M218/R) Racconto anatomico (110x135cm-43x53in) s.
    s.i.d.1959verso (I.L 4500000)

CEREZO, Mateo (attrib) (1635-1685) Spanish
£2778 $4972   (13-Mar-91 GK.Z11/R) Christ with angel holding cup (116x103cm-46x41in)
    (S.FR 7000)

CEREZO, Mateo (circle) (1635-1685) Spanish
£2800 $4732   (16-Apr-91 PH191/R) Magdalen (103x81cm-41x32in)

CERIA, Edmond (1884-1955) French
£600 $978   (5-Jul-91 APT.P102) Jardin a Evian (60x72cm-24x28in) s.d.09 board
    (F.FR 6000)
£658 $1289   (20-Nov-90 MF.P60) Bord de mer en Bretagne (27x41cm-11x16in) s.
    (F.FR 6500)
£922 $1807   (7-Nov-90 APT.P501) Village breton (27x34cm-11x13in) s. (F.FR 9000)
£1020 $2010   (16-Nov-90 LGB.P176) Le parc fleuri (59x72cm-23x28in) s.d.1909 board
    (F.FR 10000)
£1233 $2393   (8-Dec-90 LT.P86 b) Cote Bretonne (27x41cm-11x16in) s. (F.FR 12000)
£1366 $2678   (19-Nov-90 ARC.P70/R) Nu allonge (38x46cm-15x18in) s. (F.FR 13500)
£1417 $2777   (19-Nov-90 ARC.P66/R) Maisons au bord de l'eau (33x41cm-13x16in) s.
    (F.FR 14000)
£1584 $2804   (7-Apr-91 I.N65/R) Village Breton (27x35cm-11x14in) s. (F.FR 16000)
£1619 $3174   (19-Nov-90 ARC.P68/R) Port Breton (33x46cm-13x18in) s. (F.FR 16000)
£1670 $3273   (19-Nov-90 ARC.P69/R) Maree basse, le Gulvinec (33x41cm-13x16in) s.
    i.d.45 verso (F.FR 16500)
£2042 $3532   (26-May-91 ZZ.F44/R) Port Breton (25x41cm-10x16in) s. (F.FR 20500)
£7143 $14000   (21-Nov-90 NA.BA1/R) Le petit port Bretagne (65x92cm-26x36in) s.

CERMAK, Jaroslav (?) ?
£1658 $2968   (17-Mar-91 L.C87/R) Portrait d'une jeune fille orientale (58x?cm-23x?in)
    s. oval (F.FR 16500)

CERMANO, Charles Ferdinand (1829-1909) Belgian
£7470 $12923   (24-May-91 FB.P61/R) Scene pastorale (200x300cm-79x118in) s.
    (F.FR 75000)

CERMIGNANI, Vincent (20th C) Italian
£1712 $3355   (24-Nov-90 HOR.H4/R) The training ship (83x97cm-33x38in) s. (F.M 12000)

CERQUOZZI, Michelangelo (1602-1660) Italian
£6364 $12474   (19-Nov-90 CH.R134/R) Le ancelle di Diana scoprono Callisto gravida
    (75x66cm-30x26in) (I.L 14000000)
£19548 $38313   (19-Nov-90 CH.R195/R) Natura morta d'uva, fichi, melograni e meloni
    (131x92cm-52x36in) (I.L 43000000)
£36000 $70920   (31-Oct-90 S41/R) Market scene (180x145cm-71x57in)

CERQUOZZI, Michelangelo (attrib) (1602-1660) Italian
£6122 $11878   (8-Dec-90 GAB.G2046/R) Scene champetre (52x67cm-20x26in) (S.FR 15000)
£9000 $17730   (31-Oct-90 S40/R) The Rest on the Flight into Egypt (43x59cm-17x23in)

CERQUOZZI, Michelangelo (studio) (1602-1660) Italian
£3637 $7128   (19-Nov-90 CH.R139/R) Lavandaia e aiutante (37x47cm-15x19in)
    (I.L 8000000)

CERQUOZZI, Michelangelo (style) (1602-1660) Italian
£2226 $3628   (12-Jun-91 N.M299/R) Skirmish in mountainous landscape
    (71x110cm-28x43in) (DM 6500)
£4587 $9037   (14-Nov-90 SY.AM116/R) Cattle and peasants resting outside farm
    (94x132cm-37x52in) (D.FL 15000)

CERQUOZZI, Michelangelo and CODAZZI, Viviano (17th C) Italian
£61538 $120000   (11-Oct-90 SY.NY196/R) Architectural capricci with classical ruins and
    figures (95x132cm-37x52in) pair

CERRINI, Giandomenico (attrib) (1609-1681) Italian
£1198 $2000   (23-Jan-91 D.NY87) Virgin in prayer (61x48cm-24x19in) bears mono. d.1664

CERUTI, Giacomo (18th C) Italian
£55000 $95150   (24-May-91 C67/R) A girl with a cow and a sheep in a rocky landscape
    (119x91cm-47x36in)

CERUTI, Giacomo (circle) (18th C) Italian
£1910 $3132   (21-Jun-91 SY.MO269/R) La marchande d'oeufs (31x18cm-12x7in) canvas laid
    down on panel (F.FR 19000)

CERVI, Giulio (19th C) Italian
£6000 $11820   (5-Oct-90 C159/R) Il Sonetto (62x46cm-24x18in) s.i.d.1873

CESAR (1921-) French
£1000 $1950   *(18-Oct-90 S192/R) Untitled (75x55cm-30x22in) s.i.d.1978 ball point felt*
    tip collage on litho
£1601 $3011   *(19-Sep-90 KH.K119/R) Composition (18x16cm-7x6in) s.d.1978 crayon pencil*
    (D.KR 18000)

CESAR (1921-) French-cont.

£1682	$3246	(16-Dec-90 GL.P130) Arrachage (65x50cm-26x20in) s.d.1961 Indian ink wash (F.FR 16500)
£2000	$3540	(21-Mar-91 S96/R) Portrait de compression (45x33cm-18x13in) s.d.1977 wire wool pencil board
£2312	$4486	(3-Dec-90 F.M332/R) Senza titolo (45x34cm-18x13in) s.d.1977 collage pencil paniforte (I.L 5000000)
£4274	$7224	(21-Apr-91 P.V82/R) Portrait de compression (60x50cm-24x20in) s. pieces of wood crayon panel (F.FR 43000)
£4546	$8910	(20-Nov-90 BR.M106/R) Senza titolo (50x70cm-20x28in) s.d.1974 mixed media (I.L 10000000)

CESAR, Baldaccini (1921-) French

£657	$1282	(15-Oct-90 CSC.P57) Bonne annee (25x27cm-10x11in) s.i.d.1990 felt pen (F.FR 6500)
£809	$1577	(15-Oct-90 CSC.P59/R) Boite d'allumettes et visage (21x30cm-8x12in) s.i.d.1981 Indian ink (F.FR 8000)
£910	$1775	(15-Oct-90 CSC.P58/R) La poulette (26x28cm-10x11in) s.i.d.28-10-89 print Indian ink (F.FR 9000)
£1019	$1967	(10-Dec-90 LD.P23/R) Poule (27x30cm-11x12in) s.d.1985 blk.crayon (F.FR 10000)
£1104	$1778	(25-Jun-91 BG.P15) La poule (26x21cm-10x8in) s.d.1985 crayon felt pen (F.FR 11000)
£1466	$2859	(15-Oct-90 CSC.P56) Masque (23x20cm-9x8in) s.d.1983 (F.FR 14500)
£5964	$10080	(21-Apr-91 E.LA82/R) Theiere rose (45x50cm-18x20in) s. compression (F.FR 60000)

CESARI, Giuseppe (1568-1640) Italian

£17436	$34000	(11-Oct-90 SY.NY136/R) Madonna and Child with St Paul and St Peter (173x118cm-68x46in)
£75009	$147017	(20-Nov-90 F.R214/R) Diana e Callisto (88x119cm-35x47in) panel (I.L 165000000)

CESARI, Giuseppe (after) (1568-1640) Italian

£2000	$3400	(30-May-91 CE.NY86) Christ healing the Sick (75x97cm-30x38in)

CESARI, Giuseppe (attrib) (1568-1640) Italian

£4020	$6593	(22-Jun-91 CH.MO129/R) Des nymphes traversant un fleuve (57x45cm-22x18in) panel (F.FR 40000)
£5226	$8571	(21-Jun-91 SY.MO190/R) Immaculee Conception (108x89cm-43x35in) (F.FR 52000)
£930	$1600	(15-May-91 D.NY6/R) The Assumption of the Virgin (13x13cm-5x5in) pen sepia wash

CESARI, Giuseppe (circle) (1568-1640) Italian

£4103	$8000	(11-Oct-90 SY.NY30/R) Mocking of Christ (23x17cm-9x7in) copper

CESETTI, Giuseppe (1902-) Italian

£2107	$4045	(27-Nov-90 SY.MI7/R) Cavalli in Maremma (40x50cm-16x20in) s. (I.L 4600000)
£2431	$4741	(22-Oct-90 BR.M339/R) Cavalli (40x30cm-16x12in) s. (I.L 5400000)
£2476	$4829	(24-Oct-90 F.M110/R) Cavalli al pascolo (40x50cm-16x20in) s. (I.L 5500000)
£2930	$5245	(9-Apr-91 F.R119) Mucche al pascolo (59x79cm-23x31in) s. (I.L 6500000)
£3602	$7024	(22-Oct-90 BR.M199/R) Natura morta in un paesaggio (70x70cm-28x28in) s. (I.L 8000000)
£3962	$7726	(22-Oct-90 BR.M274/R) Fiori (60x80cm-24x31in) s. (I.L 8800000)
£4101	$6971	(28-May-91 SY.MI30/R) Cavalli in maremma (50x69cm-20x27in) s. (I.L 9000000)
£4126	$6767	(20-Jun-91 F.M385/R) Cavalli (40x50cm-16x20in) s. (I.L 9000000)
£12477	$24080	(13-Dec-90 F.M475/R) Bagnanti (32x76cm-13x30in) s.d.1931 (I.L 27000000)

CESTARO, Jacopo (18th C) Italian

£8183	$16038	(20-Nov-90 F.R74) Santa Caterina (90x63cm-35x25in) (I.L 18000000)

CEULEN, Cornelis Janssens van see JONSON, Cornelis

CEYTAIRE, Jean-Pierre (1946-) French

£1951	$3902	(7-Feb-91 R.P183/R) Homme a la tete de chien (41x27cm-16x11in) s.d.87 (F.FR 19200)
£2033	$4065	(10-Feb-91 CC.P17) La vie moderne (55x46cm-22x18in) s. (F.FR 20000)
£2410	$4723	(24-Nov-90 AB.L99/R) 2 belles, apero cacahuetes (41x27cm-16x11in) s.i.d.80stretcher (S.FR 6000)
£2518	$4104	(16-Jun-91 CC.P76) Histoire de famille (39x47cm-15x19in) s. i. verso oil sable (F.FR 25000)
£2749	$5416	(29-Oct-90 LC.P134/R) Doux baiser, piece dans le port-monnale (41x27cm-16x11in) s. oil gold sheet (F.FR 27000)
£2795	$5589	(7-Feb-91 R.P150/R) Sans culotte avec lame de raspoir et Arista couronne (42x56cm-17x22in) s. (F.FR 27500)
£2819	$5046	(14-Apr-91 R.P162/R) L'homme compte sur ses doigts les femmes qu'il a eues (41x27cm-16x11in) s. (F.FR 28500)
£3452	$6800	(6-Oct-90 GL.P100/R) Madame attend le feu (73x60cm-29x24in) s.d.1986 (F.FR 35000)
£3874	$7476	(16-Dec-90 GL.P70) Madame S.P.A. Phile, laisse verte dans les dents (73x60cm-29x24in) s.i. stretcher (F.FR 38000)

CEYTAIRE, Jean-Pierre (1946-) French-cont.

£4077	$7870	(16-Dec-90 GL.P143) Madame S.P.A. Phile, Boite a Susucre (73x60cm-29x24in) s. i. stretcher (F.FR 40000)
£5444	$10615	(28-Oct-90 R.P185/R) Dans les bras l'un de l'autre (73x60cm-29x24in) s. (F.FR 54000)
£6116	$11804	(16-Dec-90 GL.P195) Rendez-vous amoureux (135x97cm-53x38in) s. (F.FR 60000)
£6122	$11878	(8-Dec-90 GAB.G2441/R) Les amoureux (65x55cm-26x22in) s. gold sheet on canvas (S.FR 15000)
£1003	$1956	(11-Oct-90 QWA.P75/R) La priere (32x21cm-13x8in) s.d.1989 goauche (F.FR 10000)
£1512	$2949	(28-Oct-90 R.P160) Homme et femme bras en l'air (32x25cm-13x10in) s. gouache card (F.FR 15000)
£5607	$10821	(16-Dec-90 GL.P86/R) Methode rose (100x120cm-39x47in) s. i. verso mixed media (F.FR 55000)

CEZANNE, Paul (1839-1906) French

£61665	$119630	(9-Dec-90 E.LA151/R) Bord de riviere (92x77cm-36x30in) (F.FR 600000)
£100000	$161000	(25-Jun-91 S18/R) Portrait d'homme (48x36cm-19x14in) indis.init.
£147808	$283792	(26-Nov-90 GL.P48/R) Les deux enfants (55x46cm-22x18in) (F.FR 1450000)
£1600000	$2576000	(24-Jun-91 C11/R) La maison du jas de bouffan (60x73cm-24x29in)
£3299492	$6500000	(12-Nov-90 SY.NY7/R) Le Jas de Bouffan (74x55cm-29x22in)
£2359	$4600	(10-Oct-90 SY.NY3/R) Sketch of praying figure (10x8cm-4x3in) pencil paper on board
£20231	$35000	(9-May-91 CH.NY106/R) Madame Cezanne, pot au lait en metal (23x15cm-9x6in) i. pencil
£24277	$42000	(9-May-91 CH.NY109/R) La Montagne Sainte-Victoire. Etude d'arbres (32x48cm-13x19in) pencil recto W/C over pencil verso double-sided
£27972	$54266	(7-Dec-90 GB.B5759/R) Study of black male nude and male head (46x30cm-18x12in) c.1865 chl htd white (DM 80000)
£28902	$50000	(7-May-91 SY.NY3/R) Etude de fruits. Etude de peches (27x21cm-11x8in) W/C over pencil double-sided
£28902	$50000	(7-May-91 SY.NY6/R) Arbres et feuillages. Incomplete study of horse (21x27cm-8x11in) W/C over pencil pencil double-sided
£31423	$60647	(12-Dec-90 F.M40/R) Ritratto maschile (29x21cm-11x8in) pencil (I.L 68000000)
£37572	$65000	(7-May-91 SY.NY5/R) Arbres pres d'un sentier. Study of two bathers (27x21cm-11x8in) W/C over pencil pencil double-sided
£43353	$75000	(7-May-91 SY.NY4/R) Route tournante. Study of landscape (27x21cm-11x8in) W/C over pencil double-sided
£61162	$117431	(26-Nov-90 GL.P12/R) Paysage provencal (40x32cm-16x13in) W/C (F.FR 600000)
£150000	$291000	(4-Dec-90 C124/R) Vue prise de l'Atelier des Lauves (30x44cm-12x17in) W/C pencil
£180000	$289800	(26-Jun-91 S213) Arbres se refletant dans l'eau (31x45cm-12x18in) W/C pencil

CHABANIAN, Arsene (20th C) French

£498	$862	(26-May-91 ZZ.F2/R) Coucher de soleil sur Venise (38x45cm-15x18in) s. pastel (F.FR 5000)

CHABANNES LA PALICE, Jean Pierre Charles (1862-?) French

£860	$1444	(25-Apr-91 D.V120/R) Clouds in sky (31x39cm-12x15in) s.d.81 pastel (A.S 18000)

CHABAS, Maurice (1862-1947) French

£1205	$2229	(4-Mar-91 ARC.P101) Coucher de soleil (46x38cm-18x15in) s. (F.FR 12000)
£1507	$2969	(30-Oct-90 I.N66/R) Apparition (22x27cm-9x11in) s. (F.FR 14800)
£1515	$2970	(12-Feb-91 HC.P47) Promeneur a la riviere (39x55cm-15x22in) st.mono. (F.FR 15000)
£2243	$4328	(14-Dec-90 ARC.P15/R) Barque sur la riviere (71x99cm-28x39in) s. (F.FR 22000)
£2530	$4960	(25-Nov-90 ZZ.F30/R) Pecheurs sur la Seine (73x60cm-29x24in) s. (F.FR 25000)
£3947	$7737	(25-Nov-90 LC.P147/R) Les trois graces aupres de la riviere (55x33cm-22x13in) s. (F.FR 39000)
£4975	$8607	(12-May-91 T.B83/R) Paysage a la riviere (54x73cm-21x29in) s. (F.FR 50000)
£25304	$49595	(25-Nov-90 GL.P17/R) Les deux amies (81x64cm-32x25in) s. (F.FR 250000)

CHABAS, Paul (1869-1937) French

£1531	$3000	(21-Nov-90 NA.BA17/R) Portrait de femme en robe blanche (95x80cm-37x31in) s. oval
£2457	$4792	(12-Oct-90 APT.P106/R) Baigneuse (81x62cm-32x24in) s. (F.FR 24500)
£7000	$11480	(21-Jun-91 C33/R) Jeunes filles au coquillage (152x103cm-60x41in) s.

CHABAUD, Auguste (1882-1955) French

£683	$1121	(19-Jun-91 JM.P126) Interieur a la table (22x16cm-9x6in) board (F.FR 6800)
£1485	$2629	(7-Apr-91 I.N67) Paysage aux Cypres (33x24cm-13x9in) s. board laid down on canvas (F.FR 15000)
£1703	$3286	(12-Dec-90 CH.AM63) Croisement au bout de l'allee (26x38cm-10x15in) s. board (D.FL 5500)
£5653	$10966	(7-Dec-90 GL.P189/R) Chemin vers la Juverte (76x106cm-30x42in) s. board laid down on panel (F.FR 55000)

CHABIN, Elisabeth (20th C) French?
£1376 $2642   (2-Dec-90 ZZ.F80) Le baiser (10x81cm-4x32in) s.i.d.1989 (F.FR 13500)

CHABLYKINE, Uri (1932-) Russian
£503 $965   (18-Feb-91 ARC.P221/R) Le panier de champignons (78x100cm-31x39in) s.
                  (F.FR 5000)

CHABOT, Hendrik (1894-?) Dutch
£1220 $2341   (27-Nov-90 SY.AM3806/R) Village in winter (45x60cm-18x24in) s.d.49verso
                  (D.FL 4000)

CHADWICK, Emma (1855-1932) Swedish
£752 $1482   (13-Nov-90 AB.S446/R) Lake landscape with mother and daughter
                  (23x38cm-9x15in) s. panel (S.KR 8200)
£10000 $19200   (28-Nov-90 S130/R) Afternoon tea in garden (51x62cm-20x24in) s. mono.

CHADWICK, Ernest Albert (1876-1955) British
£460 $814   (21-Mar-91 CSK66) The estuary, Barmouth (18x28cm-7x11in) s.d.1923 i.
                  verso pencil W/C
£580 $945   (13-Jun-91 CSK145) Doorway at Whitbourn, Hertfordshire (18x25cm-7x10in)
                  s. s.i.verso pencil W/C htd white
£760 $1269   (5-Jun-91 PHK86) Garth House, Edgbaston (17x25cm-7x10in) s. W/C
£900 $1701   (26-Sep-90 S287/R) The Hill, Hampstead (35x25cm-14x10in) s. W/C
£920 $1739   (26-Sep-90 S288/R) Garden path (27x36cm-11x14in) s. W/C
£1200 $2004   (5-Jun-91 PHK85/R) Figure standing by Garth House. Girl staning by Garth
                  House, Edgbaston (26x18cm-10x7in) s. W/C pair
£1400 $2282   (14-Jun-91 C134/R) East Garston, E.Berkshire (27x38cm-11x15in) s.
                  i.verso pencil W/C scratching out
£1800 $2934   (14-Jun-91 C138/R) Old farmhouse near Rowington (38x54cm-15x21in) s.i.
                  pencil W/C htd.white

CHADWICK, Henry D (19th C) British
£2600 $4238   (14-Jun-91 C338/R) Macbeth and the Witches (98x153cm-39x60in) s.

CHADWICK, Lynn (1914-?) British
£550 $886   (28-Jun-91 CSK253/R) Untitled (60x47cm-24x19in) s.d.66 pen brush ink
£785 $1539   (20-Nov-90 L.K179/R) Sitting couple (59x41cm-23x16in) i.verso sepia wash
                  W/C (DM 2300)
£800 $1560   (10-Oct-90 S222/R) Figure study (60x47cm-24x19in) s.d.62 ink
£1017 $1698   (8-Jun-91 HN.H65) Composition (62x48cm-24x19in) s.d.1962 ink W/C
                  (DM 3000)
£1020 $2000   (12-Feb-91 SY.NY458/R) Sitting Electra (41x53cm-16x21in) s.d.68 pencil
                  ball point indian ink wash W/C

CHADWICK, W (19/20th C) American
£500 $1000   (10-Feb-91 LIT.L47) Venetian scene (36x46cm-14x18in) s. i. verso board
£510 $1000   (27-Jan-91 LIT.L9a) Venetian scene (36x46cm-14x18in) s. i.verso board

CHADWICK, William (20th C) American
£1269 $2500   (18-Nov-90 JRB.C134/R) Houses by river (20x28cm-8x11in) s. canvas on
                  board
£1424 $2450   (15-May-91 SY.NY131/R) Rocks and surf (36x46cm-14x18in) s. board

CHAGALL (1887-1985) French/Russian
£3271 $5658   (21-May-91 DUR.M47/R) Untitled (46x55cm-18x22in) (S.P 600000)

CHAGALL, Marc (1887-1985) French/Russian
£80000 $128800   (25-Jun-91 C177/R) Mere et enfant au bouquet (35x24cm-14x9in) s.
£157343 $303671   (12-Dec-90 WE.MU205/R) The lovers (26x20cm-10x8in) s. panel
                  (DM 450000)
£193727 $371956   (27-Nov-90 BU.S56/R) Le peintre en veste rouge (42x32cm-17x13in)
                  s.d.1981verso tempera panel (S.KR 2100000)
£314721 $620000   (14-Nov-90 SY.NY425/R) Village a neige (58x60cm-23x24in) s.d.950
£380711 $750000   (14-Nov-90 SY.NY424/R) Les amoureux (46x38cm-18x15in) s.
£462428 $800000   (8-May-91 CH.NY27/R) Les roses (52x67cm-20x26in) s.
£520231 $900000   (8-May-91 CH.NY15/R) Les deux bouquets (100x73cm-39x29in) s.d.926
£583756 $1150000   (13-Nov-90 SY.NY64/R) La parade au village (47x56cm-19x22in) s.
£600000 $1164000   (3-Dec-90 C58/R) La nappe mauve (74x61cm-29x24in) s.
£634518 $1250000   (13-Nov-90 SY.NY63/R) Les cerises (100x49cm-39x19in) s.d.1956
£700000 $1127000   (25-Jun-91 S13/R) Les amoureux de St. Paul-de-Venice (50x72cm-20x28in)
                  s.
£900000 $1746000   (4-Dec-90 S36/R) Couple sur Found Rouge (81x65cm-32x26in) s. s.verso
£913706 $1800000   (14-Nov-90 CH.NY46/R) La chevre de Vence (52x63cm-20x25in) s.
£1472081 $2900000   (12-Nov-90 SY.NY33/R) Hommage a Paris, Notre Dame (76x100cm-30x39in)
                  s.d.1953-54
£2538071 $5000000   (14-Nov-90 CH.NY18/R) Le buveur - le saoul (83x114cm-33x45in) s.d.910
£1051 $1818   (22-May-91 CH.AM792) Jewish girl (32x24cm-13x9in) s. col.felt-tip pens
                  (D.FL 3500)
£2607 $4250   (12-Jun-91 SY.NY61/R) Bird and tree (42x32cm-17x13in) s.i.d.1972 black
                  marker
£3303 $5715   (23-May-91 SY.AM77/R) Figures and bouquet of flowers (31x23cm-12x9in)
                  s.i.d.71 col.crayons ball point pen (D.FL 11000)
£3800 $7410   (17-Oct-90 S168/R) Portrait of V.S. Eliashev (23x35cm-9x14in) s.d.1916
                  by Alexander Housky pencil
£5198 $8525   (19-Jun-91 GK.B251/R) La famille (23x17cm-9x7in) s.i.d.1928 ink pen
                  bister (S.FR 13100)

CHAGALL, Marc (1887-1985) French/Russian-cont.

£5405	$9189	(28-May-91 KF.M516/R) Nuages et personnage (16x31cm-6x12in) s.i.d.1956/57 W/C indian ink (DM 16000)
£6122	$12000	(15-Feb-91 SY.NY97/R) La peintre a son chevalet (25x18cm-10x7in) s.i.d.1946 pen ink W/C on frontispiece of book
£6607	$11429	(23-May-91 SY.AM71/R) Moses and angel (35x50cm-14x20in) s.i.d.1965 col.crayons (D.FL 22000)
£7808	$13508	(22-May-91 CH.AM531/R) Tu es fou (13x16cm-5x6in) s.i. pen W/C (D.FL 26000)
£8000	$12880	(24-Jun-91 CSK97/R) Le reve du peintre (27x41cm-11x16in) s.i.d.1967 col.crayons pen ink wash
£8108	$13784	(28-May-91 KF.M515/R) Vase de fleurs et deux femmes (17x9cm-7x4in) s.i. indian ink pen W/C board (DM 24000)
£10000	$17700	(20-Mar-91 S62/R) La descente de croix (32x25cm-13x10in) s. pen indian ink wash
£10000	$17700	(20-Mar-91 S63/R) Le Christ au village (65x50cm-26x20in) s.d.1981 brush ink chl
£10194	$19572	(29-Nov-90 ZZ.F19/R) Scene d'interieur Russe (17x22cm-7x9in) ink wash htd.W/C (F.FR 100000)
£18000	$29340	(1-Jul-91 APT.P309/R) Le peintre et sa nature morte au vase fleuri (34x25cm-13x10in) s.d.1951 W/C (F.FR 180000)
£19000	$30590	(25-Jun-91 C264/R) Les amoureux (27x20cm-11x8in) s.i.d.1952 gouache brush ink
£19782	$35410	(14-Apr-91 GL.P216/R) Rabbin a la Thora (33x28cm-13x11in) s. Indian ink wash W/C (F.FR 200000)
£27919	$55000	(14-Nov-90 SY.NY174/R) Peintre au chevalet - la Mariee (14x9cm-6x4in) s. col.crayon indian ink pencil lined paper
£30204	$59502	(16-Nov-90 GK.Z5208/R) Paysan russe chevauchant un boeuf (32x25cm-13x10in) s. W/C gouache (S.FR 74000)
£30612	$60000	(15-Feb-91 SY.NY98/R) Moses receiving the Tablets of the Lord (38x28cm-15x11in) s. gouache india ink pencil
£35000	$67900	(4-Dec-90 C206/R) Arbres et personnages (27x23cm-11x9in) s.d.1969 gouache pencil
£39249	$76928	(23-Nov-90 VG.B59/R) To my father (31x24cm-12x9in) s. indian ink pen brush wash (DM 115000)
£45685	$90000	(2-Oct-90 CH.NY132/R) Bouquet a la vache (29x23cm-11x9in) s. ink W/C over pencil
£46107	$90369	(11-Nov-90 ZZ.F145/R) Le juif vert (38x28cm-15x11in) s. pastel Indian ink (F.FR 450000)
£52000	$92040	(19-Mar-91 C85/R) Le peintre crucifie (38x56cm-15x22in) s.d.941-942 pencil pastel W/C gouache
£55000	$106700	(5-Dec-90 S358/R) La Noce (30x22cm-12x9in) s. W/C gouache crayon pen Indian ink
£62000	$99820	(26-Jun-91 S250/R) L'homme au parapluie (39x29cm-15x11in) s. W/C pen ink over pencil
£65990	$130000	(14-Nov-90 SY.NY173/R) Rebecca a la fontaine (38x28cm-15x11in) s. gouache pastel
£66474	$115000	(9-May-91 CH.NY156/R) Fleurs et fruits (70x55cm-28x22in) s. W/C chlks.col.wax crayons pastel over pencil
£68342	$112080	(20-Jun-91 APT.P33/R) Vence - Nature morte aux fruits (48x58cm-19x23in) s.d.1949 mixed media paper laid down on canvas (F.FR 680000)
£80972	$158704	(25-Nov-90 GL.P87/R) La paysanne au parapluie (62x48cm-24x19in) s. ink wash (F.FR 800000)
£85256	$166249	(9-Oct-90 CSC.P36/R) Le cirque (56x68cm-22x27in) s. Indian ink (F.FR 850000)
£120000	$232800	(5-Dec-90 S385/R) Couple et deux Bouquets (99x61cm-39x24in) s. W/C gouache
£121827	$240000	(14-Nov-90 SY.NY175/R) Bouquet de fleurs devant la lune (44x29cm-17x11in) s. gouache
£130952	$214762	(21-Jun-91 GK.B14/R) Couple d'amoureux et le violoniste dans un village russe avec fleurs (76x56cm-30x22in) s. bodycol W/C over chk (S.FR 330000)
£131980	$260000	(15-Nov-90 CH.NY173/R) Le violoniste (98x63cm-39x25in) s.s. W/C brush ink paper on paper on canvas
£141700	$277733	(25-Nov-90 GL.P86/R) Les reflets verts (96x67cm-38x26in) W/C (F.FR 1400000)
£150289	$260000	(7-May-91 SY.NY45/R) Bouquet et village au soleil levant (60x48cm-24x19in) s. gouache W/C pastel
£167630	$290000	(8-May-91 SY.NY207/R) The red tree (67x48cm-26x19in) s. gouache W/C pastel paper mounted on canvas
£173410	$300000	(8-May-91 CH.NY55/R) Vase de fleurs (61x49cm-24x19in) s. gouache W/C pastel paper laid down on board
£200000	$388000	(5-Dec-90 S343/R) La Bicyclette (65x50cm-26x20in) s. gouache
£203046	$400000	(14-Nov-90 SY.NY170/R) Le mariage (50x66cm-20x26in) s. gouache pastel
£210000	$407400	(5-Dec-90 S382/R) Trapeziste (62x50cm-24x20in) s. gouache pen wax crayon
£241117	$475000	(14-Nov-90 SY.NY171/R) Paysan Russe (63x48cm-25x19in) s. gouache paper on canvas
£243655	$480000	(14-Nov-90 SY.NY265/R) Vase de fleurs avex coq et lune (63x48cm-25x19in) s. W/C pastel gouache
£294416	$580000	(15-Nov-90 CH.NY176/R) Autobiographie (51x76cm-20x30in) s. gouache W/C col.chk over pencil board
£304569	$600000	(15-Nov-90 CH.NY145/R) Nuit d'hiver (67x51cm-26x20in) s. gouache paper on board
£310000	$601400	(5-Dec-90 S379/R) Souvenir D'Une Soiree (94x64cm-37x25in) s. gouache crayon W/C

CHAGALL, Marc (after) (1887-1985) French/Russian
£1600 $2832   (21-Mar-91 BEL931) Untitled gouache sold with W/C portrait

CHAGNIOT, Alfred (1905-) French
£503 $986   (27-Jan-91 FE.P93) Le marche Tarnais (55x46cm-22x18in) s. (F.FR 5000)
£503 $965   (24-Feb-91 FE.P69) Ete (46x55cm-18x22in) s. (F.FR 5000)
£650 $1092   (28-Apr-91 FE.P92) Plein air (46x55cm-18x22in) s. (F.FR 6500)
£753 $1212   (30-Jun-91 FE.P108) Bord de l´etang (60x73cm-24x29in) s. (F.FR 7500)

CHAHINE, Edgar (1874-1947) French
£1506 $2786   (6-Mar-91 APT.P3) Jeune fille a l´eventail (54x45cm-21x18in) s. pastel
      (F.FR 15000)
£6886 $13359   (5-Dec-90 ZZ.F174/R) Portrait de femme (58x46cm-23x18in) s.d.1936
      gouache (F.FR 67000)

CHAIGNEAU, Jean Ferdinand (1830-1906) French
£1109 $1963   (5-Apr-91 LGB.P163/R) Berger et ses moutons (18x24cm-7x9in) s. panel
      (F.FR 11200)

CHAIGNEAU, Paul (20th C) French
£1089 $1928   (7-Apr-91 I.N68) Moutons s´abreuvant au coucher du soleil
      (34x42cm-13x17in) s. (F.FR 11000)
£2446 $4697   (1-Dec-90 PER.M1134/R) les moutons a la mare (33x41cm-13x16in) s.
      (F.FR 24000)
£2752 $5284   (1-Dec-90 PER.M110/R) Le berger et son troupeau a Barbizon
      (33x41cm-13x16in) s. (F.FR 27000)

CHAISSAC, Gaston (1910-1964) French
£32587 $64196   (29-Oct-90 FB.P34/R) Composition (46x63cm-18x25in) s. paper laid down on
      canvas (F.FR 320000)
£410 $803   (11-Nov-90 ZZ.F221/R) Sans titre (26x21cm-10x8in) s. ink (F.FR 4000)
£548 $905   (10-Jul-91 FB.P56) Personnages (21x13cm-8x5in) s.d.8-5-55 col.crayons
      (F.FR 5500)
£561 $1076   (30-Nov-90 CB.P12) Personnage s.d.5.11.61 ball-pen (F.FR 5500)
£748 $1234   (10-Jul-91 FB.P53/R) Personnage (27x21cm-11x8in) s. drawing (F.FR 7500)
£950 $1596   (28-Apr-91 FE.P13) Composition (19x25cm-7x10in) s. board (F.FR 9500)
£1000 $1670   (5-Jun-91 HC.P343) Madame la Dame (22x13cm-9x5in) s.i.d.15.12.58 crayon
      (F.FR 10000)
£1085 $2137   (1-Oct-90 CC.P13) La mise en bouteille de la camisole de force
      (31x24cm-12x9in) s. ink collage (F.FR 11000)
£1118 $2236   (10-Feb-91 CC.P9) Composition a un personnage (16x10cm-6x4in) s. Indian
      ink (F.FR 11000)
£1223 $2361   (15-Dec-90 D.P16/R) Composition (14x14cm-6x6in) s.d.13/7/55 s.verso
      collage ink (F.FR 12000)
£1381 $2720   (1-Oct-90 CC.P11) Untitled (28x24cm-11x9in) s. col.felt pens blotting
      paper (F.FR 14000)
£1381 $2720   (1-Oct-90 CC.P12) Tablettes Rennie (65x64cm-26x25in) s. felt pen card
      (F.FR 14000)
£1529 $2951   (16-Dec-90 GL.P177) Personnages (19x27cm-7x11in) s.d.1961 ink
      (F.FR 15000)
£2024 $3968   (22-Nov-90 ZZ.F46/R) Dr Kle-Holert, medecine illegale (20x27cm-8x11in)
      s.i. W/C (F.FR 20000)
£3874 $7476   (16-Dec-90 GL.P18/R) Sans titre (26x20cm-10x8in) s.d.2.10.55 collage
      Indian ink (F.FR 38000)
£4523 $8095   (11-Mar-91 GL.P184/R) Personnage (31x24cm-12x9in) s. gouache
      (F.FR 45000)
£4878 $9756   (10-Feb-91 CC.P18/R) Tete (19x18cm-7x7in) s. collage paper murals Indian
      ink (F.FR 48000)
£5930 $9725   (20-Jun-91 APT.P68/R) Dimanche de mai (25x20cm-10x8in) s.d.1958
      col.crayons (F.FR 59000)
£10101 $19798   (14-Feb-91 GL.P1/R) Personnage (31x23cm-12x9in) s. Indian ink collage
      (F.FR 100000)
£15275 $30092   (29-Oct-90 FB.P33/R) Composition (50x65cm-20x26in) s.d.1.1.62 gouache
      (F.FR 150000)
£37849 $64343   (30-May-91 FB.P43/R) Personnage (66x100cm-26x39in) s.d.9.12.61 collage
      Indian ink map wallpaper (F.FR 380000)

CHALE, Gertrudis (19/20th C) Latin American
£591 $1100   (5-Sep-90 V.BA33) Paisaje con figuras (40x50cm-16x20in)

CHALLE, Charles Michelange (1718-1778) French
£1711 $3250   (8-Jan-91 SY.NY11/R) The head of a woman wearing a laurel crown
      (43x26cm-17x10in) red chk.htd.white chk.
£2900 $5568   (18-Feb-91 S244/R) Interior with two stairways. Fountain in front of
      colonnade (18x22cm-7x9in) s. pen ink wash over chk pair
£3083 $5982   (7-Dec-90 CN.P64/R) Interieur de Palais (54x67cm-21x26in) pierre noire
      pen wash (F.FR 30000)
£5263 $10000   (8-Jan-91 SY.NY82/R) Architectural composition with elaborate staircases
      and palaces. Altar (14x22cm-6x9in) i. verso ink wash double-sided

CHALLE, Charles Michelange (attrib) (1718-1778) French
£2783 $4704   (18-Apr-91 APT.P132/R) Flore et Zephir (32x40cm-13x16in) (F.FR 28000)

CHALLENER, Frederick (1869-1959) Canadian
£789 $1555   (30-Oct-90 SY.T147/R) Shore, east of Toronto, Scarborough, with paddle
      steamer beyond (20x31cm-8x12in) s.d.1891 i.verso board (C.D 1800)

CHALLIE, Jean Laurent (1880-1943) French
£907 $1769 (26-Oct-90 APT.P87) Vase de fleurs (65x81cm-26x32in) s. (F.FR 9000)
£3061 $6031 (16-Nov-90 FB.P136/R) Village de la Clarte (54x65cm-21x26in) s. bears
st.slg. stretcher (F.FR 30000)

CHALON, Henry Bernard (1770-1849) British
£4500 $7425 (12-Jul-91 C103/R) Sligo Waxy, bay racehorse, with bulldog by wall and
kennel (61x76cm-24x30in) s.i.d.1824
£11976 $20000 (7-Jun-91 SY.NY38/R) Mare and foal (112x145cm-44x57in) s.d.1799

CHALON, Henry Bernard (after) (1770-1849) British
£800 $1560 (15-Jan-91 B88/R) Wasp, child and Billy (49x60cm-19x24in)

CHALON, Henry Bernard (attrib) (1770-1849) British
£10180 $17000 (7-Jun-91 SY.NY41/R) A King Charles Spaniel (51x63cm-20x25in)

CHALON, Henry Bernard (circle) (1770-1849) British
£2000 $3800 (1-Mar-91 C62/R) Fallow deer and water spaniel in landscape
(51x61cm-20x24in)

CHALON, Louis (1687-1741) French
£1014 $1723 (27-May-91 L.K189/R) River landscapes (26x42cm-10x17in) W/C htd.white
pair in the style of Griffier (DM 3000)

CHALOU (1942-) French
£659 $1305 (3-Feb-91 LT.P111/R) Le petit aigle (50x61cm-20x24in) s.d.89 l. verso
board (F.FR 6500)

CHAMAILLARD, Ernest (1862-1930) French
£1900 $3686 (6-Dec-90 CSK30) Paysage d'eau (61x74cm-24x29in) s.d.1899
£4893 $9443 (16-Dec-90 T.B107/R) Chaumieres pres de la Cote (55x44cm-22x17in) s.
(F.FR 48000)
£5040 $9829 (28-Oct-90 GRA.P13/R) Le parc (60x73cm-24x29in) s. (F.FR 50000)
£713 $1404 (29-Oct-90 CSC.P76) Paysage aux deux tours (15x22cm-6x9in) s. W/C
(F.FR 7000)
£746 $1291 (12-May-91 T.B32) Le Mont St-Michel (18x24cm-7x9in) s. W/C (F.FR 7500)
£764 $1505 (29-Oct-90 CSC.P62/R) Le chateau fort (12x16cm-5x6in) init. W/C
(F.FR 7500)

CHAMBAS, Jean Paul (1947-) French
£402 $647 (25-Jun-91 BG.P16) Puccini (42x29cm-17x11in) s.i.d.Nov 81 gouache W/C
(F.FR 4000)
£655 $1278 (23-Oct-90 CSC.P93/R) Smoking Ops (101x71cm-40x28in) s.i.d.Octobre 1978
gouache crayon (F.FR 6500)
£4656 $9126 (20-Nov-90 BG.P20/R) La traviata et Lautrec (64x50cm-25x20in) s.i.d.1979
pastel chl.crayon (F.FR 46000)

CHAMBERLIN, Frank Tolles (1873-1961) American
£918 $1800 (13-Feb-91 B.SF2059/R) Rome, 1910 (81x53cm-32x21in) mono.
£1276 $2500 (13-Feb-91 B.SF2065/R) Still life with fruit and jug (51x61cm-20x24in)
mono.d.1931
£2821 $5500 (10-Oct-90 B.SF508/R) Still life with white roses (48x63cm-19x25in)
mono.d.42 board

CHAMBERLIN, Mason (18/19th C) British
£1300 $2145 (10-Jul-91 S131/R) Portrait of Doctor Hornby of West Drayton, Windsor,
standing (70x90cm-28x35in)

CHAMBERS, G (19th C) British
£3500 $6895 (15-Nov-90 CSK12/R) Landscape in the West Indies (79x53cm-31x21in)
s.d.65

CHAMBERS, George (19th C) British
£600 $1152 (20-Feb-91 CSK153) Coastal landscape with fisherfolk unloading fishing
boats (21x30cm-8x12in) s.d.70
£650 $1151 (18-Mar-91 FEN88) Fishing boats in a heavy swell (18x15cm-7x6in) s.
verso panel
£3500 $6055 (22-May-91 S59/R) Ship wreck. Hove to (39cm-15ins circular) s.d.1834
pair
£4000 $7520 (8-Aug-90 PHP118/R) Fishing boats and paddle steamer in choppy seas off
coastline (65x87cm-26x34in)
£850 $1471 (22-May-91 S20) Margate (15x22cm-6x9in) init.d.35 W/C

CHAMBERS, George (attrib) (19th C) British
£750 $1440 (16-Aug-90 B247/R) Brig and other shipping off coastline
(63x76cm-25x30in)
£4023 $7000 (27-Mar-91 B.SF4228/R) Bristol Harbour (61x91cm-24x36in)

CHAMBERS, George (jnr) (19th C) British
£1500 $2595 (20-May-91 PH123) Greenwich from Thames (64x177cm-25x70in) W/C
£4800 $8592 (9-Apr-91 C159/R) Boating scenes on the lake, St James's Park
(36x53cm-14x21in) s.d.71 pencil W/C htd.white pair

CHAMBERS, Sir William (?) British
£7500 $14475 (11-Dec-90 C211/R) Design for a villa at Llanaeron (36x59cm-14x23in) l.
ink W/C htd.white

CHAMBERT, Eric (20th C) ?
£660 $1142   (22-May-91 BA.S331/R) Composition (55x46cm-22x18in) s. panel (S.KR 7000)

CHAMERSKI, Richard (20th C) Australian
£541 $1065   (13-Nov-90 J.M189) Sydney Harbour (29x59cm-11x23in) s. canvas board
               (A.D 1400)

CHAMINADE (20th C) French
£754 $1237   (21-Jun-91 G.Z288) Composition (65x49cm-26x19in) s.d.1959 (S.FR 1900)
£952 $1562   (21-Jun-91 G.Z289) Abstraction (81x100cm-32x39in) s.d.1959 (S.FR 2400)

CHAMINADE, Albert (1923-) French
£2245 $4422   (16-Nov-90 EA.Z311) Untitled (65x81cm-26x32in) s.d.1959 (S.FR 5500)

CHAMPAGNE, Horace (?) Canadian
£438 $745   (27-May-91 HO.ED275) Defourneau leduc (43x57cm-17x22in) s. s.i.d.1983
               pastel (C.D 850)
£515 $876   (27-May-91 HO.ED330/R) Laurentian countryside, Quebec, near Ripon,
               Quebec (61x76cm-24x30in) s. s.i.d.1981verso pastel board (C.D 1000)
£1485 $2925   (12-Nov-90 HO.ED285) Devil's Rock Pile, Mount Schaeffer, Lake O'Hara
               (100x126cm-39x50in) s. pastel (C.D 3400)

CHAMPAIGNE, Philippe de (1602-1674) Flemish
£71942 $139568   (7-Dec-90 CH.MO352/R) L'Annonciation (95x129cm-37x51in) (F.FR 700000)
£80402 $131859   (22-Jun-91 CH.MO161/R) Scene de la vie de Saint Benoit
               (93x148cm-37x58in) (F.FR 800000)
£89021 $159347   (9-Apr-91 APT.P31/R) Portrait de Louis XIII en buste (74x62cm-29x24in)
               oval (F.FR 900000)
£120000 $231600   (12-Dec-90 S58/R) The Visitation (114x88cm-45x35in)

CHAMPAIGNE, Philippe de (attrib) (1602-1674) Flemish
£1469 $2880   (6-Nov-90 GF.L2307/R) Crucifixion (127x79cm-50x31in) (S.FR 3600)
£2447 $4600   (22-Sep-90 WOL.C60) Saint Paul (48x38cm-19x15in) canvas on panel

CHAMPAIGNE, Philippe de (circle) (1602-1674) Flemish
£1369 $2300   (17-Jul-91 SY.NY113/R) Portrait of a gentleman (56x49cm-22x19in)

CHAMPAIGNE, Philippe de (school) (1602-1674) Flemish
£3518 $6754   (19-Feb-91 ARC.P14/R) Portrait du Cardinal Mazarin (65x50cm-26x20in)
               (F.FR 35000)

CHAMPAIGNE, Philippe de (studio) (1602-1674) Flemish
£3200 $5664   (22-Mar-91 BG.P9/R) Saint-Jacques le Majeur (61x52cm-24x20in)
               (F.FR 32000)

CHAMPAIGNE, Philippe de (style) (1602-1674) Flemish
£800 $1304   (4-Jul-91 CSK228/R) Portrait of cleric in robe and cap, holding book
               (76x63cm-30x25in) with sig.i.d.1658
£1700 $2873   (18-Apr-91 C32/R) Portrait of Prince Henry of Nassau, half length
               (69x56cm-27x22in)
£2196 $3733   (27-May-91 L.K24) Portrait of cardinal Richelieu (73x59cm-29x23in)
               (DM 6500)
£17059 $29000   (30-May-91 SY.NY14/R) Christ (64x54cm-25x21in) i.verso panel oval

CHAMPEAUX, Bertrand de (19/20th C) French
£697 $1206   (26-May-91 ZZ.F79/R) Fillette dans le jardin de fleurs (50x65cm-20x26in)
               s. (F.FR 7000)

CHAMPIN, Jean Jacques (1796-1860) French
£2959 $5830   (14-Nov-90 FB.P328/R) Le chateau de Pierre fonds vu depuis l'etang
               (16x23cm-6x9in) s. (F.FR 29000)

CHAMPION, Theo (1887-1952) German
£822 $1340   (15-Jun-91 L.K119) Trees by the river (15x23cm-6x9in) s. board
               (DM 2400)
£1122 $1807   (26-Jun-91 KM.K1411) Lower Rhine landscape (45x64cm-18x25in) s.
               (DM 3300)
£1507 $2456   (15-Jun-91 L.K120) Landscape (9x15cm-4x6in) s. board (DM 4400)
£5479 $8932   (15-Jun-91 L.K118/R) Lower Rhine landscape with rainbow
               (45x37cm-18x15in) s.d.1927 (DM 16000)

CHAMPNEY, Benjamin (1817-1907) American
£529 $1000   (27-Sep-90 CH.NY34/R) White mountains, New Hampshire (7x9cm-3x4in)
               s.i.mount paper laid down on board
£1755 $3300   (11-Aug-90 COL.M234/R) Mt.Chocorua (25x36cm-10x14in) s.d.188/
£4624 $8000   (10-May-91 S.BM29/R) From the top of little Rattlesnake Mountain, autumn
               (51x41cm-20x16in) s.d.84 s.i.d.verso
£13873 $24000   (10-May-91 S.BM44 d/R) Afternoon of fishing, autumn landscape in the
               White Mountains (56x91cm-22x36in) s.d.1869

CHAMPNEY, James Wells (1843-1903) American
£695 $1300   (30-Aug-90 MFA.C237) View of Edouard Frere House (30x36cm-12x14in)
               s.c.1883
£703 $1300   (8-Mar-91 S.BM160/R) Cinderella (28x23cm-11x9in) s. panel
£1221 $2100   (15-May-91 SY.NY13/R) Portrait of young woman (59x49cm-23x19in) pastel
               board

CHANETIE, A (19th C) ?
£1600 $3072   (29-Nov-90 B109/R) The new doll (45x35cm-18x14in) s.d.73

CHANTEREAU, Jerome Francois (?-1757) French
£15075 $24724   (22-Jun-91 CH.MO18/R) Deux jeunes paysans debout, portant des chapeaux
(22x19cm-9x7in) with i. col.chk (F.FR 150000)

CHANTEREAU, Jerome Francois (attrib) (?-1757) French
£1025 $2008   (7-Nov-90 APT.P413/R) Dresseur de chien (19x17cm-7x7in) sanguinne
(F.FR 10000)

CHANTRE, Fleury (1806-?) French
£3667 $7040   (18-Dec-90 GM.B4015/R) Bouquet de fleurs (51x68cm-20x27in) s. W/C
(B.FR 220000)

CHANTRELLE, Lucien (1890-?) French
£1488 $2560   (19-May-91 LT.P3/R) Passants a Montmartre (61x73cm-24x29in) s.
(F.FR 15000)

CHANTRON, Alexandre Jacques (1842-1918) French
£502 $929   (4-Mar-91 ARC.P103) Nu allonge (33x46cm-13x18in) s. (F.FR 5000)
£1650 $2772   (26-Apr-91 NM.P13/R) Musicienne au pre (38x80cm-15x31in) s. pastel
(F.FR 16500)

CHAPEL, A de (?) ?
£2333 $4619   (30-Jan-91 APT.P290/R) Paysage montagneux (97x132cm-38x52in) s.d.1855
(F.FR 23000)

CHAPELAIN-MIDY, Roger (1904-) French
£2041 $4000   (12-Feb-91 SY.NY99/R) Paysage de Nancray Loiset (51x74cm-20x29in) s.l.
£2490 $4308   (26-May-91 ZZ.F123/R) Champs de Bles pres de Nancray (50x73cm-20x29in)
s. (F.FR 25000)
£2976 $5119   (19-May-91 ZZ.F115/R) Petit port de Volendam (65x81cm-26x32in) s.
(F.FR 30000)
£3313 $6130   (6-Mar-91 APT.P87) Bouquet de vase bleu (81x60cm-32x24in) s.
(F.FR 33000)
£4082 $8000   (12-Feb-91 SY.NY181/R) Still life with pears (81x13cm-32x5in) s.
£6042 $9849   (15-Jun-91 FB.P62 a/R) Nature morte aux fruits (60x73cm-24x29in) s.
(F.FR 60000)
£609 $1205   (3-Feb-91 I.N41) Paysage (30x48cm-12x19in) s.i.d.64 lead pencil
(F.FR 6000)

CHAPELET, Marie (19th C) French
£1000 $1690   (1-May-91 GD.B148/R) Inn interior with peasants playing cards
(49x63cm-19x25in) s.d.1863 (S.FR 2500)

CHAPELET, Roger (1902-) French
£1644 $3190   (6-Dec-90 CB.P86/R) Ketch en fuite par gros temps (46x61cm-18x24in) s.
(F.FR 16000)

CHAPELLE, Suzanne J (20th C) French
£673 $1204   (8-Apr-91 CR.P118 b) Le controleur (120x125cm-47x49in) s. (F.FR 6800)
£791 $1416   (8-Apr-91 CR.P119) Retour de peche (190x150cm-75x59in) s. (F.FR 8000)

CHAPIN, Bryant (19/20th C) American
£1243 $2300   (8-Mar-91 S.BM166/R) Vine ripened (56x38cm-22x15in) s.d.'10
£1677 $2800   (26-Jul-91 E.EDM74/R) Still life of apples (30x46cm-12x18in) s.d.1907

CHAPIRO, Jacques (1887-?) Russian
£949 $1585   (5-Jun-91 DO.H2542/R) Two women seated at table (64x53cm-25x21in) s.
(DM 2800)
£989 $1771   (14-Apr-91 GL.P180/R) Poivrons et tomatoes (60x92cm-24x36in)
s.d.23.XI.1939-1940 (F.FR 10000)
£1286 $2302   (14-Apr-91 GL.P183/R) Nature morte a la langouste (97x130cm-38x51in) s.
d.1939 verso (F.FR 13000)
£1462 $2850   (18-Jan-91 GL.P54) Le jardin potager (73x54cm-29x21in) s. verso
(F.FR 14500)
£1613 $3145   (18-Jan-91 GL.P49) L'interieur au bouquet (92x65cm-36x26in) s.d.1947
(F.FR 16000)

CHAPLAIN, Jules Clement (1839-1909) French
£769 $1500   (26-Oct-90 SY.NY151/R) Portrait of Madame Vallet (48x38cm-19x15in)
s.i.d.1881 pencil chk

CHAPLIN, Charles (1825-1891) French
£556 $1100   (1-Feb-91 S.W2921) Portrait of lady (41x33cm-16x13in) init.d.1878
£755 $1450   (27-Nov-90 PO.BA7) Desnudo recostado (42x34cm-17x13in) s.
£1053 $2000   (27-Feb-91 SY.NY57/R) Portrait of boy (46x38cm-18x15in) s.
£1792 $2922   (1-Jul-91 AAA.S144) Portrait of a young woman (39x31cm-15x12in)
(A.D 3800)
£1835 $3541   (14-Dec-90 ARC.P112) Jeune fille a la rose (41x32cm-16x13in) s. panel
(F.FR 18000)
£3600 $6444   (12-Mar-91 PH72/R) After the masked ball (71x43cm-28x17in) s.
indis.i.d.1874
£3659 $7171   (6-Nov-90 SY.AM171/R) Letter (41x25cm-16x10in) s. (D.FL 12000)

CHAPLIN, Charles (1825-1891) French-cont.
£5071	$10041	(30-Jan-91 APT.P151/R) Allegorie du Sommeil (88x83cm-35x33in) s. (F.FR 50000)
£6316	$12000	(28-Feb-91 CH.NY8/R) The letter (42x27cm-17x11in) s.
£8500	$16320	(28-Nov-90 S284/R) Girl with cat (72x50cm-28x20in) s.
£482	$776	(28-Jun-91 LC.P55) La beaute decouverte par l'amour (16x28cm-6x11in) s.i. sanguinne (F.FR 4800)
£3878	$7639	(14-Nov-90 FB.P66/R) Coupe de fleurs (71x54cm-28x21in) s. gouache (F.FR 38000)

CHAPLIN, Henry (fl.1855-1879) British
£700	$1211	(22-May-91 CSK191) Figures by the Thames (30x45cm-12x18in) s.

CHAPMAN, Carlton Theodore (1860-1926) American
£462	$800	(10-May-91 S.BM115/R) Gloucester Harbour, portrait of ship (48x30cm-19x12in) s. i.verso pastel graphite paper on canvas

CHAPMAN, Conrad Wise (1842-1910) American
£3646	$7000	(30-Nov-90 CH.NY16/R) The trump card (53x65cm-21x26in)

CHAPMAN, Frederic A (1818-1891) American
£25773	$50000	(5-Dec-90 D.NY13/R) The Fourth of July (41x61cm-16x24in) s.

CHAPMAN, John Gadsby (1808-1889) American
£4800	$9456	(15-Nov-90 CSK30/R) Ruins of Jamestown, Virginia, America (28x36cm-11x14in) i.verso panel
£1474	$2800	(9-Jan-91 CH.NY103/R) Games. Sold with works by J.Walker, H.J.Morton and C.Wimar s.d.1860 pencil

CHAPMAN, Max (1911-) British
£1500	$2775	(8-Mar-91 C199/R) Composition (105x95cm-41x37in) s.d.64 s.stretcher
£650	$1222	(20-Sep-90 CSK165/R) Collage noye (119x74cm-47x29in) s.d.1959 s.i.d.verso collage masonite
£1000	$1960	(9-Nov-90 C261/R) Emersion exit rigth (122x107cm-48x42in) s.d.64 s.stretcher oil emulsion canvas

CHAPOVAL, Youla (1919-1951) French/Russian
£1264	$2465	(15-Oct-90 CSC.P62/R) Composition (22x34cm-9x13in) s.d.1950 paper (F.FR 12500)
£3604	$6234	(23-May-91 SY.AM277/R) Composition (60x81cm-24x32in) s. (D.FL 12000)
£6042	$9849	(11-Jun-91 CSC.P44/R) Composition (54x65cm-21x26in) s. d.8.9.1949 (F.FR 60000)
£602	$1114	(6-Mar-91 HC.P30) Composition geometrique (32x24cm-13x9in) bears st.d.1950 pierre noire (F.FR 6000)
£1193	$2016	(21-Apr-91 E.LA185) Composition abstraite (16x13cm-6x5in) s. oil crayon (F.FR 12000)
£1292	$2184	(21-Apr-91 E.LA188) Abstraction (19x16cm-7x6in) s. W/C (F.FR 13000)

CHAPPELL, R (1870-1940) British
£2900	$5191	(10-Apr-91 S153/R) Bay hunters in stables (57x74cm-22x29in) s. pair
£531	$898	(2-May-91 RAS.V312) Sailship 'Elise of Thuro' (39x53cm-15x21in) s. gouache (D.KR 6000)

CHAPPELL, Reuben (1870-1940) British
£1400	$2380	(30-May-91 C108/R) Schooner Ethel Edith off white cliffs of Dover (51x76cm-20x30in) s.i.
£450	$765	(30-May-91 C34/R) Bess Mitchell (35x53cm-14x21in) init.i. W/C bodycol
£500	$975	(18-Oct-90 SC3048/R) The Sarah Lightfoot of Fowey (36x54cm-14x21in) s.i.
£600	$1038	(22-May-91 CSK71) SS Cornish Merchant of Falmouth off Eddystone Lighthouse (33x54cm-13x21in) s.i. pencil W/C bodycol
£600	$1176	(22-Jan-91 ZZ.B368/R) Ship portrait, Terrier of Dartmouth (36x53cm-14x21in) s.
£650	$1248	(16-Aug-90 B229) Ada Cane of Harwich (37x53cm-15x21in) W/C
£850	$1471	(22-May-91 S26/R) Topsail schooner Martha Edmonds (35x52cm-14x20in) s.i. W/C htd bodycol pair
£865	$1678	(22-Aug-90 RAS.K579/R) Ships portrait of 'Dorothea of Marstal' (37x55cm-15x22in) s. gouache (D.KR 10000)
£1084	$2103	(5-Dec-90 DO.H2003) Danish three master Confidentia near white cliffs (41x67cm-16x26in) mono.i. W/C bodycol (DM 3100)

CHAPRON, Nicolasc (attrib) (1612-C.1656) French
£7368	$14000	(8-Jan-91 SY.NY71/R) Diana and huntress with her nymphs (34x29cm-13x11in) ink wash over blk.chk.

CHAPUIS, H (19th C) French
£1034	$1800	(27-Mar-91 B.SF4207/R) Rocking the baby (47x62cm-19x24in) s.

CHAPUIS, Michel (1925-) French
£1172	$2262	(12-Dec-90 D.P155) Guardomar (100x73cm-39x29in) s.d.1987 (F.FR 11500)
£1223	$2361	(12-Dec-90 D.P156) La coiffe d'arbre (100x61cm-39x24in) s. d.1989 verso (F.FR 12000)

CHARAVEL, Paul (1877-1961) French
£1188	$2103	(7-Apr-91 I.N71/R) Apres le bain (73x60cm-29x24in) s.d.53 panel (F.FR 12000)

CHARAVEL, Paul (1877-1961) French-cont.
| £1286 | $2533 | (14-Nov-90 I.N122/R) Etang en foret de Montmorency (76x92cm-30x36in) s. (F.FR 12600) |

CHARCHOUNE (1888-?) Russian
| £2548 | $4893 | *(2-Dec-90 M.V50/R) Composition (26x38cm-10x15in) s. gouache (F.FR 25000)* |

CHARCHOUNE, Serge (1888-1975) Russian
£1307	$2339	(11-Mar-91 GL.P150) Isba (17x12cm-7x5in) s.d.23 III (F.FR 13000)
£1307	$2339	(11-Mar-91 GL.P152) Les traces brouillees (15x20cm-6x8in) s.d.1930 board pasted on canvas (F.FR 13000)
£1357	$2429	(11-Mar-91 GL.P174) Eau morte (17x27cm-7x11in) s. (F.FR 13500)
£1407	$2519	(11-Mar-91 GL.P171) Eau vive (9x16cm-4x6in) s. board pasted on canvas (F.FR 14000)
£1608	$2878	(11-Mar-91 GL.P173) Ondes de choc (23x34cm-9x13in) s.d.1930 (F.FR 16000)
£1709	$3058	(11-Mar-91 GL.P164) Petits jeux d'eaux (21x13cm-8x5in) s. board pasted on wood (F.FR 17000)
£1809	$3238	(11-Mar-91 GL.P172) Paysage ornemental, Printemps (15x35cm-6x14in) s.d.1930 (F.FR 18000)
£1809	$3238	(11-Mar-91 GL.P160) Tormente (13x21cm-5x8in) board (F.FR 18000)
£1809	$3238	(11-Mar-91 GL.P163) La barque de Dante (18x29cm-7x11in) s.d.1930 (F.FR 18000)
£1822	$3571	(22-Nov-90 ZZ.F33/R) Composition (20x25cm-8x10in) s. panel (F.FR 18000)
£1859	$3328	(11-Mar-91 GL.P157) Nasse (20x21cm-8x8in) s. (F.FR 18500)
£1910	$3418	(11-Mar-91 GL.P143) Trombe coloree (15x25cm-6x10in) s. (F.FR 19000)
£2000	$3260	(3-Jul-91 CSC.P86) Mozart concerto pour basson (33x55cm-13x22in) s. i.d. verso (F.FR 20000)
£2010	$3598	(11-Mar-91 GL.P148) Paysage ornemental no.2 (15x53cm-6x21in) s.d.1930 (F.FR 20000)
£2111	$3778	(11-Mar-91 GL.P156) Nympheas (16x19cm-6x7in) s. (F.FR 21000)
£2211	$3958	(11-Mar-91 GL.P170) Bourrasdque d'ete (15x52cm-6x20in) s.d.1930 (F.FR 22000)
£2412	$4318	(11-Mar-91 GL.P158) Trouble mystique (19x33cm-7x13in) s. (F.FR 24000)
£2513	$4497	(11-Mar-91 GL.P155/R) Plumet d'or (20x22cm-8x9in) s.d.XII 44 (F.FR 25000)
£2513	$4497	(16-Mar-91 APT.P68/R) La pipe (15x53cm-6x21in) s.d.1929 (F.FR 25000)
£2613	$4285	(20-Jun-91 APT.P62) La ville engloutie (24x35cm-9x14in) s.d.50-111 panel (F.FR 26000)
£2814	$5037	(11-Mar-91 GL.P169/R) Contact (22x16cm-9x6in) s. (F.FR 28000)
£3015	$5397	(11-Mar-91 GL.P161/R) Blue moon (14x30cm-6x12in) s. (F.FR 30000)
£3015	$5397	(11-Mar-91 GL.P141) Derviche Tourneur (22x27cm-9x11in) s.d.I 46 (F.FR 30000)
£3116	$5577	(11-Mar-91 GL.P165/R) La lune est couchee (14x39cm-6x15in) s.d.1928 (F.FR 31000)
£3116	$5577	(11-Mar-91 GL.P149/R) L'amur masque (24x19cm-9x7in) s.d.XI.42 board (F.FR 31000)
£3280	$5544	(21-Apr-91 P.V7/R) Composition. Paysage s. d.1929 verso double-sided (F.FR 33000)
£3417	$6117	(11-Mar-91 GL.P166/R) Rapsodie Espagnole II (14x21cm-6x8in) s.d.1945 board (F.FR 34000)
£3668	$6566	(11-Mar-91 GL.P154/R) Vibrations (14x24cm-6x9in) s. (F.FR 36500)
£3893	$7631	(11-Nov-90 ZZ.F152/R) Portrait d'homme (53x37cm-21x15in) s.d.1940 (F.FR 38000)
£4000	$7800	(10-Oct-90 C371/R) Composition (30x40cm-12x16in) s.d.27
£4098	$8033	(11-Nov-90 ZZ.F186/R) Composition - tendre, timide, contemplatif (32x25cm-13x10in) s. i. verso (F.FR 40000)
£4200	$6846	(4-Jul-91 GL.P180/R) Evasion (31x55cm-12x22in) s.d.III 43 paper laid down on canvas (F.FR 42000)
£4348	$8478	(15-Oct-90 CSC.P61/R) Composition en 4 parties (32x42cm-13x17in) s.d.58 i. verso (F.FR 43000)
£4523	$7417	(20-Jun-91 APT.P63/R) Formes plastiques (41x33cm-16x13in) s. (F.FR 45000)
£4587	$8853	(16-Dec-90 P.V9/R) Composition (19x36cm-7x14in) s.d.1930 (F.FR 45000)
£4623	$8275	(11-Mar-91 GL.P142/R) Tornade (27x27cm-11x11in) s. (F.FR 46000)
£4824	$7912	(20-Jun-91 APT.P72/R) Beethoven, 7 symphonie 2 mouvement (60x120cm-24x47in) s. (F.FR 48000)
£5070	$8568	(21-Apr-91 P.V40/R) Autoportrait (53x37cm-21x15in) s.d.decembre 1945 (F.FR 51000)
£5573	$10755	(12-Dec-90 CH.AM362/R) Brahms - concerto pour violin (46x61cm-18x24in) s. (D.FL 18000)
£5841	$9521	(11-Jun-91 CSC.P48/R) Recif de corail (73x60cm-29x24in) s. panel (F.FR 58000)
£6192	$11950	(12-Dec-90 CH.AM363/R) Nature morte (34x47cm-13x19in) s.d.26 panel (D.FL 20000)
£6533	$10714	(20-Jun-91 APT.P60/R) Clef de l'arabesque (35x24cm-14x9in) s. panel (F.FR 65000)
£6552	$12777	(28-Oct-90 GRA.P14/R) Paysage (38x46cm-15x18in) s.d.31 XI board laid down on panel (F.FR 65000)
£6572	$12816	(21-Oct-90 P.V49/R) Composition inspiree par La Marche Funebre de Beethoven (50x100cm-20x39in) s.d.XI-59 i. verso (F.FR 65000)
£6834	$11208	(20-Jun-91 APT.P61/R) Nature mortoe blanche (38x46cm-15x18in) s.d.44-45 panel (F.FR 68000)
£7035	$12593	(16-Mar-91 APT.P67/R) Figure de proue (54x81cm-21x32in) s.d.50 (F.FR 70000)
£7035	$11538	(20-Jun-91 APT.P59/R) Coupe celadon (27x35cm-11x14in) s.d.26 (F.FR 70000)

CHARCHOUNE, Serge (1888-1975) Russian-cont.

£8217	$16023	(23-Oct-90 C.A327/R) Composition (46x38cm-18x15in) s.d.1942 panel (B.FR 500000)
£9849	$16153	(20-Jun-91 APT.P58/R) Nature morte (33x46cm-13x18in) s.d.1939 (F.FR 98000)
£9900	$17128	(12-May-91 T.B84/R) L'eclaircie (38x46cm-15x18in) s.d.37 (F.FR 99500)
£14113	$27520	(28-Oct-90 GL.P33/R) Cantate St Thomas de Bach (73x116cm-29x46in) s.d.57-60 l.d.VII-57 IV-60 verso (F.FR 140000)
£15075	$24724	(20-Jun-91 APT.P57/R) Nature morte decorative (27x41cm-11x16in) init. (F.FR 150000)
£19368	$37187	(27-Nov-90 APT.P131/R) Violon blanc (54x73cm-21x29in) s. (F.FR 190000)
£450	*$779*	*(23-May-91 SY.AM341/R) Untitled (29x21cm-11x8in) s. pastel (D.FL 1500)*
£708	*$1380*	*(15-Oct-90 CSC.P60) Composition bleue et blanche (21x27cm-8x11in) s. gouache (F.FR 7000)*
£828	*$1400*	*(20-Apr-91 WOL.C382/R) Beethoven no. 7 (51x43cm-20x17in) s.num.7 pastel oil paper*
£1005	*$1799*	*(11-Mar-91 GL.P175/R) Neptune (23x24cm-9x9in) s.d.1948 W/C paper pasted on canvas (F.FR 10000)*
£1307	*$2339*	*(11-Mar-91 GL.P177) Composition (34x26cm-13x10in) s. gouache (F.FR 13000)*
£1307	*$2339*	*(11-Mar-91 GL.P176) Etude pour le cycle marin (15x24cm-6x9in) i. W/C paper pasted non canvasd (F.FR 13000)*

CHARDIN, Jean Baptiste Simeon (style) (1699-1779) French

| £1297 | $2504 | (12-Dec-90 BU.S122/R) Still life of vegetables (19x25cm-7x10in) panel (S.KR 14000) |
| £1700 | $3281 | (11-Dec-90 PH231/R) Portrait of Auguste-Gabriel Godefroy watching a top spin (66x53cm-26x21in) |

CHARLAP, Peter (20th C) American

| £655 | $1100 | (24-Apr-91 B.SF4572/R) Two nudes (213x135cm-84x53in) |

CHARLEMAGNE, Paul (1892-1972) French

| £966 | $1854 | (1-Dec-90 SA.A2463/R) Egyptian woman (116x81cm-46x32in) s. (DM 2800) |

CHARLEMONT, Hugo (1850-1939) Austrian

£782	$1485	(28-Feb-91 D.V74/R) The lace maker (46x36cm-18x14in) s. board (A.S 16000)
£1342	$2617	(13-Oct-90 KRA.D184/R) At the well (30x21cm-12x8in) s. panel (DM 4000)
£1470	$2910	(31-Jan-91 D.V84/R) Bay of Monfalcone with Doberdo near Triest (36x25cm-14x10in) s. panel (A.S 30000)
£2450	$4851	(31-Jan-91 D.V136/R) The rest (48x42cm-19x17in) s. panel (A.S 50000)
£4054	$7703	(14-Sep-90 SA.A1156 a/R) Lower Austrian village street, afternoon (34x28cm-13x11in) s.d.1872 panel (DM 12000)

CHARLES, J (1851-1906) British

| £1200 | $2244 | (2-Aug-90 RBB589) Young woman wearing long dress and raking grass (43x36cm-17x14in) |

CHARLES, James (1851-1906) British

£650	$1151	(21-Mar-91 CSK251) Shooting crows (48x58cm-19x23in)
£1200	$2352	(22-Jan-91 PH100/R) Feeding the chickens (30x44cm-12x17in) s.d.1886 panel
£1450	$2422	(22-Jul-91 SWS957/R) Catching butterflies near Bosham (39x60cm-15x24in) s.
£1500	$2955	(13-Nov-90 PH72/R) Hide and seek (47x31cm-19x12in) s.d.1886
£1550	$2589	(5-Jun-91 S220/R) Fetching water (30x23cm-12x9in) s.
£2700	$4509	(4-Jun-91 PH29 a/R) Dappled sunlight (55x42cm-22x17in) s.d.1890
£2800	$5264	(19-Sep-90 PHC278/R) Portrait of little girl (30x41cm-12x16in) s.
£3000	$5070	(1-May-91 PHL123/R) Picking fruit (42x38cm-17x15in) s.d.1892

CHARLET (?) ?

| £1984 | $3413 | (19-May-91 ZZ.F3/R) La nouvelle invention (32x40cm-13x16in) trace sig. (F.FR 20000) |

CHARLET, Frans (1862-1928) Belgian

£1808	$3525	(23-Oct-90 C.A328/R) Sheep on the plain (50x62cm-20x24in) (B.FR 110000)
£1150	*$2243*	*(23-Oct-90 C.A330/R) Mother and child (67x49cm-26x19in) s. W/C (B.FR 70000)*
£1150	*$2243*	*(23-Oct-90 C.A331/R) Children with lanterns (58x45cm-23x18in) s. W/C (B.FR 70000)*
£2629	*$5127*	*(23-Oct-90 C.A329/R) Child with an orange (39x48cm-15x19in) s. W/C (B.FR 160000)*

CHARLET, Nicolas Toussaint (1792-1845) French

£930	*$1814*	*(17-Oct-90 LC.P49/R) Apres le souper (34x23cm-13x9in) s. (F.FR 9200)*
£668	*$1296*	*(6-Dec-90 ARC.P29/R) L'Empereur sur un dromadaire (16x20cm-6x8in) W/C htd.gouache (F.FR 6500)*
£1118	*$2236*	*(4-Feb-91 PLF.P29/R) La lecture (20x15cm-8x6in) s. W/C (F.FR 11000)*

CHARLIER, A (19/20th C) ?

| £1164 | $2083 | (12-Mar-91 GM.B1000) Vue de Nieuwport (100x140cm-39x55in) s. (B.FR 70000) |

CHARLIER, Jacques (18th) French
£3469 $6835   *(13-Nov-90 CH.G257) Couple of young lovers by a woodland pool (6x8cm-2x3in) min. gilt-wood frame rounded corners (S.FR 8500)*

CHARLOT, Jean (1898-1979) French
£1913 $3750   (12-Feb-91 SY.NY264/R) Lavandera (20x25cm-8x10in) s.d.37
£3488 $6000   (15-May-91 CH.NY183/R) Desnudo en el Bosque (35x28cm-14x11in) s.
£3571 $7000   (20-Nov-90 CH.NY119/R) Trabajadores (37x28cm-15x11in) s. indist.d.
£9694 $19000   (20-Nov-90 CH.NY123/R) Madre y nino (71x56cm-28x22in)

CHARLOT, Louis (1878-1951) French
£789 $1554   (6-Oct-90 GL.P109) Paysage (38x54cm-15x21in) s. board (F.FR 8000)
£815 $1574   (12-Dec-90 APT.P77) Lumiere d'autommne en Morvan (81x99cm-32x39in) s. (F.FR 8000)
£1282 $2526   (6-Oct-90 GL.P105) Le peintre sur le motif (92x73cm-36x29in) s.d.1915 (F.FR 13000)

CHARLOT, Paul (19/20th C) French
£633 $1246   (18-Nov-90 H.A100) Le prunellier (24x19cm-9x7in) s.l. d.70 verso (F.FR 6200)
£950 $1549   (5-Jul-91 APT.P104) Les Baliveaux (61x46cm-24x18in) s.d.56 l. verso (F.FR 9500)
£1643 $2843   (26-May-91 ZZ.F151/R) L'epine noire (73x58cm-29x23in) s. (F.FR 16500)
£1835 $3523   (2-Dec-90 M.V100/R) La plage (38x61cm-15x24in) s.d.1947 panel (F.FR 18000)

CHARLTON, John (1849-1917) British
£600 $1074   (14-Mar-91 B73) At the water's edge (53x36cm-21x14in) s. indist.d.

CHARLTON, William Henry (1846-1918) British
£1300 $2236   (13-May-91 CG202/R) Eyemouth Harbour, Berwickshire (63x76cm-25x30in) s. l. stretcher

CHARMAN, Rodney (20th C) American
£1854 $3616   (9-Oct-90 CH.HK1357/R) China tea clipper Norman Court at anchor in Foochow, with other shipping (71x91cm-28x36in) s.d.76 l.verso (HK.D 28000)

CHARMY, Emilie (1877-1974) French
£5020 $9287   (4-Mar-91 ARC.P104) Nu (89x137cm-35x54in) s. (F.FR 50000)

CHARNAY, Armand (1844-1916) French
£580 $1137   (14-Feb-91 CSK55) The Old Church, Pavillac (23x33cm-9x13in) s.indist.l. stretcher verso

CHAROVA, Elena (1931-) Russian
£896 $1558   (25-Mar-91 ARC.P152) L'orchestre (29x36cm-11x14in) s. board (F.FR 9000)
£1393 $2424   (25-Mar-91 ARC.P153) Samovar (80x60cm-31x24in) s. (F.FR 14000)
£1692 $2943   (25-Mar-91 ARC.P151/R) Musique au jardin (50x70cm-20x28in) s. board (F.FR 17000)

CHARPENTIER, Constance-Marie (1767-1849) French
£10277 $19938   (7-Dec-90 CH.MO337/R) Les cinq sens (90x120cm-35x47in) (F.FR 100000)
£15416 $29908   (7-Dec-90 CH.MO335/R) Une mere et sa fille (81x103cm-32x41in) (F.FR 150000)

CHARPENTIER, Jean Baptiste (18/19th C) French
£4868 $9639   (30-Jan-91 APT.P269/R) Le verre d'eau (32x23cm-13x9in) s. panel (F.FR 48000)
£130653 $214271   (21-Jun-91 SY.MO20/R) Portrait presume de la Princesse de Lamballe assise dans un parc (114x90cm-45x35in) (F.FR 1300000)

CHARPENTIER, Philippe (194?-) French
£1767 $3463   (24-Nov-90 AB.L51/R) Composition (139x138cm-55x54in) mono.d.1987 mixed media collage paper on canvas (S.FR 4400)

CHARRETIE, Anna Maria (1819-1875) British
£1731 $2943   (28-May-91 F.R78/R) Bambina in un interno (46x35cm-18x14in) s.d.73 (I.L 3800000)

CHARRETON, Victor (1864-1937) French
£4767 $9438   (28-Jan-91 PPB.P17/R) Rue de village (26x34cm-10x13in) s.l. panel (F.FR 47000)
£5578 $10710   (17-Dec-90 AGS.P23/R) Verger au printemps (38x47cm-15x19in) s. board (F.FR 55000)
£6042 $9849   (14-Jun-91 AGS.P21/R) La riviere (60x73cm-24x29in) s. (F.FR 60000)
£6116 $11804   (12-Dec-90 APT.P78/R) Printemps (38x45cm-15x18in) bears studio st. board laid down on canvas (F.FR 60000)
£7030 $12443   (7-Apr-91 I.N72/R) Une rue du village d'Autezat (46x39cm-18x15in) s. panel (F.FR 71000)
£8459 $13789   (14-Jun-91 AGS.P22/R) Village d'Auvergne (60x73cm-24x29in) s. (F.FR 84000)
£8621 $15000   (27-Mar-91 B.SF4185/R) Le printemps (61x72cm-24x28in) s.
£8647 $16343   (30-Sep-90 E.LA170/R) Paysage aux grands arbres (41x32cm-16x13in) s. panel (F.FR 85000)
£8673 $17000   (15-Feb-91 SY.NY28/R) Bord de la riviere (46x55cm-18x22in) s.l. board

CHARRETON, Victor (1864-1937) French-cont.

£8673	$17000	(14-Feb-91 CH.NY24/R) Pommiers en fleurs dans les pres mouilles (46x55cm-18x22in) s.
£9645	$19000	(3-Oct-90 SY.NY185/R) Paysage en hiver (48x65cm-19x26in) s.
£9677	$18581	(2-Dec-90 GAB.G1567/R) Hameau en automne (46x60cm-18x24in) s. (S.FR 24000)
£9677	$18581	(2-Dec-90 GAB.G1570/R) Paysage de neige (65x78cm-26x31in) s. (S.FR 24000)
£9816	$16000	(12-Jun-91 SY.NY21/R) Spring landscape with village (67x92cm-26x36in) s.
£11224	$22000	(14-Feb-91 CH.NY20/R) Neige au soleil a Saint-Victor pres du Mont Dore (68x90cm-27x35in) s.
£17000	$33150	(19-Oct-90 C214/R) Maison et Verger a l'automne (61x73cm-24x29in) s.
£17857	$35000	(7-Nov-90 B.SF1078/R) Un village en Auvergne (89x116cm-35x46in) s.
£18552	$35621	(27-Nov-90 APT.P31/R) Neuge a Murols, le four (72x89cm-28x35in) s. board (F.FR 182000)
£19057	$37161	(9-Oct-90 CSC.P33/R) Le Parc du Luxembourg (46x37cm-18x15in) s. board (F.FR 190000)
£20305	$40000	(2-Oct-90 CH.NY58/R) Maison a Ploare (59x73cm-23x29in) s. board
£22843	$45000	(2-Oct-90 CH.NY67/R) Rue de village ensoleillee (54x65cm-21x26in) s.

CHARTRAND, Esteban (19th C) Spanish

| £2143 | $4200 | (20-Nov-90 CH.NY88/R) Puesta de sol (45x61cm-18x24in) s.d.1883 |

CHARUVI, Samuel (1897-1965) Israeli

| £576 | $1100 | (1-Jan-91 GG.TA297/R) Seashore and palm trees (35x29cm-14x11in) s. canvas on board |

CHAS-LABORDE (1886-1941) French

| *£2543* | *$4807* | *(25-Sep-90 FB.P250/R) L'aube (26x44cm-10x17in) s.d.1912 gouache wax crayon (F.FR 25000)* |

CHASE, Adelaide (1869-1944) American

| £694 | $1200 | (21-May-91 GRO.B97/R) Still life of calla lilly (20x10cm-8x4in) mono. panel |

CHASE, Frank Swift (1886-1958) American

| £2320 | $4500 | (5-Dec-90 D.NY118/R) The green barn (30x41cm-12x16in) s. i.verso board |

CHASE, Henry (1853-1889) American

| £729 | $1400 | (17-Dec-90 SY.NY38/R) Winter along river (30x51cm-12x20in) s.d.76 |
| £1283 | $2400 | (4-Aug-90 LIT.L174) Yarmouth, Maine (76x43cm-30x17in) s.d.89 |

CHASE, John (1810-1879) British

£765	$1500	(21-Nov-90 NA.BA70) Escena de pueblo (57x75cm-22x30in) s.d.1878
£400	*$692*	*(20-May-91 PH151) Figures in interior (70x99cm-28x39in) W/C*
£400	*$692*	*(20-May-91 PH150) Hall of Justice, Courtrai, Belgium (70x99cm-28x39in) s.i.verso W/C*

CHASE, William Merritt (1849-1916) American

£3125	$5250	(28-Apr-91 HG.C35) Cow at barn door (51x41cm-20x16in) s.init.d.1869
£4469	$8000	(14-Mar-91 CH.NY56/R) Head of girl (20x15cm-8x6in) s.
£7813	$15000	(30-Nov-90 CH.NY51/R) Portrait of German boy (46x38cm-18x15in) board
£9249	$16000	(23-May-91 SY.NY40/R) Lady at window - portrait study of Madame E.H. Bensel (51x41cm-20x16in) bears sig.
£11640	$22000	(26-Sep-90 SY.NY142/R) Portrait of lady with rose (122x91cm-48x36in) s.
£12291	$22000	(12-Apr-91 SY.NY47/R) Landscape with sheep (92x122cm-36x48in) s.
£14451	$25000	(23-May-91 SY.NY45/R) Little red bowl - still life (76x51cm-30x20in) s. board
£17188	$33000	(29-Nov-90 SY.NY65/R) A Gypsy swell - a Spanish Gypsy (51x41cm-20x16in) s. s.d.1905verso
£18878	$37189	(14-Nov-90 FB.P295/R) La belle Munichoise (70x54cm-28x21in) s.d.1873 (F.FR 185000)
£24566	$42500	(23-May-91 SY.NY53/R) Shinnecock landscape (27x32cm-11x13in) s. panel
£25140	$45000	(12-Apr-91 SY.NY71/R) Ponte Vecchio (22x31cm-9x12in) s. panel
£69364	$120000	(22-May-91 CH.NY242/R) Child on a garden path (28x18cm-11x7in) s. panel
£135417	$260000	(30-Nov-90 CH.NY102/R) Shinnecock Hills (45x61cm-18x24in) s.i.d.1891 panel
£12717	*$22000*	*(22-May-91 CH.NY139/R) Reclining nude (28x50cm-11x20in) s. pastel canvas*
£12821	*$25000*	*(26-Oct-90 S.W2601/R) Shinnecock landscape (53x64cm-21x25in) s. pastel paper laid on canvas*

CHASSARD, Marcel (20th C) French

| £597 | $1039 | (31-Mar-91 FE.P116) Renarde et petite merle (65x50cm-26x20in) s. (F.FR 6000) |

CHASSELAT, Pierre (1753-1814) French

| *£854* | *$1401* | *(19-Jun-91 LC.P27/R) Charles Cosse-Brissac, Comte de Cosse (7cm-3ins circular) min.s. (F.FR 8500)* |

CHASSERIAU, Theodore (1819-1856) French

£128205	$250000	(23-Oct-90 SY.NY38/R) Deux jeunes de Constantine bercant un enfant (57x47cm-22x19in) s.d.1851
£356426	$573845	(26-Jun-91 CB.P75/R) Odalisque couchee (210x340cm-83x134in) s.d.1853 panel (F.FR 3550000)
£2261	*$4386*	*(8-Dec-90 SY.MO400/R) Etude pour une jeune femme assise (21x13cm-8x5in) pencil pen (F.FR 22000)*

CHASSERIAU, Theodore (attrib) (1819-1856) French
£571 $1109   (8-Dec-90 GAB.G2172) Portrait de jeune femme (77x62cm-30x24in) i.
     stretcher (S.FR 1400)
£3043 $6024   (30-Jan-91 APT.P296/R) La femme du desert (134x111cm-53x44in)
     (F.FR 30000)

CHASTEL, Roger (1897-?) French
£3916 $7244   (4-Mar-91 ARC.P105/R) La petite fille en rose (130x81cm-51x32in) s.
     (F.FR 39000)
£2488   *$4328*   *(25-Mar-91 PLF.P27/R) Les iris (116x89cm-46x35in) s.d.42 gouache oil*
     (F.FR 25000)

CHATAUD, Marc-Alfred (1833-1908) French
£1868 $3250   (27-Mar-91 B.SF4074/R) Algerian horsemen in forest clearing
     (35x27cm-14x11in) s.
£4437 $8696   (24-Nov-90 SA.A638/R) Harem ladies on palace steps (52x38cm-20x15in) s.
     (DM 13000)
£13158 $25789   (20-Nov-90 APT.P258/R) Lallecture du Coran (55x46cm-22x18in) s.
     (F.FR 130000)

CHATEIGNON, Ernest (19th C) French
£808 $1592   (14-Nov-90 RAS.K198) Afternoon landscape in autumn (38x55cm-15x22in) s.
     (D.KR 9000)
£4913 $8500   (8-May-91 RO.BA12/R) En moisson (46x61cm-18x24in) s.

CHATELAIN, Jean Baptiste Claude (1710-1771) French
£900   *$1485*   *(11-Jul-91 S72/R) Italianate landscape (18x25cm-7x10in) pencil pen ink*
     wash

CHATELET, Claude Louis (1753-1794) French
£5102 $10051   (12-Nov-90 CSC.P6/R) Paysage a la cascade anime de promeneurs et
     lavandieres (36x48cm-14x19in) (F.FR 50000)
£15826 $28328   (9-Apr-91 APT.P53/R) Promeneurs dans un parc (49x70cm-19x28in) traces
     sig.d.1773 (F.FR 160000)
£27136 $44503   (21-Jun-91 SY.MO149/R) Paysages avec cascades (83x55cm-33x22in) pair
     (F.FR 270000)
£653   *$1071*   *(18-Jun-91 APT.P74) Vue de Tivoli (19x29cm-7x11in) indian ink wash*
     (F.FR 6500)
£1233   *$2393*   *(6-Dec-90 ARC.P30) Vue d'un parc avec escalier anime de personnages*
     (26x40cm-10x16in) W/C pen (F.FR 12000)
£3000   *$4890*   *(1-Jul-91 S105/R) Figures in landscape by Mount Etna (22x34cm-9x13in)*
     i.verso pen W/C
£3392   *$6580*   *(7-Dec-90 CN.P84/R) Vue d'une grotte, pres de l'abbaye de San Vito de*
     Polignano (16x24cm-6x9in) pen W/C (F.FR 33000)
£3500   *$6755*   *(11-Dec-90 C82/R) View of the Temples of Agrigenta (22x35cm-9x14in) i.*
     blk.chk.ink W/C
£3700   *$7178*   *(7-Dec-90 CN.P82/R) Vue prise dans la vallee de Caudium (21x36cm-8x14in)*
     pen W/C (F.FR 36000)

CHATELET, Claude Louis (circle) (1753-1794) French
£1316   *$2500*   *(8-Jan-91 SY.NY124) Acqueduct with figures in a sailboat and an*
     extensive landscape (54x42cm-21x17in) ink. W/C over blk.chk.

CHATILLON, Charles de (18th C) French
£3333 $6500   (11-Oct-90 SY.NY37/R) Figure at foot of overgrown staircase in
     Italianate park (77x65cm-30x26in) s.

CHATILLON, Pierre (1885-1974) Swiss
£516 $892   (22-May-91 GS.B2059) Still life with jug, bowl, teapot and fruit on
     cloth (47x62cm-19x24in) s. W/C over chl (S.FR 1300)
£520 $879   (1-May-91 GD.B150/R) Houses with snow at the Aare (37x44cm-15x17in) s.
     W/C (S.FR 1300)
£675 $1167   (22-May-91 GS.B2061) View of Bern with Herrengasse and Munster
     (44x36cm-17x14in) s.i.d.13 W/C over chl (S.FR 1700)
£794 $1373   (22-May-91 GS.B2060) Metzgergasse in Bern (44x58cm-17x23in) s.i.d.49 W/C
     over chl (S.FR 2000)

CHATTERTON, Clarence K (1880-1973) American
£872 $1500   (15-May-91 SY.NY186/R) Kennebunk houses (20x25cm-8x10in) s. canvasboard

CHAUDET, Antoine Denis (1763-1810) French
£1799   *$3489*   *(6-Dec-90 ARC.P28) Buste de Napoleon vu de profil (24cm-9ins circular)*
     pen (F.FR 17500)

CHAUDET, Jeanne Elisabeth (1767-1832) French
£15578 $25548   (17-Jun-91 ARC.P30/R) Le Roi de Rome enfant (92x72cm-36x28in)
     (F.FR 155000)

CHAUTARD, Victor Saint Just (19th C) French
£714 $1377   (14-Dec-90 ARC.P115) Portrait de jeune fille (61x50cm-24x20in) s.d.1881
     (F.FR 7000)

CHAUVEL, Theophile Narcisse (1831-1910) French
£548 $948   (26-May-91 ZZ.F10/R) Chemin de Saint-James a Saint Benoit
     (26x21cm-10x8in) s. d.1856 verso (F.FR 5500)

CHAUVEL, Theophile Narcisse (1831-1910) French-cont.

£548	$948	(26-May-91 ZZ.F8/R) La clairiere en foret (39x30cm-15x12in) s. board laid down on canvas (F.FR 5500)
£548	$948	(26-May-91 ZZ.F14/R) Lac de l'Ancien Parc de Neuilly (25x33cm-10x13in) s. d.1857 verso (F.FR 5500)
£645	$1109	(19-May-91 ZZ.F36/R) Chemin dans la foret de Barbizon (32x27cm-13x11in) d.1864 verso (F.FR 6500)
£694	$1194	(19-May-91 ZZ.F90/R) Jeune fille lisant sous les arbres (30x25cm-12x10in) s. (F.FR 7000)
£794	$1365	(19-May-91 ZZ.F28/R) Rocher a royat (47x33cm-19x13in) s. l.1853 verso (F.FR 8000)

CHAUVIN (?) ?

| £1484 | $2656 | (9-Apr-91 BG.P20) Composition abstraite (47x30cm-19x12in) s. chl. (F.FR 15000) |
| £1484 | $2656 | (9-Apr-91 BG.P21) Composition abstraite (47x30cm-19x12in) s. chl. (F.FR 15000) |

CHAUVIN, Jean (1889-1976) French

£552	$889	(25-Jun-91 BG.P19/R) Composition (49x32cm-19x13in) s. lead pencil (F.FR 5500)
£552	$889	(25-Jun-91 BG.P18/R) Composition (49x32cm-19x13in) s. lead pencil (F.FR 5500)
£683	$1338	(24-Nov-90 AB.L41/R) Composition abstraite (49x30cm-19x12in) s. chl (S.FR 1700)

CHAUVIN, Pierre Athanase (attrib) (1774-1832) French

| £2513 | $4121 | (21-Jun-91 SY.MO347/R) Paysage (32x24cm-13x9in) (F.FR 25000) |

CHAVANNES, Alfred (1836-1894) Swiss

| £996 | $1713 | (14-May-91 GF.L2489/R) Torrent in mountain landscape (33x46cm-13x18in) Indis.s. (S.FR 2500) |

CHAVAZ, Albert (1907-) Swiss

| £637 | $1243 | (24-Oct-90 GD.B217/R) Interieur (24x33cm-9x13in) tempera (S.FR 1600) |
| £5306 | $10294 | (8-Dec-90 GAB.G2448/R) Bouquet de fleurs (41x49cm-16x19in) board (S.FR 13000) |

CHAVET, Victor Joseph (1822-1906) French

| £800 | $1576 | (4-Oct-90 CSK194/R) An artist in his studio (23x16cm-9x6in) s. |

CHAVEZ, Gerardo (20th C?) French

| £713 | $1404 | (31-Oct-90 ZZ.F112/R) Le minotaure (38x47cm-15x19in) s. panel (F.FR 7000) |
| £649 | $1259 | (5-Dec-90 AB.S7050/R) Le guetteur de l'ancien chaos (130x97cm-51x38in) s.d.74 pastel canvas (S.KR 7000) |

CHAVEZ, Jose (?) Spanish

| £2972 | $5796 | (23-Oct-90 DUR.M49) En la taberna (50x38cm-20x15in) (S.P 550000) |

CHAVIGNAUD, Georges (1865-1944) Canadian

| £524 | $874 | (4-Jun-91 FB.M132) After the rain (61x84cm-24x33in) s. (C.D 1000) |

CHAVRIER, A (?) ?

| £1531 | $3015 | (16-Nov-90 LGB.P178/R) La voliere (100x64cm-39x25in) s. (F.FR 15000) |

CHAZALY (?) ?

| £804 | $1439 | (17-Mar-91 L.C8/R) Les plaisirs de la mer (46x55cm-18x22in) s. panel (F.FR 8000) |

CHEADLE, A (19th C) ?

| £650 | $1164 | (11-Mar-91 HS244) Wooded landscape with figures gathering sticks and river valley beyond (50x75cm-20x30in) s.d.1881 |

CHEADLE, Henry (1852-1910) British

| £1050 | $2058 | (13-Feb-91 S66/R) Scene by weir, near old bar house, Steventon Road, Ludlow, Salop (44x36cm-17x14in) s.d.1888 s.l.d.verso |

CHEASE, Stephen A (19th C) British

| £1359 | $2568 | (27-Sep-90 D.V164/R) Landscape with windmill on rock (51x68cm-20x27in) s.d.1877 (A.S 28000) |

CHECA Y SANZ, Ulpiano (1860-1916) Spanish

£1412	$2274	(27-Jun-91 EP.M38/R) Un rincon de Toledo (40x20cm-16x8in) s.d.1890 panel (S.P 260000)
£2322	$4481	(11-Dec-90 FER.M192/R) Aguadora veneciana (27x21cm-11x8in) s. panel (S.P 425000)
£1739	$3078	(3-Apr-91 ANS.M147/R) Roma incendiada (47x58cm-19x23in) s. W/C (S.P 320000)

CHELIUS, Adolf (1856-?) German

| £616 | $1103 | (12-Mar-91 FN.S2311/R) Hunter with dog in snowy wooded landscape (40x28cm-16x11in) s.i.d.1923 board (DM 1800) |
| £1565 | $2519 | (28-Jun-91 BM.B649/R) Cattle grazing with shepherd girl near house (63x51cm-25x20in) s.d.1899 (DM 4600) |

CHELMINSKI, Jan van (1851-1925) Polish
£900	$1773	(5-Oct-90 C91/R) Despatch from Napoleon (30x23cm-12x9in) s. panel
£1297	$2115	(10-Jun-91 W.T1417/R) Gallant and girl riding in woodlands (25x32cm-10x13in) s.d.1875 (C.D 2400)
£2200	$4334	(1-Nov-90 TE666/R) Afternoon ride (23x28cm-9x11in) s. panel
£5789	$11000	(27-Feb-91 SY.NY311/R) Moonlight drive (91x56cm-36x22in) s.

CHELMONSKI, Josef (1849-1914) Polish
| £2217 | $4212 | (2-Mar-91 PSA.W1) River landscape (19x33cm-7x13in) canvas on panel (P.Z 40000000) |

CHEMETOV, Boris (1908-1982) Russian
£507	$1004	(3-Feb-91 I.N44/R) Composition animee (38x55cm-15x22in) s. (F.FR 5000)
£515	$911	(7-Apr-91 I.N73) Personnages dans la ville (46x82cm-18x32in) s. (F.FR 5200)
£624	$1018	(16-Jun-91 LT.P72/R) Commposition au cercle rouge (46x38cm-18x15in) s. (F.FR 6200)
£655	$1067	(16-Jun-91 LT.P50/R) Le port (51x65cm-20x26in) s. (F.FR 6500)

CHEMIAKIN, Mikhail (1943-) Russian
£863	$1700	(13-Nov-90 CE.NY163/R) La divinite du silence (25x23cm-10x9in) mono. pen ink W/C
£1156	$2000	(22-May-91 D.NY117 a) Apocalypse (112x76cm-44x30in) s.d.1987 pastel
£1387	$2400	(22-May-91 D.NY118 a) Carcass (60x40cm-24x16in) s.d.1979 gouache
£1775	$3497	(6-Oct-90 GL.P110/R) Les courtisans (31x31cm-12x12in) s.mono.d.1977 W/C ink (F.FR 18000)
£6018	$11735	(11-Oct-90 QWA.P71/R) Carnaval de St Petersbourg (50x35cm-20x14in) s. mixed media (F.FR 60000)

CHEMIAKINE, Dorothee (20th C) ?
| £605 | $1179 | (28-Oct-90 M.V170) Le romantique (63x48cm-25x19in) s. mixed media (F.FR 6000) |

CHEMIELINSKI, W T (20th C) European
| £1488 | $2500 | (28-Apr-91 HG.C422) Troika scene (58x89cm-23x35in) s. |

CHEN, Hilo (20th C) American
£1786	$3500	(6-Nov-90 CE.NY311/R) Ssun bath 1-0 (92x92cm-36x36in) s.l. verso acrylic
£2041	$4000	(6-Nov-90 CE.NY310/R) Bath room 35 (142x154cm-56x61in) s.l.d.88 verso acrylic
£2179	$4250	(10-Oct-90 SY.NY363/R) Bathroom 20 (137x203cm-54x80in) s.verso

CHENARD-HUCHE, Georges (1864-1937) French
| £502 | $929 | (4-Mar-91 ARC.P109) Marine (35x41cm-14x16in) s. (F.FR 5000) |
| £665 | $1190 | (12-Mar-91 C.A38) Windmill and boat in landscape (46x38cm-18x15in) s.d.1906 (B.FR 40000) |

CHENEY, Russell (1881-1945) American
| £1131 | $1900 | (28-Apr-91 HG.C2) Coahulla valley (74x91cm-29x36in) s. |

CHERET, Jules (1836-1933) French
£1639	$3213	(11-Nov-90 ZZ.F43/R) Jeune femme lisant dans la campagne (22x15cm-9x6in) s. panel (F.FR 16000)
£2500	$4750	(14-Sep-90 DM.D2025/R) Harlequin figure (53x38cm-21x15in) s.
£3179	$5500	(21-May-91 CE.NY318/R) Harlequin (53x38cm-21x15in) s.
£3762	$6659	(6-Apr-91 GL.P39/R) Elegante au chapeau (74x43cm-29x17in) s. panel (F.FR 38000)
£3791	$7430	(11-Nov-90 ZZ.F8/R) Elegante au chapeau fleuri (20x25cm-8x10in) s. panel (F.FR 37000)
£5020	$9287	(6-Mar-91 APT.P88/R) Les trois grisettes (45x38cm-18x15in) s. (F.FR 50000)
£427	$854	(6-Feb-91 LD.P31) Elegante (34x18cm-13x7in) s. crayon htd.white chk. (F.FR 4200)
£600	$978	(5-Jul-91 QWA.P5/R) Femme de profil (40x24cm-16x9in) s. sanguinne htd.pastel (F.FR 6000)
£615	$1205	(7-Nov-90 APT.P460) Femme a la mandoline (39x23cm-15x9in) s. sanguinne (F.FR 6000)
£615	$1205	(7-Nov-90 APT.P462) Femme a la mandoline (32x23cm-13x9in) s. sanguinne oval (F.FR 6000)
£650	$1060	(5-Jul-91 QWA.P6/R) Coquette (40x24cm-16x9in) s. sanguinne (F.FR 6500)
£714	$1377	(14-Dec-90 ARC.P16) Femme a la mandoline (33x21cm-13x8in) s.d.1909 crayon htd white (F.FR 7000)
£820	$1607	(7-Nov-90 APT.P458) Jeune femme (37x24cm-15x9in) s. sanguinne oval (F.FR 8000)
£1537	$3012	(7-Nov-90 APT.P454) L'elegante au chapeau (38x24cm-15x9in) s. blk.crayon (F.FR 15000)
£2412	$3956	(19-Jun-91 JM.P76/R) Farandole de musiciens (50x33cm-20x13in) s.i.d.15/2/88 gouache blk.crayon (F.FR 24000)
£2439	$4878	(6-Feb-91 LD.P32/R) Farandole de polichinelles (84x42cm-33x17in) s. pastel (F.FR 24000)
£2591	$5183	(6-Feb-91 LD.P34/R) Femme a la mandoline (36x25cm-14x10in) pastel (F.FR 25500)
£4370	$8740	(6-Feb-91 LD.P35/R) La farandole (36x30cm-14x12in) s. pastel (F.FR 43000)
£4611	$9037	(7-Nov-90 APT.P457/R) Sur la plage (32x54cm-13x21in) s. pastel (F.FR 45000)

CHERET, Jules (1836-1933) French-cont.
£5020	$8082	(28-Jun-91 ARC.P9/R) La cantiniere (165x83cm-65x33in) s. W/C gouache (F.FR 50000)
£5755	$11165	(5-Dec-90 ZZ.F134/R) Elegante a l'eventail (79x45cm-31x18in) s. pastel canvas (F.FR 56000)
£6098	$12195	(6-Feb-91 LD.P29/R) Danseuse aux masques (62x35cm-24x14in) s. pastel canvas (F.FR 60000)
£6166	$11963	(5-Dec-90 ZZ.F132/R) Femme et fillette aux biscuits (98x50cm-39x20in) pastel canvas (F.FR 60000)
£7400	$14356	(5-Dec-90 ZZ.F131/R) Farandole (73x31cm-29x12in) s. pastel (F.FR 72000)
£10277	$19938	(5-Dec-90 ZZ.F133/R) Couple a la mandoline (78x48cm-31x19in) s. pastel (F.FR 100000)

CHERKES, Constantine (1919-) American
£1006	$1700	(1-May-91 B.SF5206/R) Tribal elders (51x61cm-20x24in) s.d.87

CHERON, Louis (1660-1715) French
£1900	$3135	(11-Jul-91 S5/R) Venus and Adonis (25cm-10ins circular) pen ink htd.white

CHERUBINI, Andrea (19th C) Italian
£2972	$5736	(12-Dec-90 WE.MU104/R) Still life with melons (62x74cm-24x29in) s.i.d.1873 (DM 8500)

CHERUBINI, Giuseppe (19/20th C) Italian
£1600	$2672	(4-Jun-91 SWS1673/R) Fishing village, Capri (25x44cm-10x17in) s.i.d.1885 panel
£2542	$4905	(12-Dec-90 F.M58) Ritratto di signora (211x103cm-83x41in) s. (I.L 5500000)

CHESTAKOVA, Vera (1912-) Russian
£500	$840	(26-Apr-91 ARC.P130/R) Les lilas (70x70cm-28x28in) s. (F.FR 5000)
£625	$1075	(15-May-91 AGB.P76/R) Roses de Crimee (38x45cm-15x18in) s. board (F.FR 6300)

CHESTER, G (1813-1897) British
£550	$946	(16-May-91 CSK77) Figure on coastal path (76x122cm-30x48in) s.d.1888

CHETWOOD-AIKEN, Walter (1866-c.1899) British
£43519	$83991	(12-Dec-90 CH.E147/R) Le Pardon de Saint Barbe au Faouet et La Fete du Saint Sacrement (188x115cm-74x45in) s. (E.P 47000)

CHEVAL, Bertrand (1932-1966) French
£1018	$2006	(31-Oct-91 ZZ.F100/R) Toi et Moi (126x130cm-50x51in) s.i. verso (F.FR 10000)

CHEVALIER, Adolf (1831-?) German
£949	$1547	(3-Jul-91 WE.MU67/R) Alpine village street (50x70cm-20x28in) s. (DM 2800)

CHEVALIER, Louis Auguste (19/20th C) French
£950	$1530	(27-Jun-91 CG23) Washerwomen on the banks of a river (27x41cm-11x16in) s.

CHEVALIER, Nicholas (1828-1902) Australian
£900	$1773	(15-Nov-90 CSK97/R) A Falconer (56x46cm-22x18in) s.
£1100	$2145	(24-Oct-90 S116/R) A capriccio mountain landscape (56x39cm-22x15in) s.d.1891 W/C traces pencil stopping out
£3952	$6679	(17-Apr-91 DS.W35) River scene with Maori Waka and figures (18x35cm-7x14in) s.d.1870 W/C (NZ.D 11500)
£4124	$6969	(17-Apr-91 DS.W34/R) Maori party on track above Frankton Arm, Queenstown (20x34cm-8x13in) s.d.1870 W/C (NZ.D 12000)

CHEVALIER, Peter (20th C) ?
£1385	$2341	(3-May-91 SA.A826/R) Evening light (63x92cm-25x36in) s.d.1987 (DM 4100)
£3468	$6000	(7-May-91 CE.NY228/R) Hund mit wagen (249x199cm-98x78in) s.d.83-84 verso
£4500	$7965	(21-Mar-91 C225/R) Madonna und Pferd (221x240cm-87x94in) s. i.d.'84 verso
£753	$1228	(14-Jun-91 L.K813) Untitled (43x61cm-17x24in) s.d.1983 W/C chk (DM 2200)

CHEVILLIARD, Vincent Jean Baptiste (1841-?) French
£1500	$2580	(17-May-91 C24/R) Sunday wig (19x14cm-7x6in) s. panel
£1086	$1835	(16-Apr-91 J.M26/R) The Spill (20x15cm-8x6in) s. W/C (A.D 2400)

CHEVIOT, Lilian (20th C) British
£1500	$2925	(15-Jan-91 C9/R) Silver Persian kittens playing (51x61cm-20x24in) s.
£3200	$6304	(13-Nov-90 SWS169/R) Last year he drew the harvest home today. Today he draws the guns of war (61x73cm-24x29in) both s. pair
£12000	$23400	(15-Jan-91 C110) Royal, tricolour working springer spaniel (76x63cm-30x25in) s.

CHEVOLLEAU, Jean (1924-) French
£1600	$2608	(3-Jul-91 PLF.P11/R) Arlequin a la mandoline (55x46cm-22x18in) s. i. verso (F.FR 16000)

CHEVOLLEAU, Jean (1924-) French-cont.
£2429	$4761	(25-Nov-90 ZZ.F34/R) La Rochelle aux trois tours (65x81cm-26x32in) s. (F.FR 24000)
£2974	$5799	(28-Oct-90 M.V81/R) Tolede (65x81cm-26x32in) s. (F.FR 29500)
£3010	$5930	(18-Nov-90 H.A102) Tombee du soir sur le port (60x75cm-24x30in) s. i. verso (F.FR 29500)
£5505	$10569	(2-Dec-90 M.V120/R) Les 3 tours de la Rochelle (73x100cm-29x39in) s. i. verso (F.FR 54000)
£6018	$11735	(11-Oct-90 QWA.P107/R) Tolede, au pont San Martin (162x113cm-64x44in) s. (F.FR 60000)

CHEYSSIAL, Georges Robert (1907-) French?
£860	$1686	(23-Nov-90 PLF.P43/R) Baigneuses (74x98cm-29x39in) s. (F.FR 8500)

CHIA, Sandro (1946-) Italian
£6192	$11950	(12-Dec-90 CH.AM444/R) La face (50x100cm-20x39in) s.d.87 s.i.verso (D.FL 20000)
£7274	$14256	(20-Nov-90 BR.M75/R) Figura in un interno (70x90cm-28x35in) s.d.1989 tempera (I.L 16000000)
£12724	$21503	(18-Apr-91 BU.S19/R) Via da chi non capisce (101x80cm-40x31in) s. paper (S.KR 135000)
£16327	$32000	(15-Feb-91 SY.NY196/R) Artist with bears (152x157cm-60x62in) s.d.84 acrylic oil pastel
£21684	$42500	(7-Nov-90 SY.NY369/R) The lightening (97x130cm-38x51in) s.d.1979-80 verso
£22140	$42509	(27-Nov-90 BU.S57/R) Composition with figures (101x72cm-40x28in) s.d.1985 cardboard (S.KR 240000)
£22189	$37500	(1-May-91 SY.NY167/R) Blue man with flowers (101x74cm-40x29in) s. board
£22959	$45000	(7-Nov-90 SY.NY384/R) Untitled (256x164cm-101x65in) s.d.82 cardboard laid down on canvas
£32544	$55000	(2-May-91 CH.NY214/R) If you are born to be hanged then you will never be drowned (183x152cm-72x60in) s.d.88
£32995	$65000	(4-Oct-90 SY.NY249/R) Intrigo controluce (99x200cm-39x79in) s.d.77 verso
£1231	$2400	(10-Oct-90 SY.NY460/R) Jeunes hommes forgerons (36x28cm-14x11in) s.d.84 pencil col.crayon ink
£1529	$2951	(16-Dec-90 GL.P157/R) Maternite (32x23cm-13x9in) s.d.1984 ball-pen (F.FR 15000)
£1664	$3211	(12-Dec-90 F.M88/R) Composizione (39x29cm-15x11in) s.d.1975 ink collage (I.L 3600000)
£2451	$4141	(18-Apr-91 BU.S22/R) David with the head of Goliath (30x23cm-12x9in) s.d.1985 W/C pencil (S.KR 26000)
£2775	$5383	(3-Dec-90 F.M333/R) Figure (29x39cm-11x15in) s.d.1984 mixed media cardboard (I.L 6000000)
£4315	$8500	(4-Oct-90 SY.NY267/R) Reclining man (48x63cm-19x25in) s.d.87 W/C
£4847	$9500	(6-Nov-90 CE.NY251/R) Untitled (50x40cm-20x16in) s.i.d.1981 oil col.pencils graphite
£6410	$12500	(10-Oct-90 SY.NY465/R) Junger Mann mit Baum (89x58cm-35x23in) s.d.83 mixed media
£7500	$14625	(18-Oct-90 C443/R) Untitled (64x47cm-25x19in) s.d.88 W/C chl
£7614	$15000	(4-Oct-90 SY.NY266/R) Seated figure (75x51cm-30x20in) s.d.87 oil pastel paperboard
£10000	$19500	(18-Oct-90 C444/R) Casa (74x90cm-29x35in) s.d.85 ink gouache W/C col.crayon cardboard
£15000	$29250	(18-Oct-90 S148/R) Untitled (87x80cm-34x31in) s.d.85 pastel gouache
£28000	$54600	(18-Oct-90 C456/R) Enfant (114x92cm-45x36in) s. oil chl
£32000	$62400	(18-Oct-90 C458/R) Untitled (152x138cm-60x54in) s.d.80 gouache paper on canvas

CHIARI, Giuseppe (1654-1740) Italian
£11765	$20000	(31-May-91 CH.NY81/R) Rebecca and Eliezer at the well (62x75cm-24x30in)

CHIARI, Giuseppe (circle) (1654-1740) Italian
£6311	$11297	(8-Apr-91 CH.R46/R) Ritratto di bambina con rose (60x48cm-24x19in) (I.L 14000000)

CHIARI, Tommaso (1665-1733) Italian
£1600	$2688	(26-Apr-91 NM.P38) Vierge a l'Enfant (105x83cm-41x33in) (F.FR 16000)

CHIAROTTINI, Francesco (1748-1796) Italian
£773	$1515	(19-Nov-90 CH.R252/R) Progetto per scenografia con obelisco ed edificio porticato con colonne (24x35cm-9x14in) pencil pen ink W/C (I.L 1700000)

CHIAVETTI, Antonio (20th C) Argentinian
£809	$1400	(8-May-91 RO.BA375) Vaso con flores (89x65cm-35x26in) s.

CHICHARRO Y AGUERA, Eduardo (1873-?) Spanish
£7500	$14775	(7-Oct-90 MMB337/R) Draped lady before ornamental screen (107x97cm-42x38in) s.

CHICHESTER, Cecil (20th C) American
£888	$1500	(1-May-91 B.SF5262/R) After storm (62x90cm-24x35in) s.d.1914

CHICHKINE, Ivan Ivanovitch see SHISHKIN, Ivan Ivanovich

CHICHKO, Sergui (1911-) ?

£796	$1385	(25-Mar-91 PLF.P30) Les iris jaunes (67x37cm-26x15in) s.d.89 l. verso canvas laid down on board (F.FR 8000)
£1417	$2777	(23-Nov-90 PLF.P44/R) Les roses the (50x59cm-20x23in) s.d.79 l. verso board (F.FR 14000)
£1417	$2777	(23-Nov-90 PLF.P49) L'etang au degel (53x66cm-21x26in) s.d.55 l. verso (F.FR 14000)
£1721	$3372	(23-Nov-90 PLF.P47) Vase de fleurs, Tchernobriozi (67x37cm-26x15in) s.d.1988 l. verso canvas laid down on board (F.FR 17000)
£1822	$3571	(23-Nov-90 PLF.P45/R) Le debut du printemps (60x79cm-24x31in) s.d.48 l. verso (F.FR 18000)
£2024	$3968	(23-Nov-90 PLF.P46/R) Rue Krechatik a Kiev (57x45cm-22x18in) s.d.51 l. verso (F.FR 20000)
£2126	$4166	(23-Nov-90 PLF.P48) Vase de fleurs et tasse blanche (65x75cm-26x30in) s.d.88 l. verso (F.FR 21000)
£2189	$3809	(25-Mar-91 PLF.P29/R) La pergola en bord de mer em Crimee (40x50cm-16x20in) s.d.56 l. verso canvas laid down on board (F.FR 22000)
£2388	$4155	(25-Mar-91 PLF.P28) A la ferme de kolkhoze (51x68cm-20x27in) s.d.60 l. verso (F.FR 24000)
£3184	$5540	(25-Mar-91 PLF.P31) Vase de roses (60x63cm-24x25in) s.d.79 l. verso (F.FR 32000)

CHIERICI, Gaetano (1838-1920) Italian

£11561	$20000	(22-May-91 SY.NY288/R) At monastery well (47x58cm-19x23in) s.d.1868 canvas on masonite
£25000	$46750	(29-Aug-90 MN165/R) Welcome alms (56x79cm-22x31in) s.d.1875
£74000	$121360	(20-Jun-91 B95/R) Feeding baby (56x80cm-22x31in) s.
£127168	$220000	(22-May-91 SY.NY61/R) Tarot cards (62x80cm-24x31in) s.d.1884

CHIESA, Pietro (1876-1959) Swiss

| £1796 | $3520 | (6-Nov-90 GF.L2576/R) Madonna (140x98cm-55x39in) s.d.42 chk (S.FR 4400) |
| £2857 | $5429 | (14-Sep-90 ZOF.Z1050/R) Maternita, figure of the fresco Vita Ticinese (50x34cm-20x13in) s. pastel (S.FR 7000) |

CHIGHINE, Alfredo (1914-1974) Italian

£1110	$2153	(3-Dec-90 F.M76) Composizione (29x24cm-11x9in) d.1974 tempera (I.L 2400000)
£6754	$13170	(24-Oct-90 F.M213/R) Composizione (46x63cm-18x25in) s.d.1973verso (I.L 15000000)
£6932	$13378	(13-Dec-90 F.M423/R) Composizione (40x30cm-16x12in) s.d.1964verso (I.L 15000000)
£9628	$15789	(20-Jun-91 F.M403/R) Composizione (56x68cm-22x27in) s.d.1959 panel (I.L 21000000)

CHIGOT, Eugene (1860-1927) French

£600	$1200	(8-Feb-91 T62) Lane in St. Tropez (51x61cm-20x24in) s.l.
£1025	$2008	(11-Nov-90 ZZ.F85/R) Calais, HJotel de Guise (40x33cm-16x13in) s. panel (F.FR 10000)
£1835	$3541	(16-Dec-90 T.B109) La gardienne d'oies (73x54cm-29x21in) s.d.1896 (F.FR 18000)

CHILDS, George (19th C) British

| £480 | $811 | (29-Apr-91 HS243/R) Children and dog playing beside rocky waterfall, trees and hills beyond (60x94cm-24x37in) W/C |

CHILLIDA, Eduardo (20th C) ?

£2552	$4899	(26-Nov-90 WK.M568/R) Female nude facing back (20x27cm-8x11in) s. pencil paper on board (DM 7400)
£2759	$5297	(26-Nov-90 WK.M569/R) Hand (12x18cm-5x7in) s.c.1966 (DM 8000)
£3333	$6500	(10-Oct-90 SY.NY527/R) Untitled (18x18cm-7x7in) s. Chinese ink
£5584	$11000	(4-Oct-90 SY.NY85/R) Untitled (33x29cm-13x11in) s. chinese ink
£5641	$11000	(10-Oct-90 SY.NY525/R) Untitled (58x43cm-23x17in) s.d.1967 graphite
£6599	$13000	(4-Oct-90 SY.NY86/R) Untitled (28x19cm-11x7in) s. chinese ink
£10169	$16983	(8-Jun-91 HN.H70/R) Composition (43x32cm-17x13in) s. collage ink brush (DM 30000)
£11429	$22171	(7-Dec-90 G.Z26/R) Composition (46x34cm-18x13in) s. collage (S.FR 28000)

CHILONE, Vincenzo (attrib) (1758-1839) Italian

| £7121 | $13459 | (28-Sep-90 CSC.P5/R) Vue du Rialto (34x55cm-13x22in) (F.FR 70000) |

CHIMENTI, Jacopo (style) (1554-1640) Italian

| £25694 | $49846 | (7-Dec-90 SY.MO19/R) Interieur de cuisine (102x153cm-40x60in) (F.FR 250000) |

CHINESE SCHOOL (?) Chinese

£14570	$28411	(9-Oct-90 CH.HK1339/R) View of Victoria, Hong Kong with hulk H.M.S. Princess Charlotte and American, British, Dutch and Dan (44x78cm-17x31in) l. (HK.D 220000)
£5400	$10368	(20-Feb-91 HAR442/R) Portrait of seated high priest holding sceptre (112x71cm-44x28in) s. W/C on silk
£14570	$28411	(9-Oct-90 CH.HK1254/R) Official's investiture. Procession (94x141cm-37x56in) bodycol pair c.1800 (HK.D 220000)

CHINESE SCHOOL, 19th C Chinese

£1987	$3874	(9-Oct-90 CH.HK1270/R) Extensive river landscape with figures crossing bridge to village with pagoda, family group to fore (76x112cm-30x44in) (HK.D 30000)
£2318	$4520	(9-Oct-90 CH.HK1321/R) Folly fort on Peiho River with junks (84x127cm-33x50in) (HK.D 35000)
£2649	$5166	(9-Oct-90 CH.HK1347/R) China tea clipper Northampton off Hong Kong flying signal flags of H.J.Q.F (44x58cm-17x23in) (HK.D 40000)
£2737	$5392	(30-Oct-90 BU.S308/R) Macao landscape (45x78cm-18x31in) (S.KR 30000)
£3974	$7748	(9-Oct-90 CH.HK1258/R) Elderly gentleman listening to flautist in interior (46x57cm-18x22in) (HK.D 60000)
£6623	$12914	(9-Oct-90 CH.HK1268/R) Mandarin's family in pavilions overlooking garden ponds (51x64cm-20x25in) pair (HK.D 100000)
£6623	$12914	(9-Oct-90 CH.HK1266/R) Ladies playing cards in pavilion with three children by side (51x64cm-20x25in) (HK.D 100000)
£7600	$14667	(12-Dec-90 BU.S145/R) Panoramic view of Wampoa harbour (44x77cm-17x30in) (S.KR 82000)
£7653	$15000	(24-Nov-90 RB.HY51/R) American clipper ship at anchor in Hong Kong harbour (74x102cm-29x40in)
£7755	$15278	(30-Oct-90 BU.S307/R) Sailship off Hong Kong (45x75cm-18x30in) (S.KR 85000)
£8712	$16814	(12-Dec-90 BU.S146/R) Panoramic view of Hong Kong harbour (44x77cm-17x30in) (S.KR 94000)
£12000	$23400	(24-Oct-90 S70/R) The Bund at Shanghai (47x105cm-19x41in)
£13500	$22140	(20-Jun-91 DLY201/R) American, European and Oriental shipping before factories (51x107cm-20x42in) linen
£19868	$38742	(9-Oct-90 CH.HK1438/R) View of Singapore from roads with merchant barque and merchant brig and other shipping (26x56cm-10x22in) (HK.D 300000)
£21192	$41325	(9-Oct-90 CH.HK1318/R) View of Whampoa Anchorage from Jardine Point on Dane's Island (44x76cm-17x30in) (HK.D 320000)
£24000	$46800	(24-Oct-90 S72/R) Singapore (44x77cm-17x30in) i.
£25166	$49073	(9-Oct-90 CH.HK1437/R) View of Singapore with American, French and British shipping (44x76cm-17x30in) i. (HK.D 380000)
£3974	$7748	(9-Oct-90 CH.HK1328/R) Foreign factories on waterfront at Canton (46x59cm-18x23in) bodycol (HK.D 60000)
£4305	$8394	(9-Oct-90 CH.HK1316/R) Temple of Mazhu in Macao. View of Howqua's garden in Canton with figures (35x48cm-14x19in) bodycol pair (HK.D 65000)
£5960	$11623	(9-Oct-90 CH.HK1348/R) United States naval corvette at anchor in Hong Kong, under plain sail and in storm (44x59cm-17x23in) bodycol three (HK.D 90000)
£7285	$14205	(9-Oct-90 CH.HK1360/R) Various stages in manufacture and selling of tea (15x27cm-6x11in) bodycol (HK.D 110000)

CHINI, Galileo (1873-1956) Italian

£15587	$25563	(20-Jun-91 F.M440/R) Festa a Bangkok (68x81cm-27x32in) (I.L 34000000)
£3377	$6585	(22-Oct-90 BR.M254/R) Il sogno di una notte di mezza estate (46x34cm-18x13in) s. s.d.1911/12verso W/C (I.L 7500000)

CHINNERY, George (1774-1852) British

£800	$1552	(6-Dec-90 CG38) Chinese fisherfolk (18x22cm-7x9in)
£12583	$24536	(9-Oct-90 CH.HK1277/R) Portrait of lady, seated and daughter, seated by side holding book (45x40cm-18x16in) (HK.D 190000)
£19868	$38742	(9-Oct-90 CH.HK1276/R) Chinese family by beached sampan in Macao landscape (19x26cm-7x10in) (HK.D 300000)
£464	$904	(9-Oct-90 CH.HK1304/R) View of St. Joseph's church from harbour, Macao (21x30cm-8x12in) i.num.63 pencil (HK.D 7000)
£500	$825	(9-Jul-91 C74) Cattle watering at river with cottage and mountains beyond (14x22cm-6x9in) pencil pen ink W/C
£530	$1033	(9-Oct-90 CH.HK1283/R) Macao - Guia Fort with Chapel of Nossa Senhora da Guia seen from below (18x27cm-7x11in) i.d.1834 num.5 pencil (HK.D 8000)
£662	$1291	(9-Oct-90 CH.HK1284/R) Junks at anchor. Three figure studies (18x25cm-7x10in) i.d.1832 pencil double-sided (HK.D 10000)
£700	$1155	(9-Jul-91 C73/R) Studies of young Tanka girl (20x16cm-8x6in) i.d.1839 pencil pen ink
£750	$1343	(9-Apr-91 C86/R) Study for portrait of mother and three children with draped column beyond (14x10cm-6x4in) pencil pen ink W/C
£800	$1576	(1-Nov-90 S28/R) Portrait of gentleman wearing high-collared coat (6x?cm-2x?in) min. gold frame oval
£900	$1485	(9-Jul-91 C76 a) Indian figures collecting water below bridge (17x25cm-7x10in) pen ink
£1000	$1650	(9-Jul-91 C76/R) Indian figures and cattle outside hut (17x25cm-7x10in) pen ink
£1060	$2066	(9-Oct-90 CH.HK1279/R) Macao - view across Praya Grande with Penha Hill in distance (20x27cm-8x11in) i.d.1837 num.16 (HK.D 16000)
£1126	$2195	(9-Oct-90 CH.HK1280/R) View of St. Joseph's church from quayside, Macao and three small figure studies (27x20cm-11x8in) d.1837 num.32 pencil (HK.D 17000)
£1457	$2841	(9-Oct-90 CH.HK1285/R) Street vendors outside church of St. Dominic, Macao (27x20cm-11x8in) i.d.1839 pencil (HK.D 22000)
£1457	$2841	(9-Oct-90 CH.HK1301/R) Studies of pigs, mother and child and others. Studies of street vendors, pig and others (20x28cm-8x11in) i.d.1836 pencil two sheetu (HK.D 22000)
£1474	$2800	(9-Jan-91 CH.NY55/R) Indian Temple, Macao (16x21cm-6x8in) bears sig.i. ink W/C over pencil

CHINNERY, George (1774-1852) British-cont.
£2318	$4520	(9-Oct-90 CH.HK1278/R) View of fortress by lake in Macao landscape with figure in foreground (7x12cm-3x5in) W/C (HK.D 35000)
£3800	$7410	(24-Oct-90 S74/R) Chinese fishermen on the shore (17x24cm-7x9in) i.d.1848 verso W/C over traces pencil
£4200	$8190	(24-Oct-90 S75/R) The corner of a Macao street (27x20cm-11x8in) init.d.1848 verso pen W/C over pencil
£4600	$7590	(11-Jul-91 S261/R) Portrait of Captain James Stewart Fraser (9x?cm-4x?in) min.i.d.1814verso oval ivory case
£8500	$14025	(9-Jul-91 C75/R) Mother with two children and dog (15x10cm-6x4in) pen ink W/C

CHINNERY, George (circle) (1774-1852) British
£1192	$2325	(9-Oct-90 CH.HK1312/R) Portrait of lady, standing wearing dress and wrap, by column (47x37cm-19x15in) on copper (HK.D 18000)
£2000	$3740	(3-Aug-90 PHM73) Portrait of gentleman wearing black coat, and woman seated (46x38cm-18x15in)

CHINNERY, George (school) (1774-1852) British
£3161	$5500	(27-Mar-91 B.SF4042/R) Ships at battle. Ships in harbour (36x28cm-14x11in) canvas laid down oval pair

CHINNERY, George (style) (1774-1852) British
£1325	$2583	(9-Oct-90 CH.HK1307/R) Figures gambling by boat house (24x28cm-9x11in) (HK.D 20000)
£3311	$6457	(9-Oct-90 CH.HK1309/R) Village scene near Canton with figures in rowing boats (51x64cm-20x25in) (HK.D 50000)

CHINTREUIL, Antoine (1816-1873) French
£552	$1022	(6-Mar-91 APT.P89) Baigneuse (27x22cm-11x9in) s. (F.FR 5500)
£900	$1512	(18-Jul-91 CSK56) Wooded river landscape with fishermen pulling in net in punt (30x46cm-12x18in) s.
£1633	$3216	(15-Oct-90 ARC.P63) Paysage (25x39cm-10x15in) s. panel (F.FR 16000)
£1658	$2968	(13-Mar-91 ARC.P34/R) Ruisseau courant sur des rochers au oin du bois d'Igny (24x31cm-9x12in) s. i. paper laid down on canvas (F.FR 16500)
£3568	$6850	(1-Dec-90 PER.M138/R) Le printemps a l'oree du bois (26x37cm-10x15in) s. panel (F.FR 35000)
£5500	$10560	(27-Nov-90 PH78/R) Harvesters in the field (42x60cm-17x24in) s.

CHIRIACKA, Ernest (1920-) American
£979	$1900	(5-Dec-90 D.NY59/R) Wounded Knee hostiles, South Dakota (61x91cm-24x36in) s.
£979	$1900	(5-Dec-90 D.NY61/R) Friend or foe (51x58cm-20x23in) i. masonite
£2320	$4500	(5-Dec-90 D.NY56/R) The Indian scout (41x48cm-16x19in) i.verso masonite

CHIRICO, Giorgio de (1888-1978) Italian
£5497	$10553	(27-Nov-90 SY.MI129/R) Costume pour une femme de la foule (34x25cm-13x10in) s. tempera paper (I.L 12000000)
£14943	$26000	(27-Mar-91 B.SF4151/R) Portrait of John Moxom (49x40cm-19x16in) s.i.d.1950
£17669	$30745	(26-Mar-91 F.M118/R) Contadina in costume (34x23cm-13x9in) s. board (I.L 39000000)
£18484	$35675	(12-Dec-90 F.M47/R) Piazza d'Italia (20x30cm-8x12in) tempera board (I.L 40000000)
£22843	$45000	(3-Oct-90 SY.NY113 b/R) Autoritratto (40x30cm-16x12in) s.i. canvasboard
£24365	$48000	(2-Oct-90 CH.NY143/R) Cavaliere e zebra sulla spiagia (33x41cm-13x16in) s. burlap
£25287	$44000	(27-Mar-91 B.SF4152/R) Autoritratto (49x40cm-19x16in)
£28902	$50000	(9-May-91 CH.NY256/R) Dopa la battaglia (27x36cm-11x14in) s. i. verso canvas laid down on board
£35533	$70000	(14-Nov-90 SY.NY430/R) Vita silente de frutta in un paese (40x50cm-16x20in) s.
£39648	$77313	(24-Oct-90 EA.M466/R) Fruit with cityscape in background (35x50cm-14x20in) s. (C.D 90000)
£40323	$70161	(26-Mar-91 F.M79/R) Allegoria con guerriero (35x55cm-14x22in) s. (I.L 89000000)
£42000	$81480	(4-Dec-90 C359/R) Lampo (40x49cm-16x19in) s.
£45925	$89554	(24-Oct-90 F.M246/R) Autoritratto (50x40cm-20x16in) s. (I.L 102000000)
£50761	$100000	(15-Nov-90 CH.NY280/R) Natura morta (40x50cm-16x20in) s.
£54913	$95000	(9-May-91 CH.NY276/R) Piazza d'Italia (30x40cm-12x16in) s.
£63452	$125000	(3-Oct-90 SY.NY112/R) Natura silente (46x55cm-18x22in) s. oil tempera
£67621	$121041	(9-Apr-91 F.R229/R) Uomo che regge un cavallo alla briglia (37x56cm-15x22in) s. panel (I.L 150000000)
£71060	$116539	(20-Jun-91 F.M496/R) Piazza d'Italia (40x50cm-16x20in) s.d.1955 (I.L 155000000)
£73604	$145000	(3-Oct-90 SY.NY121/R) Piazza d'Italia (40x50cm-16x20in) s. s.i.verso
£76248	$147158	(13-Dec-90 F.M422/R) Ritratto di Vivi Gioi (70x90cm-28x35in) s. (I.L 165000000)
£80000	$128800	(25-Jun-91 C183/R) Piazza d'Italia (51x61cm-20x24in) s.
£86294	$170000	(15-Nov-90 CH.NY277/R) Natura morta (62x49cm-24x19in) s.d.1915
£112701	$201736	(9-Apr-91 F.R218/R) Cavalli antichi (80x60cm-31x24in) s. (I.L 250000000)
£121827	$240000	(3-Oct-90 SY.NY113/R) Natura morta con frutta e scultura. Self portrait (45x55cm-18x22in) s. oil tempera double-sided
£137755	$270000	(15-Feb-91 SY.NY45/R) Vita silente (46x63cm-18x25in) s.d.1923 tempera

CHIRICO, Giorgio de (1888-1978) Italian-cont.

£146574 $281422   (27-Nov-90 SY.MI207/R) Il Trovatore (50x40cm-20x16in) s.
     (I.L 320000000)

£154915 $263356   (28-May-91 SY.MI203/R) Gladiateurs a l'ecole (46x38cm-18x15in) s.
     s.i.verso (I.L 340000000)

£162437 $320000   (15-Nov-90 CH.NY249/R) La romana (72x55cm-28x22in) s.

£184843 $356747   (13-Dec-90 F.M438/R) Ettore e Andromaca (80x60cm-31x24in) s.
     s.i.d.1965verso (I.L 400000000)

£184971 $320000   (8-May-91 CH.NY47/R) Le Muse inquietanti (90x70cm-35x28in) s. i. verso

£269036 $530000   (14-Nov-90 SY.NY431/R) Cavalli in riva al mare (89x65cm-35x26in) s.

£867052 $1500000   (8-May-91 CH.NY22/R) Gli archeologi (146x114cm-57x45in) s.d.decembre
     1927

£3000   *$5850*   *(19-Oct-90 C190) Pala frenieze (16x12cm-6x5in) i. s.verso W/C pencil*
     board

£3606   *$6456*   *(9-Apr-91 F.R98/R) Figura di donna (15x11cm-6x4in) s. pencil*
     (I.L 8000000)

£3800   *$7410*   *(19-Oct-90 C158/R) Cavallo e cavaliere (24x16cm-9x6in) s.*
     s.i.d.1944verso crayon pencil W/C

£4959   *$8876*   *(9-Apr-91 F.R92/R) Cavallino (10x15cm-4x6in) s. graphite pastel*
     (I.L 11000000)

£6000   *$11700*   *(17-Oct-90 S185/R) Les bacchantes, costume design for Apollo*
     (32x15cm-13x6in) s.i. gouache pencil

£6000   *$11640*   *(4-Dec-90 C177/R) Etude pour Danae (14x21cm-6x8in) pen crayon*

£6500   *$12675*   *(19-Oct-90 C159/R) Cavallo e cavaliere (24x16cm-9x6in) s.*
     s.i.d.1944verso crayon pencil W/C

£8780   *$16945*   *(12-Dec-90 F.M3/R) Due cavalieri (20x25cm-8x10in) s. i.d.1967verso*
     pastel paper on cardboard (I.L 19000000)

£9645   *$19000*   *(3-Oct-90 SY.NY122/R) Centauro e donne. Figure drappeggiate. Toro.*
     Cavalieri. Cavaliere e toro (13x16cm-5x6in) s. pencil pen ink paper on
     board

£11820   *$23166*   *(20-Nov-90 BR.M97/R) Caricatura di De Pisis (14x18cm-6x7in) s.i.d.1916*
     mixed media (I.L 26000000)

£16948   *$32539*   *(27-Nov-90 SY.MI168/R) Uomo che abbevera il suo cavallo (24x33cm-9x13in)*
     s. gouache (I.L 37000000)

£200000   *$322000*   *(24-Jun-91 C30/R) Trophee (103x73cm-41x29in) s.d.1926 pastel*

CHITARIN, Traiano (1864-1935) Italian

£909 $1755   (12-Dec-90 N.M460/R) Houses by canal, possibly Venice (31x50cm-12x20in)
     s. canvas on board (DM 2600)

CHITTENDEN, Alice B (1860-1934) American

£2051 $4000   (10-Oct-90 B.SF500/R) Still life of lilacs and peonies (61x71cm-24x28in)
     s.

CHMIELINSKI, H T (?) ?

£672 $1344   (6-Feb-91 RAS.K82) Winter's day in an East European town
     (60x80cm-24x31in) s. (D.KR 7500)

CHMIELINSKI, W T (19th C) Polish?

£1100 $2156   (14-Feb-91 CSK91/R) Soldiers in sleighs in a winter landscape
     (51x36cm-20x14in) s.

CHMIELINSKI, Wladyslaw (?) Polish

£616 $1035   (23-Apr-91 RAS.K218) Monumental building by water (35x51cm-14x20in) s.
     (D.KR 7000)

CHMIELOWSKI, M (20th C) Polish

£1594 $2741   (14-May-91 GF.L2607/R) Sailing boat in harbour (99x99cm-39x39in)
     s.d.1932 (S.FR 4000)

CHOCARNE-MOREAU, Paul Charles (1855-1931) French

£2610 $4829   (6-Mar-91 APT.P88 b) Repetition generale (100x81cm-39x32in) s.d.1925
     (F.FR 26000)

£3897 $7638   (19-Nov-90 ARC.P37/R) Enfants de choeur jouant au corquet
     (49x60cm-19x24in) s. (F.FR 38500)

£10246 $20082   (11-Nov-90 ZZ.F48/R) Gamins de Paris, place des Ternes (86x65cm-34x26in)
     s. (F.FR 100000)

£10251 $16812   (20-Jun-91 APT.P13/R) Fillettes dans un parc (176x109cm-69x43in)
     s.d.1893 (F.FR 102000)

£26633 $43678   (20-Jun-91 APT.P14/R) La fete au pain d'epices sur les grands boulevards
     a Paris (159x123cm-63x48in) s.d.98 (F.FR 265000)

CHODOWIECKI, Daniel (1726-1801) German

£7692   *$14923*   *(7-Dec-90 GB.B5443/R) Portrait of boy (55x43cm-22x17in) i. ochre*
     (DM 22000)

CHOUBRAC, Alfred (1853-1902) French

£12450 $21165   (27-May-91 APT.P257/R) Scene de harem (129x90cm-51x35in) s.d.1878
     (F.FR 125000)

CHOULTSE, Ivan Fedorovich (fl.1880-1920) Russian

£2703 $4405   (10-Jun-91 W.T1420/R) Starlit snow covered alping view (61x65cm-24x26in)
     s. (C.D 5000)

£4865 $7930   (10-Jun-91 W.T1419/R) Winter sulight on an Alpine road (64x81cm-25x32in)
     s.d.1885 (C.D 9000)

£5000 $8200   (19-Jun-91 S91/R) Moonlight on Mediterranean (54x65cm-21x26in) s.

CHOULTSE, Ivan Fedorovich (fl.1880-1920) Russian-cont.
£6358 $11000   (21-May-91 CE.NY297/R) Garden in bloom by lake (51x61cm-20x24in) s.

CHRETIEN, Rene Louis (1867-1942) French
£579 $1100   (14-Sep-90 S.BM125/R) Woman and child at a table in an interior
        (71x53cm-28x21in) s.
£2039 $3935   (14-Dec-90 ARC.P116/R) Nature morte a la soupiere et aux marrons
        (46x38cm-18x15in) s. (F.FR 20000)
£2191 $4273   (24-Oct-90 GD.B218/R) Still life with copper kettle and garlic
        (38x46cm-15x18in) s. (S.FR 5500)
£2994 $5030   (23-Apr-91 SY.AM73/R) Interior with mother and child (65x53cm-26x21in)
        s. (D.FL 10000)

CHRIST, Josef (1732-1788) German
£559 $1085   (7-Dec-90 GB.B5457/R) The Birth of Mary (13x9cm-5x4in) pen wash
*   htd.white pencil (DM 1600)*

CHRIST, Martin Alfred (1900-1979) Swiss
£1508 $2518   (5-Jun-91 SY.Z144/R) Rhine landscape near Basle (95x102cm-37x40in) s.
        (S.FR 3800)

CHRISTENSEN, Antonore (1849-1926) Danish
£623 $1171   (18-Sep-90 BU.K2/R) Bouquet of beechleaves and fruit blossom
        (28x34cm-11x13in) mono.d.1881 (D.KR 7000)
£673 $1326   (14-Nov-90 RAS.K279) Flowering cacti 1872 (29x38cm-11x15in) mono.i.
        (D.KR 7500)
£754 $1228   (13-Jun-91 RAS.V525) Lily, forget-me-nots and insects (47x37cm-19x15in)
        mono. (D.KR 8500)
£884 $1662   (10-Aug-90 RAS.V444) White roses and rowanberries (40x28cm-16x11in)
        mono.d.1921 (D.KR 10000)
£1268 $2155   (28-May-91 AB.S4748/R) Still life of spirea and Ibuebells
        (35x31cm-14x12in) s.d.1887 panel (S.KR 13500)
£2873 $5659   (14-Nov-90 RAS.K659/R) Peach coloured rose bush (47x38cm-19x15in)
        mono.d.1917 (D.KR 32000)

CHRISTENSEN, Dan (1942-?) American
£1429 $2800   (6-Nov-90 CE.NY183/R) Sea max (77x204cm-30x80in) acrylic
£3061 $6000   (7-Nov-90 SY.NY215/R) Cloudless sulphur (183x335cm-72x132in) s.i.d.July
        1968 verso acrylic

CHRISTENSEN, John (1896-1940) Danish
£543 $1049   (12-Dec-90 RAS.K251) The family (97x79cm-38x31in) s.d.32 (D.KR 6000)

CHRISTENSEN, Kay (1899-?) Danish
£537 $1052   (13-Feb-91 KH.K45) Ship on the fjord (54x65cm-21x26in) s. (D.KR 6000)
£622 $1225   (31-Oct-90 KH.K22) Girl in red room (50x65cm-20x26in) i.d.1961verso
        (D.KR 7000)
£718 $1415   (14-Nov-90 KH.K23) In love (50x65cm-20x26in) s.d.1955 (D.KR 8000)
£748 $1459   (10-Oct-90 RAS.K197) Picking fruit in the field (75x95cm-30x37in)
        s.d.1924 (D.KR 8500)
£979 $1840   (18-Sep-90 BU.K128/R) Still life of potted plant (72x51cm-28x20in)
        s.d.1919 (D.KR 11000)

CHRISTIANSEN, Christian (19th C) Scandinavian
£323 $645   (6-Feb-91 RAS.K524) View from Frederiksholm Canal (21x26cm-8x10in)
*   init.d.1828 pencil W/C (D.KR 3600)*

CHRISTIANSEN, Nils H (1876-1903) Swedish
£800 $1576   (1-Nov-90 TE620/R) Lake scene by moonlight (61x107cm-24x42in) s.
£1000 $1670   (4-Jun-91 SWS1875) Stag in winter. Stag at dusk (24x36cm-9x14in) s. pair
£2183 $4127   (27-Sep-90 D.V152/R) Deer in wooded lake landscape, winter
        (91x61cm-36x24in) s. (A.S 45000)

CHRISTIANSEN, Professor Hans (1866-1945) German
£1314 $2575   (22-Nov-90 L.K875) Rocky coastal landscape (51x41cm-20x16in) mono.
        (DM 3850)
£533 $955   (12-Apr-91 AW.H955/R) Palace twined with vine (25x34cm-10x13in) mono.
*   i.verso W/C paper on board (DM 1600)*

CHRISTIANSEN, Rasmus (1863-1940) Danish
£538 $1075   (6-Feb-91 RAS.K490/R) Self teaching school - artists in school
        (32x45cm-13x18in) (D.KR 6000)
£859 $1400   (5-Jul-91 S.W3066/R) Peasant with cow along path (119x155cm-47x61in)
        init.i.d.1891 canvas laid on board

CHRISTIANSEN, Soren (1858-1937) Danish
£962 $1723   (9-Apr-91 RAS.K2044) Children playing on ice (71x100cm-28x39in) mono.
        (D.KR 11000)

CHRISTIANSEN, Ursula Reuter (20th C) Danish
£440 $757   (15-May-91 RAS.K4) Burning mirror (98x64cm-39x25in) init.d.83 collage
*   mirror wool (D.KR 5000)*

CHRISTIE, C (20th C) ?
£500 $865   (22-May-91 CSK226) The evening story (61x81cm-24x32in) s.d.1909

CHRISTIE, James Elder (1847-1914) British

£508	$1000	(18-Nov-90 JRB.C50/R) Children playing ball (41x51cm-16x20in) s.
£2500	$4350	(27-Mar-91 PHS869/R) Fairy Knowe (84x109cm-33x43in) s. i.verso

CHRISTMANN, Gunther (1936-) German

£2056	$3351	(16-Jun-91 SY.ME85) Terra Mater (168x137cm-66x54in) s.d.1985 verso acrylic canvas (A.D 4400)

CHRISTO (1935-) Rumanian

£3223	$5253	(16-Jun-91 CC.P29/R) Volcan VI (47x121cm-19x48in) s.d.1959 mixed media panel (F.FR 32000)
£5405	$9351	(23-May-91 SY.AM298/R) Store fronts, empaquetages, volumen temporale, design of catalogue (27x27cm-11x11in) i. pencil set of 12 (D.FL 18000)
£7107	$14000	(5-Oct-90 CH.NY101/R) Abu Dhabi Mastaba - project for UAE (30x25cm-12x10in) s.i.d.1978 col crayon W/C graphite board
£7653	$15000	(8-Nov-90 CH.NY148/R) Otterlo Mastaba, Project for the Kroller-Muller Museum Holland 1975 (36x45cm-14x18in) s.i.d.1975 graphite chl.enamel col.crayons board
£9184	$18000	(7-Nov-90 SY.NY222/R) Packed coast - Project for Australia (70x55cm-28x22in) s.i.d.1969 collage on photograph
£10135	$17534	(25-May-91 N.M42/R) Untitled (64x38cm-25x15in) s.d.1960 collage mixed media (DM 30000)
£13776	$27000	(7-Nov-90 SY.NY326/R) Running fence - Project for Sonoma and Marin Counties California (60x71cm-24x28in) s.i.d.1975 graphite ink map collage paperboard
£14000	$22540	(27-Jun-91 S59/R) Packed coast, project for Little Bay near Sydney NSW Australia (71x56cm-28x22in) s.i.d.1969 crayons chk fabric string collage
£15000	$29250	(18-Oct-90 S134/R) Wrapped Reichstag, project for Berlin (56x71cm-22x28in) s.i.d.1977 fabric string col.crayon pencil card
£16000	$28320	(21-Mar-91 C241/R) Pont Neuf wrapped (56x71cm-22x28in) s. i.d.1977 collage col.crayon pencil string
£16751	$33000	(4-Oct-90 SY.NY138/R) Wrapped walk ways - two parks project - Sonsbeek, Holland and Veno Park, Tokoyo, Japan (72x61cm-28x24in) s.d.1970 graphite col.pencil collage
£18174	$35802	(30-Oct-90 F.R247/R) The wall, project for wrapped Roman Wall, Porta Pinciana (70x50cm-28x20in) s.d.1973 pastel graphite collage cotton thread (I.L 40000000)
£23985	$46052	(27-Nov-90 BU.S59/R) The Pont Neuf, wrapped - project for Paris (56x72cm-22x28in) s.d.1985 mixed media collage diptych (S.KR 260000)
£24112	$47500	(4-Oct-90 SY.NY130/R) Gates - project for Central Park, New York City (71x88cm-28x35in) s.d.1983 graphite pastel collage paperboard
£24235	$47500	(7-Nov-90 SY.NY193/R) Wrapped trees - Project for the avenue des Champs Elysees in Paris (56x71cm-22x28in) s.i.d.1969 polyethylene mixed media board
£25510	$50000	(7-Nov-90 SY.NY320/R) Running fence - Project for Sonoma and Marin County (56x164cm-22x65in) s.i.d.1976 mixed media paperboard four panels
£25510	$50000	(15-Feb-91 SY.NY167/R) Surrounded islands, project for Biscayne Bay, Greater Miami, Florida (71x87cm-28x34in) s.i.d.1981 collage paper fabric pastel graphite
£25510	$50000	(8-Nov-90 CH.NY337/R) Orange storefront s.d.65 mixed media sheet steel nails panel
£25862	$49655	(26-Nov-90 WK.M18/R) 1566 oil drums for Institut of Contemporary Art, Philadelphia (53x71cm-21x28in) s.i.d.1968 oil chk over pencil collage board (DM 75000)
£26531	$52000	(8-Nov-90 CH.NY170/R) Wrapped monument to Cristobal Colon, project for Barcelona 1976 (70x56cm-28x22in) s.i.d.1976 fabric col.chks.chl.graphite board
£28061	$55000	(7-Nov-90 SY.NY236/R) The Pont Neuf wrapped - Project for Paris (88x71cm-35x28in) s.i.d.1979 collage photo-collage paperboard
£32348	$62431	(13-Dec-90 F.M467/R) Wrapped Reichstag, project for West Berlin (76x58cm-30x23in) s.i.d.1972 pastel tempera string collage board (I.L 70000000)
£36290	$70766	(23-Oct-90 CSC.P60/R) Wrapped trees - Porject for the avenue and rond point Champs Elysees (69x54cm-27x21in) s.i.d.1969 crayon collage photo string plastic (F.FR 360000)
£36779	$62157	(21-Apr-91 P.V72/R) Fauteuil de bureau empaquete (75x62cm-30x24in) s.i.d.1966 mixed media collage canvas (F.FR 370000)
£40000	$64400	(27-Jun-91 S58/R) Yellow store front, project from Merrin Pant Co (127x92cm-50x36in) s.i.d.1965 enamel chl wax crayon collage
£41423	$80774	(23-Oct-90 F.M51/R) Wrapped trees project for Avenue des Champs Elysees (71x56cm-28x22in) s.i.d.1969 mixed media collage (I.L 92000000)
£43000	$76110	(21-Mar-91 S77/R) Wrapped reichstag - project for Berlin (109x245cm-43x96in) s.i.d.1988 collage i. pencil chl pastel pair
£44379	$75000	(2-May-91 CH.NY146/R) Surrounded islands - project for Biscayne Bay Greater Miami, Florida-Venetian Causeway (71x56cm-28x22in) s.d.1982 col.crayon graphite paper fabric board
£46000	$89700	(18-Oct-90 S131/R) Wrapped Reichstag, project for Berlin (99x99cm-39x39in) s.i.d.1986 one i. pencil chl pastel two
£66000	$128700	(18-Oct-90 C437/R) The umbrellas - joint project for Japan and USA (78x?cm-31x?in) s. i.d.1989 collage fabric col.crayons gouache
£71006	$120000	(2-May-91 CH.NY208/R) Umbrellas - project for Japan and Western USA (67x109cm-26x43in) s.d.1990 col.crayon fabric map board two panels
£73980	$145000	(14-Feb-91 CH.NY79/R) The umbrellas, project for Japan and Western USA (67x78cm-26x31in) col.crayons fabric board on panel

CHRISTO (1935-) Rumanian-cont.
£75000 $146250   *(18-Oct-90 C407/R) The umbrellas - joint project for Japan and USA*
        (97x77cm-38x30in) .i.d.1988 collage fabric col.crayon gouache
£85000 $164900   *(6-Dec-90 C552/R) Umbrellas - joint project for Japan and USA*
        (97x77cm-38x30in) s.d.1988 fabric col.crayon gouache pencil card

CHRISTOFFERSEN, Frede (1919-) Danish
£1246 $2342   (19-Sep-90 KH.K133) Evening, March-April 1968 (62x99cm-24x39in)
        init.d.68 (D.KR 14000)
£1404 $2386   (29-May-91 KH.K213/R) Evening (50x50cm-20x20in) init.d.70 (D.KR 16000)

CHRISTOFOROU, John (20th C) Australian
£3309 $6487   (13-Feb-91 KH.K46/R) Songe aux ailes noires (66x46cm-26x18in) s.
        (D.KR 37000)
£740 $1457   *(1-Oct-90 CC.P18) Personnage (30x26cm-12x10in) s.d.1979 gouache*
        (F.FR 7500)

CHRISTOPHE (?) ?
£1613 $3145   (28-Oct-90 R.P247) Lecon de tango (145x130cm-57x51in) s.d.89 acrylic
        (F.FR 16000)

CHRISTY, Howard Chandler (1873-1952) American
£900 $1800   (6-Feb-91 D.NY16) A portrait of Ellen Thompson Mason (168x122cm-66x48in)
        s.
£1222 $2371   (4-Dec-90 R.T144/R) Portrait of young woman seated in wicker chair
        (100x86cm-39x34in) s.d.1902 (C.D 2750)
£2296 $4455   (25-Aug-90 LIT.L27) Portrait of young man in riding costume
        (86x61cm-34x24in) s.d.1921
£3575 $6400   (11-Apr-91 FA.PH934/R) Blue water landscape (74x64cm-29x25in) s.i.
£4335 $7500   (21-May-91 CE.NY574/R) Entrance fountain (91x61cm-36x24in) s.i.
£7937 $15000   (27-Sep-90 CH.NY329/R) The edge of the lake (76x63cm-30x25in) s.d.1943
£15873 $30000   (27-Sep-90 CH.NY324/R) Bill of rights (52x101cm-20x40in) s.i.d.1942
£24566 $42500   (23-May-91 SY.NY95/R) Nude on bearskin rug (129x100cm-51x39in) s.
£11176 $19000   *(1-Jun-91 IH.NY60/R) Woman by automobile (99x74cm-39x29in) s.d.1919*
        gouache

CHU TEH CHUN (1922-) Chinese
£2915 $5217   (11-Mar-91 GL.P232) Clarte Nocturne II (81x65cm-32x26in) s.d.1984 i.
        verso (F.FR 29000)
£3670 $7083   (16-Dec-90 GL.P191/R) Le buisson ardent (65x92cm-26x36in) s. num.546
        verso (F.FR 36000)
£9174 $17615   (29-Nov-90 ZZ.F49/R) Composition s. d.1961 verso (F.FR 90000)
£11078 $18056   (16-Jun-91 CC.P36/R) Sans titre (195x244cm-77x96in) s. dyptich
        (F.FR 110000)

CHURBERG, Fanny Maria (1845-1892) Finnish
£12894 $25401   (17-Nov-90 BU.H22/R) Coastal landscape from Kimito (16x25cm-6x10in)
        s.d.79 panel (F.M 90000)

CHURCH, Frederic Edwin (1826-1900) American
£9827 $17000   (22-May-91 CH.NY89/R) Twilight on Isthmus of Panama (16x22cm-6x9in)
        init. s.i.d.1883 verso paper on canvas

CHURCH, Frederick Stuart (1842-1924) American
£781 $1500   (18-Aug-90 S.BM339/R) Springtime - portrait of young girl on pony
        (117x112cm-46x44in) s.d.1916
£2000 $3900   (21-Oct-90 HG.C56) Girl and flamingos (51x69cm-20x27in) s.d.1916
£635 $1200   *(25-Sep-90 CE.NY276/R) Pushing a hay cart into the yard*
        (32x49cm-13x19in) s. gouache en grisaille pen ink laid down board
£1176 $2000   *(1-Jun-91 IH.NY159/R) Tiger having eaten professor smoking*
        (38x58cm-15x23in) W/C

CHURCH, Katharine (1910-) British
£1650 $3102   (20-Sep-90 C58/R) Back of farm (61x72cm-24x28in) s.d.38

CHURCHILL, Sir Winston (1874-1965) British
£9500 $17575   (7-Mar-91 C14/R) Still life with red peppers and aubergines on tray
        (61x75cm-24x30in) init.
£11500 $22540   (8-Nov-90 C26/R) Classical landscape (61x74cm-24x29in) init.
£18000 $35280   (7-Nov-90 S127/R) The Thames from Taplow (75x63cm-30x25in) init.
£27000 $52920   (8-Nov-90 C25/R) Amsterdam harbour from Lord Beaverbrook's yacht
        (33x48cm-13x19in) init. board

CHURCHILL, William W (1858-1926) American
£573 $1100   (18-Aug-90 S.BM210) Canoeing in Rockies (91x114cm-36x45in) s.d.22
£3757 $6500   (10-May-91 S.BM110/R) Fishing at Jamaica Pond, Boston scene
        (56x66cm-22x26in) s.d.1919 i.verso

CHUTE, Desmond Macready (fl.1914) British
£1500 $2610   *(27-Mar-91 S52/R) Portrait of Ezra Pound (32x23cm-13x9in) init.i.d.1929*
        pencil

CHWALA, Adolf (1836-?) ?
£530 $1060   (9-Feb-91 BU.O31) Landscape (56x45cm-22x18in) s. oval (N.KR 6000)
£569 $1018   (9-Apr-91 RAS.K2046) Man fishing by moonlight (40x79cm-16x31in) s. panel
        (D.KR 6500)

CHWALA, Adolf (1836-?) ?-cont.
£894	$1771	(31-Jan-91 RAS.V471/R) Austrian mountain lake landscape with boats (70x106cm-28x42in) s. (D.KR 10000)
£1525	$2486	(3-Jul-91 WE.MU48/R) Summer (42x64cm-17x25in) s. (DM 4500)
£1734	$3000	(21-May-91 CE.NY226/R) Mother and children in field (42x63cm-17x25in) init.
£2122	$4160	(6-Nov-90 GF.L2149/R) Moonlit river landscape (61x90cm-24x35in) s. (S.FR 5200)
£2890	$5000	(21-May-91 CE.NY114/R) View of Konigisee, Baiun (62x105cm-24x41in) s.

CHWALA, Fritz (19/20th C) Austrian
£816	$1600	(6-Nov-90 GF.L2357/R) Mountainous lake landscape (68x106cm-27x42in) s. (S.FR 2000)

CIACELLI, Arturo (20th C) Italian
£2041	$4020	(12-Nov-90 YC.P48/R) Port a Cancale (65x81cm-26x32in) s. d.1928 verso (F.FR 20000)
£2041	$4020	(12-Nov-90 YC.P49) Village mediterraneen (66x83cm-26x33in) s. d.1928 verso board (F.FR 20000)
£6762	$12104	(9-Apr-91 F.R185/R) Natura morta con chitarra (76x78cm-30x31in) mono.d.916 s.d.verso (I.L 15000000)

CIAMPANTI, Ansano (16th C) Italian
£18421	$35000	(11-Jan-91 CH.NY39/R) Saint Julian murdering his parents in their sleep and Martyrdom ofSaint Catherine (34x47cm-13x19in) tempera panel

CIANI, Cesare (1854-1925) Italian
£1000	$1790	(12-Apr-91 BM.B574/R) View of Venice with scene of Doge's marriage with the sea on Grand Canal (101x74cm-40x29in) s. (DM 3000)
£4621	$8919	(11-Dec-90 CH.R132/R) Mercato a Firenze (13x20cm-5x8in) s. board (I.L 10000000)
£9092	$17820	(22-Nov-90 SY.MI78/R) 'In San Frediano' (24x42cm-9x17in) s.d.1912 panel (I.L 20000000)

CIAPPA, Mario (20th C) Italian
£1143	$2240	(6-Nov-90 GF.L2068/R) La Sibilla (104x77cm-41x30in) i. after Giovanni Francesco Romanelli (S.FR 2800)

CIARDI (19th C) Italian
£1815	$3538	(28-Oct-90 M.V62/R) Vue de Venise (33x46cm-13x18in) s. panel (F.FR 18000)

CIARDI, Beppe (1875-1932) Italian
£5545	$10702	(11-Dec-90 CH.R188/R) Dogana (15x22cm-6x9in) s.d.1931 panel (I.L 12000000)
£6470	$12486	(11-Dec-90 CH.R181/R) Canale e Venezia (39x30cm-15x12in) s. board (I.L 14000000)
£8183	$16038	(22-Nov-90 SY.MI68/R) Sera Piovosa (47x80cm-19x31in) s. (I.L 18000000)
£14000	$27000	(18-Oct-90 F.M35/R) Luce diffusa (49x59cm-19x23in) s.i.verso (I.L 31000000)
£16000	$31000	(18-Oct-90 F.M1/R) Tramonto a Venezia (50x62cm-20x24in) s.i.verso (I.L 35000000)
£17222	$29105	(16-Apr-91 CH.R200/R) Marina di Burano (65x90cm-26x35in) s. s.i.d.1928verso (I.L 38000000)
£19000	$37000	(18-Oct-90 F.M46/R) Case sulla laguna (68x45cm-27x18in) s. s.i.verso (I.L 42000000)

CIARDI, E (19th C) Italian
£703	$1300	(10-Mar-91 H.C23) Boy selling fruit (81x61cm-32x24in) after Murillo

CIARDI, Emma (1879-1933) Italian
£2773	$5351	(11-Dec-90 CH.R148) Lettura nel parco (22x18cm-9x7in) s. board (I.L 6000000)
£3284	$5484	(6-Jun-91 F.M88) San Giorgio, Venezia (13x20cm-5x8in) s. i.d.1914verso board (I.L 7200000)
£4332	$7235	(6-Jun-91 F.M127) La festa (50x40cm-20x16in) s. i.verso (I.L 9500000)

CIARDI, Guglielmo (attrib) (1842-1917) Italian
£502	$838	(6-Jun-91 F.M54) Baite (28x37cm-11x15in) s. board (I.L 1100000)

CIBOT, Edouard (1799-1877) French
£1733	$3327	(1-Dec-90 PER.M122/R) Cavaliers au pied du chateau (54x65cm-21x26in) s. (F.FR 17000)

CICERI, Eugene (1813-1890) French
£7862	$15253	(5-Dec-90 F.M128/R) Sulle rive della Senna (23x43cm-9x17in) s.d.49 panel (I.L 17000000)
£8000	$15360	(28-Nov-90 S251/R) Figures in river landscape (49x67cm-19x26in) s.d.58
£988	*$1700*	*(18-May-91 W.W7/R) Figures by the river (25x43cm-10x17in) s. W/C*
£1629	*$3210*	*(30-Oct-90 I.N167) Le berger. L'Orage (25x35cm-10x14in) both mono.d.1866 W/C pair (F.FR 16000)*

CICOGNARA, Antonio (fl.1480-1500) Italian
£105350	$202272	(29-Nov-90 F.M160/R) Madonna con il Bambino, Santa Caterina d'Alessandria e Santa Agnese (169x122cm-67x48in) s. (I.L 230000000)

CIESIELSKI, Ladislaus (19th C) Polish
£2429 $4761   (23-Nov-90 PLF.P50/R) Peintre a Charenton (46x32cm-18x13in) s.d.1873
                 (F.FR 24000)

CIESLEWICZ, Roman (1930-) Polish
*£2789 $4741   (2-Jun-91 GL.P30) Projet original pour l'affiche et le catalogue
                 Paris-Berlin (61x50cm-24x20in) s.d.1978 gouache (F.FR 28000)*

CIFRONDI, Antonio (attrib) (17/18th C) Italian
£1676 $3000   (16-Mar-91 W.W7/R) Knife grinder. Wine seller (58x46cm-23x18in) second
                 canvas mounted on board pair

CIFRONDI, Antonio (circle) (17/18th C) Italian
£1824 $3046   (4-Jun-91 CH.R179) Figura di campagnolo con cappello (70x61cm-28x24in)
                 (I.L 4000000)

CIGNANI, Carlo (1628-1719) Italian
*£893 $1714   (27-Nov-90 W.T1338/R) Two putti (17x13cm-7x5in) sanguine wash
                 (C.D 2000)*

CIGNANI, Carlo (after) (1628-1719) Italian
£2821 $5500   (10-Oct-90 CH.NY188/R) The triumph of love (94x138cm-37x54in)

CIGNANI, Carlo (attrib) (1628-1719) Italian
*£8183 $16038   (19-Nov-90 CH.R129/R) Nudo maschile con le braccia alzate
                 (43x29cm-17x11in) i. i.verso pencil (I.L 18000000)*

CIGNAROLI, Gianbettino (1706-1770) Italian
£15385 $30000   (10-Oct-90 CH.NY224/R) St Nicholas of Bari with two children
                 (72x101cm-28x40in) s.

CIGNAROLI, Vittorio Amedeo (1747-1793) Italian
£36368 $71281   (20-Nov-90 F.R213/R) Paesaggio con cavalieri. Paesaggio con pastori
                 (130x138cm-51x54in) pair (I.L 80000000)

CIGNAROLI, Vittorio Amedeo (attrib) (1747-1793) Italian
£10143 $18156   (8-Apr-91 F.M348 a/R) Il miracolo della mula. La raccolta dell'uva
                 (73x103cm-29x41in) (I.L 22500000)

CIGOLI, Ludovico see CARDI, Lodovico

CIKOVSKY, Niccolai (1894-1934) American
£640 $1100   (15-May-91 SY.NY211/R) Standing nude (50x41cm-20x16in) s.

CIMA da CONEGLIANO, Giovan Battista (circle) (?-1517) Italian
£15385 $30000   (10-Oct-90 CH.NY134/R) Madonna and Child before ledge with landscape
                 beyond (57x45cm-22x18in) panel

CIMAROLI, Giovanni Battista (17/18th C) Italian
£12758 $21688   (30-May-91 F.M89/R) Paesaggio fluviale con monaci e convento
                 (38x46cm-15x18in) (I.L 28000000)
£15385 $30000   (11-Oct-90 SY.NY48/R) Architectural capricci with ruins. Shepherds with
                 animals by water (62x71cm-24x28in) pair painted with studio

CIMAROLI, Giovanni Battista (attrib) (17/18th C) Italian
£60000 $101400   (16-Apr-91 PH37/R) Peasants waiting by roadside shrine, looking out
                 across river to drover approaching ford (90x122cm-35x48in)

CIMAROLI, Giovanni Battista (circle) (17/18th C) Italian
£1429 $2400   (17-Jul-91 SY.NY92/R) Classicia landscape with figures (51x76cm-20x30in)
£14000 $23660   (17-Apr-91 S173/R) Wooded river valley with figures crossing stone
                 bridge (81x115cm-32x45in) bears mono.

CIMAROLI, Giovanni Battista (studio) (17/18th C) Italian
£4508 $8069   (8-Apr-91 CH.R91/R) Paesaggio con cascatella e mandriani
                 (132x65cm-52x26in) (I.L 10000000)

CIMAROLI, Giovanni Battista (style) (17/18th C) Italian
£1500 $2445   (2-Jul-91 PH129/R) Mountainous landscape with shepherd
                 (68x101cm-27x40in)

CIMIOTTI, Gustave (1875-?) American
£588 $1100   (1-Aug-90 B.P82/R) Landscape near Manchester, Vermont (61x46cm-24x18in)
                 s.

CINTOLI, Claudio (20th C) Italian
£1908 $3759   (30-Oct-90 F.R59) Sosta nella baia (119x150cm-47x59in) s.d.1959verso
                 (I.L 4200000)

CIOCCHINI, Cleto (1899-1974) Argentinian
£609 $1200   (14-Nov-90 V.BA25) Ribera marplatense (30x40cm-12x16in)

CIOLINA, Tonio (1898-?) Swiss
£876 $1709   (24-Oct-90 GD.B219/R) Still life (33x55cm-13x22in) s.d.54 panel
                 (S.FR 2200)

CIOR, Pierre Charles (1769-?) French
£1143 $2251   (13-Nov-90 CH.G259) Portrait of young lady wearing white dress and blue
                      sash (7x?cm-3x?in) min.s. gilt-metal mount oval (S.FR 2800)

CIPOLLA, Fabio (1854-) Italian
£818 $1415   (21-May-91 DUR.M39/R) Enamorados en un camino (50x36cm-20x14in) W/C
                      (S.P 150000)

CIPPER, Giacomo Francesco (c.1670-1738) Italian
£1713 $3066   (8-Apr-91 F.M343/R) Testa di bambina (45x36cm-18x14in) (I.L 3800000)
£10910 $21384   (20-Nov-90 F.R134/R) Le bolle di sapone (88x120cm-35x47in)
                      (I.L 24000000)
£14000 $22820   (4-Jul-91 B114/R) An old pheasant and a maid at a table with bread and
                      eggs
£14000 $27020   (11-Dec-90 PH39/R) Peasant drinking from earthenware jug at table
                      (68x52cm-27x20in)
£18638 $36531   (20-Nov-90 F.R194/R) La venditrice di frutta. Giochi di bimbi
                      (74x79cm-29x31in) pair (I.L 41000000)
£22000 $42900   (26-Oct-90 C45/R) A peasant boy holding up a slice of melon in a
                      landscape (130x98cm-51x39in)

CIPPER, Giacomo Francesco (attrib) (c.1670-1738) Italian
£3600 $7020   (25-Oct-90 CSK69/R) Shepherd boy (132x95cm-52x37in)

CIPPER, Giacomo Francesco (style) (c.1670-1738) Italian
£1800 $2934   (4-Jul-91 C573) Young man, half length, writing (89x68cm-35x27in) canvas
                      on board
£2000 $4000   (7-Feb-91 CSK81/R) Man eating ham (55x43cm-22x17in) canvas on board
£2200 $4224   (29-Nov-90 CSK61/R) Boy holding hen with basket of eggs beside him
                      (74x62cm-29x24in)
£3400 $5882   (20-May-91 SWS190/R) Portrait of a man holding a bottle of wine
                      (120x95cm-47x37in) i.

CIPRIANI, Giovanni Battista (1727-1785) Italian
£750 $1238   (11-Jul-91 S56/R) Neptune and Amphitrite (18x29cm-7x11in) pen ink W/C
£800 $1432   (9-Apr-91 C39/R) Portrait of young girl (23x19cm-9x7in) pencil chk
£1100 $2123   (13-Dec-90 B50/R) Flight into Egypt (31x42cm-12x17in) pen wash

CIRINO, Antonio (1889-?) American
£1279 $2200   (15-May-91 SY.NY161/R) Lobstermen in Pigeon Cove harbour
                      (30x41cm-12x16in) s.
£1463 $2750   (11-Aug-90 COL.M181/R) Covered bridge, autumn (51x61cm-20x24in) s.
£1968 $3700   (11-Aug-90 COL.M176/R) Fisherman tending his gear (30x43cm-12x17in) s.
                      board
£5202 $9000   (10-May-91 S.BM120/R) Morning in Pigeon Cove, Rockport (64x76cm-25x30in)
                      s.
£5319 $10000   (11-Aug-90 COL.M175/R) Lobsterman's rondezvous (64x76cm-25x30in) s.

CIRY, Michel (1919-) French
£938 $1631   (26-Mar-91 JRL.S103) Boats at bay (20x29cm-8x11in) s. board (A.D 2100)
£1109 $2162   (26-Oct-90 PPB.P86/R) Bouquet au vase bleu (55x33cm-22x13in) s.d.1961
                      (F.FR 11000)
£2610 $4829   (6-Mar-91 APT.P92 b) Paysage d'Ile-de-France (106x106cm-42x42in) s.d.62
                      (F.FR 26000)
£3036 $5951   (25-Nov-90 ZZ.F35/R) Marie-Madeleine (60x38cm-24x15in) s. (F.FR 30000)
£3956 $7082   (8-Apr-91 CSC.P80) Pieta (73x54cm-29x21in) s.i.d.86 verso (F.FR 40000)
£3956 $7082   (8-Apr-91 CSC.P79) Le roi Saul (92x60cm-36x24in) s.d.85 i. verso
                      (F.FR 40000)
£761 $1500   (15-Nov-90 D.NY63/R) Eglise a Etroussat (72x105cm-28x41in) s.i.d.62
                      i.verso W/C
£1385 $2479   (8-Apr-91 CSC.P78) Hommage a Dunoyer de Segonzac (35x45cm-14x18in)
                      s.d.84 W/C ink (F.FR 14000)
£2077 $3718   (8-Apr-91 CSC.P76/R) Le parc a moutons, Normandie (75x72cm-30x28in)
                      s.d.87 W/C gouache (F.FR 21000)

CITROEN, Paul (1896-) German
£619 $1195   (12-Dec-90 CH.AM96) Bloemen (48x31cm-19x12in) s. s.i.stretcher
                      (D.FL 2000)
£1502 $2598   (22-May-91 CH.AM377/R) Loge (47x36cm-19x14in) s.i.d.1924 verso board
                      (D.FL 5000)
£2477 $4780   (13-Dec-90 SY.AM26/R) Hollandia (34x21cm-13x8in) s.d.1919 pencil
                      (D.FL 8000)

CITTADINI, Pier Francesco (attrib) (1616-1681) Italian
£5200 $8476   (4-Jul-91 C598/R) Portrait of young lady, wearing dress and elaborate
                      lace headdress (58x44cm-23x17in) oval
£32835 $54835   (4-Jun-91 CH.R142/R) Natura morta di frutta con cesto di fichi
                      (84x99cm-33x39in) (I.L 72000000)

CITTADINI, Pier Francesco (circle) (1616-1681) Italian
£2821 $5500   (10-Oct-91 CH.NY62/R) Portrait of young girl standing holding book
                      (101x78cm-40x31in)
£11500 $19895   (24-May-91 C51/R) Portrait of a boy, wearing a red tunic and a red cap,
                      a dagger on a table (64x50cm-25x20in)

CIUSSI, Carlo (1930-) Italian
£1365 $2580   (27-Sep-90 F.M126) 65-XI (98x110cm-39x43in) s.d.1965 (I.L 3000000)

CLACY, Ellen (19th C) British
£680 $1136   (24-Jul-91 CSK183) The state prisoner (61x91cm-24x36in) s.d.1876 i.
    label pencil W/C htd.white

CLAESSON, Stig (20th C) Scandinavian
£896 $1550   (22-May-91 BA.S332/R) Standing model (117x81cm-46x32in) s. (S.KR 9500)

CLAESZ, Anthony (16/17th C) Dutch
£2599 $5121   (12-Nov-90 CH.AM161) Parrot tulip (25x9cm-10x4in) black lead W/C
    (D.FL 8500)
£3058 $6024   (12-Nov-90 CH.AM160/R) Red and white tulip (24x9cm-9x4in) black lead W/C
    bodycol (D.FL 10000)

CLAESZ, Anthony I (1592-1635) Dutch
£1200 $1956   (4-Jul-91 B71/R) A variegated red and white parrot tulip (24x11cm-9x4in)
    W/C
£1700 $3281   (12-Dec-90 PH42/R) Study of tulip Gemarmerde van Kaer (26x11cm-10x4in)
    W/C
£1700 $3281   (12-Dec-90 PH43/R) Study of tulip Pochertje (25x11cm-10x4in) W/C

CLAESZ, Anthony II (attrib) (1616-1652) Dutch
£2400 $4608   (18-Feb-91 S251/R) Study of tulip (25x9cm-10x4in) W/C

CLAESZ, Pieter (1590-1661) Dutch
£24277 $42000   (10-May-91 S.BM4/R) Tempting repast (46x64cm-18x25in) mono.indis.d.16..
    panel
£32847 $64708   (30-Oct-90 BU.S238/R) Still life of wine and cooked meat
    (44x63cm-17x25in) mono.d.1650 panel (S.KR 360000)

CLAESZ, Pieter (style) (1590-1661) Dutch
£1100 $1793   (4-Jul-91 CSK179/R) Ham on pewter salver, glasses, grapes, jug, bread
    and lemon on draped table (41x63cm-16x25in)
£1400 $2688   (29-Nov-90 CSK236/R) Still life with roemer, ham and fruit on table
    (41x53cm-16x21in) panel

CLAEUW, Jacques Grief (circle) (?-1676) Dutch
£2400 $4056   (18-Apr-91 C9) A vanitas still life with a goblet and a skull crowned
    with laurel (76x75cm-30x30in) bears sig.d.1661

CLAEYS, Albert (1883-1967) Dutch
£1478 $2557   (25-May-91 KV.L41/R) Sun going down over Latem (48x60cm-19x24in) s.
    canvas on panel (B.FR 90000)
£2791 $4829   (25-May-91 KV.L459/R) Leie landscape (80x100cm-31x39in) s. (B.FR 170000)

CLAGUE, Richard (1816-1878) ?
£8500 $16575   (24-Oct-90 S12/R) Cows feeding near a river (39x55cm-15x22in) s.

CLAIR, Charles (19/20th C) French
£917 $1761   (2-Dec-90 M.V34) Paysage anime (49x65cm-19x26in) s. (F.FR 9000)
£2446 $4697   (30-Nov-90 CB.P102) La fenaison (50x66cm-20x26in) s. (F.FR 24000)
£2778 $4972   (13-Mar-91 GK.Z13/R) Three washerwomen in river landscape with outlines
    of town beyond (72x93cm-28x37in) s.indis.i.d.1880 (S.FR 7000)
£4077 $7829   (1-Dec-90 PER.M105/R) Dans la bergerie (61x81cm-24x32in) s. (F.FR 40000)

CLAIRE, Marie (?) Canadian
£661 $1289   (25-Oct-90 EA.M681) Voyageurs de nuit (61x91cm-24x36in) s.d.79 i.verso
    (C.D 1500)
£1322 $2577   (24-Oct-90 EA.M498/R) Journee de lessive a Pang (61x51cm-24x20in) s.d.89
    (C.D 3000)

CLAIRIN, Georges (1843-1919) French
£621 $1173   (27-Sep-90 BL.P65) Portrait de jeune femme (20x14cm-8x6in) s. panel
    (F.FR 6100)
£872 $1700   (26-Oct-90 SY.NY148/R) Portrait of Maurice Jambon (34x28cm-13x11in)
    i.d.1902 pencil
£4482 $7620   (27-May-91 APT.P226/R) Femmes Ouled-Nail (55x45cm-22x18in) st.sig. W/C
    gouache (F.FR 45000)

CLAIRIN, Pierre Eugene (1897-1980) French
£856 $1480   (12-May-91 T.B238) Paysage aux chasseurs (46x61cm-18x24in) s.
    (F.FR 8600)
£1194 $2066   (12-May-91 T.B239/R) Les toits de quimper s.d.71 (F.FR 12000)

CLAIRMONT, Philip (20th C) New Zealander
£619 $1045   (17-Apr-91 DS.W45) Self-portrait - Mururoa Mania on mind
    (39x23cm-15x9in) init. mixed media collage (NZ.D 1800)
£1375 $2323   (17-Apr-91 DS.W54) Self-portrait (60x45cm-24x18in) s.d.75 mixed media
    (NZ.D 4000)

CLAISSE, Genevieve (1935-) French
£2467 $4761   (15-Dec-90 D.P17/R) Unite jaune (92x73cm-36x29in) s.verso (F.FR 24200)

CLAPHAM, James T (19th C) British

£452	$850	(22-Sep-90 WOL.C116) Still life with grapes and peaches (30x41cm-12x16in) s. W/C
£1300	$2197	(29-Apr-91 HS235/R) Still life of pelargoniums, convoluulus and apple blossom and butterfly (43x40cm-17x16in) s. W/C

CLAPP, William H (1879-1954) Canadian

£1389	$2403	(6-May-91 SY.T4) Bathers. Sketch of boat being pulled to shore (30x23cm-12x9in) s. panel double-sided (C.D 2750)
£1531	$3000	(13-Feb-91 B.SF2047/R) Springtime landscape (46x38cm-18x15in) s.d.41 board
£3571	$7000	(13-Feb-91 B.SF2046/R) Oak tree in summer (38x46cm-15x18in) s.d.17/38
£6122	$12000	(13-Feb-91 B.SF2045/R) Spring flowers on flowering bank (38x46cm-15x18in) s.d.38 board

CLARE, George (19th C) British

£820	$1615	(13-Nov-90 SWS251) Still life of a bird's nest and blossom (17x22cm-7x9in) s. board
£980	$1735	(21-Mar-91 CSK189) Grapes and plums (23x33cm-9x13in) s.i. board
£1450	$2828	(17-Oct-90 PHG37/R) Still life of assorted roses in a basket (60x40cm-24x16in) s.
£1600	$3136	(22-Jan-91 PH52/R) Still lifes of primulas, blossom and bird's nest. Apples and other fruit (15x23cm-6x9in) s. pair
£1950	$3393	(27-Mar-91 RB621) Still life of flower peice with bird's nest (13x20cm-5x8in) s.
£2200	$4312	(13-Feb-91 S111/R) Roses in basket (61x51cm-24x20in) s.
£3400	$6698	(7-Oct-90 MMB241/R) Still life of apples, plums and strawberries on mossy bank (46x61cm-18x24in) s.

CLARE, O (19th C) British

£620	$1035	(7-Jun-91 BW378) Still life study of fruit on mossy ground (36x41cm-14x16in) s. board

CLARE, Oliver (19th C) British

£520	$1030	(1-Feb-91 PHE35) Still life of flowers in basket and bird's nest (22x29cm-9x11in)
£650	$1222	(20-Sep-90 SC4182) Still life of plums and strawberries (18x23cm-7x9in)
£650	$1268	(16-Jan-91 BT122/R) Still life of plums (23x18cm-9x7in) s.
£720	$1174	(14-Jun-91 DA743/R) Still life of fruit on mossy bank (30x23cm-12x9in) s.d.1894 artist's board
£760	$1269	(23-Jul-91 LW1909) Still life of grapes, peaches, plums and gooseberries on a mossy bank (33x41cm-13x16in) s.
£800	$1536	(16-Aug-90 SC4210/R) Still life of primroses and birds nest against mossy bank (28x23cm-11x9in) s.
£867	$1500	(21-May-91 CE.NY58/R) Plums and strawberries on mossy bank (25x30cm-10x12in) s.
£983	$1700	(10-May-91 S.BM52/R) Still life with wild flowers and bird's nest (20x25cm-8x10in) s.
£1200	$2124	(20-Mar-91 WI1182) Still life of fruit (33x25cm-13x10in) s. board
£1200	$2340	(17-Oct-90 PHG73/R) Still life of assorted fruit on a bank (14x20cm-6x8in) s. board pair
£1200	$2376	(28-Jan-91 HS277) Still life studies of mixed fruit on mossy banks (14x17cm-6x7in) s. board pair
£1250	$2213	(20-Mar-91 WI1180) Still life of mixed flowers against mossy bank (13x18cm-5x7in) s.d.97
£1300	$2457	(26-Sep-90 S170/R) Still life of mixed fruit (23x30cm-9x12in) s.d.90
£1300	$2535	(12-Oct-90 GSP446) Still life with plums, grapes and strawberries (25x20cm-10x8in) s.
£1300	$2145	(9-Jul-91 PH197) Still life of blossom, violets and bird's nest on grassy bank (20x25cm-8x10in) s.
£1350	$2660	(13-Nov-90 SWS262/R) Still life of a bird's nest, primulas and primroses on a mossy bank (25x20cm-10x8in) s.
£1350	$2619	(5-Dec-90 PHE7/R) A still life of rasberries, peaches and plums on a mossy bank (25x35cm-10x14in) s.
£1400	$2338	(5-Jun-91 PHK120) Still life of bird's nest. Still life of fruit by mossy bank (27x22cm-11x9in) s.d.94 board pair
£1500	$2955	(7-Oct-90 MMB323/R) Still lives of plums, grapes and strawberries (23x18cm-9x7in) s. pair
£1500	$2835	(26-Sep-90 S174/R) Still life of mixed fruit (30x25cm-12x10in) s. board
£1500	$2835	(26-Sep-90 S169/R) Still life of bird's nest, primroses and blossom (30x25cm-12x10in) s. board
£1580	$2750	(27-Mar-91 B.SF4179/R) Still life with grapes, peaches, plums and bird's nest (35x46cm-14x18in) s.
£1618	$2800	(21-May-91 CE.NY53/R) Mixed fruit on mossy bank (25x20cm-10x8in) s.
£1650	$2838	(14-May-91 SWS206/R) Still life of apples and plums. Still life of plums and gooseberries (24x19cm-9x7in) s. board pair
£1700	$2839	(7-Jun-91 BW402) Still life study of grapes, plum and other fruit on mossy ground (46x36cm-18x14in) s.
£1800	$3402	(26-Sep-90 S178/R) Still life of mixed fruit (41x35cm-16x14in) s.d.1919 canvas on board
£2100	$4137	(13-Nov-90 SWS263/R) Still life of strawberries, greengages and plums. Still life of plums, gooseberries and a peach (14x22cm-6x9in) both s. board pair
£2200	$4312	(13-Feb-91 S102/R) Mixed fruit (14x20cm-6x8in) s. board pair
£2300	$3864	(16-Jul-91 RG2654) Still life studies of fruit, flowers and bird's nest (25x33cm-10x13in) s. pair

CLARE, Oliver (19th C) British-cont.

£2500	$4900	(13-Feb-91 S117/R) Mixed fruit. Still life with Daphne (23x18cm-9x7in) s.d.95 pair
£2650	$5035	(1-Mar-91 BW444/R) Still life of fruit on mossy background. Still life of flowers (15x20cm-6x8in) s. pair
£2700	$4455	(11-Jul-91 GSP617) Still life of grapes, gooesberries and other fruit (28x23cm-11x9in) s. pair
£2900	$4988	(15-May-91 BT176/R) Still life of apples and rasberries. Still life of plums and a pear (23x33cm-9x13in) both s.d.1920 board pair
£3200	$5504	(14-Mar-91 SWS207/R) Still lifes of peaches and other fruit. Blossom and bird's nest (29x24cm-11x9in) s. pair
£3500	$6195	(21-Mar-91 CSK192/R) Fruit on a mossy bank. Crab apples and fruit on a mossy bank (20x28cm-8x11in) s. pair
£3500	$6860	(13-Feb-91 S113/R) Mixed fruits (23x31cm-9x12in) s. board pair
£3600	$7092	(1-Nov-90 CSK127/R) Still life of bird's nest and apple blossom. Still life of bird's nest and Hawthorn blossom on mossy (15x20cm-6x8in) s. pair
£4100	$6847	(22-Jul-91 SWS995/R) Still life of grapes, apples and strawberries. Still life of plumsand other fruit (35x29cm-14x11in) both s.d.1920 pair
£4469	$8000	(16-Mar-91 W.W69/R) Fruit still life ina natural setting (51x61cm-20x24in) s.
£15029	$26000	(12-May-91 H.C2/R) Still life with grapes, strawberries and other fruit on mossy ground (30x41cm-12x16in) s.d.1888

CLARE, Oliver (attrib) (19th C) British

| £500 | $805 | (24-Jun-91 HS192) Still life of mixed fruit against mossy bank (44x37cm-17x15in) bears sig. |

CLARE, Vincent (1855-1925) British

£550	$930	(3-May-91 PHE146) Still life of grapes and plums on mossy bank (17x22cm-7x9in) s.
£590	$1003	(29-May-91 PHC239) Plums and grapes on mossy bank (20x15cm-8x6in) s.
£700	$1372	(22-Jan-91 PH50) Still life of flowers (23x31cm-9x12in) s.
£780	$1318	(1-May-91 PHL225) Still life of basket of raspberries and grapes on mossy bank (22x30cm-9x12in) s.
£1000	$1700	(29-May-91 PHC179) Primroses, hawthorn and bird's nest on bank (25x20cm-10x8in) s.
£1100	$2079	(26-Sep-90 S173/R) Still life of blossom, primroses and bird's nest (25x20cm-10x8in) s.
£1600	$3152	(13-Nov-90 SWS261/R) Still life study of apples, plums, grapes and rasberries. Still lifeof peaches, grapes and a basket (22x30cm-9x12in) rries. Still
£1800	$3510	(18-Oct-90 SC3112/R) Primroses and a birds nest. Grapes and plums (21x19cm-8x7in) both s. pair
£2500	$4125	(11-Jul-91 CSK140) Primroses, blossom and bird's nest on mossy bank. Primroses and polyanthus on mossy bank (24x19cm-9x7in) s. board pair
£3200	$5440	(29-May-91 PHC151/R) Primroses and hawthorn on bank. Gooseberries and cherries (22x17cm-9x7in) s. pair
£3700	$6179	(5-Jun-91 S121/R) Still life with basket and fruit. Still life with basket and flowers (38x61cm-15x24in) s. pair
£4400	$7568	(14-May-91 SWS274/R) Chrysanthemums and primula. Plums and grapes in basket (34x43cm-13x17in) s. s.l.d.94verso pair

CLARENBACH, Max (1880-1952) German

£2282	$4450	(13-Oct-90 KRA.D185/R) Woman reading by window (40x36cm-16x14in) s.i.d.1926 (DM 6800)
£2365	$4611	(26-Oct-90 KM.K1135/R) View from Haus Clarenbach to Rhine meadows, Wittlaer early spring (50x60cm-20x24in) s. (DM 7000)
£2703	$5270	(26-Oct-90 KM.K1136/R) Frost and fog (60x70cm-24x28in) s. l.verso (DM 8000)
£2911	$4745	(15-Jun-91 L.K125/R) Lower Rhine winter landscape (38x48cm-15x19in) s. (DM 8500)
£3209	$5456	(27-May-91 L.K255/R) Lower Rhine landscape in early spring with view of Kaiserswerth (81x120cm-32x47in) s. (DM 9500)
£5068	$8615	(27-May-91 L.K256/R) River Erft landscape, winter (41x52cm-16x20in) s. (DM 15000)
£5442	$8762	(26-Jun-91 KM.K1414/R) Snowy river landscape with view of village (60x70cm-24x28in) s. (DM 16000)
£10909	$21491	(30-Oct-90 CH.AM209 a/R) Snowy river landscape with eel-fisher in rowing boat (95x125cm-37x49in) s. (D.FL 36000)

CLARK OF GREENOCK, William (1803-1883) British

| £6500 | $12675 | (18-Oct-90 CSK102/R) The barque 'Akbar' arriving off Mauritius on voyage from the Clyde (58x140cm-23x55in) s. |

CLARK, Albert (19th C) British

| £960 | $1843 | (18-Dec-90 HC254) Study of horse with harness and saddle (48x58cm-19x23in) indis.s.d. |
| £1400 | $2730 | (12-Oct-90 HC323) 'Cicero', study of race horse and jockey (48x61cm-19x24in) s.d.1909 |

CLARK, Albert (attrib) (19th C) British

| £1500 | $2505 | (22-Jul-91 SWS1016/R) Two dark by horses in a coach house (44x59cm-17x23in) |

CLARK, Alson Skinner (1876-1949) American
£510 $1000   (12-Feb-91 MOR.P73) Sky over Pacific, no.464 (18x23cm-7x9in) s. canvas on board
£3077 $6000   (10-Oct-90 B.SF520/R) Panama (53x63cm-21x25in) s.
£4103 $8000   (10-Oct-90 B.SF521/R) Spolato harbour (38x46cm-15x18in) s.
£4103 $8000   (10-Oct-90 B.SF528/R) Arroyo Seco (66x81cm-26x32in) s.
£4601 $7500   (11-Jun-91 MOR.P70 b) Women in courtyard - Granada (53x64cm-21x25in) s.
£4601 $7500   (11-Jun-91 MOR.P60 a) Landscape (46x56cm-18x22in) s.d.29

CLARK, C L (?) British
£2100 $4137   (13-Nov-90 SWS279/R) A gaslit dance floor, Highbury (63x102cm-25x40in) s.

CLARK, C Myron (20th C) American
£564 $1100   (20-Oct-90 W.¹ᴬ¹138/R) Sails in the sunset (51x71cm-20x28in) s.d.1917

CLARK, Dixon (19/20th C) British
£1300 $2496   (26-Nov-90 HS117/R) River landscape with cows and cottage beneath trees beyond (60x90cm-24x35in) s.
£2200 $4070   (7-Mar-91 CSK175/R) Evening calls the ploughman (81x104cm-32x41in) s. s.i.verso

CLARK, Eliot (1883-1980) American
£570 $1100   (10-Dec-90 BUR.F50) Palm Springs California (38x48cm-15x19in) s.
£509 $850   (9-Jun-91 LIT.L59 b) Manhattan skyline (15x25cm-6x10in) s. pastel

CLARK, Frederick Albert (19/20th C) British
£650 $1086   (22-Jul-91 SWS1017) Duke, a grey horse in a loose box (49x60cm-19x24in) s.d.1902

CLARK, J (?) British
£549 $900   (21-Jun-91 DM.D2042/R) Father and child by farmhouse (43x53cm-17x21in) s.

CLARK, J J (19th C) British
£659 $1100   (7-Jun-91 SY.NY184/R) Heeled for battle (36x28cm-14x11in) panel

CLARK, James (1858-1943) British
£550 $919   (22-Jul-91 SWS1025) A dappled grey mare in a landscape (49x60cm-19x24in)
£620 $1011   (14-Jun-91 T38) Horses and chickens by farmyard gate (41x61cm-16x24in) s.
£700 $1155   (11-Jul-91 CSK39/R) Bolting horse (51x76cm-20x30in) s.
£800 $1352   (30-Apr-91 OT472/R) Bay stallion saddled and standing in field (50x60cm-20x24in) s.d.99
£1100 $1815   (11-Jul-91 CSK125) Bay hunter in loose box (51x61cm-20x24in) s.i.
£1875 $3600   (26-Nov-90 S.SL467/R) Portraits of bay hunters (48x61cm-19x24in) s. pair

CLARK, Joseph (1834-1926) British
£3400 $5678   (5-Jun-91 S159/R) New pet (63x54cm-25x21in) s.d.1876
£5800 $11368   (13-Feb-91 S191/R) Blowing bubbles (46x56cm-18x22in) s.d.1889
£7000 $11410   (14-Jun-91 C335/R) The very image (88x67cm-35x26in) s.d.1884

CLARK, Octavius T (19th C) British?
£620 $1011   (2-Jul-91 SWS310) Somerset river landscape (49x74cm-19x29in) s.
£800 $1480   (7-Mar-91 CSK103) Figures boating in river landscape. River landscape with sheep (51x76cm-20x30in) s. pair

CLARK, Paraskeva (1898-1986) Canadian
£455 $782   (14-May-91 JOY.T4/R) Still with hyacinth (30x46cm-12x18in) s.d.'36 W/C (C.D 900)
£1047 $1749   (3-Jun-91 R.T187/R) Landscape near Canoe Lake Station (56x76cm-22x30in) s.d.56 W/C ink (C.D 2000)

CLARK, Russell (?) New Zealander?
£557 $1092   (7-Nov-90 DS.W85) Wanaka from Ruby Island (22x27cm-9x11in) s. W/C (NZ.D 1800)

CLARK, S (?) British
£1711 $3250   (27-Feb-91 SY.NY248/R) Horse in stall (51x61cm-20x24in) s.d.1868

CLARK, S J (19th C) British
£1350 $2619   (7-Dec-90 GSP446) Farmyard scenes with figures standing beside cattle, chickens and dogs (51x76cm-20x30in) s. pair
£1800 $2934   (13-Jun-91 CSK210/R) Horses, chickens and ducks in farmyard (76x63cm-30x25in) s.
£2400 $4056   (29-Apr-91 HS299/R) Farmyard with shire horses grazing, with chickens, ducks, cattle, sheep (70x90cm-28x35in) s.d.1912
£3500 $6895   (13-Nov-90 SWS304/R) Farmyard scenes (50x75cm-20x30in) one s. pair

CLARK, S Joseph (19th C) British
£825 $1600   (24-Aug-90 RB.HY112/R) John Tinde, General Smith (51x76cm-20x30in) s.d.71

CLARK, Thomas (1820-1876) British
£736 $1450   (14-Nov-90 RAS.K199) From the Scottish Highlands (52x61cm-20x24in) s.d.18 (D.KR 8200)

CLARK, Walter (1848-1917) American
£612	$1200	(11-Nov-90 LIT.L33) Corn stacks (36x51cm-14x20in) s.
£1250	$2500	(10-Feb-91 LIT.L26) On the Bronz River (41x61cm-16x24in) s.
£1276	$2500	(27-Jan-91 LIT.L10a) On Bronx river (41x61cm-16x24in) s. estate st.verso

CLARK, William (19th C) British
£6000	$10380	(22-May-91 S76/R) Dead calm (61x90cm-24x35in) canvas on board
£18500	$32005	(22-May-91 S67/R) Clipper John R Worcester (76x111cm-30x44in) s.

CLARK, William Albert (19/20th C) British
£750	$1448	(13-Dec-90 CSK206/R) Red Drake, bay hunter in landscape (51x61cm-20x24in) s.i.d.1916
£1400	$2702	(13-Dec-90 CSK352/R) Mr. Charles Henry Simmons in buggie drawn by carriage horses (51x61cm-20x24in) s.d.1917

CLARKE, James (19th C) British
£740	$1428	(12-Dec-90 SWS2132/R) Voltigeur with jockey up (35x46cm-14x18in) i.

CLARKE, John Clem (1936-) American
£4082	$8000	(6-Nov-90 CE.NY136/R) Saw mill (179x223cm-70x88in) s.i. verso

CLARKE, William Hanna (19/20th C) British
£3800	$6422	(2-May-91 CG474/R) Under cherry blossom (36x46cm-14x18in) s.d.1919

CLARY, Jean Eugene (1856-1930) French
£1735	$3417	(14-Nov-90 FB.P116/R) Bord de Seine (36x81cm-14x32in) s. (F.FR 17000)
£3000	$5910	(5-Oct-90 C73 a/R) Wooded river landscape (45x81cm-18x32in) s.

CLARY-BAROUX, Albert Adolphe (1865-1933) French
£3465	$6134	(7-Apr-91 I.N75/R) Le village (54x65cm-21x26in) s. (F.FR 35000)
£3770	$6484	(19-May-91 ZZ.F105/R) Peniche a qual sur le canal du Loing (50x61cm-20x24in) s. (F.FR 38000)
£4016	$7430	(6-Mar-91 APT.P89 b/R) Village en bord de riviere (54x73cm-21x29in) s.d.1906 (F.FR 40000)
£4893	$9443	(12-Dec-90 APT.P80/R) Paysan aux champs (51x73cm-20x29in) s. (F.FR 48000)
£4918	$9639	(11-Nov-90 ZZ.F77/R) Champ de coquelicots et village (54x66cm-21x26in) s. (F.FR 48000)
£6932	$13378	(12-Dec-90 APT.P79/R) Le Loing (50x61cm-20x24in) s. (F.FR 68000)

CLATER, Thomas (1789-1867) British
£1000	$1650	(9-Jul-91 PH70/R) Times (48x38cm-19x15in) s.i.d.1844 verso panel

CLAUBER, C (?) ?
£1489	$2814	(25-Sep-90 GM.B880) Vue de ville (50x70cm-20x28in) s. panel (B.FR 90000)

CLAUDE (17th C) French
£3800	$7296	(29-Nov-90 HB537/R) Philosophers and other figures in classical landscape with ruined temple (99x124cm-39x49in)

CLAUDE (style) (?) French
£1200	$2028	(18-Apr-91 CSK79) Adoration of Golden Calf (29x46cm-11x18in)

CLAUDE LORRAIN see GELLEE, Claude

CLAUDE, Eugene (1841-1923) French
£1800	$3186	(21-Mar-91 LC.P63/R) Nature morte aux poissons et a la fontaine de cuivre (225x142cm-89x56in) s.d.67 (F.FR 18000)
£2551	$5000	(21-Nov-90 NA.BA14/R) La corbeille de fleurs (89x69cm-35x27in) s.
£2800	$4732	(1-May-91 GD.B158/R) Still life of fruit and white rose in wine glass (45x36cm-18x14in) s.d.66 (S.FR 7000)
£3385	$6500	(27-Nov-90 PO.BA8) Naturaleza muerta (74x92cm-29x36in) s.d.1909

CLAUDIUS, Wilhelm (1854-1942) German
£805	$1570	(10-Oct-90 ZEL.L1420/R) Luneburger Heide landscape after thunderstorm with rainbows (60x87cm-24x34in) s. i.verso (DM 2400)
£12245	$19714	(28-Jun-91 BM.B774/R) Set table before North German farmhouse amongst trees with figures (83x103cm-33x41in) s.d.1922 (DM 36000)

CLAUDOT, Jean-Baptiste-Charles (1733-1805) French
£23116	$37910	(21-Jun-91 SY.MO159/R) Paysage avec ruines et personnages (98x134cm-39x53in) (F.FR 230000)

CLAUDOT, Jean-Baptiste-Charles (school) (1733-1805) French
£1832	$3242	(4-Apr-91 CK.P25) Couples de bergers passant sous des ruines avec leur troupeau (83x64cm-33x25in) (F.FR 18500)

CLAUS, Emile (1849-1924) Belgian
£903	$1562	(25-May-91 KV.L45) Two good friends (27x12cm-11x5in) paper on board (B.FR 55000)
£3284	$5681	(25-May-91 KV.L44/R) The village (38x60cm-15x24in) s. (B.FR 200000)
£7365	$12373	(23-Apr-91 C.A83/R) Haystacks beside the Leie (42x58cm-17x23in) s. (B.FR 450000)
£18288	$32735	(16-Mar-91 KV.L357 a/R) Pine trees in a landscape near Slough (43x49cm-17x19in) s.d.1915 (B.FR 1100000)

CLAUS, Emile (1849-1924) Belgian-cont.

£22000	$35420	(24-Jun-91 CSK37/R) Paysage sur La Lys, un matin de Mai (40x58cm-16x23in) s. d.1902verso
£28902	$50000	(10-May-91 S.W2525/R) Feeding her pet (74x91cm-29x36in) s. s.i.verso
£29460	$49493	(23-Apr-91 C.A78/R) Girl on the banks of the Leie (22x33cm-9x13in) s. (B.FR 1800000)
£45000	$87750	(16-Oct-90 C6/R) Un coin de mon jardin (60x74cm-24x29in) s. i.verso
£60976	$119512	(6-Nov-90 SY.AM202/R) October morning on river Leie (74x92cm-29x36in) s. (D.FL 200000)
£75000	$145500	(5-Dec-90 PH18/R) Vue de Londres (90x70cm-35x28in) s.d.1918
£9002	*$15123*	*(23-Apr-91 C.A264) Young girl (26x37cm-10x15in) s. W/C (B.FR 550000)*

CLAUS, Hugo (1929-) Belgian

£736	*$1237*	*(23-Apr-91 C.A341) Figure near a wood (40x34cm-16x13in) s. W/C (B.FR 45000)*

CLAUS, Hugo and DOTREMONT, Christian (20th C) Belgian

£1610	*$3107*	*(13-Dec-90 SY.AM332/R) Logogramme (46x61cm-18x24in) s. W/C (D.FL 5200)*

CLAUS, Josef (20th C) ?

£1196	$2069	(8-May-91 D.V44/R) Still life of flowers with plums (60x40cm-24x16in) s. (A.S 25000)

CLAUSADES, Pierre de (1910-1976) French

£650	$1099	(2-May-91 B50) Neige sur Notre-Dame (38x46cm-15x18in) s.i.d.1973 verso
£650	$1099	(2-May-91 B49/R) Venise, Ile St Georges (38x46cm-15x18in) s.i.d.'73 verso
£750	$1463	(15-Oct-90 PH32) Les bords du fleuve (45x80cm-18x31in) s.
£750	$1268	(2-May-91 B51/R) Neige au Pont Neuf, Paris (61x91cm-24x36in) s.i.d.'73 verso
£760	$1490	(20-Nov-90 RB670) En Camargue (46x79cm-18x31in) s.
£800	$1352	(2-May-91 B48) Beach in Normandy (53x65cm-21x26in) s.
£800	$1576	(13-Nov-90 SWS388/R) Cote de Bretagne (52x72cm-20x28in) s.
£900	$1755	(15-Oct-90 PH33) Peupliers sur la Loire (54x65cm-21x26in) s.
£1046	$1809	(26-May-91 ZZ.F78/R) Champs de bles en Sologne (54x65cm-21x26in) s. (F.FR 10500)
£1200	$2328	(6-Dec-90 CSK38/R) Paris en hiver (46x54cm-18x21in) s.
£2000	$3880	(6-Dec-90 CSK93/R) Au bord de la mer (50x61cm-20x24in) s.
£2000	$3720	(5-Sep-90 BT157/R) Calm lagoon (53x64cm-21x25in) s.
£2600	$4940	(13-Sep-90 GSP475) Landscape, believed to be Loire Valley (36x43cm-14x17in) s.

CLAUSELL, Joaquin (1886-1935) Mexican

£3571	$7000	(19-Nov-90 SY.NY119/R) Canada de Tlalpan (18x28cm-7x11in) s.backing board
£7143	$14000	(19-Nov-90 SY.NY118/R) Seascapes (11x21cm-4x8in) s.verso board pair
£8163	$16000	(20-Nov-90 CH.NY86/R) Paisaje (13x22cm-5x9in) s. board

CLAUSEN, C (19th C) Danish

£3191	*$6000*	*(7-Aug-90 RB.HY71/R) 'Tasso' of Newburyport, L.L.Condry Commander 1838 (51x71cm-20x28in) s. W/C*

CLAUSEN, Christian (1862-1911) Danish

£2491	$4683	(18-Sep-90 BU.K41/R) Young nude girl in the reeds (114x72cm-45x28in) mono. (D.KR 28000)

CLAUSEN, Franciska (20th C) Danish

£3591	$7074	(14-Nov-90 KH.K24/R) Composition with houses, Paris (29x16cm-11x6in) s.d.1925 tempera paper (D.KR 40000)
£7808	$13508	(23-May-91 SY.AM43/R) Composition (71x49cm-28x19in) s. (D.FL 26000)
£14085	$27465	(10-Oct-90 RAS.K172/R) Composition from boatdeck with rope, cogwheel and chains (35x27cm-14x11in) init.d.1924 (D.KR 160000)
£440	*$757*	*(15-May-91 RAS.K142) Abstract composition (26x19cm-10x7in) gouache (D.KR 6000)*
£554	*$1063*	*(27-Nov-90 AB.S4010/R) Cubist composition (30x18cm-12x7in) s.i.d.1925 pencil (S.KR 6000)*
£614	*$1044*	*(29-May-91 KH.K224) Composition (13x10cm-5x4in) crayon (D.KR 7000)*
£877	*$1491*	*(29-May-91 KH.K222/R) Model, Paris (23x31cm-9x12in) pencil (D.KR 10000)*
£1073	*$2104*	*(13-Feb-91 KH.K48/R) Composition (19x14cm-7x6in) gouache (D.KR 12000)*
£2105	*$3579*	*(29-May-91 KH.K220/R) Composition (23x31cm-9x12in) gouache (D.KR 24000)*
£2244	*$4421*	*(14-Nov-90 KH.K25/R) Composition with glove, Paris (24x15cm-9x6in) gouache (D.KR 25000)*
£2683	*$5259*	*(13-Feb-91 KH.K47/R) Composition, Paris (31x24cm-12x9in) gouache (D.KR 30000)*
£2847	*$5352*	*(19-Sep-90 KH.K81/R) Composition with glove (24x15cm-9x6in) gouache (D.KR 32000)*

CLAUSEN, Katharine Frances (attrib) (1886-1936) British

£900	$1764	(8-Nov-90 TL82/R) In the fields (33x25cm-13x10in)

CLAUSEN, Sir George (1852-1944) British

£850	$1658	(24-Oct-90 DR150/R) Plucking the chicken (43x33cm-17x13in) s.d.1904
£1800	$3528	(9-Nov-90 GSP646) Bust portrait of a Dutch girl (28x20cm-11x8in) s. i. label verso board
£8700	$14181	(11-Jun-91 ZZ.B419/R) A young farm boy resting (31x28cm-12x11in) s.
£125000	$245000	(7-Nov-90 S6/R) Schoolgirl (56x40cm-22x16in) s.d.1889 s.d.verso

CLAUSEN, Sir George (1852-1944) British-cont.

£380	$703	(6-Mar-91 ZZ.B135) Study of tree (36x25cm-14x10in) init. W/C sepia chk
£750	$1440	(26-Nov-90 SWS110/R) Thatched cottages and storm clouds (23x28cm-9x11in) s. W/C over chk
£814	$1376	(16-Apr-91 J.M114) Quintillus Villa (23x28cm-9x11in) s. W/C (A.D 1800)
£1050	$1974	(20-Sep-90 C187/R) Study for planting tree (18x19cm-7x7in) pen
£1050	$1974	(18-Sep-90 PH45/R) Country lane (30x24cm-12x9in) s. W/C gouache

CLAVE, Antoni (1913-) Spanish

£2000	$3220	(24-Jun-91 CSK198/R) Maquette de costume pour Ballabile, Ballet de Roland Petit (32x25cm-13x10in) d.1951 W/C htd.white pencil card
£2586	$4500	(27-Mar-91 B.SF4105/R) Young woman holding rooster (21x12cm-8x5in) s. board
£4356	$8450	(4-Dec-90 BA.S73/R) Harlequin playing guitar (28x16cm-11x6in) s. (S.KR 47000)
£8341	$16182	(4-Dec-90 BA.S74/R) Southern town scene (65x45cm-26x18in) s.d.45 (S.KR 90000)
£11089	$21623	(26-Oct-90 CC.P39/R) Hommage au papier froisse (76x56cm-30x22in) s.i.d.1977 verso acrylic gouache collage canvas (F.FR 110000)
£11952	$20319	(30-May-91 FB.P47/R) La fenetre (18x26cm-7x10in) s. board (F.FR 120000)
£13252	$25576	(16-Dec-90 GL.P62/R) La ville (50x61cm-20x24in) s. (F.FR 130000)
£13514	$23378	(22-May-91 CH.AM581/R) Still life with fish (56x76cm-22x30in) s.d.58 paper on canvas (D.FL 45000)
£19241	$34442	(13-Mar-91 FER.M225/R) Verde y negro (76x56cm-30x22in) s. board (S.P 3500000)
£19782	$35410	(9-Apr-91 BG.P16/R) Composition (56x76cm-22x30in) s. paper laid down on canvas (F.FR 200000)
£19833	$38476	(5-Dec-90 AB.S7051/R) Still life (54x65cm-21x26in) s.indist.d.46 (S.KR 214000)
£20000	$39000	(18-Oct-90 C319/R) Paysage (60x73cm-24x29in) s.d.44
£20408	$40000	(14-Feb-91 CH.NY70/R) Nature morte a la mandoline (55x47cm-22x19in) s.d.46
£21804	$37721	(21-May-91 DUR.M4/R) En la playa (19x24cm-7x9in) tablex (S.P 4000000)
£26351	$44797	(1-Jun-91 VG.B344/R) Passion noir (73x100cm-29x39in) s. panel (DM 78000)
£45685	$90000	(2-Oct-90 CH.NY191/R) Paysage (73x92cm-29x36in) s.
£52212	$100247	(19-Feb-91 DUR.M8) Paysage bleu (67x75cm-26x30in) (S.P 9500000)
£55668	$109109	(24-Nov-90 APT.P92/R) Arlequin (55x38cm-22x15in) s. board (F.FR 550000)
£55668	$109109	(24-Nov-90 APT.P91/R) Le roi (60x40cm-24x16in) s. paper laid down on panel (F.FR 550000)
£60606	$118788	(14-Feb-91 GL.P23/R) Roi a la pipe (72x72cm-28x28in) s. i.d.1957 verso oil materials hardboard (F.FR 600000)
£60914	$120000	(15-Nov-90 CH.NY298/R) Nature morte (60x73cm-24x29in) s.
£61162	$117431	(28-Nov-90 CSC.P83/R) La jeune fille et la cage (60x61cm-24x24in) s. (F.FR 600000)
£65413	$113164	(21-May-91 DUR.M8/R) Madre e hija (54x65cm-21x26in) tablex (S.P 12000000)
£76142	$150000	(15-Nov-90 CH.NY295/R) Femme peintre (74x60cm-29x24in) s. paper on board
£917	$1761	(29-Nov-90 QWA.P84) La bourbonnaise (22x18cm-9x7in) s. W/C gouache traces crayon (F.FR 9000)
£1224	$2376	(8-Dec-90 GAB.G2452/R) Portrait de femme au costume catalan (15x15cm-6x6in) s. W/C (S.FR 3000)
£1450	$2364	(3-Jul-91 CSC.P37) Maquette pour un decor de theatre (29x23cm-11x9in) s. gouache (F.FR 14500)
£1514	$2952	(24-Oct-90 GD.B1380/R) Composition with glove (63x77cm-25x30in) s. mixed media (S.FR 3800)
£1529	$2951	(12-Dec-90 APT.P7/R) Sans titre (21x17cm-8x7in) s. wash gouache (F.FR 15000)
£1631	$3148	(12-Dec-90 NM.P148) Composition (20x13cm-8x5in) s. i.d.1983 verso gouache acrylic board (F.FR 16000)
£3976	$7714	(6-Dec-90 D.V133/R) The present (39x31cm-15x12in) s.d.57 tempera gouache (A.S 80000)
£4000	$6440	(24-Jun-91 CSK197) Couple espagnol (35x27cm-14x11in) s.d.38 gouache collage
£4281	$8263	(12-Dec-90 NM.P147/R) Papier froisee en trompe-l'oeil (50x65cm-20x26in) s. i.d.1970 verso mixed media (F.FR 42000)
£4281	$8263	(16-Dec-90 GL.P60/R) Matador y Parajo (16x24cm-6x9in) s. gouache (F.FR 42000)
£4980	$8466	(2-Jun-91 GL.P209/R) Retour du Japon (49x33cm-19x13in) s.i.d.1987 ink collage (F.FR 50000)
£5179	$8805	(30-May-91 FB.P15/R) Sans titre (42x49cm-17x19in) s.i. mixed media collage (F.FR 52000)
£5743	$9936	(21-May-91 WK.M709 a/R) Untitled (49x38cm-19x15in) s.d.1957 mixed media collage (DM 17000)
£14000	$27300	(18-Oct-90 S70/R) Poisson (50x31cm-20x12in) s. W/C gouache Japan paint
£20387	$39144	(26-Nov-90 GL.P94/R) Guerrier a l'oeil rouge (76x56cm-30x22in) s.d.1972 mixed media collage (F.FR 200000)
£25458	$50153	(29-Oct-90 FB.P427R) Arlequin (61x45cm-24x18in) s. gouache Indian ink (F.FR 250000)
£28542	$54801	(26-Nov-90 GL.P93/R) Louis XV Roi (54x74cm-21x29in) s. oil gouache (F.FR 280000)
£31888	$62500	(15-Feb-91 SY.NY103/R) Seated man with bird cage (69x49cm-27x19in) s. gouache ink wash
£42843	$83543	(28-Oct-90 GL.P88/R) Sans titre (130x130cm-51x51in) s.d.1972 i. verso oil collage canvas (F.FR 425000)
£48000	$93600	(18-Oct-90 S79/R) Deux rois (73x103cm-29x41in) s. gouache

CLAVEL, Marie Joseph Leon see IWILL, Joseph

CLAVEL, Olivia (1955-) French
£916	$1805	(31-Oct-90 ZZ.F83/R) En ville (100x100cm-39x39in) s.d.1988 acrylic (F.FR 9000)
£1512	$2949	(28-Oct-90 R.P84 b/R) Sans titre (130x97cm-51x38in) s. acrylic (F.FR 15000)

CLAXTON, Marshall (1812-1881) British
£650	$1274	(20-Nov-90 PH130) Cupid and lovers (45x56cm-18x22in) s.d.1848 oval

CLAYDEN, James (20th C) Australian
£1495	$2437	(16-Jun-91 SY.ME23) Untitled (244x366cm-96x144in) s.d.1988 enamel board three panels (A.D 3200)

CLAYES, Berthe des (1877-1968) Canadian
£556	$1078	(3-Dec-90 R.T361/R) Red maples on river bank (30x46cm-12x18in) s. panel (C.D 1250)
£844	$1638	(4-Dec-90 P.Q91) Paysage d'ete (49x43cm-19x17in) s. board (C.D 1900)
£1010	$1737	(14-May-91 JOY.T90/R) Glory of Autumn (35x40cm-14x16in) s. panel (C.D 2000)
£2018	$3954	(20-Nov-90 JOY.T64/R) Winter scene with horse and sleigh (46x61cm-18x24in) s. (C.D 4600)
£5236	$8743	(4-Jun-91 FB.M51/R) Maple Sugar House, Rougemont (46x61cm-18x24in) s. (C.D 10000)
£556	$961	(6-May-91 SY.T132 a) Winter sleigh scene, Quebec (19x24cm-7x9in) s. pastel (C.D 1100)
£568	$1113	(5-Nov-90 FB.M105) Autumn, eastern townships (29x31cm-11x12in) s. pastel (C.D 1300)
£576	$962	(4-Jun-91 FB.M39) Returning home (35x46cm-14x18in) s. pastel (C.D 1100)
£960	$1651	(14-May-91 JOY.T10/R) Autumn ploughing (34x39cm-13x15in) s. col.chks. (C.D 1900)
£1485	$2910	(5-Nov-90 FB.M212/R) Early winter, St.Sauveur (36x36cm-14x14in) s. pastel (C.D 3400)

CLAYS, Paul Jean (1819-1900) Belgian
£818	$1375	(23-Apr-91 C.A337) Marine (24x34cm-9x13in) s. panel (B.FR 50000)
£1119	$2171	(5-Dec-90 DO.H2002/R) Fishing boats on beach (41x67cm-16x26in) s. (DM 3200)
£1156	$2000	(21-May-91 CE.NY258/R) On Scheldt (27x22cm-11x9in) s. panel
£2395	$4024	(23-Apr-91 SY.AM109) Vessels near coast (45x53cm-18x21in) s.d.70 (D.FL 8000)
£2500	$4900	(6-Nov-90 SY.AM239/R) Vessels near shore (32x51cm-13x20in) s. panel (D.FL 8200)
£6148	$12049	(11-Nov-90 ZZ.F14/R) Bateaux dans l'estuaire (59x89cm-23x35in) s. panel (F.FR 60000)

CLAYTON, Harold (1896-1979) British
£2083	$3500	(17-Jul-91 SY.NY341/R) Still life with iris, magnolia, tulips and carnations (61x51cm-24x20in) s.
£5800	$11426	(13-Nov-90 SWS450/R) Flowerpiece (44x39cm-17x15in) s.
£8200	$16154	(13-Nov-90 SWS451/R) Early summer flowers (44x49cm-17x19in) s.

CLAYTON, James Hughes (fl.1891-1929) British
£400	$708	(21-Mar-91 CSK24) A girl feeding chickens outside a cottage (36x48cm-14x19in) s. W/C bodycol.
£520	$848	(13-Jun-91 CSK147/R) Milkmaid beside seaside cottage (35x52cm-14x20in) s. pencil W/C bodycol
£580	$945	(2-Jul-91 SWS559) Feeding doves in country cottage (36x48cm-14x19in) s. W/C
£600	$1176	(22-Nov-90 CSK42) Fisherman's cottage on Penhryn Cliff, Cemeas Bay (27x49cm-11x19in) s. W/C htd white
£750	$1425	(15-Sep-90 ME171) Heavy seas at Porth Llan Lleiana, Cemaes Bay (25x53cm-10x21in) s. W/C
£900	$1728	(28-Nov-90 AH183) Afternoon conversation at Port Patrick Bay (25x69cm-10x27in) W/C
£980	$1735	(3-Apr-91 RBB950) St Ives with fishing vessels and quayside cottages (36x56cm-14x22in) s. W/C
£1700	$3315	(18-Oct-90 SC3053/R) A quiet cove, Anglesey (47x73cm-19x29in) s.
£1800	$3600	(8-Feb-91 C61) A girl feeding chickens by cottages. Fisherfolk by a beached rowing boat (20x41cm-8x16in) both s. W/C pair

CLEDAT DE LAVIGNERIE, Samuel (19th C) French
£1618	$2800	(21-May-91 CE.NY236/R) Still life with mixed fruit and flowers (81x99cm-32x39in) s.d.1891

CLEENEWERCK, Henry (19th C) French
£3500	$6825	(24-Oct-90 S124/R) A traveller in a landscape, Cuba (56x44cm-22x17in) s.d.1879

CLEMENS, Curt (1911-1947) Swedish
£376	$638	(28-May-91 AB.S5181/R) Rainy day - woman with umbrella by building (40x25cm-16x10in) s.d.32 W/C (S.KR 4000)

CLEMENS, Gustaf Adolf (1870-1918) Danish
£1246 $2342   (18-Sep-90 BU.K61/R) Two fishermen pulling in nets at sunset
       (42x63cm-17x25in) init. (D.KR 14000)

CLEMENS, Paul Lewis (1911-) American
£938 $1800   (17-Dec-90 SY.NY336/R) Self portrait (76x61cm-30x24in) s. masonite
£2299   *$4000*   *(27-Mar-91 B.SF4129/R) La voluptueuse (60x44cm-24x17in) s. pastel*

CLEMENT (?) ?
£4317   *$8374*   *(7-Dec-90 CH.MO108/R) Une vue de Porto Ferrajo (44x58cm-17x23in)*
       s.i.d.1815 lead pencil pen wash W/C (F.FR 42000)

CLEMENT, Charles (1889-) Swiss
£3469 $6731   (8-Dec-90 GAB.G2455/R) Paysage de campagne a la maisonnette
       (65x92cm-26x36in) s.d.1942 i. verso (S.FR 8500)
£571   *$1109*   *(8-Dec-90 GAB.G2454) Rovereaz (39x49cm-15x19in) s.i.d.1934 Indian ink*
       drawing wash (S.FR 1400)

CLEMENT, Felix Auguste (1826-1888) French
£1200 $2148   (14-Mar-91 B86/R) An Odalisque (37x28cm-15x11in) s.

CLEMENT-RENE, Paul Henri (20th C) French
£706   *$1376*   *(28-Oct-90 QWA.P96) Singe tenant un serpent (61x85cm-24x33in) s.*
       chl.chk. (F.FR 7000)

CLEMENT-SERVEAU see SERVEAU, Clement

CLEMENTE, Francesco (1952-) American?
£2520   *$4914*   *(26-Oct-90 CC.P122/R) Etude pour Yes - No (24x37cm-9x15in) pastel*
       ball-point pen (F.FR 25000)
£11243   *$19000*   *(2-May-91 CH.NY213/R) Untitled (67x48cm-26x19in) s.d.MCMLXXXVIII verso*
       col.chk
£20408   *$40000*   *(7-Nov-90 SY.NY355/R) Women and men no.3 (107x51cm-42x20in) W/C three*
       sheets paper
£56122   *$110000*   *(8-Nov-90 CH.NY421/R) Mother of letters (241x327cm-95x129in) i.d.'85*
       verso gouache paper linen

CLEMENTI, Maria Giovanna (attrib) (1690-1761) Italian
£4523 $7417   (21-Jun-91 SY.MO304/R) Scene de ballet (29x20cm-11x8in) copper
       (F.FR 45000)

CLEMINSON, Robert (19th C) British
£500 $860   (16-May-91 CSK147) Deer in lake landscape (76x127cm-30x50in) s.
£600 $1062   (5-Apr-91 PHE69) Day's bag (29x39cm-11x15in) s.
£700 $1365   (15-Jan-91 C114/R) Chamoise cocker spaniel with pheasant
       (61x46cm-24x18in) s.d.1868 board
£850 $1420   (4-Jun-91 SWS1844/R) Waiting for master (49x75cm-19x30in) s.
£850 $1437   (3-May-91 PHE101) Stag and hinds in the highlands (75x127cm-30x50in)
       s.d.1876
£950 $1587   (4-Jun-91 SWS1892/R) In Highlands (74x125cm-29x49in) s.
£1013 $1702   (27-Apr-91 SO.S303/R) Fox chasing duck (59x105cm-23x41in) s.
       (S.KR 10700)
£1100 $2167   (1-Nov-90 CSK117/R) Wounded stag (76x127cm-30x50in) s.d.1886
£1300 $2405   (6-Mar-91 SC4265/R) Retrievers with game (74x61cm-29x24in) s.
£2000 $3880   (3-Dec-90 SC4288/R) Spaniel with game (38x58cm-15x23in) s.
£2000 $3780   (26-Sep-90 S101/R) Putting up pheasant. Two spaniels (26x36cm-10x14in)
       s. one indist.d. pair
£2000 $3900   (11-Oct-90 CG183/R) A Llewellyn, Gordon and English Setter with the
       day's game (91x71cm-36x28in) s.d.1899

CLERC, David le (attrib) (1679-1738) Swiss
£1800   *$2970*   *(10-Jul-91 C23/R) A lady in low-cut embroidered pink dress*
       (10x?cm-4x?in) min. gilt metal frame rec.

CLERC, Pierre (20th C) French
£671 $1321   (1-Oct-90 CC.P150) Composition (45x45cm-18x18in) s. paper on canvas
       (F.FR 6800)
£5544 $10811   (26-Oct-90 CC.P109/R) Le taureau (100x100cm-39x39in) s.d.1977
       (F.FR 55000)
£994   *$1680*   *(16-Apr-91 I.N3) Composition (30x21cm-12x8in) s. gouache W/C*
       (F.FR 10000)

CLERC, Serge (1957-) French
£416   *$736*   *(6-Apr-91 CB.P211/R) Desperate times (33x38cm-13x15in) lead pencil*
       stumping (F.FR 4200)
£495   *$876*   *(6-Apr-91 CB.P215/R) Original de l'affiche de la vente (45x67cm-18x26in)*
       lead pencil col.gouache (F.FR 5000)
£495   *$876*   *(6-Apr-91 CB.P214) Uner soiree salle pleyel (29x39cm-11x15in)*
       col.gouache (F.FR 5000)
£545   *$964*   *(6-Apr-91 CB.P206) Les trois siffleurs (33x50cm-13x20in) Indian ink*
       (F.FR 5500)

CLERCK, Hendrick de (1570-1629) Flemish
£10949 $21569   (30-Oct-90 BU.S239/R) Adoration of the shepherds (106x113cm-42x44in) s.
       (S.KR 120000)
£19000 $30970   (3-Jul-91 S39/R) Adoration of shepherds (105x113cm-41x44in) s.

CLERCK, Hendrick de (after) (1570-1629) Flemish
£2441 $4150   (28-May-91 AB.S4749/R) Landscape with reclining nude woman
                  (36x53cm-14x21in) panel (S.KR 26000)

CLERCK, Hendrick de (attrib) (1570-1629) Flemish
£12000 $23160   (12-Dec-90 S132/R) Madonna and Child with St.Francis and St.James the
                    Greater (71x58cm-28x23in) panel

CLERCK, Hendrick de (style) (1570-1629) Flemish
£1220 $2341   (27-Nov-90 SY.AM3443/R) Adoration of the Shepherds (46x34cm-18x13in)
                  panel (D.FL 4000)
£3000 $4890   (4-Jul-91 C510) Adoration of Magi (145x105cm-57x41in)

CLERCK, Jan de (1881-1962) Belgian
£9288 $17926   (12-Dec-90 CH.AM336/R) Harbour of Zeebrugge, in winter (66x93cm-26x37in)
                   s. (D.FL 30000)
£35000 $68250   (16-Oct-90 C19/R) Le soir antique (37x100cm-15x39in) s. st.studio verso
                    pastel felt

CLERCQ, Alphonse de (1868-?) Belgian
£1637 $2750   (23-Apr-91 C.A386) Winter evening (70x125cm-28x49in) s. (B.FR 100000)

CLERCQ, Pieter Jan de (1891-1964) Belgian?
£762 $1494   (6-Nov-90 SY.AM110) Coastal landscape (60x81cm-24x32in) s. pasteboard
                 (D.FL 2500)
£1349 $2617   (8-Dec-90 KV.L87) Fishing boats in evening mist (50x60cm-20x24in) s.
                  panel (B.FR 80000)

CLERGE, Auguste Joseph (1891-) French
£600 $978   (3-Jul-91 PLF.P10) Nature-morte devant la fenetre ouverte
                (99x73cm-39x29in) s.d.59 (F.FR 6000)
£1010 $1788   (7-Apr-91 I.N77/R) Entree de village (54x73cm-21x29in) s. (F.FR 10200)

CLERICI, Fabrizio (1913-) Italian
£2726 $5370   (30-Oct-90 F.R86/R) San Sebastiano (11x16cm-4x6in) s.d.1949verso
                  (I.L 6000000)

CLERISSEAU, Charles Louis (1721-1820) French
£6531 $12800   (6-Nov-90 GF.L2087/R) Park landscape with ruins (49x64cm-19x25in)
                   (S.FR 16000)
£742 $1328   (10-Apr-91 CB.P3) Projet de tombeau (29x22cm-11x9in) pen wash
                 (F.FR 7500)
£6751 $12962   (14-Aug-90 SY.ME178/R) Bathing (59x46cm-23x18in) s. W/C htd.body col.
                   (A.D 16000)

CLERISSEAU, Charles Louis (attrib) (1721-1820) French
£4196 $8098   (10-Dec-90 L.K19/R) Classical view of Rome with figures
                  (49x75cm-19x30in) (DM 12000)

CLERMONT, Auguste Henri Louis de (19th C) French
£1120 $1893   (1-May-91 GD.B162/R) Fox hunting party (18x26cm-7x10in) s. panel
                  (S.FR 2800)

CLERMONT-GALLERANDE, Adhemar (?-1895) French
£2437 $4752   (17-Oct-90 LC.P52/R) Scene de chasse a courre (24x33cm-9x13in) panel
                  (F.FR 24100)

CLESSE, Louis (1889-1961) Belgian
£632 $1131   (12-Mar-91 GM.B936) Le haou et ardenne (46x65cm-18x26in) s. board
                 (B.FR 38000)
£665 $1190   (16-Mar-91 KV.L58) View of Brugge (55x65cm-22x26in) st.sig. panel
                 (B.FR 40000)
£765 $1369   (12-Mar-91 GM.B1050) Sente dans la carriere (44x65cm-17x26in) s. wood
                 (B.FR 46000)
£1043 $2054   (6-Oct-90 KV.L50/R) Still life with pheasant (60x80cm-24x31in) s.d.1946
                  (B.FR 65000)
£1068 $2083   (24-Oct-90 GM.B1127/R) Sous-bois (45x64cm-18x25in) s. wood (B.FR 65000)
£1096 $2126   (8-Dec-90 KV.L60) River scene in Flanders (45x65cm-18x26in) s.d.39 panel
                  (B.FR 65000)
£1495 $2437   (11-Jun-91 GM.B1069/R) Promenade en foret d'automne (115x132cm-45x52in)
                  s. (B.FR 90000)
£1637 $2750   (23-Apr-91 C.A342/R) River landscape (45x65cm-18x26in) s. panel
                  (B.FR 100000)
£3658 $6547   (12-Mar-91 C.A40/R) Wooded river landscape (102x130cm-40x51in) s.
                  (B.FR 220000)
£4250 $8373   (6-Oct-90 KV.L410/R) River under the snow (100x130cm-39x51in) s.d.1949
                  (B.FR 265000)

CLEVE, Cornelis van (attrib) (1520-1567) Dutch
£15060 $24247   (25-Jun-91 APT.P1/R) La Vierge a l'Enfant avec le petit Saint Jean
                    Baptiste (93x69cm-37x27in) panel (F.FR 150000)

CLEVE, Cornelis van (circle) (1520-1567) Dutch
£5988 $10120   (2-May-91 CH.AM35/R) The Madonna and Child in a landscape
                   (66x53cm-26x21in) panel (D.FL 20000)

CLEVE, Cornelis van (style) (1520-1567) Dutch
£1600 $3088   (14-Dec-90 PHM113/R) The Circumcision (48x34cm-19x13in) panel

CLEVE, Hendrick van (circle) (16th C) Flemish
£900   *$1728*   *(18-Feb-91 S85/R) Roman ruins (23x17cm-9x7in) pen ink double-sided*

CLEVE, Hendrick van III (1525-1589) Flemish
£4970 $8400   (18-Apr-91 APT.P39/R) La construction de la Tour de Babel
                              (41x454cm-16x179in) panel (F.FR 50000)
£5000   *$9500*   *(8-Jan-91 SY.NY29/R) A view of Naples (19x31cm-7x12in) bears i. verso*
                              pen col.washes

CLEVE, Joos van (1485-1540) Dutch
£160000 $260800   (5-Jul-91 C55/R) Holy Family (69x49cm-27x19in) panel

CLEVE, Joos van (circle) (1485-1540) Dutch
£2000 $3860   (11-Dec-90 PH107/R) Madonna and Child (18cm-7ins circular) panel
£13684 $26000   (11-Jan-91 CH.NY62/R) Portrait of gentleman, wearing slashed doublet,
                              fur lined cloak and cap (39x30cm-15x12in) panel arched top

CLEVE, Joos van (school) (1485-1540) Dutch
£1195 $2056   (14-May-91 GF.L2271/R) Christ and St John as children (52x68cm-20x27in)
                              panel (S.FR 3000)

CLEVE, Joos van (studio) (1485-1540) Dutch
£11765 $20000   (30-May-91 SY.NY10/R) Virgin and child before still life of fruit on
                              table, landscape beyond (66x49cm-26x19in) panel
£21053 $40000   (11-Jan-91 CH.NY65/R) Madonna of Cherries (78x55cm-31x22in) panel

CLEVE, Joos van (style) (1485-1540) Dutch
£3000 $4890   (4-Jul-91 C577/R) Portrait of man, aged 25, wearing hat and grey
                              fur-lined cloak (16x12cm-6x5in) with i.d.1509 panel

CLEVELEY, John (18th C) British
£800   *$1584*   *(30-Jan-91 S81/R) Frigate at anchor near fishing vessels*
                              (22x38cm-9x15in) W/C over pencil

CLEVELEY, John (jnr) (1747-1786) British
£4000 $7800   (26-Oct-90 C256/R) English men-of-war off the Dutch coast
                              (63x112cm-25x44in)
£13500 $26190   (7-Dec-90 CBS269) Busy harbour scene, launching ship at Chatham
                              (53x81cm-21x32in)

CLEVELEY, Robert (1747-1809) British
£1200   *$2148*   *(9-Apr-91 C142/R) Pool of London looking towards London Bridge and*
                              Southwark Cathedral (12x19cm-5x7in) s.d.1791 pencil W/C

CLEVELEY, Robert (circle) (1747-1809) British
£650   *$1274*   *(8-Nov-90 TL33/R) Portrait of schooner in three positions*
                              (41x59cm-16x23in) W/C

CLIFFORD, Edward (1844-1907) British
£1400 $2646   (26-Sep-90 S199/R) Astrologia (56x46cm-22x18in) after Sir Edward Coley
                              Burne-Jones
£600   *$1134*   *(26-Sep-90 S354/R) Asphodels (30x21cm-12x8in) i. W/C*
£1600   *$2672*   *(5-Jun-91 S334/R) Milan cathedral from Continental Hotel*
                              (24x34cm-9x13in) one i.d.2.10.1900 num.168 W/C three
£4000   *$7800*   *(12-Oct-90 K413/R) Bubbles for granny (48x61cm-19x24in) s.d.1884 W/C*

CLIME, Winfield Scott (1881-1958) American
£671 $1100   (21-Jun-91 DM.D2308/R) Barnyard scene (30x41cm-12x16in) s.

CLINT, Alfred (1807-1883) British
£2000 $3940   (1-Nov-90 C237/R) Twilight (102x155cm-40x61in) i.d.1878stretcher

CLOAR, Carroll (1913-) American
£2964   *$5750*   *(5-Dec-90 D.NY105/R) The mule herder (58x81cm-23x32in) s. tempera*
                              masonite

CLOCHARD, William Marcel (1894-?) French
£728 $1420   (21-Oct-90 L.C65/R) Village sous la neige (52x69cm-20x27in) s.
                              (F.FR 7200)

CLOSE, Chuck (20th C) ?
£22189   *$37500*   *(1-May-91 SY.NY132/R) Susan (76x56cm-30x22in) s.d.1977 pastel pencil*

CLOSS, Gustav Paul (1840-1870) German
£1739 $2939   (19-Apr-91 FN.S1684) Wooded river landscape with farmhouse and figures
                              (27x42cm-11x17in) s. (DM 5200)

CLOSTERMAN, Johann Baptist (1660-1713) German
£3000 $5370   (10-Apr-91 S109/R) Portrait of young man, standing in landscape,
                              pointing to bird (82x72cm-32x28in)

CLOSTERMAN, Johann Baptist (circle) (1660-1713) German
£820 $1517   (6-Mar-91 SC4321/R) Portrait of gentleman wearing grey coat and white neckcloth (74x61cm-29x24in) painted oval

CLOSTERMAN, Johann Baptist (style) (1660-1713) German
£4500 $7425   (12-Jul-91 C174/R) Portrait of military commander, in armour, holding baton in hand, battle scene beyond (128x102cm-50x40in)

CLOUET (style) (16th C) French
£2637 $5221   (30-Jan-91 APT.P81/R) Portrait de Marie de Lorraine, reine d'Ecosse (35x27cm-14x11in) panel (F.FR 26000)

CLOUET, Francois (1522-1572) French
£35473 $60304   (27-May-91 L.K25/R) Portrait of King Henry II of France (45x30cm-18x12in) panel (DM 105000)

CLOUET, Francois (attrib) (1522-1572) French
£10000 $19200   (18-Dec-90 C87/R) Portrait of young gentleman in gold-embroidered doublet and white ruff (6x?cm-2x?in) min. vellum gilt-metal mount oval in rec.frame
£26000 $46020   (20-Mar-91 C151/R) Portrait of nobleman in gold-embroidered coat (5x?cm-2x?in) min. vellum gold frame rose-diamonds oval

CLOUET, Francois (school) (1522-1572) French
£4592 $9000   (21-Nov-90 NA.BA80) Retrato de Marie Puchet (26x19cm-10x7in) panel

CLOUET, Francois (style) (1522-1572) French
£1156 $2000   (21-May-91 GRO.B11/R) Portrait of boy, probably Francois II (46x38cm-18x15in) cradled panel
£1200 $1956   (4-Jul-91 C580) Portrait of lady, in dress decorated with pearls, ruff and handband (37x28cm-15x11in) panel
£1791 $3116   (25-Mar-91 PLF.P96) Portrait d'un grand seigneur du regne de Charles IX (33x30cm-13x12in) panel (F.FR 18000)

CLOUET, Jean (attrib) (1486-1541) French
£14865 $25270   (27-May-91 L.K26/R) Portrait of young cavalier wearing earring in left ear (27x13cm-11x5in) i.verso panel (DM 44000)

CLOUGH, Charles (20th C) ?
£1223 $2361   (16-Dec-90 CSC.P38/R) Pinky (135x130cm-53x51in) acrylic (F.FR 12000)

CLOUGH, George L (1824-1901) American
£1786 $3000   (27-Apr-91 YFA.M63) Adirondack landscape (51x46cm-20x18in) s.
£2577 $5000   (24-Aug-90 RB.HY98/R) The sawmill (36x56cm-14x22in) s.

CLOUGH, Prunella (1919-) British
£2000 $3260   (1-Jul-91 S30/R) Red Garden 2 (63x76cm-25x30in) s.i.d.1969 stretcher

CLOUGH, Tom (1903-) British
£4000 $7560   (27-Sep-90 L291/R) Evening in the Harbour (86x140cm-34x55in) s.
£360 $684   (25-Feb-91 PH81/R) Busy street (34x25cm-13x10in) s. W/C
£460 $796   (20-May-91 PH75) Cottage by stream (39x60cm-15x24in) s. W/C
£500 $865   (10-May-91 CBS296) Autumn on Llwgg at Bettwys-y-Coed (33x51cm-13x20in) s.i.verso W/C
£580 $1003   (20-May-91 PH74) Feeding doves (54x76cm-21x30in) s.d.1910 W/C
£760 $1292   (29-May-91 PHC103/R) Cottage garden (39x52cm-15x20in) s. W/C
£1050 $1817   (10-May-91 CBS315) Thatched cottages (33x51cm-13x20in) s. W/C
£1400 $2394   (29-Jul-91 HS212/R) Village street scene with horse drawn cart, girl standing by cottage (47x71cm-19x28in) s.d.1912 W/C
£2200 $3740   (29-May-91 PHC140/R) Cornish harbour (60x90cm-24x35in) s. W/C

CLOUTIER, Albert Edward (1902-1965) Canadian
£613 $1085   (20-Mar-91 MA.V206) Baie St Paul en printemps (30x41cm-12x16in) s.d.59 (C.D 1250)
£1179 $2311   (5-Nov-90 FB.M99/R) Ungava (76x104cm-30x41in) s. (C.D 2700)

CLOUZOT, Marianne (1908-) French
£301 $557   (4-Mar-91 ARC.P32) Le couple (49x32cm-19x13in) s. pastel (F.FR 3000)

CLOVIO, Giulio (attrib) (1498-1578) Italian
£12000 $23160   (13-Dec-90 B46/R) Holy Family under oak, surrounded by border of illuminated manuscript (35x25cm-14x10in) tempera vellum on panel after Raphael

CLOWES, Daniel (19th C) British
£3600 $7020   (18-Oct-90 SC3134/R) A bay hunter in a landscape (59x85cm-23x33in) s.

CLOWES, Daniel (attrib) (18/19th C) British
£2395 $4000   (7-Jun-91 SY.NY22/R) A bay hunter in a landscape (63x76cm-25x30in)

CLUSMANN, William (1859-1927) American
£990 $1900   (1-Dec-90 LAE.L22/R) Morning on the fusel (48x66cm-19x26in) s.
£432 $800   (10-Mar-91 H.C128 a) Boat on water (46x61cm-18x24in) s. W/C

CLUVER, Bernt (1897-1941) Norwegian
£830 $1576   (11-Sep-90 UL.T181/R) Landscape (48x59cm-19x23in) (N.KR 9500)

CLUVER, Bernt (1897-1941) Norwegian-cont.
£2178 $4247 (15-Oct-90 B.O11/R) Landscape outside Stavanger (51x68cm-20x27in) s. (N.KR 25000)
£3678 $6583 (14-Mar-91 BU.O12/R) Horn of plenty (180x114cm-71x45in) s.d.1931 (N.KR 42000)

CLUYSENAAR, Alfred Jean Andre (1837-1902) Belgian
£655 $1113 (28-May-91 C.A36/R) Symphony in brown (74x60cm-29x24in) s. panel (B.FR 40000)

CLUYSENAAR, Alfred Jean Andre (after) (1837-1902) Belgian
£850 $1437 (3-May-91 PHE143) The young artist (120x100cm-47x39in) s.i.

CLYMER, John Ford (1907-) American
£1042 $2000 (17-Dec-90 SY.NY275/R) Sailboats by bridge (61x76cm-24x30in) s.
£2083 $4000 (17-Dec-90 SY.NY274/R) View of harbour (61x91cm-24x36in) s.

COADIC, Francis le (1912-) French
£806 $1313 (14-Jun-91 FB.P97/R) Neige a Montmartre (50x61cm-20x24in) s. i.d.1951 verso (F.FR 8000)

COASTER, Austin (19th C) British?
£300 $519 (7-May-91 SWS1876) Young girl with centre-parted blonde hair min. gilt frame oval

COATES, A H (20th C) British?
£600 $1170 (15-Jan-91 C58/R) Clicquot, French bulldog (36x28cm-14x11in) s.i.

COATES, Edmund C (fl.1837-57) American
£1546 $3000 (5-Dec-90 D.NY8/R) Canadian river landscape (76x64cm-30x25in) s.i.d.1855 canvas onmasonite
£3179 $5500 (22-May-91 CH.NY12/R) Oxbow (63x75cm-25x30in) s.i. oval

COATES, Edmund C (attrib) (fl.1837-57) American
£749 $1400 (30-Aug-90 MFA.C68/R) Classical landscape (64x81cm-25x32in)

COBB, David (19th C) British?
£500 $865 (22-May-91 S173/R) British destroyers in Bay of Biscay (60x76cm-24x30in) s.
£740 $1450 (12-Feb-91 SWO245) Racing yachts passing passenger liner (46x66cm-18x26in) s.
£1050 $2058 (12-Feb-91 SWO247) Sailing ship and steam ship with sails (46x66cm-18x26in) s.

COBBAERT, Jan (20th C) Belgian
£1064 $1787 (23-Apr-91 C.A344) Figures (72x52cm-28x20in) s. panel (B.FR 65000)
£1393 $2689 (12-Dec-90 CH.AM482/R) Figures (80x100cm-31x39in) s. (D.FL 4500)
£1479 $2884 (23-Oct-90 C.A95) Blue bird (73x54cm-29x21in) s. paper (B.FR 90000)
£1806 $3125 (25-May-91 KV.L476/R) Puppet show (100x90cm-39x35in) s. (B.FR 110000)
£657 $1136 (25-May-91 KV.L49) Child in a cort (54x73cm-21x29in) s. gouache (B.FR 40000)

COBBETT, Edward John (1815-1899) British
£1550 $2589 (5-Jun-91 S189/R) Apple seller (42x34cm-17x13in) s.d.1868 canvas on board

COBBS, B (?) ?
£690 $1200 (27-Mar-91 D.NY30) Yarn and needles (25x36cm-10x14in) s.

COBELLE, Charles (1902-) French
£612 $1200 (12-Feb-91 SY.NY135/R) Les promenadeurs (61x76cm-24x30in) s.
£667 $1300 (10-Oct-90 SY.NY208/R) View of the Seine (61x76cm-24x30in) s.
£667 $1300 (10-Oct-90 SY.NY207/R) View of Paris Opera (61x76cm-24x30in) s.
£872 $1700 (10-Oct-90 SY.NY289/R) View of steeple (76x61cm-30x24in) s.
£1154 $2250 (10-Oct-90 SY.NY263/R) Summer landscape (61x76cm-24x30in) s.
£1282 $2500 (10-Oct-90 SY.NY259/R) View of street (61x76cm-24x30in) s.

COBO, Chema (20th C) ?
£5190 $10016 (13-Dec-90 EP.M19/R) Untitled (92x60cm-36x24in) s.d.75 acrylic (S.P 950000)

COBURN, Frederick Simpson (1871-1960) Canadian
£979 $1665 (27-May-91 HO.ED278/R) Paysage (25x35cm-10x14in) s. s.verso board (C.D 1900)
£5263 $10368 (30-Oct-90 SY.T80/R) Logging sleigh (47x57cm-19x22in) s.d.30 (C.D 12000)
£5291 $10000 (27-Sep-90 CH.NY213/R) A sunny sleigh ride (34x41cm-13x16in) s.d.27
£6061 $10485 (6-May-91 SY.T169/R) Sunny afternoon (28x38cm-11x15in) s.d.31 (C.D 12000)
£6061 $10485 (6-May-91 SY.T127/R) Logging sleigh in winter (58x70cm-23x28in) s.d.43 (C.D 12000)
£7027 $11454 (10-Jun-91 W.T1073/R) Winter landscape with horses and log sleigh (46x191cm-18x75in) s.d.'26 board (C.D 13000)
£7407 $14000 (27-Sep-90 CH.NY214/R) Loading wood in Quebec (51x71cm-20x28in) s.d.27
£7895 $15553 (30-Oct-90 SY.T59/R) County politics (62x80cm-24x31in) s.d.46 (C.D 18000)

COBURN, Frederick Simpson (1871-1960) Canadian-cont.
£8772 $17281   (30-Oct-90 SY.T58/R) The logging team (65x88cm-26x35in) s.d.46 canvas on
                    board (C.D 20000)
£622 $1207   (4-Dec-90 P.Q31) Hauling logs (22x29cm-9x11in) s.d.31 pastel (C.D 1400)

COBURN, John (1925-) Australian
£3187 $6279   (31-Oct-90 CH.S101/R) Tree of life (106x137cm-42x54in) s. oil gold leaf
                    (A.D 8000)

COCCAPANI, Sigismondo (1583-1642) Italian
£9231 $18000   (10-Oct-90 CH.NY209/R) Winged Victory (73x58cm-29x23in)

COCCORANTE, Leonardo (1680-1750) Italian
£9231 $18000   (11-Oct-90 SY.NY176/R) Figures amidst classical ruins (77x65cm-30x26in)

COCCORANTE, Leonardo (attrib) (1680-1750) Italian
£4412 $7500   (30-May-91 CE.NY67) Figures amongst ruins beside harbour
                    (76x63cm-30x25in)

COCCORANTE, Leonardo (circle) (1680-1750) Italian
£1600 $3120   (25-Oct-90 B11) Jonah and the whale (66x94cm-26x37in)
£6667 $13000   (10-Oct-90 CH.NY63/R) Architectural capriccio of ruins with figures and
                    putti (97x74cm-38x29in)

COCCORANTE, Leonardo (school) (1680-1750) Italian
£1471 $2500   (30-May-91 CE.NY60) Figures amongst classical ruins before lake
                    (75x63cm-30x25in)

COCCORANTE, Leonardo (style) (1680-1750) Italian
£2679 $4500   (17-Jul-91 SY.NY160/R) Landscape with figures amid ruins
                    (73x135cm-29x53in)
£4200 $7098   (17-Apr-91 S98/R) Capriccio view of classical ruins (73x97cm-29x38in)

COCHEREAU, Leon Mathieu (1793-1817) French
£26131 $42854   (21-Jun-91 SY.MO162/R) Atelier de David (91x103cm-36x41in) (F.FR 260000)

COCHIN, Charles-Nicolas (18th C) French
£1529 $2936   (27-Nov-90 APT.P179/R) Portrit de l'Abbe de Guyonnet (15x10cm-6x4in)
                    i.d.1783 pierre noire stumping htd.white chamois (F.FR 15000)

COCHIN, Charles-Nicolas (attrib) (18th C) French
£5000 $8850   (22-Mar-91 APT.P24/R) La Bataille de Fontenoy (40x57cm-16x22in) pierre
                    noire wash htd.W/C (F.FR 50000)

COCHIN, Charles-Nicolas (younger) (1715-1790) French
£2500 $4750   (8-Jan-91 SY.NY6/R) Portrait of a gentleman, half length (15x10cm-6x4in)
                    s.d.1783 blk.chk.
£3421 $6500   (9-Jan-91 CH.NY55/R) Portrait of Louis-Cesar de La Baume Le Blanc, Duc
                    de Vaujours (13x9cm-5x4in) s.d.1785 black chk

COCHRAN, Allen Dean (1888-1935) American
£833 $1600   (17-Dec-90 SY.NY279/R) Summer landscape (41x51cm-16x20in) s.

COCK, Cesar de (1823-1904) Flemish
£8537 $16732   (6-Nov-90 SY.AM127/R) Farmyard (51x36cm-20x14in) s.d.1865 (D.FL 28000)
£998 $1786   (16-Mar-91 KV.L76) Cow herder in landscape (13x29cm-5x11in) s. W/C
                    (B.FR 60000)

COCK, Gilbert de (20th C) Belgian
£427 $739   (25-May-91 KV.L79) Composition (22x17cm-9x7in) s.d.61 gouache
                    (B.FR 26000)
£460 $795   (25-May-91 KV.L78) Composition (40x30cm-16x12in) s.d.67 gouache
                    (B.FR 28000)

COCK, Jan de (attrib) (?) Flemish
£36471 $62000   (31-May-91 CH.NY17/R) The Agony in the Garden (44x34cm-17x13in) indis.l.
                    panel arched top

COCK, Matthys (1509-1548) Flemish
£19737 $37500   (8-Jan-91 SY.NY31/R) An imaginary landscape with a town set in a river
                    valley (18x25cm-7x10in) bears i.d.1540 ink htd.white bodycol.

COCK, Xavier de (1818-1896) Flemish
£1473 $2475   (23-Apr-91 C.A88/R) Shepherd with his sheep (14x20cm-6x8in) s.d.1863 W/C
                    (B.FR 90000)
£1473 $2475   (23-Apr-91 C.A89/R) Girl with cattle at a watering place (14x20cm-6x8in)
                    s.d.1862 W/C (B.FR 90000)

COCKERELL, Charles Robert (1788-1863) British
£450 $743   (9-Jul-91 C95/R) Waterloo Bridge with St Paul's beyond. Central arch of
                    Waterloo Bridge (8x11cm-3x4in) i. pencil W/C double-sided
£800 $1320   (9-Jul-91 C91/R) Campo Vaccino looking towards Capitol, Rome
                    (18x37cm-7x15in) pen ink
£850 $1403   (9-Jul-91 C96/R) Piazza dei Miracoli with Battistero, Duomo and
                    Campanile, Pisa (8x10cm-3x4in) i.d.1816 pencil W/C
£1600 $2640   (9-Jul-91 C9/R) Rome (19x23cm-7x9in) s.i.d.1817 pencil pen ink

COCKERELL, Charles Robert (1788-1863) British-cont.
£4200 $6930   *(9-Jul-91 C93/R) Rome from the Trinita dei Monti (21x27cm-8x11in) i. pencil W/C htd.gold*

COCKRAM, George (1861-1950) British
£540 $999   *(6-Mar-91 SC4165) Gorse Banks, Cymmerau Bay, Anglesey (30x46cm-12x18in) s. i.verso W/C*
£560 $1064   *(15-Sep-90 ME195) 'A Silvery Morn', coastal scene Rhosneigr (30x46cm-12x18in) s.label verso W/C*
£850 $1598   *(19-Sep-90 PHC107/R) Evening (36x75cm-14x30in) s. i.label verso W/C*
£1850 $3515   *(15-Sep-90 ME142) Shore scene, low tide with sea gulls (61x91cm-24x36in) s. W/C*

COCKRILL, Maurice (1936-) British
£3000 $5850   *(9-Oct-90 B141/R) Medea (180x152cm-71x60in) s.i.d.1984 verso*

COCKX, Philibert (20th C) Belgian
£1764 $3476   *(6-Oct-90 KV.L53/R) In the restaurant (32x41cm-13x16in) s.d.1949 canvas on board (B.FR 110000)*

COCQ, Cornelis de (1815-?) Dutch
£4200 $6888   *(18-Jun-91 PH23) Portrait of eastern gentleman with seascape beyond (86x71cm-34x28in) s.d.1848*

COCTEAU, Jean (1889-1963) French
£457 $915   *(6-Feb-91 FB.P76) Profil masculin (24x19cm-9x7in) s.i.d.1957 lead pencil (F.FR 4500)*
£561 $1082   *(14-Dec-90 ARC.P21/R) Le marin joueur de cartes (25x18cm-10x7in) s. ink (F.FR 5500)*
£617 $1073   *(25-Mar-91 CR.P3) Portrait de profil (23x19cm-9x7in) s.i. lead pencil red crayon (F.FR 6200)*
£617 $1073   *(25-Mar-91 CR.P4) Lettre manuscrite (20x12cm-8x5in) s.d.19 septembre 1957 blk.crayon (F.FR 6200)*
£673 $1204   *(12-Apr-91 JM.P16) Harpiste (26x20cm-10x8in) s. ink (F.FR 6800)*
£676 $1169   *(25-May-91 N.M47) Head and king (30x21cm-12x8in) d.1952 col.pencil on letter written by artist (DM 2000)*
£676 $1284   *(14-Sep-90 SA.A1408/R) Portrait of young man (24x14cm-9x6in) s. indian ink pen velin (DM 2000)*
£683 $1264   *(7-Mar-91 D.V279/R) Head in profile (27x20cm-11x8in) s.i.d.1958 pencil (A.S 14000)*
£725 $1400   *(16-Dec-90 LIT.L58/R) Profile (66x51cm-26x20in) s. black red crayon*
£737 $1400   *(14-Sep-90 S.BM328/R) Profile (25x20cm-10x8in) s. pastel*
£751 $1300   *(7-May-91 CE.NY68/R) Deux roses (27x21cm-11x8in) s.d.1958 col.pencils*
£815 $1605   *(30-Oct-90 I.N238) Portrait de Tony Gandarillas (27x21cm-11x8in) studio st. ink (F.FR 8000)*
£900 $1746   *(5-Dec-90 PH86/R) Femme a la lampe (25x20cm-10x8in) s.verso pen ink*
£906 $1477   *(12-Jun-91 ZZ.F82) Oracle amical (26x19cm-10x7in) s.i. pen (F.FR 9000)*
£945 $1645   *(25-Mar-91 CR.P5/R) Profil (25x20cm-10x8in) i. red crayon ink (F.FR 9500)*
£960 $1622   *(1-May-91 GD.B1387) Female nudes, portrait with horse (15x17cm-6x7in) s.d.1960 pencil wash oil chk two (S.FR 2400)*
£973 $1908   *(11-Nov-90 ZZ.F228/R) Portrait de jeune homme (15x12cm-6x5in) s. ink (F.FR 9500)*
£994 $1680   *(15-Apr-91 CC.P23 b) Souvenirs de Berlin et de Jean Cocteau (49x39cm-19x15in) s.i. crayon (F.FR 10000)*
£1026 $2000   *(24-Oct-90 B.SF1484/R) Polichinelle a l'escalier (48x30cm-19x12in) s.d.1958 pastel*
£1095 $1904   *(25-Mar-91 CR.P2/R) Jeunes comediens (24x21cm-9x8in) s.i. blk.crayon pastel (F.FR 11000)*
£1098 $1800   *(19-Jun-91 B.SF1775/R) L'unicorne (72x90cm-28x35in) s. s.i.d.1949 brush ink*
£1100 $1771   *(24-Jun-91 CSK107/R) Portrait de la Comtesse de Noailles (29x21cm-11x8in) s. pencil*
£1186 $2016   *(30-May-91 EA.Z229/R) En Face (19x12cm-7x5in) s.d.1950 pencil (S.FR 3000)*
£1200 $2028   *(1-May-91 GD.B1388/R) Eve et Jean (43x33cm-17x13in) s.i.d.1953verso pastel chk (S.FR 3000)*
£1200 $1932   *(24-Jan-91 CSK208) L'homme aux yeux poisson (27x20cm-11x8in) s.i.*
£1204 $2095   *(25-Mar-91 CR.P6/R) Lettre manuscrite s.d.1er octobre 1962 ball pen (F.FR 12100)*
£1224 $2412   *(16-Nov-90 EA.Z264) Face (18x12cm-7x5in) s.d.1950 col.pencil (S.FR 3000)*
£1250 $2125   *(31-May-91 GB.B6198) Head of youth with cap in profile (25x17cm-10x7in) s. pencil brush chk board another study verso (DM 3700)*
£1272 $2403   *(30-Sep-90 E.LA194) L'orchestre (20x27cm-8x11in) s. oil crayons (F.FR 12500)*
£1281 $2510   *(11-Nov-90 ZZ.F229/R) Autoportrait (49x38cm-19x15in) s.d.1958 chl.col.crayons (F.FR 12500)*
£1300 $2093   *(24-Jun-91 CSK113) Portrait de Raymond Rodiguet (28x22cm-11x9in) s. pencil*
£1342 $2617   *(10-Oct-90 ZEL.L1263/R) Musician with pipe (22x30cm-9x12in) s. black pen (DM 4000)*
£1351 $2338   *(21-May-91 WK.M718/R) Two faces (25x19cm-10x7in) s. pencil col.pencil (DM 4000)*
£1429 $2814   *(16-Nov-90 EA.Z270) Profile (21x13cm-8x5in) s.d.1959 col.pencil (S.FR 3500)*

COCTEAU, Jean (1889-1963) French-cont.

£1526	$2884	(30-Sep-90 E.LA187) Autoportrait (26x20cm-10x8in) st.mono. drawing (F.FR 15000)
£1677	$3303	(6-Oct-90 GL.P112) Portrait de Moretti (66x46cm-26x18in) s.i.d.63 felt pen (F.FR 17000)
£1909	$3742	(20-Nov-90 BR.M53/R) Progetto per un vaso (21x27cm-8x11in) s. pastel (I.L 4200000)
£2000	$3220	(24-Jun-91 CSK108/R) Tete de faune (27x21cm-11x8in) s.d.1954 col.crayons
£2138	$4213	(30-Oct-90 I.N237/R) Autoportrait (27x21cm-11x8in) studio st. ink (F.FR 21000)
£2243	$4306	(27-Nov-90 ARC.P23/R) Autoportrait (27x21cm-11x8in) s.d.1956 felt-tip pen (F.FR 22000)
£2548	$4893	(27-Nov-90 ARC.P6/R) Orphee a la lyre (21x22cm-8x9in) s. Indian ink (F.FR 25000)
£2548	$4893	(27-Nov-90 ARC.P32/R) Orphee (18x12cm-7x5in) s. col.crayons (F.FR 25000)
£2587	$4501	(28-Mar-91 DAR.P16/R) Segrmor et la blessure incurable (29x20cm-11x8in) s. Indian ink W/C htd.gouache (F.FR 26000)
£2650	$5115	(14-Dec-90 JM.P48/R) Les spectacles du monde se transcendent a travers lui (36x26cm-14x10in) s. col.crayon rose (F.FR 26000)
£3049	$6098	(4-Feb-91 LEB.P10/R) Nijinski dans la spectre de la rose (25x24cm-10x9in) s. W/C (F.FR 30000)
£3058	$5872	(27-Nov-90 ARC.P40/R) La femme doit suivre son mari (48x61cm-19x24in) crayon tracing paper (F.FR 30000)
£3284	$5713	(28-Mar-91 DAR.P15/R) Le Testament d'Orphee (44x32cm-17x13in) s. felt pen (F.FR 33000)
£3490	$5758	(10-Jul-91 FB.P40/R) Les juristes a Oxford (54x46cm-21x18in) s.d.56 col.crayons (F.FR 35000)
£4179	$8024	(27-Nov-90 ARC.P34/R) La noce (46x58cm-18x23in) s.d.10 aout 1956 crayon tracing paper (F.FR 41000)
£4587	$8807	(27-Nov-90 ARC.P31/R) La dame aux chats i.d.1962 felt pen col.chk. (F.FR 45000)
£6588	$12978	(30-Oct-90 F.R173/R) L'eleve Dargelos masquee 'pour le XII' (65x48cm-26x19in) s. mixed media (I.L 14500000)
£7136	$13700	(27-Nov-90 ARC.P19/R) Orphee a l'oeil-poisson (27x36cm-11x14in) s.d.1961 W/C gouache (F.FR 70000)
£7339	$14092	(27-Nov-90 ARC.P18/R) Arelquin a la collerette bleue (65x50cm-26x20in) s.d.1953 pastel (F.FR 72000)
£16310	$31315	(27-Nov-90 ARC.P38/R) Orphee, la mort d'eurydice et la bataille des centaures (50x105cm-20x41in) st.mono. crayon tracing paper (F.FR 160000)
£17910	$31164	(28-Mar-91 DAR.P21/R) Jeune fille au poisson. Arlequin au crabe both s. one d.58 other 57 pastel varnish canvas (F.FR 180000)

COCTEAU, Jean and MORETTI, Raymond (19/20th C) French

£7708	$14954	(9-Dec-90 E.LA96/R) L'age de Verseau s. both artists drawing gouache (F.FR 75000)

CODAZZI, Niccolo (1648-1693) Italian

£15294	$26000	(31-May-91 CH.NY61/R) View of the Arch of Constantine, Rome, with figures (74x98cm-29x39in)

CODAZZI, Viviano (1603-1672) Italian

£31047	$52158	(23-Apr-91 F.R92/R) Edificio antico in rovina con figure (123x171cm-48x67in) figures attrib.F.Lauri (I.L 68000000)

CODAZZI, Viviano (attrib) (1603-1672) Italian

£11765	$20000	(31-May-91 CH.NY77/R) Architectural capriccio of classical ruins with soldiers (157x157cm-62x62in)

CODAZZI, Viviano (circle) (1603-1672) Italian

£6726	$12040	(10-Apr-91 CB.P40/R) La presentation de la Vierge au temple (80x110cm-31x43in) (F.FR 68000)

CODAZZI, Viviano (studio) (1603-1672) Italian

£8000	$15440	(11-Dec-90 PH117/R) Capriccio view of Roman ruins with figures, the Colosseum in distance (98x185cm-39x73in)

CODAZZI, Viviano (style) (1603-1672) Italian

£7249	$12613	(25-Mar-91 SY.F709/R) Fantasie architettoniche (108x106cm-43x42in) pair (I.L 16000000)
£24426	$43723	(14-Mar-91 D.V43/R) Construction of classical palace (100x127cm-39x50in) (A.S 500000)

CODAZZI, Viviano and CERQUOZZI, Michelangelo (17th C) Italian

£61538	$120000	(11-Oct-90 SY.NY196/R) Architectural capricci with classical ruins and figures (95x132cm-37x52in) pair

CODAZZI, Viviano and GARGIULIO, Domenico (17th C) Italian

£16080	$26372	(21-Jun-91 SY.MO121/R) Personnages dans une architecture imaginaire (101x128cm-40x50in) (F.FR 160000)
£20513	$40000	(11-Oct-90 SY.NY197/R) Figures among classical ruins (93x124cm-37x49in)

CODDE, Pieter (1599-1678) Dutch

£5574	$9476	(27-May-91 L.K27/R) Elegant party gathered around table singing and making music (42x54cm-17x21in) panel (DM 16500)
£8000	$15600	(26-Oct-90 C147/R) Two women playing cards (37x50cm-15x20in) mono. panel

CODDE, Pieter (1599-1678) Dutch-cont.
£44693 $80000   (11-Apr-91 SY.NY121/R) Dutch family in interior (38x50cm-15x20in)
       indist.s.d.1634 panel
£70588 $120000   (31-May-91 CH.NY63/R) Seated lady seen from behind before virginal
       (40x32cm-16x13in) bears init. panel

CODDE, Pieter (style) (1599-1678) Dutch
£1371 $2701   (14-Nov-90 D.V180/R) Party making music (35x50cm-14x20in) panel
       (A.S 28000)
£2083 $3500   (17-Jul-91 SY.NY83/R) Portrait of a lady in a landscape
       (43x27cm-17x11in) panel
£2800 $4732   (16-Apr-91 PH91/R) Interior with merry company seated around table
       (34x46cm-13x18in) panel

CODINA Y LANGLIN, Victoriano (1844-1911) Spanish
£5500 $8855   (27-Jun-91 CG20/R) The unwelcome suitor (26x21cm-10x8in) s.d.1880
£15000 $29400   (13-Feb-91 S22/R) At Hyde Park Corner, London (95x127cm-37x50in)
       s.d.1880

CODINO, Francesco (style) (17th C) Italian
£7968 $13705   (14-May-91 GF.L2262/R) Still life with fruit and flowers
       (57x73cm-22x29in) (S.FR 20000)

CODMAN, Charles (attrib) (1800-1842) American
£747 $1300   (29-Mar-91 E.EDM500/R) Camping in the hills (23x28cm-9x11in) board

COELENBIER, Jan (style) (17th C) Dutch
£1000 $1790   (12-Apr-91 BM.B540/R) Dutch coastal landscape with figures and shipping
       (20x26cm-8x10in) indis.i.verso panel (DM 3000)

COELHO, Jose Julho Goncalves (1866-?) Portuguese
£1800 $3456   (28-Nov-90 S135/R) View of St.Mark's Square, Venice (42x31cm-17x12in)
       s.d.1901 W/C

COELLO, Claudio (circle) (1630-1693) Spanish
£1300 $2197   (16-Apr-91 PH77/R) Portrait of Philip II of Spain (46x34cm-18x13in)
       panel
£2000 $4000   (7-Feb-91 CSK46) Mary and Joseph at table with infant Christ
       (100x74cm-39x29in)

COELLO, Claudio (style) (1630-1693) Spanish
£1700 $2771   (4-Jul-91 C609/R) Tobias and angel (107x81cm-42x32in)

COENE, Constantinus Fidelio (1780-1841) Flemish
£1500 $2460   (18-Jun-91 PH5) Midday entertainment (26x36cm-10x14in) s. panel
£6500 $12805   (5-Oct-90 C1/R) Entertainer (103x130cm-41x51in) s.d.1827 panel

COENE, J (?) Flemish
£620 $1035   (22-Jul-91 SWS1090/R) A dutch frozen landscape with skaters
       (28x36cm-11x14in) s.d.1841 panel

COENE, Jean Henri de (1798-1866) Flemish
£2000 $3280   (19-Jun-91 S28/R) Tempting morsel (53x42cm-21x17in) s.
£4011 $7500   (1-Aug-90 B.P60/R) Angry baker (89x71cm-35x28in) s.d.1833

COENEN, Otto (1907-1971) German
£1027 $1675   (15-Jun-91 L.K128) At the dyke (29x39cm-11x15in) s.d.1967 board
       (DM 3000)
£2568 $4187   (15-Jun-91 L.K127/R) Ears (79x49cm-31x19in) board (DM 7500)

COETZER, Willem H (1900-1983) South African
£576 $1106   (26-Nov-90 SY.J330) Drakensberg (26x44cm-10x17in) s.d.45 board
       (SA.R 2800)
£617 $1185   (26-Nov-90 SY.J327/R) Waterval Onder (29x40cm-11x16in) s.d.72 s.i.verso
       board (SA.R 3000)
£632 $1067   (15-Apr-91 SY.J460/R) Naby Bandolierskop (29x39cm-11x15in) s.d.48
       (SA.R 3000)
£643 $1259   (11-Feb-91 SY.J531/R) Bushveld landscape (41x31cm-16x12in) s.d.'62
       canvas laid down on board (SA.R 3200)
£658 $1264   (26-Nov-90 SY.J326/R) Lone figure in mountainous landscape
       (40x50cm-16x20in) s.d.45 (SA.R 3200)
£823 $1580   (26-Nov-90 SY.J333/R) Homestead in hills (39x44cm-15x17in) s.d.45 canvas
       on board (SA.R 4000)
£828 $1549   (27-Aug-90 SY.J87) Golden Gate, Orange Free State (29x24cm-11x9in) s.
       canvas laid down on board (SA.R 4000)
£847 $1651   (15-Oct-90 SY.J107/R) Farmlands in the valley with mountains in the
       background (29x39cm-11x15in) s. canvas laid down on board (SA.R 4200)
£932 $1742   (27-Aug-90 SY.J233) North Eastern Transvaal (39x49cm-15x19in) s.d.73
       s.i.verso board (SA.R 4500)
£932 $1742   (27-Aug-90 SY.J234/R) Table Mountain from Blaauwberg (17x25cm-7x10in)
       s.d.64 i.verso board (SA.R 4500)
£1095 $1850   (15-Apr-91 SY.J459/R) Still life with orchid in vase, beads and perfume
       bottle (37x26cm-15x10in) s.d.69 board (SA.R 5200)
£1109 $2162   (15-Oct-90 SY.J105/R) Storm clouds over the Magaliesberg
       (40x50cm-16x20in) s.d.'49 board (SA.R 5500)

COETZER, Willem H (1900-1983) South African-cont.
£1132 $2173   (26-Nov-90 SY.J334) Shepherd with sheep in Karoo landscape
      (29x30cm-11x12in) s.d.21.7.79 s.d.7.1.80 board (SA.R 5500)
£1305 $2206   (15-Apr-91 SY.J461) Simonsberg Vanaf Duinefontein, Kaapse Vlakte
      (37x50cm-15x20in) s.d.44 (SA.R 6200)
£2743 $4525   (8-Jul-91 SY.J261/R) Crossing the Drakensberg (44x72cm-17x28in) s.d.'59
      (SA.R 13000)

COFFA, Andre (19th C) Italian
£2643 $4943   (29-Aug-90 KH.K30/R) Italian family with small child by old house
      (53x31cm-21x12in) s. (D.KR 30000)

COFFERMANS, Marcellus (16th C) Flemish
£7172 $14057   (7-Nov-90 APT.P435/R) Episode de la vie de Samuel. La nativite. Le roi
      Salomon recevant lereine de Saba (12x8cm-5x3in) panel three
      (F.FR 70000)

COFFERMANS, Marcellus (attrib) (16th C) Flemish
£4595 $7489   (10-Jun-91 W.T1359/R) The crucifixion (22x13cm-9x5in) panel (C.D 8500)

COFFEY, Alfred (1869-1950) British
£763 $1465   (26-Nov-90 SY.ME52/R) On road in front of Davis boarding house, Terrigal
      (14x29cm-6x11in) s. i.verso board (A.D 1900)

COFFIN, William Haskell (1878-1941) American
£726 $1300   (14-Apr-91 JRB.C25/R) Tall ship (20x15cm-8x6in) s.

COGHETTI, Francesco (attrib) (1804-1875) Italian
£1269 $2500   (15-Nov-90 SY.NY2) The Family of Neptune (9x12cm-4x5in) bear.i. pen wash
      over graphite

COGHUF, Ernst Stocker (1905-1976) Swiss
£1984 $3433   (25-May-91 AB.L67/R) The magic garden (68x47cm-27x19in) s.i.d.1930 oil
      mixed media board (S.FR 5000)

COGNIET, Leon (1794-1880) French
£3819 $6263   (17-Jun-91 ARC.P9/R) Les Saintes femmes au tombeau (22x50cm-9x20in)
      mono. half-circle (F.FR 38000)

COGNIET, Marcel (1857-1914) French
£853 $1680   (14-Nov-90 RAS.K201) River landscape, Champagne area (34x46cm-13x18in)
      s. (D.KR 9500)

COGORNO, Santiago (1915-) Argentinian
£1345 $2650   (14-Nov-90 V.BA27) Mujer descansando (49x68cm-19x27in) mixed media

COHEN, Bernard (1933-) British
£1200 $2220   (8-Mar-91 C186/R) Hermes (244x305cm-96x120in) s. i.d.1962verso

COHEN-GAN, Pinchas (b.1942) Israeli?
£1047 $2000   (1-Jan-91 GG.TA322/R) Figure and head (61x121cm-24x48in) s.i.d.1985
      s.d.verso

COIA, Emilio (20th C) British
£650 $1099   (17-Apr-91 CG31) James Robertson Justice in Highland Dress holding a
      falcon (56x38cm-22x15in) s. pastel

COIGNARD, James (1925-) French
£828 $1549   (27-Aug-90 SY.J204) Composition 91 (30x24cm-12x9in) s. acrylic paper
      (SA.R 4000)
£850 $1386   (3-Jul-91 CSC.P53) Les oiseaux bleus (23x43cm-9x17in) s. acrylic board
      (F.FR 8500)
£1115 $1929   (21-May-91 WK.M719/R) Univers d'enfant (49x40cm-19x16in) s. s.i.verso
      board (DM 3300)
£1118 $2236   (10-Feb-91 CC.P22) Joueur de pipeau (73x54cm-29x21in) s. i. verso
      (F.FR 11000)
£1250 $2438   (15-Oct-90 SY.J51/R) Composition 95 (35x28cm-14x11in) s. acrylic paper
      (SA.R 6200)
£1339 $2571   (28-Nov-90 PH.T31/R) L'homme de parade (49x59cm-19x23in) s.i.verso
      (C.D 3000)
£1544 $3026   (10-Nov-90 FAL.M67/R) Laboureur (30x60cm-12x24in) s. (S.KR 16800)
£1698 $2938   (22-May-91 BA.S337/R) Composition AB (60x50cm-24x20in) s. (S.KR 18000)
£1743 $2963   (29-May-91 GL.P212) Composition (58x76cm-23x30in) s. (F.FR 17500)
£2037 $4012   (29-Oct-90 LC.P65/R) Paysage (33x41cm-13x16in) s. (F.FR 20000)
£2312 $4000   (7-May-91 CE.NY114/R) L'homme de parade (50x61cm-20x24in) s.
£2574 $5044   (10-Nov-90 FAL.M66/R) Composition with triangel (64x49cm-25x19in) s.
      paper (S.KR 28000)
£3058 $5933   (4-Dec-90 BA.S75/R) 'Masse' (65x54cm-26x21in) s. (S.KR 33000)
£3244 $6293   (4-Dec-90 BA.S76/R) 'La terre' (55x65cm-22x26in) s. (S.KR 35000)
£3321 $6376   (27-Nov-90 BU.S61/R) Maternite (50x65cm-20x26in) s.s.i.verso
      (S.KR 36000)
£3469 $6731   (8-Dec-90 GAB.G2462/R) Profil sur rouge (65x50cm-26x20in) s. i. verso
      (S.FR 8500)
£3676 $7206   (10-Nov-90 FAL.M64/R) Ouvertur dynamique (80x65cm-31x26in) s.
      (S.KR 40000)
£3811 $7432   (11-Oct-90 QWA.P90/R) Composition (30x60cm-12x24in) s. (F.FR 38000)

COIGNARD, James (1925-) French-cont.

£3943	$7690	(15-Oct-90 CSC.P67/R) Architectures et structures P - 5 (56x45cm-22x18in) s. paper (F.FR 39000)
£5139	$9969	(5-Dec-90 ZZ.F203/R) Carres rouges (62x87cm-24x34in) s.d.1970 (F.FR 50000)
£5147	$10088	(10-Nov-90 FAL.M63/R) Axe de tension-rouge (82x99cm-32x39in) s. (S.KR 56000)
£7645	$14679	(2-Dec-90 M.V101 b) Monolithyque (146x114cm-57x45in) s. (F.FR 75000)
£400	$652	(3-Jul-91 CSC.P82) Vision equilibree (25x19cm-10x7in) s. acrylic collages (F.FR 4000)
£441	$750	(28-May-91 AB.S5184/R) Composition (47x60cm-19x24in) s. mixed media (S.KR 4700)
£612	$1180	(16-Dec-90 GL.P31) Sans titre (19x28cm-7x11in) s.i.d.1974 Indian ink (F.FR 6000)
£706	$1376	(20-Jan-91 GL.P127/R) Irrealite (92x73cm-36x29in) s. collage acrylic canvas (F.FR 7000)
£768	$1506	(11-Nov-90 ZZ.F208/R) Compositon pyramidale (67x51cm-26x20in) s. mixed media (F.FR 7500)
£907	$1769	(28-Oct-90 M.V48/R) Composition en rouge et bleu s. mixed media (F.FR 9000)
£1509	$2611	(22-May-91 BA.S333/R) A-b, I to VII (25x40cm-10x16in) s. paper on canvas with collage (S.KR 16000)
£1835	$3541	(16-Dec-90 P.V36/R) Composition (50x23cm-20x9in) s. mixed media (F.FR 18000)
£2140	$4194	(24-Nov-90 HOR.H6/R) Blue squares (65x50cm-26x20in) s. mixed media (F.M 15000)
£2254	$3831	(28-May-91 AB.S5182/R) Deux bleu (65x51cm-26x20in) s. mixed media (S.KR 24000)
£3265	$6335	(8-Dec-90 GAB.G2464/R) 127 sous les drapeaux (55x45cm-22x18in) s. oil collage (S.FR 8000)
£3289	$6380	(5-Dec-90 ZZ.F89/R) Composition AB (40x30cm-16x12in) s. mixed media (F.FR 32000)
£3968	$6865	(25-May-91 AB.L53/R) Traces (60x72cm-24x28in) s. s.i.verso oil mixed media canvas (S.FR 10000)

COIGNARD, James and PELLEGRINI, Alfred Heinrich (20th C) French/Swiss

£640	$1248	(17-Oct-90 G.Z124) Florence, Piazza del Duomo (24x32cm-9x13in) s.i.d.1919 indian ink brush pen (S.FR 1600)

COIGNET, Gillis II (17/18th C) French

£10398	$20483	(14-Nov-90 SY.AM108/R) Orpheus charming the animals (39cm-15ins circular) s. copper (D.FL 34000)

COIGNET, L (19th C) ?

£518	$1010	(24-Oct-90 GD.B229/R) Portrait of young boy (69x57cm-27x22in) s.d.1886 pastel (S.FR 1300)

COIGNET, Marie (19th C) French

£714	$1377	(12-Dec-90 ZZ.F34/R) Bouquet de giroflees dans une jardiniere bleue (32x40cm-13x16in) s. (F.FR 7000)

COKE, Alfred Sacheverell (fl.1881-1892) British

£32000	$63040	(1-Nov-90 C304/R) Feeding the peacocks (67x199cm-26x78in) s.d.1874 s.i.verso

COL, J D and LEEMPUTTEN, Cornelis van (19th C) Belgian

£2741	$5400	(7-Oct-90 LIT.L335) Sheep and shepherds in barn (74x107cm-29x42in) s.

COL, Jan David (1822-1900) Belgian

£2333	$4480	(18-Dec-90 GM.B4021/R) Le Concours (26x33cm-10x13in) panel (B.FR 140000)

COL, Jan David and MAES, Eugene Remy (19th C) Belgian

£12000	$23040	(28-Nov-90 S69/R) Training the dog (80x65cm-31x26in) s.

COLACICCO, Salvatore (?) Italian?

£525	$1050	(10-Feb-91 LIT.L50) The Nantucket whaler, Boston (51x76cm-20x30in) s. panel
£536	$1050	(27-Jan-91 LIT.L12a) Portrait of Nantucket Whaler Boston (51x76cm-20x30in) s. panel
£677	$1300	(28-Nov-90 D.NY38) American sailing ship 'Challenge' (61x91cm-24x36in) s.i.verso board
£781	$1500	(28-Nov-90 D.NY37) American sailing ship 'Morning Star' off Malta (61x91cm-24x36in) s.i.verso board
£1000	$1950	(18-Oct-90 CSK190/R) Sailing ship 'Hurricane' off coast of Portugal. 'Eleonora' entering Genoa's Harbour (51x76cm-20x30in) s. s.i.verso board pair

COLAS, Dominique (1960-) French

£396	$708	(14-Apr-91 APT.P77) Prole (66x49cm-26x19in) s. mixed media (F.FR 4000)

COLBRANDT, Oscar (1879-1959) ?

£1314	$2273	(25-May-91 KV.L50) St Francis with a dove (93x64cm-37x25in) s. chl. (B.FR 80000)

COLDSTREAM, Sir William (1908-1987) British

£2500	$4625	(8-Mar-91 C117/R) Falmouth (30x40cm-12x16in) i.d.1978

COLE, A (1830-?) British
£1300 $2249   (22-May-91 JT1) First riding lesson (51x61cm-20x24in) s.d.1862

COLE, E (19th C) British
£680 $1149   (1-May-91 GD.B165) River landscape, spring (60x29cm-24x11in) s.
(S.FR 1700)

COLE, George (1810-1883) British
£1600 $2688   (23-Apr-91 S88/R) Setter (35x53cm-14x21in) s.indist.d.
£1868 $3250   (27-Mar-91 B.SF4183/R) Three children playing by stone gate
(34x52cm-13x20in) s. panel
£3815 $7478   (11-Feb-91 SY.J392/R) Village of Encrone, near Mortimers Cross,
Herefordshire. Clifford Castlenear Hoy, South Wales
(60cm-24ins circular) s.d.1866 pair (SA.R 19000)

COLE, George (attrib) (1810-1883) British
£640 $1184   (6-Mar-91 SC4366) Cattle in stream (33x58cm-13x23in) bears sig.

COLE, George Vicat (1833-1893) British
£1900 $3705   (18-Oct-90 SC3105/R) The bracken gatherers (49x75cm-19x30in) s.d.1865
£2200 $4334   (1-Nov-90 C254 a/R) The cottage well (31x41cm-12x16in) s.d.1860
£2367 $4000   (20-Apr-91 WOL.C83/R) Thatched house in country (51x74cm-20x29in) s.
£2500 $4825   (12-Dec-90 PHS787/R) Surrey pastoral mono.d.1877
£4000 $6520   (14-Jun-91 C245/R) Wargrave, looking from the wharf up the river
(40x61cm-16x24in) mono.d.1880
£420   *$840*   *(8-Feb-91 C39) A mountain range at sunset (18x25cm-7x10in) mono. pencil
W/C*
£550   *$1089*   *(30-Jan-91 S168/R) Late summer landscape (27x41cm-11x16in) mono. W/C
over pencil*

COLE, George Vicat (attrib) (1833-1893) British
£1600 $3024   (27-Sep-90 CSK88/R) River landscape with mill at sunset
(143x210cm-56x83in) bears.sig.d.1872

COLE, H (?) ?
£700 $1323   (27-Sep-90 CSK87/R) Departing day, view near Staines (50x76cm-20x30in)
s. s.i.verso

COLE, James (19th C) British
£1500 $2835   (27-Sep-90 CSK128/R) The model boy (40x55cm-16x22in) s.d.1880

COLE, Joseph Foxcroft (1837-1892) American
£625 $1200   (17-Dec-90 SY.NY40/R) River at dusk (30x51cm-12x20in) s.

COLE, Lillian (19th C) British
£600 $1110   (5-Mar-91 AG243) Cullercoats Bay (28x44cm-11x17in) s.d.1890 i.label
verso

COLE, Philip Tennyson (fl.1880-1930) British
£950   *$1644*   *(20-May-91 PH3) Mother and daughter (58x43cm-23x17in) s. W/C htd white*

COLE, Rex Vicat (1870-1940) British
£600 $1008   (18-Jul-91 PHX354) The Regal - on a misty morning from Hyde Park
(23x33cm-9x13in) s.i.board sketch verso
£720 $1354   (18-Sep-90 SWS706/R) Harvest time (35x53cm-14x21in) s.d.1900
£750 $1470   (8-Nov-90 PHI227) Wooded landscape with figure (47x57cm-19x22in) s.

COLEBROOKE, Robert H (1762-1808) British
£1000   *$1790*   *(9-Apr-91 C35/R) South view of Governor General's garden house at Gaude,
Barrackpur (34x56cm-13x22in) s.d.1794 i.verso pencil pen ink W/C*

COLEMAN, Alfred (?-1953) Australian
£1033 $1694   (17-Jun-91 MGS.S170) Poplars (44x55cm-17x22in) s. board (A.D 2200)

COLEMAN, E E (?) ?
£1487   *$2900*   *(21-Oct-90 HG.C43) Italian farm scene (41x58cm-16x23in) s. W/C*

COLEMAN, Edward (?-1867) British
£1500 $3000   (5-Feb-91 S21/R) Day's catch (63x76cm-25x30in) s.d.1834

COLEMAN, Enrico (1846-1911) Italian
£547   *$929*   *(28-May-91 F.R36) Casale in campagna (12x15cm-5x6in) s. W/C
(I.L 1200000)*
£1386   *$2676*   *(11-Dec-90 CH.R111) Porta Furba (25x35cm-10x14in) s. W/C (I.L 3000000)*
£2659   *$4600*   *(21-May-91 CE.NY320/R) Monk reading in garden (29x43cm-11x17in) s.i. W/C
board*
£2781   *$5200*   *(1-Aug-90 B.P62/R) Herding in Roman campagna (41x74cm-16x29in) s. W/C*

COLEMAN, Helen Cordelia see ANGELL, Helen Cordelia

COLEMAN, Michael (1946-) American
£2041 $4000   (7-Nov-90 B.SF3810/R) Indian teepee by stream (35x51cm-14x20in)
s.d.1.9.73 board

COLEMAN, R Clarkson (1884-1945) American
£736 $1200   (11-Jun-91 MOR.P12) Coastal - moonset at sunrise (36x46cm-14x18in) s.

COLEMAN, R Clarkson (1884-1945) American-cont.
£1020 $2000   (13-Feb-91 B.SF2106/R) Changing tide (35x51cm-14x20in) s. board
£1148 $2250   (12-Feb-91 MOR.P45) Over rocks (51x76cm-20x30in) s.

COLEMAN, Ralph Pallen (1892-1968) American
£941 $1600   (1-Jun-91 IH.NY42/R) Victorian couple at fence with dog
    (74x53cm-29x21in) s.

COLEMAN, William (1922-) Australian
£560 $1092   (15-Oct-90 AAA.S165) The blue tie (37x23cm-15x9in) s. board (A.D 1400)
£562 $1080   (26-Nov-90 SY.ME82/R) Seated female nude (42x27cm-17x11in) s. board
    (A.D 1400)
£660 $1076   (1-Jul-91 AAA.S200) The Old Buick (32x27cm-13x11in) s. board (A.D 1400)
£683 $1311   (26-Nov-90 SY.ME112/R) Steps (36x48cm-14x19in) s. i.verso canvas on
    board (A.D 1700)
£724 $1224   (15-Apr-91 AAA.S148) La toilet (60x76cm-24x30in) s. board (A.D 1600)
£769 $1300   (16-Apr-91 J.M579) Street people (43x58cm-17x23in) s. canvas board
    (A.D 1700)
£800 $1504   (17-Sep-90 MGS.S248 c) Young couple (28x19cm-11x7in) s. canvas on board
    (A.D 1800)
£869 $1711   (13-Nov-90 J.M109) Seated nude (59x75cm-23x30in) s. canvas on board
    (A.D 2250)
£1266 $2430   (14-Aug-90 SY.ME150/R) Nude (64x85cm-25x33in) s. (A.D 3000)
£1674 $2813   (22-Apr-91 SY.ME76/R) Sisters (70x90cm-28x35in) s. board (A.D 3600)

COLEMAN, William Stephen (1829-1904) British
£650   *$1086*   *(5-Jun-91 S283) Cottage steps (12x17cm-5x7in) s. W/C over pencil htd*
    white
£780   *$1451*   *(5-Sep-90 BT116/R) Girl in punt (51x20cm-20x8in) s. W/C htd white*
£880   *$1734*   *(1-Nov-90 D98/R) Near Cransham, Bucks - with figure on lane at sunset,*
    town beyond (10x23cm-4x9in) s. W/C bodycol
£920   *$1582*   *(14-May-91 SWS102/R) By the cottage steps (25x19cm-10x7in) init. W/C*
    htd.bodycol scratching out
£1700   *$3315*   *(18-Oct-90 SC3046/R) The dandelion clock (16x19cm-6x7in) init. W/C*
    bodycol.over pencil
£1800   *$3402*   *(26-Sep-90 S318/R) Building sand castle. Fishing (14x21cm-6x8in) s. W/C*
    over pencil htd white pair
£2200   *$4356*   *(30-Jan-91 S237/R) Cottages at Witley, Surrey (20x25cm-8x10in) init. W/C*
    htd bodycol

COLI, Giovanni and GHERARDI, Filippo (17th C) Italian
£7047 $12191   (21-May-91 SY.Mi1057/R) La visione di un santo (285x237cm-112x93in)
    i.verso (I.L 15500000)

COLIN, Alexandre Marie (1798-1873) French
£4281 $8263   (14-Dec-90 ARC.P119/R) Hameau de pecheurs sur la cote normande
    (38x70cm-15x28in) s.d.1849 (F.FR 42000)

COLIN, Gustave (1828-1910) French
£806 $1313   (11-Jun-91 I.N32) Le pecheur (35x26cm-14x10in) s. panel (F.FR 8000)
£1003 $1956   (12-Oct-90 APT.P94) Promenade dans le dunes (73x92cm-29x36in) s.
    (F.FR 10000)

COLIN, Jean (20th C) Belgian
£4491 $8847   (6-Oct-90 KV.L55/R) La lecture (100x90cm-39x35in) s. (B.FR 280000)

COLIN, P (20th C) French
£1815 $3448   (1-Mar-91 CB.P53/R) Femme voilee (117x88cm-46x35in) s. (F.FR 18000)

COLIN, Paul (1892-1985) French
£646 $1091   (20-Apr-91 HOR.H7/R) Wooded landscape with hares (25x40cm-10x16in) s.
    (F.M 4500)
£822 $1595   (7-Dec-90 GL.P62) Le bal au temps de Moliere (58x75cm-23x30in) s.
    i.d.1955 verso panel (F.FR 8000)
£1131 $2193   (7-Dec-90 GL.P26) Centenaire de Pirandello (90x75cm-35x30in) s. soaked
    panel (F.FR 11000)
£3181 $5376   (16-Apr-91 I.N95) Electornique (100x81cm-39x32in) s. (F.FR 32000)
£15905 $26879   (16-Apr-91 QWA.P7/R) Tumulte noir (78x114cm-31x45in) s. i.d.1925 verso
    panel (F.FR 160000)
£355   *$703*   *(28-Jan-91 PPB.P18) La rue de Lappe (20x29cm-8x11in) s. gouache pastel*
    (F.FR 3500)
£402   *$659*   *(21-Jun-91 D.P63) Vallee de la Sioule (35x43cm-14x17in) s. W/C gouache*
    (F.FR 4000)
£457   *$915*   *(6-Feb-91 FB.P77) L'athlete (38x27cm-15x11in) s. ink wash (F.FR 4500)*
£617   *$1196*   *(7-Dec-90 GL.P27) New York City (22x27cm-9x11in) s. gouache (F.FR 6000)*
£771   *$1495*   *(7-Dec-90 GL.P7) Composition aux instruments de musique*
    (39x29cm-15x11in) s. collage (F.FR 7500)
£925   *$1794*   *(7-Dec-90 GL.P28) Composition cubiste (53x35cm-21x14in) s. chk.chl.*
    (F.FR 9000)
£1529   *$2936*   *(30-Nov-90 ARC.P99) Personnage (33x20cm-13x8in) studio st. s. verso*
    collage chl. (F.FR 15000)
£2367   *$3858*   *(14-Jun-91 HC.P43) Projet d'affiche (120x180cm-47x71in) s. gouache paper*
    laid down on board (F.FR 23500)
£3400   *$5542*   *(1-Jul-91 APT.P156/R) Danseurs cubistes both s. gouache two*
    (F.FR 34000)

COLIN, Paul (1892-1985) French-cont.
£5424   *$10685*   (6-Oct-90 GL.P16/R) Josephine Baker (100x80cm-39x31in) s.d.1925 soaked
       panel (F.FR 55000)
£6300   *$10269*   (1-Jul-91 APT.P159/R) Orchestre de jazz, Maurice Chevalier et Vue de
       Paris (48x63cm-19x25in) s.d.25 chl.gouache pasted paper (F.FR 63000)
£8700   *$14181*   (1-Jul-91 APT.P158/R) La revue Negre (64x49cm-25x19in) s.d.1925 gouache
       ink chl. (F.FR 87000)

COLIN, Paul-Emile (1877-?) French
£625 $1200   (27-Nov-90 W.T1121) Le repos des nymphes (46x54cm-18x21in) panel
       (C.D 1400)
£1992 $3386   (29-May-91 GL.P25) La moisson (46x55cm-18x22in) studio st. verso
       (F.FR 20000)
£670   *$1186*   (21-Mar-91 LC.P205/R) Ballet negre (40x32cm-16x13in) s. bears studio st.
       oil pastel (F.FR 6700)

COLKETT, Samuel David (1806-1863) British
£1000 $1690   (19-Apr-91 K544/R) Figure in wooded landscape with tudor cottage
       (38x58cm-15x23in) s.
£1100 $2167   (31-Oct-90 S327/R) Farm near Norwich (35x47cm-14x19in) s.d.1858 panel
£1600 $2640   (9-Jul-91 PH144/R) Herding cattle to homestead (30x41cm-12x16in) s.
       s.i.d.1851 verso
£2200 $4312   (20-Nov-90 PH24/R) A shepherd with his flock in a wooded river landscape
       (28x38cm-11x15in) panel

COLL Y PI, Juan (?) Spanish
£1898 $3700   (17-Oct-90 FER.M192/R) La taberna (40x60cm-16x24in) s. (S.P 350000)

COLLE, Michel-Auguste (1872-1949) French
£800 $1504   (20-Sep-90 CSK55) Soir d'automne, bords de la Meurthe a Baccarat
       (76x52cm-30x20in) s.i.d.1902 i.verso board

COLLE, Raffaelino del (attrib) (1490-1566) Italian
£2462 $4800   (10-Oct-90 CH.NY203/R) The Annunciation (72x58cm-28x23in) panel

COLLE, de (?) ?
£1400   *$2758*   (5-Oct-90 C140/R) Rialto Bridge, Venice (30x46cm-12x18in) indist.s.
       pencil W/C

COLLEN, Henry (1798-1872) British
£450 $743   (10-Jul-91 C152) An officer, possibly Thomas Smith (9x?cm-4x?in)
       min.s.d.1840 velvet-lined wood cas rec.

COLLENIUS, Herman (1650-1720) German
£1054 $1697   (24-Jun-91 BL.P19/R) Portrait d'homme (33x27cm-13x11in) mono.
       (F.FR 10500)
£5300 $9169   (20-May-91 SWS153/R) Venus and Adonis with cupid (92x76cm-36x30in)
       s.d.1714 oval

COLLETT, Frederik (1839-1914) Norwegian
£1678 $3357   (9-Feb-91 BU.O32) Landscape with houses (39x58cm-15x23in) s.
       (N.KR 19000)

COLLIER, Alan Caswell (1911-1990) Canadian
£606 $1042   (14-May-91 JOY.T155) Woods interior (50x75cm-20x30in) s. board
       (C.D 1200)
£654 $1093   (3-Jun-91 R.T132/R) Iceberg Peter, Baffin Bay - aboard C.C.G.S.
       D'Iberville (30x40cm-12x16in) s. millboard (C.D 1250)
£1228 $2407   (20-Nov-90 JOY.T359) New ice, Eureka sound from C.C.G.S., d'Iberville
       (60x90cm-24x35in) s. (C.D 2800)
£1237 $2103   (27-May-91 HO.ED244/R) In Jones Sound (51x76cm-20x30in) s. i.verso
       (C.D 2400)
£1392 $2366   (27-May-91 HO.ED18/R) Arctic beach (61x81cm-24x32in) s. i.verso board
       (C.D 2700)
£1622 $2643   (10-Jun-91 W.T1052) October light, Near Barry's Bay, Ont.
       (76x127cm-30x50in) s. i. verso (C.D 3000)

COLLIER, Arthur Bevan (19th C) British
£545 $921   (20-Apr-91 HOR.H8/R) Shepherd and sheep (30x46cm-12x18in) s. (F.M 3800)
£900 $1692   (18-Sep-90 CSK140/R) Tamar and Endsleigh (61x91cm-24x36in) s.d.74
       s.i.d.1873verso

COLLIER, Evert (?-c.1702) Dutch
£6145 $11000   (11-Apr-91 SY.NY120/R) Trompe l'oeil of documents, combs, medallion,
       miniature and other objects (44x66cm-17x26in) init.
£7000 $13790   (31-Oct-90 S52/R) Still life of peaches on dish with tankard and other
       things on table (61x72cm-24x28in) s.d.1699
£13000 $23270   (12-Apr-91 C39/R) Vanitas still life - inkwell, pocket watch, candle,
       books, on draped table with globe behind (64x77cm-25x30in) s.d.1706
£23743 $42500   (11-Apr-91 SY.NY119/R) Trompe l'oeil of pamphlet history of Rump
       Parliament, magnifying glass and other objects (50x69cm-20x27in)
       d.indist.1663

COLLIER, Evert (style) (?-c.1702) Dutch
£1700 $3349   (31-Oct-90 S319/R) Trompe d'oeil still life of letter rack with combs
       and musical score (52x70cm-20x28in) panel

COLLIER, Evert (style) (?-c.1702) Dutch-cont.
£1900 $3800   (7-Feb-91 C68/R) A vanitas still life with candle, skull, books and set of paint brushes (76x65cm-30x26in)

COLLIER, The Hon John (1850-1934) British
£9500 $18620   (22-Nov-90 CG516/R) The child bride (137x87cm-54x34in) s.d.1883

COLLIER, Thomas (1840-1891) British
£420 $727   (20-Mar-91 SWS380/R) On the moors (24x34cm-9x13in) s.d.Augt.15th 1883 W/C over pencil
£460 $777   (1-May-91 PHL72) Figure by some trees in landscape (23x34cm-9x13in) s. col.wash
£580 $1038   (13-Mar-91 B82) Roses in a blue and whtie vase (39x28cm-15x11in) s.d.1872 WC bodycol.
£2900 $4988   (14-May-91 SWS45/R) The heart of Surrey (23x34cm-9x13in) s.d.63 i.verso W/C over pencil htd.gum arabic

COLLIER, Thomas Frederick (fl.1856-1874) British
£1500 $2940   (13-Feb-91 S104/R) Still life with blossom and bird's nest (28x23cm-11x9in) s. board
£900 $1503   (6-Jun-91 B210/R) Still life of roses. Still life of pansies (27x38cm-11x15in) s.d.1884 W/C htd white pair

COLLIGNON (19/20th C) ?
£4118 $7000   (31-May-91 CH.NY246/R) Allegories of astrology and art with woman before globe and with drawing (89x146cm-35x57in) one s.d.1762 panel shaped pair

COLLIGNON, Georges (1923-) Belgian
£11146 $21511   (12-Dec-90 CH.AM352/R) Composition rouge (125x190cm-49x75in) s.d.49 d.1949 verso (D.FL 36000)
£12831 $25277   (6-Oct-90 KV.L381/R) Le Don du Coeur (115x196cm-45x77in) s.d.1961-62 (B.FR 800000)
£1150 $2243   (23-Oct-90 C.A339) Monochrome bleu (43x57cm-17x22in) s. W/C (B.FR 70000)
£1233 $2403   (23-Oct-90 C.A338) Monochrome bleu (60x48cm-24x19in) s. W/C (B.FR 75000)
£1808 $3525   (23-Oct-90 C.A336/R) Composition (64x48cm-25x19in) s.d.1960 collage (B.FR 110000)
£2299 $3977   (25-May-91 KV.L408/R) Composition (63x47cm-25x19in) s. oil collage (B.FR 140000)
£2301 $4486   (23-Oct-90 C.A335/R) Composition (68x51cm-27x20in) s.d.1960 collage (B.FR 140000)
£2629 $5127   (23-Oct-90 C.A334/R) Composition (64x48cm-25x19in) s.d.1960 collage (B.FR 160000)

COLLIN DE VERMONT, Hyacinthe (circle) (1693-1761) French
£3479 $5880   (18-Apr-91 APT.P95/R) Diane et Endymion. Mercure et Argus pair (F.FR 35000)

COLLIN, Marcus (1882-1966) Finnish
£1862 $3669   (17-Nov-90 BU.H27/R) August evening (50x39cm-20x15in) s.d.18 (F.M 13000)
£1934 $3810   (17-Nov-90 BU.H26/R) Winter's evening (40x40cm-16x16in) s.d.17 panel (F.M 13500)
£3868 $7620   (17-Nov-90 BU.H24/R) Waiting room (60x73cm-24x29in) s.d.61 (F.M 27000)
£547 $940   (14-May-91 HOR.H23) Wood-cutter (23x30cm-9x12in) s.d.1929 pastel (F.M 3800)
£716 $1411   (17-Nov-90 BU.H186/R) A simple meal (24x31cm-9x12in) s.d.25 W/C (F.M 5000)
£716 $1411   (17-Nov-90 BU.H185/R) Interior (40x29cm-16x11in) s.d.26 W/C (F.M 5000)
£781 $1398   (14-Apr-91 BU.H102/R) Washerwomen (24x32cm-9x13in) s.d.59 pastel (F.M 5500)
£860 $1693   (17-Nov-90 BU.H187/R) Old woman on steps in street (32x25cm-13x10in) s.d.50 pastel (F.M 6000)
£1146 $2258   (17-Nov-90 BU.H189/R) Church interior (32x25cm-13x10in) s.d.58 pastel (F.M 8000)
£1218 $2399   (17-Nov-90 BU.H190/R) In the church (25x32cm-10x13in) s.d.48 pastel (F.M 8500)
£1284 $2516   (24-Nov-90 HOR.H64/R) Departure (47x62cm-19x24in) s. pastel (F.M 9000)
£1289 $2540   (17-Nov-90 BU.H188/R) Three women (32x25cm-13x10in) s.d.52 pastel (F.M 9000)
£1435 $2425   (20-Apr-91 HOR.H53/R) In the harbour (34x46cm-13x18in) s. W/C (F.M 10000)

COLLIN, Raphael (1850-1916) French
£892 $1516   (28-May-91 AB.S4750/R) Reclining nude (30x46cm-12x18in) s.d.1912 (S.KR 9500)

COLLINGS, Albert Harry (?-1947) British
£2100 $3654   (27-Mar-91 S16/R) Girl on tigerskin rug (51x40cm-20x16in) s.

COLLINI, P (19/20th C) Italian
£4858 $9522   (20-Nov-90 APT.P259/R) Salome (73x99cm-29x39in) s. hardboard (F.FR 48000)

COLLINS OF MANCHESTER, John (19th C) British
£781 $1500 (28-Nov-90 D.NY39) Fred Vickers with his spaniel (46x36cm-18x14in)
        s.i.d.1852verso board

COLLINS, Cecil (1908-1989) British
£1200 $2364 (1-Nov-90 B37/R) A fool (15x10cm-6x4in) s.d.1961 s.i.d.1961verso board
£1500 $2820 (20-Sep-90 CSK86/R) Landscape (18x25cm-7x10in) s.d.1960 s.i.d.verso
        board
£1650 $3053 (8-Mar-91 C126/R) Woman and landscape (28x32cm-11x13in) s.d.1962
        s.i.d.verso board

COLLINS, Charles (circle) (c.1680-1744) British
£2000 $3800 (1-Mar-91 C58/R) Still life of dead game with pheasant, duck, hare and
        bird in landscape (126x101cm-50x40in)

COLLINS, Charles (1851-1921) British
£800 $1568 (8-Nov-90 PHI231) Summer landscape with cows resting by pond
        (39x59cm-15x23in) s.d.1879
£850 $1615 (1-Mar-91 PHE92) Cattle resting on cliff top (49x89cm-19x35in) s.
£904 $1700 (22-Sep-90 WOL.C117) Bringing sheep and cattle home (61x91cm-24x36in) s.
£2700 $4563 (30-Apr-91 PH73/R) Timber hauling (50x76cm-20x30in) s.d.1872
£600 $1170 (15-Jan-91 SWS15) The close of winter's day (34x52cm-13x20in) s. i.verso
        W/C over pencil

COLLINS, Deborah (1967-) British
£500 $980 (13-Feb-91 B145) Botanic Road (91x122cm-36x48in) s.i.d.1990 verso

COLLINS, Earl (20th C) American
£685 $1150 (28-Apr-91 LIT.L98) Nantucket, marinescape of sidewheeler
        (61x66cm-24x26in) s.
£1809 $3400 (7-Aug-90 RB.HY270/R) Puritan 1885 (46x61cm-18x24in) s.

COLLINS, James Edgell (1820-?) British
£1400 $2478 (20-Mar-91 ZZ.B139) Portrait of Geraldine (91x71cm-36x28in) mono.d.1855
        i. verso

COLLINS, Samuel (1735-1768) British
£450 $887 (1-Nov-90 S11/R) Portrait of Mrs Long nee Lambe (4x?cm-2x?in)
        min.init.d.1760 gold mount oval

COLLINS, William (1788-1847) British
£926 $1556 (16-Jul-91 JRL.S201/R) Before the storm (33x51cm-13x20in) s. panel
        (A.D 2000)
£2486 $4600 (10-Mar-91 H.C75/R) Fisherman's goodbye (64x76cm-25x30in) s.
£700 $1253 (9-Apr-91 C147/R) Fisherfolk on beach at low tide (18x26cm-7x10in)
        pencil W/C bodycol scratching out

COLLINS, William (snr-attrib) (?) British
£720 $1382 (30-Nov-90 T120/R) Figures and boats in cove (51x76cm-20x30in)

COLLINSON, Robert (1832-?) British
£3300 $6468 (13-Feb-91 S116/R) Wild flowers by corn field (23x30cm-9x12in) s.verso
        panel

COLLIVADINO, Pio (1869-1945) Argentinian
£809 $1400 (8-May-91 RO.BA219) Mancha (25x36cm-10x14in) s.
£2394 $4500 (18-Sep-90 RO.BA33) Puente de la noria (37x54cm-15x21in) s. panel

COLLOMB, Paul (1921-) French
£578 $1000 (7-May-91 CE.NY50/R) L'arbre aux fruits (61x46cm-24x18in) s.
£1040 $1800 (7-May-91 CE.NY47/R) L'arbre devant le lac (81x65cm-32x26in) s.
£1850 $3200 (7-May-91 CE.NY100/R) Les oiseaux (81x100cm-32x39in) s.

COLLS, Ebenezer (19th C) British
£780 $1303 (22-Jul-91 SWS991/R) Off Dover (39x65cm-15x26in) s.

COLLVER, Ethel Blanchard (1875-?) American
£1676 $3100 (8-Mar-91 S.BM275/R) Gramercey Park (33x41cm-13x16in) s. canvasboard

COLMAN, G (?) ?
£924 $1784 (11-Dec-90 CH.R149) La lettera (25x17cm-10x7in) s. W/C tempera
        (I.L 2000000)

COLMAN, Samuel (1832-1920) American
£632 $1200 (14-Sep-90 S.BM192/R) The Hill of the Alhambra (33x13cm-13x5in) s. panel
£1587 $3000 (27-Sep-90 CH.NY31/R) Along the river (10x9cm-4x4in) paper laid down on
        paper oval
£6349 $12000 (26-Sep-90 SY.NY39/R) Spanish market place (51x41cm-20x16in) s.d.64
£529 $1000 (25-Sep-90 CE.NY61/R) Ausable River, Adirondacks (25x32cm-10x13in)
        s.d.1879 W/C gouache
£636 $1100 (21-May-91 CE.NY443/R) View of Naples (27x34cm-11x13in) s. pastel board
£3421 $6500 (9-Jan-91 CH.NY121/R) Eucalyptus Grove, Santa Barbara. Geniseo s.i. one
        d.69 pencil ink W/C two

COLMO, Giovanni (1867-1947) Italian
£589 $996 (16-Apr-91 CH.R171) Paesaggio alpino (27x38cm-11x15in) s. board
(I.L 1300000)
£694 $1346 (4-Dec-90 F.R56) Baita in montagna (44x30cm-17x12in) s. panel
(I.L 1500000)

COLNOT, Arnout (1887-?) Dutch
£671 $1288 (27-Nov-90 SY.AM3807) Still life of books and plant on table
(84x74cm-33x29in) s. (D.FL 2200)
£781 $1351 (22-May-91 CH.AM309) River landscape with farm (48x62cm-19x24in) s.
(D.FL 2600)
£1141 $1974 (22-May-91 CH.AM400) Sheafs of corn (55x65cm-22x26in) s. (D.FL 3800)
£1201 $2078 (22-May-91 CH.AM328) Still life of yellow roses in vase, stoneware bowl
and book (61x50cm-24x20in) s. (D.FL 4000)
£2553 $4416 (22-May-91 CH.AM369/R) Still life with tulips in vase, mixed fruit on
plates and jug, on draped table (80x100cm-31x39in) s.d.38 (D.FL 8500)

COLOGNE SCHOOL German
£7784 $13156 (2-May-91 CH.AM84/R) Pentecost (34x21cm-13x8in) c.1500 panel
(D.FL 26000)

COLOGNE SCHOOL, 16th C German
£6351 $11368 (14-Mar-91 D.V63/R) Crucifixion with St Magdalen and other figures in
landscape (130x93cm-51x37in) panel (A.S 130000)
£6461 $10919 (18-Apr-91 APT.P32/R) Le bapteme d'un roi (82x50cm-32x20in) panel pasted
on panel (F.FR 65000)

COLOM Y AGUSTI, Juan (1879-?) Spanish
£1355 $2643 (17-Oct-90 FER.M187/R) Caserio (36x48cm-14x19in) s. W/C (S.P 250000)

COLOMBI, Plinio (1873-1951) Swiss
£600 $1014 (1-May-91 GD.B167/R) Winter landscape, Inner Schweiz (63x80cm-25x31in)
s.d.31 (S.FR 1500)
*£1270 $2197 (22-May-91 GS.B2066) Lake Thun with Bluemlisalp, winter
(52x69cm-20x27in) s.d.1947 W/C (S.FR 3200)*

COLOMBO, Giovanni Battista Innocenzo (attrib) (1717-1793) Italian
£3187 $5482 (14-May-91 GF.L2080/R) Southern landscape with shepherds
(43x55cm-17x22in) (S.FR 8000)

COLOMBO, Joe (20th C) Italian?
£2476 $4829 (22-Oct-90 BR.M117/R) Composizione nucleare (50x35cm-20x14in) s.d.1958
verso board (I.L 5500000)

COLOMBO, V (19th C) Italian
*£694 $1200 (21-May-91 CE.NY245/R) Roman lovers by crypt (52x43cm-20x17in) s. W/C
gouache*

COLONE, Adam de (attrib) (fl.1622-1628) British
£8000 $13200 (10-Jul-91 S8/R) Portrait of Sir Thomas Cowdray. Lady Cowdray
(77x61cm-30x24in) bears sig.d.1621 panel pair

COLQUHOUN, Brett (20th C) Australian
£888 $1447 (16-Jun-91 SY.ME43) Spark outside (166x99cm-65x39in) init.d.1987 verso
acrylic canvas (A.D 1900)

COLQUHOUN, Ithell (1906-1988) British
£600 $984 (20-Jun-91 DLY662) Creation du monde (25x28cm-10x11in) s.d.50 i.verso
board
£700 $1365 (18-Oct-90 CSK320/R) Tendrils of sleep (57x29cm-22x11in) s.i.d.1944
verso panel
£700 $1365 (18-Oct-90 CSK319/R) Bride of the pavement (76x61cm-30x24in) s.i.d.1942
verso
£900 $1746 (6-Dec-90 CSK203/R) Genius Loci (73x65cm-29x26in) s.d.46 s.i.d.1946
verso board
£4800 $9408 (9-Nov-90 C231/R) La Cathedrale Engloutie (131x196cm-52x77in)
s.stretcher

COLQUHOUN, Robert (1914-1962) British
£2600 $4524 (27-Mar-91 S199/R) Female nude (99x74cm-39x29in) s.d.53
£3200 $6240 (10-Oct-90 S149/R) The swineherds (62x42cm-24x17in) s.d.54 W/C

COLSON (19th C) ?
£1842 $3500 (27-Feb-91 SY.NY97/R) Summer fair (34x65cm-13x26in) s.

COLSON, Pierre Theodore (1805-1877) French
£2857 $5600 (6-Nov-90 GF.L2411/R) Robber scenes (25x33cm-10x13in) s.d.1836 pair
(S.FR 7000)

COLUCCI, Gio (20th C) Italian?
£781 $1515 (5-Dec-90 ZZ.F80/R) Composition au compotier et aux fruits
(59x48cm-23x19in) s. canvas laid down on board (F.FR 7600)
*£420 $701 (5-Jun-91 HC.P339) Femmes a la fontaine (13x16cm-5x6in) mono. ink wash
(F.FR 4200)*
£607 $1190 (23-Nov-90 PLF.P51) Adam et Eve (61x41cm-24x16in) s. goauche (F.FR 6000)

COLUCCI, Gio (20th C) Italian?-cont.
£680 $1108   (5-Jul-91 APT.P7) Nu au fauteuil (48x63cm-19x25in) s. gouache
                 (F.FR 6800)

COLUNGA, Alejandro (1948-) Mexican
£7908 $15500   (19-Nov-90 SY.NY281/R) La elefanta cirquera (80x130cm-31x51in) s.d.89
                 s.d.88-89verso
£12791 $22000   (15-May-91 CH.NY196/R) Chica fea con Pajaro Malo bajo la Lluvia pero
                 Feliz (179x141cm-70x56in) mono. i.d.1988-90 verso linen
£1658 $3250   (12-Feb-91 SY.NY286/R) Untitled (46x61cm-18x24in) s.i.d.78 mixed media

COLVILLE, Alex (1920-) Canadian
£53030 $91742   (6-May-91 SY.T114/R) Coastal figure (60x136cm-24x54in) s.d.1951 glazed
                 tempera board (C.D 105000)
£1818 $3127   (14-May-91 JOY.T55/R) Study for Western Star II (14x14cm-6x6in) s. W/C
                 (C.D 3600)

COLVILLE, George Garden (1887-) Australian
£689 $1295   (17-Sep-90 SY.ME77/R) Late evening (32x35cm-13x14in) s. board
                 (A.D 1550)

COMAN, Charlotte Buell (1833-1924) American
£833 $1400   (28-Apr-91 HG.C372) The farmyard (41x69cm-16x27in) s.

COMAS, Augusto (19/20th C) Spanish
£1229 $2372   (11-Dec-90 FER.M231/R) El pueblecito (33x45cm-13x18in) s. (S.P 225000)

COMBAS (20th C) ?
£1437 $2760   (2-Dec-90 E.LA85/R) Sans titre (25x18cm-10x7in) felt-pen (F.FR 14100)

COMBAS, Robert (1957-) ?
£2548 $4918   (16-Dec-90 GL.P137/R) Sans titre (108x74cm-43x29in) s. acrylic paper
                 laid down on canvas (F.FR 25000)
£3827 $6238   (11-Jun-91 CSC.P47/R) L'homme masque (115x90cm-45x35in) s.d.86 acrylic
                 (F.FR 38000)
£4523 $8095   (15-Mar-91 FB.P83/R) L'elephant (77x83cm-30x33in) s.d.1980 board
                 (F.FR 45000)
£4586 $7567   (10-Jul-91 FB.P111/R) Briques (153x134cm-60x53in) s.i. acrylic
                 (F.FR 46000)
£6070 $10561   (25-Mar-91 CR.P74/R) Les cactus s. W/C (F.FR 61000)
£8089 $15774   (15-Oct-90 CSC.P68/R) Caca (85x90cm-33x35in) s. acrylic paper laid down
                 on canvas (F.FR 80000)
£9684 $18690   (16-Dec-90 GL.P148/R) Le magicien (145x135cm-57x53in) s.d.86 acrylic
                 (F.FR 95000)
£11089 $21623   (23-Oct-90 CSC.P85/R) Personnage a la cravate rouge (174x174cm-69x69in)
                 s.d.81 acrylic tissue (F.FR 110000)
£11834 $20000   (2-May-91 CH.NY314/R) La Douce Musique qui fait Dancer
                 (144x240cm-57x94in) s.d.1984 acrylic fabric
£12220 $24073   (31-Oct-90 ZZ.F81/R) Joueurs de cartes (170x144cm-67x57in) s.d.1983
                 acrylic (F.FR 120000)
£12245 $24122   (16-Nov-90 FB.P88/R) Combas (127x204cm-50x80in) s. (F.FR 120000)
£13065 $23387   (15-Mar-91 FB.P82/R) Bataille de couple psychopathex avec amant volaille
                 (130x195cm-51x77in) s. acrylic (F.FR 130000)
£14070 $23075   (23-Jun-91 P.V86/R) Sans titre (220x185cm-87x73in) s.d.1987 acrylic
                 (F.FR 140000)
£14201 $24000   (2-May-91 CH.NY319/R) Les Trois Grosses (232x152cm-91x60in) s.d.85
£14257 $28086   (29-Oct-90 FB.P96/R) Les guerriers (203x165cm-80x65in) s.d.86 acrylic
                 (F.FR 140000)
£15121 $29486   (28-Oct-90 GL.P103/R) Magicien guerrier (126x186cm-50x73in) s.d.87
                 acrylic (F.FR 150000)
£15879 $26042   (23-Jun-91 P.V85/R) Le coq sportif presente les hooligans
                 (200x220cm-79x87in) s.d.1985 acrylic (F.FR 158000)
£16784 $27526   (23-Jun-91 P.V83/R) Armando, l'homme sirene (200x250cm-79x98in) s.
                 acrylic (F.FR 167000)
£2055 $3988   (5-Dec-90 ZZ.F69) Personnage (30x23cm-12x9in) s.d.89 felt (F.FR 20000)
£10617 $20703   (21-Oct-90 P.V142/R) Sans titre (130x162cm-51x64in) s.d.1987 acrylic
                 collage canvas (F.FR 105000)

COMBET-DESCOMBES, Pierre (1885-1966) French
£657 $1282   (16-Oct-90 CS.L41) Deux nus accroupis (54x46cm-21x18in) bears sig. chl.
                 (F.FR 6500)
£718 $1400   (16-Oct-90 CS.L42) Nu (64x49cm-25x19in) s. pastel (F.FR 7100)
£1112 $2169   (16-Oct-90 CS.L43/R) Nu couche (55x39cm-22x15in) bears sig.d.20 avril 31
                 W/C (F.FR 11000)

COMELLI, Dante (1880-?) Italian
£780 $1396   (12-Mar-91 F.M2) Verso la Carpegna (45x56cm-18x22in) i.verso panel
                 (I.L 1700000)

COMENSOLI, Mario (1922-) Spanish?
£2811 $5510   (24-Nov-90 AB.L55/R) Untitled (122x77cm-48x30in) s.d.70 acrylic pavatex
                 (S.FR 7000)

COMERFORD, John (18/19th C) British
£300 $588   (22-Jan-91 CSK27/R) Portrait of a young man (7x?cm-3x?in) min. oval

COMERFORD, John (18/19th C) British-cont.
£1800 $3456   *(18-Dec-90 C148/R) Portrait of Paul Helsham (7x?cm-3x?in) min.s.d.1798 gold frame plaited hair verso oval*

COMERRE, Leon (1850-1916) French
£7000 $11480   *(18-Jun-91 PH38/R) Innocence (60x50cm-24x20in) s.*
£10256 $20000   *(23-Oct-90 SY.NY316/R) The pretty maid (114x67cm-45x26in) s.*
£14359 $28000   *(23-Oct-90 SY.NY286/R) Eastern beauty (117x74cm-46x29in) s.*
£15087 $28966   *(29-Nov-90 ZZ.F31/R) Jeune fille mauresque (131x90cm-52x35in) s. (F.FR 148000)*

COMFORT, Charles Fraser (1900-) Canadian
£1351 $2203   *(10-Jun-91 W.T1098) North reflection (39x53cm-15x21in) s.d.'47 paper (C.D 2500)*

COMMENT, Jean-Francois (1919-) Swiss
£1587 $2746   *(25-May-91 AB.L102/R) Ecrit sur le soir (74x85cm-29x33in) s.d.1984 (S.FR 4000)*

COMMERE, Jean (1920-) French
£1600 $3008   *(20-Sep-90 CSK133) Les ombelliffers (89x129cm-35x51in) s.d.1969*
£9100 $17745   *(17-Oct-90 ARC.P67/R) Champ de ble (73x60cm-29x24in) s. (F.FR 90000)*
£1394 $2371   *(29-May-91 GL.P6) Bord de mer (104x73cm-41x29in) s. W/C (F.FR 14000)*

COMMERE, Yves (20th C) ?
£1381 $2720   *(6-Oct-90 GL.P18) Maison de pecheur (33x19cm-13x7in) s.d.1953 (F.FR 14000)*
£1417 $2777   *(22-Nov-90 ZZ.F64) Paysage (24x33cm-9x13in) s. panel (F.FR 14000)*
£1070 $2066   *(14-Dec-90 ARC.P24/R) Paysage (42x53cm-17x21in) s.d.52 W/C (F.FR 10500)*
£2024 $3968   *(22-Nov-90 ZZ.F62/R) Bouquets de fleurs et chaise (103x73cm-41x29in) s. W/C (F.FR 20000)*
£2024 $3968   *(22-Nov-90 ZZ.F63/R) Pecheurs (73x103cm-29x41in) s. W/C (F.FR 20000)*
£3239 $6348   *(22-Nov-90 ZZ.F65) Le Thoureil (71x98cm-28x39in) s.i.d.1980 W/C (F.FR 32000)*

COMMUNAL, Joseph (1876-1962) French
£1112 $2169   *(16-Oct-90 CS.L20/R) Il Monte del Forno, lago di Carloccio (72x92cm-28x36in) s. board (F.FR 11000)*

COMPARD, Emile (1900-) French
£992 $1716   *(25-May-91 AB.L101/R) Composition (100x80cm-39x31in) s. (S.FR 2500)*
£1580 $3049   *(12-Dec-90 APT.P81) Bateaux de peche a quai (73x60cm-29x24in) s. (F.FR 15500)*

COMPTE-CALIX, Francois Claudius (1813-1880) French
£1012 $1700   *(17-Jul-91 SY.NY250/R) Casualties of war (35x43cm-14x17in) s. panel*
£3878 $7639   *(14-Nov-90 FB.P9797/R) Scenes Galantes (22x30cm-9x12in) s. panel pair (F.FR 38000)*

COMPTON, E T (1849-1921) British
£7102 $12713   *(14-Apr-91 BU.H121/R) Italian alpine landscape (71x115cm-28x45in) s. (F.M 50000)*

COMPTON, Edward Harrison (1881-1960) British
£1104 $1800   *(5-Jul-91 S.W3082/R) Castle on the cliff, early spring (69x97cm-27x38in) s.*
£1689 $3294   *(26-Oct-90 BM.B755/R) Mountainous wooded landscape (70x95cm-28x37in) s. (DM 5000)*
£1701 $3010   *(20-Mar-91 KM.K1135/R) View of Alpine landscape (69x95cm-27x37in) s.d.1927 (DM 5000)*
£2273 $4386   *(12-Dec-90 WE.MU65/R) Farmhouse with Untersberg (70x85cm-28x33in) s.i. i.verso (DM 6500)*
£2534 $4941   *(26-Oct-90 BM.B757/R) Winter landscape with houses and figures, Schwendiberg (70x96cm-28x38in) s. i.verso (DM 7500)*
£2622 $5087   *(4-Dec-90 FN.S1788 a/R) Mountainous river landscape with farmhouse and old saw mill (19x25cm-7x10in) s.d.1882 panel (DM 7500)*
£2972 $5736   *(12-Dec-90 N.M462/R) Sella mountain range in the Dolomites (79x105cm-31x41in) s. (DM 8500)*
£3072 $5805   *(25-Sep-90 FN.S2134/R) Karersee with view of Rosengarten on summer's day (60x80cm-24x31in) s. (DM 9000)*
£3209 $6258   *(26-Oct-90 BM.B756/R) View of village in the mountains with figures (70x96cm-28x38in) s. (DM 9500)*
£3671 $7086   *(14-Dec-90 BM.B722/R) Konigsee landscape, autumn (63x90cm-25x35in) s.i. i.verso (DM 10500)*
£4000 $7880   *(13-Nov-90 SWS405/R) A Bavarian landscape (88x140cm-35x55in) s.d.1907 i. stretcher*
£342 $650   *(28-Feb-91 D.V104/R) Mountain landscape (22x26cm-9x10in) s.i. W/C (A.S 7000)*
£582 $1100   *(27-Sep-90 D.V243) View from cloister to garden (27x37cm-11x15in) s.i.d.32 W/C (A.S 12000)*
£685 $1226   *(13-Mar-91 N.M290/R) Cloister, Steingaden I (28x37cm-11x15in) s.d.1932 i.verso W/C htd.white over pencil (DM 2000)*
£839 $1636   *(10-Oct-90 WE.MU193/R) Mountain lake landscape with sheep (28x38cm-11x15in) s. W/C (DM 2500)*
£1024 $1935   *(25-Sep-90 FN.S2135/R) Dolomites landscape with rising fog (23x33cm-9x13in) s. i.verso W/C (DM 3000)*

COMPTON, Edward Harrison (1881-1960) British-cont.
£1027 $1839   (12-Mar-91 FN.S2317) Sicilian coastal landscape near Taormina, evening
       (19x30cm-7x12in) s. W/C (DM 3000)
£1329 $2379   (11-Apr-91 D.V295/R) View of town in the Alto Adige (26x36cm-10x14in) s.
       W/C (A.S 28000)
£1337 $2606   (11-Oct-90 D.V174/R) Village in Bavaria (28x42cm-11x17in) s.i.d. W/C
       (A.S 28000)
£1370 $2452   (12-Mar-91 FN.S2318) Alpine landscape with Schesaplana, Vorarlberg
       (20x32cm-8x13in) s. W/C (DM 4000)
£1541 $2512   (12-Jun-91 N.M225) High mountain landscape in spring (35x27cm-14x11in)
       s.i. W/C bodycol over pencil (DM 4500)
£1541 $2759   (12-Mar-91 FN.S2319/R) Lake landscape with Bernina Pass (21x33cm-8x13in)
       s. i.verso W/C (DM 4500)

COMPTON, Edward Theodore (1849-1921) British
£5758 $9904   (16-May-91 D.V187/R) Fjord landscape (76x51cm-30x20in) s.d.1880 i.verso
       (A.S 120000)
£7328 $13923   (28-Feb-91 D.V66/R) Summer at the Gotzenalp (41x65cm-16x26in) s.d.1916
       i.verso (A.S 150000)
£9790 $18895   (12-Dec-90 SY.MU53/R) View of Heiligenblut and Grossglockner
       (42x61cm-17x24in) s.d.1881 (DM 28000)
£13586 $25677   (27-Sep-90 D.V34/R) View of Trafoi with Ortler (76x101cm-30x40in)
       s.d.1913 (A.S 280000)
£19000 $31160   (19-Jun-91 S54/R) Alpine lake (71x115cm-28x45in) s.
£21834 $41266   (27-Sep-90 D.V35/R) Brenta mountain range in the Dolomites
       (113x163cm-44x64in) s. (A.S 450000)
£548 $981   (13-Mar-91 N.M293) Mountain range with remaining snow, possibly
       Silvretta (10x17cm-4x7in) s. W/C over pencil htd.white (DM 1600)
£612 $1206   (15-Nov-90 EA.Z154) By the mountain stream (27x33cm-11x13in) s.d.1903
       W/C (S.FR 1500)
£612 $1206   (15-Nov-90 EA.Z159) Mountain lake landscape (37x27cm-15x11in) s. W/C
       (S.FR 1500)
£685 $1226   (13-Mar-91 N.M291/R) Mountain valley with house by stream
       (23x33cm-9x13in) s. W/C (DM 2000)
£1027 $1839   (13-Mar-91 N.M292) Alpine landscape with farmhouses beneath trees and
       cattle (24x35cm-9x14in) s. W/C htd.white board (DM 3000)
£1050 $2048   (11-Oct-90 D.V228/R) Coach drawn by five horses in snow storm
       (17x29cm-7x11in) mono W/C grisaille (A.S 22000)
£1433 $2407   (25-Apr-91 D.V196/R) Lago Negro Ampezzo (23x30cm-9x12in) s.i.d.12 W/C
       (A.S 30000)
£1433 $2407   (25-Apr-91 D.V197/R) Mountain landscape near Cortina d'Ampezzo
       (23x30cm-9x12in) s.d.12 W/C (A.S 30000)
£2443 $4641   (28-Feb-91 D.V120/R) Swiss lake landscape (12x22cm-5x9in) s.d.72 W/C
       (A.S 50000)

COMPTON, Edward Thomas (19/20th C) British
£800 $1384   (22-May-91 WIN727) Swiss mountain valley with fir trees and stream
       (25x36cm-10x14in) s.d.1878 W/C
£1550 $3069   (30-Jan-91 S222/R) Matterhorn (45x32cm-18x13in) s.d.1879 W/C
£1700 $3366   (30-Jan-91 S217/R) Deer in Alps (45x31cm-18x12in) mono.d.1879 W/C over
       pencil

COMTE, Pierre Charles (1823-1895) French
£15600 $26364   (1-May-91 GD.B168/R) Woman seated in French interior listening to caged
       birds (77x53cm-30x21in) s. panel (S.FR 39000)

CONCA, Sebastiano (1676-1764) Italian
£21176 $36000   (30-May-91 SY.NY41/R) Saint Cecilia playing harp (47x35cm-19x14in)
£730 $1291   (19-Mar-91 F.M299/R) Angelo in volo (26x19cm-10x7in) i. black white chk
       (I.L 1600000)

CONCA, Sebastiano (attrib) (1676-1764) Italian
£2308 $4500   (11-Oct-90 SY.NY193/R) The Holy Family (19x13cm-7x5in) copper

CONCA, Sebastiano (circle) (1676-1764) Italian
£1801 $3512   (23-Oct-90 CH.R115) S.Cecilia mentre suona l'arpa (42x32cm-17x13in)
       (I.L 4000000)
£2154 $4200   (10-Oct-90 CH.NY4/R) Moses and the daughters of Jethro (30x41cm-12x16in)
       bears indis.sig.
£3815 $6143   (27-Jun-91 APT.P34/R) Vierge et l'enfant avec Saint Charles Borromee et
       Saint Ignace de Loyola (171x102cm-67x40in) (F.FR 38000)
£1000 $1690   (16-Apr-91 C99/R) The Presentation in the Temple (18x15cm-7x6in)
       blk.chk.ink wash htd.white

CONCA, Sebastiano (style) (1676-1764) Italian
£1700 $3400   (7-Feb-91 C20/R) The Madonna and child (28x21cm-11x8in) copper
£1800 $3420   (13-Sep-90 CSK324/R) Adoration of shepherds (80x58cm-31x23in)
£7000 $11830   (17-Apr-91 S12/R) Alexander the Great in the Temple of Jerusalem. The
       Idolatry of Solomon (98x137cm-39x54in) pair

CONCA, Tommaso (?-1815) Italian
£1200 $2400   (7-Feb-91 C139) Saint Joseph (74x61cm-29x24in) indist.s.i. stretcher
       oval

CONCHA, Jerry (20th C) American
£513 $1000   (24-Oct-90 B.SF1591/R) Oo-Wa-Tie (75x102cm-30x40in) s.i.d.1980 verso

CONCONI, L (1852-1917) Italian
£2400 $4704   (14-Feb-91 CSK180) The young pianist (71x84cm-28x33in) s. board

CONCONI, Luigi (1852-1917) Italian
£2090 $4117   (29-Oct-90 SY.F680) Figura femminile reclina (57x147cm-22x58in)
            (I.L 4600000)
£2544 $4935   (5-Dec-90 F.M62/R) Nastaglo degli Onesti (59x30cm-23x12in) s.
            (I.L 5500000)
£3210 $5746   (12-Mar-91 F.M82/R) Figura femminile (50x18cm-20x7in) s. panel
            (I.L 7000000)
£3648 $6093   (6-Jun-91 F.M224/R) Testa di giovane donna (50x45cm-20x18in) s.d.1890
            (I.L 8000000)
£2775 $5383   (5-Dec-90 F.M2) Paesaggio (44x71cm-17x28in) s. W/C (I.L 6000000)
£5929 $9901   (6-Jun-91 F.M226/R) Lezione di piano (45x41cm-18x16in) s. W/C
            (I.L 13000000)

CONDAMY, Charles Fernand de (19th C) French
£1437 $2500   (27-Mar-91 B.SF4087/R) Sounding the horn for the hounds. Rapid approach
            (30x47cm-12x19in) s. one d.1911 W/C

CONDER, C (1868-1909) British
£680 $1326   (15-Oct-90 AAA.S112) Spring stroll (34x49cm-13x19in) bears sig.
            (A.D 1700)

CONDER, Charles (1868-1909) British
£7171 $14127   (31-Oct-90 CH.S106/R) Landscape (24x14cm-9x6in) bears sig. board
            (A.D 18000)
£1004 $1978   (13-Nov-90 J.M292/R) On the terrace (16x24cm-6x9in) s.d.98 pastel
            (A.D 2600)
£2400 $4680   (24-Oct-90 S96/R) Fan design (17x55cm-7x22in) s. W/C silk fan-shaped
£3111 $5849   (17-Sep-90 SY.ME79/R) Memories from Chinese garden (22x41cm-9x16in)
            s.d.1899 W/C silk (A.D 7000)
£3861 $7606   (13-Nov-90 J.M268/R) Romantic garden with figures (36x47cm-14x19in) s.
            W/C (A.D 10000)

CONDO, George (20th C) American
£2551 $5000   (12-Feb-91 SY.NY472/R) Brown clown composition (46x38cm-18x15in)
£2551 $5000   (6-Nov-90 CE.NY276/R) Composition with flower (63x46cm-25x18in)
            s.i.d.7-19-87
£2601 $4500   (7-May-91 CE.NY298/R) King. Queen (27x22cm-11x9in) s.d.84-9 verso
            s.d.9-84 verso acrylic pair
£3024 $5897   (26-Oct-90 CC.P123/R) Arrangement (24x18cm-9x7in) s.i.d.1984 verso
            (F.FR 30000)
£714 $1400   (6-Nov-90 CE.NY275/R) Untitled (25x19cm-10x7in) s.d.86-1 brush col.inks
£1276 $2500   (12-Feb-91 SY.NY430/R) Screwdriver (51x71cm-20x28in) s.d.83 oil stick
£1276 $2500   (12-Feb-91 SY.NY393/R) Untitled (86x56cm-34x22in) s.d.81verso oil stick
£1531 $3000   (12-Feb-91 SY.NY429/R) Scissors (51x71cm-20x28in) s.d.83 oil stick
£1734 $3000   (7-May-91 CE.NY287/R) Carlyle (41x33cm-16x13in) s. s.d.87 stretcher oil
            paper collage canvas
£3061 $6000   (7-Nov-90 SY.NY345/R) Three drawings pencil crayon three drawings
£5020 $8082   (25-Jun-91 BG.P20) Composition (155x113cm-61x44in) s.d.83 oil gouache
            (F.FR 50000)

CONDY, Nicholas (1793-1857) British
£1150 $1944   (3-May-91 PHE103/R) View of Falmouth Harbour taken above Sailor's Creek
            (17x25cm-7x10in) i.verso panel
£3196 $6201   (9-Dec-90 ZZ.F18/R) Fregate et Vapeur (16x20cm-6x8in) s. panel pair
            (F.FR 31100)
£6000 $11820   (14-Nov-90 S64/R) Tea time with grandfather (34x45cm-13x18in) s. panel
£1250 $2163   (20-May-91 SWS365) Shipping in Plymouth Sound, Munt Edgcumbe beyond
            (12x17cm-5x7in) W/C htd.bodycol.

CONDY, Nicholas (attrib) (1793-1857) British
£751 $1300   (12-May-91 H.C12/R) HMS Rodney struck by lighting off Malta with HMS
            Pembroke and Dido beyond (30x43cm-12x17in) d.1838

CONDY, Nicholas Matthew (1816-1851) British
£1800 $3114   (22-May-91 S18/R) British men-of-war (22x30cm-9x12in) s. board
£2400 $3912   (14-Jun-91 K494) Man of war and other figures in colonial bay
            (23x28cm-9x11in) s.
£4600 $8556   (5-Sep-90 BT163/R) Naval frigates off coast (20x28cm-8x11in) s.
            millboard pair
£6000 $10380   (22-May-91 S6/R) Thousand guinea match between Water Witch and schooner
            Galatea (30x40cm-12x16in) s.d.1837 i.verso panel
£7000 $13650   (18-Oct-90 SC3060/R) Nap hand (46x59cm-18x23in) s.d.1828 panel

CONELY, William B (1830-1911) American
£1250 $2400   (28-Nov-90 D.NY40) The burial of Minisink (91x132cm-36x52in) s.

CONEY, John (1786-1833) British
£600 $1188   (30-Jan-91 S86) South Transept of York Minster from North Transept
            (58x49cm-23x19in) s. W/C over pencil

CONFORTINI, Jacopo (17th C) Italian
£1900 $3211   (16-Apr-91 C157/R) Studies of a seated woman (16x19cm-6x7in) i. verso
            red chk.

CONGDON, Thomas R (1862-1917) American
£898 $1500   (26-Jul-91 E.EDM156/R) At grandmother's (53x66cm-21x26in) s.
£452 $850   (22-Sep-90 WOL.C213/R) Interior scene (30x46cm-12x18in) s. W/C

CONGDON, William (1912-) American
£2519 $4837   (27-Nov-90 SY.MI50/R) Piazza Venice 5 (104x122cm-41x48in) d.51
     s.d.1951verso panel (I.L 5500000)

CONGIU, Sylvia Corinne (1953-) French
£1039 $1859   (14-Apr-91 APT.P41) Sans titre (25x25cm-10x10in) s.d.janvier 1989
     acrylic paper (F.FR 10500)

CONGNET, Gillis (attrib) (1538-1599) Dutch
£7200 $12168   (17-Apr-91 S23/R) Leda and the Swan (96x126cm-38x50in) panel

CONINCK, David de (1636-1699) Flemish
£6839 $12242   (14-Mar-91 D.V79/R) Hunting still life with dog (93x105cm-37x41in)
     (A.S 140000)
£11055 $18131   (21-Jun-91 SY.MO139/R) Rapaces attaquant des poules et des coqs dans un
     large paysage (115x231cm-45x91in) (F.FR 110000)
£14286 $28143   (15-Nov-90 EA.Z219/R) Poultry, hare and squirrel (47x63cm-19x25in)
     (S.FR 35000)
£32000 $54080   (17-Apr-91 S140/R) Still life of birds and game with spaniel and musket
     in landscape (114x163cm-45x64in)
£70000 $135100   (12-Dec-90 S70/R) Still life of fruit on silver dish, with rabbits,
     monkey, negro page and parrot (122x175cm-48x69in)

CONINCK, David de (circle) (1636-1699) Flemish
£3529 $6000   (30-May-91 CE.NY43/R) Game and birds with spaniel in landscape
     (70x95cm-28x37in)
£4500 $7335   (5-Jul-91 C293/R) Cat pulling eel from net and spaniel guarding dead
     bird (109x56cm-43x22in) with indist.sig

CONINCK, David de (studio) (1636-1699) Flemish
£12000 $19560   (3-Jul-91 S237/R) Cat surprising chickens, pigeons and rabbits in
     landscape (90x124cm-35x49in)

CONINCK, David de (style) (1636-1699) Flemish
£4158 $8233   (30-Jan-91 APT.P56/R) Paon et animaux de basse-cour dans un parc
     (57x72cm-22x28in) (F.FR 41000)

CONINXLOO, Gillis van (attrib) (16/17th C) Flemish/Dutch
£15385 $30000   (11-Oct-90 SY.NY45/R) Wooded landscape with hunters and village beyond
     (115x151cm-45x59in)
*£3000 $5310   (22-Mar-91 APT.P28) Paysage anime par une scene religieuse
     (12x18cm-5x7in) i. pen wash (F.FR 30000)*

CONINXLOO, Gillis van (style) (16/17th C) Flemish/Dutch
*£917 $1807   (12-Nov-90 CH.AM11) Hilly wooded landscape, town on hill beyond
     (28x39cm-11x15in) with i. black lead pen wash (D.FL 3000)*

CONINXLOO, Gillis van III (1544-1607) Flemish
£6200 $11966   (11-Dec-90 PH145/R) River landscape with Diana and her nymphs bathing in
     river (30x40cm-12x16in) panel

CONNARD, Philip (1875-1958) British
£13000 $25480   (7-Nov-90 S5/R) The boat trip (81x80cm-32x31in) s.
£720 $1354   (18-Sep-90 PH64/R) Beach, Dieppe (26x34cm-10x13in) s. W/C over pencil

CONNAWAY, Jay Hall (1893-1970) American
£1000 $2000   (7-Feb-91 B.P123/R) Winter, Monhegan (61x91cm-24x36in) s.
£1027 $1900   (8-Mar-91 S.BM208/R) Winter village (51x61cm-20x24in) s.indist.d.
£1073 $1900   (22-Mar-91 S.W2476/R) Autumn, Vermont (30x41cm-12x16in) s. i.verso

CONNELLY, Gordon (1956-) British
£360 $706   (13-Feb-91 B141) Petrified city II (58x76cm-23x30in) s.d.87 mixed media

CONNOR, Kevin (1932-) Australian
£881 $1665   (25-Sep-90 JRL.S186/R) Picnic 4 (61x76cm-24x30in) s.d.61 (A.D 2000)
£1402 $2285   (16-Jun-91 SY.ME97) Figure in wilderness (122x122cm-48x48in) s.d.64
     board (A.D 3000)
£2025 $3889   (14-Aug-90 SY.ME100/R) Haymarket landscape (60x90cm-24x35in) s.d.'64 i.
     verso board (A.D 4800)
£3012 $5783   (27-Nov-90 JRL.S211/R) Enclosed figures, early morning
     (121x121cm-48x48in) s. composition board (A.D 7500)
£3271 $5332   (16-Jun-91 SY.ME73) Oxford Street looking west, 1972 (121x153cm-48x60in)
     board (A.D 7000)
£8879 $14472   (16-Jun-91 SY.ME87/R) Portrait of Sydney (244x397cm-96x156in) s.d.70
     composition board three panels (A.D 19000)
*£321 $617   (26-Nov-90 SY.ME132) Officer (24x29cm-9x11in) s. i.verso ink wash
     (A.D 800)*
*£622 $1195   (27-Nov-90 JRL.S24/R) Ray Crooke's garden, Balmain (53x53cm-21x21in)
     s.d.72 pastel (A.D 1550)*

CONOR, William (1881-1968) Irish
£3500 $5845   (6-Jun-91 C106/R) Still life (51x41cm-20x16in) s.

CONOR, William (1881-1968) Irish-cont.
£3800	$7372	(5-Dec-90 PHE27/R) Evening shadows on the Minnow burn. Early spring, the river Lagan (27x31cm-11x12in) s. board two
£9500	$17005	(10-Apr-91 LJ167/R) The point to point finishing post (127x152cm-50x60in) s.
£1000	*$1950*	*(18-Oct-90 SC3045/R) The gypsy women (49x35cm-19x14in) s. W/C col.chk.*
£2000	*$3880*	*(5-Dec-90 PHE95/R) At the end of the shift (42x35cm-17x14in) s. pastel*
£2800	*$5460*	*(10-Oct-90 S21/R) Walking couple (41x27cm-16x11in) s. col.chk*

CONRAD, Albert (1837-1887) German
| £578 | $1023 | (20-Mar-91 KM.K1136/R) The Red Baron, I World War battle scene with aeroplanes (70x90cm-28x35in) s.d.1935 panel (DM 1700) |

CONRAD-KICKERT see KICKERT, Conrad

CONRADE, Alfred Charles (1863-1955) British
£450	*$797*	*(21-Mar-91 CSK100/R) A capriccio of various Roman buildings (38x30cm-15x12in) pencil ink W/C htd.white*
£500	*$835*	*(5-Jun-91 S266/R) Statue of Rameses II (33x24cm-13x9in) s. gouache over pencil*
£1000	*$1670*	*(22-Jul-91 SWS841/R) The Trevi fountain. Figures ina temple (46x57cm-18x22in) boths.d.1918 one i. W/C pencil*

CONROY, Stephen (1964-) British
£600	$1134	(27-Sep-90 CG21) Seated female nude (43x29cm-17x11in) s. chl brush ink W/C
£800	$1512	(27-Sep-90 CG20) Self portrait with hat (48x34cm-19x13in) s. brush col ink
£1400	$2366	(17-Apr-91 CG17/R) Head study (29x19cm-11x7in) s. pencil col.chk.crayon
£1500	$2925	(10-Oct-90 PHG83) Seated nude (49x35cm-19x14in) s. conte
£1500	$2895	(12-Dec-90 PHG125/R) Seated female nude (49x34cm-19x13in) s. conte crayon
£2600	$4914	(27-Sep-90 CG19/R) Bespectacled figure (46x36cm-18x14in) s. W/C htd white
£3300	$6435	(10-Oct-90 PHG66/R) Profile of young man wearing hat (27x17cm-11x7in) s. mixed media

CONSAGRA, Pietro (1920-) Italian
£818	*$1604*	*(20-Nov-90 BR.M4/R) Composizione (46x34cm-18x13in) s.d.1960 gouache paper on canvas (I.L 1800000)*
£1631	*$3148*	*(16-Dec-90 GL.P98) Composition (52x61cm-20x24in) s.d.1958 oil gouache hardboard (F.FR 16000)*
£4077	*$7870*	*(16-Dec-90 GL.P102) Composition (122x122cm-48x48in) s.d.58 oil gouache hardboard (F.FR 40000)*

CONSTABLE (19/20th C) British
| £1050 | $2016 | (17-Aug-90 K506) River scene with figures, sheep and cottage (18x23cm-7x9in) sketch |

CONSTABLE, John (1776-1837) British
£30000	$50700	(30-Apr-91 PH61/R) East Bergholt Church and West Lodge from behind Golding Contstable's house (17x24cm-7x9in) card on panel
£38000	$62700	(10-Jul-91 S83/R) Study of clouds over the sea, Brighton (16x23cm-6x9in)
£9800000	$19306000	(14-Nov-90 S128/R) The lock (142x120cm-56x47in)
£3400	$5610	(11-Jul-91 S162/R) View across wood (8x11cm-3x4in) pencil
£3800	$6270	(11-Jul-91 S163/R) Path between rocks and trees (13x21cm-5x8in) wash over pencil
£6000	$10740	(9-Apr-91 C110/R) Derwent valley with Chatsworth beyond (22x32cm-9x13in) i.d.1801verso pencil wash
£7800	$13962	(11-Apr-91 S41/R) Wooded lane. Sketch of woman and two children (16x25cm-6x10in) d.1823 wash over pencil double-sided
£8000	$14320	(11-Apr-91 S40/R) View near Hursley, Hampshire (14x20cm-6x8in) d.1804 W/C black chk bodycol
£13000	$25610	(15-Nov-90 S68/R) Woodcote Grove near Epsom, Surrey (10x17cm-4x7in) pencil W/C

CONSTABLE, John (after) (1776-1837) British
| £3400 | $6698 | (31-Oct-90 S338/R) The cornfield (140x120cm-55x47in) |

CONSTABLE, John (attrib) (1776-1837) British
| £1853 | $3577 | (12-Dec-90 WE.MU92/R) Wooded landscape (51x42cm-20x17in) panel (DM 5300) |

CONSTABLE, John (style) (19th C) British
| £2827 | $4750 | (17-Jul-91 SY.NY156/R) Promenade on a summer day (103x159cm-41x63in) s.l. |

CONSTABLE, Lionel (1828-1884) British
| £2200 | $4334 | (31-Oct-90 S365/R) Cloud study (19x25cm-7x10in) paper |

CONSTANT (1920-) Dutch
£2786	$5378	(12-Dec-90 CH.AM351/R) Baigneuses (50x65cm-20x26in) s. (D.FL 9000)
£8359	$16133	(13-Dec-90 SY.AM222/R) Untitled (24x19cm-9x7in) s. (D.FL 27000)
£12384	$23901	(13-Dec-90 SY.AM225/R) Untitled (24x30cm-9x12in) s.d.49 (D.FL 40000)
£16099	$31071	(13-Dec-90 SY.AM226/R) Untitled (35x45cm-14x18in) s.d.50 (D.FL 52000)

CONSTANT (1920-) Dutch-cont.
£20124	$38839	(13-Dec-90 SY.AM214/R) Paarse vorm of Geel Fond (65x100cm-26x39in) s.d.53 (D.FL 65000)
£1502	$2598	(22-May-91 CH.AM743) Flowers (26x35cm-10x14in) s. pastel W/C (D.FL 5000)
£2786	$5378	(12-Dec-90 CH.AM471/R) Figure (29x20cm-11x8in) s. W/C htd white (D.FL 9000)
£3003	$5195	(13-Dec-90 SY.AM256 g/R) Vogel met kindje in ovaal (24x14cm-9x6in) s.d.48 ink collage (D.FL 10000)
£3096	$5975	(13-Dec-90 SY.AM372/R) Untitled (35x44cm-14x17in) s.d.75 W/C (D.FL 10000)
£5000	$8500	(29-May-91 KH.K5/R) Fantasy animal (22x26cm-9x10in) s.d.48 gouache (D.KR 57000)
£6502	$12548	(13-Dec-90 SY.AM216/R) Untitled (25x35cm-10x14in) s.d.47 gouache ink (D.FL 21000)
£9009	$15586	(23-May-91 SY.AM256 n/R) Vogel (42x32cm-17x13in) s.i.d.1949 gouache (D.FL 30000)
£12456	$23416	(19-Sep-90 KH.K15/R) Composition (43x32cm-17x13in) s.d.49 W/C gouache crayon indian ink (D.KR 140000)
£15480	$29876	(13-Dec-90 SY.AM208/R) Untitled (44x54cm-17x21in) s.i.d.49 gouache (D.FL 50000)
£15789	$30474	(13-Dec-90 SY.AM209/R) Untitled (48x54cm-19x21in) s.d.51 gouache (D.FL 51000)

CONSTANT, Benjamin (1845-1902) French
£5984	$11489	(17-Dec-90 ARC.P99/R) La belle Orientale (65x46cm-26x18in) s. (F.FR 59000)
£7179	$14000	(23-Oct-90 SY.NY285/R) The favourite (127x91cm-50x36in) s.d.1880
£9694	$19097	(13-Nov-90 ARC.P178/R) La belle odalisque (59x84cm-23x33in) s. panel (F.FR 95000)
£12308	$24000	(24-Oct-90 CH.NY83/R) The palace guard with two leopards (100x62cm-39x24in) s.i.

CONSTANT, Benjamin (attrib) (1845-1902) French
£6923	$13500	(23-Oct-90 SY.NY287/R) Harem beauty (96x115cm-38x45in) bears sig.

CONSTANTIN, Jean Antoine (1756-1844) French
£1173	$2312	(14-Nov-90 FB.P132/R) Moines en priere (73x55cm-29x22in) (F.FR 11500)

CONSTANTINE, G H (1878-?) British
£630	$1241	(5-Oct-90 BW37) Unloading the catch (64x41cm-25x16in) W/C

CONSTANTINE, G Hamilton (1878-?) British
£900	$1521	(1-May-91 PHL16) Loading hay wagon (18x25cm-7x10in) s. wash htd white pair
£900	$1701	(26-Sep-90 S228) Ploughing in autumn (17x25cm-7x10in) s.i. W/C
£900	$1503	(5-Jun-91 S225/R) Bamborough Castle (30x45cm-12x18in) s.i. W/C htd white
£1500	$2970	(30-Jan-91 S186/R) Poor catch, near Fowey. Unloading cobbles (35x25cm-14x10in) s.i. W/C htd white pair
£2500	$4875	(18-Oct-90 SC3051/R) Bringing in the harvest. Gathering in the hay (25x35cm-10x14in) both s. pair
£3000	$5940	(30-Jan-91 S187/R) Near Balbriggan. Near Wicklow Head (36x51cm-14x20in) s.i. W/C htd white pair

CONSTANTINI, Giuseppe (19th C) Italian
£13636	$26318	(12-Dec-90 WE.MU113/R) An exciting story (34x52cm-13x20in) s.d.1877 panel (DM 39000)

CONTE, Jacopino del (attrib) (1510-1598) Italian
£31822	$62371	(19-Nov-90 CH.R176/R) Ritratto di religioso con libro (71x55cm-28x22in) panel (I.L 70000000)

CONTE, Meiffren (1630-1705) French
£38934	$76311	(11-Nov-90 M.V51/R) Nature morte sur fond de paysage panel (F.FR 380000)

CONTE, Nicolas Jacques (1755-1805) French
£2024	$3968	(20-Nov-90 APT.P225/R) Says ou Palefrenier (34x24cm-13x9in) s.i. W/C (F.FR 20000)

CONTE, P (19th C) ?
£9000	$15030	(22-Jul-91 SWS1052/R) A view across the bay, Naples (61x106cm-24x42in) s.d.1861

CONTENCIN, Charles Henry (20th C) French
£956	$1645	(14-May-91 GF.L2569/R) View of Wetterhorn (33x46cm-13x18in) s. (S.FR 2400)

CONTENOTTE, Bruno (1922-) Italian
£991	$1932	(22-Oct-90 BR.M118/R) Immagine (40x50cm-16x20in) s.d.1973 mixed media silicone polyester canvas (I.L 2200000)

CONTI, Bernardino de (attrib) (1450-1525) Italian
£16923	$33000	(11-Oct-90 SY.NY20/R) Madonna and Child (42x30cm-17x12in) panel

CONTI, Cosimo (1825-1893) Italian
£947 $1800   (27-Feb-91 SY.NY368/R) Portrait of young Italian girl (56x67cm-22x26in)
       init.

CONTI, Primo (1900-?) Italian
£8632 $17006   (30-Oct-90 F.R223/R) Tacchino bianco (116x88cm-46x35in) s.d.44
       (I.L 19000000)

CONTI, Tito (1842-1924) Italian
£588 $1100   (30-Aug-90 MFA.C138 f) Flirtation (20x18cm-8x7in) s. board
£867 $1500   (21-May-91 CE.NY61/R) Flirtation (22x18cm-9x7in) s. panel
£3265 $6400   (6-Nov-90 GF.L2131/R) The boozer (41x31cm-16x12in) s. (S.FR 8000)
£5780 $10000   (23-May-91 CH.NY169/R) The white rose (53x41cm-21x16in) s.
£6200 $12214   (5-Oct-90 C155/R) Good book (62x48cm-24x19in) s.
£7200 $14184   (13-Nov-90 SWS363/R) A Spanish beauty (51x41cm-20x16in) s.
£20000 $38400   (30-Nov-90 C31/R) The introduction (78x103cm-31x41in) s.
£2811 $4750   (20-Apr-91 WOL.C103/R) Conversation (56x41cm-22x16in) s. board

CONTINENTAL SCHOOL (?) European
£1700 $2941   (9-May-91 CSK113) Still life of mixed flowers o pedestal, mixed fruit on
       table, landscape with monkey and birds (76x101cm-30x40in)
£3464 $6200   (16-Mar-91 W.W12/R) Solon and Croesus (119x157cm-47x62in) c.1800-1900
£6704 $12000   (11-Apr-91 SY.NY149/R) Portrait of lady with parrot (207x143cm-81x56in)
       c.1800

CONTINENTAL SCHOOL, 16th C European
*£3800 $6384   (22-Apr-91 PH115/R) Portrait of Guillaume Bude (9x?cm-4x?in) min. black
       wood frame rec.*

CONTINENTAL SCHOOL, 17th C European
£5028 $9000   (11-Apr-91 SY.NY68/R) William Tell shooting apple from his son's head
       (87x117cm-34x46in) panel
£9827 $17000   (10-May-91 S.BM1/R) Aaron, High Priest of the Israelites
       (97x74cm-38x29in)

CONTINENTAL SCHOOL, 18th C European
£1071 $1800   (17-Jul-91 SY.NY133/R) Portrait of a woman in a landscape
       (58x46cm-23x18in) paper laid down on masonite
£1900 $3287   (20-May-91 SWS68/R) Landscape with a deer hunt (68x129cm-27x51in)
£3300 $5577   (30-Apr-91 AG297) Woman playing lute with putto looking on
       (73x64cm-29x25in)
*£2500 $4125   (11-Jul-91 S265/R) Portrait of Sophia, Electoress of Hanover
       (13x?cm-5x?in) min.card laid down giltwood frame oval*

CONTINENTAL SCHOOL, 18th/19th C European
£1580 $2750   (27-Mar-91 B.SF4213/R) Floral still life (61x51cm-24x20in)
£1734 $3000   (10-May-91 S.BM7/R) Monkeys playing backgammon (36x46cm-14x18in)
£2209 $3800   (18-May-91 W.W4/R) Portrait of an elegantly dressed woman
       (91x71cm-36x28in)

CONTINENTAL SCHOOL, 19th C European
£1040 $1800   (21-May-91 CE.NY330/R) Woman wearing white hat (47x39cm-19x15in)
       indist.s.
£1184 $2250   (27-Feb-91 SY.NY280/R) Still life with fruit (80x100cm-31x39in)
£1526 $2900   (27-Feb-91 SY.NY281/R) Next chapter (27x30cm-11x12in) indist.s. canvas
       on masonite
£1711 $3250   (27-Feb-91 SY.NY279/R) Floral still life with bird's nest
       (100x71cm-39x28in)
£1788 $3200   (16-Mar-91 W.W23/R) Contemplative man on a rock with Jerusalem in the
       distance (81x114cm-32x45in)
£1899 $3400   (16-Mar-91 W.W15/R) St. Barbara (104x71cm-41x28in)
£2232 $3750   (17-Jul-91 SY.NY219/R) Two pekinese (56x76cm-22x30in) indist.s.d.18
£2763 $5250   (27-Feb-91 SY.NY278/R) Lap-dog on red pillow (54x65cm-21x26in)
£2795 $4500   (26-Jun-91 D.NY22) Young lady sitting at clavier (137x86cm-54x34in)
£2938 $5700   (8-Dec-90 W.W72/R) Women at the baths (104x147cm-41x58in)
£3200 $5376   (18-Jul-91 CSK186/R) Italianate landscape with classical ruins with
       figures by stream (200x200cm-79x79in)
£3400 $5576   (20-Jun-91 B91 h) Mother and child (66x56cm-26x22in)
£3468 $6000   (21-May-91 CE.NY66/R) Elegant lady seated with basket of flowers
       (114x66cm-45x26in) indist.s.
£3631 $6500   (11-Apr-91 FA.PH652) Madonna and Child encircled by wreath of flowers
       (74x61cm-29x24in)
£5263 $10000   (27-Feb-91 SY.NY299/R) Girl with shepherd. Boy with corgi
       (107x91cm-42x36in) pair
*£1272 $2200   (21-May-91 CE.NY323/R) Portrait of Princess Colonna (76x60cm-30x24in)
       indist.s.d.1895 pastel oval*

CONTINENTAL SCHOOL, 19th/20th C European
£1200 $1968   (18-Jun-91 PH85) Still life with flowers, teapot and cup and saucer on
       table (60x45cm-24x18in) indis.s.

COOGHEN, Leendert van der (1610-1681) Dutch
£15000 $24450   (3-Jul-91 S48/R) Group of figures, including old woman removing necklace
       from child, in landscape (131x167cm-52x66in)

COOK OF PLYMOUTH, Samuel (1806-1859) British
£800 $1336   (5-Jun-91 S223/R) Polperro (32x56cm-13x22in) s. W/C

COOK OF PLYMOUTH, William (fl.1870-1880) British
£900 $1467   (14-Jun-91 C158/R) Salvaging the hulk (37x68cm-15x27in) mono.d.79 pencil
                             W/C htd white

COOK, Adel Agini (?) Australian?
£618 $1217   (13-Nov-90 J.M1094 a) The daughter (32x22cm-13x9in) s. panel (A.D 1600)

COOK, Beryl (1926-) British
£550 $957   (28-Mar-91 CSK236/R) Flamingo clown. Artist's son (61x23cm-24x9in) s.
                             board double-sided
£2500 $4350   (28-Mar-91 CSK235/R) Window dressers, No. 1 (33x58cm-13x23in) s. i.verso
                             board
£3500 $6580   (20-Sep-90 CSK194/R) Ladies' bowling team. Girls playing pick-a-back by
                             river (38x57cm-15x22in) s.i.verso board double-sided
£6500 $12220   (20-Sep-90 CSK195/R) Noah's Ark (61x75cm-24x30in) s.i.verso board

COOK, Ebenezer Wake (1843-1926) British
£700 $1239   (21-Mar-91 CSK175) Fisherfolk on a rocky coast (46x61cm-18x24in)
                             mono.d.1887
£450 $900   (8-Feb-91 C6/R) Girls feeding pigeons in the Doges' courtyard, Venice
                             (28x38cm-11x15in) s. pencil W/C
£558 $938   (22-Apr-91 SY.ME114) Lake Orta from Sacro Monte (32x47cm-13x19in) s. W/C
                             (A.D 1200)
£643 $1234   (26-Nov-90 SY.ME57/R) Picturesque view (29x40cm-11x16in) s.d.1870 W/C
                             (A.D 1600)
£800 $1288   (27-Jun-91 CG5/R) Dunkeld, Perthshire (58x39cm-23x15in) s. pencil W/C
                             htd.white
£800 $1536   (17-Dec-90 PH26/R) Old Palace, Florence (24x12cm-9x5in) s. W/C over
                             pencil
£1000 $1960   (8-Nov-90 TL37/R) Grasmere - after a shower (39x56cm-15x22in) s.d.86 W/C
£1300 $2236   (13-May-91 CG170/R) Mussel sorting on the Conway, North Wales
                             (25x44cm-10x17in) s.d.1873 i. verso W/C
£1350 $2619   (6-Dec-90 CG1/R) Isola Bella, Lake Maggiore (18x30cm-7x12in) s.d.89 W/C
£1488 $2500   (22-Apr-91 SY.ME115) Red Bluff (21x41cm-8x16in) s.d.1868 W/C (A.D 3200)

COOK, Howard (1901-1980) American
£789 $1500   (15-Sep-90 S.W1628/R) Under the El (46x33cm-18x13in) s. crayon pencil
£1627 $2750   (1-May-91 B.SF5291/R) Skyscraper no.1 (44x20cm-17x8in) s. gouache ink

COOK, William (fl.1877-1879) British
£450 $900   (8-Feb-91 C40) Figures on a rocky shore (25x43cm-10x17in) mono.d.74 W/C
£680 $1204   (22-Mar-91 T180/R) Drakes Island and St Michael's mount (20x43cm-8x17in)
                             mono.d.'74

COOK, William Delafield (snr) (1861-1931) Australian
£1026 $1815   (18-Mar-91 MGS.S272/R) Dandenongs landscape (59x48cm-23x19in) s. board
                             (A.D 2400)

COOK, William Edwards (1881-?) American
£484 $900   (9-Sep-90 LIT.L282) Island fishing (25x33cm-10x13in) s.d.1915 gouache

COOKE, Edward William (1811-1880) British
£850 $1386   (13-Jun-91 CSK288/R) Capri (24x34cm-9x13in) s.i.verso
£3800 $6574   (22-May-91 S17/R) Calm anchorage (9x19cm-4x7in) bears i.stretcher canvas
                             on panel
£4800 $7920   (10-Jul-91 S84/R) Convent at Amalfi (29x44cm-11x17in) s.d.1846
                             i.stretcher paper on canvas
£6000 $11760   (20-Nov-90 PH222/R) Beached fishing vessels (21x29cm-8x11in) s.d.1854
                             board
£19000 $36480   (30-Nov-90 C40/R) Thou has the sunset's glow .... (45x92cm-18x36in)
                             s.d.1849
£469 $900   (20-Feb-91 D.NY21) Breezy harbour (28x41cm-11x16in) s.d.1833 W/C
£500 $840   (15-Jul-91 PH95) Mast house, Blackwall (19x29cm-7x11in) s.i.d.1827
                             pencil
£900 $1773   (13-Nov-90 C116) Studies of fishermen's baskets, prawn gins and lobster
                             pots (13x18cm-5x7in) s.i.d.34 pencil W/C three in one frame
£4200 $7056   (22-Apr-91 PH244/R) Beaching a Dutch Pink (23x34cm-9x13in) s.d.1868
                             pastel

COOKE, John Percy (20th C) British
£650 $1125   (10-May-91 CBS338) Daphne (76x58cm-30x23in) s.

COOKE, William Edward (fl.1880-1886) British
£1000 $1670   (5-Jun-91 S76/R) Duck pond (17x25cm-7x10in) mono. board

COOKESLEY, Margaret Murray (19th C) British
£1300 $2171   (5-Jun-91 S177/R) Friends (25x36cm-10x14in) init. oil over printed base
                             panel

COOKSEY, May Louise Greville (1878-?) British
£1100 $2112   (29-Nov-90 B35/R) The House at Bethany (122x152cm-48x60in) s.d.1906

COOLIDGE, Cassius M (1844-1934) American
£2601 $4500   (10-May-91 S.W2463/R) The big bluff (71x56cm-28x22in) s.

COOMBS, Delbert Dana (1850-1938) American
£621 $1000   (25-Jun-91 JRB.C109/R) Mountain scene with cows (51x76cm-20x30in)
   s.d.1890

COOP, Hubert (1872-1953) British
£570 $1083   (15-Sep-90 ME148) Conway Castle from the south (36x51cm-14x20in)
   s.d.1894 W/C
£650 $1274   (8-Nov-90 PHI52) Moored boats at evening (22x34cm-9x13in) s.d.1937 W/C
£820 $1369   (22-Jul-91 SWS837/R) Beached boats, North Wales (24x34cm-9x13in) s.
£980 $1637   (22-Jul-91 SWS836/R) Fishing boat near Conway Castle (29x60cm-11x24in)
   s.
£2500 $4075   (13-Jun-91 CGC203/R) St Ives, Huntingdon, Canbridgeshire, sunset over
   river (25x48cm-10x19in) s.i. W/C

COOPER, Abraham (1787-1868) British
£2000 $3580   (10-Apr-91 S185/R) Richard the Lionheart at Battle of Ascalon in act of
   unhorsing Saladin (32x45cm-13x18in)
£7000 $13650   (26-Oct-90 C283/R) Fidele - A Blenheim spaniel with a bullfinch
   (30x38cm-12x15in) panel

COOPER, Abraham (attrib) (1787-1868) British
£1800 $3096   (16-May-91 CSK87) Slave trader (45x61cm-18x24in) panel
£3000 $5807   (26-Oct-90 C307/R) Thomas rounding on Spankerway (43x51cm-17x20in)
   indist.i.d.1841 stretcher

COOPER, Alexander Davis (19th C) British
£1600 $3120   (15-Jan-91 C115/R) Golden retriever (51x41cm-20x16in) mono.d.1881
£3000 $5850   (15-Jan-91 C37/R) Cairn terrier and Norfolk terrier near Highland loch
   (70x90cm-28x35in) mono.d.1878

COOPER, Alfred Egerton (1883-1974) British
£700 $1218   (28-Mar-91 CSK39/R) South Kensington from Carlton Tower
   (79x99cm-31x39in) mono. s.i.verso
£2700 $4779   (19-Mar-91 SHER98/R) Portrait of Lady Murial Ashton (117x89cm-46x35in)
   i.verso

COOPER, Alfred Heaton (1864-1929) British
£1650 $2723   (9-Jul-91 PH187/R) Corn stooks (71x91cm-28x36in) s.d.1896
£1900 $3363   (20-Mar-91 JT150 a) Early snow, Coniston (91x122cm-36x48in)
£400 $652   (13-Jun-91 CG20) Sheep in mist covered glen (25x36cm-10x14in) s.d.1924
   W/C
£560 $1075   (16-Aug-90 SC4077) Goats in winter sunshine, Zermatt (25x36cm-10x14in)
   s. W/C scratching out
£650 $1281   (1-Nov-90 TE564/R) Windermere from Low Wood (20x25cm-8x10in) s. W/C
£720 $1368   (10-Sep-90 PH110) Hilly landscape (38x55cm-15x22in) s.d.1910 W/C
£900 $1548   (14-May-91 SWS70/R) By the fireside (35x49cm-14x19in) s. W/C
£950 $1872   (1-Nov-90 TE565/R) The shore of Grasmere (36x53cm-14x21in) s. W/C

COOPER, Astley D M (1856-1924) American
£541 $1000   (8-Mar-91 S.BM142 a) Indian encampement (15x28cm-6x11in) s.
£1604 $3000   (1-Aug-90 B.P95/R) Buffalo hunt (76x102cm-30x40in) s.d.1909
£3155 $5900   (1-Aug-90 B.P96/R) Day's end (102x76cm-40x30in) s.d.1910

COOPER, Byron (19/20th C) British
£780 $1529   (13-Feb-91 S27/R) Whitby (51x91cm-20x36in) s.d.1901

COOPER, Colin Campbell (1856-1937) American
£695 $1300   (4-Aug-90 LIT.L175) Dutch scene with windmill (30x38cm-12x15in) s.d.1890
£2023 $3500   (21-May-91 CE.NY529/R) Sailboats (54x42cm-21x17in) s.
£2308 $4500   (10-Oct-90 B.SF609/R) Road to Mission (33x35cm-13x14in) s. board
£2398 $4700   (16-Feb-91 W.W54/R) Cafes by the canal (38x46cm-15x18in) s.
£2514 $4500   (14-Mar-91 CH.NY68/R) Grand Canal (41x54cm-16x21in) s.d.1897 canvas on
   board
£3198 $5500   (18-May-91 W.W108/R) Travelling alone (58x36cm-23x14in) s.d.1890
£583 $950   (11-Jun-91 MOR.P14) Landscape - lake (10x18cm-4x7in) init.d.1923 gouache
£3571 $7000   (13-Feb-91 B.SF2114/R) Building at San Diego Fair, 1916
   (27x35cm-11x14in) s. gouache board

COOPER, Derek (20th C) ?
£909 $1764   (4-Dec-90 FN.S1567/R) Bathers (25x35cm-10x14in) (DM 2600)

COOPER, Edward (attrib) (19th C) British
£2542 $4296   (19-Apr-91 FN.S1686/R) Pastoral wooded river landscape with shepherd and
   domestic animals (50x52cm-20x20in) canvas laid down (DM 7600)

COOPER, Edwin (1785-1833) British
£2300 $3864   (23-Apr-91 RG2238) Study of racehorse and greyhounds, outside stable
   (43x58cm-17x23in) s.d.1817

COOPER, Gerald (20th C) British
£3100 $5177   (22-Jul-91 SWS1110/R) Apples (49x59cm-19x23in) s.
£3800 $6346   (3-Jun-91 PHB40/R) Still life of summer blooms (61x51cm-24x20in) s.
   board

COOPER, Gerald (20th C) British-cont.
| £4300 | $7181 | (22-Jul-91 SWS1107/R) Still life of mixed flowers (59x49cm-23x19in) s. |
| £5200 | $9776 | (20-Sep-90 C109/R) Moss roses and irises in glass vase on stone ledge (51x41cm-20x16in) s.d.1951 s.i.verso board |

COOPER, Henry (early 20th C) British
| £808 | $1600 | (1-Feb-91 S.W2373/R) English river views (51x76cm-20x30in) s. pair |
| £816 | $1608 | (15-Nov-90 EA.Z164) Scottish landscape (51x76cm-20x30in) s. (S.FR 2000) |

COOPER, J D (19th C) ?
| £1829 | $3000 | (21-Jun-91 DM.D2017/R) Indians and ranchmen (58x76cm-23x30in) s.d.1896 |

COOPER, Joseph (1682-1743) British
| £19000 | $34010 | (10-Apr-91 S50/R) Still life of fruit (95x123cm-37x48in) s. |

COOPER, R B (20th C) American
| £592 | $1000 | (21-Apr-91 DU.E225) Gloucester Harbour, Cape Cod (58x89cm-23x35in) s. |

COOPER, Richard (jnr) (1740-1814) British
| *£900* | *$1485* | *(11-Jul-91 S87/R) Castelnuovo, Italy (29x48cm-11x19in) i. pen ink wash* |

COOPER, Robert (19th C) British
| *£540* | *$940* | *(27-Mar-91 PHS911) Evening after gale, Isle of Arran (74x124cm-29x49in) s.i.verso W/C* |

COOPER, Samuel (1609-1672) British
| *£8000* | *$13200* | *(10-Jul-91 C192/R) A gentleman wearing a breastplate with gilt studs (6x?cm-2x?in) min.init.d.1645 vellum gilt-metal frame oval* |
| *£12000* | *$19800* | *(11-Jul-91 S244) Portrait of lady, called Elizabeth, Countess of Morton (7x?cm-3x?in) min. gilt metal frame* |

COOPER, T S (1803-1902) British
| £705 | $1177 | (6-Jun-91 RAS.K231) Watering the cattle (40x60cm-16x24in) s.d.1876 (D.KR 8000) |

COOPER, Thomas George (19th C) British
| £2500 | $4875 | (18-Oct-90 SC3116/R) Sheep and cattle resting by a shady river (59x89cm-23x35in) s.d.1897 |

COOPER, Thomas Sidney (1803-1902) British
£650	$1229	(27-Sep-90 L210/R) Cattle resting by the wayside (51x61cm-20x24in) s.d.1876
£900	$1773	(15-Nov-90 WI1091/R) Longhorn cattle at rest in sunny landscape (33x23cm-13x9in) s.d.1871 board
£982	$1886	(27-Nov-90 W.T1029 a) Sheep at rest (63x76cm-25x30in) s. (C.D 2200)
£1300	$2210	(29-May-91 PHC183) Sheep on heath (30x42cm-12x17in) bears sig.
£1350	$2660	(13-Nov-90 SWS234/R) Cattle in meadow (27x21cm-11x8in) s.d.1835 panel
£1437	$2500	(27-Mar-91 B.SF4202/R) Sheep in snowy field (43x53cm-17x21in) s.
£1450	$2697	(5-Sep-90 BT177/R) Cattle watering (25x33cm-10x13in) s. indist.i.verso board
£1600	$3024	(26-Sep-90 S119/R) Kent scene (40x56cm-16x22in) s.i.d.1890 board
£1900	$3743	(13-Nov-90 SWS291/R) Cattle and sheep grazing (34x29cm-13x11in) s.d.1871 panel
£2370	$4100	(21-May-91 CE.NY127/R) Cattle and sheep resting (25x41cm-10x16in) s.d.1862 panel
£2900	$4843	(5-Jun-91 S93/R) Sheep and cow on high ground (37x47cm-15x19in) s.d.1853 panel
£3400	$5576	(20-Jun-91 B119/R) Catle in sunlit landscape (43x53cm-17x21in) s.d.1875 panel
£3720	$6250	(28-Apr-91 HG.C73) Off the Kentish coast (61x91cm-24x36in) s.d.1861
£3947	$7500	(28-Feb-91 CH.NY173 a/R) Cow, sheep and goats in meadow (45x61cm-18x24in) s.d.1857 panel
£4000	$6680	(5-Jun-91 S44/R) Goats in Highlands (50x71cm-20x28in) s.d.1854 panel
£4737	$9000	(28-Feb-91 CH.NY173/R) Sheep resting in river landscape (82x107cm-32x42in) s.
£4800	$9408	(22-Nov-90 CSK186/R) Cattle in extensive river landscape (55x43cm-22x17in) s.d.1836
£5200	$8476	(14-Jun-91 C312/R) Cattle and sheep in a water meadow (69x104cm-27x41in) s.d.1881
£5500	$9185	(5-Jun-91 S32/R) Road to field (43x53cm-17x21in) s.d.1889 board
£5946	$9692	(10-Jun-91 W.T1341/R) Cows and sheep on Canterbury meadows (53x90cm-21x35in) s.d.1854 panel (C.D 11000)
£6000	$11700	(18-Oct-90 SC3135/R) The lifting mist (74x112cm-29x44in) s.d.1874
£6122	$9857	(26-Jun-91 KM.K1415/R) Sheep resting in fields and cows grazing beyond (77x107cm-30x42in) s. (DM 18000)
£9000	$15210	(30-Apr-91 PH70/R) Cattle and sheep resting in meadow (75x108cm-30x43in) s.d.1887
£9000	$15210	(30-Apr-91 PH75/R) Scapegoat and goat shall bear upon him all iniquities into land not inhabited - Leviticus XVI, V.22 (122x183cm-48x72in) st.stretcher
£22321	$42857	(27-Nov-90 W.T1086) Sunny afternoon (122x183cm-48x72in) s.d.1852 (C.D 50000)
£600	*$1182*	*(1-Nov-90 C176) Ewes in stable (15x20cm-6x8in) s. pencil W/C*
£1750	*$3500*	*(8-Feb-91 C53/R) Cattle and sheep in an open landscape (25x36cm-10x14in) s.d.1888 pencil W/C*

COOPER, Thomas Sidney (1803-1902) British-cont.
£2500 $4925   (1-Nov-90 C80/R) Cattle grazing on river bank (43x69cm-17x27in) s.d.1863 pencil W/C

COOPER, Thomas Sidney (attrib) (1803-1902) British
£1300 $2561   (1-Nov-90 D49/R) Cattle beside river (23x30cm-9x12in) s.d.1881 panel
£2312 $4486   (4-Dec-90 F.R142) Gregge (38x59cm-15x23in) (I.L 5000000)

COOPER, Thomas Sidney (circle) (1803-1902) British
£880 $1434   (13-Jun-91 CSK258/R) Cattle with sheep watering by stream, open landscape beyond (91x71cm-36x28in)

COOPER, Thomas Sidney (style) (1803-1902) British
£3500 $6615   (26-Sep-90 S114/R) Bringing last cows home (108x157cm-43x62in) bears sig.d.1876

COOPER, Thomas Sidney and PYNE, James Baker (19th C) British
£5000 $8950   (12-Apr-91 C61/R) Wooded landscape, with drover, cattle and goats on path (48x74cm-19x29in) s.d.1844

COOPER, William Heaton (1903-?) British
£440 $814   (5-Mar-91 AG77) Clouds above a Lakeland hill (27x37cm-11x15in) s. W/C
£450 $725   (24-Jun-91 HS91) Corrie Ghreta, Isle of Skye - extensive view (28x39cm-11x15in) s. i.verso W/C
£550 $1067   (7-Dec-90 PHM7) The East face of Pillar Rock, Lake District (38x28cm-15x11in) s. W/C over pencil
£550 $1056   (26-Nov-90 SWS119/R) Boys fishing from boat (27x37cm-11x15in) s.d.1921 W/C
£850 $1590   (31-Aug-90 PHM45) At the circus (27x38cm-11x15in) s. W/C htd white

COOPER, William Sidney (1854-1927) British
£550 $919   (24-Jul-91 CSK28) The Kennell at Brimpton (41x36cm-16x14in) s.d.84 i. verso
£1000 $1630   (13-Jun-91 CSK214/R) Evening at Herne, Kent (60x91cm-24x36in) s.d.1907 s.i.verso
£1500 $2505   (4-Jun-91 SWS1699/R) Gypsy camp (44x74cm-17x29in) s.d.1888
£1700 $2924   (14-May-91 SWS178/R) On the Stour (85x110cm-33x43in) s.d.04 i.stretcher
£1800 $3528   (13-Feb-91 S132/R) Gypsy camp (46x76cm-18x30in) s.d.1888
£2000 $3540   (20-Mar-91 WI1128/R) Sheep beside grassy knoll (43x58cm-17x23in) s.
£2200 $4224   (14-Aug-90 GA82/R) View of Herne Mill with flock of sheep to fore (33x38cm-13x15in) s.d.1914
£3500 $6720   (30-Nov-90 DA675) Morning on the Stowe, cattle watering (53x84cm-21x33in) s.d.1902
£400 $740   (6-Mar-91 SC4140) Sheep resting in spring meadow (23x36cm-9x14in) s.d.1919 W/C over pencil
£600 $1062   (3-Apr-91 RBB912/R) Thames barges with figures (23x41cm-9x16in) s.d.1884 i.verso W/C
£650 $1274   (21-Nov-90 B117) Sheep on moorland (25x36cm-10x14in) s.d.1921 W/C
£1150 $2162   (20-Sep-90 M3) Cattle resting in field (33x48cm-13x19in) W/C

COOPSE, Pieter (style) (?-1677) Dutch
£1101 $2169   (13-Nov-90 AB.S874/R) Vessel near coastal cliffs in stormy weather (49x64cm-19x25in) (S.KR 12000)

COORTE, Adriaen (1685-1723) Dutch
£28571 $56286   (15-Nov-90 EA.Z227/R) Gathering of ducks (85x72cm-33x28in) (S.FR 70000)

COOSEMANS, Alexander (1627-1689) Flemish
£16842 $32000   (10-Jan-91 SY.NY27/R) Still life of mixed fruit and walnute in bowl, other fruit and ewer all on stone ledge (55x84cm-22x33in)
£27695 $49575   (8-Apr-91 ARC.P32/R) Nature morte aux fruits, legumes, papillons et lezard (80x115cm-31x45in) traces sig. (F.FR 280000)

COOSEMANS, Joseph (1828-1904) Belgian
£3187 $5482   (14-May-91 GF.L2110/R) Wooded landscape (142x214cm-56x84in) s.d.1886 (S.FR 8000)

COPE, Charles West (1811-1890) British
£360 $637   (21-Mar-91 CSK27/R) The Cardinal's blessing (46x58cm-18x23in) pencil W/C

COPE, Charles West (circle) (1811-1890) British
£2800 $5292   (27-Sep-90 CSK119/R) Architect Sansavino discussing plans for the Biblioteca, Venice (132x163cm-52x64in)

COPE, Sir Arthur Stockdale (1857-1940) British
£500 $960   (19-Feb-91 SWS28) Portrait of George W Palmer MP seated (124x99cm-49x39in) s.d.1903
£600 $1152   (19-Feb-91 SWS26) Portrait of Eleanor Barrett Palmer seated with spaniel Rajah (126x100cm-50x39in) s.d.1905

COPLEY, Billy (1946-) American
£3568 $6886   (16-Dec-90 CSC.P39 b) Its 1954 (72x97cm-28x38in) mixed media (F.FR 35000)

COPLEY, John Singleton (1737-1815) American
£1788 $3200   (14-Mar-91 CH.NY1/R) Study of child (30x42cm-12x17in) s.i.d.1752 chl white chk

COPLEY, John Singleton (attrib) (1737-1815) American
£559 $1000   (14-Apr-91 JRB.C17/R) Judith (36x30cm-14x12in)

COPLEY, William Nelson (1919-) American
£3046 $6000   (4-Oct-90 SY.NY207 a/R) Profumo affair (89x117cm-35x46in) s.d.63 d.63 verso
£3221 $5250   (12-Jun-91 SY.NY186/R) Cinzano (96x129cm-38x51in)
£4592 $9000   (6-Nov-90 CE.NY38/R) The studio (65x100cm-26x39in)
£6633 $13000   (12-Feb-91 SY.NY465/R) They're playing a tune in McGuffy's saloon, from New Year's Eve (147x114cm-58x45in) s.d.67
£6754 $13170   (23-Oct-90 F.M71/R) Lips that touch liquor must never touch mine (89x116cm-35x46in) s.d.66 l.verso acrylic (I.L 15000000)
£8589 $14000   (12-Jun-91 SY.NY185/R) Liberation sur l'herbe (161x129cm-63x51in) s. d.1956 verso
£10714 $21000   (12-Feb-91 SY.NY466/R) He's dancing with a girl called Muckluck Mag from the Man from Eldorado (147x114cm-58x45in) s.d.67 l.verso
£983 $1700   (7-May-91 CE.NY179/R) Lovers (59x45cm-23x18in) s.d.72 chl
£3333 $6500   (10-Oct-90 SY.NY425/R) Hand with women (81x66cm-32x26in) s.d.82 oil mixed media on canvas
£3807 $7500   (4-Oct-90 SY.NY145/R) Untitled (76x101cm-30x40in) s.d.62 oil fabric collage canvas

COPPE, Roger (c.1928-) French
£407 $813   (6-Feb-91 LD.P43/R) Nu allonge (33x26cm-13x10in) s.d.82 Indian ink (F.FR 4000)

COPPEDE, Carlo (1868-?) Italian
£13500 $25920   (28-Nov-90 S159/R) Bacchanalian scene (92x129cm-36x51in) s.i.d.1907

COPPEDGE, Fern Isabel (1888-1951) American
£893 $1500   (27-Apr-91 YFA.M71) Panoramic landscape (30x30cm-12x12in) s. board
£4639 $9000   (5-Dec-90 D.NY120/R) Winter on The Delaware (76x76cm-30x30in) s.
£5319 $10000   (11-Aug-90 COL.M47/R) Rigatta at Gloucester, ME (46x51cm-18x20in) s.
£8380 $15000   (14-Mar-91 CH.NY103/R) Snow covered hills (63x76cm-25x30in) s.

COPPEE (19th C) ?
£1637 $2782   (28-May-91 C.A39) Marine (30x40cm-12x16in) s.d.1846 (B.FR 100000)

COPPENOLLE, Jacques van (1915-) French
£1195 $2331   (24-Oct-90 GD.B236/R) Farmyard with chickens (65x50cm-26x20in) s. (S.FR 3000)
£1223 $2349   (1-Dec-90 PER.M80) La Basse-cour (15x21cm-6x8in) s. panel (F.FR 12000)

COPPENS, Frans (1895-1975) Belgian
£2245 $4423   (6-Oct-90 KV.L57) Farm in snowy landscape (125x150cm-49x59in) s. (B.FR 140000)

COPPENS, Omer (19/20th C) Belgian
£599 $1071   (16-Mar-91 KV.L60) Jour d'hiver- Parc Solvay (29x23cm-11x9in) s. panel (B.FR 36000)

COPPERE, van (?) ?
£1616 $3168   (11-Feb-91 D.L3) Le dresseur de chien s. (F.FR 16000)

COPPERMAN, Mildred Tuner (20th C) American
£2123 $3800   (14-Mar-91 CH.NY197/R) Bright lights, New York (77x63cm-30x25in) s.

COPPING, Harold (1863-1932) British
£850 $1428   (19-Jul-91 CBB323) The finding of Moses (41x25cm-16x10in) s. W/C

COPPINI, Fausto Eliseo (1870-1945) Italian
£798 $1380   (8-May-91 V.BA23) Paisaje (22x28cm-9x11in)
£2653 $5200   (21-Nov-90 NA.BA76) Naturaleza muerta (45x90cm-18x35in) s.

COPPOLA-CASTALDO, F (1845-) Italian
£680 $1149   (16-Apr-91 CH.R16) Pescatori nel golfo di Napoli (45x31cm-18x12in) s. tempera cardboard (I.L 1500000)

COPPOLA-CASTALDO, Francesco (1845-?) Italian
£800 $1536   (27-Nov-90 PH255) Mending the nets (30x58cm-12x23in) s. gouache

COPSLAIN, J le (?) ?
£3200 $6016   (18-Sep-90 CSK145) Hermitage in storm, St.Peter's. St.Clement's bay, Jersey (26x35cm-10x14in) s. W/C pair

COQUES, Gonzales (1614-1684) Flemish
£5935 $10623   (10-Apr-91 CB.P21 b/R) Reunion musicale sur la terrasse d'un palais (41x53cm-16x21in) panel (F.FR 60000)
£13000 $21970   (19-Apr-91 C82/R) The artist's studio with the artist painting Daniel Seghers (41x36cm-16x14in) panel

COQUES, Gonzales (attrib) (1614-1684) Flemish
£800 $1544   (14-Dec-90 PHM123/R) Portrait of gentleman wearing black dress and lace collar (14x11cm-6x4in) copper oval
£2400 $3912   (2-Jul-91 PH58/R) Portrait of young woman in dress trimmed with lace (11x8cm-4x3in) metal

COQUES, Gonzales (style) (1614-1684) Flemish
£900 $1467   (4-Jul-91 C774) Youth drinking from jug (25x20cm-10x8in) panel

CORBELLINI, Luigi (1901-1968) French
£531 $1029   (8-Dec-90 GAB.G2471/R) Portrait d'enfant (61x46cm-24x18in) s. (S.FR 1300)
£675 $1100   (12-Jun-91 SY.NY104/R) Arlequin surpris (41x33cm-16x13in) s.stretcher
£735 $1425   (8-Dec-90 GAB.G2474/R) L'Ecuyere (37x54cm-15x21in) s. (S.FR 1800)
£798 $1300   (14-Jun-91 W.W27/R) Fleurs (61x46cm-24x18in) s.
£813 $1626   (6-Feb-91 FB.P79/R) La fille au chapeau (35x27cm-14x11in) s. (F.FR 8000)
£923 $1800   (10-Oct-90 SY.NY203/R) Moulin de la Galette (38x56cm-15x22in) s.i.d.1948
£956 $1865   (24-Oct-90 GD.B238/R) View of Italian town (53x68cm-21x27in) s. (S.FR 2400)
£982 $1600   (12-Jun-91 SY.NY106/R) Young boy (33x24cm-13x9in) s.
£1071 $2100   (12-Feb-91 SY.NY204/R) Storm clouds, Paris (64x81cm-25x32in) s.i.
£1102 $2138   (8-Dec-90 GAB.G2470/R) Nature morte aux fruits (45x59cm-18x23in) (S.FR 2700)
£1122 $2200   (7-Nov-90 D.NY21) Young girl with floral bouquet (64x46cm-25x18in)
£1276 $2500   (12-Feb-91 SY.NY220/R) Girl with vase of flowers (61x46cm-24x18in) s.
£1380 $2250   (12-Jun-91 SY.NY109/R) Young girl with anemones (65x46cm-26x18in) s.
£1534 $2500   (12-Jun-91 SY.NY108/R) Harlewuln children (41x27cm-16x11in) s. pair
£1733 $3345   (14-Dec-90 ARC.P25/R) Nu assis (61x38cm-24x15in) s. (F.FR 17000)
£3893 $7631   (7-Nov-90 APT.P503/R) Femme a la mondoline (65x81cm-26x32in) s. (F.FR 38000)
£3893 $7631   (7-Nov-90 APT.P502/R) Le modele assis (84x65cm-33x26in) s. (F.FR 38000)
£6479 $11014   (28-May-91 AB.S5186/R) Femme assise (54x45cm-21x18in) s. (S.KR 69000)

CORBET, Edouard (1815-?) French
£850 $1675   (1-Nov-90 CSK5/R) Short-horned Roan cow (40x51cm-16x20in) s.d.1877

CORBET, Edouard Joseph (1772-1825) ?
£360 $637   (20-Mar-91 C47) Portrait of gentleman in mauve coat and white waistcoat (8x?cm-3x?in) min.s.d.1818 gilt-metal frame locks of hair oval

CORBET, Jean (1926-) French
£652 $1271   (8-Oct-90 MJ.P56) Dame cueillant des roses (55x46cm-22x18in) s. panel (F.FR 6500)
£702 $1369   (8-Oct-90 MJ.P44) La cueillette pres de Rochetaille (73x54cm-29x21in) s. panel (F.FR 7000)

CORBET, Matthew Ridley (1850-1902) British
£1250 $2038   (14-Jun-91 C142/R) Laundry women at the washing well, San gimignano, Italy (63x35cm-25x14in) s.d.1898 pencil W/C

CORBINO, Jon (1905-1964) American
£695 $1300   (1-Aug-90 B.P103/R) Summer riders (30x41cm-12x16in) s. board
£950 $1700   (11-Apr-91 FA.PH946/R) Wild horses (46x51cm-18x20in) s.
£1065 $1800   (1-May-91 B.SF5273/R) Children's beach party (35x25cm-14x10in) s. panel

CORBOULD, Alfred (fl.1831-1875) British
£2000 $3940   (31-Oct-90 S389/R) Mr W James Holden with favourite hunter in landscape (62x75cm-24x30in) i.verso

CORBOULD, Edward Henry (1815-1905) British
£1900 $3667   (12-Dec-90 PHS796/R) In nick of time (91x183cm-36x72in) s.i.d.1900
£1800 $3546   (13-Nov-90 SWS18/R) Edward II King of England and France and his son the Prince of Wales (90x60cm-35x24in) s.i. label verso

CORBUSIER, le (1887-1965) French
£21959 $37331   (1-Jun-91 VG.B302/R) Composition (40x59cm-16x23in) mono.d.1952 paper on canvas (DM 65000)
£126904 $250000   (14-Nov-90 SY.NY441/R) Taureau I (168x97cm-66x38in) s.d.52 plywood
£1976 $3360   (30-May-91 EA.Z246/R) L - C (20x19cm-8x7in) casein (S.FR 5000)
£3400 $6630   (17-Oct-90 G.Z81/R) Couple (34x24cm-13x9in) s.i.d.1952 col.pencil (S.FR 8500)
£3800 $7372   (5-Dec-90 PH87/R) Ubu-bois (31x22cm-12x9in) init.d.42 59 i.verso collage brush ink
£5000 $8050   (25-Jun-91 C258/R) Tapisserie chandigarh (46x54cm-18x21in) init. gouache pencil collage
£5500 $8855   (24-Jun-91 CSK159/R) Le pigney (48x64cm-19x25in) s.i.d.1935 W/C
£6024 $10120   (24-Apr-91 G.Z40/R) Nature morte (34x25cm-13x10in) mono.d.1963 mixed media collage (S.FR 15000)
£6081 $10520   (25-May-91 N.M211/R) Nature morte, siphons et bocks (27x21cm-11x8in) s.d.1928 chk over pencil (DM 18000)
£6352 $12006   (28-Sep-90 S.Z109/R) Nature morte a la guitare vermillon (24x31cm-9x12in) mono.d.1950 indian ink collage (S.FR 15500)
£7107 $14000   (3-Oct-90 SY.NY109/R) Nudes (21x31cm-8x12in) s.d.1935 W/C pencil paper on board
£7143 $14071   (17-Nov-90 S.Z30/R) Untitled (27x22cm-11x9in) d.1924 pencil (S.FR 17500)

CORBUSIER, le (1887-1965) French-cont.
£8163 $16000   *(15-Feb-91 SY.NY78/R) Two female figures standing on the rocks. Two standing nudes one s.i.d.1930 silverpoint W/C pen ink two*
£14000 $27300   *(19-Oct-90 C147/R) Composition avec une femme (58x38cm-23x15in) s. s.d.51 newspaper collage gouache brush ink*

CORCHON Y DIAQUE, Federico (19th C) Spanish
£2754 $4628   (23-Apr-91 SY.AM259/R) View of Barcelona (27x48cm-11x19in) s. (D.FL 9200)

CORCHON, Jose (19th C) Spanish
£1899 $3133   (8-Jul-91 SY.J172/R) Still life with vegetables and fish. Still life with vegetables and rooster (61x81cm-24x32in) s.d.1848 pair (SA.R 9000)

CORCOS, Vittorio (1859-1933) Italian
£3077 $6000   (23-Oct-90 SY.NY428/R) Portrait of gentleman said to be Emile Zola (46x38cm-18x15in) s.
£6000 $11520   (28-Nov-90 S171/R) The dark and the fair (57x36cm-22x14in) one s. pair
£13681 $22848   (6-Jun-91 F.M262/R) Visita al museo (49x57cm-19x22in) s. (I.L 30000000)

CORDERO, Francisco (19th C) Mexican
£1600 $2624   (18-Jun-91 PH90) Landscape (38x66cm-15x26in) s.
£2044 $3536   (21-May-91 DUR.M43/R) Paisaje (55x93cm-22x37in) (S.P 375000)
£2056 $3455   (23-Apr-91 DUR.M2/R) Paisaje (53x83cm-21x33in) (S.P 375000)
£3298 $6331   (19-Feb-91 DUR.M11) Paisaje (55x93cm-22x37in) (S.P 600000)

CORDERO, Ricardo V (?) Spanish
£1635 $2829   (21-May-91 DUR.M44/R) Nino pastor (80x50cm-31x20in) (S.P 300000)

CORDIER, Jacques (?) French?
£2738 $5422   (3-Feb-91 I.N48/R) Plage d'Ostende (60x73cm-24x29in) s. (F.FR 27000)
£2851 $5617   (30-Oct-90 I.N106/R) Les tuileries sous la neige (60x70cm-24x28in) s. (F.FR 28000)
£3259 $6420   (30-Oct-90 I.N289) Les barques bleues (81x100cm-32x39in) s.i.d.73 (F.FR 32000)
£3367 $6634   (14-Nov-90 I.N35/R) Lumiere bleue (81x100cm-32x39in) s. d.1973 verso (F.FR 33000)
£1939 $3819   *(14-Nov-90 I.N36/R) Les voiliers (50x65cm-20x26in) s. W/C (F.FR 19000)*

CORDIVIOLA, Luis Adolfo (1892-1967) Argentinian
£591 $1100   (5-Sep-90 V.BA29) Invierno (24x33cm-9x13in)
£812 $1600   (14-Nov-90 V.BA34) En el corral (30x40cm-12x16in)
£1563 $3000   (27-Nov-90 PO.BA3) Paisaje con cabras (50x60cm-20x24in) s.
£2234 $4200   (18-Sep-90 RO.BA38/R) Junto a la pirca (50x70cm-20x28in) s.d.964

CORDREY, John (fl.1765-1825) British
£950 $1872   (31-Oct-90 S401/R) Horse drawn coach in landscape (36x52cm-14x20in)

CORELLI (?) Italian
£2048 $3850   *(19-Sep-90 N.M791) Bay of Napels with fishing boats and Vesuv mountain beyond (39x65cm-15x26in) s. gouache (DM 6000)*

CORELLI, Augusto (1853-?) Italian
£3000 $4890   (1-Jul-91 LGB.P2/R) Songeuse au bord de l'eau (35x100cm-14x39in) s. (F.FR 30000)
£1600 $3072   *(28-Nov-90 S137/R) View of Naples from Posillipo (28x45cm-11x18in) s. gouache*

CORELLI, G (16th C) Italian
£720 $1159   *(24-Jun-91 HS79/R) Vesuvius from Bay of Naples (40x60cm-16x24in) s.i.d.1903 gouache*

CORELLI, Giuseppe (19/20th C) Italian
£2694 $4660   (6-May-91 ZEL.L1633/R) Bay of Naples with Vesuvius beyond, morning (32x51cm-13x20in) s.i.d.1897 panel (DM 8000)

CORENZIO, Belisario (attrib) (1558-1640) Greek
£1529 $2600   (31-May-91 CH.NY232/R) The Presentation in the Temple (39x71cm-15x28in) panel

CORIA, C (?) ?
£1086 $1835   *(15-Apr-91 AAA.S57) The Cavallier (66x49cm-26x19in) s. W/C (A.D 2400)*

CORINTH, Lovis (1858-1925) German
£9091 $17545   (12-Dec-90 SY.MU71/R) In the pig sty (58x78cm-23x31in) s. canvas on board (DM 26000)
£25338 $43074   (30-May-91 SY.BE1/R) The rose, portrait of Lucie Mainzer (60x43cm-24x17in) s.d.1914 (DM 75000)
£39000 $75660   (4-Dec-90 C285 a/R) Das Homerische Gelachter II (60x72cm-24x28in) s.i.d.1919 paper on panel
£60811 $105203   (25-May-91 N.M48/R) Forest interior near Bernried (94x110cm-37x43in) s.i.d.1892 (DM 180000)
£106780 $178322   (6-Jun-91 HN.H217/R) Cornflowers (40x26cm-16x10in) s.d.1912 (DM 315000)

CORINTH, Lovis (1858-1925) German-cont.

£121622	$210405	(25-May-91 N.M49/R) Beneath the chandelier, Charlotte Berend-Corinth and Dr Robert Richter (94x78cm-37x31in) s.d.1905 (DM 360000)
£586	$1126	(26-Nov-90 WK.M161) Butcher's shop. Sketch of bull (27x41cm-11x16in) s.i.d.1911 pencil col.chk double-sided (DM 1700)
£780	$1302	(6-Jun-91 HN.H219/R) Leda (24x31cm-9x12in) s. chk. (DM 2300)
£845	$1436	(1-Jun-91 VG.B467/R) Feamle nude in pensive mood (30x15cm-12x6in) mono. pencil ochre dr.verso (DM 2500)
£897	$1721	(26-Nov-90 WK.M160/R) Woman writing (10x17cm-4x7in) s.d.1911 pencil (DM 2600)
£897	$1721	(28-Nov-90 KF.M623/R) Portrait of Mr. Blaas from Zurich reading (30x23cm-12x9in) s.i.d.1885 W/C over pencil (DM 2600)
£1014	$1753	(25-May-91 N.M50/R) Two girls holding raised hands (52x33cm-20x13in) s.d.1892 pencil (DM 3000)
£2241	$4303	(28-Nov-90 KF.M625/R) Female nude and priest (27x22cm-11x9in) s.c.1920 chk (DM 6500)
£2797	$5399	(12-Dec-90 SY.MU6/R) Charlotte with flowers (21x14cm-8x6in) s.d.1919 chl (DM 8000)
£3041	$5169	(1-Jun-91 VG.B115/R) House in Urfeld (31x24cm-12x9in) s.i.d.1919 pencil col.chk double-sided vellum (DM 9000)
£3547	$6030	(28-Nov-90 KF.M538/R) Portrait of painter Crampe (42x32cm-17x13in) s.d.1921 chk col.pencil (DM 10500)
£6419	$10912	(1-Jun-91 VG.B119/R) The rape of Proserpina. Study for male nude and three arms (31x34cm-12x13in) s.mono.d.1917 W/C htd.white pencil double-sided (DM 19000)
£37162	$63176	(31-May-91 VG.B28/R) Walchensee landscape in fog (36x51cm-14x20in) s.i.d.1921 W/C board (DM 110000)

CORKOLE, Auguste (1829-1875) Flemish

| £3000 | $5850 | (15-Jan-91 GM.B391/R) Couple d'amoureux (55x42cm-22x17in) s. wood (B.FR 180000) |

CORMON, Fernand (1845-1924) French

£2510	$4041	(24-Jun-91 ARC.P20/R) Jeune femme de profil (126x80cm-50x31in) s.d.1904 (F.FR 25000)
£475	$850	(12-Apr-91 JM.P17/R) Salome et David (42x30cm-17x12in) bl.crayon W/C (F.FR 4800)
£769	$1500	(26-Oct-90 SY.NY105/R) Soldier (41x28cm-16x11in) init.d.97 pencil chk

CORNEAU, Eugene (1894-1976) French

| £655 | $1067 | (11-Jun-91 I.N33) Le repos sous les arbres (22x27cm-9x11in) s. panel (F.FR 6500) |
| £853 | $1672 | (24-Nov-90 N.M107/R) Still life with cherries and apricots (24x41cm-9x16in) s. (DM 2500) |

CORNEILLE (1922-) Dutch

£1868	$3512	(19-Sep-90 KH.K107/R) Deux femmes (45x33cm-18x13in) s.d.73 acrylic paper on canvas (D.KR 21000)
£2535	$4310	(28-May-91 AB.S5187/R) Composition (65x50cm-26x20in) s.d.70 acrylic paper on canvas (S.KR 27000)
£3559	$6690	(19-Sep-90 KH.K83/R) Femme et oiseau (25x27cm-10x11in) indist.s. acrylic paper (D.KR 40000)
£3947	$6711	(29-May-91 KH.K116/R) Femme (30x20cm-12x8in) s.d.69 acrylic paper on canvas (D.KR 45000)
£4286	$7929	(5-Mar-91 RAS.K1/R) Composition with three men (70x100cm-28x39in) s.d.73-88 acrylic paper on canvas (D.FL 48000)
£4561	$7754	(29-May-91 KH.K59/R) Femme et oiseau (30x20cm-12x8in) s.d.69 acrylic paper on canvas (D.KR 52000)
£5405	$9351	(23-May-91 SY.AM252/R) Aux bords de l'ocean (17x32cm-7x13in) s.d.56 i.d.verso paper on board (D.FL 18000)
£15477	$27705	(15-Mar-91 FB.P41/R) Entre terre et ciel (61x61cm-24x24in) s.d.60 i. verso (F.FR 154000)
£17959	$34841	(7-Dec-90 G.Z102/R) Composition (64x83cm-25x33in) s.d.1947 (S.FR 44000)
£21021	$36366	(22-May-91 CH.AM629/R) La fleur verte du mal (147x60cm-58x24in) s.d.69 (D.FL 70000)
£23220	$44814	(13-Dec-90 SY.AM230/R) Le domaine de l'Abeille (52x79cm-20x31in) s.d.62 (D.FL 75000)
£24768	$47802	(12-Dec-90 CH.AM399/R) Jeux de l'ete (45x35cm-18x14in) s.d.51 s.i.d.verso board (D.FL 80000)
£25801	$48505	(19-Sep-90 KH.K6/R) Bain de soleil (120x120cm-47x47in) s.d.68 i.verso (D.KR 290000)
£28529	$49354	(22-May-91 CH.AM603/R) Dans les rochers l'ete (61x61cm-24x24in) s.d.61 s.i.d.verso (D.FL 95000)
£35604	$68715	(13-Dec-90 SY.AM261/R) Les deux oiseaux (159x128cm-63x50in) s.d.69 (D.FL 115000)
£539	$1061	(14-Nov-90 KH.K26) Buste de femme (28x20cm-11x8in) s.d.78 Indian ink wash (D.KR 6000)
£702	$1193	(29-May-91 KH.K16) Figure composition (69x100cm-27x39in) s.d.73 acrylic on lithograph (D.KR 8000)
£721	$1247	(22-May-91 CH.AM706) Woman, birds and rainbow (31x31cm-12x12in) s.d.73 bodycol over printed base (D.FL 2400)
£1053	$1789	(29-May-91 KH.K120/R) Deux femmes (45x33cm-18x13in) s.d.73 acrylic W/C on lithograph (D.KR 12000)
£1068	$2007	(19-Sep-90 KH.K21) Composition (30x24cm-12x9in) s.d.76 Indian ink wash gouache (D.KR 12000)
£1100	$2145	(18-Oct-90 C346) Untitled (32x41cm-13x16in) s.d.61 pencil W/C ink

CORNEILLE (1922-) Dutch-cont.

£1134	$1951	(13-May-91 CH.R30/R) Untitled (21x30cm-8x12in) s.d.1961 gouache (I.L 2500000)
£1201	$2078	(22-May-91 CH.AM750) Isla (20x29cm-8x11in) s.i.d.20-8-68 felt-tip pen W/C (D.FL 4000)
£1316	$2579	(22-Nov-90 ZZ.F6/R) Composition aux oiseaux (20x29cm-8x11in) s.d.84 ink htd.gouache (F.FR 13000)
£1320	$2575	(10-Oct-90 RAS.K154) Woman and bird (40x39cm-16x15in) s.d.79 gouache over lithograph (D.KR 15000)
£1393	$2689	(12-Dec-90 CH.AM457) Mother and child (26x23cm-10x9in) s.d.50 brush ink (D.FL 4500)
£1512	$2843	(19-Sep-90 KH.K32/R) Composition (30x22cm-12x9in) s.d.50 Indian ink (D.KR 17000)
£1585	$3090	(10-Oct-90 RAS.K156/R) Composition with snakes (67x97cm-26x38in) s.d.73-88 gouache over lithograph (D.KR 18000)
£1585	$3090	(10-Oct-90 RAS.K156 a/R) Man and bird (67x97cm-26x38in) s.d.73-88 gouache over lithograph (D.KR 18000)
£1633	$3216	(16-Nov-90 FB.P298/R) Composition (21x26cm-8x10in) s.d.mars 1967 col.crayons (F.FR 16000)
£1721	$3372	(22-Nov-90 ZZ.F4/R) L'enfant et le cameleon (23x23cm-9x9in) s.i.d.50 ink (F.FR 17000)
£1754	$2982	(29-May-91 KH.K103/R) Composition (12x28cm-5x11in) s.d.54 crayon (D.KR 20000)
£1838	$3603	(10-Nov-90 FAL.M70/R) Composition with figures (70x101cm-28x40in) s.d.73-75 mixed media (S.KR 20000)
£1858	$3585	(12-Dec-90 CH.AM479/R) Les aventures de Pinocchio (70x100cm-28x39in) s.d.73 gouache over printed base (D.FL 6000)
£1859	$3327	(13-Apr-91 FAL.M54/R) Composition with face and bird with yellow background (70x101cm-28x40in) s.d.73-88 mixed media (S.KR 20000)
£1868	$3512	(19-Sep-90 KH.K49/R) La mere terre (43x90cm-17x35in) s.d.78 gouache lithograph (D.KR 21000)
£1878	$3682	(13-Feb-91 KH.K49/R) L'Amazone intrepide (24x31cm-9x12in) s.d.78 gouache (D.KR 21000)
£1972	$3886	(1-Oct-90 CC.P20) Untitled (13x27cm-5x11in) s.d.1957 gouache pastel (F.FR 20000)
£2135	$4014	(19-Sep-90 KH.K100/R) Femme et oiseau (26x19cm-10x7in) s.d.76 W/C pencil crayon (D.KR 24000)
£2167	$4183	(12-Dec-90 CH.AM508/R) Woman and bird (65x50cm-26x20in) s.d.73 W/C over printed base (D.FL 7000)
£2252	$3896	(23-May-91 SY.AM232/R) Untitled (23x30cm-9x12in) s.d.66 gouache (D.FL 7500)
£2313	$4349	(19-Sep-90 KH.K98/R) Pinoccio (68x98cm-27x39in) s.d.73-75 gouache (D.KR 26000)
£2367	$4663	(1-Oct-90 CC.P19/R) Untitled (20x26cm-8x10in) s.d.1957 gouache pastel (F.FR 24000)
£2500	$4425	(21-Mar-91 C201 a) Les deux baigneuses (223x29cm-88x11in) s.d.63 gouache paper mounted on canvas
£3096	$5975	(13-Dec-90 SY.AM196/R) Untitled (24x33cm-9x13in) s.d.66 gouache (D.FL 10000)
£3425	$5582	(14-Jun-91 L.K827/R) Snakes (70x100cm-28x39in) s.d.73 W/C indian ink brush (DM 10000)
£3566	$6990	(24-Nov-90 HOR.H7/R) Woman with bird (40x40cm-16x16in) s.d.1987 gouache (F.M 25000)
£4000	$7800	(18-Oct-90 C342/R) Untitled (32x43cm-13x17in) s.d.60 W/C ink
£4133	$8059	(26-Oct-90 CC.P6/R) Sans titre (30x43cm-12x17in) s.d. W/C Japan paper (F.FR 41000)
£4500	$8775	(18-Oct-90 C341/R) Untitled (29x36cm-11x14in) s.d.67 ink W/C pencil
£4570	$8958	(20-Nov-90 GO.G318/R) Composition with black bird (70x100cm-28x39in) s.d.73 gouache (S.KR 50000)
£4601	$8973	(23-Oct-90 C.A341/R) The beauties who visit Amsterdam (38x30cm-15x12in) s.d.1975 gouache (B.FR 280000)
£5030	$8500	(2-May-91 CH.NY110/R) Untitled (26x75cm-10x30in) s.d.55 gouache
£5263	$8947	(29-May-91 KH.K22/R) Composition (21x36cm-8x14in) s.d.57 gouache W/C (D.KR 60000)
£5961	$11564	(5-Dec-90 I.N41) Sans titre (81x116cm-32x46in) s. mixed media (F.FR 58000)
£6117	$11867	(4-Dec-90 BA.S77/R) La reine des baigneuses (49x66cm-19x26in) s.d.63 gouache (S.KR 66000)
£6306	$10910	(22-Nov-90 CH.AM596/R) Composition (66x85cm-26x33in) s.d.65 gouache (D.FL 21000)
£6572	$12816	(15-Oct-90 CSC.P69/R) Femme aux deux oiseaux (65x44cm-26x17in) s.d.81 gouache (F.FR 65000)
£12012	$20781	(23-May-91 SY.AM256 e/R) Vier spielende kinderen (49x65cm-19x26in) s.d.51 gouache (D.FL 40000)

CORNEILLE DE LYON (school) (?-1574) Flemish

| £4183 | $7112 | (31-May-91 LD.P34/R) Portrait d'homme sous le regne (14x10cm-6x4in) panel (F.FR 42000) |

CORNEILLE, C (20th C) ?

| £1873 | $3634 | (4-Dec-90 UL.T193/R) Composition in colour (49x32cm-19x13in) W/C (N.KR 21000) |

CORNEILLE, Jean Baptiste (1649-1695) French

| £1614 | $2743 | (27-May-91 OD.P15/R) Triomphe d'un general romain (23cm-9ins circular) i. pen wash htd.gouache pierre noire round (F.FR 16200) |

CORNEILLE, Jean Baptiste (attrib) (1649-1695) French
£2811 $4526   (27-Jun-91 APT.P167/R) La Vierge protegeant les marins (65x54cm-26x21in)
    (F.FR 28000)

CORNEILLE, Michel (17th C) French
£400 $708   (22-Mar-91 APT.P29) Homme nu assis (42x25cm-17x10in) sanguinne after
    Carrache (F.FR 4000)
£750 $1448   (11-Dec-90 C65/R) Studies of heads (10x12cm-4x5in) s. ink
£1200 $2028   (16-Apr-91 C213/R) The Lapidation of Saint Stephen (24x15cm-9x6in) i.
    verso blk.lead ink wash htd.bodycol
£1508 $2472   (22-Jun-91 CH.MO6/R) Nymphes et satyre pres d'une fontaine
    (23x32cm-9x13in) with i. num.57 verso black chk pen (F.FR 15000)
£1600 $2608   (2-Jul-91 C316/R) Judgement of Midas (26x37cm-10x15in) with i. black chk
    pen wash
£2200 $3586   (2-Jul-91 C315/R) Wooded landscape with frog physician attending
    diseased frog and family (29x44cm-11x17in) black chk pen wash

CORNEILLE, Michel (attrib) (17/18th C) French
£1587 $2730   (19-May-91 ZZ.F78/R) L'Annonciation (61x52cm-24x20in) (F.FR 16000)
£1300 $2301   (22-Mar-91 APT.P30) La fuite en Egypte (42x27cm-17x11in) sanguinne
    (F.FR 13000)

CORNEILLE, Michel (younger) (1642-1708) French
£498 $847   (27-May-91 OD.P39) Autel antique formant frontispice (37x26cm-15x10in)
    i. pen wash pierre noire (F.FR 5000)
£508 $864   (27-May-91 OD.P26) Feuille d'etudes de tetes (27x17cm-11x7in) pen
    (F.FR 5100)
£747 $1270   (27-May-91 OD.P38) Venus et Adonis (29x24cm-11x9in) i. pierre noire pen
    wash gouache (F.FR 7500)
£817 $1388   (27-May-91 OD.P27) Feuille d'etudes de tetes (30x19cm-12x7in) pen
    (F.FR 8200)
£847 $1439   (27-May-91 OD.P25) Tete de jeune homme (34x25cm-13x10in) i. sanguinne
    (F.FR 8500)
£1572 $3018   (21-Dec-90 DAR.P46/R) Le Triomphe de Bacchus (18x24cm-7x9in) pen wash
£2590 $4402   (27-May-91 OD.P24/R) Feuille d'etudes (21x23cm-8x9in) i. sanguinne
    (F.FR 26000)

CORNELIUS, Peter (circle) (1783-1867) German
£1096 $1786   (12-Jun-91 N.M406/R) Fiat Lux (58x40cm-23x16in) i.d.1849 en grisaille
    (DM 3200)

CORNELL, Joseph (1903-1973) American
£1531 $3000   (6-Nov-90 CE.NY33/R) Quiet anutumnal (13x18cm-5x7in) i. col.felt-tip
    pens paper collage greeting card
£6599 $13000   (4-Oct-90 SY.NY91/R) The bust (30x23cm-12x9in) d.9.16.69 verso ink paper
    on board
£9184 $18000   (8-Nov-90 CH.NY127/R) Untitled (39x32cm-15x13in) s. verso collage
    masonite
£9184 $18000   (8-Nov-90 CH.NY142/R) Belgique (40x32cm-16x13in) s. verso graphite
    collage of various items

CORNER, Thomas C (1865-1938) American
£2320 $4500   (7-Dec-91 S.W2680/R) Still life with cherries (36x43cm-14x17in) s.d.1886
    i.verso

CORNET, A (19th C) French
£1496 $2678   (12-Mar-91 C.A41) Girl with basket of fruit (39x30cm-15x12in) s.d.1871
    panel (B.FR 90000)

CORNET, Alphonse (1814-1874) French
£1496 $2678   (12-Mar-91 C.A42) Girl with a pony (39x30cm-15x12in) s.d.1871 panel
    (B.FR 90000)
£4429 $7484   (2-May-91 RAS.V26/R) Young woman wearing renaissance costume holding
    helmet (149x109cm-59x43in) s.d.1879 (D.KR 50000)

CORNICELIUS, Georg (1825-1898) German
£8000 $13520   (1-May-91 GD.B171/R) Gypsies (120x87cm-47x34in) s. (S.FR 20000)

CORNOYER, Paul (1864-1925) American
£657 $1300   (1-Feb-91 S.W2363/R) Promenade in park (20x25cm-8x10in) s.
£1380 $2250   (5-Jul-91 S.W3089/R) Spring landscape (30x41cm-12x16in) s. i. verso
    canvasboard
£1546 $3000   (5-Dec-90 D.NY44/R) Sailboats in dock (20x25cm-8x10in) s. board
£15625 $30000   (29-Nov-90 SY.NY94/R) The New York Public Library (30x41cm-12x16in) s.
    board

CORNU, P (1895-?) French
£2357 $4596   (13-Oct-90 H.AP3/R) Les sablettes a Toulon (33x46cm-13x18in) s.
    (F.FR 23500)

CORNU, Pierre (1895-?) French
£612 $1200   (12-Feb-91 SY.NY223/R) Femme lisant (46x53cm-18x21in) s.
£1468 $2877   (25-Nov-90 LC.P83/R) Le modele lisant sur le canape (33x46cm-13x18in) s.
    (F.FR 14500)

CORNU, Pierre (1895-?) French-cont.

£1937	$3719	(30-Nov-90 ARC.P136/R) Rosine sur le divan rouge (61x46cm-24x18in) s. (F.FR 19000)
£2037	$4012	(29-Oct-90 LC.P133) Jeune femme ecrivant (46x55cm-18x22in) s. (F.FR 20000)
£2333	$4619	(3-Feb-91 LT.P57/R) Nu au canape orange (55x46cm-22x18in) s. (F.FR 23000)
£2467	$4785	(8-Dec-90 LT.P45/R) Jeune femme au deshabille bleu (46x38cm-18x15in) s. (F.FR 24000)
£2518	$4104	(11-Jun-91 I.N173/R) Le modele au chapeau jaune (61x50cm-24x20in) s. (F.FR 25000)
£2540	$4368	(19-May-91 LT.P7/R) Modele a la tenture jaune (38x55cm-15x22in) s. (F.FR 25600)
£2548	$4893	(29-Nov-90 QWA.P213) Apres-midi d'ete (46x55cm-18x22in) s. studio st. verso (F.FR 25000)
£2574	$4556	(7-Apr-91 I.N82/R) Jeune fille assoupie (46x55cm-18x22in) s. (F.FR 26000)
£2648	$5216	(29-Oct-90 LC.P127/R) Jeune femme a la robe bleue (65x54cm-26x21in) s. (F.FR 26000)
£3353	$6606	(6-Oct-90 GL.P113) Jeunes filles sur un canape (50x61cm-20x24in) s. (F.FR 34000)
£3469	$6835	(18-Nov-90 H.A108/R) Le corsage rouge (55x46cm-22x18in) s. (F.FR 34000)
£3488	$6802	(17-Oct-90 LT.P162/R) Antonine sur le canape (50x61cm-20x24in) s. (F.FR 34500)
£400	$652	(4-Jul-91 LT.P150) Le modele au fauteuil vert (52x32cm-20x13in) s. W/C (F.FR 4000)
£400	$652	(4-Jul-91 LT.P144) Jeune femme accoudee (36x40cm-14x16in) s. W/C (F.FR 4000)
£495	$876	(7-Apr-91 LT.P169) Le modele au gilet vert (48x48cm-19x19in) s. W/C (F.FR 5000)
£495	$876	(7-Apr-91 LT.P172) Nu au bouquet (45x58cm-18x23in) s. W/C (F.FR 5000)
£505	$894	(7-Apr-91 LT.P171) Le modele au sofa (42x52cm-17x20in) s. W/C (F.FR 5100)
£614	$1087	(7-Apr-91 I.N83) Jeune femme aux fruits (40x49cm-16x19in) s. W/C (F.FR 6200)
£752	$1332	(7-Apr-91 LT.P170) Le modele au gilet rouge (40x52cm-16x20in) s. W/C (F.FR 7600)

CORNWELL, Dean (1892-1960) American

£2344	$4500	(17-Dec-90 SY.NY245/R) Oriental mother and child (114x81cm-45x32in) mono.d.29
£5085	$9000	(24-Mar-91 LIT.L53) Nicodemus coming to Jesus at night (91x71cm-36x28in) mono.
£8235	$14000	(1-Jun-91 IH.NY87/R) Group of men aboard boat one repairing nets (86x114cm-34x45in) init.d.1952
£11340	$22000	(5-Dec-90 D.NY94/R) The Den of Iniquity (91x66cm-36x26in) s.d.18 i.verso
£1176	$2000	(1-Jun-91 IH.NY168/R) Woman in 18th century costume feeding birs (76x119cm-30x47in) chl

COROMALDI, Umberto (1870-1948) Italian

£729	$1239	(28-May-91 F.R9) Sulla spiaggia (15x21cm-6x8in) s. panel (I.L 1600000)
£906	$1532	(16-Apr-91 CH.R69) Pittrice al cavalletto (45x30cm-18x12in) s. canvas on board (I.L 2000000)
£924	$1784	(11-Dec-90 CH.R90) Bambina con mazzetto di rose (58x48cm-23x19in) s. (I.L 2000000)
£1201	$2319	(11-Dec-90 CH.R136) Scorcio di paese con ragazzi (54x63cm-21x25in) (I.L 2600000)

CORONA, Poul (1872-1945) Scandinavian

£1500	$2460	(19-Jun-91 S260/R) Lady in red (46x40cm-18x16in) s.d.1922

CORONEL, Pedro (1923-) Mexican

£3316	$6500	(19-Nov-90 SY.NY212/R) Mujer extrana (45x38cm-18x15in) s.d.61verso
£10204	$20000	(19-Nov-90 SY.NY211/R) Los Perfiles Cruzados (80x60cm-31x24in) s.
£14286	$28000	(20-Nov-90 CH.NY170/R) Serie ano uno luna (234x53cm-92x21in) s.i.d.69 verso acrylic sand canvas
£22093	$38000	(15-May-91 CH.NY104/R) Tamayana (95x130cm-37x51in) s. i. verso acrylic sand

CORONEL, Rafael (1932-) Mexican

£9184	$18000	(20-Nov-90 CH.NY127/R) Charlie Chaplin (140x90cm-55x35in) s.d.68 acrylic linen
£9694	$19000	(20-Nov-90 CH.NY128/R) A la vuelta de la esquina no. 2 (100x120cm-39x47in) s. acrylic canvas
£11735	$23000	(19-Nov-90 SY.NY84/R) Para Caravaglo (100x75cm-39x30in) s.d.70
£12755	$25000	(19-Nov-90 SY.NY158/R) De Paseo (120x100cm-47x39in) s.
£14286	$28000	(19-Nov-90 SY.NY74/R) Untitled (150x100cm-59x39in) s.

COROT (school) (19th C) French

£1394	$2719	(24-Oct-90 GD.B242/R) River landscape with figures (46x61cm-18x24in) (S.FR 3500)

COROT, Jean Baptiste Camille (1796-1875) French

£1190	$2000	(28-Apr-91 HG.C52) Landscape with harbour (25x38cm-10x15in) s. panel sold with artist's letter

COROT, Jean Baptiste Camille (1796-1875) French-cont.

£12036	$23470	(12-Oct-90 APT.P54/R) Effet du soir (21x14cm-8x6in) s. panel (F.FR 120000)
£16129	$30968	(2-Dec-90 GAB.G1573/R) Baigneuses au bord d'un lac (81x100cm-32x39in) s. (S.FR 40000)
£24277	$42000	(23-May-91 CH.NY218/R) Moulin a Montmartre (23x32cm-9x13in) st.sig. st.seal verso
£26000	$41860	(25-Jun-91 C101/R) Ligne d'Arbres dans la campagne (9x14cm-4x6in) s. board
£33333	$65000	(24-Oct-90 CH.NY36/R) Environs d'Arras, bords de la Scarpe (32x42cm-13x17in) st.sig. seal verso panel
£34000	$65280	(28-Nov-90 S248/R) Church overlooking valley (23x37cm-9x15in)
£34682	$60000	(22-May-91 D.NY31/R) Le marais des Donzelles, pres de la scarpe (39x47cm-15x19in) s.
£34682	$60000	(22-May-91 SY.NY7/R) Prairies de Sainte Catherine-Lez-Arras (24x29cm-9x11in) s. cradled panel
£43353	$75000	(23-May-91 CH.NY219/R) Jeune marchand d'oranges Napolitain (18x11cm-7x4in) panel
£46243	$80000	(22-May-91 SY.NY12/R) Batelier au bord de la rive, le soir (25x40cm-10x16in) s.
£78035	$135000	(23-May-91 CH.NY221/R) Clairiere du Bois Pierre, aux Evaux pres Chateau Thierry (32x25cm-13x10in) s.
£78035	$135000	(23-May-91 CH.NY222/R) La vachere dans la vallee (23x30cm-9x12in) s.
£82051	$160000	(24-Oct-90 CH.NY33/R) Dunkerque, une pecheuse de crevettes (26x46cm-10x18in) s. panel
£87179	$170000	(24-Oct-90 CH.NY34/R) Une allee ombrageuse a Saint-Cloud, Ville d'Avray (27x32cm-11x13in) s.
£89474	$170000	(28-Feb-91 CH.NY58/R) Le batelier pres des vieux chenes (25x41cm-10x16in) s. panel
£101215	$198381	(25-Nov-90 GL.P3/R) Saint Lo (26x46cm-10x18in) s. (F.FR 1000000)
£110000	$177100	(24-Jun-91 C2/R) Les hauteurs de sevres, le chemin troyon (23x37cm-9x15in)
£134078	$240000	(11-Apr-91 FA.PH1006/R) La Rencontre sur le chemin (46x56cm-18x22in) s.
£165829	$271960	(17-Jun-91 ARC.P32/R) Un chemin dans les bois de Saint-Cloud (73x53cm-29x21in) s. (F.FR 1650000)
£213873	$370000	(22-May-91 SY.NY8/R) Les Evaux, pres Chateau-Thierry (42x61cm-17x24in) s.i.
£220000	$360800	(19-Jun-91 S124/R) Le chevrier traversant un ruisseau - paysage Italien (56x45cm-22x18in) s.
£222672	$436437	(25-Nov-90 GL.P1/R) L'arc de Constantin et le Forum - 1843 (28x39cm-11x15in) s. (F.FR 2200000)
£245000	$470400	(28-Nov-90 S10/R) Souvenir de l'Ecluze, pres Douai (40x53cm-16x21in) s.
£289017	$500000	(23-May-91 CH.NY220/R) Souvenir de Cayeux (42x61cm-17x24in) s.
£302564	$590000	(24-Oct-90 CH.NY32/R) Venise, gondole sur le Grand Canal, St Georges Majeur au fond (29x41cm-11x16in) bears sig.st.sig. vente seal verso
£1221	*$2307*	*(30-Sep-90 P.V5) De grotta ferrata a Frascati (11x20cm-4x8in) i. lead pencil stumping (F.FR 12000)*
£2062	*$4000*	*(8-Dec-90 W.23/R) Le Danube de Vienne a l'Ouest (46x69cm-18x27in) s.i.d.1823 chl pencil htd white*
£3551	*$6853*	*(11-Dec-90 FER.M21/R) Paisaje con arboles. Jinete en el bosque init. chl dr two (S.P 650000)*
£4625	*$8972*	*(7-Dec-90 GL.P101/R) Paysage a Mortefontaine (15x24cm-6x9in) s. chl. (F.FR 45000)*
£6200	*$12028*	*(5-Dec-90 PH6 a/R) Cavalier et Bucheron. Paysage (43x28cm-17x11in) st.device pencil double-sided*

COROT, Jean Baptiste Camille (attrib) (1796-1875) French

£865	$1410	(10-Jun-91 W.T1373) Near Fontainebleau (25x40cm-10x16in) s. (C.D 1600)
£1195	$2331	(24-Oct-90 GD.B241/R) Autumn landscape with farmhouse and peasant woman (46x3cm-18x1in) bears sig. (S.FR 3000)
£2000	$3380	(1-May-91 GD.B173/R) River landscape (26x18cm-10x7in) i. panel (S.FR 5000)
£3265	$6400	(6-Nov-90 GF.L2150/R) Wooded landscape (21x28cm-8x11in) bears sig. panel (S.FR 8000)
£3400	$5746	(1-May-91 GD.B174/R) Landscape with cattle grazing and peasant woman (19x26cm-7x10in) s. (S.FR 8500)
£3984	$7769	(24-Oct-90 GD.B240/R) River landscape with anglers and roofs of village beyond (25x35cm-10x14in) bears sig. (S.FR 10000)

COROT, Jean Baptiste Camille (style) (1796-1875) French

£2232	$4286	(27-Nov-90 W.T1131/R) Landscape, evening (63x113cm-25x44in) st.studio (C.D 5000)
£3869	$6500	(17-Jul-91 SY.NY210/R) Brunoy, Acacias pres de la ferme, dans le parc de M. Louis Dubuisson (101x82cm-40x32in) bears sig.

CORPORA, Antonio (1909-) Italian

£2726	$5370	(30-Oct-90 F.R95/R) Mattina d'estate (69x48cm-27x19in) s.d.71 paper laid down on canvas (I.L 6000000)
£3316	$6500	(12-Feb-91 SY.NY365/R) Untitled (99x81cm-39x32in) s.d.62
£3571	$7000	(12-Feb-91 SY.NY404/R) Verde corrotto (64x81cm-25x32in) s.d.62 s.i.d.stretcher
£4126	$6767	(20-Jun-91 F.M312/R) Senza titolo (61x59cm-24x23in) s. d.1965verso (I.L 9000000)
£5403	$10536	(22-Oct-90 BR.M130/R) Il tramonto di allora (81x100cm-32x39in) s. s.d.1973 verso (I.L 12000000)

CORPORA, Antonio (1909-) Italian-cont.
£6303	$12292	(22-Oct-90 BR.M81/R) Luce improvvisa (81x100cm-32x39in) s.d.1972 (I.L 14000000)
£7500	$14625	(9-Oct-90 B177) Mare del Nord (130x97cm-51x38in) s.d.54
£8340	$14928	(9-Apr-91 F.R242/R) Untitled (100x80cm-39x31in) s.d.63 (I.L 18500000)
£11270	$20174	(9-Apr-91 F.R213/R) Composizione in blu (81x65cm-32x26in) s.d.50 (I.L 25000000)
£20711	$40387	(22-Oct-90 BR.M11/R) Composizione (146x114cm-57x45in) s.d.1970 (I.L 46000000)
£879	*$1705*	*(3-Dec-90 F.M68) Composizione (46x30cm-18x12in) s. W/C (I.L 1900000)*
£1082	*$1937*	*(9-Apr-91 F.R58) Composizione (49x64cm-19x25in) s. pastel velvet paper (I.L 2400000)*
£1367	*$2324*	*(28-May-91 SY.MI80/R) Composizione (63x47cm-25x19in) s. pastel board (I.L 3000000)*
£1367	*$2324*	*(28-May-91 SY.MI54/R) Composizione (44x61cm-17x24in) s. pastel board (I.L 3000000)*
£2499	*$4923*	*(30-Oct-90 F.R70) Untitled (68x47cm-27x19in) s.d.60 mixed media sand board (I.L 5500000)*
£2927	*$5707*	*(24-Oct-90 F.M172/R) Una verde speranza (50x70cm-20x28in) s. s.d.1972verso mixed media canvas (I.L 6500000)*

CORRADINI, F (?) Italian
£1900	$3724	(15-Feb-91 C77/R) Flirtation (82x62cm-32x24in) s.

CORRADINI, P C A (19th C) Italian
£1300	$2496	(27-Nov-90 PH180/R) The artist's model (42x33cm-17x13in) s.i.

CORREDOYRA Y RUIZ DE BARO, Maria del Carmen (19th C) Spanish
£2540	$4953	(22-Oct-90 ANS.M91/R) Campesina (100x60cm-39x24in) s. (S.P 470000)

CORREGE (after) (?-1787) French
£12048	$19398	(25-Jun-91 APT.P49/R) Danane (54x65cm-21x26in) (F.FR 120000)

CORREGGIO (after) (16th C) Italian
£850	$1471	(20-May-91 SWS195/R) The Madonna adoring the Christ Child (78x61cm-31x24in)
£880	$1522	(20-May-91 SWS37/R) La Notte (48x36cm-19x14in) panel
£898	$1500	(23-Jan-91 D.NY19) Mystic marriage of Saint Catherine (28x23cm-11x9in)
£1300	$2119	(4-Jul-91 CSK72) Io embracing Jupiter (42x32cm-17x13in)
£2035	$3500	(15-May-91 D.NY39) Holy Night (99x74cm-39x29in) canvas on board

CORREGGIO (style) (16th C) Italian
£1400	$2660	(28-Feb-91 B19/R) Virgin and Child with St. Anne, St. John the Baptist, archangel Michael (35x26cm-14x10in) on copper

CORREGGIO, Antonio Allegri (style) (1494-1534) Italian
£996	$1713	(14-May-91 GF.L2270/R) Holy Family (97x77cm-38x30in) (S.FR 2500)
£1838	*$3603*	*(6-Nov-90 BA.S365/R) Jupiter and Io (15x21cm-6x8in) Indian ink wash htd white (S.KR 20000)*

CORREGGIO, Joseph (1870-?) German
£1712	$3065	(12-Mar-91 FN.S2322/R) Hubertus Hunt, group of hunters on horseback and dogs in landscape (41x57cm-16x22in) s.d.1923 (DM 5000)
£2800	$5516	(4-Oct-90 CSK25/R) A mallard, a partridge, finches, a lobster, corn, a pumpkin and grapeson a ledge (63x79cm-25x31in) s.
£2848	$5097	(11-Apr-91 D.V77/R) Still lifes of fruit with butterfly (19x21cm-7x8in) s.d.1863 pair (A.S 60000)
£4196	$8098	(12-Dec-90 SY.MU58/R) Still life of fruit (59x74cm-23x29in) s. (DM 12000)

CORREGGIO, Ludwig (1846-?) German
£769	$1485	(12-Dec-90 N.M464/R) Mountain lake landscape with couple in boat (24x30cm-9x12in) s.d.1885 panel (DM 2200)
£946	$1608	(28-May-91 KF.M147/R) Hilly landscape with castle and monastery (28x38cm-11x15in) s. s.verso canvas on board (DM 2800)
£1178	$2039	(6-May-91 ZEL.L1634/R) Mountain lake landscape near Mittenwald (19x25cm-7x10in) s.d.1882 panel (DM 3500)
£1573	$3052	(4-Dec-90 FN.S1789/R) Barmsee landscape near Mittenwald (19x25cm-7x10in) s.d.1882 panel (DM 4500)

CORRI, F J (19th C) Italian?
£320	*$573*	*(13-Mar-91 B23) An Italian lake with figures fishing from rowing boats (31x48cm-12x19in) s.d.1872 W/C*

CORRODI, Hermann David Salomon (1844-1905) Italian
£1250	$2350	(18-Sep-90 SWS629/R) Praying at the shrine (18x15cm-7x6in) s.i. panel
£1650	$2954	(14-Mar-91 B125/R) A coastal landscape (17x32cm-7x13in) s.i. board
£3846	$7423	(10-Dec-90 L.K403/R) Italian coastal landscape with fishermen (55x100cm-22x39in) s. (DM 11000)
£3882	$7336	(27-Sep-90 D.V167/R) Seascape with fishermen's chapel on rock (36x70cm-14x28in) s.i. (A.S 80000)
£4061	$8000	(15-Nov-90 D.NY16/R) Cattle watering by river (88x166cm-35x65in) s.i.
£4200	$7518	(12-Mar-91 PH62/R) Classical ruins at sunset with Rome beyond (128x75cm-50x30in) s.i.
£4737	$9000	(27-Feb-91 SY.NY345/R) Wishful thinking (71x43cm-28x17in) s.i.

CORRODI, Hermann David Salomon (1844-1905) Italian-cont.
£5888 $11305   (29-Nov-90 D.V60/R) Wine tasting outside monastery (36x59cm-14x23in)
       s.i. (A.S 120000)
£7568 $12335   (10-Jun-91 W.T1401/R) Girl on a floral balcony (99x62cm-39x24in) s.
       (C.D 14000)
£7796 $13956   (12-Mar-91 F.M21/R) Messa alla Pieve (101x67cm-40x26in) s.
       (I.L 17000000)
£9249 $16000   (23-May-91 CH.NY161/R) On the banks of the Nile (102x59cm-40x23in) s.
£13500 $22140   (19-Jun-91 S352/R) Buffalo by lake (87x165cm-34x65in) s.i.
£15262 $29609   (4-Dec-90 F.R156/R) La Madonna dei pescatori (125x63cm-49x25in) s.
       (I.L 33000000)
£34000 $55760   (21-Jun-91 C87/R) Neapolitan fisherfolk, Mergellina, Naples
       (86x165cm-34x65in) s.

CORRODI, Salomon (1810-1892) Swiss
£5001 $9801   (22-Nov-90 SY.MI22) Veduta della costa con rovine (50x71cm-20x28in)
       s.d.1853 gouache paper laid down on canvas (I.L 11000000)
£5910 $11583   (22-Nov-90 SY.MI23/R) Veduta della costa (50x71cm-20x28in) s.d.1853
       gouache paper laid down on canvas (I.L 13000000)
£7000 $13440   (27-Nov-90 PH266/R) Piazza San Marco and Doge's Palace, Venice
       (36x53cm-14x21in) s.d.1850 W/C over pencil

CORSI, Giacomo (?) Italian
£1359 $2365   (25-Mar-91 SY.F662) Marina al Tramonto (98x158cm-39x62in) s.d.86
       (I.L 3000000)

CORSI, Nicolas de (1882-1956) Italian
£997 $1685   (16-Apr-91 CH.R179) Porto di Napoli (13x19cm-5x7in) s. canvas on board
       (I.L 2200000)
£3210 $5746   (12-Mar-91 F.M72/R) Barche sulla laguna (50x55cm-20x22in) s.d.1926 board
       (I.L 7000000)

CORSIA, Gilbert (1915-) French
£585 $1140   (28-Oct-90 M.V163) Paysage cubiste (31x38cm-12x15in) s. mixed media
       (F.FR 5800)

CORSINI, Raffaele (19th C) Italian
£1500 $2925   (11-Oct-90 CG8/R) Brig 'Jessie Greig', Captain David Jarvis, leaving
       Smyrna Bay 1862 (46x69cm-18x27in) s.i. gouache
£1650 $3218   (15-Jan-91 SWS43/R) Ianthe, J Stapledon entering Smyrna Bay
       (45x66cm-18x26in) s.i.d.1864 gouache
£1800 $3114   (22-May-91 S12/R) Ianthe J. Stapleton entering Smyrna Bay
       (44x65cm-17x26in) s.i.d.1864 gouache

CORT, Hendrik Frans de (1742-1810) Dutch
£13000 $21970   (19-Apr-91 C67/R) A view in a Dutch town with a bakery and a tavern by a
       canal (49x65cm-19x26in) panel
£900 $1773   (13-Nov-90 C11/R) View in Whitehall, demolition of Richmond House and
       other buildings (20x33cm-8x13in) i. pencil wash

CORTAZZO, Oreste (1836-?) Italian
£1295 $2240   (24-May-91 FB.P174/R) Scene de magie (13x18cm-5x7in) s. panel
       (F.FR 13000)
£3000 $4920   (19-Jun-91 S365/R) Taking peek (46x37cm-18x15in) s.d.1871

CORTE, Gabriel de la (1648-1694) Spanish
£6294 $12147   (10-Dec-90 L.K21/R) Still life of flowers with roses, tulips and peonies
       (58x40cm-23x16in) i.d.1675 canvas laid down (DM 18000)

CORTE, Juan de la (1597-1660) Spanish
£17645 $33526   (28-Feb-91 EP.M8/R) Anibal contra Escipion (52x113cm-20x44in) s.d.1636
       (S.P 3200000)
£40223 $72000   (10-Apr-91 HF.NY18/R) Bullfight. Tournament of lances
       (103x139cm-41x55in) pair

CORTELEZZI, Pietro (1898-?) Italian
£5550 $10767   (5-Dec-90 F.M97/R) Il muratorino (119x79cm-47x31in) s. (I.L 12000000)

CORTES, Andre (19th C) Spanish
£514 $920   (12-Mar-91 FN.S2323) Cattle and horse grazing with boy watching
       (16x21cm-6x8in) s. panel (DM 1500)

CORTES, Antonio (19th C) Spanish
£1355 $2330   (14-May-91 GF.L2464/R) Shepherds with cattle, sheep and donkey
       (45x55cm-18x22in) s. (S.FR 3400)

CORTES, Antonio Cordero (1827-1908) Spanish
£1594 $3108   (24-Oct-90 GD.B245/R) Landscape with peasant woman, cattle and sheep by
       pond (40x65cm-16x26in) s. (S.FR 4000)

CORTES, Edouard (1882-1969) French
£956 $1567   (18-Jun-91 FN.S1798) Paris boulevard with figures, evening
       (27x40cm-11x16in) s. panel (DM 2800)
£1687 $2901   (19-May-91 ZZ.F18/R) Place de la Madeleine animee a la tombee du jour
       (66x93cm-26x37in) s. (F.FR 17000)
£1777 $3500   (16-Nov-90 S.BM122/R) Notre Dame (15x23cm-6x9in) s. panel

414

CORTES, Edouard (1882-1969) French-cont.

£2900	$4727	(3-Jul-91 LGB.P91/R) Une place animee a Paris (38x46cm-15x18in) s. (F.FR 29000)
£3333	$6500	(21-Oct-90 HG.C56 a) Paris street scene (30x36cm-12x14in) s.
£3800	$7372	(5-Dec-90 AB.S7053/R) Paris view with Champs Elysees and the Triumphal Arch, rainy day (33x46cm-13x18in) s. (S.KR 41000)
£4103	$8000	(10-Oct-90 SY.NY84/R) Quai de la Seine (33x46cm-13x18in) s.
£4200	$8064	(28-Nov-90 S300/R) On the Place de la Concorde, Paris (23x32cm-9x13in) s.
£4464	$7500	(28-Apr-91 HG.C81) Parisian street scene (46x53cm-18x21in) s.
£5000	$9800	(15-Feb-91 C2/R) La Madeleine, Paris, in winter (24x33cm-9x13in) s. panel
£5030	$8500	(20-Apr-91 WOL.C199 a/R) Parisian street scene (48x56cm-19x22in) s.
£5500	$9845	(12-Mar-91 PH90/R) Avenue de la Madeleine, early evening (33x46cm-13x18in) s.
£5612	$11000	(12-Feb-91 SY.NY113/R) Place de la Republique (33x46cm-13x18in) s.
£5653	$10966	(8-Dec-90 SY.MO386/R) L'Arc de Triomphe, le soir (27x35cm-11x14in) s. (F.FR 55000)
£5780	$10000	(21-May-91 CE.NY352/R) Champs Elysees with view of Arc de Triomphe (33x46cm-13x18in) s.
£5780	$10000	(21-May-91 CE.NY355/R) View of Madeleine (33x46cm-13x18in) s.
£5800	$9512	(19-Jun-91 S212/R) View of opera, Paris (16x22cm-6x9in) s. panel
£5800	$9512	(19-Jun-91 S213/R) View of Place Vendome, Paris (16x22cm-6x9in) s. panel
£5800	$9976	(17-May-91 C1/R) Gare de l'Est, Paris (24x33cm-9x13in) s.
£5835	$11495	(14-Nov-90 RAS.K51/R) Arch de Triumphe, Paris (33x46cm-13x18in) s. (D.KR 65000)
£6345	$12500	(7-Oct-90 DU.E250/R) Paris street after the rain (51x61cm-20x24in) s.
£6500	$10660	(19-Jun-91 S220/R) Quai St. Michel, Paris (37x55cm-15x22in) s. panel
£6579	$12895	(19-Nov-90 ARC.P48) Le Boulevard Bonne Nouvelle (24x33cm-9x13in) s. (F.FR 65000)
£6883	$13490	(19-Nov-90 ARC.P47) Place de la Madeleine (24x33cm-9x13in) s. (F.FR 68000)
£6883	$13490	(19-Nov-90 ARC.P45/R) L'Arc de Triomphe (24x33cm-9x13in) s. (F.FR 68000)
£6936	$12000	(21-May-91 CE.NY362/R) Paris street scene with view of Notre Dame (33x46cm-13x18in) s.
£7000	$13790	(1-Nov-90 B34/R) View of La Madeleine in Paris after rain (46x56cm-18x22in) s.
£7181	$14147	(14-Nov-90 RAS.K52/R) Prospect views of Paris, Vendome Place and The Opera (16x22cm-6x9in) s. panel pair (D.KR 80000)
£7200	$11808	(21-Jun-91 C41/R) L'Opera, Paris (33x46cm-13x18in) s.
£7225	$12500	(22-May-91 D.NY80/R) La Place de la Bastille (33x46cm-13x18in) s.
£7538	$14472	(24-Feb-91 P.V14/R) La porte Saint Denis sous la neige (27x46cm-11x18in) s. (F.FR 75000)
£7692	$15077	(19-Nov-90 ARC.P44/R) L'avenue de l'opera (65x91cm-26x36in) s. (F.FR 76000)
£7895	$15474	(19-Nov-90 ARC.P46/R) La Place de la Republique sous la neige (24x33cm-9x13in) s. (F.FR 78000)
£7927	$13000	(19-Jun-91 B.SF1747/R) Notre Dame, Vue de la Rive Gauche (38x55cm-15x22in) s.
£7949	$15500	(10-Oct-90 SY.NY82/R) Parisian street (33x46cm-13x18in) s.
£7975	$13000	(12-Jun-91 SY.NY51/R) Cafe de la Paix (33x46cm-13x18in) s.
£8000	$15360	(28-Nov-90 S299/R) Figures on Avenue de l'Opera, Paris (32x45cm-13x18in) s.
£8092	$14000	(21-May-91 CE.NY351/R) Winter evening in Paris (25x34cm-10x13in) s.
£8163	$16000	(12-Feb-91 SY.NY111/R) L'Opera (33x46cm-13x18in) s.
£8200	$13448	(21-Jun-91 C40/R) La Place de la Republique, Paris (25x35cm-10x14in) s.
£8205	$16000	(10-Oct-90 SY.NY85/R) L'Arc de Triomphe (33x46cm-13x18in) s.
£8205	$16000	(10-Oct-90 SY.NY264/R) Winter evening stroll through the boulevards (33x46cm-13x18in) s.
£8222	$15951	(8-Dec-90 SY.MO387/R) Marche aux fleurs a La Madeleine (27x35cm-11x14in) s. (F.FR 80000)
£8380	$15000	(16-Mar-91 W.W114/R) View of the Arc de Triomphe at dusk (33x46cm-13x18in) s.
£8500	$16320	(28-Nov-90 S302/R) The Boulevard Madeleine in winter, Paris (33x46cm-13x18in) s.
£8500	$16745	(1-Nov-90 B49/R) View of La Madeleine on snowy afternoon (33x46cm-13x18in) s.
£8671	$15000	(12-May-91 H.C56/R) Paris street scene with the Porte St Denis (33x46cm-13x18in) s.
£8673	$17000	(7-Nov-90 B.SF1068/R) Pantheon (33x46cm-13x18in) s.
£8878	$17489	(14-Nov-90 FB.P300/R) La place de la Bastille en hiver (46x33cm-18x13in) s. (F.FR 87000)
£9000	$17730	(5-Oct-90 C69/R) Les Champs Elysees, Paris (26x35cm-10x14in) s.
£9146	$15000	(19-Jun-91 B.SF1746/R) Quai de la messagerie (38x55cm-15x22in) s. i.verso
£9202	$15000	(12-Jun-91 SY.NY50/R) View of Sacre Coeur (33x46cm-13x18in) s.
£9500	$16815	(22-Mar-91 BG.P87/R) Le theatre du Gymnase (50x65cm-20x26in) s. (F.FR 95000)
£9744	$19000	(10-Oct-90 SY.NY100/R) Place Vendome (33x46cm-13x18in) s.
£9800	$16072	(21-Jun-91 C39/R) La Place de la Republique, Paris (33x46cm-13x18in) s.
£9827	$17000	(12-May-91 H.C55/R) Les Invalides, Paris (61x51cm-24x20in) s.
£10204	$20000	(12-Feb-91 SY.NY114/R) Place Vendome (33x46cm-13x18in) s.
£10345	$18000	(27-Mar-91 B.SF4110/R) Horse carriage and flowercart near La Madeleine (34x46cm-13x18in) s.
£10429	$17000	(12-Jun-91 SY.NY53/R) Paris in snow (66x53cm-26x21in) s.
£11043	$18000	(12-Jun-91 SY.NY52/R) Place de La Bastille, Paris (33x46cm-13x18in) s.

CORTES, Edouard (1882-1969) French-cont.
£11224 $22000 (12-Feb-91 SY.NY112/R) Marche au fleurs, Eglise de la Madeleine (33x46cm-13x18in) s.
£11656 $19000 (12-Jun-91 SY.NY54/R) Rue Royale (46x56cm-18x22in) s.
£11836 $23079 (9-Oct-90 CSC.P31/R) Quais a Paris (33x45cm-13x18in) s. (F.FR 118000)
£12200 $19886 (5-Jul-91 APT.P108/R) Paris, les grands boulevards sous la neige (33x46cm-13x18in) s. (F.FR 122000)
£13000 $25480 (15-Feb-91 C1/R) L'Arc de Triomphe, Paris (33x46cm-13x18in) s.
£13500 $26595 (1-Nov-90 B33/R) La Poste St Denis (46x56cm-18x22in) s.
£15135 $28000 (10-Mar-91 H.C58/R) Vendome Column (46x53cm-18x21in) s.
£3635 $6289 (26-May-91 ZZ.F49/R) Les Halles de Paris et Saint-Eustache (19x28cm-7x11in) s. gouache (F.FR 36500)
£6000 $11520 (28-Nov-90 S301/R) Notre Dame from the Quai St.Michel, Paris (37x54cm-15x21in) s. gouache

CORTES, Edouard (attrib) (1882-1969) French
£6599 $13000 (12-Nov-90 SG.M537) Street scene in Paris (30x43cm-12x17in) s.
£6853 $13500 (12-Nov-90 SG.M538) Street scene in Paris (30x43cm-12x17in) s.

CORTESE, F (?) Italian
£2493 $4213 (16-Apr-91 CH.R111) Lavandaie sugli scogli (27x55cm-11x22in) s. (I.L 5500000)

CORTESE, Federico (1829-1913) Italian
£1202 $2333 (4-Dec-90 F.R78) Le paludi pontine (27x55cm-11x22in) s. (I.L 2600000)
£2200 $3608 (18-Jun-91 PH177) Figures on mountain road, Bay of Naples (31x51cm-12x20in) s.

CORTESE, Guglielmo (1628-1679) Italian
£789 $1500 (8-Jan-91 SY.NY41/R) A crowd gathering around a standing figure (19x26cm-7x10in) red chk.
£30000 $48900 (2-Jul-91 C112/R) Sacrifice of Aaron (36x27cm-14x11in) with i. black chk pen wash htd white squared

CORTI, Jean (1907-1946) Swiss
£1388 $2692 (8-Dec-90 GAB.G2483/R) Sur le chemin de la messe (21x28cm-8x11in) s.d.1945 W/C gouache (S.FR 3400)

CORTIJO, Manuel (20th C) Spanish
£1898 $3700 (17-Oct-90 FER.M233/R) Dos mujeres (100x78cm-39x31in) s.d.1962-63 tablex (S.P 350000)

CORTONA, Pietro da (1596-1669) Italian
£2054 $3943 (27-Nov-90 W.T1339/R) Man in cape kneeling (31x20cm-12x8in) sanguine (C.D 4600)
£6500 $12545 (11-Dec-90 C4/R) Abraham and Hagar (11x14cm-4x6in) i. ink
£18000 $29340 (2-Jul-91 C32/R) Studies of four men in togas and angel. Expulsion from Paradise and angel (18x27cm-7x11in) chk pen ink wash
£29474 $56000 (8-Jan-91 SY.NY146/R) The adoration of the shepherds (24x20cm-9x8in) ink wash htd.white blk.chk.
£55000 $89650 (2-Jul-91 C29/R) Assembly of the Gods, design for ceiling decoration (24x60cm-9x24in) i.chk pen ink wash htd.white octagonal
£65000 $105950 (2-Jul-91 C28/R) Wooded river landscape with fishermen drawing net and washerwomen (28x43cm-11x17in) chk brush ink
£65000 $105950 (2-Jul-91 C31/R) St Ivo intervening on behalf of the poor, Christ with saints above (43x31cm-17x12in) chk wash htd.white squared
£175000 $285250 (2-Jul-91 C30/R) Christ on the Cross with Virgin Mary, St John and the Magdalen (40x26cm-16x10in) i. chk pen ink wash htd.white squared oval
£240000 $391200 (2-Jul-91 C27/R) Wooded river landscape with cascades and men dragging net (28x42cm-11x17in) chk brush ink wash

CORTONA, Pietro da (circle) (1596-1669) Italian
£3000 $5910 (30-Oct-90 PH24/R) The Marriage of Isaac and Rebecca (65x56cm-26x22in) arched top

CORTONA, Pietro da (school) (1596-1669) Italian
£2243 $4328 (14-Dec-90 LEB.P97) Les quatres Saisons (20x17cm-8x7in) i. pen wash pierre noire (F.FR 22000)

CORTONA, Pietro da (style) (1596-1669) Italian
£1100 $1793 (4-Jul-91 B143) The Madonna and Child with a supplicant female Saint bearing flowers (131x90cm-52x35in)
£3289 $6380 (7-Dec-90 SY.MO119/R) Renaud et Armide (71x87cm-28x34in) (F.FR 32000)
£7800 $13182 (19-Apr-91 C3/R) The Madonna and Child (122x86cm-48x34in)

CORVI, Domenico (1721-1803) Italian
£1316 $2500 (8-Jan-91 SY.NY191/R) Standing male nude seen from behind, holding a stick (55x39cm-22x15in) i. chk.

CORVI, Domenico (attrib) (1721-1803) Italian
£950 $1824 (18-Feb-91 S204/R) Male nude seen from behind holding arms outstretched (56x40cm-22x16in) chk htd.white

CORWIN, Charles Abel (1857-1938) American
£1183 $2000 (1-May-91 B.SF5061/R) Milking time, Beekmantown, N.Y (46x66cm-18x26in) s.

CORZAS, Francisco (1936-1983) Mexican
£9302 $16000   (15-May-91 CH.NY176/R) Rittratto di Testaccio Petto il Morante
                                 (90x75cm-35x30in) s.d.72 i. verso linen
£15116 $26000   (15-May-91 CH.NY177/R) Retrato de Pablo (100x80cm-39x31in) s.
                                 i.d.ottobre 1971 verso linen
£18605 $32000   (15-May-91 CH.NY108/R) Los Mendigos (124x150cm-49x59in) s.d.1963
£48469 $95000   (20-Nov-90 CH.NY42/R) Cavallerizzi fiorentini (194x250cm-76x98in) s.d.72

COSENZA, Giuseppe (1847-?) Italian
£2312 $4000   (21-May-91 CE.NY282/R) Fishing off coast (16x28cm-6x11in) s.i. panel
£4335 $7500   (21-May-91 CE.NY99/R) Fishing boats in Bay of Naples (24x19cm-9x7in)
                              s.i.d.83 panel

COSGROVE, Stanley Morel (1911-) Canadian
£1228 $2407   (20-Nov-90 JOY.T271) Winter landscape (25x30cm-10x12in) s. (C.D 2800)
£1404 $2751   (20-Nov-90 JOY.T377) Still life (40x50cm-16x20in) s. canvasboard
                              (C.D 3200)
£1485 $2910   (5-Nov-90 FB.M218) Landscape (31x41cm-12x16in) s. (C.D 3400)
£1577 $3027   (20-Feb-91 EA.M500 a) Forest interior (20x23cm-8x9in) s. masonite
                              (C.D 3500)
£1747 $3424   (5-Nov-90 FB.M189) Landscape with trees (41x51cm-16x20in) s. (C.D 4000)
£2183 $4279   (5-Nov-90 FB.M179) Sous-bois (51x41cm-20x16in) s. (C.D 5000)
£2261 $3912   (22-May-91 EA.M402 a) Le ciel jaune, Hudson Quebec (41x51cm-16x20in)
                              s.d.82 board (C.D 4500)
£2486 $4053   (10-Jun-91 W.T1047/R) Still life on brown table (20x25cm-8x10in) s.
                              board (C.D 4600)
£2486 $4053   (10-Jun-91 W.T1046/R) Still life with lemon and red jug (24x22cm-9x9in)
                              s.d.'52 board (C.D 4600)
£4167 $8208   (30-Oct-90 SY.T114/R) Trees by lake (80x70cm-31x28in) s.d.71 (C.D 9500)
£4386 $8596   (20-Nov-90 JOY.T1/R) Still life with yellow vase (60x80cm-24x31in)
                              s.d.52 board (C.D 10000)
£5240 $10271   (5-Nov-90 FB.M162) On the way to La Tuque (71x91cm-28x36in) s.
                              (C.D 12000)
£5263 $10316   (20-Nov-90 JOY.T147/R) Forest clearing (62x80cm-24x31in) s. (C.D 12000)
£463 $902   (24-Oct-90 EA.M418/R) Nude (43x33cm-17x13in) s. chl (C.D 1050)
£482   *$946*   *(23-Jan-91 EA.M531 a) Reclining nude (31x41cm-12x16in) s.d.'81 pastels*
                              (C.D 1100)
£969   *$1890*   *(24-Oct-90 EA.M413/R) Woman (29x45cm-11x18in) s.d.67 sanguine*
                              (C.D 2200)
£1140   *$2235*   *(23-Jan-91 EA.M411) Views of a forest (36x46cm-14x18in) s. pastel*
                              (C.D 2600)

COSMADOPOULOS, Georges (1899-?) Greek
£1800 $3474   (12-Dec-90 SWS2173/R) Landscape (45x54cm-18x21in) s. board

COSSAAR, Jan (1874-1966) Dutch
£947 $1600   (20-Apr-91 WOL.C208/R) Mont Val by Paris (46x61cm-18x24in) s.
£1124 $1900   (20-Apr-91 WOL.C207/R) French street scene (61x46cm-24x18in) s. canvas
                              on panel

COSSIAU, Jan Joost von (1660-1732) Dutch
£10024 $17041   (30-May-91 F.M90/R) Paesaggio con pastori e armenti (70x84cm-28x33in)
                              (I.L 22000000)

COSSIAU, Jan Joost von (circle) (1660-1732) Dutch
£3077 $6000   (10-Oct-90 CH.NY17/R) Mountainous river landscape with shepherds and
                              city on hill beyond (69x84cm-27x33in)
£4790 $8096   (2-May-91 CH.AM106/R) An Italianate landscape with peasant women on a
                              path, village beyond (67x77cm-26x30in) (D.FL 16000)

COSSIERS, Jan (1600-1671) Flemish
£40000   *$65200*   *(2-Jul-91 C65/R) Head of young boy looking up (20x15cm-8x6in) i. chk*

COSSINGTON-SMITH, Grace (20th C) Australian
£2667 $5013   (17-Sep-90 MGS.S248 a) Downs in haze (36x48cm-14x19in) s.d.1950 board
                              (A.D 6000)

COSSIO (20th C) ?
£981 $1609   (17-Jun-91 DUR.M1444) Marina (55x70cm-22x28in) s. (S.P 180000)

COSSIO, Pancho (1898-1970) Spanish
£655   *$1133*   *(8-May-91 FER.M106/R) Toro (32x25cm-13x10in) s.i.d.1977 gouache*
                              (S.P 120000)

COSSON, Marcel (1878-1956) French
£989 $1771   (12-Apr-91 JM.P41/R) Ballerines a la loge (27x19cm-11x7in) s. hardboard
                              (F.FR 10000)
£1004 $1616   (28-Jun-91 ARC.P72) Au foyer de l'Opera (27x16cm-11x6in) s.i.d.45 panel
                              (F.FR 10000)
£1521 $3012   (3-Feb-91 I.N54/R) La loge des ballerines (13x18cm-5x7in) s. panel
                              (F.FR 15000)
£1835 $3541   (14-Dec-90 ARC.P29) Ballerines en bas de l'escalier (27x35cm-11x14in) s.
                              panel (F.FR 18000)
£1974 $3868   (25-Nov-90 ZZ.F226) Scene de bar (11x19cm-4x7in) s. board (F.FR 19500)
£1984 $3749   (30-Sep-90 E.LA101/R) Ballerines a la barre (73x60cm-29x24in) s.
                              (F.FR 19500)

COSSON, Marcel (1878-1956) French-cont.

£2022	$3943	(17-Oct-90 ARC.P65/R) Scene de ballet (26x34cm-10x13in) s. panel (F.FR 20000)
£2024	$3968	(20-Nov-90 BG.P25/R) La fosse d'orchestre (27x22cm-11x9in) s. panel (F.FR 20000)
£2294	$4427	(12-Dec-90 D.P158/R) Danseuses et abonnes (33x41cm-13x16in) s. board (F.FR 22500)
£2601	$4500	(22-May-91 D.NY85/R) Ballerines au foyer (33x40cm-13x16in) s. l.stretcher
£2650	$5115	(14-Dec-90 ARC.P28/R) Femmes au cafe (35x27cm-14x11in) s. panel (F.FR 26000)
£2814	$4615	(18-Jun-91 APT.P181/R) Le foyer de l'Opera (33x41cm-13x16in) s. board (F.FR 28000)
£2821	$5500	(10-Oct-90 SY.NY332 a/R) Standing dancers (53x46cm-21x18in) s. board
£2860	$5634	(6-Oct-90 GL.P118) Bouquet de fleurs (61x50cm-24x20in) (F.FR 29000)
£2868	$5135	(12-Apr-91 JM.P40/R) Ballerines au foyer (54x65cm-21x26in) s. (F.FR 29000)
£2915	$4780	(18-Jun-91 APT.P182) L'escalier de l'Opera (22x33cm-9x13in) s. (F.FR 29000)
£2920	$4760	(11-Jun-91 I.N178/R) Le cabaret (45x55cm-18x22in) s. panel (F.FR 29000)
£3036	$5951	(20-Nov-90 BG.P27/R) Les elegants (33x46cm-13x18in) s. (F.FR 30000)
£3062	$4930	(24-Jun-91 PR.P105 a) Danseuses au foyer (19x27cm-7x11in) s. panel (F.FR 30500)
£3239	$6348	(25-Nov-90 ZZ.F38/R) Le foyer de l'Opera (22x27cm-9x11in) s. panel (F.FR 32000)
£3518	$5769	(18-Jun-91 APT.P180/R) Avant le spectacle (36x45cm-14x18in) s. (F.FR 35000)
£3571	$7000	(12-Feb-91 SY.NY148) Jumping the hedge (38x46cm-15x18in) s. s.verso board
£3597	$6978	(5-Dec-90 ZZ.F16/R) Ballerines et admirateurs a l'Opera (41x33cm-16x13in) s. (F.FR 35000)
£3618	$6476	(13-Mar-91 ARC.P36) Lecon de danse (38x46cm-15x18in) s. canvas laid down on board (F.FR 36000)
£3629	$7077	(26-Oct-90 APT.P89/R) Danseuses et abonnes (33x46cm-13x18in) s. (F.FR 36000)
£3803	$7377	(9-Dec-90 E.LA74) Femmes dans un interieur (50x65cm-20x26in) s. board (F.FR 37000)
£4315	$8500	(13-Nov-90 CE.NY101/R) Aux courses (38x46cm-15x18in) s. canvasboard
£4464	$7679	(19-May-91 ZZ.F126/R) Le restaurant (38x61cm-15x24in) s. panel (F.FR 45000)
£5123	$10041	(11-Nov-90 ZZ.F121/R) Le foyer de l'Opera (38x46cm-15x18in) s. (F.FR 50000)
£5865	$11436	(17-Oct-90 LT.P155/R) Le foyer de l'opera (46x55cm-18x22in) s. (F.FR 58000)
£6131	$10974	(17-Mar-91 L.C12/R) Le foyer des danseuses (48x52cm-19x20in) s. panel (F.FR 61000)
£6572	$12816	(17-Oct-90 LT.P16/R) Dejeuner en plein air (54x65cm-21x26in) s. (F.FR 65000)
£6876	$13407	(17-Oct-90 LT.P52/R) Le the sous les ombrages (46x55cm-18x22in) s. panel (F.FR 68000)
£6944	$11944	(19-May-91 ZZ.F111/R) Les coulisses du cirque Medrano (60x73cm-24x29in) s. (F.FR 70000)
£7085	$13887	(25-Nov-90 ZZ.F37/R) L'escalier de l'Opera (41x33cm-16x13in) s. panel (F.FR 70000)
£7099	$14057	(3-Feb-91 I.N53/R) Le foyer de l'opera (27x35cm-11x14in) s. board (F.FR 70000)
£8133	$15045	(6-Mar-91 APT.P90/R) Le foyer de l'Opera (56x46cm-22x18in) s. board (F.FR 81000)
£8726	$17016	(9-Oct-90 CSC.P30/R) Scene de cabaret (45x61cm-18x24in) s. (F.FR 87000)
£10194	$19572	(27-Nov-90 APT.P83/R) La loge (92x65cm-36x26in) s. (F.FR 100000)
£10194	$19572	(27-Nov-90 APT.P82/R) Au pesage (60x73cm-24x29in) s. (F.FR 100000)

COSTA, Angelo Maria (18th C) Italian

£45000	$77850	(24-May-91 C86/R) A panoramic view of Naples with Posillipo and the Castel dell'Ovo, shipping in the foreground (63x147cm-25x58in) s.i.d.1721

COSTA, Antonio (1847-1915) Italian

£1915	*$3390*	*(19-Mar-91 F.M122/R) Angelo che suona la lira (36x27cm-14x11in) s. ink W/C over pencil (I.L 4200000)*

COSTA, Catharina da (fl.1712-1730) British

£1407	*$2308*	*(21-Jun-91 D.P43/R) Le ramassage des legumes, pres d'un puits (32x24cm-13x9in) s.d.1718 gouache (F.FR 14000)*

COSTA, Claudio (1942-) Italian

£413	*$677*	*(20-Jun-91 F.M357/R) Dalla serie Il Tempo Rotolando (24x18cm-9x7in) s.i.d.c.1980verso collage canvas (I.L 900000)*
£688	*$1128*	*(20-Jun-91 F.M400/R) Magus (72x50cm-28x20in) s.i.d.1981verso polimaterico collage board (I.L 1500000)*
£1261	*$2458*	*(23-Oct-90 F.M9/R) Composizione con utensile (60x80cm-24x31in) s.d.1975verso mixed media collage canvas (I.L 2800000)*

COSTA, E (?) Italian

£1017	*$1962*	*(11-Dec-90 CH.R141) Paesaggio lacustre (29x43cm-11x17in) s.d.74 W/C (I.L 2200000)*

COSTA, G (1833-1903) Italian
£2000 *$3280* *(19-Jun-91 S345/R) Views of Naples (32x51cm-13x20in) s. W/C over pencil htd gouache four*

COSTA, Giovanni (1833-1903) Italian
£3252 $6276 (14-Dec-90 ZOF.Z934./R) Flower girl (74x58cm-29x23in) s. (S.FR 8000)
£5000 $8600 (17-May-91 C240/R) La bella in Maschera (63x50cm-25x20in) s.
£6000 $11520 (27-Nov-90 PH172/R) The orange seller (74x58cm-29x23in) s.
£7500 $12300 (19-Jun-91 S346/R) Young violinist (121x73cm-48x29in) s.
£72000 $141000 (18-Oct-90 F.M55/R) Una sera alle Cascine, Firenze (38x68cm-15x27in) s. panel (I.L 160000000)
£1020 *$2010* *(14-Nov-90 FB.P250/R) Rocher pres du bord de mer (52x35cm-20x14in) s. W/C (F.FR 10000)*

COSTA, Giovanni Battista (1818-?) Italian
£5325 *$9000* *(19-Apr-91 DM.D1039/R) 19th century sailing ship and steam ship flying American and British flags (81x46cm-32x18in) s. W/C gouache*

COSTA, Lorenzo (circle) (1460-1535) Italian
£7500 $12675 (18-Apr-91 C59/R) The circumcision (67x54cm-26x21in) panel

COSTA, Luigi da (19th C) Italian
£1974 $3750 (27-Feb-91 SY.NY342/R) La corte di contrabbando (41x63cm-16x25in) s.

COSTA, Olga (1913-) German
£1734 $3000 (10-May-91 S.BM150/R) Portrait of Marta Adams (61x51cm-24x20in) s.i.
£6633 $13000 (20-Nov-90 CH.NY110/R) Celosfas (65x85cm-26x33in) s.d.82 i.verso s.d.82 stretcher
£8140 $14000 (15-May-91 CH.NY178/R) Paisaje de Guanajuato (40x70cm-16x28in) s.d.77

COSTA, Oreste (1851-?) Italian
£1316 $2500 (27-Feb-91 SY.NY381/R) Still life with fruit on table (56x43cm-22x17in) s.d.1872
£1850 $3200 (21-May-91 CE.NY278/R) Cupid (80x63cm-31x25in) s.i.
£2200 $4290 (17-Oct-90 PHG78) Still life of fruit and dead game (75x63cm-30x25in) s.d.1870 oval

COSTANTINI, G (19/20th C) Italian
£872 $1404 (27-Jun-91 D.V46) The shoemaker (23x14cm-9x6in) s.d.1874 panel (A.S 18000)

COSTANTINI, Virgile (1882-) Italian
£7000 $11480 (19-Jun-91 S428/R) La bauja (120x99cm-47x39in) s.d.1928 s.stretcher

COSTANZI, Placido (1690-1759) Italian
£22000 $35860 (5-Jul-91 C98/R) Saint Catherine of Genoa in hospital of Genoa (257x199cm-101x78in) s.i.d.1738
£650 *$1099* *(16-Apr-91 C179/R) Roman charity (28x21cm-11x8in) i. blk.white chk.*

COSTANZI, Placido (circle) (1690-1759) Italian
£1100 $1793 (2-Jul-91 PH252/R) The apotheosis of heroine, bozetto for ceiling decoration (97x48cm-38x19in)

COSTE CRASNIER, Gin (1928-) French
£500 $815 (1-Jul-91 ZZ.F70) Un soir, une plante seductrice (55x46cm-22x18in) s. (F.FR 5000)
£500 $815 (1-Jul-91 ZZ.F59) L'heure (73x50cm-29x20in) s. (F.FR 5000)
£500 $815 (1-Jul-91 ZZ.F47) Les cariatides (65x54cm-26x21in) s. (F.FR 5000)
£600 $978 (1-Jul-91 ZZ.F71/R) Materialisme et spiritualisme (65x54cm-26x21in) s. (F.FR 6000)
£600 $978 (1-Jul-91 ZZ.F46/R) Fleurs aux rubis (55x46cm-22x18in) s. (F.FR 6000)
£650 $1060 (1-Jul-91 ZZ.F64/R) La nymphe tatouee (130x97cm-51x38in) s. (F.FR 6500)
£650 $1060 (1-Jul-91 ZZ.F79) L'arbre chatelain (92x73cm-36x29in) s. (F.FR 6500)
£710 $1157 (1-Jul-91 ZZ.F57/R) Arbre vivant - La libellule (50x70cm-20x28in) s. (F.FR 7100)
£750 $1223 (1-Jul-91 ZZ.F76/R) Le bois aux hamadryades (50x70cm-20x28in) s. (F.FR 7500)
£760 $1239 (1-Jul-91 ZZ.F74/R) Hamadryade - L'attente (65x54cm-26x21in) s. (F.FR 7600)
£800 $1304 (1-Jul-91 ZZ.F62/R) La nymphe et l'hamadryade (73x60cm-29x24in) s. (F.FR 8000)
£800 $1304 (1-Jul-91 ZZ.F72/R) Les hamadryades (65x54cm-26x21in) s. (F.FR 8000)
£850 $1386 (1-Jul-91 ZZ.F65/R) L'arbre du temps (130x97cm-51x38in) s. (F.FR 8500)
£950 $1549 (1-Jul-91 ZZ.F78/R) La naiade au crapaud d'or (73x60cm-29x24in) s. (F.FR 9500)
£1000 $1630 (1-Jul-91 ZZ.F51/R) La captive (55x46cm-22x18in) s. (F.FR 10000)
£1000 $1630 (1-Jul-91 ZZ.F61/R) L'arbre sorcier (73x60cm-29x24in) s. (F.FR 10000)
£1750 $2853 (1-Jul-91 ZZ.F59/R) La roche femme (92x73cm-36x29in) s. (F.FR 17500)
£2100 $3423 (1-Jul-91 ZZ.F77/R) La nymphe du lac (73x60cm-29x24in) s. (F.FR 21000)

COSTE, Albert (1895-1985) French
£806 $1573 (27-Oct-90 LT.P67/R) Le chant d'automne (146x89cm-57x35in) s.d.1962 (F.FR 8000)

COSTE, L (18th C) French
£12563 $22487   (17-Mar-91 M.V140/R) Vase de fleurs sur un entablement de marbre
                                  (42x32cm-17x13in) s.i. (F.FR 125000)

COSTE, Victor (1844-?) French
£1365 $2676   (24-Nov-90 SA.A627./R) Coastal harbour scene, calm day (23x33cm-9x13in)
                                  s. panel (DM 4000)

COSTER, Adam de (1586-1643) Flemish
£1327 $2613   (12-Nov-90 CSC.P5) L'enfant a la bougie (51x38cm-20x15in) (F.FR 13000)
£2982 $5040   (18-Apr-91 APT.P51/R) Chanteur a la chandelle (68x54cm-27x21in)
                                  (F.FR 30000)

COSTER, Anne Vallayer see VALLAYER-COSTER, Anne

COSTER, Jan (17th C) Dutch
£2695 $4554   (2-May-91 CH.AM75/R) A dog watching dead game on a rock in a landscape
                                  (81x116cm-32x46in) s.d.1664 (D.FL 9000)

COSTIGAN, John E (1888-1972) American
£833 $1600   (17-Dec-90 SY.NY363/R) Sun bathers (30x36cm-12x14in) s. board
£872 $1500   (15-May-91 SY.NY259/R) Still life with hydrangeas and zinnias
                                  (76x61cm-30x24in) s.
£885 $1700   (17-Dec-90 SY.NY362/R) Group of figures (30x38cm-12x15in) s. s.d.1965
                                  verso board
£957 $1800   (22-Sep-90 WOL.C351/R) By river (20x28cm-8x11in) s. panel
£2035 $3500   (15-May-91 SY.NY180/R) Bathers (41x51cm-16x20in) s. s.i.verso
                                  canvasboard
£5026 $9500   (27-Sep-90 CH.NY281/R) Mother and children (109x127cm-43x50in) s.
£872   *$1500*   *(15-May-91 SY.NY182 a/R) Mother and child with lamb (56x69cm-22x27in) s.*
                                  W/C oil

COSWAY, Richard (1742-1821) British
£2200 $3630   (12-Jul-91 C160/R) Portrait of Elizabeth, Dowager Countess of Erroll,
                                  leaning on right hand (76x65cm-30x26in) i.verso
£800   *$1416*   *(20-Mar-91 C131/R) Portrait of Col.William Wasey of the Lifeguards*
                                  (3x?cm-1x?in) min. gold frame oval
£950   *$1568*   *(9-Jul-91 C54) Portrait of Princess Michael Cleophus Oginska standing on*
                                  terrace (19x12cm-7x5in) s.d.1793 pencil W/C
£1200   *$2124*   *(20-Mar-91 C130/R) Portrait of gentleman in plum-coloured coat with*
                                  pearl buttons (5x?cm-2x?in) min. gilt metal frame blue enamel rim oval
£1800   *$2970*   *(10-Jul-91 C145/R) A gentleman in blue coat with large brown buttons*
                                  (7x?cm-3x?in) min.s.d.1793 verso silvered frame oval
£1800   *$2970*   *(10-Jul-91 C144/R) A gentleman in blue coat and gold buttons*
                                  (5x?cm-2x?in) min. gold frame plait of hair verso oval
£2500   *$4125*   *(11-Jul-91 S279/R) Portrait of two ladies with linked arms (9x?cm-4x?in)*
                                  min.s.d.1792 gold frame oval
£2568   *$4187*   *(12-Jun-91 N.M393/R) Portrait of Andrew Stuart of Craigthorn*
                                  (7x6cm-3x2in) min.i.d.1790 W/C gouache oval (DM 7500)
£3200   *$6144*   *(18-Dec-90 C127/R) Portrait of Major General Stuart (5x?cm-2x?in)*
                                  min.gold bracelet clasp frame oval
£3400   *$5610*   *(11-Jul-91 S57/R) Heavenly orchestra (11x22cm-4x9in) pencil*
£3500   *$5775*   *(9-Jul-91 C84/R) Portrait of Lady Heathcote standing by urn in garden*
                                  (28x22cm-11x9in) s. pencil W/C
£4200   *$6930*   *(11-Jul-91 S272/R) Portrait of lady wearing gown with fur wrap*
                                  (7x?cm-3x?in) min. gold frame plaited hair oval
£9500   *$18715*   *(1-Nov-90 S24/R) Portrait of Isabella Anne, Marchionness of Hertford*
                                  (7x?cm-3x?in) min.s.d.1802verso gold/pearl frame oval

COSWAY, Richard (after) (1742-1821) British
£420   *$743*   *(19-Mar-91 CSK54) Portrait of lady wearing white dress with sash*
                                  (6x?cm-2x?in) min. gold frame enamel border oval
£1000   *$1650*   *(11-Jul-91 S291/R) Misses Aston and Hedges as Ceres and Flora bearing*
                                  laden basket (?x8cm-?x3in) min. gilt metal frame oval

COSWAY, Richard (attrib) (1742-1821) British
£1350 $2498   (6-Mar-91 SC4246/R) Portrait of lady seated holding sketch pad and
                                  pencil (71x58cm-28x23in)

COSWAY, Richard (circle) (1742-1821) British
£550   *$974*   *(19-Mar-91 CSK61) Portrait of lady in white dress (8x?cm-3x?in) min.*
                                  pearl border memorial scene verso oval

COSYN, Pieter (1630-1663) Dutch
£12243 $24119   (14-Nov-90 D.V105/R) River landscape with anglers and village with ruins
                                  (44x64cm-17x25in) mono. panel (A.S 250000)

COTE, Bruno (1940-) Canadian
£592 $1161   (23-Jan-91 EA.M482) Baie de Fundy (89x107cm-35x42in) s. panel
                                  (C.D 1350)

COTES, Francis (1725-1770) British
£812 $1600   (7-Oct-90 DU.E19/R) Mr Vesty of Leeds (76x64cm-30x25in)
£2821 $5500   (10-Oct-90 CH.NY194/R) Portrait of lady said to be Mrs Joah Bates
                                  standing by statuette of Cupid (122x84cm-48x33in)

COTES, Francis (1725-1770) British-cont.

£3600	$5940	(10-Jul-91 S117/R) Portrait of David Gavin of Langton House, Berwickshire (74x61cm-29x24in) s.d.1764
£4500	$8550	(1-Mar-91 C12/R) Portrait of lady standing by urn and landscape beyond (127x102cm-50x40in)
£6000	$11820	(14-Nov-90 S40/R) Portrait of Miss Dorothea Mercer wearing Van Dyck dress and plumed hat (70x60cm-28x24in) oval
£9000	$14850	(10-Jul-91 S24/R) Portrait of Lady Sarah March seated leaning on table (87x70cm-34x28in)
£550	$1084	(13-Nov-90 C101) Portrait of lady in blue decollette dress with lace trimmings and wrap (58x43cm-23x17in) pastel
£750	$1343	(9-Apr-91 C46) Portrait of young man in lace collar and cloak (54x39cm-21x15in) pastel
£1026	$2000	(11-Oct-90 SY.NY156/R) Portrait of Sir Francis James Buchanan (58x43cm-23x17in) s.d.1754 pastel
£2200	$4070	(7-Mar-91 D106/R) Portrait of lady wearing dress with laced bodice (58x43cm-23x17in) s.d.1756 pastel

COTES, Francis (circle) (1725-1770) British

£941	$1600	(31-May-91 CH.NY93/R) Portrait of lady said to be Emilia, Duchess of Leinster (60x49cm-24x19in) oval
£3000	$5370	(10-Apr-91 S127/R) Portrait of Anne, Countess of Drogheda, with son (83x68cm-33x27in)

COTES, Francis (style) (1725-1770) British

£750	$1238	(10-Jul-91 S108) Portrait of lady wearing dress with sash (80x67cm-31x26in)

COTES, Samuel (1734-1818) British

£400	$708	(20-Mar-91 C138/R) Portrait of gentleman in brown coat, white shirt and stock (5x?cm-2x?in) min. turned black wood frame oval
£3000	$4950	(11-Jul-91 S257/R) Portrait of gentleman wearing coat, waistcoat and lace jabot (4x?cm-2x?in) min.s.d.178.enamel mounted on lid of box oval

COTES, Samuel (attrib) (1734-1818) British

£1200	$2304	(18-Dec-90 C102/R) Portrait of lady in fur-trimmed mauve dress (4x?cm-2x?in) min.gold frame split-pearl border oval

COTMAN, Frederick George (1850-1920) British

£920	$1582	(14-May-91 SWS371/R) Edwarton Beach looking towards Harwich (23x39cm-9x15in) s.d.1914 board
£2400	$4536	(26-Sep-90 S193/R) Rest from mending (33x28cm-13x11in) s.
£600	$978	(4-Jul-91 PHI141) A family of ducks on a river beside a farmstead (26x38cm-10x15in) s.d.1887 W/C
£620	$1011	(4-Jul-91 PHI136/R) Pykenham Gateway, Ipswich, under rain (45x32cm-18x13in) s.d.1909 W/C
£620	$1011	(4-Jul-91 PHI129) Sheep grazing in a Suffolk landscape (27x51cm-11x20in) s.d.1913 W/C
£700	$1141	(4-Jul-91 PHI138) The river at Hemingford grey (28x44cm-11x17in) s.d.1904 W/C

COTMAN, John Joseph (1814-1878) British

£600	$1170	(12-Oct-90 K399/R) Gunton Park (25x36cm-10x14in) s.i. W/C
£850	$1700	(8-Feb-91 C31) A faggot gatherer on a country lane (41x66cm-16x26in) s.d.1870 i. verso pencil W/C
£850	$1386	(14-Jun-91 K337) Wooded river scene at sunset with cattle grazing (33x48cm-13x19in) W/C

COTMAN, John Sell (1782-1842) British

£12000	$21480	(12-Apr-91 C67/R) River landscape with angler and dog (43x35cm-17x14in)
£2700	$4833	(14-Mar-91 ZZ.B80/R) Sailing vessels in a swell (23x35cm-9x14in) s. W/C
£4800	$9456	(15-Nov-90 S99/R) Wolterton Hall, Norfolk (18x28cm-7x11in) s.d.1818 pencil wash
£8500	$15215	(9-Apr-91 C109/R) Tan-y-Bwlch, Merionethshire (20x29cm-8x11in) s.d.1801 i.verso pencil W/C gum arabic
£9200	$15180	(11-Jul-91 S142/R) St Mary Redcliffe, Bristol, Sommerset (15x23cm-6x9in) W/C
£17000	$33490	(15-Nov-90 S73/R) The Cow Tower, Norwich (35x27cm-14x11in) W/C over pencil

COTTAAR, Piet (1878-1950) Dutch

£957	$1656	(8-May-91 D.V87/R) Sunflowers (100x80cm-39x31in) s. (A.S 20000)

COTTAVOZ (20th C) French

£2200	$3586	(4-Jul-91 GL.P302) Portrait de Jacques (73x50cm-29x20in) s. (F.FR 22000)

COTTAVOZ, Andre (1922-) French

£754	$1236	(18-Jun-91 APT.P183) Nu aux bras leves (35x24cm-14x9in) s.d.72 i. verso panel (F.FR 7500)
£794	$1365	(15-May-91 CN.P82) Le chat (30x58cm-12x23in) s.d.50 paper laid down on canvas (F.FR 8000)
£806	$1313	(11-Jun-91 I.N182) Nature morte aux fruits (22x34cm-9x13in) s. (F.FR 8000)
£893	$1536	(15-May-91 CN.P80) Menton (24x50cm-9x20in) s. i.d.1952 verso paper laid down on canvas (F.FR 9000)

COTTAVOZ, Andre (1922-) French-cont.

£942	$1621	(15-May-91 CN.P81) Rue de la poste de la glaciere (26x41cm-10x16in) s.d.48 panel (F.FR 9500)
£1429	$2771	(8-Dec-90 GAB.G2486) Le phare (15x22cm-6x9in) board (S.FR 3500)
£1488	$2560	(15-May-91 CN.P79) Le jardin public (46x55cm-18x22in) s. (F.FR 15000)
£1910	$3132	(19-Jun-91 JM.P127/R) Cueillette des cerises (33x46cm-13x18in) s.d.59 l. verso (F.FR 19000)
£2016	$3931	(26-Oct-90 APT.P93) Dame Grise (65x40cm-26x16in) s.d.53 l. verso (F.FR 20000)
£2071	$4080	(1-Oct-90 CC.P151) Nature morte (32x50cm-13x20in) paper (F.FR 21000)
£2165	$3529	(11-Jun-91 I.N181/R) Marina (46x38cm-18x15in) s. i.d.1971 verso (F.FR 21500)
£2446	$4722	(10-Dec-90 LD.P125/R) Le dos sur la plage (24x33cm-9x13in) s. i.d.7/56 verso canvas laid down on board (F.FR 24000)
£2752	$5284	(2-Dec-90 M.V133/R) Les collines de Certaldo (27x35cm-11x14in) s.d.59 (F.FR 27000)
£3175	$5460	(15-May-91 CN.P78/R) Venise, le grand canal (50x70cm-20x28in) s.d.82 (F.FR 32000)
£3374	$5500	(12-Jun-91 SY.NY157/R) Vue de Golfe Juan (38x56cm-15x22in) s. s.d.1965 verso
£3685	$6265	(29-May-91 GL.P139/R) Nature morte au bouquet d'iris (45x54cm-18x21in) s. panel (F.FR 37000)
£3968	$6825	(19-May-91 ZZ.F159/R) Boulevard raspail (33x46cm-13x18in) s.d.1975 (F.FR 40000)
£6110	$12037	(30-Oct-90 I.N154/R) Nu allonge (50x73cm-20x29in) s.d.76 (F.FR 60000)
£12398	$24299	(11-Nov-90 ZZ.F143/R) Nature morte a la coupe de fruits (73x91cm-29x36in) s. (F.FR 121000)
£1724	*$3414*	*(3-Feb-91 I.N56) Vue de Venise (29x49cm-11x19in) s. mixed media (F.FR 17000)*

COTTET, Charles (1863-1924) French

£796	$1377	(12-May-91 T.B245) Nocturne sur le port (32x29cm-13x11in) s. panel (F.FR 8000)
£1100	$1804	(19-Jun-91 CSK200) Old fisherman (80x64cm-31x25in) s. board
£1520	$2584	(31-May-91 GB.B5722) River landscape with barges (31x47cm-12x19in) s. panel (DM 4500)
£2041	$4000	(21-Nov-90 NA.BA4) Bateaux de peche, Venise (44x55cm-17x22in) s. board
£7114	$12308	(12-May-91 T.B90/R) Le Port de Camaret - Sardiniers (54x81cm-21x32in) s. (F.FR 71500)
£753	*$1393*	*(4-Mar-91 ARC.P33) Barques echouees (25x31cm-10x12in) s.d.91 pastel (F.FR 7500)*
£1580	*$3049*	*(12-Dec-90 CD.P41) Ville d'Afrique du nord (80x54cm-31x21in) s. pastel (F.FR 15500)*

COTTINGHAM, Robert (1935-) American

£21429	*$42000*	*(8-Nov-90 CH.NY350/R) Tip top (244x183cm-96x72in) s.i.d.1981 verso*
£5102	*$10000*	*(14-Feb-91 CH.NY22/R) Hall's Diner (52x71cm-20x28in) s.i.d.1988verso gouache*

COTTRAU, Felix (1799-1852) French

£1005	$1648	(21-Jun-91 SY.MO349/R) La priere du soir (115x80cm-45x31in) s.d.1832 1833 (F.FR 10000)

COTTRELL, H S (fl.1840/60) British

£2200	$4290	(15-Jan-91 C79/R) Floss, favourite spaniel (58x76cm-23x30in) s.i.

COUBINE, Othon (1883-1969) Czechoslovakian

£751	$1472	(24-Nov-90 N.M108) Still life with apples, Chinese bowl and pot plant (33x41cm-13x16in) s. (DM 2200)
£865	$1686	(23-Oct-90 DUR.M39) Florero (65x53cm-26x21in) (S.P 160000)
£1403	$2750	(12-Feb-91 SY.NY107/R) Landscape with red poppies (53x66cm-21x26in) s.
£5097	$9786	(2-Dec-90 M.V45) Vase de fleur (91x74cm-36x29in) s. (F.FR 50000)
£372	*$632*	*(28-May-91 KF.M569) Female nude (27x21cm-11x8in) s. pen (DM 1100)*

COULDERY, Horatio H (1832-1893) British

£811	$1581	(23-Oct-90 DUR.M41) Un festin (13x19cm-5x7in) panel (S.P 150000)
£1068	$2083	(24-Oct-90 GM.B1346) Chiots (51x78cm-20x31in) s. wood (B.FR 65000)
£1550	$2527	(11-Jun-91 LW1737/R) Three pug dogs seated at kennel door (36x30cm-14x12in) mono.
£1750	$2923	(22-Jul-91 SWS1059/R) Pug puppies and a tabby cat (40x56cm-16x22in) s.
£2100	$4137	(13-Nov-90 SWS329/R) A tabby kitten in a green vase (22x18cm-9x7in) mono. card laid down on panel
£2300	$3887	(30-Apr-91 PH117/R) Study of spaniel's head. Study of cat (11x8cm-4x3in) one mono. panel one init. board pair
£3800	$6384	(16-Jul-91 C54/R) Kittens up to mischief (41x51cm-16x20in) s.
£4500	$7560	(16-Jul-91 C55/R) Mischief makers (46x61cm-18x24in) s. s.i.stretcher

COULTER, William Alexander (1849-1936) American

£2168	$4250	(13-Feb-91 B.SF2016 a/R) Ship in Arctic (46x79cm-18x31in) s.d.1881
£2308	$4500	(10-Oct-90 B.SF444/R) Clipper ship off Land's End (91x152cm-36x60in) s.d.1880
£3316	$6500	(13-Feb-91 B.SF2017/R) Ships in Arctic (51x76cm-20x30in) s.d.1896
£8673	$17000	(7-Nov-90 B.SF3723/R) Moniter (61x91cm-24x36in) s.

COUNHAYE, Charles (20th C) French

£2786	$5378	(13-Dec-90 SY.AM91/R) Nude (54x46cm-21x18in) s.d.14 (D.FL 9000)

COUNIHAN, Noel Jack (1913-) Australian

£2083	$3500	(16-Jul-91 JRL.S237) Cleaning and reclaiming bricks from the ruins of Warsaw for the reconstruction (14x21cm-6x8in) s. board (A.D 4500)
£2326	$3907	(22-Apr-91 SY.ME125/R) Miner (83x83cm-33x33in) s.d.1979 (A.D 5000)
£3668	$7226	(13-Nov-90 J.M266/R) The yearning of the virgins (80x121cm-31x48in) s.d.71 board (A.D 9500)
£7722	$15212	(13-Nov-90 J.M48/R) Wharfies playing cards (54x73cm-21x29in) s.d.61 board (A.D 20000)
£524	$938	(9-Apr-91 CH.ME10) Nude with arms raised (70x47cm-28x19in) s.d.64 crayon (A.D 1200)
£656	$1293	(13-Nov-90 J.M951/R) George Bell (37x24cm-15x9in) s.d.34 pencil (A.D 1700)
£1267	$2141	(16-Apr-91 J.M96) Nude (75x56cm-30x22in) s.d.'71 chl. (A.D 2800)
£1357	$2294	(16-Apr-91 J.M126) Helen (100x75cm-39x30in) s.i.d.'73 chl. (A.D 3000)

COUR, Janus Ia (1837-1909) Danish

£623	$1214	(19-Oct-90 RAS.V468/R) Between the hills at Neissum (45x75cm-18x30in) s.d.99 (D.KR 7000)
£636	$1233	(5-Dec-90 KH.K18/R) Autumn morning at Floistrup beach (44x75cm-17x30in) s.d.1893 (D.KR 7000)
£718	$1415	(14-Nov-90 RAS.K182/R) Snowcovered mountains near Murren, Switzerland (30x38cm-12x15in) init.d.1868 (D.KR 8000)
£718	$1415	(14-Nov-90 RAS.K180/R) Evening in Dyrehaven (38x45cm-15x18in) s.d.1878 (D.KR 8000)
£749	$1251	(6-Jun-91 RAS.K116) Beached boats, Napoli (31x46cm-12x18in) init.i.d.1874 (D.KR 8500)
£763	$1503	(14-Nov-90 RAS.K556/R) The beach at Hals (45x75cm-18x30in) s.d.89 (D.KR 8500)
£974	$1647	(1-May-91 KH.K32) River landscape, summer (44x64cm-17x25in) s.d.92 (D.KR 11000)
£1038	$2014	(22-Aug-90 RAS.K298/R) Landscape (46x75cm-18x30in) s.d.1875 (D.KR 12000)
£1063	$1796	(2-May-91 RAS.V28/R) Danish coastal landscape with slopes and trees (65x100cm-26x39in) s.d.1882 (D.KR 12000)
£1526	$3006	(14-Nov-90 RAS.K623/R) Spring day by Himmelbjerget (45x75cm-18x30in) s.d.1880 (D.KR 17000)
£1700	$2788	(19-Jun-91 S263/R) Woodland lake (45x75cm-18x30in) s.d.1880
£1779	$3345	(18-Sep-90 BU.K33/R) Coastal landscape with large stones (45x75cm-18x30in) s.d.1882 (D.KR 20000)
£2321	$4388	(25-Sep-90 RAS.K116/R) Alpine landscape sketch (44x75cm-17x30in) s.d.1898 (D.KR 26000)
£2569	$4341	(2-May-91 RAS.V27/R) Southern coastal landscape with moutains and houses (81x77cm-32x30in) s.d.1879 (D.KR 29000)
£2746	$4640	(1-May-91 KH.K31/R) Arcadian landscape (94x128cm-37x50in) (D.KR 31000)
£3200	$6304	(5-Oct-90 C129/R) Villa d'Este, Tivoli (44x68cm-17x27in) s.i.d.29.6.1902
£3203	$6021	(18-Sep-90 BU.K70/R) Bare trees and blue sky, wood anemones in flowers (50x77cm-20x30in) init.d.1863 (D.KR 36000)
£7821	$14000	(10-Apr-91 HF.NY38/R) View of Arhus Bay, near Moesgard, Jutland (104x155cm-41x61in) s.d.1865

COURANT, Maurice (1847-1925) French

£2551	$5026	(16-Nov-90 NM.P7/R) Marine (F.FR 25000)
£3239	$6348	(25-Nov-90 ZZ.F39/R) Scene de port (38x55cm-15x22in) s.d.1901 (F.FR 32000)

COURBET, Gustave (1819-1877) French

£8671	$15000	(23-May-91 CH.NY252/R) Rocky landscape with ravine (55x66cm-22x26in) bears sig. painted with studio
£20548	$36781	(13-Mar-91 N.M465/R) Promenade en bateau (47x56cm-19x22in) s. (DM 60000)
£24476	$47238	(10-Dec-90 L.K404/R) Mill on the Charente with two young women on road (50x60cm-20x24in) s. (DM 70000)
£27668	$47036	(27-May-91 GK.Z5156/R) Seascape (28x36cm-11x14in) mono. (S.FR 70000)
£86032	$168623	(24-Nov-90 APT.P47/R) Renard dans la neige pris au piege (81x100cm-32x39in) s. (F.FR 850000)
£102564	$200000	(23-Oct-90 SY.NY22/R) La Vague (113x145cm-44x57in) s.
£495951	$972065	(25-Nov-90 GL.P4/R) Le chateau de Chillon (81x100cm-32x39in) s. (F.FR 4900000)
£4032	$7742	(2-Dec-90 GAB.G1575/R) La corrida (19x28cm-7x11in) s.i.d.76 lead pencil (S.FR 10000)

COURBET, Gustave (studio) (1819-1877) French

£4049	$7935	(19-Nov-90 ARC.P35/R) Forge sur la Loue (59x73cm-23x29in) bears sig. (F.FR 40000)

COURBET, Gustave (style) (1819-1877) French

£1581	$2688	(27-May-91 GK.Z5015) Young boy running in wooded landscape and procession beyond (36x24cm-14x9in) canvas on panel (S.FR 4000)

COURBET, Gustave and ORDINAIRE, Marcel (19th C) French

£13158	$25000	(28-Feb-91 CH.NY46/R) Le Ruisseau entre les rochers (81x65cm-32x26in) bears sig.d.76
£14359	$28000	(24-Oct-90 CH.NY70/R) Paysage (57x71cm-22x28in) bears sig. canvas on board

COURBET, Gustave and PATA, Cherubino (19th C) French
£7895 $15000   (28-Feb-91 CH.NY45/R) Cascade en foret, paysage des Alpes
     (72x53cm-28x21in) bears sig.
£11282 $22000   (24-Oct-90 CH.NY71/R) Mountainous stream (46x38cm-18x15in) s.
£15203 $25845   (27-May-91 L.K254/R) Alpine landscape with hut in valley
     (54x64cm-21x25in) i. (DM 45000)

COURDOUAN, Vincent-Joseph-Francois (1810-1893) French
£4800 $7872   (19-Jun-91 S147/R) Drawing in nets (49x74cm-19x29in) s.d.1884
£5159 $8873   (19-May-91 ZZ.F34/R) Les lavandieres (40x68cm-16x27in) s.d.1879
     (F.FR 52000)
£1064 $1969   (6-Mar-91 APT.P4) Paysage mediterraneen (27x42cm-11x17in) s.i. gouache
     (F.FR 10600)

COURSELLES-DUMONT, Henri (1856-1918) French
£1915 $3735   (28-Oct-90 QWA.P100) Acteon devore par ses chiens (63x84cm-25x33in)
     s.d.1908 (F.FR 19000)
£2823 $5504   (28-Oct-90 QWA.P101/R) Le lion amoureux (77x58cm-30x23in) (F.FR 28000)

COURT, Emily G (?-1957) British
£650 $1287   (29-Jan-91 PH175) Playing on beach (64x83cm-25x33in) s.
£960 $1622   (1-May-91 PHL199/R) Figures promenading on terrace by fountain, with
     parkland beyond (30x38cm-12x15in) init. canvasboard
£1700 $2839   (3-Jun-91 PHB38/R) Savoy. Chelsea in snow (13x14cm-5x6in) s. i.d.1909/10
     verso board pair

COURT, Joseph-Desire (1797-1865) French
£1789 $3024   (18-Apr-91 APT.P146/R) Portrait presume de l'architecte Lenepveu en
     compagnie de ses amis (42x35cm-17x14in) mono. (F.FR 18000)

COURTAT, Louis (?-1909) French
£2465 $4141   (23-Apr-91 RAS.K80/R) Reclining nude by lake in wood (38x61cm-15x24in)
     s. (D.KR 28000)

COURTEN, Comte Angelo de (1848-?) Italian
£3800 $7296   (27-Nov-90 PH189/R) Unwelcome suitors (81x102cm-32x40in) s.
£5978 $11478   (18-Dec-90 DUR.M6) Es una ganga (131x86cm-52x34in) (S.P 1100000)
£378 $700   (8-Mar-91 S.BM192/R) En Toscane fillette tressant la paillie
     (46x28cm-18x11in) s. i. W/C

COURTENS, Franz (1854-1943) Belgian
£800 $1568   (14-Feb-91 CSK96) Dutch girls on a dyke, a canal and village beyond
     (51x61cm-20x24in) s.
£1012 $1963   (4-Dec-90 C.A64) Marine (33x44cm-13x17in) s. panel (B.FR 60000)
£1037 $2032   (6-Nov-90 SY.AM155) Moored rowing boats (36x50cm-14x20in) s. panel
     (D.FL 3400)
£1497 $2605   (26-Mar-91 VN.R16/R) Fishing boats on the shore (37x51cm-15x20in) s.
     panel (D.FL 5000)
£1531 $3015   (14-Nov-90 CN.P114/R) Femme (55x46cm-22x18in) s. (F.FR 15000)
£1951 $3824   (6-Nov-90 SY.AM243/R) Samenloop van Dender en Schelde (36x46cm-14x18in)
     s. (D.FL 6400)
£2629 $5127   (23-Oct-90 C.A343/R) On the towpath (32x49cm-13x19in) s. panel
     (B.FR 160000)

COURTENS, Hermann (1884-1956) Belgian
£1163 $1895   (12-Jun-91 GM.B4035) Les pots de fleurs (55x70cm-22x28in) s.
     (B.FR 70000)
£2273 $4477   (30-Oct-90 CH.AM41/R) Derniers preparatifs (46x38cm-18x15in) s.i. panel
     (D.FL 7500)
£5128 $10000   (24-Oct-90 CH.NY268/R) The summer bonnet (70x60cm-28x24in) s.i.

COURTIN, Jacques Francois (1672-1752) French
£4893 $9394   (30-Nov-90 APT.P97/R) Jeune femme au masque (92x73cm-36x29in)
     (F.FR 48000)
£6030 $9889   (17-Jun-91 ARC.P19/R) La lecon de musique (130x98cm-51x39in)
     (F.FR 60000)

COURTIN, Jacques Francois (studio) (1672-1752) French
£1039 $1859   (12-Apr-91 AGS.P7) Jeune femme a la collerette (73x59cm-29x23in) oval
     (F.FR 10500)

COURTOIS (circle) (?) French
£1711 $3336   (23-Oct-90 CH.R187) Gentiluomo a cavallo (38x46cm-15x18in)
     (I.L 3800000)

COURTOIS, Guillaume (1628-1679) French
£6819 $13365   (19-Nov-90 CH.R174/R) Gioco di putti - Allegoria dell'elemento Acqua e
     dell'elemento Terra (139x62cm-55x24in) pair (I.L 15000000)

COURTOIS, Jacques (1621-1676) French
£5467 $9240   (18-Apr-91 APT.P107/R) Scene de bataille (47x64cm-19x25in) (F.FR 55000)
£6231 $11154   (8-Apr-91 ARC.P8/R) Chocs de cavalerie (11x17cm-4x7in) panel pair
     (F.FR 63000)
£6939 $13600   (6-Nov-90 GF.L2036/R) Battle scene (69x85cm-27x33in) (S.FR 17000)
£10500 $17745   (17-Apr-91 S8/R) Cavalry skirmish (28x49cm-11x19in)
£41044 $68544   (4-Jun-91 CH.R543/R) Battaglia (95x110cm-37x43in) (I.L 90000000)

COURTOIS, Jacques (attrib) (1621-1676) French
£1053 $2000   (15-Sep-90 S.W2397/R) Battle scene (89x142cm-35x56in)
£2800 $5516   (31-Oct-90 S142/R) Battle by fort (33x43cm-13x17in)

COURTOIS, Jacques (circle) (1621-1676) French
£4303 $8434   (11-Nov-90 M.V46/R) Choc de cavalier (56x74cm-22x29in) (F.FR 42000)

COURTOIS, Jacques (school) (1621-1676) French
£1531 $3000   (7-Nov-90 B.SF1006/R) Naval battle at Lepanto (91x145cm-36x57in)

COURTOIS, Jacques (studio) (1621-1676) French
£10774 $21224   (14-Nov-90 D.V26/R) Skirmish between Christian soldiers and Turks
   (33x91cm-13x36in) (A.S 220000)

COURTOIS, Jacques (style) (1621-1676) French
£1100 $2200   (7-Feb-91 CSK80) Cavalry skirmish (42x58cm-17x23in) panel
£2400 $4560   (13-Sep-90 CSK339/R) Cavalry skirmish (58x97cm-23x38in)
£4200 $8064   (29-Nov-90 CSK183/R) Crusader skirmish (34x91cm-13x36in)
£6000 $9780   (4-Jul-91 C530/R) Cavalry engagement (38x61cm-15x24in)
£6000 $10140   (18-Apr-91 C112/R) A cavalry skirmish (81x119cm-32x47in)

COURTWRIGHT, Robert (20th C) American
£769 $1500   (10-Oct-90 SY.NY523/R) Untitled CXIII (79x81cm-31x32in) s.d.78 s.d.verso
   paper collage board

COUSE, E Irving (1866-1936) American
£1702 $3200   (22-Sep-90 WOL.C167/R) Apres le peche (46x61cm-18x24in) s.
£1955 $3500   (14-Mar-91 CH.NY135 b/R) Indian with blanket (40x20cm-16x8in) canvas on
   board
£2296 $4500   (7-Nov-90 B.SF3761/R) Village scenes (23x18cm-9x7in) s. four
£2367 $4000   (1-May-91 B.SF5059/R) Shepherd watering flock (61x74cm-24x29in) s.
£2367 $4000   (1-May-91 B.SF5189/R) Benito (15x13cm-6x5in) s. i.verso board
£3352 $6000   (14-Mar-91 CH.NY135 c/R) Indian camp (46x61cm-18x24in)
£3968 $7500   (26-Sep-90 SY.NY84/R) The treaty (30x41cm-12x16in) s. canvasboard
£4337 $8500   (7-Nov-90 B.SF3794/R) Indian drinking by moonlight (25x20cm-10x8in) s.
   board
£9375 $18000   (30-Nov-90 CH.NY93/R) The badger skin (31x41cm-12x16in) s.
£52023 $90000   (22-May-91 CH.NY215/R) The skin painter (61x74cm-24x29in) s.i.

COUSIN, Charles (19/20th C) French
£732 $1428   (12-Oct-90 ZZ.F20) Martigues (60x98cm-24x39in) s. paper laid down board
   (F.FR 7300)
£798 $1500   (19-Sep-90 B.SF2705/R) In a gondola (56x46cm-22x18in) s.

COUSTOU, Jean (1719-1791) French
£20101 $32965   (21-Jun-91 SY.MO254/R) Trompe l'oeil a la gravure et aux dessins
   (44x29cm-17x11in) pair (F.FR 200000)

COUSTRY, Therese (20th C) French?
£1164 $2281   (25-Nov-90 ZZ.F81/R) Le chat et l'escargot (50x60cm-20x24in) s.
   (F.FR 11500)

COUSTURIER, Lucie (1876-1925) French
£2245 $4422   (16-Nov-90 FB.P139/R) Portrait de jeune fille (61x50cm-24x20in)
   (F.FR 22000)

COUTAUD, Lucien (1904-) French
£714 $1377   (11-Dec-90 ARC.P136/R) Nu allonge (10x18cm-4x7in) (F.FR 7000)
£755 $1231   (14-Jun-91 FB.P40/R) Fleurs (233x46cm-92x18in) s.d.42 i. verso
   (F.FR 7500)
£815 $1574   (11-Dec-90 ARC.P138/R) Marine 2 (27x46cm-11x18in) s.d.45 (F.FR 8000)
£917 $1771   (11-Dec-90 ARC.P147/R) Personnages ponctues la nuit, ou nocturne
   (29x43cm-11x17in) s.d.48 (F.FR 9000)
£994 $1680   (17-Apr-91 LGB.P50/R) Depart de l'ombre (24x16cm-9x6in) s.d.3/46 verso
   (F.FR 10000)
£1121 $2164   (11-Dec-90 ARC.P177) En rase campagne (31x47cm-12x19in) s.d.72 board
   (F.FR 11000)
£1172 $2262   (11-Dec-90 ARC.P148/R) Baigneurs aux points noirs (38x46cm-15x18in)
   s.d.50 (F.FR 11500)
£1325 $2558   (11-Dec-90 ARC.P150/R) Oreilles et eau (50x61cm-20x24in) s.d.52
   (F.FR 13000)
£1325 $2558   (11-Dec-90 ARC.P157/R) Paysage au navire (38x61cm-15x24in) s.d.55
   (F.FR 13000)
£1376 $2656   (11-Dec-90 ARC.P152/R) Mer par temps vert (46x55cm-18x22in) s.d.49
   (F.FR 13500)
£1427 $2754   (11-Dec-90 ARC.P141/R) Un des permiers essais du frere de la porteuse de
   pain (27x16cm-11x6in) s.d.44 (F.FR 14000)
£1631 $3148   (11-Dec-90 ARC.P140/R) Visage par temps gris (46x27cm-18x11in) s.d.45
   (F.FR 16000)
£1835 $3541   (11-Dec-90 ARC.P154/R) Autres faucheurs de vagues (61x38cm-24x15in)
   s.d.61 (F.FR 18000)
£1937 $3738   (11-Dec-90 ARC.P130/R) Jeune homme (22x16cm-9x6in) s.d.38 (F.FR 19000)
£1937 $3738   (11-Dec-90 ARC.P155/R) Devise rouge et blanche (65x92cm-26x36in) s.d.57
   (F.FR 19000)
£1937 $3738   (11-Dec-90 ARC.P144/R) Premiere nature morte aux pains (50x61cm-20x24in)
   s.d.47 (F.FR 19000)

COUTAUD, Lucien (1904-) French-cont.

£2039	$3935	(11-Dec-90 ARC.P137/R) Le modele (81x65cm-32x26in) s.d.47 (F.FR 20000)
£2141	$4131	(11-Dec-90 ARC.P167/R) Suerte des trois yeux (60x73cm-24x29in) s.d.67 (F.FR 21000)
£2243	$4328	(11-Dec-90 ARC.P162/R) Souvenir d'un voyage (60x73cm-24x29in) s.d.63 (F.FR 22000)
£2243	$4328	(11-Dec-90 ARC.P172/R) Il y avait aussi quelques oiseaux de nuit (73x92cm-29x36in) s.d.72 (F.FR 22000)
£2243	$4328	(11-Dec-90 ARC.P158/R) Personnage du cheval de brique (73x53cm-29x21in) d.1955 studio st. verso (F.FR 22000)
£2345	$4525	(11-Dec-90 ARC.P169/R) Tours aimaient l'arbre (65x92cm-26x36in) s.d.68 (F.FR 23000)
£2345	$4525	(11-Dec-90 ARC.P176/R) Petit interieur normand (46x55cm-18x22in) s.d.73 (F.FR 23000)
£2446	$4722	(11-Dec-90 ARC.P134/R) Le couteau de nacre (19x33cm-7x13in) s.d.3.40 (F.FR 24000)
£2446	$4722	(11-Dec-90 ARC.P175/R) Los toreros, en souvenir de la Feria de Nimes (81x100cm-32x39in) s.d.11.7.70 (F.FR 24000)
£2446	$4722	(11-Dec-90 ARC.P129/R) Femme allongee (65x91cm-26x36in) s. (F.FR 24000)
£2548	$4918	(11-Dec-90 ARC.P128/R) Le malade (72x90cm-28x35in) s. (F.FR 25000)
£2548	$4918	(11-Dec-90 ARC.P161/R) Jeune parisienne (73x54cm-29x21in) s.d.66 (F.FR 25000)
£2650	$5115	(11-Dec-90 ARC.P132/R) Nature morte en ville (46x55cm-18x22in) s.d.2.40 panel (F.FR 26000)
£2650	$5115	(11-Dec-90 ARC.P160/R) Le pavillon violace (73x100cm-29x39in) s.d.57 (F.FR 26000)
£2650	$5115	(11-Dec-90 ARC.P159/R) Jour ferie au cheval de brique (73x92cm-29x36in) s.d.57 (F.FR 26000)
£2854	$5509	(11-Dec-90 ARC.P168/R) Autre torero cathare (73x60cm-29x24in) s.d.68 (F.FR 28000)
£2854	$5509	(11-Dec-90 ARC.P149/R) Le chateau de marquis (50x61cm-20x24in) s.d.48 (F.FR 28000)
£3058	$5902	(11-Dec-90 ARC.P133/R) Le femme torero (35x22cm-14x9in) s.d.43 i. verso (F.FR 30000)
£3109	$6001	(11-Dec-90 ARC.P174/R) Corrida lunaire (46x55cm-18x22in) s.d.72 (F.FR 30500)
£3262	$6296	(11-Dec-90 ARC.P170/R) Peinture a l'huile (97x130cm-38x51in) s.d.1970 (F.FR 32000)
£3364	$6492	(11-Dec-90 ARC.P164/R) Nimes (100x81cm-39x32in) s.d.64 (F.FR 33000)
£3466	$6689	(11-Dec-90 ARC.P171/R) Plage des metamorphoses (73x92cm-29x36in) s.d.66 (F.FR 34000)
£3619	$6984	(11-Dec-90 ARC.P173/R) Pentecote sans Corrida (81x99cm-32x39in) s.d.73 (F.FR 35500)
£3925	$7574	(11-Dec-90 ARC.P153/R) Souvenir (73x116cm-29x46in) s.d.49 (F.FR 38500)
£4281	$8263	(11-Dec-90 ARC.P166/R) Templier de nimes (99x81cm-39x32in) s.d.65 (F.FR 42000)
£5607	$10821	(11-Dec-90 ARC.P165/R) Un fauteuil nimois (97x130cm-38x51in) s.d.64 (F.FR 55000)
£6524	$12591	(11-Dec-90 ARC.P145/R) L'armoire chaire de la porteuse de pain (81x100cm-32x39in) s.d.47 (F.FR 64000)
£7136	$13772	(11-Dec-90 ARC.P139/R) Les sept fers (114x146cm-45x57in) s.d.44 (F.FR 70000)
£7849	$15149	(11-Dec-90 ARC.P127/R) La bicyclette (73x94cm-29x37in) s.d.1929 (F.FR 77000)
£15596	$30101	(11-Dec-90 ARC.P163/R) Quelques dames de deauville (146x114cm-57x45in) s.d.61 (F.FR 153000)
£17329	$33445	(11-Dec-90 ARC.P156/R) Plage de l'eroticomagie (162x130cm-64x51in) s.d.4.54 (F.FR 170000)
£561	$1082	(11-Dec-90 ARC.P115/R) C'etait un ami (32x49cm-13x19in) s.d.74 gouache (F.FR 5500)
£561	$1082	(11-Dec-90 ARC.P53/R) Trois squelettes de fruits avec un personnage qui se dissimule (17x20cm-7x8in) s.d.42 i. verso gouache (F.FR 5500)
£571	$1102	(11-Dec-90 ARC.P65/R) Femme verte (46x31cm-18x12in) s.d.23.07.45 W/C gouache (F.FR 5600)
£610	$1154	(25-Sep-90 FB.P258/R) La rencontre Fontvieille (16x24cm-6x9in) s.d.43 i. verso gouache (F.FR 6000)
£612	$1180	(11-Dec-90 ARC.P81/R) Arlequin (21x14cm-8x6in) s.d.50 gouache (F.FR 6000)
£612	$1174	(2-Dec-90 M.V111 b) Elle aimait la mer (46x60cm-18x24in) s.d.63 gouache (F.FR 6000)
£612	$1180	(11-Dec-90 ARC.P114/R) Juin 1968 (40x48cm-16x19in) s.d.68 gouache (F.FR 6000)
£612	$1180	(11-Dec-90 ARC.P38/R) Tete fleurie (40x33cm-16x13in) gouache (F.FR 6000)
£612	$1180	(11-Dec-90 ARC.P80/R) La porteuse de pain s'eclaire (41x31cm-16x12in) s.i.d.46 W/C (F.FR 6000)
£612	$1180	(11-Dec-90 ARC.P77/R) Deux personnages marins (22x27cm-9x11in) s.d.46 gouache (F.FR 6000)
£632	$1220	(11-Dec-90 ARC.P76/R) Toujours les environs de F (33x41cm-13x16in) s.i.d.1946 W/C gouache (F.FR 6200)
£663	$1279	(11-Dec-90 ARC.P101/R) C'etait le dernier dimanche d'octobre (47x62cm-19x24in) s.d.60 gouache (F.FR 6500)
£663	$1279	(11-Dec-90 ARC.P92/R) Pres de St Bernard (38x46cm-15x18in) s.d.58 i. verso gouache (F.FR 6500)
£663	$1279	(11-Dec-90 ARC.P45/R) La machine agricole (38x61cm-15x24in) s.d.39 gouache (F.FR 6500)

COUTAUD, Lucien (1904-) French-cont.

£673	$1298	(11-Dec-90 ARC.P75/R) Le pere de la porteuse de pain inquiet par la rencontre de sa fille (34x27cm-13x11in) s.d.46 gouache (F.FR 6600)
£714	$1377	(11-Dec-90 ARC.P113/R) Lundi de pentecote (41x49cm-16x19in) s.d.68 gouache (F.FR 7000)
£714	$1377	(11-Dec-90 ARC.P118/R) Elles se regardent (37x52cm-15x20in) s.d.73 gouache (F.FR 7000)
£714	$1377	(11-Dec-90 ARC.P41/R) La machine agricole (34x42cm-13x17in) s.d.36 gouache (F.FR 7000)
£714	$1377	(11-Dec-90 ARC.P103/R) Le vainqueur du tournoi (32x26cm-13x10in) s.d.61 gouache (F.FR 7000)
£714	$1377	(11-Dec-90 ARC.P82/R) Deuxieme interieur Breton (29x43cm-11x17in) s.d.48 gouache (F.FR 7000)
£714	$1377	(11-Dec-90 ARC.P64/R) Femme (43x29cm-17x11in) s.d.44 gouache (F.FR 7000)
£714	$1377	(11-Dec-90 ARC.P93/R) Arbre et cathares (46x38cm-18x15in) s.d.60 gouache (F.FR 7000)
£724	$1397	(11-Dec-90 ARC.P102/R) Mesdames automne (37x45cm-15x18in) s.d.60 gouache (F.FR 7100)
£761	$1500	(13-Nov-90 CE.NY164/R) Comediens a la campagne (46x61cm-18x24in) s.d.33 i.d.verso gouache board
£765	$1476	(11-Dec-90 ARC.P52/R) Noix, grenade et figures (18x17cm-7x7in) s.d.2.40 gouache (F.FR 7500)
£765	$1476	(11-Dec-90 ARC.P73/R) Rencontres pres de F (32x40cm-13x16in) W/C gouache (F.FR 7500)
£765	$1476	(11-Dec-90 ARC.P117/R) Toutes etaient ainsi (31x47cm-12x19in) s.d.73 gouache (F.FR 7500)
£815	$1574	(11-Dec-90 ARC.P111/R) Ils venaient souvent le soir (36x45cm-14x18in) s.d.61 gouache (F.FR 8000)
£815	$1574	(11-Dec-90 ARC.P88/R) Le chatelain de lacoste (43x29cm-17x11in) s.d.1948 gouache (F.FR 8000)
£815	$1574	(11-Dec-90 ARC.P105/R) Les deux nouveaux (59x46cm-23x18in) s.d.61 wash W/C (F.FR 8000)
£815	$1574	(11-Dec-90 ARC.P35/R) Interieur au clairon (16x24cm-6x9in) s.d.34 gouache panel (F.FR 8000)
£907	$1769	(28-Oct-90 M.V147/R) Elle aimait la mer (46x60cm-18x24in) s.d.63 i.verso gouache (F.FR 9000)
£917	$1771	(11-Dec-90 ARC.P116/R) Fin septembre (37x52cm-15x20in) s.d.73 gouache (F.FR 9000)
£917	$1771	(11-Dec-90 ARC.P109/R) Plage d'aout 74 (32x49cm-13x19in) s.d.74 gouache (F.FR 9000)
£917	$1771	(11-Dec-90 ARC.P119/R) Interieur normand (36x51cm-14x20in) s.d.73 gouache (F.FR 9000)
£941	$1665	(5-Apr-91 LGB.P84/R) Hommage a Raymond Roussel (61x36cm-24x14in) s. W/C (F.FR 9500)
£968	$1869	(11-Dec-90 ARC.P107/R) Jeune torero (61x50cm-24x20in) s.d.63 gouache (F.FR 9500)
£1019	$1967	(11-Dec-90 ARC.P69/R) Jeune monegasque (65x50cm-26x20in) s.d.45 W/C (F.FR 10000)
£1019	$1967	(11-Dec-90 ARC.P39/R) Paysage provencal (36x54cm-14x21in) s.d.35 gouache (F.FR 10000)
£1019	$1967	(11-Dec-90 ARC.P61/R) La chevre (17x25cm-7x10in) s.d.43 gouache (F.FR 10000)
£1019	$1967	(11-Dec-90 ARC.P98/R) Trouville (38x47cm-15x19in) s. gouache (F.FR 10000)
£1019	$1967	(11-Dec-90 ARC.P94/R) Plage aux oiseaux (33x41cm-13x16in) s.d.52 gouache (F.FR 10000)
£1019	$1967	(11-Dec-90 ARC.P36/R) Sous une table (50x68cm-20x27in) s.d.1934 gouache (F.FR 10000)
£1019	$1967	(11-Dec-90 ARC.P86/R) Les demoiselles trianon (23x29cm-9x11in) s.d.18.3.51 gouache (F.FR 10000)
£1121	$2164	(11-Dec-90 ARC.P57/R) La porte et la fenetre (45x60cm-18x24in) s.d.43 gouache (F.FR 11000)
£1121	$2164	(11-Dec-90 ARC.P32/R) Interieur a la locomotive (38x46cm-15x18in) s.d.33 gouache panel (F.FR 11000)
£1121	$2164	(11-Dec-90 ARC.P78/R) Jeune fille abandonnee (64x49cm-25x19in) s.d.46 gouache (F.FR 11000)
£1172	$2262	(11-Dec-90 ARC.P42/R) Le mouton dans la ferme (37x47cm-15x19in) s.d.36 gouache (F.FR 11500)
£1223	$2361	(11-Dec-90 ARC.P71/R) Avant l'infini (65x50cm-26x20in) s.d.45 W/C iron (F.FR 12000)
£1274	$2459	(11-Dec-90 ARC.P108/R) Je songe a nimes (49x59cm-19x23in) s.i.d.63 ink wash (F.FR 12500)
£1325	$2558	(11-Dec-90 ARC.P99/R) Les trois pensees (36x44cm-14x17in) s.d.58 gouache (F.FR 13000)
£1376	$2656	(11-Dec-90 ARC.P46/R) L'amie de la soeur (35x23cm-14x9in) s.d.38 gouache (F.FR 13500)
£1427	$2754	(11-Dec-90 ARC.P70/R) Fantomes de fer (66x50cm-26x20in) s.i.d.45 gouache iron (F.FR 14000)
£1427	$2754	(11-Dec-90 ARC.P33/R) La pianiste (25x32cm-10x13in) s.d.34 gouache (F.FR 14000)
£1427	$2754	(11-Dec-90 ARC.P90/R) Couple a la Corrida (43x34cm-17x13in) s.d.57 gouache (F.FR 14000)
£1529	$2951	(11-Dec-90 ARC.P58/R) L'armoire ouverte (73x54cm-29x21in) s.d.43 gouache (F.FR 15000)
£1580	$3049	(11-Dec-90 ARC.P72/R) Armoires champetres (50x66cm-20x26in) s.d.46 i.verso W/C gouache (F.FR 15500)

COUTAUD, Lucien (1904-) French-cont.

£1631	$3148	(11-Dec-90 ARC.P84/R) Hommage aux surrealistes (25x17cm-10x7in) s. gouache (F.FR 16000)
£1682	$3246	(11-Dec-90 ARC.P89/R) La pentecote (27x35cm-11x14in) s.d.53 gouache (F.FR 16500)
£1733	$3345	(11-Dec-90 ARC.P59/R) Le melon du crepuscule (55x74cm-22x29in) s.d.43 gouache (F.FR 17000)
£1733	$3345	(11-Dec-90 ARC.P40/R) La jeune couturiere (22x28cm-9x11in) s.d.35 i. verso gouache (F.FR 17000)
£1784	$3443	(11-Dec-90 ARC.P100/R) Femmes pensees (29x39cm-11x15in) s.d.59 gouache (F.FR 17500)
£1835	$3541	(11-Dec-90 ARC.P62/R) L'astrologue (52x37cm-20x15in) s.d.44 gouache (F.FR 18000)
£1937	$3738	(11-Dec-90 ARC.P95/R) Le dernier personnage s'en va (33x45cm-13x18in) s.d.52 gouache (F.FR 19000)
£2039	$3935	(11-Dec-90 ARC.P51/R) Couple a la bicyclette (18x18cm-7x7in) s.d.3/40 gouache (F.FR 20000)
£2039	$3935	(11-Dec-90 ARC.P54/R) Deuxieme vaisseau (51x70cm-20x28in) s.d.41 gouache (F.FR 20000)
£2039	$3935	(11-Dec-90 ARC.P63/R) Interieur a la chaise (36x51cm-14x20in) s.d.23.04.44 gouache (F.FR 20000)
£2090	$4033	(11-Dec-90 ARC.P43/R) Souvenir (51x70cm-20x28in) s.d.37 gouache (F.FR 20500)
£2090	$4033	(11-Dec-90 ARC.P120/R) Agreables estivantes (64x49cm-25x19in) s.d.74 gouache (F.FR 20500)
£2243	$4328	(11-Dec-90 ARC.P47/R) Premier vaisseau (51x70cm-20x28in) s.d.39 gouache (F.FR 22000)
£2345	$4525	(11-Dec-90 ARC.P49/R) Personnages sur le port (25x35cm-10x14in) s. goauche (F.FR 23000)
£2497	$4820	(11-Dec-90 ARC.P48/R) Piano par temps gris (51x70cm-20x28in) s.d.1937 gouache (F.FR 24500)
£2548	$4918	(11-Dec-90 ARC.P44/R) Madame et Monsieur violon (42x34cm-17x13in) s.d.1937 gouache (F.FR 25000)
£4281	$8263	(11-Dec-90 ARC.P97/R) L'eau (56x72cm-22x28in) s.d.53 gouache (F.FR 42000)
£7021	$13691	(11-Oct-90 QWA.P79/R) Vive Mozart (15x30cm-6x12in) s.d.41 i. verso gouache (F.FR 70000)
£7136	$13772	(11-Dec-90 ARC.P55/R) La lettre, ou autoportrait (85x115cm-33x45in) s.d.12.42 gouache (F.FR 70000)

COUTTS, Gordon (1880-1937) British/American

£1982	$3250	(21-Jun-91 DM.D2021/R) Crossing plains (61x71cm-24x28in) s.
£2035	$3500	(15-May-91 SY.NY45/R) Evening (56x91cm-22x36in) s.

COUTURE, Thomas (1815-1879) French

£10277	$19938	(8-Dec-90 SY.MO316/R) Scene allegorique (54x45cm-21x18in) s. (F.FR 100000)

COUTURE, Thomas (attrib) (1815-1879) French

£1400	$2744	(22-Nov-90 CSK183/R) Tethered horse in village landscape (33x47cm-13x19in) init.

COUTURE, Thomas (school) (1815-1879) French

£3499	$6718	(17-Dec-90 AGS.P26/R) Les Romains de la Decadence (92x154cm-36x61in) (F.FR 34500)

COUTURIER, Leon Antoine Lucien (1842-1935) French

£1673	$2810	(23-Apr-91 RAS.K326/R) French soldiers repairing a brickwall (62x50cm-24x20in) s. (D.KR 19000)

COUTURIER, Philibert Leon (1823-1901) French

£1429	$2743	(28-Nov-90 PH.T27/R) The barn door (65x53cm-26x21in) s. (C.D 3200)
£1835	$3523	(1-Dec-90 PER.M82/R) Scene de Basse-cour (23x32cm-9x13in) s. panel (F.FR 18000)
£2154	$4244	(14-Nov-90 RAS.K605/R) Rabbits, chickens and magpie on steps (65x68cm-26x27in) s. (D.KR 24000)
£16488	$31657	(19-Feb-91 DUR.M29) Bodegon de caza (204x354cm-80x139in) (S.P 3000000)

COUTY, Jean (1907-) French

£815	$1574	(12-Dec-90 CD.P31/R) Lyon, le port de Beze (60x73cm-24x29in) s. (F.FR 8000)
£1542	$2991	(3-Dec-90 CS.L57/R) La passerelle duLycee a Lyon (60x73cm-24x29in) s. (F.FR 15000)

COUVELET, Jean Baptiste (1772-1830) French

£2500	$4075	(3-Jul-91 PLF.P52/R) Portraits d'un mineralogiste et de sa femme (60x49cm-24x19in) first s.d.1814 other s.d.1824 pair (F.FR 25000)

COUVEN, Ferdinand Wilhelm von (1786-1866) German

£13986	$26993	(10-Dec-90 L.K405/R) Altmuhl valley landscape with monastery, Franconia (58x72cm-23x28in) s. (DM 40000)

COUVER, J van (1836-1909) Dutch

£501	$982	(12-Feb-91 GM.B643) Marche aux fleurs (49x69cm-19x27in) s. wood (B.FR 30000)

COUVER, Jan van see also KOEKKOEK, Hermanus (Jnr)

COUVER, Jan van (1836-1909) Dutch
£1700 $3332   (14-Feb-91 CSK65) Alkmaar, Holland (76x102cm-30x40in) s.
£1800 $3546   (4-Oct-90 CSK49/R) The windmill (87x112cm-34x44in) s.

COUWENBERG, Christiaan van (1604-1667) Dutch
£40493 $68028   (23-Apr-91 RAS.K16/R) Young man seated at table with wine, fruit and
                        bread (66x84cm-26x33in) (D.KR 460000)

COVARRUBIAS, Miguel (1904-1957) Mexican
£8721   *$15000*   *(15-May-91 CH.NY158/R) Balinesa con Frutas (42x47cm-17x19in) s. W/C*
                        pastel blk.crayon
£9884   *$17000*   *(15-May-91 CH.NY157/R) Dos Balinesas (54x34cm-21x13in) s. W/C pastel*
                        blk.crayon

COVENTRY, Gertrude Mary (1886-) British
£900 $1548   (14-May-91 SWS405/R) Preparing for the fishing (45x60cm-18x24in) s.
                        indis.i.verso
£1000 $2000   (5-Feb-91 S168/R) Unloading catch (51x61cm-20x24in) s.

COVENTRY, J (19th C) British
£750   *$1478*   *(1-Nov-90 TE542/R) Highland landscape with figures by loch, and castle*
                        (51x74cm-20x29in) s.d.1866 W/C

COVENTRY, Robert McGown (1855-1914) British
£700 $1365   (11-Oct-90 CG113) Fishermen on rocks (30x51cm-12x20in) s.
£500   *$885*   *(22-Mar-91 PHE46) The return of the fleet (26x36cm-10x14in) s. W/C*
£550   *$1073*   *(11-Oct-90 CG81) Arrival of the boats (38x56cm-15x22in) s. W/C htd white*

COWARD, Sir Noel (1900-1973) British
£3800 $7144   (20-Sep-90 C149/R) On beach in Jamaica (51x41cm-20x16in) s. board
£4000 $6680   (6-Jun-91 C44/R) Jamaican Bay (51x41cm-20x16in) s.
£4000 $7520   (20-Sep-90 CSK198/R) The fruit market (30x20cm-12x8in) s. canvas-board
£4800 $9024   (20-Sep-90 C148/R) On Jamaican coast (56x71cm-22x28in) s.
£1000   *$1880*   *(20-Sep-90 CSK199/R) Theatrical designs - woman on terrace*
                        (27x22cm-11x9in) W/C
£1700   *$3196*   *(20-Sep-90 CSK201/R) The red sailingboat (14x20cm-6x8in) s. oil gouache*
                        panel
£3500   *$5915*   *(2-May-91 C24/R) View from artist's home, Firefly, Jamaica*
                        (23x32cm-9x13in) s. pencil W/C bodycol htd white

COWEN, Lionel J (19th C) British
£1629 $2753   (16-Apr-91 J.M24/R) Making the bouquet (90x49cm-35x19in) s.i.
                        (A.D 3600)

COWEN, William (1797-1860) British
£3083 $5982   (8-Dec-90 SY.MO382/R) Soiree d'ete en baie de Naples (63x76cm-25x30in)
                        s.d.1847 (F.FR 30000)

COWIE, James (1886-1956) British
£650   *$1066*   *(19-Jun-91 PHG83) Portrait study (55x37cm-22x15in) pencil conte drawing*
£1600   *$3024*   *(27-Sep-90 CG15/R) Girl's head (22x23cm-9x9in) s. W/C htd white*

COWIESON, Agnes M (fl.1882-1940) British
£500 $1000   (5-Feb-91 CG68) Spring flowers (25x30cm-10x12in) s. s.i.verso board
£800 $1344   (23-Apr-91 S155/R) Spring flowers (26x31cm-10x12in) s. i.verso board
£1000 $1680   (23-Apr-91 S154/R) Still life with anemones in vase (30x40cm-12x16in) s.

COWLES, Fleur (20th C) American
£1142   *$2250*   *(15-Nov-91 SY.NY63/R) Neighbours (12x8cm-5x3in) s.d.1959 s.verso gouache*

COX, Albert Scott (1863-?) American
£842 $1600   (28-Feb-91 MFA.C122) Cottage scene (56x71cm-22x28in) s.

COX, D (19th C) British
£780   *$1482*   *(15-Sep-90 ME86) Welsh figures in boat with cattle on riverbank*
                        (25x33cm-10x13in) s. W/C

COX, David (19th C) British
£1156 $2000   (21-May-91 CE.NY83/R) Homewards (21x31cm-8x12in) s.
£1786 $3500   (7-Nov-90 B.SF1185/R) Outskirts of wood (71x93cm-28x37in)
£3200 $6304   (31-Oct-90 S325/R) Cowherds with cattle near Harlech Castle
                        (27x38cm-11x15in) s.d.1849
£4500 $8055   (10-Apr-91 S28/R) Landscape with distant view of Bolton Abbey, Yorkshire
                        and River Wharfe (40x58cm-16x23in) s. panel
£440   *$752*   *(30-Jul-91 SWS401) A horeman and cattle crossing a bridge at dusk*
                        (22x34cm-9x13in) s.d.1843 W/C over pencil scratching out
£560   *$1098*   *(23-Jan-91 JT51) Snowdonia (33x48cm-13x19in) s.d.1859 W/C*
£600   *$1008*   *(22-Apr-91 PH240) Sea piece (14x23cm-6x9in) W/C htd white*
£750   *$1478*   *(13-Nov-90 C138) Berry Pomeroy Castle, Devon (28x41cm-11x16in) i.verso*
                        pencil W/C
£800   *$1344*   *(17-Jul-91 ME1) Boats and figures on shore (20x30cm-8x12in) s. W/C*
£850   *$1675*   *(1-Nov-90 C69) Harlech Castle with cattle and figures (10x15cm-4x6in)*
                        s.d.1809 W/C
£1000   *$1980*   *(30-Jan-91 S151/R) Moss troopers (16x23cm-6x9in) W/C over pencil*

COX, David (19th C) British-cont.

£1050	$2079	(30-Jan-91 S149/R) Mill near Kenilworth, Warwickshire (18x26cm-7x10in) i. pencil
£1200	$2016	(15-Jul-91 PH80) Stepping stones, Bolton Woods (18x27cm-7x11in) W/C over pencil
£1450	$2813	(5-Dec-90 PHL.58/R) Snowdon (29x47cm-11x19in) s. pencil co. washes
£1500	$2955	(15-Nov-90 S13/R) Dolbadern Castle, North Wales (17x28cm-7x11in) i.d.1824verso W/C over pencil gum arabic
£1500	$2685	(11-Apr-91 S82/R) Knaresborough Castle, Yorkshire (29x37cm-11x15in) s.d.1845 W/C over pencil htd bodycol
£2600	$5122	(15-Nov-90 S110/R) The Thames at Greenwich (15x22cm-6x9in) W/C over pencil
£2800	$5544	(30-Jan-91 S121) Hay barge on river (18x26cm-7x10in) W/C over pencil
£3000	$4950	(11-Jul-91 S195/R) Travellers in Welsh valley (36x54cm-14x21in) s.d.1852 W/C over pencil
£3000	$5880	(20-Nov-90 RB679/R) Going to hayfield (20x30cm-8x12in) s. W/C
£3400	$5678	(22-Jul-91 SWS802/R) Off Greenwish (12x17cm-5x7in) s.d.1828 W/C scratching out htd.bodycol.
£3800	$7486	(13-Nov-90 C137/R) Evening, Lancaster Sands (18x25cm-7x10in) s.d.1837 pencil W/C htd.white
£4500	$8055	(9-Apr-91 C113/R) Lancaster Sands (20x28cm-8x11in) s.d.1827 pencil W/C
£5500	$10835	(15-Nov-90 S128/R) Women on country road near stream (18x27cm-7x11in) s.d.1834 W/C over pencil htd.bodycol
£6000	$10740	(11-Apr-91 S74/R) Salmon trap (52x72cm-20x28in) W/C over pencil htd bodycol

COX, David (jnr) (1809-1885) British

£400	$708	(21-Mar-91 CSK52/R) Figures at the edge of the wood (36x53cm-14x21in) s.d.1854 pencil W/C htd.white
£750	$1478	(13-Nov-90 C71/R) Mounted guardsmen on road approaching Windsor Castle (18x13cm-7x5in) pencil W/C
£950	$1596	(17-Jul-91 ME2) Bolton Abbey with figure and dog to foreground (25x38cm-10x15in) s. W/C

COX, David (snr) (1783-1859) British

£350	$627	(9-Apr-91 C107 a) Procession of monks below monastery (11x18cm-4x7in) chk W/C
£600	$1074	(9-Apr-91 C114) Figures and cattle in woodland clearing (37x54cm-15x21in) s. pencil W/C
£1100	$1969	(9-Apr-91 C113 a) Hunter in rocky gorge (27x36cm-11x14in) s. pencil chk W/C
£1100	$2123	(10-Dec-90 PHB18/R) Ludford church (28x37cm-11x15in) s.d.1852 pencil W/C
£3800	$6802	(9-Apr-91 C116/R) Peat gatherers near Bettws-y-Coed, North Wales (47x74cm-19x29in) s. chk W/C
£10000	$17900	(9-Apr-91 C115/R) Pont-y-Cysylty with the Dee and Chirk Aqueduct beyond (27x37cm-11x15in) s.i.d.1833 pencil W/C htd.bodycol

COX, David (snr-attrib) (1783-1859) British

| £3396 | $6419 | (27-Sep-90 D.V139/R) River landscape with shepherd driving flock over bridge (60x90cm-24x35in) (A.S 70000) |

COX, Garstin (1892-?) British

£550	$1045	(28-Feb-91 DLY166/R) Horse and cart passing a woodland pond (64x76cm-25x30in) s.
£600	$1002	(4-Jun-91 SWS1876/R) Farm buildings at blossom time (50x61cm-20x24in) s.
£650	$1151	(18-Mar-91 FEN90) The colourful Cornish coast (51x61cm-20x24in) s. board
£800	$1504	(19-Sep-90 ZZ.B764) Kynance Cove (51x61cm-20x24in) s. board
£900	$1611	(14-Mar-91 L155/R) Road to sea, Cornwall - thatched cottages amidst trees, in distance sea (69x91cm-27x36in) s.
£920	$1748	(28-Feb-91 DLY134) Sunset on the Cornish coast (64x76cm-25x30in) s.

COX, Kenyon C (1856-1919) American

| £2105 | $4000 | (9-Jan-91 CH.NY206) Bookplate for Jeannette Prentiss Cox. Torso of Hope both s. one i.d.07 ink board one i.pencil |

COYLE, Thomas (20th C) British?

| £520 | $879 | (17-Apr-91 CG126) Autumn fields (89x122cm-35x48in) s. board |

COYPEL (style) (17/18th C) French

| £1487 | $2900 | (21-Oct-90 HG.C3) Bacchanal in graden (69x97cm-27x38in) |

COYPEL, Antoine (1661-1722) French

| £2000 | $3260 | (2-Jul-91 C156/R) Angel (12x18cm-5x7in) red white chk squared |
| £7839 | $12856 | (21-Jun-91 SY.MO264/R) Tete d'enfant (275x239cm-108x94in) pierre noire sanguinne pastel (F.FR 78000) |

COYPEL, Antoine (attrib) (1661-1722) French

| £647 | $1120 | (22-May-91 PLF.P25) Jupiter assis (34x25cm-13x10in) sanguinne pierre noire htd.white chk. (F.FR 6500) |

COYPEL, Antoine (circle) (1661-1722) French

| £5860 | $10490 | (8-Apr-91 CH.R105/R) Vertunno e Pomona (66x91cm-26x36in) (I.L 13000000) |

COYPEL, Antoine (style) (1661-1722) French

| £5778 | $9649 | (6-Jun-91 D.V26/R) Bacchus and Ariadne on Naxos (63x80cm-25x31in) (A.S 120000) |

COYPEL, Charles Antoine (1694-1752) French
£1300 $2509   (11-Dec-90 C77/R) A scene from the Commedia dell'arte (19x15cm-7x6in) red chk.
£1325 $2558   (14-Dec-90 LEB.P22) L'arrivee de visiteurs (43x62cm-17x24in) oil crayon sanguinne (F.FR 13000)

COYPEL, Charles Antoine (style) (1694-1752) French
£1900 $3648   (29-Nov-90 CSK34/R) Diana and Callisto (65x81cm-26x32in)

COYPEL, Noel (attrib) (1628-1707) French
£9455 $18343   (7-Dec-90 SY.MO172/R) Triomphe d'Apollon (74x79cm-29x31in) (F.FR 92000)

COYPEL, Noel Nicolas (1690-1734) French
£113052 $219322   (5-Dec-90 APT.P75/R) Venus et l'amour (126x108cm-50x43in) s.d.1725 (F.FR 1100000)

COYPEL, Noel Nicolas (circle) (1690-1734) French
£842 $1600   (9-Jan-91 CH.NY39 a/R) Triton with arms raised (54x38cm-21x15in) black red chk htd white stumped

COZAR (1944-) Spanish
£1100 $2200   (6-Feb-91 ANS.M85/R) Paisaje (75x150cm-30x59in) s. s.d.1940verso (S.P 200000)

COZENS, Alexander (?-1786) British
£750 $1238   (9-Jul-91 C31/R) Italianate landscape with waterfall (18x24cm-7x9in) s.d.1751 i.verso wash sold with another W/C
£1500 $2475   (9-Jul-91 C30/R) Coastal landscape (17x21cm-7x8in) s. wash sold with two other drawings
£2400 $4032   (22-Apr-91 PH216) Temple by lake (15x19cm-6x7in) s. wash
£2600 $4290   (9-Jul-91 C32 a) Coastal landscape (95x14cm-37x6in) pen ink wash

COZENS, John Robert (1752-1799) British
£4000 $6600   (9-Jul-91 C89/R) Convent from Mirabella (25x37cm-10x15in) pencil W/C
£52000 $93080   (11-Apr-91 S19/R) In gardens of villa Pamphili, Rome (24x18cm-9x7in) W/C over pencil
£100000 $179000   (11-Apr-91 S78/R) Cetara on Gulf of Salerno (36x52cm-14x20in) s. W/C over pencil

COZZENS, F S (1856-1928) American
£474 $900   (3-Mar-91 LIT.L202) Schooners at Anchor (33x23cm-13x9in) s.d.1900 W/C
£575 $1150   (10-Feb-91 LIT.L39/R) Tugboat and scooner (48x33cm-19x13in) W/C
£587 $1150   (27-Jan-91 LIT.L13a) Tugboat and schooner (48x33cm-19x13in) s. W/C

COZZENS, Frederick Schiller (1856-1928) American
£749 $1400   (30-Aug-90 MFA.C99/R) Whaling crew (23x46cm-9x18in) canvas laid down
£476 $800   (27-Apr-91 YFA.M73/R) Sailing off Lighthouse point (18x28cm-7x11in) s.d.1903 W/C
£503 $850   (17-Apr-91 D.NY42/R) Brig on swell (20x33cm-8x13in) s.d.90 W/C cardboard
£529 $1000   (25-Sep-90 CE.NY40/R) Full sail (39x62cm-15x24in) s.d.07 W/C pencil board
£703 $1300   (8-Mar-91 S.BM242/R) Off shore, Sunset (46x36cm-18x14in) s.d.94 W/C
£798 $1500   (7-Aug-90 RB.HY47/R) Tug 'Ajax' (36x58cm-14x23in) s.d.07 W/C
£1058 $2000   (25-Sep-90 CE.NY17/R) Finish of the Race, Friday the 13th (35x54cm-14x21in) s.d.93 W/C paper laid down on board

CRABEELS, Florent (1829-1896) Flemish
£1855 $3599   (8-Dec-90 KV.L69/R) Shepherd with flock (28x36cm-11x14in) s. panel (B.FR 110000)

CRABETH, Wouter II (1593-1644) Dutch
£5128 $10000   (11-Oct-90 SY.NY143/R) Jacob and Esau (109x146cm-43x57in)

CRADOCK, Marmaduke (1660-1717) British
£1550 $2496   (25-Jun-91 AG404/R) Peacock, hawk and poultry in the grounds of country house (49x67cm-19x26in)
£1600 $3040   (1-Mar-91 C59/R) Ducks on river (31x36cm-12x14in)
£5500 $9845   (12-Apr-91 C79/R) Two cockerels, hen and other fowl in landscape (81x122cm-32x48in)
£11500 $18745   (2-Jul-91 PH84/R) Farmyard fowl and peacock before house in landscape (73x92cm-29x36in)
£12000 $19800   (10-Jul-91 S55/R) Still life of exotic birds in landscape (74x62cm-29x24in) s.

CRADOCK, Marmaduke (attrib) (1660-1717) British
£24706 $42000   (31-May-91 CH.NY113/R) Two peacocks, doves, chickens and rooster in park (89x128cm-35x50in) bears init.

CRADOCK, Marmaduke (circle) (1660-1717) British
£2821 $5500   (10-Oct-90 CH.NY114 a/R) Peacock, rooster, chickens and other birds in river landscape (63x76cm-25x30in)

CRADOCK, Marmaduke (school) (1660-1717) British
£2471 $4200   (30-May-91 CE.NY61) Peahens, ducks and other birds by pond (63x77cm-25x30in)

CRADOCK, Marmaduke (style) (1660-1717) British
£2695 $4500   (23-Jan-91 D.NY83) Pigeons in coop (112x91cm-44x36in)

CRAESBEECK, Joos van (1606-1654) Flemish
£9891 $17705   (9-Apr-91 APT.P14/R) Un buveur pres d'un poele (43x344cm-17x135in) panel
             (F.FR 100000)

CRAESBEECK, Joos van (attrib) (1606-1654) Flemish
£1505 $2934   (10-Oct-90 APT.P470/R) Scene de sorcellerie (30x25cm-12x10in) panel
             (F.FR 15000)
£1926 $3216   (6-Jun-91 D.V80/R) The merry drinker (14x11cm-6x4in) panel (A.S 40000)
£1954 $3498   (14-Mar-91 D.V253/R) Pipe smoker with memento mori (20x16cm-8x6in) panel
             (A.S 40000)

CRAFFONARA, Aurelio (1875-1945) Italian
£589 $996   (16-Apr-91 CH.R108) Casolari (48x34cm-19x13in) s.d.1915 W/C board
*   (I.L 1300000)*

CRAFT, Percy R (1856-?) British
£3287 $6377   (22-Aug-90 RAS.K50/R) Pretty Polly (83x58cm-33x23in) s.d.1893-94
             (D.KR 38000)

CRAIG, Frank (1874-1918) British
£2874 $5000   (27-Mar-91 B.SF4238/R) Lady arriving on Graceyard Street
             (60x60cm-24x24in) s.d.1902

CRAIG, Henry Robertson (1916-1984) British
£926 $1787   (12-Dec-90 CH.E121/R) In the forest, Chantilly (60x81cm-24x32in) s.
             i.verso (E.P 1000)

CRAIG, Isaac Eugene (19th C) American
£807 $1300   (26-Jun-91 D.NY23) Among archives (84x64cm-33x25in) s.i.
£876 $1700   (5-Dec-90 D.NY4/R) Girl in a Florentine library (84x64cm-33x25in) s.i.

CRAIG, J Humbert (?-1944) British
£563 $1098   (10-Oct-90 WO.CO4) River Lagan (20x28cm-8x11in) s. (E.P 625)
£650 $1274   (24-Jan-91 CSK47) Landscape with trees (24x34cm-9x13in) s. panel
£2000 $3920   (23-Jan-91 WO.CO11) Cattle grazing (23x33cm-9x13in) s. (E.P 2200)
£2593 $5004   (12-Dec-90 CH.E171/R) Cattle in sunlit landscape (38x51cm-15x20in) s.
             (E.P 2800)
£3000 $5850   (10-Oct-90 S3/R) Fishermen on the Antrim coast (38x51cm-15x20in) s.
£4000 $7800   (26-Oct-90 CG98/R) Creek near Dundalk, Co Louth (30x47cm-12x19in) s.
             panel
£6000 $11820   (13-Nov-90 SWS446/R) Galway fisherfolk (49x59cm-19x23in) s.
£10000 $19600   (7-Nov-90 S99/R) Mayo lough (51x62cm-20x24in) s.

CRAIG, James Stevenson (19th C) British
£3500 $6265   (14-Mar-91 L185/R) Love letter - young man secretly giving letter to
             girl at spinning wheel (84x109cm-33x43in) s.d.1864

CRAIG, Sybil (19/20th C) Australian?
£803 $1542   (26-Nov-90 SY.ME68/R) Still life with marigolds (39x39cm-15x15in) s.
             artist's board (A.D 2000)
£849 $1673   (13-Nov-90 J.M270/R) Evening boats, Half Moon Bay (42x37cm-17x15in) s.
             canvas on board (A.D 2200)
£995 $1682   (16-Apr-91 J.M120/R) Gladioli (75x61cm-30x24in) s. canvas on board
             (A.D 2200)
£1116 $2198   (31-Oct-90 CH.S5) Still life (59x48cm-23x19in) s. card (A.D 2800)
£1176 $1988   (16-Apr-91 J.M249/R) Christmas Lillies (68x56cm-27x22in) s. canvas on
             board (A.D 2600)
£656 $1293   (13-Nov-90 J.M53) Family group (48x37cm-19x15in) s. gouache (A.D 1700)
£1055 $2025   (14-Aug-90 SY.ME1/R) Colour translation (40x50cm-16x20in) s.i. gouache
*   (A.D 2500)*

CRAIG, Thomas (19th C) ?
£1054 $1750   (11-Jan-91 DM.D2153/R) Landscape scene (23x43cm-9x17in) s.

CRAIG, Thomas Bigelow (1849-1924) American
£698 $1250   (11-Apr-91 FA.PH804) Summer morning (15x20cm-6x8in) s. board
£1105 $2100   (15-Sep-90 S.W2752/R) Below the old saw mill (25x36cm-10x14in) s.
             s.d.1910 verso
£1105 $2100   (15-Sep-90 S.W2753/R) By the mill pond (25x36cm-10x14in) s.
£1282 $2500   (20-Oct-90 W.W78/R) October in the catskills, woodland valley
             (61x86cm-24x34in) s. s.i.d.1902verso
£1337 $2500   (30-Aug-90 MFA.C94/R) Autumn scene (46x36cm-18x14in) s.d.1888
£1378 $2700   (9-Nov-90 DOU.M2) A corner of the meadow (33x23cm-13x9in)

CRAIG, William Marshall (1788-1828) British
£1037 $1700   (19-Jun-91 B.SF1910/R) English fisherfolk (34x24cm-13x9in) s. W/C board

CRAIG-WALLACE, Robert (fl.1910-1914) British
£700 $1309   (28-Aug-90 S979/R) Narrows of the Kyles of Bute (49x74cm-19x29in) s.
             board

CRALI, Tullio (20th C) Italian
£871 $1429   (20-Jun-91 F.M366/R) Composizione (10x15cm-4x6in) s. panel
                          (I.L 1900000)
£2272 $4475   (30-Oct-90 F.R187/R) I naufragi (80x70cm-31x28in) s. s.d.36verso panel
                          (I.L 5000000)
£871 $1429   (20-Jun-91 F.M367/R) Composizione (11x16cm-4x6in) s. mixed media panel
                          (I.L 1900000)

CRAM, Allen G (1886-1947) American
£561 $1100   (13-Feb-91 B.SF2110/R) Gathering, Santa Barbara fiesta (61x71cm-24x28in)
                          s.

CRAMER, Hendrik Willem (1809-?) Dutch
£2988 $5827   (24-Oct-90 GD.B249/R) Dutch interior with figures (49x63cm-19x25in) s.
                          (S.FR 7500)

CRAMOYSAN, Marcel (20th C) French
£650 $1131   (28-Mar-91 CSK154/R) Les enfants de Nazare (65x50cm-26x20in) s.
                          s.i.verso
£729 $1428   (25-Nov-90 L.C5/R) Le port de Rouen (58x80cm-23x31in) s. hardboard
                          (F.FR 7200)
£1120 $2207   (4-Nov-90 FE.P112) Marine a la Rochelle (55x38cm-22x15in) s.
                          (F.FR 11000)

CRANACH, Lucas (15/16th C) German
£30070 $58035   (10-Dec-90 L.K22/R) River landscape with town and castle on rock
                          (43x29cm-17x11in) panel fragment (DM 86000)

CRANACH, Lucas (circle) (15/16th C) German
£3279 $6164   (19-Sep-90 GK.Z812) Portrait of cleric (17x12cm-7x5in) panel (S.FR 8000)

CRANACH, Lucas (elder) (1472-1553) German
£63508 $113679   (14-Mar-91 D.V65/R) Madonna and Child seated before velvet drapes
                          (79x56cm-31x22in) s.snake device panel (A.S 1300000)
£120603 $197789   (22-Jun-91 CH.MO114/R) L'Adoration des Bergers (15x20cm-6x8in) s. panel
                          (F.FR 1200000)
£260000 $449800   (24-May-91 C4/R) Charity (49x33cm-19x13in) s.serpent device inset panel

CRANACH, Lucas (elder-studio) (1472-1553) German
£3425 $6130   (13-Mar-91 N.M394/R) Johann der Bestandige, Kurfurst von Sachsen
                          (13x12cm-5x5in) i. panel (DM 10000)
£23464 $42000   (11-Apr-91 SY.NY187/R) The god Mercury waking Paris to judge the contest
                          of the Golden Apple (61x40cm-24x16in) i.mono. panel
£38000 $73340   (12-Dec-90 S19/R) Portraits of John the Steadfast and Frederic the Wise,
                          Electors of Saxony (20x14cm-8x6in) one s.d.1533 panel pair

CRANACH, Lucas (elder-style) (1472-1553) German
£2938 $5788   (14-Nov-90 D.V326/R) Christ and the Woman Taken in Adultery
                          (48x76cm-19x30in) panel (A.S 60000)
£7500 $12225   (3-Jul-91 S243/R) Reclining water nymph (18x23cm-7x9in) bears i.d.1657
                          verso panel

CRANACH, Lucas (style) (15/16th C) German
£1232 $2070   (23-Apr-91 RAS.K219/R) Madonna and Child with St.John (23x17cm-9x7in)
                          (D.KR 14000)
£1351 $2297   (27-May-91 L.K29/R) Madonna and Child (17x13cm-7x5in) panel after
                          Cranach (DM 4000)
£2647 $4500   (30-May-91 CE.NY52/R) Portrait of Philip Melanchthon wearing fur trimmed
                          robe (32x22cm-13x9in) bears i. panel
£4200 $6846   (2-Jul-91 PH102/R) Portrait of lady standing with young boy dressed in
                          gown edged in ermine (59x42cm-23x17in) panel
£7647 $13000   (31-May-91 CH.NY138/R) Venus (37x21cm-15x8in) panel

CRANACH, Lucas (younger) (1515-1586) German
£19474 $37000   (11-Jan-91 CH.NY36/R) Portrait of Caspar Cruciger, holding book
                          (36x23cm-14x9in) s. panel
£34000 $65620   (11-Dec-90 PH73/R) Madonna and Child with St.Anne, seated in landscape
                          (42x27cm-17x11in) panel
£37849 $73805   (24-Oct-90 GD.B250/R) Rechtfertigung des Sunders durch den Glauben
                          (19x25cm-7x10in) c.1550 i.with snake and wing panel (S.FR 95000)

CRANACH, Lucas (younger-after) (1515-1586) German
£10135 $17230   (31-May-91 GB.B5098) Portrait of Martin Luther (50x40cm-20x16in) s.with
                          snake device panel (DM 30000)

CRANBOURNE, D (?) British?
£850 $1505   (21-Mar-91 CSK198/R) A dark hunter and a grey hunter in a coastal
                          landscape (61x76cm-24x30in)

CRANCH, Christopher Pearse (1813-1892) American
£1042 $2000   (17-Dec-90 SY.NY41/R) Autumn landscape with boy fishing
                          (66x91cm-26x36in) s.

CRANE, Bruce (1857-1934) American
£532 $1000   (19-Sep-90 B.SF2801/R) Landscape with pond (26x36cm-10x14in) s.
£613 $1000   (5-Jul-91 S.W2637) Walk through the stone weall (13x23cm-5x9in) s. panel

CRANE, Bruce (1857-1934) American-cont.
£625	$1050	(28-Apr-91 LIT.L131) Spring landscape with cottage (20x25cm-8x10in) s. panel
£698	$1200	(19-May-91 LIT.L174) Across fields (20x25cm-8x10in) s. board
£714	$1200	(28-Apr-91 LIT.L131 a) Bronxville, New York landscape (25x36cm-10x14in) s. panel
£806	$1500	(9-Sep-90 LIT.L298) Old Lyme landscape (28x33cm-11x13in) s. d.1927 verso board
£1563	$3000	(17-Dec-90 SY.NY82/R) Grey lowlands (36x51cm-14x20in) s.d.1923
£2910	$5500	(27-Sep-90 CH.NY220/R) Boats on shore (51x76cm-20x30in) s.
£3352	$6000	(14-Mar-91 CH.NY177/R) Morning in November (46x61cm-18x24in) s.
£3590	$7000	(21-Oct-90 HG.C50) Autumn morning (33x48cm-13x19in) s. board
£4167	$7000	(28-Apr-91 HG.C13) First snow (64x76cm-25x30in) s.
£5491	$9500	(12-May-91 H.C112/R) Landscape with flowering apple trees (61x104cm-24x41in) s.
£10825	$21000	(5-Dec-90 D.NY25/R) Country landscape with lily pond (58x91cm-23x36in) s.i.
£1221	*$2100*	*(15-May-91 SY.NY79/R) Winter landscape (30x39cm-12x15in) s. W/C*

CRANE, Frederick (1847-1915) American
| £710 | $1200 | (1-May-91 B.SF5253/R) Mountain stream in spring (30x41cm-12x16in) s. |

CRANE, Walter (1845-1915) British
£10256	$20000	(24-Oct-90 CH.NY345/R) L'Art et la vie (153x90cm-60x35in) mono.d.MCMVII
£500	*$970*	*(6-Dec-90 S353/R) Symbolic figures approaching young woman seated on throne (17x34cm-7x13in) mono.d.98 ink dr*
£2200	*$4268*	*(6-Dec-90 S354/R) Illustrations for John Lane editions of 'Mother Hubbard's Picture Book' (27x23cm-11x9in) ink dr set of four*
£8000	*$13040*	*(14-Jun-91 C10/R) Sketch for 'The Fate of Persephone' (21x45cm-8x18in) mono.d.1877 W/C bodycol.*

CRANENBURGH, Hendrik van (1754-1832) Dutch
| £898 | $1751 | (25-Oct-90 VN.R20/R) Figures in a churchyard (48x61cm-19x24in) s.d.1832 W/C after van Heyden (D.FL 3000) |

CRASH (1961-) American
| £6078 | $11853 | (22-Oct-90 BR.M56/R) Untitled (130x79cm-51x31in) s.verso acrylic (I.L 13500000) |

CRAUSAZ, Max (19th C) ?
| £1036 | $2020 | (24-Oct-90 GD.B251/R) Le marche au betail a Carouge (70x105cm-28x41in) s. (S.FR 2600) |

CRAWFORD, Edmund Thornton (1806-1885) British
£600	$1008	(23-Apr-91 S20) Wayside chat (28x39cm-11x15in) s. panel
£800	$1560	(11-Oct-90 CG141) Dutch shipping (25x36cm-10x14in) s.i.label verso
£1500	$2520	(23-Apr-91 S19/R) Canal scene, near Hague (30x45cm-12x18in) s.verso board
£1600	$3120	(16-Oct-90 CG204/R) Evening coastal scene with beached fishing boats and figures (41x51cm-16x20in) s.
£1800	$3510	(16-Oct-90 CG205/R) West Pans, Firth of Forth (36x53cm-14x21in) s. i.d.1861verso
£6000	$9660	(27-Jun-91 CG25/R) Scheveningen, fishing boats landing fish (68x91cm-27x36in) s.d.1857 i. stretcher

CRAWFORD, John Gardiner (20th C) British
| £1500 | $2925 | (10-Oct-90 PHG41) Harvest House (58x89cm-23x35in) s. acrylic board |

CRAWFORD, Ralston (1906-) American
| £12291 | $22000 | (12-Apr-91 SY.NY88/R) Net (33x46cm-13x18in) s. |

CRAWFORD, Robert C (19th C) British
| £2700 | $4509 | (5-Jun-91 S125/R) Still life of roses (53x35cm-21x14in) init. |

CRAWHALL, Joseph (1861-1913) British
| *£2400* | *$4728* | *(1-Nov-90 B130 a) The goat (16x12cm-6x5in) s.i. W/C* |
| *£11000* | *$21560* | *(22-Nov-90 CG545/R) Fluffy (45x29cm-18x11in) i. pen brush ink W/C htd.bodycol* |

CRAWSHAW, Thomas (19th C) British
| £2000 | $3780 | (27-Sep-90 CSK93/R) Harvest time (60x91cm-24x36in) s.d.1864 |

CRAXTON, John (1922-?) British
£4500	$7515	(6-Jun-91 C207/R) Lanzarote landscape (82x82cm-32x32in) s. acrylic tempera lava board
£55000	$92950	(1-May-91 S53/R) Boy, girl and cat (203x117cm-80x46in) s.d.48-49
£900	*$1503*	*(6-Jun-91 C203/R) Drinking lion (45x56cm-18x22in) s.d.70 pen brush ink gouache board*
£5200	*$9620*	*(8-Mar-91 C110/R) Man playing bouzouki (28x21cm-11x8in) s.d.56 gouache*

CRAYER, Gaspar de (circle) (1584-1669) Flemish
| £977 | $1749 | (14-Mar-91 D.V272/R) Christ as Man of Sorrow (36x26cm-14x10in) (A.S 20000) |

CRAYER, Gaspar de (style) (1584-1669) Flemish
£2000 $3900   (25-Oct-90 CSK94/R) Saint John the Evangelist. Saint James the Greater (122x88cm-48x35in) i. canvas on board pair

CREBASSA, Paul Edouard (1870-1912) French
£2988 $5169   (24-May-91 FB.P164/R) Le bal (38x46cm-15x18in) s. (F.FR 30000)

CREBER, Frank (1959-) British
£800 $1568   (13-Feb-91 B129/R) Flower border (101x142cm-40x56in) s.i.d.1990 verso

CRECCOLINI, Giovanni Antonio see GRECOLINI, Giovanni Antonio

CREFFIELD, Dennis (1931-) British
£550 $930   (2-May-91 C133/R) York Minster, East window (85x61cm-33x24in) chl

CREHAY, Gerard Antoine (1844-1936) Belgian
£1600 $2688   (16-Jul-91 C93/R) Tiger breaking cover in the jungle (63x101cm-25x40in) s.d.1893

CREIXAMS (1893-1965) Spanish
£3472 $5972   (19-May-91 ZZ.F150/R) La veillee des gitans (100x100cm-39x39in) s. (F.FR 35000)

CREIXAMS, Pierre (1893-1965) Spanish
£1807 $2910   (24-Jun-91 PR.P107/R) L'Espagnole a la mantille (73x60cm-29x24in) s. (F.FR 18000)
£2590 $4402   (29-May-91 GL.P124) Mere et enfants (100x81cm-39x32in) s. (F.FR 26000)
£2597 $5116   (30-Oct-90 I.N79/R) Joueuse de mandoline (61x450cm-24x177in) s. (F.FR 25500)
£2722 $5307   (28-Oct-90 M.V145/R) Jeune homme a la chemise bleue (55x38cm-22x15in) s. (F.FR 27000)
£3517 $6752   (2-Dec-90 M.V46/R) Femme nue allongee (54x65cm-21x26in) s. (F.FR 34500)
£3629 $7077   (26-Oct-90 APT.P94/R) La corrida (65x92cm-26x36in) s. (F.FR 36000)
£4383 $8416   (2-Dec-90 M.V110/R) Nu allonge (73x92cm-29x36in) s. (F.FR 43000)

CREMA, Giovanni Battista (1883-1964) Italian
£1360 $2298   (16-Apr-91 CH.R165) Peschereccio armato in caccia somergibili, il flottiglia (50x55cm-20x22in) s.i.verso panel (I.L 3000000)
£14594 $24371   (6-Jun-91 F.M297/R) La vanga (92x120cm-36x47in) s. (I.L 32000000)

CREMER, Jan (1940-) Dutch
£1238 $2390   (13-Dec-90 SY.AM393) Untitled (92x30cm-36x12in) s.d.verso s.stretcher (D.FL 4000)
£2102 $3637   (23-May-91 SY.AM284/R) Untitled (48x68cm-19x27in) s.d.1959 board (D.FL 7000)
£2703 $4676   (23-May-91 SY.AM289/R) Hirosjima (42x114cm-17x45in) s.d.58 s.i.d.verso hessian (D.FL 9000)
£3715 $7170   (13-Dec-90 SY.AM268/R) Untitled (120x50cm-47x20in) s.d.61 (D.FL 12000)
£3003 $5195   (23-May-91 SY.AM283/R) Crisiszee (86x110cm-34x43in) s.d.59 i.verso (D.FL 10000)

CREMERS, P (19/20th C) European
£1000 $1790   (14-Mar-91 B48/R) A still life of yellow roses (71x83cm-28x33in) s.

CREMIEUX, Edouard (1856-?) French
£650 $1060   (5-Jul-91 APT.P110) Bord de mer Mediterraneen (32x33cm-13x13in) s. (F.FR 6500)

CREMONA, Italo (1905-) Italian
£4585 $7519   (20-Jun-91 F.M320/R) Nudo disteso in un interno (60x50cm-24x20in) s.d.1947 (I.L 10000000)

CREMONESE SCHOOL (?) Italian
£2200 $3806   (20-May-91 SWS105/R) A lady spinning (26x21cm-10x8in) c.1600

CREMONESE SCHOOL, 16th C Italian
£1000 $1630   (1-Jul-91 S185) Three putti in chariot drawn by two lions (13x18cm-5x7in) red black chk

CREMONESI, Giovanni (19th C) Italian
£686 $1351   (14-Nov-90 F.M29/R) Trompe l'oeil con carta geografica dell'Arciducato d'Austria (42x52cm-17x20in) s. W/C (I.L 1500000)

CREMONINI, Leonardo (1925-) Italian
£4337 $8500   (12-Feb-91 SY.NY330/R) Lutte de taureaux (71x127cm-28x50in) s.d.54 s.i.d.verso canvas on masonite
£18299 $32755   (9-Apr-91 BG.P106 o/R) Mon cap a la mer (90x66cm-35x26in) (F.FR 185000)
£599 $1000   (26-Jul-91 E.EDM137/R) Bagnante Scott Acqua (30x48cm-12x19in) ink

CREPIN, Louis Philippe (1772-1851) French
£4111 $7975   (7-Dec-90 SY.MO174/R) Paysages (45x55cm-18x22in) bears i.verso pair (F.FR 40000)

CRESPI, Daniele (1590-1630) Italian
£1500 $2535   (16-Apr-91 C122/R) Studies of a standing Bishop (24x29cm-9x11in) i. blk.chk.ink wash

CRESPI, Daniele (1590-1630) Italian-cont.
£1850 $3016   (1-Jul-91 S163/R) *Study of kneeling bishop holding book, skull on floor beside him (15x12cm-6x5in) bears i. brush ink wash htd white over blk chk*
£7368 $14000   (8-Jan-91 SY.NY182/R) *St.Jerome in penitence (20x18cm-8x7in) ink wash*

CRESPI, Giovanni Battista (attrib) (1557-1633) Italian
£3352 $6000   (11-Apr-91 SY.NY158/R) Boy restraining dog (64x51cm-25x20in)
£1800 $2934   (1-Jul-91 S3/R) *Study for pendentive with figures of Christ and putto (32x20cm-13x8in) bears i. black chk pen wash htd white*

CRESPI, Giuseppe Maria (1665-1747) Italian
£38764 $64736   (4-Jun-91 CH.R565/R) Donna con due bambini che bisticciano (51x36cm-20x14in) (I.L 85000000)
£50201 $80823   (25-Jun-91 APT.P9/R) Bergere endormie (22x16cm-9x6in) copper (F.FR 500000)
£85000 $138550   (3-Jul-91 S56/R) Peasant girl (37x27cm-15x11in) copper
£6840 $12107   (19-Mar-91 F.M202/R) Strage degli innocenti (43x34cm-17x13in) sanguine (I.L 15000000)
£28000 $45640   (1-Jul-91 S16/R) *Young man teaching bird to sing (24x39cm-9x15in) red chk*

CRESPI, Giuseppe Maria (attrib) (1665-1747) Italian
£6154 $12000   (10-Oct-90 CH.NY217/R) The Holy Family (30x40cm-12x16in)

CRESPI, Giuseppe Maria (circle) (1665-1747) Italian
£1131 $1900   (17-Jul-91 SY.NY57/R) The Holy Family (46x36cm-18x14in)

CRESPI, Giuseppe Maria (studio) (1665-1747) Italian
£2705 $4842   (8-Apr-91 CH.R74/R) Scene satirice di vecchie che ne curano un altra con clistere. Presso unfocolare (26x37cm-10x15in) pair (I.L 6000000)

CRESPI, Giuseppe Maria (style) (1665-1747) Italian
£1700 $2941   (20-May-91 SWS207) Saint Peter (62x46cm-24x18in)
£9000 $17730   (31-Oct-90 S170/R) Hecuba blinding Polymnestor (191x179cm-75x70in)

CRESPI, Luigi (attrib) (1710-1779) Italian
£9529 $18581   (10-Oct-90 APT.P471) La flagellation du Christ (29x38cm-11x15in) panel oval (F.FR 95000)

CRESTON, Rene Yves (20th C) French
£786 $1533   (28-Oct-90 G.SB163/R) Le dechargement de la peche (50x61cm-20x24in) s. (F.FR 7800)

CRESWICK, T (1811-1869) British
£500 $815   (13-Jun-91 LE344) Springtime wooded glade with bridge and stream and view of distant castle (51x41cm-20x16in) s. i.verso board
£1450 $2842   (23-Nov-90 CBB87) Woodland scene with sheep (43x69cm-17x27in)

CRESWICK, Thomas (1811-1869) British
£638 $1250   (11-Nov-90 LIT.L32) Going home (30x51cm-12x20in) s.
£1050 $1806   (14-May-91 SWS182/R) The meeting of the waters (18x15cm-7x6in) init. i.verso panel
£1500 $2955   (13-Nov-90 PH58/R) Waiting by the gate (24x20cm-9x8in) board
£1596 $3000   (19-Sep-90 B.SF2667/R) Fishermen on a river (89x110cm-35x43in)
£2500 $4875   (18-Oct-90 SC3078/R) A farmstead in Surrey (39x59cm-15x23in) s.d.1849
£3800 $7486   (14-Nov-90 S123/R) The young anglers (41x50cm-16x20in) s.
£6000 $11340   (26-Sep-90 S93/R) Girl and dog on woodland path (61x50cm-24x20in) indist.s. panel
£11000 $21670   (14-Nov-90 S113/R) View of Windsor Castle (96x147cm-38x58in) s.
£11795 $23000   (24-Oct-90 CH.NY306/R) The nearest way in summer (117x111cm-46x44in)

CRESWICK, Thomas (attrib) (1811-1869) British
£600 $1026   (30-Jul-91 SWS50) Figures and cattle on a woodland path (32x39cm-13x15in)

CRETAN SCHOOL, 18th C Greek
£11765 $20000   (31-May-91 CH.NY150/R) Madonna and Child with two saints (49x67cm-19x26in) indis.i. embossed gold ground panel

CRETEN-GEORGES (1887-1966) Belgian
£624 $1079   (25-May-91 KV.L53) Girl in a green dress (42x32cm-17x13in) s.d.1925 board (B.FR 38000)
£818 $1375   (23-Apr-91 C.A85/R) Self-portrait (93x78cm-37x31in) s. panel (B.FR 50000)
£3287 $6409   (23-Oct-90 C.A344/R) Seated half-nude (100x80cm-39x31in) s.d.1925 (B.FR 200000)
£657 $1136   (25-May-91 KV.L54) *Woman resting (34x26cm-13x10in) s.d.1920 chl. (B.FR 40000)*
£788 $1364   (25-May-91 KV.L55) *Figure (65x53cm-26x21in) s.d.1920 chl. (B.FR 48000)*

CRETI, Donato (1671-1749) Italian
£5263 $10000   (8-Jan-91 SY.NY79/R) Two choir boys (33x26cm-13x10in) bears i. verso paper
£1186 $2098   (19-Mar-91 F.M288/R) *Figura in raccoglimento (12x11cm-5x4in) bistre ink (I.L 2600000)*

CRETI, Donato (1671-1749) Italian-cont.

£1500	$2445	(2-Jul-91 C284/R) Sleeping child holding apple (18x24cm-7x9in) with i. pen
£1824	$3228	(19-Mar-91 F.M269/R) Figura di giovane giacente. Studio per la stessa figura (24x34cm-9x13in) sanguine double-sided (I.L 4000000)
£1915	$3390	(19-Mar-91 F.M291/R) Sacra Famiglia con San Giovannino (16x12cm-6x5in) ink oval (I.L 4200000)
£3158	$6000	(9-Jan-91 CH.NY20/R) Studies of heads with vase. Studies of heads (25x19cm-10x7in) pen double-sided
£4560	$8071	(19-Mar-91 F.M292/R) Testa di guerriero (22x18cm-9x7in) pencil (I.L 10000000)
£5000	$8150	(2-Jul-91 C116/R) Saint Jerome attended by angels (24x16cm-9x6in) pen
£5016	$8878	(19-Mar-91 F.M233/R) Due studi per una scena allegorica con Amore in catene (26x41cm-10x16in) ink (I.L 11000000)
£8000	$13040	(1-Jul-91 S98/R) Landscape with two women conversing in foreground, boy seated under tree (34x23cm-13x9in) pen

CRETIEN, L (19th C) French

£1404	$2738	(12-Oct-90 ZZ.F61/R) Eglise sur la colline (59x73cm-23x29in) s. (F.FR 14000)

CREUTZ, Magnus (1909-) Swedish

£623	$1077	(22-May-91 BA.S27/R) Woman on balcony (80x65cm-31x26in) s. (S.KR 6600)

CRIPPA, Luigi (1921-) Italian

£1306	$2560	(6-Nov-90 GF.L2678/R) Vicolo N 4 (99x43cm-39x17in) s.d.1962 s.i.d.verso (S.FR 3200)

CRIPPA, Roberto (1921-1972) Italian

£1092	$2064	(27-Sep-90 F.M112) Spirali (43x41cm-17x16in) s. acrylic paper (I.L 2400000)
£1501	$2838	(27-Sep-90 F.M119/R) Untitled (50x30cm-20x12in) s.d.50 tempera panel (I.L 3300000)
£4351	$8355	(27-Nov-90 SY.MI140/R) Composizione (69x56cm-27x22in) s.d.55 (I.L 9500000)
£5038	$9674	(27-Nov-90 SY.MI174/R) Composizione (70x90cm-28x35in) s.d.1953verso (I.L 11000000)
£5043	$8270	(20-Jun-91 F.M391/R) Totem (100x70cm-39x28in) s.d.55 s.verso masonite (I.L 11000000)
£5437	$9460	(26-Mar-91 F.M74/R) Composizione (78x98cm-31x39in) s.verso (I.L 12000000)
£5550	$10767	(3-Dec-90 CH.R185/R) Composizione (70x50cm-28x20in) s.d.1950 panel (I.L 12000000)
£6189	$10150	(20-Jun-91 F.M338/R) Spirali (81x100cm-32x39in) s.d.verso (I.L 13500000)
£6303	$12292	(24-Oct-90 F.M217/R) Galleria di pittura (100x120cm-39x47in) s.d.1948verso (I.L 14000000)
£6834	$11619	(28-May-91 SY.MI189/R) Composizione (100x80cm-39x31in) s.d.56 (I.L 15000000)
£7400	$14356	(3-Dec-90 CH.R72/R) Spirali (70x90cm-28x35in) s.d.1952 (I.L 16000000)
£7794	$12782	(20-Jun-91 F.M516/R) Spirali (109x170cm-43x67in) s.d.1952 (I.L 17000000)
£8104	$15804	(24-Oct-90 F.M287/R) Composizione (70x99cm-28x39in) s.d.950 (I.L 18000000)
£8780	$16945	(13-Dec-90 F.M480/R) Composizione, totem (130x97cm-51x38in) s.d.55-56 s.d.verso (I.L 19000000)
£11270	$20174	(9-Apr-91 F.R212/R) Spirali (130x130cm-51x51in) s.d.52verso (I.L 25000000)
£13057	$25462	(24-Oct-90 F.M221/R) Spirali (98x98cm-39x39in) s.d.1949verso acrylic (I.L 29000000)
£18010	$35119	(22-Oct-90 BR.M25/R) Spirali (130x75cm-51x30in) s.d.1952 verso (I.L 40000000)
£19835	$35505	(9-Apr-91 F.R197/R) Spirali (170x200cm-67x79in) s.d.1951verso (I.L 44000000)
£1374	$2638	(27-Nov-90 SY.MI38/R) Composizione (70x50cm-28x20in) s. collage board (I.L 3000000)
£1452	$2497	(13-May-91 CH.R74/R) Senza titolo (54x65cm-21x26in) s.verso mixed media (I.L 3200000)
£2029	$3631	(9-Apr-91 F.R182/R) Chimera (45x54cm-18x21in) s.d.951verso cork collage panel (I.L 4500000)
£2551	$5000	(12-Feb-91 SY.NY407/R) Landscape (130x97cm-51x38in) s.d.1966verso casein asbestos board
£2927	$5707	(22-Oct-90 BR.M227/R) Landscape (46x38cm-18x15in) s.d.1966verso cork collage panel (I.L 6500000)
£3096	$5976	(13-Dec-90 F.M380/R) Arc en ciel (46x54cm-18x21in) s.i.d.1970verso cork (I.L 6700000)
£3697	$7135	(13-Dec-90 F.M374/R) Landscape (50x40cm-20x16in) s.i.d.1963 cork on panel (I.L 8000000)
£4728	$9219	(24-Oct-90 F.M183/R) Origine (40x49cm-16x19in) s.d.1961 cork mixed media panel (I.L 10500000)
£6932	$13378	(13-Dec-90 F.M407/R) Composizione (81x100cm-32x39in) s.verso cork panel (I.L 15000000)
£7654	$14926	(22-Oct-90 BR.M288/R) Lazard (73x92cm-29x36in) s.d.1971verso cork gold collage panel (I.L 17000000)
£9905	$19316	(22-Oct-90 BR.M332/R) Sole (116x90cm-46x35in) s.d.1971verso cork collage panel (I.L 22000000)

CRIPPA, Roberto and SAITO, Yoshishige (20th C) Italian/Japanese
£6754 $13170   (22-Oct-90 BR.M189/R) Untitled (91x117cm-36x46in) s.d.1961verso sand oil panel (I.L 15000000)

CRISCIMANNO, Nicola (19th C) Italian
£6000 $10200   (30-May-91 C157/R) Ironclad H.M.S. Swiftsure or H.M.S. Triumph in Grand Harbour, Valetta (28x47cm-11x19in) s.d.1878 board

CRISP, Frank E F (?-1915) British
£1700 $3043   (14-Mar-91 ZZ.B239/R) Portrait of Arundel Theophilla Copland-Griffiths, her dog by her side (127x102cm-50x40in)

CRISPE, Sara M (19th C) Continental
£2368 $4500   (27-Feb-91 SY.NY304/R) Gathering flowers (110x75cm-43x30in) s.

CRISTALL, J (1767-1847) British
£420 $701   (7-Jun-91 BW219) Study of country girl (56x41cm-22x16in) s. W/C

CRISTOFANO, Francesco di see FRANCIABIGIO

CRITZ (19th C) ?
£2900 $5655   (18-Oct-90 SC3165/R) By the well (118x84cm-46x33in) s.i.d.1896

CRITZ, Emmanuel de (circle) (17th C) British
£1250 $2438   (22-Oct-90 SWS1325/R) Portrait of Francis, Lord Cottingham, wearing doublet and hose, hand on sword (127x101cm-50x40in) i.

CRITZ, John de (elder-school) (1555-1641) British
£2353 $4000   (31-May-91 CH.NY114/R) Portrait of lady, possibly Arabella Stuart, in costume with lace collar (57x44cm-22x17in)

CRIVELLI, Angelo Maria (17/18th C) Italian
£4196 $8098   (10-Dec-90 L.K23/R) Waterbirds by banks of lake (36x52cm-14x20in) canvas laid down (DM 12000)
£4781 $8223   (14-May-91 GF.L2079/R) Ducks on pond (94x71cm-37x28in) (S.FR 12000)
£5578 $9594   (14-May-91 GF.L2078/R) Eagle in eyrie (94x71cm-37x28in) (S.FR 14000)
£18499 $35889   (7-Dec-90 SY.MO12/R) Vue de pigeonnier (117x147cm-46x58in) (F.FR 180000)
£32123 $57500   (11-Apr-91 SY.NY157/R) Peacock, pheasants and rabbits in landscape. Turkeys and chickens eating grapes in barnyard (117x146cm-46x57in) pair

CRIVELLI, Carlo (style) (1435-1493) Italian
£1786 $3000   (17-Jul-91 SY.NY64/R) Ecce homo (24x16cm-9x6in) i. panel

CRIVELLI, Giovanni (15th C) Italian
£4281 $8220   (30-Nov-90 APT.P32/R) Combat de chiens et de taureaux (92x118cm-36x46in) (F.FR 42000)
£5221 $8406   (27-Jun-91 APT.P61/R) Nature morte au gibier avec un chien en arret (107x139cm-42x55in) (F.FR 52000)
£6762 $12104   (8-Apr-91 F.M345/R) Anatre. Fagiani (75x75cm-30x30in) pair (I.L 15000000)

CRIVELLI, Vittorio (1440-1502) Italian
£120000 $195600   (5-Jul-91 C75/R) Lamentation (104x72cm-41x28in) tempera panel

CRIVELLI, Vittorio (style) (1440-1502) Italian
£4479 $8779   (20-Nov-90 GO.G405/R) Saint Katarina of Alexandria (72x52cm-28x20in) tempera htd gold panel (S.KR 49000)

CROCHEPIERRE, Andre (1860-?) French
£5183 $8500   (19-Jun-91 B.SF1718/R) La femme au livre (46x39cm-18x15in) s.d.1887 shaped

CROCKER, Andrew (1962-) British
£800 $1568   (13-Feb-91 B123) Whenever I take my walks abroad (127x107cm-50x42in) s.
£850 $1666   (13-Feb-91 B120/R) Eau dear (146x98cm-57x39in) acrylic paper on panel
£850 $1666   (13-Feb-91 B124/R) Unkindly (105x92cm-41x36in)

CROCKFORD, Duncan (1920-) Canadian
£619 $1052   (27-May-91 HO.ED305) High tide at Crescent Beach, B.C. (46x62cm-18x24in) s.d.1969 (C.D 1200)
£619 $1052   (27-May-91 HO.ED268/R) Spray lake (41x51cm-16x20in) s. d.1960verso canvas board (C.D 1200)
£655 $1290   (12-Nov-90 HO.ED324/R) Mountain fastness - Mount Bident and Consolation Lake, Alta (46x61cm-18x24in) s.i.d.1969 (C.D 1500)
£670 $1139   (27-May-91 HO.ED297) December gale on Tugboat Island, B.C. (62x76cm-24x30in) s.d.1969 (C.D 1300)
£961 $1893   (12-Nov-90 HO.ED274/R) A lane in old Barkerville, B.C. (46x61cm-18x24in) s.i.d. (C.D 2200)

CRODEL, Charles (1894-1973) French
£546 $1070   (24-Nov-90 N.M109) Mountain landscape (52x41cm-20x16in) s.d.1925 W/C over pen (DM 1600)

438

CROEGAERT, Georges (1848-1923) French
£692	$1357	(21-Nov-90 GM.B1181) Jeune femme a la rose (24x19cm-9x7in) s. wood (B.FR 42000)
£1397	$2500	(16-Mar-91 W.W52/R) Gypsy girl (28x20cm-11x8in) s.i. panel
£3200	$5152	(27-Jun-91 CG82/R) The letter (35x27cm-14x11in) s.i. panel
£3333	$6500	(24-Oct-90 CH.NY2/R) The dressing table (46x33cm-18x13in) s.i.
£4000	$7680	(18-Dec-90 GM.B4074) La lettre (32x25cm-13x10in) s. panel (B.FR 240000)

CROFTS, Ernest (1847-1911) British
| £579 | $1100 | (27-Feb-91 SY.NY273/R) After Flodden September 9, 1513 (51x79cm-20x31in) s.d.77 |
| £850 | $1666 | (13-Feb-91 S195/R) Banner of guild (35x25cm-14x10in) board |

CROLL, Carl Robert (1800-1842) German
| £560 | $946 | (1-May-91 GD.B1039) View through arched window of riverside town (18x30cm-7x12in) s.d.1830 W/C (S.FR 1400) |

CROMBIE, Peggy (20th C) Australian
| £618 | $1217 | (13-Nov-90 J.M169) Flowers on pink chair (64x51cm-25x20in) s. board (A.D 1600) |

CROME (17/18th C) British
| £1111 | $2189 | (14-Nov-90 WO.CO2) Wooded landscape (38x46cm-15x18in) (E.P 1200) |

CROME, John (attrib) (1768-1821) British
| £550 | $930 | (17-Apr-91 ZZ.B98) Figures on woodland path (44x42cm-17x17in) bears sig.i.verso |

CROME, John Berney (1794-1842) British
| £513 | $1000 | (20-Oct-90 FA.PH904/R) Foggy morning (127x76cm-50x30in) s.d.1838 i.stretcher |
| £4040 | $6990 | (6-May-91 ZEL.L1636/R) Wooded landscape with figures, animals and old mill (75x111cm-30x44in) s.d.1831 (DM 12000) |

CROME, John Berney (attrib) (1794-1842) British
| £2450 | $4851 | (31-Jan-91 D.V31/R) Moonlit river landscape (39x56cm-15x22in) (A.S 50000) |

CROME, William Henry (1806-1873) British
| £1100 | $1969 | (14-Mar-91 ZZ.B129) St. Benet's Abbey by moonlight (44x38cm-17x15in) s.d.1844 panel |

CROME, William Henry (attrib) (1806-1873) British
| £900 | $1773 | (31-Oct-90 S336/R) Wooded landscape with figure walking towards village and estuary beyond (32x42cm-13x17in) s. |

CROMEK, Thomas Hartley (1809-1873) British
| £5500 | $9075 | (11-Jul-91 S229/R) Interior of St Peter's Rome (45x58cm-18x23in) W/C over pencil htd.bodycol |

CROMPTON, C C (1870-1945) British
| £378 | $700 | (10-Mar-91 H.C93) Still life with fruit (25x33cm-10x13in) s.d.1904 W/C |

CROMPTON, James Shaw (1853-1916) British
£580	$1027	(21-Mar-91 CSK21/R) Pansies, that's for thoughts (51x36cm-20x14in) s.d.1885 i. pencil W/C
£720	$1274	(21-Mar-91 CSK20/R) Had we but world enough and time, this coyness, lady, were no crime (51x36cm-20x14in) s.d.1887 i. pencil W/C
£2545	$4428	(26-Mar-91 JRL.S94/R) The wedding party (57x77cm-22x30in) s. W/C (A.D 5700)

CRONNAKIWSKY, A (?) ?
| £1959 | $3801 | (8-Nov-90 GAB.G2177/R) Scene de souk (80x60cm-31x24in) s. (S.FR 4800) |

CRONQVIST, Lena (1938-) Swedish
£927	$1798	(5-Dec-90 AB.S7054/R) Island - coastal landscape (39x44cm-15x17in) s. (S.KR 10000)
£1066	$2068	(5-Dec-90 AB.S7055/R) Storm, Kalvo - archipelago (39x44cm-15x17in) s.d.88 (S.KR 11500)
£1205	$2337	(4-Dec-90 BA.S79/R) Pile of stones (39x41cm-15x16in) s.d.1977 (S.KR 13000)
£1934	$3346	(22-May-91 BA.S339/R) Baboon in cage (110x98cm-43x39in) s.d.65 (S.KR 20500)

CROOKE, Ray Austin (1922-) Australian
£563	$924	(17-Jun-91 MGS.S101) Villager with basket of fruit (45x35cm-18x14in) s. canvas on board (A.D 1200)
£618	$1217	(13-Nov-90 J.M93) Stockmen at Bore, Northern Queensland (44x60cm-17x24in) s. board (A.D 1600)
£640	$1248	(15-Oct-90 AAA.S137) Islander with fruit (41x51cm-16x20in) s. board (A.D 1600)
£660	$1076	(1-Jul-91 AAA.S174) Family group (40x50cm-16x20in) s. board (A.D 1400)
£683	$1311	(26-Nov-90 SY.ME160) Islander resting in shade of palm (39x50cm-15x20in) s. board (A.D 1700)
£694	$1167	(16-Jul-91 JRL.S328) Islander resting on verandah (37x47cm-15x19in) s. board (A.D 1500)

CROOKE, Ray Austin (1922-) Australian-cont.

£720	$1404	(15-Oct-90 AAA.S75) Native fisherman (51x40cm-20x16in) s. (A.D 1800)
£741	$1244	(16-Jul-91 JRL.S259) Villagers gossiping (50x39cm-20x15in) s. (A.D 1600)
£772	$1521	(13-Nov-90 J.M17) Islander relaxing on verandah (44x60cm-17x24in) s. board (A.D 2000)
£772	$1521	(13-Nov-90 J.M101) Islander with vase of flowers (54x65cm-21x26in) s. board (A.D 2000)
£778	$1525	(19-Nov-90 MGS.S265) Islander by hut (39x50cm-15x20in) s. (A.D 2000)
£802	$1307	(1-Jul-91 AAA.S78) Islanders on the beach (41x51cm-16x20in) s. board (A.D 1700)
£814	$1376	(16-Apr-91 J.M59) Villagers relaxing in shade (49x39cm-19x15in) s. (A.D 1800)
£860	$1453	(1-Jul-91 AAA.S144) Island scene (40x50cm-16x20in) s. board (A.D 1900)
£876	$1727	(31-Oct-90 CH.S187) Rocky landscape, North Queensland (62x90cm-24x35in) s. canvas on board (A.D 2200)
£880	$1716	(15-Oct-90 AAA.S51) Lizard Island (76x61cm-30x24in) s. (A.D 2200)
£896	$1461	(1-Jul-91 AAA.S151) Islanders near the beach (61x45cm-24x18in) s. board (A.D 1900)
£934	$1830	(19-Nov-90 MGS.S176) Burnt scrub (37x48cm-15x19in) s. board (A.D 2400)
£940	$1664	(18-Mar-91 MGS.S121) Islander, study for print (44x54cm-17x21in) s. board (A.D 2200)
£950	$1606	(15-Apr-91 AAA.S80) Islander with basket of fruit (61x46cm-24x18in) s. board (A.D 2100)
£960	$1872	(15-Oct-90 AAA.S150) Rockhampton Hinterland (61x91cm-24x36in) s. (A.D 2400)
£1041	$1759	(15-Apr-91 AAA.S73) Islander in village scene (41x51cm-16x20in) s. (A.D 2300)
£1048	$1876	(9-Apr-91 CH.ME312) Woman with vase of flwoers (39x49cm-15x19in) s. (A.D 2400)
£1092	$1954	(9-Apr-91 CH.ME207) Tropical panorama (59x74cm-23x29in) s. (A.D 2500)
£1116	$2198	(31-Oct-90 CH.S197) Horsemen at old mine (61x76cm-24x30in) s. (A.D 2800)
£1120	$2184	(15-Oct-90 AAA.S69) Islander with vase of flowers (40x50cm-16x20in) s. (A.D 2800)
£1132	$1845	(1-Jul-91 AAA.S160 i) Islander in a tropical landscape (120x85cm-47x33in) s. board (A.D 2400)
£1167	$2288	(19-Nov-90 MGS.S229) Islander working by the hut (60x75cm-24x30in) s. (A.D 3000)
£1205	$2313	(26-Nov-90 SY.ME88/R) Islander by lagoon (49x33cm-19x13in) s. canvas on board (A.D 3000)
£1221	$2002	(17-Jun-91 MGS.S99) Islanders working in garden (39x50cm-15x20in) s. (A.D 2600)
£1226	$1999	(1-Jul-91 AAA.S124) Islander with bowl of fruit (41x51cm-16x20in) s. (A.D 2600)
£1228	$2136	(26-Mar-91 JRL.S191) Islander with basket of fruit (74x59cm-29x23in) s. (A.D 2750)
£1244	$2340	(17-Sep-90 MGS.S241) Anthills, Cape York (76x101cm-30x40in) s. (A.D 2800)
£1267	$2141	(16-Apr-91 J.M202 a/R) Thursday Island (38x48cm-15x19in) s. canvas on board (A.D 2800)
£1538	$2723	(18-Mar-91 MGS.S260) Islanders gossiping (45x60cm-18x24in) s. (A.D 3600)
£1556	$2924	(17-Sep-90 MGS.S166) Island woman with date basket (40x50cm-16x20in) s. (A.D 3500)
£1584	$2676	(16-Apr-91 J.M161/R) Islander with basket of fruit and flowers (60x75cm-24x30in) (A.D 3500)
£1606	$3084	(26-Nov-90 SY.ME251) Family group (59x75cm-23x30in) s. board (A.D 4000)
£1688	$3241	(14-Aug-90 SY.ME247) Family group (76x60cm-30x24in) s. (A.D 4000)
£1719	$2906	(15-Apr-91 AAA.S122) Islanders chatting (45x55cm-18x22in) s. (A.D 3800)
£1767	$2969	(22-Apr-91 SY.ME65) Fijian village (60x75cm-24x30in) s. artist's board (A.D 3800)
£1899	$3646	(14-Aug-90 SY.ME218) Islanders relaxing in hut (49x68cm-19x27in) s. board (A.D 4500)
£1925	$3157	(17-Jun-91 MGS.S327) Islanders in sun (59x75cm-23x30in) s. (A.D 4100)
£1941	$3727	(14-Aug-90 SY.ME109/R) North Queensland landscape (60x90cm-24x35in) s. board (A.D 4600)
£2066	$3388	(17-Jun-91 MGS.S100) Islanders relaxing near hut (60x75cm-24x30in) s. (A.D 4400)
£2233	$3751	(22-Apr-91 SY.ME159/R) Islanders (59x75cm-23x30in) s. canvas on board (A.D 4800)
£2262	$3824	(16-Apr-91 J.M394) Northern Queensland (58x88cm-23x35in) s. canvas on board (A.D 5000)
£2321	$4456	(14-Aug-90 SY.ME313/R) Bora Bora (76x101cm-30x40in) s. oil acryllic board (A.D 5500)
£2376	$4015	(15-Apr-91 AAA.S89) Islanders relaxing (76x101cm-30x40in) s. (A.D 5250)
£2594	$4229	(1-Jul-91 AAA.S140) Late afternoon, Thursday Island (76x101cm-30x40in) s. (A.D 5500)
£2610	$5012	(27-Nov-90 JRL.S213/R) Islanders resting (93x133cm-37x52in) s. (A.D 6500)
£2662	$4472	(16-Jul-91 JRL.S305) The view of the lagoon, Thursday Island (60x75cm-24x30in) s. (A.D 5750)
£2743	$5266	(14-Aug-90 SY.ME287/R) Stockman by the river (59x75cm-23x30in) s. (A.D 6500)
£3187	$6279	(31-Oct-90 CH.S194/R) Two women, Thursday Island (74x59cm-29x23in) s. canvas board (A.D 8000)

CROOKE, Ray Austin (1922-) Australian-cont.
£3414	$6554	(27-Nov-90 JRL.S217/R) Islander threading frangipani (87x117cm-34x46in) s. (A.D 8500)
£3488	$5860	(22-Apr-91 SY.ME323/R) Island still life (75x100cm-30x39in) s. (A.D 7500)
£3519	$5911	(16-Jul-91 JRL.S243/R) Natives at rest (60x90cm-24x35in) s. (A.D 7600)
£3846	$6500	(16-Apr-91 J.M122/R) Thursday Island native making lei (87x117cm-34x46in) s. (A.D 8500)
£4000	$7520	(17-Sep-90 SY.ME13/R) Village scene (97x74cm-38x29in) s. canvas on board (A.D 9000)
£1606	*$3084*	*(26-Nov-90 SY.ME247/R) Woman at table. Islanders in forest (60x75cm-24x30in) s. board double-sided (A.D 4000)*
£1737	*$3423*	*(13-Nov-90 J.M83) Island village (41x52cm-16x20in) s. mixed media (A.D 4500)*

CROOS, Anthony Jansz van der (1606-1662) Dutch
£3000	$5790	(11-Dec-90 PH250/R) View of riverside town with figures and boats in foreground (9x20cm-4x8in) panel
£3911	$7000	(11-Apr-91 SY.NY15/R) Manor house on river, small village in distance (43x47cm-17x19in)
£4000	$6520	(2-Jul-91 PH55/R) Peasants unloading goods from ferry before ruined castle (33x43cm-13x17in) s.d.1661 panel
£6387	$12582	(30-Oct-90 BU.S241/R) Landscape with Pan and Syrinx (49x72cm-19x28in) s.d.1636 panel (S.KR 70000)

CROOS, Anthony Jansz van der (style) (1606-1662) Dutch
£1100	$2090	(13-Sep-90 CSK204/R) River landscape with windmill overlooking town (56x75cm-22x30in)

CROOS, Jacob van der (17th C) Dutch
£5500	$8965	(5-Jul-91 C346/R) Wooded landscape with drover leading cattle, figures on riverbank, village (66x81cm-26x32in) s.d.1664

CROPSEY, Jasper Francis (1823-1900) American
£2097	$3900	(9-Sep-90 LIT.L318) Moonlit lake scene with fishermen and moored boat (23x18cm-9x7in) s. masonite
£4762	$9000	(27-Sep-90 CH.NY33/R) High bridge in Autumn (15x11cm-6x4in) s.d.1874 board
£8380	$15000	(14-Mar-91 CH.NY22/R) Ships in storm (15x30cm-6x12in) s.d.1875
£8939	$16000	(14-Mar-91 CH.NY27/R) Along Delaware Water Gap (32x57cm-13x22in) s.d.1884
£9827	$17000	(23-May-91 SY.NY17/R) Amalfi, Italy (53x39cm-21x15in) s.l.d.1848
£11173	$20000	(14-Mar-91 CH.NY26/R) View of Delaware (30x51cm-12x20in) s.d.1889
£11458	$22000	(29-Nov-90 SY.NY7/R) Lake George, New York (36x61cm-14x24in) s.d.1892
£11640	$22000	(27-Sep-90 CH.NY29/R) Greenwood lake (32x52cm-13x20in) s.d.1875
£15029	$26000	(22-May-91 CH.NY157/R) Autumn, Fort Putnam on the Hudson (23x42cm-9x17in) init.d.1856
£20231	$35000	(23-May-91 SY.NY4/R) Autumn landscape (36x61cm-14x24in) s.d.1879 s.stretcher
£46243	$80000	(22-May-91 CH.NY9/R) Quiet valley (83x127cm-33x50in) s.d.1856
£8380	*$15000*	*(12-Apr-91 SY.NY26/R) From Kingston (30x47cm-12x19in) s.d.1891 i.verso W/C*
£16402	*$31000*	*(26-Sep-90 SY.NY43/R) Springtime on the Hudson (41x66cm-16x26in) s.d.1891 W/C gouache pencil*

CROS, Cesar Isidore Henri (1840-1907) French
£1606	*$2972*	*(4-Mar-91 ARC.P39/R) Nu au tissu jaune (40x20cm-16x8in) col.wax panel (F.FR 16000)*

CROSATO, Giovanni Battista (attrib) (1697-1756) Italian
£4518	$7274	(27-Jun-91 APT.P71/R) Alexandre recevant les clefs de Babylone (52x46cm-20x18in) (F.FR 45000)

CROSATO, Giovanni Battista (circle) (1697-1756) Italian
£21053	$40000	(11-Jan-91 CH.NY34/R) The nurturing of Jupiter (65x82cm-26x32in)

CROSBIE, William (1915-) British
£1200	$2028	(17-Apr-91 CG117/R) Still life with green bowl (30x36cm-12x14in) s. canvasboard
£1350	$2282	(17-Apr-91 CG112) World of Political Integration (37x43cm-15x17in) s.d. verso canvasboard

CROSBY, Gordon (1885-1943) British
£520	*$879*	*(2-May-91 B41/R) Air ambulance resuce (42x66cm-17x26in) s. chl.white bodycol.*
£750	*$1268*	*(2-May-91 B40/R) An Avro Manchester at dispersal (39x65cm-15x26in) s. chl.white bodycol.*

CROSBY, William (19th C) British
£1100	$2156	(20-Nov-90 PH118) Bo peep (29x23cm-11x9in) s.d.1868 i. verso
£2095	$3750	(15-Mar-91 DM.D2074/R) Girl with fan (61x51cm-24x20in) s.d.1869 board

CROSLAND, Enoch (19th C) British
£1445	$2500	(10-May-91 S.W2482/R) The leaves are paling yellow fast turning into red (51x76cm-20x30in) s. i.verso

CROSS, Alison (1952-) British

£700	$1372	(13-Feb-91 B155) Anyone who's been to hell and back rides vincent black shadow (76x76cm-30x30in) s.d.1989 verso acrylic canvas
£2000	$3920	(13-Feb-91 B153/R) Dance (112x152cm-44x60in) s.d.1989 verso
£800	*$1392*	(28-Mar-91 CSK93/R) Woman by window - blue bird (168x183cm-66x72in) s.d.1986-90 mixed media

CROSS, H H (1837-1918) American

£1396	$2750	(7-Oct-90 DU.E110/R) Buffalo grazing on the Cody Ranch (76x127cm-30x50in) s.d.1901

CROSS, Henri Edmond (1856-1910) French

£4624	$8000	(9-May-91 CH.NY212/R) Fleurs (23x14cm-9x6in) st.init. panel
£9041	$17358	(27-Nov-90 BU.S62/R) La Baie de Caraliere (27x35cm-11x14in) paper (S.KR 98000)
£242915	$476113	(25-Nov-90 GL.P30/R) La promenade au Bois de Moulogne (73x92cm-29x36in) s. (F.FR 2400000)
£250000	$485000	(3-Dec-90 C18/R) Rio San Trovaso, Venice (73x93cm-29x37in) s. i.stretcher
£250000	$485000	(3-Dec-90 C20/R) Une pinede - Provence (81x100cm-32x39in) s.
£280000	$543200	(4-Dec-90 S11/R) Cypres - Avril (72x91cm-28x36in) s.
£490	$950	(8-Dec-90 GAB.G2493) Etude de nu (28x20cm-11x8in) studio st. crayon (S.FR 1200)
£513	$1000	(10-Oct-90 SY.NY9/R) Figural studies (48x36cm-19x14in) st.studio graphite chl.
£759	$1488	(20-Nov-90 BG.P28/R) Etudes de personnages chl. three same mount (F.FR 7500)
£2157	$4250	(3-Oct-90 SY.NY58/R) Etudes pour un paysage (25x32cm-10x13in) st.init. pen ink wash pencil htd.W/C
£2500	$4425	(20-Mar-91 S2/R) Pins au bord de la mer (18x26cm-7x10in) st.init. W/C pencil
£6853	$13500	(3-Oct-90 SY.NY49/R) Cote provencale (28x38cm-11x15in) s.i.d.09 W/C paper on board

CROSS, Henry H (1837-1918) American

£1021	$1980	(25-Aug-90 LIT.L70) Florence (46x64cm-18x25in) d.1885
£1354	$2600	(17-Dec-90 SY.NY163/R) Chief Red Cloud (91x74cm-36x29in) s.i.d.1862 i.verso

CROSS, Peter (1645-1724) British

£1900	*$3648*	(18-Dec-90 C80/R) Portrait of lady in decollete white dress and blue stole (8x?cm-3x?in) min.mono.card gold frame spiral cresting oval
£3200	*$6144*	(18-Dec-90 C84/R) Portrait of gentleman, probably Robert King (8x?cm-3x?in) min.mono.i.d.1700 card gilt-metal frame oval

CROSS, Peter (after) (1645-1724) British

£600	*$1152*	(19-Feb-91 CSK34/R) Portrait of James Scott, Duke of Monmouth (8x?cm-3x?in) min.oval gilt mount on rec.black wood frame

CROSS, Roy (20th C) British

£994	$1600	(26-Jun-91 D.NY24) Nantucket wahler Atlas sending off boats (66x91cm-26x36in) s.d.c.1980

CROSSE, Richard (1742-1810) British

£400	*$788*	(1-Nov-90 S12/R) Portrait of gentleman wearing coat embroidered with gold (3x?cm-1x?in) min. gold slide frame oval
£480	*$850*	(20-Mar-91 C139/R) Portrait of young girl in white dress and lace bonnet (3x?cm-1x?in) min. gilt-wood mount oval
£650	*$1151*	(20-Mar-91 C117/R) Portrait of Katharine Stephens, Countess of Essex (5x?cm-2x?in) min.gold frame lock of hair verso oval
£850	*$1403*	(10-Jul-91 C80/R) Possibly Edward Crosse (7x?cm-3x?in) min. gilt-metal frame oval
£850	*$1403*	(10-Jul-91 C111/R) A gentleman in green coat with brown buttons (5x?cm-2x?in) min. gold frame bright cut border oval
£1200	$2124	(20-Mar-91 C146) Portrait of gentleman in dark green coat and waistcoat (5x?cm-2x?in) min. gold frame lock of hair verso oval
£3000	$4950	(10-Jul-91 C134/R) A gentleman in blue coat (7x?cm-3x?in) min. gold frame bright-cut border oval

CROSSE, Richard (attrib) (1742-1810) British

£380	*$654*	(15-May-91 BT53/R) A young lady, head and shoulders, with a long plait wearing a white dress min. gold slip frame oval
£680	*$1170*	(15-May-91 BT55/R) An officer, head and shoulders, wearing a powdered wig en queue min. gold slip frame oval
£880	*$1478*	(22-Apr-91 PH109/R) Portrait of gentleman, probably Sir Adam Gordon (4x?cm-2x?in) min. gilt metal brooch frame oval

CROTTI, Jean (1878-1958) French

£2010	$3598	(11-Mar-91 GL.P98) Transparence (30x23cm-12x9in) s. board (F.FR 20000)
£3936	$7714	(24-Nov-90 AB.L125/R) Deux tetes (42x50cm-17x20in) s. panel (S.FR 9800)
£5056	$9858	(21-Oct-90 L.C67/R) Les masques (54x45cm-21x18in) s.d.43 panel (F.FR 50000)
£7853	$13271	(21-Apr-91 E.LA168) Rosee du matin (66x54cm-26x21in) s.d.1924 verso (F.FR 79000)
£13769	$22581	(19-Jun-91 JM.P121/R) Composition au visage feminin (65x54cm-26x21in) s. (F.FR 137000)

CROTTI, Jean (1878-1958) French-cont.
| £1205 | $2229 | (6-Mar-91 APT.P5) La belle Didita (47x31cm-19x12in) s.i. col.crayons (F.FR 12000) |
| £1400 | $2338 | (5-Jun-91 HC.P338) Visage de femme (38x23cm-15x9in) s. gouache (F.FR 14000) |

CROUCH, William (fl.1817-40) British
| £620 | $1011 | (14-Jun-91 K294) View to the North of Naples (20x33cm-8x13in) i.verso W/C |
| £1000 | $1920 | (17-Aug-90 K480/R) In the mountains of ancient Attica (30x46cm-12x18in) i.d.1836verso W/C |

CROUSE, M (19th C) British
| £1750 | $2923 | (22-Jul-91 SWS990/R) Doublas Harbour (44x68cm-17x27in) i. stretcher |

CROWELL, Tom (20th C) British
| £956 | $1865 | (24-Oct-90 GD.B253/R) Still life of roses with grapes and plums and view of park (59x49cm-23x19in) s. panel (S.FR 2400) |
| £1040 | $1758 | (1-May-91 GD.B175/R) Still life with roses, tulips and other spring flowers (50x39cm-20x15in) s. panel (S.FR 2600) |

CROWLEY, Grace (20th C) Australian/British
| £1847 | $3547 | (26-Nov-90 SY.ME53) Grandmother's dress (56x42cm-22x17in) s.d.42 i.verso canvas on board (A.D 4600) |

CROWLEY, Nicholas Joseph (1813-1857) British
| £580 | $945 | (13-Jun-91 CSK301/R) Stolen treasure (33x43cm-13x17in) s.i.verso board |
| £800 | $1320 | (9-Jul-91 PH87) Cup tossing (70x78cm-28x31in) |

CROWTHER, H (20th C) British?
| £650 | $1268 | (15-Jan-91 C105) Earlswood Rex, Irish setter (37x29cm-15x11in) s.i.d.1933 |

CROXFORD, William Edwards (fl.1874-1905) British
| £550 | $1045 | (27-Feb-91 MMB155) Cornish harbour scene (46x74cm-18x29in) s.d.1897 |
| £650 | $1235 | (27-Feb-91 MMB154) Cornish fishing village with figures by a horse and cart (46x74cm-18x29in) s.d.1898 |

CROZIER, William (1930-) British
| £600 | $966 | (28-Jun-91 CSK62/R) Ayrshire landscape, 1960 (63x63cm-25x25in) s. s.i.d.1960 verso paper on board |
| £1000 | $1870 | (28-Aug-90 S1104/R) Untitled (53x63cm-21x25in) s. W/C acrylic |

CRUICKSHANK, William (1848-1922) British
£1750	$3010	(13-May-91 CG200/R) A hedgesparrow's nest and may blossom. A nest and apple blossom (9x12cm-4x5in) both s. ivory oval pair
£650	$1086	(5-Jun-91 S299/R) Still life of summer flowers in jug (21x15cm-8x6in) s. W/C gold paint on ivory
£1300	$2171	(5-Jun-91 S289/R) Flowers in jug. Flowers in vase (19x14cm-7x6in) s. W/C on ivory pair

CRUIKSHANK, George (1792-1878) British
| £1300 | $2327 | (9-Apr-91 C70/R) Parliamentary borough election (14x19cm-6x7in) s. pencil pen ink W/C |

CRUSSENS, Anton (17th C) Flemish
| £1682 | $3313 | (12-Nov-90 CH.AM81/R) Winter landscape with peasants gathering wood, windmill beyond (13x13cm-5x5in) s. d.1665 verso black chk pen on vellum (D.FL 5500) |

CRUYL, Lieven (c.1640-1720) Belgian
£1835	$3615	(12-Nov-90 CH.AM111/R) Shipping in estuary (21cm-8ins circular) s. pen wash (D.FL 6000)
£2141	$4217	(12-Nov-90 CH.AM110/R) View of Tivoli with Temple of Sybils (11x11cm-4x4in) init. black chk pen wash i.circle on vellum (D.FL 7000)
£2569	$4985	(7-Dec-90 CN.P76/R) Vue d'un port imaginaire et encadrements a vues maritimes (27x46cm-11x18in) s.d.1690 Indian ink wash parchment triptych (F.FR 25000)
£3670	$7229	(12-Nov-90 CH.AM109/R) Campidoglio, Rome (11x11cm-4x4in) init. black chk pen wash on vellum (D.FL 12000)
£7500	$12225	(1-Jul-91 S33/R) Fantastic view of town and harbour (15x22cm-6x9in) s. pen wash over black chk vellum

CRUZ HERRERA, Jose Herrerilla (1890-) Spanish
| £811 | $1581 | (23-Oct-90 DUR.M56) Morito (41x32cm-16x13in) (S.P 150000) |

CRUZ HERRERA, Juan (20th C) Spanish
| £705 | $1374 | (17-Oct-90 FER.M123/R) Con flores en el pelo (33x25cm-13x10in) s. (S.P 130000) |
| £2982 | $5815 | (17-Oct-90 FER.M213/R) Rabinos (39x46cm-15x18in) s. (S.P 550000) |

CRUZ PRENDES, Julio (20th C) Spanish
| £977 | $1926 | (15-Nov-90 ANS.M54/R) Sin titulo (81x100cm-32x39in) s.d.1981 (S.P 180000) |

CRUZ-DIEZ, Carlos (1923-) Venezuelan
£2806 $5500   *(20-Nov-90 CH.NY177/R) Physiochromie no. 348 (60x119cm-24x47in)*
                       s.i.d.1967 verso mixed media panel

CSAKY, Josef (1888-1971) Hungarian/French
£592 $1166   (6-Oct-90 GL.P119) La famille (50x30cm-20x12in) s.d.58 lead pencil
                      (F.FR 6000)
£2261 $4386   (7-Dec-90 GL.P199) Femme au miroir (31x24cm-12x9in) s. W/C crayon
                      (F.FR 22000)

CSATO, Georges (1910-) Hungarian
£1972 $3886   (1-Oct-90 CC.P153) Composition no.128 (120x60cm-47x24in) s.d.1972
                      (F.FR 20000)
£1972 $3886   (1-Oct-90 CC.P152) Composition no.30 (120x60cm-47x24in) s.d.1975
                      (F.FR 20000)

CUARTIELLES, R (19th C) Spanish
£1361 $2219   (11-Jun-91 ANS.M61/R) Galanteo (32x41cm-13x16in) s. (S.P 250000)

CUBELLS Y RUIZ, Enrique Martinez (1874-1917) Spanish
£11795 $23000   (23-Oct-90 SY.NY422/R) Horses on the docks (49x63cm-19x25in) s.
£12000 $23640   (5-Oct-90 C148/R) Waiting for boat (50x40cm-20x16in) s.
£20169 $34892   (21-May-91 EP.M21/R) Barca con pescadores (54x69cm-21x27in) s.
                      (S.P 3700000)
£20652 $39652   (19-Dec-90 ANS.M48/R) El estudio del pintor (59x74cm-23x29in) s.
                      (S.P 3800000)
£25641 $50000   (23-Oct-90 SY.NY421/R) Fishing boats at the pier (54x65cm-21x26in) s.s.
£35897 $70000   (23-Oct-90 SY.NY116/R) Return from fishing (109x104cm-43x41in) s.

CUBLEY, Henry Hadfield (19th C) British
£600 $1074   (12-Mar-91 N264) Near Inversnaid with cattle and drover
                      (58x91cm-23x36in) s.d.1887

CUCCHI, Enzo (1950-) Italian
£9704 $18729   (13-Dec-90 F.M449/R) Senza titolo (23x69cm-9x27in) s.d.1978verso
                      cardboard (I.L 21000000)
£11784 $22743   (13-Dec-90 F.M434/R) Allegoria (69x65cm-27x26in) s. canvas laid down on
                      board (I.L 25500000)
£2692 $4442   *(10-Jul-91 FB.P104/R) Composition fantastique (45x16cm-18x6in) s.d.1984*
                      verso pastel lead pencil (F.FR 27000)

CUCUEL, Edward (1875-1951) American
£2123 $3800   (14-Mar-91 CH.NY195/R) Train yard in winter (51x61cm-20x24in) s.verso
£4233 $8000   (26-Sep-90 SY.NY163/R) Lady with fan (65x47cm-26x19in) s. i.label verso
£5763 $9393   (3-Jul-91 WE.MU218/R) Still life of flowers (40x38cm-16x15in) s.
                      (DM 17000)
£10922 $21406   (24-Nov-90 N.M110/R) Artist's house beneath trees, autumn
                      (90x100cm-35x39in) (DM 32000)
£12925 $22878   (20-Mar-91 KM.K1137/R) Young lady wearing straw hat seated in rowing
                      boat in the midday sun (55x47cm-22x19in) s. board on board
                      (DM 38000)
£15511 $30557   (30-Oct-90 BU.S310/R) Autumn (80x65cm-31x26in) s. (S.KR 170000)
£15734 $30367   (12-Dec-90 SY.MU74/R) The secret landing place (70x54cm-28x21in) s.
                      (DM 45000)
£17123 $27911   (12-Jun-91 SY.MU137/R) Under the trees (63x78cm-25x31in) s.
                      s.i.stretcher (DM 50000)
£22337 $43780   (16-Feb-91 GF.H7/R) In October (101x101cm-40x40in) s. i.verso
                      (DM 65000)
£25685 $41866   (12-Jun-91 SY.MU136/R) By the lake (79x79cm-31x31in) s. s.verso
                      s.stretcher (DM 75000)
£1005 $1900   *(25-Sep-90 CE.NY73/R) Woman by the sea (48x44cm-19x17in) s.i.d. '27 W/C*
                      gouache

CUDENNEC, Patrice (?) ?
£567 $981   (12-May-91 T.B92/R) Priere bretonne (55x33cm-22x13in) s. (F.FR 5700)

CUECO, Henri (1929-?) French?
£859 $1676   *(15-Oct-90 CSC.P72/R) Mur de petites briques (54x67cm-21x26in) s.*
                      col.crayons (F.FR 8500)

CUELLAR, Teresa (1934-) Colombian
£3571 $7000   *(20-Nov-90 CH.NY163/R) Citrus (130x150cm-51x59in) s.d.87 pastel*

CUENI, August (1883-1966) Swiss
£833 $1392   (7-Jun-91 ZOF.Z1297) Geraniums in terracotta pot (50x39cm-20x15in)
                      s.d.1918 board (S.FR 2100)
£880 $1487   (1-May-91 GD.B176) Ferden in Lotschental (32x29cm-13x11in) s.d.1943
                      pavatex (S.FR 2200)

CUEVAS, Jose Luis (1934-) Mexican
£592 $1166   *(1-Oct-90 CC.P21) Autoretratto en el Pere Lachaise (30x22cm-12x9in)*
                      s.d.1979 pen Indian ink wash (F.FR 6000)
£918 $1800   *(20-Nov-90 CH.NY258/R) Untitled (33x48cm-13x19in) s.i.d.1962 pen wash*
£1224 $2400   *(20-Nov-90 CH.NY262/R) Funeral de un dictador (50x66cm-20x26in) s.d.59*
                      i.d.verso brush ink wash

CUEVAS, Jose Luis (1934-) Mexican-cont.
£1531 $3000   *(20-Nov-90 CH.NY260/R) Frequenters of 42nd Street (28x35cm-11x14in)
s.i.d.1968 pen wash W/C*
£3061 $6000   *(20-Nov-90 CH.NY257/R) El Obrador de Juan Carreno - autopotrait au
marche de Hamburg (74x99cm-29x39in) s.i.d.73 col.pencil pen*
£3827 $7500   *(19-Nov-90 SY.NY290/R) Victimas (121x79cm-48x31in) s.d.27/II/1983 pencil*

CUGAT, Delia (1935-) Argentinian
£6977 $12000   *(15-May-91 CH.NY132/R) Mise en scene (97x146cm-38x57in) s. l.stretcher*

CUGAT, Xavier (1898-1990) Spanish
£605 $1210   *(6-Feb-91 ANS.M163/R) Manuel Fraga (48x32cm-19x13in) s. col.dr
(S.P 110000)*

CUITT, George (circle) (18/19th C) British
£1200 $2148   *(14-Mar-91 ZZ.B188) Figures in an extensive lake landscape, possibly
Ireland (60x84cm-24x33in)*

CUITT, George (elder) (1743-1818) British
£2600 $4654   *(9-Apr-91 C102/R) Lancaster from the river Lune. Lancaster Castle and
Priory (44x57cm-17x22in) W/C bodycol pair*

CUITT, George (style) (18/19th C) British
£1600 $2864   *(10-Apr-91 S177/R) View of Knaresborough Castle from River Nidd
(78x109cm-31x43in)*

CUIXART, Modest (1925-) Spanish
£8333 $14417   *(25-May-91 AB.L58/R) Untitled (92x73cm-36x29in) s.d.1958 oil filler
(S.FR 21000)*
£380 $740   *(17-Oct-90 FER.M59/R) Cabezas (20x23cm-8x9in) init.d.75 ink (S.P 70000)*
£646 $1092   *(15-Apr-91 CC.P26/R) 1954 (37x29cm-15x11in) s.d.1954 W/C (F.FR 6500)*
£3777 $6384   *(15-Apr-91 CC.P119/R) Composition (47x33cm-19x13in) s.d.1956-1957 verso
oil collage canvas (F.FR 38000)*
£19742 $33167   *(25-Apr-91 EP.M17/R) Sin titulo (90x67cm-35x26in) s.i.d.59verso mixed
media oil canvas (S.P 3600000)*

CULL, Alma Burlton (fl.1906-1927) British
£550 $1073   *(18-Oct-90 CSK49/R) Ship-of-the-line, probably H.M.S. Victory, becalmed
(32x53cm-13x21in) s.d.1926 pencil W/C*

CULLBERG, Erland (1931-) Swedish
£823 $1612   *(20-Nov-90 GO.G39) Figures (98x77cm-39x30in) s. (S.KR 9000)*
£943 $1632   *(22-May-91 BA.S347/R) Rain forest (116x73cm-46x29in) s. (S.KR 10000)*
£1390 $2697   *(4-Dec-90 BA.S80 a/R) Composition (116x89cm-46x35in) s. (S.KR 15000)*
£1415 $2448   *(22-May-91 BA.S341/R) Fantasy, Parisian blue and silver
(182x122cm-72x48in) s. (S.KR 15000)*
£1602 $2708   *(18-Apr-91 BU.S34/R) Model (210x135cm-83x53in) s. (S.KR 17000)*
£1622 $3146   *(4-Dec-90 BA.S82/R) Green figure (135x160cm-53x63in) s. (S.KR 17500)*
£2642 $4570   *(22-May-91 BA.S343/R) Figures (130x130cm-51x51in) (S.KR 28000)*

CULLEN, Maurice Galbraith (1866-1934) Canadian
£1645 $3240   *(30-Oct-90 SY.T121/R) Raft on the St Lawrence (20x34cm-8x13in)
s.i.d.95verso panel (C.D 3750)*
£3070 $6048   *(30-Oct-90 SY.T98/R) Winter landscape with mountains and river
(37x46cm-15x18in) s. panel (C.D 7000)*
£7071 $12232   *(6-May-91 SY.T60/R) Wild Cat Creek (45x37cm-18x15in) s. (C.D 14000)*
£9596 $16601   *(6-May-91 SY.T61/R) Winter landscape with lake (44x55cm-17x22in) s.
(C.D 19000)*

CULVER, Charles (?) ?
£405 $700   *(21-May-91 BG.M878/R) Winter landscape with figures (36x48cm-14x19in)
s.d.1941 W/C*
£462 $800   *(21-May-91 BG.M877/R) Barn owls (69x51cm-27x20in) s.d.1951 W/C htd white*

CULVERHOUSE, Johann Mongels (fl.1849-18⌐1) Dutch
£1429 $2800   *(16-Feb-91 W.W11/R) View of family by candlelight with moon beyond
(61x81cm-24x32in) s.d.67*
£2604 $5000   *(17-Dec-90 SY.NY116/R) Night market (25x36cm-10x14in) s.d.62 panel*
£3479 $6750   *(5-Dec-90 D.NY7/R) Grand Canal, Venice by moonlight (76x137cm-30x54in)
s.d.1870*
£5897 $11500   *(25-Oct-90 GRO.B77/R) Evening market place (102x81cm-40x32in) s.d.1874*

CUMBRAE-STEWART, J A (1885-1960) Australian
£720 $1174   *(2-Jul-91 SWS527) Portrait of young girl, half-draped (35x25cm-14x10in)
s. pastel*

CUMBRAE-STEWART, Janet Agnes (1885-1960) Australian
£633 $1071   *(16-Apr-91 J.M1080) Venetian canal (37x45cm-15x18in) s.d.'26 pastel
(A.D 1400)*
£1520 $2964   *(15-Oct-90 AAA.S98) The green bowl (41x31cm-16x12in) s.d.'27 pastel
(A.D 3800)*
£2124 $4183   *(13-Nov-90 J.M6/R) Young girl (36x27cm-14x11in) s.d.21 pastel
(A.D 5500)*
£3586 $7064   *(31-Oct-90 CH.S62/R) Nude woman with chiffon stole (44x35cm-17x14in)
s.d.19 pastel (A.D 9000)*

CUMBRAE-STEWART, Janet Agnes (1885-1960) Australian-cont.
£5485 $10532   (14-Aug-90 SY.ME197/R) Portrait of a young girl-weary (36x26cm-14x10in)
                     s.d.'21 i. verso pastel (A.D 13000)

CUNAEUS, Conradyn (1828-1895) Dutch
£1364 $2686   (30-Oct-90 CH.AM273/R) Portrait of borzoi dog, Fairy (43x61cm-17x24in)
                     s. panel (D.FL 4500)
£2500 $4300   (17-May-91 C69/R) Lurcher and chocolate retriever in interior
                     (48x67cm-19x26in) s. panel
£2532 $4861   (14-Aug-90 SY.ME173/R) Two huntsmen with retrievers (21x31cm-8x12in)
                     board (A.D 6000)

CUNDALL, Charles (1890-1971) British
£960 $1622   (1-May-91 PHL147/R) Bears at zoo (34x42cm-13x17in) s.d.1932 i.verso
                     panel
£1000 $1960   (24-Jan-91 CSK159/R) Demolition of Old St. Thomas's (63x112cm-25x44in)
                     s.
£1150 $2231   (7-Dec-90 K541/R) Irish farmyard, County Wicklow (43x56cm-17x22in) s.
£3200 $6272   (22-Nov-90 CG562/R) View of Edinburgh looking towards Edinburgh Castle
                     from Calton Hill (50x61cm-20x24in) s. s.i.verso panel

CUNEO, Jose (1889-?) Latin American
£6091 $12000   (1-Nov-90 GC.M3) Arroyo Conventos (80x80cm-31x31in)
£9626 $18000   (1-Aug-90 BAV.M5) Lago de Albano (92x88cm-36x35in)
£14706 $27500   (1-Aug-90 BAV.M4) Paisaje de Minas (270x220cm-106x87in)
£618 $1050   (27-May-91 GC.M381) Tuna y nido de Hornero (28x23cm-11x9in) s. pastel

CUNEO, Rinaldo (1877-1935) American
£918 $1800   (13-Feb-91 B.SF2152/R) Desert and mountains (28x31cm-11x12in) s. board
£1276 $2500   (13-Feb-91 B.SF2160/R) Fort Point, San Francisco Bay (28x32cm-11x13in)
                     s.
£3333 $6500   (10-Oct-90 B.SF642/R) Thunder and lightning (51x61cm-20x24in) s.
£3590 $7000   (10-Oct-90 B.SF473/R) Figures on San Francisco coast (61x74cm-24x29in)
                     s.
£3846 $7500   (10-Oct-90 B.SF484/R) Vulcan's playground (58x61cm-23x24in) s. panel
£4103 $8000   (10-Oct-90 B.SF485/R) Calling home fishermen (61x74cm-24x29in) s.d.1913
£4872 $9500   (10-Oct-90 B.SF647/R) Still life with pears and squash (60x74cm-24x29in)
                     s.

CUNEO, Terence (1907-) British
£1300 $2197   (2-May-91 C65/R) Armstrong Siddeley (59x72cm-23x28in) s.

CUNLIFFE, D (19th C) British
£1000 $1960   (22-Jan-91 PH103/R) Man selling cherries (30x35cm-12x14in) s.d.1827
                     s.i.verso

CUNNINGHAM, John (1926-) British
£800 $1512   (27-Sep-90 CG125) Coastal landscape (76x91cm-30x36in) s.

CUNSOLO, Victor J (1898-1937) Argentinian
£9574 $18000   (18-Sep-90 RO.BA28/R) Chilecito (68x94cm-27x37in) s.d.932

CUNY, Francois Eugene (1839-1876) French
£2100 $3444   (18-Jun-91 PH55/R) The reading lesson (65x110cm-26x43in) s.d.1874

CUNZ, Martha (1876-?) Swiss
£1067 $2006   (20-Sep-90 D.V200/R) Portrait of a child (58x45cm-23x18in) oil tempera
                     double-sided (A.S 22000)

CUPRIEN, Frank W (1871-1948) American
£612 $1200   (12-Feb-91 MOR.P54) Coastal Silvery Light-Monterey (41x53cm-16x21in) s.
                     masonite
£816 $1600   (12-Feb-91 MOR.P60) Seascape at sunset (25x36cm-10x14in) s. board

CURLING, Peter (?) Irish?
£1600 $3120   (18-Oct-90 CSK288/R) Mares grazing in the paddock (61x76cm-24x30in) s.
£3000 $5850   (18-Oct-90 CSK283/R) The steeplechasers (101x153cm-40x60in) s.

CURNOCK, James Jackson (1839-?) British
£1500 $2925   (18-Oct-90 SC3125/R) Country folk (37x35cm-15x14in) s.d.1860 i. verso
                     panel
£1200 $2400   (8-Feb-91 C59/R) Sunshine after rain (46x61cm-18x24in) s.d.1881
                     indist.i. pencil W/C

CURNOCK, James Jackson and WAINEWRIGHT, Thomas Francis (19th C) British
£450 $734   (14-Jun-91 C61 a/R) Anglers on a riverbank (36x53cm-14x21in) s.d.1860
                     pencil W/C htd. bodycol.

CURRADI, Francesco (1570-1661) Italian
£4098 $7705   (19-Sep-90 GK.Z813/R) Salome with head of St John the Baptist
                     (85x65cm-33x26in) painted with studio (S.FR 10000)
£1000 $1930   (11-Dec-90 C268) A young boy holding a staff (27x19cm-11x7in) i. chk.
£1733 $3067   (19-Mar-91 F.M271/R) Cristo e l'adultera (34x23cm-13x9in) black and
                     white chk (I.L 3800000)
£2500 $4800   (18-Feb-91 S78/R) Standing draped male figure holding book and quill
                     (38x21cm-15x8in) chk

CURRADI, Francesco (1570-1661) Italian-cont.
£2900 $5597   *(11-Dec-90 C33/R) A page from behind, wearing a feathered hat, pointing with his left arm (19x23cm-7x9in) chk.*

CURRAN, Charles Courtney (1861-1942) American
£569 $950   (5-Jun-91 D.NY23) Mountain top (25x30cm-10x12in) s. s.l. board
£651 $1250   (29-Nov-90 MFA.C178) Nasturtiums (15x30cm-6x12in) s.
£833 $1600   (29-Nov-90 MFA.C168) Cloudy day (30x41cm-12x16in) s. board
£1026 $2000   (21-Oct-90 HG.C51) Study of wood nymph (41x25cm-16x10in) s.
£1337 $2300   (19-May-91 LIT.L150) Coming shower (30x76cm-12x30in) s. panel
£1628 $2800   (19-May-91 LIT.L60) Fox and eagle (23x30cm-9x12in) s. board
£1919 $3300   (19-May-91 LIT.L160) Across Grand Canal s.d.1926 canvasboard
£2384 $4100   (19-May-91 LIT.L70) Boulders on Bear cliff - Conference (38x76cm-15x30in) s.d.1934 board
£4535 $7800   (19-May-91 LIT.L120) Waltzing clouds (46x56cm-18x22in) s.d.1925 board
£6358 $11000   (22-May-91 CH.NY241/R) The glow of sunset (51x23cm-20x9in) s.d.'97
£7345 $13000   (22-Mar-91 S.W2826/R) Figures by lake - nocturnal view (56x46cm-22x18in) s.d.1902
£9012 $15500   (19-May-91 LIT.L100) Shawangunk Mountains in Catskills (76x102cm-30x40in) s.d.1928
£10000 $17200   (19-May-91 LIT.L50) High clouds, Cragsmoor (64x76cm-25x30in) s.d.1928
£13021 $25000   (29-Nov-90 SY.NY80/R) Pink parasol (64x76cm-25x30in) s.d.1927 i.verso
£13402 $26000   (7-Dec-90 S.W2659/R) Far away thoughts (56x46cm-22x18in) s. s.l.verso
£16927 $32500   (29-Nov-90 SY.NY54/R) Children fishing (46x81cm-18x32in) s.d.1897 i.stretcher
£50265 $95000   (26-Sep-90 SY.NY138/R) On the cliff (76x76cm-30x30in) s.d.1910

CURRIE, Ken (20th C) ?
£1000 $1950   *(10-Oct-90 PHG13/R) Riley in Warsaw (151x104cm-59x41in) i.d.Nov.80 conte*

CURRIE, Sidney (fl.1892-1930) British
£300 $537   *(14-Mar-91 L19) Willows on river near Tewkesbury (23x33cm-9x13in) s. W/C*

CURRIER, J Frank (1843-1909) American
£2926 $5500   (19-Sep-90 B.SF2782/R) Storm clouds (74x117cm-29x46in) canvas laid down

CURRY, Robert F (1872-1945) American
£872 $1701   (13-Oct-90 KRA.D188) Winter landscape at sunset, evening glow (64x80cm-25x31in) s. board (DM 2600)
£884 $1424   (26-Jun-91 KM.K1416/R) Snowy Alpine mountain landscape (60x75cm-24x30in) s. (DM 2600)

CURSITER, Stanley (1887-1976) British
£22000 $41140   (28-Aug-90 S1004/R) The seamstress (51x61cm-20x24in) s.d.1923
£3800 $6118   *(27-Jun-91 CG7/R) The Japanese Pring collection (56x76cm-22x30in) s.d.1911 W/C*

CURTIS, George (19th C) American
£867 $1500   (21-May-91 CE.NY285/R) By bookstalls on Seine (41x27cm-16x11in) s.i.d.1899

CURTIS, James Waltham (19/20th C) Australian
£579 $1141   (13-Nov-90 J.M317) Digging for water (40x66cm-16x26in) s.d.93 board (A.D 1500)

CURTIS, Jenny C (19th C) American
£1371 $2700   (16-Nov-90 DM.D2118/R) Hat full of cherries (56x69cm-22x27in) s. canvas on board

CURTIS, William Fuller (1873-?) American
£508 $1000   (3-Nov-90 S.BM149/R) Swallow and apple blossoms. Portrait of young woman (76x61cm-30x24in) s.d.1911 oil metallic panel double-sided

CURZON, Paul Alfred de (1820-1895) French
£4000 $6880   (17-May-91 C18 b/R) Scene in Tuscany (32x42cm-13x17in) s.

CUSACHS Y CUSACHS, J (1851-1908) Spanish
£1499 $2458   (17-Jun-91 DUR.M1408/R) Hipica (37x60cm-15x24in) bears sig. panel (S.P 275000)

CUSACHS Y CUSACHS, Jose (1851-1908) Spanish
£8163 $16082   (14-Nov-90 FB.P258/R) Revue militaire (75x120cm-30x47in) s. (F.FR 80000)
£601 $1039   *(8-May-91 FER.M19/R) Soldado de espaldas saludando (39x26cm-15x10in) s. chl dr (S.P 110000)*
£978 $1574   *(25-Jun-91 FER.M5/R) Soldado descansando al pie del canon (9x15cm-4x6in) s. pencil dr W/C (S.P 180000)*

CUSATI, Gaetano (18th C) Italian
£14070 $23075   (21-Jun-91 SY.MO109/R) Nature morte aux fleurs, fruits et chien (17x28cm-7x11in) copper (F.FR 140000)

CUSTER, Edward L (1837-1880) American
£726 $1300   (14-Apr-91 JRB.C109/R) Autumnal landscape with pond and cows (18x28cm-7x11in) s.d.1868 board
£1117 $2000   (14-Apr-91 JRB.C110/R) White mountains landscape (15x23cm-6x9in) mono. board

CUSTIS, Eleanor Parke (1897-1983) American
£1117 $2100   (11-Aug-90 COL.M90/R) Marketplace (48x64cm-19x25in) s. gouache
£1510 $2900   (29-Nov-90 MFA.C149/R) Albanian street scene (48x64cm-19x25in) s. gouache

CUTRONE, Ronnie (20th C) American
£1786 $3500   (6-Nov-90 CE.NY314/R) When you wish upon a star (105x75cm-41x30in) s.d.1988 i. verso acrylic graphite silver foil

CUVENES, Johannes (attrib) (17th C) German
£1803 $3228   (8-Apr-91 CH.R153/R) Natura morta con pesci, contenitore e canne da pesca (40x50cm-16x20in) panel (I.L 4000000)

CUYC, A (?) ?
£756 $1474   (24-Oct-90 GM.B1064) Betail le long de la riviere (30x40cm-12x16in) s. wood (B.FR 46000)

CUYLENBORCH, Abraham van (1620-1658) Dutch
£2167 $3618   (6-Jun-91 D.V310/R) Diana bathing (65x96cm-26x38in) panel (A.S 45000)
£3041 $5139   (3-May-91 SA.A1621/R) Diana and her followers bathing (59x81cm-23x32in) panel (DM 9000)
£3333 $6500   (10-Oct-90 CH.NY45/R) Maidens bathing in grotto (50x72cm-20x28in) s. panel
£3846 $7500   (11-Oct-90 SY.NY115/R) Diana and nymphs bathing in grotto (43x51cm-17x20in) s.d.1644 panel

CUYLENBORCH, Abraham van (attrib) (1620-1658) Dutch
£2039 $3914   (30-Nov-90 APT.P49/R) La Madeleine en priere dans un site rocheux (50x70cm-20x28in) panel (F.FR 20000)

CUYLENBORCH, Abraham van (circle) (1620-1658) Dutch
£5200 $8476   (2-Jul-91 PH158/R) Diana resting from the hunt (50x82cm-20x32in) panel

CUYLENBURGH, Cornelis van (1758-1827) Dutch
£1700 $3145   (5-Mar-91 SWS1426/R) Dutch interior with figures (39x48cm-15x19in) s.d.1818 panel

CUYLENBURGH, van (19th C) ?
£746 $1260   (18-Apr-91 APT.P75) Portrait d'un homme en habit noir a travers un oculus (26x21cm-10x8in) s.d.1813 panel (F.FR 7500)

CUYP, Aelbert (1620-1691) Dutch
£21176 $36000   (31-May-91 CH.NY141/R) Landscape with white horse and cart by farmhouse and figures (41x53cm-16x21in) s. panel
£102775 $199383   (7-Dec-90 CH.MO311/R) Paysage aux trois moulins (61x82cm-24x32in) s. panel (F.FR 1000000)

CUYP, Aelbert (circle) (1620-1691) Dutch
£15294 $26000   (31-May-91 CH.NY155/R) River landscape with figures on the shore (54x93cm-21x37in) bears sig. panel

CUYP, Aelbert (style) (1620-1691) Dutch
£833 $1400   (17-Jul-91 SY.NY124/R) Landscape with cows by the shore (28x41cm-11x16in) panel

CUYP, Benjamin Gerritsz (1612-1652) Dutch
£7000 $11410   (3-Jul-91 PLF.P56/R) L'operation de la loupe (65x82cm-26x32in) s. (F.FR 70000)

CUYP, Benjamin Gerritsz (attrib) (1612-1652) Dutch
£1223 $2410   (14-Nov-90 SY.AM79/R) Annunciation to the Shepherds (69x92cm-27x36in) panel (D.FL 4000)
£2309 $3718   (27-Jun-91 APT.P117/R) Combat de cavaliers (65x81cm-26x32in) bears traces sig. panel (F.FR 23000)

CUYP, Jacob Gerritsz (1594-1651) Dutch
£950 $1606   (18-Apr-91 C6/R) Portrait of a young boy, half length, holding a nest of fledglings (71x60cm-28x24in)

CUYP, Jacob Gerritsz (attrib) (1594-1651) Dutch
£19133 $37500   (7-Nov-90 B.SF1023/R) Portrait of young girl with red coral necklace and bracelets holding rattle (71x51cm-28x20in) cradled panel

CUYP, Jacob Gerritsz (circle) (1594-1651) Dutch
£3077 $6000   (10-Oct-90 CH.NY78/R) Sheep in landscape (75x110cm-30x43in) s. panel
£4103 $8000   (10-Oct-90 CH.NY10/R) Portrait of young boy as shepherd standing in landscape (133x104cm-52x41in) bears mono.
£8235 $14000   (30-May-91 SY.NY23/R) Portrait of girl (75x52cm-30x20in)

CUYP, Jacob Gerritsz (style) (1594-1651) Dutch
£2096 $3542   (2-May-91 CH.AM62/R) Portrait of a young boy, holding a basket with pears (74x56cm-29x22in) panel oval (D.FL 7000)

CUZCO SCHOOL (?) ?
£707 $1357   (18-Dec-90 DUR.M40) Virgen de la Almudena (85x68cm-33x27in) (S.P 130000)

CUZCO SCHOOL (?) ?-cont.
£707 $1357   (18-Dec-90 DUR.M44) Virgen de la Almudena (85x68cm-33x27in)
                    (S.P 130000)
£824 $1583   (19-Feb-91 DUR.M37) Arcangel (57x40cm-22x16in) (S.P 150000)

CUZCO SCHOOL, 17th C South American
£647 $1100   (27-May-91 GC.M399/R) La Virgen con el Nino (37x25cm-15x10in) gold
                    ground panel

CUZCO SCHOOL, 18th C South American
£1588 $2700   (27-May-91 GC.M398) Virgen de la Paz (51x37cm-20x15in) oil htd gold

CYR, Georges (20th C) French
£2024 $3968   (25-Nov-90 B.PA46) Place de la halle a Caudebec en Caux
                    (55x46cm-22x18in) s. (F.FR 20000)

CZACKA, Beata (?-1824) Polish
£1160 $2320   (10-Feb-91 FDN.W1) Portrait of a girl (43x34cm-17x13in) s.d.179...
                    (P.Z 22000000)

CZAJKOWSKI, Stanislaw (1878-1954) Polish
£590 $1156   (25-Jan-91 REM.W2) Autumn (25x32cm-10x13in) s.d.1931 plywood
                    (P.Z 11000000)

CZARNIKOW (1816-1891) Polish
£717 $1405   (10-Nov-90 FAL.M71/R) Portrait of woman (74x62cm-29x24in) s.d.1846
                    (S.KR 7800)

CZECH, Emil (1862-1929) Austrian
£5763 $9393   (3-Jul-91 WE.MU138/R) Girl by stream in landscape (77x58cm-30x23in)
                    s.d.1903 (DM 17000)

CZENE, Bela (1911-) Hungarian
£2027 $3426   (3-May-91 SA.A779/R) Picnic by the stream (96x67cm-38x26in) s.
                    (DM 6000)

CZERNOTZKY, Ernst (1869-?) ?
£909 $1573   (6-May-91 ZEL.L1637/R) Interior still life with clock and other things
                    on draped table (57x78cm-22x31in) s. (DM 2700)

CZINOBER, Nicolas (20th C) ?
£706 $1229   (25-Mar-91 CR.P76) Boulevard Bonne Nouvelle (46x55cm-18x22in) sig.
                    (F.FR 7100)
£706 $1229   (25-Mar-91 CR.P75) Bouquet de fleurs (60x47cm-24x19in) studio st. verso
                    (F.FR 7100)

D'ALIGNY, Theodore Caruelle see CARUELLE D'ALIGNY, Theodore

D'ARPINO see CESARI, Giuseppe

D'EGVILLE, James Herve (c.1810-1880) British
£550 $1073   (16-Jan-91 CSK48) Fishing craft on Venetian lagoon (28x53cm-11x21in)
                    mono.d.1869 pencil W/C htd.white
£650 $1164   (13-Mar-91 B56) Venice, August 1864 (30x50cm-12x20in) mono.i.d. W/C

D G (?) ?
£1300 $2327   (14-Mar-91 ZZ.B121/R) Figures and a timber cart on a country lane
                    (76x63cm-30x25in) init.d.1876

DAALHOFF, Hermanus Antonius van (1867-1953) Dutch
£690 $1200   (27-Mar-91 B.SF4276/R) Country home in autumn with pond
                    (40x60cm-16x24in) s.

DABO, Leon (1868-1960) American
£988 $1700   (18-May-91 W.W162/R) Bouquet on blue (61x76cm-24x30in) s.
£1163 $2000   (18-May-91 W.W201/R) Trees and rocks (51x41cm-20x16in) s. canvasboard
£1582 $3100   (16-Feb-91 W.W137/R) Artist's wife (61x41cm-24x16in) canvas on masonite
£1628 $2800   (18-May-91 W.W172/R) Shades of fall afternoon (61x76cm-24x30in)
£2514 $4500   (14-Mar-91 CH.NY181/R) Harbour night (68x91cm-27x36in) s.
£8466 $16000   (27-Sep-90 CH.NY190 a/R) Winter evening (53x71cm-21x28in) st.sig. l.
                    stretcher

D'ACERVIA, Bruno (20th C) Italian
£2521 $4917   (22-Oct-90 BR.M162/R) Venere e Amore (60x80cm-24x31in) s.d.1989
                    (I.L 5600000)

DACHAUER, Wilhelm (1881-1951) Austrian
£537 $993   (7-Mar-91 D.V92/R) Wooded landscape (18x22cm-7x9in) board (A.S 11000)

DADAMAINO (20th C) ?
£740 $1436   (3-Dec-90 F.M160) Disegno ottico dinamico (40x40cm-16x16in)
                    s.i.d.1964/65verso ink W/C (I.L 1600000)

DADD, Frank (1851-1929) British
£2800	$4732	(3-May-91 PHE160/R) Her lawyer (46x60cm-18x24in) s.d.1892
£680	$1326	(8-Oct-90 PH97) Feeding rabbits (26x35cm-10x14in) s.d.1919 W/C over pencil
£1040	$1800	(22-May-91 D.NY42/R) King George's visit, India (36x27cm-14x11in) s.i.d.1911 W/C en grisaille cardboard

DADD, Richard (1819-1887) British
£4000	$7880	(1-Nov-90 C165/R) Fantasie Egyptienne (25x18cm-10x7in) s.i.d.1865 W/C htd.white
£8000	$15760	(1-Nov-90 C164/R) Death of Richard II (36x25cm-14x10in) s.i.d.1852 W/C

DADDI, Bernardo (1312-1350) Italian
£320000	$617600	(12-Dec-90 S13/R) St.Catherine of Alexandria (76x42cm-30x17in) tempera panel gold ground

DADE, Ernest (19th C) British
£560	$1002	(11-Mar-91 HS88) Whitby Harbour with trawlers and abbey beyond (34x51cm-13x20in) s.d.1887 W/C
£600	$1170	(16-Jan-91 CSK65/R) Fishing fleet off Staithes, Yorkshire (30x48cm-12x19in) s. pencil W/C htd.white
£950	$1796	(26-Sep-90 B132/R) Bathers on beach (99x124cm-39x49in) s. W/C

DADO (1933-) Yugoslavian
£3084	$6014	(21-Oct-90 P.V70/R) Sans titre (65x81cm-26x32in) s.d.1982-83 verso (F.FR 30500)
£5976	$10159	(2-Jun-91 GL.P197/R) Baby (145x113cm-57x44in) (F.FR 60000)
£992	$1706	(19-May-91 ZZ.F209/R) Composition (76x50cm-30x20in) collage paper laid down on canvas (F.FR 10000)
£2988	$5080	(2-Jun-91 GL.P196/R) Le geant (148x116cm-58x46in) s.d.1950 crayon (F.FR 30000)
£6067	$11830	(21-Oct-90 P.V69/R) La fete Saint-Hubert (115x166cm-45x65in) s.i. mixed media collage (F.FR 60000)

DADO, Miodrag Djuric (1933-) Yugoslavian
£4791	$9247	(10-Dec-90 LD.P50/R) Geant (148x115cm-58x45in) s.d.50 crayon (F.FR 47000)

DAEL, J F van (1764-1840) Dutch
£817	$1568	(18-Dec-90 GM.B893) Nature morte au Hanap (50x40cm-20x16in) s. board (B.FR 49000)
£1661	$2708	(12-Jun-91 GM.B4082/R) Nature morte aux fleurs dans une niche (75x62cm-30x24in) (B.FR 100000)

DAEL, Jan Frans van (1764-1840) Dutch
£24706	$42000	(31-May-91 CH.NY14/R) Peonies, dahlias, epergne of plums and other fruit with flowers on ledge (83x64cm-33x25in) s.d.1814 panel
£52261	$93548	(17-Mar-91 M.V138/R) Vase de fleurs pose sur un entablement (46x37cm-18x15in) s. panel (F.FR 520000)
£206030	$368794	(17-Mar-91 M.V139/R) Composition florale et fruits sur un entablement (106x83cm-42x33in) s.d.1814 (F.FR 2050000)
£4356	$7318	(24-Apr-91 BA.S45 a/R) Still life of flowers, bird's nest and butterflies (78x60cm-31x24in) s. gouache (S.KR 46000)

DAELE, E van den (19th C) Belgian
£917	$1760	(18-Dec-90 GM.B834) Jeune fille et son chien (57x50cm-22x20in) s. board (B.FR 55000)

DAELE, van den (?) ?
£1304	$2334	(9-Apr-91 GM.B597/R) Jeune fille et son chien (57x50cm-22x20in) s. wood (B.FR 80000)

DAENS, A (20th C) Belgian
£524	$901	(14-May-91 GM.B563) Haie de peupliers (53x77cm-21x30in) s. (B.FR 32000)

DAFFINGER, Moritz Michael (1790-1849) Austrian
£7534	$12281	(12-Jun-91 SY.MU24/R) Holy Family with St Elizabeth and St John Baptist (22x16cm-9x6in) s.d.1824verso metal after Raphael (DM 22000)
£716	$1203	(25-Apr-91 D.V193/R) Magdalena Hruschka as Grafin Terzky in Schillers Wallenstein (19x13cm-7x5in) i. W/C indian ink pen (A.S 15000)
£2500	$4750	(12-Sep-90 CSK140/R) Tokens of love (23x18cm-9x7in) s.d.1818 pencil W/C htd white pair
£4000	$6600	(10-Jul-91 C53/R) Princess Clementine Melterwich (8x?cm-3x?in) min.s. gilt-metal mount velvet stand oval
£5822	$9490	(12-Jun-91 N.M395/R) Portrait of lady wearing ruff (7x5cm-3x2in) min.s. W/C gouache oval (DM 17000)
£7500	$12375	(10-Jul-91 C52/R) A lady in low-cut white dress (8x?cm-3x?in) min.s. gilt-metal mount ormolu frame oval
£7500	$14400	(18-Dec-90 C40) Portrait of Lieutenant-Colonel Peter Delancey (8x?cm-3x?in) s.oval chased ormolu in rec.leather mount
£9965	$19233	(12-Dec-90 N.M466/R) Young girl with fur stole and rose (9x8cm-4x3in) s. W/C gouache ivory (DM 28500)

DAFFINGER, Moritz Michael (circle) (1790-1849) Austrian
£1337	$2246	(25-Apr-91 D.V295/R) Portrait of lady with black curls and clouds (7x6cm-3x2in) min. W/C ivory oval (A.S 28000)

D'AGAGGIO (1937-) French
£2039 $3935   (14-Dec-90 RY.P17/R) Antumalal - au coeur du paradis, 1988
(100x100cm-39x39in) s. (F.FR 20000)

D'AGESSY, Therese (19th C) French
£1121 $2164   (12-Dec-90 ZZ.F13/R) Jete de roses (31x40cm-12x16in) s. (F.FR 11000)

DAGIU, Francesco (1714-1784) Italian
£9231 $18000   (10-Oct-90 CH.NY216/R) St Joseph and the infant Christ (81x63cm-32x25in)
£26816 $48000   (10-Apr-91 HF.NY3/R) St. John the Baptist preaching (80x130cm-31x51in)

DAGNAN-BOUVERET, Pascal Adolphe Jean (1852-1929) French
£620 $1035   (22-Jul-91 SWS1081/R) Portrait of Gildys (80x63cm-31x25in) s.d.1910
£4103 $8000   (23-Oct-90 SY.NY271/R) Jeune homme Breton (42x25cm-17x10in) s.d.1887

DAGNAUX, Albert Marie (1861-1933) French
£750 $1260   (18-Jul-91 CSK121) Autumn (60x106cm-24x42in) s.

DAHL, Chrix (1906-) Norwegian?
£2003 $3907   (15-Oct-90 B.O13/R) On the bridge (73x102cm-29x40in) s.d.32 (N.KR 23000)

DAHL, Hans (1849-1937) Norwegian
£804 $1577   (20-Nov-90 GO.G406) After Aine - portrait of girl (27x21cm-11x8in)
s.d.1898 (S.KR 8800)
£1413 $2827   (9-Feb-91 BU.O34) Fjord landscape with rowingboat (19x29cm-7x11in) s.
panel (N.KR 16000)
£4615 $9000   (23-Oct-90 SY.NY160/R) The daughters of Ran (92x144cm-36x57in) s.
£6696 $12522   (29-Aug-90 KH.K33/R) The dairy-woman's Sunday (66x100cm-26x39in) s.
(D.KR 76000)
£7008 $11773   (24-Apr-91 BA.S41/R) Returning home - view from Balestrand
(66x69cm-26x27in) s. (S.KR 74000)
£7031 $11742   (4-Jun-91 BU.O12/R) West coast landscape with harvesting girl
(95x60cm-37x24in) s. (N.KR 81000)
£8800 $16896   (30-Nov-90 C56/R) A summer's day in Norway (83x117cm-33x46in) s.i.

DAHL, Hans Andreas (1881-1919) Norwegian
£2620 $4978   (11-Sep-90 UL.T182/R) Norwegian fjord landscape with red house in
background (50x65cm-20x26in) s. (N.KR 30000)
£3591 $7074   (14-Nov-90 RAS.K592/R) Norwegian fjord landscape with men mooring
rowingboat (98x65cm-39x26in) s. (D.KR 40000)
£4401 $7394   (23-Apr-91 RAS.K111/R) Norwegian fjord landscape with girl by fence
(55x80cm-22x31in) s. (D.KR 50000)
£9800 $18816   (28-Nov-90 S106/R) Woman in mountainous landscape (127x153cm-50x60in) s.
£9898 $18706   (25-Sep-90 FN.S2139/R) Norwegian mountain landscape with figure and view
of fjord (66x100cm-26x39in) s. (DM 29000)

DAHL, I (19th C) Danish
£1971 $3943   (6-Feb-91 RAS.K137/R) Ships portrait 'Casper of Dagoe' (60x85cm-24x33in)
s.d.1876 (D.KR 22000)

DAHL, J (1827-1902) German
£1320 $2218   (23-Apr-91 RAS.K322/R) Seascape with sailing vessel in Sundet
(60x85cm-24x33in) s.d.1879 (D.KR 15000)

DAHL, J C C (1788-1857) Norwegian
£3390 $6576   (4-Dec-90 UL.T194/R) Vesuvius seen from Cartellanese (7x11cm-3x4in)
s.d.1847 (N.KR 38000)
£7136 $13845   (4-Dec-90 UL.T195/R) The Elbe in moonlight (14x22cm-6x9in) (N.KR 80000)

DAHL, Johan Christian Clausen (1788-1857) Norwegian
£16107 $31409   (13-Oct-90 KRA.D190/R) Moonlit Italian landscape (66x92cm-26x36in) s.
(DM 48000)
£32000 $61440   (28-Nov-90 S1/R) The coastal road, Copenhagen (62x77cm-24x30in) s.d.1812
£38000 $62320   (19-Jun-91 S241/R) Boats carrying wood across river (62x98cm-24x39in)
s.d.1822

DAHL, Jorgen (19th C) Danish
£996 $1923   (10-Dec-90 BU.K11/R) Seascape with sailship (60x83cm-24x33in) s.d.1879
(D.KR 11000)
*£850 $1682   (31-Jan-91 RAS.V472/R) Shipsportrait of 'Helge' off Kronborg
(52x78cm-20x31in) s.d.1874 W/C (D.KR 9500)*

DAHL, Michael (1656-1743) Swedish
£1600 $3120   (26-Oct-90 C211/R) Portrait of a lady and child in an archway and
landscape beyond (127x102cm-50x40in)
£2353 $4000   (31-May-91 CH.NY207/R) Portrait of lady as shepherdess leaning against
tree in landscape (100x126cm-39x50in)
£3400 $5610   (10-Jul-91 S113/R) Portrait of Mrs Sarah Finch standing
(123x100cm-48x39in) i.
£7000 $11550   (12-Jul-91 C10/R) Portrait of Gilbert, 4th Earl of Coventry, in
Coronation robes (244x148cm-96x58in) s. with i.
*£2400 $3960   (11-Jul-91 S33/R) Portrait study of head of gentleman (31x25cm-12x10in)
chk*

DAHL, Michael (circle) (1656-1743) Swedish
£1100	$1947	(21-Mar-91 CSK228/R) Portrait of a naturalist, seated, holding an open book in an interior (89x71cm-35x28in)
£1200	$1956	(4-Jul-91 B31) Portrait of a lady, three-quarter length, seated wearing a red dress (128x102cm-50x40in)
£1500	$2685	(12-Apr-91 C120/R) Portrait of Richard Guinness, in jacket and collar (76x63cm-30x25in) in painted oval
£2500	$4125	(9-Jul-91 PH42/R) Portrait of gentleman, said to be Sir George Thomas, Bart, standing (124x102cm-49x40in)
£5000	$9750	(26-Oct-90 C216/R) Portrait of the Misses Woodgate, one holding a spaniel on her lap (127x102cm-50x40in)

DAHL, Michael (style) (1656-1743) Swedish
| £2600 | $5122 | (31-Oct-90 S264/R) Portrait of Anne Borlase wearing dress with blue robes (71x59cm-28x23in) i.verso oval |

DAHL, Niels-Carl-Flindt (1812-1865) Danish
| £12238 | $23741 | (5-Dec-90 DO.H2006/R) Marseille harbour (64x98cm-25x39in) s.i.c.1855 (DM 35000) |

DAHL, Peer Lorentz (1915-) Norwegian
| £890 | $1719 | (13-Dec-90 BU.O2/R) Man on horseback with figures (81x100cm-32x39in) s. s.i.verso (N.KR 10000) |
| £1606 | $3132 | (11-Oct-90 BU.O18/R) Girl carrying bucket (116x82cm-46x32in) s. (N.KR 18500) |

DAHL, Peter (1934-) Swedish
£1384	$2657	(27-Nov-90 BU.S67/R) Interior with three figures (25x33cm-10x13in) s.d.1974 paper (S.KR 15000)
£2039	$3956	(4-Dec-90 BA.S83/R) Still life of fruit and plant (45x53cm-18x21in) init.d.55 (S.KR 22000)
£2583	$4959	(27-Nov-90 BU.S65/R) Gymnastics (73x91cm-29x36in) s.d.1967 (S.KR 28000)
£2828	$4779	(18-Apr-91 BU.S40/R) Couple dancing (132x89cm-52x35in) s.d.1964 (S.KR 30000)
£3875	$7439	(27-Nov-90 BU.S64/R) The models (100x80cm-39x31in) s.d.1967 (S.KR 42000)
£4717	*$8160*	*(22-May-91 BA.S349/R) Couple making love (29x42cm-11x17in) s. W/C (S.KR 50000)*

DAHLEN, Paul (1881-?) German
| £833 | $1492 | (12-Apr-91 AW.H1294/R) Oberwesel on the Rhine with Schonburg (43x50cm-17x20in) s.i. (DM 2500) |
| £1115 | $2174 | (26-Oct-90 KM.K1140) Standard roses in Chiemsee landscape (49x42cm-19x17in) s.d.1911 (DM 3300) |

DAHLGREN, Carl Christian (1841-1920) American
| £686 | $1344 | (20-Nov-90 GO.G408) Seascape with sailing vessel in rough seas (60x102cm-24x40in) s. (S.KR 7500) |

DAHLMAN, Helge (1924-1979) Finnish
£2068	$4054	(24-Nov-90 HOR.H69/R) The harbour (21x27cm-8x11in) s.d.1953 (F.M 14000)
£2149	$4234	(17-Nov-90 BU.H146/R) Breakfast table (40x48cm-16x19in) s.d.62 panel (F.M 15000)
£2568	$5033	(24-Nov-90 HOR.H66/R) Cattle grazing (22x27cm-9x11in) s.d.1979 (F.M 18000)
£3566	$6990	(24-Nov-90 HOR.H67/R) Farm in winter (54x65cm-21x26in) s. (F.M 25000)

DAHLSKOG, Evald (1894-1950) Swedish
| £1549 | $2634 | (28-May-91 AB.S5190/R) Parkview with trees (65x80cm-26x31in) s.d.39 (S.KR 16500) |
| £2736 | $4733 | (22-May-91 BA.S30/R) View from Slottsbacken (73x54cm-29x21in) (S.KR 29000) |

DAHM, Helen (1878-1968) German
£533	*$1007*	*(28-Sep-90 S.Z110) Untitled (70x100cm-28x39in) s.d.1963 gouache (S.FR 1300)*
£988	*$1680*	*(27-May-91 GK.Z5318) Flowering branches (41x30cm-16x12in) s. pastel (S.FR 2500)*
£1061	*$2091*	*(16-Nov-90 GK.Z5346) Geraniums (56x33cm-22x13in) s. s.i.verso pastel chk over gouache board (S.FR 2600)*
£1061	*$2091*	*(16-Nov-90 GK.Z5349) Portrait of woman surrounded by magnolias. Flowers (61x50cm-24x20in) s. pastel double-sided (S.FR 2600)*
£3265	*$6433*	*(16-Nov-90 EA.Z327/R) Egyptian queen (75x59cm-30x23in) s. mixed media pavatex (S.FR 8000)*

DAHMEN, Karl-Fred (1917-1981) German
£2740	$4466	(14-Jun-91 L.K828/R) Stadtbild (24x27cm-9x11in) s.i.d.1955 panel (DM 8000)
£2911	$4745	(14-Jun-91 L.K829/R) Untitled (31x25cm-12x10in) s.d.56 (DM 8500)
£5068	*$8767*	*(21-May-91 WK.M14/R) Composition (62x40cm-24x16in) s. paper (DM 15000)*
£897	*$1721*	*(26-Nov-90 WK.M589/R) Composition (26x3cm-10x1in) s. s.d.1975verso col.pencil pencil board (DM 2600)*
£1706	*$3345*	*(20-Nov-90 L.K199/R) Metaphysische Gedanken (38x36cm-15x14in) s.d.1976 s.i.d.verso col.chk (DM 5000)*
£5424	*$9058*	*(8-Jun-91 HN.H72/R) Collage (38x29cm-15x11in) s. mixed media (DM 16000)*

DAHMEN, Karl-Fred (1917-1981) German-cont.
£5500	$10725	(18-Oct-90 S105/R) Untitled (65x50cm-26x20in) s. s.i.d.1964verso paper collage oil board
£5802	$11372	(24-Nov-90 VG.B363/R) Untitled (40x32cm-16x13in) s.d.1980verso mixed media (DM 17000)
£6757	$11689	(21-May-91 WK.M13/R) Roter Akzent (64x41cm-25x16in) s.d.1960 s.i.d.1960verso mixed media collage (DM 20000)
£6780	$11322	(8-Jun-91 HN.H73/R) Collage (45x32cm-18x13in) s. mixed media (DM 20000)
£7458	$12454	(8-Jun-91 HN.H77/R) Composition (130x120cm-51x47in) gouache chk. (DM 22000)
£9153	$15285	(8-Jun-91 HN.H74/R) Collage (59x45cm-23x18in) s. mixed media (DM 27000)
£10847	$18115	(8-Jun-91 HN.H75/R) Collage (61x51cm-24x20in) s.d.1961 material picture on corrugated paper (DM 32000)
£14000	$27300	(18-Oct-90 C352/R) Untitled (110x94cm-43x37in) s. s.d.1963verso oil composition canvas
£15700	$30771	(24-Nov-90 VG.B368/R) Untitled (46x64cm-18x25in) s.d.1960 mixed media board (DM 46000)
£16216	$27568	(31-May-91 VG.B78/R) Composition grey (72x60cm-28x24in) s.indis.d.19.. i.d.1962verso mixed media canvas (DM 48000)
£22034	$36797	(8-Jun-91 HN.H71/R) Haldenzone (135x110cm-53x43in) s. sand sgraffitti acrylic tempera (DM 65000)
£34130	$66894	(23-Nov-90 VG.B92/R) Death of the matador (120x110cm-47x43in) s.d.1963 s.d.verso mixed media (DM 100000)

DAHN, Walter (20th C) ?
£8673	$17000	(6-Nov-90 CE.NY192/R) Untitled (260x171cm-102x67in) acrylic linen
£3988	$6500	(12-Jun-91 SY.NY187/R) Man crying - capitalism most barbaric of religions, creates and tolerate world hunger (250x150cm-98x59in) s.d.1984 verso spray paint canvas
£6164	$10048	(14-Jun-91 L.K836/R) The revolution (200x150cm-79x59in) s.i.d.1982verso dispersion cotton (DM 18000)

DAINGERFIELD, Elliott (1859-1932) American
£960	$1900	(1-Feb-91 S.W2586/R) Fishing by moonlight (20x28cm-8x11in) s. board

DAINI, Augusto (19th C) Italian
£2300	$3956	(14-May-91 SWS328/R) Recital by the young Mozart (40x63cm-16x25in) s.i.

DAINTREY, Adrian (1902-1988) British
£600	$1152	(21-Feb-91 B5) London to Paris (51x63cm-20x25in) init.

DAJEWSKI, Pawel (1889-?) ?
£979	$1890	(14-Dec-90 BM.B724) Portrait of peasant woman with milk bowl and cat drinking (108x101cm-43x40in) s. (DM 2800)

DAKE, Carel Lodewijk (Jnr) (1886-1946) Dutch
£1524	$2988	(6-Nov-90 SY.AM2/R) View on sawa in Indonesia (67x117cm-26x46in) s. (D.FL 5000)

DAKE, Carel Lodewyk (19/20th C) Dutch
£2195	$4215	(27-Nov-90 SY.AM3596 a) Sawa at sunset (68x119cm-27x47in) s. (D.FL 7200)

DAL, Harald (1901-1972) Norwegian
£1390	$2349	(4-May-91 BU.O17) Summer landscape (60x73cm-24x29in) s. panel (N.KR 16000)
£1606	$2682	(4-Jun-91 BU.O27/R) Landscape (60x73cm-24x29in) s.d.44 panel (N.KR 18500)

DALBONO, Eduardo (1841-1915) Italian
£1300	$2132	(18-Jun-91 PH154/R) Fishing in Mediterranean harbour (12x27cm-5x11in) s. panel
£4211	$8000	(27-Feb-91 SY.NY350/R) Young boy with violin (40x21cm-16x8in) s. panel
£5000	$10000	(18-Oct-90 F.M51/R) Popolana al verone (25x14cm-10x6in) s. panel (I.L 11000000)
£7169	$13907	(4-Dec-90 F.R160/R) Campagna con case rustiche a Portici (46x64cm-18x25in) s. (I.L 15500000)
£9000	$17280	(27-Nov-90 PH176/R) Fishing in continental harbour (44x74cm-17x29in) s.
£9250	$17945	(5-Dec-90 F.M98/R) Marina con pescatori (34x45cm-13x18in) s. panel (I.L 20000000)
£2273	$4455	(22-Nov-90 SY.MI7/R) Torre in un parco (25x17cm-10x7in) s. W/C gouache (I.L 5000000)

DALBY OF YORK, David (1794-1836) British
£740	$1280	(20-May-91 SWS318/R) A dark bay hunter in a stable s.d.1829
£1000	$1720	(16-May-91 CSK65) Saddled bay hunter with groom and dog in landscape (58x71cm-23x28in) with sig.
£1500	$2925	(18-Oct-90 SC3119/R) On the scent (21x30cm-8x12in) s.d.1855 panel
£2595	$5008	(11-Dec-90 FER.M181/R) Preparando los caballos (90x124cm-35x49in) s.d.1882 (S.P 475000)

DALBY OF YORK, David (attrib) (1794-1836) British
£1500	$2955	(31-Oct-90 S384/R) Hunter in stable yard (68x89cm-27x35in)
£2395	$4000	(7-Jun-91 SY.NY89/R) A chestnut bay in a loose box (44x58cm-17x23in)

DALBY, John (19th C) British
£2500	$4125	(12-Jul-91 C107/R) Huntsman fallen from bay hunter and another huntsman in landscape (32x40cm-13x16in) s.d.1841
£4500	$8865	(16-Nov-90 C106/R) Coming home from the fair (25x38cm-10x15in) s. i.d.1790verso
£4800	$8592	(12-Apr-91 C86/R) Coach and four on country road (23x30cm-9x12in) i.verso board

DALE (?) ?
| £800 | $1560 | (15-Jan-91 C72/R) Pekingese in country garden (56x81cm-22x32in) s. |

DALEN, Jan (circle) (17th C) Flemish
| £1835 | $3615 | (13-Nov-90 CH.AM58/R) Shipping on Maas near Dordrecht, with elegant figures strolling on quay (54x78cm-21x31in) with sig. panel (D.FL 6000) |

DALEN, Jan van II (1611-c.1677) Dutch
| £3413 | $6451 | (25-Sep-90 FN.S2140/R) Vanitas still life with books, globe, scull and violin on table (66x95cm-26x37in) s.d.1663 panel (DM 10000) |

DALENS, Dirk II (1659-1688) Dutch
| £3600 | $6912 | (18-Feb-91 S207/R) Woodland scene with peasant, huntsmen and animals (38x28cm-15x11in) gouache |

D'ALESI, Hugo (1849-1906) French
| £1000 | $1680 | (24-Apr-91 MJ.P114/R) La mer de glace (77x112cm-30x44in) (F.FR 10000) |

DALGAS, Carlo (1820-1851) Danish
| £525 | $940 | (9-Apr-91 RAS.K2050) Sheep on heath with view of Skarritso (52x75cm-20x30in) (D.KR 6000) |

DALGLISH, William (1860-1909) British
| £1000 | $1870 | (28-Aug-90 S765/R) St Monance (65x40cm-26x16in) s.i. |

D'ALHEIM, Jean (1894-?) Russian
| £900 | $1476 | (18-Jun-91 PH80) The fisherman's retreat (48x60cm-19x24in) s. panel |

DALI, Louis (20th C?) French?
| £677 | $1165 | (14-May-91 GF.L2665/R) Paysage de l'Ille de France (50x61cm-20x24in) s. i.verso (S.FR 1700) |

DALI, Salvador (1904-1989) Spanish
£25381	$50000	(2-Oct-90 CH.NY144/R) Verre de vin et bateau (20x26cm-8x10in) s.d.1956
£121827	$240000	(2-Oct-90 CH.NY183/R) Saint-Georges et le dragon (23x31cm-9x12in) s.d.1962
£140987	$229809	(15-Jun-91 FB.P53/R) Saint-Georges et le dragon (23x31cm-9x12in) s.d.1962 (F.FR 1400000)
£210299	$412187	(22-Nov-90 EP.M22/R) Anatomias (50x64cm-20x25in) s.d.1937 board laid down on panel (S.P 39000000)
£219653	$380000	(8-May-91 CH.NY44/R) Trois femmes imitant les mouvements d'un voilier (51x65cm-20x26in) s.d.1940
£243655	$480000	(15-Nov-90 CH.NY276/R) Portrait of Mrs Jack Warner (111x95cm-44x37in) s.
£541	$935	(22-May-91 CH.AM777) Nude woman (34x36cm-13x14in) s. black crayon (D.FL 1800)
£867	$1500	(21-May-91 GRO.B196/R) Astrologer (25x18cm-10x7in) pen double-sided with letter
£2284	$4500	(13-Nov-90 CE.NY153/R) Tete de femme (35x43cm-14x17in) pen
£2500	$4425	(19-Mar-91 C136/R) Etude d'anges (26x19cm-10x7in) s. ballpoint pen on headed stationery
£2500	$4025	(24-Jun-91 CSK182/R) Personnage surrealiste (25x19cm-10x7in) s.i.d.1942 pen ink
£3000	$5850	(17-Oct-90 S181/R) Les cocus du vieil art moderne (17x11cm-7x4in) s.i.d.1953 pen ink
£3213	$5944	(6-Mar-91 APT.P7/R) Pion d'echec (72x57cm-28x22in) s. pen (F.FR 32000)
£3553	$7000	(2-Oct-90 CH.NY188/R) Taburete bar (29x39cm-11x15in) i. ball-point pen pencil board
£4082	$8000	(15-Feb-91 SY.NY111/R) Aquacade, Eleanor Holm (23x18cm-9x7in) s.i. india ink pencil card laid down
£4103	$8000	(10-Oct-90 SY.NY55/R) The world of Salvador dali, dedication page (28x48cm-11x19in) s.i.d.1964 ball point pen
£4625	$8972	(9-Dec-90 E.LA137/R) Moise sauve des eaux (50x65cm-20x26in) s. W/C pen (F.FR 45000)
£5076	$10000	(2-Oct-90 CH.NY186/R) Dali noche (24x31cm-9x12in) s. Indian ink over pencil
£5102	$10000	(15-Feb-91 SY.NY110/R) Eleanor Holm (23x18cm-9x7in) s.i. india ink card on board
£5137	$8373	(15-Jun-91 L.K135/R) Female dancer (16x10cm-6x4in) s. indian ink pen (DM 15000)
£5584	$11000	(2-Oct-90 CH.NY185/R) Mesas-canapes (32x41cm-13x16in) s.i.d.1957 ball-point pen pencil
£6149	$10453	(28-May-91 KF.M584/R) Self portrait as hermaphrodite (27x21cm-11x8in) ball point pen pencil col.pencil (DM 18200)
£6853	$13500	(15-Nov-90 D.NY74/R) Aliyah - land come to life (56x38cm-22x15in) s.d.1967 num.4 verso mixed media
£7653	$15000	(15-Feb-91 SY.NY113/R) Eleanor Holm (23x18cm-9x7in) s. india ink pencil card laid down

DALI, Salvador (1904-1989) Spanish-cont.

£8629	$17000	(2-Oct-90 CH.NY172/R) Final study for Family of Marsupial Centaurs (41x33cm-16x13in) s.d.1941 pencil Indian ink paper laid down board
£8844	$15831	(16-Mar-91 APT.P45/R) Portrait de Gala (60x44cm-24x17in) s.d. drawing stumping (F.FR 88000)
£10000	$16100	(25-Jun-91 C268/R) Femme nue flottant (152x102cm-60x40in) mono.d.1974 st.d.verso W/C wax crayon pencil
£10152	$20000	(2-Oct-90 CH.NY187/R) Les trois cornes de rhinoceros (50x65cm-20x26in) s.i.d.1957 ball-point pen
£10152	$20000	(2-Oct-90 CH.NY173/R) Preliminary study for Family of Marsupial Centaurs (47x35cm-19x14in) s.d.1940 pencil Indian ink paper laid down board
£10405	$18000	(9-May-91 CH.NY174/R) San Jorque luchando con el pulpo (50x65cm-20x26in) s.i.d.1963 W/C gouache wash ink over pencil
£11224	$22000	(14-Feb-91 CH.NY66/R) Personnages (44x55cm-17x22in) s.d.1938 brush ink paper on buvard
£12000	$23280	(4-Dec-90 C191/R) Angel of Alchemy (76x56cm-30x22in) s. gouache gold paint
£14213	$28000	(2-Oct-90 CH.NY184/R) Dali noche (32x41cm-13x16in) s.i. oil ball pen plastic overlaid on paper
£14451	$25000	(8-May-91 SY.NY226/R) Standing woman (25x25cm-10x10in) s.d.1961 oil gouache W/C Indian ink board
£18010	$35119	(24-Oct-90 F.M210/R) Gala (61x47cm-24x19in) s. mixed media board (I.L 40000000)
£18349	$35229	(26-Nov-90 GL.P34/R) Le telephone aphrodisiaque (71x56cm-28x22in) s. gouache felt ink (F.FR 180000)
£19000	$33630	(19-Mar-91 C92/R) Mai (51x22cm-20x9in) s.i.d.1949 W/C pen paper on board
£20000	$38800	(4-Dec-90 C220/R) The Phoenix (76x56cm-30x22in) s.d.1974 gouache pen
£22843	$45000	(3-Oct-90 SY.NY177/R) Self portrait (33x41cm-13x16in) s.d.1957 W/C collage pen ink pencil
£25381	$50000	(15-Nov-90 CH.NY193/R) The zebra cavalier (76x100cm-30x39in) s.d.1963 pen brush col.ink board
£38000	$73720	(4-Dec-90 C221/R) Le char d'or (56x40cm-22x16in) s.d.1971 oil pen
£45000	$72450	(26-Jun-91 S268/R) Un chevalier (76x51cm-30x20in) s.i.d.1953 pen indian ink red ink card
£87217	$150886	(21-May-91 DUR.M9/R) Angel en extasis (150x100cm-59x39in) mixed media (S.P 16000000)
£106599	$210000	(14-Nov-90 SY.NY157/R) Adolescence (45x30cm-18x12in) s.d.1942 gouache brush ink
£121387	$210000	(8-May-91 SY.NY193/R) Mysterious mouth appearing in the back of my nurse (45x30cm-18x12in) s.d.1941 gouache

DALIGE DE FONTENAY, Leonard Alexis (1813-1892) French

£870	$1478	(27-May-91 GK.Z5016) Mountain lake landscape with farmhouses in valley (30x52cm-12x20in) s. (S.FR 2200)

DALL, Nicolas Thomas (?-1777) Danish

£11000	$18150	(10-Jul-91 S68/R) View of Rock Hall, Great Haywood, Staffordshire (89x135cm-35x53in)
£12000	$21480	(12-Apr-91 C46/R) View of Fountains Abbey, Yorkshire, with figures and cattle to fore (91x122cm-36x48in)

DALLAIRE, Jean Philippe (1916-1965) Canadian

£717	$1385	(12-Dec-90 EA.M656/R) Garcon-boucher s.d.62 paper (C.D 1600)
£702	$1375	(20-Nov-90 JOY.T346) Carnaval Cagnois (13x27cm-5x11in) s.d.62 gouache (C.D 1600)
£800	$1552	(4-Dec-90 P.Q35) L'ange Destructeur (59x38cm-23x15in) s.d.1938 chl. (C.D 1800)
£1644	$3190	(4-Dec-90 P.Q42/R) Nature Morte (17x15cm-7x6in) s.d.50 gouache (C.D 3700)
£2456	$4814	(20-Nov-90 JOY.T60/R) Head of clown (27x22cm-11x9in) s.d.1952 gouache (C.D 5600)

DALL'OCA BIANCA, Angelo (1858-1942) Italian

£2463	$4261	(25-May-91 KV.L61) The fish seller (159x64cm-63x25in) s. (B.FR 150000)
£11553	$22297	(11-Dec-90 CH.R219/R) Nel porto di Torri (80x90cm-31x35in) s. (I.L 25000000)

DALMATIAN SCHOOL, 15th C European

£12000	$23640	(31-Oct-90 S8/R) St John and St Peter (78x45cm-31x18in) panel

DALMATIAN SCHOOL, 18th C European

£17000	$34000	(7-Feb-91 CSK62/R) Madonna and Child enthroned (106x61cm-42x24in) panel

DALSGAARD, Christen (1824-1907) Danish

£4488	$8842	(14-Nov-90 RAS.K42/R) Young girl writing (64x48cm-25x19in) s.i.d.1871 (D.KR 50000)

DALSGAARD, Sven (1914-) Danish

£792	$1545	(10-Oct-90 RAS.K63) A problem for some of the guests at Hotel Globe (70x56cm-28x22in) s.d.1968verso (D.KR 9000)
£968	$1888	(10-Oct-90 RAS.K62/R) Disappearing summer (43x67cm-17x26in) s. d.1959-60verso (D.KR 11000)
£1056	$1817	(15-May-91 RAS.K6) The green room (56x76cm-22x30in) s.d.1955verso (D.KR 12000)
£1496	$2918	(10-Oct-90 RAS.K60) Dinner (66x66cm-26x26in) s.d.1964 (D.KR 17000)

DALY, Kathleen (1898-) Canadian
£1310 $2581   (12-Nov-90 HO.ED84/R) Portrait of an Indian boy (48x44cm-19x17in) s. (C.D 3000)

DALZIEL, Herbert (1858-?) British
£727 $1368   (20-Sep-90 D.V29/R) Swan by a lake at evening (70x91cm-28x36in) s.d.1899 (A.S 15000)

DALZIEL, James (19th C) British
£741 $1281   (6-May-91 ZEL.L1639/R) Coastal landscape with town beyond (31x47cm-12x19in) s.d.1894 (DM 2200)

DAMERET, Luca (17th C) French
£42000 $68460   (5-Jul-91 C70/R) Bacchus and Ariadne (142x219cm-56x86in)

DAMERON, Emile Charles (1848-1908) French
£959 $1563   (12-Jun-91 N.M396) Shepherd and flock on woodland path (46x38cm-18x15in) s. (DM 2800)
£1651 $3253   (13-Nov-90 AB.S878/R) Summer landscape with watercourse (73x101cm-29x40in) s. (S.KR 18000)

DAMIAN, Horia (20th C) Rumanian
£1952   *$3377*   *(22-May-91 CH.AM703/R) Comme un tapis de Prieres - Zoals een Gebedentapijt (161x130cm-63x51in) s.d.62 i.d.1962 num.2 stretcher oil mixed media (D.FL 6500)*

DAMISCH, Gunter (1958-) Austrian
£526 $911   (8-May-91 D.V234/R) Der Garten der Frau Holle (30x23cm-12x9in) i.verso acrylic (A.S 11000)
£746 $1446   (6-Dec-90 D.V161/R) Untitled s.d.80/1 two parts (A.S 15000)
£2871 $4967   (8-May-91 D.V227/R) Untitled (145x120cm-57x47in) mono.d.84 (A.S 60000)

DAMM, Johan Frederik (1820-1894) Danish
£1600 $3136   (22-Nov-90 CSK96/R) Still life of mixed fruit on vine leaves (33x40cm-13x16in) s.d.1847

DAMME, Frans van (1860-?) Flemish
£722 $1250   (25-May-91 KV.L295) The boathouse (43x60cm-17x24in) s. (B.FR 44000)

DAMME-SYLVA, Emile van (1853-1935) Belgian
£907 $1777   (21-Nov-90 GM.B908) Vaches au pre (48x65cm-19x26in) s. (B.FR 55000)
£1300 $2561   (4-Oct-90 CSK86/R) Cattle in a meadow (60x76cm-24x30in) s.
£1524 $3002   (6-Oct-90 KV.L269/R) In the Polders (56x78cm-22x31in) s. (B.FR 95000)

DAMOYE, Eugene (19th C) French
£2207 $4303   (12-Oct-90 ZZ.F82/R) Scene pastorale (46x73cm-18x29in) s.d.1890 (F.FR 22000)
£2508 $4890   (12-Oct-90 ZZ.F85/R) Paysage (50x73cm-20x29in) s. (F.FR 25000)

DAMOYE, Pierre Emmanuel (1847-1916) French
£1884 $3372   (13-Mar-91 N.M466/R) Reapers on field near village (38x56cm-15x22in) canvas on panel (DM 5500)
£2041 $4000   (6-Nov-90 GF.L2166/R) French river landscape (50x73cm-20x29in) s.d.1905 (S.FR 5000)
£2200 $3608   (18-Jun-91 PH45) Wooded landscape (66x110cm-26x43in) s.d.1892
£2200 $4334   (5-Oct-90 C34/R) Windmill in extensive landscape (33x60cm-13x24in) s.d.79 panel
£2800 $4816   (17-May-91 C10/R) Cattle grazing in pasture (33x60cm-13x24in) s.d.82

DAMRON, J C (20th C) American
£1000 $1700   (1-Jun-91 IH.NY179/R) Boy leaning against window of pet shop (56x46cm-22x18in) s. board

DAMSCHROEDER, Jan Jac Matthys (1825-1905) German
£729 $1400   (29-Nov-90 MFA.C90/R) Kitchen scene (25x36cm-10x14in) s. panel
£1297 $2115   (10-Jun-91 W.T1402) Children gathering firewood (38x48cm-15x19in) s. (C.D 2400)
£1503 $2600   (22-May-91 D.NY11/R) Afternoon nap (26x35cm-10x14in) s. panel
£1734 $3000   (21-May-91 CE.NY235/R) Lesson (56x83cm-22x33in) s. canvas on board
£1927 $3795   (13-Nov-90 AB.S879/R) Interior with man comforting his crying wife (100x125cm-39x49in) s. (S.KR 21000)
£2054 $3348   (10-Jun-91 W.T1404/R) Teatime (44x37cm-17x15in) init.sig. (C.D 3800)

DAN JACOBSON (20th C) ?
£1222 $2407   (30-Oct-90 ZZ.F102/R) Le declin d'une epoque (81x100cm-32x39in) s. (F.FR 12000)

DAN PIEL (20th C) ?
£2224 $4338   (18-Oct-90 CB.P7/R) James Dean (250x140cm-98x55in) s. acrylic (F.FR 22000)

DAN, Lars (20th C) Danish
£979 $1840   (19-Sep-90 KH.K135) Figure composition (120x100cm-47x39in) s.d.1987verso (D.KR 11000)

DAN, Theodore (1917-1981) Rumanian
£1372 $2744   (10-Feb-91 YC.P52 b) Mai 1978 - no.5 (54x65cm-21x26in) s. (F.FR 13500)

DANBY, Francis (1793-1861) British
£2725 $4687   (14-May-91 GF.L2148/R) The left lover (32x40cm-13x16in) s. (S.FR 6840)
£8500 $14365   (30-Apr-91 PH44/R) Figures at stream before terraced houses
                     (40x50cm-16x20in) s.
*£1700 $2788   (18-Jun-91 OT458/R) View of River Avon and King Road from Clifton Down
                     (16x27cm-6x11in) i.verso W/C*

DANBY, J (19th C) British
£748 $1205   (28-Jun-91 BM.B654/R) Hilly landscape with red deer by river
                   (26x39cm-10x15in) s. canvas on panel (DM 2200)

DANBY, James Francis (1816-1875) British
£1000 $1650   (10-Jul-91 S140/R) Waiting for master (24x29cm-9x11in)
£4500 $8730   (6-Dec-90 CG31/R) St Malo, sketch from nature (46x77cm-18x30in) s.d.1870

DANBY, Ken (1940-) Canadian
£3070 $6018   (20-Nov-90 JOY.T171/R) Victory (32x49cm-13x19in) s.d.83 W/C (C.D 7000)
£4545 $7818   (14-May-91 JOY.T85/R) Toward Fergus (52x67cm-20x26in) s.d.'79 W/C
                   (C.D 9000)

DANCE, George (jnr) (1741-1825) British
*£600 $1182   (13-Nov-90 C98/R) Portrait of Thomas King seated (25x18cm-10x7in)
                   s.i.d.1797 pencil*
£900 $1485   (11-Jul-91 S102/R) Portrait of James Cobb (24x18cm-9x7in) i. pencil
*£8000 $13200   (11-Jul-91 S69/R) Portrait of Joseph Mallord William Turner
                     (21x16cm-8x6in) d.1792 pencil W/C oval*

DANCE, Nathaniel (1734-1811) British
£592 $1000   (20-Apr-91 WOL.C13/R) Garrick as Richard the Third (58x41cm-23x16in)
£32000 $52800   (12-Jul-91 C20/R) Portrait of gentleman, said to be Joseph Mansel, left
                     arm on plinth (76x61cm-30x24in) i.verso
£55000 $98450   (12-Apr-91 C26/R) Portrait of Herbert Newton Jarrett, standing, holding
                     cricket bat and ball, in landscape (167x115cm-66x45in) i.verso

DANCKERTS, Hendrick (1625-1679) Dutch
£30000 $50700   (30-Apr-91 PH24/R) Views of Windsor Castle with figures and vessels on
                     river Thames and animals (54x86cm-21x34in) pair
*£1300 $2327   (9-Apr-91 C22 a) Caerphilly Castle. View of part of the castle from the
                   North East (28x43cm-11x17in) i. pen ink wash double-sided*

DAND, Louis (?) French
£2345 $4502   (30-Nov-90 APT.P79/R) Portrait de Charles I et de sa femme Henriette
                   (67x81cm-26x32in) i.verso (F.FR 23000)

DANDINI, Cesare (1595-1658) Italian
£992 $1775   (8-Apr-91 CH.R5) Busto di santa (46x32cm-18x13in) (I.L 2200000)
£3182 $6237   (19-Nov-90 CH.R55/R) La Maddalena (71x56cm-28x22in) (I.L 7000000)
£4959 $8876   (8-Apr-91 CH.R53/R) Allegoria della Commedia (87x66cm-34x26in)
                   (I.L 11000000)
£6000 $10140   (17-Apr-91 S123/R) St Agnes (73x61cm-29x24in)
£6667 $13000   (10-Oct-90 CH.NY21/R) Allegory of Vanity (82x65cm-32x26in)
£7471 $13000   (27-Mar-91 B.SF4011/R) Flora crowned with flowers and holding rose
                   (84x66cm-33x26in) oval

DANDINI, Cesare (circle) (1595-1658) Italian
£2513 $4121   (21-Jun-91 SY.MO201/R) Saint Jean Baptiste (71x57cm-28x22in)
                   (F.FR 25000)
£4200 $8274   (1-Nov-90 D147/R) Sibyl (147x58cm-58x23in)

DANDINI, Cesare (style) (1595-1658) Italian
£1500 $3000   (7-Feb-91 C57) A young woman wearing her hands over a brazier
                   (65x50cm-26x20in) oval
£2400 $4056   (18-Apr-91 C56/R) Esther swooning with two attendants (60x74cm-24x29in)

DANDINI, Ottaviano (18th C) Italian
*£2600 $5018   (11-Dec-90 C47/R) The ehad of a girl in profile to the right
                   (26x25cm-10x10in) i. chk.*

DANDINI, Pietro (1646-1712) Italian
£22000 $37180   (19-Apr-91 C142/R) Selmiramis called to arms (98x139cm-39x55in)
*£420 $814   (7-Dec-90 GB.B5105/R) Male nude bending down. Study of hand, arm and
                   heads (42x27cm-17x11in) chl htd.white double-sided (DM 1200)*

DANDRE BARDON, Michel (attrib) (1700-1778) French
*£1200 $2124   (22-Mar-91 APT.P33) L'enterrement d'Abel (32x26cm-13x10in) pen wash
                   (F.FR 12000)*

DANDRIDGE, Bartholomew (style) (17/18th C) British
£770 $1301   (1-May-91 PHL99) Portrait of young girl, seated with flowers and lamb on
                   lap (76x63cm-30x25in)

DANEDI, Stefano (1608-1689) Italian
£10000 $19000   (1-Mar-91 C173/R) Joseph and Potiphar's Wife (172x133cm-68x52in)

DANEKE, Wilfried (20th C) German
£896 $1524   (29-May-91 RCJ.P132/R) La fonderie (97x135cm-38x53in) s. panel
           (F.FR 9000)

DANERI, Eugenio (1881-1970) Argentinian
£1117 $2200   (14-Nov-90 V.BA37/R) Naturaleza muerta (38x48cm-15x19in)
£1590 $2750   (8-May-91 V.BA26) Barcas (35x45cm-14x18in)
£1720 $3200   (5-Sep-90 V.BA37) Natureleza muerta (36x46cm-14x18in)
£2312 $4000   (8-May-91 RO.BA25/R) Tarde en el Riachuelo (56x77cm-22x30in) s.d.29
           panel
£2796 $5200   (5-Sep-90 V.BA35) Canasta con pescado y verduras (60x70cm-24x28in)

DANFORTH, Mosely Isaac (1800-1862) American
£684   *$1300*   (9-Jan-91 CH.NY94/R) Crowning of the Republic (20x26cm-8x10in) init.ink
           board sold w.dr attrib.to J.MacDonough

DANGELO, Sergio (1931-) Italian
£683 $1162   (28-May-91 SY.MI22/R) Attendez, Pietons (50x60cm-20x24in) s.d.1961
           (I.L 1500000)
£2071 $4039   (22-Oct-90 BR.M120/R) Toi (80x100cm-31x39in) s.verso oil wood
           (I.L 4600000)
£1981   *$3863*   (22-Oct-90 BR.M155/R) Ambers, La Mantide (80x120cm-31x47in) s. oil
           collage canvas (I.L 4400000)

DANGER, Henri (1857-1937) French
£743 $1449   (26-Oct-90 KM.K1141) River landscape with anglers, evening
           (26x36cm-10x14in) s. panel (DM 2200)

DANHAUSER, Josef (1805-1845) Austrian
£2569 $4985   (7-Dec-90 CH.MO360/R) Portrait d'une Dame de qualite (92x74cm-36x29in)
           (F.FR 25000)
£1216   *$2068*   (31-May-91 GB.B5724/R) Lady seated (26x24cm-10x9in) pencil htd.white
           (DM 3600)
£1923   *$3750*   (26-Oct-90 SY.NY115/R) Study of spaniel (18x18cm-7x7in) s.d.1834 pencil

DANICHE, Mademoiselle (18th C) French
£1300 $2600   (7-Feb-91 CSK98) Portrait of Helene Chouart, seated holding letter.
           Portrait of clergyman (81x65cm-32x26in) one with sig.d.1787 verso pair

DANIEL, Abraham (?-1806) British
£1050   *$1733*   (10-Jul-91 C120/R) A lady in decollete white dress. Gentleman in blue
           coat (5x?cm-2x?in) min. gold frame double-sided oval
£1200   *$2124*   (20-Mar-91 C137/R) Portrait of Infantry officer in scarlet uniform
           (5x?cm-2x?in) min. gold frame oval
£2700   *$4455*   (10-Jul-91 C155/R) An officer wearing the scarlet uniform of the 65th
           Foot (8x?cm-3x?in) min. gilt-metal frame oval
£3000   *$4950*   (10-Jul-91 C75/R) Masters Charles and Samuel Black (11x?cm-4x?in) min.
           gilt-metal mount blk.wood frame oval
£6000   *$9900*   (11-Jul-91 S290/R) Portrait of two sisters seated upon bench, one child
           wearing hat (8x?cm-3x?in) min. gold frame split pearl border oval

DANIELL, Thomas (1747-1840) British
£9000 $14850   (10-Jul-91 S80/R) The rock cut temple at Kanheri, Salsette Island,
           Bombay (62x74cm-24x29in)

DANIELL, William (1769-1837) British
£1400   *$2758*   (13-Nov-90 C43/R) Hindu temples at Tritchencore (10x15cm-4x6in) i.
           pencil W/C
£1700   *$3349*   (13-Nov-90 C44/R) Deserted houses of Patan Chiefs at Old Delhi
           (10x15cm-4x6in) i. pencil W/C
£2000   *$3580*   (9-Apr-91 C127/R) Wexford Harbour (11x17cm-4x7in) pencil W/C
£7000   *$11550*   (11-Jul-91 S82/R) Indian soldier with torader and adya katti
           (35x28cm-14x11in) W/C over pencil

DANIELS, Alfred (20th C) ?
£600 $1062   (20-Mar-91 ZZ.B199) The Pavilion, the gardens and the school brass band,
           Brighton (61x101cm-24x40in) s.d.1980
£1500 $2910   (7-Dec-90 PHM80) Bank Station, City of London (70x90cm-28x35in) s. board

DANIELS, Andries (attrib) (1580-?) Flemish
£5000 $8150   (2-Jul-91 PH318/R) Still life of basket of spring flowers
           (22x41cm-9x16in) panel

DANIELSON-GAMBOGI, Elin (1861-1919) Finnish
£4137 $8108   (24-Nov-90 HOR.H70/R) Old woman (36x31cm-14x12in) s. (F.M 29000)
£9843 $19292   (24-Nov-90 HOR.H71/R) Reading by lamplight (29x40cm-11x16in) s.
           (F.M 69000)
£18651 $31521   (20-Apr-91 HOR.H60/R) Sailing (51x75cm-20x30in) s. (F.M 130000)

DANIELSSON, Carl (1866-1945) Finnish
£746 $1261   (20-Apr-91 HOR.H58/R) Selling fish at Aura River (50x40cm-20x16in) s.
           (F.M 5200)

DANIFER, Sigurd (1894-1958) Norwegian
£579 $1117   (12-Dec-90 BU.09/R) Summer's day (65x78cm-26x31in) s. i.verso
           (N.KR 6500)

DANILOV, Anatoli (1944-) Russian
£397 $683   *(15-May-91 AGB.P68/R) Katia (49x64cm-19x25in) s. pastel (F.FR 4000)*
£398 $693   *(25-Mar-91 ARC.P159) Fillette a la robe (55x45cm-22x18in) s. pastel*
             (F.FR 4000)
£446 $768   *(15-May-91 AGB.P67/R) Nu a genoux (50x64cm-20x25in) s. pastel*
             (F.FR 4500)
£458 $796   *(25-Mar-91 ARC.P158) Une blonde (50x64cm-20x25in) s. pastel (F.FR 4600)*
£796 $1385   *(25-Mar-91 ARC.P157/R) Fin du bronzage (49x62cm-19x24in) s. pastel*
             (F.FR 8000)

DANILOWATZ, Josef (1877-1945) Austrian
£369 $739   *(7-Feb-91 D.V24/R) Grossauge (36x24cm-14x9in) s.d.30 chk W/C (A.S 7500)*

DANISH SCHOOL (?) Danish
£1020 $1806   (20-Mar-91 KM.K1140/R) Portrait of lady wearing black hat
             (72x72cm-28x28in) c.1900 (DM 3000)
£1499 $2593   (21-May-91 DUR.M11/R) Bodegon con esparragos (48x66cm-19x26in) panel
             (S.P 275000)
£1408 $2366   *(23-Apr-91 RAS.K451/R) Frigate Freija defending it's convoy against*
             English frigates (26x47cm-10x19in) gouache (D.KR 16000)

DANISH SCHOOL, 18th C Danish
£1257 $2250   (11-Apr-91 SY.NY191/R) Portrait of prince (78x63cm-31x25in)
£1515 $2712   (14-Mar-91 RAS.V734/R) Portrait of Duchess Louise Augusta of
             Augustenborg (67x54cm-26x21in) oval (D.KR 17000)
£1012 $1701   *(22-Apr-91 BU.K90/R) Portrait of Princess Louise Augusta*
             (7cm-3ins circular) min. gold medallion with locks of hair
             (D.KR 11500)

DANISH SCHOOL, 19th C Scandinavian
£925 $1545   (6-Jun-91 RAS.K214) Neapolitan fisher family on beach (83x92cm-33x36in)
             (D.KR 10500)
£1094 $1958   (9-Apr-91 RAS.K2224/R) Wooded bank with ferns and flowers and swallow
             (74x94cm-29x37in) (D.KR 12500)
£1361 $2190   (26-Jun-91 KM.K1417/R) Still life of flowers on marble ledge
             (45x66cm-18x26in) indis.s. (DM 4000)
£1613 $3226   (6-Feb-91 RAS.K333/R) Basket of roses and summer flowers on tree trunk
             (34x39cm-13x15in) (D.KR 18000)
£1613 $3226   (6-Feb-91 RAS.K34/R) Frederiksborg Palace (52x76cm-20x30in) (D.KR 18000)
£2379 $3973   (6-Jun-91 RAS.K172/R) Basket of lilacs and other flowers
             (32x41cm-13x16in) (D.KR 27000)
£1436 $2829   *(14-Nov-90 RAS.K782/R) Ships portrait - Caroline Cecilie Pauline*
             (50x71cm-20x28in) W/C (D.KR 16000)

DANLOUX, Henri Pierre (1753-1809) French
£2008 $3233   (27-Jun-91 APT.P209/R) Les soins maternels (45x38cm-18x15in) panel
             (F.FR 20000)
£2895 $5500   (11-Jan-91 CH.NY87/R) Portrait of a young man, half length, wearing a
             brown jacket (76x63cm-30x25in) s.d.1795
£3479 $5880   (18-Apr-91 APT.P141/R) Portrait de Francois Antoine Herman, consul de
             France en Angleterre (76x83cm-30x33in) s.d.1793 oval (F.FR 35000)

DANNECKER, Arnold (1939-) German
£1104 $1865   (19-Apr-91 FN.S1689) Chiemsee landscape with figures and Frauenchiemsee
             beyond (11x26cm-4x10in) s. panel (DM 3300)

DANNER, Sara Kolb (1894-1969) American
£833 $1600   (1-Dec-90 LAE.L30/R) Cape Cod (51x61cm-20x24in) s. board
£2041 $4000   (13-Feb-91 B.SF2111/R) Bathers (86x91cm-34x36in) s.

D'ANNO, Alessandro (18th C) Italian
£15769 $31066   *(30-Oct-90 EP.M16/R) Taberna en la Bahia de Napoles (54x74cm-21x29in)*
             s.d.1786 gouache (S.P 2900000)

DANS, Maria Antonia (20th C) Spanish
£1772 $3065   (21-May-91 DUR.M41/R) La Tertulia (61x74cm-24x29in) (S.P 325000)
£2453 $4244   (21-May-91 DUR.M38/R) Las Quincalleras (76x100cm-30x39in) (S.P 450000)
£1036 $1792   *(21-May-91 DUR.M35/R) Pueblo (53x76cm-21x30in) gouache (S.P 190000)*
£1635 $2829   *(21-May-91 DUR.M40/R) Puerto (53x76cm-21x30in) gouache (S.P 300000)*

DANSAERT, L (1830-1909) Belgian
£631 $1029   (11-Jun-91 GM.B947) Reservation de place pour la Corrida
             (25x34cm-10x13in) s. (B.FR 38000)

DANSAERT, Leon (1830-1909) Belgian
£7606 $15061   (30-Jan-91 APT.P84/R) Scene paysanne (42x54cm-17x21in) s. (F.FR 75000)

DANSAERT, Leon (attrib) (1830-1909) Belgian
£850 $1666   (8-Nov-90 TL76/R) The dinner party (38x27cm-15x11in) bears indist.sig.
             panel

DANTON, Ferdinand (jnr) (1849-1908) American
£573 $1100   (28-Nov-90 D.NY41/R) Still life of money (43x30cm-17x12in) s.d.94

D'ANTY, Henry (1910-) French
£507 $877   (25-May-91 N.M8) Le coq (55x45cm-22x18in) s. l.stretcher (DM 1500)

D'ANTY, Henry (1910-) French-cont.

£575	$1000	(27-Mar-91 B.SF4300/R) Madonna and Child (76x48cm-30x19in) s.
£605	$1149	(1-Mar-91 CB.P83 k) Le repas en famille (46x55cm-18x22in) s. (F.FR 6000)
£605	$1149	(1-Mar-91 CB.P83 j) Le perroquet (46x55cm-18x22in) s. (F.FR 6000)
£655	$1278	(28-Oct-90 M.V140/R) Nature morte aux fruits (29x35cm-11x14in) s. (F.FR 6500)
£704	$1259	(17-Mar-91 L.C15/R) Les musiciens (55x48cm-22x19in) s. (F.FR 7000)
£708	$1380	(17-Oct-90 ARC.P55) Village sous la neige (46x55cm-18x22in) s. (F.FR 7000)
£717	$1398	(24-Oct-90 GD.B92) Musical clown (65x54cm-26x21in) s. (S.FR 1800)
£765	$1468	(2-Dec-90 M.V99) Bouquet de fleurs (28x35cm-11x14in) s. (F.FR 7500)
£806	$1313	(10-Jun-91 NM.P39 b/R) Maison aux tois rouges (65x81cm-26x32in) s. (F.FR 8000)
£813	$1626	(6-Feb-91 FB.P9/R) Le petit clown (65x50cm-26x20in) s. (F.FR 8000)
£904	$1455	(24-Jun-91 PR.P89) Les bateaux de peche (80x100cm-31x39in) s. (F.FR 9000)
£910	$1775	(17-Oct-90 ARC.P56) Fleurs dans un vase (60x73cm-24x29in) s. (F.FR 9000)
£915	$1756	(24-Feb-91 P.V30) Village sous la neige (46x56cm-18x22in) s. (F.FR 9100)
£925	$1794	(8-Dec-90 LT.P88/R) Paysage enneige (46x55cm-18x22in) s. (F.FR 9000)
£964	$1552	(30-Jun-91 FE.P62) Caleche a Montmartre (46x55cm-18x22in) s. (F.FR 9600)
£995	$1731	(31-Mar-91 FE.P66) Promenade sur lea quais (46x55cm-18x22in) s. (F.FR 10000)
£1018	$2006	(30-Oct-90 I.N229) La diligence (14x18cm-6x7in) s. (F.FR 10000)
£1099	$2077	(30-Sep-90 FE.P63) Le clown musicien (55x46cm-22x18in) s. studio st. verso (F.FR 10800)
£1250	$2038	(4-Jul-91 LT.P88) Bouquet de fleurs (55x46cm-22x18in) s. (F.FR 12500)
£1250	$2100	(28-Apr-91 FE.P49) Paysage de neige (46x55cm-18x22in) s. (F.FR 12500)
£1300	$2184	(28-Apr-91 FE.P52) La diligence de Paris (46x55cm-18x22in) s. (F.FR 13000)
£1394	$2719	(24-Oct-90 GD.B91/R) Still life of anemones in vase (60x73cm-24x29in) s. (S.FR 3500)
£1406	$2263	(24-Jun-91 PR.P88) Les chaumieres aux toits rouges (80x100cm-31x39in) s. (F.FR 14000)
£1475	$2788	(30-Sep-90 FE.P62) Le galop (46x55cm-18x22in) s. studio st. (F.FR 14500)
£1494	$2540	(2-Jun-91 LT.P141/R) Retour de peche (73x60cm-29x24in) s. d.49 verso (F.FR 15000)
£1692	$2926	(12-May-91 L.C30/R) Rue de vieux Montmartre (38x55cm-15x22in) s.d.1948 i. verso (F.FR 17000)
£1729	$3319	(24-Feb-91 FE.P45) Montmartre (46x55cm-18x22in) s. (F.FR 17200)
£1780	$3365	(30-Sep-90 FE.P64) Les musiciens (55x46cm-22x18in) s. (F.FR 17500)
£2398	$4724	(14-Nov-90 I.N120/R) La course de chevaux (60x73cm-24x29in) s. studio st. verso (F.FR 23500)
£2764	$4947	(17-Mar-91 L.C14) La maison de Mimi Pinson (73x91cm-29x36in) s. (F.FR 27500)

DANUBE SCHOOL, 16th C European

£1370	$2233	(12-Jun-91 N.M405/R) Mary's Crowning in glory with putti and mountain landscape beneath (95x71cm-37x28in) gold ground panel (DM 4000)
£13000	$21970	(19-Apr-91 C49/R) Saint Catherine with Maxentius and the fifty philosophers. The Martyrdom of Saint Catherine (46x23cm-18x9in) panel laid down on board
£4800	*$7824*	*(2-Jul-91 C176/R) Christ and woman of Samaria (21x15cm-8x6in) with i. pen htd white*
£5000	*$8150*	*(2-Jul-91 C182/R) Wooded river landscape with fortified farms and town beyond (21x32cm-8x13in) num.2 pen bodycol htd white*
£16000	*$26080*	*(2-Jul-91 C180/R) Agony on garden (15x12cm-6x5in) with i. pen htd white*

DANVIN, Victor Marie Felix (1802-1842) French

£1427	$2740	(30-Nov-90 ARC.P115) Hameau en bordure de la Seine, en Normandie, anime de personnages (42x64cm-17x25in) s. (F.FR 14000)

DANZINGER, Itzhak (1916-1977) Israeli

£576	*$1100*	*(1-Jan-91 GG.TA284/R) Images (33x43cm-13x17in) s.i.d.1945-46 ink*
£785	*$1500*	*(1-Jan-91 GG.TA283/R) Cover drawing for Kav 8 (24x33cm-9x13in) d.1968 pen*
£995	*$1900*	*(1-Jan-91 GG.TA282/R) Enclosure, temporary structure in the landscape (20x31cm-8x12in) d.1962 ink*

D'APVRIL, Edouard (19th C) French

£2224	$4338	(16-Oct-90 CS.L15/R) Les deux soeurs (92x51cm-36x20in) s.d.1915 (F.FR 22000)

DARBASQUE, Barbarine (?) Swiss

£1143	$2217	(8-Dec-90 GAB.G2179) Montreux, le Leman et dents-du-Mide (47x68cm-19x27in) s. (S.FR 2800)

DARBOVEN, Hanne (1941-) German

£1714	*$3342*	*(20-Jan-91 CSC.P23/R) Sans titre (29x20cm-11x8in) s. Indian ink (F.FR 17000)*
£2520	*$4914*	*(20-Jan-91 CSC.P25) Diptyque (58x42cm-23x17in) Indian ink (F.FR 25000)*
£3831	*$7470*	*(20-Jan-91 CSC.P24/R) Triptyque (87x42cm-34x17in) d.1972 Indian ink (F.FR 38000)*

D'ARCANGELO, Allan (1930-) American

£4046	$7000	(7-May-91 CE.NY175/R) Highway no.4 (218x152cm-86x60in) s.d.1965 verso s.num.4 stretcher acrylic canvas

D'ARCANGELO, Allan (1930-) American-cont.
£9184 $18000   (6-Nov-90 CE.NY75/R) Landscape (102x91cm-40x36in) s.i.d.1967 verso

DARDEL, Nils (1888-1943) Swedish
£6573 $11174   (28-May-91 AB.S5193/R) Town scene from Tunisa (60x81cm-24x32in) s.d.1914
                            (S.KR 70000)
£23005 $39108   (28-May-91 AB.S5192/R) The coctail party (81x65cm-32x26in) s.
                            (S.KR 245000)
£84871 $162952   (27-Nov-90 BU.S68/R) The girl and the peacock (133x97cm-52x38in)
                            s.d.1919 (S.KR 920000)
£619718 $1053521   (28-May-91 AB.S5191/R) The dying Dandy (140x180cm-55x71in) s.d.1918
                            (S.KR 6600000)
*£3429 $6652   (5-Dec-90 AB.S7056/R) View from the studio over Nybroplan
                            (48x36cm-19x14in) W/C (S.KR 37000)*
£3745 $6442   (14-May-91 BU.S89/R) Columbi egg W/C pencil sketch (S.KR 40000)
*£11993 $23026   (27-Nov-90 BU.S70/R) David Sprengel (49x36cm-19x14in) s.d.1918 W/C
                            (S.KR 130000)*

DAREL, Georges (1892-1943) Swiss
£3571 $5964   (5-Jun-91 SY.Z121/R) Interior (118x90cm-46x35in) s. i.d.1936verso
                            (S.FR 9000)

DARET, Ernesto (attrib) (17th C) Italian
£2479 $4438   (8-Apr-91 CH.R79) Paesaggio con pastorelli e bestiame (35x47cm-14x19in)
                            (I.L 5500000)

DARET, Jean (1613-1668) Flemish
*£533 $1045   (24-Jan-91 AGS.P98) Etude d'homme agenouille sur le genou gauche, le
                            corps tourne vers ladroite (30x24cm-12x9in) i. verso sanguinne
                            (F.FR 5300)*

DAREY, Louis (1863-1914) French
£728 $1376   (27-Sep-90 D.V133/R) Portrait of dog (21x16cm-8x6in) s. board
                            (A.S 15000)

DARGELAS, Andre Henri (1828-1906) French
£1923 $3712   (12-Dec-90 N.M467/R) Small female street sweeper standing shivering in
                            snowy street (49x37cm-19x15in) s. (DM 5500)
£3158 $6000   (28-Feb-91 CH.NY16/R) L'embuscade (33x25cm-13x10in) s. panel

DARGENT, Edouard van (1824-1889) French
*£398 $689   (12-May-91 T.B41) Enfants sur un rocher (32x47cm-13x19in) init. wash
                            (F.FR 4000)*
*£438 $757   (12-May-91 T.B40) L'accident de Chariot (47x32cm-19x13in) init. wash
                            (F.FR 4400)*

DARGIE, Sir William (1912-) Australian
£700 $1344   (21-Feb-91 B49) Killing Ground (45x56cm-18x22in)
£844 $1620   (14-Aug-90 SY.ME81/R) Groves at Megera (35x44cm-14x17in) i. verso board
                            (A.D 2000)

DARIEN, Henri Gaston (1864-1926) French
£16189 $31730   (11-Nov-90 ZZ.F36/R) Fecamp, le marche aux poissons (140x250cm-55x98in)
                            s.d.1909 (F.FR 158000)

DARIO, Ruben (20th C) Spanish
£1237 $2214   (13-Mar-91 FER.M202/R) Comitiva (51x72cm-20x28in) s. tempera
                            (S.P 225000)

DARLEY, Felix O C (1822-1888) American
£2023 $3500   (22-May-91 CH.NY113/R) Touchstone and Audrey (69x56cm-27x22in) s.d.1886

DARLING, William (1856-1933) American
£765 $1500   (13-Feb-91 B.SF2145/R) Ghost town, Bodie, California (46x56cm-18x22in)
                            s.
£1026 $2000   (10-Oct-90 B.SF626/R) Desert foothills (41x51cm-16x20in) s. board
£1658 $3250   (13-Feb-91 B.SF2146/R) Palm Springs (51x61cm-20x24in) s.

DARMS, Israel (1808-1887) Swiss
£3154 $5961   (27-Sep-90 D.V100/R) Pub dispute (41x55cm-16x22in) s. i.verso
                            (A.S 65000)

DARNAUT, Hugo (1851-1937) Austrian
£1698 $3210   (27-Sep-90 D.V59/R) View from the Merkenstein woods with ox-drawn cart
                            and peasant (31x39cm-12x15in) s. i.verso board (A.S 35000)
£2427 $3981   (20-Jun-91 D.V66/R) Summer landscape (34x47cm-13x19in) mono. canvas on
                            board (A.S 50000)
£4746 $8495   (11-Apr-91 D.V287/R) Laurentiuskapelle in Markersdorf near Neulengbach
                            (46x61cm-18x24in) s. board (A.S 100000)
£8637 $14856   (16-May-91 D.V161/R) Landscape with stream (40x51cm-16x20in) s.
                            (A.S 180000)
£8654 $16875   (25-Oct-90 D.V15/R) Corn stooks (46x61cm-18x24in) s. board (A.S 180000)
£9814 $18842   (29-Nov-90 D.V26/R) Beech woods (105x81cm-41x32in) s.d.1890
                            (A.S 200000)
*£525 $883   (25-Apr-91 D.V116/R) Hirschhorn am Nekar (23x30cm-9x12in) s.i.d.1873
                            pencil (A.S 11000)*

DARRIEUX, Charles Rene (1879-?) French
£2143 $3600   (17-Jul-91 SY.NY255/R) Peripateticiens du Luxembourg (105x200cm-41x79in)
                s.d.33

D'ARTHOIS, Jacques (1613-1686) Flemish
£5800 $11310   (26-Oct-90 C121/R) A wooded landscape with travellers on a track, a
                hamlet beyond (25x34cm-10x13in) panel
£5976 $10279   (14-May-91 GF.L2277/R) Rider and traveller on riverside path
                (51x66cm-20x26in) (S.FR 15000)
£7339 $14459   (13-Nov-90 AB.S876/R) Wooded landscape with figures on road by
                watercourse (62x82cm-24x32in) s. (S.KR 80000)
£10000 $16900   (17-Apr-91 S80/R) Wooded landscape with waggon and elegant figures on
                path near lake (57x91cm-22x36in)
£12291 $22000   (11-Apr-91 SY.NY42/R) Landscape with travellers on country road, castle
                and river beyond (53x82cm-21x32in) s.
£19388 $38194   (18-Nov-90 P.V26) Paysans couversant dans la campagne panel
                (F.FR 190000)

D'ARTHOIS, Jacques (attrib) (1613-1686) Flemish
£620 $998   (24-Jun-91 HS283) Cavalry skirmish with wounded figures in foreground
                (12x15cm-5x6in) metal panel

D'ARTHOIS, Jacques (circle) (1613-1686) Flemish
£2446 $4820   (13-Nov-90 CH.AM41/R) Mountainous landscape in winter with travellers on
                snowy path, monastry beyond (72x87cm-28x34in) (D.FL 8000)
£7000 $13650   (26-Oct-90 C49/R) An extensive woodland landscape with huntsmen on a
                path (83x98cm-33x39in)

D'ARTHOIS, Jacques (school) (1613-1686) Flemish
£1862 $3500   (22-Sep-90 WOL.C59) Outdoor scene with figures (76x64cm-30x25in)

D'ARTHOIS, Jacques (style) (1613-1686) Flemish
£1529 $3012   (13-Nov-90 CH.AM176) Travellers on road passing hermit, in landscape
                (36x50cm-14x20in) panel (D.FL 5000)
£2446 $4820   (13-Nov-90 CH.AM75/R) Peasants and travellers on road in landscape
                (25x36cm-10x14in) panel (D.FL 8000)

DARWIN, Sir Robin (1910-1974) British
£700 $1372   (24-Jan-91 CSK61/R) Fishmongers (91x122cm-36x48in) s.d.50
£700 $1344   (21-Feb-91 B50 c) Reclining female nude (63x76cm-25x30in) s.d.48

DASBURG, Andrew (1887-1979) American
£1788 $3200   (14-Mar-91 CH.NY212/R) Winter landscape with barn (41x51cm-16x20in) s.
                s.d.1910 verso
£9249 $16000   (22-May-91 CH.NY293/R) Still life with fruit (43x61cm-17x24in) s.d.'46
£529 $1000   (25-Sep-90 CE.NY222/R) Nancy Lane (50x40cm-20x16in) s.d.29 pencil
£1066 $2100   (7-Oct-90 DU.E113/R) Taos Pueblo and Taos church (38x58cm-15x23in)
                s.d.1942 chl
£4762 $9000   (26-Sep-90 SY.NY188/R) October landscape (44x56cm-17x22in) s.d.62 pastel
                ink

DAUBIGNY, Charles (attrib) (1740-1830) French
£589 $1002   (28-May-91 C.A47) Landscape (60x93cm-24x37in) s. (B.FR 36000)

DAUBIGNY, Charles Francois (1817-1878) French
£1117 $2200   (16-Nov-90 S.BM89/R) House through field - landscape study
                (13x20cm-5x8in) s. board
£2594 $5084   (24-Nov-90 SA.A719/R) Landscape (32x24cm-13x9in) s. (DM 7600)
£2982 $5815   (17-Oct-90 FER.M203/R) Paisaje al atardecer (24x45cm-9x18in) s. panel
                (S.P 550000)
£3093 $6000   (8-Dec-90 W.W60/R) River landscape (18x38cm-7x15in) s. panel
£6743 $11396   (20-Apr-91 HOR.H9/R) Walking by the river (40x61cm-16x24in) s.
                (F.M 47000)
£7000 $11480   (19-Jun-91 S143/R) Landscape with stream (40x67cm-16x26in) panel
£7347 $14473   (16-Nov-90 GK.Z5152/R) Les Sablieres pres de Valmondois
                (26x41cm-10x16in) s. panel (S.FR 18000)
£7500 $14400   (28-Nov-90 S249/R) Sunset over river (47x80cm-19x31in) s. board
£14388 $27914   (7-Dec-90 GL.P134/R) Bord de riviere (29x61cm-11x24in) s. panel
                (F.FR 140000)
£15000 $28800   (28-Nov-90 S252/R) Bord de riviere, pecheur a la barque
                (33x56cm-13x22in) s.d.1871 panel
£17000 $27880   (21-Jun-91 C9/R) Troupeau de moutons au bord de la riviere
                (37x66cm-15x26in) s.d.1875 panel
£19653 $34000   (23-May-91 CH.NY239/R) Landscape with fieldworkers (17x32cm-7x13in)
                s.d.1858 panel
£22000 $36080   (19-Jun-91 S135/R) Bord de mer pres de Villerville (63x98cm-25x39in)
£27746 $48000   (23-May-91 CH.NY238/R) La Seine a Conflans (41x70cm-16x28in) s.d.1876
                panel
£607 $1183   (15-Oct-90 APT.P61) Vue d'un village (24x35cm-9x14in) pierre noire
                (F.FR 6000)
£791 $1416   (12-Apr-91 JM.P18/R) Bord d'etang (24x34cm-9x13in) s. pierre noire
                htd.white chk.chamois paper (F.FR 8000)
£1100 $1859   (30-Apr-91 HS44) Landscape (15x23cm-6x9in) s.d. wash pencil
£1800 $3456   (27-Nov-90 PH247/R) Two peasants (16x13cm-6x5in) s.st.sig. pencil

DAUBIGNY, Karl (1846-1886) French
£710	$1363	(19-Dec-90 LD.P147 a) Paysan et sa vache au bord de la riviere (6x10cm-2x4in) s. panel (F.FR 7000)
£1004	$1616	(28-Jun-91 ZZ.F91) Paysage (37x27cm-15x11in) (F.FR 10000)
£1502	$2943	(24-Nov-90 SA.A720/R) Flooded landscape in thunderstorm (19x31cm-7x12in) s. panel (DM 4400)
£1525	$2547	(6-Jun-91 HN.H258/R) Bord de Riviere (23x56cm-9x22in) s. panel (DM 4500)
£1965	$3400	(21-May-91 CE.NY24/R) Country village (20x23cm-8x9in) s. estate st.verso panel
£4791	$9199	(1-Dec-90 PER.M127/R) Les jardins pres du hameau (50x65cm-20x26in) (F.FR 47000)
£4861	$8361	(19-May-91 ZZ.F31/R) Eglise et village dominant la riviere (28x50cm-11x20in) s. panel (F.FR 49000)
£6474	$11200	(24-May-91 FB.P111/R) La promenade en barque (35x58cm-14x23in) s.d.1882 panel (F.FR 65000)

DAUBIGNY, Pierre (1793-1858) French
£1600	*$3072*	*(28-Nov-90 S259/R) Portrait of young officer (54x42cm-21x17in) s.d.16.9.1815 chl oval*

DAUCHEZ, Andre (1870-1943) French
£602	$1114	(4-Mar-91 ARC.P113) Les ormes (29x41cm-11x16in) s.d.39 panel (F.FR 6000)
£896	$1549	(12-May-91 T.B95/R) Sur les Bords de L'Odet (38x46cm-15x18in) s. panel (F.FR 9000)
£1085	$1876	(12-May-91 T.B250/R) Route vers les dunes (38x46cm-15x18in) s. panel (F.FR 10900)
£1095	$1894	(12-May-91 T.B93/R) Les Rives de l'Odet (38x55cm-15x22in) s. (F.FR 11000)
£1642	$2840	(12-May-91 T.B94) Paysage au lavoir et au Moulin (53x73cm-21x29in) s. (F.FR 16500)

DAUCHOT, Gabriel (1927-?) French
£527	$890	(21-Apr-91 E.LA196) Nature morte aux instruments de musique (22x27cm-9x11in) s. panel (F.FR 5300)
£655	$1067	(14-Jun-91 FB.P45/R) Bouquet de fleurs (92x73cm-36x29in) s. (F.FR 6500)
£704	$1154	(18-Jun-91 APT.P186) 14 Juillet, le kiosque (19x47cm-7x19in) s. (F.FR 7000)
£939	$1849	(18-Nov-90 H.A111) L'esplanade animee (38x46cm-15x18in) s. (F.FR 9200)
£1055	$2026	(24-Feb-91 P.V129/R) Femme au chapeau (100x50cm-39x20in) s. (F.FR 10500)
£1066	$2100	(15-Nov-90 SY.NY34) Head of a clown (27x22cm-11x9in) s.
£1400	$2632	(20-Sep-90 CSK119/R) Le paddock (81x99cm-32x39in) s.
£1795	$3500	(10-Oct-90 SY.NY205/R) Paris street (74x91cm-29x36in) s.d.51
£1820	$3549	(17-Oct-90 ARC.P71) Bord de lac anime (40x80cm-16x31in) s. (F.FR 18000)
£2108	$3395	(28-Jun-91 ARC.P79) Le couple de maries (27x22cm-11x9in) s. (F.FR 21000)
£3807	$7500	(15-Nov-90 SY.NY38) Harlequin (132x81cm-52x32in) s.

DAUDELIN, Charles (1920-) Canadian
£661	$1289	(25-Oct-90 EA.M705) Abstract composition (91x61cm-36x24in) s.d.45 (C.D 1500)

DAUDIN, Henry-Charles (19/20th C) French
£708	$1380	(16-Oct-90 CS.L21) Jeune femme au miroir (46x55cm-18x22in) s. board (F.FR 7000)

DAUFIN, Jacques (1930-) French
£1142	$2250	(15-Nov-90 SY.NY36) Fleurs dans une vase blanche (27x16cm-11x6in) s. masonite
£1208	$1970	(11-Jun-91 I.N39) Les maisons au bord de la mer (60x73cm-24x29in) s. (F.FR 12000)
£1521	$3012	(3-Feb-91 I.N59/R) La tuilerie (81x100cm-32x39in) s. (F.FR 15000)
£1629	$3210	(30-Oct-90 I.N300/R) Le village (100x81cm-39x32in) s. (F.FR 16000)
£2041	$4020	(14-Nov-90 I.N115/R) Les genets (81x100cm-32x39in) s. (F.FR 20000)
£2284	$4500	(15-Nov-90 SY.NY42/R) Vase of flowers (120x60cm-47x24in) s.

DAUJAC, Chloe (20th C) French
£728	*$1420*	*(15-Oct-90 CSC.P75/R) Lever de lune (101x111cm-40x44in) s.d.88 oil gouache collage (F.FR 7200)*

DAUMIER, Honore (1808-1879) French
£45000	$72450	(26-Jun-91 S100/R) Deux avocats (28x24cm-11x9in) init.
£450	*$806*	*(12-Apr-91 AW.H570) Street sweepers (22x18cm-9x7in) mono. pencil wash (DM 1350)*
£1459	$2859	(24-Jan-91 AGS.P96/R) Croquis fait sur une lettre de Pierre Veron (7x10cm-3x4in) i. verso pierre noire (F.FR 14500)
£2767	$5423	(24-Jan-91 AGS.P100) Deux avocats (25x21cm-10x8in) drawing (F.FR 27500)
£6091	$12000	(3-Oct-90 SY.NY7/R) Mere et enfant (32x29cm-13x11in) chl pencil
£10405	$18000	(9-May-91 CH.NY102/R) Tete d'homme (9x8cm-4x3in) chk.brush wash over pencil paper laid down board
£26000	*$50440*	*(5-Dec-90 S300/R) La lecture - Etude pour une Foule (14x20cm-6x8in) init. pencil double sided*
£27000	*$43470*	*(25-Jun-91 C202/R) La parade. Scene de tribunal, deux avocats plaidant (11x17cm-4x7in) one W/C pen ink one pen ink*
£32995	*$65000*	*(15-Nov-90 CH.NY109/R) Don Quixote et Sancho Pansa (22x25cm-9x10in) init. wash chk*

DAUMIER, Honore (1808-1879) French-cont.
£40609 $80000   (15-Nov-90 CH.NY107/R) Une grand' maman (24x30cm-9x12in) init. wash pen ink
£72254 $125000   (9-May-91 CH.NY101/R) Trois spectateurs (11x16cm-4x6in) W/C gouache over pen
£147208 $290000   (14-Nov-90 SY.NY104/R) Un avocat plaidant (20x34cm-8x13in) init. wash chl pencil
£290000 $562600   (5-Dec-90 S303/R) Les trois Commeres (26x18cm-10x7in) s. pen Indian ink W/C htd gouache

D'AURIA, V (19th C) Italian
£2500 $4300   (17-May-91 C214/R) Fishermen's return, Capri (99x149cm-39x59in) s.

DAUZATS, Adrien (1804-1868) French
£1410 $2750   (26-Oct-90 SY.NY41/R) Study of courtyard (29x35cm-11x14in) st.studio pencil W/C

DAVEY, Randall (1887-1964) American
£781 $1500   (17-Dec-90 SY.NY259/R) Road in woods (30x46cm-12x18in) s. paper
£1272 $2200   (21-May-91 CE.NY649/R) Jockey's leaving track (81x66cm-32x26in) s. board
£1667 $3250   (21-Oct-90 HG.C47) Jockeys and grooms (51x76cm-20x30in) s. masonite
£1955 $3500   (14-Mar-91 CH.NY170/R) Smoker (61x51cm-24x20in)
£3468 $6000   (21-May-91 CE.NY647/R) Rainy day at track (54x65cm-21x26in) s. masonite
£1953 $3750   (17-Dec-90 SY.NY184/R) Seated female nude on patterned sofa (56x41cm-22x16in) s. chl

DAVID, Euphemide Therese (1823-?) French
£1497 $2515   (23-Apr-91 SY.AM305/R) Broken flowerpot (41x32cm-16x13in) s. panel (D.FL 5000)

DAVID, Gerard (style) (1450-1523) French
£7353 $12500   (30-May-91 CE.NY31/R) Madonna and Child seated in landscape (52x42cm-20x17in) panel

DAVID, Gustave (1824-1891) French
£460 $768   (22-Jul-91 SWS894/R) A simple breakfast (28x22cm-11x9in) s. W/C pencil

DAVID, Hermine (1886-1970) French
£1042 $1792   (17-May-91 LGB.P155/R) Eglise Sainte Marie des Monts a Rome (65x54cm-26x21in) s. d.1950 verso (F.FR 10500)
£1217 $2410   (3-Feb-91 I.N61) Labourage a Saint-Benoit-sur-Loire (46x55cm-18x22in) s. (F.FR 12000)
£4032 $7863   (28-Oct-90 M.V85/R) Bouquet de fleurs (81x65cm-32x26in) s. panel (F.FR 40000)
£592 $1166   (6-Oct-90 GL.P19) Jeune femme alanguie (20x26cm-8x10in) s.d.11 aout 1946 lead pencil stumping (F.FR 6000)
£1120 $2207   (30-Oct-90 I.N67/R) Sur la Place d'Ostie s. W/C (F.FR 11000)
£2459 $4820   (11-Nov-90 ZZ.F75/R) Marche aux fleurs a Versailles sous en ciel d'orage (79x59cm-31x23in) s. gouache oil panel (F.FR 24000)

DAVID, Jacques-Louis (1748-1825) French
£3518 $5769   (18-Jun-91 APT.P104/R) Tete de femme (13x11cm-5x4in) s. blk.crayon (F.FR 35000)
£10050 $16482   (22-Jun-91 CH.MO33/R) Tetes de Guerrier et de roi. Deux tetes de femmes (8x13cm-3x5in) black chk pen wash pair (F.FR 100000)

DAVID, Jacques-Louis (school) (1748-1825) French
£8750 $14700   (22-Apr-91 PO.BA12) Homero recitando a los griegos (105x147cm-41x58in)

DAVID, Jacques-Louis (style) (1748-1825) French
£4000 $8000   (7-Feb-91 C162) Portrait of Emperor Napoleon I in Coronation robes carrying his hatand sceptre (276x178cm-109x70in)

DAVID, Jean-Louis (1792-1868) French
£918 $1809   (17-Nov-90 OD.P82/R) L'Amazone (30x25cm-12x10in) s. W/C (F.FR 9000)

DAVID-NILLET, Germain (1861-1932) French
£663 $1279   (16-Dec-90 T.B278) Au centre de la place (73x91cm-29x36in) s. (F.FR 6500)

DAVIDENKOVA, Lidia (1939-) Russian
£1307 $2509   (18-Feb-91 ARC.P195/R) Marins a Leningrad (65x124cm-26x49in) s.d.65 verso (F.FR 13000)

DAVIDSON, Alexander (1838-1887) British
£1543 $2900   (22-Sep-90 WOL.C109/R) Somebody's coming (76x51cm-30x20in) s.d.1877

DAVIDSON, Allan Douglas (1873-1932) British
£700 $1365   (15-Jan-91 SWS215/R) The bather (18x6cm-7x2in) s. panel
£700 $1295   (6-Mar-91 ZZ.B151) Standing nude (94x50cm-37x20in)
£800 $1584   (29-Jan-91 PH34/R) Solitude (19x14cm-7x6in) s. board
£800 $1568   (23-Jan-91 ZZ.B226) Standing nude (94x50cm-37x20in)
£1200 $2040   (29-May-91 GA176) Portrait of female nude, holding robe and looking away (31x15cm-12x6in) s. panel
£2200 $4136   (18-Sep-90 PH140/R) Model (26x19cm-10x7in) s. board
£2400 $4512   (18-Sep-90 PH139/R) The Pose (30x18cm-12x7in) s. panel

DAVIDSON, Archibald M (?) British
£1050 $1785   (29-May-91 ZZ.B100) Portrait of E. Boyce Podmore, Master of Vine Foxhounds, in hunting pink (239x124cm-94x49in) s.i.verso

DAVIDSON, Bessie (1880-?) British
£741 $1244   (16-Jul-91 JRL.S144) Breton Scene (24x24cm-9x9in) s. board (A.D 1600)
£1200 $2328   (6-Dec-90 CSK76/R) Coastal landscape (21x26cm-8x10in) s. panel
£2398 $4724   (14-Nov-90 CN.P69) Vase de fleurs (37x29cm-15x11in) s. board (F.FR 23500)
£10000 $19400   (6-Dec-90 CSK18/R) Magnolia blossom in glass jug (55x46cm-22x18in) s. board
£13000 $25220   (6-Dec-90 CSK11/R) Interior (91x73cm-36x29in) s. board

DAVIDSON, Charles (1824-1902) British
£2000 $3700   (8-Mar-91 S.BM207/R) Autumn dawn. Winter twilight (30x51cm-12x20in) both s. two
£1000 $1680   (15-Jul-91 PH114/R) Gathering hay (45x72cm-18x28in) W/C
£1450 $2842   (20-Nov-90 RB683) Late autumn, Windsor Park (58x89cm-23x35in) i.verso W/C

DAVIDSON, Clara D (1874-) American
£853 $1613   (25-Sep-90 FN.S1936) Still life of summer flowers in copper kettle (52x78cm-20x31in) s.d.1902 (DM 2500)

DAVIDSON, Ezechial (1792-?) Dutch
£1982 $3884   (6-Nov-90 SY.AM172/R) Bitter medicine (57x43cm-22x17in) s.d.1851 (D.FL 6500)

DAVIDSON, J O (19th C) American
£1299 $2300   (4-Apr-91 BG.M384/R) Porter's gunboat fleet below Vicksburg (30x41cm-12x16in) s.d.1863 bears i. tempera paper

DAVIDSON, Jeremiah (attrib) (1695-1745) British
£850 $1675   (31-Oct-90 S254/R) Portrait of Lady Robina Crawford wearing dress inset with silver brocade (73x61cm-29x24in) i. i.verso painted oval
£1500 $2415   (27-Jun-91 CG61/R) Portrait of a man, in a full bottomed wig and red coat with breeches (116x94cm-46x37in)
£2564 $5000   (10-Oct-90 CH.NY49/R) Portrait of gentleman said to be Sir George Dashwood standing (127x104cm-50x41in)

DAVIDSON, Jeremiah (circle) (1695-1743) British
£1100 $1969   (12-Apr-91 C128/R) Group portrait of James, 13th Earl of Morton and family (59x71cm-23x28in)

DAVIDSON, Majel (20th C) British
£1600 $2688   (23-Apr-91 S234/R) Normandy girl (73x59cm-29x23in)

DAVIDSON, Maria (1926-) Russian
£534 $870   (10-Jun-91 ZZ.F51/R) Danseuse tzigane (140x120cm-55x47in) s. (F.FR 5300)

DAVIDSON, Thomas (19th C) British
£3500 $6895   (1-Nov-90 C303/R) Caractacus being paraded by the Emperor Claudius, A.D. 50 (128x102cm-50x40in) s.

DAVIE, Alan (1920-) British
£1600 $3120   (18-Oct-90 C377) Objects excited by blue sound (42x53cm-17x21in) s.d.59 i.d.verso paper
£3000 $5850   (18-Oct-90 C379/R) Let's fly to some hot place (42x53cm-17x21in) paper on board
£3000 $4890   (1-Jul-91 S52/R) Village myths - Opus 01028 (152x122cm-60x48in) s.i.d.8/83 verso
£3500 $5845   (7-Jun-91 C295/R) Clams meditation no 1 (43x55cm-17x22in) s.d.60
£9000 $15930   (21-Mar-91 S86/R) Witch Way (51x61cm-20x24in) s.d.1961 verso
£350 $609   (28-Mar-91 CSK29) Two parrotts (25x37cm-10x15in) s.d.1966 brush ink
£400 $652   (3-Jul-91 CSC.P44) Personnages jouant sous la lune (27x37cm-11x15in) s.d.1/1968 ink brush (F.FR 4000)
£2900 $4727   (1-Jul-91 S63/R) Tumbler's idea (51x76cm-20x30in) s.d.Aug.1963 W/C
£5000 $9750   (9-Oct-90 B172/R) Untitled (170x168cm-67x66in) fabric dye linen
£15000 $24450   (1-Jul-91 S54 a/R) Portrait of Sonny Rollins (152x183cm-60x72in) s.i.d.64-Nov 1966 verso acrylic enamel canvas

DAVIES, Arthur B (1862-1928) American
£1250 $2400   (17-Dec-90 SY.NY209/R) Listening to boozle (36x46cm-14x18in) s.d.1905
£1395 $2400   (15-May-91 SY.NY111/R) Female nude in landscape (46x66cm-18x26in) s.
£2659 $4600   (12-May-91 H.C157/R) Half draped nude in forest (38x30cm-15x12in) s.
£2865 $5500   (17-Dec-90 SY.NY208/R) Phantasie Hill (66x102cm-26x40in) canvas on panel
£4948 $9500   (30-Nov-90 CH.NY175/R) Aspiration (36x28cm-14x11in) s.
£5208 $10000   (17-Dec-90 SY.NY207/R) Cosmic recesses (43x56cm-17x22in) s.
£549 $950   (10-May-91 S.BM90/R) Landscapes (25x64cm-10x25in) s. W/C gouache
£885 $1700   (17-Dec-90 SY.NY189/R) Fiesole (23x30cm-9x12in) s. W/C pastel
£1481 $2800   (25-Sep-90 CE.NY155/R) Satyr and dancing nymphs (20x32cm-8x13in) s. W/C
£2214 $4250   (17-Dec-90 SY.NY190/R) San Gimigniano (23x30cm-9x12in) s.d.1926 W/C pastel pencil

DAVIES, Arthur E (1893-) British
£700 $1365   (12-Oct-90 K451) Old boats on the River Wensum, Lenwade, Norfolk (30x36cm-12x14in) s.
£600 $1164   (7-Dec-90 K207/R) St Augustine's Gate (30x41cm-12x16in) s. W/C
£620 $1011   (14-Jun-91 K452/R) Marsh mill at Runham, Great Yarmouth, Norfolk (28x38cm-11x15in) s. W/C
£680 $1149   (19-Apr-91 K519/R) Brancaster Staithe, Norfolk (28x38cm-11x15in) s. W/C
£700 $1400   (8-Feb-91 K452) Blakeney Hill (48x56cm-19x22in) s. W/C
£700 $1358   (7-Dec-90 K205/R) Horning ferry (28x41cm-11x16in) s. W/C

DAVIES, David (1862-1939) Australian
£814 $1376   (16-Apr-91 J.M133) Moonlit Farmhouse (25x20cm-10x8in) s. board (A.D 1800)
£4633 $9127   (13-Nov-90 J.M264/R) Moonrise (21x42cm-8x17in) canvas board (A.D 12000)
£1400 $2730   (16-Oct-90 HAR281) Still life with flowers (36x28cm-14x11in) s.
£1931 $3803   (13-Nov-90 J.M148 a) At the wharf. Dieppe landscape (21x26cm-8x10in) s. W/C (A.D 5000)

DAVIES, Harold Christopher (20th C) American
£893 $1500   (24-Apr-91 B.SF4567/R) Untitled (76x102cm-30x40in) s.d.58 i. verso

DAVIES, Henry Eason (1831-1868) British
£3167 $5353   (16-Apr-91 J.M220/R) Looking towards the Dandenongs (56x82cm-22x32in) s.d.1885 W/C (A.D 7000)

DAVIES, J (19th C) British
£800 $1560   (18-Oct-90 SC3077/R) The Emma Alice 83 tonne schooner built by John Evans in 1867 (71x102cm-28x40in) s.i.d.1906

DAVIES, Norman Prescott (1862-1915) British
£800 $1512   (27-Sep-90 CSK125/R) A summer afternoon (48x73cm-19x29in) s.d.1913
£3684 $7000   (27-Feb-91 SY.NY238/R) Piping wistful song (71x92cm-28x36in) s.d.1904

DAVIES, William (1826-1910) British
£1300 $2431   (28-Aug-90 S761/R) Glenstrae, Argyleshire (53x33cm-21x13in) s.d.1890 s.i.d.verso
£3500 $5880   (23-Apr-91 S14/R) Mist clearing, Loch Long, Argyllshire (61x91cm-24x36in) s.d.1907 s.i.verso

DAVILA, Fernando (1953-) Colombian
£4847 $9500   (20-Nov-90 CH.NY238/R) Hombre Leyendo El Periodico (168x223cm-66x88in) s. s.d.1983 verso diptych

DAVILA, Jose Antonio (1935-) Venezuelan
£1403 $2750   (12-Feb-91 SY.NY267/R) Paisaje (53x64cm-21x25in) s.

DAVIS, A (?) ?
£1300 $2236   (16-May-91 CSK78/R) River landscape with sheep on bank (51x76cm-20x30in) s.

DAVIS, Arthur A (19th C) British
£700 $1218   (26-Mar-91 PH132/R) Gone to ground (51x77cm-20x30in) s.d.1888 i. verso

DAVIS, Arthur H (attrib) (19th C) British
£683 $1100   (26-Jun-91 D.NY24 a) Waiting for master (30x51cm-12x20in) i.verso

DAVIS, Charles Harold (1856-1933) American
£4233 $8000   (27-Sep-90 CH.NY104/R) Twilight on the water (33x53cm-13x21in) s.

DAVIS, Cornelia Cassady (1870-1920) American
£1890 $3250   (15-May-91 SY.NY120/R) Navajo (52x43cm-20x17in) s.d.1897

DAVIS, Edward (19th C) British
£1400 $2730   (18-Oct-90 SC3151/R) A lady by a woodland pool (21x14cm-8x6in) init.d.1860 board

DAVIS, Gene (1920-) American
£4167 $7000   (24-Apr-91 B.SF4639/R) Lincoln Center 1971 (183x102cm-72x40in) acrylic

DAVIS, Gladys Rockmore (1901-1967) American
£536 $900   (28-Apr-91 HG.C373) Pensive lady (61x51cm-24x20in) s.
£1302 $2200   (17-Apr-91 D.NY27/R) Day dreams (61x51cm-24x20in) s.

DAVIS, Harry (?) British
£500 $815   (3-Jul-91 RBB776/R) View of Bridgnorth High Town from river (48x33cm-19x13in) s. W/C

DAVIS, Henry William Banks (1833-1914) British
£1053 $2000   (12-Sep-90 D.NY15/R) Laundresses along river (51x81cm-20x32in) s.
£2000 $4000   (8-Feb-91 C151/R) Twilight (28x51cm-11x20in) s.d.1870
£3553 $6750   (27-Feb-91 SY.NY222/R) Going home (81x150cm-32x59in) s.d.1890

DAVIS, Henry William Banks (attrib) (1833-1914) British
£820 $1607   (13-Feb-91 S203/R) Pas de Calais (14x18cm-6x7in) d.63 i.verso board

DAVIS, John Scarlett (1804-1845) British
£3200 $6304   *(13-Nov-90 C84/R) Figures at prayer in Church of St Sulpice, Paris (25x15cm-10x6in) init.i.d.1836 pencil W/C*

DAVIS, Lucien (1860-1941) British
£1600 $3136   *(21-Nov-90 B36/R) Reflective moment (59x39cm-23x15in) s. W/C bodycol*

DAVIS, Richard Barrett (1782-1854) British
£1186 $2300   (8-Dec-90 W.W183/R) Stalking the fox (30x36cm-12x14in) s.d.1833 board
£1500 $2925   (26-Oct-90 C309/R) The King's favourite, Minos, a hound (13x18cm-5x7in) board
£3400 $5542   (4-Jul-91 B18/R) Three feral horses standing in a rocky tropical landscape (63x76cm-25x30in) s.d.1827

DAVIS, Richard Barrett (circle) (1782-1854) British
£1058 $2063   (25-Oct-90 D.V32/R) Horse in stable interior (46x61cm-18x24in) (A.S 22000)

DAVIS, Ron (1937-) American
£1637 $2750   *(24-Apr-91 B.SF4654/R) Two cube float (48x69cm-19x27in) s.i.d.1988 W/C*

DAVIS, Stark (1885-?) American
£1995 $3750   (19-Sep-90 B.SF2775/R) Parrot with lemons (91x91cm-36x36in) s.

DAVIS, Stuart (1894-1964) American
£10053 $19000   (27-Sep-90 CH.NY252/R) Gloucester landscape with rooster and ducks (47x57cm-19x22in) s.
£3646 $7000   *(17-Dec-90 SY.NY187/R) Boating party (25x36cm-10x14in) s.d.1912 W/C pencil*

DAVIS, Thomas R (fl.1826) British
£1300 $2535   (26-Oct-90 C314/R) Philip Payne, huntsman to the Duke of Beaufort on Cherrington (69x103cm-27x41in)

DAVIS, Val (1854-?) British
£686 $1215   (20-Mar-91 MA.V168) A peaceful retreat (25x36cm-10x14in) s. (C.D 1400)

DAVIS, W (?) British?
£550 $1056   (19-Feb-91 SWS7) Mail coach on open road (42x64cm-17x25in) s.

DAVIS, W R (20th C) American
£1796 $3000   (25-Jul-91 E.EDM319 a/R) Yachting off Nantucket (20x30cm-8x12in) s. board

DAVIS, Warren B (1865-1928) American
£553 $1050   (15-Sep-90 S.W2103) The letter (41x30cm-16x12in) s.

DAVIS, William R (1952-) American
£977 $1700   (29-Mar-91 E.EDM308/R) Ship David C Meyer (38x56cm-15x22in) s.

DAVRINGHAUSEN, Heinrich Maria (1894-1970) German
£642 $1110   (21-May-91 WK.M787/R) Composition with full and half moons (33x41cm-13x16in) mono. s.i.d.1959verso panel (DM 1900)
£11945 $23413   (24-Nov-90 VG.B258/R) Portrait of mother (91x81cm-36x32in) s.c.1922 (DM 35000)
£439 $760   *(21-May-91 WK.M788/R) Composition (50x64cm-20x25in) s.d.1950 chk (DM 1300)*
£1829 $3530   *(14-Dec-90 ZOF.Z936/R) Composition (45x56cm-18x22in) s.d.1960 mixed media (S.FR 4500)*

DAWBARN, Joseph Yelverton (fl.1890-1930) British
£549 $950   (10-May-91 S.W2150/R) Cattle in Devonshire (30x41cm-12x16in) s.d.1913 board

DAWE, Georg (1781-1829) British
£8000 $13200   (12-Jul-91 C31/R) Portrait of Major General Sir George Adam Wood, in uniform (93x73cm-37x29in)

DAWS, Frederick Thomas (1878-?) British
£900 $1755   (15-Jan-91 B371) The Dachshund Venus sitting in chair (41x61cm-16x24in) s.i.d.10
£950 $1758   (6-Mar-91 RBB742/R) Portrait of springer spaniel Ch Longmynd Calon Fach amongst rushes (25x33cm-10x13in) s.i.d.1909 board

DAWS, Lawrence (1927-) Australian
£763 $1465   (26-Nov-90 SY.ME40/R) Anakie landscape (52x52cm-20x20in) s. s.i.verso board (A.D 1900)
£1013 $1944   (14-Aug-90 SY.ME125) Hills of my childhood I (44x59cm-17x23in) s. i. verso (A.D 2400)
£2000 $3880   (6-Dec-90 CSK57/R) Aeroplane over Outback (159x157cm-63x62in) s.
£2570 $4189   (16-Jun-91 SY.ME56) Omen bird (120x135cm-47x53in) s. board (A.D 5500)
£602 $1157   *(27-Nov-90 JRL.S210) Yam Creek II (30x43cm-12x17in) s.d.62 oil W/c cardboard (A.D 1500)*
£1860 $3126   *(22-Apr-91 SY.ME162/R) Lovers on beach 1 (122x122cm-48x48in) s.d.63 mixed media (A.D 4000)*

DAWS, Lawrence (1927-) Australian-cont.
£2103 $3428   (16-Jun-91 SY.ME83) Sketch for Big Mountain, 1977 (63x74cm-25x29in) s.
                                gouache (A.D 4500)

DAWSON, Alfred (19th C) British
£720 $1332   (7-Mar-91 D160/R) Mother and children on farm lane in landscape
                                (18cm-7ins circular) s.d.1886 panel

DAWSON, Henry (1811-1878) British
£780 $1498   (16-Aug-90 B252/R) Hulks in estuary (41x61cm-16x24in) s.indist.d.
£900 $1764   (15-Feb-91 N336) View near Strelley (20x28cm-8x11in) s. i.verso panel

DAWSON, Janet (1935-) Australian
£2191 $4317   (31-Oct-90 CH.S12) We are here, the altar of good fortune number one
                                (150x200cm-59x79in) s.i.d.1987verso acrylic (A.D 5500)

DAWSON, Mabel (fl. 1880's) British
£800 $1576   (13-Nov-90 SWS148/R) Fantails (27x41cm-11x16in) s. W/C gouache linen

DAWSON, Montague (1895-1973) British
£700 $1379   (13-Nov-90 SWS423/R) Convoy (22x59cm-9x23in) grisaille canvas laid down
                                on board
£950 $1872   (13-Nov-90 SWS424/R) Swedish baltic fleet (30x49cm-12x19in) grisaille
                                board
£1445 $2500   (21-May-91 GRO.B83/R) Fleet minesweepers of Bangor Class
                                (36x51cm-14x20in) s. board en grisaille
£1447 $2750   (27-Feb-91 SY.NY266/R) Cease-fire at sea (30x46cm-12x18in) s. board en
                                grisaille
£1500 $2550   (30-May-91 C159/R) H.M.S. Norfolk (23x61cm-9x24in) s. en grisaille board
£1711 $3250   (27-Feb-91 SY.NY267/R) U-boat caught (36x53cm-14x21in) s. board en
                                grisaille
£1850 $3200   (21-May-91 CE.NY187/R) Cutting axis lines to Egypt (40x58cm-16x23in) s.
                                masonite
£2632 $5000   (27-Feb-91 SY.NY265/R) Battleship under attack (51x76cm-20x30in) s.
                                engrisaille
£2821 $5500   (24-Oct-90 CH.NY356/R) The Queen Mary at Southampton (41x62cm-16x24in)
                                s. s.i.d.1936verso
£3658 $6547   (12-Mar-91 GM.B1078) Le bateau blanc (92x60cm-36x24in) s. (B.FR 220000)
£4600 $8832   (16-Aug-90 B415/R) Clipper on open sea (60x109cm-24x43in)
£5587 $10000   (15-Mar-91 DM.D2006/R) Yacht race off cliffs (41x58cm-16x23in) s. en
                                grisaille canvas on masonite
£6500 $11245   (22-May-91 S150/R) Squally weather - racing cruisers on Christchurch Bay
                                (79x40cm-31x16in) s. canvasboard
£6500 $12675   (18-Oct-90 CSK198/R) Evening shadows (71x107cm-28x42in)
£7000 $12110   (22-May-91 S108/R) H.M.S. Broke - Evans of Broke ramming German
                                destroyer in channel (51x76cm-20x30in) s.
£8163 $16000   (15-Feb-91 DM.D2019/R) Clipper ship South Australian at sea
                                (61x91cm-24x36in) s. i.verso
£9500 $16150   (29-May-91 PHC168/R) Wind abeam (51x76cm-20x30in) s.
£10983 $19000   (23-May-91 CH.NY217/R) The Pacific Combers on the open seas
                                (51x76cm-20x30in) s.
£11377 $19000   (7-Jun-91 SY.NY151/R) The old galleon (71x107cm-28x42in) s.
£13000 $24440   (8-Aug-90 PHP152/R) The winning tack (51x61cm-20x24in) s.i.label verso
£13772 $23000   (25-Jul-91 E.EDM360/R) Arabia of Boston (61x91cm-24x36in) s.
£14970 $25000   (7-Jun-91 SY.NY150/R) Blue Horizon, the Tea clipper Spindrift
                                (61x91cm-24x36in) s. i. stretcher
£15075 $26080   (22-May-91 EA.M465/R) Billowing sails (51x76cm-20x30in) s. (C.D 30000)
£25449 $42500   (7-Jun-91 SY.NY149/R) Glittering seas - The Windsor Castle
                                (102x127cm-40x50in) s.
£46000 $79580   (22-May-91 S131/R) Taking in reef (76x101cm-30x40in) s.
£55000 $95150   (22-May-91 S139/R) Flying Lightning on high seas (101x127cm-40x50in) s.
£2023 $3500   (21-May-91 GRO.B82/R) In morning watch, jumping thru chop
                                (30x48cm-12x19in) s. W/C gouache board
£8205 $16000   (24-Oct-90 CH.NY354/R) Ship Lightening making landfall in summer weather
                                (51x76cm-20x30in) s. W/C
£10256 $20000   (24-Oct-90 CH.NY353/R) Harbour scenes with shipping (39x44cm-15x17in) s.
                                three i.verso gouache one board set of four
£13000 $22490   (22-May-91 S159/R) On run (41x53cm-16x21in) s. gouache

DAWSON, Montague (attrib) (1895-1973) British
£850 $1632   (17-Aug-90 T85/R) East Indiaman 'Sumatra' (97x84cm-38x33in) canvas on
                                metal

DAWSON, Norman (1902-1960) British
£500 $805   (24-Jun-91 LR249 a) Men, women and children dancing in landscape
                                (91x119cm-36x47in) board
£1000 $1610   (24-Jun-91 LR250) Patroclus (132x150cm-52x59in) gouache board

DAWSON-WATSON, Dawson see WATSON, Dawson

DAXHELET, Paul (?) ?
£714 $1407   (13-Nov-90 ARC.P153/R) Famille congolaise (70x70cm-28x28in) s.
                                (F.FR 7000)

DAY (?) ?
£3077 $6000 (11-Oct-90 SY.NY173/R) Still life of flowers in bowl, strawberries in basket and fruit on ledge (55x70cm-22x28in) s.

DAY, Alexander (jnr) (1773-1841) British
£2000 $3300 (11-Jul-91 S262/R) Venus emerging from tranquil sea. Antinous standing in coastal landscape (19x?cm-7x?in) min.s.i.d.1793 gilt metal mount rec.pair case

DAY, Brian E (?) British
£420 $710 (19-Apr-91 K507/R) Wren and Jubilee flags at Burnham (25x20cm-10x8in) s. W/C

DAY, Francis (1863-?) American
£3704 $7000 (27-Sep-90 CH.NY116/R) Storytime (102x76cm-40x30in) s.

DAY, Melvin (1923-) New Zealander
£893 $1510 (17-Apr-91 DS.W53) Wellington harbour (149x118cm-59x46in) s.d.76 (NZ.D 2600)
£1375 $2323 (17-Apr-91 DS.W19) Somes Island, Wellington harbour (138x230cm-54x91in) s.i. (NZ.D 4000)
£687 $1162 (17-Apr-91 DS.W46) Vision of hermit (61x61cm-24x24in) s.d.69 mixed media (NZ.D 2000)

DAYES, Edward (1763-1804) British
£750 $1485 (30-Jan-91 S56/R) Rochester Castle from Medway (32x46cm-13x18in) indist.s. pen W/C over pencil
£900 $1782 (30-Jan-91 S110/R) Part of castle wall near bridge, Rochester, Kent (20x27cm-8x11in) col.wash over pencil with drawing by A.Devis
£2200 $3630 (11-Jul-91 S103/R) Binham Priory, Norfolk (14x21cm-6x8in) indis.s.d.verso W/C over pencil

DAYEZ, Georges (1907-) French
£1000 $1740 (28-Mar-91 CSK207/R) Les batisseurs (65x50cm-26x20in) s. paper on canvas
£1088 $1948 (8-Apr-91 CSC.P82) Camaret (24x41cm-9x16in) s. l.d.68 verso (F.FR 11000)
£1397 $2500 (16-Mar-91 W.W103/R) Nature mrote a l'azalic (33x41cm-13x16in) s. i. verso
£1583 $2833 (8-Apr-91 CSC.P81/R) Saint Paul de Vence (40x67cm-16x26in) s. paper (F.FR 16000)
£2123 $3800 (16-Mar-91 W.W108/R) La pianiste (38x56cm-15x22in) s.d.'50
£2393 $3948 (10-Jul-91 FB.P2/R) Nature morte a l'Azalee (33x41cm-13x16in) s. l.d.1/46 verso (F.FR 24000)
£3354 $5500 (19-Jun-91 B.SF1794/R) La cafetiere et le plat d'etain (65x49cm-26x19in) s.

DEAKIN, Edwin (1838-1923) American
£765 $1500 (13-Feb-91 B.SF2058/R) Church interior Westminster Abbey (61x41cm-24x16in) s.d.1877

DEAN, Frank (1865-?) British
£900 $1692 (20-Sep-90 C175/R) Resting on hillside, Granada (36x48cm-14x19in) s.i.d.1900 board

DEAN, Walter Lofthouse (1854-1912) American
£812 $1600 (16-Nov-90 S.BM160/R) Old fish tales (76x102cm-30x40in) s.
£1641 $3200 (25-Oct-90 GRO.B56/R) Tugboat and sailboats off coast (66x99cm-26x39in) s.d.1909

DEANE, William Wood (1825-1873) British
£1200 $2400 (8-Feb-91 C81/R) A view of Florence with pilgrims at a shrine in the foreground (51x76cm-20x30in) s.d.1858 pencil W/C

DEARMAN, John (?-1857) British
£2000 $3920 (8-Nov-90 TL70/R) The end of the day. The resting place one s.d.1846 one s.d.1847 panel

DEARTH, Henry Golden (1864-1918) American
£581 $1000 (15-May-91 SY.NY108/R) Russet and gold (89x117cm-35x46in) s.

DEBACQ, Charles Alexandre (1804-1853) French
£1429 $2814 (12-Nov-90 CSC.P11 b) La lecon (42x33cm-17x13in) s. (F.FR 14000)

DEBAT-PONSAN, Edouard-Bernard (1847-1913) French
£4762 $8000 (17-Jul-91 SY.NY236/R) Tending the herd (66x93cm-26x37in) s.d.1897

DEBELLE, Alexandre (1805-1897) French
£4514 $8801 (9-Oct-90 GGL.L3/R) Vue de Chambery (40x54cm-16x21in) s.d.1829 (F.FR 45000)

DEBERGUE, Tony (19th C) French
£2159 $3520 (12-Jun-91 GM.B4117) Les indiscrets (44x36cm-17x14in) s. wood (B.FR 130000)

DEBERITZ, Per (1880-1945) Norwegian
£1357 $2430 (14-Mar-91 BU.O17/R) Man reading (54x46cm-21x18in) s.i.d.17 (N.KR 15500)

DEBERITZ, Per (1880-1945) Norwegian-cont.
£1489 $2665   (14-Mar-91 BU.O16/R) Portrait of woman (91x70cm-36x28in) s.d.23
     (N.KR 17000)
£1692 $3265   (12-Dec-90 BU.O11/R) Landscape, Telemark, Norway (50x60cm-20x24in)
     s.d.44 panel (N.KR 19000)
£4103 $8000   (23-Oct-90 SY.NY222/R) Summer landscape (68x81cm-27x32in) s.d.'43 board
£4340 $7248   (3-Jun-91 B.O18/R) Archipelago (74x86cm-29x34in) s.d.36 (N.KR 50000)
£5521 $10655   (12-Dec-90 BU.O10/R) Landscape (85x100cm-33x39in) s.d.30 (N.KR 62000)
£7180 $12853   (14-Mar-91 BU.O15/R) Woman seated on veranda steps (120x100cm-47x39in)
     s.d.1933 (N.KR 82000)

DEBILLEMONT-CHARDON, Gabrielle (1860-1957) French
£650 $1151   (21-Mar-91 CSK3/R) Lady in a floral dress seated by a table with flowers
*   in a vase (18x15cm-7x6in) s.indist.d.95 W/C ivory laid down on board*

DEBRE, Olivier (1920-) French
£1172 $2251   (30-Nov-90 CB.P119) Esquisse tricolore (22x27cm-9x11in) mono.d.86 i.
     verso (F.FR 11500)
£2170 $4274   (1-Oct-90 CC.P154/R) Composition (19x24cm-7x9in) mono. s.d.1957 verso
     (F.FR 22000)
£2793 $5000   (16-Mar-91 W.W108 a/R) Environs d'Amsterdam (51x69cm-20x27in) s.
     i.d.1950 verso
£2883 $4872   (21-Apr-91 P.V5/R) Trait jaune (38x55cm-15x22in) s.i.d.1976 verso
     (F.FR 29000)
£3066 $5489   (14-Apr-91 APT.P43/R) Petite rose violet de Loire (38x46cm-15x18in)
     s.i.d.1982 verso (F.FR 31000)
£3469 $6835   (15-Nov-90 I.N21/R) Petite epave jaune doree (18x24cm-7x9in) s.i.d.1988
     verso (F.FR 34000)
£3589 $5922   (10-Jul-91 FB.P54/R) Environs d'Amsterdam (51x69cm-20x27in) s. i.d.1950
     verso (F.FR 36000)
£4032 $7863   (26-Oct-90 CC.P101/R) Blanc, taches vives, Royan (38x46cm-15x18in)
     mono.d.1982 i. verso (F.FR 40000)
£4487 $7403   (10-Jul-91 FB.P72/R) Blanche, buee, touches vives (100x100cm-39x39in)
     s.i.d.85 verso acrylic (F.FR 45000)
£4871 $8232   (15-Apr-91 CSC.P1/R) Ouverture d'espoir (200x380cm-79x150in)
     (F.FR 49000)
£5123 $10041   (11-Nov-90 ZZ.F184/R) Composition - blanche avec taches vives
     (100x100cm-39x39in) s. (F.FR 50000)
£5607 $10765   (27-Nov-90 APT.P146/R) Jerusalem (46x55cm-18x22in) init.d.72 i. verso
     (F.FR 55000)
£5829 $9560   (23-Jun-91 P.V7/R) Composition (51x74cm-20x29in) mono.d.1948 board
     pasted on panel (F.FR 58000)
£6014 $11608   (16-Dec-90 P.V35/R) Brun rouge, traits orange (38x55cm-15x22in) mono.
     i.d.1948 verso (F.FR 59000)
£6113 $10332   (21-Apr-91 P.V26/R) Gris-bleute de Loire (100x100cm-39x39in) s.i.d.1987
     verso (F.FR 61500)
£6116 $11804   (14-Dec-90 RY.P34) Untitled, 1982 (100x100cm-39x39in) (F.FR 60000)
£8526 $16625   (11-Oct-90 QWA.P98/R) Brume d'automne (46x60cm-18x24in) s.i.d.84 verso
     (F.FR 85000)
£10111 $19717   (21-Oct-90 P.V48/R) Sombre d'automne (100x100cm-39x39in) s.i.d.1981
     (F.FR 100000)
£18349 $35413   (16-Dec-90 GL.P169/R) Automne (100x100cm-39x39in) init. s.i.d.1970 verso
     (F.FR 180000)

DEBRUS, Alexandre (19th C) French
£900 $1764   (22-Nov-90 CSK91/R) Still life of mixed flowers in urn on ledge
     (31x23cm-12x9in) s.d.1877 panel
£3100 $6045   (15-Jan-91 SWS187/R) Roses beside river (99x74cm-39x29in) s.d.1890

DEBUCOURT, Philibert Louis (1755-1832) French
£3819 $6263   (21-Jun-91 SY.MO299/R) Portrait presume d'Hubert Robert (14x11cm-6x4in)
     panel (F.FR 38000)

DEBUCOURT, Philibert Louis (attrib) (1755-1832) French
£5000 $9750   (26-Oct-90 C60/R) A promenade in the Gardens of the Palais-Royal with
     the Duc de Chartres (12x22cm-5x9in)

DEBUS-DIGNEFFE, M (20th C) German
£1137 $1922   (19-Apr-91 FN.S1690) Bunch of summer flowers with roses and lilies in
     glass vase (60x50cm-24x20in) s. (DM 3400)

DEBUS-DIGNEFFE, Maria (20th C) German
£667 $1193   (12-Apr-91 BM.B717/R) Three female nudes on river bank (57x43cm-22x17in)
     s. board (DM 2000)
£874 $1687   (12-Dec-90 WE.MU171/R) English Garden, Munich (44x55cm-17x22in) s.
     i.verso panel (DM 2500)

DECAISNE, Henri (1799-1852) Belgian
£1007 $1963   (10-Oct-90 WE.MU235/R) Commander with family (30x30cm-12x12in) s. panel
     (DM 3000)

DECAMPS, Alexandre Gabriel (1803-1860) French
£5202 $9000   (23-May-91 CH.NY225/R) Landscape with figure at watering hole
     (33x41cm-13x16in) indis.s.
£355 $703   (3-Feb-91 I.N62) Les experts blagueurs (13x18cm-5x7in) s. pen
*   (F.FR 3500)*

DECAMPS, Alexandre Gabriel (1803-1860) French-cont.
£522	$966	(6-Mar-91 HC.P39) Le pecheur a la ligne (18x13cm-7x5in) mono. W/C varnish (F.FR 5200)
£668	$1296	(8-Dec-90 SY.MO410/R) Etude de paysan, de dos (37x24cm-15x9in) s. chl htd col.crayons (F.FR 6500)
£1131	$2193	(7-Dec-90 CN.P102/R) Soldat Albanais (19x17cm-7x7in) s. W/C (F.FR 11000)
£1387	$2692	(7-Dec-90 CN.P103/R) Groupe de personnages Arabes (28x40cm-11x16in) init. chl.htd.white (F.FR 13500)

DECAMPS, Alexandre Gabriel (attrib) (1803-1860) French
| £595 | $969 | (10-Jun-91 W.T1493) Cavalrymen on a mountain road (18x23cm-7x9in) (C.D 1100) |

DECAMPS, Alexandre Gabriel (style) (1803-1860) French
| £1697 | $3344 | (13-Nov-90 AB.S881/R) Rider with pair of horses (48x117cm-19x46in) (S.KR 18500) |

DECAMPS, Maurice (1892-1953) French
£730	$1358	(5-Sep-90 MMB277) Still life of foxgloves and other flowers in a vase (53x64cm-21x25in) s.
£760	$1414	(5-Sep-90 MMB269) Still life of carnations in a glass vase (46x56cm-18x22in) s.
£880	$1716	(15-Jan-91 SWS181/R) Still life with mixed roses in vase (45x53cm-18x21in) s.
£1706	$3345	(24-Nov-90 SA.A842/R) Still life of flowers in vase (65x100cm-26x39in) s. (DM 5000)

DECHAR, Peter (20th C) American?
| £1333 | $2600 | (10-Oct-90 SY.NY501/R) Pears 68-7 (91x132cm-36x52in) s.i.stretcher |

DECAUX, Vicomtesse Iphigenie see MILET-MOREAU, Iphigenie

DECK, Leo (1908-) Swiss
| £1111 | $1922 | (22-May-91 GS.B2069) Sunflowers (141x82cm-56x32in) s.d.81 s.i.verso (S.FR 2800) |

DECK, Theodore (?) ?
| £15625 | $30469 | (28-Oct-90 QWA.P107) Coq japonais au papillon bears st.s. three each made up of eight panels (F.FR 155000) |

DECKER, Cornelis (style) (1651-1709) Dutch
| £1000 | $1920 | (29-Nov-90 CSK262/R) River landscape with ferrymen (32x46cm-13x18in) panel |

DECKER, Cornelis Gerritsz (1643-1678) Dutch
| £2000 | $3700 | (5-Mar-91 PH97/R) Horse standing before dead tree (39x31cm-15x12in) |
| £25000 | $48250 | (12-Dec-90 S86/R) Farmhouse by stream, with peasant girl feeding pig (73x82cm-29x32in) indist.s.mono. |

DECKER, Cornelis Gerritsz (attrib) (1643-1678) Dutch
| £1346 | $2653 | (14-Nov-90 RAS.K262/R) Travellers outside an inn (38x49cm-15x19in) panel (D.KR 15000) |
| £2857 | $5429 | (14-Sep-90 ZOF.Z751/R) Wooded landscape with farmstead and figures (74x66cm-29x26in) s. (S.FR 7000) |

DECKER, Georg (1818-1894) Hungarian
| £2695 | $5336 | (31-Jan-91 D.V53/R) Portrait of Crown Prince Rudolf wearing uniform at the age of 17 (79x63cm-31x25in) s. (A.S 55000) |

DECKER, Paul (elder) (1677-1713) German
| £765 | $1468 | (27-Nov-90 APT.P79) Projet de plafond (50x42cm-20x17in) pen wash htd.W/C blk.crayon (F.FR 7500) |
| £3700 | $6031 | (1-Jul-91 S211/R) View of Monplaisir Palace (36x53cm-14x21in) pen wash |

DECKERS, Emile (20th C) Belgian
| £4251 | $8332 | (20-Nov-90 APT.P232/R) Portraits de quatre jeunes algeriennes (56x85cm-22x33in) s.d.1930 mixed media (F.FR 42000) |

DECLER, F C (?) ?
| £3100 | $5363 | (20-May-91 SWS154/R) Landscapes with travellers by a tower (16x21cm-6x8in) both s. verso panel pair |

DECORCHEMONT (20th C) French?
| £822 | $1595 | (7-Dec-90 GL.P64) Paysage (50x61cm-20x24in) s.d.1954 (F.FR 8000) |
| £1439 | $2791 | (7-Dec-90 GL.P63) Nature morte aux fleurs (46x61cm-18x24in) s.d.1956 (F.FR 14000) |

DECORCHEMONT, Francois (1880-1971) French
| £1189 | $2200 | (10-Mar-91 H.C53/R) Lavender roses (38x56cm-15x22in) s. |

DEDREUX, Alfred (attrib) (1810-1860) French
| £4000 | $6760 | (1-May-91 GD.B185/R) Rider resting with dog and horse tied to wayside cross (50x60cm-20x24in) (S.FR 10000) |

DEDREZ, D (?) ?
£734 $1446   (13-Nov-90 AB.S882/R) Officer on horseback (36x26cm-14x10in) s. panel
                        (S.KR 8000)

DEFAUX, Alexandre (1826-1900) French
£635 $1074   (17-Apr-91 WE.MU189/R) Feeding the chickens (27x33cm-11x13in) s.
                        (DM 1900)
£1156 $2000   (21-May-91 GRO.B46/R) Water carriers (56x41cm-22x16in) s.
£1242 $2000   (25-Jun-91 JRB.C26/R) Canal Scene, Northern Europe (48x66cm-19x26in)
                        s.d.1854 board
£1600 $2704   (1-May-91 GD.B186/R) Shepherd and flock by the edge of wood
                        (48x38cm-19x15in) s. (S.FR 4000)
£1842 $3500   (27-Feb-91 SY.NY109/R) Figures in wheat field with approaching storm
                        (28x55cm-11x22in) s.d.1866
£3158 $6000   (11-Sep-90 PO.BA24) Gallinero (26x35cm-10x14in) s. panel
£4040 $6990   (6-May-91 ZEL.L1640/R) Poultry before chicken house in wooded landscape
                        (50x77cm-20x30in) s. (DM 12000)
£6320 $12135   (1-Dec-90 PER.M71/R) Le marche devant Saint-Eustache (39x69cm-15x27in)
                        s. (F.FR 62000)

DEFESCHE, Pieter (1921-) Dutch
£610 $1171   (27-Nov-90 SY.AM3820/R) Untitled (49x64cm-19x25in) s.d.74 (D.FL 2000)

DEFOREST, Roy see FOREST, Roy de

DEFOSSEZ, Alfred (20th C) ?
£753 $1393   (6-Mar-91 APT.P95) Le modele (38x46cm-15x18in) s. (F.FR 7500)
£913 $1807   (3-Feb-91 I.N63) Jeune femme au bouquet (51x40cm-20x16in) s. panel
                        (F.FR 9000)

DEFREGGER, Franz von (1835-1921) German
£2098 $4049   (10-Dec-90 L.K406/R) Portrait of hunter wearing costume and hat
                        (17x14cm-7x6in) s. panel (DM 6000)
£4196 $8098   (12-Dec-90 N.M471/R) Staller Nantl, South Tyrolean peasant seated on
                        chair (32x23cm-13x9in) s.d.1865 (DM 12000)
£5017 $8478   (19-Apr-91 FN.S1691/R) Head of girl with long blonde hair
                        (16x12cm-6x5in) s. panel (DM 15000)
£6294 $12147   (12-Dec-90 SY.MU40/R) Portrait of farmer (56x43cm-22x17in) s.d.05
                        (DM 18000)
£7458 $12454   (5-Jun-91 DO.H2201/R) Tyrolean peasant with hat (41x34cm-16x13in) s.
                        canvas on board (DM 22000)
£7692 $14923   (4-Dec-90 FN.S1792/R) Portrait of girl in Tyrolean costume
                        (50x40cm-20x16in) s. panel (DM 22000)
£7905 $13439   (27-May-91 GK.Z5017/R) Portrait of young peasant (33x24cm-13x9in)
                        s.d.1872 canvas on panel (S.FR 20000)
£8446 $14274   (3-May-91 SA.A1660/R) Lenel (57x46cm-22x18in) s.d.1884 board
                        (DM 25000)
£8500 $13940   (18-Jun-91 PH129/R) Portrait of young girl wearing scarf (24x18cm-9x7in)
                        s. panel
£9122 $15507   (28-May-91 KF.M148/R) Alpine farm interior with visitors
                        (31x41cm-12x16in) s. (DM 27000)
£9589 $17164   (13-Mar-91 N.M468/R) Portrait of young huntsman with pipe
                        (62x48cm-24x19in) s.d.1880 i.stretcher (DM 28000)
£10067 $19631   (10-Oct-90 ZEL.L1432/R) Portrait of young lady with rose
                        (44x32cm-17x13in) s.indis.i.d.1883verso (DM 30000)
£19231 $37115   (12-Dec-90 N.M470/R) Zither player and two girls wearing costume in
                        peasant interior (94x74cm-37x29in) (DM 55000)
£22727 $43864   (12-Dec-90 SY.MU34/R) Poachers in Alpine hut (38x49cm-15x19in) s.
                        (DM 65000)
£32313 $52024   (28-Jun-91 BM.B656/R) Interior with figures and young man in Tyrolean
                        costume playing zither (80x70cm-31x28in) (DM 95000)
£97902 $188951   (12-Dec-90 N.M469/R) Peasant family gathered round table admiring
                        musical box (92x120cm-36x47in) s.d.1890 panel (DM 280000)
£612   *$1188*   *(7-Dec-90 G.Z451) Male nude (47x33cm-19x13in) s.st.sig. pencil dr.*
                        (S.FR 1500)
£678   *$1105*   *(3-Jul-91 WE.MU201/R) Portrait of Sepp B (34x27cm-13x11in) s.*
                        (DM 2000)
£839   *$1620*   *(12-Dec-90 WE.MU3/R) Lady standing in parlour (32x19cm-13x7in) s.d.1866*
                        chl (DM 2400)
£860   *$1444*   *(25-Apr-91 D.V68/R) View of village. Figure studies (17x13cm-7x5in)*
                        indian ink pen (A.S 18000)
£1003   *$1696*   *(17-Apr-91 WE.MU285/R) Portrait of peasant (27x22cm-11x9in) s.d.1887*
                        pencil (DM 3000)
£1070   *$1809*   *(17-Apr-91 WE.MU284/R) Portrait of hunter (29x20cm-11x8in) s.i.d.1888*
                        (DM 3200)
£2483   *$4767*   *(28-Nov-90 KF.M330/R) Portrait of girl (47x36cm-19x14in) s.d.1895 chl*
                        (DM 7200)
£3679   *$6217*   *(19-Apr-91 FN.S1692/R) The unexpected visitor (28x18cm-11x7in) s. W/C*
                        (DM 11000)

DEGAS (after) (1834-1917) French
£1158   *$2200*   *(9-Jan-91 D.NY18/R) At gallery (64x46cm-25x18in) bears sig. pastel paper*
                        on board

DEGAS, Edgar (1834-1917) French

£28902	$50000	(9-May-91 CH.NY104/R) Tete d'un enfant chantant. Une esquisse de Dante (29x20cm-11x8in) thinned oil paper double-sided
£55668	$109109	(25-Nov-90 GL.P8/R) Etude de chevaux (16x21cm-6x8in) s. panel (F.FR 550000)
£78125	$150000	(27-Nov-90 PO.BA9) Paisage d'Italie (24x31cm-9x12in) paper
£550000	$885500	(25-Jun-91 S4/R) Portrait de jeune femme (60x46cm-24x18in) st.sig.
£710660	$1400000	(12-Nov-90 SY.NY9/R) Pagans et le Pere de Degas (81x84cm-32x33in)
£5500000	$8855001	(24-Jun-91 C7/R) Les chevaux de courses, sortie du pesage (32x40cm-13x16in) s. panel
£550	$886	(24-Jun-91 CSK17) Etude pour un Larron crucifie (22x14cm-9x6in) st.studio verso pencil after Mantegna
£600	$966	(24-Jun-91 CSK16) Autoportrait (17x13cm-7x5in) pencil after Filippino Lippi
£4337	$8500	(14-Feb-91 CH.NY16/R) Cheval et cavalier. Etude de cheval de dos (25x26cm-10x10in) one st. panel pair
£4592	$9000	(14-Feb-91 CH.NY15/R) Jockey a cheval de dos (27x22cm-11x9in) st. pencil
£5102	$10000	(14-Feb-91 CH.NY8/R) Cavalier regardant vers la droite (23x18cm-9x7in) st. pencil
£5584	$11000	(2-Oct-90 CH.NY1/R) Etudes des chevaux (33x17cm-13x7in) studio st. gouache ink pencil
£6345	$12500	(15-Nov-90 CH.NY102/R) Etudes (16x19cm-6x7in) st.studio pen ink pencil
£6599	$13000	(2-Oct-90 CH.NY2/R) Etude de cheval (13x20cm-5x8in) studio st. pencil
£7200	$11592	(26-Jun-91 S206/R) Cavalier (21x29cm-8x11in) st.sig. chl
£13873	$24000	(8-May-91 SY.NY104/R) Jockey (29x24cm-11x9in) st.sig.studio st. chl.htd.pastel laid on board
£16244	$32000	(15-Nov-90 CH.NY105/R) Cheval selle et etude de cavalier (19x28cm-7x11in) st.studio pencil paper on paper
£26000	$41860	(26-Jun-91 S207/R) Le sommeil (31x23cm-12x9in) st.sig. pencil
£30457	$60000	(15-Nov-90 CH.NY114/R) La danseuse (47x31cm-19x12in) st.studio st.studio verso pastel
£32995	$65000	(12-Nov-90 SY.NY2/R) Etude de Nu (56x42cm-22x17in) st.sig. chl.
£41908	$72500	(8-May-91 SY.NY114/R) Danseuses en Maillot (48x39cm-19x15in) st.sig. chl.paper laid down on board
£52023	$90000	(9-May-91 CH.NY108/R) Danseuse (38x29cm-15x11in) s.i. chl.htd.white chk.
£53299	$105000	(14-Nov-90 SY.NY260/R) Portrait de jeune femme (36x27cm-14x11in) st.sig. pastel
£58000	$112520	(4-Dec-90 C110/R) Danseuse a la barre (31x20cm-12x8in) studio st. pencil paper on card
£59524	$97619	(21-Jun-91 GK.B23/R) Scene de ballet (49x63cm-19x25in) st.sig. st.studio verso chl pastel (S.FR 150000)
£70000	$123900	(19-Mar-91 C14/R) Les danseuses (81x65cm-32x26in) pastel paper on canvas
£81218	$160000	(14-Nov-90 SY.NY106/R) Danseuse a la barre (31x23cm-12x9in) st.sig.i. pastel chl
£111675	$220000	(15-Nov-90 CH.NY111/R) Trois danseuses (47x51cm-19x20in) s.i. chl pastel paper on paper
£151822	$297571	(25-Nov-90 GL.P21/R) Modistes garnissant un chapeau (60x92cm-24x36in) st.sig. pastel sketch three parts of paper (F.FR 1500000)
£203046	$400000	(12-Nov-90 SY.NY8/R) La femme au chien - Le Reveil (26x31cm-10x12in) s. pastel over monotype in ink
£222672	$436437	(25-Nov-90 GL.P20/R) Trois danseuses (75x54cm-30x21in) st.sig. chl.htd. (F.FR 2200000)
£231214	$400000	(7-May-91 SY.NY2/R) La sortie du bain (21x16cm-8x6in) s. pastel over monotype ink china paper
£404624	$700000	(7-May-91 SY.NY10/R) Loge d'actrices (16x23cm-6x9in) s. pastel over etching
£456853	$900000	(13-Nov-90 SY.NY23/R) Apres le bain, femme s'essuyant (47x60cm-19x24in) st.sig. pastel chl
£549133	$950000	(7-May-91 SY.NY9/R) Le bain (38x28cm-15x11in) s. pastel over monotype paper
£736041	$1450000	(12-Nov-90 SY.NY10/R) La Toilette (63x49cm-25x19in) s. pastel
£924856	$1600000	(8-May-91 CH.NY10/R) Femme a sa toilette (47x52cm-19x20in) s. pastel joined paper attached to board
£1167513	$2300000	(13-Nov-90 SY.NY22/R) Danseuses sur la scene (38x27cm-15x11in) s. pastel monotype in black ink
£1218274	$2400000	(14-Nov-90 CH.NY10/R) Trois danseuses, jupes jaunes, corsages rouges (65x52cm-26x20in) st.sig. pastel joined paper laid down on board
£1300000	$2093000	(25-Jun-91 S5/R) Femmes accoudee a une balustrade - sur le bateau (57x83cm-22x33in) pastel

DEGENHARDT, Gertrude (1940-) German

£769	$1492	(4-Dec-90 FN.S1571/R) Idyllic Sunday scene with Marx and Lenin (49x34cm-19x13in) s.d.1979 W/C indian ink pen (DM 2200)
£839	$1628	(4-Dec-90 FN.S1572/R) At our home (49x34cm-19x13in) indian ink pen W/C (DM 2400)

DEGER, Ernst (1809-1885) German

£878	$1493	(27-May-91 L.K191/R) Annuciation (38x42cm-15x17in) s. pencil (DM 2600)

DEGLER, Johann (1666-1729) German

£709	$1206	(28-May-91 KF.M37/R) Holy Family with angels and Godfather in cloud (20x13cm-8x5in) mono.d.1709 pen W/C (DM 2100)

DEGNER, Artur (1887-1972) German

£1092	$2141	(24-Nov-90 VG.B485/R) Fishing village at the Baltic Sea (60x80cm-24x31in) c.1960 (DM 3200)

DEGNER, Artur (1887-1972) German-cont.
£2972 $5766   (7-Dec-90 GB.B6444/R) Pierrot with guitar (66x51cm-26x20in) s.c.1930
                       bodycol W/C (DM 8500)

DEGOLLARD (20th C) French?
£1325 $2544   (2-Dec-90 M.V177) Paysage (46x38cm-18x15in) s.d.57 (F.FR 13000)

DEGOTTEX, Jean (1918-1988) French
£4885 $8061   (10-Jul-91 FB.P78/R) Horshere (105x75cm-41x30in) s.d.12.65 acrylic paper
                       (F.FR 49000)
£8569 $16709   (26-Oct-90 CC.P40/R) Dia - collor - Umber 1 (75x75cm-30x30in)
                       s.d.18-3-1979 i. verso acrylic pasted cotton (F.FR 85000)
£8569 $16709   (27-Oct-90 BG.P25/R) Horsphere J IV (120x80cm-47x31in) s. verso
                       (F.FR 85000)
£11869 $21246   (9-Apr-91 BG.P109 s/R) Suite rose noire XIV (120x80cm-47x31in) s. verso
                       (F.FR 120000)
£17472 $33895   (4-Dec-90 I.N52/R) Hagakure III (83x110cm-33x43in) s.i.d.1957 board laid
                       down on canvas (F.FR 170000)
£20253 $39089   (13-Dec-90 CH.BR153/R) Les alliances (162x114cm-64x45in) s.d.1960
                       s.i.d.20-7-1960 verso (B.FR 1200000)
£50917 $100306   (29-Oct-90 FB.P23/R) Antee III, Juillet 1956 (205x135cm-81x53in) s.d.56
                       i. verso (F.FR 500000)
£879 $1705   (3-Dec-90 F.M186) Composizione (50x65cm-20x26in) s.d.1963 W/C
                       (I.L 1900000)
£1115 $2151   (13-Dec-90 SY.AM296/R) Untitled (64x25cm-25x10in) s.d.1960 ink
                       (D.FL 3600)
£3640 $7098   (21-Oct-90 P.V37/R) Media gris (100x75cm-39x30in) s.i.d.23/12/1973 verso
                       acrylic Indian ink (F.FR 36000)
£8569 $16709   (27-Oct-90 BG.P23/R) Composition - les alliances (75x106cm-30x42in)
                       s.d.1959 gouache (F.FR 85000)

DEGOUVE DE NUNCQUES, William (1867-1935) Belgian
£2322 $4481   (12-Dec-90 CH.AM331/R) View of gateway (35x44cm-14x17in) init.d.12 board
                       (D.FL 7500)
£6707 $13146   (6-Nov-90 SY.AM237/R) Mediterranean nights (43x33cm-17x13in) init.d.12
                       canvas on board (D.FL 22000)
£12613 $21820   (22-May-91 CH.AM506/R) Nuit de lune a campanano, Baleares
                       (53x73cm-21x29in) init.indist.d. (D.FL 42000)
£1643 $3205   (23-Oct-90 C.A350/R) The small harbour (44x65cm-17x26in) mono. pastel
                       (B.FR 100000)
£28000 $54600   (16-Oct-90 C17/R) Crepuscule a Munster (39x98cm-15x39in) s.d.96 pastel

DEGRAIN, Antonio Munoz see MUNOZ-DEGRAIN, Antoine

DEGREEF, J B (1852-1894) Belgian
£824 $1616   (21-Nov-90 GM.B991) Etang de Groenendael (38x57cm-15x22in) s.
                       (B.FR 50000)
£907 $1777   (21-Nov-90 GM.B1100/R) Charrettes dans la foret (43x62cm-17x24in) s.
                       (B.FR 55000)
£1484 $2908   (21-Nov-90 GM.B1103/R) Nature morte aux fruits (45x70cm-18x28in) s.
                       (B.FR 90000)

DEGROSSI, Adelchi (19th C) Italian
£580 $974   (18-Jul-91 CSK39/R) Italian beauty in festive costume (53x36cm-21x14in)
                       s.i. pencil W/C htd white
£750 $1470   (22-Nov-90 CSK83) On Tiber, Castel St. Angelo and St. Peter's beyond
                       (26x36cm-10x14in) s. pencil W/C htd white
£3800 $7486   (13-Nov-90 SWS9/R) Cavaliers merrymaking (37x54cm-15x21in) s.i.d.87 W/C
                       over pencil

DEHN, Adolf (1895-1968) American
£415 $800   (10-Dec-90 H.C1054) Caribbean merchants (33x48cm-13x19in) s. W/C gouache
£471 $800   (1-Jun-91 LAE.L27/R) Carribean village with natives (38x53cm-15x21in)
                       s.d.'56 W/C
£698 $1200   (15-May-91 SY.NY225/R) Landscape with barn by pond (53x31cm-21x12in)
                       s.indist.d. W/C
£1036 $2000   (10-Dec-90 BUR.F60 a) Farm landscape (36x46cm-14x18in) s. W/C
£1036 $2000   (10-Dec-90 BUR.F60) Two farms (53x71cm-21x28in) s. W/C

DEHODENCQ, Alfred (1822-1882) French
£38462 $75385   (20-Nov-90 APT.P263/R) Les fils du Pacha (145x95cm-57x37in) s.
                       (F.FR 380000)
£724 $1397   (14-Dec-90 ARC.P122) Femme portant un vase (23x21cm-9x8in) W/C
                       (F.FR 7100)

DEHOY, Charles (1872-1940) Belgian
£904 $1763   (23-Oct-90 C.A145) In Antwerp Harbour (62x40cm-24x16in) s. (B.FR 55000)

DEICHMANN, Christine (1869-?) Danish
£705 $1318   (29-Aug-90 KH.K225) Eskimo woman with two children (86x64cm-34x25in) W/C
                       (D.KR 8000)

DEIKER, Carl Friedrich (1836-1892) German
£680 $1204   (20-Mar-91 KM.K1143) Hunting scene with stag and two other animals
                       (39x32cm-15x13in) s. panel (DM 2000)
£839 $1620   (12-Dec-90 N.M472/R) Group of deers (38x49cm-15x19in) s. (DM 2400)

DEIKER, Carl Friedrich (1836-1892) German-cont.
£1014	$1723	(28-May-91 KF.M150/R) Fox in landscape (31x40cm-12x16in) s. (DM 3000)
£1486	$2824	(14-Sep-90 SA.A1183/R) The clever hunting dog (48x38cm-19x15in) s. oval (DM 4400)
£1531	$3015	(14-Nov-90 FB.P298) La Chasse au cerf (32x50cm-13x20in) s.d.1875 (F.FR 15000)
£1871	$3311	(20-Mar-91 KM.K1144/R) Last minute rescue with cat escaping from dogs (46x29cm-18x11in) s. (DM 5500)

DEIKER, Johannes (1822-?) German
| £1531 | $2464 | (26-Jun-91 KM.K1420/R) Hunting still life with head of six ender (40x32cm-16x13in) s.d.1870 (DM 4500) |
| £2013 | $3926 | (13-Oct-90 KRA.D193/R) Hunting dog tracking down rabbit (63x85cm-25x33in) s. (DM 6000) |

DEITERS, Heinrich (1840-1916) German
| £3885 | $7576 | (26-Oct-90 KM.K1148/R) Hunting party gathering in Westfalian country estate at dawn (105x79cm-41x31in) s. (DM 11500) |
| £4795 | $7815 | (12-Jun-91 N.M399/R) Westphalian farmhouse with children playing by pond (70x60cm-28x24in) i.verso (DM 14000) |

DEJONGHE, Leon (?) Belgian
| £633 | $1216 | (18-Dec-90 GM.B831) Dame dans son salon (50x40cm-20x16in) s. board (B.FR 38000) |

DEKKER, Henk (1897-?) Dutch
| £1283 | $2528 | (6-Oct-90 KV.L73/R) Beach scene with fishing boats (50x70cm-20x28in) s.d.1933 (B.FR 80000) |

DEKKERT, Eugene (1865-1956) German
£671	$1309	(10-Oct-90 ZEL.L1434/R) Stettin harbour with shipping, hazy morning (35x30cm-14x12in) s. i.verso board (DM 2000)
£1074	$2094	(10-Oct-90 WE.MU149/R) Peasant woman by stream near village (44x49cm-17x19in) s. (DM 3200)
£1350	$2619	(5-Dec-90 PHE78/R) Leaving harbour (64x80cm-25x31in) s. board
£1477	$2879	(10-Oct-90 ZEL.L1435/R) Busy market day in Chioggia (28x35cm-11x14in) s.d.1906 i.verso (DM 4400)
£1510	$2945	(10-Oct-90 ZEL.L1436/R) Stettin harbour scene, morning (69x89cm-27x35in) s. board (DM 4500)
£2685	$5235	(10-Oct-90 ZEL.L1433/R) Ladies drinking coffee with children, sunny autumn day (34x42cm-13x17in) s. board (DM 8000)

DELABORDE, Henri (1811-1899) French
| £1906 | $3716 | (12-Oct-90 APT.P91) Orphee (74x59cm-29x23in) s.d.1849 (F.FR 19000) |
| £4313 | $8410 | (12-Oct-90 APT.P90) Pres de la fontaine (74x58cm-29x23in) s.d.1846 panel oval (F.FR 43000) |

DELACAZETTE, Sophie Clemence (1774-1854) French
| £1224 | *$2412* | *(13-Nov-90 CH.G265) Portrait of gentleman wearing black coat (11x?cm-4x?in) min.s.d.1821 gilt-bronze frame oval (S.FR 3000)* |

DELACROIX, C F see LACROIX DE MARSEILLE, C F

DELACROIX, Eugene (1798-1863) French
£163205	$292137	(12-Apr-91 JM.P43/R) Charles VI et Odette de Champdivers (35x27cm-14x11in) s. (F.FR 1650000)
£1012146	$1983806	(25-Nov-90 GL.P5/R) Madeleine - 1843 (55x45cm-22x18in) s. (F.FR 10000000)
£561	*$1082*	*(12-Dec-90 APT.P9) Etude de chevaux (20x29cm-8x11in) lead pencil (F.FR 5500)*
£582	*$938*	*(28-Jun-91 LC.P23) Croquis pour le plafond d'Appolon (24x36cm-9x14in) i. blk.crayon (F.FR 5800)*
£633	*$1018*	*(28-Jun-91 LC.P7) Gladiateur terrasse par un lion (25x37cm-10x15in) blk.crayon (F.FR 6300)*
£653	*$1051*	*(28-Jun-91 LC.P36) Etude pour la justice, caisson du plafond du salon du Roi (10x26cm-4x10in) blk.crayon tracing paper (F.FR 6500)*
£703	*$1132*	*(28-Jun-91 LC.P22) Projet de pendentif non execute pour la bibliotheque du Palais Bourbon (31x19cm-12x7in) blk.crayon (F.FR 7000)*
£803	*$1293*	*(28-Jun-91 LC.P19) Etude pour le plafond du salon de la paix de l'hotel de ville (38x24cm-15x9in) i. (F.FR 8000)*
£803	*$1293*	*(28-Jun-91 LC.P24) Etude pour Attila dans l'Hemicycle de la guerre a la chambre des deputes (30x27cm-12x11in) blk.crayon (F.FR 8000)*
£815	*$1574*	*(12-Dec-90 CD.P5) Numa et Egerie (21x29cm-8x11in) lead pencil (F.FR 8000)*
£853	*$1374*	*(28-Jun-91 LC.P17) Hercule enchainant neree (26x32cm-10x13in) blk.crayon tracing paper (F.FR 8500)*
£853	*$1374*	*(28-Jun-91 LC.P234) Etude pour la guerre, caisson du plafond du salon du roi (10x26cm-4x10in) blk.crayon pasted tracing paper (F.FR 8500)*
£924	*$1487*	*(28-Jun-91 LC.P38) Etude pour la figure en Neptune au salon du Roi (25x38cm-10x15in) blk.crayon (F.FR 9200)*
£924	*$1487*	*(28-Jun-91 LC.P37) Etude pour l'industrie, caisson du plafond du salon du Roi (10x25cm-4x10in) blk.crayon pasted tracing paper (F.FR 9200)*
£1104	*$1778*	*(28-Jun-91 LC.P35) Etude pour l'agriculture, caisson du plafond du salon du Roi (10x26cm-4x10in) blk.crayon pasted tracing paper (F.FR 11000)*
£1104	*$1778*	*(28-Jun-91 LC.P33) Etude pour le plafond du salon du Roi a la chambre des deputes (17x22cm-7x9in) blk.crayon (F.FR 11000)*

DELACROIX, Eugene (1798-1863) French-cont.

£1106	$1813	(17-Jun-91 ARC.P1/R) Bacchus (20x15cm-8x6in) pen (F.FR 11000)
£1121	$2164	(12-Dec-90 CD.P4) Deux etudes d'ange pour le Christ au jardin des Oliviers (16x12cm-6x5in) dr (F.FR 11000)
£1180	$1971	(7-Jun-91 AGS.P22) Etude d'apres un fleuve antique (13x22cm-5x9in) blk.crayon tracing paper (F.FR 11800)
£1255	$2021	(28-Jun-91 LC.P47) Etudes de lion (31x48cm-12x19in) blk.crayon (F.FR 12500)
£1255	$2021	(28-Jun-91 LC.P14) Croquis de bateaux et de pendus (19x24cm-7x9in) blk.crayon (F.FR 12500)
£1272	$2200	(21-May-91 CE.NY20/R) Figure studies - Justinian drafting laws (24x30cm-9x12in) pencil
£1355	$2182	(28-Jun-91 LC.P45) Deux couvertures de missles anciens (11x20cm-4x8in) W/C blk.crayon (F.FR 13500)
£1355	$2182	(28-Jun-91 LC.P15) Hercule et le centaure Nessus (19x27cm-7x11in) i. blk.crayon (F.FR 13500)
£1406	$2263	(28-Jun-91 LC.P16) Hercule portant le sanglier d'erymanthe. Hercule et le centaure Nessus (20x30cm-8x12in) blk.crayon (F.FR 14000)
£1506	$2425	(28-Jun-91 LC.P42) Projets de vitraux representant Sainte Victoire et Saint Jean pour l'eglise d'eu (39x9cm-15x4in) pen blk.crayon tracing paper (F.FR 15000)
£1524	$2500	(19-Jun-91 B.SF1833/R) Etudes pour l'enfant St Jean (24x19cm-9x7in) st.studio pencil pen ink wash
£1606	$2586	(28-Jun-91 LC.P10) La mort du lion (20x37cm-8x15in) d.8 mai 55 blk.crayon (F.FR 16000)
£1606	$2586	(28-Jun-91 LC.P25) Etude pour le salon du Roi a la chambre des deputes (19x28cm-7x11in) blk.crayon (F.FR 16000)
£1707	$2748	(28-Jun-91 LC.P41) La tentation du Christ (17x21cm-7x8in) blk.crayon wash (F.FR 17000)
£1800	$3024	(26-Apr-91 NM.P12/R) Theodose (29x21cm-11x8in) lead pencil (F.FR 18000)
£1807	$2910	(28-Jun-91 LC.P40) Saint Paul terrasse par sa vision (24x37cm-9x15in) d.19 fevrier 60 i. blk.crayon (F.FR 18000)
£1807	$2910	(28-Jun-91 LC.P48) Etudes d'une figure d'Arabe (19x25cm-7x10in) i. pen lead pencil (F.FR 18000)
£1807	$2910	(28-Jun-91 LC.P26) Etude pour la justice, caisson du plafond du salon du Roi (19x27cm-7x11in) blk.crayon (F.FR 18000)
£2008	$3233	(28-Jun-91 LC.P9) Etudes de personnages d'apres Masaccio et Andrea del Sarto (19x23cm-7x9in) i. verso pen (F.FR 20000)
£2008	$3233	(28-Jun-91 LC.P39/R) Etudes d'amours et d'un personnage (19x29cm-7x11in) i. pen (F.FR 20000)
£2170	$4274	(6-Oct-90 GL.P120) Arabes d'Oran (13x19cm-5x7in) st.mono. lead pencil (F.FR 22000)
£2400	$4608	(28-Nov-90 S243/R) Study of seated male nude (15x18cm-6x7in) st.init. ink
£2811	$4526	(28-Jun-91 LC.P30) Etude pour la guerre, caisson du salon du Roi (11x27cm-4x11in) trace mono. blk.crayon pasted tracing paper (F.FR 28000)
£2811	$4526	(28-Jun-91 LC.P46) La justice (24x31cm-9x12in) blk.crayon pen wash (F.FR 28000)
£3179	$5500	(21-May-91 CE.NY19/R) Arab scene - studies of robed figures and landscape (30x27cm-12x11in) st.init. pencil W/C
£3200	$5664	(22-Mar-91 APT.P34/R) Etude de femme et esquisse pour un Neptune (23x36cm-9x14in) studio st. pen (F.FR 32000)
£3213	$5173	(28-Jun-91 LC.P27) Etude pour la justice, caisson du plafond du salon du Roi (13x29cm-5x11in) blk.crayon pasted tracing paper (F.FR 32000)
£3500	$6720	(28-Nov-90 S244/R) Studies of Arabs and raven (10x13cm-4x5in) st. pencil W/C
£3514	$5658	(28-Jun-91 LC.P29) Etude pour l'agriculture, caisson du plafond ud salon du Roi (12x27cm-5x11in) blk.crayon pasted tracing paper (F.FR 35000)
£3916	$6304	(28-Jun-91 LC.P12/R) Etude de cheval (16x23cm-6x9in) pen (F.FR 39000)
£4791	$9247	(12-Dec-90 ARC.P33/R) Feuille d'etudes, academies d'hommes (20x31cm-8x12in) lead pencil (F.FR 47000)
£7200	$13968	(5-Dec-90 PH6/R) Etudes pur Medee (23x18cm-9x7in) init. pencil double-sided
£7229	$11639	(28-Jun-91 LC.P11/R) Etudes de tigres et de personnages (11x31cm-4x12in) d.9 janvier 59 pen (F.FR 72000)
£7692	$15000	(23-Oct-90 SY.NY11/R) Etude de chevaux (15x25cm-6x10in) st.init. pencil
£7731	$12447	(28-Jun-91 LC.P13/R) Etude de cavaliers (21x33cm-8x13in) pen (F.FR 77000)
£8032	$12932	(28-Jun-91 LC.P32/R) Etude pour le plafond du salon du Roi a la chambre des deputes (19x30cm-7x12in) blk.crayon ink (F.FR 80000)
£10542	$16973	(28-Jun-91 LC.P44/R) Episode de guerre en Grece ou en Afrique du nord (20x30cm-8x12in) blk.crayon (F.FR 105000)
£13052	$21014	(28-Jun-91 LC.P43/R) Etude pour la prise de Constantinople par les Croises (21x34cm-8x13in) i. blk.crayon (F.FR 130000)
£15416	$29908	(6-Dec-90 NM.P3/R) Portrait d'homme (29x23cm-11x9in) st. pierre noire wash (F.FR 150000)
£26721	$51840	(8-Dec-90 SY.MO318/R) Palikare de dos (13x8cm-5x3in) s. W/C htd gouache (F.FR 260000)
£81218	$160000	(13-Nov-90 SY.NY1/R) Chef Maure assis sur un divan et fumant (16x15cm-6x6in) s. W/C gouache

DELACROIX, Eugene (attrib) (1798-1863) French

£1212	$2400	(1-Feb-91 S.W2579/R) Portrait of bearded man (23x10cm-9x4in) bears sig.d.1805 pastel

DELACROIX, Eugene (attrib) (1798-1863) French-cont.
*£2243 $4328   (12-Dec-90 ARC.P32/R) Etude de figures d'Apotres, d'apres Rubens
                (38x24cm-15x9in) blk.crayon (F.FR 22000)*

DELACROIX, Victor (1842-?) Belgian
£4076 $7826   (18-Dec-90 DUR.M9) La toilette matinal (24x20cm-9x8in) (S.P 750000)

DELACROIX-GARNIER, Pauline (1863-1912) French
£4335 $7500   (23-May-91 CH.NY24/R) Sunlit garden (46x61cm-18x24in) s.

DELAFORGUE, Franz (1887-?) ?
£612 $1084   (20-Mar-91 KM.K1145) Lower Rhine landscape with church, possibly
                Stiftskirche in Kleve (40x60cm-16x24in) s. panel (DM 1800)

DELAHAUT, Jo (1911-) Belgian
£3325 $5952   (16-Mar-91 KV.L399/R) Geometry (60x80cm-24x31in) s.d.57 (B.FR 200000)

DELAHAYE, Ernest Jean (1855-?) French
£6250 $12000   (17-Dec-90 SY.NY60/R) Colonel Roosevelt in Cuba, near San Juan
                (107x76cm-42x30in) s.d.1902

DELAHOGUE, Alexis-Auguste (1867-c.1930) French
£1096 $1863   (27-May-91 APT.P265/R) Les enfants de l'oued (46x33cm-18x13in) s.
                (F.FR 11000)
£1793 $3048   (27-May-91 APT.P264/R) Le marche a Biskra (51x65cm-20x26in) s.d.1912
                (F.FR 18000)

DELAISTRE, Madame (18th C) Swiss?
*£4898 $9649   (13-Nov-90 CH.G225/R) Portrait of young boy seated in landscape,
                caressing his spaniel (6cm-2ins circular) min.s.gilt-metal frame
                (S.FR 12000)*

DELAMARE (18th C) ?
*£2041 $4020   (13-Nov-90 CH.G207/R) Portrait of Count Peter S. Saltykov (4x?cm-2x?in)
                min.s.d.1770 enamel gold mount silver base oval (S.FR 5000)*

DELAMARRE, Jacques Barthelemy (18th C) French
£1116 $2209   (30-Jan-91 APT.P311/R) Portrait du chien Pompon (22x27cm-9x11in) i.
                verso (F.FR 11000)

DELAMARRE, Patricia (20th C) ?
£630 $1260   (7-Feb-91 R.P236/R) Salomon et la reine de Saba (89x116cm-35x46in) s.
                acrylic (F.FR 6200)
£813 $1626   (7-Feb-91 R.P204/R) Goya almait une sorciere (116x89cm-46x35in) s.
                acrylic (F.FR 8000)
£1512 $2949   (28-Oct-90 R.P126/R) L'Infante et Velasquez (89x116cm-35x46in) s.
                acrylic (F.FR 15000)
*£305 $610   (7-Feb-91 R.P51/R) La paloma et Mel Ferrer (108x54cm-43x21in) s. Indian
                ink magazines (F.FR 3000)*

DELAMOTTE, William (1775-1863) British
*£3000 $5370   (11-Apr-91 S97/R) Promenade, Brighton, looking east from Adelaide
                Crescent and Brunswick lawns (28x49cm-11x19in) W/C over pencil htd
                bodycol*
*£3000 $5370   (11-Apr-91 S98/R) Looking west from Lewes Crescent, Kemp Town, towards
                Chain Pier, Brighton (28x49cm-11x19in) W/C over pencil htd bodycol*

DELAMOTTE, William (circle) (1775-1863) British
£3200 $5216   (4-Jul-91 B3/R) A wooded landscape with barges and swimmers in a river
                (91x123cm-36x48in)

DELANCE, Paul (1848-1924) French
£500 $815   (12-Jun-91 ZZ.B69) Les Ophelin's de Bayeux (16x21cm-6x8in) s. panel

DELANCE-FEURGARD, Julie (1859-1892) French
£16080 $26372   (20-Jun-91 APT.P16/R) Le gouter dans le jardin (192x115cm-76x45in) s.
                (F.FR 160000)

DELANEY, Arthur (?) ?
£780 $1326   (29-May-91 PHC172) Manchester street in winter (27x20cm-11x8in) s.

DELANOY, Hippolyte Pierre (1849-1899) French
£1010 $2000   (30-Jan-91 GRO.B31/R) Floral still life (51x61cm-20x24in) s.d.1874

DELAPIERRE, Roger (1935-) Swiss
£1446 $2429   (24-Apr-91 G.Z113/R) Pont de l'Ile Rousseau, Geneve (46x61cm-18x24in) s.
                (S.FR 3600)
£1594 $3108   (24-Oct-90 GD.B272) Ciel d'orage sur Geneve (46x61cm-18x24in) s.
                s.d.1990verso (S.FR 4000)
£1796 $3484   (7-Dec-90 G.Z168/R) La lagune venise (46x55cm-18x22in) s. (S.FR 4400)

DELAPUENTE, Fernando (1909-1975) Spanish
£1575 $3102   (15-Nov-90 ANS.M40/R) Lunas de Cuernavaca (40x53cm-16x21in) s. panel
                (S.P 290000)

DELARIVA, Nicolas Louis Albert (circle) (1755-1818) French
£750 $1500   (7-Feb-91 C31/R) A man helping a woman dismount outside a booth (32x27cm-13x11in) panel

DELAROCHE, Paul (1797-1856) French
£41026 $80000   (24-Oct-90 CH.NY20/R) Les enfants d'Edouard (89x107cm-35x42in)
£1282 $2500   (26-Oct-90 SY.NY30/R) Portrait of actor in Renaissance dress (19x20cm-7x8in) pencil

DELASALLE, Angele (1867-1938) French
£3163 $6232   (14-Nov-90 FB.P158/R) Promenade a cheval dans le bois (53x72cm-21x28in) s. (F.FR 31000)

DELATOUR, Elizabeth Marie (attrib) (1750-1834) Flemish
£1000 $1650   (10-Jul-91 C51/R) Camille Desmoulins (7cm-3ins circular) min.s. gilt-metal frame

DELATTRE, Joseph (1858-1912) French
£4757 $9324   (25-Nov-90 B.PA58 a/R) Bouquet de fleurs (41x33cm-16x13in) s. (F.FR 47000)

DELAULNE, Etienne (attrib) (c.1518-c.1583) French
£3772 $7279   (14-Dec-90 LEB.P13) L'Annonciation, avec en haut au centres les armes de France (19x27cm-7x11in) pierre noire pen wash htd.white chamois paper (F.FR 37000)

DELAUNAY, Jules (?-1906) French
£595 $1000   (17-Jul-91 SY.NY246/R) Cavalrymen (55x46cm-22x18in) s.

DELAUNAY, Jules Elie (1828-1891) French
£593 $1008   (27-May-91 GK.Z5018/R) Reclining nymph (22x35cm-9x14in) s.i.verso (S.FR 1500)

DELAUNAY, Pierre (1675-1774) French
£785 $1539   (22-Nov-90 L.K887) Villa Borghese (17x25cm-7x10in) mono.i.d.1912 panel (DM 2300)

DELAUNAY, Robert (1885-1941) French
£12639 $24646   (17-Oct-90 DL.P27/R) Fleurs (53x34cm-21x13in) s. (F.FR 125000)
£380000 $611800   (25-Jun-91 S30/R) Formes circulaires, soleil no 3 (81x65cm-32x26in) s.d.1912-1913 i.verso
£12139 $21000   (8-May-91 SY.NY181/R) Rythme (19x11cm-7x4in) init. gouache W/C rice paper
£86705 $150000   (9-May-91 CH.NY223/R) Portugaise au potiron (128x96cm-50x38in) encaustic canvas

DELAUNAY, Robert (attrib) (1885-1941) French
£1190 $2000   (28-Apr-91 HG.C484) Composition (46x30cm-18x12in) s.d.1924 W/C wash

DELAUNAY, Sonia (1885-1979) French
£9091 $15727   (6-May-91 ZEL.L1642/R) Composition (44x36cm-17x14in) s. (DM 27000)
£335 $671   (6-Feb-91 FB.P86) Composition (26x20cm-10x8in) gouache (F.FR 3300)
£402 $647   (25-Jun-91 BG.P21) Projet de tisu (11x11cm-4x4in) gouache (F.FR 4000)
£407 $813   (6-Feb-91 FB.P87) Projets de tisu (15x14cm-6x6in) gouache (F.FR 4000)
£427 $854   (6-Feb-91 FB.P88) Projets de tissu (21x13cm-8x5in) gouache (F.FR 4200)
£500 $885   (22-Mar-91 BG.P93) Projet de tissue (35x27cm-14x11in) W/C gouache (F.FR 5000)
£810 $1320   (3-Jul-91 CSC.P108/R) Projet pour tissu (18x18cm-7x7in) s. gouache (F.FR 8100)
£821 $1600   (10-Oct-90 SY.NY136/R) Design for textile (25x20cm-10x8in) i. st.sig.verso tempera india ink
£1220 $2000   (19-Jun-91 B.SF1811/R) Projet de tissu (10x9cm-4x4in) gouache
£1220 $2000   (19-Jun-91 B.SF1808/R) Projet de tissu (25x20cm-10x8in) i. gouache
£1372 $2250   (19-Jun-91 B.SF1809/R) Quatre petits projets de tissu gouache pencil
£1600 $3120   (17-Oct-90 S203/R) Projet de tissu (99x99cm-39x39in) one i. one i.st.studio W/C gouache two
£2041 $4000   (15-Feb-91 SY.NY77/R) Costume de sport (43x29cm-17x11in) s.d.1924 W/C over pencil
£2048 $4014   (22-Nov-90 L.K888) Composition, projet de Tissus (18x13cm-7x5in) c.1925 W/C bodycol (DM 6000)
£2055 $3988   (7-Dec-90 GL.P119) Disque lumiere (18x23cm-7x9in) s.d.1913 col.crayons (F.FR 20000)
£2284 $4500   (3-Oct-90 SY.NY94/R) Projet de costume bleu-vert (35x26cm-14x10in) s.d.1924 pastel over pencil
£2538 $5000   (3-Oct-90 SY.NY92/R) Dessin pour costume et chapeau en tissu jazz (36x50cm-14x20in) s.d.1922 W/C over pencil
£2538 $5000   (3-Oct-90 SY.NY91/R) Costume simultane (36x29cm-14x11in) s.d.1924 gouache pastel chl over pencil
£2538 $5000   (3-Oct-90 SY.NY98/R) Rythme couleur (27x19cm-11x7in) s.i. gouache
£2551 $5000   (15-Feb-91 SY.NY76/R) Costume marron et vert (34x5cm-13x2in) s.d.1924 pastel over pencil
£2792 $5500   (3-Oct-90 SY.NY93/R) Costume geometrique (35x26cm-14x10in) s.d.1924 pastel over pencil
£3046 $6000   (3-Oct-90 SY.NY97/R) Projet de tissu, zig-zag en noir, rouge, bleu et vert (48x39cm-19x15in) s.i. gouache india ink

DELAUNAY, Sonia (1885-1979) French-cont.

£3083 $5982   *(7-Dec-90 GL.P118) Montreux aux rochers de Naye (27x20cm-11x8in) s.i. col.crayons (F.FR 30000)*

£4082 $8041   *(16-Nov-90 EA.Z341/R) Design for fabric (45x30cm-18x12in) s.d.1917 chk paper on canvas (S.FR 10000)*

£4824 $7912   *(20-Jun-91 APT.P51/R) Rythme couleur (52x35cm-20x14in) s.d.1972 gouache lead pencil (F.FR 48000)*

£5587 $10000   *(15-Mar-91 DM.D2014/R) Two joined figures (51x69cm-20x27in) s.d.61 gouache*

£8217 $16023   *(23-Oct-90 C.A351/R) Le jouet portugais (65x51cm-26x20in) s.d.1951 gouache (B.FR 500000)*

£9137 $18000   *(3-Oct-90 SY.NY95/R) Composition (31x52cm-12x20in) s.i.d.69 gouache crayon*

£12000 $23400   *(17-Oct-90 G.Z57/R) Esquisse (30x23cm-12x9in) d.1954 gouache (S.FR 30000)*

£12085 $19698   *(16-Jun-91 GL.P66/R) Danseus (37x21cm-15x8in) s.i. gouache crayon Indian ink (F.FR 120000)*

£20101 $35980   *(17-Mar-91 GL.P35/R) Projet original pour la Prose du Transsiberien - de Blaise Cendrars i. W/C oil pastel three same mount (F.FR 200000)*

£20809 $36000   *(8-May-91 SY.NY184/R) Composition (57x76cm-22x30in) s.d.1954 gouache over pencil wove paper*

DELAVAL, Pierre Louis (1790-?) French

£1284 $2530   (13-Nov-90 CH.AM103/R) Portrait of young lady, wearing dress, wrap and tiara in hair (65x54cm-26x21in) s.d.1816 (D.FL 4200)

DELAVALLEE, Henri (1862-1943) French

£4027 $7771   (16-Dec-90 T.B279) L'Estuaire de l'Aven (38x55cm-15x22in) s. (F.FR 39500)

£4179 $7230   (12-May-91 T.B96/R) Homme assis de dos (30x26cm-12x10in) s. panel (F.FR 42000)

DELBLE (20th C) ?

£1416 $2760   (15-Oct-90 CSC.P76/R) Fougeres (146x114cm-57x45in) s.i. verso acrylic (F.FR 14000)

DELBOS, C E (20th C) ?

£709 $1389   (20-Nov-90 MF.P65) Odalisque (38x55cm-15x22in) s.d.1919 (F.FR 7000)

DELBOS, Julius (1879-?) American

£885 $1700   (29-Nov-90 MFA.C137 a) Santa Fe Mission (81x102cm-32x40in) s.

DELDERENE, Leon (1864-1921) Belgian

£818 $1408   (14-May-91 GM.B526/R) Vaches au paturage (78x110cm-31x43in) s. (B.FR 50000)

£843 $1636   (4-Dec-90 C.A92/R) Wooded landscape (90x75cm-35x30in) s. (B.FR 50000)

DELE, Jean Baptiste (19th C) Belgian

£6500 $12480   (28-Nov-90 S85/R) Still life of flowers and grapes on ledge (67x51cm-26x20in) s. panel

DELEN, Dirk van (1605-1671) Dutch

£6200 $10106   (2-Jul-91 PH13/R) Elegant figures in pillared courtyard of palace (80x66cm-31x26in) figures painted by another artist

DELEN, Dirk van (circle) (1605-1671) Dutch

£20000 $38600   (12-Dec-90 S199/R) Portrait of young girl wearing red and green dress (61x47cm-24x19in) panel

DELERIVE, N (18th C) French

£2857 $5600   (6-Nov-90 GF.L2327/R) Robber scenes (26x19cm-10x7in) s. panel pair (S.FR 7000)

DELESCLUZE, Edmond (1905-) Belgian

£1330 $2381   *(16-Mar-91 KV.L85) Hunting scene (53x69cm-21x27in) s.d.1932 W/C (B.FR 80000)*

DELFAUER, C (19th C) ?

£5000 $9850   (5-Oct-90 C42/R) Extensive lake landscape (111x159cm-44x63in) s.

DELFF, Cornelis Jacobsz (1571-1643) Dutch

£17000 $28730   (17-Apr-91 S78/R) Still life of fruit and shells (54x75cm-21x30in) s. panel

DELFGAAUW, Gerard Johannes (1882-1947) Dutch

£599 $1168   (25-Oct-90 VN.R23) Harbour scene (40x58cm-16x23in) s. (D.FL 2000)

£622 $1200   (14-Dec-90 DM.D2274/R) Horse-drawn cart (41x61cm-16x24in) s.

£719 $1365   (11-Sep-90 CH.AM91) Man in rowboat in river landscape near windmills (30x40cm-12x16in) s. (D.FL 2400)

£958 $1868   (25-Oct-90 VN.R22/R) Ships on a canal with windmill nearby (28x38cm-11x15in) s. (D.FL 3200)

£1363 $2686   (6-Oct-90 KV.L76/R) Rotterdam Harbour (60x101cm-24x40in) s. (B.FR 85000)

DELFS, Moritz (1823-1906) German

£2041 $3286   (26-Jun-91 KM.K1421/R) Coastal landscape with children and cattle (91x129cm-36x51in) s. (DM 6000)

DELGADO RAMOS, Alvaro (1922-) Spanish
£1359 $2405 (3-Apr-91 ANS.M113/R) Pastor con cordero (46x38cm-18x15in) s. (S.P 250000)
£1743 $2998 (16-May-91 ANS.M65/R) Francisco de Goya (41x33cm-16x13in) s. s.d.1978verso tablex (S.P 320000)
£2199 $3936 (13-Mar-91 FER.M233/R) Albama de Navia (36x86cm-14x34in) panel (S.P 400000)
£3003 $5195 (8-May-91 FER.M168/R) Tejados de Navia (60x74cm-24x29in) s. (S.P 550000)
£3259 $5247 (27-Jun-91 EP.M80/R) Gallina (60x73cm-24x29in) s. (S.P 600000)
£1222 $1968 (25-Jun-91 FER.M271/R) Perdiz roja captada en el momento de la carrera (61x44cm-24x17in) s. chl wax (S.P 225000)
£1229 $2125 (8-May-91 FER.M169/R) Cabeza de ciervo (43x59cm-17x23in) s. gouache (S.P 225000)
£1765 $2842 (25-Jun-91 FER.M270/R) La embestida del jabali (73x100cm-29x39in) s. chl wax (S.P 325000)

DELGADO, Alvaro (1922-) Spanish
£3298 $6331 (19-Feb-91 DUR.M16) Arlequin (61x45cm-24x18in) (S.P 600000)

DELIN, J (?) ?
£986 $1923 (24-Oct-90 GM.B1135/R) Dame de qualite (60x50cm-24x20in) s. (B.FR 60000)

DELIN, N J (18/19th C) Flemish
£856 $1687 (13-Nov-90 CH.AM43) Portrait of Adriana Johanna de Pineda, seated at table, holding letter (87x76cm-34x30in) s.d.1792 (D.FL 2800)

DELINCOURT, Charles (19th C) Continental
£4211 $8000 (27-Feb-91 SY.NY285/R) Odalisque (124x74cm-49x29in) s.

DELINCOURT, O F (19th C) French
£9000 $14760 (19-Jun-91 S187/R) Oriental beauty (122x75cm-48x30in) s.

DELITZ, Leo (1882-1966) Yugoslavian
£718 $1242 (8-May-91 D.V64/R) By the edge of the wood (61x80cm-24x31in) s.i.d.1920 (A.S 15000)

DELL, Adolf (1890-1977) German
£1342 $2617 (13-Oct-90 KRA.D368/R) Wood clearing with farmstead (42x59cm-17x23in) board (DM 4000)

DELL, Etheline (fl.1855-1891) British
£600 $1134 (26-Sep-90 S289/R) Under blossom (27x42cm-11x17in) s. W/C htd bodycol
£1500 $2580 (14-May-91 SWS108/R) On the Cornish coast (23x19cm-9x7in) s. W/C bodycol over pencil

DELL, John H (1836-1888) British
£1200 $2340 (24-Oct-90 HS303/R) Landscape with girl beside gate and cattle, Exminster Marshes, Devon (23x31cm-9x12in) i.verso panel
£3200 $6304 (13-Nov-90 PH31/R) Farmyard scene (43x53cm-17x21in) mono.d.56 panel

DELL'ACQUA, Cesare Felix Georges (1821-1904) Austrian
£1800 $3061 (28-May-91 C.A66) La belle Orientale (90x70cm-35x28in) s. (B.FR 110000)
£2926 $5500 (19-Sep-90 B.SF2633/R) Welcome. Arrival of the invites. Departure for the chase (110x162cm-43x64in) all s. three
£8205 $16000 (26-Oct-90 SY.NY107/R) Changing horses (67x98cm-26x39in) s.d.1845

DELL'ACQUA, Cesare Felix Georges (attrib) (1821-1904) Austrian
£663 $1300 (24-Nov-90 RB.HY195/R) The clock watcher, interior scene with lady (20x28cm-8x11in) s.d.74 panel

DELLEANI, Lorenzo (1840-1908) Italian
£8787 $17047 (4-Dec-90 F.R163/R) Mucca al pascolo (30x45cm-12x18in) s.d.1904 panel (I.L 19000000)
£14000 $26000 (18-Oct-90 F.M101/R) La casa di la dal torrente (42x32cm-17x13in) d.93 panel (I.L 30000000)
£14337 $27814 (5-Dec-90 F.M47/R) Luci intense d'estate, dintorni di Pollone (37x25cm-15x10in) d.1885 panel (I.L 31000000)

DELL'ERA, Giovan Battista (1765-1798) Italian
£684 $1211 (19-Mar-91 F.M157/R) Scena di storia antica (39x54cm-15x21in) pen W/C ink over pencil sanguine (I.L 1500000)

DELLGRUEN, Franziskus (1901-1984) German
£759 $1457 (1-Dec-90 SA.A2451/R) Still life with teddy and toys (83x105cm-33x41in) s. (DM 2200)
£1724 $3310 (1-Dec-90 SA.A2450/R) Die Geschwister (151x79cm-59x31in) s. (DM 5000)

DELMOTTE (20th C) French
£950 $1872 (4-Oct-90 CSK138) An artist in her studio (33x41cm-13x16in) s.

DELMOTTE, Marcel (1901-1984) French
£1829 $3273 (12-Mar-91 C.A56) Dieu au visage inconnu (183x122cm-72x48in) s.d.1963 panel (B.FR 110000)
£3625 $5909 (11-Jun-91 CSC.P49/R) Mere et enfant (91x122cm-36x48in) s. i. verso panel (F.FR 36000)

DELMOTTE, Marcel (1901-1984) French-cont.
£4023 $7000   (27-Mar-91 B.SF4147/R) La vue, l'age du futur (91x122cm-36x48in) s. s.i.verso board

DELOBBE, Francois Alfred (1835-1920) French
£3210 $6259   (12-Oct-90 ZZ.F43) Le gouter (93x61cm-37x24in) s. (F.FR 32000)
£7895 $15000   (28-Feb-91 CH.NY2/R) The heart's awakening (61x74cm-24x29in) s.
£11282 $22000   (24-Oct-90 CH.NY129/R) The offering (131x97cm-52x38in) s.d.1892

DELOOPER, William (1932-) American
£2448 $4750   (7-Dec-90 S.W2732/R) Untitled (183x173cm-72x68in) s.i.verso acrylic canvas

DELORME, Marguerite (1876-1946) French
£1108 $1806   (11-Jun-91 I.N41) Ville Marocaine (36x45cm-14x18in) s. panel (F.FR 11000)

DELORME, Pierre Claude Francois (1783-1857) French
£1400 $2758   (4-Oct-90 CSK222/R) A cavalry skirmish (78x103cm-31x41in) s.

DELORME, Raphael (20th C) French
£2923 $5701   (26-Oct-90 APT.P96/R) Femme oiseau (46x61cm-18x24in) s. panel (F.FR 29000)
£3024 $5897   (26-Oct-90 APT.P97/R) Sirenes (61x46cm-24x18in) s. panel (F.FR 30000)

DELORT, Charles Edouard (1841-1895) French
£3200 $5504   (17-May-91 C25/R) Going to market (32x21cm-13x8in) s. panel
£7895 $15000   (27-Feb-91 SY.NY70/R) Precious cargo (91x65cm-36x26in) s.
£8671 $15000   (23-May-91 CH.NY27/R) The red umbrella (74x65cm-29x26in) s.

DELPECH, Hermann (1865-1918) French
£969 $1910   (14-Nov-90 CN.P106/R) Baigneuses (78x98cm-31x39in) s. (F.FR 9500)
£1268 $2510   (3-Feb-91 LT.P54/R) Vue de Bassin d'Arachon (60x81cm-24x32in) s. (F.FR 12500)

DELPLANQUE, Georges Emile (1903-) French
£517 $895   (12-May-91 T.B252 b/R) GTrebeurden (33x46cm-13x18in) s.d.47 (F.FR 5200)

DELPRAT, Paul Ashton (1942-) Australian
£598 $1177   (31-Oct-90 CH.S150/R) Balmoral beach (19x24cm-7x9in) s. canvas board (A.D 1500)

DELPY, Hippolyte Camille (1842-1910) French
£503 $824   (21-Jun-91 SY.MO359/R) Marine (27x46cm-11x18in) s. panel (F.FR 5000)
£761 $1500   (15-Nov-90 D.NY19/R) River landscape under blue skies (38x63cm-15x25in) s. panel
£1474 $2800   (3-Mar-91 LIT.L16) Summer landscape lake with small boats and roof tops of houses (36x61cm-14x24in) s.
£1760 $2974   (1-May-91 GD.B189/R) Moonlit river landscape with windmills (35x60cm-14x24in) s. (S.FR 4400)
£3364 $6459   (1-Dec-90 PER.M128/R) Crepuscule pres de Vernon (25x45cm-10x18in) s.d.73 panel (F.FR 33000)
£3625 $5909   (16-Jun-91 GL.P85/R) Lavandieres au bod de l'eau (24x41cm-9x16in) s.d.71 wood (F.FR 36000)
£4283 $7409   (24-May-91 FB.P99/R) Bord de riviere (34x62cm-13x24in) s. panel (F.FR 43000)
£4694 $9247   (14-Nov-90 FB.P169/R) Au bord de l'eau (34x60cm-13x24in) s.d.76 panel (F.FR 46000)
£5025 $9648   (24-Feb-91 FE.P79) Vue de Mantes la jolie (55x38cm-22x15in) s. panel (F.FR 50000)
£814   *$1538*   *(30-Sep-90 FE.P16) Paysage anime (37x25cm-15x10in) s. W/C (F.FR 8000)*

DELPY, Hippolyte Camille (attrib) (1842-1910) French
£785 $1539   (24-Nov-90 SA.A717/R) River landscape with anglers, evening (23x18cm-9x7in) i.verso panel (DM 2300)

DELPY, J H (1877-1957) French
£990 $1623   (18-Jun-91 FN.S1806) Wooded river landscape (13x22cm-5x9in) panel (DM 2900)

DELPY, Jacques-Henry (1877-1957) French
£865 $1688   (25-Oct-90 D.V229/R) River landscape (14x25cm-6x10in) s. panel (A.S 18000)
£866 $1664   (1-Dec-90 PER.M178/R) Lavandieres au bord de la riviere (29x35cm-11x14in) s. panel (F.FR 8500)
£903 $1760   (12-Oct-90 ZZ.F68) Paysage (33x55cm-13x22in) s. panel (F.FR 9000)
£1004 $1857   (6-Mar-91 D.P33/R) Barque au bord de la riviere (24x33cm-9x13in) s. panel (F.FR 10000)
£1714 $3360   (6-Nov-90 GF.L2184/R) Vieux Pont l'Isle Adam (55x81cm-22x32in) s. i.verso panel (S.FR 4200)

DELPY, Lucien Victor (1898-1966) French
£1233 $2381   (16-Dec-90 T.B116/R) Concarneau (50x61cm-20x24in) s. (F.FR 12100)
£1294 $2238   (12-May-91 T.B99/R) Lavandieres pres du rivage (73x92cm-29x36in) s. (F.FR 13000)

DELPY, Lucien Victor (1898-1966) French-cont.
£2388 $4131   (12-May-91 T.B100/R) Retour des Thoniers (73x92cm-29x36in) s.
            (F.FR 24000)

DELSAUX, Willem (1862-?) Belgian
£660 $1293   (21-Nov-90 GM.B1041/R) Paysage automnal (150x100cm-59x39in) s.
            (B.FR 40000)

DELTOMBE, Paul (1878-1971) French
£655 $1278   (27-Oct-90 ZZ.F18/R) La Marionniere (38x46cm-15x18in) s. (F.FR 6500)
£2200 $4268   (6-Dec-90 CSK138/R) Still life of fruit and bottles on table
            (46x55cm-18x22in) s.

DELUERMOZ, Henri (1876-1943) French
£706 $1376   (28-Oct-90 QWA.P109) Tete de lion (46x38cm-18x15in) paper laid down on
            canvas (F.FR 7000)

DELVAL, Robert (20th C) French
£655 $1100   (23-Apr-91 C.A405) Flowering chestnut trees in the Bois de Boulogne
            (73x93cm-29x37in) s. (B.FR 40000)
£681 $1137   (4-Jun-91 R.T237/R) Les Soucis - marigolds (65x54cm-26x21in) s.
            (C.D 1300)
£2551 $5026   (17-Nov-90 HC.P47) Fleurs (61x50cm-24x20in) s. (F.FR 25000)

DELVAUX, Paul (1898-) Belgian
£362538 $590937   (15-Jun-91 FB.P19/R) Aphrodite (150x130cm-59x51in) s.d.6.69
            (F.FR 3600000)
£650000 $1261000   (4-Dec-90 S31/R) La Tentation de Saint Antoine (114x147cm-45x58in)
            s.d.12-45
£650000 $1046500   (24-Jun-91 C33/R) L'eveil de la foret (171x225cm-67x89in) s.d.39
£722543 $1250000   (8-May-91 CH.NY32/R) La ville endormie (150x175cm-59x69in) s.d.5-38
£3604 $6234   (23-May-91 SY.AM40/R) Paysage (32x44cm-13x17in) s.indis.d.24 W/C
            (D.FL 12000)
£5486 $9820   (16-Mar-91 KV.L457/R) L'Habilleuse (30x24cm-12x9in) mono.d.1933
            chk.pencil (B.FR 330000)
£8210 $14204   (25-May-91 KV.L406/R) Nu assis (26x17cm-10x7in) s. chk. (B.FR 500000)
£8669 $16731   (13-Dec-90 SY.AM49/R) Dunes, Middelkerke (60x79cm-24x31in) d.7-36 W/C
            (D.FL 28000)
£9092 $17820   (20-Nov-90 BR.M71/R) Due figure (17x21cm-7x8in) s.d.1945 W/C paper on
            cardboard (I.L 20000000)
£16038 $31596   (6-Oct-90 KV.L373/R) Le Sommeil (18x24cm-7x9in) s. W/C over pen
            (B.FR 1000000)
£24938 $44638   (16-Mar-91 KV.L386/R) Nude woman with hat covered in flowers
            (34x26cm-13x10in) s. W/C pen (B.FR 1500000)
£27919 $55000   (15-Nov-90 CH.NY187/R) Femme nue assise (35x27cm-14x11in) init.d.48 pen
            brush india ink over pencil
£29010 $56860   (24-Nov-90 VG.B307/R) Loving couple (37x52cm-15x20in) s.d.1942 pen W/C
            board (DM 85000)
£50000 $88500   (20-Mar-91 S57/R) Femme assise (36x54cm-14x21in) s.d.23.2.60 pen W/C

DELVIN (19th C) Belgian
£1495 $2437   (11-Jun-91 GM.B919) Le soir, apres le travail (244x169cm-96x67in) s.
            (B.FR 90000)

DEMACHY, Pierre Antoine (1723-1807) French
£3916 $6304   (27-Jun-91 APT.P191/R) Vue imaginaire de Paris (23x35cm-9x14in)
            (F.FR 39000)
£2200 $3894   (22-Mar-91 APT.P42/R) Vue de l'Ecurie du Pape Jules II (26x17cm-10x7in)
            pen wash sanguine (F.FR 22000)
£3186 $6181   (7-Dec-90 CN.P67/R) Personnages dans des ruines (34x25cm-13x10in) s.
            pierre noire wash (F.FR 31000)

DEMACHY, Pierre Antoine (studio) (1723-1807) French
£1750 $2923   (7-Jun-91 AGS.P48) Temple rond et ruines (37x29cm-15x11in) gouache
            (F.FR 17500)

DEMARNE, Jean Louis (1744-1829) French
£4762 $8190   (19-May-91 ZZ.F68/R) Scene champetre (40x51cm-16x20in) (F.FR 48000)
£6352 $12451   (7-Nov-90 APT.P439/R) Le passage du gue (26x30cm-10x12in) panel
            (F.FR 62000)
£7028 $11315   (27-Jun-91 APT.P162/R) Bergere et son galant avec son troupeau
            (49x61cm-19x24in) s. (F.FR 70000)
£23739 $42493   (9-Apr-91 APT.P64/R) La foire au Village ou le Taureau Furieux
            (47x67cm-19x26in) panel (F.FR 240000)

DEMARSTLAND, L (19th C) German
£1300 $2327   (12-Mar-91 PH16/R) Travellers in river landscape and town beyond
            (55x70cm-22x28in) s.

DEMAY, Jean Francois (1798-1850) French
£3874 $7437   (1-Dec-90 PER.M159/R) A l'affut pres de la ferme (17x25cm-7x10in) s.
            panel (F.FR 38000)

DEMETROPOULOS, Charles (1912-1976) American
£609 $1200   (18-Nov-90 JRB.C97/R) The State House (53x74cm-21x29in) d.1974 W/C
£660 $1300   (18-Nov-90 JRB.C195/R) Boston Gardens (51x74cm-20x29in) d.1973/4 W/C

482

DEMETROPOULOS, Charles (1912-1976) American-cont.
£812 $1600   *(18-Nov-90 JRB.C199/R) Boston Commons (53x74cm-21x29in) d.1974 W/C*

DEMETZ, Karl (1909-1986) German
£1678 $3256   (4-Dec-90 FN.S1794/R) River landscape with shepherd and flock, autumn
                           (66x82cm-26x32in) s. l.verso (DM 4800)
£2363 $4230   (12-Mar-91 FN.S2330/R) Peasant leading horses on village street
                           (40x50cm-16x20in) s. l.verso (DM 6900)

DEMIN, Giovanni (1786-1859) Italian
£2736 $4843   *(19-Mar-91 F.M353/R) Rappresentazione allegorica della disfatta di
                           Napoleone alla Beresina (27x40cm-11x16in) s. pen W/C in htd white
                           (I.L 6000000)*

DEMING, Edwin Willard (1860-1943) American
£694 $1200   (21-May-91 CE.NY515/R) Fremont Lake, Windriver, Wyoming
                           (25x34cm-10x13in) mono. board
£719 $1200   (26-Jul-91 E.EDM122/R) Fawn in landscape (25x33cm-10x13in) s. panel
£947 $1600   (1-May-91 B.SF5281/R) Buffalo and calf (30x44cm-12x17in) s.
£1479 $2500   (1-May-91 B.SF5180/R) Indian on horseback (14x20cm-6x8in) mono. board

DEMONGIN, V (20th C) French
£2901 $5686   (24-Nov-90 SA.A654/R) Cats and the hot mush ... (46x55cm-18x22in) s.
                           (DM 8500)

DEMONT, Adrien (1851-1928) French
£1300 $2548   (14-Feb-91 CSK56/R) In the meadow (30x58cm-12x23in) s. panel

DEMONT-BRETON, Virginie (1859-1935) French
£15029 $26000   (22-May-91 SY.NY173/R) Lady on beach mending fishing net
                           (32x42cm-13x17in) s.i.d.1899

DEMUTH, Charles (1883-1935) American
£223958 $430000   (29-Nov-90 SY.NY95/R) Sail - in two movements (41x51cm-16x20in) s.d.1919
                           init.d.verso tempera board
£10417   *$20000*   *(30-Nov-90 CH.NY182/R) Ta Nana (20x25cm-8x10in) init.i.d.1916 W/C pencil*
£18229   *$35000*   *(30-Nov-90 CH.NY186/R) Spray of flowers (46x30cm-18x12in) s. W/C*

DENCKER, August (19th C) ?
£575 $1000   (27-Mar-91 B.SF4325/R) Landscape with houses and road (55x70cm-22x28in)
                           s.d.1943

DENIS, H (19th C) ?
£4046 $7000   (21-May-91 CE.NY326/R) Chrysanthemums in oriental vase
                           (125x77cm-49x30in) s.

DENIS, Jose (19th C) Spanish
£2717 $5217   (18-Dec-90 DUR.M45) Musico callejero (65x37cm-26x15in) (S.P 500000)
£2717 $5217   (18-Dec-90 DUR.M41) Musico callejero (65x37cm-26x15in) (S.P 500000)

DENIS, Maurice (1870-1943) French
£2650 $5115   (12-Dec-90 APT.P85) Scene de chemin de croix (60x96cm-24x38in) s.d.1917
                           (F.FR 26000)
£6533 $10714   (20-Jun-91 APT.P26/R) La Mare de la Foret de Marly (47x61cm-19x24in) s.
                           panel (F.FR 65000)
£7049 $11490   (16-Jun-91 GL.P53/R) Nu pour Nausicaa (55x44cm-22x17in) s. (F.FR 70000)
£13930 $24100   (12-May-91 T.B105/R) Personnage dans un cloitre 1913 (54x44cm-21x17in)
                           mono. (F.FR 140000)
£14000 $24780   (20-Mar-91 S53/R) Village des Pyrenees (33x24cm-13x9in) st.mono. board
£15182 $29757   (25-Nov-90 GL.P16/R) L'Annonce faite a Marie (36x25cm-14x10in) s. board
                           (F.FR 150000)
£18090 $32382   (17-Mar-91 GL.P6/R) Arbre de vie (158x133cm-62x52in) mono. (F.FR 180000)
£29532 $58177   (29-Oct-90 CSC.P83/R) Etude pour la piazetta a Venise (22x17cm-9x7in) s.
                           board (F.FR 290000)
£51741 $89512   (12-May-91 T.B104/R) Baigneuses dans les bois du Huelgoat
                           (72x106cm-28x42in) s. (F.FR 520000)
£58704 $115061   (25-Nov-90 GL.P14/R) Religieuses et fillettes en rose sur la terrasse de
                           Saint-Germain (26x37cm-10x15in) board (F.FR 580000)
£483   *$788*   *(14-Jun-91 FB.P46/R) Religieuse breton (40x24cm-16x9in) s. chl.pastel
                           (F.FR 4800)*
£956   *$1854*   *(9-Dec-90 ZZ.F40/R) Le peintre et le modele (53x41cm-21x16in) mono. chl
                           crayon board (F.FR 9300)*
£1692   *$2926*   *(12-May-91 T.B193/R) Personnages au jardin (18x26cm-7x10in) s. W/C
                           (F.FR 17000)*
£2546   *$5015*   *(29-Oct-90 CSC.P88) Paysage de Bretagne (23x30cm-9x12in) s. W/C
                           (F.FR 25000)*
£2600   *$4186*   *(24-Jun-91 CSK3/R) Mere et enfant (42x32cm-17x13in) st.mono. pencil*
£2854   *$5509*   *(16-Dec-90 T.B361) La passage de la riviere (38x46cm-15x18in) s. gouache
                           (F.FR 28000)*
£4995   *$9640*   *(16-Dec-90 T.B25/R) Les Postulantes (24x17cm-9x7in) mono. W/C
                           (F.FR 49000)*

DENISART, Jacques (17th C) ?
£10000 $16900   (17-Apr-91 S100/R) Wooded landscapes with figures (61x84cm-24x33in)
                           indis.s. pair

DENLEY, L D (19th C) ?
£1307 $2548   (15-Oct-90 B.O146/R) Seated monk (61x45cm-24x18in) s.d.1885 (N.KR 15000)

DENNER, Balthasar (1685-1749) German
£797 $1347   (1-May-91 KH.K51/R) Head of old man with fur hat (32x25cm-13x10in) panel
           (D.KR 9000)
£1100 $2167   (30-Oct-90 PH29/R) Portrait of man wearing open jacket (41x36cm-16x14in)
           panel

DENNER, Balthasar (attrib) (1685-1749) German
£2167 $3618   (6-Jun-91 D.V227/R) Portrait of man (41x36cm-16x14in) panel (A.S 45000)

DENNIS, James (1841-1918) American
£475 $850   (15-Mar-91 DM.D2005/R) Portrait of Sarah Fisher (61x48cm-24x19in) pastel

DENON, Vivant Dominique (1747-1825) French
£402 $720   (17-Mar-91 M.V34) Autoportrait presume (31x29cm-12x11in) i. verso lead
           pencil oval (F.FR 4000)

DENONNE, Alexander (1879-1953) Belgian
£1043 $2054   (6-Oct-90 KV.L84) In the studio (55x45cm-22x18in) s. (B.FR 65000)
£1764 $3476   (6-Oct-90 KV.L83/R) Vegetable market in Brussels (60x70cm-24x28in) s.
           (B.FR 110000)
£1855 $3599   (8-Dec-90 KV.L424/R) Nature morte (70x87cm-28x34in) s. (B.FR 110000)
£1912 $3422   (16-Mar-91 KV.L447/R) The Stock Exchange in Brussels (70x80cm-28x31in)
           s. (B.FR 115000)

D'ENTRAYGUES, Charles Bertrand (1851-?) French
£1838 $3400   (10-Mar-91 H.C5/R) Domestic scene (41x56cm-16x22in) s.

DENZLER, Christian (20th C) Swiss
£1280 $2214   (10-May-91 S.Z22) Untitled (150x120cm-59x47in) s.d.1988 acrylic
           (S.FR 3200)

DEPERO, Fortunato (1892-1960) Italian
£1814 $3484   (2-Dec-90 M.V122/R) Cavalier mecanique (70x90cm-28x35in) s.d.1958
           (F.FR 17800)
£4355 $7143   (19-Jun-91 F.M17/R) Ballerina (39x28cm-15x11in) s. tempera
           (I.L 9500000)
£20841 $36263   (26-Mar-91 F.M101/R) Figure (76x78cm-30x31in) s. tempera paper
           (I.L 46000000)
£22923 $37593   (20-Jun-91 F.M481/R) Positano fine anni '20 (70x62cm-28x24in) s.verso
           panel (I.L 50000000)
£555 $1077   (3-Dec-90 F.M74/R) Deposizione (20x26cm-8x10in) mono.d.1944 pencil
           sanguine (I.L 1200000)
£1375 $2256   (19-Jun-91 F.M6/R) O la borsa o la vita (22x14cm-9x6in) s.i.d.1924 ink
           W/C (I.L 3000000)
£8183 $16038   (20-Nov-90 BR.M165/R) Figura (62x73cm-24x29in) s. mixed media
           (I.L 18000000)
£9250 $17945   (3-Dec-90 CH.R51/R) Bottiglie (64x76cm-25x30in) tempera W/C ind.ink
           pencil pap.on canvas arched (I.L 20000000)

DEPETRIS, Giovanni (1890-1940) Italian
£547 $914   (6-Jun-91 F.M93/R) Paesaggio montano (30x43cm-12x17in) s.d.1920 panel
           (I.L 1200000)

DEQUENE, Albert Charles (1897-1973) French
£1122 $2211   (13-Nov-90 ARC.P113/R) Taui (46x33cm-18x13in) s.i.d.9.33 chl.sanguinne
           (F.FR 11000)

DERAIN, Andre (1880-1954) French
£1315 $2564   (24-Oct-90 GD.B278/R) Couple in costumes (64cm-25ins circular) st.studio
           tempera (S.FR 3300)
£1664 $2978   (14-Mar-91 BU.O18/R) Still life of fruit and clay pots (46x56cm-18x22in)
           s. panel (N.KR 19000)
£4900 $7987   (5-Jul-91 ZZ.F9/R) Femme nue assise au bord d'une plage (26x23cm-10x9in)
           s. (F.FR 49000)
£7614 $15000   (14-Nov-90 SY.NY259/R) Les bras croises (33x54cm-13x21in) s.
£7890 $15542   (6-Oct-90 GL.P20/R) Deux baigneuses (16x17cm-6x7in) s. panel
           (F.FR 80000)
£8543 $14010   (21-Jun-91 OD.P9/R) Buste de jeune femme brune (37x32cm-15x13in) s.
           (F.FR 85000)
£10553 $18889   (16-Mar-91 APT.P35/R) Nu assis (60x73cm-24x29in) s. (F.FR 105000)
£11282 $22000   (10-Oct-90 SY.NY70/R) Standing nude (41x20cm-16x8in) s.
£14170 $27773   (20-Nov-90 BG.P29/R) Visage de femme (32x31cm-13x12in) s. (F.FR 140000)
£14286 $28000   (15-Feb-91 SY.NY51/R) Le costume bleu (73x40cm-29x16in) s.
£15000 $29250   (17-Oct-90 S57/R) Nature morte a la cruche e a la coupe
           (25x34cm-10x13in) s.
£15029 $26000   (8-May-91 SY.NY202 a/R) Paysage avec figures (47x26cm-19x10in) s. verso
£18072 $29096   (24-Jun-91 ARC.P41/R) Les baigneuses (32x33cm-13x13in) s. (F.FR 180000)
£18782 $37000   (2-Oct-90 CH.NY101/R) Poires, pechhes et raisins (29x30cm-11x12in) s.
£20000 $39000   (17-Oct-90 S163/R) Paysage de l'Ile de France (33x44cm-13x17in) s.
£20305 $40000   (3-Oct-90 SY.NY154/R) Buste al la fleur (62x56cm-24x22in) s.
£34000 $65960   (4-Dec-90 C325/R) Vase de zinnies (55x46cm-22x18in) s.
£50000 $97000   (4-Dec-90 C314/R) Paysage de Chambourcy (73x92cm-29x36in) s.

DERAIN, Andre (1880-1954) French-cont.
£498	$866	(25-Mar-91 PLF.P34) Etude d'homme nu (31x23cm-12x9in) st.sig. crayon (F.FR 5000)
£558	$1088	(24-Oct-90 GD.B280/R) Still life with bowl (14x29cm-6x11in) st.studio brush brown indian ink (S.FR 1400)
£677	$1321	(24-Oct-90 GD.B1416/R) Female nude seated on chair (27x20cm-11x8in) st.studio pencil (S.FR 1700)
£677	$1321	(24-Oct-90 GD.B279/R) Still life (20x24cm-8x9in) st.studio brush dr. (S.FR 1700)
£694	$1346	(8-Dec-90 GAB.G2506/R) Le personnage couronne (18x16cm-7x6in) studio st. W/C (S.FR 1700)
£736	$1200	(12-Jun-91 SY.NY2/R) Tete du femme. Study of female nude (41x32cm-16x13in) s. chl double-sided
£1000	$1680	(24-Apr-91 MJ.P93/R) Visages (20x13cm-8x5in) blk.crayon htd.pastel (F.FR 10000)
£1004	$1857	(6-Mar-91 HC.P44) Nu allonge (25x33cm-10x13in) bears studio st. ink (F.FR 10000)
£1020	$1980	(8-Dec-90 GAB.G2505/R) Personnage de profil (18x16cm-7x6in) studio st. W/C (S.FR 2500)
£1223	$2349	(2-Dec-90 M.V79/R) Personnages costumes (21x15cm-8x6in) studio st. wash (F.FR 12000)
£1835	$3541	(15-Dec-90 D.P6/R) Jeune femme etendue (46x60cm-18x24in) s. sanguine (F.FR 18000)
£2051	$4000	(10-Oct-90 SY.NY1/R) Standing nude (61x46cm-24x18in) s. red chk.
£2174	$3696	(27-May-91 GK.Z5560) Paysage (27x37cm-11x15in) st.studio sepia pen (S.FR 5500)
£2277	$4031	(5-Apr-91 LGB.P86/R) Academie d'homme, de dos (56x39cm-22x15in) s. sanguinne (F.FR 23000)
£2800	$4508	(24-Jun-91 CSK25/R) Femme nue assise (63x48cm-25x19in) s. sanguine
£3586	$7029	(7-Nov-90 APT.P468/R) Nu assis (50x35cm-20x14in) s. sanguinne (F.FR 35000)
£4435	$8516	(2-Dec-90 GAB.G1584/R) Paysage a la maison jaune (37x43cm-15x17in) studio st. W/C (S.FR 11000)
£13873	$24000	(9-May-91 CH.NY136/R) Arlequin, Pierrot et Colombine (48x63cm-19x25in) s. gouache brush Indian ink
£19153	$37349	(14-Jan-91 YC.P165/R) Village au bord de la mer (38x51cm-15x20in) s.d.1900 Indian ink crayon (F.FR 190000)

DERBECQ, Germaine (20th C) ?
£1923	$3731	(4-Dec-90 FN.S1573/R) Bathers (32x40cm-13x16in) s.d. panel (DM 5500)

DERBIZOVA, Praskovia (1920-) Russian
£500	$840	(26-Apr-91 ARC.P177/R) Bouquet de fleurs champetres (60x49cm-24x19in) s. (F.FR 5000)
£560	$941	(26-Apr-91 ARC.P176/R) Nature morte a la grenade (69x100cm-27x39in) s. (F.FR 5600)
£810	$1361	(26-Apr-91 ARC.P175/R) Le vase bleu (57x72cm-22x28in) s.d.57 (F.FR 8100)

DERFLA, R (19th C) ?
£561	$993	(20-Mar-91 KM.K1146) Horse market (18x31cm-7x12in) s. panel one of pair (DM 1650)
£561	$993	(20-Mar-91 KM.K1147) Peasant couple in horse-drawn coach and foal (18x31cm-7x12in) s. panel one of pair (DM 1650)

DERKERT, Siri (1888-1973) Swedish
£4449	$8630	(4-Dec-90 BA.S93/R) Sewing (100x55cm-39x22in) s. panel (S.KR 48000)
£845	$1437	(28-May-91 AB.S5194/R) Mustard tree and birds from heaven (46x117cm-18x46in) s.d.1959 collage oil (S.KR 9000)
£2224	$4315	(5-Dec-90 AB.S7059/R) People feeding birds (98x84cm-39x33in) collage oil (S.KR 24000)

DERKINDEREN, Antonius Johannes (1859-1935) Dutch
£788	$1552	(30-Oct-90 CH.AM52/R) Saint John the Baptist in mountains (112x170cm-44x67in) s. (D.FL 2600)

DEROME, Albert Thomas (1885-1959) American
£613	$1000	(11-Jun-91 MOR.P31) Evening - mouth of Carmel River (15x20cm-6x8in) s. d.38 verso
£765	$1500	(12-Feb-91 MOR.P82) Near Los Laurellos Adobe up Carmel Valley (25x36cm-10x14in) s. canvas on board with book illustration
£859	$1400	(11-Jun-91 MOR.P30 a) Lupine - near Elkhorn, May 15, '44 (15x20cm-6x8in) s.
£1020	$2000	(12-Feb-91 MOR.P83) Ripple and Egan Avenues - Pacific Grove, California (25x36cm-10x14in) s. canvas on board with book illustration

DEROP, Leonardus Willebrordus (1839-1872) Dutch
£1796	$3018	(23-Apr-91 SY.AM304/R) Anglers by brook (41x59cm-16x23in) s.d.71 (D.FL 6000)

DEROY, Isidore (1797-1886) French
£1700	$3349	(4-Oct-90 CSK151/R) The harvest girl (56x46cm-22x18in) s. oval

DERUET, Claude (attrib) (1588-1662) French
£3689	$7230	(7-Nov-90 APT.P4387/R) Portrait d'un jeune garcon au col de dentelle (34x26cm-13x10in) panel (F.FR 36000)

DERUET, Claude (circle) (1588-1662) French
£2931 $5247   (14-Mar-91 D.V352/R) Portrait of Anna of Austria (77x63cm-30x25in) oval
                  (A.S 60000)

DERUET, Claude (studio) (1588-1662) French
£2141 $4131   (10-Dec-90 BL.P14/R) Vierge a l'Enfant (76x64cm-30x25in) (F.FR 21000)

DESACHE, Herve (20th C) French
£655 $1278   (14-Jan-91 YC.P167) Les quatre saisons (60x80cm-24x31in) s.i.d.90 verso
                  mixed media hardboard panel (F.FR 6500)

DESCAMPS, Jean Baptiste (attrib) (1706-1791) French
£9548 $15658   (21-Jun-91 SY.MO295/R) Allegorie de la decouverte de l'Amerique
                  (133x189cm-52x74in) (F.FR 95000)

DESCH, Auguste-Theodore (1877-?) French
£5607 $10821   (12-Dec-90 ZZ.F38/R) La loge (104x112cm-41x44in) s. (F.FR 55000)

DESCHAMPS, Gabriel (1919-) French
£1000 $1940   (6-Dec-90 CSK64/R) Beaulieu looking towards Villefranche
                  (46x56cm-18x22in) s.
£1479 $2500   (20-Apr-91 WOL.C424 a/R) Chickens in yard (61x74cm-24x29in) s.
£1900 $3686   (6-Dec-90 CSK63/R) Mas Provence (65x54cm-26x21in) s.

DESCHAMPS, Gerard (1937-) French
£1007 $1641   (11-Jun-91 CSC.P50/R) Petites roses (44x45cm-17x18in) s.i.d.1989 verso
                  mixed media (F.FR 10000)
£10956 $18625   (30-May-91 FB.P69/R) Sans titre (60x75cm-24x30in) s.d.1964 verso
                  materials canvas in plexiglass (F.FR 110000)

DESCHAMPS, L H (1846-1902) French
£950 $1700   (15-Mar-91 DM.D2277/R) Young girl (41x33cm-16x13in) s.

DESCHENES, Francois (1938-) French
£800 $1344   (27-Apr-91 MJ.P38/R) Reflets bleus (46x62cm-18x24in) s. (F.FR 8000)

DESCHMACKER, Paul Alex (1889-1973) ?
£478 $827   (26-May-91 ZZ.F172/R) Nu en buste (42x31cm-17x12in) st.sig. pastel
                  (F.FR 4800)

DESFLACHES (19th C) ?
£6667 $13000   (26-Oct-90 SY.NY144/R) The connoisseur (61x51cm-24x20in) s.

DESFRICHES, Aignan (1715-1800) French
£3364 $6492   (12-Dec-90 ARC.P70/R) Paysage anime de personnages (16x21cm-6x8in) pen
                  wash (F.FR 33000)

DESGOFFE, Blaise (1830-1901) French
£2411 $4750   (15-Nov-90 D.NY24/R) Cherries in tazza (35x27cm-14x11in) s.
£14070 $23075   (21-Jun-91 SY.MO169/R) Porcelaines de saxe, calice et autres objects de
                  la collection du Comte Welles de la valette (123x100cm-48x39in)
                  s.d.1873 (F.FR 140000)

DESHAYES, Charles Felix Edouard (1831-1895) French
£2800 $5488   (15-Feb-91 C23/R) Watering horses (130x90cm-51x35in) s.d.1890
£3187 $6215   (24-Oct-90 GD.B282/R) Castle surrounded by water with figures
                  (130x90cm-51x35in) s. (S.FR 8000)
£3262 $6296   (16-Dec-90 DA.R3) Le lac Saint James a Paris (38x61cm-15x24in) both s.
                  two (F.FR 32000)

DESHAYES, Eugene (1828-1890) French
£752 $1467   (12-Oct-90 ZZ.F8) Le campement nomade (21x60cm-8x24in) s. (F.FR 7500)
£764 $1505   (30-Oct-90 I.N119) Marine (32x40cm-13x16in) s. (F.FR 7500)
£785 $1538   (24-Nov-90 HOR.H8/R) Interior (18x30cm-7x12in) s. (F.M 5500)
£847 $1465   (26-May-91 ZZ.F32/R) Bord de canal (19x24cm-7x9in) s. (F.FR 8500)
£1199 $1954   (12-Jun-91 N.M400/R) Peasant women before windmill (54x72cm-21x28in) s.
                  (DM 3500)
£1204 $2347   (12-Oct-90 ZZ.F7) Repos sur la terrasse (39x78cm-15x31in) s.d.1901
                  (F.FR 12000)
£1215 $2381   (20-Nov-90 APT.P261) Femmes au campement (35x100cm-14x39in) s. board
                  (F.FR 12000)
£1259 $2442   (4-Dec-90 FN.S1796/R) Rising thunderstorm in lake landscape with
                  peasants conversing (20x31cm-8x12in) s. panel (DM 3600)
£2475 $4381   (7-Apr-91 I.N93/R) Bord de riviere (50x130cm-20x51in) s. (F.FR 25000)
£2535 $5020   (3-Feb-91 I.N65/R) Bord de riviere (73x100cm-29x39in) s. (F.FR 25000)

DESHAYES, Frederic Leon (1883-?) French
£559 $1000   (16-Mar-91 W.W94/R) Still life with peaches, a pineapple and flowers in
                  a gray vase (53x81cm-21x32in) s.

DESIDE, Ramon (20th C) Spanish
£1626 $3172   (17-Oct-90 FER.M246/R) Impronta en negro y blanco (70x100cm-28x39in) s.
                  s.d.80verso paper (S.P 300000)
£1898 $3700   (17-Oct-90 FER.M247/R) Abstraccion gris (116x89cm-46x35in) s.d.79
                  (S.P 350000)

DESIRE-LUCAS, Louis-Marie (1869-1949) French
£1105 $2100   (27-Feb-91 SY.NY58/R) Sewing by morning light (33x41cm-13x16in) s.d.1935
£1336 $2592   (7-Dec-90 GL.P65) Le pont rouge (38x46cm-15x18in) s. (F.FR 13000)
£1508 $2472   (21-Jun-91 CK.P108/R) Falaises (81x100cm-32x39in) s. (F.FR 15000)
£1529 $2951   (16-Dec-90 T.B118) Pont Croix a Maree haute (38x47cm-15x19in) s.
      (F.FR 15000)
£1791 $3099   (12-May-91 T.B254) Les Martigues (38x46cm-15x18in) s. (F.FR 18000)
£2161 $4171   (16-Dec-90 T.B117/R) La rue rose (46x38cm-18x15in) s. (F.FR 21200)
£2600 $4368   (26-Apr-91 ARC.P56/R) Alentours de Tolede,Espagne, l'eglise de St Jean
      des rois (80x100cm-31x39in) s. (F.FR 26000)
£2604 $5027   (16-Dec-90 T.B281/R) Plage du Vergac'h a Camaret (54x65cm-21x26in) s.
      (F.FR 25550)
£2786 $4820   (12-May-91 T.B106/R) Camaret - Le Rocher des Anglais (54x65cm-21x26in)
      s. (F.FR 28000)
£3383 $5853   (12-May-91 T.B255) Barque sur le rivage (46x54cm-18x21in) s.
      (F.FR 34000)
£3500 $5880   (26-Apr-91 ARC.P55/R) Sur la route de Talavera, Espagne
      (62x80cm-24x31in) s. (F.FR 35000)

DESJARDINS, S (19th C) French
£1005 $1648   (21-Jun-91 SY.MO388/R) Pot de fleurs (31x23cm-12x9in) s. W/C vellum
*   (F.FR 10000)*
£1608 $2637   (21-Jun-91 SY.MO339/R) Bouquet de fleurs (31x23cm-12x9in) s. W/C vellum
*   (F.FR 16000)*

DESLANDES, E A (19th C) French
£3851 $6701   (25-Mar-91 SY.F753/R) Veduta di S.Giorgio Maggiore a chiaro di luna
      (70x115cm-28x45in) s. (I.L 8500000)

DESMAREES, George (studio) (1697-1776) Swedish
£7143 $11500   (26-Jun-91 KM.K1330/R) Portrait of Maria Amalia (85x71cm-33x28in) one of
      pair (DM 21000)
£7143 $11500   (26-Jun-91 KM.K1331/R) Portrait of Karl Albrecht, Kurfurst von Bayern
      (85x71cm-33x28in) one of pair (DM 21000)

DESMAREES, George (style) (1697-1776) Swedish
£800 $1384   (20-May-91 SWS14/R) Portrait of a gentleman,half lenght, wearing a blue
      coat with armour (86x71cm-34x28in) canvas laid on board
£2797 $5399   (10-Dec-90 L.K24/R) Portrait of Kurfurst Karl Theodor von der Pfalz with
      insignia (105x77cm-41x30in) (DM 8000)

DESMARETS, Pierre (18/19th C) French
£450 $797   (22-Mar-91 APT.P35) Portrait de Madame Recamier (17x13cm-7x5in) s.
*   blk.crayon (F.FR 4500)*

DESMARQUAIS, Charles Hippolyte (1823-?) French
£866 $1664   (1-Dec-90 PER.M189/R) La clairiere (26x40cm-10x16in) s.d.1884 panel
      (F.FR 8500)
£1004 $1616   (30-Jun-91 FE.P127) Fete a St Germain s. (F.FR 10000)

DESMEDT, Lucien (1919-) French
£400 $676   (1-May-91 GD.B192) Place du Theatre (45x61cm-18x24in) W/C bodycol
*   (S.FR 1000)*

DESMET, Leon see SMET, Leon de

DESMOULINS, Amedee Auguste (19th C) French
£923 $1800   (26-Oct-90 SY.NY140/R) L'atelier (19x25cm-7x10in) s.d.1830 W/C

DESNITSKAYA, Olga (1922-) Russian
£600 $1008   (26-Apr-91 ARC.P96/R) Le jardin de Gethsemani I (79x59cm-31x23in) s.
      verso (F.FR 6000)

DESNOYER, Francois (1894-1972) French
£1775 $3497   (6-Oct-90 GL.P121) Village de campagne (24x33cm-9x13in) s.d.'33 wood
      (F.FR 18000)
£2006 $3912   (11-Oct-90 QWA.P33/R) 14 Juillet (24x35cm-9x14in) s. (F.FR 20000)
£2010 $3859   (24-Feb-91 P.V50) Vue de village (24x33cm-9x13in) s. panel (F.FR 20000)
£12060 $19779   (21-Jun-91 OD.P10/R) Un port (50x73cm-20x29in) s. (F.FR 120000)
£422 $692   (19-Jun-91 JM.P134) Etude pour le portrait de femme (42x23cm-17x9in) s.
*   gouache (F.FR 4200)*
£771 $1495   (7-Dec-90 GL.P30) Personnages (42x35cm-17x14in) s. collage (F.FR 7500)

D'ESPAGNAT (1870-1950) French
£8638 $17276   (4-Feb-91 LEB.P9/R) Nature morte aux fleurs dans un pichet
      (64x54cm-25x21in) init. (F.FR 85000)

D'ESPAGNAT, Georges (1870-1950) French
£3525 $5745   (14-Jun-91 AGS.P24/R) Mere et enfant (73x92cm-29x36in) init.
      (F.FR 35000)
£5075 $8830   (25-Mar-91 CR.P81/R) Mere et enfants a la campagne (46x55cm-18x22in) s.
      (F.FR 51000)
£5076 $10000   (15-Nov-90 SY.NY32/R) Nature morte aux fruits (23x32cm-9x13in) init.
      board
£5841 $9521   (14-Jun-91 MB.P31/R) Baigneuse sur un rocher (33x40cm-13x16in) s. board
      (F.FR 58000)

D'ESPAGNAT, Georges (1870-1950) French-cont.

£5865	$11436	(15-Oct-90 APT.P56/R) Femme a la chemise rose (46x38cm-18x15in) init. (F.FR 58000)
£6122	$12000	(14-Feb-91 CH.NY43/R) Vase de fleurs (46x38cm-18x15in) init.
£6599	$13000	(13-Nov-90 CE.NY44/R) Vase de fleurs et fruit (35x30cm-14x12in) init. canvas on board
£7200	$12168	(1-May-91 GD.B177/R) Sailing boats (32x54cm-13x21in) mono. (S.FR 18000)
£8163	$16000	(14-Feb-91 CH.NY37/R) Jeune fille allongee (60x74cm-24x29in) init.
£9000	$17550	(19-Oct-90 C135/R) Fillette accoudee (56x46cm-22x18in) init.
£9137	$18000	(13-Nov-90 CE.NY43/R) Portrait de jeune fille (63x63cm-25x25in) init.
£10000	$19500	(19-Oct-90 C134/R) Bouquet des fleurs (56x46cm-22x18in) init.
£12690	$25000	(15-Nov-90 SY.NY30/R) Vase de roses (46x38cm-18x15in) init.
£12755	$25000	(15-Feb-91 SY.NY20/R) Jacinthes et bouquet (81x65cm-32x26in) init.
£12897	$22183	(19-May-91 ZZ.F91/R) Le port Mediterranen (46x55cm-18x22in) s. (F.FR 130000)
£14042	$27382	(11-Oct-90 QWA.P88/R) Bouquet d'anemones (38x47cm-15x19in) mono. panel (F.FR 140000)
£18782	$37000	(15-Nov-90 D.NY69/R) Femme assise dans le jardin (73x93cm-29x37in) init. indist.i.stretcher
£19527	$37883	(7-Dec-91 GL.P152/R) Jeune femme dans un interieur (58x65cm-23x26in) init. (F.FR 190000)
£40609	$80000	(15-Nov-90 SY.NY31/R) Deux vases de fleurs sur la table jaune (46x37cm-18x15in) init. panel
£42008	$82336	(11-Nov-90 ZZ.F96/R) Jeune fille a sa toilette (92x73cm-36x29in) s. (F.FR 410000)
£71066	$140000	(2-Oct-90 CH.NY53/R) Enfants dans le parc (82x100cm-32x39in) init.
£1309	*$2134*	*(14-Jun-91 MB.P14/R) Poules pres d'une ferme. Enfants jouant pres du village (24x32cm-9x13in) mono. W/C traces Indian ink pair (F.FR 13000)*
£1793	*$3102*	*(26-May-91 ZZ.F93/R) La lecon de lecture (17x20cm-7x8in) init. W/C (F.FR 18000)*

D'ESPARBES, Jean (1898-1968) French

£789	$1554	(6-Oct-90 GL.P128) Le repas de mariage (46x55cm-18x22in) s. (F.FR 8000)
£1109	$2162	(26-Oct-90 APT.P98) Arlequin a la contrebasse (55x46cm-22x18in) s. (F.FR 11000)
£1721	$3372	(25-Nov-90 ZZ.F55/R) Le repas campagnard (50x61cm-20x24in) s. (F.FR 17000)

DESPEAUX, Howard (20th C) American

£781	$1500	(17-Dec-90 SY.NY271/R) Chimney corner (81x66cm-32x26in) s. s.i.d.1930-31 verso

DESPIAU, Charles (1874-1946) French

£604	*$985*	*(14-Jun-91 FB.P48) Femme nue assise (26x33cm-10x13in) s. crayon (F.FR 6000)*
£1007	*$1963*	*(12-Oct-90 AW.H2214/R) Femme nue couchee (25x35cm-10x14in) s. ochre (DM 3000)*
£1012	*$1984*	*(20-Nov-90 BG.P30/R) Nu debout (46x31cm-18x12in) s. sanguinne (F.FR 10000)*

D'ESPIC, Christian (20th C) ?

£2665	$5250	(15-Nov-90 SY.NY73/R) Rooster (64x81cm-25x32in) s.d.60

DESPIERRE, Jacques (1912-) French

£1314	$2563	(17-Oct-90 ARC.P73/R) Trois cavaliers (41x81cm-16x32in) s. (F.FR 13000)
£1830	$3275	(8-Apr-91 CSC.P83) Saronicos (100x100cm-39x39in) s. l. verso (F.FR 18500)
£2671	$4780	(8-Apr-91 CSC.P84/R) Desserte (130x130cm-51x51in) s. i.d.1982 verso (F.FR 27000)
£2868	$5135	(8-Apr-91 CSC.P85) Le printemps (130x130cm-51x51in) s. i. verso (F.FR 29000)
£3279	$6426	(11-Nov-90 ZZ.F170/R) Vase d'anemones et coupe de fruits (81x65cm-32x26in) s. (F.FR 32000)

DESPORTES, Alexandre-Francois (1661-1743) French

£2400	$4440	(5-Mar-91 PH9/R) Bonne, Nonne and Ponne, dogs from the mews of Louis XIV with partridge inlandscape (96x132cm-38x52in)
£87571	$155000	(22-Mar-91 CH.NY653/R) Flowers in a sculpted urn with a bowl of wild strawberries and hareon a ledge (101x80cm-40x31in) s.d.1715

DESPORTES, Alexandre-Francois (attrib) (1661-1743) French

£25000	$40750	(3-Jul-91 PLF.P59/R) Portrait presume de Monsieur Paris, fermier general du Dauphine entenue de chasseur (146x112cm-57x44in) (F.FR 250000)
£70352	$115377	(21-Jun-91 SY.MO153/R) Chien assis sur un coussin (61x73cm-24x29in) (F.FR 700000)

DESPORTES, Alexandre-Francois (school) (1661-1743) French

£3529	$6000	(31-May-91 CH.NY204/R) Dogs stalking partridges (55x65cm-22x26in)

DESPORTES, Alexandre-Francois (studio) (1661-1743) French

£6166	$11963	(7-Dec-90 SY.MO190/R) Nature morte aux gibier et fruit (68x57cm-27x22in) (F.FR 60000)
£8500	$14365	(19-Apr-91 C105/R) A whippet and a spaniel watching over a game bag at the foot of a tree (109x153cm-43x60in)

DESPORTES, Claude Francois (attrib) (1695-1774) French
£1623 $3213   (30-Jan-91 APT.P283/R) Chat s'emparant d'une huitre (66x100cm-26x39in)
                   (F.FR 16000)

DESPORTES, Francois (studio) (18th C) French
£1217 $2410   (30-Jan-91 APT.P272/R) L'elephant et le lievre (48x30cm-19x12in) panel
                   (F.FR 12000)

DESPORTES, Jean Francois (style) (18th C) French
£1949 $3293   (1-May-91 KH.K52/R) Bird and squirrel on ledge with jug, flowers and
                   fruit (117x69cm-46x27in) (D.KR 22000)
£2059 $3500   (30-May-91 CE.NY37) Dogs stalking pheasants (55x65cm-22x26in)

DESPREZ, Louis Jean (1743-1804) French
£3244 $6260   (12-Dec-90 BU.S11/R) Inside Colosseum (50x88cm-20x35in) Indian ink W/C
                   (S.KR 35000)

DESRAIS, Claude Louis (1746-1816) French
£600 $1152   (18-Feb-91 S26/R) Merry drinker (18x14cm-7x6in) pen ink wash htd.white
                   over chk

DESSI, Gianni (20th C) ?
£1359 $2365   (26-Mar-91 F.M20/R) Campo di Marte (40x35cm-16x14in) s.d.1983verso
                   collage oil canvas (I.L 3000000)

DESSONS, Pierre (20th C) French
£1018 $2006   (31-Oct-90 ZZ.F99/R) Les rencontres (141x114cm-56x45in) s. l.d.1986
                   verso (F.FR 10000)

DESSOULAVY, Thomas (19th C) British
£10000 $17200   (17-May-91 C205/R) View of Rome from Villa Madama (53x79cm-21x31in)
                   s.d.1846
£11561 $20000   (22-May-91 SY.NY26/R) Roman campagna (76x114cm-30x45in) s.d.1842

DESSOUSLAVY, Georges (1898-1952) ?
£556 $961   (22-May-91 GS.B2074) Femme costumee dans la porte ouverte
                   (60x40cm-24x16in) s.indis.d. i.verso (S.FR 1400)

D'ESTE, N (19th C) ?
£5202 $9000   (21-May-91 CE.NY106/R) Carnivale (73x64cm-29x25in) s.

DESTOUCHES, Johanna von (1869-?) German
£5137 $8373   (12-Jun-91 SY.MU133/R) White lilies and larkspur (69x83cm-27x33in) s.l.
                   (DM 15000)

DESTREE, Johannes Josephus (1827-1888) Belgian
£1497 $2515   (23-Apr-91 SY.AM242/R) Summer landscape with figures in boat by farm
                   (22x32cm-9x13in) s. panel (D.FL 5000)

DESUBLEO, Michele (school) (1601-1676) Flemish
£882 $1500   (30-May-91 CE.NY64) St John the Baptist (63x51cm-25x20in)

DESUBLEO, Michele (style) (1601-1676) Flemish
£1318 $2611   (30-Jan-91 APT.P170/R) Vierge a l'Enfant (90x76cm-35x30in) (F.FR 13000)

DESVARREUX-LARPENTEUR, James (1847-1947) American
£1300 $2548   (14-Feb-91 CSK45/R) Cattle and sheep in a woodland glade
                   (132x160cm-52x63in) s.

DETAILLE, Edouard (1848-1912) French
£718 $1400   (26-Oct-90 SY.NY157/R) Sketch of fireman's ladder (21x15cm-8x6in) mono.
£4257 $7536   (7-Apr-91 I.N94/R) Scene de Guerre (140x112cm-55x44in) s.d.1885
                   (F.FR 43000)
£17341 $30000   (22-May-91 SY.NY46/R) General of First Empire (85x68cm-33x27in) s.d.1892
£1800 $3546   (5-Oct-90 C46 a/R) French cuirassiers proceeding to battle
                   (33x23cm-13x9in) s.d.1900 pencil W/C
£2179 $4250   (26-Oct-90 SY.NY104/R) Study of cavalry officer (32x23cm-13x9in)
                   s.i.d.1885 W/C
£2586 $4500   (27-Mar-91 B.SF4076/R) The charge (63x48cm-25x19in) s.d.1887 W/C
£4103 $8000   (26-Oct-90 SY.NY98/R) La charge, dragons de L'Imperatrice Garde
                   Imperiale 1806-14 (67x47cm-26x19in) s.d.1893 gouache

DETESTE (20th C) ?
£2039 $3935   (10-Dec-90 LD.P111/R) Mise en scene (73x81cm-29x32in) s. acrylic
                   (F.FR 20000)

DETHOMAS, Maxime (1867-?) French
£612 $1180   (14-Dec-90 JM.P78/R) L'attente (63x48cm-25x19in) mono. chl (F.FR 6000)

DETMOLD, Edward Julian (1883-1957) British
£800 $1304   (14-Jun-91 C165/R) Blue Tit and a Wren (17x21cm-7x8in) pencil W/C htd
                   gum arabic

DETOUCHE, Henry Julien (1854-1913) French
£311 $576   (4-Mar-91 ARC.P7/R) La correspondance du modele (41x44cm-16x17in) s.
                   chl. (F.FR 3100)

DETROY, Leon (1857-1955) French
£683	$1223	(13-Mar-91 ARC.P39/R) Paysage du midi (93x65cm-37x26in) s. (F.FR 6800)
£1263	$2475	(17-Feb-91 E.LA26) Paysage de la Creuse (57x79cm-22x31in) s. (F.FR 12500)
£2039	$3935	(12-Dec-90 APT.P87) Golfe de St-Tropez (60x93cm-24x37in) s. (F.FR 20000)
£352	$630	(11-Mar-91 GL.P45) L'atelier de poterie (45x60cm-18x24in) s. pastel (F.FR 3500)

DETTI, Cesare Auguste (1847-1914) Italian
£714	$1371	(27-Nov-90 W.T1102 a) Gallants and ladies (20x15cm-8x6in) s. (C.D 1600)
£2312	$4000	(21-May-91 CE.NY319/R) Masterpiece (51x35cm-20x14in) s.d.90
£4046	$7000	(23-May-91 CH.NY166/R) The duet (40x25cm-16x10in) s. panel
£4852	$9365	(11-Dec-90 CH.R116/R) Concerto (46x60cm-18x24in) s.d.1873 panel (I.L 10500000)
£11561	$20000	(22-May-91 SY.NY67/R) Departure (84x67cm-33x26in) s.

DEULLY, Eugene Auguste Francois (1860-?) French
£1479	$2500	(20-Apr-91 WOL.C98/R) Cherubs gathering fruit (30x46cm-12x18in) s.

DEURS, Caroline van (1860-1932) Danish
£704	$1183	(23-Apr-91 RAS.K386) Irises in flower by farmhouse (37x56cm-15x22in) mono.d.1915 (D.KR 8000)

DEUSSER, August (1870-1942) German
£1115	$2174	(26-Oct-90 KM.K1150/R) Cavalry soldiers resting in landscape (54x72cm-21x28in) s. (DM 3300)

DEUTMANN, Frans (1867-1915) Dutch
£2316	$4400	(3-Mar-91 LIT.L19) Still life of fruit with Delft plate (99x74cm-39x29in) init.

DEUTSCH, Ludwig (1855-1935) French
£5500	$10835	(5-Oct-90 C109/R) La toilette (46x36cm-18x14in) s.d.1918 s.d.1917 panel oval
£60000	$115200	(30-Nov-90 C70/R) The milk seller, Cairo (53x46cm-21x18in) s.i.d.1886 panel

DEVADE, Marc (1943-1983) French
£4234	$8256	(23-Oct-90 CSC.P73/R) Composition - 1974 (150x150cm-59x59in) s. verso (F.FR 42000)

DEVAL, Pierre (1897-?) French
£2130	$4217	(3-Feb-91 I.N66/R) Le Port de Toulon (54x65cm-21x26in) s. (F.FR 21000)
£351	$650	(6-Mar-91 HC.P51) La Seine a Paris (24x32cm-9x13in) s. W/C (F.FR 3500)
£396	$701	(7-Apr-91 I.N99) Villa Abd-el-Tif (25x32cm-10x13in) s. W/C gouache (F.FR 4000)
£416	$736	(7-Apr-91 I.N110) Nu etendu (38x28cm-15x11in) s. gouache (F.FR 4200)
£446	$789	(7-Apr-91 I.N109) Jeune fille a la liane (38x25cm-15x10in) s. gouache (F.FR 4500)
£594	$1051	(7-Apr-91 I.N108) La lecture (23x43cm-9x17in) s. W/C (F.FR 6000)
£1521	$3012	(3-Feb-91 I.N67) Nu allonge (48x26cm-19x10in) s. pastel (F.FR 15000)
£1782	$3154	(7-Apr-91 I.N107/R) La ballerine (51x35cm-20x14in) s. pastel (F.FR 18000)
£1919	$3762	(17-Feb-91 E.LA18) Jeune fille mangeant des cerises (50x50cm-20x20in) s. pastel (F.FR 19000)
£2178	$3855	(7-Apr-91 I.N106/R) Nu allonge (34x38cm-13x15in) s. pastel (F.FR 22000)
£2277	$4031	(7-Apr-91 I.N102/R) Portrait de jeune fille (55x40cm-22x16in) s. pastel (F.FR 23000)
£2475	$4381	(7-Apr-91 I.N104/R) Jeune fille etendue (50x62cm-20x24in) s. pastel (F.FR 25000)
£2535	$4486	(7-Apr-91 I.N101/R) Les ballerines (63x49cm-25x19in) s. pastel (F.FR 25600)
£3119	$5520	(7-Apr-91 I.N105/R) Nu endormi (33x48cm-13x19in) s. pastel (F.FR 31500)

DEVAMBEZ, Andre (1867-1943) French
£732	$1200	(19-Jun-91 B.SF1869/R) Le guitariste (42x93cm-17x37in) s.
£904	$1455	(28-Jun-91 ZZ.F119) La roulotte en foret (46x33cm-18x13in) s. (F.FR 9000)
£1556	$2506	(28-Jun-91 ZZ.F120) Les enfants a la fontaine (9x13cm-4x5in) s. panel (F.FR 15500)
£2510	$4041	(24-Jun-91 ARC.P13/R) La ville endormie (18x21cm-7x8in) s. board (F.FR 25000)
£884	$1635	(4-Mar-91 ARC.P41) L'arracheur de dents (25x14cm-10x6in) s. W/C (F.FR 8800)

DEVAS, Anthony (1911-) British
£1500	$2610	(28-Mar-91 CSK124) Nude on chaise longue (45x59cm-18x23in) s.
£8000	$15040	(20-Sep-90 C1/R) Camilla and Mark Sykes (49x58cm-19x23in) s.

DEVAUX (19th C) French
£1304	$2543	(12-Oct-90 APT.P76) La petite fileuse (32x24cm-13x9in) s. panel (F.FR 13000)

DEVAUX, Jules Ernest (1837-?) French
£8000	$14320	(12-Mar-91 PH93/R) Birthday celebrations (55x46cm-22x18in) s. panel pair

DEVEDEUX, Louis (1820-1874) French
£807	$1444	(11-Apr-91 D.V110/R) The wreath of flowers (36x27cm-14x11in) s. panel (A.S 17000)
£4000	$7880	(5-Oct-90 C32/R) Fete Champetre (56x43cm-22x17in) s. canvas on panel
£5061	$9919	(20-Nov-90 APT.P265/R) Les amoureux (56x36cm-22x14in) s. (F.FR 50000)

DEVER, Alfred (fl.1859-1876) British
| £5200 | $10192 | (13-Feb-91 S121/R) Drop of bitter in cup of joy (46x36cm-18x14in) mono.d.1860 indist.i.stretcher |

DEVEREUX, J (?) ?
| £940 | $1833 | (22-Oct-90 SWS66/R) Storytime (79x63cm-31x25in) indist.s. |

DEVERIA, Eugene (1808-1865) French
| £1485 | $2629 | (4-Apr-91 PPB.P25/R) La presentation (31x25cm-12x10in) s.d.1822 W/C (F.FR 15000) |
| £2200 | $3894 | (22-Mar-91 APT.P32/R) Portrait d'une jeune femme portant un chale (59x48cm-23x19in) s.d.56 pastel (F.FR 22000) |

DEVERIA, Eugene (attrib) (1808-1865) French
| £10880 | $19476 | (12-Apr-91 AGS.P20/R) Odalisque (65x54cm-26x21in) (F.FR 110000) |

DEVEZ, del (1910-1982) French
| £805 | $1577 | (27-Jan-91 FE.P112) La caleche devant le Moulin de la Galette (43x55cm-17x22in) s. panel (F.FR 8000) |

DEVIS, Anthony (1729-1817) British
£1800	$2970	(9-Jul-91 PH8/R) Extensive mountainous landscape with goats in foreground (42x54cm-17x21in) init.
£550	$985	(9-Apr-91 C32/R) Figures in wooded landscape (22x32cm-9x13in) chk pen ink W/C
£600	$1074	(9-Apr-91 C31/R) Ruined castle on cliff top (22x31cm-9x12in) pen ink W/C
£1300	$2327	(9-Apr-91 C33/R) Children and monkeys on camel at the Exeter 'Change (13x20cm-5x8in) pencil pen ink W/C

DEVIS, Arthur (1708-1787) British
| £10588 | $18000 | (30-May-91 SY.NY67/R) Portrait of gentleman said to be Dr. Young, seated under willow tree (73x61cm-29x24in) |

DEVIS, Arthur William (1763-1822) British
| £9000 | $17730 | (16-Nov-90 C29/R) Portrait of young boy holding bow and arrow in landscape (145x112cm-57x44in) |

DEVIS, Arthur William (circle) (1763-1822) British
| £5200 | $9308 | (10-Apr-91 S134/R) Portrait of Colonel John Hill of Hawkestone, holding charger, landscape (237x152cm-93x60in) |
| £7000 | $11830 | (30-Apr-91 PH58/R) Portrait of young drummer boy, standing beside brother seated at low table holding book (127x101cm-50x40in) |

DEVOLL, Frederick Usher (1873-1941) American
£508	$1000	(16-Nov-90 S.BM152/R) Clam diggers (15x20cm-6x8in) canvasboard
£2235	$4000	(14-Mar-91 CH.NY93/R) Sunset on Hudson (31x41cm-12x16in) s. board
£2312	$4000	(21-May-91 CE.NY531/R) New York docks (41x51cm-16x20in) s.i.
£761	$1500	(16-Nov-90 S.BM120/R) Montmartre, 1927 (38x48cm-15x19in) estate st.verso pastel

DEVOS, Leon (20th C) Belgian
£532	$952	(12-Mar-91 GM.B951) Nature morte aux roses (46x38cm-18x15in) s. (B.FR 32000)
£765	$1369	(12-Mar-91 GM.B1015) Langoustines (45x60cm-18x24in) s. (B.FR 46000)
£914	$1637	(16-Mar-91 KV.L108) Red rooftops (40x49cm-16x19in) s.d.29 (B.FR 55000)
£1081	$1934	(12-Mar-91 GM.B914/R) Golfe de St-Tropez et campeurs (65x80cm-26x31in) (B.FR 65000)
£2244	$4017	(16-Mar-91 KV.L107) Femme en Raccourci (92x70cm-36x28in) s. (B.FR 135000)
£2328	$4166	(16-Mar-91 KV.L452/R) Seated nude (91x69cm-36x27in) s. (B.FR 140000)

DEWASNE, Jean (1921-) French
| £2105 | $4000 | (28-Feb-91 MFA.C66/R) Composition (61x109cm-24x43in) metal |
| £8065 | $15726 | (23-Oct-90 CSC.P68/R) Composition (50x65cm-20x26in) s.d.1956 gouache (F.FR 80000) |

DEWHURST, Wynford (1864-?) British
£900	$1755	(15-Jan-91 SWS201/R) Coastal scene (32x39cm-13x15in) s. i.stretcher
£947	$1800	(27-Feb-91 SY.NY241/R) Afternoon stroll (81x61cm-32x24in) s.
£1250	$2213	(18-Mar-91 WHB147) Continental scene, with two boys fishing by village pond (28x41cm-11x16in) s.d.90
£2400	$4008	(6-Jun-91 C20/R) Stooks in meadow (33x46cm-13x18in) s.d.1898
£2500	$4800	(21-Feb-91 B50/R) Mountain lake (73x59cm-29x23in) s.

DEWING, Thomas W (1851-1938) American
£4046	$7000	(22-May-91 CH.NY121/R) Antoinette (30x20cm-12x8in) s. panel
£10241	$17000	(11-Jan-91 DM.D2005/R) Semi-nude girl seated with violin (38x23cm-15x9in) s. panel
£30208	$58000	(30-Nov-90 CH.NY128/R) June (51x23cm-20x9in) s.

DEWING, Thomas W (1851-1938) American-cont.
£4190 $7500   (14-Mar-91 CH.NY51/R) Pink wrap (36x28cm-14x11in) s.num.201 pastel paper on board

DEWS, J Steven (1949-) British
£10500 $20475   (18-Oct-90 CSK197/R) 'Shamrock V' and 'Velsheda' racing in the Solent in 1934 (61x61cm-24x24in) s.
£15000 $25950   (22-May-91 S204/R) Stars and Stripes and Kookaburra (61x91cm-24x36in) s.

DEXEL, Walter (1890-1973) German
£3767 $6140   (15-Jun-91 L.K146/R) Near Assisi (57x34cm-22x13in) s.d.13 s.i.d.verso board (DM 11000)
£4623 $7536   (15-Jun-91 L.K147/R) Black cross, yellow square (46x31cm-18x12in) s.d.1924/64 s.d.verso board (DM 13500)
£9247 $15072   (15-Jun-91 L.K148/R) With yellow square (71x60cm-28x24in) s.i.d.1968 (DM 27000)
£9492 $15851   (6-Jun-91 HN.H265/R) Composition (67x54cm-26x21in) s.d.1967 verso (DM 28000)
£10847 $18115   (7-Jun-91 HN.H15/R) Composition with red square (46x50cm-18x20in) s.i.d.1926-30 verso (DM 32000)
£12969 $25420   (24-Nov-90 VG.B283/R) Figuration senkrecht rot (72x55cm-28x22in) s.i.d.1923/1965verso (DM 38000)
£990 $1940   (22-Nov-90 L.K894) Townscapes (34x26cm-13x10in) i.d.1920/21 pencil dr. (DM 2900)
£1017 $1698   (6-Jun-91 HN.H270/R) Composition (33x25cm-13x10in) st.sig.d.1920-21 pencil (DM 3000)
£1500 $2595   (10-May-91 S.Z23/R) Composition (47x49cm-19x19in) s.d.1968 gouache fabriano (S.FR 3750)
£4778 $9365   (24-Nov-90 VG.B289/R) Composition schwarz-senkrecht-waagrecht (60x50cm-24x20in) s.d.1929 s.i.d.1929 collage board (DM 14000)
£4778 $9365   (24-Nov-90 VG.B287/R) 2 rote Scheiben, angeschnitten (37x26cm-15x10in) s.d.1930 collage board (DM 14000)
£4778 $9365   (24-Nov-90 VG.B288/R) S schrag verkehrt (59x48cm-23x19in) s.d.1929 gouache indian ink htd.white board (DM 14000)
£5424 $9058   (6-Jun-91 HN.H266/R) He'le scheibe und rotes kreuz (31x31cm-12x12in) s.d.1926 gouache (DM 16000)
£7119 $11888   (6-Jun-91 HN.H267/R) Composition (40x28cm-16x11in) s.d.1927 tempera collage (DM 21000)
£8793 $16883   (26-Nov-90 WK.M19/R) Mit blauer Scheibe (39x30cm-15x12in) s.d.1926 s.i.d.verso gouache pencil board (DM 25500)

DEYM, Marten Pietersz (1566-1626) Dutch
£4800 $9120   (1-Mar-91 C117/R) Portrait of lady aged 69 wearing white ruff and linen headdress (61x49cm-24x19in) mono.indis.i.d.1634 panel

DEYNUM, Guilliam van (17th C) Flemish
£19500 $31785   (5-Jul-91 C298/R) Mixed fruit and Facon de Venise wine glass on draped ledge (28x23cm-11x9in) i. panel

DEYROLLE, Jean (1911-1967) French
£2493 $4113   (9-Jul-91 ARC.P26) Elzear opus 536 (65x54cm-26x21in) s. (F.FR 25000)
£2809 $4831   (14-May-91 BU.S92/R) 'Ange-20P' (76x36cm-30x14in) s. i.verso (S.KR 30000)
£4307 $7408   (14-May-91 BU.S91/R) Mary (55x46cm-22x18in) s. (S.KR 46000)
£1104 $2043   (6-Mar-91 APT.P96) Composition geometrique (50x31cm-20x12in) s. mixed media panel (F.FR 11000)
£4412 $8647   (10-Nov-90 FAL.M77/R) Composition in yellow (75x57cm-30x22in) s. mixed media (S.KR 48000)

DEYROLLE, Theophile-Louis (1844-1923) French
£995 $1721   (12-May-91 T.B258) Le pardon - la procession (15x11cm-6x4in) s. panel (F.FR 10000)
£1662 $2875   (12-May-91 T.B260) Le sechage des filets (11x9cm-4x4in) s. panel (F.FR 16700)
£2090 $3615   (12-May-91 T.B108) Danse bretonne (11x15cm-4x6in) s. panel (F.FR 21000)
£2289 $3959   (12-May-91 T.B109) La Partie de Campagne (15x11cm-6x4in) s. panel (F.FR 23000)
£2500 $4750   (27-Feb-91 SY.NY61/R) Daily chores (62x92cm-24x36in) s.
£2597 $4493   (12-May-91 T.B110/R) La Cueillette des Pommes (38x45cm-15x18in) s. (F.FR 26100)
£4776 $8263   (12-May-91 T.B259/R) Jeunes bretonnes au lavoir (62x92cm-24x36in) s. (F.FR 48000)
£4893 $9443   (16-Dec-90 T.B120) Gardienne de Brebis a la Quenouille (80x61cm-31x24in) s. (F.FR 48000)
£8826 $17212   (14-Oct-90 D.L90/R) Jeux d'enfants (87x147cm-34x58in) s. (F.FR 88000)
£9453 $16353   (12-May-91 T.B111) Bretonnes de Pont Aven pres de la Fontaine (80x65cm-31x26in) s.d.1905 (F.FR 95000)

DEZAUNAY, Emile (1854-1940) French
£1990 $3443   (12-May-91 T.B114) Marine a l'Ile de Brehat (26x35cm-10x14in) s. wood (F.FR 20000)
£3781 $6541   (12-May-91 T.B262/R) Jeune bretonne en coiffe (61x50cm-24x20in) s. (F.FR 38000)
£10703 $20657   (16-Dec-90 T.B123/R) Port de Sauzon a maree basse (54x65cm-21x26in) s. (F.FR 105000)

DEZAUNAY, Emile (1854-1940) French-cont.
£1376 $2656   (16-Dec-90 T.B370) Jeunes bretonnes en coiffe (40x30cm-16x12in) s. W/C
    (F.FR 13500)
£1815 $3538   (28-Oct-90 GRA.P18) Les deux femmes (39x30cm-15x12in) s. W/C
    (F.FR 18000)
£1833 $3611   (29-Oct-90 CSC.P94/R) Bretons en costume de Plougastel (32x40cm-13x16in)
    s.i. W/C (F.FR 18000)
£1833 $3611   (29-Oct-90 CSC.P80) Bretons devant l'eglise (31x39cm-12x15in) s. W/C
    (F.FR 18000)
£5092 $10031   (29-Oct-90 CSC.P70/R) Bretonnes a la voile rouge (30x38cm-12x15in) s.
    W/C (F.FR 50000)

DEZENTJE, Eugene (20th C) ?
£1557 $2616   (23-Apr-91 SY.AM317) People in rice field (55x85cm-22x33in) s.d.49
    (D.FL 5200)

DEZIRE, Henri (1878-1965) French
£650 $1092   (26-Apr-91 ARC.P61/R) Les baigneurs (37x43cm-15x17in) s.d.1953
    (F.FR 6500)

D'HAESE, Roel (1921-) Belgian
£641 $1238   (13-Dec-90 CH.BR138/R) Untitled (31x24cm-12x9in) s.d.5.11.59 pen
    (B.FR 38000)
£675 $1303   (13-Dec-90 CH.BR140/R) Untitled (31x24cm-12x9in) s.d.1959 pen wash
    (B.FR 40000)
£759 $1466   (13-Dec-90 CH.BR141/R) Untitled (31x24cm-12x9in) s.d.1959 pen wash
    (B.FR 45000)
£928 $1792   (13-Dec-90 CH.BR139/R) Untitled (31x24cm-12x9in) s.d.1959 pen wash
    (B.FR 55000)

D'HAUTERIVES, Arnaud (1944-) French
£965 $1931   (6-Feb-91 FB.P170/R) Paysge sous l'orage (73x116cm-29x46in) s.d.68
    (F.FR 9500)

DHAWAN, Rajendra (1936-) Indian
£2022 $3943   (18-Oct-90 CB.P62/R) Sans titre (89x116cm-35x46in) s.d.1990 (F.FR 20000)

DIANO, Giacinto (1730-1803) Italian
£7728 $15147   (19-Nov-90 CH.R87/R) L'adorazione dei pastori (130x76cm-51x30in)
    (I.L 17000000)

DIANO, Giacinto (attrib) (1730-1803) Italian
£1500 $3000   (7-Feb-91 C11/R) Tobias and the angel (27x19cm-11x7in) copper oval

DIAO, David (1943-) American
£1784 $3443   (16-Dec-90 CSC.P40/R) Sieg uber die Sonne, Hanover (53x45cm-21x18in)
    acrylic (F.FR 17500)

DIAZ CARRENO, Francisco (c1840-1903) Spanish
£652 $1252   (18-Dec-90 DUR.M19) Joven con abanico (36x19cm-14x7in) W/C (S.P 120000)

DIAZ DE LA PENA, Narcisse-Virgile (1807-1876) French
£800 $1432   (12-Mar-91 PH92) Forest clearing by moonlight (28x24cm-11x9in) st.sig.
    panel
£865 $1410   (10-Jun-91 W.T1381) Faggot gatherers in a forest (42x52cm-17x20in) s.
    (C.D 1600)
£947 $1600   (20-Apr-91 WOL.C22/R) Floral still life (53x33cm-21x13in) s. panel
£1186 $1934   (3-Jul-91 WE.MU62/R) At the Bievre near Fontainebleau (12x19cm-5x7in) s.
    panel (DM 3500)
£1325 $2558   (12-Dec-90 APT.P94) Les trois amis (16x10cm-6x4in) bears studio st.
    board (F.FR 13000)
£1361 $2273   (4-Jun-91 R.T243/R) Faggot gatherer in forest interior (48x64cm-19x25in)
    panel (C.D 2600)
£1470 $2910   (31-Jan-91 D.V32/R) Foret de Fontainebleau (19x35cm-7x14in) i.verso
    (A.S 30000)
£1622 $2643   (10-Jun-91 W.T1368) Figues reclining under a tree (24x18cm-9x7in) s.
    panel (C.D 3000)
£1709 $2802   (21-Jun-91 SY.MO340/R) Bouquet de fleurs (40x32cm-16x13in) s. panel
    (F.FR 17000)
£1800 $3456   (27-Nov-90 PH52/R) Figure in wooded landscape (34x26cm-13x10in) s. panel
£2113 $3549   (22-Apr-91 BU.K27/R) Reclining nude woman seen from behind in wooded
    glade (27x35cm-11x14in) s.d.1870 panel (D.KR 24000)
£2390 $4661   (24-Oct-90 GD.B289) Male and female nude in arcadian landscape
    (33x41cm-13x16in) s. (S.FR 6000)
£2676 $4522   (17-Apr-91 WE.MU133/R) Washer women in forest of Fontainbleau
    (46x38cm-18x15in) s. (DM 8000)
£2890 $5000   (22-May-91 SY.NY147/R) Interieur de foret - gros rochers avec fagotiere
    (33x42cm-13x17in) s.d.47 cradled panel
£3074 $6025   (7-Nov-90 APT.P506/R) Sous-bois (38x29cm-15x11in) panel (F.FR 30000)
£3158 $6000   (28-Feb-91 CH.NY47/R) Faggot gatherer in landscape (29x54cm-11x21in)
    s.d.48 panel
£3262 $6263   (1-Dec-90 PER.M89/R) Les dernieres larmes (21x14cm-8x6in) s. panel
    (F.FR 32000)
£3468 $6000   (21-May-91 CE.NY26/R) Floral still life (27x20cm-11x8in) s. panel
£3500 $6265   (12-Mar-91 PH81/R) Cattle in stormy landscape (32x40cm-13x16in) s.

DIAZ DE LA PENA, Narcisse-Virgile (1807-1876) French-cont.

£4077	$7829	(1-Dec-90 PER.M87/R) La promenade de la chatelaine (28x18cm-11x7in) s. (F.FR 40000)
£4103	$8000	(23-Oct-90 SY.NY288/R) Famille de bohemiens (44x29cm-17x11in)
£4191	$7250	(22-May-91 SY.NY146/R) La penetration dans les bois (24x32cm-9x13in) s. panel
£4624	$8000	(23-May-91 CH.NY226/R) Man and hounds, Fontainebleau Forest (42x33cm-17x13in) s. panel
£4913	$8500	(23-May-91 CH.NY229/R) Tete de femme, vue de profil (30x25cm-12x10in) st.sig. panel
£5000	$9500	(28-Feb-91 CH.NY48/R) Faggot gatherer in wooded landscape (32x41cm-13x16in) s. panel
£5263	$10000	(28-Feb-91 CH.NY51/R) Still life of assorted flowers (43x34cm-17x13in) bears sig.d.1857verso painted oval
£5800	$9512	(19-Jun-91 S153/R) Oriental women and children playing in forest (36x29cm-14x11in) s.
£5912	$11352	(1-Dec-90 PER.M67/R) Nymphe dans la foret de Fontainebleau (19x41cm-7x16in) s. panel (F.FR 58000)
£6069	$10500	(21-May-91 GRO.B44/R) Toilet of Venus (36x23cm-14x9in) s. panel
£6200	$10106	(3-Jul-91 PLF.P60/R) Sous-bois (23x34cm-9x13in) s. panel (F.FR 62000)
£6728	$12917	(1-Dec-90 PER.M68/R) Paysage boise a Fontainebleau (33x44cm-13x17in) mono. l. verso panel (F.FR 66000)
£8138	$15381	(30-Sep-90 FE.P127) Gathering wild flowers (24x32cm-9x13in) s. panel (F.FR 80000)
£10983	$19000	(22-May-91 SY.NY133/R) La favorite du Sultan (61x74cm-24x29in) s.d.64
£11282	$22000	(24-Oct-90 CH.NY39/R) Le rageur (71x93cm-28x37in) s.d.1862
£1020	*$2010*	*(16-Nov-90 LGB.P96) Sous-bois a l'etang (10x16cm-4x6in) init. W/C (F.FR 10000)*

DIAZ DE LA PENA, Narcisse-Virgile (attrib) (1807-1876) French

£683	$1100	(26-Jun-91 D.NY26) Washerwoman by stream (15x25cm-6x10in) panel
£889	$1724	(4-Dec-90 P.Q171/R) Le Foret de Fontainebleau (61x92cm-24x36in) s. canvas on board (C.D 2000)
£1667	$3233	(4-Dec-90 P.Q70) Faggot gathering in the forest (50x68cm-20x27in) (C.D 3750)
£1743	$3434	(13-Nov-90 AB.S883/R) Wooded landscape with mill (102x76cm-40x30in) bears sig. (S.KR 19000)
£2373	$4248	(11-Apr-91 D.V137/R) Roses (38x46cm-15x18in) panel (A.S 50000)
£3212	$6200	(10-Dec-90 H.C1170/R) Entree du Bas Breau (48x71cm-19x28in) s.d.54

DIBBETS, Jan (20th C) ?

£4734	*$8000*	*(1-May-91 SY.NY95/R) San Casciano ceiling (73x73cm-29x29in) s.d.1979 col.photographs pencil*
£6754	*$13170*	*(23-Oct-90 F.M37/R) Water structure (45x45cm-18x18in) s.i.d.1975 composition with photographs (I.L 15000000)*

DIBDIN, Thomas Colman (1810-1893) British

£410	*$709*	*(20-May-91 SWS326/R) A French town with figures by a church entrance in the foreground (55x37cm-22x15in) s.d.1878 pen W/C htd.bodycol.*
£800	*$1432*	*(13-Mar-91 B62/R) Rouen in the precincts of the Cathedral (133x77cm-52x30in) s.d.1884 i. verso W/C*
£1500	*$2970*	*(30-Jan-91 S96/R) Travellers in lane. Labourers resting in field (18x13cm-7x5in) s.d.1876 W/C over pencil htd bodycol pair*

DICEY, Frank (?-1888) British

£10678	$20929	(25-Nov-90 B.PA61/R) Le garden party (117x98cm-46x39in) s. (F.FR 105500)

DICHTL, Erich (1890-1955) Austrian

£1697	$3191	(20-Sep-90 D.V117/R) Roaring stag (70x57cm-28x22in) s. (A.S 35000)
£1723	$3447	(7-Feb-91 D.V26/R) Capercaillie performing courtship dance (100x80cm-39x31in) s. (A.S 35000)

DICKERHOF, Urs (1941-) Swiss

£720	*$1217*	*(1-May-91 GD.B1407/R) Aswan cats, composition of 6 pictures (80x60cm-31x24in) st.studio verso wax crayons (S.FR 1800)*

DICKERSON, Robert (1924-) Australian

£542	$1041	(27-Nov-90 JRL.S233) Wistful child (30x24cm-12x9in) s. composition board (A.D 1350)
£641	$1135	(18-Mar-91 MGS.S174) Wistful child (30x24cm-12x9in) s. board (A.D 1500)
£928	$1782	(14-Aug-90 SY.ME87) Harlequin (45x37cm-18x15in) s. board (A.D 2200)
£1606	$3084	(27-Nov-90 JRL.S117/R) The Mother - Picasso (122x91cm-48x36in) s. canvas on composition board (A.D 4000)
£7907	$13284	(22-Apr-91 SY.ME258/R) Family group (120x135cm-47x53in) s.d.3.11.60 board (A.D 17000)
£386	*$761*	*(13-Nov-90 J.M898) Pensive figure (76x54cm-30x21in) s. chl (A.D 1000)*
£480	*$936*	*(15-Oct-90 AAA.S131) Girl with a cat (56x37cm-22x15in) s. pastel (A.D 1200)*
£480	*$936*	*(15-Oct-90 AAA.S79) Pensive (57x37cm-22x15in) s. pastel (A.D 1200)*
£543	*$918*	*(16-Apr-91 J.M11) The Lover (66x78cm-26x31in) s. pastel (A.D 1200)*
£568	*$1016*	*(9-Apr-91 CH.ME35) Mother and child (56x38cm-22x15in) s. pastel (A.D 1300)*
£573	*$1082*	*(25-Sep-90 JRL.S109/R) Look to the future (77x66cm-30x26in) s. pastel (A.D 1300)*
£573	*$1082*	*(25-Sep-90 JRL.S112) The glance (56x36cm-22x14in) s. pastel (A.D 1300)*

DICKERSON, Robert (1924-) Australian-cont.
£588	$994	(16-Apr-91 J.M299) The Angry lady (53x34cm-21x13in) s. pastel (A.D 1300)
£617	$1166	(25-Sep-90 JRL.S115) The street, evening (58x77cm-23x30in) s. pastel (A.D 1400)
£618	$1217	(12-Nov-90 CH.ME406) Cousins (53x73cm-21x29in) s. chl pastel (A.D 1600)
£618	$1217	(12-Nov-90 CH.ME403) Thinking of home (72x53cm-28x21in) s. chl pastel (A.D 1600)
£618	$1217	(13-Nov-90 J.M91) In thought (72x53cm-28x21in) s. pastel (A.D 1600)
£625	$1088	(26-Mar-91 JRL.S258) Two faces (77x56cm-30x22in) s. chl (A.D 1400)
£633	$1215	(14-Aug-90 SY.ME136/R) Mother and child (72x53cm-28x21in) s. chl. (A.D 1500)
£641	$1135	(18-Mar-91 MGS.S139) Students (54x72cm-21x28in) s. pastel (A.D 1500)
£661	$1249	(25-Sep-90 JRL.S126) The Siamese cat (54x71cm-21x28in) s. pastel (A.D 1500)
£699	$1251	(9-Apr-91 CH.ME95) East and west (55x74cm-22x29in) s. pastel (A.D 1600)
£769	$1300	(16-Apr-91 J.M105) Watching the traffic (54x75cm-21x30in) s. pastel (A.D 1700)
£814	$1376	(16-Apr-91 J.M101) Time to gossip (72x53cm-28x21in) s. pastel (A.D 1800)
£814	$1376	(15-Apr-91 AAA.S137) Friends (54x74cm-21x29in) s. pastel (A.D 1800)
£849	$1384	(1-Jul-91 AAA.S121) Twins (55x74cm-22x29in) s. pastel (A.D 1800)
£849	$1673	(13-Nov-90 J.M97) Geisha with daughter (74x55cm-29x22in) s. pastel (A.D 2200)
£849	$1384	(1-Jul-91 AAA.S50 f) Girl with a cat (75x56cm-30x22in) s. pastel (A.D 1800)
£920	$1499	(1-Jul-91 AAA.S137) Girl with long hair (76x55cm-30x22in) s. pastel (A.D 1950)
£930	$1563	(22-Apr-91 SY.ME150) Sketch for committee meeting (56x77cm-22x30in) s. chl (A.D 2000)
£983	$1740	(18-Mar-91 MGS.S159) Mother and son (74x54cm-29x21in) pastel (A.D 2300)
£995	$1682	(15-Apr-91 AAA.S147) Japanese sisters (73x55cm-29x22in) s. pastel (A.D 2200)
£1023	$1719	(22-Apr-91 SY.ME75) Father and son (73x54cm-29x21in) s. pastel (A.D 2200)

DICKINSON, Anson (1779-1852) American
| £700 | $1239 | (20-Mar-91 C112/R) Portrait of girl in white dress with high ruff collar (8x?cm-3x?in) min. gilt-metal frame oval |

DICKINSON, Edwin (1891-1978) American
£5291	$10000	(27-Sep-90 CH.NY307/R) Marsh at Blackfish Creek (40x50cm-16x20in) s.d.1941 i. verso
£1491	$2400	(30-Jun-91 LIT.L64) Sannery sur mer (25x36cm-10x14in) s.d.1938 chl.
£1553	$2500	(30-Jun-91 LIT.L63) Portrait (25x30cm-10x12in) s. chl.

DICKINSON, J Reed (fl.1867-1881) British
| £580 | $1079 | (3-Sep-90 SWS1409) Cottage interior (50x71cm-20x28in) s. W/C bodycol |

DICKINSON, Lowes Cato (attrib) (1819-1908) British
| £880 | $1478 | (23-Apr-91 SWS290) Portrait of Princess Louise of Hesse (63x43cm-25x17in) |

DICKINSON, Preston (1891-1930) American
| £5291 | $10000 | (27-Sep-90 CH.NY297/R) Village (61x43cm-24x17in) s. W/C pencil paper laid down on board |

DICKSEE, Herbert (1862-1942) British
| £600 | $1062 | (21-Mar-91 CSK37/R) A polar bear on an ice flow (41x61cm-16x24in) pencil chl. white chk. |

DICKSEE, Thomas Francis (1819-1895) British
| £1400 | $2772 | (30-Jan-91 CSK244) Ophelia (28x25cm-11x10in) mono.d.1861 i. label verso panel oval |

DIDAY, Francois (1802-1877) Swiss
£1606	$3149	(21-Nov-90 SY.Z19/R) Study of plant (35x50cm-14x20in) board (S.FR 4000)
£2041	$4000	(6-Nov-90 GF.L2214/R) Les beigneuses au lac de Brienz (32x46cm-13x18in) (S.FR 5000)
£15000	$24600	(19-Jun-91 S44/R) View of Lake Geneva, la Tour-de-Peliz and Vevey (93x119cm-37x47in) s.
£316	$600	(27-Feb-91 SY.NY188/R) Alpine landscape (56x69cm-22x27in) s.d.1846 pencil white chk

DIDDAERT, Henri (fl.1845-1866) Belgian
| £950 | $1786 | (21-Sep-90 PHM71) Figures in an interior (57x69cm-22x27in) s.d.1856 |

DIDIER, Clovis Francois Auguste (1858-) French
| £960 | $1622 | (1-May-91 GD.B205/R) Gardener watering vegetables (90x130cm-35x51in) s.d.1889 (S.FR 2400) |

DIDIER, J (19th C) French
| £1300 | $2249 | (9-May-91 CSK156/R) Visitor (30x46cm-12x18in) s. |

DIDIER, Luc (20th C) ?
| £609 | $1205 | (3-Feb-91 LT.P88) L'entree de Cambremer (55x45cm-22x18in) s. (F.FR 6000) |

DIDIER, Luc (20th C) ?-cont.
£706	$1376	(20-Jan-91 CB.P110) La plage de Pourville (27x41cm-11x16in) s. (F.FR 7000)
£822	$1595	(8-Dec-90 LT.P73/R) La garette a trigau en vendee (46x61cm-18x24in) s. (F.FR 8000)
£1150	$1875	(4-Jul-91 LT.P55/R) Bord de Sevres a Maille (54x65cm-21x26in) s.
£1159	$2261	(27-Oct-90 LT.P60/R) Riviere en Vendee (38x55cm-15x22in) s. (F.FR 11500)
£1205	$2229	(10-Mar-91 LT.P121/R) Effet de ciel a Tronoen (46x61cm-18x24in) s. (F.FR 12000)
£1215	$2381	(25-Nov-90 ZZ.F232/R) Paysage aux peupliers (47x61cm-19x24in) s. (F.FR 12000)
£1248	$2108	(5-May-91 LT.P88) Chemin a Villebert (27x41cm-11x16in) s. (F.FR 12500)
£1397	$2361	(5-May-91 LT.P58/R) Quelques maisons a Aureille (50x65cm-20x26in) s. (F.FR 14000)
£1494	$2540	(2-Jun-91 LT.P43/R) Chemin a Mirabeau en soiree (50x65cm-20x26in) s. (F.FR 15000)
£1494	$2585	(26-May-91 ZZ.F68/R) Barque dans les roseaux (50x66cm-20x26in) s. (F.FR 15000)
£1597	$2699	(5-May-91 LT.P78/R) Barques amarrees sur la riviere (38x55cm-15x22in) s. (F.FR 16000)
£1597	$2699	(5-May-91 LT.P68/R) Campagne autour de la Rigane (38x55cm-15x22in) s. (F.FR 16000)
£1796	$3036	(5-May-91 LT.P98/R) Barque a Dissay (26x41cm-10x16in) s. (F.FR 18000)
£1896	$3205	(5-May-91 LT.P48/R) Champs de coquelicots a Champigny, Vendee (50x65cm-20x26in) s. (F.FR 19000)
£1942	$3302	(2-Jun-91 LT.P160/R) Village en vallee sous le soliel (73x92cm-29x36in) s. (F.FR 19500)
£2292	$4538	(3-Feb-91 LT.P66/R) Ruelle a Angles-sur-l'Anglin (50x65cm-20x26in) s. (F.FR 22600)
£2067	*$4030*	*(27-Oct-90 LT.P43/R) Le rhododendron (46x61cm-18x24in) s. (F.FR 20500)*

DIDIER-POUGET, William (1864-1959) French
£526	$1037	(30-Oct-90 MA.V548) Vallee de la montane (33x56cm-13x22in) (C.D 1200)
£658	$1296	(30-Oct-90 MA.V549) Le matin, Bruyeres, en fleurs, Pyrenes (36x66cm-14x26in) s. (C.D 1500)
£676	$1318	(26-Oct-90 KM.K1180) Wooded landscape with pond near Fontainebleau, evening (103x182cm-41x72in) s.d.89 canvas laid down (DM 2000)
£2105	$4000	(27-Feb-91 SY.NY63/R) Vallee de la Creuse - environs du pin (54x65cm-21x26in) s. mono.i.num.010-131 verso
£2128	$4000	(19-Sep-90 B.SF2688/R) Le Matin-Blugeres en fleurs-Vallee du Doubs (58x100cm-23x39in) s. d.i. verso

DIEBENKORN, Richard (1922-) American
£2601	*$4500*	*(7-May-91 CE.NY153/R) Untitled (61x46cm-24x18in) chl*
£3846	*$6500*	*(1-May-91 SY.NY202/R) Untitled - Berkeley (27x25cm-11x10in) init.d.54 ink*
£4592	$9000	(12-Feb-91 SY.NY454/R) Portraits (41x33cm-16x13in) chl pair
£9137	$18000	(4-Oct-90 SY.NY151/R) Woman dressing (43x33cm-17x13in) init.d.63 pencil
£11480	$22500	(7-Nov-90 SY.NY125 a/R) Standing nude (60x48cm-24x19in) init.d.67 chl.
£56122	$110000	(7-Nov-90 SY.NY202/R) Untitled no.4 (86x56cm-34x22in) init.d.81 gouache crayon

DIEBOLT, Jean Michel (1779-?) French
£1049	$2024	(12-Dec-90 N.M482/R) Shepherdess and cattle in mountainous southern river landscape (24x33cm-9x13in) s. panel (DM 3000)

DIEBSCHLAG, Hans (20th C) German
£556	$1100	(1-Feb-91 S.W2934) Ladies lift your skirts we are going through hell (69x86cm-27x34in) s.d.85 board

DIECK, Jacob von (1805-1852) German
£1680	$3158	(10-Aug-90 RAS.V448/R) Biedermeier interior with family (77x61cm-30x24in) s.d.1847 (D.KR 19000)

DIEFENBACH, Karl Wilhelm (1851-1931) German
£4392	$8345	(14-Sep-90 SA.A1397/R) Anbetung (192x99cm-76x39in) s. i.verso (DM 13000)

DIEFFENBACH (19th C) German
£1223	$2300	(9-Aug-90 E.EDM249/R) Woman and child near harbor (38x46cm-15x18in) s.d.1871

DIEFFENBACH, Anton Heinrich (1831-1914) German
£898	$1760	(6-Nov-90 GF.L2389/R) The fortune teller (61x46cm-24x18in) s.d.1877 (S.FR 2200)
£1748	$3392	(4-Dec-90 FN.S1799) Kid sniffing rose (24x37cm-9x15in) s.d.1867 (DM 5000)

DIEGHEM, Jacob van (19th C) Dutch?
£928	$1550	(9-Jun-91 LIT.L359) Sheep with two sleeping lambs (41x61cm-16x24in) s.d.1870 board
£1190	$2107	(20-Mar-91 KM.K1183/R) Landscape with sheep resting in field (16x24cm-6x9in) s.d.77 panel (DM 3500)

DIEHL, Arthur (1870-1929) American
£533 $900   (20-Apr-91 WOL.C181) Ocean spray (28x69cm-11x27in) s.panel
£878 $1650   (7-Aug-90 RB.HY271/R) A tough rescue (41x74cm-16x29in) s.d.1925 artist's
                 board
£900 $1692   (18-Sep-90 SWS685/R) On the Lagoon, Venice (49x90cm-19x35in) s.d.1892
£1160 $2250   (24-Aug-90 RB.HY86/R) Sand and sea (30x61cm-12x24in) s.
£1272 $2200   (21-May-91 CE.NY585/R) Seascape (103x184cm-41x72in) s.d.1915
£1893 $3200   (20-Apr-91 WOL.C185/R) Fisherman's scene with windmills
                 (28x46cm-11x18in) s. pair

DIEHL, Gosta (1899-1964) Finnish
£719 $1388   (15-Dec-90 BU.H34) Vase of flowers (46x38cm-18x15in) s. (F.M 5000)
£1062   *$1794*   *(20-Apr-91 HOR.H62/R) Summer's day (31x38cm-12x15in) s.d.1945 W/C*
                 (F.M 7400)
£1854   *$3635*   *(24-Nov-90 HOR.H72/R) Sketch for 'Old, new, eternal- mosaic in FBF in*
                 Bjorneborg (40x65cm-16x26in) s.d.1961 W/C (F.M 13000)

DIEHLE, Alwin (1854-?) German
£3167 $5668   (12-Apr-91 BM.B586/R) Lake landscape with two young women in rowing boat
                 amongst reeds (108x66cm-43x26in) s.d.1895 (DM 9500)
£8333 $14917   (12-Apr-91 BM.B588/R) Upper Bavarian landscape with skaters on frozen
                 lake (60x88cm-24x35in) s.i. (DM 25000)

DIELITZ, Konrad (1845-1933) German
£828 $1622   (7-Nov-90 N.M858/R) Upper Bavarian interior (39x43cm-15x17in) s.i.d.1871
                 canvas on board (DM 2400)

DIELMAN, Pierre Emmanuel (Jnr) (1821-1893) Belgian
£1361 $2190   (26-Jun-91 KM.K1433/R) Landscape with sheep (50x68cm-20x27in) s.d.1850
                 panel (DM 4000)

DIEM, Peter Karl (1890-1956) German/American
£1134 $2200   (5-Dec-90 D.NY92/R) Times Square 1939 (102x86cm-40x34in) s.
£1183 $2000   (17-Apr-91 D.NY77/R) Four roses, Times Square (91x76cm-36x30in) s.
                 i.stretcher

DIEMER, Michael Zeno (1867-1939) German
£2055 $3678   (12-Mar-91 FN.S2333/R) Marine with three-masters in calm sea before
                 Sicilian coast (102x144cm-40x57in) s. (DM 6000)
£408   *$657*   *(28-Jun-91 BM.B661/R) Harbour scene with shipping and steam ship,*
                 possibly Hamburg (17x29cm-7x11in) s. W/C gouache (DM 1200)

DIEMER, Th Zeno (19th C) German
£898 $1768   (14-Nov-90 RAS.K580/R) Glacier in mountain landscape (128x172cm-50x68in)
                 s.d.1897 (D.KR 10000)

DIEPENBECK, Abraham van (1596-1675) Flemish
£6098 $10000   (19-Jun-91 B.SF1658/R) Allegory of the Suffering of Christ
                 (147x137cm-58x54in)

DIEPENBECK, Abraham van (attrib) (1596-1675) Flemish
£2390 $4112   (14-May-91 GF.L2283/R) Angels blowing bubbles (65x53cm-26x21in)
                 (S.FR 6000)
£800   *$1536*   *(18-Feb-91 S103/R) Saints and martyrs standing at balustrade with putti*
                 flying above (11x42cm-4x17in) pen ink wash over chk

DIER, Erhard Amadeus (1893-1969) Austrian
£730 $1431   (24-Jan-91 D.V149/R) Girls bathing in river (34x31cm-13x12in) s. board
                 (A.S 15000)
£365   *$715*   *(24-Jan-91 D.V53/R) Allegory of love (31x23cm-12x9in) s.d.1914 pen*
                 indian ink (A.S 7500)

DIERCKX, Pierre Jacques (1855-?) Belgian
£650 $1287   (30-Jan-91 CSK270) A moment's peace (33x46cm-13x18in) s.
£1496 $2678   (12-Mar-91 C.A80/R) Waiting for the fishermen to return
                 (70x90cm-28x35in) s. (B.FR 90000)
£2698 $5234   (4-Dec-90 C.A112/R) The hot soup (75x60cm-30x24in) s. panel
                 (B.FR 160000)

DIESNER, Gerhild (1915-) Austrian
£3349 $5794   (8-May-91 D.V136/R) Southern landscape (48x63cm-19x25in) s.d.72 board
                 (A.S 70000)
£10669 $20058   (20-Sep-90 D.V202/R) Red bird (64x74cm-25x29in) (A.S 220000)
£1942   *$3184*   *(20-Jun-91 D.V219/R) Sunset in the Provence (14x18cm-6x7in) s.i. pencil*
                 W/C (A.S 40000)

DIEST, Adriaen van (1655-1704) Dutch
£2471 $4200   (27-May-91 GC.M408/R) Paisaje Montanoso con cascada y dos figuras
                 (38x64cm-15x25in) s.
£5500 $8965   (2-Jul-91 PH1/R) British man of war and other shipping in coastal waters
                 (39x47cm-15x19in) s.
£10000 $19000   (1-Mar-91 C111/R) Mediterranean coast at dawn with shipping and
                 fishermen raising net (41x149cm-16x59in) mono.s.

DIEST, Adriaen van (circle) (1655-1704) Dutch
£1500 $3000   (7-Feb-91 CSK137/R) Wooded mountainous landscape with mother and
                         children on path (35x44cm-14x17in) panel

DIEST, Frans van (?) Belgian
£2800 $4956   (20-Mar-91 DL.P161/R) Berger pres d'une chaumiere en foret. Relais de
                         poste sous la neige (100x151cm-39x59in) both s. pair (F.FR 28000)

DIEST, John van (fl.1695-1757) British
£4000 $7160   (12-Apr-91 C123/R) Portrait of Anthony Browne, 6th Viscount Montague,
                         turning at wood (119x101cm-47x40in)

DIETER, Hans (1881-?) German
£2357 $4077   (6-May-91 ZEL.L1662/R) View of Lake Untersee with Swiss mountain ranges
                         beyond (50x65cm-20x26in) s. (DM 7000)

DIETERLE, Marie (1856-1935) French
£2695 $5336   (31-Jan-91 D.V119/R) Cows in landscape (60x48cm-24x19in) s. (A.S 55000)

DIETHE, Alfred (1836-1919) German
£2517 $4859   (10-Dec-90 L.K415/R) Portrait of the Birkner children from Dresden in
                         landscape (51x59cm-20x23in) s.d.1858 (DM 7200)

DIETLER, Johann Friedrich (1804-1874) Swiss
£9524 $15619   (19-Jun-91 GK.B95/R) Grandfather, mother and child (47x38cm-19x15in) s.
                         (S.FR 24000)

DIETMANN, Erik (1937-) Swedish
£1975 $3890   (14-Nov-90 KH.K30) Vacances a Laessoe (59x74cm-23x29in) s. iron
                         (D.KR 22000)

DIETRICH, Adelheid (1827-) German
£7023 $11870   (19-Apr-91 FN.S1696/R) Still life of fruit in basket with butterfly and
                         fly in niche (44x52cm-17x20in) s.i.d.1848 (DM 21000)

DIETRICH, Adolf (1877-1957) Swiss
£513 $1000   (13-Oct-90 LAE.L133/R) Mountain landscape with hay stacks
                         (38x58cm-15x23in) s.
£5928 $11500   (24-Aug-90 RB.HY206/R) Still life with fiddlehead ferns
                         (61x46cm-24x18in) s.d.49 canvas laid down on board
£13834 $23518   (27-May-91 GK.Z5319/R) Berlingen (28x39cm-11x15in) s.d.1951 panel
                         (S.FR 35000)
£18072 $35422   (21-Nov-90 SY.Z73/R) View of Untersee from Weissen Felsen
                         (41x60cm-16x24in) s.d.1930 board (S.FR 45000)
£3213   *$6297*   *(21-Nov-90 SY.Z63/R) Untersee (18x26cm-7x10in) s.d.18 pastel (S.FR 8000)*
£3213   *$6297*   *(21-Nov-90 SY.Z62/R) Untersee (18x26cm-7x10in) s. pastel (S.FR 8000)*

DIETRICH, Christian Wilhelm Ernst (1712-1774) German
£1861 $3666   (14-Nov-90 D.V295/R) Head of old bearded man (51x39cm-20x15in)
                         (A.S 38000)
£2200 $3586   (2-Jul-91 PH124 a) Diana and Actean (58x79cm-23x31in)
£2480 $4266   (19-May-91 ZZ.F66/R) Le musicien galant (33x29cm-13x11in) panel
                         (F.FR 25000)
£3420 $6121   (14-Mar-91 D.V359/R) Descent from the Cross (63x46cm-25x18in)
                         s.indis.d.17.. copper (A.S 70000)
£4012 $7823   (10-Oct-90 APT.P474/R) Ermite dans la foret (55x65cm-22x26in)
                         (F.FR 40000)
£19000 $30970   (3-Jul-91 S149/R) Lovers surprised (79x61cm-31x24in) s.
£699   *$1357*   *(7-Dec-90 GB.B5483/R) Coastal landscape with ruins (21x33cm-8x13in) pen
                         wash (DM 2000)*

DIETRICH, Christian Wilhelm Ernst (attrib) (1712-1774) German
£700 $1211   (20-May-91 SWS187/R) Study of an elderly bearded man (20x17cm-8x7in)
                         paper laid on panel
£957 $1800   (22-Sep-90 WOL.C68) Old scholar (28x23cm-11x9in) panel
£1976 $3360   (27-May-91 GK.Z5023/R) Comedia del arte in park landscape
                         (33x27cm-13x11in) panel (S.FR 5000)
£450   *$806*   *(12-Apr-91 AW.H440/R) Shepherd with dog resting beneath tree and cattle
                         watering (20x27cm-8x11in) brush over pencil (DM 1350)*

DIETRICH, Christian Wilhelm Ernst (circle) (1712-1774) German
£750 $1223   (4-Jul-91 C555) Portrait of gentleman, seated at casement
                         (23x17cm-9x7in) panel
£1198 $2024   (2-May-91 CH.AM57/R) A woman small half length, at a niche
                         (29x21cm-11x8in) panel (D.FL 4000)

DIETRICH, Christian Wilhelm Ernst (school) (1712-1774) German
£1221 $2186   (14-Mar-91 D.V347/R) Bearded man holding gold coin in his hand
                         (49x45cm-19x18in) (A.S 65000)

DIETRICH, Christian Wilhelm Ernst (style) (1712-1774) German
£3183 $6271   (14-Nov-90 D.V366/R) Southern harbour with boats and figures
                         (81x121cm-32x48in) (A.S 65000)

DIETRICHSON, Mathilde (1837-1921) Scandinavian
£2404 $4640   (10-Dec-90 B.O18/R) By the fence (34x43cm-13x17in) s.d.1907 (N.KR 27000)

DIETTERLIN, Bartholomaeus (c.1590-?) French
£6500 $10985   (16-Apr-91 C265/R) View of the Terrace of a Palazzo with a central
                   projection (12x18cm-5x7in) s.d.1638 ink bodycol. vellum laid down
                   panel
£11000 $18590   (16-Apr-91 C266/R) The Parterre of a Palazzo of nine bays
                   (12x18cm-5x7in) s.d.1638 ink bodycol vellum laid down on panel

DIETZI, Hans (1864-1929) Swiss
£1000 $1970   (4-Oct-90 CSK226/R) Statue dei Dioscuri Castore e Polluce in Piazza del
                   Quinnale, Rome (62x50cm-24x20in) s.d.96

DIETZSCH, Barbara Regina (1706-1783) German
£1399 $2699   (10-Dec-90 L.K244/R) Goldfinch perched on branch (28x20cm-11x8in)
                   indis.i.verso gouache (DM 4000)
£1818 $3509   (10-Dec-90 L.K243/R) Finch perched on branch (28x20cm-11x8in) s.verso
                   gouache (DM 5200)

DIETZSCH, Barbara Regina (attrib) (1706-1783) German
£1850 $3552   (18-Feb-91 S301/R) Two studies of carnations with butterflies
                   (27x19cm-11x7in) gouache pair

DIETZSCH, Johann Christoph (1710-1790) German
£3000 $5070   (16-Apr-91 C267/R) Travellers on a road through a village. Skaters on a
                   canal bodycolour vellum two

DIETZSCH, Johann Christoph (attrib) (1710-1790) German
£1370 $2233   (12-Jun-91 N.M228/R) Hilly river landscape with shepherds and animals
                   (16x20cm-6x8in) i.verso gouache (DM 4000)

DIETZSCH, Johann Siegmund (1707-1775) German
£2098 $4070   (7-Dec-90 GB.B5488/R) Landscape with town before mountains in
                   thunderstorm (16x22cm-6x9in) gouache (DM 6000)

DIEVENBACH, Hendricus Anthonius (1872-1946) Dutch
£1220 $2390   (6-Nov-90 SY.AM288) Teasing baby (39x49cm-15x19in) s. (D.FL 4000)

DIGHTON, Robert (1752-1814) British
£550 $1040   (26-Sep-90 B149/R) Portrait of Sir Robert Peel (47x38cm-19x15in)
                   s.d.1807 W/c
£1700 $3043   (11-Apr-91 S9/R) Landowner visiting one of farms. Pedlar trudging past
                   farm and tinkers (16x26cm-6x10in) indist.s. pen W/C pair

DIGHTON, Robert (attrib) (1752-1814) British
£6500 $12805   (13-Nov-90 C103/R) Return of Louis XVI to Paris, 6 October 1789
                   (66x99cm-26x39in) pencil pen ink W/C

DIGNIMONT, Andre (1891-1965) French
£380 $740   (17-Oct-90 FER.M90/R) Jarron con flores (33x23cm-13x9in) s. W/C
                   (S.P 70000)
£400 $652   (5-Jul-91 APT.P10) La robe verte (41x28cm-16x11in) s.d.1933 gouache
                   (F.FR 4000)
£514 $874   (27-May-91 GK.Z5320/R) Femme au chapeau vert (54x44cm-21x17in) s. W/C
                   (S.FR 1300)
£554 $1081   (22-Oct-90 MJ.P88) La pensionnaire Danoise (65x50cm-26x20in) st. W/C
                   (F.FR 5500)
£554 $1081   (22-Oct-90 MJ.P104/R) Sous la futaie (50x65cm-20x26in) st. W/C
                   (F.FR 5500)
£554 $1081   (22-Oct-90 MJ.P86) La detente de Dany (50x65cm-20x26in) st. W/C
                   (F.FR 5500)
£554 $1081   (22-Oct-90 MJ.P75) Devant le miroir (65x50cm-26x20in) st. W/C
                   (F.FR 5500)
£554 $1081   (22-Oct-90 MJ.P55/R) Pensive Sandra (65x50cm-26x20in) st. W/C
                   (F.FR 5500)
£565 $1101   (22-Oct-90 MJ.P43) Nina Falbala pensive (50x65cm-20x26in) st. W/C
                   (F.FR 5600)
£585 $1140   (22-Oct-90 MJ.P62) Pensive Anouchka (50x65cm-20x26in) st.W/C (F.FR 5800)
£603 $1158   (24-Feb-91 P.V82) Femme au chapeau (54x43cm-21x17in) s. W/C (F.FR 6000)
£605 $1179   (22-Oct-90 MJ.P78/R) La couture (50x65cm-20x26in) s. W/C (F.FR 6000)
£605 $1179   (22-Oct-90 MJ.P102/R) Dans le parc (50x65cm-20x26in) st. W/C (F.FR 6000)
£605 $1179   (22-Oct-90 MJ.P76) La tenue de theatre (65x50cm-26x20in) st. W/C
                   (F.FR 6000)
£605 $1179   (22-Oct-90 MJ.P50/R) La Blue Bell girl (65x50cm-26x20in) s. W/C gouache
                   (F.FR 6000)
£615 $1199   (22-Oct-90 MJ.P44) Jenny au chapeau fleuri (65x50cm-26x20in) st. W/C
                   (F.FR 6100)
£655 $1278   (22-Oct-90 MJ.P96) Adele au canape violet (50x43cm-20x17in) st.s. W/C
                   gouache (F.FR 6500)
£655 $1278   (22-Oct-90 MJ.P70) Pulpeuse Sonia (50x65cm-20x26in) st.W/C (F.FR 6500)
£655 $1278   (22-Oct-90 MJ.P49) Aloha, la Tahitienne (50x32cm-20x13in) s. W/C
                   (F.FR 6500)
£655 $1278   (22-Oct-90 MJ.P94) La Jarretelle (65x50cm-26x20in) st. W/C gouache
                   (F.FR 6500)
£655 $1278   (22-Oct-90 MJ.P83) Jeune femme a l'eventail (50x65cm-20x26in) st. W/C
                   (F.FR 6500)
£683 $1099   (24-Jun-91 BL.P32) Bouquet (50x63cm-20x25in) s.i.d.31 octobre 44 W/C
                   gouache (F.FR 6800)

DIGNIMONT, Andre (1891-1965) French-cont.

£706	$1376	(22-Oct-90 MJ.P90) Lecture d'automne (50x65cm-20x26in) st. W/C (F.FR 7000)
£706	$1376	(22-Oct-90 MJ.P79) Helga la Prussienne (60x50cm-24x20in) st. W/C gouache (F.FR 7000)
£706	$1376	(22-Oct-90 MJ.P20) Irma la Rousse (36x26cm-14x10in) st. W/C (F.FR 7000)
£755	$1231	(12-Jun-91 ZZ.F74) Jeune femme, chemise ouverte (47x34cm-19x13in) s. indian ink stumping (F.FR 7500)
£756	$1474	(22-Oct-90 MJ.P68) Ulla a l'eventail rose (50x65cm-20x26in) st. W/C (F.FR 7500)
£776	$1343	(12-May-91 L.C15/R) Jeune femme au canape (32x40cm-13x16in) s. W/C (F.FR 7800)
£803	$1486	(10-Mar-91 LT.P185) Le modele au sofa bleu (49x64cm-19x25in) st.sig. W/C (F.FR 8000)
£806	$1573	(22-Oct-90 MJ.P81) L'attente de Virginie (50x65cm-20x26in) st. W/C (F.FR 8000)
£815	$1574	(16-Dec-90 T.B26) Elegante a l'ombrelle (64x48cm-25x19in) s. W/C gouache (F.FR 8000)
£822	$1595	(8-Dec-90 LT.P131) Lola au canape bleu (50x65cm-20x26in) st.sig. W/C (F.FR 8000)
£857	$1671	(22-Oct-90 MJ.P38/R) Caressante Edna (37x60cm-15x24in) st. W/C (F.FR 8500)
£907	$1769	(22-Oct-90 MJ.P40) La chemise rouge de Magda (50x65cm-20x26in) st. W/C (F.FR 9000)
£925	$1794	(8-Dec-90 LT.P132) Fanny au Chignon (50x65cm-20x26in) st.sig. W/C (F.FR 9000)
£941	$1665	(7-Apr-91 I.N112) Vase de fleurs (49x63cm-19x25in) s.d.1954 gouache W/C (F.FR 9500)
£1008	$1966	(22-Oct-90 MJ.P54/R) Lascive Arlette (65x65cm-26x26in) st. W/C gouache (F.FR 10000)
£1025	$2008	(11-Nov-90 ZZ.F110/R) Jeune femme au turban bleu (63x49cm-25x19in) s. W/C gouache (F.FR 10000)
£1058	$2064	(22-Oct-90 MJ.P80/R) Mireille au chapeau fleuri (50x65cm-20x26in) st. W/C gouache (F.FR 10500)
£1076	$2109	(11-Nov-90 ZZ.F255/R) Jeune femme sur le canape (49x63cm-19x25in) s. W/C (F.FR 10500)
£1158	$1888	(11-Jun-91 I.N48/R) Nu assis (59x46cm-23x18in) s. pastel ink wash col.crayons (F.FR 11500)
£1210	$2359	(22-Oct-90 MJ.P59/R) La belle Ursula (50x65cm-20x26in) d.1957 W/C gouache (F.FR 12000)
£1336	$2592	(5-Dec-90 ZZ.F15/R) Bouquet a l'atelier (59x46cm-23x18in) s. W/C gouache (F.FR 13000)
£1411	$2752	(28-Oct-90 G.SB29/R) Jeune femme a sa coiffure (64x49cm-25x19in) st.sig. W/C (F.FR 14000)
£1512	$2949	(22-Oct-90 MJ.P103/R) Apres la moisson (42x57cm-17x22in) s. W/C (F.FR 15000)
£1512	$2949	(22-Oct-90 MJ.P58/R) Marlene la Prussienne (65x50cm-26x20in) s. W/C (F.FR 15000)
£1518	$2976	(19-Nov-90 ARC.P12/R) Femme assise (60x44cm-24x17in) st.sig. Indian ink W/C (F.FR 15000)
£2083	$3583	(19-May-91 LT.P1/R) Jeune femme au fauteuil (46x49cm-18x19in) s. W/C (F.FR 21000)

DILL, Laddie John (1943-) American

£1538	$3000	(24-Oct-90 B.SF1588/R) Untitled, 1987 (152x91cm-60x36in) cement glass acrylic emulsion on wood

DILL, Ludwig (1848-1940) German

£514	$837	(12-Jun-91 N.M414) Fishing boats in calm sea (29x36cm-11x14in) s. canvas on board (DM 1500)
£574	$976	(27-May-91 L.K259) The seamstresses (12x16cm-5x6in) s. board (DM 1700)
£650	$1274	(24-Jan-91 CSK36) Fishermen with fishing boats (67x58cm-26x23in) s.
£1020	$1643	(28-Jun-91 BM.B662/R) Fishing boats before Venice (55x40cm-22x16in) s. (DM 3000)
£1082	$2100	(8-Dec-90 W.W125/R) Moored fishing boats (66x84cm-26x33in) s. board backed by panel
£1275	$2487	(10-Oct-90 WE.MU214/R) Fishing boats in harbour (45x61cm-18x24in) s. board (DM 3800)
£1419	$2767	(26-Oct-90 KM.K1183) Harbour scene with shipping and figures, Padua in Chioggia (49x64cm-19x25in) s. i.verso board (DM 4200)
£1505	$2543	(17-Apr-91 WE.MU227/R) Fishing boats in lagoon (65x85cm-26x33in) s. board (DM 4500)
£2397	$3908	(12-Jun-91 N.M412/R) Venetian fishing boats in lagoon with view of town beyond (64x48cm-25x19in) s. i.stretcher (DM 7000)
£2833	$5354	(25-Sep-90 FN.S2148/R) Wooded Amper landscape near Dachau in late summer after rainfalls (36x52cm-14x20in) s. i.verso canvas on board (DM 8300)
£4027	$7852	(12-Oct-90 AW.H2216/R) Landscape with stream in Dachauer Moos (50x65cm-20x26in) s. i.verso board (DM 12000)
£4196	$8140	(4-Dec-90 FN.S1804/R) Seascape with figures in fishing boats and other shipping in lagoon (31x50cm-12x20in) s. (DM 12000)
£8784	$14932	(28-May-91 KF.M597/R) Poplars in moor landscape (71x91cm-28x36in) s.i.d.1910 tempera paper on board (DM 26000)
£8784	$14932	(28-May-91 KF.M598/R) Men leading horses (102x120cm-40x47in) s.d.1918 (DM 26000)

DILL, Ludwig (attrib) (1848-1940) German
£949 $1585   (8-Jun-91 FN.S721/R) Moonlit lake landscape with thunderstorm rising and
                                fishermen in boat (22x31cm-9x12in) s. panel (DM 2800)

DILL, Otto (1884-1957) German
£685 $1116   (15-Jun-91 L.K154) Beduin tent in Sahara (24x30cm-9x12in) s. tempera oil
                                paper (DM 2000)
£2703 $4676   (21-May-91 WK.M795 a/R) Two rider in woodlands (36x49cm-14x19in) s.
                                s.stretcher (DM 8000)
£4068 $6793   (6-Jun-91 HN.H272/R) By the race track (49x69cm-19x27in) s.d.1922 board
                                (DM 12000)
£4281 $7663   (13-Mar-91 N.M475/R) African lions attacking (70x101cm-28x40in) s.d.1941
                                (DM 12500)
£4561 $7708   (3-May-91 SA.A760/R) The horse race (50x70cm-20x28in) s. (DM 13500)
£4778 $9365   (22-Nov-90 L.K900/R) Arabic camel riders (67x98cm-26x39in) s. board
                                (DM 14000)
£5017 $8478   (19-Apr-91 FN.S1506/R) Horse with jockey nr 2 beneath trees with race
                                course beyond (70x90cm-28x35in) s. s.i.d.1931verso board (DM 15000)
£6993 $13497   (12-Dec-90 SY.MU76/R) The horse race (58x78cm-23x31in) s.d.1923
                                (DM 20000)
£8741 $16871   (12-Dec-90 WE.MU149/R) At the start (61x80cm-24x31in) s.d.1935 panel
                                (DM 25000)
*£769 $1492   (7-Dec-90 GB.B6452) Tigers playing (31x23cm-12x9in) s.i.d.1928 indian
                                ink pen (DM 2200)*

DILLENS, Adolphe Alexander (1821-1877) Belgian
£1800 $3061   (28-May-91 C.A85) Le mariage (73x55cm-29x22in) s. (B.FR 110000)

DILLENS, Hendrick Joseph (1812-1872) Belgian
£1900 $3724   (22-Nov-90 CSK215/R) Returning from market (97x79cm-38x31in) s.d.1862

DILLER, Burgoyne (1906-1965) American
*£2551 $5000   (7-Nov-90 SY.NY179/R) First theme no 82-113 (35x28cm-14x11in) init.d.62
                                pastel col.pencil graphite*
*£6122 $12000   (7-Nov-90 SY.NY113/R) Second theme (27x27cm-11x11in) pastel crayon
                                vellum*

DILLER, Richard (1890-) ?
£1466 $2785   (28-Feb-91 D.V42/R) View of Linz (50x76cm-20x30in) s.d.1919 (A.S 30000)

DILLEY, Ramon (20th C) ?
£713 $1404   (29-Oct-90 LC.P153) La troika a Crans Montana (38x55cm-15x22in) s.d.87
                                i. verso (F.FR 7000)
£1633 $3167   (8-Dec-90 GAB.G2512/R) Vue de l'atelier a Bois-le-Vent (46x61cm-18x24in)
                                s. (S.FR 4000)
£4419 $8573   (8-Dec-90 LT.P75/R) Ceux du cote de Saint-Tropez (39x61cm-15x24in)
                                s.d.72 hardboard (F.FR 43000)
£5341 $9561   (8-Apr-91 CSC.P86/R) Celle des cures marines (46x55cm-18x22in) s.d.87 i.
                                verso (F.FR 54000)

DILLIS, Johann Georg von (1759-1841) German
*£586 $1126   (28-Nov-90 KF.M344/R) Southern landscape with viaduct and fortification,
                                possibly Grottaferrata (23x37cm-9x15in) pencil (DM 1700)*
*£793 $1523   (28-Nov-90 KF.M348) Young man with rapier and three cornered hat
                                (24x12cm-9x5in) W/C over pencil (DM 2300)*
*£828 $1589   (28-Nov-90 KF.M347) Landscape with farmhouses and figures
                                (15x22cm-6x9in) brush ober pencil (DM 2400)*
*£862 $1655   (28-Nov-90 KF.M351) Balthasar Kirchmaier (13x9cm-5x4in) W/C over pencil
                                (DM 2500)*
*£897 $1721   (28-Nov-90 KF.M342/R) Scene outside town walls (20x27cm-8x11in) chk
                                (DM 2600)*
*£1241 $2383   (28-Nov-90 KF.M343/R) Flight to Egypt in arcadian landscape
                                (21x26cm-8x10in) pen over pencil (DM 3600)*
*£1588 $2699   (28-May-91 KF.M153/R) View of Schloss Harlaching on the Isar. Study of
                                tree and woodlands (21x29cm-8x11in) mono. pen over pencil wash, pencil
                                double-sided (DM 4700)*
*£4054 $6892   (31-May-91 GB.B5496/R) Huntsman with dog (19x15cm-7x6in) indis.i. pencil
                                W/C (DM 12000)*
*£4138 $7945   (28-Nov-90 KF.M340/R) Lake Tegernsee with view of St Quirin and
                                monastery (24x32cm-9x13in) d.1825 pencil chk (DM 12000)*
*£17241 $33103   (28-Nov-90 KF.M338/R) Bridge over the Isar (24x37cm-9x15in) s.c.1806 W/C
                                over pen (DM 50000)*
*£43448 $83421   (28-Nov-90 KF.M337/R) Graf Rumford and Grafin Baumgarten with party in
                                wooded landscape (28x20cm-11x8in) s.d.1791 W/C over chk pencil
                                (DM 126000)*

DILLON, Gerard (1917-1971) Irish
£11111 $21444   (12-Dec-90 CH.E55/R) Dun Aengus, Aran Boat (40x50cm-16x20in) s. board
                                (E.P 12000)
£648 $1251   (12-Dec-90 CH.E28/R) Cat (15x26cm-6x10in) s. W/C (E.P 700)
£648 $1251   (12-Dec-90 CH.E29) Sleeping cat (28x36cm-11x14in) s. bodycol. (E.P 700)

DILOS, Giovanni (19/20th C) Italian
*£1199 $2146   (12-Mar-91 FN.S2335/R) Elegant party playing games in park landscape
                                (63x96cm-25x38in) s.indis.d. W/C (DM 3500)*

DINE, Jim (1935-) American
£7653	$15000	(14-Feb-91 CH.NY16/R) Untitled (101x96cm-40x38in) s.verso
£2033	$4065	(5-Feb-91 CSC.P86/R) Corner Brace (58x46cm-23x18in) s.i.d.1962 lead pencil (F.FR 20000)
£3553	$7000	(5-Oct-90 CH.NY46/R) Jet beads (76x56cm-30x22in) s.i.d.1961 W/C graphite
£3846	$6500	(2-May-91 CH.NY125/R) Screwdriver (75x51cm-30x20in) s.d.1962 graphite col.crayons
£4061	$8000	(5-Oct-90 CH.NY45/R) Three chairs (56x78cm-22x31in) s.i.d.1963 paper collage gouache graphite
£4082	$8000	(8-Nov-90 CH.NY144/R) Cucumber (35x28cm-14x11in) s.i.d.1972 W/C graphite
£4315	$8500	(5-Oct-90 CH.NY25/R) Untitled (121x90cm-48x35in) s.d.1960 gouache corrugated paper
£5584	$11000	(5-Oct-90 CH.NY49/R) Jessie sitting in 1979 (127x97cm-50x38in) s.d.1979 i.verso chl chk
£7107	$14000	(5-Oct-90 CH.NY41/R) Two ties (46x61cm-18x24in) s.d.1961 acrylic chl
£16272	$27500	(1-May-91 SY.NY260 a/R) Hearts (57x72cm-22x28in) s.d.1972 W/C
£19811	$38631	(23-Oct-90 F.M61/R) Untitled (76x114cm-30x45in) s.d.1988 mixed media cardboard (I.L 44000000)
£89286	$175000	(7-Nov-90 CH.NY36/R) Painting fortress for the heart (213x305cm-84x120in) s.i.d.1981 verso acrylic synth.resin on canvas

DINET, Etienne (1861-1929) French
£1376	$2656	(10-Dec-90 LD.P68/R) Rue Chardala la nuit (23x30cm-9x12in) s.d.1885 (F.FR 13500)
£7968	$13546	(27-May-91 APT.P266/R) La halte de la caravane (32x41cm-13x16in) s. hardboard (F.FR 80000)
£20513	$40000	(24-Oct-90 CH.NY95/R) Arab women and children (66x102cm-26x40in) s.
£28398	$54523	(17-Dec-90 ARC.P93/R) Les adieux (100x81cm-39x32in) s. (F.FR 280000)
£49595	$97206	(20-Nov-90 APT.P266/R) Costume de fete (81x100cm-32x39in) s.d.1907 (F.FR 490000)
£1318	$2531	(17-Dec-90 ARC.P11/R) Khadra, danesuese Ouled Nail (17x12cm-7x5in) s. gouache (F.FR 13000)
£2028	$3895	(17-Dec-90 ARC.P12/R) Tete d'homme (13x10cm-5x4in) s. crayon W/C gouache (F.FR 20000)

DINGENEN, Ferdinand van (19/20th C) Belgian?
£1227	$2087	(28-May-91 C.A326/R) The steamboat President Bunge (63x90cm-25x35in) s.d.1908 (B.FR 75000)

DINGLINGER, Georg Friedrich (1666-1720) German
£6531	$12865	(13-Nov-90 CH.G205/R) Augustus II the Strong, Elector of Saxony and King of Poland (4x?cm-2x?in) min. enamel gilt-metal bezel oval (S.FR 16000)

DINGLINGER, Georg Friedrich (attrib) (1666-1720) German
£800	$1536	(18-Dec-90 C34) Portrait of gentleman in purple coat with gold-laced buttons (7x?cm-3x?in) min.enamel gilt-metal frame oval

DIODATI, Francesco Paolo (1864-?) Italian
£500	$820	(18-Jun-91 PH162 b) The coast of Capri (46x57cm-18x22in) s. s.i.d.1921verso

DIOMEDE, Miguel (1902-1974) Argentinian
£780	$1350	(8-May-91 V.BA32) Baradero (18x32cm-7x13in)
£1447	$2850	(14-Nov-90 V.BA45) Paseantes en la ribera (22x35cm-9x14in)
£1882	$3500	(5-Sep-90 V.BA40) Hermanitas (49x23cm-19x9in)
£2861	$4950	(8-May-91 V.BA31/R) Sandia (40x50cm-16x20in)

DIRCKINCK-HOLMFELD, Helmuth (1835-1912) Danish
£890	$1673	(18-Sep-90 BU.K21/R) Herring fishing from Kullen, autumn afternoon (30x45cm-12x18in) i. (D.KR 10000)

DIRCKX, Anton (1878-1927) Dutch
£629	$1056	(23-Apr-91 SY.AM18) Dutch landscape (73x99cm-29x39in) s. (D.FL 2100)

DIRIKS, Edvard Karl (1855-1930) Norwegian
£935	$1805	(15-Dec-90 BU.H311) Small harbour (44x64cm-17x25in) s. (F.M 6500)
£963	$1724	(11-Mar-91 B.O20/R) Seated woman reading letter (46x38cm-18x15in) s.i.d.1903 panel (N.KR 11000)
£1226	$2194	(11-Mar-91 B.O19/R) French landscape (45x58cm-18x23in) s.d.1908 panel (N.KR 14000)
£1336	$2578	(12-Dec-90 BU.O12/R) Landscape with house (46x55cm-18x22in) s. (N.KR 15000)
£1655	$3227	(15-Oct-90 B.O19/R) Landscape, Oslo fjord (46x55cm-18x22in) s.d.1925 (N.KR 19000)
£1736	$3385	(11-Oct-90 BU.O21/R) Boats by harbour (28x40cm-11x16in) s. (N.KR 20000)
£2178	$4247	(15-Oct-90 B.O17/R) Cabin by the fjord (46x55cm-18x22in) s. panel (N.KR 25000)
£2491	$4858	(15-Oct-90 B.O16/R) Reclining female nude (35x43cm-14x17in) s. panel (N.KR 28600)
£3065	$5486	(14-Mar-91 BU.O20/R) Jetty in Drobak (45x64cm-18x25in) s.d.84 (N.KR 35000)
£3144	$5974	(11-Sep-90 UL.T187/R) In the garden (46x56cm-18x22in) (N.KR 36000)
£3472	$6771	(11-Oct-90 BU.O20/R) Autumn, Kristianiafjord (95x129cm-37x51in) s.i.d.1912 (N.KR 40000)
£4427	$7393	(3-Jun-91 B.O21/R) Bergen seen from Hotel Norge (97x125cm-38x49in) s.i.d.1912 (N.KR 51000)

DIRIKS, Edvard Karl (1855-1930) Norwegian-cont.
£4514 $8802   (11-Oct-90 BU.O22/R) Jetty in Drobak (80x125cm-31x49in) s.i.verso
                            (N.KR 52000)
£5343 $10312   (10-Dec-90 B.O19/R) Vessels in a calm, morning (56x70cm-22x28in) s.
                            (N.KR 60000)

DIRKS, Andreas (1866-1922) German
£816 $1314   (26-Jun-91 KM.K1434) Shipping off harbour (45x67cm-18x26in) s.
                            (DM 2400)
£1748 $3374   (10-Dec-90 L.K416) Frisian harbour (73x107cm-29x42in) s. (DM 5000)
£2081 $4057   (13-Oct-90 KRA.D200/R) North Sea coastal landscape with fishing boats
                            (100x140cm-39x55in) s. (DM 6200)

DISCEPOLI, Giovanni Battista (1590-1660) Italian
£3631 $6500   (11-Apr-91 SY.NY33/R) Saint Catherine (80x65cm-31x26in)
£638 $1130   (19-Mar-91 F.M160/R) Figura femminile che suona il violino. Studio di
                            busto e di braccio (26x17cm-10x7in) black chk white chk double-sided
                            (I.L 1400000)

DISCHLER, Hermann (1866-1935) German
£3000 $5070   (1-May-91 GD.B207/R) Sunrise (56x87cm-22x34in) s.d.1914 st.studio verso
                            (S.FR 7500)

DISEN, Andreas (1845-1923) Norwegian
£701 $1254   (11-Mar-91 B.O21/R) Alpine mountain landscape (66x99cm-26x39in) s.d.1916
                            (N.KR 8000)
£2819 $5582   (29-Jan-91 UL.T155/R) Norwegian river landscape (57x87cm-22x34in)
                            (N.KR 32000)
£3281 $6431   (24-Nov-90 HOR.H9/R) Foaming waterfall (50x68cm-20x27in) s.d.1891
                            (F.M 23000)

DISLER, Martin (1948-) Dutch?
£1878 $3699   (17-Nov-90 S.Z35) Untitled (120x88cm-47x35in) s.d.1984 acrylic
                            (S.FR 4600)
£8065 $15726   (26-Oct-90 CC.P117/R) Sans titre (162x292cm-64x115in) s. (F.FR 80000)
£325 $628   (15-Dec-90 S.Z80) Untitled (29x42cm-11x17in) s.d.1978 indian ink ball
                            point pen (S.FR 800)
£816 $1608   (16-Nov-90 GK.Z5351 a) Die wie ein Leopold gefleckte Insel
                            (21x29cm-8x11in) s.i.d.1973 W/C pencil (S.FR 2000)
£841 $1455   (22-May-91 CH.AM752) Head (27x37cm-11x15in) bodycol (D.FL 2800)
£1557 $2943   (28-Sep-90 S.Z117) Untitled (36x45cm-14x18in) s.d.82 pastel gouache
                            pencil (S.FR 3800)
£1837 $3618   (17-Nov-90 S.Z34) Untitled (29x42cm-11x17in) s.d.1982 gouache
                            (S.FR 4500)
£2179 $4250   (10-Oct-90 SY.NY463/R) Two faces (74x109cm-29x43in) s.d.84 chl gouache
£2449 $4824   (17-Nov-90 S.Z36/R) Untitled (70x70cm-28x28in) d.1980 acrylic indian ink
                            board (S.FR 6000)
£2449 $4824   (16-Nov-90 EA.Z319/R) Untitled (75x109cm-30x43in) s.d.84 mixed media
                            (S.FR 6000)
£2653 $5227   (16-Nov-90 GK.Z5351/R) Composition (56x76cm-22x30in) s.d.1982 gouache
                            (S.FR 6500)
£3200 $6240   (17-Oct-90 GG.Z59/R) Untitled (100x70cm-39x28in) s.d.1978 indian ink
                            brush (S.FR 8000)

DISMORR, Jessica (1885-1939) British
£1300 $2262   (27-Mar-91 S134/R) Hastings (41x32cm-16x13in) i. s.verso

DISNEY, Walt (studio) (20th C) American
£1156 $2000   (10-May-91 S.BM157/R) Scene from Snow White and the Seven Dwarfs
                            (30x33cm-12x13in) gouache

DITTRICH, Simon (1940-) ?
£541 $935   (21-May-91 WK.M797 a/R) Leuchtpistole (74x100cm-29x39in) s.
                            s.i.d.1970stretcher acrylic (DM 1600)

DIULGHEROFF, Nicolas (1901-1982) Bulgarian/Italian
£2000 $3920   (20-Nov-90 BR.M29/R) Dal ciclo Medea (38x57cm-15x22in) s.
                            s.i.d.1930verso tempera board (I.L 4400000)
£555 $1077   (3-Dec-90 F.M232/R) Autoritratto (37x22cm-15x9in) s.d.1924 indian ink
                            (I.L 1200000)
£2161 $4214   (22-Oct-90 BR.M330/R) Composizione (35x49cm-14x19in) s. collage tempera
                            board (I.L 4800000)

DIX, Otto (1891-1969) German
£6164 $10048   (15-Jun-91 L.K156/R) Portrait of painter Gortitz (47x34cm-19x13in)
                            s.i.d.1963 paper (DM 18000)
£10239 $20068   (24-Nov-90 VG.B117/R) Road in wooded landscape (48x41cm-19x16in)
                            s.d.1912/6 canvas on panel (DM 30000)
£15203 $26301   (21-May-91 WK.M16/R) Winter landscape with view of Schloss Osterstein,
                            evening (43x28cm-17x11in) s.d.1908 (DM 45000)
£17065 $33447   (24-Nov-90 VG.B119/R) Sachsenallee, Dresden (47x40cm-19x16in)
                            s.d.1912/17 (DM 50000)
£21959 $37331   (30-May-91 SY.BE56/R) Landscape with cart carrying wood
                            (54x73cm-21x29in) mono.d.46 (DM 65000)
£43919 $74662   (1-Jun-91 VG.B268/R) Flowering tree at banks of Lake Constance
                            (73x54cm-29x21in) mono.d.1951 panel (DM 130000)

DIX, Otto (1891-1969) German-cont.

£81081	$137838	(31-May-91 VG.B49/R) Village street in autumn, Hemmenhofen (81x100cm-32x39in) mono.d.1962 (DM 240000)
£579	$1100	(9-Jan-91 CH.NY248/R) Untitled (28x28cm-11x11in) s. chl
£1186	$2016	(27-May-91 GK.Z5562/R) Study of pilgrim (33x24cm-13x9in) mono.i.d.1942 pencil (S.FR 3000)
£1186	$2016	(27-May-91 GK.Z5563) Angel (31x22cm-12x9in) mono.d.1941 pencil (S.FR 3000)
£2712	$4529	(5-Jun-91 DO.H2568/R) Thugny I (32x28cm-13x11in) s.i.d.1915 chl (DM 8000)
£3041	$5169	(1-Jun-91 VG.B201/R) Portrait of chubby-cheeked young woman. Portrait of couple (33x27cm-13x11in) s. i.verso pencil double-sided (DM 9000)
£3968	$6508	(19-Jun-91 GK.B363/R) Old Anna II. Two female nudes (65x50cm-26x20in) s.d.1923 carpenter's pencil double-sided (S.FR 10000)
£4096	$8027	(22-Nov-90 L.K907/R) Alpine mountain range, spring (32x48cm-13x19in) W/C over pencil (DM 12000)
£4437	$8696	(22-Nov-90 L.K910/R) Village, Bethari (28x28cm-11x11in) s.i.d.1916 black chk (DM 13000)
£5461	$10703	(22-Nov-90 L.K906/R) View of Insel Reichenau (17x26cm-7x10in) W/C (DM 16000)
£5461	$10703	(22-Nov-90 L.K908/R) View across lake towards Steckborn (32x48cm-13x19in) W/C over pencil (DM 16000)
£6207	$11917	(28-Nov-90 KF.M679/R) Portrait of Ursus (59x45cm-23x18in) s.d.1930 ochre htd.white (DM 18000)
£6419	$10912	(30-May-91 SY.BE93/R) Portrait of woman (59x46cm-23x18in) mono.d.1930 ochre (DM 19000)
£7106	$11654	(19-Jun-91 F.M24/R) Nudo femminile (47x56cm-19x22in) d.1933 tempera chk (I.L 15500000)
£7143	$11714	(19-Jun-91 GK.B362/R) Stairs to shelter, west front (40x38cm-16x15in) s.d.1918 indian ink brush over pencil (S.FR 18000)
£8135	$13341	(19-Jun-91 GK.B365/R) Church of Samaden, Engadin (27x34cm-11x13in) mono.d.1938 i.verso W/C (S.FR 20500)
£8673	$17000	(14-Feb-91 CH.NY47/R) Bildnis der tanzerin Marianne Vogelsang (61x47cm-24x19in) mono.d.1931 gouache col.chk
£9122	$15780	(21-May-91 WK.M19/R) Annunciation (39x32cm-15x13in) mono. pastel paper on board (DM 27000)
£9122	$15780	(21-May-91 WK.M18/R) Study for St Lukas painting Madonna, selfportrait (42x34cm-17x13in) s. gouache pencil board squared for transfer (DM 27000)
£9215	$18061	(24-Nov-90 VG.B248/R) Susu I (52x35cm-20x14in) s.i.d.1964 pencil col.chk (DM 27000)
£10922	$21406	(22-Nov-90 L.K909/R) Untersee landscape (51x69cm-20x27in) s.d.55 W/C (DM 32000)
£10983	$19000	(9-May-91 CH.NY121/R) Hafen (49x37cm-19x15in) s.d.Dix 22/195 W/C gouache brush ink over pencil
£13652	$26758	(24-Nov-90 VG.B160/R) Dr Mayer-Hermann, face of demon (35x26cm-14x10in) s.i.d.1928 W/C bodycol gouache board (DM 40000)
£17347	$34000	(15-Feb-91 SY.NY73/R) Zwei Madchen (48x40cm-19x16in) s.d.22 i.verso W/C pencil
£27304	$53515	(22-Nov-90 L.K902/R) Portrait of Paula Kohler (84x65cm-33x26in) mono.i.d.1938 mixed media panel (DM 80000)
£32653	$64327	(16-Nov-90 GK.Z5177/R) Girl's head (33x28cm-13x11in) s.d.1922 W/C over indian ink brush pencil (S.FR 80000)
£68259	$133788	(22-Nov-90 L.K904/R) Elegant passing lady (49x39cm-19x15in) s.i.d.1922 W/C indian ink pen pencil (DM 200000)

DIXON, Alec R (20th C) ?

£3500	$6055	(22-May-91 S151/R) Sailing off Capetown (102x209cm-40x82in) s.d.1954 board shaped corners

DIXON, Anna (?-1959) British

£1200	$2328	(6-Dec-90 TL97/R) Evening on beach at Portobello, Edinburgh (30x40cm-12x16in) s.
£2400	$4032	(23-Apr-91 S131/R) Donkey ride (30x41cm-12x16in) s.

DIXON, Arthur P (fl.1884-1917) British

£1600	$3200	(5-Feb-91 S95/R) Gardener's daughter (34x25cm-13x10in) s.

DIXON, Charles (1872-1934) British

£1158	$2200	(15-Sep-90 S.W2402/R) Clipper ship in choppy seas (74x71cm-29x28in) s.d.1928
£1800	$3114	(22-May-91 S177/R) Gib (35x51cm-14x20in) s.i.d.1928
£2700	$5265	(15-Jan-91 SWS212/R) The bombardment of Lowestoft (35x98cm-14x39in) s.d.1918 pair
£300	$570	(25-Feb-91 PH98) Manitoba in blizzard (15x25cm-6x10in) s.i.d.94 W/C over pencil
£390	$722	(5-Mar-91 AG2561/R) The steam ship 'Deborah' ploughing through storm (45x73cm-18x29in) s.d.1917 monochrome gouache
£580	$1131	(15-Jan-91 SWS58/R) Low tide, Itchenor (13x8cm-5x3in) s. W/C bodycol
£650	$1118	(14-May-91 SWS32/R) Leaving the dock (34x24cm-13x9in) s.d.94 W/C
£750	$1410	(7-Aug-90 HS53) Three masted sailing ship in fresh sea (28x36cm-11x14in) s. W/C
£800	$1344	(24-Apr-91 MMB262/R) Shipping on Thames (28x18cm-11x7in) s.d.92 W/C
£800	$1384	(22-May-91 S142/R) Portsmouth (23x71cm-9x28in) s.d.09 W/C over pencil
£880	$1725	(8-Nov-90 PHI102/R) New York harbour at dusk (14x23cm-6x9in) s.d.94 W/C over pencil

DIXON, Charles (1872-1934) British-cont.

£950	$1872	*(13-Nov-90 SWS80/R) Battersea reach (18x54cm-7x21in) s.d.1914 W/C gouache*
£950	$1824	*(28-Nov-90 AH157) Cairo bridge (25x23cm-10x9in) d.1907 W/C*
£1200	$2304	*(26-Nov-90 SWS67/R) The Thames, Westminster (34x21cm-13x8in) s.d.92 W/C*
£1250	$2375	*(10-Jan-91 B66/R) Houses of Parliament with shipping on the Thames (34x24cm-13x9in) s.d.95 W/C htd.white*
£1300	$2184	*(15-Jul-91 PH126/R) On Lower Thames (26x76cm-10x30in) s.i.d.06 W/C bodycol*
£1350	$2322	*(15-May-91 BT97/R) Off Tilbury Docks (25x76cm-10x30in) s.i.d.1901 W/C*
£1350	$2322	*(15-May-91 BT96/R) Off Deptford (25x76cm-10x30in) s.i.d.'02 W/C*
£1400	$2338	*(4-Jun-91 SWS2124/R) Inland sea, Japan. Havana - views of Empress of Australia (36x53cm-14x21in) s.i.d.1928 W/C gouache over pencil pair*
£1750	$3325	*(27-Feb-91 MMB160/R) The Ship Inn, Itchenor (25x38cm-10x15in) s.i.d.1932 bodycol.*
£1900	$3173	*(22-Jul-91 SWS846/R) Constantinople (27x79cm-11x31in) s.i.d.1910 W/C htd.bodycol.*
£2000	$3400	*(30-May-91 C60/R) Shipping in Thames estuary (23x71cm-9x28in) s.d.98 pencil W/C htd white*
£2000	$3960	*(30-Jan-91 S198/R) View of Houses of Parliament from Embankment (36x52cm-14x20in) s.d.1930 W/C*
£2300	$4554	*(30-Jan-91 S195/R) St Paul's from Thames (36x52cm-14x20in) s.d.1928 W/C htd bodycol*
£2400	$4152	*(22-May-91 S201/R) In Mersey (39x56cm-15x22in) s.i.d.98 W/C htd white*
£2800	$5460	*(18-Oct-90 CSK64/R) The Lower Pool (23x71cm-9x28in) s.i.d.02 pencil W/C htd white*
£3000	$5700	*(27-Feb-91 MMB159/R) Yachts racing off a South Coast town (18x41cm-7x16in) s.d.1931 bodycol.over pencil*
£3000	$5760	*(26-Nov-90 SWS70/R) The Thames at St Paul's (38x27cm-15x11in) s.i.d.06 W/C*
£3200	$5536	*(22-May-91 S202/R) Loading (39x56cm-15x22in) s.i.d.98 W/C htd white*
£4200	$8274	*(12-Nov-90 PH54/R) The Lower Pool (26x61cm-10x24in) s.i.d.'09 W/C*
£5000	$8400	*(23-Apr-91 GAM161/R) Big class finishing, RNYC regatta with Britannia in left background (49x75cm-19x30in) s.d.05 i.verso W/C bodycol*
£5800	$11136	*(26-Nov-90 SWS71/R) The farewell (76x55cm-30x22in) s.d.34 W/C*
£8500	$14705	*(22-May-91 S117/R) Pool of London (70x126cm-28x50in) s.d.1903 W/C htd bodycol*

DIXON, Emily (fl.1885-1886) British

£1050	$2058	*(22-Jan-91 PH51) Picking flowers (58x40cm-23x16in) s.*

DIXON, Gertrude Nellie (20th C) British

£890	$1575	*(19-Mar-91 SHER39/R) Babe in woods - little girl in sunlit wood (48x58cm-19x23in) s.*

DIXON, Leng (1916-1968) South African

£1771	$3010	*(27-May-91 SY.J615/R) Panorama of Cape Town (38x148cm-15x58in) s.d.1947 pen W/C htd.white (SA.R 8500)*

DIXON, Maynard (1875-1946) American

£65089	$110000	*(1-May-91 B.SF5182/R) Navajo women in Canyon de Chelly, Arizona (127x102cm-50x40in) s.d.1915*
£2423	$4750	*(7-Nov-90 B.SF3788 a/R) Indian mother and child (20x13cm-8x5in) s.d.1904 pastel W/C*
£4847	$9500	*(13-Feb-91 B.SF2139/R) Palominos (42x98cm-17x39in) s.d.1941 gouache*

DIXON, Otto Murray (19/20th C) British

£1000	$1680	*(15-Jul-91 PH167/R) Spring in fens - snipe and teal (46x35cm-18x14in) s.d.1914 W/C bodycol*

DIXON, William (attrib) (18/19th C) British

£1800	$3546	*(31-Oct-90 S370/R) The Moonlight Battle of St Vincent, January 16th, 1780 (68x89cm-27x35in) after Richard Paton*

DIZIANI, Antonio (18th C) Italian

£18974	$37000	*(11-Oct-90 SY.NY118/R) Scenes from the story of Bertoldino (53x70cm-21x28in) pair*
£20513	$40000	*(11-Oct-90 SY.NY128/R) Landscape with the episode of Balaam and the Ass (94x134cm-37x53in)*

DIZIANI, Antonio (circle) (18th C) Italian

£2449	$4824	*(14-Nov-90 D.V234/R) River landscape with figures in boat and village with tower beyond (75x96cm-30x38in) (A.S 50000)*

DIZIANI, Gaspare (1689-1767) Italian

£7000	$13510	*(11-Dec-90 PH195/R) The Martyrdom of St.Stephen (66x42cm-26x17in)*
£22000	$35860	*(3-Jul-91 S6/R) Adoration of magi (95x77cm-37x30in)*
£24000	$40560	*(19-Apr-91 C133/R) The rest on the flight into Egypt (18x128cm-7x50in)*
£39082	$69956	*(14-Mar-91 D.V27/R) The Return of the Arc of Covenant (47x81cm-19x32in) (A.S 800000)*
£52632	$100000	*(11-Jan-91 CH.NY31/R) Hercules, Deianeira and Centaur Nessus (79x97cm-31x38in)*
£1094	$1937	*(19-Mar-91 F.M236/R) L'Ultima Cena (36x20cm-14x8in) pen bistre W/C ink htd white (I.L 2400000)*
£1106	$1813	*(18-Jun-91 APT.P40/R) Adoration des mages (16x24cm-6x9in) ink wash (F.FR 11000)*

DIZIANI, Gaspare (1689-1767) Italian-cont.
£1140 $2018   (19-Mar-91 F.M278/R) Studio per soffitto con figure allegoriche (42x29cm-17x11in) ink W/C squared (I.L 2500000)
£1368 $2421   (19-Mar-91 F.M335/R) Due episodi della vita di Ercole. Studio per il rartto di Dejanira (36x25cm-14x10in) ink W/C chk double-sided (I.L 3000000)
£2100 $3423   (1-Jul-91 S208/R) Allegorical figure in clouds (28x26cm-11x10in) pen wash over red chk
£2800 $4732   (16-Apr-91 C183/R) The Adoration of the Magi (57x41cm-22x16in) i. ink wash htd.white
£2800 $4732   (16-Apr-91 C98/R) The Sacrifice of Isaac (20x16cm-8x6in) ink
£3192 $5650   (19-Mar-91 F.M176/R) Presentazione al Tempio. Studio di nudo maschile visto di schiena (27x19cm-11x7in) pen W/C ink sanguine double-sided (I.L 7000000)

DIZIANI, Gaspare (attrib) (1689-1767) Italian
£2041 $3959   (8-Dec-90 GAB.G2059/R) Vierge a l'enfant, St Michel terrassant le dragon, St Sebastien et St Jacques (61x39cm-24x15in) (S.FR 5000)
£450 $797   (21-Mar-91 LC.P5/R) Moise faisant jaillir la source du rocher (18x26cm-7x10in) pen crayon (F.FR 4500)

DIZIANI, Gaspare (circle) (1689-1767) Italian
£1149 $2000   (27-Mar-91 B.SF4023/R) The marble cutters (14x22cm-6x9in) panel
£4560 $7616   (4-Jun-91 CH.R131/R) Ercole e Onfale (135x96cm-53x38in) (I.L 10000000)

DIZIANI, Gaspare (style) (1689-1767) Italian
£950 $1549   (2-Jul-91 PH197) Mountainous river landscape with shepherdess and sheep and riders beyond (61x74cm-24x29in)

DMITRIENKO, Pierre (1920-) French
£3838 $6333   (10-Jul-91 FB.P61/R) Casque (27x22cm-11x9in) s. d.1969 verso (F.FR 38500)
£6275 $10667   (2-Jun-91 LT.P112/R) Usine (100x81cm-39x32in) s.d.53 (F.FR 63000)
£6552 $12777   (28-Oct-90 GL.P42/R) Composition (38x46cm-15x18in) s.d.53 (F.FR 65000)
£6751 $13030   (13-Dec-90 CH.BR136/R) Composition (65x81cm-26x32in) s.d.54 (B.FR 400000)
£11256 $20149   (17-Mar-91 GL.P88/R) Auvergne (130x97cm-51x38in) s.d.1958 i. verso (F.FR 112000)
£25628 $42030   (23-Jun-91 P.V25/R) Presence opalisante (100x81cm-39x32in) s. verso (F.FR 255000)
£1608 $2637   (21-Jun-91 OD.P1/R) Composition (63x47cm-25x19in) s.d.1957 W/C (F.FR 16000)
£3163 $6232   (15-Nov-90 I.N94/R) Presence (26x19cm-10x7in) s.d.1970 W/C (F.FR 31000)
£3528 $6880   (26-Oct-90 CC.P5/R) Sans titre (53x44cm-21x17in) s.d. goauche (F.FR 35000)

DMITRIEV-ORENBURGSKY, Nikolai (1838-1898) Russian
£6000 $11520   (27-Nov-90 C50/R) The blessing of the waters (48x74cm-19x29in) s.i.d.1785

DOBASHI, Jun (1917-) Japanese/French
£610 $1220   (10-Feb-91 CC.P22 a) Nebuleuse (21x26cm-8x10in) s. gouache (F.FR 6000)

DOBBIN, John (19th C) British
£620 $1172   (27-Sep-90 PHF196/R) Figures in Chapel of Santiago, Toleda Cathedral, Spain (74x62cm-29x24in) s.i.d.1869 label verso W/C
£620 $1178   (12-Sep-90 CSK202/R) Figures in continental square, cathedral beyond (58x41cm-23x16in) s.d.1875 W/C htd white

DOBELI, Johann Othmar (1874-1922) Swiss
£960 $1622   (1-May-91 GD.B209/R) Farmhouse on the Geishubel near Rothrist (23x28cm-9x11in) s.d.1915 i.verso board (S.FR 2400)
£1040 $1758   (1-May-91 GD.B210/R) Farmhouse on the Schneckenberg (23x28cm-9x11in) s.d.1915 i.verso board (S.FR 2600)
£1071 $1789   (7-Jun-91 ZOF.Z1305) Farmhouse near Zofingen (23x29cm-9x11in) d.1911 i.st.studio verso board (S.FR 2700)
£1116 $2175   (24-Oct-90 GD.B295) Farmhouses with well and tree (25x36cm-10x14in) s.d.1915 panel (S.FR 2800)
£1349 $2253   (7-Jun-91 ZOF.Z1300) Allemanic house near Bottenwil, winter (60x75cm-24x30in) s.d.1917 (S.FR 3400)
£1389 $2319   (7-Jun-91 ZOF.Z1302) Farmhouse by the edge of wood (60x75cm-24x30in) s.d.1919 (S.FR 3500)
£1508 $2518   (7-Jun-91 ZOF.Z1303/R) Winter landscape in Gland near Vordemwald s.d.1919 (S.FR 3800)
£1548 $2585   (7-Jun-91 ZOF.Z1299) Woodland path (75x60cm-30x24in) s.d.1921 (S.FR 3900)
£1746 $2916   (7-Jun-91 ZOF.Z1301) Farmhouse in Saget (59x75cm-23x30in) s.d.1917 (S.FR 4400)
£2143 $3579   (7-Jun-91 ZOF.Z1304/R) Autumn fire, Zofinger Heiternplatz (78x122cm-31x48in) s.d.1917 (S.FR 5400)

DOBELL, Sir William (1899-1970) Australian
£1415 $2307   (1-Jul-91 AAA.S129) Storm regatta (9x18cm-4x7in) s. verso board (A.D 3000)
£2679 $4661   (26-Mar-91 JRL.S181/R) Study of Florence Bertwistle (25x20cm-10x8in) board (A.D 6000)

DOBELL, Sir William (1899-1970) Australian-cont.

£3620	$6118	(16-Apr-91 J.M163/R) Study for the Rock Fisherman (16x18cm-6x7in) board (A.D 8000)
£3785	$7456	(31-Oct-90 CH.S103/R) Farm (8x26cm-3x10in) s. board (A.D 9500)
£6773	$13343	(31-Oct-90 CH.S81/R) Boating, Lake Macquarie (20x29cm-8x11in) s. board (A.D 17000)
£18605	$31256	(22-Apr-91 SY.ME224/R) Aspen trees, 1940 (32x36cm-13x14in) s. board (A.D 40000)
£19277	$37012	(26-Nov-90 SY.ME257/R) Harvest (26x34cm-10x13in) s. board (A.D 48000)
£55814	$93767	(22-Apr-91 SY.ME332/R) Smoko (76x69cm-30x27in) s.indist.d.50 board (A.D 120000)
£1275	$2512	(31-Oct-90 CH.S104/R) Aviaries at Nondugl (11x19cm-4x7in) s.i. gouache (A.D 3200)
£3286	$5390	(17-Jun-91 MGS.S318) Reclining nude (23x35cm-9x14in) gouache (A.D 7000)

DOBIASCHOFSKY, Frantz (1818-1867) Austrian

| £26508 | $52221 | (14-Nov-90 F.M50/R) Ritratto di due ragazzi in un paesaggio (147x118cm-58x46in) s.d.1849 (I.L 58000000) |

DOBOUJINSKY, Mstislav (1875-1957) Russian

| £5128 | $10000 | (10-Oct-90 SY.NY121/R) City by the river (69x173cm-27x68in) s.i.d.1919 W/C gouache graphite |

DOBRINSKY, Yitzhak (1891-1973) Russian

£890	$1593	(14-Apr-91 GL.P164) Garçonnet en bleu (25x27cm-10x11in) s. i.d.1950-1951 verso (F.FR 9000)
£890	$1593	(14-Apr-91 GL.P168) Garçonnet sur fond gris (35x27cm-14x11in) s. (F.FR 9000)
£1152	$2200	(1-Jan-91 GG.TA280/R) Portrait of woman with hat (66x44cm-26x17in) s. board
£1204	$2300	(1-Jan-91 GG.TA281/R) Nude (38x61cm-15x24in) s.

DOBROWOLSKI, Waclaw (1890-1969) Russian

| £747 | $1270 | (29-May-91 RCJ.P142/R) Guerre contre l'analphabetisme (92x130cm-36x51in) s.d.1949 (F.FR 7500) |

DOBROWSKY, Josef (1889-1962) Austrian

£1553	$2548	(20-Jun-91 D.V154/R) Blue jug with flowers (30x19cm-12x7in) mono. panel (A.S 32000)
£4850	$9117	(20-Sep-90 D.V199/R) The Danube near Ybbs (50x70cm-20x28in) mono. board (A.S 100000)
£5742	$9933	(8-May-91 D.V122/R) Corn stooks in hilly landscape (54x76cm-21x30in) mono. panel (A.S 120000)
£5789	$11288	(18-Oct-90 D.V157/R) Landscape, Niederosterreich (47x71cm-19x28in) s. panel (A.S 120000)
£5825	$9553	(20-Jun-91 D.V155/R) Kohlgraben (60x69cm-24x27in) mono. i.verso oil tempera (A.S 120000)
£7455	$14463	(6-Dec-90 D.V104/R) Still life with fish (74x100cm-29x39in) mono.d.44 (A.S 150000)
£579	$1129	(18-Oct-90 D.V118/R) Maria Lichtmess (50x44cm-20x17in) s.d.35 chk W/C gouache (A.S 12000)
£584	$1145	(24-Jan-91 D.V161/R) Portrait of woman (55x41cm-22x16in) pastel (A.S 12000)
£675	$1100	(14-Jun-91 W.W21) Village by the river (48x66cm-19x26in) s.d.50 gouache
£681	$1335	(24-Jan-91 D.V164/R) Portrait of lady (67x49cm-26x19in) mono. pastel (A.S 14000)
£728	$1194	(20-Jun-91 D.V97/R) Self portrait (59x42cm-23x17in) s.i.d.1938 chk (A.S 15000)
£736	$1200	(14-Jun-91 W.W20/R) August meadow (48x66cm-19x26in) s.d.50 gouache
£795	$1543	(6-Dec-90 D.V126/R) Portrait of girl with plaits (53x47cm-21x19in) s. s.d.1932 pastel (A.S 16000)
£886	$1773	(7-Feb-91 D.V29/R) Portrait of woman (56x41cm-22x16in) pastel (A.S 18000)
£973	$1908	(24-Jan-91 D.V176/R) Reclining female nude (47x63cm-19x25in) mono. pastel (A.S 20000)
£1074	$1986	(7-Mar-91 D.V207/R) Portrait of lady wearing hat with veil (93x48cm-37x19in) mono. pastel (A.S 22000)
£1359	$2229	(20-Jun-91 D.V111/R) Portrait of young woman (63x48cm-25x19in) s.d.43 pastel (A.S 28000)
£1557	$3052	(24-Jan-91 D.V189/R) Danube near Grein (50x67cm-20x26in) s.d.53 W/C gouache (A.S 32000)
£1818	$3145	(8-May-91 D.V123/R) St Margarethen, Burgenland (50x70cm-20x28in) W/C gouache (A.S 38000)
£1818	$3145	(8-May-91 D.V124/R) Woodland path in St Margarethen (49x64cm-19x25in) s. W/C gouache (A.S 38000)
£2485	$4821	(6-Dec-90 D.V68/R) Female nude with blue cap and fur cape (72x57cm-28x22in) mono. pastel (A.S 50000)
£2670	$4379	(20-Jun-91 D.V108/R) Two jugs with flowers (62x44cm-24x17in) s. W/C gouache (A.S 55000)
£2670	$4379	(20-Jun-91 D.V109/R) Gladiolies (64x50cm-25x20in) mono. W/C gouache (A.S 55000)
£2913	$4777	(20-Jun-91 D.V103/R) Yellow house in winter landscape (48x63cm-19x25in) s.d.39 W/C gouache (A.S 60000)
£3398	$5573	(20-Jun-91 D.V107/R) Gladiolies (60x45cm-24x18in) s. W/C gouache (A.S 70000)

DOBROWSKY, Josef (1889-1962) Austrian-cont.
£3641 $5971   (20-Jun-91 D.V106/R) White peonies (61x46cm-24x18in) s.d.1960 W/C
                  gouache (A.S 75000)
£3883 $6369   (20-Jun-91 D.V105/R) Tulips and other spring flowers in jug
                  (62x48cm-24x19in) s. W/C gouache (A.S 80000)
£4369 $7165   (20-Jun-91 D.V104/R) Two jugs with flowers (70x55cm-28x22in) s.d.37 W/C
                  gouache (A.S 90000)
£4970 $9642   (6-Dec-90 D.V90/R) Harvest near St Margarethen in Burgenland
                  (46x62cm-18x24in) s.d.61 mixed media (A.S 100000)

DOBSON, Frank (1888-1963) British
£320 $557   (28-Mar-91 CSK19) Reclining nude (38x30cm-15x12in) pencil
£600 $1176   (24-Jan-91 CSK131/R) Seated female nude (47x30cm-19x12in) pastel chl
£650 $1274   (25-Jan-91 C7/R) Kinsley, Hampshire (24x34cm-9x13in) s.d. pencil brush
                  ink gouache
£1000 $1940   (6-Dec-90 CSK21/R) Standing female nude (51x35cm-20x14in) s.d.34 brown
                  chk
£1200 $2328   (6-Dec-90 CSK61/R) Landscape with vineyards (33x49cm-13x19in) s.d.31
                  soft pencil W/C

DOBSON, Henry John (1858-?) British
£950 $1862   (22-Nov-90 CG596/R) Grandma peeling potatoes (36x46cm-14x18in) s.
£1300 $2561   (1-Nov-90 CSK132/R) Grandfather's pet. Indoor cat (46x36cm-18x14in) s.
                  pair

DOBSON, Robert (19th C) British
£340 $609   (13-Mar-91 B84) Harvesters in a coastal field (28x40cm-11x16in) s.d.1879
                  W/C
£515 $876   (27-May-91 HO.ED61/R) Scottish rainbow (60x91cm-24x36in) s.d. W/C paper
                  on board (C.D 1000)

DOBSON, W (1610-1646) British
£966 $1623   (27-Apr-91 SO.S307/R) Girl with jug s. oval (S.KR 10200)

DOBSON, William (circle) (1610-1646) British
£1300 $2171   (3-Jun-91 PHB83/R) Portrait of Jacob, Lord Astley wearing armour
                  (79x71cm-31x28in)

DOBSON, William (style) (1610-1646) British
£1600 $3120   (22-Oct-90 SWS1317/R) Portrait of gentleman, wearing jerkin and sash
                  (75x62cm-30x24in)

DOBSON, William Charles Thomas (1817-1898) British
£1176 $1988   (16-Apr-91 J.M28/R) Young boy (31x26cm-12x10in) mono.d.1883 (A.D 2600)
£1750 $2940   (24-Apr-91 MMB414/R) Young girl reading book in interior
                  (43x36cm-17x14in) mono.
£9000 $17010   (26-Sep-90 S293/R) Mother's care (65x50cm-26x20in) mono.d.1872 W/C htd
                  bodycol

DOBYASCHOFSKY, Franz Joseph (1818-1867) Austrian
£2500 $4750   (14-Sep-90 SA.A1155/R) The little narcissus (61x77cm-24x30in) oval
                  (DM 7400)

DOCHARTY, A Brownlie (1862-1940) British
£1300 $2431   (28-Aug-90 S748/R) Early summer in the Highlands (61x91cm-24x36in) s.

DOCHARTY, James (1829-1878) British
£600 $1014   (3-May-91 PHE161) The temple at Philae (30x61cm-12x24in) i.verso
£1000 $1950   (17-Oct-90 PHG38) A dangerous pool, Glen Etive (45x60cm-18x24in) s.

DOCKREE, Mark Edwin (19th C) British
£600 $1002   (4-Jun-91 SWS1748) Vaynor Wood, Montgomery (21x29cm-8x11in) s. s.i.verso

DODD, Arthur Charles (fl.1878-1890) British
£900 $1665   (4-Mar-91 PHB48/R) Old Covert hack (61x46cm-24x18in) s. i.num.25 verso

DODD, Francis (1874-1949) British
£1000 $1880   (20-Sep-90 C150/R) Saturday afternoon (70x84cm-28x33in) s.indist.d.

DODD, J (19th C) ?
£2493 $4213   (16-Apr-91 CH.R23) The Forum Rome, now Campo Vaccino (42x71cm-17x28in)
                  s.i.d.1886 W/C (I.L 5500000)

DODD, Joseph Josiah (1809-1880) British
£1050 $1995   (15-Sep-90 ME172) Plas Llanfair, Bangor (28x41cm-11x16in) s. W/C

DODD, Louis (20th C) British
£2000 $3460   (22-May-91 S105/R) New Bedford whalers in Arctic Ocean, 1865
                  (43x63cm-17x25in) s. panel
£2000 $3460   (22-May-91 S104/R) Nyria close hauled in good breeze (65x105cm-26x41in)
                  s. panel
£4200 $7266   (22-May-91 S107/R) American armed merchant ship saluting St. George's
                  Castle from Commerce Square, Lisbon (48x79cm-19x31in) s. panel

DODD, Louis (attrib) (20th C) British
£650 $1073   (9-Jul-91 PH3) Figures and sailing vessels on coast (46x63cm-18x25in)
                   panel

DODD, Robert (1748-1816) British
£5000 $8500   (30-May-91 C81/R) Battle of Glorious First of June 1794
                   (62x91cm-24x36in)

DODDERIDGE, Christopher (1946-) British
£750 $1470   (13-Feb-91 B177) In my room (71x84cm-28x33in) s.i.d.1990 verso panel

DODEIGNE, Eugene (20th C) French
£305 $610   (6-Feb-91 FB.P93) Personnages (57x46cm-22x18in) s. chl.htd.oil crayon
                   (F.FR 3000)
£473 $912   (13-Dec-90 CH.BR53/R) Deux nus (62x48cm-24x19in) s.d.1961 pencil
                   (B.FR 28000)
£844 $1629   (13-Dec-90 CH.BR28) Elegante assise (75x55cm-30x22in) s. chl
                   (B.FR 50000)

DODERIQUE (20th C) Belgian?
£592 $1154   (23-Oct-90 C.A197) Figures (110x75cm-43x30in) s.d.1970 drawing
                   (B.FR 36000)

DODSON, Tom (20th C) British
£1800 $3528   (6-Nov-90 CD594/R) Crowd watching rugby league match at Salford Stadium
                   (48x58cm-19x23in) s.d.1975
£2600 $5096   (6-Nov-90 CD593/R) Street scene with numerous figures moving towards
                   Swinton rugby football ground (48x58cm-19x23in) s.d.1975

DOERNER, Adolf (1892-?) German
£833 $1492   (12-Apr-91 BM.B723/R) Bowl with fruit and vase with summer flowers on
                   table (64x78cm-25x31in) mono.d.23 i.verso (DM 2500)

DOERR, Charles Augustin Victor (1815-1894) French
£8657 $15063   (27-Mar-91 CN.P75/R) Le chien d'Alcibiade (97x130cm-38x51in)
                   (F.FR 87000)

DOES, Simon van der (1653-1717) Dutch
£1014 $1976   (26-Oct-90 BM.B712/R) Hilly landscape with fountain, shepherds with
                   flocks and view of village (41x51cm-16x20in) s. panel (DM 3000)
£1224 $2412   (14-Nov-90 D.V185/R) Shepherds with flock in landscape (36x45cm-14x18in)
                   one of pair (A.S 25000)
£1567 $3087   (14-Nov-90 D.V186/R) Shepherd scene in wooded landscape
                   (36x45cm-14x18in) one of pair (A.S 32000)
£3175 $5684   (14-Mar-91 D.V224/R) Shepherd scene in the Roman Campagna
                   (41x51cm-16x20in) s.d.1711 panel (A.S 65000)

DOESBURG, Theo van (attrib) (1883-1931) Dutch
£706 $1376   (18-Jan-91 GL.P171) Groom assis (16x11cm-6x4in) s.d.1911 W/C lead pencil
                   (F.FR 7000)

DOESER, Jacobus (1884-1969) Dutch
£900 $1611   (14-Mar-91 L299/R) Potatoe pickers beneath sunny skies (89x99cm-35x39in)
                   s. i.verso

DOFFEGNIES, Thomasine Adrienne (1865-1937) Dutch
£1257 $2188   (26-Mar-91 VN.R19) Still life of flowers (46x62cm-18x24in) s.
                   (D.FL 4200)

DOGARTH, E J (1927-) Austrian
£550 $952   (22-May-91 CSK246) Still life of mixed flowers in glass bowl on marble
                   ledge (41x29cm-16x11in) s. board

DOGARTH, Oskar Robert (1898-1961) Austrian
£1440 $2476   (16-May-91 D.V28/R) Still life of flowers (40x30cm-16x12in) s. panel
                   (A.S 30000)

DOGGETT, Ruth T (fl.1915-1938) British
£600 $1032   (15-May-91 BT232/R) Long Melford, Suffolk (38x76cm-15x30in) s.i.d.1934
                   stretcher

DOHANOS, Stevan (1907-) American
£10588 $18000   (1-Jun-91 IH.NY34/R) New Year's Day clean up in Times Square
                   (76x61cm-30x24in) s. board
£719 $1200   (26-Jul-91 E.EDM199/R) Water hunters (41x43cm-16x17in) s. casein paper
£1676 $3000   (14-Mar-91 CH.NY123/R) Dunhams of Maine (63x75cm-25x30in) s. gouache W/C
                   pencil paper on board
£2910 $5500   (25-Sep-90 CE.NY288/R) Bookbinder's Saloon, Philadelphia
                   (60x128cm-24x50in) s. brush ink gouache en grisaille board

DOHLMANN, Augusta (1847-1914) Austrian
£836 $1405   (22-Apr-91 BU.K47/R) Still life of fruit, jug and books on table
                   (59x47cm-23x19in) mono.d.1881 (D.KR 9500)
£884 $1662   (10-Aug-90 RAS.V450/R) Still life of roses in vase on table
                   (45x36cm-18x14in) mono.d.89 (D.KR 10000)

DOHLMANN, Augusta (1847-1914) Austrian-cont.
£1038 $2014   (22-Aug-90 RAS.K185) Still life of oysters and lemons (51x64cm-20x25in) mono. (D.KR 12000)
£1326 $2493   (10-Aug-90 RAS.V449/R) Still life of flowers in vase on stone ledge (68x50cm-27x20in) (D.KR 15000)
£1346 $2653   (14-Nov-90 RAS.K625/R) Chrysanthemums (105x83cm-41x33in) s.d.93 (D.KR 15000)
£2513 $4952   (14-Nov-90 RAS.K85 a/R) Dahlias and beech leaves in vase (67x51cm-26x20in) (D.KR 28000)
£3028 $5874   (22-Aug-90 RAS.K105/R) Still life of blue iris and lilacs in clear vase (75x55cm-30x22in) s.d.93 (D.KR 35000)

DOIGNEAU, Edouard Edmond de (1865-1954) French
£2143 $4221   (13-Nov-90 ARC.P162/R) Campement. Deux chameaux (47cm-19ins circular) both s. pair round (F.FR 21000)
£3061 $6031   (13-Nov-90 ARC.P168/R) Campement (50x61cm-20x24in) s. board (F.FR 30000)
£609 $1168   (17-Dec-90 ARC.P27) A la fontaine (54x65cm-21x26in) init. W/C (F.FR 6000)
£918 $1809   (13-Nov-90 ARC.P108) Berberes aubec attatichs. Deux chevaux (46x42cm-18x17in) mono. W/C gouache crayon double-sided (F.FR 9000)
£1268 $2434   (17-Dec-90 ARC.P18/R) Marocains a cheval (31x39cm-12x15in) init. W/C gouache (F.FR 12500)
£1521 $2921   (17-Dec-90 ARC.P26/R) Retour du marche (61x50cm-24x20in) s. gouache paper laid down on board (F.FR 15000)

DOKOUPIL, Jiri Georg (1954-) Czechoslovakian
£1695 $2831   (8-Jun-91 HN.H88/R) Composition (100x100cm-39x39in) mono.d.1983 verso acrylic (DM 5000)
£3571 $7000   (6-Nov-90 CE.NY239/R) Untitled (61x50cm-24x20in) s.d.1987 verso acrylic
£6091 $12000   (4-Oct-90 SY.NY252/R) Untitled (216x251cm-85x99in) init.d.83 acrylic canvas
£591 $1158   (20-Nov-90 BR.M124/R) Foresta (30x41cm-12x16in) mono.d.1988 chl (I.L 1300000)
£818 $1604   (20-Nov-90 BR.M99/R) Julio (30x42cm-12x17in) mono.d.1988 ink (I.L 1800000)
£2143 $4200   (14-Feb-91 CH.NY73/R) Untitled (68x50cm-27x20in) s.i. col.chk

DOLCI, Carlo (1616-1686) Italian
£2443 $4372   (14-Mar-91 D.V12/R) Christ Child as Salvator Mundi (18x8cm-7x3in) copper (A.S 50000)
£11000 $17930   (5-Jul-91 C234/R) Virgin annunciate (65x54cm-26x21in) painted oval
£22000 $38060   (24-May-91 N.C53/R) Saint Matthew (40x27cm-16x11in) l. verso panel
£2027 $3446   (31-May-91 GB.B5109/R) Study of young man's head (15x11cm-6x4in) chk ochre (DM 6000)

DOLCI, Carlo (after) (17th C) Italian
£1400 $2800   (7-Feb-91 C29/R) The Mater Dolorosa (82x67cm-32x26in)
£2200 $4180   (13-Sep-90 CSK311) Portrait of woman, wearing laurel wreath (55x42cm-22x17in)

DOLCI, Carlo (attrib) (1616-1686) Italian
£4200 $6846   (5-Jul-91 C225/R) Saint Agatha (68x53cm-27x21in)
£956 $1873   (24-Jan-91 AGS.P114) Tete d'homme (13x9cm-5x4in) sanguinne pierre noire (F.FR 9500)

DOLCI, Carlo (studio) (17th C) Italian
£2800 $5516   (31-Oct-90 S74/R) St Cecilia (68x53cm-27x21in)

DOLCI, Carlo (style) (17th C) Italian
£889 $1724   (4-Dec-90 R.T309/R) Virgin and Child (99x74cm-39x29in) (C.D 2000)
£1150 $1990   (20-May-91 SWS185/R) Poetry (54x39cm-21x15in)
£3400 $6460   (1-Mar-91 C151/R) St John the Evangelist (113x93cm-44x37in) painted octagon

DOLININA, Antonia (1925-) Russian
£996 $1693   (29-May-91 ARC.P182/R) Sur le tapis (52x62cm-20x24in) s. verso (F.FR 10000)

DOLL, Anton (1826-1887) German
£1284 $2439   (14-Sep-90 SA.A1172/R) Bavarian inn interior with peasants merrymaking (24x32cm-9x13in) s.i. (DM 3800)
£2034 $3315   (3-Jul-91 WE.MU30/R) Alpine landscape (21x33cm-8x13in) rem.sig. (DM 6000)
£2517 $4908   (10-Oct-90 WE.MU91) Winter landscape with figures (73x105cm-29x41in) s.i. (DM 7500)
£2712 $4420   (3-Jul-91 WE.MU345) Fun on the ice (13x26cm-5x10in) s.i. panel (DM 8000)
£3767 $6140   (12-Jun-91 N.M416/R) View of Watzmann with cattle grazing and peasant outside Alpine farm (18x30cm-7x12in) s.i. i.verso panel (DM 11000)
£4196 $8098   (12-Dec-90 N.M487/R) Mountain lake landscape with skaters and village (15x25cm-6x10in) s.i. panel (DM 12000)
£4281 $7663   (13-Mar-91 N.M477/R) St Anna Vorstadt in moon light, Munich (21x41cm-8x16in) s.i. i.stretcher (DM 12500)
£5034 $9815   (10-Oct-90 WE.MU94/R) Upper Bavarian lake landscape with fishing boats (26x34cm-10x13in) s.i. (DM 15000)

DOLL, Anton (1826-1887) German-cont.

£5479	$8932	(12-Jun-91 N.M415/R) Schaffhausen street in snow storm (40x31cm-16x12in) s.i. i.verso panel (DM 16000)
£5594	$10797	(12-Dec-90 WE.MU47/R) Alpine frozen river landscape with figures on the ice (28x40cm-11x16in) s. panel (DM 16000)
£5944	$11472	(12-Dec-90 SY.MU52/R) Figures on rozen river in mountain village (71x107cm-28x42in) s.i. (DM 17000)
£5973	$11706	(24-Nov-90 SA.A694/R) Pegnitz landscape with view of Nurnberg (31x56cm-12x22in) s.i. (DM 17500)
£6107	$11909	(10-Oct-90 WE.MU90/R) Winter landscape with figures on frozen river (28x40cm-11x16in) s. board (DM 18200)
£6993	$13497	(12-Dec-90 N.M486/R) Horse-drawn haycart before farmhouse (67x82cm-26x32in) s.i. (DM 20000)
£7692	$14846	(12-Dec-90 WE.MU46/R) Snowy lake landscape (57x92cm-22x36in) s.i. i.verso (DM 22000)
£8361	$14130	(17-Apr-91 WE.MU113/R) Cattle market near Sixdorf (32x49cm-13x19in) s.i. (DM 25000)
£8361	$14130	(17-Apr-91 WE.MU112/R) Target shooting (32x49cm-13x19in) s.i. (DM 25000)
£9247	$16551	(13-Mar-91 N.M476/R) Mountain farm with peasant woman and view of river valley (70x117cm-31x46in) s. (DM 27000)
£537	*$1047*	*(12-Oct-90 AW.H1410/R) Street scene with view of St Peter's Church, Munich (24x15cm-9x6in) s.i. pencil W/C vellum (DM 1600)*
£2218	*$4171*	*(19-Sep-90 N.M793/R) Kremsthal railway in Kremsmunster with station and view of abbey (38x55cm-15x22in) s.i. W/C (DM 6500)*

DOLL, Anton (attrib) (1826-1887) German

| *£854* | *$1529* | *(11-Apr-91 D.V305/R) Sendlinger Tor, Munich (14x23cm-6x9in) mono. W/C (A.S 18000)* |

DOLLA, Noel (20th C) ?

| £5544 | $10811 | (23-Oct-90 CSC.P72/R) Composition (231x225cm-91x89in) s. verso (F.FR 55000) |
| *£1517* | *$2958* | *(15-Oct-90 CSC.P78/R) Composition (68x48cm-27x19in) s.d.75 verso W/C (F.FR 15000)* |

DOLLERSCHELL, Eduard (1887-1948) German

| £1546 | $2938 | (2-Mar-91 KRA.D475/R) Mountain village s.d.1927 (DM 4500) |

DOLLEY, Pierre (1877-1955) French

| £2000 | $3340 | (9-Jun-91 DA.R2/R) Les vendanges (146x184cm-57x72in) s. (F.FR 20000) |

DOLLMAN, John Charles (1851-1934) British

£2500	$4175	(5-Jun-91 S59/R) Home sweet home (51x61cm-20x24in) s.d.1901 s.i.d.verso
£1138	*$1900*	*(26-Jul-91 E.EDM145/R) Tigers. Lions (25x64cm-10x25in) s. W/C pair*
£2600	*$5070*	*(15-Jan-91 SWS27/R) The walk home (35x57cm-14x22in) s.d.04 W/C*

DOLLMAN, Ruth (fl.1905-1928) British

| *£500* | *$960* | *(21-Feb-91 BEL958) Sunlit haze, haymaking s. W/C* |
| *£1100* | *$2112* | *(19-Feb-91 CHAP305) Meadow landscape (33x66cm-13x26in) s.d.* |

DOLLOND, W Anstey (fl.1880-1911) British

£1585	$2662	(23-Apr-91 RAS.K380/R) Portrait of girl wearing lacy dress (53x43cm-21x17in) s. (D.KR 18000)
£1040	*$1800*	*(21-May-91 CE.NY12 a/R) Offering (51x35cm-20x14in) s. W/C paperboard*
£2800	*$5292*	*(26-Sep-90 S339/R) Grape harvest (51x33cm-20x13in) s. W/C*

DOLPH, John Henry (1835-1903) American

| £1579 | $3000 | (14-Sep-90 S.BM122/R) The master's chair (51x38cm-20x15in) s. panel |
| £1724 | $3000 | (29-Mar-91 E.EDM752/R) Landscapes (20x41cm-8x16in) s. pair |

DOMBA, R (?) ?

| £900 | $1665 | (7-Mar-91 CSK63) Constantinople (51x81cm-20x32in) |

DOMELA, Cesar (1900-) Dutch

£1502	$2598	(22-May-91 CH.AM783) Abstract composition (27x21cm-11x8in) s. bodycol (D.FL 5000)
£1712	$2791	(15-Jun-91 L.K169/R) Composition (46x60cm-18x24in) gouache spray technique (DM 5000)
£2012	$3884	(13-Dec-90 SY.AM28/R) Composition (65x50cm-26x20in) s.verso pastel crayon (D.FL 6500)
£2834	$5555	(22-Nov-90 ZZ.F34/R) Composition (47x63cm-19x25in) gouache collage (F.FR 28000)
£5916	$11537	(23-Oct-90 C.A371/R) Composition (46x62cm-18x24in) s.d.1963 verso gouache (B.FR 360000)

DOMENCHIN DE CHAVANNE, Pierre Salomon (1673-1744) French

| £30000 | $50700 | (19-Apr-91 C103/R) The four seasons (72x89cm-28x35in) four |

DOMENCHIN DE CHAVANNE, Pierre Salomon (attrib) (1673-1744) French

| £2209 | $3556 | (27-Jun-91 APT.P59/R) Moines autour d'un feu pres de ruines (62x77cm-24x30in) (F.FR 22000) |

DOMENICHINO (1581-1641) Italian

| *£2500* | *$4225* | *(16-Apr-91 C152/R) A wooded river landscape with figures gazing up at a flock of birds (13x20cm-5x8in) i. watermark pen oval* |

DOMENICHINO (1581-1641) Italian-cont.
£18000 $29340   (2-Jul-91 C20/R) Four infants making music with subsidiary study of
                       figure (11x17cm-4x7in) i. chk pen ink wash

DOMENICHINO (after) (1581-1641) Italian
£820 $1337   (4-Jul-91 CSK64) Samian Sybil (138x98cm-54x39in)
£836 $1497   (13-Apr-91 FAL.M64/R) Revelation of St. John (92x73cm-36x29in)
                       (S.KR 9000)
£982 $1600   (5-Jul-91 S.W3391/R) Il Concerto (157x119cm-62x47in)
£1100 $2123   (14-Dec-90 PHM28/R) Landscape with fishermen, hunters and washerwomen
                       (67x8cm-26x3in)
£1100 $1859   (19-Apr-91 C2) The Cumaean Sibyl (315x226cm-124x89in)
£1600 $3200   (7-Feb-91 C12) A sybil (113x103cm-44x41in)
£2000 $3920   (20-Nov-90 F.R69) Martirio di Sant'Andrea (120x180cm-47x71in)
                       (I.L 4400000)
£2705 $4842   (8-Apr-91 CH.R7/R) Testa di Sibilla (47x35cm-19x14in) (I.L 6000000)

DOMENICHINO (attrib) (1581-1641) Italian
£684 $1211   (19-Mar-91 F.M243/R) Paesaggio con alberi e rovine. Studio di nudo
                       maschile (19x14cm-7x6in) bistre ink double-sided (I.L 1500000)

DOMENICHINO (circle) (1581-1641) Italian
£1700 $2771   (2-Jul-91 PH111/R) Italianate river landscape with drovers leading
                       animals along path (48x57cm-19x22in)

DOMENICHINO (style) (1581-1641) Italian
£750 $1268   (18-Apr-91 CSK38) Persian Sibyl (63x51cm-25x20in) with i.
£3500 $7000   (7-Feb-91 CSK67/R) Annunciation (173x119cm-68x47in)

DOMENJOZ, Raoul (1896-) Swiss
£1469 $2851   (8-Dec-90 GAB.G2514/R) Bateaux de peche (50x61cm-20x24in) s.d.1934
                       (S.FR 3600)

DOMERGUE, J G (1889-1962) French
£7085 $13887   (25-Nov-90 B.PA54) Elegante (32x46cm-13x18in) s. panel (F.FR 70000)

DOMERGUE, Jean Gabriel (1889-1962) French
£1600 $2960   (5-Mar-91 SWS1397/R) Kuca la blonde (32x23cm-13x9in) s. i.verso board
£1809 $2967   (21-Jun-91 D.P90/R) Jeune femme a la voilette (24x19cm-9x7in) s. board
                       (F.FR 18000)
£2000 $3260   (4-Jul-91 GL.P251) Jeune femme au buste nu (33x24cm-13x9in) s. hardboard
                       (F.FR 20000)
£2087 $3528   (21-Apr-91 E.LA122/R) L'Andalouse dans l'atelier (33x41cm-13x16in)
                       studio st. (F.FR 21000)
£2103 $3638   (22-May-91 GS.B2352/R) Portrait of woman with yellow scarf
                       (23x19cm-9x7in) s. pavatex (S.FR 5300)
£2282 $4518   (3-Feb-91 LT.P76) Portrait de jeune femme (23x19cm-9x7in) s. hardboard
                       (F.FR 22500)
£2300 $4462   (6-Dec-90 CSK129/R) Narcisse (41x33cm-16x13in) s. i.stretcher
£2400 $4008   (5-Jun-91 HC.P346) Les yeus pers (24x19cm-9x7in) s. i. verso board
                       (F.FR 24000)
£2513 $4497   (11-Mar-91 GL.P46) La femme au boa rose (23x19cm-9x7in) s.d.1933
                       (F.FR 25000)
£2600 $4238   (4-Jul-91 GL.P260/R) Femme nue (33x23cm-13x9in) s. hardboard
                       (F.FR 26000)
£2600 $4238   (4-Jul-91 GL.P253) Danseuse nue (46x38cm-18x15in) s. hardboard
                       (F.FR 26000)
£2653 $5227   (16-Nov-90 LGB.P186/R) Gilli (24x19cm-9x7in) s. hardboard (F.FR 26000)
£2714 $5210   (24-Feb-91 P.V89/R) Gilda (24x19cm-9x7in) s. panel (F.FR 27000)
£2800 $4508   (24-Jun-91 CSK163/R) Jeune fille a la robe blanche (33x22cm-13x9in) s.
                       board
£2935 $5753   (25-Nov-90 ZZ.F42/R) Femme au turban (33x41cm-13x16in) s. (F.FR 29000)
£3012 $5572   (6-Mar-91 APT.P97) Portrait de Rafa (23x19cm-9x7in) s. panel
                       (F.FR 30000)
£3041 $5260   (21-May-91 WK.M823 a/R) Portrait of young lady in Paris landscape
                       (50x40cm-20x16in) s.d.1961 (DM 9000)
£3514 $5658   (28-Jun-91 ARC.P75/R) Portarit d'une jeune fille brune (24x19cm-9x7in)
                       s. hardboard (F.FR 35000)
£3586 $7029   (11-Nov-90 ZZ.F101/R) Portrait de jeune femme au foulard rouge
                       (25x20cm-10x8in) s. panel (F.FR 35000)
£3597 $6978   (9-Dec-90 E.LA80/R) Lucita (33x24cm-13x9in) s. hardboard (F.FR 35000)
£3762 $6659   (7-Apr-91 I.N114/R) Goergina (33x24cm-13x9in) s. board (F.FR 38000)
£3927 $6402   (11-Jun-91 I.N192/R) Jeune femme au chapeau (35x27cm-14x11in) s.
                       (F.FR 39000)
£3968 $6825   (19-May-91 ZZ.F134/R) Le bal a Venise (55x38cm-22x15in) s. i.d.1914
                       verso (F.FR 40000)
£4000 $6520   (3-Jul-91 PLF.P18/R) Portrait de femme au chapeau de plumes rouges
                       (55x46cm-22x18in) s. (F.FR 40000)
£4018 $7714   (27-Nov-90 W.T1126/R) Laura (53x43cm-21x17in) s. board (C.D 9000)
£4133 $8059   (14-Jan-91 YC.P168/R) Elegante au noeud rose (41x33cm-16x13in) s.
                       hardboard (F.FR 41000)
£4225 $7140   (21-Apr-91 E.LA114/R) Scenes galantes (60x72cm-24x28in) studio st. verso
                       laid down hardboard oval pair (F.FR 42500)
£4406 $8635   (11-Nov-90 ZZ.F125/R) Couple a l'Opera (32x24cm-13x9in) s. panel
                       (F.FR 43000)
£4563 $7849   (15-May-91 CN.P85/R) Clarita (54x46cm-21x18in) s. (F.FR 46000)

DOMERGUE, Jean Gabriel (1889-1962) French-cont.

£4573	$7728	(21-Apr-91 E.LA120) La ballerine (47x38cm-19x15in) s. (F.FR 46000)
£4667	$8960	(18-Dec-90 GM.B4041) Femme au miroir (65x54cm-26x21in) s. (B.FR 280000)
£5500	$10725	(19-Oct-90 C206/R) La lettre d'amour (41x33cm-16x13in) s. panel
£5517	$10593	(28-Nov-90 KF.M686/R) Grand Miroir (46x37cm-18x15in) s. isorel (DM 16000)
£5528	$9894	(16-Mar-91 APT.P52/R) Femme au chapeau (55x46cm-22x18in) s. panel (F.FR 55000)
£5584	$11000	(13-Nov-90 CE.NY175/R) Portrait d'elegante (46x38cm-18x15in) s.
£6355	$10739	(19-Apr-91 FN.S1512/R) Portrait of Paulette (55x46cm-22x18in) s. i.verso (DM 19000)
£6568	$11363	(25-May-91 KV.L412 a/R) Marie-Paule (46x38cm-18x15in) s. panel (B.FR 400000)
£7136	$13772	(12-Dec-90 APT.P90/R) Femme a la voilette (45x38cm-18x15in) s. board (F.FR 70000)
£7553	$12311	(12-Jun-91 ZZ.F72/R) Femme aux gants noirs (41x33cm-16x13in) s. panel (F.FR 75000)
£7645	$14679	(27-Nov-90 APT.P95/R) Femme au collier de perles (81x65cm-32x26in) s. (F.FR 75000)
£7853	$13271	(21-Apr-91 E.LA108/R) La danseuse de Moulin Rouge (81x63cm-32x25in) s.d.26 hardboard (F.FR 79000)
£9684	$18593	(27-Nov-90 APT.P97/R) Antonia (65x46cm-26x18in) s. (F.FR 95000)
£10152	$20000	(13-Nov-90 CE.NY173/R) La caline (55x46cm-22x18in) s.d.32
£11640	$22814	(20-Nov-90 PPB.P33/R) Le repos sur le canape bleu (80x65cm-31x26in) s.d.30 board (F.FR 115000)
£12232	$23486	(27-Nov-90 APT.P90/R) Caroline cherie (72x60cm-28x24in) s. panel (F.FR 120000)
£13110	$25695	(6-Nov-90 SY.AM272/R) Reclining nude (57x117cm-22x46in) s. (D.FL 43000)
£13761	$26560	(13-Dec-90 QWA.P45/R) Elegante a l'Opera (65x54cm-26x21in) s. board (F.FR 135000)
£16444	$31901	(7-Dec-90 GL.P194/R) Josephine Baker nue (228x161cm-90x63in) s. (F.FR 160000)
£25000	$42000	(24-Apr-91 MJ.P116/R) Femme allongee sur la branche d'un eucalyptus (178x199cm-70x78in) s. canvas on gold sheet (F.FR 250000)
£31792	$55000	(7-May-91 CE.NY143/R) Nu allonge (96x129cm-38x51in) s.
£40775	$78287	(29-Nov-90 ZZ.F30/R) Le parasol vert (160x130cm-63x51in) s. (F.FR 400000)
£497	*$840*	*(21-Apr-91 E.LA110) Rousse aux yeux bleus (29x20cm-11x8in) s.d.1917 oil crayons (F.FR 5000)*
£696	*$1176*	*(21-Apr-91 E.LA126) Femme a sa toilette (18x21cm-7x8in) s. pastel oil crayons (F.FR 7000)*
£746	*$1260*	*(21-Apr-91 E.LA107) Elegante (79x59cm-31x23in) studio st. verso chl.laid down on canvas (F.FR 7500)*
£795	*$1344*	*(21-Apr-91 E.LA111) Giky (30x22cm-12x9in) s. W/C gouache (F.FR 8000)*
£1093	*$1848*	*(21-Apr-91 E.LA106/R) Elegante souriant (79x59cm-31x23in) studio st. verso chl. canvas (F.FR 11000)*
£1100	*$1793*	*(1-Jul-91 APT.P67) Chapeau au ruban rouge (31x33cm-12x13in) s. W/C gouache (F.FR 11000)*
£1100	*$1793*	*(1-Jul-91 APT.P68) Chapeau bleu (29x22cm-11x9in) s. W/C gouache (F.FR 11000)*
£1441	*$2436*	*(21-Apr-91 E.LA104) Femme dans une loge (32x24cm-13x9in) s. W/C gouache (F.FR 14500)*
£1889	*$3192*	*(21-Apr-91 E.LA112/R) Fete a Venise (45x30cm-18x12in) s.d.27 W/C gouache (F.FR 19000)*
£1988	*$3360*	*(21-Apr-91 E.LA103/R) Elegante au chapeau et gants verts (32x24cm-13x9in) s. W/C (F.FR 20000)*
£2388	*$4155*	*(28-Mar-91 DAR.P1/R) Femme au paravent (31x46cm-12x18in) s.d.21 crayon W/C (F.FR 24000)*
£2982	*$5040*	*(21-Apr-91 E.LA115/R) Pierrot et Colombine (29x46cm-11x18in) s.d.26 W/C gouache (F.FR 30000)*

DOMERGUE, Jean Gabriel (attrib) (1889-1962) French

£920	*$1500*	*(14-Jun-91 W.W13/R) Comely brunette (25x18cm-10x7in) indis.i. W/C gouache chl*

DOMICENT, Martin (1823-1898) Flemish

£520	$900	(21-May-91 CE.NY213/R) Checkmate (22x27cm-9x11in) s. panel

DOMINGO Y FALLOLA, Roberto (1867-1956) Spanish

£776	*$1528*	*(18-Nov-90 H.A23) La mise a mort (21x30cm-8x12in) s. Indian ink W/C (F.FR 7600)*
£2077	*$4070*	*(24-Jan-91 EP.M52/R) La herreria (19x47cm-7x19in) s. W/C board (S.P 380000)*

DOMINGO Y MARQUES, Francisco (1842-1920) Spanish

£7147	$12793	(13-Mar-91 FER.M183/R) Tarde de recreo en el parque con personajes velazquenos (21x35cm-8x14in) s. panel (S.P 1300000)

DOMINGO Y MUNOZ, Jose (1815-1894) Spanish

£2404	$4688	(25-Oct-90 D.V94/R) In der Waffenschmiede (27x39cm-11x15in) s.i. (A.S 50000)

DOMINGO, Roberto (1867-?) Spanish

£1621	$3161	(23-Oct-90 DUR.M27) Picadores (32x43cm-13x17in) board (S.P 300000)
£815	*$1565*	*(18-Dec-90 DUR.M1) Garrochistas (18x38cm-7x15in) W/C (S.P 150000)*

DOMINGO, Roberto (1867-?) Spanish-cont.

£1038	$2003	(11-Dec-90 FER.M139/R) Tirando de la carreta (15x49cm-6x19in) s. oil gouache (S.P 190000)
£1093	$2109	(11-Dec-90 FER.M138/R) Cogida en la salida de una vara (16x23cm-6x9in) s. gouache (S.P 200000)
£1688	$2904	(16-May-91 ANS.M16/R) Rejoneador (25x50cm-10x20in) s. col.dr gouache (S.P 310000)
£1772	$2905	(17-Jun-91 DUR.M71/R) Picadores (21x26cm-8x10in) s. gouache (S.P 325000)
£1772	$2905	(17-Jun-91 DUR.M77/R) Capea (22x26cm-9x10in) s. gouache (S.P 325000)
£2474	$4428	(13-Mar-91 FER.M184/R) Quitando los arreos al caballo del picador ante la mirada de la cuadrilla (20x34cm-8x13in) s. gouache (S.P 450000)

DOMINGUEZ BECQUER, Valeriano see BECQUER, Valeriano

DOMINGUEZ NEIRA, Pedro (1894-1970) Argentinian

| £1579 | $3000 | (11-Sep-90 PO.BA41) Paisaje (69x90cm-27x35in) s. tempera |

DOMINGUEZ, Oscar (1906-1958) Spanish

£1500	$2445	(3-Jul-91 LGB.P92) Paysage a la pyramide (12x18cm-5x7in) (F.FR 15000)
£6122	$12061	(16-Nov-90 FB.P147/R) Figure de profil (46x33cm-18x13in) s. peinture a l'essence hardboard (F.FR 60000)
£6452	$12387	(2-Dec-90 GAB.G1588/R) Le chevalier (44x43cm-17x17in) s. panel (S.FR 16000)
£6848	$11162	(16-Jun-91 CC.P7/R) Composition (32x40cm-13x16in) s.d.1952 (F.FR 68000)
£7645	$14755	(16-Dec-90 GL.P65/R) Nture morte a la lampe (15x19cm-6x7in) s.i. (F.FR 75000)
£10682	$20188	(30-Sep-90 E.LA134/R) La machine a coudre (52x73cm-20x29in) s. board (F.FR 105000)
£10890	$17751	(11-Jun-91 ANS.M84/R) Composicion con pera (18x26cm-7x10in) (S.P 2000000)
£11089	$21623	(28-Oct-90 M.V65/R) Composition (61x46cm-24x18in) s. panel (F.FR 110000)
£11305	$21932	(9-Dec-90 E.LA124/R) Paysage surrealiste (48x38cm-19x15in) s.d.1938 (F.FR 110000)
£12097	$23226	(2-Dec-90 GAB.G1587/R) Composition (65x54cm-26x21in) s.d.1943 (S.FR 30000)
£13225	$24995	(30-Sep-90 E.LA133 b/R) Personnage dans un paysage surrealiste (27x35cm-11x14in) s.d.1937 (F.FR 130000)
£16281	$26702	(20-Jun-91 APT.P48/R) Nature morte au prisme (50x61cm-20x24in) s.d.1943 (F.FR 162000)
£21169	$41280	(28-Oct-90 GL.P89/R) Paysage (50x65cm-20x26in) s. board (F.FR 210000)
£31517	$61459	(24-Oct-90 F.M240/R) Le cerf volant (41x27cm-16x11in) s.d.50 tempera oil (I.L 70000000)
£80884	$158533	(22-Nov-90 EP.M23/R) Tauromaquia (60x81cm-24x32in) s.d.1950 (S.P 15000000)
£804	$1544	(24-Feb-91 P.V124/R) Guerrier (57x46cm-22x18in) s. pen drawing (F.FR 8000)
£1106	$2123	(24-Feb-91 P.V128/R) Paysage surrealiste (26x34cm-10x13in) s. gouache (F.FR 11000)
£1113	$2182	(25-Nov-90 ZZ.F44/R) Neptune (42x28cm-17x11in) s. pen W/C (F.FR 11000)
£1372	$2744	(10-Feb-91 CC.P23) Tauromachie (24x15cm-9x6in) s. gouache (F.FR 13500)
£1494	$2405	(25-Jun-91 FER.M52/R) Toro (20x29cm-8x11in) s. ink dr (S.P 275000)
£1694	$3252	(2-Dec-90 GAB.G1589/R) Guerriers (35x48cm-14x19in) s. W/C (S.FR 4200)
£1721	$3372	(25-Nov-90 ZZ.F43/R) Le crabe (221x16cm-87x6in) mono. W/C (F.FR 17000)
£2049	$4016	(11-Nov-90 ZZ.F217/R) Composition surrealiste (20x14cm-8x6in) s. lead pencil (F.FR 20000)
£4933	$9570	(7-Dec-90 GL.P31) Le taureau dans l'arene (30x41cm-12x16in) s. studio st. verso gouache (F.FR 48000)
£5907	$11401	(13-Dec-90 CH.BR122/R) Corrida - taureau agenouille dans l'arene (49x63cm-19x25in) s.d.1951 ink pencil (B.FR 350000)
£5907	$11401	(13-Dec-90 CH.BR123/R) Corrida (56x74cm-22x29in) s.d.1951 ink pencil (B.FR 350000)
£6312	$10667	(16-Apr-91 I.N47/R) Composition (51x37cm-20x15in) s.d.1950 gouache (F.FR 63500)
£8155	$15739	(16-Dec-90 GL.P76 b/R) Paysage fantastique (26x45cm-10x18in) (F.FR 80000)
£8155	$15739	(16-Dec-90 GL.P63/R) La corde a sauter (14x21cm-6x8in) s.i. d.1952 verso gouache Indian ink (F.FR 80000)

DOMINICI, Antonio de (c.1730-c.1800) Italian

| £5456 | $9439 | (21-May-91 SY.MI1002/R) Il Ratto di Europa (60x76cm-24x30in) panel (I.L 12000000) |

DOMINICIS, Achille de (19th C) Italian

| £1800 | $3456 | (27-Nov-90 PH258/R) Vilerbo (35x52cm-14x20in) s.i. W/C over pencil pair |

DOMINICUS (18th C) ?

| £3600 | $6840 | (1-Mar-91 C164/R) Jacob watering Rachel's sheep. Tending Laban's flock. Wrestling with theAngel. Reconciled with Esau (40x83cm-16x33in) three s.d.1775stretchers set of four |

DOMINQUE, Maurice (1918-) Canadian

| £641 | $1077 | (17-Jul-91 EA.M640) Mtl. - St. Henri, rue Notre Dame (53x74cm-21x29in) s. W/C (C.D 1250) |

DOMMERSEN, Cornelis Christian (1842-1928) Dutch

£1100	$1771	(27-Jun-91 CG35/R) A Dutch canal scene with figurs and boats (28x23cm-11x9in) s.d.1898 panel
£1796	$3126	(26-Mar-91 VN.R20/R) Montelbantoren in Amsterdam (20x15cm-8x6in) s. panel (D.FL 6000)
£9249	$16000	(22-May-91 SY.NY207/R) View of Amiens (37x46cm-15x18in) s.d.1880 s.verso panel

DOMMERSEN, Cornelis Christian (style) (1842-1928) Dutch

| £1200 | $2028 | (1-May-91 PHL142/R) Busy Dutch port (78x114cm-31x45in) |

DOMMERSEN, Pieter Christian (1834-1908) Dutch

£1201	$2246	(27-Aug-90 SY.J167/R) Coastal view with fishing vessels (23x34cm-9x13in) s. panel (SA.R 5800)
£1818	$2982	(18-Jun-91 VN.R57) Shipwreck on a rocky coast (120x175cm-47x69in) s.d.1878 (D.FL 6000)
£1965	$3400	(12-May-91 H.C20/R) By the Zuider Zee (20x25cm-8x10in) s.d.1891 panel
£1965	$3400	(12-May-91 H.C19/R) Scrooskerken, Holland (20x25cm-8x10in) s.d.1891
£2000	$3700	(6-Mar-91 RBB746/R) Fishing boat and two masted sailing ship close to shore with figures (43x74cm-17x29in) s.i.verso
£2100	$3612	(14-May-91 SWS323/R) On the river Spaarn. Utrecht (18x24cm-7x9in) init.d.88 indis.i.verso panel pair
£2222	$4311	(4-Dec-90 P.Q61/R) Kampen on the Zuiderzee, Holland (30x40cm-12x16in) s.d.1895 board (C.D 5000)
£2727	$5373	(30-Oct-90 CH.AM292/R) Off Pampas, on Zuiderzee (27x38cm-11x15in) s.d.1887 i.verso panel (D.FL 9000)
£2800	$5376	(27-Nov-90 PH20/R) View of the Charles Bridge, Prague (76x63cm-30x25in) s.d.1869
£3200	$6144	(16-Aug-90 B405/R) On the Louwer, Holland (29x41cm-11x16in) s.d.1890 i.verso panel
£3400	$6630	(15-Jan-91 SWS185/R) Oestuizen on the Zuiderzee, Holland (27x37cm-11x15in) indis.s.d.1884 i.verso panel
£3500	$5740	(19-Jun-91 S20/R) Preparing for sea (31x41cm-12x16in) s.d.1902 st.init.verso panel
£4042	$7033	(26-Mar-91 VN.R21/R) Shipwreck on a rocky coastline (120x175cm-47x69in) s.d.1878 (D.FL 13500)
£4500	$7740	(17-May-91 C70/R) On Bornisse, Holland. Vessels offshore in choppy sea (20x25cm-8x10in) s.i.d.1897 st.verso panel pair
£4500	$7785	(22-May-91 S36/R) Wrecked (101x152cm-40x60in) s.d.1878
£4500	$7650	(30-May-91 C142/R) Harbour of Goes on Isle of Walcheren (40x61cm-16x24in) s.d.1884 i.st.verso panel
£7000	$11480	(19-Jun-91 S21/R) Volendam on Zuiderzee. Bronkenburg house on Waal (40x61cm-16x24in) one s.d.1886 one s.d.1885 panel pair
£8000	$13120	(19-Jun-91 S31/R) Capricious view of Lutheran Church, Amsterdam (75x126cm-30x50in) s.d.1885 s.verso
£8000	$13120	(19-Jun-91 S14/R) Street scene by canal (49x39cm-19x15in) s.d.1874

DOMMERSEN, Pieter Christian (attrib) (1834-1908) Dutch

| £1100 | $1903 | (22-May-91 CSK288) Fishing boats and other shipping in stormy seas in estuary (28x39cm-11x15in) panel |

DOMMERSEN, Pieter Christian (style) (1834-1908) Dutch

| £1200 | $2076 | (9-May-91 CSK70/R) Dutch river landscape with barge and windmills (38x47cm-15x19in) |

DOMMERSEN, W (?-1927) Dutch

| £1974 | $3750 | (27-Feb-91 SY.NY228/R) View of Amsterdam (67x102cm-26x40in) s. canvas on masonite |
| £3158 | $6000 | (27-Feb-91 SY.NY230/R) De Zaand Street, Amsterdam, Holland (51x41cm-20x16in) s. mono.d.34 verso |

DOMMERSEN, William (?-1927) Dutch

£620	$1042	(18-Jul-91 CSK91) River estuary at low tide (30x61cm-12x24in)
£680	$1340	(13-Nov-90 SWS350/R) Cappico, Italy (28x39cm-11x15in) s. i. verso
£700	$1316	(6-Aug-90 SWS72) Peasants outside villa by lake (29x44cm-11x17in) s. canvas laid down on panel
£780	$1349	(9-May-91 CSK191/R) Figures by Lago Magglore (30x46cm-12x18in) s. canvas backed board
£780	$1310	(23-Apr-91 SWS355/R) Evereux Cathedral (61x40cm-24x16in) s. oval
£800	$1568	(8-Nov-90 PHI206/R) On the Senno, Brussels (39x29cm-15x11in) s.i.verso
£850	$1522	(12-Mar-91 PH3) Near Palermo (61x50cm-24x20in) s.i.verso
£980	$1686	(14-May-91 SWS322/R) Italian coastal town with travellers (49x75cm-19x30in) s.
£1031	$2000	(8-Dec-90 W.W116/R) View of Modena (41x61cm-16x24in) s. i.verso
£1100	$2145	(15-Jan-91 SWS172/R) Place de Abe, Rouen. On the River Amstel, Amsterdam, Holland (19x14cm-7x6in) mono. i.verso panel pair
£1200	$2004	(3-Jun-91 PHB80/R) Zonnerburgh, on Spaare, Holland (28x38cm-11x15in) s. i.verso
£1300	$2249	(9-May-91 CSK188/R) On Tiber, Italy. Iviza, Italy (30x51cm-12x20in) s.i.verso pair
£1372	$2689	(6-Nov-90 SY.AM180/R) Town scene (59x49cm-23x19in) s. (D.FL 4500)
£1400	$2408	(14-May-91 SWS321/R) Lighthouse at Tholen on the Scheldt, Holland (39x60cm-15x24in) s.i.verso
£1400	$2758	(13-Nov-90 SWS351/R) Kampell, Holland (19x39cm-7x15in) s. i. verso board
£1450	$2436	(16-Jul-91 RG2657) Dutch coastal scenes - Thulen on Scheldt. Kampen, Holland (51x74cm-20x29in) s.i.verso pair

DOMMERSEN, William (?-1927) Dutch-cont.
£1500	\$2520	(18-Jul-91 CSK198/R) Modena, Italy. Cattaro, Italy (41x61cm-16x24in) s. pair
£1500	\$2595	(9-May-91 CSK77/R) Near Alkmar in Netherlands (51x75cm-20x30in) s.
£1500	\$2820	(6-Aug-90 SWS60/R) St.John's Church, Breda (59x44cm-23x17in) s. s.i.verso
£1600	\$3136	(22-Jan-91 PH97/R) The flower market, Caen (51x40cm-20x16in) s. l.verso
£1600	\$3152	(13-Nov-90 SWS349/R) Unloading the catch, Kampen, Holland (60x90cm-24x35in) s. i. verso
£1600	\$3072	(16-Aug-90 B387/R) Schiedam on the Scheldt, Holland (51x76cm-20x30in) s. i.
£1700	\$3349	(4-Oct-90 CSK252/R) Tarranto, Italy. Ischia, Italy (30x51cm-12x20in) both s. two
£1700	\$3332	(14-Feb-91 CSK115/R) Rue Latour, Rouen and Utrecht, Holland (61x51cm-24x20in) s. i. verso
£1734	\$3000	(22-May-91 D.NY32/R) Town beside river with figures (51x76cm-20x30in) s.
£1800	\$3024	(18-Jul-91 CSK89/R) Tholen on Scheldt, Holland (51x76cm-20x30in) s.
£1900	\$3724	(22-Nov-90 CG510) Zierkszee on the Scheldt. Tholen on the Scheldt (30x41cm-12x16in) s. pair
£1990	\$3323	(4-Jun-91 FB.M172) Amalfi, Italy (46x81cm-18x32in) s. (C.D 3800)
£2500	\$4475	(12-Mar-91 PH11/R) Barges and moored sailing vessels in river landscape (51x76cm-20x30in) s.d.1881
£2695	\$4527	(23-Apr-91 SY.AM132/R) On River Amstel, Holland (50x75cm-20x30in) s. (D.FL 9000)
£2800	\$4844	(22-May-91 S91/R) Tollhouse, Enkhuizen, Holland (40x61cm-16x24in) s. s.i.verso

DOMMERSEN, William (attrib) (?-1927) Dutch
| £926 | \$1556 | (16-Jul-91 JRL.S228 d) Unloading a barge on the Maas (35x52cm-14x20in) s. (A.D 2000) |

DOMOTO, Hisao (1928-) Japanese
£4204	\$7273	(23-May-91 SY.AM278/R) Untitled (46x65cm-18x26in) s.d.57 s.verso (D.FL 14000)
£18000	\$31860	(21-Mar-91 S12/R) Espace B (114x145cm-45x57in) s.d.56-57 s.d.1956-7 verso
£20408	\$40000	(6-Nov-90 CE.NY78/R) Untitled (163x124cm-64x49in) s.d.1966 verso oil acrylic

DOMOTO, Insho (1891-?) Japanese
| £10239 | \$20068 | (24-Nov-90 VG.B381/R) Tableau no.4 (60x120cm-24x47in) s.i.d.1958verso (DM 30000) |

DOMUS, J I (18th C) ?
| *£1737* | *\$3421* | *(14-Nov-90 F.M23/R) Trompe l'oeil con incisione della scuola di Rembrandt e fogli di musica (39x28cm-15x11in) s.i.d.1795 W/C (I.L 3800000)* |

DON, Martino del (19th C) Italian?
| *£3000* | *\$5160* | *(17-May-91 C227/R) St. Peter's, Rome (59x43cm-23x17in) s. pencil W/C htd white* |

DONA, Lydia (20th C) American
| £2296 | \$4500 | (6-Nov-90 CE.NY254/R) The new Biochemical Essays (147x213cm-58x84in) s.i.d.1986 verso |

DONADINI, Ermenegildo Carlo Giovanni (1876-1936) Austrian
| £1531 | \$2464 | (28-Jun-91 BM.B663/R) Bisons watering in wooded landscape, possibly Tierpark Radebeul, evening (86x114cm-34x45in) s. (DM 4500) |

DONADONI, Stefano (1844-1911) Italian
| *£733* | *\$1224* | *(4-Jun-91 R.T272/R) Roma (56x77cm-22x30in) s.i.d.1893 W/C ink over graphite (C.D 1400)* |

DONALD, John Milne (1819-1866) British
£500	\$840	(23-Apr-91 S129) Country lane (23x35cm-9x14in) s.d.53
£1000	\$1690	(3-May-91 PHE78/R) On the shore at Cardross (45x65cm-18x26in) s.i.d.1858
£1300	\$2197	(2-May-91 CG495) On Arnon, Glen Falloch (58x91cm-23x36in) s.d.1860 s.i.d.1860 verso

DONALDSON, Andrew Benjamin (1840-?) British
| £1500 | \$2580 | (14-May-91 SWS253/R) Musicians by fountain (53x122cm-21x48in) s.d.1870 |

DONAS, Marthe (1885-1967) Belgian
£2993	\$5357	(16-Mar-91 KV.L397/R) Intuition (70x60cm-28x24in) s.d.1957 panel (B.FR 180000)
£3003	\$5195	(22-May-91 CH.AM540/R) Cartes a jouer (75x100cm-30x39in) s. s.i.d.1953 verso (D.FL 10000)
£90000	*\$175500*	*(16-Oct-90 C60/R) La Musique (77x52cm-30x20in) s. s.i.verso oil collage board*

DONAT, F R (19th C) Belgian
| £7000 | \$13720 | (14-Feb-91 CSK171/R) Awaiting the reply. Reading the news (51x41cm-20x16in) s. panel pair |

DONAT, Friederich Reginald (1830-1907) ?
£1049 $2035   (8-Dec-90 WK.M368/R) News from foreign countries (52x41cm-20x16in) s. panel (DM 3000)
£1364 $2645   (8-Dec-90 WK.M369/R) A good day (52x41cm-20x16in) s. panel (DM 3900)

DONAT, M (?) ?
£1000 $1710   (31-Jul-91 HUN220) Landscapes (15x23cm-6x9in) s. pair

DONATH, Gabriel Ambrosius (1684-1760) German
£11888 $22944   (10-Dec-90 L.K33/R) Church interior with figures (46x61cm-18x24in) s. (DM 34000)

DONATI, Enrico (1909-) American
£2128 $4000   (21-Sep-90 BG.M747/R) Red Reef (102x76cm-40x30in) s.
£3067 $5000   (12-Jun-91 SY.NY197/R) Quartz (127x127cm-50x50in) s. l.d.63 verso oil sand canvas

DONATI, F R (19th C) Italian
£1756 $3389   (11-Dec-90 CH.R133) Famiglia di pescatori (52x40cm-20x16in) panel (I.L 3800000)

DONCK, Gerrit (c.1610-c.1640) Flemish
£1835 $3615   (13-Nov-90 CH.AM69/R) Portrait of gentleman, standing by draped table in interior (49x32cm-19x13in) on copper (D.FL 6000)

DONCKER, Herman Mijnerts (17th C) Dutch
£5578 $9594   (14-May-91 GF.L2040/R) Cavalier standing in landscape (51x39cm-20x15in) panel (S.FR 14000)

DONDUCCI, Giovanni Andrea (1575-1655) Italian
£228628 $386382   (19-Apr-91 CSC.P9/R) Fete champetre (99x120cm-39x47in) (F.FR 2300000)

DONDUCCI, Giovanni Andrea (style) (1575-1655) Italian
£1600 $3200   (7-Feb-91 CSK26/R) Flight into Egypt (35x46cm-14x18in)
£1600 $3072   (29-Nov-90 CSK248/R) Rest on the Flight into Egypt (87x72cm-34x28in)
£4500 $8640   (29-Nov-90 CSK9/R) Rest on the Flight to Egypt (99x74cm-39x29in)

DONGEN, Kees van (1877-1968) French
£4359 $8500   (10-Oct-90 SY.NY61/R) Environs de overschie Hollande (23x30cm-9x12in) s. s.i.verso cardboard on board
£6811 $13146   (12-Dec-90 CH.AM324/R) Houses and factory along road (25x32cm-10x13in) s. panel (D.FL 22000)
£12628 $24751   (22-Nov-90 L.K919/R) Portrait of woman (50x40cm-20x16in) s. canvas laid down (DM 37000)
£25153 $41000   (12-Jun-91 SY.NY16/R) Portrait of Mrs, Mannheimer (65x54cm-26x21in) s. l.verso
£30000 $58500   (17-Oct-90 S93/R) Le petit chien (37x44cm-15x17in) s.
£33401 $65466   (24-Nov-90 APT.P71/R) Portrait de femme (36x29cm-14x11in) board oval (F.FR 330000)
£42000 $67620   (26-Jun-91 S140/R) Au cirque Medrano (50x65cm-20x26in) s.
£43147 $85000   (2-Oct-90 CH.NY174/R) Courses (33x41cm-13x16in) s.
£46243 $80000   (9-May-91 CH.NY273/R) Cannes sous la pluie (36x27cm-14x11in) s. masonite
£80000 $130400   (1-Jul-91 APT.P347/R) Le cannet,vue de la mer (50x65cm-20x26in) s. (F.FR 800000)
£80972 $158704   (25-Nov-90 GL.P50/R) La chute d'Icare (217x168cm-85x66in) (F.FR 800000)
£90000 $174600   (5-Dec-90 S198/R) Portrait de Madame G. (55x33cm-22x13in) s.
£100000 $194000   (5-Dec-90 S156/R) Au desert Egyptien (79x98cm-31x39in) s.
£102775 $199383   (5-Dec-90 ZZ.F162/R) Le jardin du Luxembourg (100x81cm-39x32in) s. (F.FR 1000000)
£160000 $310400   (4-Dec-90 S20/R) Les enfants au Bord de la Mer (38x54cm-15x21in) s.
£170000 $329800   (5-Dec-90 S150/R) Cannes, le Casino (50x65cm-20x26in) s.
£200000 $322000   (25-Jun-91 S25/R) Nu assis (50x65cm-20x26in) s.
£375722 $650000   (8-May-91 CH.NY19/R) Deauville - Joie de vivre (53x65cm-21x26in) s.
£394737 $773684   (25-Nov-90 GL.P36/R) Nu - Marie Gabrielle (65x54cm-26x21in) s. l. verso (F.FR 3900000)
£450000 $873000   (3-Dec-90 C22/R) Jeune fille au robe rouge - Dolly van Dongen (100x81cm-39x32in) s.
£1300000 $2522000   (3-Dec-90 C24/R) Femme fatale (82x61cm-32x24in) s.
£450 $779   *(23-May-91 SY.AM69) Oude haven (12x19cm-5x7in) init.i. pencil (D.FL 1500)*
£450 $779   *(23-May-91 SY.AM70) Montmartre (9x15cm-4x6in) s.i. pencil (D.FL 1500)*
£661 $1143   *(23-May-91 SY.AM65/R) Place de l'Opera (10x16cm-4x6in) s.i. pencil (D.FL 2200)*
£721 $1247   *(23-May-91 SY.AM63/R) Honfleur (17x22cm-7x9in) s.i. chl (D.FL 2400)*
£1081 $1870   *(23-May-91 SY.AM66/R) Paris (19x31cm-7x12in) init.i.d.99 chl paper on card (D.FL 3600)*
£1270 $2541   *(6-Feb-91 LD.P162/R) Nu couche (25x33cm-10x13in) s. blk.crayon (F.FR 12500)*
£1351 $2338   *(23-May-91 SY.AM68) Portrait of Dolly (12x9cm-5x4in) s. W/C over pencil card (D.FL 4500)*
£2041 $3959   *(8-Dec-90 GAB.G2979) Nu feminin agenouille (30x24cm-12x9in) s. oil chk. (S.FR 5000)*
£2792 $5500   *(13-Nov-90 CE.NY215/R) Tete de femme (14x12cm-6x5in) s. W/C col.wax crayons ink paper on board*
£3287 $6409   *(23-Oct-90 C.A463/R) The orchid (45x36cm-18x14in) s.d.1946 W/C (B.FR 200000)*

DONGEN, Kees van (1877-1968) French-cont.
| £6006 | $10390 | (23-May-91 SY.AM47/R) Musiciens (25x41cm-10x16in) s. pastel crayon (D.FL 20000) |

£6006 $10390   (23-May-91 SY.AM47/R) Musiciens (25x41cm-10x16in) s. pastel crayon (D.FL 20000)

£8130 $16260   (6-Feb-91 LD.P163/R) Chevaux au champs de meules (27x45cm-11x18in) s.d.1901 blk.crayon htd.W/C (F.FR 80000)

£12469 $22319   (16-Mar-91 KV.L426/R) L'Avant scene (45x28cm-18x11in) s. W/C (B.FR 750000)

£13000 $23010   (20-Mar-91 S50/R) Courtisane assise (44x28cm-17x11in) s. W/C gouache

£16000 $25760   (26-Jun-91 S215/R) Au Bois de Boulogne. Woman and horse (29x49cm-11x19in) s.i. pencil W/C gouache oil chl double-sided

£19920 $34462   (25-May-91 GL.P14/R) Nu couche (24x34cm-9x13in) s. gouache (F.FR 200000)

£25000 $48750   (17-Oct-90 S132/R) Modigliani a la terasse du cafe La Rotonde a Paris (31x22cm-12x9in) s.i. W/C over pencil

DONGHI, Antonio (1897-1963) Italian

£21808 $42962   (30-Oct-90 F.R228/R) Piazza di paese (45x45cm-18x18in) s.d.43 (I.L 48000000)

£3271 $6444   (30-Oct-90 F.R150/R) Vaso di fiori (30x21cm-12x8in) s. pencil (I.L 7200000)

£4773 $9356   (20-Nov-90 BR.M190/R) Tamburino (24x34cm-9x13in) s. pencil paper on canvas (I.L 10500000)

DONINO, Agnolo di (1466-?) Italian

£7000 $11410   (2-Jul-91 C70/R) Standing man, seen from behind, wearing cloak (20x11cm-8x4in) silverpoint htd white

DONNER, Carl (?) ?

£560 $946   (19-Apr-91 K512/R) Pintail on Hickling Broad (33x51cm-13x20in) s. W/C

DONNER, Georg Raphael (attrib) (1692-1741) Austrian

£500 $895   (12-Apr-91 AW.H442/R) Design for monument to Feldmarschall Prinz Eugen von Savoyen (35x18cm-14x7in) pen wash indian ink over pencil (DM 1500)

DONOSO, Jose Ximenez (1628-1690) Spanish

£11000 $20900   (1-Mar-91 C143/R) St Thomas Aquinas. Saint, possibly St Augustine (127x60cm-50x24in) one s.d.1.66 pair

DONZE, Numa (1885-1952) Swiss

£612 $1200   (6-Nov-90 GF.L2599/R) The Rape of the Sabine women (43x48cm-17x19in) s.d.1909 canvas on board (S.FR 1500)

DOOMS, Vic (?) Belgian

£589 $990   (23-Apr-91 C.A433) View of Latem (30x35cm-12x14in) s. panel (B.FR 36000)

DOOYEWAARD, Jacob (1876-?) Dutch

£854 $1639   (27-Nov-90 SY.AM3601/R) Interior with child (18x14cm-7x6in) s. panel (D.FL 2800)

DOOYEWAARD, Willem (1892-?) Dutch

£1257 $2389   (11-Sep-90 CH.AM404) The Palace of the Living Buddah at Urga, Mongolia (60x74cm-24x29in) s.d.1929 pastel chk (D.FL 4200)

DORAZIO, Piero (1927-) Italian

£2500 $4901   (20-Nov-90 BR.M191/R) Senza titolo (78x58cm-31x23in) s.d.1988 tempera paper on canvas (I.L 5500000)

£2778 $4806   (25-May-91 AB.L60/R) Untitled (20x18cm-8x7in) s.verso i.stretcher acrylic (S.FR 7000)

£2909 $5702   (20-Nov-90 BR.M37/R) Composizione (36x45cm-14x18in) s.d.1970 tempera paper (I.L 6400000)

£6364 $12474   (20-Nov-90 BR.M112/R) Composizione (70x50cm-28x20in) s.d.1965 tempera (I.L 14000000)

£6569 $11431   (26-Mar-91 F.M124/R) Mandala VII (41x62cm-16x24in) s.d.1976verso (I.L 14500000)

£9073 $15606   (13-May-91 CH.R101/R) Senza titolo (202x56cm-80x22in) panel (I.L 20000000)

£9704 $18729   (13-Dec-90 F.M493/R) Diapason I (70x90cm-28x35in) s.i.d.1985verso (I.L 21000000)

£10806 $21072   (22-Oct-90 BR.M68/R) Al colmo (90x70cm-35x28in) s.d.1982 verso (I.L 24000000)

£11706 $22828   (23-Oct-90 F.M33/R) Zag I (39x83cm-15x33in) s.d.1970verso (I.L 26000000)

£11846 $20139   (28-May-91 SY.MI164/R) Piccola elegia (63x44cm-25x17in) s.d.54 s.d.1954verso (I.L 26000000)

£12000 $21240   (21-Mar-91 C208/R) Soave Paura (65x55cm-26x22in) s.d.58 l. verso

£15712 $30323   (13-Dec-90 F.M432/R) Roma B 00805 I (119x55cm-47x22in) s.d.1970verso (I.L 34000000)

£22540 $40347   (9-Apr-91 F.R236/R) Composito 3/4 - Siparlo (180x60cm-71x24in) s.d.1984verso (I.L 50000000)

£34000 $58820   (10-May-91 S.Z27/R) Kalomathi (200x150cm-79x59in) s.d.1980verso (S.FR 85000)

£38000 $74100   (18-Oct-90 S93/R) Sine die (100x81cm-39x32in) s.i.d.1963verso

£49208 $83654   (28-May-91 SY.MI188/R) Balance and counter balance (197x270cm-78x106in) s.i.d.1965verso (I.L 108000000)

£72040 $140477   (22-Oct-90 BR.M150/R) Pandora (140x180cm-55x71in) s.verso (I.L 160000000)

DORAZIO, Piero (1927-) Italian-cont.

£1714	$3326	(7-Dec-90 G.Z24/R) Astrazione (34x49cm-13x19in) s.d.1986 pastel (S.FR 4200)
£4585	$7519	(19-Jun-91 F.M109/R) Composizione (52x72cm-20x28in) s.d.1965 W/C (I.L 10000000)
£7400	$14356	(3-Dec-90 CH.R93/R) Senza titolo (48x31cm-19x12in) s.d.1957 gouache (I.L 16000000)

DORE, Gustave (1832-1883) French

£1913	$3119	(16-Jun-91 GL.P49/R) L'oeuvre (20x47cm-8x19in) s.i. board (F.FR 19000)
£2312	$4000	(22-May-91 D.NY21/R) Don Quixote (61x51cm-24x20in) init.indist.i.
£4044	$7887	(17-Oct-90 LC.P68/R) Village en Engadine (73x48cm-29x19in) studio st. (F.FR 40000)
£7078	$13802	(17-Oct-90 ARC.P74/R) Le cerf dans la clairiere (100x150cm-39x59in) mono.d.1879 (F.FR 70000)
£7692	$15000	(23-Oct-90 SY.NY26/R) Souvenir d'ecosse (112x184cm-44x72in) s.d.1879
£9000	$14760	(21-Jun-91 C22/R) Mountain torrent in Highlands (53x78cm-21x31in) s.
£10313	$20111	(17-Oct-90 LC.P69/R) La petite marchande de fleurs (140x84cm-55x33in) studio st. (F.FR 102000)
£15167	$29575	(17-Oct-90 LC.P70/R) La fee Viviane et l'enchanteur Merlin (170x122cm-67x48in) s. (F.FR 150000)
£35897	$70000	(23-Oct-90 SY.NY27/R) Castle on the Isle of Skye (113x196cm-44x77in) s.d.1877 st.decive
£449	$871	(8-Dec-90 GAB.G2187/R) Scene biblique (29x41cm-11x16in) s. chl.htd.gouache (S.FR 1100)
£612	$1188	(8-Dec-90 GAB.G2816/R) Le retour d'Helene (32x25cm-13x10in) crayon board (S.FR 1500)
£612	$1188	(8-Dec-90 GAB.G2185) Le chasseur (29x41cm-11x16in) s. chl.thd.crayon (S.FR 1500)
£663	$1307	(14-Nov-90 FB.P41/R) Saint-Augustin et Sainbe-Monique (56x39cm-22x15in) s.i. chl. (F.FR 6500)
£688	$1341	(17-Oct-90 LC.P67) Allegorie de la victoire (57x87cm-22x34in) studio st. crayon wash htd.white (F.FR 6800)
£950	$1682	(5-Apr-91 LGB.P88) Renaud et Armide (25x19cm-10x7in) init.i. Indian ink wash htd.gouache four panels (F.FR 9600)
£4587	$8853	(14-Dec-90 ARC.P129/R) Biches dans un sous-bois (56x36cm-22x14in) s. W/C (F.FR 45000)
£4893	$9394	(29-Nov-90 ZZ.F5/R) Rixe nocturne a l'entree d'un estaminet londonien (34x24cm-13x9in) s.d.1869 ink wash white gouache (F.FR 48000)
£5000	$9850	(14-Nov-90 FB.P41 a) Les elegantes (35x25cm-14x10in) s.d.1875 W/C wash (F.FR 49000)
£5587	$10000	(10-Apr-91 HF.NY79/R) Geneva with Mt. Blanc in background (47x67cm-19x26in) s. W/C

DOREN, Emile van (1865-1949) Belgian

£3287	$6409	(23-Oct-90 C.A464/R) Sunset (90x150cm-35x59in) s. (B.FR 200000)

DORET, E (19th C) Continental

£2730	$4750	(27-Mar-91 B.SF4306 a/R) The concert (58x79cm-23x31in) s.

DORET, L (18/19th C) Swiss

£818	$1341	(17-Jun-91 DUR.M624) Joven en un jardin (81x35cm-32x14in) s. (S.P 150000)

DORFFMEISTER, Stephan (1729-1797) Hungarian

£4407	$8683	(14-Nov-90 D.V15/R) St Nepomuk and King Wenzel's wife surrounded by angels (168x96cm-66x38in) (A.S 90000)

DORIGNY, Michel (1617-1665) French

£13000	$25090	(11-Dec-90 PH136/R) Mercury seated, with Venus and Cupid (152x119cm-60x47in)
£2200	$3894	(22-Mar-91 APT.P38) Etude de jeune homme (29x20cm-11x8in) pierre noire sanguinne (F.FR 22000)

DORIGNY, Michel (attrib) (1617-1665) French

£400	$708	(22-Mar-91 APT.P37) Apparition d'un ange. Combat de guerriers (18x26cm-7x10in) wash sanguinne double-sided (F.FR 4000)
£618	$1068	(22-May-91 PLF.P31) Muse (27x38cm-11x15in) pierre noire (F.FR 6200)
£2105	$4000	(9-Jan-91 CH.NY8/R) Head of young woman looking to right (13x12cm-5x5in) black chk htd white

DORING, Adam Lude (1925-) ?

£608	$1052	(21-May-91 WK.M823/R) Hands (42x34cm-17x13in) s.d.1969 s.d.verso (DM 1800)

DORING, Rudolf (19th C) German

£655	$1258	(26-Nov-90 WK.M607/R) Composition (42x42cm-17x17in) s.d.1972 s.d.verso mixed media (DM 1900)

DORNBERGER, Karl Johannes (1864-1940) Norwegian

£742	$1410	(11-Sep-90 UL.T189/R) Sailing vessel in Oslo fjord 1910 (38x42cm-15x17in) (N.KR 8500)
£1042	$1740	(3-Jun-91 B.O25/R) Gang of gypsies (49x59cm-19x23in) s.d.1936 panel (N.KR 12000)
£1259	$2102	(3-Jun-91 B.O24/R) Winter landscape with house and trees (55x45cm-22x18in) s.d.1903 (N.KR 14500)

DORNBERGER, Karl Johannes (1864-1940) Norwegian-cont.
£1322	$2471	(29-Aug-90 KH.K49/R) Children on stone pier (35x45cm-14x18in) s.d.1904 panel (D.KR 15000)
£1828	$3235	(19-Mar-91 UL.T160/R) The sun shining on Hammersborg (67x60cm-26x24in) (N.KR 21000)
£2176	$3851	(19-Mar-91 UL.T159/R) Naughty girl (50x46cm-20x18in) (N.KR 25000)
£2364	$4232	(11-Mar-91 B.O24/R) Bright winter's day in Son (38x47cm-15x19in) s.i.d.1906 panel (N.KR 27000)
£3659	$7134	(15-Oct-90 B.O20/R) The gravedigger (92x60cm-36x24in) s.d.1889-95 (N.KR 42000)
£3765	$6740	(11-Mar-91 B.O23/R) Sunday devotion (100x80cm-39x31in) s.i.d.1903 (N.KR 43000)
£426	*$719*	*(29-Apr-91 B.O30/R) Jolly company (33x42cm-13x17in) s.d.1909 W/C (N.KR 4900)*

DORNER, Johann Jakob (18/19th C) German
£1858	*$3159*	*(28-May-91 KF.M155/R) Landscape with ruins of Hilgartsberg (29x41cm-11x16in) pen over pencil W/C (DM 5500)*

DORNER, Johann Jakob (elder) (1741-1813) German
£4027	$7852	(10-Oct-90 ZEL.L1466/R) The chemist (50x40cm-20x16in) i.d.verso one of pair (DM 12000)

DORNER, Johann Jakob (elder-circle) (1741-1813) German
£1923	$3712	(12-Dec-90 N.M364/R) The four apostles with attributes and angel (136x192cm-54x76in) (DM 5500)

DORNER, Johann Jakob (younger) (1775-1852) German
£18581	$31588	(27-May-91 L.K260/R) Upper Bavarian mountain landscape with farmhouse and figures (83x73cm-33x29in) s.indis.d.184. (DM 55000)
£570	*$1112*	*(12-Oct-90 AW.H1411/R) Italianate hilly landscape with traveller resting (20x20cm-8x8in) s.i.verso indian ink pen wash brush (DM 1700)*

DORNER, Johann Jakob (younger-attrib) (1775-1852) German
£699	$1350	(12-Dec-90 N.M489) Alpine landscape with mill (31x36cm-12x14in) i.stretcher paper on canvas (DM 2000)
£1049	$2024	(12-Dec-90 N.M488/R) Mountain valley with waterfall, farmhouse and figures (77x64cm-30x25in) (DM 3000)

DORPH, Anton (1831-?) Danish
£8977	$17684	(14-Nov-90 RAS.K82/R) Autumn harvesting scene (90x130cm-35x51in) s.d.1869 (D.KR 100000)

DORR, Ferdinand (1880-1968) German
£638	$1243	(12-Oct-90 AW.H2233/R) View from Feldberg to Titisee (24x30cm-9x12in) s. board (DM 1900)
£651	$1165	(14-Mar-91 N.M2643/R) View of lake Titisee (60x80cm-24x31in) s. (DM 1900)

DORSCH, Ferdinand (1875-1938) German
£1351	$2635	(26-Oct-90 KM.K1184) Portrait of young lady standing before chest of drawers (95x76cm-37x30in) s. oval (DM 4000)

DORSER, Jacobus (1884-?) Dutch?
£854	$1622	(26-Feb-91 VN.R91) Sunflowers (90x69cm-35x27in) s. (D.FL 2800)

DORSET, Gerald (20th C) ?
£1396	$2750	(15-Nov-90 SY.NY69) Interior with guitar (26x35cm-10x14in) s.d.64

DORSEY, William (20th C) American
£1538	$3000	(10-Oct-90 B.SF613/R) Orchards near Santa Barbara coast (102x127cm-40x50in) s.

DOSSI, Dosso (after) (1479-1542) Italian
£1275	$2193	(14-May-91 GF.L2436/R) Portrait of young Italian woman (67x54cm-26x21in) (S.FR 3200)

DOSSI, Dosso (style) (1479-1542) Italian
£2289	$3845	(23-Apr-91 RAS.K261/R) Religious scene with Madonna, Josef and Child with woman (50x32cm-20x13in) (D.KR 26000)

DOTREMONT, Christian (1922-1979) Belgian
£719	$1172	(15-Jun-91 L.K171/R) Logogram (26x20cm-10x8in) india ink brush (DM 2100)
£534	*$1004*	*(19-Sep-90 KH.K22) Composition (40x40cm-16x16in) Indian ink (D.KR 6000)*
£789	*$1342*	*(29-May-91 KH.K87/R) Caeur en criant (40x40cm-16x16in) s.d.1977 Indian ink (D.KR 9000)*

DOTREMONT, Christian and BALLE, Mogens (20th C) Belgian/Scandinavian
£965	*$1640*	*(29-May-91 KH.K2) Et si le brouillard c'etais l'entente (53x76cm-21x30in) s.d.69 W/C gouache (D.KR 11000)*

DOTREMONT, Christian and CLAUS, Hugo (20th C) Belgian
£1610	*$3107*	*(13-Dec-90 SY.AM332/R) Logogramme (46x61cm-18x24in) s. W/C (D.FL 5200)*

DOTTORI, Gerardo (1884-1977) Italian

£5452	$10741	(30-Oct-90 F.R186/R) Aeropaesaggio (30x22cm-12x9in) s.d.1935 board (I.L 12000000)
£7862	$15253	(3-Dec-90 CH.R135/R) Paesaggio (32x100cm-13x39in) s.d.1932 masonite (I.L 17000000)
£2044	$3537	(7-May-91 F.M112/R) Montagne (35x50cm-14x20in) s. W/C cardboard (I.L 4500000)
£2311	$4459	(12-Dec-90 F.M67/R) Montagne (35x50cm-14x20in) s. i.verso W/C board (I.L 5000000)
£2728	$5346	(20-Nov-90 BR.M28/R) Composizione (70x49cm-28x19in) s. pastel wax (I.L 6000000)
£3438	$5639	(20-Jun-91 F.M372/R) Tempesta mare (22x27cm-9x11in) s. mixed media graffito masonite (I.L 7500000)
£4180	$8234	(30-Oct-90 F.R152/R) Studio per 'Apocalisse' (35x48cm-14x19in) s. crayon tempera (I.L 9200000)
£4298	$8294	(12-Dec-90 F.M52/R) Paesaggio Futurista (49x33cm-19x13in) s. mixed media board (I.L 9300000)

DOU, Gerard (after) (1613-1675) Dutch

£500	$845	(3-May-91 PHE138) The herring woman (38x35cm-15x14in)

DOU, Gerard (attrib) (1613-1675) Dutch

£1984	$3313	(7-Jun-91 ZOF.Z1017/R) The herring seller (48x61cm-19x24in) (S.FR 5000)

DOU, Gerard (school) (1613-1675) Dutch

£872	$1500	(19-May-91 LIT.L129) Fisherman with dog and child (41x30cm-16x12in)

DOU, Gerard (style) (1613-1675) Dutch

£750	$1223	(4-Jul-91 CSK230) Musician at window ledge (36x25cm-14x10in) panel
£1389	$2403	(22-May-91 GS.B2353) St Hieronymus praying before altar (42x35cm-17x14in) i.verso panel (S.FR 3500)
£1800	$3510	(25-Oct-90 CSK63/R) Alchemist in laboratory (45x35cm-18x14in) panel
£1800	$3600	(7-Feb-91 C94/R) A man at a niche holding pipe (26x20cm-10x8in) copper

DOUBEK, F B (1865-?) ?

£970	$1834	(27-Sep-90 D.V91/R) Lazarus rising from the dead (89x67cm-35x26in) s. (A.S 20000)

DOUCET, Jacques (1924-) French

£2775	$5383	(5-Dec-90 HC.P59) Composition (54x38cm-21x15in) s. panel (F.FR 27000)
£2853	$4935	(22-May-91 CH.AM722) Abstract composition (62x47cm-24x19in) s. acrylic oil paper (D.FL 9500)
£3303	$5715	(22-May-91 CH.AM723/R) Abstract composition (62x47cm-24x19in) s. acrylic oil paper (D.FL 11000)
£6306	$10910	(23-May-91 SY.AM279/R) Vivre l'ete Indien (65x92cm-26x36in) s.i.verso (D.FL 21000)
£6800	$13260	(18-Oct-90 C335/R) Untitled (38x46cm-15x18in) s. i.d.1956verso
£9073	$17692	(28-Oct-90 GL.P74/R) Naissance du mouvement (73x60cm-29x24in) s. (F.FR 90000)
£2632	$5079	(12-Dec-90 CH.AM388/R) Playing figures (46x26cm-18x10in) s.i. brush ink (D.FL 8500)
£2789	$4741	(2-Jun-91 GL.P217/R) Composition (54x38cm-21x15in) s. gouache pastel (F.FR 28000)
£3486	$5926	(2-Jun-91 GL.P219/R) Composition (64x49cm-25x19in) s. gouache paper pasted on board (F.FR 35000)
£5306	$10453	(16-Nov-90 EA.Z338/R) Untitled (18x23cm-7x9in) s. mixed media collage board (S.FR 13000)
£6122	$12061	(15-Nov-90 I.N45/R) Composition (65x50cm-26x20in) s. gouache paper on panel (F.FR 60000)

DOUDELET, Charles (1861-1938) Belgian

£1238	$2390	(12-Dec-90 CH.AM22) View of conventgarden with praying nuns (24x33cm-9x13in) mono. (D.FL 4000)

DOUFFET, Gerard (1594-1660) Flemish

£15911	$31185	(19-Nov-90 CH.R24/R) S.Giacomo Apostolo (80x70cm-31x28in) (I.L 35000000)

DOUGHERTY, Paul (1877-1947) American

£651	$1250	(29-Nov-90 MFA.C144) Rocky coast (43x64cm-17x25in) s.
£918	$1800	(13-Feb-91 B.SF2105/R) Sea cliff (32x42cm-13x17in) s.d.05 board
£3316	$6500	(13-Feb-91 B.SF2083/R) Freshening gale (66x91cm-26x36in) sold with letter
£4615	$9000	(10-Oct-90 B.SF479/R) Point Lobos (61x71cm-24x28in) s.
£5102	$10000	(13-Feb-91 B.SF2074/R) California coast (61x84cm-24x33in) s.

DOUGHTY, Thomas (1793-1856) American

£3222	$6250	(5-Dec-90 D.NY15/R) View of Lake George (30x41cm-12x16in) panel
£3836	$7250	(26-Sep-90 SY.NY11/R) Passage of the Delaware through the Blue Mountain (35x51cm-14x20in) s.i.d.1827
£4688	$9000	(30-Nov-90 CH.NY17/R) Landscape with anglers and sailboats (36x51cm-14x20in) s.
£14525	$26000	(14-Mar-91 CH.NY12/R) View of Hudson (74x91cm-29x36in) s.

DOUGLAS, Edward Algernon Stuart (1850-c.1920) British
£1579 $3000   (27-Feb-91 SY.NY208/R) E'en sober Dobbin lifss clumsy heel, and kicks, disdainful of dirty wheel (71x127cm-28x50in) s.d.1906 s.stretcher
£600   *$1200*   *(8-Feb-91 C111) Calling the hounds (13x20cm-5x8in) s.d.1893 pencil W/C*
£925   *$1526*   *(10-Jul-91 GC448/R) Hunting scenes with riders jumping a hedge and a fence, with hounds (20x28cm-8x11in) s.d.1893 1894 W/C two*

DOUGLAS, Edwin (1848-1914) British
£3000 $5040   (16-Jul-91 C156/R) Collie, the guardian of the flock (66x56cm-26x22in) s.d.1908
£3500 $6265   (11-Mar-91 HS263/R) The crofter's collie - study of dog beside fireplace with cauldron (50x60cm-20x24in) s.d.1900

DOUGLAS, James (1858-1911) British
£500   *$815*   *(14-Jun-91 C74 a) Anglers in a punt (45x29cm-18x11in) s. pencil W/C htd. white gum arabic*
£780   *$1537*   *(1-Nov-90 C117) Princes Street gardens, Edinburgh (28x38cm-11x15in) s. pencil W/C htd.white*
£7000   *$11760*   *(16-Jul-91 PHC794/R) Driving from the second tee, North Berwick (43x29cm-17x11in) W/C*

DOUGLAS, Sir William Fettes (1822-1891) British
£1200 $2016   (23-Apr-91 S57/R) Thoughts of home (37x30cm-15x12in) s.d.1874
£2000 $3740   (28-Aug-90 S852/R) The panelled room (30x61cm-12x24in) s.

DOUGLAS, William (attrib) (1780-1832) British
£800   *$1536*   *(18-Dec-90 C96/R) Portrait of young girl beside plumed black hat (18x?cm-7x?in) min.gilt-wood frame rec.*

DOULAIN, Dominique (20th C) ?
£857 $1671   (28-Oct-90 R.P37) Sains titre (52x68cm-20x27in) s. acrylic cardboard (F.FR 8500)

DOUMET, Zacharie Felix (1761-1818) French
£2814   *$4615*   *(18-Jun-91 APT.P83/R) Vue de Bastia, prise du Cap Corse. Vue de Bastia, prise du chemin de Corte (28x24cm-11x9in) both s. gouache round pair (F.FR 28000)*

DOUST, Jan van (?) ?
£2646 $5000   (24-Sep-90 S.SL502/R) Still lifes depicting vase of flowers on ledge (81x61cm-32x24in) s. pair

DOUST, W H (19th C) British
£2400 $4128   (15-May-91 BT259/R) A warship shortening sail (46x61cm-18x24in) s.d.1854

DOUTRELEAU, Pierre (19th C) French
£769 $1500   (10-Oct-90 SY.NY317/R) Moored boats (46x61cm-18x24in) s.
£2232 $3839   (13-May-91 PPB.P8/R) Marine (54x73cm-21x29in) s. (F.FR 22500)

DOUVEN, Bartholomeus (1688-1726) German
£4200 $7980   (1-Mar-91 C122/R) Euterpe (132x139cm-52x55in)

DOUVEN, Jan Frans van (style) (1656-1727) German
£1399 $2699   (10-Dec-90 L.K34) Portrait of Kurfurst Johann Wilhelm von der Pfalz wearing ermine coat (84x68cm-33x27in) (DM 4000)

DOUW, Simon Johannes van (1630-1677) Flemish
£1910 $3666   (19-Feb-91 ARC.P12) Choc de cavalerie (58x81cm-23x32in) s. panel (F.FR 19000)
£7179 $14000   (11-Oct-90 SY.NY132/R) Battle scene (58x83cm-23x33in) s. panel

DOUZETTE, Louis (1834-1924) German
£805 $1352   (27-Apr-91 SO.S309/R) Moonlit landscape with house (24x34cm-9x13in) s.d.1917 panel (S.KR 8500)
£979 $1890   (12-Dec-90 N.M490/R) Moonlit landscape with sailing ship offshore (30x40cm-12x16in) s. (DM 2800)
£2449 $4800   (6-Nov-90 GF.L2119/R) Moonlit landscape (50x76cm-20x30in) s. (S.FR 6000)

DOVA, Gianni (1925-) Italian
£1063 $2051   (13-Dec-90 F.M301) Composizione (50x37cm-20x15in) s. tempera paper (I.L 2300000)
£1351 $2634   (24-Oct-90 F.M187/R) Composizione geometrica (45x35cm-18x14in) s.d.50 tempera panel (I.L 3000000)
£1374 $2638   (27-Nov-90 SY.MI121/R) Composizione (18x24cm-7x9in) s. (I.L 3000000)
£1592 $3010   (27-Sep-90 F.M105) Composizione (95x70cm-37x28in) s.d.61 tempera paper (I.L 3500000)
£1815 $3121   (13-May-91 CH.R180/R) Composizione (40x50cm-16x20in) s.d.1950 (I.L 4000000)
£1832 $3518   (27-Nov-90 SY.MI141/R) Composizione nucleare (40x60cm-16x24in) s.d.55 (I.L 4000000)
£1903 $3311   (26-Mar-91 F.M89/R) Composizione geometrica (50x40cm-20x16in) s.d.50 panel (I.L 4200000)
£1909 $3742   (20-Nov-90 BR.M126/R) Composizione (50x75cm-20x30in) d.1989 tempera (I.L 4200000)
£2364 $4633   (20-Nov-90 BR.M51/R) Gabbiano (50x75cm-20x30in) s. tempera paper on canvas (I.L 5200000)

DOVA, Gianni (1925-) Italian-cont.

£3697	$7135	(13-Dec-90 F.M479/R) Nucleare (90x70cm-35x28in) s.d.53verso (I.L 8000000)
£3736	$6352	(28-May-91 SY.MI60/R) Composizione (62x47cm-24x19in) s.d.1970verso (I.L 8200000)
£3832	$6859	(9-Apr-91 F.R77) Composizione (100x70cm-39x28in) i.verso acrylic paper laid down on canvas (I.L 8500000)
£4625	$8972	(3-Dec-90 CH.R64/R) Composizione fantastica (75x100cm-30x39in) s. acrylic (I.L 10000000)
£4998	$9846	(30-Oct-90 F.R131/R) Interno con acquario (100x80cm-39x31in) s. (I.L 11000000)
£5267	$10114	(27-Nov-90 SY.MI193/R) Composizione (100x100cm-39x39in) s.d.56 (I.L 11500000)
£5853	$11414	(22-Oct-90 BR.M226/R) In giardino (60x70cm-24x28in) s. s.d.1960verso (I.L 13000000)
£6379	$10844	(28-May-91 SY.MI136/R) Tre vortici (137x200cm-54x79in) tempera paper laid down on canvas (I.L 14000000)
£6834	$11619	(28-May-91 SY.MI138/R) Forme nere (160x130cm-63x51in) s.d.61verso (I.L 15000000)
£7329	$14071	(27-Nov-90 SY.MI39/R) Uccello di fuoco (160x130cm-63x51in) s. (I.L 16000000)
£9230	$17999	(24-Oct-90 F.M211/R) Composizione (70x60cm-28x24in) s.d.62 (I.L 20500000)
£10356	$20194	(22-Oct-90 BR.M270/R) In giardino tra i fiori (50x60cm-20x24in) s. (I.L 23000000)
£694	$1346	(3-Dec-90 F.M90) Composizione (24x18cm-9x7in) s. mixed media (I.L 1500000)
£1274	$2408	(27-Sep-90 F.M13/R) Personaggio (72x49cm-28x19in) mixed media (I.L 2800000)
£1619	$3140	(3-Dec-90 F.M329/R) Composizione (49x74cm-19x29in) s. gouache (I.L 3500000)
£1820	$3439	(27-Sep-90 F.M118/R) Totem (73x48cm-29x19in) s. tempera enamel paper (I.L 4000000)
£2312	$4486	(3-Dec-90 F.M240/R) Composizione spaziale (36x69cm-14x27in) s.d.1957 mixed media paper on faesite (I.L 5000000)

DOVASTON, Margaret (fl.1908-1913) British

£632	$1200	(14-Sep-90 DM.D2016) Looking out (41x30cm-16x12in) s.d.1922
£1111	$2155	(4-Dec-90 R.T265/R) Gossips (35x30cm-14x12in) s.d.1928 i.verso (C.D 2500)
£1451	$2786	(27-Nov-90 W.T1057/R) The rightful heir (36x56cm-14x22in) s. (C.D 3250)
£1800	$3474	(13-Dec-90 CSK183/R) New venture (51x69cm-20x27in) s.

DOVE, Arthur G (1880-1946) American

£2381	$4500	(27-Sep-90 CH.NY243/R) Across the Harbor (22x30cm-9x12in) s.d.1930 indist.i. W/C ink
£3073	$5500	(14-Mar-91 CH.NY228/R) Centrepoint series No. 20A (12x18cm-5x7in) s. W/C chl pencil paper on board
£4211	$8000	(14-Sep-90 S.BM330/R) Study for 'Summer' (13x20cm-5x8in) s. W/C ink pair
£4510	$8750	(5-Dec-90 D.NY100/R) Abstract landscape (13x20cm-5x8in) s.d.41 W/C
£4510	$8750	(5-Dec-90 D.NY101/R) Distant mountains (15x20cm-6x8in) s. W/C
£4510	$8750	(5-Dec-90 D.NY102/R) Abstract still life (15x20cm-6x8in) s. W/C
£4639	$9000	(5-Dec-90 D.NY99/R) Blazing sun (13x20cm-5x8in) s. W/C
£4639	$9000	(5-Dec-90 D.NY108/R) Life (13x15cm-5x6in) s. W/C

DOVERA, Achille (1838-1895) Italian

£5550	$10767	(5-Dec-90 F.M1/R) Marina al chiaro di luna (50x107cm-20x42in) s. (I.L 12000000)

DOW, Arthur W (1857-1922) American

£15135	$28000	(8-Mar-91 S.BM211/R) A bright sky with a breeze (84x137cm-33x54in) s.i.d.1918

DOWNIE, John P (1871-1945) British

£1100	$2057	(30-Aug-90 CG106) Quiet hours (41x51cm-16x20in) s. i.label verso

DOWNIE, Patrick (1854-1945) British

£700	$1365	(11-Oct-90 CG189) Ducks by pond (25x36cm-10x14in)
£880	$1734	(30-Oct-90 SC141/R) Bellhaven Bay, Dunbar. (26x34cm-10x13in) s.i.d.1925 i.d.verso board
£950	$1606	(3-May-91 PHE82) September, Firth of Clyde (36x54cm-14x21in) s.i.verso board
£1000	$1970	(1-Nov-90 B125/R) Sorting the catch (25x35cm-10x14in) s. board
£2000	$4000	(5-Feb-91 S205/R) Old White Hart Hotel, Cathcart Square, Greenock (38x28cm-15x11in) s. s.i.d.1927 verso
£2800	$5236	(28-Aug-90 S948/R) Gathering wrack (101x127cm-40x50in) s.
£600	$1182	(30-Oct-90 SC11/R) Snowy street scene (29x19cm-11x7in) s. W/C oil pencil scratching out
£650	$1086	(26-Jul-91 PHE131) In full sail (35x52cm-14x20in) s. W/C
£800	$1344	(23-Apr-91 S110/R) Paris (37x27cm-15x11in) s.i.d.94 d.verso W/C
£1000	$1680	(23-Apr-91 S61/R) Greenock (29x19cm-11x7in) s. W/C htd white
£1200	$2028	(2-May-91 CG434/R) Saltmarket, Glasgow, 1887 (35x25cm-14x10in) s.d.1887 s.i.d.1887 verso W/C htd bodycol

DOWNING, Delapoer (fl.1886-1902) British

£640	$1094	(30-Jul-91 SWS14/R) The barber shop (60x90cm-24x35in) s.

DOWNING, Delapoer (fl.1886-1902) British-cont.
£680 $1258   (6-Mar-91 SC4341/R) Distressing news (74x89cm-29x35in) s.

DOWNMAN, John (1750-1824) British
£650 $1300   (7-Feb-91 CSK173) Portrait of gentleman, with arms folded
       (16x13cm-6x5in) painted oval on copper
£1100   *$1815*   *(9-Jul-91 C56/R) Portrait of young girl playing mechanical zither*
       (28x39cm-11x15in) s.d.1784 chk stump W/C paper on linen oval
£6500   *$10725*   *(9-Jul-91 C55/R) Portrait of Queen Charlotte seated by table with*
       landscape beyond (53x34cm-21x13in) s.d.1784 chk stump W/C paper on
       linen
£7500   *$12375*   *(11-Jul-91 S46/R) Wedding portrait of Sir William Jarvis Twysden of*
       Roydon Hall and wife (52x36cm-20x14in) s.d.1786 chk W/C htd.white

DOWNMAN, John (attrib) (1750-1884) British
£1000 $1950   (16-Oct-90 CG228/R) Portrait of Archibald Neilson in jacket with
       waistcoat seated by window (25x20cm-10x8in) panel painted oval

DOWNS, Edgar (1876-?) British
£620 $1147   (5-Mar-91 SWS1395) Evening at the lock (76x94cm-30x37in) i.verso

DOWSON, Russell (fl.1880-1911) British
£680 $1306   (17-Aug-90 K332) River scene 'Windsor Castle' (38x53cm-15x21in) s.
       gouache

DOYLE, Charles Altamont (1832-1893) British
£800 $1352   (2-May-91 CG439/R) Demon's stack (28x45cm-11x18in) s.d.1883 i.verso pen
       W/C
£1100 $1859   (2-May-91 CG438/R) Springtime (27x61cm-11x24in) pen W/C
£1350 $2660   (12-Nov-90 PH91/R) Girl being serenaded on a snow covered branch
       (40x25cm-16x10in) ink W/C
£2100 $3549   (2-May-91 CG442/R) Dancing lesson (20x33cm-8x13in) s.i.d.1883 pen W/C
£8500 $14365   (2-May-91 CG436/R) Dance round moon (25x39cm-10x15in) pen W/C

DOYLE, Richard (1824-1883) British
£2600 $4992   (26-Nov-90 SWS76/R) The altar cup in Aagerup (25x35cm-10x14in) mono. W/C
       over pen ink

DOYLE, William M S (1769-1828) American
£700 $1155   (10-Jul-91 C65/R) Miss Mary Eliza Byrne (9x?cm-4x?in) gilt-wood frame
       rec.

D'OYLY, Sir Charles (attrib) (19th C) British
£1105 $2100   (27-Feb-91 SY.NY207/R) Marquess of Lansdowne hunting tigers
       (60x72cm-24x28in)

DOZEMAN, Roelof (1924-) Dutch
£1149 $1989   (25-May-91 KV.L105) Town scene (40x50cm-16x20in) s. (B.FR 70000)

DRACHMANN, Holger (1846-1908) Danish
£769 $1485   (14-Dec-90 BM.B605/R) Sailing ships at Blankenese with steam ship beyond
       (22x29cm-9x11in) s.d.94 (DM 2200)
£893 $1688   (25-Sep-90 RAS.K55/R) Seascape with sailship and steamship
       (66x94cm-26x37in) init.d.78 (D.KR 10000)
£900 $1530   (30-May-91 C131) Passing lighthouse (88x127cm-35x50in) s.d.74
£928 $1745   (10-Aug-90 RAS.V454/R) Seascape with vessels (24x35cm-9x14in) s.
       (D.KR 10500)
£968 $1627   (23-Apr-91 RAS.K283) Off the harbour at Ramsgate (30x41cm-12x16in)
       s.d.71 (D.KR 11000)
£1158 $2269   (22-Nov-90 RAS.V705/R) Seascape with sailship, Oresund, artist by
       beached boats (37x56cm-15x22in) init.d.1867 (D.KR 13000)
£1762 $2943   (6-Jun-91 RAS.K121/R) Norwegian archipelago, Hellesund (43x68cm-17x27in)
       s.d.1908 (D.KR 20000)
£11201 $22401   (6-Feb-91 RAS.K292/R) View from Grenens point (63x115cm-25x45in) s.
       (D.KR 125000)

DRACHMANN, Holger and SUNDT-HANSEN, Carl (19th C) Danish/Norwegian
£4053 $6768   (6-Jun-91 RAS.K61/R) Stormy weather by the ocean with mermaid washed
       ashore (90x150cm-35x59in) s.d.1895 (D.KR 46000)

DRAHONET, Alexandre Jean Dubois (1791-1834) French
£6024 $9699   (27-Jun-91 APT.P247/R) Portrait d'une dame avec des fleurs rouges dans
       les cheveux (65x55cm-26x22in) mono.d.1821 (F.FR 60000)

DRAKES, Tom (19th C) ?
£1143 $2228   (17-Oct-90 LC.P53/R) Portrait de cheval - a moi Saint Hubert
       (95x71cm-37x28in) s. (F.FR 11300)
£1822 $3571   (21-Nov-90 CB.P44/R) Tigre du Bengale (237x173cm-93x68in) s.
       (F.FR 18000)

DRAPER, Herbert James (1864-1920) British
£12821 $25000   (23-Oct-90 SY.NY394/R) The water nymph (61x114cm-24x45in) s.

DRASCHE-WARTINBERG, Richard (1850-1923) Austrian
£965 $1881   (18-Oct-90 D.V146/R) Wiener Ebene, evening (36x56cm-14x22in) s. i.verso
       canvas on board (A.S 20000)

DRATHMANN, Christopher (1856-1931) German
£2200 $4224   (27-Nov-90 PH148/R) Deer in landscape (67x101cm-26x40in) s.

DREBER, Heinrich (1822-1875) German
£16892   *$28716*   *(31-May-91 GB.B5741/R) Olevano (44x57cm-17x22in) i. pencil pen sepia wash (DM 50000)*

DREGER, Tom von (1868-1949) Austrian
£570 $1019   (11-Apr-91 D.V113/R) The old violin player (81x61cm-32x24in) s.d.1919 (A.S 12000)

DREHER, A (19th C) German
£1104 $1898   (16-May-91 D.V84/R) Kittens (17x24cm-7x9in) s. panel (A.S 23000)

DRESSLER, August Wilhelm (1886-1970) German
£1224 $2374   (7-Dec-90 GB.B6470) Italian landscape (60x70cm-24x28in) s.mono. (DM 3500)
£946   *$1608*   *(31-May-91 GB.B6239/R) In the morning, female nude standing before window mono. i.verso enkaustik board (DM 2800)*

DREUX, Alfred de (1810-1860) French
£4183 $7237   (24-May-91 FB.P160/R) Le cavalier (24x33cm-9x13in) s. (F.FR 42000)
£8588 $14084   (21-Jun-91 SY.MO321/R) L'envolee sur l'obstacle (33x41cm-13x16in) s. (F.FR 85450)
£10000 $19700 ·   (5-Oct-90 C39/R) Stallions fighting in stormy landscape (84x112cm-33x44in) s.
£14388 $27914   (8-Dec-90 SY.MO315/R) Cavaliere avec son cheval et son levrier (64x47cm-25x19in) s. (F.FR 140000)
£32335 $54000   (7-Jun-91 SY.NY45/R) Chevaux a l'exercise (43x65cm-17x26in) s.
£2935   *$5753*   *(19-Nov-90 ZZ.F2) Venus Ordonne aux amours de forger des fleches (29x40cm-11x16in) gouache parchment oval (F.FR 29000)*
£13720   *$27439*   *(4-Feb-91 PLF.P39/R) Couse de chevaux en liberte (27x40cm-11x16in) s.d.1832 W/C (F.FR 135000)*

DREUX, Alfred de (attrib) (1810-1860) French
£4200 $7266   (9-May-91 CSK98/R) Pasha's pride (59x73cm-23x29in)

DREUX, Alfred de (school) (19th C) French
£2130 $4089   (17-Dec-90 AGS.P27/R) L'amazone (60x73cm-24x29in) (F.FR 21000)

DREUX, Alfred de (style) (1810-1860) French
£1005 $1648   (21-Jun-91 D.P52/R) Chevaux a l'entrainement (72x92cm-28x36in) (F.FR 10000)
£3000 $4920   (18-Jun-91 PH53) Hounds on the chase (130x164cm-51x65in)

DREW, Clement (1807-1889) American
£1135 $2100   (8-Mar-91 S.BM173/R) Ship sounding off Cape Horn (36x56cm-14x22in) s.i.d.1885
£1491 $2400   (25-Jan-91 JRB.C21/R) Empress of China (61x91cm-24x36in)
£1604 $3000   (1-Aug-90 B.P11/R) Boston harbour and Brewster Isainds from Brewster Channel (46x76cm-18x30in) s. d.verso
£2793 $5250   (7-Aug-90 RB.HY208/R) Fisherman passing Thatcher Island Light south east gale (46x76cm-18x30in) s. s.d.1884 verso

DREW, George W (1875-?) American
£632 $1200   (14-Sep-90 DM.D2121/R) The road to home, Conn. (51x76cm-20x30in) s.
£777 $1500   (10-Dec-90 H.C1073/R) New England homestead (58x91cm-23x36in) s.
£1073 $1900   (22-Mar-91 S.W2475/R) Road to home, Connecticut (51x76cm-20x30in) s. i.stretcher

DREWES, Werner (1899-1985) American
£538 $1050   (20-Oct-90 BRA.N12) Abstract landscape d.1931
£744 $1450   (20-Oct-90 BRA.N74) Chartres d.1929 panel
£761 $1500   (18-Nov-90 JRB.C190/R) Sunday morning, Rhone valley (56x81cm-22x32in) s. s.d.59verso i.stretcher
£795 $1550   (20-Oct-90 BRA.N11) Farm landscape d.1936
£1168 $2300   (7-Oct-90 DU.E70/R) Abstract with sailboat (30x56cm-12x22in) s. d.1945verso
£3590 $7000   (20-Oct-90 BRA.N78) Yellow on green d.1935
£4615 $9000   (20-Oct-90 BRA.N50) Composition 256 d.1941 linen
£4615 $9000   (20-Oct-90 BRA.N75) Abstract landscape d.1935 panel
£5897 $11500   (20-Oct-90 BRA.N49) Geometric abstraction d.1934
£885   *$1700*   *(17-Dec-90 SY.NY389 a) Untitled no. 509 (15x15cm-6x6in) s.d.80 collage gouache*

DREXEL, Hans Christoph (1886-1979) German
£2931 $5628   (26-Nov-90 WK.M199/R) Female dancer (66x51cm-26x20in) s. panel (DM 8500)

DREYER, Dankvart (1816-1852) Danish
£692 $1343   (22-Aug-90 RAS.K187) Wooded landscape with roof of house (15x27cm-6x11in) (D.KR 8000)
£1795 $3537   (14-Nov-90 RAS.K282/R) Danish heath landscape (18x30cm-7x12in) (D.KR 20000)
£2201 $3697   (22-Apr-91 BU.K52/R) Landscape with deer, riders in background (52x65cm-20x26in) (D.KR 25000)

DREYER, Paul Uwe (1939-) German
£1160 $2274   (20-Nov-90 L.K208/R) Stutzgerust abgeblockt (85x80cm-33x31in)
             s.i.d.1970verso (DM 3400)
£1438 $2345   (14-Jun-91 L.K849) Phasenemblem (100x95cm-39x37in) s.i.d.1970verso
             (DM 4200)

DRIAN, A (19/20th C) French
£700 $1218   (28-Mar-91 CSK129/R) Harlequin and ballerina (37x38cm-15x15in) board

DRIAN, Etienne (1885-1961) French
£1106 $1813   (19-Jun-91 JM.P82) L'athlete noir (62x48cm-24x19in) s. pastel
             (F.FR 11000)

DRIESSCHE, Ernest van den (1894-1985) Belgian
£542 $937   (25-May-91 KV.L298) The Flight into Egypt (35x46cm-14x18in) s. panel
                    (B.FR 33000)
£655 $1113   (28-May-91 C.A318) St Niklaas (50x60cm-20x24in) s. (B.FR 40000)
£740 $1442   (23-Oct-90 C.A935) Carnival (60x60cm-24x24in) s. panel (B.FR 45000)

DRING, William (1904-1990) British
£550 $941   (1-Aug-91 CSK119) Double portrait of young man and woman
                    (61x52cm-24x20in) s.d.1927

DRINKWATER, Albert M (19th C) British
£1000 $1670   (4-Jun-91 SWS1663/R) Salisbury. River scene with cattle watering
                    (60x91cm-24x36in) s. one d.1894 one d.1895 pair

DRINKWATER, Milton (19/20th C) British
£1300 $2301   (20-Mar-91 JT150) Lake Ullswater (76x127cm-30x50in) s.d.1905

DROESE, Felix (1950-) German
£1024 $2007   (20-Nov-90 L.K209/R) Effecteren (50x65cm-20x26in) s.d.1985 mixed media
                    double-sided (DM 3000)

DROLLING, Martin (1752-1817) French
£1205 $1940   (27-Jun-91 APT.P220/R) Un jeune paysan ramenant un fagot de la grange
                    (26x18cm-10x7in) i. verso (F.FR 12000)
£1012 $1700   (17-Jul-91 SY.NY31/R) The music lesson (46x37cm-18x15in) W/C gouache
                    over blk.chk. paper laid down board
£2051 $4000   (26-Oct-90 SY.NY70/R) Two studies of man seen from behind
                    (26x22cm-10x9in) st.sig. chk

DRONSFIELD, John (1900-1951) British/South African
£1553 $2904   (27-Aug-90 SY.J250/R) Street corner conversation (60x50cm-24x20in) s.
                    (SA.R 7500)

DROOCHSLOOT, Joost Cornelisz (1586-1666) Dutch
£5500 $10615   (11-Dec-90 PH1/R) Peasants merrymaking around table (47x70cm-19x28in)
                    panel
£7500 $14475   (13-Dec-90 B98/R) Peasants merrymaking in village street
                    (47x70cm-19x28in) s.d.1648 panel
£7692 $15000   (10-Oct-90 CH.NY77/R) The Pool of Bethseda (103x142cm-41x56in) s.d.
£8815 $17365   (14-Nov-90 D.V87/R) Peasants merrymaking in wooded landscape
                    (48x61cm-19x24in) panel (A.S 180000)
£11558 $19995   (22-May-91 EA.M498/R) Numerous peasants and townfolk in busy street
                    (47x71cm-19x28in) mono.d.1648 panel (C.D 23000)
£13712 $27013   (14-Nov-90 D.V88/R) Village scene at the end of day (38x60cm-15x24in)
                    mono.d.1643 panel one of pair (A.S 280000)
£14388 $27914   (7-Dec-90 CB.P7/R) Une rue de village (84x115cm-33x45in) panel
                    (F.FR 140000)
£18184 $35640   (20-Nov-90 F.R166/R) L'elemosina ai poveri (87x115cm-34x45in) rem.sig.
                    (I.L 40000000)
£19878 $39159   (14-Nov-90 SY.AM94/R) Village landscape (72x106cm-28x42in) s.d.1631
                    panel (D.FL 65000)
£20408 $40000   (6-Nov-90 GF.L2003/R) Village street with figures (60x84cm-24x33in)
                    s.d.1658 panel (S.FR 50000)
£21407 $42171   (14-Nov-90 SY.AM126/R) Village street scene with soldiers and other
                    figures (74x107cm-29x42in) s.d.1633 panel (D.FL 70000)
£22105 $42000   (11-Jan-91 CH.NY13/R) Village street scene with figures
                    (73x112cm-29x44in) mono. panel
£35473 $60304   (27-May-91 L.K37/R) Village fair with figures (54x76cm-21x30in) mono.
                    panel (DM 105000)
£35971 $69784   (7-Dec-90 CH.MO309/R) Une vue d'une rue eoncombree d'un village
                    (59x97cm-23x38in) mono.d.1644 panel (F.FR 350000)

DROOCHSLOOT, Joost Cornelisz (style) (1586-1666) Dutch
£12000 $23640   (31-Oct-90 S91/R) Village scene (99x141cm-39x56in)

DROUAIS, Francois Hubert (circle) (1727-1775) French
£21298 $42170   (30-Jan-91 APT.P116/R) L'enfant aux cerises (55x45cm-22x18in)
                    (F.FR 210000)

DROUAIS, Francois Hubert (school) (1727-1775) French
£1223 $2349   (30-Nov-90 APT.P116/R) Portrait de femme tenant un chat sur ses genoux
                    (81x65cm-32x26in) (F.FR 12000)

DROUAIS, Francois Hubert (studio) (1727-1775) French
£2941 $5000   (31-May-91 CH.NY159/R) Portrait of lady said to be Mme Oudrey seated
                    holding muff (64x53cm-25x21in)

DROUAIS, Francois Hubert (style) (1727-1775) French
£1000 $1630   (4-Jul-91 CSK256/R) Portrait of lady, seated in dress and bonnet,
                    embroidering cushion (91x71cm-36x28in)
£1054 $1697   (27-Jun-91 APT.P188/R) Portrait de Herault de Sechelles
                    (38x31cm-15x12in) oval (F.FR 10500)
£1500 $2880   (29-Nov-90 CSK199/R) Putti fighting by plinth (46x36cm-18x14in) en
                    grisaille

DROUGGE, Mauritz (1874-1949) Scandinavian?
£870 $1540   (19-Mar-91 UL.T157) Portrait of dog (100x160cm-39x63in) (N.KR 10000)
£1576 $2821   (11-Mar-91 B.O22/R) Capercaillie at play (110x136cm-43x54in) s.
           (N.KR 18000)

DROUIN, J (19th C) French
£1100 $2145   (18-Oct-90 CSK92/R) French barque-rigged ship 'Celeste'
           (46x65cm-18x26in) s.d.1857

DRUCK VON STOCKMAYER, Elise (1862-1934) German
£870 $1470   (19-Apr-91 FN.S1699/R) Sunlit wood clearing (61x79cm-24x31in) s.
           (DM 2600)

DRUCK, Hermann (1856-?) German
£1304 $2204   (19-Apr-91 FN.S1700/R) Snowy village street with figures, sunny day
           (20x30cm-8x12in) s.i.verso board (DM 3900)

DRUILLET, Phillipe (1944-) French
£1067   *$2134*   (6-Feb-91 LD.P56/R) Personnage fantastique (90x69cm-35x27in) s. Indian
           ink gouache (F.FR 10500)

DRULMAN, Marinus Johannes see JONGERE, Marinus de

DRUM, David Clayton (1944-) Canadian
£811 $1322   (10-Jun-91 W.T1090) Pagoda pines (91x104cm-36x41in) s.d.'90 l. verso
           (C.D 1500)
£982 $1886   (27-Nov-90 W.T861/R) Les nympheas (61x89cm-24x35in) s.d.90 canvas on
           board (C.D 2200)
£865   *$1410*   (10-Jun-91 W.T1059/R) Silver Birch (107x135cm-42x53in) s. i. verso mixed
           media board (C.D 1600)

DRUMMOND, Arthur (1871-1951) British
£6000 $11700   (18-Oct-90 SC3069/R) The finest in the shop (61x100cm-24x39in) s.d.1901
£11000 $17930   (14-Jun-91 C254/R) Blossoms (76x55cm-30x22in) s.d.1890

DRUMMOND, J Nelson (fl.1882-1896) British
£300   *$576*   (20-Feb-91 B33) A foggy evening (58x44cm-23x17in) s. pastel

DRUMMOND, James (1816-1877) British
£750   *$1275*   (29-May-91 PHC26) Entertaining baby (61x45cm-24x18in) s. W/C
£1400 $2772   (30-Jan-91 S196/R) United service (69x51cm-27x20in) s.d.1873
           indist.s.i.verso W/C

DRUMMOND, Julian E (19/20th C) British
£660   *$1228*   (5-Sep-90 MMB160/R) A panoramic view of Whitby harbour (23x53cm-9x21in)
           s.d.1905
£750   *$1208*   (27-Jun-91 RS30) Whitby Harbour towards St Mary's church
           (23x53cm-9x21in) s.d.1905 W/C

DRUMMOND, Malcolm (1880-1945) British
£1250 $2350   (20-Sep-90 C185/R) Landscape, Donegal (29x39cm-11x15in) panel
£1700 $2958   (27-Mar-91 S29/R) Tea in the garden of Boyne Hill Vicarage near
           Maidenhead (38x56cm-15x22in) s.d.1919

DRYBERGH, Charles (1932-) Belgian
£986 $1923   (23-Oct-90 C.A199/R) Manipulation (120x130cm-47x51in) s.d.1969
           (B.FR 60000)
£1315 $2564   (23-Oct-90 C.A198) Composition (142x133cm-56x52in) s.d.1969 verso
           (B.FR 80000)

DRYDEN, Helen (19/20th C) American
£2353   *$4000*   (1-Jun-91 IH.NY55/R) Lady being courted by masked man (48x38cm-19x15in)
           s. gouache W/C

DRYSDALE, Alexander John (1870-1934) American
£651 $1100   (1-May-91 B.SF5248/R) Sunrise on Bayou, Southern Louisiana
           (58x89cm-23x35in) s. board
£635   *$1200*   (25-Sep-90 CE.NY157/R) October morning on the road to Lafayette,
           Louisana (51x76cm-20x30in) s.d.1926 W/C gouache board

DRYSDALE, Sir George Russell (1912-1981) Australian
£3488 $5860   (22-Apr-91 SY.ME223/R) Head of young woman (24x14cm-9x6in) s. canvas on
           board (A.D 7500)
£17674 $29693   (22-Apr-91 SY.ME290 a/R) Still life, 1939 (39x49cm-15x19in) s.
           (A.D 38000)
£21395 $35944   (22-Apr-91 SY.ME248/R) Girl holding flower (60x50cm-24x20in) s.i. canvas
           on board (A.D 46000)
£84337 $161928   (26-Nov-90 SY.ME215/R) Grandma's Sunday walk (75x126cm-30x50in) s.
           i.d.1972 verso (A.D 210000)
£759   *$1458*   (14-Aug-90 SY.ME2) Washing gold (23x14cm-9x6in) s.i.d.Xmas 1976 pen ink
           wash (A.D 1800)
£905   *$1529*   (16-Apr-91 J.M118/R) Brother and Sister (14x9cm-6x4in) s. W/C
           (A.D 2000)
£1013   *$1944*   (14-Aug-90 SY.ME32) Old rosie init.i.d.'61 pen (A.D 2400)
£1200 $2328   (6-Dec-90 CSK39/R) Interior with nude (25x34cm-10x13in) st.sig. studio
           st.verso pen brush

DRYSDALE, Sir George Russell (1912-1981) Australian-cont.
£1471 $2485   (16-Apr-91 J.M280/R) Men yarning (18x33cm-7x13in) s. W/C ink (A.D 3250)

DUBASTY, Adolphe Henri (1814-1884) French
£650 $1248   (29-Nov-90 B162/R) Young woman in an interior (35x26cm-14x10in) s.d.1884
    panel

DUBAUT, Pierre (1886-1968) French
£398 $693   (25-Mar-91 PLF.P35) L'attelage (23x34cm-9x13in) st.sig. Indian ink W/C
    (F.FR 4000)
£418 $727   (25-Mar-91 PLF.P36) La partie de polo (24x38cm-9x15in) st.sig. Indian
    ink W/C (F.FR 4200)
£517 $900   (25-Mar-91 PLF.P40) Verification de la sangle (29x23cm-11x9in) st.sig.
    crayon W/C gouache (F.FR 5200)
£517 $900   (25-Mar-91 PLF.P37/R) Dans les stalles (22x28cm-9x11in) st.sig. W/C ink
    wash (F.FR 5200)
£553 $1085   (26-Jan-91 ZZ.F38/R) Joueurs de Polo (20x30cm-8x12in) st.sig. wash ink
    (F.FR 5500)
£629 $1207   (17-Dec-90 ZZ.F37) Polo pendant le jeu (30x43cm-12x17in) W/C (F.FR 6200)
£705 $1149   (12-Jun-91 ZZ.F109) Promenade au bois de Boulogne (20x26cm-8x10in)
    s.d.1927 lead pencil W/C (F.FR 7000)
£755 $1479   (26-Jan-91 ZZ.F42) Preparations a la course (24x29cm-9x11in) s. W/C
    (F.FR 7500)

DUBBELS, Hendrik (1620-1676) Dutch
£6500 $12805   (1-Nov-90 CSK62/R) Frigate dropping anchor with smacks, fishing boats
    and figures on beach (68x86cm-27x34in) s.
£7500 $15000   (7-Feb-91 C8/R) A merchantman clawing off a rocky lee shore in a storm
    (80x99cm-31x39in) s.
£55000 $89650   (5-Jul-91 C50/R) Galjoot on reach, Weyschult on starboard tack and other
    shipping in choppy seas on IJ (46x57cm-18x22in)

DUBBELS, Hendrik (attrib) (1620-1676) Dutch
£2988 $5827   (24-Oct-90 GD.B300/R) Lake landscape with fishermen returning
    (41x54cm-16x21in) panel (S.FR 7500)

DUBERT, J J (?) ?
£4500 $7335   (2-Jul-91 PH173/R) Village kermesse with figures merry making in inn
    yard (18x24cm-7x9in) s.d.1872 panel pair

DUBISSON, Jean Baptiste (attrib) (c.1660-1735) ?
£3606 $6456   (8-Apr-91 CH.R189/R) Vaso di fiori (35x30cm-14x12in) (I.L 8000000)

DUBLIN, Jacques (1901-1978) Swiss
£2857 $5429   (14-Sep-90 ZOF.Z1061/R) Village in winter, Leuenplatz in Therwil
    (65x61cm-26x24in) s.d.35 l.verso (S.FR 7000)

DUBOIS (?) ?
£1667 $2800   (16-Jul-91 JRL.S133/R) King Frederick and Voltaire s. ivory triptych
    (A.D 3600)

DUBOIS, Ambroise (attrib) (1543-1614) French
£5410 $9683   (8-Apr-91 CH.R171/R) Il sacrificio di un giovane condottiero
    dell'antichita (205x141cm-81x56in) (I.L 12000000)

DUBOIS, Charles-Edouard (1847-1885) French
£1710 $3249   (28-Feb-91 D.V71/R) Wooded landscape with pond (39x32cm-15x13in) s.
    panel (A.S 35000)

DUBOIS, Francois (1790-1871) French
£4880 $8443   (24-May-91 FB.P45/R) Scene antique (196x130cm-77x51in) s.d.1853
    (F.FR 49000)

DUBOIS, Jean (1789-1849) Swiss
£1800 $3546   (5-Oct-90 C106/R) View of Lungfrau from Wengern. View of Mont Blanc from
    Col de Balme (56x39cm-22x15in) s.l. bodycol pair

DUBOIS, Louis (1830-1880) Belgian
£1319 $2585   (21-Nov-90 GM.B1029/R) Dunes a Kalmthout (45x83cm-18x33in) (B.FR 80000)
£1319 $2585   (21-Nov-90 GM.B1149) Mare aux Cigognes (45x83cm-18x33in) s. (B.FR 80000)
£2406 $4739   (6-Oct-90 KV.L102/R) Still life with dead hare (80x60cm-31x24in)
    s.d.1870 (B.FR 150000)

DUBOIS, Paul-Elie (1886-1949) French
£7470 $12699   (27-May-91 APT.P267/R) Femme du Hoggar (103x78cm-41x31in) s. hardboard
    (F.FR 75000)

DUBOIS, Raphael (1888-?) Belgian
£1330 $2381   (12-Mar-91 GM.B1033) Nu assis (90x55cm-35x22in) s. (B.FR 80000)

DUBOIS-PILLET, Albert (1845-1890) French
£37186 $66563   (16-Mar-91 APT.P9/R) Nature morte aux fruits et poissons
    (59x72cm-23x28in) s. (F.FR 370000)

DUBORD, Jean Pierre (c.1949-) French
£526 $1000   (14-Sep-90 DM.D2321) La Gelee Blanche, snow scene in Paris
                               (46x64cm-18x25in)
£600 $978   (4-Jul-91 LT.P87/R) La plage de Blonville (50x61cm-20x24in) s.
                               (F.FR 6000)
£697 $1212   (31-Mar-91 FE.P132) Paysage (46x55cm-18x22in) s. (F.FR 7000)
£700 $1141   (4-Jul-91 LT.P48) Rouen vue du Mont Gargan (50x65cm-20x26in) s.
                               (F.FR 7000)
£792 $1402   (7-Apr-91 LT.P126) Le depart des pecheurs (46x55cm-18x22in) s.
                               (F.FR 8000)
£811 $1606   (3-Feb-91 LT.P131) Sur la Dune a Oleron (46x55cm-18x22in) s. (F.FR 8000)
£862 $1707   (3-Feb-91 LT.P157) Le Mont Gargan en hiver (50x61cm-20x24in) s.
                               (F.FR 8500)
£898 $1518   (5-May-91 LT.P103/R) Un dimanche a Saint-Valery (46x61cm-18x24in) s.
                               (F.FR 9000)
£898 $1769   (18-Nov-91 H.A114) Le jardin au printemps (50x60cm-20x24in) s. i. verso
                               (F.FR 8800)
£900 $1512   (28-Apr-91 FE.P108) Maree basse en Charente (46x55cm-18x22in) s.
                               (F.FR 9000)
£906 $1541   (2-Jun-91 LT.P148) Les escaliers de Montmartre (55x74cm-22x29in) s.
                               (F.FR 9100)
£950 $1549   (4-Jul-91 LT.P96/R) Le 14 Juillet dans le port de Rouen
                               (50x61cm-20x24in) s. (F.FR 9500)
£1028 $1737   (5-May-91 LT.P72/R) La Touque a Trouville (54x65cm-21x26in) s.
                               (F.FR 10300)
£1028 $1994   (8-Dec-90 LT.P181) Le sciff (38x55cm-15x22in) s. (F.FR 10000)
£1098 $1855   (5-May-91 LT.P47) Honfleur, les regates dans l'estuaire
                               (60x73cm-24x29in) s. (F.FR 11000)
£1107 $2169   (27-Jan-91 B.PA2/R) La Seine a Croisset en hiver (54x73cm-21x29in) s.
                               (F.FR 11000)
£1148 $1940   (5-May-91 LT.P29/R) Duclair, chemin en bord de Seine (60x73cm-24x29in)
                               s. (F.FR 11500)
£1150 $1875   (4-Jul-91 LT.P78/R) L'ile aux cerises (54x73cm-21x29in) s. (F.FR 11500)
£1158 $1956   (5-May-91 LT.P83/R) La sortie du port (50x60cm-20x24in) s. (F.FR 11600)
£1297 $2193   (5-May-91 LT.P93/R) La sortie des voiliers (50x61cm-20x24in) s.
                               (F.FR 13000)
£1397 $2361   (5-May-91 LT.P39/R) Promeneurs dans un rue a Montmartre
                               (65x54cm-26x21in) s. (F.FR 14000)
£1597 $2699   (5-May-91 LT.P60/R) Les hauteurs d'Houlgate (54x65cm-21x26in) s.
                               (F.FR 16000)

DUBOUCHET, G (19th C) ?
£700 $1176   (16-Jul-91 C103/R) Playful kittens (65x54cm-26x21in) s.

DUBOURCQ, Pierre Louis (1815-1873) Dutch
£14000 $22960   (21-Jun-91 C74/R) L'Argo Romano (83x120cm-33x47in) s.d.1849 i.verso
                               panel

DUBOURG, Augustin (fl.1790) ?
£500   *$960*   *(18-Dec-90 C51/R) Portrait of lady in decollete brown dress*
                               (5x?cm-2x?in) min.silver-gilt mount paste-diamond frame oval

DUBOURG, Victoria see FANTIN-LATOUR, Victoria

DUBOUT, Albert (1906-) French
£973   *$1908*   *(7-Nov-90 APT.P471/R) Documents historiques (21x26cm-8x10in) s. pen*
                               (F.FR 9500)
£1004   *$1968*   *(7-Nov-90 APT.P469) La nouvelle riche (22x27cm-9x11in) s. pen wash*
                               (F.FR 9800)
£1127   *$2209*   *(7-Nov-90 APT.P472/R) Un incident (25x48cm-10x19in) pen (F.FR 11000)*
£1639   *$3213*   *(7-Nov-90 APT.P470/R) Marqueta (23x31cm-9x12in) s. W/C (F.FR 16000)*

DUBOVSKOY, Nicolay Nikanorovich (1859-1918) Russian
£1195 $2342   (6-Nov-90 BA.S39/R) Church in winter sun (25x35cm-10x14in) s.indist.d.
                               (S.KR 13000)

DUBUC, Roland (1924-) Swiss
£1131 $2193   (9-Dec-90 E.LA132) Paris, place Pigalle (50x65cm-20x26in) s.
                               (F.FR 11000)
£1316 $2579   (25-Nov-90 ZZ.F47/R) Honfleur, bateaux a quai (50x65cm-20x26in) s.
                               (F.FR 13000)
£1327 $2613   (17-Nov-90 HC.P67) Vue du Sacre-Coeur (64x52cm-25x20in) s. (F.FR 13000)
£1512 $2873   (1-Mar-91 CB.P175/R) La place Furstenberg (60x73cm-24x29in) s.
                               (F.FR 15000)
£1529 $2936   (2-Dec-90 ZZ.F89) Montmartre sous la neige (50x61cm-20x24in) s.
                               (F.FR 15000)
£1620 $3175   (27-Jan-91 FE.P115) Le Sacre Coeur sous la neige (60x73cm-24x29in) s.
                               (F.FR 16100)
£1663 $3243   (28-Oct-90 M.V40/R) Montmartre sous la neige (60x73cm-24x29in) s.
                               (F.FR 16500)
£1775 $3514   (3-Feb-91 LT.P83/R) Kiosque a Montmartre (60x73cm-24x29in) s.
                               (F.FR 17500)
£1966 $3735   (1-Mar-91 CB.P179) Le moulin de la Galette (73x92cm-29x36in) s.
                               (F.FR 19500)

DUBUFE, Claude Marie (1790-1864) French
£1807 $2910   (27-Jun-91 APT.P216/R) Portrait d'une jeune femme a sa fenetre
                          (73x60cm-29x24in) (F.FR 18000)
£11055 $18131   (21-Jun-91 SY.MO163/R) Le matin (90x118cm-35x46in) s. (F.FR 110000)
£14070 $23075   (19-Jun-91 LC.P53/R) Portrait de la Princese de Beauvau
                          (130x97cm-51x38in) s. (F.FR 140000)

DUBUFE, Claude Marie (attrib) (1790-1864) French
£1154 $2238   (4-Dec-90 FN.S1810) Female nude resting in shade of tree with view of
                          mountainous landscape (28x24cm-11x9in) metal (DM 3300)

DUBUFE, Edouard Louis (1820-1883) French
£6500 $12740   (22-Nov-90 CG527/R) Portrait of Mrs Douglas Baird standing in evening
                          dress holding eyeglass (131x93cm-52x37in) s.d.1858

DUBUFE, Edouard Louis (circle) (1820-1883) French
£2814 $5403   (19-Feb-91 ARC.P22/R) Portrait de fillette en robe blanche sautant a la
                          corde (129x96cm-51x38in) (F.FR 28000)

DUBUFE, Edouard Marie Guillaume (1853-1909) French
£612   *$1180*   *(12-Dec-90 D.P65/R) Etude de trois nus feminins tenant une couronne.*
                          Cinq etudes de bras (49x60cm-19x24in) st. chl (F.FR 6000)
£612   *$1180*   *(12-Dec-90 D.P62/R) Marianne drapee dans les couleurs de La France*
                          (50x31cm-20x12in) st. chl (F.FR 6000)
£1019   *$1967*   *(12-Dec-90 D.P66) Une Vierge a l'enfant (57x23cm-22x9in) bears studio*
                          st. chl (F.FR 10000)
£1223   *$2361*   *(12-Dec-90 D.P64/R) Etude decorative pour l'hotel de Ville de Paris*
                          (49x50cm-19x20in) studio st. chl (F.FR 12000)
£1427   *$2754*   *(12-Dec-90 D.P63/R) Fillette debout au ruban dans les chevaux*
                          (58x40cm-23x16in) st. sanguine (F.FR 14000)
£2650   *$5115*   *(12-Dec-90 D.P61) La verite interrogeant un miroir (56x46cm-22x18in)*
                          studio st. crayon sanguine (F.FR 26000)

DUBUFFET, Jean (1901-1985) French
£22358 $44715   (10-Feb-91 CC.P25/R) Assemblage d'empreintes (30x23cm-12x9in) s.
                          (F.FR 220000)
£43367 $85000   (7-Nov-90 SY.NY198/R) Site avec 4 personnages (49x66cm-19x26in)
                          init.d.81 acrylic paper mounted on canvas
£80000 $155200   (6-Dec-90 S59/R) Mire G 79 - Kowloon (67x100cm-26x39in) init.d.83
                          acrylic on paper on canvas
£101523 $200000   (5-Oct-90 CH.NY52/R) Fabulation du Lavabo (100x81cm-39x32in) s.d.65
                          acrylic paper on canvas
£153061 $300000   (7-Nov-90 SY.NY196/R) Mire G 107 (134x200cm-53x79in) init.d.83 acrylic 4
                          sheets paper laid on canvas
£279188 $550000   (13-Nov-90 SY.NY50/R) Riant ete (89x116cm-35x46in) s.d.54 s.i.d.54 verso
£513595 $837160   (15-Jun-91 FB.P49/R) Mademoiselle mine orange (73x65cm-29x26in) s.d.1950
                          oil cement pasted hardboard (F.FR 5100000)
£1012146 $1983806   (21-Nov-90 CL.E23/R) J'operai pour l'erreur (114x146cm-45x57in)
                          s.d.1963 (F.FR 10000000)
£1045918 $2050000   (6-Nov-90 SY.NY7 a/R) Vaches au pre (81x99cm-32x39in) s. i.d.aout 54
                          verso
£1224490 $2400000   (6-Nov-90 SY.NY29/R) Maison fondee (116x89cm-46x35in) s.d.61
£3082   *$5208*   *(21-Apr-91 P.V43/R) Image K 164 (27x21cm-11x8in) mono. felt pen*
                          (F.FR 31000)
£3486   *$5926*   *(30-May-91 FB.P49/R) La vache (24x32cm-9x13in) mono.d.54 (F.FR 35000)*
£3846   *$7500*   *(10-Oct-90 SY.NY457/R) Figuration i (30x20cm-12x8in) init.d.74 black*
                          marker pencil paper collage
£5076   *$10000*   *(4-Oct-90 SY.NY75 a/R) Trois arbres (32x24cm-13x9in) init.d.71 marker*
                          paper on wrapping paper
£5491   *$9500*   *(7-May-91 CE.NY163/R) La cafetiere (25x16cm-10x6in) init.d.66*
                          col.felt-tip pens
£6154   *$12000*   *(10-Oct-90 SY.NY458/R) Recit XXVII (36x41cm-14x16in) init.d.74 mark*
                          paper collage
£6599   *$13000*   *(5-Oct-90 CH.NY34/R) Personnage costume (46x33cm-18x13in) init.d.73*
                          felt-tip pen
£6939   *$13669*   *(17-Nov-90 S.Z39/R) Dessin pour un monument (30x21cm-12x8in) mono.d.1970*
                          felt tip pen paper on paper (S.FR 17000)
£6972   *$11853*   *(30-May-91 FB.P41/R) Paysage avec un personnage (41x35cm-16x14in)*
                          init.d.80 Indian ink (F.FR 70000)
£7143   *$14000*   *(8-Nov-90 CH.NY103/R) Le Capitaliste (25x16cm-10x6in) init.d.66*
                          col.felt-tip pens
£7514   *$13000*   *(9-May-91 CH.NY160/R) Porte de l'oasis avec traces de pas dans le sable*
                          (35x26cm-14x10in) s.d.48 col.wax crayons
£7692   *$15000*   *(10-Oct-90 SY.NY381/R) Le demarcheur (25x15cm-10x6in) init.d.66*
                          col.markers
£8000   *$14160*   *(21-Mar-91 C222) Portrait II (27x20cm-11x8in) s.i. col.felt pen*
£8122   *$16000*   *(14-Nov-90 SY.NY305/R) Personnage (25x34cm-10x13in) init.d.60 India ink*
£8978   *$17328*   *(13-Dec-90 SY.AM283/R) Paysage avec personnages, maisons, champs et*
                          chemins (23x33cm-9x13in) s.d.57 gouache (D.FL 29000)
£9137   *$18000*   *(5-Oct-90 CH.NY30/R) Le convie (25x16cm-10x6in) init.d.66 col felt-tip*
                          pens
£9250   *$17945*   *(9-Dec-90 CC.P7/R) Situation XLI (35x25cm-14x10in) mono.d.1978 blk.felt*
                          pen pasted paper (F.FR 90000)
£9645   *$19000*   *(5-Oct-90 CH.NY50/R) Situation C (35x25cm-14x10in) init.d.79 felt-tip*
                          pen collage

DUBUFFET, Jean (1901-1985) French-cont.

£10152	$20000	(4-Oct-90 SY.NY77/R) Personnage (42x19cm-17x7in) s.d.73 d.73 verso W/C paper collage board
£10660	$21000	(14-Nov-90 SY.NY302/R) Piano (29x21cm-11x8in) init.d.66 felt marker
£12245	$24000	(14-Feb-91 CH.NY9/R) Element mythique (32x48cm-13x19in) init.d. col.felt tip pens paper collage
£12329	$20096	(14-Jun-91 L.K859/R) Le clef (25x16cm-10x6in) mono.d.1966 col.felt tip pen (DM 36000)
£12755	$25000	(15-Feb-91 SY.NY133/R) Sans titre, terres radieuses (50x64cm-20x25in) s.d.52 india ink
£13198	$26000	(5-Oct-90 CH.NY5/R) Personnage dans un paysage (30x23cm-12x9in) init.d.60 i.verso pen
£14940	$25398	(30-May-91 FB.P37/R) Personnages (45x31cm-18x12in) s.d.55 ink wash collage (F.FR 150000)
£15244	$30488	(10-Feb-91 CC.P24/R) Assemblage d'empreintes (41x26cm-16x10in) s.d.1957 collage Indian ink (F.FR 150000)
£19000	$37050	(18-Oct-90 C435/R) Sequence VII (35x25cm-14x10in) init.d.79 acrylic paper collage card
£21000	$33810	(27-Jun-91 S4/R) Paysage avec personnages, maisons, champs et chemins (23x34cm-9x13in) s.d.57 gouache
£22843	$45000	(15-Nov-90 CH.NY181/R) Chameau et soleil (34x26cm-13x10in) s.d.48 W/C col.wax crayons pen ink over pencil
£24900	$42331	(30-May-91 FB.P20/R) Baigneuse nue dans le rochers de Cassis (19x24cm-7x9in) s.i.d.VII 43 gouache board (F.FR 250000)
£25000	$40250	(27-Jun-91 S3/R) L'ambulant (24x34cm-9x13in) s.d.57 gouache
£36000	$57960	(25-Jun-91 C263/R) Vue de Paris avec quatre arbres et trois personnages Place de l'Estrapade (37x30cm-15x12in) s.i. gouache
£74000	$119140	(27-Jun-91 S23/R) Culotte de peau (50x20cm-20x8in) s.d.59 s.i.d.verso leaves gouache paper on card
£78000	$125580	(27-Jun-91 S6/R) Le philosophe (60x50cm-24x20in) s.d.59 cabbage fig leaves gouache board
£92000	$148120	(27-Jun-91 S5/R) L'heureux de peu (62x68cm-24x27in) s.d.57 s.i.d.verso oil paper collage on canvas
£170000	$329800	(6-Dec-90 C550/R) Partition (73x100cm-29x39in) s.d.65 vinyl paper on canvas
£198980	$390000	(6-Nov-90 SY.NY13/R) Paysage tricolore IV (195x130cm-77x51in) init.d.74 i. verso vinyl canvas
£228426	$450000	(13-Nov-90 SY.NY52/R) Sourieuse Rose (46x34cm-18x13in) mixed media canvas
£279188	$550000	(13-Nov-90 SY.NY51/R) Astravagale (73x43cm-29x17in) s.d.56 s.i.d.56 verso oil collage canvas
£540000	$869400	(27-Jun-91 S21/R) Cingria blanc sur champ sombre (146x114cm-57x45in) i.stretcher oil mixed media canvas
£800000	$1552000	(6-Dec-90 C527/R) Monsieur Macadam (73x60cm-29x24in) paste lead oxide tar gravel canvas

DUBUFFET, Jean (attrib) (1901-1985) French

£536	$1050	(27-Jan-91 LIT.L67) Clown smoking (53x46cm-21x18in) s. cradled panel
£1429	$2400	(28-Apr-91 HG.C497) Fiat (23x36cm-9x14in) s.i.d.1951 ink wash
£2440	$4100	(28-Apr-91 HG.C490) Abstract (20x36cm-8x14in) s.d.53 mixed media

DUBUIS, George S (19/20th C) American

| £2616 | $4500 | (15-May-91 SY.NY172/R) New life on old turnpike (61x91cm-24x36in) s.d.1907 |

DUBUISSON, Albert Lucien (1850-1937) French

| £1325 | $2558 | (16-Dec-90 T.B283/R) L'Entree du Port de Pornic (50x61cm-20x24in) s. (F.FR 13000) |

DUCAIRE, Maryse (20th C) French

| £1842 | $3500 | (15-Sep-90 S.W2685/R) Seated nudes (25x20cm-10x8in) s. pair |

DUCAJU, Dominicus (1802-1867) Belgian

| £3000 | $4950 | (10-Jul-91 C54/R) A lady in low-cut embroidered white dress edged in lace (10cm-4ins circular) min.s. gilt-metal frame paste surround |

DUCHAMP, Marcel (1887-1968) French

| £8122 | $16000 | (14-Nov-90 SY.NY160/R) Portrait of Florine Stettheimer (51x35cm-20x14in) s.i. chl |
| £9137 | $18000 | (14-Nov-90 SY.NY161/R) Portrait of John Quinn (20x13cm-8x5in) s.i.d.15 pen |

DUCHAMP, Suzanne (1889-1963) French

£706	$1376	(20-Jan-91 GL.P171) Portrait de Jean Crotti (55x46cm-22x18in) s.d.56 (F.FR 7000)
£1527	$3009	(30-Oct-90 I.N215/R) Vase de fleurs (73x60cm-29x24in) s. (F.FR 15000)
£1872	$3670	(19-Nov-90 CSC.P54/R) La femme aux pigeons (59x72cm-23x28in) s. (F.FR 18500)
£816	$1600	(12-Feb-91 SY.NY53/R) Interior with vase of flowers (64x48cm-25x19in) s. W/C gouache indian ink

DUCHATEL, Marie (attrib) (17th C) Dutch

| £7000 | $11550 | (10-Jul-91 C26/R) A lady, believed to be Maria Anna Louisa de Medici (6x?cm-2x?in) min. vellum silver frame engraved verso oval |

DUCHESNE, Charles (19th C) French
£6166 $11963   (8-Dec-90 SY.MO312/R) Portrait du Comte d'Escars Pair de France
                              (65x54cm-26x21in) s.d.1820 (F.FR 60000)

DUCK, Jacob (1600-1660) Dutch
£9265 $15102   (10-Jun-91 AGB.P83/R) Soldat endormi aupres d'une table a jeu
                              (36x50cm-14x20in) s. panel (F.FR 92000)

DUCK, Jacob (style) (1600-1660) Dutch
£3200 $6080   (13-Sep-90 CSK302/R) Ladies and gentleman of pleasure making music in
                            interior (51x43cm-20x17in)

DUCK, Jan le (attrib) (1630-1676) Dutch
£3529 $6000   (31-May-91 CH.NY132/R) Cavaliers in interior (31x45cm-12x18in) bears
                            sig. panel

DUCK, Johann Franz (?) ?
£1700 $3230   (13-Sep-90 CSK238/R) Yacht with coastal shipping in estuary, town beyond
                            (23x33cm-9x13in) with sig. panel

DUCKER, Eugene Gustav (1841-1916) German
£976 $1912   (6-Nov-90 SY.AM95) View of estate with children in park
                          (39x58cm-15x23in) s. pasteboard (D.FL 3200)
£1351 $2297   (27-May-91 L.K262) Shrimpfisher by the Baltic Sea with fishing boats
                            beyond (25x32cm-10x13in) s.d.1913 (DM 4000)

DUCMELIC, Zdravko (1923-1958) Argentinian
£1040 $1800   (8-May-91 V.BA34) Mujer joven con manzana (34x22cm-13x9in) mixed media

DUCREUX, Joseph (1735-1802) French
£38000 $73340   (12-Dec-90 S2/R) Self-portrait (46x38cm-18x15in)

DUCREUX, Joseph (circle) (1735-1802) French
£5294 $9000   (30-May-91 SY.NY49/R) Man gesturing for silence (59x49cm-23x19in)

DUCREUX, Joseph (style) (1735-1802) French
£977 $1749   (14-Mar-91 D.V346/R) Portrait of Maria Theresia in widow's costume
                          (62x48cm-24x19in) (A.S 20000)

DUCROS, Abraham Louis Rodolphe (circle) (1748-1810) Swiss
£700 $1211   (20-May-91 SWS329/R) The Arch of Constantine (41x57cm-16x22in) pen W/C
£4200 $8106   (11-Dec-90 C97/R) The cascades beneath the Villa of Maecenas,Tivoli
*   (53x75cm-21x30in) blk.chk. W/C*

DUCROS, Abraham Louis Rodolphe and VOLPATO, Giovanni (18th C) Swiss/Italian
£780 $1279   (19-Jun-91 B1/R) Temple of Cecilia Metella, Rome (30x43cm-12x17in) W/C

DUCROS, Abraham Louis Rodolphe and VOLPATO, Giovanni (attrib (18th C) Swiss/Ital
£35714 $61786   (22-May-91 GS.B2355/R) Coastal landscape with figures, evening
                                (64x98cm-25x39in) pair (S.FR 90000)

DUDA, Mizon (20th C) Polish
£598 $1165   (24-Oct-90 GD.B304/R) Le village (46x55cm-18x22in) s. (S.FR 1500)

DUDANT, Roger (1929-) Belgian
£655 $1100   (23-Apr-91 C.A441) Composition (39x54cm-15x21in) s.d.1959 (B.FR 40000)

DUDGEON, T (19th C) British
£2600 $4368   (23-Apr-91 S12/R) River Clyde (42x60cm-17x24in) s.d.1867 paper on board

DUDICOURT, J A (fl.1881-1893) ?
£3800 $6536   (17-May-91 C32/R) Harem guard (77x54cm-30x21in) s.d.86

DUDLEY, Arthur (fl.1890-1907) British
£750 $1328   (21-Mar-91 CSK43/R) Grapes, oranges and carage on a ledge. Fruit and
*   sweetcorn and a jaron a ledge (25x74cm-10x29in) both s.d.'96 pencil*
*   W/C htd.gum arabic*
£780 $1349   (21-May-91 CD60/R) Still life with apples, grapes and vase
*   (25x74cm-10x29in) s. W/C*

DUDLEY, Charles (19th C) ?
£1900 $3287   (10-May-91 CBS286/R) Terriers in barn (89x69cm-35x27in) s.
£1900 $3287   (10-May-91 CBS287/R) Terriers in barn (89x69cm-35x27in) s.

DUDLEY, Frank V (1868-?) American
£761 $1500   (7-Oct-90 DU.E197/R) Peace of snow clad hills (69x76cm-27x30in) s.

DUDLEY, Robert (fl.1880-1893) British
£1000 $1970   (12-Nov-90 PH35/R) The Bridge of the Dance of Death at Lucerne
*   (34x44cm-13x17in) s.d.1875 i. verso W/C*

DUDOVICH, Marcello (1878-1962) Italian
£601 $1166   (3-Dec-90 F.M354/R) Torero (66x48cm-26x19in) s. pastel (I.L 1300000)
£879 $1705   (3-Dec-90 F.M235/R) Borsalino antica casa (71x49cm-28x19in) s. W/C
*   (I.L 1900000)*

DUDOVICH, Marcello (1878-1962) Italian-cont.
£1000 $1969   (30-Oct-90 F.R83) Signora a passeggio (46x38cm-18x15in) s. mixed media (I.L 2200000)
£1984 $3551   (9-Apr-91 F.R68/R) La coppia elegante (66x48cm-26x19in) s. chl white paint (I.L 4400000)

DUDREVILLE, Leonardo (1885-1974) Italian
£1834 $3007   (20-Jun-91 F.M325/R) Paesaggio (28x36cm-11x14in) s.d.1934 i.verso panel (I.L 4000000)
£3180 $6265   (30-Oct-90 F.R89/R) Paesaggio montano (56x74cm-22x29in) s.d.26 (I.L 7000000)

DUERINCKX, Adrien Paul Francois (1888-?) Belgian
£854 $1400   (19-Jun-91 B.SF1863/R) Rue de Dieghem, vieux coin a Bruxelles (32x24cm-13x9in) s.d.1927 board

DUEZ, Ernest Ange (1846-1896) French
£21893 $37000   (1-May-91 D.NY30) Black hat (112x66cm-44x26in) s.

DUFAUD, Georges Achille (1831-?) French
£814 $1538   (27-Sep-90 BL.P66) Bord de mer en normandie (72x99cm-28x39in) (F.FR 8000)

DUFAUX, Frederic II (1852-1943) Swiss
£657 $1282   (24-Oct-90 GD.B309/R) La route (27x35cm-11x14in) s. (S.FR 1650)
£1040 $1758   (1-May-91 GD.B224/R) Portrait of young woman (33x25cm-13x10in) s. (S.FR 2600)
£2400 $4056   (1-May-91 GD.B222/R) The bathers (34x29cm-13x11in) s. (S.FR 6000)
£2976 $4970   (5-Jun-91 SY.Z89/R) Nu au lit (50x61cm-20x24in) s.d.1920 (S.FR 7500)
£5200 $9984   (27-Nov-90 PH131/R) Lady sitting at table overlooking the sea (27x35cm-11x14in) s.
£6911 $13337   (14-Dec-90 ZOF.Z1161/R) Female nude in boudoir (54x65cm-21x26in) s. (S.FR 17000)

DUFEU, Edouard (1840-1900) French
£2872 $4853   (3-May-91 SA.A1825/R) Santa Maria della Salute (41x50cm-16x20in) s. panel (DM 8500)

DUFF, John Robert Keitley (1862-?) British
£500 $845   (30-Apr-91 AG132/R) Cattle by stone bridge (26x37cm-10x15in) s. W/C

DUFFAUT, Prefete (1923-) Haitian
£1429 $2800   (19-Nov-90 SY.NY306/R) City by the sea (61x91cm-24x36in) s.d.1963 panel

DUFFIELD, M E (1819-1914) British
£500 $980   (15-Feb-91 CBB278) Still life of fruit and roses (15x30cm-6x12in) s.
£900 $1511   (27-Apr-91 SO.S310/R) Still life of fruit (42x50cm-17x20in) s.d.1872 (S.KR 9500)

DUFFIELD, Mary Elizabeth (1819-1914) British
£1000 $1670   (5-Jun-91 S295/R) Still life of mixed flowers (30x39cm-12x15in) s.d.1868 W/C htd white

DUFFIELD, William (1816-1863) British
£680 $1258   (6-Mar-91 SC4269) Still life of birds (28x43cm-11x17in) s.
£800 $1376   (14-May-91 SWS205/R) Still life of grapes and oranges (30x25cm-12x10in) bears sig. paper on canvas
£3400 $6698   (13-Nov-90 PH75/R) The kitchen maid (61x51cm-24x20in) s.d.1839
£5500 $10780   (13-Feb-91 S100/R) Winter game (65x100cm-26x39in) s.d.1859

DUFFIELD, William (style) (1816-1863) British
£840 $1436   (30-Jul-91 SWS292) Still life of dead pheasants (60x49cm-24x19in)

DUFOUR, Bernard (1922-) French
£1000 $1630   (5-Jul-91 APT.P113) Sans titre (116x81cm-46x32in) s.d.56 (F.FR 10000)
£2300 $4485   (18-Oct-90 C302/R) Composition (146x114cm-57x45in) s.d.56
£3819 $6836   (15-Mar-91 FB.P56/R) Femme (100x81cm-39x32in) s.d.72 i. verso (F.FR 38000)

DUFOUR, Camille (1841-?) French
£867 $1500   (21-May-91 CE.NY147/R) River town (38x56cm-15x22in) s.

DUFRESNE, Charles (1876-1934) French
£2011 $3500   (27-Mar-91 B.SF4299/R) La modele (75x50cm-30x20in) s.verso board
£2465 $4857   (6-Oct-90 GL.P31) Scene champetre (18x27cm-7x11in) s. paper laid down on canvas (F.FR 25000)
£4925 $8076   (19-Jun-91 JM.P138/R) Baigneuse etendue (60x73cm-24x29in) s. (F.FR 49000)
£10194 $19674   (15-Dec-90 D.P9/R) L'enlevement d'Europe (36x104cm-14x41in) (F.FR 100000)
£797 $1355   (29-May-91 GL.P148/R) Suzanne au bain (28x34cm-11x13in) s. gouache (F.FR 8000)
£1526 $2884   (30-Sep-90 E.LA29) Ville orientale (17x15cm-7x6in) s. W/C gouache (F.FR 15000)
£2025 $3909   (13-Dec-90 CH.BR117/R) Les baigneuses (33x27cm-13x11in) s.d.30 gouache W/C (B.FR 120000)

DUFRESNE, Charles (1876-1934) French-cont.
£3452	$6800	(6-Oct-90 GL.P30/R) Apollon et Daphne (58x48cm-23x19in) oil gouache paper laid down on canvas (F.FR 35000)

DUFY, Jean (1888-1964) French
£3571	$7000	(12-Feb-91 SY.NY63/R) Circus (23x15cm-9x6in) s.
£3904	$6754	(23-May-91 SY.AM67/R) Harbour scene. Ships in harbour s. panel pair (D.FL 13000)
£4847	$9500	(12-Feb-91 SY.NY60/R) Le port (46x61cm-18x24in) st.sig.
£4960	$9721	(25-Nov-90 ZZ.F49/R) La maison dans les arbres (55x46cm-22x18in) bears studio st. (F.FR 49000)
£5010	$9820	(25-Nov-90 ZZ.F51/R) Le port du Havre (13x35cm-5x14in) s. panel (F.FR 49500)
£5128	$10000	(10-Oct-90 SY.NY161/R) Les fleurs (25x20cm-10x8in) s.
£5183	$8500	(19-Jun-91 B.SF1778/R) Promeneurs, cavaliers et caleches (38x22cm-15x9in) s.
£5357	$10500	(14-Feb-91 CH.NY53/R) Fruits et bouteille (38x47cm-15x19in) s.
£5491	$9500	(7-May-91 CE.NY97/R) Vase de fleurs (21x16cm-8x6in) s.
£5584	$11000	(13-Nov-90 CE.NY133/R) Les musiciens au cirque (24x34cm-9x13in) s.
£6599	$13000	(2-Oct-90 CH.NY222/R) Quartier de Paris, vue sur le Sacre-Coeur (27x35cm-11x14in) s.
£6780	$11322	(6-Jun-91 HN.H284/R) Le Havre (38x46cm-15x18in) s.d.1930 (DM 20000)
£7107	$14000	(13-Nov-91 CE.NY106/R) Vue de Paris (39x47cm-15x19in) s. paper on canvas
£8511	$16000	(22-Sep-90 WOL.C334/R) Bateaux au port (56x33cm-22x13in) s.
£8600	$15222	(20-Mar-91 S79/R) Cavaliers et caleches vers le bois de Boulogne (44x53cm-17x21in) s.
£8671	$15000	(7-May-91 CE.NY53/R) Paris, Place de la Concorde (49x20cm-19x8in) s.
£8673	$17000	(15-Feb-91 SY.NY121/R) Les courses (33x41cm-13x16in) s. paper on canvas
£9054	$17746	(26-Jan-91 ZZ.F44/R) Cavaliers au bois (54x73cm-21x29in) s. (F.FR 90000)
£9184	$18000	(15-Feb-91 SY.NY58/R) Paysage a Preuilly-sur-Claise (55x66cm-22x26in) s.
£9391	$18500	(2-Oct-90 CH.NY221/R) Avenue de l'Opera (47x56cm-19x22in) s.
£9694	$19000	(15-Feb-91 SY.NY59/R) Nu couche (38x46cm-15x18in) s.d.28
£10000	$19500	(10-Oct-90 SY.NY102/R) Sevilla (56x33cm-22x13in) s.
£10204	$20000	(12-Feb-91 SY.NY62/R) La Seine (33x41cm-13x16in) s.
£10976	$18000	(19-Jun-91 B.SF1779/R) Aux courses de Longchamps (46x58cm-18x23in) s.
£11043	$18000	(12-Jun-91 SY.NY23/R) Moulin Rouge (38x46cm-15x18in) s.
£11494	$20000	(27-Mar-91 B.SF4140/R) Sacre coeur avec de flacres (47x56cm-19x22in) s.
£11494	$20000	(27-Mar-91 B.SF4141/R) La Madeleine, vue de la Place de la Concorde (46x55cm-18x22in) s.
£11683	$20679	(7-Apr-91 I.N117/R) Le cirque (46x55cm-18x22in) s. (F.FR 118000)
£11735	$23000	(15-Feb-91 SY.NY120/R) Au cirque, parade equestre (46x55cm-18x22in) s.
£13198	$26000	(15-Nov-90 D.NY85/R) Le concert (61x46cm-24x18in) s.
£14031	$27500	(15-Feb-91 SY.NY52/R) Femme assise au chat (73x60cm-29x24in) s.d.26
£14213	$28000	(15-Nov-90 D.NY86/R) Parc bois de Boulogne (38x54cm-15x21in) s.
£14721	$29000	(3-Oct-90 SY.NY160/R) Au Lido (38x55cm-15x22in) s.
£15306	$30000	(7-Nov-90 B.SF1055/R) Le Havre (65x81cm-26x32in) s.d.30
£18274	$36000	(3-Oct-90 SY.NY159/R) Au cirque (46x55cm-18x22in) s. canvas on board
£21320	$42000	(3-Oct-90 SY.NY83/R) Retour de peche (89x130cm-35x51in) s.
£22000	$35420	(25-Jun-91 C171/R) Le havre (65x81cm-26x32in) s.d.30
£485	$950	(12-Feb-91 SY.NY19/R) Landscape with view of city (41x56cm-16x22in) st.studio graphite paper on board
£513	$1000	(10-Oct-90 SY.NY36/R) Toledo (25x38cm-10x15in) st.sig.i. blue ball point pen
£559	$1118	(6-Feb-91 LD.P58/R) Le port de Camret (30x25cm-12x10in) st.sig. W/C (F.FR 5500)
£676	$1284	(14-Sep-90 SA.A1401/R) Scene in town park (40x56cm-16x22in) st.studio pencil (DM 2000)
£690	$1360	(6-Oct-90 GL.P123/R) Copenhague (30x41cm-12x16in) st.sig. ball-pen (F.FR 7000)
£871	$1707	(11-Nov-90 ZZ.F168/R) Maison du midi (25x18cm-10x7in) st.sig. gouache (F.FR 8500)
£1381	$2720	(6-Oct-90 GL.P32) L'orchestre (54x77cm-21x30in) s. wash (F.FR 14000)
£1742	$3414	(11-Nov-90 ZZ.F237/R) L'orchestre (54x78cm-21x31in) s. sepia (F.FR 17000)
£1786	$3500	(12-Feb-91 SY.NY51/R) La chasse (28x18cm-11x7in) s. gouache
£1795	$3500	(10-Oct-90 SY.NY39/R) Nature morte (38x69cm-15x27in) s. ink
£1809	$2967	(18-Jun-91 APT.P16/R) Port sur la riviera (37x56cm-15x22in) s. gouache (F.FR 18000)
£1815	$3538	(20-Jan-91 GL.P11/R) Paysage du midi (54x42cm-21x17in) s.d.23 W/C (F.FR 18000)
£2312	$4000	(7-May-91 CE.NY4/R) Maison et jardin (55x44cm-22x17in) s. W/C paper on board
£2459	$4820	(11-Nov-90 ZZ.F123/R) Canal a Venise (25x19cm-10x7in) s. W/C (F.FR 24000)
£2538	$5000	(13-Nov-90 CE.NY249/R) La Tour Eiffel vue de loin (25x20cm-10x8in) s. W/C paper on board
£2601	$4500	(7-May-91 CE.NY90/R) Nature morte aux fleurs et pommes (53x41cm-21x16in) st.sig. gouache W/C
£2915	$5217	(11-Mar-91 GL.P6) Au cirque (28x22cm-11x9in) s. gouache (F.FR 29000)
£2976	$5119	(15-May-91 CN.P47/R) Choice quality (59x47cm-23x19in) s. W/C (F.FR 30000)
£3468	$6000	(7-May-91 CE.NY89/R) Bateaux au port (43x63cm-17x25in) s.d.1924 W/C
£3543	$6943	(25-Nov-90 ZZ.F50/R) L'entree du port du Havre (56x66cm-22x26in) s. W/C gouache (F.FR 35000)
£3578	$6405	(9-Apr-91 GO.G203/R) Flowers (45x45cm-18x18in) s.d.24 W/C (S.KR 38500)

DUFY, Jean (1888-1964) French-cont.

£3785	\$6434	(29-May-91 GL.P7/R) Paysage de riviere (44x54cm-17x21in) s. W/C paper laid down on canvas (F.FR 38000)
£3800	\$6118	(24-Jun-91 CSK158/R) Promenade au bois (27x20cm-11x8in) s.i. gouache
£4221	\$7556	(11-Mar-91 GL.P7) Au bois (22x36cm-9x14in) s. gouache (F.FR 42000)
£4592	\$9000	(15-Feb-91 SY.NY54/R) Au cirque, les clowns musiciens (45x56cm-18x22in) s. gouache
£4598	\$8000	(27-Mar-91 B.SF4131/R) Gonflans d'Honorine (34x47cm-13x19in) s.i.d.1920 W/C paper on canvas
£4601	\$7500	(12-Jun-91 SY.NY4/R) In garden (64x49cm-25x19in) s.d.1904 W/C pencil paper on canvas
£4980	\$8616	(26-May-91 ZZ.F116/R) Les clowns musiciens (24x39cm-9x15in) s. gouache (F.FR 50000)
£5102	\$10000	(14-Feb-91 CH.NY103/R) Le Pont-Neuf (48x60cm-19x24in) s.d.1947 gouache
£5584	\$11000	(13-Nov-90 CE.NY144/R) Vue de village (47x62cm-19x24in) s. gouache paper on canvas
£5952	\$10238	(19-May-91 ZZ.F142/R) Caleche et cavaliers (21x32cm-8x13in) s. gouache (F.FR 60000)
£6349	\$10921	(19-May-91 ZZ.F130/R) Les ecuyeres au cirque (24x40cm-9x16in) s. gouache (F.FR 64000)
£6633	\$13000	(14-Feb-91 CH.NY89/R) Montmartre, le Sacre-Coeur (48x64cm-19x25in) s. gouache paper on board
£6972	\$12062	(26-May-91 ZZ.F94/R) Cavaliers et Caleche a l'oree du bois (27x40cm-11x16in) s. gouache (F.FR 70000)
£7614	\$15000	(2-Oct-90 CH.NY217/R) Paris, place Clichy (50x60cm-20x24in) s. goauche
£10152	\$20000	(3-Oct-90 SY.NY162/R) Vue de Paris (49x65cm-19x26in) s. gouache W/C paper on canvas varnished
£13095	\$22524	(19-May-91 ZZ.F119/R) Bords de Seine et Notre-Dame (46x66cm-18x26in) s. gouache (F.FR 132000)
£14475	\$27792	(27-Nov-90 APT.P93/R) Clowns musiciens (44x54cm-17x21in) s. gouache (F.FR 142000)

DUFY, Jean (attrib) (1888-1964) French

£1036	\$2000	(10-Dec-90 H.C1203/R) Sailboats (13x23cm-5x9in) s.

DUFY, Raoul (1877-1953) French

£4893	\$9394	(27-Nov-90 APT.P81/R) Etude pour une grille (65x81cm-26x32in) bears studio st. (F.FR 48000)
£9500	\$16815	(19-Mar-91 C134/R) Le fenaison (38x61cm-15x24in) s.
£13065	\$23387	(16-Mar-91 APT.P50 b/R) Kiosque sur la cote (49x64cm-19x25in) s. W/C (F.FR 130000)
£23618	\$38734	(21-Jun-91 OD.P11/R) Le port de Deauville (17x46cm-7x18in) s. (F.FR 235000)
£36000	\$57960	(26-Jun-91 S162/R) Le peintre et son modele sur la terrasse a Caldas de Montbuy (42x53cm-17x21in) s. panel
£40775	\$78287	(26-Nov-90 GL.P60/R) Instruments de musique (18x50cm-7x20in) s. panel (F.FR 400000)
£41000	\$79540	(5-Dec-90 S164/R) Nature morte au sucrier bleu (79x64cm-31x25in) s.
£45685	\$90000	(14-Nov-90 SY.NY418/R) Saint-Jeannet (46x55cm-18x22in) s.
£49133	\$85000	(9-May-91 CH.NY224/R) Vue de la fenetre de l'atelier de la rue Seguier (72x59cm-28x23in) s.
£52000	\$83720	(26-Jun-91 S164/R) Nu dans un paysage (54x44cm-21x17in) s.
£70850	\$138866	(23-Nov-90 PLF.P64/R) Le pont d'Asnieres (49x107cm-19x42in) s. i. verso stretcher (F.FR 700000)
£72000	\$115920	(26-Jun-91 S139/R) L'orchestre (46x55cm-18x22in) s.d.1942
£75000	\$120750	(24-Jun-91 C41/R) Reception (23x38cm-9x15in) s. panel
£76142	\$150000	(14-Nov-90 SY.NY269/R) La fenetre ouverte (37x46cm-15x18in) s.i.d.1938
£81218	\$160000	(14-Nov-90 SY.NY421/R) La route de Saint-Jeannet (65x81cm-26x32in) s.
£104046	\$180000	(8-May-91 SY.NY147/R) La Place d'Hyeres-l'Obelisque et le Kiosque a musique (46x55cm-18x22in) s.
£109562	\$189542	(25-May-91 GL.P47/R) Courses a Auteuil (50x73cm-20x29in) s. (F.FR 1100000)
£131579	\$257895	(25-Nov-90 GL.P32/R) Le port (29x35cm-11x14in) s. (F.FR 1300000)
£131980	\$260000	(14-Nov-90 SY.NY442/R) Le quintette rouge (34x47cm-13x19in) s.
£155000	\$300700	(5-Dec-90 S195/R) Beethoven (15x38cm-6x15in) s.d.41 panel
£173410	\$300000	(8-May-91 SY.NY142/R) Les marchandes des quatre saisons (89x116cm-35x46in) s.d.1905
£354251	\$694332	(25-Nov-90 GL.P28/R) Le Port du Havre (54x65cm-21x26in) s. (F.FR 3500000)
£393401	\$775000	(14-Nov-90 SY.NY270/R) La Place D'Hyeres - L'Obelisque et le Kiosque a Musique (129x161cm-51x63in) s.
£323	\$629	(20-Jan-91 GL.P13/R) Pecheur japonais relevant son filet (44x47cm-17x19in) gouache chamois paper laid down on canvas (F.FR 3200)
£500	\$815	(5-Jul-91 ZZ.F13) Nu couche (50x66cm-20x26in) lead pencil (F.FR 5000)
£500	\$815	(5-Jul-91 ZZ.F22/R) Composition de carres (48x36cm-19x14in) mono. lead pencil W/C (F.FR 5000)
£600	\$978	(5-Jul-91 ZZ.F14) Arago (60x50cm-24x20in) pen wash indian ink htd.gouache (F.FR 6000)
£650	\$1060	(5-Jul-91 ZZ.F15) Galilee (65x50cm-26x20in) s. indian ink htd.gouache (F.FR 6500)
£700	\$1127	(24-Jun-91 CSK98) Tete d'hommes (54x35cm-21x14in) st.studio pencil
£700	\$1141	(5-Jul-91 ZZ.F17) Sans titre (12x18cm-5x7in) mono. lead pencil (F.FR 7000)
£750	\$1500	(7-Feb-91 B.P96/R) Nude reading (23x46cm-9x18in) s. pencil
£850	\$1369	(24-Jun-91 CSK101/R) Homme assis (66x50cm-26x20in) st.studio pencil

536

DUFY, Raoul (1877-1953) French-cont.

£1050	$1712	(5-Jul-91 ZZ.F18) Sans titre (20x31cm-8x12in) studio st. indian ink (F.FR 10500)
£1527	$3009	(29-Oct-90 LC.P61/R) Le repas des moissonneurs (31x50cm-12x20in) studio st. crayon lead pencil (F.FR 15000)
£1531	$3015	(16-Nov-90 FB.P148/R) Pablo Casals (16x10cm-6x4in) bears st. crayon (F.FR 15000)
£1600	$3120	(19-Oct-90 C113/R) Portrait d'Ambroise Vollard (55x45cm-22x18in) st.studio brush ink wash
£1831	$3461	(25-Sep-90 FB.P267/R) Bonne sante (30x22cm-12x9in) s.i.d. W/C gouache (F.FR 18000)
£2055	$3988	(5-Dec-90 HC.P33) Composition florale rose et bleue (51x48cm-20x19in) st.sig. gouache W/C ink (F.FR 20000)
£2121	$4158	(12-Feb-91 HC.P56) La Vague (48x63cm-19x25in) s.i. pen (F.FR 21000)
£2336	$3948	(21-Apr-91 E.LA155) Vue de village (33x50cm-13x20in) init. drawing (F.FR 23500)
£2982	$5040	(21-Apr-91 E.LA45) Composition florale (58x44cm-23x17in) st.init. verso gouache (F.FR 30000)
£3058	$5872	(30-Nov-90 ARC.P102/R) Marine (64x48cm-25x19in) s. Indian ink (F.FR 30000)
£3082	$5208	(21-Apr-91 E.LA154/R) Le bel ete (43x53cm-17x21in) facsimile sig. Indian ink (F.FR 31000)
£3600	$5868	(5-Jul-91 ZZ.F19/R) Regates a Cowes (47x64cm-19x25in) s. lead pencil (F.FR 36000)
£3827	$7500	(12-Feb-91 SY.NY18/R) Portrait of fillette (61x46cm-24x18in) s.i.d.1920 sepia ink W/C pencil
£4000	$6440	(24-Jun-91 CSK100/R) Chevaux et cavaliers (49x64cm-19x25in) s.i. pen ink
£4743	$8063	(30-May-91 EA.Z270) Textile design (45x40cm-18x16in) mixed media (S.FR 12000)
£4762	$8190	(19-May-91 ZZ.F144/R) Nature morte aux prunes et aux melons (38x46cm-15x18in) s. sanguinne (F.FR 48000)
£6067	$11830	(17-Oct-90 ARC.P20 b) Projet de tissu a decor de fleurs (76x59cm-30x23in) bears st.mono. gouache (F.FR 60000)
£6599	$13000	(2-Oct-90 CH.NY209/R) Paris, Place de la Concorde (51x66cm-20x26in) s. gouache
£8000	$12880	(25-Jun-91 C241/R) Dans l'atelier (27x20cm-11x8in) s.i.d.1944 gouache
£8056	$13132	(11-Jun-91 CSC.P4/R) La Seine (44x56cm-17x22in) s. W/C (F.FR 80000)
£10660	$21000	(2-Oct-90 CH.NY137/R) La flotille (50x66cm-20x26in) s. W/C
£10913	$18770	(15-May-91 CN.P48/R) Les oliviers (46x61cm-18x24in) s. W/C (F.FR 110000)
£10956	$18954	(25-May-91 GL.P5/R) Corrida a Tolede (49x65cm-19x26in) s. W/C (F.FR 110000)
£12000	$20160	(26-Apr-91 NM.P23/R) Paysage mediterraneen (50x61cm-20x24in) s. W/C (F.FR 120000)
£12085	$19698	(16-Jun-91 GL.P65/R) Nature morte au bord de la mer (28x49cm-11x19in) s. W/C (F.FR 120000)
£13944	$24124	(25-May-91 GL.P13/R) Berthe nue, vue de dos (50x65cm-20x26in) W/C (F.FR 140000)
£14000	$24780	(19-Mar-91 C124/R) L'arlequin au violon (20x26cm-8x10in) s. gouache W/C pen
£14500	$23345	(26-Jun-91 S258/R) Fenetre ouverte sur la Madeleine (72x37cm-28x15in) st.sig. gouache pencil paper on card
£14500	$23345	(26-Jun-91 S259/R) Fenetre ouverte sur le Pantheon (72x39cm-28x15in) st.sig. gouache pencil
£16185	$28000	(22-May-91 D.NY58/R) Vue panoramique de Florence (49x63cm-19x25in) s. W/C
£18497	$32000	(9-May-91 CH.NY164/R) Taormina (49x63cm-19x25in) s. W/C gouache paper laid down on board
£21574	$42500	(14-Nov-90 SY.NY191/R) Anemones au vase vert (50x66cm-20x26in) s. W/C
£22908	$39631	(25-May-91 GL.P6/R) Deauville - les drags (49x64cm-19x25in) s. W/C (F.FR 230000)
£23121	$40000	(8-May-91 SY.NY208/R) Paysage avec village (50x66cm-20x26in) s. W/C paper affixed to board
£24000	$46560	(5-Dec-90 S346/R) Palmiers et Bateaux (57x46cm-22x18in) s. W/C gouache
£25000	$48500	(5-Dec-90 S349/R) La Residence du Val D'Esquieres (49x65cm-19x26in) s. W/C gouache
£25000	$44250	(19-Mar-91 C133/R) Les rameurs a Henley (50x65cm-20x26in) s.i. W/C
£25000	$48500	(5-Dec-90 S350/R) Le Jardin de la Residence (50x56cm-20x22in) s. W/C
£25586	$49125	(29-Nov-90 ZZ.F21/R) Orchestre champetre (52x110cm-20x43in) st.sig. crayon tracing paper (F.FR 251000)
£27919	$55000	(15-Nov-90 CH.NY171/R) Chevaux (47x63cm-19x25in) s. W/C over pencil
£36000	$69840	(5-Dec-90 S345/R) Nice, Le Tournant de Roba Capeu (50x66cm-20x26in) s.d.1934 W/C gouache
£40609	$80000	(14-Nov-90 SY.NY268/R) Dimanche a Perpignan (50x65cm-20x26in) s. W/C gouache
£46243	$80000	(8-May-91 SY.NY205/R) La famile Kessler a cheval (48x63cm-19x25in) s. W/C paper laid down on board
£55000	$106700	(5-Dec-90 S360/R) Vase D'Anemones (49x66cm-19x26in) s. W/C
£71066	$140000	(14-Nov-90 SY.NY195/R) La course a Goodward (50x65cm-20x26in) s. W/C
£147208	$290000	(14-Nov-90 SY.NY192/R) Elegantes a Epsom (50x65cm-20x26in) s.i.d.39 gouache W/C

DUFY, Raoul and Jean (circle) (20th C) French

| £5544 | $10811 | (28-Oct-90 PLF.P219/R) Autodrome de Linas-Monthlery (111x197cm-44x78in) panel (F.FR 55000) |

DUGHET, Gaspard (1615-1675) French
£4359 $8500 (11-Oct-90 SY.NY36/R) Classical landscape with two shepherds reclining by lake (49x66cm-19x26in)
£604 *$1183* (24-Jan-91 AGS.P118) Paysage anime aux alentours de la porta Ostiense (7x9cm-3x4in) i. pen wash (F.FR 6000)
£1000 *$1930* (11-Dec-90 C64) A wooded landscape with a castle on a hill (33x47cm-13x19in) blk.white chk.

DUGHET, Gaspard (attrib) (1615-1675) French
£10000 $17000 (31-May-91 CH.NY227/R) Italianate landscape with figures by river (61x86cm-24x34in)
£14000 $27020 (12-Dec-90 S141/R) Classical landscape (100x134cm-39x53in)
£1332 *$2611* (7-Nov-90 APT.P422/R) Paysage anime (30x41cm-12x16in) pen sanguinne wash Indian ink (F.FR 13000)
£2100 *$3717* (21-Mar-91 LC.P7/R) Chemin en lisiere de foret (30x39cm-12x15in) sanguinne (F.FR 21000)

DUGHET, Gaspard (circle) (1615-1675) French
£1400 $2688 (29-Nov-90 CSK230/R) Italianate landscape with castle on hillside and shepherd playing pipes (72x94cm-28x37in)
£2000 $3260 (3-Jul-91 DAR.P25/R) Paysage avec cote maritime italienne (59x76cm-23x30in) (F.FR 20000)
£8621 $15000 (27-Mar-91 B.SF4041/R) River landscape with figures (72x150cm-28x59in)

DUGHET, Gaspard (studio) (1615-1675) French
£4283 $7666 (8-Apr-91 CH.R102/R) Paesaggio collinare con due astanti (77x100cm-30x39in) (I.L 9500000)

DUGHET, Gaspard (style) (1615-1675) French
£800 $1304 (2-Jul-91 PH293) Landscape with figures running along banks of river (38x46cm-15x18in)
£1800 $2934 (4-Jul-91 CSK75/R) Wooded Italianate landscape with travellers resting on track (46x63cm-18x25in)
£2200 $4180 (13-Sep-90 CSK335/R) View of Tivoli. Mountainous Italianate landscape with monastry above waterfall (91x71cm-36x28in) pair
£2780 $5366 (12-Dec-90 BU.S124/R) Italian landscape with hunters and cattle (74x134cm-29x53in) (S.KR 30000)
£3000 $6000 (7-Feb-91 CSK114) Classical Italianate landscape with herdsman and goats on track (73x96cm-29x38in)
£3500 $6720 (29-Nov-90 CSK227/R) River landscape with peasants by lake (79x96cm-31x38in)
£3600 $6840 (13-Sep-90 CSK345) Italianate river landscape with washerwoman by waterfall, village beyond (49x73cm-19x29in)
£7000 $13790 (30-Oct-90 PH67/R) Fortified Italian town with figure. River landscape with villa on hill (74x50cm-29x20in) pair
£1329 *$2564* (10-Dec-90 L.K323/R) Southern river landscape with mountains (21x33cm-8x13in) i.d.1650verso pen sepia wash (DM 3800)

DUGMORE, Arthur Radclyffe (1870-1955) American
£1443 $2800 (5-Dec-90 D.NY82/R) Moonlight march of the African elephants (71x91cm-28x36in) s.

DUHEM, Henri Aime (1860-1941) French
£1336 $2592 (7-Dec-90 GL.P66) Marais de Planques au printemps (72x98cm-28x39in) s. (F.FR 13000)

DUIFHUIZEN, Pieter Jacobsz (1608-1677) Dutch
£7770 $13209 (27-May-91 L.K39/R) Interior with peasant filling pipe and other figures (39x51cm-15x20in) panel (DM 23000)

DUJARDIN, Karel (1622-1678) Dutch
£8532 $14760 (22-May-91 GS.B2360) Pastoral wooded landscape with shepherd and animals resting (126x98cm-50x39in) s.d.1670 (S.FR 21500)
£11213 $21641 (12-Dec-90 ARC.P80/R) La Crucifixion (57x45cm-22x18in) s. (F.FR 110000)
£13183 $25839 (20-Nov-90 F.R158/R) Paesaggio con sosta dal mandiscalco (112x144cm-44x57in) (I.L 29000000)
£146707 $247934 (2-May-91 CH.AM77/R) The Flagellation (69x61cm-27x24in) indist.s. (D.FL 490000)

DUJARDIN, Karel (attrib) (1622-1678) Dutch
£1486 $2423 (10-Jun-91 W.T1353) Rural figures and animals (39x50cm-15x20in) mono. canvas laid down (C.D 2750)
£1946 $3172 (10-Jun-91 W.T1352) Travellers in a landscape (30x41cm-12x16in) sig. panel (C.D 3600)
£2027 $3446 (27-May-91 L.K38/R) Shepherd couple with cattle by ruin (52x67cm-20x26in) i.d.1658 (DM 6000)
£8000 $13040 (3-Jul-91 S161/R) Portrait of man, wearing fur edged coat, lace collar and hat and sword (81x64cm-32x25in)

DUJARDIN, Karel (style) (1622-1678) Dutch
£800 $1352 (18-Apr-91 C87) Portrait of a gentleman in costume writing at a table (22x17cm-9x7in) i. verso copper
£904 $1455 (27-Jun-91 APT.P140/R) Jeune bergere et son troupeau (32x41cm-13x16in) (F.FR 9000)
£976 $1873 (27-Nov-90 SY.AM3448/R) Cattle beneath tree (84x108cm-33x43in) (D.FL 3200)

DUJARDIN, Karel (style) (1622-1678) Dutch-cont.
£1000 $1630   (4-Jul-91 CSK157/R) Hermit assaulting shepherdess by grotto
                (71x91cm-28x36in)
£1150 $2208   (29-Nov-90 CSK225/R) Italianate landscape with traveller and peasant
                woman at ford (24x32cm-9x13in) panel
£1850 $3423   (5-Mar-91 PH113) Horseman drinking outside inn (42x33cm-17x13in)

DUKE, A (19th C) British
£950 $1872   (4-Oct-90 RBB829/R) Hunting scene with pack of hounds jumping hedge
                followed by huntsmen (41x28cm-16x11in) s.

DUKE, Alfred (19th C) British
£720 $1274   (21-Mar-91 CSK210) The baby sitters (30x41cm-12x16in) s.
£800 $1344   (16-Jul-91 C130/R) In full cry (30x41cm-12x16in) s.
£1700 $2805   (9-Jul-91 PH241/R) Comfort. Misery (36x25cm-14x10in) s. i.verso pair

DUKE, Peder (1938-) Scandinavian
£1115 $1996   (13-Apr-91 FAL.M66/R) Blue contrasts (115x115cm-45x45in) s.d.1989verso
                (S.KR 12000)
£1297 $2517   (4-Dec-90 BA.S97/R) Press (116x113cm-46x44in) s.d.84-85verso
                (S.KR 14000)
£1384 $2657   (27-Nov-90 BU.S73/R) Flash of sunshine (133x115cm-52x45in)
                s.l.d.1976verso (S.KR 15000)
£1483 $2877   (5-Dec-90 AB.S7065/R) The light (108x120cm-43x47in) s.d.1982verso
                (S.KR 16000)
£1854 $3596   (5-Dec-90 AB.S7064/R) Wing-beat (102x129cm-40x51in) s.d.1989verso
                (S.KR 20000)

DULMEN KRUMPELMAN, Erasmus Bernhard van (1897-?) Dutch
£1051 $1818   (23-May-91 SY.AM13 a) Bathing girls (93x62cm-37x24in) s.d.69 (D.FL 3500)

DULUARD, Hippolyte Francois Leon (1871-?) French
£3324 $5750   (22-May-91 SY.NY184/R) Portrait of Boyard (81x64cm-32x25in) s. panel

DUMARESQ, Armand see ARMAND-DUMARESQ, Edouard Charles

DUMBRELL, Lesley (1941-) Australian
£3738 $6093   (16-Jun-91 SY.ME38/R) Still green (198x198cm-78x78in) s.d.1979 verso
                acrylic canvas (A.D 8000)

DUMESNIL, Pierre Louis (younger) (c.1698-1781) French
£22111 $36261   (21-Jun-91 SY.MO277/R) Conversation de salon (37x45cm-15x18in)
                (F.FR 220000)

DUMINIL, Frank (1933-) French
£717 $1406   (11-Nov-90 ZZ.F202/R) Composition (81x65cm-32x26in) s. (F.FR 7000)
£809 $1577   (15-Oct-90 CSC.P80) Sans titre (100x81cm-39x32in) s. (F.FR 8000)
£874 $1695   (8-Dec-90 LT.P52/R) Fremissements (100x81cm-39x32in) s. (F.FR 8500)
£965 $1931   (7-Feb-91 R.P189/R) Composition (81x100cm-32x39in) s. (F.FR 9500)
£1008 $1966   (28-Oct-90 R.P211) Composition (100x81cm-39x32in) s. (F.FR 10000)
£1063 $2083   (25-Nov-90 LC.P70/R) Composition (100x81cm-39x32in) s. (F.FR 10500)
£1109 $2162   (28-Oct-90 R.P259/R) Composition (130x89cm-51x35in) s. (F.FR 11000)
£1260 $2457   (27-Oct-90 LT.P81/R) Composition gestuelle au fond blanc
                (100x81cm-39x32in) s. (F.FR 12500)
£1270 $2541   (7-Feb-91 R.P238/R) Composition (130x97cm-51x38in) s. (F.FR 12500)
£1273 $2508   (29-Oct-90 LC.P20) Composition (130x97cm-51x38in) s. (F.FR 12500)

DUMITRESCO, Natalie (1915-) French
£1210   *$2359*   *(28-Oct-90 M.V146/R) Composition (43x53cm-17x21in) s. gouache*
                (F.FR 12000)

DUMOND, Frank Vincent (1865-1951) American
£2682 $4800   (14-Mar-91 CH.NY52/R) Dancing children (33x32cm-13x13in) s.i.

DUMONSTIER, Daniel (attrib) (1574-1646) Italian
£7500 $12225   (3-Jul-91 S173/R) Portrait of lady, wearing richly embroidered dress
                with flowers in hair (57x48cm-22x19in)

DUMONSTIER, Etienne (1520-1603) French
£5097   *$9837*   *(12-Dec-90 ARC.P41/R) Portrait de dame blonde (24x19cm-9x7in)*
                col.crayons (F.FR 50000)

DUMONT, Francois (18/19th C) French
£6592 $13053   (30-Jan-91 APT.P293/R) Portrait de Marie-Antoinette serrant des lys sur
                son coeur (67x54cm-26x21in) s.d.1815 (F.FR 65000)

DUMONT, Henry (1859-?) French
£810 $1587   (20-Nov-90 MF.P69) Paysage aux fleurs (73x60cm-29x24in) s. (F.FR 8000)

DUMONT, Jean (attrib) (1701-1781) French
£2243   *$4328*   *(12-Dec-90 ARC.P57/R) Adoration des bergers (23cm-9ins circular) pen*
                sanguinne round (F.FR 22000)

DUMONT, P (1884-1936) French
£1363 $2235   (17-Jun-91 DUR.M551/R) Odaliscas (74x100cm-29x39in) s. (S.P 250000)

DUMONT, P (1884-1936) French-cont.
£6073 $11903   (25-Nov-90 B.PA56/R) Nature morte aux pommes (61x50cm-24x20in) s. (F.FR 60000)

DUMONT, Pierre (1884-1936) French
£1000 $1690   (30-Apr-91 AG318/R) Nofir aus Helsingfors (49x39cm-19x15in) s. l.verso panel
£2600 $4992   (21-Feb-91 B57/R) Pont Neuf (57x73cm-22x29in) s.
£3265 $6433   (16-Nov-90 NM.P29/R) Lac et sous-bois (71x59cm-28x23in) s. (F.FR 32000)
£4061 $8000   (13-Nov-90 CE.NY32/R) Le Sacre-Coeur (81x65cm-32x26in) s.
£6533 $10714   (21-Jun-91 OD.P12/R) La cathedrale de Beauvais (65x54cm-26x21in) s. (F.FR 65000)

DUMOULIN, Romeo (1883-1944) Belgian
£900 $1530   (28-May-91 C.A99/R) After the funeral (32x35cm-13x14in) s. W/C (B.FR 55000)

DUN, Nicholas Francois (1764-1832) ?
£700 $1239   (20-Mar-91 C92/R) Portrait of young girl, possibly H.J.Dunlop (8x?cm-3x?in) min.rec.in fitted leather case

DUNCAN (?) British
£504 $827   (20-Jun-91 F.M327/R) Primavera (70x94cm-28x37in) paper on masonite (I.L 1100000)

DUNCAN, Audrey (?) American?
£1142 $2250   (15-Nov-90 SY.NY44) Pink carnations (26x15cm-10x6in) init.

DUNCAN, Edward (1803-1882) British
£8000 $15600   (18-Oct-90 SC3062/R) Fishing boats in a busy channel (73x110cm-29x43in) s.d.1852
£900 $1485   (11-Jul-91 S188) Langston Harbour, Hampshire (44x59cm-17x23in) s.d.1875 W/C over pencil htd.bodycol
£1000 $1980   (30-Jan-91 S189) Off Nore (20x49cm-8x19in) s.d.1858 W/C over pencil
£1400 $2506   (9-Apr-91 C146/R) Fishing boats off the Cornish coast (36x60cm-14x24in) s.d.1871 pencil W/C htd.white scratching out
£1900 $3534   (5-Sep-90 BT153/R) Going to meet fleet (38x71cm-15x28in) s.d.1838 W/C
£2200 $3630   (11-Jul-91 S204/R) Richmond Hill from the Thames (22x33cm-9x13in) s.d.1844 W/C over pencil htd.white
£2800 $4704   (15-Jul-91 PH130/R) On Sussex Downs (33x50cm-13x20in) s.d.1859 W/C over pencil htd white
£3800 $6460   (30-May-91 C32/R) Beached fleet at low tide (29x62cm-11x24in) s.d.1857 pencil W/C

DUNCAN, George Bernard (1904-1974) New Zealander
£522 $1002   (27-Nov-90 JRL.S148 b) Before spring came (40x50cm-16x20in) s. composition board (A.D 1300)
£1101 $2081   (25-Sep-90 JRL.S182/R) Hill church, Spain (24x34cm-9x13in) s. hessian on board (A.D 2500)
£1145 $2165   (25-Sep-90 JRL.S170/R) Stablemates (70x91cm-28x36in) s. board (A.D 2600)
£2532 $4861   (14-Aug-90 SY.ME272/R) Cow pastures newa Botany (70x91cm-28x36in) s. (A.D 6000)

DUNCAN, James D (1806-1881) Canadian
£15152 $26212   (6-May-91 SY.T155/R) Sleigh de poste de Monsieur et Madame de Puibusque verse sur la route de Quebec, 11 Janvier 1850 (34x44cm-13x17in) s.l. (C.D 30000)
£19192 $33202   (6-May-91 SY.T156/R) Scieurs et labourteurs de glace sur le St. Laurent, Montreal, Canada, 1849 (34x43cm-13x17in) s.l. (C.D 38000)

DUNCAN, Jo (20th C) British?
£574 $1027   (14-Apr-91 R.P40) Composition (100x150cm-39x59in) s. mixed media (F.FR 5800)

DUNCAN, John (1866-1945) British
£4800 $8064   (23-Apr-91 S184/R) Proposal (122x79cm-48x31in) s.d.1906
£450 $797   (22-Mar-91 PHE14) Still life of vase with white roses (16x14cm-6x6in) s.d.1916 W/C

DUNCAN, Laurence (fl.1860-1891) British
£580 $1131   (16-Jan-91 CSK149) Returning home across the moor (53x76cm-21x30in) s.d.1874 s.i.verso pencil W/C

DUNCAN, Walter (fl.1880-c.1910) British
£1000 $1730   (22-May-91 S113/R) Boat ride (19x29cm-7x11in) s.d.1882 W/C

DUNCANSON, Robert S (1821-1872) American
£1744 $3000   (15-May-91 SY.NY64/R) Landscape with criver and cascade (26x41cm-10x16in) s.
£9524 $18000   (26-Sep-90 SY.NY6/R) The falls (86x74cm-34x29in) s.d.1871 l.stretcher

DUNCANSON, Robert S (attrib) (1821-1872) American
£1923 $3250   (17-Apr-91 D.NY15/R) Wooded river landscape (76x64cm-30x25in) bears sig.

DUNDAS, Douglas Robert (1900-1981) Australian
£655	$1172	(9-Apr-91 CH.ME183/R) Canberra landscape (55x70cm-22x28in) (A.D 1500)
£755	$1230	(1-Jul-91 AAA.S90 g) Barns at Wilberforce (51x61cm-20x24in) s. (A.D 1600)
£1048	$1876	(9-Apr-91 CH.ME243/R) Dahlias (37x45cm-15x18in) s.d.39 board (A.D 2400)
£1395	$2344	(22-Apr-91 SY.ME120/R) Farm and fells, Cumberland (60x75cm-24x30in) s.d.77 (A.D 3000)
£1860	$3126	(22-Apr-91 SY.ME164/R) Tuscan Hill town, Italy, 1928 (44x54cm-17x21in) (A.D 4000)
£3256	$5470	(22-Apr-91 SY.ME94/R) Peg Oldfield in red cap (59x49cm-23x19in) s. (A.D 7000)
£3256	$5470	(22-Apr-91 SY.ME89/R) Summer weather (45x60cm-18x24in) s.d.44 (A.D 7000)

DUNHAM, Carroll (1949-) American
£9184	$18000	(7-Nov-90 SY.NY344/R) Untitled (89x61cm-35x24in) s.d.June July Aug 1987 i.verso acrylic 2 panels
£12245	$24000	(8-Nov-90 CH.NY160/R) Three (86x53cm-34x21in) s.i.d.9/25/84 gouache graphite chl.ink veneers
£12755	$25000	(8-Nov-90 CH.NY174/R) Six (91x58cm-36x23in) s.i.d.9/15/84 gouache chl.graphite tape veneers
£22189	$37500	(1-May-91 SY.NY162/R) First pine (145x122cm-57x48in) s.d.1982 verso casein pigment pencil chl wood

DUNINGTON, A (19/20th C) American
£559	$1000	(16-Mar-91 W.W49 a/R) Approaching evening, goatfell, Brodick Bay on the Island of Arran, Scotland (41x61cm-16x24in) s.i.

DUNKER, Balthasar Anton (1746-1807) German
£1205	$2361	(21-Nov-90 SY.Z12/R) Peasant woman in landscape (23x19cm-9x7in) s.d.1790 W/C pencil (S.FR 3000)
£1517	$2913	(28-Nov-90 KF.M106/R) Southern landscape with traveller drinking from fountain (31x23cm-12x9in) s. W/C indian ink brush over pen (DM 4400)

DUNLOP, Brian James (1938-) Australian
£1992	$3924	(31-Oct-90 CH.S3/R) Copper jug (58x49cm-23x19in) s. (A.D 5000)
£2191	$4317	(31-Oct-90 KF.S76/R) Irises and nasturtium (59x49cm-23x19in) s. (A.D 5500)
£3012	$5783	(26-Nov-90 SY.ME311/R) Reclining nude (66x94cm-26x37in) s. i.verso canvas on board (A.D 7500)
£888	$1447	(16-Jun-91 SY.ME76) Streetcar named Desire (47x37cm-19x15in) s.d.60 pen wash (A.D 1900)
£1495	$2437	(16-Jun-91 SY.ME3) Roman rooftops (62x50cm-24x20in) s. W/C pencil (A.D 3200)

DUNLOP, Ronald Ossory (1894-1973) British
£720	$1231	(30-Jul-91 SWS11/R) Cutty Sark Tavern (34x44cm-13x17in) s.
£750	$1440	(26-Nov-90 SWS153/R) Mister Humphrey of Aldingbourne, oldest shepherd in Sussex (50x36cm-20x14in) s. i.verso
£820	$1607	(20-Nov-90 RB681) Impressionist study of Paris street (30x38cm-12x15in) s.
£880	$1514	(14-May-91 SWS431/R) Spring by the Thames (60x90cm-24x35in) s. i.stretcher
£900	$1512	(18-Jul-91 B59/R) Estuary, Weston-Super-Mare (63x76cm-25x30in) s.
£950	$1786	(20-Sep-90 C165/R) Trees by Wey (49x60cm-19x24in) s.
£1100	$2145	(15-Jan-91 SWS205/R) Shepperton weir (49x75cm-19x30in) s.
£1200	$2364	(1-Nov-90 B84/R) Still life with fruit (51x61cm-20x24in) s. board
£1300	$2262	(27-Mar-91 S28/R) Village in winter (40x50cm-16x20in) s. board
£1300	$2496	(21-Feb-91 B55/R) Banks of Seine (46x54cm-18x21in) s.
£1400	$2366	(1-May-91 PHL172/R) La Place, St. Tropez (76x103cm-30x41in) s. i.stretcher
£1800	$3132	(27-Mar-91 S25/R) At Welford-on-Avon mill (76x63cm-30x25in) s.
£600	$1158	(11-Dec-90 HS10) Head portrait of Norah (33x30cm-13x12in) s. gouache canvas

DUNN, Harvey (1884-1952) American
£1658	$3250	(7-Nov-90 B.SF3838/R) Boxers (20x72cm-8x28in) s. indist.d. board

DUNNING, Robert Spear (1829-1905) American
£1734	$3000	(21-May-91 GRO.B56/R) Landscape with hunters (10x20cm-4x8in) init.d.81 s.d.1881 verso board
£3906	$7500	(30-Nov-90 CH.NY28/R) Roses, peaches and cherries (33x22cm-13x9in) s.d.1891verso

DUNOYER DE SEGONZAC, Andre (1884-1974) French
£1927	$3700	(17-Dec-90 AGS.P28/R) Paysage (55x46cm-22x18in) s.d.24 (F.FR 19000)
£3316	$6500	(12-Feb-91 SY.NY22/R) Le petit panier (23x33cm-9x13in) s.init. s.i.verso panel
£3819	$7333	(24-Feb-91 P.V28/R) Paysage (55x46cm-22x18in) s.d.1924 (F.FR 38000)
£10152	$20000	(3-Oct-90 SY.NY44/R) Nature morte, souplere et bouteille de lait (55x81cm-22x32in) s.
£11224	$22000	(12-Feb-91 SY.NY45/R) La route de Saint-Nom (89x71cm-35x28in) s.
£450	$797	(20-Mar-91 DL.P118/R) Modele au fauteuil (35x25cm-14x10in) s. pen (F.FR 4500)
£455	$891	(17-Feb-91 E.LA22) Paysage (25x34cm-10x13in) s. Indian ink (F.FR 4500)
£615	$1200	(10-Oct-90 SY.NY54/R) Sleeping nymph (28x48cm-11x19in) s. india ink

DUNOYER DE SEGONZAC, Andre (1884-1974) French-cont.

£653	$1051	(26-Jun-91 CB.P44) Lapin de choux (20x26cm-8x10in) s.i. pen wash (F.FR 6500)
£753	$1212	(26-Jun-91 CB.P43) Le chat echaude (12x16cm-5x6in) s. ink wash (F.FR 7500)
£782	$1526	(10-Oct-90 ARC.P32/R) Personnage (23x15cm-9x6in) s. Indian ink W/C (F.FR 7800)
£873	$1502	(13-May-91 PPB.P9) Paysage de St.Tropez (27x42cm-11x17in) s. Indian ink (F.FR 8800)
£976	$1600	(19-Jun-91 B.SF1855/R) Paysage en automne (30x46cm-12x18in) s. pen ink
£1347	$2613	(8-Dec-90 GAB.G2520/R) Les pecheurs de la Marne (36x49cm-14x19in) s. pen crayon (S.FR 3300)
£1410	$2750	(10-Oct-90 SY.NY52/R) Reclining draped figure (38x56cm-15x22in) s. W/C india ink
£2590	$4402	(29-May-91 GL.P101/R) La Seine a Paris (30x48cm-12x19in) s. Indian ink (F.FR 26000)
£3067	$5000	(12-Jun-91 SY.NY58/R) Landscape (38x60cm-15x24in) s. pen wash
£3147	$6200	(13-Nov-90 CE.NY3/R) Le fond du golfe (39x58cm-15x23in) s. pen ink brush wash
£3224	$5546	(19-May-91 ZZ.F143/R) Vue sur la baie de Saint-Tropez (38x57cm-15x22in) s. sepia (F.FR 32500)
£4121	$7912	(24-Feb-91 P.V67/R) Vue de village (38x56cm-15x22in) s. pen ink wash (F.FR 41000)
£4281	$8263	(14-Dec-90 JM.P88/R) Place de village (47x62cm-19x24in) s. indian ink W/C pen (F.FR 42000)
£4500	$7245	(24-Jun-91 CSK104/R) Le Chateau de Grimaud (52x59cm-20x23in) s.i. thinned oil pen ink canvas
£7614	$15000	(2-Oct-90 CH.NY127/R) Le port de Saint-Tropez (45x79cm-18x31in) s. W/C over pen Indian ink
£8359	$13624	(14-Jun-91 AGS.P3/R) Vignes pres de Grimaud en hiver (50x76cm-20x30in) s. W/C (F.FR 83000)
£9000	$17460	(5-Dec-90 S355/R) Eglise de Grimaud (56x76cm-22x30in) s. pen W/C
£11318	$22411	(3-Feb-91 I.N74/R) Bacchus (65x82cm-26x32in) s. W/C chl. (F.FR 111600)
£20305	$40000	(15-Nov-90 CH.NY192/R) Le pichet de gres (58x80cm-23x31in) s. W/C pen ink over pencil paper on board
£22843	$45000	(12-Nov-90 SY.NY34/R) Nature Morte (56x78cm-22x31in) s. W/C India in paper on board
£31762	$62254	(7-Nov-90 APT.P476/R) La baie de Saint Tropez (55x76cm-22x30in) s. W/C gouache (F.FR 310000)

DUNSMORE, John Ward (1856-1945) British

£1100	$2079	(27-Sep-90 CSK144/R) The recital (30x38cm-12x15in) s.d.1885

DUNSTAN, Bernard (1920-) British

£750	$1478	(1-Nov-90 B7) Wet beach, Fairbourne (23x30cm-9x12in) init. board
£1000	$1950	(9-Oct-90 B39/R) Council meeting, Royal Academy (22x24cm-9x9in) init. i.verso
£1000	$1980	(29-Jan-91 PH176) Garden table (19x23cm-7x9in) init. i.verso board
£1300	$2418	(5-Sep-90 BT251/R) In front of Duomo, Siena (28x20cm-11x8in) init. i.verso board
£1300	$2093	(28-Jun-91 CSK191) Interior Pavia (29x21cm-11x8in) init. s.i.d.8.9.76 verso
£1400	$2730	(10-Oct-90 S163/R) Nude in bathroom (20x28cm-8x11in) init. s.verso board
£1700	$3315	(16-Oct-90 WW339) Making up (23x18cm-9x7in) init. panel
£1700	$3315	(16-Oct-90 WW333) Trumpet lesson (15x23cm-6x9in) init. panel
£4000	$7880	(13-Nov-90 SWS449/R) The blue towel (108x101cm-43x40in) init. s.i. verso
£1800	$3006	(6-Jun-91 C36/R) Summer evening (46x43cm-18x17in) init. s.i.d.1986verso pastel

DUNTON, W Herbert (1878-1936) American

£8939	$16000	(12-Apr-91 SY.NY42/R) Cowboy in desert (76x51cm-30x20in) s.

DUNTZE, Johannes Bertholomaus (1823-1895) German

£4286	$8314	(8-Dec-90 GAB.G2919/R) Les jeux hivernaux (64x96cm-25x38in) s. (S.FR 10500)
£4500	$8865	(4-Nov-90 CSK66/R) A village in winter with figures skating on a nearby river (35x49cm-14x19in) s.d.1881

DUPAIN, Edmond (1847-) French

£1003	$1956	(12-Oct-90 APT.P81) Venise - le palais vanAxel (92x73cm-36x29in) s. (F.FR 10000)
£1053	$2054	(12-Oct-90 APT.P82) Galants au repos a l'auberge du coq hardi (97x131cm-38x52in) s.d.1927 (F.FR 10500)

DUPARC, Francoise (1705-1778) French

£10000	$19300	(11-Dec-90 PH79/R) Portrait of young girl seated on bench knitting a sock (76x64cm-30x25in)

DUPAS, Jean (1882-1964) French

£7913	$14164	(9-Apr-91 APT.P4/R) Apres le bain (37x46cm-15x18in) s.d.1924 panel (F.FR 80000)
£3213	$5398	(24-Apr-91 G.Z46/R) Jeune femme aux oiseaux (39x30cm-15x12in) mono. pastel (S.FR 8000)

DUPASQUIER, Joseph (1893-1987) Swiss
£816 $1584   (8-Dec-90 GAB.G2523/R) Poya (66x185cm-26x73in) s. pavatex panel
                     (S.FR 2000)

DUPERAC, Etienne (1525-1604) French
*£1049 $2024   (10-Dec-90 L.K249/R) Forum Romanum with figures (19x27cm-7x11in) s.verso
                     ochre dr. (DM 3000)*

DUPLESSI-BERTAUX, Jean (1747-1819) French
£2535 $5020   (30-Jan-91 APT.P140/R) Paysages de riviere (23x37cm-9x15in) pair
                     (F.FR 25000)

DUPLESSI-BERTAUX, Jean (style) (1747-1819) French
£1400 $2282   (4-Jul-91 CSK136/R) Elegant hawking party about to depart
                     (23x28cm-9x11in)

DUPLESSIS, Joseph Siffrein (1725-1802) French
£11952 $20558   (14-May-91 GF.L2065/R) Landscapes with soldiers (24x32cm-9x13in) s.
                     panel pair (S.FR 30000)

DUPLESSIS, Joseph Siffrein (circle) (1725-1802) French
£841 $1505   (12-Apr-91 AGS.P8/R) Portrait presume de Monsieur Coqueley de
                     Chaussepierre (55x46cm-22x18in) (F.FR 8500)
£1471 $2824   (17-Dec-90 ARC.P51/R) Portrait de jeune femme en robe rose dans une
                     bibliotheque (45x38cm-18x15in) oval (F.FR 14500)

DUPLESSIS, Joseph Siffrein (studio) (1725-1802) French
£3800 $6194   (1-Jul-91 LGB.P27) Portrait du Roi Louis XVI (80x64cm-31x25in) oval
                     (F.FR 38000)

DUPLESSIS, Michel (18th C) French
£1500 $2535   (16-Apr-91 PH150/R) Military convoy on hill overlooking valley
                     (18x27cm-7x11in) panel
£3015 $4945   (19-Jun-91 LC.P41/R) Scene de port (16x21cm-6x8in) panel (F.FR 30000)
£3586 $7029   (11-Nov-90 M.V43) Convois militaires (15x29cm-6x11in) wood (F.FR 35000)

DUPONT, Gainsborough (1754-1797) British
£1282 $2500   (11-Oct-90 SY.NY98/R) Cottage door with mothers tending their children
                     at play (49x59cm-19x23in)
£1676 $3000   (11-Apr-91 SY.NY94/R) Portrait of lady (75x62cm-30x24in) in painted oval

DUPONT, Gainsborough (circle) (1754-1797) British
£3352 $6000   (11-Apr-91 SY.NY142/R) Travellers on path in wooded landscape
                     (90x108cm-35x43in)

DUPRA, Giorgio Domenico (1689-1770) Italian
£1500 $2535   (3-May-91 PHE106/R) Portrait of John Drummond, Duke of Perth
                     (64x48cm-25x19in)

DUPRAT, A F (1882-?) Italian
£2407 $4694   (12-Oct-90 ZZ.F64/R) La lagune (56x73cm-22x29in) s. (F.FR 24000)

DUPRAT, Albert Ferdinand (1882-?) Italian
£1190 $2048   (15-May-91 CN.P87) La lagune (33x46cm-13x18in) s. (F.FR 12000)

DUPRAY, Henry-Louis (1841-1909) French
£883 $1580   (13-Apr-91 FAL.M67/R) Cavalry battle (35x27cm-14x11in) s. (S.KR 9500)
£919 $1801   (6-Nov-90 BA.S40/R) French soldier (31x23cm-12x9in) panel (S.KR 10000)
£1427 $2754   (14-Dec-90 ARC.P133) L'inspection des chevaux de l'armee
                     (36x46cm-14x18in) s.d.1890 (F.FR 14000)

DUPRE, Jules (1811-1889) French
£592 $1000   (21-Apr-91 DU.E167) Coming storm (41x84cm-16x33in) s.
£1429 $2471   (22-May-91 GS.B2361/R) Peasants working in landscape (17x25cm-7x10in) s.
                     (S.FR 3600)
£2453 $4711   (29-Nov-90 D.V14/R) Farmhouse at dusk (73x60cm-29x24in) s. paper on
                     canvas (A.S 50000)
£2564 $5000   (24-Oct-90 CH.NY50/R) Cattle watering in wooded river landscape
                     (47x56cm-19x22in) s.
£2639 $4539   (16-May-91 D.V225/R) Before the thunderstorm (53x64cm-21x25in) s.
                     (A.S 55000)
£3213 $5944   (6-Mar-91 APT.P100) Vaches pres de la mare (22x27cm-9x11in) s.
                     (F.FR 32000)
£3421 $6500   (27-Feb-91 SY.NY65/R) Landscape (18x28cm-7x11in) s. cradled panel
£4286 $8443   (16-Nov-90 NM.P52/R) Cour de ferme (30x56cm-12x22in) sig. apocryphe
                     (F.FR 42000)
£4895 $9448   (12-Dec-90 WE.MU72/R) At the pond (31x50cm-12x20in) s. (DM 14000)
£5000 $9500   (27-Feb-91 SY.NY85/R) Returning home before storm (47x38cm-19x15in) s.
£5224 $10136   (8-Dec-90 GAB.G2912) Paysage (111x130cm-44x51in) s. (S.FR 12800)
£6200 $11904   (27-Nov-90 PH50/R) View of house before estuary (35x47cm-14x19in) s.
£6936 $12000   (23-May-91 CH.NY232/R) Le ravin (64x53cm-25x21in) s.
£6972 $12062   (24-May-91 FB.P147/R) Nature morte au pot bleu (51x61cm-20x24in) s.
                     (F.FR 70000)
£9000 $14760   (19-Jun-91 S151/R) Cattle by pond (65x81cm-26x32in) s.
£1019 $1957   (1-Dec-90 PER.M24) Les grands chenes (33x48cm-13x19in) chl. (F.FR 10000)

DUPRE, Jules (attrib) (1811-1889) French
£1067 $2069   (4-Dec-90 P.Q170) Cattle watering by a stream (26x36cm-10x14in) board
                        (C.D 2400)

DUPRE, Julien (1851-1910) French
£1300 $2496   (29-Nov-90 B60/R) Milkmaid with cattle and sheep in a meadow
                        (53x45cm-21x18in) s.
£3784 $6168   (10-Jun-91 W.T1384/R) La bergere et ses vaches sous arbre
                        (55x65cm-22x26in) s. (C.D 7000)
£6040 $11779   (10-Oct-90 WE.MU177/R) Young peasant woman and cows in landscape
                        (47x63cm-19x25in) s.d.1890 (DM 18000)
£8671 $15000   (22-May-91 SY.NY22/R) Shepherdess (56x46cm-22x18in) s.
£18000 $34560   (28-Nov-90 S23/R) Girl with farm animals in extensive landscape
                        (54x81cm-21x32in) s.
£23121 $40000   (22-May-91 SY.NY19/R) La fermiere (55x81cm-22x32in) s.
£27457 $47500   (22-May-91 D.NY29/R) Le fenaison (66x81cm-26x32in) s.
£109827 $190000   (22-May-91 SY.NY11/R) La recolte des foins (135x230cm-53x91in) s.d.1881
£796 $1385   (28-Mar-91 DAR.P23 b) Cheval de Halage (28x34cm-11x13in) s.i. oil crayon
*   pastel (F.FR 8000)*

DUPRE, Louis (1789-1837) French
£4103 $8000   (26-Oct-90 SY.NY45/R) Portrait of composer Cavaliere Rossini
*   (41x27cm-16x11in) s.i. pen W/C*

DUPRE, Victor (1816-1879) French
£1202 $2344   (25-Oct-90 D.V165/R) Trees in river landscape (33x25cm-13x10in) indis.s.
                        panel (A.S 25000)
£1364 $2686   (30-Oct-90 CH.AM114) Faggot-gatherer on edge of forest (21x27cm-8x11in)
                        s. (D.FL 4500)
£1638 $3193   (20-Jan-91 AG.W1) Country afternoon (28x27cm-11x11in) s. (P.Z 30000000)
£1707 $3056   (17-Mar-91 UNI.W1) Country afternoon (28x27cm-11x11in) s.
                        (P.Z 30000000)
£1850 $3200   (21-May-91 CE.NY31/R) Cattle grazing by stream (27x36cm-11x14in) s.
£2226 $3985   (13-Mar-91 N.M478/R) Peasant woman with cows grazing in landscape
                        (10x20cm-4x8in) s. panel (DM 6500)
£2273 $4477   (30-Oct-90 CH.AM108/R) Cattle watering in landscape (27x41cm-11x16in) s.
                        (D.FL 7500)
£2775 $5383   (8-Dec-90 SY.MO373/R) Troupeau s'abreuvant (24x32cm-9x13in) s.d.53 panel
                        (F.FR 27000)
£3051 $4973   (3-Jul-91 WE.MU346/R) Landscape near Barbizon (35x56cm-14x22in) s.d.1879
                        (DM 9000)
£3200 $5728   (12-Mar-91 PH100/R) Cattle watering in landscape (35x56cm-14x22in) s.
£4213 $8215   (12-Oct-90 ZZ.F42/R) Environs de Caen (18x36cm-7x14in) s. panel
                        (F.FR 42000)
£5641 $11000   (23-Oct-90 SY.NY268/R) Paturage au printemps (27x43cm-11x17in) s. panel
£7509 $14717   (24-Nov-90 N.M132/R) Moor landscape with shepherdess and cattle
                        (31x42cm-12x17in) s.d.1872 (DM 22000)
£15087 $28966   (1-Dec-90 PER.M125/R) Paturage dans le Bercy (45x74cm-18x29in) s.d.1855
                        (F.FR 148000)

DUPUIS, Francois (fl.1795-1802) French
£703 $1132   (27-Jun-91 APT.P250) Enfant soufflant des bulles de savon
                        (24x32cm-9x13in) s. (F.FR 7000)

DUPUIS, Pierre (1610-1682) French
£58824 $100000   (31-May-91 CH.NY76/R) Fruit in bowl and basket on table draped with rug
                        before curtain (88x121cm-35x48in)

DUPUY, Gilles Marie (20th C) ?
£1822 $3571   (25-Nov-90 ZZ.F54) Plage no. 19 (81x65cm-32x26in) s. (F.FR 18000)

DUPUY, Louis (19th C) French
£653 $1254   (24-Feb-91 FE.P90) Paysage de neige (65x40cm-26x16in) s. (F.FR 6500)
£768 $1506   (11-Nov-90 ZZ.F52/R) Paysannes au bord de la riviere (16x22cm-6x9in) s.
                        panel (F.FR 7500)
£804 $1544   (24-Feb-91 P.V94/R) Paysage (15x22cm-6x9in) s. panel (F.FR 8000)

DUPUY, Paul Michel (1869-?) French
£3381 $6627   (11-Nov-90 ZZ.F84/R) Jeunes enfants au bord de la plage
                        (34x56cm-13x22in) s. (F.FR 33000)
£3500 $6020   (14-May-91 SWS342/R) On the terrace (81x54cm-32x21in) s.d.1911

DUQUESNOY, Francois (1594-1643) Flemish
£800 $1304   (1-Jul-91 S222) Study of putto and study of hand (39x28cm-15x11in) black
*   chk htd white red chk*

DURA, Alberto (1888-1958) South American
£6684 $12500   (1-Aug-90 BAV.M7) Vista de Montevideo (130x100cm-51x39in)

DURA, Gaetano (19th C) Italian
£446 $789   (5-Apr-91 DAR.P33/R) Le Marchand de tamourins (20x16cm-8x6in) s. W/C
*   traces pen (F.FR 4500)*
£722 $1400   (8-Dec-90 W.W50) Sailors at sunset on Mediterranean (28x41cm-11x16in) s.
*   W/C gouache*

DURACK, Elizabeth (1916-) Australian
£350 $686   (19-Nov-90 MGS.S205) Aboriginal girls (50x70cm-20x28in) s.d.48 W/C
                   (A.D 900)
£498 $841   (16-Apr-91 J.M705) Aboriginal schoolyard (53x73cm-21x29in) s.d.'48 W/C
                   (A.D 1100)

DURAMEAU, Louis Jean (attrib) (1733-1796) French
£4111 $7975   (7-Dec-90 CH.MO338) La lecon particuliere (46x32cm-18x13in) (F.FR 40000)
£2854 $5509   (12-Dec-90 ARC.P58/R) La veillee (22x25cm-9x10in) sanguinne htd.white
                   (F.FR 28000)

DURAMEAU, Louis Jean (circle) (1733-1796) French
£704 $1154   (21-Jun-91 CK.P14/R) Le bon samaritain (31x23cm-12x9in) pen wash sketch
                   in pierre noire verso (F.FR 7000)

DURAN, A (fl.1886-1900)?
£10053 $19000   (27-Sep-90 CH.NY24/R) Time is money (41x51cm-16x20in) s.indist.d.

DURAN, Carolus (20th C) French
£5417 $9100   (28-Apr-91 HG.C72) Afternoon call (74x99cm-29x39in) panel

DURANCAMPS, Rafael (20th C) Spanish
£4049 $7935   (23-Nov-90 PLF.P62/R) Rue d'une ville de province (38x46cm-15x18in) s.
                   (F.FR 40000)

DURAND, Asher Brown (attrib) (1796-1886) Austrian
£4464 $7500   (28-Apr-91 LIT.L39) Hudson river scene with ships in background
                   (61x46cm-24x18in)

DURAND, C (?)?
£1263 $2400   (9-Jan-91 D.NY20) Thais Valley (69x91cm-27x36in) s.

DURAND, Jean (1894-1977) French
£2923 $5701   (28-Oct-90 QWA.P113/R) Panthere marchant s.d.55 panel (F.FR 29000)
£585 $1140   (28-Oct-90 QWA.P115) Panthere (19x26cm-7x10in) pen htd.white gouache
                   (F.FR 5800)
£2520 $4914   (28-Oct-90 QWA.P114) Panthere en marche (44x106cm-17x42in) s.d.
                   chl.sanguinne crayon htd.wash (F.FR 25000)

DURAND-BRAGER (1814-1879) French
£1835 $3523   (2-Dec-90 M.V132) Marine (39x61cm-15x24in) s. (F.FR 18000)

DURAND-BRAGER, Jean Baptiste Henri (1814-1879) French
£2929 $5682   (6-Dec-90 CB.P92/R) Long-courrier drosse par gros temps sur la jetee du
                   port de Montevideo (40x70cm-16x28in) s. d.1866 verso (F.FR 28500)

DURANEL, Jean (20th C) French
£742 $1328   (14-Apr-91 R.P142/R) Les pietons et les murs (118x92cm-46x36in) s. mixed
                   media canvas (F.FR 7500)

DURENNE, Eugene Antoine (1860-1944) French
£1188 $2103   (7-Apr-91 I.N120) Vallee de la Seine a Houdedonville (54x73cm-21x29in)
                   s. (F.FR 12000)
£1208 $1970   (11-Jun-91 I.N195) Cote d'Amfreville (33x45cm-13x18in) s.d.23
                   (F.FR 12000)
£1274 $2459   (12-Dec-90 APT.P95) Chambre a coucher (65x54cm-26x21in) s.d.25
                   (F.FR 12500)
£2117 $4128   (26-Oct-90 APT.P101) Entre les oliviers (50x65cm-20x26in) s. l. verso
                   (F.FR 21000)
£2419 $4718   (26-Oct-90 APT.P103/R) Entree de, Marseille (50x65cm-20x26in) s. l.
                   verso (F.FR 24000)
£2564 $5000   (10-Oct-90 SY.NY20/R) Jeune fille au piano (53x64cm-21x25in) s.
£2722 $4600   (1-May-91 D.NY31) La reunion mucicale (61x74cm-24x29in) s. s.l.stretcher
£3831 $7470   (26-Oct-90 APT.P102) Vue de Cagnes, le matin (50x65cm-20x26in) s.d. l.
                   verso (F.FR 38000)

DURER (school) (16th C) German
£2397 $4291   (13-Mar-91 N.M403/R) Circumcision of Christ in church interior
                   (48x58cm-19x23in) c.1600 after Goltzius (DM 7000)

DURER, Albrecht (circle) (1471-1528) German
£16000 $27680   (24-May-91 C2/R) The Adoration of the Shepherds, the Annunciation to the
                   Shepherds beyond (17x12cm-7x5in) panel

DUREY, Rene (1890-1959) French
£553 $989   (11-Mar-91 GL.P48) Le barrage (46x55cm-18x22in) s. (F.FR 5500)
£566 $979   (22-May-91 BA.S33/R) Vue vers Paris (33x46cm-13x18in) s. (S.KR 6000)
£1972 $3886   (6-Oct-90 GL.P34) Paysage maritime au pin parasol (60x73cm-24x29in)
                   s.d.12 (F.FR 20000)
£2548 $4918   (16-Dec-90 T.B125/R) Paysage a la tour (60x73cm-24x29in) s. (F.FR 25000)

DURHAM, Cornelius Bevis (style) (fl.1825-1865) British
£450 $770   (30-Jul-91 CSK10) Matilda Jane Pelham Clinton (11x?cm-4x?in) min.l.
                   verso gilt-metal frame oval

DURIAU, Alfred (1877-1958) Belgian
£1146 $1925   (23-Apr-91 C.A447) Sunny farm scene (57x76cm-22x30in) s. (B.FR 70000)

DURIG, Rolf (1926-) Swiss
£980 $1900   (8-Dec-90 GAB.G2524) Le Saint (50x61cm-20x24in) s.d.1949 verso
     (S.FR 2400)
£1143 $2217   (8-Dec-90 GAB.G2525) Bompre - nature morte aux peches (50x61cm-20x24in)
     s.d.1950 verso (S.FR 2800)
£1394 $2719   (24-Oct-90 GD.B305/R) Nocturne (73x91cm-29x36in) s.d.90 (S.FR 3500)
£1918 $3722   (8-Dec-90 GAB.G2526) Le chemin de Bompre (100x65cm-39x26in) s.d.1950
     verso (S.FR 4700)

DURM, Leopold (1878-1918) German
£1356 $2210   (3-Jul-91 WE.MU228/R) Woman doing toilet (101x95cm-40x37in) s.
     (DM 4000)
£1695 $2763   (3-Jul-91 WE.MU227/R) After the bath (181x100cm-71x39in) s. (DM 5000)

DUROCHER, Renee (1919-) Canadian
*£408 $690   (17-Apr-91 EA.M490) Heure d'ouverture (76x76cm-30x30in) s. s.d.90 verso
     mixed media (C.D 800)*

DURR, Louis (1896-1973) Swiss
£640 $1082   (1-May-91 GD.B218/R) Sunrise over the Wallis mountains (52x63cm-20x25in)
     s.d.37 (S.FR 1600)
£657 $1282   (24-Oct-90 GD.B307/R) Lake Geneva with view of Grammont (17x25cm-7x10in)
     mono. (S.FR 1650)
£797 $1554   (24-Oct-90 GD.B308/R) Alpine mountain range landscape (35x43cm-14x17in)
     s.d.56 (S.FR 2000)

DURRIE, George Henry (1820-1863) American
£35417 $68000   (30-Nov-90 CH.NY5/R) Winter at Jones Inn (46x61cm-18x24in) init.

DURRIE, George Henry (attrib) (1820-1863) American
£707 $1400   (1-Feb-91 S.W2557/R) Winter scene (36x53cm-14x21in)

DURST, J (?) ?
£2041 $3286   (26-Jun-91 KM.K1441) Still life of flowers with peonies, lilac, larkspur
     and butterflies (39x32cm-15x13in) s. (DM 6000)

DURSTON, Arthur (1897-1938) American
£2179 $4250   (10-Oct-90 B.SF643/R) Street car, Santa Monica (63x76cm-25x30in) s.d.38
     i.verso

DURY-VASSELON, Hortense (19th C) French
£10100 $17877   (21-Mar-91 LC.P56/R) Bouquet de roses dans un vase a monture debronze
     (92x73cm-36x29in) s. (F.FR 101000)

DUSART, Cornelis (1660-1704) Dutch
£11173 $20000   (11-Apr-91 SY.NY131/R) Fiddler and peasants outside an inn
     (38x30cm-15x12in) s.
*£795 $1566   (12-Nov-90 CH.AM132) Adoration of shepherds (24x36cm-9x14in) s.d.1702
     black lead wash (D.FL 2600)*
*£2599 $5121   (12-Nov-90 CH.AM131/R) In Liefde Vry - Rhetoricians with merry company
     in tavern (36x46cm-14x18in) i. black lead wash ink after Jan Steen
     (D.FL 8500)*

DUSART, Cornelis (attrib) (1660-1704) Dutch
£4407 $8683   (14-Nov-90 D.V188/R) Peasant family before house in wooded landscape
     (66x52cm-26x20in) (A.S 90000)
£4897 $9647   (14-Nov-90 D.V91/R) Peasants in liquor shop (60x48cm-24x19in) panel
     (A.S 100000)

DUSART, Cornelis (school) (1660-1704) Dutch
£4286 $8443   (16-Nov-90 PLF.P4/R) Assemblee villageoise (56x46cm-22x18in) panel
     (F.FR 42000)

DUSART, Cornelis (style) (17th C) Dutch
£1071 $1800   (17-Jul-91 SY.NY195/R) Peasants in moonlight (34x29cm-13x11in) s.
£1690 $2873   (28-May-91 AB.S4754/R) Farmbuildings and figures (60x73cm-24x29in) bears
     sig.d.1695 panel (S.KR 18000)
£1800 $3510   (26-Oct-90 C145/R) A family in a cottage (44x35cm-17x14in) panel

DUSAUSSAY, Jules Louis (1828-?) French
£1223 $2361   (12-Dec-90 ZZ.F42/R) Scene champetre dans la vallee de la Seine
     (57x85cm-22x33in) s. (F.FR 12000)

DUSEIN, Gilles (20th C) French?
£2520 $4914   (20-Jan-91 CSC.P61/R) Les ready made appartiennent a tout le monde
     (97x130cm-38x51in) acrylic (F.FR 25000)

DUSSAU, Georges (1947-) ?
*£424 $708   (6-Jun-91 HW.H2987) Untitled (28x22cm-11x9in) s.d.1979 bodycol chk over
     pencil (DM 1250)*

DUSSEK, Eduard Adrian (1871-?) Hungarian

£1300	$2510	(13-Dec-90 SY.AM97) Reclining nude (90x86cm-35x34in) s.d.1921 (D.FL 4200)

DUSWALD (19th C) German

£5179	$8908	(14-May-91 GF.L2087/R) View over Grand Canal to Doge's Palace, Venice (76x105cm-30x41in) s.d.1879 (S.FR 13000)

DUTCH NAIVE SCHOOL, 19th C

£1500	$2595	(9-May-91 CSK52/R) Farmstead with distant church (61x78cm-24x31in)

DUTCH SCHOOL (?)

£958	$1610	(23-Apr-91 SY.AM221) Still life with fruit and porcelain on table (100x100cm-39x39in) c.1900 (D.FL 3200)
£963	$1608	(6-Jun-91 D.V286/R) Still life of fruit (22x29cm-9x11in) c.1800 (A.S 20000)
£1000	$1650	(10-Jul-91 C21) A gentleman in black coat (8cm-3ins circular) min. c.1660 oil copper gilt frame
£1154	$2262	(21-Nov-90 GM.B1017) Marchand de Grains (55x67cm-22x26in) (B.FR 70000)
£1154	$2262	(21-Nov-90 GM.B1020) Village au bord de l'Estuaire (24x33cm-9x13in) wood (B.FR 70000)
£1164	$2083	(12-Mar-91 GM.B1104/R) Tempete en mer (100x130cm-39x51in) (B.FR 70000)
£1361	$2408	(20-Mar-91 KM.K1041/R) Hunting scene with gun, dog, dead game and view of mountain landscape (59x96cm-23x38in) c.1700 (DM 4000)
£1450	$2683	(5-Mar-91 PH165) Ferry crossing river before town (59x87cm-23x34in) c.1800 bears sig. W van Bemmel
£1486	$2898	(23-Oct-90 DUR.M43) Barcos de guerra (135x200cm-53x79in) (S.P 275000)
£1488	$2500	(28-Apr-91 HG.C50) Floral still life (104x8cm-41x3in) oval
£1514	$2604	(14-May-91 GF.L2276/R) Portrait of gentleman with son (80x66cm-31x26in) c.1700 (S.FR 3800)
£1540	$2680	(25-Mar-91 SY.F583) La toilette (72x62cm-28x24in) c.1700 (I.L 3400000)
£1548	$2600	(28-Apr-91 HG.C75) Still life with jug and fruit (91x74cm-36x29in)
£1724	$3000	(27-Mar-91 B.SF4055/R) Fishing boats preparing for the morning sail (19x25cm-7x10in) c.1800 init. panel
£1765	$3000	(27-May-91 GC.M402) Flores y centro de metal (60x70cm-24x28in)
£1765	$3000	(27-May-91 GC.M403) Flores y centro de metal (60x70cm-24x28in)
£2365	$4020	(27-May-91 L.K82) Crucifixion (104x83cm-41x33in) c.1600 panel (DM 7000)
£2471	$4200	(27-May-91 GC.M401/R) Copon con flores (100x80cm-39x31in)
£2600	$4238	(4-Jul-91 C505/R) Extensive Dutch landscape with shepherd and shepherdess making music (41x96cm-16x38in) c.1750
£2700	$5265	(22-Oct-90 SWS1435/R) Classical landscape with figures and dogs in foreground (79x119cm-31x47in) c.1700
£2789	$4797	(14-May-91 GF.L2049/R) Landscape with figures (61x81cm-24x32in) c.1700 (S.FR 7000)
£3571	$6393	(13-Mar-91 GK.Z45/R) Portrait of gentleman wearing black costume and white collar (114x92cm-45x36in) c.1700 (S.FR 9000)
£5179	$8908	(14-May-91 GF.L2289/R) Italianate harbour landscape (80x115cm-31x45in) c.1700 (S.FR 13000)
£5574	$9476	(27-May-91 L.K86/R) Still life of grapes and peaches on blue velvet bow (37x32cm-15x13in) i. (DM 16500)
£5976	$10279	(14-May-91 GF.L2298/R) Mythological scene (61x77cm-24x30in) c.1700 (S.FR 15000)
£11824	$23057	(26-Oct-90 KM.K1042/R) River landscape with figures and view of country estate (272x178cm-107x70in) c.1800 (DM 35000)
£11824	$23057	(26-Oct-90 KM.K1041/R) View of Dutch town with shipping and figures (272x178cm-107x70in) c.1800 (DM 35000)
£14558	$23439	(27-Jun-91 APT.P104/R) Marines c.1650 copper pair (F.FR 145000)
£1600	*$3072*	*(18-Feb-91 S199/R) Cupid awakening Psyche from deadly sleep (35x47cm-14x19in) c.1600 chk W/C*
£2500	*$4800*	*(18-Dec-90 C59/R) Winter landscape with ice-skaters on river (6cm-2ins circular) min.c.1700 s.verso card pierced ormolu frame*
£4500	*$7335*	*(2-Jul-91 C217/R) Naval engagement with man-o'-war sinking and others firing (14x28cm-6x11in) pen wash*
£6000	*$9780*	*(2-Jul-91 C211/R) Oriental boy, wearing turban and holding hawk, in profile to left (24x10cm-9x4in) black chk pen wash c.1620*

DUTCH SCHOOL, 15th C

£34653	$61337	(4-Apr-91 CK.P22/R) La Trinite entre Saint-Jacques, Saint-Pierre, Saint Christophe, Saint Hubert et donatrice (60x120cm-24x47in) panel (F.FR 350000)

DUTCH SCHOOL, 16th C

£1800	$3114	(20-May-91 SWS178) Portrait of a lady (91x72cm-36x28in) coat of arms panel
£2397	$3908	(12-Jun-91 N.M325/R) St Hieronymus (92x66cm-36x26in) panel (DM 7000)
£4600	$7958	(20-May-91 SWS5/R) Portrait of a gentleman wearing amour (90x64cm-35x25in) i. panel
£4706	$8000	(31-May-91 CH.NY183/R) Susannah and the Elders (97x67cm-38x26in)
£2600	*$4238*	*(1-Jul-91 S167/R) Martyrdom of female saint (28x20cm-11x8in) pen brush wash*
£3846	*$7423*	*(10-Dec-90 L.K309/R) Presentation of Jesus in the Temple (14x20cm-6x8in) pen wash dr.htd.white (DM 11000)*

DUTCH SCHOOL, 17th C

£963	$1608	(6-Jun-91 D.V337/R) Flight Into Egypt (28x42cm-11x17in) canvas on panel (A.S 20000)
£963	$1608	(6-Jun-91 D.V341/R) Portrait of lady (57x45cm-22x18in) panel (A.S 20000)
£1000	$1770	(20-Mar-91 C17/R) Portrait of gentleman in black habit with lace-bordered collar (5x?cm-2x?in) min. oil copper oval
£1020	$1806	(20-Mar-91 KM.K1035) Genre scene with couple feeding traveller (62x81cm-24x32in) (DM 3000)
£1150	$1921	(4-Jun-91 SWS1799) King with two women (60x84cm-24x33in) panel
£1154	$2227	(12-Dec-90 N.M396/R) Still life with meat, leman and clay pot with vegetable (52x63cm-20x25in) l. panel (DM 3300)
£1199	$2146	(12-Mar-91 FN.S2685/R) Portrait of Helena von Munchhausen (84x65cm-33x26in) oval (DM 3500)
£1275	$2193	(14-May-91 GF.L2279) Mary surrounded by wreath of flowers (16x14cm-6x6in) copper oval (S.FR 3200)
£1293	$2081	(26-Jun-91 KM.K1336) Village fair (38x56cm-15x22in) en grisaille panel (DM 3800)
£1327	$2613	(18-Nov-90 P.V21) Personnages contemplant un parc panel (F.FR 13000)
£1386	$2453	(5-Apr-91 DAR.P41) Les joeurs de cartes (47x38cm-19x15in) panel (F.FR 14000)
£1400	$2282	(4-Jul-91 B100 b) A mediterranean harbour scene with figures on the quayside (56x68cm-22x27in)
£1400	$2282	(4-Jul-91 B120) Actaeon discovering Diana and her Nymphs (72x108cm-28x43in)
£1400	$2660	(28-Feb-91 B34/R) Study of shepherd with shepherdess holding bird's nest (49x37cm-19x15in) canvas on panel
£1469	$2834	(12-Dec-90 N.M379/R) Esther before Ahasverus asking for pardon (106x145cm-42x57in) (DM 4200)
£1488	$2500	(17-Jul-91 SY.NY107/R) Tobias and the angel (57x75cm-22x30in)
£1497	$2649	(20-Mar-91 KM.K1036) Seascape with frigates engaged in battle and sinking rowing boat (50x95cm-20x37in) (DM 4400)
£1633	$2890	(20-Mar-91 KM.K1037) The Last Supper (98x155cm-39x61in) (DM 4800)
£1644	$2942	(13-Mar-91 N.M422) Portrait of young man standing by remnants of column (23x19cm-9x7in) panel (DM 4800)
£1683	$2844	(1-May-91 KH.K131/R) Birds and fruit on ledge by ruins (76x63cm-30x25in) (D.KR 19000)
£1737	$3022	(26-Mar-91 VN.R33) People seated around a table near a farmhouse (38x48cm-15x19in) panel (D.FL 5800)
£1800	$3097	(14-May-91 GM.B605/R) Vieil homme lisant (104x88cm-41x35in) (B.FR 110000)
£1900	$3287	(20-May-91 SWS93) A river landscape with figures by a cottage (25x30cm-10x12in) indist.s.d.1650 panel
£2027	$3446	(27-May-91 L.K85) Still life of roses, narcissi and peonies in basket (32x40cm-13x16in) (DM 6000)
£2027	$3426	(3-May-91 SA.A1626/R) Portrait of a young nobleman (50x40cm-20x16in) l. (DM 6000)
£2060	$3543	(14-May-91 BU.S84/R) Harbour view with vessel (47x62cm-19x24in) panel (S.KR 22000)
£2115	$3447	(10-Jun-91 AGB.P73) Portrait de femme a la coiffe de dentelle (95x70cm-37x28in) l. (F.FR 21000)
£2345	$4525	(12-Dec-90 ARC.P83/R) Bouquet de fleurs aux papillons et aux insectes (61x50cm-24x20in) (F.FR 23000)
£2390	$4112	(14-May-91 GF.L2029/R) Storm in mountainous landscape (45x60cm-18x24in) (S.FR 6000)
£2400	$4056	(1-May-91 GD.B413/R) Fortified harbour town with shipping and figures (75x101cm-30x40in) (S.FR 6000)
£2536	$4895	(10-Dec-90 BU.K63/R) Cavalry battle (60x84cm-24x33in) init. panel (D.KR 28000)
£2600	$5122	(31-Oct-90 S161/R) Vanitas still life (44x36cm-17x14in)
£2728	$5346	(20-Nov-90 F.R22/R) Interno di osteria (33x43cm-13x17in) rem.sig. (I.L 6000000)
£2740	$4904	(12-Mar-91 FN.S2684) Hunting party resting in wooded hilly landscape (167x240cm-66x94in) (DM 8000)
£2789	$4797	(14-May-91 GF.L2309/R) Adoration of the Child (70x92cm-28x36in) (S.FR 7000)
£2941	$5765	(6-Nov-90 BA.S351/R) Market outside Panthenon (64x89cm-25x35in) (S.KR 32000)
£2962	$5035	(30-May-91 F.M93) Scena di battaglia navale (63x103cm-25x41in) (I.L 6500000)
£3074	$6025	(11-Nov-90 M.V52/R) Bateaux dans la tempete (52x66cm-20x26in) (F.FR 30000)
£3081	$5176	(23-Apr-91 RAS.K1/R) Seascpae with sailingvessels off harbour (38x52cm-15x20in) init. panel oval (D.KR 35000)
£3196	$5369	(23-Apr-91 F.R62) Scena di mercato (27x63cm-11x25in) panel (I.L 7000000)
£3200	$6080	(13-Sep-90 CSK85/R) Allegory of Christ Good Shepherd saving Protestant souls as Catholics and infidels burn souls (72x103cm-28x41in) i.d.1618 panel
£3232	$6366	(14-Nov-90 RAS.K5/R) Portrait of elegant lady with small dog on table (110x90cm-43x35in) (D.KR 36000)
£3279	$6426	(7-Nov-90 APT.P442/R) Portrait d'une enfant en robe blanche (68x57cm-27x22in) mono.d. oval (F.FR 32000)
£3321	$6543	(14-Nov-90 RAS.K108/R) Stormy night with shipwreck off coastal cliffs (105x140cm-41x55in) indist.s. (D.KR 37000)

DUTCH SCHOOL, 17th C -cont.

£3602	$7024	(23-Oct-90 CH.R471/R) Scena di banchetto (49x64cm-19x25in) panel (I.L 8000000)
£3647	$6200	(31-May-91 CH.NY217/R) Basket of cherries, bread and objects with food on table and dog (74x94cm-29x37in)
£3800	$6422	(29-Apr-91 HS308/R) Still life of glass, mixed fruit and prawns on table top, scroll beyond (27x22cm-11x9in) i. panel
£3800	$7486	(31-Oct-90 S213/R) Church interior (35x54cm-14x21in) bears sig.d.1642 panel
£3825	$7497	(24-Jan-91 EP.M28/R) Retrato de una dama (108x86cm-43x34in) i. (S.P 700000)
£3955	$7832	(30-Jan-91 APT.P204/R) Portrait d'un enfant tenant un oiseau (116x92cm-46x36in) (F.FR 39000)
£3984	$6853	(14-May-91 GF.L2278/R) Landscape with view across plain (70x87cm-28x34in) (S.FR 10000)
£4000	$6760	(1-May-91 GD.B414/R) Still lifes with roses, tulips, iris and bluebells (55x43cm-22x17in) pair (S.FR 10000)
£4111	$7975	(7-Dec-90 CH.MO307/R) Une scene campagnarde avec des voyageurs et des marchands (29x41cm-11x16in) panel (F.FR 40000)
£4196	$8098	(12-Dec-90 N.M377/R) Amor taking young girl's children shoes off (163x105cm-64x41in) panel (DM 12000)
£4217	$6789	(26-Jun-91 CB.P106) Le Concert (48x39cm-19x15in) (F.FR 42000)
£4281	$8220	(30-Nov-90 APT.P70/R) Assemblee dans un paysage de ville avec ruines antiques (63x74cm-25x29in) (F.FR 42000)
£4469	$8000	(11-Apr-91 SY.NY110/R) Still life of flowers in glass vase resting on stone ledge (32x23cm-13x9in)
£5068	$9882	(26-Oct-90 KM.K1030/R) Portrait of gentleman by balustrade (121x102cm-48x40in) indis.s.d.1653 (DM 15000)
£5123	$10041	(11-Nov-90 M.V48/R) Marine (54x84cm-21x33in) (F.FR 50000)
£6291	$10695	(28-May-91 AB.S4843/R) The nymph Syrinx (45x34cm-18x13in) panel (S.KR 67000)
£6643	$12822	(10-Dec-90 L.K83/R) View of The Hague with figures (69x112cm-27x44in) canvas laid down (DM 19000)
£7035	$11538	(21-Jun-91 SY.MO270/R) Le chemin du marche (68x97cm-27x38in) bears trace sig. (F.FR 70000)
£7179	$14000	(10-Oct-90 CH.NY112/R) Silver plate with fruit, roemer and wineglass on draped ledge (73x62cm-29x24in) c.1670 bears init.
£7755	$15200	(6-Nov-90 GF.L2037/R) Deer hunt at dawn (85x133cm-33x52in) (S.FR 19000)
£9000	$15210	(17-Apr-91 S171/R) Shipping scene (67x99cm-26x39in) indis.s.d.16.5 panel
£11621	$22893	(14-Nov-90 SY.AM91/R) Fishermen returning to the shore (33x53cm-13x21in) panel (D.FL 38000)
£30488	$60976	(4-Feb-91 LEB.P7/R) Pivoines et roses dans un vase pose sur un entablement (65x52cm-26x20in) s.d.1675 (F.FR 300000)
£845	*$1436*	*(31-May-91 GB.B5191/R) The Finding of Moses (20x17cm-8x7in) pen wash (DM 2500)*
£1050	*$1712*	*(1-Jul-91 S72) Study of man with sword (23x20cm-9x8in) black chk htd white chk*
£1100	*$1793*	*(1-Jul-91 S125) Study of tulip (25x10cm-10x4in) W/C*
£2500	*$4200*	*(22-Apr-91 PH114/R) Portrait of Baron Sohler de Warmerhuysen (7x?cm-3x?in) min.copper set in enamelled locket oval*
£7951	*$15664*	*(12-Nov-90 CH.AM96/R) View of city of Amersfoort (10x30cm-4x12in) black chk ink (D.FL 26000)*

DUTCH SCHOOL, 17th/18th C

£1541	$2512	(12-Jun-91 N.M331/R) Shepherd with cattle in wooded landscape with view of mountains beyond (61x83cm-24x33in) i. (DM 4500)
£3082	$5517	(13-Mar-91 N.M423/R) River landscape with buildings, mill and figures (56x74cm-22x29in) (DM 9000)
£4079	$7750	(15-Sep-90 S.W2774/R) Pastoral scene with sheep (74x94cm-29x37in)
£4079	$7750	(15-Sep-90 S.W2773/R) Pastoral scene with cows (74x94cm-29x37in)
£4795	$7815	(12-Jun-91 N.M332) Village street with peasants, cattle and horse-drawn cart (29x42cm-11x17in) (DM 14000)

DUTCH SCHOOL, 18th C

£1004	$1616	(26-Jun-91 CB.P102) Vertumne et Pomone (64x80cm-25x31in) (F.FR 10000)
£1014	$2008	(30-Jan-91 APT.P231/R) Troupeau pres d'une riviere (47x62cm-19x24in) panel (F.FR 10000)
£1050	$1995	(28-Feb-91 B39/R) Shepherdess with sheep and cattle in wooded river landscape (34x40cm-13x16in) panel
£1087	$1892	(25-Mar-91 SY.F575) Velieri in burrasca (42x60cm-17x24in) panel (I.L 2400000)
£1100	$1771	(25-Jun-91 ACA738/R) Still life with flowers oval
£1190	$2000	(17-Jul-91 SY.NY94/R) Landscape with horseman (63x76cm-25x30in)
£1429	$2400	(17-Jul-91 SY.NY198/R) Ice skaters on a canal (28x46cm-11x18in) panel
£1587	$2841	(13-Mar-91 GK.Z50) Couple making music surrounded by spectators (33x39cm-13x15in) (S.FR 4000)
£1600	$2704	(1-May-91 GD.B415/R) Hunting still life (71x95cm-28x37in) (S.FR 4000)
£1617	$3153	(25-Oct-90 VN.R43/R) Huntsmen in landscape (40x40cm-16x16in) (D.FL 5400)
£1640	$2788	(30-May-91 F.M34) Ritratto di fanciulla (28x21cm-11x8in) (I.L 3600000)
£1700	$2941	(20-May-91 SWS48/R) Interior with a man at a table laden with game and kitchen utensils (48x46cm-19x18in) bears mono. panel
£1700	$2771	(4-Jul-91 C772/R) Travellers outside country inn (37x46cm-15x18in) indist.s. panel
£1700	$2889	(27-May-91 GK.Z5048) Italian landscape with fortified castle and figures (47x66cm-19x26in) panel (S.FR 4300)

DUTCH SCHOOL, 18th C -cont.

£1710	$3061	(14-Mar-91 D.V218/R) Fire raging at night, powder explosion in Delft (26x47cm-10x19in) i.d.1654 panel (A.S 35000)
£1722	$2996	(25-Mar-91 SY.F597) Cacciatori in un paesaggio (42x48cm-17x19in) (I.L 3800000)
£1984	$3552	(13-Mar-91 GK.Z47/R) Hermit in wooded landscape with ruin (60x83cm-24x33in) (S.FR 5000)
£2231	$4418	(30-Jan-91 APT.P219/R) Marine par temps calme (28x38cm-11x15in) (F.FR 22000)
£2390	$4112	(14-May-91 GF.L2295/R) Riders in encampment (46x53cm-18x21in) mono. (S.FR 6000)
£2500	$4325	(22-May-91 GS.B2402/R) River landscape with windmill and church (43x54cm-17x21in) (S.FR 6300)
£2551	$5000	(21-Nov-90 NA.BA56) La Virgen y el Nino (92x71cm-36x28in) init.
£2705	$4842	(8-Apr-91 CH.R142/R) Marina con traghetto (31x27cm-12x11in) panel (I.L 6000000)
£2752	$5422	(13-Nov-90 AB.S1010/R) Town scene with figures, Amsterdam (65x82cm-26x32in) (S.KR 30000)
£2800	$4732	(17-Apr-91 S151/R) Capriccio landscape with figures fishing beside classical ruins (176x100cm-69x39in)
£2897	$5185	(13-Mar-91 GK.Z48) Skirmish in river landscapes (12x15cm-5x6in) brass pair (S.FR 7300)
£3183	$6271	(14-Nov-90 D.V200/R) Sailing ships in calm sea with fortified castle beyond (46x64cm-18x25in) i. panel (A.S 65000)
£3634	$6250	(15-May-91 D.NY63/R) Still life of peonies, roses, carnations and other flowers in vase (94x71cm-37x28in)
£3800	$7410	(10-Oct-90 C198/R) Portrait of man, said to Tsar Peter the Great as a ship's carpenter in Zaandam, 1697 (74x59cm-29x23in)
£4077	$7870	(12-Dec-90 ARC.P90/R) Jeux d'enfants (104x82cm-41x32in) (F.FR 40000)
£4639	$9000	(8-Dec-90 W.W12/R) Flowers and fruit on stone ledge (56x48cm-22x19in) panel
£4911	$8250	(17-Jul-91 SY.NY67/R) Still life with flowers in a vase (63x46cm-25x18in)
£6300	$11151	(21-Mar-91 LC.P47/R) Navires et galeres au pied d'un chateau fort (53x82cm-21x32in) (F.FR 63000)
£6704	$12000	(11-Apr-91 SY.NY49/R) Still life of flowers in vase (72x58cm-28x23in)
£1500	*$2445*	*(2-Jul-91 C358/R) Studies of arms and heads of putti, probably for assumption (31x39cm-12x15in) num.210 black white chk*
£2600	*$4238*	*(1-Jul-91 S135/R) Floral still life (57x46cm-22x18in) W/C gouache gum arabic vellum*
£2878	*$5583*	*(7-Dec-90 CN.P112/R) Portrait de chien (38x53cm-15x21in) W/C (F.FR 28000)*

DUTCH SCHOOL, 18th/19th C

£1053	$2021	(18-Feb-91 SY.J302/R) Fishing boat in a choppy sea (36x57cm-14x22in) indist.s. (SA.R 5200)
£1370	$2452	(13-Mar-91 N.M426/R) Shepherds and flocks watering (65x54cm-26x21in) canvas on panel (DM 4000)
£5612	$11056	(18-Nov-90 P.V16) Bouquet de fleurs (F.FR 55000)

DUTCH SCHOOL, 19th C

£928	$1559	(23-Apr-91 SY.AM164) Farmer with pig looking for truffles (29x37cm-11x15in) panel (D.FL 3100)
£1000	$1720	(14-May-91 SWS296/R) The wedding (76x63cm-30x25in) indis.s.d.1879
£1014	$2008	(30-Jan-91 APT.P223/R) Nature morte de fruits (73x72cm-29x28in) panel octagonal (F.FR 10000)
£1027	$1675	(12-Jun-91 N.M468) Moonlit landscape with fishermen in boats on river (31x43cm-12x17in) i.verso panel (DM 3000)
£1048	$1760	(23-Apr-91 SY.AM216) Wooded landscape with figures on path (25x37cm-10x15in) init. panel (D.FL 3500)
£1100	$1903	(20-May-91 SWS163) A southern river landscape with figures (26x39cm-10x15in) panel
£1224	$2376	(8-Dec-90 GAB.G2096/R) Paysage hivernal avec patineurs sur un lac gele (36x54cm-14x21in) mono.d.1879 (S.FR 3000)
£1331	$2183	(18-Jun-91 FN.S2191/R) Family seated around table praying grace (26x34cm-10x13in) panel (DM 3900)
£1414	$2446	(6-May-91 ZEL.L1749/R) Inn interior with figures dancing (82x115cm-32x45in) indis.mono. (DM 4200)
£1441	$2738	(3-Mar-91 REM.W16) Beggars (24x27cm-9x11in) s. panel (P.Z 26000000)
£1497	$2649	(20-Mar-91 KM.K1384) Market scene with peasant woman offering ware by shine of oil lamp (46x37cm-18x15in) panel (DM 4400)
£1541	$2512	(12-Jun-91 N.M531/R) Tinker working outside tavern (36x28cm-14x11in) metal (DM 4500)
£1850	$3090	(22-Jul-91 SWS1060) Still life of mixed flowers in an urn on a ledge (65x54cm-26x21in)
£1919	$3301	(16-May-91 D.V157/R) Canal scene in winter (19x22cm-7x9in) panel (A.S 40000)
£2073	$3980	(27-Nov-90 SY.AM3613) Party in artist's studio (75x102cm-30x40in) (D.FL 6800)
£2232	$3750	(17-Jul-91 SY.NY193/R) The fish sellers (23x30cm-9x12in) indist.s.panel
£2300	$3979	(20-May-91 SWS7/R) Still life of various fruits in a basket with nuts and a butterfly (37x47cm-15x19in) panel
£2551	$5000	(21-Nov-90 NA.BA78) Scene d'interieur (35x29cm-14x11in) parchment
£2729	$4585	(23-Apr-91 RAS.K40/R) Hunter and dog with girl by entrance to house (61x72cm-24x28in) indist.s. panel (D.KR 31000)

DUTCH SCHOOL, 19th C -cont.
£3316 $6500   (7-Nov-90 B.SF1187/R) Young boy sleeping (96x136cm-38x54in) indist.mono. d.18
£4676 $9072   (6-Dec-90 CB.P46/R) Escadre de vaisseaux par mauvais temps (27x38cm-11x15in) mono.EH d.1805 (F.FR 45500)
£7542 $13500   (10-Apr-91 HF.NY77/R) Street scene (32x44cm-13x17in) indist.s. panel

DUTCH SCHOOL, 20th C (?)
£2535 $4868   (19-Dec-90 LD.P135) Ville au bord d'une riviere (97x120cm-38x47in) (F.FR 25000)
£3049 $5000   (19-Jun-91 B.SF1669/R) Floral still lifes (107x81cm-42x32in) init. pair

DUTEIL, Jean Claude (1950-) French
£756 $1474   (27-Oct-90 ZZ.F63 b) Contre-jour a Trouville (27x35cm-11x14in) (F.FR 7500)
£1366 $2678   (25-Nov-90 ZZ.F240/R) Les quais en fete a Trouville (60x81cm-24x32in) s. (F.FR 13500)
£1512 $2949   (28-Oct-90 M.V154/R) La terrasse, Dinard (50x65cm-20x26in) s. (F.FR 15000)

DUTEURTRE, Pierre Eugene (1911-) French
£615 $1205   (11-Nov-90 ZZ.F262/R) Paysage aux Marais (33x41cm-13x16in) s. (F.FR 6000)

DUTHIE, William (fl.1889-1894) British
£950 $1606   (2-May-91 CG501/R) Portrait of artist's wife (34x43cm-13x17in)
£1000 $1690   (2-May-91 CG502) Wooded river landscape with bridge. Cottage on banks of river (41x52cm-16x20in) s. one canvas on panel pair

DUTTOT, A (?) ?
£6000 $9780   (3-Jul-91 PLF.P61/R) Scenes de chasse a courre (92x152cm-36x60in) both s.d.77 pair (F.FR 60000)

DUVAL (?) ?
£1531 $3015   (16-Nov-90 LGB.P194) Nature morte aux peches (66x92cm-26x36in) s. (F.FR 15000)

DUVAL LECAMUS, Pierre (1790-1854) French
£1644 $2942   (12-Mar-91 FN.S2343/R) Farmhouse interior with figures and view of garden through open door (46x55cm-18x22in) s.d.1831 canvas on board (DM 4800)

DUVAL, Beatrice (1880-1973) French?
£3920 $7016   (13-Mar-91 ARC.P42/R) Ferme a Arcy sur Cure (45x33cm-18x13in) s.i. paper laid down on canvas (F.FR 39000)

DUVAL, Charles Allen (1808-1872) British
£4360 $7500   (15-May-91 D.NY60) Justice and divine vengeance punishing crime (130x163cm-51x64in) s.i. after Prudhon

DUVAL, Edward J (fl.1876-1901) British
£600 $1170   (10-Oct-90 CSK104) Cattle watering in Highland lake (36x58cm-14x23in) s.d.1879 pencil W/C htd white

DUVAL, Etienne (1824-1914) Swiss
£616 $1103   (12-Mar-91 FN.S2342/R) View from St Mark's to San Giorgio (24x38cm-9x15in) s. board (DM 1800)

DUVAL, Serge (?) ?
£2736 $4570   (6-Jun-91 F.M43/R) Ingresso di una citta orientale (60x90cm-24x35in) s. (I.L 6000000)

DUVAL-GOZLAN, Leon (1853-1941) French
£3015 $5397   (17-May-91 L.C20/R) La route de grand camp (51x78cm-20x31in) s. (F.FR 30000)
£3262 $6296   (16-Dec-90 T.B127) Village enBretagne (51x78cm-20x31in) s. (F.FR 32000)
£663 $1279   (14-Dec-90 JM.P93) Bord d'etang au pecheur (32x49cm-13x19in) s. gouache (F.FR 6500)

DUVALL, John (1816-1892) British
£1010 $1747   (6-May-91 ZEL.L1668/R) Arab horse in stable interior (40x50cm-16x20in) s. (DM 3000)

DUVALL, John (attrib) (1816-1892) British
£1700 $2924   (14-May-91 SWS196/R) Maltese terrier on red cushion (24x29cm-9x11in)

DUVAUX, Jules Antoine (1818-1884) French
£694 $1367   (14-Nov-90 FB.P47/R) Vue du theatre de Dijon (34x64cm-13x25in) s. pen wash (F.FR 6800)

DUVENECK, Frank (1848-1919) American
£2564 $5000   (13-Oct-90 LAE.L146/R) Red sail in harbour of Venice (28x46cm-11x18in) mono.d.1884 W/C with letter

DUVENECK, Frank (attrib) (1848-1919) American
£1117 $2100   (22-Sep-90 WOL.C278/R) Standing nude (89x43cm-35x17in) canvas on board

DUVERGER, Theophile Emmanuel (1821-1886) French
£1342	$2617	(13-Oct-90 KRA.D203) Milking goats (68x79cm-27x31in) s. (DM 4000)
£1586	$3093	(24-Oct-90 EA.M543/R) Hear it tick (41x32cm-16x13in) s. panel (C.D 3600)
£2105	$4000	(27-Feb-91 SY.NY59/R) Jeune fille jouant dans un interieur (32x24cm-13x9in) s.
£2956	$5705	(14-Dec-90 ARC.P136) Deux jeunes filles aux colombes (65x53cm-26x21in) s. panel (F.FR 29000)
£3160	$6099	(14-Dec-90 ARC.P135) La cueillette des coquelicots (46x37cm-18x15in) s. (F.FR 31000)
£3179	$5500	(21-May-91 CE.NY60/R) Sewing lesson (33x25cm-13x10in) s. panel
£3800	$6802	(12-Mar-91 PH86/R) The young musician (40x32cm-16x13in) s. panel
£3827	$6238	(16-Jun-91 P.V11/R) Les coquelicots (46x38cm-18x15in) s. (F.FR 38000)
£4000	$7880	(5-Oct-90 C80 b/R) Backstage (46x38cm-18x15in) s. panel
£4624	$8000	(23-May-91 CH.NY37/R) The sewing lesson (33x24cm-13x9in) s. panel
£4913	$8500	(23-May-91 CH.NY38/R) The bandaged finger (32x24cm-13x9in) s. panel
£5200	$9308	(12-Mar-91 PH107/R) The schoolroom (40x58cm-16x23in) s. panel

DUVERGNE, Paul (19th C) French
| £773 | $1500 | (8-Dec-90 W.W53/R) The Customs House, Venice (97x84cm-38x33in) s. |

DUVERT, Bernard (20th C) French?
| £762 | $1524 | (7-Feb-91 R.P72/R) Karajan (100x100cm-39x39in) s. (F.FR 7500) |

DUVIEUX, Henri (19th C) French
£800	$1312	(18-Jun-91 PH76) The duck shoot (21x34cm-8x13in) s. panel
£1116	$2142	(19-Dec-90 LD.P142) Voiliers sur le Bosphore devant Istambul (40x65cm-16x26in) s. (F.FR 11000)
£1805	$3521	(12-Oct-90 ZZ.F83/R) Venise (40x65cm-16x26in) s. (F.FR 18000)
£1882	$3200	(27-May-91 GC.M409/R) Vista de Constantinopla (21x34cm-8x13in) s. panel
£2200	$3674	(9-Jun-91 DA.R3/R) Venise, le palais des Doges (65x40cm-26x16in) s. (F.FR 22000)
£2450	$4851	(31-Jan-91 D.V63/R) Boats off Venice (13x21cm-5x8in) s. board (A.S 50000)
£2659	$4600	(21-May-91 CE.NY244/R) View of Venice (51x91cm-20x36in) s.
£3281	$5577	(27-May-91 GK.Z5026/R) Carneval party on promenade before Doge's Palace, Venice (46x76cm-18x30in) s. (S.FR 8300)

DUVILLIER, Rene (1919-) French
£911	$1785	(25-Nov-90 LC.P163) Jouissance de l'espace (73x92cm-29x36in) s. i.d.1975 verso (F.FR 9000)
£2000	$3360	(24-Apr-91 MJ.P120/R) Aspirer a l'extreme dilatation (40x80cm-16x31in) s.i.d.59 verso (F.FR 20000)
£2500	$4200	(24-Apr-91 MJ.P121/R) Vision rebescente (73x100cm-29x39in) s.i.d.11/67 verso (F.FR 25000)
£3870	$7623	(31-Oct-90 ZZ.F34/R) Cycle aerien (130x194cm-51x76in) s. i.d.11/64 verso acrylic (F.FR 38000)

DUXA, C (1871-1937) Austrian
| £753 | $1349 | (14-Mar-91 N.M2645) Boy with pipe and newspaper (31x31cm-12x12in) s. panel (DM 2200) |

DUXA, Carl (1871-1937) Austrian
| £634 | $1174 | (7-Mar-91 D.V67/R) Canal in the north of Germany (33x48cm-13x19in) s.l. canvas on board (A.S 13000) |

DUYNEN, Isaac van (attrib) (?-1688) Flemish
| £1468 | $2892 | (13-Nov-90 CH.AM35/R) Haddock in basket (30x35cm-12x14in) panel (D.FL 4800) |
| £3043 | $6024 | (30-Jan-91 APT.P222/R) Nature morte d'huitres, de poissons et de verres (37x45cm-15x18in) (F.FR 30000) |

DUYSTER, Willem Cornelisz (1600-1635) Dutch
| £5800 | $11194 | (11-Dec-90 PH160/R) Man seated, holding wine glass (44x31cm-17x12in) panel |

DUYSTER, Willem Cornelisz (style) (1600-1635) Dutch
| £2307 | $4498 | (10-Oct-90 APT.P475/R) Scene d'auberge (53x67cm-21x26in) panel (F.FR 23000) |

DYCK, Abraham van (1635-1672) Dutch
| £24000 | $46320 | (12-Dec-90 S194/R) Old woman with a staff (71x54cm-28x21in) panel |

DYCK, Albert van (20th C) Belgian?
| £9852 | $17044 | (25-May-91 KV.L403/R) Gusta in a hat (74x61cm-29x24in) s. (B.FR 600000) |
| *£493* | *$852* | *(25-May-91 KV.L309) Gusta at the table (32x28cm-13x11in) st.sig. sanguine dr. (B.FR 30000)* |

DYCK, Philip van (1680-1753) Flemish
| £15789 | $30000 | (10-Jan-91 SY.NY93/R) Elegant lady playing lute at window with young boy holding food to bird (37x32cm-15x13in) s. panel |

DYCK, Sir Anthony van (1599-1641) Flemish
| £1284 | $2530 | (13-Nov-90 CH.AM34) Portrait of artist Pieter de Jode I, standing on balcony (24x19cm-9x7in) en grisaille panel (D.FL 4200) |

DYCK, Sir Anthony van (1599-1641) Flemish-cont.

£2000	$4000	(7-Feb-91 C155) An equestrian portrait of Charles I with M. de St. Antoine (121x81cm-48x32in)
£18000	$35460	(14-Nov-90 S24/R) Portrait of Thomas Wentworth standing wearing armour (101x84cm-40x33in) painted with studio
£9000	*$14670*	*(2-Jul-91 C200/R) Paris (40x25cm-16x10in) black white chk*

DYCK, Sir Anthony van (after) (1599-1641) Flemish

£983	$1700	(12-May-91 H.C33) Deposition of Christ (61x41cm-24x16in) panel
£1200	$2400	(7-Feb-91 CSK169/R) Portrait of King Charles I in armour (76x63cm-30x25in)
£1500	$2535	(18-Apr-91 CSK131) Sir Thomas Wentworth and secretary Sir Phillip Mainwaring (132x146cm-52x57in)
£1538	$3000	(10-Oct-90 CH.NY33/R) Portraits of Andrew Colyns de Nole with classical bust. Martin Pepyn (25x20cm-10x8in) en grisaille panel pair
£1600	$2640	(10-Jul-91 S102/R) Equestrian portrait of Charles I (124x98cm-49x39in)
£1954	$3498	(14-Mar-91 D.V263/R) Samson and Delila (101x175cm-40x69in) (A.S 40000)
£2599	$5121	(14-Nov-90 SY.AM107/R) Portrait of Prince Frederik Hendrik of Orange (25x19cm-10x7in) grisaille panel (D.FL 8500)
£2938	$5788	(14-Nov-90 D.V170/R) Portrait of noble woman with fan (129x93cm-51x37in) (A.S 60000)
£6000	$11820	(31-Oct-90 S259/R) Portrait of Thomas Killigrew wearing breast plate and sash with mastiff (101x82cm-40x32in)

DYCK, Sir Anthony van (attrib) (1599-1641) Flemish

£18824	$32000	(31-May-91 CH.NY100/R) Rider mounting horse (31x26cm-12x10in) panel en grisaille

DYCK, Sir Anthony van (circle) (1599-1641) Flemish

£1000	$1900	(1-Mar-91 C3/R) Portrait of gentleman thought to be Thomas Wentworth, Earl of Strafford (43x32cm-17x13in) panel
£1190	$2000	(17-Jul-91 SY.NY207/R) Portrait of a lady, possibly a Beguine (44x32cm-17x13in)
£1400	$2282	(2-Jul-91 PH303) The Christ Child with the infant St John the Baptist (75x61cm-30x24in)
£2353	$4000	(31-May-91 CH.NY124/R) Saint Mary Magdalene (64x49cm-25x19in) panel
£2500	$4925	(30-Oct-90 PH41/R) Studies of head of bearded man (49x65cm-19x26in)
£2600	$5070	(16-Oct-90 CG223/R) Portrait of Lady Henrietta Wentworth with dog (112x81cm-44x32in)
£4283	$7666	(8-Apr-91 CH.R224/R) Ritratto di fanciulla con collana di perle (61x50cm-24x20in) (I.L 9500000)
£6936	$12000	(8-May-91 RO.BA4/R) Portrait de Martin Pepyn (81x64cm-32x25in)
£15511	$30557	(30-Oct-90 BU.S242/R) Study of dog (95x74cm-37x29in) (S.KR 170000)
£750	*$1223*	*(2-Jul-91 C351/R) Decius Mus dedicated to Underworld (25x30cm-10x12in) brush ink*

DYCK, Sir Anthony van (school) (1599-1641) Flemish

£797	$1371	(14-May-91 GF.L2284/R) Portrait of Thomas Wentworth (76x62cm-30x24in) (S.FR 2000)
£1128	$2200	(10-Oct-90 CH.NY52 a) Study of man's head, possibly for Crowning with Thorns (32x25cm-13x10in) paper on panel
£1128	$2200	(10-Oct-90 CH.NY148/R) Portrait of lady (62x52cm-24x20in)
£1389	$2750	(1-Feb-91 S.W2555/R) Portrait of two youths canvas on panel
£15385	$30000	(10-Oct-90 CH.NY104/R) King Charles I on horseback (309x231cm-122x91in)

DYCK, Sir Anthony van (studio) (1599-1641) Flemish

£4412	$7500	(31-May-91 CH.NY190/R) Portrait of Jan van Montfort wearing costume with ruff and gold chain (52x39cm-20x15in) paper on canvas
£9000	$15210	(16-Apr-91 PH90/R) Boar hunter (85x104cm-33x41in)
£11952	$20558	(14-May-91 GF.L2058/R) St Hieronymus (81x71cm-32x28in) (S.FR 30000)
£13333	$26000	(11-Oct-90 SY.NY189/R) Portrait of Cardinal Rivarola (104x81cm-41x32in)
£19000	$31350	(10-Jul-91 S14/R) Portrait of Katherine, Countess of Chesterfield standing and Lucy, Countess of Huntingdon seated hold (124x156cm-49x61in)
£34000	$56100	(12-Jul-91 C6/R) Portrait of Mary Villiers, Duchess of Lennox and Richmond, by column (218x127cm-86x50in)

DYCK, Sir Anthony van (style) (1599-1641) Flemish

£800	$1304	(2-Jul-91 PH218) The Crucifixion with the two Marys and St John (55x42cm-22x17in) panel
£1100	$1793	(4-Jul-91 CSK229/R) Portrait of lady, standing in embroidered dress, on terrace (100x93cm-39x37in)
£1347	$2653	(15-Nov-90 EA.Z177/R) Head of apostle (47x36cm-19x14in) (S.FR 3300)
£1406	$2263	(27-Jun-91 APT.P136/R) Portrait d'homme (33x25cm-13x10in) paper laid down on panel (F.FR 14000)
£1600	$3200	(7-Feb-91 CSK45/R) Crucifixion (140x91cm-55x36in)
£1605	$3129	(10-Oct-90 APT.P476) Portrait d'homme en armure (87x71cm-34x28in) panel (F.FR 16000)
£1959	$3859	(14-Nov-90 D.V161/R) Mary and Child with St Dorothea (117x152cm-46x60in) (A.S 40000)
£2000	$3460	(20-May-91 SWS198/R) The Crucifixion (139x96cm-55x38in)
£2400	$3912	(4-Jul-91 C711/R) Penitent Magdalen (86x62cm-34x24in) panel
£3000	$4950	(10-Jul-91 S101/R) Portrait of Mr Wollaston. His wife (74x62cm-29x24in) l. pair sold with another painting
£3400	$6460	(1-Mar-91 C5/R) Portrait of Queen Henrietta Maria seated wearing pearl necklace (127x102cm-50x40in)

DYCK, Sir Anthony van (style) (1599-1641) Flemish-cont.
£3800 $6422   (18-Apr-91 CSK31) Susannah and elders (190x145cm-75x57in)
£5060 $8500   (17-Jul-91 SY.NY190/R) James Stuart, Duke of Lenox and Richmond
                     (180x124cm-71x49in)
£8205 $16000   (11-Oct-90 SY.NY14/R) Lamentation of Christ (131x247cm-52x97in)
£9000 $17100   (1-Mar-91 C161/R) Dominican saint reviving youth (297x182cm-117x72in)
                     c.1630 fragment
£27000 $51300   (1-Mar-91 C123/R) Rinaldo and Armida (198x201cm-78x79in)

DYCK, van (after) (16/17th C) Flemish
£6053 $11500   (12-Sep-90 D.NY20) Children of Charles I (130x157cm-51x62in)

DYCK, van (school) (16/17th C) Flemish
£963 $1908   (30-Jan-91 APT.P201) Allegorie du printemps et de l'ete
                    (41x29cm-16x11in) (F.FR 9500)
£1453 $2500   (15-May-91 D.NY57) Portrait of Carolus Scribani (109x86cm-43x34in)
                    canvas on masonite
£6231 $11154   (8-Apr-91 ARC.P19/R) Portrait de quatre jeunes garcons (98x80cm-39x31in)
                    (F.FR 63000)
£43165 $83741   (7-Dec-90 CH.MO313/R) Portrait equestre d'un gentilhomme accompagne de
                    son page et de son chien (280x160cm-110x63in) (F.FR 420000)

DYCK, van (style) (16/17th C) Flemish
£1628 $2800   (15-May-91 D.NY41) Suzannah and the Elders (53x41cm-21x16in)
£2200 $3586   (4-Jul-91 B100 s) The Deposition (136x208cm-54x82in)

DYCKMANS, Josephus Laurentius (1811-1888) Flemish
£1198 $2275   (11-Sep-90 CH.AM303/R) Old woman pouring milk for a cat in an interior
                    (18x17cm-7x7in) s. panel (D.FL 4000)
£2300 $4117   (12-Mar-91 PH1/R) A stitch in time (43x37cm-17x15in) s.d.1843 panel
£4000 $7440   (4-Sep-90 SC3/R) La brodeuse (48x38cm-19x15in) s. panel

DYE, Clarkson (1869-?) American
£613 $1000   (11-Jun-91 MOR.P100) Landscape (46x61cm-18x24in) s.
£1410 $2750   (10-Oct-90 B.SF628/R) Desert palms (58x85cm-23x33in) s. board

DYER, Geoff (1947-) Australian
£407   *$688*   *(16-Apr-91 J.M27) Pinnicle, Mount Wellington (100x71cm-39x28in) s. W/C*
                    (A.D 900)
£430   *$726*   *(16-Apr-91 J.M1137) Towards Queenstown (71x101cm-28x40in) s. gouache*
                    (A.D 950)

DYER, H Anthony (1872-1943) American
£447   *$800*   *(14-Apr-91 JRB.C70/R) The glories of Lake Thun (53x74cm-21x29in) s. W/C*
£756   *$1300*   *(18-May-91 W.W190/R) Harbor view (43x58cm-17x23in) gouache*

DYF, Marcel (1899-1985) French
£838 $1651   (6-Oct-90 GL.P125) Discussion autour du (46x55cm-18x22in) s.
                    (F.FR 8500)
£1403 $2750   (12-Feb-91 SY.NY138 a/R) Booksellers along the Seine (38x46cm-15x18in)
                    s.
£1786 $3500   (12-Feb-91 SY.NY160/R) Flamingo dancers (46x38cm-18x15in) s. pair
£1929 $3800   (13-Nov-90 CE.NY298/R) Bouquet de fleurs (35x27cm-14x11in) s.
£2000 $3280   (18-Jun-91 PH47/R) Figures seated in Le Jardin des Tuileries, Paris
                    (37x46cm-15x18in) s.
£2041 $4000   (12-Feb-91 SY.NY102/R) Landscape with two children walking along path
                    (53x46cm-21x18in) s.
£2157 $4250   (15-Nov-90 D.NY115/R) Young girl in black seated at table
                    (56x44cm-22x17in) s.
£2157 $4250   (15-Nov-90 D.NY114/R) Young girl in yellow seated at table
                    (56x46cm-22x18in) s.
£2437 $4800   (13-Nov-90 CE.NY73/R) Jeune femme assise (46x55cm-18x22in) s.
£2486 $4600   (10-Mar-91 H.C59/R) Scene de campagne (74x58cm-29x23in) s.
£2600 $5070   (15-Jan-91 SWS220/R) Gipsy encampment (44x53cm-17x21in) s.
£2601 $4500   (7-May-91 CE.NY46/R) Les gitans (46x55cm-18x22in) s.
£3138 $6150   (25-Nov-90 B.PA59) Le port (38x46cm-15x18in) s. (F.FR 31000)
£3571 $7000   (12-Feb-91 SY.NY137/R) Promenadeurs dans un parc (46x53cm-18x21in) s.
£3590 $7000   (10-Oct-90 SY.NY224/R) Young girl with Siamese cat (64x53cm-25x21in) s.
£4000 $7880   (13-Nov-90 SWS404/R) Landscape near Arles (44x58cm-17x23in) s.
£4188 $8250   (15-Nov-90 D.NY62/R) Steeplechase (46x55cm-18x22in) s.
£4400 $8580   (15-Jan-91 SWS180/R) Enfant rousse and marguerites (63x52cm-25x20in) s.
£4592 $9000   (12-Feb-91 SY.NY182/R) Fleurs au pot rose (3x46cm-1x18in) s.
                    st.sig.d.1981stretcher
£5319 $10000   (22-Sep-90 WOL.C374/R) Distant village (81x71cm-32x28in) s.
£5400 $9288   (14-May-91 SWS447/R) Bateaux en Bretagne (46x55cm-18x22in) s.
£5400 $9018   (22-Jul-91 SWS1128/R) Golf de la Napoule (44x53cm-17x21in) s.
£5400 $10638   (13-Nov-90 SWS402/R) Claudine a St. Paul de Vence (53x44cm-21x17in) s.
£5491 $9500   (7-May-91 CE.NY5/R) Bouquet de fleurs (55x48cm-22x19in) s.
£5612 $11000   (12-Feb-91 SY.NY221/R) Fille aux fruits (74x61cm-29x24in) s.
                    st.sig.d.1967verso
£5617 $10953   (14-Oct-90 D.L101/R) Le repos (53x64cm-21x25in) s. (F.FR 56000)
£6122 $12000   (7-Nov-90 B.SF1097/R) Reflection of trees (46x56cm-18x22in) s.
£7000 $13580   (5-Dec-90 PH73/R) Fete champetre (73x92cm-29x36in) s.
£7143 $14000   (12-Feb-91 SY.NY98/R) Champs d'Avoine (61x74cm-24x29in) s.
                    st.sig.d.1981stretcher
£7200 $12024   (22-Jul-91 SWS1127/R) La chambre rouge - Jacqueline (71x58cm-28x23in) s.

554

DYF, Marcel (1899-1985) French-cont.
£7200	$14184	(13-Nov-90 SWS401/R) Maison Rose enDordogne (45x54cm-18x21in) s.
£7471	$13000	(27-Mar-91 B.SF4104/R) Reine marguerites (73x60cm-29x24in) s.
£8500	$16575	(15-Jan-91 SWS221/R) Portrait de femme au chapeau noir (76x60cm-30x24in) s.
£10000	$16300	(2-Jul-91 CD407/R) Promeneuses dans les Bles (61x74cm-24x29in) s.
£10000	$19500	(26-Oct-90 STR467) Portrait of Claudine with flowers in hair (64x53cm-25x21in) s.
£10574	$17236	(11-Jun-91 I.N196/R) Le marche aux fruits (60x73cm-24x29in) s. (F.FR 105000)

DYKE, Samuel P (19th C) American
£800	$1600	(6-Feb-91 D.NY23) Palisades of Nockamixon on the Upper Delawre River (71x130cm-28x51in) s.i.d.1874
£872	$1500	(18-May-91 W.W95/R) Boaters on a lake in autumn (56x91cm-22x36in) s.
£982	$1600	(5-Jul-91 S.W3094/R) Delaware river view in autumn (71x127cm-28x50in) s.d.1874

DYKSTRA, Johan (1896-1978) Dutch
£1610	$3107	(13-Dec-90 SY.AM4/R) View of Niehove (50x70cm-20x28in) s. (D.FL 5200)
£2105	$4063	(13-Dec-90 SY.AM6/R) River landscape with sailing boat (50x76cm-20x30in) (D.FL 6800)
£4334	$8365	(12-Dec-90 CH.AM94/R) Oogsten in Groningen (60x90cm-24x35in) s. l.verso (D.FL 14000)
£5573	$10755	(13-Dec-90 SY.AM87/R) Landscape (47x57cm-19x22in) s.d.24 (D.FL 18000)
£6502	$12548	(13-Dec-90 SY.AM76/R) Landscape (50x71cm-20x28in) s. (D.FL 21000)
£601	*$1039*	*(22-May-91 CH.AM327) Shaded lane (32x41cm-13x16in) atelier mark black chk W/C (D.FL 2000)*
£901	*$1559*	*(22-May-91 CH.AM314) View of small village, Groningen (28x47cm-11x19in) s. col.crayons (D.FL 3000)*

DYRING, Moya (?) ?
£633	$1215	(14-Aug-90 SY.ME89/R) Place Lucien Herr (58x79cm-23x31in) s. (A.D 1500)

DYSON, J H (19th C) British?
£560	$946	(1-May-91 PHL175) Fortune telling (76x103cm-30x41in) s.d.1899

DYTON, Michael (20th C) British?
£1050	$1712	(3-Jul-91 RBB789/R) Study of head of child, as used in U.N. posters for Year of Child (91x61cm-36x24in) s.d.76
£1450	$2436	(19-Jul-91 CBB80) Badminton 1979, Niels Hargesson on Camicarn s.

DZIGURSKI, Alex (1910-) American
£533	$900	(21-Apr-91 DU.E157) Seascape (58x89cm-23x35in) s. num.691 verso
£570	$1100	(10-Dec-90 H.C1105) Seascape (61x91cm-24x36in) s.
£591	$1100	(7-Sep-90 H.C638/R) Seascape (61x91cm-24x36in) s.
£660	$1300	(7-Oct-90 DU.E56/R) Painted desert (61x76cm-24x30in) s.
£860	$1600	(7-Sep-90 H.C637/R) Waves at sunset (71x122cm-28x48in) s.

DZUBAS, Friedel (1915-) American
£2197	$3800	(7-May-91 CE.NY251/R) Scherazade (72x108cm-28x43in) s.d.1988 verso acrylic canvas
£2821	$5500	(24-Oct-90 B.SF1554/R) Ajax (183x183cm-72x72in) s.d.1977 verso acrylic canvas
£3681	$6000	(12-Jun-91 SY.NY206/R) Saints Passion (102x102cm-40x40in) s.d.1976 acrylic canvas
£7614	$15000	(5-Oct-90 CH.NY76/R) Vermont green (209x171cm-82x67in) s.l.d.64verso
£1939	*$3800*	*(6-Nov-90 CE.NY88/R) Orono (60cm-24ins circular) s.i.d.70 verso magna canvas round*
£8629	*$17000*	*(5-Oct-90 CH.NY89/R) Argonaut drive (244x245cm-96x96in) s.i.d.72 magna canvas*

EADIE, Robert (1877-1954) British
£540	*$929*	*(14-May-91 SWS132/R) Boys fishing (34x23cm-13x9in) s. W/C over pencil*
£580	*$980*	*(17-Apr-91 CG41/R) Tewkesbury, Gloucestershire (29x39cm-11x15in) s.d.1936 pencil W/C htd.bodycol.*
£600	*$1002*	*(26-Jul-91 PHE25/R) Glasgow university (27x37cm-11x15in) s. W/C*

EADIE, William (fl.1880-1894) British
£806	$1613	(6-Feb-91 RAS.K62/R) School boys drawing (36x27cm-14x11in) s.d.1892 panel (D.KR 9000)

EAKINS, Thomas (1844-1916) American
£15625	$30000	(29-Nov-90 SY.NY23/R) Study for the Meadows, Gloucester, New Jersey (26x35cm-10x14in) panel

EARDLEY, Joan (1921-1963) British
£4500	$8505	(27-Sep-90 CG84/R) Lighthouse, sea and sun 1963 (30x34cm-12x13in)
£5500	$10670	(5-Dec-90 PHE57/R) Fairground (23x83cm-9x33in) s. board
£6500	$13000	(5-Feb-91 S210/R) Old woman with dog (91x61cm-36x24in) s.
£12000	$23280	(5-Dec-90 PHE37/R) Evening sky, Catterline (70x75cm-28x30in)

EARDLEY, Joan (1921-1963) British-cont.

£50000	$100000	(5-Feb-91 S209/R) Children in Glasgow back Street (72x137cm-28x54in) s. s.i.stretcher
£400	$668	(26-Jul-91 PHE134) Landscape, yellow sky (16x24cm-6x9in) pastel
£1500	$2940	(22-Nov-90 CG544/R) Two Samson children (12x9cm-5x4in) pastel W/C
£1800	$3024	(23-Apr-91 S186/R) Summertime (17x10cm-7x4in) s. pastel
£2200	$4268	(5-Dec-90 PHE73/R) Portrait of a boy (23x15cm-9x6in) pastel
£2400	$4800	(5-Feb-91 S218/R) Glasgow children (10x12cm-4x5in) s. s.i.verso W/C ink htd bodycol
£3800	$7410	(16-Oct-90 WW328) Field and cottages, Catterline (25x30cm-10x12in) col.chk.
£4000	$6680	(26-Jul-91 PHE128/R) Boy in overcoat (74x44cm-29x17in) s. pastel
£4500	$8415	(28-Aug-90 S1073/R) Cuddling the child (27x23cm-11x9in) col chk
£5000	$9700	(5-Dec-90 PHE89/R) Pat Samson (28x22cm-11x9in) pastel

EARL, James (1761-1796) American

£9000	$17730	(16-Nov-90 C19/R) Portrait of lady wearing lace-trimmed dress seated on terrace (75x62cm-30x24in)

EARL, Maud (?-1943) British

£595	$1000	(17-Jul-91 SY.NY364/R) Portrait of a hound (51x66cm-20x26in) s.d.1934 board
£1656	$3097	(27-Aug-90 SY.J181/R) Dignity and impudence (45x60cm-18x24in) s. (SA.R 8000)
£1900	$3705	(15-Jan-91 B390/R) Dignity and Impudence (46x61cm-18x24in) s.
£2000	$3900	(16-Jan-91 BT100/R) Retrieved (61x69cm-24x27in) s.d.90
£2156	$3600	(26-Jul-91 E.EDM110/R) Pheasant alone on branch with valley below (66x112cm-26x44in) s. board
£4000	$7800	(15-Jan-91 B423/R) Inquisitive look (51x66cm-20x26in) s.d.1932 board
£8000	$15600	(15-Jan-91 C140/R) In the slips, two black and white greyhounds (122x152cm-48x60in) s.
£13500	$26325	(15-Jan-91 C141/R) Brindle and brindle and white greyhound in landscape (103x129cm-41x51in) s.

EARL, Percy (20th C) British

£1500	$2880	(18-Dec-90 HC313) 1930 Grand National (69x89cm-27x35in) s.i.
£1800	$3564	(30-Jan-91 S270/R) Prominent colours and jockeys, 1900 (38x56cm-15x22in) init.d.1900 gouache

EARL, Thomas (attrib) (19th C) British

£1800	$3510	(15-Jan-91 B408) Dinmont wearing blue ribbon (19x17cm-7x7in) bears sig.verso board

EARL, Thomas (fl.1836-1885) British

£850	$1658	(15-Jan-91 C30/R) Head of West Highland terrier (25x8cm-10x3in) board on panel
£1500	$2910	(3-Dec-90 B61/R) Nap-time visitor (46x61cm-18x24in)
£4500	$8865	(1-Nov-90 C263/R) The reward (66cm-26ins circular) s.d.54

EARL, Thomas P (fl.1900-1930) British

£3892	$6500	(7-Jun-91 SY.NY51/R) Enfield with jockey up (46x61cm-18x24in) s.i.

EARLE, Charles (?-1893) British

£1800	$3024	(22-Apr-91 PH278/R) Water meadows at Canterbury (33x60cm-13x24in) s. W/C htd white
£1800	$2934	(14-Jun-91 C113/R) Evening - Elegant figures by a country house (56x34cm-22x13in) s. pencil W/C htd.white

EARLE, Eyvind (1916-) American

£1124	$1900	(20-Apr-91 WOL.C440/R) California landscape (56x76cm-22x30in) s.d.1968 W/C ink

EARLE, John (1955-) Australian?

£1563	$2719	(26-Mar-91 JRL.S301) Seascape (180x320cm-71x126in) (A.D 3500)

EARP, Henry (19th C) British

£526	$1011	(18-Feb-91 SY.J292/R) Cows in a rural path (75x54cm-30x21in) s.d.1901 W/C (SA.R 2600)

EARP, Henry (snr) (1831-1914) British

£460	$787	(30-Jul-91 SWS480) Breaking the ice (23x51cm-9x20in) s. W/C over pencil htd.white
£550	$1045	(12-Sep-90 CSK134) Cattle resting in sunlit river landscape (33x51cm-13x20in) s.d.1869 W/C htd white
£550	$1084	(13-Nov-90 SWS24/R) Cattle watering (69x53cm-27x21in) s. W/C htd.white
£850	$1675	(1-Nov-90 C96/R) Waggon on lane with harvesters at work (56x41cm-22x16in) s. pencil W/C htd.white

EAST, F W F (?) ?

£700	$1372	(24-Jan-91 CSK168) Old woodcutter (35x24cm-14x9in) s.

EAST, H (?) British

£684	$1300	(14-Sep-90 DM.D1310/R) Landscape and river scene (51x76cm-20x30in)

EAST, Sir Alfred (1849-1913) British

£1100	$1837	(5-Jun-91 S72/R) Miller's pool (46x61cm-18x24in) s.

EAST, Sir Alfred (1849-1913) British-cont.
£1200	$2304	(21-Feb-91 B38/R) Stormy landscape (71x91cm-28x36in) s.
£2500	$4875	(10-Oct-90 S17/R) Poplars (122x153cm-48x60in) s.
£3000	$5220	(27-Mar-91 S26/R) Frosty morning (107x127cm-42x50in) s.d.XIII
£3000	$5850	(12-Oct-90 K448/R) Figures and cattle in river landscape (48x74cm-19x29in) s.
£3000	$4890	(14-Jun-91 C309) A glade near Oxford (122x152cm-48x60in) s.indis.d.
£3179	$5500	(21-May-91 CE.NY78/R) Market Place, Cairo, Egypt (70x101cm-28x40in) s.
£4068	$6631	(3-Jul-91 WE.MU126/R) Oriental market scene (72x101cm-28x40in) s. (DM 12000)
£6000	$12000	(8-Feb-91 C137/R) September sunshine (102x152cm-40x60in) s.
£10500	$19845	(26-Sep-90 S167/R) Spring morning (69x107cm-27x42in) s.d.1881 s.i.verso
£300	$531	(21-Mar-91 CSK53) Swans on the River Arun at Horsham, Sussex (33x51cm-13x20in) s. pencil W/C htd.white
£550	$1078	(19-Nov-90 SWS660) Segovia (52x68cm-20x27in) s. W/C over pencil
£600	$1188	(30-Jan-91 S138) Moorish aquaduct, Alecires, Spain (23x33cm-9x13in) s. W/C over pencil
£719	$1200	(5-Jun-91 D.NY30) Mist lifting off the canal, Dordrecht, Holland (51x66cm-20x26in) s. s.i.verso W/C
£780	$1318	(1-May-91 PHL86/R) Grey morning in Savoy (53x65cm-21x26in) s.i.d.1902 verso col.wash
£1300	$2119	(14-Jun-91 T150/R) Sheep in meadow at Rye (23x33cm-9x13in) s. W/C
£2200	$3894	(22-Mar-91 PHE43/R) Passing shower at Streatley on Thames (57x90cm-22x35in) s.d. W/C
£2200	$3674	(5-Jun-91 S288/R) Passing shower at Streatley (57x91cm-22x36in) s.d.85 i.verso W/C

EASTLAKE, Sir Charles Lock (1793-1865) British
| £1200 | $2148 | (10-Apr-91 S198/R) View near Naples (23x34cm-9x13in) paper on canvas |

EASTMAN, Seth (1808-1875) American
| £4737 | $9000 | (9-Jan-91 CH.NY149/R) Cavern on Lake Superior. Mississippi River, Site of Keokuk both s. one d.1841 one W/C one pencil |

EASTMAN, Seth (style) (1808-1875) American
| £2116 | $4000 | (27-Sep-90 CH.NY3/R) The betrothal of Hiawatha (64x54cm-25x21in) |

EASTON, Reginald (1807-1893) British
| £350 | $599 | (30-Jul-91 CSK8/R) Lady Susan Hamilton Douglas (10x?cm-4x?in) min. rec.gilt-metal frame oval |

EATON, Charles Harry (1850-1901) American
| £1458 | $2800 | (17-Dec-90 SY.NY137/R) Landscape with cows (41x61cm-16x24in) s. |

EATON, Charles Warren (1857-1934) American
£632	$1200	(28-Feb-91 MFA.C108/R) The hilltop Colebrook pines (51x61cm-20x24in) s.
£745	$1400	(22-Sep-90 WOL.C150/R) Haystacks (51x76cm-20x30in) s.d.1894
£750	$1500	(6-Feb-91 D.NY24) Sun setting over Spring time pastures (51x61cm-20x24in) s.
£1395	$2400	(15-May-91 SY.NY87/R) Sunset pines (77x92cm-30x36in) s.d.1904
£2646	$5000	(26-Sep-90 SY.NY153/R) Winter landscape with stream (76x91cm-30x36in) s.
£3179	$5500	(21-May-91 CE.NY420/R) Sunset (61x51cm-24x20in) s.
£2381	$4500	(27-Sep-90 CH.NY231/R) Mountain snows (76x71cm-30x28in) s. pastel canvas

EBEL, Fritz (1835-1895) German
| £1100 | $1892 | (14-May-91 SWS289/R) Figure on path in landscape with harvesters (42x65cm-17x26in) s.d.1892 |
| £3885 | $7576 | (26-Oct-90 BM.B774/R) Wooded landscape with woman and child collecting herbs (74x108cm-29x43in) s.d.1889 (DM 11500) |

EBEL, Henri (1849-1921) ?
£402	$659	(21-Jun-91 CK.P114) Coucher de soleil (53x43cm-21x17in) s.d.1899 gouache (F.FR 4000)
£452	$742	(21-Jun-91 CK.P109) Lever de soleil (27x36cm-11x14in) s.d.10 gouache (F.FR 4500)
£452	$742	(21-Jun-91 CK.P110) La lanterne (35x45cm-14x18in) s.d.1900 gouache (F.FR 4500)
£623	$1022	(21-Jun-91 CK.P111) La salle a manger (57x45cm-22x18in) s.d.08 gouache (F.FR 6200)

EBELING, N (19th C) German?
| £1225 | $2425 | (31-Jan-91 D.V130/R) Pixendorf in Niederosterreich (41x53cm-16x21in) s. (A.S 25000) |

EBERHARD, Heinrich (1884-?) German
£1641	$3200	(10-Oct-90 SY.NY168/R) Verkundigung (33x251cm-13x99in) s. one d.1917 one d.1922 board pair
£2051	$4000	(10-Oct-90 SY.NY167/R) Soldaten (33x43cm-13x17in) s.d.1912 board
£2389	$3918	(18-Jun-91 FN.S1574/R) Saint, possibly St Sebastian (34x43cm-13x17in) s.d.1912 panel (DM 7000)

EBERHARD, Konrad (attrib) (1768-1859) German
| £759 | $1457 | (28-Nov-90 KF.M356) Allocution Gregors XVI, 10th December 1837 (44x31cm-17x12in) i. pen pencil (DM 2200) |

EBERL, Francois (1887-1962) French
£547	$924	(21-Apr-91 E.LA55) Portrait d'homme (35x27cm-14x11in) s. panel (F.FR 5500)
£1217	$2410	(3-Feb-91 I.N79) Nu allonge (44x76cm-17x30in) s. (F.FR 12000)
£1729	$3269	(30-Sep-90 E.LA163) Fille au cafe (55x46cm-22x18in) s. (F.FR 17000)
£2419	$4718	(28-Oct-90 M.V134/R) Ferme au bord de l'eau (44x36cm-17x14in) s. (F.FR 24000)
£2783	$4704	(21-Apr-91 E.LA61) Brune pensive (46x38cm-18x15in) s. (F.FR 28000)
£3579	$6048	(21-Apr-91 E.LA56/R) Jeune fille a la chemise verte (46x38cm-18x15in) s. (F.FR 36000)
£3976	$6720	(21-Apr-91 E.LA60/R) Nu accoude (55x46cm-22x18in) s. (F.FR 40000)
£1690	*$2856*	*(21-Apr-91 E.LA53/R) Les danseurs (39x30cm-15x12in) s. W/C (F.FR 17000)*

EBERL, Josef (1792-1880) Austrian?
£1800	*$3042*	*(1-May-91 GD.B1046/R) View of Gmunden and mountain range beyond (44x58cm-17x23in) s.d.1835 gouache (S.FR 4500)*

EBERLE, Adolf (1843-1914) German
£18456	$35990	(10-Oct-90 ZEL.L1472/R) Interior scene with grandmother and children by cradle (55x69cm-22x27in) s.i. panel (DM 55000)
£21834	$41266	(27-Sep-90 D.V83/R) The youngest member of the family (60x68cm-24x27in) s.i. (A.S 450000)
£30100	$50870	(19-Apr-91 FN.S1703/R) Domestic animals in barn interior with mother and children (54x73cm-21x29in) s.i. panel (DM 90000)

EBERLE, Robert (1815-1860) Swiss
£4483	$8607	(28-Nov-90 KF.M268/R) The way up to the alpine pastures (72x64cm-28x25in) s. (DM 13000)

EBERLIN, Jonna (19th C) ?
£1512	$2843	(18-Sep-90 BU.K30/R) Bouquet of rose, anemones and other flowers (23x33cm-9x13in) s.d.1876verso panel (D.KR 17000)

EBERS, Emil (1807-1884) Polish
£1877	$3679	(24-Nov-90 SA.A684/R) Slavic figures inviting hunter (63x88cm-25x35in) s. (DM 5500)

EBERSBACH, Hartwig (1940-) German
£642	*$1091*	*(28-May-91 KF.M618) Primborium (73x51cm-29x20in) mono.i.d.1988 W/C gouache (DM 1900)*
£2730	*$5352*	*(24-Nov-90 N.M133/R) Dream of youth (121x79cm-48x31in) mono.d.1987 oil collage panel (DM 8000)*

EBERT, Anton (1845-1896) German
£887	$1455	(18-Jun-91 FN.S1816/R) Woman and child collecting berries on woodland path (59x46cm-23x18in) s.l.verso (DM 2600)
£909	$1755	(12-Dec-90 N.M494/R) Portrait of young lady wearing renaissance dress (57x42cm-22x17in) s. panel (DM 2600)
£1672	$2826	(19-Apr-91 FN.S1704/R) Reclining young woman with bare breast (18x24cm-7x9in) s.i.d.1879 panel (DM5000)
£4200	$7056	(18-Jul-91 CSK123/R) Spring. Autumn (79x63cm-31x25in) s.d.1869 oval pair

EBERT, Carl (1821-1885) German
£1229	$2322	(25-Sep-90 FN.S2159/R) Study of arched bridge in campagna (22x32cm-9x13in) i.verso board (DM 3600)
£1538	$2985	(4-Dec-90 FN.S1814/R) Wooded landscape with cattle returning (16x13cm-6x5in) i.d.1882verso panel (DM 4400)
£2797	$5427	(4-Dec-90 FN.S1813/R) Peasant woman collecting wood (38x59cm-15x23in) s.i.d.1874 (DM 8000)
£5802	$10908	(19-Sep-90 N.M463/R) Chiemsee lake landscape with farmhouse and peasants (36x50cm-14x20in) s.i.d.1852 panel (DM 17000)
£6143	$11611	(25-Sep-90 FN.S2158/R) Mountainous lake landscape with children near farmhouse (22x32cm-9x13in) s. panel (DM 18000)
£9556	$18061	(25-Sep-90 FN.S2157/R) Wooded landscape with peasant girl by well (24x37cm-9x15in) s.d.1879 i.d.verso canvas on board (DM 28000)
£11224	$18071	(28-Jun-91 BM.B664/R) Wooded landscape with cattle and driver and village with church beyond (71x103cm-28x41in) s.i. (DM 33000)

EBERT, Charles H (1873-1959) American
£588	$1100	(30-Aug-90 MFA.C140) Marsh scene (30x41cm-12x16in) s.verso board
£2023	$3500	(21-May-91 CE.NY409/R) Spring in Connecticut (69x63cm-27x25in) s. artist's st.verso

EBERZ, Josef (1830-?) German
£3082	$5517	(12-Mar-91 FN.S1955/R) Ravine near Assisi (78x70cm-31x28in) mono.c.1920 (DM 9000)
£373	*$623*	*(6-Jun-91 HN.H287) Olive grove near Assisi (24x33cm-9x13in) s.d.1920 ink brush (DM 1100)*
£1541	*$2759*	*(12-Mar-91 FN.S1956/R) Southern landscape with buildings (49x34cm-19x13in) s. W/C (DM 4500)*

EBLE, Theo (1899-1974) Swiss
£1984	$3433	(25-May-91 AB.L77/R) It is turning (99x99cm-39x39in) s.d.65 (S.FR 5000)
£635	*$1098*	*(25-May-91 AB.L76/R) Composition in green and blue (38x26cm-15x10in) s.d.59 W/C (S.FR 1600)*

EBURNE, Emma see OLIVER, Emma Sophie

ECH, N (20th C) ?
£1497 $2530   (29-Apr-91 LGB.P98) Fleurs (80x60cm-31x24in) s. verso (F.FR 15000)

ECHAURRI, Miguel Angel (1927-) Spanish
£924 $1635   (3-Apr-91 ANS.M145/R) Paisaje (50x62cm-20x24in) s. (S.P 170000)

ECHENA, Jose (1845-1909) Spanish
£1363 $2358   (21-May-91 DUR.M37/R) El abanderado del tercio (67x47cm-26x19in) W/C
(S.P 250000)

ECKARDT, C (1832-1914) Danish
£772 $1498   (5-Dec-90 KH.K33) Seascape with sailship, summer's day (43x68cm-17x27in)
s.d.1868 (D.KR 8500)

ECKARDT, Christian (1832-1914) Danish
£663 $1247   (10-Aug-90 RAS.V455/R) Coastal landscape with sailship in evening sun
(25x37cm-10x15in) s.d.77 (D.KR 7500)
£887 $1739   (24-Nov-90 SA.A795/R) Oriental harbour scene, evening (22x33cm-9x13in)
s.d.1875 (DM 2600)
£1057 $1766   (6-Jun-91 RAS.K37) Seascape with several vessels (21x31cm-8x12in)
s.indist.d.18 pair (D.KR 12000)
£1298 $2517   (22-Aug-90 RAS.K190/R) Italian coastal landscape with fishermen
returning (38x62cm-15x24in) s.d.1878 (D.KR 15000)
£3584 $7168   (6-Feb-91 RAS.K91/R) On the shore of the Tyne at ebb tide, North
Shields, England (95x155cm-37x61in) s.d.1883 (D.KR 40000)
£3591 $7074   (14-Nov-90 RAS.K106/R) Seascape with frigate and fishingboats
(68x101cm-27x40in) s.d.1868 (D.KR 40000)

ECKART, Christian (20th C) American?
£10204 $20000   (8-Nov-90 CH.NY393/R) Anadachtsbild (245x169cm-96x67in) s.i.d.1987 verso
gold leaf panel

ECKELBOOM, Hendrik Daniel (1806-1847) Dutch
£1220 $2390   (6-Nov-90 SY.AM213) Peasant family resting (25x32cm-10x13in) s.d.1841
panel (D.FL 4000)

ECKENBRECHER, Themistocles von (1842-1921) German
£908 $1762   (22-Aug-90 RAS.K191/R) Norwegian landscape from Ulafoss, Gudbrandsdalen
(47x34cm-19x13in) s.i.d.03 (D.KR 10500)
£3333 $6500   (24-Oct-90 CH.NY185/R) Naero fjord (61x91cm-24x36in) s.
£7000 $13440   (28-Nov-90 S226/R) View of snowy peaks of Romsdal (92x138cm-36x54in)
s.d.94
£372 $632   (31-May-91 GB.B5742) Street scene in Cairo (36x26cm-14x10in) s.d.1885
W/C pen (DM 1100)

ECKENER, Alexander (1870-1944) German
£819 $1343   (18-Jun-91 FN.S1818) Hunting lodge at Wedingmoor with figures
(34x52cm-13x20in) s.d.1943 board (DM 2400)
£819 $1343   (18-Jun-91 FN.S1819/R) Horse-drawn cart outside smithy (28x48cm-11x19in)
s. i.verso board (DM 2400)
£856 $1533   (12-Mar-91 FN.S2345/R) Ruined peasant cottages amongst trees
(29x60cm-11x24in) bears sig. i.d.1922verso board (DM 2500)
£925 $1655   (12-Mar-91 FN.S2346) Dune landscape with view of village amongst trees
(38x57cm-15x22in) s.d.1915 (DM 2700)
£1644 $2942   (12-Mar-91 FN.S2344/R) Fishing village Holm near Schleswig, evening
(36x50cm-14x20in) s.i.d.1930 (DM 4800)

ECKENER, Alexander (attrib) (1870-1944) German
£514 $920   (12-Mar-91 FN.S2347) View to Sipplinger Hohe near Bodman, Lake Constance
(21x35cm-8x14in) bears sig. (DM 1500)

ECKENFELDER, Friedrich (1861-?) German
£3567 $5849   (18-Jun-91 FN.S1820/R) Peasant and horses ploughing with farmhouses
beyond (24x34cm-9x13in) s. (DM 18000)
£6020 $10174   (19-Apr-91 FN.S1705/R) Peasants and horses ploughing, spring
(24x30cm-9x12in) s. (DM 18000)
£7534 $13486   (12-Mar-91 FN.S2348/R) Peasant leading four horses pulling harrow and
view of Steinachtal (34x68cm-13x27in) s. (DM 22000)

ECKERSBERG, C W (1783-1853) Danish
£2249 $4363   (22-Aug-90 RAS.K18/R) Procession leaving Italian church
(61x49cm-24x19in) (D.KR 26000)
£5526 $9891   (14-Mar-91 RAS.V643/R) The farmer and mermaid at Samso (62x47cm-24x19in)
init.d.1847 (D.KR 62000)
£5835 $11495   (14-Nov-90 RAS.K16/R) Autumn girl waering antique costume
(38x23cm-15x9in) (D.KR 65000)
£25686 $43410   (1-May-91 KH.K55/R) Corvette being built (39x36cm-15x14in) (D.KR 290000)
£528 $887   (23-Apr-91 RAS.K455) Stern of sailship (33x22cm-13x9in) pencil wash
(D.KR 6000)
£531 $1010   (14-Sep-90 RAS.V768) Sailor carrying barrel (12x7cm-5x3in) init.d.1830
pencil (D.KR 6000)
£573 $1147   (6-Feb-91 RAS.K532) Deputation of Duke Adolph (11x8cm-4x3in) Indian ink
W/C sketch (D.KR 6400)

ECKERSBERG, C W (1783-1853) Danish-cont.
£1057	$1977	(29-Aug-90 KH.K227/R) Art critics (14x15cm-6x6in) pen Indian ink wash (D.KR 12000)
£1320	$2218	(23-Apr-91 RAS.K447/R) Sketch of draped female figures (17x25cm-7x10in) s. pencil wash (D.KR 15000)
£3524	$6590	(29-Aug-90 KH.K226/R) Landscape from Ilsenstein (22x18cm-9x7in) pen Indian ink wash (D.KR 40000)

ECKERSBERG, Christoffer Wilhelm (1783-1853) Danish
£4500	$7740	(17-May-91 C130/R) Women in doorway (34x26cm-13x10in)
£30769	$60000	(23-Oct-90 SY.NY133/R) Sailing ships (39x54cm-15x21in) d.1825

ECKERSBERG, Christoffer Wilhelm (school) (1783-1853) Danish
£1211	$2349	(22-Aug-90 RAS.K192/R) Murdering the babies in Bethlehem (107x90cm-42x35in) (D.KR 14000)
£2657	$4491	(1-May-91 KH.K56/R) Seascape with sailship off coast (37x44cm-15x17in) (D.KR 30000)

ECKERSBERG, Johan Fredrik (1822-1870) Norwegian
£2865	$4784	(3-Jun-91 B.O26/R) Landscape with church (34x52cm-13x20in) s.d.1850 (N.KR 33000)

ECKERT, Georg Maria (1828-1903) German
£567	$1014	(12-Apr-91 AW.H582/R) View of Heidelberg Schloss (31x48cm-12x19in) board (DM 1700)
£367	$656	(12-Apr-91 AW.H584/R) View of Gengenbach in the Black Forest (33x44cm-13x17in) s.i.verso indian ink pencil W/C htd.white (DM 1100)

ECKL, Vilma (1892-) Austrian
£777	$1274	(20-Jun-91 D.V91/R) Mother and child (54x45cm-21x18in) s. chl pastel (A.S 16000)
£795	$1543	(6-Dec-90 D.V118/R) Child writing (36x45cm-14x18in) s. pastel (A.S 16000)
£1214	$1990	(20-Jun-91 D.V90/R) Mother and child (61x50cm-24x20in) s.i. chl pastel (A.S 25000)
£1456	$2388	(20-Jun-91 D.V89/R) Woman with blue head scarf (59x45cm-23x18in) s.i. pastel (A.S 30000)

ECKMANN, Otto (1865-1902) German
£1027	$1675	(12-Jun-91 N.M419/R) Student flirting with two young ladies in interior (46x63cm-18x25in) s.i.d.1887 (DM 3000)

EDDELIEN, Heinrich (1802-1852) Danish
£6176	$11982	(5-Dec-90 KH.K36/R) Nausikaa and her maids bringing clothes to the shipwrecked Odysseus (150x130cm-59x51in) (D.KR 68000)

EDDIS, Eden Upton (1812-1901) British
£2890	$5000	(21-May-91 CE.NY71 a/R) Young vegetable seller (162x101cm-64x40in) s.
£8000	$15360	(29-Nov-90 B116/R) Portrait of a brother and sister with dog in landscape (147x113cm-58x44in)

EDE, Frederick Charles Vipond (1865-?) American
£1531	$3000	(21-Nov-90 NA.BA31) Scene d'hiver (73x61cm-29x24in) s.

EDELFELT, Albert (1854-1905) Finnish
£9182	$15518	(20-Apr-91 HOR.H63/R) Duke Karl offending Klas Fleming's corpse (33x28cm-13x11in) s. grisaille (F.M 64000)
£27422	$53748	(20-Nov-90 GO.G411/R) Reading - interior of artist's sisters Annie and Berta by lamplight bears init.d.88 (S.KR 300000)
£32110	$63257	(13-Nov-90 AB.S885/R) Ships pilot (66x54cm-26x21in) s.d.1894 (S.KR 350000)
£62500	$111875	(14-Apr-91 BU.H24/R) Woman on balcony (72x59cm-28x23in) s.d.84 (F.M 440000)
£242511	$475321	(24-Nov-90 HOR.H74/R) The mercenary and the girl (65x54cm-26x21in) s.d.1879 (F.M 1700000)
£469	$839	(14-Apr-91 BU.H103/R) On horseback (9x19cm-4x7in) s. Indian ink (F.M 3300)
£716	$1411	(17-Nov-90 BU.H191/R) Bellman singing (30x41cm-12x16in) Indian ink dr sketch (F.M 5000)
£1727	$3332	(15-Dec-90 BU.H215) Flowers in vase (35x40cm-14x16in) W/C (F.M 12000)
£8559	$16776	(24-Nov-90 HOR.H75/R) At sea (15x24cm-6x9in) s.d.c.1890 W/C (F.M 60000)

EDELMANN, Charles Auguste (1879-) French
£520	$920	(21-Mar-91 CSK44/R) The flower sellers (43x48cm-17x19in) s. chl.W/C bodycol.

EDELMANN, Jean (1916-) French
£1223	$2361	(14-Dec-90 RY.P36/R) Dormeuse au bord de la mer (85x98cm-33x39in) s.d.89 acrylic Isorel (F.FR 12000)

EDELMANN, Yrjo (1941-) Swedish
£2768	$5314	(27-Nov-90 BU.S75/R) Composition (60x70cm-24x28in) s.d.1988 (S.KR 30000)
£3244	$6293	(4-Dec-90 BA.S99/R) Parcel (100x100cm-39x39in) s.d.80 (S.KR 35000)
£3321	$6376	(27-Nov-90 BU.S74/R) Backside of a front (100x100cm-39x39in) s.d.1983 (S.KR 36000)

EDELMANN, Yrjo (1941-) Swedish-cont.
£1690　　$2873　　(28-May-91 AB.S5196/R) Gentleman in costume (52x42cm-20x17in) s.d.74
　　　　　　　　　gouache (S.KR 18000)

EDEMA, Gerard van (1652-1700) Dutch
£1231　　$2068　　(24-Apr-91 BA.S44/R) River landscape with figures (37x25cm-15x10in) s.
　　　　　　　　　(S.KR 13000)

EDEN, Denis William (1878-1949) British
£1600　　$3136　　(13-Feb-91 S202/R) Pilgrim (56x51cm-22x20in) indist.s.d. arched top

EDENS, Henning (1885-1943) German
£1259　　$2429　　(14-Dec-90 BM.B726/R) Fishing boat in Hamburg harbour (32x42cm-13x17in)
　　　　　　　　　s. l.d.1946verso board (DM 3600)

EDER, Gyula (1875-1945) Hungarian
£933　　$1557　　(7-Jun-91 ZOF.Z1077) Virgin with unicorn. Centaur with faun
　　　　　　　　　(35x26cm-14x10in) s.d.1903 and 1905 panel pair (S.FR 2350)

EDER, Hans (1883-?) Rumanian
£7586　　$14566　　(1-Dec-90 SA.A2359/R) Portrait of Heinrich Mann (49x55cm-19x22in)
　　　　　　　　　mono.indis.d. (DM 22000)

EDGAR, F (20th C) French
£637　　$1243　　(24-Oct-90 GD.B319/R) Chickens and cockerel (31x27cm-12x11in) s. board
　　　　　　　　　(S.FR 1600)

EDGREN, Jac (1899-1980) Swedish
£398　　$668　　(27-Apr-91 SO.S312/R) The outing (16x22cm-6x9in) s. mixed media
　　　　　　　　　(S.KR 4200)

EDKINS, Cathleen Elizabeth (1922-) Australian
£3861　　$7606　　(13-Nov-90 J.M90/R) After a days toil (64x89cm-25x35in) s. (A.D 10000)
£4072　　$6882　　(16-Apr-91 J.M38/R) Flint Pebbles,Carpenters Rocks, South Australia
　　　　　　　　　(59x74cm-23x29in) s. canvas on board (A.D 9000)

EDRIDGE, Henry (1769-1821) British
£300　　$537　　(9-Apr-91 C120) Le Pont Volant at Lyons (28x48cm-11x19in) i.d.1818
　　　　　　　　　pencil
£300　　$531　　(20-Mar-91 C29) Portrait of gentleman, probably of the Vansittart family
　　　　　　　　　(5x?cm-2x?in) min. gilt-metal frame oval
£400　　$768　　(18-Dec-90 C124/R) Portrait of lady in white dress and matching turban
　　　　　　　　　(7x?cm-3x?in) min.gilt-metal frame hairpiece verso oval
£550　　$974　　(20-Mar-91 C107/R) Portrait of Captain Rowland Bevan (8x?cm-3x?in)
　　　　　　　　　min.mono. gold frame plaited hair oval
£1000　　$1790　　(9-Apr-91 C118 a) Notre Dame and Pont Marie from Pont du Jardin du Roy,
　　　　　　　　　Paris (25x42cm-10x17in) i.d.1819 pencil

EDSON, Allan (1846-1888) Canadian
£800　　$1552　　(3-Dec-90 R.T364/R) Figures seated under trees in hay field
　　　　　　　　　(35x26cm-14x10in) s. panel (C.D 1800)
£1310　　$2568　　(5-Nov-90 FB.M204) Pathway through the forest (69x50cm-27x20in) s.d.1885
　　　　　　　　　W/C (C.D 3000)

EDUARDO, Jorge (20th C) South American
£4082　　$8000　　(20-Nov-90 CH.NY226/R) Ilha da Boa Viagem (59x102cm-23x40in) i.d.89
　　　　　　　　　s.i.d.verso masonite

EDWARDS, G W (?) ?
£543　　$918　　(16-Apr-91 J.M840) Salisbury Cathedral (73x54cm-29x21in) W/C (A.D 1200)

EDWARDS, George (1694-1773) British
£1200　　$1980　　(11-Jul-91 S2/R) Barbados turtledove and peacock butterfly
　　　　　　　　　(27x22cm-11x9in) s.i. W/C bodycol

EDWARDS, George Wharton (1859-?) American
£833　　$1600　　(28-Nov-90 D.NY45) Old Breton House, Morbihan, Brittany
　　　　　　　　　(76x76cm-30x30in) s.i.verso
£1289　　$2500　　(5-Dec-90 D.NY75/R) Outside the old city gate, Paris (51x61cm-20x24in)
　　　　　　　　　s.
£1632　　$3100　　(14-Sep-90 S.BM196/R) Ponte Vecchia (51x61cm-20x24in) s.i.
£2460　　$4600　　(30-Aug-90 MFA.C98/R) Bridge at Albi (51x61cm-20x24in) s. board
£6443　　$12500　　(5-Dec-90 D.NY74/R) Market day in an old Breton town (69x53cm-27x21in)
　　　　　　　　　s.i. board

EDWARDS, Harry C (1868-1922) American
£789　　$1500　　(9-Jan-91 CH.NY225/R) Leaving the old home. Sold with W/C dr by Harry A.
　　　　　　　　　Linnell (47x33cm-19x13in) s.d.04 gouache en grisaille ink wash

EDWARDS, John (19th C) British
£700　　$1365　　(16-Oct-90 WW347) Conversation (20x25cm-8x10in) s. i.verso board

EDWARDS, Lionel (1878-1966) British
£6500　　$11310　　(27-Mar-91 S43/R) The Blankney (61x92cm-24x36in) s.i.d.1953
£10500　　$20685　　(1-Nov-90 TE663/R) Brood mares and foals in wooded landscape
　　　　　　　　　(51x76cm-20x30in) s.d.1953

EDWARDS, Lionel (1878-1966) British-cont.
£12500	$24625	(1-Nov-90 TE662/R) 'Lady Electra' with groom in open landscape (51x76cm-20x30in) s.i.d.1944
£15000	$29550	(1-Nov-90 TE664/R) Rounding the bend, Pontefract Races (51x76cm-20x30in) s.i.d.1944
£300	*$585*	*(15-Jan-91 C70/R) Pekingese (15x12cm-6x5in) pencil pen ink scraperboard*
£720	*$1404*	*(22-Oct-90 SWS316/R) Spirit of chase (34x51cm-13x20in) s.d.08 grisaille*
£900	*$1764*	*(22-Nov-90 CSK13/R) Canal Turn, Grand National, March 07 (33x51cm-13x20in) s.i.d.07 pencil W/C htd white*
£1000	*$1960*	*(25-Jan-91 C119/R) October evening, Glen Garry (33x53cm-13x21in) s. pencil W/C bodycol*
£1050	*$1754*	*(22-Jul-91 SWS870/R) An ounce of blood is worth a pound of bone (22x27cm-9x11in) s.i. pencil ink*
£1150	*$2254*	*(22-Jan-91 SWS1226) Studies of a famous veteran, golden miller (34x51cm-13x20in) init.i.d.1950 W/C bodycol.over blk.chk.*
£2500	$4825	(10-Dec-90 PHB24/R) Get on to the end, Hursley (42x32cm-17x13in) s.d.53 i.verso W/C
£2500	$4225	(2-May-91 C45/R) North Cotswold hounds at Snowshill (18x33cm-7x13in) s.i.d.1905 pencil W/C bodycol
£3200	$5920	(6-Mar-91 DR23/R) Huntsmen and hounds (27x44cm-11x17in) s. W/C bodycol
£5500	$10780	(8-Nov-90 C1/R) Cub hunting in the Ashford valley (37x52cm-15x20in) s.i.d.1949 W/C bodycol.

EDY-LEGRAND, Edouard Leon Louis (1892-1970) French
£1531	$3015	(14-Nov-90 CN.P109/R) Repos sous les arbres (50x65cm-20x26in) s. board (F.FR 15000)
£2551	$5026	(14-Nov-90 CN.P117) Chanteuses chirates dans les jardins du Caid (100x130cm-39x51in) s.i. verso (F.FR 25000)

EDZARD, Dietz (1893-1963) German
£549	$950	(7-May-91 CE.NY8/R) Bouquet de fleurs (44x29cm-17x11in) s.d.45
£1061	$1900	(16-Mar-91 W.W109/R) Mademoiselle (28x20cm-11x8in) s. panel
£1320	$2600	(15-Nov-90 D.NY103/R) Pont de Rialto (27x35cm-11x14in) s. i.d.1960 stretcher
£1474	$2860	(25-Aug-90 LIT.L29) Portrait of ballerina (64x53cm-25x21in) s.
£2308	$4500	(10-Oct-90 SY.NY231/R) L'attente (81x61cm-32x24in) s.
£2312	$4000	(7-May-91 CE.NY101/R) L'attente (81x60cm-32x24in) s.
£2436	$4750	(10-Oct-90 SY.NY230/R) La poire aux quatros caminos (150x89cm-59x35in) s.
£2455	$4714	(27-Nov-90 W.T1145/R) Still life of roses (24x18cm-9x7in) s. panel pair (C.D 5500)
£3426	$6750	(15-Nov-90 D.NY116/R) Comediens sur la Piazzetta (51x61cm-20x24in) s. i.stretcher
£3553	$7000	(13-Nov-90 CE.NY120/R) Jeune femme (100x80cm-39x31in) s.d.51
£3590	$7000	(10-Oct-90 SY.NY236/R) Ballet dressing room (15x99cm-6x39in) s.d.45 canvas on board
£4188	$6995	(4-Jun-91 FB.M94/R) La petite fille aux roses (61x50cm-24x20in) s. (C.D 8000)
£5076	$10000	(15-Nov-90 D.NY117/R) Premier (65x54cm-26x21in) s. i.stretcher
£6091	$12000	(15-Nov-90 D.NY120/R) Ballet des petites modistes (124x99cm-49x39in) s.

EECKE, Constantin van and GAREMYN, Jan Anton (18th C) Flemish
£45000	$86850	(12-Dec-90 S99/R) Peasants feasting near castle with Dudzele, near Bruges, in background (250x480cm-98x189in) s.d.1772 and 1773

EECKHOUDT, Jean van den (1875-1946) Belgian
£2791	$4829	(25-May-91 KV.L454/R) La blonde au chapeau noir (49x41cm-19x16in) mono. (B.FR 170000)
£927	*$1799*	*(8-Dec-90 KV.L289) Portrait of two children (33x35cm-13x14in) s.d.1909 pastel (B.FR 55000)*

EECKHOUT, Gerbrand van den (1621-1674) Dutch
£75000	$129750	(24-May-91 C19/R) The children of Altetus Tolling and Aleid Jansson in pastoral dress (143x170cm-56x67in) s.d.1667
£4500	$7335	(2-Jul-91 C215/R) Circumcision (9x14cm-4x6in) pen wash

EECKHOUT, Victor (1821-1879) Flemish
£600	*$978*	*(2-Jul-91 C345) Pastoral concert in wood, medieval castle beyond (23x31cm-9x12in) s. ink on papier glace*

EEKMAN, Nicolaas (1889-1973) Belgian
£915	*$1756*	*(27-Nov-90 SY.AM3828) The violonplayer (69x54cm-27x21in) s.i.d.1929 pencil (D.FL 3000)*
£985	*$1704*	*(25-May-91 KV.L108/R) Peasant couple (91x71cm-36x28in) s.d.1932 chk. W/C (B.FR 60000)*
£1780	*$3187*	*(12-Apr-91 JM.P20/R) Le passeur (97x112cm-38x44in) s.i.d.21 blk.crayon paper laid down on canvas (F.FR 18000)*

EELKEMA, Elke Jelles (1788-1839) Dutch
£1679	$2889	(16-May-91 D.V172/R) Still life of fruit (37x32cm-15x13in) mono. panel (A.S 35000)

EEMANS, Marc (20th C) French?
£2226	*$3628*	*(15-Jun-91 L.K177/R) Abstract composition (40x32cm-16x13in) s.d.24 W/C pencil (DM 6500)*

562

EERELMAN, Otto (1839-1926) Dutch
£13636 $26864   (30-Oct-90 CH.AM325/R) View in town in winter with elegant lady in
                       horse-drawn sledge (60x90cm-24x35in) s. (D.FL 45000)
£732 $1434   (6-Nov-90 SY.AM136) St. Bernhard family (23x30cm-9x12in) s. pencil
                       (D.FL 2400)

EERTVELT, Andries van (1590-1652) Flemish
£5020 $8082   (27-Jun-91 APT.P103/R) Combat naval (50x81cm-20x32in) panel (F.FR 50000)

EERTVELT, Andries van (attrib) (1590-1652) Flemish
£9128 $18073   (30-Jan-91 APT.P46/R) Combat en mer (50x80cm-20x31in) panel (F.FR 90000)

EFIMOV (20th C) Russian
£2250 $3983   (20-Mar-91 DL.P165/R) Le Marechal Vorochilov pratiquant le ski de fond
                       (140x181cm-55x71in) (F.FR 22500)

EFREMOV, Kim see   IEFREIMOV, Kim

EGAN, Eloise (20th C) American
£872 $1500   (15-May-91 SY.NY179/R) Summer picnic (58x70cm-23x28in) s.

EGEDIUS, Halfdan (1877-1899) Norwegian
£1313 $2351   (14-Mar-91 BU.O23/R) Raspberries (19x21cm-7x8in) init.d.88 (N.KR 15000)
£2277 $4075   (14-Mar-91 BU.O22/R) Landscape (19x21cm-7x8in) indist.d.92 canvas on
                       panel (N.KR 26000)
£4340 $7248   (4-Jun-91 BU.O54/R) Horses in the mountains (17x24cm-7x9in) canvas on
                       panel (N.KR 50000)
£13535 $26123   (10-Dec-90 B.O23/R) Landscape from Telemark, 1893 (40x58cm-16x23in) s.
                       (N.KR 152000)
£353 $707   (9-Feb-91 BU.O44) Horse and house (25x15cm-10x6in) s. pencil (N.KR 4000)

EGERSDORFER, Heinrich (1853-1915) South African
£301 $590   (11-Feb-91 SY.J466/R) Wild dog attaching a Kudr (19x26cm-7x10in) s. W/C
                       (SA.R 1500)

EGERSDORFER, Konrad (1868-?) German
£1409 $2748   (10-Oct-90 WE.MU255/R) In the parlour (24x36cm-9x14in) s. pair
                       (DM 4200)

EGERTON, Daniel Thomas (attrib) (1800-1842) British
£5233 $9000   (15-May-91 CH.NY63/R) Castillo de Chapultepec (18x25cm-7x10in) sepia ink
                       wash gouache

EGG, Augustus Leopold (1816-1863) British
£1500 $2445   (14-Jun-91 C307/R) The Cartoon Gallery,Knowle (25x31cm-10x12in)
                       s.i.verso
£7500 $13425   (10-Apr-91 S53/R) Victim - scene from Le Diable Boiteux
                       (61x75cm-24x30in) s.d.1842

EGGENBERG, Hans (1911-) Swiss
£556 $961   (22-May-91 GS.B2079) Busy street scene (61x46cm-24x18in) s. board
                       (S.FR 1400)

EGGENHOFER, Nick (1897-?) American
£4233 $8000   (26-Sep-90 SY.NY70/R) Pony express station (41x51cm-16x20in) s. board
£1788 $3200   (14-Mar-91 CH.NY133/R) Santa Fe wagons fording Cimarron
                       (38x51cm-15x20in) s. gouache pencil
£2116 $4000   (27-Sep-90 CH.NY170/R) Mountain men under attack (38x49cm-15x19in) s.
                       gouache pencil board
£3198 $5500   (15-May-91 SY.NY115/R) White man's weapons (41x66cm-16x26in) s.d.1968
                       gouache board

EGGER, Hans (1908-) Swiss
£610 $1000   (19-Jun-91 B.SF1936/R) Circus performers (76x61cm-30x24in) s.

EGGER-LIENZ, Albin (1868-1926) Swiss
£2365 $4493   (14-Sep-90 SA.A1393/R) Der Namenlose (57x52cm-22x20in) board (DM 7000)
£27260 $53703   (30-Oct-90 F.R189/R) Rose di Pentecoste (49x57cm-19x22in) s. panel
                       (I.L 60000000)
£34791 $67495   (6-Dec-90 D.V73/R) The spring (61x90cm-24x35in) s. board (A.S 700000)
£102226 $201386   (30-Oct-90 F.R224/R) Mittagessen, Zwelte Fassung (55x80cm-22x31in) s.
                       panel (I.L 225000000)
£874 $1696   (7-Dec-90 GB.B6473) Portrait of bearded man looking down
                       (48x34cm-19x13in) s.c.1884 chl (DM 2500)
£9940 $19284   (6-Dec-90 D.V70/R) Head of first peasant, partial repeat from Totentanz
                       (31x36cm-12x14in) s.i.d.1920 W/C paper on board (A.S 200000)

EGGINTON, Frank (1908-?) British
£1852 $3648   (14-Nov-90 WO.CO4) Donkey resting (38x53cm-15x21in) s. (E.P 2000)
£640 $1069   (22-Jul-91 SWS917/R) A Connemara Lough (36x52cm-14x20in) s.
£950 $1853   (26-Oct-90 CG3) On the Atlantic Drive, Co Donegal (26x35cm-10x14in)
                       s.d.1931 W/C
£1100 $2167   (17-Nov-90 TA.B2) The eagles' nest, Killarney (36x53cm-14x21in) s.
£1150 $1921   (22-Jul-91 SWS915/R) Early morning, Lough Fee, Connemara
                       (35x52cm-14x20in) s.d.'73

EGGINTON, Frank (1908-?) British-cont.
£1200	$2400	(8-Feb-91 C41/R) Homeward bound, a loaded gig on an Irish Country Lane (51x74cm-20x29in) s. W/C
£1200	$2340	(26-Oct-90 CG1) Donkey by shed, Connemara (38x53cm-15x21in) s. W/C
£1350	$2633	(15-Jan-91 SWS80/R) Wet day near Fallcarragh, Co.Donegal (52x75cm-20x30in) s. W/C
£1455	$2851	(23-Jan-91 WO.CO14) Below Muckish, Co. Donegal (36x53cm-14x21in) s.d.1976 W/C (E.P 1600)
£1500	$2925	(26-Oct-90 CG54) Caragh Lake, Co Kerry (53x76cm-21x30in) s. i.verso W/C
£1600	$2672	(3-Jun-91 PHB25/R) Sunlight and shadow, Craigard, Co. Down (52x75cm-20x30in) s. i.verso W/C
£1800	$3006	(22-Jul-91 SWS916/R) Ballacony Bay (53x75cm-21x30in) s.
£1800	$3510	(26-Oct-90 CG2/R) The bridge (53x76cm-21x30in) s. W/C
£1850	$3608	(15-Jan-91 SWS81/R) Wash day near Durnish, Rossshire (52x75cm-20x30in) s. W/C
£2037	$4013	(14-Nov-90 WO.CO3) The Bog Road to Maam, Connemara (38x53cm-15x21in) s. W/C (E.P 2200)
£2182	$4145	(12-Sep-90 WO.CO2) Sunset, Vale of Clara, Co. Wicklow (36x51cm-14x20in) s. W/C (E.P 2400)

EGGINTON, Wycliffe (1875-1951) British
£1250	$2088	(4-Jun-91 SWS1831/R) Dales Voe, Shetland Isles. Feeding pony (39x59cm-15x23in) mono.i.verso one s.d.1899 one s.d.1900 pair
£320	$566	(19-Mar-91 OT438/R) Extensive moorland landscape (52x71cm-20x28in) s. W/C
£430	$727	(20-Apr-91 TA.B504) Dartmoor landscape (25x36cm-10x14in) s. W/C
£480	$782	(13-Jun-91 CSK89/R) Near two bridges, Dartmoor (33x51cm-13x20in) s.d.22 s.i.verso W/C
£550	$1073	(26-Oct-90 CG55) Common by the sea (27x37cm-11x15in) s. W/C
£580	$969	(22-Jul-91 SWS918/R) Primula (53x38cm-21x15in) s.
£700	$1365	(26-Oct-90 CG56) Cattle grazing by stream (26x37cm-10x15in) s. W/C htd.white
£710	$1164	(19-Jun-91 AH255) View of Peckforton (61x91cm-24x36in) W/C
£926	$1824	(14-Nov-90 WO.CO5) Low tide (25x38cm-10x15in) s. W/C (E.P 1000)
£1000	$1680	(22-Apr-91 PH322/R) Road across moor (51x71cm-20x28in) s. W/C
£1091	$2073	(12-Sep-90 WO.CO4) Ponies in bogland (36x53cm-14x21in) s. W/C (E.P 1200)
£1400	$2646	(26-Sep-90 S257/R) Driving home sheep (60x90cm-24x35in) s. W/C
£1441	$2811	(10-Oct-90 WO.CO5) Driving home the sheep (36x53cm-14x21in) s. W/C (E.P 1600)

EGGLI, Johann Jakob (1812-1880) Swiss
| £913 | $1524 | (7-Jun-91 ZOF.Z1312/R) Rheinauerthor with villagers watching artists (43x46cm-17x18in) s. gouache (S.FR 2300) |

EGLEY, William (1798-1870) British
| £2800 | $4620 | (11-Jul-91 S286/R) Bracelet with 5 miniatures of the children of William, 6th Baron Monson (3x?cm-1x?in) min.gold slide frames hinged with pins oval |

EGLEY, William Maw (c.1827-1916) British
| £500 | $825 | (10-Jul-91 ZZ.B202) Portrait of pensive young lady by window (77x65cm-30x26in) s.d.1870 |
| £900 | $1764 | (22-Jan-91 PH93/R) Adeline ... faintly smiling, Adeline, scarce of earth nor all divine (25x17cm-10x7in) s.d.1863 s.i.verso board |

EGMONT, Justus van (1601-1674) Flemish
| £5474 | $10785 | (30-Oct-90 BU.S243/R) Portrait of Queen Kristina as Diana (117x85cm-46x33in) (S.KR 60000) |

EGNELL, Allan (1884-1960) Swedish
| £1700 | $3333 | (10-Nov-90 FAL.M82/R) Helsinge Regiment in the battle of Holowezin in 1708 (65x174cm-26x69in) s. (S.KR 18500) |

EGNER, Marie (1850-1940) Austrian
£1946	$3815	(24-Jan-91 D.V29/R) Jetty (13x23cm-5x9in) s. panel (A.S 40000)
£4271	$7646	(11-Apr-91 D.V171/R) Wooded landscape with path leading to farmstead (41x31cm-16x12in) i.verso paper on panel (A.S 90000)
£716	$1396	(11-Oct-90 D.V220/R) Landscape with farmhouse (19x24cm-7x9in) s. W/C (A.S 15000)
£1367	$2528	(7-Mar-91 D.V213/R) Landscape with clouds (27x37cm-11x15in) s. W/C paper on board (A.S 28000)

EGOROV, Alexei Yegorovitch (1776-1851) Russian
| £397 | $687 | (22-May-91 GS.B2364/R) Wooded landscape with two horse-drawn sledges in snow (33x49cm-13x19in) s. gouache (S.FR 1000) |
| £397 | $687 | (22-May-91 GS.B2363/R) Wooded river landscape, winter (30x47cm-12x19in) s. gouache (S.FR 1000) |

EGOROV, Andrei see YEGOROV, Andrei

EGOROV, Andrey Simonoviev (1861-1924) Russian
| £530 | $938 | (18-Mar-91 ARC.P163/R) Nature morte aux fleurs (23x29cm-9x11in) s.d.1911 W/C gouache (F.FR 5300) |

EGTER VAN WISSEKERKE, Anna (1872-1969) Dutch
£557 $1076   (12-Dec-90 CH.AM181) Still life of michaelmas daisies in vase
                        (28x30cm-11x12in) init.d.1949 (D.FL 1800)
£991 $1912   (12-Dec-90 CH.AM184/R) Still life of strawberries on dish and teapot and
                        cup on draped table (25x32cm-10x13in) s.d.1952 (D.FL 3200)

EGUSQUIZA, Rogelio (1845-1913) Spanish
£18786 $32500   (22-May-91 SY.NY66/R) Unexpected visitors (65x55cm-26x22in) s. panel

EHLERS, Ernest H (?) ?
£520 $962   (5-Mar-91 SWS1430) The retreat (33x44cm-13x17in) s. i.verso board

EHLINGER, Maurice Ambrose (1896-1981) French
£714 $1377   (12-Dec-90 D.P170/R) Jeune femme au chapeau, le sein gauche decouvert
                        (61x50cm-24x20in) s. (F.FR 7000)

EHMSEN, Heinrich (1886-?) German
£732 $1354   (7-Mar-91 D.V173/R) Taganrog (45x53cm-18x21in) s.d.1944 i.verso board
                        (A.S 15000)
£488 $903   (7-Mar-91 D.V121/R) Pilot boat, Scheveningen (48x62cm-19x24in) s. mixed
                        media board (A.S 10000)

EHNERT, G V (?) ?
£987 $1945   (14-Nov-90 RAS.K203) Mountain landscape with river (70x108cm-28x43in) s.
                        (D.KR 11000)

EHNINGER, John W (1827-1889) American
£5422 $9000   (11-Jan-91 DM.D1350/R) Young girl with arms round negro boy, another
                        negro boy playing banjo (46x36cm-18x14in) s.d.1864

EHRENBERG, Paul (1876-1949) German
£676 $1318   (26-Oct-90 KM.K1197/R) Harbour scene with beached fishing boats and
                        horsedrawn cart (90x146cm-35x57in) s. (DM 2000)

EHRENSTRAHL, David Klocker von (1629-1698) German
£6387 $12582   (30-Oct-90 BU.S16/R) Portrait of Kristian Albrecht, Duke of Holstein
                        Gottorp (150x122cm-59x48in) (S.KR 70000)

EHRENSTRAHL, David Klocker von (after) (1629-1698) German
£2060 $3543   (14-May-91 BU.S6/R) Labour vanitas (140x120cm-55x47in) (S.KR 22000)

EHRENSTRAHL, David Klocker von (attrib) (1629-1698) German
£558 $998   (13-Apr-91 FAL.M70/R) Portrait of Ulrika Eleonora (73x59cm-29x23in) oval
                        (S.KR 6000)

EHRENSTRAHL, David Klocker von (studio) (1629-1698) German
£2434 $4187   (14-May-91 BU.S5/R) Ulrika Eleonora with her family (174x124cm-69x49in)
                        (S.KR 26000)
£3568 $6958   (21-Oct-90 BU.M477) Portrait of Karl XI (135x115cm-53x45in) (S.KR 39000)

EHRET, Georg Dyonis (1710-1770) British
£1600 $2640   (11-Jul-91 S3/R) Yellow hammer (26x20cm-10x8in) s.i.d.1757 W/C htd.white
£3472 $5972   (19-May-91 ZZ.F69/R) Natures mortes aux fruits (32x45cm-13x18in)
                        s.d.1749 s. gouache pair (F.FR 35000)
£5000 $8250   (9-Jul-91 C51/R) Rubus (52x37cm-20x15in) s.i.d.1744 pencil W/C bodycol
                        vellum
£9000 $14850   (9-Jul-91 C49/R) Cistus (52x37cm-20x15in) s.i.d.1743 pencil W/C bodycol
                        vellum
£11000 $18150   (9-Jul-91 C47/R) Martagon (53x38cm-21x15in) s.i.d.1745 pencil W/C vellum
£12000 $19800   (9-Jul-91 C52/R) Cistus (52x78cm-20x31in) s.i.d.1743 pencil W/C bodycol
                        vellum
£12000 $19800   (9-Jul-91 C46/R) Cedrus (52x37cm-20x15in) s.i.d.1745 pencil W/C bodycol
                        vellum
£12000 $19800   (9-Jul-91 C50/R) Cistus (53x37cm-21x15in) s.i.d.1747 pencil W/C bodycol
                        vellum
£26000 $42900   (9-Jul-91 C48/R) Bignonia (52x37cm-20x15in) s.i. pencil W/C bodycol
                        vellum
£65000 $107250   (9-Jul-91 C45/R) Magnolia (52x37cm-20x15in) s.i. pencil W/C bodycol
                        vellum

EHRHARDT, Paul W (1872-?) German
£1074 $2094   (10-Oct-90 WE.MU227/R) Young woman sewing in interior (56x47cm-22x19in)
                        s. (DM 3200)

EHRLICH, Georg (1897-1966) Austrian
£534 $876   (20-Jun-91 D.V93/R) Ollersbach (31x48cm-12x19in) st.sig.i.verso pen
                        indian ink W/C (A.S 11000)
£1068 $1751   (20-Jun-91 D.V94/R) Zinkenbach, Salzkammergut (32x50cm-13x20in) s.i. pen
                        indian ink W/C (A.S 22000)

EIBISCH, Eugeniusz (1896-1987) Polish
£1747 $3406   (20-Jan-91 AG.W3) Still life of flowers (45x37cm-18x15in) s.
                        (P.Z 32000000)
£2412 $4728   (26-Jan-91 PSA.W6) Town scene (48x57cm-19x22in) s.d.1930 (P.Z 45000000)

EIBNER, Friedrich (1825-1877) German
£4196 $8140   (4-Dec-90 FN.S1816/R) Strassburg Munster with figures (74x55cm-29x22in)
       s.d.1873 (DM 12000)

EICHEL, G (18th C) ?
£11000 $21670   (16-Nov-90 C93/R) Partridge shooting. Hare shooting (16x2cm-6x1in)
       init.s.d.1768 pair

EICHENBERGER, Paul (1891-?) Swiss?
£598 $1165   (24-Oct-90 GD.B323) Winter landscape with view from Wengernalp to
       Lauterbrunnen and Breithorn (75x100cm-30x39in) s. l.d.1925verso
       (S.FR 1500)

EICHENS, Friedrich Eduard (1804-1877) German
*£9744 $19000   (26-Oct-90 SY.NY47/R) Conversation piece with artist's family
       (54x72cm-21x28in) s.d.1826 chk*

EICHHORN, Alfred (1909-1972) Austrian
£1329 $2578   (4-Dec-90 FN.S1589) Lanterns (60x43cm-24x17in) s.d.1966 acrylic board
       (DM 3800)
£1370 $2452   (12-Mar-91 FN.S1959/R) Composition (40x54cm-16x21in) s.d.1949 panel
       (DM 4000)
£1748 $3392   (4-Dec-90 FN.S1584) Impression (38x54cm-15x21in) s.d.1961 paper
       (DM 5000)
£1923 $3731   (4-Dec-90 FN.S1585/R) Composition with flowers (49x35cm-19x14in)
       s.d.1947 paper (DM 5500)
*£648 $1226   (25-Sep-90 FN.S1944) Ibiza (50x65cm-20x26in) s.l.d.1961 gouache
       (DM 1900)*
*£699 $1357   (4-Dec-90 FN.S1588) Network (37x57cm-15x22in) s.d.1959 pen dr.
       (DM 2000)*
*£751 $1419   (25-Sep-90 FN.S1941) Masks (45x36cm-18x14in) s.d.1949 gouache
       (DM 2200)*
*£819 $1548   (25-Sep-90 FN.S1940) Composition (44x58cm-17x23in) s.d.1961 gouache
       (DM 2400)*
*£979 $1899   (4-Dec-90 FN.S1590) Zeichen (25x46cm-10x18in) s. indian ink wash W/C
       (DM 2800)*
*£1126 $2129   (25-Sep-90 FN.S1938/R) Composition (51x38cm-20x15in) s.d.1949 gouache
       (DM 3300)*
*£1351 $2338   (25-May-91 N.M74/R) Tachistisches Zeichen (33x47cm-13x19in) s.d.1954
       mixed media oil gouache board (DM 4000)*
*£1365 $2580   (25-Sep-90 FN.S1942) Explosion nr 1 (60x47cm-24x19in) s.d.1960 gouache
       (DM 4000)*
*£1689 $2922   (25-May-91 N.M75/R) Rote vegetative Form (61x46cm-24x18in) s.d.1969 oil
       gouache gold bronze board (DM 5000)*
*£1853 $3595   (4-Dec-90 FN.S1583) Schilf Impressionen (62x47cm-24x19in) s.d.1960
       gouache (DM 5300)*
*£1923 $3731   (4-Dec-90 FN.S1587) Composition with red sun (56x43cm-22x17in) s.d.1963
       gouache (DM 5500)*
*£2028 $3934   (4-Dec-90 FN.S1586/R) Carneval (33x47cm-13x19in) s.d.1947 chk board
       (DM 5800)*

EICHHORN, P (18th C) German
£683 $1283   (21-Sep-90 N.M3166/R) Peasant couple outside house (7x9cm-3x4in) s.
       panel (DM 2000)
£769 $1485   (13-Dec-90 N.M2678/R) Chiemsee landscape with fishermen
       (30x40cm-12x16in) s. board (DM 2200)

EICHINGER, E (19th C) Austrian
£655 $1100   (19-Jul-91 DM.D2005/R) Bavarian man holding a wine glass
       (25x20cm-10x8in) s. board

EICHINGER, Erwin (19th C) Austrian
£650 $1268   (15-Jan-91 SWS166/R) The end of the game (46x26cm-18x10in) s.l. panel
£670 $1126   (16-Jul-91 RB494) Man with blue jug. Man with wine (25x20cm-10x8in) pair
£900 $1476   (18-Jun-91 PH139) Portrait of man smoking pipe (27x21cm-11x8in) s. panel
£947 $1800   (27-Feb-91 SY.NY155/R) Tyrolean men with tankards (27x20cm-11x8in) s.
       board pair
£1500 $2445   (4-Jul-91 PHI190/R) Contemplation (42x52cm-17x20in) s.l. panel
£2600 $4264   (19-Jun-91 S109/R) Good hand. Quiet smoke (20x15cm-8x6in) s.l. panel
       pair
£2600 $4264   (19-Jun-91 S108/R) Returning from shoot. Peaceful moment (20x15cm-8x6in)
       s.l. panel pair
£3100 $6107   (13-Nov-90 SWS371/R) The dice players (47x36cm-19x14in) s.l. panel
£5000 $8350   (3-Jun-91 PHB55/R) Music lesson (61x50cm-24x20in) s.l.

EICHINGER, Otto (1922-) Austrian
£500 $845   (3-May-91 PHE95) A good book (26x20cm-10x8in) s. panel
£898 $1509   (23-Apr-91 SY.AM233/R) Portrait of rabbi (27x20cm-11x8in) s. panel
       (D.FL 3000)
£3158 $6000   (27-Feb-91 SY.NY152/R) Rabbi with manuscript. Rabbi with book
       (26x20cm-10x8in) s. panel pair

EICKELBERG, W H (1845-1920) Dutch
£788 $1292   (18-Jun-91 VN.R59) Scene in an old Dutch town (39x23cm-15x9in) panel
       (D.FL 2600)

EIEBAKKE, August (1867-1938) Norwegian
£980 $1890   (10-Dec-90 B.O24/R) Portrait of brother and sister (55x57cm-22x22in)
                 init.d.1921 (N.KR 11000)
£1259 $2102   (4-Jun-91 BU.O87/R) Figures in garden (32x52cm-13x20in) init. s.l.verso
                 (N.KR 14500)
£1519 $2537   (3-Jun-91 B.O28/R) Mother and child (55x42cm-22x17in) mono.d.1918
                 (N.KR 17500)
£2865 $4784   (3-Jun-91 B.O27/R) Church and red house (100x100cm-39x39in) mono.
                 (N.KR 33000)

EIKAAS, Ludvig (1920-) Norwegian
£781 $1305   (3-Jun-91 B.O29/R) Interior (42x69cm-17x27in) s.d.69 (N.KR 9000)
£1215 $2370   (11-Oct-90 BU.O24/R) Composition (38x46cm-15x18in) s.d.75 (N.KR 14000)
£1401 $2508   (14-Mar-91 BU.O24/R) Male figures (54x65cm-21x26in) s. (N.KR 16000)
£2582 $4984   (13-Dec-90 BU.O11/R) Spring evening (67x81cm-26x32in) s. (N.KR 29000)
£3117 $6015   (13-Dec-90 BU.O10/R) Self portrait (96x55cm-38x22in) s. (N.KR 35000)
£3918 $7562   (13-Dec-90 BU.O12/R) Rain (110x95cm-43x37in) s. (N.KR 44000)
£4809 $9280   (13-Dec-90 BU.O15/R) Cows in rain (50x68cm-20x27in) s. (N.KR 54000)

EILERSEN, Eiler Rasmussen (1827-1912) Danish
£984 $1948   (31-Jan-91 RAS.V513/R) Wooded landscape near the sea (110x156cm-43x61in)
                 s.d.1866 (D.KR 11000)
£1000 $1960   (23-Nov-90 PHM106) A wooded landscape at dawn (80x111cm-31x44in)
                 mono.d.1866
£3000 $5160   (17-May-91 C244/R) Sorrento (44x65cm-17x26in) s.i.d.76

EILSHEMIUS, Louis M (1864-1942) American
£798 $1300   (5-Jul-91 S.W2666/R) Calm day (25x33cm-10x13in) s. board
£1065 $1800   (20-Apr-91 WOL.C173/R) Nudes in landscape (36x53cm-14x21in) s.d.1910
£1744 $3000   (15-May-91 SY.NY194/R) Boy seated on fence (48x37cm-19x15in) s. board
£1823 $3500   (17-Dec-90 SY.NY343/R) Afternoon idylls - bathers (76x64cm-30x25in)
                 s.d.1896

EINARSSON, Gudmundur (1895-1963) Icelandic
£634 $1224   (12-Dec-90 RAS.K223) Snowcovered mountains (44x49cm-17x19in) init.d.1924
                 (D.KR 7000)

EINBECK, Georg (1870-1951) French
£522 $1023   (24-Nov-90 AB.L242/R) Le mistral (34x26cm-13x10in) s. i.d.1909 W/C
*   tempera (S.FR 1300)*

EINSLE, Anton (1801-1871) Austrian
£574 $976   (28-May-91 KF.M157) Head of blonde girl (20x15cm-8x6in) board
                 (DM 1700)

EINSLE, Joseph (1794-?) German
£1000 $1650   (10-Jul-91 C39/R) A young boy seated beside his wooden cart
*   (64cm-25ins circular) min.s.d.1821 gilt-metal mount wood frame*

EISELE, C (19/20th C) American
£595 $1000   (16-Jul-91 BG.M875/R) Mountainous lake landscape (56x91cm-22x36in) s.

EISEN, Charles (18th C) French
£8040 $13186   (22-Jun-91 CH.MO147/R) Une allegorie des arts (84x134cm-33x53in)
                 (F.FR 80000)

EISEN, Charles-Dominique-Joseph (1720-1778) French
£1529 $2936   (27-Nov-90 APT.P71/R) Etudes de soldats (23x15cm-9x6in) one s.d.1755
*   blk.crayon (F.FR 15000)*
£1529 $2936   (27-Nov-90 APT.P70/R) Deux etudes de soldats portant un fusil
*   (23x14cm-9x6in) both s.d.1755 crayon pair (F.FR 15000)*
£2111 $3461   (18-Jun-91 APT.P55/R) Allegorie des arts et des sciences
*   (25x15cm-10x6in) s.d.1762 pen indian ink wash (F.FR 21000)*

EISEN, Charles-Dominique-Joseph (after) (1720-1778) French
£1946 $3756   (12-Dec-90 BU.S125/R) Children playing (48x93cm-19x37in) (S.KR 21000)
£1978 $3541   (8-Apr-91 ARC.P9 b) Jeux d'enfants (38x26cm-15x10in) pair (F.FR 20000)

EISEN, Charles-Dominique-Joseph (attrib) (1720-1778) French
£540 $1037   (18-Feb-91 S254/R) Allegory of winter with putti around fire
*   (18x24cm-7x9in) indis.i. pen ink wash htd.white over chk*

EISEN, Francois (1695-1778) Flemish
£2180 $3750   (15-May-91 D.NY70) Tavern scene with boors carousing (38x51cm-15x20in)
                 s.indis.d.177. panel
£4762 $8000   (17-Jul-91 SY.NY175/R) Three children playing with a dog
                 (91x79cm-36x31in)

EISEN, Francois (attrib) (1695-1778) Flemish
£2500 $4075   (2-Jul-91 PH182/R) Children watching magician playing trick
                 (64x80cm-25x31in)

EISEN, Jean Francois (style) (?) French?
£1121 $2153   (30-Nov-90 APT.P126/R) Une ronde d'enfants (64x56cm-25x22in)
                 (F.FR 11000)

EISENDIECK, Suzanne (1908-?) German

£670	$1300	(8-Dec-90 W.W153/R) Tete de femme (41x33cm-16x13in) s.
£914	$1800	(13-Nov-90 CE.NY91/R) Jeune femme (35x27cm-14x11in) s.
£919	$1498	(10-Jun-91 W.T1407) Tete de jeune ballerine (33x23cm-13x9in) s. (C.D 1700)
£1156	$2000	(7-May-91 CE.NY6/R) Le premier bouquet (46x38cm-18x15in) s.
£1220	$2000	(19-Jun-91 B.SF1865/R) Jardin a Apremont (41x33cm-16x13in) s.
£1293	$2250	(27-Mar-91 B.SF4285/R) Two young girls wearing hats (50x61cm-20x24in) s.
£1548	$2988	(13-Dec-90 SY.AM98/R) Parasol a Ramatuelle (65x54cm-26x21in) s. (D.FL 5000)
£1777	$3500	(15-Nov-90 D.NY121/R) Avant les debute (61x48cm-24x19in) s. i.num.211 stretcher
£1800	$3456	(21-Feb-91 B43/R) La modiste (51x66cm-20x26in) s.l.verso
£1827	$3600	(15-Nov-90 D.NY118/R) La Loge (54x46cm-21x18in) s. l.verso
£1829	$3000	(19-Jun-91 B.SF1867/R) Concert champetre (55x46cm-22x18in) s.
£1829	$3000	(19-Jun-91 B.SF1866/R) Gathering wildflowers (46x56cm-18x22in) s.
£1933	$3750	(7-Dec-90 S.W2706/R) Essayage au theatre de Verdure (46x56cm-18x22in) s.
£2011	$3500	(27-Mar-91 B.SF4286/R) Jeune fille a la plage (46x61cm-18x24in) s.
£2284	$4500	(15-Nov-90 D.NY119/R) Le beau Dimanche (50x60cm-20x24in) s. l.verso
£2543	$4400	(22-May-91 D.NY86/R) Aux courses (51x61cm-20x24in) s. l.verso
£2659	$4600	(22-May-91 D.NY87/R) Plage a maree basee (49x51cm-19x20in) s. l.verso
£2700	$4644	(14-May-91 SWS442/R) La modiste (65x49cm-26x19in) s. l.verso
£2941	$5676	(13-Dec-90 SY.AM90/R) Couple dans la brasserie (56x46cm-22x18in) s. (D.FL 9500)
£3243	$5286	(10-Jun-91 W.T1405) Petite fille et petit garcon d'honneur (41x23cm-16x9in) s. pair (C.D 6000)

EISENHUT, Ferencz (1857-1903) Hungarian

£52000	$85280	(18-Jun-91 PH102/R) The captive princess (159x320cm-63x126in) s.i.d.1889

EISENSCHER, Yaacov (1896-1980) Israeli

£1675	$3200	(2-Jan-91 GG.TA524/R) Figures at shop entrance (60x73cm-24x29in) s.
£2945	$4800	(12-Jun-91 GG.TA387/R) Parrots in cage (74x100cm-29x39in) s.
£495	*$945*	*(1-Jan-91 GG.TA15/R) Village outskirts in Galilee (49x63cm-19x25in) s. gouache*

EISENSCHITZ, Willy (1889-1974) French

£898	$1760	(6-Nov-90 GF.L2580/R) Port catalan (46x61cm-18x24in) s.d.1949 s.l.verso board (S.FR 2200)
£905	$1619	(11-Mar-91 GL.P49) Le canal St-Martin (60x73cm-24x29in) s. (F.FR 9000)
£1437	$2500	(27-Mar-91 B.SF4322/R) Canal Saint Martin (65x81cm-26x32in) s.d.1955
£2055	$3988	(8-Dec-90 LT.P161) Paysage de montagne au pont (61x73cm-24x29in) s.d.31 (F.FR 20000)
£2490	$4233	(2-Jun-91 LT.P84) Village dans les champs (73x92cm-29x36in) s.d.25 (F.FR 25000)
£3046	$6000	(13-Nov-90 CE.NY40/R) Paysage de Provence (81x99cm-32x39in) s.
£3179	$5500	(7-May-91 CE.NY43/R) Paysage (65x80cm-26x31in) s.
£1527	*$3009*	*(30-Oct-90 I.N126) Paysage de Provence (36x49cm-14x19in) s. W/C (F.FR 15000)*
£1589	*$3130*	*(30-Oct-90 I.N127/R) Oliviers en Provence (38x52cm-15x20in) s. W/C (F.FR 15600)*

EISERMANN, Richard (19th C) German

£895	$1700	(27-Feb-91 SY.NY172/R) Farewell (48x31cm-19x12in) s.l. panel

EISLER, Georg (1928-) Austrian

£973	$1908	(24-Jan-91 D.V254/R) Winter landscape (30x60cm-12x24in) s.d.87 (A.S 20000)
£2392	$4139	(8-May-91 D.V134/R) Interior with three figures (60x80cm-24x31in) s.d.65-66 (A.S 50000)
£633	*$1240*	*(24-Jan-91 D.V255/R) Cafe (59x45cm-23x18in) s.d.16-18 pastel (A.S 13000)*
£861	*$1490*	*(8-May-91 D.V235/R) Coffee shop (24x33cm-9x13in) s.d.86 pastel (A.S 18000)*

EISMANN, Johann Anton (1604-1698) German

£4546	$8910	(19-Nov-90 CH.R56/R) Insenatura marina con torre e viandante (35x50cm-14x20in) (I.L 10000000)

EISSNER, F (?) ?

£1718	$3368	(16-Feb-91 GF.H11/R) Beneath the cherry tree (73x97cm-29x38in) (DM 5000)

EITNER, Ernst (1867-1955) German

£2797	$5427	(5-Dec-90 DO.H2514/R) Gotthardsau (80x70cm-31x28in) s.d.1910 (DM 8000)
£559	*$1085*	*(7-Dec-90 GB.B6480/R) Still life of flowers (30x17cm-12x7in) s. W/C (DM 1600)*

EITNER, Ernst (attrib) (1867-1955) German

£2902	$5601	(12-Dec-90 N.M496) Portrait of young lady. Study of old man in armchair (100x70cm-39x28in) double-sided (DM 8300)

EJNDEN, L van (?) ?

£1700	$3400	(7-Feb-91 CSK107) Graces (34x79cm-13x31in) s. panel after Guido Reni

EKBLAD, F (19th C) American
£1190 $2000   (19-Jul-91 DM.D2065/R) A road by the river (69x114cm-27x45in) s.

EKDAHL, Inger (1922-) Swedish
£649 $1259   (4-Dec-90 BA.S102/R) Spontaneous composition (27x24cm-11x9in) init.
     s.d.1958verso panel (S.KR 7000)
£973 $1888   (4-Dec-90 BA.S100/R) Spontaneous composition (100x73cm-39x29in) s.d.60
     (S.KR 10500)

EKEGARDH, Hans (1891-1962) Swedish
£1274 $2446   (2-Dec-90 M.V49/R) Les toits de Paris (33x41cm-13x16in) init. panel
     (F.FR 12500)

EKELAND, Arne (1908-) Norwegian
£1158 $2234   (13-Dec-90 BU.O4/R) Wooded landscape (32x33cm-13x13in) s. paper
     (N.KR 13000)
£1562 $2609   (4-Jun-91 BU.O75/R) Harbour scene (46x54cm-18x21in) s. panel
     (N.KR 18000)
£2691 $4494   (3-Jun-91 B.O32/R) Paralysed (34x26cm-13x10in) s.d.39 panel (N.KR 31000)
£4167 $6958   (3-Jun-91 B.O31/R) Landscape with woman (60x49cm-24x19in) s. panel
     (N.KR 48000)
£4553 $8151   (11-Mar-91 B.O25/R) The homecoming (46x51cm-18x20in) s. panel
     (N.KR 52000)
£5699 $10999   (13-Dec-90 BU.O23/R) Refugees (48x60cm-19x24in) s. (N.KR 64000)
£6233 $12030   (13-Dec-90 BU.O24/R) Fallen warrior (126x145cm-50x57in) s.l.
     (N.KR 70000)
£6768 $13061   (13-Dec-90 BU.O25/R) Washing day I (104x109cm-41x43in) s. (N.KR 76000)
£7658 $14780   (13-Dec-90 BU.O26/R) The child (100x90cm-39x35in) s. l.verso
     (N.KR 86000)
£7812 $15234   (11-Oct-90 BU.O25/R) The dream (61x50cm-24x20in) init. (N.KR 90000)
£18229 $30443   (3-Jun-91 B.O30/R) The battle (170x120cm-67x47in) s. (N.KR 210000)
£32986 $64323   (11-Oct-90 BU.O26/R) Sunday at the factory (121x150cm-48x59in) s.
     (N.KR 380000)
£623 $1203   (13-Dec-90 BU.O3/R) The night (29x38cm-11x15in) init.i. pastel
     (N.KR 7000)
£839 $1678   (9-Feb-91 BU.O51) Night (29x38cm-11x15in) s. pastel (N.KR 9500)
£883 $1767   (9-Feb-91 BU.O52) Composition (19x27cm-7x11in) s. pastel (N.KR 10000)
£1215 $2030   (3-Jun-91 B.O33/R) Composition in blue and white (65x50cm-26x20in) s.
     gouache pencil paper on panel (N.KR 14000)

EKELS, Jan (18th C) Dutch
£3800 $6194   (5-Jul-91 C302/R) Street in Dutch town, with man selling fruit to maid,
     church by canal (55x45cm-22x18in)

EKELUND, Poul (1920-1976) Danish
£626 $1227   (13-Feb-91 KH.K53) Autumn landscape (63x75cm-25x30in) s.d.63 (D.KR 7000)
£1268 $2447   (12-Dec-90 RAS.K218) Sea and vessels (50x80cm-20x31in) (D.KR 14000)

EKELUND, Ragnar (1892-1960) Scandinavian
£4155 $8185   (17-Nov-90 BU.H33/R) Beach huts (47x55cm-19x22in) s. (F.M 29000)
£4585 $9032   (17-Nov-90 BU.H32/R) French street scene (54x64cm-21x25in) s.
     (F.M 32000)
£5563 $10904   (24-Nov-90 HOR.H77/R) The birdge (39x46cm-15x18in) s. (F.M 39000)
£5739 $9699   (20-Apr-91 HOR.H64/R) Chevreuse (65x82cm-26x32in) s.d.1953 (F.M 40000)

EKENAES, Jahn (1847-1920) Norwegian
£8681 $14497   (4-Jun-91 BU.O66/R) Figures fishing in lake from rowingboats
     (76x121cm-30x48in) s.d.1911 (N.KR 140000)
£16000 $30720   (28-Nov-90 S92/R) Family fishing trip (58x104cm-23x41in) s.d.1895
£23438 $45703   (11-Oct-90 BU.O27/R) Washing clothes on the ice (68x108cm-27x43in)
     s.d.1891 (N.KR 270000)

EKMAN, Emil (1880-1951) Swedish
£657 $1117   (28-May-91 AB.S4610/R) Seascape with vessel on fire and men in lifeboat
     (127x202cm-50x80in) s.d.1942 (S.KR 7000)
£754 $1274   (21-Apr-91 BU.M290) Fishing place at sunset (80x130cm-31x51in) s.
     (S.KR 8000)
£823 $1612   (20-Nov-90 GO.G41) Seascape with man in rowingboat (72x100cm-28x39in)
     s.d.1930 (S.KR 9000)
£929 $1664   (9-Apr-91 GO.G30) Seascape with fisherman at sunset (69x114cm-27x45in)
     s.d.1927 (S.KR 10000)
£929 $1664   (9-Apr-91 GO.G31) Seascape with fishingboat (73x106cm-29x42in) s.d.1934
     (S.KR 10000)
£1162 $2079   (9-Apr-91 GO.G29) Seascape with fishingboats at dawn (65x110cm-26x43in)
     s.indist.d.1920 (S.KR 12500)
£1468 $2892   (13-Nov-90 AB.S349/R) Fishingboats in sunshine (77x98cm-30x39in)
     s.d.1935 (S.KR 16000)

EKMAN, Henri (?) ?
£1222 $2407   (31-Oct-90 ZZ.F122/R) Composition sur fond rouge (162x129cm-64x51in) s.
     d.semptember 89-mai 90 verso (F.FR 12000)

EKMAN, Robert Wilhelm (1808-1873) Finnish
£8427 $14494   (14-May-91 BU.S7/R) Dutch interior (73x92cm-29x36in) s.d.1838
     (S.KR 90000)

EKMAN, Robert Wilhelm (1808-1873) Finnish-cont.
£2149 $4234   (17-Nov-90 BU.H192/R) Lovers in moonlight. River landscape at sunset (31x46cm-12x18in) s.d.1864 pastel pair (F.M 15000)

EKSERGIAN, Carnig (19th C) Turkish
£2500 $4750   (27-Feb-91 SY.NY286/R) Fortune teller (55x42cm-22x17in) s.indist.d.

EKSTROM, Per (1844-1935) Swedish
£2817 $4732   (23-Apr-91 RAS.K161 a/R) Sunset over the sea, Vikleby (38x75cm-15x30in) s. (D.KR 32000)
£3005 $5108   (28-May-91 AB.S4615/R) Red evening landscape with view of sea through trees (45x64cm-18x25in) s. (S.KR 32000)
£3019 $5223   (22-May-91 BA.S565 a/R) Trees in twilight (56x81cm-22x32in) s. (S.KR 32000)
£3493 $6846   (6-Nov-90 BA.S50/R) 'Oland scene' (41x60cm-16x24in) s. (S.KR 38000)
£4596 $9007   (6-Nov-90 BA.S49/R) Sunset by the sea (36x45cm-14x18in) s. (S.KR 50000)
£4688 $9188   (6-Nov-90 BA.S50 a/R) Sunset over wet field (58x81cm-23x32in) s. (S.KR 51000)
£4912 $9480   (12-Dec-90 BU.S16/R) Landscape from Djurholm (57x86cm-22x34in) s. (S.KR 53000)
£5337 $9180   (14-May-91 BU.S8/R) Farm at sunset (70x110cm-28x43in) s. (S.KR 57000)
£5474 $10785   (30-Oct-90 BU.S25/R) Farm at sunset (60x92cm-24x36in) s. (S.KR 60000)
£6893 $13511   (6-Nov-90 BA.S47/R) French landscape with peasants (40x65cm-16x26in) s. (S.KR 75000)
£7386 $12409   (24-Apr-91 BA.S47/R) Evening sun (61x51cm-24x20in) s. (S.KR 78000)
£7629 $14952   (6-Nov-90 BA.S48/R) Restenas island (60x72cm-24x28in) s. (S.KR 83000)
£7755 $15278   (30-Oct-90 BU.S21/R) Landscape at sunset (64x98cm-25x39in) s. (S.KR 85000)
£8029 $15818   (30-Oct-90 BU.S19/R) Flooded landscape at dusk (77x128cm-30x50in) s.d.1903 (S.KR 88000)
£8212 $16177   (30-Oct-90 BU.S20/R) Moonlit sea (80x117cm-31x46in) s. (S.KR 90000)
£8716 $17170   (13-Nov-90 BA.S353/R) Summer landscape from Sartrouville by Seine (41x65cm-16x26in) s. indist.d.1888verso (S.KR 95000)
£8837 $16437   (9-Sep-90 BU.M612) Sunset over farm, Segerstrand Oland (67x100cm-26x39in) s. (S.KR 95000)
£9124 $17974   (30-Oct-90 BU.S18/R) Reflection of sunlight (67x102cm-26x40in) s. (S.KR 100000)
£10493 $20671   (30-Oct-90 BU.S23/R) Autumn landscape (29x37cm-11x15in) s. panel (S.KR 115000)
£11029 $21618   (6-Nov-90 BA.S44/R) Evening sun through trees (82x67cm-32x26in) s.d.1899 (S.KR 120000)
£11121 $21464   (12-Dec-90 BU.S15/R) Lake landscape (55x73cm-22x29in) s. (S.KR 120000)
£11468 $22592   (13-Nov-90 AB.S351/R) Wooded landscape with watercourse at dusk in summer (100x72cm-39x28in) s. (S.KR 125000)
£14085 $23944   (28-May-91 AB.S4612/R) French evening landscape (27x40cm-11x16in) s.d.1881 (S.KR 150000)
£21779 $42034   (12-Dec-90 BU.S13/R) French landscape with figures (65x80cm-26x31in) s. (S.KR 235000)
£32864 $55869   (28-May-91 AB.S4611/R) Morning sun through the trees with men in rowingboat on lake (100x72cm-39x28in) s. (S.KR 350000)

EKSTROM, Thea (1920-1989) Swedish
£1019 $1978   (4-Dec-90 BA.S104/R) Conversation (46x55cm-18x22in) s.d.1958 panel (S.KR 11000)

EKVALL, Emma (1838-1925) Swedish
£758 $1273   (24-Apr-91 BA.S50/R) Still life of roses (32x46cm-13x18in) s. panel (S.KR 8000)
£2757 $5404   (6-Nov-90 BA.S51/R) Lady from medieval times (32x23cm-13x9in) s. (S.KR 30000)
£2966 $5724   (12-Dec-90 BU.S17/R) Breakfast (41x24cm-16x9in) s. (S.KR 32000)

EKVALL, Knut (1843-1912) Swedish
£2390 $4684   (6-Nov-90 BA.S53/R) Hunting in winter (91x68cm-36x27in) mono. (S.KR 26000)
£8044 $15766   (20-Nov-90 GO.G43/R) Flirting by the wood, young boy and girl in national costume (70x53cm-28x21in) s. (S.KR 88000)

ELAND, Leonardus Joseph (1884-1952) Dutch
£778 $1479   (11-Sep-90 CH.AM237) Workers in a sawa, Indonesia (60x90cm-24x35in) s. (D.FL 2600)

ELANDER, Kristina A (1952-) Scandinavian
£563 $958   (28-May-91 AB.S5197/R) Desperate living s. d.1988verso triptych (S.KR 6000)

ELDERSHAW, John Roy (1892-1973) Australian
£656 $1293   (13-Nov-90 J.M576 a) Convict Ruins, Stanley, Tasmania (28x37cm-11x15in) s.d.36 W/C (A.D 1700)

ELDRED, Lemeul D (1848-1921) American
£658 $1250   (1-Mar-91 RB.HY26/R) Seascape with sailboats (25x36cm-10x14in) s.d.81
£773 $1500   (24-Aug-90 RB.HY70/R) The caravan (30x41cm-12x16in) s.
£773 $1500   (24-Aug-90 RB.HY17/R) Clamming, New Bedford shore (18x28cm-7x11in) s.
£928 $1800   (24-Aug-90 RB.HY57/R) Full moon rising (23x36cm-9x14in) s.d.74

ELDRED, Lemuel D (1848-1921) American-cont.
£1031 $2000   (24-Aug-90 RB.HY92/R) New England coastal scene (25x38cm-10x15in)
                  s.d.1868
£1031 $2000   (24-Aug-90 RB.HY32/R) The Twin Ships, Grand Manan Island
                  (56x91cm-22x36in) s.

ELESZKIEWICZ, Stanislas (1900-1963) Polish
£663 $1272   (2-Dec-90 M.V51) La parade (50x61cm-20x24in) s. (F.FR 6500)

ELFFERS, Dick (1919-1991) Dutch
£571 $987   (22-May-91 CH.AM676) Groep te katendrecht (60x50cm-24x20in) s.d.48
                 (D.FL 1900)

ELFVEN, Erik (1921-) Swedish
£649 $1259   (4-Dec-90 BA.S108/R) The Elfven couple on holiday (43x54cm-17x21in) s.
                 (S.KR 7000)

ELGOOD, George Samuel (1851-1943) British
£550   *$1084*   *(1-Nov-90 C115) The Temple of Castor and Pollux, Girgenti*
                    (25x36cm-10x14in) s.i.d.94 pencil W/C
£750   *$1425*   *(12-Sep-90 CSK142) Garden that I love (23x18cm-9x7in) s. s.i. W/C htd*
                    white
£950   *$1549*   *(13-Jun-91 CSK161/R) Peacocks in walled garden (23x35cm-9x14in) s.d.1903*
                    i.verso pencil W/C
£1000   *$1960*   *(21-Nov-90 B83) Piper's walk, Barncluith (34x24cm-13x9in) s.d.1906 W/C*
£3900   *$7683*   *(13-Nov-90 SWS112/R) Bulwick - the gateway (32x50cm-13x20in) s.d.1893 i.*
                    label verso
£9000   *$14670*   *(14-Jun-91 C61/R) Compton Wynyates from the moat (36x53cm-14x21in)*
                    s.d.1890 pencil W/C
£11000   *$17930*   *(14-Jun-91 C60 a/R) Compton Wynyates, Warwickshire (36x53cm-14x21in)*
                    s.d.1890 pencil W/C

ELIA, P (19th C) ?
£2046 $4010   (22-Nov-90 SY.MI11) Fiori (76x60cm-30x24in) s.d.1883 (I.L 4500000)

ELIAERTS, J F (1761-1848) Belgian
£926 $1509   (11-Jun-91 ANS.M105/R) Bodegon de frutas (28x35cm-11x14in) s.
                 (S.P 170000)

ELIAS, Nicolaes (attrib) (1590-1656) Dutch
£1825 $3595   (30-Oct-90 BU.S244/R) Portrait of elderly man with ruff
                  (57x45cm-22x18in) panel (S.KR 20000)

ELIE, Aglae (19th C) French?
£1200 $2124   (21-Mar-91 LC.P54/R) Portrait d'une jeune femme assise
                  (100x81cm-39x32in) s.d.1816 (F.FR 12000)

ELIM, Frank (20th C) French
£520 $868   (6-Jun-91 CSK81) Le Prodige, dark bay racehorse with O'Neill up on
                  racecourse (32x40cm-13x16in) s.d.1922 panel
£1019 $1967   (10-Dec-90 BL.P46/R) L'arrivee de la Reine sur le champ de course
                  d'Ascot (48x60cm-19x24in) s.d.1949 panel (F.FR 10000)
£1265 $2480   (22-Nov-90 D.P3) Cheval au pre (80x64cm-31x25in) s.d.1910 panel
                  (F.FR 12500)

ELIOT, Maurice (1864-?) French
£2800 $5516   (5-Oct-90 C65/R) Sur la barriere (50x67cm-20x26in) s.d.87

ELK, Gerard Pieter van (1941-) Dutch
£6607   *$11429*   *(23-May-91 SY.AM300/R) Pushing nose sculpture (140x200cm-55x79in)*
                    s.i.d.1981 oil photo collage (D.FL 22000)

ELLIGER, Ottmar (17/18th C) Swedish
£4098 $8033   (11-Nov-90 M.V16/R) Antoine decouvrant le corps de Cleopatre
                  (58x69cm-23x27in) (F.FR 40000)
£7167 $14048   (24-Nov-90 SA.A571/R) Banquet with Alexander the Great after the
                  conquest of Babylon (55x67cm-22x26in) s. (DM 21000)

ELLIGER, Ottmar (circle) (17/18th C) Swedish
£11055 $18131   (21-Jun-91 SY.MO186/R) Le passage du Granique (27x46cm-11x18in) copper
                  (F.FR 110000)

ELLIGER, Ottmar I (1633-1679) Swedish
£12213 $21861   (14-Mar-91 D.V80/R) Still life of peaches, grapes, currants and pears
                  with butterfly and bugs (48x33cm-19x13in) panel (A.S 250000)

ELLIOT, Thomas (fl.1790-1800) British
£1450 $2683   (6-Mar-91 SC4380) Sailing vessels near Portsmouth Harbour
                  (30x46cm-12x18in) s.
£17964 $30000   (7-Jun-91 SY.NY141/R) Man O'War in Portsmouth harbour (88x141cm-35x56in)

ELLIOTT, Frederic (19/20th C) Australian
£350   *$686*   *(19-Nov-90 MGS.S217) Shipping in Darling Harbour (31x58cm-12x23in) W/C*
                   (A.D 900)
£402   *$699*   *(26-Mar-91 JRL.S246) The tug, Sydney Harbour (36x25cm-14x10in) s. W/C*
                   (A.D 900)

ELLIOTT, Frederic (19/20th C) Australian-cont.
£482	$925	(27-Nov-90 JRL.S89) Tramp steamer and tug (37x54cm-15x21in) s. W/C (A.D 1200)
£543	$918	(16-Apr-91 J.M660) Pushing off the wharf (34x22cm-13x9in) s. W/C (A.D 1200)
£694	$1167	(16-Jul-91 JRL.S46) Wartime Liberty Ship, Sydney Harbour (25x36cm-10x14in) s. W/C (A.D 1500)

ELLIOTT, Ric (1933-) Australian
| £613 | $1000 | (1-Jul-91 AAA.S79) Miners' reunion (41x51cm-16x20in) s. board (A.D 1300) |
| £855 | $1513 | (18-Mar-91 MGS.S259 n) Paddington street scene (31x90cm-12x35in) s.d.1972 board (A.D 2000) |

ELLIS, Edwin (1841-1895) British
£550	$930	(30-Apr-91 PH127) Beached sailing vessels in cove (51x91cm-20x36in) s.
£600	$1110	(7-Mar-91 CSK142) Crowland Abbey (51x76cm-20x30in) s. l.stretcher
£700	$1183	(30-Apr-91 PH129) Young mariner (72x92cm-28x36in) s.
£717	$1398	(24-Oct-90 GD.B324) Figures waiting for the return of the fishermen (45x81cm-18x32in) s. (S.FR 1800)
£850	$1658	(18-Oct-90 CSK158/R) Crab catching, Sands End Yorkshire (42x61cm-17x24in) s. s.l.verso
£900	$1521	(30-Apr-91 PH125/R) Bridlington Quay (45x81cm-18x32in) s. l.stretcher

ELLIS, Fremont F (1897-?) American
£1479	$2500	(1-May-91 B.SF5200/R) Cotton woods (23x30cm-9x12in) s.d.27 panel
£1596	$3000	(19-Sep-90 B.SF2797/R) Cottonwoods (23x30cm-9x12in) s.d.27 board
£4233	$8000	(27-Sep-90 CH.NY197/R) Aspen and Spruce (76x101cm-30x40in) s.d.1926
£5917	$10000	(1-May-91 B.SF5199/R) Santa Fe autumn (56x71cm-22x28in) s.
£6633	$13000	(7-Nov-90 B.SF3816/R) Galisteo (76x102cm-30x40in) s.

ELLIS, Joseph F (1783-1848) British
| £552 | $950 | (18-May-91 W.W60/R) Ships entering a harbour (20x25cm-8x10in) s. panel |

ELLIS, Paul H (fl.1882-1908) British
| £1400 | $2310 | (9-Jul-91 PH225) Mosque of Sultan Achmet, Constantinople (35x51cm-14x20in) s.l. |

ELLIS, Tristram (1844-1922) British
£300	$531	(21-Mar-91 CSK77/R) Fishing vessels in Tromso harbour (23x53cm-9x21in) s.i.d.1903 pencil W/C
£440	$717	(2-Jul-91 SWS464) Constantinople (25x52cm-10x20in) s.i.d.1903 W/C
£1800	$2934	(2-Jul-91 SWS465) Harbour, Constantinople (24x54cm-9x21in) one s.d.1909 W/C pair

ELLIS, William (1747-1810) British
| £632 | $1200 | (14-Sep-90 DM.D2230) Boy fishing (48x41cm-19x16in) s.d.1856 |

ELLMINGER, Ignaz (1843-1894) Austrian
£949	$1699	(11-Apr-91 D.V204/R) Danube landscape (14x24cm-6x9in) board (A.S 20000)
£2273	$4386	(12-Dec-90 N.M497/R) Young peasant woman with child resting in wooded river landscape (25x31cm-10x12in) s. panel (DM 6500)
£15702	$30147	(29-Nov-90 D.V113/R) Preparations for Corpus Christi Procession (88x130cm-35x51in) s. (A.S 320000)

ELLYS, John (attrib) (1700-1757) British
| £7500 | $13425 | (10-Apr-91 S73/R) Portrait of Mrs. Hester Booth, dancer (120x74cm-47x29in) l. |

ELMER, Stephen (1717-1796) British
£1315	$2235	(28-May-91 AB.S4755/R) Still life of dead birds (76x64cm-30x25in) s. (S.KR 14000)
£3000	$5370	(12-Apr-91 C75/R) Red grouse in extensive river landscape (38x46cm-15x18in)
£4200	$7518	(12-Apr-91 C74/R) Covey of partridges in extensive wooded landscape, house beyond (28x46cm-11x18in) s.

ELMER, Stephen (attrib) (1717-1796) British
| £4600 | $9062 | (14-Nov-90 S68/R) Great crested grebe by lake (63x76cm-25x30in) |
| £5600 | $11032 | (14-Nov-90 S67/R) White pheasant in landscape (64x76cm-25x30in) i.d.1761 |

ELMER, Stephen (style) (1717-1796) British
| £1650 | $2838 | (15-May-91 BT240/R) Partridges in a landscape (51x58cm-20x23in) |

ELMORE, Alfred (1815-1881) British
| £3179 | $5500 | (21-May-91 CE.NY77/R) Return home (61x73cm-24x29in) s. |

ELOUT, Franchoys (attrib) (1597-c.1641) Dutch
| £76453 | $150612 | (14-Nov-90 SY.AM37/R) Still life of two glasses, bread, nuts, lemon and knife on ledge (37x55cm-15x22in) panel (D.FL 250000) |

ELSAS, Paul (1896-) German
| £1329 | $2578 | (4-Dec-90 FN.S1594/R) Melodie picturale, hommage a Arthur Honegger (50x100cm-20x39in) s.i.verso paper collage panel (DM 3800) |
| £444 | $728 | (18-Jun-91 FN.S1577/R) Melodie picturale, hommage a Arthur Honegger (50x100cm-20x39in) s.i.verso paper collage panel (DM 1300) |

ELSASSER, Friedrich August (1810-1845) German
£950 $1862 (22-Jan-91 SWS958) A service in St. Peter's Rome (72x63cm-28x25in) s.i.d.35

ELSEN, Alfred (1850-1900) Belgian
£2312 $4000 (10-May-91 S.BM41/R) Approaching storm (127x94cm-50x37in) s.

ELSHEIMER, Adam (studio) (1574-1620) German
£3637 $7128 (19-Nov-90 CH.R21/R) Paesaggio con Cristo che risana il cieco (25x41cm-10x16in) panel (I.L 8000000)

ELSHEIMER, Adam (style) (1574-1620) German
£550 $1084 (13-Nov-90 CH.AM63) Rest on Flight into Egypt (25x30cm-10x12in) panel (D.FL 1800)
£2041 $3959 (7-Dec-90 G.Z214/R) Il contento (28x39cm-11x15in) copper (S.FR 5000)
£2635 $4480 (27-May-91 L.K40/R) Glorification of the Cross (50x37cm-20x15in) copper (DM 7800)

ELSNER, Franz (1898-1977) Austrian
£727 $1368 (20-Sep-90 D.V188/R) House amongst the trees (59x80cm-23x31in) s. (A.S 15000)

ELSNER, Otto (20th C) German?
£716 $1203 (25-Apr-91 D.V249/R) View over rooftops of Rothenburg ob der Tauber (37x31cm-15x12in) s.d.22 W/C (A.S 15000)

ELTEN, Hendrik Dirk Kruseman van (1829-1904) Dutch
£1010 $2000 (1-Feb-91 S.W2395/R) Landscape (36x53cm-14x21in) s.
£1020 $1643 (26-Jun-91 KM.K1444) Mountain landscape with view of village and church (33x55cm-13x22in) s. (DM 3000)
£8092 $14000 (22-May-91 CH.NY49/R) Picnic in Westchester county (68x106cm-27x42in) s.
£2211 $4200 (9-Jan-91 CH.NY123/R) Adirondack (33x49cm-13x19in) s.i.d.68 pencil.Sold w.work by Russell Smith

ELTZNER, Adolph (19th C) German
£909 $1764 (5-Dec-90 DO.H2087) View of Hamburg (35x50cm-14x20in) s.d.1881 W/C indian ink pen (DM 2600)

ELWELL, Frederick William (1870-1958) British
£2545 $4810 (28-Sep-90 DA709/R) An old Palace, Venice (38x28cm-15x11in) s. board
£7200 $14040 (17-Oct-90 PHL200/R) The workshop interior (102x127cm-40x50in) s.d.1920

ELWELL, Mary (1874-?) British
£780 $1498 (30-Nov-90 DA662) Sketch for interior of St Mary's Close (36x25cm-14x10in) i.verso panel

ELWYN, John (1916-) British
£620 $1215 (25-Jan-91 C162/R) Conversation (70x90cm-28x35in) s.d.54
£800 $1568 (25-Jan-91 C163/R) Wool dyers (51x76cm-20x30in) s.
£380 $752 (29-Jan-91 PH87) Gale havoc (30x40cm-12x16in) s. gouache

EMANUEL, Frank Lewis (1865-1948) British
£581 $1150 (1-Feb-91 S.W2607/R) Le Portel (25x33cm-10x13in) i.verso board

EMILIAN SCHOOL, 14th C Italian
£15778 $28243 (8-Apr-91 CH.R180/R) Nativita con l'annuncio ai pastori e l'arrivo dei Re Magi (20x21cm-8x8in) gold ground panel (I.L 35000000)

EMILIAN SCHOOL, 15th C Italian
£10526 $20000 (11-Jan-91 CH.NY4/R) Deposition (45x28cm-18x11in) tempera gold ground panel

EMILIAN SCHOOL, 16th C Italian
£3851 $6701 (25-Mar-91 SY.F717) S.Caterina di Alessandria (42x30cm-17x12in) panel (I.L 8500000)
£6937 $13459 (3-Dec-90 SY.F1039/R) Ritratto di Portia Margani (86x68cm-34x27in) i. panel (I.L 15000000)
£7022 $12219 (25-Mar-91 SY.F577 a) Madonna e Bambino e San Giovannino (56x44cm-22x17in) panel (I.L 15500000)
£7692 $15000 (11-Oct-90 SY.NY72/R) Holy Family with infant St John the Baptist in landscape (39x30cm-15x12in) indis.i. panel
£1003 $1776 (19-Mar-91 F.M41/R) Camino. Portale con lo stemma della famiglia della Rovere pen W/C ink two mounted on album leaf (I.L 2200000)
£4200 $6846 (1-Jul-91 S18/R) Holy Family with St. John the Baptist and putti (27x23cm-11x9in) pen wash htd white

EMILIAN SCHOOL, 17th C Italian
£2273 $3933 (23-May-91 F.M485) Maddalena (73x58cm-29x23in) (I.L 5000000)
£2945 $5124 (25-Mar-91 SY.F720) Mose e il popolo ebreo durante la caduta della manna (34cm-13ins circular) panel (I.L 6500000)
£3000 $5070 (17-Apr-91 S128/R) The Death of St John the Baptist (163x122cm-64x48in)
£3189 $5422 (30-May-91 F.M23) Deposizione (128x102cm-50x40in) (I.L 7000000)
£4799 $9454 (13-Nov-90 F.M116/R) Ritratto di gentildonna. Ritratto di gentiluomo (102x88cm-40x35in) pair (I.L 10500000)
£7664 $13718 (8-Apr-91 F.M346) Vanitas (76x101cm-30x40in) (I.L 17000000)

EMILIAN SCHOOL, 17th C Italian-cont.
£13669 $23237   (30-May-91 F.M75/R) Natura morta con composizione floreali, frutta e uccelli (85x113cm-33x44in) (I.L 30000000)

EMILIAN SCHOOL, 18th C Italian
£4625 $8972   (3-Dec-90 SY.F1019/R) Erminia tra i pastori (74x87cm-29x34in) (I.L 10000000)
£4625 $8972   (3-Dec-90 SY.F1020/R) Scena con musicanti (42x56cm-17x22in) (I.L 10000000)

EMMENEGGER, Hans (1866-?) Swiss
£1786 $2982   (5-Jun-91 SY.Z82/R) Ruin of Castello di Cannero (51x81cm-20x32in) s. (S.FR 4500)
£2008 $3936   (24-Nov-90 AB.L176/R) Nature morte (24x37cm-9x15in) s.d.1911 i.stretcher (S.FR 5000)

EMMERIK, Govert van (1808-1882) Dutch
£900 $1476   (18-Jun-91 PH34) Dutch barges moored before harbour town (45x65cm-18x26in) s.
£906 $1748   (10-Dec-90 BU.K4/R) Sailship off the Dutch coast (46x65cm-18x26in) s. (D.KR 10000)
£1652 $3221   (20-Oct-90 CH.AM150 a) Shipping on choppy sea near jetty with two-master beyond (58x73cm-23x29in) s.indis.d.1825 (D.FL 5500)
£2036 $3543   (26-Mar-91 VN.R22/R) Shipping moored near a village (55x72cm-22x28in) s. (D.FL 6800)

EMMET, Lydia Field (1866-1952) American
£10000 $19700   (1-Nov-90 C307/R) Portrait of boy seated in chair (157x106cm-62x42in) s.

EMMETT, Rowland (1906-1990) British
£650   *$1073*   *(10-Jul-91 CSK142) He said if he took camouflage job on he'd have to do it his own way (18x25cm-7x10in) s.i. pen wash*
£750   *$1238*   *(10-Jul-91 CSK146/R) Upside down lantern lecture (28x23cm-11x9in) s. pen wash*
£800   *$1320*   *(10-Jul-91 CSK145) Pierhead revellers (23x28cm-9x11in) s. pen wash*
£850   *$1403*   *(10-Jul-91 CSK141/R) Any more for Roman Villa (30x36cm-12x14in) s. pencil pen htd white*
£1400   *$2702*   *(12-Dec-90 CSK33/R) Gas works to Hang dog Heath (48x33cm-19x13in) s.i. pen wash htd white*

EMMONS, Dorothy Stanley (1891-?) American
£812 $1600   (18-Nov-90 JRB.C82/R) Men and fishing boats (20x25cm-8x10in) s. board

EMMS, John (1843-1912) British
£780 $1521   (17-Oct-90 PHL294) Portrait of a lap dog (31x40cm-12x16in) s.d.1878
£872 $1700   (26-Oct-90 S.W2230/R) On the scent (36x30cm-14x12in) s.
£1000 $1950   (15-Jan-91 C55 a) Rough-haired collie (43x69cm-17x27in)
£1100 $1793   (14-Jun-91 DA746/R) Terriers rabbiting by lanternlight (46x38cm-18x15in) s.d.85
£1200 $1968   (20-Jun-91 B27/R) Horse in stable interior (61x76cm-24x30in) s.d.94
£1300 $2444   (18-Sep-90 SWS739) Hunting on the heath (47x64cm-19x25in) s.
£1500 $2910   (7-Dec-90 CBS285) Two dogs guarding dead game (38x58cm-15x23in) s.
£1600 $3152   (13-Nov-90 PH67/R) Awaiting his master (19x28cm-7x11in) s. board
£1900 $3705   (15-Jan-91 B367/R) The smooth haired fox terrier Peter (38x42cm-15x17in) s.i.d.1899
£2300 $3841   (5-Jun-91 S83/R) Waiting for mistress (52x70cm-20x28in) s.d.89
£3000 $5850   (24-Oct-90 SWS345/R) Fox up tree (53x46cm-21x18in) s.
£3300 $6435   (15-Jan-91 C36/R) Sharp, Irish terrier (53x66cm-21x26in) s.i.d.1897
£3800 $6384   (16-Jul-91 C88/R) Shot and his friends (38x56cm-15x22in) s.d.76 i.verso
£4755 $7750   (5-Jul-91 S.W3020/R) Portraits of Foller and another fox terrier (23x23cm-9x9in) first s.i.d.1873 other i.d.1873 verso pair board
£5400 $8802   (13-Jun-91 L95/R) In full cry (48x66cm-19x26in) s.
£13772 $23000   (7-Jun-91 SY.NY97/R) In the kennel (43x53cm-17x21in) s.
£14970 $25000   (7-Jun-91 SY.NY180/R) Waiting for master (71x91cm-28x36in) s.d.1897
£15500 $30225   (15-Jan-91 C138/R) Fox hounds and smooth-haired fox terrier at kennel door (91x71cm-36x28in) s.d.1853
£26000 $50700   (15-Jan-91 C132/R) Foxhounds in kennel at the end of the day (101x127cm-40x50in) s.

EMMS, John (style) (1843-1912) British
£1400 $2758   (1-Nov-90 TE635) Unseated (76x51cm-30x20in)

EMPI, Maurice (?) ?
£1050 $1858   (7-Apr-91 LT.P243) Montmartre (37x45cm-15x18in) s. paper laid down on board (F.FR 10600)

EMPRESS OF PRUSSIA, Victoria (1840-1901) British
£800   *$1384*   *(20-May-91 PH147) Still life (32x47cm-13x19in) s.d.1873 W/C bodycol over pencil*

EMSLIE, Alfred Edward (1848-1918) British
£1800 $3402   (26-Sep-90 S127/R) Punch and Judy (56x76cm-22x30in) s.

ENCKELL, Rabbe (20th C) Scandinavian
£1079 $2083   (15-Dec-90 BU.H36) Tempel (19x27cm-7x11in) s. (F.M 7500)

ENCKELL, Torger (1901-) Finnish
£1151 $2222   (15-Dec-90 BU.H37) Woman reading (39x46cm-15x18in) s. (F.M 8000)

ENDARA CROW, Gonzalo (1936-) Ecuadorian
£11224 $22000   (20-Nov-90 CH.NY240/R) Untitled (80x90cm-31x35in) init.d.87 acrylic
         canvas

ENDE, Edgar (1901-1965) German
£1531 $3000   (12-Feb-91 SY.NY103/R) The Alps (89x119cm-35x47in) s.d.31 canvas on
         board
£2372 $4032   (27-May-91 GK.Z5173/R) Surrealistic composition (58x74cm-23x29in)
         s.d.1949 canvas on pavatex (S.FR 6000)
£2568 $4187   (15-Jun-91 L.K178/R) The vine (47x62cm-19x24in) s.d.47 board (DM 7500)
£7797 $13020   (6-Jun-91 HN.H291/R) The flying ship (70x90cm-28x35in) s.d.1933
         (DM 23000)
*£591 $1023   (21-May-91 WK.M834/R) The rest (50x65cm-20x26in) s.i.d.1931 pencil W/C
         board (DM 1750)*

ENDE, Hans am (1864-?) German
£3448 $6621   (28-Nov-90 KF.M693/R) Mountain solitude (76x126cm-30x50in) s.
         s.i.stretcher (DM 10000)
£4797 $9355   (26-Oct-90 BM.B633/R) Thunderstorm at Weyerberg (46x67cm-18x26in) mono.
         board (DM 14200)
£5102 $8214   (28-Jun-91 BM.B562/R) Moor landscape with treelined stream, evening
         (39x54cm-15x21in) mono. board (DM 15000)
£15517 $29793   (26-Nov-90 WK.M22/R) Fisherman's hut (60x50cm-24x20in) s. (DM 45000)

ENDE, Jacobus van den (1849-?) Dutch
£4682 $7913   (19-Apr-91 FN.S1706/R) Wooded river landscape with figures transporting
         wood (61x98cm-24x39in) rem.sig. i.verso (DM 14000)

ENDER, Axel Hjalmar (1853-1920) Norwegian
£2500 $4300   (17-May-91 C143/R) Making hay (85x85cm-33x33in) s.
£2500 $4300   (17-May-91 C145/R) Moment's rest (75x51cm-30x20in) s.
£2582 $4984   (12-Dec-90 BU.O15/R) Mother and baby (55x37cm-22x15in) s. (N.KR 29000)
£2800 $4816   (17-May-91 C144/R) Hunting party (73x53cm-29x21in) s.d.1911
£3853 $6897   (11-Mar-91 B.O26/R) The dairy maid (52x42cm-20x17in) s. (N.KR 44000)
£4014 $7788   (4-Dec-90 UL.T201/R) Trout fishing (43x33cm-17x13in) (N.KR 45000)
£6589 $12718   (12-Dec-90 BU.O14/R) Children skating (50x70cm-20x28in) s. i.verso
         (N.KR 74000)

ENDER, Eduard (1822-1883) Austrian
£3500 $6860   (15-Feb-91 C38/R) Inheritance (55x44cm-22x17in) s.d.1851 panel

ENDER, Johann Nepomuk (1793-1854) Austrian
*£525 $1024   (11-Oct-90 D.V127/R) Portrait of lady seated wearing straw hat
         (27x22cm-11x9in) s. W/C (A.S 11000)*
*£860 $1444   (25-Apr-91 D.V180/R) Portrait of young Habsburg, son of Erzherzog Karl
         (26x20cm-10x8in) s. W/C pencil (A.S 18000)*
*£1337 $2606   (11-Oct-90 D.V125/R) Portrait of Erzherzogin Maria Elisabeth seated
         (24x19cm-9x7in) s.d.1833 W/C (A.S 28000)*

ENDER, Thomas (1793-1875) Austrian
*£621 $1043   (25-Apr-91 D.V65/R) View of Oberranna (16x22cm-6x9in) s.i. pencil W/C
         (A.S 13000)*
*£1199 $1954   (12-Jun-91 N.M232/R) Hirschkogel near Gastein (19x23cm-7x9in) s. i.verso
         W/C (DM 3500)*
£1433 $2407   (25-Apr-91 D.V172/R) View of Lucca (17x22cm-7x9in) i. W/C (A.S 30000)
*£2000 $3280   (19-Jun-91 S52/R) Figures by Uffizi Gallery, Florence (16x23cm-6x9in) s.
         W/C*
*£5500 $10835   (15-Nov-90 CSK20/R) Hunting party in the Brazilian jungle
         (77x56cm-30x22in) s. W/C bodycol*
*£7163 $12034   (25-Apr-91 D.V173/R) The Lofer valley, Tyrol (34x50cm-13x20in) s.verso
         W/C (A.S 150000)*

ENDER, Thomas (attrib) (1793-1875) Austrian
£959 $1716   (13-Mar-91 N.M481/R) Landscape near Meran with view of mountains
         (37x23cm-15x9in) indis.d.3. i.verso paper (DM 2800)

ENDOGOUROV, Ivan (1861-1898) Russian
£6116 $11804   (16-Dec-90 CL.E3/R) Deput de printemps (61x102cm-24x40in) s.
         (F.FR 60000)

ENEA, Giuseppe (1863-?) Italian
*£2800 $5488   (22-Nov-90 CSK65) Study for frieze - cherubs in Arcadia
         (87x225cm-34x89in) s.i.d.1901 pastel*

ENFIELD, Henry (1849-1908) British
£800 $1320   (9-Jul-91 PH219) Moored sailing vessels on fjord (72x117cm-28x46in) s.

ENGALIERE, Marius (1824-1857) French
£2834 $5555   (23-Nov-90 PLF.P66) Vue de Grenade, avec voiture de voyageurs au premier
         plan (67x105cm-26x41in) (F.FR 28000)

ENGARD, Robert Oliver (1915-) American
£847 $1600   *(25-Sep-90 CE.NY118/R) Smokestacks at the lumbermill (37x28cm-15x11in)*
         s.i. verso W/C pencil

ENGBERG, Gabriel Karl (1872-1953) Finnish
£1439 $2777   (15-Dec-90 BU.H39) River landscape (25x75cm-10x30in) s. (F.M 10000)
£1576 $3105   (17-Nov-90 BU.H35/R) Green shore (53x64cm-21x25in) s. (F.M 11000)
£1719 $3387   (17-Nov-90 BU.H37/R) Wind blowing on beach (42x53cm-17x21in) s.d.1917
         panel (F.M 12000)
£1791 $3528   (17-Nov-90 BU.H36/R) Autumn wood (52x32cm-20x13in) s.d.1918 panel
         (F.M 12500)

ENGEL, Johann Friedrich (1844-?) German
£1053 $2000   (9-Jan-91 D.NY24) Young boy wearing lederhosen (33x23cm-13x9in) s.i.
         panel
£1300 $2327   (12-Mar-91 PH28/R) Portrait of young girl holding apple
         (34x26cm-13x10in) s.i. panel
£1627 $2652   (3-Jul-91 WE.MU155/R) Portrait of peasant girl (35x27cm-14x11in) s.i.
         panel (DM 4800)
£1700 $3043   (12-Mar-91 PH24/R) Portrait of young boy (26x18cm-10x7in) s.i. panel

ENGEL, Johanna (20th C) German
£2800 $5516   (5-Oct-90 C104/R) Seasons (210x105cm-83x41in) one s.d.1910 three

ENGEL, Otto Heinrich (1866-1949) German
£1084 $2103   (5-Dec-90 DO.H2520/R) Schloss Glucksburg (34x50cm-13x20in) s.i.d.1935
         panel (DM 3100)

ENGEL-PAK, Ernest (1885-1965) Belgian
£1479 $2914   (6-Oct-90 GL.P126) Composition (54x39cm-21x15in) s.d.1937 board
         (F.FR 15000)

ENGELBACH, Florence (1872-1951) British
£700 $1365   (18-Oct-90 CSK318/R) Still life with roses and foxgloves
         (102x76cm-40x30in) s.d.1945

ENGELBERTSZ, Pieter Cornelisz (1490-?) Dutch
£28000 $45640   *(2-Jul-91 C62/R) Seven Acts of Mercy, ransoming prisoners*
         (23x17cm-9x7in) i.d.1532 chk pen ink

ENGELBRECHTSZ, Cornelisz (attrib) (1468-1533) Dutch
£8222 $15951   (5-Dec-90 APT.P4/R) La Crucifixion (90x58cm-35x23in) panel arched
         (F.FR 80000)

ENGELBRECHTSZ, Cornelisz (style) (1468-1533) Dutch
£4167 $7000   (17-Jul-91 SY.NY95/R) The Deposition of Christ (66x49cm-26x19in) panel
         laid down on board

ENGELEN, Louis van (1856-?) Belgian
£1473 $2504   (28-May-91 C.A329/R) Washday (55x45cm-22x18in) s. (B.FR 90000)
£2128 $3617   (28-May-91 C.A328/R) Near the farm (70x100cm-28x39in) s. (B.FR 130000)

ENGELHARDT, Edna (20th C) American
£1860 $3200   (18-May-91 W.W208/R) Winter brook (102x122cm-40x48in) s.

ENGELHARDT, Georg (1823-1883) German
£2465 $4141   (23-Apr-91 RAS.K132/R) Summer landscape with horses in field
         (40x57cm-16x22in) s.d.1851 (D.KR 28000)
£2879 $4952   (16-May-91 D.V208/R) Wooded mountainous landscape with stream
         (71x103cm-28x41in) indis.s. (A.S 60000)

ENGELHARDT, Maja Lisa (20th C) Scandinavian
£898 $1768   (14-Nov-90 KH.K37) Composition (116x89cm-46x35in) init.d.86 (D.KR 10000)
£979 $1840   (19-Sep-90 KH.K141) Composition (146x114cm-57x45in) init.d.85
         (D.KR 11000)
£1167 $2299   (14-Nov-90 KH.K36) Composition (146x144cm-57x57in) init.d.85
         (D.KR 13000)
£1290 $2425   (19-Sep-90 KH.K142) Composition (116x89cm-46x35in) init.d.87
         (D.KR 14500)

ENGELHART, Josef (1864-1941) Austrian
£1740 $3375   (6-Dec-90 D.V6/R) Portrait of lady seated on bear rug (24x38cm-9x15in)
         i. panel (A.S 35000)
£582 $1094   *(20-Sep-90 D.V5/R) The harpist Baumann and his daughter*
         (34x38cm-13x15in) s.chk. (A.S 12000)
£777 $1274   (20-Jun-91 D.V70/R) Monte Carlo (25x34cm-10x13in) s.i.d.1926 pencil
         (A.S 16000)
£1071 $2098   *(24-Jan-91 D.V1/R) Design for wall decoration for Somossy Theatre,*
         Budapest (25x22cm-10x9in) d.1893 mixed media (A.S 22000)

ENGELMANN, Ernst Julius (1820-1902) German
£748 $1324   (20-Mar-91 KM.K1195) Alpine landscape with two women on path near
         village (48x60cm-19x24in) i.d.870 (DM 2200)

ENGELSBERG, Leon (?) Israeli
£4188 $8000   (1-Jan-91 GG.TA227/R) Judean Hills (55x76cm-22x30in) s.

ENGELSBERG, Leon (?) Israeli-cont.
£4294	$7000	(12-Jun-91 GG.TA388/R) Environs of Jerusalem (60x98cm-24x39in) s.
£1534	$2500	(12-Jun-91 GG.TA390/R) Dove and landscape. Dove and flowers on window-sill (35x35cm-14x14in) s. W/C double-sided

ENGELSTED, Malthe (1852-1930) Danish
£1630	$3147	(10-Dec-90 BU.K75/R) Boys merrymaking in wood (65x77cm-26x30in) init.d.1885 (D.KR 18000)

ENGELUND, Svend (1908-) Danish
£1404	$2386	(29-May-91 KH.K232/R) Spring fields, Vra 1962 (73x100cm-29x39in) init.d.62 (D.KR 16000)
£1779	$3345	(19-Sep-90 KH.K143/R) Fields, Vra (42x70cm-17x28in) init.88 (D.KR 20000)

ENGER, Erling (1899-) Norwegian
£1649	$2754	(4-Jun-91 BU.O16/R) Wooded landscape (38x46cm-15x18in) s.d.44 panel (N.KR 19000)
£1693	$3301	(11-Oct-90 BU.O28/R) Landscape (38x46cm-15x18in) s. panel (N.KR 19500)
£2404	$4640	(13-Dec-90 BU.O5/R) River landscape (50x70cm-20x28in) s.d.42 panel (N.KR 27000)
£3524	$6978	(29-Jan-91 UL.T157/R) Wooded landscape 1969 (65x80cm-26x31in) (N.KR 40000)

ENGERT, Erasmus von (1796-1871) Austrian
£1442	$2813	(25-Oct-90 D.V117/R) Farmhouse by pond (27x45cm-11x18in) s. (A.S 30000)

ENGERT, Ernst M (1892-?) German
£751	$1231	(18-Jun-91 FN.S1825) Still life with primulas on white table cloth before statue (66x50cm-26x20in) s. (DM 2200)
£1024	$1679	(18-Jun-91 FN.S1826) Still life with azalea and primulas on white table cloth before jug (66x50cm-26x20in) s. (DM 3000)

ENGLEHEART, George (1752-1829) British
£400	$672	(15-Jul-91 PH30) Gentleman, with powdered hair en queue, in coat, waistcoat and cravat (3x?cm-1x?in) min. gilt metal slide frame oval
£420	$706	(22-Apr-91 PH90) Portrait of gentleman wearing blue coat and white cravat (5x?cm-2x?in) min. oval frame
£450	$743	(10-Jul-91 C101/R) A gentleman in blue-bordered brown coat (3x?cm-1x?in) min. gilt-metal frame oval
£450	$743	(10-Jul-91 C136) A gentleman in mole-coloured coat (4x?cm-2x?in) min.mono. verso gold frame plaited hair oval
£620	$1042	(22-Apr-91 PH92) Portrait of lady wearing white dress and bonnet (7x?cm-3x?in) min. s.d.1799verso papier-mache frame oval
£820	$1378	(16-Jul-91 SWS1951/R) Gentleman, with powdered hair, wearing jacket and white stock and shirt (5x?cm-2x?in) min. gold frame opaline plaited hair panel oval
£1100	$2167	(1-Nov-90 S26/R) Portrait of lady wearing string of pearls in hair (8x?cm-3x?in) min.s.init.d.1806verso gilt metal frame oval
£1150	$1932	(15-Jul-91 PH31/R) Lady, with powdered hair, wearing low-cut dress, trimmed with lace (5x?cm-2x?in) min. gilt frame oval
£1250	$2100	(22-Apr-91 PH107/R) Portrait of Mrs. Emma Chalmers (5x?cm-2x?in) min.oval mounted within tortoiseshell box
£1300	$2496	(18-Dec-90 C125/R) Portrait of Edward Preston Long of Hampton Lodge (5x?cm-2x?in) min.gold frame plaited hair verso oval
£1300	$2145	(10-Jul-91 C148/R) Colonel Black (4x?cm-2x?in) min. gold frame plaited hair verso oval
£1500	$2475	(10-Jul-91 C174/R) A gentleman in black coat (8x?cm-3x?in) min.init. gold frame hair panel verso oval
£1700	$3264	(18-Dec-90 C131/R) Portrait of Officer in red uniform of Fencible Infantry (7x?cm-3x?in) min. gold frame lock of hair verso oval
£1800	$3186	(20-Mar-91 C127/R) Portrait of gentleman in blue coat with large gold buttons (5x?cm-2x?in) min. gold frame plaited hair verso oval
£2000	$3300	(10-Jul-91 C167/R) Mrs Tennant (5x?cm-2x?in) min. gold frame plaited hair verso oval
£2800	$4620	(10-Jul-91 C138/R) Mr and Mrs Stewart (6x?cm-2x?in) min.d.1781 card gilt-metal moutns oval two
£4000	$7680	(18-Dec-90 C128/R) Portrait of lady in decollete white dress with blue side panel (5x?cm-2x?in) min.gold frame split-pearl border hair oval
£4200	$8064	(18-Dec-90 C129/R) Portrait of gentleman in dark blue coat, frilled white shirt and cravat (9x?cm-4x?in) min.init.s.d.1803verso fitted leather case oval
£4600	$8142	(20-Mar-91 C129/R) Portrait of Captain Philip Brown (8x?cm-3x?in) min.s.d.April 1800 gold frame oval
£5000	$8250	(10-Jul-91 C108/R) Two girls both in white low-cut dresses facing each other (4x?cm-2x?in) min. double-sided gold locket plaited hair oval

ENGLEHEART, George (attrib) (1752-1829) British
£500	$840	(22-Apr-91 PH81/R) Portrait of Officer of the Guard (8x?cm-3x?in) min.gold frame split pearl surround oval

ENGLEHEART, George (circle) (1752-1829) British
£600	$984	(18-Jun-91 CSK9/R) Mrs Hamilton wearing large brimmed black plumed hat (5x?cm-2x?in) min. silver pendant frame oval

ENGLEHEART, George (style) (1752-1829) British
£320 $525   (18-Jun-91 CSK28/R) Lady facing left in frilled white dress and bonnet with blue ribbon (6x?cm-2x?in) min. oval

ENGLEHEART, John Cox Dillman (1782-1862) British
£750 $1238   (10-Jul-91 C60/R) A gentleman, wearing spectacles and black coat (8x?cm-3x?in) min.s.d.1827 verso blk.wood frame rec.
£2400 $3960   (10-Jul-91 C59/R) The Rev. James Kevill. Portrait of a lady, presumably his wife (8x?cm-3x?in) min.s.d.1815 ormolu frames pair

ENGLERTH (20th C) ?
£5000 $9850   (5-Oct-90 C84/R) Reclining nude (76x101cm-30x40in) s.i.d.1920

ENGLERTH, Emil (1887-?) Austrian
£872 $1701   (10-Oct-90 ZEL.L1474/R) Still life of fruit with decanter and glasses on lace table cloth (60x75cm-24x30in) s. (DM 2600)

ENGLISH PRIMITIVE SCHOOL, 19th C
£1050 $1943   (6-Mar-91 DR187/R) Portrait of prize cow (41x56cm-16x22in)
£6400 $10496   (18-Jun-91 SWS270/R) Stag hunting in grounds of castellated mansion (62x182cm-24x72in)

ENGLISH PROVINCIAL SCHOOL (?)
£1550 $2542   (18-Jun-91 SWS271/R) Classical river landscape with figures crossing bridge (97x123cm-38x48in)
£8600 $14362   (22-Jul-91 SWS1031/R) The Gibson children in the garden of the house at Southall, Middlesex (54x64cm-21x25in) c.1849

ENGLISH PROVINCIAL SCHOOL, 18th C
£2300 $4117   (14-Mar-91 ZZ.B145) A double portrait of two young children, one holding a goldfinch (118x98cm-46x39in)
£6000 $11820   (16-Nov-90 C48/R) Prospect of town with cattle and herdsmen (70x129cm-28x51in) canvas on panel

ENGLISH PROVINCIAL SCHOOL, 19th C
£1400 $2338   (22-Jul-91 SWS945/R) A gentleman in a gig on Wimbledon Common (49x59cm-19x23in)
£1500 $2460   (20-Jun-91 B23/R) Mr Thos. Cleman's South Down Wether won premium at Smithfield, 1833 (28x36cm-11x14in) i.verso
£1900 $3211   (30-Apr-91 PH65/R) Portrait of young girl teaching dog to beg (24x51cm-9x20in)
£2800 $5516   (1-Nov-90 CSK52/R) Barber's shop (76x65cm-30x26in) canvas on panel
£6200 $12214   (31-Oct-90 S349/R) Limestone quarries and lead workings at Dimminsdale, Leicestershire (68x89cm-27x35in) c.1810

ENGLISH SCHOOL (?)
£1400 $2310   (12-Jul-91 C172/R) Portrait of lady, by column and curtain, landscape beyond (121x96cm-48x38in) c.1660
£1400 $2436   (26-Mar-91 PH76/R) Portrait of a young child, holding a cap and two apples in a landscape with a still life at his feet (123x90cm-48x35in) c.1800
£1484 $2656   (8-Apr-91 ARC.P10) Paysage anime de personnages (51x61cm-20x24in) (F.FR 15000)
£1964 $3378   (14-May-91 GM.B459) Pique-nique dans le bois (190x252cm-75x99in) (B.FR 120000)
£2000 $3220   (27-Jun-91 CG63/R) Portrait of a young girl in a blue dress and pink waistband (96x71cm-38x28in) c.1820
£2000 $3800   (1-Mar-91 C19/R) Portrait of sportsman wearing waistcoat and dog in landscape (127x102cm-50x40in) c.1800
£2000 $3840   (18-Dec-90 C13/R) Portrait of Mary Killigrew (5x?cm-2x?in) min.c.1600 i.verso card gold frame oval
£2600 $4264   (19-Jun-91 CSK211) Young girl with elves in bower (144x86cm-57x34in) c.1870
£3000 $5070   (30-Apr-91 PH3/R) Figures by river with cattle before village (76x122cm-30x48in) c.1770
£3052 $5250   (15-May-91 D.NY53) Portrait of lady in pastoral landscape (127x102cm-50x40in) c.1700
£3300 $5577   (30-Apr-91 PH42/R) Portrait of young man holding rifle and pigeon. Young man beside carnations in sculpted pot (91x80cm-36x31in) c.1735 pair
£3800 $7410   (15-Jan-91 C91 a) Blenheim spaniel on cushion, landscape beyond (63x55cm-25x22in)
£4000 $6520   (4-Jul-91 PHI201/R) Norwich Cathedral Close (64x76cm-25x30in) c.1800
£8000 $14320   (12-Apr-91 C1/R) Portrait of Sir John Popham, in legal robes (91x80cm-36x31in) with i.
£8000 $13520   (30-Apr-91 PH33/R) Portrait of gentleman playing doodlesack, seated at table with two ladies (81x137cm-32x54in) c.1625
£8638 $14944   (21-May-91 SY.MI1003/R) Ritratti di fanciulle, una con un coniglio, l'altra con piccioni (27x37cm-11x15in) c.1800 pair (I.L 19000000)
£13000 $21970   (30-Apr-91 PH5/R) Figures by river before ruined castle. Figures and sailing vessels on river. Cattle resting by river (61x91cm-24x36in) c.1790 three
£18972 $32253   (27-May-91 GK.Z5028/R) Pack of hunting dogs in wooded landscape (92x116cm-36x46in) c.1800 (S.FR 48000)
£909 $1573   (21-May-91 SY.MI252/R) Ritratto di una giovane gentildonna vestita in una gonna gialla (5x?cm-2x?in) min.c.1700 oval (I.L 2000000)

ENGLISH SCHOOL (?) -cont.

£1050	$1733	(10-Jul-91 C93/R) Elizabeth and Marianne Austen as children (8x?cm-3x?in) min.c.1805 gilt-metal frame blk.wood frame oval
£1050	$1806	(15-May-91 BT54/R) Young lady, head and shoulders, wearing straw bonnet min. c.1800 gold frame hair plait back oval
£1300	$2249	(20-May-91 SWS407/R) A college from interior (25x38cm-10x15in) c.1850 W/C htd.bodycol.
£1387	$2692	(3-Dec-90 SY.F1001/R) Trompe-d'oeil con cartoline che rappresentano figure e paesaggi (35x45cm-14x18in) c.1800 W/C (I.L 3000000)
£2400	$3960	(10-Jul-91 C38/R) An officer perhaps Lt-Col.Georg von der Decken (3x?cm-1x?in) min.mounted in designed bangle with locket oval

ENGLISH SCHOOL, 16th C

£963	$1608	(6-Jun-91 D.V324/R) Portrait of gentleman (71x55cm-28x22in) panel (A.S 20000)
£5000	$8250	(10-Jul-91 S91/R) Portrait of Miss Peacocke holding prayer book (47x35cm-19x14in) l.d.1597 panel
£5294	$9000	(31-May-91 CH.NY116/R) Portrait of lady holding fan (61x77cm-24x30in)

ENGLISH SCHOOL, 17th C

£2938	$5788	(14-Nov-90 D.V275/R) Portrait of William Shakespeare aged 40 (46x37cm-18x15in) l. (A.S 60000)
£24000	$42960	(10-Apr-91 S67/R) Portrait of Thomas Butler, Earl of Ossory, standing by table (267x115cm-105x45in) l.
£1500	$2475	(11-Jul-91 S239/R) Portrait of gentleman with moustache wearing lace collar (3x?cm-1x?in) min.d.1628 card oval

ENGLISH SCHOOL, 17th/18th C

| £3800 | $7486 | (1-Nov-90 D148/R) Heraldic shield surmounted by helm on hillside, country house below (71x104cm-28x41in) l. |

ENGLISH SCHOOL, 18th C

£1100	$2156	(22-Jan-91 ZZ.B391) Three-quarter length portrait of a young girl holding flowers (89x66cm-35x26in)
£1156	$2000	(10-May-91 S.W2537/R) Portrait of William III (124x102cm-49x40in)
£1200	$2220	(4-Mar-91 PHB72) Portrait of lady, said to be Judith Weston, wife of John Norris (128x100cm-50x39in)
£1236	$2213	(10-Apr-91 CB.P28) Deux enfants lisant (38x47cm-15x19in) (F.FR 12500)
£1395	$2400	(15-May-91 D.NY92 a) Portrait of young girl with dog in garden (84x58cm-33x23in)
£1700	$2771	(4-Jul-91 B33) Portrait of a gentleman, three-quarter length, wearing a red waistcoat (122x94cm-48x37in)
£2005	$3930	(12-Feb-91 GM.B583/R) Cormoran devant une ville chinoise (78x60cm-31x24in) (B.FR 120000)
£2046	$3539	(21-May-91 SY.MI1024) Ritratto di gentiluomo a tre quarti di figura (110x91cm-43x36in) (I.L 4500000)
£2179	$4250	(24-Oct-90 D.NY42) On the way to market (38x64cm-15x25in) panel
£2793	$5000	(11-Apr-91 SY.NY177/R) Portrait of Major General Richard Montgomery (74x61cm-29x24in) in painted oval
£3000	$5700	(1-Mar-91 C17/R) Portrait of gentleman holding letter and landscape beyond (122x96cm-48x38in) c.1760 shaped top
£3175	$5683	(13-Mar-91 GK.Z17/R) Dogs and cat scrapping in wine cellar (71x91cm-28x36in) (S.FR 8000)
£3189	$5422	(30-May-91 F.M8) Ritratto di gentiluomo. Ritratto di gentildonna (76x65cm-30x26in) pair (I.L 7000000)
£3743	$6250	(23-Jan-91 D.NY66/R) Knight of Order of Garter (76x64cm-30x25in)
£4000	$6600	(12-Jul-91 C104/R) Equestrian portrait of gentleman, in landscape (82x90cm-32x35in) l.
£909	$1573	(21-May-91 SY.MI228/R) Ritratto di una madre e figlio, la donna vestita in bianco e blu (7cm-3ins circular) min. (I.L 2000000)
£1000	$1650	(11-Jul-91 S90/R) Indians attacking schooner upon lake Erie in which they were defeated (22x34cm-9x13in) l. pen ink W/C over pencil
£1000	$1650	(11-Jul-91 S295/R) Portrait of Captain Sir Jacob Wheate (4x?cm-2x?in) min. gold frame oval
£1500	$2955	(1-Nov-90 S20) Five portraits of gentlemen with tightly curled wigs min. oil on copper gilt frame one oval
£1800	$2970	(9-Jul-91 C33 a/R) Marble Palace, St Petersberg (41x59cm-16x23in) l.verso pencil W/C
£2400	$4296	(9-Apr-91 C41) Study of man writing (21x16cm-8x6in) c.1730 chk
£2400	$3960	(9-Jul-91 C44/R) Prospect of Vanbrugh Castle with shipping. St Luke's Church Charlton (43x67cm-17x26in) pencil pen ink W/C two

ENGLISH SCHOOL, 18th/19th C

£1906	$3279	(16-May-91 ANS.M99/R) Retrato de joven (76x60cm-30x24in) (S.P 350000)
£3401	$5476	(28-Jun-91 BM.B627/R) Portrait of greyhound standing in landscape (85x130cm-33x51in) l. (DM 10000)
£3741	$6024	(28-Jun-91 BM.B627 a/R) Portrait of greyhound standing in landscape (85x130cm-33x51in) l. (DM 11000)

ENGLISH SCHOOL, 19th C

£986	$1676	(28-May-91 AB.S4840/R) Man and donkey by building with children and dogs (45x36cm-18x14in) panel (S.KR 10500)
£1000	$1680	(26-Apr-91 ARC.P13/R) La jeune laitiere (120x108cm-47x43in) (F.FR 10000)
£1000	$1950	(15-Jan-91 C133/R) Otter hounds (46x61cm-18x24in) canvas on board
£1000	$1770	(21-Mar-91 CSK174) Greenwich from the hill (30x43cm-12x17in)

ENGLISH SCHOOL, 19th C -cont.

£1000	$1630	(4-Jul-91 B12/R) A terrier standing beside a rabbit (37x45cm-15x18in) panel
£1000	$1850	(4-Mar-91 PHB29/R) Corn mill (50x61cm-20x24in)
£1043	$1700	(5-Jul-91 S.W3023/R) Portrait of a bulldog (28x36cm-11x14in) indist.sig. panel
£1100	$1793	(13-Jun-91 CSK312) Portrait of lady, standing in garden with dog and flamengo at side (248x164cm-98x65in)
£1122	$2200	(21-Nov-90 NA.BA66) Portrait of a lady (146x114cm-57x45in) after Reynolds
£1143	$2217	(8-Dec-90 GAB.G2089) Portrait d'une elegante (76x63cm-30x25in) (S.FR 2800)
£1150	$1898	(9-Jul-91 PH189) Brathe Hall, near Furness (71x92cm-28x36in) l.verso
£1156	$2000	(21-May-91 CE.NY117/R) Full sail (28x40cm-11x16in) mono.d.1859
£1183	$2000	(20-Apr-91 WOL.C191 a/R) Preparing game (74x53cm-29x21in)
£1200	$2280	(1-Mar-91 C92/R) Capriccio of ruined abbey with visitors (96x71cm-38x28in) c.1840
£1200	$2220	(7-Mar-91 D59/R) Portrait of officer in red tunic (74x61cm-29x24in)
£1200	$2220	(4-Mar-91 PHB74) Portrait of Caroline Lady Stamer and son, Lovelace (148x114cm-58x45in)
£1221	$2100	(17-May-91 WOL.C277/R) Portrait of a young girl with a dove (36x28cm-14x11in) s.d.1860 panel
£1272	$2200	(21-May-91 CE.NY80/R) Extensive river landscape with houses in distance (62x76cm-24x30in)
£1329	$2166	(12-Jun-91 GM.B4101) Troupeau se desalterant (80x100cm-31x39in) (B.FR 80000)
£1400	$2478	(21-Mar-91 CSK252/R) The slave market (51x41cm-20x16in) indist.sig.
£1500	$2685	(10-Apr-91 CSK330/R) The wounded soldier (132cm-52ins circular)
£1514	$2604	(14-May-91 GF.L2470/R) Travelling artist with animals (54x64cm-21x25in) (S.FR 3800)
£1521	$3012	(30-Jan-91 APT.P310/R) L'accordeur de violon (23x30cm-9x12in) l. panel (F.FR 15000)
£1600	$2640	(9-Jul-91 PH137) Portrait of Clementine Cooper and sister, daughters of Edwin Butler (92x72cm-36x28in)
£1600	$2608	(3-Jul-91 PLF.P64/R) Portrait de jeune femme sous un arbre sur fond de paysage (118x93cm-46x37in) (F.FR 16000)
£1600	$3040	(1-Mar-91 C95/R) Prospect of Midlands village (63x91cm-25x36in) indis.s.d.1855
£1608	$3087	(19-Feb-91 ARC.P24) Cheval au pre (64x79cm-25x31in) (F.FR 16000)
£1700	$2788	(20-Jun-91 B19/R) Italianate landscape (73x91cm-29x36in)
£1800	$2934	(13-Jun-91 CSK196) Chestnut foal in landscape (114x140cm-45x55in)
£1812	$3153	(25-Mar-91 SY.F659) La colazione (62x83cm-24x33in) panel (I.L 4000000)
£2000	$3900	(15-Jan-91 C62/R) Portrait of little boy seated holding wild rose with spitz in landscape (76x95cm-30x37in) canvas on board
£2000	$3300	(9-Jul-91 PH185) Figures resting in extensive landscape, sea beyond (58x77cm-23x30in) indist.l.verso
£2000	$3260	(13-Jun-91 CSK285/R) Ponte della Paglia, with Palazzo Ducale and Bridge of Sighs, Venice (61x91cm-24x36in) with sig.
£2200	$3630	(10-Jul-91 S156/R) Sir Robert Hamilton's Camp, Dewas, India c.1857 (25x35cm-10x14in) l.verso board
£2200	$3674	(24-Jul-91 CSK39 a) Portrait of Lt J Scott Hodgson of the Shropshire Yeomanry (239x145cm-94x57in)
£2500	$4750	(1-Mar-91 C46/R) Portrait of George Simmons with servants, lurchers and fox in landscape (106x136cm-42x54in) s.i.d.1845verso
£2500	$4075	(3-Jul-91 PLF.P68/R) La caleche (59x73cm-23x29in) s.d.1873 (F.FR 25000)
£2865	$5530	(12-Dec-90 F.M298) Cascata di Tivoli (63x92cm-25x36in) (I.L 6200000)
£2917	$4958	(27-May-91 SY.J606/R) Man-of-war in Table Bay (29x40cm-11x16in) gouache (SA.R 14000)
£3200	$6272	(15-Feb-91 N375/R) Brother and sister on garden terrace with dog (69x61cm-27x24in) c.1825
£3400	$6698	(16-Nov-90 C23/R) Portrait of Lord Godolphin as child holding branch with dog in landscape (129x101cm-51x40in)
£3500	$6895	(1-Nov-90 CSK51/R) Fighting cock (61x91cm-24x36in)
£3800	$7410	(24-Oct-90 S132/R) A Negro smoking a pipe standing beside a tierce (44x29cm-17x11in) panel
£3800	$7410	(18-Oct-90 CSK75/R) The 'Kongen af Danmark' and other frigates, thought to be in Bombay Harbour (68x92cm-27x36in)
£3800	$6384	(16-Jul-91 C168/R) Bichon frise (63x81cm-25x32in)
£3968	$7103	(13-Mar-91 GK.Z17 a/R) Brown stallion in wooded landscape (100x125cm-39x49in) (S.FR 10000)
£5800	$11426	(1-Nov-90 CSK25/R) In hot pursuit of fox (102x127cm-40x50in)
£5890	$10248	(25-Mar-91 SY.F668) Ritratto di donna (212x147cm-83x58in) (I.L 13000000)
£6000	$11700	(26-Oct-90 C274/R) A coach and four on a country lane with Burton Constable beyond (52x107cm-20x42in)
£12717	$22000	(22-May-91 D.NY6/R) Young girl with spaniel (152x102cm-60x40in) bears sig.d.1812
£13185	$26105	(30-Jan-91 APT.P145/R) Anne Boleyn (129x162cm-51x64in) (F.FR 130000)
£909	*$1782*	*(22-Nov-90 SY.MI28/R) Paesaggio con figure (38x54cm-15x21in) s. W/C (I.L 2000000)*
£1000	*$1650*	*(9-Jul-91 C101) Cintra (18x24cm-7x9in) pencil W/C htd.gum arabic*
£1050	*$1806*	*(15-May-91 BT146/R) View from the terrace, Dale Park, Sussex (58x99cm-23x39in) W/C*
£1096	*$1841*	*(23-Apr-91 CH.R103/R) Venere seduta su un drappo con amorini con ghirlande (16x?cm-6x?in) min. ivory (I.L 2400000)*

ENGLISH SCHOOL, 19th C -cont.

£1200	$2364	(13-Nov-90 C79/R) Incident in the Peninsular War (61x114cm-24x45in) c.1815 pencil pen ink W/C
£2000	$3360	(26-Apr-91 ARC.P8/R) Promenade dans la campagne (47x87cm-19x34in) s. crayon W/C (F.FR 20000)
£2569	$4985	(9-Dec-90 ZZ.F9/R) Portrait de femme (59x44cm-23x17in) pastel oval (F.FR 25000)
£2742	$5402	(14-Nov-90 F.M31/R) Trompe l'oeil con testate di giornali, carte da gioco e strumenti (51x72cm-20x28in) W/C (I.L 6000000)
£3000	$5850	(18-Oct-90 CSK35/R) H.M.S. Tartar (86x108cm-34x43in) i. pencil pen W/C

ENGLISH SCHOOL, 19th/20th C

£957	$1800	(18-Sep-90 RO.BA193) Landscape with animals (33x46cm-13x18in)
£5851	$11000	(18-Sep-90 RO.BA19/R) Hunting dogs (53x64cm-21x25in) two

ENGLISH SCHOOL, 20th C

£1500	$2925	(15-Jan-91 B149/R) White Lap dog in interior (30x41cm-12x16in)
£2260	$4000	(22-Mar-91 S.W2885) Floral still life (130x89cm-51x35in)
£1087	$1892	(25-May-91 SY.F611) Barca a vapore (46x78cm-18x31in) gouache (I.L 2400000)

ENGLISH, F F (1854-1922) American

£783	$1300	(11-Jan-91 DM.D2264/R) Farm wagon (38x74cm-15x29in) s. W/C

ENGLISH, Frank F (1854-1922) American

£342	$650	(28-Feb-91 MFA.C196) Summer lake scene (33x58cm-13x23in) s. W/C
£526	$1000	(28-Feb-91 MFA.C93) Horse and buggy on a country road (33x58cm-13x23in) s. W/C
£983	$1700	(21-May-91 CE.NY400/R) Dawn (76x50cm-30x20in) s. W/C paper on board
£2402	$4300	(11-Apr-91 FA.PH942/R) Hay wagon (36x74cm-14x29in) s. W/C
£2821	$5500	(20-Oct-90 FA.PH902/R) Converting apples into cider (51x71cm-20x28in) s. gouache

ENGSTROM, Albert (1869-1940) Swedish

£402	$720	(17-Mar-91 BU.M204) Comic drawing (28x41cm-11x16in) s. i.verso Indian ink (S.KR 4300)
£2294	$4518	(13-Nov-90 AB.S358/R) Skipper Mattson and painting of ship (57x70cm-22x28in) s. pastel (S.KR 25000)

ENGSTROM, Leander (1886-1927) Swedish

£5535	$10627	(27-Nov-90 BU.S81/R) Town scene (62x43cm-24x17in) s.d.1913 (S.KR 60000)
£6458	$12399	(27-Nov-90 BU.S80/R) Palace chappel in Jonkoping (54x43cm-21x17in) panel (S.KR 70000)
£7841	$15055	(27-Nov-90 BU.S79/R) Fjord landscape. Still life of fruit in bowl (59x68cm-23x27in) s. double-sided (S.KR 85000)
£12915	$24797	(27-Nov-90 BU.S78/R) Bunch of rays over the town (53x68cm-21x27in) s. (S.KR 140000)
£29194	$56636	(4-Dec-90 BA.S116/R) Nude woman (89x113cm-35x44in) s.d.1911 (S.KR 315000)
£32437	$62929	(4-Dec-90 BA.S117/R) Landscape, Salangenfjord (87x74cm-34x29in) s. panel (S.KR 350000)
£91752	$177998	(4-Dec-90 BA.S115/R) Nude girl on the shore by mountain lake (92x73cm-36x29in) s. (S.KR 990000)
£1038	$1795	(22-May-91 BA.S38/R) Harbour in Viareggio (86x104cm-34x41in) s.d.1922 pencil (S.KR 11000)
£2780	$5394	(4-Dec-90 BA.S118/R) Three women. Dancers (49x45cm-19x18in) s. W/C pair (S.KR 30000)

ENGSTROM, Martin (1952-) Scandinavian

£1698	$2938	(22-May-91 BA.S358/R) 'Peon' (167x121cm-66x48in) s.d.1988 (S.KR 18000)

ENJOLRAS, Delphin (1857-1945) French

£1980	$3505	(6-Apr-91 GL.P43/R) La bulle de savon (21x16cm-8x6in) s. panel (F.FR 20000)
£1980	$3505	(6-Apr-91 GL.P42/R) Le deshabille (22x16cm-9x6in) s. panel (F.FR 20000)
£5780	$10000	(21-May-91 CE.NY339/R) Tea at dusk (61x73cm-24x29in) s.
£6018	$11735	(10-Oct-90 ARC.P65/R) Odalisque au miroir (60x93cm-24x37in) s. (F.FR 60000)
£6579	$12895	(25-Nov-90 P.V36/R) Premiers apprets (46x33cm-18x13in) s. (F.FR 65000)
£7455	$12599	(21-Apr-91 DA.R2) La soiree sur la terrasse (60x73cm-24x29in) s. (F.FR 75000)
£6219	$12126	(12-Oct-90 APT.P97/R) Ballerine dans sa loge (53x36cm-21x14in) s. pastel (F.FR 62000)
£6219	$12126	(12-Oct-90 APT.P96/R) L'elixir (53x36cm-21x14in) s. pastel (F.FR 62000)

ENNEKING, J J (1841-1916) American

£600	$1200	(10-Feb-91 LIT.L51) Landscape (30x51cm-12x20in) s.
£612	$1200	(27-Jan-91 LIT.L15a) Landscape (30x51cm-12x20in) s.

ENNEKING, John J (1841-1916) American

£550	$1100	(7-Feb-91 B.P73/R) Skating at sunset (20x43cm-8x17in) s.d. panel
£938	$1800	(17-Dec-90 SY.NY42/R) Autumn landscape (25x46cm-10x18in) s. board
£960	$1900	(30-Jan-91 GRO.B51/R) The bridge at twilight (46x61cm-18x24in) s. i. stretcher
£1065	$1800	(17-Apr-91 D.NY48/R) North shore at twilight (20x30cm-8x12in) s.d.78 board

ENNEKING, John J (1841-1916) American-cont.
£1269	$2500	(16-Nov-90 S.BM145/R) Forest brook (51x61cm-20x24in)
£1546	$3000	(24-Aug-90 RB.HY151/R) Autumn sunset (30x36cm-12x14in) s. panel
£1795	$3500	(25-Oct-90 GRO.B131/R) Summer landscape (36x51cm-14x20in) s.
£2023	$3500	(10-May-91 S.BM82/R) Apple blossoms (23x36cm-9x14in) s. l.verso board
£2734	$5250	(17-Dec-90 SY.NY51/R) Sailing in Venice (36x56cm-14x22in) s.indist.d.
£3299	$6500	(16-Nov-90 S.BM107/R) Potatoe harvesters (46x66cm-18x26in) s.d.77
£3727	$6000	(25-Jun-91 JRB.C6/R) December thaw (30x36cm-12x14in) s. board
£3827	$7500	(24-Nov-90 RB.HY215/R) Autumn landscape (51x61cm-20x24in) s.
£4054	$7500	(8-Mar-91 S.BM167/R) Still life with zinnias (56x46cm-22x18in) s.d.'77
£4211	$8000	(14-Sep-90 S.BM229/R) Autumnal woods (51x61cm-20x24in) s.
£4290	$7250	(17-Apr-91 D.NY88) Unfinished symphony (71x102cm-28x40in) s. l.stretcher
£5030	$8500	(20-Apr-91 WOL.C31/R) Fall landscape at dusk (61x84cm-24x33in) s.d.78
£7107	$14000	(16-Nov-90 S.BM96/R) Apple and cherry blossoms (56x76cm-22x30in) s.d.01
£15625	$30000	(30-Nov-90 CH.NY70/R) Evening glow (107x159cm-42x63in) s.d.91

ENNEKING, Joseph Elliot (20th C) American
| £535 | $1000 | (30-Aug-90 MFA.C105) Harbour scene (36x28cm-14x11in) s. board |

ENNESS, Augustus William (1876-1948) British
| £580 | $945 | (3-Jul-91 RBB756) Children close to haystacks beside country lane, Pulborough (23x33cm-9x13in) s.d.1919 l.verso panel |
| £1305 | $2558 | (11-Feb-91 SY.J420/R) St. James Park (62x75cm-24x30in) s. (SA.R 6500) |

ENNION, Eric (?) ?
| £1400 | $2688 | (19-Feb-91 C108/R) Pintail (38x53cm-15x21in) s. pencil W/C htd.white |

ENNS, Maureen (1943-) Canadian
| £1092 | $2151 | (12-Nov-90 HO.ED322) Heavenly daze II (127x91cm-50x36in) s.l.indist.d.1975 acrylic (C.D 2500) |

ENOCK, Arthur Henry (fl.1869-1910) British
£400	$672	(18-Jul-91 PHX396/R) Calm on the River Dark, Nr.Dittisham (33x51cm-13x20in) s. W/C
£400	$716	(13-Mar-91 B103) Sunrise over the river Dart (33x51cm-13x20in) s. W/C htd.white
£400	$708	(22-Mar-91 T156) Near Poundsgate, Dartmoor (43x64cm-17x25in) s.
£550	$1056	(17-Dec-90 PH9) Teignmouth Harbour, S Devon (34x52cm-13x20in) s. l.verso W/C
£600	$1074	(13-Mar-91 B102) A view across the river Dart (33x51cm-13x20in) s. W/C htd.white
£1300	$2574	(30-Jan-91 S212/R) Totnes on Dart, twilight (51x75cm-20x30in) s. indist.s.l.verso W/C

ENOTRIO (20th C) ?
| £772 | $1522 | (30-Oct-90 F.R76) Paesaggio calabrese (60x50cm-24x20in) s. panel (I.L 1700000) |

ENRIQUE, J (19th C) ?
| £1300 | $2535 | (22-Oct-90 SWS26/R) In the park (30x53cm-12x21in) s.d.1880 |

ENS, Carl (style) (1802-1865) German
| £1573 | $3037 | (12-Dec-90 N.M502/R) Hunting party resting (50x57cm-20x22in) l. (DM 4500) |

ENSLER, J (19th C) Austrian
| £1120 | $1893 | (1-May-91 GD.B246/R) Mill by the edge of wood (67x105cm-26x41in) s. (S.FR 2800) |

ENSOR, James (1860-1949) Belgian
£36007	$60491	(23-Apr-91 C.A100/R) Sourires d'oeillets, caresses de marguerites (16x22cm-6x9in) s. panel (B.FR 2200000)
£52588	$102547	(23-Oct-90 C.A372/R) The dying Christ (50x60cm-20x24in) s. (B.FR 3200000)
£83333	$160000	(18-Dec-90 GM.B4117/R) Nature morte a l'eventail japonais (47x66cm-19x26in) s. (B.FR 5000000)
£1000	$1690	(1-May-91 GD.B1426/R) Wettrennen skuriler Gestalten (13x18cm-5x7in) s. pencil (S.FR 2500)
£1929	$3800	(13-Nov-90 CE.NY224/R) Poupeline, Demoiselle de Magasin (27x23cm-11x9in) s.i.d.1911 wax crayons over pencil
£3944	$7691	(23-Oct-90 C.A374/R) Figures au silex (14x22cm-6x9in) s.d.1920 coloured drawing (B.FR 240000)
£11457	$19247	(23-Apr-91 C.A101/R) The game of chess (19x27cm-7x11in) s. colour dr. (B.FR 700000)
£15358	$30102	(24-Nov-90 VG.B101/R) Josua arretant le soleil (17x22cm-7x9in) s.d.1885 pencil (DM 45000)
£18000	$28980	(25-Jun-91 C218/R) Etude de jeune garcon (57x47cm-22x19in) s.d.90 chl W/C wash

ENSOR, Mary (19th C) British
| £680 | $1108 | (2-Jul-91 SWS265/R) Turkeys, chickens and ducks in farmyard (58x89cm-23x35in) s.d.1862 |
| £1000 | $1960 | (13-Feb-91 S115/R) Bird's nest (23x31cm-9x12in) s. board |

ENZINGER, Hans (1889-1972) Austrian
| £634 | $1174 | (7-Mar-91 D.V188/R) The coach trip (8x8cm-3x3in) s. panel (A.S 13000) |

582

ENZINGER, Hans (1889-1972) Austrian-cont.
£750 $1208   (27-Jun-91 CG94/R) Austrian cavalryman in a farmyard (9x12cm-4x5in) s. panel
£868 $1693   (18-Oct-90 D.V112/R) Horse-drawn coach with figures before farmstead (8x8cm-3x3in) s. tempera panel (A.S 18000)
£1053 $1821   (8-May-91 D.V63/R) Horse-drawn cart in village street (11x14cm-4x6in) s. panel (A.S 22000)
£1061 $2069   (18-Oct-90 D.V113/R) Outing in horse-drawn sledge (8x9cm-3x4in) s. tempera panel (A.S 22000)
£1460 $2861   (24-Jan-91 D.V135/R) End of the shoot (14x18cm-6x7in) s. panel (A.S 30000)
£1460 $2861   (24-Jan-91 D.V134/R) The wood transport (14x18cm-6x7in) s. panel (A.S 30000)
£2879 $4952   (16-May-91 D.V3/R) Village scene (17x29cm-7x11in) s.d.1907 panel (A.S 60000)
£955   *$1862*   *(11-Oct-90 D.V209/R) Perchtoldsdorf covered in snow (21x27cm-8x11in) s.d.39 W/C htd.white (A.S 20000)*
£1363   *$2671*   *(24-Jan-91 D.V133/R) Arrival (17x8cm-7x3in) s. mixed media panel (A.S 28000)*

EPP, Rudolf (1834-1910) German
£3265 $6400   (6-Nov-90 GF.L2101/R) Portrait of young girl (56x47cm-22x19in) s.d.93 (S.FR 8000)
£3322 $6411   (12-Dec-90 N.M504/R) Bavarian girl wearing costume with hat and bunch of violets (56x37cm-22x15in) s.d.1909 (DM 9500)
£5594 $10797   (10-Dec-90 L.K417/R) Young woman and child watching boy holding goat (33x25cm-13x10in) s. (DM 16000)
£5897 $11500   (23-Oct-90 SY.NY354/R) Portrait of peasant girl (29x22cm-11x9in) s. panel
£7895 $15000   (28-Feb-91 CH.NY79/R) Feeding the lamb (96x67cm-38x26in) s.
£12238 $23619   (12-Dec-90 N.M503/R) Young peasant woman and baby seated at table with small daughter (71x58cm-28x23in) s.d.1856 (DM 35000)
£13873 $24000   (22-May-91 SY.NY39/R) Intruder (81x61cm-32x24in) s.d.97

EPPER, Ignaz (1892-1969) Swiss
£15079 $25183   (5-Jun-91 SY.Z101/R) Landscape with railway track and tunnel (60x50cm-24x20in) mono. double-sided (S.FR 38000)
£476   *$795*   *(7-Jun-91 ZOF.Z1315) Das Abendmahl (19x26cm-7x10in) chl (S.FR 1200)*
£514   *$874*   *(27-May-91 GK.Z5574) Supper (32x28cm-13x11in) s. chl (S.FR 1300)*
£556   *$928*   *(5-Jun-91 SY.Z106/R) Southern landscape with steam train (31x43cm-12x17in) s.d.32 W/C (S.FR 1400)*
£791   *$1344*   *(27-May-91 GK.Z5571) Railway track with view of town (33x25cm-13x10in) s. col.pencil (S.FR 2000)*
£880   *$1716*   *(17-Oct-90 G.Z9/R) Harbour (28x32cm-11x13in) col.pencil (S.FR 2200)*
£952   *$1648*   *(25-May-91 AB.L181/R) Boats in harbour (18x24cm-7x9in) col.pencil (S.FR 2400)*
£1143   *$2171*   *(14-Sep-90 ZOF.Z1064/R) Beach landscape near La Spezia (24x42cm-9x17in) s.d.1931 W/C (S.FR 2800)*
£1186   *$2016*   *(27-May-91 GK.Z5323/R) Harbour town (38x50cm-15x20in) s.d.1924 pastel (S.FR 3000)*
£1205   *$2024*   *(24-Apr-91 G.Z52/R) Landwasser in Davos (38x49cm-15x19in) s.d.1923 pastel (S.FR 3000)*
£1347   *$2653*   *(16-Nov-90 GK.Z5352) Riverside town (28x32cm-11x13in) s. col.pencil (S.FR 3300)*
£1448   *$2506*   *(25-May-91 AB.L182/R) Fair with carousel (26x19cm-10x7in) chl (S.FR 3650)*

EPSTEIN, Henri (1892-1944) Polish
£1542 $2991   (8-Dec-90 LT.P127/R) Rue animee aupres de Notre-Dame (56x46cm-22x18in) s. (F.FR 15000)
£1692 $3300   (10-Oct-90 SY.NY156/R) Man with hat (61x46cm-24x18in) s.
£1841 $3203   (25-Mar-91 PLF.P43/R) Nature morte aux fruits (54x73cm-21x29in) s. (F.FR 18500)
£2077 $3718   (14-Apr-91 GL.P202) La famille (50x65cm-20x26in) s. (F.FR 21000)
£2176 $3895   (14-Apr-91 GL.P182) Paysanne allongee (50x61cm-20x24in) s. (F.FR 22000)
£2371 $4030   (2-Jun-91 LT.P81/R) Paysage aux promeneurs (65x81cm-26x32in) s. (F.FR 23800)
£2488 $4328   (25-Mar-91 PLF.P44/R) Paysage (65x81cm-26x32in) s. (F.FR 25000)
£3579 $6048   (17-Apr-91 LGB.P53/R) Le village (46x61cm-18x24in) s.d.1917 (F.FR 36000)
£5200 $10192   (26-Jan-91 PSA.W7) Self-portrait (61x46cm-24x18in) s. (P.Z 97000000)
£397   *$683*   *(17-May-91 LGB.P125) Un port (50x64cm-20x25in) s. W/C (F.FR 4000)*
£825   *$1625*   *(29-Oct-90 LC.P126) Hameau breton en bordure de mer (33x55cm-13x22in) s. W/C traces crayon (F.FR 8100)*

EPSTEIN, Jehudo (1870-1946) Polish
£989 $1771   (14-Apr-91 GL.P193) Canal a Venise la nuit (64x77cm-25x30in) s. panel (F.FR 10000)
£1227 $2000   (12-Jun-91 GG.TA18/R) Seascape (85x56cm-33x22in) s.
£1952 $3612   (7-Mar-91 D.V83/R) Violin player with daughter (40x26cm-16x10in) s.d.1903 (A.S 40000)
£3000 $5160   (17-May-91 C46/R) Recital (75x109cm-30x43in) s.d.1922
£4337 $8500   (12-Feb-91 SY.NY105/R) Studying the Torah (89x81cm-35x32in) s.d.1926
£8042 $15521   (12-Dec-90 WE.MU111/R) The melon seller (168x233cm-66x92in) s.d.1910 (DM 23000)

EPSTEIN, Sir Jacob (1880-1959) British

£480	$811	(3-May-91 PHE112/R) Portrait study of Jackie (56x44cm-22x17in) s. pencil
£480	$811	(3-May-91 PHE113/R) Portrait study of Jackie with apple (57x43cm-22x17in) s. pencil
£520	$998	(21-Feb-91 B25) Portrait of Ernest Gye (30x23cm-12x9in) s. pencil
£675	$1167	(25-May-91 AB.L132/R) Two heads (34x28cm-13x11in) s. pencil (S.FR 1700)
£682	$1295	(12-Sep-90 WO.CO6) In the park (53x69cm-21x27in) gouache (E.P 750)
£800	$1392	(28-Mar-91 CSK21/R) Reclining female nude (37x56cm-15x22in) s. chl brown chk
£850	$1437	(2-May-91 C127/R) Song of songs (35x45cm-14x18in) pencil
£900	$1755	(18-Oct-90 CSK263/R) Portrait of the artist's son, Jackie (58x44cm-23x17in) s. pencil
£1350	$2282	(2-May-91 C126/R) Christmas tree (53x40cm-21x16in) s. gouache sequins paper on canvas
£1500	$2535	(2-May-91 C125/R) Epping Forest (43x56cm-17x22in) s. gouache
£1500	$2535	(3-May-91 PHE77/R) Study of fir trees (57x44cm-22x17in) s. pencil W/C
£1500	$2535	(3-May-91 PHE76/R) Still life of red and yellow roses (57x44cm-22x17in) s. pencil W/C
£1500	$2610	(27-Mar-91 S75/R) Reclining nude (43x56cm-17x22in) s. pencil
£1700	$2873	(2-May-91 C124/R) Theydon Bois, Epping forest (56x43cm-22x17in) s. gouache
£1800	$3132	(27-Mar-91 S76/R) Reclining nude (41x56cm-16x22in) s. pencil W/C
£1909	$3627	(12-Sep-90 WO.CO5) The Valley Farm (56x66cm-22x26in) gouache (E.P 2100)
£2200	$4136	(20-Sep-90 C130/R) Flowers (56x43cm-22x17in) s. gouache
£2500	$4225	(1-May-91 PHL91/R) Magnolia (56x43cm-22x17in) s. gouache
£2500	$4725	(24-Sep-90 CSK257/R) Hollyhocks (56x43cm-22x17in) s. W/C
£2700	$4563	(3-May-91 PHE110/R) Epping Forest (57x44cm-22x17in) s. pencil W/C
£2900	$5684	(6-Nov-90 PH106/R) White roses (56x43cm-22x17in) s. gouache
£3000	$5550	(7-Mar-91 C62/R) Epping forest (56x43cm-22x17in) s. gouache
£3500	$6090	(27-Mar-91 S86/R) Epping Forest (56x43cm-22x17in) s. gouache
£3800	$7448	(6-Nov-90 PH105/R) Peonies and poppies (56x44cm-22x17in) s. gouache
£4200	$7896	(20-Sep-90 C108/R) Roses and summer flowers (56x42cm-22x17in) s. gouache
£4500	$7830	(28-Mar-91 CSK169/R) Dahlias (56x38cm-22x15in) s. pencil bodycol W/C
£8000	$15600	(10-Oct-90 S42/R) Poppies, anemones and peonies. Poppies and stocks (56x43cm-22x17in) s. gouache pair
£10000	$19600	(6-Nov-90 PH108/R) Study for Birth (62x52cm-24x20in) pencil chk

EPWORTH, Hans (after) (?) ?

£1600	$3072	(29-Nov-90 HB530/R) Thomas Cromwell, Earl of Essex, seated at writing table (198x147cm-78x58in) l.

EQUIPO CRONICA (20th C) Spanish

£41130	$69098	(25-Apr-91 EP.M23/R) El expresionismo en la calle (200x200cm-79x79in) s.d.71 acrylic (S.P 7500000)

ERAM, O (18th C) ?

£1589	$3084	(5-Dec-90 KH.K38) Romantic landscapes with gods and shepherds (53x77cm-21x30in) s.d.1793 pair (D.KR 17500)

ERAUD, Marius (20th C) French

£786	$1533	(26-Oct-90 PPB.P93) Entree du Port de Marseille (15x21cm-6x8in) s. (F.FR 7800)

ERB, Erno (20th C) Polish?

£643	$1273	(1-Feb-91 DE.B4) Market scene (28x38cm-11x15in) s. board (P.Z 12000000)
£1373	$2430	(23-Mar-91 HO.P1) View of the Tatra Mountains (60x80cm-24x31in) s.d. (P.Z 23500000)

ERBA, Carlo (1884-1917) Italian

£1623	$2905	(9-Apr-91 F.R104/R) Studio di nudo (31x24cm-12x9in) s. pencil (I.L 3600000)
£3403	$5852	(13-May-91 CH.R13/R) Notturno (22x25cm-9x10in) mono. chl (I.L 7500000)

ERBE, Paul (1894-1972) German

£1104	$1865	(19-Apr-91 FN.S1707) Still life of fished on plate, bread, litre jug and glass on cloth (40x50cm-16x20in) s. canvas on board (DM 3300)

ERBE, Robert (1844-1903) German

£671	$1309	(10-Oct-90 WE.MU196/R) Chasing off the intruder (24x32cm-9x13in) s.d.1888 W/C (DM 2000)

ERBEN, Ulrich (1940-) German

£1024	$2007	(20-Nov-90 L.K211/R) Birten 83 IV (137x96cm-54x38in) s.d.1983 paper collage (DM 3000)

ERBSLOH, Adolf (1881-1947) German

£8621	$16552	(28-Nov-90 KF.M702/R) Park with roof of Calenberg school (24x34cm-9x13in) board (DM 25000)

ERCHOV, Youri (1927-) Russian

£765	$1468	(29-Nov-90 YC.P168/R) Au marche (73x105cm-29x41in) s.d.1953 (F.FR 7500)

ERDMANN, Moritz (1845-1919) Austrian

£1509	$2611	(22-May-91 BA.S542 a/R) Harvest time (30x44cm-12x17in) s. mixed media (S.KR 16000)

ERDMANN, Otto (1834-1905) German
£2048 $3870   (25-Sep-90 FN.S2162/R) Gentleman holding lady's hand in interior of
     castle (69x53cm-27x21in) s.i. (DM 6000)

ERDTMANN, Elias (1862-1945) Swedish
£872 $1717   (13-Nov-90 AB.S360/R) Ljungberg in evening, Halland skerries
     (78x132cm-31x52in) s.d.1918 (S.KR 9500)
£1376 $2711   (13-Nov-90 AB.S359/R) Landscape from Vastervik's skerries, summer
     sunshine (52x112cm-20x44in) s. (S.KR 15000)

ERFMANN, Ferdinand (1908-1968) Dutch
£1786 $3500   (12-Feb-91 SY.NY68/R) Nightclub (69x66cm-27x26in) s.d.1943

ERHARDT, Johann Christoph (1795-1822) German
£372 $632   (31-May-91 GB.B5751) Traveller by farmstead in mountains (16x21cm-6x8in)
     s.i. pencil (DM 1100)
£507 $861   (31-May-91 GB.B5750) Three women in garden by well (15x19cm-6x7in)
     i.d.1812 pencil (DM 1500)
£567 $1014   (12-Apr-91 AW.H588/R) Wooded rock with view of Danube (18x20cm-7x8in)
     s.d.1818 pencil (DM 1700)

ERICHSEN, Thorvald (1868-1939) Norwegian
£2120 $4240   (9-Feb-91 BU.O53) Landscape (31x41cm-12x16in) s. panel (N.KR 24000)
£2137 $4125   (12-Dec-90 BU.O16/R) Landscape (32x41cm-13x16in) s.d.1916 (N.KR 24000)
£2315 $4468   (12-Dec-90 BU.O17/R) Landscape with animal (31x38cm-12x15in) s.d.1915
     panel (N.KR 26000)
£2315 $4468   (10-Dec-90 B.O27/R) Landscape from Kviteseid (26x35cm-10x14in) init.
     panel (N.KR 26000)
£3299 $5509   (3-Jun-91 B.O36/R) Landscape from Holmsbu (46x53cm-18x21in) s.d.1936
     panel (N.KR 38000)
£8205 $16000   (23-Oct-90 SY.NY221/R) An interior at Lillehammer (37x46cm-15x18in)
     init.d.'29 board
£9231 $18000   (23-Oct-90 SY.NY219/R) Landscape at Stoa (64x80cm-25x31in) s.d.1919
£14000 $22960   (19-Jun-91 S325/R) Village in autumn (60x72cm-24x28in) s.d.39
£19625 $38073   (4-Dec-90 UL.T205/R) Landscape from Dovre wood 1927 (75x93cm-30x37in)
     (N.KR 220000)
£20000 $34400   (17-May-91 C170/R) Wooded lake landscape (90x101cm-35x40in) s.d.1910
£33072 $58538   (19-Mar-91 UL.T162/R) Tulips (82x65cm-32x26in) (N.KR 380000)

ERICHSEN, Vigilius (1722-1782) Danish
£1795 $3537   (14-Nov-90 RAS.K830/R) Portrait of Katharina the Great of Russia
     (23x18cm-9x7in) s. red chk (D.KR 20000)

ERICHSEN, Vigilius (attrib) (1722-1782) Danish
£16000 $31200   (10-Oct-90 C199/R) Portrait of Catherine the Great wearing the Sash and
     Diamond Star of Order of St.Andrew (66x52cm-26x20in)

ERICSON, Johan (1849-1925) Swedish
£1278 $2148   (24-Apr-91 BA.S51/R) Visby town wall (55x45cm-22x18in) s.d.1898 panel
     (S.KR 13500)
£1371 $2687   (20-Nov-90 GO.G49) Bohuslan coastal landscape with figures
     (38x60cm-15x24in) s.d.1919 (S.KR 15000)
£1463 $2867   (20-Nov-90 GO.G47) Lake landscape with cottage in moonlight
     (55x45cm-22x18in) s.d.1890 panel (S.KR 16000)
£2102 $4121   (20-Nov-90 GO.G50) Street scene from Marstrand with Carlsten Castle
     (61x50cm-24x20in) s.d.1918 panel (S.KR 23000)
£2194 $4300   (20-Nov-90 GO.G46) Winter landscape with Carlsten Castle, Marstrand
     (31x38cm-12x15in) s. panel (S.KR 24000)
£4388 $8600   (20-Nov-90 GO.G52/R) Westcoast scene with boats by boathouses
     (55x75cm-22x30in) s.d.24 (S.KR 48000)
£5119 $10033   (20-Nov-90 GO.G51 a/R) Boats and boathouses - fishing village from the
     westcoast (50x73cm-20x29in) s.d.1920 (S.KR 56000)
£5941 $11645   (20-Nov-90 GO.G53/R) Coastal landscape with houses (55x72cm-22x28in) s.
     (S.KR 65000)
£5948 $10647   (9-Apr-91 GO.G35/R) Walking in the avenue, Meudon, France
     (55x45cm-22x18in) s. panel (S.KR 64000)
£5948 $10647   (9-Apr-91 GO.G33/R) Fishing village, Bohuslan (75x120cm-30x47in)
     s.d.1919 (S.KR 64000)
£6250 $10500   (24-Apr-91 BA.S52/R) Farmhouses in Marstrand (61x91cm-24x36in) s.
     (S.KR 66000)
£7353 $14412   (6-Nov-90 BA.S55/R) Field of flowers with Marstrand church in background
     (89x71cm-35x28in) s.d.1909 (S.KR 80000)

ERIKSEN, Bjarne (1882-1970) Norwegian?
£890 $1719   (10-Dec-90 B.O28/R) Landscape from Filtvedt (50x61cm-20x24in) s.d.1944
     panel (N.KR 10000)
£1043 $1762   (4-May-91 BU.O31) Garden seat by the sea (53x40cm-21x16in) s. panel
     (N.KR 12000)
£4007 $7814   (15-Oct-90 B.O23/R) Landscape (118x113cm-46x44in) s.d.1911 (N.KR 46000)
£4378 $7837   (14-Mar-91 BU.O26/R) Woman and man in landscape (108x119cm-43x47in) s.
     (N.KR 50000)

ERIKSEN, Hans (20th C) Scandinavian
£619 $1164   (10-Aug-90 RAS.V458/R) Interior from Nyborg Palace (60x60cm-24x24in)
     init. (D.KR 7000)
£2000 $3440   (17-May-91 C138/R) Interior (61x61cm-24x24in) mono. s.d.1940 verso board

ERIKSEN, Lars (?) Norwegian
£573	$1134	(29-Jan-91 UL.T159) Spring (81x101cm-32x40in) (N.KR 6500)

ERIKSEN, Sigurd (1884-1976) Norwegian?
£521	$870	(3-Jun-91 B.O38/R) House and garden (57x67cm-22x26in) s.d.1927 (N.KR 6000)
£521	$881	(4-May-91 BU.O39) Two children in landscape (50x55cm-20x22in) s. (N.KR 6000)
£565	$954	(4-May-91 BU.O36) Winter (38x46cm-15x18in) s. panel (N.KR 6500)
£608	$1028	(4-May-91 BU.O38) Landscape (40x55cm-16x22in) s. panel (N.KR 7000)
£608	$1028	(4-May-91 BU.O37) Archipelago (38x46cm-15x18in) s. panel (N.KR 7000)
£712	$1375	(13-Dec-90 BU.O8/R) View from Akershus (47x42cm-19x17in) s.d.1955 (N.KR 8000)
£781	$1305	(3-Jun-91 B.O40/R) View of Akers river (55x66cm-22x26in) s.d.1959 (N.KR 9000)
£876	$1567	(14-Mar-91 BU.O28/R) Winter landscape (32x42cm-13x17in) s.d.1941 panel (N.KR 10000)
£883	$1767	(9-Feb-91 BU.O56) Summer landscape 1956 (38x46cm-15x18in) s. panel (N.KR 10000)
£963	$1724	(14-Mar-91 BU.O29/R) Landscape from Lommedalen (55x66cm-22x26in) s.d.1966 (N.KR 11000)
£963	$1724	(11-Mar-91 B.O29/R) Landscape with woman wearing blue dress (54x52cm-21x20in) s. landscape verso (N.KR 11000)
£972	$1943	(9-Feb-91 BU.O55) Winter landscape (33x41cm-13x16in) s. panel (N.KR 11000)
£1135	$2157	(11-Sep-90 UL.T194) By the porch (47x42cm-19x17in) s.d.1955 (N.KR 13000)
£1259	$2454	(11-Oct-90 BU.O31/R) From Lommedalen (83x70cm-33x28in) s.d.1936 i.verso (N.KR 14500)
£1270	$2273	(14-Mar-91 BU.O27/R) Coastal landscape (48x55cm-19x22in) s. (N.KR 14500)
£1302	$2539	(11-Oct-90 BU.O33/R) Two figures on rocks (36x45cm-14x18in) s. (N.KR 15000)
£1336	$2578	(13-Dec-90 BU.O9/R) From Asgardstrand (38x45cm-15x18in) s.d.1964 i.verso panel (N.KR 15000)
£1476	$2878	(11-Oct-90 BU.O32/R) Landscape in green and blue (50x56cm-20x22in) s. (N.KR 17000)
£1781	$3437	(13-Dec-90 BU.O7/R) Woman in landscape (99x84cm-39x33in) s.d.1919 (N.KR 20000)
£1959	$3781	(10-Dec-90 B.O30/R) Sailboat by jetty (55x67cm-22x26in) s.d.1952 (N.KR 22000)
£2404	$4640	(10-Dec-90 B.O29/R) Red house by the sea (66x73cm-26x29in) s.d.1948 (N.KR 27000)
£2787	$5436	(15-Oct-90 B.O24/R) Street scene, Storgaten, Oslo (73x87cm-29x34in) s.d.1939 (N.KR 32000)
£3125	$6094	(11-Oct-90 BU.O30/R) Street scene, Son, Norway (73x62cm-29x24in) s.d.1936 (N.KR 36000)
£8905	$17186	(13-Dec-90 BU.O6/R) In the garden (112x128cm-44x50in) s.d.1943 i.verso (N.KR 100000)

ERIXSON, Sven (1899-1970) Scandinavian
£927	$1798	(4-Dec-90 BA.S120/R) Theater couple (43x34cm-17x13in) s. panel (S.KR 10000)
£1131	$1911	(21-Apr-91 BU.M6) Boy resting (32x40cm-13x16in) s.d.43 panel (S.KR 12000)
£1384	$2657	(27-Nov-90 BU.S85/R) Evening, Nybroviken (30x38cm-12x15in) s. (S.KR 15000)
£1502	$2554	(28-May-91 AB.S5199/R) Stones on beach (40x57cm-16x22in) s. (S.KR 16000)
£1509	$2611	(22-May-91 BA.S50 a/R) Field of flowers (24x34cm-9x13in) s. (S.KR 16000)
£1604	$2775	(22-May-91 BA.S45/R) Alley in Paris (65x50cm-26x20in) s.d.29 cardboard (S.KR 17000)
£1871	$3349	(17-Mar-91 BU.M80) Woman in garden (45x37cm-18x15in) s. panel (S.KR 20000)
£2066	$3512	(28-May-91 AB.S5200/R) Composition with margueritas (32x40cm-13x16in) s. panel (S.KR 22000)
£2264	$3917	(22-May-91 BA.S44/R) Still life of flowers (31x30cm-12x12in) s.d.43 panel (S.KR 24000)
£2273	$3818	(27-Apr-91 SO.S325/R) Evening view with Arc de Triumphe (45x54cm-18x21in) s. (S.KR 24000)
£2317	$4495	(4-Dec-90 BA.S128/R) Roadwork in Urvadersgrand (31x23cm-12x9in) s.d.32 panel (S.KR 25000)
£2453	$4243	(22-May-91 BA.S44 a/R) Harvesters at work (54x55cm-21x22in) s. (S.KR 26000)
£2583	$4959	(27-Nov-90 BU.S84/R) Driving coal (71x70cm-28x28in) s.d.1950 (S.KR 28000)
£2595	$5034	(4-Dec-90 BA.S129/R) The new water tower (31x43cm-12x17in) s. (S.KR 28000)
£2830	$4896	(22-May-91 BA.S42/R) Katarina bridge (51x62cm-20x24in) s. (S.KR 30000)
£3019	$5223	(22-May-91 BA.S43/R) Kaseberga harbour (47x66cm-19x26in) s. (S.KR 32000)
£3707	$7192	(4-Dec-90 BA.S127/R) Lilan and her dad stealing logs (38x36cm-15x14in) s.d.40 panel (S.KR 40000)
£4053	$6809	(27-Apr-91 SO.S324/R) Figures on the beach (53x70cm-21x28in) s.d.50 (S.KR 42800)
£4078	$7911	(4-Dec-90 BA.S125/R) Spiral staircase in Alcala (73x57cm-29x22in) s.d.1935 (S.KR 44000)
£4078	$7911	(5-Dec-90 AB.S7070/R) Evening landscape with white house by road (73x92cm-29x36in) s.d.1930 (S.KR 44000)

ERIXSON, Sven (1899-1970) Scandinavian-cont.
£4263	$8271	(4-Dec-90 BA.S126/R) Prince of the North (52x45cm-20x18in) s.d.34 panel (S.KR 46000)
£5472	$9466	(22-May-91 BA.S50 b/R) Harvesting landscape (63x74cm-25x29in) s.d.29 (S.KR 58000)
£6919	$13284	(27-Nov-90 BU.S82/R) Coastal landscape, East Skane (65x81cm-26x32in) s.d.1934 (S.KR 75000)
£8764	$16827	(27-Nov-90 BU.S83/R) Canal lock. Interior (106x122cm-42x48in) s. l.verso double-sided (S.KR 95000)
£10565	$20497	(4-Dec-90 BA.S123/R) Irma in her pram in October (65x54cm-26x21in) s.d.37 (S.KR 114000)
£455	$764	(27-Apr-91 SO.S326/R) Still life of flowers (23x31cm-9x12in) s. W/C (S.KR 4800)
£660	$1142	(22-May-91 BA.S48/R) Shore scene from above (25x33cm-10x13in) s. W/C (S.KR 7000)
£708	$1224	(22-May-91 BA.S50/R) In the garden (28x33cm-11x13in) s.d.68 gouache (S.KR 7500)
£1158	$2247	(4-Dec-90 BA.S119/R) Gondolas (34x43cm-13x17in) s.d.1930 gouache (S.KR 12500)
£1174	$1995	(28-May-91 AB.S5201/R) Composition with figures (25x33cm-10x13in) s.d.1949 mixed media (S.KR 12500)
£1321	$2285	(22-May-91 BA.S46/R) Northern power-lines (45x60cm-18x24in) s.d.65 mixed media (S.KR 14000)
£1390	$2697	(5-Dec-90 AB.S7071/R) Fire in spring (61x68cm-24x27in) s. mixed media (S.KR 15000)
£1761	$3416	(4-Dec-90 BA.S121/R) Shore scene with boats and figures (36x56cm-14x22in) s.d.68 gouache (S.KR 19000)

ERLER, Erich (1870-1946) German
£870	$1427	(18-Jun-91 FN.S1578/R) Shepherd and goats by gate with village and mountain range at sunset (100x85cm-39x33in) s. (DM 2550)
£1689	$2922	(25-May-91 N.M79/R) Sunday, seated peasant women in interior of Alpine dairy farm (96x96cm-38x38in) s. (DM 5000)

ERLER, Fritz (1868-1940) German
£878	$1520	(25-May-91 N.M80) Young girl with rose (56x44cm-22x17in) s. (DM 2600)

ERMELS, Georg Paul (17/18th C) German
£20000	$33800	(17-Apr-91 S3/R) Arcadian landscapes with figures near classical ruins (35x36cm-14x14in) panel painted circles made up corners pair

ERNI, Hans (1909-?) Swiss
£5556	$9278	(5-Jun-91 SY.Z159/R) Cat with tabouret (58x96cm-23x38in) s.d.53 s.l.d.verso (S.FR 14000)
£7738	$13310	(19-May-91 ZZ.F184/R) Couple jouant (48x53cm-19x21in) s.d.1967 (F.FR 78000)
£516	$892	(25-May-91 AB.L191/R) Dancer from Balette Russe (25x18cm-10x7in) s.l. W/C pen (S.FR 1300)
£632	$1075	(27-May-91 GK.Z5577) Portrait of girl (21x14cm-8x6in) ink (S.FR 1600)
£680	$1149	(1-May-91 GD.B1429/R) Orpheus, poster study for International Music Festival, Luzern 1964 (65x50cm-26x20in) s.d.62 indian ink brush (S.FR 1700)
£1036	$2020	(24-Oct-90 GD.B1451/R) Female faces (29x26cm-11x10in) s. white dr. (S.FR 2600)
£1315	$2564	(24-Oct-90 GD.B1454/R) Figure of male without shoes (54x22cm-21x9in) s.d.43 india ink (S.FR 3300)
£2538	$5000	(13-Nov-90 CE.NY151/R) Danseuse (53x42cm-21x17in) s.d.64 W/C
£10612	$20800	(6-Nov-90 GF.L2276/R) Archimede et Alethee (66x97cm-26x38in) s.d.41 mixed media (S.FR 26000)

ERNI, Paul (1917-) Swiss
£677	$1321	(24-Oct-90 GD.B1461/R) Wetterhorner (26x17cm-10x7in) mono.l. d.1983verso pentel wash (S.FR 1700)

ERNST, Alfred von (1799-1850) Swiss
£1275	$2486	(24-Oct-90 GD.B328/R) View of Po plain (54x82cm-21x32in) s.d.1888 (S.FR 3200)

ERNST, Helge (1916-) Danish
£789	$1342	(29-May-91 KH.K234/R) Composition (48x54cm-19x21in) init. (D.KR 9000)
£848	$1569	(5-Mar-91 RAS.K38) Still life (38x55cm-15x22in) s.d.1989verso (D.KR 9500)
£890	$1745	(22-Nov-90 RAS.V818/R) Town by the Mediterranean (65x100cm-26x39in) s. (D.KR 10000)
£890	$1673	(19-Sep-90 KH.K114) 'Strommende former' (115x163cm-45x64in) init. (D.KR 10000)
£890	$1745	(22-Nov-90 RAS.V817/R) Composition (65x88cm-26x35in) init.i.d. (D.KR 10000)
£974	$1851	(14-Sep-90 RAS.V726/R) Table by window (81x54cm-32x21in) init. s.d.1976verso (D.KR 11000)
£2105	$3579	(29-May-91 KH.K233/R) Still life (60x73cm-24x29in) init. (D.KR 24000)
£2952	$5785	(13-Feb-91 KH.K56/R) Still life (73x100cm-29x39in) s. (D.KR 33000)

ERNST, Jimmy (1920-?) American
£867	$1700	(12-Feb-91 SY.NY363/R) Red blue sound (20x25cm-8x10in) s.l.d.67verso masonite

ERNST, Jimmy (1920-?) American-cont.

£582	$1100	(25-Sep-90 CE.NY266/R) Illumination No 4 (20x30cm-8x12in) s.d.71 gouache
£613	$1000	(12-Jun-91 SY.NY191/R) Quasars II (62x62cm-24x24in) s.d.67 mixed media assemblage
£794	$1500	(25-Sep-90 CE.NY265/R) Dayscape I (46x61cm-18x24in) s.d.64 i. verso gouache
£952	$1800	(25-Sep-90 CE.NY263/R) Abstract (20x15cm-8x6in) s.d.52 W/C gouache ink paper laid down on board
£1481	$2800	(25-Sep-90 CE.NY264/R) High water (57x77cm-22x30in) s.d.57 W/C gouache pen

ERNST, Max (1891-1976) German

£62712	$104729	(7-Jun-91 HN.H16/R) Fleurs (19x24cm-7x9in) s. (DM 185000)
£92486	$160000	(7-May-91 SY.NY32/R) Foret (61x46cm-24x18in) s.
£104995	$201590	(28-Nov-90 CSC.P79/R) Nautile, coquillage sur fond vert (39x44cm-15x17in) s. (F.FR 1030000)
£122867	$240819	(23-Nov-90 VG.B60/R) Fleurs sur fond vert (65x81cm-26x32in) s.d.1928 canvas laid down (DM 360000)
£130000	$209300	(25-Jun-91 C34/R) Soleil esquimau (55x46cm-22x18in) s.d.56 s.i.d.verso
£152284	$300000	(13-Nov-90 SY.NY57/R) Alice envole des messages aux poissons (102x83cm-40x33in) s.d.64
£173410	$300000	(8-May-91 CH.NY45/R) La mare aux grenouilles (60x73cm-24x29in) s. i. verso
£210000	$338100	(24-Jun-91 C34/R) Vol nuptial (81x65cm-32x26in) s.i. i.d.1931verso
£240000	$386400	(25-Jun-91 S35/R) Landscape with lake and chimeras (51x66cm-20x26in) s.
£444162	$875000	(13-Nov-90 SY.NY55/R) Le cimetiere des oiseaux (100x81cm-39x32in) s.
£480000	$772800	(25-Jun-91 S31/R) Foret et soleil (81x100cm-32x39in) s.
£3000	$5850	(19-Oct-90 C156 c/R) Les chiens ont soif (41x29cm-16x11in) s. felt pen wax crayon
£3000	$5850	(19-Oct-90 C156 b/R) Motif d'oiseau (39x32cm-15x13in) s. chl.frottage
£3553	$7000	(2-Oct-90 CH.NY189/R) Tete d'homme (33x26cm-13x10in) s. col.wax crayons
£8219	$13397	(15-Jun-91 L.K181/R) Head (29x25cm-11x10in) s. pastel frottage (DM 24000)
£8428	$16349	(7-Dec-90 GL.P204/R) Sans titre (16x12cm-6x5in) s. gouache crayon (F.FR 82000)
£9122	$15507	(30-May-91 SY.BE101/R) Illustration for cover of Bousquet's and Ernst's Partition (27x22cm-11x9in) s.d.49 collage indian ink pen (DM 27000)
£11451	$21986	(27-Nov-90 SY.MI205/R) Untitled, Per Lewis Carroll (38x31cm-15x12in) s. frottage paper (I.L 25000000)
£15291	$29511	(16-Dec-90 GL.P53/R) Entre deux eaux (35x28cm-14x11in) pastel paper laid down on canvas (F.FR 150000)
£17919	$31000	(8-May-91 SY.NY171/R) La comete affolee (32x49cm-13x19in) s.d.51 pastel
£34682	$60000	(8-May-91 SY.NY190/R) Huits portraits sectraux (60x49cm-24x19in) s.i. pencil W/C oil collage
£39054	$75766	(5-Dec-90 ZZ.F207/R) La porte du ciel s.d.1974 rubbing col.chk. pastel (F.FR 380000)

ERNST, Otto (1884-1967) Swiss

£1673	$2878	(14-May-91 GF.L2558/R) Cherry blossoms near Barmelhof (46x61cm-18x24in) s. (S.FR 4200)

ERNST, Rudolph (1854-1932) Austrian

£2105	$4000	(27-Feb-91 SY.NY150/R) Pearl necklace (79x61cm-31x24in) s.d.1880
£4500	$8865	(5-Oct-90 C176/R) Study of tiger (28x36cm-11x14in) panel
£5172	$9931	(17-Dec-90 ARC.P135/R) La fileuse, Maroc (33x23cm-13x9in) s. panel (F.FR 51000)
£11500	$22080	(28-Nov-90 S212/R) On guard (50x61cm-20x24in) s. panel
£20000	$37200	(4-Sep-90 OT403/R) Antique dealers - Arab street bazaar scene (60x49cm-24x19in) s. board
£25126	$41206	(19-Jun-91 ZZ.F57/R) L'Ecole Arabe (93x70cm-37x28in) s. panel (F.FR 250000)
£27457	$47500	(22-May-91 SY.NY49/R) Evening prayer (81x63cm-32x25in) s. panel

ERRO (1932-) Icelandic

£4532	$7387	(16-Jun-91 CC.P84) Sans titre (100x69cm-39x27in) s.d.1989 verso acrylic (F.FR 45000)
£7560	$14743	(26-Oct-90 CC.P58/R) Moyen - Orient (150x195cm-59x77in) acrylic (F.FR 75000)
£8222	$15951	(9-Dec-90 CC.P58/R) Sans titre (115x100cm-45x39in) s.d.1987-1988 verso acrylic (F.FR 80000)
£480	$782	(4-Jul-91 GL.P207) Comment developper votre memoire (31x23cm-12x9in) s.d.1959 collage (F.FR 4800)

ERRO, Gudmundur (1932-) Icelandic

£3036	$5951	(20-Nov-90 BG.P34 b/R) Composition Leger-Picasso (30x42cm-12x17in) s.d.1985 verso acrylic (F.FR 30000)
£3041	$5017	(10-Jul-91 FB.P118/R) La justice (100x73cm-39x29in) s.d.1988 verso acrylic (F.FR 30500)
£3061	$6031	(16-Nov-90 FB.P411/R) Ardy Castle (100x65cm-39x26in) s.i.d.1980 verso acrylic (F.FR 30000)
£4247	$8281	(21-Oct-90 P.V74/R) Sans titre (100x65cm-39x26in) s.d.1989 verso oil lacquered (F.FR 42000)
£4286	$8443	(16-Nov-90 FB.P86/R) Serie Wonder Woman (100x73cm-39x29in) s.i. verso acrylic (F.FR 42000)
£4482	$7620	(2-Jun-91 GL.P190/R) Personnages aux bulles (100x73cm-39x29in) s.d.1989 verso (F.FR 45000)

ERRO, Gudmundur (1932-) Icelandic-cont.

£4800	$7824	(5-Jul-91 APT.P116/R) Superman (64x99cm-25x39in) s.i.d.1982 verso acrylic (F.FR 48000)
£5080	$8635	(2-Jun-91 GL.P198/R) Appetit Kandinsky (86x75cm-34x30in) s.d.sept.63 acrylic (F.FR 51000)
£5102	$10051	(16-Nov-90 FB.P71/R) Of the fantastic four (100x73cm-39x29in) s.d.1987 verso acrylic (F.FR 50000)
£18330	$36110	(29-Oct-90 FB.P90/R) All power (195x130cm-77x51in) s.d.1974 verso (F.FR 180000)
£602	$970	(30-Jun-91 I.N8) Sans titre (14x12cm-6x5in) s. collage board (F.FR 6000)
£688	$1349	(21-Nov-90 C.P27/R) Save our child (100x65cm-39x26in) s.d.1958 verso gouache (F.FR 6800)
£771	$1495	(5-Dec-90 HC.P82/R) Programme spatial, 1976 (37x22cm-15x9in) collage (F.FR 7500)
£925	$1794	(5-Dec-90 HC.P81/R) Pinocchio et Modigliani (26x39cm-10x15in) s.d.1960 collage (F.FR 9000)
£961	$1873	(15-Oct-90 CSC.P82) Porgramme spacial (21x33cm-8x13in) s.d.1975 collage board (F.FR 9500)
£1815	$3538	(23-Oct-90 CSC.P90/R) Sans titre (57x77cm-22x30in) s.d.8/9/89 felt pen paper laid down on panel (F.FR 18000)

ERTE (1892-1990) Russian

£1363	$2358	(7-May-91 F.M115) Final, la femme (34x24cm-13x9in) s. i.verso tempera (I.L 3000000)
£495	$876	(6-Apr-91 GL.P23) La soubrette (29x24cm-11x9in) s. gouache (F.FR 5000)
£516	$887	(13-May-91 PPB.P10) Lumiere noire (13x20cm-5x8in) s. gouache (F.FR 5200)
£1386	$2453	(6-Apr-91 GL.P14) Robe de cocktail (37x26cm-15x10in) s. gouache (F.FR 14000)
£1400	$2366	(3-May-91 S270/R) Shop window design for Holproof Hosiery, USA (7x11cm-3x4in) gouache
£1526	$2961	(3-Dec-90 F.M308/R) Si voux voyagez par chemin de fer. Si vous voyagez par auto (17x17cm-7x7in) s.d.1923 i.verso indian ink cardboard pair (I.L 3300000)
£2168	$4250	(12-Feb-91 SY.NY78/R) Waltzer Traum (36x28cm-14x11in) s. i.d.1958verso gouache pencil
£2374	$4250	(15-Mar-91 DM.D1348/R) Cosmopolitan illustration depicting single figure of man, couple behind (15x8cm-6x3in) s. st.ink board
£2821	$5500	(10-Oct-90 SY.NY127/R) Joseph, cadre de scene et rideau (25x38cm-10x15in) s.i.d.1944 st.studio verso gouache
£2959	$5830	(18-Nov-90 S.S43/R) Jean Foucaud, auberge du chat coiffe (27x22cm-11x9in) s. gouache (F.FR 29000)
£3061	$6031	(18-Nov-90 S.S42/R) Orchester feminin (36x26cm-14x10in) s. gouache (F.FR 30000)
£4190	$7500	(15-Mar-91 DM.D1349/R) Harper's Bazaar illustration depicting five art deco style women (30x25cm-12x10in) s. st.ink
£5918	$11659	(18-Nov-90 S.S38/R) Lucky doll - wishbone (37x29cm-15x11in) s. d.1926 vero (F.FR 58000)

ERTE (studio) (1892-1990) Russian

£407	$813	(6-Feb-91 FB.P110) Hercule (37x27cm-15x11in) i. verso gouache studio of Erte (F.FR 4000)
£457	$915	(6-Feb-91 FB.P111) Les nouvelles, la nouvelle caldeonie (37x26cm-15x10in) i. verso gouache studio do Erte (F.FR 4500)

ERTE, Romain de Tirtoff (1892-1990) Russian

£2200	$3586	(1-Jul-91 APT.P6/R) Les fleurs d'oranger (38x27cm-15x11in) s.i. gouache (F.FR 22000)
£2500	$4075	(1-Jul-91 APT.P11/R) L'eunuque, les derniers jours de Don Juan (30x23cm-12x9in) s. i. verso gouache (F.FR 25000)
£2700	$4401	(1-Jul-91 APT.P7/R) L'Opera Fedora (33x29cm-13x11in) s. gouache (F.FR 27000)
£3500	$5705	(1-Jul-91 APT.P13/R) Princesse (39x23cm-15x9in) s. d.Avril 1921 verso gouache (F.FR 35000)
£3800	$6194	(1-Jul-91 APT.P10/R) Femme fatale, esclave de Salomon (38x29cm-15x11in) s. i.d.1926 verso (F.FR 38000)
£4000	$6520	(1-Jul-91 APT.P1) Le roi des legendes (39x29cm-15x11in) s. i.d.1919 verso gouache (F.FR 40000)
£4000	$6520	(1-Jul-91 APT.P2/R) La princesse Aline (29x20cm-11x8in) s. gouache (F.FR 40000)
£4000	$6520	(1-Jul-91 APT.P1/R) Lucky doll, four-feal clover-trefle (39x31cm-15x12in) s. i.d.1926 verso gouache (F.FR 40000)
£4028	$6566	(12-Jun-91 ZZ.F118) Costume pour Maitresse de ceremonies (29x27cm-11x11in) s. i.d.21 avril 1922 verso gouache (F.FR 40000)
£4028	$6566	(12-Jun-91 ZZ.F111) Costume pour Gaby Deslys (36x27cm-14x11in) s. i.d.1915 verso gouache (F.FR 40000)
£4200	$6846	(1-Jul-91 APT.P3/R) Robe de soiree (43x29cm-17x11in) s. d.1927 verso gouache (F.FR 42000)
£4800	$7824	(1-Jul-91 APT.P19/R) Contes Hindou (29x39cm-11x15in) s. gouache (F.FR 48000)
£5000	$8150	(1-Jul-91 APT.P16) Martha (29x22cm-11x9in) s. i.d.XI 1924 verso gouache (F.FR 50000)
£7000	$11410	(1-Jul-91 APT.P5/R) Conte Hindou (29x47cm-11x19in) s. i.d.1922 verso gouache (F.FR 70000)
£7000	$11410	(1-Jul-91 APT.P4/R) Rideau de scene, Ave Maria (26x37cm-10x15in) s. gouache (F.FR 70000)
£11000	$17930	(1-Jul-91 APT.P15/R) Femme (37x27cm-15x11in) s. gouache (F.FR 110000)

ERTEL, Hans (19th C) ?
£749 $1251   (6-Jun-91 RAS.K41/R) Small boy smoking at the greengrocer's (80x53cm-31x21in) s. (D.KR 8500)

ES, Jacob van (1596-1666) Flemish
£41176 $70000   (31-May-91 CH.NY83/R) Plate with prawns and roll, bowl with olives and glass on table (32x40cm-13x16in) s. copper

ES, Jacob van (circle) (1596-1666) Flemish
£5128 $10000   (11-Oct-90 SY.NY52/R) Still life of bread, olives and game on plates and glass of wine on table (26x38cm-10x15in) panel

ES, Jacob van (style) (1596-1666) Flemish
£2200 $4180   (13-Sep-90 CSK313/R) Still life of fruit, cooked lobster, silver beaker and flagon on drapedtable (46x89cm-18x35in) panel
£3000 $5790   (11-Dec-90 PH240/R) Still life of bowl of walnuts with roemer, strawberries and grapes on ledge (48x56cm-19x22in)

ESAM, Arthur (1850-?) Australian
£1086   *$1835*   *(16-Apr-91 J.M83) The coach stop (19x30cm-7x12in) s.d.1887 W/C (A.D 2400)*
£1176   *$1988*   *(16-Apr-91 J.M34/R) Bailed up (22x37cm-9x15in) s.d.1887 W/C (A.D 2600)*
£1357   *$2294*   *(16-Apr-91 J.M290/R) Coach and Horse Hotel (25x42cm-10x17in) s.d.1885 W/C (A.D 3000)*

ESCHARD, Charles (1748-1810) French
£714   *$1370*   *(27-Nov-90 APT.P221/R) Paysage anime de personnages (26x29cm-10x11in) i. pen wash (F.FR 7000)*

ESCHBACH, Paul Andre Jean (1881-1961) French
£500 $815   (4-Jul-91 LT.P21) Les grandes voiles (50x61cm-20x24in) s. (F.FR 5000)
£711 $1423   (6-Feb-91 FB.P112/R) Eglise sous la neige (53x45cm-21x18in) s. (F.FR 7000)
£813 $1505   (6-Mar-91 APT.P104) Honfleur, la sortie du port a maree basse (50x62cm-20x24in) s. (F.FR 8100)
£1095 $1894   (12-May-91 T.B117/R) Honfleur, voiliers rentrant au port (50x61cm-20x24in) s. (F.FR 11000)
£1631 $3148   (16-Dec-90 T.B128/R) Retour de peche a Concarneau (61x81cm-24x32in) s. (F.FR 16000)

ESCHER, E A von (20th C) ?
£664 $1282   (13-Dec-90 N.M2681) View of St Moritz (54x70cm-21x28in) s.d.1933 i.verso (DM 1900)

ESCHKE, Hermann (1823-1900) German
£1149 $2240   (26-Oct-90 BM.B775/R) View out to the sea with figures, Rugen (32x49cm-13x19in) s.i.d.85 board (DM 3400)

ESCHKE, Richard-Hermann (1859-1944) German
£1000 $1960   (8-Nov-90 PHI201) Goats in mountain landscape (91x120cm-36x47in) s.
£2027 $3446   (31-May-91 GB.B5757/R) Girl picking flowers in the Spreewald (49x70cm-19x28in) s. (DM 6000)
£4907 $9421   (29-Nov-90 D.V12/R) Sprewald landscape, evening (63x90cm-25x35in) s.d.96 i.verso (A.S 100000)

ESCHWEGE, Elmar von (1856-1935) German
£874 $1687   (14-Dec-90 BM.B606 a/R) Goats and shepherdess returning from the summer farm in the mountains (65x89cm-26x35in) s. s.i.verso board (DM 2500)
£5137 $9195   (13-Mar-91 N.M483/R) Riders hunting falcons in wooded lake landscape (105x220cm-41x87in) s.d.1884 (DM 15000)

ESKILSON, Per (1820-1872) Swedish
£1195 $2342   (10-Nov-90 FAL.M89/R) Boy on rocky shore (37x44cm-15x17in) s. (S.KR 13000)
£2000 $3440   (17-May-91 C155/R) Portrait (36x45cm-14x18in) s. with photograph pair

ESMONDE-WHITE, Eleanore (1914-) South African
£864 $1659   (26-Nov-90 SY.J363/R) Two women with cloth (39x50cm-15x20in) s. (SA.R 4200)

ESPALTER Y RULL, Joaquin (1809-1880) Spanish
£8197 $16066   (24-Jan-91 EP.M34/R) Retrato de Manuel y Matilde Alvarez Amoros (140x80cm-55x31in) s.d.1853 (S.P 1500000)

ESPERLING, Joseph (1707-1775) Swiss
£22750 $44363   (17-Oct-90 LC.P44/R) L'Adoration des mages. L'Adoration des bergers (60x42cm-24x17in) both s. pair (F.FR 225000)

ESPINOSA, Juan Bautista de (attrib) (fl.1616-1626) Spanish
£28205 $55000   (11-Oct-90 SY.NY58/R) Still life of meat pie, fruit and knife on table and fruit hanging above (58x81cm-23x32in)

ESPLANDIU, Juan (1901-1978) Spanish
£1502 $2598   (8-May-91 FER.M88/R) Corrida en la plaza del pueblo (60x71cm-24x28in) s.d.1958 (S.P 275000)

ESPOSITO, Gaetano (1858-1911) Italian
£1375 $2694   (16-Feb-91 GF.H12) Italian landscape with view of village and mountains beyond (32x45cm-13x18in) s. (DM 4000)

ESPOY, Angel (20th C) American
£1020 $2000   (13-Feb-91 B.SF2090/R) Sunset at sea (66x81cm-26x32in) s.
£1403 $2750   (13-Feb-91 B.SF2148/R) Desert foothills (76x102cm-30x40in) s.

ESQUIVEL, Antonio Maria de (1806-1857) Spanish
£1450 $2523   (25-Mar-91 SY.F664) Ritratto di dama con cagnolino (210x146cm-83x57in) l. (I.L 3200000)
£1626 $3172   (17-Oct-90 FER.M149/R) Retrato de nino (50x41cm-20x16in) (S.P 300000)
£2595 $5008   (11-Dec-90 FER.M182/R) Tobias y el Angel (183x127cm-72x50in) (S.P 475000)
£2602 $5075   (17-Oct-90 FER.M148/R) Retrato de joven (61x50cm-24x20in) s. (S.P 480000)
£19241 $34442   (13-Mar-91 FER.M167/R) La caida de Luzbel (274x202cm-108x80in) s.d.1840 (S.P 3500000)

ESSCHE, Maurice van (1906-1977) South African
£1055 $1741   (8-Jul-91 SY.J296/R) Five Congolese women (50x39cm-20x15in) s. board (SA.R 5000)
£1793 $2959   (8-Jul-91 SY.J295) Congolese women with pots (90x72cm-35x28in) s. (SA.R 8500)
£1263 $2135   (15-Apr-91 SY.J473/R) Three women in landscape (50x36cm-20x14in) s.d.66 gouache (SA.R 6000)

ESSELENS, Jacob (1626-1687) Dutch
£1529 $3012   (12-Nov-90 CH.AM37/R) Mountainous river landscape with monastery, city beyond (17x20cm-7x8in) black chk pen (D.FL 5000)

ESSELENS, Jacob (attrib) (1626-1687) Dutch
£7485 $12650   (2-May-91 CH.AM80/R) A coastal landscape with a huntsman conversing with a peasant woman (38x59cm-15x23in) (D.FL 25000)

ESSEN, Cornelis van (17/18th C) Dutch
£1500 $3000   (7-Feb-91 C101/R) A hunting party on a path at the edge of a wood (29x37cm-11x15in) init.
£1600 $2704   (16-Apr-91 PH175/R) Horsemen outside farrier's shop (21x23cm-8x9in) panel
£4000 $7800   (26-Oct-90 C110/R) Carthorses offered fodder outside a village inn (82x101cm-32x40in) init.
£4200 $6846   (3-Jul-91 S250/R) Peasants and riders by inn (58x73cm-23x29in) s.

ESSEN, Johannes Cornelis (1854-1936) Dutch
£599 $1138   (11-Sep-90 CH.AM18/R) Sheep by a stream in dune landscape (56x90cm-22x35in) s. (D.FL 2000)

ESTALELLA, Ramon (20th) Spanish
£2716 $4373   (25-Jun-91 FER.M232/R) Braojos (54x64cm-21x25in) s.d.1971 tablex (S.P 500000)

ESTEVE, Maurice (1904-?) French
£19881 $33598   (21-Apr-91 E.LA93/R) Coin de table a la bouteille (46x38cm-18x15in) s. (F.FR 200000)
£28884 $49104   (2-Jun-91 GL.P165/R) Lumiere sur la fenetre (73x60cm-29x24in) s. i.d.1942 verso (F.FR 290000)
£34000 $54740   (27-Jun-91 S18/R) Tricornu (46x38cm-18x15in) s.d.59 s.i.d.1959verso
£40775 $78695   (16-Dec-90 GL.P77/R) Le bouquet mecanique (50x61cm-20x24in) s.d.74 l. verso (F.FR 400000)
£48241 $79116   (19-Jun-91 CL.E17/R) Nohant Vicq (60x49cm-24x19in) s.d.1954 (F.FR 480000)
£5179 $8805   (2-Jun-91 GL.P153/R) Composition (41x30cm-16x12in) s. W/C (F.FR 52000)
£5528 $9065   (23-Jun-91 P.V18/R) Composition (20x26cm-8x10in) s. W/C (F.FR 55000)
£5607 $10821   (16-Dec-90 GL.P13/R) Esquisse pour une dame sculpteur (30x23cm-12x9in) i. W/C Indian ink (F.FR 55000)
£8502 $16664   (22-Nov-90 ZZ.F50/R) Petit cornu de nuit (39x24cm-15x9in) s.d.65 pastel ink collage (F.FR 84000)
£12663 $20768   (23-Jun-91 P.V16/R) Composition (36x49cm-14x19in) S.D.1967 W/C (F.FR 126000)
£16080 $26372   (19-Jun-91 CL.E18/R) 882A (50x37cm-20x15in) s.d.1964 W/C (F.FR 160000)
£22000 $42900   (18-Oct-90 C323/R) Untitled (41x31cm-16x12in) s.d.52 W/C
£26689 $45372   (31-May-91 VG.B72/R) Composition (65x49cm-26x19in) s.d.1964 W/C (DM 79000)

ETCHEVERRY, Denis (1867-1950) French
£867 $1500   (21-May-91 CE.NY289/R) Marigolds in vase (41x33cm-16x13in) s.
£2030 $4000   (15-Nov-90 D.NY32/R) La Nourrice (76x38cm-30x15in) s.d.1900

ETEVE, Felix Raoul (20th C) French
£1276 $2500   (21-Nov-90 NA.BA41) Vieilles maisons et ponts sur la Coussane a Estaing (45x38cm-18x15in) s.
£1633 $3200   (21-Nov-90 NA.BA55) Vista de Ciudad (50x45cm-20x18in) s.

ETHOFER, Theodor J (1849-1915) Austrian
£1083 $2166   (7-Feb-91 D.V38/R) Lungau costume (66x41cm-26x16in) s.i.d.MCMV mixed media board (A.S 22000)
£1477 $2954   (7-Feb-91 D.V39/R) Tennengau costume (66x41cm-26x16in) s.i.d.MCMV mixed media board (A.S 30000)

ETNIER, Stephen (1903-1984) American
£1000 $2000   (7-Feb-91 B.P128/R) Study for Basin Point in winter, Harpswell (41x23cm-16x9in) s. masonite
£1497 $2800   (1-Aug-90 B.P111/R) Rocks on Coast of Maine (56x91cm-22x36in) s. masonite
£2000 $4000   (7-Feb-91 B.P131/R) Boats at dock, morning (41x61cm-16x24in) s.d.50 i.verso
£2193 $4100   (1-Aug-90 B.P88/R) Three carriages (41x74cm-16x29in) s.

ETTY, William (1787-1849) British
£2700 $4833   (10-Apr-91 S128/R) Portrait of Elizabeth Singleton. Portrait of Rebecca, sister (28x20cm-11x8in) board pair
£4000 $7160   (10-Apr-91 S97/R) Portraits of Rebecca Singleton and Elizabeth, sister (65x53cm-26x21in) panel oval
£4624 $8000   (23-May-91 NY201/R) Academic male nude (63x48cm-25x19in) board
£900 $1701   (26-Sep-90 S357/R) Portrait of male nude (38x26cm-15x10in) pencil

ETTY, William (attrib) (1787-1849) British
£1300 $2561   (31-Oct-90 S306/R) The letter (37x24cm-15x9in) paper
£1972 $3845   (17-Oct-90 LC.P42/R) Jeune femme au lit (21x27cm-8x11in) canvas laid down on panel (F.FR 19500)

EUGEN (1865-1947) Swedish
£5243 $9019   (14-May-91 BU.S9/R) Sketch for 'Hoare-frost' (28x46cm-11x18in) s.d.1908 s.i.d.1939verso (S.KR 56000)
£398 $668   (24-Apr-91 BA.S301/R) Gustav III's garden pavilion (20x21cm-8x8in) s.d.1906 red chk (S.KR 4200)
£2746 $4614   (24-Apr-91 BA.S300/R) Harvesting time, Ostgota fields (27x45cm-11x18in) s.d.1933 gouache (S.KR 29000)
£41026 $80000   (23-Oct-90 SY.NY199/R) A view from the Park at Dala Manor (32x57cm-13x22in) s.i.d.1911 W/C gouache

EULER, Carl (1815-?) German
£836 $1413   (19-Apr-91 FN.S1708/R) Bavarian landscape with village and figures in thunderstorm (65x75cm-26x30in) s. canvas laid down (DM 2500)

EURICH, Richard (1903-?) British
£1900 $3306   (27-Mar-91 S109/R) Cornish coast (41x51cm-16x20in) s.d.36 board
£2600 $4524   (27-Mar-91 S130/R) The old boathouse on the Beaulieu River (71x91cm-28x36in) s.d.77 s.i.d.verso board
£2600 $5148   (29-Jan-91 PH84/R) Three bridges (61x106cm-24x42in) s.
£400 $672   (24-Apr-91 CSK231) Figures on beach - rainbow (21x29cm-8x11in) s.d.1975 pencil paper on board

EUROPEAN SCHOOL (?) European
£5581 $9377   (22-Apr-91 SY.ME206/R) Mercury, Cupid and Venus (29x25cm-11x10in) c.1800 (A.D 12000)

EUROPEAN SCHOOL, 17th C European
£2100 $4200   (7-Feb-91 B.P95/R) Figures in landscape (28x36cm-11x14in) cradled panel
£2100 $4200   (7-Feb-91 B.P94/R) Figures in landscape (28x36cm-11x14in) panel
£2555 $5033   (30-Oct-90 BU.S303/R) Harvesting landscape (17x23cm-7x9in) panel (S.KR 28000)

EUROPEAN SCHOOL, 18th C European
£1974 $3750   (15-Sep-90 S.W2398/R) Allegorical figural scene (74x48cm-29x19in) canvas on panel
£3409 $6683   (19-Nov-90 CH.R63/R) Ritratto di dama (80x64cm-31x25in) (I.L 7500000)

EUSTACE, Alfred William (19/20th C) Australian
£618 $1217   (13-Nov-90 J.M733) Northern Victorian landscapes (9x12cm-4x5in) s.verso board pair (A.D 1600)
£2262 $3824   (16-Apr-91 J.M279/R) The river crossing, North Eastern Victoria (39x55cm-15x22in) (A.D 5000)

EUSTACHE, Charles Francois (1820-1870) French
£712 $1346   (27-Sep-90 BL.P101) Plage (21x41cm-8x16in) panel (F.FR 7000)

EUSTACHE, Robert (19th C) French
£1068 $2019   (27-Sep-90 BL.P134) Interieur d'atelier au Caire (64x80cm-25x31in) s.d.89 (F.FR 10500)
£2747 $5191   (27-Sep-90 BL.P129) Le cuisinier noir et la servante (64x90cm-25x35in) s. (F.FR 27000)

EVANS DE SCOTT (1847-1898) American
£1775 $3000   (1-May-91 B.SF5099/R) Still life with jonquils (109x61cm-43x24in) s.d.1885
£1994 $3250   (11-Jun-91 MOR.P95) Interior scene - sketching Kitty (51x41cm-20x16in) s.indist.d.
£3550 $6000   (20-Apr-91 WOL.C40/R) Paper doll (28x41cm-11x16in) s.d.87 panel

EVANS DE SCOTT (1847-1898) American-cont.
£4624 $8000   (10-May-91 S.W2455/R) Dorothy (91x61cm-36x24in) s. s.i.stretcher

EVANS OF ETON, William (1798-1877) British
£750 $1478   (15-Nov-90 S5) Otter hunt in Scotland (23x46cm-9x18in) indis.s. W/C over
       pencil htd.white
£1100 $1848   (15-Jul-91 PH86) Three Horseshoes on road to Windsor (28x45cm-11x18in)
       W/C bodycol
£1800 $3024   (15-Jul-91 PH87/R) Mill on Thames (51x67cm-20x26in) W/C over pencil

EVANS OF ETON, William (attrib) (1798-1877) British
£2400 $3960   (12-Jul-91 C121/R) Ciew of Windsor Castle, with figures walking by
       Thames and others rowing (52x87cm-20x34in) copper

EVANS, Bernard (1848-1922) British
£460 $851   (6-Mar-91 SC4149) The Mill Lane, Fountains Abbey, Yorkshire
       (69x46cm-27x18in) s. s.i.verso W/C
£700 $1365   (18-Oct-90 SC3024/R) Rievaulx Abbey, Yorkshire (39x75cm-15x30in) s.
£1600 $3120   (18-Oct-90 SC3027/R) Bolton Abbey, Yorkshire (41x76cm-16x30in) s. i.
       label verso
£1650 $2756   (22-Jul-91 SWS808/R) A view of Knaresborough (39x73cm-15x29in) s. W/C
       pencil
£3000 $5910   (1-Nov-90 TE544/R) Fountains Abbey (69x102cm-27x40in) s. W/C

EVANS, Bruce (20th C) American?
£1179 $2300   (10-Oct-90 SY.NY500/R) Turn the screw II (91x127cm-36x50in)
       s.i.d.82verso acrylic

EVANS, Donald (20th C) ?
£1923 $3750   (10-Oct-90 SY.NY486/R) Pear of Achterduk (15x10cm-6x4in) i.d.1972 W/C
       paper on printed postcard
£3550 $6000   (1-May-91 SY.NY136/R) Song-Ting (29x21cm-11x8in) four W/C paper in
       philatelic sheet
£3604 $6234   (22-May-91 CH.AM709/R) Tourist stamps from Yteke (13x18cm-5x7in)
       init.i.d.74 ten handpainted stamps W/C envelope (D.FL 12000)
£4805 $8312   (22-May-91 CH.AM708/R) Vegetales of Jantar (21x18cm-8x7in) init.d.73 25
       handpainted stamps W/C one sheet (D.FL 16000)

EVANS, F M (19/20th C) British
£1750 $3290   (21-Sep-90 CBB238) Amateur musician (41x36cm-16x14in) s.verso W/C

EVANS, Frederick M (fl.1888-c.1928) British
£1600 $2864   (14-Mar-91 L380/R) Sailors tale - young boy listening to old sea dog
       (38x28cm-15x11in) s. W/C

EVANS, Jane (20th C) Australian?
£619 $1214   (7-Nov-90 DS.W66) Seated figure in garden (55x37cm-22x15in) s.d.79 W/C
       (NZ.D 2000)
£681 $1335   (7-Nov-90 DS.W45) In garden (50x42cm-20x17in) s.d.78 W/C (NZ.D 2200)
£681 $1335   (7-Nov-90 DS.W20) Double portrait (56x75cm-22x30in) s. gouache
       (NZ.D 2200)
£928 $1568   (17-Apr-91 DS.W26) Woman in hat (55x37cm-22x15in) s.d.1985 gouache
       (NZ.D 2700)
£1237 $2091   (17-Apr-91 DS.W21) Girl in flower red hat (37x55cm-15x22in) s.d.87
       gouache (NZ.D 3600)
£1703 $3337   (7-Nov-90 DS.W11/R) Poppies (55x74cm-22x29in) s.d.85 W/C (NZ.D 5500)

EVANS, Merlyn (1910-1973) British
£1300 $2171   (6-Jun-91 C227/R) Two figures (46x41cm-18x16in) s.d.50 s.i.stretcher
£1600 $3024   (24-Sep-90 CSK260/R) Two heads (53x43cm-21x17in) s.d.1947

EVANS, T S (20th C) British
£680 $1149   (16-Apr-91 HAR358) Still life with flowers (76x64cm-30x25in) s.d.1947

EVARD, Andre (1876-1972) French
£2041 $3959   (8-Dec-90 GAB.G2533/R) Composition au verre a pied (35x27cm-14x11in)
       s.d.1925 panel (S.FR 5000)

EVE, Jean (1900-1968) French
£1148 $2250   (12-Feb-91 SY.NY130/R) La ferme lepine de Dampmesnil au printemps
       (46x53cm-18x21in) s. s.i.d.1953verso
£3815 $6143   (26-Jun-91 CB.P59/R) L'allee des platanes (55x46cm-22x18in) s.d.1931
       (F.FR 38000)

EVERARD, J B (19th C) British
£2500 $4100   (18-Jun-91 SWS280/R) Yorkshire sow (36x46cm-14x18in) s.i.d.1819

EVERBROECK, Frans van (style) (17th C) Flemish
£6200 $12214   (31-Oct-90 S114/R) Still life of grapes, figs and hazelnuts
       (44x34cm-17x13in)

EVERDINGEN, A van (1832-1910) Dutch
£580 $952   (18-Jun-91 FN.S1827/R) Wooded lower Rhine landscape with reapers
       (21x31cm-8x12in) s. canvas on panel (DM 1700)

EVERDINGEN, Adriaen van (1832-1912) Dutch
£1030 $2030   (30-Oct-90 CH.AM63) Cows in meadow, at dawn (32x42cm-13x17in) s. panel
                    (D.FL 3400)

EVERDINGEN, Allart (1621-1675) Dutch
£3517 $6928   (14-Nov-90 SY.AM18/R) Mountainous landscape with figures by torrent
                    (89x71cm-35x28in) bears sig. (D.FL 11500)
£4380 $8628   (30-Oct-90 BU.S245/R) Landscape with pines and waterfall
                    (100x86cm-39x34in) (S.KR 48000)
£6728 $13254   (13-Nov-90 CH.AM170/R) Waterfall in rocky wooded landscape with
                    watermill nearby, churchspire beyond (38x33cm-15x13in) panel
                    (D.FL 22000)
£7000 $11410   (3-Jul-91 S181/R) Nordic landscape with figures near stream
                    (41x53cm-16x21in) bears sig. panel
£1000   *$1920*   *(18-Feb-91 S143/R) Village scene with church and peasants conversing on*
                    blustery day (18x28cm-7x11in) init. wash over chk
£2599   *$5121*   *(12-Nov-90 CH.AM93/R) Path on outskirts of village with horseman by*
                    cottage (8x12cm-3x5in) init. black chk brush ink (D.FL 8500)
£4281   *$8434*   *(12-Nov-90 CH.AM92/R) Waggon outside farmhouse, extensive panorama*
                    beyond (18x30cm-7x12in) init. black chk wash (D.FL 14000)

EVERDINGEN, Allart (attrib) (1621-1675) Dutch
£7086 $11975   (2-May-91 RAS.V37/R) Norwegian landscape with waterfall and figures
                    (106x114cm-42x45in) (D.KR 80000)
£769   *$1300*   *(19-Apr-91 FN.S1447/R) Landscape with fishing and sailing boats off*
                    island with church (5x8cm-2x3in) sepia dr. (DM 2300)
£769   *$1300*   *(19-Apr-91 FN.S1448/R) Fun on the ice (5x8cm-2x3in) sepia dr.*
                    (DM 2300)

EVERETT, Walter Hunt (1880-1946) American
£1294 $2200   (1-Jun-91 IH.NY84/R) Couple on hillside with horse beyond
                    (58x76cm-23x30in) oil chl

EVERGOOD, Phillip (1901-1973) American
£7407 $14000   (26-Sep-90 SY.NY191/R) What's the weather going to be (89x63cm-35x25in)
                    s.
£741   *$1400*   *(25-Sep-90 CE.NY201/R) Mother love (77x57cm-30x22in) s.i. W/C chl.*
£1376   *$2600*   *(25-Sep-90 CE.NY140/R) Men and machines (100x76cm-39x30in) s. i. verso*
                    pencil gouache
£2604   *$5000*   *(17-Dec-90 SY.NY424/R) Female nude (74x53cm-29x21in) s.d.63 gouache*

EVERS, Ivar Elis (1866-?) American
£537 $950   (22-Mar-91 S.W2470/R) Young girl with straw hat (91x76cm-36x30in)
                    s.d.1902

EVERSDYCK, Cornelis Willemsz (1590-1644) Dutch
£12500 $20375   (5-Jul-91 C351/R) Cat watching over dead game on draped ledge
                    (163x207cm-64x81in) with sig. i.

EVERSEN, Adrianus (1818-1897) Dutch
£1716 $2900   (20-Apr-91 WOL.C114/R) Belgian street scene (28x20cm-11x8in) s. panel
£1900 $3648   (29-Nov-90 B119/R) Dutch street scene (22x18cm-9x7in) s. panel
£2000 $3920   (22-Nov-90 CSK152/R) Figures in street (25x21cm-10x8in) s. panel
£3030 $5970   (30-Oct-90 CH.AM47/R) Market in Dutch town (19x14cm-7x6in) s. panel
                    (D.FL 10000)
£3125 $6094   (25-Oct-90 D.V11/R) Market scene in Dutch town (25x30cm-10x12in) mono.
                    panel (A.S 65000)
£3333 $6567   (30-Oct-90 CH.AM74/R) View in town with peasant selling vegetables near
                    entrance of church (44x36cm-17x14in) s. panel (D.FL 11000)
£4116 $8067   (6-Nov-90 SY.AM182/R) Market in Dutch town (27x21cm-11x8in) s. panel
                    (D.FL 13500)
£8639 $14427   (4-Jun-91 FB.M82/R) View of a Dutch town (44x45cm-17x18in) s. board
                    (C.D 16500)
£10000 $19000   (28-Feb-91 CH.NY150/R) Village street (32x42cm-13x17in) s.
£15569 $26156   (23-Apr-91 SY.AM156/R) Figures in street of Dutch town (40x35cm-16x14in)
                    s.d.1852 panel (D.FL 52000)
£16185 $28000   (22-May-91 SY.NY24/R) Winter street scene (66x51cm-26x20in) s.
£1527   *$2979*   *(11-Oct-90 D.V154/R) View of Belgian town with figures (31x38cm-12x15in)*
                    s.d.65 W/C (A.S 32000)

EVERSEN, Johannes Hendrik (1906-) Dutch
£1500 $2880   (27-Nov-90 PH27) Still life with shells and lemon (41x51cm-16x20in)
                    s.d.1953 canvas on board

EWAN, Frances (fl.1892-1929) British
£1600 $2624   (20-Jun-91 DLY77) Cornish village (51x61cm-20x24in) indist.s.

EWBANK, John Wilson (attrib) (1799-1847) British
£2419 $4718   (15-Oct-90 SY.J14/R) View on the Clyde (39x60cm-15x24in) (SA.R 12000)

EWBANK, John Wilson (style) (1799-1847) British
£2600 $5200   (5-Feb-91 S37/R) Stirling Castle and River Forth. Huntly Castle and
                    River Tay (45x61cm-18x24in) canvas on panel pair

EWBANK, Thomas John (19th C) British
£3600 $5940   (11-Jul-91 GSP636) The sister's kiss (69x86cm-27x34in) mono.d.1859

594

EWERS, Heindrich (1817-1885) German
£10135 $17230   (27-May-91 L.K268 a/R) Herzoge Christian Ludwig and Friedrich von
                   Mecklenburg in picture galleryof Schloss Schwerin (100x126cm-39x50in)
                   s.d.1881 (DM 30000)

EWORTH, Hans (16th C) British
£12000 $23640   (16-Nov-90 C7/R) Portrait of gentleman ages 27 in doublet with fur
                   trimmed cloak by table (108x80cm-43x31in) mono.i.d.1556

EXNER, Julius (1825-1910) Danish
£717 $1434   (6-Feb-91 RAS.K491/R) Portrait of small girl. Kitchen interior
                   (32x25cm-13x10in) s.d.1845 init.d.1846verso double-sided (D.KR 8000)
£880 $1479   (23-Apr-91 RAS.K351/R) Interior with young man lighting cigar from
                   candle (40x35cm-16x14in) s. (D.KR 10000)
£974 $1647   (1-May-91 KH.K59/R) Children playing in yard (28x37cm-11x15in) s.d.77
                   (D.KR 11000)
£1075 $2151   (6-Feb-91 RAS.K61/R) Small girl wearing Fano costume (26x19cm-10x7in)
                   s.d.1854 (D.KR 12000)
£1125 $2182   (22-Aug-90 K195) Woman from Refsnaes (21x18cm-8x7in) s. (D.KR 13000)
£1346 $2653   (14-Nov-90 RAS.K393/R) Young girl reading by candlelight
                   (28x30cm-11x12in) s.d.1900 (D.KR 15000)
£2553 $4289   (22-Apr-91 BU.K31/R) Practising the celebration song (30x38cm-12x15in)
                   s.d.1906 (D.KR 29000)
£2688 $5376   (6-Feb-91 RAS.K209/R) The artist in his studio (67x60cm-26x24in)
                   s.d.1910 (D.KR 30000)
£3047 $6093   (6-Feb-91 RAS.K410/R) Interior with small girl reading (38x47cm-15x19in)
                   s.d.1901 (D.KR 34000)

EYCK, Charles (1897-?) Dutch
£1347 $2560   (11-Sep-90 CH.AM418) Snowy landscape (65x54cm-26x21in) (D.FL 4500)
£1037   *$1990*   *(27-Nov-90 SY.AM3829/R) Montmartre with Sacre Coeur beyond
                   (44x68cm-17x27in) s.i.d.29 gouache (D.FL 3400)*

EYCK, Gaspard van (1613-1673) Flemish
£1350 $2592   (18-Feb-91 S128/R) Lisbon Harbour (15x37cm-6x15in) bears i. pen ink wash

EYCK, Jan van (style) (15th C) Flemish
£1900 $3610   (13-Sep-90 CSK124/R) Donor adoring Madonna and Child (45x28cm-18x11in)
                   panel

EYCKEN, Charles van den (jnr) (1859-1923) Belgian
£1700 $2856   (16-Jul-91 C51/R) Les artistes dans les coulisses (36x27cm-14x11in)
                   s.i.d.1916
£2800 $4704   (16-Jul-91 C50/R) Artist's studio (45x34cm-18x13in) s.
£3200 $5376   (16-Jul-91 C48/R) Signed and sealed (34x46cm-13x18in) s.d.1907
£4400 $8580   (15-Jan-91 C13/R) Kittens playing in sewing basket (35x45cm-14x18in)
                   s.d.1905
£5500 $9240   (16-Jul-91 C47/R) Tabby cat (38x50cm-15x20in) s.d.1920
£6000 $10080   (16-Jul-91 C49/R) Circus entertainers (43x46cm-17x18in) s.d.1890
                   indis.i.verso

EYCKEN, van den (19th C) Belgian
£1167 $2240   (18-Dec-90 GM.B776/R) Portrait de chien (51x42cm-20x17in) s.
                   (B.FR 70000)

EYMER, Arnoldus Johannes (1803-1863) Dutch
£8537 $16732   (6-Nov-90 SY.AM99/R) Winter landscape with moored vessels and figures
                   with sledge on frozen river (63x84cm-25x33in) s.d.1850 (D.FL 28000)

EYRE, Gladstone (1863-1933) Australian
£519 $846   (1-Jul-91 AAA.S93) Govetts Leap (67x120cm-26x47in) s. W/C (A.D 1100)
£720 $1404   (15-Oct-90 AAA.S49) Ships in Sydney Harbour (31x58cm-12x23in) s. W/C
                   (A.D 1800)
£798 $1309   (17-Jun-91 MGS.S186) Milson Island, Hawkesbury River (30x58cm-12x23in)
                   s. W/C (A.D 1700)
£1197 $2118   (18-Mar-91 MGS.S250) Hawkesbury landscape (58x106cm-23x42in) s. W/C
                   (A.D 2800)
£7393 $14490   (19-Nov-90 MGS.S244/R) Sydney skyline from Hungry Bay (59x114cm-23x45in)
                   s.d.1890 W/C (A.D 19000)

EYSDEN, Robert van (1810-1890) Dutch
£1951 $3824   (6-Nov-90 SY.AM143) Johan van Oldenbarneveldt informed about sentence
                   (65x77cm-26x30in) s. panel (D.FL 6400)

EYSKENS, Felix (19th C) Belgian
£736 $1252   (28-May-91 C.A105) Landscape (45x64cm-18x25in) s. (B.FR 45000)

EYSMOND, Stanislaw (1894-1939) Polish
*£526 $1000   (3-Mar-91 REM.W3) Mimosa and cyclamen (70x50cm-28x20in) s. W/C board
                   (P.Z 9500000)*

EYTEL, Carl A (1862-1925) American
£632 $1100   (29-Mar-91 E.EDM501/R) Cattle herding (76x152cm-30x60in)

F W C (?) ?
£3500 $6895   (30-Oct-90 PH28/R) Stone masons working on palace forecourt. Riders
                          dismounting by palace (32x41cm-13x16in) indis.init. panel pair

FABBI, Fabio (1861-1946) Italian
£550 $985   (12-Mar-91 PH67) Desert tribesman mounted on camel (29x19cm-11x7in) s.
                          panel
£4615 $9000   (23-Oct-90 SY.NY416/R) The slave market (100x70cm-39x28in) s.
£7556 $14658   (4-Dec-90 R.T289/R) Arabian village festival (121x160cm-48x63in) s.
                          (C.D 17000)
£7692 $15000   (23-Oct-90 SY.NY415/R) Wedding cortege (61x90cm-24x35in) s.
£1000 $1900   (15-Sep-90 S.W2790/R) Harem interior (41x25cm-16x10in) s. W/C

FABBRI, Laurina (19th C) Italian
£737 $1400   (15-Sep-90 S.W2404/R) Italian industry (58x76cm-23x30in) s.

FABER DU FAUR, Hans von (1863-1949) German
£669 $1130   (19-Apr-91 FN.S1709/R) Race course with jockeys on galopping horses
                          (14x18cm-6x7in) mono. i.verso baord (DM 2000)
£619 $1046   (19-Apr-91 FN.S1710/R) The morning ride (13x21cm-5x8in) ono.d.1915 W/C
                          (DM 1850)
£845 $1436   (1-Jun-91 VG.B525/R) Study of riders (10x16cm-4x6in) s.d.1922 W/C
                          bodycol (DM 2500)
£1182 $2010   (30-May-91 SY.BE82/R) Horseriding on the beach (13x16cm-5x6in)
                          mono.d.1916 W/C (DM 3500)
£2196 $3733   (30-May-91 SY.BE84/R) The ride (21x27cm-8x11in) d.1920 W/C gouache over
                          pencil (DM 6500)

FABER DU FAUR, Otto von (1828-1901) German
£669 $1130   (19-Apr-91 FN.S1712/R) Feldherrnhugel near Koniggratz (12x24cm-5x9in)
                          i.verso board (DM 2000)
£1027 $1839   (13-Mar-91 N.M485/R) Arab holding death watch before convicts heads
                          hanging from wall (46x27cm-18x11in) s.i. (DM 3000)

FABER, Johann (19th C) German
£26481 $44222   (6-Jun-91 D.V91/R) Interior of tobacco merchant with figures
                          (85x99cm-33x39in) s.i.d.1760 (A.S 550000)

FABER, Johann Theodor (1772-1852) German
£1553 $2934   (27-Sep-90 D.V154/R) View of Dresden (34x43cm-13x17in) i.d.1808verso
                          board (A.S 32000)

FABER, John (elder) (c.1650-1721) Dutch
£1500 $2475   (11-Jul-91 S19/R) Portrait of Major General John Hill (12x10cm-5x4in)
                          s.d.1709 plumbago on vellum oval

FABER, Martin Hermansz (attrib) (1587-1648) German
£18564 $33229   (14-Mar-91 D.V49/R) The Adoration of the Shepherds before the town walls
                          of Rome (122x199cm-48x78in) (A.S 380000)

FABER, Will (20th C) German?
£1358 $2186   (25-Jun-91 FER.M147/R) Hagal (50x65cm-20x26in) s. s.d.75verso
                          (S.P 250000)
£407 $785   (14-Dec-90 ZOF.Z939) Composition vert (45x33cm-18x13in) s. mixed media
                          board (S.FR 1000)

FABIEN, Louis (20th C?) Flemish?
£1053 $2000   (14-Sep-90 DM.D2003/R) Street scene at St.Tropez (61x74cm-24x29in)
                          s.d.76
£1387 $2400   (22-May-91 D.NY118) Jeune fille heureuse (135x102cm-53x40in) s.d.69
£1640 $2755   (28-Apr-91 FE.P127) Chemin a Porquerolles (60x73cm-24x29in) s.
                          (F.FR 16400)

FABIUS, Jan (1820-1889) Dutch
£610 $1171   (27-Nov-90 SY.AM3639) Children in interior (17x21cm-7x8in) s. panel
                          (D.FL 2000)
£2000 $3280   (18-Jun-91 VN.R66/R) The doll seller (51x62cm-20x24in) s. panel
                          (D.FL 6600)

FABIUS-BREST see BREST, Fabius

FABRE, Francois-Xavier (1766-1837) French
£23000 $45310   (14-Nov-90 S56/R) Portrait of John Henry Petty Earl Wycombe wearing coat
                          and waistcoat (73x60cm-29x24in) s.d.1795 painted oval

FABRI, Willem Adrianus (?) Dutch
£599 $1138   (11-Sep-90 CH.AM124) Peasants digging by a pond in moorland
                          (106x93cm-42x37in) s. (D.FL 2000)

FABRIANO, Gentile da (after) (1370-1450) Italian
£4615 $9000   (10-Oct-90 CH.NY130/R) St Mary Magdalene (155x44cm-61x17in) gold ground
                          panel shaped top

FABRIS, Jacobo (1689-1761) Italian
£22000 $35860   (3-Jul-91 S177/R) View in Roman forum (71x99cm-28x39in) s.

FABRIS, Pietro (18th C) Italian
£14154 $23778   (23-Apr-91 F.R54/R) Paesaggio con l'Arco di Traiano e figure
               (63x76cm-25x30in) s. (I.L 31000000)
£15075 $24724   (21-Jun-91 SY.MO124/R) Les danseurs de Tarentelle. Repas de chasse dans
               un paysage (39x44cm-15x17in) paper laid down on canvas pair
               (F.FR 150000)
£49000 $84770   (24-May-91 C90/R) Santa Lucia with the Castel dell'Ovo and the
               Pizzofalcone Barracks (42x76cm-17x30in) s.

FABRIS, Pietro (circle) (18th C) Italian
£12000 $23160   (11-Dec-90 PH172/R) Figures in grotto on coast (53x86cm-21x34in)
£800 $1352   (16-Apr-91 C193) A natural arch with cacti and other vegetation and
               travellers on rocks in the river below (27x46cm-11x18in) bodycolour

FABRIS, Pietro (style) (18th C) Italian
£4500 $7335   (2-Jul-91 PH264/R) View of Spanish port with town. Causeway across
               harbour with shipping (36x65cm-14x26in) pair

FABRO, Rosina del (1874-1946) Austrian
£868 $1693   (18-Oct-90 D.V8/R) Girl with duckling (69x47cm-27x19in) s. board
               (A.S 18000)

FABRY, Suzanne (20th C) French?
£2857 $5629   (15-Nov-90 ZZ.F3) Les trois femmes (117x92cm-46x36in) s.d.1942
               (F.FR 28000)

FACCHINETTI, Carlo (1870-?) Italian
£4000 $6560   (19-Jun-91 S369/R) Proud young mother (69x49cm-27x19in) s.

FACCINI, Pietro (attrib) (1560-1602) Italian
£4800 $7824   (2-Jul-91 C103/R) Putto seen from below and study of hand
               (15x13cm-6x5in) red chk

FACCINI, Pietro (style) (1560-1602) Italian
£1221 $2186   (14-Mar-91 D.V181/R) The Holy Family (24x18cm-9x7in) (A.S 25000)

FACCIOLI, Raffaele (1846-?) Italian
£1000 $1730   (9-May-91 CSK159/R) Portrait of lady, in high bonnet (32x23cm-13x9in) s.
               panel

FACCIOLI, Silvio (19th C) Italian
£1043 $1700   (5-Jul-91 S.W2639/R) After the concert (38x30cm-15x12in) s. canvas laid
               on board

FACKERE, Jef van de (1879-?) Belgian
£1081 $1934   (16-Mar-91 KV.L284) Dahlias and bowl of fruit (89x78cm-35x31in) s.
               pastel (B.FR 65000)

FADER, Fernando (1882-1935) Argentinian
£6915 $13000   (18-Sep-90 RO.BA27/R) Camiseta colorada (40x33cm-16x13in) s.d.1913
£13830 $26000   (18-Sep-90 RO.BA25/R) Descanso en el cerro (58x80cm-23x31in)
£14894 $28000   (18-Sep-90 RO.BA26/R) Carreton de circo (34x48cm-13x19in) panel
£15029 $26000   (8-May-91 SY.NY110/R) A lady watching the plough (130x90cm-51x35in)
               s.d.03
£16489 $31000   (18-Sep-90 RO.BA24/R) De Tarde (100x120cm-39x47in)
£17919 $31000   (8-May-91 RO.BA20/R) Mi hijo en el atelier (107x91cm-42x36in)
£32500 $61750   (11-Sep-90 PO.BA6) Tarde apacible (88x140cm-35x55in) s.
£1908 $3300   (8-May-91 V.BA37) Retrato (17cm-7ins circular) W/C

FADINE, Igor (1939-) Russian
£503 $965   (18-Feb-91 ARC.P220/R) Sur le quai du port (60x88cm-24x35in) s.
               (F.FR 5000)
£598 $1016   (29-May-91 ARC.P181/R) Brumes matinales (60x120cm-24x47in) s.
               (F.FR 6000)
£704 $1351   (18-Feb-91 ARC.P218/R) La promenade (60x70cm-24x28in) s.d.79 (F.FR 7000)
£784 $1505   (18-Feb-91 ARC.P219/R) Attelage pres de la Volga (74x92cm-29x36in)
               s.d.63 (F.FR 7800)

FAED, James (19/20th C) British
£500 $990   (1-Feb-91 PHE63) Two worthies (14x12cm-6x5in) s. panel
£2098 $4070   (4-Dec-90 FN.S1821/R) Two boys fishing in ice hole (45x35cm-18x14in)
               (DM 6000)

FAED, James (Jnr) (1847-1920) British
£800 $1496   (28-Aug-90 S890) River in Spate (20x26cm-8x10in) s. panel
£825 $1361   (10-Jul-91 GC496) A scottish moorland scene with heather
               (25x28cm-10x11in) s.d.1903 panel
£1000 $1650   (10-Jul-91 GC518) A highland glen with sheep in the foreground
               (61x91cm-24x36in) s.d.1892
£1150 $2151   (2-Aug-90 RBB585) Boulder strewn stream with heather and mountains
               beyond (33x51cm-13x20in) s.d.1903 l.verso
£1600 $2992   (28-Aug-90 S767/R) Moorland heather. Moorland Lochan (15x25cm-6x10in) s.
               one d.1911 panel pair
£1900 $3724   (22-Nov-90 CG599/R) Invercomrie Burn, Perthshire (36x53cm-14x21in)
               s.d.1908 s.i.verso
£2800 $5236   (28-Aug-90 S775/R) November (55x76cm-22x30in) s.i.

FAED, John (1820-1902) British
£800 $1304   (13-Jun-91 MO408/R) Interior scene, father instructing young child time
    on longcase clock (41x33cm-16x13in) s. W/C

FAED, Thomas (1826-1900) British
£510 $903   (20-Mar-91 KM.K1205) Woman seated with baby by open door in kitchen
    interior (45x61cm-18x24in) s.d.1899 (DM 1500)
£950 $1606   (2-May-91 CG493) Sewing (40x30cm-16x12in) panel
£1263 $2134   (20-Apr-91 HOR.H12/R) Time for reading (34x25cm-13x10in) s. (F.M 8800)
£1650 $2690   (10-Jun-91 TAY835/R) Portrait of girl with basket by feet
    (30x23cm-12x9in) s.
£2400 $4176   (27-Mar-91 PHS861/R) Highland Lassie (23x18cm-9x7in) s. board
£3000 $5070   (2-May-91 CG492/R) Mother and child gathering berries (30x40cm-12x16in)
    s.
£9000 $15030   (5-Jun-91 S140/R) Home and homeless (36x51cm-14x20in) s. panel
£9500 $19000   (5-Feb-91 S47/R) Only herself (51x35cm-20x14in) s.d.1868

FAES, Pieter (style) (1750-1814) Belgian
£1678 $3272   (13-Oct-90 KRA.D207) Still life of flowers in glass vase
    (50x40cm-20x16in) panel (DM 5000)

FAESI, Ernst (1917-) Swiss
£794 $1373   (25-May-91 AB.L78/R) Totemwald (45x64cm-18x25in) s. st.studio
    i.d.1968stretcher (S.FR 2000)

FAGAN, Robert (1745-1816) British
£24000 $42960   (10-Apr-91 S104/R) Portrait of Anna Maria Ferri, artist's first wife
    (73x61cm-29x24in)

FAGAN, Robert (circle) (1745-1816) British
£2400 $4704   (20-Nov-90 PH162/R) Portrait of a young girl presumed wife of Major John
    Cliffe, Governor of Carlisle (84x64cm-33x25in)

FAGERKVIST, Thor (1884-?) Swedish
£2736 $4733   (22-May-91 BA.S51/R) Boy with roses (66x47cm-26x19in) s.d.12
    (S.KR 29000)

FAGET-GARMIN, P (20th C) ?
£896 $1558   (25-Mar-91 CR.P87) Le port d'Alger (51x125cm-20x49in) s.d.1930 panel
    (F.FR 9000)

FAGNANI, Giuseppe (1819-1873) Italian
£2000 $3940   (13-Nov-90 SWS337/R) A shepherdess (141x100cm-56x39in) s.

FAHEY, Edward Henry (1844-1907) British
£560 $969   (20-May-91 PH174) Pine trees near Pesquiers, mountains in distance
    (33x56cm-13x22in) s. i.verso W/C

FAHLCRANTZ, Axel-Erik-Valerius (1851-1925) Swedish
£3493 $6846   (6-Nov-90 BA.S59/R) Morning mist (40x75cm-16x30in) s.d.1894 (S.KR 38000)

FAHLCRANTZ, Carl Johan (1774-1861) Swedish
£750 $1470   (22-Nov-90 CSK150/R) Coastal windmill (27x37cm-11x15in) s.d.1836
£947 $1591   (24-Apr-91 BA.S55/R) Mill at Waldemarsudde (27x37cm-11x15in) s.d.1836
    (S.KR 10000)
£2482 $4864   (10-Nov-90 FAL.M91/R) Romantic landscape (112x146cm-44x57in) s.d.1851
    (S.KR 27000)
£3500 $5740   (19-Jun-91 S242/R) Wooded landscape overlooking river (86x115cm-34x45in)
£4312 $8494   (13-Nov-90 AB.S364/R) Landscape, Sparreholm (90x117cm-35x46in) s.d.1837
    (S.KR 47000)

FAHLSTROM, Oyvind (1928-) Scandinavian
£28746 $48582   (18-Apr-91 BU.S15/R) Pentagon Puzzle (79x102cm-31x40in) painting
    magnetic element acrylic vinyl shaped (S.KR 305000)
£1981 $3427   (22-May-91 BA.S360/R) That's what you believed (27x35cm-11x14in) s.
    mixed media (S.KR 21000)
£13902 $26969   (5-Dec-90 AB.S7073/R) 'Kvalstersangen' (29x42cm-11x17in) s. d.1958verso
    mixced media (S.KR 150000)

FAHNLE, Hans (1903-1968) German
£753 $1349   (12-Mar-91 FN.S1962) Coastal landscape, Liguria (65x46cm-26x18in) s.
    board (DM 2200)

FAHNRICH, Ferdinand (18th C) ?
£382 $642   (25-Apr-91 D.V125/R) Design for fortified town (48x69cm-19x27in)
    s.i.d.1751 Indian ink pen grisaille (A.S 8000)

FAHR-EL-NISSA-ZEID (c,1900-) Turkish?
£1400 $2730   (15-Oct-90 PH104) Exploration (71x180cm-28x71in) s.

FAHRBACH, Carl Ludwig (1835-1902) German
£2852 $5562   (13-Oct-90 KRA.D208/R) Venusteich im Dusseldorfer Malkastenpark
    (84x112cm-33x44in) s.d.1876 (DM 8500)
£4452 $7969   (13-Mar-91 N.M485 a/R) View of Heidelberg (64x90cm-25x35in) s.d.1897
    (DM 13000)

FAHRBACH, Carl Ludwig (1835-1902) German-cont.
£8042 $15521   (12-Dec-90 N.M508/R) View of Dillenburg, Hesse (71x102cm-28x40in)
          s.d.1866 (DM 23000)

FAHRBACH, W A (20th C) German?
£874 $1687   (12-Dec-90 N.M509/R) Hunting party gathering round dead bear in snowy
          wood clearing (64x106cm-25x42in) s. (DM 2500)

FAHRINGER, Carl (1874-1952) Austrian
£873 $1641   (20-Sep-90 D.V113/R) Portrait of a woman (62x50cm-24x20in) s.d.1934
          (A.S 18000)
£1212 $2279   (20-Sep-90 D.V112/R) Flowering branch (51x40cm-20x16in) s. (A.S 25000)
£317   *$587*   *(7-Mar-91 D.V16/R) Illustration for fairy tale Der goldene Rehbock*
          (14x13cm-6x5in) pen brush indian ink htd.white paper on board
          (A.S 6500)
£681   *$1335*   *(24-Jan-91 D.V37/R) Oriental street scene (25x32cm-10x13in) i. pencil*
          W/C gouache (A.S 14000)

FAIJA, Guglielmo (1803-?) Italian
£539 $900   (3-Jun-91 GRO.B230 a/R) Portrait of seated artist with palette and
          portrait (13x10cm-5x4in) s.d.1825 on ivory miniature

FAIRCHILD, Elizabeth Nelson (19th C) British
£677 $1300   (17-Aug-90 DM.D2003/R) Full cry (51x66cm-20x26in) s.

FAIRHOLME, Adele (fl.1899-1936) British
£700 $1344   (21-Feb-91 B249) Sisters in nursery (87x72cm-34x28in) s.d.1916

FAIRLESS, T K (1825-1853) British
£1500 $2940   (20-Nov-90 RB641) Extensive Yorkshire landscapes, with stream, cattle,
          figures and church (51x79cm-20x31in) s. pair

FAIRMAN, Frances C (1836-1923) British
£600   *$1170*   *(15-Jan-91 C92) Clumber spaniel puppies (36x51cm-14x20in) s. pencil W/C*

FAIRMAN, G (19th C) ?
£1579 $3000   (27-Feb-91 SY.NY344/R) Orsini Palace Venice (41x79cm-16x31in) s.

FAIRMAN, James (1826-1904) American
£1607 $2700   (17-Jul-91 SY.NY372/R) Middle Eastern coastal town (44x76cm-17x30in)
          s.d.83
£1823 $3500   (17-Dec-90 SY.NY112/R) Landscape with classical temple and figures
          (81x114cm-32x45in) s.d.77
£7500 $14700   (22-Nov-90 CG520/R) Entrance of Bonnie Prince Charlie to Edinburgh, 17th
          September 1745 (82x115cm-32x45in) s.d.83

FAIRWEATHER, Ian (1891-1974) Australian
£2233 $3751   (22-Apr-91 SY.ME200) Portrait (20x17cm-8x7in) init. paper (A.D 4800)
£580   *$1010*   *(26-Mar-91 JRL.S1) Cats (42x63cm-17x25in) s. ink (A.D 1300)*
£12048   *$23133*   *(26-Nov-90 SY.ME270/R) Coolie (54x44cm-21x17in) gouache (A.D 30000)*

FAISTAUER, Anton (1887-1930) Austrian
£17396 $33748   (6-Dec-90 D.V72/R) Pensive young woman seated in armchair
          (62x53cm-24x21in) s.d.1918 panel (A.S 350000)
£18000 $34920   (5-Dec-90 PH90/R) Die Eberjagd (72x54cm-28x21in) s.d.1928 s.l.verso
£1699   *$2786*   *(20-Jun-91 D.V51/R) Portrait of woman with hair put up (43x33cm-17x13in)*
          mono.d.1920 pastel (A.S 35000)
£2392   *$4139*   *(8-May-91 D.V58/R) Female nude seated (48x30cm-19x12in) mono.d.1912 chl*
          W/C (A.S 50000)
£2427   *$3981*   *(20-Jun-91 D.V50/R) Woman sewing (42x33cm-17x13in) s.d.15 pastel*
          (A.S 50000)
£2440   *$4514*   *(7-Mar-91 D.V120/R) Girl in white shirt (47x30cm-19x12in) mono.d.1921*
          chk (A.S 50000)
£2670   *$4379*   *(20-Jun-91 D.V52/R) Portrait of pensive looking woman (55x44cm-22x17in)*
          s.d.1929 chl pastel (A.S 55000)

FAISTENBERGER, Anton (1663-1708) Austrian
£13011 $23290   (13-Apr-91 FAL.M72/R) The finding of Moses (124x174cm-49x69in) s.
          (S.KR 140000)

FAIVRE, Jules-Abel (1867-1945) French
£1644 $3190   (9-Dec-90 ZZ.F25) Nymphes au bain (90x117cm-35x46in) s. (F.FR 16000)

FALAT, Julian (1853-?) Austrian
£776   *$1474*   *(3-Mar-91 PPB.K6) Forest path (50x80cm-20x31in) s. W/C (P.Z 14000000)*

FALCHETTI (19/20th C) Italian
£794 $1405   (22-Mar-91 EA.Z971) View of Castello d'Angeli (40x51cm-16x20in) s.d.1887
          (S.FR 2000)

FALCHETTI, Giuseppe (1843-1918) Italian
£750 $1470   (14-Feb-91 CSK185) A figure praying at a wayside shrine
          (46x30cm-18x12in) s. other painting by same hand two

FALCIATORE, Filippo (18th C) Italian
£34099 $58991   (21-May-91 SY.MI1077/R) Scena galante (60x42cm-24x17in) oval
                   (I.L 75000000)
£77290 $133712   (21-May-91 SY.MI1076/R) Concerto dei contadini. Concerto dei signori
                   (60x43cm-24x17in) pair oval (I.L 170000000)

FALCINELLI (?) ?
£1121 $2164   (12-Dec-90 ZZ.F43/R) Reines-marguerites dans une coupe (46x55cm-18x22in)
                   s. (F.FR 11000)

FALCK, Jarl (1901-1983) Finnish
£935 $1805   (15-Dec-90 BU.H45) Cattle in field near sea (21x28cm-8x11in) s.d.1961
                   panel (F.M 6500)

FALCO, Filippo de (1852-?) Italian
£1387 $2692   (4-Dec-90 F.R83/R) Piazza Municipio a Napoli (30x37cm-12x15in) s. panel
                   (I.L 3000000)

FALCO, Paolo de (attrib) (18th C) Italian
£2374 $4250   (11-Apr-91 SY.NY111/R) Noli me tangere (28x20cm-11x8in) copper

FALCON, M E (?) ?
£1000 $1630   (4-Jul-91 C614) Pieta (80x115cm-31x45in) s. after Jusepe Ribera

FALCONE, Aniello (1607-1656) Italian
£1824 $3228   (19-Mar-91 F.M336/R) Scena di battaglia (13x19cm-5x7in) pen bistre ink
                   W/C over pencil (I.L 4000000)
£4200 $6846   (1-Jul-91 S27/R) Head of boy seen in profile (27x21cm-11x8in) bears i.
                   red chk

FALCONE, Aniello (attrib) (1607-1656) Italian
£6843 $13481   (30-Oct-90 BU.S246/R) Cavalry skirmish by bridge (59x74cm-23x29in)
                   (S.KR 75000)

FALCONE, Aniello (style) (1607-1656) Italian
£2600 $4940   (13-Sep-90 CSK343) Cavalry engagement (56x70cm-22x28in)
£3000 $4890   (4-Jul-91 CSK101/R) Muleteers on track, hilltop village beyond
                   (56x71cm-22x28in)

FALCONER, Douglas (?) British
£550 $897   (13-Jun-91 CG95) The river Tay, Pertshire (51x76cm-20x30in) s. s.l.verso

FALCONER, Ian (20th C) American?
£2041 $4000   (6-Nov-90 CE.NY285/R) Butch, arms folded (91x75cm-36x30in) acrylic

FALCONNER, John M (1820-1903) American
£1474 $2800   (9-Jan-91 CH.NY96/R) Ruins. The fruit seller one i. one init.d.51 W/C
                   pencil three

FALCUCCI, Robert (1900-1982) ?
£2520 $4914   (28-Oct-90 PLF.P196/R) La 40 Chevaux sport (27x20cm-11x8in) s. gouache
                   (F.FR 25000)

FALDI, Arturo (1856-1911) Italian
£6250 $12250   (6-Nov-90 BA.S60/R) Washerwomen (43x66cm-17x26in) s.d.1882 (S.KR 68000)

FALERO, Luis Riccardo (1851-1896) Spanish
£5179 $8959   (21-May-91 DUR.M13/R) Momentos ociosos (40x20cm-16x8in) pair
                   (S.P 950000)
£13000 $24960   (30-Nov-90 C77/R) La coquette (161x84cm-63x33in) s.d.1879

FALK, Gathie (20th C) Canadian
£1404 $2751   (20-Nov-90 JOY.T9/R) Artist's garden (59x28cm-23x11in) s. board
                   (C.D 3200)

FALK, Hans (1918-) Swiss
£1107 $1881   (30-May-91 EA.Z167/R) Three little fish (28x44cm-11x17in) (S.FR 2800)
£2041 $4020   (16-Nov-90 EA.Z306/R) New York (27x34cm-11x13in) s.d.79 mixed media
                   collage (S.FR 5000)
£1061 $2091   (13-Nov-90 GF.L5323/R) Street sweeper with market woman Rina Gebhart in
                   Lenzburg (28x37cm-11x15in) s.i.d.1968 pencil col.pencil (S.FR 2600)
£1639 $3098   (28-Sep-90 S.Z134/R) Number 9 (56x90cm-22x35in) s.d.1960 mixed media
                   (S.FR 4000)
£1976 $3360   (27-May-91 GK.Z5325) Stromboli (45x73cm-18x29in) s.i.d.1963verso mixed
                   media canvas (S.FR 5000)
£5556 $9111   (21-Jun-91 G.Z77/R) Composition (81x122cm-32x48in) mixed media collage
                   (S.FR 14000)

FALK, Hjalmar (1856-1938) Scandinavian
£1136 $1909   (27-Apr-91 SO.S330/R) Coastal view with rocks and breakers
                   (21x42cm-8x17in) s.d.1910 W/C (S.KR 12000)
£1618 $3171   (10-Nov-90 FAL.M92/R) Coastal landscape, Blekinge (26x52cm-10x20in)
                   s.d.1933 W/C (S.KR 17600)

FALK, Lars-Erik (1922-) Scandinavian
£923 $1771   (27-Nov-90 BU.S87/R) Geometrical composition (81x60cm-32x24in)
                    s.d.1951-83verso panel (S.KR 10000)
£1661 $3188   (27-Nov-90 BU.S86/R) Painting (50x84cm-20x33in) s.i.d.1973verso
                    (S.KR 18000)

FALK, Ragnar (1903-1977) Swedish
£750 $1469   (20-Nov-90 GO.G59) Still life (50x61cm-20x24in) s. (S.KR 8200)

FALK, Robert Rafailovich (1886-1958) Russian
£1106 $1813   (19-Jun-91 ARC.P197/R) Monastere de Zagorsk (49x56cm-19x22in) mono.
                    board (F.FR 11000)
£2600 $4186   (24-Jun-91 CSK72) Summer landscape (59x79cm-23x31in) s.

FALK, Robert Rafailovich (attrib) (1886-1958) Russian
£811 $1322   (10-Jun-91 W.T1421) Blessing of the house (30x41cm-12x16in) board
                    (C.D 1500)

FALKENSTEIN, V v (19th C) ?
£1541 $2512   (12-Jun-91 N.M421/R) The storming of the Duppeler Schanzen in
                    German-Danish War of 1864 (33x42cm-13x17in) s. board (DM 4500)

FALL, George (c.1848-1925) British
*£780 $1513   (5-Dec-90 PHL29) Figures in boats on the river at Knareborough
                    (14x23cm-6x9in) s. col. washes*

FALSEN, Mimi (1861-1957) Norwegian
£2170 $4232   (11-Oct-90 BU.O34/R) Woman watering flowers (54x68cm-21x27in) s.
                    (N.KR 25000)

FALTER, John P (1910-1982) American
£8854 $17000   (30-Nov-90 CH.NY222/R) The fair (61x91cm-24x36in) s.

FANCELLI, Pietro (1764-1850) Italian
*£800 $1304   (2-Jul-91 C307) Statue of wisdom holding book and staff
                    (54x41cm-21x16in) i. black white chk*
*£912 $1614   (19-Mar-91 F.M275/R) Studio per Giasone e Medea (40x53cm-16x21in) ink
                    squared (I.L 2000000)*
£1200 $1956   (2-Jul-91 C306/R) Study of seated woman (56x37cm-22x15in) col.chk

FANELLI, Francesco (19th C) Italian
£593 $990   (6-Jun-91 F.M32) Viareggio (32x40cm-13x16in) s.d.16 i.verso
                    (I.L 1300000)
£924 $1784   (11-Dec-90 CH.R168) Paesaggio lacustre (23x32cm-9x13in) s. panel
                    (I.L 2000000)
£1091 $2138   (21-Nov-90 F.M88) Giovane boscaiola (66x41cm-26x16in) (I.L 2400000)

FANGOR, Wojciech (1922-) Polish
£613 $1000   (12-Jun-91 SY.NY209/R) M9 (122x122cm-48x48in) s.d.1970 verso
£1096 $1786   (14-Jun-91 L.K861/R) E 27 (71x71cm-28x28in) s.i.d.1966verso (DM 3200)
£1531 $3000   (6-Nov-90 CE.NY87/R) M57 (135x275cm-53x108in) s.i.d.1969 verso

FANNEN, J (fl.1890-1900) British
*£600 $1152   (16-Aug-90 B200/R) The S.S. 'Helen Newton' of Hull (47x81cm-19x32in)
                    s.d.1880 gouache*

FANNEN, John (fl.1890-1900) British
£1800 $3456   (16-Aug-90 B393/R) The Barque 'Tongoy' off coastline (51x76cm-20x30in)
                    init.d.1897
£1900 $3610   (10-Jan-91 B120/R) The barque Tongoy off coastline (51x76cm-20x30in)
                    init.d.1897

FANNER, Alice (1865-1930) British
£740 $1458   (5-Oct-90 ZZ.B225) Donkeys on beach (23x33cm-9x13in) s.

FANTIN-LATOUR, Henri (1836-1904) French
£1707 $3158   (6-Mar-91 APT.P106) Esquisse pour - Reflets d'Orient (24x28cm-9x11in)
                    paper laid down on canvas (F.FR 17000)
£2259 $4179   (6-Mar-91 APT.P105) Reverie, petit paysage (14x24cm-6x9in) s.
                    (F.FR 22500)
£8000 $13120   (19-Jun-91 S152/R) Le crepuscule (20x32cm-8x13in) s.
£10000 $19500   (19-Oct-90 C56/R) Troubadour et sa dame (24x17cm-9x7in) s. paper on
                    canvas
£12253 $20830   (27-May-91 GK.Z5154/R) Deux baigneuses sous bois (15x25cm-6x10in) s.
                    (S.FR 31000)
£14286 $28000   (14-Feb-91 CH.NY3/R) Fleurs, cyclamens (20x15cm-8x6in) s.
£50761 $100000   (14-Nov-90 SY.NY359/R) Roses (23x30cm-9x12in) s.d.84
£60302 $98894   (20-Jun-91 APT.P5/R) La tentation de Saint Antoine (62x76cm-24x30in) s.
                    (F.FR 600000)
£75000 $120750   (24-Jun-91 C3/R) Bouquet de fleurs, pensees (26x30cm-10x12in) s.d.83
£101523 $200000   (15-Nov-90 CH.NY205/R) Vase de roses (28x28cm-11x11in) s.d.80
£115607 $200000   (8-May-91 SY.NY118/R) Grand bouquet de roses (43cm-17ins circular)
                    s.d.86
£152284 $300000   (15-Nov-90 CH.NY202/R) Grand bouquet de chrysanthemes (42x45cm-17x18in)
                    s.d.1873
£196532 $340000   (7-May-91 SY.NY11/R) Oeillets d'Inde (46x50cm-18x20in) s.d.93

FANTIN-LATOUR, Henri (1836-1904) French-cont.
£663	$1279	(14-Dec-90 JM.P104) Etudes de nymphes (25x14cm-10x6in) black crayon tracing paper (F.FR 6500)
£750	$1223	(5-Jul-91 APT.P17) Baigneuse (14x8cm-6x3in) bears studio st. chl.htd.white chk. (F.FR 7500)
£1579	$3000	(28-Feb-91 CH.NY31/R) Etude des mains. Figure study after Michelangelo st.sig. crayon paper on board two
£1600	$2576	(24-Jun-91 CSK11/R) Etudes de nus debouts et couches (15x24cm-6x9in) st.sig. pencil paper on paper set of three
£1700	$2737	(24-Jun-91 CSK9/R) Etudes de nus et cupidons. Etude de nus (18x26cm-7x10in) st.sig. pencil paper on paper two
£2200	$3894	(19-Mar-91 C7/R) Etudes de nus (25x16cm-10x6in) st.sig. soft pencil tracing paper
£31000	$60140	(4-Dec-90 C102/R) La lecture (21x26cm-8x10in) s. chl

FANTIN-LATOUR, Henri (attrib) (1836-1904) French
£1523	$3000	(12-Nov-90 SG.M564) Nude on a rock in the forest (25x13cm-10x5in) s. panel
£6215	$11000	(18-Mar-91 SG.M1190) A vase of roses (56x43cm-22x17in) s.

FANTIN-LATOUR, Theodore (1805-1872) French
£814	$1335	(21-Jun-91 D.P67/R) Fillette au noeud rose (58x46cm-22x18in) s. pastel oval (F.FR 8100)
£2700	$5184	(27-Nov-90 PH243/R) Dark haired beauty (66x56cm-26x22in) s. pastel oval
£2700	$5184	(27-Nov-90 PH240/R) Portrait of lady (66x56cm-26x22in) s. pastel oval

FANTIN-LATOUR, Victoria (1840-1926) French
£2800	$4508	(24-Jun-91 CSK56/R) Vase de roses jaunes (45x65cm-18x26in) s.

FARA, Teresio (1929-1986) Argentinian
£780	$1350	(8-May-91 V.BA38) Boquense 2 (18x26cm-7x10in)
£1345	$2650	(14-Nov-90 V.BA52) Palsaje de Italia (57x77cm-22x30in)
£1345	$2650	(14-Nov-90 V.BA53) Jarra y huevos (39x49cm-15x19in)
£1774	$3300	(5-Sep-90 V.BA49) Naturaleza muerta (48x73cm-19x29in)
£1882	$3500	(5-Sep-90 V.BA50/R) Casas de Peralta Ramos (40x70cm-16x28in)

FARASYN, Edgard (1858-1938) Belgian
£736	$1252	(28-May-91 C.A106) Fishing boats in the surf (36x53cm-14x21in) s. (B.FR 45000)
£1164	$2083	(12-Mar-91 C.A89/R) Scene in Venice (46x57cm-18x22in) s. (B.FR 70000)
£1700	$3264	(27-Nov-90 PH28) Picking flowers (81x60cm-32x24in) s.l.d.1898
£499	$893	(12-Mar-91 C.A90) Fishing boats on the beach (36x53cm-14x21in) s. gouache (B.FR 30000)

FARASYN, L (1822-1899) Belgian
£684	$1300	(27-Feb-91 SY.NY135) Descent from cross (129x96cm-51x38in) s.d.1865
£2738	$4600	(17-Jul-91 SY.NY356/R) Sir Thomas More (152x112cm-60x44in) s.d.1876

FARAULT, Andre (20th C) ?
£557	$1091	(25-Nov-90 ZZ.F56/R) La bisquine cancalaise a Granville (31x39cm-12x15in) s. W/C (F.FR 5500)

FARBER, Manny (20th C) American
£3550	$6000	(1-May-91 B.SF5142/R) Carpenters (66x86cm-26x34in) s.d.1940 verso

FARELLI, Giacomo (1624-1706) Italian
£9092	$17820	(19-Nov-90 CH.R32/R) Giuseppe e la moglie di Putifarre (109x142cm-43x56in) (I.L 20000000)

FARENGHI, G (19th C) Italian
£3814	$6750	(22-Mar-91 S.W2805/R) Figures conversing outside Roman gates (71x53cm-28x21in) s. W/C

FARFA (1881-1964) Italian
£2071	$4039	(22-Oct-90 BR.M312/R) Castello (53x43cm-21x17in) s. oil collage mixed media board (I.L 4600000)

FARGUE, Paulus Constantin la (1732-1782) Dutch
£797	$1378	(22-May-91 PLF.P134/R) Homme fumant la pipe dans un paysage. Femme allant au marche (11x8cm-4x3in) both s. gouache vellum pair (F.FR 8000)

FARHI (?) ?
£2123	$4141	(15-Oct-90 CSC.P83/R) Composition (62x122cm-24x48in) s. oil plaster panel (F.FR 21000)

FARIN, Yvonne (?) ?
£1080	$1760	(11-Jun-91 GM.B963) Scene allegorique (170x222cm-67x87in) s. (B.FR 65000)

FARINATI, Giambattista Zelotti (1526-1578) Italian
£1003	$1776	(19-Mar-91 F.M322/R) Studio di profeta per pennacchio di volta (10x8cm-4x3in) ink htd white over pencil (I.L 2200000)

FARINATI, Glambattista Zelotti (attrib) (1526-1578) Italian
£553 $907   (21-Jun-91 CK.P40/R) Deux etudes de femme pour une alleogrie de
                 l'abondance (27x27cm-11x11in) i. verso wash ink htd.white (F.FR 5500)

FARINATI, Paolo (1524-1606) Italian
£57895 $110000   (11-Jan-91 CH.NY27/R) Forge of Vulcan (33x44cm-13x17in) on copper
£1700 $2873   (16-Apr-91 C113/R) A Ssibyl holding a tablet (27x13cm-11x5in) watermark
                 red chk.ink wash
£34737 $66000   (8-Jan-91 SY.NY128/R) The dead Christ supported by putti
                 (42x35cm-17x14in) ink wash htd.white traces blk.chk

FARINATI, Paolo (circle) (1524-1606) Italian
£1450 $2799   (14-Dec-90 PHM18) Christ at the pillar with the penitent St Peter and
                 town beyond (22x17cm-9x7in) copper

FARINGTON, Joseph (1747-1821) British
£5400 $10638   (31-Oct-90 S328/R) Landscape with view of Lincoln Castle with Lucy Tower
                 (60x72cm-24x28in) i.
£1000 $1680   (22-Apr-91 PH220) At Hastings in Sussex, fishing boats (27x59cm-11x23in)
                 s.d.1785 W/C over pencil ink
£1800 $2970   (11-Jul-91 S51/R) Grange near Keswick, Cumberland (14x23cm-6x9in) s.
                 i.verso pencil wash

FARKAS, Hazy (20th C) Hungarian
£1224 $2400   (6-Nov-90 GF.L2204/R) Interior with still life (100x73cm-39x29in) s.
                 (S.FR 3000)

FARLEY, Richard Blossom (1875-1951) American
£2835 $5500   (6-Dec-90 FA.PH646/R) Crows watching sunrise in November
                 (64x81cm-25x32in) s.

FARMER, Emily (1826-1905) British
£720 $1368   (12-Sep-90 CSK122/R) Daisy chain (56x36cm-22x14in) s.d.1873 W/C htd
                 white

FARNDON, Walter (1876-1964) American
£1091 $1800   (13-Jul-91 YFA.M65/R) Boatyard (36x46cm-14x18in) s. board
£1105 $1900   (15-May-91 SY.NY206/R) House by arched bridge in winter
                 (51x61cm-20x24in) s. board

FARNSWORTH, Jerry (1895-?) American
£781 $1500   (17-Dec-90 SY.NY340/R) Thoughtful child (61x51cm-24x20in) s. s.d.1944
                 stretcher masonite
£2646 $5000   (26-Sep-90 SY.NY183 a/R) The spring hat (51x42cm-20x17in) s.

FARQUHARSON, David (1839-1907) British
£500 $895   (10-Apr-91 CSK252) Wooded landscape with deer (46x33cm-18x13in) s.d.1906
£700 $1372   (21-Nov-90 JT194) Flowering pasture (46x76cm-18x30in) s.d.1903
£1020 $2010   (16-Nov-90 NM.P58) Paysage de neige (20x31cm-8x12in) panel (F.FR 10000)
£1105 $1900   (18-May-91 W.W81/R) Walking on the moors (30x46cm-12x18in) s.d.1896
£1200 $2244   (28-Aug-90 S799/R) The peep of day (54x71cm-21x28in) s.s.i.on stretcher
£1700 $3332   (22-Nov-90 CG601/R) The Allan Water, Stirlingshire (21x36cm-8x14in)
                 s.i.d.83 panel
£2400 $4032   (23-Apr-91 S108/R) Hoddum Castle on Annan (41x61cm-16x24in) s.d.89
                 mono.i.verso
£3200 $6144   (26-Nov-90 SWS170/R) Sennen Coe, Cornwall (34x59cm-13x23in) s.d.1897
                 i.verso
£4000 $7480   (28-Aug-90 S794/R) Hoeing the fields (31x51cm-12x20in) s.d.1883
£9000 $17640   (22-Nov-90 CG602/R) The morning breeze, Dordrecht (102x183cm-40x72in)
                 s.d.89 i.verso
£450 $734   (14-Jun-91 C136) The Seine from St Cloud (21x33cm-8x13in) s.d.83 W/C gum
                 arabic
£480 $850   (22-Mar-91 PHE20) A bit of the tweed (32x22cm-13x9in) s.d.95 W/C

FARQUHARSON, Joseph (1846-1935) British
£950 $1843   (6-Dec-90 CG92) Portrait of girl in brown dress (46x30cm-18x12in) s.
£1300 $2418   (5-Sep-90 BT169/R) In Glen Garry (28x43cm-11x17in) s. canvas on panel
£2423 $4700   (8-Dec-90 W.W219/R) The Trossachs in May (51x91cm-20x36in) s.d.84
£2800 $5600   (5-Feb-91 S26/R) Cauld blows wind frae east to west (30x46cm-12x18in) s.
£3200 $6400   (5-Feb-91 S65/R) Loch Howin (77x103cm-30x41in) s. i.stretcher
£3500 $7000   (8-Feb-91 C143/R) In the garden (46x30cm-18x12in) s.
£4000 $6760   (2-May-91 CG494/R) Sheep on snow bound road (49x43cm-19x17in) s.
£5000 $9800   (22-Nov-90 CG582/R) Winter river landscape with sheep (72x107cm-28x42in)
                 s.
£5200 $10400   (5-Feb-91 S32/R) Egyptian market (46x72cm-18x28in) s.
£5500 $9240   (23-Apr-91 S51/R) Corner of garden, Finzean (49x35cm-19x14in) s.
£5500 $10725   (17-Oct-90 PHG84/R) Gathering firewood (66x101cm-26x40in) s.
£6500 $12740   (22-Nov-90 CG578/R) Leaving the hills (41x65cm-16x26in) s.
£8500 $16660   (22-Nov-90 CG580/R) Sheep in winter landscape (30x46cm-12x18in) s.
£9000 $17640   (22-Nov-90 CG581/R) Sheep in winter landscape, evening (31x46cm-12x18in)
                 s.
£16000 $31360   (22-Nov-90 CG579/R) The joyless winter day (61x107cm-24x42in) s.
                 i.stretcher
£44000 $82280   (28-Aug-90 S786/R) Sheep in the snow (50x75cm-20x30in) s.
£4500 $9000   (5-Feb-91 CG24/R) Sketch for joyless winter day (36x69cm-14x27in) W/C
                 htd white

FARREN, Robert (1832-?) British
£5000 $9800   (13-Feb-91 S65/R) Donkeys and geese (76x127cm-30x50in) s.d.1891

FARRER, Henry (1843-1903) American
£2222 $4200   (27-Sep-90 CH.NY91/R) Twilight (31x46cm-12x18in) s.d.1896 W/C pencil
                       paper laid down on board

FARRER, Thomas Charles (1831-1891) British
£635 $1200   (25-Sep-90 CE.NY18/R) Study of a tree (21x19cm-8x7in) s.d.59 pencil
                       gouache

FARRERAS, Francisco (1927-) Spanish
£2097 $3607   (16-May-91 ANS.M89/R) Serie pequeno formato B/IV (42x34cm-17x13in)
                       s.d.87 collage board (S.P 385000)
£2622 $5061   (11-Dec-90 FER.M256/R) Cascada de piedra rosa (43x32cm-17x13in) s.d.87
                       collage board (S.P 480000)

FARRIER, Robert (1796-1879) British
£1579 $3000   (27-Feb-91 SY.NY256/R) Tragedy (66x83cm-26x33in) panel on masonite

FARUFFINI, Federico (1831-1869) Italian
£1368 $2600   (27-Feb-91 SY.NY328/R) Visit (42x35cm-17x14in) s.
£3004 $5797   (11-Dec-90 CH.R146/R) Paggio con liuto (34x23cm-13x9in) cardboard on
                       canvas (I.L 6500000)

FASANOTTI, Gaetano (1831-1882) Italian
£1201 $2319   (11-Dec-90 CH.R190/R) Paesaggio (22x47cm-9x19in) s. (I.L 2600000)
£2371 $3960   (6-Jun-91 F.M125) Ritorno dai campi (39x66cm-15x26in) s.d.1876
                       (I.L 5200000)

FASOLO, Giovanni Antonio (1530-1572) Italian
£27000 $44010   (5-Jul-91 C78/R) Girl adoring Christ Child on Madonna's lap, landscape
                       beyond (96x82cm-38x32in)

FASSBENDER, Josef (1903-1974) German
£1233 $2010   (14-Jun-91 L.K862/R) Vor mir (40x47cm-16x19in) s. indian ink brush pen
                       (DM 3600)
£1918 $3126   (14-Jun-91 L.K863/R) Untitled (65x92cm-26x36in) s.d.59 mixed media board
                       (DM 5600)

FASSIANOS, Aleco (1935-) Greek
£1276 $2513   (16-Nov-90 FB.P384/R) L'homme au cigare (25x25cm-10x10in) s.
                       (F.FR 12500)
£2111 $3778   (11-Mar-91 GL.P238) Le fumeur (42x33cm-17x13in) s. (F.FR 21000)
£4016 $6466   (25-Jun-91 BG.P25/R) Le sommeil qui arrive s.d.1970 i. stretcher
                       (F.FR 40000)
£4482 $7620   (30-May-91 FB.P52/R) Celui qui vent du monde (92x73cm-36x29in) s.d.71
                       (F.FR 45000)
£455 $891   (12-Feb-91 HC.P88) Le microphone. Tete d'homme (25x21cm-10x8in) s.i.
                       verso gouache copper double-sided (F.FR 4500)
£2390 $4064   (29-May-91 GL.P219/R) Le fumeur rose (36x26cm-14x10in) s. gouache board
                       laid down on canvas (F.FR 24000)
£4032 $7863   (20-Jan-91 GL.P132) Trois personnages sur fond bleu (34x53cm-13x21in) s.
                       gouache paper laid down on canvas (F.FR 40000)
£5183 $10366   (10-Feb-91 CC.P26/R) Le couple cycliste rouge (116x76cm-46x30in) s.
                       gouache pasted paper (F.FR 51000)

FATTORI, Giovanni (1825-1908) Italian
£10033 $16755   (6-Jun-91 F.M257/R) Marina livornese (13x23cm-5x9in) s. panel
                       (I.L 22000000)
£20179 $36120   (12-Mar-91 F.M81/R) Autunno (9x18cm-4x7in) s. panel (I.L 44000000)
£45861 $82091   (12-Mar-91 F.M119/R) Cortile rustico con contadina in costume da
                       ciociara e galline (43x34cm-17x13in) (I.L 100000000)
£59000 $115000   (18-Oct-90 F.M92/R) Bastimenti nel porto di Livorno (19x32cm-7x13in) s.
                       panel (I.L 130000000)
£100894 $180601   (12-Mar-91 F.M120/R) Paesaggio alberato, con tre monache e case sullo
                       sfondo (22x55cm-9x22in) panel (I.L 220000000)
£105480 $188810   (12-Mar-91 F.M118/R) La Punta del Romito, con barche di pescatori
                       (22x56cm-9x22in) (I.L 230000000)
£160514 $287319   (12-Mar-91 F.M111/R) Manovre di artiglieria (30x59cm-12x23in) s.
                       (I.L 350000000)
£909 $1782   (21-Nov-90 F.M130/R) Soldato con carro e cavalli. Studio per zampe di
                       cavallo (9x14cm-4x6in) pencil double-sided (I.L 2000000)
£21275 $41273   (5-Dec-90 F.M109/R) Veduta di Castiglioncello (12x38cm-5x15in) i.verso
                       W/C (I.L 46000000)

FATTORI, Giovanni (style) (1825-1908) Italian
£1813 $3064   (16-Apr-91 CH.R85) Mucche nella stalla (21x33cm-8x13in) i. panel
                       (I.L 4000000)

FAUBERT, Jean (20th C) French
£1004 $1616   (30-Jun-91 FE.P150) Femme a la guitare (112x58cm-44x23in) s. panel
                       (F.FR 10000)

FAUCONNIER, Henri le (1881-1946) French
£805	$1570	(10-Oct-90 ZEL.L1612/R) Female nude seated by table with vase of flowers (73x52cm-29x20in) s.verso (DM 2400)
£1007	$1963	(10-Oct-90 ZEL.L1613/R) Still life of marguerites in jug, tea pot, bottle of wine by curtain (61x65cm-24x26in) s.d.1939verso (DM 3000)
£1220	$2341	(27-Nov-90 SY.AM3830) Still life with sculpture and flowers (76x51cm-30x20in) init. (D.FL 4000)
£781	*$1351*	*(22-May-91 CH.AM348) Still life with flowers (84x45cm-33x18in) mono. chl W/C (D.FL 2600)*
£9655	$18538	(28-Nov-90 KF.M1034/R) Composition aux plaieuls (101x68cm-40x27in) mono.c.1920 W/C chl (DM 28000)

FAUERHOLDT, Viggo (1832-1883) Danish
£5338	$10036	(18-Sep-90 BU.K7/R) View of Dampskibsbroen with vessels, early spring morning (80x116cm-31x46in) s.d.1861 (D.KR 60000)

FAULKNER, Frank (20th C) British
£1538	$3000	(10-Oct-90 SY.NY559/R) Untitled (163x104cm-64x41in) s.d.1979erso acrylic

FAULKNER, H W (1860-?) American
£1058	*$2064*	*(28-Oct-90 M.V45) Venise (19x37cm-7x15in) s. W/C (F.FR 10500)*

FAULKNER, John (19th C) British
£1852	$3574	(12-Dec-90 CH.E148) Rathfarnham Castle Gate (45x65cm-18x26in) s.verso (E.P 2000)
£500	*$990*	*(30-Jan-91 CSK131) Cattle watering beside a highland loch (43x76cm-17x30in) s.d.1876 pencil W/C htd.white*
£600	*$978*	*(13-Jun-91 CSK95) Fox Warren, Byfleet, Surrey (44x75cm-17x30in) s.i. pencil W/C*
£700	*$1211*	*(9-May-91 B175/R) Kenilworth Castle (46x81cm-18x32in) s.i. W/C scratching out*
£720	*$1418*	*(30-Oct-90 SC99) Loch Shiel, Argyllshire (60x100cm-24x39in) s.i. W/C pencil paper on canvas*
£880	*$1470*	*(22-Jul-91 SWS806/R) Byfleet,Surrey (44x73cm-17x29in) s.i. W/C over pencil htd.bodycol.*
£900	*$1485*	*(11-Jul-91 GSP591) A shepherd's home (46x97cm-18x38in) s. W/C*
£950	*$1786*	*(19-Sep-90 PHC78) Corurck, North Wales (46x81cm-18x32in) s. i.verso W/C*
£1000	*$1950*	*(18-Oct-90 SC3041/R) Over Swavesey, Cambridgeshire (47x96cm-19x38in) s.i. W/C pencil*
£1200	*$2364*	*(13-Nov-90 SWS64/R) Near Rickmansworth, Hertfordshire (47x97cm-19x38in) s.i.W/C htd.bodycol.*
£1250	*$2363*	*(27-Sep-90 PHF195/R) Irish moorland landscape with figure on track (43x76cm-17x30in) s.d.1878 W/C*
£1500	*$3000*	*(8-Feb-91 C17/R) Cottages at Cambus o'May, Aberdeenshire (43x76cm-17x30in) s.d.1878 i. verso pencil W/C htd.white*
£1850	*$3201*	*(20-May-91 SWS394/R) The Grand Junction canal at Cowley near Uxbridge (44x83cm-17x33in) s. W/C over pencil htd.bodycol.scratching out*
£2000	*$3340*	*(3-Jun-91 PHB5) Farmpond (44x75cm-17x30in) s. W/C*
£2200	*$3674*	*(22-Jul-91 SWS807/R) Roundstone Road, County Galway (47x98cm-19x39in) s. W/C*
£3500	*$6545*	*(28-Aug-90 S779/R) Grouse shooting (77x132cm-30x52in) s. W/C over pencil htd white*
£4000	*$7800*	*(26-Oct-90 CG28/R) The old bridge of Arda, Co Donegal (51x103cm-20x41in) s.d.1876 W/C*

FAURE, Elisabeth (1906-1964) ?
£2755	$5428	(13-Nov-90 ARC.P157/R) Marche aux boeufs, Madagascar (100x144cm-39x57in) s. (F.FR 27000)
£4260	$8178	(17-Dec-90 ARC.P61/R) Marchandes de poissons (100x144cm-39x57in) s. (F.FR 42000)
£40609	$80000	(15-Nov-90 SY.NY50/R) Les anemones (85x56cm-33x22in) s.d.1955 oil sand

FAURE, Germain (1884-) French
£594	*$1051*	*(5-Apr-91 DAR.P4 a) Projet de monument aux morts (82x58cm-32x23in) crayon pen W/C (F.FR 6000)*
£1040	*$1840*	*(5-Apr-91 DAR.P6/R) Projet pour une fontaine monumentale dont le Jugement (108x62cm-43x24in) pen wash (F.FR 10500)*
£1188	*$2103*	*(5-Apr-91 DAR.P5/R) Elevation et coupe longitudinale pen W/C two on same mount (F.FR 12000)*
£2079	*$3680*	*(5-Apr-91 DAR.P8/R) Facade Louis XVI (55x148cm-22x58in) pen wash (F.FR 21000)*
£2178	*$3855*	*(5-Apr-91 DAR.P3/R) Facade. Plan au sol W/C drawing (F.FR 22000)*

FAUSTNER, Luitpold (1845-?) German
£1092	$2053	(21-Sep-90 N.M3173/R) Two women at the banks of lake Chiemsee (12x16cm-5x6in) s. panel (DM 3200)

FAUTRIER, Jean (1898-1964) French
£5478	$9313	(2-Jun-91 GL.P156/R) Sans titre (50x64cm-20x25in) s. blotting paper (F.FR 55000)
£5478	$9313	(2-Jun-91 GL.P151/R) Sans titre (65x50cm-26x20in) s. blotting paper (F.FR 55000)
£9628	$15789	(20-Jun-91 F.M486/R) Claudette (24x27cm-9x11in) s. (I.L 21000000)
£12232	$23486	(26-Nov-90 GL.P91/R) Jeune femme a sa toilette (46x38cm-18x15in) s. (F.FR 120000)
£15936	$27092	(2-Jun-91 GL.P166/R) Les raisins noirs (26x34cm-10x13in) s. paper laid down on canvas (F.FR 160000)

FAUTRIER, Jean (1898-1964) French-cont.
£19920	$33865	(30-May-91 FB.P26/R) Inepties (89x116cm-35x46in) s.d.59 paper laid down on canvas (F.FR 200000)
£24900	$42331	(2-Jun-91 GL.P161/R) Tete (27x22cm-11x9in) s.d.1942 paper laid down on canvas (F.FR 250000)
£43000	$83850	(18-Oct-90 S40/R) Nature morte (38x46cm-15x18in) s.
£66000	$106260	(27-Jun-91 S9/R) Variations chromatiques (27x46cm-11x18in) s.d.58 oil pigment paper on canvas
£100000	$194000	(6-Dec-90 C500/R) Tranches d'orange (27x35cm-11x14in) s. oil pigment paper on canvas
£370000	$595700	(27-Jun-91 S36/R) Grandes etendues (73x92cm-29x36in) s.d.57 oil pigment paper on hessian
£2393	*$3948*	*(10-Jul-91 FB.P51/R) Nu (29x35cm-11x14in) ink (F.FR 24000)*
£4394	*$8524*	*(3-Dec-90 F.M343/R) Composizione (12x17cm-5x7in) mono.d.1957 gouache cardboard (I.L 9500000)*
£6000	*$10620*	*(21-Mar-91 C202/R) Untitled (20x35cm-8x14in) s. ink chl.*
£6000	*$10620*	*(21-Mar-91 C203/R) Untitled (20x35cm-8x14in) s. ink chl.*
£6263	*$12275*	*(14-Feb-91 GL.P6/R) Nu couche (22x34cm-9x13in) s. lead pencil (F.FR 62000)*
£6877	*$11278*	*(19-Jun-91 F.M75/R) Nudo femminile (27x33cm-11x13in) s.d.1943 pencil (I.L 15000000)*
£7396	*$14571*	*(6-Oct-90 GL.P38/R) Modele nu, accroupi (34x30cm-13x12in) wash stumping (F.FR 75000)*
£18330	*$36110*	*(29-Oct-90 FB.P8/R) Composition (49x64cm-19x25in) mono. gouache (F.FR 180000)*

FAUVEL, Georges (19th C) French
| £2008 | $3233 | (24-Jun-91 BL.P24) Chiens de chasse (99x80cm-39x31in) s.d.18 (F.FR 20000) |

FAVAI, Gennaro (1882-) Italian?
| £609 | $1200 | (13-Nov-90 CE.NY23/R) Il Canale Grande di Venezia (58x65cm-23x26in) s. |
| £711 | $1423 | (6-Feb-91 FB.P115) Palais Venitien (47x53cm-19x21in) s. panel (F.FR 7000) |

FAVANNE, Henri de (attrib) (1668-1752) French
| £10500 | $17115 | (4-Jul-91 C780/R) Discovery of Callisto (65x94cm-26x37in) |

FAVEN, Antti (1882-1948) Finnish
| £3409 | $6102 | (14-Apr-91 BU.H27/R) Summer's day (60x46cm-24x18in) s.d.1927 (F.M 24000) |
| £5014 | $9878 | (17-Nov-90 BU.H38/R) Landscape view from Brunnsparken (90x130cm-35x51in) s.d.1931 (F.M 35000) |

FAVEROT, Joseph (1862-?) French
| £1376 | $2683 | (12-Oct-90 AW.H2286/R) Shepherd with flock (55x47cm-22x19in) s. (DM 4100) |

FAVIER, Philippe (1957-) French
£2493	$4113	(10-Jul-91 FB.P108/R) Sans titre (11x9cm-4x4in) s.d.27/7/88 glass (F.FR 25000)
£3789	$6251	(10-Jul-91 FB.P105 a/R) Sans titre (13x7cm-5x3in) s.d.85 glass (F.FR 38000)
£4133	$8059	(26-Oct-90 CC.P115/R) Vent (15x22cm-6x9in) s.i.d.1988 enamel paint glass (F.FR 41000)
£5179	$8805	(30-May-91 FB.P96/R) Vent bleu fonce (15x19cm-6x7in) s.d.6.8.88 glass (F.FR 52000)
£1004	*$1616*	*(25-Jun-91 BG.P23) Paysage (12x10cm-5x4in) s.d.9/1/82 mixed media (F.FR 10000)*
£5976	*$10159*	*(30-May-91 FB.P95/R) Hommage aux demoiselles (11x19cm-4x7in) s.i.d.20.5.86 oil collage glass triptych (F.FR 60000)*

FAVORIN, Ellen (1853-1919) Finnish
£994	$1780	(14-Apr-91 BU.H28/R) Coastal landscape (12x14cm-5x6in) s. panel (F.M 7000)
£1871	$3610	(15-Dec-90 BU.H47) Landscape from Ruokolaks (21x28cm-8x11in) s. panel (F.M 13000)
£2152	$3637	(20-Apr-91 HOR.H68/R) 'Punkaharju' (12x16cm-5x6in) s. (F.M 15000)
£2292	$4516	(17-Nov-90 BU.H41/R) Winter arriving (27x19cm-11x7in) s. (F.M 16000)
£2853	$5592	(24-Nov-90 HOR.H79/R) Landscape from Punkaharju (12x16cm-5x6in) s. (F.M 20000)
£3295	$6491	(17-Nov-90 BU.H40/R) Landscape, Vintervy (14x22cm-6x9in) s. (F.M 23000)
£3424	$6710	(24-Nov-90 HOR.H83/R) Lake landscape (39x26cm-15x10in) s. (F.M 24000)
£3424	$6710	(24-Nov-90 HOR.H80/R) Fishing (16x21cm-6x8in) s. (F.M 24000)
£5421	$10625	(24-Nov-90 HOR.H81/R) View of the lake (54x39cm-21x15in) s. (F.M 38000)

FAVORY, Andre (1888-1937) French
£610	$1220	(6-Feb-91 FB.P116) Moret sur Loing (50x65cm-20x26in) mono. l. verso panel (F.FR 6000)
£754	$1236	(18-Jun-91 APT.P194) Le modele (38x55cm-15x22in) s. (F.FR 7500)
£1947	$3816	(11-Nov-90 ZZ.F103/R) Nu assis au chapeau (65x46cm-26x18in) s. (F.FR 19000)
£3651	$7229	(3-Feb-91 I.N86/R) Du dans un paysage (81x125cm-32x49in) s. (F.FR 36000)

FAVRAY, Antoine de (1706-1791) French
£9000 $17100   (1-Mar-91 C139/R) Portrait of Emmanuel, Prince de Rohan, Bishop of Malta
                                and other clerics (49x70cm-19x28in)
£48304 $93710   (7-Dec-90 SY.MO193/R) Dames de Malte se faisant visite (48x64cm-19x25in)
                                (F.FR 470000)

FAVRAY, Antoine de (circle) (1706-1791) French
£6030 $9889   (21-Jun-91 SY.MO22/R) Portrait de gentilhomme europeen en perse
                                (53x33cm-21x13in) canvas laid down on board (F.FR 60000)

FAY, Hans (1888-1957) German
£839 $1636   (12-Oct-90 AW.H2287/R) Boys bathing in sea (27x30cm-11x12in) s. i.on
                                card verso (DM 2500)
£3333 $5967   (12-Apr-91 AW.H1395/R) View over Bad Durkheim towards the Rhine valley
                                (61x81cm-24x32in) s. board (DM 10000)

FAY, Joseph (1813-1875) German
£1361 $2300   (20-Apr-91 WOL.C122/R) In fields (53x71cm-21x28in) s.d.64
£1497 $2649   (20-Mar-91 KM.K1206) Italian landscape with figures making music and
                                dancing (31x42cm-12x17in) s. (DM 4400)

FAY, Ludwig Benno (1859-1906) German
£5374 $10210   (28-Feb-91 D.V4/R) Mare and foal (52x69cm-20x27in) s. (A.S 110000)

FAYARD, A (19th C) ?
£867 $1500   (21-May-91 CE.NY219/R) Gathering seaweed (66x92cm-26x36in) s.i.

FAYARD, R (19th C) ?
£2299 $4000   (27-Mar-91 B.SF4306/R) The farewell (65x93cm-26x37in) s.

FAYRAM, John (attrib) (18th C) British
£2800 $5516   (13-Nov-90 PH102/R) Portrait of lady wearing satin dress with cloak and
                                straw hat (91x72cm-36x28in)

FAYRAM, John (circle) (18th C) British
£3500 $6475   (4-Mar-91 PHB73) Portrait of naval officer, with warship beyond
                                (126x110cm-50x43in)

FEARNLEY, Thomas (1802-1842) Norwegian
£25000 $48000   (28-Nov-90 S2/R) Norwegian river landscape (62x80cm-24x31in) s.d.1820

FEBVRE, Edouard (20th C) French
£900 $1467   (5-Jul-91 APT.P119) Bal du 14 juillet (46x55cm-18x22in) s. (F.FR 9000)
£1217 $2410   (3-Feb-91 I.N88/R) Paysage de neige (46x56cm-18x22in) s. panel
                                (F.FR 12000)
£1471 $2912   (3-Feb-91 I.N87) Montmartre sous la neige (55x46cm-22x18in) s.
                                (F.FR 14500)
£1744 $3400   (10-Oct-90 SY.NY105/R) Jardin Luxembourg (38x53cm-15x21in) s.d.1924
                                s.i.d.1924verso

FEBVRE, le (?) ?
£600   *$1158*   *(11-Dec-90 C72/R) An extensive hilly landscape with a traveller and*
                                mules on a path (15x19cm-6x7in) bodycol. vellum laid down on panel

FECHIN, Nicolai (1881-1955) American/Russian
£3846   *$6500*   *(1-May-91 B.SF5187/R) Portrait of man in hat (44x32cm-17x13in) s. chl*

FEDARB, Daphne (fl.1934-1940) British
£3200 $6016   (20-Sep-90 C117/R) Anchor (56x77cm-22x30in) s.

FEDDEN, A Romilly (1875-1939) British
£380   *$661*   *(28-Mar-91 CSK134) Saint-Jean-Pied-de-Port (25x34cm-10x13in) s. W/C*
                                bodycol

FEDDEN, Mary (1915-) British
£700 $1344   (21-Feb-91 B47/R) Maltese landscape (40x51cm-16x20in) board
£750 $1478   (1-Nov-90 B69/R) View of village (41x51cm-16x20in) s.d.1964
£800 $1392   (28-Mar-91 CSK199/R) Checked mug (15x20cm-6x8in) s.d.1987 s.i.verso
                                board
£800 $1568   (25-Jan-91 C68/R) Black dish (51x40cm-20x16in) s.d.1989 s.i.stretcher
£950 $1786   (20-Sep-90 CSK137/R) Stormy weather (40x29cm-16x11in) s.d.1983 s.i.verso
£1000 $1740   (27-Mar-91 S236/R) Still life IV (91x117cm-36x46in) s.d.1962 i.verso
                                board
£1400 $2632   (20-Sep-90 C100/R) The Meeting (51x61cm-20x24in) s.d.1988
£1400 $2436   (27-Mar-91 S182/R) Sheep (46x61cm-18x24in) s.d.1989 s.i.verso board
£2000 $3920   (6-Nov-90 PH145/R) The black table (30x40cm-12x16in) s.d.1971
£2500 $4225   (2-May-91 B99/R) Window, Valletta (50x61cm-20x24in) s.d.1958 i. verso
£2500 $4625   (8-Mar-91 C197/R) Still life with fruit (61x51cm-24x20in) s.d.1988
£2800 $5264   (20-Sep-90 C111/R) Striped dish (51x61cm-20x24in) s.d.1986
£3200 $6016   (20-Sep-90 C35/R) Lulu (50x40cm-20x16in) s.d.1989 s.i.verso board
£4500 $8820   (9-Nov-90 C217/R) Still life of flowers and fruits on blue table
                                (46x54cm-18x21in) s.d.1952 s.i.stretcher
£420   *$731*   *(28-Mar-91 CSK226/R) Butterflies (20x13cm-8x5in) s.d.1986 collage W/C*
£500   *$870*   *(27-Mar-91 S197/R) Shrimping (25x20cm-10x8in) s.d.1988 W/C gouache*
£950   *$1862*   *(25-Jan-91 C60/R) Cat on harbour wall (21x16cm-8x6in) s.d.1981 W/C*
                                bodycol

FEDDER, Otto (1873-1919) German
£847 $1381   (3-Jul-91 WE.MU15/R) Shepherd returning with flock (25x33cm-10x13in)
     s.d.1902 (DM 2500)
£900 $1611   (12-Apr-91 BM.B591/R) Skaters in winter landscape, possibly Netherlands
     (17x17cm-7x7in) s.i. panel (DM 2700)
£970 $1834   (27-Sep-90 D.V165/R) Winter landscape at sunset (25x43cm-10x17in) s.
     (A.S 20000)
£1017 $1658   (3-Jul-91 WE.MU14/R) Winter landscape (24x43cm-9x17in) s. (DM 3000)
£1224 $2362   (12-Dec-90 WE.MU80/R) Gossip at the wayside (10x14cm-4x6in) s. board
     (DM 3500)
£1370 $2233   (12-Jun-91 N.M422) Upper Bavarian peasant couples with cow on road after
     rain (6x9cm-2x4in) s. panel (DM 4000)
£1433 $2709   (25-Sep-90 FN.S2163) Snowy river landscape with farmhouses and figures,
     evening (34x53cm-13x21in) s. (DM 4200)

FEDDERSEN, Hans Peter (younger) (1848-1941) Danish
£4899 $9552   (26-Oct-90 BM.B778/R) Graben im ... (35x46cm-14x18in) s.d.1897
     rem.i.verso (DM 14500)

FEDELER, Carl Justus Harmen (1799-1858) German
£2048 $4014   (24-Nov-90 SA.A642/R) Regenstein, Harz (90x125cm-35x49in) s.i.
     (DM 6000)

FEDER, Adolphe (1886-1945?) French
£890 $1593   (14-Apr-91 GL.P71) Nu dans l'atelier (66x50cm-26x20in) s. (F.FR 9000)
£1224 $2386   (10-Oct-90 ARC.P73) Nature morte aux tulipes (100x66cm-39x26in) s.d.38
     (F.FR 12200)
£1407 $2308   (18-Jun-91 APT.P195) Portrait de femme (100x81cm-39x32in) s.
     (F.FR 14000)
£593 $1062   (14-Apr-91 GL.P69) Maternite (44x30cm-17x12in) s.i. W/C (F.FR 6000)

FEDERICO, Cavalier Michele (1884-?) Italian
£625 $1200   (27-Nov-90 W.T1104) Breakers and rocky shore, Capri (66x88cm-26x35in) s.
     (C.D 1400)
£700 $1379   (13-Nov-90 SWS353/R) Fisherman tending his nets, Facaglioni
     (24x39cm-9x15in) s.i. i.d.1905 label verso

FEDERLE, Aegidius (1810-1876) Swiss
£720 $1217   (1-May-91 GD.B256/R) View from Gindelwaldtal to Wellhorn and Wetterhorn
     (69x91cm-27x36in) s. W/C (S.FR 1800)

FEDERLE, Helmut (1944-) Swiss
£15306 $30000   (8-Nov-90 CH.NY387/R) Women standing in the doorframe
     (241x213cm-95x84in) s.i.d.83 verso dispersion linen

FEDI, Guiseppe (attrib) (?) ?
£2972 $5766   (5-Dec-90 DO.H2041/R) Ship portrait Vesta von Flensburg
     (46x68cm-18x27in) W/C gouache over indian ink pen dr. (DM 8500)

FEDIER, Franz (1922-) ?
£675 $1167   (25-May-91 AB.L98/R) Untitled (80x55cm-31x22in) s.d.1980verso acrylic
     panel (S.FR 1700)

FEDOROFF, Michel (19th C) Russian
£1406 $2263   (27-Jun-91 APT.P148/R) Danseurs devant une datcha. Jeunes filles jouant
     a la balancoire devant une datcha (26x35cm-10x14in) s.d.28 juillet-9
     aout 1843 pair (F.FR 14000)

FEDOROV, Alexei (1927-) Russian
£503 $965   (18-Feb-91 ARC.P61/R) L'embarcadere (36x66cm-14x26in) s. canvas laid
     down on panel (F.FR 5000)
£503 $965   (18-Feb-91 ARC.P55) Le Grand Rostov (80x60cm-31x24in) s. (F.FR 5000)
£503 $965   (18-Feb-91 ARC.P58/R) A l'usine (80x64cm-31x25in) s. (F.FR 5000)
£520 $874   (26-Apr-91 ARC.P81/R) Le tourneur (74x114cm-29x45in) s. d.54 verso
     (F.FR 5200)
£854 $1640   (18-Feb-91 ARC.P59) Remorqueurs sur la Neva (41x95cm-16x37in) s.
     (F.FR 8500)
£1357 $2605   (18-Feb-91 ARC.P60/R) Reunion technique (50x76cm-20x30in) s.d.52
     (F.FR 13500)

FEDOROVA, Maria (1859-1934) ?
£739 $1322   (14-Apr-91 BU.H123/R) Wood interior (34x25cm-13x10in) s. panel
     (F.M 5200)
£1218 $2399   (17-Nov-90 BU.H223/R) In the farmyard (32x47cm-13x19in) s. (F.M 8500)
£3152 $6209   (17-Nov-90 BU.H222/R) Harvesting scene (40x59cm-16x23in) s. (F.M 22000)
£4011 $7903   (17-Nov-90 BU.H221/R) On the lake shore (71x56cm-28x22in) s.
     (F.M 28000)

FEDOTOV, Pavel Andreevich (1815-1852) Russian
£6000 $11700   (10-Oct-90 C204/R) Portrait of young man (25x20cm-10x8in) s.verso card

FEEDERLE, Carl (1832-1881) German
£1525 $2486   (3-Jul-91 WE.MU58/R) View of Eibsee with Zugspitze (14x26cm-6x10in)
     mono. panel (DM 4500)

FEELEY, Paul (1913-) American
£3807 $7500 (5-Oct-90 CH.NY21/R) Orange and blue (122x153cm-48x60in) acrylic
£4061 $8000 (5-Oct-90 CH.NY18/R) Acrab (153x152cm-60x60in) s.i.d.64 acrylic

FEHDMER, Richard (1860-?) German
£2136 $3823 (11-Apr-91 D.V278/R) Winter landscape, evening (28x45cm-11x18in)
s.d.1893 (A.S 45000)

FEHR, Friedrich (1862-?) German
£1107 $2159 (12-Oct-90 AW.H2294/R) Wooded landscape (34x50cm-13x20in) indis.s. board
(DM 3300)

FEHR, Henri (19/20th C) Swiss?
*£408 $804 (16-Nov-90 GK.Z5354) Portrait d'une Espagnole (49x32cm-19x13in) s.
pastel (S.FR 1000)*

FEID, Josef (1806-1870) Austrian
£2373 $4248 (11-Apr-91 D.V4/R) River landscape with cattle watering
(53x68cm-21x27in) s.d.1857 (A.S 50000)

FEIERTAG, Karl (19/20th C) German
£380 $680 (11-Apr-91 D.V333/R) We congratulate (26x17cm-10x7in) s. W/C (A.S 8000)

FEIKL, Stanislaw (?) ?
£623 $1246 (6-Feb-91 N.M595/R) View of Prague Castle seen from Karlsbrucke at dawn
(71x100cm-28x39in) s. (DM 1800)

FEIKS, Alfred (1880-?) Hungarian
£3589 $6208 (8-May-91 D.V60/R) Bull fight (56x70cm-22x28in) s.d.924 (A.S 75000)

FEILER, Paul (1918-) British
£620 $1035 (4-Jun-91 PH83/R) Orbis XXVIII (15x20cm-6x8in) s.i.d.1968 verso
£1400 $2590 (8-Mar-91 C167/R) Little orange rocks III (23x30cm-9x12in) s.d.53
i.d.verso board
£2100 $3906 (5-Sep-90 BT238/R) Boboli Gardens, Florence (38x53cm-15x21in) s.
s.i.d.18.10.53 verso board
£2200 $4312 (6-Nov-90 PH177) Related forms, grey IV (46x46cm-18x18in)
s.i.d.1966/67verso
£2200 $3586 (1-Jul-91 S23/R) Untitled (56x76cm-22x30in) s.d.60 oil pastels col.chks.

FEININGER (20th C) German
£1600 $2672 (7-Jun-91 BW211) Aquadukt (41x46cm-16x18in) s. W/C

FEININGER, Lyonel (1871-1956) German
£27304 $53515 (23-Nov-90 VG.B8/R) Farmhouse with orchard (37x61cm-15x24in) s.d.1907
canvas on board (DM 80000)
£88737 $173925 (23-Nov-90 VG.B43/R) Wellenkamm und Gegenbild (51x76cm-20x30in) s.d.1952
canvas laid down (DM 260000)
£121622 $206757 (28-May-91 KF.M627/R) Shadow of dissolution (91x76cm-36x30in) s.
s.i.d.1953stretcher (DM 360000)
£153584 $290273 (25-Sep-90 FN.S1947/R) Seascape (33x56cm-13x22in) s. s.i.d.1947stretcher
(DM 450000)
£170648 $334471 (23-Nov-90 VG.B41/R) Visiting (53x35cm-21x14in) i.d.1917stretcher
(DM 500000)
£409556 $802730 (23-Nov-90 VG.B42/R) Stars over the city, night (91x101cm-36x40in)
s.d.21 s.i.d.verso (DM 1200000)
*£814 $1359 (6-Jun-91 HN.H310/R) Two illustrations to Norwegian folk stories
(31x24cm-12x9in) i. pen chk.bodycol. (DM 2400)*
*£845 $1436 (28-May-91 KF.M629/R) Beach scene with boats (14x22cm-6x9in) d.1929
pencil (DM 2500)*
*£1014 $1723 (1-Jun-91 VG.B528/R) Stroller in coastal landscape (14x22cm-6x9in)
d.1924 pencil (DM 3000)*
*£1486 $2527 (1-Jun-91 VG.B527/R) Warrior from the Middle Ages with gun. Study of
seated woman (18x13cm-7x5in) s.d.1901 gouache ink pen pencil
double-sided (DM 4400)*
*£2000 $3220 (24-Jun-91 CSK156/R) Strand Heringsdorf (16x20cm-6x8in) s.i.d.1912
pencil paper on card sold with 2 W/C*
*£2200 $3542 (24-Jun-91 CSK157/R) View from artist's studio (10x16cm-4x6in) i.d.11
pencil paper on board sold with two W/C*
*£2397 $3908 (15-Jun-91 L.K201/R) Stagsegel, schooner (18x28cm-7x11in) s.i.d.1930
indian ink pen (DM 7000)*
*£3220 $5378 (6-Jun-91 HN.H320/R) Little ghost (15x8cm-6x3in) s. W/C over pen
(DM 9500)*
*£3390 $5661 (6-Jun-91 HN.H318/R) Silent city (28x44cm-11x17in) s.d.1953 chl.
(DM 10000)*
*£4061 $8000 (3-Oct-90 SY.NY136/R) Ghosties (99x99cm-39x39in) one s.d.1954 one
s.d.1955 W/C pen ink*
*£4061 $8000 (3-Oct-90 SY.NY135/R) Summer skies (19x31cm-7x12in) s.i.d.1953 W/C pen
ink*
*£4778 $9365 (22-Nov-90 L.K933/R) Coastal landscape (23x29cm-9x11in) s.i. indian nk
pen (DM 14000)*
*£4822 $9500 (3-Oct-90 SY.NY137/R) Powder tower (32x48cm-13x19in) s.d.44 W/C chl pen
ink*
*£5076 $10000 (15-Nov-90 CH.NY149/R) Mole (30x48cm-12x19in) s.i.d.28 pen ink W/C paper
on board*

FEININGER, Lyonel (1871-1956) German-cont.

£5076	$10000	(15-Nov-90 CH.NY137/R) Mole II (30x46cm-12x18in) s.i.d.25 pen ink W/C paper on board
£5085	$8492	(6-Jun-91 HN.H316/R) Ships and lighthouse (27x18cm-11x7in) s.d.1938 pen (DM 15000)
£6048	$11794	(23-Oct-90 CSC.P7/R) La locomotive (8x15cm-3x6in) s.i. W/C Indian ink (F.FR 60000)
£6122	$11878	(7-Dec-90 G.Z69/R) Gabendorf with church in yellow sunlight (23x31cm-9x12in) s.d.1955 W/C chl indian ink pencil (S.FR 15000)
£6599	$13000	(3-Oct-90 SY.NY133/R) All directions (31x47cm-12x19in) s.d.51 W/C pen ink
£7770	$13209	(1-Jun-91 VG.B287/R) Silhouette of town by the river (15x25cm-6x10in) s.i.d.1945 W/C indian ink pen (DM 23000)
£8163	$16000	(15-Feb-91 SY.NY72/R) Street in Treptow (31x24cm-12x9in) s.i.d.52 W/C india ink
£8446	$14358	(1-Jun-91 VG.B285/R) Four little ghosties (16x11cm-6x4in) s.d.1954 i.verso W/C indian ink pen (DM 25000)
£8475	$14153	(6-Jun-91 HN.H314/R) Sailing boat (20x29cm-8x11in) s.i.d.1934 W/C pen (DM 25000)
£9538	$16500	(9-May-91 CH.NY135/R) Seascape (30x48cm-12x19in) s.d.1952 W/C pen
£10135	$17230	(1-Jun-91 VG.B286/R) The stroller (15x23cm-6x9in) s.d.1951 W/C indian ink pen over chk (DM 30000)
£11149	$18953	(1-Jun-91 VG.B284/R) Clouds above the sea (27x44cm-11x17in) s.d.1950 W/C indian ink pen (DM 33000)
£13959	$27500	(14-Nov-90 SY.NY169/R) Scattered gold (32x48cm-13x19in) s.d.51 W/C pen
£14189	$24122	(28-May-91 KF.M628/R) Stadt Tor II (3x23cm-1x9in) s.i.d.1923 W/C pen (DM 42000)
£15228	$30000	(15-Nov-90 CH.NY184/R) Sheer nostalgia (29x44cm-11x17in) s.d.44 W/C pen ink paper on board
£15593	$26041	(6-Jun-91 HN.H311/R) Mellingen I (23x31cm-9x12in) s.i.d.1914 chl. (DM 46000)
£16382	$32109	(24-Nov-90 VG.B252/R) Houses in Luneburg (23x30cm-9x12in) s.i.d.1932 pen W/C (DM 48000)
£18182	$35273	(7-Dec-90 GB.B6493/R) Jolly offshore II (31x47cm-12x19in) s.i.d.1942 W/C pen (DM 52000)
£28716	$48530	(3-May-91 SA.A811/R) Nermsdorf I (24x38cm-9x15in) s.d.1924 W/C (DM 85000)
£37572	$65000	(8-May-91 SY.NY166/R) Pariser hauser (32x23cm-13x9in) s.i.d.Sunday July 14.1912 ink laid on paper
£58376	$115000	(3-Oct-90 SY.NY134/R) Composition, gables 5 (38x61cm-15x24in) s. s.i.d.1934stretcher oil pencil crayon burlap
£68966	$132414	(1-Dec-90 SA.A2442/R) Old gables in Luneburg (45x31cm-18x12in) s.i. d.1934verso W/C (DM 200000)
£145270	$246959	(31-May-91 VG.B52/R) Vita nova (80x100cm-31x39in) s. i.d.1946/47stretcher oil chk canvas (DM 430000)
£202703	$344595	(30-May-91 SY.BE13/R) Eichelborn II (24x32cm-9x13in) s.i.d.1916 indian ink pen W/C (DM 600000)

FEINT, Adrian (1894-?) Australian

£600	$1170	(15-Oct-90 AAA.S87) Floral still life (13x20cm-5x8in) s.d.1961 board (A.D 1500)
£600	$1170	(15-Oct-90 AAA.S117) Camellia (24x19cm-9x7in) s. board (A.D 1500)
£934	$1830	(19-Nov-90 MGS.S196/R) Still life with flowers and jug (23x19cm-9x7in) s.d.1962 board (A.D 2400)
£1250	$2175	(26-Mar-91 JRL.S233 a) Still life of flowers (44x39cm-17x15in) s. board (A.D 2800)
£1266	$2430	(14-Aug-90 SY.ME291/R) Pittwater (29x24cm-11x9in) s.d.1955 board (A.D 3000)
£1408	$2310	(17-Jun-91 MGS.S285) Tulips and camellias (24x44cm-9x17in) s.d.1961 (A.D 3000)
£1600	$3008	(17-Sep-90 MGS.S218 a) Roses and irises in blue and white vase (29x17cm-11x7in) s.d. board (A.D 3600)

FEITH, Gustav (1875-?) Austrian

£621	$1210	(11-Oct-90 D.V194/R) Purple field flowers in glass (15x15cm-6x6in) s.d.1920 gouache board (A.S 13000)
£859	$1675	(11-Oct-90 D.V193/R) Violet (14x12cm-6x5in) s.d.1929 W/C (A.S 18000)
£1051	$1765	(25-Apr-91 D.V247/R) Spring flowers in glass (27x20cm-11x8in) s.d.1925 W/C (A.S 22000)
£1194	$2006	(25-Apr-91 D.V246/R) Bunch of spring flowers (29x21cm-11x8in) s.d.1938 W/C paper on board (A.S 25000)
£1337	$2246	(25-Apr-91 D.V248/R) Autumn leaves in vase (25x18cm-10x7in) s.d.1925 W/C (A.S 28000)

FEITO, Luis (1929-) Spanish

£3400	$6018	(21-Mar-91 S24/R) Composition (65x51cm-26x20in) s. paper
£4732	$8754	(5-Mar-91 RAS.K72/R) 'Base' (100x81cm-39x32in) s.d.1961verso (D.KR 53000)
£4946	$9497	(19-Feb-91 DUR.M30) Composicion en negro (100x81cm-39x32in) (S.P 900000)
£5083	$9811	(13-Dec-90 F.M484/R) Composizione (45x54cm-18x21in) s.d.1969 (I.L 11000000)
£6000	$11700	(18-Oct-90 S68/R) Composition (54x74cm-21x29in) s. cardboard
£7059	$13907	(15-Nov-90 ANS.M20/R) Pintura (56x76cm-22x30in) s. s.d.1972verso panel (S.P 1300000)

FEITO, Luis (1929-) Spanish-cont.

£8689	$17116	(15-Nov-90 ANS.M21/R) Composicion (46x55cm-18x22in) s. s.d.1961verso (S.P 1600000)
£9893	$18994	(19-Feb-91 DUR.M14) Composicion (130x97cm-51x38in) (S.P 1800000)
£9960	$16932	(30-May-91 FB.P51/R) Composition (130x196cm-51x77in) s. d.1975 verso (F.FR 100000)
£11562	$22431	(3-Dec-90 CH.R74/R) Untitled (45x55cm-18x22in) tempera paper on canvas (I.L 25000000)
£12490	$24605	(15-Nov-90 ANS.M22/R) Composicion en amarillo (94x127cm-37x50in) s. s.d.1970verso (S.P 2300000)
£15296	$29522	(13-Dec-90 EP.M9/R) Cuadro 830 (146x114cm-57x45in) s. s.d.1971verso (S.P 2800000)
£26106	$50124	(19-Feb-91 DUR.M13) Composicion (98x130cm-39x51in) (S.P 4750000)
£2982	*$5815*	*(17-Oct-90 FER.M252/R) Abstracto (32x43cm-13x17in) mixed media (S.P 550000)*
£5190	*$10016*	*(11-Dec-90 FER.M258/R) Abstracto (57x71cm-22x28in) s. mixed media paper laid down on canvas (S.P 950000)*

FELBER, Carl (1880-1932) Swiss

£574	$994	(25-May-91 N.M85/R) Santa Maria della Salute (60x80cm-24x31in) s.i. s.i.verso (DM 1700)

FELDBAUER, Max (1869-1948) German

£621	*$1192*	*(28-Nov-90 KF.M733/R) Schwabinger Nebenberuf (68x51cm-27x20in) gouache (DM 1800)*

FELDHUTTER, Ferdinand (1842-1898) German

£803	$1357	(17-Apr-91 WE.MU142/R) Konigsee landscape (25x45cm-10x18in) panel (DM 2400)
£1070	$1809	(17-Apr-91 WE.MU141/R) Mountain lake (25x45cm-10x18in) s.d.1883 panel (DM 3200)
£1399	$2699	(10-Dec-90 L.K420) Alpine landscape with hunter and dog by lake (42x67cm-17x26in) s. (DM 4000)
£1442	$2813	(25-Oct-90 D.V166/R) Konigsee landscape (24x16cm-9x6in) s.i. panel (A.S 30000)
£2183	$4127	(27-Sep-90 D.V158/R) View of Alpine landscape, possibly Konigssee (25x18cm-10x7in) s.i. panel (A.S 45000)
£2273	$4386	(10-Dec-90 L.K419/R) Lake Garda with fishermen pulling boats ashore (42x66cm-17x26in) s. (DM 6500)
£2879	$4952	(16-May-91 D.V196/R) Lake Hallstatt, evening (64x80cm-25x31in) s. (A.S 60000)
£3396	$6419	(27-Sep-90 D.V129/R) Alpine river landscape (68x87cm-27x34in) mono. (A.S 70000)

FELDMANN, Karel Albert (1894-1966) Dutch

£557	$1076	(12-Dec-90 CH.AM199/R) Church interior in Amsterdam (47x37cm-19x15in) mono.d.1945 (D.FL 1800)

FELDMANN, Wilhelm (1859-1932) German

£765	$1369	(12-Mar-91 GM.B1087/R) Paysage de Plaine (100x150cm-39x59in) s. (B.FR 46000)

FELGENTREFF, Paul (1854-1933) German

£1580	$2750	(27-Mar-91 B.SF4192/R) The young lady's lesson (21x18cm-8x7in) s.i.
£1818	$3509	(12-Dec-90 WE.MU133/R) Female nude facing back (84x69cm-33x27in) s. (DM 5200)

FELIX, Eugen (1837-1906) Austrian

£4200	$8064	(28-Nov-90 S198/R) Guarding the baby (65x79cm-26x31in) s.

FELIX, Isidor (?) ?

£1800	$3546	(4-Oct-90 CSK142/R) Elegant ladies on the coast (79x62cm-31x24in) both s. pair

FELIXMULLER, Conrad (1897-1977) German

£8621	$16552	(28-Nov-90 KF.M734/R) Wooded landscape with stream (85x61cm-33x24in) (DM 25000)
£9122	$15507	(1-Jun-91 VG.B232/R) View from Wustenhain to Gnadstein (55x67cm-22x26in) s.d.1943 panel (DM 27000)
£41379	$79448	(26-Nov-90 WK.M25/R) Portrait of Carl Sternheim (85x80cm-33x31in) s.i.d.1928 s.i.stretcher (DM 120000)
£54608	$107031	(23-Nov-90 VG.B39/R) Portrait of Alois Erbach (78x75cm-31x30in) s.d.1920 i.verso (DM 160000)
£751	*$1472*	*(22-Nov-90 L.K938) Boy reading (65x50cm-26x20in) s.i.d.1932 indian ink brush (DM 2200)*

FELL, Clara (19th C) British?

£1600	$3120	(16-Oct-90 CG212) Maid of Athens (46x41cm-18x16in) s.d.1868 s.i.verso

FELL, Sheila (1931-?) British

£1550	$2914	(20-Sep-90 C57/R) Farm (30x41cm-12x16in) s. i.d.1977 verso sold with pencil drawing
£3800	$6574	(7-May-91 PH83/R) Cumberland landscape I (102x127cm-40x50in) s. s.i.d.1967 stretcher

FENASSE, Paul (20th C) French
£12170 $23367   (17-Dec-90 ARC.P88/R) Panorama de la baie d'Alger (74x164cm-29x65in) s.
     (F.FR 120000)

FENDI, Peter (1796-1842) Austrian
£1600 $2688   (18-Jul-91 CSK23) Chasing mouse (6x6cm-2x2in) pencil W/C

FENENGA, T G G (19th C) ?
£1783 $3459   (5-Dec-90 DO.H2001/R) Norwegian Brigg Vestaline rescued by Maria
     Catharina near Doggersbank (43x64cm-17x25in) s.i.d.1889 W/C gouache
     (DM 5100)

FENETTI, F (19/20th C) Italian
£564 $1100   (25-Oct-90 GRO.B137) Still life of yellow roses and pansies
     (53x38cm-21x15in) s.

FENN, Harry (1845-1911) American
£474 $900   (9-Jan-91 CH.NY182/R) House of Samuel Colman, Newport (30x46cm-12x18in)
     mono. ink pencil htd white en grisaille
£1368 $2600   (9-Jan-91 CH.NY204) Frisco Mill, Coeur D'Alene, Idaho. F.L.Higginson and
     C.A.Whittier houses, Boston one mono.ink wash board one ink gouache
     two

FENSON, R (19/20th C) British?
£600 $1188   (28-Jan-91 HS269) Peaceful river landscape with ducks beside pond,
     shepherd and sheep s.d.1901

FENSON, Robert (19/20th C) British
£550 $1018   (7-Mar-91 CSK164) Hay cart on bridge in river landscape
     (61x106cm-24x42in) s.d.95

FENSON, Robin (19/20th C) British
£638 $1200   (22-Sep-90 WOL.C205) Country landscape (20x25cm-8x10in) s.

FERAT, Serge (1881-1958) Russian
£2759 $5297   (26-Nov-90 WK.M213/R) Mother and child (73x54cm-29x21in) s.c.1939
     gouache over pencil paper on board (DM 8000)
£3210 $6259   (11-Oct-90 QWA.P97/R) Nature morte (11x15cm-4x6in) s. gouache
     (F.FR 32000)

FERAUD, Louis (20th C) French
£12085 $19698   (10-Jun-91 NM.P66/R) Femme a l'echarpe et a l'oiseau (146x114cm-57x45in)
     s. (F.FR 120000)

FERDINANDI, Margaretha (19th C) Austrian
£1195 $2341   (24-Nov-90 SA.A713/R) Forest flowers (40x59cm-16x23in) mono. (DM 3500)

FERENCHICH, Gabor von (19/20th C) Continental
£550 $902   (18-Jun-91 PH93) Portrait of young girl wearing blue ribbon in hair
     (25x15cm-10x6in) s.d.1902 bears sig.d. panel

FERG, Franz de Paula (1689-1740) Austrian
£3333 $6500   (10-Oct-90 CH.NY83/R) River landscapes with figures dancing
     (16x60cm-6x24in) panel pair
£4898 $9600   (6-Nov-90 GF.L2090/R) Travellers on road in hilly landscape
     (33x27cm-13x11in) copper (S.FR 12000)
£5500 $9295   (19-Apr-91 C44/R) Peasants at cards and brawling by an Italianate
     farmhouse, castle beyond (69x94cm-27x37in) copper
£7000 $11830   (19-Apr-91 C43/R) A gypsy encampment with a traveller having his pocket
     picked as his fortune is told (71x99cm-28x39in) s. copper
£7328 $13117   (14-Mar-91 D.V52/R) River landscape with village, windmill and figures
     (38x47cm-15x19in) one of pair (A.S 150000)
£9790 $18895   (10-Dec-90 L.K38/R) Hunting party in mountainous landscape
     (26x20cm-10x8in) s. copper (DM 28000)
£12000 $19560   (3-Jul-91 S182/R) Italianate landscape with drovers and animals by ruins
     (29x35cm-11x14in) mono. copper
£27000 $44010   (3-Jul-91 S72/R) Italian landscape with Virgil's tomb (76x135cm-30x53in)
     s.
£44118 $75000   (31-May-91 CH.NY56/R) Mountainous river landscape with figures
     (77x65cm-30x26in) pair
£2231 $4418   (30-Jan-91 APT.P262/R) Bergers pres d'un obelisque (27x38cm-11x15in)
     gouache (F.FR 22000)

FERG, Franz de Paula (attrib) (1689-1740) Austrian
£18779 $31925   (28-May-91 AB.S4756/R) Ferry place with figures and cattle
     (32x46cm-13x18in) mono. copper (S.KR 200000)

FERG, Franz de Paula (circle) (1689-1740) Austrian
£1371 $2701   (14-Nov-90 D.V311/R) Peasants before inn (22x19cm-9x7in) panel one of
     pair (A.S 28000)
£1371 $2701   (14-Nov-90 D.V310/R) Peasants before inn (23x19cm-9x7in) panel one of
     pair (A.S 28000)

FERG, Franz de Paula (style) (1689-1740) Austrian
£1600 $2608   (4-Jul-91 CSK126/R) Extensive landscape with traveller watering horse by
     footbridge (43x62cm-17x24in) panel

FERGOLA DA MIGLIARINO, F (19th C) Italian
£1812 $3153   (25-Mar-91 SY.F738) Napoli da Margellina (35x48cm-14x19in) s.d.1838
                   gouache two (I.L 4000000)

FERGOLA, Francesco (19th C) Italian
£5892 $9957   (16-Apr-91 CH.R60/R) Paesaggio con la Reggia di Caserta
                   (54x81cm-21x32in) s.d.1847 (I.L 13000000)
£6345 $10723   (16-Apr-91 CH.R61/R) Paesaggio lacustre con templetto (54x81cm-21x32in)
                   s.d. (I.L 14000000)

FERGOLA, Salvatore (1799-1877) Italian
£2945 $5124   (25-Mar-91 SY.F675) Veduta di torre del greco (41x82cm-16x32in) s.
                   (I.L 6500000)
£7631 $14804   (4-Dec-90 F.R138/R) La Badia di Cava dei Tirreni (53x66cm-21x26in) s.
                   (I.L 16500000)

FERGUSON, Henri A (1842-1911) American
£1618 $2800   (22-May-91 CH.NY102/R) Near Troy, New York (26x46cm-10x18in) s.stretcher
£10582 $20000   (26-Sep-90 SY.NY54/R) Glen Falls on the Hudson (39x65cm-15x26in) s.

FERGUSON, Henry (1675-1730) French
£3550 $6000   (1-May-91 B.SF5102/R) Pallanza (58x104cm-23x41in) s.

FERGUSON, William Gowe (1632-1695) British
£900 $1467   (13-Jun-91 CSK297/R) Hunting still life with birds on ledge
                   (61x48cm-24x19in)
£3000 $5370   (10-Apr-91 S49/R) Still life with various birds (61x74cm-24x29in)
                   s.d.1661
£5200 $8788   (17-Apr-91 S59/R) Still life of game (59x47cm-23x19in) s.d.1684

FERGUSON, William Gowe (circle) (1632-1695) British
£2446 $4820   (13-Nov-90 CH.AM49/R) Pigeon hanging from nail above ledge with
                   goldfinch and powder horn (47x53cm-19x21in) (D.FL 8000)

FERGUSSON, John Duncan (1874-1961) British
£7000 $13580   (5-Dec-90 PHE28/R) Flora (34x26cm-13x10in) s. verso panel
£7500 $14550   (5-Dec-90 PHE102/R) Head with white rose (24x19cm-9x7in) s. verso board
£13000 $21970   (3-May-91 PHE154/R) Figures in park (22x27cm-9x11in) board
£15000 $29100   (6-Dec-90 CG213/R) Avenue de L'Observatoire, Paris, moonlight
                   (27x35cm-11x14in) s. i.d.1907verso board
£19000 $36860   (6-Dec-90 CG216/R) The cloche hat (35x28cm-14x11in) s.i.d.1916 board
£30000 $58200   (6-Dec-90 CG218/R) Thorenc, afternoon (76x66cm-30x26in) s.i.d.1929verso
£35000 $67900   (6-Dec-90 CG211/R) Towards Juan from Cap d'Antibes (56x61cm-22x24in)
                   s.verso
£40000 $77600   (6-Dec-90 CG215/R) The pink box, portrait of Margaret Morris
                   (61x56cm-24x22in) s.d.1929verso
£50000 $97000   (6-Dec-90 CG212/R) Bouquet de fleurs (61x51cm-24x20in) s.i.verso board
£400 $668   (26-Jul-91 PHE107) Eden Roc, Chateau des Enfants, Juan Les Pins
                   (33x25cm-13x10in) i. chl wash
£420 $701   (26-Jul-91 PHE109) Study of female head in profile (33x26cm-13x10in) i.
                   pencil
£420 $701   (26-Jul-91 PHE108) Paris 1931 (18x12cm-7x5in) crayon
£420 $701   (26-Jul-91 PHE112) Juan Les Pins, 1924 (17x10cm-7x4in) pencil wash
£450 $752   (26-Jul-91 PHE103) Eden Roc, Chateau des enfants, Juan Les Pins, summer
                   1924 (32x25cm-13x10in) chl wash
£480 $802   (26-Jul-91 PHE106) Eden Roc, Chateau des Enfants, Juan Les Pins, summer
                   1924 (25x32cm-10x13in) wash
£500 $835   (26-Jul-91 PHE105/R) La femme au canape, 1910 (31x21cm-12x8in) chl
£580 $969   (26-Jul-91 PHE115) Cap D'Antibes, 1926 (20x12cm-8x5in) chl wash
£580 $969   (26-Jul-91 PHE104) Cap D'Antibes 1926 (17x12cm-7x5in) wash
£580 $969   (26-Jul-91 PHE118) Cloche hat (34x26cm-13x10in) i.verso pencil
£600 $1002   (26-Jul-91 PHE110) Juan Les Pins, 1924 (15x20cm-6x8in) wash
£650 $1099   (17-Apr-91 CG30) Seated nude (25x19cm-10x7in) chl.wash buff paper
£700 $1169   (26-Jul-91 PHE116/R) Leaving la petite farandole, Cap D'Antibes,
                   September 1914 (21x29cm-8x11in) pencil
£750 $1268   (17-Apr-91 CG29) Woman with a rose, Cafe d'Harcourt, Paris
                   (22x13cm-9x5in) col.chks. buff paper
£750 $1253   (26-Jul-91 PHE102/R) Christmas 1937 (24x19cm-9x7in) pencil wash
£800 $1352   (17-Apr-91 CG26) A Fir Tree, Thorenc W/C pair
£900 $1746   (6-Dec-90 CG207/R) The cliffs, Thorenc (18x15cm-7x6in) pencil W/C
£900 $1800   (5-Feb-91 S113/R) Botanic gardens, Glasgow (14x11cm-6x4in) W/C
£900 $1800   (5-Feb-91 S115/R) Botanic gardens, May 40, Glasgow (11x15cm-4x6in) W/C
£1200 $2028   (17-Apr-91 CG25/R) Margaret Morris, Thorenc. Eden Rock, Cap D'Antibes
                   latter d.4 Aout 30 i. pencil W/C pair
£1200 $2400   (5-Feb-91 S118/R) Flowers (16x11cm-6x4in) W/C over black chk
£1200 $2028   (17-Apr-91 CG27) Standing nude (16x11cm-6x4in) d.20 Aug 57 pencil W/C
£1300 $2522   (6-Dec-90 CG202/R) Fir tree and buildings, Thorenc (19x15cm-7x6in) W/C
                   pair
£1300 $2431   (28-Aug-90 S1041/R) Sketch for La terrasse (15x10cm-6x4in) W/C over
                   pencil
£1400 $2800   (5-Feb-91 S119/R) Flowers (16x11cm-6x4in) i. W/C
£1400 $2800   (5-Feb-91 S122/R) Restaurant, 1925, Antibes (16x11cm-6x4in) W/C over
                   black chk
£1400 $2800   (5-Feb-91 S120/R) Restaurant, 1925, Antibes (16x11cm-6x4in) i. W/C over
                   black chk
£1500 $2910   (6-Dec-90 CG206/R) Towards Cap d'Antibes (19x23cm-7x9in) W/C

FERGUSSON, John Duncan (1874-1961) British-cont.

£1500	$3000	(5-Feb-91 S117/R) Self-portrait (15x10cm-6x4in) W/C
£1500	$3000	(5-Feb-91 S116/R) View from Queen Margaret's Drive, Glasgow (11x16cm-4x6in) W/C over black chk
£1500	$3000	(5-Feb-91 S112/R) View from Queen Margaret's Drive (15x11cm-6x4in) W/C
£1700	$3400	(5-Feb-91 S121/R) Antibes, 1925 (16x11cm-6x4in) i. W/C over black chk
£1800	$3366	(28-Aug-90 S1044/R) Paris from Parc Monsonry. Houses through the trees (15x11cm-6x4in) one i.d.1930verso W/C pair
£1900	$3553	(28-Aug-90 S1042/R) Looking down to the quay (16x11cm-6x4in) W/C over pencil
£1900	$3211	(2-May-91 CG447) Nude, cushion and peach (33x25cm-13x10in) i. chl W/C
£2000	$3740	(28-Aug-90 S1040/R) Study of the quai, Dinard (17x11cm-7x4in) i. W/c over chk htd bodycol
£2000	$3880	(5-Dec-90 PHE62/R) Still life of flowers (15x20cm-6x8in) pencil W/C
£2000	$4000	(5-Feb-91 S123/R) Antibes (16x11cm-6x4in) W/C over black chk
£2200	$4268	(6-Dec-90 CG201/R) Mixed flowers in vase (24x17cm-9x7in) i.d.29verso W/C
£3000	$5820	(6-Dec-90 CG209/R) Margaret Morris, Cap d'Antibes. Margaret Morris, Thorenc (19x15cm-7x6in) pencil W/C pair
£3000	$5610	(28-Aug-90 S1043/R) Portrait studies of Mademoiselle 'E' (20x12cm-8x5in) chk three
£3400	$6358	(28-Aug-90 S1035/R) Studies of female figures (33x25cm-13x10in) i. black chk pencil five
£5000	$8450	(2-May-91 CG446/R) Nude on canape (27x38cm-11x15in) mono. s.i.d.1910 verso mixed media
£5000	$8350	(26-Jul-91 PHE60/R) La Terrasse, Duex Rives, Dinard, 1931 (15x20cm-6x8in) W/C chk

FERNANDEZ, Alejo (circle) (c.1470-1543) Spanish

£10000	$16300	(5-Jul-91 C246/R) Male warrior saints (100x37cm-39x15in) i. parts altarpiece pair

FERNANDEZ, Angel (?) Spanish

£2331	$3916	(23-Apr-91 DUR.M20) Arbol de Goyan (33x27cm-13x11in) (S.P 425000)

FERNANDI, Francesco see IMPERIALI, Francesco

FERNELEY, Claude Lorraine (1822-1892) British

£3593	$6000	(7-Jun-91 SY.NY46/R) The Early of Jersey's Riddlesworth with J. Robinson up (25x30cm-10x12in) init.d.1841 i. label stretcher

FERNELEY, John (jnr) (1815-1862) British

£630	$1128	(11-Mar-91 HS174/R) Study of stallion and groom in landscape with cattle and horses beyond (62x74cm-24x29in) s.d.1854
£800	$1352	(29-Apr-91 HS336/R) Mares and foals in landscape, with oak trees and mountains beyond (70x90cm-28x35in)
£1900	$3401	(10-Apr-91 S155/R) Bay racehorse with groom in stable (61x73cm-24x29in) s.
£2000	$3940	(13-Nov-90 PH120/R) Huntsman with hounds, possibly Mr Warkwell on grey hunter Magie (46x61cm-18x24in) s. i.verso
£2300	$3956	(15-May-91 BT242/R) Portrait of a race horse in a Rutland landscape (58x71cm-23x28in)
£3800	$6422	(30-Apr-91 PH17/R) Figures and horses in courtyard, town beyond (46x61cm-18x24in) s.indist.d.
£4200	$8274	(16-Nov-90 C66/R) Mounted officer of Bundelkand Legion with cavalry in hilly landscape (46x61cm-18x24in)
£5000	$8250	(10-Jul-91 S61/R) Mr Markwell, huntsman to the Cheshire on Magic (43x60cm-17x24in) s.

FERNELEY, John (jnr-attrib) (1815-1862) British

£7500	$12375	(12-Jul-91 C100/R) Mr. Barton of Straffan House, Co. Kildare, on hunter (53x72cm-21x28in)

FERNELEY, John (snr) (1781-1860) British

£5912	$9992	(3-May-91 SA.A1781/R) Brown racehorse in wooded meadow landscape (64x77cm-25x30in) s.d.1848 (DM 17500)
£9231	$18000	(24-Oct-90 CH.NY320/R) Golden chestnut hunter in landscape (87x112cm-34x44in) s.i.d.1853
£9231	$18000	(24-Oct-90 CH.NY321/R) Cecil, favourite hunter of the Earl of Jersey in landscape (88x107cm-35x42in) s.d.1811
£11000	$21670	(14-Nov-90 S94/R) Harlequin, dark bay hunter in stable (73x107cm-29x42in) s.d.1829
£11000	$21670	(14-Nov-90 S93/R) Bay hunter owned by H G Surtees of Frenchay in loosebox with terrier (73x104cm-29x41in) s.d.1844
£13772	$23000	(7-Jun-91 SY.NY56/R) Lady Middleton's Benedict in a stable (86x107cm-34x42in) s.d.1858
£19461	$32500	(7-Jun-91 SY.NY52/R) Buckle, the first Lord Chesham's hunter in a landscape (72x91cm-28x36in) s.d.1830
£25000	$44750	(12-Apr-91 C94/R) Cigar, Mr. W.L. Sterling Crawford's hunter, in stable (84x110cm-33x43in) s.d.1841
£35928	$60000	(7-Jun-91 SY.NY57/R) Three hunters belonging to John Sidebottom, Esq (114x153cm-45x60in) s.d.1851
£38000	$64220	(30-Apr-91 PH51/R) Morning - Hyde Park (91x83cm-36x33in) s.d.1833
£47904	$80000	(7-Jun-91 SY.NY53/R) Wycombe Abbey with Johnny Wilmer, John Cross and the 1st Lady Carrington's favourite hack (114x160cm-45x63in) s.i.d.1832

FERNELEY, John (snr) (1781-1860) British-cont.
£83832　$140000　(7-Jun-91 SY.NY58/R) A racehorse with jockey up in the colours of Lord Elcho (86x107cm-34x42in) s.d.1838

FERNELEY, John (snr-circle) (1781-1860) British
£1100　$2200　(7-Feb-91 CSK175/R) Portrait of young man, seated at table, holding open book in wooded landscape (53x48cm-21x19in)

FERNELEY, Sarah (1812-1903) British
£4000　$6600　(12-Jul-91 C81/R) Extensive river landscape, with woman sketching, girl and dog by tree (63x76cm-25x30in) indist.s.

FERNELEY, Sarah (circle) (1812-1903) British
£3000　$5010　(3-Jun-91 PHB70) Figures seated in garden of country house (51x61cm-20x24in)

FERNHOUT, Edgar (1912-?) Dutch
£1198　$2275　(11-Sep-90 CH.AM433/R) Young woman in a hat (60x50cm-24x20in) s.d.49 (D.FL 4000)
£2012　$3884　(12-Dec-90 CH.AM18/R) Landscape in spring (60x72cm-24x28in) init.d.41 s.d.verso (D.FL 6500)
£4025　$7768　(13-Dec-90 SY.AM86/R) Landschap by Bergen (65x100cm-26x39in) s.d.55 (D.FL 13000)

FERON, Eloi Firmin (19th C) French?
£3800　$7486　(5-Oct-90 C76/R) Ambush (33x41cm-13x16in) s.d.44

FERON, William (1858-1894) Swedish
£852　$1432　(27-Apr-91 SO.S331/R) Woman in garden (60x48cm-24x19in) s. (S.KR 9000)

FERONI, Giuseppe (19th C) Italian
£2218　$4348　(24-Nov-90 SA.A625/R) View of Florence (81x86cm-32x34in) s.indis.i.d.1848 (DM 6500)
£2534　$4282　(3-May-91 SA.A1822/R) Panoramic view of Florence (81x86cm-32x34in) s.d.1848 (DM 7500)

FERRAGUTI, Arnaldo (1862-1925) Italian
£947　$1800　(27-Feb-91 SY.NY377/R) Peasant girl with basket (95x65cm-37x26in) s.d.87 pastel

FERRAJUOLI, Nunzio (attrib) (1661-1735) Italian
£22730　$44551　(19-Nov-90 CH.R157/R) Paesaggio con tempio e il Ratto di Proserpina. Paesaggio lacustre con bagnanti (72x99cm-28x39in) pair (I.L 50000000)

FERRANDIZ Y BADENES, Bernardo (1835-1890) Spanish
£22000　$36080　(21-Jun-91 C93/R) In courtyard (46x71cm-18x28in) s.

FERRANT Y FISCHERMANS, Alejandro (1843-1917) Spanish
£2322　$4481　(11-Dec-90 FER.M189/R) Hidalgo (48x32cm-19x13in) s. W/C (S.P 425000)

FERRANTI, C (?) ?
£1580　$2750　(27-Mar-91 B.SF4194/R) I pescatori (83x53cm-33x21in) s.i.

FERRANTI, Carlo (19th C) Italian
£880　$1690　(19-Feb-91 SWS59/R) Seduction (44x33cm-17x13in) s.

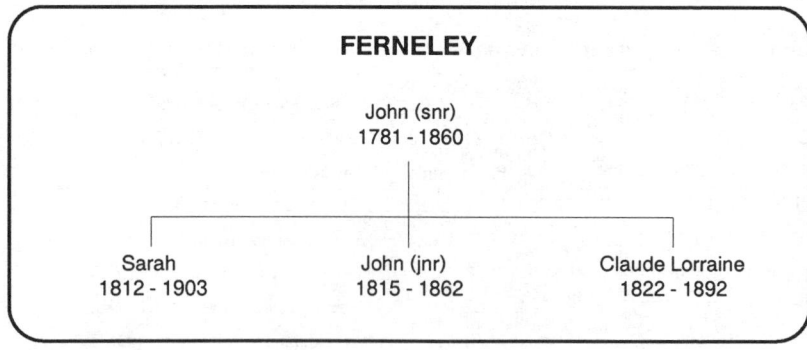

FERNELEY

John (snr)
1781 - 1860

Sarah
1812 - 1903

John (jnr)
1815 - 1862

Claude Lorraine
1822 - 1892

615

FERRANTI, Carlo (19th C) Italian-cont.
£930 $1600   (17-May-91 DM.D1998/R) Calm harvesters (61x74cm-24x29in) s.
£2800 $5516   (4-Oct-90 CSK24/R) Still life of mixed fruit with a salver on a table
                 (45x60cm-18x24in) s.

FERRARESE SCHOOL (?) Italian
£3000 $5790   (11-Dec-90 PH206/R) St. Jerome in wilderness. Cartouche with decorative
                 scroll work (100x41cm-39x16in) c.1500 panel double-sided

FERRARESE SCHOOL, 15th C Italian
£4800 $8112   (19-Apr-91 C120/R) Saint Sebastian (51x36cm-20x14in) panel
£12060 $19779   (21-Jun-91 SY.MO179/R) Vierge a l'enfant (56x36cm-22x14in) panel oval
                 (F.FR 120000)
£44000 $71720   (1-Jul-91 GL.P30/R) Le chariot (17x8cm-7x3in) gold sheet on paper
                 (F.FR 440000)

FERRARESE SCHOOL, 16th C Italian
£3182 $6237   (20-Nov-90 F.R11/R) Cristo tra i simboli degli Evangelisti.
                 Crocefissione (16x41cm-6x16in) tempera paper on panel two in one frame
                 (I.L 7000000)
£5473 $9139   (4-Jun-91 CH.R290) Nativita in un paesaggio (29x31cm-11x12in) panel
                 (I.L 12000000)
£6871 $13192   (29-Nov-90 F.M54/R) Ultima cena (65x111cm-26x44in) (I.L 15000000)
£15327 $27436   (8-Apr-91 CH.R173/R) La caccia al cervo (26x26cm-10x10in) panel
                 octagonal (I.L 34000000)

FERRARI, Agostino (20th C) Italian
£3602 $7024   (22-Oct-90 BR.M188/R) Viva (120x160cm-47x63in) acrylic sand
                 (I.L 8000000)

FERRARI, Antoine (1910-) French
£653 $1157   (7-Apr-91 I.N127) Paysage Provencal (45x30cm-18x12in) s. panel
                 (F.FR 6600)
£990 $1752   (7-Apr-91 I.N126) La place des Licesd a Saint-Tropez (54x65cm-21x26in)
                 s. (F.FR 10000)
£1378 $2714   (18-Nov-90 H.A119) Nature morte au violon et au pichet bleu
                 (50x60cm-20x24in) s. i. verso hardboard (F.FR 13500)

FERRARI, Arturo (1861-1932) Italian
£684 $1142   (6-Jun-91 F.M24/R) Lungo il Naviglio (16x24cm-6x9in) s. board
                 (I.L 1500000)
£1661 $2973   (11-Apr-91 D.V227/R) Certeso de Pavia (30x50cm-12x20in) s. (A.S 35000)
£2789 $4797   (14-May-91 GF.L2469/R) View of Villa d'Este in Cernobbio
                 (45x35cm-18x14in) s. (S.FR 7000)
£4856 $9421   (5-Dec-90 F.M32/R) Piazza San Marco, Venezia (32x48cm-13x19in) s.
                 (I.L 10500000)
£530 $1050   (1-Feb-91 S.W2594/R) Figures among ruins (38x25cm-15x10in) s. W/C
*£684 $1142   (6-Jun-91 F.M241) Naviglio in campagna (27x39cm-11x15in) s. W/C paper on
                 board (I.L 1500000)*
*£1368 $2285   (6-Jun-91 F.M269/R) Cascina presso il Lambro meridionale
                 (53x69cm-21x27in) s. W/C board (I.L 3000000)*

FERRARI, Berto (20th C) Italian
£1368 $2285   (6-Jun-91 F.M33) Primo caldo, Nervi (42x50cm-17x20in) s.d.1939 board
                 (I.L 3000000)

FERRARI, Ettore (1849-1929) Italian
£410 $697   (28-May-91 F.R46) Paesaggio (70x53cm-28x21in) mono. pastel (I.L 900000)
*£591 $1158   (21-Nov-90 F.M160) Cortile di palazzo veronese (28x21cm-11x8in)
                 i.d.1885verso W/C (I.L 1300000)*

FERRARI, Gaudenzio (style) (1484-1546) Italian
£3000 $5850   (26-Oct-90 C3/R) The Adoration of the Shepherds (43x55cm-17x22in) panel

FERRARI, Giovanni Andrea de (1598-1669) Italian
£502 $808   (27-Jun-91 APT.P19) Tete d'apotre (48x39cm-19x15in) (F.FR 5000)
£4959 $8876   (8-Apr-91 CH.R137/R) Compianto sul Cristo morto (96x121cm-38x48in)
                 (I.L 11000000)
*£342 $605   (19-Mar-91 F.M305/R) Salome con la testa del Battista. Studio per la
                 stessa composizione (18x15cm-7x6in) sanguine (I.L 750000)*

FERRARI, Giovanni Battista (1829-1906) Italian
£1800 $3528   (14-Feb-91 CSK62/R) A river landscape with huntsmen in a punt
                 (46x69cm-18x27in) s.d.1872

FERRARI, Gregorio de (1647-1726) Italian
*£6840 $12107   (19-Mar-91 F.M206/R) Santa Rosa da Lima, il Bambino e San Vincenzo
                 Ferreri (37x25cm-15x10in) ink htd white (I.L 15000000)*
*£9500 $15485   (2-Jul-91 C113/R) Madonna of Loreto appearing to two saints
                 (32x33cm-13x13in) black chk pen wash htd white*

FERRARI, Luca (1605-1654) Italian
£5410 $9683   (8-Apr-91 CH.R126/R) San Giovanni Battista giovane (93x67cm-37x26in)
                 (I.L 12000000)

FERRARI, Luca (school) (1605-1654) Italian
£1195 $2056   (14-May-91 GF.L2255/R) Madonna with Child (80x60cm-31x24in) (S.FR 3000)

FERRARI, Orazio de (attrib) (1605-1657) Italian
£7099 $14057   (30-Jan-91 APT.P164/R) La Charite (112x89cm-44x35in) (F.FR 70000)

FERRARI, Teodoro Wolf (1876-1945) Italian
£1458 $2479   (28-May-91 F.R93) Paesaggio (50x60cm-20x24in) s. l.d.1930verso panel
                     (I.L 3200000)
£4104 $6854   (6-Jun-91 F.M287/R) Paesaggio lacustre (56x88cm-22x35in) s.d.1917
                     (I.L 9000000)
£5017 $8378   (6-Jun-91 F.M288/R) Salice e cipressi (57x88cm-22x35in) s.d.1917
                     (I.L 11000000)

FERRARINI, Pier Giuseppe (1852-1887) Italian
£3600 $5904   (18-Jun-91 PH163 a) Dante and Beatrice (123x98cm-48x39in) indis.s.

FERRARIS, Arthur (1856-?) Hungarian
£12821 $25000   (23-Oct-90 SY.NY46/R) L'aveugle a la mosquee (63x46cm-25x18in)
                     s.l.indis.d. panel

FERRER CARBONELL, Juan (1892-?) Spanish
£1925 $3849   (6-Feb-91 ANS.M79/R) Tarde de mayo en Zarate (54x73cm-21x29in) s.l.verso
                     (S.P 350000)

FERRER Y PALLOJA, J (19th C) Spanish?
£3500 $6860   (15-Feb-91 C5/R) La Place de la Concorde, Paris (38x55cm-15x22in)
                     s.d.1886

FERRER, Jose (younger) (1746-1815) Spanish
£7222 $12061   (6-Jun-91 D.V50/R) Still life of flowers in porcelain bowl
                     (26x39cm-10x15in) (A.S 150000)

FERRERO, J (20th C) Italian
£3000 $5910   (4-Oct-90 CSK249/R) Fishing boats on the Venetian lagoon
                     (43x57cm-17x22in) s.

FERRERO, Lorenzo (19th C) Italian
£1371 $2701   (14-Nov-90 F.M21/R) Trompe l'oeil con icisioni all'acquatinta dei
                     dintorni di Napoli (49x60cm-19x24in) s.d.1819 W/C (I.L 3000000)

FERRETTI, Gian Domenico (1692-1766) Italian
£3597 $6978   (7-Dec-90 SY.MO87/R) Scene de la comedia dell'arte (45x32cm-18x13in)
                     (F.FR 35000)

FERRETTI, Odoardo (20th C) Italian
£1155 $2230   (11-Dec-90 CH.R59) Una via di Gaeta dalla finestra (40x62cm-16x24in)
                     s.d.1931 (I.L 2500000)

FERRI, Augusto (1829-1895) Italian
£1505 $2513   (6-Jun-91 F.M79/R) Nespole e ciliege (31x50cm-12x20in) s. (I.L 3300000)

FERRI, Ciro (1634-1689) Italian
£365 $646   (19-Mar-91 F.M154/R) Studio di due angeli su nubi (9x13cm-4x5in)
                     sanguine (I.L 800000)
£4104 $7264   (19-Mar-91 F.M300/R) Pallade strappa l'adolescenza dalle braccia di
                     Venere (28x42cm-11x17in) pencil ink (I.L 9000000)
£26000 $42380   (2-Jul-91 C50/R) Julius Caesar preferring his Agrarian Law
                     (23x31cm-9x12in) chk pen ink wash lead
£32000 $52160   (2-Jul-91 C49/R) Allegory of the labours of Hercules (23x36cm-9x14in)
                     lead pen ink wash
£35000 $57050   (2-Jul-91 C51/R) The meeting of St Francis and St Dominic
                     (26x39cm-10x15in) chk htd.white squared

FERRI, Ciro (attrib) (1634-1689) Italian
£2400 $4680   (25-Oct-90 CSK32/R) Madonna and Child with Infant Saint John the Baptist
                     (98x119cm-39x47in)

FERRI, Ciro (circle) (1634-1689) Italian
£5000 $8450   (16-Apr-91 PH26/R) Raising of Lazarus (94x123cm-37x48in)

FERRIER, James (19th C) British
£700 $1379   (30-Oct-90 SC69/R) Herding sheep on mountain path (26x36cm-10x14in) s.
                     W/C bodycol
£1300 $2522   (6-Dec-90 CG6) Salmon fishing in the Highlands (61x99cm-24x39in) s. W/C
                     htd.bodycol

FERRO-LA-GREE (1941-) French
£658 $1289   (25-Nov-90 ZZ.F248/R) Fleurs fleurs fleurs (46x55cm-18x22in) s.
                     (F.FR 6500)

FERRO-LA-GREE, G (1941-) French
£815 $1605   (30-Oct-90 ZZ.F88 b) Champ de coquelicots (55x46cm-22x18in) s.
                     (F.FR 8000)

FERRO-LA-GREE, Georges (1941-) French
£634 $1242   (27-Jan-91 FE.P145) Bord de Seine sous la neige (65x50cm-26x20in) s.
                  (F.FR 6300)

FERRON, Marcelle (20th C) ?
£786 $1541   (5-Nov-90 FB.M232) Abstract (64x48cm-25x19in) s.d.1963 mixed media
                  (C.D 1800)

FERRONI, Egisto (1835-1912) Italian
£655 $1100   (27-Apr-91 YFA.M94/R) First rose (81x36cm-32x14in) s.
£9092 $17820   (22-Nov-90 SY.MI79/R) Il carro - tramonto (80x44cm-31x17in) s.d.1910
                  (I.L 20000000)

FERRONI, Gianfranco (1927-) Italian
£918 $1800   (12-Feb-91 SY.NY185/R) Composition with buildings (69x48cm-27x19in)
                  s.d.1955
£6877 $11278   (19-Jun-91 F.M240/R) Racconto di un interno (70x90cm-28x35in) s.d.1962
                  i.d.verso (I.L 15000000)
£1294 $2497   (12-Dec-90 F.M81/R) Paesaggio (20x20cm-8x8in) s.d.66 indian ink
                  (I.L 2800000)
£1375 $2256   (19-Jun-91 F.M210/R) Figura seduta (34x24cm-13x9in) s.d.1966 pencil
                  (I.L 3000000)
£3209 $5263   (19-Jun-91 F.M230/R) Senza titolo (47x52cm-19x20in) s.d.1963 mixed media
                  paper on canvas (I.L 7000000)
£5501 $9022   (19-Jun-91 F.M98/R) Composizione con molti oggetti (26x22cm-10x9in)
                  s.d.1986 pencil (I.L 12000000)

FERRONI, Riccardo Tommasi (1934-) Italian
£9174 $17706   (16-Dec-90 CL.E24/R) Pittore e modella (120x140cm-47x55in) (F.FR 90000)
£10194 $19674   (16-Dec-90 CL.E25/R) Ritratto di Giovannino come Angioletto Romano
                  (100x140cm-39x55in) s. verso (F.FR 100000)
£832 $1615   (3-Dec-90 F.M223) Battaglia (30x42cm-12x17in) s. ink W/C (I.L 1800000)

FERRY, Jules Jean (1844-?) French
£9000 $16920   (18-Sep-90 PH200/R) Off to hunt, Chateau de la Valade beyond
                  (185x194cm-73x76in) decorative cycle six

FERY, John (1865-1934) American/Hungarian
£703 $1350   (23-Feb-91 YFA.M61/R) Lake Twitchell (28x53cm-11x21in) s.

FESTA, G (18th C) Italian
£6137 $12029   (20-Nov-90 F.R127/R) Natura morta con pane, cipolle, uova e olive
                  (33x44cm-13x17in) s. s.d.1783 (I.L 13500000)

FESTA, Tano (1938-1988) Italian
£900 $1756   (24-Oct-90 F.M155) Palme (50x90cm-20x35in) s.d.1987verso (I.L 2000000)
£955 $1806   (27-Sep-90 F.M48) Paesaggio (70x60cm-28x24in) s.d.1973 verso
                  (I.L 2100000)
£1192 $1955   (20-Jun-91 F.M304) Figura (80x60cm-31x24in) s.d.1983 (I.L 2600000)
£1441 $2810   (24-Oct-90 F.M131) Finestra (90x60cm-35x24in) s.d.1986verso
                  (I.L 3200000)
£1513 $2481   (20-Jun-91 F.M406/R) Piazza d'Italia (80x114cm-31x45in) s.i.d.1982verso
                  acrylic canvas emulsion (I.L 3300000)
£1631 $2838   (26-Mar-91 F.M1) Figura (70x80cm-28x31in) s.d.1986verso (I.L 3600000)
£1650 $2707   (20-Jun-91 F.M351) Omaggio al colore, Degas (100x100cm-39x39in) s.d.1981
                  (I.L 3600000)
£1803 $3228   (9-Apr-91 F.R128) Finestra (100x70cm-39x28in) s.d.86verso wood acrylic
                  (I.L 4000000)
£2029 $3631   (9-Apr-91 F.R163/R) Dal 'Peccato originale' (50x110cm-20x43in)
                  s.d.1978verso acrylic emulsioned canvas (I.L 4500000)
£2039 $3547   (26-Mar-91 F.M41) Figura (70x80cm-28x31in) s.d.1986verso (I.L 4500000)
£2930 $5245   (9-Apr-91 F.R172/R) Untitled (160x130cm-63x51in) s.d.1985verso acrylic
                  coriander seeds (I.L 6500000)
£3152 $6146   (22-Oct-90 F.M88/R) Degas (120x120cm-47x47in) s.d.1984 verso acrylic
                  (I.L 7000000)
£3180 $6265   (30-Oct-90 F.R240/R) Untitled (160x130cm-63x51in) s.d.85verso acrylic
                  confetti (I.L 7000000)
£4277 $8341   (22-Oct-90 BR.M39/R) Monet (100x100cm-39x39in) s.d.1981 verso acrylic
                  (I.L 9500000)
£4728 $9219   (22-Oct-90 BR.M75/R) Lampada (60x80cm-24x31in) s.d.1976 acrylic
                  (I.L 10500000)
£5628 $10975   (22-Oct-90 BR.M125/R) Paesaggio (100x80cm-39x31in) s.d.1975 verso
                  acrylic (I.L 12500000)
£8104 $15804   (23-Oct-90 F.M20/R) Le stanze del Vaticano, particolare
                  (65x81cm-26x32in) s.i.d.1962verso panel (I.L 18000000)
£10774 $17669   (20-Jun-91 F.M513/R) Nero e rosso n. 28 (130x148cm-51x58in)
                  s.i.d.1961verso acrylic paper wood on canvas (I.L 23500000)
£12157 $23706   (22-Oct-90 BR.M178/R) La porta del Duomo (81x64cm-32x25in) s.d.1962
                  verso panel (I.L 27000000)
£546 $1032   (27-Sep-90 F.M116) Estate (100x70cm-39x28in) s.d.1973 pen (I.L 1200000)
£636 $1247   (20-Nov-90 BR.M66/R) La nuovola rosa (70x100cm-28x39in) s.i.d.1972 felt
                  tip pens (I.L 1400000)
£675 $1317   (24-Oct-90 F.M107) Personaggio (70x55cm-28x22in) s.d.1978 oil mixed
                  media canvas (I.L 1500000)
£728 $1376   (27-Sep-90 F.M74) Marina (70x100cm-28x39in) s.d.1982 mixed media
                  (I.L 1600000)

FESTA, Tano (1938-1988) Italian-cont.

£1605 $2632   (20-Jun-91 F.M359/R) Coriandoli (130x160cm-51x63in) s.d.1985verso collage (I.L 3500000)

£2795 $5003   (9-Apr-91 F.R158) Ritratti di Catherine Deneuve e di Marcello Mastroianni (80x60cm-31x24in) s. one d.1973 one d.1975 enamel acrylic pair (I.L 6200000)

£3176 $5462   (13-May-91 CH.R61/R) Il periodo rosa (81x65cm-32x26in) s. i.d.1968verso enamel acrylic canvas (I.L 7000000)

£4585 $7519   (20-Jun-91 F.M398/R) Omaggio al colore (161x130cm-63x51in) s.i.d.1972verso enamel acrylic panel (I.L 10000000)

£4953 $9658   (22-Oct-90 BR.M102/R) Persiana (80x120cm-31x47in) s.d.1963 verso enamel wood (I.L 11000000)

£8245 $15830   (27-Nov-90 SY.MI217/R) Il periodo rosa n.5 dal Peccato Originale - Michelangelo Secondo Tano Festa (100x81cm-39x32in) s.d.68verso enamel canvas (I.L 18000000)

£9087 $17901   (30-Oct-90 F.R271/R) Finestra (100x80cm-39x31in) s.d.1963verso enamel panel (I.L 20000000)

FETI, Domenico (after) (1589-1624) Italian

£2400 $4056   (18-Apr-91 C62/R) Hero and Leander (67x88cm-26x35in)

FETTING, Rainer (1949-) German

£1241 $2383   (26-Nov-90 WK.M616/R) Untitled portrait (29x21cm-11x8in) s. s.i.d.1978verso board (DM 3600)

£8122 $16000   (4-Oct-90 SY.NY275/R) Prisoner (230x160cm-91x63in) s.d.83 verso

£10204 $20000   (7-Nov-90 SY.NY338/R) Head (183x152cm-72x60in) s.i.d.84 verso

£12000 $21240   (21-Mar-91 S81/R) Mad Max (180x250cm-71x98in) s.verso

£14000 $22540   (27-Jun-91 C60/R) Bugler VII (230x200cm-91x79in) s.i.d.83 verso acrylic canvas

£15000 $29250   (18-Oct-90 S161/R) Green mountain Indian (250x120cm-98x47in) s.i.d.82verso diptych two canvases

£15930 $30904   (9-Dec-90 CC.P43/R) Tuxedo man and Doberman (229x184cm-90x72in) s.i.d.1984 wood (F.FR 155000)

£1216 $2104   (21-May-91 WK.M851/R) The kiss (21x29cm-8x11in) s.d.1978 gouache (DM 3600)

£1877 $3679   (24-Nov-90 VG.B506/R) Male nude (100x70cm-39x28in) s.d.1983 gouache (DM 5500)

£2600 $5070   (18-Oct-90 S199/R) Untitled (70x100cm-28x39in) s.d.83 gouache

£11735 $23000   (7-Nov-90 SY.NY353 a/R) Holsbild (228x183cm-90x72in) oil wood canvas laid down on board

FEUCHT, Theodore (1867-?) German

£2181 $4253   (13-Oct-90 KRA.D376/R) Village stret in St Arnoult near Paris (76x51cm-30x20in) s. i.verso (DM 6500)

FEUERBACH, Anselme (1829-1880) German

£2879 $4952   (16-May-91 D.V97/R) Narciss by spring (18x23cm-7x9in) canvas on panel (A.S 60000)

£11888 $22944   (10-Dec-90 L.K421/R) Portrait of young girl with flowers in hair resting chin on hand (49x41cm-19x16in) (DM 34000)

£27972 $53986   (12-Dec-90 SY.MU62/R) Peonies (99x78cm-39x31in) (DM 80000)

£1133 $2029   (12-Apr-91 AW.H597/R) Prospero and Ariel (28x48cm-11x19in) indian ink over pencil (DM 3400)

FEURE, Georges de (1868-1943) French

£804 $1544   (24-Feb-91 P.V18) Maison en Hollande (28x33cm-11x13in) s. gouache (F.FR 8000)

£900 $1467   (1-Jul-91 APT.P43) Paysage de Hollande (35x52cm-14x20in) s. gouache (F.FR 9000)

FEURE, le (18th C) ?

£600 $990   (10-Jul-91 C24/R) Lady in low-cut white dress (4cm-2ins circular) min. vellum gilt-metal brooch frame

FEVRET DE ST MEMIN, Charles (1770-1852) American

£1676 $3000   (11-Apr-91 FA.PH969/R) Portrait of John Morgan Price (48x36cm-19x14in) pencil chk

£3684 $7000   (9-Jan-91 CH.NY92/R) Portrait of gentleman (56x39cm-22x15in) chl crayon sold with pencil dr by G.W.Flagg

FEYEN, Jacques Eugene (1815-1908) French

£1657 $2800   (20-Apr-91 WOL.C91/R) After concert (18x25cm-7x10in) s. board

£2789 $4825   (24-May-91 FB.P83/R) La cueillette des pommes (56x66cm-22x26in) s. (F.FR 28000)

£3000 $5910   (5-Oct-90 C53/R) Les Ramasseuses de Coquillages (61x98cm-24x39in) s.

FEYEN-PERRIN, Francois Nicolas Augustin (1826-1888) French

£1272 $2200   (21-May-91 CE.NY131/R) Fisherfolk by sea (75x107cm-30x42in) init.

£3532 $6111   (12-May-91 T.B58) Nu de dos (32x45cm-13x18in) s. pastel (F.FR 35500)

FIAMMINGO, Paolo (style) (1540-1596) Flemish

£3200 $6144   (29-Nov-90 CSK4/R) St John the Baptist in the Wildnerness (81x64cm-32x25in) panel

FIASELLA, Domenico (1589-1669) Italian
£3606 $6456   (8-Apr-91 CH.R149/R) Cristo fra angeli che incorona Santa Teresa d'Avila
       (59x38cm-23x15in) (I.L 8000000)
£27048 $48417   (8-Apr-91 CH.R208/R) Scena mitologica con personaggio femminile che
       piange sul corpo dell' amante (173x223cm-68x88in) (I.L 60000000)
£79412 $135000   (31-May-91 CH.NY8/R) Carlo and Ubaldo rescuing Rinaldo from Armida
       (187x256cm-74x101in)

FIASELLA, Domenico (attrib) (1589-1669) Italian
£1600 $3040   (13-Sep-90 CSK188) Samson and Delilah (91x143cm-36x56in)

FICHEL, Benjamin Eugene (1826-1895) French
£3000 $5010   (3-Jun-91 PHB56/R) Critics (25x17cm-10x7in) s.d.1871 l.verso panel
£4000 $6680   (3-Jun-91 PHB57/R) Game of chess (24x33cm-9x13in) s.d.1881 panel
£5408 $10654   (14-Nov-90 FB.P148/R) Le club (37x55cm-15x22in) s.d.1883 panel
       (F.FR 53000)
£5800 $11426   (5-Oct-90 C49/R) Musical party. Card party (21x27cm-8x11in) one s.d.1862
       one s.d.1856 panel pair
£1004 $1857   (4-Mar-91 ARC.P45) Parade militaire (38x28cm-15x11in) s. gouache
       (F.FR 10000)

FICHEL, Eugene (19th C) French
£867 $1500   (21-May-91 CE.NY49/R) On guard (24x14cm-9x6in) s. panel
£2833 $5552   (24-Nov-90 SA.A813/R) The astonished harlequin (22x14cm-9x6in) s.d.1857
       panel (DM 8300)
£580 $1027   (22-Mar-91 PHE36) Figures in tavern interior (25x36cm-10x14in) s.d.1880
       W/C
£1100 $1903   (9-May-91 CSK10/R) Selection from menu (25x35cm-10x14in) s.d.1880 pencil
       W/C htd white

FICHERELLI, Felice (after) (1605-1660) Italian
£2600 $5122   (30-Oct-90 PH44/R) Tarquin and Lucretia (118x149cm-46x59in)

FICHTL, A (?) ?
£884 $1565   (20-Mar-91 KM.K1209) Still life of flowers (40x30cm-16x12in) s. copper
       (DM 2600)

FIDANI, Orazio (attrib) (1610-1656) Italian
£4771 $8064   (18-Apr-91 APT.P7/R) Le retour du chasseur (97x134cm-38x53in)
       (F.FR 48000)

FIDANZA, Francesco (1747-1819) Italian
£4283 $7666   (8-Apr-91 CH.R73/R) Notturno con l'incendio di un borgo
       (73x60cm-29x24in) (I.L 9500000)
£6834 $11619   (30-May-91 F.M125/R) Marina con pescatori e barca (57x75cm-22x30in)
       (I.L 15000000)

FIDLER, Anton (19th C) Austrian
£1282 $2500   (24-Oct-90 D.NY70/R) Bird with flowers and fruit on ledge
       (53x43cm-21x17in) s.indis.d.18.7

FIDLER, Harry (?-1935) British
£700 $1358   (6-Dec-90 CSK153) Plough team (25x30cm-10x12in) s.
£782 $1501   (26-Nov-90 SY.J282/R) Cows grazing in pasture (36x49cm-14x19in) init.
       board (SA.R 3800)
£1100 $1837   (22-Jul-91 SWS1140/R) Cattle and chickens in a farmyard
       (77x91cm-30x36in) s.
£1300 $2444   (20-Sep-90 PHS616/R) Harvesting scene (36x43cm-14x17in) mono.
£1479 $2500   (20-Apr-91 WOL.C189/R) Carting hay (30x36cm-12x14in) s.
£1862 $3500   (22-Sep-90 WOL.C209/R) Carting hay (30x36cm-12x14in) s.
£820 $1574   (18-Dec-90 HC12) Life on Salisbury Plain (18x20cm-7x8in) s. W/C

FIDUS (1868-1948) German
£569 $961   (19-Apr-91 FN.S1515/R) Wooded river landscape with girl seated on swing
       pushed by boy (72x125cm-28x49in) (DM 1700)
£6081 $11554   (14-Sep-90 SA.A1373/R) Hohe Wacht (150x100cm-59x39in) s.d.1894
       (DM 18000)

FIEBIG, Carl Rudolph (1812-1874) Danish
£4167 $8042   (10-Dec-90 BU.K70/R) Portrait of Fredrik VII wearing uniform
       (112x65cm-44x26in) s. oval (D.KR 46000)

FIEDLER, Arnold (1900-) ?
£476 $767   (28-Jun-91 BM.B895) Untitled (25x31cm-10x12in) s.d.1961 mixed media
       (DM 1400)
£548 $981   (12-Mar-91 FN.S1964) Untitled (24x31cm-9x12in) s.d.1964 mixed media
       (DM 1600)
£1100 $1771   (28-Jun-91 CSK44) Paysage. Personnages (33x46cm-13x18in) one s.d.56 one
       s.d.1958 gouache board pair
£1695 $2831   (6-Jun-91 HN.H332/R) Garden view (50x69cm-20x27in) s.d.1934 gouache
       (DM 5000)

FIEDLER, Bernhard (1816-1904) German
£1573 $3037   (12-Dec-90 N.M512/R) Ruins of Balbek, Libanon (103x197cm-41x78in) s.
       (DM 4500)

FIEDLER, Herbert (1891-1962) Dutch
£781 $1351   (23-May-91 SY.AM53/R) Winterlandschap met fietsers (50x80cm-20x31in) s.
(D.FL 2600)

FIEDLER, Marianne (1864-1904) German
£936 $1583   (19-Apr-91 FN.S1714) Autumn still life of fruit and flowers with view of
landscape (79x63cm-31x25in) s. (DM 2800)

FIELD, Isabel Jane (1867-1950) ?
£2405 $4065   (17-Apr-91 DS.W37) River and southern alps landscape (71x50cm-28x20in)
s.d.99 W/C (NZ.D 7000)

FIELD, Robert (19th C) Canadian
£500 $825   (10-Jul-91 C66) A lady in low-cut white dress trimmed with lace
(7x?cm-3x?in) min.init.d.1803 gold frame plaited hair oval

FIELD, Walter (1837-1901) British
£3800 $6194   (14-Jun-91 C224/R) The gentle wind bloweth.... (76x122cm-30x48in)
s.d.1870 i.verso
£1900 $3762   (30-Jan-91 S225/R) Hay in meadows opposite Shiplake (35x52cm-14x20in)
s.d.1881 W/C

FIELDING, Anthony Vandyke Copley (1787-1855) British
£2011 $3500   (27-Mar-91 B.SF4054/R) Dunstaffnage Castle (20x25cm-8x10in) panel
£17000 $28050   (10-Jul-91 S78/R) Distant view of Rievaulx Abbey near Helmsley,
Yorkshire (35x44cm-14x17in) s.d.1847 i.verso panel
£320 $614   (20-Feb-91 B64) Llanberis, Snowdonia (16x25cm-6x10in) s. W/C htd.white
£800 $1344   (22-Apr-91 PH234/R) On road to Arundel (17x25cm-7x10in) s.d.1845 W/C htd
white
£850 $1445   (29-May-91 PHC76) Grange, Barrowdale (17x24cm-7x9in) s. W/C
£1200 $2364   (15-Nov-90 S109/R) Near Llangollen, Denbighshire (12x17cm-5x7in) s. W/C
over pencil
£1642 $2775   (15-Apr-91 SY.J395/R) Loch Eil and Ben Nevis (56x68cm-22x27in) s. W/C
(SA.R 7800)
£1700 $3349   (13-Nov-90 C76) Fishing boats off port in squall (23x30cm-9x12in) s.
pencil W/C
£1800 $2970   (11-Jul-91 S185/R) Sailbarge in choppy waters at mouth of estuary
(29x39cm-11x15in) s.d.1831 W/C scratching out
£2100 $4137   (15-Nov-90 S120/R) Fishing boats in rough seas off jetty
(21x32cm-8x13in) s. W/C scratching out
£2218 $4325   (15-Oct-90 SY.J22/R) Loch Fyne (35x47cm-14x19in) s.indist.d. W/C
(SA.R 11000)
£2600 $4290   (9-Jul-91 C123/R) Arundel Castle at dusk (62x53cm-24x21in) s.d.1849 W/C
htd.gum arabic scratching out
£2600 $4602   (22-Mar-91 PHE32/R) Dunderawe Castle on Loch Fyne (26x36cm-10x14in) s.
W/C
£3000 $4950   (11-Jul-91 S199/R) Cattle grazing near Ben Lomond (48x34cm-19x13in)
s.d.1840 W/C over pencil with gum arabic

FIELDING, Anthony Vandyke Copley (attrib) (1787-1855) British
£620 $1011   (13-Jun-91 CSK122) Fishing smack at low tide (10x14cm-4x6in) init.d.1831
pencil W/C

FIELDING, C (?) ?
£500 $835   (7-Jun-91 BW47) Highland loch (38x58cm-15x23in) s.d.1846
£1250 $2425   (7-Dec-90 BW304) Distant view of Chepstow (20x28cm-8x11in) s. W/C

FIELDING, G (19th C) British
£750 $1410   (7-Aug-90 HS7/R) Gipsy encampment with horses in wood (61x89cm-24x35in)
s.

FIELDING, Nathan Theodore (fl.1775-1815) British
£750 $1238   (9-Jul-91 C67) Farm labourers outside inn (31x42cm-12x17in) s.d.1777 pen
ink W/C

FIELDING, Newton Limbird Smith (1799-1856) British
£800 $1576   (15-Nov-90 S102) Old cottages by stream with church beyond
(21x30cm-8x12in) W/C htd.bodycol gum arabic scratching out
£864 $1728   (4-Feb-91 PLF.P30/R) Deux chiens dans un paysage boise (26x38cm-10x15in)
s.d.1832 W/C gouache (F.FR 8500)
£1000 $1970   (13-Nov-90 C119/R) Stag and other deer beside river (15x20cm-6x8in)
s.indis.d.183. W/C gum arabic
£1067 $2134   (4-Feb-91 PLF.P31/R) Chasse au sanglier (20x29cm-8x11in) s.d.1833 W/C
(F.FR 10500)

FIENE, Ernest (1894-1965) American
£833 $1400   (28-Apr-91 HG.C368) Approaching storm (66x84cm-26x33in) s. board
£1047 $1800   (15-May-91 SY.NY187/R) Summer evening, Lancaster, PA (33x41cm-13x16in)
s.panel
£1744 $3000   (15-May-91 SY.NY209/R) Snowy night - Eastside (61x51cm-24x20in)
s.d.54.55 s.stretcher
£3704 $7000   (27-Sep-90 CH.NY262/R) New snow (66x92cm-26x36in) s.
£4469 $8000   (14-Mar-91 CH.NY222/R) Girl with black hat (61x41cm-24x16in) s.
£503 $950   (25-Sep-90 CE.NY231/R) Lillies (30x23cm-12x9in) s. W/C gouache
£812 $1600   (18-Nov-90 JRB.C149/R) Mountain landscape (36x56cm-14x22in) s.d.35 W/C

FIERAVINO, Francesco (17th C) Italian
£13408 $24000   (10-Apr-91 HF.NY4/R) Still life with flowers and silver jug (76x103cm-30x41in)

FIERAVINO, Francesco (attrib) (17th C) Italian
£24426 $43723   (14-Mar-91 D.V38/R) Still lifes on tables draped with Oriental carpets with fruit and jewels (65x128cm-26x50in) rem.sig. pair (A.S 500000)

FIERAVINO, Francesco (circle) (17th C) Italian
£6030 $9889   (22-Jun-91 CH.MO127 a/R) Nature morte aux paniers de fruits et de fleurs sur un entablement (69x95cm-27x37in) (F.FR 60000)
£7000 $13300   (1-Mar-91 C171/R) Silver vessels and other utensils on table draped with carpet (91x111cm-36x44in)
£7784 $13156   (2-May-91 CH.AM98 a/R) A lute leaning against a chair, gilt ewers and other objects on adraped ledge (72x94cm-28x37in) (D.FL 26000)
£8000 $15360   (29-Nov-90 CSK152/R) Spaniel on cushion on draped table (90x128cm-35x50in)
£9500 $18335   (11-Dec-90 PH43/R) Still life of musical instruments and score on stone ledge (72x96cm-28x38in)

FIETZ, Gerhard (1910-) ?
£1233 $2010   (14-Jun-91 L.K864/R) Untitled (33x48cm-13x19in) s.d.53 pastel chk (DM 3600)

FIGARI, Andrea (?) Italian
£1140 $1904   (6-Jun-91 F.M70/R) Costa ligure (19x25cm-7x10in) s. panel (I.L 2500000)

FIGARI, Pedro (1861-1938) Uruguayan
£3571 $7000   (21-Nov-90 NA.BA88/R) Los musicos (32x39cm-13x15in) s. board
£4142 $7000   (20-Apr-91 WOL.C255/R) Dance (38x48cm-15x19in) s. panel
£5020 $9287   (4-Mar-91 ARC.P129/R) Lavanderas (33x40cm-13x16in) s.d.1919 verso board (F.FR 50000)
£5102 $10000   (20-Nov-90 CH.NY256/R) Condombe (16x25cm-6x10in) i.num 133 Serie XXXIII E.e. verso board
£5523 $9500   (15-May-91 CH.NY187/R) La Carreta (34x48cm-13x19in) s.d.1921 i. verso board
£6633 $13000   (20-Nov-90 CH.NY254/R) El mate (35x50cm-14x20in) s. s.d.1926 verso board
£6977 $12000   (15-May-91 CH.NY127/R) Bochadores (33x39cm-13x15in) s. i. verso board
£7763 $14750   (11-Sep-90 PO.BA7) De paseo (50x69cm-20x27in) board
£7868 $15500   (1-Oct-90 GC.M5) El Tango (50x70cm-20x28in) board
£8122 $16000   (1-Oct-90 GC.M4) El Ultimo Partido (35x50cm-14x20in) board
£8883 $17500   (1-Nov-90 GC.M4) En el llano (40x33cm-16x13in) board
£10714 $21000   (19-Nov-90 SY.NY31/R) El Circo (50x69cm-20x27in) s. board
£10882 $18500   (27-May-91 GC.M377/R) Hacia la Casa del Gobernador (33x70cm-13x28in) s. board
£11224 $22000   (20-Nov-90 CH.NY162/R) Baile criollo (33x40cm-13x16in) s. num.33 verso board
£16279 $28000   (15-May-91 CH.NY110/R) Matinal (53x69cm-21x27in) s. i. verso board
£16279 $28000   (15-May-91 CH.NY23/R) Reunion Colonial (69x99cm-27x39in) s. board
£17059 $29000   (27-May-91 GC.M376/R) Diligencia en la Estancia (54x69cm-21x27in) s. board
£17347 $34000   (19-Nov-90 SY.NY30/R) Corrida de toros (40x50cm-16x20in) s. board
£21429 $42000   (20-Nov-90 CH.NY18/R) Hacia la Plaza (98x34cm-39x13in) s. i.num.743 verso board
£21472 $35000   (1-Jul-91 GC.M1) El Minuet (100x70cm-39x28in) board
£23121 $40000   (8-May-91 SY.NY148/R) Enganchando (53x68cm-21x27in) s.i. label verso board
£24235 $47500   (19-Nov-90 SY.NY4/R) La Espera (70x100cm-28x39in) s. board

FIGINI, Arturo (20th C) Italian
£1617 $3122   (13-Dec-90 SY.MI208/R) Ballerine (130x120cm-51x47in) masonite (I.L 3500000)

FIGINO, Giovanni Ambrogio (attrib) (1550-1595) Italian
£1200 $2304   (18-Feb-91 S25/R) Study for figure of Christ in Pieta (34x21cm-13x8in) chk squared all corners cut

FIGLIO, Vivo de (19th C) Italian
£1800 $3456   (27-Nov-90 PH178/R) Portraits of hunting dogs (67x55cm-26x22in) s. oval pair

FIKENTSCHER, Otto Clemens (1831-1880) German
£1049 $2035   (4-Dec-90 FN.S1829/R) Skirmish scene, German French War (37x44cm-15x17in) d.1870/71 bears sig. canvas laid down (DM 3000)
£4054 $6851   (3-May-91 SA.A1773/R) Blucher being rescued by Ajutant Nostiz at Quatrebras (42x66cm-17x26in) s.d.1862 (DM 12000)

FILARSKI, Dirk Herman Willem (1885-) Flemish
£1858 $3585   (12-Dec-90 CH.AM51) View on castle in South of Spain (67x82cm-26x32in) s. (D.FL 6000)
£1976 $3360   (30-May-91 EA.Z191/R) Place Blanche, Paris (81x65cm-32x26in) s. (S.FR 5000)
£2102 $3637   (22-May-91 CH.AM308/R) Still life with painter's equipment (55x70cm-22x28in) s.d.1911 (D.FL 7000)
£3303 $5715   (23-May-91 SY.AM4) Schin op geul (54x65cm-21x26in) s.d.40 i.verso (D.FL 11000)

FILARSKI, Dirk Herman Willem (1885-) Flemish-cont.
£8108 $14027   (23-May-91 SY.AM28/R) 't Oude Hof in Bergen (54x65cm-21x26in) s.d.1940
                   (D.FL 27000)

FILHOL, Sophie Antoinette (1806-1854) French
£1143   *$2251*   *(13-Nov-90 CH.G274/R) Portrait of young girl wearing pleated white*
                   off-the-shoulder dress (5x?cm-2x?in) min.s.d.1845 gilt-metal mount
                   wood frame oval (S.FR 2800)

FILIGER, Charles (1863-1928) French
£1910   *$3418*   *(11-Mar-91 GL.P9) La vierge a l'enfant (8x6cm-3x2in) W/C gouache gilded*
                   paint (F.FR 19000)

FILIMONOV, Vladimir (1873-1934) Russian
£653 $1071   (19-Jun-91 ARC.P196/R) Nature morte a la pasteque (97x120cm-38x47in) s.
                   (F.FR 6500)

FILIPKIEWICZ, Stefan (1879-1944) Polish
£965 $1891   (26-Jan-91 PSA.W8) Winter landscape (70x80cm-28x31in) s.d.1911
                   (P.Z 18000000)

FILIPOV, Konstantin Nikolaivich (1830-1878) Russian
£3200 $6304   (4-Oct-90 CSK69) Setters' homestead in the caucasian foothills
                   (39x51cm-15x20in) s.d.1873

FILIPPELLI, Cafiero (1889-?) Italian
£866 $1447   (6-Jun-91 F.M233) Paese (29x39cm-11x15in) s. i.d.1952verso panel
                   (I.L 1900000)
£1824 $3046   (6-Jun-91 F.M44/R) Nudo femminile di schiena (112x70cm-44x28in) s.d.1940
                   panel (I.L 4000000)

FILIPPI, Fernando de (1940-) Italian
£2431 $4741   (22-Oct-90 BR.M111/R) Spesso attraverso gli anni ricorderai quel canto
                   (110x100cm-43x39in) s.d.1989 verso acrylic (I.L 5400000)
£729   *$1239*   *(28-May-91 SY.MI111) Studio per all'ombra delle fanciulle in fiore*
                   (100x70cm-39x28in) s.d.65 mixed media canvas (I.L 1600000)

FILKUKA, Anton (1888-1947) Austrian
£679 $1276   (20-Sep-90 D.V73/R) Path through alpine meadow (80x90cm-31x35in) s.
                   (A.S 14000)
£6200 $11904   (30-Nov-90 C48/R) Ice breakers in a winter landscape
                   (205x300cm-81x118in) s.

FILLA, Emil (1882-1953) Czechoslovakian
£3800 $6118   (24-Jun-91 CSK146) Nature morte aux fruits et fleurs (65x53cm-26x21in)
                   s.d.32 indis.i.verso board
£4500 $7245   (24-Jun-91 CSK145/R) Nature morte a la trompette, et aux fruits
                   (26x66cm-10x26in) s.d.48
£7509 $14717   (24-Nov-90 N.M155/R) Still life (31x87cm-12x34in) s.d.1936 s.d.stretcher
                   (DM 22000)
£10239 $19352   (25-Sep-90 FN.S1948/R) Still life with mandolin and fruit
                   (27x30cm-11x12in) s. (DM 30000)

FILLARD, F (?) ?
£629 $1188   (25-Sep-90 GM.B1089) Portrait de dame (50x40cm-20x16in) s. panel
                   (B.FR 38000)
£667 $1280   (18-Dec-90 GM.B829) Dames admirant des bijoux (60x50cm-24x20in) s. board
                   (B.FR 40000)
£1654 $3127   (25-Sep-90 GM.B1024) Dame portant un toast (50x40cm-20x16in) s. panel
                   (B.FR 100000)
£1654 $3127   (25-Sep-90 GM.B1029) Jeune femme jouant de l'epinette (50x40cm-20x16in)
                   s. panel (B.FR 100000)

FILLATREAU, Benoist (1843-?) French
£1399 $2713   (4-Dec-90 FN.S1830/R) Still life of flowers with fan, glass bowl and
                   jewellery (46x55cm-18x22in) s. canvas laid down (DM 4000)

FILLEAU, Emery A (fl.1890-1910) American
£2162 $4000   (10-Mar-91 H.C130/R) Boy watering horse (91x152cm-36x60in) s.d.94

FILLIA (1904-1936) Italian
£7702 $13402   (26-Mar-91 F.M100/R) L'attesa (40x50cm-16x20in) s. (I.L 17000000)

FILLIARD, Ernest (1868-1933) French
£638 $1200   (18-Sep-90 RO.BA382) Vase avec fleurs (14x12cm-6x5in) s.
£416   *$736*   *(7-Apr-91 I.N130) Bouquet d'Oeillets (27x38cm-11x15in) s. W/C*
                   (F.FR 4200)
£816   *$1445*   *(20-Mar-91 KM.K1210) Still life of flowers in vase (56x48cm-22x19in)*
                   s.d.1927 W/C (DM 2400)

FILLIARD, F (?) ?
£1083 $2080   (18-Dec-90 GM.B801) Femme a l'orchidee (60x40cm-24x16in) s. board
                   (B.FR 65000)
£1489 $2814   (25-Sep-90 GM.B873) Lecture de la lettre (50x60cm-20x24in) s. panel
                   (B.FR 90000)

FILLIOU, Robert (1926-) ?
£1224 $2412   *(17-Nov-90 S.Z45/R) Pink spaghetti (30x22cm-12x9in) d.1965 s.i. pink spaghetti mixed media (S.FR 3000)*

FILLON, Arthur (1900-) French
£1210 $2359   (26-Oct-90 APT.P109) Remorqueur a quai (22x27cm-9x11in) s. panel (F.FR 12000)
£1310 $2555   (26-Oct-90 APT.P108) La route (60x73cm-24x29in) s. (F.FR 13000)
£2117 $4128   (26-Oct-90 APT.P107) Paris - bateaux a quai (50x65cm-20x26in) s. (F.FR 21000)
£2238 $4230   (30-Sep-90 E.LA67) Paris - le parc Montsouris (60x73cm-24x29in) s. (F.FR 22000)
£2319 $4521   (26-Oct-90 APT.P106/R) Notre Dame de Paris (81x65cm-32x26in) s. (F.FR 23000)
£661   *$1321*   *(6-Feb-91 FB.P118/R) Au cabaret (30x46cm-12x18in) s. gouache (F.FR 6500)*
£1619   *$3174*   *(25-Nov-90 ZZ.F58/R) Le Pont-Neuf a Paris (37x54cm-15x21in) s. W/C (F.FR 16000)*

FILMUS, Tully (20th C) American
£657 $1300   (1-Feb-91 S.W1865/R) Student (23x30cm-9x12in) s.
£1148 $2250   (12-Feb-91 SY.NY104/R) Two rabbis reading the Torah (51x66cm-20x26in) s.

FILONOV, Pavel (1883-) Russian
£51000 $99450   (17-Oct-90 S113/R) The Magi (46x35cm-18x14in) i.d.1913verso tempera paper on board

FILONOV, Pavel (studio) (1883-?) Russian
£1524   *$3049*   *(10-Feb-91 YC.P71) L'attente (38x30cm-15x12in) gouache pasted paper (F.FR 15000)*

FILOSA, Giovanni B (1850-1935) Italian
£950   *$1530*   *(24-Jun-91 CSK70/R) La passegiata (81x59cm-32x23in) s.*
£575   *$1000*   *(27-Mar-91 B.SF4077/R) Ritratto di una fianculla (30x27cm-12x11in) s. W/C board*
£682   *$1337*   *(21-Nov-90 F.M147) Profilo di giovane pastore (37x27cm-15x11in) s. W/C (I.L 1500000)*
£3700   *$7178*   *(4-Dec-90 F.R40/R) Confidenze (67x49cm-26x19in) s. W/C paper on panel (I.L 8000000)*

FIMA (1916-) Israeli
£733 $1400   (2-Jan-91 GG.TA413/R) Around Jerusalem (46x55cm-18x22in) s. s.i.verso

FINART, Noel Dieudonne (1797-1852) French
£1300 $2535   (24-Oct-90 S225/R) An Arab encampment (23x31cm-9x12in) s.d.1834

FINCH, A W (1854-?) Belgian
£4161 $7032   (20-Apr-91 HOR.H69/R) Red flowers (58x76cm-23x30in) s. (F.M 29000)

FINCH, Alfred William (1854-?) Belgian
£5278 $10345   (24-Nov-90 HOR.H84/R) The old bridge (27x32cm-11x13in) s. (F.M 37000)

FINCH, Francis Oliver (1802-1862) British
£900   *$1728*   *(26-Nov-90 SWS2/R) Cattle grazing by castle ruins (22x33cm-9x13in) W/C htd.gum arabic scratching out*

FIND, Ludvig (1869-?) Scandinavian
£692 $1343   (22-Aug-90 RAS.K102/R) Road through the village (85x100cm-33x39in) s.d.1904 (D.KR 8000)

FINDENIGG, Franz Paul (circle) (1726-1771) Austrian
£2198 $3935   (14-Mar-91 D.V330/R) After the battle (43x66cm-17x26in) (A.S 45000)

FINES, Eugene Francois (1826-1882) French
£3413 $6689   (24-Nov-90 SA.A751/R) Girl playing bubbles in interior (68x46cm-27x18in) s. (DM 10000)

FINETTI, Gino Ritter von (1877-?) Italian
£6345 $11737   (7-Mar-91 D.V156/R) Garbin auf Brioni (46x62cm-18x24in) s. i.verso (A.S 130000)

FINGESTEN, Michel (20th C) German?
£3716 $6318   (31-May-91 GB.B6279/R) Landscape with female nude seated beneath trees (51x60cm-20x24in) s. (DM 11000)

FINI, Leonor (1908-?) Italian
£1172 $2262   (10-Dec-90 LD.P54/R) Portrait de jeune femme (30x20cm-12x8in) s. (F.FR 11500)
£4052 $7902   (22-Oct-90 BR.M204/R) Figure (36x46cm-14x18in) s.d.1931 tempera paper on canvas (I.L 9000000)
£11558 $20688   (16-Mar-91 APT.P58/R) Madame X (93x65cm-37x26in) s. (F.FR 115000)
£13145 $25632   (17-Oct-90 DL.P37/R) Jeune femme au collier bleu (81x54cm-32x21in) s.d.1942 (F.FR 130000)
£13514 $22973   (1-Jun-91 VG.B315/R) Le rendez-vous (39x57cm-15x22in) s. (DM 40000)
£15000 $24150   (26-Jun-91 S173/R) Les deux femmes aux chapeau (56x39cm-22x15in) s.
£40000 $70800   (19-Mar-91 C106/R) L'Escarpolette I (118cm-46ins circular) s. s.stretcher

FINI, Leonor (1908-?) Italian-cont.

£415	$744	(8-Apr-91 CSC.P95) Ecuyers (46x30cm-18x12in) s. gouache W/C Indian ink (F.FR 4200)
£553	$907	(18-Jun-91 APT.P18) Portrait de femme (32x24cm-13x9in) s. Indian ink htd.gouache (F.FR 5500)
£653	$1267	(8-Dec-90 GAB.G2541/R) Etude de femmes (28x15cm-11x6in) s. (S.FR 1600)
£692	$1364	(30-Oct-90 I.N310) Femme et hibou (24x17cm-9x7in) s. ink (F.FR 6800)
£714	$1377	(10-Dec-90 LD.P11/R) Ecuyere fantastique (27x20cm-11x8in) s. Indian ink (F.FR 7000)
£814	$1538	(30-Sep-90 E.LA188) Cesar Borgia et son page (40x30cm-16x12in) s. gouache (F.FR 8000)
£872	$1701	(12-Oct-90 AW.H2328/R) Les quatre dames (42x32cm-17x13in) s.i. indian ink pen (DM 2600)
£1309	$2200	(23-Apr-91 C.A455/R) Mother and child (20x26cm-8x10in) s. wash (B.FR 80000)
£1500	$2415	(24-Jan-91 CSK166/R) Tete de femme (27x20cm-11x8in) s.i. gouache
£1837	$3618	(16-Nov-90 FB.P152) Portail s. ink W/C (F.FR 18000)
£2959	$5828	(6-Oct-90 GL.P130) Portrait de jeune femme (39x22cm-15x9in) s. W/C pastel (F.FR 30000)

FINK, Aaron (20th C) American?

| £636 | $1100 | (12-May-91 H.C209) Red hat on green (152x122cm-60x48in) s.d.1988verso |
| £636 | $1100 | (12-May-91 H.C210) Head (112x107cm-44x42in) acrylic |

FINK, Hans (1873-?) Austrian

| £2425 | $4559 | (20-Sep-90 D.V15/R) Portrait of a woman in her walking out clothes (122x63cm-48x25in) s.d.1907 (A.S 50000) |

FINKELSTEIN, Anna (20th C) ?

| £1121 | $2153 | (2-Dec-90 M.V158) Bouquet de fleurs (55x46cm-22x18in) mono. canvas-board (F.FR 11000) |

FINLEY, Elizabeth R (19th C) American?

| £1026 | $1950 | (3-Mar-91 LIT.L20) Woman in green kimono (33x46cm-13x18in) s. panel |

FINN, Herbert John (1860-?) British

| £543 | $918 | (16-Apr-91 J.M222/R) Plymouth Sound (50x67cm-20x26in) s.d.1920 W/C (A.D 1200) |
| £840 | $1579 | (20-Sep-90 SC4135/R) Barges on Thames (53x76cm-21x30in) s.d.1922 W/C |

FINNBERG, Gustaf Wilhelm (1784-1833) Swedish

| £3852 | $7549 | (24-Nov-90 HOR.H87/R) Alexander and guards visiting Diogenes (114x92cm-45x36in) (F.M 27000) |
| £4137 | $8108 | (24-Nov-90 HOR.H86/R) Family group, Abo cathedral in background (31x19cm-12x7in) mixed media (F.M 29000) |

FINNE, Henrik (1898-?) Norwegian

| £521 | $870 | (3-Jun-91 B.O42/R) Spanish town scene with people (40x60cm-16x24in) s.d.36 (N.KR 6000) |
| £2189 | $3919 | (11-Mar-91 B.O31/R) Nude woman seen from behind (78x61cm-31x24in) s.d.28 (N.KR 25000) |

FINNE-GRONN, Hans (1903-) Norwegian

| £1380 | $2664 | (13-Dec-90 BU.O11/R) Skottevik near Kristiansand (73x92cm-29x36in) s. s.i.verso panel (N.KR 15500) |

FINNEMORE, Joseph (1860-1939) British

| £500 | $855 | (30-Jul-91 SWS103) Hard times (110x83cm-43x33in) s.d.1881 |

FINOGLIA, Paolo (?-1656) Italian

| £12769 | $21325 | (4-Jun-91 CH.R444/R) La regina di Saba reca i doni a Salomone (141x179cm-56x70in) (I.L 28000000) |

FINSON, David (1597-?) Dutch

| £6533 | $10714 | (21-Jun-91 SY.MO180/R) Scene de la vie a Troie (140x224cm-55x88in) s.d.1642 (F.FR 65000) |

FINSTER, Howard (20th C) American

| £606 | $1200 | (30-Jan-91 GRO.B108/R) Coca Cola (89x25cm-35x10in) s.i.d.Nov 17.89 acrylic panel |
| £1272 | $2200 | (7-May-91 CE.NY300/R) Stay off cocaine. Coca Cola (86x25cm-34x10in) s.i.d.1988 verso acrylic panel pair |

FIOCCA (19th C) Italian

| £1939 | $3819 | (14-Nov-90 FB.P251/R) Les Azalees (31x18cm-12x7in) s.d.1874 i. verso panel (F.FR 19000) |

FIORAVANTI, Benedetto (circle) (17th C) Italian

| £2000 | $3800 | (13-Sep-90 CSK144/R) Still life with oysters in pan, artichokes, fish, bread, olives, fruit on table (32x41cm-13x16in) |

FIORAVANTI, Benedictus (attrib) (18th C) Italian

| £9363 | $16105 | (14-May-91 BU.S83/R) Still life of flowers with rabbits and dog (93x64cm-37x25in) pair (S.KR 100000) |

FIORENTINO, Pier Francesco see PIER FRANCESCO

FIORENZO DI LORENZO (c.1445-1525) Italian
£1112 $2169   (15-Oct-90 APT.P78/R) Saint Sebastien (20x15cm-8x6in) panel oval
       (F.FR 11000)

FIORENZO DI LORENZO (style) (c.1445-1525) Italian
£10882 $18500   (31-May-91 CH.NY244/R) Madonna and Child surrounded by mandorla of
       seraphim (72x73cm-28x29in) panel

FIORI, Mario da see NUZZI, Mario

FIRLE, Walter (1859-1929) German
£1027 $1839   (13-Mar-91 N.M486/R) Madonna and Child in autumnal landscape. Portrait
       of gentleman (75x63cm-30x25in) s. board double-sided (DM 3000)
£2000 $3580   (12-Apr-91 BM.B593/R) Kitchen interior with seated little girl cleaning
       copper kettle (68x58cm-27x23in) (DM 6000)
£2041 $3612   (20-Mar-91 KM.K1211/R) Still life of asters, dahlias and other flowers
       in glass vase (105x75cm-41x30in) s. paper on panel (DM 6000)
£3586 $6992   (24-Oct-90 GD.B345/R) Interior with two women needle working and child
       playing on floor (74x100cm-29x39in) s. board (S.FR 9000)
£6294 $12147   (12-Dec-90 SY.MU56/R) Tea party (61x84cm-24x33in) s. (DM 18000)

FIRMIN, Claude (1864-?) French
£7225 $12500   (22-May-91 SY.NY174/R) Dans le jardin (55x46cm-22x18in) s.d.1899

FIRMIN-GIRARD see GIRARD, Marie Firmin

FIRTH-SMITH, John (1943-) Australian
£930 $1563   (22-Apr-91 SY.ME128) Untitled (56x152cm-22x60in) s.d.1969 card on board
       (A.D 2000)
£7009 $11425   (16-Jun-91 SY.ME65/R) Over time, 1981 (185x367cm-73x144in) linen
       (A.D 15000)
£602 $1157   (27-Nov-90 JRL.S220/R) Untitled (79x119cm-31x47in) s.d.79 mixed media
       (A.D 1500)
£602 $1157   (27-Nov-90 JRL.S206/R) Fragmented time No.1 (63x99cm-25x39in) s.d.81
       mixed media paper (A.D 1500)

FISCH, Hans Ulrich I (1583-1647) Swiss
£6000 $9780   (2-Jul-91 C185/R) Christian virtues - design for stained glass
       (19x30cm-7x12in) s.i.d.1641 pen wash htd white

FISCH, Istvan (1922-) ?
£1183 $2331   (1-Oct-90 CC.P155) Untitled (100x70cm-39x28in) s.d.1978 paper on board
       (F.FR 12000)
£1183 $2331   (1-Oct-90 CC.P156) Untitled (100x70cm-39x28in) s.d.1978 paper on board
       (F.FR 12000)

FISCHBACH, Johann (1797-1871) German
£10779 $21342   (31-Jan-91 D.V22/R) Mountain view with Untersberg, Hohe Goll and
       Tennengebirge (31x42cm-12x17in) s.d.1850 (A.S 220000)
£655 $1258   (28-Nov-90 KF.M364) View of Salzburg with Monchsberg (19x30cm-7x12in)
       pencil wash htd.white (DM 1900)

FISCHBECK, Ludwig (1866-?) German
£769 $1485   (14-Dec-90 BM.B529) North German farmhouse (51x82cm-20x32in) s.
       (DM 2200)
£1224 $2362   (14-Dec-90 BM.B530/R) Seascape with Westurm, Wangerooge and steam ship
       beyond (69x102cm-27x40in) s. (DM 3500)
£1224 $2362   (14-Dec-90 BM.B528/R) Wooded landscape with pond (60x86cm-24x34in) s.
       panel (DM 3500)

FISCHER, Amandus Julius (1859-?) Australian
£746 $1261   (20-Apr-91 HOR.H13/R) Hay harvest (33x43cm-13x17in) mono.d.1897
       (F.M 5200)

FISCHER, Anton Otto (1882-1962) American
£765 $1300   (1-Jun-91 IH.NY23/R) Eskimos breaking open barrels, winter camp
       (46x66cm-18x26in) s.d.1927
£804 $1543   (27-Nov-90 W.T1158 a) Trouble on board (61x91cm-24x36in) s. (C.D 1800)

FISCHER, August (1854-1921) Danish
£621 $1012   (13-Jun-91 RAS.V534/R) Northern Italian lake landscape (50x81cm-20x32in)
       s.d.1880 (D.KR 7000)
£754 $1228   (13-Jun-91 RAS.V533/R) Canal view, Nuremberg (55x65cm-22x26in) s.d.1890
       (D.KR 8500)
£893 $1688   (25-Sep-90 RAS.K60) Italian women in market, summer's day
       (38x26cm-15x10in) s.i. (D.KR 10000)
£1298 $2517   (22-Aug-90 RAS.K199/R) View from Nurnberg (39x54cm-15x21in) s.d.1918
       (D.KR 15000)
£1330 $2168   (13-Jun-91 RAS.V535/R) Canal landscape, Palazzo Salriati, Venice
       (58x44cm-23x17in) s.d.90 (D.KR 15000)
£1712 $2791   (12-Jun-91 N.M423/R) Synagog of Nuremberg seen from Insel Schutt
       (37x52cm-15x20in) s.i. (DM 5000)
£2313 $4349   (18-Sep-90 BU.K8/R) View from Copenhagen with old Knippel's bridge
       (57x85cm-22x33in) s.d.1896 (D.KR 26000)
£2911 $5211   (13-Mar-91 N.M487/R) View of Nuremberg with Henkersteg (40x54cm-16x21in)
       s.i.d.1918 (DM 8500)

FISCHER, Hans Christian (1849-1886) Danish
£3925 $7537   (29-Nov-90 D.V68/R) Wooded river landscape (68x94cm-27x37in) s.d.1880
(A.S 80000)

FISCHER, Holger (20th C) Danish
£1057 $2072   (10-Nov-90 FAL.M94/R) Still life of fruit and flowers (89x129cm-35x51in)
s.d.1921 (S.KR 11500)

FISCHER, Johann Georg Paul (1786-1875) German
£1900 $3743   *(1-Nov-90 S9/R) Portraits, probably of Sir Jonathan Wathen Waller and of*
Sir Thomas Wathen Waller min.s.d.1830 gilt gesso frames rec.two

FISCHER, Johannes (19th C) German?
£970 $1823   (20-Sep-90 D.V109/R) Landscape (40x50cm-16x20in) i.verso board
(A.S 20000)
£1196 $2069   (8-May-91 D.V95/R) Lake landscape, Upper Engadin (107x130cm-42x51in) s.
i.verso hessian (A.S 25000)

FISCHER, Joseph (1769-1822) Austrian
£1300 $2197   *(16-Apr-91 C272/R) Hollyhock, morning glories, roses and other flowers*
in an urn on a ledge (65x91cm-26x36in) s. blk.chk.bodycol.

FISCHER, Leopold (1813-1864) Austrian
£1337 $2606   *(11-Oct-90 D.V124/R) Portrait of Grafin Schaffgottsch with fur trimmed*
wrap seated at table (27x22cm-11x9in) s.d.837 W/C (A.S 28000)

FISCHER, Lothar (1933-) German
£397 $710   *(16-Mar-91 S.Z107) Untitled (44x31cm-17x12in) s.d.1987 indian ink*
(S.FR 1000)
£1858 $3159   *(28-May-91 KF.M648) Composition Spur (62x49cm-24x19in) s.i. gouache*
(DM 5500)
£1858 $3159   *(28-May-91 KF.M649/R) Eva (60x42cm-24x17in) s. s.i.d.72 W/C (DM 5500)*

FISCHER, Ludwig Hans (1848-1915) German
£825 $1600   *(8-Dec-90 W.W91/R) View of Paris (23x36cm-9x14in) s.i. W/C paper backed*
by panel

FISCHER, Mark (20th C) American
£698 $1200   (15-May-91 SY.NY142 a/R) Country landscape (34x51cm-13x20in)

FISCHER, Oskar (1892-) German
£3413 $6689   (24-Nov-90 N.M164/R) Composition (77x57cm-30x22in) mono. panel
(DM 10000)

FISCHER, Paul (1860-1934) Danish
£572 $961   (23-Apr-91 RAS.K310) Road through town at night (27x38cm-11x15in) s.
(D.KR 6500)
£620 $1048   (1-May-91 KH.K62) Woman standing wearing Amager costume
(41x27cm-16x11in) s. (D.KR 7000)
£704 $1183   (23-Apr-91 RAS.K309/R) Mother going to town, children and maid waving
goodbye (31x25cm-12x10in) mono. (D.KR 8000)
£973 $1898   (12-Oct-90 AW.H1775/R) Geraniums at window (80x75cm-31x30in) s.
(DM 2900)
£1125 $2182   (22-Aug-90 RAS.K204/R) Three children and snowman with Christmas tree
(21x14cm-8x6in) (D.KR 13000)
£1254 $2509   (6-Feb-91 RAS.K364/R) Graveyard in Pompei (75x57cm-30x22in) s.i.
(D.KR 14000)
£1726 $3348   (5-Dec-90 KH.K40/R) Mother and daughter walking by Pebling lake
(19x25cm-7x10in) s. grisaille (D.KR 19000)
£2022 $3963   (6-Nov-90 BA.S64/R) Horse and carriage by Scala (12x17cm-5x7in) panel
(S.KR 22000)
£2203 $3678   (6-Jun-91 RAS.K101/R) Portrait of the artist's daughter
(46x40cm-18x16in) s.d.93 (D.KR 25000)
£2244 $4421   (14-Nov-90 RAS.K657/R) Town hall square, evening (20x25cm-8x10in) s.
panel (D.KR 25000)
£2330 $4659   (6-Feb-91 RAS.K461/R) View from Nyhavn with cargo boat (32x39cm-13x15in)
s.d.1924 (D.KR 26000)
£2379 $4448   (29-Aug-90 KH.K57/R) Soldier guarding the fortress (39x56cm-15x22in) s.
(D.KR 27000)
£2513 $4952   (14-Nov-90 RAS.K658/R) Entrance to Kongen's Have on corner of
Gothersgade (20x25cm-8x10in) s. panel (D.KR 28000)
£2513 $4952   (14-Nov-90 RAS.K567/R) Portrait of Swedish peasant girl wearing head
scarf (38x31cm-15x12in) s. (D.KR 28000)
£2855 $5538   (22-Aug-90 RAS.K202/R) Young girl reading in deckchair by sea
(34x40cm-13x16in) s. (D.KR 33000)
£3000 $4920   (19-Jun-91 S299/R) Kongenshave in winter (19x24cm-7x9in) s. panel
£3260 $5444   (6-Jun-91 RAS.K70/R) Two bathing nymphs in the shadow of trees
(39x54cm-15x21in) s. (D.KR 37000)
£3591 $7074   (14-Nov-90 RAS.K80/R) From Dante's Plads with view towards
Videnskabernes Selskab (22x35cm-9x14in) s. panel (D.KR 40000)
£3893 $7552   (22-Aug-90 RAS.K61/R) View of Kongens Nytorv on rainy winter's day
(32x39cm-13x15in) s. (D.KR 48000)
£4225 $7099   (23-Apr-91 RAS.K103/R) Elsa and Inga, Bastad (54x38cm-21x15in) s.d.1915
(D.KR 48000)
£4401 $7394   (23-Apr-91 RAS.K123/R) Young mother and boy earthing potatoes, Dalarne
(66x120cm-26x47in) s.d.1887 (D.KR 50000)

FISCHER, Paul (1860-1934) Danish-cont.

£4451	$7477	(24-Apr-91 BA.S60/R) Winter's day in Copenhagen (20x25cm-8x10in) s. panel (S.KR 47000)
£4488	$8842	(14-Nov-90 RAS.K117/R) Summer's day at Langelinie (32x22cm-13x9in) s. panel (D.KR 50000)
£4596	$9007	(6-Nov-90 BA.S63/R) View from Aarhus (32x39cm-13x15in) s.d.1926 panel (S.KR 50000)
£4842	$8134	(23-Apr-91 RAS.K61/R) View of Nytorv with the Court-house (32x39cm-13x15in) s. panel (D.KR 55000)
£5000	$9600	(28-Nov-90 S109/R) Street scene in Copenhagen (37x28cm-15x11in) s. panel
£5566	$10964	(14-Nov-90 RAS.K181/R) Two girl bathing (38x53cm-15x21in) s. (D.KR 62000)
£5783	$10872	(18-Sep-90 BU.K90/R) Kongen's Nytorv with Royal Theatre in background (25x32cm-10x13in) s. (D.KR 65000)
£5882	$11412	(22-Aug-90 RAS.K78/R) Copenhagen view, Nyboder with Chr IV's statue (32x39cm-13x15in) s. (D.KR 68000)
£7048	$13181	(29-Aug-90 KH.K55/R) Interior with young woman reading (39x55cm-15x22in) s.d.1916 (D.KR 80000)
£7353	$14412	(6-Nov-90 BA.S62/R) By Central Station, Copenhagen (20x25cm-8x10in) s. panel (S.KR 80000)
£7630	$15031	(14-Nov-90 RAS.K30/R) Fjord landscape with two children playing on pier (40x55cm-16x22in) s. (D.KR 85000)
£7630	$15031	(14-Nov-90 RAS.K119/R) Girl cyclist looking at flowers at Hojbro Plads (32x38cm-13x15in) s. panel (D.KR 85000)
£8000	$13760	(17-May-91 C192/R) On tram (39x32cm-15x13in) s. panel
£9874	$19452	(14-Nov-90 RAS.K78/R) Guards in snow outside Amalieborg (57x51cm-22x20in) s. (D.KR 110000)
£10000	$16400	(19-Jun-91 S295/R) Figures in snowy wood (48x38cm-19x15in) s.d.1908 panel
£10417	$17500	(24-Apr-91 BA.S58/R) Flower market (39x32cm-15x13in) s.d.1928 panel (S.KR 110000)
£11670	$22989	(14-Nov-90 RAS.K79/R) View from Kongen's Nytorv with Hotel d'Angleterre (39x56cm-15x22in) s. (D.KR 130000)
£12324	$20704	(23-Apr-91 RAS.K58/R) The flower sellers at Hojbro Plads (24x31cm-9x12in) s. panel (D.KR 140000)
£16904	$31779	(18-Sep-90 BU.K34/R) Sunbathing - two nude girls on beach (58x75cm-23x30in) s.d.1916 (D.KR 190000)
£20000	$32800	(19-Jun-91 S297/R) Osterbrogade in winter (37x53cm-15x21in) s.d.1918
£33708	$57978	(14-May-91 BU.S10/R) By the jetty (95x80cm-37x31in) s.d.1891 (S.KR 360000)
£62837	$123788	(14-Nov-90 RAS.K65/R) Figures on Queen Louise's Bridge seen from Norrebro Street (64x105cm-25x41in) s.d.1888 (D.KR 700000)
£730	$1423	(19-Oct-90 RAS.V475/R) From Klampenborg race-course (29x23cm-11x9in) s. pen W/C (D.KR 8200)
£808	$1592	(14-Nov-90 RAS.K800/R) Education. Why have they cut her arms off. Because she sucked her thumbs (27x20cm-11x8in) mono. grisaille (D.KR 9000)
£1268	$2447	(10-Dec-90 BU.K52/R) Lady wearing red dress crossing Town Hall Square (40x19cm-16x7in) s. W/C pen (D.KR 14000)

FISCHER, Richard Johann Christian (attrib) (1826-?) German

£676	$1318	(26-Oct-90 KM.K1207) Park landscape with young woman holding bunch of flowers walking (62x88cm-24x35in) s. (DM 2000)

FISCHER-HANSEN, Else (20th C) Danish

£667	$1254	(19-Sep-90 KH.K145/R) Composition (85x67cm-33x26in) init.d.1951verso (D.KR 7500)

FISCHER-KOYSTRAND, Carl (1861-1918) Austrian

£1200	$2304	(28-Nov-90 S232/R) Design for poster (53x41cm-21x16in) s.d.98 W/C gold paint
£9000	$17280	(28-Nov-90 S241/R) Portrait of Leonore Rellee, opera singer (96x47cm-38x19in) s. pastel

FISCHER-TRACHAU, Otto (1878-1958) German

£5898	$9850	(5-Jun-91 DO.H2633/R) The faraway town, Stade (110x80cm-43x31in) mono.d.1919 tempera (DM 17400)

FISCHETTI, Fedele (1734-1789) Italian

£1182	$2317	(19-Nov-90 CH.R221/R) Narciso alla fonte. Eco piange la morte di Narciso (99x99cm-39x39in) i. pencil ink pen W/C pair (I.L 2600000)
£3800	$6194	(2-Jul-91 C287/R) Bacchus and nymph seated on cloud with putti (59x44cm-23x17in) with i. red black chk pen wash

FISCHHOF, Georg (1859-1914) Austrian

£1510	$2945	(10-Oct-90 ZEL.L1482/R) Bust of Dante Alighieri with laurel wreath (111x70cm-44x28in) s. (DM 4500)
£1519	$2719	(11-Apr-91 D.V290/R) Roedeer in landscape. Ducks by pond (53x42cm-21x17in) s.d.1895 panel pair (A.S 32000)

FISCHL, Eric (1948-) American

£5612	$11000	(8-Nov-90 CH.NY210/R) Untitled (51x42cm-20x17in) s.d.85 paper
£13018	$22000	(2-May-91 CH.NY179/R) Untitled (93x96cm-37x38in) glassine
£22189	$37500	(1-May-91 SY.NY168/R) Untitled - bather (117x84cm-46x33in) s.d.86 paper
£89286	$175000	(6-Nov-90 SY.NY70/R) Untitled (101x114cm-40x45in) s.d.1986 verso

FISCHL, Eric (1948-) American-cont.
£100592 $170000   (30-Apr-91 SY.NY67/R) Untitled (241x287cm-95x113in) s.d.1989 verso two
                                         parts

FISH, Anne Harriet (20th C) British
£400 $652   (13-Jun-91 L232) Tabby cat amidst roses (36x41cm-14x16in) s. W/C

FISH, George G (fl.1846-1880) American
£452 $800   (22-Mar-91 S.W2252/R) Helping grandmother knit (61x51cm-24x20in)
                                         s.d.1869 pastel

FISH, Janet (1938-) American
£1026 $2000   (10-Oct-90 SY.NY435/R) Self portrait (38x51cm-15x20in) s.d.1964 paper
£4061 $8000   (4-Oct-90 SY.NY160/R) Pink jug (99x74cm-39x29in) s.d.1987 W/C
£4082 $8000   (14-Feb-91 CH.NY23/R) Red glasses (77x60cm-30x24in) s.i.d.77 col.chk
£6122 $12000   (15-Feb-91 SY.NY170/R) Painted glasses (56x94cm-22x37in) s.d.1974 pastel
£6213 $10500   (2-May-91 CH.NY147/R) Star map (75x106cm-30x42in) s.d.1986 col.chk
                                         acrylic paper

FISHER, Anna S (?-1942) American
£613 $1000   (5-Jul-91 S.W2660/R) Still life of nasturtiums (64x76cm-25x30in) s.

FISHER, Harrison (1875-1936) American
£1294 $2200   (1-Jun-91 IH.NY47/R) Woman with muff (41x25cm-16x10in) init.d.1897 pen
                                         ink
£3000 $5910   (12-Nov-90 PH83/R) A romantic dinner (72x52cm-28x20in) s.d.1911 W/C
                                         bodycol.over pencil

FISHER, Hugo (1867-1916) American
£339 $600   (22-Mar-91 S.W2250/R) Watering cows (51x74cm-20x29in) s. W/C
£447 $800   (15-Mar-91 DM.D2188/R) Winter woodland road (74x53cm-29x21in) s. W/C
                                         gouache

FISHER, Janet C (fl.1891-1925) British
£1500 $2820   (17-Sep-90 WHB58/R) Landscape with boys bathing in pool
                                         (43x58cm-17x23in) s.

FISHER, P Harland (1865-1944) British
£720 $1418   (1-Nov-90 C319/R) Collie and pug in garden (41x56cm-16x22in)
£1600 $3152   (1-Nov-90 C318/R) Young student (76x63cm-30x25in)
£2100 $3969   (27-Sep-90 L165/R) The telegram (79x91cm-31x36in) s.
£2200 $4334   (1-Nov-90 C317/R) Best of friends (76x63cm-30x25in) s.
£4000 $7840   (13-Feb-91 S182/R) Under blossom (68x64cm-27x25in) s.
£5200 $9828   (26-Sep-90 S165/R) Girl with bay hunter (141x101cm-56x40in) s.
£6400 $12096   (26-Sep-90 S166/R) Boy with West Highland White (142x101cm-56x40in) s.
                                         s.stretcher
£620 $1066   (14-May-91 SWS130/R) Young traveller (58x42cm-23x17in) s. col.chk
£620 $1221   (1-Nov-90 C15 a) Portrait of lady wearing black shawl and hat
                                         (76x64cm-30x25in) rem.sig. pastel

FISHER, Samuel Melton (1860-1939) British
£2600 $4342   (5-Jun-91 S153/R) Washday companion (80x61cm-31x24in) s.d.1887
£6500 $10855   (5-Jun-91 S150/R) Necklace (149x117cm-59x46in) s.

FISHER, Vernon (20th C) American
£5076 $10000   (4-Oct-90 SY.NY182/R) Looking for Judd (239x241cm-94x95in) init.d.76
                                         acrylic laminated paper
£2296 $4500   (12-Feb-91 SY.NY394/R) Cows (71x51cm-28x20in) s.i.d.77 graphite two
                                         sheets

FISHER, William Mark (1841-1923) British
£856 $1600   (30-Aug-90 MFA.C138 c/R) Tending the cattle (51x76cm-20x30in) s.
£1200 $2088   (28-Mar-91 CSK135/R) Cattle by pond in orchard (56x79cm-22x31in) s.
£1700 $3315   (18-Oct-90 CSK277/R) The Lock, Sawbridgeworth (50x67cm-20x26in) s.i.
                                         labels stretcher
£1800 $3528   (25-Jan-91 C105/R) Sheep shearing in barn (43x62cm-17x24in) s.
£2312 $4000   (21-May-91 CE.NY542/R) Cows grazing in afternoon (77x118cm-30x46in)
                                         s.d.83
£3000 $4890   (11-Jun-91 ZZ.B405/R) Shepherd and his sheep (53x78cm-21x31in) s.
£950 $1824   (26-Nov-90 SWS11/R) In the meadow (29x23cm-11x9in) s. W/C

FISK, William Henry (1827-1884) British
£1216 $2371   (23-Oct-90 DUR.M29) Camino de la iglesia (71x76cm-28x30in) (S.P 225000)

FISKE, Gertrude (1879-1961) American
£508 $1000   (18-Nov-90 JRB.C128/R) Sunlit dunes (20x25cm-8x10in) st.studio verso
                                         board

FITLER, William Crothers (1857-1915) American
£581 $1000   (15-May-91 SY.NY102/R) Early morning on farm (25x38cm-10x15in) s.d.92
                                         W/C board

FITS, Louis (?) Belgian?
£622 $1070   (14-May-91 GM.B625/R) Place animee (60x45cm-24x18in) s. (B.FR 38000)

FITTKE, A (?) ?
£703 $1350   (18-Dec-90 BG.M1001/R) Female nude in garden of roses (99x145cm-39x57in)

FITZGERALD, Florence (19th C) British
£1000 $1920   (14-Aug-90 GA61/R) Daisy chain - two young girls on steps to old English garden of cottage (46x30cm-18x12in) s.
£1800 $3528   (13-Feb-91 S187/R) Daisy chain (46x30cm-18x12in) s.

FITZGERALD, Frederick R (19/20th C) British
£500 $865   (22-May-91 S172/R) Fleet at anchor (29x49cm-11x19in) s.d.1902 board

FITZGERALD, Gerald (1873-1935) Australian
£1181 $2268   (14-Aug-90 SY.ME13/R) Girl with hoola-hoop (24x34cm-9x13in) s.d.1909 W/C (A.D 2800)

FITZGERALD, John Austen (1832-1906) British
£5000 $9850   (1-Nov-90 C274 c/R) Christmas (40x35cm-16x14in) s.
£26000 $42380   (14-Jun-91 C256/R) Original sketch for 'The Fairy's Banquet'. Giving alms (23x28cm-9x11in) s.i. double-sided board
£900 $1782   (30-Jan-91 S298/R) Fairy providers (38x27cm-15x11in) pen grisaille

FITZGERALD, Lionel Lemoine (1890-1956) Canadian
£1515 $2606   (14-May-91 JOY.T130/R) Field and sky (19x22cm-7x9in) s. canvas laid down on board (C.D 3000)
£429 $738   (14-May-91 JOY.T52/R) Haystacks (28x37cm-11x15in) init. pencil (C.D 850)
£464 $789   (27-May-91 HO.ED236/R) West coast landscape (21x29cm-8x11in) ink (C.D 900)
£464 $789   (27-May-91 HO.ED109/R) Abstract composition (15x22cm-6x9in) init. col.pencil (C.D 900)
£556 $961   (6-May-91 SY.T219) Trees of spring (29x21cm-11x8in) d.c.1948 verso pencil (C.D 1100)
£909 $1564   (14-May-91 JOY.T43/R) Nude (54x38cm-21x15in) init. col.chks. (C.D 1800)
£1228 $2407   (20-Nov-90 JOY.T2/R) From dining room window (36x27cm-14x11in) init. pencil (C.D 2800)

FITZGERALD, M (?) British
£700 $1295   (7-Mar-91 CSK191) The farmers distraction (53x43cm-21x17in) init. canvas on panel

FITZPATRICK, Arthur (19th C) British
£1768 $3324   (10-Aug-90 RAS.V462) Visiting the sweet shop (71x91cm-28x36in) s. (D.KR 20000)

FITZPATRICK, Mary (1968-) British
£350 $686   (13-Feb-91 B108) Landscape (61x61cm-24x24in) s.verso oil collage
£480 $941   (13-Feb-91 B107/R) Sensual world (108x108cm-43x43in) s.verso oil collage canvas

FIUME, Salvatore (1915-) Italian
£4159 $8027   (13-Dec-90 F.M318/R) Tre figure a cavallo (27x36cm-11x14in) s. masonite (I.L 9000000)
£4351 $8355   (27-Nov-90 SY.MI47/R) Illustrazione per le Poesie di Essenin (35x54cm-14x21in) s. panel (I.L 9500000)
£4728 $9219   (22-Oct-90 BR.M213/R) Isola di statue (27x18cm-11x7in) s. faesite (I.L 10500000)
£5695 $9682   (28-May-91 SY.MI195/R) Ritratto di Bunty Gozdava-Piotrowsky (100x72cm-39x28in) s.i.d.1958 board laid down on panel (I.L 12500000)
£5853 $11414   (22-Oct-90 BR.M305/R) Crocefissione (33x27cm-13x11in) s. faesite (I.L 13000000)
£5906 $11636   (30-Oct-90 F.R211/R) Paesaggio con figura femminile e cavallo (35x53cm-14x21in) s. faesite (I.L 13000000)
£9169 $15037   (20-Jun-91 F.M468/R) Isola (47x135cm-19x53in) s.d.1953 canvas on panel (I.L 20000000)
£9500 $18525   (17-Oct-90 S101/R) Ritratto di donna (168x70cm-66x28in) s.d.1958 board
£694 $1346   (3-Dec-90 F.M21) Dalla serie L'Asino d'oro (24x16cm-9x6in) s.c.1940 i.verso ink (I.L 1500000)

FIVIAN, Bendicht (1940-) Swiss
£476 $824   (25-May-91 AB.L142/R) Three heads (49x69cm-19x27in) s.d.1968 mixed media tempera pencil (S.FR 1200)

FIX-MASSEAU, Pierre-Felix (1869-1937) French
£1149 $2000   (27-Mar-91 B.SF4343/R) Bouquet de fleurs (61x46cm-24x18in) s.

FIZELLE, Rah (1891-1964) Australian
£480 $860   (9-Apr-91 CH.ME215/R) Nude study for sculpture (75x54cm-30x21in) i. pencil (A.D 1100)
£584 $1144   (19-Nov-90 MGS.S223/R) South of France (33x43cm-13x17in) s. W/C (A.D 1500)
£670 $1165   (26-Mar-91 JRL.S203) Landscape (33x43cm-13x17in) s. W/C (A.D 1500)
£996 $1962   (31-Oct-90 CH.S118) The punt, Sydney harbour (31x41cm-12x16in) s. W/C (A.D 2500)

FJAESTAD, Gustaf (1868-1948) Swedish

£1376	$2711	(13-Nov-90 AB.S366/R) Reflections in water - sketch (17x22cm-7x9in) s.i. panel (S.KR 15000)
£6197	$10535	(28-May-91 AB.S4618/R) Sunlit beach in winter frost (90x103cm-35x41in) s.d.45 (S.KR 66000)
£10110	$19816	(6-Nov-90 BA.S65/R) Winter shore with snowcovered boat (120x147cm-47x58in) s.d.09 (S.KR 110000)
£11861	$23367	(30-Oct-90 BU.S28/R) Ski-track in snow (124x99cm-49x39in) s.d.1936 panel (S.KR 130000)

FJELL, Kai (1907-1989) Norwegian

£1215	$2030	(3-Jun-91 B.O43/R) Landscape from Telemark (32x42cm-13x17in) s. panel (N.KR 14000)
£2493	$4812	(10-Dec-90 B.O33/R) The curse of Job (60x59cm-24x23in) s.d.30 (N.KR 28000)
£3384	$6531	(10-Dec-90 B.O32/R) Market, Elverum (49x51cm-19x20in) s.d.1925 panel (N.KR 38000)
£4181	$8153	(15-Oct-90 B.O27/R) Story with bird's nest (51x45cm-20x18in) s.d.31 panel (N.KR 48000)
£4452	$8593	(13-Dec-90 BU.O14/R) Female nude (52x46cm-20x18in) s.d.46 panel (N.KR 50000)
£6987	$13275	(11-Sep-90 UL.T200/R) Madonna (32x23cm-13x9in) (N.KR 80000)
£8727	$16842	(13-Dec-90 BU.O27/R) The confirmation-candidate 1952 (60x50cm-24x20in) s.d.52 (N.KR 98000)
£9115	$17773	(11-Oct-90 BU.O37/R) Woman and cat (33x24cm-13x9in) s. panel (N.KR 105000)
£13021	$21745	(4-Jun-91 BU.O20/R) Woman and rider (50x45cm-20x18in) s.d.58 (N.KR 150000)
£18700	$36091	(10-Dec-90 B.O31/R) Mother and child (81x91cm-32x36in) s. (N.KR 210000)
£24454	$46463	(11-Sep-90 UL.T198/R) Interior with woman (60x49cm-24x19in) (N.KR 280000)
£25000	$43000	(17-May-91 C173/R) Figures in harbour (81x92cm-32x36in) s.d.59
£438	$784	(14-Mar-91 BU.O34/R) Woman and locomotive (20x29cm-8x11in) s.d.79 W/C Indian ink (N.KR 5000)
£438	$784	(14-Mar-91 BU.O31/R) Zeus and Io (20x28cm-8x11in) s.i.d.80 W/C Indian ink (N.KR 5000)
£442	$883	(9-Feb-91 BU.O59) Mountain man (27x20cm-11x8in) s. Indian ink W/C (N.KR 5000)
£521	$881	(29-Apr-91 B.O56/R) The toll of bells, evening (20x28cm-8x11in) s.i.d.79 Indian ink W/C (N.KR 6000)
£521	$881	(29-Apr-91 B.O57/R) Solitary party (19x28cm-7x11in) s.i.d.81 Indian ink W/C (N.KR 6000)
£530	$1060	(9-Feb-91 BU.O58) Lazarus and Abraham (28x40cm-11x16in) s. Indian ink W/C (N.KR 6000)
£569	$1019	(14-Mar-91 BU.O33/R) Mary and Venus (20x29cm-8x11in) s.i.d.80 W/C Indian ink (N.KR 6500)
£569	$1019	(14-Mar-91 BU.O32/R) The doctor (21x28cm-8x11in) s.i.d.81 W/C Indian ink (N.KR 6500)
£608	$1015	(3-Jun-91 B.O44/R) Women and horses in landscape (20x28cm-8x11in) s.d.81 W/C Indian ink (N.KR 7000)
£617	$1221	(29-Jan-91 UL.T163) Summer's day (20x28cm-8x11in) W/C (N.KR 7000)
£652	$1101	(29-Apr-91 B.O55) Woman sleeping (20x28cm-8x11in) s.d.78 Indian ink W/C (N.KR 7500)
£663	$1325	(9-Feb-91 BU.O60) Puppies (27x20cm-11x8in) s. Indian ink W/C (N.KR 7500)
£663	$1325	(9-Feb-91 BU.O61) Artist and model (21x28cm-8x11in) s. Indian ink W/C (N.KR 7500)
£744	$1332	(14-Mar-91 BU.O30/R) Wanderer (29x40cm-11x16in) s.i.d.81 W/C Indian ink (N.KR 8500)
£751	$1502	(9-Feb-91 BU.O57) Figures and birds 1981 (28x41cm-11x16in) s. Indian ink W/C (N.KR 8500)
£6114	$11616	(11-Sep-90 UL.T199/R) Woman with town in background (60x45cm-24x18in) mixed media (N.KR 70000)

FLAD, Georg (1853-1913) German

| £839 | $1636 | (10-Oct-90 ZEL.L1484/R) Wooded landscape with woman collecting wood, late summer (62x91cm-24x36in) s. (DM 2500) |

FLAGG, George Whiting (1816-1897) American

| £3684 | $7000 | (9-Jan-91 CH.NY92/R) A young woman, Marguerite (29x23cm-11x9in) bears sig.pencil board sold w.dr by Saint-Memin |

FLAGG, James Montgomery (1877-1960) American

£3776	$7250	(17-Dec-90 SY.NY339/R) Ham fisher with three nudes (127x157cm-50x62in) s.
£952	$1800	(25-Sep-90 CE.NY309/R) The hold up (49x70cm-19x28in) s. W/C pencil
£1176	$2000	(1-Jun-91 IH.NY70/R) Standing couple near lifeboat (64x43cm-25x17in) s. pencil W/C

FLAHERTY, James Thorp (19th C) American?

| £593 | $1150 | (6-Dec-90 FA.PH640) Washing clothes in river (38x64cm-15x25in) s.d.1874 board |

FLAMENG, Francois (1856-1923) French

| £5607 | $10821 | (10-Dec-90 BL.P55/R) Portrait de Cleo de Merode (92x73cm-36x29in) s. (F.FR 55000) |

FLAMENG, Francois (1856-1923) French-cont.
£7400 $14356   (9-Dec-90 ZZ.F32/R) New York (62x52cm-24x20in) s.d.1909 board
                 (F.FR 72000)

FLAMM, Albert (1823-1906) German
£962 $1875   (25-Oct-90 D.V103/R) Street with Myla house (39x53cm-15x21in) s.d.872
                 (A.S 20000)
£3082 $5024   (12-Jun-91 N.M424/R) Brush wood collector in woodland clearing with
                 stream (57x75cm-22x30in) s.d.1843 (DM 9000)

FLANDIN, Eugene Napoleon (1803-1876) French
£1748 $3392   (4-Dec-90 FN.S1832/R) Shipping in distress in stormy sea
                 (32x40cm-13x16in) (DM 5000)

FLANDRIN, Jean Hippolyte (1809-1864) French
£1351 $2297   (27-May-91 L.K270) The Samaritan (16x22cm-6x9in) (DM 4000)
£2179 $4250   (26-Oct-90 SY.NY16/R) Sketch of young man's head (41x30cm-16x12in) paper
                 on canvas

FLANDRIN, Jules (1871-1947) French
£961 $1873   (16-Oct-90 CS.L24/R) La baie de Frejus (46x61cm-18x24in) s. (F.FR 9500)
£1000 $1610   (24-Jun-91 CSK112/R) Le quatres femmes de la Paix (40x50cm-16x20in) s.
                 paper on board
£1366 $2678   (23-Nov-90 PLF.P67) Hameau en montagne (27x46cm-11x18in) s. (F.FR 13500)

FLASSCHOEN, Gustave (1868-?) Belgian
£2463 $4261   (25-May-91 KV.L117/R) View of the Bab-Mansourh of Menkes, Morocco
                 (35x50cm-14x20in) s. (B.FR 150000)

FLATAU, Joanna (20th C) ?
£508 $1016   (7-Feb-91 R.P129/R) Daisy (107x75cm-42x30in) s. pastel oil paper laid
                 down on canvas (F.FR 5000)

FLATZ, Gebhard (1800-1881) German
£900 $1764   (22-Nov-90 CSK222) Ecstasy of Saint Francis (137x96cm-54x38in)
                 s.i.d.1864

FLAUBERT, Paul (1928-) French
£542 $1003   (10-Mar-91 LT.P161) Le dejeuner au jardin (30x25cm-12x10in) s. panel
                 (F.FR 5400)
£700 $1141   (4-Jul-91 LT.P130) La cueillette des Boutons d'or (38x46cm-15x18in) s.
                 panel (F.FR 7000)
£796 $1385   (31-Mar-91 FE.P159) Le marche en Provence (27x36cm-11x14in) s. panel
                 (F.FR 8000)
£992 $1706   (19-May-91 ZZ.F136/R) Vue de Grand Canal a Venise (33x46cm-13x18in) s.
                 panel (F.FR 10000)
£998 $1687   (5-May-91 LT.P36/R) Conversation aupres d'un lac (37x55cm-15x22in) s.
                 panel (F.FR 10000)
£1040 $1840   (7-Apr-91 LT.P91/R) Les environs de Rouen (46x55cm-18x22in) s. panel
                 (F.FR 10500)
£1222 $2407   (30-Oct-90 I.N301) Venise, le Grand Canal (38x45cm-15x18in) s. panel
                 (F.FR 12000)
£1339 $2304   (19-May-91 ZZ.F98/R) Plage animee (29x42cm-11x17in) s. panel
                 (F.FR 13500)

FLAXMAN, John (1755-1826) British
£700 $1351   (11-Dec-90 C220/R) Design for the stem of a candelabrum (23x17cm-9x7in)
                 i. pencil ink wash
£1100 $1815   (9-Jul-91 C16/R) Charity (28x47cm-11x19in) pencil pen ink wash
£1700 $3349   (13-Nov-90 C18/R) Prometheus attacked by Jupiter. Achilles mourning over
                 Patroclus (23x23cm-9x9in) pencil pen ink two
£3000 $5910   (13-Nov-90 C91/R) Mercury uniting hands of Britain and France
                 (25x33cm-10x13in) i. pencil pen ink wash

FLECHEMULLER, Jacques (1945-) American?
£867 $1500   (7-May-91 CE.NY233/R) Texas style (208x140cm-82x55in) s. acrylic canvas

FLECK, Karl Anton (1928-) Austrian
£443 $886   (7-Feb-91 D.V50) Landscape (23x29cm-9x11in) mono.d.77 pencil W/C
                 (A.S 9000)
£634 $1174   (7-Mar-91 D.V280/R) Head behind bars (31x22cm-12x9in) mono. pencil
                 (A.S 13000)

FLEGEL, Georg (16/17th C) German
£72000 $117360   (3-Jul-91 S30/R) Still life of sweets in pewter dish, glass of wine,
                 mouse, cheese, all lit by candle (22x16cm-9x6in) panel
£72000 $117360   (3-Jul-91 S57/R) Still life of carnations in glass vase, kutrolff white
                 wine and cherries (24x16cm-9x6in) mono. panel
£121053 $230000   (10-Jan-91 SY.NY98/R) Still life with mixed flowers in vase, crayfish on
                 plate, mixed fruit on dish, jug, all on marble l (62x46cm-24x18in)

FLEGEL, Georg (style) (16/17th C) German
£2994 $5060   (2-May-91 CH.AM68) A breakfast still life with sausages on pewter
                 plates, knife and otherobjects on a draped table (38x49cm-15x19in)
                 panel (D.FL 10000)

FLEISCHMANN, Adolf (1892-1969) German

£22000	$42900	(18-Oct-90 C356/R) Comp-567 (89x101cm-35x40in) s. s.i.d.1961verso
£28276	$54290	(28-Nov-90 KF.M754/R) Composition (76x63cm-30x25in) mono.d.1959 (DM 82000)
£3072	$6020	*(20-Nov-90 L.K217/R) Composition (45x30cm-18x12in) s.d.1964 gouache two small dr.verso (DM 9000)*
£4096	$8027	*(24-Nov-90 VG.B296/R) Composition (32x49cm-13x19in) mono. i.d.1946/15verso gouache htd.white board (DM 12000)*
£5500	$9735	*(21-Mar-91 C245/R) C 110 (39cm-15ins circular) init. collage gouache*
£6102	$10190	*(6-Jun-91 HN.H334/R) Composition (36x24cm-14x9in) s. W/C (DM 18000)*
£6897	$13241	*(26-Nov-90 WK.M624/R) Composition (62x47cm-24x19in) s.c.1958 gouache (DM 20000)*

FLEISCHMANN, August (19/20th C) German

£444	$728	*(22-Jun-91 WK.M1387/R) Portrait of Georg Deller (33x32cm-13x13in) s. pastel paper on panel (DM 1300)*

FLEISCHMANN, Trude (20th C) ?

£1427	$2754	*(16-Dec-90 GL.P54) Composition sur fond noir (24x31cm-9x12in) s. pastel gouache (F.FR 14000)*

FLEMAL, Bertholet I (attrib) (1614-1675) Flemish

£4625	$8972	(5-Dec-90 APT.P68/R) Le Christ mort pleure par la Vierge et les anges (62x76cm-24x30in) (F.FR 45000)

FLEMISH SCHOOL (?)

£654	$1282	(27-Jan-91 FE.P121) Grand bouquet (81x65cm-32x26in) (F.FR 6500)
£1000	$1730	(20-May-91 SWS149/R) The penitent Magdalen (52x40cm-20x16in) panel
£1146	$1948	(28-May-91 C.A369) Promenade (50x66cm-20x26in) panel (B.FR 70000)
£1320	$2218	(23-Apr-91 RAS.K260/R) Lucretia's suicide (54x43cm-21x17in) panel (D.KR 15000)
£1359	$2365	(25-Mar-91 SY.F560) Trittico con la Sacra Famiglia e due santi (23x19cm-9x7in) c.1800 panel triptych (I.L 3000000)
£1495	$2437	(11-Jun-91 GM.B964/R) Judith et Holopherne (170x105cm-67x41in) (B.FR 90000)
£1700	$3400	(7-Feb-91 C.C181/R) Peeled lemon and wine glass and cover on tray with grapes above (34x44cm-13x17in)
£1786	$3000	(17-Jul-91 SY.NY97/R) The Crucifixion with the Virgin and Saint John (92x68cm-36x27in) c.1600 panel
£1884	$3372	(12-Mar-91 FN.S2682) Classical scene with Adonis and dogs and other figures in landscape (180x146cm-71x57in) c.1600 (DM 6500)
£1900	$3211	(18-Apr-91 C120/R) Esther and Ahasuerus (141x223cm-56x88in)
£1908	$3071	(27-Jun-91 APT.P98/R) Le retour du troupeau (36x51cm-14x20in) c.1800 panel (F.FR 19000)
£2051	$4000	(11-Oct-90 SY.NY88/R) Classical female figure (85x67cm-33x26in) c.1700
£2289	$3845	(23-Apr-91 RAS.K267/R) Still life of roses and tulips surrounding landscape (65x54cm-26x21in) (D.KR 26000)
£2339	$4585	(12-Feb-91 GM.B690) Vierge a l'enfant (47x37cm-19x15in) wood (B.FR 140000)
£2600	$4498	(20-May-91 SWS76) Mercury and a female allegorical figure (53x50cm-21x20in) c.1800 panel octagonal
£2638	$5171	(21-Nov-90 GM.B1188) Cour de ferme anime (91x123cm-36x48in) s. (B.FR 160000)
£2700	$4563	(18-Apr-91 CSK113/R) Wooded river landscape with peasants on track, fishermen in rowing boats and town beyond (47x73cm-19x29in) panel c.1700
£2726	$5370	(29-Oct-90 SY.F645) Susanna e i vecchioni (81x103cm-32x41in) (I.L 6000000)
£3000	$6000	(7-Feb-91 C145/R) Orange, plums peaches on silver platter, with grapes and glasses (48x38cm-19x15in)
£3035	$5889	(4-Dec-90 C.A456) St Sebastian (185x117cm-73x46in) (B.FR 180000)
£3161	$5500	(27-Mar-91 B.SF4035/R) Still life with flowers, grapevine and peaches in basket (100x81cm-39x32in) c.1800
£3200	$6400	(7-Feb-91 C74) Wild strawberries and carnation in bowl with cherries and currants (35x46cm-14x18in) panel
£3213	$5173	(27-Jun-91 APT.P139/R) Pecheurs aupres d'un batiment fortifie (97x130cm-38x51in) (F.FR 32000)
£3420	$6121	(14-Mar-91 D.V204/R) Bunch of flowers in glass vase standing in stone niche (100x70cm-39x28in) (A.S 70000)
£3547	$6030	(27-May-91 L.K140/R) Christ and the Devil in wooded landscape (26x32cm-10x13in) panel (DM 10500)
£4500	$7785	(20-May-91 SWS69/R) An extensive southern landscape with huntsmen despatching a stag beforea classical ruin (96x159cm-38x63in)
£5500	$10560	(29-Nov-90 CSK305) Landscape with sledges outside town wall. River landscape with ferry (24x33cm-9x13in) panel pair
£6796	$11825	(25-Mar-91 SY.F703/R) Paesaggio con montagne e fiume (44x57cm-17x22in) c.1700 (I.L 15000000)
£8000	$13520	(17-Apr-91 S91/R) The Annunciation (51x43cm-20x17in) c.1500 panel
£9000	$15210	(18-Apr-91 C84/R) The Madonna and Child (47x36cm-19x14in) panel
£14000	$22820	(3-Jul-91 S219/R) Still lifes of flowers in baskets (55x46cm-22x18in) pair c.1700
£3670	$7229	*(12-Nov-90 CH.AM21/R) Mountainous wooded river landscape with travellers near village (20x38cm-8x15in) i. pen (D.FL 12000)*

FLEMISH SCHOOL, 15th C

£5017	$8378	(4-Jun-91 CH.R482/R) Deposizione (62x46cm-24x18in) panel (I.L 11000000)

FLEMISH SCHOOL, 16th C

£1200	$1956	(2-Jul-91 PH284) Portrait of man wearing fur trimmed jacket and hat before landscape (27x21cm-11x8in) panel
£2273	$4455	(19-Nov-90 CH.R83/R) Paesaggio boschivo con casolari (34x24cm-13x9in) panel (I.L 5000000)
£2500	$4075	(2-Jul-91 PH356/R) Crucifixion with the Virgin and St John (63x44cm-25x17in) panel
£3568	$6850	(30-Nov-90 APT.P44/R) Vanite (28x42cm-11x17in) panel (F.FR 35000)
£3754	$7358	(24-Nov-90 SA.A565/R) Mountain valley with comestic animals and figures (101x126cm-40x50in) canvas laid down (DM 11000)
£3953	$6719	(27-May-91 GK.Z5032/R) Portrait of noble lady wearing diadem, possibly member of Hohenemb family (28x21cm-11x8in) panel (S.FR 10000)
£4281	$8220	(30-Nov-90 APT.P41/R) Vierge avec Christ sur ses genoux, entouree d'anges (115x88cm-45x35in) three panels (F.FR 42000)
£4625	$8972	(7-Dec-90 SY.MO160/R) Portrait d'homme (17x14cm-7x6in) panel (F.FR 45000)
£5000	$8450	(17-Apr-91 S101/R) St Martha. St Margaret of Antioch (76x30cm-30x12in) panel pair
£5025	$8241	(21-Jun-91 SY.MO182/R) La mise au tombeau. La Resurrection (45x27cm-18x11in) panel pair (F.FR 50000)
£5179	$8908	(14-May-91 GF.L2028/R) Christ in Limbo (25x34cm-10x13in) copper (S.FR 13000)
£6006	$10390	(8-May-91 FER.M264 J/R) El sueno del caballero (75x101cm-30x40in) panel (S.P 1100000)
£6704	$12000	(11-Apr-91 SY.NY172/R) Members of the Van Brade Family. Stories of Jonah and Ezekiel (101x32cm-40x13in) panel wings of altarpiece double-sided two
£7647	$13000	(31-May-91 CH.NY152/R) Adoration of the Magi. Adoration of the Shepherds (128x69cm-50x27in) panel pair
£8638	$14944	(21-May-91 SY.MI1061/R) Il concerto - un'allegoria dei cinque sensi (98x65cm-39x26in) panel (I.L 19000000)
£10374	$17947	(8-May-91 FER.M264 I/R) La bendicion del hijo (31x100cm-12x39in) panel (S.P 1900000)
£11500	$19435	(17-Apr-91 S87/R) The Annunciation (115x85cm-45x33in) panel
£12000	$20280	(17-Apr-91 S137/R) Christ on the Road to Calvary. The Resurrection (64x28cm-25x11in) panel pair arched top
£13686	$26962	(30-Oct-90 BU.S296/R) Resurrection panel triptych (S.KR 150000)
£14000	$23660	(17-Apr-91 S90/R) Christ and the Woman of Samaria (123x96cm-48x38in) l. panel two parts
£16410	$32000	(10-Oct-90 CH.NY175/R) The Adoration of the Shepherds (60x47cm-24x19in) panel arched top
£20000	$32600	(3-Jul-91 S21/R) Deposition (80x99cm-31x39in) panel
£22000	$42460	(12-Dec-90 S159/R) Virgin and Child with Saint Anne (67x51cm-26x20in) panel
£113052	$219322	(7-Dec-90 CN.P150/R) Vue de la Place du Capitole et de l'eglise Santa Maria in Aracoeli (134x186cm-53x73in) (F.FR 1100000)
£1793	*$3102*	*(22-May-91 CD.P2/R) L'Assomption d'un Saint (27x26cm-11x10in) pen wash (F.FR 18000)*
£2000	*$3260*	*(1-Jul-91 S188/R) Figures watching procession of Roman soldiers (22x30cm-9x12in) pen wash over black chk*

FLEMISH SCHOOL, 16th/17th C

£1923	$3712	(12-Dec-90 N.M368 a/R) Ceres with wreath of ears and sickle (51x38cm-20x15in) panel (DM 5500)

FLEMISH SCHOOL, 17th C

£1000	$1630	(2-Jul-91 PH352) Crucifixion with St John and the two Marys (49x39cm-19x15in) canvas on panel oval
£1005	$1648	(21-Jun-91 D.P58/R) Scene de bataille contre les infideles (24x32cm-9x13in) copper (F.FR 10000)
£1020	$1643	(26-Jun-91 KM.K1356) Adoration of the Magi (94x121cm-37x48in) panel (DM 3000)
£1061	$2059	(8-Dec-90 GAB.G2028/R) Scene de la vie quotidienne dans un bourg (47x64cm-19x25in) panel (S.FR 2600)
£1110	$1854	(3-Jun-91 RY.P19/R) Crucifixion (24x19cm-9x7in) copper (F.FR 11100)
£1163	$2000	(15-May-91 D.NY58) Portrait of Admiral Blake (69x61cm-27x24in) i.d.1652 i.stretcher
£1208	$1970	(10-Jun-91 AGB.P88/R) Le savetier et le fileuse (68x89cm-27x35in) (F.FR 12000)
£1233	$2207	(13-Mar-91 N.M405/R) Zeitgott Chronos entfuhrt die Wahrheit (77x92cm-30x36in) mono. (DM 3600)
£1406	$2263	(27-Jun-91 APT.P93) L'adoration des bergers (35x29cm-14x11in) copper (F.FR 14000)
£1429	$2400	(17-Jul-91 SY.NY78/R) Portrait of a gentleman (77x60cm-30x24in) i.
£1524	$2500	(19-Jun-91 B.SF1656/R) The Lamentation (105x71cm-41x28in) panel
£1531	$2709	(20-Mar-91 KM.K1079) Expulsion from Paradise (58x73cm-23x29in) panel (DM 4500)
£1600	$2960	(5-Mar-91 PH87) The Finding of Moses (86x153cm-34x60in)
£1600	$2768	(20-May-91 SWS29/R) Adam and Eve (26x21cm-10x8in) panel
£1693	$2878	(31-May-91 LD.P16/R) Ecce Homo (96x60cm-38x24in) panel (F.FR 17000)
£1748	$3374	(12-Dec-90 N.M370/R) River landscape with boat and peasants (46x39cm-18x15in) panel (DM 5000)
£1786	$3000	(17-Jul-91 SY.NY168/R) A Palace garden (95x155cm-37x61in) canvas laid down on masonite
£1789	$3024	(18-Apr-91 APT.P53/R) L'Annonciation (179x139cm-70x55in) (F.FR 18000)

634

FLEMISH SCHOOL, 17th C -cont.

£1892	$3216	(27-May-91 L.K141) Tobias and the Angel in hilly wooded landscape (77x93cm-30x37in) panel (DM 5600)
£2028	$4016	(30-Jan-91 APT.P213/R) Vierge a l'Enfant (52x41cm-20x16in) panel (F.FR 20000)
£2051	$4000	(10-Oct-90 CH.NY146/R) Mystic Marriage of St Catherine with female saints in park of palace (44x32cm-17x13in) panel
£2187	$3696	(18-Apr-91 APT.P35/R) La sacrifice d'Isaac (72x104cm-28x41in) panel (F.FR 22000)
£2199	$3936	(13-Mar-91 FER.M151/R) En el fragor de la batalla (25x33cm-10x13in) panel (S.P 400000)
£2381	$4000	(17-Jul-91 SY.NY80/R) Portrait of Gerard Beeckman (77x60cm-30x24in) i.
£2436	$4750	(25-Oct-90 GRO.B20/R) Adoration of the Holy Family (135x221cm-53x87in)
£2446	$4820	(14-Nov-90 SY.AM34/R) The Entombment (40x31cm-16x12in) panel (D.FL 8000)
£2449	$4800	(6-Nov-90 GF.L2021/R) Holy Family with St John the Baptist and two angels (25x18cm-10x7in) panel (S.FR 6000)
£2450	$4092	(7-Jun-91 AGS.P54) L'onction de David (59x76cm-23x30in) copper (F.FR 24500)
£2492	$4336	(25-Mar-91 SY.F736) Ritratto di dama (68x50cm-27x20in) (I.L 5500000)
£2492	$4061	(12-Jun-91 GM.B4130) Scene de guerre (120x170cm-47x67in) (B.FR 150000)
£2500	$4075	(1-Jul-91 GL.P19/R) Saint Antoine Abbe, Saint Roch et Saint Antoine de Padoue (42x27cm-17x11in) sketch (F.FR 25000)
£2500	$4875	(26-Oct-90 C87/R) Solomon's idolatry (64x77cm-25x30in)
£2548	$4893	(30-Nov-90 APT.P61/R) Une halte de cavaliers (48x69cm-19x27in) (F.FR 25000)
£2705	$4842	(8-Apr-91 F.M328) L'imbarco (71x115cm-28x45in) (I.L 6000000)
£2742	$4635	(19-Apr-91 FN.S1912/R) Turmbau zu Babel (48x63cm-19x25in) panel (DM 8200)
£2766	$5422	(11-Nov-90 M.V38/R) Paysage anime (30x37cm-12x15in) panel (F.FR 27000)
£2854	$5480	(30-Nov-90 APT.P64/R) Le porteur d'eau (29x21cm-11x8in) panel (F.FR 28000)
£2985	$5194	(29-Mar-91 CJ.N5/R) Mise au tombeau (68x86cm-27x34in) copper (F.FR 30000)
£3200	$6304	(31-Oct-90 S151/R) The Crucifixion (45x32cm-18x13in) panel after Michelangelo
£3235	$5500	(31-May-91 CH.NY110/R) Dido and Aenas (114x89cm-45x35in)
£3262	$6263	(30-Nov-90 APT.P62/R) Marines (15x19cm-6x7in) on bronze pair (F.FR 32000)
£3343	$5750	(15-May-91 D.NY84) Portrait of gentleman (74x61cm-29x24in) bears sig.d.1647 panel
£3550	$7028	(30-Jan-91 APT.P198/R) L'adoration des Bergers (49x63cm-19x25in) (F.FR 35000)
£3579	$6048	(18-Apr-91 APT.P68/R) Soldats a l'auberge (61x89cm-24x35in) (F.FR 36000)
£3625	$6307	(25-Mar-91 SY.F551/R) Estate (57x53cm-22x21in) copper (I.L 8000000)
£3645	$6197	(30-May-91 F.M81) Il martirio di Santa Caterina d'Alessandria (125x98cm-49x39in) (I.L 8000000)
£3651	$7229	(30-Jan-91 APT.P206/R) Le fils prodigue (49x76cm-19x30in) (F.FR 36000)
£3800	$7030	(6-Mar-91 DR106/R) Peasants travelling on country road. Travellers by lake with fisherman (17x25cm-7x10in) one copper one panel pair
£3800	$6194	(3-Jul-91 S230/R) Saint Pieter. Archangel Gabriel. Saint Elizabeth of Hungary. Virgin annunciate (49x13cm-19x5in) panel double-sided two wings altarpiece
£3851	$6701	(25-Mar-91 SY.F732) Andorazione dei Magi (22x27cm-9x11in) slate (I.L 8500000)
£3854	$7631	(30-Jan-91 APT.P220/R) Bateaux au mouillage (41x72cm-16x28in) panel (F.FR 38000)
£4175	$7056	(18-Apr-91 APT.P44/R) Scene pastorale dans un paysage de riviere (61x83cm-24x33in) (F.FR 42000)
£4665	$9237	(30-Jan-91 CSC.P13/R) Scene de bivouac (50x68cm-20x27in) panel (F.FR 46000)
£4689	$9050	(12-Dec-90 ARC.P77/R) L'hommage a Venus (36x61cm-14x24in) panel (F.FR 46000)
£4790	$8096	(2-May-91 CH.AM133/R) Peasants merry-making in an italianate landscape (90x122cm-35x48in) panel (D.FL 16000)
£5000	$9650	(12-Dec-90 S121/R) Woodcutters on forest path with landscape beyond (35x66cm-14x26in) panel
£5017	$8378	(4-Jun-91 CH.R296) Interno di galleria (71x62cm-28x24in) (I.L 11000000)
£5187	$8974	(8-May-91 FER.M264 c/R) Caceria en el bosque. Conversacion en el camino a la vista de los ciervos (24x34cm-9x13in) panel pair (S.P 12000000)
£5456	$9439	(21-May-91 SY.MI1013/R) Veduta di porto (93x134cm-37x53in) (I.L 12000000)
£5473	$9139	(4-Jun-91 CH.R305/R) Adorazione del serpente (51x70cm-20x28in) (I.L 12000000)
£5533	$10844	(11-Nov-90 M.V36/R) Scene villageoise (51x59cm-20x23in) (F.FR 54000)
£5600	$9688	(20-May-91 SWS219/R) Pyramus and Thisbe (145x203cm-57x80in)
£5606	$10988	(21-Nov-90 GM.B1051) Scene de siege d'une ville (105x200cm-41x79in) (B.FR 340000)
£5964	$10080	(18-Apr-91 APT.P60/R) Nature morte aux fruits sur un entablement (51x90cm-20x35in) (F.FR 60000)
£6000	$11820	(31-Oct-90 S116/R) Madonna and Child encircled by garland of flowers (64x51cm-25x20in)
£6116	$11743	(30-Nov-90 APT.P56/R) Les oeuvres de misericorde (59x87cm-23x34in) panel (F.FR 60000)
£6667	$13000	(10-Oct-90 CH.NY151/R) Esther accusing Haman before Ahasuerus in architectural courtyard (108x163cm-43x64in)

FLEMISH SCHOOL, 17th C -cont.

£7263	$13000	(11-Apr-91 SY.NY188/R) Expulsion of Adam and Eve. Creation of birds and fishes (58x77cm-23x30in) pair
£7263	$13000	(11-Apr-91 SY.NY62/R) Rebecca and Eliezer at the well (39x47cm-15x19in) copper
£7692	$15000	(10-Oct-90 CH.NY89/R) Allegory of War (91x117cm-36x46in)
£7821	$14000	(11-Apr-91 SY.NY18/R) Mountain pass with travellers feasting at inn, valley beyond (120x89cm-47x35in)
£8184	$14158	(23-May-91 F.M523/R) Scena di vita cittadina (104x158cm-41x62in) s. (I.L 18000000)
£9800	$18914	(12-Dec-90 S146/R) The rest on the flight into Egypt (43x64cm-17x25in) panel
£11200	$18928	(1-May-91 GD.B265/R) Hunting still life with dead game, fruit, food and cat (51x96cm-20x38in) panel (S.FR 28000)
£11305	$21932	(7-Dec-90 SY.MO140/R) La marchande de legumes (110x220cm-43x87in) (F.FR 110000)
£12000	$19560	(3-Jul-91 S248/R) Extensive wooded river landscape with Abraham banishing Hagar and Ishmael (61x103cm-24x41in) panel
£13000	$25090	(12-Dec-90 S180/R) Cowherd, milkmaid and cows in front of farm (15x24cm-6x9in) copper
£16901	$28732	(28-May-91 AB.S4842/R) Scenes from the life of Mary (65x48cm-26x19in) copper three (S.KR 180000)
£17568	$29865	(27-May-91 L.K142) Rest on the Flight to Egypt (160x116cm-63x46in) (DM 52000)
£26000	$43940	(17-Apr-91 S84/R) Village scene in winter (75x75cm-30x30in) i. panel painted circle
£50000	$96500	(12-Dec-90 S11/R) Still life of fruit in Wan-Li bowl on table (40x57cm-16x22in) bears sig.d.1625 panel
£1450	$2364	(1-Jul-91 S65/R) Study of hands and drapery of elegantly posed gentleman (25x19cm-10x7in) black white chk
£1700	$2771	(2-Jul-91 C204/R) Head of bearded man, looking down to left (29x21cm-11x8in) black red white chk
£5528	$9065	(18-Jun-91 APT.P7/R) Adam et Eve au paradis terrestre (19x25cm-7x10in) gouache vellum (F.FR 55000)
£6133	$10977	(8-Apr-91 ARC.P2) La chasse au faucon (14x21cm-6x8in) s. gouache (F.FR 62000)

FLEMISH SCHOOL, 17th/18th C

| £1311 | $2530 | (11-Dec-90 FER.M73/R) Caceria (105x162cm-41x64in) (S.P 240000) |
| £2436 | $4750 | (25-Oct-90 GRO.B21/R) Peasant feast in landscape (99x140cm-39x55in) |

FLEMISH SCHOOL, 18th C

£983	$1898	(11-Dec-90 FER.M69/R) Escena costumbrista con representacion teatral (30x40cm-12x16in) panel (S.P 180000)
£988	$1700	(15-May-91 D.NY33) Sorrows of the Virgin (18x13cm-7x5in) panel
£1190	$2000	(17-Jul-91 SY.NY171/R) Child hunters in a landscape (48x184cm-19x72in) en grisaille
£1200	$2076	(20-May-91 SWS44/R) Interior with an old lady spinning (59x84cm-23x33in)
£1313	$2272	(12-May-91 L.C61) Le troupeau (31x41cm-12x16in) (F.FR 13200)
£1318	$2611	(30-Jan-91 APT.P69/R) Paysage anime (33x40cm-13x16in) panel (F.FR 13000)
£1410	$2298	(10-Jun-91 AGB.P74) Paysage anime de personnages pres d'une riviere (24x24cm-9x9in) panel (F.FR 14000)
£1429	$2814	(15-Nov-90 EA.Z187/R) Military encampment and village beyond (45x75cm-18x30in) (S.FR 3500)
£1506	$2425	(27-Jun-91 APT.P99/R) Interieur d'etable (48x64cm-19x25in) panel (F.FR 15000)
£1700	$2941	(20-May-91 SWS130/R) Figures resting by a bridge (21x28cm-8x11in) panel
£1700	$2941	(20-May-91 SWS157/R) Landscape with travellers on a country path with figures resting bya cottage in the foreground (47x63cm-19x25in)
£1800	$2934	(4-Jul-91 C617/R) Last Supper (87x139cm-34x55in)
£2287	$3750	(19-Jun-91 B.SF1664/R) Pursuing the game (95x132cm-37x52in)
£2500	$4325	(20-May-91 SWS75/R) Narcissus. Diana and Actaeon (37x27cm-15x11in) pair
£2518	$4104	(16-Jun-91 P.V42/R) Troupeau dans un paysge boise (57x72cm-22x28in) bears sig.d.92 (F.FR 25000)
£2600	$4992	(29-Nov-90 CSK218) Flora (179x58cm-70x23in)
£2700	$5265	(22-Oct-90 SWS1510) Southern port scene with figures (82x118cm-32x46in)
£2900	$5017	(20-May-91 SWS202/R) Juno asking Argus to guard Io. Juno with Diana and Callisto changed intoa bear (93x67cm-37x26in) canvas laid on panel pair
£3000	$5550	(5-Mar-91 PH67) The rape of the Sabine women (54x70cm-21x28in) after Pietro Berretini
£3100	$5363	(20-May-91 SWS92/R) A village scene with figures merrymaking outside an inn (52x65cm-20x26in) panel
£3100	$6045	(26-Oct-90 PHM54/R) Peasants playing boules (87x114cm-34x45in)
£3337	$6507	(21-Oct-90 L.C42) Portrait de l'Empereur Charles Quint, vu a mi corps, portant l'amure (128x98cm-50x39in) (F.FR 33000)
£3424	$5753	(23-Apr-91 F.R52) Cacciagione e cani su sfondo di paesaggio (57x81cm-22x32in) mono. (I.L 7500000)
£3770	$6296	(7-Jun-91 ZOF.Z1014/R) King Louis XIV riding on horse with troops before town (44x61cm-17x24in) (S.FR 9500)
£3900	$6747	(20-May-91 SWS212/R) Achilles among the daughters of Lycomedes (119x134cm-47x53in)
£4322	$7736	(17-Mar-91 L.C98/R) Les noceos de Cana (92x104cm-36x41in) panel (F.FR 43000)
£4464	$7500	(17-Jul-91 SY.NY179/R) Afternoon idyll (72x141cm-28x56in) s.indist.d. shaped

636

FLEMISH SCHOOL, 18th C -cont.

£4473	$7560	(18-Apr-91 APT.P43/R) Paysages animes (50x73cm-20x29in) two (F.FR 45000)
£4872	$9500	(24-Oct-90 D.NY72/R) Flowers in urns on ledges (46x30cm-18x12in) pair
£6116	$11804	(12-Dec-90 CD.P25) Paysans attables a l'exterieur d'auberge. Servante au puits pres auberge (27x38cm-11x15in) panel pair (F.FR 60000)
£6660	$13053	(11-Nov-90 M.V41/R) Vase de fleurs sur un entablement (108x69cm-43x27in) (F.FR 65000)
£8442	$13845	(21-Jun-91 D.P55/R) Scene de bal et scene de banquet (49x57cm-19x22in) pair (F.FR 84000)

FLEMISH SCHOOL, 19th C

| £2700 | $5184 | (27-Nov-90 PH24/R) Reading the news (49x61cm-19x24in) indis.i.d.verso panel |
| £3955 | $7832 | (30-Jan-91 APT.P234/R) Une de fleurs et nid sur un entablement (57x72cm-22x28in) (F.FR 39000) |

FLEMISH SCHOOL, 20th C

| £1494 | $2585 | (26-May-91 ZZ.F59/R) Les Grands Boulevards et la place de la Republique (30x40cm-12x16in) indist.sig. panel (F.FR 15000) |

FLEMISH-GERMAN SCHOOL, 16th C

| £13000 | $21190 | (2-Jul-91 C183/R) David and Bathsheba (17x21cm-7x8in) black chk pen wash |

FLERS, Camille (1802-1868) French

| £2141 | $4131 | (12-Dec-90 D.P173/R) Lavandiere et pecheur a l'epervier en barque, pres d'un moulin (38x54cm-15x21in) s.d.1850 board (F.FR 21000) |
| £815 | $1566 | (1-Dec-90 PER.M12/R) Au bord de l'etang (31x44cm-12x17in) s.d.1859 pastel paper laid down on canvas (F.FR 8000) |

FLETCHER, Blythe (?) New Zealander?

| £412 | $697 | (17-Apr-91 DS.W95) Munster cathedral (45x31cm-18x12in) s.d.24 W/C (NZ.D 1200) |

FLETCHER, Edwin (1857-1945) British

£500	$895	(14-Mar-91 L174) Shipping in Thames Basin (51x41cm-20x16in) s.
£650	$1248	(16-Aug-90 B310/R) Shipping on the Lower Thames (41x62cm-16x24in) bears inits.
£750	$1238	(9-Jul-91 PH213) Shipping on Thames (40x61cm-16x24in)
£1100	$2156	(22-Jan-91 PH2/R) Shipping on the Thames (51x76cm-20x30in) s.
£1100	$2079	(26-Sep-90 S67) River Thames (51x76cm-20x30in)
£2300	$4416	(16-Aug-90 B410/R) Outward bound (76x127cm-30x50in) s. s.l.verso
£3000	$4950	(9-Jul-91 PH211/R) Shipping on River Thames, St. Paul's beyond. Shipping on Thames, Tower Bridge beyond (51x76cm-20x30in) s. pair

FLETCHER, William (1924-1983) Australian

£1772	$3403	(14-Aug-90 SY.ME84/R) Gompholobium and banksia (54x43cm-21x17in) board (A.D 4200)
£723	$1388	(26-Nov-90 SY.ME101/R) Hakea Purpurea (45x35cm-18x14in) s.d.73 gouache (A.D 1800)
£797	$1570	(31-Oct-90 CH.S176/R) Hibbertia (40x30cm-16x12in) s.d.74 gouache (A.D 2000)
£844	$1620	(14-Aug-90 SY.ME35/R) Rhododendrum (45x36cm-18x14in) s.d.'73 gouache (A.D 2000)

FLEURY, Albert Francois (1848-1925) American

| £2800 | $4816 | (17-May-91 C17 c/R) At seaside (24x32cm-9x13in) s.d.83 board |

FLEURY, Francois-Antoine (1804-1858) French

| £996 | $1723 | (24-May-91 FB.P103/R) La ferme (29x36cm-11x14in) s. paper laid down on canvas (F.FR 10000) |

FLEURY, J V de (19th C) British

| £1000 | $1950 | (15-Jan-91 SWS122/R) Looking from Palanza, Maggiore towards the Simplon, North Italy (39x49cm-15x19in) s. l.verso |

FLEURY, V de (19th C) French

| £825 | $1600 | (8-Dec-90 W.W84/R) On the banks of Lake Garda (51x76cm-20x30in) s.d.indist. |

FLICKE, Gerlach (style) (16th C) British?

| £2500 | $4225 | (30-Apr-91 PH41/R) Portrait of Archbishop Cranmer holding bible (40x32cm-18x13in) panel |

FLIEHER, Karl (1881-1958) Austrian

£570	$1019	(11-Apr-91 D.V48/R) Mountain landscape (52x69cm-20x27in) s.i.d.1932 (A.S 12000)
£634	$1174	(7-Mar-91 D.V74/R) Wayside shrine (33x26cm-13x10in) s. board (A.S 13000)
£878	$1625	(7-Mar-91 D.V73/R) Flakerhof in Gumpendorf (30x45cm-12x18in) s.i.d.1909 board (A.S 18000)
£1329	$2379	(11-Apr-91 D.V92/R) Wachau landscape (23x31cm-9x12in) s. board (A.S 28000)
£1538	$3000	(25-Oct-90 D.V13/R) Mountain landscape with view of Bad Gastein on way to Kaffee Gamskar (39x29cm-15x11in) s.l. paper on canvas (A.S 32000)
£1941	$3668	(27-Sep-90 D.V5/R) Old village street, Radelbach at the Danube, Wachau (32x36cm-13x14in) s. l.verso board (A.S 40000)

FLIEHER, Karl (1881-1958) Austrian-cont.
£573 $1117   (11-Oct-90 D.V223/R) View of Hohen Tauern, Zell am See, from arched
                verandah (23x18cm-9x7in) s.i.d.1932 W/C chk (A.S 12000)
£1193 $2327   (11-Oct-90 D.V208/R) Tyrolean landscape near Grins, Landeck, with view
                of Parseier (28x37cm-11x15in) s.i. mixed media (A.S 25000)

FLIER, Helmert Richard van der (1827-1899) Dutch
£1701 $2738   (26-Jun-91 KM.K1456/R) Rider resting in landscape with horse and dog
                (45x59cm-18x23in) s. (DM 5000)

FLIGHT, Claude (1881-1955) British
£480 $835   (28-Mar-91 CSK166) Punt (34x49cm-13x19in) s. chl W/C

FLINCK, Govaert (circle) (1615-1660) Dutch
£4422 $7827   (20-Mar-91 KM.K1018/R) Elegant hunting party (154x164cm-61x65in)
                (DM 13000)

FLINT, Francis Russell (1915-) British
£400 $688   (15-May-91 BT147/R) Foreshore terrace, Puerto Pollensa (25x23cm-10x9in)
                s. i. backboard W/C

FLINT, S (19/20th C) British
£943 $1584   (24-Apr-91 N.M515 a/R) Willow trees along stream (45x70cm-18x28in) s.
                (DM 2800)

FLINT, Sir William Russell (1880-1969) British
£1300 $2444   (18-Sep-90 PH72) Alberta (19x12cm-7x5in) init.i.
£4103 $8000   (23-Oct-90 SY.NY399 b) The golden stool (99x99cm-39x39in)
£4103 $8000   (23-Oct-90 SY.NY399 a) Model for goddess (99x99cm-39x39in)
£470 $893   (28-Feb-91 DLY15/R) Spanish dancers (25x36cm-10x14in) init.
£550 $1067   (8-Dec-90 B185) New Cross Friesole (16x24cm-6x9in) s.i.d.1912 pencil
£800 $1552   (8-Dec-90 B181) Washing hair (17x14cm-7x6in) s. pencil
£800 $1552   (8-Dec-90 B169/R) 18th Century artist holding palette and brush
                (22x11cm-9x4in) s. sanguine chk
£820 $1386   (3-May-91 T240/R) Study of two girls (25x36cm-10x14in) init. red chk
£900 $1755   (10-Oct-91 S75/R) The intruder (24x16cm-9x6in) s. W/C htd.white
£980 $1646   (23-Apr-91 SWS425) The dilettante (22x35cm-9x14in) s. red chk.
£1100 $1892   (18-May-91 B128/R) Patricia Dascot (16x11cm-6x4in) s.i.d.1.12.48
                sanguine chk with two letters
£1190 $2000   (28-Apr-91 HG.C264) Seated woman (36x23cm-14x9in) s.d.1953
£1200 $2340   (10-Oct-90 S105/R) Woodland path, Ardlui (32x48cm-13x19in) s. i.verso
                W/C
£1300 $2522   (8-Dec-90 B177/R) Study of girl wearing flounced Spanish skirt
                (25x18cm-10x7in) init. col.chk wash
£1351 $2338   (25-May-91 N.M89) Scottish village amongst trees (37x50cm-15x20in) s.
                W/C (DM 4000)
£1450 $2494   (14-May-91 SWS138/R) Black Frost, Kincraig (37x53cm-15x21in) s.d.1910
                i.verso W/C
£1607 $2700   (28-Apr-91 HG.C273) Amalfi balcony scene (33x30cm-13x12in) s. W/C
£1700 $3332   (25-Jan-91 C24/R) Nude rolling hoop (32x43cm-13x17in) s. pencil W/C
£1800 $3024   (23-Apr-91 S121/R) April shower (24x30cm-9x12in) s. W/C
£1900 $3705   (10-Oct-90 S104/R) Golden bracken, Lochiel (24x34cm-9x13in) s.d.1901
                i.verso W/C
£2000 $3780   (27-Sep-90 L249/R) Semi nude female (33x23cm-13x9in) s. chk.
£2000 $3880   (6-Dec-90 CSK131/R) Reclining nude (20x35cm-8x14in) s. brown chk chl
£2000 $3880   (8-Dec-90 B187/R) Porch of St. Martin, Segovia (35x25cm-14x10in) s.
                i.d.16/6/21 verso W/C
£2000 $3880   (8-Dec-90 B198/R) Madame du Barry playing blind man's buff
                (38x22cm-15x9in) s.i. col.chk
£2200 $4312   (25-Jan-91 C16/R) The pretty gypsy in the stocks (24x34cm-9x13in) s.
                s.i.verso red chk
£2500 $4175   (26-Jul-91 PHE71/R) At water's edge, Gareloch (24x33cm-9x13in) s.
                s.i.verso W/C
£2800 $5460   (18-Oct-90 SC3014/R) Draped dancer resting. Nude study (28x21cm-11x8in)
                s. verso chk. double-sided
£2900 $5626   (8-Dec-90 B165/R) Natalia nude (21x33cm-8x13in) s.num. chk
£2900 $5655   (10-Oct-90 S100/R) Catalina Alvarez (33x20cm-13x8in) s. red chk
£2900 $4843   (22-Jul-91 SWS932/R) Holiday river (26x36cm-10x14in) s.i. verso
£3000 $5880   (25-Jan-91 C17/R) Evangeline (29x16cm-11x6in) s. s.i.verso red chk
£3000 $5640   (20-Sep-90 C7/R) Sleeping nude (24x42cm-9x17in) s. col.crayon
£3000 $5880   (25-Jan-91 C14/R) The passing barge, Petit Audely on the Seine
                (19x27cm-7x11in) s. s.i.verso W/C bodycol
£3200 $6272   (6-Nov-90 PH22) Evening on the Rhone from La Voulte (19x27cm-7x11in) s.
                s.i.d.1967verso W/C
£3400 $6392   (20-Sep-90 C8/R) Reclining nude (23x35cm-9x14in) s. col.chk
£4000 $7520   (20-Sep-90 C9/R) Study for fountain figure (24x42cm-9x17in) s.i.
                col.crayon pencil
£4000 $7760   (8-Dec-90 B191/R) Four backs (22x36cm-9x14in) s. s.i.verso col.chk
£4200 $8232   (25-Jan-91 C15/R) Pyrennean rendezvous (12x27cm-5x11in) s. s.i.d.verso
                W/C
£4359 $8500   (23-Oct-90 SY.NY399/R) Carlotta's mop of hair (44x29cm-17x11in) s.i. chk
£4600 $7912   (18-May-91 B134/R) Gendarmerie, Quimperle (40x32cm-16x13in)
                s.i.d.20.6.32 s.i.verso pen W/C
£5000 $9800   (6-Nov-90 PH24/R) Standing nude (35x25cm-14x10in) s. col.chk
£5000 $8350   (6-Jun-91 C4/R) Abigail (33x45cm-13x18in) s. s.i.d.61verso red chk

FLINT, Sir William Russell (1880-1969) British-cont.

£5200	$9776	(20-Sep-90 M4) Still life of Diana (28x18cm-11x7in) s.d.August 1952 chl pencil W/C wash
£5200	$9048	(27-Mar-91 S121/R) The fisher girl (29x37cm-11x15in) s. W/C
£5200	$10088	(8-Dec-90 B197/R) Pompadour two-piece (27x18cm-11x7in) s.d.9.8.67 s.i.verso red chk
£5600	$9632	(15-May-91 BT105/R) Veronica (33x46cm-13x18in) s.i. verso col.chks.
£6250	$12000	(28-Nov-90 PH.T112/R) The gull (24x33cm-9x13in) s. W/C bodycol (C.D 14000)
£6500	$11635	(14-Mar-91 ZZ.B70/R) And so she went with the wind roaring and yelling .... (28x22cm-11x9in) s.d.MCMXI W/C
£6800	$11696	(18-May-91 B127/R) Fiametta (27x55cm-11x22in) s. s.i.verso red chk
£7000	$13580	(8-Dec-90 B190/R) Model with newspaper (29x44cm-11x17in) s. col.chk
£7179	$14000	(23-Oct-90 SY.NY398/R) Reclining nude (26x42cm-10x17in) s. chk
£7800	$14664	(20-Sep-90 C6/R) To Anthea, lying in bed (24x39cm-9x15in) s. col.chk
£8000	$13760	(18-May-91 B126/R) Josefina (33x33cm-13x13in) s. sanguine chk
£8500	$14620	(18-May-91 B138/R) Rendezvous, Ardisa (37x56cm-15x22in) s. s.i.verso W/C
£8671	$15000	(22-May-91 SY.NY125/R) Two bathers (49x67cm-19x26in) s. W/C board
£9000	$15030	(6-Jun-91 C53/R) Lakeside in Arcady (23x38cm-9x15in) s. s.i.d.1960verso W/C
£9500	$18620	(8-Nov-90 C33/R) Lochside Caprice (35x53cm-14x21in) s. i. verso W/C bodycol.
£9800	$19208	(6-Nov-90 PH21/R) Illustration for The Canterbury Tales (27x21cm-11x8in) s.d.1912 W/C over pencil
£10000	$16100	(27-Jun-91 CG9/R) Advance guard at circus,Tarascon, France (49x67cm-19x26in) s. i. verso W/C htd.bodycol.
£10000	$19400	(8-Dec-90 B193) Bathers in Loire (36x54cm-14x21in) s. W/C
£11000	$21340	(8-Dec-90 B170/R) Natalia and Yvette, servants' courtyard, St. Crivot (37x55cm-15x22in) s. W/C
£12000	$20040	(6-Jun-91 C2/R) Ballerinas (30x25cm-12x10in) s. W/C
£12500	$24250	(6-Dec-90 CG9/R) Posies of the Loire (37x55cm-15x22in) s. s.i.verso W/C
£14000	$23380	(6-Jun-91 C5/R) Afternoon idleness, Banborough (48x66cm-19x26in) s. W/C
£14141	$28000	(30-Jan-91 GRO.B117/R) Contrasts (51x69cm-20x27in) s.i. W/C gouache
£14368	$25000	(27-Mar-91 B.SF4112/R) Trembling leaves (49x67cm-19x26in) s. s.i.verso W/C
£14493	$27101	(27-Aug-90 SY.J190/R) San Geremia, Grand Canal, Venice (49x68cm-19x27in) s. s.i.verso W/C (SA.R 70000)
£14500	$28130	(6-Dec-90 CG8/R) Under the sundial, Cobonne (49x67cm-19x26in) s. s.i.verso W/C
£15000	$25050	(6-Jun-91 C3/R) Cecilia as Julia (10x24cm-4x9in) s. s.i.d.1964verso W/C
£16000	$31040	(8-Dec-90 B172/R) Cousin from Valence (38x54cm-15x21in) s. s.i.verso W/C
£16000	$31040	(8-Dec-90 B171/R) Blue and silver (33x60cm-13x24in) s. s.i.verso W/C bodycol
£16000	$27040	(1-May-91 S61/R) The bathers (51x67cm-20x26in) s. W/C
£17000	$32980	(6-Dec-90 CG7/R) The girl called Marisa, Provence (49x67cm-19x26in) s. s.i.verso W/C
£17000	$33320	(8-Nov-90 C35/R) Cecilia (27x37cm-11x15in) s.d.1961 i. backboard W/C
£17949	$35000	(23-Oct-90 SY.NY395/R) Disputation at the well (53x71cm-21x28in) s. s.i.verso W/C board
£18000	$30060	(6-Jun-91 C54/R) Disputation at the well (51x70cm-20x28in) s. s.i.verso W/C bodycol
£23000	$38410	(6-Jun-91 C56/R) Gossip in park (56x38cm-22x15in) s. s.i.d.1955verso W/C
£26000	$50960	(8-Nov-90 C43/R) Belle poseuse (47x62cm-19x24in) s. i.d.1968 backboard W/C
£26000	$48100	(7-Mar-91 C27/R) Vignette, Cecilia (24x33cm-9x13in) s. s.i.d.1956verso W/C
£28000	$48160	(15-May-91 BT106/R) Cecilia contemplating Europa (38x30cm-15x12in) s.i.d.March 1964 verso W/C
£38000	$73720	(8-Dec-90 B199/R) Silver and white (30x55cm-12x22in) s. s.i.d.1958 verso W/C
£43000	$71810	(6-Jun-91 C55/R) Silver shade, Languedoc (48x68cm-19x27in) s. s.i.verso W/C

FLIPART, Charles Joseph (attrib) (1721-1797) French

| £1988 | $3360 | (18-Apr-91 APT.P134/R) Le maître de musique (35x45cm-14x18in) (F.FR 20000) |

FLOCH, Josef (1895-1977) American/Austrian

£1190	$2000	(28-Apr-91 HG.C8) The window (56x38cm-22x15in) s.
£1212	$2279	(20-Sep-90 D.V183/R) House in the dunes (46x61cm-18x24in) s. (A.S 25000)
£1421	$2700	(27-Feb-91 BG.M811/R) Spectators (46x46cm-18x18in) s.
£1607	$2700	(28-Apr-91 HG.C6) View from the roof (61x51cm-24x20in) s.
£1726	$2900	(28-Apr-91 HG.C7) The peninsula (51x76cm-20x30in) s.
£5467	$10606	(6-Dec-90 D.V19/R) Woman on roof terrace (89x45cm-35x18in) st.studio (A.S 110000)
£6220	$10761	(8-May-91 D.V107/R) Two models in studio interior (80x60cm-31x24in) s. (A.S 130000)
£583	$955	(20-Jun-91 D.V85/R) Bridge (40x51cm-16x20in) st.sig.i.verso mixed media (A.S 12000)
£1214	$1990	(20-Jun-91 D.V83/R) Before the window (43x31cm-17x12in) s. pastel (A.S 25000)
£1359	$2229	(20-Jun-91 D.V84/R) Female nude (54x36cm-21x14in) s. i.verso chk wash (A.S 28000)

FLOCH, Lionel (20th C) French
£1325 $2558   (16-Dec-90 T.B286) Le marche aux Cochons (38x46cm-15x18in) s. board
        (F.FR 13000)
£1478 $2853   (16-Dec-90 T.B130/R) Burlage duGoemon sur la dune (50x61cm-20x24in) s.
        (F.FR 14500)
£4791 $9247   (16-Dec-90 T.B129/R) Les naufrageurs (110x165cm-43x65in) s. (F.FR 47000)

FLOCKEMANN, August (1849-1915) German
£1679 $2889   (16-May-91 D.V159/R) Woodland path, winter (34x25cm-13x10in) s.d.1889
        panel (A.S 35000)

FLOCKENHAUS, H (20th C) German
£1233 $2207   (12-Mar-91 FN.S2358) Wooded river landscape and snow storm rising
        (43x32cm-17x13in) s.i. (DM 3600)

FLOCKENHAUS, Heinz (20th C) German
£872 $1701   (13-Oct-90 KRA.D211/R) Landscape with windmill, evening (32x23cm-13x9in)
        s. panel (DM 2600)
£1361 $2408   (20-Mar-91 KM.K1213) Snowy river landscape at sunset (44x33cm-17x13in)
        s. (DM 4000)
£1846 $3599   (13-Oct-90 KRA.D210/R) Winter landscape, evening (46x37cm-18x15in)
        s.i.d.1882 (DM 5500)
£2551 $4107   (26-Jun-91 KM.K1458/R) Lower Rhine landscape with view of village and
        mill (39x50cm-15x20in) s.i. panel (DM 7500)

FLODIN, Hilda (1877-1958) Finnish
£927 $1817   (24-Nov-90 HOR.H88/R) Water-lilies (27x36cm-11x14in) s. (F.M 6500)
£1213 $2377   (24-Nov-90 HOR.H89/R) Girl with plaits (35x28cm-14x11in) s.d.1918
        (F.M 8500)
£374   *$722*   *(15-Dec-90 BU.H226) Cleaning the nets (42x31cm-17x12in) s.d.1919 W/C*
        (F.M 2600)

FLOGNY, Eugene Victor de (1825-?) French
£3093 $5876   (2-Mar-91 KRA.D308/R) River landscape with anglers and figures resting
        (50x61cm-20x24in) s. (DM 9000)

FLORA, Paul (1922-) Austrian
£488   *$903*   *(7-Mar-91 D.V250/R) Verliebte Kentauren (43x61cm-17x24in) s.d.55 pen*
        indian ink (A.S 10000)
£535   *$1049*   *(24-Jan-91 D.V303/R) Fantastic bird (48x65cm-19x26in) s. pen indian ink*
        (A.S 11000)
£680   *$1115*   *(20-Jun-91 D.V205/R) 1987 (12x16cm-5x6in) s.i.d. pen indian ink*
        col.pencil (A.S 14000)
£680   *$1115*   *(20-Jun-91 D.V204/R) Kasperltheater (12x16cm-5x6in) s.i.d.89 pen indian*
        ink col.pencil (A.S 14000)
£728   *$1194*   *(20-Jun-91 D.V202/R) Acrobatic carneval figure (12x16cm-5x6in) s.i.d.85*
        pen indian ink col.pencil (A.S 15000)
£728   *$1194*   *(20-Jun-91 D.V206/R) Meine Verehrung (12x16cm-5x6in) s.i.d.87 pen indian*
        ink col.pencil (A.S 15000)
£777   *$1274*   *(20-Jun-91 D.V197/R) Duell der Konige (47x64cm-19x25in) s.i.d.1973 pen*
        indian ink (A.S 16000)
£874   *$1433*   *(20-Jun-91 D.V199/R) Flight meeting (24x31cm-9x12in) s.i.d.78 pen indian*
        ink W/C (A.S 18000)
£971   *$1592*   *(20-Jun-91 D.V196/R) Schreckliche Annaherung (48x61cm-19x24in) s.i. pen*
        indian ink (A.S 20000)
£971   *$1592*   *(20-Jun-91 D.V198/R) Der Bergmaher (38x53cm-15x21in) s.i.d.76 pen indian*
        ink (A.S 20000)
£1068   *$1751*   *(20-Jun-91 D.V203/R) Carnevale Veneziano (12x16cm-5x6in) s.i.d.1981*
        indian ink col.pencil (A.S 22000)
£1214   *$1990*   *(20-Jun-91 D.V201/R) By the railway (32x47cm-13x19in) s.i.d.1975 pen*
        indian ink (A.S 25000)
£1456   *$2388*   *(20-Jun-91 D.V200/R) Haunted house (48x62cm-19x24in) s. pen indian ink*
        (A.S 30000)

FLORAVANTI, Benedictus (attrib) (18th C) Italian
£7000 $11830   (16-Apr-91 PH189/R) Still life of vase of flowers standing on bank
        surrounded by fruit (73x97cm-29x38in)

FLOREIN, Jan (?) ?
£1329 $2166   (11-Jun-91 GM.B940) Adoration des rois mages (46x55cm-18x22in) triptych
        after Memling (B.FR 80000)

FLOREN, Lars (1889-?) Scandinavian
£669 $1198   (13-Apr-91 FAL.M74/R) View of Stockholm (65x73cm-26x29in) s. (S.KR 7200)

FLORENT, Willems (?) ?
£759 $1458   (14-Aug-90 SY.ME165) Interior scene (56x44cm-22x17in) s. board
        (A.D 1800)

FLORENTINE SCHOOL Italian
£1350 $2336   (20-May-91 SWS208/R) The Annunciation (50x53cm-20x21in) panel
£1685 $2814   (6-Jun-91 D.V21/R) View across Arno to Florence (17x26cm-7x10in) c.1800
        panel (A.S 35000)
£4800 $9264   (13-Dec-90 B54/R) Frieze with reclining youths and decorative cartouches
        (13x62cm-5x24in) i. panel

FLORENTINE SCHOOL Italian-cont.

£5020	$8082	(27-Jun-91 APT.P15/R) La lapidation de Saint Etienne (178x137cm-70x54in) c.1610 (F.FR 50000)
£5500	$10725	(25-Oct-90 CSK58) Madonna and Child (55x33cm-22x13in) panel arched top
£5714	$11200	(6-Nov-90 GF.L2303/R) Portrait of gentleman (88x70cm-35x28in) c.1700 rem.i.verso (S.FR 14000)
£6475	$12561	(3-Dec-90 SY.F1055/R) Ninfe in un paesaggio (53x107cm-21x42in) c.1700 pair (I.L 14000000)
£8000	$13360	(3-Jun-91 RY.P21/R) Vierge a l'enfant et Saint Jean Baptiste (68x40cm-27x16in) c.1500 panel (F.FR 80000)
£28000	$45640	(5-Jul-91 C91/R) Angel appearing to Hagar (144x173cm-57x68in) c.1650
£1000	*$1630*	*(2-Jul-91 C82/R) Portrait of Monsieur d'Artus, in profile to left (22x17cm-9x7in) black chk c.1540*

FLORENTINE SCHOOL, 14th C Italian

£2500	$4875	(26-Oct-90 C11/R) Saint Mary Magdalen kneeling by the Cross (24x18cm-9x7in) panel
£9960	$16932	(31-May-91 LD.P44 b/R) La Vierge a l'Enfant entre deux Saints tempera sheet of gold on panel tryptich (F.FR 100000)

FLORENTINE SCHOOL, 15th C Italian

£2443	$4372	(14-Mar-91 D.V145/R) Portrait of young man wearing laurel wreath (45x37cm-18x15in) panel (A.S 50000)

FLORENTINE SCHOOL, 16th C Italian

£1400	$2282	(4-Jul-91 C751/R) Madonna and child with infant Saint John the Baptist (73x55cm-29x22in) panel
£2265	$3942	(25-Mar-91 SY.F578/R) Madonna con Bambino (63x48cm-25x19in) panel (I.L 5000000)
£4111	$7975	(7-Dec-90 CN.P149/R) La Vierge et l'enfant Jesus, Sainte Elisebeth et Saint Jean-Baptiste (137x108cm-54x43in) panel (F.FR 40000)
£5452	$10741	(29-Oct-90 SY.F596/R) Ritratto di Ferdinando I de Medici (110x95cm-43x37in) (I.L 12000000)
£7500	$12225	(1-Jul-91 LGB.P18/R) Vierge a l'Enfant, Saint Jean Baptiste et un donateur (67cm-26ins circular) round (F.FR 75000)
£9092	$17820	(20-Nov-90 F.R111/R) Madonna col Bambino e angeli, Santi Domenico e Francesco e donatore (35x25cm-14x10in) panel (I.L 20000000)
£1233	*$2208*	*(12-Apr-91 AW.H296/R) Kindermord zu Bethlehem (27x27cm-11x11in) pen brush (DM 3700)*
£1500	*$2895*	*(11-Dec-90 C1/R) Rebecca at the well, Study for a Last Judgement (26x20cm-10x8in) i. blk.chk.ink red chk.wash double-sided*
£2000	*$3260*	*(1-Jul-91 S169) Design for base of bowl, salt-cellar or fountain, with tritons, nereids blowing horns (15x15cm-6x6in) bears i. pen*
£2081	*$4038*	*(3-Dec-90 SY.F1011/R) Studio di nudo (38x26cm-15x10in) sanguine (I.L 4500000)*
£3158	*$6000*	*(8-Jan-91 SY.NY39/R) Costume studies (28x42cm-11x17in) i. ink over blk.chk. double-sided*

FLORENTINE SCHOOL, 17th C Italian

£1163	$2000	(15-May-91 D.NY79) David with the Head of Goliath (112x71cm-44x28in)
£2254	$4035	(8-Apr-91 CH.R89) Tre cani presso un muretto (60x45cm-24x18in) fragment (I.L 5000000)
£2518	$4104	(13-Jun-91 CSC.P4/R) Le portement de croix (17x22cm-7x9in) (F.FR 25000)
£3287	$5523	(23-Apr-91 F.R12/R) Predica del Battista (137x90cm-54x35in) (I.L 7200000)
£5028	$9000	(11-Apr-91 SY.NY55/R) Youth wearing a helmet (49x39cm-19x15in)
£6122	$12000	(6-Nov-90 GF.L2043/R) Esther before Ahasveurus. Salomon and the Queen of Shaba (153x110cm-60x43in) pair (S.FR 15000)
£6796	$11825	(25-Mar-91 SY.F708) Allegoria della vanita (159x176cm-63x69in) (I.L 15000000)
£6800	$11492	(17-Apr-91 S15/R) Venus and Cupid (56x77cm-22x30in)
£1055	*$1731*	*(19-Jun-91 LC.P17/R) Etude de main ecrivant (17x25cm-7x10in) crayons (F.FR 10500)*

FLORENTINE SCHOOL, 18th C Italian

£10000	$19700	(31-Oct-90 S107/R) The Bath of Bathsheba (142x201cm-56x79in)

FLORES, Pedro (1897-1967) Spanish

£1413	$2501	(3-Apr-91 ANS.M139/R) Cabeza de mujer (42x32cm-17x13in) s. paper (S.P 260000)
£2172	$4279	(15-Nov-90 ANS.M39/R) Marina bretona (46x55cm-18x22in) s. (S.P 400000)
£2184	$3778	(8-May-91 FER.M91/R) La maja y el torero (63x48cm-25x19in) s. tablex (S.P 400000)
£3003	$5195	(8-May-91 FER.M90/R) Personajes goyescos (63x49cm-25x19in) s. tablex (S.P 550000)
£654	*$1124*	*(16-May-91 ANS.M28/R) Figuras junto al arbol (27x21cm-11x8in) W/C (S.P 120000)*
£1209	*$2237*	*(5-Mar-91 ANS.M383/R) El pintor (45x31cm-18x12in) W/C (S.P 220000)*
£1522	*$2693*	*(3-Apr-91 ANS.M153/R) Bateau Surrealiste (33x43cm-13x17in) gouache (S.P 280000)*

FLORIAN, Mark (1908-) American

£430	*$727*	*(20-Apr-91 HOR.H14/R) Nude resting (42x55cm-17x22in) s. pastel (F.M 3000)*

FLORIAN, Maximilian (1901-) Austrian
£1435 $2483   (8-May-91 D.V131/R) Portrait of gentleman with book (110x90cm-43x35in)
s.d.1959 (A.S 30000)

FLORIDO BERNILS, Enrique (1873-1929) Spanish
£815 $1443   (3-Apr-91 ANS.M127/R) Paisaje (41x33cm-16x13in) s. tablex (S.P 150000)
£1491 $2907   (17-Oct-90 FER.M181/R) Pescadores llegando al puerto (50x31cm-20x12in)
s. (S.P 275000)
£1491 $2907   (17-Oct-90 FER.M180/R) Puerto de Malaga (50x31cm-20x12in) s.
(S.P 275000)
£3276 $5667   (8-May-91 FER.M143/R) Barcos pesqueros frente a la costa de Malaga
(60x100cm-24x39in) s. (S.P 600000)

FLORIDO, E (19th C) Spanish
£1094 $2100   (27-Nov-90 PO.BA10) Barcos en el puerto (60x100cm-24x39in) s.

FLORIDO, Francisco (20th C) Spanish
£1036 $1699   (17-Jun-91 DUR.M1426/R) Vista de Malaga (80x100cm-31x39in) s.d.1957
(S.P 190000)

FLORIS, Frans (16/17th C) Flemish
£1450 $2364   (1-Jul-91 S165/R) Allegorical figure of Concord (26x14cm-10x6in) bears
i. num.7 pen wash htd white

FLORIS, Frans (circle) (16/17th C) Flemish
£2372 $4032   (30-May-91 EA.Z327/R) The Judgement of Midas (61x98cm-24x39in)
(S.FR 6000)

FLORIS, Frans (studio) (16/17th C) Flemish
£4555 $8927   (19-Nov-90 ZZ.F11/R) Le portement de croix (74x101cm-29x40in) panel
(F.FR 45000)
£5729 $10999   (19-Feb-91 ARC.P16/R) Le songe d'herodiade (98x78cm-39x31in) panel
(F.FR 57000)

FLORIS, Frans (style) (16/17th C) Flemish
£1500 $3000   (7-Feb-91 C134/R) The Last Supper (62x84cm-24x33in) copper
£4749 $8500   (11-Apr-91 SY.NY173/R) Saints Catherine and Helena and two kneeling nuns
(91x32cm-36x13in) i. panel wings of altarpiece two

FLOUQUET, Pierre Louis (19/20th C) French
£1180 $2290   (8-Dec-90 KV.L122/R) Jacob et L'Ange aux Joueurs de Cartes
(71x96cm-28x38in) (B.FR 70000)
£3287 $6409   (23-Oct-90 C.A377/R) Portrait of the architect Victor Bourgeois
(80x60cm-31x24in) s.d.1920 (B.FR 200000)

FLOWER, Cedric (1920-) Australian
£1023 $1719   (22-Apr-91 SY.ME202) Girl arranging flowers (50x34cm-20x13in) s. ink oil
board (A.D 2200)

FLUCK, Martin Peter (1935-) Swiss
£757 $1476   (24-Oct-90 GD.B347) Brienzersee landscape, winter (35x60cm-14x24in) s.
panel (S.FR 1900)

FLUELER, Anton (1898-1960) Swiss
£816 $1600   (6-Nov-90 GF.L2595/R) La muse en detresse (36x23cm-14x9in) s.
i.d.1936verso panel (S.FR 2000)

FLUGGEN, Hans (1875-1942) German
£816 $1314   (28-Jun-91 BM.B779/R) Portrait of lady before window with view of
landscape (38x30cm-15x12in) s.indis.d.1928 panel (DM 2400)

FLUGGEN, Josef (1842-1906) German
£7509 $14717   (24-Nov-90 SA.A835/R) Beach scene with figures, evening
(95x190cm-37x75in) s.d.1870 (DM 22000)

FLUMIANI, Ugo (1876-1938) Italian
£650 $1300   (7-Feb-91 B.P80/R) Mounatin stream (48x64cm-19x25in) s.
£1683 $3281   (25-Oct-90 D.V133/R) Seascape with sailing ship (65x50cm-26x20in) s.
(A.S 35000)
£1708 $3160   (7-Mar-91 D.V44/R) Fishing boats, sunny evening (60x90cm-24x35in) s.i.
(A.S 35000)

FLYCKT, Manfred (1893-1956) Swedish
£658 $1290   (20-Nov-90 GO.G66) Big farmer (65x57cm-26x22in) s. (S.KR 7200)
£790 $1414   (9-Apr-91 GO.G39) Landscape with barn (49x60cm-19x24in) s. panel
(S.KR 8500)
£868 $1702   (20-Nov-90 GO.G67) Trees by watercourse (51x62cm-20x24in) s. panel
(S.KR 9500)

FOCARDI, Piero (1889-) Italian
£730 $1219   (6-Jun-91 F.M128) Lago di Garda (19x31cm-7x12in) s. i.verso panel
(I.L 1600000)
£866 $1447   (6-Jun-91 F.M130) Bosco d'autunno (18x29cm-7x11in) s. board on panel
(I.L 1900000)

FOCARDI, Ruggero (1864-1934) Italian
£2964 $4950   (6-Jun-91 F.M252) Castagni a Pelago (38x51cm-15x20in) s.d.1920 l.verso
                  panel (I.L 6500000)

FOERSTER, Emil (1822-1906) American
£578 $1000   (21-May-91 CE.NY569/R) Portrait of artist's grand-daughter, Elsa
                  (91x63cm-36x25in)

FOGARTY, Thomas (1873-1938) American
£6704 $12000   (14-Mar-91 CH.NY126/R) Summer picnic (122x194cm-48x76in) s.d.1937

FOGGIA, Mario Moretti (1882-) Italian
£546 $1069   (21-Nov-90 F.M109) Temporale estivo (47x36cm-19x14in) s.d.34 s.i.verso
                  W/C paper on board (I.L 1200000)

FOGGIE, David (1878-1948) British
£475 $803   (1-May-91 PHL70) Figures in hayfield (37x54cm-15x21in) s.d.18 col.wash
£637 $1128   (20-Mar-91 MA.V425) Seated woman washing (36x23cm-14x9in) s. W/C
                  (C.D 1300)

FOHN, Emanuel (1881-1966) German
£541 $935   (25-May-91 N.M90/R) Place de la Concorde with Tuilleries
                  (46x62cm-18x24in) s.d.1932 W/C over pen (DM 1600)
£2237 $4339   (6-Dec-90 D.V92/R) Coastal landscape, South of France (50x65cm-20x26in)
                  s. mixed media oil paper on board (A.S 45000)

FOHR, Karl Philipp (1795-1818) German
£629 $1221   (7-Dec-90 GB.B5809/R) Four painters in German costumes one pointing to
                  another one crying (10x15cm-4x6in) pen htd.white (DM 1800)

FOLCKER, Goran (1920-) Swedish
£377 $653   (22-May-91 BA.S364/R) Composition with collage (61x61cm-24x24in) s.d.58
                  mixed media (S.KR 4000)

FOLEY, H (19th C) British
£1300 $2444   (21-Sep-90 CBB100/R) Anne Hathaway's cottage near Stratford-on-Avon
                  (25x20cm-10x8in) s.i.verso

FOLEY, Henry (19th C) British
£750 $1448   (13-Dec-90 CSK84/R) Venetian capriccio (46x81cm-18x32in) s.
£1100 $1848   (23-Apr-91 S35/R) Edinburgh Castle (46x25cm-18x10in) s. indist.i.d.verso

FOLINSBEE, John F (1892-1972) American
£1183 $2200   (9-Sep-90 LIT.L299) Alsatian village bazaar, the Green, August 23rd
                  (76x61cm-30x24in) init.
£1270 $2400   (27-Sep-90 CH.NY235/R) Baby girl (21x26cm-8x10in) s. board
£8247 $16000   (5-Dec-90 D.NY123/R) Autumn rain (51x41cm-20x16in) s. s.i.verso
£10417 $20000   (30-Nov-90 CH.NY144/R) Winter Sunlight (41x51cm-16x20in) s. l.stretcher

FOLKESTAD, Bernhard (1879-1933) Norwegian
£788 $1411   (11-Mar-91 B.O34/R) Seated boy with berries (47x54cm-19x21in)
                  (N.KR 9000)
£3299 $6432   (11-Oct-90 BU.O40/R) Girl with Christmas decorations (63x52cm-25x20in)
                  init.d.08 (N.KR 38000)
£4729 $8464   (14-Mar-91 BU.O35/R) Still life of flowers in vase and bowls
                  (72x100cm-28x39in) s.d.1918, female nude verso (N.KR 54000)

FOLLAK, Alex (1915-) Russian
£1017 $1658   (3-Jul-91 WE.MU75/R) Goats in Alpine landscape (50x70cm-20x28in) s.
                  (DM 3000)

FOLLI, Luigi (19th C) Italian
£1395 $2400   (17-May-91 WOL.C334 k) Interior scene with mother and children
                  (25x33cm-10x13in) s.d.1873 canvas laid on board

FOLLINI, Carlo (1848-1938) Italian
£521 $1000   (27-Nov-90 PO.BA11) Paisaje con personajes (23x30cm-9x12in) s. panel
£1992 $3426   (14-May-91 GF.L2476/R) Stormy day by the seaside (50x63cm-20x25in) s.
                  (S.FR 5000)
£5087 $9870   (5-Dec-90 F.M80/R) Tramonto (23x34cm-9x13in) s. panel (I.L 11000000)

FOLMER, Georges (1899-?) French
£1409 $2423   (13-May-91 PPB.P11/R) Sans titre (35x27cm-14x11in) s. gouache pastel
                  wash (F.FR 14200)

FOLTYN, Francois (20th C) ?
£9250 $17945   (9-Dec-90 CC.P26/R) Composition (92x65cm-36x26in) (F.FR 90000)

FOLTYN, Frantisek (1891-1976) ?
£18000 $34920   (4-Dec-90 C304/R) Abstract composition (92x60cm-36x24in) s.d.1926

FOMISON, Tony (20th C) New Zealander?
£836 $1638   (7-Nov-90 DS.W82) Portrait (30x22cm-12x9in) s.d.16.12.72 (NZ.D 2700)

FONCHE, T (19th C) European
£600 $1074   (14-Mar-91 B17) A Venetian street (46x81cm-18x32in) s.d.'77

FONDA, Enrico (1892-1929) Italian
£1952	$3612	(7-Mar-91 D.V33/R) Capagna, Castua-Fiume (50x70cm-20x28in) s. i.verso board (A.S 40000)

FONSECA, Gonzalo (1922-) Uruguayan
£1142	$2250	(1-Nov-90 PO.M1) Naturaleza muerta (43x59cm-17x23in) board
£1320	$2600	(1-Oct-90 GC.M6) Puerto de Mikonos (36x48cm-14x19in) board

FONSECA, Reynaldo (19/20th C) Argentinian
£2168	$4250	(12-Feb-91 SY.NY295/R) Mother and child (74x61cm-29x24in) s.d.1977

FONTAINE, Gabriel (1945-) French
£545	$964	(7-Apr-91 LT.P125) Rocher dans le causse (50x61cm-20x24in) s. i. verso (F.FR 5500)
£549	$928	(5-May-91 LT.P124) Pins dans la cause (65x54cm-26x21in) s. (F.FR 5500)
£550	$897	(4-Jul-91 LT.P107) Le petit village (46x61cm-18x24in) s. (F.FR 5500)
£699	$1356	(8-Dec-90 LT.P177) Symphonie Provencale (65x81cm-26x32in) s. (F.FR 6800)

FONTAINE, Paul (19th C) ?
£820	$1542	(20-Sep-90 SC4223/R) Still life of apples and pears in basket on ledge (48x69cm-19x27in) s.d.

FONTAINE, Pierre Francois Leonard (1762-1853) French
£400	$708	(22-Mar-91 BG.P23/R) Projet pour une grande salle (7x11cm-3x4in) pierre noire wash W/C (F.FR 4000)
£420	$743	(22-Mar-91 BG.P45/R) Projets pour une coupe et deux vases a the i. pierre noire wash W/C (F.FR 4200)
£450	$797	(22-Mar-91 BG.P22/R) Reunion familiale (7cm-3ins circular) wash round (F.FR 4500)
£450	$797	(22-Mar-91 BG.P33/R) Projet de chaise pierre noire W/C two drawings on same mount (F.FR 4500)
£450	$797	(22-Mar-91 BG.P25/R) Projets de chaises et etude d'un bas-relief antique (16x9cm-6x4in) i. pierre noire wash (F.FR 4500)
£500	$885	(22-Mar-91 BG.P50) Projet pour une frise (7x23cm-3x9in) i. pierre noire W/C (F.FR 5000)
£500	$885	(22-Mar-91 BG.P24/R) Projet d'elements de mobilier i. pierre noire wash (F.FR 5000)
£500	$885	(22-Mar-91 BG.P49/R) Porjet pour la decoration d'un plafond (12x11cm-5x4in) i. pierre noire pen W/C (F.FR 5000)
£550	$974	(22-Mar-91 BG.P44/R) Projet de cheminee et de vase a the i. pierre noire wash (F.FR 5500)
£550	$974	(22-Mar-91 BG.P60/R) Etude pour un fauteuil de bureau (15x23cm-6x9in) pierre noire W/C (F.FR 5500)
£550	$974	(22-Mar-91 BG.P30/R) Projets d'elements de mobilier (17x9cm-7x4in) i. pierre noire W/C (F.FR 5500)
£550	$974	(22-Mar-91 BG.P57/R) Etude pour un fauteuil (21x16cm-8x6in) pierre noire W/C (F.FR 5500)
£600	$1062	(22-Mar-91 BG.P28/R) Projets d'elements de mobilier (12x20cm-5x8in) pierre noire W/C (F.FR 6000)
£750	$1328	(22-Mar-91 BG.P29/R) Projet de mobilier (11x20cm-4x8in) i. pierre noire W/C (F.FR 7500)
£750	$1328	(22-Mar-91 BG.P36/R) Projets d'elements de mobilier (15x8cm-6x3in) i. pierre noire wash (F.FR 7500)
£800	$1416	(22-Mar-91 BG.P37/R) Projet de fontaine (15x6cm-6x2in) i. pierre noire wash (F.FR 8000)
£850	$1505	(22-Mar-91 BG.P31/R) Projet pour deux chaises et une console (17x8cm-7x3in) i. pierre noire W/C (F.FR 8500)
£900	$1593	(22-Mar-91 BG.P59/R) Etude pour une chaise (16x23cm-6x9in) pierre noire W/C (F.FR 9000)
£1000	$1770	(22-Mar-91 BG.P55/R) Projet de bureau plat (10x19cm-4x7in) i. pierre noire pen W/C (F.FR 10000)
£1100	$1947	(22-Mar-91 BG.P34/R) Vase egyptian, lampe a huile i. pierre noire W/C (F.FR 11000)
£1200	$2124	(22-Mar-91 BG.P58/R) Etude pour un fauteuil (21x16cm-8x6in) pierre noire W/C (F.FR 12000)
£1200	$2124	(22-Mar-91 BG.P56/R) Etude pour un fauteuil (21x16cm-8x6in) pierre noire W/C (F.FR 12000)
£1200	$2124	(22-Mar-91 BG.P51/R) Projet de decoration pour une chambre (10x8cm-4x3in) i. pierre noire pen W/C (F.FR 12000)
£1500	$2655	(22-Mar-91 BG.P42/R) Vue de l'escalier de Richard Mique (12x13cm-5x5in) pierre noire wash (F.FR 15000)
£1600	$2832	(22-Mar-91 BG.P52/R) Projet de decoration murale a motifs egyptiens (8x12cm-3x5in) pierre noire W/C (F.FR 16000)
£1600	$2832	(22-Mar-91 BG.P43/R) Projet pour une salle a manger i. pierre noire wash W/C (F.FR 16000)
£1700	$3009	(22-Mar-91 BG.P41/R) Etude pour une deocration pompeienne (23x16cm-9x6in) pierre noire W/C (F.FR 17000)
£1800	$3186	(22-Mar-91 BG.P53/R) Projet pour une salle a manger (12x20cm-5x8in) pierre noire W/C (F.FR 18000)
£1800	$3186	(22-Mar-91 BG.P48/R) Projet pour le salon du General Moreau pierre noire W/C (F.FR 18000)
£2400	$4248	(22-Mar-91 BG.P35/R) Trepied et vase antiques W/C (F.FR 24000)
£4000	$7080	(22-Mar-91 BG.P32/R) Projet de chaise et dessin d'une lampe a huile pierre noire wash (F.FR 40000)
£4000	$7080	(22-Mar-91 BG.P61/R) Etude pour un siege a deux places (16x23cm-6x9in) pierre noire W/C wash gold (F.FR 40000)

FONTAINE, Pierre Francois Leonard (1762-1853) French-cont.
£5000	$8850	(22-Mar-91 BG.P46/R) Projet pour une table a the (9x12cm-4x5in) i. pierre noire W/C (F.FR 50000)
£5200	$9204	(22-Mar-91 BG.P54/R) Projet pour une chambre a coucher (13x19cm-5x7in) pierre noire W/C (F.FR 52000)
£5200	$9204	(22-Mar-91 BG.P38/R) Projet pour une salle de theatre (11x12cm-4x5in) pierre noire W/C (F.FR 52000)
£6000	$10620	(22-Mar-91 BG.P47/R) Projet pour un canape (8x17cm-3x7in) i. pierre noire W/C (F.FR 60000)
£8947	$17000	(9-Jan-91 CH.NY81/R) Piazza della Signoria, Florence. Baths of Caracalla, Rome (63x94cm-25x37in) s.d.1792 black chk W/C bodycol htd white pair

FONTAINE, Pierre Francois Leonard and PERCIER, Charles (18th C) French
£4000	$7080	(22-Mar-91 BG.P16/R) Interieur de la cour du Palais Lancellotti pres la Strada de Coronari (29x20cm-11x8in) pierre noire pen W/C (F.FR 40000)
£4221	$6923	(17-Jun-91 ARC.P3/R) Vue du Palais de la Villa d'Este pris du cote de l'entree dans le Parterre (15x23cm-6x9in) i. pen wash indian ink (F.FR 42000)
£4800	$8496	(22-Mar-91 BG.P14/R) Interieurs, palais et maisons pierre noire pen W/C (F.FR 48000)
£7500	$13275	(22-Mar-91 BG.P18/R) Vue de la cour du Palais de la Chancellerie (17x29cm-7x11in) pierre noire pen W/C (F.FR 75000)
£9000	$15930	(22-Mar-91 BG.P21/R) Vue de l'interieur de l'eglise San-Lorenzo fuiro della mura (28x24cm-11x9in) pierre noire pen W/C (F.FR 90000)
£9000	$15930	(22-Mar-91 BG.P19/R) Vue du grand escalier du Palais Corsini (19x32cm-7x13in) pierre noire pen W/C (F.FR 90000)
£9000	$15930	(22-Mar-91 BG.P15/R) Ajustement d'un puits dans le couvent diGesuiti Penitenzieri... (26x18cm-10x7in) pierre noire pen W/C (F.FR 90000)
£9500	$16815	(22-Mar-91 BG.P17/R) Vue de la cour du Palais Mattei (30x20cm-12x8in) pen W/C (F.FR 95000)
£17000	$30090	(22-Mar-91 BG.P20/R) Vue de la nouvelle entree du Museum de Vatican en 1790 (26x33cm-10x13in) pierre noire pen wash (F.FR 170000)

FONTAINEBLEAU SCHOOL, 16th C French
£8736	$16948	(5-Dec-90 APT.P9/R) La remise de la lettre ou l'entremetteuse (103x75cm-41x30in) (F.FR 85000)
£8815	$17365	(14-Nov-90 D.V37/R) Cleopatra with snake in landscape (58x95cm-23x37in) c.1590 panel (A.S 180000)
£10000	$17000	(30-May-91 SY.NY1/R) Diana, said to be Diane de Poitiers, reclining in landscape with stag (37x53cm-15x21in) panel
£23116	$37910	(21-Jun-91 SY.MO105/R) La femme entre deux ages (91x111cm-36x44in) (F.FR 230000)
£44737	$85000	(11-Jan-91 CH.NY41/R) Lovers (90x82cm-35x32in)
£1047	$1780	(31-May-91 GB.B5142/R) Pegasus crowned with wreath by Hecate and Artemis (25x20cm-10x8in) pen wash (DM 3100)
£4000	$6520	(1-Jul-91 S13/R) Judith and Holofernes (22x18cm-9x7in) pen wash

FONTAN, Leo (1884-1965) French
£1266	$2089	(8-Jul-91 SY.J207/R) Port Beaulieu (32x40cm-13x16in) s. (SA.R 6000)

FONTANA, Carlo (circle) (fl.1700-1711) Italian?
£2400	$4632	(12-Dec-90 PH329/R) Facade of S Giovanni in Laterno (23x33cm-9x13in) pen ink wash sold with other drawings

FONTANA, Ernesto (19/20th C) Swiss
£9172	$16418	(12-Mar-91 F.M63/R) Il segnale amoroso (90x61cm-35x24in) s.d.1904 (I.L 20000000)
£1212	$2388	(30-Oct-90 CH.AM442/R) Portrait of lady in spanish costume (63x40cm-25x16in) s.d.1886 pastel (D.FL 4000)

FONTANA, Lavinia (1552-1614) Italian
£20000	$38600	(12-Dec-90 S25/R) Portrait of Pope Gregory XIII (116x97cm-46x38in) i.

FONTANA, Lavinia (after) (1552-1614) Italian
£1182	$2317	(20-Nov-90 F.R44) Cristo e la Samaritana (102x75cm-40x30in) (I.L 2600000)

FONTANA, Lavinia (attrib) (1552-1614) Italian
£1819	$3146	(21-May-91 SY.MI222/R) Ritratto di una gentildonna vestito con collana e orecchini in perla min. rec. (I.L 4000000)

FONTANA, Lucio (1899-1968) Italian
£38934	$74753	(27-Nov-90 SY.MI172/R) Concetto spaziale (30x55cm-12x22in) s.d.49 (I.L 85000000)
£45000	$87300	(6-Dec-90 S42/R) Concetto Spaziale (62x53cm-24x21in) s. s.i.verso
£52000	$100880	(6-Dec-90 C501/R) Concetto spaziale (50x60cm-20x24in) s.d.53 s.i.d.1953 verso pigment glass canvas
£53299	$105000	(14-Nov-90 SY.NY317/R) Concetto Spaziale - Attese (55x47cm-22x19in) s.i.verso
£60000	$103800	(10-May-91 S.Z32) Concetto spaziale (81x81cm-32x32in) s.d.1960verso (S.FR 150000)
£76531	$150000	(7-Nov-90 SY.NY217 a/R) Concetto spaziale (81x65cm-32x26in) s.i. mixed media graph panel laid down on wood
£90000	$144900	(27-Jun-91 S54/R) Concetto spaziale (60x50cm-24x20in) s.d.55 s.d.verso oil pebbles canvas

FONTANA, Lucio (1899-1968) Italian-cont.

£106580	$206766	(4-Dec-90 BA.S136/R) Concetto Spaziale, attese (81x65cm-32x26in) s.verso (S.KR 1150000)
£140000	$225400	(27-Jun-91 C10/R) Concetto spaziale (146x114cm-57x45in) s.
£150000	$291000	(6-Dec-90 S36/R) Concetto Spaziale (81x60cm-32x24in) s.
£866	$1472	(28-May-91 SY.MI113) Nudo di donna (26x19cm-10x7in) s.d.44 Indian ink (I.L 1900000)
£1546	$3029	(20-Nov-90 BR.M40/R) Figura femminile (20x27cm-8x11in) s.d.1946 ballpoint pen (I.L 3400000)
£1622	$2757	(1-Jun-91 VG.B535/R) Untitled (12x9cm-5x4in) s.d.1951 ball point pen board on board (DM 4800)
£1637	$3208	(20-Nov-90 BR.M176/R) Senza titolo (29x23cm-11x9in) gouache (I.L 3600000)
£2953	$5818	(30-Oct-90 F.R162/R) Concetto spaziale (25x35cm-10x14in) s. Indian ink holes (I.L 6500000)
£6871	$13192	(27-Nov-90 SY.MI112/R) Concetto spaziale (45x35cm-18x14in) s. ink holes board (I.L 15000000)
£7062	$12006	(28-May-91 SY.MI159/R) Progetto per ambiente spaziale (60x41cm-24x16in) s.d.53 ink pencil gouache (I.L 15500000)
£8556	$16599	(3-Dec-90 F.M342/R) Lotta di centauri (31x49cm-12x19in) s.i.d.1955 gouache paper on masonite triptych (I.L 18500000)
£9161	$17589	(27-Nov-90 SY.MI236/R) Concetto spaziale (49x57cm-19x22in) s. holes blotting paper (I.L 20000000)
£34000	$54740	(27-Jun-91 S61/R) Concetto spaziale (54x45cm-21x18in) s.i.verso waterpaint canvas
£43147	$85000	(5-Oct-90 CH.NY6/R) Concetto spaziale (54x65cm-21x26in) s.s.i.d.1954verso collage col chk canvas
£47782	$93652	(23-Nov-90 VG.B76/R) Concetto spaziale attesa (55x46cm-22x18in) s.i.d.1967verso dispersion paint cut canvas (DM 140000)
£56000	$108640	(6-Dec-90 S43/R) Concetto Spaziale (65x54cm-26x21in) s.i. verso waterpaint on canvas
£292661	$570689	(22-Oct-90 BR.M116/R) Concetto spaziale (70x80cm-28x31in) s.d.1956 s.i.verso oil mixed media lustre (I.L 650000000)

FONTANA, Prospero (1512-1597) Italian

| £21538 | $42000 | (11-Oct-90 SY.NY81/R) Madonna, infant St John the Baptist and bishop saint (79x68cm-31x27in) panel |
| £550 | $930 | (16-Apr-91 C16) Hercules and the Nemean Lion (11x8cm-4x3in) bk.chk.ink wash |

FONTANA, Roberto (1844-1907) Italian

| £1088 | $1838 | (16-Apr-91 CH.R98) Busto di ragazza (12x8cm-5x3in) s. board (I.L 2400000) |
| £8094 | $15702 | (5-Dec-90 F.M54/R) Ritratto di giovane donna nello studio del pittore (32x13cm-13x5in) s.d.1883 canvas on panel (I.L 17500000) |

FONTANAROSA, Lucien (1912-1975) French

£1250	$2038	(5-Jul-91 APT.P121) La colline (43x65cm-17x26in) s. paper laid down on canvas (F.FR 12500)
£4734	$9325	(6-Oct-90 GL.P131/R) Les deux ballerines (73x50cm-29x20in) s. (F.FR 48000)
£5216	$10171	(9-Oct-90 GGL.L16/R) L'enfant aux fruits (46x75cm-18x30in) s.d.1957 (F.FR 52000)
£7236	$13893	(24-Feb-91 P.V140/R) Jeune violoncelliste (51x74cm-20x29in) s. i. verso (F.FR 72000)

FONTANESI, Antonio (1818-1882) Italian

£9064	$15318	(16-Apr-91 CH.R190/R) Figura nel paesaggio (21x30cm-8x12in) s.verso panel (I.L 20000000)
£14800	$28711	(5-Dec-90 F.M39/R) Vallata solitaria (32x26cm-13x10in) board arched (I.L 32000000)
£956	$1865	(24-Oct-90 GD.B1063) Landscape with peasants (33x50cm-13x20in) mono.d.71 i.verso chl htd.white (S.FR 2400)

FONTEBASSO, Francesco (1709-1769) Italian

£11000	$21670	(31-Oct-90 S35/R) Daniel in the Lions' Den (74x58cm-29x23in)
£13000	$25610	(31-Oct-90 S33/R) The Sacrifice of Aaron (74x58cm-29x23in)
£14000	$27580	(31-Oct-90 S32/R) The Meeting of Abraham and Melchizedek (74x58cm-29x23in)
£17000	$28730	(19-Apr-91 C151/R) Cloelia and her companions escaping from Lars Porsena (43x55cm-17x22in)
£1500	$2445	(1-Jul-91 S104) Studies of dead Christ supported by angels and priest (24x35cm-9x14in) pen
£13000	$25090	(11-Dec-90 C49/R) The martyrdom of Saint Andrew (27x24cm-11x9in) chk.ink.wash

FONTEBASSO, Francesco (attrib) (1709-1769) Italian

| £1100 | $1859 | (16-Apr-91 C186/R) A river God and studies of a nude (28x20cm-11x8in) i. verso watermark ink |

FONTEBASSO, Francesco (circle) (1709-1769) Italian

| £8233 | $13255 | (27-Jun-91 APT.P78/R) Cleopatre dans son palais recoit le serpent qui va la tuer (83x119cm-33x47in) (F.FR 82000) |

FONTEBASSO, Francesco (style) (1709-1769) Italian
£3000 $4890   (4-Jul-91 C640/R) Aeneas and Creusa extinguishing flames above
                  Ascanius's head (43x60cm-17x24in)

FONTENAY, Andre (1913-) French
£500 $1000   (6-Feb-91 D.NY31) Restaurant des Aiglons (58x74cm-23x29in) s.
£613 $1000   (12-Jun-91 SY.NY42 a/R) Des Aiglons (60x73cm-24x29in) s.

FONTENAY, Jean Baptiste Belin de (1653-1715) French
£7347 $14400   (6-Nov-90 GF.L2054/R) Still life of flowers (67x100cm-26x39in)
                  (S.FR 18000)

FONTENAY, Leonard Alexis de see DALIGE DE FONTENAY, Leonard Alexis

FOO FAT, Dulcie (1946-) Canadian?
£3535 $6116   (6-May-91 SY.T115/R) Kananaskis autumn (155x112cm-61x44in) s. d.1983
                  verso (C.D 7000)

FOOTE, Mary (1847-1938) American
£1198 $2000   (26-Jul-91 E.EDM190/R) Raining Mountain, portrait of Indian boy
                  (104x74cm-41x29in) s.
*£1368 $2600   (9-Jan-91 CH.NY228/R) Royal Bay, British Columbia. Homesteaders one i.
                  pencil wash two*

FOOTE, Will Howe (1874-1965) American
£578 $1000   (21-May-91 GRO.B99/R) Sunny walls (30x41cm-12x16in) s. canvasboard
£599 $1150   (29-Nov-90 MFA.C220) Sponge boats, Nassau (18x23cm-7x9in) panel
£872 $1500   (18-May-91 W.W200/R) The White House (18x23cm-7x9in) s. board
£1289 $2500   (5-Dec-90 D.NY54/R) Old prospector, Gold Bar Mine, Arizona
                  (76x76cm-30x30in) s.i.

FORABOSCO, Gerolamo (circle) (1605-1679) Italian
£1392 $2352   (18-Apr-91 APT.P16) Portrait d'homme (46x38cm-18x15in) (F.FR 14000)

FORABOSCO, Gerolamo (studio) (1605-1679) Italian
£2705 $4842   (8-Apr-91 CH.R150/R) Ritratto di gentildonna (83x68cm-33x27in)
                  (I.L 6000000)

FORABOSCO, Gerolamo (style) (1605-1679) Italian
£5000 $9600   (29-Nov-90 CSK6/R) Head of young woman with laurel wreath in hair
                  (43x36cm-17x14in) panel

FORAIN, Jean Louis (1852-1931) French
£1777 $3500   (13-Nov-90 CE.NY166/R) Mere et son enfant (55x65cm-22x26in) s.
£3568 $6850   (29-Nov-90 ZZ.F6/R) Femme aux bras croises (33x24cm-13x9in) panel
                  (F.FR 35000)
£5330 $10500   (13-Nov-90 CE.NY46/R) Danseuses (63x48cm-25x19in) s. panel
£5641 $11000   (23-Oct-90 SY.NY303/R) In the wings (61x74cm-24x29in)
£5882 $11294   (17-Dec-90 AGS.P29/R) Mere et enfant (61x50cm-24x20in) mono.
                  (F.FR 58000)
£6633 $13000   (14-Feb-91 CH.NY14/R) La loge (81x65cm-32x26in) init.
£7614 $15000   (13-Nov-90 CE.NY99/R) Scene de couloir au Palais (60x73cm-24x29in) s.
£17857 $35000   (14-Feb-91 CH.NY13/R) Cafe Maxim, Paris (60x74cm-24x29in) init.
£20000 $38800   (4-Dec-90 C270/R) Au bar (66x82cm-26x32in) s.
*£321 $594   (6-Mar-91 APT.P9 b) Apres le vote (36x51cm-14x20in) s.d.24 chl.
                  (F.FR 3200)*
*£422 $780   (6-Mar-91 APT.P10) L'annexion (25x36cm-10x14in) s. pen htd.W/C
                  (F.FR 4200)*
*£531 $1029   (8-Dec-90 GAB.G2549) Juges s'habillant (27x30cm-11x12in) Indian ink
                  drawing (S.FR 1300)*
*£550 $974   (22-Mar-91 BG.P67) Deux personnages sur la jete (24x38cm-9x15in) ink
                  wash col.crayons (F.FR 5500)*
*£756 $1474   (14-Jan-91 YC.P185) Sortie de bal (37x32cm-15x13in) s.d.1902 chl.
                  tracing paper (F.FR 7500)*
*£800 $1512   (27-Sep-90 CG3/R) Baiser dans le coulisses (41x27cm-16x11in) s.i. chl
                  brush ink*
£866 $1672   (12-Dec-90 APT.P12) A l'otel (32x23cm-13x9in) s. col.crayons (F.FR 8500)
*£946 $1637   (22-May-91 PLF.P124) Les femmes sont rosses (26x18cm-10x7in) s.i. wash
                  W/C (F.FR 9500)*
*£994 $1680   (15-Apr-91 CC.P11/R) Jeune femme etendue sur un lit (25x36cm-10x14in) s.
                  sanguinne chl. (F.FR 10000)*
£1000 $1610   (24-Jun-91 CSK2/R) La deshabillee (27x19cm-11x7in) s. crayon
*£1012 $1984   (20-Nov-90 BG.P39/R) La lecture du journal (19x20cm-7x8in) Indian ink
                  (F.FR 10000)*
*£1272 $2403   (30-Sep-90 E.LA43) Le peintre et son modele (31x25cm-12x10in) s.i. ink
                  col.crayons (F.FR 12500)*
*£1827 $3600   (13-Nov-90 CE.NY36/R) Danseuse (31x25cm-12x10in) s.i. W/C brush ink
                  paper on board*
*£1837 $3563   (8-Dec-90 GAB.G2548/R) Le couple (29x22cm-11x9in) s.i. wash pen
                  (S.FR 4500)*
*£2049 $4016   (7-Nov-90 APT.P474/R) Femme assoupie (27x42cm-11x17in) s. col.crayons
                  (F.FR 20000)*
*£32000 $62080   (4-Dec-90 C114/R) Chez la modiste (55x46cm-22x18in) pastel paper on
                  board*

FORBES, Elizabeth Adela (1859-1912) British
£1350 $2552   (27-Sep-90 L105/R) The lute player (43x30cm-17x12in) s. W/C chl.
£9000 $17280   (21-Feb-91 B61/R) Pied Piper (63x89cm-25x35in) s. W/C gouache
£9200 $17664   (26-Nov-90 SWS135/R) Driving home the geese (44x31cm-17x12in) s. W/C
                gouache over chk

FORBES, Helen K (1891-1945) American
£510 $1000   (13-Feb-91 B.SF2157/R) Wells Fargo ruin (86x102cm-34x40in)
£513 $1000   (10-Oct-90 B.SF640/R) Mesa land (61x102cm-24x40in) s.
£615 $1200   (10-Oct-90 B.SF641/R) Death Vaslley II (92x82cm-36x32in)

FORBES, John Colin (1846-?) Canadian
£505 $869   (14-May-91 JOY.T47/R) Cattle watering (34x45cm-13x18in) s. board
               (C.D 1000)
£1515 $2621   (6-May-91 SY.T172/R) Bird sanctuary, Bonaventure Island, Perce Rock
               (23x31cm-9x12in) s. board (C.D 3000)

FORBES, Stanhope Alexander (1857-1947) British
£680 $1285   (27-Sep-90 L199) The Greengrocers (61x76cm-24x30in) s.
£1500 $2850   (28-Feb-91 DLY279/R) Cutting hay (28x41cm-11x16in) s.
£1850 $3182   (14-May-91 SWS369/R) Topping and tailing turnips (42x25cm-17x10in) s.
               canvas on board
£5000 $9450   (27-Sep-90 L150/R) The story book (79x61cm-31x24in) s.d.1888
£5102 $10000   (7-Nov-90 B.SF1165/R) Resting by fire (46x58cm-18x23in) s.
£5800 $11310   (15-Jan-91 SWS214/R) Cornish lane (50x60cm-20x24in) s.d.1917
£12000 $20280   (1-May-91 S5/R) At noonday (122x102cm-48x40in) s.d.1918
£14000 $25900   (7-Mar-91 C26/R) Street harmony (76x61cm-30x24in) s.d.1921
               s.i.d.stretcher
£17500 $34300   (8-Nov-90 DLY287/R) Children playing on old quay (61x76cm-24x30in)
               s.d.1931
£23000 $43470   (27-Sep-90 L304/R) The old weighing house, Penzance, Cornwall
               (61x76cm-24x30in) s.

FORBES, Stanhope Alexander (attrib) (1857-1947) British
£500 $895   (14-Mar-91 L105) Portrait of young man holding oar (71x56cm-28x22in)

FORBES, Stanhope Alexander (style) (1857-1947) British
£1300 $2561   (1-Nov-90 CSK130/R) Day's bag (108x87cm-43x34in)

FORCELLA, N (?) ?
£1439 $2834   (16-Nov-90 LGB.P196) Scene de marche (68x93cm-27x37in) s. (F.FR 14100)

FORD, Henry Chapman (1828-1894) American
£851 $1600   (19-Sep-90 B.SF2781) Pastoral landscape (56x91cm-22x36in) s.d.1874
£988 $1700   (15-May-91 SY.NY60/R) California landscape (58x43cm-23x17in) s.d.1879

FORD, John (fl.1875-1885) British
£740 $1251   (2-May-91 HB469) Self portrait of artist in full wig and cloak
               (74x56cm-29x22in) s.d.1885 verso painted oval after W.Aikman

FORD, Ruth Vansickel (1897-1980) American
£888 $1500   (21-Apr-91 DU.E152/R) New England town (91x74cm-36x29in) s.

FORD, William (19th C) British
£2532 $4861   (14-Aug-90 SY.ME308/R) Harvest Scene (41x66cm-16x26in) s. (A.D 6000)

FOREAU, Henri (1866-1938) French
£803 $1542   (27-Nov-90 JRL.S248) Winter street, Paris (49x39cm-19x15in) s. panel
               (A.D 2000)
£480 $850   (20-Mar-91 DL.P120) Moutons et bergers pres de la riviere
               (26x36cm-10x14in) s. W/C gouache (F.FR 4800)

FOREST, Jean Baptiste (1635-1712) French
£1706 $3345   (24-Nov-90 SA.A567/R) Pastoral landscape (60x72cm-24x28in) canvas laid
               down (DM 5000)

FOREST, Pierre (1881-1971) French
£405 $689   (28-May-91 KF.M653) Ferme de la Fauconniere (34x21cm-13x8in) s. pastel
               board (DM 1200)

FOREST, Roy de (1930-) American
£1939 $3800   (6-Nov-90 CE.NY171/R) Untitled (53x42cm-21x17in) s.d.1976 verso acrylic
£2041 $4000   (12-Feb-91 SY.NY468/R) Abstraction (56x56cm-22x22in) s.verso
£615 $1200   (24-Oct-90 B.SF1530/R) Dog and figure in landscape (56x75cm-22x30in)
               s.d.1976 pastel crayon pencil
£1488 $2500   (24-Apr-91 B.SF4641/R) Kate Van Horn series (51x74cm-20x29in) s.i.d.1969
               oil col.crayon pencil
£1531 $3000   (6-Nov-90 CE.NY170/R) Dog with a very long tail (89x123cm-35x48in)
               s.d.1984 col.chk.crayon pencil acrylic paper
£1786 $3000   (24-Apr-91 B.SF4640/R) Drawing 60 (56x76cm-22x30in) s.d.1979 pastel
£1935 $3250   (24-Apr-91 B.SF4642/R) Drawing 102 (56x76cm-22x30in) s.d.1975 pastel

FOREST, Wesner la (?-1965) Haitian
£3571 $7000   (19-Nov-90 SY.NY305/R) Homme assis (43x45cm-17x18in) s. board

FORESTIER, Henri Joseph de (1790-1868) French
£12871 $22782 (5-Apr-91 DAR.P63/R) Ulysse massacrant les pretendants de Penelope
(114x148cm-45x58in) (F.FR 130000)

FORG, Gunther (1952-) American
£8876 $15000 (2-May-91 CH.NY283/R) Farbfeld (200x60cm-79x24in) s.i.d.1986 B-9 verso
acrylic wood
£12245 $24000 (7-Nov-90 SY.NY330/R) Bleibild (180x250cm-71x98in) s.d.1987 verso
acrylic lead over two wood panels
£18935 $32000 (2-May-91 CH.NY291/R) Untitled (60x50cm-24x20in) s.d.89 num verso
acrylic wood six panels

FORGIOLI, Attilio (1933-) Italian
£910 $1720 (27-Sep-90 F.M55) Paesaggio (60x68cm-24x27in) s.d.67 (I.L 2000000)
£2109 $3459 (20-Jun-91 F.M309/R) Isola (100x90cm-39x35in) s. (I.L 4600000)

FORLI (school) (?) Italian
*£7000 $11410 (2-Jul-91 C114/R) Bird's eye view of town of Forli (56x42cm-22x17in) l.
black chk pen wash two joined sheets c.1600*

FORMOZOV, Valerian (1921-) Russian
£1479 $2914 (3-Oct-90 QWA.P18) Interieur chez Aralov (70x94cm-28x37in) (F.FR 15000)
£1627 $3206 (3-Oct-90 QWA.P9/R) Des fraises (50x70cm-20x28in) board (F.FR 16500)
£1677 $3303 (3-Oct-90 QWA.P19) Plein air (100x58cm-39x23in) board (F.FR 17000)
£1726 $3400 (3-Oct-90 QWA.P7/R) Une conversation entre filles (60x70cm-24x28in)
board (F.FR 17500)

FORNARA, Carlo (1871-1968) Italian
£2590 $5025 (5-Dec-90 F.M91/R) Paesaggio collinare (16x22cm-6x9in) init. panel
(I.L 5600000)
£7796 $13956 (12-Mar-91 F.M108/R) Valle Vigezzo (23x30cm-9x12in) mono. s.verso
(I.L 17000000)
£9172 $16418 (12-Mar-91 F.M84/R) Rose in un vaso bianco (37x28cm-15x11in) s. i.verso
panel (I.L 20000000)
£45787 $88826 (5-Dec-90 F.M103/R) Giardino con ciliego in fiore (50x40cm-20x16in) s.
panel (I.L 99000000)

FORNARA, Sallustio (1852-1922) Italian
£4856 $9421 (5-Dec-90 F.M73/R) Case al sole, Venezia (23x39cm-9x15in) s. i.verso
panel (I.L 10500000)

FORNER, Raquel (1902-1990) Argentinian
£4451 $7700 (8-May-91 V.BA41) Mujer de pueblo (46x45cm-18x18in)

FORREST, Archie (20th C) British
*£1400 $2366 (17-Apr-91 CG37/R) Sharp plants and heat haze, Monterosso, Italy
(71x96cm-28x38in) s.i.d.82 verso gouache*

FORREST, Captain J Haughton (1825-1925) Australian
£926 $1556 (16-Jul-91 JRL.S309) Tasmanian coast (11x12cm-4x5in) board (A.D 2000)
£1174 $2195 (27-Aug-90 SY.ME146/R) River sunset (21x30cm-8x12in) s. canvas on board
(A.D 2700)
£1584 $2676 (16-Apr-91 J.M63) The pilot boat (28x45cm-11x18in) board (A.D 3500)
£1923 $3250 (16-Apr-91 J.M176) Lake Scene (29x44cm-11x17in) init. board (A.D 4250)
£2262 $3824 (16-Apr-91 J.M23) Lake scene (28x44cm-11x17in) s. board (A.D 5000)
£2489 $4206 (16-Apr-91 J.M116/R) On the Derwent (22x46cm-9x18in) s. board
(A.D 5500)
£3586 $6886 (14-Aug-90 SY.ME202/R) Sailing off the coast (29x44cm-11x17in) s. board
(A.D 8500)
£3614 $6940 (26-Nov-90 SY.ME232/R) Tasmanian landscape (30x45cm-12x18in) s.d.1920
board (A.D 9000)
£4600 $8970 (24-Oct-90 S82/R) The Derwent Lighthouse, Tasmania (31x46cm-12x18in)
init. i. verso board
£8734 $15633 (9-Apr-91 CH.ME225/R) Mt Ben Lomond from South Esk River, Tasmania
(96x72cm-38x28in) s. (A.D 20000)

FORREST, Captain J Haughton (attrib) (1825-1925) Australian
£695 $1369 (13-Nov-90 J.M603) Scottish lake (29x44cm-11x17in) board (A.D 1800)

FORRESTALL, Thomas de Vany (1936-) Canadian
£1586 $3093 (24-Oct-90 EA.M497/R) Boat club (41x71cm-16x28in) s. s.i.d.1975 verso
egg tempera panel (C.D 3600)

FORSBERG, Carl Johan (1868-1938) Swedish
*£925 $1730 (29-Aug-90 KH.K58/R) Vesuv's eruption (39x36cm-15x14in) s.i.d.99 W/C
(D.KR 10500)*

FORSBERG, Nils (19/20th C) ?
£596 $1175 (13-Nov-90 AB.S367/R) View from Versailles with balustrade and pond
(30x40cm-12x16in) s.d.1882 panel (S.KR 6500)
£1368 $2367 (22-May-91 BA.S539/R) Playing chess (34x44cm-13x17in) s.d.10 i. panel
(S.KR 14500)

FORSMAN, Erik (1916-1976) Swedish
*£618 $1187 (27-Nov-90 AB.S4018) Happy joke (22x15cm-9x6in) s. gouache W/C
(S.KR 6700)*

FORSMAN, Erik (1916-1976) Swedish-cont.
£849 $1630   *(27-Nov-90 AB.S4019) Father Christmas' helpers coming with presents*
(22x15cm-9x6in) s. gouache W/C (S.KR 9200)
£1384 $2657   *(27-Nov-90 AB.S4015) Preparing for Christmas (43x87cm-17x34in) s.*
gouache W/C (S.KR 15000)
£1430 $2745   *(27-Nov-90 AB.S4016/R) Christmas atmosphere (39x69cm-15x27in) s. gouache*
W/C (S.KR 15500)
£1937 $3720   *(27-Nov-90 AB.S4017) Pixies dancing (36x65cm-14x26in) s. gouache W/C*
(S.KR 21000)

FORSSELL, Victor (1846-1931) Swedish
£2737 $5392   (30-Oct-90 BU.S30) From Palsundet III (27x36cm-11x14in) s. panel
(S.KR 30000)
£3244 $6260   (12-Dec-90 BU.S20/R) Landscape from Torne Trask (34x41cm-13x16in) s.
panel (S.KR 35000)

FORSSLUND, Jonas (attrib) (1754-1809) Swedish
£3745 $6442   *(14-May-91 BU.S11/R) Portrait of Lorents Gorges and Hedvig Elisabeth*
Gorges (70x54cm-28x21in) pastel pair (S.KR 40000)

FORSTER, G (19th C) American
£6932 $13309   (1-Dec-90 PER.M156/R) L'Equipage. La chasse a courre (41x61cm-16x24in)
both s. one d.1863 panel pair (F.FR 68000)

FORSTER, George (19th C) American?
£2211 $4200   (14-Sep-90 S.BM170/R) Still life with grapes, strawberries and apple
(23x30cm-9x12in) s.d.1871
£3179 $5500   (21-May-91 CE.NY385/R) Grapes and peaches. Grapes and plums
(15x18cm-6x7in) pne s.d.1853 panel pair
£6145 $11000   (14-Mar-91 CH.NY21/R) Still life with currants, mouse, lady bug and
grasshopper (25x20cm-10x8in) s.d.1869

FORSTER, Thomas (18th C) British
£1000 $1650   *(11-Jul-91 S30/R) Portrait of gentleman wearing cravat and full bottomed*
wig (11x9cm-4x4in) indis.s. plumbago on vellum oval
£1200 $2304   *(18-Dec-90 C83/R) Portrait of Sir Thomas Pope Blount (11x?cm-4x?in)*
min.s.d.1700 plumbago black wood frame rec.

FORT, Jean Antoine Simeon (1793-1861) French
£427 $854   *(4-Feb-91 PLF.P32) Vue d'une maison a la lisiere d'un bois*
(27x35cm-11x14in) s.d.1832 W/C (F.FR 4200)

FORTE, Luca (18th C) Italian
£36484 $60928   (4-Jun-91 CH.R564/R) Natura morta con uva (84x101cm-33x40in)
(I.L 80000000)

FORTE, Luca (attrib) (18th C) Italian
£20080 $32329   (25-Jun-91 APT.P35/R) Bouquet de fleurs dans un vase (75x58cm-30x23in)
(F.FR 200000)

FORTE, Luca (school) (18th C) Italian
£23196 $45000   (7-Dec-90 S.W2683/R) Still life of fruit and flowers with bird and
butterfly (58x170cm-23x67in)

FORTESCUE, William B (?-1924) British
£550 $919   (4-Jun-91 SWS1674/R) Driving cattle (69x51cm-27x20in) s.
£3200 $6016   (20-Sep-90 CSK118/R) Winter draweth nigh (91x71cm-36x28in) s.s.i.verso
£1200 $2148   *(14-Mar-91 L256/R) Unloading cart before Sloop Inn, St. Ives*
(23x28cm-9x11in) s. W/C

FORTESCUE-BRICKDALE, Eleanor see   BRICKDALE, Eleanor Fortesque

FORTI, Ettore (19th C) Italian
£4906 $8487   (21-May-91 DUR.M28/R) Dias tranquilos en las afueras de Pompeya
(60x101cm-24x40in) (S.P 900000)
£8671 $15000   (22-May-91 D.NY9/R) Flirtatious doves (56x95cm-22x37in) s.

FORTIN, Marc-Aurele (1888-1970) Canadian
£804 $1543   (27-Nov-90 W.T852) Harbour scene (22x34cm-9x13in) s.verso board
(C.D 1800)
£1579 $3095   (20-Nov-90 JOY.T368/R) Village au coucher du soleil (22x37cm-9x15in) s.
panel (C.D 3600)
£8811 $17181   (24-Oct-90 EA.M434/R) Paysage laurentien (66x81cm-26x32in) s.
(C.D 20000)
£9424 $15738   (4-Jun-91 FB.M56/R) Port de Montreal, construction du pont Jacques
Cartier (56x71cm-22x28in) s. board (C.D 18000)
£9948 $16613   (4-Jun-91 FB.M165/R) Montagnes vertes (68x133cm-27x52in) s. board
(C.D 19000)
£10965 $21601   (30-Oct-90 SY.T69/R) Ste Rose, winter, Quebec (44x59cm-17x23in) s. board
(C.D 25000)
£15707 $26230   (4-Jun-91 FB.M58/R) Ombres sur Hochelaga (42x64cm-17x25in) s. board
(C.D 30000)
£1096 $2149   *(21-Nov-90 EA.M641 a) Hochelaga (25x34cm-10x13in) s. W/C (C.D 2500)*
£1223 $2397   *(5-Nov-90 FB.M106) Landscape Ste.Rose (27x19cm-11x7in) s. col.crayon*
(C.D 2800)

FORTIN, Marc-Aurele (1888-1970) Canadian-cont.
£1735 $2932 (17-Apr-91 EA.M505) View of stone Quebecois farmhouse (54x68cm-21x27in)
    s. W/C (C.D 3400)
£3275 $6419 (5-Nov-90 FB.M164/R) Barques sur la Greve, Perce (38x56cm-15x22in) s.
    W/C (C.D 7500)
£3922 $6941 (20-Mar-91 EA.M506/R) View of Quebecois village (65x100cm-26x39in) s.
    W/C (C.D 8000)
£5045 $9737 (12-Dec-90 EA.M639/R) River landscape (51x66cm-20x26in) s. W/C
    (C.D 11250)
£5066 $9879 (24-Oct-90 EA.M506/R) Hochelaga (33x50cm-13x20in) s. W/C (C.D 11500)
£8040 $13910 (22-May-91 EA.M414/R) Ma vieille maison grise (56x71cm-22x28in) s. chl
    W/C wash (C.D 16000)
£8794 $15214 (22-May-91 EA.M450 a/R) Piedmont (71x56cm-28x22in) s. W/C (C.D 17500)
£9091 $15727 (6-May-91 SY.T167/R) Etude a Ste. Rose (55x70cm-22x28in) s.i. W/C crayon
    (C.D 18000)

FORTUNATI, F (?) Italian
£1155 $2230 (11-Dec-90 CH.R89) La morra (30x76cm-12x30in) s. (I.L 2500000)

FORTUNE, Euphemia Charlton (1885-1969) American
£7558 $13000 (15-May-91 SY.NY136/R) Boats in harbour (42x30cm-17x12in) s.
£10256 $20000 (10-Oct-90 B.SF571/R) Sunny morning, St. Tropez (32x41cm-13x16in) panel

FORTUNEY (19/20th C) French
£724 $1187 (21-Jun-91 D.P71/R) Andalouse (40x32cm-16x13in) s. pastel (F.FR 7200)
£915 $1829 (6-Feb-91 LD.P64/R) Scenes symbolistes (63x24cm-25x9in) s. pastel two
    (F.FR 9000)
£1020 $2010 (14-Nov-90 CN.P17/R) Ballerine (47x63cm-19x25in) s.d.1900 pastel
    (F.FR 10000)
£1992 $3386 (2-Jun-91 LT.P29/R) L'elegante au bouquet (52x34cm-20x13in) s. pastel
    (F.FR 20000)

FORTUNY (?) ?
£951 $1826 (18-Dec-90 DUR.M25) En la taberna (29x44cm-11x17in) panel (S.P 175000)
£1365 $2239 (18-Jun-91 FN.S1582/R) Meeting at the ball (50x32cm-20x13in) s. pastel
    (DM 4000)

FORTUNY Y CARBO, Mariano (1838-1874) Spanish
£750 $1230 (18-Jun-91 PH203/R) Gentleman with cane (28x22cm-11x9in) s.d.1869 pen
    ink

FORTUNY Y CARBO, Mariano (attrib) (1838-1874) Spanish
£750 $1470 (14-Feb-91 CSK184) Faust and Margarite (23x30cm-9x12in) board

FORTUNY Y MARSAL, Mariano (19th C) Spanish
£1619 $3140 (4-Dec-90 F.R89) Ritratto di Francesco di Borbone (60x46cm-24x18in)
    s.d.1870 pencil bodycol (I.L 3500000)

FORTUNY, Mariano (19th C) Spanish
£1038 $2003 (11-Dec-90 FER.M58/R) Retrato de senor con sombrero (10x9cm-4x4in)
    plumilla dr (S.P 190000)
£2336 $4182 (13-Mar-91 FER.M106/R) Escena teatral en el pequeno callejon
    (26x11cm-10x4in) s. ink W/C (S.P 425000)
£2702 $5269 (23-Oct-90 DUR.M46) Figuras junto a la puerta (26x19cm-10x7in) W/C
    sketch (S.P 500000)
£4641 $8029 (8-May-91 FER.M122/R) Carnaval en Roma (12x8cm-5x3in) W/C (S.P 850000)
£5463 $10544 (11-Dec-90 FER.M197/R) El trovador (36x25cm-14x10in) s. W/C
    (S.P 1000000)
£6506 $12686 (17-Oct-90 FER.M163/R) Novicia (41x22cm-16x9in) s. W/C (S.P 1200000)

FOSCHI (?) Italian
£8661 $14117 (11-Jun-91 ZZ.F2/R) Paysage de neige (49x66cm-19x26in) (F.FR 86000)

FOSCHI, Francesco (18th C) Italian
£6200 $10106 (2-Jul-91 PH16/R) Rocky river landscape under snow with travellers on
    road (21x30cm-8x12in)

FOSCHI, Francesco (circle) (18th C) Italian
£1700 $3230 (13-Sep-90 CSK370/R) Extensive italianate winter landscape with skaters
    and travellers (53x72cm-21x28in)

FOSCHI, Giambattista (attrib) (17th C) Italian
£6856 $13506 (14-Nov-90 D.V35/R) Bacchus and Ariadne (177x190cm-70x75in) bears sig.
    after Titian (A.S 140000)

FOSELLI, A (19th C) Italian
£700 $1253 (14-Mar-91 B28/R) Both hands hffull (27x35cm-11x14in) s.

FOSIE, Johanna (1726-1764) Danish
£484 $968 (6-Feb-91 RAS.K535/R) Cavalry battle (20x24cm-8x9in) gouache (D.KR 5400)

FOSS, Harald (1843-1922) Danish
£632 $1200 (27-Feb-91 SY.NY315/R) Impending summer storm (40x58cm-16x23in) s.d.1875
£749 $1251 (6-Jun-91 RAS.K45) Afternoon at Kolding fjord, autumn
    (126x189cm-50x74in) s.d.1879 (D.KR 8500)

FOSS, Harald (1843-1922) Danish-cont.
| £880 | $1479 | (23-Apr-91 RAS.K275) Early September morning, Bruunshaab near Viborg (93x153cm-37x60in) s. (D.KR 10000) |
| £1105 | $2133 | (10-Dec-90 BU.K19/R) Lake landscape (58x87cm-23x34in) init.d.1863 (D.KR 12200) |

FOSSE, Jean Baptiste Adolphe la (1810-1879) French
| £5000 | $8200 | (21-Jun-91 C4/R) Portrait of child resting on draped high back chair (31x23cm-12x9in) s.d.1847 panel oval |

FOSSI, Paolo (?) Italian
| £1200 | $2052 | (30-Jul-91 SWS68) Self Portrait of the artist (75x59cm-30x23in) i. after Elizabeth Vigee Lebrun |

FOSSOUX, Claude (1946-) French
£898	$1518	(5-May-91 LT.P51) Sur le banc (46x55cm-18x22in) s. (F.FR 9000)
£990	$1752	(7-Apr-91 LT.P81/R) Le vent (50x61cm-20x24in) s. (F.FR 10000)
£996	$1693	(2-Jun-91 LT.P82/R) Aupres du bouleau blanc (54x73cm-21x29in) s. (F.FR 10000)
£1542	$2991	(8-Dec-90 LT.P94/R) L'apres-midi au jardin (55x60cm-22x24in) s. (F.FR 15000)

FOSTER, Frederick Lucas (1842-1899) Canadian
| £1082 | $1840 | (27-May-91 HO.ED301/R) Qu'Appelle Valley (50x77cm-20x30in) s.d.1893 (C.D 2100) |

FOSTER, Hal (1892-1982) American
| *£1118* | *$1900* | *(1-Jun-91 IH.NY102/R) Prince Valian, adventure strip (86x58cm-34x23in) s. pen ink* |

FOSTER, Herbert Wilson (fl.1881-1917) British
| *£420* | *$685* | *(13-Jun-91 CSK165) Lazy afternoon's fishing on River by abbey ruins (19x27cm-7x11in) s. pencil W/C* |
| *£900* | *$1764* | *(21-Nov-90 B53/R) Village green (38x55cm-15x22in) s.d.1914 W/C* |

FOSTER, John Ernest (1877-?) British
| £5100 | $8772 | (14-May-91 SWS441/R) Azaleas (126x101cm-50x40in) s. i.verso |

FOSTER, Myles Birket (1825-1899) British
£440	*$739*	*(22-Apr-91 PH254) Vesuvius (4x8cm-2x3in) W/C htd white*
£520	*$988*	*(27-Feb-91 MMB169) Cottages near the Downs (5x10cm-2x4in) with bodycol.*
£780	*$1482*	*(12-Sep-90 CSK197/R) Children playing on fallen tree (10x15cm-4x6in) with mono. pencil W/C*
£880	*$1716*	*(17-Oct-90 PHL165/R) A view of Richmond, North Yorkshire (9x14cm-4x6in) mono. col.washes*
£1300	*$2132*	*(19-Jun-91 B65/R) Changing pastures (9x16cm-4x6in) mono. W/C over red chk*
£1400	*$2296*	*(19-Jun-91 B67/R) At cottage door (11x15cm-4x6in) mono. pencil W/C*
£1600	*$2864*	*(13-Mar-91 B144/R) Craigmillar castle (13x24cm-5x9in) mono.i. W/C*
£1900	*$3401*	*(13-Mar-91 B87/R) On the Thames (15x23cm-6x9in) mono. bodycol.*
£2500	*$4875*	*(18-Oct-90 SC3039/R) York Minster from the river (11x15cm-4x6in) mono. W/C*
£3600	*$7056*	*(21-Nov-90 JT201) In a garden in Sorrento (30x20cm-12x8in) mono. W/C*
£3800	*$7296*	*(26-Nov-90 SWS106/R) Cullercoats on Tyne (20x34cm-8x13in) mono. W/C*
£4000	*$7080*	*(18-Mar-91 WHB163/R) Young girls haymaking and taking rest (33x53cm-13x21in) mono. W/C htd white*
£4000	*$7880*	*(12-Nov-90 PH47/R) Feeding the geese (22x31cm-9x12in) mono. W/C htd.bodycol.*
£4600	*$7682*	*(5-Jun-91 S234/R) Harvest in Highlands - left in charge (20x28cm-8x11in) mono. s.i.verso W/C htd bodycol*
£4800	*$9600*	*(8-Feb-91 C33/R) A highland cottage (18x23cm-7x9in) s. pencil W/C htd.white*
£4800	*$8016*	*(5-Jun-91 S316/R) Girl with donkey and young child (16x13cm-6x5in) mono. W/C htd white*
£4800	*$8064*	*(22-Apr-91 PH299/R) In garden at Sorrento (30x21cm-12x8in) mono. W/C bodycol.*
£5000	*$8150*	*(14-Jun-91 C92/R) The young angler (21x28cm-8x11in) mono. pencil W/C htd.bodycol.*
£5400	*$10638*	*(13-Nov-90 SWS114/R) Church of San Barnaba Apostolo, Venice (28x21cm-11x8in) mono. W/C over pencil htd.bodycol.*
£6000	*$11820*	*(12-Nov-90 PH66/R) Feeding the peacocks (24x45cm-9x18in) mono. W/C bodycol.*
£6500	*$12480*	*(26-Nov-90 SWS107/R) The lily pond (17x12cm-7x5in) mono. W/C bodycol*
£7000	*$13230*	*(26-Sep-90 S266/R) Children by well (20x15cm-8x6in) mono. W/C htd bodycol*
£7500	*$12225*	*(4-Jul-91 PHI48/R) Birdnesting (15x22cm-6x9in) mono. W/C htd.bodycol.*
£8000	*$15120*	*(26-Sep-90 S265/R) Woodman by country cottage (21x33cm-8x13in) mono. W/C htd bodycol*
£10000	*$19800*	*(30-Jan-91 S216/R) Cottage in Trossachs (28x38cm-11x15in) s. W/C htd bodycol over pencil*
£11000	*$20790*	*(26-Sep-90 S252/R) Old Shoreham bridge (34x60cm-13x24in) mono.i. W/C htd bodycol*
£12000	*$24000*	*(8-Feb-91 C72/R) The Bridge of Sighs, Venice (30x23cm-12x9in) mono.i. s. verso pencil W/C htd.white*
£12000	*$22680*	*(26-Sep-90 S253/R) Young drover (35x60cm-14x24in) mono. W/C htd bodycol*

FOSTER, Myles Birket (attrib) (1825-1899) British
£840 $1630 (5-Dec-90 PHL83/R) Craigmillar Castle (14x24cm-6x9in) bears.mono.i.
         pencil col. washes

FOSTER, William Gilbert (1855-1906) British
£360 $644 (13-Mar-91 B88) Ducks by a pond (25x36cm-10x14in) s.i.d.1890 W/C

FOTHERGILL, George Algernon (1868-?) British
£300 $585 (15-Jan-91 C121) Cumberland trail hound (51x66cm-20x26in) i.d. pencil
         W/C bodycol

FOUACE, Charles (19th C) French
£2653 $5227 (16-Nov-90 LGB.P197) Les constructeurs (65x81cm-26x32in) s.d.1868
         (F.FR 26000)

FOUACE, Guillaume Romain (1827-1895) French
£1796 $3413 (11-Sep-90 CH.AM76/R) Still life with pumpkin (47x65cm-19x26in) s.
         (D.FL 6000)
£2439 $4780 (6-Nov-90 SY.AM295/R) Still life with peaches in basket
         (53x64cm-21x25in) s.d.1875 (D.FL 8000)
£3425 $6130 (13-Mar-91 N.M488/R) Hunting still life with dead game and vessel on
         table (85x130cm-33x51in) s. (DM 10000)

FOUCHE, Nicolas (attrib) (1653-1733) French
£19095 $31317 (22-Jun-91 CH.MO149/R) L'allegorie de la jeunesse. Allegorie de la
         fortune (63cm-25ins circular) pair (F.FR 190000)

FOUGERON, Andre (1913-) French
£2096 $3542 (29-Apr-91 LGB.P101/R) Nu allonge (65x81cm-26x32in) s.d.1945
         (F.FR 21000)

FOUJITA (1886-1968) French/Japanese
£766 $1493 (10-Oct-90 WO.CO6) Girl with kitten (38x46cm-15x18in) s. W/C (E.P 850)

FOUJITA, Tsuguharu (1886-1968) Japanese
£4000 $7800 (17-Oct-90 S207/R) Portrait de femme (36x24cm-14x9in) s. canvas on board
£15000 $29250 (17-Oct-90 S91/R) Nu assis dans un atelier (28x22cm-11x9in) s.d.1945
£30457 $60000 (15-Nov-90 CH.NY259/R) Grez-sur-Loing (27x35cm-11x14in) s.s.d.1931
£35533 $70000 (15-Nov-90 CH.NY261/R) Le ballon (27x35cm-11x14in) s.s.d.1931
£35533 $70000 (2-Oct-90 CH.NY98/R) Cour de la Delambre, effet de neige
         (27x35cm-11x14in) s. d.1918 verso
£38071 $75000 (15-Nov-90 CH.NY260/R) Enfant devant une maison (27x35cm-11x14in)
         s.s.d.1931
£38793 $67500 (27-Mar-91 B.SF4117/R) Portrait of young girl (32x23cm-13x9in) s.
£40000 $78000 (17-Oct-90 S74/R) Paysage a Cagnes (35x27cm-14x11in) s. s.i.
£41837 $82000 (14-Feb-91 CH.NY56/R) Le bebe (27x19cm-11x7in) s.
£46231 $75819 (20-Jun-91 APT.P31/R) Nature mrote a l'encrier (27x35cm-11x14in)
         s.d.1930 (F.FR 460000)
£63452 $125000 (3-Oct-90 SY.NY167/R) Fillette aux raisins (22x16cm-9x6in) s. s.i.verso
£72254 $125000 (8-May-91 SY.NY234/R) Trompe l'oeil (22x27cm-9x11in) s.d.1956
£73604 $145000 (2-Oct-90 CH.NY196/R) Jumelles (14x10cm-6x4in) s.i.d.1952
£76142 $150000 (2-Oct-90 CH.NY134/R) Tete de femme (26x23cm-10x9in) s.d.1949
£88710 $170323 (2-Dec-90 GAB.G1609/R) Portrait de jeune femme (41x33cm-16x13in)
         s.d.1927 (S.FR 220000)
£89641 $155080 (25-May-91 GL.P26/R) Nature morte a la cuvette (81x65cm-32x26in)
         s.d.1914 (F.FR 900000)
£91371 $180000 (3-Oct-90 SY.NY168/R) Deux soeurs (16x22cm-6x9in) s. s.verso
£101215 $198381 (25-Nov-90 GL.P82/R) Petite fille devant la maison de Foujita
         (18x14cm-7x6in) s.d.XII.60 verso (F.FR 1000000)
£105000 $169050 (26-Jun-91 S148/R) Pieta (81x100cm-32x39in) s.
£110000 $177100 (26-Jun-91 S147/R) A l'ecole (24x19cm-9x7in) s. s.d.1957 verso
£145000 $281300 (5-Dec-90 S174/R) Nature morte (63x46cm-25x18in) s.
£151822 $297571 (25-Nov-90 GL.P45/R) Portrait de fillette (41x33cm-16x13in) s.
         (F.FR 1500000)
£182186 $357085 (25-Nov-90 GL.P77/R) Fillette a la marionnette (35x27cm-14x11in)
         s.d.1950 (F.FR 1800000)
£202429 $396761 (25-Nov-90 L.C61/R) La fille de la concierge (27x22cm-11x9in) s.
         (F.FR 2000000)
£213198 $420000 (15-Nov-90 CH.NY248/R) Jeune fille au chat (73x54cm-29x21in) s.s.d.1923
£222672 $436437 (25-Nov-90 GL.P78/R) Portrait de famille (18x13cm-7x5in) s.d.1954 i.
         verso canvas laid down on panel (F.FR 2200000)
£230000 $446200 (5-Dec-90 S154/R) Deux fillettes a la poupee (46x38cm-18x15in) s.
£468128 $809861 (25-May-91 GL.P28/R) Vierge a l'enfant (41x33cm-16x13in) s. with gold
         sheet (F.FR 4700000)
£583756 $1150000 (14-Nov-90 SY.NY403/R) Enfant egaree (57x44cm-22x17in) s.
£867 $1700 (12-Feb-91 SY.NY17/R) Head of young child (20x13cm-8x5in) s.i.d.1931
         pencil
£956 $1865 (24-Oct-90 GD.B1477/R) Portrait of woman with short hair
         (25x18cm-10x7in) s. pencil chl over litho (S.FR 2400)
£1008 $1935 (2-Dec-90 GAB.G1596/R) Portrait de Yozo (24x17cm-9x7in) s.i.d.1035
         crayon (S.FR 2500)
£2306 $4428 (27-Nov-90 AB.S4021) Buste de jeune femme (15x21cm-6x8in) s.d.1926
         Indian ink (S.KR 25000)
£2388 $4155 (25-Mar-91 QWA.P159/R) Tete de chat (8x9cm-3x4in) s. ink crayon
         (F.FR 24000)

FOUJITA, Tsuguharu (1886-1968) Japanese-cont.

£2543	$4807	(25-Sep-90 FB.P274/R) Petite fille, Kermesse aux etoiles (22x18cm-9x7in) s.i.d. ink (F.FR 25000)
£2569	$4985	(7-Dec-90 GL.P111) Le chat (15x21cm-6x8in) s.bears i.d.1953 Indian ink (F.FR 25000)
£3083	$5982	(7-Dec-90 GL.P115) La boite de jazz (22x15cm-9x6in) s. Indian ink (F.FR 30000)
£3715	$7170	(13-Dec-90 SY.AM70/R) Petite fille a bouteille. Garconnet au livre. Petite fille a casserole (16x12cm-6x5in) s. pen W/C three (D.FL 12000)
£3715	$6872	(6-Mar-91 HC.P66) Le cave de jazz (23x15cm-9x6in) s. Indian ink (F.FR 37000)
£3905	$7577	(7-Dec-90 GL.P122/R) La tour Eiffel (23x15cm-9x6in) s. Indian ink (F.FR 38000)
£4028	$6566	(16-Jun-91 GL.P6/R) Deux profils (46x36cm-18x14in) s.d.1926 ink (F.FR 40000)
£4032	$7863	(26-Oct-90 APT.P9/R) Chat (20x25cm-8x10in) s.i.d.15.6.53 crayon (F.FR 40000)
£4111	$7975	(7-Dec-90 GL.P116) Le chat et la cle (23x15cm-9x6in) s. Indian ink (F.FR 40000)
£4200	$7434	(19-Mar-91 C114/R) Bebe endormi (22x27cm-9x11in) s.d.1926 brush ink
£4310	$7500	(27-Mar-91 B.SF4121/R) When I was young (27x23cm-11x9in) s.i. brush ink
£4728	$9172	(5-Dec-90 HC.P28/R) Nu feminin (61x39cm-24x15in) s. crayon (F.FR 46000)
£5097	$9786	(27-Nov-90 APT.P47/R) Echassier et ses petits (23x13cm-9x5in) s. Indian ink htd.white gouache (F.FR 50000)
£5139	$9969	(7-Dec-90 GL.P112) Amour moqueur (33x33cm-13x13in) s. lead pencil stumping (F.FR 50000)
£7136	$13772	(12-Dec-90 CD.P43/R) Jeune femme en buste de profil (30x24cm-12x9in) s.d.1928 indian ink (F.FR 70000)
£8665	$16636	(28-Nov-90 CSC.P49/R) Jeune femme en buste de trois-quarts (61x57cm-24x22in) crayon (F.FR 85000)
£9174	$17615	(2-Dec-90 M.V61/R) Tete de Christ (44x38cm-17x15in) s.d.66 wash W/C (F.FR 90000)
£9615	$18846	(24-Nov-90 APT.P21/R) Le bebe chinois (26x21cm-10x8in) s.d.1934 W/C (F.FR 95000)
£9645	$19000	(3-Oct-90 SY.NY161/R) Le chats (25x34cm-10x13in) s.s. india ink wash pair
£10070	$16415	(16-Jun-91 GL.P5/R) Portrait d'Olivette (33x26cm-13x10in) s.d.1928 ink stumping (F.FR 100000)
£19462	$37757	(4-Dec-90 BA.S141/R) Girl wearing stripy jersey (64x48cm-25x19in) s.d.1938 W/C (S.KR 210000)
£20000	$38800	(5-Dec-90 PH21/R) Tete de femme (25x21cm-10x8in) s.i.d.1939 pencil W/C
£20408	$40204	(16-Nov-90 FB.P156 a/R) Le lutteur (115x96cm-45x38in) s. crayon stumping (F.FR 200000)
£21912	$42729	(24-Oct-90 GD.B354/R) Reclining female nude with yellow hair (40x50cm-16x20in) s.d.1932 pen gouache (S.FR 55000)
£26012	$45000	(8-May-91 SY.NY237/R) La mere et l'enfant (37x24cm-15x9in) s. W/C paper laid down on board
£29562	$56758	(26-Nov-90 GL.P9/R) Madeleine (40x35cm-16x14in) s.d.1935 W/C (F.FR 290000)
£30242	$58065	(2-Dec-90 GAB.G1599/R) Portrait de jeune femme aux levres peintes (27x24cm-11x9in) s.i.d.1939 Indian ink htd.W/C (S.FR 75000)
£32258	$61935	(2-Dec-90 GAB.G1594/R) Jeune fille a la cape bleue (23x17cm-9x7in) s.d.1951 Indian ink col.chk. (S.FR 80000)
£32995	$65000	(15-Nov-90 CH.NY153/R) Autoportrait au chat (40x31cm-16x12in) s.s.d.1931 pen ink graphite
£35838	$62000	(9-May-91 CH.NY132/R) Roses (31x24cm-12x9in) s. d.1922 verso W/C ink gold leaf
£38071	$75000	(15-Nov-90 CH.NY141/R) Deux femmes nues (48x37cm-19x15in) s.s.i.d.1928 pen ink graphite htd.paper on mat
£38071	$75000	(14-Nov-90 SY.NY198/R) Young girl with Mexican doll (30x21cm-12x8in) s.d.1949 W/C pen wash paper on board
£40000	$78000	(17-Oct-90 S82/R) Portrait de femme (42x33cm-17x13in) s. s.d.1932 pen ink W/C paper on card
£40486	$79352	(25-Nov-90 GL.P56/R) L'Annonciation (85x99cm-33x39in) s.d.1927 lead pencil stumping parchment (F.FR 400000)
£54435	$104516	(2-Dec-90 GAB.G1598/R) Nu (53x85cm-21x33in) s.d.1927 lead pencil (S.FR 135000)
£81218	$160000	(15-Nov-90 CH.NY147/R) Mere et enfant (23x17cm-9x7in) s.i. W/C pen ink gold leaf paper on board
£82000	$159080	(5-Dec-90 S352/R) Vierge et L'Enfant (30x21cm-12x8in) s.d.59 pen gouache W/C gold-leaf

FOULD, Consuelo (1862-1927) French

£7368	$14000	(28-Feb-91 CH.NY41/R) Un passage risque (185x105cm-73x41in) s.

FOUQUERAY, Charles (1872-1956) French

£969	$1910	(13-Nov-90 ARC.P101/R) Scene de rue, Jerusalem (48x63cm-19x25in) s.d.1919 chl.gouache (F.FR 9500)

FOUQUES, Robert Henry (1892-?) French

£1150	$1944	(30-Apr-91 AG290/R) La Pointe de Treboul - Finistere (112x143cm-44x56in) s.d.1939

FOUQUET, Jean (style) (18th C) French

£952	$1600	(17-Jul-91 SY.NY115/R) Portrait of a young man in a red cap (46x33cm-18x13in) panel

FOUQUET, Louis Vincent (1803-1869) French
£1837 $3618   (15-Oct-90 ARC.P71/R) Couple surpris par l'orage (69x51cm-27x20in) panel
                    (F.FR 18000)

FOUQUIER, Jacques (1580-1659) French
£25100 $40412   (25-Jun-91 APT.P17/R) L'ete ou les moissons (49x75cm-19x30in) i. verso
                    panel (F.FR 250000)

FOUR, Victor (20th C) ?
£2102 $3637   (23-May-91 SY.AM348/R) I am grateful for this opportunity to enter in to
                    your breakfast hour (146x55cm-57x22in) s.d.1966 panel (D.FL 7000)

FOURIE, Albert Auguste (1854-?) French
£1908 $3300   (8-May-91 RO.BA7) Les brumes du soir (61x81cm-24x32in) s.
£612   *$1180*   *(12-Dec-90 ZZ.F47/R) Jeunes baigneuses dans un parc (23x31cm-9x12in) s.*
                    pastel (F.FR 6000)

FOURMOIS, Theodore (1814-1871) Belgian
£502 $808   (24-Jun-91 PR.P125/R) Paysans sur la route (21x32cm-8x13in) s. panel
                    (F.FR 5000)

FOURNIER (?) ?
£1500 $2940   (14-Feb-91 CSK167/R) The kitchen maid (74x99cm-29x39in) s.

FOURNIER, Alexis Jean (1865-1948) American
£1479 $2500   (20-Apr-91 WOL.C157/R) Clearing after rain (41x51cm-16x20in) s.d.1911
                    canvas on panel
£3704 $7000   (27-Sep-90 CH.NY84/R) Niagara Falls by moonlight (71x97cm-28x38in)
                    s.85/R

FOURNIER, Alfred Victor (19/20th C) French
£9425 $18568   (14-Nov-90 RAS.K185/R) Summer's day by the sea (55x64cm-22x25in) s.
                    (D.KR 105000)

FOURNIER, Charles (1803-1854) French
£4970 $8400   (18-Apr-91 APT.P155/R) Portrait de la comtesse de Solancy et de son fils
                    (117x89cm-46x35in) s. (F.FR 50000)

FOURNIER, Jean Baptiste Fortune de (1798-1864) French
£4111   *$7975*   *(8-Dec-90 SY.MO399/R) Vue interieure de la Tribune de Florence, Salle*
                    des Medicis (46x59cm-18x23in) W/C (F.FR 40000)

FOURNIER, Victor (1872-1924) French
£806 $1573   (14-Jan-91 YC.P186/R) Marche Breton (50x61cm-20x24in) s.d.1921
                    (F.FR 8000)

FOUS, Jean (1901-1971) French
£504 $821   (14-Jun-91 FB.P56) La Bastille (38x45cm-15x18in) s. board (F.FR 5000)
£600 $1062   (20-Mar-91 DL.P133/R) Mariage (49x64cm-19x25in) s. (F.FR 6000)
£765 $1508   (18-Nov-90 S.S48/R) Retour de chasse (27x35cm-11x14in) s. (F.FR 7500)

FOWERAKER, A Moulton (1873-1942) British
£450   *$797*   *(22-Mar-91 T249) Moonlight, Constantine Bay, Cornwall (23x28cm-9x11in)*
                    s.
£450   *$761*   *(3-May-91 T220/R) Strete Church, Dartmouth (23x28cm-9x11in) s. W/C*
£600   *$1176*   *(23-Jan-91 B122) Shepherd and sheep in downland landscape*
                    (23x28cm-9x11in) s. W/C
£650   *$1151*   *(22-Mar-91 T174) Moonlit street scene with figures (20x25cm-8x10in) s.*
£660   *$1109*   *(18-Jul-91 PHX390/R) Cottages at Newton St.Cyres, Nr.Exeter*
                    (36x53cm-14x21in) s.i.label verso W/C
£680   *$1136*   *(22-Jul-91 SWS828/R) The convent (21x26cm-8x10in) s. i. verso*
£700   *$1183*   *(3-May-91 T241) French landscape (36x46cm-14x18in) s. W/C*
£750   *$1470*   *(21-Nov-90 B57/R) Figures in Spanish square (23x28cm-9x11in) s. W/C*
£750   *$1298*   *(20-May-91 PH183) Antequera, Spain - middle of day (35x53cm-14x21in) s.*
                    i.verso W/C
£780   *$1537*   *(13-Nov-90 SWS99) Mill pond, Old Swanage (23x28cm-9x11in) s.*
£780   *$1482*   *(10-Sep-90 PH98/R) Moonlight - Algeciras (23x27cm-9x11in) s. i.verso W/C*
£800   *$1376*   *(14-May-91 SWS74/R) Spanish village at night (52x35cm-20x14in) s. W/C*
£800   *$1600*   *(8-Feb-91 T228) Figure with lantern in street, bay beyond*
                    (20x28cm-8x11in) s. W/C
£850   *$1675*   *(1-Nov-90 C143/R) Valley near Cordes, Tarn, France (36x51cm-14x20in) s.*
                    i.verso pencil W/C htd.white
£850   *$1675*   *(13-Nov-90 SWS100/R) Evening, Godlingston Farm, Swanage (24x34cm-9x13in)*
                    s.i.
£850   *$1607*   *(26-Sep-90 S233) Mediterranean fishing village (25x35cm-10x14in) s. W/C*
£900   *$1773*   *(13-Nov-90 SWS101/R) A Spanish hillside town (25x35cm-10x14in) s.*
£1000   *$1980*   *(30-Jan-91 S209) St Ives, Cornwall. In Cork woods, Almoraima*
                    (25x35cm-10x14in) s. one i.verso W/C htd white pair
£1050   *$2069*   *(5-Oct-90 T155) Moonlit courtyard with figures (51x36cm-20x14in) s. W/C*
£1400   *$2772*   *(30-Jan-91 S208/R) Blown with wind (33x43cm-13x17in) s. W/C*

FOWLER, Daniel (1810-1894) British?
£568   *$925*   *(10-Jun-91 W.T1028/R) European town square (47x30cm-19x12in) s.d.1809*
                    W/C (C.D 1050)
£595   *$969*   *(10-Jun-91 W.T1035) Street scene with crucifix (32x48cm-13x19in)*
                    s.d.1883 W/C (C.D 1100)

FOWLER, Robert (1853-?) British
£1100	$2112	(16-Aug-90 SC4070/R) Dreamland (51x36cm-20x14in) s. s.i.label frame
£1250	$2150	(14-May-91 SWS238/R) Pale light on the coast (59x120cm-23x47in) s.
£2500	$4900	(20-Nov-90 PH141/R) Nymphs bathing (166x228cm-65x90in) s.
£3179	$5500	(21-May-91 CE.NY303/R) Classical lady by shore (71x93cm-28x37in) s.

FOWLER, Robert (attrib) (1853-?) British
| £5000 | $8350 | (5-Jun-91 S176/R) Diana (152x85cm-60x33in) |

FOWLER, William II (fl.1825-1867) British
| £1300 | $2301 | (21-Mar-91 CSK104/R) An extensive lakeland landscape of Windermere with figures and cattle (46x61cm-18x24in) s.d.1845 I. verso |
| £1700 | $3009 | (21-Mar-91 CSK107) An extensive lakeland landscape of Derwentwater with cattle and a bridge (46x61cm-18x24in) s.d.1845 I. verso |

FOWLES, Arthur W (c.1815-1878) British
| £6500 | $11245 | (22-May-91 S50/R) Esmeralda, schooner yacht, strong breeze Alderney Roads, off Cap Hague. Esmerelda, schooner yacht (30x46cm-12x18in) s.i.d.1861 pair |
| £8000 | $13840 | (22-May-91 S3/R) Royal yacht Victoria and Albert II passing Royal yacht squadron, Cowes (76x137cm-30x54in) s.i.d.1867 |

FOWLES, Arthur W (attrib) (c.1815-1878) British
| £751 | $1300 | (12-May-91 H.C74/R) Shipwreck scenes (25x38cm-10x15in) pair |

FOWLES, Joseph (19th C) Australian
| £1158 | $2282 | (13-Nov-90 J.M748) The storm (28x36cm-11x14in) s. (A.D 3000) |

FOX, B (?) ?
| £620 | $1073 | (20-May-91 SWS317/R) Old hunters, the property of the Rev. J R Holden (61x74cm-24x29in) s.i. |

FOX, Charles James (1860-?) British
£1000	$1960	(13-Feb-91 S149/R) Williton in Somerset (41x51cm-16x20in)
£1047	$1749	(4-Jun-91 FB.M99) Portrait of a literary figure (12x86cm-5x34in) after Sir Joshua Reynolds (C.D 2000)
£2000	$3780	(26-Sep-90 S312/R) Winding river (79x125cm-31x49in) s.

FOX, E P (1865-1915) Australian
| £708 | $1153 | (1-Jul-91 AAA.S90 j) Vue de Mentone (19x26cm-7x10in) s. panel (A.D 1500) |

FOX, Edwin M (19th C) British
| £2607 | $4250 | (5-Jul-91 S.W3022/R) Gipsy King - Greyhound (30x36cm-12x14in) s.i.d.1855 board |

FOX, Emanuel Phillips (1865-1915) Australian
£2941	$4971	(15-Apr-91 AAA.S189) Garden scene (31x18cm-12x7in) s. (A.D 6500)
£4072	$6882	(16-Apr-91 J.M42/R) A brilliant morning (36x43cm-14x17in) s. (A.D 9000)
£6962	$13367	(14-Aug-90 SY.ME302/R) Cliff and sea (36x43cm-14x17in) s. i. verso (A.D 16500)
£12236	$23494	(14-Aug-90 SY.ME200/R) Lady with rhodendrons (49x39cm-19x15in) s. verso (A.D 29000)

FOX, Ethel Carrick (1876-1952) Australian
£543	$918	(16-Apr-91 J.M838) La Madelaine (58x49cm-23x19in) (A.D 1200)
£800	$1560	(15-Oct-90 AAA.S96 j) Floral still life (30x23cm-12x9in) s. (A.D 2000)
£1131	$1912	(16-Apr-91 J.M35/R) Still life (49x39cm-19x15in) s. canvas on board (A.D 2500)
£1964	$3418	(26-Mar-91 JRL.S157/R) Castor oil trees, Brisbane (26x35cm-10x14in) s. (A.D 4400)
£2390	$4709	(31-Oct-90 CH.S127/R) Lourdes (16x22cm-6x9in) s. board (A.D 6000)
£3057	$5472	(9-Apr-91 CH.ME252) Beach scene (23x27cm-9x11in) s. board c.1908 (A.D 7000)
£3275	$5862	(9-Apr-91 CH.ME274/R) Family outing, Chinamans Beach (42x58cm-17x23in) s. canvas on board (A.D 7500)
£4054	$7986	(13-Nov-90 J.M140/R) Summer at Brittany (15x22cm-6x9in) s. board (A.D 10500)

FOX, George (19th C) British
| £1216 | $1982 | (10-Jun-91 W.T1316/R) Huntsman at the tailor's shop (53x42cm-21x17in) s. canvas laid down (C.D 2250) |

FOX, H C (1860-?) British
| *£580* | *$951* | *(19-Jun-91 AH215/R) Cows in winter landscape (36x53cm-14x21in) W/C* |

FOX, Henry Charles (1860-?) British
£851	$1600	(18-Sep-90 RO.BA191) Shepherd with his flock (75x55cm-30x22in) s.d.1912 tempera
£851	$1600	(18-Sep-90 RO.BA192) People beside river (75x55cm-30x22in) s.d.1912 tempera
£440	*$757*	*(15-May-91 BT73/R) Cattle watering (33x51cm-13x20in) s.d.1909 W/C htd.bodycol.*
£450	*$734*	*(13-Jun-91 CSK27/R) Huntsman and hounds heading for home (27x37cm-11x15in) s.d.1927 pencil W/C htd white*

FOX, Henry Charles (1860-?) British-cont.

£470	$766	(2-Jul-91 SWS512/R) Cattle grazing above valley (41x60cm-16x24in) s.d.1902 W/C bodycol
£500	$835	(22-Jul-91 SWS813/R) To the harvest field (36x51cm-14x20in) s.d.1907 W/C gouache
£500	$845	(19-Apr-91 K505/R) Figure herding sheep in country lane with hayrick and shed (38x28cm-15x11in) s. W/C
£500	$840	(18-Jul-91 PHX235/R) Romany family watering the horses (36x53cm-14x21in) s.d.1904 W/C
£510	$831	(14-Jun-91 K464) Cattle on lane, Ringmere, Sussex (36x53cm-14x21in) s.d.1922 W/C
£530	$864	(14-Jun-91 T206) River landscape with boats (36x53cm-14x21in) s.d.1900 W/C
£540	$880	(2-Jul-91 SWS586) Figure and two horses on country road (37x55cm-15x22in) s.d.1918 W/C htd gouache
£548	$1080	(30-Oct-90 MA.V583) Village landscape with sheep (36x30cm-14x12in) s. W/C (C.D 1250)
£550	$1040	(26-Sep-90 B64/R) Silver birch by pond, cows under tree (56x38cm-22x15in) s.d.1908 W/C htd white
£570	$1123	(30-Oct-90 MA.V585) Country lane with rider (36x28cm-14x11in) s. W/C (C.D 1300)
£570	$1123	(30-Oct-90 MA.V584) Cattle grazing by river (28x36cm-11x14in) s. W/C (C.D 1300)
£570	$1123	(30-Oct-90 MA.V586) Farm lane with horses (25x36cm-10x14in) s. W/C (C.D 1300)
£620	$1197	(10-Dec-90 PHB32) The farm pool (36x54cm-14x21in) s.d.1905
£620	$1153	(5-Sep-90 MMB186) Shepherd and flock on a wooded lane (51x33cm-20x13in) s.d.1926 bodycol.
£650	$1164	(11-Apr-91 GSP481) Bringing home the flock (25x36cm-10x14in) s.d.1924 W/C
£680	$1340	(1-Nov-90 C90/R) Figure in barge on river with cottage and hills beyond (41x56cm-16x22in) s.d.1899 W/C htd.white
£700	$1211	(20-May-91 PH11) Pulborough (53x73cm-21x29in) s.d. W/C bodycol
£720	$1210	(22-Apr-91 PH284) River landscape (37x54cm-15x21in) s.d.93 W/C
£740	$1458	(13-Nov-90 SWS22/R) Watering horses at Bosham, near Chichester (51x74cm-20x29in) s.d.1902 W/C gouache
£750	$1418	(26-Sep-90 B72/R) Pond at Tolworth farm, Surrey (52x73cm-20x29in) s.d.1903 W/C
£750	$1478	(1-Nov-90 C88/R) Cottage beside river with ducks near Cookham-on-Thames (36x53cm-14x21in) s. W/C htd.white
£750	$1343	(14-Mar-91 ZZ.B104) The end of the day (36x54cm-14x21in) s.d.1923 W/C bodycol.
£800	$1584	(30-Jan-91 S252/R) Homeward bound (25x35cm-10x14in) s.d.1900 W/C
£850	$1615	(27-Feb-91 MMB163) Extensive wooded landscape with cattle on path by a river and barge (33x51cm-13x20in) s.d.1903 htd.white
£850	$1522	(11-Apr-91 GSP444) Cattle at pond, farm buildings and distant church (33x51cm-13x20in) sd.1925 W/C
£850	$1598	(20-Sep-90 M14) Hemingford Grey on the Ouse (51x74cm-20x29in) W/C
£860	$1668	(24-Aug-90 CBB215) Watering the horse (56x36cm-22x14in) s.d.1906 W/C
£900	$1755	(24-Oct-90 DR80/R) Near Dedham (57x38cm-22x15in) s.d.1915 i.verso W/C
£900	$1611	(11-Apr-91 GSP445) The Thames at Windsor with figures and horses (36x53cm-14x21in) s.d.1919 W/C
£900	$1773	(5-Oct-90 T295) The ford (38x53cm-15x21in) s.d.1922 W/C
£920	$1840	(8-Feb-91 T180/R) Cattle in country lane (33x53cm-13x21in) s.d.1919 W/C
£1150	$2162	(20-Sep-90 M2) Returning to the farm (51x74cm-20x29in) s. W/C
£1150	$1886	(19-Jun-91 B128/R) Bringing in hay (37x55cm-15x22in) s.d.1910 W/C pair
£1250	$2500	(8-Feb-91 K326) Drover and cattle in wooded landscapes, returning home (38x25cm-15x10in) s.d.1922 W/C pair
£1450	$2755	(25-Feb-91 PH88/R) On Thames, near Wargrave (52x75cm-20x30in) s.d.1904 W/C
£1900	$3743	(13-Nov-90 SWS61/R) Cattle grazing beside a river. Returning home (48x74cm-19x29in) both s.d.1920 W/C gouache pair
£2400	$4800	(8-Feb-91 C24/R) Horses and a cart in a lande beside a farm and cattle watering (36x53cm-14x21in) s.d.1911 W/C htd.white

FOX, John R (1927-) Canadian

£961	$1883	(5-Nov-90 FB.M187) Still life with books and flower vase (61x51cm-24x20in) s. (C.D 2200)

FOX, R Atkinson (19th C) Canadian

£1163	$2000	(15-May-91 SY.NY58/R) Rushing stream in mountains (71x91cm-28x36in) s.

FOX, T M (fl.1843-1846) British

£300	$531	(20-Mar-91 C91) Portrait of lady wearing pink dress and pink bonnet (8x?cm-3x?in) min.s.d.1846 oval gilt metal rec.frame

FRACANZANO, Francesco (style) (17th C) Italian

£1800	$3510	(25-Oct-90 CSK96/R) Saint Joseph with Christ Child (69x86cm-27x34in) i.verso

FRADGLEY, Ellen (fl.1923-1940) British

£500	$990	(30-Jan-91 S274/R) Rose arbour and old well, Venice (39x26cm-15x10in) mono. W/C

FRAGIACOMO, Pietro (1856-1922) Italian
£632 $1075   (27-May-91 GK.Z5151) Harbour landscape, evening (16x26cm-6x10in) s. (S.FR 1600)
£1386 $2676   (11-Dec-90 CH.R147) Barcaiolo in laguna (10x17cm-4x7in) s. cardboard (I.L 3000000)
£2052 $3427   (6-Jun-91 F.M218) Marina (16x22cm-6x9in) s. i.d.1913verso board (I.L 4500000)
£2428 $4200   (22-May-91 D.NY39/R) Boating in lagoon (23x49cm-9x19in) s. panel
£12069 $21000   (27-Mar-91 B.SF4070) Boys fishing on the banks of the Venetian Lagoon (25x45cm-10x18in) s. panel
£13000 $21320   (19-Jun-91 S384/R) Boats on Venetian lagoon (36x65cm-14x26in) s.
£25416 $49053   (11-Dec-90 CH.R212/R) Venezia povera (35x55cm-14x22in) s.c.1885 (I.L 55000000)
£34000 $66000   (18-Oct-90 F.M47/R) Veduta di Venezia dalla Laguna (37x60cm-15x24in) s. (I.L 75000000)

FRAGIACOMO, Pietro (attrib) (1856-1922) Italian
£1360 $2298   (16-Apr-91 CH.R67) Laguna veneta (12x20cm-5x8in) s. board (I.L 3000000)

FRAGIACOMO, Pietro (circle) (1856-1922) Italian
£3928 $7581   (11-Dec-90 CH.R226) Dopo la pesca (17x28cm-7x11in) i. canvas on panel (I.L 8500000)

FRAGONARD (circle) (18/19th C) French
£2243 $4306   (30-Nov-90 APT.P137/R) Nativite (40x32cm-16x13in) (F.FR 22000)

FRAGONARD (school) (18/19th C) French
£814 $1400   (15-May-91 D.NY16/R) Profile of wood nymph (53x43cm-21x17in) pastel oval

FRAGONARD, Alexandre Evariste (attrib) (1780-1850) French
£3279 $6426   (11-Nov-90 I.N25/R) Marie-Therese presentant son fils aux hongrois (76x97cm-30x38in) (F.FR 32000)

FRAGONARD, Jean Honore (1732-1806) French
£18079 $32000   (22-Mar-91 CH.NY660/R) Spring - Two cupids (16x22cm-6x9in)
£30832 $59815   (7-Dec-90 CH.MO342/R) La recompense (26x34cm-10x13in) paper pasted on panel (F.FR 300000)
£50000 $85000   (31-May-91 CH.NY36/R) The performance (29x39cm-11x15in) board
£118191 $229291   (7-Dec-90 SY.MO49/R) Paysage au champ de ble et au charriot attele dit les moissonneurs au repos (55x65cm-22x26in) (F.FR 1150000)
£1316 $2500   (8-Jan-91 SY.NY10/R) Study of a girl on a donkey (16x24cm-6x9in) red chk.
£3800 $6194   (2-Jul-91 C162/R) Angel appearing to Saint Jerome (29x20cm-11x8in) i. black chk after Johann Liss
£10000 $19000   (9-Jan-91 CH.NY63/R) Departure of flock (12x19cm-5x7in) black chk wash
£18079 $32000   (22-Mar-91 CH.NY618/R) The card trick (22x31cm-9x12in) i. blk.chk.wash
£25126 $41206   (18-Jun-91 APT.P72/R) Le temple dans le parc (32x37cm-13x15in) sanguinne (F.FR 250000)
£50000 $96500   (11-Dec-90 C89/R) The interior of a Roman building (47x37cm-19x15in) s.d.1759 red chk.
£50251 $82412   (21-Jun-91 SY.MO13/R) Portrait de jeune fille assise (35x23cm-14x9in) bears artist st. sanguinne (F.FR 500000)
£326198 $629562   (12-Dec-90 ARC.P60/R) Renaud dans les jardins d'Armide (35x46cm-14x18in) pierre noire wash (F.FR 3200000)

FRAGONARD, Jean Honore (after) (1732-1806) French
£2260 $4000   (22-Mar-91 CH.NY631) The Fountain of Pomona at the Villa d'Este, Tivoli (48x36cm-19x14in) red chk.

FRAGONARD, Jean Honore (attrib) (1732-1806) French
£3568 $6850   (30-Nov-90 APT.P138/R) Le feu aux poudres (15x21cm-6x8in) canvas on board (F.FR 35000)
£8543 $14010   (22-Jun-91 CH.MO145/R) Sapho inspiree par l'amour (55x45cm-22x18in) with studio (F.FR 85000)

FRAGONARD, Jean Honore (circle) (1732-1806) French
£2051 $4000   (11-Oct-90 SY.NY148/R) The amorous courtesan (31x39cm-12x15in)
£8040 $13186   (21-Jun-91 SY.MO297/R) Sainte Famille (59x76cm-23x30in) (F.FR 80000)
£890 $1593   (10-Apr-91 CB.P8) Paysage anime (16x20cm-6x8in) gouache oval (F.FR 9000)

FRAGONARD, Jean Honore (school) (1732-1806) French
£1497 $2500   (23-Jan-91 D.NY72) Young goatherd coming in from field (89x127cm-35x50in)

FRAGONARD, Theophile Evariste (1806-1876) French
£1600 $2832   (22-Mar-91 APT.P50/R) L'amoureuse decue (24x18cm-9x7in) s.d.1849 W/C traces blk.crayon (F.FR 16000)

FRAILE, Alfonso (1930-) Spanish
£4348 $8348   (19-Dec-90 ANS.M82/R) Sobre gris (90x80cm-35x31in) s.d.1966 (S.P 800000)
£10926 $21087   (13-Dec-90 EP.M16/R) Agrupacion autorizada (120x110cm-47x43in) s.d.1976 s.d.verso (S.P 2000000)
£1374 $2543   (5-Mar-91 ANS.M378/R) Paisaje con toro (44x53cm-17x21in) s. gouache (S.P 250000)

FRAMA (20th C) ?
£4082 $8041   *(14-Nov-90 CN.P43/R) Hommage a Arthur Rimbaud (62x48cm-24x19in) s.d.89*
                   ink htd.col.crayons (F.FR 40000)
£11202 $22067   *(31-Oct-90 ZZ.F129/R) Hommage (47x61cm-19x24in) s.d.1989 col.crayons*
                   (F.FR 110000)
£11593 $22606   *(28-Oct-90 R.P48 b) Sans titre (61x47cm-24x19in) s. drawing htd.cols*
                   (F.FR 115000)

FRAME, Robert Aaron (1924-) American
£774 $1300   (24-Apr-91 B.SF4568/R) Window at Newport (122x152cm-48x60in) s.

FRAN-BARO (1926-) French
£2008 $3715   (10-Mar-91 LT.P140/R) Notre-Dame, la Seine (24x33cm-9x13in) s. panel
                  (F.FR 20000)

FRANCAIS, Anne (1909-) French
£958 $1867   (28-Oct-90 M.V128) Un soir tres vert sur la Seine (50x66cm-20x26in) s.
                  (F.FR 9500)
£1008 $1966   (28-Oct-90 M.V129/R) Cannes, clarte du printemps (50x61cm-20x24in) s.
                  (F.FR 10000)
£1417 $2777   (25-Nov-90 ZZ.F61/R) Cannes, les palmiers du Grand Hotel
                  (50x61cm-20x24in) s. (F.FR 14000)

FRANCAIS, Francois Louis (1814-1897) French
£804 $1319   (19-Jun-91 JM.P145/R) Crepuscule,Auvers (29x39cm-11x15in) s.d.1855 panel
                  (F.FR 8000)
£2039 $3914   (1-Dec-90 PER.M153/R) Le torrent (71x48cm-28x19in) s.d.1866 (F.FR 20000)

FRANCES, Esteban (20th C) Spanish/American
£2132   *$4200   (13-Nov-90 CE.NY160/R) Composicion surrealista (47x63cm-19x25in)*
                   s.d.1944 pen ink gouache

FRANCES, Juana (1926-) Spanish
£522   *$935   (13-Mar-91 FER.M146/R) Abstracto en negro y amarillo (50x66cm-20x26in)*
                   s. gouache (S.P 95000)

FRANCES, P (19th C) ?
£4055 $7259   *(12-Apr-91 JM.P48/R) La farandole (90x125cm-35x49in) s.d.1878*
                  (F.FR 41000)

FRANCESCHI, Mariano de (1849-1896) Italian
£600   *$1032   (14-May-91 SWS8/R) Outside the city walls (35x50cm-14x20in) s.i. W/C*
£720   *$1411   (22-Jan-91 SWS1233) Figures by the ruins of the forum of Nerva*
                   (73x51cm-29x20in) s.i.
£950   *$1644   (9-May-91 CSK35/R) Peasant woman with donkeys under Arch of Titus*
                   (62x47cm-24x19in) s.i. pencil W/C htd white gum arabic

FRANCESCHINI (attrib) (17/18th C) Italian
£5473 $9139   (4-Jun-91 CH.R326/R) Maddalena in paesaggio con putti
                  (162x122cm-64x48in) (I.L 12000000)

FRANCESCHINI, Baldassare (1611-1689) Italian
£6820 $11798   (23-May-91 F.M517/R) S. Michele Arcangelo (72x55cm-28x22in)
                  (I.L 15000000)
£1000   *$1930   (12-Dec-90 PH52/R) Studies of two arms and hand (19x25cm-7x10in) red chk*
£1182   *$2010   (31-May-91 GB.B5144) Study of bearded man holding book (27x38cm-11x15in)*
                   ochre (DM 3500)

FRANCESCHINI, Baldassare (attrib) (1611-1689) Italian
£1305   *$2518   (14-Dec-90 LEB.P105) La vision de Saint-Ignace de Loyola*
                   (33x25cm-13x10in) sanguinne (F.FR 12800)

FRANCESCHINI, Marco Antonio (1648-1729) Italian
£24000 $41520   (24-May-91 C61/R) The Rape of Europa (116x152cm-46x60in)
£64706 $110000 (30-May-91 SY.NY36/R) Drunkeness of Pan (113x147cm-44x58in)

FRANCESCHINI, Marco Antonio (studio) (1648-1729) Italian
£6000 $10380   (20-May-91 SWS78 J/R) The penitent Magdalen in a landscape surrounded by
                  angels (121x162cm-48x64in)

FRANCESCO DI SIMONE DA SANTA CROCE (attrib) (14th C) Italian
£698 $1200   (15-May-91 D.NY37) The cup found in Benjamin's sack (94x119cm-37x47in)

FRANCESE, Franco (1920-) Italian
£2521 $4135   *(19-Jun-91 F.M213/R) Studio per cinemascope (64x53cm-25x21in) s.d.1958*
                  s.i.d.verso (I.L 5500000)
£917 $1504   *(19-Jun-91 F.M209/R) Nudo di donna (70x50cm-28x20in) s.d.1955 chl*
                  (I.L 2000000)
£1467 $2406   *(19-Jun-91 F.M208/R) Interno con figure (39x49cm-15x19in) s.d.1955 mixed*
                  media cardboard (I.L 3200000)

FRANCHI, Francesco (18th C) Italian
£2194   *$4322   (14-Nov-90 F.M26/R) Trompe l'oeil con incisioni raffiguranti antichita*
                   classiche (37x53cm-15x21in) s.i.d.1778 W/C (I.L 4800000)

FRANCHOYS, Lucas (style) (16/17th C) Flemish
£2500 $4225   (18-Apr-91 CSK124/R) Portrait of lady, in dress with lace collar
(63x52cm-25x20in) i.

FRANCIA, Alexandre T (1820-1884) French
£3125 $6094   (25-Oct-90 D.V16/R) Marine (37x56cm-15x22in) s. (A.S 65000)
£1500   *$2940*   *(8-Nov-90 TL46/R) The Embarkation (53x94cm-21x37in) s. W/C*
£1950   *$3198*   *(19-Jun-91 S149/R) View of Santa Maria della Salute, Venice*
(52x93cm-20x37in) s. W/C over pencil
£1970   *$3880*   *(30-Oct-90 CH.AM440/R) Ballachulish sur la Cote d'Ecosse*
(43x70cm-17x28in) s. i.verso pencil W/C bodycol (D.FL 6500)

FRANCIA, Francesco (attrib) (17/18th C) Italian
£4392 $7466   (31-May-91 GB.B5145/R) Study of male nudes (14x19cm-6x7in) indian ink
brush over chk (DM 13000)

FRANCIA, Francesco (style) (17/18th C) Italian
£2000 $3260   (2-Jul-91 PH305/R) Virgin and Child with St John the Evangelist and St
Dominic (73x56cm-29x22in) panel

FRANCIA, Francesco di Marco (attrib) (1450-1517) Italian
£11765 $20000   (31-May-91 CH.NY1/R) Madonna and Child in landscape (81x66cm-32x26in)
panel

FRANCIA, Francois Louis Thomas (1772-1839) French
£4663 $8020   (19-May-91 ZZ.F38/R) Bateau a la sortie du port (37x56cm-15x22in) s.
(F.FR 47000)

FRANCIA, Giacomo (1486-1557) Italian
£17804 $31869   (9-Apr-91 APT.P3/R) La Vierge a l'Enfant avec Saint Catherine
(57x49cm-22x19in) panel (F.FR 180000)

FRANCIA, Giacomo (attrib) (1486-1557) Italian
£4556 $7746   (30-May-91 F.M13/R) San Francesco (54x39cm-21x15in) panel
(I.L 10000000)

FRANCIABIGIO (1482-1525) Italian
£9500   *$15485*   *(2-Jul-91 C73/R) Head of man in profile to left, wearing hat*
(10x7cm-4x3in) red chk

FRANCINI, Mauro (1924-) Italian
£1531 $3000   (20-Nov-90 CH.NY178/R) Pesce rosso (43x53cm-17x21in) s.d.52 s.i.d.1952
verso board
£1633 $3200   (20-Nov-90 CH.NY179/R) Pesce bianco (54x67cm-21x26in) s.d.53 s.i.d.1953
verso board

FRANCIS, Dorothea (?) ?
£724 $1224   (16-Apr-91 J.M682) Ballet dancers (44x34cm-17x13in) init. (A.D 1600)

FRANCIS, Ivor Pengelly (1906-) Australian
£837 $1407   (22-Apr-91 SY.ME101) Balanced king size (76x60cm-30x24in) s.d.66
s.i.verso canvas on board (A.D 1800)

FRANCIS, John F (1808-1886) American
£5491 $9500   (22-May-91 CH.NY153/R) Still life with apples and chestnuts
(28x36cm-11x14in) board

FRANCIS, Sam (1923-) American
£7101 $12000   (1-May-91 SY.NY233/R) Untitled (48x35cm-19x14in) acrylic paper
£8163 $16000   (6-Nov-90 CE.NY73/R) Untitled (22x10cm-9x4in) s. verso acrylic paper
£8876 $15000   (1-May-91 SY.NY237/R) Untitled (48x35cm-19x14in) acrylic paper
£9174 $17706   (16-Dec-90 GL.P114/R) Sans titre (45x60cm-18x24in) acrylic paper laid
down on canvas (F.FR 90000)
£9403 $18337   (21-Oct-90 P.V56/R) Composition (49x35cm-19x14in) s.d.1979 verso acrylic
(F.FR 93000)
£11224 $22000   (7-Nov-90 SY.NY242/R) Untitled (23x31cm-9x12in) s. verso acrylic paper
£12333 $23926   (9-Dec-90 CC.P65/R) Sans titre (45cm-18ins circular) s. verso acrylic
round (F.FR 120000)
£15228 $30000   (4-Oct-90 SY.NY117/R) Untitled (48x39cm-19x15in) s.d.1977 verso acrylic
paper
£15873 $26032   (21-Jun-91 GK.B31/R) Tokyo (38x56cm-15x22in) s.i.d.verso acrylic paper
(S.FR 40000)
£16174 $31215   (13-Dec-90 F.M466/R) From Tokyo I (70x103cm-28x41in) s.verso acrylic
canvas paper (I.L 35000000)
£17766 $35000   (4-Oct-90 SY.NY108/R) Untitled (56x76cm-22x30in) acrylic paper
£18367 $36000   (14-Feb-91 CH.NY68/R) Untitled (56x76cm-22x30in) s.d.1973verso acrylic
paper
£21825 $35794   (21-Jun-91 GK.B30/R) Cross colours (45x60cm-18x24in) s.d.1978erso
acrylic paper (S.FR 55000)
£25381 $50000   (4-Oct-90 SY.NY110 a/R) Untitled (79x60cm-31x24in) acrylic paper
£26627 $45000   (2-May-91 CH.NY190/R) Untitled (56x76cm-22x30in) s.d.1976 verso acrylic
paper
£26650 $52500   (14-Nov-90 SY.NY298/R) As for appearance VII (33x24cm-13x9in) s.verso
£41420 $70000   (2-May-91 CH.NY207/R) Untitled (161x122cm-63x48in) s.d.1971 verso
acrylic paper on canvas

FRANCIS, Sam (1923-) American-cont.

£41667	$68333	(21-Jun-91 GK.B28/R) As for appearance, IV (27x22cm-11x9in) s.verso (S.FR 105000)
£53254	$90000	(2-May-91 CH.NY160/R) Untitled (131x163cm-52x64in) s.verso acrylic canvas
£59172	$100000	(2-May-91 CH.NY164./R) Untitled (122x91cm-48x36in) s.verso acrylic canvas
£63776	$125000	(7-Nov-90 SY.NY211/R) Augustus image and word (170x211cm-67x83in) s.i.d.1987 verso acrylic
£71429	$140000	(7-Nov-90 SY.NY204/R) Resurrection (91x205cm-36x81in) s.d.1988 verso acrylic
£88757	$150000	(1-May-91 SY.NY246 b/R) Krator 10 (174x174cm-69x69in) acrylic canvas
£88832	$175000	(4-Oct-90 SY.NY104/R) Untitled (198x137cm-78x54in) acrylic canvas
£91837	$180000	(8-Nov-90 CH.NY330/R) Untitled (121x162cm-48x64in) acrylic paper mounted canvas
£96000	$154560	(27-Jun-91 S63/R) Composition no 6 (182x152cm-72x60in) acrylic
£102041	$200000	(8-Nov-90 CH.NY347/R) Santa Monica I (163x104cm-64x41in) acrylic
£151210	$294859	(28-Oct-90 GL.P90/R) Sans titre (107x350cm-42x138in) s.d.1979 verso acrylic paper laid down on canvas (F.FR 1500000)
£238095	$390476	(21-Jun-91 GK.B26/R) Over red (184x95cm-72x37in) s.i.d.1959 acrylic paper on canvas (S.FR 600000)
£433673	$850000	(7-Nov-90 CH.NY8/R) Untitled (185x197cm-73x78in) s.d.56verso
£3303	*$5715*	*(23-May-91 SY.AM265/R) Untitled (47x31cm-19x12in) s.d.1960verso W/C (D.FL 11000)*
£9249	*$16000*	*(7-May-91 CE.NY162/R) Untitled no.20 (35x51cm-14x20in) W/C gouache*
£10081	*$19657*	*(28-Oct-90 GL.P18/R) Tryptich II 1 (38x29cm-15x11in) s.i. verso gouache (F.FR 100000)*
£19133	*$37500*	*(7-Nov-90 SY.NY209/R) Untitled (101x71cm-40x28in) s.i.d.June 1966 verso gouache*
£21429	*$42000*	*(8-Nov-90 CH.NY151/R) Untitled (21x47cm-8x19in) s. verso acrylic*
£28000	*$49560*	*(21-Mar-91 S52/R) Untitled (31x24cm-12x9in) gouache oil paper*
£43367	*$85000*	*(15-Feb-91 SY.NY135/R) Untitled (51x68cm-20x27in) s.verso W/C acrylic paper on board*
£59524	*$97619*	*(21-Jun-91 GK.B27/R) Firework (56x75cm-22x30in) s.i.d.1962 bodycol W/C (S.FR 150000)*

FRANCISCO, J Bond (1863-1931) American

£1026	$2000	(10-Oct-90 B.SF553/R) Sunset in Sierras (18x25cm-7x10in) s. board

FRANCK, Adolf (1841-1929) German

£13287	$25643	(10-Dec-90 L.K423/R) Tavern interior with figures at table drinking red wine near Bozen (85x113cm-33x44in) s. canvas on panel (DM 38000)

FRANCK, Albert Jacques (1899-1973) Canadian

£657	$1129	(14-May-91 JOY.T152/R) Peggy's cove (25x29cm-10x11in) canvas laid down on board (C.D 1300)
£918	$1552	(15-Apr-91 L.V3) Grey houses on Lowther St (25x30cm-10x12in) board (C.D 1800)
£1122	$1897	(15-Apr-91 L.V1) Scolland Street 58 (25x30cm-10x12in) board (C.D 2200)
£1316	$2592	(30-Oct-90 SY.T23/R) Victoria College gate (29x24cm-11x9in) s.d.68 i.verso board (C.D 3000)
£2018	$3954	(20-Nov-90 JOY.T312/R) Behind Denison Avenue (30x25cm-12x10in) s.d.67 board (C.D 4600)
£2062	$3505	(27-May-91 HO.ED279/R) Grand River, Paris, Ontario (61x91cm-24x36in) s.d.1963 i.verso board (C.D 4000)
£3070	$6048	(30-Oct-90 SY.T90/R) Behind Ontario Street (49x39cm-19x15in) s.d.69 i.verso board (C.D 7000)
£3070	$6048	(30-Oct-90 SY.T134/R) 15 Berryman Street (30x25cm-12x10in) s.d.68 i.verso board (C.D 7000)
£657	*$1129*	*(14-May-91 JOY.T107/R) Lane off of Sackville St. (16x12cm-6x5in) s.d.'65 W/C (C.D 1300)*
£658	*$1296*	*(30-Oct-90 SY.T3/R) Backyard on Gerrard Street East (18x14cm-7x6in) s.d.66 i.verso W/C (C.D 1500)*
£658	*$1296*	*(30-Oct-90 SY.T127/R) Back of Parliament Street (20x14cm-8x6in) s.d.71 i.verso W/C (C.D 1500)*
£702	*$1382*	*(30-Oct-90 SY.T129/R) Howard Street (30x25cm-12x10in) s. i.verso W/C (C.D 1600)*
£3070	*$6018*	*(20-Nov-90 JOY.T20/R) Wellesley E. at parliament (61x50cm-24x20in) s.d.68 W/C (C.D 7000)*

FRANCK, Christoffel Frederik (1758-1816) Dutch

£3000	$5910	(31-Oct-90 S197/R) Figures standing outside cottage by river (38x54cm-15x21in)

FRANCK, Philipp (1860-1944) German

£3633	$7266	(6-Feb-91 N.M597/R) Peasant and women harvesting potatoes (82x98cm-32x39in) s.d.1905 (DM 10500)
£8741	$16958	(7-Dec-90 GB.B6518/R) Lake landscape, Lugano (85x100cm-33x39in) s.d.1925 (DM 25000)

FRANCKEN (studio) (16/17th C) Flemish

£1300	$2301	(20-Mar-91 DL.P105) Nativite (31x24cm-12x9in) copper (F.FR 13000)

FRANCKEN, Ambrosius (attrib) (16/17th C) Flemish

£5781	$11446	(30-Jan-91 APT.P218/R) Salomon accueillant la Reine de Saba (88x192cm-35x76in) panel (F.FR 57000)

FRANCKEN, Ambrosius (circle) (16/17th C) Flemish
£2204 $4341   (14-Nov-90 D.V146/R) The Last Supper (25x33cm-10x13in) panel
                    (A.S 45000)

FRANCKEN, Ambrosius (style) (16/17th C) Flemish
£1900 $3705   (26-Oct-90 PHM89/R) Christ bound (106x74cm-42x29in) panel

FRANCKEN, Frans (attrib) (16/17th C) Flemish
£2185 $4217   (11-Dec-90 FER.M172/R) Salome presentando la cabeza del Bautista
                    (36x29cm-14x11in) copper (S.P 400000)
£5929 $9901   (4-Jun-91 CH.R349/R) L'Annunciazione (36x29cm-14x11in) copper
                    (I.L 13000000)

FRANCKEN, Frans (circle) (16/17th C) Flemish
£4000 $6720   (26-Apr-91 NM.P64/R) Scene d'auberge, les joueurs de tric-trac
                    (54x73cm-21x29in) panel (F.FR 40000)

FRANCKEN, Frans (style) (16/17th C) Flemish
£2204 $4341   (14-Nov-90 D.V162/R) Christ being shown to the people (35x44cm-14x17in)
                    copper (A.S 45000)
£5663 $9854   (25-Mar-91 SY.F716/R) Scena di ballo (51x82cm-20x32in) panel
                    (I.L 12500000)

FRANCKEN, Frans I (circle) (1542-1616) Flemish
£1695 $2763   (3-Jul-91 WE.MU182/R) Biblical scene (38x42cm-15x17in) (DM 5000)

FRANCKEN, Frans II (1581-1642) Flemish
£1250 $2438   (26-Oct-90 PHM36/R) Noli me tangere (62x48cm-24x19in) panel
£1300 $2197   (18-Apr-91 CSK1/R) Christ on Road to Calvary (32x23cm-13x9in) on copper
£4091 $8019   (19-Nov-90 CH.R180/R) Duello fra Minerva e Marte alla presenza di
                    Mercurio (56x85cm-22x33in) s. (I.L 9000000)
£7000 $11830   (16-Apr-91 PH113/R) Putti supporting garland of flowers enclosing Holy
                    Trinity (38x29cm-15x11in) on copper
£7485 $12650   (2-May-91 CH.AM112/R) Christ preaching on the sea of Galilee
                    (41x64cm-16x25in) s. panel (D.FL 25000)
£12758 $21688   (30-May-91 F.M92/R) Le opere di misericordia (50x76cm-20x30in) panel
                    (I.L 28000000)
£17085 $28020   (22-Jun-91 CH.MO102/R) La legende de virgile et de la fille de
                    l'empereur (59x80cm-23x31in) panel (F.FR 170000)
£19553 $35000   (11-Apr-91 SY.NY63/R) Flight into Egypt, with stag in distant forest
                    (38x41cm-15x16in) panel
£23445 $45015   (30-Nov-90 APT.P50/R) L'adoration des mages (55x80cm-22x31in) s. panel
                    on canvas (F.FR 230000)

FRANCKEN, Frans II (attrib) (1581-1642) Flemish
£3670 $7229   (13-Nov-90 AB.S889/R) The rich man and Lasarus (44x63cm-17x25in)
                    indist.s. panel (S.KR 40000)
£4317 $8374   (7-Dec-90 SY.MO143/R) Cresus et Solon (52x28cm-20x11in) panel
                    (F.FR 42000)

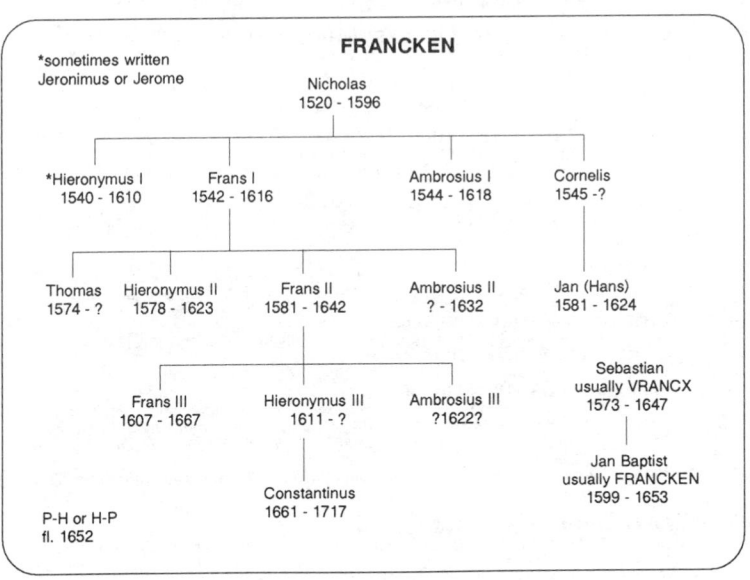

FRANCKEN

*sometimes written Jeronimus or Jerome

Nicholas 1520 - 1596

*Hieronymus I 1540 - 1610   Frans I 1542 - 1616   Ambrosius I 1544 - 1618   Cornelis 1545 -?

Thomas 1574 - ?   Hieronymus II 1578 - 1623   Frans II 1581 - 1642   Ambrosius II ? - 1632   Jan (Hans) 1581 - 1624

Frans III 1607 - 1667   Hieronymus III 1611 - ?   Ambrosius III ?1622?

Sebastian usually VRANCX 1573 - 1647

Jan Baptist usually FRANCKEN 1599 - 1653

Constantinus 1661 - 1717

P-H or H-P fl. 1652

FRANCKEN, Frans II (attrib) (1581-1642) Flemish-cont.
£5500 $10725 (26-Oct-90 C83/R) The conversion of Saul (55x70cm-22x28in) copper

FRANCKEN, Frans II (circle) (1581-1642) Flemish
£1122 $1807 (26-Jun-91 KM.K1325 a) Jesus before Pilate (57x73cm-22x29in) copper
(DM 3300)
£1500 $2955 (30-Oct-90 PH9/R) The Idolatry of Solomon (40x59cm-16x23in) panel
£1959 $3859 (14-Nov-90 D.V191/R) The Presentation in the Temple (16x13cm-6x5in)
copper (A.S 40000)
£2800 $4564 (4-Jul-91 CSK35/R) Christ at supper with Simon the Pharasee
(116x159cm-46x63in)
£3041 $5169 (27-May-91 L.K42/R) Scene from the Old Testament with woman accusing
feasting king (13x16cm-5x6in) copper (DM 9000)
£4500 $8550 (1-Mar-91 C175/R) The martyrdom of St Ursula and her companions
(57x49cm-22x19in) panel

FRANCKEN, Frans II (studio) (1581-1642) Flemish
£1521 $3012 (30-Jan-91 APT.P217/R) Alexandre et Diogene (42x28cm-17x11in) pnel
(F.FR 15000)

FRANCKEN, Frans II (style) (1581-1642) Flemish
£1348 $2251 (6-Jun-91 D.V303/R) Adoration of the Shepherds (15x12cm-6x5in) copper
(A.S 28000)
£2200 $4180 (13-Sep-90 CSK201/R) Adoration of Magi (74x105cm-29x41in) panel
£3670 $7229 (13-Nov-90 CH.AM206/R) Ananias falls dead as berated by Saint Peter for
deceitfulness (52x74cm-20x29in) panel (D.FL 12000)

FRANCKEN, Frans II and LAANEN, Jasper van (17th C) Flemish
£58000 $94540 (3-Jul-91 S46/R) Expulsion of Hagar and Ishmael (79x115cm-31x45in) s.
panel

FRANCKEN, Frans II and MARLIER, Philippe de (17th C) Flemish
£420000 $810600 (12-Dec-90 S8/R) Still life of flowers in metal vase painted with The
Rape of Deijanara (60x48cm-24x19in) panel

FRANCKEN, Frans III (1607-1667) Flemish
£3968 $6825 (19-May-91 ZZ.F80/R) Le joyeux festin (22x29cm-9x11in) copper
(F.FR 40000)

FRANCKEN, Frans III (attrib) (1607-1667) Flemish
£900 $1665 (5-Mar-91 PH6/R) Interior of artist's studio with artist, model and
spectators (35x28cm-14x11in) copper
£979 $1929 (14-Nov-90 D.V193/R) Noli me tangere (7x20cm-3x8in) copper one of pair
(A.S 20000)
£979 $1929 (14-Nov-90 D.V194/R) Washing the Feet of Christ (7x20cm-3x8in) copper
one of pair (A.S 20000)

FRANCKEN, Frans and MOMPER, Joos de (16/17th C) Flemish
£4337 $8500 (7-Nov-90 B.SF1014/R) Temptation of Christ, castle in background
(50x53cm-20x21in) panel

FRANCKEN, Hieronymus (attrib) (16/17th C) Flemish
£917 $1760 (18-Dec-90 GM.B785) Sermon du Christ (127x83cm-50x33in) board
(B.FR 55000)
£3183 $6271 (14-Nov-90 D.V192/R) Moses and the Miracle of the Water from the
Mountain (72x95cm-28x37in) panel (A.S 65000)

FRANCKEN, Hieronymus (style) (16/17th C) Flemish
£1800 $2934 (4-Jul-91 C636/R) Elegant company dancing at feast in interior
(72x97cm-28x38in) d.1.6.1.6.

FRANCKEN, Hieronymus I (studio) (1540-1610) Flemish
£6325 $10184 (27-Jun-91 APT.P96/R) Les Noces de Cana (72x105cm-28x41in) panel
(F.FR 63000)

FRANCKEN, Ruth (20th C) ?
£2022 $3943 (21-Oct-90 P.V126/R) La berceuse s.d.1974 mixed media (F.FR 20000)

FRANCO Y CORDERO, Jose (19th C) Spanish
£1223 $2164 (3-Apr-91 ANS.M118/R) Paisaje con edificios (59x38cm-23x15in) s.
(S.P 225000)

FRANCO, Giovanni Battista (1510-1580) Italian
*£1100 $2123 (12-Dec-90 PH262/R) River god, reclining torso and centurians. Design
for altar decoration (24x39cm-9x15in) pen ink laid down double-sided*
*£1800 $2934 (1-Jul-91 S221) Study of leg and of bearded head seen in profile
(22x13cm-9x5in) pen*
*£3158 $6000 (9-Jan-91 CH.NY5/R) Battle of Lapiths and Centaurs (14x43cm-6x17in) pen
wash*

FRANCO, Giovanni Battista (style) (1510-1580) Italian
*£1200 $2316 (12-Dec-90 PH260/R) Studies of walking woman with billowing robe and
women. Study of column (26x13cm-10x5in) ink over chk double-sided*

FRANCO-FLEMISH SCHOOL. 18th C French/Flemish
£1000 $1730 (20-May-91 SWS79/R) Mars and Venus (58x75cm-23x30in)

FRANCO-FLEMISH SCHOOL, 18th C French/Flemish-cont.
| £3700 | \$6401 | (20-May-91 SWS136/R) An Italianate landscape with drovers near classical ruins (66x82cm-26x32in) |

FRANCO-ITALIAN SCHOOL, 18th C French/Italian
| £2479 | \$4438 | (8-Apr-91 CH.R82) Paesaggio classico con pastori (46x56cm-18x22in) (I.L 5500000) |

FRANCOIS, Andre (1915-) French
| £797 | \$1355 | (2-Jun-91 GL.P33) Le cuirasse (27x22cm-11x9in) s. lead pencil W/C pebble manuscript (F.FR 8000) |

FRANCOIS, Gustave see BARRAUD, Gustave Francois

FRANCOIS, Guy (1580-1650) French
| £20588 | \$35000 | (31-May-91 CH.NY13/R) St John the Baptist (97x74cm-38x29in) |

FRANCOIS, Joseph (19/20th C) Belgian?
£636	\$1233	(5-Dec-90 KH.K41/R) River through the woods (51x75cm-20x30in) s. (D.KR 7000)
£709	\$1198	(2-May-91 RAS.V41/R) River through wood (51x75cm-20x30in) s. (D.KR 8000)
£1164	\$2083	(12-Mar-91 GM.B984/R) Vallee du Flavion (86x100cm-34x39in) mono. (B.FR 70000)

FRANCOIS, Pierre (20th C) French
| £521 | \$1000 | (20-Feb-91 D.NY34) Canal village at Chateau Thierry (76x102cm-30x40in) s. |

FRANCOIS, Pierre Joseph C (1759-1851) Flemish
| £6500 | \$10660 | (21-Jun-91 C1/R) Death of Marcus Curtius (66x51cm-26x20in) s. with i.verso panel |

FRANCQ, Colin le (19/20th C) French
| £544 | \$963 | (20-Mar-91 KM.K1337) Still life with fruit in basket, pewter vessel and glass (46x55cm-18x22in) s. (DM 1600) |

FRANCUCCI, Innocenzo (studio) (1494-1550) Italian
| £6500 | \$13000 | (7-Feb-91 C17/R) The Holy Family with Saint Elizabeth and the Infant Saint John theBaptist (65x51cm-26x20in) panel |

FRANG, Felix (1862-1932) Finnish
| £2009 | \$3395 | (20-Apr-91 HOR.H74/R) Afternoon in the skerries (35x29cm-14x11in) s.d.1907 (F.M 14000) |
| £2439 | \$4122 | (20-Apr-91 HOR.H73/R) Waterfall (30x42cm-12x17in) s.d.1888 (F.M 17000) |

FRANGIAMORE, Salvatore (20th C) British
| £6936 | \$12000 | (23-May-91 CH.NY214/R) The unveiling (62x50cm-24x20in) s.i. canvas on board |

FRANK WILL (1900-1951) French
£923	\$1799	(10-Oct-90 ARC.P60) Nature morte (46x55cm-18x22in) board (F.FR 9200)
£1578	\$3108	(6-Oct-90 GL.P132) Notre Dame sous la neige (19x24cm-7x9in) s. board (F.FR 16000)
£2871	\$5082	(4-Apr-91 PPB.P48/R) Colmar (55x38cm-22x15in) s. (F.FR 29000)
£3134	\$6112	(17-Oct-90 ARC.P135/R) La cathedrale de Chartres (35x27cm-14x11in) s.i. (F.FR 31000)
£3175	\$5460	(19-May-91 ZZ.F102/R) Marche sur la place de l'eglise (66x55cm-26x22in) s. (F.FR 32000)
£3640	\$7098	(17-Oct-90 ARC.P134/R) Le marche aux fleurs et la Conciergerie (35x27cm-14x11in) s. (F.FR 36000)
£4587	\$8807	(2-Dec-90 M.V130) Notre Dame et les bouquinistes (46x55cm-18x22in) s. (F.FR 45000)
£5746	\$11205	(26-Oct-90 APT.P111) Paris - le Moulin Rouge (46x65cm-18x26in) s. (F.FR 57000)
£6552	\$12777	(26-Oct-90 APT.P110/R) Paris - place Blanche, rue Lepic (46x61cm-18x24in) s. (F.FR 65000)
£720	\$1426	(3-Feb-91 LT.P16) Vue de Notre-Dame (20x30cm-8x12in) s.d.19 Indian ink (F.FR 7100)
£761	\$1500	(15-Nov-90 D.NY83) Fishing along Seine (22x30cm-9x12in) s.i. W/C over black chk
£942	\$1621	(15-May-91 CN.P27/R) Notre Dame vue des quais de Bercy (23x33cm-9x13in) s. crayon W/C (F.FR 9500)
£1040	\$1800	(7-May-91 CE.NY22/R) Scene de port (18x22cm-7x9in) s. W/C black chk
£1172	\$2262	(12-Dec-90 APT.P15) Paris, une rue sous la neige (26x35cm-10x14in) s. W/C (F.FR 11500)
£1182	\$2293	(5-Dec-90 ZZ.F10/R) Le marche au Treport (24x29cm-9x11in) s. W/C (F.FR 11500)
£1188	\$2103	(7-Apr-91 I.N136) La Concorde (25x37cm-10x15in) s. W/C chl. (F.FR 12000)
£1223	\$2361	(12-Dec-90 APT.P14) Rouen (35x23cm-14x9in) s. W/C (F.FR 12000)
£1310	\$2555	(26-Oct-90 APT.P11) Mantes, la place du marche (30x24cm-12x9in) s.i. W/C (F.FR 13000)
£1316	\$2579	(20-Nov-90 MF.P13/R) Saint-Malo (47x54cm-19x21in) s. W/C (F.FR 13000)
£1345	\$2326	(26-May-91 ZZ.F82/R) Vieille porte a Chartres (26x38cm-10x15in) s. W/C (F.FR 13500)
£1491	\$2520	(21-Apr-91 E.LA95/R) Fecamp - le port et les bateaux (33x26cm-13x10in) s. W/C (F.FR 15000)

FRANK WILL (1900-1951) French-cont.

£1558	$2555	(18-Jun-91 APT.P20) Paris, rue Lepic (44x53cm-17x21in) s. W/C (F.FR 15500)
£1582	$3116	(15-Oct-90 ARC.P48) Montmartre vue de Saint-Ouen (18x39cm-7x15in) s.i. W/C (F.FR 15500)
£1587	$2730	(17-May-91 LGB.P127/R) La Seine a Rouen (23x32cm-9x13in) s. W/C (F.FR 16000)
£1606	$2586	(24-Jun-91 PR.P131/R) La Concorde (50x65cm-20x26in) s.d.1928 W/C (F.FR 16000)
£1606	$2586	(24-Jun-91 PR.P129) La cociergerie (50x65cm-20x26in) s.d.1928 W/C (F.FR 16000)
£1650	$2756	(5-Jun-91 HC.P350) Le Moulin Rouge (54x45cm-21x18in) s. W/C crayon (F.FR 16500)
£1667	$3250	(10-Oct-90 SY.NY113/R) Place Pigalle (23x33cm-9x13in) s.i. W/C
£1693	$2929	(26-May-91 ZZ.F115/R) La tour de l'horloge et Notre-Dame a Paris (37x29cm-15x11in) s. W/C chl. (F.FR 17000)
£1714	$3326	(8-Dec-90 GAB.G3000/R) Les quais de Paris (50x40cm-20x16in) s.d.1928 W/C (S.FR 4200)
£1759	$3377	(24-Feb-91 P.V13) Le treport (22x30cm-9x12in) s. W/C crayon (F.FR 17500)
£1822	$3571	(25-Nov-90 ZZ.F251/R) Voiliers au Treport (20x28cm-8x11in) s. W/C (F.FR 18000)
£1910	$3666	(24-Feb-91 P.V24/R) L'entree du port (32x84cm-13x33in) s. W/C (F.FR 19000)
£2100	$3507	(7-Jun-91 LD.P4/R) Les bouquinistes face a Notre Dame de Paris (46x55cm-18x22in) s. W/C (F.FR 21000)
£2211	$3626	(18-Jun-91 APT.P19/R) Paris, la Seine, le Chevet de Notre Dame (44x53cm-17x21in) s. W/C (F.FR 22000)
£2254	$4418	(11-Nov-90 ZZ.F66/R) Vue de Treport (24x30cm-9x12in) s. W/C (F.FR 22000)
£2309	$3718	(24-Jun-91 PR.P128/R) La Seine et le Pont-Neuf (50x65cm-20x26in) s.d.1928 W/C (F.FR 23000)
£2345	$4502	(2-Dec-90 M.V32/R) Paris, le Moulin Rouge (44x54cm-17x21in) s. W/C (F.FR 23000)
£2510	$4041	(28-Jun-91 ARC.P19/R) La conciergerie (45x53cm-18x21in) s. W/C (F.FR 25000)
£2610	$4203	(28-Jun-91 ARC.P18/R) Le pont Neuf (45x53cm-18x21in) s. W/C (F.FR 26000)
£2650	$5115	(10-Dec-90 BL.P30/R) Amiens, la cathedrale (48x60cm-19x24in) s. W/C gouache (F.FR 26000)
£2711	$5015	(6-Mar-91 APT.P12/R) Paris, Montmartre, la place du Tertre (45x54cm-18x21in) s. W/C (F.FR 27000)
£2733	$5356	(25-Nov-90 ZZ.F63/R) Montmartre sous la neige (26x33cm-10x13in) s. W/C (F.FR 27000)
£2820	$4596	(11-Jun-91 I.N207/R) Le Port de Cassis (44x54cm-17x21in) s.i. W/C (F.FR 28000)
£2857	$5629	(15-Oct-90 ARC.P49/R) Le port de Fecamp (44x60cm-17x24in) s.i. W/C (F.FR 28000)
£2869	$5623	(11-Nov-90 ZZ.F104/R) Le port de fecamp (30x45cm-12x18in) s. W/C (F.FR 28000)
£3236	$6309	(17-Oct-90 ARC.P50) Notre-Dame et les quais (48x63cm-19x25in) s.d.1925 W/C (F.FR 32000)
£3380	$5712	(21-Apr-91 E.LA94) Paris - Notre-Dame, la Seine et les peniches (53x63cm-21x25in) s. W/C (F.FR 34000)
£3819	$7333	(24-Feb-91 P.V37/R) Paris, Notre Dame et la Seine (50x66cm-20x26in) s. W/C (F.FR 38000)
£3846	$7538	(25-Nov-90 ZZ.F64/R) Remorqueur sur la Seine a Paris (32x47cm-13x19in) s. W/C (F.FR 38000)
£3878	$7639	(17-Nov-90 HC.P71) Honfleur (45x31cm-18x12in) s. W/C (F.FR 38000)
£4536	$8846	(26-Oct-90 PPB.P22) Place de la Concorde (44x53cm-17x21in) s. W/C (F.FR 45000)
£4816	$9439	(11-Nov-90 ZZ.F124/R) La place du tertre sous la neige (30x41cm-12x16in) s. W/C (F.FR 47000)
£4839	$9435	(26-Oct-90 APT.P10/R) Notre-Dame sous la neige (61x77cm-24x30in) s. W/C (F.FR 48000)
£4858	$9522	(25-Nov-90 ZZ.F62/R) La Seine a Paris (50x60cm-20x24in) s. W/C (F.FR 48000)
£7026	$13842	(30-Oct-90 I.N203/R) La Madeleine (51x64cm-20x25in) s. W/C (F.FR 69000)

FRANK, Dale (1958-) Australian

£386	$761	(13-Nov-90 J.M666) So art was the quotation (101x121cm-40x48in) s.d.87 collage (A.D 1000)
£679	$1147	(16-Apr-91 J.M286/R) Burnt landscape (90x74cm-35x29in) mixed media (A.D 1500)
£1195	$2355	(31-Oct-90 CH.S14) Autumn nocturne and the symphonic green (200x180cm-79x71in) d.1987 acrylic mixed media plastic (A.D 3000)

FRANK, Edvard (1909-) German

£507	$877	(21-May-91 WK.M860 a/R) Six figures (48x62cm-19x24in) s. s.i.d.1949 W/C over pencil (DM 1500)
£612	$1084	(23-Mar-91 WK.M193/R) Houses and trees (22x32cm-9x13in) s.d.1931 gouache paper on board (DM 1800)
£612	$1084	(23-Mar-91 WK.M194/R) Treelined street (25x32cm-10x13in) s.d.1931 gouache paper on board (DM 1800)
£833	$1492	(12-Apr-91 AW.H1442/R) Hilly landscape with cypresses, South of France (44x58cm-17x23in) s. W/C (DM 2500)

FRANK, Ellen (fl.1889-1912) British

£500	$820	(20-Jun-91 B7/R) Gossip in 'thirties (26x38cm-10x15in) s.

FRANK, Ellen (fl.1889-1912) British-cont.
£330	$627	(25-Feb-91 PH5) Pink and sulphur crested cockatoo (24x29cm-9x11in) s. W/C

FRANK, Friedrich (1871-1945) Austrian
£430	$722	(25-Apr-91 D.V221/R) View of Graz (26x19cm-10x7in) s.i. mixed media (A.S 9000)
£1432	$2792	(11-Oct-90 D.V182/R) Island of Philae, Egypt (34x50cm-13x20in) s.d.1931 W/C (A.S 30000)
£1671	$2808	(25-Apr-91 D.V239/R) Belvedere, Vienna (17x23cm-7x9in) s.i. W/C htd.white (A.S 35000)
£1815	$3049	(25-Apr-91 D.V241/R) Stephanskirche, Vienna (38x26cm-15x10in) s.i. W/C (A.S 38000)
£2148	$4189	(11-Oct-90 D.V187/R) Jerusalem street scene with shepherd and flock (44x49cm-17x19in) s.i.d.1931 W/C (A.S 45000)
£2149	$3610	(25-Apr-91 D.V240/R) Flower market with Hof, Vienna (23x17cm-9x7in) s. W/C htd.white (A.S 45000)
£2627	$4413	(25-Apr-91 D.V237/R) Ringstrasse with Parliament and Town Hall, Vienna (31x47cm-12x19in) s.i. W/C (A.S 55000)
£3103	$6050	(11-Oct-90 D.V248/R) Busy street scene with trams and fiakers on Ringstrasse by Oper (18x23cm-7x9in) s.i. W/C htd.white (A.S 65000)
£3103	$6050	(11-Oct-90 D.V249/R) Ringstrasse in Vienna with trams, cars and fiaker (18x23cm-7x9in) s. W/C (A.S 65000)

FRANK, Hans (younger) (1925-) Austrian
£781	$1445	(7-Mar-91 D.V180/R) Mondsee landscape in thunderstorm (60x50cm-24x20in) s. bears d.22 board (A.S 16000)

FRANK, Lucien (1857-1920) Belgian
£848	$1672	(30-Oct-90 CH.AM21) Figures on quay, Dordrecht (36x27cm-14x11in) s.i.verso panel (D.FL 2800)
£1164	$2083	(12-Mar-91 C.A101/R) In the harbour (30x40cm-12x16in) s. board (B.FR 70000)
£1473	$2475	(23-Apr-91 C.A106) Park scene (38x53cm-15x21in) s.d.1918 paper (B.FR 90000)
£3713	$7166	(13-Dec-90 CH.BR114/R) Promenade (32x40cm-13x16in) s. panel (B.FR 220000)
£11457	$19247	(23-Apr-91 C.A104/R) Orchard in spring (76x106cm-30x42in) s. (B.FR 700000)

FRANK-BOGGS (1855-1926) French
£2604	$5000	(17-Dec-90 SY.NY216/R) Hotel de Ville, Paris (38x56cm-15x22in) s.
£2840	$4800	(20-Apr-91 WOL.C146/R) Cityscape (41x51cm-16x20in) s.
£3198	$5500	(15-May-91 SY.NY48/R) Crossing river (56x38cm-22x15in) s.
£3200	$5216	(5-Jul-91 APT.P95/R) Calfatage (56x38cm-22x15in) s. (F.FR 32000)
£3200	$5216	(4-Jul-91 GL.P271/R) La Seine quai Conti (33x41cm-13x16in) s.d.1889 board (F.FR 32000)
£3439	$6500	(24-Sep-90 S.SL503/R) Honfleur, entree du port (58x71cm-23x28in) s.
£3704	$7000	(27-Sep-90 CH.NY106/R) The pont royal (38x55cm-15x22in) s.
£4694	$9106	(8-Dec-90 GAB.G2393/R) La Conciergerie vue de la Seine (29x46cm-11x18in) s. (S.FR 11500)
£5233	$9000	(15-May-91 SY.NY21/R) On Seine (36x53cm-14x21in) s.d.1897
£5567	$10911	(23-Nov-90 PLF.P35/R) Debut d'incendie a bord d'un paquebot americain (60x82cm-24x32in) s. (F.FR 55000)
£5729	$11000	(29-Nov-90 SY.NY26/R) Dieppe (58x81cm-23x32in) s.d.81
£5730	$11346	(3-Feb-91 I.N26/R) Voiliers a quai (56x38cm-22x15in) s. (F.FR 56500)
£922	$1807	(11-Nov-90 ZZ.F26/R) Voiliers en mer (18x23cm-7x9in) s.d.1899 chl.W/C (F.FR 9000)
£1060	$1770	(5-Jun-91 HC.P349/R) Bord de Seine (26x43cm-10x17in) s.d.17 fevrier 1908 W/C crayon (F.FR 10600)
£1091	$1877	(15-May-91 CN.P28/R) Montmartre (40x26cm-16x10in) s. crayon W/C wash (F.FR 11000)
£1190	$2048	(15-May-91 CN.P33/R) Les regates (28x44cm-11x17in) s. W/C (F.FR 12000)
£1215	$2381	(25-Nov-90 ZZ.F18) Vue de Harfleur (23x14cm-9x6in) s.d.1900 (F.FR 12000)
£1290	$2218	(15-May-91 CN.P31/R) Honfleur (44x28cm-17x11in) s. W/C (F.FR 13000)
£1290	$2218	(15-May-91 CN.P29/R) Le Moulin de la Galette (21x30cm-8x12in) s. crayon W/C (F.FR 13000)
£1438	$2474	(15-May-91 CN.P30/R) L'eglise de Houdan (27x40cm-11x16in) s. crayon W/C (F.FR 14500)
£1468	$2877	(25-Nov-90 B.PA4 a) La Seine a Paris (31x40cm-12x16in) s. W/C (F.FR 14500)
£1488	$2560	(17-May-91 LGB.P126/R) Le Palais de Justice a Paris (45x31cm-18x12in) s. W/C (F.FR 15000)
£1531	$3015	(14-Nov-90 FB.P58/R) La cathedrale de Reims (38x46cm-15x18in) s.d.1914 W/C (F.FR 15000)
£1531	$3015	(16-Nov-90 FB.P128/R) Le port de Dunkerque (38x46cm-15x18in) s. W/C chl. (F.FR 15000)
£1587	$2730	(15-May-91 CN.P32/R) Rue de Bercy (33x41cm-13x16in) s. crayon W/C (F.FR 16000)
£1733	$3327	(2-Dec-90 M.V38) Bord de Seine (26x43cm-10x17in) s.d.17.02.1908 W/C (F.FR 17000)
£1736	$2986	(15-May-91 CN.P34/R) L'Institut vu des quais du Louvre (26x39cm-10x15in) s. crayon W/C (F.FR 17500)
£1775	$3000	(1-May-91 B.SF5106/R) Pont a Dinaut (25x39cm-10x15in) s. W/C chl
£1966	$3833	(28-Oct-90 M.V76/R) La place du Marche (56x39cm-22x15in) s.d.1912 W/C pastel (F.FR 19500)

FRANK-BOGGS (1855-1926) French-cont.

£2180	$3750	(15-May-91 SY.NY100/R) Venice (39x55cm-15x22in) s.d.1902 W/C chl paper on board
£2277	$4031	(7-Apr-91 I.N45) Le Pont Neuf (22x41cm-9x16in) s.d.1905 W/C chl. (F.FR 23000)
£2291	$3894	(2-Jun-91 LT.P25/R) Animation aupres de l'eglise (31x39cm-12x15in) s.d.1902 W/C (F.FR 23000)
£2345	$4502	(2-Dec-90 M.V37/R) Paris, le Seine les quais le remorqueur (27x40cm-11x16in) s. W/C (F.FR 23000)
£3468	$6000	(22-May-91 CH.NY126/R) La Portr St. Denis, Paris (54x38cm-21x15in) s.i. W/C chl

FRANK-KRAUSS, Robert (1893-1950) German

£680	$1204	(22-Mar-91 GRA.B2608/R) Black Forest girl (21x16cm-8x6in) s. panel (DM 2000)
£782	$1385	(22-Mar-91 GRA.B2609) Old man threading needle (21x16cm-8x6in) s. panel (DM 2300)
£1027	$1675	(12-Jun-91 N.M426/R) Dachau peasant seated at table reading letter (21x16cm-8x6in) s. i.d.1932verso panel (DM 3000)
£1301	$2121	(12-Jun-91 N.M427/R) Portrait of young Dachau woman (49x38cm-19x15in) s. panel (DM 3800)

FRANKE, Heinrich (after) (1738-1792) German

| £743 | $1264 | (27-May-91 L.K43) Friedrich II von Preussen on horseback in landscape (28x21cm-11x8in) (DM 2200) |

FRANKEN, Ian (1896-?) Dutch

| £1074 | $1986 | (7-Mar-91 D.V182/R) Child in red high chair (81x60cm-32x24in) s.d.24 (A.S 22000) |

FRANKEN, Pierre Antoine (?-1928) French

| £815 | $1574 | (12-Dec-90 ZZ.F49/R) La rue de Moulin de Beurre a Paris (61x43cm-24x17in) s.d.1924 (F.FR 8000) |

FRANKENTHAL SCHOOL, 17th C German

| £12060 | $19779 | (21-Jun-91 SY.MO231/R) Paysage fluvial (50x72cm-20x28in) panel (F.FR 120000) |
| £13158 | $25000 | (10-Jan-91 SY.NY37/R) Three Graces beside sleeping eros (34x40cm-13x16in) on copper |

FRANKENTHALER, Helen (1928-) American

£5917	$10000	(1-May-91 SY.NY232/R) London memos no.2 (57x72cm-22x28in) s.d.71 acrylic paper
£6599	$13000	(4-Oct-90 SY.NY101/R) Untitled (192x16cm-76x6in) s.d.74 acrylic canvas
£19133	$37500	(7-Nov-90 SY.NY203/R) Earth watch (232x331cm-91x130in) s.i.d.March 1978 verso
£24365	$48000	(5-Oct-90 CH.NY99/R) Brooding light (81x190cm-32x75in) s.s.i.d.1974verso acrylic
£25148	$42500	(1-May-91 SY.NY234/R) Ore (79x166cm-31x65in) s. s.d.1978 verso acrylic canvas
£30612	$60000	(7-Nov-90 SY.NY200/R) Years later (213x137cm-84x54in) s.d.1980 verso acrylic
£32995	$65000	(5-Oct-90 CH.NY92/R) Kashmir (194x159cm-76x63in) s.s.i.d.1979verso acrylic
£38071	$75000	(4-Oct-90 SY.NY97/R) Aladdin (129x117cm-51x46in) s. s.d.79 verso acrylic canvas
£43367	$85000	(14-Feb-91 CH.NY48/R) Golden day (236x207cm-93x81in) s.d.67 acrylic

FRANKL, Franz (1881-) German

| £651 | $1165 | (13-Mar-91 N.M490/R) Poplars by stream and village (81x101cm-32x40in) s.i. (DM 1900) |
| £1149 | $2000 | (27-Mar-91 B.SF4281/R) View of the town steeple (43x48cm-17x19in) s.i. canvas laid down |

FRANKY BOY see SEVEHON, Francky Boy

FRANS, Paul (20th C) French

| £797 | $1371 | (14-May-91 GF.L2603/R) La Promenade a Dieppe (38x55cm-15x22in) s. (S.FR 2000) |

FRANSIOLI, Thomas Adrian (1906-) American

| £578 | $1000 | (21-May-91 CE.NY473/R) October (36x79cm-14x31in) s. |

FRANZ, E R (1845-1907) Italian

| £440 | $779 | (5-Apr-91 BW17) Study of Italian girl (33x15cm-13x6in) s. W/C |

FRANZ, Ettore Roesler (1845-1907) Italian

£893	$1500	(21-Jul-91 LIT.L142) Roman landscape (43x71cm-17x28in) s.
£550	$952	(9-May-91 CSK27) Roman campagna (26x44cm-10x17in) s.i. pencil W/C
£2400	$4680	(22-Oct-90 SWS322/R) Faggot gatherers in wood (33x45cm-13x18in) s.i. W/C over pencil
£3000	$5910	(5-Oct-90 C138/R) Extensive landscape in Roman Campagna (39x75cm-15x30in) s. pencil W/C

FRAPPA, Jose (1854-1904) French

| £1750 | $3448 | (13-Nov-90 SWS370/R) The latest scandal (49x61cm-19x24in) s. |

FRASER, A (19th C) British
£550 $897   (13-Jun-91 CSK300) Preparing vegetables (25x20cm-10x8in) s.d.1810 panel

FRASER, Alec (fl.1902-1912) British
£1000 $1960   (22-Nov-90 CG595/R) Scottish fishing village (35x53cm-14x21in) s.

FRASER, Alexander (19/20th C) British
£650 $1216   (28-Aug-90 S805/R) Autumn morning, Cadzow Forest (30x50cm-12x20in) s.s.i.verso panel
£680 $1340   (30-Oct-90 SC225) Outside the croft (30x49cm-12x19in) s.
£700 $1176   (23-Apr-91 S242/R) Near Almeria (20x29cm-8x11in) init.d.91 s.i.d.1991 verso board
£1000 $1870   (28-Aug-90 S847/R) Old well near Hamilton (28x33cm-11x13in) s.indist.d. s.i.verso board
£850 $1649   (6-Dec-90 CG12) Workhorse and two figures by water trough (51x66cm-20x26in) s. W/C

FRASER, Alexander (attrib) (19/20th C) British
£1500 $2805   (28-Aug-90 S851/R) Reading lesson (63x76cm-25x30in)

FRASER, Alexander (jnr) (1828-1899) British
£3000 $5040   (23-Apr-91 S7/R) Autumn among Surrey hills (76x107cm-30x42in) s.d.1867 s.i.verso

FRASER, Arthur Anderson (fl.1882-1894) British
£600 $1134   (26-Sep-90 S218) Riverside village (16x50cm-6x20in) mono.d.1893 W/C

FRASER, Donald Hamilton (1929-) British
£500 $845   (2-May-91 C135/R) Blue seascape (23x18cm-9x7in) paper on panel
£800 $1568   (25-Jan-91 C175/R) Landscape, Biesse no. 1 (75x49cm-30x19in) s. s.i.overlap
£1800 $3006   (7-Jun-91 C299/R) Agdistis III (91x71cm-36x28in) s.i.d.1964
£2200 $3674   (7-Jun-91 C92/R) Landscape (70x89cm-28x35in)
£3700 $6179   (7-Jun-91 C293/R) Landscape (121x89cm-48x35in) s.d.1967verso
£750 $1305   (28-Mar-91 CSK157) Still life with bowl and coffee pot (51x40cm-20x16in) s. gouache acrylic

FRASER, Garden William see GARDEN, William Fraser

FRASER, George Gordon (19th C) British
£780 $1342   (14-May-91 SWS63/R) Hunter at the edge of river (35x25cm-14x10in) s. W/C htd.bodycol.paper on card
£1100 $2145   (18-Oct-90 SC3012/R) On the river at dusk (33x51cm-13x20in) s.d.1888

FRASER, John (1858-1927) British
£1800 $3456   (16-Aug-90 B401/R) Shipping, possibly off the Azores (61x107cm-24x42in)
£580 $1143   (5-Oct-90 T292) Loo Castle (38x56cm-15x22in) s.i. W/C

FRASER, R W (19/20th C) British
£550 $1073   (12-Oct-90 GSP423) At Walton (18x36cm-7x14in) s.d. W/C

FRASER, Robert Winchester (1872-1930) British
£540 $956   (22-Mar-91 T264) On the Ouse (23x36cm-9x14in) s.d.'75
£780 $1396   (14-Mar-91 ZZ.B50) On the Stour (24x43cm-9x17in) s.i. W/C htd.bodycol. pair
£850 $1386   (4-Jul-91 PHI128) Harleston, Norfolk (24x53cm-9x21in) s.i. W/C
£1450 $2828   (18-Oct-90 SC3013/R) Figures on a riverside path. The old lock (23x49cm-9x19in) s.d.87 pair

FRASER, Robert Winter (fl.1870-1899) British
£400 $676   (18-Apr-91 B245/R) A river landscape with figures on a path and a church beyond (18x39cm-7x15in) s.d.'96 W/C
£940 $1617   (15-May-91 BT136/R) Estbrook (18x38cm-7x15in) s.i.d.'99 W/C

FRASER, William Miller (19th C) British
. £1200 $2028   (15-Apr-91 WW61/R) Sea sketch - Machrihamish (25x35cm-10x14in) s. with i.verso canvasboard
£1700 $2856   (23-Apr-91 S146/R) Children playing on beach (25x35cm-10x14in) s. i.d.1933 verso canvasboard

FRAST, Karoline (1841-1902) Austrian
£720 $1238   (16-May-91 D.V37/R) Portrait of Kaiserin Elisabeth (68x54cm-27x21in) s. (A.S 15000)

FRATER, William (1890-) British/Australian
£830 $1485   (9-Apr-91 CH.ME349/R) Portrait of Elna Hellene Watt (65x55cm-26x22in) s. board (A.D 1900)
£1013 $1944   (14-Aug-90 SY.ME72/R) The hillside (49x60cm-19x24in) s. board (A.D 2400)
£1737 $3423   (13-Nov-90 J.M178/R) In Central Australia (50x60cm-20x24in) s. board (A.D 4500)
£1810 $3059   (15-Apr-91 AAA.S149) Seated nude (66x60cm-26x24in) s. board (A.D 4000)
£1965 $3517   (9-Apr-91 CH.ME324) Figure beside fence (50x55cm-20x22in) s. canvasboard (A.D 4500)
£2172 $3671   (16-Apr-91 J.M44/R) Susanna (90x76cm-35x30in) s. board (A.D 4800)

FRATTA, Domenico Maria (1696-1763) Italian
£2000 $3380   *(16-Apr-91 C178/R) The Rape of Amphitrite (30x43cm-12x17in) ink*

FRATTA, Domenico Maria (attrib) (1696-1763) Italian
£550 $1062   *(11-Dec-90 C308) Saint Rosalia and a woman in a cave attended by angels (27x20cm-11x8in) i. blk.chk. ink wash*

FRAU, Jose (1898-1976) Spanish
£1594 $3109   (22-Oct-90 ANS.M93/R) Paisaje (21x27cm-8x11in) s. board (S.P 295000)
£2070 $3560   (16-May-91 ANS.M64/R) Interior (60x81cm-24x32in) s. (S.P 380000)

FRAZER, William Miller (1864-1961) British
£600 $1164   (6-Dec-90 CG89) St Ives, Huntingdonshire (25x36cm-10x14in) s.l. panel
£650 $1151   (5-Apr-91 PHE65) Cattle on country path (25x34cm-10x13in) s.
£650 $1216   (28-Aug-90 S965) Pittendynie (24x34cm-9x13in) s. i.d.1923verso board
£650 $1151   (5-Apr-91 PHE76) Spate on Dochart, Killin (39x59cm-15x23in) s.
£700 $1365   (17-Oct-90 PHG61) Sheep in an autumn landscape (45x70cm-18x28in) s.i.d.'96
£750 $1260   (23-Apr-91 S101) Farm by sea (24x34cm-9x13in) s. canvas on board
£780 $1451   (7-Sep-90 PHE62) Cattle grazing in meadow (27x34cm-11x13in) s.
£780 $1537   (2-Nov-90 PHE59) Highland cattle amongst the heather (44x34cm-17x13in) s. W/C
£789 $1500   (14-Sep-90 S.BM265/R) Children on the shore (25x36cm-10x14in) s. canvasboard
£900 $1683   (28-Aug-90 S969/R) On the Garry, near Struan (46x61cm-18x24in) s.i.
£900 $1773   (31-Oct-90 LV131/R) A fen farm, Lincolnshire (23x33cm-9x13in) s.
£1100 $2057   (28-Aug-90 S932) Landscape with sheep (51x61cm-20x24in) s.d.1912
£1100 $2200   (5-Feb-91 S58/R) Watermeadow (46x35cm-18x14in) s.
£1200 $2016   (23-Apr-91 S169/R) Moonlit path (32x23cm-13x9in) s. board
£1200 $2400   (5-Feb-91 S62/R) River landscape (47x38cm-19x15in) s.
£1300 $2431   (28-Aug-90 S956/R) Quiet river (46x60cm-18x24in) s.
£1400 $2730   (17-Oct-90 PHG40/R) Summer clouds (34x44cm-13x17in) s.
£1400 $2366   (1-May-91 RBB692) Shore at Machrihanish, Mull of Kintyre, Argyllshire, with children (38x48cm-15x19in) s.
£1500 $2910   (5-Dec-90 PHE104/R) Boatman by the mill (35x45cm-14x18in) s.
£1600 $3200   (5-Feb-91 S72/R) Macrinhanish (25x35cm-10x14in) s. canvasboard
£1600 $2992   (28-Aug-90 S863/R) Whitekirk (62x75cm-24x30in) s.i.
£1800 $2898   (27-Jun-91 CG18/R) Harvesting, East Lothian (46x61cm-18x24in) s.
£1800 $3492   (5-Dec-90 PHE12/R) East Lothian pasture (25x45cm-10x18in) s.d.'15
£1800 $3492   (5-Dec-90 PHE84/R) On the Tyne, East Linton (34x45cm-13x18in) s.
£2000 $4000   (5-Feb-91 S80/R) Shepherd with flock (64x77cm-25x30in) s.
£2500 $4225   (3-May-91 PHE136) By the sea (25x35cm-10x14in) s. board
£2800 $5600   (5-Feb-91 S48/R) Mill pond (84x127cm-33x50in) s.
£3200 $5152   (27-Jun-91 CG19) Cattle grazing by a river, East Lothian (71x91cm-28x36in) s.d.04
£3500 $6790   (5-Dec-90 PHE74) Beached fishing boats (50x68cm-20x27in) s.

FRAZETTA, Frank (1928-) American
£1059 $1800   *(1-Jun-91 IH.NY138) Johnny and Sparky meet with foul play, comic strips (10x43cm-4x17in) s. pen ink pair*

FRAZIER, John Robinson (1889-1966) American
£595 $1100   (8-Mar-91 S.BM200/R) The pink grave yard (51x61cm-20x24in) s.d. verso

FRECHKOP, L (1897-1982) Belgian
£633 $1216   (18-Dec-90 GM.B837) Portrait de femme (70x50cm-28x20in) s. (B.FR 38000)

FRECHKOP, Leonid (1897-1982) Belgian
£2277 $4417   (8-Dec-90 KV.L126/R) Model in the artist's studio (92x73cm-36x29in) s.d.44 (B.FR 135000)

FRECKLETON, Harry (20th C) British
£579 $950   (19-Jun-91 B.SF1944/R) In the orchard, Attenborough (63x76cm-25x30in) s.
£800 $1392   (28-Mar-91 CSK50/R) First day of summer (63x67cm-25x26in) s.

FREDDIE, Wilhelm (1909-?) Danish
£1068 $2007   (19-Sep-90 KH.K104/R) Landscape (28x46cm-11x18in) s. panel (D.KR 12000)
£1423 $2676   (19-Sep-90 KH.K94) Landscape, Kulhuse (32x43cm-13x17in) s. panel (D.KR 16000)
£1495 $2885   (12-Dec-90 RAS.K182/R) Melancholy (24x19cm-9x7in) s.d.1939 masonite (D.KR 16500)
£1878 $3682   (13-Feb-91 KH.K60/R) Picture intended for execution in effegie (56x47cm-22x19in) s.d.52 (D.KR 21000)
£2046 $3847   (19-Sep-90 KH.K102/R) Still life of flowers and book on table (84x56cm-33x22in) s. panel (D.KR 23000)
£3081 $5299   (15-May-91 RAS.K73/R) Reclining woman (50x70cm-20x28in) s.d.1959 (D.KR 35000)
£3737 $7025   (19-Sep-90 KH.K110/R) Flowers in vase (61x51cm-24x20in) s.d.30 tempera panel (D.KR 42000)
£4472 $8766   (13-Feb-91 KH.K59/R) Trotsky's death (64x100cm-25x39in) s.d.60 (D.KR 50000)
£623 $1171   *(19-Sep-90 KH.K93) Composition (21x19cm-8x7in) s.d.52 pencil (D.KR 7000)*
£898 $1768   *(14-Nov-90 KH.K191) Composition (33x28cm-13x11in) s.d.80 W/C crayon collage (D.KR 10000)*
£968 $1888   *(10-Oct-90 RAS.K115) Composition (39x29cm-15x11in) s.d.84 crayon gouache (D.KR 11000)*

FREDDIE, Wilhelm (1909-?) Danish-cont.
£1042 $2010   *(12-Dec-90 RAS.K120/R) Portrait (46x55cm-18x22in) s.d.1964verso painting collage (D.KR 11500)*
£1056 $2060   *(10-Oct-90 RAS.K116) Composition (39x29cm-15x11in) s.d.84 crayon gouache (D.KR 12000)*
£2224 $4181   *(19-Sep-90 KH.K101/R) Composition (34x26cm-13x10in) s.d.79 collage W/C (D.KR 25000)*
£2244 $4421   *(14-Nov-90 KH.K45/R) Composition, Olympia (62x49cm-24x19in) s.d.81 collage crayon (D.KR 25000)*

FREDERIKSEN, Aksel (?) ?
£720 $1411   *(23-Nov-90 PHM104) A farmyard scene (42x56cm-17x22in) s.d.'07*

FREDERIKSEN, Arne Skottenborg (?) Danish
£1250 $2363   *(25-Sep-90 RAS.K197/R) Danish men-o-war at anchor, 5th April 1849 (67x98cm-26x39in) s.d.89 (D.KR 14000)*

FREDRIKS, Johannes Hendrik (1751-1822) Dutch
£40000 $65200   *(5-Jul-91 C42/R) Mixed flowers, bird's nest and cabbage leaves on marble ledge with insects (70x59cm-28x23in) panel*
£42000 $68460   *(5-Jul-91 C41/R) Mixed fruit, mixed flowers, chestnuts, corncob on stone ledge with mouseand insects (70x59cm-28x23in) s. panel*

FREEBAIRN, Robert (attrib) (1765-1808) British
£580 $1038   *(14-Mar-91 PHX351) Figures sketching withing Italianate ruins (58x76cm-23x30in)*

FREEDMAN, Barnett (1901-1958) British
£850 $1598   *(20-Sep-90 CSK54) Farmstead (46x56cm-18x22in) s.d.33*

FREEMAN, Don (?) ?
£3175 $6000   *(26-Sep-90 SY.NY202/R) Plights of stardom (107x164cm-42x65in) s.*

FREEMAN, G (?) ?
£789 $1500   *(12-Sep-90 D.NY27) Mixed fruit on ledge (97x66cm-38x26in) indist.s.d.*

FREEMAN, R (18th C) British
£850 $1658   *(15-Jan-91 SWS39/R) HMS Dutton off Dover (42x67cm-17x26in) s.d.1787*
£1600 $2768   *(22-May-91 S11/R) Ship Dutton in three positions off DFover (40x67cm-16x26in) s.d.1787 W/C*

FREEMAN, William Philip Barnes (1813-1897) British
£2200 $4400   *(8-Feb-91 C145/R) Thorpe reach on the river Yare. A view possibly on the river Orwell pair*

FREESE, N (fl.1794-1814) ?
£700 $1344   *(18-Dec-90 C134/R) Portrait of lady in decollete black dress with white rim (7x?cm-3x?in) min.gilt-metal oval mount black wood frame rec.*

FREGERE, C F (20th C) ?
£642 $1264   *(30-Oct-90 I.N299/R) La repetition (60x73cm-24x29in) s. (F.FR 6300)*

FREGERE, Claude (20th C) French
£609 $1205   *(3-Feb-91 I.N97/R) Guitare et trompette (73x54cm-29x21in) s. (F.FR 6000)*

FREGEVIZE, Frederic (1770-1849) Swiss
£1796 $3484   *(8-Dec-90 GAB.G2194/R) La danse paysanne (81x101cm-32x40in) (S.FR 4400)*
£4949 $8116   *(18-Jun-91 FN.S1844/R) Upper Rhine landscape with figures and snowy mountain range beyond (56x81cm-22x32in) s.d.1822 (DM 14500)*

FREIDHOF, Franz (20th C) German
£600 $1074   *(12-Apr-91 AW.H1444/R) View of Wurzburg (54x42cm-21x17in) s.i.d.1922 W/C board (DM 1800)*

FREIMAN, Lillian (1908-1986) Canadian
£558 $1071   *(27-Nov-90 W.T812) Village square in winter (30x23cm-12x9in) s. board (C.D 1250)*
£1010 $1747   *(6-May-91 SY.T20/R) Village square in winter (30x22cm-12x9in) s. panel (C.D 2000)*
£412 $701   *(27-May-91 HO.ED108/R) Orchestra 12 (46x46cm-18x18in) pastel mixed media oval (C.D 800)*

FREITAG, Karl (20th C) German
£683 $1264   *(7-Mar-91 D.V153/R) Dachau moor landscape (60x70cm-24x28in) s. i.verso (A.S 14000)*

FREIXANES, Jose (1953-) Spanish
£1512 $2949   *(26-Oct-90 CC.P113/R) Faro mareante (140x140cm-55x55in) s.i.d. verso (F.FR 15000)*

FREMY, Jacques Noel Marie (1782-1867) French
£1421 $2700   *(8-Jan-91 SY.NY144) Portrit of Monsieur Chateaubrillant (10x7cm-4x3in) s.i. graphite*

FRENCH IMPRESSIONIST SCHOOL (?)
£2327 $4513   *(8-Dec-90 GAB.G2331/R) Paysage (81x100cm-32x39in) (S.FR 5700)*

FRENCH SCHOOL (?)

£618	$1217	(13-Nov-90 J.M1160) Farmyard (23x34cm-9x13in) indis.s.i. (A.D 1600)
£998	$1786	(12-Mar-91 C.A104) The seduction (47x90cm-19x35in) (B.FR 60000)
£1000	$1690	(18-Apr-91 C15) Mixed flowers in an urn on a shaped ledge (65x55cm-26x22in) board
£1163	$1895	(11-Jun-91 GM.B1028) Mere allaitant (82x90cm-32x35in) (B.FR 70000)
£1195	$1959	(18-Jun-91 FN.S2172/R) Bacchanale in wooded mountainous landscape with stone bridge (26x33cm-10x13in) c.1800 panel oval (DM 3500)
£1220	$2000	(19-Jun-91 B.SF1700) Lot and his daughters (47x64cm-19x25in) c.1700 oval
£1351	$2297	(27-May-91 L.K45) Scene from the Old Testament with Potiphars wife courting Joseph (36x47cm-14x19in) c.1800 panel (DM 4000)
£1424	$2549	(11-Apr-91 D.V136/R) Diana and Callisto (11x15cm-4x6in) panel after F Boucher (A.S 30000)
£1424	$2549	(11-Apr-91 D.V135/R) Leda and the swan (11x15cm-4x6in) c.1800 panel after F Boucher (A.S 30000)
£1450	$2509	(20-May-91 SWS51/R) Still life of game in a landscape (87x74cm-34x29in) c.1800
£1457	$2390	(19-Jun-91 LC.P49/R) Bouquet de fleurs dans une corbeille (81x65cm-32x26in) oval (F.FR 14500)
£1497	$2649	(20-Mar-91 KM.K1021) Portrait of noble man wearing wig and armour (78x62cm-31x24in) c.1700 (DM 4400)
£1686	$3272	(4-Dec-90 C.A145) Portrait of a nobleman (91x71cm-36x28in) (B.FR 100000)
£1700	$2771	(4-Jul-91 CSK166/R) Noble family in grounds of chateau (76x91cm-30x36in)
£1829	$3273	(12-Mar-91 GM.B938) L'ecrivain (100x120cm-39x47in) (B.FR 110000)
£1900	$3287	(20-May-91 SWS10/R) A still life of flowers in a vase on a ledge (62x52cm-24x20in) c.1800
£1903	$3311	(25-Mar-91 SY.F644) Due donne sdraiate (99x141cm-39x56in) c.1900 (I.L 4200000)
£1988	$3360	(18-Apr-91 APT.P80/R) Laban cherchant les idoles (64x76cm-25x30in) c.1700 (F.FR 20000)
£1992	$3426	(14-May-91 GF.L2449/R) Riverside pigeon house (29x38cm-11x15in) c.1800 (S.FR 5000)
£1992	$3426	(14-May-91 GF.L2324/R) Still life of flowers (51x40cm-20x16in) c.1800 rem.sig. (S.FR 5000)
£2149	$3632	(16-Apr-91 J.M258) Spring afternoon on the Seine (36x54cm-14x21in) indist.sig. (A.D 4750)
£2200	$3718	(1-May-91 GD.B300/R) Bouquet of flowers and Chinese porcelain (45x63cm-18x25in) c.1900 indis.s. (S.FR 5500)
£2500	$4075	(3-Jul-91 S148/R) Portrait of actor, said to be Francois Charles Racot de Grandval (48x40cm-19x16in) c.1730
£2510	$4041	(27-Jun-91 APT.P206/R) Jeune page jouant de la guitare (80x66cm-31x26in) c.1810 (F.FR 25000)
£2711	$4364	(27-Jun-91 APT.P254/R) Panneau decoratif representant un heron et un perroquet dans un encadrement de fleurs (330x184cm-130x72in) c.1840 (F.FR 27000)
£2941	$5000	(27-May-91 GC.M404/R) Escena de batalla (36x48cm-14x19in)
£2941	$5000	(27-May-91 GC.M405) Escena de batalla (36x48cm-14x19in)
£3015	$4945	(21-Jun-91 SY.MO273/R) Paysage (57x71cm-22x28in) c.1700 (F.FR 30000)
£3073	$5500	(11-Apr-91 SY.NY189/R) Still life of flowers, peaches, grapes, plums and other fruit in urn (116x100cm-46x39in) oval
£4394	$8524	(3-Dec-90 SY.F1014) Nature morte con frutta (31x41cm-12x16in) c.1800 tempera glass pair (I.L 9500000)
£4500	$7605	(18-Apr-91 CSK158/R) Mixed flowers in vase with mixed fruit on marble ledge (86x102cm-34x40in)
£4625	$8972	(7-Dec-90 SY.MO204/R) Enfants jouant au cerf-volant devant un chateau (64x82cm-25x32in) c.1800 (F.FR 45000)
£5102	$10051	(16-Nov-90 LGB.P152) Scene allegorique (46x55cm-18x22in) (F.FR 50000)
£5944	$11472	(10-Dec-90 L.K257/R) The martyrdom of St Peter (10x20cm-4x8in) c.1600 gouache (DM 17000)
£6200	$12214	(31-Oct-90 S134/R) Portrait of gentleman in armour (55x44cm-22x17in) c.1600 canvas on panel
£6343	$11037	(25-Mar-91 SY.F727/R) Cinque putti (98x129cm-39x51in) c.1800 oval (I.L 14000000)
£7530	$12123	(27-Jun-91 APT.P170/R) Le printemps (90x90cm-35x35in) c.1640 wood (F.FR 75000)
£9200	$18124	(31-Oct-90 S165/R) David and Abigail (89x119cm-35x47in) c.1700
£9548	$15658	(21-Jun-91 SY.MO16/R) Allegorie de la musique (40x41cm-12x16in) c.1800 (F.FR 95000)
£1106	$1813	(19-Jun-91 LC.P18/R) Les admiratrices, ou le fait d'armes (50x38cm-20x15in) c.1790 pen wash indian ink htd.gouache oval (F.FR 11000)
£1318	$2611	(30-Jan-91 APT.P285/R) Paysage anime avec ruines et pyramide (18x26cm-7x10in) bears mono.d. (F.FR 13000)
£1500	$2955	(1-Nov-90 S3/R) Portrait of nobleman with brown curled wig and lace jabot (9x?cm-4x?in) min.c.1700 gilt gesso frame oval
£1600	$3152	(1-Nov-90 S4/R) Portrait of gentleman with embroidered coat and lace jabot (9x?cm-4x?in) min.c.1700 gilt gesso frame oval
£3000	$4890	(2-Jul-91 C138/R) Extensive rocky river landscape with figures on path. Hilly landscape, with brawl by inn (15x20cm-6x8in) black chk pen wash pair
£3077	$6000	(26-Oct-90 SY.NY43/R) Etude de jeune homme (41x30cm-16x12in) chk estampe
£3200	$6144	(18-Feb-91 S291/R) Male nude striding with stick and two studies of hands (37x25cm-15x10in) c.1700 chk htd.white
£3333	$6500	(26-Oct-90 SY.NY42/R) Etudes de jeune homme (36x28cm-14x11in) chk estampe double-sided

FRENCH SCHOOL (?) -cont.
£14689 $26000   (22-Mar-91 CH.NY617/R) *A woman playing a guitar and a girl dancing with a dog* (49x42cm-19x17in) c.1770 bodycolour
£50000 $81500   (1-Jul-91 S38/R) *Elegant family group-gentleman standing, wife seated, child, nurse, baby* (39x31cm-15x12in) W/C gouache over graphite col.chk vellum c.1790

FRENCH SCHOOL, 14th C
£7000 $11410   (2-Jul-91 C134/R) *Pope Gregory IX handing down Decretals, flanked by Clergy and Laity* (9x19cm-4x7in) with i.verso bodycol gold vellum panel

FRENCH SCHOOL, 15th C
£4020 $6593   (17-Jun-91 ARC.P15/R) *Les prophetes tenant des phylacteres* (81x59cm-32x23in) two parts of a triptych panel (F.FR 40000)
£9000 $17370   (12-Dec-90 S201/R) *Saint Sebastian* (85x52cm-33x20in) tempera gold ground panel

FRENCH SCHOOL, 16th C
£1114 $1939   (25-Mar-91 PLF.P106) *Le Christ aux enfers* (105x73cm-41x29in) panel (F.FR 11200)
£2028 $4016   (30-Jan-91 APT.P79/R) *Portrait d'un homme age de 40 ans* (52x49cm-20x19in) i. panel (F.FR 20000)
£2333 $4619   (30-Jan-91 APT.P243/R) *Portrait de Dame Barbe Guyffart* (43x32cm-17x13in) i.d.1598 panel (F.FR 23000)
£2449 $4751   (8-Dec-90 GAB.G2030/R) *Portrait d'une elegante* (50x37cm-20x15in) panel (S.FR 6000)
£2840 $5623   (30-Jan-91 APT.P82/R) *Portrait d'homme barbu a la toque noire* (25x20cm-10x8in) bears i.d.1576 (F.FR 28000)
£7542 $13500   (11-Apr-91 SY.NY84/R) *Portrait of lady, said to be Dame de Noixces* (67x50cm-26x20in) i. panel
£13000 $21190   (5-Jul-91 C261/R) *Portrait of Charles de Bourbon, wearing tunic, fur-edged cloak and hat* (16x11cm-6x4in) with i.verso shaped panel

FRENCH SCHOOL, 17th C
£994 $1680   (18-Apr-91 APT.P84/R) *Portrait de Georges Langlois* (75x60cm-30x24in) i. (F.FR 10000)
£1020 $1806   (20-Mar-91 KM.K1019) *Abraham and Sarah sending Hagar and her son Ismael away* (94x135cm-37x53in) (DM 3000)
£1037 $1795   (8-May-91 FER.M60/R) *Retrato de caballero* (40x32cm-16x13in) (S.P 190000)
£1217 $2410   (30-Jan-91 APT.P80/R) *Portrait de femme a la collerette, vue en buste* (58x42cm-23x17in) (F.FR 12000)
£1250 $2100   (17-Jul-91 SY.NY144/R) *Portrait of a woman said to be Marie Foubair* (104x80cm-41x31in)
£1394 $2371   (31-May-91 LD.P30/R) *La Circoncision* (100x65cm-39x26in) panel (F.FR 14000)
£1508 $2894   (19-Feb-91 ARC.P10) *Portrait d'une jeune fille en robe bleue* (40x33cm-16x13in) oval (F.FR 15000)
£1606 $2586   (24-Jun-91 BL.P17) *Deploration du Christ* (42x34cm-17x13in) (F.FR 16000)
£1800 $2934   (3-Jul-91 OD.P71) *Portrait de Louis XIV* (41x33cm-16x13in) (F.FR 18000)
£2028 $4016   (30-Jan-91 APT.P89/R) *Le Christ apparaissant a Saint Bruno. Le Christ apparaissant a Saint Louis* (24x18cm-9x7in) panel two (F.FR 20000)
£2551 $5000   (7-Nov-90 B.SF1033/R) *Expulsion of Hagar* (63x63cm-25x25in) circular
£2629 $5126   (19-Oct-90 MB.P29/R) *Portrait d'homme* (41x32cm-16x13in) oval (F.FR 26000)
£2693 $5306   (14-Nov-90 D.V269/R) *Elegant party in palace* (103x83cm-41x33in) (A.S 55000)
£2814 $4615   (17-Jun-91 ARC.P14/R) *Portrait de jeune femme entouree de quatre putti* (74x78cm-29x31in) (F.FR 28000)
£2854 $5480   (30-Nov-90 APT.P95/R) *Dame de qualite vue a mi-corps, assise presque de face, avec petit chien* (99x80cm-39x31in) (F.FR 28000)
£3024 $5412   (13-Mar-91 FER.M157/R) *El descanso de los soldados junto a las ruinas clasicas* (126x102cm-50x40in) (S.P 550000)
£3360 $5711   (27-May-91 GK.Z5034/R) *Portrait of Anna von Osterreich seated wearing dress decorated with lace* (144x105cm-57x41in) (S.FR 8500)
£3757 $6500   (10-May-91 S.W2497/R) *Young prince in armour with the goddess Minerva* (196x135cm-77x53in)
£3984 $6853   (14-May-91 GF.L2035/R) *Portrait of lady* (89x68cm-35x27in) (S.FR 10000)
£4023 $7000   (27-Mar-91 B.SF4027/R) *Holy Family with St John the Baptist* (155x118cm-61x46in)
£4103 $8000   (10-Oct-90 CH.NY179/R) *Soldiers on patio before classical building* (73x75cm-29x30in)
£4406 $8635   (11-Nov-90 M.V12/R) *Jeune femme en buste* (33x24cm-13x9in) panel (F.FR 43000)
£4564 $9037   (30-Jan-91 CSC.P15/R) *Scene mythologique* (114x124cm-45x49in) (F.FR 45000)
£4625 $8972   (7-Dec-90 CH.MO330/R) *Portrait de Henri de la Tour d'Auvergne, Marechal de France, 1611-1675* (60x48cm-24x19in) (F.FR 45000)
£5635 $11045   (11-Nov-90 I.N7/R) *Portrait de jeune homme en habit rouge* (48x38cm-19x15in) (F.FR 55000)
£5707 $9588   (23-Apr-91 F.R32/R) *Venere e Enea* (128x87cm-50x34in) (I.L 12500000)
£5829 $10434   (17-Mar-91 L.C99) *Legende de Junon, Io et Argus* (128x147cm-50x58in) (F.FR 58000)
£7347 $14400   (6-Nov-90 GF.L2035/R) *Heroic landscape* (82x101cm-32x40in) (S.FR 18000)
£9045 $14834   (21-Jun-91 SY.MO185/R) *Josue arretant le soleil* (103x136cm-41x54in) (F.FR 90000)

672

FRENCH SCHOOL, 17th C -cont.

£9200	$15548	(17-Apr-91 S162/R) The Holy Family (92x99cm-36x39in)
£10000	$19700	(31-Oct-90 S112/R) Still life of samovar and other metal objects on table draped with carpet (108x150cm-43x59in)
£11305	$21932	(7-Dec-90 CH.MO354/R) Scene tiree de l'histoire de Jacob (152x154cm-60x61in) (F.FR 110000)
£26000	$50180	(12-Dec-90 S33/R) Coriolanus with his wife and mother (95x133cm-37x52in)
£46249	$89723	(7-Dec-90 CH.MO349/R) Le mariage de la vierge (112x173cm-44x68in) (F.FR 450000)
£1054	$1697	(27-Jun-91 APT.P180) Neptune et Amphirite (29x15cm-11x6in) gouache (F.FR 10500)
£1500	$2535	(16-Apr-91 C218/R) Studies of pediments (43x28cm-17x11in) i. watermark blk.chk.ink wash double-sided
£2800	$4564	(2-Jul-91 C150/R) Orpheus charming animals (27x22cm-11x9in) black chk pen wash vellum
£5460	$10647	(21-Oct-90 L.C29) Figure allegorique (46x39cm-18x15in) sanguinne htd.white (F.FR 54000)
£6667	$13000	(11-Oct-90 SY.NY53/R) Rest on the Flight into Egypt within garland of flowers (25x33cm-10x13in) gouache vellum laid on panel

FRENCH SCHOOL, 17th/18th C

£2932	$5718	(21-Oct-90 DA.R5/R) Femme au chapeau et a la tasse de chocolat (81x65cm-32x26in) (F.FR 29000)
£5561	$10732	(12-Dec-90 BU.S127/R) Minerva and the Muses on Helikon mountain (133x108cm-52x43in) (S.KR 60000)

FRENCH SCHOOL, 18th C

£1000	$1630	(4-Jul-91 B177) An Italianate landscape with travellers watering at a river (28x37cm-11x15in)
£1000	$1680	(26-Apr-91 ARC.P12) Portrait d'une princesse (65x54cm-26x21in) oval (F.FR 10000)
£1014	$2008	(30-Jan-91 APT.P97) La Madeleine (73x98cm-29x39in) (F.FR 10000)
£1014	$2008	(30-Jan-91 APT.P270/R) La cour de l'auberge (43x33cm-17x13in) (F.FR 10000)
£1014	$2008	(30-Jan-91 APT.P121/R) Portrait d'un ecclesiastique (65x54cm-26x21in) (F.FR 10000)
£1014	$2008	(30-Jan-91 APT.P276/R) Paysage a la riviere (25x32cm-10x13in) panel (F.FR 10000)
£1020	$2000	(21-Nov-90 NA.BA23) Vase aux fleurs (66x51cm-26x20in)
£1071	$1800	(17-Jul-91 SY.NY161/R) Classical landscape with figures (55x63cm-22x25in)
£1087	$1892	(25-Mar-91 SY.F602) Ritratto di uomo (47x38cm-19x15in) panel (I.L 2400000)
£1100	$1837	(7-Jun-91 AGS.P52) La Sainte Famille (101x81cm-40x32in) (F.FR 11000)
£1137	$2036	(12-Apr-91 AGS.P3) Portrait d'un Magistrat (70x63cm-28x25in) (F.FR 11500)
£1176	$2000	(31-May-91 CH.NY212/R) The Agony in the Garden (102x77cm-40x30in)
£1193	$2016	(18-Apr-91 APT.P97/R) Scene de la Jerusalem Delivree (54x43cm-21x17in) (F.FR 12000)
£1217	$2410	(30-Jan-91 APT.P256/R) L'Amour endormi (44x56cm-17x22in) (F.FR 12000)
£1224	$1971	(28-Jun-91 BM.B628/R) Tete a tete in park landscape with figures (81x104cm-32x41in) (DM 3600)
£1229	$2372	(11-Dec-90 FER.M180/R) Venus y Vulcano (47x56cm-19x22in) bears i. (S.P 225000)
£1240	$2096	(2-May-91 RAS.V156/R) Religious scene (102x76cm-40x30in) (D.KR 14000)
£1287	$2278	(5-Apr-91 DAR.P40/R) Le petit pecheur (54x64cm-21x25in) (F.FR 13000)
£1307	$2143	(21-Jun-91 D.P45) Portrait de dame de qualite (41x33cm-16x13in) oval (F.FR 13000)
£1350	$2336	(20-May-91 SWS40) A wedding feast (90x120cm-35x47in) oval
£1360	$2216	(10-Jun-91 AGB.P79) Portrait d'homme tenant un livre (87x68cm-34x27in) oval (F.FR 13500)
£1385	$2479	(8-Apr-91 ARC.P33/R) Portrait de dame de qualite en robe blanche et cape bleue (80x64cm-31x25in) (F.FR 14000)
£1400	$2688	(18-Dec-90 C15/R) Portrait of lady in gold-figured green dress (6x?cm-2x?in) min.copper gilt-metal mount silver frame oval
£1407	$2519	(17-Mar-91 L.C97) Portrait d'un jeune officier (74x57cm-29x22in) (F.FR 14000)
£1500	$2445	(4-Jul-91 C775/R) Young woman, head and shoulders, en deshabille (58x46cm-23x18in)
£1500	$2445	(4-Jul-91 B100 h) Joseph welcoming his brothers into Egypt (63x75cm-25x30in)
£1506	$2425	(24-Jun-91 BL.P22/R) Allegorie de l'innocence (53x43cm-21x17in) (F.FR 15000)
£1508	$2472	(21-Jun-91 SY.MO287/R) Paysage avec rivieres (32x49cm-13x19in) paper laid down on canvas (F.FR 15000)
£1511	$2462	(13-Jun-91 CSC.P3/R) Portrait de jeune femme en buste (65x53cm-26x21in) oval (F.FR 15000)
£1521	$3012	(30-Jan-91 APT.P114/R) Portrait d'une jeune femme au serin (59x49cm-23x19in) s. (F.FR 15000)
£1550	$2682	(20-May-91 SWS132/R) Classical landscape with putti playing with a goat (103x165cm-41x65in)
£1592	$2770	(25-Mar-91 QWA.P155) Faisans et chien (86x110cm-34x43in) (F.FR 16000)
£1608	$2637	(21-Jun-91 D.P51/R) Le joueur de vielle (92x64cm-36x25in) (F.FR 16000)
£1608	$2637	(21-Jun-91 SY.MO279/R) Portrait de femme (63x52cm-25x20in) oval (F.FR 16000)

FRENCH SCHOOL, 18th C -cont.

£1663	$2976	(12-Mar-91 GM.B950) Interieur de cathedrale (118x170cm-46x67in) (B.FR 100000)
£1680	$2839	(1-May-91 GD.B272/R) Wooded river landscape with elegant party (65x79cm-26x31in) (S.FR 4200)
£1690	$2856	(18-Apr-91 APT.P104) Portrait de famille dans un jardin (17x22cm-7x9in) paper laid down on board (F.FR 17000)
£1809	$2967	(21-Jun-91 SY.MO306/R) La mort de Raymond Diocres (30x22cm-12x9in) (F.FR 18000)
£1826	$3615	(30-Apr-91 APT.P268/R) Portrait d'homme en manteau rouge (73x60cm-29x24in) (F.FR 18000)
£1873	$3221	(14-May-91 BU.S82/R) Still life of dead hare and birds (63x50cm-25x20in) (S.KR 20000)
£1910	$3132	(19-Jun-91 LC.P48/R) Portrait de jeune femme coiffe d'un bonnet aux rubans roses (51x40cm-20x16in) oval (F.FR 19000)
£1990	$3463	(25-Mar-91 PLF.P108) Portrait d'un militaire en armure (79x61cm-31x24in) oval (F.FR 20000)
£1990	$3463	(27-Mar-91 CN.P61) Allegorie de l'Aurore (54x46cm-21x18in) (F.FR 20000)
£2008	$3233	(27-Jun-91 APT.P178/R) Le Menuet dans le parc (93x134cm-37x53in) (F.FR 20000)
£2200	$3586	(4-Jul-91 B179/R) Portrait of a young girl, standing at stone ledge holding flowers (52x44cm-20x17in) indist.s.d.1768
£2231	$4418	(30-Jan-91 APT.P267/R) Portrait de jeune femme (80x65cm-31x26in) (F.FR 22000)
£2281	$3673	(25-Jun-91 FER.M180/R) Santa Catalina de Alejandria (31x24cm-12x9in) copper (S.P 420000)
£2475	$4381	(5-Apr-91 DAR.P51/R) Saint Jean Baptiste. Anges avec les instruments de la Passion (35x42cm-14x17in) pair (F.FR 25000)
£2534	$4282	(3-May-91 SA.A1634/R) Busy harbour scene at evening (188x60cm-74x24in) (DM 7500)
£2535	$5020	(30-Jan-91 APT.P128/R) Portrait d'une femme assise dans un fauteuil (88x67cm-35x26in) bears sig.d.1788 (F.FR 25000)
£2540	$4318	(31-May-91 LD.P25/R) Vase de fleurs sur en entablement avec un ecureuil (24x33cm-9x13in) panel (F.FR 25500)
£2542	$4905	(12-Dec-90 F.M361) Interno (40x33cm-16x13in) (I.L 5500000)
£2548	$4893	(30-Nov-90 APT.P139/R) Le corps de garde (44x52cm-17x20in) (F.FR 25000)
£2551	$4107	(26-Jun-91 KM.K1326/R) The Judgement of Paris (66x99cm-26x39in) (DM 7500)
£2579	$4617	(13-Mar-91 GK.Z23) Park landscape with figures making music (115x112cm-45x44in) (S.FR 6500)
£2600	$5018	(11-Dec-90 PH245/R) River landscape with traders on bank by open merchant boats (63x76cm-25x30in)
£2600	$4394	(16-Apr-91 PH135/R) Cupid (137x110cm-54x43in)
£2679	$4500	(17-Jul-91 SY.NY118/R) Portrait of Empress Maria (75x61cm-30x24in) within oval
£2793	$5000	(11-Apr-91 SY.NY25/R) Portrait of gentleman wearing white satin costume with lace collar (53x42cm-21x17in)
£2800	$5404	(12-Dec-90 S124/R) Death of Priam (54x45cm-21x18in)
£2800	$5180	(5-Mar-91 PH48/R) Elegant party hunting stag through parkland (97x151cm-38x59in)
£3043	$6024	(30-Jan-91 APT.P248/R) Paysage heroique (54x69cm-21x27in) l. (F.FR 30000)
£3200	$6304	(30-Oct-90 PH91/R) Fete champetre (88x145cm-35x57in)
£3200	$6304	(31-Oct-90 S176/R) Still life of flowers in silver urn (63x47cm-25x19in)
£3245	$6426	(30-Jan-91 APT.P91/R) Le piqueux et son chien. Chasseur chargeant son fusil (29x22cm-11x9in) panel pair (F.FR 32000)
£3253	$5303	(12-Jun-91 N.M310/R) Flora with garland of flowers and putti holding basket of flowers (83x58cm-33x23in) (DM 9500)
£3333	$6400	(18-Dec-90 GM.B4079/R) Scene allegorique (61x75cm-24x30in) (B.FR 200000)
£3392	$6580	(7-Dec-90 CN.P137/R) Berger et bergere dans un paysage (54x73cm-21x29in) (F.FR 33000)
£3517	$6787	(16-Dec-90 M.V145/R) Scene a la fontaine (60x82cm-24x32in) (F.FR 34500)
£3521	$5915	(23-Apr-91 RAS.K48/R) Boudoir-scene with courtisan at toilett, and cavalier visiting (80x125cm-31x49in) pair (D.KR 40000)
£3597	$6978	(7-Dec-90 SY.MO205/R) Le sacrifice de Manoah (80x72cm-31x28in) arched (F.FR 35000)
£3824	$7380	(11-Dec-90 FER.M174/R) Bodegon con flores y papagayo (80x120cm-31x47in) (S.P 700000)
£3846	$7500	(25-Oct-90 GRO.B25/R) La vallierre (104x137cm-41x54in)
£3956	$7082	(8-Apr-91 ARC.P15/R) Portrait d'un serviteur nain (94x80cm-37x31in) (F.FR 40000)
£4057	$8032	(30-Jan-91 APT.P257/R) Allegorie de la Peinture (103x129cm-41x51in) (F.FR 40000)
£4074	$6559	(25-Jun-91 FER.M178/R) Edificios clasicos y personajes (95x132cm-37x52in) (S.P 750000)
£4098	$8033	(11-Nov-90 I.N20/R) Portrait de femme (66x50cm-26x20in) (F.FR 40000)
£4171	$7883	(28-Sep-90 CSC.P11/R) Composition florale avec tapis, vase antique et fruits (92x120cm-36x47in) (F.FR 41000)
£4317	$8374	(7-Dec-90 CH.MO340 a/R) Un sultan et sa favorite (81x65cm-32x26in) (F.FR 42000)
£4824	$7912	(21-Jun-91 SY.MO21/R) La musicienne (31x24cm-12x9in) (F.FR 48000)
£5000	$8150	(3-Jul-91 S129/R) Portrait of Denis Diderot (141x107cm-56x42in)
£5020	$8383	(7-Jun-91 AGS.P53) Les quatre saisons (76x103cm-30x41in) four (F.FR 50200)
£5060	$8500	(17-Jul-91 SY.NY142/R) A whippet and a pomeranian in a landscape (89x120cm-35x47in)

674

FRENCH SCHOOL, 18th C -cont.

£5139	$9969	(7-Dec-90 SY.MO201/R) Scene allegorique (38x62cm-15x24in) (F.FR 50000)
£5160	$8308	(25-Jun-91 FER.M179/R) Paseando bajo las ruinas clasicas (95x132cm-37x52in) (S.P 950000)
£5528	$9065	(21-Jun-91 SY.MO303/R) Mars (182x127cm-72x50in) (F.FR 55000)
£5545	$9814	(4-Apr-91 CK.P24/R) Paysage a la riviere avec des pecheurs aux filets (91x131cm-36x52in) (F.FR 56000)
£6000	$10140	(17-Apr-91 S27/R) Still lifes of flowers with parrot in ornamental garden settings (55x95cm-22x37in) pair
£6024	$9699	(24-Jun-91 DL.P71/R) Beau trompe l'oeil, avec arte de l'Ile de Saint Domingue (50x61cm-20x24in) (F.FR 60000)
£6085	$12049	(30-Jan-91 APT.P110/R) Portrait du Roi Louis XV, enfant (125x94cm-49x37in) (F.FR 60000)
£6166	$11963	(7-Dec-90 CN.P139/R) Bal pare pendant le carnaval (80x100cm-31x39in) (F.FR 60000)
£6166	$11963	(7-Dec-90 SY.MO169/R) Chinoiserie avec oiseaux (120x100cm-47x39in) (F.FR 60000)
£6533	$10714	(21-Jun-91 SY.MO281/R) Trompe l'oeil de bas-relief (23x27cm-9x11in) bears mono.M…G.d.1789 (F.FR 65000)
£6834	$11208	(21-Jun-91 SY.MO280/R) Portraits de Dames de qualite (29x20cm-11x8in) pair (F.FR 65000)
£6915	$13000	(18-Sep-90 RO.BA17) Chaseuse (145x111cm-57x44in)
£7186	$12000	(23-Jan-91 D.NY60/R) Still life of flowers in basket on ledge (64x74cm-25x29in)
£8190	$15971	(21-Oct-90 L.C42/R) Louis XIV an armure assis sur un char marin presente par la France (149x206cm-59x81in) (F.FR 81000)
£8200	$13858	(17-Apr-91 S43/R) Still life of flowers in vase with fruit on stone ledge (119x91cm-47x36in)
£8475	$15000	(22-Mar-91 CH.NY640) Venus instructing Cupid. A Bacchante feeding grapes to infant Bacchus (63x48cm-25x19in) pastel
£8736	$16948	(7-Dec-90 CN.P142/R) Fete champetre (53x68cm-21x27in) panel (F.FR 85000)
£9359	$17689	(27-Sep-90 BL.P46) Portrait d'un homme en perruque et d'une jeune femme en robe blanche (22x16cm-9x6in) pair (F.FR 92000)
£20916	$36185	(22-May-91 CD.P5/R) La delivrance de Saint-Pierre (88x70cm-35x28in) (F.FR 210000)
£30832	$59815	(7-Dec-90 CH.MO333 a/R) Louis XIV devant le Grand Escalier de Versailles. Louis XIV devant la Grande Piece d'eau de Marly (115x176cm-45x69in) pair (F.FR 300000)
£909	$1573	(21-May-91 SY.MI242/R) Ritratto di una nobildonna vestita in celeste con mantello blu (4x?cm-2x?in) min.enamel gilded frame oval (I.L 2000000)
£909	$1573	(21-May-91 SY.MI232/R) Ritratto di gentildonna con maschera (5cm-2ins circular) min. paper pearl border frame (I.L 2000000)
£989	$1771	(10-Apr-91 CB.P6) Portrait de Pierre d'Abadie (77x59cm-30x23in) pastel (F.FR 10000)
£1005	$1648	(18-Jun-91 APT.P86/R) Architecture imaginaire - Palais antique avec personnages (26x41cm-10x16in) pen W/C wash (F.FR 10000)
£1050	$1859	(20-Mar-91 DL.P103/R) Jeune fille a l'oiseau (40x32cm-16x13in) pastel (F.FR 10000)
£1050	$1859	(22-Mar-91 APT.P54/R) Vue d'un village sous la neige et Temple sous une grotte (7x8cm-3x3in) gouache pair (F.FR 10500)
£1100	$1947	(22-Mar-91 APT.P57) Passage de gue sous l'orage (17x21cm-7x8in) gouache (F.FR 11000)
£1100	$1947	(22-Mar-91 APT.P56) Personnages dans des ruines (39x32cm-15x13in) gouache (F.FR 11000)
£1108	$1806	(14-Jun-91 AGS.P33) Paysage avec des habitations troglodytes anime de personnages (63x85cm-25x33in) gouache (F.FR 11000)
£1194	$2078	(27-Mar-91 CN.P32/R) Academie d'homme (43x29cm-17x11in) sanguine (F.FR 12000)
£1200	$2028	(16-Apr-91 C246/R) A fountain with female caryatids by a classical Portico (59x41cm-23x16in) watermark blk.chk.ink wash
£1217	$2410	(30-Jan-91 APT.P265/R) Portrait en buste de Jean Guerangal de Kervisio, Receveur des Fermes (72x58cm-28x23in) pastel (F.FR 12000)
£1224	$2412	(13-Nov-90 CH.G220/R) Portrait of Monsieur de Seze (6x6cm-2x2in) min. hair verso silver-gilt frame octagonal (S.FR 3000)
£1250	$2100	(17-Jul-91 SY.NY33/R) Landscape with lovers by a stream (16x26cm-6x10in) i.d.1770 gouache W/C board
£1300	$2301	(22-Mar-91 BG.P11/R) Scene galante dans un jardin avec cenotaphe egyptien (26x32cm-10x13in) W/C gouache (F.FR 13000)
£1400	$2478	(22-Mar-91 APT.P53) Portrait d'une jeune fille tenant une rose (54x44cm-21x17in) i. Greuze pastel oval (F.FR 14000)
£1450	$2567	(22-Mar-91 APT.P49) Combats de cavalerie (16x21cm-6x8in) gouache pair (F.FR 14500)
£1508	$2609	(22-May-91 GS.B2370) Portrait of woman dressed in Turkish costume holding letter and picture (52x61cm-20x24in) indis.s.i. pastel oval (S.FR 3800)
£1508	$2698	(17-Mar-91 DA.R1/R) Allegorie du Temps et de la Renommee ou l'Alliance des maisons royales.. traces sig.d.i. W/C vellum (F.FR 15000)
£1693	$2929	(22-May-91 PLF.P96) Etude de chien assis (45x35cm-18x14in) i. sanguinne (F.FR 17000)
£1800	$3186	(22-Mar-91 APT.P51) Naufrage d'un voilier devant l'entree d'un port (65x101cm-26x40in) W/C gouache (F.FR 18000)
£1900	$3097	(1-Jul-91 S93/R) Allegory of Catholic church flanked by Justice, Faith and Charity, receiving king (35x27cm-14x11in) black chk
£2000	$3540	(22-Mar-91 APT.P83) Trois jeunes femmes jouant aux cartes dans un parc (45x44cm-18x17in) pierre noire sanguinne pastel (F.FR 20000)

FRENCH SCHOOL, 18th C -cont.

£2008	$3233	(24-Jun-91 BL.P11) Paysans et troupeau traversant une riviere. Couple de paysans traversantun que (34x48cm-13x19in) gouache pair (F.FR 20000)
£2100	$3528	(26-Apr-91 ARC.P6/R) Nature morte aux fruits et aux fleurs avec un babouin (40x52cm-16x20in) s.d.1798 W/C (F.FR 21000)
£2400	$4056	(16-Apr-91 C243/R) A female nude, her left arm raised (22x17cm-9x7in) i. watermark red chk.
£2600	$4394	(16-Apr-91 C244/R) An Indian Cassowary observed by a native in a wooded landscape (49x65cm-19x26in) i.d.1788 watermark blk.chk.wash W/C
£2800	$4956	(22-Mar-91 APT.P52/R) Tete de femme, les yeux leves (46x36cm-18x14in) i. pastel (F.FR 28000)
£4179	$8066	(14-Dec-90 LEB.P44) Scene de bataille antique (42x41cm-17x16in) i. pen sanguinne Indian ink (F.FR 41000)
£4211	$8000	(11-Jan-91 CH.NY86/R) Portrait of a lady, half length, wearing a grey satin dress, book in hand (85x69cm-33x27in) pastel
£4830	$9371	(7-Dec-90 CN.P114/R) Portrait de la Comtesse d'Hunolstein (63x52cm-25x20in) pastel oval (F.FR 47000)
£5300	$8639	(1-Jul-91 S1/R) Seated woman in exotic costume (50x41cm-20x16in) reddish-brown chk
£5500	$8965	(1-Jul-91 S137/R) Study of seated male figure holding large bowl (30x21cm-12x8in) black chk htd white
£12105	$23000	(9-Jan-91 CH.NY67/R) Portrait of Queen Marie-Antoinette, holding rose (91x71cm-36x28in) pastel oval after Vigee-Le Brun
£15254	$27000	(22-Mar-91 CH.NY616/R) Views of the Chateau of Rambouillet (15x13cm-6x5in) bodycolour pair
£18256	$36146	(30-Jan-91 CSC.P14/R) Les thermes de Caracalla a Rome (50x68cm-20x27in) i. wash sanguinne (F.FR 180000)

FRENCH SCHOOL, 18th/19th C

£996	$1723	(22-May-91 CD.P8) Bergers et moutons dans un paysage orageux (24x32cm-9x13in) panel (F.FR 10000)
£1494	$2405	(25-Jun-91 FER.M65/R) La merienda en el bosque (107x165cm-42x65in) (S.P 275000)

FRENCH SCHOOL, 19th C

£816	$1600	(6-Nov-90 GF.L2382/R) Coastal landscape with boats (27x35cm-11x14in) rem.mono. (S.FR 2000)
£983	$1898	(11-Dec-90 FER.M94/R) Pastor con su rebano (30x32cm-12x13in) panel (S.P 180000)
£1000	$1630	(2-Jul-91 PH280) Still life of roses and other flowers in sculptured urn (57x41cm-22x16in)
£1000	$1680	(26-Apr-91 NM.P16/R) Chemin retour des lavandieres (31x40cm-12x16in) (F.FR 10000)
£1014	$2008	(30-Jan-91 APT.P148/R) La separation d'Achille et Briseis (30x45cm-12x18in) (F.FR 10000)
£1047	$1800	(18-May-91 W.W14/R) Shepherds overlooking an Arab compound (71x97cm-28x38in)
£1079	$2083	(15-Dec-90 BU.H332) Still life of flowers (24x19cm-9x7in) bears sig. panel (F.M 7500)
£1100	$1848	(18-Jul-91 CSK105) Allegory of summer (239x421cm-94x166in) oval
£1116	$1919	(14-May-91 GF.L2391) Still life of peonies and field flowers (36x46cm-14x18in) (S.FR 2800)
£1116	$2209	(30-Jan-91 CSC.P17/R) Jeune femme en buste presque de face (60x50cm-24x20in) oval (F.FR 11000)
£1195	$2056	(14-May-91 GF.L2414/R) Still life of flowers (56x73cm-22x29in) (S.FR 3000)
£1195	$2056	(14-May-91 GF.L2357/R) Shepherd couple in landscape (25x35cm-10x14in) panel (S.FR 3000)
£1200	$1956	(1-Jul-91 GL.P16) Le jeune prince (45x44cm-18x17in) oval (F.FR 12000)
£1240	$2133	(19-May-91 ZZ.F55/R) Jete de fleurs (24x30cm-9x12in) bears sig.d.1889 panel (F.FR 12500)
£1290	$2218	(19-May-91 ZZ.F51/R) Bouquet de fleurs (29x23cm-11x9in) bears indist.sig. panel (F.FR 13000)
£1393	$2424	(27-Mar-91 CN.P55/R) Portrait de jeune femme (54x44cm-21x17in) (F.FR 14000)
£1400	$2744	(14-Feb-91 CSK177) Portrait of Napoleon, bust length, in a painted cartouche (102x76cm-40x30in)
£1446	$2385	(9-Jul-91 ARC.P7) Enlevement d'une jeune fille par un centaure (40x30cm-16x12in) (F.FR 14500)
£1474	$2800	(27-Feb-91 SY.NY56/R) Portrait of gentleman (66x55cm-26x22in)
£1493	$2597	(27-Mar-91 CN.P54/R) Paysage anime (11x18cm-4x7in) (F.FR 15000)
£1500	$2595	(20-May-91 SWS218/R) A sunset scene in a harbour (15x28cm-6x11in) i.1853 panel
£1512	$2600	(17-May-91 WOL.C256 a) Landscape with putti, cherubs and a lamb (66x104cm-26x41in)
£1542	$2991	(8-Dec-90 SY.MO364/R) Tombeau de Cecilia Metella (23x32cm-9x13in) bears sig.Corot paper laid down on canvas (F.FR 15000)
£1557	$2600	(5-Jun-91 D.NY36/R) Afternoon hours (56x46cm-22x18in) s.
£1582	$3100	(21-Nov-90 NA.BA67) Cignes et geons dans un paysage (120x100cm-47x39in) s.
£1630	$2624	(27-Jun-91 EP.M21/R) Florero (57x83cm-22x33in) (S.P 300000)
£1633	$3200	(21-Nov-90 NA.BA47) Nature morte (87x145cm-34x57in)
£1744	$3000	(17-May-91 WOL.C1088) Venus and Cupid (89x117cm-35x46in)
£1890	$3250	(15-May-91 D.NY49) The curious gift (97x81cm-38x32in)
£2000	$3580	(12-Mar-91 PH105) The country feast (74x61cm-29x24in) bears sig. canvas on board oval pair

FRENCH SCHOOL, 19th C -cont.

£2010	$3296	(19-Jun-91 LC.P55/R) Le bon samaritain (54x42cm-21x17in) traces pen paper (F.FR 20000)
£2108	$3395	(28-Jun-91 ZZ.F130) Femems grecques au perroquet (100x80cm-39x31in) mono.d.1844 (F.FR 21000)
£2130	$4217	(30-Jan-91 APT.P291/R) Paysage anime de personnages (32x40cm-13x16in) (F.FR 21000)
£2168	$4250	(7-Nov-90 B.SF1010/R) Portrait of Marie Antoinette's blackamoor in fanciful dress turban (15x12cm-6x5in) panel
£2176	$3895	(12-Apr-91 AGS.P21/R) Le Pont Valentre a Cahors (52x74cm-20x29in) (F.FR 22000)
£2308	$4500	(24-Oct-90 D.NY93) Young girl wearing green turban reading book (81x66cm-32x26in)
£2400	$4128	(17-May-91 C30/R) Winter street scene (60x73cm-24x29in) indist.s.
£2424	$4752	(11-Feb-91 CSC.P19/R) Chasseur a cheval pres d'une riviere (34x44cm-13x17in) (F.FR 24000)
£2474	$4428	(13-Mar-91 FER.M182/R) Retrato de dama (32x26cm-13x10in) (S.P 450000)
£2600	$4498	(9-May-91 CSK115/R) Allegory of music (198x122cm-78x48in)
£2600	$4368	(18-Jul-91 CSK112) Mixed flowers in bowl (55x45cm-22x18in) panel pair
£2637	$5221	(30-Jan-91 APT.P297/R) Les reproches maternels (81x65cm-32x26in) (F.FR 26000)
£2705	$4842	(8-Apr-91 CH.R71/R) Ritratti del Conte de Chabrol (75x54cm-30x21in) oval pair (I.L 6000000)
£2763	$5250	(27-Feb-91 SY.NY110/R) Figures in classical landscape (63x92cm-25x36in)
£2792	$5500	(15-Nov-90 SY.NY7/R) Pink and red roses (27x22cm-11x9in) panel
£2834	$5555	(20-Nov-90 APT.P264/R) Les mamluques (45x55cm-18x22in) (F.FR 28000)
£2988	$4810	(25-Jun-91 FER.M181/R) Retrato de dama (62x47cm-24x19in) (S.P 550000)
£2992	$5744	(17-Dec-90 ARC.P63/R) Nature morte aux fruits (82x61cm-32x24in) (F.FR 29500)
£3083	$5982	(7-Dec-90 CH.MO347/R) L'Enlevement de Proserpine (24x32cm-9x13in) (F.FR 30000)
£3200	$6304	(5-Oct-90 C60/R) First Day (76x63cm-30x25in) with i.
£3347	$6627	(30-Jan-91 APT.P137/R) Portrait de femme a l'etole rouge (64x53cm-25x21in) (F.FR 33000)
£3366	$5958	(5-Apr-91 DAR.P62/R) Etude d'homme (42x31cm-17x12in) (F.FR 34000)
£3421	$6500	(27-Feb-91 SY.NY124/R) Moment of decision (97x130cm-38x51in)
£3759	$6728	(8-Apr-91 ARC.P14/R) Vue du theatre de Taormina et de l'Etna (97x130cm-38x51in) (F.FR 38000)
£3785	$6548	(24-May-91 FB.P145/R) Nature morte (36x42cm-14x17in) (F.FR 38000)
£3858	$6905	(12-Apr-91 AGS.P4) Les noces d'Alexandre et de Roxane (93x53cm-37x21in) (F.FR 39000)
£4158	$7984	(17-Dec-90 ZZ.F87/R) Le baise main (70x59cm-28x23in) (F.FR 41000)
£4200	$8190	(24-Oct-90 SWS340/R) Overdoor with silver-gilt urn draped with flowers and decorated plates either side (51x82cm-20x32in)
£4300	$7224	(26-Apr-91 NM.P63) Scenes napoleonniennes (220x330cm-87x130in) pair (F.FR 43000)
£4449	$8675	(19-Oct-90 MB.P44) Troupeau a l'abreuvoir (F.FR 44000)
£4490	$8800	(6-Nov-90 GF.L2182/R) River landscape, spring (117x100cm-46x39in) (S.FR 11000)
£4500	$7380	(19-Jun-91 S174/R) Regatta (30x52cm-12x20in)
£4578	$8652	(27-Sep-90 BL.P47) Portrait d'une jeune femme aux anglaises (74x62cm-29x24in) (F.FR 45000)
£4809	$9234	(29-Nov-90 F.M57) Natura morta con frutta e calice di vino bianco. E di vino bianco (26x22cm-10x9in) pair (I.L 10500000)
£4868	$9347	(17-Dec-90 ARC.P57) Portrait d'un enfant chassant des papillons (129x97cm-51x38in) (F.FR 48000)
£5076	$10000	(15-Nov-90 SY.NY8/R) Pink roses in landscape (24x18cm-9x7in) panel
£6154	$12000	(11-Oct-90 SY.NY137 a/R) View of the Basilica of Maxentius and Constantine and Roman Forum (56x75cm-22x30in) c.1810
£6958	$11759	(18-Apr-91 APT.P136/R) Le lecture de la lettre. La jeune affligee (56x46cm-22x18in) pair (F.FR 70000)
£7099	$13631	(17-Dec-90 ZZ.F119/R) Portrait de femme et de son chien (257x170cm-101x67in) (F.FR 70000)
£7911	$15663	(30-Jan-91 APT.P139/R) Corbeille de fleurs. Bouquet de fleurs dans un vase (60x49cm-24x19in) pair (F.FR 78000)
£8200	$15990	(16-Oct-90 WW311) Interior with a parrot, a basket of strawberries, bottle and plans (51x71cm-20x28in)
£8402	$16467	(7-Nov-90 APT.P513/R) Je jure d'etre fidele (92x73cm-36x29in) (F.FR 82000)
£8449	$14279	(18-Apr-91 APT.P148/R) Portrait de jeune fille au chapeau fleuri (123x102cm-48x40in) (F.FR 85000)
£8629	$17000	(15-Nov-90 SY.NY19/R) A white terrier (17x17cm-7x7in) board
£11952	$20677	(22-May-91 CD.P16/R) Fleurs sur un entablement (65x53cm-26x21in) both s.d.1854 pair (F.FR 120000)
£1047	*$1800*	*(15-May-91 D.NY4) Terrace l'un parc (20x28cm-8x11in) i.verso W/C*
£1150	*$1921*	*(7-Jun-91 AGS.P412) Traversee d'une riviere en barque (47x63cm-19x25in) gouache (F.FR 11500)*
£1194	*$2078*	*(27-Mar-91 CN.P51/R) Zeuxis choisissant comme modele les plus belles filles de Crotone (40x54cm-16x21in) black chk pen wash htd white (F.FR 12000)*
£1250	*$2100*	*(17-Jul-91 SY.NY208/R) Landscape with figures travelling on a road (58x45cm-23x18in) W/C gouache pen brown ink*
£5528	*$9065*	*(21-Jun-91 SY.MO310/R) Bouquets de fleurs (40x31cm-16x12in) gouache pair (F.FR 55000)*
£6800	*$11356*	*(7-Jun-91 AGS.P44) Paysages animes de personnages (38x47cm-15x19in) gouache four (F.FR 68000)*

FRENCH SCHOOL, 19th C -cont.
£10483 $20337   (7-Dec-90 CN.P39/R) Projet de Concours pour un Pavillon d'exposition (100x349cm-39x137in) ink W/C (F.FR 102000)

FRENCH SCHOOL, 20th C
£1220 $2000   (19-Jun-91 B.SF1947/R) Le cafe (38x46cm-15x18in) indis.s.
£2175 $3784   (25-Mar-91 SY.F671) Paesaggio (24x35cm-9x14in) s. (I.L 4800000)
£2964 $5040   (30-May-91 EA.Z193) Walkers in river landscape (38x46cm-15x18in) (S.FR 7500)

FRENCH, Annie (fl.1904-1921) British
£1474 $2800   (27-Feb-91 SY.NY203/R) Queen's dancing maiden (24x37cm-9x15in) s. W/C ink pencil
£3800 $7106   (28-Aug-90 S991/R) Courtly love (25x28cm-10x11in) s. pen W/C htd bodycol gold leaf

FRENCH, Leonard (1928-) Australian
£5581 $9377   (22-Apr-91 SY.ME341/R) Landscape with setting sun (74x75cm-29x30in) s. enamel hardboard (A.D 12000)
£9346 $15234   (16-Jun-91 SY.ME86/R) Raft crucifixion (181x151cm-71x59in) s.d.1969 verso enamel hessian on hardboard (A.D 20000)
£10233 $17191   (22-Apr-91 SY.ME305/R) Rainbow dragonfly (136x121cm-54x48in) s.i.d.1965-1968 verso enamel hardboard (A.D 22000)
£22326 $37507   (22-Apr-91 SY.ME345/R) Pale rider (180x180cm-71x71in) s. enamel hardboard (A.D 48000)

FRENCH, Percy (1854-1920) Irish
£850 $1590   (1-Aug-90 CSK119) Marshy mountainous landscape (23x33cm-9x13in) s. W/C

FRENCH, William Percy (19/20th C) British
£320 $634   (29-Jan-91 PH62) Dusk over loch (11x17cm-4x7in) s. W/C htd white
£600 $1170   (26-Oct-90 CG48) Fishing boats offshore (26x36cm-10x14in) indis.s. W/C
£600 $1032   (14-May-91 SWS154/R) Rustic in bog landscape (21x31cm-8x12in) init. W/C
£650 $1060   (14-Jun-91 C93) Connemara evening (17x25cm-7x10in) s. i.verso W/C
£650 $1255   (10-Dec-90 PHB33 a) Irish bog (16x23cm-6x9in) s.d.1907 W/C
£650 $1268   (26-Oct-90 CG59) Beach scene, West of Ireland (13x18cm-5x7in) s. W/C
£650 $1255   (10-Dec-90 PHB33) Ballycastle Beach, Co Antrim (15x24cm-6x9in) s.d.1905 i.verso W/C
£750 $1223   (14-Jun-91 C94) Connemara (17x25cm-7x10in) s. W/C
£800 $1584   (29-Jan-91 PH61) Road across moor (16x34cm-6x13in) s. W/C
£900 $1782   (29-Jan-91 PH60/R) Peat stacks (16x34cm-6x13in) s. W/C
£1050 $2048   (26-Oct-90 CG49) The Scrabo Monument across Strangford Lough (18x23cm-7x9in) s.d.1906 W/C

FRENCH-AUSTRIAN SCHOOL, 18th C
£1829 $3000   (19-Jun-91 B.SF1672/R) Young Joseph II von Hapsburg wearing dress uniform with order (61x47cm-24x19in)

FRENDER, Helge (1906-) Scandinavian
£823 $1612   (20-Nov-90 GO.G69) View from window with blue vase (80x61cm-31x24in) s. (S.KR 9000)

FRENKEL, Itzhak (1900-1981) Israeli
£1104 $1800   (12-Jun-91 GG.TA427/R) Vase and flowers (66x48cm-26x19in) s.d.1925 paper on canvas

FRERE, Charles Edouard (1837-1894) French
£1100 $2156   (22-Nov-90 CSK224) Young fish seller (34x44cm-13x17in) s.d.72 panel

FRERE, Charles Theodore (1814-1888) French
£1375 $2612   (2-Mar-91 KRA.D313/R) Oriental street market (33x23cm-13x9in) s. panel (DM 4000)
£3187 $5418   (27-May-91 APT.P268/R) Vue de chateau de Rumeli Hisar (37x67cm-15x26in) s. (F.FR 32000)
£3735 $6350   (27-May-91 APT.P270/R) Campement a Beni-Souef (25x40cm-10x16in) s. i. verso panel (F.FR 37500)
£4057 $7789   (17-Dec-90 ARC.P127/R) Sur les hauteurs d'Alger (41x33cm-16x13in) s. (F.FR 40000)
£4103 $8000   (24-Oct-90 CH.NY87/R) Au Caire (66x49cm-26x19in) s.i.
£4474 $8500   (27-Feb-91 SY.NY122/R) Vue du Caire (39x61cm-15x24in) s.
£4573 $7500   (19-Jun-91 B.SF1743/R) Bab Hussenieh au Caire, Egypte (34x23cm-13x9in) s. s.i.verso panel
£5128 $10000   (24-Oct-90 CH.NY89/R) Caravan approaching river (30x57cm-12x22in) s.d.1857
£6574 $11175   (27-May-91 APT.P269/R) Vue de Jerusalem (38x69cm-15x27in) s. (F.FR 66000)
£10121 $19838   (20-Nov-90 APT.P271/R) Halte d'une caravane a Latakie, Syrie. Le gue, environs d'Esne (21x37cm-8x15in) both s.i. panel pair (F.FR 100000)
£12755 $25000   (7-Nov-90 B.SF1206/R) Au Caire, Egypte (46x71cm-18x28in) s.
£15182 $29757   (20-Nov-90 APT.P272/R) Caravane a Minieh (32x50cm-13x20in) s. panel (F.FR 150000)

FRERE, Edouard (1819-1886) French
£3800 $6232   (19-Jun-91 S169/R) Decorating straw hat (54x44cm-21x17in) s.
£3800 $7296   (28-Nov-90 S272 a/R) Children gathering wood in snowy forest (32x24cm-13x9in) s.d.83 panel

FRERE, Theodore see FRERE, Charles Theodore

FRESNAYE, Roger de la (1885-1925) French

£15029	$26000	(8-May-91 SY.NY154/R) Femme nue couchee (68x105cm-27x41in)
£271357	$445025	(20-Jun-91 APT.P23/R) L'artillerie (130x162cm-51x64in) (F.FR 2700000)
£452	$836	(6-Mar-91 HC.P112) Modele assis (62x44cm-24x17in) s. chl. (F.FR 4500)
£579	$1100	(15-Sep-90 S.W2791/R) Gentleman reading in an interior (36x33cm-14x13in) s. ink dr.
£746	$1260	(15-Apr-91 CC.P2/R) Etude de nus. Etude pour Psyche (26x19cm-10x7in) st.sig. lead pencil double-sided (F.FR 7500)
£1093	$1848	(17-Apr-91 LGB.P8/R) Page d'etude pour les baigneurs (30x24cm-12x9in) st.sig. Indian ink (F.FR 11000)
£1439	$2791	(7-Dec-90 GL.P200) Femme cubiste (33x25cm-13x10in) st.sig. ink (F.FR 14000)
£1605	$3129	(10-Oct-90 ARC.P20/R) L'artiste et son modele (27x20cm-11x8in) bears studio st. Indian ink wash (F.FR 16000)
£2700	$4401	(1-Jul-91 APT.P280/R) Nature morte a la theiere (19x23cm-7x9in) st.sig. indian ink (F.FR 27000)
£4323	$8171	(30-Sep-90 E.LA146/R) Composition cubiste (43x29cm-17x11in) st.sig. chl. (F.FR 42500)
£4438	$8743	(6-Oct-90 GL.P54/R) La theiere (19x23cm-7x9in) st.sig. Indian ink (F.FR 45000)
£5375	$10428	(4-Dec-90 BA.S140/R) Landscape, Grasse (24x24cm-9x9in) s.d.20 gouache (S.KR 58000)
£7000	$11410	(1-Jul-91 APT.P284/R) Au cabaret (25x20cm-10x8in) s.d.Nov.17 W/C (F.FR 70000)
£16244	$32000	(14-Nov-90 SY.NY166/R) Les acrobates (29x22cm-11x9in) s.d.20 gouache over pencil paper on board

FREUD, Lucian (1922-?) British

£340000	$547400	(27-Jun-91 S43/R) Woman with bare breast (63x49cm-25x19in)
£5500	$8965	(1-Jul-91 S59/R) Drawing after Ahmenhotep III (30x24cm-12x9in) init. pen
£14000	$22540	(27-Jun-91 S2/R) Seaside garden (13x18cm-5x7in) init. col.crayons pencil
£19900	$34627	(28-Mar-91 DAR.P13/R) Portrait de Christian Berard (41x31cm-16x12in) s.i. crayon htd.white (F.FR 200000)
£85000	$165750	(18-Oct-90 S7/R) Rabbit on chair (45x29cm-18x11in) s.d.44 conte pencil

FREUDENBERG, Jacobus (1818-1873) Dutch

£1616	$2796	(6-May-91 ZEL.L1687/R) Skaters on frozen river landscape with village and windmill (31x40cm-12x16in) s. panel (DM 4800)
£1757	$3338	(14-Sep-91 SA.A1240/R) Fun on the ice (31x47cm-12x19in) s. panel (DM 5200)

FREUDENBERGER, Sigmund (1745-1801) Swiss

£1205	$2361	(21-Nov-90 SY.Z4/R) Mother with child and dog (7x6cm-3x2in) s.i. W/C ink (S.FR 3000)

FREUDENBERGER, Sigmund (attrib) (1745-1801) Swiss

£880	$1434	(2-Jul-91 SWS328) Elegant figures by Brandenburg Gate (47x52cm-19x20in) s. canvas on board

FREUDENTHAL, Peter (20th C) Scandinavian

£695	$1348	(5-Dec-90 AB.S7075/R) Perspective (55x67cm-22x26in) s.d.1966verso acrylic (S.KR 7500)
£1791	$3026	(18-Apr-91 BU.S42/R) Tradition (160x116cm-63x46in) s.i.d.1982-85verso (S.KR 19000)
£2828	$4779	(18-Apr-91 BU.S130/R) 'Autoritratto' (150x120cm-59x47in) s.i.d.1986verso (S.KR 30000)

FREUND, Fritz (1859-1942) German

£2644	$5156	(25-Oct-90 D.V64/R) Children playing (58x49cm-23x19in) s. (A.S 55000)

FREUNDLICH, Otto (1878-1943) German

£100000	$194000	(6-Dec-90 C526/R) Composition (65x50cm-26x20in) init.
£27304	$53515	(22-Nov-90 L.K944/R) Compositions (12x9cm-5x4in) d.1931 three mono. gouache set of five (DM 80000)

FREVILLE, Noel de (1803-?) German

£2622	$5061	(12-Dec-90 N.M514/R) Wooded landscape with cottage and boy in boat on pond (61x81cm-24x32in) s.d.1846 panel (DM 7500)

FREY, Alice (1895-1981) Belgian

£591	$1023	(25-May-91 KV.L122) Girl in a black hat (35x27cm-14x11in) s. (B.FR 36000)
£802	$1580	(6-Oct-90 KV.L112) The dance (24x20cm-9x8in) s. (B.FR 50000)
£821	$1420	(25-May-91 KV.L121) Sailing regatta (60x70cm-24x28in) s.d.1922 (B.FR 50000)
£2958	$5768	(23-Oct-90 C.A379/R) La jolie extravagante (64x53cm-25x21in) s. (B.FR 180000)

FREY, Eugene (1864-1930) French

£4020	$6593	(21-Jun-91 SY.MO356/R) Pivoines (72x99cm-28x39in) s. (F.FR 40000)

FREY, J W (1830-?) Austrian

£1884	$3372	(13-Mar-91 N.M492/R) Tyrolean inn interior with figures making music and dancing (84x115cm-33x45in) s.d.1858 (DM 5500)

FREY, Johann Jakob (1813-1865) Swiss
£1084 $2092   (10-Dec-90 L.K424) Italian coastal landscape (34x45cm-13x18in) s. canvas
laid down (DM 3100)
£24000 $39360   (19-Jun-91 S48/R) Mountainous landscape with figures and ruins. Forest
landscape with figures (96x134cm-38x53in) s.d.1859 pair

FREY, Joseph (20th C) American
£1026 $2000   (10-Oct-90 B.SF565/R) Desert scrubs and mountian landscape
(46x61cm-18x24in) s.

FREY, Wilhelm (1826-1911) German
£887 $1668   (21-Sep-90 N.M3174) Cows resting near water (70x108cm-28x43in)
s.i.d.1905 (DM 2600)

FREY-MOOCK, Adolf (1881-1954) German
£516 $862   (7-Jun-91 ZOF.Z1327) The vision (65x80cm-26x31in) (S.FR 1300)
£595 $1054   (22-Mar-91 EA.Z355/R) Sybil (45x35cm-18x14in) s. panel (S.FR 1500)
£898 $1760   (6-Nov-90 GF.L2512/R) Artist's studio (60x80cm-24x31in) s (S.FR 2200)
£940 $1832   (10-Oct-90 ZEL.L1498/R) Family scene with fauns (41x20cm-16x8in) s.
board on panel (DM 2800)

FREY-SURBECK, Marguerite (1886-1981) Swiss?
£1190 $2060   (22-May-91 GS.B2091/R) View from Junkerngasse to gardens and houses in
the Matte, March (92x60cm-36x24in) s. (S.FR 3000)

FREYMUTH, Alphons (1940-) Dutch
£619   *$1195*   *(12-Dec-90 CH.AM475) Portrait (40x33cm-16x13in) pastel (D.FL 2000)*

FREYTAG, Otto (20th C) German?
£1182 $2010   (1-Jun-91 VG.B537/R) Breakfast table in Florence (70x69cm-28x27in) s.
(DM 3500)

FREZIN, Roger (1927-) French
£700 $1176   (24-Apr-91 MJ.P41/R) Hommage a Carpeaux (65x50cm-26x20in) s.d.91 oil
acrylic (F.FR 7000)
£1286   *$2302*   *(14-Apr-91 APT.P90/R) Bottines de Chaplin (150x140cm-59x55in) s. mixed
media paper laid down on canvas (F.FR 13000)*

FRIBERG, Roj (1934-) Swedish
£1415   *$2448*   *(22-May-91 BA.S367/R) River in jungle (93x122cm-37x48in) init.d.88 mixed
media (S.KR 15000)*

FRIBOULET, Jef (1919-) French
£1194 $2341   (25-Nov-90 ZZ.F65/R) Femme pensive (46x38cm-18x15in) s. (F.FR 11800)
£7538 $12362   (17-Jun-91 D.L50/R) Les glaneuses (115x71cm-45x28in) s.d.1955
(F.FR 75000)

FRICH, Joachim (1810-1858) Norwegian
£1910 $3189   (4-Jun-91 BU.O86/R) Fjord landscape (25x33cm-10x13in) s.d.1836
(N.KR 22000)
£1926 $3448   (14-Mar-91 BU.O36/R) Landscape with figure (19x22cm-7x9in) s. paper on
panel (N.KR 22000)
£1963 $3807   (4-Dec-90 UL.T212/R) Norwegian landscape (22x31cm-9x12in) (N.KR 22000)
£2517 $4204   (3-Jun-91 B.O45/R) Mountainous landscape (14x17cm-6x7in) s.d.1847
(N.KR 29000)
£2882 $5476   (11-Sep-90 UL.T204) Landscape 1846 (27x33cm-11x13in) (N.KR 33000)
£3646 $7109   (11-Oct-90 BU.O42/R) Klemetle outfarm (24x29cm-9x11in) s.d.1848 l.verso
panel (N.KR 42000)
£4340 $8464   (11-Oct-90 BU.O43/R) Boy and old man (33x26cm-13x10in) s.d.1834
(N.KR 50000)
£7630 $15031   (14-Nov-90 RAS.K110/R) Norwegian fjord landscape with farm and field of
corn (60x67cm-24x26in) s.d.1853 (D.KR 85000)

FRICK, Paul de (1864-?) French
£1254 $2445   (12-Oct-90 ZZ.F28) Vignes au puits (100x100cm-39x39in) s. (F.FR 12500)

FRIDELL, Axel (1894-1935) Swedish
£2317 $4495   (4-Dec-90 BA.S147/R) Stockholm in winter II (41x33cm-16x13in) s.i.d.1919
panel (S.KR 25000)
£9268 $17980   (4-Dec-90 BA.S146/R) Interior with man wearing red fez (29x40cm-11x16in)
s. panel (S.KR 100000)
£741   *$1438*   *(4-Dec-90 BA.S148/R) Quai de Montebello (23x29cm-9x11in) mono.i.d.1930
pencil (S.KR 8000)*
£1799   *$3454*   *(27-Nov-90 AB.S4022/R) Gentlemen's dinner party (23x49cm-9x19in) s. W/C
Indian ink gouache (S.KR 19500)*

FRIE, Peter (?) American
£1854 $3596   (5-Dec-90 AB.S7077/R) Avenue of trees (60x80cm-24x31in) s.d.89verso
(S.KR 20000)

FRIED, Pal (1893-?) Hungarian
£536 $1029   (27-Nov-90 W.T1198) Annabella a Port St Denis (60x76cm-24x30in) s.
i.verso (C.D 1200)
£576 $962   (4-Jun-91 R.T214/R) Little ballerina (61x77cm-24x30in) s. i.verso
(C.D 1100)

FRIED, Pal (1893-?) Hungarian-cont.

| £875 | $1514 | (6-May-91 ZEL.L1459/R) Female nude (65x48cm-26x19in) s. pastel (DM 2600) |
| £973 | $1586 | (10-Jun-91 W.T1276) On a Paris Boulevard (41x51cm-16x20in) s. pastel (C.D 1800) |

FRIEDENSON, Arthur (1872-1955) British

| £1150 | $1944 | (1-May-91 RBB693/R) River view with fisherman, ancient church beyond (25x36cm-10x14in) |
| £1800 | $3510 | (17-Oct-90 PHL264/R) Spring, the primose bank (34x25cm-13x10in) s. panel pair |

FRIEDLANDER, Alfred (1860-1927) Austrian

| £956 | $1567 | (18-Jun-91 FN.S1846/R) Wooded moorlandscape with soldiers confiscating horses before plough (19x24cm-7x9in) s. l.verso panel (DM 2800) |
| £1546 | $2938 | (2-Mar-91 KRA.D314/R) Drinking session in interior (15x21cm-6x8in) s. panel (DM 4500) |

FRIEDLANDER, Camilla (1856-1928) Austrian

| £735 | $1455 | (31-Jan-91 D.V92/R) Still life (30x41cm-12x16in) s. canvas on board (A.S 15000) |

FRIEDLANDER, Friedrich (1825-1901) Austrian

| £12587 | $24294 | (10-Dec-90 L.K426/R) Girl playing zither and old man with violin and other figures in interior (48x61cm-19x24in) s.d.88 panel (DM 36000) |

FRIEDLANDER, Julius (1810-1861) Danish

| £748 | $1257 | (22-Apr-91 BU.K11/R) Russian soldier bargaining with peasant woman (29x27cm-11x11in) init.d.1850 (D.KR 8500) |

FRIEDRICH, Caspar David (1774-1840) German

| £3716 | $6280 | (3-May-91 SA.A1707/R) Morning landscape (15x27cm-6x11in) d.18 Oct paper (DM 11000) |
| £350000 | $672000 | (30-Nov-90 C15/R) Set of six scenes including five sea scenes one s.i. pencil wash htd.white six |

FRIEDRICH, Gustav-Adolf (1824-1889) German

| £1796 | $3520 | (6-Nov-90 GF.L2362/R) Augustusbrucke, Dresden (15x20cm-6x8in) board (S.FR 4400) |

FRIEDRICH, Heinz (1924-) German

| £367 | $656 | (12-Apr-91 AW.H1455/R) Bunch of summer flowers in vase (76x59cm-30x23in) s.d.1987 W/C (DM 1100) |

FRIEDRICH, Johann Christian Jacob (1746-1813) German

| £5446 | $9258 | (28-May-91 AB.S4757/R) Gentlefolk watching peasants at play (44x60cm-17x24in) s. (S.KR 58000) |

FRIEDRICH, Johann Heinrich August (1789-1843) German

| £450 | $864 | (18-Feb-91 S242/R) Study of lily with snail on leaf (28x18cm-11x7in) s.d.1817verso gouache gum arabic |

FRIEDRICH, M G (?) ?

| £1400 | $2422 | (22-May-91 S208/R) Yachts (61x91cm-24x36in) s. pair |

FRIEDRICH, Otto (1862-1937) Austrian

| £488 | $903 | (7-Mar-91 D.V17/R) Head in red (20cm-8ins circular) mono.d.99 ochre W/C (A.S 10000) |
| £1367 | $2528 | (7-Mar-91 D.V138/R) Lady seated wearing hat with veil (28x23cm-11x9in) mono.d.98 W/C gouache board (A.S 28000) |

FRIEND, Donald Stuart Leslie (1915-1989) Australian

£6977	$11721	(22-Apr-91 SY.ME288/R) Ceylon (38x48cm-15x19in) s. (A.D 15000)
£17674	$29693	(22-Apr-91 SY.ME226/R) Apotheosis of Ned Kelly, 1946 (75x100cm-30x39in) s. i.verso (A.D 38000)
£386	$761	(13-Nov-90 J.M211) In thought (34x25cm-13x10in) s.d.87 W/C (A.D 1000)
£425	$837	(13-Nov-90 J.M519) By the water of Babylon (26x35cm-10x14in) s.i. W/C (A.D 1100)
£425	$837	(13-Nov-90 J.M299) Landscape and donkey (32x47cm-13x19in) s.i. mixed media (A.D 1100)
£437	$782	(9-Apr-91 CH.ME14) Standing boy (34x28cm-13x11in) s. ink wash (A.D 1000)
£452	$765	(16-Apr-91 J.M240) Portrait of a boy (33x49cm-13x19in) init. ink (A.D 1000)
£463	$913	(13-Nov-90 J.M222) Pubescent nude (65x120cm-26x47in) s.i.d.89 mixed media (A.D 1200)
£579	$1141	(13-Nov-90 J.M46/R) Sundays (34x48cm-13x19in) s.i. W/C (A.D 1500)
£618	$1217	(13-Nov-90 J.M205) Male nude seated (76x56cm-30x22in) s.d.88 mixed media (A.D 1600)
£679	$1147	(16-Apr-91 J.M111) Dini (41x34cm-16x13in) s.i. gouache (A.D 1500)
£695	$1369	(13-Nov-90 J.M265) In the Tweed Valley (36x49cm-14x19in) s.d.83 crayon (A.D 1800)
£700	$1373	(19-Nov-90 MGS.S288) Council workers digging a Hole Woollahra (34x49cm-13x19in) s.d. ink W/C (A.D 1800)
£723	$1388	(27-Nov-90 JRL.S168/R) Australian in Paris (35x45cm-14x18in) s. mixed media paper (A.D 1800)

FRIEND, Donald Stuart Leslie (1915-1989) Australian-cont.

£769	$1300	(16-Apr-91 J.M1141) A health to King Billy (25x34cm-10x13in) s.i. W/C (A.D 1700)
£800	$1504	(17-Sep-90 SY.ME24) The youth (48x31cm-19x12in) s. ink (A.D 1800)
£814	$1376	(16-Apr-91 J.M109/R) Stroud, New South Wales (37x50cm-15x20in) s.i. mixed media (A.D 1800)
£837	$1407	(22-Apr-91 SY.ME2/R) Study at Ikerre, Nigeria (32x20cm-13x8in) s.d.1939 s.i.d.verso ink wash (A.D 1800)
£844	$1620	(14-Aug-90 SY.ME24) Settler's wife (30x46cm-12x18in) s.i.d.'5 mixed media (A.D 2000)
£849	$1673	(13-Nov-90 J.M965) Head study (33x48cm-13x19in) s.i. ink (A.D 2200)
£849	$1673	(13-Nov-90 J.M2) Boatshed at Foster (36x46cm-14x18in) s.i. W/C (A.D 2200)
£869	$1711	(13-Nov-90 J.M66) Melancholic head study (76x57cm-30x22in) s.i.d.89 W/C (A.D 2250)
£905	$1529	(16-Apr-91 J.M89) Man in chair (65x56cm-26x22in) s.d.'88 W/C gouache (A.D 2000)
£1081	$2130	(13-Nov-90 J.M314) Remembering Portofino Mare (64x102cm-25x40in) s.i. mixed media (A.D 2800)
£1156	$2172	(17-Sep-90 MGS.S153) Balinese rock carving (48x72cm-19x28in) s. ink (A.D 2800)
£1158	$2282	(13-Nov-90 J.M260/R) Moses in the Bullrushes (26x35cm-10x14in) s.i. W/C (A.D 3000)
£1161	$2020	(26-Mar-91 JRL.S133/R) Head of boy (37x27cm-15x11in) s. gouache board (A.D 2600)
£1200	$2340	(15-Oct-90 AAA.S154) Island Boy (33x41cm-13x16in) s. gouache (A.D 3000)
£1209	$2032	(22-Apr-91 SY.ME180/R) Jinin Tanjangg Hamilton - portrait of boy (39x31cm-15x12in) s.i.d.45 ink wash (A.D 2600)
£1267	$2141	(16-Apr-91 J.M40/R) The Main Street, Manilla, N.S.W. (37x50cm-15x20in) s.i. pastel (A.D 2800)
£1333	$2507	(17-Sep-90 SY.ME91/R) Two boys (31x47cm-12x19in) s.d.56 ink (A.D 3000)
£1400	$2716	(6-Dec-90 CSK31/R) Royal Navy commando (37x30cm-15x12in) s. pen wash
£1446	$2776	(26-Nov-90 SY.ME103/R) Magnetic island (40x50cm-16x20in) s.i.d.54 crayon ink W/C htd bodycol (A.D 3600)
£1448	$2447	(16-Apr-91 J.M150/R) The Prodigals return (44x54cm-17x21in) s.i. mixed media (A.D 3200)
£1448	$2447	(16-Apr-91 J.M243) Horse and birds (50x65cm-20x26in) s.i.d.'88 W/C gouache (A.D 3200)
£1526	$2930	(26-Nov-90 SY.ME189/R) Boy with celadon jar (62x47cm-24x19in) i. ink (A.D 3800)
£1673	$3296	(31-Oct-90 CH.S44/R) Athens (48x35cm-19x14in) s.i.d.67 ink gouache (A.D 4200)
£1688	$3241	(14-Aug-90 SY.ME34/R) The old shops (27x36cm-11x14in) s.d.'48 i. verso ink W/C (A.D 4000)
£1872	$3539	(25-Sep-90 JRL.S53/R) Theme and variations for three flutes (60x47cm-24x19in) s. ink wash (A.D 4250)
£1946	$3813	(19-Nov-90 MGS.S224) Yellow sarong (76x56cm-30x22in) s.d. mixed media (A.D 5000)
£1953	$3282	(22-Apr-91 SY.ME191) Stogumber, Somerset (30x47cm-12x19in) s.i.d.1950 ink pastel wash (A.D 4200)
£2025	$3889	(14-Aug-90 SY.ME266/R) Circus (26x34cm-10x13in) s.i. W/C htd.ink body col. (A.D 4800)
£2110	$4051	(14-Aug-90 SY.ME3/R) Garden party, Ceylon (33x49cm-13x19in) s.i. pen W/C (A.D 5000)
£2209	$4241	(26-Nov-90 SY.ME206/R) Bali boys (49x73cm-19x29in) s.i. mixed media paper on board (A.D 5500)
£2532	$4861	(14-Aug-90 SY.ME242/R) Monkeys, Bali (55x76cm-22x30in) s.i. ink W/C (A.D 6000)
£3213	$6169	(26-Nov-90 SY.ME246/R) Melancholy of thirties (77x55cm-30x22in) s.i. mixed media paper on board (A.D 8000)
£4419	$7423	(22-Apr-91 SY.ME347/R) Titian, barbaric variations (69x100cm-27x39in) s.i. i.verso mixed media board (A.D 9500)

FRIEND, Washington F (1820-1886) British

£1257	$2098	(4-Jun-91 FB.M32/R) View towards lie d'Orleans (25x52cm-10x20in) s. W/C (C.D 2400)
£1800	$3024	(18-Jul-91 ZZ.B687) River Hudson from Fort Putnam (30x41cm-12x16in) s. W/C

FRIER, Harry (c.1849-1919) British

£1050	$2079	(30-Jan-91 HUN1) Country gentleman smoking a clay pipe (58x46cm-23x18in)
£440	$708	(26-Jun-91 HUN288) Creech Papermills (36x53cm-14x21in) s. W/C

FRIES, Bernhard (1820-1879) German

£2432	$4622	(14-Sep-90 SA.A1237/R) Italian coastal landscape (49x65cm-19x26in) s. (DM 7200)
£3142	$5970	(14-Sep-90 SA.A1238/R) View of bay, Southern Italy (49x64cm-19x25in) s. (DM 9300)

FRIES, Charles Arthur (1854-1940) American

£1104	$1800	(11-Jun-91 MOR.P24) Twixt earth and sky (36x25cm-14x10in) s.

FRIES, Ernst (1801-1833) German

£1577	$3076	(12-Oct-90 AW.H1432/R) View of Baden-Baden with figures (29x43cm-11x17in) c.1832 W/C vellum (DM 4700)

FRIES, Ernst (1801-1833) German-cont.
£3188 $6216   *(12-Oct-90 AW.H1431/R) Heidelberg Castle with washerwomen by mill (26x34cm-10x13in) c.1820 W/C gouache (DM 9500)*

FRIES, Willy (1881-1965) Swiss
£1032 $1785   (22-May-91 GS.B2094/R) Young lady dressed in Japanese costume before drapes (60x48cm-24x19in) s. canvas on pavatex (S.FR 2600)

FRIESE, Richard (1854-1918) German
£6000 $9840   (21-Jun-91 C69/R) Polar bear in Arctic landscape (89x162cm-35x64in) s.d.99

FRIESEKE, Frederick Carl (1874-1939) American
£95376 $165000   (23-May-91 SY.NY47/R) Mirror (81x81cm-32x32in) s.d.1912

FRIESIAN SCHOOL, 16th C Dutch
£15000 $28500   (1-Mar-91 C115/R) Portrait of gentleman standing by table. Portrait of wife holding gloves (95x70cm-37x28in) i.coat of arms one d.1595 one d.1596 pair

FRIESZ, Emile Othon (1879-1949) French
£1858 $3215   (25-May-91 N.M100/R) Standing female nude putting on earrings. With cloth (50x35cm-20x14in) paper one paper on board pair (DM 5500)
£1988 $3360   (17-Apr-91 CB.P43/R) Femme nue dans un sous-bois (22x16cm-9x6in) s. panel (F.FR 20000)
£2541 $5081   (4-Feb-91 LGB.P158) Femme assise en buste (65x54cm-26x21in) s. (F.FR 25000)
£3604 $6234   (23-May-91 SY.AM48/R) Nu assis (54x37cm-21x15in) s. (D.FL 12000)
£3762 $6659   (7-Apr-91 I.N138) Nu (61x50cm-24x20in) s. (F.FR 38000)
£4179 $8024   (29-Nov-90 ZZ.F24/R) Roses blanches et rouges (36x45cm-14x18in) s. (F.FR 41000)
£4230 $6894   (16-Jun-91 GL.P40/R) La baigneuse (65x54cm-26x21in) s. (F.FR 42000)
£5085 $8492   (6-Jun-91 HN.H338/R) Gorge du Sorgues (50x70cm-20x28in) s.d.1909 (DM 15000)
£5097 $9786   (29-Nov-90 ZZ.F25/R) Bouquet de fleurs (55x65cm-22x26in) s. (F.FR 50000)
£5375 $10643   (3-Feb-91 I.N98/R) Nu assis (41x24cm-16x9in) s. (F.FR 53000)
£5427 $8901   (18-Jun-91 APT.P197/R) Le couvon (73x60cm-29x24in) s. d.1924 verso (F.FR 54000)
£6091 $12000   (2-Oct-90 CH.NY95/R) Bouquet de muguets (36x27cm-14x11in) s.d.43 panel
£6200 $10354   (7-Jun-91 LD.P39/R) Saint Malo (38x46cm-15x18in) s.d.1935 (F.FR 62000)
£6972 $12062   (25-May-91 GL.P43/R) Le port du Havre (65x81cm-26x32in) s.d.1921 (F.FR 70000)
£7905 $12886   (11-Jun-91 I.N210/R) Le marche Normand (33x46cm-13x18in) s. (F.FR 78500)
£10000 $19500   (17-Oct-90 S47/R) Le port de Toulon (54x66cm-21x26in) s.
£10553 $18889   (16-Mar-91 APT.P31/R) Honfleur, la sortie du port (54x65cm-21x26in) s. (F.FR 105000)
£10843 $20060   (10-Mar-91 LT.P55/R) Le port de Creux-St-Georges (50x61cm-20x24in) s.l. (F.FR 108000)
£11156 $22089   (3-Feb-91 I.N99/R) Marines (33x19cm-13x7in) s. (F.FR 110000)
£11561 $20000   (8-May-91 SY.NY129/R) Les Baigneuse a la plage (65x81cm-26x32in) s.
£13150 $25248   (27-Nov-90 APT.P27/R) Toulon, le port (46x55cm-18x22in) s. (F.FR 129000)
£15306 $30000   (15-Feb-91 SY.NY36/R) Algier, la Place du Gouvernement (54x65cm-21x26in) s.l.d.28 l.d.verso
£16434 $28431   (25-May-91 GL.P42/R) Le port normand (65x81cm-26x32in) s. l.d.1944 verso (F.FR 165000)
£16444 $31901   (5-Dec-90 ZZ.F144/R) La ferme (41x54cm-16x21in) s.d.1901 verso (F.FR 160000)
£20101 $32965   (21-Jun-91 OD.P13/R) Un port (43x53cm-17x21in) s. (F.FR 200000)
£20408 $40204   (16-Nov-90 FB.P154/R) Le port (50x65cm-20x26in) s.d.35 (F.FR 200000)
£22366 $43390   (6-Dec-90 D.V34/R) Harbour (90x117cm-35x46in) s.d.09 (A.S 450000)
£23904 $41355   (25-May-91 GL.P20/R) Jeux de l'ete (140x45cm-55x18in) init. verso d.1940 four (F.FR 240000)
£28311 $55207   (17-Oct-90 LT.P38/R) Le Port de la Rochelle (60x73cm-24x29in) s. (F.FR 280000)
£38736 $74373   (29-Nov-90 ZZ.F26/R) La bassin du Havre (63x81cm-25x32in) s.d.06 (F.FR 380000)
£119284 $201590   (17-Apr-91 LGB.P57/R) Les environs de l'Esatque (82x60cm-32x24in) s.d.07 (F.FR 1200000)
£163968 $321377   (23-Nov-90 PLF.P70/R) Le port d'Anvers (60x80cm-24x31in) s.d.06 (F.FR 1620000)
£301 $557   *(10-Mar-91 LT.P24) La cravane (26x20cm-10x8in) mono. Indian ink drawing (F.FR 3000)*
£321 $594   *(6-Mar-91 HC.P142) Nus feminins (22x31cm-9x12in) s. ink wash chamois paper double-sided (F.FR 3200)*
£321 $594   *(6-Mar-91 HC.P144) Nus (30x23cm-12x9in) s. ink wash chamois paper double-sided (F.FR 3200)*
£571 $1109   *(8-Dec-90 GAB.G2559) Nu debout (41x21cm-16x8in) s. Indian ink drawing htd.W/C (S.FR 1400)*
£587 $1151   *(25-Nov-90 LC.P76) Nu debout (65x50cm-26x20in) bears st.sig. crayon (F.FR 5800)*
£647 $1101   *(29-May-91 GL.P11) Les deux routes a la Cote de Grace (20x27cm-8x11in) st.init. lead pencil W/C (F.FR 6500)*
£658 $1289   *(25-Nov-90 ZZ.F67) Nu couche (25x34cm-10x13in) studio st. crayon (F.FR 6500)*
£753 $1228   *(15-Jun-91 L.K218) Reclining female nude (33x53cm-13x21in) s. chk (DM 2200)*

FRIESZ, Emile Othon (1879-1949) French-cont.
£1400	$2338	(7-Jun-91 LD.P21/R) Sous-bois (44x44cm-17x17in) s.d.1939 W/C (F.FR 14000)
£1590	$2688	(15-Apr-91 CC.P5/R) Port (23x31cm-9x12in) s.d.1927 W/C (F.FR 16000)
£2016	$3931	(20-Jun-91 GL.P37) Scene d'Algerie (26x20cm-10x8in) init. Indian ink (F.FR 20000)
£2122	$4118	(8-Dec-90 GAB.G2528) Coimbra (48x37cm-19x15in) s. W/C (S.FR 5200)
£2237	$3780	(21-Apr-91 E.LA152) Le 14 Juillet (34x23cm-13x9in) st. W/C (F.FR 22500)
£2488	$4328	(25-Mar-91 PLF.P42/R) Le port de Saint Malo (36x48cm-14x19in) s. W/C (F.FR 25000)
£4000	$6440	(25-Jun-91 C236/R) Entree des barques de peche a Honfleur (30x39cm-12x15in) s. i.verso W/C paper on card
£4121	$6758	(21-Jun-91 OD.P2/R) Femme nue accroupie (43x53cm-17x21in) s. sanguinne (F.FR 41000)

FRIGERIO, R (20th C) ?
| £720 | $1339 | (3-Sep-90 SWS1266/R) Mandolin player (43x28cm-17x11in) s. canvas on board |

FRIIS, Frederick Trap (1865-1909) American
| £7263 | $13000 | (14-Mar-91 CH.NY67/R) In courtyard (74x73cm-29x29in) bears artist's estate st.stretcher |

FRINK, Elizabeth (1930-) British
£700	$1316	(20-Sep-90 CSK129/R) Man and Satyr (51x68cm-20x27in) s.d.68 pen
£1200	$2352	(25-Jan-91 C165/R) Illustration for Aesop's Fables (54x74cm-21x29in) s.d.68 W/C pencil
£1500	$2925	(9-Oct-90 B182 c) Head 1965 (77x56cm-30x22in) s.d.65 chl
£1500	$2610	(27-Mar-91 S228/R) Warrior's head (76x56cm-30x22in) s.d.64 chk
£1700	$3145	(8-Mar-91 C179/R) Head (80x57cm-31x22in) s.d.76 pencil W/C
£1800	$3006	(6-Jun-91 C277/R) Bloome dogs, Australia (42x58cm-17x23in) s.i.d.86 col.crayon pencil
£1800	$3042	(2-May-91 C121/R) Dog lying down (57x76cm-22x30in) s.d.80 pencil W/C
£1900	$3173	(7-Jun-91 C282/R) Head (80x58cm-31x23in) s.d.76 pencil W/C
£2000	$3380	(2-May-91 C120/R) Two eagles (73x49cm-29x19in) s.d.56 W/C bodycol brush ink
£2000	$3700	(8-Mar-91 C180/R) Standing dog (76x57cm-30x22in) s.d.81 pencil
£2500	$4175	(6-Jun-91 C278/R) Dog with palms, Australia (58x42cm-23x17in) s.d.86 pencil col.crayon
£2500	$4175	(7-Jun-91 C279/R) Dog with potted palms, Australia (58x42cm-23x17in) s.d.86 pencil col.crayon
£3200	$5568	(27-Mar-91 S226/R) Boar (69x49cm-27x19in) s.d.68 pencil W/C
£4600	$7682	(7-Jun-91 C283/R) Fox (67x100cm-26x39in) s.d.68 pencil W/C
£6000	$11100	(8-Mar-91 C181/R) Horse lying down (57x79cm-22x31in) s.d.78 pencil W/C

FRIPP, Alfred Downing (1822-1895) British
| £1900 | $3097 | (14-Jun-91 C64/R) Durdle Door, Dorset (48x75cm-19x30in) s.d.1890 i.verso pencil W/C htd.white |

FRIPP, George Arthur (1813-1896) British
£550	$1089	(30-Jan-91 S135) Fishing boat on Scottish loch (17x28cm-7x11in) s. W/C over pencil
£650	$1274	(21-Nov-90 B44) Magdalen Tower, Oxford, from Watermeadows (29x51cm-11x20in) W/C
£750	$1230	(19-Jun-91 B41 b) Backwater (25x39cm-10x15in) s.d.1841 W/C
£850	$1666	(22-Nov-90 CG507) Ben Sligachan, Isle of Skye (35x56cm-14x22in) s. W/C
£980	$1637	(26-Jul-91 PHE133) Shepherdess with flock by estuary (31x58cm-12x23in) s. W/C
£980	$1607	(19-Jun-91 B59/R) Drover and cattle by lake (16x25cm-6x10in) s. W/C
£1300	$2249	(20-May-91 SWS393/R) A continental river scene (35x49cm-14x19in) s.d.1846 W/C bodycol.scratching out
£1450	$2523	(27-Mar-91 HUN1) River landscape with cattle (38x53cm-15x21in) d.1886 W/C
£1650	$3053	(6-Mar-91 SC4210/R) Angler by lake at evening. Wooded river landscapes two s.d.1841 W/C gum arabic set of three
£2500	$4175	(5-Jun-91 RBB911/R) View of bay on coast of Sark, Port du Moulin with fisherman and dog (36x56cm-14x22in) s.d.1873 i.verso W/C
£2800	$5516	(13-Nov-90 C134/R) Goring-on-Thames (36x51cm-14x20in) s. i.verso pencil W/C
£3000	$4920	(19-Jun-91 B59 b) Wooded river (28x46cm-11x18in) W/C pair
£13500	$24975	(4-Mar-91 PHB21/R) Figures by waterfall (32x45cm-13x18in) W/C

FRIPP, Innes (fl.1893-1904) British
| £600 | $990 | (10-Jul-91 ZZ.B126) At blacksmith's (51x61cm-20x24in) s. |

FRIPP, Thomas William (20th C) Canadian
| £711 | $1380 | (3-Dec-90 R.T265/R) Up the Pacific Great Eastern Railway (27x36cm-11x14in) s.d.1924 i.verso W/C ink over pencil (C.D 1600) |

FRIS, Jan (attrib) (1627-1672) Dutch
| £6000 | $11820 | (1-Nov-90 CSK55/R) Still life with globe, rummer, violin, document, goblet and recorder (53x49cm-21x19in) |

FRISCH, J C (1738-1815) German
| £1012 | $1700 | (17-Jul-91 SY.NY290/R) A middle eastern town (51x76cm-20x30in) s. |

FRISIA, Donato (1883-1953) Italian
£1551 $2589   (6-Jun-91 F.M113) Ponte in costruzione, Parigi (34x47cm-13x19in) s.
             canvas on board (I.L 3400000)

FRISON, Jehan (20th C) Belgian?
£982 $1650   (23-Apr-91 C.A471/R) Arabian market (50x60cm-20x24in) s. (B.FR 60000)
£2361 $4580   (8-Dec-90 KV.L355/R) La lanterne Japonaise (102x82cm-40x32in) s.d.22
             (B.FR 140000)
£3096 $5975   (13-Dec-90 SY.AM61/R) Young girl bathing (54x44cm-21x17in) s.d.1918
             panel (D.FL 10000)

FRISTRUP, Niels (1837-1909) Danish
£718 $1415   (14-Nov-90 RAS.K645) From a south European town (62x40cm-24x16in)
             init.d.76 (D.KR 8000)

FRITH, William Powell (1819-1909) British
£3200 $5344   (5-Jun-91 S166/R) Difficult reply (34x26cm-13x10in) s.d.1891
£3500 $5705   (14-Jun-91 C303/R) Norah Creina (33x26cm-13x10in) s.d.1846 oval
£8800 $14872   (30-Apr-91 PH104/R) Flower girl (76x52cm-30x20in) s.d.
£11282 $22000   (24-Oct-90 CH.NY330/R) At my window, Boulogne (91x71cm-36x28in) s.d.1872
£12000 $24000   (8-Feb-91 C170/R) A sketch for 'Many Happy Returns of the Day'
             (41x76cm-16x30in) board

FRITZ, A (19th C) ?
£718 $1415   (14-Nov-90 RAS.K460) From Ornereden near Arhus (79x93cm-31x37in)
             s.d.1887 (D.KR 8000)

FRITZEL, Wilhelm (1870-?) German
£1419 $2696   (14-Sep-90 SA.A1307/R) Lower Rhine landscape with figures harvesting at
             village outskirts (75x100cm-30x39in) s. (DM 4200)

FRITZVOLD, Reidar (1920-) Norwegian
£1839 $3292   (11-Mar-91 B.O35/R) Mountain landscape (82x99cm-32x39in) s.d.62
             i.d.verso panel (N.KR 21000)

FRIULIAN SCHOOL, 16th C Italian
£7368 $14000   (10-Jan-91 SY.NY14/R) Saint Paul the Hermit. Saint Anthony Abbot
             (79x48cm-31x19in) panel arched top pair

FRIZE, Bernard (1949-) French
£1626 $3252   (5-Feb-91 CSC.P7/R) Nature morte aux pots casses (160x200cm-63x79in)
             s.i.d.novembre 84 verso acrylic (F.FR 16000)
£3900 $6357   (3-Jul-91 CSC.P17/R) Sans titre (146x114cm-57x45in) acrylic (F.FR 39000)

FROBENIUS, Hermann (1871-?) German
£5245 $10122   (12-Dec-90 SY.MU64/R) Ariadne abandoned (102x94cm-40x37in) s.d.1934
             i.stretcher (DM 15000)

FROBERG, Maria (1886-1962) Swedish
£2941 $5765   (6-Nov-90 BA.S73/R) Twilight over chalets (65x198cm-26x78in) s.
             (S.KR 32000)

FRODIN, Sven (1921-) Swedish
£1998 $3577   (13-Apr-91 FAL.M78/R) 'Rent spel gra' (150x140cm-59x55in) s.d.78 acrylic
             (S.KR 21500)

FROHLICH, Ernst (1810-1882) German
£1070 $1809   (17-Apr-91 WE.MU263/R) Feeding the chickens (18x24cm-7x9in) s. panel
             (DM 3200)
£1338 $2261   (17-Apr-91 WE.MU262/R) The new sledge (18x24cm-7x9in) s. panel
             (DM 4000)

FROHNER, Adolf (1934-) German
£746 $1446   (6-Dec-90 D.V233/R) Untitled (30x40cm-12x16in) s.s. panel (A.S 15000)
£535 $1049   *(24-Jan-91 D.V289) Untitled (65x50cm-26x20in) s.c.1963 pencil col.pencil*
             htd.white (A.S 11000)
£795 $1543   *(6-Dec-90 D.V222/R) The model (64x49cm-25x19in) s.d.69 pencil*
             (A.S 16000)
£994 $1928   *(6-Dec-90 D.V244/R) Female seated with one stocking on and the other off*
             (103x88cm-41x35in) s. pencil (A.S 20000)
£3349 $5794   *(8-May-91 D.V173/R) The widow (100x70cm-39x28in) s.d.71 oil graphite*
             collage canvas (A.S 70000)

FROHNERT, Emil (1884-?) German
£787 $1471   (27-Aug-90 SY.J189) Busy street scene (78x74cm-31x29in) s. (SA.R 3800)

FROLICH, Lorenz (1820-1908) Danish
£705 $1177   (6-Jun-91 RAS.K135/R) Heracles taking a satyr to be judged at Olympus
             (38x63cm-15x25in) s.d.1890 (D.KR 8000)

FROLICHER, Otto (1840-1890) Swiss
£2776 $5468   (16-Nov-90 GK.Z5357/R) Dachauer Moos landscape in rain (27x37cm-11x15in)
             mono. canvas on board (S.FR 6800)
£1581 $2688   *(27-May-91 GK.Z5327) Landscape with view of village and hills beyond*
             (26x43cm-10x17in) mono. canvas on board (S.FR 4000)

FROLOV, Serguei (1924-) Russian
£547 $952   (25-Mar-91 ARC.P206) Le Pont d'Anitchkov, Leningrd (65x89cm-26x35in) s. (F.FR 5500)
£746 $1299   (25-Mar-91 ARC.P204/R) La Place Saint-Isaac, Leningrad (65x89cm-26x35in) s. (F.FR 7500)

FROMANGER, Gerard (1939-) French
£881   *$1726*   *(21-Nov-90 C.P30/R) Plateau (65x50cm-26x20in) s.i.d.1988 oil pastel*

FROMENTIN, Eugene (1820-1876) French
£4046 $7000   (21-May-91 CE.NY269/R) Two arabs on terrace (27x20cm-11x8in) s. panel
£5491 $9500   (22-May-91 SY.NY142/R) Arabes en repos (60x89cm-24x35in) s.
£6030 $9889   (21-Jun-91 SY.MO322/R) Deux cavaliers et bergers dans un paysage (45x65cm-18x26in) s.d.73 (F.FR 60000)
£7692 $15000   (24-Oct-90 CH.NY85/R) Arabs hunting (41x26cm-16x10in) s. panel
£16393 $32131   (7-Nov-90 APT.P518/R) L'embuscade (65x46cm-26x18in) s.d.1868 panel (F.FR 160000)
£18786 $32500   (22-May-91 SY.NY138/R) Cavaliers Arabes dans un coup de vent (23x39cm-9x15in) s.d.1857 panel
£34171 $56040   (19-Jun-91 ZZ.F58/R) L'embuscade (65x46cm-26x18in) s.d.1868 panel (F.FR 340000)

FROMMHOLD, Ernst (?) ?
£912 $1733   (14-Sep-90 SA.A1310/R) View of Lubeck (61x81cm-24x32in) s. (DM 2700)

FROMUTH, Charles Henry (1861-1937) American
£1070   *$2000*   *(30-Aug-90 MFA.C150) Harbour scene (41x48cm-16x19in) s.d.1896 pastel*
£3517   *$6787*   *(16-Dec-90 T.B53/R) Sardiniers a Concarneau sechage des filets (44x22cm-17x9in) s. pastel (F.FR 34500)*

FRONIUS, Hans (1903-1988) Austrian
£3976   *$7714*   *(6-Dec-90 D.V147/R) The draw bridge (64x73cm-25x29in) s.d.77 s.i.d.verso panel (A.S 80000)*
£389   *$763*   *(24-Jan-91 D.V251/R) Die Gesellschaft im Keller, illustration for E T A Hoffmanns Erzahlung (30x21cm-12x8in) s.d.75 pen brush indian ink (A.S 8000)*
£488   *$903*   *(7-Mar-91 D.V257/R) Reclining female nude in landscape (20x29cm-8x11in) mono. chk (A.S 10000)*
£584   *$1145*   *(24-Jan-91 D.V249/R) El Greco (28x20cm-11x8in) s.d.50 chk (A.S 12000)*
£586   *$1083*   *(7-Mar-91 D.V255/R) Scene with figures (30x21cm-12x8in) s. chl chk (A.S 12000)*
£876   *$1717*   *(24-Jan-91 D.V252) Illustrations for Hoffmanns Erzahlungen (29x20cm-11x8in) s.d.1945 one i. pen indian ink wash three (A.S 18000)*

FROOD, Millie (fl.1936-1940) British
£680 $1319   (5-Dec-90 PHE85) Fruits of the harvest (50x75cm-20x30in)

FROSCHL, Carl (1848-1934) Austrian
£1027 $1839   (13-Mar-91 N.M494) Madonna with Child (30x19cm-12x7in) s. leather gold ground (DM 3000)

FROSSARD, L (?) ?
£795 $1590   (9-Feb-91 BU.O62) The singer Mimi Hauck (100x74cm-39x29in) s. (N.KR 9000)

FROST, A B (1851-1928) American
£529   *$900*   *(1-Jun-91 IH.NY140/R) Mishaps in the country heat, cartoon (28x25cm-11x10in) init. pen ink*

FROST, Anthony (1951-) British?
£550   *$1078*   *(8-Nov-90 DLY600) Savagery s.i.d.1986 verso oil collage*

FROST, Arthur Burdett (1851-1928) American
£1443 $2800   (5-Dec-90 D.NY16/R) Two boys fishing (36x30cm-14x12in) s.
£368   *$700*   *(9-Jan-91 CH.NY191) Git on yer heels, for yer toes is afire (27x27cm-11x11in) s.d.1884 ink Chinese white board*
£474   *$900*   *(9-Jan-91 CH.NY192/R) Here comes the man I've been laying for (36x37cm-14x15in) s. ink pencil board*
£561   *$1100*   *(16-Feb-91 W.W80/R) The moulders (51x36cm-20x14in) W/C gouache en grisaille*
£3421   *$6500*   *(9-Jan-91 CH.NY194/R) Den he shuck a gourd-vine flower over de pot. Backstage one s. one ink wash one W/C htd white two*

FROST, Joseph Ambrose (1953-) Australian
£2113 $3465   (17-Jun-91 MGS.S104/R) Rippon Lea (90x135cm-35x53in) s.d. (A.D 4500)
£660 $1076   (1-Jul-91 AAA.S177) Across Hyde Park (13x16cm-5x6in) s. gouache (A.D 1400)
£695 $1369   (13-Nov-90 J.M217) Summer harvest (8x26cm-3x10in) s. W/C (A.D 1800)
£695 $1369   (13-Nov-90 J.M251) The bounty at anchor, Athol Bay (8x26cm-3x10in) s. W/C (A.D 1800)
£772 $1521   (13-Nov-90 J.M81) Rose Valley (23x33cm-9x13in) s. W/C (A.D 2000)
£772 $1521   (13-Nov-90 J.M125) Farm cottages near Berrima, NSW (8x26cm-3x10in) s. W/C (A.D 2000)

FROST, Joseph Ambrose (1953-) Australian-cont.
£1179 $2040   *(21-May-91 JRL.S121) The bounty at the quay (17x26cm-7x10in) s. gouache*
           (A.D 2700)

FROST, Terry (1915-) British
£820	$1607	(25-Jan-91 C168/R) Downalong, St Ives (23x30cm-9x12in) s.verso panel
£1300	$2548	(25-Jan-91 C171/R) Cyclists Battersea, Albert Bridge Road (24x18cm-9x7in) s.i.d.47/48 panel
£1850	$3423	(8-Mar-91 C172/R) Yellow, red and black sun (66x40cm-26x16in) s.d.88
£2800	$5180	(8-Mar-91 C146/R) Battersea flower seller. Park landscape (67x31cm-26x12in) double-sided
£2800	$5488	(9-Nov-90 C277/R) Lilac and lemon (127x102cm-50x40in) s.i.d.67 verso
£3000	$5220	(27-Mar-91 S167/R) Black, green and white (46x61cm-18x24in) s.i.d.1953verso board
£3000	$5010	(7-Jun-91 C346/R) Umber and ochre (62x76cm-24x30in) s.i.d.1961verso
£3500	$6860	(9-Nov-90 C250/R) Red, black and white, September '60 (46x41cm-18x16in) s.i.d.60
£5200	$10192	(9-Nov-90 C236/R) Resting pink figure (39x39cm-15x15in) s.d.58 verso board
£6000	$11700	(10-Oct-90 S197/R) Khaki, blue and orange, autumn (76x63cm-30x25in) s.i.d.1956verso
£6500	$12740	(7-Nov-90 S181/R) North to South, Hawes (152x102cm-60x40in) s.i.d.1967verso
£7500	$13875	(8-Mar-91 C145/R) Tall red and yellow (151x63cm-59x25in) s.d.54 s.i.verso
£8200	$15170	(8-Mar-91 C144/R) Black form with blue and red (124x124cm-49x49in) board
£9500	$18620	(7-Nov-90 S180/R) Blues (183x183cm-72x72in) s.i.d.69verso
£12000	$23520	(9-Nov-90 C251/R) Black and white painting, November '59 (152x102cm-60x40in) s.verso
£420	*$706*	*(24-Apr-91 CSK96/R) Abstract (24x33cm-9x13in) d.56 pencil W/C gouache*
£540	*$891*	*(10-Jul-91 WAL225/R) P.Z. 1981 - abstract study with canvas collage (59x43cm-23x17in) s.d.Feb.76/81 collage*
£600	*$990*	*(10-Jul-91 WAL224/R) P.Z. Red and black, abstract study with inscribed letters (50x24cm-20x9in) s. crayon bodycol.*
£700	*$1372*	*(25-Jan-91 C174/R) Green for Lorca (56x38cm-22x15in) thinned oil poster paint col.crayon collage*
£800	*$1336*	*(7-Jun-91 C335/R) Untitled (39x28cm-15x11in) s.d.60 W/C brush ink*
£800	*$1504*	*(20-Sep-90 CSK163/R) Black and white pisa (77x56cm-30x22in) s.i.d.71verso collage*
£900	*$1755*	*(9-Oct-90 B56) Composition (79x58cm-31x23in) gouache paper collage*
£1050	*$1722*	*(20-Jun-91 DLY729) Composition (58x41cm-23x16in) s.d.1986 i.verso acrylic gouache collage card*
£1200	*$1968*	*(20-Jun-91 DLY726/R) Orange sun dipper (86x64cm-34x25in) s.d.1986 gouache collage*
£2400	*$4008*	*(7-Jun-91 C306/R) Laced grace (61x51cm-24x20in) s.i.d.62verso oil canvas collage leather*

FROST, William Edward (1810-1877) British
£1400 $2646   (26-Sep-90 S187/R) Vintage (20x15cm-8x6in) board oval

FROST, William Edward (attrib) (1810-1877) British
£550 $985   (10-Apr-91 CSK275/R) The Triumph of Venus (41cm-16ins circular)

FROST, William Edward (circle) (1810-1877) British
£1050 $1995   (28-Feb-91 B94) Holy Family in landscape (30x41cm-12x16in) board

FROSTERUS-SEGERSTRALE, Hanna (1867-1946) Finnish
£1284 $2516   (24-Nov-90 HOR.H85/R) Walking in the wood (34x23cm-13x9in) s.d.1938 (F.M 9000)

FRY, Anthony (1927-) British
£1500   *$2445*   *(1-Jul-91 S31/R) Nude 1 (91x137cm-36x54in) oil collage canvas*

FRY, John Hemming (1861-1946) American
£798	$1500	(22-Sep-90 WOL.C274) Lorelei (61x46cm-24x18in) s.
£851	$1600	(22-Sep-90 WOL.C247/R) Song of Pines (56x38cm-22x15in) s.
£1011	$1900	(22-Sep-90 WOL.C249/R) Elemental drift (43x86cm-17x34in)
£1170	$2200	(22-Sep-90 WOL.C272/R) Fates (76x51cm-30x20in)
£1330	$2500	(22-Sep-90 WOL.C248/R) Dryad (122x66cm-48x26in) s.
£1915	$3600	(22-Sep-90 WOL.C246/R) Orpheus and Eurydice (160x97cm-63x38in)

FRY, Roger (1866-1934) British
£2800 $4872   (27-Mar-91 S57/R) The house in the clearing (60x74cm-24x29in) s.d.26
£3200 $5568   (27-Mar-91 S95/R) Lady with pet monkey (65x47cm-26x19in) s.

FRY, Rowena (20th C) American
£829 $1600   (10-Dec-90 H.C1109) Painting class at Art Institute (114x180cm-45x71in)

FRY, Windsor (?) British?
£720 $1202   (5-Jun-91 S156/R) Blossom by Thames (77x35cm-30x14in) s. panel

FRYE, Thomas (attrib) (1710-1762) British
£3030 $5242   (6-May-91 ZEL.L1694/R) Portrait of noble man with dog in park landscape, evening (125x97cm-49x38in) (DM 9000)

FRYE, Thomas (circle) (1710-1762) British
£750 $1223   (13-Jun-91 CSK175/R) Portrait of artist, wearing coat and cravat,
     holding palette (90x65cm-35x26in) with i.verso
£1100 $2112   (20-Feb-91 CSK248) Portrait of merchant captain, holding onto telescope,
     view ship beyond (88x71cm-35x28in)

FRYE, Thomas (style) (1710-1762) British
£1000 $1970   (31-Oct-90 S271/R) Portrait of young boy standing with greyhound and
     house beyond (123x97cm-48x38in)

FRYTOM, Frederick van (?-1658) Dutch
£4895 $9448   (10-Dec-90 L.K42/R) Rider and peasant conversing in river landscape
     (41x43cm-16x17in) s. (DM 14000)

FUCHS, Alfred (1877-?) German
£550 $1045   (2-Mar-91 KRA.D485) Children at table (40x37cm-16x15in) s. wax crayon
     (DM 1600)

FUCHS, Daniel (20th C) ?
£615 $1205   (11-Nov-90 ZZ.F265/R) Le Trousale a Toussus le noble (34x55cm-13x22in)
     s. (F.FR 6000)
£820 $1607   (11-Nov-90 ZZ.F261/R) La Bartavelle des Lefebvre a Chantemerle les
     Grignan (65x100cm-26x39in) s. (F.FR 8000)

FUCHS, Ernst (1930-) Austrian
£33948 $63822   (20-Sep-90 D.V217/R) Janus (35x22cm-14x9in) s.d.1954 parchment
     (A.S 700000)
£839 $1636   (12-Oct-90 AW.H2369/R) Pascal, portrait study (35x24cm-14x9in) s.d.1981
     col.pencil (DM 2500)
£1160 $2274   (20-Nov-90 L.K226/R) W.A.Mozart The Magic Flute (28x21cm-11x8in)
     s.i.d.1969 col.chk bodycol (DM 3400)
£1367 $2528   (7-Mar-91 D.V262/R) Female prophet (18x15cm-7x6in) s. pen indian ink W/C
     (A.S 28000)
£3931 $7666   (27-Oct-90 BG.P31/R) Composition (46x33cm-18x13in) s. ink W/C
     (F.FR 39000)
£6667 $11933   (12-Apr-91 BM.B966/R) Im Blutenschmuck (77x58cm-30x23in) s.d.87 tempera
     pastel (DM 20000)

FUCHS, J H G (18th C) German
£1049 $2024   (12-Dec-90 N.M372/R) Portrait of Bernardus Schumann. Portrait of lady
     (79x67cm-31x26in) one i.d.1751verso pair (DM 3000)

FUCHS, Jacques (1922-) Swiss
£797 $1554   (24-Oct-90 GD.B382/R) Spanish landscape (38x55cm-15x22in) s.
     i.d.1965verso (S.FR 2000)

FUCHS, Lorenz (1863-?) Austrian
£621 $1210   (11-Oct-90 D.V171/R) Stubenfall near Murhausen in Otztal
     (34x24cm-13x9in) s.d.94 W/C (A.S 13000)

FUCHS, Robert (1896-1981) Austrian
£1562 $2889   (7-Mar-91 D.V181/R) Paradise (94x110cm-37x43in) s.d.1952 (A.S 32000)

FUCHS, Th (19th C) German
£769 $1485   (12-Dec-90 N.M516/R) Fjord landscape with boats (68x98cm-27x39in)
     s.i.d.1893 (DM 2200)

FUCHSEL, Hermann (1833-1915) American
£1351 $2500   (8-Mar-91 S.BM140/R) Lake Placid and whiteface Mountain
     (51x81cm-20x32in) s.i.d.20x32

FUEGER, Friedrich Heinrich (1751-1818) German
£428 $698   (12-Jun-91 N.M234/R) Ceiling painting in monastery of San Paolo in Parma
     (43x54cm-17x21in) s.i. W/C bodycol pen after Correggio (DM 1250)
£428 $698   (12-Jun-91 N.M235/R) Ceiling painting in monastery of San Paolo in Parma
     (44x55cm-17x22in) s.i. W/C bodycol pen after Correggio (DM 1250)
£525 $883   (25-Apr-91 D.V53/R) Figurengruppe nach den Stanzen in Rom
     (73x51cm-29x20in) s.i.verso ochre (A.S 11000)

FUEGER, Friedrich Heinrich (attrib) (1751-1818) German
£1224 $2412   (14-Nov-90 D.V343/R) Neptun with trident (180x131cm-71x52in)
     (A.S 25000)
£2081 $3600   (12-May-91 H.C24/R) Un bouquet des roses (36x43cm-14x17in) i.verso
     copper

FUENTES, Giorgio (1756-1821) Italian
£405 $689   (31-May-91 GB.B5668/R) Stage design with view of monuments, pyramid and
     temples (18x27cm-7x11in) pen wash (DM 1200)
£405 $689   (31-May-91 GB.B5669/R) Stage design with view of stairs and palace
     (19x27cm-7x11in) pen wash (DM 1200)
£455 $882   (7-Dec-90 GB.B5711) Interior of columned hall, stage design
     (18x25cm-7x10in) pen wash (DM 1300)

FUERTES, Louis Agassiz (1874-1927) American
£1693 $3250   (17-Dec-90 SY.N134/R) Study of two wrens in landscape. Study of head of
     Caspian Tern (30x18cm-12x7in) s. W/C pair

FUERTES, Louis Agassiz (1874-1927) American-cont.
£2907 $5000   (15-May-91 SY.NY36/R) Three eagles (49x39cm-19x15in) s. W/C paper on
                    mulberry paper
£3968 $7500   (25-Sep-90 CE.NY19/R) Birds on a branch (37x30cm-15x12in) s. gouache
                    pencil board

FUHR, Franz Xaver (1898-1973) German
£3716 $6429   (25-May-91 N.M102/R) Still life with rubber plant (94x64cm-37x25in) s.
                  (DM 11000)
£956 $1873   (24-Nov-90 N.M171/R) The bridge (59x42cm-23x17in) i.verso W/C
                  (DM 2800)

FUHRER, Kai (?) ?
£671 $1315   (13-Feb-91 KH.K62) Fine Festival (120x120cm-47x47in) s.verso (D.KR 7500)

FUJINO (20th C) Japanese
£872 $1700   (24-Oct-90 B.SF1566/R) Untitled (61x74cm-24x29in) init. acrylic canvas

FULCHIRON, Madame (19th C) French
£2008 $3233   (27-Jun-91 APT.P237/R) Bergers antiques pres d'un aqueduc
                  (54x45cm-21x18in) s. (F.FR 20000)

FULLBROOK, Samuel Sydney (1922-) Australian
£1778 $3342   (17-Sep-90 SY.ME115/R) Untitled (25x20cm-10x8in) init. board (A.D 4000)
£1869 $3047   (16-Jun-91 SY.ME67) Drover's boy, 1953 (32x22cm-13x9in) init. board
                  (A.D 4000)
£2570 $4189   (16-Jun-91 SY.ME7) Girl with sturt pea, Coobina Creek, W.A
                  (24x32cm-9x13in) s. masonite (A.D 5500)
£2743 $5266   (14-Aug-90 SY.ME186/R) Landscape (61x61cm-24x24in) init. (A.D 6500)
£3556 $6684   (17-Sep-90 SY.ME46/R) Hut in the Coolibah, Darling River series
                  (29x39cm-11x15in) init.d.1962 canvasboard (A.D 8000)
£3846 $6500   (15-Apr-91 AAA.S132 a) Sunflowers on Darling Downs (42x70cm-17x28in) s.
                  (A.D 8500)
£8000 $15040   (17-Sep-90 SY.ME19/R) Aeroplane and landscape (38x50cm-15x20in) s.d.1965
                  i.verso (A.D 18000)

FULLER, Arthur (1889-1967) American
£1183 $2000   (20-Apr-91 WOL.C154/R) Mallards in flight (102x76cm-40x30in) s.

FULLER, Edmund G (19/20th C) British
£750 $1455   (7-Dec-90 K545/R) Beach scene with fisherfolk and fishing boats
                  (61x89cm-24x35in) s.
£900 $1773   (1-Nov-90 B81/R) Gleam of light on troubled waters (63x127cm-25x50in) s.
                  s.i.verso

FULLER, Isaac (style) (1606-1672) British
£2400 $4560   (1-Mar-91 C4/R) Cavaliers watching cockfight (101x125cm-40x49in)

FULLER, Leonard John (1891-?) British
£900 $1701   (27-Sep-90 L241/R) Girl in red kimino reading Velazquez
                  (61x51cm-24x20in) i. verso
£1100 $2090   (28-Feb-91 DLY369/R) Lanhams picture framing workshop, St. Ives
                  (71x89cm-28x35in) s.d.1962

FULLEYLOVE, John (1845-1908) British
£600 $1200   (7-Feb-91 HB531) Church of St Giles, Edinburgh (25x18cm-10x7in) s. W/C

FULLWOOD, Albert Henry (1864-1930) British
£1209 $2032   (22-Apr-91 SY.ME193) Chelsea river (12x16cm-5x6in) init. i.verso panel
                  (A.D 2600)
£1395 $2344   (22-Apr-91 SY.ME174/R) Winter landscape (29x39cm-11x15in) init. canvas
                  on board (A.D 3000)
£506 $972   (14-Aug-90 SY.ME15/R) A wet boater/toujours la politesse
                  (52x35cm-20x14in) s. monochrome gouache (A.D 1200)
£698 $1172   (22-Apr-91 SY.ME134) Lane Cove River (12x25cm-5x10in) s.d.88 W/C
                  (A.D 1500)
£724 $1224   (16-Apr-91 J.M289/R) Entrance to Sydney Harbour (27x33cm-11x13in)
                  init.d.'25 W/C (A.D 1600)
£964 $1851   (26-Nov-90 SY.ME62/R) Southern Alps (18x26cm-7x10in) init.d.05 s.i.verso
                  W/C canvas (A.D 2400)

FULOP, Karoly (1893-1963) American
£1148 $2250   (13-Feb-91 B.SF2138/R) Winter landscape (65x65cm-26x26in) s.

FULTON, David (1848-1950) British
£750 $1455   (6-Dec-90 CG40) Barking the nets, Cullen (46x61cm-18x24in) s.d.1887
£800 $1336   (6-Jun-91 CSK120 a) Fishing from the rocks (46x30cm-18x12in) s.d.1887
£925 $1600   (21-May-91 CE.NY239/R) Feeding chicks (35x41cm-14x16in) s.i.
£1600 $3168   (30-Jan-91 CSK243) Gathering driftwood (51x76cm-20x30in) s.d.83
£2600 $4862   (28-Aug-90 S886/R) Lying by a cornfield (30x51cm-12x20in) s.d.82
£1200 $2016   (23-Apr-91 S65/R) Autumn in Kintyre (39x49cm-15x19in) s. W/C

FUNGAI, Bernardino (1460-1516) Italian
£36842 $70000   (11-Jan-91 CH.NY5/R) Christ supported by two angels (43x65cm-17x26in)
                  panel

FUNGAI, Bernardino (circle) (1460-1516) Italian
£40000 $78800   (31-Oct-90 S99/R) Madonna and Child (56cm-22ins circular) panel

FUNI, Achille (1890-1972) Italian
£1351 $2634   (24-Oct-90 F.M102) Natura morta (40x60cm-16x24in) s.d.1961 tempera
masonite (I.L 3000000)
£818   *$1415*   *(7-May-91 F.M127/R) Dioscuro (62x39cm-24x15in) d.1940 pencil*
(I.L 1800000)
£832   *$1615*   *(3-Dec-90 F.M80) Paesaggio (24x32cm-9x13in) s.d.1945 pencil*
(I.L 1800000)
£1295   *$2512*   *(3-Dec-90 F.M350) Paesaggio. Figura distesa s. one pencil one ink two*
(I.L 2800000)

FUNKE, Helene (1869-1957) Austrian
£2392 $4139   (8-May-91 D.V97/R) Still life with fishes (38x46cm-15x18in) s.d.20
(A.S 50000)

FURET, F (1842-1909) Swiss
£780 $1349   (9-May-91 CSK106) Grapes, peaches, chalice and knife on stoneledge
(39x29cm-15x11in) s. panel

FURET, Francois (1842-1909) Swiss
£800 $1352   (1-May-91 GD.B309/R) Boy wearing straw hat riding on donkey
(20x14cm-8x6in) s. board (S.FR 2000)
£1406 $2755   (21-Nov-90 SY.Z38/R) Pralognan, Savoie (55x46cm-22x18in) s. (S.FR 3500)

FURINI, Francesco (1604-1646) Italian
£9794 $19295   (14-Nov-90 D.V252/R) The Penitent Magdalen (114x86cm-45x34in)
(A.S 200000)
£850   *$1641*   *(11-Dec-90 C34/R) Studies of hands (16x20cm-6x8in) i. chk.*

FURINI, Francesco (attrib) (1604-1646) Italian
£4970 $8400   (18-Apr-91 APT.P13/R) Jeune courtisane (80x58cm-31x23in) (F.FR 50000)

FURINI, Francesco (style) (?) ?
£800 $1304   (4-Jul-91 C760) Angels with instruments of Passion (115x99cm-45x39in)

FURLONGER, Joseph (20th C) Australian
£1928 $3701   (27-Nov-90 JRL.S222/R) Two figures on beach (90x105cm-35x41in) init.d.87
(A.D 4800)

FUSARO, Jean (1925-) French
£1055 $1731   (18-Jun-91 APT.P198) La jetee d'Agde (22x27cm-9x11in) s. i.d.1965 verso
(F.FR 10500)
£1728 $3455   (6-Feb-91 FB.P123/R) Fete nautique (18x24cm-7x9in) s. board (F.FR 17000)
£2857 $5543   (8-Dec-90 GAB.G2562/R) Port vert de Sete (33x51cm-13x20in) paper laid
down on canvas (S.FR 7000)
£2939 $5701   (8-Dec-90 GAB.G2561/R) Port bleu de Sete (33x51cm-13x20in) paper laid
down on canvas (S.FR 7200)
£3274 $5631   (19-May-91 ZZ.F193/R) Pecheur au petit matin (33x46cm-13x18in) s. d.1968
verso (F.FR 33000)
£4146 $8084   (17-Oct-90 ARC.P79) Quai de la maree, Sete (27x41cm-11x16in) s. i.d.1965
verso (F.FR 41000)
£5510 $10690   (8-Dec-90 GAB.G2564/R) Quai a la Vitriolerie, Lyon (50x80cm-20x31in)
s.i.d.1956 verso (S.FR 13500)
£5561 $10844   (17-Oct-90 ARC.P80) Nuages sur le port (65x81cm-26x32in) s. i.d.1967
verso (F.FR 55000)
£6994 $12030   (19-May-91 ZZ.F158/R) Arc en ciel a Saint-Paul-de-Leon (50x72cm-20x28in)
s. (F.FR 70500)
£7143 $13857   (8-Dec-90 GAB.G2563/R) Bassin du Midi (80x99cm-31x39in) s. i.d.1956
verso (S.FR 17500)
£7300 $12264   (24-Apr-91 MJ.P101/R) Place de Cannes (60x92cm-24x36in) s. i. verso
(F.FR 73000)
£7855 $12804   (16-Jun-91 GL.P79/R) Port et chevaux (73x92cm-29x36in) s. (F.FR 78000)
£8061 $15881   (18-Nov-90 H.A123/R) Bouquet bleu (73x60cm-29x24in) s. (F.FR 79000)
£11256 $20149   (17-Mar-91 GL.P90/R) Venise, la lagune (65x100cm-26x39in) s.
(F.FR 112000)

FUSSELL, Charles Lewis (1840-?) American
£3704   *$7000*   *(25-Sep-90 CE.NY45/R) Children wading in a stream (60x51cm-24x20in)*
s.d.1905 W/C gouache

FUSSLI, Jean Henri (1741-1825) Swiss
£65000 $116350   (12-Apr-91 C38/R) Three witches appearing to Macbeth and Banquo
(87x112cm-34x44in)
£4000   *$7880*   *(13-Nov-90 C93/R) Spirit of Knowledge, possibly design for William*
Roscoe's The Nurse (18x23cm-7x9in) pencil wash
£11000   *$17930*   *(2-Jul-91 C191/R) Woman leaning on table gazing at nude by candlelight*
(17x9cm-7x4in) num.35 verso black chk pen wash
£19000   *$30970*   *(2-Jul-91 C193/R) Seated nudes (22x17cm-9x7in) pen double-sided*
£28000   *$45640*   *(2-Jul-91 C192/R) King David being warned by phophet Nathan. Standing*
nude, studies leg and arm (62x92cm-24x36in) i. black chk wash
double-sided

FUSSLI, Jean Henri (style) (1741-1825) Swiss
£1200 $2028   (1-May-91 GD.B307) At the death bed (34x36cm-13x14in) (S.FR 3000)

FUSSLI, Johann Melchior and PREISSLER, Johann Daniel (18th C) Swiss/German

£800	$1544	(11-Dec-90 C116/R) The storming of a city. Two figures in a storm ink wash chk. two
£800	$1544	(11-Dec-90 C118) Jonathan and Saul slaughtering Philistines. David and Goliath (29x20cm-11x8in) red chk.ink wash two

FUSSMANN, Klaus (1938-) German

£1433	$2810	(20-Nov-90 L.K235) Still life with cup, glass and bottles (43x41cm-17x16in) s.d.1981 (DM 4200)
£2020	$3394	(26-Apr-91 KM.K281/R) Still life with tumblers and tea pot (50x59cm-20x23in) s.d.73 (DM 6000)
£2759	$5297	(28-Nov-90 KF.M773/R) Still life with bowl (43x56cm-17x22in) s.i.d.1979 (DM 8000)
£2911	$4745	(14-Jun-91 L.K884/R) Still life (61x84cm-24x33in) s.d.84 (DM 8500)
£3448	$6621	(28-Nov-90 KF.M772/R) Still life with three vessels (43x56cm-17x22in) si.d.1979 (DM 10000)
£3885	$6605	(1-Jun-91 VG.B379/R) Still life of vessels on table (135x100cm-53x39in) s.d.70 (DM 11500)
£4437	$8696	(20-Nov-90 L.K234/R) Beloved pink (85x101cm-33x40in) s.i.d.1979 hessian (DM 13000)
£5479	$8932	(14-Jun-91 L.K881/R) Still life with plates (75x90cm-30x35in) s.i.d.75 (DM 16000)
£6507	$10606	(14-Jun-91 L.K882/R) Interior (120x126cm-47x50in) s.indis.i.d.1976 (DM 19000)
£6849	$11164	(14-Jun-91 L.K883/R) View across rooftops (120x131cm-47x52in) s.i.d.77 (DM 20000)
£7432	$12635	(1-Jun-91 VG.B380/R) Still life (79x72cm-31x28in) s.i.d.1974 (DM 22000)
£10690	$20524	(28-Nov-90 KF.M774/R) Bed before mirror (151x161cm-59x63in) s.i.d.1982 (DM 31000)
£13793	$26483	(28-Nov-90 KF.M771/R) Wall (145x155cm-57x61in) s.i.d.1974 (DM 40000)
£966	$1854	(28-Nov-90 KF.M779) Rhododendron (29x41cm-11x16in) s.i.d.1980 W/C (DM 2800)
£1014	$1723	(28-May-91 KF.M667/R) Group of trees in field (29x41cm-11x16in) s.d.1978 W/C poster paint indian ink (DM 3000)
£1365	$2676	(20-Nov-90 L.K239/R) Flowers in vase (30x39cm-12x15in) s.i.d.1979 W/C (DM 4000)
£1424	$2378	(8-Jun-91 HN.H117/R) View (61x71cm-24x28in) s.d.77 gouache (DM 4200)
£2414	$4634	(28-Nov-90 KF.M776/R) Studio Hardenbergstrasse 1 (66x71cm-26x28in) s.i.d.1978 gouache (DM 7000)
£2483	$4767	(28-Nov-90 KF.M777/R) Still life (61x70cm-24x28in) s.i.d.1978 W/C bodycol (DM 7200)
£2759	$5297	(28-Nov-90 KF.M775/R) Still life (75x81cm-30x32in) s.i.d.1988 oil mixed media paper on board (DM 8000)

FUSTER, Alberto (19th C) Mexican

£536	$900	(28-Apr-91 HG.C408) Still life of fan and flowers (56x33cm-22x13in) s.

FUTTERER, Joseph (1871-1930) German

£1199	$2146	(13-Mar-91 N.M495/R) Young woman seated at table decorated with flowers by window (59x71cm-23x28in) s. i.verso (DM 3500)

FYT, Jan (style) (17th C) Flemish

£2200	$4224	(29-Nov-90 CSK257) Dead nuthatch, thrush and finch with cherries by rock in landscape (40x32cm-16x13in) painted oval

G M (?) ?

£880	$1531	(27-Mar-91 EH792) Portrait of lady in shawl holding fan (61x48cm-24x19in) indist.s.
£32000	$54080	(16-Apr-91 PH45/R) Still lives of shells upon tables draped with coloured cloths (13x19cm-5x7in) init. on copper four

GAAL, Ferenc (1891-) Hungarian

£524	$1012	(12-Dec-90 N.M517/R) Gypsies resting with covered wagons in wooded landscape (61x79cm-24x31in) s. (DM 1500)
£720	$1217	(1-May-91 GD.B310/R) Sunlit park landscape with figures (58x78cm-23x31in) s.d.1934 (S.FR 1800)

GABBIANI, Antonio Domenico (1652-1726) Italian

£780	$1498	(18-Feb-91 S104/R) The Triumph of David (20x23cm-8x9in) pen ink wash
£2000	$3260	(1-Jul-91 S36/R) Prisoners before Roman leader. Studies for same composition (34x46cm-13x18in) pen wash over black chk red chk double-sided

GABE, Nicolas Edward (1814-1865) French

£2600	$5070	(15-Jan-91 SWS183/R) Harbour scene (49x73cm-19x29in) s.d.1839

GABORIAUD, Josue (1883-1955) French

£1361	$2654	(27-Oct-90 LT.P50/R) Composition a la cruche (72x84cm-28x33in) s.d.36 paper laid down on canvas (F.FR 13500)
£1420	$2811	(3-Feb-91 LT.P55/R) Barques amarrees (61x93cm-24x37in) s.d.27 (F.FR 14000)

GABORIAUD, Josue (1883-1955) French-cont.
£3364 $6459   (2-Dec-90 M.V60/R) Le grand vase d'anemones (73x60cm-29x24in) s.
(F.FR 33000)

GABRIEL, F (19th C) French
£1190 $2000   (17-Jul-91 SY.NY226/R) Still life with roses and tulips
(40x30cm-16x12in) s. panel
£1775 $3000   (1-May-91 D.NY40) Still life with flowers on stone ledge
(51x38cm-20x15in) s. board
£2232 $3750   (17-Jul-91 SY.NY225/R) Still life with flowers and fruit
(51x41cm-20x16in) s. panel
£3158 $6000   (27-Feb-91 SY.NY42/R) Floral still lifes (56x46cm-22x18in) s. panel pair

GABRIEL, Francois (19th C) French
£658 $1250   (3-Mar-91 LIT.L17) Still life with lobster, fruit and wine panel

GABRIEL, Justin J (1838-?) French
£1372 $2716   (31-Jan-91 D.V28/R) View of Venice (47x56cm-19x22in) s. (A.S 28000)

GABRIEL, M (19th C) Dutch
£598 $1028   (14-May-91 GF.L2556/R) Girl selling flowers by harbour (68x55cm-27x22in)
s.d.1871 (S.FR 1500)

GABRIEL, Paul Joseph Constantin (1828-1903) Dutch
£1220 $2390   (6-Nov-90 SY.AM260/R) Farmyard on sunny day (33x44cm-13x17in) s.d.86
canvas on panel (D.FL 4000)

GABRINI, Pietro (1865-1926) Italian
£1330 $2500   (19-Sep-90 B.SF2672/R) Seaside romance (75x84cm-30x33in) s.
£2237 $4250   (27-Feb-91 SY.NY331/R) On Venetian lagoon (137x99cm-54x39in) s.d.1914
£2390 $4135   (24-May-91 FB.P173/R) La conversation (54x84cm-21x33in) s. (F.FR 24000)
£4083 $6860   (22-Apr-91 PO.BA33) Ala fiesta (80x60cm-31x24in) s.d.1908
£5405 $8811   (10-Jun-91 W.T1400/R) Home again (64x109cm-25x43in) s. panel
(C.D 10000)
£7500 $12300   (18-Jun-91 PH150/R) On the Bay of Naples (98x74cm-39x29in) s.
£8158 $15500   (27-Feb-91 SY.NY337/R) Leaving Palazzo, Venice (80x55cm-31x22in) s.
£514   *$920*   *(13-Mar-91 N.M301) Soldier with drum before arched gate*
(49x32cm-19x13in) s.d.1878 W/C (1500)
£684   *$1300*   *(27-Feb-91 SY.NY356/R) Quenching thirst (49x72cm-19x28in) s.i. pencil*
W/C gouache
£2000   *$3840*   *(27-Nov-90 PH254/R) Venetian serenade (49x74cm-19x29in) s.i. W/C*
£3000   *$5880*   *(15-Feb-91 C90/R) Going home, Tivoli (98x62cm-39x24in) s. W/C*

GABRON, Guilliam (1619-1678) Belgian
£3183 $6271   (14-Nov-90 D.V157/R) Hunting still life with cat in wooded landscape
(100x123cm-39x48in) (A.S 65000)
£6958 $11759   (18-Apr-91 APT.P58/R) Nature morte - Trophees de chasse
(59x73cm-23x29in) s. (F.FR 70000)

GACHAL, Jozsef Eolvedi (1889-?) Hungarian
£685 $1116   (12-Jun-91 N.M429/R) View of riverside village (60x80cm-24x31in)
s.d.1939 (DM 2000)

GADAN, A (?) ?
£1385 $2479   (8-Apr-91 CR.P60) La cueillette des fruits en Algerie (60x98cm-24x39in)
s. (F.FR 14000)

GADBOIS, Louis (circle) (?-1826) French
£2000   *$3340*   *(7-Jun-91 AGS.P39/R) Paysages avec des bergers (30x40cm-12x16in) gouache*
pair (F.FR 20000)

GADDI, Angelo di Taddeo (attrib) (c.1345-1396) Italian
£88629 $149783   (19-Apr-91 FN.S1719/R) Sacra conversazione (86x50cm-34x20in) oil tempera
panel (DM 265000)

GADDI, Angelo di Taddeo (school) (c.1345-1396) Italian
£15671 $30872   (14-Nov-90 D.V31/R) Madonna with Child and saints surrounded by angels
(62x29cm-24x11in) tempera gold ground pointed arched top (A.S 320000)

GADDI, Taddeo (?-1366) Italian
£1800000 $3114000   (24-May-91 C33/R) The Bromley Davenport Altarpiece - The Man of Sorrows,
Saints Peter, Francis, Paul and Andrew tempera gold panel five

GADO, Bertil (1916-) Scandinavian?
£919 $1801   (10-Nov-90 FAL.M110/R) Morning (48x58cm-19x23in) s.d.83 (S.KR 10000)
£2045 $3660   (13-Apr-91 FAL.M79/R) Conversation in evening (96x75cm-38x30in) s.d.84
(S.KR 22000)
£2757 $5404   (10-Nov-90 FAL.M109/R) September day (95x116cm-37x46in) s.d.1984
(S.KR 30000)

GADOU-ROYER, Jeanne (attrib) (?-1907) French
£1000 $1730   (9-May-91 CSK100/R) Dame de la Halle (122x91cm-48x36in) with sig.d.1853
oval

GAEL, Adriaen II (?-1665) Dutch
£2100 $3885   (5-Mar-91 PH112/R) The triumph of Mordecai (60x84cm-24x33in) panel

GAEL, Barent (1620-1703) Dutch
£4941 $8399   (27-May-91 GK.Z5040/R) Figures resting before country inn
                 (36x49cm-14x19in) panel (S.FR 12500)

GAEL, Barent (attrib) (1620-1703) Dutch
£3425 $6130   (12-Mar-91 FN.S2368/R) Encampment with horses and figures
                 (65x81cm-26x32in) (DM 10000)

GAEL, Barent (circle) (1620-1703) Dutch
£1000 $1630   (2-Jul-91 PH224) Village scene with group of horsemen gathered outside
                 inn (52x64cm-20x25in) panel

GAEL, Barent (style) (1620-1703) Dutch
£1600 $2768   (20-May-91 SWS54/R) Revellers and figures on horseback outside an inn
                 (40x48cm-16x19in) panel
£3823 $7531   (14-Nov-90 SY.AM63/R) Poultry market (60x69cm-24x27in) (D.FL 12500)

GAERTNER, Bernard (1881-1938) German
£680 $1204   (20-Mar-91 KM.K1225) Alpine landscape, winter (85x105cm-33x41in)
                 s.d.1925 (DM 2000)

GAERTNER, Carl (1898-?) American
£5319 $10000   (22-Sep-90 WOL.C285/R) Quiet afternoon (76x89cm-30x35in) s.

GAERTNER, Christoph (1580-?) German
£56380 $100920   (9-Apr-91 APT.P16/R) Le couple inegal (94x113cm-37x44in) mono.d.1623
                 (F.FR 570000)

GAETANO, C (19th C) ?
£1700 $3315   (16-Oct-90 CG256) Monastery cloister with monks (76x56cm-30x22in)

GAFFRON, A (?) ?
£700 $1141   (13-Jun-91 CG157) The triumph of Pan (114x137cm-45x54in) s.

GAFGEN, Wolfgang (20th C) German
£750 $1328   (21-Mar-91 C266) Charlie's Canape (100x130cm-39x51in) s.d.72 pencil

GAGEN, Robert Ford (1847-1926) Canadian
£1667 $3233   (3-Dec-90 R.T264/R) Rocky Mountain view (51x68cm-20x27in) s.d.1909 W/C
                 (C.D 3750)

GAGLIARDINI, Julien Gustave (1846-1927) French
£700 $1344   (27-Nov-90 PH41) Beached rowing boat before continental harbour town
                 (38x55cm-15x22in) s.
£1000 $1920   (27-Nov-90 PH40/R) Figures on continental quayside before moored sailing
                 vessels (46x55cm-18x22in) s.
£1295 $2240   (26-May-91 ZZ.F64/R) Voilier a la sortie du port (38x62cm-15x24in) s.
                 (F.FR 13000)
£1434 $2811   (7-Nov-90 APT.P515) Voiliers au port (38x55cm-15x22in) s. panel
                 (F.FR 14000)
£3976 $7633   (29-Nov-90 QWA.P168) Bord de mer (36x54cm-14x21in) s. panel (F.FR 39000)
£8560 $13953   (14-Jun-91 AGS.P26/R) Marseille - Cannebiere et quai du Vieux Port
                 (46x65cm-18x26in) s. (F.FR 85000)

GAGLIER, D (19th C) French?
£350 $620   (20-Mar-91 C61/R) Portrait of lady in black dress and scarlet shawl
                 (15x?cm-6x?in) min. s. turned wooden frame rec.

GAGNEREAUX, Benigne (1756-1795) French
£3725 $7338   (17-Nov-90 BU.H224/R) Alexander's injury (58x83cm-23x33in) i. Indian ink
                 wash (F.M 26000)

GAGNON, Clarence A (1882-1942) Canadian
£1974 $3888   (30-Oct-90 SY.T95/R) Valle du Linthal, Suisse (16x23cm-6x9in) s.with
                 thumbprint i.d.1926 i.verso panel (C.D 4500)
£2313 $4510   (24-Oct-90 EA.M420/R) Twilight in Laurentians (12x18cm-5x7in) i.d.circa
                 1921 panel (C.D 5250)
£3022 $5863   (3-Dec-90 R.T263/R) Ice harvest (14x20cm-6x8in) studio st. num.792 verso
                 panel (C.D 6800)
£5702 $11175   (20-Nov-90 JOY.T83/R) Ferme de Charlevoix (17x24cm-7x9in) panel
                 (C.D 13000)
£21053 $41263   (20-Nov-90 JOY.T28/R) Children at play in valley (16x23cm-6x9in) panel
                 (C.D 48000)
£28947 $56737   (20-Nov-90 JOY.T93/R) Le canal du Loing, Moret (64x91cm-25x36in) s.
                 (C.D 66000)
£1263 $2184   (6-May-91 SY.T87) Man on snowshoes with dog (43x27cm-17x11in) s. W/C
                 (C.D 2500)

GAILLARDOT, Pierre (20th C) French
£792 $1402   (7-Apr-91 LT.P179) Le polo (55x46cm-22x18in) s. (F.FR 8000)
£794 $1565   (30-Oct-90 I.N247) Courses de haies (27x35cm-11x14in) s. (F.FR 7800)
£1535 $2716   (7-Apr-91 LT.P113) La course de Sulkys (81x100cm-32x39in) s.
                 (F.FR 15500)
£502 $929   (10-Mar-91 LT.P165) La course de Sulkys (49x66cm-19x26in) s.d.81 W/C
                 gouache (F.FR 5000)

GAINES, Charles (20th C) American?

£1243	$2100	(1-May-91 SY.NY93/R) Incomplete text no.6 E (56x43cm-22x17in) s.d.1978 and 1979 col.ink photo triptych
£2071	$3500	(1-May-91 SY.NY92/R) Walnut tree orchard (55x45cm-22x18in) col.ink black white photo triptych

GAINSBOROUGH, Thomas (1727-1788) British

£7179	$14000	(11-Oct-90 SY.NY1/R) Portrait of young girl (58x47cm-23x19in) oval
£8718	$17000	(11-Oct-90 SY.NY169 a/R) Portrait of Anne Furye wearing lace-trimmed dress with bows on sleeve (75x62cm-30x24in)
£10000	$19500	(26-Oct-90 C224/R) Portrait of Colonel Henry Townshend, in uniform by a marble bust (63x76cm-25x30in)
£40000	$78800	(14-Nov-90 S43/R) Portrait of Catherine Griffith wearing silver dress decorated with pearls (74x61cm-29x24in)
£46000	$90620	(14-Nov-90 S45/R) Portrait of Constantine John standing by window wearing naval uniform (126x150cm-50x59in)
£50000	$98500	(14-Nov-90 S101/R) The Suffolk plough (50x60cm-20x24in)
£60000	$118200	(16-Nov-90 C10/R) Portrait of John, 2nd Earl of Buckinghamshire in peer's robes (122x96cm-48x38in)
£78000	$139620	(10-Apr-91 S86/R) Portrait of Lady Margaret Fordyce, seated in dress lace and pearl trimmed dress and feathered hat (76x62cm-30x24in) in painted oval
£150000	$247500	(12-Jul-91 C66/R) Extensive landscape with boy tending cows, milkmaid, woodcutters and church tower through trees (71x136cm-28x54in)
£190000	$313500	(10-Jul-91 S74/R) Wooded landscape with drover and cattle and distant mansion (121x146cm-48x57in)
£210000	$346500	(10-Jul-91 S70/R) Wooded landscape with figures, donkeys, buildings and mountains beyond (35x44cm-14x17in) s.
£7200	$12888	(11-Apr-91 S15/R) Wooded landscape with horse (18x21cm-7x8in) black white chk stump
£14000	$23100	(11-Jul-91 S153/R) Figures and horses by buildings on country road (24x31cm-9x12in) chk htd.white
£15500	$27745	(11-Apr-91 S16/R) Wooded landscape with figure seated near pool (18x21cm-7x8in) black white chk stump
£560000	$924000	(9-Jul-91 C90/R) Lady walking in garden holding small child by hand (50x32cm-20x13in) chk stump htd.white oil

GAINSBOROUGH, Thomas (after) (1727-1788) British

£800	$1480	(6-Mar-91 SC4346/R) Rustic courtship (66x107cm-26x42in)
£880	$1470	(7-Jun-91 PHE99) Half length portrait of a lady in a feather hat (75x62cm-30x24in)
£1800	$3222	(10-Apr-91 S163/R) Milkmaid (70x90cm-28x35in)
£1800	$3456	(17-Dec-90 PH148) Portrait of Lady Sheffield (96x72cm-38x28in) pastel

GAINSBOROUGH, Thomas (attrib) (1727-1788) British

£2204	$4341	(14-Nov-90 D.V276/R) Portrait of gentleman (14x11cm-6x4in) board (A.S 45000)
£11000	$21670	(14-Nov-90 S46/R) Portrait of Mrs Horton later Duchess of Cumberland wearing gold shawl (37x28cm-15x11in)
£21176	$36000	(31-May-91 CH.NY208/R) Portrait of Mrs Robinson standing wearing dress with bow and shawl (221x129cm-87x51in)

GAINSBOROUGH, Thomas (circle) (1727-1788) British

£10000	$16500	(10-Jul-91 S75/R) Cattle and drovers resting by river at dusk in classical landscape (104x136cm-41x54in)

GAINSBOROUGH, Thomas (studio) (1727-1788) British

£5020	$8082	(27-Jun-91 APT.P149/R) Portrait of la Comtesse de Waldegrave (130x102cm-51x40in) (F.FR 50000)

GAINSBOROUGH, Thomas (style) (1727-1788) British

£1250	$2100	(24-Apr-91 MMB419) Wooded landscape with cart on track and figures by stile (127x102cm-50x40in)
£1500	$2685	(12-Apr-91 C142/R) Portrait of Edward Elton, in jacket and elaborate ruff (74x62cm-29x24in) oval
£6200	$11780	(1-Mar-91 C82/R) Landscape with peasants on track along cornfield (49x60cm-19x24in)

GAIPER, T E (19th C) ?

£2849	$5100	(16-Mar-91 W.W27/R) Gay Society (66x81cm-26x32in) s.

GAISSER, Jakob Emmanuel (1825-1899) German

£1238	$2427	(7-Nov-90 DS.W49) Herzdame - card players (68x72cm-27x28in) s. (NZ.D 4000)
£1429	$2400	(17-Jul-91 SY.NY305/R) The cardgame (31x39cm-12x15in) s. panel
£1627	$2717	(5-Jun-91 DO.H2282/R) Soldiers and peasant women merrymaking (40x29cm-16x11in) s. panel (DM 4800)
£1712	$2791	(12-Jun-91 N.M430/R) Roccoco couple reading with maid servant in interior (36x29cm-14x11in) s. panel (DM 5000)
£2490	$4308	(24-May-91 FB.P167/R) La partie de cartes (33x44cm-13x17in) s. panel (F.FR 25000)
£4500	$7380	(19-Jun-91 S92/R) Game of cards (31x38cm-12x15in) s. panel
£4615	$9000	(23-Oct-90 SY.NY361/R) A good joke. The letter (65x76cm-26x30in) s. pair

GAISSER, Max (1857-1922) German
£1225	$2425	(31-Jan-91 D.V98/R) Dutch interior (19x24cm-7x9in) rem.sig. panel (A.S 25000)
£1301	$2329	(12-Mar-91 FN.S2369/R) The unexpected visit, Dutch interior scene with elegant figure and maid (65x52cm-26x20in) s. panel (DM 3800)
£2397	$3908	(12-Jun-91 N.M431/R) Gentlemen eating in Dutch interior (26x35cm-10x14in) s. panel (DM 7000)
£2632	$5000	(27-Feb-91 SY.NY160/R) Taking careful account (22x28cm-9x11in) s. panel
£4281	$7663	(13-Mar-91 N.M497/R) Dutch interior with councillors conversing and eating (28x35cm-11x14in) s. panel (DM 12500)
£6643	$12822	(12-Dec-90 WE.MU109/R) Meeting between merchant men (49x61cm-19x24in) s. panel (DM 19000)
£7692	$14846	(12-Dec-90 WE.MU110/R) Gentlemen gathered round table (44x54cm-17x21in) s. panel (DM 22000)
£508	*$829*	*(3-Jul-91 WE.MU44/R) Siegestor, Munich (17x25cm-7x10in) s.d. gouache (DM 1500)*

GAL, Menchu (20th C) ?
£770	*$1378*	*(13-Mar-91 FER.M252/R) Flora marina en una burbuja (31x21cm-12x8in) s. W/C (S.P 140000)*

GALAN, Julio (1958-) Mexican
£9184	$18000	(19-Nov-90 SY.NY279/R) Clown (162x119cm-64x47in) s.
£8163	*$16000*	*(19-Nov-90 SY.NY280/R) Argentina (99x99cm-39x39in) s.d.80 oil mixed media collage canvas*

GALANTIERE, Nancy (20th C) French
£851	$1600	(19-Sep-90 B.SF2622/R) Mrs De Saint Exupery (43x61cm-17x24in) s.d.48

GALARD, Gustave de (1779-1841) French
£3083	$5982	(7-Dec-90 SY.MO113/R) Bouquet de fleurs (33x24cm-13x9in) s. (F.FR 30000)

GALBUSERA, Giovacchino (1871-1942) Italian
£2191	$3769	(14-May-91 GF.L2518/R) San Bernardino, Lago d'Ospizio (27x39cm-11x15in) s. i.verso panel (S.F.R 5500)

GALE, William (1823-1909) British
£550	$974	(21-Mar-91 CSK166) A dip on a summer's day (23x30cm-9x12in) mono. paper laid down on canvas
£650	$1229	(27-Sep-90 CSK113) A young beauty (22x17cm-9x7in) mono. board

GALEA, Luigi M (1847-1917) Maltese
£780	$1318	(3-May-91 PHE159) Mediterranean harbour (18x42cm-7x17in) s. board
£950	$1853	(18-Oct-90 CSK163/R) The Grand Harbour, Valetta, Malta (14x33cm-6x13in) s. card
£1000	$1950	(18-Oct-90 CSK162/R) H.M.S. Furious leaving Valetta Harbour (28x53cm-11x21in) s.d.1904 i.verso board
£1200	$2016	(18-Jul-91 CSK191) Valetta harbour, Malta (18x42cm-7x17in) s. board
£1300	$2561	(4-Oct-90 CSK246/R) Valetta harbour at sunset (21x54cm-8x21in) s. board
£1400	$2744	(14-Feb-91 CSK201/R) Sunset over Valletta Harbour (18x36cm-7x14in) s. board
£1650	$3218	(15-Jan-91 SWS165/R) Maltese harbour scenes (14x33cm-6x13in) s. board pair
£1900	$3268	(17-May-91 C216/R) Valetta at sunrise. Valetta at sunset (15x33cm-6x13in) s. board pair
£2550	$4335	(29-May-91 GA186) Panoramic Maltese harbour scenes at sunset and sunrise - probably Valetta (21x54cm-8x21in) s.d.1908 board pair
£2800	$5012	(12-Mar-91 PH48/R) The Grand Harbour, Valetta, Malta (22x54cm-9x21in) s. board pair
£3800	$7486	(5-Oct-90 C166/R) Valetta Harbour, Malta. Medina, Malta (29x77cm-11x30in) one s.d.1904 board pair

GALEOTA-RUSSO, Leopoldo (1868-1938) Italian
£861	$1455	(16-Apr-91 CH.R161) Studio di paese (35x51cm-14x20in) s. i.verso (I.L 1900000)

GALEOTTI, Sebastiano (1676-1746) Italian
£593	*$1049*	*(19-Mar-91 F.M277/R) Allegoria (35x25cm-14x10in) bistre ink (I.L 1300000)*

GALEOTTI, Sebastiano (circle) (1676-1746) Italian
£32000	$63040	(31-Oct-90 S193/R) David with the head of Goliath (132x94cm-52x37in)

GALES, Simon (1964-) British
£2000	$3220	(28-Jun-91 CSK196/R) College (61x53cm-24x21in) s.d.1990 polyptych

GALGARIO, Fra see GHISLANDI, Vittore

GALIEN-LALOUE, Eugene (1854-1941) French
£1156	$2000	(21-May-91 CE.NY338/R) Ships in harbour (31x23cm-12x9in) s. panel
£1445	$2500	(22-May-91 D.NY51/R) Lakeside cottage, Brittany (36x53cm-14x21in) s.
£2000	$3440	(14-May-91 SWS352/R) French harbour at sunset (35x46cm-14x18in) s.
£2800	$4564	(1-Jul-91 APT.P143/R) Boulevards animes (23x35cm-9x14in) s. panel (F.FR 28000)
£2800	$4816	(17-May-91 C8/R) Granville (49x62cm-19x24in) s.
£3077	$5200	(20-Apr-91 WOL.C200/R) Village scene (41x33cm-16x13in) s.

GALIEN-LALOUE, Eugene (1854-1941) French-cont.

£3684	$7000	(28-Feb-91 CH.NY39/R) Les forges d'Ivry (49x65cm-19x26in) s.l.d.94
£4211	$8000	(28-Feb-91 CH.NY38/R) Pont sur la Seine avec une vue sur l'ancien Trocadero (48x65cm-19x26in) s.
£6018	$11735	(12-Oct-90 APT.P60/R) Criee au crepuscule a Dieppe (47x65cm-19x26in) s. (F.FR 60000)
£1796	$3520	(6-Nov-90 GF.L2187/R) Quai du Louvre in Paris (10x13cm-4x5in) s. W/C (S.FR 4400)
£1829	$3000	(19-Jun-91 B.SF1739/R) Promenade sur le boulevard (23x33cm-9x13in) s. W/C
£3303	$6506	(13-Nov-90 AB.S890/R) Place du Chatelet, Paris (19x31cm-7x12in) s. W/C (S.KR 36000)
£3465	$6134	(7-Apr-91 I.N141) Saint-Germain-des-Pres (20x32cm-8x13in) s. gouache W/C (F.FR 35000)
£3553	$7000	(15-Nov-90 D.NY82/R) Paris in snow (23x30cm-9x12in) s. W/C gouache cardboard
£3846	$7500	(23-Oct-90 SY.NY14/R) Boulevard des Italiens, Paris (19x30cm-7x12in) s. gouache
£3878	$7639	(14-Nov-90 FB.P20/R) Pont Notre-Dame en Automne (18x30cm-7x12in) s. gouache (F.FR 38000)
£3993	$6668	(3-Jun-91 B.O46/R) Porte St.Denis, Paris (19x31cm-7x12in) s. gouache (N.KR 46000)
£4000	$7680	(28-Nov-90 S293/R) Place de la Bastille, Paris (18x30cm-7x12in) s. ink W/C htd bodycol.
£4080	$6813	(3-Jun-91 B.O47/R) Foire du Trone, Paris (19x31cm-7x12in) s. gouache (N.KR 47000)
£4100	$6847	(22-Jul-91 SWS933/R) Quai du Louvre (25x33cm-10x13in) s. gouache pencil
£4400	$7216	(19-Jun-91 S217/R) Arc de Triomphe, Paris (19x31cm-7x12in) s. gouache W/C
£4482	$7620	(29-May-91 GL.P8/R) La place de la Bastille (20x32cm-8x13in) s. gouache (F.FR 45000)
£4724	$7747	(18-Jun-91 APT.P21/R) Paris, l'eglise Saint Vincent de Paul (19x31cm-7x12in) s. gouache (F.FR 47000)
£4893	$9394	(29-Nov-90 ZZ.F2/R) Notre-Dame vue de chevet (19x31cm-7x12in) s. gouache (F.FR 48000)
£5000	$9750	(18-Oct-90 SC3019/R) Quai D'Orsay (18x30cm-7x12in) s. gouache ink
£5000	$8850	(22-Mar-91 BG.P86/R) Le theatre du Gymnase (18x31cm-7x12in) s. gouache (F.FR 50000)
£5500	$10560	(28-Nov-90 S294/R) The Porte St.Denis, Paris (18x30cm-7x12in) s. ink gouache
£5641	$11000	(23-Oct-90 SY.NY311/R) La Madeleine en hiver (33x21cm-13x8in) s. W/C
£5800	$9512	(19-Jun-91 S223/R) L'eglise St. Etienne du Mont, Paris (37x54cm-15x21in) s. gouache
£6114	$11983	(5-Nov-90 FB.M345/R) Street scene, Paris (19x31cm-7x12in) s. gouache (C.D 14000)
£6116	$11743	(2-Dec-90 M.V96/R) La Madeleine sous la neige (23x36cm-9x14in) s. gouache (F.FR 60000)
£6626	$12722	(2-Dec-90 M.V95) Notre Dame vue du quai Montbello (27x38cm-11x15in) s. gouache (F.FR 65000)
£6800	$13328	(15-Feb-91 C3/R) Boulevard du Palais, Paris (21x34cm-8x13in) s. black chk W/C bodycol
£6939	$13461	(8-Dec-90 GAB.G2565/R) Vue de la Bastille en hiver (28x42cm-11x17in) s. gouache (S.FR 17000)
£7000	$11480	(19-Jun-91 S224/R) Figures on Quay Megisserie near Place du Chatelet, Paris (18x31cm-7x12in) s. gouache
£8000	$15360	(28-Nov-90 S297/R) Flower market in Place de la Republique, Paris (18x32cm-7x13in) s. gouache
£8500	$16320	(28-Nov-90 S296/R) The Arc de Triomphe in winter, Paris (18x31cm-7x12in) s. gouache
£9000	$14670	(1-Jul-91 APT.P146/R) Boulevard anime pres de la Republique (38x57cm-15x22in) s. gouache (F.FR 90000)
£9694	$19097	(14-Nov-90 FB.P18/R) Lwe marche aux fleurs (19x31cm-7x12in) s. gouache (F.FR 95000)
£9901	$17525	(4-Apr-91 PPB.P49/R) La Place de la Madeleine (38x57cm-15x22in) s. gouache (F.FR 100000)
£10000	$16400	(19-Jun-91 S218/R) Figures by Madeleine, Paris (39x58cm-15x23in) s. pen gouache
£10000	$16400	(19-Jun-91 S215/R) Figures at dusk, Paris (39x54cm-15x21in) s. pen gouache
£12500	$20500	(19-Jun-91 S214/R) Figures by flower barrow, Paris (39x58cm-15x23in) s. pen gouache

GALIZIA, Fede (1578-1630) Italian

£4773	$9356	(20-Nov-90 F.R136/R) Ritratto di donna in veste di cacciatrice (32x25cm-13x10in) s. panel (I.L 10500000)

GALIZIA, Fede (circle) (1578-1630) Italian

£11405	$22468	(30-Oct-90 BU.S247/R) Still life of fruit (52x69cm-20x27in) (S.KR 125000)

GALL, Francois (1912-1987) French

£614	$1008	(18-Jun-91 FN.S1587/R) Busy park scene (18x22cm-7x9in) s. panel (DM 1800)
£616	$1005	(15-Jun-91 L.K219/R) Portrait of young woman (24x16cm-9x6in) s.indis.d. panel (DM 1800)

696

GALL, Francois (1912-1987) French-cont.

£853	$1672	(22-Nov-90 L.K946) River landscape with bathers (31x41cm-12x16in) s.d.1931 board (DM 2500)
£900	$1773	(13-Nov-90 SWS389/R) Quai des Grands Augustins (17x22cm-7x9in) s.l.
£1321	$2285	(22-May-91 BA.S58/R) View of the Seine (26x34cm-10x13in) s. (S.KR 14000)
£1421	$2800	(13-Nov-90 CE.NY131/R) Au bord de la Seine a Paris (22x27cm-9x11in) s.l.
£1472	$2900	(13-Nov-90 SY.NY181/R) Place du Tertre (27x38cm-11x15in) s. panel
£1538	$3000	(10-Oct-90 SY.NY316/R) Along the Seine (23x25cm-9x10in) s.
£1604	$2775	(22-May-91 BA.S57/R) Fishing by the Seine (26x34cm-10x13in) s.l. (S.KR 17000)
£1613	$3145	(27-Oct-90 LT.P52/R) Le boulevard Rochechouart (50x61cm-20x24in) s. (F.FR 16000)
£1657	$2800	(20-Apr-91 WOL.C244/R) Market scene (51x36cm-20x14in) s.
£1700	$2771	(4-Jul-91 GL.P246) Elegante a sa coiffeuse (27x22cm-11x9in) s. (F.FR 17000)
£1759	$2884	(18-Jun-91 APT.P200) Montmartre, la place du Tertre (38x46cm-15x18in) s. panel (F.FR 17500)
£1795	$3500	(10-Oct-90 SY.NY315/R) Figures on beach (23x25cm-9x10in) s.
£1984	$3433	(22-May-91 GS.B2378/R) View of town and river with railway bridge (50x60cm-20x24in) s.indis.d. hessian (S.FR 5000)
£2041	$4000	(12-Feb-91 SY.NY228/R) At the ballet (28x23cm-11x9in) s.
£2051	$4000	(10-Oct-90 SY.NY218/R) La jeune baigneuse (28x23cm-11x9in) s.
£2168	$4250	(12-Feb-91 SY.NY226/R) Argenteuil (23x25cm-9x10in) s.l.
£2224	$4315	(4-Dec-90 BA.S156/R) Walk in winter (50x65cm-20x26in) s.l. (S.KR 24000)
£2347	$4623	(16-Nov-90 FB.P156/R) Jeune femme devant la coiffeuse (27x22cm-11x9in) s. (F.FR 23000)
£2428	$4200	(7-May-91 CE.NY9/R) Danseuse assise (70x20cm-28x8in) s.l.
£2551	$5000	(12-Feb-91 SY.NY100/R) Figures in park (41x48cm-16x19in) l.d.1940
£2949	$5750	(10-Oct-90 SY.NY220/R) At the cafe (28x46cm-11x18in) s.
£3046	$6000	(15-Nov-90 D.NY98/R) Round point des Champs Elysees (46x54cm-18x21in) s.i. masonite
£3085	$5367	(28-Mar-91 DAR.P32/R) Rond-point des Champs Elysees (54x65cm-21x26in) s. (F.FR 31000)
£3179	$5500	(7-May-91 CE.NY16/R) La danseuse (27x22cm-11x9in) s.
£3179	$5500	(7-May-91 CE.NY19/R) Jeune fille au cafe (27x22cm-11x9in) s.
£3200	$5408	(1-May-91 GD.B316/R) Man leading horse with jockey up to race course (22x27cm-9x11in) s.l. pavatex (S.FR 8000)
£3299	$6500	(13-Nov-90 CE.NY53/R) Les Invalides (46x61cm-18x24in) s.l.d.46
£3353	$6606	(6-Oct-90 GL.P136/R) Sur les grands boulevards, Paris (49x61cm-19x24in) s. (F.FR 34000)
£3518	$5769	(18-Jun-91 APT.P199/R) Paris, la Seine auPont Saint Michel (64x81cm-25x32in) s.d.938 (F.FR 35000)
£3543	$6943	(25-Nov-90 ZZ.F68/R) La plage de Trouville (27x22cm-11x9in) s. (F.FR 35000)
£3550	$7028	(28-Jan-91 PPB.P22/R) Le Pont des Arts (40x50cm-16x20in) s. (F.FR 35000)
£3553	$7000	(13-Nov-90 CE.NY149/R) La plage (27x46cm-11x18in) s.
£3571	$7000	(12-Feb-91 SY.NY145/R) Au bord de la Seine (51x74cm-20x29in) s.
£3593	$6036	(23-Apr-91 SY.AM17/R) Feeding baby (27x35cm-11x14in) s.l. panel (D.FL 12000)
£3655	$7200	(13-Nov-90 CE.NY110/R) La plage d'Arcachon (27x34cm-11x13in) s.
£4000	$6760	(1-May-91 GD.B318/R) Harbour scene with fishermen unloading boats (38x46cm-15x18in) s.l. (S.FR 10000)
£4077	$7870	(14-Dec-90 ARC.P47/R) La plage (27x46cm-11x18in) s. (F.FR 40000)
£4167	$7208	(22-May-91 GS.B2377/R) View of Trouville with figures (27x46cm-11x18in) s. s.l.verso (S.FR 10500)
£4230	$6894	(11-Jun-91 I.N211) Le pont des arts (50x61cm-20x24in) s. (F.FR 42000)
£4294	$7000	(12-Jun-91 SY.NY45/R) Deauville (27x46cm-11x18in) s.
£4569	$9000	(13-Nov-90 CE.NY174/R) Nature morte (60x49cm-24x19in) s.
£5076	$10000	(15-Nov-90 D.NY99/R) Girl with red coat (47x56cm-19x22in) s. i.stretcher
£5128	$10000	(10-Oct-90 SY.NY217/R) By the kiosk (61x51cm-24x20in) s.l.
£5149	$9113	(7-Apr-91 LT.P81 b) Jeune fille au piano (61x50cm-24x20in) s. (F.FR 52000)
£5622	$10402	(10-Mar-91 LT.P57/R) Jeune femme au cafe (46x33cm-18x13in) s. (F.FR 56000)
£6773	$13207	(24-Oct-90 GD.B386/R) Young woman taking aperitif (46x33cm-18x13in) s. (S.FR 17000)
£6923	$13500	(10-Oct-90 SY.NY329/R) La belle saison (61x74cm-24x29in) s. s.l.verso
£7107	$14000	(15-Nov-90 D.NY101/R) Devant la coiffeuse (46x27cm-18x11in) s. l.verso
£7614	$15000	(13-Nov-90 CE.NY118/R) Danseuse (92x71cm-36x28in) s.
£8629	$17000	(13-Nov-90 CE.NY142/R) Cafe-Restaurant Pigalle (45x81cm-18x32in) s. s.l.verso
£12000	$20280	(1-May-91 GD.B315/R) Girl embroidering in park (40x32cm-16x13in) s. (S.FR 30000)
£594	*$1165*	*(11-Nov-90 ZZ.F65/R) Manege en bois de Martel en Quercy (17x20cm-7x8in) s. W/C (F.FR 5800)*
£2081	*$3413*	*(19-Jun-91 B.SF1820/R) La ballerina (50x58cm-20x23in) s.i. pastel chl*

GALLAGHER, Michael (20th C) American

£2538	$5000	(4-Oct-90 SY.NY117 a/R) Wood shadows study (63x58cm-25x23in) s.d.1978 verso acrylic board

GALLAIT, Louis (1810-1887) Belgian

£930	$1600	(15-May-91 D.NY54) Mother and Child (20x13cm-8x5in) s.d.69 panel
£2806	$5500	(7-Nov-90 B.SF1149/R) Minstrel boy (47x38cm-19x15in) s.d.1867 panel

GALLAND, Pierre Victor (1822-1892) French
£2051 $4000   (26-Oct-90 SY.NY170/R) Sketch of sea goddess, study for ceiling in
   Louvre (47x58cm-19x23in) st.mono.
£14617 $28503   (28-Oct-90 QWA.P132 b/R) Les trophees (310x195cm-122x77in) (F.FR 145000)

GALLARD, Michel de (20th C) French
£1005 $1648   (19-Jun-91 JM.P135/R) Arbre dans un paysage (46x38cm-18x15in) s.d.1957
   (F.FR 10000)
£1747 $2952   (29-Apr-91 LGB.P104/R) La rue (45x56cm-18x22in) s.d.1953 (F.FR 17500)
£3289 $6380   (7-Dec-90 GL.P69) Village dans la campagne (40x80cm-16x31in) s.
   (F.FR 32000)

GALLARD-LEPINAY (1842-1885) French
£621 $1000   (26-Jun-91 D.NY61) Venetian sailboat leaving port (46x74cm-18x29in) s.

GALLARD-LEPINAY, Paul Charles Emmanuel (1842-1885) French
£3500 $6580   (8-Aug-90 PHP136/R) Shipping in Mediterranean harbour (46x73cm-18x29in)
   s. pair

GALLATIN, Albert E (1882-1952) American
£3846 $7500   (20-Oct-90 W.W244/R) Contrast of forms (46x61cm-18x24in) s.
   s.i.d.1951verso canvasboard

GALLAWAY, Alexander (fl.1794-1812) British
*£900 $1485   (10-Jul-91 C109/R) A lady in grey-blue dress (6x?cm-2x?in) min.s.d.1795
   gold frame oval*

GALLE, E (19th C) ?
£2600 $4264   (19-Jun-91 S188/R) Dressing up (54x35cm-21x14in) s.d.1892

GALLEGOS Y ARNOSA, Jose (1859-1917) Spanish
£2728 $5346   (22-Nov-90 SY.MI54/R) Davanti al fuoco (27x21cm-11x8in) s.
   (I.L 6000000)
£34682 $60000   (23-May-91 CH.NY146/R) Venetian carnival (31x51cm-12x20in) s.i. panel

GALLEGOS, Fernando (school) (1440-c.1507) Spanish
£31579 $60000   (11-Jan-91 CH.NY2/R) Shooting of bull on Monte Gargano (84x60cm-33x24in)
   panel

GALLEN-KALLELA, Akseli Valdemar (1865-1931) Finnish
£6304 $12418   (17-Nov-90 BU.H43/R) Small girl on bear skin rug (38x29cm-15x11in)
   s.d.1904 canvas on panel (F.M 44000)
£6419 $12582   (24-Nov-90 HOR.H92/R) Winter afternoon (32x21cm-13x8in) s.d.1916
   (F.M 45000)
£9843 $19292   (24-Nov-90 HOR.H91/R) Winter in the wood (31x31cm-12x12in) s.d.1894
   (F.M 69000)
£10791 $20827   (15-Dec-90 BU.H50/R) Rainy street scene with man, evening
   (37x30cm-15x12in) s.indist.d.1886 panel (F.M 75000)
£21583 $41655   (15-Dec-90 BU.H49/R) The first snow (54x54cm-21x21in) s. (F.M 150000)
*£3000 $5760   (28-Nov-90 S124/R) Le Roi Deometif et la Courtisane Rhodope
   (33x20cm-13x8in) s.indist.d. gouache htd gold paint*

GALLI (1944-) German
*£685 $1116   (14-Jun-91 L.K885/R) Untitled (90x80cm-35x31in) s.i.d.83 s.i.d.verso oil
   col.chk canvas (DM 2000)*

GALLI, Eduardo (1845-?) Italian
£7000 $14000   (18-Oct-90 F.M98/R) Contadina nel bosco con capra (107x170cm-42x67in) s.
   (I.L 16000000)

GALLI, G (?) Italian
£1000 $1920   (29-Nov-90 B107/R) Reflections (34x25cm-13x10in) s.

GALLI, Giovanni Antonio (after) (17th C) Italian
£950 $1606   (19-Apr-91 C19) The Madonna sewing as Saint Anne winds yarn
   (264x335cm-104x132in)

GALLI, Giovanni Antonio (style) (17th C) Italian
£15075 $24724   (21-Jun-91 SY.MO184/R) Venus allongee (107x175cm-42x69in) (F.FR 150000)

GALLI, Riccardo -20th C (1869-1944) Italian
£1368 $2285   (6-Jun-91 F.M105/R) Alagna, sulla strada della miniera (34x49cm-13x19in)
   s. i.verso panel (I.L 3000000)
£5455 $10692   (22-Nov-90 SY.MI81/R) Ragazza alla festa (130x92cm-51x36in) s.d.1924
   oval (I.L 12000000)
£9092 $17820   (22-Nov-90 SY.MI70/R) Nella casa silenziosa (105x98cm-41x39in) s.d.1926
   (I.L 20000000)

GALLI, Sergio (20th C) ?
£816 $1584   (8-Dec-90 RU.ZU179) Roy Lichtenstein, I can see the whole room
   (120x20cm-47x8in) d.1989 (S.FR 2000)

GALLIAC, Louis (1849-1931) French
£510 $1000   (21-Nov-90 NA.BA81) La lecture (23x36cm-9x14in) s. panel
£765 $1508   (16-Nov-90 LGB.P198) Jeune femme a la lampe (35x27cm-14x11in) s. panel
   (F.FR 7500)

GALLIANI, Omar (1954-) Italian
£1534 $2500   (12-Jun-91 SY.NY252/R) Attraverso (41x41cm-16x16in) s.d.1985 verso
£1941   *$3746*   *(13-Dec-90 F.M383/R) Senza titolo (98x128cm-39x50in) s.d.80 mixed media*
                       collage (I.L 4200000)

GALLIARI, Gaspare (circle) (1761-1823) Italian
£559   *$1085*   (7-Dec-90 GB.B5714/R) View into arched hall with monuments
                       (21x30cm-8x12in) indian ink pen wash (DM 1600)

GALLIBERT, Genevieve (1888-?) French
£1500 $2955   (1-Nov-90 TE650/R) Le Cap d'Antibes (46x61cm-18x24in) s.d.51

GALLIEN-BERTHON, Marie Clotilde (1870-?) French
£1518   *$2976*   *(20-Nov-90 APT.P227/R) L'Algerienne (121x96cm-48x38in) s.d.1921 W/C*
                       (F.FR 15000)

GALLIER, Gratien Achille (1814-1871) French
£808 $1398   (6-May-91 ZEL.L1697/R) Wooded landscape with village beyond, evening
                       (38x55cm-15x22in) s. (DM 2400)

GALLINER, A (20th C) ?
£839 $1620   (13-Dec-90 N.M2696/R) Portrait of young woman from Chiemgau
                       (69x53cm-27x21in) s.d.1929 (DM 2400)

GALLIZIO, Pinot (1902-) Italian
£1068 $2007   (19-Sep-90 KH.K106/R) La rue rouge (62x50cm-24x20in) s.d.61verso
                       (D.KR 12000)
£1690 $3178   (19-Sep-90 KH.K16/R) Composition (72x60cm-28x24in) s.d.61verso
                       (D.KR 19000)
£2669 $5018   (19-Sep-90 KH.K48/R) Composition (80x140cm-31x55in) (D.KR 30000)

GALLO, Giuseppe (1954-) Italian
£3625 $6307   (26-Mar-91 F.M49/R) Dionisio (135x120cm-53x47in) s.d.1983verso
                       (I.L 8000000)
£5662 $11041   (15-Oct-90 CSC.P86/R) Agora (150x200cm-59x79in) s.i.d.84 verso
                       (F.FR 56000)

GALLON, Robert (1845-1925) British
£789 $1547   (21-Nov-90 EA.M660) Saint Michael's Mount, Cornwall (30x45cm-12x18in) s.
                       (C.D 1800)
£950 $1872   (30-Oct-90 SC164/R) Highland cattle in valley (49x75cm-19x30in) s.
£1100 $1914   (26-Mar-91 PH101/R) An angler in a wooded river landscape
                       (51x76cm-20x30in) s.
£1850 $3090   (22-Jul-91 SWS980/R) A sunny afternoon on the coast (61x126cm-24x50in)
                       s.
£3000 $4890   (14-Jun-91 C218/R) Sailing boat on an estuary (60x101cm-24x40in) s.
£4000 $7880   (1-Nov-90 C251/R) Near Farnham (61x104cm-24x41in) s.
£4500 $7335   (14-Jun-91 C217/R) Feeding the chickens (51x76cm-20x30in) s.
£5500 $10835   (1-Nov-90 C230/R) River landscape with harvesters (61x102cm-24x40in)
                       s.d.1894
£5500 $8965   (14-Jun-91 C195/R) Children playing by a river (61x101cm-24x40in)
                       s.d.1882

GALOFRE Y GIMENEZ, Baldomero (1849-1902) Spanish
£16842 $32000   (28-Feb-91 CH.NY112/R) Encampment (23x39cm-9x15in) s.i. panel
£978   *$1574*   *(25-Jun-91 FER.M110/R) Bahia de Napoles (39x53cm-15x21in) s. W/C*
                       (S.P 180000)
£4200   *$7224*   *(15-May-91 BT120/R) The storm (61x94cm-24x37in) s. W/C*

GALSTER, H L (1826-1901) Danish
£2154 $4244   (14-Nov-90 RAS.K507/R) The moment the Crownprince arrived at Toldboden
                       it started to rain (110x180cm-43x71in) s.d.1871i.verso (D.KR 24000)

GALTER, Pietro (19th C) Italian
£800 $1568   (8-Nov-90 TL83/R) Shipping in the port of Venice (23x36cm-9x14in) s.

GALVAN, Jesus Guerrero see GUERRERO GALVAN, Jesus

GAMAIN, Louis Honore Frederic (1803-1871) French
£1527 $3009   (30-Oct-90 I.N11/R) Marine (43x60cm-17x24in) s. (F.FR 15000)

GAMAREE (19th C) French
£1304 $2543   (12-Oct-90 ZZ.F62) Bouquet de fleurs (100x70cm-39x28in) s.d.1888
                       (F.FR 13000)

GAMARRA, Jose (1934-) Uruguayan
£526 $1000   (14-Sep-90 S.BM244/R) Quetzalcoatl (84x56cm-33x22in) s.

GAMBA, Enrico (1831-1883) Italian
£1200 $2148   (12-Mar-91 PH59/R) The cardinal's visit. Sweeping the floor
                       (54x43cm-21x17in) one s.d.1876 one panel pair
£1300   *$2470*   *(12-Sep-90 CSK158/R) Young spectators (56x43cm-22x17in) s. W/C*
£1500   *$2850*   *(12-Sep-90 CSK143/R) On terrace (38x23cm-15x9in) s.indist.i. pencil W/C*
                       htd white

GAMBARA, Lattanzio (1530-1574) Italian
£2063 $3570   (22-May-91 GS.B2379) Sacra conversazione (96x84cm-38x33in) (S.FR 5200)
£1800 $3042   (16-Apr-91 C116/R) Designs for a Section of a trompe l'oeil frieze
      (17x59cm-7x23in) blk.chk.ink wash htd.white two

GAMBARINI, Giuseppe (1680-1725) Italian
£2052 $3427   (4-Jun-91 CH.R289) Bottega di S.Giuseppe (66x48cm-26x19in)
      (I.L 4500000)
£23638 $45858   (7-Dec-90 SY.MO21/R) Musiciens dans un paysage (47x65cm-19x26in)
      (F.FR 230000)
£27013 $51865   (30-Nov-90 APT.P29/R) Rejouissances paysannes (137x124cm-54x49in) pair
      (F.FR 265000)
£1800 $2934   (1-Jul-91 S152/R) Figure studies (32x41cm-13x16in) brush wash htd white

GAMBARINI, Giuseppe (attrib) (1680-1725) Italian
£9500 $15485   (4-Jul-91 CSK65/R) Peasant milking cow in farmyard. Gypsy encampment
      with peasant offering food to shepherdess (71x94cm-28x37in) pair

GAMBARTES, Leonidas (1909-1963) Argentinian
£2551 $5000   (20-Nov-90 CH.NY180/R) Paye (55x37cm-22x15in) chromogesso panel
£2660 $5000   (18-Sep-90 RO.BA43) Labores campestres (72x103cm-28x41in) s. chrome
      plaster

GAMBERUCCI, Cosimo (17th C) Italian
£6937 $13459   (3-Dec-90 SY.F1056/R) Assunzione della Vergine (193x137cm-76x54in)
      s.d.1602 (I.L 15000000)

GAMBLE, John M (1863-1957) American
£859 $1400   (11-Jun-91 MOR.P16) Landscape (20x30cm-8x12in) s. canvas on board
£1276 $2500   (12-Feb-91 MOR.P124) Landscape (20x30cm-8x12in) s.
£1410 $2750   (10-Oct-90 B.SF515/R) Poppies and lupines (40x30cm-16x12in) s. board
£3077 $6000   (10-Oct-90 B.SF513/R) Lupines and poppies on spring hillside
      (30x46cm-12x18in) s.d.34
£5128 $10000   (10-Oct-90 B.SF514/R) Wild buckwheat, Demore (51x76cm-20x30in) s.
      i.verso
£6800 $13260   (24-Oct-90 S11/R) Wild buckwheat, Santa Barbara, California
      (59x90cm-23x35in) s. i. verso
£8380 $15000   (12-Apr-91 SY.NY67/R) Joyous spring (66x51cm-26x20in) s. i.stretcher
£10256 $20000   (10-Oct-90 B.SF512/R) California wildflowers (76x102cm-30x40in) s.

GAMBOGI, Emile (19th C) French
£1032 $1847   (13-Mar-91 GK.Z26) Shepherd boy and sheep in Mediterranean landscape
      with ruins (73x59cm-29x23in) s. (S.FR 2600)

GAMBONI, Domenico (18th C) ?
£4106 $8089   (30-Oct-90 BU.S248/R) Landscape with ruins (68x84cm-27x33in)
      indist.sig.d.17 (S.KR 45000)

GAMELIN, Jacques (1738-1803) French
£4771 $8064   (18-Apr-91 APT.P108/R) La mort de Darius (63x97cm-25x38in) s.
      (F.FR 48000)

GAMLEY, Andrew (?-1949) British
£588 $1141   (20-Aug-91 L.V2) Working the fields (38x48cm-15x19in) W/C (C.D 1300)
£900 $1800   (5-Feb-91 S101/R) Potato workers, East Fife (40x49cm-16x19in) s. W/C

GAMONEDA, Boris (?) ?
£605 $1082   (13-Mar-91 FER.M268/R) El duque de Alba (10x10cm-4x4in) min. s.
      polychrome wood frame (S.P 110000)

GAMP, Botho von (1894-1977) German
£505 $874   (6-May-91 ZEL.L1698/R) White lilac in vase on draped table
      (60x80cm-24x31in) mono. (DM 1500)

GAMPERT, Otto (1842-?) Swiss
£699 $1357   (8-Dec-90 WK.M375/R) Wooded river landscape (32x46cm-13x18in) mono.
      paper on panel (DM 2000)
£1034 $1986   (28-Nov-90 KF.M273/R) Wooded moor landscape (30x44cm-12x17in) s. canvas
      on board (DM 3000)
£1207 $2317   (28-Nov-90 KF.M274/R) Wooded landscape (27x36cm-11x14in) mono. board on
      board (DM 3500)
£1379 $2648   (28-Nov-90 KF.M272/R) Wooded pond landscape (46x56cm-18x22in) s.
      (DM 4000)
£1519 $2719   (11-Apr-91 D.V87/R) Still life (49x60cm-19x24in) s. board (A.S 32000)

GANDARA, Antonio de la (1862-1917) French
£624 $1104   (5-Apr-91 LGB.P116) Femme en buste, de profil a gauche (44x36cm-17x14in)
      s. pastel (F.FR 6300)

GANDOLFI, Gaetano (1734-1802) Italian
£29000 $49010   (16-Apr-91 PH38/R) St. Dominic holding rosary to Virgin Mary on High,
      whilst angel burns evil spirits from heretics at (46x30cm-18x12in)
£72968 $121856   (4-Jun-91 CH.R439/R) La cena in casa di Simone, il Fariseo
      (120x95cm-47x37in) (I.L 160000000)
£236842 $450000   (11-Jan-91 CH.NY81/R) Assumption of Virgin (95x136cm-37x54in) painted
      arch

GANDOLFI, Gaetano (1734-1802) Italian-cont.
£638	$1130	(19-Mar-91 F.M313/R) Santo in preghiera (39x29cm-15x11in) black chk htd white (I.L 1400000)
£2006	$3551	(19-Mar-91 F.M208/R) San Leonardo da Porto Maurizio libera un'ossessa (21x15cm-8x6in) i. pencil (I.L 4400000)
£2028	$3934	(7-Dec-90 GB.B5510/R) Male nude standing resting one arm and leg on rock (38x23cm-15x9in) chk htd white (DM 5800)
£2052	$3632	(19-Mar-91 F.M256/R) Studio di nudo maschile seduto (42x31cm-17x12in) black chk (I.L 4500000)
£7368	$14000	(9-Jan-91 CH.NY7/R) Joshua and Aaron (41x31cm-16x12in) chk
£8421	$16000	(8-Jan-91 SY.NY199/R) The martyrdom of St.Eusebius (30x21cm-12x8in) ink wash
£15048	$26635	(19-Mar-91 F.M203/R) Assunzione della Vergine (40x28cm-16x11in) sanguine paper laid down on album leaf (I.L 33000000)

GANDOLFI, Gaetano (circle) (1734-1802) Italian
| £8000 | $13040 | (5-Jul-91 C212/R) Bearded old man, in white coat (55x46cm-22x18in) |

GANDOLFI, Mauro (1764-1834) Italian
| £1000 | $1930 | (11-Dec-90 C52/R) Time and fame (19x15cm-7x6in) s. blk.lead wash |
| £3158 | $6000 | (8-Jan-91 SY.NY80/R) Head of a girl resting her chin in her hand and reading a book (45x34cm-18x13in) chk. |

GANDOLFI, Mauro (attrib) (1764-1834) Italian
| £1003 | $1776 | (19-Mar-91 F.M283/R) Contadina seduta (17x14cm-7x6in) ink (I.L 2200000) |

GANDOLFI, Ubaldo (1728-1781) Italian
£12327	$20710	(23-Apr-91 F.R63/R) San Camillo de Lellis (106x74cm-42x29in) (I.L 27000000)
£69238	$123937	(9-Apr-91 APT.P48/R) Hercule et le chien Cerbere (217x118cm-85x46in) (F.FR 700000)
£1000	$1630	(1-Jul-91 S110/R) Male nude posed as Farnese Hercules (43x28cm-17x11in) red chk htd white
£1003	$1776	(19-Mar-91 F.M240/R) Estasi della Maddalena (22x16cm-9x6in) pen W/C ink over sanguine (I.L 2200000)
£1600	$2608	(1-Jul-91 S206/R) Apotheosis of Dominican saint with putti and angels (38x24cm-15x9in) pen wash
£1800	$2934	(2-Jul-91 C286/R) Beheading of Saint John the Baptist (38x27cm-15x11in) red chk
£2105	$4000	(9-Jan-91 CH.NY6/R) Seven heads of grotesques (21x29cm-8x11in) black chk ink wash
£2736	$4843	(19-Mar-91 F.M264/R) Paesaggio con tre figure (21x30cm-8x12in) pen W/C ink (I.L 6000000)
£2736	$4843	(19-Mar-91 F.M221/R) Sant'Antonio col Bambino e due santi in adorazione (21x16cm-8x6in) pen W/C ink over pencil (I.L 6000000)
£2964	$5246	(19-Mar-91 F.M194/R) San Giovanni Battista (27x19cm-11x7in) pen W/C bistre ink over pencil (I.L 6500000)
£3500	$5705	(1-Jul-91 S148/R) Bishop saint healing possessed woman (37x26cm-15x10in) bears num.46 i. pen wash
£5700	$10089	(19-Mar-91 F.M205/R) Adorazione dei Magi (28x20cm-11x8in) pen W/C ink (I.L 12500000)
£5700	$10089	(19-Mar-91 F.M241/R) Studio di decorazione con due figure maschili e cartiglio ornamentale (20x30cm-8x12in) pen W/C ink pencil (I.L 12500000)
£6612	$11703	(19-Mar-91 F.M265/R) Mercurio e Argo (17x24cm-7x9in) pen W/C ink over pencil (I.L 14500000)

GANDOLFI, Ubaldo (attrib) (1728-1781) Italian
| £17241 | $33103 | (17-Dec-90 ARC.P45/R) Saint Barthelemy (92x73cm-36x29in) (F.FR 170000) |

GANDOLFI, Ubaldo (circle) (1728-1781) Italian
| £1000 | $1630 | (2-Jul-91 PH166/R) St John the Evangelist standing before niche (50x24cm-20x9in) panel |

GANDY, Herbert (?-1920) British
| £14000 | $26460 | (26-Sep-90 S196/R) Welcome (180x77cm-71x30in) s.d.08 s.i.frame |
| £16000 | $30240 | (26-Sep-90 S210/R) Jephtha's daughter (122x213cm-48x84in) s.d.31 s.i.stretcher |

GANDY, Joseph Michael (1771-1843) British
| £600 | $1158 | (11-Dec-90 C213/R) Design for a stage set for Euripides (19x31cm-7x12in) two |

GANGOLF, Paul (1879-1945) German
| £606 | $1018 | (26-Apr-91 KM.K282/R) Beach scene (23x28cm-9x11in) s.i.d.23 indian ink brush W/C paper collage (DM 1800) |
| £676 | $1149 | (31-May-91 GB.B6296/R) City street with centre island (27x43cm-11x17in) s. chinese ink (DM 2000) |

GANKEVICH, Alexandre (20th C) Russian
| £500 | $885 | (18-Mar-91 ARC.P164/R) Nature morte aux fleurs (25x19cm-10x7in) s. (F.FR 5000) |

GANTLEY, James (?) ?
| £2000 | $3840 | (17-Aug-90 K519/R) Romantic parkland settings with courting figures (76x48cm-30x19in) s. pair |

GANTNER, Bernard (1930-) French
£1800	$3186	(20-Mar-91 DL.P135) Bord de l'etang Gele (55x38cm-22x15in) s.d.68 (F.FR 18000)
£2100	$3717	(20-Mar-91 DL.P136/R) Foret en Automne (65x81cm-26x32in) s.d.69 (F.FR 21000)
£5584	$11000	(13-Nov-90 CE.NY29/R) Saint Julien en hiver (74x100cm-29x39in) s.d.80
£5641	$11000	(10-Oct-90 SY.NY265/R) Oree de foret sous la neige (74x91cm-29x36in) s.i.d.1978 i.verso
£480	$941	(23-Jan-91 ZZ.B190) Neige 1970 (22x30cm-9x12in) s.d.70 W/C bodycol
£636	$1075	(16-Apr-91 PPB.P218) Paysage de neige (39x31cm-15x12in) s.d.75 W/C (F.FR 6400)
£859	$1676	(17-Oct-90 ARC.P23) Paris sous la neige (20x20cm-8x8in) s. pastel gouache chl. (F.FR 8500)
£989	$1771	(8-Apr-91 CSC.P97) Paysage (33x50cm-13x20in) s. mixed media (F.FR 10000)
£1065	$2045	(24-Feb-91 P.V56) Vue de Paris sous la neige (221x20cm-87x8in) s. gouache (F.FR 10600)
£1923	$3750	(10-Oct-90 SY.NY116/R) Sat sur Soane (33x48cm-13x19in) s.d.74 W/C ink crayon

GANTZ, Justinian (?) ?
| £1600 | $3120 | (24-Oct-90 S58/R) The interior of the fort at Madras (31x45cm-12x18in) ink W/C over traces pencil |

GANZ, Edwin (1871-?) Swiss
| £4098 | $7705 | (19-Sep-90 GK.Z834/R) Horses Spa and Coo in park of Chateau de Laeken (89x139cm-35x55in) s.d.1903 (S.FR 10000) |

GANZONI, Vitale (1915-) Italian?
| £980 | $1930 | (16-Nov-90 GK.Z5358) Bondo (50x60cm-20x24in) s.d.1954 (S.FR 2400) |

GARAT, Francis (19th C) French
| £325 | $650 | (6-Feb-91 LD.P68) Promeneurs sur les berges (23x17cm-9x7in) s. W/C (F.FR 3200) |

GARBELL, Alexandre (1903-1970) Latvian
£1233	$2393	(5-Dec-90 ZZ.F32/R) Sur la table (24x41cm-9x16in) s.d.46 (F.FR 12000)
£1314	$2563	(17-Oct-90 ARC.P82) Plage I (21x33cm-8x13in) s. (F.FR 13000)
£1325	$2583	(17-Oct-90 ARC.P83) Composition (17x26cm-7x10in) s.d.1966 paper laid down on canvas (F.FR 13100)
£2312	$4000	(7-May-91 CE.NY119/R) Vue de Londres (89x117cm-35x46in) s.d.62
£3075	$5290	(19-May-91 ZZ.F177/R) Scene de bar (72x64cm-28x25in) s. (F.FR 31000)
£3165	$5666	(14-Apr-91 GL.P212/R) Bord de mer (103x130cm-41x51in) s.d.1968 (F.FR 32000)
£3511	$6285	(14-Apr-91 GL.P213) Le port (65x100cm-26x39in) s. (F.FR 35500)
£3945	$7771	(6-Oct-90 GL.P40/R) La plage a maree basse (80x160cm-31x63in) s.d.64 (F.FR 40000)

GARBO, Raffaellino del (style) (16th C) Italian
| £15000 | $24450 | (3-Jul-91 S235/R) Virgin and Child with Saint John (114cm-45ins circular) panel |

GARBUZ, Yair (20th C) Israeli
| £838 | $1600 | (1-Jan-91 GG.TA277/R) Figures (140x120cm-55x47in) s.d.1972 s.erso mixed media board |

GARCIA DE ACILU, Manuel (19/20th C) Spanish
| £874 | $1714 | (24-Jan-91 EP.M44/R) Figura de mujer (22x15cm-9x6in) s.d.97 W/C (S.P 160000) |

GARCIA FONS, Pierre (1928-) French
| £1456 | $2693 | (10-Mar-91 LT.P134) Les Vignes au pied de la Colline (73x60cm-29x24in) s. (F.FR 14500) |

GARCIA GUTIERREZ, J (19/20th C) Spanish
| £867 | $1500 | (8-May-91 RO.BA362) La leccion de guitarra (60x69cm-24x27in) s. |

GARCIA MARTINEZ, Emilio (1875-?) Spanish
| £1035 | $1780 | (16-May-91 ANS.M124/R) Ria de Pontevedra (31x41cm-12x16in) s.d.905 (S.P 190000) |

GARCIA OCHOA, Luis (1920-) Spanish
| £1100 | $1968 | (13-Mar-91 FER.M253/R) Floresta umbrosa (65x110cm-26x43in) s.d.45 (S.P 200000) |
| £6518 | $10494 | (25-Jun-91 FER.M259/R) Figuras en un prostibulo (81x100cm-32x39in) s. (S.P 1200000) |

GARCIA Y MARCO, Francisco (19th C) Spanish
| £1030 | $2009 | (17-Oct-90 FER.M88/R) La construccion del ferrocarril (29x46cm-11x18in) s. panel (S.P 190000) |

GARCIA Y MENCIA, A (c.1853-1915) Spanish
| £1661 | $2708 | (11-Jun-91 GM.B906/R) La surprise (45x31cm-18x12in) s. wood (B.FR 100000) |

GARCIA Y MENCIA, Antonio (c.1853-1915) Spanish
£1796 $3126   (26-Mar-91 VN.R26/R) Rendezvous in the garden (44x31cm-17x12in) s. panel
                  (D.FL 6000)

GARCIA Y RAMOS, Jose (1850-1912) Spanish
£900 $1764   (14-Feb-91 CSK146/R) The Rendez-vous (28x23cm-11x9in) panel

GARCIA Y RAMOS, Juan (?) Spanish
£2446 $4696   (18-Dec-90 DUR.M13) Escena costrumbrista (67x34cm-26x13in) (S.P 450000)

GARCIA Y RODRIGUEZ, Manuel (1863-1925) Spanish
£1084 $2114   (17-Oct-90 FER.M84/R) Patio andaluz (16x25cm-6x10in) s.d.1916 panel
                  (S.P 200000)
£1518 $2960   (17-Oct-90 FER.M173/R) Feria de Sevilla (17x26cm-7x10in) init. panel
                  (S.P 280000)
£1638 $2834   (8-May-91 FER.M135/R) Con mi borriquillo (17x21cm-7x8in) s. panel
                  (S.P 300000)
£2105 $4000   (27-Feb-91 SY.NY376/R) Parque Maria Luisa (36x26cm-14x10in) s.d.1913
£2304 $4493   (17-Oct-90 FER.M172/R) Sanlucar (28x18cm-11x7in) s. panel (S.P 425000)
£5128 $10000   (24-Oct-90 CH.NY248/R) Mother and daughter sewing on patio
                  (25x32cm-10x13in) s.indis.i. panel
£10256 $20000   (23-Oct-90 SY.NY407/R) In the courtyard (29x46cm-11x18in) s.i.d.1906
                  panel
£10405 $18000   (22-May-91 SY.NY119/R) Una Plaza del Pueblo (41x58cm-16x23in) s.
£10983 $19000   (22-May-91 SY.NY118/R) El Pozo (50x70cm-20x28in) s.d.1920
£18000 $29520   (19-Jun-91 S394/R) Garden in Seville (49x71cm-19x28in) s.d.1919

GARCIA, David (1936-?) French
£510 $1000   (7-Nov-90 D.NY31) Daybreak (61x76cm-24x30in) s.

GARCIA, Domingo (1930-) Puerto Rican
£16860 $29000   (15-May-91 CH.NY197/R) Autorretrato - El Abuelo (84x65cm-33x26in) s.
                    masonite

GARCIA, J (19th C) ?
£600 $1200   (8-Feb-91 K489) Spanish palace interior scene with courtier figures
                  (25x38cm-10x15in) s.

GARCIA-SEVILLA, Ferran (1949-) Spanish
£2551 $5000   (6-Nov-90 CE.NY195/R) Untitled (161x129cm-63x51in) acrylic
£5746 $11147   (5-Dec-90 AB.S7079/R) Composition (163x130cm-64x51in) s.verso
                  (S.KR 62000)
£2173   *$3498*   *(25-Jun-91 FER.M268/R) Composicion en marron sobre fondo naranja*
                  (75x53cm-30x21in) mixed media (S.P 400000)

GARCIA-TELLA, Jose see TELLA, Jose Garcia

GARDELL-ERICSON, Anna (1853-1939) Swedish
£539   *$965*   *(9-Apr-91 GO.G208) Coastal landscape with figures on jetty, evening*
                    (17x20cm-7x8in) s. W/C (S.KR 5800)
£1193   *$2350*   *(13-Nov-90 AB.S371/R) Coastal landscape with beached punts at sunset*
                    (24x44cm-9x17in) s. W/C (S.KR 13000)
£1284   *$2530*   *(13-Nov-90 AB.S370/R) Coastal landscape cliffs and sailingboats in*
                    moonlight (26x15cm-10x6in) s. W/C (S.KR 14000)
£1325   *$2598*   *(20-Nov-90 GO.G326/R) Landscape view (21x29cm-8x11in) s.i.d.90 W/C*
                    (S.KR 14500)
£1483   *$2862*   *(12-Dec-90 BU.S21/R) Summer landscape (25x17cm-10x7in) s. W/C*
                    (S.KR 16000)
£1887   *$3264*   *(22-May-91 BA.S542/R) Picking spring flowers (24x35cm-9x14in) s.d.81 W/C*
                    (S.KR 20000)
£2202   *$4338*   *(13-Nov-90 AB.S368/R) Lake landscape with boy fishing from punt near*
                    waterlilies (48x45cm-19x18in) s. W/C (S.KR 24000)
£2416   *$4325*   *(9-Apr-91 GO.G210/R) Coastal landscape with sailingboats*
                    (29x44cm-11x17in) s. W/C (S.KR 26000)
£2477   *$4880*   *(13-Nov-90 AB.S369/R) Spring landscape with girl on wooded path*
                    (26x38cm-10x15in) s.i. W/C (S.KR 27000)
£2602   *$4658*   *(9-Apr-91 GO.G214/R) Moonlit lake landscape (66x50cm-26x20in) s. W/C htd*
                    white (S.KR 28000)
£2834   *$5554*   *(20-Nov-90 GO.G327) Coastal landscape, Fishebackskil (35x50cm-14x20in)*
                    s. W/C (S.KR 31000)
£4082   *$8000*   *(6-Nov-90 GF.L2165/R) Swedish seascape (50x85cm-20x33in) s. W/C*
                    (S.FR 10000)
£4570   *$8958*   *(20-Nov-90 GO.G325/R) Coastal landscape from Marstrand (33x50cm-13x20in)*
                    s.d.1899 W/C htd white (S.KR 50000)
£5302   *$10391* *(20-Nov-90 GO.G331/R) Landscape from Aspen lake (34x66cm-13x26in) W/C*
                    htd white (S.KR 58000)
£6033   *$11824* *(20-Nov-90 GO.G330/R) Moonlit lakelandscape with man in rowingboat*
                    (44cm-17ins circular) s. W/C htd white (S.KR 66000)

GARDELLE, Robert (1682-1766) Swiss
£2610 $5116   (21-Nov-90 SY.Z1/R) Portrait Louis Marquis (81x64cm-32x25in)
                  s.d.1729verso (S.FR 6500)

GARDEN, W F (1856-1921) British
£560   *$1092*   *(22-Oct-90 SWS208) View across meadow to village (27x38cm-11x15in) s.*
                    W/C

GARDEN, William Fraser (1856-1921) British
£750 $1223   *(4-Jul-91 PHI129) Cottages by a river (9x13cm-4x5in) init.d. '07 W/C*
£820 $1607   *(8-Nov-90 PHI129) Hemingford grey parish church with stream*
       (11x14cm-4x6in) init.d.1900 W/C
£920 $1509   *(19-Jun-91 B122/R) Ferry Boat Inn, Holywell (18x27cm-7x11in) s.d.1908*
       W/C
£1400 $2772   *(30-Jan-91 S239/R) Quiet corner (27x37cm-11x15in) s.d.1881 W/C*
£1450 $2842   *(8-Nov-90 PHI39/R) The towpath near Hemingford on the Great Ouse*
       (14x18cm-6x7in) s.d.02 W/C
£3700 $6364   *(14-May-91 SWS64/R) The mill. Church by river (35x26cm-14x10in) s.d.1903*
       W/C pair

GARDIER, Raoul du (1871-?) French
£4814 $9388   *(12-Oct-90 APT.P55/R) Baignade en mer (54x65cm-21x26in) s. (F.FR 48000)*
£610 $1000   *(19-Jun-91 B.SF1894/R) Les bords nu Nile (41x32cm-16x13in) s. W/C*

GARDINER, Frank Joseph Henry (?) British
£615 $1200   *(26-Oct-90 S.W2217/R) U.K. frigate Chesapeake (46x61cm-18x24in) s.i. W/C*

GARDINER, Stanley (1887-?) British
£1200 $2268   *(27-Sep-90 L116) The evening rise on a cornish trout stream*
       (51x61cm-20x24in) s.

GARDNER, Daniel (1750-1805) British
£1800 $3186   *(21-Mar-91 CSK218/R) A mother playing with her infant son and his*
       hobby-horse (97x89cm-38x35in)
£400 $676   *(18-Apr-91 B218/R) Portrait of Mrs Castle, mother of the Hon. Edward*
       Bouverie (49x38cm-19x15in) pastel oval
£750 $1478   *(15-Nov-90 S81/R) Portrait of naval officer (26x21cm-10x8in) pastel*
£2800 $5012   *(11-Apr-91 S25/R) Portrait of Mrs Marton of Lancaster (106x72cm-42x28in)*
       gouache

GARDNER, Daniel (attrib) (1750-1805) British
£1250 $2325   *(5-Sep-90 MMB58) A portrait of Mrs Heneage, seated before a landscape*
       (43x36cm-17x14in) i. labels verso pastel oval

GARDNER, Daniel (circle) (1750-1805) British
£1313 $2561   *(25-Oct-90 SY.J390/R) Col. Francis Scott as young man*
       (120x100cm-47x39in) canvas on board (SA.R 6500)

GARDNER, Elisabeth Jeanne see BOUGUEREAU, Elizabeth Gardner

GARDNER, William Biscombe (c.1847-1919) British
£650 $1060   *(14-Jun-91 C85/R) Sheep by a stile in wooded landscape (15x23cm-6x9in)*
       s.d.1868 pencil W/C htd.white

GARDON, Felix J (19/20th C) French
£1157 $1944   *(16-Jul-91 JRL.S169/R) Portrait of Hans Heysen (44x34cm-17x13in) s.*
       board (A.D 2500)

GARELLE, G (?) ?
£607 $1190   *(25-Nov-90 ZZ.F255) La place de la Madeleine (26x34cm-10x13in) s. panel*
       (F.FR 6000)

GAREMYN, Jan Anton (1712-1799) Flemish
£2600 $4368   *(26-Apr-91 NM.P57) Allegorie du gout (74x181cm-29x71in) (F.FR 26000)*
£2800 $4732   *(16-Apr-91 PH140/R) Shepherdess and dog on hillside. Shepherd seated*
       beneath tree playing pipe (56x137cm-22x54in) en grisaille three

GAREMYN, Jan Anton (circle) (1712-1799) Flemish
£2400 $4056   *(18-Apr-91 C151/R) Fishermen with their catch by a river, a bridge*
       beyond (87x64cm-34x25in)

GAREMYN, Jan Anton (style) (1712-1799) Flemish
£1200 $2400   *(7-Feb-91 C28/R) The rest on the flight into Egypt (63x55cm-25x22in)*

GAREMYN, Jan Anton and EECKE, Constantin van (18th C) Flemish
£45000 $86850   *(12-Dec-90 S99/R) Peasants feasting near castle with Dudzele, near*
       Bruges, in background (250x480cm-98x189in) s.d.1772 and 1773

GARET, Jedd (20th C) American
£765 $1500   *(6-Nov-90 CE.NY132/R) Landscape with seductive glance*
       (145x185cm-57x73in) s.i.d.1984 verso acrylic
£1020 $2000   *(6-Nov-90 CE.NY131/R) Primary decor (126x203cm-50x80in) acrylic*
£1122 $2200   *(6-Nov-90 CE.NY130/R) The flying fish and it's enemies*
       (241x175cm-95x69in) s.i.d.'83 stretcher acrylic

GARGANI, L (19th C) Italian
£3242 $6355   *(24-Nov-90 SA.A612/R) Portrait of young lady seated at table holding*
       book (78x63cm-31x25in) s.d.1844 canvas laid down (DM 9500)

GARGIULIO, Domenico (1612-1679) Italian
£17647 $30000   *(30-May-91 SY.NY46/R) Christ on Road to Calvary (124x178cm-49x70in)*
£6533 $10714   *(18-Jun-91 APT.P35/R) Feuille d'etude (14x20cm-6x8in) pen (F.FR 65000)*

GARGIULIO, Domenico (attrib) (1612-1679) Italian
£1387 $2400   (10-May-91 S.W2503/R) The death of Abel (43x56cm-17x22in) painted oval
£8500 $13855   (2-Jul-91 PH267/R) Christ on the road to Jerusalem surrounded by the
                             Multitudes (112x128cm-44x50in)

GARGIULIO, Domenico and CODAZZI, Viviano (17th C) Italian
£16080 $26372   (21-Jun-91 SY.MO121/R) Personages dans une architecture imaginaire
                             (101x128cm-40x50in) (F.FR 160000)
£20513 $40000   (11-Oct-90 SY.NY197/R) Figures among classical ruins (93x124cm-37x49in)

GARIBALDI, Joseph (1863-?) French
£830 $1627   (25-Nov-90 LC.P149/R) Promeneurs aux abords du village (46x55cm-18x22in)
                        s. (F.FR 8200)
£1067 $1740   (11-Jun-91 I.N211 b) Bord de mer (21x32cm-8x13in) s. (F.FR 10600)

GARIKOV, Ivan (1918-1982) Russian
£518 $1000   (10-Dec-90 BUR.F102 c) View of Salzburg (79x107cm-31x42in) d.1949
£622 $1200   (10-Dec-90 BUR.F102 e) Mother Russia (81x61cm-32x24in) s.d.1973
£1036 $2000   (10-Dec-90 BUR.F102 a) Peter the Great mounted on white stead
                        (221x152cm-87x60in)

GARIN, Alexei (1961-) Russian
£690 $1159   (26-Apr-91 ARC.P14) La chasse a l'ours (71x100cm-28x39in) s. (F.FR 6900)

GARINEI, Max (?) ?
£1350 $2498   (5-Mar-91 AG229/R) Serving drinks to musicians (30x25cm-12x10in) s. W/C

GARINO, Angelo (1860-?) Italian
£1076 $1850   (14-May-91 GF.L2466/R) Procession in Piemont (38x53cm-15x21in) s.
                        i.d.1892verso paper on board (S.FR 2700)
£4523 $7417   (21-Jun-91 SY.MO360/R) Vue des Alpes (60x81cm-24x32in) s. (F.FR 45000)
£10500 $20160   (30-Nov-90 C53/R) Picking flowers, Nice (65x81cm-26x32in) s.i.d.1905

GARIOT, Paul Cesare (1811-?) French
£7179 $14000   (23-Oct-90 SY.NY68/R) Pandora's box (81x56cm-32x22in) s.d.1877 panel

GARLAND, Henry (fl.1854-1900) British
£3200 $6400   (8-Feb-91 C184/R) In the Vale of Glencoe (124x99cm-49x39in) s.d.1902 I.

GARLAND, Valentine Thomas (fl.1884-1903) British
£920 $1702   (4-Mar-91 PHB44) Great Expectations (21x24cm-8x9in) s. I.verso panel
£1000 $1950   (15-Jan-91 B394/R) Guarding the catch (41x30cm-16x12in) s.
£1100 $1914   (26-Mar-91 PH129/R) A Brown family (24x16cm-9x6in) s.d.1893 I. verso
                        panel
£1450 $2828   (15-Jan-91 SWS148/R) Favourite terrier (31x23cm-12x9in) s.d.1893 panel
£1600 $2672   (5-Jun-91 S90/R) Sharing (30x41cm-12x16in) s.d.1899 panel
£2200 $4070   (4-Mar-91 PHB43/R) We are seven - Welsh Terriers (25x20cm-10x8in)
                        s.i.verso panel

GARMAN, Ed (20th C) American
£2235 $4000   (14-Mar-91 CH.NY224/R) Painting No. 283-C (61x61cm-24x24in) s.d.1942
                        num.283-C verso masonite

GARNERAY, Ambroise Louis (1783-1857) French
£13500 $22005   (3-Jul-91 DAR.P30/R) Marine - rencontre du brick (89x117cm-35x46in) s.
                        (F.FR 135000)
*£3165 $5666   (8-Apr-91 ARC.P4/R) Vue du port de Bayonne (15x23cm-6x9in) s. W/C pierre
                        noire (F.FR 32000)*

GARNERAY, Auguste (1785-1824) French
*£2500 $4100   (19-Jun-91 S117/R) Lady by balustrade. Couple by tomb of Eloise and
                        Abelard (19x16cm-7x6in) s. one d.1822 one d.1817 W/C pair*

GARNEREY, Hippolyte Jean-Baptiste (1787-1858) French
*£630 $1260   (4-Feb-91 PLF.P40/R) Porche d'une eglise gothique. Maisons anciennes
                        s.i. W/C two in same mount (F.FR 6200)*

GARNIER, Jules Arsene (1847-1889) French
£2500 $4300   (17-May-91 C20/R) Romeo and Juliet (41x27cm-16x11in) st.
£5202 $9000   (23-May-91 CH.NY26/R) Courting couple (79x47cm-31x19in) d.1880

GARNIER, Michel (studio) (18th C) French
£1200 $2316   (11-Dec-90 PH138/R) Young woman seated contemplating open bird cage
                        (16x23cm-6x9in) bears sig.L.Boilly panel

GARONET, A (19th C) ?
£6073 $11903   (20-Nov-90 APT.P277/R) Fumeur de Chibouk au balcon (81x65cm-32x26in)
                        mono. (F.FR 60000)

GAROUSTE, Gerard (1946-) French
£21106 $34613   (23-Jun-91 P.V78/R) La chute de l'ange (200x180cm-79x71in) s.
                        (F.FR 210000)
*£4500 $7965   (21-Mar-91 C244/R) Goupil Le Renard (121x143cm-48x56in) s.d.Sept 1982
                        chl.pencil three sheets of paper*

GAROW, Marcel (20th C) Belgian?
£1800 $3025 (23-Apr-91 C.A473) Le faucheur (85x70cm-33x28in) s.d.1924 (B.FR 110000)

GARRAUD, Leon (1877-1961) French
£750 $1455 (3-Dec-90 CS.L75/R) Vue de Lyon avec le pont Lafayette (22x35cm-9x14in)
   s. board (F.FR 7300)

GARRETT, Thomas Balfour (1874-1952) Australian
£1131 $1912 (16-Apr-91 J.M325) Beach scene (22x90cm-9x35in) s. board (A.D 2500)
£1158 $2282 (13-Nov-90 J.M157) Sydney Harbour (29x67cm-11x26in) s. board (A.D 3000)
£452 $765 (16-Apr-91 J.M988) Deserted (24x22cm-9x9in) s.i. monotype (A.D 1000)
£814 $1376 (16-Apr-91 J.M173) Village scene (21x31cm-8x12in) s.i. monotype
   (A.D 1800)
£869 $1711 (13-Nov-90 J.M259) Morning sunlight, Old Park (26x36cm-10x14in) s. W/C
   (A.D 2250)
£905 $1529 (16-Apr-91 J.M245 a) Landscape (27x24cm-11x9in) s. W/C (A.D 2000)
£1158 $2282 (13-Nov-90 J.M136/R) The farmhouse (25x37cm-10x15in) s. W/C (A.D 3000)
£1244 $2103 (16-Apr-91 J.M158) The Bridge (26x26cm-10x10in) s. W/C (A.D 2750)
£1285 $2467 (26-Nov-90 SY.ME27) Ballet Bay (26x29cm-10x11in) s. i.verso W/C
   (A.D 3200)
£1357 $2294 (16-Apr-91 J.M167) Village scene (27x30cm-11x12in) s. W/C (A.D 3000)
£1357 $2294 (16-Apr-91 J.M67) A quiet place (26x24cm-10x9in) s.i. (A.D 3000)
£1357 $2294 (16-Apr-91 J.M276) The town square (27x32cm-11x13in) s. W/C (A.D 3000)
£1448 $2447 (16-Apr-91 J.M205/R) Mother and child in spring light (28x29cm-11x11in)
   s. W/C (A.D 3200)
£1493 $2524 (16-Apr-91 J.M2/R) The Blue Pool (27x31cm-11x12in) s. W/C (A.D 3300)
£1584 $2676 (16-Apr-91 J.M52/R) The artist's studio (32x27cm-13x11in) s. W/C
   (A.D 3500)
£1584 $2676 (16-Apr-91 J.M200) Returning home (27x38cm-11x15in) s. W/C (A.D 3500)
£1584 $2676 (16-Apr-91 J.M283/R) Figures in a bush clearing (25x33cm-10x13in) s. W/C
   (A.D 3500)
£1778 $3342 (17-Sep-90 SY.ME154) The open gate (25x31cm-10x12in). W/C (A.D 4000)
£1810 $3059 (16-Apr-91 J.M217) Asquith (23x37cm-9x15in) s.i. W/C (A.D 4000)
£1810 $3059 (16-Apr-91 J.M294/R) Village high road (26x26cm-10x10in) s.i. monotype
   (A.D 4000)

GARRI, Giorgio (circle) (?-1731) Italian
£12353 $21000 (31-May-91 CH.NY48/R) Putti playing with goat in park. Bacchanti by urn
   in landscape (118x64cm-46x25in) d.1731 pair

GARRIDO, Eduardo Leon (1856-1949) Spanish
£2530 $4250 (17-Jul-91 SY.NY380/R) Young woman before a mirror (40x22cm-16x9in) s.
   panel
£2600 $5096 (22-Nov-90 CSK260/R) Young woman dressing in front of mirror
   (33x24cm-13x9in) s. board
£2742 $4607 (23-Apr-91 DUR.M5/R) Coqueteria (38x30cm-15x12in) panel (S.P 500000)
£5498 $9841 (13-Mar-91 FER.M168/R) Modelo descansando en el estudio
   (26x34cm-10x13in) s. panel (S.P 1000000)
£8659 $15500 (10-Apr-91 HF.NY51/R) Lady in pink (81x64cm-32x25in) s. panel
£13295 $23000 (22-May-91 SY.NY80/R) Moment of reflection (55x38cm-22x15in) s.
£15607 $27000 (22-May-91 SY.NY286/R) La femme a la mandoline (61x50cm-24x20in) s.
   panel
£18000 $34560 (28-Nov-90 S144/R) Lady with basket of flowers (114x83cm-45x33in) s.
£1486 $2898 (23-Oct-90 DUR.M45) Pasos de baile (33x40cm-13x16in) W/C (S.P 275000)

GARRONE, Romolo (1891-?) Italian
£2273 $4455 (22-Nov-90 SY.MI65/R) Paesaggio montano (70x92cm-28x36in) s.d.1924
   (I.L 5000000)

GARSIDE, Oswald (1879-1942) British
£350 $620 (21-Mar-91 CSK103) Dutch fisherfolk on the coast (20x53cm-8x21in) s.
   pencil W/C
£950 $1786 (19-Sep-90 PHC79) Cart on woodland track (43x74cm-17x29in) s. W/C

GARSIDE, Thomas H (1906-1980) Canadian
£510 $862 (17-Apr-91 EA.M507) Late afternoon (11x15cm-4x6in) s. (C.D 1000)
£529 $1031 (24-Oct-90 EA.M588/R) Head Mountain (20x28cm-8x11in) s. (C.D 1200)
£611 $1198 (5-Nov-90 FB.M45) Eastern townshiplands (36x46cm-14x18in) s. board
   (C.D 1400)
£655 $1284 (5-Nov-90 FB.M249) March - Baie St.Paul (41x51cm-16x20in) s. (C.D 1500)
£807 $1558 (12-Dec-90 EA.M686 a) Winter landscape (41x51cm-16x20in) s. aluminium
   (C.D 1800)
£873 $1712 (5-Nov-90 FB.M167) Ferry crossing from Levis, Quebec, in winter
   (48x64cm-19x25in) s. pastel (C.D 2000)

GARSTIN, Alethea (1894-1978) British
£980 $1921 (8-Nov-90 DLY163/R) Mount Errigal, Co. Donegal (23x30cm-9x12in) s.
   i.verso board
£2500 $4100 (20-Jun-91 DLY311/R) Guiness's boat, Dublin (23x33cm-9x13in) s. panel

GARSTIN, Norman (1855-1926) British
£6200 $11594 (29-Aug-90 HUN2) Tangier Street scenes (23x13cm-9x5in) board pair
£1200 $2376 (30-Jan-91 S276/R) School hours, Petit Andely (17x12cm-7x5in) s. i.verso
   W/C

GARTMEIER, Hans (1910-) Swiss

£640	$1082	(1-May-91 GD.B321/R) Female nude reclining (33x53cm-13x21in) s. board (S.FR 1600)
£1116	$2175	(24-Oct-90 GD.B388/R) Lake landscape with female nude (33x57cm-13x22in) panel (S.FR 2800)
£1200	$2028	(1-May-91 GD.B323/R) Harvest scene with horse-drawn hay cart and peasant (30x21cm-12x8in) s. i.verso board (S.FR 3000)
£1600	$2704	(1-May-91 GD.B324/R) Portrait of bearded peasant (15x11cm-6x4in) s. board (S.FR 4000)
£1315	*$2564*	*(24-Oct-90 GD.B389/R) Interned cavalry soldiers (44x33cm-17x13in) s.d.1940 i.verso W/C over pencil (S.FR 3300)*

GARTNER DE LA PENA, Jose (1866-1918) Spanish

£6534	$10651	(11-Jun-91 ANS.M75/R) Marina, St.Helier, Jersey (94x174cm-37x69in) s. (S.P 1200000)

GARTNER, Fritz (1882-?) German

£2284	$4500	(7-Oct-90 DU.E161/R) Deutschland Erwache, Hitler Kundgebung (84x69cm-33x27in) s.d.1933 panel
£2411	$4750	(7-Oct-90 DU.E159/R) Hitler receiving the Oath of Office from Hindenberg (99x140cm-39x55in) s.d.1933 panel

GARTNER, J (?) German

£1300	$2561	(4-Oct-90 CSK52) An Alpine river in spate (99x71cm-39x28in) s.

GARVEY, Edmund (attrib) (?-1813) British

£1300	$2561	(31-Oct-90 S354/R) Coastal landscape with cattle and sheep and view of Lundy Island (61x91cm-24x36in)

GARZI, Luigi (1638-1721) Italian

£774	*$1300*	*(17-Jul-91 SY.NY15/R) Glorification of St. Francis (25x16cm-10x6in) blk.red chk.*

GASCAR, Henri (1635-1701) French

£4615	$9000	(10-Oct-90 CH.NY156/R) Portraits of lady seated at table. Gentleman, possibly James II asDuke of York standing (63x50cm-25x20in) pair
£11000	$18150	(10-Jul-91 S13) Portrait of Louise de Kerouaille, Duchess of Portsmouth seated (104x80cm-41x31in)
£11765	$20000	(30-May-91 SY.NY13/R) Portrait of lady (114x90cm-45x35in) s.

GASCAR, Henri (attrib) (1635-1701) French

£3525	$5745	(14-Jun-91 AGS.P42/R) Portrait d'un enfant de France portant une corbeille de fruits (72x59cm-28x23in) oval (F.FR 35000)

GASCAR, Henri (style) (1635-1701) French

£950	$1549	(4-Jul-91 CSK252/R) Portrait of sportsman, standing, holding musket in landscape (29x23cm-11x9in) panel
£2800	$5600	(7-Feb-91 C49/R) Portrait of a lady, said to be the Duchess of Burgundy a palace beyond (122x88cm-48x35in)

GASCOYNE, George (1862-1953) British

£640	$1229	(19-Feb-91 SWS48) In the shade (26x44cm-10x17in) init.d.95

GASIOROWSKI, Gerard (1930-) French

£5000	$8150	(3-Jul-91 CSC.P169/R) Exercise libre (36x158cm-14x62in) d.1980 acrylic (F.FR 50000)

GASPAR, Marta (20th C) ?

£2530	$4960	(25-Nov-90 ZZ.F34/R) Le jardin d'Eden (138x210cm-54x83in) s.d.1908 (F.FR 25000)

GASPARD, Leon (1882-1964) French

£2604	$5000	(17-Dec-90 SY.NY153/R) Russian village and church (15x33cm-6x13in) s. canvas on board
£2604	$5000	(17-Dec-90 SY.NY152/R) Barges and tugboat on Divina (23x28cm-9x11in) s. panel
£3352	$6000	(12-Apr-91 SY.NY46/R) Early winter sketch (27x22cm-11x9in) s.d.1911 canvasboard
£26455	$50000	(26-Sep-90 SY.NY76/R) In the wilderness of Siberia (86x76cm-34x30in) s.d.1926 i.verso board
£1148	*$2250*	*(7-Nov-90 B.SF3785/R) At Pueblo (14x21cm-6x8in) s. W/C*

GASQUY, Marius (?) ?

£822	*$1595*	*(7-Dec-90 CH.MO110) Le vaisseau Lyralm, commande par le Capitaine Bertrandon fils en 1838 (42x62cm-17x24in) s.i.d.1838 lead pencil pen wash W/C (F.FR 8000)*

GASSER, Henry (1909-1981) American

£531	$950	(14-Apr-91 JRB.C196/R) Cityscape (5x91cm-2x36in) s. masonite
£1395	$2400	(15-May-91 SY.NY184/R) Outskirts (51x71cm-20x28in) s.
£1734	$3000	(21-May-91 CE.NY608/R) Yellow diner (39x30cm-15x12in) s. oil on chl paper on board
£1744	$3000	(15-May-91 SY.NY190/R) Return to Thames (76x91cm-30x36in) s.
£479	*$900*	*(22-Sep-90 WOL.C400) Archway flower woman, Paris (36x20cm-14x8in) s. W/C*
£479	*$900*	*(22-Sep-90 WOL.C346) Art gallery, Paris (36x20cm-14x8in) s. W/C*
£479	*$900*	*(22-Sep-90 WOL.C419) Spanish market (25x33cm-10x13in) s. W/C*

GASSER, Henry (1909-1981) American-cont.
£559	$1050	(22-Sep-90 WOL.C399) Corner market, Paris (38x28cm-15x11in) s. W/C
£694	$1200	(21-May-91 CE.NY620/R) Industrial winter (56x66cm-22x26in) s. W/C paperboard
£698	$1200	(15-May-91 SY.NY185/R) Backyard tracks (28x36cm-11x14in) s. s.i.verso W/C board
£885	$1700	(17-Dec-90 SY.NY224/R) Drying wash (38x56cm-15x22in) s. W/C indian ink
£925	$1600	(21-May-91 CE.NY666/R) Pennsylvania country (66x99cm-26x39in) s. W/C board
£925	$1600	(21-May-91 CE.NY621/R) Hanging laundry out to dry (50x62cm-20x24in) s. W/C paper on board
£988	$1700	(15-May-91 SY.NY155/R) Gloucester harbour in winter (49x62cm-19x24in) s.gouache W/C board
£990	$1900	(17-Dec-90 SY.NY223/R) Collection (18x25cm-7x10in) s. gouache
£1198	$2300	(17-Dec-90 SY.NY220/R) Industrial vista (51x69cm-20x27in) s. W/C paper on board
£1302	$2500	(17-Dec-90 SY.NY225/R) We got pile of salvation tonight (20x25cm-8x10in) s. gouache board
£2734	$5250	(17-Dec-90 SY.NY226/R) Lord loves dancing man (20x25cm-8x10in) s. gouache

GASTINEAU, Henry (attrib) (1791-1876) British
| £340 | $629 | (6-Mar-91 SC4208) St Asaph (23x30cm-9x12in) W/C pencil |

GAT, Eliahu (1919-1987) Israeli
£838	$1600	(1-Jan-91 GG.TA279/R) Safed (49x60cm-19x24in) s.
£1047	$2000	(1-Jan-91 GG.TA278/R) Landscape (80x100cm-31x39in) s.c.1978
£1047	$2000	(2-Jan-91 GG.TA535/R) Boats (70x100cm-28x39in) s.c.1981
£1350	$2200	(12-Jun-91 GG.TA261/R) Landscape (49x69cm-19x27in) s.

GATCH, Lee (1902-1968) American
| £698 | $1200 | (15-May-91 SY.NY277/R) Untitled composition (76x61cm-30x24in) s.d.60 mixed media collage board |

GATIER, Pierre (1878-1944) French
| £815 | $1605 | (29-Oct-90 LC.P91/R) Rochers a Maree Basse - Les Sables d'Olonne (54x65cm-21x26in) s. (F.FR 8000) |

GATTA, Saverio della (?-1829) Italian
£1200	$2280	(12-Sep-90 CSK162/R) La tarantella (18x25cm-7x10in) s.d.1818 pencil W/C
£2800	$4592	(19-Jun-91 S338/R) Racing mules in Naples (15x22cm-6x9in) s.d.1814 W/C
£3000	$4920	(19-Jun-91 S337/R) Neapolitan fair (15x22cm-6x9in) s.d.1814 W/C
£3000	$4920	(19-Jun-91 S335/R) Divertimenti Napoletani (15x22cm-6x9in) s. W/C
£3200	$5248	(19-Jun-91 S336/R) Pifferari E Suonatori d'Arpa a Napoli (15x23cm-6x9in) s.d.1814 W/C
£8000	$13040	(1-Jul-91 S101/R) View of Bay of Naples seen from Certosa di San Martino (36x59cm-14x23in) s.d.1787 bears i.verso gouache
£17675	$29871	(16-Apr-91 CH.R15/R) Vedute de venditori. Festicciola in barca. Teatrino dei burattini.Bancarella sul lungomare (19x25cm-7x10in) s.d.1919 W/C set of 6 (I.L 39000000)

GATTA, Saverio della (attrib) (?-1829) Italian
| £3600 | $6444 | (13-Mar-91 B38) Banca di acquajuolo in Napoli i. pencil W/C four others |

GATTI, Annibale (1828-1909) Italian
| £1500 | $2880 | (29-Nov-90 B137/R) Galileo receiving John Milton (99x85cm-39x33in) s. |

GATTI, Bernardino (1495-1575) Italian
| £9121 | $15232 | (4-Jun-91 CH.R380/R) Sacra Famiglia (64x49cm-25x19in) (I.L 20000000) |

GATTI, Ceasare (19th C) Italian
| £1071 | $2057 | (27-Nov-90 W.T1105) View from the mountain, Capo Museno. View of Island of Toscano (57x96cm-22x38in) pair after Salvatore Rosa (C.D 2400) |

GAUDENZI, Pietro (1880-1955) Italian
| £1387 | $2692 | (4-Dec-90 F.R104/R) Caraffa di fiori su un tavolo (73x60cm-29x24in) s. (I.L 3000000) |

GAUDIER-BRZESKA, Henri (1891-1915) French
£380	$745	(25-Jan-91 C84/R) Head of man (22x11cm-9x4in) pencil
£500	$980	(25-Jan-91 C86/R) Bust of woman (26x20cm-10x8in) brush wash crayon
£680	$1278	(18-Sep-90 PH184/R) Man on bicycle (25x37cm-10x15in) pen wash
£750	$1470	(25-Jan-91 C83/R) Two nude female torsos (30x24cm-12x9in) pen ink wash crayon
£800	$1392	(27-Mar-91 S72/R) Two nude studies chk two
£1200	$2328	(6-Dec-90 CSK12) Goose (38x25cm-15x10in) chl
£1300	$2171	(6-Jun-91 C72/R) Seated female nude with knee raised (25x35cm-10x14in) s.i.d.12 purple ink
£1300	$2548	(7-Nov-90 S52/R) Standing male nude (38x23cm-15x9in) chk
£1400	$2646	(27-Sep-90 CG7/R) Portrait of man, 1914 (33x23cm-13x9in) chl
£1800	$3132	(27-Mar-91 S80/R) Woman walking. Head in profile. Three people talking. The windmill one s.d.11 chk wash pen ink set of four
£1864	$3114	(6-Jun-91 HN.H343/R) Two standing figures (27x17cm-11x7in) chl. (DM 5500)
£2000	$3880	(6-Dec-90 CSK11/R) Duck (38x25cm-15x10in) chl
£2400	$4704	(7-Nov-90 S43/R) The swan I (31x47cm-12x19in) mono. chk

GAUDIER-BRZESKA, Henri (1891-1915) French-cont.
£4200 $7770   (7-Mar-91 C35/R) *Pastiche of Michaelangelo's Night and Day*
                               (70x54cm-28x21in) s.d.13 pen ink
£6200 $12152   (7-Nov-90 S45/R) *Nude study (51x38cm-20x15in) chk*
£8500 $16660   (7-Nov-90 S50/R) *Mother and child (30x23cm-12x9in) pencil*
£11500 $22540   (7-Nov-90 S42/R) *Composition with three figures (47x31cm-19x12in) chk*
£14000 $27440   (7-Nov-90 S35/R) *Still life with teapot (38x56cm-15x22in) pastel*

GAUERMANN, Carl (1804-1829) Austrian
£3104 $5215   (25-Apr-91 D.V155/R) *Eingang zur Saurusselbrucke in Nasswald*
                               (17x23cm-7x9in) s. i.verso W/C (A.S 65000)

GAUERMANN, Friedrich (1807-1862) Austrian
£632 $1200   (12-Sep-90 D.NY30/R) *Gleaner (30x25cm-12x10in) board*
£2048 $3870   (25-Sep-90 FN.S2175/R) *View of country estate in hilly park landscape*
                               (19x33cm-7x13in) s. i.verso (DM 6000)
£2797 $5427   (7-Dec-90 GB.B5819/R) *Study of plants by stream (16x21cm-6x8in) i.verso*
                               (DM 8000)
£856 $1396   (12-Jun-91 SY.MU3/R) *Cattle watering (21x28cm-8x11in) pencil ink wash*
                               (DM 2500)
£1051 $1765   (25-Apr-91 D.V119/R) *Landscape with cattle (5x10cm-2x4in) pencil chk*
                               (A.S 22000)
£1815 $3049   (25-Apr-91 D.V67/R) *View of Alpine village (15x18cm-6x7in) i.d.1832 pen*
                               indian ink wash (A.S 38000)

GAUERMANN, Friedrich (after) (1807-1862) Austrian
£1365 $2567   (21-Sep-90 N.M3182/R) *Forge in the Ramsau (76x101cm-30x40in) i.d.*
                               (DM 4000)

GAUERMANN, Friedrich (circle) (19th C) Austrian
£2500 $4900   (22-Nov-90 CSK165/R) *Travellers at blacksmith's in mountainous landscape*
                               (76x101cm-30x40in)

GAUERMANN, Jakob (1773-1843) German
£716 $1203   (25-Apr-91 D.V83/R) *Hunter caught in fox trap (23x18cm-9x7in) c.1835*
                               pencil pen (A.S 15000)

GAUERMANN, Jakob (attrib) (1773-1843) German
£2857 $5600   (6-Nov-90 GF.L2355/R) *Retour pendant l'orage (28x33cm-11x13in) copper*
                               (S.FR 7000)

GAUGENGIGL, Ignaz Marcel (1855-1932) German
£636 $1100   (21-May-91 CE.NY376/R) *Directions (18x24cm-7x9in) s.d.1876 panel*
£8402 $14200   (20-Apr-91 WOL.C137/R) *Duet (33x25cm-13x10in) s. panel*

GAUGUIN, Paul (1848-1903) French
£90000 $175500   (17-Oct-90 S19/R) *Aux abords de la ferme (35x27cm-14x11in) s.d.74*
£97336 $190779   (7-Nov-90 APT.P519/R) *Le verger ou le mer mitoyen (31x47cm-12x19in)*
                               s.d.1881 (F.FR 950000)
£166163 $270846   (15-Jun-91 FB.P33/R) *L'abreuvoir (46x55cm-18x22in) s.d.85 (F.FR 1650000)*
£184971 $320000   (8-May-91 CH.NY2/R) *Le verger (30x47cm-12x19in) s.d.1881*
£279188 $550000   (14-Nov-90 CH.NY6/R) *Paysage d'hiver a Copenhague (46x32cm-18x13in)*
                               s.d.85
£4569 $9000   (15-Nov-90 D.NY28/R) *Woman sewing (26x20cm-10x8in) num.14 black chk*
£12183 $24000   (15-Nov-90 CH.NY104/R) *Fils de l'artiste couche (20x27cm-8x11in) chl*
                               double-sided
£14000 $24780   (19-Mar-91 C13/R) *Portrait d'Emil Gauguin age de cinq mois (5x4cm-2x2in)*
                               s.i. W/C paper on card

GAUGUIN, Pola (1883-1961) Danish
£534 $1031   (12-Dec-90 BU.O19/R) *Southern landscape (22x33cm-9x13in) s.d.26*
                               (N.KR 6000)
£1469 $2836   (10-Dec-90 B.O34/R) *Wooded landscape (79x65cm-31x26in) s. (N.KR 16500)*
£2048 $3953   (10-Dec-90 B.O35/R) *Paris and Athena, Hera and Afrodite*
                               (38x48cm-15x19in) s.d.30 (N.KR 23000)
£2170 $4232   (11-Oct-90 BU.O45/R) *Nude woman in landscape (103x84cm-41x33in) s.*
                               (N.KR 25000)
£2671 $5156   (12-Dec-90 BU.O18/R) *Summer landscape (77x73cm-30x29in) s.indist.d.13*
                               (N.KR 30000)
£3385 $6602   (11-Oct-90 BU.O44/R) *House in wood (63x55cm-25x22in) s.d.13 i.verso*
                               (N.KR 39000)

GAUL, Gilbert (1855-1919) American
£583 $950   (5-Jul-91 S.W2668/R) *Picnic at the pond (13x20cm-5x8in) s. board*
£1162 $2300   (1-Feb-91 S.W2577/R) *Chimney smoke (30x41cm-12x16in) s. board*
£1658 $3250   (15-Feb-91 DM.D2075/R) *Winter in Hackensack (46x61cm-18x24in) s. board*
£2471 $4250   (15-May-91 SY.NY67/R) *Fetching water (46x36cm-18x14in) s.d.1885*

GAUL, Winfred (1928-) German
£1570 $3077   (20-Nov-90 L.K240/R) *Composition no.8-75 (80x80cm-31x31in) s.i.d.1974*
                               thinned oil tempera (DM 4600)
£2740 $4466   (14-Jun-91 L.K886/R) *Composition (50x65cm-20x26in) s. paper (DM 8000)*
£616 $1005   (14-Jun-91 L.K891/R) *Is this you, male nude seated seen from behind*
                               (19x14cm-7x6in) s.i.d.1953 pencil (DM 1800)
£1301 $2121   (14-Jun-91 L.K890/R) *Composition (50x65cm-20x26in) s. col.oil chk board*
                               (DM 3800)

GAUL, Winfred (1928-) German-cont.
£2740 $4466   (14-Jun-91 L.K887) Composition (50x65cm-20x26in) s.d.61 s.d.verso oil
                  chk (DM 8000)

GAULD, David (1865-1936) British
£1500 $2880   (26-Nov-90 SWS169/R) In the shade (71x92cm-28x36in) s.
£1800 $3600   (5-Feb-91 S208/R) Calves (56x76cm-22x30in) s.
£2000 $3740   (28-Aug-90 S944/R) Ayrshire calves (41x61cm-16x24in) s.
£2600 $5096   (22-Nov-90 CG574/R) Two Ayrshire calves (41x51cm-16x20in) s.
£2600 $5044   (6-Dec-90 CG37/R) Farmhouse reflections (61x76cm-24x30in) s.
£2600 $5096   (22-Nov-90 CG576/R) Ayrshire calves in barn (51x76cm-20x30in) s.
£3000 $4830   (27-Jun-91 CG96/R) Three Ayrshire calves in a barn (51x76cm-20x30in) s.
£3200 $6208   (6-Dec-90 CG79/R) Ayrshire calves in barn (61x76cm-24x30in) s.

GAULLI, Giovanni Battista (1639-1709) Italian
£3200 $5216   (3-Jul-91 S198/R) Portrait of cardinal (39x32cm-15x13in)
£5000 $8150   (1-Jul-91 S8/R) Seated figures of Prudence and Fortitude (17x15cm-7x6in)
                  pen wash over black chk
£7895 $15000   (8-Jan-91 SY.NY47/R) Study of a naked slave, seated with his hands
                  behind his back (28x37cm-11x15in) bears sig. red chk.htd.white
£15000 $24450   (2-Jul-91 C58/R) Putto crowning Justice with Peace and Law, Truth below
                  (26x23cm-10x9in) chk pen ink wash htd.white oval
£15000 $24450   (2-Jul-91 C59/R) Scene of martyrdom with saint seated on pyre and
                  decapitations of monks (26x34cm-10x13in) chk pen ink wash htd.white
£100000 $163000 (2-Jul-91 C57/R) The Sacrifice of Isaac (32x23cm-13x9in) i. chk pen ink
                  wash htd.white

GAULLI, Giovanni Battista (attrib) (1639-1709) Italian
£400 $676   (16-Apr-91 C166/R) A Putto holding a cross (28x20cm-11x8in) i. red
                  chk.htd.white

GAULLI, Giovanni Battista (circle) (1639-1709) Italian
£2200 $4334   (30-Oct-90 PH99/R) Portrait of cardinal (73x60cm-29x24in)

GAULLI, Giovanni Battista (style) (1639-1709) Italian
£1600 $3072   (29-Nov-90 CSK19/R) Adam and Eve expelled from Paradise
                  (165x128cm-65x50in)

GAULT, Jean Jacques de (c.1738-1812) ?
£1000 $1920   (18-Dec-90 C56/R) The Triumph of Bacchus (7x?cm-3x?in) min.s.carved gilt
                  wood frame rec.

GAUPMANN, Rudolf (1815-1877) Austrian
£987 $1945   (14-Nov-90 RAS.K206) Madonna and Child (47x38cm-19x15in) s.d.1854 oval
                  (D.KR 11000)
£430 $722   (25-Apr-91 D.V149/R) Portrait of young man with blonde hair
                  (23x18cm-9x7in) d.1836 W/C (A.S 9000)
£573 $963   (25-Apr-91 D.V147/R) Artist seated before easel (39x32cm-15x13in)
                  s.d.1843 W/C (A.S 12000)

GAURY, Maurice (1924-) French?
£820 $1607   (11-Nov-90 ZZ.F259/R) Depart de la regate (74x60cm-29x24in)
                  (F.FR 8000)

GAUSSEN, Adolphe-Louis (1871-?) French
£996 $1723   (24-May-91 FB.P147 b) Tempete d'equinoxe, Provence (50x65cm-20x26in) s.
                  (F.FR 10000)
£1205 $1940   (28-Jun-91 ZZ.F143) Les calanques (49x63cm-19x25in) s. (F.FR 12000)
£1575 $3150   (6-Feb-91 FB.P129/R) Port de la joliette, Marseille (50x65cm-20x26in) s.
                  (F.FR 15500)

GAUSSON, Leo (1860-1944) French
£653 $1207   (6-Mar-91 D.P36/R) Au bord du chemin (50x61cm-20x24in) studio st.
                  stretcher (F.FR 6500)
£1008 $1966   (27-Oct-90 LT.P46/R) Bord de mer (28x38cm-11x15in) s.d.1883 (F.FR 10000)

GAUTHERIN, Jacques (1929-) French
£1159 $2261   (28-Oct-90 M.V52) Saint Tropez, le port (48x36cm-19x14in) s. d.57 verso
                  (F.FR 11500)
£2016 $3931   (28-Oct-90 M.V53/R) Vue sur le golfe de Saint Tropez (73x60cm-29x24in)
                  s. (F.FR 20000)
£2345 $4502   (2-Dec-90 M.V102/R) Le sentier surplombant la mer (60x73cm-24x29in)
                  s.d.53 verso (F.FR 23000)

GAUTHIER, Joachim (1897-) Canadian
£556 $956   (14-May-91 JOY.T123) Black spruce and red maples (40x50cm-16x20in) s.
                  board (C.D 1100)
£676 $1101   (10-Jun-91 W.T1044 b) Old barns at Conway March, Haliburton
                  (29x37cm-11x15in) s. i. verso board (C.D 1250)

GAUTHIER, Oscar (1921-) French
£3262 $6296   (16-Dec-90 GL.P188) Composition (116x89cm-46x35in) s. (F.FR 32000)
£3500 $6825   (18-Oct-90 C318/R) Untitled (73x92cm-29x36in) s.d.53
£4028 $6566   (16-Jun-91 LT.P66/R) Hiver (65x54cm-26x21in) s.d.52 (F.FR 40000)
£5912 $11411   (12-Dec-90 APT.P100/R) Composition (115x89cm-45x35in) s.d.58
                  (F.FR 58000)

GAUTHIER, Oscar (1921-) French-cont.

| £610 | $1220 | (10-Feb-91 CC.P27) Composition (32x50cm-13x20in) s. gouache craft paper (F.FR 6000) |
| £906 | $1477 | (16-Jun-91 LT.P41/R) Composition (32x49cm-13x19in) s. gouache wax paper laid down on panel (F.FR 9000) |

GAUTIER (attrib) (?) ?

| £1143 | $2251 | (13-Nov-90 CH.G212) Portrait of young lady wearing white dress and mob-cap (5x?cm-2x?in) min. enamel paste-set silver frame oval (S.FR 2800) |

GAUTIER D'AGOTY, Jacques Fabien (1710-1781) French

| £10920 | $19000 | (27-Mar-91 B.SF4058/R) Portrait du dauphin dressed in satin and hat with ostrich plumes (132x98cm-52x39in) s.indis.d.17.. |

GAUTIER D'AGOTY, Pierre Edouard (1775-1871) French

£3800	$7486	(30-Oct-90 PH49/R) Portrait of small girl in white dress (37x28cm-15x11in) i.d.1802stretcher
£2000	$3540	(20-Mar-91 C66) Portrait of Master Morton with his sister Cora (10x?cm-4x?in) min.s.d.1810 i.verso wood frame rec.
£7000	$12390	(20-Mar-91 C65/R) Portraits of Mrs.Mary Morton and her children, and of John Archer Morton min.one s.i.d.1810 rec. one oval

GAUVREAU, Pierre (1922-) Canadian

| £4167 | $8208 | (30-Oct-90 SY.T72/R) Un jardin et son anglais (91x76cm-36x30in) s.d.77 i.d.verso acrylic (C.D 9500) |

GAUVRIT, Jean Jacques (20th C) French?

| £871 | $1707 | (11-Nov-90 ZZ.F132/R) Barque sur l'etang au lever du jour (60x73cm-24x29in) s. (F.FR 8500) |
| £976 | $1894 | (8-Dec-90 LT.P137) Maintee sur le lac (73x92cm-29x36in) s. (F.FR 9500) |

GAVAGNIN, Natale (1851-?) Italian

| £716 | $1396 | (11-Oct-90 D.V159/R) Tranquil Venice canal scene (34x16cm-13x6in) s. W/C (A.S 15000) |

GAVANCETZI, V (?) Italian

| £1586 | $2759 | (25-Mar-91 SY.F679) Odalisca (200x109cm-79x43in) s.d.98 (I.L 3500000) |

GAVARDIE, Jean de (1909-1961) French

| £911 | $1785 | (25-Nov-90 ZZ.F69/R) Nature morte a la viole (17x25cm-7x10in) s. gouache (F.FR 9000) |

GAVARNI, Paul (1804-1866) French

£493	$957	(8-Dec-90 SY.MO412/R) Le Turc (20x14cm-8x6in) pen htd white (F.FR 4800)
£552	$889	(28-Jun-91 ARC.P7) Deux enfants (16x12cm-6x5in) W/C (F.FR 5500)
£565	$1097	(8-Dec-90 SY.MO430/R) Le dejeuner sur l'herbe (12x20cm-5x8in) s. W/C (F.FR 5500)
£633	$1134	(12-Apr-91 AW.H607/R) Mercredi des Cendres (22x32cm-9x13in) s.i. W/C bodycol over pencil (DM 1900)
£1474	$2800	(9-Jan-91 CH.NY61/R) The gardener (28x21cm-11x8in) i. ink W/C gouache pencil
£1529	$2951	(12-Dec-90 ARC.P35/R) Les deux jeunes filles (17x14cm-7x6in) s.d.1834 blk.crayon W/C (F.FR 15000)
£1689	$2872	(28-May-91 KF.M162) Pensive young man standing in landscape (26x21cm-10x8in) s.i. pen W/C htd.white (DM 5000)
£1835	$3541	(12-Dec-90 ARC.P36/R) Le pierrot gentilhomme (29x21cm-11x8in) s. pen wash htd.white (F.FR 18000)
£2000	$3800	(9-Jan-91 CH.NY62/R) Partis en Guerre Tour tuer les ennemis (33x21cm-13x8in) s.i. gouache ink
£2105	$4000	(9-Jan-91 CH.NY63/R) Revint de guerre apres sept ans et d'mi (33x46cm-13x18in) s.i. gouache ink
£10703	$20657	(12-Dec-90 ARC.P37/R) Autoportrait (16x11cm-6x4in) d.1835 blk.crayon wash (F.FR 105000)

GAVASSETTI, Camillo (?-1628) Italian

| £916 | $1759 | (29-Nov-90 F.M43) Allegoria della geometria (56x47cm-22x19in) (I.L 2000000) |

GAVIN, Malcolm (1894-?) British

| £1885 | $3148 | (4-Jun-91 FB.M79/R) Young ladies arranging daffodils (77x63cm-30x25in) s. (C.D 3600) |

GAVIN, Robert (1827-1883) British

| £720 | $1440 | (8-Feb-91 T60/R) Temptation (46x38cm-18x15in) s.i. board |
| £4500 | $8415 | (28-Aug-90 S868/R) The pet lamb (69x46cm-27x18in) s. |

GAWELL, Oskar (1888-1955) Austrian

| £341 | $668 | (24-Jan-91 D.V192) Encounter (34x24cm-13x9in) mono.i. mixed media (A.S 7000) |

GAWTHORN, Henry George (1879-1941) British

| £605 | $1179 | (15-Oct-90 SY.J17) Portrait of a gentleman (51x45cm-20x18in) s. pastel (SA.R 3000) |

GAY, August (1890-1949) American
£4592	$9000	(13-Feb-91 B.SF2051/R) Street scene (30x35cm-12x14in) s. board
£6667	$13000	(10-Oct-90 B.SF487/R) Houses in shade (37x49cm-15x19in) s. board
£7692	$15000	(10-Oct-90 B.SF489/R) Carmel Valley (29x38cm-11x15in) s. board

GAY, Edward (1837-1928) American
£958	$1600	(26-Jul-91 E.EDM136 g) Landscape with skiffs, fisherman and house (64x91cm-25x36in) s.
£1272	$2200	(21-May-91 CE.NY453/R) Twilight on East Chester Creek (20x33cm-8x13in) s. panel
£1563	$3000	(17-Dec-90 SY.NY37/R) Crossing river by raft (51x91cm-20x36in) s.indist.d.
£1739	$2800	(26-Jun-91 D.NY44) Gypsies camping along riverbank (51x91cm-20x36in) s.d.75
£2411	$4750	(18-Nov-90 JRB.C40/R) Sunset river landscape (46x91cm-18x36in) s.d.1875

GAY, George Howell (1858-1931) American
£585	$1100	(22-Sep-90 WOL.C137/R) Coastline (56x91cm-22x36in) s.d.83
£606	$1000	(13-Jul-91 YFA.M72/R) Seascape (46x76cm-18x30in) s.
£407	*$700*	*(18-May-91 W.W113/R) Spring Brook (23x48cm-9x19in) s. W/C*

GAY, Nicolai Nikolajewitsch (attrib) (1831-1894) Russian
£1054	$1698	(28-Jun-91 BM.B673/R) Portrait of bearded gentleman in profile, possibly Moses (16x14cm-6x6in) i.verso canvas on board (DM 3100)

GAY, Walter (1856-1937) American
£1472	$2900	(18-Nov-90 JRB.C53/R) Interior (61x46cm-24x18in)
£2191	$4250	(5-Dec-90 D.NY119/R) Interior view with fireplace (53x46cm-21x18in) s. board
£2775	$4800	(21-May-91 CE.NY576/R) Yellow curtains, Chateau du Breau (56x46cm-22x18in) s.
£8671	$15000	(22-May-91 CH.NY125/R) Frame maker (39x28cm-15x11in) s.i. panel

GAY, Winkworth Allen (1821-1910) American?
£2515	$4250	(1-May-91 B.SF5056/R) Salt marsh (35x61cm-14x24in) s.d.1862
£3179	$5500	(21-May-91 CE.NY618/R) View of Tokyo with Mount Fujiyama in distance (74x60cm-29x24in) s.d.1884

GAYAT, Sandra (20th C) Belgian?
£1800	$3025	(23-Apr-91 C.A109/R) Reve (55x75cm-22x30in) s. (B.FR 110000)

GAZZERA, Romano (1908-) Italian
£918	$1800	(12-Feb-91 SY.NY440/R) Locust and streliria (48x66cm-19x26in) s.
£1658	$3250	(12-Feb-91 SY.NY439/R) Christ's Baptism (66x76cm-26x30in) s. s.i.d.1958stretcher canvas on masonite

GEAR, Mabel (1900-) British
£1000	$1880	(20-Sep-90 C129/R) Vanity of vanities (62x75cm-24x30in) s. i.verso
£600	*$1170*	*(15-Jan-91 C84) Scottie with paint brush (22x20cm-9x8in) s. pencil W/C htd.white*
£1000	*$1950*	*(15-Jan-91 C23/R) West Highland terrier and two scotties (30x46cm-12x18in) s. W/C bodycol.htd.white*

GEAR, William (1915-) British
£700	$1218	(28-Mar-91 CSK220) Study (56x46cm-22x18in) s.d.60 s.i.d.60 verso
£800	$1392	(28-Mar-91 CSK217) Autumn landscape III (65x52cm-26x20in) s.d.50 s.i.d.1950 verso
£1000	$1680	(23-Apr-91 S237/R) Spring song (91x61cm-36x24in) s.d.82 s.i.d.82 verso
£1800	$3330	(8-Mar-91 C157/R) Grey landscape (38x61cm-15x24in) s. s.i.d.51verso
£2000	$3900	(9-Oct-90 B98/R) Spring frolic (74x54cm-29x21in) s.d.52 s.i.d.52 verso
£2200	$4136	(18-Sep-90 PH200) Interieur, Forme Blanche (51x61cm-20x24in) s.d.49
£4200	$7434	(21-Mar-91 S51/R) Landscape with blue (98x70cm-39x28in) s.d.1959
£650	*$1131*	*(28-Mar-91 CSK218) Paysage sauvage - Paris (28x47cm-11x19in) s.d.48 gouache*
£1379	*$2648*	*(28-Nov-90 KF.M787/R) Composition, ruins (32x48cm-13x19in) s.d.1947 gouache col.indian ink pen dr. (DM 4000)*
£1655	*$3178*	*(28-Nov-90 KF.M786/R) Composition Espagnole I (32x50cm-13x20in) s.d.1947 oil gouache (DM 4800)*

GEBAUER, C D (1777-1831) German
£2046	$3847	(18-Sep-90 BU.K52/R) Horses in landscape, deer in background (36x44cm-14x17in) s.d.1826verso (D.KR 23000)

GEBHARD, Albert (1869-1937) Finnish
£2140	$4194	(24-Nov-90 HOR.H94/R) Evening sun's reflection (24x31cm-9x12in) s. (F.M 15000)

GEBHARD, Johannes (1892-1976) Finnish
£861	$1455	(20-Apr-91 HOR.H78/R) Rocky coastal landscape, Kokar (49x64cm-19x25in) s.d.1923 (F.M 6000)
£861	$1455	(20-Apr-91 HOR.H77/R) Beach (49x63cm-19x25in) s.d.1947 (F.M 6000)
£1007	$1732	(14-May-91 HOR.H32) From Helsingfors (38x46cm-15x18in) s.d.1923 (F.M 7000)
£1433	$2822	(17-Nov-90 BU.H44/R) Sailboat in the outer skerries (46x65cm-18x26in) s.d.70 (F.M 10000)

GEBHARD, Johannes (1892-1976) Finnish-cont.
£1433 $2822   (17-Nov-90 BU.H45/R) River landscape (46x55cm-18x22in) s.d.49 panel
                 (F.M 10000)

GEBHARDT, Eduard K F von (1838-1925) German
£1347 $2330   (6-May-91 ZEL.L1701/R) Portrait of man, possible Faust (31x21cm-12x8in)
                 s.d.1920 panel (DM 4000)

GEBHARDT, Ludwig (1830-1908) German
£1027 $1839   (13-Mar-91 N.M498) Moonlit wooded landscape with bridge across stream
                 (88x73cm-35x29in) s. (DM 3000)

GEBHARDT, Wolfgang Magnus (fl.1730-1750) German
£3846 $7500   (10-Oct-90 CH.NY18/R) Figures by fountain among classical ruins and town
                 on river beyond (79x99cm-31x39in) s.indis.d.

GEBLER, Otto Friedrich (1838-1917) German
£4013 $6783   (19-Apr-91 FN.S1720/R) Pond landscape with lamb and sheep
                 (37x26cm-15x10in) panel (DM 12000)
£12587 $24294   (12-Dec-90 WE.MU54/R) An umbrella in any case (45x72cm-18x28in) s. panel
                 (DM 36000)
£13699 $22329   (12-Jun-91 N.M433/R) Sheep watering beside fence and shepherd resting
                 beyond (28x37cm-11x15in) s.mono. panel (DM 40000)

GECELLI, Johannes (1925-) German
£507 $861   (1-Jun-91 VG.B547/R) Composition no 7 (66x45cm-26x18in) s.i.d.1982
                 acrylic over pencil board (DM 1500)
£2560 $5017   (20-Nov-90 L.K242/R) Blauriss (90x100cm-35x39in) s.d.1984
                 s.i.d.stretcher acrylic (DM 7500)
£2911 $4745   (14-Jun-91 L.K892) Vorbeigang (70x100cm-28x39in) s.d.70/71 acrylic
                 (DM 8500)

GECHTOFF, Leonid (19/20th C) American
£1037 $1700   (21-Jun-91 DM.D2277/R) Mosque with figures (41x46cm-16x18in) s.d.38
                 board

GEDDES, Andrew (1783-1844) British
£3000 $4950   (12-Jul-91 C33/R) Portrait of gentleman, traditionally identified as Sir
                 David Wilkie (76x63cm-30x25in) init.d.1834

GEDLEK, Ludwig (1847-?) Austrian
£870 $1470   (19-Apr-91 FN.S1721/R) Panzerreiter und Panduren auf der Verfolgung
                 flüchtiger Janitscharen (15x20cm-6x8in) s.i. panel (DM 2600)
£1894 $3750   (30-Jan-91 GRO.B23/R) Three men on horseback (25x33cm-10x13in) s.i.
                 panel
£2885 $5625   (25-Oct-90 D.V100/R) Skirmish (16x21cm-6x8in) s.i. panel (A.S 60000)
£2895 $5500   (27-Feb-91 SY.NY176/R) Soldier's encampment (21x41cm-8x16in) s.i.
£8205 $16000   (25-Oct-90 GRO.B65/R) Riders through village (69x119cm-27x47in) s.i.

GEEFS, Fanny (1814-1883) Belgian
£578 $1121   (4-Dec-90 R.T209/R) Meditation (63x54cm-25x21in) s.i. oval (C.D 1300)

GEELEN, Christian van (elder) (1755-1826) Dutch
£1200 $1956   (4-Jul-91 CSK255) Portrait of child, standing holding map by desk, in
                 uniform (71x57cm-28x22in) s.d.1781

GEER-BERGENSTRAHLE, Marie Louise Ekman see BERGENSTRAHLE, Marie Louise de Geer

GEERTSEN, Ib (20th C) Danish
£526 $895   (29-May-91 KH.K241) Composition (85x60cm-33x24in) s.d.1949 (D.KR 6000)
£801 $1505   (19-Sep-90 KH.K150) Composition (85x101cm-33x40in) s.d.1950verso
                 (D.KR 9000)
£1053 $1789   (29-May-91 KH.K240/R) Composition (126x91cm-50x36in) s.d.1946
                 (D.KR 12000)

GEEST, Wybrand de (style) (17/18th C) Flemish
£1310 $2200   (17-Jul-91 SY.NY84/R) Portrait of a young girl playing golf
                 (33x23cm-13x9in) panel

GEEST, Wybrand-Simonsz de (elder-circle) (1592-1659) Dutch
£2800 $5180   (5-Mar-91 PH118/R) Portrait of child standing with parakeet holding
                 feathered hat (114x82cm-45x32in) panel

GEETERE, Frans de (20th C) Belgian
£783 $1449   (4-Mar-91 ARC.P47/R) Carnaval (70x54cm-28x21in) s. d.janvier 17 verso
                 Indian ink gouache board (F.FR 7800)

GEETS, Willem (1838-?) Belgian
£2361 $4580   (4-Dec-90 C.A149/R) The pot cleaner (91x135cm-36x53in) s. (B.FR 140000)
£4000 $7160   (12-Mar-91 PH12/R) The kitchen maid (91x137cm-36x54in) s.

GEFFCKEN, Walter (1872-1950) German
£554 $1107   (6-Feb-91 N.M606/R) Danae. Portrait study (50x45cm-20x18in) s.d.1913
                 board (DM 1600)
£1284 $2170   (3-May-91 SA.A1658/R) Elegant figures in a rococo interior
                 (59x76cm-23x30in) s. (DM 3800)

GEGERFELT, Wilhelm von (1844-1920) Swedish
£836	$1497	(9-Apr-91 GO.G42) Coastal cliffs (40x72cm-16x28in) s. i.verso (S.KR 9000)
£982	$1758	(17-Mar-91 BU.M81) Fishmarket (57x42cm-22x17in) s. (S.KR 10500)
£1231	$2068	(24-Apr-91 BA.S68/R) Southern street scene (52x43cm-20x17in) s. (S.KR 13000)
£1394	$2495	(9-Apr-91 GO.G46) Evening canal view, Holland (37x51cm-15x20in) s. panel (S.KR 15000)
£1487	$2662	(9-Apr-91 GO.G45) Moonlit landscape with house (41x60cm-16x24in) s. panel (S.KR 16000)
£2022	$4044	(10-Feb-91 BU.M50) Italian town by the sea (78x124cm-31x49in) s. (S.KR 22000)
£2273	$3818	(24-Apr-91 BA.S66/R) Dutch farm in winter (50x72cm-20x28in) s.d.80 (S.KR 24000)
£2564	$5000	(24-Oct-90 CH.NY182/R) Village by the sea at sunset (73x100cm-29x39in) s.
£2757	$5404	(6-Nov-90 BA.S78/R) Stranded vessel (53x45cm-21x18in) s. panel (S.KR 30000)
£3717	$6654	(9-Apr-91 GO.G43) Winter scene, coastal view with figures by boat (60x95cm-24x37in) s. (S.KR 40000)
£3745	$6442	(14-May-91 BU.S12/R) Harbour scene from Venice (46x55cm-18x22in) s. panel (S.KR 40000)
£4054	$7703	(14-Sep-90 SA.A1160/R) Village street after rain (81x60cm-32x24in) s. panel (DM 12000)
£4634	$8943	(12-Dec-90 BU.S22/R) Haze in Venice (40x56cm-16x22in) s.d.1883 (S.KR 50000)
£4647	$8318	(9-Apr-91 GO.G47/R) Women by fountain, Italy (59x34cm-23x13in) s. (S.KR 50000)
£7813	$15313	(6-Nov-90 BA.S75/R) Gondolas by Venetian bridge (44x64cm-17x25in) s. (S.KR 85000)
£20513	$40000	(23-Oct-90 SY.NY176/R) A Venetian canal (165x100cm-65x39in) s.
£24357	$47739	(6-Nov-90 BA.S74/R) Harbour scene (115x156cm-45x61in) s. (S.KR 265000)

GEHRI, Franz (1882-1960) Swiss
£683	$1338	(24-Nov-90 N.M176) Peasant girl reading on verandah (65x51cm-26x20in) s. (DM 2000)

GEHRIG, Jakob (1846-1922) German
£979	$1899	(4-Dec-90 FN.S1841) View from Canale de la Giudecca to Santa Maria della Salute, Venice (33x50cm-13x20in) s.i. (DM 2800)

GEIGER, Caspar Augustin (1847-1924) German
£933	$1671	(12-Apr-91 BM.B596/R) Venus standing in shell surrounded putti (55x53cm-22x21in) s. board (DM 2800)
£1084	$2092	(14-Dec-90 BM.B613 a/R) Park landscape with rendezvous scene (27x17cm-11x7in) s. panel (DM 3100)

GEIGER, Conrad (1751-1808) German
£854	$1529	(11-Apr-91 D.V182/R) Portrait of Johann Baptist von Roll (85x66cm-33x26in) s.i.d.1764verso (A.S 18000)

GEIGER, E (1876-1965) Swiss
£510	$1000	(7-Nov-90 D.NY32) Lake view under rolling clouds (56x64cm-22x25in) s.d.1911

GEIGER, R (?) German
£805	$1570	(13-Oct-90 KRA.D380) Scene with musician (68x55cm-27x22in) s. (DM 2400)

GEIGER, Richard (1870-) Austrian
£671	$1309	(10-Oct-90 WE.MU265/R) In the theatre (73x100cm-29x39in) s. (DM 2000)
£683	$1338	(24-Nov-90 SA.A830/R) Inn interior scene with musicians and singer (60x80cm-24x31in) s. (DM 2000)
£700	$1176	(18-Jul-91 CSK164 a) Reclining beauty (72x107cm-28x42in) s.
£749	$1257	(23-Apr-91 SY.AM174) Carnival (58x78cm-23x31in) s. (D.FL 2500)
£850	$1675	(4-Oct-90 CSK134/R) A fancy dress party (61x79cm-24x31in) s.
£1100	$2167	(4-Oct-90 CSK190 a) A game of cards (38x47cm-15x19in) s.
£1200	$2076	(9-May-91 CSK153) Backstage at cabaret (102x76cm-40x30in) s.
£1714	$3257	(14-Sep-90 ZOF.Z844/R) Cavalier surprising Bajadere in opera box (99x80cm-39x31in) s. (S.FR 4200)
£3217	$6305	(26-Jan-91 PSA.W9) Comedians (68x55cm-27x22in) s. (P.Z 60000000)

GEIGER, Rupprecht (1908-) German
£10922	$21406	(20-Nov-90 L.K241/R) Composition 759 (90x100cm-35x39in) s.i.d.83stretcher acrylic (DM 32000)
£15203	$26301	(21-May-91 WK.M35/R) White oval on yellow (150x150cm-59x59in) s.verso (DM 45000)
£676	$1169	(21-May-91 WK.M894) Red rectangle on orange (35x23cm-14x9in) s.i. wax crayons board (DM 2000)

GEIGER, T von (19th C) ?
£977	$1856	(28-Feb-91 D.V19/R) River landscape with mill (45x56cm-18x22in) s.d.1843 (A.S 20000)

GEIGER, Willi (1878-1971) German
| £544 | $876 | (28-Jun-91 BM.B900/R) Portrait of man before cactus (54x45cm-21x18in) (DM 1600) |

£1365 $2676   (24-Nov-90 KM.K507/R) Still life with pear and quince (38x60cm-15x24in) s.d.39 (DM 4000)

£1748 $3374   (12-Dec-90 WE.MU208/R) Flowers, evening (70x60cm-28x24in) mono.d.1966 i.verso (DM 5000)

£2027 $3507   (21-May-91 WK.M898/R) Vase with flowers (70x50cm-28x20in) mono.d.1962 (DM 6000)

£2617 $5104   (10-Oct-90 WE.MU139/R) House in landscape (55x70cm-22x28in) s.i. (DM 7800)

£1622 $2805   (21-May-91 WK.M899/R) Flowers (47x32cm-19x13in) s.d.1950 W/C over pencil board (DM 4800)

GEISSER, Johann Josef (1824-1894) Swiss
£595 $1065   (13-Mar-91 GK.Z31) View of sunlit Aletsch glacier (52x84cm-20x33in) s. (S.FR 1500)

£819 $1548   (25-Sep-90 FN.S2176/R) Rocky mountain landscape with peasant couple driving cattle (33x46cm-13x18in) s. board (DM 2400)

£1111 $1989   (13-Mar-91 GK.Z31 b) Peasant women in interior (42x34cm-17x13in) s. (S.FR 2800)

£1143 $2217   (8-Dec-90 GAB.G2200) Le Mont-Blanc (81x122cm-32x48in) (S.FR 2800)

£2213 $3763   (27-May-91 GK.Z5330/R) Alpine landscape with view of Breithorn range (61x84cm-24x33in) s. (S.FR 5600)

£1033 $1850   (12-Apr-91 AW.H609/R) Mountain lake with rowing boats (31x45cm-12x18in) s. pencil htd.white (DM 3100)

GEIST, August Christian (1835-1868) German
£570 $1112   (12-Oct-90 AW.H1438/R) View of Burg Bischofstein at the Moselle (22x35cm-9x14in) c.1860 pencil vellum (DM 1700)

GEIST, C F W (1870-?) German
£1373 $2320   (2-May-91 RAS.V42/R) Girl with dog (66x47cm-26x19in) s.d.1901 pastel (D.KR 15500)

GELDER, Aert de (attrib) (1645-1727) Dutch
£1974 $3750   (8-Jan-91 SY.NY175/R) Abraham and Jacob (15x14cm-6x6in) ink wash

GELDER, Nicolaes van (1620-1677) Flemish
£12587 $24294   (10-Dec-90 L.K45/R) Still life of fruit on draped table with cup, glass and clock (58x44cm-23x17in) bears i. (DM 36000)

GELDORP, Georg (attrib) (?-c.1658) Flemish
£2477 $4880   (13-Nov-90 AB.S891/R) Portrait of man wearing pointed collar (77x63cm-30x25in) mono. (S.KR 27000)

£6000 $10140   (17-Apr-91 S49/R) Portrait of young woman (83x67cm-33x26in) i.d.1624 panel

GELDORP, Gortzius (1553-1618) Flemish
£1100 $2112   (29-Nov-90 CSK175/R) The Penitent Magdalen (62x49cm-24x19in) panel

£1600 $3088   (13-Dec-90 B90/R) Portrait of young lady wearing pearl necklace and earrings (53x42cm-21x17in) mono.d.1611 panel

GELDORP, Gortzius and SNYDERS, Frans (attrib) (17th C) Flemish/Dutch
£18779 $31925   (28-May-91 AB.S4758/R) Elegant couple buying fish at the fishmarket (136x222cm-54x87in) (S.KR 200000)

GELHAY, Edouard (1856-?) French
£1000 $1680   (18-Jul-91 CSK152/R) In park (33x42cm-13x17in) s.

GELINET, Marcel (20th C) French
£1306 $2573   (16-Nov-90 EA.Z280) Le bateau bleu givre et neige au Pont de St Cloud (53x73cm-21x29in) s. (S.FR 3200)

GELISSEN, Maximilien Lambert (1786-1867) Belgian
£1100 $1859   (1-May-91 PHL189) Organ grinder with monkey and group of peasants before farm, landscape (37x48cm-15x19in) s.

GELLEE, Claude (1600-1682) French
£13559 $24000   (22-Mar-91 CH.NY635/R) A classical landscape with distant mountains. A perspective study (14x20cm-6x8in) ink wash double-sided

£3000 $5760   (18-Feb-91 S114/R) Studies of two soldiers and another figure. Landscape (14x20cm-6x8in) i. chk ink wash double-sided

£14000 $22820   (1-Jul-91 S83/R) Study of clump of trees (20x14cm-8x6in) pen wash over black chk

£17000 $27710   (2-Jul-91 C311/R) Herd of cattle ascending hill (12x18cm-5x7in) pen

£21000 $40530   (11-Dec-90 C66/R) A villa beside a harbour with anchored ships (13x20cm-5x8in) blk.chk.wash

GELLEE, Claude (after) (1600-1682) French
£1927 $3853   (6-Feb-91 RAS.K112) Ursula being pulled away by 11.000 young maids (108x147cm-43x58in) (D.KR 21500)

£4000 $6760   (18-Apr-91 C63/R) The Forum, Rome (56x72cm-22x28in)

£7692 $15000   (10-Oct-90 CH.NY177/R) Seaport at sunset with figures (117x145cm-46x57in)

GELLEE, Claude (circle) (1600-1682) French

£1376	$2711	(14-Nov-90 SY.AM118/R) Peasants by pool (58x90cm-23x35in) formerly oval (D.FL 4500)
£1809	$2967	(21-Jun-91 SY.MO225/R) Paysage avec Saint Jean Baptiste (17x22cm-7x9in) copper (F.FR 18000)
£750	*$1223*	*(2-Jul-91 C312/R) Tree (27x22cm-11x9in) black chk pen wash*
£800	*$1304*	*(2-Jul-91 C313/R) Two trees. Sketch of rocks (19x22cm-7x9in) red chk double-sided*

GELLEE, Claude (school) (1600-1682) French

| £560 | $946 | (1-May-91 GD.B543/R) Wooded landscape with party merrymaking (58x73cm-23x29in) (S.FR 1400) |

GELLEE, Claude (style) (1600-1682) French

£1200	$2340	(25-Oct-90 CSK78/R) Extensive wooded landscape with hunter and huntresses on path (65x82cm-26x32in)
£1300	$2496	(29-Nov-90 CSK317) Arcadian landscape with traveller on path (30x41cm-12x16in) panel
£1400	$2688	(29-Nov-90 CSK229/R) Italianate landscape with artist sketching ruined temple (51x63cm-20x25in)
£1471	$2500	(30-May-91 CE.NY77) Mediterranean port with figures (49x36cm-19x14in)
£1992	$3426	(14-May-91 GF.L2272/R) Mountain landscape (54x67cm-21x26in) (S.FR 5000)
£2869	$5623	(7-Nov-90 APT.P437/R) L'embarquement de Cleopatre a Tarse (38x47cm-15x19in) (F.FR 28000)
£839	*$1620*	*(10-Dec-90 L.K295) Landscape with rock (22x32cm-9x13in) i. indian ink brush sepia (DM 2400)*
£1350	*$2592*	*(18-Feb-91 S15/R) View of wall of town (16x23cm-6x9in) i. pen ink wash htd.white*
£5245	*$10122*	*(10-Dec-90 L.K296) Southern landscape with classical temple and cattle watering (23x38cm-9x15in) mono. indian ink brush sepia (DM 15000)*

GELLER, Johann Nepomuk (1860-1954) Austrian

| £570 | $1019 | (11-Apr-91 D.V212/R) The horse-drawn cart (11x14cm-4x6in) s. panel (A.S 12000) |
| *£1456* | *$2751* | *(27-Sep-90 D.V124/R) Procession outside the Jesuit Church, Krakau (40x56cm-16x22in) s. mixed media canvas on board (A.S 30000)* |

GELMO, Marianne (19th C) Austrian

| £1372 | $2716 | (31-Jan-91 D.V76/R) Still life with basket of cherries (36x44cm-14x17in) s.d.1897 panel (A.S 28000) |

GEMITO, Vincenzo (1852-1929) Italian

£3697	$7135	(11-Dec-90 CH.R5/R) Profilo di fanciulla (46x46cm-18x18in) s. tempera (I.L 8000000)
£1595	*$2711*	*(28-May-91 F.R66/R) Studio di ragazza (28x42cm-11x17in) pencil (I.L 3500000)*
£2964	*$4950*	*(6-Jun-91 F.M215/R) Autoritratto (48x36cm-19x14in) s.d.1920 tempera W/C board (I.L 6500000)*

GEMPT, Bernard de (1826-1879) Dutch

| £2312 | $4000 | (21-May-91 CE.NY158/R) Catch (82x105cm-32x41in) s. |
| *£1667* | *$3283* | *(30-Oct-90 CH.AM483/R) Honi soit qui mal y pense (61x98cm-24x39in) s.i.d.1859 chl (D.FL 5500)* |

GEN-PAUL (1895-1975) French

£602	$1114	(4-Mar-91 ARC.P131) Montmartre (16x22cm-6x9in) s. board (F.FR 6000)
£2024	$3968	(25-Nov-90 LC.P119) Le garconnet en salopette (41x27cm-16x11in) s. panel (F.FR 20000)
£2284	$4500	(13-Nov-90 CE.NY286/R) Cavalier a cheval (41x27cm-16x11in) s. masonite
£2590	$4402	(29-May-91 GL.P68/R) Le guitariste (33x22cm-13x9in) s. hardboard (F.FR 26000)
£2888	$4997	(26-May-91 ZZ.F134/R) Cavalier (41x27cm-16x11in) s. panel (F.FR 29000)
£3046	$6000	(13-Nov-90 CE.NY130/R) Le cavalier a cheval (41x27cm-16x11in) s. masonite
£4049	$7935	(25-Nov-90 LC.P103/R) Bouquet de fleurs (61x50cm-24x20in) s. (F.FR 40000)
£7049	$11490	(16-Jun-91 GL.P62/R) Les courses (50x65cm-20x26in) s.d.3 mai 49 (F.FR 70000)
£7614	$15000	(15-Nov-90 D.NY92/R) Le course aux chevaux (50x65cm-20x26in) s.
£7645	$14755	(12-Dec-90 APT.P102/R) L'enfant au taxi (73x50cm-29x20in) s. (F.FR 75000)
£8569	$16709	(28-Oct-90 M.V54/R) Le pianiste (55x38cm-22x15in) s. (F.FR 85000)
£10194	$19572	(27-Nov-90 APT.P92/R) Voitures a cheval (65x81cm-26x32in) s. (F.FR 100000)
£11628	$22674	(17-Oct-90 LT.P48/R) Les cavaliers (50x65cm-20x26in) s. (F.FR 115000)
£12690	$25000	(15-Nov-90 SY.NY51/R) Violinist (40x22cm-16x9in) s.
£14286	$28143	(16-Nov-90 FB.P170/R) Bouquet de fleurs (68x54cm-27x21in) s. (F.FR 140000)
£15306	$30153	(16-Nov-90 FB.P171/R) Les mesnils, Seine et Oise (81x65cm-32x26in) s.d.25 i. verso (F.FR 150000)
£15873	$27302	(19-May-91 ZZ.F161/R) La gare de la frette sur Oise (65x81cm-26x32in) s. (F.FR 160000)
£18367	$36184	(16-Nov-90 FB.P169/R) La queue en Yvelines (50x61cm-20x24in) s. i. verso (F.FR 180000)
£21939	$43219	(16-Nov-90 FB.P166/R) La croix rouge a Fourquey (65x81cm-26x32in) s. i. verso (F.FR 215000)

GEN-PAUL (1895-1975) French-cont.

£22449	$44224	(16-Nov-90 FB.P167/R) La plage de cette (65x81cm-26x32in) s. i. verso (F.FR 220000)
£22959	$45230	(16-Nov-90 FB.P165/R) Le Joueur de banjo (81x60cm-32x24in) s. (F.FR 225000)
£23618	$42276	(17-Mar-91 L.C23/R) Les cyclistes (73x92cm-29x36in) s. (F.FR 235000)
£423	$826	(20-Jan-91 GL.P17/R) Le theatre de l'Atelier a Montmartre (27x38cm-11x15in) s. oil pastel (F.FR 4200)
£457	$915	(6-Feb-91 FB.P140) L'accordeoniste (41x28cm-16x11in) s. pastel (F.FR 4500)
£528	$913	(26-May-91 ZZ.F198/R) Cavalier (50x65cm-20x26in) s. indian ink wash (F.FR 5300)
£585	$1140	(20-Jan-91 CB.P39) Don quichotte (21x27cm-8x11in) s. pastel (F.FR 5800)
£605	$1179	(26-Oct-90 APT.P13) L'accordeoniste (42x27cm-17x11in) s.d.dec. 60 pen htd.crayolor (F.FR 6000)
£605	$1179	(20-Jan-91 CB.P77) Nu au fauteuil rose (28x22cm-11x9in) s. pastel felt-pen (F.FR 6000)
£609	$1200	(13-Nov-90 CE.NY219/R) Les courses (34x42cm-13x17in) s. col.chk wax crayons
£609	$1200	(13-Nov-90 CE.NY214/R) Notre-Dame de Paris (49x65cm-19x26in) s. brush ink
£609	$1200	(13-Nov-90 CE.NY157/R) Les courses (30x42cm-12x17in) s. col.wax crayons paper on board
£609	$1200	(13-Nov-90 CE.NY216/R) Les courses (49x65cm-19x26in) s. brush ink
£609	$1200	(13-Nov-90 CE.NY217/R) Caleche (49x65cm-19x26in) s. brush ink
£612	$1188	(8-Dec-90 GAB.G2573/R) Le violoniste (40x27cm-16x11in) s. col.oil crayons (S.FR 1500)
£612	$1206	(18-Nov-90 S.S51/R) Les courses a Enghien (18x41cm-7x16in) s. col.crayon (F.FR 6000)
£612	$1188	(8-Dec-90 GAB.G2572/R) La clarinettiste (38x28cm-15x11in) s. col.oil crayons (S.FR 1500)
£617	$1196	(7-Dec-90 GL.P114) L'embarcadere a Geneve (35x50cm-14x20in) s. crayolor (F.FR 6000)
£624	$1104	(7-Apr-91 LT.P88) Le cycliste (20x12cm-8x5in) s. gouache (F.FR 6300)
£650	$1060	(4-Jul-91 GL.P142/R) Cavalier (39x27cm-15x11in) s. pastel (F.FR 6500)
£653	$1051	(26-Jun-91 CB.P37) L'Accordeoniste (41x29cm-16x11in) s.d.9.6.61 pastel (F.FR 6500)
£663	$1279	(12-Dec-90 APT.P19) Voiture a cheval (25x34cm-10x13in) s.i. crayolor (F.FR 6500)
£663	$1279	(12-Dec-90 APT.P20) Le saxophoniste (40x28cm-16x11in) s. crayolor (F.FR 6500)
£692	$1239	(12-Apr-91 JM.P21) L'accordeoniste (28x20cm-11x8in) s. crayolor (F.FR 7000)
£705	$1149	(14-Jun-91 FB.P62) Les joueurs de musique (41x29cm-16x11in) s. col.crayons (F.FR 7000)
£706	$1376	(26-Oct-90 APT.P12) Le picador (20x24cm-8x9in) s. ink crayolor (F.FR 7000)
£726	$1379	(1-Mar-91 CB.P35) L'accordeoniste (41x29cm-16x11in) s.d.6.9.61 col.crayons (F.FR 7200)
£732	$1463	(6-Feb-91 LD.P71) Enghien (29x39cm-11x15in) s. pastel (F.FR 7200)
£814	$1538	(25-Sep-90 FB.P283/R) Cavalier (29x20cm-11x8in) s.i.d.53 ball pen col.crayons (F.FR 8000)
£814	$1538	(25-Sep-90 FB.P279/R) Le trompettiste (42x33cm-17x13in) s. col.crayons (F.FR 8000)
£815	$1605	(30-Oct-90 I.N222) Les cavaliers au bois (48x61cm-19x24in) s. W/C Indian ink (F.FR 8000)
£816	$1584	(8-Dec-90 GAB.G2571/R) La danseuse (43x50cm-17x20in) s. gouache col.oil crayons (S.FR 2000)
£840	$1420	(1-May-91 GD.B1473/R) Portrait of Chantal seated (42x26cm-17x10in) s.d.33 pencil (S.FR 2100)
£863	$1597	(6-Mar-91 HC.P74) La Paix, 8 mai 1945 (24x21cm-9x8in) s.i. gouache (F.FR 8600)
£866	$1672	(12-Dec-90 APT.P17) Aux courses (28x39cm-11x15in) s. crayolor (F.FR 8500)
£918	$1800	(12-Feb-91 SY.NY123/R) Saxophone player (41x28cm-16x11in) s. pastel
£996	$1723	(26-May-91 ZZ.F205/R) Cavalier (28x20cm-11x8in) s. pastel (F.FR 10000)
£1007	$1641	(14-Jun-91 FB.P63/R) Don quichotte (45x40cm-18x16in) s. gouache col.oil crayons (F.FR 10000)
£1016	$2033	(6-Feb-91 LD.P70/R) Clowns musiciens (63x47cm-25x19in) s. gouache (F.FR 10000)
£1020	$1980	(8-Dec-90 GAB.G2574/R) Le violoncelliste (45x35cm-18x14in) s. gouache col.oil crayons (S.FR 2500)
£1071	$2111	(14-Nov-90 CN.P26/R) Les jockeys (27x38cm-11x15in) s. crayon pastel (F.FR 10500)
£1120	$2207	(30-Oct-90 I.N178) Mistinguet (40x30cm-16x12in) s. pastel (F.FR 11000)
£1172	$2262	(12-Dec-90 APT.P18) A bicyclette (30x41cm-12x16in) s. crayolor (F.FR 11500)
£1188	$2103	(7-Apr-91 I.N150) Le cavalier (28x20cm-11x8in) s. pastel (F.FR 12000)
£1310	$2555	(25-Oct-90 CB.P22) Geneve (26x35cm-10x14in) s. pastel (F.FR 13000)
£1393	$2424	(25-Mar-91 CR.P31 b) Clown accodeoniste (28x20cm-11x8in) s. gouache pastel (F.FR 14000)
£1508	$2894	(24-Feb-91 P.V105) Le Moulin Rouge (31x41cm-12x16in) s. pastel (F.FR 15000)
£1511	$2462	(11-Jun-91 I.N64) La partie de cartes (19x12cm-7x5in) s. ink gouache (F.FR 15000)

GEN-PAUL (1895-1975) French-cont.

£1624	$3200	(13-Nov-90 CE.NY154/R) Les cavaliers (48x63cm-19x25in) s. gouache W/C brush ink
£1777	$3500	(13-Nov-90 CE.NY195/R) Aux courses (41x53cm-16x21in) s. gouache board
£2041	$4020	(16-Nov-90 FB.P173) Le guitariste (48x62cm-19x24in) s. W/C oil crayon (F.FR 20000)
£2137	$4167	(25-Oct-90 CB.P26/R) Moulin Rouge (48x63cm-19x25in) s. crayolor pastel (F.FR 21200)
£2258	$4335	(2-Dec-90 GAB.G1615/R) Chevaux de course (47x62cm-19x24in) s. gouache crayons (S.FR 5600)
£2289	$4326	(30-Sep-90 FE.P28) La course de chevaux (50x65cm-20x26in) s. W/C gouache (F.FR 22500)
£2429	$4761	(25-Nov-90 ZZ.F70/R) Les clowns (44x33cm-17x13in) s. pastel (F.FR 24000)
£2485	$4200	(21-Apr-91 E.LA76) Le concert (52x65cm-20x26in) s. gouache (F.FR 25000)
£2530	$4960	(19-Nov-90 CSC.P64/R) Les courses (47x63cm-19x25in) s. pastel ink (F.FR 25000)
£2800	$4676	(5-Jun-91 HC.P355) Le Port de Dinard (49x66cm-19x26in) s. gouache blk.crayon (F.FR 28000)
£2811	$5201	(6-Mar-91 HC.P78) Match de Polo a Bagatelle (48x62cm-19x24in) s.i. crayon blk.felt pen (F.FR 28000)
£2959	$5830	(16-Nov-90 FB.P175/R) Les amoureux a cheval (49x63cm-19x25in) s. gouache (F.FR 29000)
£2959	$5830	(16-Nov-90 FB.P174/R) Les caleches (48x63cm-19x25in) s. gouache (F.FR 29000)
£3112	$5758	(6-Mar-91 HC.P79) Scene de cafe (43x55cm-17x22in) s.d.27 gouache (F.FR 31000)
£3138	$6150	(25-Nov-90 ZZ.F71/R) Trotteurs en course (50x65cm-20x26in) s. gouache (F.FR 31000)
£3287	$5686	(22-May-91 CD.P24/R) Orchestre de jazz sous l'enseigne d'une guinguette marquee (48x63cm-19x25in) s. gouache (F.FR 33000)
£3373	$5802	(19-May-91 ZZ.F170/R) Baigneuses et baigneurs (48x62cm-19x24in) s. W/C gouache (F.FR 34000)
£3414	$6315	(6-Mar-91 HC.P80) Rue de village (49x64cm-19x25in) s.i. gouache crayon (F.FR 34000)
£3465	$6134	(7-Apr-91 I.N149) Les cavaliers (48x103cm-19x41in) s. gouache (F.FR 35000)
£3561	$6729	(30-Sep-90 E.LA100) Clowns musiciens (64x48cm-25x19in) s.d.50 gouache (F.FR 35000)
£3586	$7029	(11-Nov-90 ZZ.F173/R) La course attelee (47x62cm-19x24in) s. W/C gouache (F.FR 35000)
£3644	$7142	(25-Nov-90 LC.P100/R) Les joueurs de boules chez la mere Paille a Montmartre (48x63cm-19x25in) s.d. W/C gouache (F.FR 36000)
£3673	$7237	(16-Nov-90 FB.P179/R) Le quatuor (48x63cm-19x25in) s. gouache (F.FR 36000)
£3678	$6216	(21-Apr-91 DA.R3/R) Trotteurs en course (50x65cm-20x26in) s. gouache (F.FR 37000)
£3878	$7639	(16-Nov-90 FB.P178/R) Le picador (48x63cm-19x25in) s. gouache (F.FR 38000)
£4082	$8000	(12-Feb-91 SY.NY122/R) Figures on beach. Tunisian strollers (48x64cm-19x25in) one s. gouache chl pair
£4082	$8041	(16-Nov-90 FB.P176/R) L'orchestre (48x63cm-19x25in) s. gouache paper laid down on panel (F.FR 40000)
£4592	$9046	(16-Nov-90 FB.P177/R) Le pere labille (63x48cm-25x19in) s.i.d.29 gouache W/C (F.FR 45000)
£4663	$8020	(19-May-91 ZZ.F187/R) La course de haies (49x65cm-19x26in) s. gouache (F.FR 47000)
£5086	$9613	(30-Sep-90 E.LA99/R) Les courses (46x60cm-18x24in) s. gouache (F.FR 50000)
£6071	$11961	(14-Nov-90 I.N2/R) Port d'Ondaroa (48x64cm-19x25in) s. gouache W/C (F.FR 59500)
£17893	$30239	(17-Apr-91 LGB.P13/R) La terrasse de Greolot (49x65cm-19x26in) s.d.27 gouache W/C laid down on canvas (F.FR 180000)

GENABETH, Eleonore Eugenie van (1819-1891) Dutch

| £1199 | $1954 | (12-Jun-91 N.M434/R) Shepherdess with cattle on path amongst trees (56x95cm-22x37in) s.d.1887 (DM 3500) |

GENAILLE, Felix Francois Barthelemy (1826-?) French

| £1096 | $1863 | (31-May-91 LD.P5) La belle italienne (32x24cm-13x9in) s.d.1862 panel (F.FR 11000) |

GENBERG, Anton (1862-1939) Swedish

£1654	$3243	(6-Nov-90 BA.S84/R) Farm yard in Skane (50x71cm-20x28in) s.d.1933 panel (S.KR 18000)
£1743	$3434	(13-Nov-90 AB.S376/R) Norwegian mountain landscape with farm in winter (54x74cm-21x29in) s.i.d.92 (S.KR 19000)
£1878	$3192	(28-May-91 AB.S4623/R) Mountain landscape with huts in winter (45x38cm-18x15in) s. panel (S.KR 20000)
£1989	$3341	(24-Apr-91 BA.S71/R) Late summer in the bay (50x74cm-20x29in) s.d.1914 (S.KR 21000)
£2058	$3684	(17-Mar-91 BU.M110) Mountainous winterlandscape, Storulvastugan (50x74cm-20x29in) s. (S.KR 22000)
£2206	$4324	(6-Nov-90 BA.S85/R) Hogfors works in Varmland (50x73cm-20x29in) s.d.1920 (S.KR 24000)
£2233	$4153	(9-Sep-90 BU.M664) Mountain landscape with farm (50x72cm-20x28in) s.d.1922 (S.KR 24000)

GENBERG, Anton (1862-1939) Swedish-cont.

£2595	$5008	(12-Dec-90 BU.S26/R) Landscape with angler (70x90cm-28x35in) s.d.1928 (S.KR 28000)
£3058	$5903	(12-Dec-90 BU.S25/R) Winter landscape with skiers (81x115cm-32x45in) s.d.1913 (S.KR 33000)
£3676	$7206	(6-Nov-90 BA.S82/R) Winter, Bjornange (50x74cm-20x29in) s.l.d.1919 (S.KR 40000)
£5474	$10785	(30-Oct-90 BU.S32/R) Summer landscape with girl on road (45x61cm-18x24in) s.d.1892 (S.KR 60000)

GENEGEN, Jos van (?) Belgian

| £914 | $1637 | (12-Mar-91 C.A280) Farm beside the water (55x90cm-22x35in) s. (B.FR 55000) |
| £1349 | $2617 | (8-Dec-90 KV.L293) Mother and children in the snow (55x80cm-22x31in) s.d.1897 (B.FR 80000) |

GENELLI, Bonaventura (1798-1868) German

| £769 | $1492 | (7-Dec-90 GB.B5821) Woman seated and another woman squatting facing back (26x32cm-10x13in) pencil dr paper on paper (DM 2200) |
| £862 | $1655 | (28-Nov-90 KF.M368) Scene from the Old Testament (26x40cm-10x16in) pencil (DM 2500) |

GENERALIC, Ivan (1914-) Yugoslavian

| £408 | $804 | (16-Nov-90 EA.Z237) Still life with flowers in vase (40x30cm-16x12in) s. indian ink (S.FR 1000) |

GENERALIC, Josip (1936-) Yugoslavian

| £973 | $1908 | (24-Jan-91 D.V308/R) Stork carrying baby (34x24cm-13x9in) s.d.1988 oil glass (A.S 20000) |

GENERALIC, Milan (1941-) Yugoslavian

| £535 | $1049 | (24-Jan-91 D.V210/R) Pheasant flying (32x37cm-13x15in) s.d.1986 oil glass (A.S 11000) |

GENET, A (19th C) French

| £759 | $1472 | (4-Dec-90 C.A153) Near the farm (51x63cm-20x25in) s.d.1873 (B.FR 45000) |

GENILLION, Jean Baptiste Francois (1750-1829) French

| £7136 | $13772 | (12-Dec-90 ARC.P15/R) Vue de l'Ile de la cite, du Pont-Neuf, et de la petite Galerie du Louvre (28x43cm-11x17in) pierre noire wash Indian ink (F.FR 70000) |

GENIN, Lucien (1894-1958) French

£995	$1731	(25-Mar-91 PLF.P47) Le Mouline de la Galette (32x41cm-13x16in) s. board (F.FR 10000)
£1700	$2771	(3-Jul-91 PLF.P14) Le Moulin Rouge (18x22cm-7x9in) s. (F.FR 17000)
£2337	$4675	(4-Feb-91 LGB.P159/R) Une place animee en Provence (35x27cm-14x11in) s. (F.FR 23000)
£3466	$6689	(12-Dec-90 APT.P103) Paris, Montmartre sous la neige (60x73cm-24x29in) s. (F.FR 34000)
£3827	$6238	(11-Jun-91 CSC.P6/R) Le port de St-Tropez (38x46cm-15x18in) s. canvas laid down on board (F.FR 38000)
£6000	$11700	(19-Oct-90 C198/R) Devant le theatre (60x72cm-24x28in) s.
£6116	$11743	(29-Nov-90 ZZ.F12/R) La butte Montmartre (46x55cm-18x22in) s. (F.FR 60000)
£6231	$10219	(19-Jun-91 JM.P131) Montmartre, consulat d'Auvergne (73x61cm-29x24in) s. (F.FR 62000)
£6983	$13407	(2-Dec-90 M.V123/R) Place Clichy (56x80cm-22x31in) s. board (F.FR 68500)
£7034	$13575	(10-Dec-90 BL.P52/R) Paris, la place Pigalle (60x73cm-24x29in) s. (F.FR 69000)
£7238	$13968	(10-Dec-90 BL.P51/R) Montmartre, la place du Tertre (60x73cm-24x29in) s. (F.FR 71000)
£7685	$14985	(17-Oct-90 ARC.P87/R) Notre Dame de Paris (60x73cm-24x29in) s. (F.FR 76000)
£9480	$18297	(10-Dec-90 BL.P53/R) Paris, la Tour St-Jacques (73x60cm-29x24in) s. (F.FR 93000)
£9950	$17313	(25-Mar-91 PLF.P55/R) Nogent, le dimanche (60x72cm-24x28in) s. (F.FR 100000)
£10102	$19901	(16-Nov-90 FB.P164/R) La tour St-Jacques (73x60cm-29x24in) s. (F.FR 99000)
£12639	$24646	(17-Oct-90 LT.P51/R) La Porte Saint-Denis (60x73cm-24x29in) s. (F.FR 125000)
£13433	$23373	(25-Mar-91 PLF.P46/R) Guinguette a Bry-sur-Marne (60x73cm-24x29in) s. (F.FR 135000)
£15291	$29358	(2-Dec-90 M.V161 b/R) La place duTertre (59x72cm-23x28in) s. (F.FR 150000)
£15547	$30316	(11-Oct-90 QWA.P51/R) La passerelle des Arts a Paris, animee de personnages (60x73cm-24x29in) s. (F.FR 155000)
£16327	$32163	(17-Nov-90 HC.P54) Theatre de l'atelier (54x65cm-21x26in) s. (F.FR 160000)
£553	$907	(18-Jun-91 APT.P23) Paris, rue Galande (26x20cm-10x8in) s. gouache (F.FR 5500)
£657	$1282	(17-Oct-90 ARC.P25) Place du tertre (23x30cm-9x12in) s.d.1922 gouache (F.FR 6500)
£896	$1558	(25-Mar-91 PLF.P56) L'Eglise Saint Germain des Pres (40x33cm-16x13in) s. gouache board (F.FR 9000)

GENIN, Lucien (1894-1958) French-cont.

£995	$1731	(25-Mar-91 PLF.P60) Le Sacre-Coeur (41x33cm-16x13in) s. gouache board (F.FR 10000)
£1017	$1923	(25-Sep-90 FB.P278/R) Place animee a Montmartre (22x26cm-9x10in) s. gouache (F.FR 10000)
£1028	$1994	(9-Dec-90 E.LA130) Rue l.epic (23x33cm-9x13in) s. gouache (F.FR 10000)
£1205	$2229	(6-Mar-91 APT.P14) Paris, le pont St Michel (32x39cm-13x15in) s. gouache (F.FR 12000)
£1214	$2112	(25-Mar-91 PLF.P59/R) La place Vendome (32x42cm-13x17in) s. gouache board (F.FR 12200)
£1233	$2393	(8-Dec-90 LT.P67/R) La place de la Concorde (26x35cm-10x14in) s. gouache (F.FR 12000)
£1264	$2465	(17-Oct-90 ARC.P24) Le pont neuf (27x35cm-11x14in) s. goauche (F.FR 12500)
£1406	$2263	(24-Jun-91 PR.P142) Rue de l'Abreuvoir (50x65cm-20x26in) s. W/C (F.FR 14000)
£1508	$2894	(24-Feb-91 P.V110) Paris, Place de l'Opera (26x35cm-10x14in) s. oil gouache (F.FR 15000)
£1537	$3012	(11-Nov-90 ZZ.F102/R) La chambre des Deputes (32x42cm-13x17in) s. gouache (F.FR 15000)
£1613	$3145	(28-Oct-90 M.V57) Montmartre, le Moulin Rouge (23x19cm-9x7in) s. W/C (F.FR 16000)
£1693	$2929	(26-May-91 ZZ.F96/R) La Place du Tertre (223x31cm-88x12in) s. gouache (F.FR 17000)
£1700	$2771	(3-Jul-91 PLF.P13) Le restaurant de Coucou (33x41cm-13x16in) s. gouache board (F.FR 17000)
£1937	$3719	(2-Dec-90 ZZ.F39) L'Eglise St.Germain des pres (23x30cm-9x12in) s. gouache (F.FR 19000)
£2041	$4020	(17-Nov-90 HC.P53) L'Hotel de ville (25x34cm-10x13in) s. gouache (F.FR 20000)
£2123	$4141	(21-Oct-90 DA.R6/R) Paris, les Champs Elysees, l'Arc de Triomphe (27x21cm-11x8in) s. gouache (F.FR 21000)
£2328	$4563	(20-Nov-90 BG.P41/R) Les Champs Elysees (23x31cm-9x12in) s. goauche (F.FR 23000)
£2427	$4732	(21-Oct-90 L.C73/R) L'angle de la rue Marcadet et du Mont Cenis (45x54cm-18x21in) s. gouache (F.FR 24000)
£2653	$5227	(16-Nov-90 FB.P163/R) La Place Pigalle (48x59cm-19x23in) s. gouache board (F.FR 26000)
£2761	$5440	(6-Oct-90 GL.P41/R) La place du Tertre (54x44cm-21x17in) s. goauche (F.FR 28000)
£3058	$5902	(12-Dec-90 APT.P21 b) Place de l'Opera a la Liberation (45x54cm-18x21in) s. gouache (F.FR 30000)
£3061	$6031	(17-Nov-90 HC.P52) Le theatre de l'atelier (31x23cm-12x9in) s. gouache (F.FR 30000)
£3417	$6117	(11-Mar-91 GL.P10/R) Le marche (46x54cm-18x21in) s. goauche board (F.FR 34000)
£3511	$6846	(9-Oct-90 CSC.P6/R) Lal place de l'eglise (32x40cm-13x16in) s. gouache (F.FR 35000)
£3511	$6846	(9-Oct-90 CSC.P8/R) L'Escalier de Montmartre (25x20cm-10x8in) s. gouache (F.FR 35000)
£3649	$7188	(6-Oct-90 GL.P138) Cafe de la Tourelle, Montmartre (48x59cm-19x23in) s. goauche (F.FR 37000)
£4057	$8032	(3-Feb-91 I.N100/R) La place du tertre (44x59cm-17x23in) s. gouache (F.FR 40000)
£4714	$9193	(9-Oct-90 CSC.P11/R) Notre Dame de Paris (44x56cm-17x22in) s. goauche (F.FR 47000)
£5092	$10031	(30-Oct-90 I.N61/R) La place du tertre (46x55cm-18x22in) s. gouache paper laid down on canvas (F.FR 50000)
£6048	$11794	(28-Oct-90 M.V56/R) Bry sur Marne (50x61cm-20x24in) s. W/C (F.FR 60000)

GENIN, Robert (1884-1939) French

£5068	$8767	(21-May-91 WK.M35 a/R) The widow (201x188cm-79x74in) s. (DM 15000)

GENIS, Rene (1922-) French

£3265	$6335	(8-Dec-90 GAB.G2583/R) Les eglantines (60x60cm-24x24in) s. (S.FR 8000)

GENISSON, Jules Victor (1805-1860) Belgian

£1349	$2617	(4-Dec-90 C.A154/R) Interior scene (55x45cm-22x18in) s.d.1853 panel (B.FR 80000)
£1515	$2985	(30-Oct-90 CH.AM169/R) View in Gothic church, looking east, with service taking place (74x94cm-29x37in) s.d.1851 (D.FL 5000)
£2039	$3935	(14-Dec-90 ARC.P161) Interieur de cathedrale (36x29cm-14x11in) s. panel (F.FR 20000)
£2359	$4600	(14-Oct-90 H.C443/R) Church interior (51x43cm-20x17in) s.

GENKINGER, Fritz (1934-) German

£1081	$1838	(28-May-91 KF.M680/R) Portrait of gambler II (78x33cm-31x13in) mono.d.1968 i.verso resin panel (DM 3200)

GENN, Robert (1936-) Canadian

£567	$964	(27-May-91 HO.ED83/R) Cariboo pattern (28x36cm-11x14in) s. s.i.verso (C.D 1100)
£1360	$2679	(30-Oct-90 MA.V101) Hilltop entrance (91x122cm-36x48in) s.d.1977 (C.D 3100)
£1809	$3130	(22-May-91 MA.V222) Morning at Nehatlatch Lake (71x86cm-28x34in) (C.D 3600)

GENNARI, Bartolomeo (1594-1661) Italian
£1803 $3228   (8-Apr-91 CH.R40/R) Salome (93x76cm-37x30in) (I.L 4000000)

GENNARI, Benedetto (attrib) (16/17th C) Italian
£2564 $5000   (11-Oct-90 SY.NY33/R) Judith with the head of Holofernes and maidservant
                    (120x97cm-47x38in)
£40000 $65200   (3-Jul-91 S62/R) Portrait of young man holding drawing (60x48cm-24x19in)

GENNARI, Benedetto (circle) (16/17th C) Italian
£1889 $3192   (18-Apr-91 APT.P12/R) Sainte Marie Madeleine (76x62cm-30x24in)
                    (F.FR 19000)

GENNARI, Benedetto (style) (16/17th C) Italian
£913 $1807   (30-Jan-91 APT.P163) La mort de Saint Joseph (70x96cm-28x38in)
                    (F.FR 9000)

GENNARI, Cesare (attrib) (1637-1688) Italian
£2100 $3885   (5-Mar-91 PH108) The Magdalen (105x84cm-41x33in)

GENOESE SCHOOL (?) Italian
£1722 $2996   (25-Mar-91 SY.F576) Naufragio (79x112cm-31x44in) (I.L 3800000)
£7820 $14000   (11-Apr-91 SY.NY112 a/R) Joseph with the Christ Child, two angels
                    looking on (87x112cm-34x44in) c,1700

GENOESE SCHOOL, 17th C Italian
£2564 $5000   (10-Oct-90 CH.NY154/R) Mountainous river landscape with shepherd resting
                    by ravine (73x83cm-29x33in)
£2593 $4356   (16-Jul-91 JRL.S163/R) St Jeronimus (95x70cm-37x28in) (A.D 5600)
£2700 $5265   (22-Oct-90 SWS1357/R) Madonna and Child (73x60cm-29x24in)
£3182 $6237   (20-Nov-90 F.R113/R) Paesaggio con Susanna al bagno (43x46cm-17x18in)
                    (I.L 7000000)
£3417 $5809   (30-May-91 F.M40) Giuseppe e la moglie di Putifarre (110x129cm-43x51in)
                    (I.L 7500000)
£3911 $7000   (11-Apr-91 SY.NY71/R) Holy Family with an adoring saint
                    (117x89cm-46x35in)
£4546 $8910   (19-Nov-90 CH.R108/R) Ritratto di gentildonna (201x112cm-79x44in)
                    (I.L 10000000)
£6012 $11664   (3-Dec-90 SY.F1061/R) Ritratto di gentildonna (129x87cm-51x34in)
                    (I.L 13000000)
£6937 $13459   (3-Dec-90 SY.F1043/R) Cristo e la Samaritana al pozzo (89x129cm-35x51in)
                    (I.L 15000000)
£8155 $14190   (25-Mar-91 SY.F730) Tempeste sul mare (73x100cm-29x39in) pair
                    (I.L 18000000)
£8500 $16405   (12-Dec-90 S205/R) Portrait of Paolo Giovanni Spinola (119x90cm-47x35in)
                    i.
£8736 $16948   (7-Dec-90 SY.MO73/R) Le Christ et la femme adultere (98x133cm-39x52in)
                    (F.FR 85000)
£9891 $17705   (10-Apr-91 CB.P36/R) Paysage anime avec ruines (89x129cm-35x51in)
                    (F.FR 100000)
*£1003 $1776   (19-Mar-91 F.M225) Madonna col Bambino e San Giovannino (26x20cm-10x8in)
                    tempera W/C paper laid down on panel (I.L 2200000)*
*£4523 $7417   (18-Jun-91 APT.P42/R) Cavalier bondissant (42x29cm-17x11in) pen wash
                    htd.white (F.FR 45000)*

GENOESE SCHOOL, 18th C Italian
£3864 $7574   (20-Nov-90 F.R37/R) Paesaggio con Agar e l'angelo (73x95cm-29x37in)
                    (I.L 8500000)

GENOVES, Juan (1930-) Spanish
£3600 $7020   (18-Oct-90 S198/R) Tres historias (125x90cm-49x35in) s.d.66

GENSA, L (?) ?
£760 $1482   (22-Oct-90 SWS100/R) Summer flowers (53x38cm-21x15in) s. panel

GENSCHOW, Georg (1828-1902) German
£2273 $4409   (4-Dec-90 FN.S1842/R) Engstlensee landscape with cows watering and
                    figures, Switzerland (87x126cm-34x50in) s.l. (DM 6500)

GENTH, Lillian (1876-1953) American
£6105 $10500   (15-May-91 SY.NY109/R) Promenading along river (66x51cm-26x20in) s.

GENTILESCHI, Artemisia (1597-1651) Italian
£35000 $57050   (5-Jul-91 C88/R) Judith and maidservant and head of Holofernes
                    (110x137cm-43x54in)

GENTILESCHI, Artemisia (after) (1597-1651) Italian
£1359 $2365   (25-Mar-91 SY.F563) Madonna con bambino (61x44cm-24x17in) panel
                    (I.L 3000000)

GENTILESCHI, Artemisia (style) (1597-1651) Italian
£850 $1437   (16-Apr-91 PH101) Virgin and Child (28x20cm-11x8in) panel

GENTILINI, Franco (1909-1981) Italian
£5215 $8500   (12-Jun-91 SY.NY107/R) Le streghe (45x35cm-18x14in) s.d.1944 s.i.d.verso
£9230 $17999   (24-Oct-90 F.M216/R) La Giustizia (48x33cm-19x13in) s. (I.L 20500000)

GENTILINI, Franco (1909-1981) Italian-cont.
£10819 $19367   (9-Apr-91 F.R214/R) Natura morta con grappoli d'uva (35x59cm-14x23in)
           (I.L 24000000)
£14993 $29537   (30-Oct-90 F.R222/R) Giuditta (40x30cm-16x12in) s.d.69 (I.L 33000000)
£33769 $65849   (22-Oct-90 BR.M218/R) Cattedrale nera (60x90cm-24x35in) s.
           (I.L 75000000)
£36245 $63066   (26-Mar-91 F.M86/R) Il garage (110x75cm-43x30in) s.d.52 (I.L 80000000)
£1262 $2259   (9-Apr-91 F.R89/R) Figure in piazza (37x30cm-15x12in) s.d.45 mixed media
           (I.L 2800000)
£1367 $2324   (28-May-91 SY.MI28/R) Madre con bambino (32x23cm-13x9in) s. gouache
           (I.L 3000000)
£1590 $3133   (30-Oct-90 F.R82) Autoritratto (28x22cm-11x9in) s.d.1941 ink
           (I.L 3500000)
£4277 $8341   (22-Oct-90 BR.M326/R) Gatto (36x44cm-14x17in) s. wax oil board
           (I.L 9500000)

GENTZ, Ismael (1862-1914) German
£500 $895   (13-Mar-91 B34) An old man at his prayers (20x15cm-8x6in) s.d.Juli '86
           gouache

GEOFFROY, Henry Jules Jean (1853-1924) French
£2808 $5476   (12-Oct-90 APT.P9/R) Fillette a sa lecture (54x40cm-21x16in) s.l.d.16
           mai 1875 (F.FR 28000)
£3611 $7041   (12-Oct-90 APT.P15/R) Les jeunes ecoliers (25x35cm-10x14in) s.i.d.
           (F.FR 36000)
£4213 $8215   (12-Oct-90 APT.P12/R) Il a bouge (57x43cm-22x17in) s. panel (F.FR 42000)
£4359 $8500   (24-Oct-90 CH.NY97/R) Give me a bite (37x26cm-15x10in) s.d.1883
£5641 $11000   (24-Oct-90 CH.NY98/R) Sharing a meal (55x47cm-22x19in) s.
£9228 $17994   (12-Oct-90 APT.P11/R) Ressemblance non garantie (56x38cm-22x15in)
           s.d.1879 (F.FR 92000)
£14544 $28360   (12-Oct-90 APT.P8/R) La fessee (72x54cm-28x21in) s.d.1886 panel
           (F.FR 145000)

GEORGE, Ernest (1839-1922) British
£580 $1143   (1-Nov-90 C35/R) Piazza Cavalli, Piacenza (20x28cm-8x11in) s.i. pencil
           W/C board
£620 $1221   (1-Nov-90 C33/R) Entrance to Pazzi Chapel, Florence (43x30cm-17x12in)
           init.indis.i. i.verso pencil W/C
£750 $1478   (1-Nov-90 C37/R) Siena, washerwomen at work (36x25cm-14x10in) s.i.
           pencil W/C
£800 $1568   (22-Nov-90 CSK71) Castle of St. Angelo, Rome (29x41cm-11x16in) s.i.
           i.verso pencil W/C

GEORGE-JULLIARD, Jean Philippe (1818-1888) Swiss
£876 $1709   (24-Oct-90 GD.B403/R) Wetterhorn, evening (27cm-11ins circular) s.
           i.verso board (S.FR 2200)
£898 $1742   (8-Dec-90 GAB.G2201/R) Paysage de montagne (65x92cm-26x36in) s.
           (S.FR 2200)
£996 $1713   (14-May-91 GF.L2496/R) Lauterbrunnental with view of Jungfrau
           (46x65cm-18x26in) s. (S.FR 2500)
£1502 $2553   (30-May-91 EA.Z334) Scene on the Vierwaldstattersee with the Urirostock
           (33x46cm-13x18in) s. (S.FR 3800)
£5159 $8615   (5-Jun-91 SY.Z36/R) Le Karrenstock dans le Canton de Glaris
           (75x100cm-30x39in) s. (S.FR 13000)

GEORGES, Claude (1929-) French
£1506 $2425   (30-Jun-91 I.N126/R) Composition (92x73cm-36x29in) s.d.1958 (F.FR 15000)
£1631 $3148   (16-Dec-90 GL.P178) Abstraction (92x73cm-36x29in) s.d.1955 (F.FR 16000)
£2347 $4623   (16-Nov-90 FB.P330/R) Composition (92x72cm-36x28in) s.d.58 (F.FR 23000)
£4088 $6745   (10-Jul-91 FB.P60/R) Metal elliptique (161x129cm-63x51in) s.d.57
           (F.FR 41000)
£1850 $3589   (4-Dec-90 I.N63/R) Composition (38x45cm-15x18in) s. mixed media paper
           laid down on canvas (F.FR 18000)

GEORGES-MICHEL, Michel (1883-?) French
£1523 $3000   (15-Nov-90 SY.NY64/R) Still life (30x23cm-12x9in) s.d.1942 i.verso
           canvasboard

GEORGET, Jean (1763-1823) French
£1835 $3523   (30-Nov-90 APT.P125) Rivage anime de pecheurs. Scene de chasse a courre
           (19x30cm-7x12in) panel pair (F.FR 18000)

GEORGI, Friedrich Otto (1819-1874) German
£1316 $2500   (27-Feb-91 SY.NY140/R) Sandstorm at sphinx (62x85cm-24x33in) s.d.1867
£1429 $2471   (22-May-91 GS.B2380) Landscape with castle on rock and snowy mountain
           range beyond (97x82cm-38x32in) s.d.1866 (S.FR 3600)

GEORGIUS, R (19th C) ?
£6800 $11152   (19-Jun-91 S76/R) Sultan and concubine (151x170cm-59x67in) s.i. after
           Emile Jacobs

GERALIS, Apostolos (1886-?) Greek
£5594 $10797   (12-Dec-90 WE.MU117/R) The cheeky little dog (114x77cm-45x30in) s.
           (DM 16000)

GERARD, Baron Francois (1770-1837) French
£45317 $73867   (14-Jun-91 MB.P10/R) Portrait de Pulcherie de Montmorency, marquise de Mortemart (63x52cm-25x20in) (F.FR 450000)

GERARD, Baron Francois (style) (1770-1837) French
£5738 $11246   (7-Nov-90 APT.P441/R) Portrait de jeune femme (60x49cm-24x19in) (F.FR 56000)

GERARD, Marguerite (1761-1837) French
£2055 $3988   (7-Dec-90 SY.MO176/R) Cupidon dans un parc (21x15cm-8x6in) panel (F.FR 20000)
£100410 $196803   (7-Nov-90 APT.P440/R) La lecon du dessin (48x40cm-19x16in) s. board (F.FR 980000)

GERARD, Marguerite (circle) (1761-1837) French
£1538 $3000   (26-Oct-90 SY.NY108/R) Portrait of lady with turban (33x25cm-13x10in) panel

GERARD, Marguerite (style) (1761-1837) French
£3568 $6850   (30-Nov-90 APT.P151/R) Mere venant voir enfants (46x39cm-18x15in) (F.FR 35000)

GERARD, Pascal (20th C) French?
£815 $1566   (2-Dec-90 M.V48/R) Le promenade (54x61cm-21x24in) s. (F.FR 8000)
£853 $1579   (10-Mar-91 LT.P151) Promenade sur le front de mer (54x65cm-21x26in) s. (F.FR 8500)
£922 $1807   (11-Nov-90 ZZ.F271) Paris, la Place Vendome (65x54cm-26x21in) s. (F.FR 9000)
£1076 $2109   (11-Nov-90 ZZ.F159/R) Enfants sur la plage (54x65cm-21x26in) s. (F.FR 10500)
£1109 $2107   (1-Mar-91 CB.P157) Le port (50x61cm-20x24in) s. (F.FR 11000)

GERARD, Theodore (1829-1895) French
£714 $1200   (17-Jul-91 SY.NY280/R) Interior with nursing mother (29x22cm-11x9in) s. panel
£1325 $2544   (30-Nov-90 ARC.P144/R) La partie de cartes (35x66cm-14x26in) s. (F.FR 13000)
£2500 $4100   (19-Jun-91 S170/R) Nursing mother (32x23cm-13x9in) s.d.1867 panel
£4000 $7680   (28-Nov-90 S67/R) Friendly encounter (95x62cm-37x24in) s.d.1873
£4500 $8820   (15-Feb-91 C25/R) Keeping lookout (56x49cm-22x19in) s.d.60 panel
£7692 $15000   (23-Oct-90 SY.NY32/R) The country children (59x89cm-23x35in) s.i.d.1875 panel

GERASCH, August (1822-1894) Austrian
£678 $1092   (27-Jun-91 D.V59) High mountain landscape (15x20cm-6x8in) s. panel (A.S 14000)

GERBEAUD, Catalyn (?) ?
£629 $1188   (25-Sep-90 GM.B904) Chats sur le bureau (50x60cm-20x24in) s. panel (B.FR 38000)

GERE, Charles M (1869-1957) British
£460 $750   (2-Jul-91 SWS520) Evening in Umbria (35x39cm-14x15in) mono. W/C

GERE, Margaret (1878-1965) British
£850 $1649   (6-Dec-90 CSK196) Nativity (37x39cm-15x15in) s.
£3600 $7056   (7-Nov-90 S15/R) Jean Valjean at the bishop's table (31x51cm-12x20in) s.d.1907 W/C over pencil

GERELL, Greta (1898-1982) Swedish
£798 $1572   (13-Nov-90 AB.S378/R) Hay harvest, landscape with figures and horses (45x55cm-18x22in) s.d.38 (S.KR 8700)
£3396 $5875   (22-May-91 BA.S59/R) Girl wearing red jacket (41x35cm-16x14in) s. panel (S.KR 36000)
£2132 $4135   (4-Dec-90 BA.S157/R) Chinese girl with lantern (34x28cm-13x11in) s. gouache (S.KR 23000)

GERGELY, Imre (1868-1914) Hungarian
£650 $1274   (22-Nov-90 CSK270/R) On Amalfi coast (33x44cm-13x17in) s.

GERHARD, Adolf (1910-1975) German?
£1034 $1986   (26-Nov-90 WK.M641/R) City street (90x121cm-35x48in) s.d.1972 (DM 3000)

GERHARDI, Ida (1867-1927) German
£1706 $3345   (24-Nov-90 N.M177/R) Girl reading (47x47cm-19x19in) mono.d.1924 (DM 5000)

GERHARDINGER, Constantin (1888-1970) German
£514 $837   (12-Jun-91 N.M435/R) Portrait of Hilmar Binter, director of the Munich Marionettentheater (41x38cm-16x15in) s. (DM 1500)
£1843 $3023   (18-Jun-91 FN.S1851) Village street with trees and figures, evening, Lilienberg (29x35cm-11x14in) s.i. board (DM 5400)
£3754 $6157   (18-Jun-91 FN.S1850) Village street with gas lanterns and figures (48x66cm-19x26in) s.d.1914 (DM 11000)
£4362 $8507   (10-Oct-90 WE.MU309/R) Cyclamen (35x50cm-14x20in) s. (DM 13000)

GERICAULT, Theodore (1791-1824) French
£12000 $19560   (2-Jul-91 C168/R) Bacchus and Ariadne on leopard. Study of Chevaux de
                           Marly and landscape (26x21cm-10x8in) black chk pen wash double-sided
£308325 $598150   (8-Dec-90 SY.MO308/R) Le Colonel Bro a Saint Domingue (21x31cm-8x12in)
                           s. pen W/C (F.FR 3000000)

GERICAULT, Theodore (style) (1791-1824) French
£1272 $2200   (21-May-91 CE.NY1/R) Head of man (61x51cm-24x20in)

GERICKE, Willi and ZANK, Hans (20th C) German
£946 $1797   (14-Sep-90 SA.A1293/R) Summer's day at the Havel (60x68cm-24x27in) s.
                         (DM 2800)

GERINI, Niccolo di Pietro (attrib) (?-1415) Italian
£5179 $8908   (14-May-91 GF.L2243/R) St Paul (107x39cm-42x15in) panel (S.FR 13000)

GERINI, Niccolo di Pietro (studio) (?-1415) Italian
£50000 $96500   (12-Dec-90 S15/R) St. Peter and St. Benedict, Angel of the Annunciation
                         above (66x38cm-26x15in) tempera gold ground panel pointed top

GERLACH, Georg (1874-1962) German
£1703 $3338   (24-Jan-91 D.V6/R) Graben in Vienna decorated for victory parade
                         (32x24cm-13x9in) s.d.1915 board (A.S 35000)

GERMAIN, Jacques (1915-) French
£1314 $2563   (18-Oct-90 CB.P74/R) Composition (50x38cm-20x15in) s.d.1956 paper laid
                         down on canvas (F.FR 13000)
£1837 $3618   (16-Nov-90 FB.P324/R) Composition (73x53cm-29x21in) s. d.88 verso paper
                         laid down on canvas (F.FR 18000)
£1972 $3886   (1-Oct-90 CC.P157/R) Composition (33x41cm-13x16in) s.d.1955 (F.FR 20000)
£2584 $4368   (15-Apr-91 CC.P108/R) Composition (61x50cm-24x20in) s.d.1956
                         (F.FR 26000)
£2962 $4769   (30-Jun-91 I.N33/R) Composition (64x49cm-25x19in) s.d.1989 paper laid
                         down on canvas (F.FR 29500)
£3543 $6943   (22-Nov-90 ZZ.F35/R) Composition (61x54cm-24x21in) s.d.75 paper pasted
                         canvas (F.FR 35000)
£3571 $7036   (16-Nov-90 FB.P296/R) Composition (43x64cm-17x25in) s.d.56 (F.FR 35000)
£4689 $9050   (16-Dec-90 GL.P184/R) Composition (85x87cm-33x34in) s.d.1955
                         (F.FR 46000)
£6030 $10794   (15-Mar-91 FB.P61/R) Composition (73x92cm-29x36in) s.d.68 (F.FR 60000)
£7143 $14071   (14-Nov-90 CN.P91/R) Composition (71x50cm-28x20in) s. (F.FR 70000)
£9694 $19097   (15-Nov-90 I.N33/R) Composition (60x73cm-24x29in) s.d.1975 (F.FR 95000)

GERMAN SCHOOL (?)
£1000 $1730   (9-May-91 CSK169 a/R) Portrait of huntsman (110x80cm-43x31in)
£1010 $1747   (6-May-91 ZEL.L1658/R) Ducks on pond (25x41cm-10x16in) c.1900
                         (DM 3000)
£1027 $1675   (12-Jun-91 N.M301/R) Portrait of duchess standing by table holding habit
                         and view of monastery (90x105cm-35x41in) c.1700 (DM 3000)
£1123 $2009   (17-Mar-91 BU.M50) The feast at Emmaus (120x125cm-47x49in) (S.KR 12000)
£1233 $2207   (13-Mar-91 N.M395/R) Gregoriusmesse (60x69cm-24x27in) c.1500 panel
                         (DM 3600)
£1250 $2100   (28-Apr-91 HG.C53) Mountain landscape with man and cattle
                         (76x117cm-30x46in)
£1406 $2263   (27-Jun-91 APT.P83/R) Vierge a l'enfant entre deux anges musiciens
                         (34x25cm-13x10in) (F.FR 14000)
£1423 $2419   (27-May-91 GK.Z5020) Study of angel (57x31cm-22x12in) c.1500 panel
                         (S.FR 3600)
£1469 $2834   (12-Dec-90 N.M398/R) Crucifixion in mountainous landscape
                         (34x24cm-13x9in) c.1500 panel (DM 4200)
£1689 $2872   (27-May-91 L.K31/R) Nude women in bathhouse (28x22cm-11x9in) c.1600
                         (DM 5000)
£1850 $3016   (1-Jul-91 GL.P13) Paysage a la briqueterie (26x39cm-10x15in) c.1780
                         panel (F.FR 18500)
£1898 $3170   (8-Jun-91 FN.S772/R) Ceres and Proserpina in park landscape with
                         fountain (135x136cm-53x54in) c.1700 (DM 5600)
£2189 $3786   (6-May-91 ZEL.L1647/R) Portrait of elegant lady wearing velvet cap with
                         feather (77x63cm-30x25in) c.1800 canvas on panel (DM 6500)
£2872 $4882   (27-May-91 L.K32/R) Southern landscape with sepherd and flock and woman
                         riding donkey (81x114cm-32x45in) c.1700 (DM 8500)
£3083 $5982   (7-Dec-90 SY.MO93/R) La Transfiguration du Christ (58x39cm-23x15in) on
                         bronze c.1600 after Raphael (F.FR 30000)
£4200 $6846   (4-Jul-91 C588/R) Trompe l'oeil-feigned carvings, emblematic pictures
                         below. Portrait of M. Maier (24x47cm-9x19in) panel en grisaille verso
                         double-sided c.1617
£5068 $8615   (27-May-91 L.K257/R) View of Mainz Cathedral with figures
                         (30x42cm-12x17in) c.1800 panel (DM 15000)
£8566 $16619   (4-Dec-90 FN.S2165/R) Portrait of duke wearing armour and ermine cloak
                         (246x165cm-97x65in) c.1800 canvas laid down (DM 24500)
£13500 $22815   (17-Apr-91 S154/R) Town square with market (51x67cm-20x26in) c.1700
£1000 $1650   (11-Jul-91 S259/R) Family group of father, mother and five children
                         gathered at table (?x15cm-?x6in) min.c.1800 giltwood frame oval
£1000 $1730   (9-May-91 CSK21/R) Fork in road, town beyond (14x27cm-6x11in) i. pencil
                         W/C bodycol

GERMAN SCHOOL, 15th C

£2564	$5000	(11-Oct-90 SY.NY168/R) Christ as the Man of Sorrows (23x37cm-9x15in) gold ground panel
£4634	$8943	(12-Dec-90 BU.S139/R) On the road to Mount Calvary (50x58cm-20x23in) panel (S.KR 50000)
£7171	$12335	(14-May-91 GF.L2005/R) Crucifixion (47x33cm-19x13in) panel (S.FR 18000)
£10490	$20245	(10-Dec-90 L.K89/R) Christ standing before cross with Mary and apostles and view of landscape (39x26cm-15x10in) panel (DM 30000)
£6000	*$9780*	*(2-Jul-91 C173/R) Lamentation (18x14cm-7x6in) black chk pen wash*

GERMAN SCHOOL, 16th C

£1208	$2356	(13-Oct-90 KRA.D164/R) Mary with Christ Child (64x49cm-25x19in) panel (DM 3600)
£1500	$2445	(3-Jul-91 S168) Portrait of gentleman, wearing green embroidered tunic and hat (35x30cm-14x12in) panel
£1500	$2595	(20-May-91 SWS203) The Crucifixion (31x23cm-12x9in) copper
£2967	$5312	(8-Apr-91 ARC.P16/R) La Resurrection du Christ (108x41cm-43x16in) panel (F.FR 30000)
£3322	$6411	(10-Dec-90 L.K90/R) Pieta in mountainous landscape with town (64x45cm-25x18in) panel (DM 9500)
£3800	$6422	(16-Apr-91 PH135/R) Virgin and child with St. Anne seated before window (48x35cm-19x14in) i. panel
£4057	$8032	(30-Jan-91 APT.P240/R) Portrait de Sigismond 1er de Pologne (23x16cm-9x6in) panel (F.FR 40000)
£4103	$8000	(10-Oct-90 CH.NY19/R) Ecce Homo (127x114cm-50x45in)
£7059	$12000	(31-May-91 CH.NY250/R) The Entombment. The Resurrection (39x27cm-15x11in) panel pair
£10747	$19238	(14-Mar-91 D.V70/R) Portrait of noble lady holding carnation at the age of 30 (63x50cm-25x20in) i.d.1566 panel (A.S 220000)
£17000	$32810	(11-Dec-90 PH184/R) Virgin and Child enthroned before gold damask curtain (30x20cm-12x8in) panel
£160839	$310420	(10-Dec-90 L.K25/R) Still life of flowers in vase on stone ledge with dragonfly and fly (43x31cm-17x12in) panel (DM 460000)
£1600	*$3088*	*(11-Dec-90 C110/R) Joseph and Potiphar's wife (185cm-73ins circular) mono. ink wash round*
£4200	$6846	(2-Jul-91 C179/R) Two saints (21x17cm-8x7in) black chk pen wash

GERMAN SCHOOL, 17th C

£1163	$2000	(15-May-91 D.NY17) The three fates (76x94cm-30x37in) i.
£1450	$2509	(20-May-91 SWS211/R) The Holy family with the infant Saint John (20x26cm-8x10in) copper octagonal
£1884	$3372	(13-Mar-91 N.M399/R) Ecce Homo (130x96cm-51x38in) (DM 5500)
£1900	$3097	(2-Jul-91 PH233/R) Lamentation over the Dead Christ at the Foot of the Cross (51x94cm-20x37in) panel embellished with gold
£2191	$3769	(14-May-91 GF.L2030/R) Still life with fishes and fishing utensils (68x95cm-27x37in) (S.FR 5500)
£2600	$5122	(31-Oct-90 S211/R) Cleobis and Biton (56x48cm-22x19in)
£2945	$5124	(25-Mar-91 SY.F724) Conversione di S.Paolo. Assedio di una citta (20x30cm-8x12in) panel oval pair (I.L 6500000)
£3142	$5970	(14-Sep-90 SA.A1103/R) Municipal official writing with figures and view of town, Netherlands (55x47cm-22x19in) panel (DM 9300)
£3210	$6259	(10-Oct-90 APT.P458) Portrait d'homme barbu (92x74cm-36x29in) i. (F.FR 32000)
£3600	$6084	(19-Apr-91 C46/R) Portrait of a military Commander holding a marshal's baton (292x236cm-115x93in) i.d.1615
£8736	$15113	(8-May-91 FER.M264 d/R) El baile de un dia de mercado. Cruce de carros en el camino (25x39cm-10x15in) copper pair (S.P 1600000)
£14626	$23548	(26-Jun-91 KM.K1321/R) Portrait of lady aged 20 in black dress with white collar (69x59cm-27x23in) i.d.1630 (DM 43000)
£1263	*$2400*	*(9-Jan-91 CH.NY100/R) Gladiators fighting observed by mounted soldiers (15x20cm-6x8in) i. black chk pen wash htd white*

GERMAN SCHOOL, 17th/18th C

£1712	$2791	(12-Jun-91 N.M302/R) River landscape with guards before classical building near woods (36x59cm-14x23in) (DM 5000)

GERMAN SCHOOL, 18th C

£1031	$1959	(2-Mar-91 KRA.D255/R) Death of Lucretia (104x157cm-41x62in) (DM 3000)
£1063	$1796	(1-May-91 KH.K189/R) Romantic landscape with castle by river (65x82cm-26x32in) (D.KR 12000)
£1075	$1924	(14-Mar-91 D.V319/R) Conversation outside tavern (29x32cm-11x13in) panel (A.S 22000)
£1176	$2000	(31-May-91 CH.NY219/R) Portrait of girl said to be Anna Sophia Burckhard, aged 9, with nosegay (83x64cm-33x25in)
£1176	$2000	(30-May-91 CE.NY42) Lady seated at clavicord (91x70cm-36x28in) indis.i. i.stretcher
£1200	$2076	(20-May-91 SWS15/R) Portrait of a lady, half length, wearing a pink dress and red sash (76x64cm-30x25in) canvas laid donw on board
£1221	$2186	(14-Mar-91 D.V208/R) Still life of fruit (14x21cm-6x8in) (A.S 25000)
£1284	$2170	(3-May-91 SA.A1631/R) Portrait of a nobleman in armour (78x62cm-31x24in) (DM 3800)
£1300	$2405	(5-Mar-91 PH103/R) Elegant horsemen riding in river landscape beside ruined villa (131x105cm-52x41in)
£1349	$2253	(7-Jun-91 ZOF.Z1011/R) The Way to Emmaus (85x115cm-33x45in) indis.s. (S.FR 3400)

GERMAN SCHOOL, 18th C -cont.

£1500	$2445	(2-Jul-91 PH213) Portrait of young girl holding rose with parents and grandparents (40x52cm-16x20in) i.
£1575	$2820	(13-Mar-91 N.M400/R) Venus and Amor with attendants in landscape (110x153cm-43x60in) (DM 4600)
£1700	$2771	(2-Jul-91 PH169) Christ before Caiphas (43x81cm-17x32in) bears indis.sig.l.d.1542 panel
£1728	$3455	(4-Feb-91 LEB.P3/R) Paysage fluvial anime (27x38cm-11x15in) panel (F.FR 17000)
£1858	$3159	(27-May-91 L.K35/R) Portrait of lady with basket of flowers in landscape (84x65cm-33x26in) (DM 5500)
£2000	$3460	(20-May-91 SWS107) Still life of fruit and game (105x86cm-41x34in)
£2191	$3769	(14-May-91 GF.L2325/R) Village scene with figures, winter (21x28cm-8x11in) panel (S.FR 5500)
£2231	$4418	(30-Jan-91 APT.P93/R) Un lievre sur fond de paysage (61x78cm-24x31in) (F.FR 22000)
£2365	$4611	(26-Oct-90 BM.B731/R) Der Lauf der Zeit (60x77cm-24x30in) (DM 7000)
£2448	$4724	(10-Dec-90 L.K706) Christ and Mary (49x49cm-19x19in) (DM 7000)
£2467	$4785	(7-Dec-90 CB.P3) Le passage du gue (64x84cm-25x33in) (F.FR 24000)
£2508	$4890	(14-Oct-90 D.L87 a) Bouquets de fleurs (F.FR 25000)
£2600	$5070	(22-Oct-90 SWS1434/R) Stag hunt in winter landscape (36x49cm-14x19in) panel
£2800	$4564	(3-Jul-91 S152) Cavalry skirmish (18x19cm-7x7in) panel
£2911	$5211	(13-Mar-91 N.M400 a/R) Trompe l'oeil with dead birds, portrait, fruit and branch with birds (80x59cm-31x23in) one of pair (DM 8500)
£2911	$5211	(13-Mar-91 N.M400 b/R) Trompe l'oeil with portrait, dead birds, grapes on board and book (80x59cm-31x23in) one of pair (DM 8500)
£3000	$5910	(31-Oct-90 S159/R) Portrait of gentleman (70x54cm-28x21in) painted oval
£3183	$6271	(14-Nov-90 D.V286/R) Terrace by river in palace grounds (53x183cm-21x72in) (A.S 65000)
£3409	$5727	(24-Apr-91 BA.S235/R) Still life of fruit, lobster and wine (61x45cm-24x18in) (S.KR 36000)
£4000	$7720	(12-Dec-90 S197/R) Hawking party and other sportsmen in landscape (19x26cm-7x10in) copper
£4200	$8274	(31-Oct-90 S205/R) Cavalry battles (75x103cm-30x41in) pair
£4400	$7172	(3-Jul-91 S186/R) Capriccio view of Turin in winter, with cathedral of S.Giovanni Battista (16x21cm-6x8in) copper
£4500	$7785	(20-May-91 SWS140) A battle scene (120x160cm-47x63in)
£4933	$9570	(7-Dec-90 SY.MO155/R) Paysage Anthropomorphie (40x53cm-16x21in) panel (F.FR 48000)
£5000	$9750	(23-Oct-90 SWS493/R) Portrait of commander standing holding hat with battle scene beyond (143x104cm-56x41in)
£5051	$8737	(6-May-91 ZEL.L1644/R) Portrait of prince standing at table with pet dog and landscape beyond (135x84cm-53x33in) (DM 15000)
£5200	$10244	(31-Oct-90 S14/R) View of Dresden (41x76cm-16x30in)
£6000	$9780	(3-Jul-91 S146/R) Still lifes of fruit (37x28cm-15x11in) pair
£6500	$12805	(31-Oct-90 S124/R) The Temptation of Adam and Eve (124x100cm-49x39in)
£8042	$15601	(4-Dec-90 FN.S2155/R) Portrait of Duke wearing armour (210x168cm-83x66in) canvas laid down (DM 23000)
£11009	$21688	(14-Nov-90 SY.AM20/R) Capriccio views of sea and mountains with figures (40x54cm-16x21in) copper pair (D.FL 36000)
£14000	$22820	(3-Jul-91 S179/R) Still lifes of flowers with putti in landscapes (38x51cm-15x20in) pair
£28000	$54040	(12-Dec-90 S131/R) Mountainous river landscapes with buildings and cattle, and with horsemen (44x59cm-17x23in) i.verso copper pair
£822	*$1603*	*(12-Oct-90 AW.H1256/R) River landscape with shepherds near Pirna (15x23cm-6x9in) c.1780 gouache (DM 2450)*
£1421	*$2700*	*(9-Jan-91 CH.NY101/R) Trompe l'oeil with musical instruments, scores and map (21x32cm-8x13in) pen W/C*
£1900	*$3667*	*(11-Dec-90 C121/R) The boudoir of the Grafin Vitzhum in Priztitz (19x28cm-7x11in) i. verso blk.chk.ink W/C*
£2000	*$3860*	*(11-Dec-90 C122/R) A dance in the park (24x30cm-9x12in) s.d.1782,1785 ink W/C*
£2034	*$3600*	*(22-Mar-91 CH.NY632/R) Two youths and a young lady dancing in a garden with fountains (18x23cm-7x9in) i. bodycolour*
£2245	*$4422*	*(13-Nov-90 CH.G223/R) La lectrice pudique (5x7cm-2x3in) min. mounted on velvet gilt-wood frame (S.FR 5500)*
£5025	*$8241*	*(22-Jun-91 CH.MO45/R) Le lever de Venus (36x28cm-14x11in) gouache vellum (F.FR 50000)*
£7708	*$14954*	*(7-Dec-90 CN.P83/R) Vue d'une ideale (48x83cm-19x33in) pierre noire W/C (F.FR 75000)*

GERMAN SCHOOL, 19th C

£963	$1608	(6-Jun-91 D.V236/R) Christ on Mount of Olives (29x23cm-11x9in) panel (A.S 20000)
£979	$1890	(12-Dec-90 N.M491/R) Wooded rocky landscape with waterfall (45x49cm-18x19in) i.verso paper on board (DM 2800)
£988	$1680	(30-May-91 EA.Z304) The falconer (25x30cm-10x12in) board (S.FR 2500)
£1020	$1806	(20-Mar-91 KM.K1166) Coastal landscape with threemaster in choppy seas and figures (75x100cm-30x39in) (DM 3000)
£1024	$1679	(22-Jun-91 WK.M1368/R) Two girls by spring (24x30cm-9x12in) metal (DM 3000)
£1037	$1700	(19-Jun-91 B.SF1879/R) The music lesson (30x23cm-12x9in) bears sig. board
£1116	$1919	(14-May-91 GF.L2344/R) Still life with flowers, fruit, book and wine glass (50x40cm-20x16in) panel (S.FR 2800)

GERMAN SCHOOL, 19th C -cont.

£1200	$1968	(18-Jun-91 PH127) Weighing up the odds (71x91cm-28x36in)
£1224	$2167	(20-Mar-91 KM.K1149) Portrait of Caroline Freifrau von Schwentz zu Schweinb. (60x49cm-24x19in) (DM 3600)
£1300	$2535	(15-Jan-91 C90) German pointer with day's bag (93x70cm-37x28in) mono.d.1866
£1399	$2699	(12-Dec-90 N.M477) St Anna Selbdritt (48x35cm-19x14in) panel (DM 4000)
£1445	$2500	(21-May-91 CE.NY65/R) Nymph in forest with tambourine (51x34cm-20x13in) indist.s. d.64
£1500	$2460	(18-Jun-91 PH138) Portrait of young girl (68x60cm-27x24in)
£1500	$2685	(12-Apr-91 BM.B580/R) Figures in peasant interior (95x74cm-37x29in) indis.s. (DM 4500)
£1507	$2457	(13-Jun-91 RAS.V623/R) Interior with family at dinner table (36x45cm-14x18in) (D.KR 17000)
£1538	$2969	(12-Dec-90 N.M476) Rocky landscape with peasant girl standing in mountain stream (34x28cm-13x11in) (DM 4400)
£1596	$2601	(13-Jun-91 RAS.V624/R) Interior with mother and children playing with kittens (37x45cm-15x18in) (D.KR 18000)
£1712	$2791	(12-Jun-91 N.M402/R) Annunciation (47x31cm-19x12in) panel (DM 5000)
£1753	$3015	(14-May-91 GF.L2368/R) Noli me tangere (53x34cm-21x13in) panel (S.FR 4400)
£1823	$3098	(28-May-91 F.R126) Natura morta con lepre su sfondo di paesaggio (127x94cm-50x37in) (I.L 4000000)
£1842	$3500	(27-Feb-91 SY.NY146/R) Panoramic view of Rhine river (65x95cm-26x37in) indist.s.
£2055	$3349	(12-Jun-91 SY.MU33/R) Artist sketching (27x35cm-11x14in) panel (DM 6000)
£2600	$5018	(13-Dec-90 B71) Madonna and Child (44x35cm-17x14in) bears init. l.verso panel
£2667	$4773	(12-Apr-91 BM.B584/R) Coastal landscape with portrait of the ship Bolke (60x91cm-24x36in) indis.i.d.1880 (DM 8000)
£2752	$5284	(30-Nov-90 APT.P77/R) Le bain des nymphes (35x44cm-14x17in) on bronze (F.FR 27000)
£2797	$5399	(10-Dec-90 L.K414) Still life of flowers with roses, carnations and lilac (65x53cm-26x21in) (DM 8000)
£2800	$4592	(19-Jun-91 S74/R) Still life of roses (51x41cm-20x16in) indist.s.d.
£3010	$5087	(17-Apr-91 WE.MU253/R) Bourgeois interior scene (51x68cm-20x27in) (DM 9000)
£3425	$5582	(12-Jun-91 SY.MU19/R) View of the Ungenberg (33x46cm-13x18in) (DM 10000)
£4500	$8055	(12-Mar-91 PH35) Shipping in Mediterranean harbour (47x69cm-19x27in) bears sig.
£5000	$9800	(15-Feb-91 C45/R) Personification of music (117x173cm-46x68in) en grisaille
£5528	$9065	(21-Jun-91 SY.MO337/R) Etudiant a sa table de travail (57x71cm-22x28in) bears sig.d.1860 (F.FR 55000)
£6471	$11000	(31-May-91 CH.NY184/R) Triumphal return to the Temple of Athena in classical landscape (102x127cm-40x50in)
£6522	$11087	(27-May-91 GK.Z5021/R) Rhine landscape with view of Siebengebirge and Insel Nonnenwerth (183x98cm-72x39in) (S.FR 16500)
£22936	$45183	(13-Nov-90 AB.S1025/R) Winter landscape with figures on wooden bridge (100x137cm-39x54in) (S.KR 250000)
£1306	*$2573*	*(13-Nov-90 CH.G275/R) Portrait of Grand-Duke Charles of Baden (6x?cm-2x?in) min. gilt-metal mount oval (S.FR 3200)*
£14925	*$25970*	*(27-Mar-91 CN.P50/R) Vue de chateau de Willemshohe a Cassel. Vue de la Gerbe et de la fontaine de l'Hercule (61x83cm-24x33in) gouache pair (F.FR 150000)*

GERMAN SCHOOL, 19th/20th C

£2081	$4100	(12-Nov-90 SG.M522) Grain harvesting (58x61cm-23x24in) s.

GERMAN SCHOOL, 20th C

£1028	$1747	(30-May-91 EA.Z141) Das Massenlager (37x31cm-15x12in) s.d. board (S.FR 2600)
£1697	$3191	(20-Sep-90 D.V110/R) Landscape on the Jagst (63x70cm-25x28in) s. (A.S 35000)
£2184	$4040	(10-Mar-91 AG.W11) Reading (60x70cm-24x28in) (P.Z 39000000)

GERMAN Y LLORENTE, Bernardo (1680-1759) Spanish

£10926	$21087	(11-Dec-90 FER.M177/R) Nacimiento (107x158cm-42x62in) (S.P 2000000)

GERMAN-FLEMISH SCHOOL, 15th C

£5996	$10373	(21-May-91 DUR.M23/R) Virgen con nino (35x24cm-14x9in) panel (S.P 1100000)

GERNEZ, Paul Elie (1888-1948) French

£2460	$4551	(10-Mar-91 LT.P61/R) Apres les moissons (51x73cm-20x29in) s. (F.FR 24500)
£4625	$8972	(7-Dec-90 GL.P162) Voiliers au port (46x55cm-18x22in) s.d.1913 board laid down on panel (F.FR 45000)
£5617	$10953	(11-Oct-90 QWA.P36/R) Nature morte (46x55cm-18x22in) s. (F.FR 56000)
£7500	$12075	(24-Jun-91 CSK40/R) Le jardin d'Eden (89x115cm-35x45in) s.
£9265	$15102	(16-Jun-91 GL.P84/R) Le Port de Honfleur (54x81cm-21x32in) s. wood (F.FR 92000)
£9567	$15594	(16-Jun-91 GL.P82/R) Paysage (80x64cm-31x25in) s.d.1918 board (F.FR 95000)

GERNEZ, Paul Elie (1888-1948) French-cont.

£765	$1476	(16-Dec-90 T.B34/R) Nu de dos (30x39cm-12x15in) s.d.25 W/C (F.FR 7500)
£1807	$2910	(28-Jun-91 ARC.P32/R) Sallenelles (29x48cm-11x19in) d.25-10-34 W/C (F.FR 18000)
£2400	$4008	(7-Jun-91 LD.P12/R) La brune endormie (47x72cm-19x28in) s. pastel (F.FR 24000)
£3494	$6779	(7-Dec-90 GL.P132/R) Deauville, la plage (29x55cm-11x22in) s. W/C (F.FR 34000)
£3514	$5658	(28-Jun-91 ARC.P30/R) Honfleur (35x53cm-14x21in) s. W/C (F.FR 35000)
£4980	$8466	(29-May-91 GL.P49/R) Les falaises de la Roque (48x71cm-19x28in) s.d.25 pastel (F.FR 50000)

GEROME, Francois (20th C) French?

£609	$1200	(7-Oct-90 DU.E131/R) Le Madelene, Paris (61x76cm-24x30in) s.
£2449	$4653	(14-Sep-90 ZOF.Z845/R) Sunday coach trip on the Champs-Elysees (58x70cm-23x28in) s.i. (S.FR 6000)

GEROME, Jean Leon (1824-1904) French

£3205	$6250	(26-Oct-90 SY.NY17/R) Portrait of man (17x11cm-7x4in) board
£13295	$23000	(22-May-91 SY.NY132/R) Une fontaine a Rome (37x35cm-15x14in) s.d.1852
£14451	$25000	(22-May-91 SY.NY166/R) Personnage - Louis XIII (33x24cm-13x9in) s.
£30000	$57600	(30-Nov-90 C67/R) The Iliad. The Odyssey (98x78cm-39x31in) both i. pair
£46243	$80000	(22-May-91 SY.NY86/R) Madeleine Juliette Gerome et ses poupees (85x64cm-33x25in)
£54913	$95000	(23-May-91 CH.NY44/R) The grand white eunuch (61x51cm-24x20in) s.
£69231	$135000	(23-Oct-90 SY.NY44/R) Dispute d'arabes (30x23cm-12x9in) s. panel
£92486	$160000	(23-May-91 CH.NY18/R) Venus rising, the star (129x79cm-51x31in) s.
£184615	$360000	(23-Oct-90 SY.NY47/R) Bashi-Bazouk and his dog (36x25cm-14x10in) s. panel
£420	$710	(16-Apr-91 C71) A seated nude seen from behind (36x23cm-14x9in) red chk.
£703	$1300	(6-Mar-91 APT.P15) La lumiere (56x33cm-22x13in) s.i. lead pencil htd.gouache (F.FR 7000)
£1505	$2934	(12-Oct-90 APT.P84/R) Etude de femme antique (64x34cm-25x13in) s.i. lead pencil drawing (F.FR 15000)
£5780	$10000	(22-May-91 SY.NY130/R) Bashi-bazouk dancing - Pyrrhic dance (36x23cm-14x9in) s. pencil

GEROME, Jean Leon (attrib) (1824-1904) French

£612	$1200	(27-Jan-91 LIT.L9) Bearded penitent (58x33cm-23x13in) s.
£1351	$2635	(26-Oct-90 KM.K1227) Oriental scene with figures and view through town gate to hill (82x61cm-32x24in) mono. (DM 4000)

GERRITSEN, G (20th C) ?

£959	$1716	(13-Mar-91 N.M501) Bunch of asters in vase (95x72cm-37x28in) s.d.1929 (DM 2800)

GERRY, Samuel Lancaster (1813-1891) American

£1098	$1900	(22-May-91 CH.NY70/R) Mount Desert Island, Maine (48x28cm-19x11in) s.

GERSON, Wojciech (1831-1901) Polish

£3756	$6724	(17-Mar-91 UNI.W2) Head of a young man (40x35cm-16x14in) s.d.1889 (P.Z 66000000)

GERSTMEYER, Joseph (1801-1870) Austrian

£577	$1125	(25-Oct-90 D.V124/R) In the monastery (39x54cm-15x21in) s. (A.S 12000)
£854	$1529	(11-Apr-91 D.V259/R) Courtyard of monastery at night (55x68cm-22x27in) s. (A.S 18000)

GERTLER, Mark (1892-1939) British

£4400	$7348	(6-Jun-91 C99/R) Nice (32x40cm-13x16in) s.d.23 s.i.verso panel
£6000	$11700	(10-Oct-90 S130/R) The mandolin player (43x41cm-17x16in)
£21000	$41160	(7-Nov-90 S103/R) Still life with benin head (74x94cm-29x37in) s.d.37
£2200	$4290	(10-Oct-90 S62/R) Female nudes (99x99cm-39x39in) one s.d.27 one s.d.37 chk two

GERVAIS, Lise (1933-) Canadian

£1067	$2069	(3-Dec-90 R.T252/R) Onde de corail (73x91cm-29x36in) s.d.59 (C.D 2400)
£1244	$2414	(3-Dec-90 R.T251/R) La soudure des chats (91x92cm-36x36in) s.i.d.69 stretcher (C.D 2800)
£1675	$2798	(3-Jun-91 R.T204/R) Le soleil encercle (101x101cm-40x40in) s.d.64 (C.D 3200)
£1754	$3456	(30-Oct-90 SY.T24/R) Les jeux scolaires (102x76cm-40x30in) s.d.64 i.verso (C.D 4000)
£2273	$3932	(6-May-91 SY.T194/R) Les caves de Clyford (152x152cm-60x60in) s. acrylic canvas (C.D 4500)

GERVEX, Henri (1852-1929) French

£1172	$2251	(2-Dec-90 M.V104) Portrait de femme (24x19cm-9x7in) s. (F.FR 11500)
£1429	$2400	(17-Jul-91 SY.NY234/R) Pret a Partir (58x46cm-23x18in) s.
£2649	$4741	(13-Apr-91 FAL.M82/R) Portrait of woman (46x38cm-18x15in) s.d.1877 (S.KR 28500)
£2857	$5629	(14-Nov-90 FB.P123/R) Esquisse pour le plafond du restaurant le train bleu (62cm-24ins circular) s. panel round (F.FR 28000)

GERVEX, Henri and STEVENS, Alfred (20th C) Austrian
£11735 $23117   (14-Nov-90 FB.P125/R) Le panorama du siecle (196x251cm-77x99in) s. both
                  artists (F.FR 115000)

GERZSO, Gunther (1915-) Mexican
£1913 $3750   (19-Nov-90 SY.NY184/R) Paisaje (27x29cm-11x11in) s.d.69 acrylic paper
£2041 $4000   (12-Feb-91 SY.NY280/R) F Variacion 12 a (41x36cm-16x14in) s.d.70 acrylic
                  paper
£2551 $5000   (19-Nov-90 SY.NY183/R) Naranja-Azul-Rojo-Verde (26x47cm-10x19in) s.d.73
                  acrylic paper
£8719 $17090   (19-Nov-90 SY.NY182/R) Azul-Amarillo-Blanco (43x46cm-17x18in) s.d.69
                  masonite
£13265 $26000   (20-Nov-90 CH.NY69/R) Naranja-azul-blanco (63x63cm-25x25in) s.d.71
                  s.i.d.IX.71 verso masonite
£18605 $32000   (15-May-91 CH.NY101/R) Paisaje Verde y Azul (37x55cm-15x22in) s.d.65 i.
                  verso masonite
£20349 $35000   (15-May-91 CH.NY85/R) Personaje-Agua (38x48cm-15x19in) s.d.47 i. verso
                  masonite
£22093 $38000   (15-May-91 CH.NY47/R) Paisaje de Chiapas (58x110cm-23x43in) s.d.IX-77 i.
                  verso oil sand

GESELSCHAP, Eduard (1814-1878) Dutch
£3860 $7604   (14-Nov-90 RAS.K157/R) Interior with mother and child (60x46cm-24x18in)
                  s.d.1864 (D.KR 43000)
£5405 $10270   (14-Sep-90 SA.A1271/R) The unwelcome bath (20x15cm-8x6in) s. panel
                  (DM 16000)

GESSI, Francesco (1588-1649) Italian
£13720 $22500   (19-Jun-91 B.SF1683/R) Allegory of Charity (79x99cm-31x39in)

GESSNER, Conrad (1764-1826) Swiss
£683 $1338   (24-Nov-90 SA.A606/R) Mountainous river landscape, evening
                  (48x63cm-19x25in) indis.s. i.stretcher canvas laid down (DM 2000)
£3974 $7750   (24-Oct-90 D.NY63/R) Full cry (102x145cm-40x57in) s.d.1797
£4418 $8659   (21-Nov-90 SY.Z15/R) Rider in stormy night (29x41cm-11x16in)
                  (S.FR 11000)
£15261 $29912   (21-Nov-90 SY.Z16/R) Horses and cows watering (83x100cm-33x39in)
                  (S.FR 38000)

GESSNER, Richard (1894-1988) German
£676 $1318   (26-Oct-90 KM.K1231) View of industrial area with chimneys, towers and
                  gas container (63x92cm-25x36in) s.i. canvas on board (DM 2000)
£1190 $1917   (26-Jun-91 KM.K1471/R) View of south German town, possibly Dachau
                  (98x92cm-39x36in) s. (DM 3500)

GESSNER, Robert S (1908-) Swiss
*£2131 $4028   (28-Sep-90 S.Z151) Untitled (28x45cm-11x18in) s.d.47 mixed media
                  (S.FR 5200)*

GESSNER, Salomon (1730-1788) Swiss
*£10317 $17230   (5-Jun-91 SY.Z18/R) Arcadian landscape (28x40cm-11x16in) s.d.1785
                  gouache (S.FR 26000)*

GESTEL, Fik van (20th C) Belgian
£1972 $3846   (23-Oct-90 C.A969/R) Culto-stock (200x245cm-79x96in) s. acrylic
                  (B.FR 120000)

GESTEL, Leo (1881-1941) Dutch
£743 $1434   (12-Dec-90 CH.AM11) Peasant and horse (22x30cm-9x12in) with i.verso
                  paper (D.FL 2400)
£7508 $12988   (22-May-91 CH.AM489/R) Roses (47x28cm-19x11in) s.d.04 (D.FL 25000)
£35604 $68715   (12-Dec-90 CH.AM293/R) Mallorca (55x69cm-22x27in) s.i.d.1914
                  (D.FL 115000)
£61920 $119505 (12-Dec-90 CH.AM298/R) Gitana (120x104cm-47x41in) s.i. (D.FL 200000)
£71207 $137430 (12-Dec-90 CH.AM297/R) Still life of flowers in vase, Colenbrander vase
                  and fruit bol on draped table (91x64cm-36x25in) s.d.12 (D.FL 230000)
*£511 $883   (22-May-91 CH.AM366) Cows in landscape (28x36cm-11x14in) s.d.39 pastel
                  (D.FL 1700)*
£610 $1171   (27-Nov-90 SY.AM3837) Begonia (63x52cm-25x20in) s.d.16 chk (D.FL 2000)
*£1198 $2275   (11-Sep-90 CH.AM436 a) Reclining nude under the moon (61x45cm-24x18in)
                  s.d.31 pastel (D.FL 4000)*
*£1201 $2078   (22-May-91 CH.AM346) View of flemish river landscape (50x60cm-20x24in)
                  s.i. pastel (D.FL 4000)*
*£2043 $3944   (13-Dec-90 SY.AM1/R) Woman and horse (49x58cm-19x23in) studio st.
                  gouache (D.FL 6600)*
*£4204 $7273   (22-May-91 CH.AM485/R) Seated Gitana (57x47cm-22x19in) s.i. pastel
                  (D.FL 14000)*

GETTE, Paul Armand (1927-) French
*£1011 $1972   (15-Oct-90 CSC.P87 b/R) Sans titre (92x60cm-36x24in) s.d.1961 wood panel
                  (F.FR 10000)*

GEVEL, Jan van der (19/20th C) Dutch
£548 $981   (12-Mar-91 FN.S2375) Shepherd couple and sheep on path in hilly wooded
                  landscape (60x82cm-24x32in) s. board (DM 1600)

GEYER, Alexius (1816-1883) German
£5179 $8908   (14-May-91 GF.L2086/R) Turkish Churchyard near Rome (57x94cm-22x37in) s. (S.FR 13000)

GEYER, Georg (1823-1912) Austrian
£580 $1091   (19-Sep-90 N.M799) *Fruit market in Bulak near Cairo (33x46cm-13x18in) s.d.872 i.verso W/C (DM 1700)*
£683 $1283   (19-Sep-90 N.M797/R) *Lake landscape, possibly Zurich See (32x44cm-13x17in) s.d.872 i.verso W/C (DM 2000)*

GEYLING, Carl (attrib) (1814-1880) Austrian
£949 $1699   (11-Apr-91 D.V104/R) Salzkammergut landscape (48x62cm-19x24in) (A.S 20000)

GEYP, Adriaan Marinus (1855-1926) Dutch
£1051 $2050   (20-Oct-90 CH.AM152/R) Peasant woman walking in forest with church beyond, autumn (65x95cm-26x37in) s. (D.FL 3500)
£1737 $2917   (23-Apr-91 SY.AM116) Cows in polder landscape (68x91cm-27x36in) s. (D.FL 5800)

GHEDUZZI, Cesare (1894-1944) Italian
£6007 $11594   (11-Dec-90 CH.R228) Veduta di Genova (61x90cm-24x35in) s. panel (I.L 13000000)

GHEDUZZI, Giuseppe (1889-1957) Italian
£1637 $3208   (21-Nov-90 F.M61) Paesaggio della Val d'Aosta (50x65cm-20x26in) s. panel (I.L 3600000)
£2500 $4901   (21-Nov-90 F.M135/R) Mietitura dei campi (40x70cm-16x28in) s. panel (I.L 5500000)
£3182 $6237   (21-Nov-90 F.M102/R) Laboratorio di calzoleria (32x44cm-13x17in) s. panel (I.L 7000000)

GHEE, Robert Edgar Taylor (1872-1951) Australian
£541 $1065   (13-Nov-90 J.M332) Captain Cook's cottage (24x29cm-9x11in) s. board (A.D 1400)
£786 $1407   (9-Apr-91 CH.ME301) Princes Bridge, Melbourne (24x37cm-9x15in) s. board (A.D 1800)
£1116 $1875   (22-Apr-91 SY.ME38) Evening, Melbourne (26x16cm-10x6in) s. canvasboard (A.D 2400)
£1810 $3059   (16-Apr-91 J.M145) The Prospectors Tent (23x29cm-9x11in) s. board (A.D 4000)

GHEERAERTS, Marcus (younger) (1561-1636) British
£18000 $35460   (16-Nov-90 C3/R) Portrait of Charles Hoskins aged 26 in doublet with ruff and cloak (65x52cm-26x20in) i.d.1629 i.verso painted oval panel

GHEERAERTS, Marcus (younger-attrib) (1561-1636) British
£2200 $3630   (10-Jul-91 S96/R) Portrait of John Graves of Beamsley seated (90x68cm-35x27in) i. panel
£3908 $6996   (14-Mar-91 D.V87/R) Portrait of noble lady as Magdalen (67x48cm-26x19in) i.d.1545 panel (A.S 80000)

GHEERAERTS, Marcus (younger-circle) (1561-1636) British
£4469 $8000   (11-Apr-91 SY.NY161/R) Double portrait of man and woman (90x109cm-35x43in)

GHEERAERTS, Marcus (younger-studio) (1561-1636) British
£11000 $18150   (10-Jul-91 S10/R) Portrait of Robert Devereux wearing Garter Robes (75x62cm-30x24in) bears i. panel

GHELARDINI, Albert (20th C) French?
£502 $808   (24-Jun-91 PR.P143) Le village de Cucuron au printemps (46x55cm-18x22in) s. (F.FR 5000)

GHELLIN, von (19th C) ?
£915 $1793   (6-Nov-90 SY.AM123/R) Merry company with horse-sledge on ice (54x73cm-21x29in) s. (D.FL 3000)

GHERARDI, Filippo and COLI, Giovanni (17th C) Italian
£7047 $12191   (21-May-91 SY.MI1057/R) La visione di un santo (285x237cm-112x93in) i.verso (I.L 15500000)

GHERARDI, Giuseppe (19th C) Italian
£453 $788   (25-Mar-91 SY.F749) Veduta di Fiesole (28x44cm-11x17in) s. pencil (I.L 1000000)

GHERARDINI, Giovanni (1654-1725) Italian
£4598 $8000   (27-Mar-91 B.SF4031/R) View of boatyard on estuary at sunrise with bathing figures (84x136cm-33x54in) s.

GHESQUIERRE, Napoleon Francois (1812-1862) Belgian
£3030 $5091   (24-Apr-91 BA.S72/R) Idyllic family scene (48x59cm-19x23in) s.d.1859 panel (S.KR 32000)

GHEYN, Jacob de (younger) (1565-1629) Dutch
£3000 $4890   (2-Jul-91 C206/R) Diablerie - witch and corpses of humans and horse in
                souterrain (9x13cm-4x5in) pen
£13761 $27110 (12-Nov-90 CH.AM69/R) Mars - warrior holding lance sitting on drum
                (15x12cm-6x5in) pen (D.FL 45000)
£30581 $60245 (12-Nov-90 CH.AM68/R) V polver neerstampt - soldier ramming powder and
                bullet into barrel (26x19cm-10x7in) num.27 pen wash (D.FL 100000)
£39000 $63570 (1-Jul-91 S58/R) Fisherman's wife (12x17cm-5x7in) pen wash

GHEZZI, Pier Leone (1674-1755) Italian
£16410 $32000 (10-Oct-90 CH.NY65/R) Portrait of Pope Clement XI seated wearing papal
                robes holding letter (19x80cm-7x31in) s.i.
£89474 $170000 (11-Jan-91 CH.NY23/R) Portrait of young lady seated holding kitten
                (72x59cm-28x23in)
£789 $1500   (8-Jan-91 SY.NY164/R) Male robed figure in a landscape (26x14cm-10x6in)
                ink over blk.chk.
£1019 $1967   (14-Dec-90 LEB.P127/R) Caricature d'un abbe (31x20cm-12x8in) i. verso
                pen (F.FR 10000)
£2200 $3586   (2-Jul-91 C117/R) Principe d'Avellino with Don Ciccio (32x22cm-13x9in)
                i. black chk pen
£3600 $5868   (2-Jul-91 C291/R) Surrender of Messina to Spanish in 1680 - design for
                fanmount (15x50cm-6x20in) with i. black chk pen wash shaped

GHIDONI, Matteo see PITOCCHI, Matteo de

GHIGLIA, Oscar (1876-1945) Italian
£1231 $2056   (6-Jun-91 F.M232/R) Fiore (26x18cm-10x7in) i.verso (I.L 2700000)

GHIGLIA, Paulo (20th C) Italian
£727 $1432   (29-Oct-90 SY.F485/R) Ritratto di Aldo Fabrizi (99x70cm-39x28in) s.
                (I.L 1600000)

GHIGLIA, Valentino (1903-1960) Italian
£818 $1604   (21-Nov-90 F.M48) Natura morta con cacclagione e vischio
                (70x50cm-28x20in) s. board (I.L 1800000)
£1182 $2317   (21-Nov-90 F.M114/R) Stella di natale (70x50cm-28x20in) s. board
                (I.L 2600000)

GHIGLION-GREEN, Maurice (1913-) ?
£590 $962   (5-Jul-91 APT.P127) Le gardien de square au vert galant
                (38x46cm-15x18in) s. (F.FR 5900)
£714 $1400   (12-Feb-91 SY.NY131/R) Paysage de Haute-Provence au chasseur
                (51x61cm-20x24in) s. s.i.stretcher
£923 $1800   (10-Oct-90 SY.NY77/R) Fleurs des champs (33x46cm-13x18in) s.

GHIKA, Nicolas (1906-) French
£7500 $12075 (24-Jun-91 CSK137/R) The bathers (30x35cm-12x14in) s.d.46 canvas board
£19000 $30590 (24-Jun-91 CSK136/R) Approaching moonlit port (63x76cm-25x30in) s.d.67
                s.i.d.verso
£25000 $48500 (4-Dec-90 C360/R) Wandering moon over streets of Hydra (60x40cm-24x16in)
                s.d.56 board
£720 $1159   (24-Jun-91 CSK135) Landscape (47x44cm-19x17in) s.i. brush ink

GHIRARDINI, Stefano (1696-1756) Italian
£30000 $48900 (3-Jul-91 S7/R) Peasants dancing and making music in landscape
                (82x111cm-32x44in)

GHIRLANDAIO, Domenico (style) (1449-1494) Italian
£7895 $15000 (10-Jan-91 SY.NY3/R) St. Martin dividing cloak. Tobias and angel
                (13x26cm-5x10in) panel pair

GHIRLANDAIO, Michele di Ridolfo del see TOSINI, Michele

GHIRLANDAIO, Ridolfo (style) (1483-1561) Italian
£3571 $6000   (17-Jul-91 SY.NY59/R) Holy Family with infant Saint John the Baptist and
                male Saint (83x70cm-33x28in) panel

GHISLANDI, Vittore (1655-1743) Italian
£23000 $37490 (5-Jul-91 C208/R) Portrait of young gentleman, wearing breastplate over
                doublet, hand on hip (100x86cm-39x34in) painted oval
£2931 $5247   (14-Mar-91 D.V147/R) Portrait of young man with baret (43x33cm-17x13in)
                pastel (A.S 60000)

GHISLANDI, Vittore (circle) (1655-1743) Italian
£1856 $3323   (14-Mar-91 D.V148/R) Portrait of noble man (81x63cm-32x25in)
                (A.S 38000)
£2179 $4250   (11-Oct-90 SY.NY182/R) Portrait of gentleman (70x52cm-28x20in)

GHISLANDI, Vittore (school) (1655-1743) Italian
£4794 $8054   (23-Apr-91 F.R44/R) Ritratto del pittore Gilardi e del musicista
                Marcantonio Bernardi (77x60cm-30x24in) (I.L 10500000)

GHISOLFI, Giovanni (1632-1683) Italian
£3864 $7574   (19-Nov-90 CH.R114/R) Architettura con scena classica (73x59cm-29x23in)
                (I.L 8500000)

GHISOLFI, Giovanni (1632-1683) Italian-cont.
£11173 $20000   (11-Apr-91 SY.NY36/R) Artemesia toasting statue of her dead husband
           Mausolus with wine mixed with his ashes (80x106cm-31x42in) mono.
£14837 $26558   (9-Apr-91 APT.P5/R) Paysage avec le Campo Vaccino (96x129cm-38x51in)
           (F.FR 150000)

GHISOLFI, Giovanni (circle) (1632-1683) Italian
£16000 $30400   (1-Mar-91 C174/R) Capricci of classical ruins, water carriers,
           philosophers and noblemen (99x74cm-39x29in) pair

GHISOLFI, Giovanni (style) (1632-1683) Italian
£1800 $2934   (4-Jul-91 C744/R) Capriccio of Roman ruins with beggar and philosopher
           (71x58cm-28x23in)
£2200 $3718   (18-Apr-91 C72) Christ and the Centurion (36x59cm-14x23in)

GHITI, Pompeo (1631-1703) Italian
£750 $1223   (1-Jul-91 S87/R) Design for pendentive with bishop and two putti
           (18x16cm-7x6in) pen htd white

GIACOMETTI, Alberto (1901-1966) Swiss
£1815 $3538   (25-Oct-90 CB.P51/R) Composition (24x17cm-9x7in) s.d.1935 ink
           (F.FR 18000)
£3789 $6251   (10-Jul-91 FB.P8/R) Personnages (51x38cm-20x15in) s.i.d.1951 lead pencil
           (F.FR 38000)
£4000 $7800   (17-Oct-90 S187/R) Vase de fleurs (30x21cm-12x8in) s.d.1952 pen ink
£8122 $16000   (14-Nov-90 SY.NY145/R) Projet pour Jean-Michel Frank (25x18cm-10x7in)
           s.i. gouache pencil
£8868 $15342   (21-May-91 WK.M36/R) Fauteuil. Armchair (31x23cm-12x9in) s.d.1943 pencil
           board double-sided (DM 26250)
£9016 $16139   (9-Apr-91 F.R99/R) Figura femminile (50x32cm-20x13in) s.d.1924 pencil
           (I.L 20000000)
£9249 $16000   (9-May-91 CH.NY138/R) Paysage (23x29cm-9x11in) s.d.1919 W/C over pencil
           paper laid on board
£9628 $15789   (19-Jun-91 F.M59/R) Ritratto di Mosieur A Rosenbaum (21x25cm-8x10in)
           s.i.d.1963 ink (I.L 21000000)
£10946 $18936   (21-May-91 WK.M37/R) Arbre a Stampa (50x32cm-20x13in) s.d.1951 board
           pencil (DM 32400)
£11561 $20000   (9-May-91 CH.NY139/R) Etude de sculpture. Tete de femme
           (50x32cm-20x13in) s. pencil double-sided
£13959 $27500   (14-Nov-90 SY.NY178/R) Trois tetes. Portrait de la mere del'artiste
           (20x17cm-8x7in) s. pencil double-sided
£14286 $23429   (21-Jun-91 GK.B37/R) Bouquet des fleurs et journal sur une table de
           l'atelier a Stampa (36x24cm-14x9in) s.i.d.1956 ink pen (S.FR 36000)
£20305 $40000   (14-Nov-90 SY.NY179/R) Tete de femme (47x30cm-19x12in) s.d.1947 pencil
£22222 $36444   (21-Jun-91 GK.B38/R) Nature morte avec trois verres (32x25cm-13x10in)
           s.d.1962 pencil (S.FR 56000)
£22843 $45000   (15-Nov-90 CH.NY188/R) Tete d'homme (50x32cm-20x13in) s.d.1963 ball
           point pen
£27000 $43470   (26-Jun-91 S265/R) Bustes dans l'atelier (50x32cm-20x13in) s.d.1959
           pencil paper on card

GIACOMETTI, Augusto (1877-1947) Swiss
£3265 $6433   (16-Nov-90 GK.Z5359) Bergellerin (35x28cm-14x11in) s. chl (S.FR 8000)
£10516 $17246   (19-Jun-91 GK.B424/R) Roses (20x24cm-8x9in) mono. s.i.d.1935verso
           (S.FR 26500)
£13889 $23194   (5-Jun-91 SY.Z78/R) Abstract (25x32cm-10x13in) pastel (S.FR 35000)
£2778 $4639   (5-Jun-91 SY.Z72/R) Abstract studies pastel four (S.FR 7000)
£2778 $4639   (5-Jun-91 SY.Z71/R) Abstract studies pastel set of three (S.FR 7000)
£3213 $6297   (21-Nov-90 SY.Z60/R) Design for the magician (43x32cm-17x13in)
           mono.d.1925 chl chk (S.FR 8000)
£4762 $7952   (5-Jun-91 SY.Z73/R) Abstract studies pastel three (S.FR 12000)
£6349 $10603   (5-Jun-91 SY.Z75/R) Abstract studies pastel four (S.FR 16000)
£6746 $11266   (5-Jun-91 SY.Z74/R) Abstract studies one i. pastel four (S.FR 17000)
£7540 $12591   (5-Jun-91 SY.Z76/R) Abstract studies pastel three (S.FR 19000)

GIACOMETTI, Giovanni (1868-1934) Swiss
£21429 $37071   (22-May-91 GS.B2099/R) Winter landscape near Maloja with peasant
           (41x44cm-16x17in) mono. s.i.d.1924verso board (S.FR 54000)
£49407 $83992   (27-May-91 GK.Z5332/R) The red house in Stampa (73x65cm-29x26in)
           mono.s.i.verso (S.FR 125000)
£65217 $110870   (27-May-91 GK.Z5331/R) Montaccio (90x141cm-35x56in) s.d.1894
           (S.FR 165000)
£70000 $135800   (3-Dec-90 C7/R) Giovane Madre (65x56cm-26x22in) init.d.1910
           init.stretcher i.verso
£83333 $136667   (21-Jun-91 GK.B42/R) View of Albignatal in Bergell with waterfall seen
           from Septimerpass (93x135cm-37x53in) mono. s.i.d.1932-3verso
           (S.FR 210000)
£7738 $12690   (19-Jun-91 GK.B425/R) Stables in Capolago near Maloja, winter
           (23x29cm-9x11in) mono. W/C over chl (S.FR 19500)
£8163 $16082   (16-Nov-90 GK.Z5360/R) Toeletta della Sera II (19x18cm-7x7in) s. indian
           ink pen over pencil (S.FR 20000)

GIACOMOTTI, Felix Henri (1828-1909) French
£1383 $2600   (18-Sep-90 RO.BA16) I primi fiori (37x27cm-15x11in) s. panel
£4624 $8000   (23-May-91 CH.NY25/R) The courtship (72x46cm-28x18in) s. pair

GIALLINA, Angelos (1857-?) Greek
£850 $1471   *(9-May-91 CSK24/R) Citadel, Corfu (15x31cm-6x12in) s. pencil W/C*
£1200 $2340   *(24-Oct-90 S162/R) Toldeo from the Tajo, Spain (19x44cm-7x17in) s. W/C*
£1700 $3315   *(24-Oct-90 S158) A fisherman off the coast. Fishing boats at sea*
                      (43x19cm-17x7in) both s. W/C traces pencil pair
£1858 $3159   *(27-May-91 L.K196) Southern park landscape (71x39cm-28x15in) s. W/C*
                      (DM 5500)
£2200 $4290   *(24-Oct-90 S169/R) Coastal view, Corfu (38x73cm-15x29in) s.d.86 W/C*
£3000 $5160   *(17-May-91 C218/R) View from village of Peleca, Corfu (40x74cm-16x29in)*
                      s. pencil W/C paper on board
£4500 $7740   *(17-May-91 C223/R) Pondikonisi and Vlakherne off Kanoni. View of Corfu*
                      town (27x44cm-11x17in) s.d.93 i.mount W/C pair

GIALLINA, Angelos (attrib) (1857-?) Greek
£2400 $4680   *(24-Oct-90 S168/R) View of Corfu (38x69cm-15x27in) s. W/C over pencil*

GIAMBOLOGNA (after) (c.1529-1608) Italian
£1800 $3474   *(11-Dec-90 C35/R) Venus bathing (27x20cm-11x8in) red chk.*

GIAMPETRI, Chevalier Septimio (19th C) Italian
£450 $779   *(9-May-91 CSK37/R) Forum, Rome (34x51cm-13x20in) s.i. pencil W/C*

GIANCELLO, G (19/20th C) Italian
£508 $900   *(22-Mar-91 S.W1577) Beggar (56x36cm-22x14in) s.*

GIANI, Felice (1760-1823) Italian
£9000 $14670   *(2-Jul-91 PH46/R) Telemachus and Eucharis before Calypso. Telemachus and*
                      Mentor (30x22cm-12x9in) pair painted oval
£684 $1300   *(8-Jan-91 SY.NY204/R) Putti and Nymphs (19x25cm-7x10in) ink*
£684 $1211   *(19-Mar-91 F.M29/R) Studi di erme e cariatide (22x30cm-9x12in) ink W/C*
                      joined paper (I.L 1500000)
£1368 $2421   *(19-Mar-91 F.M306/R) Scene storiche (29x20cm-11x8in) W/C ink*
                      (I.L 3000000)
£2964 $5246   *(19-Mar-91 F.M193/R) Giove e Minerva creano l'uomo pen W/C ink over*
                      pencil (I.L 6500000)
£3876 $6860   *(19-Mar-91 F.M199/R) La Vergine appare a devoti (35x30cm-14x12in) ink*
                      W/C (I.L 8500000)
£7313 $14406   *(14-Nov-90 F.M56/R) Zefiro per comando d'Amore trasporta Psiche*
                      (405x595cm-159x234in) d.1794 pen ink W/C (I.L 16000000)
£7313 $14406   *(14-Nov-90 F.M55/R) Psiche e adorata come Venere (405x595cm-159x234in)*
                      d.1794 pen ink W/C (I.L 16000000)

GIANI, Felice (attrib) (1760-1823) Italian
£388 $686   *(19-Mar-91 F.M321/R) Circoncisione (28x21cm-11x8in) pen bistre ink W/C*
                      htd white (I.L 850000)
£593 $1049   *(19-Mar-91 F.M304/R) Minerva impedisce che Achille uccida Agamennone*
                      (20x37cm-8x15in) i. ink W/C (I.L 1300000)

GIANI, Giovanni (1866-1937) Italian
£1848 $3567   *(11-Dec-90 CH.R197/R) Scena galante (65x55cm-26x22in) s.d.1930*
                      (I.L 4000000)

GIANI, Hugo (19/20th C) Italian
£2134 $3500   *(19-Jun-91 B.SF1956/R) Street in Egypt (51x76cm-20x30in) s.*

GIANLISI, Antonio (circle) (1652-1727) Italian
£18000 $29340   *(5-Jul-91 C203/R) Draped table with peaches, books, cup and flowers.*
                      Draped table with clock, flowers and fruit (76x100cm-30x39in) with
                      sig.d.1664 pair

GIANLISI, Francesco (attrib) (?) Italian
£3192 $5331   *(4-Jun-91 CH.R16) Natura morta con piatto di pesche e pappagallo*
                      (65x90cm-26x35in) (I.L 7000000)

GIANNETTI, Raffaele (1832-1916) Italian
£6000 $11520   *(28-Nov-90 S161/R) The pet bird (40x51cm-16x20in) s.d.1878 panel*
£8671 $15000   *(22-May-91 SY.NY276/R) Nu au pastorale (49x69cm-19x27in) s.d.1883*

GIANNI (?) Italian
£1151 $1991   *(22-May-91 GS.B2381) Still life of fruit, jug, glass, lobster and rabbit*
                      on draped table (80x110cm-31x43in) s. (S.FR 2900)

GIANNI, G (19th C) Italian
£424 $750   *(22-Mar-91 S.W2244) Monks viewing Amalfi Coast (48x28cm-19x11in)*
                      s.d.1893 gouache

GIANNI, Gerolamo (1837-?) Italian
£6030 $9889   *(21-Jun-91 SY.MO167/R) Deux vues de Malte (22x53cm-9x21in) s.d.1882*
                      paper laid down on canvas pair (F.FR 60000)
£6500 $11180   *(17-May-91 C248/R) Grand Harbour, Malta (21x68cm-8x27in) s.d.1875*
£9000 $17640   *(15-Feb-91 C66/R) Quarantine harbour from Casa Critien, Malta*
                      (51x38cm-20x15in) s.d.1872
£10500 $20580   *(15-Feb-91 C65/R) Valetta from Casa Critien Sliemann, Malta*
                      (74x38cm-29x15in) s.d.1872
£11000 $18040   *(18-Jun-91 PH151/R) View of Valletta, Malta, from Manoel Island*
                      (38x102cm-15x40in) s.d.1870

GIANNI, Gerolamo (1837-?) Italian-cont.
£11500 $22540   (15-Feb-91 C64/R) St. Paul's Bay, Malta (38x74cm-15x29in) s.d.1872
£23638 $45858   (8-Dec-90 SY.MO334/R) Vues de Naples (39x61cm-15x24in) one s. pair
                 (F.FR 230000)
£8000   *$13120*   *(19-Jun-91 S388/R) View of Quarantine harbour, Valletta. H.M.S. Lord*
                 Wardon steaming out of Grand Harbour, Valletta (37x102cm-15x40in)
                 s.d.1870 gouache canvas pair

GIANNI, Gian (19th C) Italian
£800 $1568   (14-Feb-91 CSK193) A Neapolitan terrace. A terrace on the Amalfi coast
                 (28x43cm-11x17in) s.
£2695 $4500   (5-Jun-91 D.NY40) Piazza overlooking the Bay of Naples (38x74cm-15x29in)
                 s.d.1871
£3200 $6144   (16-Aug-90 B422/R) Shipping in Valetta Harbour (32x53cm-13x21in) s.
                 board
£622   *$1170*   *(17-Sep-90 SY.ME4) Bay of Naples (30x44cm-12x17in) s. gouache*
                 (A.D 1400)

GIANNI, J (20th C) Italian
£377   *$614*   *(12-Jun-91 N.M237) Flower market in Naples with view of Vesuvio*
                 (42x18cm-17x7in) s. gouache board (DM 1100)

GIANNI, M (19th C) Italian
£460   *$754*   *(18-Jun-91 PH235) On the Neapolitan coast (29x47cm-11x19in) s. gouache*
                 pair

GIANNI, Y (18th C) Italian
£420   *$727*   *(9-May-91 CSK42) Napoli dalla Viadi Possillipo (48x30cm-19x12in) s.*
                 bodycol

GIANNINI, Giovanni (1930-) Czechoslovakian
£2077 $3718   (14-Apr-91 APT.P119) 4 Rond point (116x89cm-46x35in) s. (F.FR 21000)

GIANOLI, Pietro Francesco (attrib) (1620-1690) Italian
£6413 $12312   (29-Nov-90 F.M20/R) La cacciata dal Paradiso terrestre
                 (98x137cm-39x54in) (I.L 14000000)

GIANPIETRINO (16th C) Italian
£35000 $60550   (24-May-91 C47/R) The Madonna and Child with Saint John the Baptist and
                 a Deacon Martyr (89x72cm-35x28in) panel
£110000 $179300   (3-Jul-91 S17/R) Salome with head of John the Baptist (62x47cm-24x19in)
                 panel

GIANPIETRINO (circle) (16th C) Italian
£5410 $9683   (8-Apr-91 CH.R30/R) La Madonna col Bimbo e i Santi Gerolamo e Michele
                 (60x76cm-24x30in) (I.L 12000000)

GIANPIETRINO (style) (16th C) Italian
£1710 $3061   (14-Mar-91 D.V144/R) Portrait of lady in red dress (41x36cm-16x14in)
                 (A.S 35000)
£3081 $5361   (25-Mar-91 SY.F566) Madonna con Bambino (48x37cm-19x15in) panel
                 (I.L 6800000)

GIAQUINTO, Corrado (1690-1765) Italian
£10277 $19938   (5-Dec-90 APT.P14/R) L'Immaculee conception (66x42cm-26x17in)
                 (F.FR 100000)
£18263 $30681   (23-Apr-91 F.R64/R) Morte di San Giuseppe (96x63cm-38x25in)
                 (I.L 40000000)
£1186   *$2098*   *(19-Mar-91 F.M255/R) Studio di composizione per soffitto*
                 (19x26cm-7x10in) ink (I.L 2600000)
£1824   *$3228*   *(19-Mar-91 F.M280/R) Mose e il serpente di bronzo (19x13cm-7x5in) ink*
                 W/C (I.L 4000000)

GIAQUINTO, Corrado (attrib) (1690-1765) Italian
£44000 $74360   (19-Apr-91 C25/R) Aneneas before Dido (124x254cm-49x100in)
£502   *$888*   *(19-Mar-91 F.M252/R) Episodio della vita di Alessandro Magno. Studio di*
                 due figure di carnefici (25x20cm-10x8in) bistre ink W/C pencil
                 double-sided (I.L 1100000)

GIAQUINTO, Corrado (circle) (1690-1765) Italian
£1700 $3400   (7-Feb-91 C23) A woman and stayr in a landscape with a sleeping child
                 (178x128cm-70x50in)

GIAQUINTO, Corrado (studio) (1690-1765) Italian
£9000 $17100   (1-Mar-91 C172/R) Moses and the Brazen Serpent. Moses Striking the Rock
                 (63x51cm-25x20in) pair

GIAQUINTO, Corrado (style) (1690-1765) Italian
£1300 $2600   (7-Feb-91 CSK60) Lot and daughters (83x70cm-33x28in)
£1488 $2500   (17-Jul-91 SY.NY100/R) Saint Cecelia (40x32cm-16x13in)
£1676 $3000   (11-Apr-91 SY.NY88/R) Saint Nicholas of Bari discovering the source of
                 water (127x73cm-50x29in)

GIARDIELLO, C (?) ?
£1650 $3251   (15-Nov-90 SC4156) Friendly chat. Courtship (53x36cm-21x14in) s. pair

GIARDIELLO, Giovanni (19th C) Italian
£2800	$5488	(15-Feb-91 C92/R) On Neapolitan coast (28x46cm-11x18in) s.
£2900	$4843	(22-Jul-91 SWS1099/R) A view across the bay of Naples with fishermen pulling in their boats.Fishermen tending their boats, (26x42cm-10x17in) both s. pair
£3500	$6860	(15-Feb-91 C74/R) Capri (53x34cm-21x13in) s. canvas on board

GIARDIELLO, Giuseppe (?) Italian?
£2800	$5488	(15-Feb-91 C73/R) Street scene, Naples (40x25cm-16x10in) s.
£5500	$10835	(5-Oct-90 C128/R) La Tarantella, Naples (50x104cm-20x41in) s.

GIBB, H W Phelan (1870-1948) British
£1100	$2156	(8-Nov-90 DLY553/R) Resting (51x38cm-20x15in) s.d.1914 i.verso board

GIBB, John (19th C) British
£2921	$4936	(17-Apr-91 DS.W91 b) Kaikoura's from coast (49x74cm-19x29in) s.d.1885 (NZ.D 8500)

GIBB, Robert (1845-1932) British
£650	$1216	(28-Aug-90 S846/R) Portrait of David Robertson (38x29cm-15x11in)
£8000	$15760	(14-Nov-90 S110/R) The Vale of Leven, Dumbartonshire, with Alexandria (64x93cm-25x37in) s.d.1833

GIBB, Thomas Henry (19th C) British
£1500	$2940	(22-Nov-90 CSK184/R) Soldiers rustling Highland cattle (76x127cm-30x50in) s.d.1882

GIBBON, G (19th C) British
£1450	$2683	(5-Mar-91 SWS1443/R) Mother and child. Children with dog in landscape and country house beyond (112x87cm-44x34in) s.d.1819 pair

GIBBONS, W (19th C) British?
£2000	$3460	(22-May-91 S101/R) Pulling in wreckage (51x76cm-20x30in) s.d.1883

GIBBONS, William (19th C) British
£350	$620	(18-Mar-91 FEN132) The Plymouth fishing fleet off the Barbican (20x33cm-8x13in) s.d.1885 W/C
£1800	$3510	(18-Oct-90 CSK51/R) Plymouth. Fishermen unloading their catch (40x61cm-16x24in) one s.i.d.1881 one s.d.1883 pencil W/C pair

GIBBS, Charles C (19th C) British
£2800	$4564	(14-Jun-91 C314/R) On the hill (76x57cm-30x22in) s.d.1892

GIBRAN, Kahlil (1883-1931) American/Syrian
£2020	$4000	(1-Feb-91 S.W2578/R) Untitled (25x20cm-10x8in) i. pencil
£4802	$8500	(22-Mar-91 S.W2835/R) Woman with red hair (33x33cm-13x13in) i. pencil sepia wash

GIBSON, Charles Dana (1867-1944) American
£794	$1500	(25-Sep-90 CE.NY286/R) Dinner party (42x70cm-17x28in) s. pen brush ink pencil board

GIBSON, Gael (1963-) British
£520	$1019	(13-Feb-91 B119) Attraction of opposites (81x66cm-32x26in) mixed media collage on board

GIBSON, John (19th C) British
£800	$1432	(9-Apr-91 C7/R) Widow and children mourning fallen warrior (2x18cm-1x7in) s. pen ink wash
£1600	$2640	(9-Jul-91 C15/R) Cupid and Psyche (19x30cm-7x12in) pen ink htd.white

GIBSON, Richard (1615-1690) British
£1100	$1815	(11-Jul-91 S241/R) Portrait of gentleman wearing gold studded armour (8x?cm-3x?in) min. gilt metal frame scroll surmount oval
£14000	$26880	(18-Dec-90 C89/R) Portrait of Elizabeth Capell, Countess of Carnarvon (8x?cm-3x?in) min.mono.s.i.d.1657 vellum gold frame oval

GIBSON, William Alfred (1866-1931) British
£650	$1248	(26-Nov-90 SWS167/R) River scene in winter (20x26cm-8x10in) s. panel
£660	$1300	(30-Oct-90 SC226) In Ross-shire (25x35cm-10x14in) s.i.verso canvas on board

GID, Raymond (1905-) French?
£2823	$5504	(28-Oct-90 PLF.P201/R) Dimanche auto (40x62cm-16x24in) s.d.1928 gouache (F.FR 28000)

GIEL, Frans van (1892-1975) Belgian
£998	$1786	(12-Mar-91 C.A281/R) Landscape in Wechelterzande (32x37cm-13x15in) s. (B.FR 60000)
£1518	$2944	(8-Dec-90 KV.L294) Kempish farm under the snow (50x60cm-20x24in) s. (B.FR 90000)

GIEL, Frans van (attrib) (1892-1975) Belgian
£1214	$2355	(4-Dec-90 C.A400) Still life (100x90cm-39x35in) s. (B.FR 72000)
£2192	$4253	(4-Dec-90 C.A401) Still life (90x100cm-35x39in) s. (B.FR 130000)

GIEROWSKI, Stefan (1925-) Polish
£714 $1400   (12-Feb-91 SY.NY364/R) Composition XCIX (132x97cm-52x38in) s.

GIERSING, Harald (1881-?) Danish
£2054 $3799   (5-Mar-91 RAS.K160/R) Wooded landscape (61x51cm-24x20in) mono.
                   (D.KR 23000)
£4440 $8748   (31-Oct-90 KH.K25/R) Seated model, portrait of Ellen Sandholt
                   (92x78cm-36x31in) compoboard (D.KR 50000)

GIES, Emil (1872-?) German
£1336 $2618   (22-Nov-90 RAS.V714/R) Young girl in deep thought while working
                   (99x74cm-39x29in) s.d.1913 (D.KR 15000)

GIETL, Josua von (1847-1922) German
£1224 $2400   (6-Nov-90 GF.L2446/R) River landscape (23x32cm-9x13in) s. (S.FR 3000)
£1913 $3750   (7-Nov-90 B.SF1011/R) Harvesters (24x32cm-9x13in) s. board

GIFFARD, Alexandre S (19th C) Canadian
£889 $1724   (4-Dec-90 P.Q128) The hunters and their prey (26x39cm-10x15in) board
                   (C.D 2000)

GIFFORD, Charles H (1839-1904) American
£595 $1100   (8-Mar-91 S.BM141/R) Black Mountain, Lake George, New York
                   (18x30cm-7x12in) s.i.
£900 $1800   (7-Feb-91 B.P114/R) New Bedford fishermen (18x25cm-7x10in) s.d.
£1031 $2000   (5-Dec-90 D.NY113/R) Gay head, looking toward The Elizabeth Islands
                   (23x43cm-9x17in) s. board
£1031 $2000   (24-Aug-90 RB.HY31/R) Grand Manan, Bay of Fundy (13x46cm-5x18in) paper
                   laid down on cardboard
£1198 $2000   (26-Jul-91 E.EDM136 b/R) Sunset lake scene (23x36cm-9x14in) s.d.74
£1289 $2500   (24-Aug-90 RB.HY90/R) 'East Side', fog rolling over lake in peaceful
                   mountain valley (23x36cm-9x14in) s.d.1878
£1387 $2400   (10-May-91 S.BM46 a/R) Supper by moonlight, shore view with fishermen
                   and ruins (61x46cm-24x18in) s.d.1885 indis.i.verso
£1546 $3000   (24-Aug-90 RB.HY69/R) Campground at Oak Bluffs (13x15cm-5x6in) s.d.66
                   paper laid down on cardboard
£1933 $3750   (24-Aug-90 RB.HY131/R) Clearing up (20x25cm-8x10in) s.d.92
£2890 $5000   (10-May-91 S.BM44/R) Sailing about the harbour (61x46cm-24x18in)
                   s.d.1885
£3316 $6500   (24-Nov-90 RB.HY131/R) Coastal view with fishing boats and large sailing
                   ship with beach (33x46cm-13x18in) s.d.1887
£4211 $8000   (1-Mar-91 RB.HY40/R) Double rainbow over Fairhaven, Mass
                   (46x33cm-18x13in) s.d.1880
£4639 $9000   (24-Aug-90 RB.HY56/R) Hauling nets (23x36cm-9x14in) s.d.1867
£12690 $25000   (16-Nov-90 S.BM76/R) Striped bass on shores of Cuttyhunk Island, fishing
                   stand used by Cuttyhunk club (89x152cm-35x60in) s.d.1870
£1134   *$2200*   *(24-Aug-90 RB.HY91/R) Early morning (15x28cm-6x11in) s.d.99 W/C*

GIFFORD, John (19th C) British
£1000 $1950   (15-Jan-91 C100/R) Gordon setter and English setter with game basket.
                   Setters on the moor (29x39cm-11x15in) s. pair
£2428 $4200   (21-May-91 CE.NY178/R) Day's bag (91x69cm-36x27in) s.
£3593 $6000   (7-Jun-91 SY.NY6/R) At the end of the day (127x102cm-50x40in) s.

GIFFORD, R Swain (1840-1905) American
£2312 $4000   (22-May-91 CH.NY128/R) Sun-up (76x102cm-30x40in) s.
£3784 $7000   (8-Mar-91 S.BM219/R) Sand dunes, Naushon (46x76cm-18x30in) s.d.1881
£9827 $17000   (22-May-91 CH.NY19/R) Beach and cliffs at Nonquitt (44x69cm-17x27in)
                   s.d.1863

GIFFORD, Sandford R (1823-1880) American
£3911 $7000   (14-Mar-91 CH.NY16/R) Woodland hunter (29x24cm-11x9in) s.d.66
£4469 $8000   (14-Mar-91 CH.NY13/R) Mount Merino (28x56cm-11x22in)
£5000 $9500   (9-Jan-91 CH.NY162/R) Country stroll (13x17cm-5x7in) init.d..4 paper
                   laid down on canvas
£5026 $9500   (26-Sep-90 SY.NY29/R) Isolo San Julio, Lago d'Orta (22x39cm-9x15in)
                   st.verso
£7813 $15000   (29-Nov-90 SY.NY3/R) Tongue Mountain, Lake George (13x18cm-5x7in) init.
                   panel
£8333 $16000   (29-Nov-90 SY.NY12 a/R) The river bank (30x41cm-12x16in) s. i.verso
£13757 $26000   (27-Sep-90 CH.NY51/R) On the sea-shore, looking eastward at sunset
                   (22x40cm-9x16in) s. i. verso board

GIGANTE, Ercole (19th C) Italian
£5200 $10036   (13-Dec-90 CSK360/R) Il convento dei capuccini, Amalfi with Gulf of
                   Salerno beyond (51x76cm-20x30in) s.d.1853

GIGANTE, Giacinto (1806-1876) Italian
£3303 $6506   (13-Nov-90 AB.S892/R) Italian palace building with figures on steps
                   (43x33cm-17x13in) s.d.1840 (S.KR 36000)
£39000   *$63960*   *(19-Jun-91 S389/R) View of Ischia and Palazzo of King Ladislav, Gaeta*
                   (36x59cm-14x23in) s.d.1860 s.i.d.1856 W/C htd bodycol pair

GIGER, Hans-Rudolf (1940-) Swiss
£1837 $3618   (17-Nov-90 S.Z52/R) Mask (48x33cm-19x13in) s.d.1983 acrylic board
                   (S.FR 4500)

GIGER, Hans-Rudolf (1940-) Swiss-cont.

£1633 $3216   *(16-Nov-90 GK.Z5362/R) Biomechanische Landschaft no 540 (48x34cm-19x13in) s.d.1983 s.verso spray technique (S.FR 4000)*

£2857 $5629   *(16-Nov-90 EA.Z308/R) Untitled (78x69cm-31x27in) s.d.1964 mixed media paper on panel (S.FR 7000)*

GIGLI (?) Italian

£475 $950   *(6-Feb-91 D.NY34) Peasant girl beside a well (48x33cm-19x13in) s. W/C*

GIGLI, R (?) Italian

£414 $700   *(20-Apr-91 WOL.C106/R) Woman at edge of shore (56x43cm-22x17in) s. W/C*

£900 $1728   *(27-Nov-90 PH256) Figures before flower stall (73x48cm-29x19in) s.i. W/C*

GIGNON, Louis (20th C) ?

£1650 $3250   *(15-Nov-90 SY.NY47) Flowers (35x27cm-14x11in) s.d.1939*

GIGNOUS, Eugenio (1850-1906) Italian

£7705 $13021   *(16-Apr-91 CH.R94/R) Veduta lagunare (17x26cm-7x10in) s. panel (I.L 17000000)*

£10089 $18060   *(12-Mar-91 F.M114/R) Porticciolo di Calde sul lago Maggiore (54x97cm-21x38in) s. (I.L 22000000)*

£10637 $20636   *(5-Dec-90 F.M105/R) Paesaggio boschivo (39x58cm-15x23in) s. (I.L 23000000)*

£16650 $32300   *(5-Dec-90 F.M83/R) Veduta di Feriolo, Lago Maggiore (49x74cm-19x29in) s. (I.L 36000000)*

£25900 $50245   *(5-Dec-90 F.M13/R) Veduta di Suna e Pallanza, Lago Maggiore (38x62cm-15x24in) s.d.86 (I.L 56000000)*

£1596 $2666   *(6-Jun-91 F.M19/R) Paesaggi lacustre. Paesaggio montano (13x21cm-5x8in) one s. W/C set of three (I.L 3500000)*

GIGNOUS, Lorenzo (19th C) Italian

£12487 $24225   *(4-Dec-90 F.R161/R) L'isola dei pescatori sul lago di Como. Veduta di Sesto Calende (89x148cm-35x58in) s. pair (I.L 27000000)*

GIGNOUX, Francois Regis (1816-1882) American/French

£899 $1700   *(27-Sep-90 CH.NY37/R) Winter promenade (12x16cm-5x6in) canvas laid down on panel*

£9249 $16000   *(22-May-91 CH.NY8/R) Lush spring (101x149cm-40x59in) s.d.1853*

GIGNOUX, Francois Regis (attrib) (1816-1882) American/French

£1272 $2200   *(21-May-91 CE.NY381 a/R) Frozen river (65x91cm-26x36in)*

GIGOUX DE GRANDPRE, Pierre Emile (1826-?) French

£1858 $3140   *(3-May-91 SA.A1821/R) Ferry on the Bosphorus (35x55cm-14x22in) s.d.1860 (DM 5500)*

GIHON, Clarence M (1871-1929) American

£900 $1503   *(7-Jun-91 LD.P27) Boulevard a Paris (25x33cm-10x13in) s. board (F.FR 9000)*

£1100 $1837   *(7-Jun-91 LD.P29) Tour a La Rochelle (34x41cm-13x16in) s. board (F.FR 11000)*

£1937 $3738   *(10-Dec-91 LD.P77/R) Vue de Pont Neuf (54x65cm-21x26in) s. (F.FR 19000)*

£4700 $7849   *(7-Jun-91 LD.P30) Les tours du port de La Rochelle (132x97cm-52x38in) s. (F.FR 47000)*

£5000 $8350   *(7-Jun-91 LD.P30 b) La mer entre Brehat et Paimpol (100x102cm-39x40in) s. (F.FR 50000)*

GIL SALA, Ignacio (1912-) Spanish

£5460 $9446   *(8-May-91 FER.M264 q/R) Reparando las redes bajo el ardiente sol (73x92cm-29x36in) s. (S.P 1000000)*

GILADI, Aharon (?) Israeli

£798 $1300   *(12-Jun-91 GG.TA259/R) Figures (73x60cm-29x24in) s.*

GILARDI, Piero (1924-) Italian

£1531 $2985   *(22-Oct-90 BR.M176/R) Cachi (50x50cm-20x20in) s.d.1986 verso expanded polyurethane (I.L 3400000)*

GILBERT (?) ?

£956 $1645   *(14-May-91 GF.L2552/R) Fishing boats in coastal landscape (18x36cm-7x14in) s. panel (S.FR 2400)*

GILBERT and GEORGE (20th C) British

£8876 $15000   *(2-May-91 CH.NY215/R) Scout cross (110x79cm-43x31in) s.d.1981 sixteen postcards on board*

£12755 $25000   *(14-Feb-91 CH.NY78/R) Just married (117x112cm-46x44in) s.i.d.1981 postcard collage board*

£13198 $26000   *(5-Oct-90 CH.NY110/R) Red William murder (112x81cm-44x32in) s.i.d.1981 25 postcards on board*

£50000 $97000   *(6-Dec-90 S60/R) Hands up (241x401cm-95x158in) s.d.1984 photographic collage*

GILBERT, Arthur (1819-1895) British

£920 $1730   *(18-Sep-90 SWS668/R) In the valley, near Strata Florida, N. Wales (52x80cm-20x31in) s.d.1893*

GILBERT, Arthur (1819-1895) British-cont.
£1550 $2604   (24-Apr-91 MMB413/R) Travellers, sheep and shepherd on sandy lane
                   (51x76cm-20x30in) s.d.1879

GILBERT, Arthur Hill (1894-1970) American
£1837 $3600   (24-Nov-90 RB.HY134/R) Rocky coastal landscape with flowers and trees
                   and view of Pacific (86x114cm-34x45in) s.d.1929
£2564 $5000   (10-Oct-90 B.SF549/R) River (61x76cm-24x30in) s.

GILBERT, C Allan (1873-1929) American
£1412 $2400   (1-Jun-91 IH.NY163/R) Young woman holding hand mirror (48x36cm-19x14in)
                   s.d.1899 gouache en grisaille

GILBERT, F (?) ?
£1027 $1839   (14-Mar-91 N.M2652/R) Lake Eibsee (68x105cm-27x41in) s.i. (DM 3000)
£1164 $2084   (12-Mar-91 FN.S2378/R) View of harbour town with shipping
                   (68x55cm-27x22in) s. (DM 3400)

GILBERT, Horace W (1855-?) British
£2300 $4508   (13-Feb-91 S159/R) On mid Surrey hills. Early autumn day, May Hill,
                   Gloucesterhire (46x61cm-18x24in) s.d.1893 i.frame pair

GILBERT, John (19th C) British
£442 $848   (26-Nov-90 SY.ME165) Challenger (30x46cm-12x18in) s. gouache (A.D 1100)

GILBERT, Rene Joseph (1858-1914) French
£2613 $4285   (18-Jun-91 APT.P23 b/R) Pecheur en barque (73x92cm-29x36in) s.d.1887
                   pastel (F.FR 26000)

GILBERT, Sir John (1817-1897) British
£800 $1576   (31-Oct-90 S318/R) Duke of Wellington leading troops in battle
                   (32x39cm-13x15in) board
£1000 $1640   (21-Jun-91 CBB6) Standard bearer (66x41cm-26x16in) bears sig.d.1875

GILBERT, Stephen (1910-) British
£1393 $2689   (12-Dec-90 CH.AM456) Composition (20x13cm-8x5in) s.d.50 W/C pair
                   (D.FL 4500)

GILBERT, Victor (1847-1933) French
£1188 $2103   (7-Apr-91 LT.P41) Interieur (33x41cm-13x16in) s. (F.FR 12000)
£3468 $6000   (22-May-91 SY.NY159/R) L'Indolence (56x48cm-22x19in) s.
£4762 $7667   (26-Jun-91 KM.K1473/R) Young woman with basket and milk churns in Paris
                   street (46x37cm-18x15in) s.d.1894 (DM 14000)
£10405 $18000   (23-May-91 CH.NY23/R) Au marche aux fleurs (47x39cm-19x15in) s.
£28000 $45920   (21-Jun-91 C38/R) Vegetable stand, at Les Halles Centrales, Paris
                   (46x54cm-18x21in) s.d.1878
£109827 $190000   (22-May-91 SY.NY73/R) Le marche aux legumes (90x131cm-35x52in) s.d.1878

GILBERT, W J (19th C) British
£880 $1637   (3-Sep-90 SWS1247/R) Equestrian portrait of gentleman on dapple grey
                   hunter (61x74cm-24x29in) s.d.1838

GILDEMEESTER, Anna (1867-?) Dutch
£1061 $2089   (30-Oct-90 CH.AM408/R) Bien etonnes de se trouver ensemble
                   (36x58cm-14x23in) s. black col.chk (D.FL 3500)

GILDEMEISTER, Gustav (1876-1915) German
£1802 $3117   (22-May-91 CH.AM552) Landleute mit musikanten (68x87cm-27x34in)
                   (D.FL 6000)
£3904 $6754   (22-May-91 CH.AM547/R) Jungling in der landschaft (85x172cm-33x68in)
                   s.d.09 (D.FL 13000)
£4505 $7793   (22-May-91 CH.AM551/R) Erntearbeiter (87x102cm-34x40in) (D.FL 15000)

GILDOR, Jacob (1948-) Israeli
£920 $1500   (12-Jun-91 GG.TA255/R) Mimi (101x73cm-40x29in) s.d.1987 paper on canvas
£661 $1321   (6-Feb-91 FB.P144/R) Le cafe (62x90cm-24x35in) s. mixed media board
                   (F.FR 6500)
£671 $1100   (19-Jun-91 B.SF1842/R) L'embrasse (63x48cm-25x19in) s.i.d.1987 W/C
                   pastel
£1263 $2475   (17-Feb-91 E.LA13) Pluie a Paris (75x105cm-30x41in) s. mixed media
                   (F.FR 12500)

GILE, Seldon Connor (1877-1947) American
£2821 $5500   (10-Oct-90 B.SF486/R) Pots, path and trestle (35x41cm-14x16in) board
£3590 $7000   (10-Oct-90 B.SF483/R) Purple and pink hills (30x39cm-12x15in) s.d.1916

GILES, James William (1801-1870) British
£12000 $23520   (22-Nov-90 CG567/R) Prospect of Aberdeen from Drumthwacket
                   (102x152cm-40x60in) s.d.1851

GILI, Anna Caterina (fl.1729-1751) Italian
£7200 $12168   (17-Apr-91 S60/R) Garlands of flowers with peacock and fruit in
                   landscape (63x49cm-25x19in)

GILIOLI, Emile (1911-1977) French
£453 $739   (16-Jun-91 CC.P20) Figure (50x33cm-20x13in) s.i. chl.crayon (F.FR 4500)

GILIOLI, Emile (1911-1977) French-cont.
£2039 $3935   *(16-Dec-90 GL.P151) Nu allonge (41x51cm-16x20in) s.d.46 chl. (F.FR 20000)*
£2055 $3988   *(4-Dec-90 I.N65) Composition (64x47cm-25x19in) s.d.1954 chl. (F.FR 20000)*

GILL, Edmund (1820-1894) British
£1000 $2000   (5-Feb-91 CG72/R) Cleghorn mills in ruins, Lanark (46x61cm-18x24in) s.d.1865 s.i.d.1865 verso
£1030 $2030   (30-Oct-90 CH.AM99) Glenn Affric, Scotland (45x61cm-18x24in) s.d.1877 (D.FL 3400)
£1400 $2478   (21-Mar-91 CSK159/R) Falls on the Greta, Westmorland. Scandel Beck Falls, Westmorland (28x23cm-11x9in) s.i.d.1890 pair

GILL, Eric (1882-1940) British
£700 $1316   *(20-Sep-90 CSK1/R) Reclining nude (30x28cm-12x11in) s.d.27 pencil col crayon*

GILL, F (19th C) ?
£2859 $5574   *(10-Oct-90 ARC.P46/R) Paysage anime de personnages (64x97cm-25x38in) s.d.1852 (F.FR 28500)*

GILL, Naylor (1873-?) Australian
£543 $918   (16-Apr-91 J.M504) Landscape (43x68cm-17x27in) s. canvas on board (A.D 1200)

GILL, Samuel Thomas (1818-1890) Australian
£814 $1376   *(16-Apr-91 J.M5) On the River Murray (16x26cm-6x10in) init. W/C (A.D 1800)*
£1351 $2662   *(13-Nov-90 J.M287) Windmill at Waverley (10x20cm-4x8in) init. W/C (A.D 3500)*
£3213 $6169   *(26-Nov-90 SY.ME234/R) Bee hunter, Aboriginal of Australia (17x29cm-7x11in) init.i.d.1874 W/C (A.D 8000)*
£3571 $6214   *(26-Mar-91 JRL.S84/R) Incident in the outback (38x67cm-15x26in) init. W/C (A.D 8000)*

GILLARD, William (1812-?) British
£1800 $3402   (26-Sep-90 S86/R) Menai Straits (67x106cm-26x42in) s.

GILLEMANS, Jan Pauwel (17th C) Flemish
£9462 $16370   (26-May-91 E.LA23) Nature morte de fruits (69x79cm-27x31in) (F.FR 95000)
£17206 $33725   (19-Nov-90 ZZ.F20/R) Nature morte aux fruits et singe sur un entablement. Fruits, orfevrerie,perroquet et ecureuils (48x64cm-19x25in) both s. pair (F.FR 170000)

GILLEMANS, Jan Pauwel (circle) (17th C) Flemish
£2051 $4000   (11-Oct-90 SY.NY138 a/R) Still life of fruit on fountain (114x82cm-45x32in)
£5800 $9802   (16-Apr-91 PH132/R) Still life of fruit on table with gilt covered chalice (59x92cm-23x36in)

GILLEMANS, Jan Pauwel (elder) (1618-1675) Flemish
£10002 $17304   (21-May-91 SY.MI1029/R) Natura morta con festone di frutta e pappagallo (48x75cm-19x30in) s. (I.L 22000000)
£52920 $104252   (30-Oct-90 BU.S249/R) Still life of lobster and ham on table (56x82cm-22x32in) s.d.1655 (S.KR 580000)

GILLEMANS, Jan Pauwel (younger) (1651-1704) Flemish
£6500 $10595   (3-Jul-91 S111/R) Still life of bread with roemer, lemon, nuts, oyster, shrimps, in stone ledge with garland fruit (76x64cm-30x25in)
£11236 $19326   (14-May-91 BU.S77/R) Cupids playing among garlands of fruit (68x85cm-27x33in) s. (S.KR 120000)
£12213 $21861   (14-Mar-91 D.V201/R) Garland of flowers and fruit with putti before castle (61x74cm-24x29in) (A.S 250000)
£19000 $36670   (12-Dec-90 S138/R) Putti playing beside swag of fruit in landscape (82x120cm-32x47in)

GILLEMANS, Jan Pauwel (younger-circle) (1651-1704) Flemish
£11000 $17930   (2-Jul-91 PH357/R) Nymphs crowning personification of summer and cherubs holding garlands (104x70cm-41x28in)

GILLER, Joseph Isaacovich (1912-) Russian
£503 $824   (19-Jun-91 ARC.P15/R) Le bapteme du chalutier (105x180cm-41x71in) s. (F.FR 5000)

GILLES, Eugene (?-1909) French
£663 $1307   (17-Nov-90 HC.P2) Paysage (80x100cm-31x39in) s. (F.FR 6500)

GILLES, Werner (1894-1961) German
£2226 $3628   (15-Jun-91 L.K224/R) Still life with doll. Landscape (46x62cm-18x24in) s. double-sided (DM 6500)
£2703 $4595   (1-Jun-91 VG.B334/R) Crashing angel (49x66cm-19x26in) s. (DM 8000)
£4437 $8696   (22-Nov-90 L.K955/R) Home of Orpheus, Ischia (60x75cm-24x30in) s. i.d.1931stretcher (DM 13000)
£1034   *$1986*   *(28-Nov-90 KF.M796/R) Beached fishing boats (22x30cm-9x12in) indian ink brush over pencil (DM 3000)*

GILLES, Werner (1894-1961) German-cont.

£1195	$2341	(22-Nov-90 L.K957/R) Coastal landscape (32x43cm-13x17in) s.d.59 W/C (DM 3500)
£1379	$2648	(26-Nov-90 WK.M221) Archaische Begegnung (26x39cm-10x15in) s.d.1952 mixed media (DM 4000)
£1525	$2547	(6-Jun-91 HN.H354/R) Beach ghost (32x43cm-13x17in) i.verso W/C (DM 4500)
£1586	$3046	(28-Nov-90 KF.M795/R) Ischia (32x43cm-13x17in) s.d.1959 W/C bodycol (DM 4600)
£1712	$3065	(12-Mar-91 FN.S1975/R) Ischia (20x24cm-8x9in) s.d.1956 W/C (DM 5000)
£2027	$3446	(1-Jun-91 VG.B274/R) Mountains, Ischia (30x43cm-12x17in) bears i.d.1961verso W/C (DM 6000)
£2192	$3573	(15-Jun-91 L.K225/R) Street of passion s.d.48 i.verso W/C pen (DM 6400)
£2389	$4683	(22-Nov-90 L.K956/R) Rock before Sant'Angelo II (32x21cm-13x8in) c.1950 W/C brush double-sided (DM 7000)
£2432	$4135	(28-May-91 KF.M687/R) Ischia landscape (32x45cm-13x18in) s.i.d.1956 W/C (DM 7200)
£2881	$4812	(6-Jun-91 HN.H353/R) The Harbour of Sant Angelo d'Ischia (47x61cm-19x24in) s. W/C (DM 8500)
£4054	$6892	(28-May-91 KF.M685/R) Landscape (42x60cm-17x24in) s. mixed media board (DM 12000)
£4730	$8041	(28-May-91 KF.M686/R) Boats in Porto d'Ischia (48x67cm-19x26in) s.d.1938 W/C double-sided (DM 14000)
£4730	$8041	(1-Jun-91 VG.B273/R) Still life with fishes (49x63cm-19x25in) s. i.verso W/C gouache over chk (DM 14000)

GILLES-MURIQUE, Jeannine (1924-) French

£559	$1118	(7-Feb-91 R.P32/R) L'orientale (97x130cm-38x51in) s. (F.FR 5500)

GILLESPIE, George (?) Irish

£811	$1581	(10-Oct-90 WO.CO7) Reflections, Kylemore, Connemara (48x74cm-19x29in) s. (E.P 900)
£864	$1641	(12-Sep-90 WO.CO9) Cushendun, Co. Antrim (38x71cm-15x28in) s. (E.P 950)
£909	$1727	(12-Sep-90 WO.CO8) April morning among the 12 pins (43x74cm-17x29in) s. (E.P 1000)
£909	$1727	(12-Sep-90 WO.CO7) April morning among the 12 pins (43x74cm-17x29in) s. (E.P 1000)

GILLESPIE, George K (1924-) British

£800	$1560	(26-Oct-90 CG172) Children on beach (41x51cm-16x20in) s.
£1364	$2673	(23-Jan-91 WO.CO18) Children on beach, Gortahork, Co. Donegal (61x91cm-24x36in) s. (E.P 1500)

GILLESPIE, Gregory (1936-) American

£3827	$7500	(6-Nov-90 CE.NY127/R) The morbid man (102x62cm-40x24in) s.
£2806	$5500	(12-Feb-91 SY.NY483/R) Double image in Easthampton, Mass. studio (58x53cm-23x21in) oil alkyd photo collage panel

GILLET (?) ?

£1159	$2261	(25-Oct-90 CB.P103) Composition (51x40cm-20x16in) s. (F.FR 11500)

GILLET, Numa (1868-?) French

£416	$736	(5-Apr-91 LGB.P96/R) Solitudo refugium (29x33cm-11x13in) s.i. W/C htd.gold (F.FR 4200)

GILLET, Roger Edgar (1924-) French

£1000	$1680	(24-Apr-91 MJ.P124/R) Composition (65x92cm-26x36in) s.d.59 (F.FR 10000)
£1850	$3589	(3-Dec-90 CH.R54/R) Personnage (89x129cm-35x51in) s.d.1965verso (I.L 4000000)
£1857	$3583	(13-Dec-90 CH.BR134/R) Composition (64x46cm-25x18in) s.d.58 (B.FR 110000)
£4016	$6466	(25-Jun-91 BG.P26/R) Composition (163x115cm-64x45in) s.d. (F.FR 40000)
£5102	$10051	(15-Nov-90 I.N2/R) Composition (50x39cm-20x15in) s.d.1953 panel (F.FR 50000)
£305	$610	(6-Feb-91 FB.P148/R) Composition (21x32cm-8x13in) s.d.59 gouache (F.FR 3000)
£452	$810	(11-Mar-91 GL.P192) Composition rouge et noire (41x46cm-16x18in) gouache Indian ink (F.FR 4500)
£503	$899	(11-Mar-91 GL.P191) Sans titre (43x55cm-17x22in) s. gouache (F.FR 5000)
£603	$1079	(11-Mar-91 GL.P189) Sans titre (64x50cm-25x20in) s.d.1952 gouache (F.FR 6000)
£653	$1169	(11-Mar-91 GL.P188) Composition brune et noire (46x64cm-18x25in) s.d.1960 Indian ink gouache (F.FR 6500)

GILLIES, Sir William George (1898-1973) British

£2800	$4704	(23-Apr-91 S177/R) Four pots (52x59cm-20x23in) s.
£3500	$6790	(5-Dec-90 PHE68 a) Still life on white ground (69x69cm-27x27in) s.
£5500	$10780	(22-Nov-90 CG632/R) Still life on white ground (71x86cm-28x34in) s.
£15000	$29400	(22-Nov-90 CG631/R) Kippford (63x91cm-25x36in) s.
£500	$845	(17-Apr-91 CG51) Farm near Middleton (25x36cm-10x14in) s. W/C
£780	$1303	(26-Jul-91 PHE90) Near Romanno Bridge (25x34cm-10x13in) s. W/C
£1700	$3179	(28-Aug-90 S1094/R) Near Temple (28x38cm-11x15in) s.s.i.verso W/C
£2100	$4116	(22-Nov-90 CG561/R) Durnish near Kyle (25x32cm-10x13in) s. pen ink W/C
£2800	$4732	(2-May-91 CG457/R) Near temple (55x78cm-22x31in) s. s.i.verso pen W/C
£2800	$5488	(22-Nov-90 CG560/R) Wester Ross (48x63cm-19x25in) s. W/C

GILLIES, Sir William George (1898-1973) British-cont.

£4000	$7840	(22-Nov-90 CG559/R) Laide (56x77cm-22x30in) s. pencil W/C
£4200	$7854	(28-Aug-90 S1095/R) Farmhouse in the trees (55x70cm-22x28in) s. W/C over pencil
£4500	$8820	(22-Nov-90 CG557/R) Lower Temple (51x67cm-20x26in) s. pen ink W/C
£5000	$9800	(22-Nov-90 CG555/R) Near Balmacara (55x70cm-22x28in) pencil W/C
£5500	$10780	(22-Nov-90 CG558/R) Balmacara (47x56cm-19x22in) s. pen ink W/C
£9000	$17640	(22-Nov-90 CG556/R) Kippford (51x70cm-20x28in) s.d.1948 s.i.verso pen ink W/C

GILLIG, Jacob (attrib) (1636-1701) Dutch

£1116	$2076	(9-Sep-90 BU.M187) Still life of fish (42x31cm-17x12in) panel (S.KR 12000)
£3364	$6627	(13-Nov-90 CH.AM158/R) Mixed fish and baskets on seashore, village on dune beyond (59x82cm-23x32in) indist.s. (D.FL 11000)

GILLING, Otto (?) ?

£440	$788	(13-Mar-91 B13) A view of Taormina, Sicily (15x24cm-6x9in) s. W/C htd.white

GILLIS, Marcel (20th C) ?

£2551	$5000	(12-Feb-91 SY.NY66/R) Procession (107x119cm-42x47in) s.d.1934 s.i.d.verso

GILLON, Jean Francois le (1739-1797) French

£1856	$3137	(2-May-91 CH.AM117/R) A cow resting in a stable with a peasant coversing with a milk-maid (22x29cm-9x11in) s. panel (D.FL 6200)
£3352	$6000	(10-Apr-91 HF.NY30/R) Rocky landscape with goatherds and animals (37x47cm-15x19in) s.

GILLOT, Claude (1673-1722) French

£2600	$4238	(2-Jul-91 C155/R) Figures from Commedia dell'Arte (17x20cm-7x8in) black lead pen
£10500	$17115	(2-Jul-91 C154/R) Feste de Diane, troublee par des satyres (16x37cm-6x15in) black lead red chk

GILLOT, Claude (attrib) (1673-1722) French

£854	$1400	(19-Jun-91 B.SF1699/R) Les mendicants (33x25cm-13x10in) sanguine
£4893	$9443	(12-Dec-90 ARC.P43/R) Bacchanale (19x20cm-7x8in) trace pierre noire pen wash sepia (F.FR 48000)

GILLOT, Eugene Louis (1868-1925) French

£1212	$2388	(30-Oct-90 CH.AM112) View in French town (65x86cm-26x34in) s. (D.FL 4000)
£1600	$2752	(17-May-91 C13/R) Gondolas on Grand Canal, Venice (39x59cm-15x23in) s. board
£2000	$3440	(17-May-91 C14/R) La Salute, Venice (44x52cm-17x20in) s.

GILPIN, Sawrey (1733-1807) British

£1000	$1970	(1-Nov-90 TE600/R) Portrait of chestnut mare with 'Shark' the terrier (48x64cm-19x25in) s.d.1795 i.backing
£1300	$2301	(21-Mar-91 CSK204/R) Fighting horses (46x61cm-18x24in)
£22754	$38000	(7-Jun-91 SY.NY30/R) A groom offering a feeding sieve to a pony in a wooded landscape (98x131cm-39x52in)
£25449	$42500	(7-Jun-91 SY.NY15/R) Three greyhounds (63x76cm-25x30in) s.d.1783

GILPIN, Sawrey (circle) (1733-1807) British

£6500	$11635	(10-Apr-91 S40/R) Rough haired retriever with ptarmigan in landscape (106x132cm-42x52in)

GILPIN, Sawrey and BARRET, George (late 18th C) British

£3316	$6500	(21-Nov-90 NA.BA13/R) Landscape with cattle and sheep (63x76cm-25x30in) s.

GILROY, John William (fl.1890-1904) British

£1600	$2960	(5-Mar-91 AG307/R) Unloading the catch (45x60cm-18x24in) s.

GILSOUL, Victor (1867-?) Belgian

£1397	$2724	(23-Oct-90 C.A508/R) River landscape (32x41cm-13x16in) s. panel (B.FR 85000)
£5183	$10159	(6-Nov-90 SY.AM225) Poppy field (26x54cm-10x21in) s. panel (D.FL 17000)
£8191	$16055	(22-Nov-90 L.K958/R) View of canal in Brugge (80x100cm-31x39in) s.d.1903 (DM 24000)

GILSOUL-HOPPE, Ketty (1868-?) Belgian

£914	$1637	(12-Mar-91 C.A106) Beguinage (54x70cm-21x28in) s. W/C (B.FR 55000)
£1560	$2699	(25-May-91 KV.L128) In the Begijnhof (55x70cm-22x28in) s. gouache (B.FR 95000)

GIMENEZ Y MARTIN, Juan (1858-?) Spanish

£1223	$2348	(18-Dec-90 DUR.M20) La carta (49x32cm-19x13in) W/C (S.P 225000)

GIMIGNANI, Giacinto (1611-1681) Italian

£9016	$16139	(8-Apr-91 CH.R132/R) Gloria di S.Tommaso di Villanova con la figura allegorica della Carita (100x75cm-39x30in) (I.L 20000000)
£10526	$20000	(11-Jan-91 CH.NY70/R) Mars and Venus (84x62cm-33x24in)

GIMIGNANI, Giacinto (1611-1681) Italian-cont.

£57471	$100000	(27-Mar-91 B.SF4060/R) Alessandro. Alessandro con Diogene (117x122cm-46x48in) one s. pair
£7000	*$11410*	*(2-Jul-91 C41/R) Horatius slaying sister Horatia outside walls of Rome, ceiling design (23x37cm-9x15in) i. chk pen ink wash htd.white*

GIMIGNANI, Lodovico (1643-1697) Italian

£4104	*$7264*	*(19-Mar-91 F.M244/R) Enea riceve l'ordine di lasciare Cartagine (55x42cm-22x17in) sanguine bistre W/C (I.L 9000000)*

GIMMI, Wilhelm (1886-1965) Swiss

£670	$1200	(16-Mar-91 W.W89/R) Nude study (25x23cm-10x9in)
£1496	$2468	(10-Jul-91 FB.P33/R) Nu assis (27x22cm-11x9in) s. (F.FR 15000)
£1581	$2688	(27-May-91 GK.Z5337) Nu assis dans un fauteuil (41x33cm-16x13in) s. (S.FR 4000)
£1959	$3801	(8-Dec-90 GAB.G2597/R) Nu assis (41x33cm-16x13in) s. (S.FR 4800)
£3265	$6335	(8-Dec-90 GAB.G2594/R) Pont-Marie, Paris (55x46cm-22x18in) s. (S.FR 8000)
£4800	$8112	(1-May-91 GD.B341/R) The wine connoisseur (65x53cm-26x21in) s.d.45 (S.FR 12000)
£4819	$9446	(21-Nov-90 SY.Z44/R) Bois de Boulogne, groupe de cavaliers (27x35cm-11x14in) s. board (S.FR 12000)
£6122	$12000	(6-Nov-90 GF.L2252/R) Sempachersee landscape (46x55cm-18x22in) s. (S.FR 15000)
£8835	$14843	(24-Apr-91 G.Z86/R) Portrait de James Joyce (41x33cm-16x13in) s.d.1942 board (S.FR 22000)
£11067	$18814	(27-May-91 GK.Z5336/R) Self portrait (73x60cm-29x24in) s.d.1918 (S.FR 28000)
£12000	$23400	(17-Oct-90 G.Z99/R) Demi nu au peignoir (46x55cm-18x22in) s.d.1924 (S.FR 30000)
£15079	$25183	(5-Jun-91 SY.Z113/R) La loge (46x38cm-18x15in) s. (S.FR 38000)
£449	*$871*	*(8-Dec-90 GAB.G2596/R) Nu de dos (30x23cm-12x9in) s. lead pencil drawing (S.FR 1100)*
£476	*$781*	*(19-Jun-91 GK.B427) La loge au theatre du Palais Royal a Paris (25x27cm-10x11in) s. chk (S.FR 1200)*
£794	*$1302*	*(19-Jun-91 GK.B428) Nude young girl drying foot (35x24cm-14x9in) s. pencil (S.FR 2000)*
£960	*$1872*	*(17-Oct-90 G.Z100) Female nude seated (27x25cm-11x10in) s.d.37 pencil (S.FR 2400)*
£1061	*$2059*	*(8-Dec-90 GAB.G2591) Scene d'auberge (27x22cm-11x9in) s.d.1914 W/C (S.FR 2600)*
£2823	*$5419*	*(2-Dec-90 GAB.G1619/R) Le repose de modele (30x42cm-12x17in) s. mixed media htd.oil panel (S.FR 7000)*

GIN COSTE-CRASNIER see COSTE CRASNIER, Gin

GINDERTAEL, Roger van (1899-1982) Belgian

£5916	*$11537*	*(23-Oct-90 C.A382/R) The woman (37x31cm-15x12in) s. gouache (B.FR 360000)*

GINNER, Charles (1878-1952) British

£3590	$7072	(1-Nov-90 B77/R) Rooftops, Le Havre (28x20cm-11x8in) s. board
£5000	$9250	(7-Mar-91 C40/R) Boscastle Harbour (20x28cm-8x11in) board
£2000	*$3700*	*(7-Mar-91 C41/R) London Bridge (30x23cm-12x9in) s. pen ink W/C*
£3200	*$5920*	*(7-Mar-91 C42/R) In the Vale of Health, Hampstead, The Lodge (28x40cm-11x16in) s. pen ink W/C*
£3600	*$7056*	*(7-Nov-90 S30/R) Farm in valley (29x41cm-11x16in) s. pen ink W/C*
£3800	*$6346*	*(6-Jun-91 C75/R) Village in the New Forest (33x48cm-13x19in) s. W/C pen ink*
£5500	*$10780*	*(7-Nov-90 S29/R) The fir tree (27x16cm-11x6in) s. pen indian ink W/C*

GINOVSZKY, Joseph (1800-1857) Austrian

£4915	$8012	(3-Jul-91 WE.MU348) Lipizzaner (35x38cm-14x15in) s.l.d.1825 pair (DM 14500)
£7692	$14846	(12-Dec-90 WE.MU100/R) Lipizzaner (35x38cm-14x15in) s.l.d.1825 pair (DM 22000)

GIOBBI (20th C) American

£510	*$1000*	*(6-Nov-90 CE.NY128/R) Mycenae C (81x71cm-32x28in) s.d.1979 verso oil graphite panel and canvas*

GIOJA, Belisario (1829-1906) Italian

£859	*$1400*	*(5-Jul-91 S.W2676/R) The chess game (36x51cm-14x20in) s. W/C*
£928	*$1800*	*(7-Dec-90 S.W2727/R) Chess game (36x48cm-14x19in) s. W/C*
£2746	*$4750*	*(10-May-91 S.W2492/R) Garden party (64x41cm-25x16in) s.i. W/C*
£2746	*$4750*	*(10-May-91 S.W2493/R) Garden party (64x41cm-25x16in) s.i. W/C*

GIOJA, Camillo (?) Italian

£1600	$3136	(14-Feb-91 CSK204/R) On the grand canal. On the Venetian Lagoon (28x48cm-11x19in) s. board pair
£400	*$716*	*(13-Mar-91 B4/R) The young watercarrier (56x39cm-22x15in) s.i. W/C*

GIOJA, Edoardo (1862-?) Italian

£3200	$6240	(18-Oct-90 SC3140/R) Intimate moments. The proposal (47x32cm-19x13in) both s.i. one d.1883 pair

GIOJA, G (19th C) Italian
£430 $705   *(21-Jun-91 HC4) Continental scene with two peasant figures leaning against pillars (51x36cm-20x14in) s.i. W/C*

GIOLI, Francesco (1849-1922) Italian
£3172 $5361   (16-Apr-91 CH.R166) Paese al tramonto (23x23cm-9x9in) s. panel
                  (I.L 7000000)
£13000 $21840   (18-Jul-91 CSK174/R) Crossing stream (66x39cm-26x15in) s.d.1873

GIOLI, Luigi (1854-1947) Italian
£1368 $2285   (6-Jun-91 F.M94/R) Campagna pisana (12x21cm-5x8in) s. panel
                  (I.L 3000000)
£1505 $2513   (6-Jun-91 F.M118) Marina pisana (13x22cm-5x9in) s. panel (I.L 3300000)
£9000 $18000   (18-Oct-90 F.M38/R) Veduta di campagna toscana (46x66cm-18x26in) s.
                  (I.L 20000000)
£13225 $22086   (6-Jun-91 F.M261/R) Buttero a cavallo (53x37cm-21x15in) s.
                  (I.L 29000000)

GIONIMA, Antonio (1697-1732) Italian
£5700 $10089   *(19-Mar-91 F.M172/R) Studio di figure (41x26cm-16x10in) sanguine over pencil (I.L 12500000)*

GIONIMA, Antonio (circle) (1697-1732) Italian
£5028 $9000   (11-Apr-91 SY.NY72/R) Pharoah's daughter pulling the infant Moses from the waters (105x148cm-41x58in)

GIORDA, Patrice (1952-) French
£6209 $12046   (5-Dec-90 AB.S7080/R) La promenade no.7 - le petit cimetiere (165x203cm-65x80in) s.d.85verso acrylic (S.KR 67000)

GIORDANI, Italo (19/20th C) Italian
£713 $1404   (30-Oct-90 I.N248) Environs de Paris (45x59cm-18x23in) s. panel
                  (F.FR 7000)
£2428 $4200   (8-May-91 RO.BA355) Mercato di fiore (40x60cm-16x24in) s. panel

GIORDANI, Monaldo (1879-?) Italian
£5461 $10703   (24-Nov-90 SA.A637/R) Livorno harbour (59x117cm-23x46in) s. (DM 16000)

GIORDANO (school) (?) Italian
£1748 $3374   (12-Dec-90 WE.MU28/R) Satyr and family asleep (50x37cm-20x15in) canvas on board (DM 5000)
£2632 $5158   (20-Nov-90 PPB.P26) Homme a demi etendu, tenant une lanterne (67x155cm-26x61in) (F.FR 26000)

GIORDANO DI PALMA, Leon Jean (1882-?) Italian
£810 $1587   *(23-Nov-90 PLF.P121/R) Port mediterranneen (66x55cm-26x22in) s. crayon W/C (F.FR 8000)*

GIORDANO, Felice (1880-1964) Italian
£521 $1000   (20-Feb-91 D.NY41) Positano (69x89cm-27x35in) s.
£592 $1000   (1-May-91 D.NY42) Harbour view (30x38cm-12x15in) s. board
£785 $1350   (17-May-91 DM.D2228/R) Beach scene (58x81cm-23x32in) s.
£1173 $2100   (16-Mar-91 W.W98/R) Village on the coast (71x102cm-28x40in) s.
£2266 $3830   (16-Apr-91 CH.R113) Natura morta di pesci con bilancia (100x90cm-39x35in) s. (I.L 5000000)
£2736 $4570   (6-Jun-91 F.M26/R) Capri (74x118cm-29x46in) s. (I.L 6000000)

GIORDANO, Luca (1632-1705) Italian
£5000 $8150   (5-Jul-91 C232/R) Adoration of shepherds (58x117cm-23x46in) panel
£7692 $15000   (10-Oct-90 CH.NY76/R) The Assumption of the Virgin (180x127cm-71x50in)
£9500 $18525   (26-Oct-90 C1/R) The presentation of the Virgin in the Temple (107x135cm-42x53in)
£12048 $19398   (25-Jun-91 APT.P6/R) La Circoncision (180x233cm-71x92in) (F.FR 120000)
£12274 $24057   (19-Nov-90 CH.R159/R) Filosofo leggente (117x99cm-46x39in) (I.L 27000000)
£14691 $28942   (14-Nov-90 D.V45/R) Samson and Delila (124x99cm-49x39in) (A.S 300000)
£22000 $42460   (12-Dec-90 S208/R) The conversion of Saul (102x121cm-40x48in)
£29981 $51867   (21-May-91 EP.M9/R) La Adoracion de los pastores (208x170cm-82x67in) (S.P 5500000)
£36842 $70000   (10-Jan-91 SY.NY54/R) Diana adoring sleeping Endymion (155x208cm-61x82in) s.
£145488 $251694   (21-May-91 SY.MI1069/R) La morte di Giuliano l'Apostata (249x359cm-98x141in) (I.L 320000000)
£1600 $3088   *(12-Dec-90 PH138/R) Two bearded men strolling before colonnade (20x12cm-8x5in) chk wash*
£2000 $3260   *(1-Jul-91 S5/R) Dream of Solomon (43x32cm-17x13in) bears init.verso red chk*
£3000 $5070   *(16-Apr-91 C165/R) The agony in the garden (18x22cm-7x9in) watermark red chk. inscribed oval*
£3800 $6194   *(1-Jul-91 S174/R) Rinaldo and Armida (44x64cm-17x25in) red chk*

GIORDANO, Luca (after) (1632-1705) Italian
£6000 $9780   (5-Jul-91 C223/R) Rape of Helen (159x206cm-63x81in)

GIORDANO, Luca (attrib) (1632-1705) Italian
£8205 $16000   (10-Oct-90 CH.NY20/R) Salome with head of St John the Baptist
                 (170x280cm-67x110in)
£10553 $17307   (22-Jun-91 CH.MO128/R) Des musiciennes (74x115cm-29x45in) (F.FR 105000)
£11500 $22655   (31-Oct-90 S128/R) The Rape of Helen (28x34cm-11x13in) glass
*£1053 $2000   (8-Jan-91 SY.NY185/R) A kneeling figure draped in a long robe
                 (23x18cm-9x7in) chk.*
*£4211 $8000   (8-Jan-91 SY.NY2/R) Christ among the doctors (38x54cm-15x21in) pen over
                 traces blk.chk. laid down album page*

GIORDANO, Luca (circle) (1632-1705) Italian
£1000 $1920   (29-Nov-90 CSK28/R) The Judgement of Solomon (51x78cm-20x31in)
£1937 $3719   (30-Nov-90 APT.P20/R) L'alchimiste (100x74cm-39x29in) (F.FR 19000)
£2900 $5655   (26-Oct-90 PHM79/R) The Adoration of the shepherds (36x45cm-14x18in)
£3182 $6237   (19-Nov-90 CH.R70/R) S.Benedetto accoglie Totila (73x143cm-29x56in)
                 (I.L 7000000)
£6000 $11700   (26-Oct-90 C20/R) The dream of Joseph (67x81cm-26x32in)
£13917 $23519   (18-Apr-91 APT.P5/R) La Sainte Famille au desert (117x162cm-46x64in)
                 (F.FR 140000)

GIORDANO, Luca (studio) (1632-1705) Italian
£13529 $23000   (30-May-91 SY.NY74/R) Departure of Rebecca (109x142cm-43x56in)

GIORDANO, Luca (style) (1632-1705) Italian
£820 $1607   (24-Jan-91 EP.M9/R) El descanso en la huida a Egipto (140x200cm-55x79in)
                 (S.P 150000)
£1000 $2000   (7-Feb-91 CSK17) Franciscan saint performing miracle (51x51cm-20x20in)
£1000 $1900   (13-Sep-90 CSK276/R) Annunciation (51x58cm-20x23in)
£2938 $5788   (14-Nov-90 D.V263/R) Triumph of Amphitrite (39x53cm-15x21in) panel
                 (A.S 60000)
£3200 $5408   (18-Apr-91 C20/R) The death of Cleopatra (116x98cm-46x39in)
£13000 $21970   (17-Apr-91 S126/R) Democritus (113x86cm-44x34in)

GIORGI, A (1781-?) Spanish
£600 $1032   (16-May-91 CSK121) Posy (49x34cm-19x13in) s.d.1879

GIORGIONE (after) (1477-1510) Italian
£750 $1268   (18-Apr-91 CSK26) Man holding recorder (56x46cm-22x18in)

GIORGIONE (style) (1477-1510) Italian
£1800 $3510   (25-Oct-90 CSK33/R) Wooded landscape with shepherdess by pool
                 (33x25cm-13x10in)

GIORNI, G (?) Italian
£555 $1077   (4-Dec-90 F.R2) Campagna romana (17x50cm-7x20in) s. W/C (I.L 1200000)

GIOVANNI DI PAOLO (15th C) Italian
£311558 $510955 (17-Jun-91 ARC.P16/R) La Vierge et l'Enfant en trone dans une mandorle
                 de seraphins ...... (69x59cm-27x23in) tempera panel painted with
                 studio (F.FR 3100000)

GIOVANNI DI SAN GIOVANNI (attrib) (1592-1636) Italian
*£946 $1608   (27-May-91 L.K197/R) Allegorical scene with the triumph of victorious
                 navy hero (31x34cm-12x13in) i. ochre (DM 2800)*

GIOVANNI, Luigi di (1856-?) Italian
£4784 $8133   (28-May-91 F.R101/R) Bimbo col tamburo (125x69cm-49x27in) s.d.1889
                 (I.L 10500000)
*£729 $1239   (28-May-91 F.R47) Ritratto di bimbo (44x35cm-17x14in) s.d.1889 pastel
                 (I.L 1600000)*

GIOVANNINI (attrib) (?) Italian
£3289 $6380   (8-Dec-90 SY.MO338/R) Vue du Forum Romain (47x72cm-19x28in) s.
                 (F.FR 32000)

GIOVANNINI, Vincenzo (19th C) Italian
£6007 $11594   (11-Dec-90 CH.R79/R) Campagna romana con contadini e mandrie di cavalli
                 (40x93cm-16x37in) s.d.1887 (I.L 13000000)
£8684 $16500   (27-Feb-91 SY.NY362/R) Via Appia (48x96cm-19x38in) s.i.d.1875
£8684 $16500   (27-Feb-91 SY.NY361/R) Roman landscape with aqueduct (48x96cm-19x38in)
                 s.indist.i.d.1875
£11163 $18977   (28-May-91 F.R116/R) Butteri nella campagna romana. Sul fiume
                 (38x91cm-15x36in) s.d.1884 pair (I.L 24500000)

GIOVANNINI, Vincenzo (attrib) (19th C) Italian
£5789 $11000   (27-Feb-91 SY.NY358/R) Coaches departing Rome (48x71cm-19x28in)

GIRAN, Christian (1942-) French?
£1223 $2349   (2-Dec-90 FE.P133) Masque a Venise (80x40cm-31x16in) s. (F.FR 12000)

GIRAN-MAX, Leon (1867-1927) French
£1012 $1984   (20-Nov-90 MF.P77) Village provencal (94x155cm-37x61in) s.d.1920
                 (F.FR 10000)
£7591 $14879   (20-Nov-90 MF.P71) Bords de Seine a Conflans (143x83cm-56x33in) s.d.1917
                 (F.FR 75000)

GIRARD, Johan-Peter (1769-1851) Swiss
£2551 $5026   (14-Nov-90 FB.P265/R) Vue de l'ile Saint-Pierre sur le lac de Bienne (35x49cm-14x19in) s. gouache (F.FR 25000)

GIRARD, Marie Firmin (1838-1921) French
£2976 $5000   (17-Jul-91 SY.NY254/R) Summer outing (16x22cm-6x9in) s. panel
£9231 $18000   (24-Oct-90 CH.NY65/R) Le moulin de Gatellier (63x86cm-25x34in) s.
£28947 $55000   (28-Feb-91 CH.NY12/R) Promenade on autumn day (74x104cm-29x41in) s.

GIRARDET, Abraham (attrib) (1764-1823) Swiss
£1480 $2915   (14-Nov-90 FB.P82/R) Semira et Semino (25x30cm-10x12in) wash (F.FR 14500)

GIRARDET, Edouard-Henri (1819-1880) Swiss
£797 $1554   (24-Oct-90 GD.B407/R) Entrance to castle with elegant lady meeting gentleman (41x32cm-16x13in) s. panel (S.FR 2000)

GIRARDET, Eugene Alexis (1853-1907) French
£911 $1785   (20-Nov-90 APT.P274/R) Anier dans la montagne (26x40cm-10x16in) s. panel (F.FR 9000)
£1923 $3769   (20-Nov-90 APT.P273/R) En descendant vers l'oued (21x32cm-8x13in) s. panel (F.FR 19000)
£1992 $3426   (14-May-91 GF.L2149/R) Paysage a El-Kanthara (38x55cm-15x22in) s. (S.FR 5000)
£2335 $3923   (23-Apr-91 SY.AM189/R) Washerwoman and man on donkey in North African landscape (26x41cm-10x16in) s. panel (D.FL 7800)
£4361 $8635   (3-Feb-91 I.N102) La carvane (40x62cm-16x24in) s. (F.FR 43000)
£5179 $8805   (27-May-91 APT.P276/R) La priere (54x40cm-21x16in) s. (F.FR 52000)
£5976 $10159   (27-May-91 APT.P272/R) Paysage de Kabylle (49x82cm-19x32in) s. (F.FR 60000)
£14940 $25398   (27-May-91 APT.P273/R) Les lavandieres au bord du Nil (68x110cm-27x43in) s. (F.FR 150000)

GIRARDET, Eugene Alexis (attrib) (1853-1907) French
£1020 $2010   (13-Nov-90 ARC.P203/R) Deux soeurs devant leur maison (21x32cm-8x13in) (F.FR 10000)

GIRARDET, Jules (1856-?) French
£518 $1010   (24-Oct-90 GD.B409) The rose (35x52cm-14x20in) s. W/C over pencil (S.FR 1300)

GIRARDET, Karl (1813-1871) Swiss
£635 $1137   (13-Mar-91 GK.Z35 a) View of mountains and Lake Brienz (19x25cm-7x10in) board (S.FR 1600)
£1224 $2400   (6-Nov-90 GF.L2470/R) Forest stream (30x34cm-12x13in) mono. st.studio verso board (S.FR 3000)
£3811 $7432   (12-Oct-90 APT.P27/R) Le retour du troupeau (11x32cm-4x13in) bears init. studo st. verso board (F.FR 38000)
£16867 $33060   (21-Nov-90 SY.Z22/R) Vierwaldstattersee landscape (50x93cm-20x37in) s. (S.FR 42000)

GIRARDIN, Julien (19th C) French
£2191 $3791   (24-May-91 FB.P150/R) Fleurs de pavots (148x94cm-58x37in) s.d.1894 (F.FR 22000)

GIRARDOT, Ernest Gustave (fl.1860-1893) British
£1050 $1817   (22-May-91 S61/R) Aye, ready (57x44cm-22x17in) s.d.1902 s.i.d.1902 verso

GIRAUD, L H (?) ?
£1506 $2786   (4-Mar-91 ARC.P132/R) Jeune femme a l'eventail (80x55cm-31x22in) s. (F.FR 15000)

GIRAUD, P (?) French
£1400 $2744   (22-Nov-90 CSK92/R) Still life of summer flowers in vase on table (71x57cm-28x22in) s.

GIRAUD, Sebastien Charles (1819-1892) French
£4798 $8253   (16-May-91 D.V46/R) Still life of flowers (71x57cm-28x22in) s. (A.S 100000)
£23000 $37720   (21-Jun-91 C103/R) Preparing hookah (53x39cm-21x15in) s. panel

GIRAUD, Victor (after) (1840-1871) French
£2010 $3296   (19-Jun-91 ZZ.F59) Un marchand d'esclaves (60x94cm-24x37in) (F.FR 20000)

GIRAULT, Gaston (20th C) French?
£1215 $2381   (25-Nov-90 ZZ.F72/R) Le port de Honfleur (64x80cm-25x31in) s.d.55 (F.FR 12000)

GIRIER, Jean-Aime (1837-1912) French
£1233 $2393   (3-Dec-90 CS.L113/R) Paysage des Dombes (27x54cm-11x21in) s. (F.FR 12000)

GIRKE, Raimund (1930-) German
£3767 $6140   (14-Jun-91 L.K898) Untitled (90x80cm-35x31in) s.i.d.1964 egg tempera cotton (DM 11000)
£4452 $7257   (14-Jun-91 L.K897/R) On white (55x55cm-22x22in) tempera (DM 13000)

GIRKE, Raimund (1930-) German-cont.
£6143	$12041	(20-Nov-90 L.K243/R) Structurbild (35x80cm-14x31in) s.d.1961stretcher oil tempera (DM 18000)
£7877	$12839	(14-Jun-91 L.K899) Untitled (60x60cm-24x24in) d.1967 (DM 23000)
£683	$1338	*(20-Nov-90 L.K244/R) Untitled (38x28cm-15x11in) s.d.1974verso gouache (DM 2000)*
£751	$1472	*(20-Nov-90 L.K245) Untitled (27x19cm-11x7in) d.1980 W/C (DM 2200)*
£1138	$2185	*(26-Nov-90 WK.M647/R) Progression horizontal (31x25cm-12x10in) s.d.1970verso W/C over pencil (DM 3300)*
£2568	$4187	(14-Jun-91 L.K902) White structures (25x32cm-10x13in) s.d.1963verso mixed media (DM 7500)
£2568	$4187	(14-Jun-91 L.K903) Untitled (101x72cm-40x28in) s.d.71 spray technique pencil board (DM 7500)
£3425	$5582	(14-Jun-91 L.K901/R) White structures (34x54cm-13x21in) s.d.1961 s.i.d.verso mixed media (DM 10000)
£4623	$7536	(14-Jun-91 L.K900/R) White structures (34x48cm-13x19in) s.d.60 mixed media (DM 13500)

GIRODET DE ROUCY TRIOSON, Anne Louis (1767-1824) French
£13065	$21427	(21-Jun-91 SY.MO24/R) Portrait d'Antoine-Etienne Girodet de Roussy (53x44cm-21x17in) oval (F.FR 130000)
£18090	$29668	(21-Jun-91 SY.MO26/R) Le vigneron (40x32cm-16x13in) (F.FR 180000)
£60302	$98894	(21-Jun-91 SY.MO28/R) Etude pour le visage de Galatee (46x38cm-18x15in) (F.FR 600000)
£130653	$214271	(21-Jun-91 SY.MO27/R) Portrait en buste de la Reine Hortense (61x50cm-24x20in) (F.FR 1300000)

GIRODET DE ROUCY TRIOSON, Anne Louis (attrib) (1767-1824) French
| £1300 | $2301 | *(22-Mar-91 APT.P85) Le repos du guerrier (14x22cm-6x9in) i. pen wash blk.crayon htd.white gouache (F.FR 13000)* |

GIROL, Paul (1911-) French
| £742 | $1328 | (8-Apr-91 CR.P168) Sainte Marine (81x100cm-32x39in) s. (F.FR 7500) |
| £4000 | $7760 | (6-Dec-90 CSK188/R) L'Itimite (98x131cm-39x52in) s. s.l.verso |

GIRON, Charles (1850-1914) Swiss
| £5500 | $10835 | (5-Oct-90 C38/R) Diana and Actaeon (70x114cm-28x45in) s.d.1879 |

GIRONCOLI, Bruno (1936-) Austrian
| £2485 | $4821 | *(6-Dec-90 D.V198/R) Untitled (75x55cm-30x22in) s.d.1970/72 mixed media collage (A.S 50000)* |

GIRONES, Ramon Anton Pichot see PICHOT GIRONES, Ramon Antonio

GIROUD, P (19th C) French
| £2232 | $3750 | (17-Jul-91 SY.NY260/R) The Procession (111x89cm-44x35in) s. |

GIROUST, Jean Antoine Theodore (1753-1817) French
| £68966 | $132414 | (17-Dec-90 ARC.P55/R) Oedipe a colonne (160x193cm-63x76in) (F.FR 680000) |

GIROUX, Ernest (1851-?) Italian/French
| £14800 | $28711 | (5-Dec-90 F.M76/R) Veduta di piazza londinese (77x97cm-30x38in) s. (I.L 32000000) |

GIRTIN, Thomas (1775-1802) British
| £4000 | $6600 | *(11-Jul-91 S168/R) Westminster from Adelphi Terrace (29x22cm-11x9in) pen ink over pencil wash* |
| £17000 | $30430 | *(9-Apr-91 C112/R) Paris, looking towards Montmartre (16x23cm-6x9in) i.verso pencil W/C* |

GIRTIN, Thomas (after) (1775-1802) British
| £3500 | $6790 | (5-Dec-90 PHL79) An overshot mill (39x56cm-15x22in) col. washes |

GISCHARD, Th (19th C) Swiss
| £1786 | $3161 | (22-Mar-91 EA.Z585) Lake landscape with town, possibly Brienz (122x202cm-48x80in) s.i.d.1889 one of pair (S.FR 4500) |

GISCHIA, Leon (1903-) French
£960	$1661	(10-May-91 S.Z37) Composition (60x81cm-24x32in) s.d.1973 (S.FR 2400)
£1016	$2033	(10-Feb-91 CC.P28) Composition (38x54cm-15x21in) s. d.1956 verso (F.FR 10000)
£1529	$2951	(16-Dec-90 GL.P88) Composition (48x38cm-19x15in) s. (F.FR 15000)
£1529	$2951	(16-Dec-90 GL.P80) Composition (55x38cm-22x15in) s.d.75 (F.FR 15000)
£1580	$3049	(16-Dec-90 GL.P144) Composition (46x38cm-18x15in) s.d.74 (F.FR 15500)
£2039	$3935	(16-Dec-90 GL.P106) Composition (73x60cm-29x24in) s. (F.FR 20000)
£2273	$4455	(20-Nov-90 BR.M36/R) Composizione (76x55cm-30x22in) s. tempera board (I.L 5000000)
£2341	$4566	(22-Oct-90 BR.M228/R) Composition (38x46cm-15x18in) s. d.1975verso (I.L 5200000)
£2811	$4526	(30-Jun-91 I.N20) Composition (38x46cm-15x18in) s. (F.FR 28000)
£2945	$5124	(26-Mar-91 F.M144/R) Les Objets sur la table (80x65cm-31x26in) s. d.1967verso (I.L 6500000)
£5128	$10103	(1-Oct-90 CC.P160/R) Le vase verre (65x50cm-26x20in) s.d.1953 (F.FR 52000)
£10703	$20657	(14-Dec-90 RY.P45/R) Alberi i murali, 1956 (100x72cm-39x28in) s. (F.FR 105000)

GISCHIA, Leon (1903-) French-cont.
£1631 $3148   (16-Dec-90 GL.P82) Composition (53x75cm-21x30in) s.d.73 gouache
                (F.FR 16000)

GISELA, Josef (1851-1899) Austrian
£5802 $10908   (19-Sep-90 N.M494/R) Pub interior with landlord and guests
                 (41x50cm-16x20in) s. (DM 17000)
£668 $1303   (11-Oct-90 D.V74/R) The evening prayers (27x34cm-11x13in) s. chl
                 (A.S 14000)

GISIKO-SPARCK, Ida (1859-1940) Swedish
£566 $979   (22-May-91 BA.S546/R) Boats in the bay in summer (31x55cm-12x22in)
                 s.d.79 (S.KR 6000)

GISLANDER, William (1890-1937) Swedish
£597 $1171   (10-Nov-90 FAL.M119/R) Seascape (60x80cm-24x31in) s.d.1919 (S.KR 6500)
£644 $1275   (31-Jan-91 RAS.V477/R) Bird of prey with catch in landscape
                 (82x100cm-32x39in) s.d.1929 (D.KR 7200)
£796 $1544   (22-Aug-90 RAS.K209/R) Heath landscape with snipe (76x97cm-30x38in)
                 s.d.1929 (D.KR 9200)
£822 $1594   (22-Aug-90 RAS.K210/R) Landscape with duck and ducklings
                 (80x100cm-31x39in) s.d.1928 (D.KR 9500)
£952 $1846   (22-Aug-90 RAS.K211/R) Three swans in flight over ocean
                 (55x55cm-22x22in) s.d.1929 (D.KR 11000)
£974 $1647   (1-May-91 KH.K70) Swans in flight over coast, winter (115x130cm-45x51in)
                 s.d.1931 (S.KR 11000)
£1103 $2206   (10-Feb-91 BU.M39) Swans swimming (95x142cm-37x56in) s. (S.KR 12000)
£1125 $2182   (22-Aug-90 RAS.K208/R) Landscape with swans in flight (85x119cm-33x47in)
                 s.d.1928 (D.KR 13000)
£1149 $2252   (10-Nov-90 FAL.M118/R) Pheasant in winter landscape (92x73cm-36x29in)
                 s.d.1931 (S.KR 12500)
£1301 $2329   (13-Apr-91 FAL.M89/R) Boggy landscape with snipe (78x99cm-31x39in)
                 s.d.1929 (S.KR 14000)
£1884 $3693   (10-Nov-90 FAL.M116/R) Swans (55x65cm-22x26in) s.d.1924 (S.KR 20500)
£2206 $4324   (10-Nov-90 FAL.M114/R) Family of swans on glittering lake
                 (111x120cm-44x47in) s.d.1927 (S.KR 24000)
£2649 $4741   (13-Apr-91 FAL.M87/R) Duck and ducklings (81x100cm-32x39in) s.d.1928
                 (S.KR 28500)
£3768 $7386   (10-Nov-90 FAL.M115/R) Swans in flight over sea (88x133cm-35x52in)
                 s.d.1927 (S.KR 41000)

GISSING, Roland (1895-1967) Canadian
£526 $1032   (20-Nov-90 JOY.T335/R) Kananaskis range (30x40cm-12x16in) canvasboard
                 (C.D 1200)
£702 $1382   (30-Oct-90 MA.V100) Bow Lake and Crawford Glacier (30x36cm-12x14in) s.
                 board (C.D 1600)
£773 $1314   (27-May-91 HO.ED93) Scene near Proctor, Alec Garner's House
                 (30x41cm-12x16in) s. s.i.d.verso board (C.D 1500)
£786 $1548   (12-Nov-90 HO.ED35/R) Bow lake and Bow peak (41x51cm-16x20in) s.i.
                 (C.D 1800)
£789 $1547   (20-Nov-90 JOY.T288) Winter sunset (45x60cm-18x24in) s. (C.D 1800)
£877 $1719   (20-Nov-90 JOY.T254/R) River in mountains (60x75cm-24x30in) s.
                 (C.D 2000)
£942 $1574   (3-Jun-91 R.T112/R) Winter stream (50x61cm-20x24in) s. (C.D 1800)
£965 $1891   (20-Nov-90 JOY.T414/R) Black Rock Mountain and Ghost River
                 (45x60cm-18x24in) s. (C.D 2200)
£1053 $2063   (20-Nov-90 JOY.T365) Valley of Ten Peaks (55x75cm-22x30in) s.
                 (C.D 2400)
£1082 $1840   (27-May-91 HO.ED68) Autumn sun (46x61cm-18x24in) s. s.i.verso
                 (C.D 2100)
£1179 $2323   (12-Nov-90 HO.ED215/R) On Sheep River (41x56cm-16x22in) s.i. (C.D 2700)
£1201 $2126   (20-Mar-91 MA.V193) The Kananaskis river (41x51cm-16x20in) s.
                 (C.D 2450)
£1340 $2278   (27-May-91 HO.ED37/R) Harvest, Bow Valley (46x61cm-18x24in) s. i.verso
                 (C.D 2600)
£1443 $2454   (27-May-91 HO.ED322/R) Reflections, Lake Minnewanka (51x76cm-20x30in) s.
                 s.i.d.1951verso (C.D 2800)
£1572 $3097   (12-Nov-90 HO.ED327/R) Bow river near Bow lake (51x66cm-20x26in)
                 s.i.d.1952 (C.D 3600)
£1753 $2979   (27-May-91 HO.ED335) Oil rig (91x76cm-36x30in) s. (C.D 3400)
£2165 $3680   (27-May-91 HO.ED273/R) Winter sunset (61x76cm-24x30in) s. i.verso
                 (C.D 4200)
£2533 $4990   (12-Nov-90 HO.ED278/R) Alberta harvest (46x61cm-18x24in) s.i.d.
                 (C.D 5800)
£2729 $5377   (12-Nov-90 HO.ED298/R) New Valley Well (61x76cm-24x30in) s.i. board
                 (C.D 6250)
£2964 $5039   (27-May-91 HO.ED95/R) Mid Royal Well (60x76cm-24x30in) s.d.1938 i.verso
                 board (C.D 5750)

GISSON, Andre (20th C) American
£518 $1000   (10-Dec-90 H.C1212) Femme nue se coiffant (51x41cm-20x16in) s.
£533 $900   (20-Apr-91 WOL.C375) Paris street scene (23x30cm-9x12in) s.
£564 $1100   (10-Oct-90 SY.NY221/R) The laundresses (23x30cm-9x12in) s.
£667 $1300   (10-Oct-90 SY.NY301/R) Floral still life (51x41cm-20x16in) s.
£710 $1200   (20-Apr-91 WOL.C376/R) Paris Arch of Triumph (41x51cm-16x20in) s.
£761 $1500   (13-Nov-90 CE.NY41/R) Mere avec son enfant (23x30cm-9x12in) s.

GISSON, Andre (20th C) American-cont.
£767	$1250	(5-Jul-91 S.W3061/R) Parisian street scene (30x41cm-12x16in) s.
£767	$1250	(5-Jul-91 S.W3062) Figures strolling near the Arc de Triomphe (30x41cm-12x16in) s.
£821	$1600	(10-Oct-90 SY.NY173/R) Stroll on the beach (61x76cm-24x30in) s.
£863	$1700	(7-Oct-90 DU.E127/R) Carousel (23x30cm-9x12in) s.
£888	$1500	(20-Apr-91 WOL.C377) Harbour (28x38cm-11x15in) s.
£914	$1800	(7-Oct-90 DU.E249/R) Flowers on ledge (30x41cm-12x16in) s.
£915	$1500	(23-Jun-91 H.C988) Paris street scene (61x91cm-24x36in) s.
£933	$1800	(10-Dec-90 H.C1209/R) Arc de Triomphe (51x61cm-20x24in) s.
£942	$1574	(4-Jun-91 R.T238/R) In Tuilleries (77x61cm-30x24in) s. (C.D 1800)
£957	$1800	(22-Sep-90 WOL.C413/R) Poplars along Seine (61x76cm-24x30in) s.
£1011	$1900	(22-Sep-90 WOL.C412/R) Boats on Seine (61x76cm-24x30in) s.
£1168	$2300	(13-Nov-90 CE.NY38/R) Mere et enfant dans la campagne (41x51cm-16x20in) s.
£1276	$2500	(12-Feb-91 SY.NY140/R) Parisian street scene (23x30cm-9x12in) s.
£1282	$2500	(10-Oct-90 SY.NY256/R) Place de la Concorde (36x91cm-14x36in) s.
£1330	$2500	(22-Sep-90 WOL.C405/R) By Seine (61x91cm-24x36in) s.
£1385	$2700	(10-Oct-90 SY.NY225/R) Mother and child (41x51cm-16x20in) s.
£1403	$2750	(12-Feb-91 SY.NY139/R) Promenade sur le Quai des Tuleries (61x91cm-24x36in) s.
£1421	$2800	(13-Nov-90 CE.NY42/R) Rue de Paris (61x92cm-24x36in) s.
£1524	$2500	(19-Jun-91 B.SF1948/R) The merry-go-round (61x91cm-24x36in) s. board
£1534	$2500	(12-Jun-91 SY.NY49/R) Notre Dame (46x61cm-18x24in) s.
£1534	$2500	(12-Jun-91 SY.NY116/R) Portrait of young girl (23x30cm-9x12in) s.
£1538	$3000	(10-Oct-90 SY.NY257/R) Notre Dame (61x91cm-24x36in) s.
£1777	$3500	(16-Nov-90 DM.D2020/R) Carousel (61x91cm-24x36in) s.
£2083	$4000	(26-Nov-90 S.SL471/R) River landscape with couple seated on grass and boat drawn up on bank (61x91cm-24x36in) s.
£2147	$3500	(12-Jun-91 SY.NY141/R) Patio (76x61cm-30x24in) s.

GITTARD, Alexandre (1832-1904) French
£789	$1547	(25-Nov-90 ZZ.F73) Lavandiere sous le pont (26x21cm-10x8in) s. panel (F.FR 7800)

GIUDICI, Reinaldo (1853-1921) Argentinian
£1156	$2000	(8-May-91 RO.BA370) Veleros en la costa (40x65cm-16x26in) s.

GIUFFRIDA, Nino (1924-) Italian
£907	$1769	(28-Oct-90 M.V138) Theatre future (60x73cm-24x29in) s. acrylic oil (F.FR 9000)

GIULI, Niccola (attrib) (1720-1784) Italian
£6166	$11963	(7-Dec-90 SY.MO109/R) Oiseaux et tortue dans un paysage (54x80cm-21x31in) (F.FR 60000)

GIULIANO, Bartolomeo (1829-1909) Italian
£3378	$5709	(3-May-91 SA.A1843/R) Dreaming by the sea (78x63cm-31x25in) s.d.1872 (DM 10000)
£4625	$8972	(5-Dec-90 F.M70/R) Una vittima del feudalesimo (103x90cm-41x35in) s.d.1855 (I.L 10000000)
£12000	$24000	(18-Oct-90 F.M44/R) Pastorella con gregge (35x27cm-14x11in) s. (I.L 27000000)
£18344	$32837	(12-Mar-91 F.M66/R) Alla fonte (100x85cm-39x33in) s.d.1882 (I.L 40000000)
£31449	$61012	(5-Dec-90 F.M78/R) La Mignon (151x104cm-59x41in) s.d.1892 (I.L 68000000)

GIUNTA, Joseph (1911-) Canadian
£830	$1626	(5-Nov-90 FB.M240/R) Sous bois (61x51cm-24x20in) s.d.1961 board (C.D 1900)

GIUNTA, Marc (1954-) French
£502	$808	(24-Jun-91 PR.P147) Les flamands roses (135x182cm-53x72in) s.d.dec.87 (F.FR 5000)
£1305	$2101	(24-Jun-91 PR.P145) Les voitures (110x148cm-43x58in) s.d.August 88 (F.FR 13000)

GIUSTI, Guglielmo (1824-1916) Italian
£2719	$4596	(16-Apr-91 CH.R117/R) Costiera napoletana (72x96cm-28x38in) s. (I.L 6000000)
£850	$1632	(17-Dec-90 PH154) Napoli da Capadimonte (22x33cm-9x13in) s. i.verso gouache
£850	$1632	(17-Dec-90 PH156) Sorrento (34x43cm-13x17in) s. i.verso gouache
£950	$1824	(17-Dec-90 PH155/R) Napoli da Posilipos (33x43cm-13x17in) s. i.verso gouache
£1800	$3546	(5-Oct-90 C126/R) Napoli da Capodimonte. Ischia (33x17cm-13x7in) s. one i.verso bodycol pair
£1900	$3724	(22-Nov-90 CSK77/R) Peasants on path overlooking Bay of Sorrento (32x45cm-13x18in) s. bodycol

GIUSTO, Andrea di (late 15th C) Italian
£84211	$160000	(11-Jan-91 CH.NY41/R) Madonna and child. The Nativity with the angel of the Annunciation. The Crucifixion bears i. tempera on gold panel triptych

GIUSTO, Faust (?) Italian
£2500 $4925   (5-Oct-90 C73/R) Le Boulevard St. Denis, Paris (44x70cm-17x28in) s.

GIUTTI, G (19th C) Italian
£694   *$1200*   *(10-May-91 S.W2559) Along the Amalfi coast (33x46cm-13x18in) s. gouache*

GLACKENS, William (1870-1938) American
£1515 $3000   (30-Jan-91 GRO.B55/R) Bridge over the river (36x51cm-14x20in) s. verso
   i. stretcher
£4734 $8000   (20-Apr-91 WOL.C178/R) Floral still life (33x41cm-13x16in) s.
£13372 $23000   (18-May-91 W.W178/R) Road near Cannes (33x41cm-13x16in) init. i. verso
   canvasboard
£15385 $26000   (19-Apr-91 DM.D2038/R) Baie St. Paul, Quebec (30x41cm-12x16in)
   canvasboard
£17341 $30000   (22-May-91 CH.NY260/R) Alice Mumford (76x63cm-30x25in)
£57803 $100000   (22-May-91 CH.NY266/R) A portrait of Penny (60x57cm-24x22in) s.
£549   *$950*   *(10-May-91 S.BM72/R) Seated woman (13x8cm-5x3in) s. chl*
£893   *$1714*   *(27-Nov-90 W.T1249) New York street scene (23x18cm-9x7in) init. pencil*
   chl (C.D 2000)
£1082   *$2100*   *(7-Dec-90 S.W2686/R) Woodland and mountain stream (36x41cm-14x16in) s.*
   pastel
£1163   *$2000*   *(18-May-91 W.W170/R) Nude leaning (25x20cm-10x8in) pastel*
£1198   *$2300*   *(17-Dec-90 SY.NY229/R) You are Mrs. Nolan (28x30cm-11x12in) s. indian*
   ink col.pencil
£1339   *$2571*   *(27-Nov-90 W.T1249 a) The stolen crown, study for May day*
   (18x15cm-7x6in) init. pencil W/C (C.D 3000)
£1474   *$2800*   *(9-Jan-91 CH.NY237/R) A tune in court (39x35cm-15x14in) s. chl Chinese*
   white ink en grisaille
£3158   *$6000*   *(9-Jan-91 CH.NY238/R) The Trevinos (31x40cm-12x16in) s. gouache wash en*
   grisaille

GLAIN, Pascal Leon (18th C) French
£1521   *$3012*   *(30-Jan-91 APT.P122/R) Portrait de femme vue en buste (60x51cm-24x20in)*
   s.i. verso pastel (F.FR 15000)
£1631   *$3131*   *(27-Nov-90 APT.P151/R) Portrait d'homme (66x54cm-26x21in) s.d.1755*
   pastel (F.FR 16000)

GLAIZE, Auguste Barthelemy (1807-1893) French
£2490 $4308   (24-May-91 FB.P3/R) L'apparition (130x200cm-51x79in) s.d.1884
   (F.FR 25000)
£697   *$1206*   *(24-May-91 FB.P25/R) Tristesse (53x35cm-21x14in) lead pencil (F.FR 7000)*
£1263   *$2400*   *(27-Feb-91 SY.NY46/R) Study of seated woman in classical dress*
   (45x32cm-18x13in) s.i. chl white chk

GLANSDORFF, Hubert (1877-1964) Belgian
£2566 $5055   (6-Oct-90 KV.L117/R) Flowers in a vase (80x100cm-31x39in) s.d.44
   (B.FR 160000)

GLANTSCHNIGG, Ulrich (attrib) (1661-1722) Italian
£1221 $2186   (14-Mar-91 D.V368/R) Mary and Child (28x22cm-11x9in) copper (A.S 25000)

GLARNER, Fritz (1899-1972) Swiss
£25794 $43075   (5-Jun-91 SY.Z180/R) Relational painting (41x33cm-16x13in) s.d.43
   (S.FR 65000)

GLASS, William Mervyn (1885-1965) British
£2800 $5236   (28-Aug-90 S942/R) Iona (62x92cm-24x36in) init.s.i.

GLASSON, Lancelot Myles (1894-?) British
£2100 $4158   (29-Jan-91 PH37/R) Model (73x96cm-29x38in) s.d.1932

GLATT, Karl (1912-) Swiss
£2245 $4265   (14-Sep-90 ZOF.Z1078/R) Maison a Froidevaux (96x146cm-38x57in) s.
   (S.FR 5500)

GLATZ, Hans (1878-?) Austrian
£1007 $1963   (10-Oct-90 WE.MU268/R) The birth s. (DM 3000)

GLAUBER, Jan (1656-1703) Dutch
£4000 $7800   (26-Oct-90 C153/R) Diana and nymphs bathing (57x46cm-22x18in) s. canvas
   laid down on board
£7297 $12186   (4-Jun-91 CH.R297/R) Figure in un paesaggio (68x98cm-27x39in)
   (I.L 16000000)

GLAUBER, Jan (attrib) (1656-1703) Dutch
£1644 $3190   (7-Dec-90 SY.MO116/R) Paysage Italien (49x64cm-19x25in) (F.FR 16000)

GLAUBER, Johannes (1646-1726) Dutch
£1856 $3137   (2-May-91 CH.AM109) A waterfall with sherpherdesses resting and a
   traveller (45x64cm-18x25in) s. (D.FL 6200)
£8500 $15725   (5-Mar-91 PH96/R) Peasants unloading vessels on quay before coastal
   Roman landscape (51x71cm-20x28in)
£2446   *$4820*   *(12-Nov-90 CH.AM115/R) Figures on road in Arcadian landscape in storm*
   (24x37cm-9x15in) red chk (D.FL 8000)

GLAUBER, Johannes (circle) (1646-1726) Dutch
£2701 $5268   (23-Oct-90 CH.R452/R) Paesaggio con arco trionfale e la raccolta
            dell'uva (74x100cm-29x39in) (I.L 6000000)

GLEESON, James Timothy (1915-) Australian
£578 $1086   (17-Sep-90 MGS.S252 a) Cadmus (17x14cm-7x6in) s. board (A.D 1300)
£791 $1328   (22-Apr-91 SY.ME175) Portent (23x29cm-9x11in) s. s.i.verso paper on
            board (A.D 1700)
£1004 $1928   (27-Nov-90 JRL.S195) St Sebastian (33x21cm-13x8in) s. panel (A.D 2500)
£935   *$1523*   *(16-Jun-91 SY.ME98) Fantasy in figure 1 (49x37cm-19x15in) s. ink W/C*
            (A.D 2000)

GLEGHORN, Thomas (1925-) Australian
£633 $1215   (14-Aug-90 SY.ME64/R) Dog trap - landscape (59x90cm-23x35in) indist.sig.
            s.i. verso (A.D 1500)
£695   *$1369*   *(13-Nov-90 J.M25) Kakadu Theme (8x12cm-3x5in) mixed media panel of*
            sixteen images (A.D 1800)

GLEHN, Jane de (fl.1905-1940) British
£2000 $3480   (27-Mar-91 S27/R) Wylye Mill (51x61cm-20x24in) s.d.1932

GLEHN, Wilfred Gabriel de (1870-1951) British
£3000 $4890   (13-Jun-91 L399/R) The Helford Creek, Cornwall (46x61cm-18x24in) bears
            studio st. stretcher
£3000 $4890   (13-Jun-91 L398/R) At Helford - A cornish cornfield (46x61cm-18x24in) s.
£9000 $17010   (27-Sep-90 L50/R) The picnic (64x76cm-25x30in) bears studio st.
            stretcher
£800   *$1352*   *(2-May-91 C72/R) Venetian sunset (40x51cm-16x20in) W/C pencil*
£950   *$1606*   *(2-May-91 C76/R) Helford River, Cornwall (33x51cm-13x20in) W/C pencil*
£950   *$1606*   *(2-May-91 C75/R) St. Anthony-in-Meneage, Cornwall (40x51cm-16x20in) W/C*
            pencil
£1000   *$1690*   *(2-May-91 C73/R) River landscape with church tower (41x51cm-16x20in) W/C*
            pencil

GLEICH, John (1879-?) German
£1492 $2491   (5-Jun-91 DO.H2011/R) Hamburg Harbour with steamship (51x70cm-20x28in)
            s. (DM 4400)

GLEICHMANN, Otto (1887-1963) German
£3051   *$5095*   *(6-Jun-91 HN.H355/R) Harrende der eigenen Traurigkeit s.d.1921 W/C*
            bodycol. (DM 9000)

GLEIZES, Albert (1881-1953) French
£11000 $17710   (25-Jun-91 C113/R) Bord de riviere (48x65cm-19x26in) s.d.06
£13293 $21668   (11-Jun-91 I.N216/R) Le pont de Neuilly le soir (54x65cm-21x26in)
            (F.FR 132000)
£41833 $72371   (25-May-91 GL.P7/R) Femmes a Barcelone (38x46cm-15x18in) s.d.1916
            (F.FR 420000)
£47945 $78151   (15-Jun-91 L.K230/R) Abstract composition (73x60cm-29x24in) s.
            (DM 140000)
£75145 $130000   (8-May-91 SY.NY176/R) Les musiciens (119x94cm-47x37in) s.d.1920
£136986 $223288   (15-Jun-91 L.K229/R) Peinture familiere (102x77cm-40x30in) s.d.24
            (DM 400000)
£753   *$1228*   *(15-Jun-91 L.K231/R) Vanite (27x19cm-11x7in) s.i. indian ink pen*
            (DM 2200)
£918   *$1809*   *(16-Nov-90 FB.P179 c/R) Le printemps, l'ete, l'automne (16x34cm-6x13in)*
            lead pencil tracing paper (F.FR 9000)
£1205   *$2229*   *(6-Mar-91 HC.P72/R) Les Mejades - l'oie (20x15cm-8x6in) s.i.d.42 pen*
            htd.wash (F.FR 12000)
£1233   *$2393*   *(7-Dec-90 GL.P123) Le cirque (24x19cm-9x7in) s.d.1914 lead pencil*
            (F.FR 12000)
£2170   *$4274*   *(6-Oct-90 GL.P42) Les femmes qui cousent (13x9cm-5x4in) s.i.d.1913 lead*
            pencil ink (F.FR 22000)
£3223   *$5253*   *(16-Jun-91 CC.P2/R) Composition (20x14cm-8x6in) s.d.1914 indian ink*
            (F.FR 32000)
£3960   *$7010*   *(4-Apr-91 PPB.P50/R) Composition (23x18cm-9x7in) s.d.24 gouache*
            (F.FR 40000)
£5600   *$9128*   *(4-Jul-91 GL.P214/R) Crucifixion (39x25cm-15x10in) s.i.d.1922 gouache*
            (F.FR 56000)
£5935   *$10623*   *(9-Apr-91 BG.P24/R) Composition abstraite (15x11cm-6x4in) s.d.22 gouache*
            (F.FR 60000)
£7553   *$12311*   *(16-Jun-91 GL.P63/R) Paysage des Bermudes (24x22cm-9x9in) s.d.1917 W/C*
            (F.FR 75000)
£7839   *$14032*   *(17-Mar-91 GL.P31/R) Composition (22x17cm-9x7in) gouache (F.FR 78000)*
£8980   *$17420*   *(7-Dec-90 G.Z52/R) Nature morte cubiste (27x21cm-11x8in) s.d.1923*
            gouache (S.FR 22000)
£9654   *$19309*   *(10-Feb-91 CC.P29/R) Composition cubiste (38x27cm-15x11in) s.d.1916*
            Indian ink (F.FR 95000)
£10040   *$16165*   *(24-Jun-91 ARC.P33/R) Composition (35x27cm-14x11in) s. gouache*
            (F.FR 100000)
£10116   *$17500*   *(9-May-91 CH.NY129/R) Cubiste composition (30x23cm-12x9in) s.d.21*
            gouache
£13595   *$22160*   *(11-Jun-91 CSC.P8/R) Composition cubiste (37x26cm-15x10in) s. gouache*
            (F.FR 135000)
£14000   *$24780*   *(20-Mar-91 S41/R) La musicienne (48x32cm-19x13in) s.d.21 gouache W/C*
            over pencil

GLEIZES, Albert (1881-1953) French-cont.
*£101523 $200000   (15-Nov-90 CH.NY269/R) Composition (146x115cm-57x45in) s.d.1930 casein
              canvas*

GLENAVY, Lady Beatrice (1883-1970) British
£1481 $2859   (12-Dec-90 CH.E166/R) Driftwood (35x45cm-14x18in) mono. s.l.verso
                      (E.P 1600)

GLENDENING, Alfred (19th C) British
£2100 $3969   (26-Sep-90 S63/R) Cottage path (15x20cm-6x8in) s.d.1882
*£1500 $2970   (30-Jan-91 S246/R) Near Henley. Footbridge (32x23cm-13x9in) mono.d.1896
                      W/C htd bodycol oval pair*
£4200 $7938   (26-Sep-90 S346/R) Flower arranging (74x49cm-29x19in) mono.d.1897 W/C

GLENDENING, Alfred Augustus (19th C) British
£800 $1568   (20-Nov-90 PH61/R) View of the Thames (40x76cm-16x30in) init.d.1878
£1297 $2115   (10-Jun-91 W.T1473) View on the thames (39x75cm-15x30in) init.d.1878
                      (C.D 2400)
£1800 $3546   (1-Nov-90 CSK121/R) At Sunbury-on-Thames (39x29cm-15x11in) s.
£1800 $3546   (13-Nov-90 PH48/R) Figures on river bank (25x41cm-10x16in) init.d.98
£2500 $4900   (8-Nov-90 RBB712) Mountain landscape with sheep grazing near river
                      (28x53cm-11x21in) s.
£2800 $5516   (1-Nov-90 D173/R) Man in punt on river at sunset, with church tower and
                      cottages beyond (25x41cm-10x16in) mono.d.94
£3313 $6195   (27-Aug-90 SY.J164/R) Swans on upper Thames (61x107cm-24x42in) init.d.91
                      (SA.R 16000)
£3400 $6698   (1-Nov-90 D172/R) Alfriston, Sussex (28x48cm-11x19in) mono.d.1893
£4000 $6520   (14-Jun-91 C329/R) Wooded river landscape with shepherd and his flock
                      (61x107cm-24x42in) s.d.07
£5000 $9750   (18-Oct-90 SC3081/R) Cattle in a shady stretch of river
                      (39x65cm-15x26in) s.
£6000 $9780   (14-Jun-91 C317/R) View of Wrexham, N.Wales (45x76cm-18x30in) s.
£6200 $12152   (13-Feb-91 S42/R) River Rother, Grassmere, Rydal Water
                      (61x107cm-24x42in) s.d.07 indist.l.stretcher
£7000 $13230   (26-Sep-90 S97/R) Fishing by lock. Herding cattle, sunset
                      (30x51cm-12x20in) init.d.89 pair
£7200 $14400   (8-Feb-91 C150/R) Near Thursby, Yorkshire. Near Pevensey, Sussex
                      (25x41cm-10x16in) one init.d.95.6 other init.d.98
£7514 $13000   (22-May-91 SY.NY250 a/R) Fishing by mill (72x112cm-28x44in) s.
£15500 $25885   (5-Jun-91 S49/R) Harvest (61x91cm-24x36in) s.d.66

GLENDENING, Alfred Augustus (Jnr) (1861-1907) British
£3500 $6895   (1-Nov-90 C222/R) Highland lake landscape with cattle (40x66cm-16x26in)
                      s.
£3600 $7056   (8-Nov-90 PH1224/R) Near Thursby, Yorks. Near Pevensey, Sussex
                      (24x39cm-9x15in) init.d.98 pair
£3600 $7056   (8-Nov-90 PH1223/R) The angler (29x39cm-11x15in) init.d.98
£7800 $15366   (1-Nov-90 C221/R) Hay time near Hailsham, Sussex (41x76cm-16x30in)
                      s.d.1901
*£2000 $3260   (11-Jun-91 HS42) Squire's daughter (41x30cm-16x12in) bears mono. d.1895
                      W/C*

GLENDENING, Alfred Augustus (snr) (?-c.1910) British
£1000 $1630   (13-Jun-91 CSK243) Extensive wooded landscape with woman and dog
                      crossing stream (46x36cm-18x14in) init.d.71

GLETTE, Erich (1896-1920) German
£743 $1286   (25-May-91 N.M105) Still life of flowers (43x36cm-17x14in) board
                      (DM 2200)

GLEYRE, Charles (1806-1874) Swiss
*£1300 $2119   (2-Jul-91 C171/R) Poet playing lyre - possibly Homer (40x21cm-16x8in)
                      pencil*

GLEYRE, Charles (attrib) (1806-1874) Swiss
£804 $1319   (21-Jun-91 SY.MO348/R) Allegorie de la Republique drapee du drapeau
                      tricolore (62x44cm-24x17in) (F.FR 8000)

GLIKSBERG, Haim (1904-1970) Israeli
£5215 $8500   (12-Jun-91 GG.TA256/R) Bare tree on way to Jerusalem (40x46cm-16x18in)
                      s.
£9509 $15500   (12-Jun-91 GG.TA257/R) Interior (66x88cm-26x35in) s.
*£2086 $3400   (12-Jun-91 GG.TA258/R) Still life of vase, flowers and fruit
                      (34x44cm-13x17in) s. W/C*

GLINDEN, Frank (?) ?
£1100 $2079   (26-Sep-90 S125/R) Making garlands (80x109cm-31x43in) s.

GLINDONI, Henry Gillard (1852-1913) British
£714 $1371   (27-Nov-90 W.T1042 a) The toast (23x18cm-9x7in) s. panel (C.D 1600)
£800 $1352   (30-Apr-91 PH107/R) Beyond his last (21x26cm-8x10in) s. s.l.verso panel
£4464 $8571   (27-Nov-90 W.T1053/R) The first impression (89x115cm-35x45in) s.
                      (C.D 10000)
£4500 $8820   (13-Feb-91 S120/R) Loyal toast (86x127cm-34x50in) s.d.1896
£5500 $8965   (14-Jun-91 C264/R) Fan flirtation (86x111cm-34x44in) s.d.1908

GLINDONI, Henry Gillard (1852-1913) British-cont.
| £700 | $1379 | (15-Nov-90 SC4032/R) Toast (69x89cm-27x35in) s.d.1897 W/C paper on canvas |
| £950 | $1824 | (26-Nov-90 SWS91/R) The connoisseur (36x25cm-14x10in) s. W/C |

GLOCKLER, J D (17th C) German
| £5245 | $10122 | (10-Dec-90 L.K46/R) Portrait of Herzog Friedrich Wilhelm von Sachsen-Altenburg and wife (19x32cm-7x13in) s. copper (DM 15000) |

GLOERSEN, Jakob (1852-1912) Norwegian
| £1850 | $3663 | (29-Jan-91 UL.T167) Norwegian landscape with farmyard 1907 (75x98cm-30x39in) (N.KR 21000) |
| £1997 | $3334 | (3-Jun-91 B.O51/R) Summer landscape from Rollag (82x65cm-32x26in) s.d.1904 (N.KR 23000) |

GLOUKHOV, Victor (1946-) Russian
| £789 | $1554 | (3-Oct-90 QWA.P24) Nature morte fleurs (80x90cm-31x35in) (F.FR 8000) |
| £1085 | $2137 | (3-Oct-90 QWA.P23) Le monastere Saint-Jean (73x90cm-29x35in) (F.FR 11000) |

GLOVER, John (1767-1849) British
£4800	$8592	(10-Apr-91 S21/R) Before storm (54x70cm-21x28in)
£15000	$29400	(8-Nov-90 RBB666/R) Mountainous lake landscape with figures and animals grazing (89x130cm-35x51in)
£300	$588	(23-Jan-91 B128) Kenilworth Castle (22x32cm-9x13in) W/C
£850	$1683	(30-Jan-91 S23/R) Bayham Abbey, Sussex, near Tunbridge Wells (28x41cm-11x16in) s.i.verso W/C over pencil with gum arabic
£1000	$1730	(20-May-91 SWS386/R) Doune Castle, Perthshire (52x73cm-20x29in) i. verso W/C over pencil scratching out
£1600	$2640	(11-Jul-91 S125) Ruined castle overlooking valley (18x29cm-7x11in) W/C gum arabic sold with another W/C
£2889	$5431	(17-Sep-90 SY.ME51/R) Landscape with cattle (25x54cm-10x21in) W/C (A.D 6500)
£3400	$6698	(15-Nov-90 S89/R) Cows grazing near lake (20x30cm-8x12in) W/C over pencil htd.gum arabic
£5622	$10795	(26-Nov-90 SY.ME278/R) Landscape with waterfall (58x88cm-23x35in) W/C (A.D 14000)
£10222	$19218	(17-Sep-90 SY.ME71/R) Windsor Castle (76x115cm-30x45in) W/C (A.D 23000)

GLOVER, John (style) (1767-1849) British
| £1300 | $2249 | (20-May-91 SWS294/R) A lakeland landscape with figures on a country path and town beyond (66x91cm-26x36in) |

GLUCK (?) ?
| £620 | $1215 | (8-Nov-90 DLY96/R) Cornish landscape (5x10cm-2x4in) init. W/C |

GLUCKMANN, Grigory (1898-?) Russian
£1026	$2000	(10-Oct-90 SY.NY111/R) Seated nude (41x33cm-16x13in) s.d.1929 panel
£1707	$3158	(6-Mar-91 D.P46/R) Baigneuses et amour (81x112cm-32x44in) s.d.1934 panel (F.FR 17000)
£2000	$3260	(1-Jul-91 APT.P147/R) Les trois animes (22x46cm-9x18in) s.d.11 panel (F.FR 20000)
£2436	$4750	(10-Oct-90 SY.NY86/R) Autumn in Venice (48x61cm-19x24in) s. panel
£2437	$4800	(13-Nov-90 CE.NY71/R) Avant le spectacle (32x51cm-13x20in) s. panel on panel
£2890	$5000	(7-May-91 CE.NY37/R) Corps de ballet (49x63cm-19x25in) s. panel
£988	$1700	(19-May-91 LIT.L11) Portrait of female nude (38x30cm-15x12in) s. d.1929 verso W/C parchment
£1456	$2693	(4-Mar-91 ARC.P50/R) Nu assis (32x20cm-13x8in) s.d.1934 W/C (F.FR 14500)

GLYDE, Henry George (1906-) Canadian
| £1834 | $3613 | (12-Nov-90 HO.ED38/R) Spray Lake no 2, near Canmore (46x61cm-18x24in) s.i.d. board (C.D 4200) |
| £1965 | $3871 | (12-Nov-90 HO.ED249/R) Kent village of Wittersham (61x76cm-24x30in) s.i.d. (C.D 4500) |

GMELIN, Friedrich Wilhelm (1760-1820) German
| £1667 | $2883 | (22-May-91 GS.B4041) Lago di Varano with shepherd. View of Sorrento and Capri beyond (53x75cm-21x30in) one s.i.d.1789 pencil sepia wash pair (S.FR 4200) |

GMELIN, Johann (1810-1854) German
| £20000 | $32800 | (19-Jun-91 S43/R) View of Bay of Naples (85x118cm-33x46in) s.d.1841 |

GNEHM, Peter (1712-1799) Swiss
| £1116 | $2175 | (24-Oct-90 GD.B412/R) Alpine river landscape (61x61cm-24x24in) i.verso (S.FR 2800) |

GNOLI, Domenico (1933-1970) Italian?
£4509	$7800	(12-May-91 H.C65/R) Marketplace, Napoli (46x69cm-18x27in) i.verso pen ink W/C wash htd.white
£7746	$13168	(28-May-91 SY.MI135/R) Paesaggio (33x54cm-13x21in) mono.d.60 ink gouache board (I.L 17000000)
£10163	$20325	(10-Feb-91 CC.P30/R) Pistolero (65x40cm-26x16in) s.d.1963 tempera sable collage canvas (F.FR 100000)

GOBATOW, Konstantin (1876-1946) Russian
£676 $1169   (25-May-91 N.M106/R) Kinsk in winter (38x49cm-15x19in) s. gouache W/C
                          bodycol (DM 2000)

GOBAUT, Gaspard (1814-1882) French
£1233 $2393   (8-Dec-90 SY.MO395/R) La Place de la Concorde (12x18cm-5x7in) s. bears
                          i.verso W/C (F.FR 12000)
£1233 $2393   (8-Dec-90 SY.MO396/R) L'Arc de Triomphe (12x18cm-5x7in) s. bears i.verso
                          W/C (F.FR 12000)

GOBBI, Dario (20th C) Italian
£912 $1523   (6-Jun-91 F.M96) Ciociara tra i fiori (50x40cm-20x16in) s.d.1944 board
                          (I.L 2000000)

GOBBIS, Giuseppe de (18th C) Italian
£47059 $80000   (30-May-91 SY.NY56/R) Elegant figures in interior (82x114cm-32x45in)

GOBERT, Pierre (1662-1744) French
£3083 $5982   (7-Dec-90 SY.MO179/R) Portrait de femme (82x65cm-32x26in) (F.FR 30000)
£3781 $6579   (27-Mar-91 CN.P64/R) Portrait de Louise-Adelaide d'Orleans, Abbesse de
                          Chelles (145x114cm-57x45in) (F.FR 38000)

GOBERT, Pierre (studio) (1662-1744) French
£2579 $4437   (19-May-91 ZZ.F73/R) Portrait d'un jeune prince (78x62cm-31x24in)
                          (F.FR 26000)

GOBILLARD, Paule (1869-1946) French
£806 $1573   (26-Oct-90 APT.P115) Portrait de femme (73x60cm-29x24in) s. (F.FR 8000)
£1411 $2752   (26-Oct-90 APT.P114) Femma a sa couture dans un jardin (61x50cm-24x20in)
                          s. (F.FR 14000)

GOBL, Camilla (1871-1965) Austrian
£1174 $2290   (10-Oct-90 ZEL.L1506/R) Still life of summer flowers in landscape
                          (75x105cm-30x41in) s. (DM 3500)

GOBLE, Warwick (?-1943) British
£400 $740   (6-Mar-91 DR28) Geisha girl (33x23cm-13x9in) s. W/C
£1700 $3400   (8-Feb-91 C102/R) An illustratin of the 'Water-Babies' (33x23cm-13x9in)
                          s. ink W/C htd.white
£1700 $3400   (8-Feb-91 C101/R) An illustration of the 'Water-Babies'
                          (33x48cm-13x19in) s. ink W/C htd.white

GODARD, Gabriel (1933-) ?
£732 $1200   (19-Jun-91 B.SF1952/R) Bord de mer (100x82cm-39x32in) s.d.1972 i.verso
£853 $1662   (10-Oct-90 ARC.P112/R) Nature morte a la dentelle (116x80cm-46x31in)
                          s.d.62 (F.FR 8500)
£915 $1500   (19-Jun-91 B.SF1951/R) Barques (129x130cm-51x51in) s.d.73

GODCHAUX (?) ?
£1121 $2164   (14-Dec-90 ARC.P166) Le torrent de montagne (67x92cm-26x36in) s.
                          (F.FR 11000)
£1295 $2240   (24-May-91 FB.P98/R) Paysage alpestre (68x92cm-27x36in) s. (F.FR 13000)
£1385 $2479   (12-Apr-91 JM.P49) Oeillets, pivoines (49x65cm-19x26in) s. (F.FR 14000)
£1469 $2880   (6-Nov-90 GF.L2386/R) Chicken in farmyard (92x65cm-36x26in) s.
                          (S.FR 3600)
£1633 $3216   (14-Nov-90 FB.P149/R) Pecheurs au bord du lac (48x61cm-19x24in) s.
                          (F.FR 16000)
£2347 $4623   (14-Nov-90 FB.P152/R) Marines (16x27cm-6x11in) s. pair (F.FR 23000)
£3000 $5370   (14-Mar-91 ZZ.B157/R) A vase of roses (71x98cm-28x39in) s.
£3200 $5504   (17-May-91 C7 h/R) Peonies and delphiniums in basket with other flowers
                          in vase (72x100cm-28x39in) s.

GODCHAUX, Alfred (1835-1895) French
£1587 $2730   (19-May-91 ZZ.F6/R) Barques et voiliers au crepuscule (65x92cm-26x36in)
                          s. (F.FR 16000)
£3021 $4924   (12-Jun-91 ZZ.F27/R) Barques sur la plage (55x100cm-22x39in) s.d.1875
                          two (F.FR 30000)

GODCHAUX, C (19th C) French
£1581 $2688   (27-May-91 GK.Z5042/R) French wooded landscape with female figure and
                          farmstead beyond (22x40cm-9x16in) s. panel (S.FR 4000)

GODCHAUX, Emil (1860-?) Austrian?
£1020 $2010   (14-Nov-90 CN.P110/R) Bateaux sur la greve (60x73cm-24x29in) s.
                          (F.FR 10000)
£1551 $3040   (6-Nov-90 GF.L2370/R) Still life with grapes and pears (33x41cm-13x16in)
                          s. (S.FR 3800)
£1608 $2878   (17-Mar-91 DA.R2/R) Berger et ses moutons dans un paysage valonne
                          (92x73cm-36x29in) s. (F.FR 16000)

GODEFROY, Felix de (?-1848) French
£3590 $7000   (26-Oct-90 SY.NY137/R) Artist drawing from male model (38x28cm-15x11in)
                          s.

GODEFROY, Jean Joseph (?) French
£1028 $1994   (7-Dec-90 CN.P21/R) Projet de Fontaine (47x33cm-19x13in) s.i. verso pen wash (F.FR 10000)

GODET, Julius (19th C) British
£690 $1200   (27-Mar-91 B.SF4235/R) Inquiring the way (77x107cm-30x42in) s. s.i.verso

GODET, Pierre Philippe (1876-1951) Swiss
£1878 $3642   (8-Dec-90 GAB.G2600/R) Jardin breton (60x73cm-24x29in) s.d.1909 (S.FR 4600)

GODEWOLS, Ludwig (1870-1926) German
£2389 $4515   (29-Sep-90 GRA.B2284 a/R) Cottages by the Teutoburger Forest near Werther (75x100cm-30x39in) s.d.1925 (DM 7000)

GODFRINON, Ernest (20th C) Belgian?
£665 $1190   (16-Mar-91 KV.L129) Het verstelwerk (38x27cm-15x11in) s. panel (B.FR 40000)
£1667 $3200   (18-Dec-90 GM.B4023) Nature morte aux citrons (35x48cm-14x19in) s. (B.FR 100000)
£1833 $3520   (18-Dec-90 GM.B4018) Vase de fleurs (60x50cm-24x20in) s. (B.FR 110000)

GODIHAUS, Al (19th C) ?
£961 $1873   (21-Oct-90 L.C51) Scene de peche (45x65cm-18x26in) s. (F.FR 9500)

GODLEK, L (19th C) European
£1700 $3043   (12-Mar-91 PH38) Magyar cavalry (21x26cm-8x10in) s.i. panel

GODLEVSKY, Ivan (1908-) Russian
£508 $864   (29-May-91 ARC.P74/R) Les ruches (59x80cm-23x31in) s. (F.FR 5100)
£518 $880   (29-May-91 ARC.P50/R) Dans la barque (71x92cm-28x36in) s. (F.FR 5200)
£518 $880   (29-May-91 ARC.P116/R) Les ruches (78x90cm-31x35in) s. (F.FR 5200)
£518 $880   (29-May-91 ARC.P101/R) Le pont aux lions, Leningrad (60x79cm-24x31in) s. (F.FR 5200)
£538 $914   (29-May-91 ARC.P127/R) Le bateau de croisiere (60x80cm-24x31in) s. (F.FR 5400)
£548 $931   (29-May-91 ARC.P42/R) Paysage de montagne (48x65cm-19x26in) s. (F.FR 5500)
£548 $931   (29-May-91 ARC.P119/R) La nappe verte (50x69cm-20x27in) s. board (F.FR 5500)
£548 $931   (29-May-91 ARC.P91/R) La colonne rostrale (60x79cm-24x31in) s. (F.FR 5500)
£548 $931   (29-May-91 ARC.P143) Place du Tertre (60x81cm-24x32in) s. (F.FR 5500)
£548 $931   (29-May-91 ARC.P99/R) Village de Ladoga (59x79cm-23x31in) s. (F.FR 5500)
£548 $931   (29-May-91 ARC.P37/R) Sur le seuil de la porte (69x92cm-27x36in) s.d.58 (F.FR 5500)
£548 $931   (29-May-91 ARC.P88/R) L'eglise de Zagorsk (80x60cm-31x24in) s. (F.FR 5500)
£568 $965   (29-May-91 ARC.P131/R) le club de voile (69x92cm-27x36in) s. (F.FR 5700)
£578 $982   (29-May-91 ARC.P69/R) Les toits rouges (59x79cm-23x31in) s. (F.FR 5800)
£588 $999   (29-May-91 ARC.P78/R) La petite rouge (59x79cm-23x31in) s. (F.FR 5900)
£598 $1016   (29-May-91 ARC.P13/R) Le port de Pilau (69x93cm-27x37in) s. (F.FR 6000)
£598 $1016   (29-May-91 ARC.P112/R) Le bouquet (90x69cm-35x27in) s.d.55 (F.FR 6000)
£598 $1016   (29-May-91 ARC.P125/R) La forteresse de Novgorod (68x92cm-27x36in) s. (F.FR 6000)
£598 $1016   (29-May-91 ARC.P22/R) Village au bord de la riviere (70x92cm-28x36in) s. (F.FR 6000)
£598 $1016   (29-May-91 ARC.P40/R) Pris dans la glace (60x80cm-24x31in) s. (F.FR 6000)
£598 $1016   (29-May-91 ARC.P17/R) Leningrad, la premiere neige (70x92cm-28x36in) s. (F.FR 6000)
£598 $1016   (29-May-91 ARC.P132/R) La ville de Borisogleb (70x93cm-28x37in) s.d.59 (F.FR 6000)
£598 $1016   (29-May-91 ARC.P65/R) Canal au printemps, Leningrad (59x80cm-23x31in) s. (F.FR 6000)
£603 $1158   (18-Feb-91 ARC.P5) Le port de plaisance (59x79cm-23x31in) s. (F.FR 6000)
£608 $1033   (29-May-91 ARC.P136) Matinee dans le port (59x73cm-23x29in) s. board (F.FR 6100)
£618 $1050   (29-May-91 ARC.P109/R) La ville d'eau (70x93cm-28x37in) s. (F.FR 6200)
£627 $1067   (29-May-91 ARC.P77/R) Bateaux de peche (59x80cm-23x31in) s. (F.FR 6300)
£647 $1101   (29-May-91 ARC.P83/R) Les volles blanches (61x79cm-24x31in) s.d.58 (F.FR 6500)
£647 $1101   (29-May-91 ARC.P33/R) Les rives de la Neva (70x89cm-28x35in) s. (F.FR 6500)
£647 $1101   (29-May-91 ARC.P105/R) La vedette (50x70cm-20x28in) s. board (F.FR 6500)
£647 $1101   (29-May-91 ARC.P7/R) Sur la plage (60x79cm-24x31in) s. panel (F.FR 6500)
£647 $1101   (29-May-91 ARC.P71/R) Paysage d'hiver (69x93cm-27x37in) s. (F.FR 6500)
£667 $1134   (29-May-91 ARC.P144) Le manege a Montmartre (81x60cm-32x24in) s. (F.FR 6700)
£677 $1151   (29-May-91 ARC.P41/R) Neige en Crimee (60x80cm-24x31in) s. (F.FR 6800)
£677 $1151   (29-May-91 ARC.P34/R) Voilier a quai (70x93cm-28x37in) s. (F.FR 6800)
£697 $1185   (29-May-91 ARC.P98/R) Le port de Simferpol (59x80cm-23x31in) s. (F.FR 7000)
£697 $1185   (29-May-91 ARC.P114/R) L'atelier des locomotives (69x93cm-27x37in) s. (F.FR 7000)

GODLEVSKY, Ivan (1908-) Russian-cont.

£697	$1185	(29-May-91 ARC.P15/R) Embarcadere sur la Neva (69x93cm-27x37in) s. (F.FR 7000)
£697	$1185	(29-May-91 ARC.P87/R) Monastere de Petchora (70x53cm-28x21in) s.d.58 (F.FR 7000)
£697	$1185	(29-May-91 ARC.P28/R) Le port de Leningrad (69x92cm-27x36in) s. (F.FR 7000)
£697	$1185	(29-May-91 ARC.P120/R) L'ecole de voile (60x79cm-24x31in) s. (F.FR 7000)
£697	$1185	(29-May-91 ARC.P57/R) Paysage aux grands arbres (70x93cm-28x37in) s. (F.FR 7000)
£697	$1185	(29-May-91 ARC.P38/R) Village en hiver (60x79cm-24x31in) s. (F.FR 7000)
£697	$1185	(29-May-91 ARC.P58/R) Journee d'Octobre (70x93cm-28x37in) s. (F.FR 7000)
£697	$1185	(29-May-91 ARC.P122/R) Le vieux Ladoga (69x93cm-27x37in) s. (F.FR 7000)
£697	$1185	(29-May-91 ARC.P121/R) Les trotteurs (49x65cm-19x26in) s.d.58 board (F.FR 7000)
£697	$1185	(29-May-91 ARC.P62/R) La premiere neige (60x80cm-24x31in) s. board (F.FR 7000)
£697	$1185	(29-May-91 ARC.P67/R) Le port animee (59x80cm-23x31in) s. (F.FR 7000)
£697	$1185	(29-May-91 ARC.P93/R) Le port de Yalta (70x93cm-28x37in) s. (F.FR 7000)
£717	$1219	(29-May-91 ARC.P20/R) Le phare (60x79cm-24x31in) s. (F.FR 7200)
£747	$1270	(29-May-91 ARC.P142/R) Retour au port (60x79cm-24x31in) s. (F.FR 7500)
£747	$1270	(29-May-91 ARC.P32/R) Paysage d'automne (69x93cm-27x37in) s. (F.FR 7500)
£777	$1321	(29-May-91 ARC.P140/R) La maison du berger (60x79cm-24x31in) s. (F.FR 7800)
£797	$1355	(29-May-91 ARC.P138) L'orangerie (69x92cm-27x36in) s. (F.FR 8000)
£797	$1355	(29-May-91 ARC.P43/R) Le remorqueur (70x89cm-28x35in) s.d.58 (F.FR 8000)
£797	$1355	(29-May-91 ARC.P56/R) Village pres de la riviere (70x93cm-28x37in) s. (F.FR 8000)
£797	$1355	(29-May-91 ARC.P111/R) La vallee d'Alupka (69x93cm-27x37in) s. (F.FR 8000)
£797	$1355	(29-May-91 ARC.P133/R) Le petit port, Gourzouf (65x93cm-26x37in) s. (F.FR 8000)
£804	$1544	(18-Feb-91 ARC.P6) Entree de l'eglise (59x79cm-23x31in) s. (F.FR 8000)
£827	$1405	(29-May-91 ARC.P44/R) Nature morte a la carafe (70x92cm-28x36in) s. d.50 verso (F.FR 8300)
£837	$1422	(29-May-91 ARC.P59/R) Composition aux iris (93x70cm-37x28in) s. (F.FR 8400)
£847	$1439	(29-May-91 ARC.P1/R) Le parasol rouge (80x60cm-31x24in) s. (F.FR 8500)
£847	$1439	(29-May-91 ARC.P76/R) La maison du cap (59x80cm-23x31in) s. (F.FR 8500)
£847	$1439	(29-May-91 ARC.P79/R) Cargo a quai (60x80cm-24x31in) s. (F.FR 8500)
£847	$1439	(29-May-91 ARC.P66/R) Les marronniers enfleurs (60x80cm-24x31in) s. (F.FR 8500)
£847	$1439	(29-May-91 ARC.P46/R) L'attelage (69x92cm-27x36in) s.d.58 (F.FR 8500)
£847	$1439	(29-May-91 ARC.P118/R) Buisson de fleurs (60x80cm-24x31in) s.d.56 (F.FR 8500)
£876	$1490	(29-May-91 ARC.P54/R) L'eglise rose (70x93cm-28x37in) s. (F.FR 8800)
£876	$1490	(29-May-91 ARC.P48/R) L'ecluse (60x80cm-24x31in) s. (F.FR 8800)
£896	$1524	(29-May-91 ARC.P5/R) La maison du lac (69x93cm-27x37in) s. (F.FR 9000)
£896	$1524	(29-May-91 ARC.P19/R) Voiliers sur la plage (60x80cm-24x31in) s. (F.FR 9000)
£905	$1737	(18-Feb-91 ARC.P4/R) La terrasse (67x92cm-26x36in) s. (F.FR 9000)
£946	$1609	(29-May-91 ARC.P47/R) Le port (60x80cm-24x31in) s. (F.FR 9500)
£996	$1693	(29-May-91 ARC.P53/R) Les pommiers en fleurs (60x80cm-24x31in) s. (F.FR 10000)
£996	$1693	(29-May-91 ARC.P45/R) Voiliers pres du rivage (69x92cm-27x36in) s. (F.FR 10000)
£996	$1693	(29-May-91 ARC.P21/R) Gourzouf, le soleil de midi (59x79cm-23x31in) s. (F.FR 10000)
£996	$1693	(29-May-91 ARC.P26/R) Leningrad, matinee d'hiver (70x89cm-28x35in) s. (F.FR 10000)
£996	$1693	(29-May-91 ARC.P80/R) Pavots et iris (80x59cm-31x23in) s.d.57 (F.FR 10000)
£1046	$1778	(29-May-91 ARC.P31/R) La petite plage (94x70cm-37x28in) s. (F.FR 10500)
£1096	$1863	(29-May-91 ARC.P30/R) Printemps a Leningrad (70x92cm-28x36in) s. (F.FR 11000)
£1155	$1964	(29-May-91 ARC.P81/R) Lever de soleil sur la Neva (60x79cm-24x31in) s. (F.FR 11600)
£1195	$2032	(29-May-91 ARC.P11/R) Le quai rouge (80x60cm-31x24in) s. (F.FR 12000)
£1195	$2032	(29-May-91 ARC.P29/R) Le yacht-club (59x79cm-23x31in) s. board (F.FR 12000)
£1195	$2032	(29-May-91 ARC.P3/R) Le retour du paquebot (70x93cm-28x37in) s. (F.FR 12000)
£1295	$2201	(29-May-91 ARC.P89/R) L'embarcadere (59x80cm-23x31in) s.d.50 (F.FR 13000)
£1394	$2371	(29-May-91 ARC.P70/R) Voiliers sur la plage (66x101cm-26x40in) s. (F.FR 14000)
£1394	$2371	(29-May-91 ARC.P115/R) Bateaux a l'ancrage (80x60cm-31x24in) s. (F.FR 14000)
£1494	$2540	(29-May-91 ARC.P108/R) Le vieux Gourzouf (68x92cm-27x36in) s. (F.FR 15000)
£1494	$2540	(29-May-91 ARC.P145/R) L'eglise du Kremlin (105x140cm-41x55in) s. (F.FR 15000)
£1508	$2894	(18-Feb-91 ARC.P1/R) Lever du soleil sur la Neva (59x80cm-23x31in) s. (F.FR 15000)
£1544	$2625	(29-May-91 ARC.P137/R) Panorama sur Batumi (60x79cm-24x31in) s. board (F.FR 15500)

GODLEVSKY, Ivan (1908-) Russian-cont.

£1544	$2625	(29-May-91 ARC.P8/R) Les iris (70x92cm-28x36in) s. (F.FR 15500)
£1544	$2625	(29-May-91 ARC.P113/R) Le port de Yalta (69x93cm-27x37in) s. (F.FR 15500)
£1544	$2625	(29-May-91 ARC.P104/R) Le cafe a Samarkand (92x69cm-36x27in) s.d.53 (F.FR 15500)
£1594	$2709	(29-May-91 ARC.P4/R) Gourzouf, les pins rouges (60x80cm-24x31in) s. (F.FR 16000)
£1594	$2709	(29-May-91 ARC.P106/R) Le coucher de soleil a Sevastopol (48x65cm-19x26in) s. (F.FR 16000)
£1643	$2794	(29-May-91 ARC.P2/R) Coucher de soleil sur la Neva (60x80cm-24x31in) s. (F.FR 16500)
£1793	$3048	(29-May-91 ARC.P90/R) Les pins rouges (60x80cm-24x31in) s. (F.FR 18000)
£1843	$3132	(29-May-91 ARC.P75/R) Chemin dans les oliviers (60x80cm-24x31in) s. (F.FR 18500)
£2010	$3859	(18-Feb-91 ARC.P2/R) L'amandier en fleurs (70x92cm-28x36in) s. (F.FR 20000)
£2540	$4318	(29-May-91 ARC.P107/R) Les champs du sud (69x93cm-27x37in) s. (F.FR 25500)

GODWARD, John William (1858-1922) British

£4046	$7000	(23-May-91 CH.NY213/R) Looking seaward (33x22cm-13x9in) s.d.90
£5051	$8737	(6-May-91 ZEL.L1711/R) Portrait of young woman (45x45cm-18x18in) s.d.1892 (DM 15000)
£7200	$14184	(1-Nov-90 CSK134/R) Arrival (84x65cm-33x26in) s.
£7692	$15000	(24-Oct-90 CH.NY347 a/R) Classical beauty (91x71cm-36x28in) d.1890
£9000	$17280	(28-Nov-90 S29/R) An idle hour (59x22cm-23x9in) s.d.90 canvas board
£12821	$25000	(23-Oct-90 SY.NY75/R) Classical beauty (53x43cm-21x17in) s.
£21387	$37000	(22-May-91 SY.NY95/R) Innocent amusement (76x46cm-30x18in) s.d.1891
£24566	$42500	(22-May-91 SY.NY96/R) Draped nude (77x38cm-30x15in) s.d.1909
£80000	$157600	(1-Nov-90 TE640/R) Absence makes the heart grow fonder (130x79cm-51x31in) s.d.1912 s.i.verso

GODWARD, John William (circle) (1858-1922) British

£2800	$5516	(1-Nov-90 CSK135/R) Centurion's return (56x30cm-22x12in)

GODWARD, John William (style) (1858-1922) British

£2400	$4728	(1-Nov-90 CSK136/R) Idle moments (85cm-33ins circular) with sig. d.1910

GODWIN, Ted (1933-) Canadian

£873	$1721	(12-Nov-90 HO.ED289/R) Late fall (91x61cm-36x24in) s.i. tempera board (C.D 2000)

GOEBEL, Carl (1824-1899) Austrian

£875	$1566	(9-Apr-91 RAS.K2058) Flowers on ledge (50x40cm-20x16in) s. panel (D.KR 10000)
£1297	$2400	(10-Mar-91 H.C14/R) Reading newspaper (25x33cm-10x13in) s.d.1892 panel

GOEBEL, Carl (1824-1899) Austrian-cont.
£430 $722   *(25-Apr-91 D.V156/R) Hospital garden (32x48cm-13x19in) s. W/C htd.white* (A.S 9000)
£686 $1358   *(31-Jan-91 D.V167/R) Hunter with dead stag and dog in wooded landscape (29x48cm-11x19in) s. W/C (A.S 14000)*
£1100 $2090   *(12-Sep-90 CSK230/R) Stroll on waterfront, Cadiz (18x43cm-7x17in) s. pencil W/C htd white*
£1432 $2792   *(11-Oct-90 D.V148) Austrian cavalry regiment moving out (42x60cm-17x24in) s. W/C (A.S 30000)*
£1528 $2567   *(25-Apr-91 D.V177/R) Winter landscape with mill and horse-drawn sledge (48x68cm-19x27in) s. W/C (A.S 32000)*

GOEBEL, Hermann (1885-1945) German
£3253 $5824   *(12-Nov-90 FN.S2381/R) River landscape with view of town and church spires (80x91cm-31x36in) s.d.1912 (DM 9500)*

GOEBEL, Rod (20th C) American
£2147 $3500   *(11-Jun-91 MOR.P97 a) Late night - Pacific Grove (61x76cm-24x30in) s.*

GOENEUTTE, Norbert (1854-1894) French
£6965 $12119   *(25-Mar-91 CR.P95) L'ancre (46x38cm-18x15in) s. (F.FR 70000)*
£21000 $34440   *(19-Jun-91 S226/R) Young woman in meadow (24x32cm-9x13in) s.*
£10000 $16400   *(19-Jun-91 S194/R) Victorine Meurent by bath (53x36cm-21x14in) s.d.1888 pastel*

GOEPFERT, Hermann (1926-) ?
£1884 $3070   *(14-Jun-91 L.K904) Weissbild W 67 (100x66cm-39x26in) s.i.d.1961verso (DM 5500)*
£2730 $5352   *(20-Nov-90 L.K247/R) Weissbild (100x65cm-39x26in) s.i.d.1961 (DM 8000)*

GOEREE, Jan (1670-1731) Dutch
£400 $676   *(16-Apr-91 C254) Cannibals dancing around the head of a victim and preparing the corpse (13x18cm-5x7in) i. red chk.wash*

GOERG, Edouard (1893-1969) French
£2072 $4040   *(24-Oct-90 GD.B414/R) Dans le jardin (41x33cm-16x13in) s. i.verso (S.FR 5200)*
£2480 $4860   *(25-Nov-90 LC.P99/R) Les fleurs du mal (38x28cm-15x11in) mono.i. gouache (F.FR 24500)*
£3571 $7000   *(12-Feb-91 SY.NY236/R) La tentation (46x56cm-18x22in) s.d.45 s.i.d.45verso*
£3700 $6179   *(7-Jun-91 LD.P51/R) Profil brun (41x33cm-16x13in) s. i.d.Aout-Semptembre 52 verso (F.FR 37000)*
£4049 $7935   *(23-Nov-90 PLF.P71/R) Les rivaux (41x33cm-16x13in) s.d.45 i. verso (F.FR 40000)*
£4281 $8263   *(12-Dec-90 APT.P108/R) Deux jeunes femmes emues (46x38cm-18x15in) s.d.48 i.d.Nov-Dec 48 verso (F.FR 42000)*
£5653 $10966   *(9-Dec-90 CC.P27/R) Les fleurs des champs (81x65cm-32x26in) s.i. verso (F.FR 55000)*
£5917 $11657   *(6-Oct-90 GL.P43/R) Un petit bouquet d'anniversaire (65x54cm-26x21in) s. i.d. verso (F.FR 60000)*
£8163 $16082   *(14-Nov-90 CN.P79/R) Deux nus au clair de lune (55x46cm-22x18in) s.i.d.Avril Mai 58 (F.FR 80000)*
£8709 $17070   *(7-Nov-90 APT.P521/R) La jeune mere aux deux jumeaux (61x50cm-24x20in) s.d.1950 i. verso (F.FR 85000)*
£12755 $25128   *(14-Nov-90 CN.P80/R) Quant le paradis etait terrestre (100x81cm-39x32in) s. i.d.Juillet 57 verso (F.FR 125000)*
£596 $1008   *(15-Apr-91 CC.P7/R) Femme nue allongee (37x27cm-15x11in) s. Indian ink (F.FR 6000)*
£661 $1321   *(6-Feb-91 FB.P153) Jeunes filles aux fleurs (32x25cm-13x10in) s.i.d.1963 ink wash (F.FR 6500)*
£911 $1785   *(22-Nov-90 ZZ.F1/R) Le baiser (32x23cm-13x9in) s. chl. (F.FR 9000)*
£1113 $2182   *(22-Nov-90 ZZ.F2/R) Deux jeunes filles (31x23cm-12x9in) s. chl. (F.FR 11000)*
£1183 $2331   *(6-Oct-90 GL.P145/R) Les Champs Elysees (50x32cm-20x13in) s.i.d.55 pen wash Indian ink (F.FR 12000)*
£2823 $5504   *(26-Oct-90 APT.P16) Plage de Bretagne (31x48cm-12x19in) s.d.48 gouache (F.FR 28000)*

GOETZ, Gottfried Bernhard (1708-1774) German
£606 $1048   *(6-May-91 ZEL.L1462/R) Karl VII seated on throne (9x6cm-4x2in) s. pen wash htd.white (DM 1800)*

GOETZ, Henri (1909-1989) American
£1417 $2777   *(25-Nov-90 LC.P121) Composition (22x27cm-9x11in) s.d.56 (F.FR 14000)*
£1700 $2771   *(3-Jul-91 CSC.P64/R) Aigalier (38x55cm-15x22in) s. i.d.1968 verso (F.FR 17000)*
£2435 $4116   *(15-Apr-91 CC.P95) Composition (32x24cm-13x9in) s. board (F.FR 24500)*
£2510 $4041   *(30-Jun-91 I.N152/R) Composition (65x81cm-26x32in) s. (F.FR 25000)*
£2548 $4918   *(16-Dec-90 GL.P83/R) Composition (38x46cm-15x18in) s. hardboard (F.FR 25000)*
£2590 $4402   *(29-May-91 GL.P208/R) Composition verte (59x73cm-23x29in) s.d.1964 (F.FR 26000)*
£2789 $4741   *(2-Jun-91 GL.P205/R) Composition (38x55cm-15x22in) s.d.1962 (F.FR 28000)*
£2834 $5555   *(25-Nov-90 LC.P91/R) Paysage (27x41cm-11x16in) s.d.61 i. verso (F.FR 28000)*

GOETZ, Henri (1909-1989) American-cont.

£2959	$5830	(16-Nov-90 FB.P46/R) Composition (54x65cm-21x26in) s. (F.FR 29000)
£3036	$5951	(20-Nov-90 MF.P78/R) Composition (22x30cm-9x12in) s. papyrus (F.FR 30000)
£3074	$6025	(11-Nov-90 ZZ.F197/R) Composition (46x56cm-18x22in) s. paper laid down on canvas (F.FR 30000)
£3112	$5758	(6-Mar-91 APT.P113/R) Complicite nocturne (65x54cm-26x21in) s.i.d.56 verso (F.FR 31000)
£3262	$6296	(16-Dec-90 GL.P174/R) Nature motre (65x81cm-26x32in) s. (F.FR 32000)
£3262	$6296	(16-Dec-90 GL.P100/R) Paysage (65x81cm-26x32in) s.d.74 (F.FR 32000)
£3287	$5686	(26-May-91 ZZ.F156/R) Paysage astral (31x80cm-12x31in) s. (F.FR 33000)
£3568	$6886	(16-Dec-90 GL.P104/R) Sans titre (38x46cm-15x18in) s.d.1953 board (F.FR 35000)
£3842	$7492	(15-Oct-90 CSC.P89/R) Composition (33x41cm-13x16in) s. (F.FR 38000)
£3874	$7476	(16-Dec-90 GL.P164/R) Interieur a Montpellier (65x81cm-26x32in) s.d.75 (F.FR 38000)
£4536	$8755	(16-Dec-90 P.V18/R) Composition (50x65cm-20x26in) s. (F.FR 44500)
£5102	$10051	(15-Nov-90 I.N24/R) Composition (81x65cm-32x26in) s.i. (F.FR 50000)
£5157	$10056	(17-Oct-90 LT.P81/R) Composition (46x55cm-18x22in) s.d.56 (F.FR 51000)
£5204	$10252	(16-Nov-90 FB.P33/R) Composition (74x93cm-29x37in) s.d.58 (F.FR 51000)
£6122	$12061	(15-Nov-90 I.N31/R) Composition (65x100cm-26x39in) s. (F.FR 60000)
£8767	$16919	(15-Dec-90 D.P65 a/R) Composition (89x116cm-35x46in) s.d.70 (F.FR 86000)
£9184	$18092	(18-Nov-90 S.S52/R) Nature morte (33x41cm-13x16in) s.d.43 (F.FR 90000)
£9394	$18412	(14-Feb-91 GL.P73/R) Composition (73x92cm-29x36in) s.d.1958 (F.FR 93000)
£9808	$19125	(17-Oct-90 LT.P97/R) Composition (89x116cm-35x46in) s. (F.FR 97000)
£14257	$28086	(31-Oct-90 ZZ.F56/R) Composition abstraite (54x73cm-21x29in) s.d.54 (F.FR 140000)
£404	$792	(17-Feb-91 E.LA99) Composition (50x65cm-20x26in) s. pastel heated laid down on canvas (F.FR 4000)
£554	$1081	(20-Jan-91 GL.P138) Composition sur fond noir (48x57cm-19x22in) s. pastel paper laid down on canvas (F.FR 5500)
£565	$1097	(9-Dec-90 E.LA159) Composition (56x68cm-22x27in) s. gouache lithograph (F.FR 5500)
£586	$1148	(17-Feb-91 E.LA15) Abstraction (56x68cm-22x27in) s. W/C gouache lithograph (F.FR 5800)
£617	$1196	(9-Dec-90 E.LA157) Composition (32x38cm-13x15in) s.d.81 pastel (F.FR 6000)
£746	$1260	(15-Apr-91 CC.P31/R) Composition (33x47cm-13x19in) s.d.1950 pastel (F.FR 7500)
£900	$1467	(4-Jul-91 GL.P184/R) Composition abstraite (23x30cm-9x12in) s. pastel (F.FR 9000)
£1100	$1793	(4-Jul-91 GL.P185/R) Composition abstraite (23x31cm-9x12in) s. pastel (F.FR 11000)
£1108	$1806	(16-Jun-91 LT.P78/R) Composition au fond jaune (48x56cm-19x22in) s. pastel (F.FR 11000)
£1158	$2247	(5-Dec-90 AB.S7081/R) Plage a Riva-Bella (25x32cm-10x13in) s. mixed media cardboard (S.KR 12500)
£1486	$2572	(21-May-91 WK.M911/R) Composition (28x40cm-11x16in) mixed media (DM 4400)
£1491	$2520	(21-Apr-91 P.V2/R) Composition (57x48cm-22x19in) s. heated pastel (F.FR 15000)
£2041	$3959	(8-Dec-90 GAB.G2603/R) Les Hauts de Monte-Carlo (48x62cm-19x24in) s. pastel (S.FR 5000)
£2209	$3556	(30-Jun-91 I.N133/R) Composition (48x58cm-19x23in) s. pastel (F.FR 22000)
£2427	$4732	(17-Oct-90 LT.P111/R) Composition (23x22cm-9x9in) s.d.48 pastel (F.FR 24000)
£2730	$5324	(21-Oct-90 P.V24/R) Composition (66x48cm-26x19in) s. pastel (F.FR 27000)
£4077	$7870	(16-Dec-90 P.V20/R) Composition (50x65cm-20x26in) s. oil pastel (F.FR 40000)
£5500	$10725	(18-Oct-90 S13/R) Untitled (99x99cm-39x39in) s. one d.56 pastel set of three

GOFF, Frederick E J (1855-1931) British

£500	$925	(4-Mar-91 PHB8) Nuneham-on-the-Thames, Oxfordshire (11x15cm-4x6in) s.i. W/C
£600	$1170	(15-Jan-91 SWS35/R) Salisbury (11x15cm-4x6in) s.i. W/C
£680	$1217	(10-Apr-91 CSK76/R) Barges under Westminster Bridge with Houses of Parliament beyond (13x15cm-5x6in) s.i. W/C htd.bodycol.white
£750	$1230	(19-Jun-91 B118/R) Shipping before Tower Bridge (11x15cm-4x6in) s.i. W/C
£750	$1463	(18-Oct-90 CSK65) Blackfriars Bridge (18x25cm-7x10in) s.i. pencil W/C htd white
£880	$1514	(14-May-91 SWS25/R) Cleopatra's Needle. Barque in tow off Greenwich (14x10cm-6x4in) s.i. W/C htd.bodycol pair
£880	$1663	(26-Sep-90 S230/R) Westminster from Thames (11x15cm-4x6in) s.i. W/C
£1000	$1720	(14-May-91 SWS24/R) Westminster from the Thames. View of London Bridge (11x15cm-4x6in) s.i. W/C htd.bodycol pair
£1000	$1640	(19-Jun-91 B125) On Avon (26x71cm-10x28in) s.i. W/C
£1200	$2280	(12-Sep-91 CSK212/R) Barges at Westminster Bridge, Houses of Parliament beyond (53x71cm-21x28in) s.i. W/C htd white
£1400	$2646	(26-Sep-90 S231/R) Westminster (11x15cm-4x6in) s.i. W/C htd bodycol
£1400	$2646	(26-Sep-90 S229/R) St. Pauls from bankside (15x11cm-6x4in) s.i. W/C htd bodycol
£1700	$2924	(14-May-91 SWS26/R) Thames from Blackfriars Bridge (26x71cm-10x28in) s.i. i.verso W/C htd.bodycol
£1800	$3510	(18-Oct-90 SC3055/R) Docks at twilight (20x38cm-8x15in) both s. pair

GOGARTEN, H (1850-1911) German
£751 $1412   (21-Sep-90 N.M3184) Winter landscape with windmill (13x18cm-5x7in) s. board (DM 2200)

GOGARTEN, Heinrich (1850-1911) German
£952 $1686   (20-Mar-91 KM.K1233) South Italian coastal landscape (32x24cm-13x9in) s.d.79 (DM 2800)
£1062 $1730   (12-Jun-91 N.M437/R) View from Alpsee to Hohenschwangau and Neuschwanstein (51x41cm-20x16in) s.i.d.1890 (DM 3100)
£1884 $3372   (13-Mar-91 N.M505 a/R) Winter landscape at sunset (44x64cm-17x25in) s.d.1887 (DM 5500)
£2273 $4409   (7-Dec-90 GB.B5826/R) View from Bellevue over the Alster to Poseldorf at sunset (23x41cm-9x16in) s.d.1888 panel (DM 6500)

GOGH, Vincent van (1853-1890) Dutch
£43344 $83653   (12-Dec-90 CH.AM258/R) Two hands (29x18cm-11x7in) canvas on panel (D.FL 140000)
£282258 $541936   (2-Dec-90 GAB.G1734/R) Jeune femme assise devant une porte ouverte, pelant des pommes-de-terre (36x25cm-14x10in) canvas laid down on wood (S.FR 700000)
£702703 $1300000   (10-Mar-91 H.C7/R) Still life with flowers (41x33cm-16x13in) init.summer 1886
£20124 $38839   (12-Dec-90 CH.AM254/R) Jacob Meyer's daughter (42x30cm-17x12in) with sig.i. pencil after Hans Holbein (D.FL 65000)
£59000 $94990   (25-Jun-91 C205/R) Le Champ de Ble, Saint Remy (25x33cm-10x13in) pencil
£123839 $239009   (12-Dec-90 CH.AM253/R) Sien and child under umbrella (45x25cm-18x10in) s. pencil htd white (D.FL 400000)
£133127 $256935   (12-Dec-90 CH.AM255/R) Sien's mother's house from backyard (45x29cm-18x11in) s. pencil pen htd white (D.FL 430000)
£232794 $456275   (24-Nov-90 APT.P4/R) Sur la plage de Scheveningen, automne 1882 (27x45cm-11x18in) W/C (F.FR 2300000)
£3857868 $7600000   (14-Nov-90 CH.NY14/R) Jardin de fleurs (61x49cm-24x19in) s. quill and reed pen over pencil Whatman paper

GOGH, Vincent van and KERSSEMAKERS, Anton (19th C) Dutch
£38700 $74690   (12-Dec-90 CH.AM261/R) Wooden barn in forest (15x23cm-6x9in) s. panel (D.FL 125000)

GOGO, Felix (19/20th C) Belgian
£655 $1113   (28-May-91 C.A124) Fishing boats by a jetty (75x100cm-30x39in) s. (B.FR 40000)
£843 $1636   (4-Dec-90 C.A160) St Andries Church in Antwerp (125x100cm-49x39in) s. (B.FR 50000)

GOLA, Emilio (1852-1923) Italian
£2508 $4189   (6-Jun-91 F.M111) Nudo femminile seduto (50x35cm-20x14in) paper on board (I.L 5500000)
£693 $1338   (12-Dec-90 F.M172/R) Figura femminile (52x37cm-20x15in) pastel pencil (I.L 1500000)

GOLDBERG, Eric (?) Canadian?
£541 $1038   (20-Feb-91 EA.M451 a) Mother and child (46x36cm-18x14in) masonite (C.D 1200)

GOLDBERG, Fred (20th C) American
£969 $1900   (13-Feb-91 B.SF2163/R) Cable cars along Market Street (76x102cm-30x40in) s.

GOLDBERG, Michael (1924-) American
£3673 $7200   (6-Nov-90 CE.NY54/R) End of summer (216x236cm-85x93in) s.i.d.65 verso acrylic

GOLDIE, Charles Frederick (20th C) New Zealander
£3096 $6068   (7-Nov-90 DS.W24/R) Kapi Kapi (20x14cm-8x6in) s. i.verso (NZ.D 10000)
£4651 $7814   (22-Apr-91 SY.ME360/R) Relics of bygone age - Mere Werohia (29x24cm-11x9in) s.d.1933 i.verso (A.D 10000)
£5000 $9750   (24-Oct-90 S111/R) Portrait of a Maori (61x51cm-24x20in) s.d.08

GOLDMANN, Hias (1859-?) Austrian
£776 $1467   (27-Sep-90 D.V52/R) Washerwoman (33x22cm-13x9in) indis.s. board (A.S 16000)

GOLDSCHMIEDT, Milan (1931-) Italian?
£1294 $2497   (13-Dec-90 F.M397) Lylgfed CBA (50x50cm-20x20in) s.verso nitro-acrylic masonite (I.L 2800000)

GOLDSTEIN, Jack (1945-) American
£1538 $2600   (2-May-91 CH.NY227/R) Untitled (244x91cm-96x36in) s.d.1984 stretcher acrylic canvas
£2367 $4000   (2-May-91 CH.NY312/R) Untitled (91x244cm-36x96in) acrylic canvas
£2890 $5000   (7-May-91 CE.NY268/R) Untitled (152x152cm-60x60in)

GOLDTHWAIT, Harold (19th C) British
£1459 $2379   (10-Jun-91 W.T1331/R) Thatched tudor cottage and gypsy caravan (51x76cm-20x30in) (C.D 2700)

GOLIK, Frans von (19th C) ?
£580 $1119   (12-Dec-90 SWS2175) Dutch frozen winter landscape (69x119cm-27x47in)
indist.s. d.1886

GOLL VAN FRANKENSTEIN, Johann (18th C) Dutch
£2000   *$3260*   *(2-Jul-91 C361/R) Winter landscape with figures by bridge over frozen
canal and skaters (40x32cm-16x13in) s.d.1763 black chk pen wash W/C*
£4000   *$6520*   *(2-Jul-91 C360/R) Amstelveenseweg - wooded avenue with carriages and
milkmaid (40x32cm-16x13in) s.d.1763 black chk W/C ink*

GOLLER, Bruno (1901-) German
£6419 $10912   (1-Jun-91 VG.B230/R) Summer landscape with hay stooks (73x64cm-29x25in)
s.d.1922 (DM 19000)
£13014 $21212   (15-Jun-91 L.K232/R) Garden by the Berstig (74x65cm-29x26in) s.
(DM 38000)
£19795 $38799   (20-Nov-90 L.K250/R) Portrait of woman (60x41cm-24x16in) s.d.1947
(DM 58000)
£22184 $43481   (23-Nov-90 VG.B66/R) The little fire (66x51cm-26x20in) s. (DM 65000)
£55932 $93407   (7-Jun-91 HN.H21/R) Two cups (100x105cm-39x41in) s. (DM 165000)
£66553 $130444   (23-Nov-90 VG.B67/R) Two hats (100x120cm-39x47in) s.d.1956 i.verso
(DM 195000)
£15541   *$26419*   *(1-Jun-91 VG.B231/R) Female nude with cloth (55x40cm-22x16in) s. i.verso
pastel gouache linen (DM 46000)*

GOLLINGS, William Elling (1878-1932) American
£599 $1150   (1-Dec-90 LAE.L44/R) Indian encampment (43x38cm-17x15in) s.d.1922 canvas
on board
£2439   *$4000*   *(21-Jun-91 DM.D2016/R) Cowboy on horse with steer (30x25cm-12x10in)
s.d.1911 W/C*

GOLTZIUS, Hendrik (attrib) (1558-1616) Dutch
£1937   *$3738*   *(14-Dec-90 LEB.P84) Divinite mythologique, debout casquee. Etude d'un
cavalier (38x24cm-15x9in) pen oil crayon double-sided (F.FR 19000)*

GOLTZIUS, Hendrik (circle) (1558-1616) Dutch
£2941 $5824   (30-Jan-91 APT.P65/R) Mars ou l'Allegorie de la Guerre (29x38cm-11x15in)
panel (F.FR 29000)
£3600 $6084   (19-Apr-91 C9595/R) Saint Paul (109x86cm-43x34in)

GOLUB, Leon Albert (1922-) American
£1538 $3000   (10-Oct-90 SY.NY360/R) Chiang Kai-Shek, 1974 (36x38cm-14x15in)
s.i.d.1976 burlap
£3163 $6200   (6-Nov-90 CE.NY24/R) Head XV (43x33cm-17x13in) s. i.d.8/8/59 verso
£3374 $5500   (12-Jun-91 SY.NY251/R) Hunger (124x232cm-49x91in) s. acrylic graphite
canvas
£5612 $11000   (6-Nov-90 CE.NY125/R) The Prodigal Sphinx (82x130cm-32x51in) s. oil
latex

GOMAR Y GOMAR, Antonio (1853-1911) Spanish
£8177 $14146   (21-May-91 DUR.M24/R) Madrid visto desde la Casa de Campo
(110x175cm-43x69in) (S.P 1500000)

GOMEZ CORNET, Ramon (1898-1964) Argentinian
£4133 $7150   (8-May-91 V.BA46) Magnolias (50x40cm-20x16in)
£4624 $8000   (8-May-91 RO.BA216) Vaso con flores (45x35cm-18x14in) s.

GOMEZ EL VIEJO, Martin (fl.1526-1562) Spanish
£27189 $53562   (30-Oct-90 EP.M1/R) La Sagrada Familia con San Juanito (76x55cm-30x22in)
panel (S.P 5000000)

GOMEZ Y GIL, Guillermo (1862-1942) Spanish
£585 $1100   (18-Sep-90 RO.BA190) Atardecer en la ribera (18x27cm-7x11in) s. panel —
£3543 $6130   (21-May-91 DUR.M21/R) Laguna tranquila (62x88cm-24x35in) (S.P 650000)

GOMEZ, Paul Pierre (19th C) French
£1734 $3000   (10-May-91 S.W2500/R) Unloading the day's catch (53x64cm-21x25in) s.

GOMOT, L Pierre (19th C) French
£1849 $3106   (23-Apr-91 RAS.K161/R) Young girl at prayer (170x67cm-67x26in) s.
(D.KR 21000)

GONDOUIN, E (1883-1934) French
£14113 $27520   (26-Oct-90 PPB.P95/R) Portrait d'Octave Mirbeau (114x152cm-45x60in)
s.d.1919 (F.FR 140000)

GONDOUIN, Emmanuel (1883-1934) French
£2345 $4525   (16-Dec-90 T.B134) Paysage maritime cubiste (39x47cm-15x19in) studio st.
verso (F.FR 23000)
£346 $691   (4-Feb-91 LGB.P128 e) Jeune femme a mi-corps (28x23cm-11x9in) studio st.
chl. (F.FR 3400)
£376 $752   (4-Feb-91 LGB.P128 a) Tete de jeune fille (56x44cm-22x17in) studio st.
blk.crayon (F.FR 3700)
£417 $833   (4-Feb-91 LGB.P128 c) Tete d'homme (56x44cm-22x17in) s. lead pencil
(F.FR 4100)
£450 $734   (3-Jul-91 LGB.P71 b) Tete de femme a la frange (54x42cm-21x17in) chl.
(F.FR 4500)

GONIN, Francesco (1808-1889) Italian
£8201 $13942   (30-May-91 F.M19/R) Natura morta con vaso di ceramica e fiori
           (54x43cm-21x17in) i. panel (I.L 18000000)
£10819 $19367   (8-Apr-91 CH.R41/R) Scherzi di amorini con fiori (105x90cm-41x35in) two
           s.d.1882 set of 3 (I.L 24000000)

GONNE, Christian F (1813-1906) German
£4192 $7000   (7-Jun-91 SY.NY199/R) The polo match (61x96cm-24x38in) s.d.96 W/C

GONSCHIOR, Kuno (1935-) German
£1458 $2479   (28-May-91 SY.MI97) Vibration magenta - blau- grun (80x80cm-31x31in)
           s.d.71/73verso acrylic (I.L 3200000)
£3413 $6689   (20-Nov-90 L.K251/R) Blue (126x105cm-50x41in) s.d.1986 hessian
           (DM 10000)

GONTCHAROVA, Natalia (1881-1962) Russian
£1200 $1932   (24-Jun-91 CSK196/R) Stage design (19x25cm-7x10in) s. W/C chl paper on
           card
£1520 $2630   (21-May-91 WK.M914 a/R) Composition (36x25cm-14x10in) s. s.d.1912verso
           pastel over pencil (DM 4500)
£5200 $8476   (1-Jul-91 APT.P91) Le Talmud (41x30cm-16x12in) s. W/C (F.FR 52000)

GONTIER (?) French
£2006 $3912   (12-Oct-90 APT.P73) La partie de cartes (97x130cm-38x51in) s.
           (F.FR 20000)

GONTIER, Clement (19th C) French
£3200 $6144   (28-Nov-90 S274/R) Geraniums and nasturtiums on window sill
           (89x61cm-35x24in) s.

GONTIER, Pierre Camille (1840-?) French
£7600 $12844   (1-May-91 GD.B345/R) Birds on flowering cherry branch feeding young
           (92x74cm-36x29in) (S.FR 19000)

GONZALES, Eva (1849-1883) French
£27888 $48247   (24-May-91 FB.P140/R) Les pivoines et le hanneton (23x36cm-9x14in) s.
           (F.FR 280000)
£34000 $65960   (5-Dec-90 S103/R) Portrait de profil de Jeanne Gonzales (22x15cm-9x6in)
           board

GONZALES, Julio (1876-1942) Spanish
£712 $1346   (25-Sep-90 FB.P289/R) Marie-Therese au fichu (19x13cm-7x5in) lead pencil
           (F.FR 7000)
£6897 $13241   (26-Nov-90 WK.M222/R) Monsieur Cactus (25x11cm-10x4in) mono.d.1939 mixed
           media (DM 20000)

GONZALEZ PASCUAL, Alejandro (1930-) Spanish
£605 $1119   (5-Mar-91 ANS.M370/R) Bodegon con tazas (53x81cm-21x32in) s.d.79 tablex
           (S.P 110000)

GONZALEZ VELAZQUEZ, Antonio (1723-1793) Spanish
£4057 $7262   (8-Apr-91 CH.R125/R) Paride invita Elena a fuggire (32x39cm-13x15in)
           (I.L 9000000)

GONZALEZ, Jeanne (1868-1908) French
£3077 $6000   (24-Oct-90 CH.NY1/R) Still life with peaches (38x46cm-15x18in) s.

GONZALEZ, Juan Antonio (1842-?) Spanish
£3533 $6253   (3-Apr-91 ANS.M109/R) Sorprendidas (60x80cm-24x31in) s. (S.P 650000)
£9249 $16000   (23-May-91 CH.NY150/R) The presentation (61x51cm-24x20in) s.d.77

GONZALEZ, Julio (1876-1942) Spanish
£12690 $25000   (14-Nov-90 SY.NY280/R) Femme assise se Coiffant (24x15cm-9x6in)
           init.d.1936 crayon India ink pencil
£14807 $24875   (25-Apr-91 EP.M3/R) Femme (24x14cm-9x6in) init.d.1931 ink pencil pastel
           wax (S.P 2700000)

GOOCH, Thomas (fl.1777-1802) British
£2600 $4290   (10-Jul-91 S139/R) Black hunter in landscape. Carthorse in brewers yard
           (36x44cm-14x17in) indis.s. pair oval

GOOD, Thomas Sword (1787-1872) British
£650 $1248   (20-Dec-90 CSK71) Gentleman seated in chair reading a newspaper
           (30x23cm-12x9in) panel

GOODALL, E A (1819-1908) British
£851 $1396   (17-Jun-91 L.V4) Bruge Cathedral (51x33cm-20x13in) W/C (C.D 1600)

GOODALL, Edward Alfred (1819-1908) British
£1500 $2445   (14-Jun-91 C144/R) Notre Dame from the Left Bank by moonlight
           (36x57cm-14x22in) s.d.1864 pencil W/C htd.bodycol.

GOODALL, Frederick (1822-1904) British
£800 $1536   (29-Nov-90 B36/R) An Arab warrior (55x34cm-22x13in) mono.
£950 $1796   (26-Sep-90 S212/R) Pyramids (19x53cm-7x21in) mono.d.1871
£1100 $2079   (27-Sep-90 CSK109/R) An Arab beauty (53x38cm-21x15in) mono.d.1871

GOODALL, Frederick (1822-1904) British-cont.

£1500	$2970	(30-Jan-91 CSK279) A mother and child (43x28cm-17x11in) mono.d.1875-89 panel
£1842	$3500	(27-Feb-91 SY.NY237/R) Cutting rushes in Nile (61x127cm-24x50in) s.
£2058	$3951	(26-Nov-90 SY.J277/R) Watering sheep and camels on Nile (80x183cm-31x72in) mono.d.1896 (SA.R 10000)
£4196	$8098	(12-Dec-90 WE.MU57/R) Sugar cane harvest (20x55cm-8x22in) mono.d.1869 (DM 12000)
£5202	$9000	(22-May-91 SY.NY260/R) Afterglow (102x89cm-40x35in) s.d.1901
£6154	$12000	(26-Oct-90 SY.NY85/R) Portrait of F E Lewis in Turkish costume (53x39cm-21x15in)
£12000	$23520	(22-Nov-90 CG513/R) Dream of paradise (147x185cm-58x73in) mono.d.1889

GOODALL, John Strickland (1908-) British

£700	$1141	(14-Jun-91 C118/R) On the way to the beach (18x20cm-7x8in) s. pencil W/C htd white
£700	$1141	(14-Jun-91 C119/R) Young girls reading in an orchard (15x18cm-6x7in) s. pencil W/C htd.white
£1300	$2145	(10-Jul-91 CSK131/R) Packing up - ferry crossing and at seaside souvenir shop (13x18cm-5x7in) s.pencil W/C htd white double-sided two sheets

GOODALL, Walter (1830-1889) British

£1000	$1670	(5-Jun-91 S278/R) Sea urchins (32x46cm-13x18in) s.d.1875 W/C
£2000	$3340	(22-Jul-91 SWS826/R) The lottery list (60x98cm-24x39in) s.d.1874 i. verso W/C over pencil htd.bodycol.

GOODMAN, Bertram (1904-) American

£635	$1200	(25-Sep-90 CE.NY101/R) Fisherman going home (60x52cm-24x20in) s.d.41 gouache pencil

GOODMAN, George (19th C) British

£1050	$2048	(15-Jan-91 SWS149) Rabbits and chickens by barn (30x40cm-12x16in) s.
£2800	$5488	(13-Feb-91 S108/R) Bird's nest and butterflies (25x33cm-10x13in) s.d.1862

GOODMAN, John Reginald (1878-?) British

£1400	$2744	(8-Nov-90 PHI133/R) Broadlands scene at sunset, possibly Ranworth (52x76cm-20x30in) s. W/C

GOODMAN, Maude (1860-1938) British

£1103	$2151	(9-Oct-90 GGL.L4/R) Fillette au chat (76x61cm-30x24in) s. (F.FR 11000)

GOODMAN, Robert Gwelo (1871-1939) British

£1863	$3484	(27-Aug-90 SY.J228/R) Isipingo lagoon (22x29cm-9x11in) init. (SA.R 9000)
£4762	$8905	(27-Aug-90 SY.J227/R) Cape Dutch homestead with slave-bell (50x45cm-20x18in) init. (SA.R 23000)
£402	$787	(11-Feb-91 SY.J525/R) View from the valley to the peaks (36x33cm-14x13in) s. W/C (SA.R 2000)
£506	$835	(8-Jul-91 SY.J284) The Blue Pool, sunset (27x33cm-11x13in) init. pastel (SA.R 2400)
£522	$1023	(11-Feb-91 SY.J524/R) Autumn landscape (35x43cm-14x17in) init. W/C (SA.R 2600)
£580	$1084	(27-Aug-90 SY.J82) Roadway to homestead beneath mountains (29x35cm-11x14in) init. pastel (SA.R 2800)

GOODMAN, Sydney (1936-) American

£7107	$14000	(4-Oct-90 SY.NY153/R) Portrait of five figures (132x183cm-52x72in) s.d.73-74

GOODNOUGH, Robert (1917-) American

£736	$1200	(12-Jun-91 SY.NY192/R) Bright colours on pale grey (183x183cm-72x72in) s.d.72 verso oil acrylic graphite
£751	$1300	(12-May-91 H.C222/R) Silver grey (91x152cm-36x60in) s.i.d.1971verso s.i.d.stretcher acrylic oil
£974	$1900	(10-Oct-90 SY.NY388/R) Spring (41x51cm-16x20in) s.
£1282	$2500	(10-Oct-90 SY.NY391/R) Colour chips on grey (198x198cm-78x78in) s. d.1973verso acrylic oil
£1327	$2600	(12-Feb-91 SY.NY367/R) Pastel statement II (102x102cm-40x40in) s.d.71 s.i.d.1971verso acrylic oil
£1531	$3000	(12-Feb-91 SY.NY415 a/R) Colours with red on green (147x198cm-58x78in) s.i.d.1975verso acrylic oil
£2761	$4500	(12-Jun-91 SY.NY196/R) Pocahontas II (194x194cm-76x76in) s.d.60 s.verso
£2806	$5500	(6-Nov-90 CE.NY59/R) Sheridan square (102x152cm-40x60in) s.
£3333	$6500	(10-Oct-90 SY.NY390/R) Abduction (152x152cm-60x60in) s. s.i.verso acrylic
£667	$1300	(10-Oct-90 SY.NY379/R) Black sticks (30x36cm-12x14in) s. paper collage

GOODRICH, James B (fl.1853-58) British

£5000	$9500	(10-Jan-91 B163/R) Three-masted schooner England's Rose shown dressed up and down (35x53cm-14x21in) s.d.1858

GOODWIN, Albert (1845-1932) British

£700	$1372	(22-Jan-91 PH17/R) Bucks Mill, North Devon (33x51cm-13x20in) s.i. board
£1950	$3705	(10-Jan-91 GSP601) Lifeboat fromn the Old Chain Pier, Brighton (41x46cm-16x18in) s.
£583	$1125	(10-Dec-90 L.V1) Forest landscape (28x33cm-11x13in) W/C (C.D 1300)

GOODWIN, Albert (1845-1932) British-cont.

£600	$1176	(21-Nov-90 B93) Hastings (16x21cm-6x8in) init.i.d.89 W/C
£600	$1008	(24-Apr-91 MMB272) Westminster (18x25cm-7x10in) s.i. W/C
£610	$1000	(19-Jun-91 B.SF1926/R) View of street in Chester (21x27cm-8x11in) s. W/C
£657	$1300	(30-Jan-91 GRO.B110/R) Charles river, Boston (18x25cm-7x10in) s.i. W/C gouache
£680	$1217	(13-Mar-91 B112) Dordrecht (25x40cm-10x16in) s.i.d.82 ink W/C
£800	$1584	(30-Jan-91 S171/R) Ilfracombe, Devon (21x23cm-8x9in) s.i. W/C pen
£1000	$1640	(19-Jun-91 B93/R) Hills over Hastings (20x27cm-8x11in) s.i.d.1906 W/C bodycol
£1000	$1680	(15-Jul-91 PH124) Noston (11x17cm-4x7in) s.i. W/C over pencil htd white
£1000	$1670	(5-Jun-91 S257/R) Maidstone (29x45cm-11x18in) s.i.d.88 W/C htd scratching out
£1000	$1980	(30-Jan-91 S248/R) Shepherd (25x35cm-10x14in) s.i.d.1875/1931 i.verso W/C htd scratching out
£1100	$2200	(8-Feb-91 C128/R) The coast of Ilfracombe, North Devon (25x36cm-10x14in) s.d.78 indist.i. verso pencil W/C htd.white
£1300	$2327	(13-Mar-91 B125/R) Grenada, West Indies (21x27cm-8x11in) s.i. W/C bodycol.
£1400	$2744	(21-Nov-90 B87) Sandwich (18x25cm-7x10in) init.i.d.89 W/C
£1500	$2505	(5-Jun-91 S258/R) Rye (22x28cm-9x11in) s.i. W/C pastel
£1500	$2835	(26-Sep-90 S222/R) Palermo (19x25cm-7x10in) s.i. W/C bodycol
£1500	$2445	(14-Jun-91 C40/R) Woolacombe Sands, N. Devon (19x24cm-7x9in) s.i. W/C bodycol
£1650	$3267	(30-Jan-91 S174/R) Valley of Silvaplana, Switzerland (25x37cm-10x15in) s.i. W/C over pencil with bodycol
£1800	$3546	(12-Nov-90 PH40/R) Canterbury (24x36cm-9x14in) s.i. ink W/C scratching out
£1800	$3474	(10-Dec-90 PHB14/R) Gathering blossom (25x35cm-10x14in) s.indis.i. W/C scratching out
£1800	$2934	(13-Jun-91 L90/R) Crossing the ford (33x51cm-13x20in) s.d.1879
£2000	$3720	(5-Sep-90 BT84/R) Burgenstock from Stens (18x23cm-7x9in) s.i. W/C htd bodycol
£2000	$3360	(15-Jul-91 PH125/R) In dust of bazaar, Cairo (34x49cm-13x19in) s.i.d.1875/1911 W/C over pencil
£2200	$3784	(14-May-91 SWS142/R) Capetown docks by moonlight (30x46cm-12x18in) s.i.d.1917 W/C bodycol
£2400	$4800	(8-Feb-91 C70/R) The Lagoons near Chioggia, Venice (33x51cm-13x20in) s.i.d.1917 W/C bodycol.
£2500	$4200	(22-Apr-91 PH274/R) Gloucester (25x37cm-10x15in) s.i.d.1904 W/C bodycol.
£2500	$4825	(10-Dec-90 PHB15/R) Windsor (25x36cm-10x14in) s.i.d.1912 W/C scratching out
£2800	$5600	(8-Feb-91 C71/R) Sunrise from Baveno, Lago Maggiore (25x36cm-10x14in) s.i.d.1911 pencil W/C htd.white board
£3600	$6192	(14-May-91 SWS140/R) Bristol Docks (25x36cm-10x14in) s.i.d.1900 W/C scratching out
£4200	$8232	(21-Nov-90 B119/R) Bristol - when day's work is done (25x37cm-10x15in) s.i.d.1901 pen W/C
£6400	$12544	(21-Nov-90 B120/R) Boulac - Nile ferry (25x37cm-10x15in) s.i.d.1909 W/C bodycol

GOODWIN, Arthur C (1866-1941) American

£758	$1500	(30-Jan-91 GRO.B79/R) Berkshire mountains (33x38cm-13x15in) s. panel
£1189	$2200	(8-Mar-91 S.BM236/R) Sailing into the twilight (102x112cm-40x44in) s.
£2762	$4750	(15-May-91 SY.NY154/R) Harbour scene (87x99cm-34x39in)
£3476	$6500	(30-Aug-90 MFA.C166/R) City street scene (64x76cm-25x30in) s.
£3723	$7000	(22-Sep-90 WOL.C236/R) Boston Street scene (64x76cm-25x30in) s.
£4595	$8500	(8-Mar-91 S.BM226/R) T Wharf, winter (61x76cm-24x30in) s.
£4865	$9000	(8-Mar-91 S.BM223/R) Winter view across Boston common to the State House (58x71cm-23x28in) s.
£7821	$14000	(14-Mar-91 CH.NY184/R) Boston harbour (84x99cm-33x39in) s.
£694	$1200	(10-May-91 S.BM73/R) New York harbour scene (33x48cm-13x19in) s. s.i.verso pastel
£1734	$3000	(10-May-91 S.BM76/R) Looking down Mt Vernon towards the river (33x48cm-13x19in) s. i.verso pastel board ·
£2168	$3750	(21-May-91 GRO.B148/R) Central Park, New York. Portrait head of man (43x53cm-17x21in) s. pastel board double-sided
£3046	$6000	(18-Nov-90 JRB.C104/R) Frog pond, public gardens, Boston (30x46cm-12x18in) s. pastel

GOODWIN, Betty (20th C) American?

£613	$1000	(12-Jun-91 SY.NY241/R) Stone eater (47x69cm-19x27in) i.d.87 indist.num. oilstick pastel metal

GOODWIN, Harry (?-1925) British

£600	$1134	(26-Sep-90 S234/R) Lakeside road, Switzerland (52x34cm-20x13in) mono.d.1906 W/C over pencil
£1700	$2771	(14-Jun-91 C46/R) Fribourg, Switzerland (33x50cm-13x20in) mono.d.1892-4 pencil W/C

GOODWIN, Herbert (19th C) ?

£2200	$4290	(18-Oct-90 CSK114/R) H.M.S. Diana in Plymouth (61x91cm-24x36in) init.d.1880 bears sig.i.label verso

GOODWIN, Phillip R (1882-1935) American
£8671 $15000   (10-May-91 S.BM133/R) We're going home, genre scene with bears and skunk
        (61x84cm-24x33in) s. i.verso
£8671 $15000   (10-May-91 S.BM134/R) In trouble, genre scene with bears and porcupine
        (61x84cm-24x33in) s. i.verso
*£882 $1500   (1-Jun-91 IH.NY25/R) Toting venison under difficulties, man and horse in
        mountains (8x13cm-3x5in) s. gouache pencil*

GOODWIN, Richard Labarre (1840-1910) American
£7732 $15000   (7-Dec-90 S.W2673/R) Greater scaup ducks hanging on cabin door
        (107x69cm-42x27in) s.

GOODWIN, Robin (20th C) British
£1200 $2364   (1-Nov-90 TE654/R) The red stole (38x43cm-15x17in) s. s.i.d.1949verso

GOOILRE, M S van (?) ?
£917 $1760   (18-Dec-90 GM.B881) Les bouleaux (80x102cm-31x40in) s. board
        (B.FR 55000)

GOOKINS, James F (1840-1904) ?
£711 $1400   (7-Oct-90 DU.E68/R) View near Kufstein, Tyrol (71x122cm-28x48in)
        s.d.1880

GOOL, Jan van (1685-1763) Dutch
£3500 $5705   (5-Jul-91 C329/R) Peasants herding animals along hillside path
        (34x48cm-13x19in) s. panel
£6200 $10478   (19-Apr-91 C70/R) Peasants with sheep and cows by a wood
        (53x72cm-21x28in) s.d.1716 panel

GOOL, Jan van (after) (1685-1763) Dutch
£2395 $4479   (1-Sep-90 CH.AM142/R) Italiante landscape with shepherds and animals
        (51x77cm-20x30in) pair (D.FL 8000)

GOOL, Jan van (style) (1685-1763) Dutch
£5500 $9295   (18-Apr-91 C90/R) A farm by a track with a drover and his dogs resting
        by a tree (40x63cm-16x25in) panel

GOOS, Berend (1815-1885) German
£2817 $4732   (23-Apr-91 RAS.K407/R) Distant view of Hamburg (28x42cm-11x17in)
        (D.KR 32000)

GOOSSENS, Josse (1876-1929) German
£3846 $7423   (12-Dec-90 WE.MU204/R) Street cafe (46x55cm-18x22in) s. (DM 11000)
£8785 $16252   (7-Mar-91 D.V157/R) Kasperltheater (60x79cm-24x31in) s.i.d.1923verso
        (A.S 180000)

GORANSSON, Ake (1902-1942) Swedish
£5283 $9140   (22-May-91 BA.S74/R) Still life of bottle and fruit (40x27cm-16x11in)
        st.sig. (S.KR 56000)
£5720 $10982   (27-Nov-90 BU.S113/R) Female nude, green background (98x68cm-39x27in)
        st.sig. (S.KR 62000)

GORBATOFF, K (19/20th C) Russian
£3673 $7200   (6-Nov-90 GF.L2175/R) Russian village, early spring (77x91cm-30x36in)
        s.d.1923 (S.FR 9000)

GORBATOFF, Konstantin (19/20th C) Russian
£7000 $13650   (10-Oct-90 C232/R) View of Pskov (80x110cm-31x43in) s.d.1922
*£950 $1853   (10-Oct-90 C224/R) First snow in Moscow (40x50cm-16x20in) s. W/C htd
        white paper laid down on board*

GORBONOV, Vladimir (1950-) Russian
£511 $915   (9-Apr-91 GO.G170) Composition with female figures (54x65cm-21x26in) s.
        (S.KR 5500)
£731 $1433   (20-Nov-90 GO.G413) St George and the Dragon (62x46cm-24x18in) s.
        (S.KR 8000)

GORDER, Levon (19/20th C) American
£2012 $3400   (20-Apr-91 WOL.C65/R) In village (64x89cm-25x35in) s.d.1895

GORDIGIANI, Edoardo (1866-1961) Italian
£997 $1685   (16-Apr-91 CH.R119) Nel parco (25x33cm-10x13in) s.i.d.1931 panel
        (I.L 2200000)

GORDILLO, Luis (20th C) Spanish
£24530 $40229   (18-Jun-91 EP.M15/R) Caballero cubista aux larmes (160x106cm-63x42in)
        s.d.73 acrylic (S.P 4500000)
£27420 $46065   (25-Apr-91 EP.M24/R) Magmatica (92x73cm-36x29in) i.d.1964verso canvas on
        panel (S.P 5000000)
*£4097 $7908   (13-Dec-90 EP.M18/R) Dibujo con dos seres (70x100cm-28x39in) s.d.19-1-75
        gouache col.crayons ink pencil (S.P 750000)*

GORDON, Arthur (19th C) British
£1000 $1670   (5-Jun-91 S62/R) Early morning, Kew Bridge (51x76cm-20x30in) s.d.1898

GORDON, G (?) ?
£1600 $3024   (26-Sep-90 S184/R) Fortune teller (76x127cm-30x50in) s.

GORDON, Grigori (1909-) Russian
£519 $897   (8-May-91 FER.M234/R) El lago de Sinej (40x60cm-16x24in) s.
  s.i.d.1962verso board (S.P 95000)
£601 $1039   (8-May-91 FER.M245/R) La catedral de Pereslavizalesski (50x70cm-20x28in)
  s.i.d.1971verso canvas laid down on board (S.P 110000)
£601 $1039   (8-May-91 FER.M244/R) Paisaje de invierno (50x60cm-20x24in) s.
  s.i.d.1979verso (S.P 110000)
£601 $1039   (8-May-91 FER.M247/R) Encaladora descansando (50x51cm-20x20in) s.
  s.i.d.1958verso board (S.P 110000)
£710 $1228   (8-May-91 FER.M249/R) El pantano Jlebnicovskoe (50x70cm-20x28in) s.
  s.i.d.1975verso board (S.P 130000)
£792 $1370   (8-May-91 FER.M248/R) Embarcadero en el mar Blanco (40x59cm-16x23in) s.
  s.i.d.1965verso board (S.P 145000)
£874 $1511   (8-May-91 FER.M250/R) Aldea a las afueras de Moscu (50x81cm-20x32in) s.
  board (S.P 160000)
£874 $1511   (8-May-91 FER.M251/R) Monasterio Danilovski (50x80cm-20x31in) s.
  s.i.d.1965verso board (S.P 160000)
£956 $1653   (8-May-91 FER.M246/R) Retrato de muchacha de Yakutia (80x60cm-31x24in)
  s. s.i.d.1979verso (S.P 175000)
£1365 $2361   (8-May-91 FER.M254/R) Terraza con jarron de lilas (75x100cm-30x39in) s.
  s.i.d.1982 (S.P 250000)
£1502 $2598   (8-May-91 FER.M253/R) Jarron con lilas (90x72cm-35x28in) s.
  s.i.d.1986verso (S.P 275000)

GORDON, J (19th C) British
£548 $981   (12-Mar-91 FN.S2386 a) Horses grazing in landscape. Two horses in stable
  interior (40x50cm-16x20in) s. panel (DM 1600)

GORDON, Robert James (19th C) British
£1050 $1775   (30-Apr-91 AG304/R) Betty (44x34cm-17x13in)

GORDON, Sir John Watson (1788-1864) British
£540 $923   (30-Jul-91 SWS75/R) Portrait of Elizabeth Rogerson, wife of William
  Rollo (75x62cm-30x24in) s.i. verso
£600 $1038   (22-May-91 CSK265) Study of child eating (37x29cm-15x11in) board
£700 $1176   (23-Apr-91 S60/R) Study for portrait of Lady Murray (30x20cm-12x8in)
  d.1831 verso board
£850 $1615   (28-Feb-91 B78/R) Portrait of Amelia Frances Pellatt, with river
  landscape beyond (76x63cm-30x25in) bears i.verso

GORDON, Sir John Watson (circle) (1788-1864) British
£2200 $4312   (22-Nov-90 CG526/R) Portrait of Robert Baird of Auchmedden standing with
  top hat in landscape (147x119cm-58x47in)

GORDON-CUMMING, Constance Frederika (19th C) ?
*£993 $1937   (9-Oct-90 CH.HK1405/R) Fujiyama and Hakoni Lake from Atami Pass
  (38x61cm-15x24in) s.i.d.1879 pencil W/C (HK.D 15000)*

GORDY, Dudley (20th C) British
£1650 $3053   (5-Mar-91 AG273/R) Her path (49x59cm-19x23in) s.d.1917 i.verso panel

GORE, Frederick (1913-) British
£2300 $3956   (14-May-91 SWS444/R) Landscape, late afternoon, Provence
  (51x60cm-20x24in) s.d.48 double-sided
£3500 $6475   (8-Mar-91 C220/R) Sunflowers, Bonnieux (49x58cm-19x23in) s.d.89
  s.i.d.stretcher
£3800 $7410   (10-Oct-90 S134/R) Mountain pool (64x82cm-25x32in) s.
£4000 $7520   (20-Sep-90 C173/R) Rhone at Arles (75x101cm-30x40in) s.
£5000 $8450   (2-May-91 C90/R) Field of flowers, St. Remy (61x81cm-24x32in) s.d.55
  s.i.d. 1955 verso
£7000 $13160   (20-Sep-90 C49/R) View from artist's window (57x47cm-22x19in) s.

GORE, Hon Charles (1729-1807) British
*£3000 $5370   (9-Apr-91 C27/R) Colosseum with Martyr's Memorial and House of the
  Societas Gonfalonis (24x41cm-9x16in) s.i.d.1776 pencil pen ink W/C*

GORE, S F (1878-1914) British
£2545 $4836   (12-Sep-90 WO.CO10) Portrait of girl by a mirror (33x43cm-13x17in) s.
  (E.P 2800)

GORE, William Henry (fl.1880-1916) British
£720 $1332   (7-Mar-91 CSK115/R) Reeding (29x44cm-11x17in) s.
£2000 $3480   (27-Mar-91 S5/R) The rising moon (61x91cm-24x36in) s.
£460 $773   (15-Jul-91 PH149/R) Who's afraid (14x9cm-6x4in) init. W/C bodycol
£920 $1546   (15-Jul-91 PH153/R) In disgrace (14x9cm-6x4in) init. W/C bodycol

GORI, Alessandro (17th C) Italian
£8718 $17000   (11-Oct-90 SY.NY68/R) Dead game in landscape with still life of fruit
  (60x73cm-24x29in) s.

GORIN, Jean (1899-1981) French
£1282 $2526   (1-Oct-90 CC.P31/R) Composition au carre bleu (32x31cm-13x12in)
  mono.d.1964 gouache (F.FR 13000)

GORIN, Jean (1899-1981) French-cont.
£1282 $2526   (1-Oct-90 CC.P34) Composition no.7 (24x24cm-9x9in) s.d.63 verso gouache
                      (F.FR 13000)
£1282 $2526   (1-Oct-90 CC.P32) Composition no.1 (24x24cm-9x9in) s.d.63 verso gouache
                      (F.FR 13000)
£1282 $2526   (1-Oct-90 CC.P33/R) Composition no.9 (24x24cm-9x9in) s.d.63 verso
                      gouache (F.FR 13000)

GORKUM, Jacobus van (1827-1880) Dutch
£1257 $2188   (26-Mar-91 VN.R27) Shipping on a town canal (21x29cm-8x11in) s. panel
                      (D.FL 4200)

GORKY, Arshile (1905-1948) American
£1429 $2800   (6-Nov-90 CE.NY10/R) Untitled (22x19cm-9x7in) graphite
£1531 $3000   (6-Nov-90 CE.NY11/R) Untitled (14x22cm-6x9in) s. felt-tip pen
£1538 $3000   (10-Oct-90 SY.NY339/R) Figure studies (23x28cm-9x11in) bears sig.d.1934
                      graphite
£2381 $4000   (24-Apr-91 B.SF4630/R) Head study (33x20cm-13x8in) s. crayon pen
£3077 $6000   (10-Oct-90 SY.NY342/R) Drawing of male head (23x28cm-9x11in) bears
                      sig.s.d.1932 crayon
£4569 $9000   (4-Oct-90 SY.NY14/R) Untitled (40x30cm-16x12in) s. crayon ink
                      double-sided
£5102 $10000   (7-Nov-90 SY.NY105/R) Vase of flowers (60x45cm-24x18in) s. pastel paper
                      laid down on board
£6231 $11154   (17-Mar-91 GL.P21/R) Sans titre (33x27cm-13x11in) lead pencil
                      (F.FR 62000)
£23669 $40000   (2-May-91 CH.NY106/R) Untitled (48x63cm-19x25in) s. graphite
£25510 $50000   (8-Nov-90 CH.NY125/R) Untitled (58x74cm-23x29in) pen
£96447 $190000   (4-Oct-90 SY.NY18/R) Untitled (51x67cm-20x26in) s.d.44 graphite crayon
£165680 $280000   (1-May-91 CH.NY3/R) Untitled (48x64cm-19x25in) s.d.44 col.crayons
                      graphite

GORP, Henri Nicolas van (attrib) (c.1756-c.1819) French
£1103 $2151   (10-Oct-90 APT.P488/R) Portrait d'un jeune homme en habit noir
                      (28x23cm-11x9in) panel (F.FR 11000)

GORSON, Aaron Henry (1872-1933) American
£1034 $1850   (11-Apr-91 FA.PH924/R) Bay with tree (28x36cm-11x14in)
£4050 $7250   (11-Apr-91 FA.PH801/R) Hudson yacht basin looking toward Palisades
                      (61x76cm-24x30in) s.
£8092 $14000   (22-May-91 CH.NY286/R) The smoke stcks of industry (89x101cm-35x40in) s.
£9249 $16000   (23-May-91 SY.NY62/R) Pittsburgh Mills (77x96cm-30x38in) s.
£12169 $20000   (26-Sep-90 SY.NY166/R) Pittsburgh Mills at night (91x122cm-36x48in) s.

GORTER, Arnold Marc (1866-1933) Dutch
£526 $1037   (30-Oct-90 MA.V553) Cattle at stream (36x36cm-14x14in) mono.d.1911 panel
                      (C.D 1200)
£854 $1673   (6-Nov-90 SY.AM144) Trees along water (36x25cm-14x10in) s. panel
                      (D.FL 2800)
£1048 $2054   (5-Nov-90 FB.M341) Apple blossom (36x48cm-14x19in) s. (C.D 2400)
£1437 $2501   (26-Mar-91 VN.R28) Farmstead with well in the yard (46x64cm-18x25in) s.
                      (D.FL 4800)
£1579 $3000   (27-Feb-91 SY.NY24/R) Autumn landscape with cows (51x65cm-20x26in) s.
£1676 $3000   (11-Apr-91 FA.PH683/R) Cattle grazing by pond (69x53cm-27x21in)
£1890 $3591   (26-Feb-91 VN.R112) Wooded landscape (50x38cm-20x15in) (D.FL 6200)
£2395 $4551   (11-Sep-90 CH.AM221/R) Cattle by a lake in autumn (33x53cm-13x21in) s.
                      (D.FL 8000)
£2730 $4750   (27-Mar-91 B.SF4084/R) Wooded pond with cattle on the Veluwe
                      (68x84cm-27x33in) s.
£2994 $5030   (23-Apr-91 SY.AM97) Figure with cattle at Vordense Beek
                      (37x48cm-15x19in) s. (D.FL 10000)
£3293 $5533   (23-Apr-91 SY.AM146/R) View of Vordense Beek (61x80cm-24x31in) s.
                      (D.FL 11000)
£3426 $6750   (7-Oct-90 DU.E5/R) Apple blossoms (66x84cm-26x33in) s.

GORUS, Pieter (1881-1941) Belgian
£1413 $2530   (16-Mar-91 KV.L131/R) The white farmhouse (50x52cm-20x20in) s.
                      (B.FR 85000)
£1829 $3273   (16-Mar-91 KV.L349/R) Sunny avenue (32x40cm-13x16in) s. (B.FR 110000)
£3627 $7110   (21-Nov-90 GM.B1179) Verger en fleurs (60x80cm-24x31in) s. (B.FR 220000)

GOS, Albert (1852-1942) Swiss
£516 $923   (13-Mar-91 GK.Z36) View from hill to village, Wallis (46x55cm-18x22in)
                      s. (S.FR 1300)
£1633 $3167   (8-Dec-90 GAB.G2615) Paysage de montagne avec lac (68x81cm-27x32in) s.
                      mono. verso (S.FR 4000)
£1714 $3326   (7-Dec-90 G.Z568/R) Cross in mountain landscape (80x65cm-31x26in) s.
                      (S.FR 4200)

GOS, Francois (1880-1968) Swiss
£1429 $2714   (14-Sep-90 ZOF.Z1079/R) View of Ligerz with church and Lake Biel
                      (75x58cm-30x23in) s. (S.FR 3500)

GOSCHEL, Eberhard (1943-) German
£2872 $4968   (25-May-91 N.M107/R) Aufschwung (180x145cm-71x57in) s.d. (DM 8500)

GOSER, Karl (1803-1858) German
£1095 $2157   (30-Oct-90 BU.S313/R) Kitchen interior (24x33cm-9x13in) s.d.1834 copper (S.KR 12000)

GOSLING, William (1824-1883) British
£550 $897   (4-Jul-91 PHI34/R) Near Henley-on-Thames (35x68cm-14x27in) s. i. verso W/C
£620 $1035   (3-Jun-91 PHB6/R) Pangbourne on Thames (24x47cm-9x19in) s. W/C

GOSSAERT, Jan (1478-1533) Flemish
£22000 $35860   (2-Jul-91 C194/R) Saint John on Patmos experiencing Vision of Virgin and child (21cm-8ins circular) black chk pen squared

GOSSAERT, Jan (circle) (1478-1533) Flemish
£1100 $2123   (11-Dec-90 PH277) Lucretia, three quarter length (46x32cm-18x13in) panel
£3083 $5982   (7-Dec-90 SY.MO146/R) Vierge a l'enfant (30x24cm-12x9in) panel (F.FR 30000)

GOSSE, Sylvia (1881-1968) British
£2000 $3700   (7-Mar-91 C50/R) Bon voyage (67x44cm-26x17in) s.
£6500 $12740   (8-Nov-90 C84/R) A street in Dieppe (39x29cm-15x11in) s.

GOTCH, Bernard Cecil (1876-?) British
£520 $894   (14-May-91 H280) View of Winchester College (28x38cm-11x15in) s. W/C

GOTCH, Thomas Cooper (1854-1931) British
£2174 $4065   (27-Aug-90 SY.J187/R) Spring garden (49x38cm-19x15in) s. (SA.R 10500)
£2400 $4512   (18-Sep-90 PH32/R) View of Gretton, near Kettering (41x51cm-16x20in) s.
£3800 $6574   (7-May-91 PH4/R) The sailor's farewell (102x69cm-40x27in) s.d.1887
£4800 $8880   (7-Mar-91 C16/R) Flanders poppies (49x39cm-19x15in) s. s.i.stretcher
£5000 $8150   (13-Jun-91 L400/R) The Sailors' farewell (102x69cm-40x27in) s.d.1887
£5800 $10382   (14-Mar-91 L200/R) Silver morning - panoramic view of Penzance from Chywoone Hill, Newlyn (28x48cm-11x19in) s.
£14500 $27405   (27-Sep-90 L250/R) Time was (53x43cm-21x17in) s.
£980 $1842   (18-Sep-90 PH125/R) Study of young girl (50x40cm-20x16in) chl

GOTLIB, Henryk (1890-1966) Polish
£1154 $2238   (4-Dec-90 FN.S1844) French town (63x78cm-25x31in) s.d.1926 (DM 3300)

GOTLIEB, Jules (1897-?) American
£882 $1500   (1-Jun-91 IH.NY208/R) Modern girl of the 1930s and other woman (56x58cm-22x23in) en grisaille

GOTSCH, Friedrich Karl (1900-1984) Danish
£1573 $3052   (7-Dec-90 GB.B6552/R) Elba (24x30cm-9x12in) mono.d.1962 (DM 4500)
£24828 $47669   (26-Nov-90 WK.M27/R) Artistinnen III (53x99cm-21x39in) mono. s.i.d.1958verso i.stretcher (DM 72000)
£1049 $2035   (7-Dec-90 GB.B6553/R) By the dyke, possibly St Peter (30x40cm-12x16in) s.i.d.1925 W/C bodycol (DM 3000)
£1520 $2584   (30-May-91 SY.BE71/R) Ste Maries de la Mer (31x47cm-12x19in) s.i.d.29 W/C (DM 4500)
£1700 $3043   (12-Apr-91 BM.B839/R) Landscape with house (55x76cm-22x30in) mono. s.i.d.50 W/C gouache (DM 5100)
£2080 $4036   (5-Dec-90 DO.H2573/R) Teenager (65x41cm-26x16in) mono.s.d.1957 gouache (DM 5950)
£2500 $4475   (12-Apr-91 BM.B838/R) Munch geht um in Aassaard Strand (57x69cm-22x27in) mono.i.d.1964-67 gouache (DM 7500)

GOTTFRIED, Oswald (1869-?) German
£526 $1000   (9-Jan-91 D.NY33) Sycamores under grey skies (71x99cm-28x39in) s. s.indist.i.stretcher

GOTTLIEB, Adolph (1903-1974) American
£2959 $5000   (1-May-91 D.NY45) Objects on table (43x30cm-17x12in) s. s.i.verso canvas on board
£4082 $8000   (14-Feb-91 CH.NY4/R) Green foreground (21x23cm-8x9in) s.d.1970 i.d.1972verso acrylic
£19133 $37500   (15-Feb-91 SY.NY150/R) Above and below no 2 (61x76cm-24x30in) s.i.d.1965verso
£4734 $8000   (1-May-91 SY.NY181/R) Untitled (25x20cm-10x8in) s.i.d.1962 W/C
£5102 $10000   (14-Feb-91 CH.NY10/R) Untitled (48x61cm-19x24in) s. W/C

GOTTLIEB, Harry (1895-?) American
£694 $1200   (21-May-91 CE.NY580/R) Mine workers (60x76cm-24x30in) s.
£1875 $3750   (6-Feb-91 D.NY37) Steel Mill, Western Pennsylvania (71x99cm-28x39in) s.i.

GOTTLIEB, Leopold (1883-1934) Polish
£1840 $3000   (12-Jun-91 GG.TA401/R) Nude in bathroom (40x33cm-16x13in) s. board
£1152 $2200   (1-Jan-91 GG.TA266/R) Bathers (42x52cm-17x20in) s. pastel htd.white
£1288 $2100   (12-Jun-91 SY.NY31/R) Group of seated figures (50x38cm-20x15in) s.d. gouache oil paper

GOTTSCHALK, Albert (1866-1906) Danish
£636 $1233   (5-Dec-90 KH.K45) Outskirts of wood (45x62cm-18x24in) (D.KR 7000)
£1031 $1980   (27-Dec-90 RAS.V32/R) Country road in winter (42x60cm-17x24in) (D.KR 11500)

GOTTWALD, Frederick C (1860-1941) American
£523 $900   (18-May-91 W.W148/R) Evening light on the Castello (66x84cm-26x33in) s. i. backing

GOTZ, Karl Otto (1914-) Swiss
£8219 $13397   (14-Jun-91 L.K908/R) Roter Wimpel (46x68cm-18x27in) s.d.46 tempera board (DM 24000)
£1775 $3478   (24-Nov-90 N.M180/R) Composition (26x19cm-10x7in) mono. s.d.1957verso indian ink brush (DM 5200)
£2568 $4187   (14-Jun-91 L.K910/R) Untitled (30x41cm-12x16in) s. gouache (DM 7500)
£3925 $7693   (20-Nov-90 L.K249/R) Untitled (28x22cm-11x9in) s. gouache (DM 11500)
£5631 $11038   (20-Nov-90 L.K248/R) Untitled (62x93cm-24x37in) s.i.d. gouache board (DM 16500)
£10274 $16747   (14-Jun-91 L.K909/R) Untitled (55x70cm-22x28in) s. s.i.d.1955verso mixed media canvas (DM 30000)

GOTZELMANN, E (1830-1903) Austrian
£890 $1594   (13-Mar-91 N.M503/R) Father and son returning home on haycart (26x47cm-10x19in) s. panel (DM 2600)

GOTZELMANN, Edward (1830-1903) Austrian
£1367 $2446   (12-Apr-91 BM.B599/R) Russian wedding procession in winter landscape (31x48cm-12x19in) s. i.verso panel (DM 4100)

GOTZINGER, Hans (1867-?) Austrian
£1050 $2048   (11-Oct-90 D.V201/R) View of Ennsberg near Enns (29x38cm-11x15in) s.d.1921 i.verso W/C (A.S 22000)

GOTZLOFF, Carl (1799-1866) German
£3767 $6743   (13-Mar-91 N.M505/R) View of Vesuvio with Monte Somma, evening (39x61cm-15x24in) s. (DM 11000)
£9091 $17545   (12-Dec-90 N.M524/R) Bay of Sorrent near Vico at sunset (50x76cm-20x30in) s. i.verso (DM 26000)
£46075 $86621   (19-Sep-90 N.M497/R) Neapolitan market scene before Castel Nuovo (104x164cm-41x65in) s.i. (DM 135000)
£541 $919   (31-May-91 GB.B5773/R) Olevano seen from Serpentara with view of church and Casa Baldi (28x20cm-11x8in) i.d.1822 pencil (DM 1600)
£743 $1264   (31-May-91 GB.B5775/R) View of Capri with Certosa seen from Monte Solaro (22x35cm-9x14in) d.1823 pencil (DM 2200)
£1824 $3101   (28-May-91 KF.M164/R) Capri seen from Sorrento (24x33cm-9x13in) s. W/C (DM 5400)

GOTZSCHE, Kai G (1886-?) Danish
£750 $1470   (22-Nov-90 CSK278/R) Arch of Titus, Rome (80x65cm-31x26in) s.i.d.1911

GOUBAU, Antoni (1616-1698) Dutch
£2534 $4307   (27-May-91 L.K48/R) Figures and two horses before tavern (37x49cm-15x19in) panel (DM 7500)
£25295 $49073   (4-Dec-90 C.A163/R) The market (125x250cm-49x98in) (B.FR 1500000)
£78163 $139912   (14-Mar-91 D.V48/R) Roman fun fair (125x250cm-49x98in) (A.S 1600000)

GOUBAU, Antoni (style) (1616-1698) Dutch
£3000 $5850   (25-Oct-90 CSK103/R) Peasants by fountain outside Rome (84x112cm-33x44in)

GOUBIE, Jean Richard (1842-1899) French
£3072 $5805   (25-Sep-90 FN.S2182) Young lady riding in wooded landscape (32x41cm-13x16in) s.d.1896 (DM 9000)
£8929 $15000   (19-Jul-91 DM.D2007/R) Landy on horseback with artist, easel and dog (36x28cm-14x11in) s.d.1890
£9231 $18000   (24-Oct-90 CH.NY124/R) Afternoon ride (38x50cm-15x20in) s.d.1879
£19000 $30590   (27-Jun-91 CG128/R) Startled by steam (48x70cm-19x28in) s.d.1877

GOUDIE, Alexander (19th C) British
£500 $840   (23-Apr-91 S168) Flight into Egypt (71x107cm-28x42in) s.d.55
£950 $1596   (23-Apr-91 S167/R) Marriage of Cana (91x122cm-36x48in) s. s.i.verso board
£2000 $3380   (17-Apr-91 CG144/R) Anisa II (102x96cm-40x38in) s.

GOUDT, Hendrik (1585-1630) Dutch
£1542 $2991   (7-Dec-90 CH.MO212/R) Un homme enveloppe dans un manteau et tenant un baton (196x115cm-77x45in) pen (F.FR 15000)

GOUETSKI, Semen (1902-1972) Russian
£680 $1204   (18-Mar-91 ARC.P142/R) Les bergers (90x130cm-35x51in) (F.FR 6800)

GOUGET, Tal (20th C) French
£2016 $3931   (20-Jan-91 CB.P129/R) Vase de fleurs (65x81cm-26x32in) s. (F.FR 20000)

GOUGIS, Jacqueline (20th C) French
£505 $990   (17-Feb-91 E.LA42) Lecture au bord de l'Epte (38x46cm-15x18in) s. (F.FR 5000)

GOULD, Alexander Carruthers (1870-?) British
£500 $865   (7-May-91 PH121) Horner Woods and Dunkery Beacon (64x76cm-25x30in) s.

GOULD, John (attrib) (1804-1881) British?
£420 $806   (19-Feb-91 C12) Study of cream coloured courser (10x28cm-4x11in) pencil W/C htd.white

GOULDING, H J (?) ?
£1800 $3564   (30-Jan-91 CSK275/R) The Doge's Palace, VENICE (51x81cm-20x32in) s.

GOULIAIEV, Alexandre (1917-) Russian
£503 $965   (18-Feb-91 ARC.P189/R) La crique en Crimee (81x100cm-32x39in) s. (F.FR 5000)
£503 $965   (18-Feb-91 ARC.P190/R) Pecheur du lac Baikal (108x67cm-43x26in) s. verso (F.FR 5000)
£600 $1008   (26-Apr-91 ARC.P188/R) Nature morte a la theiere rouge (98x68cm-39x27in) s. (F.FR 6000)
£603 $1158   (18-Feb-91 ARC.P186/R) Pecheur au filet (86x70cm-34x28in) s.d.50 (F.FR 6000)
£653 $1254   (18-Feb-91 ARC.P185/R) Cavaliers de l'Armee Rouge (82x140cm-32x55in) s. (F.FR 6500)
£900 $1512   (26-Apr-91 ARC.P186/R) Confidence sur le banc (90x69cm-35x27in) s. (F.FR 9000)
£1307 $2509   (18-Feb-91 ARC.P187/R) Nature morte aux pommes (86x64cm-34x25in) s.d.46 (F.FR 13000)
£1407 $2702   (18-Feb-91 ARC.P191/R) Nature morte au samovar (90x100cm-35x39in) s.d.72 (F.FR 14000)
£3317 $6368   (18-Feb-91 ARC.P188/R) Le gouter de fruits (68x112cm-27x44in) s. verso (F.FR 33000)

GOUNARO, Georges (20th C) French
£4281 $8220   (30-Nov-90 CB.P121/R) Nu assis (80x60cm-31x24in) s. (F.FR 42000)

GOUPIL, Jules Adolphe (1839-1883) French
£2143 $4200   (21-Nov-90 NA.BA34) Tete ideale (67x41cm-26x16in) s. panel

GOURDAULT, Pierre (1880-1915) French
£1436 $2541   (7-Apr-91 I.N154) Cours d'eau en Bretagne (46x55cm-18x22in) s. (F.FR 14500)

GOURDET, Adam (19th C) ?
£1618 $3155   (19-Oct-90 MB.P53) L'hallali (114x272cm-45x107in) s.d.1856 (F.FR 16000)

GOURDON, A (?) ?
£1258 $2415   (17-Dec-90 ZZ.F95) Bouquet de pivoines dans un vase (98x75cm-39x30in) s. (F.FR 12400)

GOURGUE, Enguerrand-Jean (1930-) Haitian
£1276 $2500   (19-Nov-90 SY.NY309/R) La vendeuse de mais (70x56cm-28x22in) s. masonite
£3061 $6000   (19-Nov-90 SY.NY300/R) Toussaint l'Ouverture. Petion (61x51cm-24x20in) s. masonite two
£3061 $6000   (19-Nov-90 SY.NY299 a/R) Dessalines and le Roi Henri Christophe (61x51cm-24x20in) s. masonite two

GOUTEL (19th C) French
£1297 $2542   (24-Nov-90 SA.A581/R) Still life of fruit (53x66cm-21x26in) s.i.d.1805 (DM 3800)

GOUVRANT, Gerard (1946-) French
£577 $998   (12-May-91 L.C36/R) Clowns au saxo (55x46cm-22x18in) s. (F.FR 5800)
£713 $1404   (4-Nov-90 FE.P155) Personnage au bouquet (55x46cm-22x18in) s. (F.FR 7000)
£1194 $2078   (31-Mar-91 FE.P174) Les clowns (60x73cm-24x29in) s. (F.FR 12000)
£4995 $9640   (13-Dec-90 QWA.P1012/R) Le charivari (81x100cm-32x39in) s. (F.FR 49000)
£7614 $15000   (15-Nov-90 D.NY125/R) Le gendarme (60x74cm-24x29in) s.

GOUWE, Adriaan Herman (1875-1965) Dutch
£867 $1673   (12-Dec-90 CH.AM8) Camel in desert (38x80cm-15x31in) s.d.1922 (D.FL 2800)

GOUWELOOS, Jean (1865-?) Belgian
£1663 $2976   (16-Mar-91 KV.L425/R) Young woman in an interior (80x60cm-31x24in) s. (B.FR 100000)

GOVAERTS, Abraham (circle) (1589-1626) Flemish
£2353 $4000   (31-May-91 CH.NY201/R) The Good Samaritan (75x99cm-30x39in) panel
£5000 $8150   (4-Jul-91 C669/R) Rocky landscape with gypsy encampment by river (49x74cm-19x29in) panel

GOVAERTS, Abraham (studio) (1589-1626) Flemish
£5120 $8244   (27-Jun-91 APT.P87/R) Paysage de foret avec le Sacrifice d'Isaac (23x30cm-9x12in) panel (F.FR 51000)

GOVAERTS, Hendrik (1669-1720) Flemish
£4192 $7000   (23-Jan-91 D.NY82) Twelfth night (69x86cm-27x34in) wax seal Coat of Arms
£6667 $12800   (18-Dec-90 GM.B4102/R) L'artiste dans son atelier (49x58cm-19x23in) (B.FR 400000)

GOVAERTS, Hendrik (school) (1669-1720) Flemish
£1826 $3615   (30-Jan-91 APT.P73/R) Le pase de danse (50x60cm-20x24in) (F.FR 18000)

GOVAERTS, Hendrik (style) (1669-1720) Flemish
£1450 $2509   (20-May-91 SWS43/R) A musical soiree (48x68cm-19x27in)

GOW, Andrew Carrick (1848-1920) British
£400 $716   (10-Apr-91 CSK57/R) Florence from the Arno at dusk (25x36cm-10x14in) pencil W/C
£420 $752   (10-Apr-91 CSK58) Rock pools at low tide (25x36cm-10x14in) s.i.d.1912 pencil W/C htd.white
£500 $895   (10-Apr-91 CSK55) Fishing boats beached at low tide (36x25cm-14x10in) s.i.d.1913 pencil W/C htd.white

GOW, Mary L (1851-1929) British
£1250 $2088   (22-Jul-91 SWS830) Mrs S P Hall with her daughter (35x19cm-14x7in) W/C htd.white

GOYA Y LUCIENTES, Francisco Jose de (1746-1828) Spanish
£750 $1268   (16-Apr-91 PH119) Portrait of lady, said to be Maria Louisa of Parma, before landscape (76x63cm-30x25in)
£374966 $712435   (28-Feb-91 EP.M12/R) Retrato de dama con mantilla (61x51cm-24x20in) (S.P 68000000)
£294118 $500000   (30-May-91 SY.NY83/R) Maja and Celestina (5x5cm-2x2in) min. carbon black wash htd graffito on ivory

GOYA Y LUCIENTES, Francisco Jose de (circle) (1746-1828) Spanish
£1093 $1848   (18-Apr-91 APT.P22/R) Portrait d'un gentilhomme en jabot (30x23cm-12x9in) zinc oval (F.FR 11000)
£8500 $14365   (19-Apr-91 C112/R) Portrait of General Jose Rebolledo de Palafox y Melci (72x56cm-28x22in)

GOYA Y LUCIENTES, Francisco Jose de (style) (1746-1828) Spanish
£794 $1421   (13-Mar-91 GK.Z37) Seated women and children (20x38cm-8x15in) (S.FR 2000)
£2000 $3260   (4-Jul-91 C596/R) Portrait of young man, in coat, waistcoat and stock (63x51cm-25x20in)
£2679 $4500   (17-Jul-91 SY.NY130/R) Portrait of Helena Franze-Ghae (89x69cm-35x27in) i.

GOYEN, Jan van (1596-1665) Dutch
£20000 $32600   (5-Jul-91 C323/R) Winter landscape with numerous skaters and horsedrawn sledge outside inn (28x21cm-11x8in) with sig. panel oval
£22610 $43864   (5-Dec-90 APT.P57/R) Marine (37x62cm-15x24in) mono.d.1635 panel (F.FR 220000)
£26500 $51145   (11-Dec-90 ACA832) Landscape with travellers outside inn (32x53cm-13x21in) mono.d.1633
£33639 $66269   (13-Nov-90 CH.AM128/R) Travellers resting at foot of oak tree near sandy track, farm nearby (45x61cm-18x24in) s.d.1633 panel (D.FL 110000)
£50000 $95000   (10-Jan-91 SY.NY22/R) Landscape with figures beneath large oak tree, village in distance (35cm-14ins circular) s.d.1630 panel
£50000 $96500   (12-Dec-90 S97/R) Castle on bank of inland water (36x50cm-14x20in) s.d.1642 panel
£62000 $119660   (12-Dec-90 S91/R) River landscape with castle (43x70cm-17x28in) s.d.1635 panel
£78947 $150000   (10-Jan-91 SY.NY59/R) Extensive river landscape with church and sailboats in distance (40x63cm-16x25in) mono.d.1644 panel
£370588 $630000   (31-May-91 CH.NY12/R) River estuary with boats docked by shore (36x51cm-14x20in) init.d.1655 panel
£1366 $2636   (11-Dec-90 FER.M19/R) La cabana (17x28cm-7x11in) pencil dr (S.P 250000)
£4300 $7009   (1-Jul-91 S20/R) River landscape with drawbridge (11x18cm-4x7in) s. black chk wash
£5600 $9128   (1-Jul-91 S147/R) Landscape with peasants at well (11x20cm-4x8in) s. black chk
£9800 $15974   (1-Jul-91 S60/R) Travellers on road by river (18x28cm-7x11in) s.d.1653 black chk wash
£19878 $39159   (12-Nov-90 CH.AM72/R) Twisted tree by fence with two travellers resting near road, cottages beyond (10x14cm-4x6in) pen (D.FL 65000)
£21053 $40000   (8-Jan-91 SY.NY156/R) River landscape with peasants beside a water mill (18x28cm-7x11in) d.1653 blk.chk.wash

GOYEN, Jan van (after) (1596-1665) Dutch
£1198 $2240   (1-Sep-90 CH.AM143) Cowherd driving cattle towards barn near a farm (41x65cm-16x26in) panel (D.FL 4000)

GOYEN, Jan van (attrib) (1596-1665) Dutch
£5460 $9500   (27-Mar-91 B.SF4018/R) Estuary with buildings and fishermen dragging in nets (57x80cm-22x31in) panel
£5823 $9376   (27-Jun-91 APT.P123/R) Paysge fluvial (21x34cm-8x13in) bears mono.d.16.. panel (F.FR 58000)
£17930 $35143   (11-Nov-90 M.V39/R) Vue d'un estuaire (42x65cm-17x26in) bears mono. panel (F.FR 175000)

770

GOYEN, Jan van (circle) (1596-1665) Dutch
£4893 $9639   (13-Nov-90 CH.AM23/R) River landscape with fishermen unloading catch, travellers by inn (27x25cm-11x10in) bears sig.d.1634 panel (D.FL 16000)

GOYEN, Jan van (school) (1596-1665) Dutch
£1034 $1800   (27-Mar-91 B.SF4211/R) Estuary (33x42cm-13x17in)

GOYEN, Jan van (style) (1596-1665) Dutch
£850 $1386   (4-Jul-91 CSK149/R) River landscape with fishermen laying nets by ruined tower (34x39cm-13x15in) panel
£1223 $2410   (14-Nov-90 SY.AM137/R) River landscape (31x45cm-12x18in) panel (D.FL 4000)
£1224 $2412   (14-Nov-90 D.V199/R) River landscape with boats and church (40x70cm-16x28in) panel (A.S 25000)
£1300 $2119   (4-Jul-91 CSK152/R) Peasnats in winter landscape (18x27cm-7x11in) indist.i. en grisaille panel
£2200 $4290   (26-Oct-90 C126/R) A wooded river landscape with a cottage, a church in the distance (31x47cm-12x19in) panel
£4000 $6520   (4-Jul-91 C714/R) View of possibly Deventer with shipping (45x80cm-18x31in) panel
£4790 $8096   (2-May-91 CH.AM51) Small ships under sail on a river with fishermen drawing in their nets (36x49cm-14x19in) panel (D.FL 16000)
£11000 $18590   (18-Apr-91 C167/R) River landscape with fishermen hauling in nets, windmill beyond (57x83cm-22x33in) sig.d.1636 panel

GOYEN, van (style) (1596-1665) Dutch
£2448 $4724   (10-Dec-90 L.K87/R) River landscape with three man in boat and village (26x41cm-10x16in) panel (DM 7000)

GOZLAN, Claude (1930-) Tunisian
£1506 $2786   (10-Mar-91 LT.P127/R) Soir de Carnaval a Venise (53x44cm-21x17in) s.d.77 (F.FR 15000)

GOZZARD, J W (?) ?
£580 $945   (13-Jun-91 LE404) Stream with silver birch and sheep grazing (23x15cm-9x6in) W/C
£580 $1027   (22-Mar-91 T140/R) Gleaners resting at the stile (30x41cm-12x16in) s.i.

GOZZI, Marco (1759-1839) Italian
£7831 $12608   (27-Jun-91 APT.P82/R) Paysage de foret avec bergers et leurs troupeaux pres d'une riviere (99x57cm-39x22in) i. verso panel (F.FR 78000)

GOZZOLI, Benozzo (attrib) (1420-1497) Italian
£23158 $44000   (10-Jan-91 SY.NY1/R) Annunciation (24cm-9ins circular) tempera panel

GRAAT, Barend (1628-1709) Flemish
£2685 $5235   (10-Oct-90 ZEL.L1509/R) Mythological scene with figures before statue decorated with flowers (44x34cm-17x13in) (DM 8000)
£9770 $17489   (14-Mar-91 D.V130/R) Portrait of married couple dressed as Venus and Adonis (136x163cm-54x64in) (A.S 200000)

GRAB, Walter (1927-) Swiss
£2600 $4498   (10-May-91 S.Z38/R) Verlogener Strand (22x69cm-9x27in) s.d.1960 panel (S.FR 6500)

GRABACH, John R (1886-?) American
£751 $1300   (21-May-91 CE.NY607/R) Man with pipe (69x69cm-27x27in) s.
£1042 $2000   (28-Nov-90 D.NY51) Under the bridge (20x28cm-8x11in) s. panel
£1878 $3700   (16-Nov-90 S.BM211/R) Japanese lantern (48x46cm-19x18in) s.
£3352 $6000   (14-Mar-91 CH.NY198/R) Last Stand (90x107cm-35x42in) s.
£3488 $6000   (15-May-91 SY.NY238/R) Lineman (108x91cm-43x36in) s.panel
£756 $1300   (15-May-91 SY.NY240/R) Entering harbour (48x61cm-19x24in) s. W/C

GRABAR, Igor (1872-1960) Russian
£10000 $19500   (10-Oct-90 C233/R) Sharp frost at end of day (85x89cm-33x35in) s.d.1907

GRABAR, Igor (attrib) (1872-1960) Russian
£616 $1035   (23-Apr-91 RAS.K328/R) Flowers in basket by window (64x50cm-25x20in) (D.KR 7000)
£1167 $2299   (14-Nov-90 RAS.K680/R) Flowers in woven basket by window (64x50cm-25x20in) (D.KR 13000)

GRABER, Otto (1885-1952) German
£872 $1701   (12-Oct-90 AW.H2412/R) Still life of azalea and pansies (65x54cm-26x21in) s. i.verso (DM 2600)

GRABHEIN, Wilhelm (1859-?) German
£1190 $2107   (20-Mar-91 KM.K1240) Hunting dog seated before hut and fawn eating from his bowl with rabbits (55x76cm-22x30in) s.d.99 (DM 3500)

GRABMAYER, Franz (1927-) German
£994 $1928   (6-Dec-90 D.V237/R) Sandgrube (67x89cm-26x35in) s.i.d.1970verso hessian (A.S 20000)

GRABONE, Arnold (1896-1981) German

£510	$821	(26-Jun-91 KM.K1478) Waxenstein with Zugspitze (70x60cm-28x24in) s. (DM 1500)
£510	$821	(26-Jun-91 KM.K1480/R) Morning light in the Hohe Tauern (80x70cm-31x28in) s. (DM 1500)
£514	$920	(12-Mar-91 FN.S2389) Alpine landscape with farmhouse and wayside memorial, Marmolada (81x71cm-32x28in) s. i.verso (DM 1500)
£548	$981	(12-Mar-91 FN.S2388/R) Farmhouse on hill with view of Wilde Kaiser range (60x80cm-24x31in) s. (DM 1600)
£582	$1042	(14-Mar-91 N.M2656/R) Chapel in wooded mountain landscape (61x80cm-24x31in) s.i. (DM 1700)
£638	$1243	(10-Oct-90 ZEL.L1511/R) Dutch harbour with shipping, evening (70x80cm-28x31in) s.i.verso (DM 1900)
£671	$1309	(10-Oct-90 WE.MU162/R) Farmstead in Dachstein mountains (80x71cm-31x28in) s.i. (DM 2000)
£671	$1309	(10-Oct-90 WE.MU107/R) Wayside cross in the Alpine landscape (50x60cm-20x24in) s. (DM 2000)
£676	$1318	(26-Oct-90 KM.K1235) Moor landscape near Murnau and Alpine range beyond (100x90cm-39x35in) s. i.verso (DM 2000)
£680	$1204	(20-Mar-91 KM.K1234) Karwendel mountain landscape (117x97cm-46x38in) s. (DM 2000)
£683	$1290	(25-Sep-90 FN.S2183/R) Haff seascape with fishing boats (30x50cm-12x20in) s. i.verso (DM 2000)
£683	$1290	(25-Sep-90 FN.S2184) Wooded landscape with view of snowy mountain range (70x80cm-28x31in) s. (DM 2000)
£796	$1592	(6-Feb-91 N.M611/R) Fishing boats, evening (60x80cm-24x31in) s. i.verso (DM 2300)
£874	$1687	(12-Dec-90 WE.MU180/R) Dachstein mountain range (100x90cm-39x35in) s. (DM 2500)
£936	$1583	(17-Apr-91 WE.MU137/R) Way side memorial in mountain landscape (80x100cm-31x39in) mono. (DM 2800)
£956	$1806	(25-Sep-90 FN.S2185/R) Wooded landscape with cattle grazing near stream, autumn (82x70cm-32x28in) s. i.verso (DM 2800)
£1229	$2015	(18-Jun-91 FN.S1862/R) Farmhouse at the foot of Karwendel mountain (65x81cm-26x32in) s. (DM 3600)

GRABWINKLER, Paul (1880-1946) Austrian

£505	$874	(6-May-91 ZEL.L1715/R) Lake Chiemsee landscape with view of Fraueninsel and Herzogstand (70x100cm-28x39in) s. (DM 1500)
£584	$1145	(24-Jan-91 D.V120/R) Zellersee with Kitzsteinhorn, Salzkammergut (70x100cm-28x39in) s. (A.S 12000)

GRACE, Alfred Fitzwalter (1844-1903) British

£550	*$1056*	*(29-Nov-90 PHX327/R) Haymaking at Amberley (36x56cm-14x22in) s.i. W/C*

GRACE, James Edward (1851-1908) British

£1000	$1740	(26-Mar-91 PH94/R) Where birchen bough and the hazels mingle (61x91cm-24x36in) s. i. verso

GRACHT, Gommaer van der (1590-C.1639) Flemish

£16554	$28142	(27-May-91 L.K49/R) Still life of fruit and vegetables on mossy ground and squirrel in tree (125x208cm-49x82in) (DM 49000)

GRADA, Raffaele de (1885-?) Italian

£1028	$1747	(27-May-91 GK.Z5338) Landscape near Lugano (34x40cm-13x16in) s. (S.FR 2600)
£1181	$2327	(30-Oct-90 F.R87) Natura morta con cacciagione (35x45cm-14x18in) s. panel (I.L 2600000)
£1815	$3121	(13-May-91 CH.R171/R) Paesaggio (36x51cm-14x20in) s. (I.L 4000000)
£2726	$5262	(13-Dec-90 F.M371/R) Paesaggio. Il paese (35x49cm-14x19in) s. canvas on masonite double-sided (I.L 5900000)
£2840	$5453	(27-Nov-90 SY.MI49/R) Paesaggio Toscano (35x45cm-14x18in) s. canvas laid down on masonite (I.L 6200000)
£4531	$7883	(26-Mar-91 F.M17/R) Natura morta con ciliegie (29x38cm-11x15in) s. panel (I.L 10000000)
£5468	$9295	(28-May-91 SY.MI123/R) Paesaggio invernale (50x60cm-20x24in) s. (I.L 12000000)
£8201	$13942	(28-May-91 SY.MI115/R) Porto (67x80cm-26x31in) s. (I.L 18000000)

GRADL, Hermann (1883-?) German

£2174	$3674	(17-Apr-91 WE.MU127/R) River landscape (38x32cm-15x13in) s. board (DM 6500)
£2389	$4683	(24-Nov-90 SA.A762/R) Lake Chiemsee with view of Fraueninsel (50x70cm-20x28in) s.d.1927 (DM 7000)

GRAECEN, Edmund (1877-1949) American

£5028	$9000	(12-Apr-91 SY.NY63/R) Southport harbour (51x41cm-20x16in)

GRAEFF, Werner (1901-1964) German

£1186	*$1981*	*(6-Jun-91 HN.H358/R) Composition (6x12cm-2x5in) s.i. temper pen (DM 3500)*

GRAEFLE, Albert (1807-1889) German

£800	$1536	(27-Nov-90 PH132) Portrait of woman wearing Tyrolean costume (48x39cm-19x15in) s. s.verso

GRAEME, Colin (19th C) British

£700	$1155	(9-Jul-91 PH124) Timber hauling (61x92cm-24x36in) s.d.84
£800	$1552	(5-Dec-90 PHL211/R) A spaniel retrieving a mallard (61x46cm-24x18in) s.
£800	$1584	(30-Jan-91 CSK217/R) Julius - a saddled grey hunter in a loose box (46x58cm-18x23in) s.i.d.'88
£900	$1467	(13-Jun-91 CSK192/R) Head of bay mare with English setter and hound in open landscape (40x35cm-16x14in) s.d.1900
£950	$1682	(21-Mar-91 CSK215/R) The heads of a Gordon Setter and an English Setter. The heads of Pointers (28x23cm-11x9in) s. pair
£1100	$2156	(20-Nov-90 PH67) Timber hauling (61x92cm-24x36in) s.d.'84
£1300	$2431	(28-Aug-90 S811/R) Otter hounds (40x56cm-16x22in) s.d.95
£1500	$2580	(14-May-91 SWS200/R) Pointers on moor (34x52cm-13x20in) s. one d.91 pair
£1900	$3097	(4-Jul-91 PHI178/R) Minding the day's bag (51x76cm-20x30in) s.d.'98
£1900	$3097	(13-Jun-91 CSK200/R) End of day (61x51cm-24x20in) s.
£1900	$3705	(15-Jan-91 C63/R) Don Puggles, pug on bear skin rug (25x30cm-10x12in) s.i.d.86
£2000	$3580	(12-Mar-91 HS267/R) Two dogs with dead game on heather-clad rocky outcrop and lake beyond (43x60cm-17x24in) s.
£6200	$11594	(28-Aug-90 S751/R) Waiting for the guns (61x91cm-24x36in) s.d.1896

GRAESER, Camille (1892-?) French?

| £7290 | $12393 | (28-May-91 SY.MI186/R) Komplementare beziehung (54x36cm-21x14in) s.d.1963-65verso (I.L 16000000) |

GRAF, Anton (19th C) German

| £3500 | $5705 | (3-Jul-91 S127/R) Portrait of gentleman, said to be Freiherr Berlepsch (84x67cm-33x26in) |

GRAF, Franz (1840-?) German

| £1184 | $1989 | (24-Apr-91 BA.S73/R) Still life of late summer flowers in vase (90x60cm-35x24in) s. (S.KR 12500) |

GRAF, Gerhard (1883-1960) German

| £559 | $934 | (5-Jun-91 DO.H2668) Travemunde (69x59cm-27x23in) s. i.verso (DM 1650) |
| £2211 | $3913 | (20-Mar-91 KM.K1241) View of Danzig with Kranentor and boats (87x115cm-34x45in) s. (DM 6500) |

GRAF, Gottfried (1881-1938) German?

| £1603 | $3079 | (26-Nov-90 WK.M226/R) Figuration (21x15cm-8x6in) d.1917 W/C over pencil (DM 4650) |

GRAF, Johann (1653-1710) Austrian

| £5944 | $11472 | (12-Dec-90 WE.MU21/R) Fair, Vienna (40x56cm-16x22in) (DM 17000) |

GRAF, Johann (attrib) (1653-1710) Austrian

| £4397 | $7870 | (14-Mar-91 D.V326/R) Town square with figures (25x35cm-10x14in) panel (A.S 90000) |

GRAF, Karl (1902-1984) German

| £1007 | $1963 | (12-Oct-90 AW.H2414/R) Saartal, autumn (70x110cm-28x43in) s. i.d.1940verso panel (DM 3000) |

GRAF, Ludwig Ferdinand (1868-1932) Austrian

| £542 | $1083 | (7-Feb-91 D.V69) Sailing boats in harbour (64x46cm-25x18in) s.d.03 mixed media (A.S 11000) |

GRAF, Urs (circle) (1485-1527) Swiss

| £1700 | $3281 | (11-Dec-90 C111/R) A bear dressed as a soldier with a shield with three fleur-de-lys (24x15cm-9x6in) i. ink |

GRAF, Urs (school) (1485-1527) Swiss

| £4000 | $6520 | (2-Jul-91 C178/R) Standard bearer of Canton of Lucerne. Standard Bearer of Canton of Berne (15x10cm-6x4in) with i. pen pair |

GRAFF, Anton (1736-1813) German

£3373	$6038	(13-Mar-91 GK.Z38/R) Portrait of Leipzig gentleman (75x59cm-30x23in) s.i.d.1806verso (S.FR 8500)
£5479	$8932	(12-Jun-91 SY.MU7/R) Self portrait (53x43cm-21x17in) (DM 16000)
£5743	$9706	(3-May-91 SA.A1632/R) Portrait of a man in red velvet jacket with fur collar (62x50cm-24x20in) (DM 17000)
£13986	$26993	(10-Dec-90 L.K48/R) Portrait of Graf Johann Hilmar von Schonfeld seated at table with book (85x63cm-33x25in) canvas laid down (DM 40000)
£23891	$44915	(19-Sep-90 N.M366/R) Selfportrait seated with easel (59x51cm-23x20in) s.d.1776 i.verso (DM 70000)

GRAFF, Anton (attrib) (1736-1813) German

| £544 | $963 | (20-Mar-91 KM.K1024) Portrait of gentleman opening book (73x60cm-29x24in) (DM 1600) |
| £2018 | $3976 | (13-Nov-90 AB.S893/R) Portrait of Bengt Sparre (63x53cm-25x21in) oval (S.KR 22000) |

GRAFF, Anton (circle) (1736-1813) German

| £800 | $1304 | (2-Jul-91 PH317/R) Portrait of lady (73x56cm-29x22in) painted oval |
| £1800 | $3042 | (19-Apr-91 C54 a/R) Portrait of a lady, half length, wearing a lilac dress (185x142cm-73x56in) i. |

GRAFFIONE, Giovanni (1455-1527) Italian
£35294 $60000   (30-May-91 SY.NY2/R) Madonna and child adored by four angels
                    (96cm-38ins circular) tempera panel

GRAFTON, R (?) ?
£538 $1050   (21-Oct-90 HG.C248) Woman and calf by shed (43x64cm-17x25in) s.

GRAHAM, Anne Marie (20th C) Australian
£618 $1217   (13-Nov-90 J.M23) Pumpkin flowers (44x34cm-17x13in) s.d.81 board
                 (A.D 1600)
£1131 $1912   (16-Apr-91 J.M46/R) Laycock School (40x50cm-16x20in) s.d.'88 (A.D 2500)

GRAHAM, George (1881-1949) British
£1400 $2730   (17-Oct-90 PHL270/R) Durmani Bridge (50x61cm-20x24in) s. i.d.1910 verso

GRAHAM, John (18/19th C) British
£1000 $2000   (7-Feb-91 CSK177/R) Portrait of General John Burgoyne in uniform
                  (37x29cm-15x11in) i.verso
£8671 $15000   (22-May-91 D.NY59/R) Egg and hat rack (81x115cm-32x45in) s.d.30

GRAHAM, Peter (1836-1921) British
£1150 $2185   (10-Jan-91 B126/R) Coastal scene (101x144cm-40x57in) s.d.1868
£1600 $3104   (5-Dec-90 PHL230/R) Highland cattle (122x109cm-48x43in)
£1800 $3024   (23-Apr-91 S72) Highland cattle (124x110cm-49x43in) s.d.1875
£3500 $7000   (8-Feb-91 C177/R) A rising tide (137x185cm-54x73in) s.d.1899
£6000 $11220   (28-Aug-90 S817/R) Sea-girt crags (60x91cm-24x36in) s.d.1886
£8000 $13040   (14-Jun-91 C249/R) The seabird's resting place (108x166cm-43x65in)
                   s.d.1879

GRAHAM, Robert Alexander (1873-1946) American
£4103 $8000   (10-Oct-90 B.SF577/R) Boats Lake Union (76x91cm-30x36in) s.d.1931

GRAILLY, Victor de (1804-1889) French
£769 $1500   (25-Oct-90 GRO.B66/R) Cottage by river (38x51cm-15x20in)

GRAILLY, Victor de (attrib) (1804-1889) French
£765 $1300   (1-Jun-91 LAE.L41/R) Landscape with cottage with two figures
                 (38x51cm-15x20in)
£919 $1700   (8-Mar-91 S.BM121/R) Bucolic pastures, late afternoon (53x51cm-21x20in)
                 i.

GRAM, Lennart (1910-) Swedish
£1019 $1978   (4-Dec-90 BA.S158/R) The red dressing-gown (92x65cm-36x26in) s.d.1939
                  (S.KR 11000)

GRAMATTE, Walter (19/20th C) ?
£4266   *$8362*   *(24-Nov-90 VG.B159/R) Self portrait, Barcelona (48x37cm-19x15in)*
                    s.d.1924 W/C over pencil board (DM 12500)

GRAMATYKA, Antoni (1841-1922) Polish
£526 $930   (23-Mar-91 HO.P2) By the pond (41x50cm-16x20in) s. board (P.Z 9000000)

GRAMMATICA, Antiveduto (attrib) (1571-1626) Italian
£6531 $12865   (15-Nov-90 EA.Z213/R) Judith and servant leaving the tent of Holofernes
                   (76x87cm-30x34in) (S.FR 16000)

GRAN, B (19th C) ?
£1187 $2124   (11-Apr-91 D.V133/R) Lake Zell with Kitzsteinhorn (60x47cm-24x19in)
                  s.d.64 (A.S 25000)

GRAN, Halfdan (1869-1930) Norwegian
£1202 $2320   (10-Dec-90 B.O38/R) Hunting scene (76x121cm-30x48in) s.d.1904
                  (N.KR 13500)

GRANADA SCHOOL, 17th C Spanish
£9783 $17315   (3-Apr-91 ANS.M101/R) Virgen con el Nino (165x130cm-65x51in)
                   (S.P 1800000)

GRANADOS, Miguel (?) Spanish
£1090 $1886   (21-May-91 DUR.M14/R) Fuente de los Tritones, Jardines de la Granja
                  (67x113cm-26x44in) (S.P 200000)

GRANDE, Severin (1869-1934) Norwegian
£1432 $2392   (3-Jun-91 B.O53/R) Still life of fruit, flowers and wine
                  (45x54cm-18x21in) s.d.29 (N.KR 16500)
£2189 $3919   (14-Mar-91 BU.O38/R) Apple blossom (77x67cm-30x26in) s.d.1920 i.verso
                  (N.KR 25000)
£2257 $3769   (4-Jun-91 BU.O6/R) Summer landscape with red house (69x79cm-27x31in)
                  s.d.32 i.verso (N.KR 26000)
£2257 $4401   (11-Oct-90 BU.O46/R) Anemones and lilies in vase (55x46cm-22x18in)
                  s.d.18 (N.KR 26000)
£3853 $6897   (14-Mar-91 BU.O37/R) Children playing ludo, Christmas 1917
                  (69x78cm-27x31in) s.d.17 i.verso (N.KR 44000)
£5590 $10620   (11-Sep-90 UL.T207/R) Woman doing embroidery (100x90cm-39x35in)
                   (N.KR 64000)

GRANDGERARD, Colette (20th C) ?
£495 $885   *(14-Apr-91 R.P128/R) Deambulation (100x150cm-39x59in) s. mixed media*
           paper laid down on canvas (F.FR 5000)
£508 $1016   *(7-Feb-91 R.P229/R) L'attente (160x100cm-63x39in) s. mixed media paper*
           laid down on canvas (F.FR 5000)

GRANDGERARD, Lucien Henri (1880-1965) French
£680 $1149   *(30-Apr-91 B63/R) Apres La pose (32x44cm-13x17in) s.d.'58 panel*

GRANDI, Francesco (1831-1891) Italian
£5403 $10536   *(23-Oct-90 CH.R393/R) Riposo durante la fuga in Egitto con angeli in*
           adorazione (183x260cm-72x102in) s.d.1880 (I.L 12000000)

GRANDI, Mario Dario (1918-1971) Argentinian
£867 $1500   *(8-May-91 RO.BA511) La cantante (53x38cm-21x15in) s. pastel*

GRANDIO, Constantino (1923-1977) Spanish
£1924 $3444   *(13-Mar-91 FER.M261/R) Cabeza de asno (62x50cm-24x20in) (S.P 350000)*
£2199 $3936   *(13-Mar-91 FER.M262/R) Las llaves de Adan y Eva (200x80cm-79x31in)*
           (S.P 400000)
£3524 $6872   *(17-Oct-90 FER.M255/R) La abutarda (92x65cm-36x26in) s.d.1968*
           (S.P 650000)
£5223 $9349   *(13-Mar-91 FER.M263) Jugador de golf (158x53cm-62x21in) s.d.1965*
           (S.P 950000)
£656 $1265   *(11-Dec-90 FER.M55/R) Los abuelos. Gatos. Caballos. Con el saco a*
           cuestas s. pastel four dr in one frame (S.P 120000)
£872 $1509   *(21-May-91 DUR.M51/R) En el cafe (69x49cm-27x19in) W/C sketch*
           (S.P 160000)
£872 $1509   *(21-May-91 DUR.M50/R) Pescador (69x49cm-27x19in) W/C sketch*
           (S.P 160000)
£927 $1603   *(21-May-91 DUR.M53/R) Rostros (59x44cm-23x17in) wax crayon dr*
           (S.P 170000)
£1100 $1968   *(13-Mar-91 FER.M260/R) Los payasos nacen por la cabeza (40x31cm-16x12in)*
           s.d.1964 W/C (S.P 200000)

GRANDJEAN, Edmond Georges (1844-1908) French
£12500 $20500   *(19-Jun-91 S192/R) Changing horses (172x206cm-68x81in) s.d.1882*

GRANDMAISON, Nickola de (1892-1978) Canadian/Russian
£1425 $2808   *(30-Oct-90 SY.T103/R) Portrait of Indian (30x25cm-12x10in) s. board*
           (C.D 3250)
£3608 $6134   *(27-May-91 HO.ED96/R) Blood Indian, Cardston, Alberta (65x51cm-26x20in)*
           s. s.i.verso canvas board (C.D 7000)
£1425 $2808   *(30-Oct-90 SY.T105/R) Indian mother with papoose (40x32cm-16x13in) s.*
           pastel dr. (C.D 3250)
£1754 $3439   *(20-Nov-90 JOY.T6/R) Indian warrior (64x49cm-25x19in) s. col.chk*
           (C.D 4000)
£1754 $3456   *(30-Oct-90 SY.T104/R) Indian girl (29x22cm-11x9in) s. pastel dr.*
           (C.D 4000)
£1864 $3672   *(30-Oct-90 SY.T108/R) Indian boy (29x22cm-11x9in) s. pastel dr.*
           (C.D 4250)
£2000 $3880   *(3-Dec-90 R.T233/R) Indian warrior (46x34cm-18x13in) s. i.verso col.chk*
           (C.D 4500)
£3351 $5696   *(27-May-91 HO.ED317/R) Cree from Saskatchewan (51x37cm-20x15in) s. bears*
           i.d.1951verso pastel sand paper (C.D 6500)
£3930 $7742   *(12-Nov-90 HO.ED316/R) Jim Knife - Peigan from Brockett*
           (42x33cm-17x13in) s. bears i.d.1954 verso pastel sandpaper (C.D 9000)

GRANDMAISON, Oreste de (1932-1985) Canadian
£1340 $2278   *(27-May-91 HO.ED71/R) The homestead, late autumn (56x76cm-22x30in) s.*
           s.i.verso canvas board (C.D 2600)

GRANDVILLE, Jean Ignace (1803-1847) French
£553 $907   *(21-Jun-91 CK.P75) Cupidon jouant du violon pour les anes*
           (29x27cm-11x11in) pen wash W/C (F.FR 5500)

GRANELLO, Nicolosio (16th C) Italian
£4000 $7720   *(12-Dec-90 PH144/R) The penitent Magdalen, study for pendentive*
           (41x24cm-16x9in) pen ink wash shaped

GRANELLO, Nicolosio (attrib) (1567-1593) Italian
£579 $1100   *(8-Jan-91 SY.NY125/R) Study of a seated male figure (27x21cm-11x8in) ink*
£3500 $5705   *(1-Jul-91 S207/R) Design for pendentive with male figure, possibly St.*
           John Evangelist (28x25cm-11x10in) pen

GRANER Y ARRUFI, Luis (1867-1929) Spanish/Brazilian
£9249 $16000   *(23-May-91 CH.NY154/R) The iron works (100x120cm-39x47in) s.*
£18678 $32500   *(27-Mar-91 B.SF4092/R) View of spring (86x63cm-34x25in) s.*
£22000 $43120   *(15-Feb-91 C60/R) Girls with lantern (91x94cm-36x37in) s.*

GRANER, Ernst (1865-1943) Austrian
£602 $1017   *(19-Apr-91 FN.S1451) Vienna street scene with horse-drawn cab*
           (28x43cm-11x17in) s.d.1911 W/C (DM 1800)
£631 $1192   *(27-Sep-90 D.V203/R) Street in Salzburg with view of St Peter*
           (35x25cm-14x10in) s. W/C (A.S 13000)

GRANER, Ernst (1865-1943) Austrian-cont.

£635	$1207	(28-Feb-91 D.V84/R) Courtyard of Wiener Freihaus (22x32cm-9x13in) W/C pencil (A.S 13000)
£764	$1489	(11-Oct-90 D.V246/R) View of Maria am Gestade with figures (73x60cm-29x24in) W/C htd.white (A.S 16000)
£980	$1910	(26-Oct-90 BM.B786/R) Karlskirche in winter, Vienna (49x37cm-19x15in) s. W/C paper on board (DM 2900)
£1432	$2792	(11-Oct-90 D.V244/R) Rennbahn in der Krieau mit Rotunde (30x58cm-12x23in) s.d.27 W/C (A.S 30000)

GRANERI (?) Italian

£39761	$67197	(18-Apr-91 APT.P24/R) Une prisee dans le Piemont (99x135cm-39x53in) s.d.1741 (F.FR 400000)

GRANET, Francois Marius (1775-1849) French

£1710	$3352	(24-Jan-91 AGS.P163) Le graveur (22x19cm-9x7in) s. pen wash Indian ink oil crayon (F.FR 17000)

GRANFELT, Erik (1919-1990) Finnish

£1563	$2797	(14-Apr-91 BU.H31/R) Model resting (54x73cm-21x29in) s. (F.M 11000)
£3152	$6209	(17-Nov-90 BU.H150/R) Still life of glasses and bottle (50x61cm-20x24in) s.d.77 (F.M 22000)
£716	$1411	(17-Nov-90 BU.H193/R) Disney pendant (39x28cm-15x11in) s. collage (F.M 5000)

GRANINGER, Leopold (19/20th C) Austrian

£759	$1359	(11-Apr-91 D.V73/R) Mill by mountain stream (78x66cm-31x26in) s.d.96 (A.S 16000)
£489	$928	(28-Feb-91 D.V86/R) Stiege in Alt Wien (35x24cm-14x9in) s. gouache (A.S 10000)
£1075	$2042	(28-Feb-91 D.V103/R) Village street with horse-drawn cart (24x34cm-9x13in) s. W/C (A.S 22000)
£1466	$2785	(28-Feb-91 D.V79/R) Street in old Vienna (35x24cm-14x9in) s. gouache (A.S 30000)

GRANSOW, Helmut (1921-) Canadian

£524	$1027	(5-Nov-90 FB.M88) Evening, Charlevoix (56x76cm-22x30in) s.d.1987 (C.D 1200)

GRANT, Carlton (fl.1885-1899) British

£520	$884	(29-May-91 PHC86) Figures on coastal path, North Wales (17x37cm-7x15in) s.d.1889 W/C
£900	$1530	(29-May-91 PHC68/R) Little girl with ducks beside pond (28x45cm-11x18in) s.d.1889 W/C

GRANT, Duncan (1885-1975) British

£550	$919	(6-Jun-91 C93/R) Three female nudes (59x119cm-23x47in) board
£650	$1229	(26-Sep-90 RB666) Still life of jugs and apples (30x38cm-12x15in) s. board
£1500	$2535	(1-May-91 S27/R) Portrait of Adrian Stephen (41x33cm-16x13in) i.verso
£1600	$3136	(25-Jan-91 C114/R) Boy asleep on railway carriage (25x35cm-10x14in) board
£1700	$3332	(25-Jan-91 C145/R) St Paul's Cathedral (61x41cm-24x16in) s. board
£1800	$3528	(7-Nov-90 S70/R) Portrait of Henrietta (61x46cm-24x18in) i.verso
£1923	$3769	(19-Nov-90 ARC.P36/R) Jeune homme assis (50x41cm-20x16in) s.d.1950 hardboard (F.FR 19000)
£2200	$4312	(7-Nov-90 S68/R) The Turkish bath (74x102cm-29x40in) paper
£2400	$4704	(7-Nov-90 S69/R) Towards Monaco from Cap St Martin (79x56cm-31x22in) board
£2600	$4888	(20-Sep-90 C134/R) Still life with bottles (51x44cm-20x17in) s.d.72 paper
£2800	$5460	(10-Oct-90 S33/R) Thorpe-le-Soken (56x77cm-22x30in) s.d.72 board
£3000	$5550	(7-Mar-91 C68/R) Sleeping man (44x59cm-17x23in) s.
£3200	$5408	(1-May-91 S32/R) The barn at Charleston (44x53cm-17x21in) paper
£3400	$5916	(27-Mar-91 S99/R) Towards Monaco from Cap St Martin (61x51cm-24x20in) init.verso
£4200	$8232	(7-Nov-90 S62/R) Acrobats (76x53cm-30x21in) s.d.68 paper
£4200	$8232	(7-Nov-90 S56/R) Landscape sketch with barn (51x61cm-20x24in) s.i.verso
£4500	$8820	(6-Nov-90 PH79/R) Girl in bathtub (42x30cm-17x12in) s. board
£5000	$8450	(1-May-91 S21/R) Self portrait (46x36cm-18x14in) s.d.67 board
£5200	$8788	(1-May-91 S25/R) Perugia (61x51cm-24x20in) s. board
£5500	$10780	(25-Jan-91 C143/R) Endymion (36x55cm-14x22in) paper
£5500	$10780	(7-Nov-90 S60/R) Quentin, Olivier and Julian Bell in the studio at Charleston (142x122cm-56x48in) s.d.53
£6500	$12025	(7-Mar-91 C67/R) Still life with vase and envelopes (80x63cm-31x25in) s.d.23
£7500	$12675	(1-May-91 S24/R) Still life in cabinet (53x53cm-21x21in) s.d.56 board
£8000	$15680	(6-Nov-90 PH80/R) Under the vine (76x51cm-30x20in) s.d.46
£8000	$15040	(20-Sep-90 C106/R) Chrysanthtmums and dahlias in vase (65x46cm-26x18in) s.d.68 s.i.d.1968 verso board
£9000	$17640	(7-Nov-90 S82/R) Still life of leaves in omega jug (63x50cm-25x20in) s. board
£18000	$35280	(7-Nov-90 S55/R) Vanessa Bell at Charleston (84x69cm-33x27in)
£460	$777	(2-May-91 C32) Sleeping figure (56x38cm-22x15in) s.d.48 pencil red crayon wash

GRANT, Duncan (1885-1975) British-cont.

£540	$999	(5-Mar-91 SWS1620/R) Charles Laughton as Nero (23x23cm-9x9in) s. W/C over pencil
£550	$1073	(18-Oct-90 CSK261/R) Reclining male nude (58x43cm-23x17in) init. W/C gouache pencil
£1500	$2940	(7-Nov-90 S63/R) Two studies of Pan (25x99cm-10x39in) init. pen ink W/C pair
£1600	$2784	(27-Mar-91 S94) Male nude (38x56cm-15x22in) init.d.57 pencil W/C gouache
£2800	$5488	(25-Jan-91 C146/R) Still life with plate, apples and beaker in front of tapestry (57x48cm-22x19in) W/C pastel
£3200	$5920	(7-Mar-91 C65/R) Still life with black jug (52x32cm-20x13in) s.d.73 black crayon oil paper on board
£4200	$7770	(7-Mar-91 C69/R) Paul Roche in uniform (44x61cm-17x24in) s.d.52 gouache paper on canvas
£4500	$8820	(7-Nov-90 S49/R) Seated male nude (55x69cm-22x27in) s.d.33 pastel

GRANT, Dwinell (1912-) American

| £925 | $1600 | (21-May-91 CE.NY694/R) Contrathemis (22x28cm-9x11in) init.d.41 collage crayon pencil tissue paper |
| £1117 | $2000 | (14-Mar-91 CH.NY226/R) Contrathemis (21x28cm-8x11in) init.d.41 paper collage col.pencil tissue paper |

GRANT, Frederick M (1886-1959) American

£754	$1350	(11-Apr-91 FA.PH770/R) Festival (76x76cm-30x30in) s.
£1331	$2250	(1-May-91 B.SF5133/R) Still life (117x76cm-46x30in) s.
£7101	$12000	(20-Apr-91 WOL.C153/R) At shore (53x53cm-21x21in) s.

GRANT, Gordon (1875-1962) American

£751	$1300	(21-May-91 CE.NY584/R) Squarerigger off Mystic (71x91cm-28x36in) s. i.verso
£751	$1300	(10-May-91 S.BM121/R) Portrait of sailing ship, sundown (48x38cm-19x15in) s. canvas board
£1351	$2500	(8-Mar-91 S.BM234/R) A sea wind (46x56cm-18x22in) s. i. verso masonite
£2474	$4750	(17-Dec-90 SY.NY255/R) Wind in harness (71x91cm-28x36in) s.stretcher
£446	$875	(27-Jan-91 LIT.L17a) Travellers at sea (36x53cm-14x21in) W/C
£459	$900	(27-Jan-91 LIT.L16a) Storm coming (36x53cm-14x21in) W/C
£565	$1000	(22-Mar-91 S.W2488/R) Lobstermen (28x41cm-11x16in) s. W/C
£747	$1300	(29-Mar-91 E.EDM184/R) Fishing boat at dock (33x48cm-13x19in) s.i.d.1939 W/C
£1534	$2900	(25-Sep-90 CE.NY104/R) Harbour scenes with boats (40x58cm-16x23in) both s. W/C pencil two

GRANT, J (?) ?

| £1923 | $3769 | (22-Nov-90 D.P4 b/R) Le jocket S. Manne montant Grand Carlos (48x65cm-19x26in) s.d.1892 (F.FR 19000) |

GRANT, J A (?) ?

| £350 | $672 | (19-Feb-91 C41 a) Bullfinches (38x28cm-15x11in) s. pencil W/C htd.white |

GRANT, Matilde (20th C) ?

£593	$1062	(14-Apr-91 R.P204/R) Voyage aquatique (100x100cm-39x39in) s. acrylic (F.FR 6000)
£610	$1220	(7-Feb-91 R.P33/R) La dame a l'aquarium (49x55cm-19x22in) s. acrylic (F.FR 6000)
£630	$1260	(7-Feb-91 R.P83/R) La coiffe magique (80x80cm-31x31in) s. acrylic (F.FR 6200)
£711	$1423	(7-Feb-91 R.P14) Tetes de femme (48x57cm-19x22in) s. mixed media panel (F.FR 7000)

GRANT, Sir Francis (1810-1878) British

£1300	$2561	(31-Oct-90 S329/R) Equestrian portrait of young lady seated on bay horse in river landscape (24x19cm-9x7in)
£1800	$3222	(12-Apr-91 C132/R) Portrait of Frances, Lady Smith, in fur-trimmed gown holding book (79x63cm-31x25in) i.verso
£2200	$4290	(26-Oct-90 C269/R) Portrait of Sir Francis Geary (35x25cm-14x10in) i. verso board
£2400	$4560	(1-Mar-91 C35/R) Portrait of Mr Simms wearing bow-tie. Portrait of Mrs Simms (76x63cm-30x25in) pair
£3600	$6444	(10-Apr-91 S138/R) Portrait of Hon. Lewis Alexander Grant, standing in landscape (90x65cm-35x26in)
£4400	$7876	(10-Apr-91 S139/R) Portrait of Miss Gower, seated in river landscape (72x60cm-28x24in)
£13000	$25610	(16-Nov-90 C33/R) Portrait of Seymour Sydney Hyde in landscape with poodle and spaniel (76x60cm-30x24in)

GRANT, Sir Francis (attrib) (1810-1878) British

| £1100 | $1859 | (3-May-91 PHE73/R) Portrait of young lady and pet spaniel (240x150cm-94x59in) |

GRAS, Francisco (19/20th C) Spanish

| £4359 | $8500 | (23-Oct-90 SY.NY424/R) Fisherwoman on the beach (97x86cm-38x34in) s.d.XXI |

GRAS, Jean Pierre (20th C) French

| £917 | $1761 | (29-Nov-90 QWA.P198) Le ventoux (50x73cm-20x29in) s. (F.FR 9000) |

GRASHOF, Otto (after) (1812-1876) German
£4737 $9000   (11-Sep-90 PO.BA25) La doma en tiempo de Rosas (67x79cm-26x31in)

GRASSE, Wolfgang (20th C) Australian
£1600 $3008   (17-Sep-90 MGS.S286) Spring (181x136cm-71x54in) s.d.1978 board
        (A.D 3600)

GRASSEL, Franz (1861-1948) German
£8725 $17013   (10-Oct-90 ZEL.L1512/R) Ganseliesel, shepherd girl with geese in
        landscape with village beyond (24x38cm-9x15in) s. i.verso panel
        (DM 26000)
£8904 $14514   (12-Jun-91 N.M440/R) Ducks and ducklings by stream (43x63cm-17x25in) s.
        (DM 26000)

GRASSET, Eugene (after) (1841-1917) Swiss
£891 $1577   (6-Apr-91 GL.P35) A la place Clichy (458x200cm-180x79in) (F.FR 9000)

GRASSI, Nicola (attrib) (1662-1748) Italian
£2400 $4056   (19-Apr-91 C122/R) A Saint explaining the Trinity to a group of peasants
        (35x23cm-14x9in)

GRASSIS, Giuseppe (1870-1949) Italian
£2500 $4901   (21-Nov-90 F.M153/R) Torrente di montagna (85x125cm-33x49in) s.
        (I.L 5500000)

GRASSL (20th C) German
£719 $1287   (12-Mar-91 FN.S2392) Fun on the ice in snowy river landscape with
        village beyond (24x30cm-9x12in) s.i. panel (DM 2100)

GRASSY, Giuseppe (1755-1838) Austrian
£9106 $16301   (16-Mar-91 AL.W1) Woman wearing a turban (70x57cm-28x22in)
        (P.Z 160000000)
£12333 $23926   (7-Dec-90 SY.MO52/R) Portrait de Gothard Andreas Graf Mannteuffell
        (63x49cm-25x19in) s.d. oval (F.FR 120000)

GRASSY, Giuseppe (attrib) (1755-1838) Austrian
£4000 $7600   (13-Sep-90 CSK46/R) Portrait of Duchess Maria Christine Lichnowsky, hand
        on Grecian urn (79x61cm-31x24in) s. oval

GRATCHEV, Mikhail (1913-) Russian
£1000 $1680   (26-Apr-91 ARC.P230/R) Le vase de clochettes bleues (130x89cm-51x35in)
        s. (F.FR 10000)
£1000 $1680   (26-Apr-91 ARC.P232/R) Nature morte au homard (71x93cm-28x37in) s.
        (F.FR 10000)
£1000 $1680   (26-Apr-91 ARC.P229/R) Le panier de lilas (99x68cm-39x27in) s. verso
        (F.FR 10000)
£1400 $2352   (26-Apr-91 ARC.P231/R) Bouquet champetre (99x71cm-39x28in) s.
        (F.FR 14000)
£1500 $2520   (26-Apr-91 ARC.P233/R) Les beaux lilas (79x99cm-31x39in) s. (F.FR 15000)

GRAU, Enrique (1920-) Colombian
£8673   *$17000*   *(20-Nov-90 CH.NY252/R) George Sand (100x70cm-39x28in) s.d.71 black*
        crayon pencil pen

GRAU-SALA, Emile (1911-1975) Spanish
£4592 $9000   (12-Feb-91 SY.NY227/R) Young woman in garden (28x23cm-11x9in) s.
        s.i.d.1960verso
£4872 $9500   (10-Oct-90 SY.NY181/R) Young woman seated at table (23x28cm-9x11in) s.
        masonite
£5149 $9113   (7-Apr-91 I.N155/R) La plage (18x36cm-7x14in) s. (F.FR 52000)
£5250 $8820   (22-Apr-91 PO.BA13) Payasos musicales (33x55cm-13x22in) s.
£5357 $10500   (12-Feb-91 SY.NY153/R) Young girl with flowers and fruit
        (23x28cm-9x11in) s. s.d.1964verso
£6124 $9860   (24-Jan-91 ARC.P40/R) Jeune fille au chat (45x38cm-18x15in) s. panel
        (F.FR 61000)
£7868 $15500   (13-Nov-90 CE.NY145/R) Le balcon a Barcelona (61x38cm-24x15in) s.
        s.i.d.1968
£7890 $15542   (6-Oct-90 GL.P148/R) Sur la terrasse (48x64cm-19x25in) s. paper laid
        down on canvas (F.FR 80000)
£7975 $13000   (12-Jun-91 SY.NY144/R) At racecourse (38x46cm-15x18in) s.d.57
£8241 $13516   (20-Jun-91 APT.P39/R) Le Havre (27x46cm-11x18in) s. d.1960 verso
        (F.FR 82000)
£9645 $19000   (13-Nov-90 CE.NY126/R) Jeune fille avec fleurs (38x46cm-15x18in) s.
        s.i.d.69verso
£9694 $19000   (12-Feb-91 SY.NY156/R) Pensive woman in interior (46x38cm-18x15in) s.
        s.d.1938verso
£9694 $19097   (16-Nov-90 FB.P179 d/R) Cafe billard (46x38cm-18x15in) s.i. (F.FR 95000)
£9919 $19441   (20-Nov-90 MF.P79/R) Femme a sa fenetre (46x55cm-18x22in) s. hardboard
        (F.FR 98000)
£10902 $18861   (21-May-91 DUR.M3/R) Nina en la ventana (46x38cm-18x15in) (S.P 2000000)
£11480 $22500   (12-Feb-91 SY.NY150/R) Jeune fille assise dans un paddock
        (61x71cm-24x28in) s. s.i.d.1969verso
£11542 $20084   (25-Mar-91 CR.P94/R) Scene d'interieur (50x61cm-20x24in) s.
        (F.FR 116000)
£11558 $20688   (15-Mar-91 FB.P13/R) Le foyer de danse (49x63cm-19x25in) s. board
        (F.FR 115000)

GRAU-SALA, Emile (1911-1975) Spanish-cont.

£12000	$20040	(7-Jun-91 LD.P48/R) Mere et fillette au gouter (38x46cm-15x18in) s. d.1964 verso (F.FR 120000)
£12036	$23470	(9-Oct-90 GGL.L15/R) Avant le Depart (48x64cm-19x25in) s. (F.FR 120000)
£12060	$19779	(20-Jun-91 APT.P41/R) Fillette aux fleurs (73x60cm-29x24in) s. d.1963 verso (F.FR 120000)
£12195	$20000	(19-Jun-91 B.SF1758/R) La plage (51x100cm-20x39in) s. s.i.d.1972verso
£12903	$24774	(2-Dec-90 GAB.G1622/R) Sous la lampe (38x46cm-15x18in) s. d.1960 verso (S.FR 32000)
£14031	$27500	(12-Feb-91 SY.NY155/R) Trouville, Normandie (58x71cm-23x28in) s. s.i.d.1965verso
£14451	$25000	(7-May-91 CE.NY55/R) Le marche (74x60cm-29x24in) s. s.d.1960 verso
£15416	$29908	(7-Dec-90 GL.P178/R) Le gouter des enfants (55x46cm-22x18in) s. i. verso (F.FR 150000)
£15897	$31000	(10-Oct-90 SY.NY192/R) Lady at dressing table (91x74cm-36x29in) s.
£16194	$31741	(19-Nov-90 ARC.P64/R) L'etang aux nenuphars (63x80cm-25x31in) s.d.1959 (F.FR 160000)
£16444	$31901	(9-Dec-90 E.LA122/R) Interieur rouge sous la lampe (60x73cm-24x29in) s. (F.FR 160000)
£17418	$34139	(11-Nov-90 ZZ.F116/R) Terrasse sur la baie de Cadaques au crepuscule (60x73cm-24x29in) s.d.1966 (F.FR 170000)
£17745	$30699	(8-May-91 FER.M164/R) Cabeza de nina (46x38cm-18x15in) s. s.i.d.1968verso (S.P 3250000)
£17766	$35000	(13-Nov-90 CE.NY246/R) Au bois (53x63cm-21x25in) s. s.i.d.verso
£18293	$30000	(19-Jun-91 B.SF1757/R) Fete en Catalogne (58x72cm-23x28in) s. s.i.d.1964verso
£19236	$36933	(19-Feb-91 DUR.M6) La costurera (46x38cm-18x15in) (S.P 3500000)
£19289	$38000	(13-Nov-90 CE.NY128/R) La fleuriste (60x74cm-24x29in) s. s.d.1952verso
£19289	$38000	(13-Nov-90 CE.NY115/R) Fleurs et maternite (91x73cm-36x29in) s. s.i.d.69
£19527	$37883	(5-Dec-90 HC.P19/R) Plage en Normandie (50x100cm-20x39in) s. d.1961 verso (F.FR 190000)
£20060	$39117	(9-Oct-90 CSC.P44/R) Courses (38x46cm-15x18in) s. i.d.1971 verso (F.FR 200000)
£20555	$39877	(7-Dec-90 GL.P182/R) L'enfant au cheval de bois (73x50cm-29x20in) s. (F.FR 200000)
£23167	$40079	(21-May-91 DUR.M6/R) Llansa, Costa Brava (54x65cm-21x26in) (S.P 4250000)
£23227	$45061	(5-Dec-90 ZZ.F29/R) Les cavaliers avant la course (36x73cm-14x29in) s.d.1957 (F.FR 226000)
£23358	$44847	(19-Feb-91 DUR.M7) Jardin (46x55cm-18x22in) (S.P 4250000)
£23955	$45994	(27-Nov-90 APT.P103/R) Portrait de femme au chapeau (100x73cm-39x29in) s. (F.FR 235000)
£29337	$57500	(7-Nov-90 B.SF1072/R) Paris, la nuit (72x91cm-28x36in) s. board
£30653	$54869	(16-Mar-91 APT.P49/R) Le rond-point des Champs-Elysees en 1900 (81x116cm-32x46in) s. i. verso (F.FR 305000)
£41220	$79143	(19-Feb-91 DUR.M10) La lampe verte (80x100cm-31x39in) (S.P 7500000)
£448	$762	(29-May-91 GL.P96) El Rastro (50x40cm-20x16in) s. Indian ink (F.FR 4500)
£540	$1054	(22-Oct-90 ANS.M176/R) La visita (14x11cm-6x4in) s. W/C ink (S.P 100000)
£1028	$1994	(5-Dec-90 HC.P17) La partie de carte (19x13cm-7x5in) s. W/C (F.FR 10000)
£1028	$1994	(5-Dec-90 HC.P14/R) Promenade au bord de mer (19x13cm-7x5in) s. W/C (F.FR 10000)
£1028	$1994	(5-Dec-90 HC.P16) Femme devant un metier a tisser (19x13cm-7x5in) s. W/C (F.FR 10000)
£1086	$1749	(25-Jun-91 FER.M135/R) Dama recostada (19x26cm-7x10in) s. W/C (S.P 200000)
£1197	$2250	(19-Sep-90 B.SF2652/R) On the porch (20x14cm-8x6in) s. W/C
£1330	$2500	(19-Sep-90 B.SF2651/R) Reading by a light (20x14cm-8x6in) s. W/C
£1387	$2692	(5-Dec-90 HC.P18) La lettre (19x13cm-7x5in) s. W/C (F.FR 13500)
£1490	$2891	(5-Dec-90 HC.P15) La promenade (19x13cm-7x5in) s. W/C (F.FR 14500)
£1494	$2405	(27-Jun-91 EP.M64/R) Paisaje (24x32cm-9x13in) pastel (S.P 275000)
£1518	$2976	(19-Nov-90 ARC.P17/R) Etang aux nenuphars (20x26cm-8x10in) s. gouache (F.FR 15000)
£1542	$2991	(7-Dec-90 GL.P35) Jeune fille au miroir (32x23cm-13x9in) s. W/C (F.FR 15000)
£1596	$3000	(19-Sep-90 B.SF2653/R) Standing by the window (20x14cm-8x6in) s. W/C
£1619	$3174	(19-Nov-90 ARC.P19/R) Honfleur (20x26cm-8x10in) s.d.62 gouache (F.FR 16000)
£1835	$3541	(12-Dec-90 APT.P23/R) Printemps en Provence (39x49cm-15x19in) s. pastel (F.FR 18000)
£2010	$3296	(18-Jun-91 APT.P24) Deux clowns (34x26cm-13x10in) bears trace sig. pastel (F.FR 20000)
£2024	$3968	(19-Nov-90 ARC.P18/R) Deauville, les planches (20x26cm-8x10in) s. gouache (F.FR 20000)
£3988	$6580	(10-Jul-91 FB.P11/R) Mere et enfant (63x50cm-25x20in) s.d.55 W/C htd.gouache (F.FR 40000)
£4985	$8125	(11-Jun-91 I.N218/R) Le paddock (31x48cm-12x19in) s. mixed media (F.FR 49500)
£9045	$16191	(15-Mar-91 FB.P8/R) Aux courses (49x62cm-19x24in) s. gouache (F.FR 90000)
£10194	$19572	(27-Nov-90 APT.P104/R) Femme a l'eventail (49x64cm-19x25in) s. oil gouache (F.FR 100000)
£15800	$30336	(27-Nov-90 APT.P102/R) Le dejeuner des enfants (91x92cm-36x36in) s. pastel (F.FR 155000)

GRAUBNER, Gotthard (1930-) German
£2252	$3896	(23-May-91 SY.AM307/R) Untitled (73x57cm-29x22in) s.d.1964 paper (D.FL 7500)
£9247	$15072	(14-Jun-91 L.K913/R) Fliessblatt (64x40cm-25x16in) s.d.73 oil cellulose (DM 27000)
£11263	$22075	(20-Nov-90 L.K252/R) Fliessblatt (66x40cm-26x16in) s.d.73 creased tissue paper (DM 33000)
£1351	*$2338*	*(23-May-91 SY.AM306/R) Untitled (42x34cm-17x13in) s.d.74 dye (D.FL 4500)*
£2703	*$4676*	*(22-May-91 CH.AM788/R) Composition - rose (65x49cm-26x19in) s.d.1963 W/C (D.FL 9000)*
£8136	*$13586*	*(8-Jun-91 HN.H120/R) Composition (64x49cm-25x19in) s.i.d.1963 sponge gouache cushion (DM 24000)*

GRAUMANN, Erwin (1902-) German
£1423	$2676	(19-Sep-90 KH.K65/R) Garden paths (32x42cm-13x17in) s.d.33 (D.KR 16000)

GRAVE, Josua de (17/18th C) Dutch
£550	*$1056*	*(18-Feb-91 S213/R) View of Monastery at Hocht (10x15cm-4x6in) i.d.1669 chk wash*
£900	*$1728*	*(18-Feb-91 S124/R) Figures harvesting hillside field with church of Grand-Hallet beyond (9x16cm-4x6in) bears i. pen ink wash*

GRAVELOT, Hubert Francois (1699-1773) French
£553	*$907*	*(21-Jun-91 CK.P20/R) Les trois sultanes (136x86cm-54x34in) s. pen wash (F.FR 5500)*
£6842	*$13000*	*(9-Jan-91 CH.NY46 a/R) Allegory (27x39cm-11x15in) red black chk pen wash*

GRAVEROL, Jeanne (1907-1984) Belgian
£1643	$3205	(24-Oct-90 GM.B952) Serres chaudes (47x41cm-19x16in) s. (B.FR 100000)

GRAVES, Abbott Fuller (1859-1936) American
£1176	$2200	(1-Aug-90 B.P110/R) Kennebunkport cottage (25x36cm-10x14in) s.verso board
£2030	$4000	(16-Nov-90 S.BM49/R) Goin' fishin' (33x41cm-13x16in) s.
£3000	$6000	(7-Feb-91 B.P74/R) Roses (51x61cm-20x24in) s.
£4190	$7500	(14-Mar-91 CH.NY182/R) Model boat (51x61cm-20x24in) s.
£7821	$14000	(12-Apr-91 SY.NY61/R) Still life with roses and ginger jar (51x61cm-20x24in) s.
£10417	$20000	(29-Nov-90 SY.NY40/R) Still life with flowers and fan (75x51cm-30x20in) s.d.87
£23699	$41000	(10-May-91 S.BM107/R) Tending the garden with cottages and ocean beyond (61x76cm-24x30in) s.
£1270	*$2400*	*(25-Sep-90 CE.NY75/R) The garden (30x46cm-12x18in) W/C*

GRAVES, Morris (1910-?) American
£2051	*$4000*	*(24-Oct-90 B.SF1481/R) Bird and egg (32x43cm-13x17in) s.d.54 chl*

GRAVES, Nancy (1940-) American
£5102	*$10000*	*(6-Nov-90 CE.NY249/R) Honokohau (112x127cm-44x50in) W/C*

GRAVIER, A du (?) ?
£950	$1644	(9-May-91 CSK168/R) French huntsmen on heath (27x47cm-11x19in) s. panel

GRAVINA (?) ?
£1325	$2544	(2-Dec-90 FE.P138) La Tamise (50x60cm-20x24in) s. (F.FR 13000)

GRAY, Cleve (1918-) American
£816	$1600	(12-Feb-91 SY.NY366/R) Woman tree 3 (208x132cm-82x52in) s.d.68 liquitex gesso on canvas
£510	*$1000*	*(6-Nov-90 CE.NY52/R) Untitled (58x47cm-23x19in) s.d.62 col.chks. ink*

GRAY, George (18/19th C) British
£680	$1204	(21-Mar-91 CSK186) Still life of melon, grapes, peaches and other fruit (43x51cm-17x20in) s.
£720	$1411	(13-Feb-91 S125/R) Working in garden (35x53cm-14x21in) s.
£1500	$2805	(28-Aug-90 S744/R) Fly fishing (77x127cm-30x50in) s.

GRAY, H Barnard (19/20th C) British?
£850	$1386	(14-Jun-91 C258/R) Woodpigeon with robin nearby (30x46cm-12x18in) s.d.1856

GRAY, Henry Percy (1869-1952) American
£3827	$7500	(13-Feb-91 B.SF2038/R) Oak tree, Marin (41x51cm-16x20in) s. canvasboard
£10204	$20000	(13-Feb-91 B.SF2035/R) Aetna springs landscape (61x76cm-24x30in) s. with letter
£11538	$22500	(10-Oct-90 B.SF459/R) Marin landscape (63x76cm-25x30in) s.
£14103	$27500	(10-Oct-90 B.SF458/R) Mount Tamalpais (56x71cm-22x28in) s.
£888	*$1500*	*(1-May-91 D.NY46) Dusk (15x20cm-6x8in) s. W/C*
£2564	*$5000*	*(10-Oct-90 B.SF465/R) Lucas Valley and farm (24x34cm-9x13in) s. W/C*
£3061	*$6000*	*(13-Feb-91 B.SF2020/R) View of Mount Tamalpais (22x30cm-9x12in) s.d.1924 W/C*
£3061	*$6000*	*(13-Feb-91 B.SF2021/R) Barn on hillside (24x33cm-9x13in) s.d.1907 W/C*
£3333	*$6500*	*(10-Oct-90 B.SF470/R) Monterey coast (29x39cm-11x15in) s. W/C*
£4615	*$9000*	*(10-Oct-90 B.SF452/R) Eucalyptus grove beside lake (35x25cm-14x10in) s.d.1919 W/C*
£5102	*$10000*	*(13-Feb-91 B.SF2037/R) Eucalyptus Grove (36x53cm-14x21in) s.d.1924 W/C*

GRAY, Henry Percy (1869-1952) American-cont.
£8673	$17000	(13-Feb-91 B.SF2036/R) Lupine and poppies, Carmel Valley (40x50cm-16x20in) s.d.1925 W/C paper on board
£11538	$22500	(10-Oct-90 B.SF457/R) Landscape with poppies and lupines (39x49cm-15x19in) s. W/C

GRAY, Jack L (1927-1981) American
£1796	$3000	(25-Jul-91 E.EDM320/R) Fishing schooner and dorymen (76x102cm-30x40in) s.
£2663	$4500	(1-May-91 B.SF5094/R) Still morning, Blue Rocks, N.S. 1959 (61x91cm-24x36in) s.
£3027	$5600	(10-Mar-91 H.C166/R) Two lobstermen laying traps (76x102cm-30x40in) s.
£5325	$9000	(17-Apr-91 D.NY49/R) Muriel Isabel, home from banks (76x56cm-30x22in) s. i.stretcher
£6509	$11000	(20-Apr-91 WOL.C404/R) Nova Scotia fishing scene (76x102cm-30x40in) s.

GRAY, James (?-1947) British
£550	$1073	(17-Oct-90 PHG83) Still life of sweet peas (45x63cm-18x25in) s. W/C
£700	$1169	(26-Jul-91 PHE58) Still life of bowl of roses (34x49cm-13x19in) s. W/C
£1100	$2057	(28-Aug-90 S1079/R) Still life of flowers (51x72cm-20x28in) s. W/C over chk
£1500	$2805	(28-Aug-90 S902/R) Sweet peas (45x60cm-18x24in) s. W/C

GRAY, Kate (19th C) British
£1050	$1806	(14-May-91 SWS260/R) Dress for dolly (75x62cm-30x24in) s.d.1876

GRAY, W (19th C) British
£1064	$1830	(14-May-91 GM.B598/R) Rochers sur la plage (55x90cm-22x35in) s. (B.FR 65000)
£550	$1034	(21-Sep-90 CBB307) Italian lake scene with figures and boats (18x38cm-7x15in) s. W/C

GRAZIANI (circle) (17/18th C) Italian
£4052	$7902	(23-Oct-90 CH.R388/R) Battaglia fra cristiani e turchi (72x98cm-28x39in) (I.L 9000000)

GRAZIANI, Ciccio (17th C) Italian
£4332	$7235	(4-Jun-91 CH.R159) Battaglia (26x48cm-10x19in) (I.L 9500000)

GRAZIANI, Ercole (17/18th C) Italian
£2083	$3500	(17-Jul-91 SY.NY102/R) The devout Canetoli refusing the Archibishop (124x76cm-49x30in)

GRAZIANI, Ercole (elder) (1651-1726) Italian
£8718	$17000	(10-Oct-90 CH.NY97/R) The Finding of Moses (86x112cm-34x44in)

GRAZIANI, Pietro (17/18th C) Italian
£5200	$8788	(17-Apr-91 S67/R) Cavalry engagements (20x34cm-8x13in) canvas on panel pair
£7213	$12911	(8-Apr-91 CH.R25/R) Battaglia di cavalieri sul Ponte Nomentano presso Roma (31x49cm-12x19in) (I.L 16000000)

GREACEN, Edmund William (1877-1949) American
£1649	$3100	(22-Sep-90 WOL.C295/R) Floral still life (51x41cm-20x16in) s. canvasboard
£6250	$12000	(30-Nov-90 CH.NY106/R) Still life with lilacs (76x63cm-30x25in) st.studio st.studio verso

GREACEN, Nan (20th C) American
£588	$1000	(1-Jun-91 LAE.L42/R) Peace roses (36x53cm-14x21in) s. W/C

GREASON, William (1884-?) American
£518	$1000	(14-Dec-90 DM.D997/R) River boats, Manistee, Michigan (74x53cm-29x21in) s.

GREATOREX, Kathleen Honora (1851-?) American
£600	$1200	(6-Feb-91 D.NY38) Floral still life (58x43cm-23x17in) s.i.d.1880 W/C gouache

GREAVES, Derrick (1927-) British
£2800	$5488	(7-Nov-90 S170/R) The siesta (91x122cm-36x48in) s.

GREAVES, Walter (1846-1930) British
£1098	$1900	(21-May-91 CE.NY153/R) Running brook (29x43cm-11x17in) s.d.78
£700	$1365	(10-Oct-90 S70/R) Riverside landing stage Old Swan, Chelsea (35x48cm-14x19in) s. W/C over pen ink

GREAVES, William (fl.1882-1920) British
£740	$1273	(14-May-91 CHAP298/R) Maltongate, Thornton le Dale, South End (30x51cm-12x20in) s.d.1889
£800	$1376	(14-May-91 CHAP299/R) Maltongate, Thornton le Dale, North End (30x46cm-12x18in) s.
£800	$1432	(11-Apr-91 MO417) Woodland scene with horse drawn cart (64x76cm-25x30in) s.
£900	$1611	(11-Apr-91 MO418/R) A hay meadow in a woodland landscape (41x51cm-16x20in) s.d.1933

GREBBER, Fransz Pieter and BRIZE, Cornelis (17th C) Dutch
£2262 $3823 (21-Apr-91 BU.M313) Allegory of Peace (105x88cm-41x35in) s.d.1654
(S.KR 24000)

GREBE, Fritz (1850-?) German
£3469 $6592 (14-Sep-90 ZOF.Z846/R) Fjord landscape with fishing harbour at night
(66x96cm-26x38in) s. (S.FR 8500)

GRECO, El (1541-1614) Spanish
£1105263 $2100000 (11-Jan-91 CH.NY78/R) The Coronation of the Virgin (57x76cm-22x30in) in
a painted oval
£1522567 $2999456 (30-Oct-90 EP.M11/R) El expolio (139x165cm-55x65in) (S.P 280000000)

GRECO, El (attrib) (1541-1614) Spanish
£76471 $130000 (31-May-91 CH.NY58/R) Adoration of the Shepherds (24x19cm-9x7in) panel
shaped top

GRECO, El (studio) (1541-1614) Spanish
£15294 $26000 (31-May-91 CH.NY194/R) The Virgin and St Anne (54x65cm-21x26in)

GRECO, El (style) (1541-1614) Spanish
£1104 $1778 (27-Jun-91 APT.P38/R) Un apotre (82x65cm-32x26in) (F.FR 11000)
£14103 $27500 (11-Oct-90 SY.NY117/R) St Francis of Assisi in Ecstasy
(107x81cm-42x32in)
£19231 $37500 (11-Oct-90 SY.NY59/R) St Francis of Assisi having the Vision of the
Flaming Torch (102x70cm-40x28in) i.

GRECO, Emilio (1913-) Italian
£615 *$1200* *(10-Oct-90 SY.NY350) Head of woman (48x33cm-19x13in) s.i.d.1954 india*
ink
£1090 *$2148* *(30-Oct-90 F.R73) Nudo seduto (45x30cm-18x12in) s.d.1949 Indian ink*
(I.L 2400000)
£1094 *$1859* *(28-May-91 SY.MI15/R) Donna seduta (66x46cm-26x18in) s.d.1960 ink*
(I.L 2400000)
£1727 *$3386* *(20-Nov-90 BR.M48/R) Nudo di donna (50x69cm-20x27in) s.d.1972 ink*
(I.L 3800000)

GRECO, Gennaro (1663-1714) Italian
£8939 $16000 (11-Apr-91 SY.NY35/R) Figures among classical ruins near southern port
(46x72cm-18x28in)

GRECO, Gennaro (attrib) (1663-1714) Italian
£889 $1724 (4-Dec-90 R.T302/R) Capricci of Mediterranean port (56x72cm-22x28in)
(C.D 2000)

GRECOLINI, Giovanni Antonio (1675-1725) Italian
£3200 *$6176* *(11-Dec-90 C43/R) The head of a young girl (30x22cm-12x9in) i. col.chks.*
£4000 *$7720* *(11-Dec-90 C42/R) Saint John the Baptist (30x23cm-12x9in) i. col.chks.*

GREEN, Albert van Nesse (20th C) American
£2515 $4250 (17-Apr-91 D.NY83/R) Pennsylvania corner (71x76cm-28x30in) s.

GREEN, Alfred H (fl.1844-1862) British
£700 $1204 (14-May-91 SWS252/R) The see-saw (14x20cm-6x8in) mono.d.1861 board
£1169 $2280 (15-Oct-90 SY.J20/R) Harvest time (75x62cm-30x24in) mono. (SA.R 5800)
£1300 $2457 (26-Sep-90 S142/R) Inspecting catch (76x63cm-30x25in)

GREEN, Anthony (1939-) British
£1000 *$1960* *(6-Nov-90 PH118/R) Self portrait seated in father's chair*
(85x87cm-33x34in) s.d.67 pencil

GREEN, Charles (1840-1898) British
£800 *$1536* *(26-Nov-90 SWS94/R) Spilt ink (15x14cm-6x6in) mono. W/C htd.bodycol*
£1550 *$2527* *(14-Jun-91 C108/R) A game of chess (18x25cm-7x10in) inits.d.1874 prncil*
W/C htd.white
£3000 *$5760* *(26-Nov-90 SWS102/R) Captain Cuttle and Florence Dombey*
(46x59cm-18x23in) s.d.1886 i.verso W/C

GREEN, Charles Lewis (1844-?) American
£660 $1300 (18-Nov-90 JRB.C125/R) Woman and child by cottage (33x25cm-13x10in) s.
panel

GREEN, Elizabeth Shippen (1871-1954) American
£1587 $3000 (25-Sep-90 CE.NY278/R) A good book (68x40cm-27x16in) s. chl. board

GREEN, Gertrude (1904-) American
£1164 $2200 (25-Sep-90 CE.NY249/R) Collage - brown abstract (30x36cm-12x14in) s.d.36
paper collage

GREEN, James (1771-1834) British
£2800 $5012 (12-Apr-91 C146/R) Portrait of artist's daughter, looking over right
shoulder, falcon on arm (91x70cm-36x28in)
£2200 *$3894* *(20-Mar-91 C133/R) Portrait of gentleman in maroon coat and white*
waistcoat (5x?cm-2x?in) min. gold frame plaited hair verso oval

GREEN, Mike (1941-) New Zealander
£1131 $1912   (16-Apr-91 J.M256 a) The Stair-case (118x78cm-46x31in) s. mixed media
                        (A.D 2500)

GREEN, Mrs James (attrib) (1776-1845) British
£500 $960   (18-Dec-90 C100) Portrait of lady in frilled white dress (8x?cm-3x?in)
                        min. silver frame oval

GREEN, Nathaniel Everett (fl.1880-1896) British
£460 $851   (6-Mar-91 SC4170/R) Bath (30x48cm-12x19in) s.i.d.1886 W/C
£500 $990   (30-Jan-91 S108) View of Bellaggio (23x49cm-9x19in) s.i. W/C over pencil
                        htd bodycol

GREEN, Richard Crafton (19th C) British
£680 $1333   (8-Nov-90 PHI219) Autumnal river landscape (90x136cm-35x54in) init.d.87
£850 $1666   (8-Nov-90 PHI225) Figures on path in continental coastal landscape
                        (90x136cm-35x54in) s.d.1880
£4500 $8820   (13-Feb-91 S36/R) Italian Bay (137x234cm-54x92in) s.d.1880

GREEN, Roland (1896-1972) British
£450 $864   (19-Feb-91 C24/R) Goldfinches in winter (23x28cm-9x11in) s. pencil W/C
                        htd.white
£480 $782   (13-Jun-91 CSK35) Cock and hen pheasants in snow (22x28cm-9x11in) s.
                        pencil W/C htd white
£560 $1120   (8-Feb-91 K446/R) Mallard rising from pool (46x33cm-18x13in) s. W/C
£600 $1152   (19-Feb-91 C101) Swans in flight (25x36cm-10x14in) s. pencil W/C
                        htd.white
£620 $1048   (19-Apr-91 K518/R) Reed pheasant (25x18cm-10x7in) s.i.d.1927 W/C
£620 $1048   (19-Apr-91 K517/R) Long tailed tits (23x15cm-9x6in) s. W/C
£880 $1487   (15-Apr-91 WW160) Snipe. Wild duck (10x14cm-4x6in) s. W/C pair
£900 $1800   (8-Feb-91 K448/R) Pheasant in autumnal woodland clearing
                        (25x36cm-10x14in) s. W/C
£1300 $2119   (14-Jun-91 C166/R) Snipe over the marshes. Teal in flight
                        (26x37cm-10x15in) s. pencil W/C htd white pair
£2200 $4224   (19-Feb-91 C21/R) Goldfinches. Blue tits. Coal tits (33x23cm-13x9in) s.
                        pencil W/C htd.white set of three

GREEN-EMMOTT, Louisa Mary (19th C) Australian
£3400 $6630   (24-Oct-90 S88/R) The Gold Commissioner's station at Timbarra, New South
                        Wales (75x110cm-30x43in)

GREENAWAY, Kate (1846-1901) British
£1000 $1940   (6-Dec-90 S369/R) Girl lying asleep in wood (22x19cm-9x7in) W/C
£1100 $2134   (6-Dec-90 S373/R) 'A very happy dream' - girl asleep on cloud
                        (7x15cm-3x6in) init.d.1884 W/C dr
£1500 $2910   (6-Dec-90 S375/R) Eight children on village green playing 'Ring a Ring
                        of Roses' (15x24cm-6x9in) pencil W/C dr
£1700 $3298   (6-Dec-90 S372/R) Two girls standing in bonnets and cloaks on way to
                        school (10cm-4ins circular) init. ink W/C dr
£1800 $3492   (6-Dec-90 S374/R) Row of four jumping girls (7x15cm-3x6in) ink W/C dr
                        sold with sketch and proof
£2200 $4268   (6-Dec-90 S371/R) Girl seated by garden wall (10x11cm-4x4in) init. ink
                        W/C dr
£4624 $8000   (22-May-91 SY.NY258/R) Through white flowers (36x53cm-14x21in) s.d.1891
                        W/C card

GREENBLAT, Rodney Alan (20th C) American?
£1020 $2000   (6-Nov-90 CE.NY270/R) Head Dress II (54x48cm-21x19in) init. gouache
                        col.pencils
£1122 $2200   (6-Nov-90 CE.NY268/R) Headdresses (54x48cm-21x19in) init.i.d.May 20,
                        1984 gouache col.pencils

GREENE, Anne Alison (?) Australian?
£1266 $2430   (14-Aug-90 SY.ME285/R) Place du Marche, Cherbourg, France
                        (37x44cm-15x17in) s. board (A.D 3000)

GREENE, Balcomb (1904-) American
£3343 $5750   (15-May-91 SY.NY267/R) Abstract collage (25x22cm-10x9in) s.num.C34-21
                        mixed media collage

GREENE, Gertrude (1911-1956) American?
£698 $1200   (15-May-91 SY.NY270/R) Abstract collage (16x18cm-6x7in) s.d.39-5 paper
                        collage

GREENHALGH, Thomas (?) ?
£700 $1148   (19-Jun-91 B76) View of Salute, Venice after rain (25x36cm-10x14in) s.
                        W/C
£1000 $1950   (18-Oct-90 SC3002/R) Magdalen Bridge, Oxford (50x70cm-20x28in) s. W/C
                        pencil

GREENHAM, Robert Duckworth (1906-1975) British
£700 $1183   (2-May-91 C83/R) Jilly Cooper (91x44cm-36x17in) s.d.73 s.i.verso
£900 $1692   (20-Sep-90 C195/R) Girl in front of mirror (15x11cm-6x4in) init.d.56
                        board
£900 $1764   (25-Jan-91 C12/R) Jesse Matthews (25x20cm-10x8in) s.d.34 board

GREENHAM, Robert Duckworth (1906-1975) British-cont.

£1100	$2068	(20-Sep-90 C197/R) Girl in white headscarf (21x16cm-8x6in) init.d.66 board
£1600	$3008	(20-Sep-90 C196/R) Flowers and apples, No. 2 (46x35cm-18x14in) s.d.28 s.i.verso
£2100	$3948	(20-Sep-90 C198/R) Girl in white hat (24x10cm-9x4in) init. d.1964 verso board
£3000	$5940	(29-Jan-91 PH137/R) Bank Holiday (38x49cm-15x19in) s.d.45 board
£3200	$6016	(20-Sep-90 C201/R) Iris and rhododendrons (44x29cm-17x11in) s.d.53
£3500	$6580	(20-Sep-90 C199/R) Parisian girl (19x14cm-7x6in) init.d.74 s.i.verso board
£4200	$7014	(6-Jun-91 C26/R) Ann Todd as Lottie Dundas (56x39cm-22x15in) s.d.43 s.i.verso
£850	*$1598*	*(20-Sep-90 CSK131/R) Study for a painting of Jessie Matthews (20x21cm-8x8in) s. i.verso gouache brush ink chk pencil*

GREENHILL, Harold (1914-) Australian

£683	$1311	(26-Nov-90 SY.ME127/R) Castle circuit (58x52cm-23x20in) s.i. cardboard (A.D 1700)

GREENLEAF, Jacob (1887-1968) American

£510	$1000	(24-Nov-90 YFA.M59/R) Autumn in village (56x71cm-22x28in) s.

GREENMAN, Frances (1890-1982) American

£578	$1000	(12-May-91 H.C160/R) Child in costume (64x53cm-25x21in) s.
£1042	$1750	(19-Jul-91 DM.D2062/R) Portrait of a seated girl (64x51cm-25x20in) s.

GREENWOOD, George Parker (19th C) British

£559	$1000	(16-Mar-91 W.W38/R) The S S Shakespeare (51x91cm-20x36in) s.

GREENWOOD, John (1727-1792) American

£1684	*$3200*	*(9-Jan-91 CH.NY101/R) Harbor scene in blow (18x24cm-7x9in) mono.i.ink sold w.works byR.Hinshelwood,A.Fisher*

GREENWOOD, Joseph H (1857-1927) American

£615	$1200	(14-Oct-90 H.C399/R) Midsummer (38x48cm-15x19in) s.d.16
£1015	$2000	(16-Nov-90 S.BM95/R) Autumn evening (38x48cm-15x19in) s.d.22

GREENWOOD, Orlando (1892-1989) British

£650	$1268	(11-Oct-90 CSK203/R) The crystal well (33x39cm-13x15in) s.i.
£650	$1268	(11-Oct-90 CSK206/R) Pastoral (47x51cm-19x20in) s.i.
£650	$1268	(11-Oct-90 CSK52/R) View across town to the castle (63x76cm-25x30in)
£650	$1268	(11-Oct-90 CSK207/R) The pedlar (57x61cm-22x24in) s.i.
£650	$1268	(11-Oct-90 CSK64/R) Houses at foot of hills (40x51cm-16x20in)
£650	$1268	(11-Oct-90 CSK212/R) Cwellyn (56x74cm-22x29in) i.
£700	$1365	(11-Oct-90 CSK175/R) Three village girls (61x66cm-24x26in) s.
£700	$1365	(11-Oct-90 CSK78/R) Durham (60x51cm-24x20in) i.verso
£700	$1365	(11-Oct-90 CSK193/R) Horses (112x141cm-44x56in)
£700	$1365	(11-Oct-90 CSK241/R) Red, yellow and mauve tulips in yellow jug (68x46cm-27x18in)
£700	$1365	(11-Oct-90 CSK81/R) Criccieth (51x61cm-20x24in) s.i.
£700	$1365	(11-Oct-90 CSK56/R) Bridges under snow (53x61cm-21x24in)
£700	$1365	(11-Oct-90 CSK132/R) Family in mourning (53x46cm-21x18in)
£700	$1365	(11-Oct-90 CSK163/R) Negro couple (46x38cm-18x15in)
£700	$1365	(11-Oct-90 CSK215/R) The knight errant (41x51cm-16x20in) s.i.
£750	$1463	(11-Oct-90 CSK53/R) St Martin de Boscherville (46x61cm-18x24in) i.
£800	$1560	(11-Oct-90 CSK229/R) Snowdrops in blue urn (39x30cm-15x12in)
£800	$1560	(11-Oct-90 CSK249/R) Self portrait with multi-coloured jacket (43x35cm-17x14in)
£800	$1560	(11-Oct-90 CSK146/R) The little provincial (39x30cm-15x12in) s.d.1924 i.
£850	$1658	(11-Oct-90 CSK195/R) Geese on pond (89x63cm-35x25in)
£850	$1658	(11-Oct-90 CSK164/R) Village with church and houses (61x66cm-24x26in)
£850	$1658	(11-Oct-90 CSK143/R) Woman reading at the piano (71x66cm-28x26in)
£850	$1658	(11-Oct-90 CSK63/R) Tow path by the canal (51x66cm-20x26in)
£900	$1755	(11-Oct-90 CSK222/R) Tulips, apples and bananas (51x66cm-20x26in)
£900	$1755	(11-Oct-90 CSK94/R) Windmill by bridge (102x86cm-40x34in) s.i.
£950	$1853	(11-Oct-90 CSK174/R) Femme couchant (52x89cm-20x35in)
£950	$1853	(11-Oct-90 CSK1045/R) House on hillside (46x56cm-18x22in)
£950	$1853	(11-Oct-90 CSK61/R) Rooftops in the mountains (46x61cm-18x24in)
£950	$1853	(11-Oct-90 CSK55/R) Boats at low tide (46x55cm-18x22in)
£950	$1853	(11-Oct-90 CSK200/R) The T'Ang Tiger (33x39cm-13x15in) s.i.
£950	$1853	(11-Oct-90 CSK230/R) Snowdrops in glass vase on windowsill (35x30cm-14x12in)
£1000	$1950	(11-Oct-90 CSK239/R) Irises and daffodils in blue and white vase (61x51cm-24x20in)
£1000	$1950	(11-Oct-90 CSK218/R) Pineapple (33x39cm-13x15in) s.i.
£1000	$1950	(11-Oct-90 CSK160/R) Self portrait in the mirror (41x51cm-16x20in)
£1000	$1950	(11-Oct-90 CSK198/R) Ringstone Hill (61x51cm-24x20in) i.
£1000	$1670	(22-Jul-91 SWS1134/R) A busy street scene at night (75x45cm-30x18in) mono.d.1920
£1000	$1950	(11-Oct-90 CSK190/R) Gazelles on the run (61x76cm-24x30in)
£1000	$1950	(11-Oct-90 CSK238/R) Still life with chrysanthemums and daisies in vase (56x76cm-22x30in)
£1000	$1950	(11-Oct-90 CSK208/R) Hagar and Ishmael (60x46cm-24x18in) i.
£1100	$2145	(11-Oct-90 CSK231/R) Roses in pot on table (58x51cm-23x20in)
£1100	$2145	(11-Oct-90 CSK217/R) Emigrants (56x53cm-22x21in) s.s.i.on stretcher

GREENWOOD, Orlando (1892-1989) British-cont.

£1200	$2340	(11-Oct-90 CSK248/R) The blunderbuss (112x86cm-44x34in) s.i.verso
£1200	$2340	(11-Oct-90 CSK234/R) Tulips (61x43cm-24x17in) s.i.
£1200	$2340	(11-Oct-90 CSK219/R) Apples (35x56cm-14x22in) s.s.i.verso
£1200	$2340	(11-Oct-90 CSK221/R) Orange and lemon on checked tablecloth (23x30cm-9x12in)
£1300	$2535	(11-Oct-90 CSK237/R) Summer still life in copper vase (63x56cm-25x22in) s.
£1300	$2535	(11-Oct-90 CSK145/R) Standing female nude. Putti (127x71cm-50x28in) pair
£1300	$2535	(11-Oct-90 CSK93/R) Fold (56x46cm-22x18in) i.
£1400	$2730	(11-Oct-90 CSK153/R) The M.M.Club (56x61cm-22x24in) i.
£1400	$2730	(11-Oct-90 CSK118/R) Bridge in landscape, trees and mountains beyond (56x46cm-22x18in)
£1500	$2925	(11-Oct-90 CSK223/R) Onions (46x38cm-18x15in) s.i.
£1500	$2925	(11-Oct-90 CSK233/R) Carnations (63x51cm-25x20in) s.i.
£1500	$2925	(11-Oct-90 CSK169/R) Judgement of Paris (43x127cm-17x50in) i.
£1600	$3120	(11-Oct-90 CSK220/R) Crimson bramleys on green and white checked tablecloth (30x39cm-12x15in)
£1600	$3120	(11-Oct-90 CSK232/R) Roses in blue and white vase on table (66x51cm-26x20in)
£1600	$3120	(11-Oct-90 CSK98/R) Pendle (56x66cm-22x26in) i.verso
£1800	$3510	(11-Oct-90 CSK106/R) Mountainous landscape (46x53cm-18x21in)
£2000	$3900	(11-Oct-90 CSK65/R) Barrowford locks (56x76cm-22x30in) s.i.
£2200	$4290	(11-Oct-90 CSK214/R) Plough team (43x127cm-17x50in)
£2400	$4680	(11-Oct-90 CSK112/R) Cottage by hillside road (38x46cm-15x18in)
£2400	$4680	(11-Oct-90 CSK228/R) Tulips and other flowers in jug on patterned tablecloth (68x46cm-27x18in)
£2600	$4654	(11-Mar-91 HS286/R) The antique shop - street scene with figures (97x128cm-38x50in) mono.d.1918
£2800	$5460	(11-Oct-90 CSK120/R) Cowgirl in meadow (66x61cm-26x24in) s. on stretcher
£2800	$5460	(11-Oct-90 CSK80/R) Boulby Bank (56x46cm-22x18in) s.s.i.on stretcher
£2800	$5460	(11-Oct-90 CSK154/R) Little girl in blue with corn-coloured hair (43x37cm-17x15in)
£3000	$5850	(11-Oct-90 CSK186/R) Piano solo (74x61cm-29x24in) i.verso
£3500	$6825	(11-Oct-90 CSK227/R) Tulips in blue vase on table set for tea (81x66cm-32x26in) s.
£3500	$6825	(11-Oct-90 CSK138/R) 'La Messe' (91x122cm-36x48in) mono.d.1920 s.i.on stretcher
£3500	$6825	(11-Oct-90 CSK242/R) Still life of autumn flowers (76x91cm-30x36in) i.
£3800	$7410	(11-Oct-90 CSK225/R) Pears (46x51cm-18x20in) s.i.
£4200	$8190	(11-Oct-90 CSK235/R) Delphiniums and other flowers in vase (84x71cm-33x28in)
£550	*$1073*	*(11-Oct-90 CSK26/R) The nomads (53x71cm-21x28in) mono.d.1922 W/C*
£650	*$1268*	*(11-Oct-90 CSK21/R) The old market, Whitby (56x76cm-22x30in) mono.d.1922 W/C*
£750	*$1463*	*(11-Oct-90 CSK31/R) Cotton factory (32x74cm-13x29in) pastel*
£1100	*$2145*	*(11-Oct-90 CSK44/R) Night at the theatre (54x64cm-21x25in) s.d.1919 W/C*

GREER, J T (19th C) ?

£765	$1500	(16-Feb-91 W.W22/R) Portrait of Daniel Webster (48x38cm-19x15in) indis.s.

GREGOOR, Gillis Smak (1770-1843) Dutch

£2879	$5412	(22-Sep-90 CH.AM145/R) Horse-man driving cattle and woman with child by ruined fortification (70x90cm-28x35in) s. (D.FL 9500)

GREGORIO, Giuseppe de (1920-?) Italian

£773	$1462	(27-Sep-90 F.M127) Composizione (98x99cm-39x39in) s.verso (I.L 1700000)

GREGORIO, Marco de (1829-1876) Italian

£5000	$9800	(15-Feb-91 C99/R) Arab boy and negro boy smoking Hookahs (16x29cm-6x11in) s.i.

GREGORY, Arthur V (1867-1957) Australian

£464	*$891*	*(14-Aug-90 SY.ME12/R) The last lap (59x84cm-23x33in) s.i.d.1927 gouache (A.D 1100)*
£1042	*$2054*	*(13-Nov-90 J.M9) SS Rotomahana Crossing Bass Straight (30x53cm-12x21in) s.d.13 W/C (A.D 2700)*
£1097	*$2106*	*(14-Aug-90 SY.ME49/R) S. S. Melbourne (53x89cm-21x35in) s.d.'99 gouache (A.D 2600)*

GREGORY, C F (1815-1885) Australian

£2096	*$3500*	*(25-Jul-91 E.EDM369/R) American ship Rutland (46x61cm-18x24in) s. W/C*

GREGORY, Charles (19/20th C) British

£1200	*$2280*	*(27-Feb-91 MMB166) Beccles, Suffolk, with young ladies in a punt (66x33cm-26x13in) s. bears i. scratching out*

GREGORY, Dorothy Lake (1893-?) American

£523	$900	(15-May-91 SY.NY276/R) Birds (25x20cm-10x8in) s. canvasboard

GREGORY, Edward James (1850-1909) British

£600	*$1152*	*(26-Nov-90 SWS95/R) The guardroom dandy (20x16cm-8x6in) init. W/C*

GREGORY, George (1849-1938) British
£750	$1463	(18-Oct-90 CSK122/R) Fishing vessels and other shipping off south coast (35x53cm-14x21in) s.d.1901
£950	$1872	(7-Oct-90 MMB275) Rouen, street scene with figures (41x61cm-16x24in) s.d.1899 i.stretcher
£1150	$2254	(13-Feb-91 S28/R) Portsmouth (46x76cm-18x30in) s.d.1888 i.stretcher
£2600	$4940	(10-Jan-91 B130/R) Fishing boats entering harbour in breeze and other shipping beyond (51x72cm-20x28in) s.d.1896
£900	$1683	(1-Aug-90 CSK24) Shipping in storm off small quayside (23x51cm-9x20in) s.d.1889 pencil W/C htd white

GREGORY, George Frederick (?-c.1890) Australian
£781	$1359	(26-Mar-91 JRL.S86/R) The iris (40x58cm-16x23in) s.d.1881 W/C gouache (A.D 1750)
£781	$1359	(26-Mar-91 JRL.S88/R) Adieu (40x60cm-16x24in) W/C gouache (A.D 1750)
£876	$1727	(31-Oct-90 CH.S20) The S S Coorong (57x84cm-22x33in) s.d.67 gouache cardboard (A.D 2200)

GREIL, Alois (1841-1902) Austrian
| £4110 | $7356 | (13-Mar-91 N.M304/R) Artillery marching through town watched by folk, possibly Franconia (38x47cm-15x19in) s.d.1889 W/C (DM 12000) |

GREINER, Otto (1869-1916) German
£422	$717	(28-May-91 KF.M342) Nude female walking with arms raised (47x29cm-19x11in) mono. chk htd.white (DM 1249)
£439	$747	(28-May-91 KF.M352/R) Portrait of elderly woman (34x28cm-13x11in) mono.i.d.1904 col.chk chl (DM 1300)
£439	$747	(28-May-91 KF.M357) Studies of fish, arm, hand and figures (47x33cm-19x13in) chk double-sided (DM 1300)
£507	$861	(28-May-91 KF.M341) Head of woman bent backwards (26x21cm-10x8in) mono.d.1896 pen brush indian ink over pencil (DM 1500)
£541	$919	(28-May-91 KF.M339) Landscape near Florence (32x46cm-13x18in) s.i.d.1891 pen wash over chk (DM 1600)
£574	$976	(28-May-91 KF.M344/R) Male nude with arms raised (57x17cm-22x7in) ochre (DM 1700)
£676	$1149	(28-May-91 KF.M343/R) Study for title page of Klassischer Skulpturen Schatz (48x36cm-19x14in) mono.i. chl chk (DM 2000)
£743	$1264	(28-May-91 KF.M359/R) Female nude from behind. Nude child seated (58x30cm-23x12in) chl chk double-sided (DM 2200)
£743	$1264	(28-May-91 KF.M346/R) Head of woman. Heads and hands of figures (39x28cm-15x11in) s.d.1897 ochre pencil chk htd.white double-sided (DM 2200)
£872	$1701	(12-Oct-90 AW.H1448) Study for Ganymed (31x50cm-12x20in) c.1898 ochre pencil (DM 2600)
£912	$1551	(28-May-91 KF.M358) Female nude resting (16x25cm-6x10in) chk over pencil (DM 2700)
£946	$1608	(28-May-91 KF.M347) Female nude (60x44cm-24x17in) ochre col.chk (DM 2800)
£946	$1608	(28-May-91 KF.M350/R) Death of singer (15x12cm-6x5in) s.i.d.1902 pen (DM 2800)
£1081	$1838	(28-May-91 KF.M349/R) Head of young woman (46x34cm-18x13in) mono.i.d.1901 col.chk (DM 3200)
£1081	$1838	(28-May-91 KF.M355) Self portrait. Study of plants (26x37cm-10x15in) chl col.chk double-sided (DM 3200)
£1284	$2182	(28-May-91 KF.M345/R) Male nude from behind and study for hands and feet (59x31cm-23x12in) chk (DM 3800)
£7432	$12635	(28-May-91 KF.M351/R) Nude and dressed female figures riding on brooms (44x37cm-17x15in) s.d.1903 ochre pencil chl (DM 22000)

GREIS, Otto (1913-) German
| £1419 | $2455 | (21-May-91 WK.M920/R) Compositions (19x24cm-7x9in) s.d.1962 and 1965 canvas on panel (DM 4200) |

GREIVE, Johan Conrad (19th C) Dutch
| £788 | $1552 | (30-Oct-90 CH.AM46) Spankeren (44x33cm-17x13in) s. s.d.1874 verso panel (D.FL 2600) |

GREIVE, Johan Conrad (Jnr) (1837-1891) Dutch
| £8500 | $13940 | (19-Jun-91 S24/R) Dutch village by canal (44x64cm-17x25in) s. panel |

GREL, Schmit (?) ?
| £2051 | $4000 | (10-Oct-90 CH.NY173/R) Classical maidens offering garland of flowers to statue of Cupid (54x64cm-21x25in) s.indis.d. |

GRELL, Louis Frederick (1887-1960) American
| £1156 | $2000 | (12-May-91 H.C136/R) Century of progress (216x320cm-85x126in) s.i. |

GRELLET, Roger (1924-) French?
| £396 | $701 | (7-Apr-91 LT.P228) L'Eglise de Chennevieres (56x76cm-22x30in) s. gouache (F.FR 4000) |

GRENET, Edward (1857-?) French
| £1100 | $2167 | (15-Nov-90 SC4162/R) In studio (23x18cm-9x7in) s. panel |

GRENIER DE SAINT-MARTIN, Francisque Martin Francois (1793-1867) French
£904 $1455 (27-Jun-91 APT.P240) Cheval hunter dans un pre (24x32cm-9x13in) s. (F.FR 9000)
£813 $1626 (4-Feb-91 PLF.P41) Petite fille offrant une fleur a sa mere (23x18cm-9x7in) s.i.d.1838 W/C (F.FR 8000)

GRENIER, Madeleine (1929-1982) French
£937 $1846 (1-Oct-90 CC.P163/R) Lignes (116x55cm-46x22in) s.d.1958 (F.FR 9500)

GRESELY, Gabriel (1712-1756) French
£3631 $6500 (11-Apr-91 SY.NY99/R) Trompe-l'oeil still life of print, letters, pamphlet and quill (48x40cm-19x16in) s.

GRESLEY, Frank (1855-1936) British
£400 $716 (12-Mar-91 N213) In the Dales, Derbyshire with figures resting on river bank, autumn (18x25cm-7x10in) s. W/C htd.white
£500 $895 (12-Mar-91 N210) Swarkestone, Derbyshire, with sheep and figures and church beyond (18x28cm-7x11in) s. W/C htd.white
£500 $820 (21-Jun-91 CBB266) Derbyshire scene (25x15cm-10x6in) s. W/C
£520 $1019 (15-Feb-91 N277) Sheep in river landscape (30x43cm-12x17in) s.d.1892 pencil W/C htd.white
£700 $1365 (12-Oct-90 K384/R) Landscape at Swakeston (18x38cm-7x15in) s. W/C
£780 $1396 (12-Mar-91 N218) Bolton Abbey, Yorkshire, with angler and figures in evening sunlight (25x38cm-10x15in) s. W/C
£1000 $1790 (12-Mar-91 N205) Swarkestone Bridge Derbyshire with figures conversing on path (23x43cm-9x17in) s. W/C htd.white
£1250 $2238 (12-Mar-91 N224) Rest by the stream, sunlit summer scene with figures and stone bridge (41x58cm-16x23in) s. W/C htd.white
£1300 $2431 (1-Aug-90 CSK172) Cottages at Swarkeston s. s.i.label backboard W/C two
£2100 $3969 (26-Sep-90 S250/R) View near Twyford (45x76cm-18x30in) s.d.1872 W/C htd bodycol

GRESLEY, Harold (1892-1967) British
£520 $931 (12-Mar-91 N220) Summer scene with poultry and old farmhouse near Beddgelert, North Wales (28x36cm-11x14in) s. W/C
£650 $1164 (12-Mar-91 N226) Iron Tors, Dovedale, Derbyshire, with cattle watering, figures and dog (25x36cm-10x14in) s. W/C htd.white
£680 $1292 (28-Feb-91 DLY393) Thor's cave, near Derbyshire (28x38cm-11x15in) s. W/C
£720 $1289 (12-Mar-91 N211) The Stepping Stones, Dovedale, Derbyshire, summer landscape with figures (25x38cm-10x15in) s. W/C htd.white
£1050 $1880 (12-Mar-91 N232/R) Haddon Hall, Derbyshire, summer view with angler, shepherd, sheep and dog (28x38cm-11x15in) s. W/C htd.white
£1100 $1969 (12-Mar-91 N223) The Trent at Kings Mills with figures and ducks, Derbyshire (28x38cm-11x15in) s.d.1925 W/C htd.white
£1500 $2685 (12-Mar-91 N204) The Bluebell Wood, Staunton, with children on path (48x38cm-19x15in) s. W/C
£1550 $2775 (12-Mar-91 N233/R) Carter's Mill, Lathkilldale, Derbyshire, with figures and sheep (36x51cm-14x20in) s. W/C htd.white

GRESLEY, J S (1829-1908) British
£1100 $1859 (29-Apr-91 HS220) Rural landscape with figures and cattle. River landscape with cattle crossing stone bridge (21x28cm-8x11in) s. W/C pair

GRESLEY, James S (1829-1908) British
£420 $710 (15-Apr-91 WW112) Harvest time (29x40cm-11x16in) s. W/C stopping out

GRETHE, Carlos (1864-1913) South American
£2365 $4611 (26-Oct-90 BM.B798/R) Dunes landscape with rain clouds and village beyond (56x80cm-22x31in) s. i.verso (DM 7000)

GREUZE (after) (1725-1805) French
£950 $1549 (4-Jul-91 B186) Portrait of a boy (47x36cm-19x14in)
£1150 $2277 (29-Jan-91 OT511) Portrait of a young lady in disarray, holding flowers in her skirt (79x63cm-31x25in) s.indist,A...U...Fitch oval

GREUZE (school) (1725-1805) French
£769 $1500 (24-Oct-90 D.NY2/R) Mother and child in interior (28x23cm-11x9in) bears sig. wash ink
£4057 $8032 (30-Jan-91 APT.P123/R) Portrait presume de Madame Branze en buste. Portrait presume de M. Branze en buste (53x44cm-21x17in) pastel oval pair (F.FR 40000)

GREUZE (style) (1725-1805) French
£923 $1800 (10-Oct-90 D.NY31) The broken pitcher (107x76cm-42x30in) oval
£2551 $5000 (15-Feb-91 DM.D105/R) Portrait of young girl in classical garden setting (142x99cm-56x39in) oval

GREUZE, Jean-Baptiste (1725-1805) French
£21469 $38000 (22-Mar-91 CH.NY661/R) La premiere lecon d'amour (40x32cm-16x13in)
£27119 $48000 (22-Mar-91 CH.NY659/R) La Revenue (46x38cm-18x15in)
£5000 $8450 (16-Apr-91 C228/R) An old man embracing a young woman (222x18cm-87x7in) blk.chk.
£15000 $24450 (2-Jul-91 C163/R) Shepherd with dead wolf on shoulders (34x22cm-13x9in) black chk wash

GREUZE, Jean-Baptiste (1725-1805) French-cont.
£16310	$31478	*(12-Dec-90 ARC.P62/R) Academies d'hommes luttant (40x27cm-16x11in) sanguinne (F.FR 160000)*
£23684	$45000	*(9-Jan-91 CH.NY60/R) Young woman appearing from behind curtain, bringing hand to mouth (42x32cm-17x13in) s. red chk*
£121053	$230000	*(8-Jan-91 SY.NY7/R) The head of a reclining woman (43x33cm-17x13in) red chk.*

GREUZE, Jean-Baptiste (after) (1725-1805) French
£1250	$2375	(12-Sep-90 PHL174/R) La cruche cassee (79x67cm-31x26in)
£1400	$2632	(18-Sep-90 SWS713) Portrait of young girl carrying flowers (109x87cm-43x34in) painted oval
£1600	$2672	(4-Jun-91 SWS1816/R) La cruche cassee (107x86cm-42x34in) oval
£1900	$3097	(4-Jul-91 C691/R) Child with dog (60x50cm-24x20in)

GREUZE, Jean-Baptiste (attrib) (1725-1805) French
£1224	$2400	(6-Nov-90 GF.L2336/R) Portrait of gentleman (57x43cm-22x17in) (S.FR 3000)
£1800	$2934	(4-Jul-91 CH.C690/R) Boy, head and shoulders, in red shirt and grey coat (40x31cm-16x12in) panel
£5034	$9815	(10-Oct-90 ZEL.L1513/R) Portrait of young lady with marguerite (74x57cm-29x22in) oval (DM 15000)
£5410	$9683	(8-Apr-91 CH.R80/R) Busto di fanciulla discinta (41x32cm-16x13in) (I.L 12000000)
£9040	$16000	(22-Mar-91 CH.NY665/R) Portrait of a young lady, wearing a white costume (40x32cm-16x13in)
£22105	$42000	(11-Jan-91 CH.NY68/R) Bacchante (42x34cm-17x13in)
£23684	$45000	(11-Jan-91 CH.NY15/R) La Reveuse (39x31cm-15x12in)
£600	$1062	*(22-Mar-91 APT.P89) Le Paralytique (24x33cm-9x13in) i.d.1777 pen (F.FR 6000)*
£3262	$6296	*(12-Dec-90 ARC.P61/R) L'amour maternel ou la jeune mere (30x23cm-12x9in) pierre noire wash (F.FR 32000)*

GREUZE, Jean-Baptiste (circle) (1725-1805) French
£976	$1600	(19-Jun-91 B.SF1694/R) Jeune fille (34x29cm-13x11in)
£3011	$5932	(30-Oct-90 BU.S251/R) Portrait of woman with thin veil (48x38cm-19x15in) (S.KR 33000)

GREUZE, Jean-Baptiste (style) (1725-1805) French
£1300	$2197	(16-Apr-91 PH138) Interior of tavern with numerous figures (68x98cm-27x39in) indist.s.
£1700	$2941	(20-May-91 SWS108/R) Portrait of a young girl wearing a veil (39x31cm-15x12in)
£1786	$3000	(17-Jul-91 SY.NY147/R) Young girl pausing while reading (53x44cm-21x17in) oval
£2353	$4000	(31-May-91 CH.NY180/R) Portrait of young girl (47x35cm-19x14in) panel oval
£3000	$5070	(18-Apr-91 C53) Portrait of a child, bust length, with an orange and a slice of breadon a table (41x32cm-16x13in) panel
£3100	$5363	(20-May-91 SWS110/R) Portrait of a young girl, head and shoulders wearing a black cap (39x31cm-15x12in)
£1800	$3474	*(12-Dec-90 PH175/R) Study of two young girls (40x32cm-16x13in) pastel delineated oval*

GREVENBROECK, Alessandro (18th C) Italian
£1400	$2758	(30-Oct-90 PH42) Sailing ship in harbour and figures standing on rocky shore by castle (41x57cm-16x22in)

GREVENBROECK, Orazio (17/18th C) Dutch
£3550	$7028	(30-Jan-91 APT.P277/R) Scene de port mediterraneen (63x99cm-25x39in) (F.FR 35000)

GREY, Alfred (19th C) British
£1273	$2418	(12-Sep-90 WO.CO11) Highland cattle (71x97cm-28x38in) s. (E.P 1400)

GREY, James (19th C) British
£1111	$2144	(12-Dec-90 CH.E149) Cottage and roadside scene (37x58cm-15x23in) s.d.1875 (E.P 1200)

GREY-SMITH, Guy (1916-1981) Australian
£2667	$5013	(17-Sep-90 SY.ME120/R) Bayon head (119x97cm-47x38in) s.d.69 canvas on board (A.D 6000)
£2667	$5013	(17-Sep-90 SY.ME100/R) Swamp lands (59x90cm-23x35in) s.d.72 board (A.D 6000)
£2988	$5886	(31-Oct-90 CH.S179/R) By the sea (80x105cm-31x41in) s.d.65 board (A.D 7500)
£4439	$7236	(16-Jun-91 SY.ME27/R) Shrubs on salt pan (92x122cm-36x48in) s.d.74 board (A.D 9500)
£800	$1504	*(17-Sep-90 SY.ME114/R) Seated figure (60x31cm-24x12in) s.d.72 ink (A.D 1800)*
£1067	$2005	*(17-Sep-90 SY.ME37/R) Scull spring (41x58cm-16x23in) s.d.1967 W/C (A.D 2400)*

GRIBBLE, Bernard Finegan (1873-1962) British
£636	$1100	(21-May-91 CL.NY306 R) HMS Bellerophon (51x76cm-20x30in) s.
£900	$1728	(16-Aug-90 B419/R) Taking on a pilot (38x54cm-15x21in) s.

GRIBBLE, Bernard Finegan (1873-1962) British-cont.
£1000 $1790   (14-Mar-91 L350/R) Eastern dock, Dover harbour - shipping before jetty
       and white cliffs (36x43cm-14x17in) s. board
£1500 $2820   (8-Aug-90 PHP167/R) Evening in the Pool of London (70x90cm-28x35in) s.
       i.plaque
£2600 $5070   (18-Oct-90 CSK184/R) Evening in the Pool (71x91cm-28x36in) s.
£3600 $6228   (22-May-91 S156/R) St. George's Eve, 1918- inshore force setting out for
       Zeebrugge (99x173cm-39x68in) s.

GRIEB, Ludwig (1884-) German
£887 $1739   (24-Nov-90 N.M183/R) Lady from Munich (81x66cm-32x26in) s. s.i.verso
       (DM 2600)

GRIEKEN, Jef van (1950-) Belgian
£1496 $2678   (16-Mar-91 KV.L292) Itabira II (90x130cm-35x51in) s. (B.FR 90000)
£843 $1636   (8-Dec-90 KV.L297/R) Igarape-Manaus II (52x72cm-20x28in) s. pastel
       (B.FR 50000)
£998 $1786   (16-Mar-91 KV.L293/R) Ebbtide on the Solimoes (63x77cm-25x30in) s.
       pastel (B.FR 60000)
£1149 $1989   (25-May-91 KV.L311) Market in Manaus (73x95cm-29x37in) s. pastel
       (B.FR 70000)

GRIER, Louis Monro (1864-1920) Australian/British
£700 $1176   (23-Apr-91 SWS325) A meandering river (50x75cm-20x30in) s.i.

GRIER, Sir Edmond Wyly (1862-1957) British
£1257 $2098   (3-Jun-91 R.T165/R) Before ball (163x122cm-64x48in) s.d.1925 (C.D 2400)
£1361 $2273   (3-Jun-91 R.T166/R) La poudreuse (113x127cm-44x50in) s.d.1933
       (C.D 2600)
£3665 $6120   (3-Jun-91 R.T164/R) Portrait of artist's children, twins John and Sylvia
       (91x77cm-36x30in) s. (C.D 7000)

GRIERSON, Charles Iver (1864-1939) British
£560 $1098   (13-Feb-91 PHL94/R) Bridge (30x20cm-12x8in) s. col.wash
£847 $1651   (15-Oct-90 SY.J23/R) Artist and model after the sitting
       (55x77cm-22x30in) s.d.1918 W/C (SA.R 4200)
£1700 $3366   (30-Jan-91 S268/R) Picnic (28x36cm-11x14in) s.d.1921 i.verso W/C

GRIESHABER, H A P (1909-1981) German
£425 $753   (23-Mar-91 WK.M239/R) Study for peasant revolution (26x16cm-10x6in)
       s.i.d.1975 pencil (DM 1250)

GRIFFA, Giorgio (1936-) Italian
£765 $1493   (22-Oct-90 BR.M194/R) Untitled (50x45cm-20x18in) tempera (I.L 1700000)
£1603 $3078   (27-Nov-90 SY.MI77/R) Composizione (103x108cm-41x43in) s.d.1973 painted
       canvas (I.L 3500000)
£610 $1177   (15-Dec-90 S.Z124) Untitled (63x175cm-25x69in) c.1985 gouache burlap
       (S.FR 1500)

GRIFFIER, Jan (17/18th C) Dutch
£34211 $65000   (11-Jan-91 CH.NY72/R) Skaters ona frozen river before a town
       (35x47cm-14x19in) s. panel

GRIFFIER, Jan (circle) (17/18th C) Dutch
£3800 $7334   (11-Dec-90 PH185/R) View on Rhine with river boats and barges, and
       peasants (37x49cm-15x19in) indist.s. panel

GRIFFIER, Jan (elder-attrib) (1652-1718) Dutch
£1812 $3534   (12-Oct-90 AW.H989/R) Rhine landscape with shipping. Landscape
       (15x21cm-6x8in) c.1680 W/C chl. pencil double-sided (DM 5400)

GRIFFIER, Jan (elder-style) (1652-1718) Dutch
£3892 $6578   (2-May-91 CH.AM99/R) A Rhenish river valley with moored barges near a
       castle (27x35cm-11x14in) panel (D.FL 13000)

GRIFFIER, Jan (style) (17/18th C) Dutch
£900 $1800   (7-Feb-91 C172/R) A Rhenish river landscape (33x38cm-13x15in) panel
£1463 $2810   (27-Nov-90 SY.AM3460/R) Figures skating on frozen lake with walled city
       beyond (64x80cm-25x31in) (D.FL 4800)

GRIFFIER, Robert (1688-1750) British
£13712 $27013   (14-Nov-90 D.V106/R) Winter landscape with skaters and sledges on frozen
       canal (24x31cm-9x12in) (A.S 280000)

GRIFFIER, Robert (circle) (1688-1750) British
£4800 $9360   (26-Oct-90 C119/R) An extensive Rhenish landscape with shepherds
       resting, Gothicruins beyond (36x49cm-14x19in)

GRIFFIER, Robert (style) (1688-1750) British
£2400 $4440   (5-Mar-91 PH61/R) Peasants making merry outside inn in mountainous river
       landscape (40x58cm-16x23in) panel
£3000 $5070   (18-Apr-91 C108/R) An extensive Rhenish landscape with boats moored by a
       hamlet and children (41x56cm-16x22in)

GRIFFIN, T B (19th C) American
£888 $1500   (20-Apr-91 WOL.C86/R) Village by lake with mountainous backdrop
                    (41x64cm-16x25in) s.

GRIFFIN, Thomas Bailey (19th C) American
£533 $900   (1-May-91 D.NY47) Alleghany River (30x46cm-12x18in) s. s.i.verso
£938 $1800   (17-Dec-90 SY.NY140/R) Hunting dogs pointing (61x91cm-24x36in) s.
£1064 $2000   (22-Sep-90 WOL.C175/R) Landscape with stream and waterfall
                    (41x61cm-16x24in) s.

GRIFFIN, Vaughan Murray (1903-) Australian
£661 $1249   (25-Sep-90 JRL.S59/R) The bathers (52x41cm-20x16in) s. W/C (A.D 1500)

GRIFFIN, Walter (1861-1935) American
£508 $1000   (18-Nov-90 JRB.C187/R) The cove at Lynne river (30x41cm-12x16in) s.
                    i.verso canvas board

GRIFFITH, Moses (1749-1809) British
£700 $1330   (15-Sep-90 ME155) Halston House, Shropshire (28x18cm-11x7in) ink
                    col.wash W/C

GRIFFITHS, Harley Cameron (1908-) Australian
£579 $1141   (13-Nov-90 J.M77) Port in Spain (24x28cm-9x11in) s.d.68 board
                    (A.D 1500)
£1200 $2328   (6-Dec-90 CSK6/R) Queensland landscape (78x103cm-31x41in) s.d.59
£1448 $2852   (13-Nov-90 J.M342/R) Roses (49x39cm-19x15in) s.d.73 board (A.D 3750)

GRIG, Alex (20th C) ?
£1511 $2462   (12-Jun-91 ZZ.F90) Musicorama (65x92cm-26x36in) s.d.90 (F.FR 15000)

GRIGGS, Samuel W (?-1898) American
£947 $1800   (14-Sep-90 S.BM136/R) Souveniar of Lake George (53x43cm-21x17in) s. oval

GRIGORESCO, Nicolas (1838-1907) ?
£4054 $6608   (10-Jun-91 W.T1418/R) Figure with horse and cart (21x34cm-8x13in) s.
                    (C.D 7500)

GRIGORIEV, Boris (1886-1939) Russian
£1531 $3000   (12-Feb-91 SY.NY109/R) Chilean Andes (51x69cm-20x27in) s.
£6135 $10000   (12-Jun-91 SY.NY36/R) Harvest time (92x80cm-36x31in) s.d.1920 indist.i.
£420 $806   (27-Nov-90 C42/R) At the cabaret (35x31cm-14x12in) s. pencil
£1200 $2340   (10-Oct-90 C385/R) Portrait of a woman (37x26cm-15x10in) s.i.d.24 pencil
£1400 $2730   (10-Oct-90 C384/R) At the cabaret (25x27cm-10x11in) s. pencil

GRIGORIEV, Sergie Alexeyevitch (?-1989) Russian
£510 $903   (18-Mar-91 ARC.P55/R) Le Kievite (80x60cm-31x24in) (F.FR 5100)
£520 $920   (18-Mar-91 ARC.P48/R) Un livre interessant (80x60cm-31x24in) (F.FR 5200)

GRILL, Oswald (1878-1969) Austrian
£779 $1526   (24-Jan-91 D.V26/R) Portrait of Oriental wearing turban
                    (55x43cm-22x17in) i.d.02 (A.S 16000)
£965 $1881   (18-Oct-90 D.V145/R) Landscape in winter (48x70cm-19x28in) s.d.1904
                    panel (A.S 20000)
£1340 $2318   (8-May-91 D.V120/R) Wooded lake landscape (50x84cm-20x33in) s. panel
                    (A.S 28000)

GRILLON, Roger-Maurice (1881-1938) French
£867 $1673   (12-Dec-90 CH.AM76) Fishermen on sailing-boat (96x96cm-38x38in) init.
                    board (D.FL 2800)
£1531 $3000   (12-Feb-91 SY.NY49/R) Nudes in landscape (38x46cm-15x18in) s.
                    s.d.1916verso

GRIMALDI, Giovanni Francesco (1606-1681) Italian
£7179 $14000   (11-Oct-90 SY.NY42/R) Landscape with figures by banks of river
                    (30x40cm-12x16in) octagonal panel
£342 $605   (19-Mar-91 F.M315/R) Paesaggio collinare (19x27cm-7x11in) ink
                    (I.L 750000)
£850 $1632   (18-Feb-91 S14/R) View of town with river and fisherman (22x34cm-9x13in)
                    pen ink
£1500 $2895   (11-Dec-90 C2/R) An extensive river landscape at sunset (19x26cm-7x10in)
                    i. blk.chk. pen
£1600 $3072   (18-Feb-91 S1/R) Design for fresco (20x41cm-8x16in) bears i. pen ink
                    wash over chk
£6000 $9780   (2-Jul-91 C39/R) Wooded river landscape with boats and castle byeond
                    (22x32cm-9x13in) chk pen ink
£16000 $26080   (2-Jul-91 C38/R) Wooded river landscape with tree and town beyond, boat
                    on lake (22x31cm-9x12in) chk pen ink

GRIMALDI, Giovanni Francesco (attrib) (1606-1680) Italian
£2211 $4200   (9-Jan-91 CH.NY7/R) River landscape with boy with rod (20x29cm-8x11in)
                    i. chk pen wash

GRIMALDI, Giovanni Francesco (style) (1606-1680) Italian
£1400 $2688   (29-Nov-90 HB536/R) Baptism of Christ (66x97cm-26x38in)
£2200 $3718   (19-Apr-91 C149/R) The flight into Egypt (46x62cm-18x24in)

GRIMALDI, William (1751-1830) British
£1200	$1980	(10-Jul-91 C160/R) A gentleman in blue coat (7x?cm-3x?in) min.s.d.1796 gold frame blue glass verso oval
£1800	$2970	(10-Jul-91 C147) The Duke of Wellington (6x?cm-2x?in) min.s.d.1819 enamel gilt-metal frame octagonal
£2000	$3300	(10-Jul-91 C146) Sir Joshua Reynolds (13x?cm-5x?in) min.s.d.1811 enamel gilt-wood frame rec.
£2500	$4125	(10-Jul-91 C114/R) H.R.H. Frederica, Duchess of York (7x?cm-3x?in) min. gold frame lock of hair verso oval

GRIMALDI, William (school) (1751-1830) British
£300	$513	(30-Jul-91 CSK36) Lady Colchester (6x?cm-2x?in) min.with sig. oval

GRIMANI, Guido (1871-?) Italian
£2800	$5488	(15-Feb-91 C88/R) Trieste (76x50cm-30x20in) s.i. panel

GRIMELUND, Johannes Martin (1842-1917) Norwegian
£955	$1595	(4-Jun-91 BU.O82/R) Harbour with sailship (61x44cm-24x17in) s.d.1896 panel (N.KR 11000)
£1056	$1775	(23-Apr-91 RAS.K405/R) Field landscape with haystooks (33x55cm-13x22in) s. panel (D.KR 12000)
£1313	$2351	(14-Mar-91 BU.O39/R) September morning, Fjellbacka (47x65cm-19x26in) s.d.1880 i.verso (N.KR 15000)
£3206	$6187	(10-Dec-90 B.O39/R) Harbour with vessels (46x65cm-18x26in) s.d.1885 (N.KR 36000)
£8681	$16927	(11-Oct-90 BU.O47/R) Ferry quay in Kristiania fjord (66x100cm-26x39in) s.i.d.1891 (N.KR 100000)

GRIMM, Ludwig Emil (1790-1863) German
£979	$1899	(7-Dec-90 GB.B5838) Am Rhein am Rhein ... man pointing to writing on panel (20x17cm-8x7in) pen (DM 2800)

GRIMM, Ludwig Emil (attrib) (1790-1863) German
£350	$678	(7-Dec-90 GB.B5839/R) Head of girl with curly hair (28x22cm-11x9in) s.d.c.1840 pencil dr (DM 1000)

GRIMM, Luise Dorothea (1805-1850) German
£391	$743	(28-Feb-91 D.V107/R) Flowering branch (22x25cm-9x10in) mono.d.1840 gouache (A.S 8000)
£617	$1104	(11-Apr-91 D.V299/R) Roses (33x25cm-13x10in) gouache (A.S 13000)

GRIMM, Pierre (1898-) ?
£7650	$14995	(24-Jan-91 EP.M62/R) Estacion de Montreuil (65x80cm-26x31in) s.d.37 (S.P 1400000)

GRIMM, Samuel Hieronymus (1733-1794) Swiss
£1000	$1970	(15-Nov-90 S85/R) Ruined castle above river in Switzerland (28x21cm-11x8in) W/C over pencil
£3000	$5370	(11-Apr-91 S26/R) View of farmhouse in Derbyshire (35x52cm-14x20in) pen W/C over pencil

GRIMM, Walter O (1894-1919) American/German
£699	$1357	(7-Dec-90 GB.B6582) Couple dancing (37x28cm-15x11in) mono. W/C (DM 2000)

GRIMMEL, Ludwig (19th C?) German?
£541	$881	(10-Jun-91 W.T1402) Market day (36x25cm-14x10in) s. panel (C.D 1000)

GRIMMER, Abel (1573-1619) Flemish
£6085	$12049	(30-Jan-91 APT.P191/R) Scene de la vie paysanne (10x13cm-4x5in) panel (F.FR 60000)
£12232	$24098	(14-Nov-90 SY.AM32/R) Church interior (25x37cm-10x15in) s.d.1588 panel (D.FL 40000)
£18609	$36660	(14-Nov-90 D.V70/R) Flemish winter landscape with castle and figures skating on frozen pond (30x43cm-12x17in) panel (A.S 380000)
£35294	$60000	(31-May-91 CH.NY15/R) Summer, peasants harvesting wheat in landscape (25x37cm-10x15in) panel

GRIMMER, Abel (attrib) (1573-1619) Flemish
£2141	$4217	(14-Nov-90 SY.AM23/R) Church interior (33x40cm-13x16in) s.i.d.62 panel (D.FL 7000)

GRIMMER, Abel (circle) (1573-1619) Flemish
£3083	$5982	(7-Dec-90 SY.MO153/R) Paysans au puit (11x18cm-4x7in) on bronze (F.FR 30000)
£4397	$7870	(14-Mar-91 D.V273/R) The Adoration of the Magi (55x77cm-22x30in) panel (A.S 90000)

GRIMMER, Abel (style) (1573-1619) Flemish
£1606	$2586	(27-Jun-91 APT.P100/R) Decembre (28x28cm-11x11in) (F.FR 16000)
£6500	$10595	(3-Jul-91 S218/R) Landscape with Mary and Joseph arriving at inn and nativity (29x43cm-11x17in) panel

GRIMMER, Jacob (1526-1589) Flemish
£27695	$49575	(9-Apr-91 APT.P21/R) L'Automne. L'hiver panel pair (F.FR 280000)

GRIMMER, Jacob (1526-1589) Flemish-cont.

£39000	$63570	(5-Jul-91 C345/R) Wooded landscape with waggoner and drover by pond, vilage nearby (23x38cm-9x15in) panel
£66804	$129599	(7-Dec-90 CH.MO305/R) Scene de paysans aux champs (43x59cm-17x23in) s.d.1546 panel (F.FR 650000)
£1529	$3012	(12-Nov-90 CH.AM10/R) Road through village in wooded upland landscape (24x36cm-9x14in) s. with i.verso pen wash (D.FL 5000)

GRIMMER, Jacob (circle) (1526-1589) Flemish

£8000	$13040	(2-Jul-91 PH75/R) Peasants treading grapes and pouring wine in courtyard before castle (26x37cm-10x15in) panel

GRIMOU, Alexis (1680-1740) French

£8902	$15935	(9-Apr-91 APT.P43/R) Portrait d'enfant (44x35cm-17x14in) (F.FR 90000)
£20555	$39877	(7-Dec-90 SY.MO38/R) Portrait de femme au tambourin (110x86cm-43x34in) (F.FR 200000)
£23000	$37490	(3-Jul-91 PLF.P80/R) Portrait d'un acteur (92x72cm-36x28in) (F.FR 200000)

GRIMOU, Alexis (circle) (1680-1740) French

£4361	$8635	(30-Jan-91 APT.P252/R) Portrait de Mademoiselle de Sens, fille du Prince de Conde (81x65cm-32x26in) oval (F.FR 43000)

GRIMOU, Alexis (school) (1680-1740) French

£1245	$2117	(31-May-91 LD.P11) Le Buveur (15x12cm-6x5in) panel (F.FR 12500)

GRIMSHAW, Atkinson (1836-1893) British

£1600	$2864	(14-Mar-91 B42/R) A moonlit street scene (56x81cm-22x32in) s.d.1881
£4200	$8274	(1-Nov-90 C279/R) The lone heron (51x76cm-20x30in) s.indis.d.1872
£4400	$8536	(4-Dec-90 AG363/R) Figure on moonlit road (21x43cm-8x17in) s.d.1878 board
£4500	$7335	(14-Jun-91 C328/R) The trysting gate (28x44cm-11x17in) s.d.1877
£6800	$13328	(13-Feb-91 S32/R) Old Whitby (35x52cm-14x20in) s.d.1877 s.i.d.verso board
£7400	$12358	(5-Jun-91 S68/R) Autumn (61x51cm-24x20in) s.d.1878
£8000	$15600	(17-Oct-90 PHL290/R) Gloucester docks (61x92cm-24x36in) s.
£8200	$16154	(1-Nov-90 C280/R) Southwark Bridge from Blackfriars by night (35x46cm-14x18in) s.d.1881 board
£14250	$27788	(17-Oct-90 PHL365/R) The gossips, Bonchurch, Isle of Wight (43x31cm-17x12in) s.d.1889 i. backboard board
£16000	$30720	(30-Nov-90 C27/R) Reekie, Glasgow (24x29cm-9x11in) s.i. verso
£18786	$32500	(22-May-91 SY.NY104/R) Autumn, Becketts Park (40x58cm-16x23in) s.d.1882 board
£21965	$38000	(22-May-91 SY.NY105/R) Salthouse Dock, Liverpool (30x46cm-12x18in) s.
£58000	$116000	(8-Feb-91 C142/R) In the golden gloaming (51x76cm-20x30in) s.d.1883
£460	$777	(3-May-91 T238) High Ham - moonlight (20x33cm-8x13in) init.d.83 W/C

GRIMSHAW, Louis (1870-1943) British

£5300	$9222	(27-Mar-91 RB634) Thames and Houses of Parliament in moonlight (28x43cm-11x17in) s. panel
£6000	$11700	(17-Oct-90 PHL211/R) St Peter's church, Leeds (69x50cm-27x20in) s.d.9 1895

GRINO (19th C) ?

£2400	$4704	(14-Feb-91 CSK200) Maltese fishing boats off a coastline (20x25cm-8x10in) s.d.1879 board oval

GRIPS, Charles Joseph (1825-1920) Belgian

£4400	$8668	(13-Nov-90 SWS364/R) An interior scene (34x43cm-13x17in) s.d.1879 panel

GRIS, Juan (1887-1927) Spanish

£86294	$170000	(14-Nov-90 SY.NY394/R) L'enveloppe (32x19cm-13x7in) s.d.7-18
£129575	$231993	(9-Apr-91 BG.P15/R) Carafe et verre (33x19cm-13x7in) s. (F.FR 1310000)
£158259	$283284	(9-Apr-91 BG.P14/R) Carafe, cuillere et vere (33x24cm-13x9in) s.d.21 (F.FR 1600000)
£555556	$911111	(21-Jun-91 GK.B44/R) La fenetre ouverte (66x101cm-26x40in) s.d.1921 (S.FR 1400000)
£1374876	$2461029	(9-Apr-91 BG.P13/R) Guitare (73x60cm-29x24in) s.d.12-13 verso (F.FR 13900000)
£984	$1919	(16-Jan-91 FER.M36) Retrato de Ana Paulova (37x31cm-15x12in) s.d.1921 pencil dr (S.P 180000)
£1411	$2752	(26-Oct-90 APT.P19) Projet d'affiche (22x31cm-9x12in) init.i. lead pencil (F.FR 14000)
£3800	$6118	(24-Jun-91 CSK24/R) Dans la cuisine (26x26cm-10x10in) s. crayon chl ink htd.white
£4315	$8500	(13-Nov-90 CE.NY35/R) Femme devant le miroir (40x29cm-16x11in) s. brush ink wax crayon chl
£103858	$185905	(9-Apr-91 BG.P10/R) Nature morte (45x28cm-18x11in) s.d.4/18 crayon drawing (F.FR 1050000)

GRISET, Ernest (1844-1907) French

£900	$1683	(28-Aug-90 S733/R) Eagle owl (61x41cm-24x16in) s.

GRISON, Francois Adolphe (1845-1914) French

£3231	$5202	(26-Jun-91 KM.K1481/R) In time of flood (21x27cm-8x11in) s. panel (DM 9500)

GRISON, Francois Adolphe (attrib) (1845-1914) French
£1224 $2362   (12-Dec-90 N.M526/R) Gentleman in rococo clothes standing before mirror in elegant interior (22x16cm-9x6in) i. (DM 3500)

GRISOT, Pierre (19th C?) French?
£1194 $2078   (31-Mar-91 FE.P180) Jacotte et son amie s. (F.FR 12000)
£1210 $2033   (28-Apr-91 FE.P153) Trois jeunes danseuses (45x56cm-18x22in) s. (F.FR 12100)

GRISWOLD, Casimir Clayton (1834-1916) American
£6000 $11760   (15-Feb-91 C81/R) Ponte Milvio, Rome (42x84cm-17x33in) s.d.1879

GRITCHENKO, Alexis (1883-) Russian
£906 $1748   (12-Dec-90 RAS.K226/R) Still life of oysters on dish (24x40cm-9x16in) s. (D.KR 10000)

GRITTEN, Henry C (1818-1873) British
£1267 $2141   (15-Apr-91 AAA.S197) Waterfall (30x23cm-12x9in) one s. board pair (A.D 2800)
£1544 $3042   (13-Nov-90 J.M298/R) Quiet river bend (29x44cm-11x17in) s.d.1863 board (A.D 4000)

GRIVAZ, Eugene (1859-1915) Swiss
£694 $1200   (21-May-91 CE.NY175/R) Courtship (51x36cm-20x14in) s. W/C paperboard

GROBE, German (1857-1938) German
£584 $1110   (2-Mar-91 KRA.D318) Beach scene with fishing boats (31x22cm-12x9in) s. (DM 1700)
£839 $1636   (10-Oct-90 ZEL.L1514/R) Lake landscape with sailing boats (34x47cm-13x19in) s. (DM 2500)
£1049 $2024   (10-Dec-90 L.K428) Idyllic beach scene with young Frisian woman seated in grass knitting (41x50cm-16x20in) s. (DM 3000)
£1531 $2464   (26-Jun-91 KM.K1482/R) Coastal landscape with fishing boats entering harbour, evening (90x121cm-35x48in) s. (DM 4500)

GROBON, Francois Frederic (1815-1901) French
£1404 $2738   (12-Oct-90 ZZ.F65/R) Paysage a la cascade s. (F.FR 14000)
£2213 $4338   (22-Jan-91 YC.P52) Le coup de vent (151x191cm-59x75in) s. (F.FR 22000)

GROEBER, Hermann (1865-1935) German
£1294 $2497   (12-Dec-90 N.M527/R) Portrait of young boy seated in armchair (88x71cm-35x28in) s. i.d.1908verso (DM 3700)
£2740 $4904   (13-Mar-91 N.M508/R) Peasant servants seated on bench in farmhouse interior (50x43cm-20x17in) s. board (DM 8000)

GROEN, Hendrik Pieter (1886-1964) Dutch
£610 $1159   (26-Feb-91 VN.R116/R) Still life of fungi, chestnuts and fruit (59x79cm-23x31in) (D.FL 2000)

GROENESTEIN, Jan (19th C) Dutch
£1011 $1708   (15-Apr-91 SY.J423/R) Still life with artist's brushes and figure on horse (100x75cm-39x30in) s.d.57 (SA.R 4800)

GROENEVELD, Cornelius (18th C) Dutch
£628 $1049   (4-Jun-91 R.T257/R) Mother attending children in interior (60x76cm-24x30in) s. (C.D 1200)

GROENEWEGEN, A J (1874-1963) Dutch
£793 $1506   (26-Feb-91 VN.R118) Landscape (22x30cm-9x12in) panel (D.FL 2600)

GROENEWEGEN, Adrianus Johannes (1874-1963) Dutch
£1152 $2268   (30-Oct-90 CH.AM242) Cows in meadow by farm (33x43cm-13x17in) s. (D.FL 3800)
£450 $797   (22-Mar-91 PHE98) Cattle grazing in water meadow (25x34cm-10x13in) s. W/C
£480 $850   (22-Mar-91 PHE27) Milking time (26x34cm-10x13in) s. W/C
£500 $865   (9-May-91 CSK13/R) Shepherdess with flock (29x39cm-11x15in) s. pencil W/C
£560 $1042   (3-Sep-90 SWS1450) Cattle watering near windmill in Dutch river landscape (20x30cm-8x12in) s. W/C
£1078 $1811   (23-Apr-91 SY.AM224) Shepherd with flock (49x34cm-19x13in) s. W/C (D.FL 3600)
£1257 $2113   (23-Apr-91 SY.AM200/R) Cattle in meadow. Milking time (33x51cm-13x20in) one s. W/C pair (D.FL 4200)
£1557 $3036   (25-Oct-90 VN.R33/R) Milking time (25x36cm-10x14in) s. W/C (D.FL 5200)

GROENEWEGEN, Pieter Anthonisz van (?-1658) Dutch
£1684 $2912   (6-May-91 ZEL.L1717/R) Landscape with ruins and figures on road (32x40cm-13x16in) panel (DM 5000)

GROGER, Friedrich Carl (1766-1838) German
£10110 $19816   (6-Nov-90 BA.S87/R) Portraits of Emelie and J.F. Petersen (205x148cm-81x58in) s.d.1806 (S.KR 110000)

GROISEILLIEZ, Marcelin de (1837-1880) French
£820 $1517   (4-Mar-91 PHB40/R) Canal with figures (27x46cm-11x18in) s.

GROLL, Albert Lorey (1866-1952) American
£952 $1600   (28-Apr-91 HG.C15) Desert clouds (64x76cm-25x30in) s.

GROLLERON, Paul Louis Narcisse (1848-1901) French
£1786 $3000   (17-Jul-91 SY.NY247/R) On patrol (65x46cm-26x18in) s.

GROMAIRE, Marcel (1892-1971) French
£14712	$24863	(17-Apr-91 CB.P42/R) Les bords de la Dordogne (82x100cm-32x39in) s.d.1949 i. verso (F.FR 148000)
£24000	$46800	(19-Oct-90 C143/R) L'antiquaire (81x65cm-32x26in) s.d.1922
£32389	$63482	(24-Nov-90 APT.P890/R) Personnages a l'oree d'un bois (81x100cm-32x39in) s.d.1954 i. verso (F.FR 320000)
£323	$634	(17-Feb-91 E.LA55) le remorqueur (24x32cm-9x13in) s. Indian ink (F.FR 3200)
£615	$1200	(10-Oct-90 SY.NY34/R) Maison avec arbres (23x30cm-9x12in) s.d.1927 ink
£1017	$1923	(25-Sep-90 FB.P291/R) Nu a la chaise (31x23cm-12x9in) s.d.1926 Indian ink (F.FR 10000)
£1020	$2010	(16-Nov-90 LGB.P103/R) Bords de riviere et bateau (25x32cm-10x13in) s.d.1945 pen (F.FR 10000)
£1224	$2376	(8-Dec-90 GAB.G2620) Arbres au bord de l'eau (25x33cm-10x13in) s.d.1957 Indian ink (S.FR 3000)
£1292	$2184	(15-Apr-91 CC.P13/R) Femme assise de face (33x25cm-13x10in) studio st. Indian ink (F.FR 13000)
£1292	$2184	(15-Apr-91 CC.P14/R) Femme nue asise aux bas (33x25cm-13x10in) studio st. Indian ink (F.FR 13000)
£1336	$2592	(5-Dec-90 ZZ.F38) Nu (31x23cm-12x9in) Y (F.FR 13000)
£1474	$2947	(6-Feb-91 LD.P78/R) Nu etendu (24x33cm-9x13in) s.d.1954 Indian ink (F.FR 14500)
£1495	$2646	(7-Apr-91 I.N158) Nu. Paysage (24x32cm-9x13in) s. pen double-sided (F.FR 15100)
£1627	$2668	(19-Jun-91 GK.B433) Nude girl reclining on couch (22x32cm-9x13in) s.d.1929 indian ink pen (S.FR 4100)
£1721	$3372	(22-Nov-90 ZZ.F8/R) Femme allongee (24x31cm-9x12in) s. Indian ink (F.FR 17000)
£2049	$4016	(11-Nov-90 ZZ.F231/R) Bateau dans la baie (25x33cm-10x13in) s. Indian ink (F.FR 20000)
£2141	$3640	(29-May-91 GL.P94/R) Nu assis (32x25cm-13x10in) s.d.1954 Indian ink (F.FR 21500)
£2396	$4623	(15-Dec-90 D.P4/R) Jeune femme debout (27x20cm-11x8in) s.d.1957 indian ink (F.FR 23500)
£2538	$5000	(13-Nov-90 CE.NY85/R) Nu allonge (51x63cm-20x25in) s.d.1923 chl chk
£3083	$5982	(9-Dec-90 E.LA86) Nu sur une chaise (30x26cm-12x10in) s. Indian ink (F.FR 30000)
£3689	$7230	(11-Nov-90 ZZ.F220/R) Nu assis (32x24cm-13x9in) s.d.1964 Indian ink (F.FR 36000)
£4569	$9000	(2-Oct-90 CH.NY103/R) Fermier (39x32cm-15x13in) s.d.1929 gouache W/C Indian ink paper laid board
£6045	$11848	(11-Nov-90 ZZ.F174/R) Maison sur le port (32x43cm-13x17in) s.d.1954 W/C (F.FR 59000)

GRONDARD, Philippe (attrib) (19/20th C) French
£684 $1300   (9-Jan-91 D.NY35) Preparing meal (33x41cm-13x16in) bears sig. i.verso board

GRONE, Ferdinand E (fl.1888-1919) British
£1400 $2772   (30-Jan-91 S279/R) Seventy years ago, my darling, seventy years ago (34x48cm-13x19in) s. i.verso W/C

GRONHOLM, Paul (1907-) Finnish
£2354 $4613   (24-Nov-90 HOR.H98/R) The red tablecloth (55x33cm-22x13in) s.d.1957 (F.M 16500)

GRONLAND, Nelius (1859-?) French
£839	$1636	(13-Oct-90 KRA.D216/R) Still life with yellow roses in sculptured vase (60x75cm-24x30in) s.d.1913 (DM 2500)
£1715	$3395	(31-Jan-91 D.V41/R) Girl wearing Southern costume (109x65cm-43x26in) s. (A.S 35000)

GRONLAND, R (1849-?) German
£1026 $2000   (20-Oct-90 FA.PH836/R) Still life with game (79x64cm-31x25in) s.

GRONLAND, Rene (1849-?) German
£1800 $2952   (19-Jun-91 S77/R) Still life of game and fruit (78x61cm-31x24in) s.

GRONLAND, Theude (1817-1876) German
£1700	$3332	(22-Nov-90 CSK203) Cobbler (41x48cm-16x19in) s.d.1837
£3000	$5760	(27-Nov-90 PH144/R) Still lifes with roses (17x25cm-7x10in) s. board pair
£4514	$7538	(4-Jun-91 BU.O57/R) Still life of fruit (78x103cm-31x41in) s.d.1871 N.KR 52000)

GRONOW, Mortimer (19/20th C) ?
£910 $1775   (16-Oct-90 CS.L25/R) Bords du Loing - Coteaux de Nemours (60x74cm-24x29in) s. (F.FR 9000)

GRONVALL, Sven (1908-1975) Finnish
£689 $1164   (20-Apr-91 HOR.H85/R) Harvesting (44x54cm-17x21in) s. (F.M 4800)

GRONVOLD, Hendrik (1858-1940) British
£350   *$672*   *(19-Feb-91 C11/R) Desert birds of eastern Canary Islands (25x33cm-10x13in) s.i. W/C htd.white*

GRONVOLD, Marcus (1845-1929) Norwegian
£1693 $2827   (3-Jun-91 B.O56/R) The promenade (72x45cm-28x18in) s.d.1916 (N.KR 19500)

GROOMS, Red (1937-) American
£1429 $2800   (6-Nov-90 CE.NY37/R) Palermo (61x48cm-24x19in) s.i.d.1968 ink shaped paper
£1667 $3250   (10-Oct-90 SY.NY354/R) Saskia (66x51cm-26x20in) s.i.d.73 acrylic over chl
£2051 $4000   (10-Oct-90 SY.NY436/R) Traffic jam in Tortola (61x46cm-24x18in) s.d.81 W/C
£4337 $8500   (6-Nov-90 CE.NY36/R) Terrorists (58x89cm-23x35in) s.d.1969 felt-tip pen col.inks
£5584 $11000   (4-Oct-90 SY.NY223/R) Hotline (106x75cm-42x30in) s.d.80 gouache

GROOT, Frans Arnold Breuhaus de (1824-1872) Belgian
£2610 $4673   (11-Apr-91 D.V233/R) Dutch farmstead (34x40cm-13x16in) s. (A.S 55000)

GROOT, Frans Breuhaus de (1796-1875) Dutch
£719 $1365   (11-Sep-90 SY.AM31) Figures on path in wooded landscape (20x19cm-8x7in) init. panel (D.FL 2400)
£2273 $4477   (30-Oct-90 CH.AM11/R) Herds resting by watermill in forest (25x19cm-10x7in) s. panel (D.FL 7500)
£2700 $5319   (13-Nov-90 SWS335/R) A Dutch river scene with figures in a rowing boat nearing a chateau (51x61cm-20x24in) s.

GROOTERS (?) ?
£1300 $2405   (7-Mar-91 CSK186) On the Grand Canal, Venice (63x79cm-25x31in) s.

GROOTVELT, Jan Hendrik van (1808-1855) Dutch
£1515 $2985   (30-Oct-90 CH.AM172/R) Maid serving glass of wine to sportsman in inn by candlelight (29x34cm-11x13in) s.d.1834 panel (D.FL 5000)
£5200 $9984   (28-Nov-90 S48/R) Outside the inn (45x58cm-18x23in) s.d.1841 panel

GROPPE, Johanna Luise (1863-?) German
£1859 $3327   (13-Apr-91 FAL.M94/R) 'Hyade' (80x110cm-31x43in) s. (S.KR 20000)

GROPPER, William (1897-1977) American
£1183 $2000   (1-May-91 B.SF5145/R) Rabbi (25x18cm-10x7in) s. on tin
£1531 $3000   (7-Nov-90 B.SF3811/R) The West (35x66cm-14x26in) s.
£1852 $3500   (27-Sep-90 CH.NY283/R) Bill of particulars (51x41cm-20x16in) s.
£2551 $5000   (7-Nov-90 B.SF3830/R) Minority leader (41x29cm-16x11in) s. board
£4070 $7000   (19-May-91 LIT.L85) Bench worker (43x36cm-17x14in) s. masonite
£4167 $8000   (17-Dec-90 SY.NY373/R) Opera patrons (56x36cm-22x14in) s. st.verso
£13408 $24000   (12-Apr-91 SY.NY101/R) Untouchables (102x127cm-40x50in) s.
£794 $1500   (25-Sep-90 CE.NY94/R) Study for The Student (51x36cm-20x14in) s. bears st. verso pastel paper laid on board
£1628 $2800   (15-May-91 SY.NY195/R) Homework (49x34cm-19x13in) s. artist's st.verso gouache canvas on panel

GROS, Antoine Jean (circle) (1771-1835) French
£2471 $4200   (31-May-91 CH.NY218/R) Portrait of gentleman said to be Marechal Macdonald standing in uniform (64x54cm-25x21in) bears d.1808

GROS, Baron (19th C) ?
£1682   *$3246*   *(10-Dec-90 BL.P9/R) Vue d'Hacahousiatta. Lavoir public a Jalapa. Vue des environs de Mexico all s.d.1835 crayon wash three (F.FR 16500)*

GROSE, Captain Francis (1731-1791) British
£470   *$799*   *(29-May-91 PHC59) Italianate lake landscape (31x44cm-12x17in) i.verso W/C*

GROSE, D C (1865-1890) American
£920 $1600   (29-Mar-91 E.EDM760/R) Autumn landscape (38x66cm-15x26in) s.

GROSE, Daniel C (1865-1890) American
£2030 $4000   (16-Nov-90 S.BM43/R) Landscape scene with cattle grazing (66x114cm-26x45in) s.

GROSJEAN, Cl (?) ?
£750 $1342   (9-Apr-91 GM.B592/R) Vasque garnie de roses (90x70cm-35x28in) s. (B.FR 46000)

GROSJEAN, Henry (1864-1948) French
£679 $1147   (16-Apr-91 J.M891) The Valley (64x91cm-25x36in) s. (A.D 1500)
£740 $1436   (3-Dec-90 CS.L35) Paysage de Revermont (89x145cm-35x57in) s. (F.FR 7200)
£750 $1260   (26-Apr-91 ARC.P34/R) L'oree du bois (53x79cm-21x31in) s. (F.FR 7500)

GROSPERIN, Claude (1936-) Swiss?
£513 $1000   (10-Oct-90 D.NY33) Violon et fleurs (81x99cm-32x39in) s. i.verso

GROSPIETSCH, Florian (1789-1830) German
£405 $689 (31-May-91 GB.B5785/R) *Knight saying farewell before fortified castle (26x41cm-10x16in) d.1828 pen wash htd.white (DM 1200)*

GROSS, Anthony (1905-) British
£900 $1692 (18-Sep-90 PH216/R) *Fountain square (50x59cm-20x23in)* init.
£750 $1463 (9-Oct-90 B41/R) *Betty's Buckhorn Bar, New Orleans (37x57cm-15x22in)* s. pen wash
£750 $1388 (5-Mar-91 PH28) *Jupiter landscape (37x55cm-15x22in)* s. W/C pen indian ink

GROSS, Gaetano (1956-) ?
£3644 $7142 (25-Nov-90 LC.P152/R) *L'artiste et son modele (49x72cm-19x28in)* s.d.1985 panel (F.FR 36000)
£4453 $8729 (25-Nov-90 LC.P138/R) *Composition au cratere grec (70x100cm-28x39in)* s.d.1984 panel (F.FR 44000)

GROSS, Valentine see HUGO, Valentine

GROSSE, Franz Theodore (1829-1891) German
£1900 $3211 (2-May-91 CG429/R) *Portrait of Miss Hedwig Henschel, seated in evening dress, holding fan (50x37cm-20x15in)* mono.d.1884 panel

GROSSEN, E (19th C) Swiss
£556 $961 (6-May-91 ZEL.L1718/R) *View of Lauterbrunnental with Staubbachfall and Jungfrau range (12x17cm-5x7in)* s. board (DM 1650)

GROSSI, Carlo (1857-1931) Italian
£2200 $3784 (17-May-91 C229/R) *Peonies in vase (96x64cm-38x25in)* s. s.i.verso

GROSSO, Giacomo (1860-1938) Italian
£3083 $5982 (8-Dec-90 SY.MO355/R) *Fillette aux roses (150x100cm-59x39in)* (F.FR 30000)

GROSZ, George (1893-1959) German
£1554 $3000 (14-Dec-90 DM.D2020/R) *Model (23x15cm-9x6in)* s.d.1940 artist board
£3179 $5500 (21-May-91 CE.NY689/R) *Golden City (62x39cm-24x15in)* masonite
£5584 $11000 (3-Oct-90 SY.NY78/R) *Gothic wood and the nymph (81x60cm-32x24in)* indis.s. s.d.1945verso s.d.stretcher
£508 $849 (6-Jun-91 HN.H380) *Passing by (17x11cm-7x4in)* s. pencil (DM 1500)
£582 $1100 (25-Sep-90 CE.NY174/R) *George Grosz (46x61cm-18x24in)* s.i. W/C
£694 $1200 (21-May-91 CE.NY650/R) *View of New York from Central Park (17x11cm-7x4in)* W/C ink board
£952 $1562 (19-Jun-91 GK.B435) *Ile de Brehat, Bretagne (23x30cm-9x12in)* s.i. pencil (S.FR 2400)
£1195 $2032 (2-Jun-91 GL.P35/R) *Ne debout, bras leves (21x14cm-8x6in)* lead pencil (F.FR 12000)
£1276 $2450 (26-Nov-90 WK.M236) *Dune landscape, Cape Cod (36x46cm-14x18in)* s.c.1949 W/C board (DM 3700)
£1276 $2500 (12-Feb-91 SY.NY59/R) *Dr Fritz Adler (58x41cm-23x16in)* st.sig.indis.i. i.verso indian ink pencil
£1302 $2500 (17-Dec-90 SY.NY422/R) *Sea anatomy (46x36cm-18x14in)* st.sig. d.1958 estate st.verso collage board
£1351 $2297 (1-Jun-91 VG.B192/R) *Tartarin's collection of murder instruments. Study of running Egyptian (23x33cm-9x13in)* s.i. indian ink pen (DM 4000)
£1706 $3345 (24-Nov-90 VG.B291/R) *Ivan Goll, der ewige Burger (53x41cm-21x16in)* st.sig.i.d.1922 W/C pen over pencil board (DM 5000)
£2030 $4000 (13-Nov-90 CE.NY221/R) *Drei Biertrinker (59x46cm-23x18in)* s.d.38 st.studio i.verso pencil
£2030 $4000 (3-Oct-90 SY.NY74/R) *Double image (26x16cm-10x6in)* s. st.studio verso pencil
£2368 $4500 (14-Sep-90 S.BM326/R) *Street scenes (61x51cm-24x20in)* s.i. pencil double-sided
£2551 $5000 (15-Feb-91 SY.NY74/R) *Kleine Husche (54x42cm-21x17in)* s.i.d.1925 i.verso india ink
£2775 $4800 (7-May-91 CE.NY92/R) *Christmas story (58x46cm-23x18in)* s. st.num.676 verso pen pencil
£3209 $5456 (30-May-91 SY.BE23) *Portrait of Rudolf Schlichter (53x39cm-21x15in)* i. indian ink brush (DM 9500)
£3299 $6500 (3-Oct-90 SY.NY79/R) *Nocturne in minor key (44x56cm-17x22in)* s. i.st.studio verso brush ink W/C
£3500 $6195 (19-Mar-91 C76/R) *Lesende mann (22x28cm-9x11in)* st.sig. Nachlass st.num.VC 353-35 verso pencil
£3807 $7500 (13-Nov-90 CE.NY222/R) *Klienten der Prostitution (56x38cm-22x15in)* s. pen ink
£4036 $7750 (17-Dec-90 SY.NY320/R) *Blue sky, no. 3 (30x23cm-12x9in)* s. W/C
£4469 $8000 (12-Apr-91 SY.NY86/R) *New York harbour (29x43cm-11x17in)* s.d.34 W/C
£4615 $9000 (10-Oct-90 SY.NY122/R) *Standing nude (58x46cm-23x18in)* st.sig. st.studio i.verso gouache
£4762 $9000 (27-Sep-90 CH.NY273/R) *City lights (42x60cm-17x24in)* s. W/C paper laid down on canvas
£4778 $9365 (24-Nov-90 VG.B169/R) *The republic, a scarecrow (65x50cm-26x20in)* s.i. indian ink brush (DM 14000)
£5076 $10000 (13-Nov-90 CE.NY248/R) *Frauenakt (48x63cm-19x25in)* st.sig.d.1939 st.studio i.verso gouache W/C

GROSZ, George (1893-1959) German-cont.

£5076	$10000	(3-Oct-90 SY.NY76/R) Zur Schlachtbank fur's Vaterland (60x52cm-24x20in) st.sig.i.d.1924 i.st.studio verso brush ink
£5085	$8492	(6-Jun-91 HN.H377/R) Cheated (41x26cm-16x10in) s. pen (DM 15000)
£5743	$9764	(30-May-91 SY.BE25/R) Study for painting Ball Room (54x42cm-21x17in) s.d.26 indian ink pen (DM 17000)
£6143	$12041	(24-Nov-90 VG.B171/R) Moonlit night (17x30cm-7x12in) s.i. pen col.chk (DM 18000)
£6588	$11397	(21-May-91 WK.M39 a/R) Reclining female nude (37x57cm-15x22in) st.sig.d.1940 W/C (DM 19500)
£6599	$13000	(3-Oct-90 SY.NY77/R) So smells defeat (58x42cm-23x17in) s. W/C india ink
£7509	$14717	(24-Nov-90 VG.B170/R) Two women (48x67cm-19x26in) s.i. W/C over pen (DM 22000)
£7514	$13000	(9-May-91 CH.NY127/R) Mann mit Waffe. Zwei sitzende Frauen (53x46cm-21x18in) s.tsig. Indian ink double-sided
£7514	$13000	(9-May-91 CH.NY128/R) Akt mit grauen hut (64x43cm-25x17in) s. W/C
£8629	$17000	(3-Oct-90 SY.NY80/R) Ein Kindlein soll sie fuhren (48x62cm-19x24in) s.s. W/C india ink
£8669	$16731	(12-Dec-90 CH.AM314/R) Mann am tisch (38x34cm-15x13in) s.d.15 pen W/C (D.FL 28000)
£9137	$18000	(14-Nov-90 SY.NY135/R) Heroic thoughts (39x30cm-15x12in) s.d. pen
£9556	$18730	(24-Nov-90 VG.B167/R) Couple wearing riding outfit. Sketch of store (50x39cm-20x15in) s. pen dr. W/C board double-sided (DM 28000)
£9827	$17000	(9-May-91 CH.NY157/R) Attackiert (48x65cm-19x26in) W/C Indian ink
£10135	$17230	(30-May-91 SY.BE21/R) Couple undressing, brothel scene (74x55cm-29x22in) s. W/C (DM 30000)
£12000	$21240	(19-Mar-91 C69/R) Die passanten (60x46cm-24x18in) s. pencil
£12717	$22000	(9-May-91 CH.NY119/R) Strassenfeger (62x44cm-24x17in) W/C
£13198	$26000	(15-Nov-90 CH.NY150/R) Sitzender Akt (65x45cm-26x18in) s. W/C
£16216	$27568	(30-May-91 SY.BE20/R) Berlin street scene (66x48cm-26x19in) s. W/C (DM 48000)
£18782	$37000	(14-Nov-90 SY.NY137/R) Tauwetter (46x60cm-18x24in) s. W/C over pen
£20812	$41000	(14-Nov-90 SY.NY136/R) Street scene (63x49cm-25x19in) s. W/C indian ink
£21965	$38000	(9-May-91 CH.NY158/R) Study for - I am a camera (58x39cm-23x15in) s. W/C pen over pencil
£22184	$43481	(23-Nov-90 VG.B38/R) Kaschemme. Woman doing acrobatic exercise (46x30cm-18x12in) s.d.1916 pen dr. (DM 65000)
£26000	$50440	(4-Dec-90 C158/R) Berliner Strassenszene (60x46cm-24x18in) st. ink W/C oil paper
£27027	$46757	(21-May-91 WK.M39/R) Married couple (64x52cm-25x20in) s.i.d.1924 i.verso board W/C over indian ink (DM 80000)
£170000	$329800	(4-Dec-90 C149/R) Menschem im kaffeehaus (57x44cm-22x17in) s.i.d.1918 i.verso W/C ink

GROUCHKO, Boris (20th C) Russian

£503	$965	(18-Feb-91 ARC.P132) Village au bord de la Neva (88x176cm-35x69in) s. (F.FR 5000)
£804	$1544	(18-Feb-91 ARC.P134) Village de pecheurs (30x63cm-12x25in) s. board (F.FR 8000)

GROUX, Charles de (1825-1870) Belgian

£2299	$3977	(25-May-91 KV.L436/R) Les Apprets de la procession (35x42cm-14x17in) s. W/C (B.FR 140000)

GROUX, Henry de (1867-1930) Belgian

£5126	$9175	(11-Mar-91 GL.P56/R) La mort de Siegfried (120x151cm-47x59in) s.d.1899 (F.FR 51000)

GROVE, Nordahl (1822-1885) Danish

£531	$898	(2-May-91 RAS.V44) Wooded landscape with women chatting (79x124cm-31x49in) s. (D.KR 6000)
£621	$1012	(13-Jun-91 RAS.V584/R) Thatched farm on outskirts of wood, winter (47x67cm-19x26in) s.d.80 (D.KR 7000)
£661	$1104	(6-Jun-91 RAS.K54) Large beech tree in Dyrehaven (109x95cm-43x37in) s.d.1865 (D.KR 7500)
£712	$1274	(11-Apr-91 D.V209/R) Winter landscape (43x67cm-17x26in) s.d.1872 (A.S 15000)

GROVES, Mary (fl.1884-1904) British

£2200	$4158	(27-Sep-90 CSK136/R) Revelation (101x66cm-40x26in) s.

GRUAU, Rene (20th C) French?

£3500	$5705	(1-Jul-91 APT.P36/R) Femme a l'ombrelle rose (73x59cm-29x23in) s. (F.FR 35000)
£1166	$1912	(19-Jun-91 JM.P93/R) Comedien au miroir (63x47cm-25x19in) mono. ink (F.FR 11600)
£2820	$4596	(12-Jun-91 ZZ.F132/R) Femme a l'aigrette (36x19cm-14x7in) s. gouache W/C (F.FR 28000)
£3021	$4924	(12-Jun-91 ZZ.F133/R) Femme en robe noire (32x23cm-13x9in) s. gouache W/C (F.FR 30000)

GRUBACS, Carlo (19th C) German

£1400	$2758	(13-Nov-90 SWS338 a/R) The Grand canal, Venice (14x24cm-6x9in) s. panel
£2800	$5488	(22-Nov-90 CSK283/R) St. Mark's Square, Venice (20x26cm-8x10in) s.
£4490	$8710	(8-Dec-90 GAB.G2207/R) Vue de Rialtto. Vue du Palais St-Marc. Vue de la basilique Salute (20x27cm-8x11in) s. three (S.FR 11000)

GRUBACS, Carlo (19th C) German-cont.
£4800 $7872   (18-Jun-91 PH136/R) Figures in the Piazza di San Marco (37x50cm-15x20in)
                    s. pair
£9249 $16000   (23-May-91 CH.NY124/R) Carnivale at the Piazza San Marco, evening
                    (84x120cm-33x47in) s.

GRUBACS, Carlo (attrib) (19th C) German
£1800 $3510   (16-Jan-91 BT143/R) Views of St Mark's, Venice (36x51cm-14x20in) one
                    indis.s. pair
£9000 $17280   (28-Nov-90 S180/R) Figures on the Piazzetta, Venice (98x104cm-39x41in)

GRUBACS, Carlo (style) (19th C) German
£950 $1558   (18-Jun-91 PH120) View of Doge's Palace, Venice (16x23cm-6x9in) board

GRUBACS, Giovanni (1829-1919) Italian
£3200 $6144   (27-Nov-90 PH175/R) The Grand Canal, Venice (20x30cm-8x12in) s. panel
£3200 $6144   (27-Nov-90 PH174/R) View of the Doge's Palace, Venice (16x26cm-6x10in)
                    s. panel
£4200 $8232   (15-Feb-91 C98/R) Doge's Palace and Grand Canal, Venice (15x27cm-6x11in)
                    s. panel
£13500 $22140   (19-Jun-91 S356/R) View of Doge's Palace. View of San Marco, Venice
                    (15x24cm-6x9in) s. panel pair

GRUBACS, Giovanni (attrib) (1829-1919) Italian
£4800 $9312   (6-Dec-90 TL98/R) Views near St.Mark's, Venice (15x25cm-6x10in)
                    indist.s. panel pair

GRUBACS, Giovanni (circle) (1829-1919) Italian
£900 $1476   (20-Jun-91 B32) Doge's Palace, Venice (20x28cm-8x11in) panel
£1150 $2059   (14-Mar-91 B11/R) A view of the Doge's Palace, the Bridge of Sighs and
                    the Prison (15x25cm-6x10in) panel

GRUBACS, M (19th C) ?
£1300 $2561   (4-Oct-90 CSK244) Figures, pigeons, and a dog in front of the Doge's
                    palace, Venice (28x15cm-11x6in) s. panel

GRUBER, Carl (1803-1845) Austrian
£350 $678   *(7-Dec-90 GB.B5841) Parrot (40x31cm-16x12in) s. W/C (DM 1000)*

GRUBER, Francis (1912-1948) French
£147959 $291480   (18-Nov-90 H.A130/R) L'atelier du peintre (92x73cm-36x29in) s.d.1942
                    panel (F.FR 1450000)

GRUBER, Franz Xaver (1801-1862) Austrian
£4452 $7257   (12-Jun-91 N.M442/R) Primulas, anemones and other spring flowers
                    (44x36cm-17x14in) s.d.1851 panel (DM 13000)
£382 $642   *(25-Apr-91 D.V150/R) Onotera biennis and cyclamen europaeum
                    (37x26cm-15x10in) s.i. W/C (A.S 8000)*
£430 $722   *(25-Apr-91 D.V151/R) Thunbergia alata Agiasp (36x26cm-14x10in) s.i. W/C
                    (A.S 9000)*
£621 $1043   *(25-Apr-91 D.V152/R) Azalia mediflora alba (37x26cm-15x10in) s.i. W/C
                    (A.S 13000)*

GRUBER-WURFEL, Maria (1894-1965) Austrian
£1206 $2352   (18-Oct-90 D.V147/R) Ybbs an der Donau (67x92cm-26x36in) s.d.1934
                    (A.S 25000)

GRUN, Jules Alexandre (1868-1934) French
£816 $1600   (21-Nov-90 NA.BA45) Nature morte (55x46cm-22x18in) s.
£4523 $7417   (21-Jun-91 SY.MO331/R) Portrait de jeune femme (115x80cm-45x31in)
                    s.d.1916 oval (F.FR 45000)
£4850 $9117   (20-Sep-90 D.V17/R) Avant port de Le Havre (39x68cm-15x27in) s.
                    (A.S 100000)

GRUN, Maurice (1869-1947) French
£2024 $3968   (20-Nov-90 MF.P80) La fileuse (81x65cm-32x26in) s. (F.FR 20000)

GRUNBAUM, Laurent A (1760-?) Austrian
£800 $1320   *(11-Jul-91 S255/R) Portrait of officer seated wearing blue uniform
                    (9x?cm-4x?in) min.s.d.1826 gilt metal frame oval*

GRUND, Johann Jakob Norbert (1755-1812) German
£5139 $9969   (7-Dec-90 SY.MO110/R) Bouquet de fleurs (20x15cm-8x6in) panel
                    (F.FR 50000)
£11000 $21450   (26-Oct-90 C94 a/R) Mixed flowers in vases with a blue tit. Mixed
                    flowers with a cabbagewhite (23x17cm-9x7in) panel pair

GRUND, Norbert Joseph Carl (1717-1767) Czechoslovakian
£3279 $6426   (7-Nov-90 APT.P443/R) Pelerin demandant son chemin. Berger et son chien
                    (9x16cm-4x6in) zinc pair (F.FR 32000)
£9548 $15658   (21-Jun-91 SY.MO296/R) Scenes galantes dans un parc (18x24cm-7x9in) four
                    under glass (F.FR 95000)

GRUNDTVIG, Axel Valdemar (1867-1911) Danish
£890 $1673   (18-Sep-90 BU.K17/R) Seascape with sailship in rough seas
                    (81x124cm-32x49in) s.d.1889 (D.KR 10000)

GRUNENWALD, Jakob (1822-1896) German

£548	$981	(12-Mar-91 FN.S2396) Portrait study of young shepherd leaning on shovel (30x21cm-12x8in) s. board (DM 1600)
£959	$1716	(12-Mar-91 FN.S2395/R) Grape harvest, Neckar valley (15x22cm-6x9in) board (DM 2800)
£1538	$2985	(4-Dec-90 FN.S1850/R) Funeral scene with family (27x43cm-11x17in) s. (DM 4400)

GRUNER, Elioth (1882-1939) Australian

| £5333 | $10027 | (17-Sep-90 SY.ME90/R) Dewy morning (35x35cm-14x14in) s.d.1902 indis.l.verso panel (A.D 12000) |
| £6426 | $12337 | (26-Nov-90 SY.ME250/R) South coast, New South Wales (29x39cm-11x15in) s.d.1932 canvas on board (A.D 16000) |

GRUNERT, Eugen (1856-?) German

| £1463 | $2824 | (14-Dec-90 ZOF.Z953/R) Wood clearing with pond (90x74cm-35x29in) s.l. l.verso (S.FR 3600) |

GRUNEWALD, Isaac (1889-1946) Swedish

£2768	$5314	(27-Nov-90 BU.S109/R) Amaryllis and tulips (45x37cm-18x15in) s. panel (S.KR 30000)
£3019	$5223	(22-May-91 BA.S64 a/R) Amaryllis (46x38cm-18x15in) s. panel (S.KR 32000)
£3137	$6022	(27-Nov-90 BU.S107/R) Portrait of Sigrid Hjerten wearing pink dress (27x21cm-11x8in) s.d.1912 panel (S.KR 34000)
£3345	$5620	(22-Apr-91 BU.K73/R) The proposal (75x46cm-30x18in) s.d.34 (D.KR 38000)
£3707	$7192	(4-Dec-90 BA.S166/R) Flowers in vase (46x38cm-18x15in) s. (S.KR 40000)
£4151	$7970	(27-Nov-90 BU.S102/R) Still life of flowers (55x46cm-22x18in) s. panel (S.KR 45000)
£5190	$10069	(4-Dec-90 BA.S167/R) Amaryllis (54x65cm-21x26in) s. panel (S.KR 56000)
£5351	$10273	(27-Nov-90 BU.S108/R) Still life of amaryllis (66x53cm-26x21in) s. panel (S.KR 58000)
£5561	$10788	(5-Dec-90 AB.S7084/R) Katarinavagen, view from Sodermalm, Stockholm (64x53cm-25x21in) s. (S.KR 60000)
£6642	$12753	(27-Nov-90 BU.S101/R) Red crane (81x65cm-32x26in) (S.KR 72000)
£7170	$12404	(22-May-91 BA.S64/R) The old chimney (65x54cm-26x21in) s. (S.KR 76000)
£7959	$13689	(14-May-91 BU.S94/R) Thawing, Katarina Street (55x50cm-22x20in) s. (S.KR 85000)
£8395	$16118	(27-Nov-90 BU.S103/R) Still life of flowers (73x60cm-29x24in) s. (S.KR 91000)
£9082	$17529	(12-Dec-90 BU.S154/R) Amaryllis in blue vase (93x73cm-37x29in) s. (S.KR 98000)
£9225	$17712	(27-Nov-90 BU.S99/R) Still life of flowers (65x92cm-26x36in) (S.KR 100000)
£10870	$20978	(12-Dec-90 RAS.K212/R) Autumn landscape with rainbow (64x80cm-25x31in) s.d.45 (D.KR 120000)
£12547	$21707	(22-May-91 BA.S62/R) Sigrid wearing the green hat (73x54cm-29x21in) (S.KR 133000)
£15221	$29225	(27-Nov-90 BU.S98/R) The round window (81x100cm-32x39in) s. (S.KR 165000)
£43358	$83247	(27-Nov-90 BU.S97/R) Cafe Royal (100x81cm-39x32in) (S.KR 470000)
£45876	$88999	(4-Dec-90 BA.S163/R) La belle Polonaise (130x85cm-51x33in) s.d.1923 (S.KR 495000)
£1604	$2775	(22-May-91 BA.S65/R) Model (34x25cm-13x10in) s. W/C (S.KR 17000)
£2600	$4472	(17-May-91 C154/R) On Mediterranean (47x62cm-19x24in) s. W/C bodycol
£2627	$4702	(14-Mar-91 BU.O40/R) Woman in garden (36x26cm-14x10in) s. W/C paper on cardboard (N.KR 30000)
£2817	$4789	(28-May-91 AB.S5207/R) Early morning, Etretat Normandie (50x64cm-20x25in) s. gouache (S.KR 30000)
£3019	$5223	(22-May-91 BA.S64 b/R) Sketch for the curtain at Dragon Cinema (40x125cm-16x49in) s. mixed media (S.KR 32000)
£3256	$6056	(9-Sep-90 BU.M241) 'Soderkakar' view from Stockholm (64x49cm-25x19in) s. mixed media (S.KR 35000)
£4151	$7970	(27-Nov-90 BU.S106/R) Still life of flowers (66x50cm-26x20in) s. gouache oil (S.KR 45000)
£4819	$9349	(5-Dec-90 AB.S7085/R) The blue road (98x68cm-39x27in) s. pastel (S.KR 52000)
£6273	$10790	(14-May-91 BU.S95/R) View of Stockholm (65x47cm-26x19in) s. pastel (S.KR 67000)

GRUNWALD (?) ?

| £1220 | $2257 | (7-Mar-91 D.V51/R) Am Hof, Wien (25x26cm-10x10in) s.l.d.1920 canvas on board (A.S 25000) |

GRUNWALD, Carl (1907-1968) ?

| £1115 | $1895 | (28-May-91 KF.M706/R) Pleasures of winter (34x48cm-13x19in) s.d.1962 mixed media board (DM 3300) |

GRUPPE, Charles Paul (1860-1940) American

£508	$1000	(16-Nov-90 S.BM78/R) Boats at pier, morning (36x51cm-14x20in) s.
£649	$1200	(10-Mar-91 H.C114/R) Landscape with stream and cattle (36x51cm-14x20in) s.
£758	$1500	(30-Jan-91 GRO.B98) Old Lyme (30x41cm-12x16in) s. board
£1081	$2000	(10-Mar-91 H.C113/R) Rocky seacoast (30x41cm-12x16in) s. board
£1269	$2500	(16-Nov-90 S.BM102/R) Marshlands with grazing cattle (71x86cm-28x34in) s.
£1371	$2700	(16-Nov-90 S.BM161/R) Gloucester harbour (30x41cm-12x16in) s. board

GRUPPE, Charles Paul (1860-1940) American-cont.
£1452	$2700	(9-Sep-90 LIT.L271 a) Pastoral scene (51x61cm-20x24in) s.
£599	*$1006*	*(23-Apr-91 SY.AM110) Washing day (49x69cm-19x27in) W/C (D.FL 2000)*
£615	$1200	(20-Oct-90 W.W162/R) By the docks at Dordrecht (36x25cm-14x10in) s.i. W/C

GRUPPE, Emile A (1896-1978) American
£670	$1200	(14-Apr-91 JRB.C161/R) Coastal winter landscape (46x51cm-18x20in) s.
£710	$1200	(20-Apr-91 WOL.C312/R) Landscape with nude (33x33cm-13x13in) s. artist's board
£751	$1300	(10-May-91 S.BM112/R) Bathers on riverbank (25x20cm-10x8in) s. canvas board
£789	$1500	(14-Sep-90 S.BM256/R) Fishing from Bass Rocks (51x61cm-20x24in) s.
£867	$1700	(11-Nov-90 LIT.L76) Gloucester seascape (20x25cm-8x10in) s. board
£895	$1700	(3-Mar-91 LIT.L21) Coastal scene (51x61cm-20x24in) s.
£914	$1800	(7-Oct-90 DU.E62/R) Winter scene (71x97cm-28x38in) s.
£918	$1800	(24-Nov-90 YFA.M61/R) Vermont village (30x41cm-12x16in) s. board
£1000	$1900	(14-Sep-90 S.BM233/R) Along the creek in winter (41x51cm-16x20in) s. i.verso board
£1031	$2000	(24-Aug-90 RB.HY81/R) Fall, Vermont (64x76cm-25x30in) s.d.
£1070	$2000	(30-Aug-90 MFA.C114) Hunter in the woods (51x46cm-20x18in) s.
£1105	$2100	(14-Sep-90 S.BM270/R) Smith Cove, Gloucester (46x51cm-18x20in) s.
£1179	$2300	(25-Oct-90 GRO.B154/R) Fishing boats in Gloucester Harbour (46x51cm-18x20in) s.
£1183	$2000	(17-Apr-91 D.NY81/R) White birch, Vermont (46x51cm-18x20in) s.
£1198	$2300	(17-Dec-90 SY.NY213/R) Sailboats at dock (46x51cm-18x20in) s.
£1250	$2400	(17-Dec-90 SY.NY311/R) Winter landscape (76x91cm-30x36in) s.
£1323	$2500	(29-Sep-90 YFA.M33/R) Autumn in Vermont (46x51cm-18x20in) s.
£1329	$2300	(10-May-91 S.BM106/R) Sugaring Vermont (51x61cm-20x24in) s. i.verso
£1354	$2600	(17-Dec-90 SY.NY212/R) Harbour with sailboats (46x51cm-18x20in) s.
£1453	$2500	(18-May-91 W.W225/R) Morning, Tarpon Spring (64x76cm-25x30in) s. i. stretcher
£1488	$2500	(28-Apr-91 HG.C34) Last light Vermont (64x76cm-25x30in) s.
£1503	$2600	(21-May-91 CE.NY617/R) Woodstock valley in winter (64x76cm-25x30in) s. s.i.verso
£1686	$2900	(18-May-91 W.W218/R) Bahamas (76x91cm-30x36in) s. i. stretcher
£1693	$3250	(17-Dec-90 SY.NY308/R) Landscape with birch trees (76x91cm-30x36in) s.
£1734	$3000	(21-May-91 CE.NY589/R) Fishing boats at dusk (63x76cm-25x30in) s.
£1856	$3600	(5-Dec-90 D.NY116/R) Fishing boats in Gloucester Harbour (61x51cm-24x20in) s. i.d.1957 verso
£1935	$3250	(27-Apr-91 YFA.M109/R) Trout stream (76x91cm-30x36in) s.
£2105	$4000	(14-Sep-90 S.BM278/R) Morning, Rocky Neck (61x51cm-24x20in) s.
£2168	$3750	(10-May-91 S.BM132/R) After the storm (76x91cm-30x36in) s. s.i.verso
£2204	$4100	(9-Sep-90 LIT.L316) Snow scene (28x41cm-11x16in)
£2312	$4000	(10-May-91 S.BM114/R) At the pier, Gloucester Harbour (51x61cm-20x24in) s.
£2368	$4500	(14-Sep-90 S.BM276/R) Fishing off the pier (61x91cm-24x36in) s.
£2368	$4500	(14-Sep-90 S.BM274/R) Gill Netters (64x64cm-25x25in) s.
£2384	$4100	(19-May-91 LIT.L40) Vermont covered bridge, winter scene (64x76cm-25x30in) s.
£2604	$5000	(17-Dec-90 SY.NY411/R) Logging near Mt. Mansfield (76x91cm-30x36in) s.d.1955 stretcher
£2706	$5250	(24-Aug-90 RB.HY80/R) Shrimp boat yard (64x76cm-25x30in) s.
£2835	$5500	(24-Aug-90 RB.HY40/R) Sugaring on Mt.Mansfield, Vt. (76x91cm-30x36in) s.
£3351	$6500	(24-Aug-90 RB.HY124/R) Baiting the fish (51x61cm-20x24in) s.
£4142	$7000	(17-Apr-91 D.NY82/R) Rolling foot hills, spring (76x102cm-30x40in) s.

GRUST, F G (19/20th C) Dutch
£1657	$2800	(20-Apr-91 WOL.C209 c/R) By shore (66x91cm-26x36in) s.
£1775	$3000	(20-Apr-91 WOL.C209 b/R) New baby (76x102cm-30x40in) s.

GRUST, Theodor (1859-?) German
£3736	$6500	(27-Mar-91 B.SF4205/R) Mother and child (76x63cm-30x25in) s.

GRUTTEFIEN, E (19th C) German
£542	$971	(9-Apr-91 RAS.K2061) Norwegian fjordlandscape (80x120cm-31x47in) s. (D.KR 6200)

GRUTZKE, Johannes (20th C) ?
£2000	$3580	(12-Apr-91 AW.H1555/R) Portrait of Lucie Wahren (60x50cm-24x20in) i.d.1981 (DM 6000)
£4392	$7466	(1-Jun-91 VG.B365/R) The sculptor and his models (63x80cm-25x31in) mono.d.1974 i.verso (DM 13000)
£9932	$16188	(14-Jun-91 L.K914/R) Admiration (135x145cm-53x57in) mono.d.69 s.d.verso (DM 29000)
£915	*$1528*	*(8-Jun-91 HN.H127/R) Studio (49x63cm-19x25in) s.d.1982 colour pencil (DM 2700)*
£1000	*$1790*	*(12-Apr-91 AW.H1556/R) Thora (80x45cm-31x18in) .i.d.85 col.chk wash (DM 3000)*
£1186	*$1981*	*(8-Jun-91 HN.H124/R) Self-portrait (41x29cm-16x11in) mono.d.1973 graphite pencil (DM 3500)*
£1712	*$2791*	*(14-Jun-91 L.K915/R) Sei wie ich (53x48cm-21x19in) mono.d.71 s.i.d.verso col.chk pastel (DM 5000)*
£2226	*$3628*	*(14-Jun-91 L.K916/R) Hilmar Thate as Fallada (151x99cm-59x39in) s.i.d.1981 col.chk paper on canvas (DM 6500)*

GRUTZNER, Eduard von (1846-1925) German

£1361	$2190	(26-Jun-91 KM.K1486/R) Portrait of Dominican monk (49x37cm-19x15in) board (DM 4000)
£9091	$17545	(12-Dec-90 WE.MU106/R) Falstaff and the women (42x41cm-17x16in) s. (DM 26000)
£13986	$27133	(4-Dec-90 FN.S1851/R) Cardinal seated in armchair reading in elegant interior (50x40cm-20x16in) s.d.1912 (DM 40000)
£13986	$26993	(12-Dec-90 WE.MU105/R) Monk in cellar interior holding glass of wine (38x30cm-15x12in) s.d.1885 panel (DM 40000)
£18497	$32000	(22-May-91 SY.NY217/R) Der meisterbrauer (49x39cm-19x15in) s.d.1892
£37543	$70956	(25-Sep-90 FN.S2188/R) Falstaff seated in arched cellar with other figures (82x67cm-32x26in) s.d.1899 (DM 110000)
£473	$804	(28-May-91 KF.M170) Malweibchen am hellichten Tage in der Briennerstr (20x11cm-8x4in) mono.i.d.1902 chk (DM 1400)
£473	$804	(28-May-91 KF.M171) Portrait of monk (13x14cm-5x6in) s. pencil board (DM 1400)
£979	$1890	(14-Dec-90 BM.B732/R) Portrait of monk (20x16cm-8x6in) s.d.91 pencil dr. (DM 2800)
£1027	$1675	(12-Jun-91 N.M239/R) Monks conversing at table (22x34cm-9x13in) s. i.verso pecil (DM 3000)

GRUYTER, Jacob Willem (1856-1908) Dutch

£719	$1207	(23-Apr-91 SY.AM171) Marine (22x42cm-9x17in) s.d.77 panel (D.FL 2400)

GRUYTER, Willem (19th C) Dutch

£3000	$4920	(18-Jun-91 PH26/R) Shipping in calm (38x54cm-15x21in) s.d.1858 panel

GRYEFF, Adriaen de (1670-1715) Flemish

£2888	$5170	(10-Apr-91 CB.P45) Volatiles dans un parc (15x21cm-6x8in) s. panel (F.FR 29200)
£3378	$5743	(27-May-91 L.K50/R) Still life in farmyard with peasant, vegetables, game and kitchen things (42x59cm-17x23in) s. (DM 10000)
£3425	$5582	(12-Jun-91 N.M311/R) Swans, ducks and herons by water attached by bird of prey (20x28cm-8x11in) s. panel (DM 10000)
£3756	$6385	(28-May-91 AB.S4761/R) Dogs and dead game by ruins in landscape (60x76cm-24x30in) s. (S.KR 40000)
£5115	$9975	(14-Oct-90 D.L86/R) Epagneuls devant des trophees de chasse (22x17cm-9x7in) panel pair (F.FR 51000)
£8222	$15951	(7-Dec-90 CH.MO304/R) Une halte de chasse. Un chasseur sonnant de la trompe s. pair (F.FR 80000)
£24486	$48237	(14-Nov-90 D.V79/R) Hunting still lifes with figures and dogs in landscape (43x53cm-17x21in) one s. pair (A.S 500000)

GRYEFF, Adriaen de (attrib) (1670-1715) Flemish

£600	$978	(4-Jul-91 C554) Spaniel and whippet watching over game bag of partridges, finches, hare, pheasant at foot of tree (29x23cm-11x9in) paper on panel
£1077	$2122	(14-Nov-90 D.V149/R) Dog guarding bag (19x23cm-7x9in) panel (A.S 22000)
£2000	$3840	(29-Nov-90 CSK75/R) Pomegranates, grapes and other fruit with guinea pigs in landscape (15x24cm-6x9in) painted surround

GRYEFF, Adriaen de (circle) (1670-1715) Flemish

£1400	$2366	(18-Apr-91 C128) Hounds after the chase (23x32cm-9x13in) panel
£2300	$3749	(2-Jul-91 PH283/R) King Charles spaniel seated on cushion by urn of roses (47x63cm-19x25in)

GRYEFF, Adriaen de (style) (1670-1715) Flemish

£1096	$1786	(12-Jun-91 N.M312) Poultry and parrot in river landscape with sheep and cattle (21x29cm-8x11in) panel (DM 3200)

GSCHOSMANN, Ludwig (1901-) German

£881	$1437	(3-Jul-91 WE.MU73/R) Travelling circus (70x80cm-28x31in) s. i.verso (DM 2600)

GSELL, Laurent (1860-1944) French

£1195	$2068	(24-May-91 FB.P74/R) Vue de Paris (56x46cm-22x18in) s. pastel (F.FR 12000)

GUACCIMANNI, A (19/20th C) Italian

£850	$1666	(14-Feb-91 CSK178) A call to prayer (28x20cm-11x8in) indist.sig. panel

GUALA, Pier Francesco (attrib) (1698-1757) Italian

£1923	$3712	(12-Dec-90 N.M373/R) St Domenicus presented with the rosary (168x124cm-66x49in) (DM 5500)

GUALLA, Pietro (?-1760) Italian

£7222	$12061	(6-Jun-91 D.V7/R) Presentation of the rosary to St Dominic and bischof saint (168x124cm-66x49in) shaped (A.S 150000)

GUALLINO, Patrick (20th C) French

£559	$1118	(7-Feb-91 R.P116/R) Chevelure rouge baiser (130x97cm-51x38in) s. acrylic (F.FR 5500)
£579	$1159	(7-Feb-91 R.P248) Sans titre (116x89cm-46x35in) s. acrylic (F.FR 5700)
£589	$1179	(7-Feb-91 R.P57/R) Dans la foret de Broscelliande (81x116cm-32x46in) s. acrylic canvas (F.FR 5800)

GUALLINO, Patrick (20th C) French-cont.
£610 $1220   (7-Feb-91 R.P207/R) Rouge baiser et bleu d'ivresse (130x97cm-51x38in) s.
        acrylic (F.FR 6000)

GUANSE, Antonio (20th C) ?
*£1392 $2352   (16-Apr-91 I.N96) Vieille forteresse (65x50cm-26x20in) s.d.1982 mixed
        media panel (F.FR 14000)*

GUARDABASSI, Guerrino (1841-?) Italian
*£1200 $2280   (12-Sep-90 CSK157/R) In campagna. On ships (53x38cm-21x15in) s.i. pencil
        W/C pair*

GUARDI (?) Italian
£4532 $7387   (11-Jun-91 ZZ.F1/R) Le Grand Canal (11x18cm-4x7in) gouache (F.FR 45000)

GUARDI (style) (18/19th C) Italian
£1538 $2969   (13-Dec-90 N.M2956/R) View of Venice with Santa Maria della Salute
        (69x99cm-27x39in) (DM 4400)
£12500 $21250   (27-May-91 L.K135/R) View of Doge's Palace and Piazetta with figures,
        S.Maria d.Salute beyond (68x110cm-27x43in) (DM 37000)

GUARDI, Francesco (1712-1793) Italian
£14737 $28000   (11-Jan-91 CH.NY59/R) The return of a Roman warrior (71x52cm-28x20in)
£18000 $29340   (5-Jul-91 C217/R) Isola di S. Giorgio Maggiore, Venice, with gondolas,
        sandalos and barge (19x26cm-7x10in)
£28000 $45640   (3-Jul-91 S80/R) Capricci (7x9cm-3x4in) canvas on panel pair
£36181 $59337   (21-Jun-91 SY.MO128/R) Caprices Venitiens (23x17cm-9x7in) pair
        (F.FR 360000)
£52632 $100000   (11-Jan-91 CH.NY65/R) A parade in the Piazza San Marco, Venice
        (67x92cm-26x36in)
£54097 $96833   (8-Apr-91 F.M353/R) Il ridotto (70x97cm-28x38in) painted with studio
        (I.L 120000000)
£60000 $97800   (3-Jul-91 S55/R) View of Rialto Bridge, Venice (23x35cm-9x14in)
£72000 $138960   (12-Dec-90 S51/R) Venice, Santa Maria della Salute with the Punta di
        Dogana (24x35cm-9x14in) panel
£90000 $155700   (24-May-91 C80/R) The Grand Canal, Venice, with the Church of Santa
        Lucia (30x33cm-12x13in)
£100000 $173000   (24-May-91 C78/R) S. Giorgio Maggiore, Venice, with the Giudecca, the
        Church of the Zitelleand shipping (42x67cm-17x26in)
£260000 $501800   (12-Dec-90 S29/R) Church on the Lagoon (36x49cm-14x19in)
£270000 $467100   (24-May-91 C77/R) A capriccio of classical ruins with a peasant woman,
        children, youthsand a soldier admiring a statue (104x123cm-41x48in) s.
£347368 $660000   (11-Jan-91 CH.NY86/R) Piazza San Marco, Venice, looking towards S.
        Geminiano (84x128cm-33x50in)
£365974 $655094   (9-Apr-91 APT.P45/R) Vue de la Place Saint Marc (71x95cm-28x37in)
        (F.FR 3700000)
*£1800 $2934   (1-Jul-91 S9/R) Design for two frames surmounted by Marquis' coronet
        (20x17cm-8x7in) pen wash over red chk*
*£8208 $14528   (19-Mar-91 F.M308/R) Capriccio con edificio e archi (20x18cm-8x7in) pen
        bistre ink W/C (I.L 18000000)*
*£68421 $130000   (8-Jan-91 SY.NY114/R) A Capriccio view of Palladio's project for the
        Rialto bridge (28x44cm-11x17in) ink wash over traces blk.chk.*

GUARDI, Francesco (attrib) (1712-1793) Italian
£8532 $16724   (24-Nov-90 SA.A604/R) Canal scenes, Venice (26x18cm-10x7in) pair
        (DM 25000)
£9827 $17000   (10-May-91 S.BM8/R) Il Palazzo Ducale e gli Edifici adiacenti con Bacino
        di San Marco (66x109cm-26x43in)
£22105 $42000   (11-Jan-91 CH.NY19/R) A Venetian Lagoon capriccio (42x56cm-17x22in)

GUARDI, Francesco (circle) (1712-1793) Italian
£7530 $12123   (27-Jun-91 APT.P50/R) Vases fleuris presentes sur un entablement
        (66x93cm-26x37in) pair (F.FR 75000)
£20000 $38000   (11-Jan-91 CH.NY44/R) A capriccio of buildings and an arch on a lagoon
        with figures (36x50cm-14x20in)

GUARDI, Francesco (school) (1712-1793) Italian
£1637 $3208   (20-Nov-90 F.R60) Gesu Bambino (49x36cm-19x14in) (I.L 3600000)
£3077 $6000   (10-Oct-90 CH.NY87/R) View of Santa Maria dela Salute, Venice
        (47x60cm-19x24in)
£23684 $45000   (11-Jan-91 CH.NY61/R) The Piazza San Marco, Venice with the Basilica and
        the Campanile (51x94cm-20x37in)

GUARDI, Francesco (studio) (1712-1793) Italian
£4897 $9647   (14-Nov-90 D.V237/R) Venetian Campo. Venetian cappriccio with stone arch
        by lagoon (9x12cm-4x5in) canvas on panel pair (A.S 100000)
£68000 $110840   (2-Jul-91 PH78/R) View of the Piazza San Marco looking east with elegant
        figures (34x55cm-13x22in) init.

GUARDI, Francesco (style) (1712-1793) Italian
£726 $1300   (10-Apr-91 HF.NY25/R) Shipwreck (12x11cm-5x4in) panel
£850 $1428   (23-Apr-91 SWS328) Venice, the Piazza san Marco viewed from the west
        (48x57cm-19x22in)
£1200 $2304   (29-Nov-90 CSK260) Figures by ruined archway with lagoon beyond
        (43x36cm-17x14in)
£2232 $3750   (17-Jul-91 SY.NY164/R) Capriccio (47x37cm-19x15in)

GUARDI, Francesco (style) (1712-1793) Italian-cont.

£2400	$4608	(29-Nov-90 CSK146/R) Santa Maria della Salute from Grand Canal (55x71cm-22x28in)
£3000	$4890	(4-Jul-91 C625) Piazza di San Marco, Venice looking towards Basilica (47x66cm-19x26in)
£3274	$5500	(17-Jul-91 SY.NY167/R) View of canal in Venice (46x57cm-18x22in)
£3500	$6895	(1-Nov-90 CSK60/R) Still life with sculptured urn of mixed summer flowers on ledge (105x71cm-41x28in)
£3800	$7220	(13-Sep-90 CSK47/R) Dogana, Venice (23x30cm-9x12in)
£4118	$7000	(30-May-91 SY.NY78/R) View of Dogana with Santa Maria delle Salute and Grand Canal (49x68cm-19x27in)
£5200	$8788	(18-Apr-91 CSK166/R) Figures in Piazza San Marco, Venice (72x123cm-28x48in)
£5944	$11472	(10-Dec-90 L.K49/R) View of Piazza San Marco, Venice (64x80cm-25x31in) (DM 17000)
£7143	$12000	(17-Jul-91 SY.NY163/R) The Grand Canal with view of Santa Maria Della Carita. The Doges Pala ce two
£8736	$16948	(7-Dec-90 SY.MO98/R) Vues de Venise (25x35cm-10x14in) pair (F.FR 85000)
£15454	$25499	(9-Jul-91 ARC.P13/R) Le Rio du Mendicanti. La Place Saint Marc (51x77cm-20x30in) pair (F.FR 155000)
£20555	$39877	(6-Dec-90 NM.P13/R) Le Palais des Doges et la Piazetta. La Piazza San Marco et le Campanile (70x100cm-28x39in) two (F.FR 200000)

GUARDI, Giacomo (1764-1835) Italian

£5000	$8150	(2-Jul-91 PH315/R) Capricci of lagoon before tower and bridge. Gondola on canal by bridge (12x19cm-5x7in) paper on board pair
£8939	$16000	(11-Apr-91 SY.NY125/R) Distant view of Venetian lagoon (7x13cm-3x5in) paper laid down on panel
£63158	$120000	(11-Jan-91 CH.NY9/R) San Giorgio Maggiore, Venice, with the Punta della Giudecca from theBacino di San Marco (18x32cm-7x13in) panel
£2548	$4893	(27-Nov-90 APT.P46/R) Personnage dans une cour a Venise (23x18cm-9x7in) pen wash htd.W/C (F.FR 25000)
£2878	$5583	(7-Dec-90 SY.MO104/R) Vue de San Nicolo avec le Bucintorro (10x16cm-4x6in) bears i. gouache (F.FR 28000)
£4600	$7498	(1-Jul-91 S94/R) Rialto Bridge (14x25cm-6x10in) s.i.verso gouache
£5263	$10000	(8-Jan-91 SY.NY147/R) An architectural capriccio of a courtyard with figures (41x32cm-16x13in) ink wash
£7200	$11736	(1-Jul-91 S32/R) Ca' Pesaro, Venice (22x33cm-9x13in) s.i.verso gouache

GUARDI, Giacomo (after) (1764-1835) Italian

£850	$1386	(4-Jul-91 B175/R) The Equestrian monument overlooking the Venetian lagoon (17x28cm-7x11in) paper laid down on canvas

GUARDI, Giacomo (attrib) (1764-1835) Italian

£5017	$8378	(4-Jun-91 CH.R583/R) Ponte di Rialto (32x42cm-13x17in) (I.L 11000000)
£12632	$24000	(11-Jan-91 CH.NY55/R) The Punta della Dogana, Venice (11x17cm-4x7in) paper laid down on panel

GUARDI, Giacomo (style) (1764-1835) Italian

£2000	$3260	(4-Jul-91 B142/R) The Dogana and the entrance to the Grand Canal, Venice (27x30cm-11x12in) canvas laid down on panel

GUARDI, Giovanni Antonio (1698-1760) Italian

£22105	$42000	(11-Jan-91 CH.NY46/R) The interior of a harem (44x62cm-17x24in)
£27136	$44503	(21-Jun-91 SY.MO127/R) Scene d'interieur de Palais avec personnages (55x47cm-22x19in) (F.FR 270000)
£78947	$150000	(11-Jan-91 CH.NY79/R) Interior of Turksih harem (46x60cm-18x24in)
£84211	$160000	(11-Jan-91 CH.NY47/R) Fortitude (155x121cm-61x48in)
£94737	$180000	(11-Jan-91 CH.NY48/R) Temperance (155x121cm-61x48in)
£757	$1476	(24-Oct-90 GD.B1067) Study of male facing back (16x10cm-6x4in) red chk (S.FR 1900)

GUARDI, Giovanni Antonio (circle) (1698-1760) Italian

£73278	$131168	(14-Mar-91 D.V55/R) Visit of Venetian delegation in Constantinople (103x130cm-41x51in) (A.S 1500000)

GUARDI, Giovanni Antonio and Francesco (18th C) Italian

£55263	$105000	(11-Jan-91 CH.NY62/R) A rider with a musician and washerwoman resting before a fountain (84x115cm-33x45in)

GUARINO da Solofra, Francesco (1611-1654) Italian

£10001	$19602	(19-Nov-90 CH.R51/R) S.Antonio da Padova con Gesu Bambino (91x71cm-36x28in) (I.L 22000000)
£11213	$21529	(30-Nov-90 APT.P16/R) Le poete laure (75x62cm-30x24in) (F.FR 110000)

GUARINO da Solofra, Francesco (circle) (1611-1654) Italian

£1900	$3192	(26-Apr-91 NM.P42) Sainte Madeleine (98x73cm-39x29in) (F.FR 19000)

GUARNIERI, Riccardo (1933-) Italian

£864	$1634	(27-Sep-90 F.M25) Quadrati simultanei-spostamento in basso a destra n.162 (130x124cm-51x49in) s.d.1966 verso acrylic (I.L 1900000)

GUASTALLA, Pierre (1891-1968) French

£815	$1574	(16-Dec-90 T.B292/R) La terrasse (46x33cm-18x13in) s. (F.FR 8000)
£816	$1412	(12-May-91 T.B122) Paysage aux maisons jaunes (35x56cm-14x22in) s. board (F.FR 8200)

GUASTALLA, Pierre (1891-1968) French-cont.
£917	$1771	(16-Dec-90 T.B291) Sainte-Victoire (55x33cm-22x13in) s. (F.FR 9000)
£1075	$1859	(12-May-91 T.B267/R) Ramassage des foins (38x61cm-15x24in) s. (F.FR 10800)
£1784	$3443	(16-Dec-90 T.B139) Les oliviers (46x33cm-18x13in) s. panel (F.FR 17500)
£2548	$4918	(16-Dec-90 T.B137/R) Aux champs (38x55cm-15x22in) s. board (F.FR 25000)
£2886	$4992	(12-May-91 T.B123/R) Paysage de Provence (60x90cm-24x35in) s. (F.FR 29000)

GUAYASAMIN, Oswaldo (1913-) Ecuadorian
£3061	$6000	(20-Nov-90 CH.NY230/R) Guerrero (49x37cm-19x15in) s. acrylic paper
£3488	$6000	(15-May-91 CH.NY128/R) Figura Suplicante (57x57cm-22x22in) s.
£3573	*$6396*	*(13-Mar-91 FER.M219/R) Retrato de la senora Guayasamin (74x54cm-29x21in) s. gouache (S.P 650000)*

GUBBINS, Henrietta G (19th C) British
£950	$1786	(20-Sep-90 SC4203/R) Portrait of little girl with toy drum (38x25cm-15x10in) s.d.1859 board arched top

GUBLER, Ernst (1895-1958) Swiss
£516	*$862*	*(5-Jun-91 SY.Z134/R) Portrait of youth (60x48cm-24x19in) s. chl (S.FR 1300)*
£964	*$1889*	*(21-Nov-90 SY.Z51/R) Portrait of woman (44x30cm-17x12in) st.studio verso gouache (S.FR 2400)*

GUBLER, Max (1898-1973) Swiss
£3175	$5302	(5-Jun-91 SY.Z165/R) Thistle (65x54cm-26x21in) (S.FR 8000)
£7540	$12365	(19-Jun-91 GK.B437/R) Der Rutlischwur (65x54cm-26x21in) s. (S.FR 19000)
£7631	$12819	(24-Apr-91 G.Z15/R) Self portrait seated before easel (60x51cm-24x20in) s.d.1944 (S.FR 19000)
£7905	$13439	(27-May-91 GK.Z5339/R) Woman with red cloak (88x70cm-35x28in) d.1923 (S.FR 20000)
£7937	$13254	(5-Jun-91 SY.Z128/R) Interior with female nude and melon (46x64cm-18x25in) (S.FR 20000)
£8730	$14317	(21-Jun-91 G.Z88/R) Lying pheasant (97x130cm-38x51in) (S.FR 22000)
£9921	$16567	(5-Jun-91 SY.Z133/R) Woman seated with peach (111x82cm-44x32in) (S.FR 25000)
£17600	$34320	(17-Oct-90 G.Z36/R) Still life with thistles (97x130cm-38x51in) s. (S.FR 44000)
£873	*$1432*	*(21-Jun-91 G.Z39/R) The old man and the sea (48x33cm-19x13in) col.chk (S.FR 2200)*
£1837	*$3618*	*(16-Nov-90 EA.Z325/R) Female seated (88x62cm-35x24in) chl (S.FR 4500)*
£1837	*$3618*	*(16-Nov-90 EA.Z314) Woman with jug on head (60x44cm-24x17in) chl (S.FR 4500)*
£2063	*$3384*	*(19-Jun-91 GK.B438) Portrait of artist's wife (41x30cm-16x12in) st.studio col.chk (S.FR 5200)*

GUCCIONE, Piero (1925-) Italian
£771	*$1327*	*(13-May-91 CH.R11/R) Appunti per un viaggio in Africa (46x54cm-18x21in) s.i.d.1963 indian ink (I.L 1700000)*

GUDDEN, R (1863-?) German
£850	$1675	(14-Nov-90 CSK173) Vogesen Berge - view from forest to mountains (79x97cm-31x38in) s. s.l.stretcher

GUDE, H F (1825-1903) Norwegian
£5027	$9903	(14-Nov-90 RAS.K727/R) Evening river landscape with new moon (42x63cm-17x25in) s.d.1855 (D.KR 56000)

GUDE, Hans Fredrik (1825-1903) Norwegian
£2027	$3446	(31-May-91 GB.B5787/R) Norwegian landscape with view of mountain ranges (39x47cm-15x19in) (DM 6000)
£2513	$4952	(14-Nov-90 RAS.K560/R) Mountainous landscape with cabins, lake and church (20x35cm-8x14in) mono.d.48 (D.KR 28000)
£2644	$5156	(25-Oct-90 D.V142/R) Coastal landscape (36x25cm-14x10in) mono.d.1849 (A.S 55000)
£2977	$5329	(14-Mar-91 BU.O41/R) Woman hanging out washing (28x48cm-11x19in) mono.i. canvas on panel (N.KR 34000)
£3117	$6015	(12-Dec-90 BU.O22/R) Mountainous landscape (23x36cm-9x14in) s.i.d.45 indist.i.verso (N.KR 35000)
£3300	$5412	(19-Jun-91 S283/R) Sea in storm (33x49cm-13x19in) s.d.1889 board
£4054	$7905	(26-Oct-90 BM.B789/R) Coastal landscape with figures building ship in bay, Lillesand (28x55cm-11x22in) mono.i.d.58 board (DM 12000)
£5521	$10655	(12-Dec-90 BU.O21/R) In deep thought (41x22cm-16x9in) s.i.d.1882 panel (N.KR 62000)
£6773	$11649	(14-May-91 GF.L2352/R) Coastal landscape (45x67cm-18x26in) s.d.1899 (S.FR 17000)
£7583	$14710	(4-Dec-90 UL.T217/R) Fjord landscape with sailship and fishermen 1879 (20x31cm-8x12in) (N.KR 85000)
£9115	$15221	(4-Jun-91 BU.O67/R) Shipwreck near the coast (42x66cm-17x26in) s.d.1876 i.verso (N.KR 105000)
£12021	$23201	(12-Dec-90 BU.O20/R) Fishing from rowingboats, Christianiafjorden (53x77cm-21x30in) s.d.1868 (N.KR 135000)
£12238	$23619	(12-Dec-90 N.M529/R) Chiemsee lake landscape with fishermen and view of Herreninsel (100x146cm-39x57in) s.d.1886 (DM 35000)
£13000	$22360	(17-May-91 C141/R) By lake (96x159cm-38x63in) s.d.1869 d.69 verso

GUDE, Hans Fredrik (1825-1903) Norwegian-cont.

£15138	$29216	(10-Dec-90 B.O41/R) Coastal landscape (57x87cm-22x34in) s.d.1860 (N.KR 170000)
£414	*$820*	*(29-Jan-91 UL.T169 a) From Dumbarton near London, 20 June 1877 (12x17cm-5x7in) W/C (N.KR 4700)*
£1115	$2163	(4-Dec-90 UL.T220) Study with trees and flowers (28x34cm-11x13in) W/C (N.KR 12500)
£1674	$3315	(29-Jan-91 UL.T169 b) Brigatine 'Norsk Bonde'. The barque 'Betzy Gude' (24x34cm-9x13in) W/C double-sided (N.KR 19000)
£1736	$3385	(11-Oct-90 BU.O48/R) Landscape (38x50cm-15x20in) mono.i.d.43 pen W/C (N.KR 20000)
£1817	$3524	(22-Aug-90 RAS.K586/R) Landscape from Sandbakke near Honefoss (18x27cm-7x11in) s.i.d.93 pen W/C (D.KR 21000)
£2178	$4247	(15-Oct-90 B.O29/R) By the open fire (21x32cm-8x13in) mono. W/C pencil (N.KR 25000)

GUDE, Nils (1859-1908) Norwegian

| £568 | $1079 | (11-Sep-90 UL.T208/R) Roses in a Jugend flowervase (55x40cm-22x16in) s.d.1900 (N.KR 6500) |

GUDGEON, Ralston (1910-1984) British

| *£700* | *$1344* | *(19-Feb-91 C205/R) The lek, blackgame among trees (38x56cm-15x22in) s. s.i.verso pencil W/C bodycol* |

GUDIN, Henriette (1825-) French

£514	$837	(12-Jun-91 N.M443) Seascape with fishing boats, evening (14x21cm-6x8in) s. panel (DM 1500)
£982	$1669	(28-May-91 C.A128) Marine (10x16cm-4x6in) s. panel (B.FR 60000)
£1411	$2752	(26-Oct-90 PPB.P97) Voiliers (15x25cm-6x10in) s. (F.FR 14000)
£1984	$3413	(19-May-91 ZZ.F9/R) Le naufrage pres des rochers (14x21cm-6x8in) s. panel (F.FR 20000)

GUDIN, Theodore (1802-1880) French

£1037	$2032	(6-Nov-90 SY.AM312/R) Fishermen on beach at sunset (28x38cm-11x15in) s. panel (D.FL 3400)
£1715	$3395	(31-Jan-91 D.V20/R) Scottish highlands at sunset (54x39cm-21x15in) s. panel (A.S 35000)
£2424	$4776	(30-Oct-90 CH.AM160/R) Coastal landscape with moored sailing vessel (58x39cm-23x15in) s.d.1841 panel (D.FL 8000)
£3125	$5375	(19-May-91 ZZ.F8/R) Pecheurs au lever du jour (36x52cm-14x20in) s.d.1840 (F.FR 31500)
£699	*$1350*	*(12-Dec-90 WE.MU85/R) Sailing boats in bay (22x36cm-9x14in) s.d.1831 W/C (DM 2000)*

GUDMUNDSEN-HOLMGREEN, Johan (1858-1912) Danish

| £1434 | $2867 | (6-Feb-91 RAS.K310/R) Small girl with her doll (115x75cm-45x30in) s.d.1904 (D.KR 16000) |

GUDNASON, Svavar (1909-1988) Icelandic

£2536	$4895	(12-Dec-90 RAS.K191) Two figures on a pier (86x58cm-34x23in) s. (D.KR 28000)
£4386	$7456	(29-May-91 KH.K57/R) Composition (96x72cm-38x28in) s.d.55verso panel (D.KR 50000)
£6579	$11184	(29-May-91 KH.K20/R) Composition (53x47cm-21x19in) init.d.41 (D.KR 75000)
£491	*$908*	*(5-Mar-91 RAS.K69/R) 'Maneskaer' (51x34cm-20x13in) s.d.53 W/C pencil (D.KR 5500)*
£614	$1044	(29-May-91 KH.K3) Water plants (26x27cm-10x11in) s. crayon (D.KR 7000)
£614	$1044	(29-May-91 KH.K81/R) Pink bride (51x40cm-20x16in) s.d.52 W/C pencil (D.KR 7000)
£658	*$1118*	*(29-May-91 KH.K101) Light mask (41x35cm-16x14in) s.d.58 pastel (D.KR 7500)*
£836	$1631	(10-Oct-90 RAS.K24) 'Fugleslaegt' (52x66cm-20x26in) pastel (D.KR 9500)
£1163	$2279	(13-Feb-91 KH.K64/R) Through the window (50x35cm-20x14in) s. W/C (D.KR 13000)

GUE, Arthur (20th C) French

| £2000 | $3440 | (17-May-91 C3/R) In Tuileries, Paris (24x32cm-9x13in) s. panel |

GUELFENBEIN, Eduardo (1953-) Australian

| £1780 | $3187 | (14-Apr-91 APT.P68/R) Tel Aviv (81x101cm-32x40in) s.d.1991 acrylic (F.FR 18000) |
| *£396* | *$708* | *(14-Apr-91 APT.P69) Reflexion (70x50cm-28x20in) s.d.1990 gouache (F.FR 4000)* |

GUEQUIER, Georges (?) Belgian

| £1080 | $1760 | (12-Jun-91 GM.B4021) Jeune fille au piano (93x65cm-37x26in) s. (B.FR 65000) |

GUERARD, Eugene von (1811-1901) German

£3089	$6085	(13-Nov-90 J.M62 a) From our apartment in Collins Street (17x25cm-7x10in) s.i.d.1854 i.verso board (A.D 8000)
£4633	$9127	(13-Nov-90 J.M151 a) Naples (20x31cm-8x12in) i.d.1851verso board (A.D 12000)
£17269	$33157	(26-Nov-90 SY.ME223/R) Port Phillip Bay (23x34cm-9x13in) s.i.d.1857 paper on board (A.D 43000)

GUERARD, Eugene von (1811-1901) German-cont.
£176707 $339277   (26-Nov-90 SY.ME229/R) View towards Grampians from Black Range with
Mount Abrupt and Sturgeon in distance (74x125cm-29x49in) s.d.1875
(A.D 440000)

GUERASIMOVA, Valentina (1948-) Russian
£603 $1158   (18-Feb-91 ARC.P113) La repetition (90x90cm-35x35in) s. (F.FR 6000)
£854 $1640   (18-Feb-91 ARC.P114/R) Le bouquet de lilas (78x81cm-31x32in) s.d.89
(F.FR 8500)
£876 $1524   (25-Mar-91 ARC.P203) Avant la premiere (44x38cm-17x15in) s. (F.FR 8800)
£1244 $2164   (25-Mar-91 ARC.P202) Applaudissements (18x20cm-7x8in) s. board
(F.FR 12500)
£1144 $1991   (25-Mar-91 ARC.P201/R) Le cours de danse (12x13cm-5x5in) s. gouache
tempera board (F.FR 11500)

GUERCHET-JEANNIN, Anne-Marie (20th C) French
£554 $1081   (28-Oct-90 R.P262) Les vacances de Victorine Meurent (116x89cm-46x35in)
s. mixed media canvas (F.FR 5500)
£613 $1098   (14-Apr-91 R.P242) Le pied rouge (89x116cm-35x46in) s. mixed media
canvas (F.FR 6200)
£692 $1239   (14-Apr-91 R.P117/R) Les vacances de Victorine meurant no.12, Lecture
(116x89cm-46x35in) s. mixed media canvas (F.FR 7000)
£756 $1474   (28-Oct-90 R.P96/R) Les vacances de Victorine Meurent IV
(116x89cm-46x35in) s. mixed media canvas (F.FR 7500)
£793 $1585   (7-Feb-91 R.P154/R) Et sirene etait (116x89cm-46x35in) s. mixed media
canvas (F.FR 7800)
£894 $1789   (7-Feb-91 R.P87/R) Les vacances de Victorine Meurent no.3
(116x89cm-46x35in) s. mixed media canvas (F.FR 8800)

GUERCINO, Giovanni Francesco (1591-1666) Italian
£912 $1614   (19-Mar-91 F.M347/R) Studio di figura femminile (17x15cm-7x6in) ink
(I.L 2000000)
£3684 $7000   (8-Jan-91 SY.NY174/R) Study of a woman, half length, holding a bowl
(154x116cm-61x46in) ink
£4000 $7720   (11-Dec-90 C41/R) Study of a youth in profile to the left
(27x20cm-11x8in) ink chk.stylus
£5200 $8476   (4-Jul-91 B87/R) Study of a female nude, possibly Susanna
(24x19cm-9x7in) ink paper laid down on canvas
£5500 $8965   (2-Jul-91 C25/R) Wooded landscape with group of figures by farmhouse and
on cliff (21x30cm-8x12in) pen ink wash
£6316 $12000   (8-Jan-91 SY.NY112/R) Head of a bearded man (10x10cm-4x4in) ink
£7000 $11830   (16-Apr-91 C141/R) Saint Philip Neri flanked by two angels
(27x38cm-11x15in) ink wash
£9000 $14670   (2-Jul-91 C267/R) Prophet Isaiah (13x13cm-5x5in) with i. red chk
£24000 $39120   (2-Jul-91 C23/R) King David (16x13cm-6x5in) i. pen ink wash
£27632 $52500   (8-Jan-91 SY.NY3/R) An elderly bearded man looking down (26x17cm-10x7in)
pen
£28000 $45640   (2-Jul-91 C109/R) Head of man wearing fur hat, in profile to right
(27x18cm-11x7in) pen
£55000 $89650   (2-Jul-91 C24/R) Wooded upland landscape with figures outside gate of
castle (23x40cm-9x16in) pen ink
£95000 $154850   (2-Jul-91 C22/R) Reclining nude woman lifting curtain (20x24cm-8x9in)
pen ink

GUERCINO, Giovanni Francesco (after) (1591-1666) Italian
£750 $1223   (2-Jul-91 PH247) The Sybil of Samaria (35x29cm-14x11in)
£951 $1655   (25-Mar-91 SY.F562) La Maddalena col Crocifisso tre quarti di figura
(99x84cm-39x33in) (I.L 2100000)
£963 $1608   (6-Jun-91 D.V178/R) Evangelist Markus (42x34cm-17x13in) one of pair
(A.S 20000)
£963 $1608   (6-Jun-91 D.V179/R) Evangelist Matthew (42x34cm-17x13in) one of pair
(A.S 20000)
£1693 $2878   (31-May-91 LD.P26/R) Le Roi David (93x73cm-37x29in) after Giovanni
Francesco Barbieri (F.FR 17000)
£4000 $6760   (18-Apr-91 C58/R) The arrest of Christ (117x145cm-46x57in)

GUERCINO, Giovanni Francesco (attrib) (1591-1666) Italian
£816 $1584   (7-Dec-90 G.Z215/R) Ecce homo (27x18cm-11x7in) indian ink dr.
(S.FR 2000)

GUERCINO, Giovanni Francesco (circle) (1591-1666) Italian
£6707 $11000   (19-Jun-91 B.SF1675/R) Parable of the rich courtesan (133x178cm-52x70in)
£850 $1437   (16-Apr-91 C1/R) The Madonna and child (16x17cm-6x7in) red chk.
£1014 $1723   (31-May-91 GB.B5187) Head of woman looking up (19x14cm-7x6in) ochre
(DM 3000)

GUERCINO, Giovanni Francesco (school) (1591-1666) Italian
£1148 $2157   (19-Sep-90 GK.Z802) Standard bearer wearing armour and red sash
(111x87cm-44x34in) (S.FR 2800)
£1900 $3363   (22-Mar-91 APT.P90) Paysage anime de personnages (28x42cm-11x17in) pen
two on same mount (F.FR 19000)

GUERCINO, Giovanni Francesco (studio) (1591-1666) Italian
£4000 $7880   (31-Oct-90 S76/R) Angel (85x70cm-33x28in)
£7821 $14000   (11-Apr-91 SY.NY69/R) Baptism of Christ (110x168cm-43x66in)

GUERCINO, Giovanni Francesco (studio) (1591-1666) Italian-cont.
£2100 $3423   (1-Jul-91 S201/R) Salome with head of St. John the Baptist
       (23x30cm-9x12in) bears sig. black chk

GUERCINO, Giovanni Francesco (style) (1591-1666) Italian
£1521 $3012   (30-Jan-91 APT.P167/R) Judith et Holopherne (67x55cm-26x22in)
       (F.FR 15000)
£3130 $5226   (6-Jun-91 D.V171/R) Sybilla Samia (60x52cm-24x20in) (A.S 65000)
£4020 $6593   (19-Jun-91 LC.P44 b/R) Saint Jean l'Evangeliste. Saint Marc
       (86x70cm-34x28in) pair (F.FR 40000)
£4695 $7981   (28-May-91 AB.S4762/R) The Penitent Magdalen (178x167cm-70x66in)
       (S.KR 50000)
£4800 $9456   (31-Oct-90 S75/R) The Penitent Magdalene (118x94cm-46x37in)
£12587 $24294   (10-Dec-90 L.K265/R) Heads of two men (20x17cm-8x7in) pen sepia wash
       board (DM 36000)

GUERIN (?) French
£2485 $4200   (18-Apr-91 APT.P153/R) Portrait d'une jeune femme en robe blanche sur
       fond de paysage (116x88cm-46x35in) s. (F.FR 25000)

GUERIN, A M (?) French?
£655 $1278   (28-Oct-90 M.V34) Rue barree (60x72cm-24x28in) s. hardboard (F.FR 6500)

GUERIN, Armand (1913-1983) French
£510 $1000   (12-Feb-91 SY.NY134/R) La course a Longchamp (46x61cm-18x24in) s.
£513 $1000   (10-Oct-90 SY.NY177/R) Le bassin des Tuileries (66x79cm-26x31in) s.
       masonite
£705 $1149   (14-Jun-91 FB.P72/R) Le kiosque a musique (54x65cm-21x26in) s. hardboard
       (F.FR 7000)
£1020 $2010   (16-Nov-90 EA.Z292/R) Place Dancour (61x72cm-24x28in) s. acrylic pavatex
       (S.FR 2500)
£1113 $2182   (19-Nov-90 CSC.P66/R) Place de la Concorde sous la neige
       (59x72cm-23x28in) s. panel (F.FR 11000)

GUERIN, Ernest (19th C) French
£485 $859   (7-Apr-91 I.N162) Automne en Bretagne (22x33cm-9x13in) s.i. W/C
       (F.FR 4900)
£657 $1136   (12-May-91 T.B197 b) Chaumieres bretonnes en automne (27x22cm-11x9in) s.
       W/C (F.FR 6600)
£815 $1574   (16-Dec-90 T.B218/R) Sinagot dans le golfe du Morbihan (18x23cm-7x9in)
       s. W/C (F.FR 8000)
£989 $1908   (16-Dec-90 T.B221) Chaumieres en Bretagne et Barques (15x23cm-6x9in) s.
       W/C (F.FR 9700)
£1045 $1807   (12-May-91 T.B197/R) Route du pardon en Bretagne (28x36cm-11x14in) s.i.
       W/C (F.FR 10500)
£1121 $2164   (16-Dec-90 T.B33/R) Les dunes de la Baie d'Audierne (38x45cm-15x18in) s.
       W/C (F.FR 11000)
£1325 $2558   (16-Dec-90 T.B30/R) Concarneau la Ville Close (34x26cm-13x10in) s. W/C
       (F.FR 13000)
£1417 $2324   (21-Jun-90 CK.P77) Village Breton (26x34cm-10x13in) s. W/C gouache
       (F.FR 14100)
£1427 $2754   (16-Dec-90 T.B32/R) Bretonnes pres de la chaumiere. Depart pour la peche
       en Bretagne (15x9cm-6x4in) both s. W/C gouache pair (F.FR 14000)
£1631 $3148   (16-Dec-90 T.B31/R) Jour de fete a St Guenole (34x26cm-13x10in) s. W/C
       (F.FR 16000)
£3976 $7673   (16-Dec-90 T.B29/R) Retour de pardon en Bretagne (50x105cm-20x41in) s.
       W/C (F.FR 39000)

GUERIN, Ernest Pierre (1887-1952) French
£1195 $2258   (25-Sep-90 FN.S2189/R) Peasant women in Sunday costumes going to church,
       Brittany (17x23cm-7x9in) s.i. pencil W/C (DM 3500)

GUERIN, Jean Urbain (1760-1836) French
£898 $1769   (13-Nov-90 CH.G256) Portrait of young lady wearing low-cut pink dress
       (6x?cm-2x?in) min. gilt-metal mount oval in rec.frame (S.FR 2200)
£2286 $3864   (18-Apr-91 APT.P163) Portrait de J.B. Isabey dans son atelier
       (12x9cm-5x4in) s. miniature gouache vellum (F.FR 23000)

GUERIN, Joseph (19th C) American
£446 $750   (21-Jul-91 LIT.L72) New York Harbour (58x74cm-23x29in) s.

GUERIN, Jules (1866-1946) American
£900 $1800   (7-Feb-91 B.P115/R) Pier and beach scene (23x36cm-9x14in) s. pencil
£1263 $2400   (9-Jan-91 CH.NY183/R) St. John the Divine, New York. Reflections s. one
       W/C pencil board one pencil wash canvas
£1272 $2200   (10-May-91 S.BM108/R) Forest Hills Gardens, New York (76x51cm-30x20in)
       s. i.verso mixed media canvas board
£2344 $4500   (17-Dec-90 SY.NY122/R) Grand Central station (99x69cm-39x27in) s. W/C
       oil pencil chl

GUERIN, Pierre Narcisse (attrib) (1774-1833) French
£2231 $4418   (30-Jan-91 APT.P312/R) Tete d'expression (63x53cm-25x21in) (F.FR 22000)
£3877 $6552   (18-Apr-91 APT.P149/R) Academie d'homme (102x82cm-40x32in) (F.FR 39000)

GUERMACHEV, Mikhail Mikhailovich (1867-?) Russian
£750 $1478   (4-Oct-90 CSK61/R) A winter road (47x56cm-19x22in) s.

GUERNIER, Louis du II (1677-1716) French
£1100 $1793   (2-Jul-91 C412/R) Adam and Eve in Garden of Eden (14x26cm-6x10in) s.
   with i. black red chk

GUERRA, Antoine (younger-attrib) (1666-1711) French
£2752 $5422   (13-Nov-90 AB.S897/R) Portrait of Captain Jean Francois Gaudart
   (113x87cm-44x34in) i.verso (S.KR 30000)

GUERRA, Isabel (?) Spanish
£2989 $5739   (19-Dec-90 ANS.M66/R) El pilon de Valbona (100x65cm-39x26in) s.
   (S.P 550000)

GUERRERO GALVAN, Jesus (1910-1973) Mexican
£7653 $15000   (19-Nov-90 SY.NY154/R) Untitled (80x100cm-31x39in) s.d.1956
£18605 $32000   (15-May-91 CH.NY71/R) Retrato de Mujer con Mascara (74x59cm-29x23in)
   s.d.1947
£21684 $42500   (19-Nov-90 SY.NY129/R) Las dos ninas (61x46cm-24x18in) s.d.37 masonite
£24419 $42000   (15-May-91 CH.NY83/R) Maternidad (39x33cm-15x13in) s.d.1956
£36990 $72500   (19-Nov-90 SY.NY43/R) Narciso (80x105cm-31x41in) s.d.1948
£37791 $65000   (15-May-91 CH.NY6/R) Sueno de Juventud (56x71cm-22x28in) s.d.1946
£649 $1057   (10-Jun-91 W.T1281/R) Woman and a dove (55x48cm-22x19in) s.d.1951 pencil
   (C.D 1200)

GUERRERO, Jose (20th C) Spanish?
£3297 $5835   (20-Mar-91 DUR.M5) Carnaval (104x98cm-41x39in) (S.P 600000)
£4076 $7826   (19-Dec-90 ANS.M79/R) Composicion (63x48cm-25x19in) s.d.1987 paper
   (S.P 750000)
£10420 $17505   (25-Apr-91 EP.M16/R) Sin titulo (46x55cm-18x22in) s. (S.P 1900000)
£27315 $52718   (13-Dec-90 EP.M8/R) Blanco Sur (176x150cm-69x59in) s.d.1977verso
   (S.P 5000000)

GUERRESCHI, Giuseppe (1929-1985) Italian
£682 $1290   (27-Sep-90 F.M65) Testimoni (40cm-16ins circular) s.d.1962 collage mixed
   media (I.L 1500000)
£1850 $3589   (3-Dec-90 F.M340/R) Uomo (102x73cm-40x29in) s.d.1962 mixed media
   (I.L 4000000)
£2312 $4486   (3-Dec-90 F.M228/R) Figura seduta (101x72cm-40x28in) s.d.1966 mixed
   media (I.L 5000000)

GUERRIER, Raymond (1920-) French
£525 $1029   (12-Feb-91 HC.P90) L'homme dans la ville (115x88cm-45x35in) s. i. verso
   (F.FR 5200)
£586 $1148   (12-Feb-91 HC.P89) Fecamp (81x99cm-32x39in) s. verso (F.FR 5800)
£758 $1485   (12-Feb-91 HC.P91) Calanque (96x129cm-38x51in) s. i. verso (F.FR 7500)
£2275 $4072   (14-Apr-91 R.P170) La mandoline (73x100cm-29x39in) s. (F.FR 23000)

GUERTCHOV, Solomon (1906-1989) Russian
£655 $1067   (16-Jun-91 C.P30/R) Saint Jean l'evangeliste (39x29cm-15x11in) s.
   (F.FR 6500)
£1005 $1930   (18-Feb-91 ARC.P108/R) La ballerine (74x59cm-29x23in) s. board laid down
   on canvas (F.FR 10000)

GUERTICK, Wladimir see LUSSON

GUERY, Armand (1850-1912) French
£4523 $8683   (24-Feb-91 FE.P108) Village en Bourgogne (60x38cm-24x15in) s.d.1895
   (F.FR 45000)
£4689 $9050   (16-Dec-90 DA.R5/R) Sureaux et fleurs au soleil du soir a Pontigivart.
   La voyette deLoivre a L'entree de Pontigivart (28x45cm-11x18in) mono.
   panel pair (F.FR 46000)
£5662 $11041   (21-Oct-90 DA.R7/R) Bord de riviere. Les lavandieres one s. both mono.
   d.30 juillet 1908 d.1908 (F.FR 56000)

GUERZONI, Stephanie (1887-1970) Swiss
£803 $1574   (24-Nov-90 AB.L179/R) Port de la ciotat pres Marseille (46x65cm-18x26in)
   s. i.stretcher (S.FR 2000)

GUEST, D (1781-?) British
£360 $605   (15-Jul-91 PH47) Lady, wearing coral necklace and low-cut dress with
   blue shawl (6x?cm-2x?in) min. s.indist.d.1801 metal frame oval

GUET, Charlemagne Oscar (1801-1871) French
£6533 $10714   (21-Jun-91 SY.MO327/R) Jeune fille chassant les papillons
   (177x117cm-70x46in) s.d.1851 (F.FR 65000)

GUETAL, Abbe Laurent (1841-1892) French
£560 $946   (1-May-91 GD.B360/R) Hilly landscape with rocks and trees
   (38x60cm-15x24in) s.d.1884 (F.FR 1400)
£2008 $3233   (24-Jun-91 PR.P149) Bords de riviere au soleil couchant
   (38x55cm-15x22in) s.d.1887 (F.FR 20000)

GUFFENS, Godfried (1823-1901) Belgian
£2647 $5002   (25-Sep-90 GM.B941) Grand Dignitaire en habit d'Apparat
   (218x127cm-86x50in) s. (B.FR 160000)
£3354 $6573   (6-Nov-90 SY.AM60/R) Lovers in classical landscape (95x86cm-37x34in)
   s.d.1848 (D.FL 11000)

GUGEL, Karl Adolf (1820-1885) German
£1200 $2352   (14-Feb-91 CSK95) The harvesters (99x89cm-39x35in) s.d.1857

GUGGENBERGER, Theodor Otto Michael (1866-1929) German
£960 $1651   (16-May-91 D.V236/R) View of Berchtesgaden with Watzmann
     (60x80cm-24x31in) s. (A.S 20000)
£1071 $2098   (24-Jan-91 D.V121/R) Zellersee landscape (60x80cm-24x31in) s.i.
     (A.S 22000)

GUGLIELMI, O Louis (1906-1956) American
£1775 $3000   (1-May-91 B.SF5148/R) Figures in flight (93x77cm-37x30in) s.d.49
£4046 $7000   (22-May-91 CH.NY310/R) Third at Ninetieth (132x61cm-52x24in) s.d.53
£8466 $16000   (26-Sep-90 SY.NY189/R) Night windows (81x48cm-32x19in) s.d.48
     i.stretcher

GUIBERT, A (?) ?
£2231 $4284   (19-Dec-90 LD.P145) Le pas de danse (72x98cm-28x39in) s. (F.FR 22000)

GUICHARD, Joseph Benoit (1806-1880) French
£1336 $2592   (3-Dec-90 CS.L77/R) Venus et l'Amour dans le parc (33x26cm-13x10in)
     (F.FR 13000)

GUIDI, Giovanni (elder) see SCHEGGIA, Giovanni di Ser Giovanni

GUIDI, Guido (19th C) Italian
£502 $838   (6-Jun-91 F.M112) Natura morta (50x70cm-20x28in) s. (I.L 1100000)

GUIDI, Virgilio (1892-1984) Italian
£1294 $2497   (13-Dec-90 F.M354) Figura nello spazio (31x40cm-12x16in) s. i.verso
     (I.L 2800000)
£1351 $2634   (24-Oct-90 F.M190/R) Bacino San Marco (30x40cm-12x16in) s.
     (I.L 3000000)
£1375 $2256   (20-Jun-91 F.M350/R) Testa (30x24cm-12x9in) s. i.verso (I.L 3000000)
£2492 $4336   (26-Mar-91 F.M43/R) Isola di San Giorgio (35x50cm-14x20in) s.verso
     (I.L 5500000)
£9568 $16266   (28-May-91 SY.MI196/R) L'atelier (63x50cm-25x20in) panel (I.L 21000000)
£36020 $70239   (22-Oct-90 BR.M287/R) Veduta di Roma (77x64cm-30x25in) s.d.1912verso
     (I.L 80000000)
£1110   *$2153*   *(3-Dec-90 F.M247/R) Figura seduta (60x37cm-24x15in) s.c.1936 chl*
     (I.L 2400000)

GUIDOBONO, Bartolomeo (1657-1709) Italian
£4382 $7538   (14-May-91 GF.L2012/R) Venus mourning death of Adonis (78x68cm-31x27in)
     (S.FR 11000)
£53412 $95608   (8-Apr-91 ARC.P30/R) Bethsabee au bain (95x122cm-37x48in) (F.FR 540000)

GUIETTE, Rene (1893-1976) Belgian
£900 $1512   (23-Apr-91 C.A518) Composition (56x44cm-22x17in) mixed media
     (B.FR 55000)
£985 $1704   (25-May-91 KV.L132) Composition (48x38cm-19x15in) s.d.54 paper
     (B.FR 60000)
£1232 $2131   (25-May-91 KV.L133) Composition (48x38cm-19x15in) s.d.54 paper
     (B.FR 75000)
£1800 $3025   (23-Apr-91 C.A515) Composition (73x41cm-29x16in) s.d.1968 (B.FR 110000)
£1800 $3025   (23-Apr-91 C.A516) Composition (61x41cm-24x16in) s.d.1962 (B.FR 110000)
£559   *$1090*   *(24-Oct-90 GM.B960) Composition abstraite gouache (B.FR 34000)*
£714   *$1377*   *(16-Dec-90 GL.P35) Composition (48x30cm-19x12in) s.d.1957 oil gouache*
     board (F.FR 7000)
£740   *$1442*   *(23-Oct-90 C.A540) Reclining girl (46x62cm-18x24in) s.d.1921 W/C*
     (B.FR 45000)
£904   *$1763*   *(23-Oct-90 C.A542/R) Seated woman (53x40cm-21x16in) s.d.1921 W/C*
     (B.FR 55000)
£927   *$1799*   *(8-Dec-90 KV.L136) Landscape (40x50cm-16x20in) s.d.51 gouache*
     (B.FR 55000)
£1064 $1787   (23-Apr-91 C.A514) Composition (56x43cm-22x17in) s.d.1960 (B.FR 65000)
£1164 $2083   (16-Mar-91 KV.L135) Composition (48x38cm-19x15in) s.d.54 gouache W/C
     (B.FR 70000)
£1529   *$2951*   *(16-Dec-90 GL.P41) Composition (56x44cm-22x17in) s.d.1958 mixed media*
     board (F.FR 15000)
£1764   *$3476*   *(6-Oct-90 KV.L120/R) Composition (71x43cm-28x17in) s.d.64 mixed media*
     sand (B.FR 110000)
£3284   *$5681*   *(25-May-91 KV.L456/R) Danseres (60x45cm-24x18in) s. gouache*
     (B.FR 200000)
£3990   *$7142*   *(16-Mar-91 KV.L132/R) Figure couchee (36x50cm-14x20in) s. W/C gouache*
     (B.FR 240000)

GUIGON, Charles-Louis (1807-1882) Swiss
£1349 $2415   (13-Mar-91 GK.Z39) View of sunlit valley with ruins and figures
     (38x55cm-15x22in) s. (S.FR 3400)

GUIGOU, Paul (1834-1871) French
£2191 $3791   (24-May-91 FB.P13) Sans titre (9x19cm-4x7in) s.i. W/C (F.FR 22000)
£12245 $24122   (14-Nov-90 FB.P168/R) Souvenir de Provence (17x21cm-7x8in) s. i. verso
     panel (F.FR 120000)
£13944 $24124   (24-May-91 FB.P113/R) La ferme de sommeret en Seine-et-Oise
     (14x26cm-6x10in) s.d.68 i. verso panel (F.FR 140000)

GUIGOU, Paul (1834-1871) French-cont.
£34682 $60000   (22-May-91 SY.NY21/R) Paysage a Saint-Paul-Les-Durance (22x46cm-9x18in)
                     s.d.69 panel
£591   *$1135*   *(29-Nov-90 QWA.P90) L'isle sur sorgue (17x25cm-7x10in) s.d.1863*
                     col.crayons htd.white chk. (F.FR 5800)
£612   *$1206*   *(14-Nov-90 FB.P32) Paysage (10x17cm-4x7in) s. lead pencil (F.FR 6000)*
£2789   *$4825*   *(24-May-91 FB.P12/R) Les oliviers au printemps (11x20cm-4x8in) s.i.d.62*
                     blk.crayon W/C (F.FR 28000)

GUIGUET, Francois Joseph (1860-1937) French
£13566 $26319   (3-Dec-90 CS.L92/R) Montmartre, la Place Ravignan (90x106cm-35x42in)
                     s.d.1912 (F.FR 132000)
£500   *$885*   *(18-Mar-91 GGL.L3/R) Garconnet (34x23cm-13x9in) W/C (F.FR 5000)*
£582   *$1134*   *(9-Oct-90 GGL.L12/R) Sans titre s.d.1914 pencil (F.FR 5800)*
£702   *$1369*   *(9-Oct-90 GGL.L11/R) Sans titre s.d.1917 pencil (F.FR 7000)*
£720   *$1274*   *(18-Mar-91 GGL.L4/R) Meditation (30x22cm-12x9in) s.d.1935 col.crayons*
                     (F.FR 7200)
£752   *$1467*   *(9-Oct-90 GGL.L10/R) Sans titre s.indist.d. pencil (F.FR 7500)*

GUIJARRO, Antonio (20th C) Spanish
£2474 $4428   (13-Mar-91 FER.M214/R) Barco atracado en el puerto (81x100cm-32x39in) s.
                     (S.P 450000)
£2474 $4428   (13-Mar-91 FER.M215/R) Desnudo femenino recostado en el divan
                     (85x100cm-33x39in) s. (S.P 450000)

GUILBERT, Maurice (1876-1933) French?
£5000 $9750   (16-Oct-90 C54/R) Paysage en Ardennes (88x78cm-35x31in) s.

GUILBERT, Narcisse (1876-1942) French
£5617 $10953   (11-Oct-90 QWA.P8/R) Dieppe sous la brume (38x55cm-15x22in) s.
                     (F.FR 56000)

GUILLAIN, Marthe (1890-1974) Belgian
£1083 $2113   (15-Jan-91 GM.B613/R) Solitude (82x130cm-32x51in) s. (B.FR 65000)

GUILLAUME, Albert (1873-1942) French
£2126 $4166   (25-Nov-90 P.V34) Le duvet superflu (39x31cm-15x12in) s. panel
                     (F.FR 21000)
£3590 $7000   (23-Oct-90 SY.NY308/R) Le jour du mariage (42x33cm-17x13in) s. panel
£1113   *$2182*   *(20-Nov-90 MF.P17/R) La chambre d'ami (31x23cm-12x9in) s. W/C*
                     (F.FR 11000)
£2282   *$3925*   *(15-May-91 CN.P38/R) Elegants sur la terrasse (84x58cm-33x23in) s.*
                     crayon W/C (F.FR 23000)

GUILLAUME, Albert (attrib) (1873-1942) French
£714 $1193   (7-Jun-91 ZOF.Z1085) The music evening (67x100cm-26x39in) s. (S.FR 1800)

GUILLAUMET, Gustave (1840-1887) French
£1000 $1960   (14-Feb-91 CSK1218) Jerusalem (38x56cm-15x22in) s.
£15213 $29209   (17-Dec-90 ARC.P76/R) Un marche arabe en Algerie (63x96cm-25x38in) init.
                     (F.FR 150000)
£657   *$1282*   *(15-Oct-90 APT.P67) Femme orientale portant un enfant sur son dos*
                     (39x26cm-15x10in) s. pierre noire htd.white (F.FR 6500)
£800   *$1384*   *(9-May-91 CSK5/R) Levantine woman (46x28cm-18x11in) s. black white chk*

GUILLAUMIN, Armand (1841-1927) French
£5102 $10000   (14-Feb-91 CH.NY21/R) Le village de Pornic (24x33cm-9x13in)
£10660 $21000   (2-Oct-90 CH.NY23/R) Nature morte aux biscuits (55x46cm-22x18in) s.
£12000 $19320   (25-Jun-91 C119/R) Sur le hauteurs de la Sedelle (60x81cm-24x32in) s.
£12755 $25000   (15-Feb-91 SY.NY17/R) La mer a Saint Palais (60x93cm-24x37in) s.
£13706 $27000   (3-Oct-90 SY.NY30/R) Crozant barrage de Genetin (34x41cm-13x16in) s.
                     i.d.1917verso
£14721 $29000   (2-Oct-90 CH.NY35/R) Les rochers a Saint-Palais (60x73cm-24x29in) s.
                     canvas laid down on board
£16000 $25760   (25-Jun-91 C144/R) Maison dans un paysage (37x45cm-15x18in) s.
£16552 $31779   (1-Dec-90 SA.A2360/R) Portrait of young woman with hat (42x29cm-17x11in)
                     s. board (DM 48000)
£17206 $33725   (19-Nov-90 ARC.P49/R) Bord de la Creuse (38x46cm-15x18in) s.d.Juin 1916
                     (F.FR 170000)
£17472 $33895   (7-Dec-90 GL.P153/R) Barrage de Genetin a Crozant au matin
                     (61x73cm-24x29in) s. (F.FR 170000)
£19878 $38165   (27-Nov-90 APT.P19/R) Paysage de la Creuze (60x73cm-24x29in) s.
                     (F.FR 195000)
£20000 $32200   (25-Jun-91 C142/R) Arbres et fleurs, paysage a Damiette
                     (60x73cm-24x29in) s. i.stretcher
£20305 $40000   (2-Oct-90 CH.NY64/R) Le Puy Barriou, Crozant (60x73cm-24x29in) s.
£22000 $38940   (20-Mar-91 S11/R) Le village (60x73cm-24x29in) s.
£22843 $45000   (2-Oct-90 CH.NY41/R) Paysage d'automne, Crozant (60x72cm-24x28in) s.
£23121 $40000   (8-May-91 SY.NY111/R) Madame Guillaumin lisant (72x60cm-28x24in) s.
£31621 $53755   (27-May-91 GK.Z5158/R) Village (61x73cm-24x29in) s. (S.FR 80000)
£37587 $67280   (9-Apr-91 BG.P101 j/R) Bord de mer (81x66cm-32x26in) s. (F.FR 380000)
£40486 $79352   (20-Nov-90 BG.P44/R) Paysage (54x66cm-21x26in) s. (F.FR 400000)
£42800 $69763   (11-Jun-91 CSC.P11/R) La Seine a Charenton (60x73cm-24x29in) s.d.84
                     (F.FR 425000)
£55838 $110000   (15-Nov-90 CH.NY212/R) Viaduc, paysage d'Ile de France (54x63cm-21x25in)
                     s.

GUILLAUMIN, Armand (1841-1927) French-cont.
£60000 $96600   (25-Jun-91 C116/R) La Seine a Alfortville (53x72cm-21x28in) s.
£814 $1538   (25-Sep-90 FB.P293/R) Femme allongee (18x28cm-7x11in) mono.d.74 wax
      crayon (F.FR 8000)
£1282 $2500   (10-Oct-90 SY.NY197/R) Paysage a Git (43x58cm-17x23in) s.i.d.86 chl
£4644 $8963   (12-Dec-90 CH.AM318/R) Portrait of Mr. Martinez (43x35cm-17x14in) s.
      pastel (D.FL 15000)
£5888 $9951   (29-Apr-91 LGB.P32) Quai de la Rapee (54x71cm-21x28in) s.d.84 pastel
      (F.FR 59000)
£6579 $12895   (19-Nov-90 ARC.P20/R) Saint Palais (46x60cm-18x24in) s.d.93 pastel
      (F.FR 65000)
£9137 $18000   (15-Nov-90 CH.NY122/R) Paysage de la Creuse (30x45cm-12x18in) s. pastel
      paper on board
£9246 $15164   (21-Jun-91 OD.P26/R) Le Morin a Villiers (43x57cm-17x22in) s. pastel
      (F.FR 92000)
£10152 $20000   (3-Oct-90 SY.NY32/R) Les quais de la Seine a Paris (46x60cm-18x24in) s.
      pastel
£10152 $20000   (3-Oct-90 SY.NY31/R) Vallee (43x59cm-17x23in) s. pastel
£17206 $33725   (24-Nov-90 APT.P3/R) Madame Guillaumin au jardin (60x45cm-24x18in)
      s.d.98 pastel (F.FR 170000)

GUILLEMET, Jean Baptiste Antoine (1843-1918) French
£757 $1476   (24-Oct-90 GD.B432/R) Coastal landscape, Normandy (23x35cm-9x14in) s.
      panel (S.FR 1900)
£922 $1807   (11-Nov-90 ZZ.F5/R) Vue de Boulogne (18x27cm-7x11in) s. panel
      (F.FR 9000)
£1104 $1778   (24-Jun-91 PR.P150) Le chemin de campagne (55x73cm-22x29in) s.
      (F.FR 11000)
£1200 $2028   (1-May-91 GD.B367/R) Windmill in landscape (27x35cm-11x14in) s.indis.i.
      board (S.FR 3000)
£1224 $2400   (6-Nov-90 GF.L2380/R) Coastal landscape with fisher women
      (38x55cm-15x22in) s. (S.FR 3000)
£1687 $2901   (15-May-91 CN.P115) Paysage a la riviere (37x55cm-15x22in) s. panel
      (F.FR 17000)
£1800 $3546   (1-Nov-90 B91/R) Coastal view with figures on the shore
      (54x75cm-21x30in) s.d.72
£2500 $4875   (19-Oct-90 C219/R) Environs de Moret-sur-Loing (38x56cm-15x22in) s.
£5020 $9840   (11-Nov-90 ZZ.F15/R) Chaumiere sous un ciel d'orage (38x46cm-15x18in) s.
      (F.FR 49000)

GUILLEMIN, Alexandre Marie (1817-1880) French
£1488 $2560   (19-May-91 ZZ.F13/R) La demande en mariage (38x46cm-15x18in) s.
      (F.FR 15000)

GUILLEMINET, Claude (1821-1860) French
£1325 $2558   (12-Dec-90 ZZ.F58/R) Basse-Cour (21x16cm-8x6in) s. panel (F.FR 13000)
£1923 $3250   (19-Apr-91 DM.D2010/R) Barnyard scenes with chickens (15x23cm-6x9in) s.
      bevelled wood panel pair
£2191 $3769   (14-May-91 GF.L2398/R) Chicken yards (41x32cm-16x13in) s. panel pair
      (S.FR 5500)

GUILLERMET (19th C) French
£2988 $5169   (24-May-91 FB.P152) Nature morte aux pivoines (32x40cm-13x16in)
      s.i.d.1887 (F.FR 30000)

GUILLERMO, Juan (1916-1968) Spanish
£2309 $3717   (25-Jun-91 FER.M258/R) San Antonio de la Florida (65x81cm-26x32in)
      s.d.56 (S.P 425000)

GUILLERMOT, C T (19th C) French
£2243 $4306   (30-Nov-90 ARC.P124/R) Paris, sur les quais (50x61cm-20x24in) s.
      (F.FR 22000)
£2400 $3912   (5-Jul-91 APT.P129) Paris - Porte Sainte-Denis (53x46cm-21x18in) s.
      (F.FR 24000)

GUILLERY, Franz (1863-1933) German
£683 $1338   (24-Nov-90 SA.A725/R) View of Hohenburg (75x57cm-30x22in) s. (DM 2000)

GUILLET-SAGUEZ, A (19th C) French
£4847 $9500   (7-Nov-90 B.SF1138/R) Baby girl and dog (60x72cm-24x28in) s.d.1840

GUILLIBAUD, Jean Francois (1718-1799) Swiss
£2307 $4498   (10-Oct-90 APT.P489) Portraits de Henri de Martine, Pierre Daniel de
      Beausobre etJean Francois de Chesnay (86x134cm-34x53in) s.d.1720 verso
      (F.FR 23000)

GUILLON, Adrien (19th C) French
£702 $1369   (12-Oct-90 ZZ.F32) Vezelay (73x100cm-29x39in) s.d.1893 (F.FR 7000)

GUILLONNET, O D V (1872-1967) French
£725 $1422   (21-Nov-90 GM.B333) Jeunes femmes au parasol (24x18cm-9x7in) s. wood
      (B.FR 44000)

GUILLONNET, Octave Denis Victor (1872-1967) French
£1600 $3136   (22-Jan-91 SWS959/R) A lady with peacocks (67x55cm-26x22in) s.d.'22
      board

GUILLONNET, Octave Denis Victor (1872-1967) French-cont.
£2613 $5017   (24-Feb-91 P.V66/R) Le jardin de Garches (46x37cm-18x15in) s. panel
                  (F.FR 26000)
£3015 $5789   (24-Feb-91 P.V65/R) Le jardin de Garches (37x46cm-15x18in) s.i. panel
                  (F.FR 30000)

GUILLOU, Alfred (1844-1926) French
£2090 $3615   (12-May-91 T.B124) Bretonnes sur les Roches (24x33cm-9x13in) s. panel
                  (F.FR 21000)

GUILLOU, Alfred (attrib) (1844-1926) French
£572 $961   (23-Apr-91 RAS.K179/R) French summer landscape (38x63cm-15x25in) s.
                  (D.KR 6500)

GUIMARAES, Jose de (20th C) Portuguese
£657 $1136   (25-May-91 KV.L81) Composition with woman (54x37cm-21x15in) s. canvas on
                  panel (B.FR 40000)
£556   *$1080*   *(8-Dec-90 KV.L91/R) Figures (45x35cm-18x14in) s.d.1977 gouache*
                  (B.FR 33000)
£589   *$990*   *(23-Apr-91 C.A395) Figure (43x30cm-17x12in) s.d.1977 mixed media*
                  (B.FR 36000)
£655   *$1100*   *(23-Apr-91 C.A396) Composition (51x35cm-20x14in) d.1977 mixed media*
                  (B.FR 40000)

GUINIER, Henri Jules (1867-1927) French
£1276 $2513   (16-Nov-90 LGB.P202/R) La femme a l'oiseau (81x65cm-32x26in) s.
                  (F.FR 12500)

GUINOVART, Jose (1927-) Spanish
£4608 $8986   (17-Oct-90 FER.M251/R) Abstracto (81x100cm-32x39in) s.d.79 (S.P 850000)
£7065 $13565   (19-Dec-90 ANS.M80/R) Sin titulo (70x50cm-28x20in) s.d.59 panel
                  (S.P 1300000)
£9833 $18978   (13-Dec-90 EP.M24/R) Untitled (100x100cm-39x39in) s.d.80-86 barro
                  acrylic panel (S.P 1800000)
£1374   *$2460*   *(13-Mar-91 FER.M213/R) Abstracto en negro, marron y verde*
                  (23x32cm-9x13in) s. mixed media oil wax (S.P 250000)
£2891   *$4771*   *(10-Jul-91 FB.P91/R) Composition (60x60cm-24x24in) s.d.82 verso oil*
                  sable mirror canvas on panel (F.FR 29000)
£19667   *$37957*   *(13-Dec-90 EP.M14/R) Untitled (214x171cm-84x67in) s.d.79 oil chl*
                  (S.P 3600000)

GUIOT, Hector (1825-1903) French
£853   *$1374*   *(24-Jun-91 BL.P34) Jeune femme a l'eventail (118x60cm-46x24in) s.d.1887*
                  pastel (F.FR 8500)

GUIPON, Leon (1872-1910) French
£751   *$1300*   *(10-May-91 S.BM95 a/R) Scene from Juggler de Toraine (61x41cm-24x16in)*
                  s. mixed media

GUIRALDES, Alberto (1897-1961) Argentinian
£1129   *$2100*   *(5-Sep-90 V.BA57) En la lluvia (30x45cm-12x18in) W/C*

GUIRAMAND, Paul (?) French
£2665 $5250   (15-Nov-90 D.NY124/R) Les meules a Palome (73x91cm-29x36in) s.
                  i.stretcher
£5139 $9969   (5-Dec-90 ZZ.F55/R) Oliviers en Italie (73x92cm-29x36in) s. (F.FR 50000)
£5321 $9844   (6-Mar-91 APT.P114 b) Panier de fruits (81x100cm-32x39in) s.
                  (F.FR 53000)

GUIRAND DE SCEVOLA (1871-1950) French
£953 $1858   (12-Oct-90 ZZ.F52) Roses (37x46cm-15x18in) s. board (F.FR 9500)
£1400 $2282   (1-Jul-91 APT.P151/R) Nature morte au bouquet (73x92cm-29x36in) s.
                  (F.FR 14000)

GUIRAND DE SCEVOLA, Lucien (1871-1950) French
£1842 $3500   (27-Feb-91 SY.NY91/R) Still life with flowers and artist's materials
                  (65x54cm-26x21in) s.
£2245 $4422   (16-Nov-90 EA.Z323/R) Au parc (73x92cm-29x36in) s. pavatex (S.FR 5500)
£402   *$743*   *(4-Mar-91 ARC.P51) Portrait de jeune fille (42x35cm-17x14in) s. W/C*
                  (F.FR 4000)

GUISE, Pieter Jan (1814-1859) Dutch
£838 $1635   (25-Oct-90 VN.R34/R) Woman with cattle in landscape (58x77cm-23x30in)
                  s.d.1843 (D.FL 2800)
£915 $1738   (26-Feb-91 VN.R122) Woman with cattle in landscape (58x77cm-23x30in)
                  s.d.1843 (D.FL 3000)

GUITET, James (1925-) French
£905 $1619   (11-Mar-91 GL.P239 b) 12.F.6.59 (61x50cm-24x20in) s.d.1959 i. verso
                  (F.FR 9000)
£2811 $4526   (30-Jun-91 I.N145/R) Composition (61x50cm-24x20in) s.d.1959 verso
                  (F.FR 28000)
£522   *$966*   *(6-Mar-91 HC.P88) Composition abstraite sur fond bleu (27x22cm-11x9in)*
                  s.d.70 gouache (F.FR 5200)
£915   *$1829*   *(10-Feb-91 CC.P33) 50/50.10.79 (50x50cm-20x20in) s.i.d.1979 verso mixed*
                  media collage (F.FR 9000)

GUIZVILLER, S (?) ?
£2407 $4694   (10-Oct-90 APT.P491) Apparition au berger (225x161cm-89x63in) s.
                                   (F.FR 24000)

GULBRANSSON, Olaf (1873-1958) Scandinavian
£350   *$678*   *(7-Dec-90 GB.B6605) The King of Tabor (16x11cm-6x4in) s.i.c.1920 indian*
                                    ink pen over pencil board (DM 1000)
£541   *$935*   *(25-May-91 N.M402) Portrait of Karl Valentin (29x20cm-11x8in) mono.i.*
                                    indian ink (DM 1600)
£1049   *$2035*   *(7-Dec-90 GB.B6604) Adagio, mother and child in garden (16x11cm-6x4in)*
                                    s.i.c.1920 indian ink pen over pencil board (DM 3000)

GULIK, Franciscus Lodewijk van (1841-1899) Dutch
£838 $1635   (25-Oct-90 VN.R36) Winter in Rotterdam (59x46cm-23x18in) s. (D.FL 2800)
£1078 $2102   (25-Oct-90 VN.R35) A scene in Rotterdam (59x46cm-23x18in) (D.FL 3600)

GULLY, John (1819-1888) Australian
£1600   *$3120*   *(24-Oct-90 S114/R) River landscape, New Zealand (30x49cm-12x19in)*
                                    s.d.1866 W/C over pencil scratching gum arabic
£2941   *$4971*   *(16-Apr-91 J.M108/R) New Zealand high ground (37x31cm-15x12in) s. W/C*
                                    (A.D 6500)
£3265   *$5517*   *(17-Apr-91 DS.W56/R) View of colonial Nelson and Maitai river*
                                    (30x45cm-12x18in) s.d.1866 W/C (NZ.D 9500)
£8669   *$16991*   *(7-Nov-90 DS.W26) Mt Egmont and Fanthams peak (40x73cm-16x29in) s.d. W/C*
                                    (NZ.D 28000)

GUMERY, Adolphe (1861-?) French
£1121 $2164   (12-Dec-90 APT.P111) Torero dans les coulisses de l'arene
                                    (90x72cm-35x28in) s. (F.FR 11000)
£1190 $2000   (17-Jul-91 SY.NY244/R) In the orchard (67x99cm-26x39in) s. canvas laid
                                    down on board

GUMME, G de (?) ?
£635 $1244   (12-Feb-91 GM.B654) Paysage mediterraneen (60x80cm-24x31in) s.
                                    (B.FR 38000)

GUMMESSON, Per (1858-1928) Swedish
£1022 $1830   (13-Apr-91 FAL.M97/R) Autumn landscape with trees by white house
                                    (54x82cm-21x32in) s.d.1905 (S.KR 11000)

GUNDERSEN, Gunnar S (1921-1983) Norwegian
£1511 $2916   (15-Dec-90 BU.H314) Red abstract (90x80cm-35x31in) s. (F.M 10500)
£2939 $5671   (13-Dec-90 BU.O18/R) Composition 1951 (91x104cm-36x41in) init.d.51
                                    (N.KR 33000)
£5343 $10312   (13-Dec-90 BU.O15/R) Composition (101x75cm-40x30in) s. (N.KR 60000)
£6233 $12030   (13-Dec-90 BU.O17/R) Composition 1958 (100x100cm-39x39in) s.d.58
                                    (N.KR 70000)
£9115 $15221   (4-Jun-91 BU.O44/R) Composition (121x151cm-48x59in) s. (N.KR 105000)
£10240 $19764   (13-Dec-90 BU.O19/R) Regatta (121x101cm-48x40in) s. i.verso
                                    (N.KR 115000)
£1649   *$3216*   *(11-Oct-90 BU.O50/R) Composition in red and yellow s. mixed media pair*
                                    (N.KR 19000)

GUNDERSEN, Helene (1858-1934) Norwegian
£564 $942   (3-Jun-91 B.O57/R) Female nude (56x41cm-22x16in) init. (N.KR 6500)

GUNN, Herbert James (1893-1964) British
£2500 $5000   (5-Feb-91 S172/R) Bridge at Toledo (30x21cm-12x8in) s.d.1914 board
£3000 $6000   (5-Feb-91 S171/R) Park Terrace, from Kelvingrove Park (26x18cm-10x7in)
                                    board
£5000 $9250   (7-Mar-91 C28/R) Portrait of Pauline (44x59cm-17x23in) s.

GUNN, James (20th C) British
£480   *$826*   *(14-May-91 SWS160/R) Portrait of G K Chesterton (25x20cm-10x8in)*
                                    s.i.d.1932 monochrome wash

GUNNE, Carl (1893-1979) Scandinavian
£613 $1061   (22-May-91 BA.S70/R) Calm day on the West coast (54x81cm-21x32in) s.
                                    (S.KR 6500)
£868 $1502   (22-May-91 BA.S69/R) Sunset (55x81cm-22x32in) s. (S.KR 9200)

GUNSTON, William (fl.1867-1875) British
£500 $870   (26-Mar-91 PH107) The empty cage (22x15cm-9x6in) s. verso board

GUNTEN, Roger von (1933-) Swiss
£1020 $2000   (12-Feb-91 SY.NY290/R) Detras del Telon. El Turco Fantasma
                                    (41x30cm-16x12in) one s.d.84 one s.d.83 s.i.d.verso acrylic pair

GUNTHER, Margot (1937-) German
£648 $1226   (25-Sep-90 FN.S1960) Cross roads (60x80cm-24x31in) s.d.1968 paper
                                    (DM 1900)

GURLITT, Louis (1812-1897) German
£2685 $5235   (13-Oct-90 KRA.D217/R) Traveller in river landscape with view of town
                                    beyond (24x33cm-9x13in) s.d.63 (DM 8000)

GURVICH, Jose (1927-1974) Lithuanian
£2538 $5000   (1-Oct-90 GC.M7) Gente en el Bar (50x68cm-20x27in)
£4082 $8000   (19-Nov-90 SY.NY202/R) Untitled (51x60cm-20x24in) s.d.67

GUSSONI, Felice (1885-1908) Italian
£2311 $4459   (12-Dec-90 F.M158/R) Ragazza con fiori (100x63cm-39x25in) s.
                  (I.L 5000000)

GUSSONI, Vittorio (1893-1968) Italian
£546 $944   (23-May-91 F.M199) Natura morta con grappoli d'uva (30x40cm-12x16in) s.
                  (I.L 1200000)
£773 $1515   (21-Nov-90 F.M175) Sottobosco a San Romolo, Sanremo (40x50cm-16x20in) s.
                  s.i.d.1965verso (I.L 1700000)

GUSSOW, Bernard (1881-1957) American
£1302 $2500   (29-Nov-90 MFA.C206/R) Costume party in Rockport (61x76cm-24x30in) s.

GUSSOW, Karl (1843-1907) German
£1886 $3262   (6-May-91 ZEL.L1720/R) Portrait of young woman wearing flowers in hair
                  before window (57x46cm-22x18in) s.i.d.1898 (DM 5600)

GUSTAFSON, Sven (20th C) Swedish
£4315 $8500   (15-Nov-90 SY.NY35) Embracing couple (69x46cm-27x18in)

GUSTAFSSON, Erik B (1913-) Swedish
£923 $1771   (27-Nov-90 BU.S112/R) The pencil pot (73x60cm-29x24in) s.d.1977
                  (S.KR 10000)
£1384 $2657   (27-Nov-90 BU.S111/R) Still life of flowers in vase (80x61cm-31x24in)
                  s.d.1956 (S.KR 15000)

GUSTON, Philip (1913-1980) American
£16751 $33000   (14-Nov-90 SY.NY296/R) Warwick II (58x76cm-23x30in) s. s.i.d.1959 verso
                  masonite
£51020 $100000   (8-Nov-90 CH.NY370/R) Lamp (81x91cm-32x36in) s. i.d.1979 verso
£62130 $105000   (1-May-91 SY.NY135/R) Untitled (76x102cm-30x40in) paper
£193878 $380000   (7-Nov-90 CH.NY47/R) Downtown (122x152cm-48x60in) s. s.d.1969verso
£295858 $500000   (30-Apr-91 SY.NY53/R) Edge (204x315cm-80x124in) s. s.d.1976 verso
£489796 $960000   (7-Nov-90 CH.NY4/R) Summer (160x153cm-63x60in) s. s.i.d.1954verso
£5076 $10000   (14-Nov-90 SY.NY304/R) Abstract (45x61cm-18x24in) s.d.1960 ink
£12755 $25000   (8-Nov-90 CH.NY169/R) Untitled (48x61cm-19x24in) s.d. '74 ink paper
                  mounted on board

GUTERBOCK, Leopold (c.1820-1881) German
£1100 $1903   (9-May-91 CSK135/R) Bather (41x32cm-16x13in) s.

GUTERSLOH, Albert Paris (1887-1973) Austrian
£40000 $77600   (5-Dec-90 PH36/R) Bildnis der Frau E. G. (100x79cm-39x31in) init.
                  s.i.verso
£1214 $1990   (20-Jun-91 D.V7/R) Female nude seated (44x32cm-17x13in) mono.d.12 pencil
                  (A.S 25000)
£1491 $2893   (6-Dec-90 D.V134/R) The still life (11x12cm-4x5in) s.i.d.71 mixed media
                  (A.S 30000)
£1491 $2893   (6-Dec-90 D.V135/R) Discussion about picture (10x12cm-4x5in) s.i.d.68
                  mixed media (A.S 30000)
£2182 $4103   (20-Sep-90 D.V251/R) Debate over a newspaper article (11x9cm-4x4in)
                  s.d.71 pencil W/C gouache (A.S 45000)
£3110 $5380   (8-May-91 D.V139/R) Childrn greeting coffee house visitors
                  (15x20cm-6x8in) s.i.d.1968 pencil gouache (A.S 65000)

GUTHRIE, James (1859-1930) British
£2200 $4268   (5-Dec-90 PHE30/R) The peacock fan (49x37cm-19x15in) s.

GUTIERREZ RIVERA, Francisco (19/20th C) Spanish
£5503 $9851   (12-Mar-91 F.M96/R) Navi nel porto di Barcellona (113x155cm-44x61in)
                  s.d.1902 (I.L 12000000)

GUTIERREZ, Ernesto (19/20th C) Spanish
£700 $1379   (4-Oct-90 CSK172) A village street (27x18cm-11x7in) s. panel

GUTIERREZ, Jose L (1900-) Mexican
£1276 $2500   (20-Nov-90 CH.NY293/R) Entierro (61x76cm-24x30in) s.d.1950 polytec panel

GUTMAN, Nachum (1898-1978) Israeli
£1276 $2500   (12-Feb-91 SY.NY146 a/R) Fishing boats at port (58x71cm-23x28in) s.
£1534 $2500   (12-Jun-91 SY.NY78/R) Fishing boats at port (60x72cm-24x28in) s.
£6806 $13000   (2-Jan-91 GG.TA532/R) Coach (38x46cm-15x18in) s.c.1960
£576 $1100   (1-Jan-91 GG.TA40/R) Family meal and donkey's head in the window
                  (21x19cm-8x7in) s. pastel W/C
£681 $1300   (1-Jan-91 GG.TA275/R) Children in grove (19x29cm-7x11in) s. W/C
                  col.crayons
£785 $1500   (1-Jan-91 GG.TA274/R) Fisherman (19x21cm-7x8in) s. W/C
£1675 $3200   (1-Jan-91 GG.TA271/R) Landscape and figures (33x46cm-13x18in) s.d.1948
                  W/C
£1885 $3600   (1-Jan-91 GG.TA272/R) The walls of Jerusalem (49x34cm-19x13in) s. W/C
£1963 $3200   (12-Jun-91 GG.TA251/R) Galilee landscape (41x54cm-16x21in) s. W/C

GUTMAN, Nachum (1898-1978) Israeli-cont.

£2094	$4000	(1-Jan-91 GG.TA270/R) Galilee landscape, house and trees (38x56cm-15x22in) s. W/C
£2209	$3600	(12-Jun-91 GG.TA253/R) Trees (37x54cm-15x21in) s.d.1950 W/C
£2454	$4000	(12-Jun-91 GG.TA252/R) Landscape in Galilee (33x47cm-13x19in) s.d.1975 W/C
£3313	$5400	(12-Jun-91 GG.TA249/R) Midnight prayer (48x60cm-19x24in) s. gouache pastel oil paper
£3665	$7000	(1-Jan-91 GG.TA268/R) Figures in Galilee (57x77cm-22x30in) s.c.1950 pastel gouache
£3927	$7500	(1-Jan-91 GG.TA267/R) Tiberias, figures by the Sea of Galilee (49x68cm-19x27in) s.d.1951 W/C
£4450	$8500	(1-Jan-91 GG.TA269/R) Coach (48x63cm-19x25in) s. gouache pastel mixed media

GUTSCHMIDT, Richard (1861-?) German

| £1923 | $3712 | (13-Dec-90 N.M2715/R) Sailing on lake Starnberg (61x50cm-24x20in) s.i.verso board (DM 5500) |

GUTTUSO, Renato (1912-1987) Italian

£3697	$7135	(12-Dec-90 F.M1/R) Natura morta con ciotola e pomodoro (25x31cm-10x12in) s. tempera (I.L 8000000)
£6364	$12474	(20-Nov-90 BR.M60/R) Paesaggio (37x27cm-15x11in) s.d.1936 tempera paper on canvas (I.L 14000000)
£7200	$12168	(1-May-91 GD.B370/R) Natura morta con caffettiera (40x50cm-16x20in) s. (S.FR 18000)
£7204	$14048	(24-Oct-90 F.M275/R) Ragazzo di Sicilia (30x25cm-12x10in) s. s.d.1984verso (I.L 16000000)
£9514	$16555	(26-Mar-91 F.M137/R) Trulli ad Alberobello (49x64cm-19x25in) s. tempera oil board (I.L 21000000)
£11735	$23000	(12-Feb-91 SY.NY156 a/R) Woman undressing (117x18cm-46x7in) s. paper on canvas
£12302	$20914	(28-May-91 SY.MI178/R) Ritratto (116x93cm-46x37in) s. (I.L 27000000)
£14125	$24012	(28-May-91 SY.MI204/R) Omaggio a Delacroix, commento delle femmes d'Algers (54x66cm-21x26in) s.i.d.1958verso (I.L 31000000)
£20503	$34856	(28-May-91 SY.MI132/R) Aranceto (50x62cm-20x24in) s.d.56 (I.L 45000000)
£21162	$41265	(22-Oct-90 BR.M221/R) Foglie su paesaggio (70x55cm-28x22in) s. s.d.1978verso (I.L 47000000)
£23105	$44593	(13-Dec-90 F.M468/R) Ragazze in una stanza (50x80cm-20x31in) s. s.verso (I.L 50000000)
£24313	$47411	(22-Oct-90 BR.M285/R) Torre al tramonto, Torre di Velate (55x64cm-22x25in) s.d.1961 (I.L 54000000)
£29773	$57164	(27-Nov-90 SY.MI229/R) Natura morta (62x50cm-24x20in) s. s.d.61verso (I.L 65000000)
£32621	$56760	(26-Mar-91 F.M110/R) Ragazzo sdraiato sul muretto (68x120cm-27x47in) s.d.53 paper (I.L 72000000)
£786	$1525	(3-Dec-90 F.M31/R) Nudo femminile (38x26cm-15x10in) s. pen (I.L 1700000)
£971	$1884	(3-Dec-90 F.M127/R) Nudo femminile (30x25cm-12x10in) s.d.1935 ink (I.L 2100000)
£1181	$2327	(30-Oct-90 F.R63) Ritratto di Alberto Moravia (46x33cm-18x13in) s. pencil (I.L 2600000)
£1272	$2201	(7-May-91 F.M203/R) Studio per Le Ginnaste (34x46cm-13x18in) s. ink (I.L 2800000)
£1356	$2264	(8-Jun-91 HN.H131/R) Composition with three nudes (63x46cm-25x18in) s.d.1941 ink brush W/C (DM 4000)
£1387	$2692	(3-Dec-90 F.M256/R) Da Robinson Crusoe s.d.1950 indian ink pair (I.L 3000000)
£1466	$2814	(27-Nov-90 SY.MI31/R) Studio di mani (35x31cm-14x12in) s. gouache ink (I.L 3200000)
£1727	$3386	(20-Nov-90 BR.M188/R) Testa di Gericault (37x50cm-15x20in) s.d.1958 ink (I.L 3800000)
£1741	$3342	(27-Nov-90 SY.MI15/R) Donna sdraiata (103x69cm-41x27in) s. W/C ink paper laid down on canvas (I.L 3800000)
£1796	$3484	(8-Dec-90 GAB.G2628) Scene erotique - trois femmes (50x40cm-20x16in) s. Indian ink W/C (S.FR 4400)
£1817	$3144	(7-May-91 F.M328) Grottesca (51x60cm-20x24in) s.i. ink W/C (I.L 4000000)
£1908	$3759	(30-Oct-90 F.R79) Busto femminile (34x25cm-13x10in) s.d.67 col.ink (I.L 4200000)
£2734	$4647	(28-May-91 SY.MI27/R) Vegetazione (108x69cm-43x27in) s.d.25-6-70 W/C ink (I.L 6000000)
£3006	$5832	(3-Dec-90 F.M341/R) Nudi (40x35cm-16x14in) s. W/C (I.L 6500000)
£4052	$7902	(22-Oct-90 BR.M237/R) Nudo di donna (44x62cm-17x24in) s.d.1968 W/C paper on canvas (I.L 9000000)
£8201	$13942	(28-May-91 SY.MI124/R) Donna con una sedia sulle spalle (71x41cm-28x16in) oil mixed media board (I.L 18000000)

GUY, Seymour (1824-1910) British

£670	$1300	(7-Dec-90 S.W2970/R) Portrait of young girl (23x18cm-9x7in) init.
£5506	$9250	(28-Apr-91 HG.C19) Sound in the dark (28x20cm-11x8in) init. board
£8092	$14000	(22-May-91 CH.NY82/R) Bitter bite (48x36cm-19x14in) mono.i.d.1877
£23121	$40000	(22-May-91 CH.NY84/R) Knowledge is power (76x63cm-30x25in) mono. canvas on panel

GUYOMARD, Gerard (1938-) French?
£2551 $5026   (16-Nov-90 FB.P375/R) Appartement (130x162cm-51x64in) s.d.1972 verso acrylic (F.FR 25000)

GUYON, J (19th C) French
£4577 $7690   (23-Apr-91 RAS.K85/R) Young sleeping model (140x195cm-55x77in) s.d.1891 (D.KR 52000)

GUYOT (?) ?
£2183 $3754   (15-May-91 CN.P39/R) Lion (52x67cm-20x26in) s. chl. (F.FR 22000)

GUYOT, Charles Leon (19/20th C) French
£547 $925   (15-Apr-91 SY.J425/R) French Riviera (50x60cm-20x24in) s. (SA.R 2600)

GUYOT, Georges Lucien (1885-1973) French
£2035 $3845   (25-Sep-90 FB.P295/R) Lions couches (51x73cm-20x29in) s. mixed media (F.FR 20000)

GUYOT, Jacques Henri (?) French?
£800 $1344   (28-Apr-91 FE.P156) Les trois femmes (50x65cm-20x26in) s. hardboard (F.FR 8000)
£896 $1558   (31-Mar-91 FE.P184) Le bar du club (55x46cm-22x18in) s. (F.FR 9000)
£1223 $2349   (2-Dec-90 FE.P142) Le repas (91x74cm-36x29in) s. panel (F.FR 12000)

GUYS, Constantin (1802-1892) French
£522 $966   (6-Mar-91 APT.P17) Deux elegantes (21x15cm-8x6in) pen wash (F.FR 5200)
£620 $1240   (6-Feb-91 LD.P80) Cavalier (14x16cm-6x6in) blk.crayon94 (F.FR 6100)
£700 $1239   (22-Mar-91 APT.P91) Deux grisettes (20x17cm-8x7in) pen wash (F.FR 7000)
£772 $1505   (12-Oct-90 AW.H1453/R) Southern street scene (16x13cm-6x5in) pen wash over pencil vellum on board (DM 2300)
£1113 $2182   (19-Nov-90 CSC.P147 b/R) Dame a l'eventail (30x19cm-12x7in) crayon (F.FR 11000)
£1400 $2688   (29-Nov-90 B16/R) Lady in a chaise with two men riding behind (23x36cm-9x14in) s.i.d.1853 pen W/C
£1580 $3049   (14-Dec-90 ARC.P169) Le tripot (16x23cm-6x9in) pen wash lead pencil (F.FR 15500)
£1619 $3174   (19-Nov-90 CSC.P136 b/R) Promenande en caleche (18x24cm-7x9in) pen wash (F.FR 16000)
£2515 $4930   (24-Jan-91 AGS.P166/R) Jeune femme au manchon (19x15cm-7x6in) W/C (F.FR 25000)
£3968 $6508   (19-Jun-91 GK.B440/R) Coach drawn by four horses and accompanying rider at Paris street corner (17x26cm-7x10in) indian ink bister pen over pencil (S.FR 10000)
£3968 $6508   (19-Jun-91 GK.B439/R) Two riders conversing with ladies seated in landaure (15x26cm-6x10in) bister indian ink pen over pencil (S.FR 10000)
£4281 $8220   (29-Nov-90 ZZ.F4/R) Promenade en fiacre (25x39cm-10x15in) s. Indian ink wash W/C (F.FR 42000)

GUZMAN, Manuel Rodriguez de (1818-1867) Spanish
£1310 $2267   (8-May-91 FER.M136/R) Escena de taberna (63x51cm-25x20in) (S.P 240000)
£6556 $12652   (11-Dec-90 FER.M210/R) Fiesta flamenca (47x58cm-19x23in) s. panel (S.P 1200000)

GUZMAN, R de (19/20th C) Spanish
£800 $1536   (27-Nov-90 PH215) Arresting dialogue (45x65cm-18x26in) s.

GUZZI, Virgilio (1902-) Italian
£1272 $2506   (30-Oct-90 F.R137) Ritratto di ragazza (75x50cm-30x20in) s. (I.L 2800000)

GWATHMEY, Robert (1903-?) American
£1823 $3500   (17-Dec-90 SY.NY402/R) Sewing (28x18cm-11x7in) s.
£2540 $4800   (27-Sep-90 CH.NY301/R) Tending the fields (41x36cm-16x14in) s.
£3385 $6500   (17-Dec-90 SY.NY403/R) Man eating apple (36x41cm-14x16in) s.
£6349 $12000   (26-Sep-90 SY.NY224/R) Shelling peas (92x51cm-36x20in) s.

GYARFAS, Jeno (1857-1925) Hungarian
£12450 $21539   (24-May-91 FB.P171/R) Les trois ages (81x80cm-32x31in) s.d.1880 (F.FR 125000)

GYSBRECHTS, Cornelis Norbertus (17th C) Flemish
£20950 $37500   (11-Apr-91 SY.NY20/R) Trompe-l'oeil still life with lute and rebec and other objects (107x96cm-42x38in) s.d.indist.

GYSBRECHTS, Franciscus (17th C) Dutch
£3333 $6500   (11-Oct-90 SY.NY171/R) Vanitas still life with musical scores, flute and other objects on table (84x58cm-33x23in) mono.
£5500 $10615   (11-Dec-90 PH111/R) Still life of covered chalice, shell and book in stone niche (95x73cm-37x29in) s.

GYSBRECHTS, Franciscus (attrib) (17th C) Dutch
£6752 $13301   (30-Oct-90 BU.S252/R) Trompe l'oeil (63x53cm-25x21in) (S.KR 74000)

GYSELAER, Nicolas de (1590-1654) Dutch
£6461 $10919   (18-Apr-91 APT.P41/R) Un roi acceuillant un serviteur devant un palais
          (81x113cm-32x44in) panel (F.FR 65000)
£7692 $15000   (11-Oct-90 SY.NY166/R) Figures in loggia with courtyard beyond
          (77x110cm-30x43in) panel

GYSELS, Pieter (1621-1690) Flemish
£14444 $24121   (6-Jun-91 D.V34/R) Dutch canal landscape with village and figures
          (39x53cm-15x21in) (A.S 300000)
£19782 $35410   (9-Apr-91 APT.P26/R) Paysage de riviere (25x34cm-10x13in) i. verso
          copper (F.FR 200000)

GYSELS, Pieter (circle) (1621-1690) Flemish
£4500 $8550   (28-Feb-91 B35/R) Wooded river landscape with figures merrymaking to
          fore, village beyond (12x28cm-5x11in) panel pair

GYSELS, Pieter (studio) (1621-1690) Flemish
£7911 $15663   (30-Jan-91 APT.P207/R) Le repas des paysans (58x75cm-23x30in) panel
          (F.FR 78000)

GYSELS, Pieter (style) (1621-1690) Flemish
£4500 $8550   (13-Sep-90 CSK248/R) Extensive landscape with travellers on open road
          (36x45cm-14x18in)
£7000 $14000   (7-Feb-91 C174/R) A carriage on a village road by an inn, a windmill
          beyond (18x21cm-7x8in) panel

GYSIS, Nicolas (1842-1901) Greek
£872 $1700   (25-Oct-90 GRO.B46/R) Still life with fruit and fowl (97x76cm-38x30in)
£10000 $16400   (19-Jun-91 S408/R) Harmonia (55cm-22ins circular) s. canvas on board in
          painted circle
£25685 $41866   (12-Jun-91 SY.MU73/R) Mother and child (31x25cm-12x10in) s. panel
          (DM 75000)

GYSIS, Nicolas (attrib) (1842-1901) Greek
£10959 $19616   (13-Mar-91 N.M511/R) The little run-away received by family in interior
          (68x98cm-27x39in) (DM 32000)

GYURKOVICH, Karoly (1810-1874) Hungarian
£4283 $7666   (8-Apr-91 F.M351/R) Ritratti di Franz e Maria Rathauer
          (122x95cm-48x37in) (I.L 9500000)

H S (?) ?
£1500 $2940   (22-Nov-90 CSK233/R) Arranging roses (92x72cm-36x28in) mono.

H V D (?) ?
£3593 $6072   (2-May-91 CH.AM7/R) A capriccio view of a Mediterranean harbour with
          sailors in a rowing boatmaking for a three-master (58x82cm-23x32in)
          init. panel (D.FL 12000)

H V H (?) ?
£1000 $1720   (15-May-91 ZZ.B97) View of St. James' Park (19x25cm-7x10in) init. panel

HAAG, Carl (1820-1915) Swedish
£3486 $5926   (27-May-91 APT.P233/R) On the alert (51x38cm-20x15in) s.d.1876 W/C
          (F.FR 35000)
£5128 $10000   (24-Oct-90 CH.NY199/R) Shipwreck in the desert (79x136cm-31x54in)
          s.i.d.1886 i.verso W/C over pencil
£6355 $10739   (19-Apr-91 FN.S1726/R) Serenata in Cairo (100x48cm-39x19in) s.d.1893 W/C
          (DM 19000)

HAAG, Jean Paul (attrib) (19th C) French
£1500 $2940   (14-Feb-91 CSK139/R) A bed-time story (38x30cm-15x12in) s. panel

HAAGEN, Joris van der (attrib) (c.1615-1669) Dutch
£20000 $33800   (17-Apr-91 S144/R) Prospect of Dutch country house (62x192cm-24x76in)

HAAKO, Hans (1897-1984) Norwegian
£1247 $2406   (10-Dec-90 B.O59/R) From Hestervik in Malangen (75x90cm-30x35in)
          s.d.1936 (N.KR 14000)
£1259 $2454   (11-Oct-90 BU.O52/R) Landscape with houses (54x60cm-21x24in) s.
          (N.KR 14500)

HAALAND, Lars Laurits (1855-1938) Norwegian
£868 $1450   (3-Jun-91 B.O75/R) Coastal landscape with boat (24x37cm-9x15in) s.d.89
          panel (N.KR 10000)
£972 $1943   (9-Feb-91 BU.O70) Coastal landscape with sailingboat and rowingboat
          (20x30cm-8x12in) s. (N.KR 11000)
£1138 $2038   (11-Mar-91 B.O54/R) Sailing vessels and fishermen in rowingboat
          (25x37cm-10x15in) s.d.89 (N.KR 13000)
£1193 $2385   (9-Feb-91 BU.O71) Coastal landscape with rowingboat (20x34cm-8x13in) s.
          panel (N.KR 13500)

HAALAND, Lars Laurits (1855-1938) Norwegian-cont.
£1300	$2535	(18-Oct-90 CSK125/R) Fishing boat rounding rocky outcrop (46x65cm-18x26in) s.
£2096	$3983	(11-Sep-90 UL.T224) Seascape with the steamship 'Vaagen' (40x68cm-16x27in) (N.KR 24000)
£2404	$4640	(12-Dec-90 BU.O23/R) Seascape with sailship (39x55cm-15x22in) s.d.1900 (N.KR 27000)
£2939	$5671	(10-Dec-90 B.O58/R) Coastal landscape with vessel (50x78cm-20x31in) s.d.1921 (N.KR 33000)
£3348	$6629	(29-Jan-91 UL.T175) Rough seas with the fishingboat 'Royal' (47x66cm-19x26in) d.1911 (N.KR 38000)
£3493	$6638	(11-Sep-90 UL.T225) Steamship in storm 1903 (47x65cm-19x26in) (N.KR 40000)
£3646	$6089	(3-Jun-91 B.O74/R) Seascape (75x150cm-30x59in) s.d.1917 (N.KR 42000)
£4700	$8319	(19-Mar-91 UL.T175/R) Stiff breeze (58x99cm-23x39in) (N.KR 54000)
£7424	$14105	(11-Sep-90 UL.T223/R) Sailship in storm, lighthouse in background (N.KR 85000)
£8734	$16594	(11-Sep-90 UL.T221/R) Pilot boat 'Skude' 1906 (68x110cm-27x43in)
£9170	$17424	(11-Sep-90 UL.T220/R) Seascape with sailship 1903 (98x150cm-39x59in) (N.KR 105000)
£13465	$26526	(14-Nov-90 RAS.K71/R) Seascape with the vessel 'Victoria' off cliffs (100x150cm-39x59in) s.d.97 (D.KR 150000)

HAALKE, Hjalmar (1894-1964) Norwegian
£1394	$2718	(15-Oct-90 B.O41/R) Landscape (85x85cm-33x33in) s.d.1924 (N.KR 16000)
£1916	$3737	(15-Oct-90 B.O40/R) Autumn landscape (65x81cm-26x32in) s.d.37 (N.KR 22000)

HAAN, P J (?) ?
£767	$1472	(18-Dec-90 GM.B883) Canal gele (50x60cm-20x24in) s. board (B.FR 46000)

HAANEN, Adriana (1814-1895) Dutch
£3337	$6507	(21-Oct-90 L.C45) Nature morte aux fruits (62x49cm-24x19in) s.d.1866 (F.FR 33000)

HAANEN, C van (1844-c.1885) Dutch
£1049	$2024	(13-Dec-90 N.M2716/R) Portrait of young lady (115x81cm-45x32in) s.i.d.1886 (DM 3000)

HAANEN, Elizabeth Alida (1809-1845) Dutch
£689	$1157	(23-Apr-91 SY.AM64) Girl with dog (27x23cm-11x9in) s.d.1836 panel (D.FL 2300)

HAANEN, Remi van (1812-1894) Dutch
£2879	$4952	(16-May-91 D.V124/R) Snow storm (26x39cm-10x15in) mono. panel (A.S 60000)
£5068	$8615	(27-May-91 L.K274/R) Landscape with two figures by stream and church tower beyond (38x52cm-15x20in) s.d.69 panel (DM 15000)
£5254	$8564	(3-Jul-91 WE.MU36/R) Landscape with shepherd scene (63x55cm-25x22in) s.d.1834 (DM 15500)
£7360	$14132	(29-Nov-91 D.V17/R) Dutch winter landscape (43x52cm-17x20in) s.d.1849 (A.S 150000)

HAANEN, Remi van (attrib) (1812-1894) Dutch
£1409	$2748	(10-Oct-90 ZEL.L1519/R) Southern coastal landscape with beached sailing boat (30x43cm-12x17in) one of pair (DM 4200)

HAARDT, Georges van (1907-) Polish
£1100	$1771	(28-Jun-91 CSK2/R) Les Verticales, Naissance du monde (129x96cm-51x38in) s.d.57

HAARDT, Roger van (20th C) ?
£711	$1423	(10-Feb-91 CC.P34) Composition (73x60cm-29x24in) s.d.1957 (F.FR 7000)

HAARLEM, Cornelis Cornelisz van (1562-1638) Dutch
£3500	$5705	(2-Jul-91 PH22/R) Allegory of summer (28x31cm-11x12in) panel
£20513	$40000	(10-Oct-90 CH.NY103/R) Allegory of Time (33x46cm-13x18in) panel
£110000	$212300	(13-Dec-90 B101/R) St. Sebastian (43x33cm-17x13in) panel

HAARLEM, Cornelis Cornelisz van (circle) (1562-1638) Dutch
£1412	$2400	(31-May-91 CH.NY108/R) Allegory of time with old man holding hourglass (52x41cm-20x16in) canvas on panel

HAARTMAN, Axel (1877-1969) Finnish
£947	$1600	(20-Apr-91 HOR.H86/R) Old Abo (35x50cm-14x20in) s.d.1906 (F.M 6600)
£1007	$1944	(15-Dec-90 BU.H54) Birch grove (33x27cm-13x11in) s.i.d.1940 panel (F.M 7000)
£1504	$2963	(17-Nov-90 BU.H46/R) Reading (65x57cm-26x22in) s.i.d.1934 panel (F.M 10500)
£2639	$5173	(24-Nov-90 HOR.H99/R) From the artist's home (81x70cm-32x28in) s.d.1943 (F.M 18500)

HAAS, Johannes Hubertus Leonardus de (1832-1908) Flemish
£749	$1422	(11-Sep-90 CH.AM134/R) Cattle in a meadow (39x59cm-15x23in) s. (D.FL 2500)

HAAS, Johannes Hubertus Leonardus de (1832-1908) Flemish-cont.

£1078	$2102	(25-Oct-90 VN.R38) Cow in landscape (32x37cm-13x15in) s. panel (D.FL 3600)
£1176	$2200	(30-Aug-90 MFA.C180) Cows grazing (48x66cm-19x26in) s. panel
£1250	$2113	(3-May-91 PHE127/R) Feeding time (25x36cm-10x14in) s.d.62 panel
£1632	$3100	(14-Sep-90 S.BM133/R) Cattle grazing (48x74cm-19x29in) s.d.1865
£2400	$4032	(18-Jul-91 CSK69/R) Feeding cattle (25x38cm-10x15in) s.d.62 panel
£2695	$5336	(31-Jan-91 D.V128/R) Cows in landscape (39x64cm-15x25in) s. (A.S 55000)
£3147	$6073	(10-Dec-90 L.K430/R) Cows grazing and shepherdess resting with church tower beyond (46x71cm-18x28in) s. panel (DM 9000)

HAAS, M F H de (1832-1895) Dutch

£700	$1400	(10-Feb-91 LIT.L30) Marine scene (18x25cm-7x10in) s. board
£714	$1400	(27-Jan-91 LIT.L14a) Marine scene (18x25cm-7x10in) s.
£1337	$2500	(1-Aug-90 B.P7/R) Coastal scene (28x41cm-11x16in) s. panel
£1693	$3250	(17-Dec-90 SY.NY26/R) Boston lighthouse (36x58cm-14x23in) s.

HAAS, Mauritz F H de (1832-1895) Dutch

£931	$1750	(19-Sep-90 B.SF2758/R) Cornish coast (33x41cm-13x16in) s.
£1600	$3200	(4-Feb-91 S.SL190/R) Moonlit marine scene with lighthouse and boats (46x36cm-18x14in) s.
£7263	$13000	(12-Apr-91 SY.NY17/R) Sailing off coast (61x102cm-24x40in) s.

HAAS, Richard (20th C) American?

£1227	*$2000*	*(12-Jun-91 SY.NY176/R) Dakota (48x61cm-19x24in) graphite*
£1288	*$2100*	*(12-Jun-91 SY.NY173/R) Evening Post building (69x41cm-27x16in) graphite*
£1380	*$2250*	*(12-Jun-91 SY.NY172/R) 38 Row (69x46cm-27x18in) graphite*
£1380	*$2250*	*(12-Jun-91 SY.NY171/R) Old Lord and Taylor building (48x36cm-19x14in) graphite*

HAAS, T (20th C) ?

£727	$1453	(6-Feb-91 N.M614) In the coffee house (80x65cm-31x26in) s.d.1931 (DM 2100)

HAASE, Ove (19/20th C) ?

£2000	$3440	(17-May-91 C94/R) Daffodils (43cm-17ins circular) s.d.1924
£3000	$5160	(17-May-91 C93/R) Tulips and hyacinths in glass vase on marble pediment (63x54cm-25x21in) s.d.1931

HABERMANN, Hugo von (1849-1929) German

£699	$1357	(8-Dec-90 WK.M383/R) Portrait of lady wearing pearl necklace (68x56cm-27x22in) s. (DM 2000)
£898	$1760	(6-Nov-90 GF.L2448/R) Portrait of lady with hat (56x48cm-22x19in) s. board (S.FR 2200)
£608	*$1052*	*(25-May-91 N.M115/R) Portrait of lady, possibly Marianne von Willemer (38x33cm-15x13in) s. W/C bodycol over chl (DM 1800)*

HACHT/HAECHT, Tobias van see VERHAECHT, Tobias

HACKAERT, Jan (1629-1699) Dutch

£9397	$16820	(8-Apr-91 ARC.P26/R) Un carrefour dans une foret (108x83cm-43x33in) (F.FR 95000)
£968	*$1859*	*(27-Nov-90 APT.P76) Paysage vallonne avec personnages au bord d'un lac (21x26cm-8x10in) mono. pen wash (F.FR 9500)*

HACKER, Adolf (1908-) German

£1120	$2240	(6-Feb-91 RAS.K493/R) Young girl seated by Neckar River, Heidelberg (50x39cm-20x15in) s.i.d.1928 (D.KR 12500)

HACKER, Arthur (1858-1919) British

£719	$1200	(26-Jul-91 E.EDM56/R) Nude girl on knees (38x30cm-15x12in) s. panel
£1036	$2000	(10-Dec-90 H.C1137) Portrait of artist's brother (152x122cm-60x48in) s.i.d.1919 s.d.verso
£1400	$2338	(5-Jun-91 S187/R) Warmth and comfort (61x51cm-24x20in) s.d.1886
£1650	$3250	(15-Nov-90 D.NY32 a/R) Sunday morning (20x15cm-8x6in) s.d.1885 board

HACKER, Dieter (?) ?

£2538	$5000	(15-Nov-90 D.NY6/R) Der fluss (192x286cm-76x113in) s.i.d.1982 verso
£4822	$9500	(5-Oct-90 CH.NY114/R) Big splash (180x115cm-71x45in) s.i.d.1983verso
£1020	*$2000*	*(6-Nov-90 CE.NY179/R) Mon dieu 6 (107x79cm-42x31in) s.d.83 chl.*

HACKER, Horst (1842-1906) German

£1289	$2500	(6-Dec-90 FA.PH662/R) River cutting through mountains (79x132cm-31x52in) s.i.
£5102	$10000	(7-Nov-90 B.SF1178/R) Lake of Vierwaldstadt (94x123cm-37x48in) s.

HACKERT, Carl Ludwig (circle) (1740-1800) German

£2825	*$5000*	*(22-Mar-91 CH.NY628/R) A classical landscape with six girls beside a pool (28x21cm-11x8in) bodycolour*

HACKERT, Jacob Philippe (1737-1807) German

£2027	$3953	(26-Oct-90 BM.B714/R) Cow in Southern landscape (36x27cm-14x11in) mono. i.verso metal (DM 6000)
£2232	$4286	(27-Nov-90 W.T1146/R) Italianate harbour scene with townspeople (61x84cm-24x33in) (C.D 5000)

HACKERT, Jacob Philippe (1737-1807) German-cont.

£13878	$27339	(15-Nov-90 EA.Z217/R) Southern landscape with travellers (30x39cm-12x15in) indis.s. (S.FR 34000)
£19580	$37790	(10-Dec-90 L.K710/R) Grotto in mountain landscape with shepherd and goats (42x31cm-17x12in) s.d.1805 metal (DM 56000)
£1000	$1930	(11-Dec-90 C54) Figures beneath an oak on the edge of Lake Albano. View from VillaBorghese, Rome (67x50cm-26x20in) indist.s.i. pencil ink two
£1434	$2781	(7-Dec-90 GB.B5539/R) Group of trees (46x35cm-18x14in) brush over pencil pen (DM 4100)
£1500	$2535	(16-Apr-91 C262/R) View of the Lake Como with fisherman ashore (34x45cm-13x18in) s.d.1778 watermark blk.chk.wash
£6000	$11580	(11-Dec-90 C53/R) A view of the waterfall at Isola di Sora (63x82cm-25x32in) s.d.1793 blk.chk. ink wash

HACKERT, Jacob Philippe (attrib) (1737-1807) German

| £699 | $1357 | (7-Dec-90 GB.B5540) River landscape with fortified castle and classical ruins (21x30cm-8x12in) pen wash (DM 2000) |

HACKERT, Jacob Philippe (circle) (1737-1807) German

| £7213 | $12911 | (8-Apr-91 CH.R184/R) Paesaggio boschivo con torri (67x90cm-26x35in) (I.L 16000000) |
| £3000 | $5790 | (12-Dec-90 PH153/R) Travellers resting in the mouth of cave overlooking river landscape (55x79cm-22x31in) gouache |

HACKERT, Jacob Philippe (style) (1737-1807) German

£1900	$3610	(13-Sep-90 CSK16/R) Wooded river landscape with fisherman by stream, travellers and cattle in foreground (56x81cm-22x32in)
£3058	$6024	(13-Nov-90 CH.AM59/R) Travellers halting near waterfall in Italianate landscape (61x81cm-24x32in) with sig. (D.FL 10000)
£3259	$5247	(27-Jun-91 EP.M18/R) Paisaje con figuras (78x113cm-31x44in) (S.P 600000)
£5200	$9984	(28-Nov-90 S181/R) Figures on ledge below Tivoli (107x141cm-42x56in)

HACKERT, Johann Gottlieb (1744-1773) German

| £3800 | $6194 | (1-Jul-91 S197/R) View of Bay of Naples, with Vesuvius (34x46cm-13x18in) s.d.1772 pen W/C |
| £7500 | $12225 | (1-Jul-91 S198/R) View of Ponte Molle (35x47cm-14x19in) s.d.1770 pen W/C |

HACKL, Gabriel von (1843-1926) German

| £582 | $949 | (12-Jun-91 N.M444) Wedding congratulations (21x34cm-8x13in) s.d.1884 panel (DM 1700) |

HADDON, David W (19th C?) British

| £1200 | $1968 | (20-Jun-91 B71/R) Pet guinea pig (61x41cm-24x16in) s. |

HADDON, Trevor (1864-1941) British

£520	$932	(9-Apr-91 GO.G172) Landscape with washerwomen (54x74cm-21x29in) s. panel (S.KR 5600)
£520	$848	(2-Jul-91 SWS267) Country folk on Italian back street (40x60cm-16x24in) s.
£541	$881	(10-Jun-91 W.T1450) Spanish musicians at a doorway (75x45cm-30x18in) s. (C.D 1000)
£576	$962	(4-Jun-91 FB.M101/R) In conversation by the well (46x35cm-18x14in) s. (C.D 1100)
£707	$1400	(1-Feb-91 S.W2367/R) Women on Spanish terrace (51x76cm-20x30in) s.
£920	$1500	(5-Jul-91 S.W651/R) Arabian scene (36x46cm-14x18in) s.
£700	$1379	(1-Nov-90 TE552/R) While baby sleeps (66x46cm-26x18in) s. W/C

HADENGUE, Sebastien (1932-) ?

| £407 | $813 | (6-Feb-91 FB.P165) Empreinte (80x40cm-31x16in) s. verso i.d.62 stretcher mixed media canvas (F.FR 4000) |
| £427 | $854 | (6-Feb-91 FB.P167) Les shemes 4 (54x52cm-21x20in) mono.i.d.63 dec.62 col.ink (F.FR 4200) |

HADJU, Etienne (1907-) ?

| £602 | $970 | (25-Jun-91 BG.P28/R) Composition (64x42cm-25x17in) s.d.1975 ink (F.FR 6000) |

HAECK, Leopold (1868-1928) Belgian

| £736 | $1237 | (23-Apr-91 C.A519) Horse and cart in landscape (50x40cm-20x16in) s.d.1919 panel (B.FR 45000) |

HAEFELFINGER, Eugen (1898-?) Swiss

| £1406 | $2755 | (24-Nov-90 AB.L217/R) Untitled (61x51cm-24x20in) d.1931 canvas on pavatex (S.FR 3500) |

HAEFLIGER, Leopold (1929-1989) Swiss

£791	$1344	(27-May-91 GK.Z5340) Summer landscape with thunderstorm rising (24x34cm-9x13in) s.d.1988 board (S.FR 2000)
£1551	$3040	(6-Nov-90 GF.L2278/R) Winterlandscape in evening sun (47x63cm-19x25in) s.d.86 (S.FR 3800)
£2449	$4800	(6-Nov-90 GF.L2281/R) Winter landscape (110x120cm-43x47in) s.d.69 (S.FR 6000)

HAEFLIGER, Paul (1914-1982) Australian/German
£3493 $6253   (9-Apr-91 CH.ME187/R) Woman holding candlestick (89x150cm-35x59in) mono.
   board (A.D 8000)
£465 $781   *(22-Apr-91 SY.ME17) Seated nude (50x37cm-20x15in) s.d.71 ink oil paper*
   (A.D 1000)

HAEN, David de (1602-1659) Dutch
£28000 $48440   (24-May-91 C56/R) Portrait of a youth, bust length, wearing a feathered
   cap (76x62cm-30x24in) s.

HAENSBERGEN, Jan van (1642-1705) Dutch
£1765 $3000   (31-May-91 CH.NY135/R) Portrait of gentleman standing leaning on balcony
   and park beyond (48x39cm-19x15in)

HAENSBERGEN, Jan van (attrib) (1642-1705) Dutch
£950 $1758   (5-Mar-91 PH86) Nymphs bathing with two spaniels on seashore
   (22x26cm-9x10in) bears init. panel

HAES, Carlos de (1829-1898) Spanish
£2474 $4428   (13-Mar-91 FER.M173/R) Paisaje montanoso (31x47cm-12x19in) s. canvas
   laid down on board (S.P 450000)
£488 $951   *(17-Oct-90 FER.M37/R) A la vera del rio (32x23cm-13x9in) s. pencil dr*
   (S.P 90000)
£983 $1700   *(8-May-91 FER.M42/R) Paisaje rocoso con arboles (28x55cm-11x22in) s. chl*
   dr (S.P 180000)

HAES, Johannes de (?-1666) Dutch
£5000 $8150   (2-Jul-91 PH321/R) River landscape with horsemen and other figures
   before town (70x87cm-28x34in) s.

HAESAERT, Paul (1813-1893) Flemish
£1856 $3119   (23-Apr-91 SY.AM217/R) Enchanting music (54x44cm-21x17in) s.d.1842 panel
   (D.FL 6200)

HAFFER, A E (19th C) ?
£12607 $24584   (23-Oct-90 CH.R491/R) Veduta di Ischia (121x195cm-48x77in) s.d.1845
   (I.L 28000000)

HAFFNER, Leon (1881-1972) French
£565 $1097   *(6-Dec-90 CB.P97) Long-courrier gree en trois-mats carre, vu par babord*
   avant pres d'unetourelle (39x79cm-15x31in) s. gouache (F.FR 5500)

HAFSTROM, Jan (1937-) Swedish
£754 $1274   (18-Apr-91 BU.S57/R) Composition (42x47cm-17x19in) s.d.1979 acrylic
   (S.KR 8000)
£2132 $4135   (5-Dec-90 AB.S7110/R) Mine - variation (61x50cm-24x20in) s.d.1976
   (S.KR 23000)
£660 $1115   (18-Apr-91 BU.S60/R) Memory lane (44x48cm-17x19in) s.d.1979 mixed media
   collage acrylic (S.KR 7000)
£1112 $2158   (4-Dec-90 AB.S219/R) 18 January 1976 (64x50cm-25x20in) s.d.1976 gouache
   collage (S.KR 12000)
£1483 $2877   (5-Dec-90 AB.S7111/R) Untitled (45x39cm-18x15in) s. mixed media metal
   (S.KR 16000)
£1761 $3416   (5-Dec-90 AB.S7109/R) Dike - variation (64x45cm-25x18in) s.d.1979 mixed
   media (S.KR 19000)
£3582 $6053   (18-Apr-91 BU.S56/R) Fragment II (139x98cm-55x39in) s.d.1985 mixed media
   collage acrylic (S.KR 38000)

HAGARTY, Mary S (fl.1885-1930) British
£460 $782   *(29-May-91 PHC84) Cattle watering in wooded river landscape*
   (29x39cm-11x15in) s. W/C
£540 $918   *(29-May-91 PHC85) Figures by cart on village road (30x40cm-12x16in) s.*
   W/C
£850 $1615   *(10-Sep-90 PH87/R) Babbling stream (28x39cm-11x15in) s. i.verso W/C*

HAGBERG, Rune (20th C) Scandinavian
£660 $1115   *(18-Apr-91 BU.S43/R) Untitled (48x46cm-19x18in) init. mixed media*
   collage (S.KR 7000)

HAGBORG, August (1852-1925) Swedish
£735 $1441   (6-Nov-90 BA.S93/R) Model in deep thought (22x28cm-9x11in) s. panel
   (S.KR 8000)
£1502 $2554   (28-May-91 AB.S4628/R) View of the sea from sandy beach
   (31x40cm-12x16in) s. (S.KR 16000)
£1838 $3603   (6-Nov-90 BA.S92/R) Fishing village, Lysekil (40x53cm-16x21in)
   s.i.d.1873 (S.KR 20000)
£2817 $4789   (28-May-91 AB.S4627/R) Cottage interior with nude girl by window
   (58x47cm-23x19in) s. (S.KR 30000)
£3382 $6629   (20-Nov-90 GO.G82) Oyster gatherer seated on the shore (36x48cm-14x19in)
   s. (S.KR 37000)
£3590 $7000   (23-Oct-90 SY.NY161/R) Figures on a beach (60x72cm-24x28in) s.
£4106 $8089   (30-Oct-90 BU.S37/R) Hazy river landscape, Stockholm (54x72cm-21x28in)
   s. (S.KR 45000)
£5019 $8983   (9-Apr-91 GO.G51/R) Beach scene with oyster gatherer (92x64cm-36x25in)
   s. (S.KR 54000)
£5682 $9545   (24-Apr-91 BA.S78/R) Barefooted boy (100x65cm-39x26in) s. (S.KR 60000)

HAGBORG, August (1852-1925) Swedish-cont.
£6486 $12000 (10-Mar-91 H.C16/R) Two girls on beach (53x81cm-21x32in) s.
£7785 $15025 (12-Dec-90 BU.S27/R) Oyster gatherers on beach (81x115cm-32x45in) s.
               (S.KR 84000)
£11861 $23367 (30-Oct-90 BU.S36/R) Gathering oysters on Brittany beach
               (74x100cm-29x39in) s. (S.KR 130000)
£22004 $37846 (14-May-91 BU.S13/R) Washerwomen at Dalaro (149x260cm-59x102in) s.
               (S.KR 235000)

HAGEDORN, Friedrich (19th C?) German?
*£1400 $2758 (15-Nov-90 CSK25/R) Botafago, Rio de Janeiro (35x58cm-14x23in) s.
               i.verso pencil bodycol*

HAGEDORN, Karl (1889-?) British
£1350 $2646 (25-Jan-91 C138/R) Home defence (36x76cm-14x30in) s.d.40 s.i.verso panel
£1350 $2646 (25-Jan-91 C139/R) In training (30x76cm-12x30in) s.d.40 s.i.verso panel
£850 $1598 (20-Sep-90 C102/R) On the beach (20x25cm-8x10in) s.num.125 W/C chl

HAGEDORN, Winkler (19th C?) German?
£615 $1200 (26-Oct-90 S.W2202/R) Man of war at sea (56x66cm-22x26in) s.

HAGEDORN-OLSEN, Th (1902-) Danish
£572 $984 (15-May-91 RAS.K90) Winter landscape (75x100cm-30x39in) s.d.42
            (D.KR 6500)

HAGEL, Alfred (1898-) Austrian
£1460 $2861 (24-Jan-91 D.V95/R) Heuriger (38x34cm-15x13in) board (A.S 30000)

HAGEMANS, M (19/20th C) Belgian
£532 $866 (11-Jun-91 GM.B972) Vaches au pre (27x42cm-11x17in) s. wood (B.FR 32000)
£631 $1029 (11-Jun-91 GM.B1005) Pecheur au bord de l'etang (44x30cm-17x12in) s.
             (B.FR 38000)
£831 $1354 (11-Jun-91 GM.B968/R) Promeneur en Foret (43x27cm-17x11in) s.
             (B.FR 50000)
*£399 $650 (11-Jun-91 GM.B95) La Cueillette s. pastel (B.FR 24000)
£662 $1251 (25-Sep-90 GM.B1140/R) Paysanne sous la pluie s.d.86 W/C (B.FR 40000)
£720 $1239 (14-May-91 GM.B164) Rue de village animee s. gouache (B.FR 44000)*

HAGEMANS, Maurice (1852-1917) Belgian
£900 $1512 (23-Apr-91 C.A523) Children playing in an orchard (31x50cm-12x20in) s.
             panel (B.FR 55000)
£927 $1799 (8-Dec-90 KV.L139) On the quay (42x27cm-17x11in) s. canvas on panel
             (B.FR 55000)
£1227 $2062 (23-Apr-91 C.A522) October sun (29x44cm-11x17in) s. (B.FR 75000)
£1925 $3791 (6-Oct-90 KV.L397/R) Woman with cos beside the Maas (28x43cm-11x17in) s.
             panel (B.FR 120000)
*£432 $704 (11-Jun-91 GM.B1167) Vaches en pature s. gouache (B.FR 26000)
£432 $704 (11-Jun-91 GM.B1209) Homme sur l'Echelle s. W/C (B.FR 26000)
£599 $1071 (12-Mar-91 GM.B1193) Autochtone sur la Passerelle s. W/C (B.FR 36000)
£650 $1060 (4-Jul-91 PHI80) The angler (75x50cm-30x20in) s. W/C
£914 $1637 (12-Mar-91 GM.B895/R) Bergere et ses moutons s. gouache (B.FR 55000)
£1080 $1760 (11-Jun-91 GM.B115/R) Troupeau pres de la Mare s. pastel (B.FR 65000)
£1637 $2750 (23-Apr-91 C.A520/R) Cows watering (57x98cm-22x39in) s. W/C
             (B.FR 100000)*

HAGEMANS, Paul (1884-1959) Belgian
£753 $1295 (14-May-91 GM.B447) Roses blanches (58x47cm-23x19in) board (B.FR 46000)
£818 $1375 (23-Apr-91 C.A524) Before the ball (40x33cm-16x13in) s. panel
             (B.FR 50000)

HAGEMEISTER, Karl (1848-1933) German
£2730 $5352 (22-Nov-90 L.K983/R) Kitchen still life (25x33cm-10x13in) s. board
             (DM 8000)
£4778 $9365 (24-Nov-90 N.M191/R) Silver birch tree (126x75cm-50x30in) s.d.1912
             (DM 14000)
£6081 $10338 (30-May-91 SY.BE77/R) Stormy sea (77x119cm-30x47in) s. (DM 18000)
*£629 $1221 (7-Dec-90 GB.B5847/R) Landscape near Ferch (48x67cm-19x26in) mono.d.1890
             pencil dr (DM 1800)*
£1000 $1790 (12-Apr-91 BM.B840 a/R) River landscape with bridge (38x53cm-15x21in) s.
             mixed media (DM 3000)
*£1853 $3595 (7-Dec-90 GB.B5846/R) Mark lake landscape in stormy weather
             (75x110cm-30x43in) s. pastel canvas (DM 5300)
£3242 $6355 (24-Nov-90 N.M193/R) Trees at the shores of Baltic Sea
             (79x110cm-31x43in) s. pastel canvas (DM 9500)
£6040 $11779 (13-Oct-90 KRA.D387/R) Water lilies (61x88cm-24x35in) s.d.1912 pastel
             (DM 18000)
£6757 $11486 (1-Jun-91 VG.B109/R) Winter landscape (110x75cm-43x30in) s. gouache
             pastel (DM 20000)*

HAGEN, Johann van der (style) (1676-1745) Dutch
£1000 $1950 (18-Oct-90 CSK79/R) English men-o-war caught in storm off rocky headland
             (63x107cm-25x42in)

HAGEN, Theodor (1842-1919) German
£959 $1563 (12-Jun-91 N.M446/R) Hilly landscape with grass and bushes
             (28x46cm-11x18in) s. canvas on panel (DM 2800)

HAGENDORN, P H van (19th C) ?
£980 $1940 (31-Jan-91 D.V152/R) Village view (21x27cm-8x11in) s. (A.S 20000)

HAGENMULLER, N (19th C) ?
£2426 $4585 (27-Sep-90 D.V148/R) Children playing in Augarten (40x50cm-16x20in) s.
        (A.S 50000)

HAGG, Jacob (1839-1931) Swedish
£318 $569 (11-Mar-91 AB.S1027) Battle at sea (21x31cm-8x12in) s. Indian ink
        (S.KR 3400)
£412 $737 (11-Mar-91 AB.S1028) The Battle at Hogland (28x42cm-11x17in) s. Indian
        ink (S.KR 4400)
£567 $1100 (7-Dec-90 S.W2974/R) The Henry M. Clarke at full sail (51x74cm-20x29in)
        s.i.d.1881 W/C

HAGGENMACHER, Emma (19th C) ?
£4200 $8274 (4-Oct-90 CSK240/R) Venetian lovers (30x23cm-12x9in) s.d.1876 board

HAGHE, Louis (1806-1885) Belgian
£4600 $7590 (9-Jul-91 PH101/R) Council of war at Courtai (105x140cm-41x55in) s.
£500 $1000 (8-Feb-91 C51) The Baronial Hall (20x25cm-8x10in) pencil W/C htd.gum
        arabic
£545 $943 (21-May-91 DUR.M46/R) Interior de catedral (38x30cm-15x12in) W/C
        (S.P 100000)
£600 $1038 (20-May-91 PH182) Town hall, Brussels (43x28cm-17x11in) W/C over pencil

HAGN, Ludwig von (1819-1898) German
£4872 $9500 (25-Oct-90 GRO.B67/R) Passing room of Castle at Versailles
        (79x109cm-31x43in) s.i. panel

HAGUE SCHOOL (?) Dutch
£838 $1408 (23-Apr-91 SY.AM282) Fisherman in boat, village in distance
        (36x59cm-14x23in) bears sig. (D.FL 2800)

HAGUE, J Houghton (1842-?) British
£600 $1002 (6-Jun-91 CSK92) Saturday afternoon (76x110cm-30x43in) s.d.1881
        s.i.d.1880verso

HAGUE, Joshua Anderson (1850-1916) British
£718 $1415 (14-Nov-90 RAS.K135) Landscape with house by river (75x63cm-30x25in) s.
        (D.KR 8000)
£890 $1540 (7-May-91 PH11) Fishing in the brook (68x89cm-27x35in) s.
£1200 $2352 (13-Feb-91 S26/R) Breaking waves (51x76cm-20x30in) s.

HAHN, E (19th C) German?
£1541 $2759 (12-Mar-91 FN.S2401) Portrait of bearded Oriental wearing fir trimmed
        coat and turban (32x27cm-13x11in) s.d.1838 panel (DM 4500)

HAHN, Friedemann (1949-) German
£683 $1338 (20-Nov-90 L.K260/R) Marlene Dietrich (27x20cm-11x8in) s.d.81 W/C
        (DM 2000)

HAHN, Karl Wilhelm (1829-1887) German
£1712 $3065 (13-Mar-91 N.M512 a/R) Shepherd boy with horses by fountain
        (48x68cm-19x27in) s.i.d.1864 (DM 5000)
£2146 $4250 (30-Jan-91 GRO.B40/R) The horse seller (38x56cm-15x22in) s.i.d.1863
        panel
£2797 $5399 (12-Dec-90 N.M535/R) Shepherd boy with horses by well (48x68cm-19x27in)
        s.i.d.1864 (DM 8000)

HAHNISCH, Anton (1817-1897) Austrian
£1487 $2871 (13-Dec-90 D.V18/R) Portrait of lady seated in armchair wearing lace
        bonnet (28x22cm-11x9in) s.d.842 W/C (A.S 30000)

HAIER, Joseph (1816-1891) Austrian
£1000 $1940 (7-Dec-90 CBS259) The fortune teller (74x97cm-29x38in) s.

HAIG, Axel Herman (1835-1921) British
£1977 $3500 (22-Mar-91 S.W2809/R) Cathedral interior with figures (76x53cm-30x21in)
        mono.d.1885 W/C gouache

HAIG, Earl (20th C) British
£550 $957 (28-Mar-91 CSK142) Haliwell stream 3 (33x41cm-13x16in) init. panel

HAIGH, Alfred G (fl.1890-1928) British
£750 $1290 (16-May-91 CSK88) Harkaway VIII, dark bay racehorse in loose box
        (34x44cm-13x17in) s.d.1909
£880 $1628 (6-Mar-91 RBB800) Coach and four arriving at castle entrance, Lancaster
        (56x76cm-22x30in) s.d.1913
£2000 $3940 (1-Nov-90 CSK35/R) Tagalle, grey filly, in loose box (61x76cm-24x30in)
        s.d.1912

HAIGH-WOOD, C (1856-1927) British
£720 $1390 (13-Dec-90 CSK344) Portrait of gentleman, thought to be George Bernard
        Shaw, seated (142x113cm-56x44in) s.d.00

HAINE, Desire Victor Felix (1900-) Belgian
£549 $1043   (26-Feb-91 VN.R123) Town scene (69x79cm-27x31in) s. (D.FL 1800)

HAINES, Frederick Stanley (1879-1960) Canadian
£768 $1512   (30-Oct-90 SY.T153/R) Road near Glen Williams (41x51cm-16x20in) s.
        i.verso board (C.D 1750)
£890 $1486   (3-Jun-91 R.T146/R) Birches, Dark Lake (50x60cm-20x24in) s. canvasboard
        (C.D 1700)
£1010 $1747   (6-May-91 SY.T180/R) Island in Bad River (41x51cm-16x20in) s. board
        (C.D 2000)
£1514 $2467   (10-Jun-91 W.T1066/R) Autumn afternoon (76x91cm-30x36in) s. i. verso
        board (C.D 2800)

HAINES, William Henry (1812-1884) British
£1400 $2688   (29-Nov-90 B73/R) Venetian canal (63x104cm-25x41in) s

HAINS, Raymond (1926-?) French
£7500 $14625   (18-Oct-90 C396/R) Picasso vous connaissez (73x60cm-29x24in) s.
*   i.d.1971verso paper collage on canvas*

HAINZ, Johann Georg see HINZ, Johann Georg

HAITE, George Charles (1855-1924) British
£868 $1702   (20-Nov-90 GO.G414) River landscape with boats at river's edge
        (59x101cm-23x40in) s.d.96 (S.KR 9500)
£300 $537   (14-Mar-91 GSP581) Boats by quay, town beyond (10x18cm-4x7in) s. W/C
£820 $1615   (13-Nov-90 SWS62/R) Driving cattle past a mill (36x57cm-14x22in) s.
£1031 $1742   (17-Apr-91 DS.W70) Mediterranean washer woman (34x68cm-13x27in) s. W/C
*   (NZ.D 3000)*
£1200 $2016   (22-Apr-91 PH276/R) Venetian fruit stall (30x52cm-12x20in) s.d.1903 W/C
*   bodycol.*

HAJEK, Otto Herbert (1927-) German?
£683 $1338   (20-Nov-90 L.K264 a) Untitled (57x60cm-22x24in) s.d.87 indian ink brush
*   wash (DM 2000)*
£743 $1286   (21-May-91 WK.M935/R) Composition (31x30cm-12x12in) s.i.d.1960 gouache
*   board sold with two other W/C (DM 2200)*
£1575 $2568   (14-Jun-91 L.K925) Farbwege, Studie 3 (51x68cm-20x27in) s.d.72
*   s.i.d.verso mixed media (DM 4600)*

HAKAVA, Aale (1909-) Finnish
£1712 $3355   (24-Nov-90 HOR.H100/R) Northern quay (65x92cm-26x36in) s. (F.M 12000)

HALAUSKA, Ludwig (1827-1882) German
£1715 $3395   (31-Jan-91 D.V218/R) Landscape with farmhouse and pond (34x57cm-13x22in)
        s.d.872 (A.S 35000)
£2205 $4366   (31-Jan-91 D.V68/R) Village in river landscape (28x34cm-11x13in) s.
        (A.S 45000)
£3797 $6796   (11-Apr-91 D.V132/R) River landscape (45x60cm-18x24in) s.d.862
        (A.S 80000)

HALBERG-KRAUSS, Fritz (1874-1951) German
£514 $837   (12-Jun-91 N.M450) Woodlands near Dachau (42x29cm-17x11in) s. board
        (DM 1500)
£1049 $2024   (12-Dec-90 N.M537/R) Pond landscape with ducks (33x37cm-13x15in) s.
        i.verso board (DM 3000)
£1233 $2010   (12-Jun-91 N.M448/R) Schachenbach in Kanton Uri, Switzerland
        (49x67cm-19x26in) s. i.verso board (DM 3600)
£1301 $2121   (12-Jun-91 N.M449) Pond with reeds in wooded landscape (42x56cm-17x22in)
        s. board (DM 3800)
£1370 $2452   (13-Mar-91 N.M517/R) Wooded landscape with pond (24x37cm-9x15in) s.i.
        board (DM 4000)
£1370 $2452   (13-Mar-91 N.M516/R) Peasant with horse-drawn cart on path
        (21x35cm-8x14in) s. board (DM 4000)
£1409 $2748   (10-Oct-90 WE.MU92/R) Summer landscape (20x27cm-8x11in) s. board
        (DM 4200)
£1541 $2759   (12-Mar-91 FN.S2402/R) Murnau moor landscape with fisherman in boat and
        thunderstorm rising (14x30cm-6x12in) s. board (DM 4500)
£1748 $3392   (4-Dec-90 FN.S1857/R) Dachauer Moos landscape with boys playing
        (51x71cm-20x28in) s. (DM 5000)
£2098 $4049   (12-Dec-90 N.M536/R) Moor landscape near Schleissheim (36x60cm-14x24in)
        s. i.verso board (DM 6000)
£2534 $4941   (26-Oct-90 KM.K1244/R) Rising thunder storm in Alpine river landscape
        (99x969cm-39x381in) s. board on panel (DM 7500)
£2885 $5625   (25-Oct-90 D.V10/R) Winter landscape with ducks (64x105cm-25x41in) s.i.
        (A.S 60000)
£2901 $5483   (25-Sep-90 FN.S2196/R) Path with figures in wooded landscape
        (65x88cm-26x35in) s.i. (DM 8500)
£3253 $5824   (13-Mar-91 N.M513/R) View over Isar valley (80x126cm-31x50in) s.i.
        (DM 9500)
£3596 $6437   (13-Mar-91 N.M515/R) Peasant woman with cows watering in pond
        (80x100cm-31x39in) s.i. canvas on panel (DM 10500)
£4110 $7356   (13-Mar-91 N.M515 a/R) Wooded pond landscape with cows watering
        (69x99cm-27x39in) s.i. board (DM 12000)
£7000 $13790   (4-Oct-90 CSK39/R) The Frauninsel from Lake Chiem (70x100cm-28x39in)
        s.i.

HALE, Edward Matthew (1852-1924) British
£800 $1336   (5-Jun-91 S199/R) Daydreams (33x47cm-13x19in) mono. panel

HALE, Miss E Thomas (fl.1892-1919) British
£950 $1862   (22-Jan-91 PH107) Little shepherdess (18x37cm-7x15in) s.indis.d.
                   s.i.verso canvas on panel

HALE, W (19/20th C) ?
£789 $1500   (9-Jan-91 D.NY36) Sailing ships (23x41cm-9x16in) s. board backed
                   masonite

HALE, William Matthew (1837-1929) British
£350 $627   (13-Mar-91 B122) Deer in parkland (37x55cm-15x22in) W/C bodycol.

HALEY (?) ?
£1128 $2200   (24-Oct-90 D.NY35/R) Elegant lady seated in park (38x25cm-15x10in) s.
                   panel

HALICKA, Alice (1895-1975) Polish
£1104 $2043   (4-Mar-91 ARC.P134/R) L'expert (41x33cm-16x13in) s. (F.FR 11000)
£1206 $2159   (11-Mar-91 GL.P58) Danseuses (46x55cm-18x22in) s. (F.FR 12000)
£4082 $7918   (8-Dec-90 GAB.G2634/R) Composition aux instruments de musique
                   (54x65cm-21x26in) s.d.1916 (S.FR 10000)

HALIRKA (20th C) ?
£1109 $2162   (28-Oct-90 M.V161) Le Sacre Coeur vu des toits de Paris
                   (81x100cm-32x39in) s. (F.FR 11000)

HALL, Clifford (1904-1973) British
£720 $1411   (25-Jan-91 C28/R) Artist's wife (86x51cm-34x20in) s.d.46-7
£480 $811   (30-Apr-91 B80/R) Bull fight (25x36cm-10x14in) s.d.July 31st 1946 brush
                   W/C

HALL, Frederick (1860-1948) British
£982 $1886   (27-Nov-90 W.T1039) River scene with girls under Scotch pine
                   (91x71cm-36x28in) s. (C.D 2200)
£2008 $3855   (26-Nov-90 SY.ME177/R) Farm courtyard (38x31cm-15x12in) s. board
                   (A.D 5000)
£2800 $5460   (24-Oct-90 DR145/R) Evening glow, carthorses by hayrick
                   (41x32cm-16x13in) s. panel
£3000 $5820   (5-Dec-90 PHE51/R) The shepherd's cot (32x40cm-13x16in) s.i. verso board
£4800 $7824   (14-Jun-91 C298/R) Portraits of James Douglas and Lilian Fletcher
                   (102x127cm-40x50in) s.d.1909 pair
£6000 $9780   (13-Jun-91 L100/R) The Home pond (38x53cm-15x21in) s.
£8500 $14365   (1-May-91 S4/R) Ducks in farmyard at sunset (64x76cm-25x30in) s.
£9500 $15865   (4-Jun-91 PH48/R) Gaggle of geese outside Greyhound Inn, Corfe Castle,
                   Dorset (62x75cm-24x30in) s.

HALL, G L and WAINEWRIGHT (19th C) British
£590 $1044   (5-Apr-91 BW386) Returning to the fields (33x69cm-13x27in) s. W/C

HALL, George Henry (1825-1913) American
£719 $1200   (5-Jun-91 D.NY43/R) The spice market, Cairo (30x38cm-12x15in) s.verso
                   i.d.1876stretcher
£7292 $14000   (30-Nov-90 CH.NY8/R) Still life with watermelon (22x28cm-9x11in)
                   s.d.1868 panel

HALL, George Lothian (1825-1888) British
£610 $1000   (19-Jun-91 B.SF1915/R) Crammond Kirk near Edinburgh (51x76cm-20x30in) s.

HALL, George Lothian and WAINEWRIGHT, Thomas Francis (19th C) British
£600 $1014   (3-May-91 T210) Farmstead by sea with sheep and cattle (33x69cm-13x27in)
                   s. W/C

HALL, H R (fl.1895-1902) British
£650 $1229   (26-Sep-90 RB659) Highland cattle, Loch Lomond (61x91cm-24x36in) s.
£700 $1386   (30-Jan-91 CSK223) Highland cattle by Loch Tarridon in the early morning
                   (61x107cm-24x42in) s. i. verso

HALL, Harry (1814-1882) British
£714 $1200   (17-Jul-91 SY.NY362/R) Repulse (25x33cm-10x13in) i.d.1866 board
£1946 $3250   (7-Jun-91 SY.NY126/R) Macaroni, winner of the Derby 1863
                   (38x51cm-15x20in)
£3158 $6000   (28-Feb-91 CH.NY167/R) John Scott holding Daniel O'Rourke derby winner
                   with Frank Betler up (50x66cm-20x26in) indis.s.i.d.1857
£4211 $8000   (15-Sep-90 S.W2410/R) Kingston (71x91cm-28x36in) s.d.1873
£5090 $8500   (7-Jun-91 SY.NY59/R) A racehorse with jockey up (58x76cm-23x30in) s.
£10778 $18000   (7-Jun-91 SY.NY54/R) Eagle with jockey up and trainer (71x91cm-28x36in)
                   init.i.d.1846
£11976 $20000   (7-Jun-91 SY.NY55/R) West Australian with jockey up and trainer
                   (62x76cm-24x30in) s.i.d.1853
£13000 $24960   (29-Nov-90 HB509/R) Lord Falmouth's mares and foals, in Mereworth Park,
                   Maidstone (76x132cm-30x52in) s.d.1876

HALL, Harry (circle) (1814-1882) British
£900 $1467   (4-Jul-91 B58) Portrait of a racehorse in a stable (43x53cm-17x21in)
                 bears sig.

HALL, J (?) ?
£798 $1500   (7-Aug-90 RB.HY157/R) Portrait of the ship 'Vendome' under sail
                 (61x91cm-24x36in) s.

HALL, Jan Jacob Teyler van (1794-1851) Dutch
£719 $1365   (11-Sep-90 CH.AM128) Huntsmen on a wooded road, village beyond
                 (24x22cm-9x9in) s. panel (D.FL 2400)

HALL, Lindsay Bernard (1859-1935) British
£2500 $4850   (6-Dec-90 CSK28/R) Government house (69x55cm-27x22in) s. s.i.verso

HALL, Peter Adolphe (1739-1793) Swedish
£1600 $2832   *(20-Mar-91 C59/R) Portrait of lady in red dress and stole with frilled*
                 border (3x?cm-1x?in) min. gilt-metal frame oval
£1600 $3072   *(18-Dec-90 C35/R) Portrait of lady in loose grey dress, matching shawl*
                 and headdress (7cm-3ins circular) min. chased gilt-metal mount
£2449 $4824   *(13-Nov-90 CH.G217) Portrait of Alexandre Roslin (3x?cm-1x?in) min. oval*
                 mounted on gilt-metal lacquer box (S.FR 6000)

HALL, Richard (1860-?) British
£635 $1124   (22-Mar-91 EA.Z597) Little girl sewing (46x38cm-18x15in) s.d.1894 panel
                 (S.FR 1600)
£694 $1200   (8-May-91 RO.BA361) Vase ave fleurs (46x33cm-18x13in) s.d.37
£3457 $6500   (18-Sep-90 RO.BA200) Composition (60x100cm-24x39in) s.

HALL, Thomas P (19th C) British
£605 $1179   (15-Oct-90 SY.J28) Moliere reading his comedies to his housekeeper
                 (24x29cm-9x11in) s.d.1869 i. verso (SA.R 3000)

HALL, William (19th C) British
£750 $1328   (21-Mar-91 CSK142) Near Llangollen (46x64cm-18x25in) s.i. verso

HALLANDER, Gunnar (1915-1980) Swedish
£943 $1632   (22-May-91 BA.S91/R) Brown pear and grey-white utensils
                 (46x55cm-18x22in) s.d.1966 panel (S.KR 10000)
£1226 $2122   (22-May-91 BA.S90/R) Bouquet of white flowers (38x46cm-15x18in) s. panel
                 (S.KR 13000)

HALLANDER, Karl Johan (1935-) Swedish
£519 $898   (22-May-91 BA.S374/R) Regimental prayers before the next attack
                 (64x88cm-25x35in) s.d.69 (S.KR 5500)

HALLATZ, Emil (1837-1888) German
£839 $1620   (14-Dec-90 BM.B619/R) Donkey driven by man on road to mill
                 (19x15cm-7x6in) s. panel (DM 2400)

HALLE, Noel (1711-1781) French
£34619 $61968   (9-Apr-91 APT.P39/R) Allegorie du Soir (115x145cm-45x57in) (F.FR 350000)

HALLE, Noel (attrib) (1711-1781) French
£3043 $6024   (30-Jan-91 APT.P255/R) Amours jouant aux artistes (24x52cm-9x20in) panel
                 (F.FR 30000)

HALLE, Samuel Baruch (1824-1889) French
£3468 $6000   (23-May-91 CH.NY42/R) Buy my flowers (79x62cm-31x24in) s.d.1861

HALLER, Michael (19th C) Austrian
£753 $1349   (13-Mar-91 N.M518) Peasant woman and child on bridge across stream in
                 mountain landscape (68x55cm-27x22in) s. i.stretcher (DM 2200)

HALLER, Roman (1920-) Austrian
£861 $1490   *(8-May-91 D.V144/R) Untitled (54x39cm-21x15in) mono.d.52 mixed media*
                 board (A.S 18000)

HALLET, Andre (?) ?
£2619 $4452   (28-May-91 C.A130/R) Town scene (50x60cm-20x24in) s. panel (B.FR 160000)

HALLETT, Hendricks (1847-1921) ?
£974 $1900   (20-Oct-90 W.W108/R) Maine coastal view (56x91cm-22x36in) s.
£635 $1200   *(25-Sep-90 CE.NY68/R) Marblehead (34x49cm-13x19in) s. W/C*

HALLEY, Peter (20th C) American
£47337 $80000   (1-May-91 SY.NY154/R) Two conduits (178x279cm-70x110in) acrylic day-glo
                 acrylic canvas
£42899 $72500   *(1-May-91 SY.NY146/R) White cell with triple conduit*
                 (163x274cm-64x108in) s.d.1986 verso acrylic roll-a-tex canvas
£45918 $90000   *(15-Feb-91 SY.NY189/R) Two cells with circulating conduit*
                 (196x350cm-77x138in) day-glo acrylic roll-a-tex canvas

HALLIER, Theodor (1908-1982) German
£1486 $2899   (26-Oct-90 BM.B639/R) Street scene, winter evening (81x81cm-32x32in) s.
                 (DM 4400)

HALLMANN, Anton (1812-1845) German
£472 $916   (7-Dec-90 GB.B5849/R) View of Kremlin (26x21cm-10x8in) i.d. pencil dr (DM 1350)
£472 $916   (7-Dec-90 GB.B5848) Main portal of San Marco in Venice (34x26cm-13x10in) d.1836 pencil dr (DM 1350)

HALLOWELL, George Hawley (1871-1926) American
£1777 $3500   (16-Nov-90 S.BM165/R) Marine scene (71x119cm-28x47in) s.

HALLSTROM, Bjorn (1916-1982) Swedish
£621 $1205   (4-Dec-90 BA.S176/R) Reflections (46x68cm-18x27in) s.d.58 (S.KR 6700)

HALLSTROM, Eric (1893-1946) Swedish
£834 $1618   (4-Dec-90 BA.S185/R) Autumn in Lappland (20x29cm-8x11in) s. panel (S.KR 9000)
£1158 $2247   (5-Dec-90 AB.S7090/R) Still life of flowers in interior (45x30cm-18x12in) s. (S.KR 12500)
£2595 $5034   (4-Dec-90 BA.S182/R) Old town scene, Hagalund (73x82cm-29x32in) s. (S.KR 28000)
£2768 $5314   (27-Nov-90 BU.S118/R) Amaryllis (95x73cm-37x29in) s. (S.KR 30000)
£2780 $5394   (4-Dec-90 BA.S181/R) Transporting timber (72x93cm-28x37in) s. (S.KR 30000)
£3506 $6731   (27-Nov-90 BU.S116/R) Landscape near poitiers (49x61cm-19x24in) s. panel (S.KR 38000)
£4906 $8487   (22-May-91 BA.S75/R) Morning, Ytterkolksele (86x99cm-34x39in) s. (S.KR 52000)
£8434 $16361   (4-Dec-90 BA.S178/R) The school (54x65cm-21x26in) s. (S.KR 91000)
£849 $1469   (22-May-91 BA.S79/R) Street in Funchal (28x22cm-11x9in) s. W/C (S.KR 9000)
£868 $1702   (20-Nov-90 GO.G333) Summer's day (51x69cm-20x27in) s. gouache (S.KR 9500)
£1103 $2162   (10-Nov-90 FAL.M130/R) Interior with woman washing (47x54cm-19x21in) s. gouache (S.KR 12000)
£1127 $1915   (28-May-91 AB.S5213/R) Crayfish fishing (66x88cm-26x35in) s.d.40 pastel (S.KR 12000)
£1390 $2697   (4-Dec-90 BA.S183/R) Girl on balcony (60x50cm-24x20in) s.i.d.33 mixed media (S.KR 15000)

HALLSTROM, Staffan (1914-1976) Swedish
£880 $1708   (5-Dec-90 AB.S7091/R) Psychial symphony (28x35cm-11x14in) s.d.51 (S.KR 9500)
£1112 $2158   (4-Dec-90 BA.S195/R) Self portrait in the studio (46x62cm-18x24in) s. (S.KR 12000)
£1476 $2834   (27-Nov-90 BU.S126/R) Winter landscape (65x54cm-26x21in) s. (S.KR 16000)
£1854 $3596   (4-Dec-90 BA.S194/R) Winter landscape (72x78cm-28x31in) init.d.54 (S.KR 20000)
£3396 $5875   (22-May-91 BA.S370/R) Yellow still life (76x44cm-30x17in) mono. (S.KR 36000)
£4618 $7805   (18-Apr-91 BU.S92/R) Crowding (116x88cm-46x35in) i.sig. s.verso (S.KR 49000)
£5904 $11336   (27-Nov-90 BU.S123/R) In the wood I (78x65cm-31x26in) s. (S.KR 64000)
£11121 $21576   (4-Dec-90 BA.S189/R) Teaching studio (111x135cm-44x53in) init.d.1967verso (S.KR 120000)
£1080 $1836   (28-May-91 AB.S5214/R) Reading newspapers (22x16cm-9x6in) s.d.70 W/C (S.KR 11500)

HALONEN, Kalle (1899-1947) Finnish
£863 $1666   (15-Dec-90 BU.H55) Old barn (33x41cm-13x16in) s.d.1924 canvas on panel (F.M 6000)

HALONEN, Pekka (1865-1933) Finnish
£6705 $13141   (24-Nov-90 HOR.H106/R) Grey day (52x50cm-20x20in) s.d.1916 (F.M 47000)
£6906 $13329   (15-Dec-90 BU.H56/R) Beach in spring (46x38cm-18x15in) s.d.1928 (F.M 48000)
£10904 $18428   (20-Apr-91 HOR.H90/R) Turbulence in Kivikoski (62x40cm-24x16in) s.d.1922 (F.M 76000)
£11461 $22579   (17-Nov-90 BU.H49/R) Winter landscape (63x51cm-25x20in) s.d.1931 (F.M 80000)
£16833 $32993   (24-Nov-90 HOR.H103/R) Early spring (60x42cm-24x17in) s.d.1928 (F.M 118000)
£17934 $30308   (20-Apr-91 HOR.H88/R) Winter morning with hoar-frost (75x55cm-30x22in) s.d.1916 (F.M 125000)
£20086 $33945   (20-Apr-91 HOR.H87/R) Winter's day (68x53cm-27x21in) s.d.1912 (F.M 140000)
£156919 $307561   (24-Nov-90 HOR.H101/R) Approaching the enemy (155x117cm-61x46in) s.d.1896 (F.M 1100000)

HALPERT, Samuel (1884-1930) American
£691 $1300   (19-Sep-90 B.SF2742/R) Edith Halpert setting a table (61x51cm-24x20in) s.
£6061 $12000   (30-Jan-91 GRO.B92/R) Central park (76x64cm-30x25in) s.d.

HALS, Dirck (1591-1656) Dutch
£20359 $34407   (2-May-91 CH.AM85/R) Elegant companies smoking, drinking and music making in interiors (17x16cm-7x6in) panel two (D.FL 68000)

HALS, Dirck (circle) (1591-1656) Dutch
£1826 $3615   (30-Jan-91 APT.P205/R) Le dejeuner galant (40x69cm-16x27in) panel
     (F.FR 18000)

HALS, Dirck (school) (1591-1656) Dutch
£882 $1500   (30-May-91 CE.NY21) Elegant figures gathered in interior
     (46x56cm-18x22in) panel

HALS, Frans (16/17th C) Dutch
£126316 $240000   (11-Jan-91 CH.NY83/R) Portrait of a gentleman wearing black costume.
     Portrait of a lady wearing a black costume, white coll
     (63x49cm-25x19in) both mono. pair

HALS, Frans (circle) (16/17th C) Dutch
£3059 $5200   (31-May-91 CH.NY104/R) Portrait of gentleman holding roemer
     (39x27cm-15x11in) bears mono.d.1647 panel
£4103 $8000   (11-Oct-90 SY.NY162/R) Portrait of young man dressed in black
     (74x59cm-29x23in) panel
£9744 $19000   (10-Oct-90 CH.NY199/R) Portrait of lady wearing costume with ruff
     (47x42cm-19x17in)

HALS, Frans (style) (16/17th C) Dutch
£898 $1518   (2-May-91 CH.AM97) Officers merry-making in an inn (72x62cm-28x24in)
     mono. (D.FL 3000)
£1497 $2530   (2-May-91 CH.AM38/R) A jester, half length, wearing a green costume
     holding a sheet of music (76x71cm-30x28in) mono. (D.FL 5000)

HALSALL, William Formby (1841-1919) American
£990 $1900   (17-Dec-90 SY.NY22/R) Sailing off coast (30x51cm-12x20in) s.
£1005 $1900   (26-Sep-90 S.BM780) Sailing vessels in high seas off stone pier
     (74x127cm-29x50in) s.

HALSTED, F (19th C) Australian
*£1544 $3042   (13-Nov-90 J.M137) Sydney Heads looking from South Head
     (33x49cm-13x19in) s. W/C (A.D 4000)*

HALSWELLE, Keeley (1832-1891) British
£2200 $3630   (9-Jul-91 PH75/R) Roman fruit girl (69x99cm-27x39in) s.i.d.1874
     s.i.stretcher
£15000 $24450   (14-Jun-91 C216/R) Waiting for the Blessing of Pius IX at St John
     Lateran, Rome 1869 (145x233cm-57x92in) s.d.1869-78 i.verso

HALTER, Marek (?) ?
£692 $1239   (14-Apr-91 GL.P296) Bouquet de fleurs (81x61cm-32x24in) s. (F.FR 7000)

HAM, Geo (20th C) ?
*£1512 $2949   (28-Oct-90 PLF.P212/R) La coupe Deutch de la Meurthe (33x68cm-13x27in)
     mono. crayon W/C gouache (F.FR 15000)*
*£3226 $6290   (28-Oct-90 PLF.P211/R) 24 H du Mans 1952 (18x24cm-7x9in) s. gouache
     (F.FR 32000)*

HAMACHER, Willy (1865-1909) German
£559 $1080   (12-Dec-90 N.M539) Rocky coastal landscape with surf (61x95cm-24x37in)
     s. (DM 1600)
£1399 $2713   (4-Dec-90 FN.S1858/R) Venazza di Levante, coastal landscape, evening
     (140x180cm-55x71in) s. (DM 4000)

HAMALAINEN, Vaino (1876-1940) Finnish
£1367 $2351   (14-May-91 HOR.H57) Young repairer (37x30cm-15x12in) s.d.1899
     (F.M 9500)

HAMANN, Julie Caroline (1842-1916) Danish
£831 $1488   (9-Apr-91 RAS.K2063) White and pale purple lilacs (92x64cm-36x25in)
     s.d.1893 (D.KR 9500)

HAMBACH, Johann Michael (17th C) German
£3000 $5070   (16-Apr-91 PH190/R) String of thrushes hanging on wall with bird
     catcher's tools (67x54cm-26x21in) s.d.

HAMBIDGE, Jay (20th C) Australian
£1684 $3200   (9-Jan-91 CH.NY200/R) The meeting. Sold with ink dr by A.L.Brennan and
     pastel dr by J.P.Jones (45x32cm-18x13in) s. en grisaille

HAMBLETON, Richard (20th C) American
£1531 $3000   (6-Nov-90 CE.NY296/R) Untitled (222x122cm-87x48in) s. acrylic paper

HAMBOURG, Andre (1909-?) French
£1156 $2000   (12-May-91 H.C58/R) Sur la Touques (15x18cm-6x7in) s.init. i.verso
£1156 $2000   (12-May-91 H.C59) Maree basse a Trouville (13x18cm-5x7in) s.init.
     i.verso
£1156 $2000   (12-May-91 H.C60/R) Trouville (13x23cm-5x9in) s. init.i.verso
£2122 $4118   (8-Dec-90 GAB.G2635/R) Au manege (14x18cm-6x7in) s. (S.FR 5200)
£2487 $4800   (10-Dec-90 H.C1215) Basin St. Marc au printemps, Venice (20x25cm-8x10in)
     s.
£2551 $5000   (12-Feb-91 SY.NY101/R) La campagne le soir, en auge (23x36cm-9x14in) s.
     init.i.verso

HAMBOURG, Andre (1909-?) French-cont.

£2679	$4500	(16-Jul-91 BG.M983 a/R) Sunset at Trouville (13x23cm-5x9in) s.
£3262	$6296	(12-Dec-90 APT.P112) Paysage aux moulins a vent (33x54cm-13x21in) s. (F.FR 32000)
£3571	$7000	(12-Feb-91 SY.NY149/R) Fin de jour sur la plage, Trouville en aout (23x36cm-9x14in) s. init.i.verso
£3984	$6773	(29-May-91 GL.P161/R) Londres a Hyde Park (27x35cm-11x14in) s.d.1970 i.verso (F.FR 40000)
£4000	$6760	(1-May-91 GD.B373/R) Vieux belle Triers (46x65cm-18x26in) s. i.d.verso (S.FR 10000)
£4335	$7500	(12-May-91 H.C57/R) Boats on the water (46x66cm-18x26in) s.
£5097	$9837	(12-Dec-90 ZZ.F64/R) Le drapeau tricolore (27x35cm-11x14in) s.d.1957 i. verso (F.FR 50000)
£5521	$9000	(12-Jun-91 SY.NY136/R) Vent sur la plage - Trouville (27x36cm-11x14in) s.d.1985 init.verso
£7614	$15000	(13-Nov-90 CE.NY100/R) Septembre a la Carriere (60x74cm-24x29in) s. init.d.1967.68verso
£7653	$15000	(12-Feb-91 SY.NY147/R) The riding lesson (64x76cm-25x30in) s.
£8800	$14168	(24-Jun-91 CSK123/R) La plage a Trouville (38x55cm-15x22in) s. i.d.1956stretcher
£11431	$19319	(21-Apr-91 E.LA67/R) Deauville - l'entree du port (38x55cm-15x22in) s. (F.FR 115000)
£14271	$27543	(12-Dec-90 CD.P44/R) Soir de fete, Honfleur (81x100cm-32x39in) s.d.1961 init.d.verso (F.FR 140000)
£14356	$25411	(7-Apr-91 I.N165/R) Un ete, l'apres-midi, a Deauville (46x55cm-18x22in) s. (F.FR 145000)
£15873	$27302	(19-May-91 ZZ.F151/R) Cavalieres et cavaliers (60x73cm-24x29in) s. d.1967 verso (F.FR 160000)
£18725	$36700	(23-Nov-90 PLF.P77/R) Le quai Saint-Etienne a Honfleur (50x73cm-20x29in) s.d.1948 mono.i. verso (F.FR 185000)
£709	*$1389*	*(25-Nov-90 ZZ.F76) Lettre manuscrite illustree (27x21cm-11x8in) s.d.66 ink wash (F.FR 7000)*
£1503	*$2600*	*(7-May-91 CE.NY3/R) Honfleur, le vieux bassin (39x48cm-15x19in) s. col.chk pen paper on board*
£1518	*$2976*	*(23-Nov-90 PLF.P78/R) La plage (34x45cm-13x18in) s.d.49 pastel ink (F.FR 15000)*
£1619	*$3174*	*(25-Nov-90 ZZ.F75/R) L'entree du port du Honfleur (19x27cm-7x11in) s.d.1964 crayon drawing (F.FR 16000)*
£1992	*$3446*	*(26-May-91 ZZ.F95/R) Le paddock (21x28cm-8x11in) s. W/C (F.FR 20000)*

HAMBUCHEN, Georg (20th C) German

| *£638* | *$1243* | *(13-Oct-90 KRA.D129/R) Harbour entrance (40x50cm-16x20in) s. (DM 1900)* |
| *£952* | *$1686* | *(20-Mar-91 KM.K1244) View of Cologne (45x140cm-18x55in) s. pastel (DM 2800)* |

HAMBUCHEN, Wilhelm (1869-1939) German

| £687 | $1306 | (2-Mar-91 KRA.D325/R) Coastal scene with fishing boat and fishermen (36x48cm-14x19in) s. (DM 2000) |

HAMELIN, Jacques-Gustave (1809-?) French

| *£578* | *$1000* | *(21-May-91 CE.NY142/R) Portrait of M. Tallouard (32x27cm-13x11in) s.i.d.1861 black white chk* |

HAMESSE, Adolphe-Jean (1849-1925) Belgian

| £675 | $1309 | (4-Dec-90 C.A171) Woman in wooded landscape (27x40cm-11x16in) s.d.1888 (B.FR 40000) |

HAMILTON, Carl Wilhelm de (style) (1668-1754) Austrian

| £5199 | $10242 | (13-Nov-90 CH.AM89/R) Forest florr still life with wildlife, mushrooms, thistle by tree trunk on river bank (41x26cm-16x10in) panel (D.FL 17000) |

HAMILTON, Cuthbert (1885-1959) British

| *£720* | *$1253* | *(27-Mar-91 S73/R) The breakfast table (56x38cm-22x15in) i. indian ink* |

HAMILTON, Franz de (style) (17th C) German

| £2202 | $4338 | (14-Nov-90 SY.AM64/R) Hunting party (57x78cm-22x31in) (D.FL 7200) |

HAMILTON, Gavin (1723-1798) British

| £8500 | $15215 | (12-Apr-91 C32/R) Persian Sibyl (119x91cm-47x36in) after Giovanni Francesco Barbieri |
| £9500 | $17005 | (12-Apr-91 C33/R) Saul and David (146x200cm-57x79in) after Giovanni Francesco Barbieri |

HAMILTON, Hamilton (1847-1928) American

| £535 | $1000 | (30-Aug-90 MFA.C138 d) Setting sun (36x43cm-14x17in) s. |
| £2312 | $4000 | (10-May-91 S.BM87/R) The desert air (76x91cm-30x36in) s. |

HAMILTON, Helen (19/20th C) American

£1369	$2300	(28-Apr-91 LIT.L91) Shore scape with dock and lone tree (48x51cm-19x20in) s.
£4800	$9600	(10-Feb-91 LIT.L36) The old barn (64x76cm-25x30in) s.
£4898	$9600	(27-Jan-91 LIT.L18a) Old barn (64x76cm-25x30in) s.
£485	*$950*	*(11-Nov-90 LIT.L146) Houses with trees (46x56cm-18x22in) s. W/C*

HAMILTON, Hugh Douglas (1739-1808) British
£3500	$6265	(10-Apr-91 S100/R) Portrait of officer (74x61cm-29x24in) in painted oval
£600	*$1182*	*(12-Nov-90 PH1/R) Portrait of a lady, bust length, wearing a white dress (35x29cm-14x11in) indist.i. back paper pastel oval*
£2000	$3580	(9-Apr-91 C44/R) Portrait of Olivia St George, Duchess of Leinster (23x18cm-9x7in) i.verso chk pastel oval
£2800	$5516	(15-Nov-90 S60/R) Portraits of lady and gentleman (23x19cm-9x7in) s.d.1777 pastel pencil pair

HAMILTON, Hugh Douglas (attrib) (1739-1808) British
| £500 | $895 | (9-Apr-91 C45) Portrait of lady in white dress (23x18cm-9x7in) pastel oval |

HAMILTON, J B A George von (studio) (18th C) Flemish
| £28000 | $55160 | (31-Oct-90 S140/R) Tiger and lion. Tigress with cubs threatened by snake (127x175cm-50x69in) pair |

HAMILTON, James (1819-1878) American
£888	$1500	(20-Apr-91 WOL.C39/R) Children playing (43x30cm-17x12in) s. panel
£1481	$2800	(27-Sep-90 CH.NY41 a/R) Seascape (20x28cm-8x11in) s. d.1866 verso
£3704	$7000	(27-Sep-90 CH.NY52/R) Boston Harbor (36x77cm-14x30in) s.
£3911	$7000	(12-Apr-91 SY.NY6/R) Monitor and Merrimac, noon (31x51cm-12x20in) s. i.verso

HAMILTON, James Whitelaw (1860-1932) British
| £1800 | $3042 | (3-May-91 PHE74/R) View of east coast fishing village (87x100cm-34x39in) s. |
| £3500 | $6545 | (28-Aug-90 S830/R) Fisherfolk on the quay, Banff (64x76cm-25x30in) s. |

HAMILTON, Johann Georg de (1672-1737) Flemish
£836	$1413	(19-Apr-91 FN.S1728) Hunting scene with dogs and dead game in wooded hilly landscape (27x35cm-11x14in) mono. canvas laid down (DM 2500)
£4885	$8745	(14-Mar-91 D.V335/R) Bear hunt (50x64cm-20x25in) s.i.d.1732verso copper (A.S 100000)
£17804	$31869	(9-Apr-91 APT.P56/R) Un daim dans un parc (99x112cm-39x44in) (F.FR 180000)

HAMILTON, Johann Georg de (attrib) (1672-1737) Flemish
| £1567 | $3087 | (14-Nov-90 D.V324/R) Wolf and wild cat in wooded landscape (112x125cm-44x49in) (A.S 32000) |
| £1600 | $3120 | (26-Oct-90 C101/R) Forest floor still life with a snake devouring a toad. A snake, lizardssnails and butterflies (35x44cm-14x17in) |

HAMILTON, John McLure (1853-1939) American
| £19048 | $36000 | (26-Sep-90 SY.NY40/R) The young navigator (147x98cm-58x39in) s.d.1884 |

HAMILTON, Letitia (1878-1964) British
£620	$1066	(14-May-91 SWS406/R) Dalkey Island from Vigo Bay (19x24cm-7x9in) init. i.verso canvasboard
£750	$1298	(7-May-91 PH14) Landscape (18x26cm-7x10in) init.i.verso panel
£1667	$3217	(12-Dec-90 CH.E64/R) Dooks, Co. Kerry (29x45cm-11x18in) init. i.verso panel (E.P 1800)
£1800	$3510	(26-Oct-90 CG141/R) The Squirtima House (46x33cm-18x13in) s.i.verso
£1909	$3627	(12-Sep-90 WO.CO12) Harbour scene with shipping (28x38cm-11x15in) s. (E.P 2100)
£2600	$5070	(26-Oct-90 CG103/R) Slieve Donard, Co Down (43x47cm-17x19in) init. s.i.verso
£2600	$5070	(26-Oct-90 CG139/R) The monastery, Valdemosa (51x61cm-20x24in) init. s.i.verso
£3000	$5850	(26-Oct-90 CG72) Haystacks by the sea (50x60cm-20x24in) init.
£3600	$7020	(26-Oct-90 CG102/R) Dubrovnik from the walls (61x51cm-24x20in) init. s.i.verso
£4000	$7880	(13-Nov-90 SWS203/R) Venice in November (50x65cm-20x26in) init. i. label verso
£4500	$8775	(26-Oct-90 CG101/R) Bathers, Lake Maggiore (51x56cm-20x22in) init. s.i.verso

HAMILTON, Philipp Ferdinand de (attrib) (1664-1750) Flemish
£1444	$2412	(6-Jun-91 D.V205/R) Capercaillie in landscape (36x46cm-14x18in) (A.S 30000)
£1954	$3498	(14-Mar-91 D.V333/R) Bear hunt (175x214cm-69x84in) (A.S 40000)
£6849	$11164	(12-Jun-91 N.M313/R) Park landscape with stone vase and animals by trees and view of hills (110x164cm-43x65in) (DM 20000)

HAMILTON, Philipp Ferdinand de (circle) (1664-1750) Flemish
| £2167 | $3618 | (6-Jun-91 D.V343/R) Lizard and flowers by edge of wood (57x45cm-22x18in) (A.S 45000) |

HAMILTON, Philipp Ferdinand de (style) (1664-1750) Flemish
| £2200 | $4400 | (7-Feb-91 C102) Dogs in a knacker's yard (107x178cm-42x70in) |
| £13000 | $21320 | (19-Jun-91 CSK319/R) Bay stallion with black groom in landscape. Pie-bald stallion fighting with dog, black groom beyond (66x84cm-26x33in) pair |

HAMILTON, Richard (1922-?) British
£17627	$29437	(8-Jun-91 HN.H133/R) Im dreaming of a white Christmas (58x91cm-23x36in) ink on 2 plastic films and paper (DM 52000)
£79000	$127190	(27-Jun-91 S39/R) Swingeing London (67x85cm-26x33in) enamel silkscreen canvas

HAMM, Eugen (1885-1930) German
£667	$1193	(12-Apr-91 BM.B733/R) Still life with pot of tulips (55x46cm-22x18in) s.d.19 i.verso (DM 2000)
£667	$1193	(12-Apr-91 BM.B734/R) Southern coastal landscape (50x61cm-20x24in) s.d.24 i.verso (DM 2000)

HAMMAN, Edouard-Michel-Ferdinand (1850-?) French
£2105	$4000	(27-Feb-91 SY.NY84/R) Vaches pres de la mer (81x151cm-32x59in) s.

HAMMAREN, Carl Erik (1922-) Swedish
£651	$1164	(9-Apr-91 GO.G52) Portrait - metamorphosis (99x81cm-39x32in) (S.KR 7000)
£658	$1290	(20-Nov-90 GO.G83) Wooded glade (73x60cm-29x24in) init. (S.KR 7200)

HAMME, Alexis van (1818-1875) Belgian
£2693	$5305	(14-Nov-90 RAS.K145/R) Interior with girl playing music (63x75cm-25x30in) s.d.1873 (D.KR 30000)
£5789	$11000	(28-Feb-91 CH.NY138/R) Planning the meal (73x57cm-29x22in) s.d.1863 s.i.verso panel

HAMMER, Hans Jorgen (1815-1882) Danish
£2616	$4500	(15-May-91 SY.NY51/R) In cellar, autumn (44x36cm-17x14in) s.d.1876

HAMMER, Johann-J (1842-1906) German/American
£1183	$2000	(1-May-91 B.SF5282/R) Buffalo at sunset (51x76cm-20x30in) s.
£1974	$3750	(27-Feb-91 SY.NY169/R) Women in garden (88x60cm-35x24in) s.
£3679	$6217	(17-Apr-91 WE.MU244/R) The alm (86x57cm-34x22in) s.d.1879 (DM 11000)

HAMMER, William (1821-1889) German
£2334	$4598	(14-Nov-90 RAS.K524/R) Still life of fruit and tomatoes on table (55x71cm-22x28in) (D.KR 26000)
£2740	$4466	(12-Jun-91 N.M451/R) Still life of apples, quinces, hazelnuts and plum branch (18x24cm-7x9in) s.d.1851 panel (DM 8000)
£2780	$5338	(27-Dec-90 RAS.V34/R) Gundog with game and gun by oaktree (93x72cm-37x28in) s.d.1842 (D.KR 31000)

HAMMERSHOI, Svend (1873-1948) Danish
£808	$1592	(14-Nov-90 RAS.K288) Landscape, Oxford (76x64cm-30x25in) init.i.d.1925 (D.KR 9000)
£1013	$1895	(29-Aug-90 KH.K68/R) From Lincoln College (81x70cm-32x28in) (D.KR 11500)
£1779	$3470	(19-Oct-90 RAS.V482/R) View from Borsen (91x46cm-36x18in) init.d.44 (D.KR 20000)

HAMMERSHOI, Vilhelm (1864-1916) Danish
£2906	$5639	(5-Dec-90 KH.K171/R) Trees by Gentofte lake (21x27cm-8x11in) pencil (D.KR 32000)

HAMMOND, Arthur Henry Knighton (1875-1970) British
£1200	$2304	(28-Nov-90 AH160) The light that lingers in the West (23x33cm-9x13in)
£520	$848	(14-Jun-91 T269) Artist's wife and son John in the garden t Port Mourizio (36x33cm-14x13in) s.i. W/C
£520	$920	(18-Mar-91 FEN43) Eton College (46x41cm-18x16in) s. W/C
£600	$1062	(18-Mar-91 FEN38) The caretaker's daughter (58x48cm-23x19in) s.i. pastel
£775	$1488	(15-Aug-90 HAR303/R) Still life of flowers (33x48cm-13x19in) s. W/C
£800	$1312	(20-Jun-91 DLY498) Polperro (51x64cm-20x25in) s. W/C
£800	$1304	(14-Jun-91 T200/R) Le Plage, Menton (30x46cm-12x18in) s.
£900	$1521	(15-Apr-91 WW202) Summer day, figures relaxing on balcony (54x79cm-21x31in) s. W/C
£1150	$1886	(20-Jun-91 DLY499) Polperro (51x64cm-20x25in) s. W/C
£1300	$2496	(26-Nov-90 SWS124/R) On the beach, Lyme Regis (55x77cm-22x30in) s. W/C
£1400	$2716	(6-Dec-90 TL179) Polperro Harbour. Polperro Harbour Entrance (48x62cm-19x24in) s.i. W/C pair

HAMMOND, Horace (fl.1902-1939) British
£640	$1050	(19-Jun-91 AH188 a) Mailcoach and horses in the snow (30x46cm-12x18in) W/C

HAMMOND, John (1843-1939) Canadian
£758	$1311	(6-May-91 SY.T84) Landscape, Belgium (33x41cm-13x16in) s.verso board (C.D 1500)
£2525	$4369	(6-May-91 SY.T215/R) Tantramar Marsh (88x116cm-35x46in) s. (C.D 5000)

HAMMOND, Miss Gertrude Demain (1862-1953) British
£520	$868	(22-Jul-91 SWS898/R) The village fair (22x15cm-9x6in) s. W/C pencil
£1400	$2506	(14-Mar-91 ZZ.B94/R) By the firelight, a scene from the 'Mill on the Floss' (27x21cm-11x8in) s.d.1905 W/C htd.bodycol.

HAMMOND, R J (20th C) British
£1700	$3179	(28-Aug-90 S764/R) Perthshire glen. In the Trossachs (28x35cm-11x14in) i.on stretcher pair

HAMMOND, Robert John (20th C) British
| £622 | $1207 | (4-Dec-90 R.T279/R) Feeding poultry outside thatched cottage (36x53cm-14x21in) s.d.1891 (C.D 1400) |

£622 $1207 (4-Dec-90 R.T279/R) Feeding poultry outside thatched cottage (36x53cm-14x21in) s.d.1891 (C.D 1400)
£893 $1500 (17-Jul-91 SY.NY332/R) Camp at a highland stream (41x61cm-16x24in) s.
£1500 $2955 (13-Nov-90 PH35/R) Figures in landscape (67x91cm-26x36in) s.d.1903
£1548 $2600 (17-Jul-91 SY.NY333/R) On the river Severn (41x61cm-16x24in) s.
£2100 $3465 (9-Jul-91 PH183/R) Young girl feeding chickens before cottage. Faggot gatherers (40x30cm-16x12in) s.d.1897 pair
£2105 $4000 (27-Feb-91 SY.NY244/R) Path home (77x128cm-30x50in) s.d.1883

HAMON, Roland (20th C) French
£704 $1380 (27-Jan-91 LT.P4/R) Boulevard Rochechouart (33x41cm-13x16in) s. l. verso (F.FR 7000)
£712 $1346 (30-Sep-90 E.LA203) Paris - rue St. Jacques (28x36cm-11x14in) s. (F.FR 7000)
£885 $1735 (27-Jan-91 LT.P2/R) Notre-Dame, La Seine les quais (50x65cm-20x26in) s. l. verso (F.FR 8800)
£966 $1893 (27-Jan-91 LT.P5/R) Descente du Sacre-Coeur par la Rue Muller (65x50cm-26x20in) s. l. verso (F.FR 9600)
£1107 $2169 (27-Jan-91 LT.P3) Notre-Dame vue de la cites (F.FR 11000)
£1167 $2287 (27-Jan-91 LT.P1/R) Le vieux logis, Rue Lepic (50x65cm-20x26in) s. l. verso (F.FR 11600)

HAMPE, Guido (1839-?) German
£1359 $2568 (27-Sep-90 D.V50/R) House in Alpine lake landscape (41x58cm-16x23in) mono. (A.S 28000)

HAMPEL, Carl (?-1942) Australian
£772 $1521 (13-Nov-90 J.M73) Cattle grazing (52x69cm-20x27in) s. (A.D 2000)

HAMPEL, Sigmund Walter (1868-1949) Austrian
£1111 $1922 (6-May-91 ZEL.L1725/R) Spring flowers in vase (45x40cm-18x16in) s. (DM 3300)
£1196 $2069 (8-May-91 D.V46/R) In the garden (40x31cm-16x12in) board (A.S 25000)
£573 $1117 (11-Oct-90 D.V226/R) Lied der Mignon, nur wer die Sehnsucht kennt, weiss was ich leide (22x14cm-9x6in) s. W/C (A.S 12000)
£621 $1043 (25-Apr-91 D.V280/R) Lady in park with swans (25x21cm-10x8in) mono. pen indian ink pencil oil board (A.S 13000)
£1243 $2411 (6-Dec-90 D.V145/R) Milada Balda de Herrera (34x18cm-13x7in) i. mixed media (A.S 25000)

HAMPSHIRE, E L (20th C) British?
£720 $1411 (9-Nov-90 GSP626) Landscape with irises (89x64cm-35x25in) s.

HAMPSON, Albert W (1911-1990) American
£1765 $3000 (1-Jun-91 IH.NY40/R) Couple in jalopy, disastrous date (84x64cm-33x25in) s.d.1936 board

HAMSUN, Tore (1912-) Norwegian
£1336 $2578 (10-Dec-90 B.O42/R) Portrait of the artist's father, Knut Hamsun on his 90th birthday (65x50cm-26x20in) s. panel (N.KR 15000)

HAMZA, Hans (1879-1945) Austrian
£797 $1371 (14-May-91 GF.L2550/R) Woman wearing Lower Austrian costume (21x14cm-8x6in) s. panel (S.FR 2000)
£1568 $3104 (31-Jan-91 D.V79/R) Woman seated wearing lower Austrian costume reading letter (19x14cm-7x6in) s. panel (A.S 32000)

HAMZA, Johann (1850-1927) German
£1706 $3345 (24-Nov-90 SA.A731/R) The little connoisseur (48x39cm-19x15in) s. (DM 5000)
£1923 $3712 (12-Dec-90 N.M542/R) Portrait of harem's lady by window (31x31cm-12x12in) s.i. (DM 5500)
£3421 $6500 (27-Feb-91 SY.NY161/R) Woodshop (27x36cm-11x14in) s.i. paper on board
£9249 $16000 (22-May-91 SY.NY225/R) Wedding (36x27cm-14x11in) s.i. panel
£13333 $26000 (25-Oct-90 GRO.B91/R) Worshippers in cathedral (89x119cm-35x47in) s.i.

HANCOCK, Robert (1912-) Finnish
£890 $1503 (20-Apr-91 HOR.H93/R) Nude woman with red hair (69x49cm-27x19in) s.d.1947 (F.M 6200)

HAND, I (19th C) British
£3457 $6500 (7-Aug-90 RB.HY146/R) Ship 'British Empire' at anchor (56x89cm-22x35in) s.
£3590 $7000 (26-Oct-90 S.W2613/R) British Empire (56x89cm-22x35in) s. l. label stretcher

HANDLER, Richard (20th C) Austrian
£949 $1699 (11-Apr-91 D.V194/R) Still life of flowers (68x47cm-27x19in) s. (A.S 20000)
£1959 $3311 (3-May-91 SA.A1874/R) Summer flowers in a glass vase (65x52cm-26x20in) s. panel (DM 5800)

HANDLER, Rolf (1938-) German
£9556 $18730 (20-Nov-90 L.K258/R) Aufbruch, V. Fassung (179x200cm-70x79in) s.d.1989/90 s.i.d.verso (DM 28000)

HANDMANN, Emanuel (attrib) (1718-1781) Swiss
£1014 $1926   (14-Sep-90 SA.A1115/R) Portrait of noble woman (75x63cm-30x25in)
                (DM 3000)

HANFSTAENGL, Franz Seraph (1804-1877) German
£24000 $46080   (28-Nov-90 S195/R) Portrait of Theodoros Kolocotronis (33x27cm-13x11in)
                indist.s.i.

HANFT, Willy (1888-?) German
£878 $1625   (7-Mar-91 D.V41/R) Das Waldhaus (83x115cm-33x45in) s. (A.S 18000)

HANGER, M (1874-1955) German
£680 $1204   (20-Mar-91 KM.K1243 a) Chickens before stable corner in landscape
                (18x24cm-7x9in) s. panel (DM 2000)

HANGER, Max (1874-1955) German
£680 $1095   (26-Jun-91 KM.K1491/R) Cockerel with hens before stable (10x13cm-4x5in)
                s. board (DM 2000)
£680 $1095   (26-Jun-91 KM.K1490/R) Two cockerels fighting (9x13cm-4x5in) s. board
                (DM 2000)
£856 $1533   (14-Mar-91 N.M2659) Capercaillie performing courtship display
                (21x16cm-8x6in) s.i. panel (DM 2500)
£874 $1687   (14-Dec-90 BM.B617/R) Cockerel and hens in landscape (9x14cm-4x6in) s.
                panel (DM 2500)
£1007 $1963   (10-Oct-90 WE.MU195/R) Farmstead with poultry (18x24cm-7x9in) rem.sig.
                panel (DM 3000)
£1199 $2146   (13-Mar-91 N.M512/R) Chickens feeding (14x24cm-6x9in) s.i. panel
                (DM 3500)
£1279 $2213   (6-May-91 ZEL.L1721/R) Landscape with snowy mountain range beyond,
                autumn (50x40cm-20x16in) s.i. (DM 3800)
£1361 $2190   (26-Jun-91 KM.K1489/R) Chickens, peacock and ducks by lake shore
                (16x24cm-6x9in) s.i. board (DM 4000)
£1843 $3612   (24-Nov-90 SA.A672/R) Farmyard scene, spring day (18x24cm-7x9in) s.
                panel (DM 5400)
£1919 $3301   (16-May-91 D.V221/R) Game by garden fence (18x26cm-7x10in) s. board
                pencil study verso (A.S 40000)

HANGER, Max (jnr) (1898-) German
£853 $1613   (25-Sep-90 FN.S2195/R) Poultry beneath tree before fence
                (16x25cm-6x10in) s.i. panel (DM 2500)
£1014 $1976   (26-Oct-90 KM.K1241) Chicken yard (12x18cm-5x7in) s. panel (DM 3000)
£1297 $2451   (25-Sep-90 FN.S2194/R) Poultry by fence in landscape (20x25cm-8x10in) s.
                board (DM 3800)

HANICOTTE, Augustin (1870-1957) French
£1837 $3618   (14-Nov-90 FB.P323/R) Les patineurs (91x73cm-36x29in) s. (F.FR 18000)
£1822 $3571   *(20-Nov-90 MF.P18/R) Paysage aux toits rouges (32x24cm-13x9in) s. pastel*
                W/C (F.FR 18000)

HANISCH, Alois (1866-1937) Austrian
£724 $1411   (18-Oct-90 D.V111/R) View of village (40x55cm-16x22in) s.d.1907
                (A.S 15000)

HANKE, August (20th C) Austrian
£1829   *$3000*   *(21-Jun-91 DM.D2276/R) Peonies (56x46cm-22x18in) s. W/C*

HANKE, Henry Aloysius (1901-) Australian
£618 $1217   (13-Nov-90 J.M127) Parramatta River (38x45cm-15x18in) s.d.35 (A.D 1600)
£623 $1220   (19-Nov-90 MGS.S236/R) Calm weather, North Head, Sydney
                (49x60cm-19x24in) s. canvas on board (A.D 1600)

HANLEY, F (20th C) American
£706   *$1200*   *(1-Jun-91 IH.NY98/R) A hard sell, brush salesman showing custodian*
                product (43x33cm-17x13in) s. gouache

HANNAFORD, Charles (19/20th C) British
£420   *$706*   *(24-Apr-91 HUN2) Kynance Cove, Cornwall W/C*

HANNAFORD, Charles E (1863-1955) British
£550   *$1056*   *(30-Nov-90 T212) Sheep on Dartmoor (46x71cm-18x28in) s. W/C*

HANNEMAN, Adriaen (1601-1671) Dutch
£1444 $2412   (6-Jun-91 D.V325/R) Portrait of King Charles I (23x16cm-9x6in) rem.sig.
                panel (A.S 30000)

HANNEMAN, Adriaen (attrib) (1601-1671) Dutch
£4103 $8000   (11-Oct-90 SY.NY44/R) Portrait of young woman wearing silk gown standing
                on terrace (105x84cm-41x33in)

HANNEMAN, Adriaen (style) (1601-1671) Dutch
£2800 $4732   (18-Apr-91 C109) Portrait of a gentleman, wearing a white doublet,
                tuning a lute (112x99cm-44x39in)

HANNINGTON, R (19th C) British
£1182 $2247   (14-Sep-90 SA.A1207/R) Horse in stable interior (46x61cm-18x24in)
                (DM 3500)

HANNO, Carl von (1901-1953) Norwegian
£651 $1270   (11-Oct-90 BU.O53/R) Fishing boats (50x61cm-20x24in) s.d.50 panel
             (N.KR 7500)
£1427 $2769   (4-Dec-90 UL.T224/R) Landscape with red house (45x53cm-18x21in)
             (N.KR 16000)

HANNON, Theodore (1851-1916) Belgian
*£732 $1309   (16-Mar-91 KV.L138) Children by the sea (22x28cm-9x11in) mono. pastel
             (B.FR 44000)*

HANNOT, Johannes (17th C) Dutch
£16314 $26592   (14-Jun-91 AGS.P44/R) Nature morte aux fruits, crabes et verre de vin
             (57x42cm-22x17in) (F.FR 162000)

HANS, Josefus Gerardus (1826-1891) Dutch
£1818 $3582   (30-Oct-90 CH.AM3/R) Hunters in rowing-boat, at dawn (29x43cm-11x17in)
             s.d.49 panel (D.FL 6000)

HANSCH, Anton (1813-1876) Austrian
£700 $1211   (9-May-91 CSK56) Mountainous lakeland landscape (63x79cm-25x31in)
             s.d.1857
£2055 $3678   (13-Mar-91 N.M520) Mountain valley with peasant family on path by stream
             (37x53cm-15x21in) s. panel (DM 6000)
£5337 $10087   (27-Sep-90 D.V105/R) River landscape in the Dolomites (92x80cm-36x31in)
             s.d.1873 (A.S 110000)

HANSCH, Johannes (1875-C.1945) German
£606 $1048   (6-May-91 ZEL.L1722/R) Landscape with ducks on pond and village beyond,
             evening (53x72cm-21x28in) s.d.1904 (DM 1800)
£699 $1357   (4-Dec-90 FN.S1854/R) Snowy village street with figures, Spreewald
             (57x59cm-22x23in) s.d.1918 (DM 2000)

HANSEN, Adolf Heinrich Claus see HEINRICH-HANSEN, Adolf

HANSEN, Al (1927-) American
*£976 $1883   (15-Dec-90 S.Z128/R) NYC raygun for Claes (21x18cm-8x7in) s.d.1964 paper
             collage on panel (S.FR 2400)*

HANSEN, Armin Carl (1886-1957) American
£2308 $4500   (13-Oct-90 LAE.L134/R) Fisherman (23x30cm-9x12in) s.
£12821 $25000   (10-Oct-90 B.SF576/R) Clipper ship on high seas (76x80cm-30x31in) s.
£969 $1900   (13-Feb-91 B.SF2040/R) Fishing huts (42x62cm-17x24in) s.d.16 chl

HANSEN, Arne L (20th C) Danish
£623 $1214   (19-Oct-90 RAS.V636/R) Yellow, green farm, clear frozen snow
             (62x99cm-24x39in) init. (D.KR 7000)

HANSEN, Asor Henrik (1862-1929) Norwegian
£1024 $1976   (12-Dec-90 BU.O24/R) Girl by open fire wearing national costume
             (64x52cm-25x20in) s.d.07 (N.KR 11500)

HANSEN, Bjorn T (20th C) Scandinavian
£570 $969   (29-May-91 KH.K243) Composition (92x73cm-36x29in) s.d.79 (D.KR 6500)

HANSEN, C (19th C) ?
£1921 $3746   (21-Oct-90 L.C46/R) Dessinateur devant des ruines (43x36cm-17x14in)
             s.d.1833 canvas pasted panel (F.FR 19000)

HANSEN, Carel Lodewyk (1765-1840) Dutch
£1365 $2239   (18-Jun-91 FN.S1877/R) Wooded landscape with cottage and peasant woman
             with animals (18x25cm-7x10in) s. panel (DM 4000)

HANSEN, Constantin (1804-1880) Danish
£3142 $6189   (14-Nov-90 RAS.K31/R) View of Naples seen from Capri (25x36cm-10x14in)
             (D.KR 35000)
£4032 $8065   (6-Feb-91 RAS.K54/R) Domestic scene, woman with child on her knees
             (47x39cm-19x15in) init.d.1870 (D.KR 45000)

HANSEN, Ejnar (1884-1965) Danish/American
£612 $1200   (12-Feb-91 MOR.P89) Floral still life (74x61cm-29x24in) s. board
£2308 $4500   (10-Oct-90 B.SF649/R) Girl in pink skirt (107x76cm-42x30in) s.

HANSEN, Gordon (20th C) American
£914 $1800   (16-Nov-90 S.BM162/R) T Wharf (43x53cm-17x21in) s. st.verso

HANSEN, H (?) ?
£1190 $2000   (17-Jul-91 SY.NY291/R) Marketplace (53x42cm-21x17in) init.

HANSEN, Hans (1769-1828) Danish
£2509 $5018   (6-Feb-91 RAS.K74/R) Two small children playing with dog
             (80x72cm-31x28in) (D.KR 28000)

HANSEN, Hans Nikolaj (1853-1923) Danish
£792 $1331   (23-Apr-91 RAS.K357/R) Chr II leaving Copenhagen with his family in 1532
             (47x68cm-19x27in) init.d.18 (D.KR 9000)
£2200 $3784   (17-May-91 C104/R) Late arrival (47x60cm-19x24in) mono.d.94

HANSEN, Heinrich (1821-1890) Danish
£792	$1331	(23-Apr-91 RAS.K184/R) Interior with gentleman smoking pipe, Antwerp (35x44cm-14x17in) init.d.73 (D.KR 9000)
£1038	$2014	(22-Aug-90 RAS.K7/R) Catholic church interior with women praying (31x41cm-12x16in) init.d.89 (D.KR 12000)
£1937	$3254	(23-Apr-91 RAS.K378/R) Interior from Palace church, Copenhagen (35x32cm-14x13in) init. (D.KR 22000)
£3714	$6981	(10-Aug-90 RAS.V471/R) Sala della quatro porto (66x94cm-26x37in) init. (D.KR 42000)
£3911	$7000	(10-Apr-91 HF.NY64/R) Interior of Duomo, Pisa (32x36cm-13x14in) init.
£6704	$12000	(10-Apr-91 HF.NY66/R) Sala della quatre porte, Doge's Palace, Venice (66x94cm-26x37in) init.d.88

HANSEN, Henrik Asor (1862-?) Norwegian
£1069	$2062	(10-Dec-90 B.O44/R) My livingroom (86x95cm-34x37in) s.d.1903 (N.KR 12000)

HANSEN, Herman Wendelborg (1854-1924) American
£9249	$16000	(22-May-91 CH.NY208/R) Spring round-up (91x61cm-36x24in) s. W/C pencil paper laid down on board
£4734	*$8000*	*(1-May-91 B.SF5165/R) Two riders (38x48cm-15x19in) s. W/C*
£5325	*$9000*	*(1-May-91 B.SF5164/R) Bucking bronco (35x49cm-14x19in) s. W/C*
£5621	*$9500*	*(1-May-91 B.SF5166/R) Chase (29x39cm-11x15in) s.d.1922 W/C*
£22189	*$37500*	*(1-May-91 B.SF5163/R) Narrows (90x56cm-35x22in) s.d.03 W/C*

HANSEN, I T (?) Scandinavian
£1257	$2476	(14-Nov-90 RAS.K127) From an official bathing place, Pompeij (34x43cm-13x17in) s.d.1884 (D.KR 14000)
£1761	$2958	(22-Apr-91 BU.K2/R) Street in Pompei (21x28cm-8x11in) s.d.1905 (D.KR 20000)
£1938	$3237	(6-Jun-91 RAS.K48/R) Venetian canal scene (27x17cm-11x7in) s.i.d.1882 (D.KR 22000)
£2873	$5659	(14-Nov-90 RAS.K126/R) Interior from La Martorana church, Palermo (48x38cm-19x15in) s.d.1906 (D.KR 32000)

HANSEN, J R (fl.1830-1840) ?
£1783	*$3459*	*(5-Dec-90 DO.H2034/R) Brigg Robert and Mary of Newcastle (39x57cm-15x22in) s.i. bodycol pen (DM 5100)*

HANSEN, Jens Peter Helge (1934-) Danish
£671	$1315	(13-Feb-91 KH.K67) Composition (85x100cm-33x39in) s.d.71verso (D.KR 7500)

HANSEN, John F (fl.1900-1920) Danish
£698	$1200	(17-May-91 DM.D2020/R) Reindeer (56x81cm-22x32in) init.d.1914
£1453	$2500	(17-May-91 DM.D2026/R) Classical scene of girl with putti (163x89cm-64x35in)
£2907	$5000	(17-May-91 DM.D2021/R) Arabs praying to Mecca (66x91cm-26x36in) s.

HANSEN, Josef Theodor (1848-1912) Danish
£4000	$7880	(5-Oct-90 C120/R) Interior of Alhambra Palace (49x38cm-19x15in) init.
£4200	$8274	(5-Oct-90 C119/R) Interior at Rosenborg (40x51cm-16x20in) s.i.d.1909
£5800	$11368	(15-Feb-91 C70/R) Entrance to Senato, Doge's Palace, Venice (32x24cm-13x9in) s.d.1881 panel

HANSEN, Knut (1876-1926) Danish/German
£3800	$6232	(19-Jun-91 S259/R) Portrait of collector (43x34cm-17x13in) s.d.1894

HANSEN, Leon (1918-) Australian
£962	$1702	(18-Mar-91 MGS.S254) Towards Northbridge from Seaforth (50x76cm-20x30in) s. (A.D 2250)
£1544	$3042	(13-Nov-90 J.M300/R) Sydney Harbour (49x75cm-19x30in) s. (A.D 4000)

HANSEN, Niels (1880-?) Danish
£705	$1177	(6-Jun-91 RAS.K198/R) Still life of cherryblossom in vase, bowl and figurine (60x66cm-24x26in) s.d.1912 (D.KR 8000)

HANSEN, Peter (1868-1928) Danish
£1155	$2274	(31-Oct-90 KH.K28) The girl from Enghave Plads (34x28cm-13x11in) mono. (D.KR 13000)
£1335	$2509	(18-Sep-90 BU.K126/R) In the ice behind the town (32x47cm-13x19in) init. sketch (D.KR 15000)
£1421	$2799	(31-Oct-90 KH.K27/R) Having a chat (51x74cm-20x29in) init. (D.KR 16000)
£2487	$4899	(31-Oct-90 KH.K26/R) A labourer (58x75cm-23x30in) mono.d.1907 (D.KR 28000)

HANSEN, Sigvard (1859-1938) Danish
£505	$853	(1-May-91 KH.K77) Forest ranger's place (46x66cm-18x26in) init.d.1909 (D.KR 5700)
£714	$1350	(25-Sep-90 RAS.K78) Road through wood in winter (50x75cm-20x30in) s.d.1922 (D.KR 8000)
£809	$1618	(10-Feb-91 BU.M352) Winter landscape, Lillehammer (62x85cm-24x33in) s.d.1919 (S.KR 8800)
£1515	$2545	(24-Apr-91 BA.S79/R) Winter's day by Fure lake, Denmark (99x130cm-39x51in) s.d.1929 (S.KR 16000)
£2200	$4312	(22-Nov-90 CSK107/R) Day in winter (50x75cm-20x30in) s.d.1922

HANSEN, Thrine (?) ?
£720 $1202   (4-Jun-91 SWS1943) Still life of dahlias in basket (41x51cm-16x20in) s.

HANSEN-REISTRUP, K (1863-1929) Danish
£4200 $7056   (23-Apr-91 BOY853 a/R) Cavalry charge at Vorbasse in Southern Jutland
            1864 (74x127cm-29x50in) s.d.1911

HANSEN-SVANEKE, Bertel (1883-1937) Danish
£3400 $5848   (17-May-91 C101/R) Interior with bureau de dame and corner chair
            (61x46cm-24x18in) s.

HANSON, Clifford (20th C) ?
£900 $1773   (2-Nov-90 PHM64) Spanish jar and two wine carriers, delft plates
            (27x108cm-11x43in) init.d.1977 board

HANSON, Leon William (1918-) Australian
£543 $918   (16-Apr-91 J.M589) The farm, Dandenongs (49x59cm-19x23in) s. canvas
            board (A.D 1200)
£814 $1376   (16-Apr-91 J.M51) Afternoon at Vaucluse (25x50cm-10x20in) s. (A.D 1800)
£905 $1529   (16-Apr-91 J.M25) Middle harbour from Balmoral (34x70cm-13x28in) s.d.'89
            (A.D 2000)
£1000 $1940   (6-Dec-90 CSK8/R) Landscape (50x61cm-20x24in) s. board
£1158 $2282   (13-Nov-90 J.M134/R) Mosman Bay (49x75cm-19x30in) s. (A.D 3000)
£1351 $2662   (13-Nov-90 J.M308/R) Sydney Harbour from Seaforth (49x74cm-19x29in) s.
            canvas board (A.D 3500)
£1544 $3042   (13-Nov-90 J.M252/R) Lorne (60x75cm-24x30in) s. board (A.D 4000)
£1629 $2753   (16-Apr-91 J.M206/R) Sydney Harbour from Balmoral (50x75cm-20x30in)
            s.d.'86 canvas board (A.D 3600)

HANSON, R (?) ?
£616 $1005   (12-Jun-91 N.M452) Still life of flowers in vase (38x45cm-15x18in)
            s.d.1947 board (DM 1800)

HANSSEN, C (?) ?
£565 $1012   (12-Mar-91 GM.B964) La lecture de la libre Belgique (97x130cm-38x51in)
            s. (B.FR 34000)

HANSTEEN, Nils (1855-1912) Norwegian
£742 $1410   (11-Sep-90 UL.T213) River scene (12x33cm-5x13in) (N.KR 8500)
£920 $1600   (29-Mar-91 E.EDM303/R) Seascape with ship beyond s.
£1070 $1914   (14-Mar-91 RAS.V650/R) Seascape with steamship off cliffs
            (85x127cm-33x50in) s.d.1892 (D.KR 12000)
£1390 $2349   (4-May-91 BU.O64) Courtyard with woman (90x70cm-35x28in) s. (N.KR 16000)
£1883 $3370   (14-Mar-91 BU.O43/R) Sailship in harbour (16x21cm-6x8in) s.d.1881 panel
            (N.KR 21500)
£1975 $3890   (14-Nov-90 RAS.K107) Seascape with sailship off coastal cliff, fresh
            breeze (54x80cm-21x31in) s. (D.KR 22000)
£1997 $3334   (4-Jun-91 BU.O2/R) Sailboat in moonlight (50x95cm-20x37in) s.
            (N.KR 23000)
£2048 $3953   (10-Dec-90 B.O45/R) Coastal landscape with vessels (69x83cm-27x33in)
            s.d.1894 (N.KR 23000)
£3940 $7053   (14-Mar-91 BU.O42/R) Pilot boat and sailship (94x150cm-37x59in) s.
            (N.KR 45000)
£4167 $8125   (11-Oct-90 BU.O55/R) Pilotboat and sailship (63x95cm-25x37in) s.d.1891
            (N.KR 48000)
£4688 $7828   (3-Jun-91 B.O58/R) Evening seascape (81x130cm-32x51in) s. (N.KR 54000)

HANTAI, Simon (1922-?) Hungarian
£2480 $4860   (23-Nov-90 PLF.P82/R) Sans titre (23x23cm-9x9in) s.d.1951 (F.FR 24500)
£11089 $21623   (26-Oct-90 CC.P20/R) Sans titre (36x26cm-14x10in) s.d.1951 oil paper on
            canvas (F.FR 110000)
£30120 $48494   (25-Jun-91 BG.P29/R) Composition (85x102cm-33x40in) s.d.8-11-50
            (F.FR 300000)
£110887 $216230   (27-Oct-90 BG.P36/R) Sans titre (240x207cm-94x81in) s. (F.FR 1100000)
£110887 $216230   (26-Oct-90 CC.P53/R) Sans titre (240x222cm-94x87in) mono.d.73 acrylic
            (F.FR 1100000)
£1259 $2052   (16-Jun-91 CC.P11) Femme dans un interieur (29x30cm-11x12in) i.d.946 W/C
            gouache (F.FR 12500)
£1410 $2298   (16-Jun-91 CC.P10/R) Homme et cheval (28x22cm-11x9in) s.d. W/C ink
            (F.FR 14000)
£1813 $2955   (16-Jun-91 CC.P8) Jeune garcon dans un interieur (68x48cm-27x19in)
            s.d.1946 gouache W/C chk. (F.FR 18000)
£2316 $3775   (16-Jun-91 CC.P9/R) Personnage debout (58x35cm-23x14in) s.d.946 W/C
            (F.FR 23000)
£15416 $29908   (9-Dec-90 CC.P65 b/R) Sans titre (66x58cm-26x23in) mono.d.1971 W/C
            canvas (F.FR 150000)

HARA, Jacques (1933-) French
£809 $1577   (17-Oct-90 LT.P169/R) Le village en hiver (46x55cm-18x22in) s.
            (F.FR 8000)

HARASIMOWICZ, M (19th C) Polish
£803 $1574   (11-Feb-91 SY.J352/R) Portrait of Marie de Rabutin Chantal, Marquise de
            Segigne (70x56cm-28x22in) s.d.1890 (SA.R 4000)

HARBURGER, Edmund (1846-1906) German
£633 $1134   (12-Apr-91 BM.B607/R) Portrait of old man with pipe (15x11cm-6x4in) s. board on panel (DM 1900)

HARCOURT, Clewin Simon (1870-1965) Australian
£880 $1478   (18-Jul-91 B57) Figures on lakeshore (24x34cm-9x13in) s. board

HARDENBERG, Lambertus (1822-1900) Dutch
£1317 $2213   (23-Apr-91 SY.AM299) Figures near St. Bavo church, Haarlem (37x29cm-15x11in) s.d.1859 panel (D.FL 4400)
£909   *$1791*   *(30-Oct-90 CH.AM503 b/R) Fishmarket in front of De Waag on Nieumarkt, Amsterdam, Suiderkerk beyond (30x40cm-12x16in) s.i.d.48 pencil pen W/C wash (D.FL 3000)*

HARDIE, Charles Martin (1858-1916) British
£900 $1710   (27-Feb-91 MMB210/R) Young girl picking poppies in a coastal town (41x51cm-16x20in) init.d.1894
£2600 $5070   (16-Oct-90 CG202/R) Mistress Margery (251x251cm-99x99in) s.d.1879

HARDIE, Gwen (1962-) British
£1200 $2340   (9-Oct-90 B152) Totemic Woman II (99x69cm-39x27in) s.verso acrylic

HARDIE, Robert Gordon (1854-1904) American
£2260 $4000   (22-Mar-91 S.W2837/R) Le petit soldad (168x127cm-66x50in) s.d.1891

HARDIME, Pieter (1677-1758) Flemish
£8000 $13040   (2-Jul-91 PH18/R) Glass bowl of summer flowers on stone ledge (63x76cm-25x30in)
£8046 $14000   (27-Mar-91 B.SF4020/R) Still life with bouquet of mixed flowers, orange and butterfly on table (48x38cm-19x15in) s.
£26934 $53061   (14-Nov-90 D.V133/R) Still life of flowers in stone vase with view of palace gardens (146x117cm-57x46in) s.d.1727 (A.S 550000)

HARDIME, Pieter (attrib) (1677-1758) Flemish
£4615 $9000   (11-Oct-90 SY.NY60/R) Still life of flowers in urn resting on ledge (59x42cm-23x17in)

HARDIME, Pieter (style) (1677-1758) Flemish
£1500 $3000   (7-Feb-91 C147/R) Roses, hydrangeas, chrysanthemums and other flowers on a stone ledge (58x70cm-23x28in)
£3000 $5910   (30-Oct-90 PH104/R) Basket of summer flowers with peaches on stone ledge (43x54cm-17x21in)
£3100 $5363   (20-May-91 SWS106) A still life of flowers on a table (40x53cm-16x21in)
£3200 $5216   (4-Jul-91 CSK173/R) Mixed flowers in unr, vase and dish on ledge, parrot on branch, landscape beyond (85x94cm-33x37in) panel shaped
£4500 $9000   (7-Feb-91 C35/R) Mixed flowers in a basket on a stone ledge (56x66cm-22x26in)
£5000 $9600   (29-Nov-90 CSK67/R) Tulips, roses, narcissi and other flowers in vase on ledge (76x63cm-30x25in)

HARDIME, Simon (1672-1737) Flemish
£10359 $17817   (14-May-91 GF.L2077/R) Still life of flowers (97x82cm-38x32in) (S.FR 26000)

HARDING, George Perfect (circle) (1780-1853) British
£650   *$1125*   *(21-May-91 CSK149) The Earl and Countess of Sunderland (23x?cm-9x?in) min.i. rectangular pair*

HARDING, James Duffield (1798-1863) British
£800   *$1520*   *(10-Jan-91 B75/R) Whitby (31x48cm-12x19in) W/C htd.white scratching out*
£3500   *$6895*   *(15-Nov-90 S135/R) On the Italian lake (35x53cm-14x21in) s.d.1860 W/C over pencil htd.bodycol*

HARDING, James Duffield (circle) (1798-1863) British
£1400   *$2744*   *(21-Nov-90 B28/R) Florence from S. Miniato (51x76cm-20x30in) W/C*

HARDT, Ernst (1869-1917) German
£1351 $2635   (26-Oct-90 KM.K1251) Landscape with peasant ploughing, spring (88x115cm-35x45in) s. (DM 4000)

HARDY, Cyril (19th C) British
£918   *$1552*   *(15-Apr-91 L.V8) Arabian street scene (36x51cm-14x20in) W/C (C.D 1800)*
£1071   *$1811*   *(15-Apr-91 L.V9) Arabian street scene (36x51cm-14x20in) W/C (C.D 2100)*

HARDY, Dudley (1865-1922) British
£1007 $1963   (10-Oct-90 ZEL.L1525/R) The white slave (4x9cm-2x4in) s. (DM 3000)
£550 $924   (15-Jul-91 PH127/R) Carting sand (24x34cm-9x13in) s. W/C bodycol
£700 $1365   (17-Oct-90 PHL70) Landing fish, Etaples (25x36cm-10x14in) s.d.1909 i. verso col.washes htd.white
£1600 $3040   (10-Jan-91 B77/R) The morning catch (47x64cm-19x25in) s.d.92 chl W/C bodycol

HARDY, Dudley (attrib) (1865-1922) British
£1443 $2800   (8-Dec-90 W.W227/R) Middle Eastern temple scene (66x81cm-26x32in) s.

HARDY, Frederick Daniel (1826-1911) British
£900	$1548	(14-May-91 SWS254/R) The cuckoo clock (18x12cm-7x5in) s.d.1875 board
£1600	$3008	(18-Sep-90 SWS576/R) The fiddler at the cobbler's door (36x52cm-14x20in) s.d.1857 panel
£1786	$3429	(27-Nov-90 W.T1047) Bedtime (44x34cm-17x13in) s. (C.D 4000)
£2400	$4008	(5-Jun-91 S138/R) Miser (39x54cm-15x21in) s.d.1891
£2600	$5096	(22-Jan-91 PH101/R) Exchanging news (42x61cm-17x24in) s.d.1905

HARDY, Frederick Daniel (attrib) (1826-1911) British
| £2500 | $4175 | (5-Jun-91 S139/R) Blacksmith's shop (39x49cm-15x19in) |

HARDY, Heywood (1843-1933) British
£2811	$5200	(10-Mar-91 H.C77/R) Meet (48x61cm-19x24in) s.
£2994	$5000	(7-Jun-91 SY.NY95/R) In the park (36x51cm-14x20in) s.d.1893
£4103	$8000	(24-Oct-90 CH.NY327/R) Noonday taking horse to water (66x99cm-26x39in) s.d.1877 s.i.d.verso
£4600	$9016	(13-Feb-91 S78/R) Hounslow Heath (57x102cm-22x40in) s.d.1875
£6696	$12857	(28-Nov-90 PH.T93/R) Busy day at the tollgate (49x75cm-19x30in) s. (C.D 15000)
£9000	$15030	(5-Jun-91 S182/R) New puppy (48x68cm-19x27in) s.
£9744	$19000	(24-Oct-90 CH.NY326/R) The morning ride (89x71cm-35x28in) s.
£9821	$18857	(28-Nov-90 PH.T70/R) The morning ride (75x52cm-30x20in) s. (C.D 22000)
£11000	$20790	(26-Sep-90 S168/R) Donkey ride on sands (51x35cm-20x14in) s.d.1900
£12000	$19560	(14-Jun-91 C283/R) Picking up the scent (91x70cm-36x28in) s.d.1903
£12000	$23640	(13-Nov-90 PH124/R) From cover to cover (51x77cm-20x30in) s.
£13000	$21970	(30-Apr-91 PH81/R) Grouse shooting (74x104cm-29x41in) s.d.1893
£13000	$25350	(23-Oct-90 SWS498/R) Portrait of Agnes Fanny Marland Denny, aged 15 at Chiddingstone Castle (30x37cm-12x15in) s.d.1889
£14000	$27580	(1-Nov-90 C316/R) The peacemaker (64x48cm-25x19in) s.
£16174	$31215	(11-Dec-90 CH.R210/R) Incontro in campagna (81x101cm-32x40in) s.d.1885 (I.L 35000000)
£22754	$38000	(7-Jun-91 SY.NY92/R) The kill (90x115cm-35x45in) s.

HARDY, Heywood and WALTON, Frank (19th C) British
| £6316 | $12000 | (27-Feb-91 BG.M822/R) Pheasant hunt (91x61cm-36x24in) s. |

HARDY, James (19th C) British
| £3276 | $5667 | (8-May-91 FER.M116/R) Perros junto a sus presas de caza (87x113cm-34x44in) s.d.84 (S.P 600000) |
| £13650 | $23615 | (8-May-91 FER.M117/R) Caravana en el paso de la montana (71x96cm-28x38in) s.d.1854 gouache (S.P 2500000) |

HARDY, James (jnr) (1832-1889) British
£520	$848	(13-Jun-91 CSK315) Sorting vegetables (15x20cm-6x8in) s.d.59 panel
£12000	$23640	(13-Nov-90 PH125/R) 1st of October (52x73cm-20x29in) s.
£1000	$1630	(14-Jun-91 C116) Woodman and his daughter (35x27cm-14x11in) s.d.63 pencil W/C bodycol.
£2200	$4290	(15-Jan-91 C83) Highland gillie with three English setters (25x50cm-10x20in) s.d.71 pencil W/C
£3600	$6768	(18-Sep-90 CSK148/R) The day's bag (49x67cm-19x26in) s.d.1864 W/C bodycol htd white
£3757	$6500	(10-May-91 S.BM24/R) The day's bag (36x46cm-14x18in) s.d.84 W/C gouache ink
£4000	$7920	(30-Jan-91 S228/R) Day's bag (25x35cm-10x14in) s.d.86 W/C htd bodycol
£8500	$17000	(5-Feb-91 S12/R) Young huntsman with two retrievers and game (43x32cm-17x13in) s.d.69 W/C htd white

HARDY, Jeremiah Pearson (1800-1888) American
| £909 | $1700 | (1-Aug-90 B.P106/R) Portrait of lady from Maine (10x8cm-4x3in) s.verso W/C |

HARDY, T B (1842-1897) British
| £440 | $779 | (5-Apr-91 BW372) Coastal scene with fishing boats (23x51cm-9x20in) s. W/C |

HARDY, Thomas (fl.1777-1805) British
| £634 | $1104 | (25-Mar-91 SY.F546) Ritratto maschile (37x30cm-15x12in) s.d.1791 pastel (I.L 1400000) |

HARDY, Thomas Bush (1842-1897) British
£680	$1319	(3-Dec-90 TAY605) Harbour scene with boats (38x58cm-15x23in) s.d.1874
£714	$1200	(17-Jul-91 SY.NY353/R) Seascape (41x62cm-16x24in) s.d.92
£1200	$2376	(28-Jan-91 HS257) Beach scene with fishing boats setting out under stormy sky and figures (34x48cm-13x19in) s. indist.d. board
£1600	$3072	(16-Aug-90 B443/R) Continental fish market (51x81cm-20x32in) s.d.1878
£400	$668	(26-Jul-91 T270) Fishing boats returning to harbour (20x43cm-8x17in) s.d.1889 W/C
£440	$788	(11-Apr-91 GSP468) Near Artois, French coast (13x15cm-5x6in) s.i.d.1890 W/C
£450	$855	(28-Feb-91 DLY160) Beached (23x30cm-9x12in) s.d.'89 i. verso W/C
£450	$797	(22-Mar-91 PHE53) Yachts in choppy seas (19x30cm-7x12in) s. W/C
£480	$816	(30-May-91 C55) Leaving port (25x46cm-10x18in) s.d.1895 pencil W/C htd white
£550	$1089	(30-Jan-91 S142) Shipping outside harbour at Le Treport, France (15x23cm-6x9in) s. W/C over pencil htd white

HARDY, Thomas Bush (1842-1897) British-cont.

£550	$919	(24-Jul-91 CSK52) Fishing vessels in an offshore breeze (13x18cm-5x7in) s.i.d.1876 W/C htd.white
£600	$1170	(16-Jan-91 CSK18) Offshore fishing smacks (18x25cm-7x10in) s.d.1886 pencil W/C
£649	$1057	(10-Jun-91 W.T1255) Shipwreck (19x28cm-7x11in) s.d.1889 W/C (C.D 1200)
£650	$1092	(22-Apr-91 PH288/R) Dutch boats (24x33cm-9x13in) s.d.1889 W/C bodycol.
£750	$1463	(18-Oct-90 CSK63/R) Fishing fleet at Scheveningen (23x34cm-9x13in) s. pencil W/C htd white
£750	$1253	(24-Jan-91 ZZ.B148/R) Boulogne harbour - boats coming in (33x51cm-13x20in) s.i.d.1882 W/C
£780	$1521	(18-Oct-90 SC3052) On the Maas, Holland (12x17cm-5x7in) s.i.
£780	$1521	(24-Oct-90 DR42/R) Running for port (15x30cm-6x12in) s.d.93 W/C htd.bodycol
£800	$1376	(14-May-91 SWS15/R) Boulogne Pier (28x21cm-11x8in) s.i.d.1890 W/C htd.bodycol scratching out
£820	$1337	(14-Jun-91 T153) At Scarborough (28x76cm-11x30in) s.indis.d.1895 W/C
£850	$1675	(13-Nov-90 SWS69/R) Outward bound (44x70cm-17x28in) s.i.d.1895 W/C bodycol.scratching out
£865	$1410	(10-Jun-91 W.T1256) Weymouth, The Castle (44x70cm-17x28in) s.i. W/C (C.D 1600)
£880	$1434	(14-Jun-91 T170/R) Off Crail, Scotland (25x74cm-10x29in) s.i.d.1890 W/C
£900	$1755	(18-Oct-90 CSK60/R) Boulogne Harbour (38x76cm-15x30in) s.i. W/C htd white
£920	$1822	(30-Jan-91 S182/R) Beached fishing boats (20x18cm-8x7in) s.i.d.1893 W/C htd bodycol
£950	$1824	(17-Dec-90 PH44/R) Bamborough Castle (10x20cm-4x8in) s.i.d.1893 W/C
£1000	$1970	(12-Nov-90 PH58) Scarboro, The herring fishers (22x47cm-9x19in) s.i. W/C bodycol.
£1100	$1804	(18-Jun-91 OT402/R) Approach to Boulogne Harbour (57x89cm-22x35in) s.d.X96 W/C
£1100	$1804	(19-Jun-91 AH243/R) Shipping off the harbour jetty (23x51cm-9x20in) d.1891 W/C
£1150	$2128	(5-Mar-91 AG223/R) Portsmouth harbour (22x45cm-9x18in) s.i.d.1894 W/C
£1200	$2352	(8-Nov-90 DLY34/R) At mouth of harbour (25x51cm-10x20in) s.d.1887 W/C
£1200	$2028	(30-Apr-91 AG111/R) Bamburgh Castle (16x31cm-6x12in) s.i.d.1877 W/C
£1200	$2016	(22-Apr-91 PH290/R) On the Giudecca, Venice (12x17cm-5x7in) s.i. W/C bodycol.
£1250	$2450	(8-Nov-90 PHI123/R) The Yare at Gorleston (23x70cm-9x28in) s.i.d.1891 htd.white
£1300	$2184	(16-Jul-91 RG2655/R) Estuary scene with numerous sailing and steam vessels, North Shields (23x69cm-9x27in) s.d.93 W/C
£1300	$2535	(15-Jan-91 SWS55/R) Coastal scene, Broadstairs, Kent. Fisherfolk on the shore (16x51cm-6x20in) s. one i. W/C bodycol scratching out pair
£1339	$2571	(27-Nov-90 W.T1268/R) Entrance to the Guidecca, Venice (44x70cm-17x28in) s.i.d.1893 W/C (C.D 3000)
£1350	$2646	(8-Nov-90 PHI122/R) Summer shower (47x74cm-19x29in) s.i. W/C
£1400	$2688	(16-Aug-90 B234) Old Tynemouth, Northumberland (42x69cm-17x27in) s.i.d.1882 W/C
£1500	$2955	(31-Oct-90 B50/R) Shipping in coastal waters (38x56cm-15x22in) s.d.1892 W/C htd.white
£1500	$2565	(29-Jul-91 HS210/R) Near Ventnor, Isle of Wight - extensive seascape (27x55cm-11x22in) s.i.d.1896 W/C
£1600	$3104	(4-Dec-90 RG2730) A wet day, Boulogne (48x74cm-19x29in) s. W/C drawing
£1700	$3043	(13-Mar-91 B130/R) Within a mile of Venice (46x69cm-18x27in) s.i.d.1879 W/C
£1700	$2839	(4-Jun-91 RG2068/R) Beach scene with fishermen Scheveningen, boat preparing for sea (46x74cm-18x29in) s.d.1870 W/C
£1750	$3360	(17-Aug-90 T152) Coming into Yarmouth Harbour (23x53cm-9x21in) s.i.d.96 W/C
£1750	$2958	(30-Apr-91 AG112/R) Wellesley at North Shields (23x70cm-9x28in) s.i. W/C
£1800	$3024	(22-Apr-91 PH289) On Dutch coast (21x29cm-8x11in) s.i.d.1890 W/C bodycol.
£1800	$3114	(22-May-91 S143/R) H.M.S. Actaeon, off Portchester Castle (22x70cm-9x28in) s.i.d.1892 W/C
£1800	$3096	(14-May-91 SWS14/R) Scheveningen. Near Leigh, Essex (10x27cm-4x11in) s.i.d.1886 W/C pair
£1900	$3230	(30-May-91 C54/R) Pool of Thames (32x51cm-13x20in) s.i.d.94 W/C htd white
£1900	$3059	(27-Jun-91 CG1/R) Ambleteuse, Picardy (33x50cm-13x20in) s.i.d.1882 W/C htd.bodycol.
£1900	$3268	(15-May-91 BT98/R) The Pool, London (23x71cm-9x28in) s.i.d.1895 W/C htd.white
£2000	$3460	(22-May-91 S114/R) Tug with disabled vessel in tow, off Bridport (35x62cm-14x24in) s.i.d.1895 W/C htd white
£2000	$3940	(13-Nov-90 SWS70/R) Off Dieppe. Off Yarmouth (25x77cm-10x30in) both s.d. one i. W/C bodycol.scratching pair
£2200	$4290	(18-Oct-90 CSK59/R) Broadstairs Pier (38x76cm-15x30in) s.i. pencil W/C
£2300	$3864	(22-Apr-91 PH291/R) Venice (34x54cm-9x13in) s.d.1880 W/C bodycol.
£2300	$3864	(23-Apr-91 RG2271/R) Storm at Staithes, Yorkshire, with numerous figures and boats on quay (51x124cm-20x49in) s.d.1890 W/C
£2400	$4296	(13-Mar-91 B59/R) On the mouth of the Thames (23x33cm-9x13in) s.i.d.1880 W/C
£2900	$4785	(11-Jul-91 S235/R) Dutch fishing boats on the sands. Boats at Zwydrecht, Holland (12x17cm-5x7in) indis.s.d.1879 W/C over pencil bodycol.pair
£4500	$8505	(26-Sep-90 S221/R) Venice (151x105cm-59x41in) s.d.1893 W/C htd bodycol

HARE, David (1917-) American
£923 $1800   (10-Oct-90 SY.NY380/R) Untitled (20x30cm-8x12in) s.d.53 gouache

HARE, John (20th C) American
£722 $1400   (24-Aug-90 RB.HY20/R) Midwinter (61x76cm-24x30in) s.
£833 $1400   (21-Jul-91 LIT.L214) High tide (61x76cm-24x30in) s.

HARE, John Knowles (1882-1947) American
£615 $1100   (11-Apr-91 FA.PH795) Young girl eating ice cream cone on beach
(66x53cm-26x21in) s. pastel

HARE, Julius (1859-1932) British
£600 $983   (17-Jun-91 DUR.M467/R) Retrato de dama con vestido azul y estola de piel
(126x96cm-50x38in) s. (S.P 110000)
£3827 $7500   (7-Nov-90 B.SF1147/R) Mother's hat (74x56cm-29x22in) s.d.85

HAREUX, Ernest Victor (1847-1909) French
£1080 $1825   (1-May-91 GD.B375/R) Landscape with cattle grazing and peasant women
resting by haystack (35x60cm-14x24in) s.d.1877 (S.FR 2700)

HARGITT, Edward (1835-1895) British
£1100 $1848   (23-Apr-91 S18/R) On White Adder (30x45cm-12x18in) mono.d.1854 s.i.verso
board
£360 $666   (6-Mar-91 SC4218) Cattle watering at lake in mountainous landscape
(15x25cm-6x10in) init.d.63 W/C bodycol
£845 $1647   (26-Oct-90 BM.B792/R) Eridge Park, Kent (71x107cm-28x42in) s. i.verso
W/C (DM 2500)
£2000 $3580   (11-Apr-91 S87/R) Eridge Castle, Sussex (70x108cm-28x43in) s. W/C over
pencil bodycol

HARGREAVES, Thomas (1774-1846) British
£700 $1344   (18-Dec-90 C103/R) Portrait of girl in white dress with blue ribbon
(9x?cm-4x?in) min.s.d.1816/7verso ormolu oval in leather case

HARING, Keith (1958-1990) American
£1815 $3538   (26-Oct-90 CC.P121/R) Sans titre (15x14cm-6x6in) s.d.1988 felt pen red
tissue paper (F.FR 18000)
£1815 $3538   (26-Oct-90 CC.P120/R) Sans titre (26x15cm-10x6in) s.d.1989 felt on denim
(F.FR 18000)
£2312 $4000   (7-May-91 CE.NY283/R) Untitled (50x61cm-20x24in) s.i.d.89 acrylic paper
£5076 $10000   (4-Oct-90 SY.NY274/R) Untitled (15x30cm-6x12in) s.d.1982 verso board
£5565 $9349   (23-Apr-91 C.A111/R) Three figures (40x54cm-16x21in) ink dr.
(B.FR 340000)
£5641 $11000   (10-Oct-90 SY.NY511/R) Untitled (69x69cm-27x27in) s.d.1982verso acrylic
£20408 $40000   (7-Nov-90 SY.NY376/R) Untitled (76x76cm-30x30in) s.i.d.Oct. 10 1984
overlap acrylic
£25510 $50000   (7-Nov-90 SY.NY351/R) Untitled (213x213cm-84x84in) s.d.Oct.1982 verso
tarpaulin
£38462 $65000   (1-May-91 SY.NY173/R) Exploding head (185x185cm-73x73in) s.d.1983 verso
acrylic tarpaulin
£48223 $95000   (4-Oct-90 SY.NY279/R) Untitled (122x122cm-48x48in) acrylic canvas
£73469 $142531   (8-Dec-90 RU.ZU192 a) Fresco (400x280cm-157x110in) acrylic (S.FR 180000)
£655 $1278   (27-Oct-90 BG.P37/R) Lezard (29x21cm-11x8in) s. felt pen (F.FR 6500)
£806 $1313   (16-Jun-91 CC.P54) Sans titre (26x19cm-10x7in) blk.felt pen (F.FR 8000)
£1008 $1966   (26-Oct-90 CC.P124) Sans titre (26x20cm-10x8in) black market folded foil
(F.FR 10000)
£1411 $2300   (12-Jun-91 SY.NY238/R) Stacked figures with dog · signature
(22x28cm-9x11in) s.i.d.1986 black marker
£1502 $2598   (22-May-91 CH.AM673/R) Portrait of Bidet (35x28cm-14x11in) s.i.d.86
col.felt-tip pen (D.FL 5000)
£1503 $2600   (7-May-91 CE.NY284/R) Untitled (35x28cm-14x11in) s.d.86 col.felt-tip
pens
£1531 $3000   (6-Nov-90 CE.NY301/R) Act up for life (16x22cm-6x9in) s.i.d.89
col.felt-tip pens
£1531 $3000   (12-Feb-91 SY.NY450/R) Figure holding child (61x48cm-24x19in) s.d.85
marker
£1633 $3167   (8-Dec-90 GAB.G2638/R) L'homme-double s.i.d.86 felt pen (S.FR 4000)
£1658 $3250   (12-Feb-91 SY.NY455/R) Figure holding child (61x48cm-24x19in) s.d.85
marker
£1701 $2738   (28-Jun-91 BM.B1057/R) Delphin man (14x23cm-6x9in) s.d.1989 felt tip pen
(DM 5000)
£2449 $4751   (8-Dec-90 GAB.G2652/R) La trompette folle (21x29cm-8x11in) s.i.d.86 felt
pen (S.FR 6000)
£2667 $4773   (12-Apr-91 BM.B983/R) Doubleman (22x29cm-9x11in) s.d.1989 felt tip
(DM 8000)
£2806 $5500   (12-Feb-91 SY.NY449/R) Stack figures (61x48cm-24x19in) s.d.84 marker
£3518 $5769   (23-Jun-91 P.V77/R) Sans titre (57x75cm-22x30in) s.i.d.17 novembre 88
verso gouache Indian ink (F.FR 35000)
£3571 $7000   (6-Nov-90 CE.NY305/R) Untitled (58x74cm-23x29in) s.d.July 21-1988 brush
sumi ink
£3673 $7127   (8-Dec-90 RU.ZU192/R) Tower of 5 figures (68x47cm-27x19in) s.d.1984 felt
tip pen dr (S.FR 9000)
£3846 $7500   (10-Oct-90 SY.NY472/R) Untitled (28x20cm-11x8in) s.d.89 marker pair
£4438 $7500   (2-May-91 CH.NY313/R) Untitled (53x54cm-21x21in) s.d.1981 verso
col.felt-tip pen plastic film

HARING, Keith (1958-1990) American-cont.
£4592	$9000	(6-Nov-90 CE.NY272/R) Untitled (5x76cm-2x30in) s.d.27-81 verso brush sumi ink
£5612	$11000	(8-Nov-90 CH.NY214/R) Untitled (137x106cm-54x42in) s.st.d.JAN 15 1981 sumi ink vellum
£6091	$12000	(5-Oct-90 CH.NY106/R) Untitled (97x127cm-38x50in) s.d.1981 verso brush ink
£6531	$12669	(8-Dec-90 GAB.G2651/R) Le roi est mort, vive le roi (21x29cm-8x11in) s.i.d.86 felt pen (S.FR 16000)
£7614	$15000	(5-Oct-90 CH.NY139/R) Untitled (96x127cm-38x50in) s.d.82 verso brush sumi ink
£7653	$15000	(8-Nov-90 CH.NY215/R) Untitled (96x127cm-38x50in) s.d.June 1982 verso acrylic ink
£7653	$15000	(14-Feb-91 CH.NY106/R) Untitled (60x70cm-24x28in) s.d.87 s.i.d.verso sumi ink acrylic rag paper
£10152	$20000	(5-Oct-90 CH.NY141/R) Untitled (70x113cm-28x44in) s.d.82 felt-tip pen
£10152	$20000	(4-Oct-90 SY.NY272/R) Untitled (68x70cm-27x28in) s.i.d.1984 verso marker on foamcore
£10204	$20000	(7-Nov-90 SY.NY367/R) Untitled (109x109cm-43x43in) s.d.Sept.26-27 1982 verso baked enamel metal
£10909	$21382	(14-Feb-91 GL.P12/R) USA - 1982 (96x127cm-38x50in) s.d.juin 1982 verso acrylic Indian ink (F.FR 108000)
£13959	$27500	(4-Oct-90 SY.NY239/R) Untitled (99x130cm-39x51in) s.i.d.82 verso acrylic ink
£14286	$28000	(8-Nov-90 CH.NY216/R) Untitled (80x121cm-31x48in) s.d.DEC 10-1982 blk.felt-tip pen
£21429	$42000	(8-Nov-90 CH.NY213/R) Untitled (162x122cm-64x48in) s.d.1980 verso gouache sumi ink spray enamel

HARITONOFF, Nicholas B (1880-1944) American
£1224	$2400	(7-Nov-90 D.NY36) The story teller (119x203cm-47x80in) s.

HARKE, Evelyn (fl.1899-1914) British
£1700	$3332	(22-Jan-91 PH69/R) The plough team (74x126cm-29x50in) s.

HARKONEN, Eino (1886-1944) Finnish
£1007	$1944	(15-Dec-90 BU.H77) Early spring (70x53cm-28x21in) s.d.12 (F.M 7000)
£1439	$2777	(15-Dec-90 BU.H78) Girl with plait (68x40cm-27x16in) s.indist.d.38 (F.M 10000)

HARLAMOFF, Alexis (1842-?) Russian
£2250	$3668	(5-Jul-91 ZZ.F27/R) Enfant jouant aux bulles de savon (33x45cm-13x18in) trace sig. (F.FR 22500)
£3795	$7286	(27-Nov-90 W.T1164) Siesta (35x52cm-14x20in) s. (C.D 8500)
£5800	$11426	(4-Oct-90 CSK175/R) A young beauty (25x22cm-10x9in) s.i.
£11000	$18040	(21-Jun-91 C36/R) Moment's rest (38x55cm-15x22in) s.d. 1886
£24000	$39360	(19-Jun-91 S65/R) Portrait of young girl (45x37cm-18x15in) s.

HARLFINGER, Richard (1873-1943) Austrian
£1212	$2279	(20-Sep-90 D.V162/R) On the Danube Canal (63x98cm-25x39in) s.i. (A.S 25000)

HARLOFF, Guy (1933-?) French
£550	$902	(19-Jun-91 F.M55/R) Composition (19x15cm-7x6in) s.i.d.1958 mixed media (I.L 1200000)

HARLOW, George Henry (1787-1819) British
£1128	$2200	(14-Oct-90 H.C430/R) Portrait of lady (43x36cm-17x14in)
£1400	$2660	(1-Mar-91 C31/R) Portrait of Miss Caroline Dalrymple (42x35cm-17x14in)
£1538	$3000	(25-Oct-90 GRO.B27/R) Portrait of young girl holding kitten (76x64cm-30x25in)
£400	$660	(11-Jul-91 S160) Rome with the Baths of Caracalla (27x41cm-11x16in) init.d.1818 col.chk

HARLOW, Louis Kinney (1850-1930) American
£2267	$3650	(30-Jun-91 LIT.L75) Nantucket Lane (46x76cm-18x30in) s.

HARMAR, Fairlie (1876-1945) British
£880	$1716	(22-Oct-90 SWS104) Tree-lined avenue (53x74cm-21x29in) s.

HARNETT, William Michael (1851-1892) American
£41908	$72500	(23-May-91 SY.NY23 a/R) Bowl of cherries (26x19cm-10x7in) s.d.1882 panel
£49160	$85000	(22-May-91 CH.NY170/R) A gentleman's essentials (21x31cm-8x12in) mono.d.1880

HARNETT, William Michael (after) (1851-1892) American
£1149	$2000	(27-Mar-91 D.NY54) Still life with pewter mug, smoking pipe, watch and other objects (38x51cm-15x20in) bears sig. board

HARPER, Adolf Friedrich (attrib) (1725-1806) German
£1027	$1839	(12-Mar-91 FN.S2405) Rocky wooded arcadian landscape with peasants resting (54x121cm-21x48in) (DM 3000)
£1027	$1839	(12-Mar-91 FN.S2404/R) Arcadian wooded river landscape and mountain range with fortification (54x121cm-21x48in) (DM 3000)
£1105	$1900	(18-May-91 W.W1/R) Figures near a fortress by a moutain lake (69x91cm-27x36in)

HARPER, Edward Steel (1878-1951) British

£850 $1624   (4-Jan-91 BW412) Extensive coastal scene (61x91cm-24x36in) mono.

HARPER, Henry Andrew (1835-1900) British

£580   *$980*   *(18-Apr-91 B276) A quiet street, Jerusalem (23x18cm-9x7in) s.i.d.1897 W/C*

£600   *$1182*   *(15-Nov-90 SC4080) Jerusalem from North West (51x74cm-20x29in) s.i.d.1872 W/C pencil*

HARPIGNIES, Henri (1819-1916) French

£750 $1253   (5-Jun-91 HC.P359) Bord de riviere au crepuscule (18x35cm-7x14in) s.mono. (F.FR 7500)

£804 $1543   (27-Nov-90 W.T1124) Full moon over still water (43x30cm-17x12in) s.d.94 (C.D 1800)

£853 $1579   (6-Mar-91 APT.P115) Marche en Normandie (27x26cm-11x10in) s. i.d.avril 1861 verso panel (F.FR 8500)

£917 $1771   (12-Dec-90 D.P181/R) Le coucheur de soleil (16x24cm-6x9in) s.d.1908 (F.FR 9000)

£1014 $1947   (17-Dec-90 AGS.P31/R) Paysage (26x34cm-10x13in) s. panel (F.FR 10000)

£1272 $2200   (21-May-91 CE.NY39/R) Hilly landscape with village in distance (32x42cm-13x17in) init. board

£1360 $2298   (1-May-91 GD.B377/R) River landscape with houses and children playing (45x36cm-18x14in) s.d.1888 (S.FR 3400)

£2027 $3446   (27-May-91 L.K277) In the forest of Fontainebleau with young man on rock (26x41cm-10x16in) s.d.84 panel (DM 6000)

£2312 $4000   (21-May-91 CE.NY42/R) Hilly landscape (25x34cm-10x13in) s.d.62 canvas on panel

£3061 $6031   (16-Nov-90 NM.P51) Clair de lune sur l'etang (38x55cm-15x22in) s. (F.FR 30000)

£3468 $6000   (21-May-91 CE.NY29/R) Wooded river landscape (65x82cm-26x32in) bears sig.d.93

£3511 $6846   (12-Oct-90 ZZ.F11/R) Paysage des environs de Villefranche (27x44cm-11x17in) s.i.d. (F.FR 35000)

£3976 $7633   (29-Nov-90 ZZ.F7/R) Paysage (36x54cm-14x21in) s. board laid down on canvas (F.FR 39000)

£4000 $7880   (5-Oct-90 C37/R) Le chemin conduisant au lac (40x30cm-16x12in) s.d.90

£4000 $6560   (19-Jun-91 S131/R) Mother and child in woodland path (24x33cm-9x13in) s.d.83 panel

£4049 $7935   (20-Nov-90 MF.P81/R) Paysage a Saint Prive (55x38cm-22x15in) s. panel (F.FR 40000)

£5500 $9460   (17-May-91 C7 a/R) Wooded river landscape (41x31cm-16x12in) s.d.92

£5587 $10000   (11-Apr-91 FA.PH1004 a) Wooded landscape with figures (61x79cm-24x31in) s.d.1900

£16410 $32000   (23-Oct-90 SY.NY13/R) Midday in the meadows (57x77cm-22x30in) s.d.86

£412   *$663*   *(28-Jun-91 LC.P70) Paysage boise (43x28cm-17x11in) blk.crayon (F.FR 4100)*

£416   *$736*   *(7-Apr-91 I.N166) Paysage (21x28cm-8x11in) s. chl. (F.FR 4200)*

£583   *$956*   *(18-Jun-91 APT.P27) Le clocher (13x22cm-5x9in) s.d.1912 W/C (F.FR 5800)*

£704   *$1154*   *(18-Jun-91 APT.P28) Paysage a Baden (28x44cm-11x17in) s.d.1850 pen stumping (F.FR 7000)*

£751   *$1300*   *(21-May-91 CE.NY33/R) La route (12x18cm-5x7in) s.d.1912 W/C black chk textured paper*

£760   *$1239*   *(3-Jul-91 OD.P51) Estaminet du Buisson (15x20cm-6x8in) s.d.1908 i. W/C (F.FR 7600)*

£897   *$1481*   *(9-Jul-91 ARC.P16) Interieur d'eglise (28x22cm-11x9in) s. W/C wash india ink (F.FR 9000)*

£955   *$1833*   *(24-Feb-91 P.V2/R) Paysage a St Prive (26x36cm-10x14in) s.d.1886 W/C (F.FR 9500)*

£996   *$1693*   *(29-May-91 GL.P23) Le retour du troupeau (13x21cm-5x8in) s.d.1872 W/C (F.FR 10000)*

£1038   *$2003*   *(11-Dec-90 FER.M20/R) Casa rustica junto al rio (26x41cm-10x16in) s. chl dr (S.P 190000)*

£1197   *$2250*   *(19-Sep-90 B.SF2670/R) Stopping to look at an oak tree (27x41cm-11x16in) s.i.d.1847 gouache*

£1223   *$2349*   *(1-Dec-90 PER.M25) Vue de St Licq Lapopie dans le lot (12x19cm-5x7in) s.d.98 W/C (F.FR 12000)*

£1294   *$2251*   *(25-Mar-91 PLF.P49/R) Paysage au soleil couchant (24x33cm-9x13in) s.d.1866 W/C (F.FR 13000)*

£1753   *$3366*   *(30-Nov-90 ARC.P119/R) Devant la ferme (18x24cm-7x9in) s.d.84 W/C (F.FR 17200)*

£1850   *$3589*   *(8-Dec-90 SY.MO429/R) Le Cap Martin (26x37cm-10x15in) s.d.1908 W/C (F.FR 18000)*

£3518   *$5769*   *(18-Jun-91 APT.P26/R) La Bourboule (25x36cm-10x14in) s.d.1881 W/C (F.FR 35000)*

£3625   *$5909*   *(14-Jun-91 AGS.P4/R) Allee sous-bois (38x27cm-15x11in) s.d.83 W/C (F.FR 36000)*

£3947   *$7500*   *(27-Feb-91 SY.NY49/R) Paris (35x25cm-14x10in) s.d.92 W/C*

£4500   *$8640*   *(27-Nov-90 PH248/R) Quai de Bercy (36x52cm-14x20in) s.i.d.1883 W/C over pencil*

£8359   *$16133*   *(12-Dec-90 ARC.P18/R) L'ancien Pont du Carousel vu des berges de la Seine (18x27cm-7x11in) s.i.d.1881 blk.crayon W/C (F.FR 82000)*

£8560   *$13953*   *(14-Jun-91 AGS.P5/R) Bords de la Seine a Paris (36x25cm-14x10in) s.d.92 W/C (F.FR 85000)*

£15416   *$29908*   *(8-Dec-90 SY.MO324/R) Paris, Le Pavillon de Flore et le Quai d'Orsay (18x27cm-7x11in) s.d.1881 W/C (F.FR 150000)*

HARRADEN, Richard Bankes (1778-1862) British
£1300	$2145	(12-Jul-91 C134/R) View of Trinity College, Cambridge, from backs (30x45cm-12x18in) board
£1600	$2864	(12-Apr-91 C137/R) View of Ely Cathedral, with figures, sheep and cattle to fore (47x66cm-19x26in)
£1200	*$2364*	*(13-Nov-90 C129/R) Front of Emmanuel College, Cambridge (23x36cm-9x14in) pencil W/C*
£1200	*$2364*	*(13-Nov-90 C128/R) Front of Emmanuel College, Cambridge (23x36cm-9x14in) i. pencil W/C*
£1400	*$2310*	*(9-Jul-91 C100/R) Peterborough Cathedral from the Nene, the West. South-East view (13x21cm-5x8in) s. pencil W/C pair*

HARRER, Hugo Paul (1836-1876) German
£743	$1449	(26-Oct-90 KM.K1252/R) Tiber landscape near Rome (44x63cm-17x25in) i.d.1884 board (DM 2200)
£2570	$4600	(16-Mar-91 W.W32/R) Sunset over the bay of Naples (46x94cm-18x37in) s.i.

HARRINGTON, Charles (?-1943) British
£300	*$537*	*(14-Mar-91 GSP554) Valley landscape (46x64cm-18x25in) s.d.1905 W/C*
£1000	*$1680*	*(22-Apr-91 PH317) Farm in the South Downs (27x37cm-11x15in) s. W/C*

HARRINGTON, Robert (1800-1882) British
£800	$1552	(3-Dec-90 SC4298/R) Bay horse with two dogs in yard (43x58cm-17x23in) s. indist.d.

HARRINGTON, Robert (attrib) (1800-1882) British
£900	$1593	(21-Mar-91 CSK200) Hunters disturbed by a hunt (43x53cm-17x21in)

HARRIS, Edwin (19th C) British
£950	$1862	(8-Nov-90 DLY226/R) Head of fisherman s. panel
£1100	$1815	(11-Jul-91 CSK118) Skipper (45x55cm-18x22in) with sig.
£1800	$3456	(28-Nov-90 SC4240/R) Portrait of girl (18x13cm-7x5in) s. panel
£2100	$3507	(4-Jun-91 SWS1890/R) Harvest time (107x80cm-42x31in) s.

HARRIS, George (19/20th C) British
£3000	$4890	(13-Jun-91 CSK259) Glen Stapleton. Near Dorchester (76x127cm-30x50in) s.i. pair

HARRIS, J (19th C) British
£680	$1170	(14-May-91 SWS202 a) Still life of mixed fruit and jug on ledge (44cm-17ins circular) s.d.1883

HARRIS, J (jnr) (1831-1904) British
£950	*$1596*	*(24-Apr-91 CSK3) Barque Helvetia in distress off Worms Head (33x51cm-13x20in) s.i.d.1887 pencil W/C htd white*

HARRIS, James (19th C) British
£2500	$4700	(8-Aug-90 PHP151) Shipping off The Mumbles (30x56cm-12x22in) s.

HARRIS, Lawren Stewart (1885-1970) Canadian
£3947	$7776	(30-Oct-90 SY.T75/R) Abstract composition (54x74cm-21x29in) s.i.d.1957verso board (C.D 9000)
£5263	$10368	(30-Oct-90 SY.T78/R) Birches (27x29cm-11x11in) s. s.i.verso board (C.D 12000)
£6566	$11293	(14-May-91 JOY.T141/R) Deserted farm, Laurentian Mts. (37x45cm-15x18in) s. board (C.D 13000)
£7018	$13754	(20-Nov-90 JOY.T144/R) Shacks, Earlscourt (26x34cm-10x13in) panel (C.D 16000)
£7576	$13030	(14-May-91 JOY.T133/R) Abstract (129x89cm-51x35in) s. (C.D 15000)
£10811	$17622	(10-Jun-91 W.T1080/R) Algomo landscape (27x35cm-11x14in) s.init. i. verso board (C.D 20000)
£11892	$19384	(10-Jun-91 W.T1086/R) Landscape distant view of lake (27x34cm-11x13in) bears i. verso board (C.D 22000)
£12281	$24193	(30-Oct-90 SY.T41/R) Agawa Falls, Montreal river, Algoma (27x32cm-11x13in) s.i.verso board (C.D 28000)
£12500	$24000	(27-Nov-90 W.T876/R) Lake Superior, Pic Island (27x34cm-11x13in) s. board (C.D 28000)
£13393	$25714	(27-Nov-90 W.T868) Northern lake (27x34cm-11x13in) s. s.i.verso board (C.D 30000)
£13393	$25714	(27-Nov-90 W.T873/R) Northern river through screen of trees (27x34cm-11x13in) board (C.D 30000)
£14286	$27429	(27-Nov-90 W.T870) Algoma sketch (27x34cm-11x13in) s. i.erso board (C.D 32000)
£15152	$26061	(14-May-91 JOY.T94/R) Mount Sampson, Maligne Lake (26x35cm-10x14in) board (C.D 30000)
£15351	$30241	(30-Oct-90 MA.V110) Emerald Lake, Canadian Rockies (30x38cm-12x15in) s.i.verso board (C.D 35000)
£16216	$26432	(10-Jun-91 W.T1072/R) Algomo sketch LXVIII (34x27cm-13x11in) s. i. verso board (C.D 30000)
£19192	$33010	(14-May-91 JOY.T79/R) Lake Superior sketch XCIX (26x34cm-10x13in) panel (C.D 38000)
£21717	$37354	(14-May-91 JOY.T125/R) In the white mountains I (45x55cm-18x22in) s. board (C.D 43000)
£24123	$47522	(30-Oct-90 SY.T28/R) House, Centre Street, Toronto (27x34cm-11x13in) s. s.i.verso board (C.D 55000)

HARRIS, Lawren Stewart (1885-1970) Canadian-cont.

£25253	$43434	(14-May-91 JOY.T41/R) Glacier, Mt. Robson District (30x37cm-12x15in) board (C.D 50000)
£27027	$44054	(10-Jun-91 W.T1074/R) Houses Group, XIX (27x34cm-11x13in) s. l. verso board (C.D 50000)
£33514	$54627	(10-Jun-91 W.T1078/R) Lake superior (30x38cm-12x15in) s. l. verso board (C.D 62000)
£43860	$86404	(30-Oct-90 SY.T43/R) Trees in the north, Northern Paintings (81x102cm-32x40in) s. s.i.verso (C.D 100000)
£47980	$83005	(6-May-91 SY.T97/R) Second-hand store (24x34cm-9x13in) s. board (C.D 95000)
£1161	*$2229*	*(27-Nov-90 W.T866/R) Arctic bay (19x24cm-7x9in) d.1930 pencil (C.D 2600)*

HARRIS, Moses (attrib) (1731-1785) British

£800	*$1320*	*(11-Jul-91 S4/R) Butterflies and flowers (54x42cm-21x17in) i.d.1766 pen ink W/C gum arabic*

HARRIS, Patricia (1950-) ?

£4065	$8130	(6-Feb-91 FB.P168/R) Delicatesses evanscentes (81x65cm-32x26in) s. (F.FR 40000)

HARRIS, Robert (1849-1919) Canadian

£658	$1296	(30-Oct-90 SY.T113) Self portrait (18x11cm-7x4in) d.1900verso board (C.D 1500)
£556	$961	(6-May-91 SY.T7 a) From Mutch's hotel, Stanhope, P.E.I., looking west (14x20cm-6x8in) s. s.d.verso gouache board (C.D 1100)

HARRIS, Sam Hyde (1889-1977) American

£561	$1100	(12-Feb-91 MOR.P79) Smoke tree morning (46x61cm-18x24in) s. canvas on board
£675	$1100	(11-Jun-91 MOR.P69) Landscape - lake (46x61cm-18x24in) estate st. canvasboard
£816	$1600	(12-Feb-91 MOR.P31) Landscape - Bishop, CA (46x61cm-18x24in) s.
£859	$1400	(11-Jun-91 MOR.P56) Near Bishop, CA (46x61cm-18x24in) s.
£2436	$4750	(10-Oct-90 B.SF629/R) Deserted ranch (46x61cm-18x24in) s. canvasboard

HARRIS, William E (19th C) British

£680	$1149	(3-May-91 PHE145) Torrent on the Machor, North Wales (58x77cm-23x30in) s.i.d.1881verso
£2200	$3630	(9-Jul-91 PH167/R) Figures in street, Broadway, Worcestershire (49x75cm-19x30in) s.d.1892
£2800	$4620	(9-Jul-91 PH170/R) Shepherd with sheep in Broadway, Worcestershire (41x61cm-16x24in) s.d.1893
£3000	$5670	(26-Sep-90 S69/R) Road at Broadway, Worcestershire (51x76cm-20x30in) bears other sig. l.verso
£3800	$6270	(9-Jul-91 PH168) Figures and children in busy village street (49x75cm-19x30in) s.d.1893
£4400	$7260	(9-Jul-91 PH169/R) Figures with horses and carts in Broadway, Worcestershire (49x80cm-19x31in) s.d.1893

HARRISON, Birge (1853-1930) American

£663	$1300	(16-Feb-91 W.W78/R) Street scene at dusk (36x28cm-14x11in) s.d.1907 canvas on board

HARRISON, Charles Harmony (1842-1902) British

£500	*$815*	*(14-Jun-91 K450) North Tower, Great Yarmouth (36x18cm-14x7in) s.d.1897 W/C*
£500	*$820*	*(19-Jun-91 B119) Little Broad, Norfolk (27x48cm-11x19in) s.d.1887 W/C*
£780	*$1521*	*(22-Oct-90 SWS270) Sailing barges passing mill (24x51cm-9x20in) s.d.1875 W/C*
£950	*$1549*	*(4-Jul-91 PHI117) A sailing boat moored in backwater (12x28cm-5x11in) s.d.1886 W/C*
£1200	*$2352*	*(8-Nov-90 PHI37) Waterlilies on reed-lined pool (36x54cm-14x21in) s.d.1897 W/C*

HARRISON, Claude (20th C) British

£1150	$2254	(23-Jan-91 JT170) Guitar coast (38x43cm-15x17in) s.d.1969 board

HARRISON, J H (19/20th C) British

£807	*$1550*	*(27-Dec-90 RAS.V36/R) Ships portrait - 'Olga' (53x74cm-21x29in) s.i. pen W/C (D.KR 9000)*

HARRISON, John Cyril (1898-1985) British

£550	*$1100*	*(8-Feb-91 K415/R) Partridge in flight over gorge (25x33cm-10x13in) s. W/C*
£680	*$1306*	*(17-Dec-90 PH172) Rising ducks (22x28cm-9x11in) s.d.1921 W/C over pencil htd.bodycol*
£700	*$1344*	*(19-Feb-91 C151/R) Adult Madagascar fish eagle (28x20cm-11x8in) s. pencil W/C*
£800	*$1536*	*(19-Feb-91 C68/R) Swallow catching dragonfly (23x15cm-9x6in) s.i.d.1958verso pencil W/C*
£900	*$1728*	*(19-Feb-91 C119/R) Wigeon (23x33cm-9x13in) s. pencil W/C htd.white*
£1000	*$1920*	*(19-Feb-91 C150) Golden eagle in flight (43x58cm-17x23in) s. pencil W/C*
£1000	*$1920*	*(19-Feb-91 C69/R) Tern fishing (25x18cm-10x7in) s. pencil W/C htd.white*

HARRISON, John Cyril (1898-1985) British-cont.

£1100	$2112	(19-Feb-91 C71/R) Red spotted bluethroat (23x36cm-9x14in) s.i.d.1976vero pencil W/C
£1100	$2112	(17-Dec-90 PH63/R) Grouse in flight (30x48cm-12x19in) s. W/C
£1150	$2243	(12-Oct-90 K371/R) Yellow Hammers (23x15cm-9x6in) s. W/C
£1200	$2400	(8-Feb-91 K447/R) Illustration for Falcons of World (43x33cm-17x13in) s. W/C
£1200	$2304	(19-Feb-91 C70/R) Redpolls (23x18cm-9x7in) s.i.d.1975verso pencil W/C htd.white
£1300	$2496	(19-Feb-91 C120/R) Pair of pochard (18x28cm-7x11in) s. pencil W/C htd.white
£1400	$2730	(12-Oct-90 K370/R) Red legged partridges (23x13cm-9x5in) s.i. W/C
£1500	$2880	(19-Feb-91 C187/R) Woodcock in flight among trees (58x43cm-23x17in) s. pencil W/C
£1500	$2505	(22-Jul-91 SWS854/R) Winter (20x39cm-8x15in) s. W/C gouache
£1550	$3023	(12-Oct-90 K369/R) Partridges (23x13cm-9x5in) s.i. W/C
£1600	$2688	(23-Apr-91 S86/R) White fronted geese over marshes (54x74cm-21x29in) s. W/C
£1600	$2992	(28-Aug-90 S712/R) Pintail (33x23cm-13x9in) s. W/C htd bodycol
£1734	$3000	(10-May-91 S.BM25/R) Woodcock in flight (46x33cm-18x13in) s. W/C
£1800	$3492	(7-Dec-90 K488/R) Partridge over river (33x23cm-13x9in) s. W/C
£1900	$3097	(14-Jun-91 C168/R) Sheldrake in flight (34x48cm-13x19in) s. pencil W/C
£1900	$3648	(19-Feb-91 C117/R) Brent geese (53x74cm-21x29in) s. pencil W/C
£2000	$3380	(19-Apr-91 K506/R) Tide Way Wigeon (36x53cm-14x21in) s. W/C
£2800	$5376	(19-Feb-91 C67/R) Avocets at low tide (38x56cm-15x22in) s. pencil W/C
£3000	$5610	(28-Aug-90 S741 a) Pheasant taking flight (76x54cm-30x21in) s. W/C over pencil
£3000	$5610	(28-Aug-90 S741 b) Osprey with it's catch (57x74cm-22x29in) s. W/C over pencil
£3200	$6144	(19-Feb-91 C118/R) Shoveler duck (23x33cm-9x13in) s. pencil W/C htd.white
£3200	$6144	(19-Feb-91 C153/R) Osprey seizing fish from loch (43x58cm-17x23in) s. pencil W/C htd.white
£3200	$6208	(7-Dec-90 K487/R) White fronted geese flighting at Holkham Gap (46x61cm-18x24in) s. W/C
£3500	$5705	(14-Jun-91 C167/R) Red grouse in flight over moorland (34x48cm-13x19in) s. pencil W/C htd. white
£4000	$7680	(19-Feb-91 C189/R) Partridge over moorland landscape (33x48cm-13x19in) s. pencil W/C htd.white
£4200	$7854	(28-Aug-90 S724/R) Gold autumn, blackgame. Turning down the glen, grouse (33x47cm-13x19in) s. bears i.verso W/C pair
£6500	$12480	(19-Feb-91 C188/R) Red grouse in flight over moorland (33x46cm-13x18in) s. W/C bodycol

HARRISON, Mary R (1788-1875) British

| £1886 | $3640 | (10-Dec-90 BL.P10/R) Composition de fleurs et raisin (51x38cm-20x15in) s.d.1864 W/C (F.FR 18500) |

HARRISON, Sir Rex (1908-1990) British

| £622 | $1200 | (13-Dec-90 D.NY117) Straffan stud farm, County Kildare, Ireland (58x43cm-23x17in) init. l.verso |

HARRISON, Ted (1926-) Canadian

| £573 | $1117 | (24-Oct-90 EA.M438/R) Trophy (45x61cm-18x24in) s.d.1985 verso acrylic canvas (C.D 1300) |
| £705 | $1374 | (24-Oct-90 EA.M512/R) Summer wind (91x122cm-36x48in) s. acrylic (C.D 1600) |

HARRISON, Thomas Alexander (?) British?

| £2156 | $3600 | (9-Jun-91 LIT.L378) Falls at Montigny, France (71x99cm-28x39in) s. |

HARROWING, Walter (19th C) British

| £1315 | $2564 | (24-Oct-90 GD.B445/R) Horse and dog in stable interior (56x69cm-22x27in) s.d. (S.FR 3300) |

HARSHE, Robert Bartholomew (1879-?) American

| £2197 | $3800 | (21-May-91 CE.NY577/R) Girl at cafe table (77x98cm-30x39in) masonite |

HARSING, Wilhelm (1861-?) German

| £1053 | $2000 | (27-Feb-91 SY.NY178/R) Deer park in morning (67x102cm-26x40in) s. |

HART, J Laurence (fl.1882-1906) British

| £480 | $941 | (23-Jan-91 B38) Cotswolds village (60x90cm-24x35in) s.d.1895 W/C |
| £755 | $1472 | (19-Oct-90 CBB250) Anne Hathaway's cottage, Shottery (74x46cm-29x18in) s. W/C dr |

HART, James (?) British

| £744 | $1250 | (21-Jul-91 LIT.L121) Landscape with cattle (23x38cm-9x15in) s. panel |

HART, James MacDougal (1828-1901) American

| £688 | $1300 | (27-Sep-90 CH.NY36/R) Twilight (15x11cm-6x4in) s. panel |
| £4290 | $7250 | (17-Apr-91 D.NY92) Deer watering in mountain lake (28x46cm-11x18in) s.d.1891 |

HART, Kevin Pro (1928-) Australian
£513	$908	(18-Mar-91 MGS.S126) Brolgas - water birds (29x29cm-11x11in) s. board (A.D 1200)
£543	$918	(15-Apr-91 AAA.S138) Still life in abstract (61x61cm-24x24in) s. board (A.D 1200)
£613	$1000	(1-Jul-91 AAA.S84) The picnic races (26x36cm-10x14in) s. board (A.D 1300)
£633	$1071	(15-Apr-91 AAA.S126) Dragon fly (41x51cm-16x20in) s. (A.D 1400)
£708	$1153	(1-Jul-91 AAA.S131) Rabbit Trappers camp (30x47cm-12x19in) s. board (A.D 1500)
£769	$1300	(15-Apr-91 AAA.S136) Out station (30x60cm-12x24in) s. board (A.D 1700)
£849	$1384	(1-Jul-91 AAA.S70) Western landscape (46x60cm-18x24in) s. board (A.D 1800)
£905	$1529	(16-Apr-91 J.M186) The polo game (49x59cm-19x23in) s. board (A.D 2000)
£1004	$1978	(13-Nov-90 J.M123) Race day outback (50x60cm-20x24in) s. canvas board (A.D 2600)
£1321	$2153	(1-Jul-91 AAA.S138) Behind the reef (70x65cm-28x26in) s. board (A.D 2800)
£1357	$2294	(16-Apr-91 J.M287) End of season party (75x74cm-30x29in) s.d. '85 (A.D 3000)
£1448	$2447	(15-Apr-91 AAA.S132 d) Back of track (60x60cm-24x24in) s. board (A.D 3200)
£1514	$2982	(31-Oct-90 CH.S195) Country races (59x89cm-23x35in) s.i. acrylic board (A.D 3800)
£1544	$3042	(13-Nov-90 J.M255) The sand carters (44x59cm-17x23in) s. canvas board (A.D 4000)
£2140	$4195	(19-Nov-90 MGS.S308/R) Camped by the waterhole (75x100cm-30x39in) s.d.1976 (A.D 5500)
£2756	$5180	(17-Sep-90 MGS.S188/R) River country study, the drain (90x120cm-35x47in) s.i.d.1969 board (A.D 6200)

HART, Thomas (18/19th C) British
£450	$752	(6-Jun-91 B229/R) Figures clearing wreckage from beach (35x62cm-14x24in) s. W/C htd white
£520	$853	(20-Jun-91 DLY124/R) Looking out to sea (36x61cm-14x24in) s.d.1867 W/C
£620	$1215	(8-Nov-90 DLY314) Wreckers (15x25cm-6x10in) s. W/C

HART, William (fl.1882-1901) British
£1354	$2600	(17-Dec-90 SY.NY61/R) Cows in summer landscape (46x61cm-18x24in) s.
£3179	$5500	(22-May-91 CH.NY43/R) Near Tappan Zee, New York (23x45cm-9x18in) s.
£4624	$8000	(22-May-91 CH.NY161/R) Autumn by the river (32x27cm-13x11in) s.d.1874

HART, William M (1823-1894) American
£677	$1300	(17-Dec-90 SY.NY43/R) Wooded landscape (28x36cm-11x14in) s.i.d.1850 i.stretcher paper on canvas
£1000	$1900	(14-Sep-90 S.BM153/R) Cows watering at a stream (23x41cm-9x16in) s.
£1042	$2000	(17-Dec-90 SY.NY58 a/R) Landscape (10x18cm-4x7in) s.d.79 panel
£1042	$2000	(17-Dec-90 SY.NY131 a/R) Autumn landscape (18x15cm-7x6in) s. panel
£3073	$5500	(14-Mar-91 CH.NY14/R) Narrows (38x66cm-15x26in) s.
£3488	$6000	(15-May-91 SY.NY26/R) English landscape (67x91cm-26x36in) s.d.1851
£3704	$7000	(26-Sep-90 SY.NY33/R) Wooded glen (63x76cm-25x30in) s.
£3906	$7500	(17-Dec-90 SY.NY85 a/R) Conway Valley, N.H (23x38cm-9x15in) s.
£3968	$7500	(26-Sep-90 SY.NY31/R) On the Esopus (25x46cm-10x18in) s.
£4469	$8000	(12-Apr-91 SY.NY28/R) Prairie (19x36cm-7x14in) i.stretcher
£6936	$12000	(22-May-91 CH.NY18/R) Coastal sunrise (30x51cm-12x20in) s.d.61

HARTA, Felix Albrecht (1884-1970) Hungarian/Austrian
£3152	$5926	(20-Sep-90 D.V122/R) La Marianne (46x38cm-18x15in) s.d.1926 (A.S 65000)

HARTCHENKO, Boris (1927-1985) Russian
£507	$883	(25-Mar-91 ARC.P63/R) Dans le vieux Samarcande (57x42cm-22x17in) s. (F.FR 5100)
£816	$1420	(25-Mar-91 ARC.P61/R) Vacances au bord de la mer (30x48cm-12x19in) s. board (F.FR 8200)
£893	$1536	(15-May-91 AGB.P170/R) En promenade (16x22cm-6x9in) s. board (F.FR 9000)

HARTENKAMPF, Gottlieb Theodor Kempf von (1871-1956) Austrian
£1600	$2752	(17-May-91 C62/R) Frosch Konig (72x71cm-28x28in) s.

HARTIG, Hans (1873-?) German
£809	$1400	(22-May-91 D.NY44/R) On waterfront (85x79cm-33x31in) s.i.d.1910

HARTIGAN, Grace (1922-) American
£4872	$9500	(10-Oct-90 SY.NY536/R) East Hampton (71x56cm-28x22in) s.i.d.57 oil paper collage

HARTINGER, Anton (1806-1890) Austrian
£7200	$12384	(17-May-91 C42/R) Roses in vase on tiled ledge (36x29cm-14x11in) s.i. panel

HARTINGER, Anton (style) (1806-1890) Austrian
£4500	$8640	(28-Nov-90 S188/R) Still life with flowers and fruit (72x51cm-28x20in) bears sig.d.

HARTLEY, Marsden (1877-1943) American
£15625	$30000	(30-Nov-90 CH.NY207/R) Bird of paradise (51x61cm-20x24in) s.

846

HARTLEY, Marsden (1877-1943) American-cont.
£20833	$40000	(29-Nov-90 SY.NY107/R) Cyclamen (58x71cm-23x28in) i.mount
£1693	$3200	(25-Sep-90 CE.NY237/R) Compote fruit vase (46x61cm-18x24in) pencil
£1693	$3200	(25-Sep-90 CE.NY239/R) Tree on rocks (49x63cm-19x25in) i. verso pencil
£2011	$3800	(25-Sep-90 CE.NY234/R) Peaches and a pomegranate (47x62cm-19x24in) pencil
£2116	$4000	(25-Sep-90 CE.NY252/R) Bend in the road (48x61cm-19x24in) s.d.27 pencil
£2381	$4500	(25-Sep-90 CE.NY240/R) Three shells (37x29cm-15x11in) pen pencil
£3175	$6000	(27-Sep-90 CH.NY245/R) Apples (17x24cm-7x9in) s. W/C pencil paper laid down on paper
£4233	$8000	(27-Sep-90 CH.NY244/R) Fruit still life (17x24cm-7x9in) s. W/C pencil paper laid down on paper
£14286	$27000	(26-Sep-90 SY.NY187/R) Blue Hills (33x41cm-13x16in) pastel

HARTMANN, Bertram (1882-1960) American
| £2500 | $4300 | (17-May-91 C61/R) Embrace (53x52cm-21x20in) s.d.1912 W/C |

HARTMANN, Carl (1818-1857) German
| £2568 | $4598 | (13-Mar-91 N.M521/R) Allegory of autumn with putti and fruit in landscape (60x136cm-24x54in) s. i.verso (DM 7500) |

HARTMANN, Erich (1886-?) German
| £541 | $935 | (21-May-91 WK.M943/R) Female seated (61x44cm-24x17in) s. oil gouache board (DM 1600) |

HARTMANN, Hans (1845-?) German
| £10274 | $18390 | (13-Mar-91 N.M522/R) Coal market in Braunschweig (74x111cm-29x44in) s.i.d.89 i.stretcher (DM 30000) |

HARTMANN, J J (attrib) (17th C) German
| £4667 | $8960 | (18-Dec-90 GM.B4135/R) Vue de village avec personnages (25x34cm-10x13in) pair (B.FR 280000) |

HARTMANN, Johann Jacob (1680-1730) Czechoslovakian
| £13712 | $27013 | (14-Nov-90 D.V9/R) Wooded river landscape with boats and peasants near houses (24x31cm-9x12in) panel (A.S 280000) |

HARTMANN, Karl (1861-?) German
| £2027 | $3953 | (26-Oct-90 BM.B791/R) Village street with figures (40x50cm-16x20in) s. (DM 6000) |
| £2911 | $5211 | (12-Mar-91 FN.S2406/R) Peasant women on village street in Fehling, Chiemgau (40x50cm-16x20in) s. (DM 8500) |

HARTMANN, Ludwig (1835-1902) German
£640	$1082	(1-May-91 GD.B378/R) Brown stallion (31x52cm-12x20in) s.d.1878 (S.FR 1600)
£8671	$15000	(10-May-91 S.BM15/R) Peasant with team of three horses (33x64cm-13x25in) s.i. panel
£30457	$60000	(16-Nov-90 S.BM35/R) Before stables with peasants, horses and cattle (46x94cm-18x37in) s.i. cradled panel

Ludwig Hartmann (German, 1835–1902). Before the Stables, sold for $66,000, 11/16/90.

SKINNER

357 Main Street	*Auctioneers and Appraisers*	2 Newbury Street
Bolton, MA 01740	*of Antiques and Fine Art*	Boston, MA 02116
(508) 779-6241		(617) 236-1700

HARTMANN, Sven (1943-) Swiss
£653 $1287 (13-Nov-90 GF.L5354/R) C'est le ton qui fait la musique (20x17cm-8x7in)
s.d.1989 W/C indian ink pen (S.FR 1600)

HARTOGENSIS, Joseph (1822-1865) Flemish
£721 $1406 (25-Oct-90 D.V171/R) Landscape with castle ruin (41x59cm-16x23in) s.d.59
(A.S 15000)

HARTUNG, Hans (1904-1989) French
£6932 $13378 (16-Dec-90 GL.P28/R) Composition (49x70cm-19x28in) s.d.1960 card
(F.FR 68000)
£11000 $19470 (21-Mar-91 C225) P.40 1975-H 13 (75x104cm-30x41in) s.d.75 acrylic
cardboard
£16129 $30968 (2-Dec-90 GAB.G1630/R) Composition jaune et bleue (50x69cm-20x27in) s.
paper (S.FR 40000)
£31621 $53755 (30-May-91 EA.Z285/R) A 46 - 1967 (72x99cm-28x39in) s.d.67 card on
canvas (S.FR 80000)
£34000 $66300 (18-Oct-90 S50/R) T52-V46 (50x61cm-20x24in) s.d.62
£44369 $86962 (23-Nov-90 VG.B78/R) T 54 - 34 (35x24cm-14x9in) s.d.1954 (DM 130000)
£48138 $78946 (20-Jun-91 F.M463/R) T - 1961 - H 3 - 1961 (80x130cm-31x51in) s.d.61
i.verso (I.L 105000000)
£56213 $95000 (1-May-91 SY.NY187/R) T 1959-3 (65x50cm-26x20in) s.d.59
£76000 $122360 (27-Jun-91 S11/R) T 1961 - H 27 (92x150cm-36x59in) s.d.61
£126069 $245835 (22-Oct-90 BR.M26/R) T 1963 - H 18 (63x92cm-25x36in) s.d.1963
(I.L 280000000)
£155000 $302250 (18-Oct-90 S27/R) T50-45 (63x79cm-25x31in) s.d.50 i.stretcher
£230000 $407100 (21-Mar-91 S37/R) T 1951-4 (97x146cm-38x57in) s.d.51
£3003 $5195 (22-May-91 CH.AM608/R) Composition with l'art de notre temps
(31x25cm-12x10in) s.d.24-12-67 ink col.crayons over printed base
(D.FL 10000)
£5777 $9821 (30-May-91 FB.P33 b/R) Sans titre (50x73cm-20x29in) s.d.61 gouache
(F.FR 58000)
£7430 $14341 (13-Dec-90 SY.AM284/R) Untitled (64x49cm-25x19in) s.d.60 pastel
(D.FL 24000)
£8657 $14717 (28-May-91 SY.MI158/R) Composizione (56x38cm-22x15in) s.d.66 pastel
board (I.L 19000000)
£9146 $18293 (5-Feb-91 CSC.P67/R) Composition (45x55cm-18x22in) s.d.59 pastel
(F.FR 90000)
£9556 $18061 (25-Sep-90 FN.S1963) Composition with verticals (26x19cm-10x7in)
s.d.1977 enkaustik board (DM 28000)
£9677 $18581 (2-Dec-90 GAB.G1628/R) Composition (55x40cm-22x16in) s.d.40 gouache chk.
(S.FR 24000)
£11003 $18045 (20-Jun-91 F.M437/R) P 1971 - 12 - 1971 (48x71cm-19x28in) s.d.71 i.verso
crayon tempera board (I.L 24000000)
£12859 $23017 (9-Apr-91 BG.P105 m/R) Composition (52x66cm-20x26in) s.i.d.58 crayon
pastel (F.FR 130000)
£14500 $25665 (21-Mar-91 S1/R) Composition (32x22cm-13x9in) s.d.51 gouache ink
graphite
£14694 $28947 (16-Nov-90 EA.Z363/R) Untitled (32x25cm-13x10in) mono.d.1938 indian ink
chl (S.FR 36000)
£16724 $32778 (23-Nov-90 VG.B80/R) Untitled (65x48cm-26x19in) s.d.1957 chl col.chk
board (DM 49000)
£17766 $35000 (14-Nov-90 SY.NY315/R) Composition P 1961-91 (80x59cm-31x23in) s.d.61
crayon on paperboard
£19000 $37050 (18-Oct-90 S36/R) Composition (71x47cm-28x19in) s.d.60 pastel
£23649 $40203 (31-May-91 VG.B71/R) Komposition P 1961-74 (60x79cm-24x31in) s.d.1961
i.verso col.chk board (DM 70000)
£25457 $49897 (20-Nov-90 BR.M193/R) P 1973-Z 33 (73x50cm-29x20in) s.d.1973 i.verso
mixed media board (I.L 56000000)
£33769 $55381 (20-Jun-91 APT.P65/R) Composition (47x71cm-19x28in) s.d.1948 mixed media
(F.FR 336000)
£40000 $78000 (18-Oct-90 C367/R) P 1967-A 52 (73x99cm-29x39in) s.d.67 acrylic
col.crayon cardboard

HARTUNG, Heinrich (1851-1919) German
£811 $1581 (26-Oct-90 KM.K1256) Wooded river landscape, autumn (85x63cm-33x25in)
s.d.1920 i.verso (DM 2400)
£878 $1713 (26-Oct-90 KM.K1255) Grandfather and grandson walking through orchard to
farmhouse, spring (43x29cm-17x11in) mono.d.99 board (DM 2600)
£1497 $2649 (20-Mar-91 KM.K1245/R) Eifel landscape, autumn (46x67cm-18x26in) s.
(DM 4400)

HARTUNG, Johann (19th C) German
£798 $1500 (21-Sep-90 BG.M770/R) Dogs playing with a kite (33x25cm-13x10in) s.
board

HARTUNG, Julius (1836-1918) ?
£1600 $2752 (14-May-91 SWS301/R) Mischievous pugs (26x21cm-10x8in) s. pair

HARTUNG, Karl (1908-1967) German
£1216 $2068 (1-Jun-91 VG.B557/R) Composition (31x43cm-12x17in) s. i.d.1950verso chk
board (DM 3600)
£1689 $2872 (30-May-91 SY.BE97/R) Figure study (50x34cm-20x13in) s.d.49 chl over W/C
(DM 5000)

HARTWICH, Herman (1853-1926) American
£1014 $1976   (26-Oct-90 KM.K1257/R) Italian wine grower and dog watering horses (28x36cm-11x14in) s. board (DM 3000)
£1734 $3000   (21-May-91 CE.NY464/R) Ducks by stream (36x53cm-14x21in) s.
£1823 $3500   (17-Dec-90 SY.NY55/R) Haying (94x135cm-37x53in) s.
£17341 $30000 (22-May-91 CH.NY193/R) Tending geese (34x53cm-13x21in) s.
£31792 $55000 (22-May-91 CH.NY192/R) A bleachery in Lombardy (120x192cm-47x76in) s.

HARTWICK, George Gunther (fl.1847-1857) American
£859 $1400   (5-Jul-91 S.W2659/R) View on the Marne (30x51cm-12x20in) s.i. verso

HARTWIG, Max (1873-?) German
£1508 $2518   (7-Jun-91 ZOF.Z1088/R) Landscape with village (9x14cm-4x6in) mono. board (S.FR 3800)
£1529 $2936   (2-Dec-90 M.V124/R) Fleurs (51x38cm-20x15in) s. board (F.FR 15000)
£1697 $3191   (20-Sep-90 D.V164/R) View of Strobl by Wolfgangsee (70x128cm-28x50in) s. (A.S 35000)

HARVEG, Rino (1918-) Norwegian
£757 $1461   (13-Dec-90 BU.O21/R) Town musicians in Kragero 1945 (50x61cm-20x24in) s.d.45 s.i.verso panel (N.KR 8500)
£1051 $1881   (11-Mar-91 B.O40/R) Evening in Kragero Park (81x100cm-32x39in) s.d. (N.KR 12000)

HARVENG, Carl Friedrich (1832-1874) ?
£2162 $3524   (10-Jun-91 W.T1406/R) A conversation on washing day (36x50cm-14x20in) s. (C.D 4000)

HARVEY (?) ?
£888 $1500   (17-Apr-91 D.NY63/R) Flute player (91x61cm-36x24in) s.

HARVEY, George (c.1800-1878) American
£3243 $6000   (8-Mar-91 S.BM156/R) Rain Storm, Cider Mill at Reading, Connecticut (20x33cm-8x13in) s. i. verso W/C htd.white

HARVEY, Gertrude (1889-?) British
£620 $1178   (28-Feb-91 DLY146/R) Summer bunch (51x46cm-20x18in) s.
£650 $1274   (8-Nov-90 DLY276) Hillside garden (30x38cm-12x15in) s. board

HARVEY, Harold (1874-1941) British
£1800 $3456   (20-Dec-90 CSK135/R) Reading by the fire (34x29cm-13x11in) s.d.18 board
£2800 $4732   (30-Apr-91 AG268/R) Gypsy family (29x44cm-11x17in) s.d.1906
£3140 $5900   (18-Sep-90 PH26/R) Ploughing (64x76cm-25x30in) s.d.1921
£4200 $7938   (27-Sep-90 L55/R) A rest by the wayside (51x41cm-20x16in) s.d.'37
£4500 $7830   (27-Mar-91 S55/R) Mother and child (46x46cm-18x18in) s.d.26
£5800 $9454   (13-Jun-91 L110/R) The wayfarers (30x46cm-12x18in) s.d.1906
£8000 $15840 (29-Jan-91 PH30/R) Front, Newlyn (38x46cm-15x18in) s.
£11000 $21560 (6-Nov-90 PH43/R) Washday (39x29cm-15x11in) s.d.07

HARVEY, John Rabone (?-1933) British
£1700 $3315   (15-Jan-91 C26/R) Smooth-haired fox terrier on sofa (53x43cm-21x17in) s.

HARVEY, Nelly (19/20th C) British
£750 $1418   (26-Sep-90 S143/R) Girl with chicken and chicks (30x23cm-12x9in) s.d.87

HARVEY, Reginald L (1888-1963) Canadian
£722 $1227   (27-May-91 HO.ED13/R) Near Weaselhead Bridge (61x46cm-24x18in) s.d. i.verso pastel (C.D 1400)

HARVEY, Seymour Garstin (fl.1896-1906) British
£528 $887   (23-Apr-91 RAS.K318/R) The Lady of Shalot (67x48cm-26x19in) s. panel (D.KR 6000)
£980 $1920   (22-Nov-90 RAS.V719/R) The Lady of Shaloh (68x48cm-27x19in) s. (D.KR 11000)

HARVEY, W Craig (1882-?) American
£521 $1000   (18-Aug-90 S.BM370) Autumn fields (51x61cm-20x24in) s.

HARWOOD, John (1818-1871) British
£42000 $82740 (14-Nov-90 S9/R) The Shannon and Chesapeake (104x165cm-41x65in) s.d.1813

HARWOOD, John Hammond (1904-) British
£740 $1399   (27-Sep-90 ZZ.B123/R) Peregrine on rocky sea cliffs (41x30cm-16x12in) s. W/C
£1350 $2552   (27-Sep-90 ZZ.B122) Ptarmigan. Ptarmigan in winter plumage (30x41cm-12x16in) s. W/C pair

HASCH, Carl (1834-1897) Austrian
£1456 $2751   (27-Sep-90 D.V17/R) Wooded river landscape (31x52cm-12x20in) s. (A.S 30000)
£1827 $3563   (25-Oct-90 D.V173/R) Hallstatt (36x31cm-14x12in) mono. (A.S 38000)
£2399 $4127   (16-May-91 D.V87/R) River landscape (39x47cm-15x19in) s.d.1856 (A.S 50000)
£2500 $4750   (27-Feb-91 SY.NY148/R) Gathering faggots by stream (50x39cm-20x15in) s. panel

HASEGAWA, Kiyoshi (1891-1980) Japanese
£20161 $38710   (2-Dec-90 GAB.G1631/R) Bouquet de fleurs (64x54cm-25x21in) s. d.1943
                                 verso (S.FR 50000)
£1429 $2771   (8-Dec-90 GAB.G2656/R) Bateaux sur la mer (24x36cm-9x14in) s. W/C
                                   (S.FR 3500)

HASELEER, Frans (1804-?) Belgian
£3000 $4920   (19-Jun-91 S26/R) Admiring new picture (63x48cm-25x19in) s.i. panel

HASELTINE, William Stanley (1835-1900) American
£2154 $4200   (20-Oct-90 W.W38/R) Lago Maggiore, Island of the Fishermen
                                 (56x91cm-22x36in) s.
£2174 $4196   (10-Dec-90 BU.K15/R) Beached boats on the shore (36x53cm-14x21in) s.
                                 (D.KR 24000)
£2750 $5500   (7-Feb-91 B.P36/R) North African coastal village scene (48x79cm-19x31in)
                                 mono.
£9249 $16000   (22-May-91 CH.NY39/R) Coastal scene (35x57cm-14x22in)

HASLEHURST, Ernest William (1866-1949) British
£400 $652   (14-Jun-91 C29/R) Norwich Cathedral (23x35cm-9x14in) s.i.verso pencil
                               W/C
£420 $685   (14-Jun-91 C32/R) Canterbury Cathedral from Christ Church Gate
                               (23x35cm-9x14in) s.i.verso pewncil W/C
£580 $1131   (16-Jan-91 CSK37/R) Village on estuary, Devon (33x51cm-13x20in) s.
                               pencil W/C
£620 $1011   (14-Jun-91 C30/R) The gatehouse, Charlecote (23x35cm-9x14in) s.i.verso
                               pencil W/C

HASLUND, Otto (1842-1917) Danish
£3000 $5760   (28-Nov-90 S68/R) Mother and child by doorway (78x60cm-31x24in) s.d.04

HASS, Fritz (1864-?) German
£673 $1165   (6-May-91 ZEL.L1730/R) Portrait of Rudolf Christoph Eucken, Nobel Prize
                               Winner for Literature (70x65cm-28x26in) s. (DM 2000)

HASS, Sigfred (1848-1908) Danish/German
£753 $1272   (1-May-91 KH.K78) Moonlit fjord landscape, Norway (63x101cm-25x40in)
                               s.d.05 (D.KR 8500)

HASSAM, Childe (1859-1935) American
£12717 $22000   (22-May-91 CH.NY255/R) West Course, Maidstone (20x28cm-8x11in) s.d.1926
                                  panel
£13757 $26000   (27-Sep-90 CH.NY182/R) The mantle piece (19x25cm-7x10in) s.d.1912 verso
                                  panel
£26042 $50000   (30-Nov-90 CH.NY118/R) The hawk's nest (51x35cm-20x14in) s.d.1904
                                  init.d.verso
£39063 $75000   (29-Nov-90 SY.NY53/R) Church procession, Spanish Steps (32x43cm-13x17in)
                                  s.d.1883 mono.d.backing
£80925 $140000   (23-May-91 SY.NY44/R) Roses in bowl with jug, Isles of shoals
                                  (23x15cm-9x6in) s.i.d.1890 panel
£250000 $480000   (30-Nov-90 CH.NY110/R) The El, New York (46x35cm-18x14in) s.d.1894
£4046 $7000   (22-May-91 CH.NY133/R) Brick mansion, Portsmouth, New Hampshire
                                  (25x35cm-10x14in) W/C crayon
£10615 $19000   (12-Apr-91 SY.NY62/R) Brittany barns (20x28cm-8x11in) s.i. chk W/C
                                  gouache
£11458 $22000   (29-Nov-90 SY.NY52/R) Duck Island, Isles of Shoals (36x51cm-14x20in)
                                  s.d.1906 W/C paperboard
£15104 $29000   (29-Nov-90 SY.NY51/R) Portrait of lady in blue dress (53x34cm-21x13in)
                                  s.d.1906 pastel board
£20833 $40000   (29-Nov-90 SY.NY49/R) Gate of the Alhambra (50x31cm-20x12in) s.d.1883
                                  W/C gouache
£39063 $75000   (30-Nov-90 CH.NY114/R) Quai du Louvre (22x21cm-9x8in) s.i.d.1889 W/C
                                  board

HASSAN EL GLAOUI (20th C) ?
£709 $1389   (20-Nov-90 APT.P228) Fete et Cavaliers (49x75cm-19x30in) s. gouache
                                  (F.FR 7000)

HASSEBRAUK, Ernst (1905-1974) German
£946 $1608   (1-Jun-91 VG.B558/R) Still life with flagon shaped bottle
                                  (55x76cm-22x30in) s. paper (DM 2800)
£1049 $2035   (7-Dec-90 GB.B6620) Still life with oranges and lemons (46x60cm-18x24in)
                                  c.1950 (DM 3000)
£1126 $2208   (24-Nov-90 N.M200/R) Portrait of man with pipe before garden
                                  (81x60cm-32x24in) s. (DM 3300)
£1502 $2943   (24-Nov-90 N.M201/R) Still life with red cabbage and preserving jar
                                  (60x81cm-24x32in) s. i.verso (DM 4400)
£887 $1739   (22-Nov-90 L.K989/R) Still life (45x69cm-18x27in) s. d.1970verso mixed
                                  media (DM 2600)

HASSELBACH, Wilhelm (1846-?) German
£2174 $3674   (19-Apr-91 FN.S1729/R) Peasant interior with figure (67x57cm-26x22in)
                                  s.i. (DM 6500)
£3026 $5750   (15-Sep-90 S.W2767/R) The broken window (76x99cm-30x39in) s.

HASSELL, Hilton Macdonald (1910-1980) Canadian
£546 $1075   (12-Nov-90 HO.ED330/R) Hillside house, Looe, Cornwall (30x41cm-12x16in)
   s..d.1961 acrylic board (C.D 1250)

HASSELT, Willem van (1882-1963) Dutch
£802 $1555   (7-Dec-90 GL.P90) Le bateau rose (38x46cm-15x18in) s. i. verso
   (F.FR 7800)
£1336 $2592   (7-Dec-90 GL.P91) Sur le perret, Arachon (38x46cm-15x18in) s.d.1927 i.
   verso (F.FR 13000)
£3571 $7000   (7-Nov-90 B.SF1060/R) Afternoon in park (71x91cm-28x36in) s.

HASSENTEUFEL (?) ?
£800 $1352   (1-May-91 GD.B379/R) Italian woman before wall with terracotta jug
   (95x69cm-37x27in) s.i. (S.FR 2000)
£800 $1536   (27-Nov-90 PH159/R) The gypsy musician (86x70cm-34x28in) s.i.

HASSENTEUFEL, Hans (1887-) German
£680 $1095   (26-Jun-91 KM.K1494) Oriental dancer semi nude (42x30cm-17x12in)
   s.i.d.1925 (DM 2000)
£1427 $2796   (24-Nov-90 HOR.H10/R) Gypsy woman dancing (95x70cm-37x28in) s.i.
   (F.M 10000)

HASSMANN, Carl (1869-1933) Austrian
£730 $1431   (24-Jan-91 D.V104/R) The kiss (37x44cm-15x17in) mono. board (A.S 15000)

HASTAIRE (20th C) French?
£742 $1328   (14-Apr-91 R.P55/R) Les belles anonymes (92x73cm-36x29in) acrylic
   newspaper laid down on canvas (F.FR 7500)
£910 $1629   (14-Apr-91 R.P247) Les belles annees no.5 (92x73cm-36x29in) s. acrylic
   newspaper laid down on canvas (F.FR 9200)

HASTE, Edlyn (1967-) British
£750 $1470   (13-Feb-91 B122/R) Not waving (107x127cm-42x50in) s.d.90 s.d.1990 verso

HASTINGS, Edward (18/19th C) British
£420 $777   (5-Mar-91 AG213) *Double portrait of small girl and boy (34x27cm-13x11in)*
   s.d.1829 W/C
£800 $1480   (5-Mar-91 AG224/R) *Portrait of girl and her spaniel (66x54cm-26x21in)*
   s.d.1847 pastel

HATFIELD, Joseph Henry (1863-?) Canadian
£1904 $3750   (16-Nov-90 S.BM72/R) Scene with young girl on beach (41x61cm-16x24in) s.

HATHAWAY, George M (19th C) British
£670 $1300   (24-Aug-90 RB.HY23/R) Portland Head Light (15x25cm-6x10in) s. board
£1489 $2800   (11-Aug-90 COL.M171/R) Yacht off Cushing Island (25x48cm-10x19in) s.
   board
£1658 $3250   (24-Nov-90 RB.HY171/R) Schooner Nellie sailing off the coast
   (28x56cm-11x22in) s.d.1891
£1700 $3400   (7-Feb-91 B.P127/R) View of Portland harbour at sunset (15x25cm-6x10in)
   s. board
£1765 $3300   *(1-Aug-90 B.P10/R) Sunset in Portland harbour (25x36cm-10x14in) s. W/C*

HATTERSLEY, F W (19/20th C) British
£490 $818   *(4-Jun-91 SWS2040) Boats at anchor (24x34cm-9x13in) s. W/C*

HATTICH, Petrus van (17th C) Dutch
£3486 $5926   (31-May-91 LD.P28/R) Paysage avec des chevres au pied de ruines
   (103x70cm-41x28in) sig. panel (F.FR 35000)

HATTINCK, W L (?) ?
£728 $1376   (25-Sep-90 GM.B980) Canal gele (50x60cm-20x24in) s. panel (B.FR 44000)

HATZ, Felix (?) ?
£697 $1248   (9-Apr-91 GO.G54) Coastal landscape with flowers (46x55cm-18x22in) s.
   panel (S.KR 7500)
£823 $1612   (20-Nov-90 GO.G85) Boats covered in snow (60x80cm-24x31in) s.
   (S.KR 9000)

HAU, Woldemar (1816-1895) Russian
£1200 $2340   *(10-Oct-90 C180/R) Grand Duchess Ekaterina Mikhailovna, Duchess of*
   Mecklenburg-Strelitz (28x23cm-11x9in) s.d.1845 i.verso pencil W/C htd
   white card
£3200 $6240   *(10-Oct-90 C181/R) Lady in riding habit, supposedly Grand Duchess Maria*
   Nikolaevna (34x25cm-13x10in) s.d.1841 pencil W/C htd white card

HAUDEBOURT-LESCOT, Antoinette (1784-1845) French
£3469 $6731   (8-Dec-90 GAB.G2064/R) Le contrat de mariage (50x60cm-20x24in) s.
   (S.FR 8500)

HAUDEBOURT-LESCOT, Antoinette (attrib) (1784-1845) French
£2051 $4000   (26-Oct-90 SY.NY143/R) Lecon de peinture (43x36cm-17x14in)

HAUER, Leopold (1896-1984) Austrian
£1243 $2411   (6-Dec-90 D.V109/R) Landscape (31x36cm-12x14in) mono. mono.s.verso panel
   (A.S 25000)

HAUER, Leopold (1896-1984) Austrian-cont.
£1456 $2388   (20-Jun-91 D.V67/R) Houses by the water (24x34cm-9x13in) mono.s. board
(A.S 30000)

HAUG, Kristian (1862-?) Norwegian
£521 $870   (3-Jun-91 B.O60/R) Akershus shore (92x70cm-36x28in) s.d.1906 (N.KR 6000)

HAUG, Robert von (1857-1922) German
£2218 $4193   (25-Sep-90 FN.S2199) Mail coach stopping by architectural buildings
(47x64cm-19x25in) s.d.1912 board (DM 6500)

HAUGE, Marie (1864-1931) Norwegian
£569 $1019   (11-Mar-91 B.O41/R) Mountain landscape with cheesefarm (40x81cm-16x32in)
s. i.verso (N.KR 6500)
£653 $1274   (15-Oct-90 B.O32/R) Landscape from Balestrand (60x76cm-24x30in) s.
(N.KR 7500)
£757 $1461   (12-Dec-90 BU.O25/R) Still life of flowers in vase (81x45cm-32x18in)
s.i.d.06 (N.KR 8500)
£1394 $2718   (15-Oct-90 B.O30/R) Farm-yard (90x115cm-35x45in) s. (N.KR 16000)
£4355 $8493   (15-Oct-90 B.O31/R) Peasants returning home (100x82cm-39x32in) s.
(N.KR 50000)

HAUGEN-SORENSEN, Arne (1932-) Danish
£861 $1661   (12-Dec-90 RAS.K113) 'Lady-baby' (46x34cm-18x13in) init.d.74 (D.KR 9500)
£1346 $2653   (14-Nov-90 KH.K55/R) Figure on table (55x38cm-22x15in) s.d.70
(D.KR 15000)
*£934 $1756   (19-Sep-90 KH.K273) Composition (44x53cm-17x21in) s.d.79 W/C
(D.KR 10500)*

HAUGHTON, Moses (Jnr) (c.1772-1848) British
£1400 $2506   (10-Apr-91 S133/R) Mrs. Siddons at tragic muse (59x40cm-23x16in) s.panel
after Sir Joshua Reynolds

HAUKEBO, Gunnar (1909-) Norwegian
£525 $940   (11-Mar-91 B.O42/R) Landscape from Ibiza (38x48cm-15x19in) s.d.58
(N.KR 6000)

HAUNOLD, Carl (1832-1911) Austrian
£735 $1455   (31-Jan-91 D.V120/R) Mountainous river landscape (53x38cm-21x15in) mono.
board (A.S 15000)
£2136 $3823   (11-Apr-91 D.V46/R) View of Vienna valley (25x71cm-10x28in) s.
(A.S 45000)

HAUPT, Matti (1912-) Finnish
*£717 $1212   (20-Apr-91 HOR.H94/R) Nude model (34x25cm-13x10in) s. pastel (F.M 5000)
£2853 $5592   (24-Nov-90 HOR.H109/R) The model (75x56cm-30x22in) s. mixed media
(F.M 20000)*

HAUPTMANN, Ivo (1886-1973) German
£1049 $2035   (7-Dec-90 GB.B6627) Still life with fishes (73x51cm-29x20in) s.d.1928
(DM 3000)
£1351 $2338   (25-May-91 N.M123) The chess player (33x48cm-13x19in) i.d.1904verso
board (DM 4000)
*£467 $835   (12-Apr-91 AW.H1590/R) Yellow blossom before window (38x46cm-15x18in)
s.d.1964 W/C over chk (DM 1400)
£507 $861   (1-Jun-91 VG.B562/R) Shipping on the Elbe (28x43cm-11x17in) s. W/C over
chk (DM 1500)
£587 $1145   (12-Oct-90 AW.H2506/R) Alpine lake landscape with tree (8x47cm-3x19in)
s.d.1965 W/C over chk (DM 1750)
£700 $1253   (12-Apr-91 BM.B847/R) Mountain landscape with paddock and telegraph
poles (38x45cm-15x18in) s.d.1919 chl col.chk (DM 2100)
£819 $1605   (24-Nov-90 VG.B545/R) Still life with roses (38x46cm-15x18in) s.d.1964
W/C over chk (DM 2400)
£1024 $2007   (24-Nov-90 VG.B546/R) Sunflower (38x46cm-15x18in) s.d.1965 W/C over
pencil (DM 3000)
£1706 $3345   (24-Nov-90 VG.B232/R) View of Corfu (23x36cm-9x14in) s.i.d.1907 pastel
(DM 5000)
£2048 $4014   (24-Nov-90 VG.B233/R) Market in Weimar (24x37cm-9x15in) mono.i. pastel
(DM 6000)*

HAUPTMANN, Karl (1880-1947) German
£1846 $3599   (12-Oct-90 AW.H2507/R) Landscape with Black Forest farmhouses, late
summer (70x90cm-28x35in) s. (DM 5500)
£2517 $4908   (12-Oct-90 AW.H2508/R) Elztal landscape, sunny winter's day
(70x90cm-28x35in) s. s.i.stretcher (DM 7500)
£4667 $8353   (12-Apr-91 AW.H1591/R) Black Forest landscape with farmhouses and
stream, spring (80x120cm-31x47in) s. (DM 14000)

HAUPTMANN, Klaus (?) ?
£905 $1529   (16-Apr-91 J.M278/R) A Swiss Winter (69x99cm-27x39in) s.d.'36 board
(A.D 2000)

HAUSER, Carry (1895-1985) Austrian
*£1243 $2411   (6-Dec-90 D.V121/R) Two figures (20x13cm-8x5in) mono. col.pencil
(A.S 25000)*

HAUSER, John (1859-1913) American
£1156	$2000	(21-May-91 CE.NY555/R) Outside village shops (76x114cm-30x45in) s.
£1604	$3000	(1-Aug-90 B.P93/R) Chief Fire Cloud, Sioux (30x20cm-12x8in) s. board
£4878	$8000	(21-Jun-91 DM.D2015/R) Sioux hunter (53x36cm-21x14in) s.d.1912 board
£794	$1500	(25-Sep-90 CE.NY267/R) The chase (22x37cm-9x15in) s. W/C gouache pencil
£1015	$2000	(16-Nov-90 WOL.C365/R) Lookout (33x23cm-13x9in) s.d.1941 W/C
£1624	$3200	(16-Nov-90 WOL.C364/R) Cleaning gun (33x23cm-13x9in) s.d.1962 W/C

HAUSER, Renee-Yolande (1919-) Swiss
£677	$1321	(24-Oct-90 GD.B449/R) Des fraises et des framboises (55x45cm-22x18in) s. l.d.1962verso panel (S.FR 1700)

HAUSHOFER, Alfred (1872-1943) German
£542	$884	(3-Jul-91 WE.MU215/R) After the mass (30x25cm-12x10in) s. gouache (DM 1600)
£629	$1215	(12-Dec-90 WE.MU12/R) To be seen in the theatre, for Fliegende Blatter (32x25cm-13x10in) mono. gouache (DM 1800)

HAUSLEITHNER, Rudolf (1840-1918) Austrian
£1700	$3043	(14-Mar-91 ZZ.B146) Portrait of a lady, three-quarter length, in red, fur-trimmed dress (132x81cm-52x32in) s.

HAUSMANN, Gustav (1827-1899) German
£1596	$3000	(19-Sep-90 B.SF2668/R) Alpine landscape with travellers (86x122cm-34x48in) s.i.d.1891
£1923	$3712	(12-Dec-90 N.M544/R) Farmstead beneath old oak trees and peasant woman hanging up washing (79x104cm-31x41in) s. (DM 5500)

HAUSNER, Rudolf (1914-) Austrian
£4473	$8678	(6-Dec-90 D.V168/R) Head and jug (50x68cm-20x27in) s.d.46 mixed media (A.S 90000)

HAUSSER, Johann (attrib) (16/17th C) German
£9790	$18895	(10-Dec-90 L.K52/R) Ecce Homo with view of landscape (26x36cm-10x14in) copper (DM 28000)

HAUSSER, R (19th C) French
£702	$1369	(12-Oct-90 ZZ.F57) Barques sur l'etang (63x54cm-25x21in) s.d.1881 (F.FR 7000)

HAUSSMAN, Raoul (1886-1970) German?
£918	$1809	(16-Nov-90 FB.P344/R) Composition (49x65cm-19x26in) mono.d.57 tempera paper laid down on panel (F.FR 9000)

HAUSTRAETE, G (1878-1949) Belgian
£769	$1506	(12-Feb-91 GM.B426) Ramasseuse de fagots (75x100cm-30x39in) s. (B.FR 46000)

HAUSTRATE, H (19/20th C) Belgian
£5667	$10880	(18-Dec-90 GM.B4024) La reussite (79x99cm-31x39in) s. (B.FR 340000)

HAVARD, James (20th C) American
£1786	$3500	(6-Nov-90 CE.NY100/R) Cane Garden Bay (76x51cm-30x20in) s.i.d.79 acrylic board
£2051	$4000	(10-Oct-90 SY.NY553/R) Buffalo Bull's backfat (81x102cm-32x40in) s.i.d.75 acrylic
£2055	$3988	(9-Dec-90 CC.P79/R) Sans titre (93x72cm-37x28in) s.d.1984 acrylic (F.FR 20000)
£6122	$12000	(6-Nov-90 CE.NY103/R) Ute (122x122cm-48x48in) s.i.d.75 verso acrylic
£6154	$12000	(10-Oct-90 SY.NY498/R) Plegan (152x137cm-60x54in) s.d.75overlap s.i.d.75verso acrylic
£7044	$13665	(5-Dec-90 AB.S7093/R) Trompe l'oeil (94x102cm-37x40in) s.d.75verso oil acrylic (S.KR 76000)
£7143	$14000	(7-Nov-90 SY.NY241/R) Drink the juice of the stone (169x169cm-67x67in) s.i.d.75 acrylic
£8122	$16000	(4-Oct-90 SY.NY114/R) Kiowa (122x122cm-48x48in) s.d.77 s.d.77 num.verso acrylic canvas
£15292	$29666	(4-Dec-90 BA.S196/R) No 3 B.A (120x145cm-47x57in) s.d.74verso (S.KR 165000)

HAVELL, Alfred C (fl.1878-84) British
£1500	$2460	(20-Jun-91 B49/R) Sheen. Alicante (25x30cm-10x12in) s.i. pair

HAVEN, Franklin de (1856-1934) American
£565	$950	(28-Apr-91 HG.C302) Autumn landscape (61x46cm-24x18in) s.
£714	$1400	(16-Feb-91 W.W77/R) Sun drenched dunes (51x86cm-20x34in) s.
£2083	$4000	(17-Dec-90 SY.NY94/R) Along Long Island sound (51x81cm-20x32in) s.d.1890 s.i.stretcher

HAVERTY, Joseph Patrick (attrib) (1794-1864) British
£720	$1246	(20-May-91 SWS287) The fortune teller (98x124cm-39x49in)

HAVLICEK, Vincenz (1864-1914) Austrian
£728	$1376	(27-Sep-90 D.V189/R) Pond landscape with silver birches, evening (59x88cm-23x35in) s.d.1901 W/C (A.S 15000)

HAVLICEK, Vincenz (1864-1914) Austrian-cont.
£764 $1489   (11-Oct-90 D.V236/R) View of Salzburg (20x25cm-8x10in) s.i.d.1907 indian
                     ink W/C (A.S 16000)

HAVSTEEN-MIKKELSEN, Sven (1912-) Danish
£799 $1575   (31-Oct-90 KH.K31) Sunset, Faroe Islands (35x44cm-14x17in) init.
                     (D.KR 9000)

HAWKINS, H F Weaver (1893-1977) Australian/British
£694 $1167   (16-Jul-91 JRL.S228 o) Near orange (39x50cm-15x20in) s.d.1947 board
                     (A.D 1500)
£961 $1720   (9-Apr-91 CH.ME267/R) Stark trees (44x37cm-17x15in) s.d.46 canvasboard
                     (A.D 2200)
£1931 $3803   (13-Nov-90 J.M154/R) Checkers (49x69cm-19x27in) s.d.44 (A.D 5000)
£4016 $7711   (26-Nov-90 SY.ME185/R) Deck-game (69x90cm-27x35in) s.d.58 s.i.verso
                     board (A.D 10000)
£519 $846   (1-Jul-91 AAA.S1609 j) Tropical landscape (39x57cm-15x22in) s. W/C
                     (A.D 1100)
£622 $1170   (17-Sep-90 MGS.S172/R) Landscape (38x27cm-15x11in) s.d.1945 W/C
                     (A.D 1400)

HAWKINS, Louis Welden (1849-1910) British
£499 $843   (29-Apr-91 LGB.P33) Femme assise dans la campagne (44x33cm-17x13in)
                     init. blk.crayon (F.FR 5000)
£2608 $5085   (12-Oct-90 APT.P112/R) La glaneuse assoupie (73x53cm-29x21in) s. W/C
                     gouache (F.FR 26000)

HAWLEY, Hughson (19/20th C) ?
£2105 $4000   (9-Jan-91 CH.NY213/R) Union League Club, N.Y.C. Mayday at Central Park
                     one s.i.ink board one init.d.1893 gouache two

HAWORTH, Bobs Cogill (1904-) Canadian
£524 $1032   (12-Nov-90 HO.ED83/R) Sunflowers (39x57cm-15x22in) s. tempera
                     (C.D 1200)

HAWTHORNE, Charles W (1872-1930) American
£1302 $2500   (17-Dec-90 SY.NY333/R) Little boy in blue (76x64cm-30x25in) s.d.2
£2326 $4000   (18-May-91 W.W134/R) Portrait of a woman (91x81cm-36x32in) s. board
£2762 $4750   (15-May-91 SY.NY113/R) Portrait of young girl (76x63cm-30x25in) canvas
                     on board
£7101 $12000   (1-May-91 B.SF5075/R) Two women on beach (76x62cm-30x24in) s.
£8854 $17000   (29-Nov-90 SY.NY89/R) The boat steerer (152x122cm-60x48in)

HAWTHORNE, Marion C (1870-1945) American
£508 $1000   (18-Nov-91 JRB.C117/R) September morning, Venice (51x38cm-20x15in) s.
                     i.verso W/C gouache
£761 $1500   (18-Nov-91 JRB.C118/R) Cannareggio, Venice (41x36cm-16x14in) s. i.verso
                     W/C gouache

HAXTON, Elaine Alys (1909-) Australian
£724 $1224   (16-Apr-91 J.M224/R) Rhinosceros (29x37cm-11x15in) s.d.1950 board
                     (A.D 1600)
£1116 $2198   (31-Oct-90 CH.S61) Fishing, possibly near Palm Beach (29x40cm-11x16in)
                     s. (A.D 2800)
£1116 $2198   (31-Oct-90 CH.S85/R) Woman balancing urn (61x30cm-24x12in) s.d.61 board
                     (A.D 2800)
£1544 $3042   (13-Nov-90 J.M100/R) Flower girl (59x44cm-23x17in) s. board (A.D 4000)
£2791 $4688   (22-Apr-91 SY.ME328/R) Pittwater, 1958 (48x58cm-19x23in) s. board
                     (A.D 6000)

HAY, Bernard (1864-?) British
£520 $900   (21-May-91 GRO.B65/R) Capri street (23x13cm-9x5in) s. board
£694 $1200   (21-May-91 CE.NY75/R) View of Naples with Vesuvius in distance
                     (23x35cm-9x14in) s.d.1890 panel
£1224 $2400   (6-Nov-90 GF.L2412/R) Neapolitan beauty (65x43cm-26x17in) s. (S.FR 3000)
£1684 $2912   (6-May-91 ZEL.L1731/R) Coastal landscape with figures, Capri
                     (49x89cm-19x35in) s.i.d.1923 (DM 5000)

HAY, George (1831-1913) British
£734 $1300   (22-Mar-91 S.W2497/R) Wounded cavalier (76x91cm-30x36in) s.d.1866

HAY, James Hamilton (1874-1916) British
£1000 $1940   (4-Dec-90 RG2544) The Blonde Sky (64x76cm-25x30in) s.d.1909 i. verso

HAY, Peter Alexander (1866-1952) British
£1700 $3145   (4-Mar-91 PHB70) Portrait of lady holding umbrella (117x84cm-46x33in)
                     s.d.1896
£1293 $2250   (27-Mar-91 B.SF4253/R) Les papillons (50x42cm-20x17in) s.d.1922 W/C
£1900 $3724   (21-Nov-90 B35) Hundred years ago (58x48cm-23x19in) s.d.1919 W/C

HAY, Thomas Marjoribanks (1862-1921) British
£720 $1404   (15-Jan-91 SWS60/R) The storm (67x99cm-26x39in) s. W/C over pencil

HAY, William Hardie (20th C) British
£750 $1403   (28-Aug-90 S856/R) Strolling by the shore (41x61cm-16x24in) s.d.84

HAY, William M (19th C) British
£1850 $3090   (5-Jun-91 S147/R) On sand hills of Beerck-sur-Mer (63x94cm-25x37in)
                s.d.76 s.i.verso

HAYDEN, Edward Parker (?-1922) American
£1015 $2000   (16-Nov-90 S.BM142/R) Stream by forest's edge (56x79cm-22x31in) s.d.98

HAYDEN, Henri (1883-1970) French
£1295 $2201   (29-May-91 GL.P140/R) La bouteille rouge (51x65cm-20x26in) s.d.1967
                (F.FR 13000)
£1780 $3187   (14-Apr-91 GL.P195) Paysage du midi (38x52cm-15x20in) s. (F.FR 18000)
£2200 $4290   (17-Oct-90 S195/R) Gateaux fond rouge (51x65cm-20x26in) s.d.63
                i.stretcher
£2500 $4875   (17-Oct-90 S194/R) Paysage (33x46cm-13x18in) s. paper on canvas
£3066 $5489   (14-Apr-91 GL.P181/R) Portrait d'homme (47x38cm-19x15in) s. st.sig.
                verso (F.FR 31000)
£4500 $8775   (19-Oct-90 C166/R) Champs verts (32x47cm-13x19in) s.d.64 card
£5800 $11310   (17-Oct-90 S161/R) Avernes (65x81cm-26x32in) s.d.62
£7833 $14805   (30-Sep-90 E.LA159/R) Les champs s.d.69 (F.FR 77000)
£26408 $51496   (10-Oct-90 RAS.K169/R) Cubist still life (46x61cm-18x24in) s.
                d.1919verso (D.KR 300000)
£42304 $81223   (27-Nov-90 APT.P49/R) Nature morte a la palette (65x81cm-26x32in)
                s.d.1916 (F.FR 415000)
£925 $1794   (7-Dec-90 GL.P213) Bateaux a quai (31x48cm-12x19in) s.d.54 W/C Indian
                ink (F.FR 9000)
£1439 $2791   (7-Dec-90 GL.P95) Portrait de Picasso (28x22cm-11x9in) s.d.1916 lead
                pencil (F.FR 14000)
£5237 $8536   (16-Jun-91 GL.P61/R) Nature mrote au compotier (26x29cm-10x11in) s.
                gouache chl. (F.FR 52000)

HAYDON, Benjamin Robert (1786-1846) British
£19000 $34010   (10-Apr-91 S52/R) Xenophon and ten thousand (244x289cm-96x114in)

HAYE, Jeanne de la (fl.1653) ?
£950 $1824   (18-Dec-90 C70/R) Portrait of Principe Tommaso di Savoja Carignano
                (13x?cm-5x?in) min.s.d.1653 vellum gilt-metal mount rec.

HAYE, Reinier de la (1640-1684) Dutch
£900 $1467   (4-Jul-91 C687) Portrait of lady as Ceres, seated in landscape, basket
                of fruit on lap (18x14cm-7x6in) s.i.
£1557 $2600   (23-Jan-91 D.NY59) Portrait of gentleman (69x58cm-27x23in) s.i.
£2200 $3586   (5-Jul-91 C276/R) Portrait of lady, wearing red dress and green wrap,
                plucking rose (73x61cm-29x24in) s.

HAYEK, Hans von (1869-1940) Austrian
£608 $1052   (25-May-91 N.M125/R) View of Wilhelmina mountains, Sumatra
                (61x81cm-24x32in) s. (DM 1800)
£965 $1881   (18-Oct-90 D.V155/R) Kitzbuhel (65x85cm-26x33in) s. (A.S 20000)

HAYES, Edward (1797-1864) British
£600 $1176   (23-Nov-90 PHE68/R) Portrait of Mary, Anna, William and Arthur Stone
                (48x42cm-19x17in) s.i. W/C

HAYES, Edwin (1820-1904) British
£700 $1372   (15-Feb-91 N333) Lowestoft Harbour (15x25cm-6x10in) s. s.i.d.1877verso
£814 $1376   (16-Apr-91 J.M19) French fishing boats leaving Boulogne harbour
                (19x29cm-7x11in) indist.sig. board (A.D 1800)
£920 $1555   (1-May-91 PHL158/R) Sunset over fishing fleet (17x24cm-7x9in) s.
£1000 $1730   (22-May-91 S111/R) Harbour, Lowestoft, Norfolk (18x28cm-7x11in) s.i.
                board
£1041 $1759   (16-Apr-91 J.M833) Fishing boats (22x33cm-9x13in) s.d.1870 (A.D 2300)
£1600 $3120   (18-Oct-90 CSK74 c) Top's'l schooner on starboard reach with other
                shipping (20x34cm-8x13in) s. indist.d. board
£1600 $2720   (30-May-91 C135) Swansea Bay. Moored fishing boats in Dutch estuary
                (18x28cm-7x11in) s.d.70 s. board pair
£3200 $6272   (13-Feb-91 S6/R) Low tide (26x36cm-10x14in) s.d.74
£4800 $9360   (26-Oct-90 CG104/R) North Sea trawlers entering harbour, Great Yarmouth
                (43x76cm-17x30in) s. s.i.d.1888verso
£520 $900   (20-May-91 PH101) Shipping off coast (15x24cm-6x9in) s.d.1867 W/C
£520 $868   (22-Jul-91 SWS835 a/R) On the Medway (29x47cm-11x19in) s. W/C over
                pencil htd.gum arabic scratching out
£620 $1066   (14-May-91 SWS19/R) Early morning landing fish, Hastings (11x20cm-4x8in)
                s. i.verso W/C scratching out
£620 $1079   (27-Mar-91 PHS935) Sailing vessels approaching harbour (10x18cm-4x7in)
                s. W/C
£703 $1145   (10-Jun-91 W.T1243) Godstone, fishing smacks leaving harbour
                (21x32cm-8x13in) s. i. verso W/C (C.D 1300)
£1000 $1730   (21-May-91 CD52/R) Rough seascape with sailing vessel floundering, small
                boat going to help (15x25cm-6x10in) s. W/C

HAYES, Edwin (attrib) (1820-1904) British
£750 $1463   (17-Oct-90 PHG77) At the harbour mouth (24x34cm-9x13in)

HAYES, Edwin (circle) (1820-1904) British
£2200 $3586   (4-Jul-91 PH202) Figures in a rowing boat with sailing vessels beyond
                (33x46cm-13x18in)

HAYES, J W (19th C) British
£1050 $2058   (22-Jan-91 PH113/R) Distant thoughts (77x63cm-30x25in) s.indis.d.

HAYES, Janet (?) ?
£679 $1147   (16-Apr-91 J.M21) The gift (109x55cm-43x22in) s.d.'89 pastel (A.D 1500)
£724 $1224   (16-Apr-91 J.M272) Serenade (92x71cm-36x28in) s.d.'89 pastel (A.D 1600)

HAYES, John (1786-1866) British
£6500 $10920   (16-Jul-91 C82/R) He who pays the piper plays the tune (64x77cm-25x30in)
     s.

HAYET, Louis (1854-1940) French
£2888 $4910   (29-May-91 GL.P72/R) Bouquet de fleurs (34x24cm-13x9in) st.sig. board
     (F.FR 29000)
£3381 $6627   (11-Nov-90 ZZ.F86/R) Promeneurs dans la ville (18x12cm-7x5in) s. panel
     (F.FR 33000)
£5653 $10966   (5-Dec-90 ZZ.F154/R) Riviere a travers champs (46x61cm-18x24in) s.d.1903
     board laid down on canvas (F.FR 55000)
£5961 $11564   (5-Dec-90 ZZ.F159/R) Les Balmes, Grenoble (60x94cm-24x37in) st.d.1901
     (F.FR 58000)
£612 $1206   (14-Nov-90 CN.P39) Les hauts-de-forme (15x11cm-6x4in) s. chl.
     (F.FR 6000)
£1224 $2412   (14-Nov-90 CN.P57/R) L'Orchestre (15x19cm-6x7in) s. chl.htd.blue
     (F.FR 12000)

HAYEZ, Francesco (1791-1881) Italian
£24000 $40560   (16-Apr-91 PH12/R) Family of Marquis Giuseppe Sigismondo Ala, in Palazzo
     Ala-Ponzone, Cremona (86x123cm-34x48in) indist.s.
£25515 $43376   (30-May-91 F.M36/R) Ritratto di gentiluomo in veste da camera, possibly
     Manolo Nunez Falco (100x75cm-39x30in) (I.L 56000000)
£3656 $7203   (14-Nov-90 F.M46/R) Gli sponsali di Giulietta e Romeo procurati da Fra
     Lorenzo (218x285cm-86x112in) s. ink pen W/C over pencil (I.L 8000000)

HAYLLAR, James (1829-1920) British
£850 $1386   (14-Jun-91 C260) Houses at Aberdovey, N.Wales (19x28cm-7x11in) s.d.1896
     board
£4038 $6864   (28-May-91 AB.S4764/R) Enough and to spare (50x76cm-20x30in) s.
     (S.KR 43000)
£4000 $6520   (14-Jun-91 C99/R) The rose tree (36x25cm-14x10in) s.d.1870 pencil W/C
     htd.white
£6358 $11000   (22-May-91 SY.NY259/R) At theatre (29x50cm-11x20in) s.d.1866 W/C gouache

HAYLLAR, Jessica (1858-1940) British
£3800 $6194   (14-Jun-91 C261/R) Lady making posies from primroses (29x21cm-11x8in)
     s.d.1887 panel
£5000 $8150   (14-Jun-91 C262/R) An azalea in a Japanese bowl with other vases on a
     rug (28x22cm-11x9in) s.d.1887 panel
£11561 $20000   (22-May-91 SY.NY88/R) Teaching (55x45cm-22x18in) s.d.1895

HAYLS, John (attrib) (?-1679) British
£4800 $9600   (7-Feb-91 CSK153/R) Portrait of John, 2nd Baron Paulett of
     Hinton-St-George and wife (126x101cm-50x40in) pair

HAYMAN, Francis (1708-1776) British
£18462 $36000   (11-Oct-90 SY.NY54/R) Portraits of two boys said to be the sons of David
     Garrick (37x28cm-15x11in)
£20000 $35800   (12-Apr-91 C18/R) Portrait of John Barber, leaning on chair in interior.
     Portrait of Elizabeth Barber, seated on bank, (61x51cm-24x20in)
     i.verso pair

HAYMAN, Patrick (1915-) British
£500 $950   (28-Feb-91 DLY471/R) Francis and the birds (56x30cm-22x12in) s.i. board
£650 $1235   (28-Feb-91 DLY470/R) Three friends from over the sea isolated in
     eternity (18x43cm-7x17in) s.i. d.'74 verso board
£900 $1755   (10-Oct-90 S202/R) Ibsen and family (48x37cm-19x15in) s. s.i.d.1980verso
     board

HAYNES, G W (19th C) ?
£723 $1229   (28-May-91 AB.S4765/R) Coastal landscape with figures by beached boat
     (77x127cm-30x50in) s.d.1880 (S.KR 7700)

HAYNES, George (1938-) Australian
£633 $1071   (16-Apr-91 J.M1031) Studio III (42x59cm-17x23in) board (A.D 1400)

HAYNES, John William (fl.1852-1882) British
£550 $946   (14-May-91 SWS262) A quiet read (25x20cm-10x8in) s.
£650 $1268   (16-Jan-91 CSK155/R) Peeling apples (25x25cm-10x10in) s.d.1852
£800 $1512   (27-Sep-90 CSK127/R) Kindlings (36x25cm-14x10in) s. s.i.verso
£1293 $2288   (20-Mar-91 KM.K1245 a) Young girl eating meal (21x26cm-8x10in) s. paper
     (DM 3800)

HAYNES, John William (attrib) (fl.1852-1882) British
£800 $1568   (20-Nov-90 PH123) Tying the shoe (25x20cm-10x8in) board

HAYNES-WILLIAMS, John see WILLIAMS, John Haynes

HAYS, George Arthur (1854-?) American
£651	$1100	(20-Apr-91 WOL.C143/R) Florida Everglades (91x61cm-36x24in) s.
£1183	$2200	(9-Sep-90 LIT.L302) Cattle at watering place (64x76cm-25x30in) s. d.1928 verso
£2128	$4000	(11-Aug-90 COL.M214/R) Team of oxen (89x155cm-35x61in) s.

HAYTER (?) British
£1100	$2167	(15-Nov-90 WI1064/R) Deerfoot - portrait of Indian runner (61x48cm-24x19in)

HAYTER, Charles (?) British
£420	$806	(18-Dec-90 C114) Portrait of gentleman in blue coat and white waistcoat (5x?cm-2x?in) min. gold frame oval
£440	$739	(22-Apr-91 PH70/R) Portrait of mother and child, landscape background (7x?cm-3x?in) min.s.d.1812 card verso gilt metal frame rec.
£500	$985	(1-Nov-90 S17/R) Portrait of gentleman wearing blue coat and white waistcoat and cravat (5x?cm-2x?in) min. gilt-metal frame oval brooch attachment
£620	$1042	(22-Apr-91 PH71/R) Portrait of father and child (7x?cm-3x?in) min.s.d.1811 card verso gilt metal frame rec.

HAYTER, Sir George (1792-1871) British
£500	$885	(20-Mar-91 C31) Portrait of General George Henry Vansittart (13x?cm-5x?in) min.i.verso ormolu frame rec.

HAYTER, Stanley William (1901-1988) British
£5200	$8684	(7-Jun-91 C287/R) Survival of the vertebrates (24x63cm-9x25in) s.i.d.44 i.verso oil tempera board
£6680	$12960	(9-Dec-90 CC.P25/R) Composition (79x109cm-31x43in) s.d.1945 (F.FR 65000)
£10500	$20580	(6-Nov-90 PH150/R) Still life with self portrait (76x61cm-30x24in) s.
£14000	$27440	(6-Nov-90 PH149/R) The hotel (75x91cm-30x36in) s.d.39 board
£33266	$64869	(28-Oct-90 GL.P25/R) Danseurs de feu (116x81cm-46x32in) s.d.53 (F.FR 330000)
£969	$1910	(16-Nov-90 FB.P339/R) Composition (71x57cm-28x22in) s.i.d. ink W/C (F.FR 9500)
£1439	$2791	(9-Dec-90 CC.P94/R) Etudes (67x100cm-26x39in) s.d.14.6.55 col.crayons felt-pen (F.FR 14000)
£4032	$7863	(26-Oct-90 CC.P37/R) Flamme (81x100cm-32x39in) s.d.1969 i. verso acrylic crayon canvas (F.FR 40000)
£7194	$13957	(5-Dec-90 ZZ.F76/R) Composition (67x51cm-26x20in) s.d.6.4.53 gouache (F.FR 70000)

HAYTER, William (20th C) British?
£1807	$2910	(30-Jun-91 I.N150/R) Sans titre (66x49cm-26x19in) s.d.1959 mixed media (F.FR 18000)

HAYWARD, Alfred (19th C) British
£600	$1014	(30-Apr-91 ACA626) Venetian scene (58x51cm-23x20in) s.

HAYWARD, Alfred Frederick William (1856-1939) British
£750	$1440	(16-Aug-90 SC4165/R) Still life of fruits and flowers with bowls and platters on table (48x69cm-19x27in) s.

HAYWARD, Arthur (1889-?) British
£820	$1607	(8-Nov-90 DLY365) St. Ives harbour (13x23cm-5x9in) s. panel
£1550	$2589	(22-Jul-91 SWS1146/R) The Harbour, St. Ives (25x21cm-10x8in) s.d.'34 panel
£2600	$5096	(8-Nov-90 DLY164/R) St. Ives harbour (25x36cm-10x14in) s.d.30 panel
£3200	$6336	(29-Jan-91 PH21/R) Peon-Olver, St Ives (30x40cm-12x16in) s. board

HAYWARD, Joshua Henshaw (19th C) ?
£923	$1800	(20-Oct-90 W.W17/R) Portrait of Joseph P Taylor (66x53cm-26x21in)

HAZARD, Arthur Merton (1872-1930) American
£920	$1500	(11-Jun-91 MOR.P50) Landscape (76x102cm-30x40in) s.d.23

HAZEU, Arend Cornelis (1826-1888) Dutch
£853	$1613	(25-Sep-90 FN.S2200/R) Wooded lake landscape with woman collecting wood (81x64cm-32x25in) s. (DM 2500)

HAZLEHURST, Thomas (1740-1821) British
£300	$588	(22-Jan-91 CSK23/R) Portrait of gentleman (7x?cm-3x?in) min.init. gilt-metal frame, plaited hair oval
£580	$974	(22-Apr-91 PH68/R) Portrait of gentleman wearing black coat and white waistcoat (7x?cm-3x?in) min.inits. gilt metal frame oval
£780	$1287	(10-Jul-91 C116) A gentleman in black coat (6x?cm-2x?in) min.init. gold frame lock of hair verso oval
£800	$1320	(10-Jul-91 C92/R) Elizabeth Bridges (7x?cm-3x?in) min.init. maple wood frame oval
£2000	$3840	(18-Dec-90 C120/R) Portrait of Mary, Lady Feilden (8x?cm-3x?in) min.init.gold frame enamel border oval

HEADE, Martin Johnson (1819-1904) American
£7937	$15000	(27-Nov-90 CH.NY53/R) Flatlands and haystacks (23x55cm-9x22in) s. paper laid down on canvas on aluminium
£21907	$42500	(5-Dec-90 D.NY29/R) Wild roses in a glass vase (46x30cm-18x12in)

HEADE, Martin Johnson (1819-1904) American-cont.
£54913	$95000	(23-May-91 SY.NY23/R) Floral piece (51x41cm-20x16in) s. l.verso panel
£145833	$280000	(29-Nov-90 SY.NY12 b/R) Hummingbird and orchid, sun breaking through the clouds (51x38cm-20x15in) s.
£257732	$500000	(24-Aug-90 RB.HY200/R) 'Heliodore's Woodstar' with pink orchid (38x51cm-15x20in) s.

HEARD, Joseph (19th C) British
£2890	$5000	(23-May-91 CH.NY202/R) Passengers from the dismasted US Merchantman Troope being rescued (61x92cm-24x36in)

HEARMAN, Louise (20th C) Australian
£1215	$1980	(16-Jun-91 SY.ME22) Untitled, 1989 (279x279cm-110x110in) (A.D 2600)

HEARNE, Thomas (1744-1817) British
£450	$806	(9-Apr-91 C20/R) Gothic house set amongst trees (25x38cm-10x15in) pen ink wash
£5500	$9075	(11-Jul-91 S155/R) Well Cathedral, the east end, Somerset (18x25cm-7x10in) s. WC/ over pencil
£9000	$14850	(11-Jul-91 S38/R) Autumn, Palemon and Lavinia (267x31cm-105x12in) pen ink W/C oval
£30000	$49500	(11-Jul-91 S49/R) Derwentwater from Skiddaw, Cumberland (27x35cm-11x14in) s. W/C over pencil

HEATH, Adrian (1920-) British
£1500	$2445	(1-Jul-91 S29/R) Abstract (25x30cm-10x12in) s.d.'59 verso
£2200	$4268	(6-Dec-90 CSK233/R) Composition 1960 (54x75cm-21x30in) s. gouache W/C

HEATH, Frank Gascoigne (1873-1931) British
£1800	$3042	(1-May-91 GD.B382/R) Flower garden (36x25cm-14x10in) s.i.d.1916 (S.FR 4500)

HEATH, Margaret A (1886-1914) British
£600	$1128	(20-Sep-90 SC4138/R) Pool - backwater of Arun (76x53cm-30x21in) s. W/C

HEBERT, Adrien (1890-1967) Canadian
£749	$1460	(24-Oct-90 EA.M491/R) Perce, Mont Pic de Llouloire (51x38cm-20x15in) s. board (C.D 1700)
£833	$1475	(20-Mar-91 EA.M456) Quebec (38x64cm-15x25in) s. (C.D 1700)
£1004	$1969	(5-Nov-90 FB.M172) Paysage avec pont (61x81cm-24x32in) s. (C.D 2300)

HEBERT, Antoine Auguste Ernest (1817-1908) French
£1842	$3500	(27-Feb-91 SY.NY102/R) Water carriers (48x29cm-19x11in) init.
£3216	$5274	(19-Jun-91 LC.P54/R) Portrait de la Comtese de Ludre (146x96cm-57x38in) (F.FR 32000)
£35897	$70000	(23-Oct-90 SY.NY69/R) Les deux odalisques contemplant le bosphore (226x150cm-89x59in) s.d.1843

HECHT, Hendrick van der (1841-1901) Belgian
£1484	$2908	(21-Nov-90 GM.B1193) Etang aux Canards (100x126cm-39x50in) s. (B.FR 90000)
£4963	$9380	(25-Sep-90 GM.B1025/R) Vue de port (132x184cm-52x72in) s.d.74 (B.FR 300000)

HECK, Claes Dircksz van der (17th C) Dutch
£2778	$4556	(21-Jun-91 G.Z19/R) Village scene (65x83cm-26x33in) s.d.1634 (S.FR 7000)

HECK, van (20th C) ?
£1935	$3812	(30-Oct-90 I.N269/R) Vase de fleurs (116x89cm-46x35in) s. (F.FR 19000)

HECKE, Arthur van (20th C) ?
£692	$1239	(8-Apr-91 CSC.P105) Soleil blanc (54x65cm-21x26in) s. (F.FR 7000)
£768	$1506	(11-Nov-90 ZZ.F236/R) Portrait d'homme (73x54cm-29x21in) s. (F.FR 7500)
£841	$1505	(8-Apr-91 CSC.P106/R) Flandres (46x61cm-18x24in) s. (F.FR 8500)
£1127	$2209	(11-Nov-90 ZZ.F270/R) Paysage (61x50cm-24x20in) s. (F.FR 11000)

HECKE, Jan van den (elder-attrib) (1620-1684) Belgian
£1759	$3377	(19-Feb-91 ARC.P6) Navires Hollandais a l'ancre dans un port oriental (30x39cm-12x15in) s. panel (F.FR 17500)

HECKE, Willem van (1895-) Belgian
£609	$1201	(6-Oct-90 KV.L280) Structure (36x27cm-14x11in) s.d.1968 paper on panel (B.FR 38000)
£802	$1580	(6-Oct-90 KV.L281) Head of a child (13x11cm-5x4in) s.d.1953 paper double-sided (B.FR 50000)
£831	$1488	(16-Mar-91 KV.L295) Figure (30x22cm-12x9in) s.d.1968 paper (B.FR 50000)
£831	$1488	(16-Mar-91 KV.L294) Motherhood (27x19cm-11x7in) s.d.1966 paper (B.FR 50000)
£1067	$1846	(25-May-91 KV.L312/R) Figure (48x36cm-19x14in) s.d.1969 paper (B.FR 65000)
£822	$1602	(23-Oct-90 C.A974) Mother and child (19x25cm-7x10in) s.d.1966 mixed media (B.FR 50000)
£982	$1650	(23-Apr-91 C.A780) Figure (31x23cm-12x9in) s.d.1968 mixed media (B.FR 60000)

HECKEL, Erich (1883-1970) German

£204778	$401365	(23-Nov-90 VG.B18/R) Girl standing (83x40cm-33x16in) s.d.1913 s.i.d.verso (DM 600000)
£253968	$416508	(21-Jun-91 GK.B45/R) Portraits of Siddi Heckel, Walter Kaesbach and self portrait reading (94x81cm-37x32in) mono. s.verso (S.FR 640000)
£1182	*$2010*	*(31-May-91 GB.B6349) Fishing boats in Dieppe Harbour (16x23cm-6x9in) s.d.1959 W/C over pencil (DM 3500)*
£1284	*$2221*	*(21-May-91 WK.M973/R) Head of woman (16x10cm-6x4in) col.pencil (DM 3800)*
£2302	*$3775*	*(19-Jun-91 GK.B446) Portrait of Siddi Heckel (40x32cm-16x13in) s. W/C over pencil (S.FR 5800)*
£3413	*$6689*	*(24-Nov-90 KM.K553/R) Mountain landscape in winter (31x43cm-12x17in) s.i.d.61 W/C bodycol over pencil (DM 10000)*
£3912	*$6298*	*(28-Jun-91 BM.B906/R) Mountain peaks (63x48cm-25x19in) s.i.d.1961 W/C (DM 11500)*
£4054	*$6892*	*(1-Jun-91 VG.B245/R) Girl (43x31cm-17x12in) s.i.d.1948 W/C chk (DM 12000)*
£4437	*$8696*	*(24-Nov-90 N.M208/R) Mountain lake (48x63cm-19x25in) s.i.d.1962 W/C (DM 13000)*
£4500	*$7965*	*(19-Mar-91 C75/R) Berghange (50x69cm-20x27in) s.d.40 i.num.1421 verso W/C soft pencil*
£4915	*$8208*	*(6-Jun-91 HN.H390/R) By the Wattenmeer (54x70cm-21x28in) s.d.1950 W/C chk. (DM 14500)*
£5245	*$10175*	*(7-Dec-90 GB.B6636/R) Still life with precious stones and amethysts (57x42cm-22x17in) s.i.d.1960 W/C (DM 15000)*
£5743	*$9764*	*(1-Jun-91 VG.B246/R) Branches of pepper bushes (43x31cm-17x12in) s.d.1950 i.verso W/C over chk (DM 17000)*
£6294	*$12210*	*(7-Dec-90 GB.B6632/R) Bunch of marguerites (56x41cm-22x16in) s.i.d.1921 W/C bodycol over pencil (DM 18000)*
£6294	*$12210*	*(7-Dec-90 GB.B6634/R) Sand dunes, Sylt (43x67cm-17x26in) s.i.d.1935 W/C (DM 18000)*
£6734	*$11313*	*(26-Apr-91 KM.K301/R) Houses in mountainous landscape (48x63cm-19x25in) s.i.d.57 W/C pencil (DM 20000)*
£6757	*$11486*	*(1-Jun-91 VG.B154/R) Bathing female (54x65cm-21x26in) s.i.d.1920 W/C gouache pencil paper on board (DM 20000)*
£6826	*$13379*	*(24-Nov-90 VG.B192/R) Two women seated (53x69cm-21x27in) s.i.d.1935 chk wash gouache board (DM 20000)*
£7095	*$12061*	*(1-Jun-91 VG.B247/R) Forde bei Sudwind (48x67cm-19x26in) s.i.d.1938 W/C over pencil (DM 21000)*
£7143	*$11714*	*(19-Jun-91 GK.B448/R) View across dunes (48x61cm-19x24in) s.d.1922 W/C over carpenter's pencil (S.FR 18000)*
£7432	*$12635*	*(1-Jun-91 VG.B243/R) Larkspur (67x49cm-26x19in) s.i.d.1962 W/C over pencil (DM 22000)*
£7432	*$12635*	*(28-May-91 KF.M722/R) Karwendelwand (48x61cm-19x24in) s.i.d.1924 W/C pencil (DM 22000)*
£8191	*$16055*	*(24-Nov-90 VG.B183/R) Leinkraut (63x48cm-25x19in) s.i.d.1934 W/C pen dr. (DM 24000)*
£8191	*$16055*	*(24-Nov-90 VG.B184/R) Zinnia (60x46cm-24x18in) s.i.d.1933 W/C gouache over pen (DM 24000)*
£8219	*$13397*	*(15-Jun-91 L.K280/R) Still life of flowers (43x31cm-17x12in) s.i.d.1956 W/C chl (DM 24000)*
£8475	*$14153*	*(6-Jun-91 HN.H389/R) View of the shore (44x57cm-17x22in) s.d.1921 W/C over pencil (DM 25000)*
£9000	*$17550*	*(17-Oct-90 S155/R) Madchenkopf (50x33cm-20x13in) s.i.d.12 pencil*
£9524	*$15619*	*(19-Jun-91 GK.B447/R) Seaview (43x58cm-17x23in) s.i.d.1919 W/C over pencil (S.FR 24000)*
£10135	*$17230*	*(30-May-91 SY.BE51/R) Villach (55x69cm-22x27in) s.d.41 pencil W/C (DM 30000)*
£10490	*$20350*	*(7-Dec-90 GB.B6633/R) Russian woman (41x31cm-16x12in) s.i.d.1922 W/C (DM 30000)*
£10508	*$17549*	*(6-Jun-91 HN.H388/R) Nude on the beach (51x69cm-20x27in) s.d.1921 W/C over graphite (DM 31000)*
£11604	*$22744*	*(24-Nov-90 VG.B190/R) Bay with figures bathing (55x69cm-22x27in) s.i.d.1934 W/C gouache over chk (DM 34000)*
£12838	*$21824*	*(31-May-91 VG.B12/R) Young female artist (38x31cm-15x12in) s.i.d.1910 chl chk (DM 38000)*
£12969	*$25420*	*(24-Nov-90 VG.B193/R) Woman sleeping (48x62cm-19x24in) s.d.1931 W/C chk (DM 38000)*
£15017	*$29433*	*(24-Nov-90 VG.B185/R) Steep coastal landscape with nudes (47x64cm-19x25in) s.d.1921 W/C over pencil (DM 44000)*
£16047	*$27280*	*(31-May-91 GB.B6348/R) Variete. Man in sand ditch (36x28cm-14x11in) s.i.d.1909 W/C chk double-sided (DM 47500)*

HECKENDORF, Franz (1888-1962) German

£574	$976	(28-May-91 KF.M737) River landscape (27x35cm-11x14in) s.d.1917 tempera board (DM 1700)
£3716	$6318	(30-May-91 SY.BE63/R) Munich and the river Isar (50x65cm-20x26in) s.d.50 panel (DM 11000)
£4054	$6892	(30-May-91 SY.BE62/R) Landscape in Ticino, ronco supra Ascona (59x79cm-23x31in) s.d.58 (DM 12000)
£4500	$8640	(21-Feb-91 B66/R) Boats on Wahnsee (61x76cm-24x30in) s.d.29 panel
£4730	$8041	(30-May-91 SY.BE61/R) Winter landscape (60x81cm-24x32in) s.d.22 (DM 14000)
£4778	$9365	(22-Nov-90 L.K998/R) Southern lake landscape (80x99cm-31x39in) s.d.1922 (DM 14000)

HECKENDORF, Franz (1888-1962) German-cont.

£5405	$9189	(28-May-91 KF.M736/R) Still life of flowers (70x55cm-28x22in) s.d.1952 board (DM 16000)
£5802	$11372	(24-Nov-90 VG.B240/R) Lake landscape with village (40x50cm-16x20in) s. panel (DM 17000)
£5912	$10051	(1-Jun-91 VG.B241/R) Spanish landscape (98x79cm-39x31in) s.d.1925 s.l.d.verso panel (DM 17500)
£6143	$12041	(24-Nov-90 VG.B241/R) Romerbrucke in Mostar, Dalmatien (78x103cm-31x41in) s.d.1923 canvas laid down (DM 18000)
£6164	$10048	(15-Jun-91 L.K293/R) Still life with flowers and fruit (70x49cm-28x19in) s. panel (DM 18000)
£11149	$18953	(30-May-91 SY.BE49/R) Bunch of flowers (122x100cm-48x39in) s.d.20 (DM 33000)
£12587	$24420	(7-Dec-90 GB.B6647/R) Southern harbour (91x119cm-36x47in) s.d.1923 (DM 36000)
£505	*$848*	*(26-Apr-91 KM.K299) Alpine landscape, winter (40x48cm-16x19in) s.d.42 W/C bodycol over pencil (DM 1500)*
£1288	*$2151*	*(6-Jun-91 HN.H407/R) House in a park (66x47cm-26x19in) s. pastel (DM 3800)*
£1515	*$2545*	*(26-Apr-91 KM.K300/R) Beach scene (50x64cm-20x25in) s.d.51 gouache (DM 4500)*
£1520	*$2965*	*(26-Oct-90 BM.B969/R) Wannsee (29x39cm-11x15in) s.d.1925 W/C over pencil (DM 4500)*
£1745	*$3403*	*(12-Oct-90 AW.H2521/R) Storm in harbour (48x64cm-19x25in) s.l.d.1919 gouache (DM 5200)*
£4082	*$6571*	*(28-Jun-91 BM.B907/R) Southern coastal landscape with village in bay and shipping (67x91cm-26x36in) s. (DM 12000)*

HECKER, Franz (1870-1944) German

£1791	$3492	(26-Oct-90 KM.K1259/R) Pipe smokers at table (32x44cm-13x17in) s.d.1909 (DM 5300)

HEDA, Gerrit Willemsz (c.1620-1702) Dutch

£24000	$45600	(1-Mar-91 C132/R) Silver and pewter vessels with shell fish and utensils on draped table (81x101cm-32x40in)

HEDA, Willem Claesz (1594-1680) Dutch

£684211	$1300000	(10-Jan-91 SY.NY66/R) Still life with plate oysters, tazza, roemer, peeled lemon on pewter plate and other objects on drap (59x79cm-23x31in) s.d.1635 panel

HEDA, Willem Claesz (style) (1594-1680) Dutch

£12500	$21125	(17-Apr-91 S77/R) Still life of bread, cherries, lemon and roemer on draped table (54x47cm-21x19in) panel

HEDAEUS, John (1872-1967) Swedish

£732	*$1427*	*(17-Oct-90 GO.G2080) Shopping in market (21x31cm-8x12in) s. pencil W/C (S.KR 8000)*

HEDBERG, Kalle (1894-1959) Swedish

£1015	$1948	(27-Nov-90 BU.S130/R) Northern landscape (47x56cm-19x22in) s. panel (S.KR 11000)
£1205	$2337	(5-Dec-90 AB.S7094/R) Northern landscape with houses and drying-hurdles (47x60cm-19x24in) s.d.1943verso panel (S.KR 13000)
£1698	$2938	(22-May-91 BA.S85/R) The newborn (61x75cm-24x30in) s. panel (S.KR 18000)
£2317	$4495	(4-Dec-90 BA.S198/R) Mountainous landscape (84x121cm-33x48in) s. (S.KR 25000)
£3396	$5875	(22-May-91 BA.S84/R) Barbro (122x73cm-48x29in) s.d.36 panel (S.KR 36000)
£10936	$21216	(4-Dec-90 BA.S197/R) The violin player (122x91cm-48x36in) s. panel (S.KR 118000)

HEDLEY, Ralph (1851-1913) British

£1150	$2231	(4-Dec-90 AG376/R) Northumbrian Epic (40x32cm-16x13in) i.verso board
£1450	$2451	(30-Apr-91 AG310/R) Cornmarket (36x49cm-14x19in) s.d.1911
£1500	$2415	(24-Jun-91 HS176) Interior with elderly bearded man lighting pipe, dog at side, glass on table (59x43cm-23x17in) s.d.88
£1500	$2535	(30-Apr-91 AG309/R) Scottish prisoners in Tower of St. Nicholas' (163x130cm-64x51in) s.
£2000	$3700	(5-Mar-91 AG310/R) Returning home - a Durham pit lad (75x49cm-30x19in) s.d.1894
£2500	$4800	(17-Aug-90 T100/R) Miner and son at start of a day (51x30cm-20x12in) s.
£2800	$5432	(4-Dec-90 AG377/R) Early morning, going to the pit (49x29cm-19x11in) s.
£3500	$5705	(14-Jun-91 C265/R) The News-Boy (76x51cm-30x20in) s.d.78
£460	*$851*	*(5-Mar-91 AG87/R) Summer flowers in yard of cottage (23x19cm-9x7in) init. W/C*
£4400	*$8536*	*(4-Dec-90 AG250/R) The poor student (52x38cm-20x15in) s.d.1887 W/C*

HEDLUND, Alfred (1884-1930) Swedish

£597	$1171	(6-Nov-90 BA.S94/R) Willows by Stockholm river (38x46cm-15x18in) s.d.1920 (S.KR 6500)

HEDQVIST, Tage (1909-) Swedish

£741	$1438	(4-Dec-90 BA.S199 a/R) arild harbour (55x65cm-22x26in) s. l.d.1944verso (S.KR 8000)

HEEM, Cornelis de (1631-1695) Dutch

£32000	$52160	(5-Jul-91 C288/R) Mixed fruit on pewter plate, roemer, mixed fruit and hazelnut on stone ledge (14x24cm-6x9in) with indist.sig copper
£44000	$74360	(16-Apr-91 PH49/R) Still life of mixed fruit by pewter dish, glass of wine surrounded by fruit, all on draped stone led (38x55cm-15x22in) with sig.
£160000	$308800	(11-Dec-90 PH89/R) Still life of roemer, oysters, lobsters, grapes and pepper pot on ledge (36x44cm-14x17in) s. copper
£271357	$445025	(21-Jun-91 SY.MO136/R) Composition aux fleurs, fruits et crustaces (64x53cm-25x21in) s. (F.FR 2700000)

HEEM, Cornelis de (style) (1631-1695) Dutch

£1800	$2934	(4-Jul-91 CSK172) Mixed flowers in glass vase on ledge (76x63cm-30x25in) panel
£2500	$4875	(26-Oct-90 PHM57/R) Still life of fruit and a pewter plate (48x38cm-19x15in)
£2508	$4940	(14-Nov-90 SY.AM125/R) Still life of fish and fruit on plate (30x37cm-12x15in) (D.FL 8200)
£6500	$10595	(3-Jul-91 S188/R) Still life of fruit, oysters, roemer, wine glass and smoking materials, on ledge (37x48cm-15x19in)

HEEM, Jan Davidsz de (1606-1684) Dutch

£55000	$89650	(5-Jul-91 C37/R) Overturned roemer, lemon, oysters and bread on pewter plates and bowl on table (37x63cm-15x25in) s.d.1629 panel
£142105	$270000	(10-Jan-91 SY.NY29/R) Still life of mixed flowers in glass vase, on ledge with various insects (70x48cm-28x19in)
£176471	$300000	(31-May-91 CH.NY88/R) Fruit, shell fish, silver vessels and insects on ledge (55x66cm-22x26in) s.
£180000	$293400	(3-Jul-91 S74/R) Still life of mixed fruit on pewter dish, glass vessels, vine leaves, all on partly draped ledge (50x46cm-20x18in) s. panel
£184995	$358890	(5-Dec-90 APT.P39/R) Guirlandde de roses, tulipes et autres fleurs (44x54cm-17x21in) s. panel (F.FR 1800000)

HEEM, Jan Davidsz de (after) (1606-1684) Dutch

£1861	$3666	(14-Nov-90 D.V143/R) Still life of flowers in glass vase (59x45cm-23x18in) (A.S 38000)

HEEM, Jan Davidsz de (style) (1606-1684) Dutch

£1800	$3420	(13-Sep-90 CSK7/R) Mixed flowers in glass vase on ledge (57x51cm-22x20in)

HEEMSKERCK, Jacoba B van (1876-1923) Dutch

£3096	*$5975*	*(13-Dec-90 SY.AM29/R) Untitled (46x61cm-18x24in) mono. W/C (D.FL 10000)*

HEEMSKERK (attrib) (17/18th C) Dutch

£2637	$5221	(30-Jan-91 APT.P208/R) Interieur de cuisine (32x37cm-13x15in) (F.FR 26000)

HEEMSKERK, Egbert van (17/18th C) Dutch

£612	$1205	(14-Nov-90 SY.AM55/R) Two monks in discussion (13x10cm-5x4in) init. copper oval (D.FL 2000)
£1368	$2448	(14-Mar-91 D.V257/R) Peasants playing cards in pub interior (31x26cm-12x10in) (A.S 28000)
£2800	$4732	(17-Apr-91 S55/R) Boors carousing in tavern (26x20cm-10x8in) s. panel
£3400	$5542	(2-Jul-91 PH251/R) Boers playing cards and smoking in interior (94x121cm-37x48in)
£3670	$7046	(29-Nov-90 ZZ.F2/R) Scene d'Auberge (23x34cm-9x13in) (F.FR 36000)
£6000	$9780	(5-Jul-91 C303/R) Boors drinking and merrymaking in interiors (35x41cm-14x16in)
£7000	$11410	(5-Jul-91 C305/R) Boors drinking and playing cards (22x32cm-9x13in) panel pair
£500	*$815*	*(2-Jul-91 C355/R) Peasant dancing to violin outside tavern (28x42cm-11x17in) brush ink*

HEEMSKERK, Egbert van (attrib) (17/18th C) Dutch

£1437	$2500	(27-Mar-91 B.SF4016/R) The congregation (76x63cm-30x25in)
£3077	$6000	(10-Oct-90 CH.NY158/R) The Temptation of St Anthony (23x34cm-9x13in) mono. panel

HEEMSKERK, Egbert van (elder) (1610-1680) Dutch

£1150	$1944	(16-Apr-91 PH86) Three boers and young woman at table (35x27cm-14x11in) mono.
£2400	$4056	(18-Apr-91 C64/R) Boors merrymaking in an interior (26x22cm-10x9in) with sig. panel
£7000	$13650	(26-Oct-90 C141/R) Peasants carousing in an Inn (36x33cm-14x13in) mono. panel

HEEMSKERK, Egbert van (elder-style) (1610-1680) Dutch

£1000	$1920	(29-Nov-90 CSK141) Man reading letter and another holding tankard (24x21cm-9x8in) panel

HEEMSKERK, Egbert van (younger) (1634-1704) Dutch

£1892	$3217	(31-May-91 LD.P33/R) Scene de taverne - les deux chanteurs (19x25cm-7x10in) i. panel (F.FR 19000)

HEEMSKERK, Egbert van (younger-style) (1634-1704) Dutch
£6500 $12350   (13-Sep-90 CSK72/R) Apothecary shop (71x119cm-28x47in)

HEEMSKERK, Marten Jacobsz van Veen (circle) (1498-1574) Dutch
£1200 $2364   (30-Oct-90 PH4/R) Portrait of lady wearing wimple (38x29cm-15x11in)
                 panel

HEEMSKERK, Marten van (style) (17th C) Dutch
£6500 $12545   (12-Dec-90 S147/R) Baptism of Ethiopian eunuch (69x112cm-27x44in)

HEERE, Lucas de (1534-1584) Flemish
£9231 $18000   (11-Oct-90 SY.NY32/R) Allegory with Apollo and other Olympian gods
                 (119x147cm-47x58in)

HEEREBAART, Georgius (1829-1915) Dutch
£2844 $4778   (23-Apr-91 SY.AM131) Winter landscape with skaters. Summer landscape
                 with figures by church (17x23cm-7x9in) s. panel pair (D.FL 9500)

HEEREMANS, Thomas (fl.1660-1697) Dutch
£1000 $1850   (5-Mar-91 PH145) Beach scene with figures amongst the dunes and loading
                 boats on shore (29x36cm-11x14in) panel
£3000 $4890   (4-Jul-91 C572/R) Wooded river landscape with boatmen unloading baskets
                 by cottage (42x34cm-17x13in) s.indist.d. panel
£4200 $8274   (31-Oct-90 S195/R) Village on the Dort (58x81cm-23x32in)
£4469 $8000   (11-Apr-91 SY.NY115/R) Boating on estuary lined with houses
                 (58x84cm-23x33in) panel
£7179 $14000   (11-Oct-90 SY.NY26/R) Party of villagers boarding ferries on river bank
                 (65x52cm-26x20in) s.
£7500 $12225   (2-Jul-91 PH31/R) Figures in small boats moored to bank of river outside
                 inn (38x54cm-15x21in) s. panel
£12243 $24119   (14-Nov-90 D.V125/R) River landscape with boats and village with figures
                 outside inn (43x56cm-17x22in) s.d. 1682 (A.S 250000)
£15888 $26533   (6-Jun-91 D.V49/R) View of Amsterdam and Montalbaanturm with Yssel Sea
                 and skaters (25x33cm-10x13in) s. panel (A.S 330000)
£16566 $26672   (25-Jun-91 APT.P23/R) Patineurs pres d'un village (34x47cm-13x19in)
                 bears sig.d.1670 panel (F.FR 165000)

HEEREMANS, Thomas (circle) (fl.1660-1697) Dutch
£1200 $2340   (25-Oct-90 B34/R) Group of drunken villagers crossing river and others
                 dancing on bank (28x34cm-11x13in)
£2800 $5600   (7-Feb-91 C183/R) A village with peasants merrymaking by a river
                 (58x77cm-23x30in) panel

HEEREMANS, Thomas (style) (fl.1660-1679) Dutch
£2235 $3800   (30-May-91 CE.NY33) River landscape (21x27cm-8x11in) bears sig.d. panel

HEERFORDT, Anna Cathrine Christine (1839-1910) Danish
£1433 $2822   (17-Nov-90 BU.H225/R) Still life of flowers (54x43cm-21x17in) s.d.92
                 (F.M 10000)

HEERSCHOP, Hendrik (1620-1672) Flemish
£1500 $2535   (18-Apr-91 C127/R) A young man studing at a table by a window
                 (52x43cm-20x17in) s.d.1667

HEERSCHOP, Hendrik (attrib) (1620-1672) Flemish
£917 $1807   (13-Nov-90 CH.AM124) Christ on Road to Calvary (54x44cm-21x17in) panel
                 (D.FL 3000)

HEERUP, Henry (1907-) Danish
£614 $1044   (29-May-91 KH.K1) Composition (26x34cm-10x13in) s. carton (D.KR 7000)
£660 $1287   (10-Oct-90 RAS.K46) Horses (59x55cm-23x22in) s. (D.KR 7500)
£748 $1287   (15-May-91 RAS.K11) Bull (25x33cm-10x13in) s.d.56 (D.KR 8500)
£880 $1717   (10-Oct-90 RAS.K43) Mask (33x39cm-13x15in) s.d.70 (D.KR 10000)
£1068 $2007   (19-Sep-90 KH.K96) Lady with red cape (62x43cm-24x17in) s.d.1923
                 (D.KR 12000)
£1087 $2098   (12-Dec-90 RAS.K119) Tulip (34x36cm-13x14in) s.d.66 (D.KR 12000)
£1087 $2098   (12-Dec-90 RAS.K27) Palette picture (45x54cm-18x21in) s.verso
                 (D.KR 12000)
£1257 $2476   (14-Nov-90 KH.K59/R) Lovers (35x47cm-14x19in) s. (D.KR 14000)
£1607 $2973   (5-Mar-91 RAS.K87/R) Children tobogganing (51x69cm-20x27in) s.
                 (D.KR 18000)
£1761 $3028   (15-May-91 RAS.K10/R) Eye (38x34cm-15x13in) s.d.50 (D.KR 20000)
£1786 $3304   (5-Mar-91 RAS.K4/R) Seed (36x56cm-14x22in) s.d.63verso (D.KR 20000)
£1789 $3506   (13-Feb-91 KH.K69/R) Girls bathing, Bellevue 1957 (28x41cm-11x16in)
                 s.d.57 (D.KR 20000)
£2154 $4244   (14-Nov-90 KH.K58/R) Composition with dustman and blue coffee-jug
                 (80x11cm-31x4in) s. (D.KR 24000)
£2368 $4026   (29-May-91 KH.K90/R) The girl and the children (40x61cm-16x24in) s.
                 masonite (D.KR 27000)
£2402 $4156   (23-May-91 SY.AM241/R) The anchor and the egg (41x58cm-16x23in) s.
                 s.d.1964verso board (D.FL 8000)
£2411 $4460   (5-Mar-91 RAS.K82/R) Symbols of wisdom (40x45cm-16x18in) s.d.66
                 (D.KR 27000)
£2465 $4806   (10-Oct-90 RAS.K42/R) Harlequin (57x42cm-22x17in) s.d.65 (D.KR 28000)
£2857 $5286   (5-Mar-91 RAS.K8/R) Chicken (36x68cm-14x27in) s.d.69 (D.KR 32000)
£3070 $5219   (29-May-91 KH.K24/R) Woman bathing (48x55cm-19x22in) panel (D.KR 35000)

862

HEERUP, Henry (1907-) Danish-cont.

£3114	$5854	(19-Sep-90 KH.K12/R) The bicycle man (34x57cm-13x22in) s.d.80 panel (D.KR 35000)
£3170	$6119	(12-Dec-90 RAS.K32/R) Horn of plenty (51x78cm-20x31in) s.d.60 (D.KR 35000)
£3604	$6234	(23-May-91 SY.AM256 k/R) Gravesmakinen (55x93cm-22x37in) s.d.51 (D.FL 12000)
£3623	$6993	(12-Dec-90 RAS.K87/R) Bathing girl - nude from behind (99x60cm-39x24in) s.d.1951 oil on carpet (D.KR 40000)
£3947	$6711	(29-May-91 KH.K72/R) The medicine man (78x99cm-31x39in) s.d.1976 plywood (D.KR 45000)
£4076	$7867	(12-Dec-90 RAS.K114/R) Christmas picture (80x110cm-31x43in) s. (D.KR 45000)
£4225	$8239	(10-Oct-90 RAS.K100/R) Snail on road (80x100cm-31x39in) s.d.46 (D.KR 48000)
£4386	$7456	(29-May-91 KH.K8/R) United Nations (59x61cm-23x24in) s.d.45 (D.KR 50000)
£4505	$7793	(23-May-91 SY.AM244/R) The harvest workers (46x124cm-18x49in) s.d.56 board (D.FL 15000)
£4529	$8741	(12-Dec-90 RAS.K28/R) The mouth (70x80cm-28x31in) s.d.54 (D.KR 50000)
£4805	$8312	(23-May-91 SY.AM245/R) L'arbre genealogique (61x121cm-24x48in) s.d.64 board (D.FL 16000)
£5206	$10257	(14-Nov-90 KH.K57/R) Lovers (76x86cm-30x34in) s.d.48, composition by E.Ortvad verso (D.KR 58000)
£5405	$9351	(23-May-91 SY.AM325/R) Self portrait (77x101cm-30x40in) s.d.62 board (D.FL 18000)
£5516	$10370	(19-Sep-90 KH.K51/R) The Virgin and the Bull (84x84cm-33x33in) s.d.58 panel (D.KR 62000)
£7018	$11930	(29-May-91 KH.K43/R) Horse harvesting (80x100cm-31x39in) s.d.56 (D.KR 80000)
£7042	$13732	(10-Oct-90 RAS.K45/R) Policeman, gnome and nude woman (100x121cm-39x48in) s.d.1953 (D.KR 80000)
£8079	$15916	(14-Nov-90 KH.K56/R) Lovers, Acropolis (67x97cm-26x38in) s.d.54 (D.KR 90000)
£11566	$21744	(19-Sep-90 KH.K42/R) The joker and the lovers (66x182cm-26x72in) s.d.53 (D.KR 130000)
£526	*$895*	*(29-May-91 KH.K26) The artist and his muse (41x50cm-16x20in) s.d.1958 crayon pencil (D.KR 6000)*
£623	*$1171*	*(19-Sep-90 KH.K95) Birth of death (31x43cm-12x17in) s. crayon (D.KR 7000)*

HEES, Gerrit van (18th C) Flemish

| £4781 | $8223 | (14-May-91 GF.L2285/R) Haarlem landscape with gothic church (79x90cm-31x35in) panel (S.FR 12000) |

HEFFNER, Karl (1849-1925) German

£800	$1432	(12-Mar-91 PH21) Fishing boats at low tide (13x23cm-5x9in) s. canvas on panel
£1200	$2352	(14-Feb-91 CSK60) A coastal village on a hillside (79x97cm-31x38in) s.
£1350	$2282	(3-May-91 PHE129/R) Home from the fields (12x28cm-5x11in) s. board
£1473	$2400	(12-Jun-91 N.M454/R) Dutch dyke landscape (70x95cm-28x37in) s. (DM 4300)
£1706	$3225	(25-Sep-90 FN.S2201/R) Wooded river landscape with farmhouses and cattle watering (27x33cm-11x13in) s. l.verso board (DM 5000)
£1800	$3096	(14-May-91 SWS290/R) Collecting ice (24x34cm-9x13in) s.l.
£2000	$3920	(14-Feb-91 CSK61) An extensive lakeland landscape at dusk (89x135cm-35x53in) s.
£2055	$3678	(13-Mar-91 N.M524/R) Dutch harbour town with sailing boats (70x95cm-28x37in) s. (DM 6000)
£2455	$4714	(27-Nov-90 W.T1134/R) River scene with Bavarian house and buildings (36x50cm-14x20in) s. (C.D 5500)
£5461	$10703	(24-Nov-90 SA.A676/R) Moor landscape with figures getting peat (48x81cm-19x32in) s.l. (DM 16000)

HEFFNER, Karl (attrib) (1849-1925) German

| £856 | $1396 | (12-Jun-91 N.M455) Ships by river banks at sunset (25x41cm-10x16in) s.l. (DM 2500) |

HEGENBARTH, Emanuel (1868-?) German

| £1092 | $2064 | (25-Sep-90 FN.S2203/R) Dead game on draped table with flowers (72x93cm-28x37in) s. canvas on panel (DM 3200) |
| £1365 | $2676 | (24-Nov-90 N.M220/R) Cattle and peasant woman returning (70x98cm-28x39in) s. (DM 4000) |

HEGENBARTH, Josef (1884-1962) German

£473	*$804*	*(1-Jun-91 VG.B578/R) Portrait of gentleman in profile (33x30cm-13x12in) s. indian ink pen (DM 1400)*
£507	*$861*	*(1-Jun-91 VG.B577/R) Giraffes. Study of two goats (35x25cm-14x10in) s. indian ink pen brush double-sided (DM 1500)*
£508	*$849*	*(6-Jun-91 HN.H411) Dogs (24x30cm-9x12in) s. ink brush (DM 1500)*
£608	*$1034*	*(28-May-91 KF.M742) Elbe landscape. Study of mountainous landscape (50x36cm-20x14in) s.i. mixed media board double-sided (DM 1800)*
£608	*$1034*	*(28-May-91 KF.M739) Nimmersatt, Storch (49x32cm-19x13in) s.indis.d.1921 mixed media board on board (DM 1800)*
£685	*$1116*	*(15-Jun-91 L.K297/R) Poultry (31x44cm-12x17in) s. l.verso W/C boydocl double-sided (DM 2000)*

HEGENBARTH, Josef (1884-1962) German-cont.
£743	$1264	(1-Jun-91 VG.B582/R) On the beach (33x46cm-13x18in) s. indian ink pen brush (DM 2200)
£887	$1739	(22-Nov-90 L.K1004) Circus scenes (48x36cm-19x14in) s.d.1955 s.d.59verso double-sided (DM 2600)
£922	$1806	(22-Nov-90 L.K1003/R) Clown in arena (38x47cm-15x19in) s. i.d.1955verso indian ink brush (DM 2700)
£946	$1608	(28-May-91 KF.M741) Woman holding head. Conversation (36x51cm-14x20in) s. s.i.d.1925 mixed media board double-sided (DM 2800)
£946	$1608	(28-May-91 KF.M740/R) Pines (47x37cm-19x15in) s. mixed media board (DM 2800)
£1014	$1723	(1-Jun-91 VG.B581/R) Howling dog. Bathers on beach (38x50cm-15x20in) s.d.1958 indian ink pen brush double-sided (DM 3000)
£1027	$1675	(15-Jun-91 L.K296/R) Ice skating artists (36x48cm-14x19in) s.d.56 gouache brush (DM 3000)
£1233	$2010	(15-Jun-91 L.K295) Till Eulenspiegel's execution (31x39cm-12x15in) s. i.verso gouache (DM 3600)
£1706	$3345	(24-Nov-90 VG.B224/R) Im Parkett (39x33cm-15x13in) s. brush indian ink W/C board (DM 5000)
£2365	$4091	(25-May-91 N.M132/R) Three wolves in compound (37x50cm-15x20in) s. gouache (DM 7000)

HEIBERG, Jean (1884-1976) Norwegian
£803	$1558	(4-Dec-90 UL.T225) Landscape from Engeloya in Steigen (50x60cm-20x24in) (N.KR 9000)
£1226	$2194	(11-Mar-91 B.O44/R) Coastal landscape (50x61cm-20x24in) s.d.1959 (N.KR 14000)
£1336	$2578	(12-Dec-90 BU.O27/R) Coastal landscape (60x73cm-24x29in) s.d.1944 panel (N.KR 15000)
£1401	$2508	(14-Mar-91 BU.O44/R) Coastal landscape (45x54cm-18x21in) s. panel (N.KR 16000)
£2671	$5156	(12-Dec-90 BU.O26/R) Head of young girl (41x33cm-16x13in) s. (N.KR 30000)

HEICKE, Joseph (1811-1861) Austrian
£977	$1856	(28-Feb-91 D.V52/R) Shepherdess with goats in mountainous lake landscape (55x74cm-22x29in) s. metal (A.S 20000)

HEICKELL, Arthur (1873-1958) Finnish
£863	$1666	(15-Dec-90 BU.H65) Beach landscape (30x40cm-12x16in) s. (F.M 6000)
£1061	$1782	(27-Apr-91 SO.S358/R) Interior with open fireplace (43x63cm-17x25in) s. (S.KR 11200)
£1079	$1856	(14-May-91 HOR.H44) Pines on beach (40x50cm-16x20in) s. (F.M 7500)
£1151	$1980	(14-May-91 HOR.H45) Summer's day (40x50cm-16x20in) s. (F.M 8000)
£1151	$2222	(15-Dec-90 BU.H63) View of sea (35x50cm-14x20in) s. (F.M 8000)
£1151	$2222	(15-Dec-90 BU.H64) Woman by wooded glade (35x50cm-14x20in) s. (F.M 8000)
£1151	$1980	(14-May-91 HOR.H42) Spring (47x65cm-19x26in) s. (F.M 8000)
£1220	$2061	(20-Apr-91 HOR.H96/R) Autumn landscape, Esboviken (90x71cm-35x28in) s. (F.M 8500)
£1223	$2360	(15-Dec-90 BU.H62) Well (40x50cm-16x20in) s. (F.M 8500)
£1295	$2499	(15-Dec-90 BU.H61) Green beach scene (40x50cm-16x20in) s. (F.M 9000)
£1295	$2227	(14-May-91 HOR.H41) Autumn (59x80cm-23x31in) s. (F.M 9000)
£1367	$2351	(14-May-91 HOR.H43) Apple tree in bloom (40x50cm-16x20in) s. (F.M 9500)
£1435	$2425	(20-Apr-91 HOR.H97/R) Still bay (44x66cm-17x26in) s. (F.M 10000)
£1453	$2805	(15-Dec-90 BU.H60) Lake landscape (50x60cm-20x24in) s. (F.M 10100)
£1583	$3055	(15-Dec-90 BU.H59) Sunset in Bergen (50x60cm-20x24in) s. (F.M 11000)

HEIDECK, Carl Wilhelm von (1788-1861) German
£2841	$5569	(25-Jan-91 REM.W3) Rest (39x50cm-15x20in) s. panel (P.Z 53000000)

HEIDELOFF, Josef von (elder) (1743-1830) Austrian
£3582	$6017	(25-Apr-91 D.V135/R) Landscape near Heiligenkreuz (31x44cm-12x17in) mono.d.1795 W/C (A.S 75000)

HEIGEL, Franz Napoleon (1813-1888) German
£3000	$4830	(25-Jun-91 ACA743/R) Tyrolean family in group in national costume (51x41cm-20x16in) s. W/C

HEIL, Daniel van (1604-1662) Flemish
£1835	$3615	(14-Nov-90 SY.AM117) View of harbour (2x32cm-1x13in) s.init. panel (D.FL 6000)
£2020	$3960	(11-Feb-91 CSC.P24/R) Incendie nocturne (77x64cm-30x25in) (F.FR 20000)

HEIL, Daniel van (school) (1604-1662) Flemish
£1734	$3000	(8-May-91 RO.BA6/R) San Jeronimo en su gruta (71x90cm-28x35in)
£1734	$3000	(8-May-91 RO.BA5/R) Incendie de Sodome (73x96cm-29x38in)

HEIL, Daniel van (style) (1604-1662) Flemish
£900	$1557	(20-May-91 SWS137) A town on fire at night (59x76cm-23x30in) panel

HEILBUTH, Ferdinand (1826-1889) French
£1818	$3564	(22-Nov-90 SY.MI9) Omaggio al cardinale (52x90cm-20x35in) s. (I.L 4000000)
£5917	$10000	(1-May-91 D.NY50) Peaceful moment (122x79cm-48x31in) init.
£34211	$65000	(28-Feb-91 CH.NY9/R) On the Marne (91x117cm-36x46in) s. panel

HEILBUTH, Ferdinand (1826-1889) French-cont.
£1190 $2000   (17-Jul-91 SY.NY229/R) Portrait of Robert Browning (23x17cm-9x7in)
     s.d.1855 chl.white chk.pastel paper laid paper

HEILIGER, Bernhard (1915-) ?
£1638 $3211   (24-Nov-90 VG.B554/R) Drawing (100x70cm-39x28in) s.d.1957 st.studio
     i.d.verso board (DM 4800)
£2560 $5017   (24-Nov-90 VG.B555/R) Untitled (99x128cm-39x50in) s.d.1967 graphite
     htd.white wash board (DM 7500)

HEILMANN, Anton Paul (1830-1912) Austrian
£635 $1207   (28-Feb-91 D.V85/R) Park landscape in Heiligenstadt with female figure
     walking, spring (25x36cm-10x14in) s.d.897 W/C (A.S 13000)

HEILMANN, Gerhard (1859-1946) Danish
£878 $1669   (14-Sep-90 SA.A1159/R) Baltic coastal landscape with peasant ploughing
     (77x122cm-30x48in) mono. (DM 2600)

HEILMAYER, Karl (1829-1908) German
£1356 $2264   (5-Jun-91 DO.H2296/R) Moonlit Upper Bavarian village scene with
     nightwatchman by fountain (27x43cm-11x17in) s. panel (DM 4000)
£1678 $3004   (12-Mar-91 FN.S2412/R) Moonlit village view of Garmisch with
     night-watchman (55x75cm-22x30in) s. (DM 4900)
£2506 $4260   (28-May-91 F.R131/R) Sera al Pincio (61x81cm-24x32in) s.i.d.1895
     (I.L 5500000)

HEIM, Francois Joseph (1787-1865) French
£1224 $2412   (14-Nov-90 FB.P135/R) L'astronomie (18x14cm-7x6in) s. canvas pasted on
     board (F.FR 12000)
£9684 $18593   (30-Nov-90 APT.P134/R) Presentation de l'enfant Jesus au Temple
     (30x60cm-12x24in) paper on board (F.FR 95000)

HEIMBACH, Christian Wolfgang (1613-1678) German
£17000 $27710   (3-Jul-91 S197/R) Portrait of man wearing gold chain (21x16cm-8x6in)
     s.d.1642 bears i. copper painted oval
£63158 $120000   (10-Jan-91 SY.NY47/R) Interior of hall at night with people feasting
     (85x160cm-33x63in) s.i.d.1655

HEIMBACH, Christian Wolfgang (attrib) (1613-1678) German
£16000 $27040   (19-Apr-91 C47/R) Marriage portrait of a couple in a wooded landscape
     (53x69cm-21x27in) panel

HEIMBURG, E von (19th C) German
£767 $1372   (12-Apr-91 BM.B610/R) Southern landscape with rider taking farewell
     before farmhouse (43x51cm-17x20in) s. panel (DM 2300)

HEIMER, C (19th C) German
£581 $1000   (18-May-91 W.W23/R) Stormy seas (69x104cm-27x41in) s.d.1892 canvas
     mounted on board

HEIMERDINGER, Friedrich (1817-1882) Italian/German
£1520 $2965   (26-Oct-90 BM.B794/R) Circus people with horse dompteuse holding letter
     (56x69cm-22x27in) s.d.1870 (DM 4500)

HEIMERL, Josef (19/20th C) Austrian
£839 $1636   (10-Oct-90 WE.MU337) Friends (26x21cm-10x8in) s. (DM 2500)

HEIMIG, Walter (1881-?) German
£1375 $2612   (2-Mar-91 KRA.D501/R) Ball room interior (50x50cm-20x20in) s. panel
     (DM 4000)
£2703 $5270   (26-Oct-90 BM.B795/R) Portrait of young woman seated in interior
     (65x65cm-26x26in) s.d.1913 (DM 8000)

HEIN, A von (19th C) ?
£516 $892   (22-May-91 GS.B2393) Venus and entourage on cart drawn by seahorses
     (19x28cm-7x11in) s. gouache (S.FR 1300)

HEIN, Alois Raimond (1852-1936) Austrian
£1212 $2097   (6-May-91 ZEL.L1734/R) Still life with sculpted figures and lotos
     flowers in vase (30x24cm-12x9in) s. panel (DM 3600)

HEIN, Christianus Hendricus (1815-?) Dutch
£788 $1552   (30-Oct-90 CH.AM9) Travellers and sportsman on sandy path, Barchem
     (50x72cm-20x28in) s. (D.FL 2600)
£2159 $3714   (16-May-91 D.V83/R) View of church in landscape (50x72cm-20x28in) s.
     (A.S 45000)

HEIN, E (1875-?) Danish
£1573 $3052   (4-Dec-90 FN.S1862/R) Rhine landscape with view of Siebengebirge and
     Drachenfels (80x95cm-31x37in) s. (DM 4500)

HEIN, Eduard (?) German
£748 $1205   (26-Jun-91 KM.K1497) Alpine lake landscape (67x96cm-26x38in) s.
     (DM 2200)

HEIN, H (19th C) German
£822 $1471   (13-Mar-91 N.M525/R) Mill in mountain lake landscape (66x95cm-26x37in)
                 s. (DM 2400)

HEIN, Hendrik Jan (1822-1866) Dutch
£4545 $8955   (30-Oct-90 CH.AM185/R) Birds. fruit and flowers on stone ledge
                 (34x27cm-13x11in) s. panel (D.FL 15000)
£6138 $10311   (23-Apr-91 SY.AM291/R) Still life with flowers, fruit and dead game on
                 marble ledge (62x66cm-24x26in) s.d.1852 panel (D.FL 20500)

HEINE, A (19/20th C) German
£2226 $3985   (13-Mar-91 N.M526/R) Two boys playing with dog in peasant interior
                 (32x25cm-13x10in) s. board (DM 6500)

HEINE, Johann Adalbert (19th C) German
£2797 $5399   (12-Dec-90 N.M546/R) Tea break in peasant interior. Hunter and peasant
                 woman by stove (21x27cm-8x11in) s. panel pair (DM 8000)
£3000 $5910   (5-Oct-90 C103/R) Merry company (22x27cm-9x11in) s.i. panel

HEINE, Thomas Theodor (1867-?) German
£5405 $9351   (25-May-91 N.M134/R) Village street of Brunn with lovers
                 (46x32cm-18x13in) mono.d.1936 board (DM 16000)
£552   *$1059*   *(28-Nov-90 KF.M850) World champion Tunney in New York (30x26cm-12x10in)*
                 mono.i. gouache indian ink brush (DM 1600)
£1310   *$2516*   *(26-Nov-90 WK.M254) Editors in hell (36x32cm-14x13in) mono. W/C indian*
                 ink over pencil board (DM 3800)

HEINEMANN, Joseph (1825-1901) German
£606 $1048   (6-May-91 ZEL.L1735/R) Portrait of blonde boy holding flowers
                 (22x18cm-9x7in) s.d.1851 (DM 1800)

HEINISCH, Karl Adam (1847-1923) German
£2397 $3908   (12-Jun-91 N.M457/R) Shepherd couple with sheep and geese before
                 farmstead (50x71cm-20x28in) s. (DM 7000)
£4600 $9016   (15-Feb-91 C44/R) Winter landscape with shepherdess and sheep by
                 cottages (15x27cm-6x11in) s.indist.i. panel

HEINONEN, Mauri (1926-) Finnish
£642 $1258   (24-Nov-90 HOR.H113/R) Flowers in vase (53x40cm-21x16in) s.d.1979
                 (F.M 4500)

HEINRICH-HANSEN, Adolf (1859-1925) Danish
£1408 $2366   (23-Apr-91 RAS.K398/R) Poly players (53x53cm-21x21in) s. (D.KR 16000)
£1761 $2958   (23-Apr-91 RAS.K185/R) Livingroom of printer Plantin's house in Antwerp
                 (45x65cm-18x26in) s.i. (D.KR 20000)
£2000 $3440   (17-May-91 C201/R) Choir of Duomo, Siena (54x63cm-21x25in) init.d.91
£2641 $4437   (22-Apr-91 BU.K16/R) Manor house interior (60x80cm-24x31in) (D.KR 30000)
£3500 $5740   (19-Jun-91 S282/R) View of marble church from Amalien Borg Palace,
                 Copenhagen (50x68cm-20x27in) init.

HEINSIUS, Johann Ernst (1740-1812) German
£696 $1176   (18-Apr-91 APT.P57) Portrait d'une femme en robe blanche
                 (73x60cm-29x24in) s.d.1812 (F.FR 7000)

HEINSIUS, Johann Ernst (attrib) (1740-1812) German
£1529 $2936   (30-Nov-90 APT.P118/R) Portrait de jeune femme vue en buste
                 (55x45cm-22x18in) oval (F.FR 15000)

HEINTZ, Joseph (16/17th C) Swiss
£13052 $21014   (27-Jun-91 APT.P92/R) Diane et Acteon (155x223cm-61x88in) (F.FR 130000)

HEINTZ, Joseph (circle) (16/17th C) Swiss
£1800 $2934   (2-Jul-91 PH231/R) Ecce Homo (109x150cm-43x59in)

HEINTZ, Joseph (elder-circle) (1564-1609) Swiss
£1900 $3097   (4-Jul-91 C549) Rest on Flight into Egypt (22x17cm-9x7in) inset copper

HEINTZ, Joseph (style) (16/17th C) Swiss
£895 $1512   (18-Apr-91 APT.P52/R) Psyche et l'Amour (14x12cm-6x5in) panel oval
                 (F.FR 9000)
£6500 $12675   (25-Oct-90 CSK75/R) Woman's bath-house (56x78cm-22x31in) panel

HEINTZ, Joseph (younger) (1600-1678) Swiss
£6754 $13170   (23-Oct-90 CH.R490/R) Perseo libera Andromeda (124x91cm-49x36in)
                 (I.L 15000000)
£36484 $60928   (4-Jun-91 CH.R574/R) Fiera del toro (124x170cm-49x67in) (I.L 80000000)

HEINZMANN, Carl Friedrich (1795-1846) German
£3061 $6000   (6-Nov-90 GF.L2143/R) Alpine landscape with cows and traveller
                 (25x31cm-10x12in) s.d.1826 panel (S.FR 7500)
£6849 $11164   (12-Jun-91 N.M458/R) Schliersee landscape (71x83cm-28x33in) mono.d.1817
                 (DM 20000)

HEISIG, Bernhard (1925-) Polish
£10490 $20350   (4-Dec-90 FN.S1618/R) Lenin and the doubting Thomas (59x79cm-23x31in) s.
                 (DM 30000)

HEISIG, Bernhard (1925-) Polish-cont.
£1276 $2450   *(28-Nov-90 KF.M857/R) On the run (23x17cm-9x7in) s.d.1984/85 indian ink pen htd.white (DM 3700)*

HEISKA, Joonas (1873-1937) Finnish
£1367 $2638   (15-Dec-90 BU.H68) Twilight (29x22cm-11x9in) s.d.1920 panel (F.M 9500)

HEISS, Johann (1640-1704) German
£4359 $8500   (10-Oct-90 CH.NY202/R) The Death of Dido (83x116cm-33x46in)
£11765 $20000   (31-May-91 CH.NY172/R) The continence of Scipio (77x87cm-30x34in)

HEITINGER, P (19/20th C) German
£699 $1350   (12-Dec-90 N.M547/R) Zell am See (40x60cm-16x24in) s. i.stretcher (DM 2000)

HEITINGER, Paul (19/20th C) German
£856 $1533   (13-Mar-91 N.M528/R) Shore of lake with sailing boat, possibly lake Constance (35x49cm-14x19in) s. canvas on panel (DM 2500)

HEITINGER, V (20th C) German
£671 $1309   (10-Oct-90 WE.MU130/R) Boat yard at Lake Constance (31x51cm-12x20in) s. i.verso (DM 2000)

HEITMULLER, Louis (1863-?) American
£714 $1400   (16-Feb-91 W.W56/R) Boys fishing (43x64cm-17x25in) s.d.96

HEIZER, Michael (20th C) German
£765 $1500   (12-Feb-91 SY.NY415/R) Untitled black and gold (282x183cm-111x72in) oil aluminum powder canvas
£638 $1250   (12-Feb-91 SY.NY313/R) Untitled models for paintings (28x43cm-11x17in) init. pencil ink ballpoint pair
£1276 $2500   (12-Feb-91 SY.NY361/R) Untitled no 4, stone grey (183x213cm-72x84in) polyvinyl latex canvas
£3827 $7500   (15-Feb-91 SY.NY183/R) Untitled blue (244x244cm-96x96in) polyvinyl latex canvas

HEKKING, J Antonio (fl.1859-1865) American
£659 $1100   (5-Jun-91 D.NY45) The lawn behind the conservatory (30x51cm-12x20in) s.
£677 $1300   (17-Dec-90 SY.NY68/R) Landscape with cows by stream (64x102cm-25x40in) s.

HEKKING, Willem (1796-1862) Dutch
£1538 $3000   (26-Oct-90 SY.NY57/R) Study of striped pink. Study of carnation buds (99x8cm-39x3in) W/C pair

HELBERGER, Alfred Hermann (1871-1946) German
£946 $1608   (31-May-91 GB.B6366) Flowering garden before house (47x58cm-19x23in) s.d.1916 (DM 2800)

HELD, Al (1928-) American
£10651 $18000   (2-May-91 CH.NY133/R) Untitled (61x45cm-24x18in) s.d.61 acrylic paper on composition board
£2284 $4500   (4-Oct-90 SY.NY128/R) Untitled (57x89cm-22x35in) indian ink

HELD, John (jnr) (1889-1958) American
£588 $1000   (1-Jun-91 IH.NY117/R) Now-a-days in the spring a young man's fancy turns to cough drops (25x56cm-10x22in) pen ink
£706 $1200   (1-Jun-91 IH.NY116/R) Just to remind you, I like books (23x28cm-9x11in) s. pen ink

HELDNER, Knute (1886-1952) American
£532 $1000   (19-Sep-90 B.SF2829/R) In the French quarter (22x27cm-9x11in) s.
£729 $1400   (28-Nov-90 D.NY54) Landscape with birch trees (74x86cm-29x34in) s.d.1923
£791 $1400   (23-Mar-91 LAE.L45/R) Landscape (43x43cm-17x17in) s.
£1406 $2700   (17-Dec-90 SY.NY186/R) Napoleon House in New Orleans (56x61cm-22x24in) s.

HELDT, Werner (20th C) German?
£3716 $6429   (21-May-91 WK.M47 a/R) Berlin am Meer (36x49cm-14x19in) mono.d.1949 W/C paper on board (DM 11000)

HELFFERICH, Frans (1871-1941) Dutch
£1056 $1775   (23-Apr-91 RAS.K403/R) Summer's day on the beach (60x100cm-24x39in) s. panel (D.KR 12000)

HELION, Jean (1904-?) French
£1743 $2963   (29-May-91 GL.P217) Le Brabant (46x33cm-18x13in) s.i.d.2-6 sept 57 board (F.FR 17500)
£5737 $10269   (9-Apr-91 BG.P107 q/R) Le Luxembourg (100x72cm-39x28in) s.i.d.65-66 verso (F.FR 58000)
£6572 $12816   (15-Oct-90 CSC.P90/R) SDuite Metropolitaine (55x32cm-22x13in) mono.d.69 i. verso (F.FR 65000)
£11089 $21623   (23-Oct-90 CSC.P43/R) Le chemin de Kervic (72x91cm-28x36in) mono.d.60 i. verso (F.FR 110000)
£14414 $24359   (21-Apr-91 P.V51/R) .... in de Paris (130x95cm-51x37in) mono.d.Mars-Avril 1967 i. verso (F.FR 145000)

HELION, Jean (1904-?) French-cont.
£20231 $35000   (9-May-91 CH.NY250/R) Composition abstraite (38x28cm-15x11in) s.d.14 Dec 38-2 Avril 39 verso masonite
£86705 $150000   (8-May-91 CH.NY52/R) Composition (162x118cm-64x46in) s.d.1936 verso
£552 $889   *(25-Jun-91 BG.P30) Etude pour une figure tombee (23x30cm-9x12in) s.d.38 ink crayon (F.FR 5500)*
£798 $1316   *(10-Jul-91 FB.P87/R) L'accident du 6 Novembre 1981 (22x15cm-9x6in) s.d.23/IX/81 crayon ink pastel (F.FR 8000)*
£1147 $1892   *(10-Jul-91 FB.P52/R) Personnage assis (45x33cm-18x13in) d.18/10/47 ink wash (F.FR 11500)*
£1407 $2519   *(11-Mar-91 GL.P104/R) Vitrine Newyorkaise (24x34cm-9x13in) s.d.1945 W/C Indian ink (F.FR 14000)*
£1411 $2752   *(23-Oct-90 CSC.P116/R) Nature morte au chapeau (31x22cm-12x9in) s.i.d.67 pastel (F.FR 14000)*
£1542 $2991   *(9-Dec-90 CC.P90/R) L'accident (108x74cm-43x29in) s.d.1981 chl.pastel W/C double-sided (F.FR 15000)*
£1984 $3749   *(30-Sep-90 E.LA119) Couple cycliste no 2 (44x32cm-17x13in) s.d.83 W/C (F.FR 19500)*
£2872 $5600   *(10-Oct-90 SY.NY187/R) Untitled composition (69x23cm-27x9in) s.i.d.38 ink W/C*
£2956 $5705   *(10-Dec-90 LD.P15/R) Scene de rue (24x34cm-9x13in) s.d.6X70 col.crayons (F.FR 29000)*
£3800 $6118   *(24-Jun-91 CSK214/R) Composition (29x24cm-11x9in) s.d.36 W/C pencil pen ink*
£5179 $8805   *(30-May-91 FB.P28/R) Seins pales (29x21cm-11x8in) s.d.48 ink (F.FR 52000)*
£5584 $11000   *(2-Oct-90 CH.NY126/R) Composition abstraite (38x28cm-15x11in) s.d.36 W/C paper laid down on board*
£5897 $11500   *(10-Oct-90 SY.NY188/R) Figure study (38x28cm-15x11in) s.d.38 W/C ink*
£6572 $12816   *(15-Oct-90 CSC.P91/R) Suite puciere no.6, machinale, vertueuse, pluvieuse, osseuse etmilitaire (75x110cm-30x43in) mono.d.77 pastel (F.FR 65000)*

HELL, Johan van (1889-1952) Dutch
£6006 $10390   (22-May-91 CH.AM495/R) Acrobats giving performance on terrace (90x68cm-35x27in) s.d.1935 (D.FL 20000)

HELLBUSCH, Hermann (1879-?) German
£680 $1204   (20-Mar-91 KM.K1254) View of Cologne (63x87cm-25x34in) s. (DM 2000)

HELLER, Andor (?) Scandinavian?
£850 $1675   (4-Oct-90 CSK113/R) Black boots (60x50cm-24x20in) s.d.1933

HELLESEN, Hanne (?-1844) Danish
£1500 $2580   (17-May-91 C78/R) Bouquet of mixed flowers and ears of barley (24x19cm-9x7in) panel
£5282 $8873   (23-Apr-91 RAS.K88) Garland of flowers (D.KR 60000)
£6007 $9851   (18-Jun-91 FN.S1888/R) Still life of fruit and flowers on draped table (51x42cm-20x17in) s.d.1835 (DM 17600)

HELLEU, Jean (1894-) French
£500 $815   (5-Jul-91 APT.P131) La Seine a Bougival (50x73cm-20x29in) s. (F.FR 5000)
£559 $1118   (6-Feb-91 FB.P179) Marine (33x56cm-13x22in) s. (F.FR 5500)

HELLEU, Paul-Cesar (1859-1927) French
£1531 $3000   (12-Feb-91 SY.NY10/R) Two women (38x51cm-15x20in) s. pencil col.pencil
£1845 $3100   (28-Apr-91 HG.C47) Ellen (43x33cm-17x13in) s. chk htd.white
£2200 $3784   (17-May-91 C22/R) Madame Helleu (37x24cm-15x9in) s. col.chk
£2711 $4364   (24-Jun-91 ARC.P8/R) Femme a la harpe (40x28cm-16x11in) s. col.crayons (F.FR 27000)
£2834 $5555   (23-Nov-90 PLF.P79) Jeune femme a la robe de bal (50x28cm-20x11in) s. sanguinne htd.white chk. (F.FR 28000)
£3590 $7000   (23-Oct-90 SY.NY328/R) Trois etudes pour une tete de femme (40x52cm-16x20in) s. pencil chk
£5000 $9600   (30-Nov-90 C23/R) The Duchess of Marlborough seated in a chair (49x36cm-19x14in) s.i. col.chk.
£7500 $12900   (17-May-91 C21/R) Portrait of lady, seated (62x38cm-24x15in) s. col.chk
£15000 $28800   (28-Nov-90 S295/R) Studies of girls' heads (32x49cm-13x19in) s. pencil red chk
£16000 $30720   (30-Nov-90 C25/R) Madame Helleu reading (46x63cm-18x25in) s. col.chk.
£19500 $37440   (30-Nov-90 C24/R) Madame Helleu reading, with Paulette lying beside her on a sofa (30x53cm-12x21in) s. col.chk.
£38000 $62320   (21-Jun-91 C26/R) Portrait of Peggy Gillespie, holding parasol (80x65cm-31x26in) s.i. pastel canvas
£63895 $122677   (17-Dec-90 AGS.P33/R) Jeune femme a l'Hortensia (74x99cm-29x39in) s. pastel (F.FR 630000)

HELLMAN, Ake (1915-) Finnish
£2029 $3489   (14-May-91 HOR.H50) Artist and model (46x64cm-18x25in) s.d.1963-70 (F.M 14100)
£2140 $4194   (24-Nov-90 HOR.H114/R) On the table (48x34cm-19x13in) s. (F.M 15000)
£2436 $4798   (17-Nov-90 BU.H151/R) Still life of shelves (62x46cm-24x18in) s.d.72 (F.M 17000)

HELLMEIER, Otto (1908-) German
| £610 | $995 | (3-Jul-91 WE.MU106/R) Gandria, Lake Lugano (60x80cm-24x31in) s. (DM 1800) |

£678 . $1105   (3-Jul-91 WE.MU118/R) Still life with sunflowers (60x70cm-24x28in) s. s.i.verso (DM 2000)
£1017 $1658   (3-Jul-91 WE.MU107/R) Sebastiansplatz (60x79cm-24x31in) s. (DM 3000)
£1153 $1879   (3-Jul-91 WE.MU117/R) Viktualienmarkt (60x70cm-24x28in) s. s.i.verso (DM 3400)

HELLQVIST, Carl Gustav (1851-1890) Swedish
£5607 $10989   (6-Nov-90 BA.S95/R) Girl in field of wild flowers (47x56cm-19x22in) s.i.d.1884 (S.KR 61000)

HELLWAG, Rudolf (1867-1942) German
£667 $1193   (12-Apr-91 AW.H1614/R) Nightly harbour (41x53cm-16x21in) s. (DM 2000)

HELMAN, Robert (1910-) French
£594 $1051   (5-Apr-91 LGB.P167) Composition (60x73cm-24x29in) s. (F.FR 6000)
£2055 $3988   (9-Dec-90 CC.P80/R) Foret (92x73cm-36x29in) s. (F.FR 20000)
£17347 $34173   (16-Nov-90 FB.P28/R) Composition (100x81cm-39x32in) s. d.1966 verso (F.FR 170000)
£356 $711   (6-Feb-91 FB.P180) Composition (59x73cm-23x29in) s.d.63 W/C (F.FR 3500)

HELMBERGER, Adolf (1885-?) Austrian
£878 $1625   (7-Mar-91 D.V48/R) Stream in landscape (24x31cm-9x12in) s.d.1918 canvas on board (A.S 18000)

HELMBREKER, Theodor (1633-1696) Flemish
£3000 $5790   (11-Dec-90 PH264/R) Peasants making merry before castle ruins. Peasants within town (60x74cm-24x29in) pair

HELME, Helge (?) Scandinavian
£718 $1415   (14-Nov-90 RAS.K292) Girl seated on bed (28x23cm-11x9in) s. (D.KR 8000)
£990 $1862   (10-Aug-90 RAS.V589/R) Young girl playing patience (73x60cm-29x24in) s. (D.KR 11200)
£1063 $1796   (2-May-91 RAS.V177/R) Portrait of Royal dancer Kirsten Ralov at dressingtable (78x63cm-31x25in) s.d.42 (D.KR 12000)
£1077 $2122   (14-Nov-90 RAS.K291) Portrait of a ballet dancer wearing tu-tu (61x50cm-24x20in) s.d.27 (D.KR 12000)
£1322 $2471   (29-Aug-90 KH.K77) Ballet dancer tying her shoes (56x45cm-22x18in) s. (D.KR 15000)
£1384 $2685   (22-Aug-90 RAS.K231/R) Young ballet dancer tying black ribbon round her neck (33x25cm-13x10in) s. (D.KR 16000)

HELMINEN, Martta (1890-1983) Finnish
£719 $1388   (15-Dec-90 BU.H69) Shadows in landscape (46x34cm-18x13in) s. panel (F.M 5000)

HELMONT, Lucas van Gassel (circle) (c.1480-c.1570) Flemish
£1500 $2880   (29-Nov-90 CSK204/R) The Garden of Gethsemane (25x29cm-10x11in) panel fragment
£5500 $9295   (16-Apr-91 PH88/R) Saint Jerome in wilderness (56x45cm-22x18in) canvas transferred from panel

HELMONT, Lucas van Gassel (style) (c.1480-c.1570) Flemish
£2600 $4992   (29-Nov-90 CSK207/R) Ecce Homo with scene of Passion beyond (29x34cm-11x13in) panel

HELMONT, Matheus van (1623-1679) Flemish
£2767 $4704   (27-May-91 GK.Z5044/R) Peasant interior (42x56cm-17x22in) mono. (S.FR 7000)

HELNWEIN, Gottfried (1948-) Austrian
£389 $763   (24-Jan-91 D.V280/R) The boy who followed Tom Ripley (31x31cm-12x12in) s. pen indian ink (A.S 8000)
£779 $1526   (24-Jan-91 D.V279/R) Der Froschhupfer (42x32cm-17x13in) s.d.79 pen indian ink (A.S 16000)

HELST, Bartholomeus van der (1613-1670) Dutch
£1588 $3017   (14-Sep-90 SA.A1113/R) Portrait of Dutch woman (40x30cm-16x12in) s. canvas on panel (DM 4700)
£2844 $5603   (13-Nov-90 AB.S902/R) Portrait of gentleman (72x57cm-28x22in) s.d.1655 panel (S.KR 31000)
£3041 $5139   (3-May-91 SA.A1627/R) Portrait of a nun (56x70cm-22x28in) (DM 9000)

HELST, Bartholomeus van der (after) (1613-1670) Dutch
£1835 $3615   (13-Nov-90 AB.S903/R) Portrait of man holding helmet (89x72cm-35x28in) (S.KR 20000)

HELST, Bartholomeus van der (circle) (1613-1670) Dutch
£2385 $4699   (14-Nov-90 SY.AM29/R) Portrait of man aged 35 (103x80cm-41x31in) i.d.1643 (D.FL 7800)
£4190 $7500   (11-Apr-91 SY.NY176/R) Portrait of gentleman said to be Cornelis Wilten, Burgomaster of Amsterdam (84x64cm-33x25in) panel

HELSTED, Vigo (1861-1926) Danish
£927 $1817   (24-Nov-90 HOR.H11/R) Rough seascape (40x58cm-16x23in) s.d.1891 (F.M 6500)

HELT-STOCADE, Nicolaes (1614-1669) Flemish
£2000 $3260   (2-Jul-91 PH123/R) Bacchanal scene in ornamental garden with satyr filling Bacchus' cup (73x59cm-29x23in) indis.s.

HEM, Piet van der (1885-1961) Dutch
£719 $1250   (26-Mar-91 VN.R32/R) Man with a cello (100x75cm-39x30in) s. (D.FL 2400)
£1138 $1980   (26-Mar-91 VN.R31/R) A cossak with a sleeping drunken man at his feet (120x90cm-47x35in) s. (D.FL 3800)

HEMBERG, Elly (1896-?) Swedish
£741 $1438   (4-Dec-90 BA.S200/R) Waves (73x60cm-29x24in) init.d.59 panel (S.KR 8000)

HEMERET (20th C) ?
£3571 $7036   (14-Nov-90 CN.P116/R) La Serre aux fleurs rouges (73x92cm-29x36in) s. i. verso (F.FR 35000)

HEMERET, Claude (20th C) ?
£3429 $5796   (21-Apr-91 E.LA31/R) Village provencal (60x73cm-24x29in) s. (F.FR 34500)

HEMESSEN, Jan van (1504-1566) Flemish
£2006 $3912   (10-Oct-90 APT.P492) La Deposition du Christ (74x57cm-29x22in) panel (F.FR 20000)

HEMESSEN, Jan van (circle) (1504-1566) Flemish
£3000 $5790   (11-Dec-90 PH194/R) Christ and the woman taken in adultery (113x135cm-44x53in) panel after Lorenzo Lotto
£3908 $6996   (14-Mar-91 D.V117/R) St Hieronymus in interior (64x52cm-25x20in) panel (A.S 80000)

HEMESSEN, Jan van (style) (1504-1566) Flemish
£2000 $3840   (29-Nov-90 CSK280/R) Boy, possibly Ismael, reclining in landscape (22x33cm-9x13in) panel

HEMKEN, Willem de Haas (attrib) (1831-1911) Dutch
£659 $1107   (23-Apr-91 SY.AM55) Figures in Dutch town (30x23cm-12x9in) panel (D.FL 2200)

HEMMRICH, Georg (?) German?
£533 $955   (12-Apr-91 AW.H1616/R) Horse market near village (24x33cm-9x13in) s. board (DM 1600)
£1154 $2227   (12-Dec-90 WE.MU165/R) Rest at the mail station (13x17cm-5x7in) s. board (DM 3300)
£1224 $2362   (12-Dec-90 N.M549/R) Peasants harvesting potatoes (14x18cm-6x7in) s. panel (DM 3500)

HEMPFING, Wilhelm (1886-1951) German
£600 $1074   (12-Apr-91 BM.B737) Ballet dancer arranging hair before mirror (58x44cm-23x17in) s.d.1919 (DM 1800)
£685 $1226   (12-Mar-91 FN.S2416) Girl stepping into boat (67x55cm-26x22in) s. i.verso (DM 2000)
£769 $1485   (12-Dec-90 N.M550) Young woman wearing striped blouse (72x55cm-28x22in) s. st.sig.stretcher (DM 2200)
£839 $1636   (10-Oct-90 ZEL.L1529/R) Lake Constance landscape with figures (50x40cm-20x16in) s.d.1919 (DM 2500)
£1003 $1696   (19-Apr-91 FN.S1734/R) Nude woman in interior holding magnolia blossoms (104x95cm-41x37in) s.d.1947 (DM 3000)
£2203 $4251   (12-Dec-90 WE.MU93/R) Lake landscape with figures in rowing boats (55x46cm-22x18in) s. (DM 6300)

HEMSLEY, William (1819-?) British
£769 $1492   (4-Dec-90 FN.S1864/R) English coastal landscape with children and basket of fishes (20x17cm-8x7in) s. board on panel (DM 2200)
£1050 $2037   (3-Dec-90 WSW124/R) Teasing - two children and cockerel (20x15cm-8x6in) s. panel
£1100 $2090   (27-Feb-91 MMB283/R) Children playing cards (15x20cm-6x8in) s. panel
£1600 $3120   (18-Oct-90 SC3155/R) The ball of string (21x16cm-8x6in) s. board
£2100 $4074   (3-Dec-90 WSW125/R) Baby's breakfast - cottage interior (30x38cm-12x15in) s.
£2800 $4676   (5-Jun-91 S134/R) First attempt (54x43cm-21x17in) s. s.i.verso
£620 $1011   (11-Jun-91 LW1877) Grandma's sketch study of boy seated on barrel holding blackboard (23x18cm-9x7in) s. W/C

HEMSLEY, William (attrib) (1819-?) British
£1244 $2414   (4-Dec-90 R.T260/R) Majestic drive (43x58cm-17x23in) bears sig.d. i.stretcher (C.D 2800)

HEMY, Bernard Benedict (19th C) British
£740 $1443   (17-Oct-90 PHL212) Return of the fishing fleet to North Shields (51x76cm-20x30in)
£760 $1284   (30-Apr-91 AG200/R) Sail and steam coaster leaving Tyne (36x51cm-14x20in) s.d.1889 W/C

HEMY, Bernard Benedict (19th C) British-cont.
£800 $1384   (22-May-91 S130/R) Fishing harbours on North-East coast (49x72cm-19x28in) s. W/C htd bodycol pair

HEMY, Charles Napier (1841-1917) British
£4200 $8064   (27-Nov-90 OT550/R) A rocky shore (50x75cm-20x30in) s.d.1878 I. verso
£300 $537   (14-Mar-91 L276) Gentle swell off rocky foreshore (41x58cm-16x23in) s. W/C
£650 $1248   (19-Feb-91 SWS364) Rough weather (46x68cm-18x27in) init.d.1916 W/C htd.white
£800 $1432   (14-Mar-91 L129) Rough weather (46x69cm-18x27in) init.d.1916 W/C htd white
£800 $1344   (15-Jul-91 PH132/R) Riding waves (44x67cm-17x26in) init.d.1907 W/C bodycol
£1500 $2580   (14-May-91 SWS21/R) Brigatine (45x65cm-18x26in) init.d.1912 i.verso W/C htd.bodycol
£2000 $3840   (16-Aug-90 B378/R) On the crest of a wave (41x69cm-16x27in) s. W/C bodycol.
£4000 $6920   (22-May-91 S145/R) Harbour master's home, Limehouse (44x67cm-17x26in) init.d.1891 W/C htd white

HEMY, Thomas Marie (1852-1937) British
£1200 $2064   (14-May-91 SWS27/R) Fishing boats in harbour. At anchor (24x34cm-9x13in) s.d.1888 W/C pair

HENAULT, Jean-Pierre (20th C) French
£2275 $4436   (15-Oct-90 CSC.P92/R) Les escaliers blancs (80x80cm-31x31in) s. i.d. verso (F.FR 22500)
£2423 $4338   (8-Apr-91 CSC.P119) La corde jaune (80x80cm-31x31in) s. i.d.1990 verso acrylic (F.FR 24500)

HENCZ, Antal (1839-?) Hungarian
£1365 $2676   (24-Nov-90 N.M225/R) Girl reclining on sofa (29x36cm-11x14in) s.d.1912 (DM 4000)

HENDERIKSE, Jan (1937-) Dutch
£929 $1793   (13-Dec-90 SY.AM417/R) Untitled (190x190cm-75x75in) (D.FL 3000)

HENDERSON, Charles Cooper (1803-1877) British
£660 $1135   (15-May-91 BT218) The Bristol, Bath and London coach (41x41cm-16x16in) mono.
£5000 $9850   (16-Nov-90 C76/R) Wells-Lynn-London royal mail coach in storm. Mail coach at night (33x61cm-13x24in) one init. one indis.init. pair

HENDERSON, Charles Cooper (attrib) (1803-1877) British
£580 $980   (3-May-91 PHE163) Poste haste (52x75cm-20x30in)

HENDERSON, James (1871-1951) Canadian
£979 $1665   (27-May-91 HO.ED302/R) Moonrise, Qu'Appelle River, Sask. (20x25cm-8x10in) s. bears i.verso board (C.D 1900)

HENDERSON, John (1860-1924) British
£1200 $2028   (3-May-91 PHE104) Stepping stones (61x46cm-24x18in) s.
£1600 $2992   (28-Aug-90 S970/R) Picnicing (46x63cm-18x25in) s.

HENDERSON, Joseph (1832-1908) British
£1000 $1870   (28-Aug-90 S841/R) Crossing a field (46x61cm-18x24in) s.
£1900 $3553   (28-Aug-90 S930/R) Ballantrae Shore (51x61cm-20x24in) s.i.
£2100 $3759   (14-Mar-91 CG72) The sea angler (46x61cm-18x24in) s.
£2200 $4114   (28-Aug-90 S833/R) Breezy day at Ballintrae (46x61cm-18x24in) s.
£4000 $6760   (3-May-91 PHE68/R) Beside the sea (72x99cm-28x39in) s.

HENDERSON, Joseph Morris (1863-1936) British
£600 $1008   (16-Jul-91 RG2375) Extensive landscape with cattle in foreground (30x41cm-12x16in) s.
£1100 $1848   (23-Apr-91 S71/R) Narrows, Aberfoyle (43x58cm-17x23in) s.
£1500 $2910   (5-Dec-90 PHE43/R) Picking wild flowers (45x75cm-18x30in) s.
£3200 $5376   (23-Apr-91 S69/R) Playing on rocky beach (61x91cm-24x36in) s.

HENDERSON, W S P (19th C) British
£850 $1386   (14-Jun-91 C310) Relics of the olden time (16x24cm-6x9in) s. i.verso panel
£1156 $2000   (22-May-91 D.NY5/R) Morning call (51x40cm-20x16in) s.d.1857 panel

HENDERSON, William Penhallow (1877-1943) American
£1341 $2400   (14-Mar-91 CH.NY188/R) Pink twilight, 96th and Drive (28x20cm-11x8in) s.with artist's device chl pastel

HENDRICKX, Jos (1906-1971) Belgian
£736 $1237   (23-Apr-91 C.A114) Figure (191x125cm-75x49in) s.d.1953 panel (B.FR 45000)

HENDRIKS, J (19th C?) Dutch?
£1408 $2366   (23-Apr-91 RAS.K43/R) Shepherd with sheep and cattle by watermill (34x43cm-13x17in) indist.s. (D.KR 16000)

HENDRIKS, Willem (1828-1891) Dutch
£578 $1121   (4-Dec-90 R.T201) Cattle by river bend (52x72cm-20x28in) s. (C.D 1300)
£588 $1041   (20-Mar-91 MA.V464) Landscape with cattle by a pond (61x91cm-24x36in) s.
                (C.D 1200)
£838 $1399   (4-Jun-91 R.T254/R) Autumn glory (52x66cm-20x26in) s. (C.D 1600)
£978 $1897   (4-Dec-90 R.T202/R) Cattle in pasture by thatched cottage
                (51x62cm-20x24in) s. (C.D 2200)

HENDRIKS, Wybrand (1744-1831) Dutch
*£1970 $3880   (30-Oct-90 CH.AM420/R) Basket with flowers and fruit and two sparrows on
                marble ledge (43x34cm-17x13in) s. W/C bodycol (D.FL 6500)*

HENDRIKSE, Jan (1937-) Dutch
*£1201 $2078   (22-May-91 CH.AM746) K.S.268.58.50 (80x58cm-31x23in) i.verso mixed media
                canvas (D.FL 4000)*
*£1393 $2689   (12-Dec-90 CH.AM558/R) 280.1.4 (60x45cm-24x18in) s.i.stretcher mixed
                media canvas (D.FL 4500)*

HENEGONIZE, J L van (?) Belgian?
£917 $1760   (18-Dec-90 GM.B865) Moulin a Vent (70x80cm-28x31in) s. board
                (B.FR 55000)

HENGELER, Adolf (1863-?) German
£769 $1485   (12-Dec-90 WE.MU132/R) The right way (5x42cm-2x17in) s. canvas on board
                (DM 2200)
£2000 $3580   (12-Mar-91 PH19/R) Elegant figures and putti in river landscape
                (60x71cm-24x28in) s.d.1911 panel

HENKEL, Irmin (1921-) South African
£703 $1378   (11-Feb-91 SY.J555/R) Still life with a box of vegetables and a bottle
                (50x60cm-20x24in) s.d.'72 (SA.R 3500)

HENKES, Gerke (1844-1927) Dutch
£1259 $2102   (3-Jun-91 B.O62/R) Church interior (202x161cm-80x63in) s.d.80
                (N.KR 14500)
£592 $1000   (21-Apr-91 DU.E133) Shelling peas (23x30cm-9x12in) s. W/C

HENLEY, W B (?) ?
£540 $929   (15-May-91 BT210/R) A Devonshire Mill (58x89cm-23x35in) s. i. verso

HENNEKYN, Paulus (1611-1671) Dutch
£3593 $6072   (2-May-91 CH.AM40/R) Portrait of a naval officer standing on a draped
                terrace holding a baton (112x91cm-44x36in) s.d.1665 (D.FL 12000)

HENNEQUIN, Philippe Auguste (1762-1833) French
*£700 $1351   (12-Dec-90 PH59/R) Vanity, nude draped in cloak kneeling on step looking
                in mirror (33cm-13ins circular) s. pen ink wash*

HENNER (?) French
£843 $1636   (4-Dec-90 C.A176) Girl with flowers (105x77cm-41x30in) s. (B.FR 50000)

HENNER, Jean Jacques (1829-1905) French
£663 $1307   (16-Nov-90 NM.P8) La fileuse (29x21cm-11x8in) studio st. (F.FR 6500)
£769 $1500   (21-Oct-90 HG.C24) Portrait of woman in red (25x20cm-10x8in) s. panel
£1190 $2060   (22-May-91 GS.B2395) Portrait of young woman with red hair
                (26x22cm-10x9in) s. board (S.FR 3000)
£1243 $2100   (29-Apr-91 S.SL310/R) Portrait of a red haired beauty (46x33cm-18x13in)
                s.
£1369 $2300   (21-Jul-91 LIT.L85) Reclining nude (76x97cm-30x38in) s.
£1372 $2689   (6-Nov-90 SY.AM306/R) Nymph in woods (26x40cm-10x16in) s. (D.FL 4500)
£1518 $2976   (20-Nov-90 BG.P45/R) Portrait de femme (46x31cm-18x12in) mono.
                (F.FR 15000)
£1667 $3250   (26-Oct-90 SY.NY145/R) Portrait d'homme (44x32cm-17x13in) s.
£1735 $3417   (16-Nov-90 NM.P42/R) Femme allongee (27x38cm-11x15in) s. (F.FR 17000)
£1778 $3449   (4-Dec-90 R.T166/R) Profile of red-haired beauty (41x31cm-16x12in) s.
                (C.D 4000)
£1825 $3158   (22-May-91 GS.B2394) Portrait of young woman with red hair
                (28x22cm-11x9in) s. board (S.FR 4600)
£2000 $3260   (4-Jul-91 GL.P259) Portrait de jeune femme (27x21cm-11x8in) s. wood
                (F.FR 20000)
£2296 $4500   (21-Nov-90 NA.BA39/R) Tete de jeune fille au corsage rouge
                (27x23cm-11x9in) s. board
£4000 $6520   (1-Jul-91 LGB.P1/R) Nu allonge dans un paysage (26x39cm-10x15in) s.
                (F.FR 40000)
£4103 $8000   (23-Oct-90 SY.NY294/R) Tete de jeune fille (27x19cm-11x7in) s. board
£4103 $8000   (23-Oct-90 SY.NY295/R) Ideal head (30x24cm-12x9in) s. panel
£6332 $10384 (21-Jun-91 D.P97) Jeuen fille au ruban bleu (47x39cm-19x15in) s.
                (F.FR 63000)

HENNER, Jean Jacques (attrib) (1829-1905) French
£1829 $3000   (19-Jun-91 B.SF1821/R) Fete champetre (2x39cm-1x15in) st.sig. board
                after Giorgione

HENNESSEY, Frank Charles (1893-1941) Canadian
*£459 $900   (24-Nov-90 YFA.M66/R) Early spring across valley (41x51cm-16x20in) s.
                pastel*

HENNESSY, Patrick (20th C) Irish

£1150	$2162	(18-Sep-90 PH177) Red Strand, Clonakilty (63x76cm-25x30in) s.
£2593	$5107	(14-Nov-90 WO.CO6) Lake Island (51x61cm-20x24in) s. (E.P 2800)
£3600	$6768	(18-Sep-90 PH176/R) Portrait of Lady Ursula Vernon, standing in grounds of Bruree House, Co.Limerick (91x122cm-36x48in) s.
£864	*$1693*	*(23-Jan-91 WO.CO21) Riverside landscape (36x25cm-14x10in) s.d.1943 W/C (E.P 950)*

HENNIG, Albert (1896-?) German

£580	*$1137*	*(22-Nov-90 L.K1005) Fantastic houses (15x22cm-6x9in) s.d.1962 W/C pen (DM 1700)*
£648	*$1271*	*(22-Nov-90 L.K1006) Houses in landscape (15x22cm-6x9in) s.d.1975 W/C over pen (DM 1900)*
£651	*$1061*	*(14-Jun-91 L.K947) Composition with figures (16x15cm-6x6in) s.d.84 W/C over felt tip pen (DM 1900)*

HENNIG, Otto (1871-1920) Norwegian

£2627	$4702	(14-Mar-91 BU.O45/R) Woman in landscape (93x76cm-37x30in) s. (N.KR 30000)

HENNING, Gerhard (1880-1967) Swedish

£1601	*$3011*	*(18-Sep-90 BU.K132/R) Selfportrait (23x18cm-9x7in) mono.d.1900 gold paint canvas (D.KR 18000)*

HENNINGER, Manfred (1894-) German

£845	$1461	(21-May-91 WK.M993/R) In the forest (66x48cm-26x19in) s.indis.i.d.1941 W/C over chl (DM 2500)
£1115	$1929	(21-May-91 WK.M989/R) Peasant from Ticino (46x35cm-18x14in) s.d.1938 paper (DM 3300)
£1884	$3372	(12-Mar-91 FN.S2021/R) Figures amongst trees (75x105cm-30x41in) s. (DM 5500)
£4196	$8140	(4-Dec-90 FN.S1619/R) Neckar landscape III (65x85cm-26x33in) s.d.1964 i.verso (DM 12000)
£4895	$9497	(4-Dec-90 FN.S1620/R) Figures and trees (83x102cm-33x40in) s.d.1978 (DM 14000)
£6020	$10174	(19-Apr-91 FN.S1527/R) Southern summer landscape (70x90cm-28x35in) s.d.1975 (DM 18000)
£6355	$10739	(19-Apr-91 FN.S1526/R) Harbour view with figures, Heraklion, Kreta (70x90cm-28x35in) s.d.1975 (DM 19000)
£6826	$12901	(25-Sep-90 FN.S1967/R) Italianate river landscape with houses, possibly Losone near Ascona (54x73cm-21x29in) s.d.1943 (DM 20000)
£7363	$13180	(12-Mar-91 FN.S2020/R) Composition with figures (97x146cm-38x57in) s.d.1952 (DM 21500)
£669	*$1130*	*(19-Apr-91 FN.S1529/R) Mother and child seated (50x27cm-20x11in) s.i.d.1962 chl (DM 2000)*
£839	*$1628*	*(4-Dec-90 FN.S1622/R) Assembly (44x62cm-17x24in) s.d.1967 pastel (DM 2400)*
£878	*$1520*	*(21-May-91 WK.M997/R) Utoquai, Zurich (30x42cm-12x17in) s.d.1947 pastel (DM 2600)*
£1049	*$2035*	*(4-Dec-90 FN.S1621/R) Bathers (47x65cm-19x26in) s.d.1963 W/C over pencil (DM 3000)*
£1638	*$3096*	*(25-Sep-90 FN.S1972/R) Nude males beneath trees (50x64cm-20x25in) s.d.1950 pastel (DM 4800)*
£2508	*$4239*	*(19-Apr-91 FN.S1528/R) Illustration for Virgil with figures beneath trees (42x60cm-17x24in) s.d.1975 pastel (DM 7500)*

HENNINGS, Ernest Martin (1886-1956) American

£5000	$8200	(18-Jun-91 PH94/R) Portrait of young Indian woman wearing native American jewellery (68x48cm-27x19in) s.
£5291	$10000	(26-Sep-90 SY.NY82/R) Pueblo at night (61x84cm-24x33in) s.
£6122	$12000	(7-Nov-90 B.SF3780/R) Taos Pueblo girl (35x35cm-14x14in) s.
£14031	$27500	(7-Nov-90 B.SF3788/R) Indian fishing with horse hair (76x76cm-30x30in) s.

HENNINGS, J F (1838-1899) German

£956	$1797	(21-Sep-90 N.M3209) Sculptures in Nymphenburger Park (53x35cm-21x14in) s.i.indis.d.79 (DM 2800)

HENNINGSEN, Erik (1855-1930) Danish

£1408	$2366	(23-Apr-91 RAS.K400/R) The first Danish soldiers coming across border in Sonderjylland 1920 (63x70cm-25x28in) s.d.1920 (D.KR 16000)
£3500	$5740	(19-Jun-91 S296/R) Lowering colours (50x69cm-20x27in) s.d.1899

HENNINGSEN, Frants (1850-1908) Danish

£707	$1330	(10-Aug-90 RAS.V475/R) Two hussars (55x43cm-22x17in) init. (D.KR 8000)
£1651	*$3253*	*(13-Nov-90 AB.S904/R) Woman carrying fagots (60x50cm-24x20in) mono.d.85 pastel (S.KR 18000)*

HENOCQUE, Narcisse (?) French

£3160	$6099	(12-Dec-90 APT.P112 b) Peniche sur la Seine au crepuscule (54x73cm-21x29in) s. (F.FR 31000)

HENRARD, Joseph (19th C) European

£1347	$2653	(15-Nov-90 EA.Z165/R) The hunter. Cows (7x12cm-3x5in) s. panel pair (S.FR 3300)

HENRI, Robert (1865-1929) American
£1176	$2200	(4-Aug-90 LIT.L173) Artist in Brittany picnic setting (15x23cm-6x9in) s. board
£10405	$18000	(22-May-91 CH.NY263/R) Wet Road, Pennsylvania landscape (66x81cm-26x32in) s.
£11458	$22000	(30-Nov-90 CH.NY171/R) Cafe Interior. Promenade (10x15cm-4x6in) s. panel double-sided
£15029	$26000	(23-May-91 SY.NY52/R) Spanish landscape (65x81cm-26x32in) s. num.57A/1 verso
£23438	$45000	(30-Nov-90 CH.NY174/R) Mary Kate (61x51cm-24x20in) s. s.i.verso i.stretcher
£26042	$50000	(30-Nov-90 CH.NY179/R) Joble, the laughing boy (61x50cm-24x20in) s.
£26042	$50000	(29-Nov-90 SY.NY90/R) Portrait of young girl (71x51cm-28x20in) s.
£31250	$60000	(30-Nov-90 CH.NY173/R) Little girl in red stripes (61x51cm-24x20in) s. s.i.verso i.stretcher
£41667	$80000	(30-Nov-90 CH.NY172/R) Boy with green cap, Chico (61x51cm-24x20in) s. s.i.verso i.stretcher
£636	*$1100*	*(10-May-91 S.BM74/R) Indulgences, reclining woman (15x23cm-6x9in) s. ink*
£847	*$1600*	*(25-Sep-90 CE.NY76/R) Crashing waves (38x56cm-15x22in) s. W/C*
£888	*$1500*	*(1-May-91 B.SF5241/R) Study of woman (21x13cm-8x5in) st. pencil*
£930	*$1600*	*(15-May-91 SY.NY162/R) Portrait of young girl in bonnet (33x28cm-13x11in) s. chl*
£2632	*$5000*	*(9-Jan-91 CH.NY239/R) Man in top hat leading crowd (25x36cm-10x14in) init.d.1907 ink*

HENRICHSEN, Carsten (1824-1897) Danish
£549	$928	(2-May-91 RAS.V50/R) Sunset over Nordsjaelland with figures and game (72x98cm-28x39in) mono.d.1866 (D.KR 6200)
£576	$939	(13-Jun-91 RAS.V545/R) Southern landscape with houses and figures (50x72cm-20x28in) mono.d.1874 (D.KR 6500)
£758	$1356	(14-Mar-91 RAS.V652/R) Summer landscape with figures and old houses (36x56cm-14x22in) s.d.1856 (D.KR 8500)
£1232	$2070	(23-Apr-91 RAS.K288/R) View towards Radvad (50x70cm-20x28in) mono.d.1865 (D.KR 14000)

HENRIKSEN, William (1880-?) Danish
£650	$1118	(17-May-91 C115/R) Sunlight in living room (46x37cm-18x15in) s. init.i.verso
£800	$1376	(17-May-91 C122/R) Interior (41x31cm-16x12in) s.
£962	$1723	(9-Apr-91 RAS.K2069) Sitting room interior (53x48cm-21x19in) s. (D.KR 11000)
£1300	$2236	(17-May-91 C123/R) Interior (40x33cm-16x13in) s.
£1662	$2976	(9-Apr-91 RAS.K2068) Interior with sunlight coming through thin curtains (55x51cm-22x20in) s. (D.KR 19000)
£1700	$2924	(17-May-91 C112/R) Interior with sunlight (46x39cm-18x15in) s. init.i.verso
£2800	$4816	(17-May-91 C114/R) Sunshine in living room (43x37cm-17x15in) s. init.i.verso

HENRION, Armand (1875-) Belgian
£1368	$2600	(27-Feb-91 SY.NY75/R) Clowns (18x15cm-7x6in) s. panel pair

HENRY D'ARLES, Jean (1734-1784) French
£9131	$15341	(23-Apr-91 F.R53/R) Scena di naufragio (74x101cm-29x40in) (I.L 20000000)

HENRY, David Reid see REID-HENRY, David M

HENRY, E L (1841-1919) American
£1368	*$2600*	*(14-Sep-90 DM.D1303/R) 'Reading Bluebeard' (23x30cm-9x12in) s. W/C*

HENRY, Edward Lamson (1841-1919) American
£6213	$10500	(29-Apr-91 S.SL309/R) Busy street scene in rural American town with stagecoach and riverboat landing (30x38cm-12x15in) s.d.1818
£13873	$24000	(22-May-91 CH.NY117/R) On way to town (40x51cm-16x20in) s.d.1907
£28902	$50000	(23-May-91 SY.NY8/R) Departing for seat of war from New Jersey (27x41cm-11x16in) s.d.69 panel
£2000	*$3800*	*(9-Jan-91 CH.NY135/R) City Point, Virginia (25x52cm-10x20in) s.i.d.1864 W/C pencil htd white over photo.base*
£6936	*$12000*	*(22-May-91 CH.NY114/R) Waiting for ferry (38x54cm-15x21in) s.d.1902 W/C htd gouache paper on board*

HENRY, George (1859-1943) British
£1050	$1943	(6-Mar-91 DR186/R) Bridge (51x61cm-20x24in) s.
£9000	*$16830*	*(28-Aug-90 S989/R) Japanese lady (51x35cm-20x14in) s. W/C htd bodycol*

HENRY, George Morrison Reid (1891-1983) British
£320	*$614*	*(19-Feb-91 C36) Curlews and oyster catchers at Portscatho, Cornwall (13x15cm-5x6in) s.i.d.1939verso W/C htd.white*
£420	*$806*	*(19-Feb-91 C34) Dabchicks or little grebes (20x30cm-8x12in) i.verso W/C*

HENRY, Grace (1863-1953) British
£1111	$2144	(12-Dec-90 CH.E157/R) Polyanthus in a vase (65x54cm-26x21in) s. (E.P 1200)
£1600	$3120	(26-Oct-90 CG146/R) Sailing offshore at dusk (19x31cm-7x12in) s. board

HENRY, Grace (1863-1953) British-cont.

£2200 $4290   (26-Oct-90 CG145) Winter in St Stephens Green, Dublin (30x26cm-12x10in)
s. canvas board

£2600 $5070   (26-Oct-90 CG144/R) Hills of Connemara (33x41cm-13x16in) s. i.stretcher
£3600 $7020   (26-Oct-90 CG142/R) Country fair, West of Ireland (41x48cm-16x19in)

HENRY, Harry Raymond (1882-1974) American

£3846 $7500   (10-Oct-90 B.SF618/R) Landscape through wooded clearing
(102x127cm-40x50in) s.

HENRY, Maurice (1907-) French

£1386 $2676   (13-Dec-90 F.M321/R) Dans le Marecage (40x60cm-16x24in) s.d.74 s.i.verso
(I.L 3000000)

£3408 $6713   (30-Oct-90 F.R194/R) Derriere les folies (97x130cm-38x51in) s.
s.d.1970verso (I.L 7500000)

£5853 $11414   (22-Oct-90 BR.M291/R) L'inconnue (54x65cm-21x26in) s.d.1974
(I.L 13000000)

*£2292 $3759   (19-Jun-91 F.M80/R) Composizione (32x24cm-13x9in) s.d.1935 ink collage
(I.L 5000000)*

HENRY, Michel (19/20th C) French

£1004 $1929   (27-Nov-90 W.T1111) Dahlias (63x53cm-25x21in) s. (C.D 2250)

HENRY, N (19th C) ?

£556 $961   (22-May-91 GS.B2396) Portrait of young woman dressed in Spanish costume
(45x37cm-18x15in) s.d.59 oval (S.FR 1400)

HENRY, Olive (1902-) British

£800 $1560   (26-Oct-90 CG126/R) Beach huts, Costa Brava (41x76cm-16x30in) s.

HENRY, Paul (1877-1958) Irish

£2000 $3840   (17-Aug-90 K552/R) Cottages and peat stacks in Irish landscape
(25x36cm-10x14in) s.

£2100 $3927   (29-Aug-90 HUN1) Fisherman placing crab pots from curragh off rocky
shore (30x43cm-12x17in)

£12105 $23000   (27-Feb-91 SY.NY276/R) Landscape with cottages (50x55cm-20x22in) s.
panel

£13500 $22140   (21-Jun-91 HC1) Cottages beside Lake Connemara (48x58cm-19x23in)

HENRY, Pierre (1924-) French

£1195 $2032   (29-May-91 GL.P13) Printemps a Madere (31x90cm-12x35in) s. (F.FR 12000)

HENSCHE, Henry (1901-) American

£964 $1900   (16-Nov-90 S.BM180/R) Still life (76x86cm-30x34in) canvasboard

HENSE, S (19/20th C) ?

£850 $1700   (8-Feb-91 K502/R) White roses and other flowers in green vase on table
(43x58cm-17x23in)

HENSEL, Wilhelm (1794-1861) German

£19000 $31160   (21-Jun-91 C75/R) L'Acquaiolo (99x130cm-39x51in) s.d.1844

HENSELER, Ernst (1852-?) German

£4270 $8028   (18-Sep-90 BU.K119/R) Girl picking cherries (77x51cm-30x20in) s.
(D.KR 48000)

£8000 $15680   (15-Feb-91 C50/R) Rendez-vous (49x71cm-19x28in) s. board

HENSHALL, John Henry (1856-1928) British

£800 $1480   (6-Mar-91 SC4180/R) Beggars (23x13cm-9x5in) bears i.verso W/C
*£2500 $4800   (26-Nov-90 HS103/R) The day of rest, cottage interior with elderly
couple (76x55cm-30x22in) s.d.1918 W/C*

HENSHAW, Frederick Henry (1807-1891) British

£650 $1281   (31-Oct-90 CSK99) Figures fetching water amongst Roman ruins
(25x33cm-10x13in) panel

£660 $1115   (1-May-91 ZZ.B138) Gypsy encampment in wood (37x42cm-15x17in) s. board
£1300 $2509   (13-Dec-90 CSK217/R) Extensive mountainous landscape with shepherd and
sheep on track (25x38cm-10x15in) s.d.1842

£2200 $3586   (14-Jun-91 C226/R) Highland landscape with figure on a path
(91x71cm-36x28in)

£2400 $4056   (30-Apr-91 PH83/R) Kenilworth Castle, Warwickshire, twilight
(30x45cm-12x18in) s.i.d.1845 verso

£4000 $7880   (1-Nov-90 C231/R) Road to the abbey, Bolton Yorkshire. Crossing the
bridge (49x39cm-19x15in) one s.i.d.1853 panel pair

HENSHAW, Glenn Cooper (1881-1946) American

£414 $700   (21-Apr-91 DU.E89 a/R) El at Bowry (30x23cm-12x9in) s. pastel

HENSTENBURGH, Herman (1667-1726) Dutch

£3158 $6000   (9-Jan-91 CH.NY95/R) Studies (20x28cm-8x11in) one mono. pen W/C bodycol
one on vellum pair

HENTER (19th C) British?

£2237 $4250   (27-Feb-91 SY.NY260/R) Emily. Ann - marine scenes (46x63cm-18x25in) s.
pair

HENTON, George Moore (c.1859-1924) British
£1400 $2772   (30-Jan-91 S224/R) Punting (38x55cm-15x22in) s. W/C

HENTZE, Gudmund Herman Peter (1875-1948) Danish
£399 $674   (1-May-91 KH.K227/R) Young girl with basket of flowers (77x50cm-30x20in)
                                 s.d.1932 pastel (D.KR 4500)

HENTZEPETER, Theodorus (19th C) Dutch
£1200 $1968   (18-Jun-91 PH2) Shooting party resting on banks of estuary
                                 (32x40cm-13x16in) s.d.1842

HENZELL, Isaac (19th C) British
£2200 $4400   (8-Feb-91 C160/R) Off to market (30x41cm-12x16in) s.d.69
£3200 $6304   (1-Nov-90 TE638/R) Going along shore (51x41cm-20x16in) s.d.1861
£3700 $5957   (25-Jun-91 AG401/R) Fishergirls accompanied by dog on north east beach
                                 at low tide (101x133cm-40x52in) s.d.1856

HENZIROSS, Eugen (1877-1961) ?
£794 $1325   (7-Jun-91 ZOF.Z1338/R) Hilternfingen on Lake Thun (65x75cm-26x30in) s.
                                 i.verso (S.FR 2000)

HEPPE, Hortense von (1941-) German
£3181 $5376   (15-Apr-91 CSC.P11/R) Vie (140x100cm-55x39in) (F.FR 32000)

HEPPEL, H (19th C) German
£642 $1091   (27-May-91 L.K281) Upper Bavarian lake landscape (16x29cm-6x11in) s.
                                 board (DM 1900)
£811 $1378   (27-May-91 L.K280) Upper Bavarian landscape with harvesting scene beyond
                                 (25x36cm-10x14in) s. panel (DM 2400)

HEPPER, W J (?) ?
£520 $894   (15-May-91 BT246/R) A black hunter standing in a stable
                                 (48x58cm-19x23in) s.d.'81

HEPPLE, Robert Norman (1908-) British
£2800 $5460   (10-Oct-90 S92/R) The mirror (89x71cm-35x28in) s.

HEPPLE, Wilson (1854-1937) British
£820 $1320   (25-Jun-91 AG397/R) Portrait of tabby kitten (20x22cm-8x9in) s.d.1907
                                 board
£1400 $2744   (13-Feb-91 PHL185/R) Kittens at play (61x30cm-24x12in) s.d.1903
£1700 $3315   (15-Jan-91 C8/R) Artist's kittens (46x36cm-18x14in) s.
£2000 $3380   (30-Apr-91 AG313/R) Blue flowers and kittens (59x29cm-23x11in) s.d.1903
£2200 $3718   (30-Apr-91 PH118/R) Teatime (41x51cm-16x20in) s.

HEPWORTH, Dame Barbara (1903-?) British
£4000 $6960   (27-Mar-91 S176/R) Crouching figure (23x33cm-9x13in) s.d.1948 pen ink
                                 wash chk
£7500 $14625   (17-Oct-90 S108/R) Drawing in stone sculpture (23x30cm-9x12in) s.d.1942
                                 s.i.d.verso gouache W/C pencil board
£18000 $33300   (5-Mar-91 PH60/R) Interlocking forms (61x41cm-24x16in) s.d.22/1/50
                                 thinned oil pencil board
£43147 $85000   (15-Nov-90 CH.NY185/R) Duo, surgeon and sister (40x35cm-16x14in)
                                 s.d.1948 s.i.d.verso oil pencil

HER, Theodor (1838-1892) German
£2003 $3907   (15-Oct-90 B.O33/R) Picnic by edge of river (62x96cm-24x38in) s.
                                 (N.KR 23000)

HERALD, James Watterson (1859-1914) British
£820 $1382   (2-May-91 CG499) Arbroath harbour, 1903 (36x25cm-14x10in) s. canvas on
                                 panel
£950 $1606   (2-May-91 CG515) Fishing boats in Arbroath harbour (27x36cm-11x14in) s.
£450 $756   (23-Apr-91 S210) Nocturne (23x27cm-9x11in) s. pastel
£600 $1182   (1-Nov-90 B127) Figures among the trees (37x49cm-15x19in) indis.s.
                                 pastel
£720 $1238   (14-May-91 SWS131/R) Evening, Harwick (34x25cm-13x10in) W/C
£980 $1931   (13-Nov-90 SWS86/R) A Gipsy family (36x25cm-14x10in) s.d.1897
£1300 $2431   (28-Aug-90 S967/R) Arbroath harbour (18x26cm-7x10in) init. W/C
£1450 $2842   (23-Nov-90 PHE39/R) Village news (29x36cm-11x14in) s. W/C
£2200 $3586   (14-Jun-91 C155/R) The sea at Arbroath (16x34cm-6x13in) s.d.98 pencil
                                 W/C

HERAMB, Thore (1916-) Norwegian
£556 $939   (20-Apr-91 BU.O37) Composition 1958 (50x65cm-20x26in) s. panel
                                 (N.KR 6435)
£781 $1305   (3-Jun-91 B.O68/R) Autumn landscape, 1976 (38x54cm-15x21in) s.d.76
                                 (N.KR 9000)
£1345 $2247   (3-Jun-91 B.O67/R) Landscape, 1954 (49x65cm-19x26in) s.d.54 (N.KR 15500)
£1823 $3044   (3-Jun-91 B.O66/R) From Cornwall, 1972 (65x50cm-26x20in) s.d.72
                                 (N.KR 21000)
£4181 $8153   (15-Oct-90 B.O34/R) Landscape composition - towards the country
                                 (92x73cm-36x29in) s.d.75 (N.KR 48000)

HERAS, Gaetano de la (19/20th C) Spanish
£8197	$16066	(11-Nov-90 ZZ.F45/R) Scene de cafe a Paris (54x65cm-21x26in) s.d.1903 (F.FR 80000)

HERBERT, Alfred (?-1861) British
£650	$1248	(26-Nov-90 SWS60/R) Salvaging the wreck (42x83cm-17x33in) s. W/C htd.gum arabic scratching out
£650	$1268	(18-Oct-90 CSK53) Fishing yawl in storm (34x62cm-13x24in) bears sig.verso pencil W/C sold with another W/C
£1500	$2880	(26-Nov-90 SWS59/R) Unloading the catch (32x65cm-13x26in) s. W/C
£1600	$3072	(26-Nov-90 SWS66/R) The harbour entrance (43x84cm-17x33in) s. W/C scratching out
£2000	$3840	(26-Nov-90 SWS61/R) Beached boats at sunset unloading the catch (32x73cm-13x29in) s.d.1860 W/C
£2600	$4992	(26-Nov-90 SWS65/R) Dutch fishing boats beinig offloaded in rough weather (31x76cm-12x30in) W/C scratching out

HERBERT, Harold Brocklebank (20th C) Australian
£407	$688	(16-Apr-91 J.M304/R) Towards the castle (26x38cm-10x15in) s. W/C (A.D 900)
£440	$858	(15-Oct-90 AAA.S109) Early Canberra (26x23cm-10x9in) s. W/C (A.D 1100)
£463	$913	(13-Nov-90 J.M507) Through the trees (14x14cm-6x6in) s. W/C stencil (A.D 1200)
£1255	$2472	(13-Nov-90 J.M230/R) Summer shadows (25x34cm-10x13in) s. W/C (A.D 3250)
£1354	$2423	(9-Apr-91 CH.ME255/R) Couples talking beside bridge, Tasmania (31x37cm-12x15in) s. W/C (A.D 3100)
£1394	$2747	(31-Oct-90 CH.S167/R) The sandhill, Ninety Mile Beach (25x35cm-10x14in) s.d.1911 W/C (A.D 3500)
£1584	$2676	(16-Apr-91 J.M330) Country village (29x38cm-11x15in) s.d.1934 W/C (A.D 3500)
£1737	$3423	(13-Nov-90 J.M54/R) Blue hills and hay barn (34x39cm-13x15in) s.d.30 W/C (A.D 4500)
£2510	$4944	(13-Nov-90 J.M42/R) Yarra Willows, Kew (36x46cm-14x18in) s.d.1938 W/C (A.D 6500)

HERBERT, John Rogers (1810-1890) British
£5800	$11426	(1-Nov-90 CSK155/R) Vine that maketh glad heart of man (76x63cm-30x25in) init.

HERBERT, Sidney (1854-1914) British
£976	$1912	(6-Nov-90 SY.AM21) View at Kom Ombos Temple by Alexandrie, Egypt (57x88cm-22x35in) mono. (D.FL 3200)
£2200	$4334	(13-Nov-90 SWS305/R) Joan of Arc and the Dauphin gathering their army at Rheims Cathedral (138x100cm-54x39in) s.d.1878

HERBERTE, E B (19th C) British
£1000	$1850	(5-Mar-91 AG311/R) Foxhunt in full cry (44x29cm-17x11in) s.d.1886
£1488	$2500	(21-Jul-91 LIT.L151) Fox hunting (30x51cm-12x20in) s.d.1881
£3600	$5940	(9-Jul-91 PH249/R) Portrait of chestnut horse with jockey up, landscape beyond (71x91cm-28x36in) s. indist.d.
£5000	$9450	(26-Sep-90 S108/R) Meet. Drawing cover. Full cry. The kill (30x51cm-12x20in) s.d.1885 four

HERBERTE, Edward Benjamin (fl.1860-1893) British
£1000	$1770	(21-Mar-91 CSK216) A meeting on the road. Riding bare-back (28x43cm-11x17in) s.d.1886 pair
£2000	$3780	(27-Sep-90 CSK37) The lost scent. Breaking cover (35x45cm-14x18in) s.d.1880 and 1882 pair
£5500	$10395	(27-Sep-90 CSK42) The meet. Breaking cover. The fall. The kill (30x45cm-12x18in) s.d.1877 set of four
£7186	$12000	(7-Jun-91 SY.NY100/R) Full cry. The kill (46x61cm-18x24in) each s.d.1891 two
£18563	$31000	(7-Jun-91 SY.NY99/R) The meet. Drawing cover. Full cry. The kill (30x51cm-12x20in) each s.d.1885 four

HERBIG, Otto (1889-1971) German
£751	$1419	(25-Sep-90 FN.S1973/R) Wooded landscape with garden table in late summer (60x46cm-24x18in) s. mixed media (DM 2200)
£800	$1432	(12-Apr-91 AW.H1620/R) Grunewaldfenster (66x48cm-26x19in) s.d.1933 pastel (DM 2400)
£897	$1721	(1-Dec-90 SA.A2425/R) Group of trees in landscape (48x62cm-19x24in) s.d.43 W/C (DM 2600)
£1024	$2007	(24-Nov-90 VG.B562/R) Lake landscape, Mark (46x62cm-18x24in) s.d.1924 pastel chl panel (DM 3000)

HERBIN, Auguste (1882-1960) French
£1479	$2914	(6-Oct-90 GL.P152) Saint Martin de Fenouillard XII (63x48cm-25x19in) s.i.d.1918 W/C (F.FR 15000)
£6993	$13497	(14-Dec-90 BM.B737/R) Soleil, composition (40x46cm-16x18in) s.d.1947 i.d.verso (DM 20000)
£19195	$37046	(12-Dec-90 CH.AM240/R) Paysage (46x27cm-18x11in) s. panel (D.FL 62000)
£19881	$33598	(15-Apr-91 CC.P97/R) Volutes (73x82cm-29x32in) s. (F.FR 200000)
£26000	$50700	(17-Oct-90 S59/R) Nature morte aux fruits (64x84cm-25x33in) s.
£26786	$52500	(15-Feb-91 SY.NY62/R) Paysage Vaison la Romaine (73x100cm-29x39in) s.
£28000	$45080	(27-Jun-91 S17/R) Om (81x60cm-32x24in) s.i.d.1945

HERBIN, Auguste (1882-1960) French-cont.

£65306	$128653	(16-Nov-90 GK.Z5204/R) Le port (100x73cm-39x29in) s.d.1925-26 (S.FR 160000)
£65458	$106697	(11-Jun-91 CSC.P19/R) Le Port (100x73cm-39x29in) s. (F.FR 650000)
£130916	$213394	(15-Jun-91 FB.P27/R) Nature morte aux pots de fleurs (100x73cm-39x29in) s. (F.FR 1300000)
£1500	$2445	(3-Jul-91 LGB.P72/R) Composition geometrique (25x16cm-10x6in) s. gouache (F.FR 15000)
£6030	$9889	(23-Jun-91 P.V17/R) Composition (48x30cm-19x12in) s.d.1917 W/C col.crayons (F.FR 60000)
£6372	$12362	(7-Dec-90 GL.P129/R) Christ (36x25cm-14x10in) s.d.1943 gouache (F.FR 62000)
£6500	$12675	(19-Oct-90 C167/R) Une (27x35cm-11x14in) s.i.d.1949 gouache
£7119	$11888	(6-Jun-91 HN.H414/R) Abstract design stationary (29x14cm-11x6in) s. W/C pencil (DM 21000)
£8056	$13132	(15-Jun-91 FB.P28/R) Etude pour la nature morte aux pots de fleurs (32x25cm-13x10in) s. ink crayon (F.FR 80000)
£12500	$24375	(18-Oct-90 C310/R) Alouette (38x28cm-15x11in) s.i.d.1951 gouache
£12705	$24012	(28-Sep-90 S.Z175) Composition (34x29cm-13x11in) s.d.1920 gouache htd.white (S.FR 31000)
£14070	$25186	(17-Mar-91 GL.P32/R) Composition (47x35cm-19x14in) s. W/C (F.FR 140000)
£26000	$50700	(18-Oct-90 C311/R) Composition (25x32cm-10x13in) gouache

HERBO, Fernand (1905-) French

£645	$1109	(17-May-91 LGB.P154) Bord de riviere (24x33cm-9x13in) s. panel
£1042	$1792	(17-May-91 LGB.P153/R) Neige a Meziares en Drouais (50x65cm-20x26in) s. (F.FR 10500)
£1205	$2229	(10-Mar-91 LT.P90/R) Avant l'orage (23x34cm-9x13in) s. (F.FR 12000)
£2823	$5504	(28-Oct-90 GRA.P32/R) Honfleur - le port (33x46cm-13x18in) s. (F.FR 28000)
£3087	$6051	(25-Nov-90 LC.P118/R) Le port de Quimper (50x65cm-20x26in) s.d.1933 W/C (F.FR 30500)
£3317	$5937	(11-Mar-91 GL.P57) Le port de Honfleur (50x65cm-20x26in) s. (F.FR 33000)
£3869	$6655	(19-May-91 ZZ.F118/R) Vue de Honfleur (45x81cm-18x32in) s.d.1939 (F.FR 39000)
£4024	$7887	(27-Jan-91 B.PA5/R) Les voiliers (46x81cm-18x32in) s. (F.FR 40000)
£4918	$9639	(11-Nov-90 ZZ.F118/R) Neige sur la Touques a Pont-Audemer (60x81cm-24x32in) s. d.1976 verso (F.FR 48000)
£5061	$9919	(25-Nov-90 LC.P116/R) Vue du village de Duravel (50x65cm-20x26in) s.d.1935 (F.FR 50000)
£5268	$8904	(21-Apr-91 E.LA68) Bateaux a Honfleur (58x78cm-23x31in) s. (F.FR 53000)
£5478	$9477	(26-May-91 FB.F99/R) Vue du port de Honfleur (50x65cm-20x26in) s. (F.FR 55000)
£5708	$10960	(2-Dec-90 M.V171 b/R) Marine (50x65cm-20x26in) s. (F.FR 56000)
£7136	$13700	(29-Nov-90 ZZ.F16/R) Le vieux marche de Falaise (73x92cm-29x36in) s. (F.FR 70000)
£7523	$14669	(11-Oct-90 QWA.P38/R) Maree Basse au Crotoy (81x100cm-32x39in) s. i. verso (F.FR 75000)
£7523	$14669	(9-Oct-90 CSC.P24/R) Honfleur, le Port (60x81cm-24x32in) s. i. verso (F.FR 75000)
£8656	$17052	(29-Oct-90 LC.P106/R) Honfleur (60x81cm-24x32in) s. (F.FR 85000)
£9629	$18776	(9-Oct-90 CSC.P12/R) Saint-Gilles-Croix-de-Vie (45x81cm-18x32in) s. (F.FR 96000)
£675	$1160	(17-May-91 LGB.P131) Honfleur (13x20cm-5x8in) s. W/C (F.FR 6800)
£823	$1523	(4-Mar-91 ARC.P52) L'oise a Conflans (38x53cm-15x21in) s.d.avril 1929 W/C (F.FR 8200)
£853	$1579	(6-Mar-91 APT.P18) St Valery sur Somme (30x48cm-12x19in) s. W/C (F.FR 8500)
£866	$1672	(12-Dec-90 D.P128) Bateaux de peche a quai (17x25cm-7x10in) s. W/C (F.FR 8500)
£954	$1765	(6-Mar-91 APT.P19) Le Treport (30x49cm-12x19in) s. W/C (F.FR 9500)
£1215	$2381	(25-Nov-90 B.PA14 a) Quai a Honfleur (23x31cm-9x12in) s. W/C (F.FR 12000)
£1321	$2642	(6-Feb-91 FB.P183/R) Le port de Dieppe (47x62cm-19x24in) s. gouache W/C (F.FR 13000)
£1424	$2692	(25-Sep-90 FB.P298) Peniches a quai (22x30cm-9x12in) s. W/C (F.FR 14000)
£1424	$2692	(25-Sep-90 FB.P297) Peniches (21x30cm-8x12in) s. W/C (F.FR 14000)
£1637	$2815	(17-May-91 LGB.P129) Conflans Saint-Honorine (33x47cm-13x19in) s.d.1932 W/C gouache (F.FR 16500)
£1662	$2708	(11-Jun-91 I.N222) Les quais de la Seine (33x50cm-13x20in) s.d.33 W/C (F.FR 16500)
£1771	$3472	(20-Nov-90 MF.P22/R) Peniches et remorqueurs sur la Seine (22x30cm-9x12in) s. W/C (F.FR 17500)
£2024	$3968	(25-Nov-90 B.PA14/R) Camaret (65x50cm-26x20in) s. W/XC (F.FR 20000)
£2024	$3968	(25-Nov-90 LC.P117) Le port (25x33cm-10x13in) s.d.44 W/C Indian ink (F.FR 20000)
£2024	$3968	(25-Nov-90 B.PA14 b/R) La Lieutenance a Honfleur (45x30cm-18x12in) s.d.1936 W/C (F.FR 20000)
£2033	$4065	(6-Feb-91 FB.P182/R) Le port de Honfleur (29x46cm-11x18in) s.d. W/C (F.FR 20000)
£2238	$4230	(25-Sep-90 FB.P296/R) Peniches a quai (32x48cm-13x19in) s. W/C (F.FR 22000)
£2328	$4563	(25-Nov-90 ZZ.F79/R) La rade de Cherbourg (46x56cm-18x22in) s. W/C (F.FR 23000)

HERBO, Fernand (1905-) French-cont.
£2419	$4718	(28-Oct-90 GRA.P33/R) Le quai Sainte-Catherine, Honfleur (31x46cm-12x18in) s.d.1941 W/C (F.FR 24000)
£2429	$4761	(20-Nov-90 MF.P21/R) Le marais a Honfleur (50x65cm-20x26in) s. W/C (F.FR 24000)
£2429	$4761	(25-Nov-90 ZZ.F81/R) Le dechargement du bois en Seine (50x65cm-20x26in) s. W/C (F.FR 24000)
£2632	$5158	(25-Nov-90 ZZ.F80/R) Le bateau rouge des phares et balises a Honfleur (50x65cm-20x26in) s. W/C (F.FR 26000)
£2834	$5555	(25-Nov-90 ZZ.F78/R) Honfleur (23x31cm-9x12in) d.1936 W/C (F.FR 28000)
£3693	$6241	(5-May-91 LT.P87/R) Benodet (50x65cm-20x26in) s. W/C (F.FR 37000)
£4403	$8630	(25-Nov-90 LC.P114/R) Le clown (65x50cm-26x20in) s. W/C (F.FR 43500)

HERBOECHON, L J (?) Belgian
£1154	$2262	(21-Nov-90 GM.B1058) Paysage pastel (32x46cm-13x18in) s. (B.FR 70000)

HERBOSCH, L (?) Belgian?
£652	$1167	(9-Apr-91 GM.B612) Mille reflets sur l'eau (65x126cm-26x50in) s. wood (B.FR 40000)
£655	$1126	(14-May-91 GM.B607) Peuplier au bord du chemin (73x96cm-29x38in) s. (B.FR 40000)

HERBST, Adolf (1909-1983) Swiss
£2400	$4056	(1-May-91 GD.B391) Autumnal woods with mountain range beyond (38x61cm-15x24in) s. (S.FR 6000)
£3400	$5746	(1-May-91 GD.B389/R) Village in autumnal woods (73x50cm-29x20in) s. (S.FR 8500)
£3984	$6853	(14-May-91 GF.L2626/R) Mendrisiotto (38x46cm-15x18in) s. l.d.1945verso board (S.FR 10000)
£476	$781	(21-Jun-91 G.Z80) Mother with children (41x30cm-16x12in) s.d.1946 mixed media (S.FR 1200)
£595	$994	(5-Jun-91 SY.Z126/R) Female nude (29x21cm-11x8in) mono.d.46 indian ink W/C (S.FR 1500)

HERBST, Frank C (19/20th C) American
£1138	$1900	(26-Jul-91 E.EDM191/R) Outlaw, 1927 - cover for Adventure magazine (94x66cm-37x26in) s.d.27

HERBST, Thomas (1848-1915) German
£524	$1017	(7-Dec-90 GB.B5857) Fishing cutter in canal (35x41cm-14x16in) board (DM 1500)

HERBSTHOFFER, Karl (1821-1876) French
£524	$1012	(12-Dec-90 N.M552/R) Priest standing in vestry defending church treasure (39x31cm-15x12in) s.l.d.1846 panel (DM 1500)

HERDMAN, Robert (1829-1888) British
£670	$1286	(27-Nov-90 W.T1286/R) Scottish lass (30x21cm-12x8in) s. W/C htd.bodycol (C.D 1500)

HERDMAN, William Gavin (1805-1882) British
£580	$986	(29-May-91 PHC114) Figures on river bank with town beyond (37x67cm-15x26in) s. W/C
£800	$1536	(28-Nov-90 SC4093/R) Figures in street near chapel, Liverpool (30x51cm-12x20in) s.d.1853 W/C over traces of pencil

HERDTLE, Hermann (1819-1889) German
£6507	$11647	(13-Mar-91 N.M529/R) View of Stuttgart (36x51cm-14x20in) s.d.1854 board (DM 19000)

HERDTLE, Richard (1866-1943) German
£890	$1594	(12-Mar-91 FN.S2417/R) Neckar landscape with four horses and peasants (41x51cm-16x20in) s.d.1938 (DM 2700)
£903	$1526	(19-Apr-91 FN.S1736/R) Market scene, Hauptstatter Strasse, Stuttgart, evening (62x75cm-24x30in) s. (DM 2700)

HEREAU, Jules (1839-1879) French
£853	$1374	(24-Jun-91 PR.P152) Le depart des pecheurs (26x46cm-10x18in) s. (F.FR 8500)

HERFORT, L (?) ?
£1357	$2294	(16-Apr-91 J.M204) Hunting Scenes (11x24cm-4x9in) s. pair (A.D 3000)

HERING, George Edwards (1805-1879) British
£573	$1100	(20-Feb-91 D.NY45) Angler in Italianate landscape (36x30cm-14x12in) s.d.1860 board
£1104	$2165	(11-Feb-91 SY.J386/R) At the river side (45x56cm-18x22in) s. (SA.R 5500)
£1200	$1968	(20-Jun-91 B13/R) Italian lake scene (32x49cm-13x19in) s.

HERIOT, George (1766-1844) Canadian
£614	$1204	(20-Nov-90 JOY.T296/R) Derwent Water (17x27cm-7x11in) W/C pencil (C.D 1400)
£759	$1268	(4-Jun-91 FB.M27) View of Houses above the river (12x18cm-5x7in) W/C (C.D 1450)

HERKENDELL, Friedrich August (1876-?) German
£687 $1306   (2-Mar-91 KRA.D504) Summer's day at the Wannsee, Berlin
           (61x80cm-24x31in) s. (DM 2000)

HERKENRATH, Peter (1900-) German
£4096 $8027   (20-Nov-90 L.K275/R) Untitled (105x80cm-41x31in) s. (DM 12000)

HERKOMER, H (19/20th C) ?
£2890 $5000   (21-May-91 CE.NY266/R) View of Alhambra (53x41cm-21x16in) s.d.79

HERKOMER, Hubert von (1849-1914) British
£400 $716   (10-Apr-91 CSK123) The street musicians (30x23cm-12x9in) s.d.1876 pencil
           W/C
£580 $951   (19-Jun-91 B126) Woman seated in punt with man standing on nearby river
           bank (18x29cm-7x11in) init.i. W/C bodycol
£700 $1176   (22-Apr-91 PH300/R) An artesan (27x17cm-11x7in) s.d.1884 W/C
£1116 $1875   (22-Apr-91 SY.ME204/R) Tale (57x37cm-22x15in) init.d.82 gouache
           (A.D 2400)
£5000 $9450   (26-Sep-90 S320/R) Arrest of poacher in Bavarian alps (52x88cm-20x35in)
           init. s.verso W/C htd white

HERMAN, Josef (1911-) British
£550 $930   (2-May-91 B71) Women on a beach (25x35cm-10x14in) s.l.d.81 verso panel
£600 $1044   (28-Mar-91 CSK53) Man resting (28x35cm-11x14in) s.l.d.1988 panel
£750 $1463   (10-Oct-90 S102/R) Two men (36x25cm-14x10in) s.l.verso
£1000 $1670   (7-Jun-91 C353 a/R) Homewards at sundown (30x35cm-12x14in)
£1250 $2350   (20-Sep-90 C90/R) Going home (18x25cm-7x10in) panel
£1400 $2436   (27-Mar-91 S187/R) Diggers (45x63cm-18x25in) board
£1600 $3120   (10-Oct-90 S119/R) Mexican peasants with donkey (46x61cm-18x24in)
£1600 $2784   (28-Mar-91 CSK51/R) Man and woman (61x51cm-24x20in) s.l.verso

HERMAN, Sali (1898-) Swiss
£1688 $3241   (14-Aug-90 SY.ME214) Corner shop (30x37cm-12x15in) s.d.'81 (A.D 4000)
£1747 $3022   (21-May-91 JRL.S164) Forest (75x98cm-30x39in) (A.D 4000)
£1767 $2969   (22-Apr-91 SY.ME203) War (20x50cm-8x20in) s.d.1944 l.verso canvas on
           board (A.D 3800)
£2203 $4163   (25-Sep-90 JRL.S187) Bare island (32x39cm-13x15in) s.d.44-54 board
           (A.D 5000)
£5581 $9377   (22-Apr-91 SY.ME233/R) Mixed blooms (54x41cm-21x16in) s.d.1944 board
           (A.D 12000)
£6977 $11721   (22-Apr-91 SY.ME377/R) Demolition, Darlinghurst (131x101cm-52x40in)
           s.d.82 (A.D 15000)
£7442 $12502   (22-Apr-91 SY.ME379/R) Coastal landscape, Newcastle (83x106cm-33x42in)
           s.indist.d. (A.D 16000)
£7968 $15697   (31-Oct-90 CH.S178/R) Paddington street (29x37cm-11x15in) s.d.59
           (A.D 20000)
£8439 $16203   (14-Aug-90 SY.ME294/R) Terrace houses, Wooloomooloo (45x65cm-18x26in)
           s.d.'65 (A.D 20000)
£8439 $16203   (14-Aug-90 SY.ME232/R) Woolloomooloo terraces (29x37cm-11x15in) s.d.'55
           (A.D 20000)
£9639 $18506   (26-Nov-90 SY.ME286/R) Outback scene with barn (50x60cm-20x24in) s.d.46
           (A.D 24000)
£10039 $19776   (13-Nov-90 J.M55 a) Street scene, Paddington (37x50cm-15x20in) s.d.70
           (A.D 26000)
£10233 $17191   (22-Apr-91 SY.ME225/R) Revery (44x39cm-17x15in) s.d.1946 l.verso board
           (A.D 22000)
£10667 $20053   (17-Sep-90 SY.ME38/R) Victoria Street, Potts Point (40x44cm-16x17in)
           s.d.46 canvas on board (A.D 24000)
£13953 $23442   (22-Apr-91 SY.ME234/R) Street scene (40x50cm-16x20in) s.d.1947
           (A.D 30000)
£16064 $30843   (26-Nov-90 SY.ME207/R) Woolloomooloo - boys playing ball
           (80x136cm-31x54in) s.d.1976 l.verso (A.D 40000)
£17195 $29059   (16-Apr-91 J.M58/R) Outback farm buildings, Northern New South Wales
           (45x55cm-18x22in) s.d.'51 (A.D 38000)
£17674 $29693   (22-Apr-91 SY.ME231/R) House at Prymont (45x60cm-18x24in) s.d.1947
           (A.D 38000)

HERMANJAT, Abraham (1862-1932) Swiss
£757 $1476   (24-Oct-90 GD.B456/R) Jura landscape with forest (32x23cm-13x9in) s.
           canvasboard (S.FR 1900)

HERMANN, H (1813-1890) German
£576 $939   (13-Jun-91 RAS.V547/R) Figures on path by lake (70x95cm-28x37in)
           s.d.1887 (D.KR 6500)

HERMANN, Johann (attrib) (1794-1880) Austrian
£967 $1730   (12-Apr-91 AW.H631/R) Biblical scene with Joseph's brothers and Jacob
           (80x107cm-31x42in) s.d.1834verso (DM 2900)

HERMANN, Leo (1853-?) French
£1474 $2800   (12-Sep-90 D.NY33/R) Cleric playing flute (30x23cm-12x9in) s.
£1600 $3152   (4-Oct-90 CSK210/R) A good joke (42x29cm-17x11in) s.d.'76 panel
£2105 $4000   (27-Feb-91 SY.NY277/R) At fish pond (37x46cm-15x18in) s.
£2990 $4874   (12-Jun-91 GM.B4103) Le Fou-Rire (40x29cm-16x11in) s. wood (B.FR 180000)

HERMANN, Ludwig (1812-1881) German
£1400	$2408	(15-May-91 BT233/R) Abbeville (25x36cm-10x14in) s.i.d.1868 stretcher
£1500	$2580	(15-May-91 BT234/R) Riverside cottages (28x38cm-11x15in) s.
£4000	$7160	(14-Mar-91 B132/R) A town on the Rhine (67x96cm-26x38in) s.d.1880
£4124	$7835	(2-Mar-91 KRA.D329/R) River landscape with town (70x96cm-28x38in) s. (DM 12000)
£4200	$8190	(18-Oct-90 SC3083/R) A Dutch waterfront (66x95cm-26x37in) s.d.1870
£4211	$8000	(9-Jan-91 D.NY37) Skaters on frozen river before town wall (53x89cm-21x35in) s.d.1863

HERMANN, Roger (20th C) American
£893	$1500	(24-Apr-91 B.SF4560/R) Small paint cans (81x76cm-32x30in) s.d.87 verso

HERMANNS, Heinrich (1862-1942) German
£1074	$2094	(13-Oct-90 KRA.D227/R) St Werner Kapelle in Oberwesel (55x40cm-22x16in) s.d.33 i.verso (DM 3200)
£1675	$3250	(24-Aug-90 RB.HY120/R) Goldener Weiher (102x74cm-40x29in) s.
£2062	$4041	(16-Feb-91 GF.H17/R) Square with obelisk before country estate (41x60cm-16x24in) (DM 6000)

HERMANSEN, O A (1849-1897) Danish
£2741	$5153	(10-Aug-90 RAS.V476/R) Two hares in field of flowers with butterflies and insects (62x52cm-24x20in) s.d.1878 (D.KR 31000)
£3260	$5444	(6-Jun-91 RAS.K71/R) Wood anemones and cowslip beneath beechtree (67x82cm-26x32in) s.d.1875 (D.KR 37000)

HERMANSEN, Olaf August (1849-1897) Danish
£10256	$20000	(23-Oct-90 SY.NY130/R) A still life with vase, basket and parrot (122x117cm-48x46in) s.d.1874

HERMEL, Michel (1934-) French
£1122	$2211	(17-Nov-90 HC.P46) Mimi pinson (46x55cm-18x22in) s. (F.FR 11000)
£1122	$2211	(17-Nov-90 HC.P41) Quai aux fleurs sous la neige (46x55cm-18x22in) s. (F.FR 11000)

HERMELIN, Olof (1820-1913) Swedish
£558	$998	(9-Apr-91 GO.G55) Wooded landscape with figure by house (33x24cm-13x9in) s. (S.KR 6000)
£616	$1034	(24-Apr-91 BA.S85/R) Lake landscape (16x33cm-6x13in) init. (S.KR 6500)
£632	$1200	(15-Sep-90 S.W2131/R) Figures on village street (30x51cm-12x20in) s. panel
£1420	$2386	(24-Apr-91 BA.S83/R) Landscape with tree (44x27cm-17x11in) s.d.1908 (S.KR 15000)
£1654	$3243	(6-Nov-90 BA.S102/R) Autumn landscape with traveller (24x43cm-9x17in) s. panel (S.KR 18000)
£1765	$3459	(10-Nov-90 FAL.M136/R) Coastal landscape boats and beach hut (25x46cm-10x18in) s. (S.KR 19200)
£1799	$3023	(27-Apr-91 SO.S361/R) Officer's wife and children in Karlberg's Palace avenue (93x60cm-37x24in) s.d.1906 (S.KR 19000)
£1831	$3113	(28-May-91 AB.S4629/R) Sunny summer landscape with lake (47x63cm-19x25in) s.d.95 (S.KR 19500)
£1989	$3341	(24-Apr-91 BA.S84/R) Traveller at sunset, Uppsala fields (52x81cm-20x32in) s.d.1901 copper (S.KR 21000)
£2281	$4494	(30-Oct-90 BU.S38/R) Summer landscape with red cottages (54x79cm-21x31in) s.d.1908 (S.KR 25000)
£2377	$4658	(20-Nov-90 GO.G86/R) View from Montmartre, Paris (50x65cm-20x26in) s.d.1875 (S.KR 26000)
£2390	$4684	(6-Nov-90 BA.S101/R) Early spring landscape (53x80cm-21x31in) s.d.1913 (S.KR 26000)
£2834	$5554	(20-Nov-90 GO.G87/R) View towards Bohus Castle (66x93cm-26x37in) s.d.1886 (S.KR 31000)
£3211	$6326	(13-Nov-90 AB.S383/R) Mountainous landscape with Laplander's hut (54x80cm-21x31in) s. (S.KR 31000)
£3217	$6305	(6-Nov-90 BA.S99/R) Woman reading by pond with water lilies (39x65cm-15x26in) s.d.1878 (S.KR 35000)
£3401	$6665	(6-Nov-90 BA.S96 a/R) Harvesting (29x56cm-11x22in) s.d.77 (S.KR 37000)
£4136	$8107	(6-Nov-90 BA.S100/R) Tann waterfall in Jamtland (102x78cm-40x31in) s.d.1883 (S.KR 45000)
£5055	$9908	(6-Nov-90 BA.S97/R) Washerwomen on frozen river (31x42cm-12x17in) s.d.1875 (S.KR 55000)
£5303	$8909	(24-Apr-91 BA.S82/R) Spring landscape with bay (60x92cm-24x36in) s.d.1889 (S.KR 56000)
£5492	$9227	(24-Apr-91 BA.S81/R) Riders on horseback in birchwood (55x80cm-22x31in) s. (S.KR 58000)

HERMES, Erich (1881-?) Swiss
£677	$1321	(24-Oct-90 GD.B458/R) Dancing female nudes (55x46cm-22x18in) s. (S.FR 1700)

HERN, Charles E (1848-1894) Australian/British
£650	*$1086*	*(6-Jun-91 B136/R) Christchurch, Bristol (31x11cm-12x4in) s. W/C*
£675	*$1296*	*(14-Aug-90 SY.ME92) Long Bay, Middle Harbour, New South Wales (14x30cm-6x12in) s.d.1883 i. label verso W/C (A.D 1600)*

HERNANDEZ MOMPO, Manuel (1927-) Spanish
£5978	$11478	(19-Dec-90 ANS.M88/R) Hora es (23x18cm-9x7in) s.d.1955 (S.P 1100000)

HERNANDEZ MOMPO, Manuel (1927-) Spanish-cont.
£7609 $14609   (19-Dec-90 ANS.M89/R) Composicion (13x75cm-5x30in) s.d.1988
     (S.P 1400000)
£8741 $16870   (13-Dec-90 EP.M27/R) El Saludo (65x54cm-26x21in) s.d.59 (S.P 1600000)
£10870 $20870   (19-Dec-90 ANS.M87/R) Torero (39x27cm-15x11in) s.d.1955 (S.P 2000000)
£12019 $23196   (13-Dec-90 EP.M28/R) Gardener with leaves (81x65cm-32x26in) s.d.1959
     (S.P 2200000)
£16650 $32300   (3-Dec-90 CH.R52/R) Calles de un pueblo en fiesta (81x130cm-32x51in)
     s.d.1969 s.i.d.verso (I.L 36000000)
£1635   *$2682*   *(18-Jun-91 EP.M14/R) Untitled (25x18cm-10x7in) s.d.62 W/C gouache pastel*
     (S.P 300000)
£2717   *$4810*   *(3-Apr-91 ANS.M111/R) Sin titulo (27x21cm-11x8in) s.d.1967 mixed media*
     (S.P 500000)

HERNANDEZ MONJO, Francesc (20th C) Spanish
£1045 $1870   (13-Mar-91 FER.M130/R) Barco pesquero frente a la costa (17x32cm-7x13in)
     s. panel (S.P 190000)
£1223 $2348   (18-Dec-90 DUR.M24) Acantilado (32x18cm-13x7in) panel (S.P 225000)
£2321 $4014   (8-May-91 FER.M140/R) Pescadores (45x55cm-18x22in) s. (S.P 425000)
£2322 $4481   (11-Dec-90 FER.M228/R) Barcas de pescadores (45x29cm-18x11in) s.
     (S.P 425000)
£462   *$818*   *(3-Apr-91 ANS.M198/R) Marina (24x34cm-9x13in) s. W/C (S.P 85000)*

HERNANDEZ, Agustin (1931-) Spanish
£1090 $1886   (21-May-91 DUR.M12/R) Hospital de Tavera, Toledo (63x82cm-25x32in)
     (S.P 200000)
£1362 $2342   (16-May-91 ANS.M103/R) Rincon rural (81x100cm-32x39in) s. (S.P 250000)

HERNANDEZ, Daniel (1856-1932) Peruvian
£3000 $5760   (28-Nov-90 S147/R) Fair game (46x38cm-18x15in) s. panel
£4624 $8000   (23-May-91 CH.NY148/R) Lady with fan (41x33cm-16x13in) s.
£4737 $9000   (28-Feb-91 CH.NY107/R) The coquette (55x38cm-22x15in) s.
£800   *$1312*   *(19-Jun-91 S392/R) Young goatherd (56x39cm-22x15in) s.d.1880 W/C*

HERNANDEZ, J (20th C) Mexican
£976 $1600   (23-Jun-91 H.C1008) Surreal composition (155x114cm-61x45in) s.d.76

HERNANDEZ, Jose (20th C) Spanish
£489   *$963*   *(15-Nov-90 ANS.M72/R) Copa V (10x7cm-4x3in) plumilla dr (S.P 90000)*
£516   *$1016*   *(15-Nov-90 ANS.M73/R) Pluma al viento (10x7cm-4x3in) s.d.1987 plumilla*
     dr (S.P 95000)

HERNANDEZ, Vicco (fl.1880-1920) Spanish
£1827 $3563   (25-Oct-90 D.V131/R) Spanish garden landscape (38x27cm-15x11in) s.
     (A.S 38000)

HEROLD, Georg (20th C) American?
£2367   *$4000*   *(1-May-91 SY.NY160/R) Untitled (46x60cm-18x24in) init.d.87 verso buttons*
     thread primed canvas

HEROLD, Jacques (1910-1987) Rumanian
£1346 $2221   (10-Jul-91 FB.P58) Blanc-seing (27x21cm-11x8in) s. i.d.53 verso
     hardboard (F.FR 13500)
£2398 $4724   (15-Nov-90 I.N145/R) Face cachee (35x24cm-14x9in) s. (F.FR 23500)
£3160 $6099   (16-Dec-90 P.V73/R) Souvenirs d'enfance (73x92cm-29x36in) s.d.1962 i.
     stretcher (F.FR 31000)
£9184 $18092   (16-Nov-90 FB.P4/R) Portrait de Van Gogh (73x50cm-29x20in) s.
     (F.FR 90000)
£19153 $37349   (27-Oct-90 BG.P6/R) Quelquefois (130x195cm-51x77in) s. (F.FR 190000)
£866   *$1705*   *(29-Oct-90 LC.P43) Sans titre (35x27cm-14x11in) s.d.70 gouache*
     (F.FR 8500)
£1578   *$3109*   *(29-Oct-90 LC.P42/R) Sans titre (44x34cm-17x13in) s.d.69 gouache*
     (F.FR 15500)

HERON, Patrick (1920-?) British
£2600 $5070   (10-Oct-90 S201/R) Vermilion and lemon in orange (30x40cm-12x16in)
     s.i.d.62
£2800 $5460   (10-Oct-90 S177/R) The blue tablecloth (25x36cm-10x14in) s.d.47 panel
£3600 $6660   (8-Mar-91 C134/R) Figure on the road (40x50cm-16x20in) s.d.48
£12500 $23125   (5-Mar-91 PH55/R) White painting - pale squares (97x122cm-38x48in)
     s.d.1961
£30000 $48900   (1-Jul-91 S40/R) Abstract (91x71cm-36x28in) s.d.August 52
£37000 $68450   (8-Mar-91 C169/R) Black, green and yellow (152x183cm-60x72in) d.1960
£680   *$1136*   *(7-Jun-91 C360 b/R) Lemon yellow and orange (18x23cm-7x9in) gouache*
£950   *$1587*   *(7-Jun-91 C360 a/R) Cobalt blue and scarlet red (30x24cm-12x9in) gouache*
£1000   *$1960*   *(6-Nov-91 PH194/R) Studio international cover, version II*
     (30x24cm-12x9in) s.i.d.1967verso gouache

HEROULT, Antoine Desire (1802-1853) French
£864   *$1728*   *(4-Feb-91 PLF.P47/R) Cour de ferme animee (35x48cm-14x19in) s. W/C*
     gouache (F.FR 8500)
£1118   *$2236*   *(4-Feb-91 PLF.P45) L'arrive au bal du chateau (32x20cm-13x8in) s. W/C*
     gouache (F.FR 11000)
£1270   *$2541*   *(4-Feb-91 PLF.P48/R) Arrivee d'une caleche devant la maison*
     (34x48cm-13x19in) s. W/C gouache (F.FR 12500)

HEROULT, Antoine Desire (1802-1853) French-cont.
£1524 $3049   (4-Feb-91 PLF.P49/R) Vue du port d'Anvers (35x48cm-14x19in) s. W/C
                       gouache (F.FR 15000)

HERP, Willem van (17/18th C) Flemish
£13000 $25350   (26-Oct-90 C93/R) Moses trampling on Pharoah's crown (81x116cm-32x46in)
£20000 $32600   (2-Jul-91 PH50/R) Peasants merrymaking at table before open fireplace of
                       Inn (72x99cm-28x39in) panel

HERP, Willem van (elder) (1614-1677) Flemish
£8200 $13858   (19-Apr-91 C88/R) A peasant woman peeling potatoes with two children in
                       the kitchen (58x78cm-23x31in) canvas laid down on masonite
£19000 $36670   (13-Dec-90 B100/R) Elegant company merrymaking in interior with servants
                       in attendance (79x117cm-31x46in)

HERP, Willem van (elder-after) (1614-1677) Flemish
£963 $1608   (6-Jun-91 D.V368/R) Satyr with peasant family (73x103cm-29x41in)
                       (A.S 20000)

HERP, Willem van (elder-circle) (1614-1677) Flemish
£5294 $9000   (31-May-91 CH.NY144/R) St Michael triumphing over evil (68x89cm-27x35in)
                       copper

HERP, Willem van (style) (17/18th C) Flemish
£3500 $6825   (26-Oct-90 C80/R) Jacob stealing Esau's birthright (68x85cm-27x33in)
                       copper laid down on panel
£5387 $10612   (14-Nov-90 D.V190/R) Party merrymaking (62x78cm-24x31in) (A.S 110000)
£6269 $12350   (14-Nov-90 SY.AM57/R) Adoration of the shepherds (59x56cm-23x22in)
                       copper (D.FL 20500)

HERPFER, Carl (1836-1897) German
£2890 $5000   (21-May-91 CE.NY145/R) Letter (32x23cm-13x9in) s. panel
£9744 $19000   (24-Oct-90 CH.NY210/R) Wedding party in the Garden of Fontainebleau
                       (98x136cm-39x54in) s.i.

HERR, Michael (1591-1661) German
£671 $1309   (12-Oct-90 AW.H990/R) The rape of the Sabine women (12x18cm-5x7in)
                       mono.d.1626 indian ink pen wash (DM 2000)

HERRAN, Saturnino (1887-1918) Mexican
£6633 $13000   (19-Nov-90 SY.NY122/R) Tres mujeres (40x49cm-16x19in)

HERRER, Cesar de (1868-1919) Spanish
£1329 $2379   (11-Apr-91 D.V282/R) Venice (47x36cm-19x14in) s. (A.S 28000)

HERRERA BARNUEVO, Sebastian de (circle) (1619-1671) Spanish
£12000 $23160   (12-Dec-90 S31/R) Portrait of King Carlos II when a child
                       (133x98cm-52x39in)

HERRERA, Francisco (attrib) (1576-1656) Spanish
£15493 $26338   (28-May-91 AB.S4767/R) Burlesque scene with singers led by cat
                       (73x99cm-29x39in) indist.s. (S.KR 165000)

HERRFELDT, Marcel Rene von (1890-1965) French
£738 $1440   (10-Oct-90 ZEL.L1530/R) Dancing gypsy with tambourine and bear breasts
                       (80x60cm-31x24in) s. (DM 2200)
£1275 $2487   (12-Oct-90 AW.H2531/R) Female nude with tambourin (100x80cm-39x31in) s.
                       (DM 3800)

HERRICK, William Salter (19th C) British
£2400 $3912   (2-Jul-91 SWS400/R) Portrait of Mrs. and Miss Hill of Almington Hall,
                       Shropshire, and dogs (126x101cm-50x40in)

HERRIMAN, George (1880-1944) American
£3235 $5500   (1-Jun-91 IH.NY114/R) Ahoy Mousie, comic strip (56x36cm-22x14in) pen ink

HERRING (after) (19th C) British
£1631 $3148   (16-Dec-90 M.V140/R) La chasse a courre (F.FR 16000)

HERRING, Benjamin (snr) (1806-1830) British
£2800 $5516   (14-Nov-90 S77/R) Chestnut hunter with groom in landscape
                       (32x44cm-13x17in) s.
£5500 $10835   (14-Nov-90 S78/R) Captain Williamson's chestnut racehorse with jockey up
                       and bay hunter (54x74cm-21x29in) s.d.1829

HERRING, F (?) ?
£579 $1141   (13-Nov-90 J.M680) Horses at the trough (49x58cm-19x23in) s.d.1870
                       (A.D 1500)

HERRING, J F (19/20th C) British
£1600 $2704   (19-Apr-91 K546/R) Study of hunter and two dogs by stable, landscape
                       beyond (58x71cm-23x28in) s.i.d.

HERRING, J F (jnr) (1815-1907) British
£1250 $2400   (30-Nov-90 DA666/R) Horses ducks and chickens at watering place
                       (36x25cm-14x10in) s.

HERRING, John Frederick (attrib) (19/20th C) British
£1500 $2550   (28-May-91 PHG182) Riding to hounds (14x19cm-6x7in) s. panel

HERRING, John Frederick (circle) (19/20th C) British
£1200 $1968   (20-Jun-91 B29/R) Horse and hare in courtyard (28x38cm-11x15in) l.verso

HERRING, John Frederick (jnr) (1815-1907) British
£1500 $2535   (30-Apr-91 PH18/R) Portrait of bay racehorse, with jockey up, landscape beyond (23x30cm-9x12in) s.i.d.1835
£1550 $2589   (22-Jul-91 SWS1011/R) Matilda, a bay racehorse with jockey up (22x30cm-9x12in) i.
£1550 $2589   (22-Jul-91 SWS1010/R) Elis, a chesnut racehorse with jockey up (22x30cm-9x12in) i.
£1600 $2672   (22-Jul-91 SWS1013) The colonel, a chesnut racehorse with jockey up (22x30cm-9x12in) i.
£1600 $2672   (22-Jul-91 SWS1012) Rowton, a chesnut racehorse with jockey up (22x30cm-9x12in) i.
£2000 $3300   (12-Jul-91 C112/R) Cock and hen in farmyard (15x20cm-6x8in) s. panel
£2500 $4750   (1-Mar-91 C65/R) Bay horse, chickens and ducks in yard (20cm-8ins circular) s. board
£2600 $4914   (27-Sep-90 CSK59/R) Mallard, ducks and ducklings by a pool (15x19cm-6x7in) s. panel
£2800 $4620   (10-Jul-91 S146/R) Cart with team of horses in winter landscape (44x59cm-17x23in) s.
£2844 $4750   (7-Jun-91 SY.NY47/R) Lord Orford's grey colt Clearwell by Jerry and Colonel Peel's by filly Rosalie (23x30cm-9x12in) s.i.d.1835
£3600 $7020   (26-Oct-90 C239/R) A farmyard scene (70x91cm-28x36in) s.
£3600 $7020   (15-Jan-91 SWS150/R) Going to the start. Out shooting. Hunting (13cm-5ins circular) canvas on board set of three
£3600 $7056   (8-Nov-90 PHI167/R) Horses and chickens beside thatched farm buildings (24x29cm-9x11in) s. board
£4211 $8000   (14-Sep-90 DM.D2375/R) Courting couple with white horse (81x66cm-32x26in)
£4600 $9016   (8-Nov-90 TL80/R) Farmyard companions (19x19cm-7x7in) board
£5461 $10321   (25-Sep-91 FN.S2205/R) 3 horses outside farmhouses in wooded landscape (59x84cm-23x33in) s. (DM 16000)
£6500 $11635   (12-Apr-91 C100/R) Shooting. Hunting. Racing (12cm-5ins circular) canvas on millboard three
£8982 $15000   (7-Jun-91 SY.NY79/R) The water pump (46cm-18ins circular) s. round
£10000 $19700   (16-Nov-90 C83/R) Farmyard with horses, goats, chickens, cows and byre beyond (47x78cm-19x31in) s.
£10778 $18000   (7-Jun-91 SY.NY75/R) A horse, pigs, ducks and cows in a farmyard (36x41cm-14x16in) s.
£11377 $19000   (7-Jun-91 SY.NY78/R) The wheelbarrow (46cm-18ins circular) s.d.1854 round
£13772 $23000   (7-Jun-91 SY.NY80/R) The farmyard (31x46cm-12x18in) s.
£14689 $26000   (22-Mar-91 S.W2798/R) Fenland farm (61x107cm-24x42in) s.
£48000 $79200   (12-Jul-91 C91/R) Mares Queen of Trumps, Beeswing and Alice Hawthorn, with foals, river landscape (66x107cm-26x42in) s.i.d.1846 l.verso

HERRING, John Frederick (jnr) and CAFFYN, Walter Wallor (19th C) British
£9100 $17199   (26-Sep-90 RB643/R) River scene with reed cutters and horses watering s.d.1879

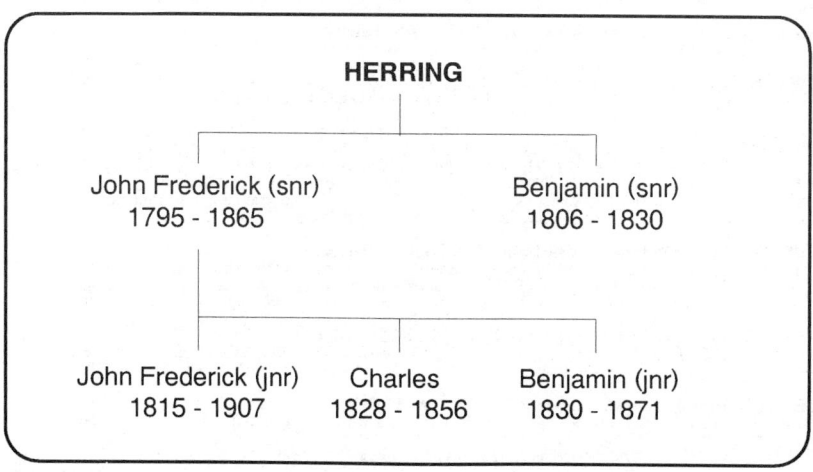

HERRING

John Frederick (snr)
1795 - 1865

Benjamin (snr)
1806 - 1830

John Frederick (jnr)
1815 - 1907

Charles
1828 - 1856

Benjamin (jnr)
1830 - 1871

HERRING, John Frederick (jnr-after) (1815-1907) British

| £1100 | $2200 | (7-Feb-91 CSK190/R) Horses, ducks, pigs and chickens in farmyard (61x91cm-24x36in) with sig. |
| £1100 | $2200 | (7-Feb-91 CSK192/R) Confidence, drawing gig driven by groom (43x63cm-17x25in) panel |

HERRING, John Frederick (jnr-circle) (1815-1907) British

| £1400 | $2282 | (4-Jul-91 D92/R) Figures and shire horses beside haystack (33x46cm-13x18in) bears sig.d.1842 panel |

HERRING, John Frederick (snr) (1795-1865) British

£1858	$3530	(14-Sep-90 SA.A1206/R) Stable horses at the rack (31x31cm-12x12in) s. panel (DM 5500)
£3468	$6000	(23-May-91 CH.NY203/R) The red fox (25x30cm-10x12in) s.d.1849 panel
£4000	$7800	(15-Jan-91 C137/R) Two lurchers (25x34cm-10x13in) init.d.1851 board
£4200	$6846	(14-Jun-91 T30/R) Horses in stable (20x30cm-8x12in) s. board
£4592	$9000	(7-Nov-90 B.SF1200/R) Bay hunter in stable (56x76cm-22x30in) s.d.1835
£5000	$9850	(16-Nov-90 C113/R) Industry, brown racehorse in stable (20x25cm-8x10in) s.i.d.1838 panel
£5090	$8500	(7-Jun-91 SY.NY71/R) Interior of a highland cottage (56x76cm-22x30in) s.d.1850
£5389	$9000	(7-Jun-91 SY.NY87/R) Beeswing in a stall (38x51cm-15x20in) s.i.
£5500	$10835	(16-Nov-90 C114/R) Bay racehorse in loosebox, traditionally identified as Miss Letty (20x25cm-8x10in) s.d.1834 panel
£6000	$11820	(16-Nov-90 C82/R) Three harnessed carthorses by well in farmyard with poultry (38x51cm-15x20in) s.d.1851
£6154	$12000	(24-Oct-90 CH.NY316/R) Mallard ducks and ducklings on river bank (28x39cm-11x15in) s.d.1863
£6200	$12090	(16-Oct-90 WW320/R) Portrait of the thoroughbred Attila in a stable interior (56x76cm-22x30in) s.i.d.1842
£6587	$11000	(7-Jun-91 SY.NY61/R) A study for steeple chase cracks (44x32cm-17x13in) init.i.d.1846
£8982	$15000	(7-Jun-91 SY.NY157/R) Two harnessed cart horses (72x91cm-28x36in) s.d.1853
£9000	$14850	(10-Jul-91 S65/R) Bay Middleton in stable (34x43cm-13x17in) s.d.1836 panel
£10204	$20000	(7-Nov-90 B.SF1222/R) Grey horse in stable (56x76cm-22x30in) s.d.1830
£11377	$19000	(7-Jun-91 SY.NY111/R) The squire's pets (36x51cm-14x20in) init.d.1852
£12575	$21000	(7-Jun-91 SY.NY110/R) Three white rabbits (27x34cm-11x13in) init.d.1851 panel
£13500	$22275	(10-Jul-91 S64/R) Pigs with dog in stable yard (34x34cm-13x13in) s.d.1847
£14500	$28565	(14-Nov-90 S95/R) Drake, ducks and ducklings on riverbank (40x35cm-16x14in) s.d.1850 panel
£16000	$28640	(12-Apr-91 C95/R) Earl of Chesterfield's filly Industry, with W. Scott up, in landscape (34x44cm-13x17in) s.d.1838
£16766	$28000	(7-Jun-91 SY.NY83/R) A chestnut race horse in a stall (56x76cm-22x30in) s.
£17964	$30000	(7-Jun-91 SY.NY44/R) Amato, winner of the 1838 Derby, with J. Chapple up (33x43cm-13x17in) s.i.
£19162	$32000	(7-Jun-91 SY.NY76/R) Lord Wilton's chestnut colt Gladiator in a loose box (35x46cm-14x18in) s.i.d.1844 panel
£65868	$110000	(7-Jun-91 SY.NY62/R) Squire Osbaldeston and his famous trotting horse Ratler (72x92cm-28x36in) s.i.d.1838
£119760	$200000	(7-Jun-91 SY.NY73/R) The farmyard (122x198cm-48x78in) init.

HERRING, John Frederick (snr-after) (1795-1865) British

| £1700 | $3349 | (31-Oct-90 S387/R) Flying Dutchman with Lord Eglinton and jockey Mr Marlow on racecourse (51x80cm-20x31in) |
| £1900 | $3743 | (31-Oct-90 S379/R) Charles Marlow on the Flying Dutchman beating Nat Flatman on Voltigeur (89x133cm-35x52in) d.1851 |

HERRING, John Frederick (snr-attrib) (1795-1865) British

£2035	$3500	(15-May-91 D.NY44) Horses and chickens in farmyard with young stable hand (71x91cm-28x36in) bears sig.d.1948 i.verso
£3743	$6250	(7-Jun-91 SY.NY156/R) A farmyard scene (70x91cm-28x36in)
£4790	$8000	(7-Jun-91 SY.NY152/R) Mr S Batson's Plenipotentiaray with Patrick Connolly up (56x76cm-22x30in) s.d.1835

HERRING, John Frederick (snr-circle) (1795-1865) British

| £2036 | $3400 | (23-Jan-91 D.NY74) Inheritress (64x76cm-25x30in) bears sig. d.1848 |
| £2200 | $3630 | (10-Jul-91 S137/R) Blacklock with jockey up in landscape (34x44cm-13x17in) panel |

HERRING, John Frederick (snr-school) (1795-1865) British

| £2096 | $3500 | (7-Jun-91 SY.NY127/R) Attila with W.Scott up (63x77cm-25x30in) bears sig.i.d.1842 |

HERRING, John Frederick (snr-style) (1795-1865) British

| £2156 | $3600 | (7-Jun-91 SY.NY49/R) D. Syntax with jockey up (41x51cm-16x20in) bears sig. |
| £2200 | $3630 | (9-Jul-91 PH62) Feeding time (71x112cm-28x44in) |

HERRLEIN, Johann Andreas (1720-1796) German

| £4000 | $6520 | (3-Jul-91 S144/R) Still life of meat and vegetables (53x67cm-21x26in) |

HERRLEIN, Johann Andreas (1720-1796) German-cont.
£15734 $30367   (12-Dec-90 N.M376/R) St Petrus awaking figure to life. St Paul healing the Lame (27x36cm-11x14in) one mono.indis.d.1782 panel pair (DM 45000)

HERRMANN, Carl Gustav (1857-?) German
£1644 $2942   (13-Mar-91 N.M530) Three peasant women conversing in village street, Klausen, South Tyrol (45x33cm-18x13in) s. i.stretcher (DM 4800)

HERRMANN, Caspar (1855-1955) Austrian
£612 $1200   (6-Nov-90 GF.L2616/R) Still life of flowers (97x72cm-38x28in) s. (S.FR 1500)

HERRMANN, Frank S (1866-1942) American
£421 $800   (28-Feb-91 MFA.C79/R) Busy street scene (48x61cm-19x24in) s. gouache

HERRMANN, Franz (1864-?) German
£777 $1515   (26-Oct-90 BM.B798/R) Horse standing in landscape (71x97cm-28x38in) s. (DM 2300)

HERRMANN, Hans (1858-1942) German
£4242 $8358   (30-Oct-90 CH.AM212 a/R) View of flower market on Singel, Amsterdam, Minttower beyond (80x60cm-31x24in) s. (D.FL 14000)

HERRMANN-LEON, Charles (1838-1908) French
£597 $1039   (25-Mar-91 QWA.P165/R) Chien terrier (45x37cm-18x15in) mono.d.1861 (F.FR 6000)
£597 $1039   (25-Mar-91 QWA.P166) Love epagneul breton (46x38cm-18x15in) s.d.1861 (F.FR 6000)
£650 $1255   (12-Dec-90 SWS2117/R) Two hounds on hill (44x60cm-17x24in) s.
£4281 $8263   (14-Dec-90 ARC.P187/R) Portrait de chiens (62x50cm-24x20in) s. (F.FR 42000)

HERRMANSTORFER, Josef (1817-1901) German
£509 $998   (25-Jan-91 REM.W4) Lake landscape (50x60cm-20x24in) s. (P.Z 9500000)

HERSCHEL, Otto (1871-?) German
£536 $1061   (1-Feb-91 DE.B5) Romantic ruins (80x114cm-31x45in) s. after Bocklin (P.Z 10000000)

HERSCHEND, Oscar (1853-1891) Danish
£704 $1183   (22-Apr-91 BU.K21/R) Coastal landscape with beached boat (41x80cm-16x31in) s.d.89 (D.KR 8000)
£931 $1517   (13-Jun-91 RAS.V546/R) Fishermen with boat on road by cliffs (43x83cm-17x33in) s.d.82 (D.KR 10500)
£1233 $2060   (6-Jun-91 RAS.K10/R) Rescuing shipwreck on the West coast (86x157cm-34x62in) init.d.88 (D.KR 14000)

HERSENT, Louise Marie Jeanne (attrib) (1784-1862) French
£2211 $3913   (20-Mar-91 KM.K1260) Portrait of young woman (64x54cm-25x21in) s. (DM 6500)

HERTEL, Albert (1843-1912) German
£514 $837   (12-Jun-91 N.M462) Olevano landscape (38x52cm-15x20in) mono.d.1873 i.verso board (DM 1500)
£950 $1701   (12-Mar-91 PH30) Still life of lute, casket and books on table covering (109x219cm-43x86in) s.d.1880

HERTER, Albert (1871-?) American
£2722 $4600   (20-Apr-91 WOL.C141/R) Romantic evening (61x51cm-24x20in) s.d.1906 panel

HERTERICH, Johann Caspar (1843-1905) German
£8446 $14358   (27-May-91 L.K283 a/R) Two young women showing young cleric love letter found in waste basket (52x68cm-20x27in) s. (DM 25000)

HERTEVIG, Lars (1830-1902) Norwegian
£2613 $5096   (15-Oct-90 B.O35/R) Wood (7x12cm-3x5in) panel (N.KR 30000)

HERTH, Francis (1943-) Belgian
£405 $782   (13-Dec-90 CH.BR70/R) Composition (47x62cm-19x24in) s.d.1968 pen wash (B.FR 24000)
£928 $1792   (13-Dec-90 CH.BR102) Composition (43x54cm-17x21in) s.d.67 num.11 ink wash (B.FR 55000)

HERTZ (?) ?
£804 $1439   (17-Mar-91 L.C31/R) L'Institut et le Pont des Arts (36x53cm-14x21in) s. (F.FR 8000)

HERTZ, Mogens (1909-1990) Danish
£546 $939   (15-May-91 RAS.K129/R) Landscape with farm (54x81cm-21x32in) s. (D.KR 6200)
£581 $1140   (13-Feb-91 KH.K71) Street scene with figures (54x81cm-21x32in) s.d.57 (D.KR 6500)
£623 $1171   (19-Sep-90 KH.K161) Harvesters, Bornholm (68x98cm-27x39in) s.d.44 (D.KR 7000)

HERTZ, Mogens (1909-1990) Danish-cont.
£1646 $3094   (19-Sep-90 KH.K160) View of red rooves, Gudhjem (85x116cm-33x46in)
             s.d.53 (D.KR 18500)

HERTZBERG, Axel Gustaf (1832-1878) Swedish
£673 $1165   (6-May-91 ZEL.L1737/R) Interior with young woman seated by window
             holding musical instrument (49x38cm-19x15in) s.d.1876 (DM 2000)

HERTZER, Else (1884-?) German
£507 $861   (31-May-91 GB.B6370) Still life of fruit (42x52cm-17x20in) s.d.1948
             (DM 1500)

HERVE, Jules R (1887-1981) French
£958 $1867   (26-Oct-90 PPB.P97 b) Le pecheur (22x27cm-9x11in) s. (F.FR 9500)
£1109 $2162   (26-Oct-90 APT.P117) Chasseur et ses chiens (27x22cm-11x9in) s.
             (F.FR 11000)
£1118 $2236   (6-Feb-91 FB.P184/R) Paris, le bassin des Tuileries (23x27cm-9x11in) s.
             (F.FR 11000)
£1166 $1900   (12-Jun-91 SY.NY47/R) In Luxembourg Gardens (27x22cm-11x9in) s.
£1257 $2098   (4-Jun-91 FB.M69/R) The club meeting (37x46cm-15x18in) s. board
             (C.D 2400)
£1260 $2457   (26-Oct-90 PPB.P97 a) Joueurs de Petanque (22x27cm-9x11in) s.
             (F.FR 12500)
£1269 $2500   (13-Nov-90 CE.NY68/R) Enfants dans le parc (24x27cm-9x11in) s. s.verso
£1320 $2600   (13-Nov-90 CE.NY65/R) Danseuses sur l' escalier (26x22cm-10x9in) s.
             canvas on masonite
£1394 $2412   (24-May-91 FB.P71/R) Vue de Paris (27x22cm-11x9in) s. board (F.FR 14000)
£1400 $2730   (15-Oct-90 PH57/R) La sortie du cafe (39x30cm-15x12in) s. canvasboard
£1434 $2811   (11-Nov-90 ZZ.F58/R) Le jardin des Tuileries (23x27cm-9x11in) s.
             (F.FR 14000)
£1487 $2900   (10-Oct-90 SY.NY106/R) Arguing the case (23x28cm-9x11in) s.i.verso
£1487 $2900   (10-Oct-90 SY.NY80/R) In the park, Paris (23x28cm-9x11in) s.i.verso
£1506 $2786   (4-Mar-91 ARC.P136) Les Champs Elysees (22x27cm-9x11in) s. (F.FR 15000)
£1534 $2500   (12-Jun-91 SY.NY46/R) Young boys fishing along Seine (42x34cm-17x13in)
             s.
£1538 $3000   (10-Oct-90 SY.NY89/R) Art vendor, Paris (28x23cm-11x9in) s.
£1569 $3075   (19-Nov-90 CSC.P71/R) Le bain de soleil (27x22cm-11x9in) s. panel
             (F.FR 15500)
£1734 $3000   (7-May-91 CE.NY59/R) Les enfants (33x41cm-13x16in) s.
£1927 $3815   (3-Feb-91 LT.P52/R) Pecheurs aupres du Pont Marie (46x39cm-18x15in) s.
             (F.FR 19000)
£1947 $3816   (11-Nov-90 ZZ.F67/R) Paris, jardin des Tuileries (22x27cm-9x11in) s.
             (F.FR 19000)
£2030 $4000   (13-Nov-90 CE.NY25/R) Les boquinistes (33x41cm-13x16in) s. s.verso
£2152 $4217   (11-Nov-90 ZZ.F60/R) Le mariage (22x27cm-9x11in) s. (F.FR 21000)
£2180 $3641   (9-Jun-91 DA.R4/R) La sortie de messe (38x46cm-15x18in) s. (F.FR 21800)
£2434 $4819   (3-Feb-91 LT.P43/R) Animation aupres de Notre-Dame (46x55cm-18x22in) s.
             (F.FR 24000)
£2490 $4308   (26-May-91 ZZ.F100/R) Les jeunes artistes (33x40cm-13x16in) s.
             (F.FR 25000)
£2551 $5000   (12-Feb-91 SY.NY232/R) Le salut (46x38cm-18x15in) s. s.verso
£2921 $5550   (2-Mar-91 KRA.D505/R) In the park (60x73cm-24x29in) s. s.verso
             (DM 8500)
£2944 $5800   (13-Nov-90 CE.NY30/R) Cavaliers en hiver (100x81cm-39x32in) s. s.verso
£3000 $5850   (15-Oct-90 PH58/R) Au bord du Fleuve (79x100cm-31x39in) s.
£3035 $5250   (22-May-91 D.NY82/R) Les Communiantes (56x46cm-22x18in) s. s.num.50429
             verso
£3072 $5038   (18-Jun-91 FN.S1604/R) Washerwomen in wooded river landscape
             (79x100cm-31x39in) s. s.verso (DM 9000)
£3077 $6000   (10-Oct-90 SY.NY81/R) Paris street (46x53cm-18x21in) s. canvas on board
£3200 $6304   (13-Nov-90 SWS397/R) Avenue Foch, Paris (52x63cm-20x25in) s.
£3590 $7000   (10-Oct-90 SY.NY104/R) Game of skittles (64x81cm-25x32in) s. canvas on
             board
£3757 $6500   (22-May-91 D.NY81) Enfant a le bassin du jardin des Tuileries
             (79x99cm-31x39in) s.
£3963 $7768   (6-Nov-90 SY.AM101/R) Children on square. Merry figures by inn
             (37x45cm-15x18in) pair (D.FL 13000)
£4569 $9000   (13-Nov-90 CE.NY245/R) La Madeleine en hiver (66x81cm-26x32in) s.
             s.verso
£4913 $8500   (22-May-91 D.NY84/R) Enfants cueillent les fleur (65x85cm-26x33in) s.
£4913 $8500   (7-May-91 CE.NY56/R) Enfants dans le parc (61x76cm-24x30in) s.
£6091 $12000   (15-Nov-90 D.NY104/R) Enfants et pigeons dans le jardin
             (80x99cm-31x39in) s.
£703   *$1300*   *(4-Mar-91 ARC.P52) Cafe la chope Normande (48x39cm-19x15in) s. gouache*
             (F.FR 7000)

HERVE-MATHE, Jules Alfred (1868-1953) French
£1490 $2891   (8-Dec-90 LT.P22/R) Ruelle animee a Annecy (55x38cm-22x15in) s.
             (F.FR 14500)
£2079 $3680   (7-Apr-91 LT.P64/R) Paris, L'Ile Saint-Louis (50x65cm-20x26in) s.
             (F.FR 21000)

HERVIAULT, Andre (1884-1969) French
£1020 $2010   (13-Nov-90 ARC.P148/R) Guerrier Kouka (92x55cm-36x22in) s.i.
             (F.FR 10000)

HERVIER, Adolphe (1818-1879) French
£1500 $2955   (4-Oct-90 CSK67) A treefeller in a wooded landscape (46x75cm-18x30in) s.

HERVIEU, August (fl.1819-1858) British
£850 $1615   (12-Sep-90 CSK133/R) *Children with toys on canopied terrace*
       (25x20cm-10x8in) s.d.1832 pencil W/C htd white

HERVIEU, Louise (1878-1954) French
£416 $736   (5-Apr-91 LGB.P108) *Plume au noeud noir (24x18cm-9x7in) s. chl.*
       (F.FR 4200)
£542 $1069   (6-Oct-90 GL.P52) *Nature morte au panier de cerises (32x50cm-13x20in) s.*
       chl. (F.FR 5500)
£641 $1263   (6-Oct-90 GL.P49) *La danseuse espagnole (51x41cm-20x16in) s. i.d. verso*
       chl. (F.FR 6500)
£888 $1749   (6-Oct-90 GL.P51) *Nature morte au bouquet d'anemones (40x50cm-16x20in)*
       s. chl. (F.FR 9000)
£968 $1869   (10-Dec-90 BL.P34) *Devant un tableau (55x41cm-22x16in) s. chl.*
       (F.FR 9500)
£996 $1962   (6-Oct-90 GL.P50) *Nature morte au bouquet de lilas (71x52cm-28x20in) s.*
       chl. (F.FR 10100)

HERVIS, Ed (?) ?
£1154 $2227   (13-Dec-90 N.M2728/R) Landscape with fortified castle (56x69cm-22x27in)
       s. (DM 3300)

HERVO, Vaino (1894-1974) Finnish
£576 $1111   (15-Dec-90 BU.H70) Rowing boat on beach (33x46cm-13x18in) s.d.39
       (F.M 4000)
£791 $1361   (14-May-91 HOR.H53) The river (61x46cm-24x18in) s.d.1956 (F.M 5500)
£935 $1609   (14-May-91 HOR.H52) The bay (60x81cm-24x32in) s.d.1957 (F.M 6500)

HERWIJNEN, Jan van (1889-1965) Dutch
£3604 $6234   (23-May-91 SY.AM20/R) Still life with chrysanthemums (101x89cm-40x35in)
       s. (D.FL 12000)

HERZ, G (19th C) ?
£1731 $2943   (28-May-91 F.R76/R) *Bambini (46x38cm-18x15in) s.indis.d.18.5*
       (I.L 3800000)

HERZMANOVSKY-ORLANDO, Fritz von (1877-1954) Austrian
£390 $722   (7-Mar-91 D.V124/R) *Two girls went into the garden (12x14cm-5x6in)*
       pencil (A.S 8000)
£488 $903   (7-Mar-91 D.V125/R) *Study for Maskenspiel der Genien (22x14cm-9x6in)*
       mono.i.d.1917verso pencil (A.S 10000)
£596 $1157   (6-Dec-90 D.V38/R) *Sphinx. Sketches (21x34cm-8x13in) pen indian ink*
       double-sided (A.S 12000)
£1068 $1751   (20-Jun-91 D.V37/R) *Sphinx (25x18cm-10x7in) pencil (A.S 22000)*
£1214 $1990   (20-Jun-91 D.V36/R) *Schaumgeborene (34x21cm-13x8in) mono.i.d.1918 pencil*
       col.pencil (A.S 25000)
£1675 $2897   (8-May-91 D.V40/R) *Deutung oder heizbarer Lindwurm (25x21cm-10x8in)*
       mono.d.30 pencil col.pencil (A.S 35000)

HERZOG, August (20th C) German
£606 $1018   (24-Apr-91 N.M538) Im Englischen Garten (46x61cm-18x24in) s.i.d.1917
       board (DM 1800)
£5763 $9393   (3-Jul-91 WE.MU28/R) View of Hopfensee and Hopfen near Fussen
       (50x69cm-20x27in) s.i.d.1921 board (DM 17000)

HERZOG, Hermann (1832-1932) American/German
£1221 $2100   (19-May-91 LIT.L107) Man in boat on lake (23x33cm-9x13in) s.
£1510 $2900   (17-Dec-90 SY.NY132/R) Looking down valley from Hundeck, Switzerland
       (28x38cm-11x15in) s. i.stretcher
£1808 $3200   (23-Mar-91 LAE.L46/R) Florida marshes (74x64cm-29x25in) s.
£1872 $3500   (1-Aug-91 B.P8/R) Near Stonington, coast of Maine (41x53cm-16x21in) s.
£2326 $4000   (15-May-91 SY.NY11/R) Fishing in rough coastal seas (46x71cm-18x28in) s.
£2398 $4700   (16-Feb-91 W.W38/R) Canal in Venice (51x41cm-20x16in) s.
£2443 $4641   (28-Feb-91 D.V21/R) Moonlit Amper landscape (13x26cm-5x10in) s. panel
       (A.S 50000)
£2663 $4500   (21-Apr-91 DU.E165/R) Southern swamp (64x53cm-25x21in) s.
£3590 $7000   (20-Oct-90 W.W165/R) Woodland scene (69x56cm-27x22in) s.
£6349 $12000   (26-Sep-90 SY.NY34/R) Landscape with carriage (44x69cm-17x27in) s.
£6936 $12000   (22-May-91 CH.NY175/R) Fishing on the Hudson River (32x52cm-13x20in) s.
£27933 $50000   (12-Apr-91 SY.NY33/R) Scene on Adams Brook, Pike County, Pennsylvania
       (103x84cm-41x33in) s.d.1882

HESS, Eugen (1824-1862) German
£7458 $12156   (3-Jul-91 WE.MU351/R) On the road (24x18cm-9x7in) s.d.1855 board
       (DM 22000)

HESS, Hieronymus (1799-1850) Swiss
£2302 $3982   (22-May-91 GS.B3221) *Als Demuth weint und Hochmuth lacht, da ward der*
       Schweizerbund gemacht (41x32cm-16x13in) s.d.1843 W/C (S.FR 5800)

HESSE, Bruno (1905-) Swiss
£797 $1554   (24-Oct-90 GD.B468/R) Landscape near Herzogenbuchsee (38x55cm-15x22in)
       mono.d.69 (S.FR 2000)

888

HESSE, Henri-Joseph (1781-1849) French

£492	$808	(19-Jun-91 LC.P43/R) Portrait d'une damme assise au chale (19x14cm-7x6in) s.i.d.1830 W/C oval (F.FR 4900)
£523	$857	(19-Jun-91 LC.P45/R) Portrait de Marie Therese Antoinette du Cluzel (19x14cm-7x6in) s.i.d.1830 W/C oval (F.FR 5200)
£553	$907	(19-Jun-91 LC.P44/R) Portrait de Marie Francoise du Cluzel (19x14cm-7x6in) s.i.d.1830 W/C oval (F.FR 5500)
£663	$1272	(27-Nov-90 APT.P176) Portrait d'homme (20x17cm-8x7in) pastel oval (F.FR 6500)
£714	$1170	(19-Jun-91 LC.P41/R) Portrait d'une dame assise en robe brune (19x14cm-7x6in) s.i.d.1830 W/C oval (F.FR 7100)
£804	$1319	(19-Jun-91 LC.P42/R) Portrait d'Esther de Cosse-Brissac, marquise d'Espinay Saint-Luc (19x14cm-7x6in) s.d.1830 W/C oval (F.FR 8000)
£1206	$1978	(19-Jun-91 LC.P40/R) Portrait de Marie-Antoinette Francoise Amelie du Cluzel (19x14cm-7x6in) s.d.1830 W/C oval (F.FR 12000)
£1518	$2489	(19-Jun-91 LC.P37/R) Portrait d'enfant Antoine de Cosse a l'age de deux ans (16x12cm-6x5in) s.d.1836 W/C (F.FR 15100)
£1960	$3214	(19-Jun-91 LC.P38/R) Portrait d'Anne-Marie Amelie du Cluzel (19x14cm-7x6in) s.d.1830 W/C oval (F.FR 19500)
£2010	$3296	(19-Jun-91 LC.P39/R) Portrait de Louis Frederic Ghislain, Comte de Merode (19x14cm-7x6in) s.d.1830 W/C oval (F.FR 20000)

HESSE, Hermann (1877-?) German

£1092	$2141	(24-Nov-90 N.M226) View of Montagnola (7x8cm-3x3in) d.1935 W/C (DM 3200)
£672	$1142	(30-May-91 EA.Z139 a) Houses (8x10cm-3x4in) ink W/C (S.FR 1700)
£887	$1739	(22-Nov-90 L.K1007/R) Im Hessischen Odenwald (14x9cm-6x4in) mono.i.d.1910 W/C pen board (DM 2600)
£2881	$4812	(6-Jun-91 HN.H415/R) Southern landscape (16x12cm-6x5in) s.d.1921 W/C over pencil (DM 8500)
£4082	$8041	(13-Nov-90 GF.L5360/R) Montagnola (17x22cm-7x9in) mono.d.1935 W/C over indian ink (S.FR 10000)
£5172	$9931	(26-Nov-90 WK.M257/R) Landscape (23x27cm-9x11in) s.d.1925 W/C (DM 15000)

HESSE, Nicolas Auguste (1795-1869) French

£2191	$3791	(24-May-91 FB.P93) Saint Joannes. Sainte Elizabeth (16x10cm-6x4in) pair (F.FR 22000)
£2191	$3791	(24-May-91 FB.P92/R) Saint Joachim. Saint Zacharias (16x10cm-6x4in) pair (F.FR 22000)
£2390	$4135	(24-May-91 FB.P95) Saint Anne. Saint Jean Baptiste (17x12cm-7x5in) pair (F.FR 24000)
£2490	$4308	(24-May-91 FB.P94/R) Saint Joseph. Saint David (16x10cm-6x4in) pair (F.FR 25000)

HESSE, Richard (1864-1910) German

| £642 | $1220 | (14-Sep-90 SA.A1215/R) Girl knitting (51x27cm-20x11in) s. i.verso (DM 1900) |
| £1329 | $2578 | (4-Dec-90 FN.S1868/R) Little girl seated by window knitting (51x26cm-20x10in) s. (DM 3800) |

HESSE, Rudolf (1871-?) German

| £856 | $1396 | (12-Jun-91 N.M464/R) Conventssitzung (55x70cm-22x28in) s.i. panel (DM 2500) |
| £1224 | $2374 | (4-Dec-90 FN.S1869/R) Antique dealer offering ware before entrance to house (52x67cm-20x26in) s. i.verso panel (DM 3500) |

HESSELBERG, Abraham (19th C) ?

| £1977 | $3400 | (17-May-91 WOL.C1127/R) Still life with basket of Flowers. Still life with squirrel and toppledflower basket both s.d.1849 gouache pair |

HESSELBOM, Otto (1848-1913) Swedish

£743	$1331	(9-Apr-91 GO.G56) Trees in winter night (42x31cm-17x12in) s.d.1912 (S.KR 8000)
£849	$1469	(22-May-91 BA.S547/R) Butterflies among roses and poppies (29x17cm-11x7in) s. (S.KR 9000)
£3650	$7190	(30-Oct-90 BU.S40/R) Sunday morning by the church (104x140cm-41x55in) s. (S.KR 40000)
£3650	$7190	(30-Oct-90 BU.S39/R) Brook through wood (110x69cm-43x27in) s.d.1893 (S.KR 40000)

HESSING, Gustav (1909-1981) Rumanian

£317	$587	(7-Mar-91 D.V249/R) Reclining female nude (47x62cm-19x24in) s. pen indian ink W/C (A.S 6500)
£365	$715	(24-Jan-91 D.V242/R) After the rain (49x61cm-19x24in) W/C (A.S 7500)
£365	$715	(24-Jan-91 D.V244/R) Wie ein Baukastendorf (48x65cm-19x26in) W/C (A.S 7500)
£533	$1003	(20-Sep-90 D.V224/R) New York (47x64cm-19x25in) s.d.65 W/C (A.S 11000)
£586	$1083	(7-Mar-91 D.V251/R) Stag (46x65cm-18x26in) W/C collage (A.S 12000)
£795	$1543	(6-Dec-90 D.V140/R) Landscape (47x64cm-19x25in) W/C (A.S 16000)

HESSL, Gustav August (1849-1926) Austrian

| £4500 | $7380 | (20-Jun-91 B102/R) Preparing meal (33x42cm-13x17in) s. panel |

HESTER, D (?) British?

| £680 | $1346 | (1-Feb-91 PHE151) On quayside (26x71cm-10x28in) s. W/C |

HESTER, Joy (20th C) Australian
£502	$964	(26-Nov-90 SY.ME90) Woman's head (29x24cm-11x9in) s. ink (A.D 1250)
£1028	$1676	(16-Jun-91 SY.ME12) Sleeping nude (26x36cm-10x14in) s. chinese ink wash paperboard (A.D 2200)
£1526	$2930	(26-Nov-90 SY.ME5/R) Woman and rose (61x47cm-24x19in) s.d.57 chl (A.D 3800)
£2169	$4164	(26-Nov-90 SY.ME295/R) Woman in robes (67x50cm-26x20in) s. W/C (A.D 5400)

HETSCH, Christian (1830-1903) Danish
£906	$1748	(10-Dec-90 BU.K67/R) Kronborg Palace 1650 (57x48cm-22x19in) s.d.1874 (D.KR 10000)

HETSCH, Philippe Friedrich von (1758-1839) German
£2676	$4522	(19-Apr-91 FN.S1737/R) Portrait of young woman with two children (97x77cm-38x30in) (DM 8000)

HETSCH, Theophiulus (?) Danish
£1344	$2688	(6-Feb-91 RAS.K132) Portrait of Miss Horstmann from Stuttgart (73x57cm-29x22in) panel oval (D.KR 15000)

HETZEL, George (1826-1899) American
£3457	$6500	(22-Sep-90 WOL.C91/R) Forest stream (91x127cm-36x50in) s.
£4469	$8000	(14-Mar-91 CH.NY46/R) Woodland stream (61x91cm-24x36in) s.d.1882
£5820	$11000	(26-Sep-90 SY.NY10/R) Still life with melons, pears and apples (56x87cm-22x34in) s.d.1882
£6548	$11000	(17-Jul-91 SY.NY225 a/R) Still life with canteloupe, peaches and grapes (30x41cm-12x16in) s.d.1864

HEUBERGER, Felix (20th C) ?
£1697	$3191	(20-Sep-90 D.V125/R) Morning mist (70x90cm-28x35in) s. board (A.S 35000)

HEUSCH, Jacob de (1657-1701) Dutch
£15902	$31327	(13-Nov-90 CH.AM204/R) Fishermen gathered on shore in Italianate coastal landscape, town beyond (38x49cm-15x19in) panel (D.FL 52000)
£20286	$36312	(8-Apr-91 CH.R161/R) Paesaggio collinare. Insenatura marina. Paesaggio roccioso (50x124cm-20x49in) set of three (I.L 45000000)
£27276	$53461	(20-Nov-90 F.R200/R) Marina con pescatori (47x96cm-19x38in) (I.L 60000000)

HEUSCH, Willem de (1638-1692) Dutch
£3716	$6318	(27-May-91 L.K53) Southern mountain landscape with travellers and donkeys on path (40x55cm-16x22in) panel (DM 11000)

HEUSCH, Willem de (attrib) (1638-1692) Dutch
£612	$1205	(12-Nov-90 CH.AM106/R) Wooded upland landscape with travellers on path (16x25cm-6x10in) with i. pen wash (D.FL 2000)

HEUSCH, Willem de (circle) (1638-1692) Dutch
£5294	$9000	(31-May-91 CH.NY131/R) Travellers resting on path in mountainous river landscape (64x77cm-25x30in) canvas on board

HEUSCH, Willem de (style) (1638-1692) Dutch
£1224	$2412	(14-Nov-90 D.V208/R) Wooded landscape with castle and figures (32x43cm-13x17in) mono. panel (A.S 25000)

HEUSER, Carl (19th C) German
£821	$1600	(25-Oct-90 GRO.B121/R) The pipe smoker (15x13cm-6x5in) s. panel

HEUSSLER, Ernst Georg (1903-) ?
£1959	$3722	(14-Sep-90 ZOF.Z1092/R) Carneval clique in Basel (81x105cm-32x41in) s.d.1934 hessian (S.FR 4800)

HEUVEL, Theodore Bernard de (1817-1906) Flemish
£2800	$5460	(18-Oct-90 SC3162/R) The village schoolroom (58x72cm-23x28in) s.

HEUZE, Edmond (1884-1967) French
£502	$929	(4-Mar-91 ARC.P142) Danseuse assise (41x33cm-16x13in) s. panel (F.FR 5000)
£602	$1114	(4-Mar-91 ARC.P139) Le cirque (33x41cm-13x16in) s. canvas laid down on board (F.FR 6000)
£800	$1344	(28-Apr-91 FE.P159) Portrait de femme (46x38cm-18x15in) s. (F.FR 8000)
£863	$1597	(4-Mar-91 ARC.P141) L'artiste (41x33cm-16x13in) s. board (F.FR 8600)
£1537	$3012	(11-Nov-90 ZZ.F157/R) Bords de Seine a Paris (66x54cm-26x21in) s. panel (F.FR 15000)
£2548	$4893	(2-Dec-90 M.V67/R) La toilette (41x33cm-16x13in) wood (F.FR 25000)
£3239	$6348	(25-Nov-90 ZZ.F83/R) Le clown dans sa loge (65x54cm-26x21in) s. board (F.FR 32000)
£332	$637	(24-Feb-91 FE.P21) Une voleuse a la X chambre (25x19cm-10x7in) s.d.1931 pastel (F.FR 3300)

HEWARD, Prudence (1896-1947) Canadian
£722	$1227	(27-May-91 HO.ED212/R) Lake reflections, Laurentians (45x30cm-18x12in) init. canvas board (C.D 1400)

HEWTON, Randolph Stanley (1888-1960) Canadian
£1096 $2160   (30-Oct-90 SY.T17/R) Quebec Village, winter (49x59cm-19x23in)
          (C.D 2500)
£1316 $2579   (20-Nov-90 JOY.T88/R) Wash day in summer (30x35cm-12x14in) (C.D 3000)

HEY, Paul (1867-1952) German
£1049 $2024   (14-Dec-90 BM.B625/R) Mountainous landscape with hunter and dog
          (32x46cm-13x18in) s. canvas on board (DM 3000)
£546   *$896*   *(22-Jun-91 WK.M1404/R) Peasant ploughing (24x40cm-9x16in) s. gouache*
          board (DM 1600)
£676   *$1318*   *(26-Oct-90 BM.B799) Landscape view from terrace in garden with figures*
          (20x14cm-8x6in) s. gouache (DM 2000)
£1356   *$2210*   *(3-Jul-91 WE.MU168/R) Garden terrace (20x13cm-8x5in) s. gouache over*
          pencil (DM 4000)
£3500   *$6265*   *(12-Apr-91 BM.B614/R) Family drinking coffee on terrace and young woman*
          watering garden (35x46cm-14x18in) s. gouache (DM 10500)

HEYBOER, Anton (1924-) Dutch
£665 $1190   (16-Mar-91 KV.L144) Creative man (52x52cm-20x20in) s. (B.FR 40000)
£4954 $9560   (13-Dec-90 SY.AM389/R) Untitled (100x130cm-39x51in) s.d.1975
          (D.FL 16000)
£549   *$982*   *(16-Mar-91 KV.L146) Four women. The hen (74x104cm-29x41in) s.d.1989*
          mixed media pair (B.FR 33000)

HEYDEN, August Jakob Theodor von (1827-1897) German
£1049 $2024   (12-Dec-90 N.M554/R) Monk reading to two elegant ladies from old
          chronicles (49x64cm-19x25in) s. i.verso panel (DM 3000)
£1351 $2297   (31-May-91 GB.B5793) Crowd before Schlosskirche Wittenberg with Luther's
          Propositions (47x95cm-19x37in) s.d.1868 (DM 4000)

HEYDEN, Johannes Hermanus van der (1825-1907) Dutch
£2061 $4059   (30-Oct-90 CH.AM50/R) View in Amsterdam with carriage on canal
          (26x37cm-10x15in) s. panel (D.FL 6800)

HEYDENDAHL, Friedrich Joseph Nicolai (1844-1906) German
£1399 $2699   (10-Dec-90 L.K441) Dutch winter landscape with figures on frozen canal
          (17x79cm-7x31in) s.d.1897 (DM 4000)
£2234 $4244   (2-Mar-91 KRA.D332/R) Winter landscape with hunters (40x50cm-16x20in) s.
          (DM 6500)

HEYDENDAHL, Friedrich Joseph Nicolai (attrib) (1844-1906) German
£2295 $4107   (12-Mar-91 FN.S2418/R) Frozen river landscape with farmhouse and female
          figure on ice (66x47cm-26x19in) s. (DM 6700)

HEYDENDAHL, L (19th C) German
£1775 $3354   (25-Sep-90 FN.S2208/R) Frozen river landscape with horse-drawn cart and
          farmhouse, evening (65x94cm-26x37in) s.d.1884 (DM 5200)

HEYER, Arthur (1872-?) German
£659 $1251   (11-Sep-90 CH.AM293/R) Reindeer in snow covered wooded landscape
          (79x93cm-31x37in) s.d.1917 (D.FL 2200)
£700 $1176   (18-Jul-91 CSK100) White Persian cats with beetle (49x70cm-19x28in) s.
£950 $1853   (15-Jan-91 C4/R) White Persian with ladybird (41x51cm-16x20in) s.
£1178 $2039   (6-May-91 ZEL.L1738/R) White Persian cat watching ladybird
          (34x43cm-13x17in) s. board (DM 3500)
£1189 $2200   (10-Mar-91 H.C3/R) Two angora cats (99x79cm-39x31in) s.
£1208 $2356   (10-Oct-90 ZEL.L1531/R) 3 cats playing in interior before curtain
          (50x38cm-20x15in) s. (DM 3600)
£1548 $2600   (28-Apr-91 LIT.L51) Mother Persian and kitten (48x69cm-19x27in) s.
£1900 $3572   (18-Sep-90 SWS650/R) An intruder (38x48cm-15x19in) s.
£2000 $3900   (15-Jan-91 C15/R) White Persian cat with kitten (52x67cm-20x26in) s.
£2000 $3360   (16-Jul-91 C137/R) Study of bull dog (79x99cm-31x39in) s.d.14
£2000 $3900   (15-Jan-91 C14/R) White Persian cat with five kittens (61x81cm-24x32in)
          s.
£2200 $4290   (15-Jan-91 C10/R) White Persian kittens with bee (51x71cm-20x28in) s.
£3000 $5040   (16-Jul-91 C124/R) Two white Persian cats with ladybird by deckchair
          (76x102cm-30x40in) s.
£3200 $5376   (16-Jul-91 C52/R) White angora kittens with beetle (55x68cm-22x27in)
          s.d.1929

HEYERDAHL, Hans Olaf (1857-1913) Norwegian
£744 $1332   (14-Mar-91 BU.O47/R) Portrait of woman (80x60cm-31x24in) s. (N.KR 8500)
£3472 $6771   (11-Oct-90 BU.O56/R) Portrait of child - Mme Dubois-Laugier
          (35cm-14ins circular) s.i.d.1881 panel (N.KR 40000)
£5254 $9405   (14-Mar-91 BU.O46/R) Summer evening by the Thames (77x51cm-30x20in) s.
          i.verso (N.KR 60000)
£8757 $15674   (11-Mar-91 B.O47/R) Girl with roses (68x44cm-27x17in) s.d.98
          (N.KR 100000)
£11384 $20377   (11-Mar-91 B.O46/R) Resting nymph with Pan (63x162cm-25x64in) s.d.91
          (N.KR 130000)
£32202 $56997   (19-Mar-91 UL.T170/R) Strandveien, Asgardstrand (107x140cm-42x55in)
          (N.KR 370000)
£35619 $68744   (10-Dec-90 B.O51/R) Landscape from Asgardstrand (101x154cm-40x61in) s.
          (N.KR 400000)
£23438   *$45703*   *(11-Oct-90 BU.O57/R) View from Asgardstrand (72x98cm-28x39in) s. gouache*
          (N.KR 270000)

HEYERMANS, Jean Arnould (1837-1892) Belgian
£800 $1312   (20-Jun-91 B108/R) Young pupil (70x56cm-28x22in) s.i.
£5734 $11123   (4-Dec-90 C.A179/R) The landlord's visit (112x147cm-44x58in) s.
                     (B.FR 340000)

HEYL, Marinus (1836-1931) Dutch
£791 $1344   (27-May-91 GK.Z5046/R) Coastal landscape with fishing boats
                     (42x26cm-17x10in) s. panel (S.FR 2000)
£2399 $4127   (16-May-91 D.V66/R) Cattle watering (115x79cm-45x31in) (A.S 50000)

HEYLIGERS, Gustaaf A F (19th C) Dutch
£12717 $22000   (22-May-91 SY.NY210/R) Sleeping cook (29x37cm-11x15in) s.d.1863 panel

HEYLIGERS, Hendrik (1877-1967) Dutch
£579 $1101   (26-Feb-91 VN.R130) Interior scene with a mother reading
                     (59x49cm-23x19in) s. (D.FL 1900)
£732 $1390   (26-Feb-91 VN.R139/R) Children in cottage interior (48x59cm-19x23in) s.
                     (D.FL 2400)

HEYMANS, A J (1839-1921) Flemish
£692 $1357   (21-Nov-90 GM.B1192) Coucher de soleil (33x42cm-13x17in) s. wood
                     (B.FR 42000)
£1484 $2908   (21-Nov-90 GM.B952/R) Moulin a vent (27x35cm-11x14in) s. wood
                     (B.FR 90000)

HEYMANS, Adriaan Josef (1839-1921) Flemish
£556 $946   (28-May-91 C.A140) Hay ship in winter (57x78cm-22x31in) s. (B.FR 34000)
£1180 $2290   (8-Dec-90 KV.L150/R) Autumn landscape (41x69cm-16x27in) s. (B.FR 70000)
£1309 $2200   (23-Apr-91 C.A121/R) Washday (36x62cm-14x24in) s. panel (B.FR 80000)
£1964 $3339   (28-May-91 C.A139/R) Sunny landscape (34x54cm-13x21in) s. panel
                     (B.FR 120000)

HEYMANS, Joseph (jnr) (?) ?
£702 $1382   (30-Oct-90 MA.V556) Shepherd and sheep (66x102cm-26x40in) s.d.1899
                     (C.D 1600)

HEYN, Auguste (1837-1920) German
£5705 $11124   (13-Oct-90 KRA.D229/R) Peasant family eating meal (93x73cm-37x29in) s.
                     (DM 17000)

HEYN, Karl (1834-1906) German
£1027 $1839   (14-Mar-91 N.M2669/R) Mountain lake landscape, Tyrol (61x100cm-24x39in)
                     s.i.d.83 (DM 3000)

HEYRAULT, Louis Robert (19th C) French
£4213 $8215   (12-Oct-90 ZZ.F35/R) Le saut d'obstacle both s.d.1852 pair (F.FR 42000)

HEYSEN, Nora (1911-) Australian
£927 $1825   (13-Nov-90 J.M96/R) Still life, interior (38x5cm-15x2in) s.d.1956 canvas
                     on board (A.D 2400)

HEYSEN, Sir Hans (1877-1968) Australian
£1533 $2499   (1-Jul-91 AAA.S99) Still life - carnations (34x43cm-13x17in) s.
                     (A.D 3250)
£2262 $3824   (16-Apr-91 J.M60/R) Carting in the hay, Mount Barker (23x29cm-9x11in) s.
                     board (A.D 5000)
£407 $688   (16-Apr-91 J.M480) Tree tops, Hahndorf (26x30cm-10x12in) s. pencil
                     (A.D 900)
£498 $841   (16-Apr-91 J.M255) Flinders ranges (16x24cm-6x9in) init. pencil
                     (A.D 1100)
£520 $1014   (15-Oct-90 AAA.S102) Post and rail fence (21x29cm-8x11in) s. chk.chl.
                     (A.D 1300)
£643 $1234   (26-Nov-90 SY.ME114) Botanical gardens (26x36cm-10x14in) s. i.d.1906
                     verso pencil conte (A.D 1600)
£708 $1153   (1-Jul-91 AAA.S96) The Big Gum, Hahndorf (16x19cm-6x7in) s. chl.white
                     (A.D 1500)
£905 $1529   (16-Apr-91 J.M326) Sheep on a hillside (20x25cm-8x10in) pencil
                     (A.D 2000)
£1603 $3078   (14-Aug-90 SY.ME83) Pastoral ambleside (29x39cm-11x15in) s. i. verso
                     chl.chk. (A.D 3800)
£3089 $6085   (13-Nov-90 J.M246/R) Nildottie (30x38cm-12x15in) s.i.d.1918/40 W/C
                     (A.D 8000)
£3167 $5353   (16-Apr-91 J.M56/R) Cattle in the early morning light (30x39cm-12x15in)
                     s. W/C (A.D 7000)
£3167 $5353   (16-Apr-91 J.M274/R) Summer flats, Guneracha (37x30cm-15x12in) s. pastel
                     (A.D 7000)
£3200 $6240   (24-Oct-90 S105/R) Sheep amidst blue gums, Ambleside (32x40cm-13x16in)
                     s.i.d.1945 W/C over pencil
£3488 $5860   (22-Apr-91 SY.ME311) Ambleside (27x35cm-11x14in) s.i.d.1924 W/C
                     (A.D 7500)
£4000 $7800   (24-Oct-90 S104/R) Cattle amongst gums (32x40cm-13x16in) s.d.1932 W/C
                     over pencil
£4247 $8367   (13-Nov-90 J.M180) Summer gums (33x41cm-13x16in) s.d.40 W/C (A.D 11000)
£4247 $8367   (13-Nov-90 J.M254) Under opal tinted saplings (38x31cm-15x12in) s.d.1915
                     W/C (A.D 11000)

HEYSEN, Sir Hans (1877-1968) Australian-cont.

£6751	$12962	(14-Aug-90 SY.ME304/R) Cattle under blue gums (31x39cm-12x15in) s.d. '24 W/C over pencil (A.D 16000)
£7240	$12235	(16-Apr-91 J.M185/R) The willow tree, Balhannah (32x40cm-13x16in) s.d.1925 W/C (A.D 16000)
£7336	$14452	(13-Nov-90 J.M24/R) Summer (32x39cm-13x15in) s.d.1952 W/C (A.D 19000)
£7722	$15212	(13-Nov-90 J.M90 a/R) Late afternoon droving (30x39cm-12x15in) s. s.i.d.1915verso W/C (A.D 20000)
£8889	$16711	(17-Sep-90 SY.ME55/R) Autumn morning, Ambleside (30x38cm-12x15in) s.d.1918 i.verso W/C (A.D 20000)
£10127	$19443	(14-Aug-90 SY.ME195/R) Valley of the Onkaparinga, overlooking Oakban, towards Mt.Charles andMt.Torrens (32x49cm-13x19in) s.d.1925 i. verso (A.D 24000)
£10970	$21063	(14-Aug-90 SY.ME275/R) Two horses grazing amongst the gums (32x40cm-13x16in) s.d.1926 W/C over pencil (A.D 26000)

HEYTMANN, Willem (20th C) Dutch

£1126	$1847	(18-Jun-91 FN.S1896/R) Busy city boulevard (60x80cm-24x31in) s. (DM 3300)

HEYWOOD-HARDY, Tom (fl.1882-1913) British

£2395	$4000	(7-Jun-91 SY.NY172/R) Obedient pets (46x61cm-18x24in) s.d.1884

HIBBARD, Aldro Thompson (1886-1972) American

£558	$1100	(16-Nov-90 S.BM168/R) New England coastline (46x64cm-18x25in) s. estate st.verso canvasboard
£726	$1300	(14-Apr-91 JRB.C163/R) Bass Rock (46x61cm-18x24in) s. i.verso
£737	$1400	(14-Sep-90 S.BM262/R) Harbour scene (30x23cm-12x9in) s. board
£773	$1500	(24-Aug-90 RB.HY79/R) Monhegan Island, Maine (46x61cm-18x24in) s. board
£1190	$2000	(27-Apr-91 YFA.M119/R) Mountain landscape (41x51cm-16x20in) s. board
£1229	$2200	(14-Apr-91 JRB.C40/R) River scene in snow (46x61cm-18x24in) s. panel
£1308	$2250	(15-May-91 SY.NY203/R) Vermont mountains (43x53cm-17x21in) s. canvasboard
£1488	$2500	(27-Apr-91 YFA.M120/R) Winter landscape (41x51cm-16x20in) s. board
£1523	$3000	(16-Nov-90 S.BM134/R) North Londonderry stream - winter landscape (61x81cm-24x32in) st.s.verso
£1676	$3000	(14-Apr-91 JRB.C204/R) Lake Louise (51x61cm-20x24in) s.
£2041	$4000	(27-Jan-91 LIT.L19a) Vermont farm at south Londonberry (46x61cm-18x24in) s. board
£2092	$4100	(11-Nov-90 LIT.L22) Winter landscape (64x76cm-25x30in) s.
£2094	$4000	(6-Jan-91 LIT.L2) Vermont Farm at South (46x61cm-18x24in) s. i. verso board
£3324	$5750	(21-May-91 GRO.B142 a/R) Winter landscape (53x66cm-21x26in) s.d.29
£3352	$6000	(14-Mar-91 CH.NY81/R) Snow-covered trees (51x86cm-20x34in) s.
£3784	$7000	(8-Mar-91 S.BM266/R) Winter morning (61x81cm-24x32in) s.
£5307	$9500	(12-Apr-91 SY.NY83/R) Winhall River, Vermont (60x107cm-24x42in) s. i.stretcher
£8629	$17000	(18-Nov-90 JRB.C139/R) Winter in Vermont (76x91cm-30x36in) s.

HIBBERT, Phyllis I (1903-) British

£450	$779	(20-May-91 PH88/R) October (36x44cm-14x17in) s. i.verso W/C over pencil

HICKEL, Joseph (attrib) (1736-1807) Austrian

£1469	$2894	(14-Nov-90 D.V323/R) Portrait of Kaiser Joseph II (64x45cm-25x18in) (A.S 30000)

HICKEY, Thomas (1741-1824) British

£2400	$4296	(10-Apr-91 S118/R) Portraits of lady of Abergavenny family and children (32x27cm-13x11in) oval four

HICKEY, Thomas (attrib) (1741-1824) British

£1300	$2145	(9-Jul-91 PH50) Portrait of Lady Clanbrassil. Portrait of Lord Clanbrassil (25x20cm-10x8in) canvas on panel pair
£4000	$7600	(1-Mar-91 C24/R) Portrait of Admiral Peter Rainier in uniform wearing spectacles (76x63cm-30x25in)

HICKEY, Thomas (circle) (1741-1824) British

£820	$1419	(20-May-91 SWS264) Portrait of Dominic Serres (59x49cm-23x19in) i. verso

HICKIN, George (19th C) British

£640	$1229	(16-Aug-90 SC4114) At Roe, near Conway, North Wales (30x25cm-12x10in) s.i.d.1849 verso
£1400	$2338	(5-Jun-91 RBB923/R) View in Bradgate Forest, Leicestershire with deer beneath ancient oaks (107x168cm-42x66in) s. i.verso

HICKLING, Michael (1968-) British

£800	$1568	(13-Feb-91 B89) Untitled I (183x183cm-72x72in) s.i.d.1990 stretcher
£900	$1764	(13-Feb-91 B90/R) Untitled II (183x183cm-72x72in)

HICKS, Edward (1780-1849) American

£468750	$900000	(29-Nov-90 SY.NY17/R) Penn's treaty (63x76cm-25x30in) i.

HICKS, George Elgar (1824-1914) British

£2200	$3674	(5-Jun-91 S164/R) Utilizing church metal. AD 1653 (46x61cm-18x24in) s.d.1868

HICKS, George Elgar (1824-1914) British-cont.
£2200 $3718   (3-May-91 PHE162/R) Portrait of Sibyl Esther Napier (90x70cm-35x28in)
                       s.d.1881
£15000 $28800   (30-Nov-90 C62/R) Portrait of the Duchess of St. Albans, seated half
                       length, with her son (91x71cm-36x28in) s.d.1875

HICKS, George Elgar (attrib) (1824-1914) British
£1100 $1793   (13-Jun-91 CSK314/R) First steps (15x13cm-6x5in) with sig.d.1866 board

HICKS, Lieutenant Colonel Edward (18th C) Canadian
£1900   *$3705*   *(24-Oct-90 S47/R) Entrance to Halifax Harbour and the town of Halifax,*
                       Nova Scotia (16x34cm-6x13in) ink W/C over traces pencil

HICKS, Nicola (1960-) British
£800   *$1504*   *(20-Sep-90 C36/R) Walking dog (100x150cm-39x59in) s.d.84 chl white chk*

HICKS, Thomas (attrib) (1823-1890) American
£900 $1548   (14-May-91 SWS258/R) Reading to grandma (30x25cm-12x10in) arched top

HIDALGO DE CAVIEDES, Hipolito (1902-) Spanish
£2749 $4920   (13-Mar-91 FER.M204/R) Los cantaros (60x48cm-24x19in) s. panel
                       (S.P 500000)
£655   *$1100*   *(27-Apr-91 YFA.M121/R) Juggler (56x33cm-22x13in) s. gouache)*

HIDALGO DE CAVIEDES, Rafael (?) Spanish
£594   *$1159*   *(22-Oct-90 ANS.M174/R) Cabeza de mujer (43x31cm-17x12in) s.d.1910 W/C*
                       (S.P 110000)

HIDALGO Y PADILLA, Felix Resurreccion (1857-1915) Spanish
£440   *$787*   *(13-Mar-91 FER.M126/R) Aldea filipina (10x17cm-4x7in) s. W/C*
                       (S.P 80000)
£495   *$886*   *(13-Mar-91 FER.M125) Marineros en la estacion de Manila (10x19cm-4x7in)*
                       s. W/C (S.P 90000)
£550   *$984*   *(13-Mar-91 FER.M124/R) Mindanao, Filipinas (13x22cm-5x9in) s. W/C*
                       (S.P 100000)

HIDDEMANN, Friedrich Peter (1829-1892) German
£1701 $3010   (20-Mar-91 KM.K1268) Black Forest girl looking into glass ball and young
                       man in park landscape (69x54cm-27x21in) s. (DM 5000)

HIDER, Frank (?) ?
£520 $868   (4-Jun-91 SWS1689) Children picking flowers by lake (41x61cm-16x24in) s.

HIDLEY, Joseph H (1830-1872) American
£2485 $4200   (20-Apr-91 WOL.C49/R) Landscape with figures (30x51cm-12x20in) pine
                       board

HIENONEN, Erkki (1933-) Finnish
£1363 $2303   (20-Apr-91 HOR.H99/R) Along the way (82x73cm-32x29in) s.d.1979
                       (F.M 9500)

HIEPES, Tomas see YEPES, Tomas

HIERSCH-MINERBI, Joachim (1834-?) Austrian
£735 $1455   (31-Jan-91 D.V142) View of Dutch town (16x20cm-6x8in) s. panel
                       (A.S 15000)
£2183 $4127   (27-Sep-90 D.V186/R) Harbour mouth (43x53cm-17x21in) s.van Hoffmann
                       (A.S 45000)

HIEZ, van (?) ?
£806 $1313   (12-Jun-91 ZZ.F4) Port des Flandres (56x89cm-22x35in) s.d.78 (F.FR 8000)

HIFTER, M (19th C) Austrian
£539 $900   (5-Jun-91 D.NY47) Song bird (30x15cm-12x6in) s. panel

HIGGINS (20th C) British
£3600   *$6984*   *(6-Dec-90 CSK159/R) St. Andrews, home of Royal and Ancient golf*
                       (81x122cm-32x48in) indist.s. gouache paper on board

HIGGINS, Eugene (1874-1958) American
£606 $1200   (1-Feb-91 S.W2918/R) Mother and child (30x48cm-12x19in) s. artist's
                       board

HIGGINS, Roma (1908-) Australian
£1255 $2472   (13-Nov-90 J.M98/R) Musical evening (60x91cm-24x36in) s. board
                       (A.D 3250)
£1351 $2662   (13-Nov-90 J.M65) At the sale yards (60x90cm-24x35in) s. board
                       (A.D 3500)

HIGGS, Cecil (1906-) South African
£1346 $2517   (27-Aug-90 SY.J253/R) Still life with bowl of grapes and apples
                       (65x44cm-26x17in) s.d.63 (SA.R 6500)
£3106 $5807   (27-Aug-90 SY.J252/R) Still life with pumpkin (50x60cm-20x24in) s.d.1945
                       verso (SA.R 15000)

HIGHMORE, Anthony (1719-1799) British
£900 $1485   (11-Jul-91 S76/R) Street musicians (11x19cm-4x7in) d.1781 pen ink W/C
    over pencil

HIGHMORE, Joseph (1692-1780) British
£1282 $2500   (10-Oct-90 CH.NY29/R) Portrait of young lady said to be Caroline Horsey
    holding fan (77x64cm-30x25in)

HIGHMORE, Joseph (attrib) (1692-1780) British
£3400 $6528   (14-Aug-90 GA60/R) Portrait of Miss Dorothea Mercer, wearing
    lace-trimmed dress and hat (71x64cm-28x25in) oval
£3800 $6802   (10-Apr-91 S119/R) Portrait of young girl, wearing dress decorated with
    ribbon and pearls (39x29cm-15x11in)

HIGHMORE, Joseph (circle) (1692-1780) British
£1100 $2167   (31-Oct-90 S278/R) Portrait of young boy (75x62cm-30x24in) painted oval
£2500 $4825   (12-Dec-90 SWS2191/R) Portrait of Elizabeth Grey, holding pet bird
    (74x61cm-29x24in)

HIGHMORE, Joseph (style) (1692-1780) British
£4000 $7160   (10-Apr-91 S116/R) Portrait of lady, seated, holding book on lap
    (123x98cm-48x39in)

HIGHTON, J (19th C) British
£580 $998   (15-May-91 BT237/R) Love Lane, Liverpool 1803 (46x61cm-18x24in)
    s.i.d.1876 board

HIGS, Richard (fl.1786-1796) British
£540 $907   (22-Apr-91 PH94) Portrait of Sophia, Duchess of Gloucester (8x?cm-3x?in)
    min. s.verso enamel oval gilt metal frame

HILAIRE, Camille (1916-1988) French
£2412 $3956   (18-Jun-91 APT.P203) Bord du cousin (33x41cm-13x16in) s. i. verso
    (F.FR 24000)
£2601 $4500   (7-May-91 CE.NY117/R) Les jockeys (24x33cm-9x13in) s.
£3161 $5500   (27-Mar-91 B.SF4088/R) Deauville (30x60cm-12x24in) s.
£3462 $6197   (8-Apr-91 CSC.P119 b/R) Jazz (24x33cm-9x13in) s. i.d.1961 verso
    (F.FR 35000)
£3590 $7000   (10-Oct-90 SY.NY293/R) Trot attele (30x61cm-12x24in) s. i.verso
    s.stretcher
£3719 $6098   (18-Jun-91 APT.P202/R) Le bouquet de printemps (65x54cm-26x21in) s. i.
    verso (F.FR 37000)
£5248 $9288   (7-Apr-91 I.N172/R) La lumiere dans la foret (46x55cm-18x22in) s.
    (F.FR 53000)
£5777 $9994   (26-May-91 ZZ.F125/R) Bateaux dans la marina de Ravene (50x73cm-20x29in)
    s. (F.FR 58000)
£5930 $9725   (19-Jun-91 ZZ.F97/R) Le printemps eclate (73x92cm-29x36in) s. i. verso
    (F.FR 59000)
£6548 $11262   (19-May-91 ZZ.F185/R) Vase de fleurs (55x46cm-22x18in) s. (F.FR 66000)
£6548 $11262   (19-May-91 ZZ.F182/R) Le coucher (61x73cm-24x29in) s. (F.FR 66000)
£6723 $11631   (26-May-91 ZZ.F136/R) La pesee des jockeys (19x33cm-7x13in) s.
    (F.FR 67500)
£6748 $11000   (12-Jun-91 SY.NY145/R) Pesage a Longchamps (72x91cm-28x36in) s. s.d.1957
    verso
£7035 $12593   (15-Mar-91 FB.P17/R) Jazz (60x73cm-24x29in) s. i. verso (F.FR 70000)
£8065 $15484   (2-Dec-90 GAB.G1633/R) Au Mayol (100x80cm-39x31in) s. d.1966 verso
    (S.FR 20000)
£17361 $29861   (19-May-91 ZZ.F166/R) Le Pesage a Deauville (88x115cm-35x45in) s.
    (F.FR 175000)
£20492 $40164   (11-Nov-90 ZZ.F154/R) Printemps en Normandie (80x130cm-31x51in) s.d.1969
    (F.FR 200000)
£888 $1749   (6-Oct-90 GL.P153) Nu (40x30cm-16x12in) s. Indian ink wash (F.FR 9000)
£1018 $2006   (29-Oct-90 LC.P109/R) Nu aux bas noirs (42x55cm-17x22in) s. W/C traces
    crayon (F.FR 10000)
£2440 $4222   (26-May-91 ZZ.F141/R) Nu allonge (50x73cm-20x29in) s. W/C (F.FR 24500)
£2465 $4857   (6-Oct-90 GL.P155) Paysage (52x72cm-20x28in) s. W/C (F.FR 25000)
£2663 $5246   (6-Oct-90 GL.P154) Personnages (74x54cm-29x21in) s. W/C (F.FR 27000)

HILAIRE, Jean Baptiste (1753-1822) French
£7136 $13772   (12-Dec-90 ARC.P68/R) Ruine de Milet et cours du Meandre
    (22x35cm-9x14in) s.i. pierre noire W/C (F.FR 70000)
£8421 $16000   (8-Jan-91 SY.NY195/R) Equestrian Turkish officer. Equestrian Turkish
    soldier (25x19cm-10x7in) both s.d.1783 W/C gouache over blk.chk. pair

HILDEBRANDT, Eduard (1818-1869) German
£949 $1585   (5-Jun-91 DO.H2302) Rocky coastal landscape with fortification
    (29x45cm-11x18in) board on canvas (DM 2800)
£1153 $1925   (5-Jun-91 DO.H2303/R) Beach and fishing boat in surf (24x45cm-9x18in)
    mono. (DM 3400)
£507 $861   (31-May-91 GB.B5796/R) Bamboo plantage in Brasil (26x36cm-10x14in)
    i.verso W/C board (DM 1500)
£508 $849   (5-Jun-91 DO.H2304) Glacier (13x18cm-5x7in) mono. W/C bodycol
    (DM 1500)
£586 $1126   (1-Dec-90 HW.H3077/R) View of Trondheim with figures (29x39cm-11x15in)
    s.c.1840i. W/C over pencil board (DM 1700)

HILDEBRANDT, Eduard (1818-1869) German-cont.
£872 $1701   (12-Oct-90 AW.H1472/R) Harbour scene with boat and cliffs beyond (23x18cm-9x7in) st.studio W/C vellum (DM 2600)

HILDEBRANDT, Friedrich Fritz (1819-1885) German
£1024 $2007   (24-Nov-90 SA.A805/R) View of Helgoland (27x40cm-11x16in) s. paper on canvas (DM 3000)

HILDEBRANDT, Fritz (1878-?) German
£743 $1449   (26-Oct-90 BM.B801/R) New cathedral with statue of Friedrich Wilhelm III, Berlin (41x51cm-16x20in) s.d.1932 (DM 2200)

HILDER, Jesse Jewhurst (1881-1916) Australian
£2489 $4206   (16-Apr-91 J.M92 a) In the clearing (24x22cm-9x9in) s.d.1912 W/C (A.D 5500)
£3089 $6085   (13-Nov-90 J.M34 a/R) The blue lagoon (14x25cm-6x10in) s.d.1907 W/C (A.D 8000)
£5116 $8595   (22-Apr-91 SY.ME269/R) Bridge (13x22cm-5x9in) s.d.1906 W/C (A.D 11000)
£6827 $13108   (26-Nov-90 SY.ME198/R) Farmhouse, Ryde (22x23cm-9x9in) s.d.1910 W/C (A.D 17000)
£8439 $16203   (14-Aug-90 SY.ME219/R) The brickmakers (28x28cm-11x11in) s.d.1911 i. label verso (A.D 20000)

HILDER, John (attrib) (19th C) British
£1171 $1978   (19-Apr-91 FN.S1738/R) Wooded river landscape with house and figures in ferry boat (31x56cm-12x22in) (DM 3500)

HILDER, Richard (1813-1848) British
£920 $1536   (22-Jul-91 SWS960/R) Landscape with two figures passing a cottage (41x57cm-16x22in)
£1000 $1950   (26-Oct-90 C299/R) A cottage in a landscape with a figure and cattle in the foreground (34x43cm-13x17in)
£2600 $4654   (10-Apr-91 S193/R) Landscape with figures by pond (33x41cm-13x16in)
£2800 $5012   (10-Apr-91 S183/R) Kentish homestead (35x50cm-14x20in) panel

HILDER, Richard (attrib) (1813-1848) British
£950 $1862   (22-Jan-91 SWS1009) Landscape with cattle and drover (43x65cm-17x26in) bears init.

HILDER, Roland (?) British
£1800 $2934   (14-Jun-91 T220/R) Filldyke, flooded fields (36x53cm-14x21in) s. W/C

HILDER, Rowland (1905-) British
£520 $1014   (15-Jan-91 SWS91/R) Coastal village (24x35cm-9x14in) s. W/C over pencil
£800 $1376   (14-May-91 SWS161/R) Crockham Hill (32x51cm-13x20in) s. i.verso pen ink W/C scratching out
£1100 $2068   (20-Sep-90 CSK63/R) River Cononish, Perthshire (26x37cm-10x15in) s. W/C htd white
£1350 $2633   (15-Jan-91 SWS92/R) The farmstead (20x30cm-8x12in) s.d.41 W/C pen ink over pencil with scratch.out

HILDESLEY, Percival T (fl.1907-1915) British
£410 $668   (2-Jul-91 SWS519) Perspective view of design for saloon in Caroline style (56x81cm-22x32in) s.indist.d. W/C over pencil htd bodycol

HILDING, Tommy (1954-) Swedish?
£566 $956   (18-Apr-91 BU.S46/R) Vittring - from the civilized world (40x60cm-16x24in) s.d.1988verso (S.KR 6000)

HILGERS, Carl (1818-1890) German
£680 $1204   (20-Mar-91 KM.K1269) Snow covered yard of monastery with monk (36x28cm-14x11in) s. (DM 2000)
£1174 $2290   (10-Oct-90 WE.MU161/R) Children collecting faggott (13x12cm-5x5in) s.d.1879 panel (DM 3500)
£2500 $4200   (18-Jul-91 CSK61/R) Winter landscape with horse drawn sleigh on track by house (52x64cm-20x25in) s.

HILL, Adrian (1897-1977) British
£710 $1200   (20-Apr-91 WOL.C196/R) Spring Tides Norfolk Coast (64x76cm-25x30in) s.

HILL, Arthur (19th C) British
£620 $1079   (27-Mar-91 PHS883) Two children in interior (30x20cm-12x8in) indist.s.

HILL, Carl Frederik (1849-1911) Swedish
£12868 $25221   (6-Nov-90 BA.S105/R) Sunset over lake (29x40cm-11x16in) (S.KR 140000)
£519 $898   (22-May-91 BA.S548/R) Three women dancing (18x20cm-7x8in) s. chk (S.KR 5500)
£915 $1784   (21-Oct-90 BU.M5) Crows in desert landscape (17x20cm-7x8in) pastel (S.KR 10000)
£1103 $2162   (6-Nov-90 BA.S368/R) Three nude men (11x7cm-4x3in) Indian ink (S.KR 12000)
£2022 $3963   (6-Nov-90 BA.S391/R) Scene from the New Testament. Man with horses (20x31cm-8x12in) mixed media Indian ink pair (S.KR 22000)
£2925 $5059   (22-May-91 BA.S586/R) Napoleon and three women (24x32cm-9x13in) ink chk (S.KR 31000)

HILL, Edward (19th C) American
£703 $1300   (8-Mar-91 S.BM128/R) Littlefield Ravine, Jackson, N.H. (51x36cm-20x14in)
                     s.d.1881

HILL, Howard (19th C) American
£1017 $1800   (22-Mar-91 S.W2474/R) Roosters and hens (38x30cm-15x12in) s. l.stretcher
£1390 $2600   (30-Aug-90 MFA.C103/R) Family of grouse (81x61cm-32x24in)

HILL, J J (1811-1882) British
£800 $1416   (21-Mar-91 CSK139) On the road to market (20x15cm-8x6in) s.d.1860 board

HILL, James John (1811-1882) British
£1000 $1900   (9-Jan-91 D.NY39/R) Afternoon visit (56x41cm-22x16in) st.d.1860 verso
£2800 $4676   (5-Jun-91 S155/R) Into field (66x56cm-26x22in) s.
£3000 $4890   (14-Jun-91 C233/R) The harvesters (48x38cm-19x15in) s.

HILL, John William (1812-1879) American
£1270 $2400   (25-Sep-90 CE.NY49/R) Mountain stream (63x48cm-25x19in) s.d.1858 W/C
                     paper laid down on board
£1719 $3300   (17-Dec-90 SY.NY130/R) Landscape with mountain stream (33x43cm-13x17in)
                     s.d.1863 W/C paper on board
£1771 $3400   (28-Nov-90 D.NY55/R) View of Niagara Falls (38x61cm-15x24in) s.d.1867
                     W/C

HILL, Nina (?) ?
£571 $1118   (24-Nov-90 HOR.H12/R) Pine trees (22x29cm-9x11in) s. (F.M 4000)

HILL, Roland Henry (1873-1952) British
£620 $1209   (17-Oct-90 PHL146) Spring ploughing (24x30cm-9x12in) s. col.washes

HILL, Rowland (1919-) British
£610 $1025   (18-Jul-91 PHX349/R) The harbour, Port-Na-Blagh, Co.Donegal, Ireland
                     (33x61cm-13x24in) s. board

HILL, Thomas (1829-1908) American
£1378 $2700   (16-Feb-91 W.W39 a/R) Yosemite scene (56x36cm-22x14in) s.
£1890 $3250   (15-May-91 SY.NY49/R) Fishing the stream (70x39cm-28x15in) s.d.1900
£2059 $3850   (1-Sep-90 LAE.L28/R) Geyser near Yellowstone Falls (36x56cm-14x22in) s.
£2806 $5500   (13-Feb-91 B.SF2001/R) Eagle Cliff, Franconia Notch, New Hampshire
                     (56x35cm-22x14in) s. paper on canvas
£3906 $7500   (17-Dec-90 SY.NY149/R) Bow River gap-Rocky Mountains view from hotel at
                     Banff, Canadian Pacific rail road (36x51cm-14x20in) s.d.1892
£4103 $8000   (10-Oct-90 B.SF433/R) Mountian stream (160x108cm-63x43in) s.d.1901
£4103 $8000   (10-Oct-90 B.SF431/R) Vernal Falls, Yosemite (76x51cm-30x20in) s.d.1903
£6186 $12000   (5-Dec-90 D.NY62/R) Yosemite Valley (61x41cm-24x16in) s.d.1890
£6977 $12000   (18-May-91 W.W96/R) Fishing in a country stream (66x91cm-26x36in)
                     s.d.1866
£7216 $14000   (5-Dec-90 D.NY63/R) Geysers in Yellowstone (76x51cm-30x20in) s.
£9744 $19000   (10-Oct-90 B.SF441/R) Fishing on stream (38x55cm-15x22in) s.
£12717 $22000   (22-May-91 CH.NY72/R) Bridal Falls, Yosemite (75x49cm-30x19in) s.
£17949 $35000   (10-Oct-90 B.SF434/R) Figures in Yosemite valley (61x51cm-24x20in)
                     s.d.1894
£25397 $48000   (26-Sep-90 SY.NY80/R) Lone fisherman in Yosemite (92x135cm-36x53in)
                     s.d.1891
£29948 $57500   (29-Nov-90 SY.NY28/R) Resting by stream (61x81cm-24x32in) s.d.1866
£500 $950   (28-Feb-91 MFA.C198) Sarah among redwoods (25x10cm-10x4in) s. W/C

HILL, Thomas (circle) (1661-1734) British
£3200 $6080   (1-Mar-91 C11/R) Portrait of Arthur Barnardiston aged 5 in classical
                     dress with parakeet (76x63cm-30x25in) i.d.1690 oval

HILLEGAERT, Pauwels van (c.1596-1640) Dutch
£2400 $4056   (16-Apr-91 PH149/R) Equestrian portrait of Prince Frederick Henry of
                     Netherlands upon hill (37x30cm-15x12in) panel

HILLEGAERT, Pauwels van (attrib) (c.1596-1640) Dutch
£3550 $7028   (30-Jan-91 APT.P75/R) Scene de bataille pres d'une ruine antique
                     (48x66cm-19x26in) traces mono. panel (F.FR 35000)

HILLER, Heinrich (19th C) German
£1130 $2023   (12-Mar-91 FN.S2420/R) River landscape with farmhouses and figures
                     returning at the end of day (52x73cm-20x29in) s. (DM 3300)
£1678 $3239   (14-Dec-90 BM.B627/R) View of Venice from harbour with shipping and
                     figures (50x115cm-20x45in) s. (DM 4800)
£2911 $5502   (27-Sep-90 D.V56/R) Venice with view of Doge's Palace (56x62cm-22x24in)
                     s. (A.S 60000)
£3356 $6544   (13-Oct-90 KRA.D230/R) View of Edinburgh (51x137cm-20x54in) s.d.1871
                     (DM 10000)

HILLER, Karol (1891-1939) Polish
£2072 $3832   (10-Mar-91 AG.W3) Monastery in Kazimierzu (101x76cm-40x30in) s.d.1929
                     (P.Z 37000000)

HILLER-FOELL, Maria (1880-1943) German
£734 $1424   (4-Dec-90 FN.S1632/R) Flowering cactus and cockatoo (86x81cm-34x32in) s.
                     (DM 2100)

HILLERN FLINSCH, Wilhelm von (1884-?) German
£777 $1321   *(28-May-91 KF.M745) Women facing each other (45x57cm-18x22in) s.d.1953 mixed media (DM 2300)*

HILLERSBERG, Lars (20th C) Swedish
£2074 $3504   *(18-Apr-91 BU.S50/R) Barcelona (199x149cm-78x59in) tempera (S.KR 22000)*

HILLERT (?) Swiss
£996 $1713   *(14-May-91 GF.L2494/R) Fortified castle in hilly landscape (28x36cm-11x14in) s. panel (S.FR 2500)*

HILLESTROM, Carl Peter (1760-1812) Swedish
£2039 $3935   *(12-Dec-90 BU.S30/R) Romantic landscape. Landscape with church (37x50cm-15x20in) s.one d.1799 W/C pair (S.KR 22000)*

HILLESTROM, Per (1732-1816) Swedish
£2757 $5404   *(6-Nov-90 BA.S108/R) The desertion of King Waldemar (42x52cm-17x20in) s. (S.KR 30000)*
£9124 $17974   *(30-Oct-90 BU.S42/R) Lady shoemaker (51x41cm-20x16in) s.d.1776 (S.KR 100000)*
£32437 $62604   *(12-Dec-90 BU.S29/R) Portrait of Carl Michael Bellman (39x32cm-15x13in) i.d.1786verso (S.KR 350000)*

HILLFON, Curt (1943-) Swedish
£827 $1621   *(10-Nov-90 FAL.M137/R) Composition in grey (73x64cm-29x25in) s. (S.KR 9000)*
£927 $1798   *(5-Dec-90 AB.S7095/R) Waiting (100x82cm-39x32in) s. tempera (S.KR 10000)*
£1020 $2000   *(10-Nov-90 FAL.M139/R) Right angel composition (82x60cm-32x24in) s.d.1978verso (S.KR 11100)*

HILLIARD, Lawrence (fl.1876-1887) British
£500 $1000   *(8-Feb-91 C27) Study in a studio (28x23cm-11x9in) s.d.1885 i. verso pencil W/C htd.white*

HILLIARD, Nicholas (circle) (1547-1619) British
£2800 $4620   *(11-Jul-91 S238/R) Portrait of lady wearing ruff and pearl jewellery (6x?cm-2x?in) min.d.1579 bears mono. gilt metal frame oval*

HILLIARD, Nicholas (school) (1547-1619) British
£10000 $16500   *(11-Jul-91 S243/R) Portrait of James I, King of England (4x?cm-2x?in) min. vellum gilt-metal frame oval*

HILLIARD, Nicholas (studio) (1547-1619) British
£1600 $3072   *(18-Dec-90 C74/R) Portrait of gentleman in white doublet with gold buttons (4x?cm-2x?in) min.vellum on card gilt-metal frame oval*

HILLIARD, Nicholas (style) (1547-1619) British
£2600 $5070   *(18-Oct-90 SC3156/R) Portrait of Queen Elizabeth the First (67x56cm-26x22in)*

HILLIARD, Nicholas and Lawrence (19th C) British
£12000 $19800   *(10-Jul-91 C193/R) A gentleman in black doublet (5x?cm-2x?in) min. vellum gold frame oval*

HILLIER, H D (?) British
£850 $1675   *(30-Oct-90 SC201/R) Corner of Loch Katrine, Perthshire (50x40cm-20x16in) s. s.i.verso*
£1000 $1630   *(2-Jul-91 SWS307/R) Rannoch Moor. Near Loch Katrine (42x32cm-17x13in) s. s.i.verso panel*

HILLIER, Tristram (1905-?) British
£950 $1843   *(6-Dec-90 CSK39/R) Snow at Pennard (25x30cm-10x12in) s. board*
£1300 $2522   *(6-Dec-90 CSK20) Pylon (49x34cm-19x13in) s. pencil*
£1400 $2716   *(6-Dec-90 CSK17/R) Sea shore (20x32cm-8x13in) s.d.1933 pencil*

HILLINGFORD, Robert Alexander (1825-1904) British
£899 $1700   *(26-Sep-90 S.BM739/R) The elopement (51x76cm-20x30in) s.*
£1127 $1915   *(28-May-91 AB.S4769/R) Battle scene (31x21cm-12x8in) s. (S.KR 12000)*
£1400 $2366   *(1-May-91 PHL190/R) Wedding - scene taken from Taming of Shrew (49x74cm-19x29in) s.*
£2200 $3674   *(5-Jun-91 S167/R) Wellington in Spain. Rescued from firing squad (20x30cm-8x12in) s.panel pair*
£2236 $4428   *(31-Jan-91 RAS.V481/R) The return from the Spanish Main (46x61cm-18x24in) s. (D.KR 25000)*
£2800 $5516   *(1-Nov-90 C259/R) News from the front (20x30cm-8x12in) s. panel*
£4737 $9000   *(28-Feb-91 CH.NY186/R) Musical gathering (95x133cm-37x52in) mono.*

HILLNER, C (19th C) ?
£3797 $6796   *(11-Apr-91 D.V170/R) Lake Konigssee (40x36cm-16x14in) s.d.1885 (A.S 80000)*

HILLS, Anna A (1882-1930) American
£532 $1000   *(22-Sep-90 WOL.C192/R) Near Laguna Beach (23x33cm-9x13in) s. artist board*
£561 $1100   *(12-Feb-91 MOR.P61) Almond blossoms - Banning, CA (25x36cm-10x14in) s.d.1922 canvas on board*

HILLS, Anna A (1882-1930) American-cont.
| £675 | $1100 | (11-Jun-91 MOR.P47) Coastal - beside sea (28x20cm-11x8in) s. canvas on board |
| £2051 | $4000 | (10-Oct-90 B.SF533/R) Pasadena (35x46cm-14x18in) s.d.13 |

HILLS, Laura Coombs (1859-?) American
£3243	$6000	(8-Mar-91 S.BM259/R) Pansies in a yellow jar (25x20cm-10x8in) s. pastel
£3684	$7000	(14-Sep-90 S.BM200/R) Roses and larkspur (53x43cm-21x17in) s. pastel
£4054	$7500	(8-Mar-91 S.BM264/R) Still life with marigolds and wildflowers (46x36cm-18x14in) s. pastel paperboard

HILLS, Robert (1769-1844) British
£360	$644	(9-Apr-91 C107) Figure with horse and cart (37x49cm-15x19in) pencil wash
£580	$951	(19-Jun-91 B56/R) Woman and children by stream (9x6cm-4x2in) W/C
£590	$1162	(1-Nov-90 D164/R) Cattle near Guildford, Surrey (23x30cm-9x12in) s. W/C
£700	$1141	(11-Jun-91 ZZ.B385) Herding sheep and cattle (37x50cm-15x20in) s.d.1804 W/C
£750	$1238	(9-Jul-91 C124/R) Drover and cattle crossing ford (51x41cm-20x16in) s.d.1817 pencil W/C
£925	$1794	(8-Dec-90 SY.MO398/R) Les laboureurs (29x42cm-11x17in) s.d.1819 W/C (F.FR 9000)
£2600	$5122	(15-Nov-90 S114/R) The farmer and his family (26x19cm-10x7in) W/C over pencil htd.bodycol gum arabic

HILLYARD, J W (19th C) British
| £1250 | $2088 | (22-Jul-91 SWS1008/R) A hunt on a country road (33x52cm-13x20in) s. |

HILSOE, Hans (?) Scandinavian
£973	$1908	(24-Jan-91 D.V208/R) Ducks and chickens (69x53cm-27x21in) s.d.21 (A.S 20000)
£1113	$2182	(22-Nov-90 RAS.V722/R) Interior with sunlit sittingroom (53x42cm-21x17in) s. (D.KR 12500)
£1500	$2580	(17-May-91 C149/R) Full bloom (56x74cm-22x29in) s.d.
£3000	$5160	(17-May-91 C108/R) Looking through to dining room (55x75cm-22x30in) s.
£3500	$6020	(17-May-91 C113/R) Interior (53x42cm-21x17in) s.

HILSON, J M (fl.1890-1900) British
| £570 | $1072 | (20-Sep-90 LJ322) Boats at Le Hocq (30x51cm-12x20in) s. W/C |

HILTON, John William (1904-1983) American
| £842 | $1600 | (12-Jan-91 LAE.L23/R) Stone dancers, Monument Valley (61x91cm-24x36in) s. board |

HILTON, Roger (1911-?) British
£3500	$6860	(6-Nov-90 PH195/R) Composition in yellow, white, black and grey (46x54cm-18x21in) s.d.53verso
£3800	$7410	(18-Oct-90 S9/R) Untitled (68x50cm-27x20in) s. s.d.1957verso paper on board
£9000	$14670	(1-Jul-91 S43/R) Untitled - green and black (63x76cm-25x30in) s.d.Dec '64 verso
£9500	$15485	(1-Jul-91 S21/R) Untitled (41x51cm-16x20in) s.d.DEC '64 verso
£11000	$20350	(8-Mar-91 C143/R) January 69 (75x75cm-30x30in) s.d.69verso
£13000	$24050	(5-Mar-91 PH59/R) Abstract composition (90x107cm-35x42in) s.d.60 verso
£16000	$26080	(1-Jul-91 S37/R) Sickle moon (63x76cm-25x30in) s.l.d.April'60 verso
£16500	$32340	(9-Nov-90 C260 a/R) May '60 (91x76cm-36x30in) s.i.d.60 verso
£18000	$29340	(1-Jul-91 S42/R) Green and brown figure (91x76cm-36x30in)
£25000	$49000	(9-Nov-90 C241/R) Untitled (140x153cm-55x60in) s.d.70 verso
£600	$1170	(9-Oct-90 B65) Untitled (34x51cm-13x20in) init.d.73 gouache
£1500	$2775	(8-Mar-91 C166/R) Woman's face (29x38cm-11x15in) s.d.73 crayon W/C gouache
£2000	$3760	(20-Sep-90 C114/R) Abstract composition (24x35cm-9x14in) init.d.14.3.73 W/C bodycol
£2600	$5096	(9-Nov-90 C257/R) Composition 1973 (37x56cm-15x22in) init.d.73 gouache chl
£2600	$5096	(9-Nov-90 C258/R) Untitled (37x30cm-15x12in) init.d.74 gouache
£3000	$5220	(27-Mar-91 S180/R) Circus nude (37x56cm-15x22in) init.d.73 chk gouache

HILTON, Rose (1931-) British
| £820 | $1345 | (20-Jun-91 DLY610/R) Woman with towel (41x33cm-16x13in) s.verso board |

HILVERDINK, Johannes (1813-1902) Dutch
| £1220 | $2390 | (6-Nov-90 SY.AM313/R) Mountainous landscape with figures by river (37x50cm-15x20in) s.d.1865 panel (D.FL 4000) |
| £4242 | $8358 | (30-Oct-90 CH.AM282/R) Mediterranean coastal view with gypsies resting on hill (101x151cm-40x59in) s.d.1878 b.stretcher (D.FL 14000) |

HIND, William George Richardson (1833-1888) Canadian
| £965 | $1891 | (20-Nov-90 JOY.T213/R) Louis, seen carrying shotgun and pack (15x17cm-6x7in) W/C pencil (C.D 2200) |

HINDENLANG, Charles (1894-1960) Swiss
£657	$1136	(25-May-91 KV.L144) Composition (100x100cm-39x39in) s.d.57 (B.FR 40000)
£3095	$5169	(5-Jun-91 SY.Z69/R) Circus menagerie (37x47cm-15x19in) s.d.23 pavatex (S.FR 7800)
£3265	$6400	(6-Nov-90 GF.L2274/R) Landscape near Lugano (41x49cm-16x19in) s. s.i.verso panel (S.FR 8000)

HINDER, Francis Henry Critchley (1906-) Australian
£2110 $4051   (14-Aug-90 SY.ME262) City buildings (89x121cm-35x48in) s.d.'61 i. verso (A.D 5000)
£3505 $5713   (16-Jun-91 SY.ME69/R) Abstract painting (70x95cm-28x37in) s.d.56 board (A.D 7500)
£573   *$1082*   *(25-Sep-90 JRL.S116/R) Abstract geometry (18x23cm-7x9in) s.d.38 W/C pair in one frame (A.D 1300)*
£695   *$1369*   *(13-Nov-90 J.M195) Nooralie (77x55cm-30x22in) s.d.63 mixed media (A.D 1800)*

HINE, Henry George (1811-1895) British
£850 $1607   (26-Sep-90 S245/R) Old Eastbourne (29x44cm-11x17in) s.i.d.1885 W/C
£1100 $1903   (20-May-91 PH59) Moonlight (14x21cm-6x8in) s.d.1871 W/C htd white
£1600 $3136   (8-Nov-90 PHI76/R) On the South Downs (28x52cm-11x20in) s.d.1850 W/C
£2100 $4116   (9-Nov-90 GSP657) An autumn evening, Horndean Valley, Lewes (46x86cm-18x34in) s.d. W/C

HINES, Frederick (19th C) British
£1800 $3546   (13-Nov-90 PH40/R) Oak grove in the New Forest, Hants (76x117cm-30x46in) s.d.1878 s.i.verso
£420 $752   (13-Mar-91 B119) A Surrey wood (27x37cm-11x15in) s. W/C bodycol.
£480 $826   (14-May-91 SWS79/R) Surrey woodside (37x26cm-15x10in) s.d.1923 W/C gouache
£520 $978   (20-Sep-90 M1) Gleaners at moonrise (20x15cm-8x6in) W/C
£580 $1079   (5-Sep-90 MMB198) Mother and child gathering wood by a stream, Burnham Beeches (25x36cm-10x14in) s. bears i. label verso bodycol.
£679 $1147   (16-Apr-91 J.M267) English landscapes (25x54cm-10x21in) both s. pair W/C (A.D 1500)
£700 $1302   (5-Sep-90 MMB197/R) Ranmore Common, Surrey (25x36cm-10x14in) s.i.d.1905 bodycol.
£919 $1498   (10-Jun-91 W.T1228) Blossom time, girls and ducks (56x38cm-22x15in) s. W/C (C.D 1700)
£1000 $1680   (24-Apr-91 MMB264) Avon valley, autumn. Crossing Commons (28x38cm-11x15in) s. gouache pair

HINES, Theodore (19th C) British
£500 $990   (1-Feb-91 PHE19) Loch Achray and trussachs church (49x79cm-19x31in) s. s.i.verso
£650 $1274   (20-Nov-90 PH81) By the edge of the pond (45x81cm-18x32in) s.
£850 $1658   (16-Jan-91 CSK302/R) Forest stream (193x323cm-76x127in) s. s.i.verso
£1100 $2112   (20-Feb-91 HAR492/R) View of Luss, Loch Lomond (48x74cm-19x29in) s.
£1300 $2301   (21-Mar-91 CSK147/R) A wooded river landscape with a woman on a bank feeding swans (76x127cm-30x50in) s.
£1400 $2730   (16-Jan-91 CSK303/R) Hastings from the croft (193x323cm-76x127in) s.i. s.i.verso
£1474 $2800   (27-Feb-91 SY.NY217/R) At Burnham Beeches (76x127cm-30x50in) s.

HINGQUA (?) Asian
£12245 $24000   (24-Nov-90 RB.HY41/R) Portrait of American ship Flying Childers at anchor in Hong Kong (71x99cm-28x39in) s.i.d.1859

HINKLE, Clarence Keiser (1880-1960) American
£1840 $3000   (11-Jun-91 MOR.P10) Coastal scene (23x30cm-9x12in) s. board
£2051 $4000   (10-Oct-90 B.SF545/R) Rockport Harbour, Maine (27x35cm-11x14in) s. panel
£3333 $6500   (10-Oct-90 B.SF532/R) Santa Barbara harbour (25x35cm-10x14in) s. i.verso panel
£10256 $20000   (10-Oct-90 B.SF504/R) Jonquils (61x76cm-24x30in) s. masonite

HINRICKSEN, Kurt (1901-) Swiss
£503 $824   (19-Jun-91 JM.P136/R) Venise San Moise (65x54cm-26x21in) s. hardboard (F.FR 5000)
£607 $1190   (25-Nov-90 ZZ.F269/R) Le lac du Bourget (40x30cm-16x12in) s. paper laid down (F.FR 6000)
£777 $1321   (2-Jun-91 LT.P164) Voiliers au port (65x54cm-26x21in) s. (F.FR 7800)
£1937 $3719   (2-Dec-90 M.V72/R) Personnages a Venise (73x44cm-29x17in) s. canvas laid down on hardboard (F.FR 19000)

HINTERMEISTER, Henry (1897-) American
£2214 $4250   (17-Dec-90 SY.NY251/R) Scout feeding girl, with dog nearby (76x58cm-30x23in) s.

HINTERREITER, Hans (20th C) ?
£1000 $1940   (5-Dec-90 PH120) Konstruktivistische Komposition (30x30cm-12x12in) tempera

HINTZE, Johann Heinrich (attrib) (1800-1860) German
£16000 $31200   (17-Oct-90 G.Z15/R) View of Berlin (72x112cm-28x44in) c.1832 (S.FR 40000)

HINZ, F (19th C) German
£1575 $2820   (12-Mar-91 FN.S2422/R) Little girl giving bunch of grapes to boy behind wooden gate (58x47cm-23x19in) s. (DM 4600)

HINZ, J G (fl.1666-1700) German
£11189 $21594   (12-Dec-90 N.M374/R) Still life of fruit and Nautilus cup on draped table (83x65cm-33x26in) s. (DM 32000)

HINZ, Johann Georg (fl.1666-1700) German
£15511 $30557   (30-Oct-90 BU.S254/R) Still life of columbine goblet and basket of fruit
                               (103x81cm-41x32in) (S.KR 170000)

HINZ, Johann Georg (style) (fl.1666-1700) German
£3058 $6024   (13-Nov-90 CH.AM144/R) Stoneware tankard, herring on pewter plate,
                               mussels, butter in bowl, glass and bun on draped table
                               (84x61cm-33x24in) (D.FL 10000)

HIPPOLYTE-LUCAS, Marie Felix (1854-1925) French
£1190 $2000   (19-Jul-91 DM.D1326/R) Walled garden (43x30cm-17x12in) s.

HIRAGA, Kamesuke (1890-1971) Japanese
£1724 $3000   (27-Mar-91 B.SF4113/R) La modele nue (66x48cm-26x19in) s.i.d.1925

HIREMY-HIRSCHL, Adolph (1860-1933) Hungarian
£681   *$1170*   *(13-May-91 CH.R37 b/R) Senza titolo (42x44cm-17x17in) pastel wax*
                               (I.L 1500000)

HIRSCH, Alphonse (1843-1884) French
£1212 $2036   (27-Apr-91 SO.S263/R) Landscape with man carrying water on road
                               (118x96cm-46x38in) s.d.69 (S.KR 12800)

HIRSCH, Joseph (1920-) American
£1453 $2600   (14-Mar-91 CH.NY220/R) Chef (65x46cm-26x18in) s.
£5026 $9500   (26-Sep-90 SY.NY223/R) Sextet (35x51cm-14x20in) s.
£7407 $14000   (27-Sep-90 CH.NY290/R) Persuasion (65x92cm-26x36in) s.d.37 masonite

HIRSCHEL, Caspar (circle) (1698-1743) German
£2800 $5516   (30-Oct-90 PH11/R) Still life of roses, convulvolus and other flowers in
                               vase on stone ledge (52x41cm-20x16in)

HIRSCHFELD, Al (1903-) American
£518   *$1000*   *(13-Dec-90 D.NY150) Kingfisher - Rex Harrison, Claudette Colbert and*
                               George Rose (43x56cm-17x22in) s.i. ink
£1235   *$2100*   *(1-Jun-91 IH.NY100/R) Junior Miss, Christmas morning in the Graves'*
                               apartment (33x61cm-13x24in) s.i. pen ink W/C

HIRSCHFELD, Emil Benediktoff (1867-1922) Russian
£1223 $2361   (16-Dec-90 T.B146/R) Thoniers au mouillage le soir (46x55cm-18x22in) s.
                               panel (F.FR 12000)
£1631 $3148   (16-Dec-90 T.B294) Jeune garcon au bord de la mer (55x38cm-22x15in) s.
                               (F.FR 16000)
£1692 $2926   (12-May-91 T.B125) Thoniers au mouillage le soir (46x55cm-18x22in) s.
                               panel (F.FR 17000)

HIRSCHFELDER, Salomon (1832-1903) German
£1440 $2434   (1-May-91 GD.B403/R) Little girl crying with jug of spilled milk
                               (66x48cm-26x19in) s.d.1876 (S.FR 3600)
£2600 $4394   (1-May-91 GD.B404/R) Returning from sledging (67x49cm-26x19in) s.d.1877
                               (S.FR 6500)
£8136 $13261   (3-Jul-91 WE.MU141/R) Love is blinding (57x49cm-22x19in) s.d.1880
                               (DM 24000)

HIRSCHING, August (1889-1962) German
£614 $1161   (25-Sep-90 FN.S1974/R) View of Stuttgart (71x55cm-28x22in) s. s.i.verso
                               panel (DM 1800)

HIRSCHMANN, Johann Baptist (1770-c.1829) German
£1723   *$2929*   *(27-May-91 L.K285/R) Portrait of Kgl Bayerischer Staatsrat Nicolaus*
                               Thaddaus von Goenner (41x33cm-16x13in) s.d.1819 pastel (DM 5100)

HIRST, Claude Raguet (1855-1942) American
£5319 $10000   (19-Sep-90 B.SF2723/R) Books, jar and copper bowl (18x25cm-7x10in) s.
£14815 $28000   (27-Sep-90 CH.NY64/R) Poems of William Cowper (20x25cm-8x10in) s.i.
£15029 $26000   (22-May-91 CH.NY158/R) Some interesting volumes (25x36cm-10x14in) s.i.
£7514   *$13000*   *(22-May-91 CH.NY169/R) A vision (37x27cm-15x11in) s.i. W/C pencil board*

HIRT, Friedrich Wilhelm (1721-1772) German
£1700 $2771   (2-Jul-91 PH142/R) Leopards attacking stag in parkland (33x33cm-13x13in)
                               s.d.1755 panel
£2000 $3860   (11-Dec-90 PH156/R) Leopards attacking stag in parkland
                               (33x33cm-13x13in) s.d.1755 panel

HIRT, Lise (20th C) ?
£771 $1495   (9-Dec-90 ZZ.F43/R) Femme au chapeau (81x54cm-32x21in) s. (F.FR 7500)

HIRTH DU FRENES, Rudolf (1846-1916) German
£683 $1119   (18-Jun-91 FN.S1896 a/R) Portrait of young girl wearing shawl
                               (29x37cm-11x15in) s. (DM 2000)
£743 $1449   (26-Oct-90 BM.B803/R) Alpine landscape with young woman on bench
                               startled by hunter (55x38cm-22x15in) s. (DM 2200)
£821 $1600   (26-Oct-90 S.W2166/R) Woman knitting outside a cottage (33x33cm-13x13in)
                               s.
£874 $1687   (14-Dec-90 BM.B628/R) Coastal landscape with boats and lighthouse
                               (37x40cm-15x16in) s. i.stretcher (DM 2500)

HIRTH DU FRENES, Rudolf (1846-1916) German-cont.
£2891 $4655 (26-Jun-91 KM.K1502/R) Alpine lake landscape with washerwomen, monk and
              children (66x89cm-26x35in) s. (DM 8500)
£5137 $8373 (12-Jun-91 SY.MU122/R) Portrait of girl (33x25cm-13x10in) s. board
              (DM 15000)

HIS, Rene Charles Edmond (1877-?) French
£750 $1290 (14-May-91 SWS436/R) La riviere (53x71cm-21x28in) s.
£765 $1468 (30-Nov-90 CB.P107) Bords de riviere (46x61cm-18x24in) (F.FR 7500)
£903 $1760 (12-Oct-90 ZZ.F47) Paysage aux moutons s. (F.FR 9000)
£1300 $2184 (18-Jul-91 CSK81/R) River landscape in spring (61x81cm-24x32in) s.
£1670 $3273 (25-Nov-90 ZZ.F84) Sous-bois (54x65cm-21x26in) s. pair (F.FR 16500)

HISCOX, George (1840-1909) British
*£450 $779 (20-May-91 PH22) St. George's Chapel and Windsor Castle, autumn breeze
              (53x73cm-21x29in) s. i.verso W/C htd white*

HISLOP, Margaret Ross (fl.1919-1940) British
£1300 $2522 (5-Dec-90 PHE105/R) Still life of flowers and shells (66x70cm-26x28in)
              s. board
£1400 $2352 (23-Apr-91 S172/R) Venice (68x56cm-27x22in) s. board

HITCHCOCK, George (1850-1913) American
£4438 $7500 (1-May-91 B.SF5072/R) Woman with white veil (56x44cm-22x17in) s.
£8376 $16500 (7-Oct-90 DU.E140/R) Dutch flower girl (91x112cm-36x44in)
£8854 $17000 (30-Nov-90 CH.NY56/R) Normandy farmhouse (40x56cm-16x22in)
£1000 $1960 (23-Jan-91 ZZ.B186) Winter garden (42x57cm-17x22in) s. pastel

HITCHCOCK, Harold (1914-) British
£380 $661 (28-Mar-91 CSK150) Ebb tide (51x61cm-20x24in) mono.d.1965 W/C bodycol

HITCHENS, Ivon (1893-1979) British
£800 $1512 (27-Sep-90 L283/R) Rolling hills (71x91cm-28x36in) s.
£4800 $8880 (8-Mar-91 C136/R) Seated girl on yellow couch (73x39cm-29x15in) s.d.68
               s.i.d.stretcher
£6200 $10354 (6-Jun-91 C261/R) Black down 2 (41x74cm-16x29in) s. s.i.d.1969stretcher
£8000 $13360 (7-Jun-91 C326/R) Foliage by water no 6 (61x137cm-24x54in) s.
               s.i.d.1962stretcher
£10000 $16700 (7-Jun-91 C325/R) Trees overhanging water (51x105cm-20x41in) s.
               s.i.stretcher
£13000 $25480 (7-Nov-90 S179/R) Geraniums and daisies (52x108cm-20x43in) s.
£15000 $27900 (5-Sep-90 BT252/R) Footbridge over marsh (38x74cm-15x29in) s.i.d.1970
               stretcher
£15000 $27750 (8-Mar-91 C107/R) Cottage interior (51x45cm-20x18in) s.
£15000 $29400 (7-Nov-90 S178/R) Land and sky spaces no.3 (46x144cm-18x57in) s.
               s.i.d.1963
£15500 $25885 (7-Jun-91 C324/R) Landscape (40x91cm-16x36in) s.
£16000 $29600 (8-Mar-91 C138/R) Trees and boathouse no 1 (51x91cm-20x36in) s.
               s.i.d.1956stretcher
£18000 $35280 (7-Nov-90 S94/R) Flowers (75x65cm-30x26in) s.d.32
£21000 $41160 (9-Nov-90 C264/R) Interior, red sunlight (56x84cm-22x33in) s. l.d.1960
               stretcher
*£5500 $10835 (1-Nov-90 TE586/R) The bridge, Grange-in-Borrowdale (25x38cm-10x15in) s.
               pencil W/C*

HITCHENS, John (1940-) British
£680 $1278 (20-Sep-90 CSK155/R) Landscape (56x84cm-22x33in) s.
£700 $1316 (20-Sep-90 CSK156) Sussex bushes (56x84cm-22x33in) s.
£780 $1498 (21-Feb-91 B236/R) Falling river pass (51x76cm-20x30in) s. s.i.d.1967
             stretcher
£900 $1728 (21-Feb-91 B235) Open Downland (52x104cm-20x41in) s.d.1964 s.i.d.verso
             board
£900 $1503 (7-Jun-91 C338) April clouds over Heyshott Downs (46x109cm-18x43in) s.i.
             s.i.d.1959stretcher

HITZLER, Franz (1946-) German
£1920 $3322 (10-May-91 S.Z40) Untitled (116x74cm-46x29in) s.d.1978 acrylic board
             (S.FR 4800)

HJERTEN, Sigrid (1885-1948) Swedish
£9268 $17980 (4-Dec-90 BA.S209/R) Still life of flowers (65x54cm-26x21in) s. panel
               (S.KR 100000)
£9363 $16105 (14-May-91 BU.S96/R) The lock (70x48cm-28x19in) s. (S.KR 100000)
£16038 $27745 (22-May-91 BA.S87/R) Landscape from Alvastra (55x73cm-22x29in) s.
               (S.KR 170000)
£18450 $35424 (27-Nov-90 BU.S134/R) Landscape with surroundings of Paris
               (64x54cm-25x21in) s. panel (S.KR 200000)
£28730 $55737 (4-Dec-90 BA.S207/R) View from the window, Saint-Paul (92x73cm-36x29in)
               s. (S.KR 310000)
£1622 $3146 (4-Dec-90 BA.S210/R) Tea-time (31x23cm-12x9in) s. W/C (S.KR 17500)

HJORTH, Bror (1894-1968) Swedish
£16605 $31882 (27-Nov-90 BU.S136/R) Hospital visit (32x39cm-13x15in) s.d.1924 i.verso
               panel (S.KR 180000)
£927 $1798 (4-Dec-90 BA.S213/R) Cessi (32x25cm-13x10in) s. pencil (S.KR 10000)
£1476 $2834 (27-Nov-90 BU.S137/R) Eve (25x17cm-10x7in) s. gouache (S.KR 16000)

HJORTH-NIELSEN, S (1901-) Danish
£799 $1575   (31-Oct-90 KH.K42) View from Rome (46x69cm-18x27in) init.d.1928
                        (D.KR 9000)
£1599 $3149   (31-Oct-90 KH.K38/R) Summer landscape (105x120cm-41x47in) init.
                        (D.KR 18000)

HJORTH-NIELSEN, Soren (1901-) Danish
£893 $1652   (5-Mar-91 RAS.K203) Landscape, Arreso (65x81cm-26x32in) init.
                        s.d.1955verso (D.KR 10000)
£1087 $2098   (12-Dec-90 RAS.K194/R) Road, houses and wood (73x93cm-29x37in) init.
                        (D.KR 12000)
£1161 $2147   (5-Mar-91 RAS.K206/R) Enghave Park (100x110cm-39x43in) s.d.1936-37verso
                        (D.KR 13000)
£1364 $2661   (10-Oct-90 RAS.K195/R) View of houses (73x85cm-29x33in) init.
                        (D.KR 15500)
£1408 $2423   (15-May-91 RAS.K130/R) Landscape (65x81cm-26x32in) init. (D.KR 16000)
£1506 $2861   (14-Sep-90 RAS.V749/R) View towards red houses in Valby
                        (91x115cm-36x45in) init. l.d.1949verso (D.KR 17000)
£4286 $7929   (5-Mar-91 RAS.K202/R) Fredensbro 1941-42 (107x130cm-42x51in) init.
                        (D.KR 48000)

HJORTZBERG, Olle (1872-1959) Swedish
£1033 $1756   (28-May-91 AB.S4632/R) Italian landscape with man on donkey
                        (38x46cm-15x18in) s.d.53 (S.KR 11000)
£1251 $2427   (5-Dec-90 AB.S7100/R) Italian coastal town (61x50cm-24x20in) s.d.1950
                        panel (S.KR 13500)
£1604 $2775   (22-May-91 BA.S552/R) Italian farm (46x55cm-18x22in) s. (S.KR 17000)
£1651 $2856   (22-May-91 BA.S551/R) Still life with white lilies (65x53cm-26x21in)
                        s.d.1942 panel (S.KR 17500)
£3883 $6523   (27-Apr-91 SO.S364/R) Bleeding-hearts (52x64cm-20x25in) s.d.1942 panel
                        (S.KR 41000)
£3903 $6987   (9-Apr-91 GO.G57/R) Still life of violets and cowslips (46x38cm-18x15in)
                        s.d.48 panel (S.KR 42000)
£4225 $7183   (28-May-91 AB.S4631/R) Still life of yellow rose in pottery vase
                        (64x49cm-25x19in) s.d.52 (S.KR 45000)
£4740 $8484   (9-Apr-91 GO.G58/R) Interior with lilies in jug (61x50cm-24x20in) s.d.58
                        panel (S.KR 51000)
£5535 $10627   (27-Nov-90 BU.S138/R) Still life of yellow roses in silver vase
                        (54x65cm-21x26in) s.d.1949 panel (S.KR 60000)
£6629 $11136   (24-Apr-91 BA.S90/R) Roses by open window (74x60cm-29x24in) s.d.1934
                        panel (S.KR 70000)
£7299 $14380   (30-Oct-90 BU.S44/R) Pink roses in silver vase (61x50cm-24x20in)
                        s.d.1952 (S.KR 80000)
£8272 $16213   (6-Nov-90 BA.S112/R) Still life of autumn leaves in vase
                        (65x54cm-26x21in) s.d.47 panel (S.KR 90000)
£9434 $16321   (22-May-91 BA.S550/R) White peonies in silver vase (61x50cm-24x20in)
                        s.d.1945 (S.KR 100000)
£13787 $27022   (6-Nov-90 BA.S110/R) Still life of wild flowers in vase
                        (65x54cm-26x21in) s.d.1946 panel (S.KR 150000)
£27462 $46136   (24-Apr-91 BA.S89/R) Still life of flowers (73x59cm-29x23in) s.d.1950
                        panel (S.KR 290000)
£3217   *$6305*   *(6-Nov-90 BA.S371/R) Yellow roses (43x29cm-17x11in) s.d.55 W/C*
                        (S.KR 35000)

HLAVACEK, Anton (1842-1926) Austrian
£3300 $5708   (6-May-91 ZEL.L1741/R) View of Reschensee and Ortler range with rising
                        thunderstorm (90x173cm-35x68in) s. (DM 9800)

HMELKO, Mikhail Ivanovitch (1919-) Russian
£500 $885   (18-Mar-91 ARC.P66/R) Lenine decrete le pouvoir sovietique
                        (46x80cm-18x31in) board (F.FR 5000)

HNIYITTI, F (?) ?
£1140   *$2234*   *(20-Nov-90 RB693) Roma Villa d'Este (38x58cm-15x23in) s. W/C*

HOARE, William (1706-1799) British
£6500 $12805   (14-Nov-90 S36/R) Portrait of Rev William Freind seated with son Robert
                        holding book (100x126cm-39x50in)
£3800   *$7486*   *(15-Nov-90 S63/R) Portrait of Anne Bristow, later Countess of Effingham*
                        (59x44cm-23x17in) i.verso pastel
£5500   *$10835*   *(15-Nov-90 S64/R) Portrait of Sir Thomas Lee wearing gold embroidered*
                        coat (57x44cm-22x17in) pastel
£7500   *$14775*   *(15-Nov-90 S61/R) Portrait of Sir William Lee wearing white and gold*
                        waistcoat with cloak (60x45cm-24x18in) pastel
£17200   *$30788*   *(11-Apr-91 S28/R) Portrait of Frederick, Prince of Wales*
                        (59x45cm-23x18in) pastel

HOBART, Clark (1880-?) American
£1658 $3250   (13-Feb-91 B.SF2050/R) Oak tree, Marin (41x51cm-16x20in) s.

HOBBEMA, Meindert (after) (1638-1709) Dutch
£3500 $6650   (13-Sep-90 CSK229/R) Village in wood with revellers returning from
                        kermesse (98x109cm-39x43in)

HOBBEMA, Meindert (school) (1638-1709) Dutch
£2941 $5000   (31-May-91 CH.NY117/R) Mill on river (44x38cm-17x15in) panel

HOBBEMA, Meindert (style) (1638-1709) Dutch
£2000	$3840	(29-Nov-90 CSK300) Wooded landscape with peasants on path and cottage beyond (58x78cm-23x31in)
£2008	$3233	(27-Jun-91 APT.P135/R) Promeneur dans la campagne au bord d'une riviere (43x66cm-17x26in) panel (F.FR 20000)
£2821	$5500	(10-Oct-90 CH.NY108/R) Wooded landscape with figures in stream before ruins (74x90cm-29x35in) bears sig.indis.d.

HOBBS, George T (1846-?) American
| £2147 | $3500 | (5-Jul-91 S.W3004/R) Tabletop still life (36x25cm-14x10in) s. panel |

HOBSON, Cecil J (1874-1918) British
| £1200 | $2376 | (30-Jan-91 S223/R) Whitby (23x29cm-9x11in) mono. W/C htd bodycol |

HOCH, Franz Xaver (1869-1916) German
£680	$1095	(26-Jun-91 KM.K1505/R) Upper Italian lake landscape with houses and church tower (53x41cm-21x16in) s. paper (DM 2000)
£769	$1485	(12-Dec-90 N.M559/R) Rocky lake landscape, possibly Fuorcla Surley with view of Bernina Group (84x120cm-33x47in) s.d.1911 i.stretcher (DM 2200)
£1122	$1807	(26-Jun-91 KM.K1506/R) View of Italian village (43x53cm-17x21in) s. paper (DM 3300)
£1267	$2268	(13-Mar-91 N.M533/R) Landscape with stream and farmhouse amongst trees (99x120cm-39x47in) s.d.1909 (DM 3700)

HOCH, Hannah (1889-1978) German
£6897	$13241	(26-Nov-90 WK.M30/R) Gefahr droht (68x77cm-27x30in) mono. s.d.1960verso (DM 20000)
£374	$602	(28-Jun-91 BM.B909/R) Faces (13x19cm-5x7in) mono.d.1966 indian ink (DM 1100)
£405	$689	(31-May-91 GB.B6374) Figure made of head, hand and glass (20x14cm-8x6in) mono.d.1973 collage (DM 1200)
£411	$670	(15-Jun-91 L.K311) Chicken yard (30x40cm-12x16in) mono. indian ink pen (DM 1200)
£420	$814	(7-Dec-90 GB.B6672) Young woman bending to the left (32x24cm-13x9in) mono.c.1925 indian ink pen (DM 1200)
£456	$775	(1-Jun-91 VG.B585/R) Composition (23x33cm-9x13in) indian ink brush W/C (DM 1350)
£514	$837	(15-Jun-91 L.K306) Christmas (30x21cm-12x8in) mono.d.1939 i.verso W/C (DM 1500)
£610	$1000	(19-Jun-91 B.SF1812/R) Spielerische Formen (15x24cm-6x9in) d.1955 ink
£690	$1324	(26-Nov-90 WK.M259/R) Girl (13x21cm-5x8in) mono.d.1967 gouache (DM 2000)
£743	$1264	(31-May-91 GB.B6376/R) The goal, composition with letter G (65x50cm-26x20in) mono. felt tip pen spray technique (DM 2200)
£853	$1672	(22-Nov-90 L.K1012/R) Selfportrait (30x17cm-12x7in) mono. st.studio verso indian ink brush (DM 2500)
£856	$1396	(15-Jun-91 L.K308) Mittellandkanal (46x65cm-18x26in) s. s.verso chl pencil (DM 2500)
£862	$1655	(26-Nov-90 WK.M259 a/R) Behutet (13x17cm-5x7in) mono.s.i.d.1938 W/C indian ink coll.pap.on board (DM 2500)
£946	$1608	(31-May-91 GB.B6375) Composition with letter W (50x65cm-20x26in) mono.s.d.1956 spray technique (DM 2800)
£1017	$1698	(6-Jun-91 HN.H427/R) Witch dance (18x20cm-7x8in) mono. pen (DM 3000)
£1220	$2038	(6-Jun-91 HN.H426/R) Composition (24x15cm-9x6in) mono. collage (DM 3600)
£1331	$2609	(24-Nov-90 VG.B571/R) Vegetabiles (49x63cm-19x25in) mono. W/C bodycol (DM 3900)
£1365	$2676	(24-Nov-90 VG.B565/R) Composition with eyes (24x24cm-9x9in) mono. s.verso W/C pen (DM 4000)
£1536	$3010	(24-Nov-90 VG.B570/R) Composition with zig zag lines (74x60cm-29x24in) mono.i. W/C (DM 4500)
£1706	$3345	(24-Nov-90 VG.B569/R) Geschwungene und spitze Formen (50x74cm-20x29in) mono.c.1960 s.verso W/C indian ink brush (DM 5000)
£2048	$4014	(24-Nov-90 VG.B292/R) Black in the middle (21x15cm-8x6in) mono. s.verso paper collage (DM 6000)
£4730	$8041	(1-Jun-91 VG.B584/R) Quarrel (28x28cm-11x11in) mono.d.1946 collage (DM 14000)
£9589	$15630	(15-Jun-91 L.K300/R) Unsere lieben Kleinen (17x13cm-7x5in) mono.d.1924 collage (DM 28000)
£24603	$40349	(19-Jun-91 GK.B469/R) The female singer (28x28cm-11x11in) s.i.d.1926 collage (S.FR 62000)

HOCHECKER, Franz (1730-1782) German
| £1923 | $3731 | (4-Dec-90 FN.S1874/R) Wooded landscape with hunting scene (20x27cm-8x11in) rem.mono. panel (DM 5500) |
| £5068 | $8615 | (27-May-91 L.K54/R) River landscape with fishermen loading barge and twon (68x105cm-27x41in) s.d.1755 (DM 15000) |

HOCHMANN, Franz Gustav (1861-?) German
| £1793 | $3084 | (14-May-91 GF.L2089/R) Pastoral Italian landscape (46x76cm-18x30in) s.i.d.1885 (S.FR 4500) |

HOCK, Daniel (1858-?) Austrian
| £6500 | $10660 | (19-Jun-91 S80/R) Still life with peppers, fruit, lobster and cat (50x120cm-20x47in) init. |

HOCKELMANN, Antonius (?) ?
£683 $1338   (20-Nov-90 L.K277 a) Female nude seated (44x39cm-17x15in) s.d.1988 mixed media (DM 2000)

HOCKEY, Patrick (?) Australian
£845 $1386   (17-Jun-91 MGS.S184) Riding brood mare (60x75cm-24x30in) s.d.73 board (A.D 1800)

HOCKNER, Rudolf (1864-1942) German
£912 $1779   (26-Oct-90 BM.B805) Path in wooded landscape (29x46cm-11x18in) s. board (DM 2700)
£1020 $1643   (28-Jun-91 BM.B787/R) River landscape with poultry and houses beyond (25x37cm-10x15in) s. board (DM 3000)
£1573 $3037   (14-Dec-90 BM.B629/R) North German landscape with mill and figures (27x45cm-11x18in) s. board (DM 4500)
£1959 $3331   (28-May-91 KF.M174/R) River landscape (48x72cm-19x28in) s.d.1913 (DM 5800)
£2667 $4773   (12-Apr-91 BM.B738/R) North German farmhouse with figures, autumn (61x91cm-24x36in) s. (DM 8000)

HOCKNEY, David (1937-) British
£74576 $124542   (8-Jun-91 HN.H156/R) Big stone (120x150cm-47x59in) mono.i.verso acrylic (DM 220000)
£240000 $386400   (27-Jun-91 S41/R) The actor (167x167cm-66x66in) acrylic
£5254 $8775   (8-Jun-91 HN.H157/R) Man in yellow coat (31x25cm-12x10in) mono.d.1963 wax crayon pencil (DM 15500)
£6122 $12000   (7-Nov-90 SY.NY321/R) Pineapple (43x35cm-17x14in) init.d.70 ink
£6667 $13000   (24-Oct-90 B.SF1506/R) Peter Schlesinger (43x35cm-17x14in) init.d.68 pen
£7500 $14625   (18-Oct-90 C380/R) Peter (31x50cm-12x20in) init.i.d.1964 pen ink
£13265 $26000   (8-Nov-90 CH.NY130/R) Boy taking a shower (40x29cm-16x11in) init.d.'62 col.pencils graphite
£42899 $72500   (1-May-91 SY.NY133/R) Grand Hotel terrace, Vittel (43x35cm-17x14in) init.d.70 col.pencil

HODE, Pierre (1889-1942) French
£1800 $2934   (4-Jul-91 GL.P250/R) Nature morte au pichet et aux fruits (27x35cm-11x14in) s. panel (F.FR 18000)
£2500 $4075   (4-Jul-91 GL.P248/R) Notre-Dame (60x73cm-24x29in) s. (F.FR 25000)
£5025 $8995   (16-Mar-91 APT.P57/R) Bouquet de fleurs et citrons (81x54cm-32x21in) s. (F.FR 50000)
£10296 $19871   (10-Dec-90 LD.P153/R) Composition mixte a la pipe (19x37cm-7x15in) s. (F.FR 101000)
£11168 $22000   (13-Nov-90 CE.NY61/R) Chatillon sur Seine (60x73cm-24x29in) s. s.i.verso
£18090 $32382   (16-Mar-91 APT.P54/R) Honfleur, la Lieutenance (65x81cm-26x32in) s. (F.FR 180000)
£23077 $45000   (10-Oct-90 SY.NY107/R) Harbour view (53x64cm-21x25in) s.

HODEL, Ernst (1881-1955) Swiss
£760 $1284   (1-May-91 GD.B405/R) Alpine landscape with sheep and Breithorn beyond, Wallis (59x80cm-23x31in) s. (S.FR 1900)
£1306 $2560   (6-Nov-90 GF.L2612/R) Winter landscape (53x66cm-21x26in) s. board (S.FR 3200)
£1306 $2560   (6-Nov-90 GF.L2617/R) View of Piz Bernina (60x73cm-24x29in) s. board (S.FR 3200)

HODEL, Ernst (elder) (1852-1902) Swiss
£518 $891   (14-May-91 GF.L2531/R) Young peasant woman in high mountains (61x58cm-24x23in) s. (S.FR 1300)
£598 $1028   (14-May-91 GF.L2529/R) Seelisberg (25x34cm-10x13in) i.verso canvas on board (S.FR 1500)
£1195 $2056   (14-May-91 GF.L2532/R) View of Lauterbrunnental with shepherd (36x27cm-14x11in) s. (S.FR 3000)

HODGES, Charles Howard (18/19th C) British
£848 $1672   (30-Oct-90 CH.AM216/R) Portrait of lady, said to be Maria van de Graff, seated on terrace (34x28cm-13x11in) pastel vellum (D.FL 2800)

HODGES, Samuel (19th C) British
£1400 $2604   (5-Sep-90 BT168/R) Loch Awe (81x119cm-32x47in) s.d.1855

HODGES, William Merrett (fl.1896-1938) British
£800 $1368   (29-Jul-91 HS269/R) Critic - interior of artist's studio with dog on stool gazing at picture (75x60cm-30x24in) s.d.1908 i.verso

HODGKIN, Howard (1932-) British
£35503 $60000   (30-Apr-91 SY.NY18/R) Girl in bed (71x91cm-28x36in) s.d.1965 stretcher
£73964 $125000   (30-Apr-91 SY.NY2/R) Family group (91x107cm-36x42in)

HODGKINS, Frances (1869-1947) New Zealander
£13502 $25924   (14-Aug-90 SY.ME177/R) Flemish street scene (42x48cm-17x19in) s. (A.D 32000)
£1000 $1980   (29-Jan-91 PH64/R) Clock tower (36x27cm-14x11in) s. W/C htd bodycol
£1050 $1712   (2-Jul-91 CD403) Still life of bowl of fruit (56x79cm-22x31in) s. mixed media
£1546 $2613   (17-Apr-91 DS.W99) Sheds, Otago init. W/C (NZ.D 4500)

HODGKINS, Frances (1869-1947) New Zealander-cont.

£1548	$3034	(7-Nov-90 DS.W175) Richmond Bridge (23x13cm-9x5in) d.30.4.01 W/C (NZ.D 5000)
£2477	$4854	(7-Nov-90 DS.W43) Harbour (17x37cm-7x15in) init. W/C (NZ.D 8000)
£5500	$10725	(10-Oct-90 S144/R) In the hills, Spain (48x36cm-19x14in) s. W/C
£6014	$10163	(17-Apr-91 DS.W109) Young girl feeding chickens (31x26cm-12x10in) init.d.93 W/C (NZ.D 17500)
£6811	$13350	(7-Nov-90 DS.W35/R) Conversation (45x55cm-18x22in) W/C (NZ.D 22000)
£7388	$12486	(17-Apr-91 DS.W64) Bedford on tone (54x37cm-21x15in) s. W/C (NZ.D 21500)
£7560	$12777	(17-Apr-91 DS.W38/R) Potters (48x48cm-19x19in) W/C gouache (NZ.D 22000)
£7904	$13357	(17-Apr-91 DS.W25/R) In hills, Spain (51x38cm-20x15in) s. W/C (NZ.D 23000)
£8591	$14519	(17-Apr-91 DS.W12/R) Walled garden with convoluulas (44x51cm-17x20in) W/C gouache (NZ.D 25000)
£15480	$30341	(7-Nov-90 DS.W17/R) Picnic (41x52cm-16x20in) s. W/C (NZ.D 50000)

HODGKINSON, Cecil Thomas (1895-1979) British

£450	$864	(19-Feb-91 C94) Shovelers in flight above the shore (25x38cm-10x15in) s. pencil W/C
£600	$1152	(19-Feb-91 C93/R) Mallard in flight above winter landscape (33x48cm-13x19in) s. pencil W/C

HODGKINSON, Frank (1919-) Australian

£2570	$4189	(16-Jun-91 SY.ME92/R) Behold scribbling worm (183x137cm-72x54in) i.verso board (A.D 5500)

HODGSON, David (1798-1864) British

£600	$978	(14-Jun-91 K475/R) On the walls of Norwich (41x30cm-16x12in) s.
£1100	$2167	(31-Oct-90 S350/R) Farm in woodland clearing (56x74cm-22x29in)

HODGSON, John Evan (1831-1895) British

£1050	$2079	(28-Jan-91 HS172/R) Village scene, with duck pond in foreground and figures in street (38x58cm-15x23in) s. W/C

HODICKE, Karl Horst (1938-) American/German

£1199	$1954	(14-Jun-91 L.K950) Ram (100x70cm-39x28in) s. tempera W/C (DM 3500)
£6143	$12041	(24-Nov-90 VG.B389/R) Dapple greys (155x190cm-61x75in) s.d.1980verso resin cotton (DM 18000)
£20137	$39468	(24-Nov-90 VG.B395/R) Boat in jungle (184x270cm-72x106in) s.d.1978 resin (DM 59000)

HODINOVA, Eva (1946-) Czechoslovakian

£675	$1317	(22-Oct-90 BR.M320/R) Veduta di Praga (60x70cm-24x28in) s. oil mixed media canvas (I.L 1500000)

HODLER, Ferdinand (1853-1918) Swiss

£21017	$35098	(7-Jun-91 HN.H25/R) Willows by the Rhone (33x24cm-13x9in) s. (DM 62000)
£23810	$39762	(5-Jun-91 SY.Z37/R) Self portrait of artist laughing with hat (28x22cm-11x9in) s.d.1873verso board (S.FR 60000)
£25763	$43024	(7-Jun-91 HN.H26/R) Head of an Italian woman (37x31cm-15x12in) s. (DM 76000)
£34137	$66908	(21-Nov-90 SY.Z40/R) Landscape with silver birch tree (26x21cm-10x8in) s. (S.FR 85000)
£99206	$165675	(5-Jun-91 SY.Z67/R) Reichenbach (52x28cm-20x11in) s. (S.FR 250000)
£108730	$181579	(5-Jun-91 SY.Z59/R) The day (61x53cm-24x21in) s. double-sided (S.FR 274000)
£119048	$195238	(21-Jun-91 GK.B48/R) Autumn landscape with the Arve near Geneva (70x89cm-28x35in) s. (S.FR 300000)
£273092	$535261	(21-Nov-90 SY.Z54/R) Wetterhorn mountains (48x65cm-19x26in) s. (S.FR 680000)
£476	$781	(19-Jun-91 GK.B464) Study of female figure seated (36x13cm-14x5in) pencil (S.FR 1200)
£794	$1325	(5-Jun-91 SY.Z61/R) Portrait of sculptor Jean Vibert (18x13cm-7x5in) chl indian ink (S.FR 2000)
£816	$1584	(8-Dec-90 GAB.G2664/R) Etude d'homme etendant son bras pour l'unanimite (32x14cm-13x6in) s. lead pencil Fabriano paper (S.FR 2000)
£949	$1613	(27-May-91 GK.Z5346) Study for L'Amour (20x14cm-8x6in) s.d.1908 pencil (S.FR 2400)
£1049	$2035	(7-Dec-90 GB.B5368) Man standing, possibly portrait of doctor (30x12cm-12x5in) mono. pencil dr squared (DM 3000)
£1190	$1988	(5-Jun-91 SY.Z60/R) Study for portrait of Madame Guenzburger-Moos (50x28cm-20x11in) pencil (S.FR 3000)
£1285	$2159	(24-Apr-91 G.Z54/R) Study for Freude an der Natur (34x40cm-13x16in) s. pencil (S.FR 3200)
£1304	$2217	(30-May-91 EA.Z165/R) Study of figure os man holding staff (52x21cm-20x8in) chk. (S.FR 3300)
£1304	$2217	(30-May-91 EA.Z162/R) Study for 'Der Tag II' (21x16cm-8x6in) s. pencil (S.FR 3300)
£1399	$2713	(7-Dec-90 GB.B5867) Female nude seated on floor (21x16cm-8x6in) s. pencil dr squared (DM 4000)
£1429	$2343	(19-Jun-91 GK.B460) The reaper (43x58cm-17x23in) chk (S.FR 3600)
£1526	$2991	(21-Nov-90 SY.Z58/R) Lady with hat (36x22cm-14x9in) pencil (S.FR 3800)
£1548	$2677	(22-May-91 GS.B2111) Study of standing female (44x27cm-17x11in) st.sig. pencil (S.FR 3900)

HODLER, Ferdinand (1853-1918) Swiss-cont.

£1573	$3052	(7-Dec-90 GB.B5865) Lansquenet with outstretched arms (30x22cm-12x9in) pencil dr squared (DM 4500)
£1680	$3276	(17-Oct-90 G.Z22/R) Calf (17x21cm-7x8in) s. pencil double-sided (S.FR 4200)
£1746	$2863	(19-Jun-91 GK.B467) Portrait of young woman (61x47cm-24x19in) s. bodycol W/C over pencil (S.FR 4400)
£1748	$3392	(7-Dec-90 GB.B5864) Lansquenet with halberd (51x21cm-20x8in) chk squared (DM 5000)
£1796	$3538	(13-Nov-90 GF.L5361/R) Study of figure, possibly for Wahrheit I (26x40cm-10x16in) mono.d.1898 pencil indian ink pen (S.FR 4400)
£1905	$3124	(19-Jun-91 GK.B463/R) Study of male swearing oath for L'Unanimite (44x39cm-17x15in) carpenter's pencil blue pen squared (S.FR 4800)
£2063	$3384	(19-Jun-91 GK.B461/R) Study of four reclining female figures (26x29cm-10x11in) s. indian ink pen over pencil (S.FR 5200)
£2063	$3384	(19-Jun-91 GK.B462) Dent du Midi (34x44cm-13x17in) chk pencil (S.FR 5200)
£2098	$4070	(7-Dec-90 GB.B5866/R) Two women walking (39x22cm-15x9in) s. pen indian ink over pencil W/C (DM 6000)
£2400	$4680	(17-Oct-90 G.Z101/R) Cow in Alpine landscape (13x22cm-5x9in) s. W/C (S.FR 6000)
£2619	$4295	(19-Jun-91 GK.B468/R) Portrait of James Vibert as warrior in 1476 in battle near Murten (40x53cm-16x21in) s.i. carpenter pencil (S.FR 6600)
£2698	$4506	(5-Jun-91 SY.Z62/R) Portrait of Berthe Hodler (15x13cm-6x5in) s. pencil indian ink (S.FR 6800)
£5556	$9111	(19-Jun-91 GK.B458/R) Study for The Day (34x29cm-13x11in) i.verso W/C over pen paper on board (S.FR 14000)
£7937	$13254	(5-Jun-91 SY.Z63/R) Figure study for Blick ins Unendliche (30x15cm-12x6in) oil gouache (S.FR 20000)

HODLER, Ferdinand (attrib) (1853-1918) Swiss

| £996 | $1942 | (24-Oct-90 GD.B474/R) Chalet near Hilterfingen (22x27cm-9x11in) i.verso (S.FR 2500) |

HOEBER, Arthur (1854-1915) American

| £1027 | $1900 | (8-Mar-91 S.BM146/R) Near Nutley N.J (30x46cm-12x18in) s. i. verso |
| £1856 | $3600 | (24-Aug-90 RB.HY181/R) Twilight (46x56cm-18x22in) s. |

HOECKE, Robert van den (1622-1668) Flemish

| £3878 | $7600 | (6-Nov-90 GF.L2053/R) Winter landscape with skaters (17x23cm-7x9in) gouache paper on panel (S.FR 9500) |

HOEF, A van (17th C) Dutch

| £5929 | $10079 | (30-May-91 EA.Z351/R) Cavalry skirmish before a fort (58x83cm-23x33in) rem.sig. panel (S.FR 15000) |

HOEFEL, Johann Nepomuk (1786-1864) Austrian

| £1075 | $2042 | (28-Feb-91 D.V26/R) Portrait of gentleman. Portrait of lady (67x53cm-26x21in) one s.d.1824 pair (A.S 22000) |

HOEFFLER, Adolf (1826-?) German

| £1678 | $3272 | (10-Oct-90 WE.MU166/R) Hunter in wooded landscape, autumn (40x34cm-16x13in) s. panel (DM 5000) |
| £1795 | $3500 | (25-Oct-90 GRO.B63/R) Horse and rider in landscape (41x74cm-16x29in) s. |

HOEHME, Gerhard (1920-1990) German

£2740	$4466	(14-Jun-91 L.K952) Two shapes on red ground (59x76cm-23x30in) s.d.55 paper (DM 8000)
£10811	$18703	(21-May-91 WK.M50/R) Kleine Welt in ocker (45x45cm-18x18in) s. s.i.d.1955 (DM 32000)
£15017	$29433	(20-Nov-90 L.K278/R) Kleine Schwarzwelt (40x60cm-16x24in) s. s.i.d.1956stretcher fabric (DM 44000)
£21233	$34610	(14-Jun-91 L.K951/R) Untitled (98x79cm-39x31in) s. canvas on panel (DM 62000)
£751	$1472	(20-Nov-90 L.K281/R) Dalmatien (25x37cm-10x15in) s.i.d.1955 indian ink pen wash dr. (DM 2200)
£1909	$3742	(20-Nov-90 BR.M115/R) Studio (28x40cm-11x16in) d.1971 pencil (I.L 4200000)
£2000	$3920	(20-Nov-90 BR.M114/R) Studio per Fenster Mediatoren (28x40cm-11x16in) d.1971 pencil mixed media (I.L 4400000)
£2730	$5352	(20-Nov-90 L.K284/R) Labanus (37x26cm-15x10in) mono.i.d.1980 W/C pencil (DM 8000)
£8532	$16724	(20-Nov-90 L.K280/R) Untitled (73x49cm-29x19in) s.d.55 mixed media paper on canvas (DM 25000)
£10239	$20068	(20-Nov-90 L.K282/R) Untitled (66x50cm-26x20in) s. oil tempera htd.white board (DM 30000)
£10616	$17305	(14-Jun-91 L.K953/R) Untitled (65x50cm-26x20in) s.d.56 oil chk board (DM 31000)
£14334	$28096	(20-Nov-90 L.K279/R) Moribundi (50x71cm-20x28in) s.d.1978 s.i.d.verso acrylic string canvas (DM 42000)

HOELLERING, Stefanie (1955-) German

| £3378 | $5743 | (28-May-91 KF.M749/R) Interior (174x183cm-69x72in) i.d.1982verso hessian (DM 10000) |

HOEN, Cornelis Peter (1814-1880) Dutch
£769	$1492	(4-Dec-90 FN.S1876) Dutch river landscape with farmstead and figures skating (23x32cm-9x13in) s. panel (DM 2200)
£976	$1912	(6-Nov-90 SY.AM72) Figures on frozen river by mill (23x29cm-9x11in) s. panel (D.FL 3200)
£1078	$2134	(31-Jan-91 D.V150/R) Winter scene on frozen canal (18x24cm-7x9in) s. panel (A.S 22000)

HOERLE, Heinrich (1895-1936) German
£6826	$13379	(24-Nov-90 VG.B301/R) Wald (38x40cm-15x16in) mono.d.1934 panel (DM 20000)
£13652	$26758	(22-Nov-90 L.K1022) Still life with pears (58x70cm-23x28in) mono.c.1927 mono. i.verso panel (DM 40000)
£18430	$36123	(22-Nov-90 L.K1024/R) Woman in woods (41x22cm-16x9in) mono.i.d.1931 paper (DM 54000)
£22526	$44150	(22-Nov-90 L.K1023/R) Woman (70x46cm-28x18in) mono. panel (DM 66000)
£2560	*$5017*	*(22-Nov-90 L.K1025/R) Torso of woman. Female nude seated (55x46cm-22x18in) mono.d.1926 st.studio mixed media double-sided (DM 7500)*
£2662	*$5218*	*(22-Nov-90 L.K1026/R) Madonna with fish (50x35cm-20x14in) mono.d.34 s.i.d.verso wax crayon board (DM 7800)*
£2740	*$4466*	*(15-Jun-91 L.K316/R) Female nude standing (27x17cm-11x7in) mono.d.1935 indian ink pen (DM 8000)*

HOESE, Jean de la (1846-1917) Belgian
| £1000 | $1680 | (18-Jul-91 CSK120/R) Summer beauty (31x23cm-12x9in) s. panel |

HOESSLIN, George von (1851-1923) Hungarian
| £751 | $1412 | (21-Sep-90 N.M3214/R) Young lady in forest (169x113cm-67x44in) s. (DM 2200) |
| £6316 | $12000 | (27-Feb-91 SY.NY289/R) Nymphen rufen Odysseus (112x188cm-44x74in) s.i. |

HOET, Gerard (17/18th C) Dutch
£2397	$3908	(12-Jun-91 N.M315/R) Easter celebrations before classical ruins (51x60cm-20x24in) (DM 7000)
£3874	$7476	(12-Dec-90 ARC.P81/R) Antoine et Cleopatre (63x66cm-25x26in) (F.FR 38000)
£4564	$9037	(30-Jan-91 APT.P216/R) le Christ et les enfants (66x84cm-26x33in) (F.FR 45000)
£13361	$25920	(5-Dec-90 APT.P44/R) Le banquet des Dieux (32x41cm-13x16in) s. panel (F.FR 130000)
£14056	$22631	(25-Jun-91 APT.P42/R) La Fete de Pomone (45x52cm-18x20in) s. (F.FR 140000)
£550	*$930*	*(16-Apr-91 C253) Athena on Mount Helicon attended by the muses (25x51cm-10x20in) blk.chk.ink wash*

HOET, Gerard (attrib) (17/18th C) Dutch
| £3785 | $6510 | (14-May-91 GF.L2299/R) Jesus Blessing the Children (29x35cm-11x14in) copper (S.FR 9500) |

HOET, Gerard (style) (17/18th C) Dutch
| £1190 | $2000 | (17-Jul-91 SY.NY89/R) Diana after the bath (29x36cm-11x14in) panel |
| £4000 | $7720 | (12-Dec-90 S125/R) Allegories of Sight and Sound (44x35cm-17x14in) pair |

HOETERICKX, Emile (1858-1923) Belgian
| *£495* | *$969* | *(21-Nov-90 GM.B1291) Au bon vieux temps s. gouache (B.FR 30000)* |

HOEYDONCK, Paul van (1925-) Belgian
£589	*$990*	*(23-Apr-91 C.A782) Composition (18x27cm-7x11in) s.d.1956 gouache (B.FR 36000)*
£1193	*$2016*	*(15-Apr-91 CC.P137) Space mirror with flying madonna (71x71cm-28x28in) s.i.d.1964 verso mixed media panel (F.FR 12000)*
£1193	*$2016*	*(15-Apr-91 CC.P138) Hidden Space-ca (70x70cm-28x28in) s.i.d.1964 verso mixed media panel (F.FR 12000)*

HOFBAUER, J (20th C) ?
| £556 | $961 | (6-May-91 ZEL.L1742) Landscape with ducks near pond and village beyond (28x38cm-11x15in) s. panel one of pair (DM 1650) |
| £556 | $961 | (6-May-91 ZEL.L1743) Poultry in farmyard (28x38cm-11x15in) s. one of pair (DM 1650) |

HOFBAUER, Ludwig (1843-?) Austrian
| *£588* | *$1164* | *(31-Jan-91 D.V196/R) Molkerbastei, Vienna (13x11cm-5x4in) s.d.1893 W/C (A.S 12000)* |
| *£1027* | *$1675* | *(12-Jun-91 N.M244/R) Am Hof, Vienna (23x38cm-9x15in) s.d.1906 W/C pen htd.white (DM 3000)* |

HOFER, Andre (20th C) French
| *£2345* | *$4525* | *(15-Dec-90 D.P8/R) Grand nu cubiste (97x146cm-38x57in) s.d.21 (F.FR 23000)* |

HOFER, Heinrich (1825-1878) German
| £4196 | $8098 | (12-Dec-90 WE.MU59/R) Lake Hintersee landscape (61x82cm-24x32in) s.i.d.1872 (DM 12000) |
| £15035 | $29017 | (12-Dec-90 WE.MU49/R) Journey home through snowy Isar landscape (60x80cm-24x31in) s.i.d.1872 (DM 43000) |

HOFER, Karl (1878-1955) German

£2534	$4307	(31-May-91 GB.B6380/R) Garden corner (50x47cm-20x19in) board (DM 7500)
£12969	$25420	(22-Nov-90 L.K1028/R) Chalk oven in Ticino (78x100cm-31x39in) mono. (DM 38000)
£12969	$25420	(24-Nov-90 VG.B272/R) Landscape, Bernau (49x69cm-19x27in) mono.c.1920 (DM 38000)
£16892	$28716	(1-Jun-91 VG.B229/R) Flowers in white vase (48x34cm-19x13in) mono. bears i.d.1932stretcher (DM 50000)
£18243	$31014	(1-Jun-91 VG.B228/R) Self portrait with straw hat (70x60cm-28x24in) mono.d.1917 (DM 54000)
£19113	$37461	(24-Nov-90 VG.B242/R) Still life with jug, bowl and fruits (43x68cm-17x27in) mono.c.1934 (DM 56000)
£20809	$36000	(9-May-91 CH.NY247/R) Malcescine (50x80cm-20x31in) init.d.37
£22184	$43481	(24-Nov-90 VG.B243/R) Three beauties (100x75cm-39x30in) mono.d.1943 (DM 65000)
£24407	$40759	(6-Jun-91 HN.H418/R) Tessin landscape (80x100cm-31x39in) mono.d.1935 (DM 72000)
£24476	$47483	(7-Dec-90 GB.B6678/R) Woman at window (90x71cm-35x28in) mono.d.43 (DM 70000)
£25676	$43392	(3-May-91 SA.A818/R) Before the night (106x81cm-42x32in) mono.d.50 (DM 76000)
£27986	$54853	(23-Nov-90 VG.B37/R) Houses in Ticino (56x68cm-22x27in) mono.c.1935 (DM 82000)
£28209	$48802	(21-May-91 WK.M51/R) Man and woman (90x70cm-35x28in) mono.d.1948 i.stretcher (DM 83500)
£30405	$51689	(30-May-91 SY.BE57/R) Figures seated round table (56x65cm-22x26in) mono. (DM 90000)
£37162	$63176	(30-May-91 SY.BE58/R) Landscape in Ticino (66x81cm-26x32in) mono.d.35 (DM 110000)
£37931	$72828	(1-Dec-90 SA.A2447/R) Female nude reclining by window (80x120cm-31x47in) mono.d.49 (DM 110000)
£1153	*$1925*	*(6-Jun-91 HN.H420/R) Two little girls (26x41cm-10x16in) mono. chl. (DM 3400)*
£1520	*$2584*	*(1-Jun-91 VG.B591/R) Female nude holding hands across head. Old woman seated (31x23cm-12x9in) mono. pen wash brush (DM 4500)*
£2196	*$3733*	*(1-Jun-91 VG.B257/R) Two female nude standing (50x36cm-20x14in) mono. indian ink brush over pencil (DM 6500)*
£2200	*$4290*	*(19-Oct-90 C101/R) Die Umarmung (38x42cm-15x17in) s.init.i. pen brush ink*

HOFF, George Raynor (20th C) ?

£602	*$1157*	*(27-Nov-90 JRL.S75/R) San Andrea della Valle, Rome (33x49cm-13x19in) pencil ink wash (A.D 1500)*

HOFF, Guy (1889-1962) American

£5294	$9000	(1-Jun-91 IH.NY184/R) Young woman in summer hat, hand on hip (76x58cm-30x23in) s.

HOFF, Jakob (1838-1892) German

£774	$1300	(28-Apr-91 HG.C356) Woman and cow (56x81cm-22x32in) s.

HOFF, Margo (1912-?) American

£983	$1700	(21-May-91 CE.NY518/R) In cathedral (76x50cm-30x20in) s. canvasboard

HOFFBAUER, Charles (1875-1957) French

£1777	$3500	(16-Nov-90 S.BM63/R) Poursuite - figures dashing through winter landscape (48x71cm-19x28in) s.
£415	*$800*	*(10-Dec-90 H.C1068) Sketch World War I (46x61cm-18x24in) s. artist's st.verso pencil W/C*

HOFFMAN, Murray (20th C) American

£970	$1600	(10-Jul-91 D.NY44) A portrait of a Venetian lady (99x74cm-39x29in) s.d.36

HOFFMAN, Nancy M (1949-) American

£1223	$2361	(16-Dec-90 CSC.P48/R) Tipped Tourmaline no.1 (135x135cm-53x53in) (F.FR 12000)

HOFFMANN, Ansen (?) ?

£1800	$3564	(30-Jan-91 CSK296) Salome (99x74cm-39x29in) s.

HOFFMANN, Anton (1863-?) German

£1119	$2159	(12-Dec-90 N.M562) Horse-drawn cart with driver resting outside farmhouse (46x75cm-18x30in) s.i. (DM 3200)
£1174	$2290	(10-Oct-90 WE.MU186/R) The curler s.i. panel (DM 3500)
£548	*$893*	*(12-Jun-91 N.M245) Die Gallier in Rom (60x80cm-24x31in) s.i. i.verso W/C bodycol board (DM 1600)*

HOFFMANN, Carl Heinrich (19th C) German

£874	*$1696*	*(4-Dec-90 FN.S1885/R) River landscape with cattle watering and shepherd girl (16x15cm-6x6in) mono. i.verso W/C (DM 2500)*

HOFFMANN, Hans (after) (16th C) German

£2184	$3800	(27-Mar-91 D.NY55) Study of squirrel (25x20cm-10x8in) bears init.d.1571 copper

HOFFMANN, Hans (style) (16th C) German
£1796 $3000   (23-Jan-91 D.NY25) Portrait of Albrecht Durer (18x13cm-7x5in) on copper

HOFFMANN, Josef (1831-1904) Austrian
£3199 $5534   (6-May-91 ZEL.L1744/R) View of Heiligenblut with figures and
                    Glossglockner range beyond, spring (125x101cm-49x40in) s.d.1885
                    (DM 9500)
£437 $717   (20-Jun-91 D.V47/R) Design (30x21cm-12x8in) mono pencil pen indian ink
                    (A.S 9000)
£1214 $1990   (20-Jun-91 D.V45/R) Design for fabric with palm branches
                    (36x29cm-14x11in) mono pencil pen brush indian ink (A.S 25000)

HOFFMANN, Kurt R see SONDERBORG, Kurt R H

HOFFMANN, Paul (19th C) German
£2300 $3772   (18-Jun-91 PH119/R) Gypsy girl smoking pipe. Gypsy girl spinning
                    (53x37cm-21x15in) s.d.1886 pair

HOFFMANN-FALLERSLEBEN, Franz (1855-1927) German
£1538 $2969   (12-Dec-90 N.M563/R) Pond in snowy wooded landscape (96x131cm-38x52in)
                    s.i.d.1883 (DM 4400)
£1748 $3374   (14-Dec-90 BM.B630/R) Wooded landscape with North German farmstead
                    (94x130cm-37x51in) s.d.07 (DM 5000)
£2218 $4348   (24-Nov-90 SA.A690/R) View of farmhouse (66x49cm-26x19in) s. (DM 6500)

HOFLAND, Thomas Christopher (attrib) (1777-1843) British
£4500 $7425   (10-Jul-91 S77/R) The Thames near Henley (48x66cm-19x26in)

HOFLEHNER, Rudolf (1916-?) German
£526 $911   (8-May-91 D.V143/R) Untitled (43x60cm-17x24in) mono.d.49 pen brush
                    col.indian ink (A.S 11000)
£616 $1005   (14-Jun-91 L.K958) Untitled (51x34cm-20x13in) mono.d.1961 indian ink pen
                    (DM 1800)
£680 $1115   (20-Jun-91 D.V117/R) Untitled (39x57cm-15x22in) W/C (A.S 14000)
£1214 $1990   (20-Jun-91 D.V116/R) Untitled (39x57cm-15x22in) s.d.49 W/C (A.S 25000)

HOFMAN-BANG, Ellen (20th C) Scandinavian
£3000 $5160   (17-May-91 C125/R) Confidante (69x60cm-27x24in) init.d.10

HOFMANN, Hans (1880-1966) American/German
£3061 $6000   (14-Feb-91 CH.NY6/R) Untitled (48x63cm-19x25in) s.d.61 paper
£12755 $25000   (8-Nov-90 CH.NY303/R) The peacock (51x42cm-20x17in) s.i.d.62 board
£16582 $32500   (7-Nov-90 SY.NY115/R) Le bouquet (42x35cm-17x14in) s.d.44 board
£18343 $31000   (1-May-91 SY.NY192/R) Landscape (63x76cm-25x30in) plywood
£178571 $350000 (6-Nov-90 SY.NY11/R) Radiant space (152x122cm-60x48in) s.d.'55 l. verso
£204082 $400000 (6-Nov-90 SY.NY4/R) Flaming earth (122x152cm-48x60in) s.d.65 l. verso
£1026 $2000   (10-Oct-90 SY.NY432/R) Head of student (46x41cm-18x16in) s.d.XXXIII
                    pencil ink
£3316 $6500   (12-Feb-91 SY.NY322/R) Untitled (28x36cm-11x14in) init.d.41 ink crayon
£3827 $7500   (15-Feb-91 SY.NY138/R) Figurative (30x20cm-12x8in) init. W/C crayon ink
£5102 $10000   (7-Nov-90 SY.NY132/R) Figurative (30x20cm-12x8in) init. W/C crayon ink
£7653 $15000   (15-Feb-91 SY.NY130/R) Untitled (60x48cm-24x19in) s. gouache
£8122 $16000   (5-Oct-90 CH.NY9/R) Fantsia in red and bue (57x72cm-22x28in) s.d.56
                    gouache
£10204 $20000   (8-Nov-90 CH.NY113/R) Untitled (28x36cm-11x14in) s. gouache graphite
£10204 $20000   (7-Nov-90 SY.NY118/R) Untitled (60x45cm-24x18in) s. gouache
£10651 $18000   (1-May-91 SY.NY217/R) Untitled (25x96cm-10x38in) s. oil gouache
                    paperboard
£11168 $22000   (4-Oct-90 SY.NY1/R) Untitled (40x32cm-16x13in) casein plywood

HOFMANN, Ludwig von (1861-1945) German
£1877 $3679   (22-Nov-90 L.K1032/R) The blue grotto with bathers (61x72cm-24x28in)
                    mono. hessian (DM 5500)
£5068 $8767   (21-May-91 WK.M55/R) Alpine landscape (40x68cm-16x27in) mono.d.1910
                    board on panel (DM 15000)
£350 $678   (7-Dec-90 GB.B6687) Female nude seated on rock (51x30cm-20x12in) mono.
                    ochre bister (DM 1000)
£408 $657   (28-Jun-91 BM.B911/R) Diabolo (24x32cm-9x13in) mono.i.d.1910 col.chk
                    over pencil (DM 1200)
£420 $814   (7-Dec-90 GB.B6685) Boys playing and fighting on beach (18x26cm-7x10in)
                    mono.c.1910 pastel over chl (DM 1200)
£510 $821   (28-Jun-91 BM.B910/R) Bathers (26x28cm-10x11in) s.mono. col.chk over
                    pencil (DM 1500)
£526 $1000   (9-Jan-91 CH.NY81/R) Study of partially draped women by mountainous
                    stream (16x25cm-6x10in) init. pastel wash
£559 $1085   (7-Dec-90 GB.B6684) Arcadian landscape with water carriers by well
                    (32x22cm-13x9in) c.1905 W/C chl sold with two other drawings
                    (DM 1600)
£872 $1701   (12-Oct-90 AW.H2554) Two bathing girls with red paradise bird
                    (16x24cm-6x9in) mono.pastel (DM 2600)
£874 $1696   (7-Dec-90 GB.B6686/R) Study of man picking up and throwing stones
                    (49x57cm-19x22in) mono.d.1906 chl (DM 2500)
£874 $1696   (7-Dec-90 GB.B6683/R) Boys and girls by woodlake (25x37cm-10x15in)
                    c.1910 pastel (DM 2500)
£1351 $2297   (31-May-91 GB.B6387/R) Female nude seen from behind seated on rock
                    (63x47cm-25x19in) s. pastel (DM 4000)

HOFMANN, Ludwig von (1861-1945) German-cont.
£16552 $31779   (26-Nov-90 WK.M31/R) Girls dancing and bathing (80x138cm-31x54in) s. paper on canvas (DM 48000)

HOFMANN, Ludwig von (attrib) (1861-1945) German
£813 $1569   (14-Dec-90 ZOF.Z958/R) Boys bathing and playing with toy sailing ships (25x43cm-10x17in) mono.i. pastel (S.FR 2000)

HOFMANN, Vlastimil (1881-?) Czechoslovakian
£789 $1396   (23-Mar-91 HO.P3) Portrait of an old man s. board (P.Z 13500000)
£804 $1591   (1-Feb-91 DE.B6) Portrait of boy in landscape (24x34cm-9x13in) s.d.1929 board (P.Z 15000000)
£1340 $2627   (26-Jan-91 PSA.W10) Angel (71x50cm-28x20in) s.d.1934 (P.Z 25000000)
£2051 $3896   (3-Mar-91 REM.W4) Youth and old age (35x51cm-14x20in) s. panel (P.Z 37000000)
£2161 $4107   (3-Mar-91 REM.W5) Nike legionow (92x73cm-36x29in) s. board (P.Z 39000000)
£3753 $7355   (26-Jan-91 PSA.W11) Bird (62x73cm-24x29in) s.d.1922 panel (P.Z 70000000)

HOFMANN-GROTZINGEN, Gustav (1889-) German
£651 $1165   (12-Mar-91 FN.S2431) Snowy wooded river landscape (51x42cm-20x17in) s. (DM 1900)

HOFMANN-ZEITZ, Ludwig (1832-1895) German
£2365 $3997   (3-May-91 SA.A1662/R) In the high alps (55x41cm-22x16in) s. (DM 7000)

HOFMEISTER, Johannes (1914-?) Danish
£671 $1315   (13-Feb-91 KH.K72 a) Houses by the sea (31x38cm-12x15in) init. masonite (D.KR 7500)
£893 $1652   (5-Mar-91 RAS.K149) View of the sea with figures and windmolle in foreground (50x61cm-20x24in) init. (D.KR 10000)
£894 $1753   (13-Feb-91 KH.K72) Evening, Hjorring Bjerge, early spring (38x45cm-15x18in) init. panel (D.KR 10000)
£1100 $1893   (15-May-91 RAS.K86) Hilly landscape with sea in background and figure in foreground (40x50cm-16x20in) init. panel (D.KR 12500)
£1167 $2299   (14-Nov-90 KH.K62) Figure in landscape (50x60cm-20x24in) init. (D.KR 13000)
£1449 $2797   (12-Dec-90 RAS.K196) View of the bay (51x62cm-20x24in) init. (D.KR 16000)

HOFSCHEN, Edgar (1941-) German
£1027 $1675   (14-Jun-91 L.K959/R) Untitled (46x48cm-18x19in) s.d.68 oil metal collage panel (DM 3000)
£1229 $2408   (20-Nov-90 L.K294/R) Untitled (72x95cm-28x37in) s.d.1973 paper collage on canvas (DM 3600)

HOGARTH (after) (18th C) British
£399 $650   (12-Jun-91 GM.B4018/R) La halte (12x15cm-5x6in) min. (B.FR 24000)

HOGARTH, William (1697-1794) British
£365000 $602250   (10-Jul-91 S33/R) The Edwards Hamilton Family on terrace in Kensington (68x86cm-27x34in)

HOGARTH, William (after) (1697-1794) British
£1100 $2123   (13-Dec-90 B11) Evening (137x126cm-54x50in)
£1150 $1990   (20-May-91 SWS286/R) The enraged musician (45x51cm-18x20in) indist.s.

HOGARTH, William (studio) (1697-1794) British
£1081 $1762   (10-Jun-91 W.T1305/R) Portrait of the artist's mother (61x52cm-24x20in) (C.D 2000)

HOGARTH, William (style) (1697-1794) British
£1500 $2850   (1-Mar-91 C41/R) Portrait of Edward Thelwall holding black tricorn hat (76x64cm-30x25in) i.d.1754 painted oval

HOGARTH, William and LAMBERT, George (18th C) British
£200000 $394000   (14-Nov-90 S98/R) Chiswick House, Middlesex (77x103cm-30x41in) s.d.1741

HOGE, Oscar (20th C) ?
£556 $935   (23-Apr-91 C.A537) Marine (35x53cm-14x21in) s. panel (B.FR 34000)

HOGER, R A (1876-1928) Austrian
£765 $1500   (15-Feb-91 DM.D2053/R) Schubert sitting in park with other figures (89x122cm-35x48in) s.

HOGER, Rudolf Alfred (1876-1928) Austrian
£2373 $4248   (11-Apr-91 D.V291/R) Bacchanale (80x160cm-31x63in) s.i.d.1913 (A.S 50000)

HOGFELDT, Robert (1894-1986) Swedish
£1158 $2247   (5-Dec-90 AB.S7107/R) Jesus in the temple (60x73cm-24x29in) s. (S.KR 12500)
£616 $1034   (24-Apr-91 BA.S277/R) Troll laughing in doorway (21x27cm-8x11in) s. W/C (S.KR 6500)

HOGFELDT, Robert (1894-1986) Swedish-cont.
£880	*$1708*	*(5-Dec-90 AB.S7104/R) The Princess and the Dragon (39x54cm-15x21in) s. W/C (S.KR 9500)*
£1838	*$3603*	*(6-Nov-90 BA.S372/R) Troll party (32x40cm-13x16in) s. W/C (S.KR 20000)*

HOGGATT, William (1880-1961) British
£700	$1211	(10-May-91 CBS238/R) Rocket House at Castletown (20x25cm-8x10in) s. board
£700	$1358	(7-Dec-90 CBS242) Landscape with geese near trees (25x23cm-10x9in) s.
£866	$1664	(2-Dec-90 M.V54) Paris, le Pont Neuf (46x33cm-18x13in) s. (F.FR 8500)
£1600	$2768	(10-May-91 CBS237) Lake at Ballasalla (33x25cm-13x10in) s. board
£1700	$2941	(10-May-91 CBS235/R) Darragh at Port Erin (46x56cm-18x22in) s. board
£1900	$3287	(10-May-91 CBS234/R) Orchard (51x61cm-20x24in) s.
£3000	$5820	(7-Dec-90 CBS284) Glendown House, Port St.Mary (43x53cm-17x21in) s.i.verso
£400	*$692*	*(10-May-91 CBS252) Smallest farm, Glen Tramman, Lezayre, Isle of Man (38x46cm-15x18in) s. W/C*
£420	*$727*	*(10-May-91 CBS257/R) Gathering seaweed (15x18cm-6x7in) s. W/C*
£460	*$796*	*(10-May-91 CBS254/R) Gathering seaweed (23x33cm-9x13in) s. W/C*
£630	*$1222*	*(7-Dec-90 CBS246) Manx Glen at crocus time (25x33cm-10x13in) s. W/C*
£630	*$1222*	*(7-Dec-90 CBS244) Weeding the vegetables (23x30cm-9x12in) s. W/C*
£800	*$1384*	*(10-May-91 CBS210/R) Unloading catch (25x36cm-10x14in) s. W/C*
£880	*$1654*	*(6-Aug-90 SWS320) Moonlight (37x46cm-15x18in) s. W/C*
£900	*$1557*	*(10-May-91 CBS255/R) Dancing waters (38x56cm-15x22in) s. W/C*
£1000	*$1950*	*(18-Oct-90 SC3001/R) Unloading the catch (24x35cm-9x14in) s. W/C scratching out*
£1050	*$2037*	*(7-Dec-90 CBS266) Manx landscape (36x46cm-14x18in) s. W/C*
£1300	*$2522*	*(7-Dec-90 CBS245) Flowering cherry trees (36x48cm-14x19in) s. col.chks*
£1400	*$2716*	*(7-Dec-90 CBS247) Manx harbour scene, unloading the catch (28x38cm-11x15in) s. W/C*
£1400	*$2716*	*(7-Dec-90 CBS267) The village church (61x76cm-24x30in) s. W/C*
£1400	*$2422*	*(10-May-91 CBS236/R) Ploughing in Manx Hills (51x61cm-20x24in) s. W/C*
£3600	*$6984*	*(7-Dec-90 CBS268) A Manx glen (53x71cm-21x28in) s. W/C*

HOGNER, F (?) ?
£727	$1453	(6-Feb-91 N.M622) Wood clearing (51x39cm-20x15in) s.d.36 (DM 2100)

HOGUET, Charles (1821-1870) French
£874	$1687	(10-Dec-90 L.K447) Peasant woman and child by stream with ducks and view of farmhouse (27x21cm-11x8in) board (DM 2500)
£878	$1493	(27-May-91 L.K286) Still life of pot on rechod and fruit on table (15x13cm-6x5in) s.d.1863 panel (DM 2600)
£1429	$2814	(15-Nov-90 EA.Z192/R) Beached fishing boats (33x44cm-13x17in) s.d.1854 (S.FR 3500)
£2692	$5250	(26-Oct-90 S.W2630/R) Die Muhle aux Norderney (20x38cm-8x15in) s.d.1865 panel
£680	*$1326*	*(22-Oct-90 SWS201/R) French street scene (22x11cm-9x4in) s. W/C over pencil htd bodycol*

HOHENBERG, Josef Wagner see WAGNER-HOHENBERG, Josef

HOHENBERG, Wagner (19th C) Austrian
£1974	$3750	(27-Feb-91 SY.NY159/R) Reunion (61x81cm-24x32in) s.

HOHENLEITER, Francisco (20th C) ?
£6552	$11335	(8-May-91 FER.M264 r/R) Paseando a caballo por las calles de Granada (60x81cm-24x32in) s.d.1941 (S.P 1200000)

HOHENLOHE, Emilie de (19th C) German
£693	$1338	(12-Dec-90 ZZ.F67/R) Roses (27x21cm-11x8in) s. bears init. panel (F.FR 6800)

HOHLWEIN, Ludwig (1879-1949) ?
£780	*$1302*	*(5-Jun-91 DO.H2741/R) Munich street scene, winter (42x54cm-17x21in) s.i. W/C (DM 2300)*

HOHNECK, Adolf (1812-1878) German
£2622	$5061	(14-Dec-90 BM.B631/R) Elbe landscape with shipping and figures and view of Dresden (32x43cm-13x17in) s. paper on board (DM 7500)

HOIN, Claude (1750-1817) French
£1300	*$2301*	*(21-Mar-91 LC.P19/R) Paysage au temple antique (15x19cm-6x7in) s. gouache (F.FR 13000)*
£8000	*$15440*	*(11-Dec-90 C84/R) A seated man resting on his arm on a table. A woman three-quarter length (49x32cm-19x13in) chk. double-sided*

HOLBECH, N P (1804-1889) Danish
£1425	$2793	(22-Nov-90 RAS.V723/R) Mountain farmer coming to Rome to sing to Madonna pictures (57x49cm-22x19in) (D.KR 16000)

HOLBEIN (after) (16th C) German
£800	$1312	(19-Jun-91 CSK214) Cardinal Wolsey (58x43cm-23x17in) panel

HOLBEIN, Eduard Carl Friedrich (1807-1875) German
£10490	$20245	(12-Dec-90 SY.MU13/R) The old pilgrim (135x153cm-53x60in) s.d.1835 arched top (DM 30000)

HOLBEIN, Hans (15/16th C) German
£1078 $1800   (23-Jan-91 D.NY26) Portrait of Erasmus (36x25cm-14x10in) i. panel

HOLBEIN, Hans (younger-after) (1497-1593) German
£2700 $5265   (25-Oct-90 CSK41/R) Portrait of Nicholas Kratzer (82x63cm-32x25in) panel

HOLBEIN, Therese (1785-1859) Austrian
£635 $1207   (28-Feb-91 D.V53/R) Landscape near Modling (31x28cm-12x11in) i.
                  (A.S 13000)

HOLBO, Halvdan (1907-) Norwegian
£608 $1185   (11-Oct-90 BU.O60/R) Chrysanthemums and red sofa (38x46cm-15x18in)
                  s.d.1954 s.i.verso (N.KR 7000)
£868 $1693   (11-Oct-90 BU.O61/R) Fruit and flowers (46x65cm-18x26in) s.d.35
                  s.i.verso (N.KR 10000)

HOLBO, Kristen (1869-1953) Norwegian
£1042 $2031   (11-Oct-90 BU.O62/R) Clouds lifting (65x82cm-26x32in) s.d.38 i.verso
                  (N.KR 12000)

HOLCK, Julius (1845-1911) Norwegian
£890 $1719   (13-Dec-90 BU.O29/R) Horns of an elk (37x146cm-15x57in) (N.KR 10000)
£1202 $2320   (13-Dec-90 BU.O30/R) Still life of fish, hare and dead game
                  (73x225cm-29x89in) (N.KR 13500)
£2344 $3914   (3-Jun-91 B.O69/R) Two ptarmigans (48x74cm-19x29in) s.d.89 (N.KR 27000)
£5877 $11343   (13-Dec-90 BU.O31/R) Midsummer-night bonfire 1890 (184x159cm-72x63in)
                  s.d.90 (N.KR 66000)
£18700 $36091   (13-Dec-90 BU.O28/R) Bergen harbour (182x286cm-72x113in) s.d.1891
                  (N.KR 210000)

HOLD, A (19th C) British
*£523 $900   (15-May-91 D.NY8) Still life with melon, grapes, peach, plums, pears and
                  figs (25x38cm-10x15in) s.d.1808 W/C*

HOLD, Abel (19th C) British
£700 $1358   (22-Aug-90 CSK314) Feeding the geese (46x37cm-18x15in) mono.d.1884
£1400 $2800   (5-Feb-91 S25/R) Grouse (57x79cm-22x31in)

HOLDER, E H (19th C) British
£1732 $3100   (11-Apr-91 FA.PH713) Whitchurch, Salop (84x30cm-33x12in) s.

HOLDER, Edward Henry (fl.1864-1917) British
£640 $1075   (23-Apr-91 SWS350/R) A valley farmstead (68x50cm-27x20in) s.d.1879
£1200 $2364   (13-Nov-90 SWS245/R) A coastal scene (49x74cm-19x29in) s.d.'75
£1368 $2599   (28-Feb-91 D.V62/R) River landscape (33x87cm-13x34in) s. (A.S 28000)
£2439 $4000   (19-Jun-91 B.SF1957/R) Mountain gorge in the highlands with fishermen
                  (60x101cm-24x40in) s.d.1872
£2800 $4676   (5-Jun-91 S144/R) Harvest time (33x86cm-13x34in) s.d.96

HOLDING, Henry James (1833-1872) British
£694 $1200   (10-May-91 S.W2484/R) Peasants along the shore (30x91cm-12x36in)

HOLDREDGE, Ransome G (1836-1899) American
£833 $1600   (17-Dec-90 SY.NY150/R) Indian encampment in Rocky Mountains
                  (76x127cm-30x50in) s. canvas on board

HOLDSTOCK, Alfred Worsley (1820-1901) Canadian
*£439 $860   (20-Nov-90 JOY.T178/R) Thousand Islands (33x51cm-13x20in) s.i. W/C
                  (C.D 1000)*
*£445 $743   (3-Jun-91 R.T124/R) La Chinque Creek, C.W (33x52cm-13x20in) s. pastel
                  (C.D 850)*
*£568 $1113   (5-Nov-90 FB.M247) The Thousand Islands from Wolfe Island
                  (31x49cm-12x19in) s. pastel (C.D 1300)*
*£628 $1049   (4-Jun-91 FB.M35/R) From Gore Island (33x50cm-13x20in) s.i. verso pastel
                  (C.D 1200)*
*£658 $1289   (20-Nov-90 JOY.T86/R) Indian encampment on Madawaska (45x69cm-18x27in)
                  i. col.chk (C.D 1500)*

HOLFELD, Hippolyte (1804-1872) French
£711 $1380   (4-Dec-90 R.T169/R) Three children praying (66x81cm-26x32in) s.d.1852
                  i.verso oval (C.D 1600)

HOLFFERICH, Frans (20th C) ?
£1400 $2758   (1-Nov-90 B44/R) Bathers at the water's edge (26x44cm-10x17in) s. panel

HOLGATE, Edwin Headley (1892-1977) Canadian
£1067 $2069   (3-Dec-90 R.T366/R) Elm tree, Morin Heights (21x27cm-8x11in) init.
                  d.c.1946 verso panel (C.D 2400)
£1754 $3456   (30-Oct-90 SY.T106/R) Portrait of Jennifer (27x22cm-11x9in)
                  init.i.d.verso panel (C.D 4000)
£1778 $3449   (4-Dec-90 P.Q37/R) Baie St Paul (14x17cm-6x7in) init. board (C.D 4000)
£10101 $17374   (14-May-91 JOY.T86/R) Woman with daffodils (52x45cm-20x18in) s.
                  (C.D 20000)

HOLIDAY, Gilbert (1879-1937) British
£1200 $2028   (2-May-91 C87/R) Farm horse (22x30cm-9x12in) s. pencil W/C

HOLIDAY, Gilbert (1879-1937) British-cont.

£1500	$2520	(24-Apr-91 MMB265/R) Team of horses at Royal Tournament (33x46cm-13x18in) pastel
£3000	$5820	(5-Dec-90 PHE61/R) A south wind and a cloudy sky (24x37cm-9x15in) s. pencil gouache W/C
£3200	$6208	(5-Dec-90 PHE21/R) Point to point (35x45cm-14x18in) s. pastel wash
£6200	$11780	(27-Feb-91 MMB170/R) Groom leading a horse from his box (28x41cm-11x16in) s. gouache
£6500	$12025	(7-Mar-91 C23/R) Gone away, Irish hunt (38x59cm-15x23in) s. pastel pencil col.crayon
£6500	$10855	(6-Jun-91 C24/R) Well turned out (38x32cm-15x13in) s. crayon W/C bodycol htd.white

HOLKERTON, Charles (?) British?

£900	$1737	(13-Dec-90 CSK303) Portrait of Hon. Mrs. Thomas in dress and feathered hat, by pillar (91x69cm-36x27in) after Thomas Gainsborough

HOLL, Frank (attrib) (1845-1888) British

£2200	$4334	(1-Nov-90 C335/R) Contemplation (56x41cm-22x16in) i.verso

HOLLAMS, F Mabel (fl.1897-1929) British

£580	$969	(22-Jul-91 SWS1037/R) Chorus girl (39x50cm-15x20in) s.i.d.'52 panel
£680	$1326	(24-Oct-90 DR190/R) Frisco, boxer (51x37cm-20x15in) s.d.49 panel
£700	$1365	(23-Oct-90 SWS497/R) Johnathan (33x46cm-13x18in) s. panel
£1200	$2340	(15-Jan-91 B410) Judy, wire haired Jack Russell pup (31x43cm-12x17in) s. board
£1500	$2460	(19-Jun-91 CSK190) Saddled bay hunter on country road. Saddled bay hunter in field. Dark bay hunter (30x43cm-12x17in) s. panel three
£1700	$3281	(10-Dec-90 PHB47/R) Study of long-haired Jack Russell (31x43cm-12x17in) s. panel
£4500	$7515	(5-Jun-91 S103/R) Thirsk. Gold Bridge. Curlew. Con Cagney (32x43cm-13x17in) s.i. panel four

HOLLAND, Dudley (20th C) British

£820	$1542	(6-Aug-90 SWS100/R) The studio corner (51x84cm-20x33in) s.d.47 i.verso

HOLLAND, James (1799-1870) British

£780	$1521	(15-Jan-91 SWS111/R) View of Greenwich Hospital (56x81cm-22x32in) canvas on board
£860	$1471	(30-Jul-91 SWS164) Coast and Martello tower, Jersey, Channel Islands (29x44cm-11x17in) s.
£900	$1764	(22-Jan-91 PH13/R) The new moon, Greenwich Hospital from the river (27cm-11ins circular) s.i.d.1852verso board
£1200	$2148	(10-Apr-91 S172/R) Dogana and Salute Church, Venice (30x42cm-12x17in) i.verso panel
£2312	$4000	(21-May-91 CE.NY103/R) View of Rialto Bridge, Venice (61x91cm-24x36in) s. canvas on masonite
£14000	$23100	(10-Jul-91 S86/R) Rua Mezericordia, Leiria, Portugal (54x38cm-21x15in) s.d.38 i.d.verso
£15000	$24750	(10-Jul-91 S87/R) Largo da se Velha, Coimbra, Portugal (53x38cm-21x15in) s.d.1838 i.verso
£400	$716	(9-Apr-91 C103) Entrance hall, Naworth Castle, Northumberland (17x23cm-7x9in) init.d.43 pencil W/C
£900	$1485	(9-Jul-91 C83/R) Boats and figures by steps of temple (10x16cm-4x6in) pencil W/C htd.white scratching out
£950	$1881	(30-Jan-91 S167/R) Venetian room at Knole, Sussex (28x41cm-11x16in) mono.i. W/C htd bodycol over pencil
£2000	$3960	(30-Jan-91 S99/R) Washerwomen below palace, Genoa (45x29cm-18x11in) mono.i.d.1868 W/C htd bodycol over pencil
£2400	$4296	(11-Apr-91 S86/R) Salute from Doge's Palace, Venice (25x17cm-10x7in) mono.d.1863 W/C over pencil bodycol
£4000	$7880	(12-Nov-90 PH32) The Bridge of Sighs, Venice (38x26cm-15x10in) init.i.d.1835 W/C

HOLLAND, John (18/19th C) British

£550	$946	(16-May-91 CSK12/R) Rocky river landscape with anglers on bank (38x55cm-15x22in) s.
£789	$1500	(27-Feb-91 SY.NY196/R) Landscape in Surrey (41x56cm-16x22in) s.
£1300	$2301	(21-Mar-91 CSK120/R) An extensive landscape with the Severn estuary beyond (46x61cm-18x24in) s.
£2000	$3460	(10-May-91 CBS317) Highlander (46x66cm-18x26in) s.
£600	$1164	(7-Dec-90 CBS302) Sugar Loaf Rock and the Calf of Man (58x89cm-23x35in) s. mono. chl
£660	$1142	(10-May-91 CBS33 a) Niarbyl (76x127cm-30x50in) s. chl monochrome

HOLLAND, John (jnr) (1830-1886) British

£750	$1440	(29-Nov-90 B63/R) Young faggot gatherers (35x53cm-14x21in) s.
£780	$1505	(10-Dec-90 PHB56) View of Kirstall, Yorkshire (76x127cm-30x50in) s.i.verso

HOLLANDER, Hendrik (1823-1884) Dutch

£1633	$3200	(6-Nov-90 GF.L2425/R) Genre scenes with ladies in interior (19x15cm-7x6in) s.d.63 panel pair (S.FR 4000)

HOLLAR, Wencelaus (1606-1677) Hungarian
£34000　$56100　(11-Jul-91 S20/R) View of Tangier with Gibraltar and coast of Spain beyond (15x62cm-6x24in) i. pen ink W/C two sheets joined

HOLLENBERG, Felix (1868-?) German
£700　$1148　(18-Jun-91 PH124) Alblandschaft (26x35cm-10x14in) init.d.14 i.verso panel

HOLLOWAY, Edward Stratton (?-1939) American
£538　$1050　(20-Oct-90 FA.PH842) Preparing the boats (76x127cm-30x50in) s.

HOLLYER, Eva (late 19th C) British
£1600　$3152　(13-Nov-90 PH80/R) The first tiff (66x41cm-26x16in) s.d.92 i.verso
£700　$1379　(5-Oct-90 T290/R) Young lady with basket of flowers (36x20cm-14x8in) s. W/C

HOLLYER, W P (19th C) British
£2100　$3927　(28-Aug-90 S758/R) On the open hill (76x112cm-30x44in) s.indist.d.

HOLM, H G F (1803-1861) Danish
£1163　$2255　(5-Dec-90 KH.K177/R) From Kongen's Nytorv seen towards Charlottenborg (11x18cm-4x7in) s. pen W/C (D.KR 12800)

HOLM, Kjell Lodberg (1919-1974) Norwegian
£521　$870　(3-Jun-91 B.O70/R) Landscape from Eggedal (64x77cm-25x30in) s.d.1963 (N.KR 6000)
£788　$1411　(11-Mar-91 B.O50/R) Church bells (64x81cm-25x32in) s.d.1858-60 panel (N.KR 9000)
£876　$1567　(11-Mar-91 B.O49/R) Composition (83x127cm-33x50in) s.d.1961-62 (N.KR 10000)

HOLM, Per Daniel (1835-1903) Swedish
£1838　$3603　(6-Nov-90 BA.S117/R) Heather covered hills (57x80cm-22x31in) s.d.1865 (S.KR 20000)

HOLMAN, Francis (attrib) (18th C) British
£4500　$8640　(16-Aug-90 B438) Ship of the Admiral of the Red (102x127cm-40x50in)

HOLMBERG-KROHN, Julie (20th C) Scandinavian
£608　$1185　(11-Oct-90 BU.O83/R) Mountain landscape in grey and green (81x93cm-32x37in) s.d.1918 (N.KR 7000)

HOLMBOE, Thorolf (1866-1955) Norwegian
£661　$1308　(29-Jan-91 UL.T174) Garden scene (96x78cm-38x31in) (N.KR 7500)
£697　$1359　(15-Oct-90 B.O39/R) Still life of peonies (85x60cm-33x24in) s. (N.KR 8000)
£788　$1411　(11-Mar-91 B.O53/R) Northern coastal landscape (46x54cm-18x21in) s. (N.KR 9000)
£876　$1567　(14-Mar-91 BU.O49/R) Cormorants in the mountains (60x100cm-24x39in) s.d.95 (N.KR 10000)
£935　$1805　(12-Dec-90 BU.O30/R) Anemones in vase (45x42cm-18x17in) s.i.d.1920 (N.KR 10500)
£957　$1695　(19-Mar-91 UL.T172) From Lofoten (64x54cm-25x21in) (N.KR 11000)
£981　$1904　(4-Dec-90 UL.T230/R) Coastal landscape, North of Norway (60x80cm-24x31in) (N.KR 11000)
£1085　$1812　(3-Jun-91 B.O72/R) Lilacs in full bloom (60x90cm-24x35in) s.d.1931 (N.KR 12500)
£1095　$1959　(14-Mar-91 BU.O50/R) Coastal landscape with sailingboat (59x72cm-23x28in) s. (N.KR 12500)
£1215　$2030　(3-Jun-91 B.O73/R) Coastal landscape (79x70cm-31x28in) s.d.04 (N.KR 14000)
£1425　$2750　(12-Dec-90 BU.O28/R) Landscape (78x94cm-31x37in) s.d.1925 (N.KR 16000)
£1519　$2962　(11-Oct-90 BU.O65/R) Summer landscape, Helgelands coast (46x66cm-18x26in) s.d.91 (N.KR 17500)
£1659　$3153　(11-Sep-90 UL.T218/R) Summer day on the beach (60x79cm-24x31in) (N.KR 19000)
£1741　$3081　(19-Mar-91 UL.T173/R) View of the fjord (70x58cm-28x23in) (N.KR 20000)
£2271　$4314　(11-Sep-90 UL.T215/R) Street scene from Asgardstrand (55x76cm-22x30in) (N.KR 26000)
£2277　$4075　(11-Mar-91 B.O51/R) Northern coastal landscape with sailingboats and cormoran (67x123cm-26x48in) s. (N.KR 26000)
£2315　$4468　(10-Dec-90 B.O54/R) Coastal landscape with sailingboat (59x100cm-23x39in) s.d.1917 (N.KR 26000)
£2404　$4640　(10-Dec-90 B.O53/R) Summer landscape from Fredriksvaern (65x70cm-26x28in) s. (N.KR 27000)
£2620　$4978　(11-Sep-90 UL.T217) View towards the fjord (67x90cm-26x35in) (N.KR 30000)
£2620　$4978　(11-Sep-90 UL.T219/R) View from Hostbjor 1931 (100x116cm-39x46in) (N.KR 30000)
£2787　$5436　(15-Oct-90 B.O36/R) Seabirds (90x110cm-35x43in) s. (N.KR 32000)
£2939　$5671　(12-Dec-90 BU.O29/R) Entrance to Fredriksvaern (66x111cm-26x44in) s. i.verso (N.KR 33000)
£4167　$6958　(4-Jun-91 BU.O50/R) Clearing land by burning (98x112cm-39x44in) s.d.1913 i.verso (N.KR 48000)
£4987　$9624　(10-Dec-90 B.O52/R) View of Asgardstrand (71x90cm-28x35in) s. (N.KR 56000)

HOLMBOE, Thorolf (1866-1955) Norwegian-cont.
£1172 $2285   (11-Oct-90 BU.O64/R) Coastal landscape (80x69cm-31x27in) s. pastel
                     (N.KR 13500)
£1576 $2821   (11-Mar-91 B.O52/R) Seabirds (56x71cm-22x28in) s. mixed media panel
                     (N.KR 18000)

HOLMCHAMP, L (?) ?
£1278 $2288   (14-Apr-91 BU.H124/R) Sheep grazing (34x93cm-13x37in) s. (F.M 9000)

HOLMES, George Augustus (?-1911) British
£2400 $4728   (1-Nov-90 C261/R) Prickly problem (51x67cm-20x26in) s.
£4600 $7682   (22-Jul-91 SWS1034/R) Colonel North's daughter and pony
                     (34x46cm-13x18in) s.

HOLMES, George Augustus (attrib) (?-1911) British
£1200 $1968   (20-Jun-91 B88) Music hath charms (76x63cm-30x25in) bears sig.

HOLMES, Mary D see ELWELL, Mary

HOLMES, Ralph (1876-1963) American
£552 $900   (11-Jun-91 MOR.P100 a) Sierra landscape (46x61cm-18x24in) s. canvasboard
£612 $1200   (13-Feb-91 B.SF2078/R) Coastal inlet (24x30cm-9x12in) s. board

HOLMES, Wilfred (?) British
£520 $931   (13-Mar-91 B78) A cottage garden in summer (36x25cm-14x10in) s. W/C

HOLMES, William H (1846-1933) American
£429 $700   (5-Jul-91 S.W2673/R) In Ucatan (30x46cm-12x18in) s.i. W/C

HOLMSTROM, Tora Vega (1880-1967) Swedish
£1069 $1913   (13-Apr-91 FAL.M115/R) Flowers in vase (48x36cm-19x14in) mono. panel
                     (S.KR 11500)
£1103 $2162   (10-Nov-90 FAL.M144/R) Spring flowers in vase (55x46cm-22x18in) s.
                     (S.KR 12000)
£1320 $2362   (13-Apr-91 FAL.M114/R) Fruit on white tablecloth (32x41cm-13x16in) mono.
                     panel (S.KR 14200)

HOLMYARD, James (1929-) Australian
£633 $1071   (16-Apr-91 J.M85) Rutted road in Normanby (29x39cm-11x15in) s. canvas on
                     board (A.D 1400)

HOLROYD, T (19th C) British
£8500 $16575   (18-Oct-90 CSK116/R) The Faraglioni, Capri (53x82cm-21x32in) s.i.d.1867

HOLSOE, Carl (1863-1935) Danish
£620 $1178   (14-Sep-90 RAS.V588/R) Interior with girl playing the piano
                     (22x15cm-9x6in) s.d.22 (D.KR 7000)
£725 $1399   (10-Dec-90 BU.K58/R) Still life of two lumpsuckers on dish
                     (46x56cm-18x22in) s. (D.KR 8000)
£779 $1510   (22-Aug-90 RAS.K243) Summer flowers by garden steps (30x37cm-12x15in)
                     (D.KR 9000)
£779 $1510   (22-Aug-90 RAS.K242) Elder flowers (43x51cm-17x20in) s. (D.KR 9000)
£880 $1479   (22-Apr-91 BU.K69/R) Trees by water's edge (58x70cm-23x28in) s.
                     (D.KR 10000)
£1298 $2517   (22-Aug-90 RAS.K240) Interior with chair and flowers on table
                     (30x18cm-12x7in) s. (D.KR 15000)
£2477 $4880   (13-Nov-90 AB.S908/R) Interior with old woman by kitchen table
                     (46x56cm-18x22in) s. panel (S.KR 27000)
£3707 $7155   (12-Dec-90 BU.S33/R) Interior (42x50cm-17x20in) s. (S.KR 40000)
£3918 $7679   (22-Nov-90 RAS.V725/R) Kitchen interior with woman by stove
                     (55x49cm-22x19in) s. (D.KR 44000)
£4640 $7795   (24-Apr-91 BA.S93/R) Interior (45x37cm-18x15in) s. panel (S.KR 49000)
£5206 $10257   (14-Nov-90 RAS.K593/R) Interior with chest of drawer and chair by open
                     door (41x32cm-16x13in) s. panel (D.KR 58000)
£6023 $10179   (1-May-91 KH.K81/R) Interior with young girl reading (47x46cm-19x18in)
                     s. (D.KR 68000)
£6358 $12334   (5-Dec-90 KH.K54/R) Interior with small girl reading (47x53cm-19x21in)
                     s. panel (D.KR 70000)
£6387 $12582   (30-Oct-90 BU.S315/R) Interior (65x54cm-26x21in) s. (S.KR 70000)
£6602 $11092   (23-Apr-91 RAS.K65/R) Giving milk to the cat (63x53cm-25x21in) s.
                     (D.KR 75000)
£7795 $13173   (1-May-91 KH.K82/R) Sunlit sitting room (48x42cm-19x17in) s.
                     (D.KR 88000)
£7923 $13310   (23-Apr-91 RAS.K137/R) Interior with lady tidying her dressing table
                     (49x39cm-19x15in) s. (D.KR 90000)
£8000 $15760   (5-Oct-90 C112/R) Woman reading in interior (32x41cm-13x16in) s.d.02
                     panel
£8000 $13760   (17-May-91 C117/R) Interior (49x38cm-19x15in) s.
£8088 $15853   (6-Nov-90 BA.S119/R) Interior with woman dressed in white
                     (86x63cm-34x25in) s. (S.KR 88000)
£8977 $17684   (14-Nov-90 RAS.K122/R) Interior with woman reading (55x46cm-22x18in) s.
                     (D.KR 100000)
£10000 $17200   (17-May-91 C131/R) Woman in interior (50x40cm-20x16in) s. canvas on
                     panel
£12000 $23040   (30-Nov-90 C57/R) A woman reading in an interior (57x51cm-22x20in) s.

HOLSOE, Carl (1863-1935) Danish-cont.
£12111 $23495   (22-Aug-90 RAS.K101/R) Interior with lady embroidering in sittingroom
                      (50x42cm-20x17in) s. (D.KR 140000)
£16869 $32725   (22-Aug-90 RAS.K39/R) Interior with Ingeborg Nordfort by open window
                      (57x38cm-22x15in) s. (D.KR 195000)
£25641 $50000   (23-Oct-90 SY.NY149/R) At the window (82x90cm-32x35in) s.
£1158 $2269   (22-Nov-90 RAS.V724/R) Interior with woman wearing white dress knitting
                      (32x25cm-13x10in) init.d.1915 pastel (D.KR 13000)

HOLSOE, Carl (attrib) (1863-1935) Danish
£640 $1254   (20-Nov-90 GO.G417) Cheers - interior with men conversing
                      (40x40cm-16x16in) (S.KR 7000)

HOLSOE, Elise (19th C) Danish
£792 $1331   (23-Apr-91 RAS.K419/R) Still life of roses, gardenias and beechleaves
                      (26x35cm-10x14in) s.d.1837verso (D.KR 9000)

HOLSOE, N (19th C) Danish
£1817 $3524   (22-Aug-90 RAS.K246) Interior with open window, door and chair
                      (50x60cm-20x24in) init. (D.KR 21000)

HOLSOE, Niels (1865-?) Danish
£2000 $3440   (17-May-91 C161/R) Sunlit interior (45x37cm-18x15in) with i. panel
£2200 $3784   (17-May-91 C107/R) White room (51x61cm-20x24in)

HOLST, Agda (1886-1976) Swedish
£548 $982   (13-Apr-91 FAL.M118/R) Roses (46x36cm-18x14in) s.d.1931 (S.KR 5900)
£689 $1351   (10-Nov-90 FAL.M145/R) Wild flowers in vase (55x46cm-22x18in) s.
                      (S.KR 7500)
£1125 $2013   (13-Apr-91 FAL.M116/R) Still life of poppies in vase (67x55cm-26x22in)
                      s.d.1939 (S.KR 12100)

HOLST, Johannes (1880-1965) ?
£1356 $2264   (5-Jun-91 DO.H2014/R) Choppy sea with cloudy sky (60x88cm-24x35in)
                      s.d.1960 (DM 4000)
£1622 $2643   (10-Jun-91 W.T1284) A three-masted schooner on rough seas
                      (76x102cm-30x40in) s.d.1929 (C.D 3000)
£1678 $3239   (14-Dec-90 BM.B632/R) Sailing ship (55x79cm-22x31in) s.d.1959
                      (DM 4800)
£3500 $6265   (12-Apr-91 BM.B740/R) Tug Simson off shore with sailing ship beyond
                      (67x104cm-26x41in) s. (DM 10500)

HOLST, Laurits (1848-1934) Danish
£550 $1018   (7-Mar-91 CSK74) Off Teneriffe (38x58cm-15x23in) s.d.1912 s.i.verso
£1317 $2200   (26-Jul-91 E.EDM83/R) Rocky seascape with lighthouse (61x91cm-24x36in)
                      s.d.88
£2000 $3460   (22-May-91 S120/R) Off Gibraltar (41x68cm-16x27in) s.d.92

HOLST, Theodore von (1810-1844) British
£2114 $4143   (10-Nov-90 FAL.M148/R) Hero and Leander (128x103cm-50x41in) s.verso
                      (S.KR 23000)
£3500 $6265   (12-Apr-91 C37/R) Hero and Leander in moonlit seascape
                      (128x101cm-50x40in) s.verso

HOLT, E F (19th C) British
£600 $1014   (17-Apr-91 ZZ.B93) Busy country road (41x61cm-16x24in) s.d.1899

HOLT, Edwin Frederick (fl.1864-1897) British
£920 $1702   (6-Mar-91 SC4361/R) Shoeing the grey mare (38x58cm-15x23in) s.d.1898
                      s.i.verso
£923 $1800   (21-Oct-90 HG.C18) Scottish hunter (41x61cm-16x24in) s.
£1000 $1730   (10-May-91 CBS302) Mare Polly in loose box (51x61cm-20x24in) s.d.1883
£1700 $2924   (14-May-91 SWS218/R) The village carter's team (49x75cm-19x30in)
                      s.d.1880 i.verso
£3000 $5670   (26-Sep-90 S163/R) Going, going, gone (71x91cm-28x36in) s.d.1863

HOLTMARK, N (?) Scandinavian
£1761 $2958   (23-Apr-91 RAS.K135/R) Two children writing 'Hayppy Christmas' on
                      steamed up window (49x32cm-19x13in) s. (D.KR 20000)

HOLTRUP, Jan (1917-) Dutch
£778 $1518   (25-Oct-90 VN.R45) Cattle in landscape (30x39cm-12x15in) s. (D.FL 2600)

HOLTY, Carl (1900-1973) American
£521 $1000   (17-Dec-90 SY.NY390/R) Ajax (33x28cm-13x11in) s. s.d.1947 verso
£781 $1500   (17-Dec-90 SY.NY401/R) Call (33x28cm-13x11in) s. s.d.1948 verso
£781 $1500   (17-Dec-90 SY.NY393/R) Rocks (36x46cm-14x18in) s. s.d.1944 verso
                      masonite
£833 $1600   (17-Dec-90 SY.NY400/R) Mountain top (46x36cm-18x14in) s. s.d.1947 verso
                      masonite
£885 $1700   (17-Dec-90 SY.NY404/R) Dutch study (36x46cm-14x18in) s. s.d.48 verso
                      masonite
£885 $1700   (17-Dec-90 SY.NY391/R) Europa II (46x36cm-18x14in) s. s.d.47 verso
                      masonite
£781 $1500   (17-Dec-90 SY.NY410 a/R) Untitled (20x18cm-8x7in) init.d.45 W/C

HOLTZ, Karl (1899-1978) German
£4054　　$6892　　(31-May-91 GB.B6395/R) Yorkstrasse with view of S-Bahnhof
　　　　　　　　　　Grossgorschenstrasse, Berlin (53x70cm-21x28in) (DM 12000)

HOLY, Adrien (1898-1979) Swiss
£757　　$1476　　(24-Oct-90 GD.B484/R) Fishing boats on Norwegian beach (35x55cm-14x22in)
　　　　　　　　　　s.d.56 paper (S.FR 1900)
£980　　$1920　　(6-Nov-90 GF.L2254/R) Summer garden (72x53cm-28x21in) s.d.41 (S.FR 2400)
£1143　　$2240　　(6-Nov-90 GF.L2253/R) Seritos (65x92cm-26x36in) s.d.61 (S.FR 2800)
£1400　　$2366　　(1-May-91 GD.B421/R) Harbour scene with fishing boats (49x71cm-19x28in)
　　　　　　　　　　s.d.57 (S.FR 3500)
£2449　　$4800　　(6-Nov-90 GF.L2263/R) Le portail rouge (65x92cm-26x36in) s.d.64
　　　　　　　　　　(S.FR 6000)
£7968　　$13705　　(14-May-91 GF.L2242/R) Self portrait (116x73cm-46x29in) s.d.1925
　　　　　　　　　　(S.FR 20000)
£595　　$1030　　(22-May-91 GS.B2113) Arendal en Norvege (36x55cm-14x22in) s.d.51 i.verso
　　　　　　　　　　gouache (S.FR 1500)

HOLYOAKE, Rowland (19th C) British
£1167　　$2299　　(14-Nov-90 RAS.K553/R) A proposal (41x50cm-16x20in) s. (D.KR 13000)

HOLYOAKE, William (1834-1894) British
£12000　　$23640　　(1-Nov-90 C36/R) The lover's vows (101x122cm-40x48in) s.

HOLZ, Johann Daniel (1867-1949) German
£753　　$1349　　(13-Mar-91 N.M535/R) Cattle in landscape (52x42cm-20x17in) s. canvas on
　　　　　　　　　　panel (DM 2200)
£1081　　$1870　　(21-May-91 WK.M1008/R) Cows in landscape (40x50cm-16x20in) s.
　　　　　　　　　　(DM 3200)
£1200　　$2040　　(29-May-91 PHC242/R) Cattle in meadow (60x51cm-24x20in) s.
£1573　　$3037　　(12-Dec-90 N.M564/R) Young cattle watering, summer morning
　　　　　　　　　　(69x102cm-27x40in) i.stretcher (DM 4500)

HOLZEL, Adolf (1853-1934) German
£3378　　$5743　　(30-May-91 SY.BE104/R) Abstract composition (15x24cm-6x9in) pencil
　　　　　　　　　　pastel (DM 10000)
£10811　　$18703　　(25-May-91 N.M138/R) Village near Dachau (69x84cm-27x33in) s.d.1901
　　　　　　　　　　(DM 32000)
£13397　　$23177　　(8-May-91 D.V15/R) Before sunset (49x59cm-19x23in) s. (A.S 280000)
£643　　$1261　　(10-Nov-90 FAL.M160/R) Composition with figures (13x11cm-5x4in) pastel
　　　　　　　　　　(S.KR 7000)
£1027　　$1675　　(15-Jun-91 L.K315) Figure (14x11cm-6x4in) i. col.chk pencil board
　　　　　　　　　　(DM 3000)
£1250　　$2163　　(21-May-91 WK.M1004/R) Composition (17x20cm-7x8in) s. W/C indian ink
　　　　　　　　　　brush over pencil (DM 3700)
£1689　　$2922　　(25-May-91 N.M140/R) Composition with figures (14x11cm-6x4in) pastel
　　　　　　　　　　col.chk pencil (DM 5000)
£1706　　$3345　　(22-Nov-90 L.K1021/R) Composition (14x11cm-6x4in) col.chk pencil
　　　　　　　　　　(DM 5000)
£1923　　$3731　　(4-Dec-90 FN.S1634/R) Farmhouse beneath blue sky (29x47cm-11x19in)
　　　　　　　　　　s.c.1896 chk bodycol (DM 5500)
£2218　　$4348　　(22-Nov-90 L.K1020) Composition (11x14cm-4x6in) pastel pencil
　　　　　　　　　　(DM 6500)
£2872　　$4882　　(28-May-91 KF.M750/R) Composition (32x21cm-13x8in) s. pencil col.chk W/C
　　　　　　　　　　egg white (DM 8500)
£3072　　$6020　　(22-Nov-90 L.K1017/R) Abstract composition (16x25cm-6x10in) col.chk over
　　　　　　　　　　pencil board (DM 9000)
£3310　　$6356　　(28-Nov-90 KF.M874/R) Composition with figures (19x23cm-7x9in) mono.
　　　　　　　　　　pastel graphite (DM 9600)
£3716　　$6318　　(1-Jun-91 VG.B290/R) Composition (15x11cm-6x4in) pastel (DM 11000)
£3716　　$6429　　(25-May-91 N.M141/R) Geometric composition (16x25cm-6x10in) pastel
　　　　　　　　　　col.chk (DM 11000)
£3767　　$6140　　(15-Jun-91 L.K314/R) Composition (22x18cm-9x7in) s. col.chk pencil
　　　　　　　　　　(DM 11000)
£4437　　$8696　　(24-Nov-90 N.M231/R) Composition with figures (11x17cm-4x7in) W/C indian
　　　　　　　　　　ink (DM 13000)
£6143　　$12041　　(22-Nov-90 L.K1019/R) Composition (37x70cm-15x28in) pastel (DM 18000)
£6143　　$12041　　(24-Nov-90 N.M229/R) Landscape composition (27x40cm-11x16in) mono.d.1914
　　　　　　　　　　W/C collage (DM 18000)
£6757　　$11689　　(25-May-91 N.M142/R) Figures in landscape (23x29cm-9x11in) pastel
　　　　　　　　　　(DM 20000)
£7095　　$12274　　(25-May-91 N.M139/R) Walking woman (16x19cm-6x7in) pastel (DM 21000)
£8191　　$16055　　(24-Nov-90 N.M230/R) Composition (16x25cm-6x10in) pastel (DM 24000)
£10811　　$18378　　(31-May-91 VG.B22/R) Composition with figures in circle
　　　　　　　　　　(25x35cm-10x14in) pastel (DM 32000)
£14189　　$24122　　(30-May-91 SY.BE100/R) Abstract composition (50x62cm-20x24in) s. pencil
　　　　　　　　　　pastel (DM 42000)

HOLZER, Brigitte (?) German
£1115　　$2174　　(26-Oct-90 KM.K1278/R) Young woman with hat and parasol walking on beach
　　　　　　　　　　(23x17cm-9x7in) s. panel (DM 3300)
£10204　　$18061　　(20-Mar-91 KM.K1274/R) Beach scene with two ladies and children playing
　　　　　　　　　　(50x70cm-20x28in) s. panel (DM 30000)

HOLZER, Jenny (1950-) American?
£3550 $6000   (2-May-91 CH.NY250/R) Untitled - from Living Series (53x58cm-21x23in)
                                enamel on metal

HOLZER, Johann Evangelist (attrib) (1719-1740) German
£11213 $21529   (27-Nov-90 APT.P68/R) Intercession de la Vierge aupres de Dieu le pere
                                et le fils (55x40cm-22x16in) pen wash htd.white (F.FR 110000)

HOLZER, Joseph (1824-1876) Austrian
£4623 $8276   (13-Mar-91 N.M536/R) Wooded landscape with wild boars watering in stream
                                (95x79cm-37x31in) s. (DM 13500)
£6645 $11894   (11-Apr-91 D.V10/R) Wood clearing with deer (59x78cm-23x31in)
                                (A.S 140000)

HOLZER, Meieli (20th C) Swiss
£516 $862   (7-Jun-91 ZOF.Z224/R) Two Siamese cats (42x31cm-17x12in) s.d.79 tempera
                                panel (S.FR 1300)

HOLZHAUSEN, Olga von (1871-1944) Austrian
£689 $1379   (7-Feb-91 D.V89/R) Portrait of lady (73x100cm-29x39in) s. (A.S 14000)

HOLZHAUSEN-MARTINY, Margarete von (1893-?) Polish
£886 $1773   (7-Feb-91 D.V90/R) Europe (46x73cm-18x29in) s. W/C paper on board
                                (A.S 18000)

HOLZL, Johann Felix (18th C) ?
£3356 $6544   (10-Oct-90 ZEL.L1534/R) Portrait of Johann Georg von Lori with wig and
                                ermine collar (90x70cm-35x28in) s.i.d.1752 (DM 10000)

HOM, Poul (1905-) Danish
£543 $1049   (12-Dec-90 RAS.K282) Young man by window (98x68cm-39x27in) s.
                                (D.KR 6000)
£663 $1247   (10-Aug-90 RAS.V593) Interior with boy (100x83cm-39x33in) s. (D.KR 7500)
£1680 $3158   (10-Aug-90 RAS.V592/R) Mother with girl and small boy (130x80cm-51x31in)
                                s. (D.KR 19000)
£2387 $4488   (10-Aug-90 RAS.V591/R) Interior with nude young woman, baby in crib
                                (92x145cm-36x57in) s.d.46 (D.KR 27000)

HOME, Robert (1752-1834) British
£340 $602   (20-Mar-91 C82/R) Portrait of Lieutenant-General Henry J.Stannus of the
                                Bengal Cavalry (13x?cm-5x?in) min. card wood rec.frame

HOMENKO, Boris (1930-) Russian
£603 $1158   (18-Feb-91 ARC.P238/R) La carrousel (82x85cm-32x33in) s. (F.FR 6000)

HOMER, Winslow (1836-1910) American
£15976 $27000   (17-Apr-91 D.NY91) Haycart (20x25cm-8x10in) init.
£5491 $9500   (23-May-91 SY.NY1/R) Bicycle race (20x26cm-8x10in) i. pencil
£7263 $13000   (14-Mar-91 CH.NY3/R) Union cavalry and artillery starting in pursuit of
                                rebels Up the Yorktown Turnpike (22x36cm-9x14in) s.d.1862 pencil
£30168 $54000   (14-Mar-91 CH.NY64/R) Boy frightening birds (23x30cm-9x12in) s.d.79
                                init. pencil htd chinese white
£115607 $200000 (23-May-91 SY.NY20/R) Fodder (33x49cm-13x19in) s.d.1887 W/C

HONDECOETER, Gillis Claesz de (1570-1638) Dutch
£11765 $20000   (31-May-91 CH.NY142/R) Wooded landscape with stags and other animals
                                (46x76cm-18x30in) panel
£40000 $65200   (3-Jul-91 S45/R) Christ healing blind man, in extensive wooded landscape
                                (97x139cm-38x55in) s.d.1608 panel
£1600 $2608   (2-Jul-91 C208/R) Outskirts of village with ruined arch (14x16cm-6x6in)
                                with i. black chk pen wash

HONDECOETER, Gysbert Gillisz de (attrib) (1604-1653) Dutch
£1745 $3403   (10-Oct-90 ZEL.L1543/R) Chicken beneath tree and exotic birds in river
                                landscape, evening (99x150cm-39x59in) (DM 5200)

HONDECOETER, Melchior de (1636-1695) Dutch
£6024 $11627   (12-Dec-90 BU.S118/R) Still life of dead hare and pheasant
                                (102x126cm-40x50in) (S.KR 65000)
£6673 $12879   (12-Dec-90 BU.S119/R) Still life of dead birds (94x121cm-37x48in)
                                (S.KR 72000)
£29052 $57232   (14-Nov-90 SY.AM99/R) Fox beside lamb and poultry in landscape with
                                shepherd and flock beyond (138x169cm-54x67in) bears sig. (D.FL 95000)
£60000 $97800   (5-Jul-91 C47/R) Poultry, Feral pigeons and yoke at edge of wood
                                (88x78cm-35x31in) s.
£70000 $121100 (24-May-91 C32/R) Poultry, ducks and a pigeon in an ornamental park
                                (102x118cm-40x46in) s.

HONDECOETER, Melchior de (after) (1636-1695) Dutch
£973 $1800   (10-May-91 H.C12/R) Chickens and ducks (71x84cm-28x33in) init.
£5988 $10120   (2-May-91 CH.AM54/R) Goats resting near a wooden fence, with chickens
                                nearby, herdsman andsheep in background (119x152cm-47x60in)
                                (D.FL 20000)

HONDECOETER, Melchior de (circle) (1636-1695) Dutch
£2051	$4000	(10-Oct-90 CH.NY34/R) Fowl in farmyard (63x95cm-25x37in) bears init.indis.d.
£4000	$8000	(7-Feb-91 C80/R) Poultry in a farmyard (124x163cm-49x64in)
£8543	$14010	(21-Jun-91 SY.MO245/R) Paon pose sur une urne de fleurs (125x130cm-49x51in) bears sig. (F.FR 85000)

HONDECOETER, Melchior de (style) (1636-1695) Dutch
£900	$1728	(20-Feb-91 CSK293) Hens and chicks in landscape (69x91cm-27x36in)
£1436	$2800	(14-Oct-90 H.C444/R) Chickens in farmyard (74x91cm-29x36in)
£2000	$3260	(4-Jul-91 C540/R) Poultry by column (76x63cm-30x25in)
£2284	$4500	(7-Oct-90 LIT.L336) Roosters (81x99cm-32x39in)
£2600	$4940	(13-Sep-90 CSK240/R) Cockerel and hens in wooded landscape (96x109cm-38x43in)
£3500	$6720	(29-Nov-90 CSK87/R) Turkey and poultry in farmyard (71x91cm-28x36in)
£3593	$6000	(23-Jan-91 D.NY76/R) Roosters, pigeons and turkeys in landscape (104x135cm-41x53in)
£5500	$11000	(7-Feb-91 C79/R) Poultry, a red squirrel and a parrot in a landscape (111x89cm-44x35in)
£6800	$13600	(7-Feb-91 C185/R) Peacocks, cocks, parrots, budgerigars and other poultry in ornamentalgardens (163x109cm-64x43in) two
£6800	$11084	(4-Jul-91 CSK145/R) Cockerells, chicks and pigeons by wall, dove-cot beyond (124x94cm-49x37in)
£13000	$21970	(19-Apr-91 C77/R) A brace of mallard, duck, curlew, snipe and other birds by a plinth (110x135cm-43x53in)

HONDIUS, Abraham (1625-1695) Dutch
£4800	$9264	(12-Dec-90 S183/R) Stork assailed by hounds among Italianate ruins in evening landscape (39x35cm-15x14in) s. panel

HONDIUS, Abraham (circle) (1625-1695) Dutch
£1900	$3515	(5-Mar-91 PH25) Hounds attacking boar (101x111cm-40x44in)

HONDIUS, Abraham (style) (1625-1695) Dutch
£800	$1384	(20-May-91 SWS38/R) Two hounds flushing a heron by a river (28x33cm-11x13in) bears indist.mono. panel
£893	$1500	(17-Jul-91 SY.NY143/R) Dogs attacking a bear (37x49cm-15x19in) s. panel
£900	$1467	(4-Jul-91 C769) Hounds putting up heron in landscape (28x33cm-11x13in) with indist.sig. panel

HONDT, Lambert de (?-1665) Flemish
£2600	$4394	(18-Apr-91 C110) A cavalry skirmish (44x67cm-17x26in)
£3300	$6105	(5-Mar-91 PH80/R) Battle scene with cavalry (29x41cm-11x16in) s.
£6000	$9780	(4-Jul-91 C679/R) Garden of Eden (52x75cm-20x30in) indist.sig.
£24000	$45600	(1-Mar-91 C135/R) Orpheus charming the animals. The flood (60x42cm-24x17in) one bears sig. pair

HONE, Evie (1894-1955) British
£750	$1463	(26-Oct-90 CG19/R) The pond at Marley (36x9cm-14x4in) s.d.1949 W/C htd.bodycol

HONE, Horace (1756-1825) British
£400	$768	(19-Feb-91 CSK50/R) Portrait of gentleman in black coat with blue collar (6x?cm-2x?in) min.gilt-metal frame plaited hair border oval
£480	$806	(22-Apr-91 PH69) Portrait of Sir Adam Gordon (8x?cm-3x?in) min.inits.d.1817 i.verso papier-mache frame oval
£500	$960	(18-Dec-90 C142/R) Portrait of lady in blue dress and white fichu (4x?cm-2x?in) min.init.d.1782 gilt-metal frame oval
£550	$908	(10-Jul-91 C130) The Hon. Charles James Fox in blue coat (4x?cm-2x?in) min.s.d.1807 verso enamel gilt-metal frame oval
£550	$952	(21-May-91 CSK167/R) Gentleman facing left (7x?cm-3x?in) min. pearl mono.plaited hair verso oval
£900	$1485	(10-Jul-91 C178) Gentleman in blue coat with brown buttons (7x?cm-3x?in) min.mono.d.1798 rec.blk.wood frame oval
£3800	$6726	(20-Mar-91 C106/R) Portrait of officer, possibly the Hon.Edward Bligh (8x?cm-3x?in) min. init.d.1789 ormolu mount velvet frame oval

HONE, Nathaniel (1718-1784) British
£659	$1252	(12-Sep-90 WO.CO13) Going home (33x23cm-13x9in) mono. (E.P 725)
£1200	$2316	(10-Dec-90 PHB54) Rocky seascape (19x29cm-7x11in) init. board
£2353	$4000	(30-May-91 CE.NY29) Young artist sketching (93x77cm-37x30in)
£3704	$7148	(12-Dec-90 CH.E131) Sunset and the winding road (63x91cm-25x36in) (E.P 4000)
£8500	$14025	(10-Jul-91 S38/R) Portrait of girl with dog (54x43cm-21x17in) s.d.1776
£650	$1248	(18-Dec-90 C24/R) Portrait of gentleman in gold-trimmed blue coat (4x?cm-2x?in) min.enamel gold frame plaited hair verso oval
£1050	$1733	(10-Jul-91 C179) Young lady dress in a blue dress. Young lady dressed in a pink dress (3x?cm-1x?in) min.both mono.d.1756 bracelet frame oval pair
£1389	$2681	(12-Dec-90 CH.E11) Two Pyramids. Palms on the Nile. Boats on the Nile W/C three in one frame (E.P 1500)
£3200	$5664	(20-Mar-91 C126/R) Portrait of Sir Thomas Wynn (5x?cm-2x?in) min.init.d.1766 gold frame oval

HONE, Nathaniel (attrib) (1718-1784) British
£2800 $5460   (26-Oct-90 C223 a/R) Portrait of Philadelphia, Lady Call, half length in a white dress (76x63cm-30x25in) i.
£591 $1023   (21-May-91 SY.MI238/R) Ritratto di un gentiluomo vestito in giacca porpora e parrucca grigia (3x?cm-1x?in) min.mono.d.1754 enamel gilded frame oval (I.L 1300000)

HONE, Nathaniel (circle) (1718-1784) British
£1200 $2304   (20-Feb-91 CSK247) Portrait of boy, in van Dyck costume, with slashed sleeved doublet (60x50cm-24x20in) i.
£1400 $2688   (20-Feb-91 CSK246) Portrait of boy, in van Dyck costume and doublet with slashed sleeves (61x51cm-24x20in) indist.i.

HONEGGER, Gottfried (1917-) Swiss
£6024 $11807   (24-Nov-90 AB.L118/R) Tableau relief PZ 32 (78x100cm-31x39in) s.i.d.1963verso oil resin (S.FR 15000)
£1016 $1961   (15-Dec-90 S.Z144/R) Untitled (78x56cm-31x22in) s. gouache beseautage (S.FR 2500)
£1124 $2204   (24-Nov-90 AB.L114/R) Composition abstraite (48x38cm-19x15in) gouache (S.FR 2800)

HONG KONG SCHOOL (?) Oriental
£3000 $5190   (22-May-91 S80/R) Two merchant ships (45x59cm-18x23in) pair

HONICH, Adriaen (?-c.1683) Dutch
£1106 $1813   (18-Jun-91 APT.P16) Paysage de bord de mer (18x24cm-7x9in) s. pen wash (F.FR 11000)

HONICH, Adriaen (attrib) (?-c.1683) Dutch
£15291 $30122   (12-Nov-90 CH.AM14/R) View of Falls at Tivoli (57x42cm-22x17in) with i. black chk pen W/C htd white (D.FL 50000)

HONTHORST, Gerrit van (1590-1656) Dutch
£39522 $77463   (6-Nov-90 BA.S120/R) King Frode Fredegod receiving his followers and kings (276x333cm-109x131in) (S.KR 430000)
£190000 $366700   (12-Dec-90 S63/R) Phryne and Xenocrates (151x207cm-59x81in) s.d.1623

HONTHORST, Gerrit van (attrib) (1590-1656) Dutch
£1026 $2000   (24-Oct-90 D.NY74/R) The Adoration of the Shepherds (142x81cm-56x32in) canvas on board
£8500 $16405   (11-Dec-90 PH154/R) Portrait of lady as Diana (44cm-17ins circular) panel

HONTHORST, Gerrit van (circle) (1590-1656) Dutch
£2500 $4225   (30-Apr-91 PH35/R) Portrait of lady standing, holding flowers in right hand (118x90cm-46x35in)

HONTHORST, Gerrit van (school) (1590-1656) Dutch
£16842 $32000   (11-Jan-91 CH.NY85/R) Mercenary love (108x136cm-43x54in)

HONTHORST, Gerrit van (studio) (1590-1656) Dutch
£1800 $2934   (2-Jul-91 PH287/R) Allegory of spring, young woman with bird's nest and crook (76x63cm-30x25in)
£3400 $5610   (10-Jul-91 S100/R) Portrait of Prince Rupert, Count Palatine of Rhine and Duke of Bavaria (73x58cm-29x23in) panel painted oval
£4500 $7425   (10-Jul-91 S16/R) Portrait of Louise, Princess Palatine wearing dress with lace collar (61x47cm-24x19in) panel oval

HONTHORST, Gerrit van (style) (1590-1656) Dutch
£2000 $3840   (29-Nov-90 CSK64/R) Four men singing (81x127cm-32x50in)

HOOCH, Charles Cornelisz de (?-1638) Dutch
£2395 $4048   (2-May-91 CH.AM128/R) Travellers admiring classical ruins ina grotto (41x54cm-16x21in) s. panel (D.FL 8000)
£21000 $34230   (5-Jul-91 C326/R) Gentleman by well in grotto by sarcophagus, abandoned arcade beyond (63x49cm-25x19in) i. panel

HOOCH, Charles Cornelisz de (attrib) (?-1638) Dutch
£659 $1100   (23-Jan-91 D.NY56) Shepherd leading flock along riverbed (53x69cm-21x27in)

HOOCH, Charles Cornelisz de (circle) (?-1638) Dutch
£3908 $6996   (14-Mar-91 D.V220/R) Southern landscape with shepherd and flock (19x25cm-7x10in) copper (A.S 80000)

HOOCH, Pieter de (circle) (1629-1681) Dutch
£3670 $7046   (29-Nov-90 ZZ.F4/R) Scene d'Auberge (50x38cm-20x15in) s. (F.FR 36000)

HOOD, Ernest (19th C) British
£700 $1351   (12-Dec-90 PHG19/R) The barmaid (19x29cm-7x11in) s. board

HOOD, Ernest Burnett (?-1988) British
£1200 $2268   (27-Sep-90 CG121) H.M.S Hood after sinking of Bismark (86x127cm-34x50in) s.

HOOD, Kenneth Edwin (1928-) Australian
£844 $1620   (14-Aug-90 SY.ME108/R) Still life (90x104cm-35x41in) s.d. '64 board (A.D 2000)

HOOG, Bernard de (1867-1943) Dutch
£1138 $1911   (23-Apr-91 SY.AM255) Interior with mother and child (29x24cm-11x9in) s. panel (D.FL 3800)
£1466 $2448   (4-Jun-91 FB.M70) A young Dutch girl (40x30cm-16x12in) s. (C.D 2800)
£2439 $4000   (21-Jun-91 DM.D2041/R) Doll's toilet (51x41cm-20x16in) s.
£2600 $4472   (14-May-91 SWS327/R) Happy days (49x39cm-19x15in) s.
£2600 $5096   (14-Feb-91 CSK161) A mother and child in an interior (38x28cm-15x11in) s.
£2618 $4372   (4-Jun-91 FB.M96/R) The new sister (51x65cm-20x26in) s. (C.D 5000)
£3000 $5820   (6-Dec-90 CG90/R) Comforting baby (63x51cm-25x20in) s.
£4000 $7840   (22-Nov-90 CG508/R) The new born (41x51cm-16x20in) s.
£4800 $9360   (17-Oct-90 PHG33/R) Maternal cares (100x80cm-39x31in) s.
£4872 $9500   (24-Oct-90 CH.NY279/R) Mother and children in interior (51x39cm-20x15in) s.
£12000 $23640   (5-Oct-90 C13/R) Little family (102x121cm-40x48in) s.

HOOGKAMER, Willem Hendrik (after) (1790-1864) Dutch
£1067   *$2049*   *(27-Nov-90 SY.AM3511/R) Door-Ijzing van eenige Koopvaardij-Schepen door het Groot Noord-HollanschKanaal (55x78cm-22x31in) i.d.1830 W/C (D.FL 3500)*

HOOGSTEYNS, Jan (?) ?
£927 $1799   (8-Dec-90 KV.L152/R) The private party (90x100cm-35x39in) s. (B.FR 55000)

HOOGSTRATEN, Samuel van (1627-1678) Flemish
£1284   *$2530*   *(12-Nov-90 CH.AM126/R) Massacre of Innocents (20x25cm-8x10in) pen (D.FL 4200)*
£4500   *$8640*   *(18-Feb-91 S135/R) Christ brought before Pilate (15x18cm-6x7in) pen ink wash*

HOOGSTRATEN, Samuel van (circle) (1627-1678) Flemish
£2200 $3586   (4-Jul-91 C651/R) Scholar studying with books, skull, candle, hour glass at desk (105x119cm-41x47in)

HOOK, James Clarke (1819-1907) British
£2600 $5200   (8-Feb-91 C174/R) The fisherman's return (64x99cm-25x39in) s.
£6200 $11718   (26-Sep-90 S209/R) Gratitude of mother of Moses for safety of child (127x82cm-50x32in) s.d.1855
£630   *$1235*   *(20-Nov-90 RB684) Salmon trappers (56x76cm-22x30in) W/C*

HOOPER, John Horace (19th C) British
£750 $1223   (13-Jun-91 CSK256/R) Summer's evening light (51x91cm-20x36in) s.
£947 $1591   (24-Apr-91 BA.S95/R) Autumn on the Arun (60x106cm-24x42in) s. (S.KR 10000)
£1550 $3007   (7-Dec-90 CBS270) Hay making near Great Marlow. River landscape at Rye, Sussex (38x66cm-15x26in) s.i.verso pair
£1700 $3332   (13-Feb-91 S69/R) Diss, Norfolk (61x101cm-24x40in) s.

HOORDE, Ernest van (19th C?) Belgian
£532 $1000   (19-Sep-90 B.SF2709/R) Rainy Paris street scene (23x15cm-9x6in) s. panel

HOORDE, Louis van (19th C?) Belgian
£1329 $2166   (12-Jun-91 GM.B4072/R) Cardinal a table (45x39cm-18x15in) s. wood (B.FR 80000)

HOPE, Robert (19th C) British
£850 $1369   (27-Jun-91 CG127) A cottage garden, East Linton (24x20cm-9x8in) init. board
£1100 $1859   (3-May-91 PHE123) The quarry at East Linton (30x45cm-12x18in) s. board
£1579 $3000   (27-Feb-91 SY.NY211/R) Rehearsal (41x51cm-16x20in) s.

HOPF, Alfred (1880-1929) German
£1237 $2091   (19-Apr-91 FN.S1745/R) Father smoking pipe and young son seated at table in peasant interior (41x34cm-16x13in) s. (DM 3700)

HOPKIN, Robert (1832-1909) American
£565 $950   (19-Jul-91 DM.D2012/R) Waiting for the tide, evening (36x61cm-14x24in) s. i. verso
£651 $1250   (18-Dec-90 BG.M940/R) Three-masted schooner in rough seas (61x91cm-24x36in) s. canvas on board
£1053 $2000   (27-Feb-91 BG.M823/R) Passing shower off Holborn Head (38x33cm-15x13in) s.
£1842 $3500   (14-Sep-90 DM.D22/R) Ocean courtesies (69x130cm-27x51in) s.d.1880
£3354 $5500   (21-Jun-91 DM.D2000/R) Off harbour bar (122x157cm-48x62in) s. d.1900 verso
£1263   *$2400*   *(27-Feb-91 BG.M825/R) In Channel (61x46cm-24x18in) s. mixed media canvas*

HOPKINS, Arthur (1848-1930) British
£700   *$1379*   *(1-Nov-90 TE550/R) Her picture (28x23cm-11x9in) s. W/C gouache*
£1100   *$2112*   *(17-Dec-90 PH157) The diver (75x55cm-30x22in) s.d.1913 s.i.verso W/C*
£3800   *$7524*   *(30-Jan-91 S265/R) Under gardner (21x16cm-8x6in) s. W/C htd white*

HOPKINS, Frances Anne (19th C) British
£3030 $5212   (14-May-91 JOY.T142/R) Among the untrodden ways (32x24cm-13x9in) init. (C.D 6000)
£833 $1633   (20-Nov-90 JOY.T275/R) Canadian swamp in autumn (17x24cm-7x9in) W/C (C.D 1900)

HOPKINS, Peter (20th C) American?
£1243 $2100   (20-Apr-91 WOL.C300/R) Walking in park (48x38cm-19x15in) s.

HOPKINS, Robert (19/20th C) American
£904 $1500   (11-Jan-91 DM.D1002/R) Sailing ship in stormy sea (48x23cm-19x9in) s.

HOPKINSON, Charles Sydney (1869-1962) American
£7487 $14000   (1-Aug-90 B.P14/R) Elinor, artist's wife, with Ibby, daughter (64x61cm-25x24in) s.
£578 $1000   (21-May-91 GRO.B143/R) View from Sharksmouth, artist's home, Manchester. Landscape (36x51cm-14x20in) init. W/C over pencil double-sided
£1214 $2100   (21-May-91 GRO.B144/R) Agave and Spanish bayonet, Bermuda (38x56cm-15x22in) s.i.d.1940 W/C double-sided

HOPPE, Erik (1897-1968) Danish
£977 $1925   (31-Oct-90 KH.K44/R) Figure in Sondermarken (35x40cm-14x16in) s. (D.KR 11000)
£1087 $2098   (12-Dec-90 RAS.K203) From the old Valby (65x81cm-26x32in) init. (D.KR 12000)
£2054 $3799   (5-Mar-91 RAS.K148/R) Landscape from Sondermark (76x82cm-30x32in) (D.KR 23000)
£2398 $4724   (31-Oct-90 KH.K43/R) Figures in Sondermarken (66x82cm-26x32in) s. (D.KR 27000)
£6338 $12359   (10-Oct-90 RAS.K293/R) Mother and sister by lamplight - dusk (110x136cm-43x54in) s. (D.KR 72000)

HOPPENBROUWERS, Johannes Franciscus (1819-1866) Dutch
£664 $1282   (14-Dec-90 BM.B633/R) Mountain landscape with house by pond and figures (35x50cm-14x20in) s. (DM 1900)
£1898 $3398   (11-Apr-91 D.V251/R) Landscape at sunset with evening glow (38x55cm-15x22in) s. (A.S 40000)

HOPPENER, Hugo see FIDUS

HOPPER, Edward (1882-1967) American
£1145833 $2200000   (29-Nov-90 SY.NY104/R) South Truro Church (74x109cm-29x43in) s.
£3704 $7000   (26-Sep-90 SY.NY179/R) Study of woman knitting (20x19cm-8x7in) pencil
£5291 $10000   (26-Sep-90 SY.NY178/R) Cat study (38x55cm-15x22in) s. chl

HOPPER, Edward (attrib) (1882-1967) American
£1163 $2000   (19-May-91 LIT.L69 a) Lighthouse at two lights (41x51cm-16x20in)

HOPPNER, John (1758-1810) British
£821 $1600   (20-Oct-90 FA.PH872) Portrait of Lady Hamilton (74x64cm-29x25in)
£1026 $2000   (24-Oct-90 D.NY91 a) Portrait of William Law snr (76x64cm-30x25in)
£1310 $2200   (17-Jul-91 SY.NY204/R) Portrait of Robert Kennedy (76x63cm-30x25in)
£1765 $3000   (31-May-91 CH.NY188/R) Portrait of Mrs John Corbett of Chetwyn in landscape (77x64cm-30x25in)
£2308 $4500   (14-Oct-90 H.C423/R) Portrait of Mrs. Wright (76x64cm-30x25in)
£2308 $4500   (14-Oct-90 H.C425/R) Portrait of Mrs. Eliot (76x64cm-30x25in)
£2976 $5000   (17-Jul-91 SY.NY188/R) William Dawson, Esq. of Craven, Yorks (76x63cm-30x25in)
£5588 $9500   (31-May-91 CH.NY200/R) Portrait of Mrs Shaw of Green's Norton standing on porch (239x146cm-94x57in)
£40000 $66000   (12-Jul-91 C35/R) Group portrait of Hon. Mrs. Grenfell, seated and son, holding hoop and hat, by draped curtain (229x152cm-90x60in)
£62000 $122140   (16-Nov-90 C15/R) Portrait of Mademoiselle Hilligsberg by window in interior (240x147cm-94x58in)
£1800 $3546   (13-Nov-90 C27/R) Mother and children (23x30cm-9x12in) pen ink wash

HOPPNER, John (attrib) (1758-1810) British
£882 $1500   (31-May-91 CH.NY187/R) Portrait of Mrs Whitbread in lace wrap, cap and scarf seated in landscape (76x63cm-30x25in)

HOPPNER, John (circle) (1758-1810) British
£833 $1400   (17-Jul-91 SY.NY185/R) Portrait of a young woman (39x32cm-15x13in)

HORACIO (1912-?) Mexican
£3316 $6500   (19-Nov-90 SY.NY294/R) Nina a caballo (59x46cm-23x18in) s.
£3571 $7000   (20-Nov-90 CH.NY307/R) Nino con caballo de juguete (60x46cm-24x18in) s.
£3699 $7250   (19-Nov-90 SY.NY293/R) Portrait of girl (60x46cm-24x18in) s.

HORDE, F (?) ?
£900 $1611   (14-Mar-91 ZZ.B156) Fisherfolk on the shore at the end of the day (67x53cm-26x21in) s. pair
£2000 $3460   (9-May-91 CSK102/R) Fisherfolk on beach (67x53cm-26x21in) s. pair

HOREBOUT, Gerard (1465-1540) Flemish
£8333 $16000   (18-Dec-90 GM.B4093/R) L'adoration des rois mages (44x74cm-17x29in) panel (B.FR 500000)

HOREMANS, Jan Josef (18th C) Flemish
£1394 $2371   (27-May-91 OD.P87) Scene de cabaret (47x57cm-19x22in) bears mono.
                  (F.FR 14000)
£500   *$960*   *(18-Feb-91 S292/R) Standing boy seen from behind (20x12cm-8x5in) chk*

HOREMANS, Jan Josef (attrib) (18th C) Flemish
£1835 $3615   (13-Nov-90 AB.S909/R) Interior with figures by sickbed (50x57cm-20x22in)
                  bears sig. (S.KR 20000)

HOREMANS, Jan Josef (elder) (1682-1759) Flemish
£3386 $5859   (22-May-91 CD.P6) La reunion musicale (56x68cm-22x27in) (F.FR 34000)
£40984 $80328   (11-Nov-90 M.V32/R) La joyeuse assemblee pair (F.FR 400000)
£1900   *$3097*   *(2-Jul-91 C222/R) Standing man, in profile to left, smoking pipe and
                  holding jug (31x17cm-12x7in) red chk*

HOREMANS, Jan Josef (elder-attrib) (1682-1759) Flemish
£673   *$1325*   *(12-Nov-90 CH.AM186/R) Study of gentleman, holding letter. Figure
                  studies (28x17cm-11x7in) with i. red chk ink double-sided (D.FL 2200)*

HOREMANS, Jan Josef (style) (18th C) Flemish
£2381 $4000   (17-Jul-91 SY.NY103/R) Hunt scenes (58x80cm-23x31in) pair
£3000 $6000   (7-Feb-91 CSK70/R) Peasants in tavern interior (75x105cm-30x41in)
£3800 $6574   (20-May-91 SWS47/R) A street scene (68x94cm-27x37in)

HOREMANS, Jan Josef (younger) (1714-1790) Flemish
£1444 $2412   (6-Jun-91 D.V360/R) The coffee break (50x59cm-20x23in) (A.S 30000)
£6500 $10595   (5-Jul-91 C308/R) Dentist at work in surgery (49x58cm-19x23in) s.

HOREMANS, Peter Jacob (1700-1776) Flemish
£2018 $3976   (14-Nov-90 SY.AM128/R) Interior with elegant company taking tea
                  (28x36cm-11x14in) copper (D.FL 6600)
£8000 $13040   (5-Jul-91 C304/R) Peasants offering rent in kind to landlord in library
                  (65x82cm-26x32in)

HOREMANS, Peter Jacob (circle) (1700-1776) Flemish
£17500 $28525   (4-Jul-91 C698/R) Roemer, earthenware jug, roll, oysters and lemons on
                  pewter plates with bowl on draped table (58x84cm-23x33in)

HORIK, Vladimir (1939-) Canadian
£570 $1118   (20-Nov-90 JOY.T419/R) Le village de St. Hilarion, en Charlevoix, Quebec
                  (75x80cm-30x31in) s. board (C.D 1300)

HORLOR, George W (19th C) British
£700 $1155   (9-Jul-91 PH93) Hawking party (63x66cm-25x26in) s.indist.d.1840
£963 $1898   (13-Nov-90 AB.S910/R) Calves, pony, dog and sheep in highland landscape
                  (66x102cm-26x40in) s. (S.KR 10500)
£1250 $2113   (30-Apr-91 AG291/R) Dogs and calves near Highland bothy
                  (49x75cm-19x30in) s.d.1887
£1488 $2500   (19-Jul-91 DM.D2064/R) Big cat (69x104cm-27x41in) s.d.1871
£3333 $6500   (24-Oct-90 CH.NY317/R) Calves feeding (40x51cm-16x20in) s.d.1856 panel
£3400 $6018   (21-Mar-91 CSK208/R) A pony and collies by a stream. Cattle and a dog
                  watering at a stream (46x61cm-18x24in) s.d.1897 pair
£4167 $7000   (17-Jul-91 SY.NY366/R) End of the day's sport (57x86cm-22x34in) s.d.1851
£4200 $8400   (8-Feb-91 C187/R) The Lords of the Isles (33x41cm-13x16in) s.d.1881 i.
                  verso

HORLOR, George W (circle) (19th C) British
£900 $1512   (16-Jul-91 C138) Spaniel with pheasant (76x63cm-30x25in) oval

HORLOR, Joseph (19th C) British
£823 $1580   (26-Nov-90 SY.J253/R) Figures on rocky coastline (29x49cm-11x19in)
                  s.d.66 (SA.R 4000)
£850 $1675   (1-Nov-90 CSK138) Timber cart on track (46x66cm-18x26in) s.d.48
£900 $1782   (30-Jan-91 CSK207/R) A figure crossing a bridge in an extensive
                  mountainous river landscape (61x102cm-24x40in) s.
£900 $1503   (5-Jun-91 S43/R) Salmon pool (46x61cm-18x24in) s.
£1202 $2344   (25-Oct-90 D.V156/R) Mountainous lake landscape (31x51cm-12x20in) s.
                  (A.S 25000)
£1500 $2790   (4-Sep-90 OT380/R) West Wales estuary scene with cattle
                  (100x150cm-39x59in) s.d.73
£2500 $4075   (3-Jul-91 PLF.P82/R) Paysage avec vachers (30x45cm-12x18in) s.
                  (F.FR 25000)
£3200 $6304   (13-Nov-90 PH56/R) Driving the cattle home (86x114cm-34x45in) s.d.64

HORMANN, Theodor von (1840-1895) Austrian
£2695 $5336   (31-Jan-91 D.V132/R) Tyrolean farmhouse (19x25cm-7x10in) panel
                  (A.S 55000)
£24534 $47105   (29-Nov-90 D.V99/R) Landscape with view of town, possibly near Znaim
                  (38x58cm-15x23in) indls.i.verso (A.S 500000)
£1051   *$1765*   *(25-Apr-91 D.V200/R) Studie zur Figur eines deutschen Landsknechts
                  (40x28cm-16x11in) W/C (A.S 22000)*

HORNE, Sir William van (1843-1915) Canadian
£1297 $2115   (10-Jun-91 W.T1058) Autumn woodland (80x127cm-31x50in) s.d.1903
                  (C.D 2400)

HORNEL, Edward Atkinson (1864-1933) British

£2400	$4056	(3-May-91 PHE120/R) Study of girl's head (12x11cm-5x4in) s.d.1920 canvas laid down
£3500	$6825	(11-Oct-90 CG138/R) Portrait of girl holding primrose (46x36cm-18x14in) s.d.1929
£4352	$8400	(10-Dec-90 H.C1144/R) Two girls on seashore (61x51cm-24x20in) s.d.1919
£6200	$12400	(5-Feb-91 S191/R) Children by sea (23x56cm-9x22in) s.d.1901 panel
£6800	$13056	(26-Nov-90 SWS174/R) The lark's song (75x34cm-30x13in) s.d.1910
£7500	$12675	(2-May-91 CG490/R) Picking perwinkles (62x51cm-24x20in) s.d.1919
£9500	$16055	(2-May-91 CG489/R) Vanity (55x23cm-22x9in) s.d.1900 canvas on panel
£9500	$18430	(5-Dec-90 PHE45/R) Japanese girls in a garden (76x34cm-30x25in) s.d.1922
£10000	$19600	(22-Nov-90 CG585/R) Gathering primroses (51x61cm-20x24in) s.d.1919
£10233	$17191	(22-Apr-91 SY.ME214/R) Scottish lass with spring blossoms (49x39cm-19x15in) s.d.1910 (A.D 22000)
£13000	$21840	(23-Apr-91 S141/R) Geisha girl (47x27cm-19x11in) s.d.1894 canvas on panel
£14000	$28000	(5-Feb-91 S189/R) Girl and pink flower (51x41cm-20x16in) s.d.1910
£19000	$35530	(28-Aug-90 S988/R) The peacock feather (102x127cm-40x50in) s.d.1916
£19000	$31920	(23-Apr-91 S151/R) Promenade (76x63cm-30x25in) s.d.1922 s.l.verso
£20000	$40000	(5-Feb-91 S180/R) Woodland elf (51x62cm-20x24in) s.d.1910
£40000	$74800	(28-Aug-90 S959/R) Spring time (127x102cm-50x40in) s.d.1916
£42000	$78540	(28-Aug-90 S958/R) Goose girl (76x91cm-30x36in) s.d.1916

HORNEMAN, Christian (1765-1844) Danish

£815	$1573	(10-Dec-90 BU.K22/R) Portrait of young girl with blue hair band (49x39cm-19x15in) s.d.1815 pastel (D.KR 9000)

HORNER, Friedrich and MULLER, Rudolf (19th C) Swiss/Austrian

£1500	$2850	(12-Sep-90 CSK204/R) Near Lausanne, Switzerland (25x38cm-10x15in) s. pencil W/C htd gum arabic

HORNER, Johan (1711-1763) Danish

£1882	$3763	(6-Feb-91 RAS.K494/R) Portrait of young gentleman (67x56cm-26x22in) (D.KR 21000)

HORNUNG, Emile (1883-1956) Swiss

£531	$1029	(8-Dec-90 GAB.G2677) Les regates a Bellerives (38x55cm-15x22in) d.36 l. stretcher (S.FR 1300)
£571	$1109	(8-Dec-90 GAB.G2673) Bouquet d'hiver (65x54cm-26x21in) s.d.45 l. stretcher (S.FR 1400)
£612	$1188	(8-Dec-90 GAB.G2668) Interieurs (65x54cm-26x21in) s.l.d.1955 stretcher (S.FR 1500)
£694	$1346	(8-Dec-90 GAB.G2672) Bouquet a Cologny (54x65cm-21x26in) s.d.45 (S.FR 1700)

HORNUNG, Preben (1919-) Danish

£581	$1140	(13-Feb-91 KH.K76) Composition (25x18cm-10x7in) s. (D.KR 6500)
£614	$1044	(29-May-91 KH.K252) Outhouse (37x43cm-15x17in) s.d.1955verso (D.KR 7000)
£616	$1202	(10-Oct-90 RAS.K105) 'B and W picture no.2' (24x42cm-9x17in) s.d.1954 tempera (D.KR 7000)
£625	$1156	(5-Mar-91 RAS.K98 a/R) Composition (48x63cm-19x25in) mono. (D.KR 7000)
£704	$1373	(10-Oct-90 RAS.K47) From my garden (38x45cm-15x18in) mono. d.73verso (D.KR 8000)
£805	$1578	(13-Feb-91 KH.K74) Etude, from the white wall (59x49cm-23x19in) mono.d.67 (D.KR 9000)
£808	$1592	(14-Nov-90 KH.K65/R) Love (54x45cm-21x18in) s. canvas on masonite (D.KR 9000)
£1087	$2098	(12-Dec-90 RAS.K21) 'Etude' - the white wall s.d.1967 (D.KR 12000)
£1096	$1864	(29-May-91 KH.K251) Variation of a free subject III (46x27cm-18x11in) mono. (D.KR 12500)
£1250	$2313	(5-Mar-91 RAS.K92) Relations - studio picture (56x79cm-22x31in) s.d.1972verso (D.KR 14000)
£1423	$2676	(19-Sep-90 KH.K164/R) Spots on the wall (43x73cm-17x29in) mono. (D.KR 16000)
£2147	$4208	(13-Feb-91 KH.K73/R) Landscape, Langebro (50x73cm-20x29in) s.d.52 (D.KR 24000)
£2224	$4181	(19-Sep-90 KH.K163/R) Composition (97x130cm-38x51in) mono. (D.KR 25000)
£2368	$4026	(29-May-91 KH.K250) Composition (98x64cm-39x25in) s.d.50 (D.KR 27000)
£2500	$4625	(5-Mar-91 RAS.K98/R) Remembrance of Valby (79x112cm-31x44in) s.d.1984verso (D.KR 28000)
£2936	$5520	(19-Sep-90 KH.K162/R) Studio picture II (79x113cm-31x44in) mono. (D.KR 33000)

HORNUNG-JENSEN, Carl (1882-1960) Danish

£661	$1301	(13-Nov-90 AB.S911/R) Danish summer landscape (77x135cm-30x53in) s. (S.KR 7200)
£1700	$3349	(4-Oct-90 CSK34/R) Hornbaek beach, North Sealand (76x92cm-30x36in) s.
£4000	$6880	(17-May-91 C183/R) Water garden (71x82cm-28x32in) s.d.1939

HORNY, Franz (1798-1824) German

£1643	$3188	(7-Dec-90 GB.B5872) Two sheep watering in lake landscape (14x12cm-6x5in) pen wash over pencil (DM 4700)
£4054	$6892	(31-May-91 GB.B5797/R) View of Olevano (27x40cm-11x16in) brush over pen pencil (DM 12000)

HORNY, Franz (attrib) (1798-1824) German
£633 $1134   (12-Apr-91 AW.H640) Albanian woman wearing basket on head (14x8cm-6x3in)
               pencil (DM 1900)

HORNYAK, Jennifer (1940-) Canadian
£528 $913   (22-May-91 EA.M403/R) Le pommier (117x71cm-46x28in) s. (C.D 1050)
£617 $1203   (24-Oct-90 EA.M416/R) Antibes - sunbathers (91x96cm-36x38in) s. d.85
               verso (C.D 1400)
£824 $1352   (19-Jun-91 EA.M620) La clocharde (107x91cm-42x36in) s. (C.D 1550)
£1345 $2596   (12-Dec-90 EA.M620 a/R) Clown (97x91cm-38x36in) s. (C.D 3000)

HORRIX, Hendrikus Mattheus (1845-1932) Dutch
£1437 $2501   (26-Mar-91 VN.R34/R) Zealand girls sewing in an interior
               (55x69cm-22x27in) s. (D.FL 4800)
£727 $1433   (30-Oct-90 CH.AM513/R) Girl in Zeeland costume reading to brother
               (32x22cm-13x9in) s. W/C bodycol htd white (D.FL 2400)

HORSCHELT, Friedrich Theodor (1824-1881) German
£629 $1221   (7-Dec-90 GB.B5873/R) Fop startling nude young woman (23x27cm-9x11in)
               s.d.1856 pencil (DM 1800)

HORSLEY, Hopkins Horsley Hobday (1807-1890) British
£1000 $1960   (19-Nov-90 SWS550/R) Snowdrift (59x90cm-23x35in) mono.d.1881 s.i.d.1881
               stretcher
£1800 $2934   (13-Jun-91 CSK222/R) On road to Stafford from Cannock Chase
               (61x91cm-24x36in) mono.d.73 s.i.stretcher verso

HORSLEY, John Callcott (1817-1903) British
£1868 $3250   (27-Mar-91 B.SF4229/R) Hunting morn (27x21cm-11x8in) s.d.1867 panel

HORSLEY, John Callcott (circle) (1817-1903) British
£1400 $2646   (26-Sep-90 S190/R) Surprised (99x79cm-39x31in)

HORST, Gerard van der (attrib) (c.1581-1629) Dutch
£780 $1498   (18-Feb-91 S257/R) Mountainous landscape with river and town beyond
               (18x27cm-7x11in) d.1608 pen ink chk vellum

HORST, Gerrit Willemsz (1612-1652) Dutch
£7179 $14000   (10-Oct-90 CH.NY132/R) Ginger jar, roemer, wineglass and plate with
               fruit on draped table (94x74cm-37x29in) panel

HORST, Jan van (attrib) (16th C) Dutch
£10986 $18676   (28-May-91 AB.S4770/R) Christ in Emmaus - kitchen scene
               (80x119cm-31x47in) indist.d. panel (S.KR 117000)

HORTON (?) ?
£1300 $2249   (22-May-91 S53/R) Schooner yacht Ethel, towing wreck of Heroine into
               Belfast Loch, 1857 (74x107cm-29x42in) s.
£3000 $5190   (22-May-91 S54/R) Schooner yacht Hisby Queen (44x63cm-17x25in) s.
               i.stretcher
£3600 $6228   (22-May-91 S58/R) Yacht Edith (40x56cm-16x22in) s. i.verso
£3800 $6574   (22-May-91 S57/R) Yacht Edith (40x58cm-16x23in) s. i.verso
£3800 $6574   (22-May-91 S56/R) Yacht Ethel (40x57cm-16x22in) s. i.stretcher
£5200 $8996   (22-May-91 S55/R) Yacht, America (40x58cm-16x23in) s. i.stretcher

HORTON, Brian (1933-) British
£900 $1503   (4-Jun-91 PH93) River valley with rainbow (42x52cm-17x20in) W/C
£1000 $1670   (7-Jun-91 C333/R) Valley thick with corn (44x53cm-17x21in) s.d.84 pencil
               W/C
£1600 $2960   (8-Mar-91 C216/R) November sunrise and wooded path (52x70cm-20x28in) s.
               W/C

HORTON, Etty (fl.1882-1905) British
£700 $1379   (13-Nov-90 SWS174) A farmyard scene (49x75cm-19x30in) s.
£1100 $1881   (30-Jul-91 SWS228) A quiet place. Figures in a river landscape
               (50x75cm-20x30in) both s. one i. verso pair

HORTON, George (1859-1950) British
£460 $851   (5-Mar-91 AG98) Riverside pub at North Shields (33x24cm-13x9in) s. W/C
£650 $1086   (24-Jul-91 CSK137) Unloading the catch (13x18cm-5x7in) s. pencil W/C

HORTON, William Samuel (1865-1936) American
£2910 $5500   (27-Sep-90 CH.NY110/R) The Seine (37x45cm-15x18in) s. board
£3179 $5500   (10-May-91 S.BM103/R) Sunset beyond the mountains (64x76cm-25x30in) s.
£5221 $9659   (4-Mar-91 ARC.P144/R) La plage (38x46cm-15x18in) s. panel (F.FR 52000)

HORWARTER, Joseph Eugene (1854-?) Austrian
£735 $1447   (15-Nov-90 EA.Z171/R) Der freche Laufbursche (45x31cm-18x12in) s. panel
               (S.FR 1800)

HOSCH, Edouard (1843-1908) Swiss
£420 $814   (7-Dec-90 GB.B5715/R) View of classical country estate (48x64cm-19x25in)
               s.d.1868 pen wash over pencil board (DM 1200)

HOSCH, Hans (1855-1902) German
£3253 $5824   (13-Mar-91 N.M534/R) Woman and children praying in church interior
                                  (95x78cm-37x31in) s.d.1884 (DM 9500)

HOSCHEDE-MONET, Blanche (1865-1947) French
£12387 $20190   (11-Jun-91 I.N224) La Meule (46x55cm-18x22in) s. (F.FR 123000)

HOSEMANN, Theodor (1807-1875) German
£2095 $3980   (14-Sep-90 SA.A1216/R) Young boy sleeping and faithful friend
                                  (27x21cm-11x8in) (DM 6200)
£705 $1374   *(12-Oct-90 AW.H1473/R) Shepherd girl knitting with geese (18x12cm-7x5in)*
                                  s.i.d.1861 W/C over pencil vellum (DM 2100)
£1520 $2584   *(1-Jun-91 VG.B599/R) Bollemann (8x11cm-3x4in) s.d.1860 W/C pencil*
                                  (DM 4500)

HOSEMANN, Theodor (attrib) (1807-1875) German
£640 $1107   (6-May-91 ZEL.L1753/R) Portrait of man wearing cap (14x12cm-6x5in)
                                  canvas on board (DM 1900)

HOSENFELDER, Christian Friedrich (1706-1780) German
£2797 $5427   (5-Dec-90 H2236/R) Prussion officers serving under King Friedrich
                                  Wilhelm I (38x52cm-15x20in) s.i.d.1738verso panel pair (DM 8000)

HOSIASSON, Philippe (1898-1978) French
£1946 $3776   (5-Dec-90 AB.S7101/R) Composition (80x64cm-31x25in) s.d.59 (S.KR 21000)
£4242 $8315   (14-Feb-91 GL.P77/R) Sans titre (80x64cm-31x25in) s.d.1960 oil pigment
                                  (F.FR 42000)
£5128 $10000   (10-Oct-90 NY.NY502/R) Composition (99x79cm-39x31in) s.d.61
£2117 $4128   *(26-Oct-90 CC.P7/R) Composition (54x45cm-21x18in) s.d.1960 oil gouache*
                                  board (F.FR 21000)
£2520 $4914   *(26-Oct-90 CC.P33/R) Sans titre (73x60cm-29x24in) s.d.1971 oil gouache*
                                  (F.FR 25000)
£4046 $7000   *(7-May-91 CE.NY156/R) Four squares (89x129cm-35x51in) s.d.62 oil dry*
                                  pigment canvas

HOSKINS, Gayle Porter (1887-1962) American
£12849 $23000   (14-Mar-91 CH.NY137/R) Shoot out. Bear attack. Lasso. Unfortunate fall
                                  (94x68cm-37x27in) s. four

HOSKINS, John (17th C) British
£3500 $6720   *(18-Dec-90 C82/R) Portrait of gentleman in armour (4x?cm-2x?in) min.card*
                                  gold filigree frame ribbon crest oval

HOSSE, Adolf (1875-?) German
£1616 $2796   (6-May-91 ZEL.L1754/R) Blacksmith interior (60x74cm-24x29in) s.
                                  (DM 4800)

HOST, Oluf (1884-1966) Danish
£528 $908   (15-May-91 RAS.K126) Hilly landscape view (54x64cm-21x25in) init.d.1915
                                (D.KR 6000)
£1687 $3324   (31-Oct-90 KH.K51/R) Landscape, Bornholm (31x38cm-12x15in) init.d.28
                                (D.KR 19000)
£2025 $3948   (10-Oct-90 RAS.K260/R) Landscape with cows (39x61cm-15x24in) init.d.
                                (D.KR 23000)
£2083 $4021   (12-Dec-90 RAS.K290/R) 'Bognemark, 14-10-42' (27x46cm-11x18in)
                                (D.KR 23000)
£2226 $4363   (22-Nov-90 RAS.V826/R) Evening landscape with farm (29x47cm-11x19in)
                                init. (D.KR 25000)
£2641 $5150   (10-Oct-90 RAS.K296/R) Hilly landscape (43x49cm-17x19in) init.d.1911
                                (D.KR 30000)
£2664 $5249   (31-Oct-90 KH.K49/R) Sunset, winter, Ostersoen (60x93cm-24x37in) init.i.
                                (D.KR 30000)
£3257 $6351   (10-Oct-90 RAS.K221/R) Osterlars church (40x53cm-16x21in) init.d.49
                                (D.KR 37000)
£3730 $7348   (31-Oct-90 KH.K50/R) Composition (50x45cm-20x18in) init. (D.KR 42000)
£4464 $8259   (5-Mar-91 RAS.K164/R) 'Bognemark' (40x63cm-16x25in) init.d.47
                                (D.KR 50000)
£32570 $56021   (15-May-91 RAS.K125/R) Mid-summer night's bonfires (81x146cm-32x57in)
                                init. (D.KR 370000)

HOSTE, Einar (1930-) Swedish
£892 $1516   (28-May-91 AB.S5215/R) O 49 - Composition in black and blue
                                  (100x70cm-39x28in) s.d.86 acrylic (S.KR 9500)

HOSTEIN, Edouard (1804-1889) French
£2956 $5676   (1-Dec-90 PER.M61/R) Le hameau (35x60cm-14x24in) s. panel (F.FR 29000)

HOT, Georges (20th C) French?
£1159 $2261   (28-Oct-90 R.P268) Sans titre (73x60cm-29x24in) acrylic (F.FR 11500)
£1426 $2809   (30-Oct-90 ZZ.F97) Sans titre (73x60cm-29x24in) s.mono. acrylic
                                  (F.FR 14000)

HOTERE, Ralph (1931-) New Zealander
£515 $871   *(17-Apr-91 DS.W62) Drawing for Ian Weddes' Pathway to Sea*
                                  (54x75cm-21x30in) s.i.d.75 W/C (NZ.D 1500)

HOTERE, Ralph (1931-) New Zealander-cont.
£557 $1092   (7-Nov-90 DS.W27) Black painting (90x44cm-35x17in) s.d.69 verso brolite lacquer (NZ.D 1800)

HOTZENDORFF, Theodor von (1898-1974) German
£1464 $2709   (7-Mar-91 D.V235) Sailing boats in lake landscape (45x53cm-18x21in) mono. (A.S 30000)

HOU, Axel (1860-?) Danish
£9000 $15480   (17-May-91 C137/R) Artist's music room (72x87cm-28x34in) s.d.1939

HOUASSE, Rene-Antoine (attrib) (1645-1710) French
£368 $700   (9-Jan-91 CH.NY9/R) Studies of women kneeling and seated (16x19cm-6x7in) red chk

HOUBEN, Charles (1871-?) Belgian
£907 $1777   (21-Nov-90 GM.B1127/R) Le pont de Montigny sur le Laing (35x50cm-14x20in) s. wood (B.FR 55000)

HOUBEN, H (1858-1931) Belgian
£1964 $3378   (14-May-91 GM.B457) Canal dans la ville (60x100cm-24x39in) s. (B.FR 120000)
£2134 $4055   (26-Feb-91 VN.R156) Rendezvous in Volendam (60x78cm-24x31in) (D.FL 7000)

HOUBEN, Henri (1858-1931) Belgian
£1600 $3152   (4-Oct-90 CSK199) Morning gossip (66x76cm-26x30in) s.
£1829 $3273   (12-Mar-91 C.A567/R) Two Zealand girls (90x64cm-35x25in) s. (B.FR 110000)
£2660 $4761   (12-Mar-91 C.A124/R) Shepherd by a river (105x160cm-41x63in) s. (B.FR 160000)
£10961 $21265   (4-Dec-90 C.A185/R) Flower market in Amsterdam (91x127cm-36x50in) s. (B.FR 650000)

HOUBRAKEN, Arnold (1660-1719) Dutch
£1677 $3220   (27-Nov-90 SY.AM3463/R) Painter in studio (56x46cm-22x18in) s. (D.FL 5500)
£2514 $4500   (11-Apr-91 SY.NY144/R) Portrait of gentleman, landscape beyond (115x92cm-45x36in) i.sig.d.1686

HOUBRAKEN, Arnold (circle) (1660-1719) Dutch
£3500 $5915   (16-Apr-91 PH184/R) Rebecca at well (86x109cm-34x43in)

HOUBRAKEN, Niccolino van (17/18th C) Italian
£26471 $45000   (31-May-91 CH.NY50/R) Fennel, salami, onions and wine bottle. Fennel, meat and wine bottle (47x63cm-19x25in) pair

HOUDIAKOV, Leonid (1915-) Russian
£904 $1672   (4-Mar-91 ZZ.F45 a) Femme en rose s. (F.FR 9000)

HOUEL, Jean (?) French
£1780 $3187   (10-Apr-91 CB.P11/R) Pecheurs pres d'un torrent (37x51cm-15x20in) gouache (F.FR 18000)
£1978 $3541   (10-Apr-91 CB.P13/R) Ruines romaines (37x51cm-15x20in) gouache (F.FR 20000)
£2275 $4072   (10-Apr-91 CB.P12/R) Paysage italien avec le transport d'une statue antique (33x52cm-13x20in) gouache (F.FR 23000)

HOUEL, Jean Pierre (1735-1813) French
£28777 $55827   (7-Dec-90 SY.MO50/R) Vue du chateau de Chanteloup - pres d'Amboise (79x125cm-31x49in) s.d.1769 (F.FR 280000)
£2814 $4615   (22-Jun-91 CH.MO42/R) Les Solfatares, Naples (29x43cm-11x17in) with i. gouache (F.FR 28000)

HOUGAARD, Henning (19/20th C) Swedish
£625 $1050   (27-Apr-91 SO.S368/R) Winter landscape with fox (43x64cm-17x25in) s. (S.KR 6600)

HOUGH, William (fl.1857-1894) British
£720 $1411   (21-Nov-90 B67/R) Still life of mixed fruit (25x35cm-10x14in) s. W/C
£1100 $1859   (2-May-91 CG412/R) Two plums. Two strawberries and peach (11x14cm-4x6in) s. W/C htd bodycol pair
£1750 $3290   (20-Sep-90 M7) Bird's nest and appleblossom (23x33cm-9x13in) W/C htd
£2000 $3960   (30-Jan-91 S291) Plums on bank. Primroses on bank (18x13cm-7x5in) s. W/C htd bodycol pair

HOUPHNIER, Franz (?) ?
£550 $924   (18-Jul-91 CSK66) Moonlit gypsy encampment by ruins of Melrose Abbey (76x122cm-30x48in) s.d.85

HOUSE, Gordon (1932-) British
£1400 $2730   (9-Oct-90 B93/R) Three arc segments (79x79cm-31x31in) s.i.d.77 verso acrylic board

HOUSEZ, Charles Gustave (1822-1880) French
£925 $1600   (22-May-91 D.NY12/R) King Alfred in Neatherd's cottage (66x81cm-26x32in) s.d.1863

928

HOUSTON, George (1869-1947) British
£800	$1288	(27-Jun-91 CG125) Dunure Castle,Ayrshire (46x61cm-18x24in) s.
£850	$1590	(28-Aug-90 S834/R) Damp Ayrshire day (46x61cm-18x24in) s.
£1000	$1690	(3-May-91 PHE81/R) On the Eck near Kilmun (45x65cm-18x26in) s.i.d.1858verso
£1100	$1859	(3-May-91 PHE79) Sunlit country road (50x60cm-20x24in) s.
£1100	$2134	(6-Dec-90 CG32) Near Dunderave Castle, Loch Fyne (34x39cm-13x15in) s. s.i.verso
£1300	$2431	(28-Aug-90 S1014) Woodland in winter (46x65cm-18x26in) s.
£1400	$2744	(22-Nov-90 CG598) Spring, Loch Awe (71x91cm-28x36in) s. i.verso
£1500	$2805	(28-Aug-90 S1012/R) Ardchonnell Castle, Loch Awe. River valley (25x35cm-10x14in) s.one i. one board pair
£1600	$3120	(17-Oct-90 PHG30/R) Harvest time (70x90cm-28x35in) s.
£1600	$3120	(17-Oct-90 PHG27/R) A road by the loch (70x90cm-28x35in) s.
£1900	$3686	(5-Dec-90 PHE69/R) Winter grazing (72x91cm-28x36in) s.
£2400	$4680	(17-Oct-90 PHG66/R) Gorse on the loch side (70x90cm-28x35in) s.
£3000	$5070	(3-May-91 PHE164/R) Children by waterfall (70x90cm-28x35in) s.
£3000	$5070	(2-May-91 CG506/R) Cottages by Loch Awe (46x61cm-18x24in) s.
£4800	$9360	(17-Oct-90 PHG17/R) Cutting cabbages (70x90cm-28x35in) s.
£5500	$10285	(28-Aug-90 S934/R) View from the artist's garden (101x152cm-40x60in) s.
£13000	$21970	(2-May-91 CG511/R) Lochgair, Loch Fyne (71x91cm-28x36in) s.
£460	*$791*	*(14-May-91 SWS133/R) Asa Japanese bridge (33x49cm-13x19in) s. W/C gouache over pencil*

HOUSTON, John (19/20th C) British
£600	$984	(19-Jun-91 PHG81) Dark sky, pale sea (75x112cm-30x44in) s.d.1977
£650	$1066	(19-Jun-91 PHG34 a) The Loch at night (49x59cm-19x23in) s.d.1960
£1000	$1870	(28-Aug-90 S1072/R) Yellow cafe (25x30cm-10x12in) s.d.1980-81 s.i.d.on stretcher
£1200	$2340	(10-Oct-90 PHG98/R) Cornfield and wood (85x110cm-33x43in) s.i.d.1953stretcher
£420	*$689*	*(19-Jun-91 PHG4) Beach, Stoer (51x75cm-20x30in) s.d.63 W/C*
£420	*$701*	*(26-Jul-91 PHE73) Before storm (24x33cm-9x13in) s. W/C*
£1300	*$2535*	*(10-Oct-90 PHG100 a) Vase of flowers (87x62cm-34x24in) s. W/C pastel*

HOUSTON, John Adam (1812-1884) British
£650	$1164	(14-Mar-91 CG134) Night (36x30cm-14x12in) s. i.d.verso panel

HOUSTON, Robert (1891-?) British
£536	$1029	(27-Nov-90 W.T1001) Driving home the flock (71x91cm-28x36in) s. (C.D 1200)
£580	$980	(3-May-91 PHE69) The stack yard (40x50cm-16x20in) s.d.1911
£2000	$3740	(28-Aug-90 S835/R) Eigg and Rhum from Arisaig (63x76cm-25x30in) s.

HOUSTOUN, Donald Mackay (1916-) Canadian
£611	$1204	(12-Nov-90 HO.ED114) The Ridge Bell's orchard, Beaver Valley (81x102cm-32x40in) s.i. oil lucite (C.D 1400)

HOUTEN, Henricus Leonardus van den (1801-1833) Dutch
£4418	$8482	(26-Nov-90 SY.ME225/R) Rural landscape with grazing sheep (29x39cm-11x15in) s.d.1875 (A.D 11000)

HOUWALD, Werner von (1901-) German
£648	$1063	(18-Jun-91 FN.S1610) View of village in hilly landscape (55x73cm-22x29in) s. (DM 1900)
£1520	$2630	(21-May-91 WK.M1009/R) Sonntagshorn landscape (80x95cm-31x37in) s. (DM 4500)

HOVE, Bartholomeus Johannes van (1790-1880) Dutch
£823	*$1580*	*(27-Nov-90 SY.AM3668) Figures in church interior (40x32cm-16x13in) s.d.1842 W/C (D.FL 2700)*

HOVE, J van (19th C) Belgian
£700	$1253	(14-Mar-91 ZZ.B153) Vessels on a canal before a town and windmills (16x23cm-6x9in) i. panel

HOW, Beatrice (1867-1932) British
£600	$1014	(1-May-91 ZZ.B199) Les huitres (24x33cm-9x13in) s. board
£653	*$1207*	*(4-Mar-91 ARC.P54/R) Mere et fillette (40x30cm-16x12in) pastel (F.FR 6500)*
£1104	*$2043*	*(4-Mar-91 ARC.P55/R) Le modele (45x54cm-18x21in) s. pastel (F.FR 11000)*

HOWANIETZ, Franz Joseph (1897-1972) Austrian
£4970	$9642	(6-Dec-90 D.V85/R) Girl with cloth (102x89cm-40x35in) s.d.1930 hessian (A.S 100000)

HOWARD, B K (19/20th C) American
£508	$1000	(16-Nov-90 S.BM144/R) Edge of forest (66x76cm-26x30in) s.d.1906
£914	$1800	(16-Nov-90 S.BM141/R) Pasture with grazing cattle (66x86cm-26x34in) s.d.1910

HOWARD, George (1843-1911) British
£750	$1418	(26-Sep-90 S202/R) Maries at Sepulchre (43x33cm-17x13in) s.d.1869 panel after Andrea Mantegna
£900	$1701	(26-Sep-90 S213/R) Marshes in Campagna (18x46cm-7x18in) panel

HOWARD, Henry (attrib) (1769-1847) British
£1600 $3040   (1-Mar-91 C77/R) Echo flying from Narcissus (137x17cm-54x7in)

HOWARD, Ken (1932-) British
£640 $1146   (14-Mar-91 L321/R) Amaryllis on window sill (61x48cm-24x19in) s.
£650 $1222   (18-Sep-90 PH153) Reclining nude in interior (22x18cm-9x7in) s. canvas
        on board
£650 $1164   (14-Mar-91 L236) View of old National School Sampford Spiney
        (48x58cm-19x23in) s.d.87 verso
£1000 $1710   (30-Jul-91 SWS89) Studio nude (49x39cm-19x15in) s.i. stretcher
£1200 $1932   (28-Jun-91 CSK195/R) Franchesca and black kimono (61x51cm-24x20in) s.
        i.stretcher
£1400 $2366   (2-May-91 C129/R) Recumbent nude (30x58cm-12x23in) s.
£1500 $2610   (27-Mar-91 S119/R) Nude in the studio (51x61cm-20x24in) s.
£1600 $2576   (28-Jun-91 CSK249) Nude model in studio (61x51cm-24x20in) s.
£1700 $2839   (6-Jun-91 C35/R) Cornish beach (51x61cm-20x24in) s.
£1700 $3145   (8-Mar-91 C224/R) Girl with parasol (59x48cm-23x19in) s.
£1800 $3042   (2-May-91 C128/R) Josie (39x29cm-15x11in) s. i.verso
£1850 $3626   (25-Jan-91 C67/R) Female nude asleep on chaise-longue (40x51cm-16x20in)
        s.
£2000 $3380   (2-May-91 C130/R) Nude by window (60x49cm-24x19in) s.
£2500 $4175   (6-Jun-91 C43/R) The red parasol (61x51cm-24x20in) s.
£2600 $4342   (6-Jun-91 C37/R) Reclining nude below window (61x51cm-24x20in) s.
£3000 $5880   (9-Nov-90 C281/R) Danny and Omani coffee pot (122x102cm-48x40in) s.i.
£3200 $5920   (8-Mar-91 C225/R) Reclining nude by wash stand (50x60cm-20x24in) s.
£3200 $6208   (6-Dec-90 CSK195/R) Sarah, winter day (61x51cm-24x20in) s.
£3600 $6768   (20-Sep-90 CSK110/R) Female nude in front of mirror (61x51cm-24x20in) s.
£4000 $7400   (8-Mar-91 C219/R) Flying the kite, Sennen Cove, Cornwall
        (98x122cm-39x48in) s.
£300   *$537*   *(14-Mar-91 L71) Marazion Beach before St Michael's Mount, Penzance,*
        Cornwall (13x18cm-5x7in) s. W/C

HOWARD, Margaret Maitland (1898-?) British
£1011 $1900   (19-Sep-90 B.SF2647/R) Leda and the swan (56x74cm-22x29in) s.

HOWARD, W (17th C) British
£1450 $2364   (14-Jun-91 SIM212) Bridge at Sonning on Thames with figures fishing and
        buildings beyond (61x91cm-24x36in) s.

HOWARD, William (17th C) British
£2200 $3674   (5-Jun-91 S61/R) Busy waterfront (76x127cm-30x50in) s.

HOWARD, William C (19/20th C) British
£300   *$555*   *(5-Mar-91 SWS1623) Gateway, Mogador (25x20cm-10x8in) s.i.d.1902 W/C over*
        pencil htd.bodycol

HOWE, B Aplin (?) British
£720 $1181   (18-Jun-91 SWS278/R) Greyhound by cottage door (43x58cm-17x23in) s.

HOWE, William Henry (1846-1929) American
£684 $1300   (28-Feb-91 MFA.C138/R) Landscape (30x41cm-12x16in) s. panel

HOWELL, Felicie (1897-1968) American
£789   *$1500*   *(14-Sep-90 S.BM264/R) Dock scene (48x64cm-19x25in) s.d.1923 gouache chl*

HOWET, Marie (1897-?) Belgian
£524   *$880*   *(23-Apr-91 C.A540) The pear tree in my garden (73x55cm-29x22in) s. W/C*
        (B.FR 32000)

HOWIE, James (1780-1836) British
£900 $1512   (23-Apr-91 S230/R) Landscape (56x63cm-22x25in) s.verso
£2000 $3360   (23-Apr-91 S231/R) Island (69x84cm-27x33in) s.d.71 verso board

HOWIE, James (attrib) (1780-1836) British
£2500 $4925   (31-Oct-90 S377/R) Croc, saddled bay hunter, held by small boy
        (51x63cm-20x25in)

HOWITT, John Newton (1885-1958) American
£765 $1300   (1-Jun-91 IH.NY205/R) Man holding Christmas presents (56x76cm-22x30in)
        s.

HOWITT, Samuel (1765-1822) British
£2335 $3900   (7-Jun-91 SY.NY118/R) Two hares (24x36cm-9x14in) s. panel
£10000 $19000   (1-Mar-91 C67/R) Leopard in tree with two passing deer in tropical
        landscape (61x51cm-24x20in) s.
£600   *$990*   *(9-Jul-91 C118 a) Partridge nesting in long grass (23x31cm-9x12in) s.*
        pencil W/C
£600   *$1182*   *(15-Nov-90 S70) Hounds pursuing stag across Thames near Windsor*
        (14x20cm-6x8in) pen ink W/C
£1600   *$3152*   *(15-Nov-90 S69/R) Hounds leaving kennels. Huntsmen and hounds*
        (10x15cm-4x6in) s. W/C pen ink pair
£6587   *$11000*   *(7-Jun-91 SY.NY82/R) The hog-deer at bay. Driving a bear out of sugar*
        canes. Peacock shooting (29x43cm-11x17in) W/C three

HOWLEY, John Richard (1931-) Australian

£588	$994	(16-Apr-91 J.M271) Williamstown after image (89x120cm-35x47in) s. board (A.D 1300)
£676	$1331	(13-Nov-90 J.M1214) Not so easy rider of the arts (47x62cm-19x24in) s.d.89 paper (A.D 1750)
£772	$1521	(13-Nov-90 J.M235) The camp of the silver visitor (30x58cm-12x23in) s.d.89 board (A.D 2000)

HOWSON, Peter (1958-) British

£5000	$9750	(10-Oct-90 PHG121/R) The policy (152x122cm-60x48in) s.
£400	$656	*(19-Jun-91 PHG89) Barrowland warriors (25x35cm-10x14in) pastel*
£400	$656	*(19-Jun-91 PHG96) The interrogation (39x30cm-15x12in) oil pastel*
£500	$975	*(10-Oct-90 PHG58) Dockyard family (51x39cm-20x15in) s. mixed media*
£680	$1142	*(23-Apr-91 S249/R) Arm wrestling II (31x40cm-12x16in) pastel*
£1000	$1680	*(23-Apr-91 S247/R) Girl and boy (37x26cm-15x10in) s. mixed media board*
£1100	$2145	*(10-Oct-90 PHG50) Eldorado (82x59cm-32x23in) s. pastel*
£1500	$2925	*(10-Oct-90 PHG21/R) Bargains galore (97x77cm-38x30in) s.d.87 pastel*

HOYER, C F (1775-1855) Danish

£952	$1846	(22-Aug-90 RAS.K34/R) Habor and Signe untied at Frejas altar (140x178cm-55x70in) (D.KR 11000)

HOYER, Christian Faedder (1775-1855) Danish

£2317	$4148	(14-Mar-91 RAS.V653/R) Habor and Signe united by Freja's altar (138x178cm-54x70in) (D.KR 26000)

HOYER, Edward (19th C?) British?

£780	$1466	(8-Aug-90 PHP134) Three masted cutter in open sea (41x61cm-16x24in) s.d.80
£1500	$2880	(16-Aug-90 B244/R) Two sailing vessels on open sea (76x127cm-30x50in) s.d.81
£4000	$7800	(24-Oct-90 S196/R) Shipping on the Bosphorus (50x75cm-20x30in)
£5500	$10725	(24-Oct-90 S193/R) Shipping at Istanbul in the moonlight (50x75cm-20x30in) s.

HOYER, H E (19th C) German

£616	$1035	(23-Apr-91 RAS.K231) Alpine landscape (67x98cm-26x39in) s.d.64 (D.KR 7000)

HOYLAND, John (1934-) British

£900	$1521	(2-May-91 C165/R) Abstract composition No. 6 (40x46cm-16x18in) s.i.verso acrylic canvas
£1156	$2000	(7-May-91 CE.NY205/R) Untitled (77x57cm-30x22in) s.d.79 acrylic paper
£1600	$2608	(1-Jul-91 S92/R) Untitled (50x71cm-20x28in) s.d.69 acrylic paper
£2000	$3700	(8-Mar-91 C193/R) Untitled (56x46cm-22x18in) s.d.74verso acrylic
£2100	$4116	(9-Nov-90 C285/R) Untitled (74x55cm-29x22in) s.d.78 oil acrylic paper
£2296	$4500	(6-Nov-90 CE.NY101/R) Untitled (76x61cm-30x24in) s.d.17.2.75 stretcher acrylic
£2300	$4255	(8-Mar-91 C192/R) Untitled (76x61cm-30x24in) s.d.76verso acrylic
£2700	$4401	(1-Jul-91 S66/R) 21.3.69 (66x101cm-26x40in) acrylic
£2800	$4676	(7-Jun-91 C336/R) Abstract composition (61x76cm-24x30in) s.d.76verso s.d.overlap
£3738	$6093	(16-Jun-91 SY.ME95/R) Billy's Blues (203x203cm-80x80in) d.6.7.79 verso (A.D 8000)
£5000	$8150	(1-Jul-91 S64/R) Untitled (183x289cm-72x114in) s.d.16.10.68 verso
£5500	$10780	(7-Nov-90 S182/R) Untitled (183x305cm-72x120in) d.67verso
£5500	$10780	(7-Nov-90 S183/R) Untitled (300x183cm-118x72in) s.d.67
£6000	$9780	(1-Jul-91 S72/R) Untitled (244x213cm-96x84in) s.d.26.11.71 verso
£550	$919	*(4-Jun-91 PH103) Untitled (47x70cm-19x28in) s.d.65 gouache*
£1200	$1956	*(1-Jul-91 S94/R) Untitled (51x88cm-20x35in) s.d.76 W/C acrylic*
£1850	$3423	*(8-Mar-91 C191/R) Abstract (54x72cm-21x28in) s.d.69 gouache acrylic paper*

HOYOLL, Philipp (1816-?) German

£745	$1200	(26-Jun-91 D.NY52) Basket of peaches (43x36cm-17x14in) s.d.1875

HOYOS, Anna Mercedes (1942-) Colombian

£4847	$9500	(20-Nov-90 CH.NY157/R) Pina (99x99cm-39x39in) s.
£7653	$15000	(19-Nov-90 SY.NY241/R) Palenqueras en Domingo III (109x109cm-43x43in) s.
£11224	$22000	(20-Nov-90 CH.NY158/R) Bazurto (100x199cm-39x78in) s.d.89
£26163	$45000	(15-May-91 CH.NY24/R) Bodegon de Palenque (150x150cm-59x59in) s.d.89

HOYTE, John Barr Clarke (1835-1913) New Zealander

£495	$971	*(7-Nov-90 DS.W52) Harrisons Cove Milford Sound (21x40cm-8x16in) indist.s. W/C (NZ.D 1600)*
£653	$1103	*(17-Apr-91 DS.W67) Lake and mountain scene with Maori canoe (18x33cm-7x13in) init. W/C (NZ.D 1900)*
£825	$1394	*(17-Apr-91 DS.W72) Mitre Peak (21x40cm-8x16in) s. W/C (NZ.D 2400)*
£900	$1764	*(20-Nov-90 PH256/R) Middle harbour with Heads, Sydney, Australia (24x58cm-9x23in) s. W/C over pencil htd.bodycol.*
£1856	$3136	*(17-Apr-91 DS.W17/R) Rangitoto from Lake Takapuna (23x46cm-9x18in) W/C (NZ.D 5400)*
£3620	$6118	*(16-Apr-91 J.M62/R) Mountain peaks, New Zealand (38x63cm-15x25in) s. W/C (A.D 8000)*

HRADECZNY, Gottlieb (1876-?) Hungarian?
£586 $1083   (7-Mar-91 D.V98/R) Still life with bunch of flowers and house plant
                     (72x42cm-28x17in) s. (A.S 12000)

HRADIL, Rudolf (1925-) Austrian
£485   *$796*   *(20-Jun-91 D.V172/R) View over rooftops of Rome (36x48cm-14x19in) s. pen*
                     indian ink (A.S 10000)
£728   *$1194*   *(20-Jun-91 D.V173/R) Farmhouse (34x52cm-13x20in) s.i.d.1975 W/C*
                     (A.S 15000)

HRDLICKA, Alfred (1928-) ?
£1164   *$1898*   *(14-Jun-91 L.K963) Composition with figures (44x55cm-17x22in) s.d.1969*
                     indian ink pen col.chk (DM 3400)
£1288   *$2151*   *(8-Jun-91 HN.H175/R) Cecil de Vere and Mac Donnell, his discoverer*
                     (32x55cm-13x22in) s.d.1980 ochre dr. sepia (DM 3800)
£1424   *$2378*   *(8-Jun-91 HN.H176/R) Cecil de Vere and Mac donnell, his dicoverer III*
                     (35x44cm-14x17in) s. ink brush sepia (DM 4200)
£1988   *$3857*   *(6-Dec-90 D.V179/R) Study of figures (46x62cm-18x24in) s.d.1961 pencil*
                     brush indian ink wash (A.S 40000)

HSIAO CHIN (1935-) Chinese
£773 $1462   (27-Sep-90 F.M57) Pittura GH (60x70cm-24x28in) s.d.59 (I.L 1700000)

HUAULT BROTHERS (17/18th C) Swiss
£500   *$960*   *(18-Dec-90 C25/R) Portrait of gentleman in damascened armour and white*
                     cravat (7x?cm-3x?in) min.enamel twisted gilt-metal frame oval
£750   *$1328*   *(20-Mar-91 C68/R) Portrait of lady in white dress with blue and yellow*
                     cloak (3x?cm-1x?in) min. enamel gold unframed oval

HUBBARD, Harlan (?) American?
£1220 $2000   (21-Jun-91 DM.D2214/R) Steamboat on river (36x64cm-14x25in) s. panel

HUBBARD, John (1931-) American
£450   *$752*   *(4-Jun-91 PH97) Abstract (52x52cm-20x20in) s.d.1976 gouache*

HUBBARD, W (?) ?
£880 $1479   (23-Apr-91 RAS.K228) Coachman running after horse and cart on country
                     road (46x71cm-18x28in) s.d.1852 (D.KR 10000)

HUBBELL, Henry Salem (1870-1949) American
£2296 $4500   (16-Feb-91 W.W101/R) Ladies in interior (76x61cm-30x24in) s.
£2471 $4250   (15-May-91 SY.NY114/R) Garden bendh (58x42cm-23x17in) s.

HUBBUCH, Karl (1891-1979) German
£87838 $149324   (31-May-91 VG.B40/R) Im Romanischen Cafe (74x74cm-29x29in) s.
                     (DM 260000)
£507   *$861*   *(31-May-91 GB.B6407) Female nude standing (45x33cm-18x13in) st.sig.*
                     pencil (DM 1500)
£541   *$919*   *(1-Jun-91 VG.B601/R) Berlin-Schoneberg in the Twenties (24x20cm-9x8in)*
                     pencil (DM 1600)
£709   *$1206*   *(1-Jun-91 VG.B600/R) Wannsee landscape (30x39cm-12x15in) s. pencil*
                     col.pencil (DM 2100)
£847   *$1415*   *(6-Jun-91 HN.H429/R) People in the Madeleine in Paris (36x49cm-14x19in)*
                     s. pen wash (DM 2500)
£853   *$1613*   *(29-Sep-90 GRA.B2342/R) Seated female nude (49x31cm-19x12in) mono. pen*
                     (DM 2500)
£1207   *$2317*   *(26-Nov-90 WK.M271/R) Die Wolgaschiffer, cinema entrance*
                     (49x41cm-19x16in) mono. pencil.col.chk board (DM 3500)
£1399   *$2713*   *(7-Dec-90 GB.B6706/R) Couple seated (33x42cm-13x17in) mono.c.1925 pencil*
                     (DM 4000)
£1554   *$3030*   *(20-Oct-90 WK.M222/R) Lady's legs (37x25cm-15x10in) s.c.1928 pencil W/C*
                     (DM 4600)
£1689   *$2872*   *(1-Jun-91 VG.B199/R) Portrait of laughing young woman in profile*
                     (27x19cm-11x7in) mono. col.chk board (DM 5000)
£1834   *$3007*   *(19-Jun-91 F.M22/R) Paesaggio urbano (33x42cm-13x17in) st.sig. ink*
                     pencil (I.L 4000000)
£1941   *$3746*   *(12-Dec-90 F.M28/R) A teatro (38x33cm-15x13in) s. pencil (I.L 4200000)*
£2069   *$3972*   *(26-Nov-90 WK.M270/R) Forty years old, female nude (68x51cm-27x20in) s.*
                     W/C over chk pen board (DM 6000)
£9459   *$16081*   *(30-May-91 SY.BE27/R) Edith (100x55cm-39x22in) s. W/C over pencil joined*
                     paper (DM 28000)

HUBER, Carl Rudolf (1839-1896) Austrian
£1715 $3395   (31-Jan-91 D.V49/R) Egyptian stone monuments (63x126cm-25x50in)
                     (A.S 35000)

HUBER, Conrad (1752-1830) German
£2685 $5235   (10-Oct-90 ZEL.L1546/R) St Paul in chains before the Romans
                     (68x89cm-27x35in) s.i.d.1819 (DM 8000)

HUBER, Ernst (1895-1960) Austrian
£1708 $3160   (7-Mar-91 D.V167/R) Winter landscape (46x54cm-18x21in) s.d.41 board
                     (A.S 35000)
£5857 $10835   (7-Mar-91 D.V168/R) View of village (60x78cm-24x31in) s.i.d.1959verso
                     (A.S 120000)

HUBER, Ernst (1895-1960) Austrian-cont.

£5964	$11571	(6-Dec-90 D.V88/R) Bunch of flowers in ceramic jug (71x58cm-28x23in) s.d.56 panel (A.S 120000)
£6958	$13499	(6-Dec-90 D.V78/R) Badgastein in winter (160x134cm-63x53in) s.d.1939 i.verso (A.S 140000)
£531	$1035	(18-Oct-90 D.V192/R) Hotel by the sea (27x41cm-11x16in) s.d.1923 W/C (A.S 11000)
£586	$1083	(7-Mar-91 D.V218/R) Winter landscape (42x56cm-17x22in) s.d.1940 W/C gouache (A.S 12000)
£683	$1264	(7-Mar-91 D.V122/R) Winter landscape (44x60cm-17x24in) W/C gouache (A.S 14000)
£1067	$2006	(20-Sep-90 D.V207/R) Gastein (45x60cm-18x24in) s. W/C gouache (A.S 22000)
£1340	$2318	(8-May-91 D.V76/R) Bunch of flower with lakrspur and marguerites (61x47cm-24x19in) s.d.46 W/C gouache (A.S 28000)
£1708	$3160	(7-Mar-91 D.V205/R) Bunch of field flowers with marguerites (49x46cm-19x18in) s. W/C (A.S 35000)
£2734	$5303	(6-Dec-90 D.V89/R) Wagrain in early spring (44x60cm-17x24in) s.d.1950 W/C (A.S 55000)
£3172	$5869	(7-Mar-91 D.V166/R) Landscape (48x57cm-19x22in) s.d.1928 mixed media canvas (A.S 65000)

HUBER, Leon (1858-1928) French

£2600	$4368	(16-Jul-91 C57/R) Waiting for more (38x54cm-15x21in) s.
£2872	$5456	(14-Sep-90 SA.A1204/R) Cats playing (47x55cm-19x22in) s. (DM 8500)
£2880	$4809	(4-Jun-91 FB.M74/R) Les chats a la marmite de cuivre (53x65cm-21x26in) s.d.1917 (C.D 5500)
£512	$840	(18-Jun-91 FN.S1905/R) Three kittens on floor before drapes (25x33cm-10x13in) s. W/C (DM 1500)

HUBER, Thomas (1700-1779) German

£3293	$5566	(2-May-91 CH.AM113/R) Portrait of probably Countess of Kavenhuller in a dark red velvet dress (65x54cm-26x21in) s.d. i. verso (D.FL 11000)

HUBERT, Jean Baptiste Louis (1801-?) French

£677	$1165	(14-May-91 GF.L2346) Fishing boat by river bank (28x39cm-11x15in) s.d.1835 W/C (S.FR 1700)

HUBERTI, Antonio (Pseudonym) (20th C) French

£351	$650	(10-Mar-91 LT.P150) Conversation sous un arbre (33x28cm-13x11in) s. W/C (F.FR 3500)
£423	$689	(10-Jun-91 NM.P92) L'homme au masque (19x15cm-7x6in) s. gouache (F.FR 4200)
£477	$806	(16-Apr-91 PPB.P248) La marchande de poissons (28x23cm-11x9in) s. W/C panel (F.FR 4800)
£1193	$2016	(16-Apr-91 PPB.P247) La femme au kimono (53x44cm-21x17in) s. gouache panel (F.FR 12000)
£1360	$2216	(10-Jun-91 NM.P91/R) Le vieil homme assis devant chez lui (39x35cm-15x14in) s. gouache (F.FR 15000)
£1491	$2520	(16-Apr-91 PPB.P249/R) L'homme a la casquette (65x54cm-26x21in) s. collage (F.FR 15000)
£1606	$2972	(10-Mar-91 LT.P109/R) Le basque a la pipe (63x52cm-25x20in) s. gouache collage (F.FR 16000)
£2039	$3914	(2-Dec-90 ZZ.F94) L'homme masque (65x54cm-26x21in) s. mixed media collage (F.FR 20000)

HUBLER (19th C) ?

£1365	$2676	(24-Nov-90 SA.A738/R) Wooded landscape in rising thunderstorm with mountains beyond (34x38cm-13x15in) s.indis.d. (DM 4000)

HUBNER, Carl Wilhelm (1814-1879) German

£680	$1204	(20-Mar-91 KM.K1276) Praying young woman with bible and rosary (107x87cm-42x34in) s.d.1870 (DM 2000)
£822	$1471	(12-Mar-91 FN.S2436) Alpine lake landscape with farmhouse amongst trees and figures (48x65cm-19x26in) s.d.1875 (DM 2400)
£952	$1600	(17-Jul-91 SY.NY298/R) Hansel and Gretel (38x30cm-15x12in) s.
£3051	$4973	(3-Jul-91 WE.MU133/R) Portrait of girl in love (104x91cm-41x36in) s. (DM 9000)
£8000	$14320	(12-Apr-91 BM.B618/R) The emigrants (58x73cm-23x29in) s.d.1862 (DM 24000)

HUBNER, Heinrich (1869-?) German

£533	$955	(12-Apr-91 BM.B619/R) Bunch of summer flowers in interior by door to balcony (71x82cm-28x32in) s. (DM 1600)

HUBNER, Julius (1842-1874) German

£5119	$10034	(24-Nov-90 SA.A614/R) Farewell scene (168x133cm-66x52in) s.d.1878 (DM 15000)

HUBNER, Louis (?) British

£3000	$5370	(10-Apr-91 S51/R) Still life of birds in landscape (69x87cm-27x34in) s.

HUBNER, Ulrich (1872-1932) German

£842	$1423	(15-Apr-91 SY.J408/R) Landungs brucken (59x80cm-23x31in) s.d.15 i.verso (SA.R 4000)

HUBNER, Ulrich (1872-1932) German-cont.
£1536 $2903   (25-Sep-90 FN.S2223/R) View of Havel canal with figures, Berlin (60x58cm-24x23in) s. (DM 4500)
£2273 $4386   (12-Dec-90 N.M565/R) Elbe landscape with shipping and harbour (65x167cm-26x66in) s. (DM 6500)

HUBNER-ANDORF, E (19th C) German
£769 $1492   (4-Dec-90 FN.S1889) Still life of draped table laid with silver ware and fruit near column (100x152cm-39x60in) s.i. (DM 2200)

HUCHTENBURGH, Jan van (1647-1733) Dutch
£1364 $2700   (1-Feb-91 S.W2368/R) Cavalry skirmish (15x20cm-6x8in) panel
£3000 $5070   (19-Apr-91 C52/R) A Cavalry skirmish (94x104cm-37x41in)
£4057 $8032   (30-Jan-91 APT.P226/R) Scene de bataille (62x89cm-24x35in) mono. panel (F.FR 40000)
£4500 $8865   (31-Oct-90 S181/R) Horsemen in landscape (48x59cm-19x23in) mono.
£4800 $9600   (7-Feb-91 C159/R) A cavalry skirmish (57x74cm-22x29in)
£7654 $12475   (10-Jun-91 AGB.P84/R) Choc de cavalerie (87x114cm-34x45in) s. (F.FR 76000)
£8383 $14168   (2-May-91 CH.AM105/R) A hunting party in an italianate landscape (65x78cm-26x31in) s. (D.FL 28000)

HUCHTENBURGH, Jan van (attrib) (1647-1733) Dutch
£1166 $2239   (27-Dec-90 RAS.V38/R) Battle scene (26x36cm-10x14in) (D.KR 13000)
£1858 $3530   (14-Sep-90 SA.A1097/R) Battle scene (35x51cm-14x20in) canvas on panel (DM 5500)
£2390 $4684   (6-Nov-90 BA.S121/R) Battle scene (54x71cm-21x28in) (S.KR 26000)
£2857 $5629   (12-Nov-90 CSC.P30/R) Choc de cavalerie (77x125cm-30x49in) (F.FR 28000)

HUCHTENBURGH, Jan van (circle) (1647-1733) Dutch
£2281 $4494   (30-Oct-90 BU.S256/R) Cavalry skirmish in wooded glade (48x56cm-19x22in) bears mono. (S.KR 25000)

HUCHTENBURGH, Jan van (style) (1647-1733) Dutch
£900 $1665   (5-Mar-91 PH65) Cavalry skirmish outside city walls (40x59cm-16x23in) panel
£1400 $2730   (26-Oct-90 C120) Ladies and gentlemen returning from the chase (58x71cm-23x28in)
£1514 $2982   (13-Nov-90 AB.S912/R) Cavalry battle (27x36cm-11x14in) panel (S.KR 16500)
£4000 $6760   (17-Apr-91 S95/R) Cavalry battle before castle (73x90cm-29x35in)
£6500 $10985   (17-Apr-91 S94/R) Cavalry engagement (81x97cm-32x38in)

HUCK, Karl (1876-1926) Austrian
£5000 $9800   (15-Feb-91 C48/R) Hunting falcon in mountainous landscape. Deer in wooded landscape (213x190cm-84x75in) s. double-sided

HUDECEK, Antonin (1872-1941) Czechoslovakian
£676 $1149   (28-May-91 KF.M760) Flower bed (25x35cm-10x14in) s.d.1898 canvas on board (DM 2000)

HUDSON, E (19th C) American
£1117 $2000   (11-Apr-91 FA.PH903 a) Man with cattle (69x89cm-27x35in) s.

HUDSON, Grace Carpenter (1865-1937) American
£10417 $20000   (17-Dec-90 SY.NY157/R) Mollie Wright's dog (13x18cm-5x7in) s.d.05 i.num.269 verso board

HUDSON, Robert (jnr) (?-1884) British
£750 $1388   (7-Mar-91 CSK201) The edge of Sherwood Forest (61x91cm-24x36in) s.i.d.1884

HUDSON, Thomas (1701-1779) British
£2400 $4728   (13-Nov-90 PH101/R) Portrait of Walter Oborne wearing coat and embroidered waistcoat (77x63cm-30x25in) i.d.1778
£3800 $6270   (10-Jul-91 S22/R) Portrait of Miss Furneaux Pelham wearing Van Dyck costume (89x68cm-35x27in)
£4000 $6600   (10-Jul-91 S23/R) Portrait of gentleman wearing velvet coat with tricorn hat under arm (125x100cm-49x39in) s.d.1749
£4018 $7714   (27-Nov-90 W.T1059/R) Portrit of James, Lord Strange in van Dyke costume (127x102cm-50x40in) (C.D 9000)
£6500 $10725   (12-Jul-91 C15/R) Portrait of Rear Admiral Richard Tyrell, in uniform, holding tricorn hat (126x101cm-50x40in)

HUDSON, Thomas (attrib) (1701-1779) British
£821 $1600   (14-Oct-90 H.C421/R) Portrait of Lady Bridget Bouverie (97x74cm-38x29in)
£994 $1600   (26-Jun-91 D.NY53) Portrait of elegant lady in red satin dress (76x64cm-30x25in)
£1000 $1970   (31-Oct-90 S274/R) Portrait of Bernard Gates wearing coat and brown embroidered waistcoat (74x61cm-29x24in)

HUDSON, Thomas (circle) (1701-1779) British
£750 $1305   (26-Mar-91 PH74) Portrait of presumably Lady Margaret Campbell, half length (77x63cm-30x25in)
£800 $1320   (9-Jul-91 PH25/R) Portrait of lady, wearing cream and blue satin dress (76x63cm-30x25in)

HUDSON, Thomas (school) (1701-1779) British
£1176 $2000   (30-May-91 CE.NY88 b) Portrait of George Frederick Handel standing
                        (50x40cm-20x16in)
£1641 $3200   (10-Oct-90 CH.NY38/R) Portrait of lady seated holding flowers
                        (126x101cm-50x40in)

HUDSON, Thomas (style) (1701-1779) British
£800 $1536   (20-Feb-91 CSK231) Portrait of gentleman, standing, holding document by
                        table (243x151cm-96x59in)
£1700 $2805   (11-Jul-91 CSK55/R) Portrait of lady, holding rose, view to landscape
                        beyond (74x61cm-29x24in) partly painted oval
£2095 $3750   (11-Apr-91 SY.NY114/R) Portrait of gentleman architect
                        (122x94cm-48x37in)

HUDSON, William (?-1847) British
*£950 $1644   (21-May-91 CSK162/R) Family portrait of mother and two children beside
                        harp (22x?cm-9x?in) min.s.d.1822 rectangular leather case*

HUE, Charles Desire (1825-?) French
£2041 $4020   (15-Nov-90 EA.Z194/R) Two rococo ladies fishing (55x45cm-22x18in) s.
                        (S.FR 5000)

HUE, Jean Francois (1751-1823) French
£3364 $6627   (13-Nov-90 CH.AM131/R) Cappriccio view of Mediterranean harbour with
                        fishermen in foreground (32x40cm-13x16in) s. (D.FL 11000)
£4374 $7392   (18-Apr-91 APT.P109/R) Paysage aux cascades (21x32cm-8x13in) s. panel
                        (F.FR 44000)

HUE, Jean Francois (attrib) (1751-1823) French
£1677 $2800   (23-Jan-91 D.NY10) Struggle after wreck (58x79cm-23x31in)

HUECK, Georges de (1904-1964) Russian
£1460 $2380   (12-Jun-91 ZZ.F98) Abstraite bleue outremer (100x73cm-39x29in) s. studio
                        st. verso (F.FR 14500)

HUEN, V (?)?
£1453 $2907   (6-Feb-91 N.M625/R) Napoleonic battle. Study of soldier
                        (67x102cm-26x40in) s. board double-sided (DM 4200)

HUET, Christophe (?-1759) French
£38235 $65000 (31-May-91 CH.NY66/R) Mother with puppies (127x146cm-50x57in) s.d.1734

HUET, Christophe (attrib) (?-1759) French
£3245 $6426   (30-Jan-91 APT.P273/R) Singe grimpe sur un tronc (63x49cm-25x19in)
                        (F.FR 32000)

HUET, Francois (1772-1813) French
£2000 $3300   (12-Jul-91 C176/R) Tethered donkey, sheep and poultry in barn
                        (37x47cm-15x19in) paper on panel

HUET, Francois (attrib) (1772-1813) French
*£380 $657   (21-May-91 CSK159) Officer of the 8th Hussars (7x?cm-3x?in) min.
                        porcelain oval*

HUET, Jacques (20th C) French?
£607 $1190   (25-Nov-90 ZZ.F270) Dieppedale (46x55cm-18x22in) s. (F.FR 6000)
£918 $1809   (18-Nov-90 S.S58) Le port de Rouen (50x60cm-20x24in) s. (F.FR 9000)
£1116 $2209   (3-Feb-91 I.N119/R) Les nenuphars a Giverny (60x73cm-24x29in) s.
                        (F.FR 11000)

HUET, Jean Baptiste (18/19th C) French
£4200 $6846   (1-Jul-91 GL.P24/R) Chinoiserie (79x39cm-31x15in) four (F.FR 42000)
£7708 $14954   (6-Dec-90 NM.P11/R) Paysage avec paon et poule sur une corniche
                        (40x32cm-16x13in) traces sig. (F.FR 75000)
£40000 $77200 (12-Dec-90 S103/R) Pastoral journey (56x99cm-22x39in) s. paper laid down
                        on board
£102775 $199383 (5-Dec-90 APT.P77/R) La guerre. La paix (112x131cm-44x52in) s.d.1790
                        pair (F.FR 1000000)
*£500 $835   (7-Jun-91 AGS.P24) Etude d'une tete d'ane (14x10cm-6x4in) s.d.1788
                        crayon wash (F.FR 5000)*
*£800 $1416   (22-Mar-91 APT.P96) Le bain d'une nymphe (9x11cm-4x4in) s.d.1783 pen
                        wash W/C oval (F.FR 8000)*
*£917 $1761   (27-Nov-90 APT.P103/R) Jeune cerf et un putti (18x16cm-7x6in) s.d.1785
                        pierre noire wash (F.FR 9000)*
*£1000 $1630   (1-Jul-91 S224) Peasant women with children and animals (24x32cm-9x13in)
                        pen wash over black chk*
£1316 $2500   (8-Jan-91 SY.NY118/R) A sheep (13x18cm-5x7in) s.d. wash htd.white
*£1500 $2655   (22-Mar-91 APT.P94/R) Jeune bergere et son troupeau (26x20cm-10x8in)
                        s.d.1780 pen W/C (F.FR 15000)*
*£1808 $3200   (22-Mar-91 CH.NY625/R) A couple inscribing linked hearts on a tree in a
                        landscape (13x15cm-7x6in) s.d.1783 blk.lead pen W/C htd.white*
*£1850 $3275   (22-Mar-91 APT.P95) Allegorie de la France (19x11cm-7x4in) pen wash
                        (F.FR 18500)*
*£1900 $3211   (16-Apr-91 C236/R) A wooded river landscape with shepherdess in a
                        clearing by a cottage (29x41cm-11x16in) s.d.1778 blk.white chk.*

HUET, Jean Baptiste (18/19th C) French-cont.

£2049	$4016	(7-Nov-90 APT.P419/R) Tetes de boucs (30x26cm-12x10in) s. pierre noire (F.FR 20000)
£2775	$5383	(6-Dec-90 ARC.P94/R) Scenes pastorales (36x26cm-14x10in) i. W/C htd.white gouache (F.FR 27000)
£3390	$6000	(22-Mar-91 CH.NY623/R) Studies of animals (8x10cm-3x4in) s. ink wash six on same mount
£3900	$7488	(18-Feb-91 S294/R) Two women and boy fishing by river with farmhouses and trees beyond (38x31cm-15x12in) s.d.1773 chk htd.white
£4587	$8807	(27-Nov-90 APT.P211/R) La bergere et son troupeau (42x36cm-17x14in) s.d.1779 pen wash W/C (F.FR 45000)
£6842	$13000	(11-Jan-91 CH.NY90/R) A shepherdess and a waterwoman resting by a tree. A shepherdess meetinga washerwoman by a farm (25x36cm-10x14in) both s.d.1780 blk.chk. W/C pair
£8947	$17000	(9-Jan-91 CH.NY71/R) Shepherdess seated on rock with goat and lamb (27x30cm-11x12in) s.d.1782 col.chk

HUET, Jean Baptiste (attrib) (18/19th C) French

£7059	$12000	(30-May-91 SY.NY77/R) Shepherdess in landscape (108x130cm-43x51in)

HUET, Nicolas (18/19th C) French

£759	$1488	(19-Nov-90 ZZ.F7/R) Jeune chevreuil (14x17cm-6x7in) blk.crayon W/C (F.FR 7500)

HUET, Nicolas (younger) (1770-?) French

£594	$1051	(4-Apr-91 PPB.P17) Pique boeuf bec corail, male (48x35cm-19x14in) s.i. W/C (F.FR 6000)
£743	$1314	(4-Apr-91 PPB.P14) Martin chasseur mignon (48x35cm-19x14in) s.i. W/C (F.FR 7500)
£1040	$1840	(4-Apr-91 PPB.P18) Grue a nuque blanche (48x35cm-19x14in) s.i. W/C (F.FR 10500)
£1040	$1840	(4-Apr-91 PPB.P19) Martin-pecheur lazuli (48x35cm-19x14in) s.i. W/C (F.FR 10500)
£1584	$2804	(4-Apr-91 PPB.P20) Coracine cephaloptere (48x35cm-19x14in) s.i. W/C (F.FR 16000)
£1782	$3154	(4-Apr-91 PPB.P15) Heron Goliat, femelle adulte (48x35cm-19x14in) s.i. W/C (F.FR 18000)
£1782	$3154	(4-Apr-91 PPB.P23/R) Tete grandeur naturelle du Catharte Condor, male (48x35cm-19x14in) s.i. W/C (F.FR 18000)

HUET, P (19th C) ?

£659	$1251	(11-Sep-90 CH.AM45) Men unloading barrels and villagers in a street (48x36cm-19x14in) s. (D.FL 2200)

HUET, Paul (1803-1869) French

£596	$1008	(21-Apr-91 E.LA204) Bord de riviere (46x55cm-18x22in) s. (F.FR 6000)
£1426	$2809	(4-Nov-90 FE.P174) Paysage (28x35cm-11x14in) s. (F.FR 14000)
£2092	$3619	(24-May-91 FB.P102/R) La cascade a Mortain-en-Marche (48x69cm-19x27in) s. (F.FR 21000)
£2243	$4306	(1-Dec-90 PER.M65/R) Le pont sur le torrent (33x41cm-13x16in) s. (F.FR 22000)
£800	$1304	(5-Jul-91 APT.P22) Vagues sur les rochers (13x23cm-5x9in) bears studio st. W/C (F.FR 8000)

HUG, Fritz Rudolf (1921-1989) Swiss

£516	$846	(21-Jun-91 G.Z491) Village street (50x65cm-20x26in) s. (S.FR 1300)
£635	$1041	(21-Jun-91 G.Z489) Mountain village (28x57cm-11x22in) s. (S.FR 1600)
£735	$1425	(7-Dec-90 G.Z134) Bellevue, Zurich (44x61cm-17x24in) s. board (S.FR 1800)
£794	$1302	(21-Jun-91 G.Z490) Winter at Bellevue (54x65cm-21x26in) s. (S.FR 2000)
£1905	$3124	(21-Jun-91 G.Z66/R) Abessinian cat (70x40cm-28x16in) s.i. (S.FR 4800)
£2449	$4751	(7-Dec-90 G.Z133/R) Owl in starry sky (35x27cm-14x11in) s. (S.FR 6000)
£754	$1259	(7-Jun-91 ZOF.Z1346) African baby (33x23cm-13x9in) s. gouache (S.FR 1900)

HUGARD DE LA TOUR, Claude-Sebastian (1818-1886) French

£2548	$4893	(1-Dec-90 PER.M64) La promenade sur l'etang (63x100cm-25x39in) s. (F.FR 25000)
£2613	$4285	(19-Jun-91 LC.P56/R) Paysage de Montagne (48x64cm-19x25in) s. (F.FR 26000)

HUGE, Jurgan Frederick (1809-1878) American

£2204	$4100	(9-Sep-90 LIT.L313) Alfred Thomas in full sail (74x97cm-29x38in) W/C
£11735	$23000	(24-Nov-90 RB.HY71/R) Emily, view of sailing ship under full sail (53x84cm-21x33in) s.i.d.1838 W/C

HUGER, Eduard (19th C) German

£2390	$4112	(14-May-91 GF.L2404/R) Still life of flowers and fruit (34x28cm-13x11in) s.d.1862 pair (S.FR 6000)

HUGGINS, W (1820-1884) British

£775	$1372	(20-Mar-91 JT198) Pastoral scene with cattle and sheep (46x61cm-18x24in) board

HUGGINS, William (1820-1884) British

£1400	$2380	(29-May-91 PHC194) Old forge (63x75cm-25x30in) s.

HUGGINS, William (1820-1884) British-cont.

£1600	$2752	(14-May-91 SWS176/R) Sheep by burn (60x44cm-24x17in) s.d.1856 paper on panel
£4800	$8112	(30-Apr-91 PH74/R) Oryx and calf in tropical landscape (69x69cm-27x27in) s.i.verso
£8200	$16154	(13-Nov-90 PH65/R) Lion and lioness resting by river (42x58cm-17x23in) s.d.1881 board
£14000	$25060	(10-Apr-91 S45/R) One of working class (73x61cm-29x24in) s.d.1864 arched top

HUGGINS, William John (1781-1845) British

£4800	$8160	(30-May-91 C95/R) Calypso, dismasted and jury-rigged after storm damage, being offered help by American brig (74x105cm-29x41in) s.d.1838
£11000	$18700	(30-May-91 C96/R) Royal Naval third-rater in full sail on starboard tack, island beyond (66x107cm-26x42in) s.d.1806
£56250	$95625	(27-May-91 SY.J603/R) The Thetis Calcutta in three positions in Table Bay (80x120cm-31x47in) s.d.1820 (SA.R 270000)

HUGGINS, William John (attrib) (1781-1845) British

| £2000 | $3400 | (30-May-91 C97/R) Royal naval frigate being hailed by fishing lugger (51x61cm-20x24in) |

HUGHES, Edward John (1913-?) Canadian

| *£1515* | *$2606* | *(14-May-91 JOY.T45/R) West coast of Vancouver Island (37x45cm-15x18in) s. W/C (C.D 3000)* |

HUGHES, Edward Robert (1851-1914) British

£5789	$11000	(27-Feb-91 SY.NY206/R) Portrait of Mrs. William Rhinelander Stewart (138x96cm-54x38in) s.d.1895
£1300	*$2496*	*(20-Feb-91 CSK25/R) Hermione - head study of young lady (22x16cm-9x6in) s. pencil col.chk*
£1700	*$3366*	*(30-Jan-91 S295/R) In corner chair (71x52cm-28x20in) s.d.1891 i.verso red chk*
£3400	*$6698*	*(1-Nov-90 C168/R) Portrait of Hilda Virtue Tebbs (61x51cm-24x20in) s.i.d.1897 chk*

HUGHES, Edwin (19th C) British

| £700 | $1344 | (20-Feb-91 CSK273) Collecting wild flowers (25x20cm-10x8in) s.d.1874 |

HUGHES, Ethel (19/20th C) British?

| *£480* | *$782* | *(13-Jun-91 GSP516) Country lane with girl feeding chickens and cottage beyond (18x23cm-7x9in) s. W/C* |
| *£1550* | *$2527* | *(13-Jun-91 GSP515/R) In the times of the roses, lady standing in cottage doorway (48x38cm-19x15in) s.i. W/C* |

HUGHES, George (19/20th C) British

| *£1000* | *$1980* | *(30-Jan-91 S275/R) Tangle of autumn, Temple Grafton, Warwickshire (30x22cm-12x9in) s. i.verso W/C* |

HUGHES, George H (fl.1894-1909) British

| £1263 | $2184 | (6-May-91 SY.T206/R) Mocassin seller (25x20cm-10x8in) bears sig. (C.D 2500) |
| *£650* | *$1105* | *(29-May-91 PHC90) Thatched cottage with garden in bloom (35x47cm-14x19in) s. W/C* |

HUGHES, J J (19th C) British

| £610 | $1171 | (27-Nov-90 SY.AM3669/R) Shepherd with flock near castle ruin (98cm-39ins circular) s.d.1851 (D.FL 2000) |
| £850 | $1522 | (10-Apr-91 CSK221) On the Trent near Nottingham (61x91cm-24x36in) s.d.1874 i.verso |

HUGHES, John Joseph (19th C) British

£594	$1159	(23-Oct-90 DUR.M26) At Claymarket, Norfolk (23x35cm-9x14in) (S.P 110000)
£964	$1889	(11-Feb-91 SY.J370/R) Gipsies in a country lane (45x59cm-18x23in) s.d.1858 (SA.R 4800)
£1200	$2220	(6-Mar-91 SC4370/R) On the Dee at Carrog near Corwen (58x91cm-23x36in) s.

HUGHES, Talbot (1869-1942) British

| £5780 | $10000 | (22-May-91 SY.NY256/R) Bountiful nature (61x51cm-24x20in) s.d.97 panel |

HUGHES, Thomas John (19th C) British

£550	$1018	(6-Mar-91 SC4250/R) The gamekeeper's daughter (58x38cm-23x15in) mono.
£750	$1290	(16-May-91 CSK81/R) Real enjoyment (32x22cm-13x9in) init. s.i.verso
£750	$1388	(6-Mar-91 SC4337/R) Portrait of Laura (33cm-13ins circular)
£2800	$4508	(27-Jun-91 CG22/R) Leaving home (62x51cm-24x20in) s.
£500	*$925*	*(6-Mar-91 SC4148/R) Sharing his lunch (66x53cm-26x21in) mono. W/C*

HUGHES, William (1842-1901) British

£1400	$2758	(13-Nov-90 PH109/R) Still life of grapes, pears and peach (35x47cm-14x19in) s.d.1864 board
£1600	$2752	(14-May-91 SWS204/R) Fresh gathered (20x30cm-8x12in) s.d.78 i.verso board
£2000	$3580	(14-Mar-91 B128/R) A still life of plums and other fruit on a mossy bank (25x41cm-10x16in) s.d.1869

HUGHES, William (1842-1901) British-cont.
£3590 $7000   (24-Oct-90 CH.NY341/R) Still life with grapes, pears, peaches, urn and butterfly (81x64cm-32x25in) s.d.1873

HUGHES-STANTON, Blair (1902-) British
£1500 $2610   (27-Mar-91 S51/R) Portrait of Nelson Illingworth (76x63cm-30x25in)
£880   *$1690*   *(21-Feb-91 B10) Fisherman's catch (28x50cm-11x20in) init.d.38 pen W/C*
£2000   *$3340*   *(22-Jul-91 SWS914/R) Figures in a boat (56x76cm-22x30in) s.d.'38 pen W/C*

HUGHES-STANTON, Sir Herbert (1870-1937) British
£800 $1376   (16-May-91 CSK43) Drover with sheep on track in open landscape (25x34cm-10x13in) s.d.1890 panel
£1200 $2328   (5-Dec-90 PHL189/R) Gathering the new peas (35x45cm-14x18in) s.d.1935 i.verso

HUGHTO, Darryl (1943-) American
£867 $1500   (7-May-91 CE.NY194/R) Monkey shines (190x142cm-75x56in) init.d.78 verso acrylic canvas

HUGO, Jean (1894-1984) French
£503 $965   (24-Feb-91 P.V51) Nature morte aux becasses et au pichet (11x15cm-4x6in) s. panel (F.FR 5000)
£1244 $2152   (12-May-91 T.B275/R) Maisons et gondole sur le lac (47x55cm-19x22in) s. (F.FR 12500)
£1800 $2898   (24-Jun-91 CSK114/R) Paysage au clair de la lune (24x33cm-9x13in) s. tempera
£614   *$1087*   *(5-Apr-91 LGB.P111) Vue de ville (10x13cm-4x5in) s. gouache (F.FR 6200)*
£644   *$1139*   *(5-Apr-91 LGB.P110) Paysage provencal (26x44cm-10x17in) s. pastel (F.FR 6500)*
£2436   *$4750*   *(10-Oct-90 SY.NY241/R) Reve a la nuit obscure (30x18cm-12x7in) s. gouache panel*
£2800   *$4508*   *(24-Jun-91 CSK174/R) Le mas provencal (29x21cm-11x8in) s. gouache paper on card*

HUGO, Valentine (1890-1968) French
£806   *$1573*   *(25-Oct-90 CB.P30) Autoportrit (57x42cm-22x17in) pastel (F.FR 8000)*

HUGO, Victor (1802-1885) French
£1200   *$2076*   *(9-May-91 CSK25) Castle in mountain landscape (13x18cm-5x7in) s. pen wash W/C*
£14915   *$24908*   *(6-Jun-91 HN.H431/R) Vision de Notre-Dame (14x23cm-6x9in) sepia dr. wash (DM 44000)*

HUGUE, Manolo (1872-1945) Spanish
£436   *$749*   *(16-May-91 ANS.M11/R) Desgranando el maiz (26x35cm-10x14in) pencil dr (S.P 80000)*
£1032   *$2033*   *(15-Nov-90 ANS.M48/R) Retrato de hombre (23x16cm-9x6in) gouache (S.P 190000)*

HUGUENIN, Paul (1870-1919) Swiss
£1189 $2306   (4-Dec-90 FN.S1890/R) Coastal landscape with figures collecting shells, Brittanny (21x41cm-8x16in) s. panel (DM 3400)

HUGUET, Victor Pierre (1835-1902) French
£2490 $4233   (27-May-91 APT.P282/R) Vue du Caire (41x65cm-16x26in) s.d.1895 (F.FR 25000)
£2988 $5080   (27-May-91 APT.P274/R) La traversee de l'oued (38x46cm-15x18in) s. panel (F.FR 30000)
£4286 $8443   (13-Nov-90 ARC.P169/R) Devant le port d'une ville algerienne (47x36cm-19x14in) s. panel (F.FR 42000)
£5000 $8850   (19-Mar-91 SHER120/R) Group of Arabs and horses beneath cedar tree (33x23cm-13x9in) s.
£5491 $9500   (23-May-91 CH.NY46/R) At the watering hole (65x85cm-26x33in) s.
£5789 $11000   (27-Feb-91 SY.NY123/R) Mounted Arabs (66x81cm-26x32in) s.

HUILLIOT, Pierre Nicolas (1674-1751) French
£8408 $15049   (8-Apr-91 ARC.P28/R) Vases de fleurs et fruits sur un entablement (88x99cm-35x39in) (F.FR 85000)
£14359 $28000   (10-Oct-90 CH.NY180/R) Flowers and fruit in silver urns on plinths before curtains oval pair

HUILLIOT, Pierre Nicolas (attrib) (1674-1751) French
£4980 $8616   (22-May-91 CD.P17/R) Nature morte de fleurs et de fruits avec un singe (110x92cm-43x36in) (F.FR 50000)

HUILLIOT, Pierre Nicolas (circle) (1674-1751) French
£4000 $8000   (7-Feb-91 C85/R) An urn adorned with flowers, gilt platters and ewers, and muscial instruments in a stone recess (50x213cm-20x84in)

HUITTI, Ilmari (1897-1960) Finnish
£935 $1805   (15-Dec-90 BU.H73) Autumn landscape (26x35cm-10x14in) s.d.54 panel (F.M 6500)
£935 $1805   (15-Dec-90 BU.H74) Huts (38x46cm-15x18in) s.d.38 panel (F.M 6500)

HULBERT, Katherine Allmond (?-1937) American
£565 $1000   (22-Mar-91 S.W2212) Boy and girl on bridge (51x41cm-20x16in) s. artist's board

HULK (19th C) Dutch?
£850 $1632   (21-Feb-91 KING322) Sailing vessels in misty seascape (53x84cm-21x33in) panel

HULK, A (19th C) Dutch
£920 $1536   (7-Jun-91 BW359) Dutch coastal scene with figures and barges (25x43cm-10x17in) s. W/C

HULK, A (jnr) (1851-1922) British
£1000 $1610   (24-Jun-91 LS595/R) Study of river view with child on bridge, cottage beyond (41x58cm-16x23in)
£1300 $2197   (29-Apr-91 HS272/R) Rural landscape with girl wlaking along track. Girl resting beneath tree (75x49cm-30x19in) s. pair
£1377 $2686   (25-Oct-90 VN.R48/R) Children in heath landscape (30x45cm-12x18in) s. (D.FL 4600)

HULK, Abraham (19th C) Dutch
£1149 $2000   (27-Mar-91 B.SF4250/R) Sailboats at anchor (18x24cm-7x9in) s. board pair
£1565 $2769   (20-Mar-91 KM.K1278/R) Coastal landscape with beached boats and ships offshore (40x60cm-16x24in) s. (DM 4600)
£1633 $3216   (15-Nov-90 EA.Z184/R) River landscape with shipping (43x81cm-17x32in) s. panel (S.FR 4000)
£3030 $5970   (30-Oct-90 CH.AM287/R) Sailing boat in choppy seas, at sunset (29x43cm-11x17in) s. panel (D.FL 10000)
£3049 $5976   (6-Nov-90 SY.AM218/R) Shipwreck (43x60cm-17x24in) s. panel (D.FL 10000)
£7179 $14000   (24-Oct-90 CH.NY285/R) Twilight sails (57x87cm-22x34in) s.
£8718 $17000   (23-Oct-90 SY.NY383/R) Fishing vessels at sunset (29x43cm-11x17in) s. pair

HULK, Abraham (attrib) (19th C) Dutch
£1408 $2394   (28-May-91 AB.S4771/R) Stormy coastal landscape with vessels (42x61cm-17x24in) s. (S.KR 15000)

HULK, Abraham (circle) (19th C) Dutch
£500 $815   (2-Jul-91 SWS284) Stiff breeze (22x30cm-9x12in) bears sig.d. panel

HULK, Abraham (jnr) (1851-1922) British
£838 $1408   (23-Apr-91 SY.AM184/R) View near Guildford (18x16cm-7x6in) i.verso board (D.FL 2800)
£2000 $3780   (26-Sep-90 S41/R) Albury pond, Surrey (102x75cm-40x30in) s. s.i.verso

HULK, Abraham (snr) (1813-1897) Dutch
£3800 $6460   (30-May-91 C125/R) Fishing boat in river estuary at end of day (20x30cm-8x12in) s. panel
£4000 $7400   (5-Mar-91 AG2961) Shipping on the Dutch coast (24x29cm-9x11in) s. panel
£4000 $6880   (14-May-91 SWS335/R) Barges off the coast at sunset (26x37cm-10x15in) s. panel
£4500 $7740   (14-May-91 SWS334/R) Dutch barges at the mouth of estuary (24x38cm-9x15in) s. panel
£5000 $9600   (16-Aug-90 B397/R) Shipping off coastline (18x25cm-7x10in) s.
£7800 $13026   (3-Jun-91 PHB77/R) Dutch fishing boats in freshening breeze (58x87cm-23x34in) s.

HULK, Abraham (snr-attrib) (1813-1897) Dutch
£750 $1268   (29-Apr-91 HS302) Coastal scene with fishing barges in foreground, coastal town beyond (19x29cm-7x11in) s.

HULK, Hendrik (1842-1937) Dutch
£976 $1912   (6-Nov-90 SY.AM22) River landscape with sailing boats (24x38cm-9x15in) s. panel (D.FL 3200)
£2500 $4875   (18-Oct-90 SC3075/R) Sailing boats on an estuary. Sailing boats in the Zuyder Zee (25x40cm-10x16in) both s. panel

HULK, John Frederick (1855-1913) Dutch
£599 $1006   (23-Apr-91 SY.AM107) Ducks by pond (28x46cm-11x18in) s.d.1906 (D.FL 2000)
£1786 $3000   (28-Apr-91 LIT.L121) Three setters in field (61x84cm-24x33in) s.

HULK, John Frederick (snr) (1829-1911) Dutch
£6707 $13146   (6-Nov-90 SY.AM93/R) Het Spaarne, Haarlem (60x91cm-24x36in) s. (D.FL 22000)

HULK, William F (19th C) British
£500 $960   (20-Feb-91 CSK213) Cattle watering in water meadow (39x49cm-15x19in) s.
£738 $1440   (10-Oct-90 ZEL.L1548/R) Landscape with cows grazing and farmhouse beneath trees beyond (30x23cm-12x9in) s. (DM 2200)
£788 $1410   (12-Mar-91 FN.S2439) Cattle grazing in wooded landscape with stream (30x23cm-12x9in) s. (DM 2300)
£1202 $2344   (25-Oct-90 D.V59/R) Sheep grazing in landscape (20x32cm-8x13in) s. board (A.S 25000)
£1500 $2505   (5-Jun-91 S51/R) Cattle, early morning (76x101cm-30x40in) s. s.i.verso

HULK, William F (19th C) British-cont.
£1667 $3283   (30-Oct-90 CH.AM76/R) Cattle near Dorking, England (102x76cm-40x30in) s.
                      s.i.verso (D.FL 5500)
£2100 $3444   (18-Jun-91 OT426/R) Quiet morning (50x74cm-20x29in) s.

HULL, Edward (19th C) British
£640 $1261   (13-Nov-90 SWS56/R) Figures boating on the Thames (28x43cm-11x17in)
                      s.indist.d.1872 W/C bodycol.over pencil

HULL, Thomas H (fl.1775-1827) British
£1050 $1733   (10-Jul-91 C163/R) A lady in white dress with brown bodice (4x?cm-2x?in)
                      min. gold swivel frame oval

HULL, William (1820-1880) British
£320 $554   (7-May-91 SWS1893/R) Gentleman with powdered hair and blue jacket min.
                      oval gold frame pearl hair opalescent verso
£1050 $2058   (23-Jan-91 JT157) Pine wood near Coniston (64x104cm-25x41in) s.d.1875
                      W/C

HULLGREN, Oscar (1869-1948) Swedish
£1147 $2259   (13-Nov-90 AB.S386/R) Seascape with breakers (40x50cm-16x20in) s.
                      (S.KR 12500)
£1149 $2252   (10-Nov-90 FAL.M155/R) Sun going to behind cloud (43x53cm-17x21in)
                      s.d.33 (S.KR 12500)
£1372 $2676   (21-Oct-90 BU.M93) Seascape with cliffs and breakers (40x50cm-16x20in)
                      s.d.32 (S.KR 15000)

HULME, Alice L (fl.1877-1890) British
£750 $1478   (13-Nov-90 SWS173/R) Christmas roses (29x40cm-11x16in) s. l. label verso

HULME, Frederick William (1816-1884) British
£3200 $6240   (18-Oct-90 SC3088/R) Junction of the Llugwy and Conway, NW Vale of
                      Bettws-Y-Coed (50x70cm-20x28in) s. l. stretcher
£4800 $9600   (8-Feb-91 C134/R) Bettws-y-Coed, North Wales (51x71cm-20x28in) s.
£15000 $25050   (5-Jun-91 S26/R) Sweet summer time (122x198cm-48x78in) s.d.1860

HULSDONCK, Gillis van (1626-1670?) Dutch
£11858 $20158   (30-May-91 EA.Z357) Still life of grapes, apricots and plums
                      (77x56cm-30x22in) s. (S.FR 30000)

HULSDONCK, Jacob van (style) (1582-1647) Flemish
£1450 $2451   (18-Apr-91 CSK162/R) Plums and grapes with bowl on ledge
                      (28x37cm-11x15in)
£5263 $10000   (10-Jan-91 SY.NY8/R) Mixed fruit in basket (51x73cm-20x29in) panel

HULST, Frans de (1610-1661) Flemish
£1982 $3250   (19-Jun-91 B.SF1660/R) Village landscape with peasants near brook and
                      church beyond (37x70cm-15x28in) s. panel
£5771 $10042   (25-Mar-91 PLF.P119/R) Vues de village en Hollande (40x53cm-16x21in)
                      both s. panel pair oval (F.FR 58000)
£6000 $11400   (1-Mar-91 C112/R) View of Rhenen with ferry boat carrying coach
                      (41x61cm-16x24in) s. panel

HULST, Frans de (attrib) (1610-1661) Flemish
£4082 $8041   (15-Nov-90 EA.Z201/R) River landscape with boats (43x70cm-17x28in) l.
                      panel (S.FR 10000)

HULSTEYN, Johan van (1860-1894) Dutch
£1829 $3585   (6-Nov-90 SY.AM209) Dutch polderlandscape (64x93cm-25x37in) s.
                      (D.FL 6000)

HULSTYN, Cornelis Johannes van (1813-1879) Dutch
£667 $1313   (30-Oct-90 CH.AM312) Seamstress (48x32cm-19x13in) s. panel (D.FL 2200)

HULSWIT, Jan (1766-1822) Dutch
£2545 $4301   (2-May-91 CH.AM129/R) A view of the Singel, Amsterdam, with a barge
                      being loaded, the Munttoren beyond (40x55cm-16x22in) s. (D.FL 8500)

HULTEN, C O (1916-) Swedish
£3770 $6371   (18-Apr-91 BU.S55/R) 'Lianmanster' (114x135cm-45x53in) s.d.1988
                      (S.KR 40000)
£7069 $11946   (18-Apr-91 BU.S93/R) 'Overvunna minnen' (200x134cm-79x53in) s.d.1989
                      (S.KR 75000)

HULTEN, Carl Otto (1916-) Swedish
£1384 $2657   (27-Nov-90 BU.S141/R) 'Kring Klotet' (54x65cm-21x26in) s.d.1988
                      (S.KR 15000)
£1668 $3236   (5-Dec-90 AB.S7102/R) Composition (81x65cm-32x26in) s. (S.KR 18000)
£2830 $4896   (22-May-91 BA.S379/R) Drawing and blue wing (63x51cm-25x20in) s.
                      (S.KR 30000)
£3151 $6113   (5-Dec-90 AB.S7103/R) 'Dogonland' (73x92cm-29x36in) s. (S.KR 34000)
£741 $1438   (4-Dec-90 BA.S217 a/R) Composition (18x32cm-7x13in) s. gouache
                      (S.KR 8000)
£1845 $3542   (27-Nov-90 BU.S140/R) Composition with figure and bird (50x39cm-20x15in)
                      s. gouache (S.KR 20000)

HUMBERT, Jacques Ferdinand (1842-1934) French
£2500 $4300   (17-May-91 C17 d/R) Diana bathing (81x109cm-32x43in) s.d.86

HUMBERT, Jean-Charles-Ferdinand (1813-1881) Swiss
£1633 $3200   (6-Nov-90 GF.L2239/R) Landscape with domestic animals (65x97cm-26x38in)
                    s.d.1852 (S.FR 4000)
£1959 $3801   (8-Dec-90 GAB.G2216) Moutons paissant (90x140cm-35x55in) s.d.1859
                    (S.FR 4800)

HUMBERT-VIGNOT (19/20th C) French
£1354 $2640   (12-Oct-90 ZZ.F39/R) La Divette (118x93cm-46x37in) s. (F.FR 13500)

HUMBLOT, George (20th C) French
£1285 $2300   (11-Apr-91 FA.PH998) Winter farm scene (36x48cm-14x19in) s.

HUMBLOT, Robert (1907-1962) French
£1154 $2250   (10-Oct-90 SY.NY261/R) Paysage Provencal (18x23cm-7x9in) s.d.56

HUMBORG, Adolf (1847-?) Austrian
£512 $840   (22-Jun-91 WK.M1411) Monk painting at easel (66x29cm-26x11in) s.i.
               (DM 1500)

HUME, Edith (19th C) British
£2800 $5516   (13-Nov-90 PH78/R) On the Dutch coast (24x31cm-9x12in) s.
               s.i.d.1908verso panel
£3300 $6501   (13-Nov-90 PH86/R) A stitch in time (24x31cm-9x12in) s. s.i.d.1908verso
               panel

HUMMEL, Theodor (1864-1939) German
£1049 $2024   (12-Dec-90 N.M566/R) Marienplatz in Munich (33x44cm-13x17in) s.d.1919
               board (DM 3000)
£1074 $2094   (10-Oct-90 WE.MU271/R) Portrait of little girl (60x50cm-24x20in) st.sig.
               (DM 3200)

HUMPHREY, Ozias (1742-1810) British
£900   *$1485*   *(10-Jul-91 C176) A gentleman in blue coat (4x?cm-2x?in) min. gold frame*
               scalloped border oval
£1200   *$2124*   *(19-Mar-91 CSK57/R) Portrait of gentleman in coat and waistcoat and*
               cravat (4x?cm-2x?in) min. gold bracelet clasp frame macasite border

HUMPHREY, Ralph (1932-) American
£4569 $9000   (4-Oct-90 SY.NY170 a/R) Untitled (183x274cm-72x108in)
£6122 $12000   (14-Feb-91 CH.NY36/R) Oval composition (137x198cm-54x78in)
               s.d.73stretcher acrylic shaped

HUMPHREY, Walter Beach (1892-1966) American
£1118 $1900   (1-Jun-91 IH.NY203/R) Woman operator handing phone message to boss
               (69x56cm-27x22in) s.
£1331 $2250   (1-May-91 B.SF5275/R) Timeless moments (74x53cm-29x21in) s.i.
£1412 $2400   (1-Jun-91 IH.NY30/R) Back at home, soldier with boy and puppies
               (64x53cm-25x21in) s.

HUMPHRIES, John Barry (1934-) Australian
£3057 $5472   (9-Apr-91 CH.ME292/R) Self portrait (50x40cm-20x16in) s. s.i.d.11.11.72
               board (A.D 7000)

HUMPHRIES, William H (fl.1881-1899) British
£500 · $820   (18-Jun-91 OT436) Lady wearing blue dress in dressing room
               (52x42cm-20x17in) s.

HUNAEUS, A (1814-1866) Danish
£779   *$1510*   (22-Aug-90 RAS.K252/R) Portrait of young girl (29x24cm-11x9in) s.d.1843
               (D.KR 9000)

HUNASTENBROOKGS, D (?) ?
£1325   *$2544*   *(30-Nov-90 CB.P50) Le port (49x72cm-19x28in) s. W/C (F.FR 13000)*

HUNDERTWASSER (1928-) Austrian
£55000 $106700   (6-Dec-90 C516/R) Spirale in gold rain (73x60cm-29x24in) s.i.d.61
               num.492 verso egg tempera gold paint
£92000   *$179400*   *(17-Oct-90 G.Z147R) Ich wohne zu nahe an der Route Nationale und ein*
               Dampfer fahrt durch die Wiese (81x116cm-32x46in) s.d.1963verso mixed
               media hessian (S.FR 230000)

HUNDERTWASSER, Friedrich (1928-) Austrian
£38845 $66036   (2-Jun-91 GL.P169/R) Bain gazon pour la spirale (48x62cm-19x24in) s. i.
               verso paper laid down on panel (F.FR 390000)
£54000 $104760   (6-Dec-90 S7/R) Occhio Del Dio Sole - Le Tir Auge des Sonnengottes - Die
               Zielscheibe (165x54cm-65x21in) s.d.1954 i.verso oil gold leaf
£60000 $96600   (27-Jun-91 S29/R) Globulant (117x77cm-46x30in) s.i.d.1956verso
£791   *$1344*   *(30-May-91 EA.Z56/R) For Sonnenstern's 80th Birthday 11 9 72*
               (86x64cm-34x25in) s. mixed media (S.FR 2000)
£1858   *$3159*   *(1-Jun-91 VG.B610/R) Survivant de Laszlo (16x12cm-6x5in) s. collage*
               col.pencil bodycol (DM 5500)
£17928   *$30478*   *(2-Jun-91 GL.P158/R) Le western oriental - ville haute ville basse*
               (48x55cm-19x22in) s.d.1955 W/C chk.zinc (F.FR 180000)

HUNDERTWASSER, Friedrich (1928-) Austrian-cont.
£20717	$40398	(24-Oct-90 GD.B497/R) Kopf mit Erdfenstern (18x27cm-7x11in) W/C over pencil (S.FR 52000)
£32000	$56640	(21-Mar-91 S72/R) Man find in Zahala (35x50cm-14x20in) s.d.1975 num.739c W/C egg oil paper on canvas
£43860	$74561	(29-May-91 KH.K253/R) Der asiatische Krieg (116x87cm-46x34in) s.d.1958 mixed media silk on canvas (D.KR 500000)
£55102	$106898	(7-Dec-90 G.Z30/R) The city is the woman's coiffure (65x50cm-26x20in) s.d.1962 mixed media W/C chk paper on canvas (S.FR 135000)

HUNG QUA (attrib) (19th C) Chinese
| £2119 | $4132 | (9-Oct-90 CH.HK1345/R) Portrait of Chinese Imperial Commisioner Kiyeng, in official robes (34x27cm-13x11in) indist.i.d.1845 verso (HK.D 32000) |

HUNN, Tom (fl.1878-1908) British
£720	$1289	(14-Mar-91 ZZ.B100) At Eashing (33x49cm-13x19in) s.d.'04 W/C
£1000	$1680	(22-Apr-91 PH315/R) At Shere (30x47cm-12x19in) s.i. W/C
£1050	$2058	(8-Nov-90 PHI60/R) The White Hart, Whitley, Surrey (31x48cm-12x19in) s.i.d.1908 W/C

HUNT, Alfred William (1830-1896) British
| £4600 | $9062 | (15-Nov-90 SJ124/R) Grape pickers near the Rhine (26x37cm-10x15in) s.i. bears i.verso W/C over pencil bodycol |

HUNT, Arthur Ackland (fl.1881-1913) British
| £540 | $913 | (15-Apr-91 WW5) Idle moments (28x20cm-11x8in) s.d.1910 canvasboard |

HUNT, Bryan (1947-) American
| £1040 | $1800 | (7-May-91 CE.NY180/R) Hoyle's dream (15x15cm-6x6in) s.d.76 stretcher gouache col.ink graphite |
| £5917 | $10000 | (2-May-91 CH.NY305/R) Untitled (238x107cm-94x42in) graphite wax oilstick |

HUNT, Cecil Arthur (1873-1965) British
| £950 | $1900 | (8-Feb-91 C68) A distant view of St.Julien, Le Puy (25x36cm-10x14in) s. pencil W/C |
| £1050 | $2016 | (17-Dec-90 PH77/R) Gibraltar (28x38cm-11x15in) s. i.verso W/C bodycol |

HUNT, Charles (1803-1877) British
£875	$1488	(27-May-91 SY.J276/R) Don't pick the flowers (24x19cm-9x7in) s.d.70 (SA.R 4200)
£1451	$2786	(27-Nov-90 W.T1035/R) After Donny Brook Fair (50x39cm-20x15in) s.d.1895 (C.D 3250)
£1600	$2608	(14-Jun-91 C292/R) The trial (16x24cm-6x9in) s.d.1866
£2308	$4500	(23-Oct-90 SY.NY392/R) No thoroughfare (71x91cm-28x36in) s.i.d.1871
£2800	$5460	(18-Oct-90 SC3123/R) Two suitors (62x91cm-24x36in) s.d.1860
£3811	$7432	(9-Oct-90 GGL.L13/R) Preparatifs de Carnaval (31x46cm-12x18in) s.d.1862 (F.FR 38000)
£5000	$9850	(1-Nov-90 C324/R) The rival suitors (91x148cm-36x58in) s.d.1876
£14451	$25000	(22-May-91 SY.NY44/R) Trial by Judge and Jury (53x83cm-21x33in) s.d.1866

HUNT, Charles (Jnr) (19th C) British
| £11500 | $22655 | (1-Nov-90 C325/R) The game of draughts (51x76cm-20x30in) s.d.91 |

HUNT, Charles Henry (20th C) Australian
| £3111 | $5849 | (17-Sep-90 SY.ME69/R) Orange blossoms (45x33cm-18x13in) s.d.1887 (A.D 7000) |

HUNT, Edgar (1876-1953) British
£3800	$6346	(5-Jun-91 S97/R) Calves and pony (28x38cm-11x15in) s. board
£4192	$7000	(7-Jun-91 SY.NY114/R) Farmyard scene (30x39cm-12x15in) s.d.1943 board
£4700	$8319	(5-Apr-91 BW408/R) Farmyard study with cockerel and chickens at feeding time (20x28cm-8x11in) s.d.1919
£5090	$8500	(7-Jun-91 SY.NY113/R) Mealtime (28x38cm-11x15in) s.d.1943 board
£5400	$9018	(5-Jun-91 S106/R) Ducks and pigeons (35x30cm-14x12in) s.d.1909
£5641	$11000	(24-Oct-90 CH.NY318/R) Chickens in barnyard (28x38cm-11x15in) s.d.1927
£5778	$11209	(4-Dec-90 R.T266/R) Goat, ducks and poultry in farmyard (28x38cm-11x15in) s.d.1922 (C.D 13000)
£6000	$10020	(5-Jun-91 S78/R) Chickens. Goats and rabbit (26x21cm-10x8in) s. board pair
£6000	$9780	(14-Jun-91 C239/R) Chicks by a basket (25x30cm-10x12in) s.d.1908
£6154	$12000	(24-Oct-90 CH.NY319/R) Donkey and chickens outside stable (57x77cm-22x30in) s.d.1921
£6200	$10974	(5-Apr-91 BW409/R) Farmyard study with chickens on barrel near barn at feeding time (28x38cm-11x15in) s.d.1925
£6316	$12000	(28-Feb-91 CH.NY172/R) Poultry in barnyard (36x30cm-14x12in) s.d.1926
£6800	$11356	(5-Jun-91 S85/R) Chickens with chicks (30x43cm-12x17in) s.d.1925
£9000	$15030	(5-Jun-91 S96/R) Ducks and goat (40x61cm-16x24in) s.d.1919
£10180	$17000	(7-Jun-91 SY.NY112/R) Chickens. Pigeons (20x28cm-8x11in) each s.d.1920 pair
£12500	$20875	(5-Jun-91 S87/R) New brood (76x63cm-30x25in) s.d.1914
£13000	$21710	(5-Jun-91 S79/R) Donkeys and chickens (40x61cm-16x24in) s.d.1919
£15500	$25885	(5-Jun-91 S98/R) Goats and chickens (91x71cm-36x28in) s.d.1914
£17000	$33490	(1-Nov-90 D178/R) Donkeys, hens and chicks in farmyard (53x74cm-21x29in) s.d.1915
£22000	$36740	(5-Jun-91 S77/R) Corner of farmyard (76x127cm-30x50in) s.d.1902

HUNT, Edward Aubrey (1855-1922) British
£1900 $3173   (22-Jul-91 SWS1125/R) Old Bridge, St. Ives, Huntingdonshire (67x87cm-26x34in) s. .d.1903 verso

HUNT, Esther (1875-1951) American
£1020 $2000   (13-Feb-91 B.SF2014/R) China town (132x61cm-52x24in) s.
£1667 $3250   (10-Oct-90 B.SF499/R) Chinese girl (56x35cm-22x14in) s.
£452 $850   (22-Sep-90 WOL.C34/R) Chinese family in temple (76x56cm-30x22in) s. W/C

HUNT, Percy Ivor (?) ?
£622 $1170   (17-Sep-90 SY.ME87/R) Boys boating (27x37cm-11x15in) s. W/C (A.D 1400)
£1600 $3008   (17-Sep-90 SY.ME26/R) Portrait of J.W.Linton (35x26cm-14x10in) s. W/C (A.D 3600)

HUNT, Rhoda H (fl.1899-1904) British
£1600 $2960   (6-Mar-91 SC4350/R) Donkey and cockerels with terrier (36x46cm-14x18in) s.d.1925

HUNT, Thomas (1854-1929) British
£1020 $2000   (13-Feb-91 B.SF2032/R) Mission (23x30cm-9x12in) artist board

HUNT, Thomas L (20th C) American
£2296 $4500   (7-Nov-90 B.SF3769/R) At the harbour (61x66cm-24x26in) s. board
£8673 $17000   (12-Feb-91 MOR.P114 a) Coastal scene (71x76cm-28x30in) s.

HUNT, Tony (?) Canadian
£897 $1731   (10-Dec-90 L.V4) N W coastal landscape (549x305cm-216x120in) board (C.D 2000)

HUNT, W (19th C) British?
£789 $1500   (27-Feb-91 SY.NY203 a) Portrait of young twins with dolls (42x32cm-17x13in) s. W/C

HUNT, Walter (1861-1941) British
£3757 $6500   (23-May-91 CH.NY210/R) Two calves in barn (40x50cm-16x20in) s. panel
£6316 $12000   (27-Feb-91 SY.NY254/R) Blowing bubbles (76x51cm-30x20in) s.d.1892
£10526 $20000   (28-Feb-91 CH.NY184/R) Horses in pasture (102x152cm-40x60in) s.d.87
£13000 $25610   (1-Nov-90 D177/R) Calves and fowl in framyard (48x74cm-19x29in) s.d.1921

HUNT, William (19th C) British
£1063 $1796   (1-May-91 KH.K83/R) Kitchen interior with boy seated (41x51cm-16x20in) s. (D.KR 12000)
£559 $1118   (4-Feb-91 LGB.P130) Scene medievale (11x8cm-4x3in) s. W/C (F.FR 5500)

HUNT, William Henry (1790-1864) British
£565 $1000   (22-Mar-91 S.W2203) Still life of fruit (36x46cm-14x18in) s.
£1200 $2352   (20-Nov-90 PH183/R) Still life of primulas, violets, blossom and a bird's nest (43x34cm-17x13in) s.d.1861
£660 $1181   (12-Mar-91 LW1496) Study of a young girl with a basket of strawberries (41x30cm-16x12in) s.
£750 $1478   (13-Nov-90 C144/R) Outside the gardener's cottage at Chatsworth (33x23cm-13x9in) bears sig. indis.i.verso pencil W/C
£850 $1394   (19-Jun-91 B46/R) Rest by wayside (42x31cm-17x12in) s. W/C
£900 $1773   (15-Nov-90 S87/R) The backs of old cottages (32x42cm-13x17in) pen ink W/C two sheets joined
£1000 $2000   (8-Feb-91 C30/R) Apple blossom and a bird's nest on a mossy bank (20x30cm-8x12in) W/C htd.white oval
£3400 $6086   (11-Apr-91 S4) Children playing in country churchyard (27x36cm-11x14in) s. W/C

HUNT, William Holman (1827-1910) British
£600 $1014   (29-Apr-91 HS189/R) Study of child wearing robes (22x13cm-9x5in) init. graphite
£600 $1002   (5-Jun-91 S332/R) Study for two sword hilts (23x15cm-9x6in) i.pencil
£900 $1521   (29-Apr-91 HS190/R) In cafe, Egypt (17x13cm-7x5in) init.i.d.1854 graphite htd white
£1700 $3349   (1-Nov-90 C172/R) William Etty in the Life School (10x13cm-4x5in) init. pencil pen ink
£8000 $15360   (28-Nov-90 S15/R) Portrait of Fanny Hunt (71x52cm-28x20in) mono.d.1866 col.chk wash paper on canvas
£28000 $45920   (19-Jun-91 S229/R) Wadi in Palestine (34x49cm-13x19in) s.i.d. W/C over pencil

HUNT, William Morris (1824-1879) American
£769 $1300   (20-Apr-91 WOL.C50) Landscape at dusk (48x58cm-19x23in) mono.

HUNTEN, Emil (1827-1902) German
£3209 $5424   (3-May-91 SA.A1770/R) A column of French prisoners during the 1870-71 war (62x80cm-24x31in) s. (DM 9500)
£3468 $6000   (23-May-91 CH.NY114/R) Der Spion (71x107cm-28x42in) s.d.1867
£5236 $9949   (14-Sep-90 SA.A1247/R) The information (73x66cm-29x26in) s.d.1865 (DM 15500)

HUNTEN, Franz Johann Wilhelm (1822-1887) German
£649 $1057   (10-Jun-91 W.T1408 a) The S.S. John Preston, Caernarvon, David Davies Master (49x71cm-19x28in) s.i. (C.D 1200)

HUNTEN, Franz Johann Wilhelm (1822-1887) German-cont.

| £848 | $1629 | (28-Nov-90 PH.T7/R) Fishing vessels in swell (56x89cm-22x35in) s.d.1881 canvas on board (C.D 1900) |

HUNTER, Colin (1841-1904) British

| £1600 | $3200 | (5-Feb-91 S176/R) Tanning herring nets (51x91cm-20x36in) s.d.1895 |
| £7500 | $12600 | (23-Apr-91 S66/R) Baiters (168x124cm-66x49in) s.d.1889 |

HUNTER, E (20th C) ?

| *£650* | *$1274* | *(8-Nov-90 CSK2) Figures in a French town (15x21cm-6x8in) s.d.1924 W/C bodycol.* |

HUNTER, George Leslie (1877-1931) British

£1400	$2800	(5-Feb-91 S133/R) Pink and red roses (23x31cm-9x12in) s. indist.s.d.verso board
£3200	$6208	(6-Dec-90 CG270/R) On the Hard, Largo (12x21cm-5x8in) s. panel
£3500	$7000	(5-Feb-91 S126/R) Distant rooftop (39x44cm-15x17in) s. board
£3800	$7106	(28-Aug-90 S1026/R) Toulon (38x46cm-15x18in) s. board
£4600	$8602	(28-Aug-90 S1038) Still life of roses (26x27cm-10x11in) s. board
£5102	$10000	(7-Nov-90 B.SF1064/R) Still life with portrait of Infanta by Velasquez (46x35cm-18x14in) s.
£6500	$12610	(6-Dec-90 CG271/R) Pink roses in Chinese glue and white gu-shaped vase (35x25cm-14x10in) s. canvas board
£7000	$11830	(2-May-91 CG522/R) Still life with lemon, carnations and fan on table (25x51cm-10x20in) s. canvasboard
£8500	$15895	(28-Aug-90 S1025/R) Toulon (50x61cm-20x24in) s. board
£11000	$21340	(6-Dec-90 CG262/R) Mixed dahlias in green vase with book on chequered tablecloth (56x46cm-22x18in) s.
£14000	$27160	(6-Dec-90 CG266/R) Le Pont Neuf, Paris (38x46cm-15x18in) s.
£18000	$34920	(6-Dec-90 CG267/R) Apples in white fruitbowl and pink rose in vase (40x45cm-16x18in) s. board
£19000	$36860	(6-Dec-90 CG265/R) The black hat (43x35cm-17x14in) s. board
£19000	$36860	(6-Dec-90 CG263/R) Grapes and other fruit in silver dish with wine glasses and bread (51x41cm-20x16in) s.
£20000	$38800	(6-Dec-90 CG264/R) The brown jug (53x43cm-21x17in) s. l.verso
£25000	$50000	(5-Feb-91 S108/R) Black vase (69x76cm-27x30in) s. board
£26000	$48620	(28-Aug-90 S1023/R) Roses (68x50cm-27x20in) s. board
£2800	*$5488*	*(22-Nov-90 CG546/R) Girl at scullery table (42x38cm-17x15in) s. W/C htd.white*
£5500	*$10670*	*(6-Dec-90 CG261/R) Juan-les-Pins (30x39cm-12x15in) s. brush ink col.crayons*

HUNTER, George Sherwood (1850-1919) British

£600	$1170	(18-Oct-90 CSK113/R) Figures by a balustrade overlooking the Grand Canal (23x61cm-9x24in)
£600	$1044	(27-Mar-91 RB674) Study of peasant girl in traditional costume (33x41cm-13x16in) i.
£600	$1170	(18-Oct-90 CSK178/R) The artist's greenhouse under snow (25x30cm-10x12in) d.December 12 1903
£650	$1268	(18-Oct-90 CSK13/R) A Dutch farmstead (21x27cm-8x11in)
£650	$1268	(18-Oct-90 CSK176/R) Banter, Newlyn (30x46cm-12x18in) i. stretcher
£650	$1268	(18-Oct-90 CSK187/R) A young woman at a window (29x23cm-11x9in)
£700	$1365	(18-Oct-90 CSK51/R) A faggot gatherer, winter time, Scotland (22x28cm-9x11in)
£700	$1365	(18-Oct-90 CSK10/R) A harbour welcome (76x51cm-30x20in)
£700	$1365	(18-Oct-90 CSK24/R) Salmon netting on the east coast of Scotland (23x28cm-9x11in)
£700	$1365	(18-Oct-90 CSK5/R) A sunlit church (18x36cm-7x14in) indist.i.d.May 13, 1888
£700	$1365	(18-Oct-90 CSK114/R) Santa Maria della Salute from the Canal (30x38cm-12x15in)
£700	$1365	(18-Oct-90 CSK81/R) Trawling for shrimps, near Port Bruns (18x36cm-7x14in) i.d.1907
£700	$1365	(18-Oct-90 CSK174/R) Everybody loves a sailor, Newlyn lighthouse and St.Michael's Mountbeyond (15x23cm-6x9in)
£700	$1365	(18-Oct-90 CSK56/R) On the Finhorn path (76x51cm-30x20in) init.i.d.1881 stretcher
£700	$1365	(18-Oct-90 CSK76/R) A religious festival inside a church (30x45cm-12x18in)
£750	$1463	(18-Oct-90 CSK43/R) Stacking whiskey casks on the North East coast of Scotland (21x27cm-8x11in)
£750	$1463	(18-Oct-90 CSK115/R) A view of Venice from Guidecca (25x51cm-10x20in)
£750	$1463	(18-Oct-90 CSK112/R) The Doge's Palace, with Santa Maria delle Salute in the distance (28x45cm-11x18in)
£750	$1463	(18-Oct-90 CSK39/R) A young boy playing in the sand, a clipper beyond (27x22cm-11x9in)
£800	$1560	(18-Oct-90 CSK37/R) Homewards, Aberdeen beach (51x76cm-20x30in) s.i.d.1877 stretcher
£850	$1658	(18-Oct-90 CSK20/R) A little Dutch girl waiting on the quay (46x30cm-18x12in) init.d.1890
£900	$1755	(18-Oct-90 CSK186/R) A mother with her baby in a Cornish cottage (21x28cm-8x11in)
£900	$1755	(18-Oct-90 CSK19/R) Funeral of a Fisherman's child, Volendam (48x71cm-19x28in)
£950	$1853	(18-Oct-90 CSK111/R) Figures promenading on the Piazzetta, Venice (32x44cm-13x17in)

HUNTER, George Sherwood (1850-1919) British-cont.

£950	$1853	(18-Oct-90 CSK195/R) Newlyn, George V's Coronation Procession on the new road returning from Penzance (30x46cm-12x18in) i. stretcher
£950	$1853	(18-Oct-90 CSK161/R) H.M.S. Renard and Torpedo-Catcher H.M.S. Ferret off Newlyn pier (20x27cm-8x11in) init.i.d.13 June 1896
£957	$1656	(8-May-91 D.V12/R) Venice, Ponte della Paglia (36x31cm-14x12in) (A.S 20000)
£1000	$1950	(18-Oct-90 CSK47/R) Aberdeen (25x51cm-10x20in)
£1000	$1950	(18-Oct-90 CSK138/R) A fountain in the Dolomites, Pieve di Ladore (65x51cm-26x20in)
£1100	$2145	(18-Oct-90 CSK88/R) Figures on a beach in Brittany (22x27cm-9x11in) s.d.1881
£1100	$2145	(18-Oct-90 CSK180/R) Fishermen by the harbour (21x27cm-8x11in)
£1200	$2340	(18-Oct-90 CSK119/R) Venice in the early morning from the public gardens (16x30cm-6x12in) i. verso card
£1300	$2535	(18-Oct-90 CSK93) An orchard in bloom (32x41cm-13x16in) s.i. stretcher
£1300	$2535	(18-Oct-90 CSK109/R) Figures on the Ponte delle Paglia, Venice (39x32cm-15x13in)
£1500	$2925	(18-Oct-90 CSK125/R) Feeding the birds. The bridge of Sighs (51x25cm-20x10in)
£1500	$2925	(18-Oct-90 CSK140/R) The last days of the carnival, via Flamina, Rome (30x23cm-12x9in) init.i.d.1876 stretcher
£1600	$3120	(18-Oct-90 CSK126/R) A gondolier in the lagoon (25x51cm-10x20in) s.
£1700	$3315	(18-Oct-90 CSK106/R) The Embankment, London (18x36cm-7x14in) init.indist.i.d.1886
£2000	$3900	(18-Oct-90 CSK67/R) The artist painting amongst trees under a white umbrella (21x27cm-8x11in)
£2200	$4290	(18-Oct-90 CSK12/R) Enjoying life, Volendam, Zuider Zee (46x30cm-18x12in) s.i. verso
£2800	$5460	(18-Oct-90 CSK3/R) Lighting Up, Volendam (76x51cm-30x20in) d.1862 i. stretcher
£3000	$5850	(18-Oct-90 CSK121/R) Venetian fisherman awaiting daybreak (121x72cm-48x28in) s.d.1877
£4000	$7800	(18-Oct-90 CSK94/R) Figures on a beach, Brittany (32x46cm-13x18in)
£1000	$1950	(18-Oct-90 CSK11/R) A marken girl, Holland (44x30cm-17x12in) s.d.1890 pastel
£1200	$2340	(18-Oct-90 CSK79/R) The red umbrella (46x29cm-18x11in) pastel
£1300	$2535	(18-Oct-90 CSK107/R) The Piazzetta, Venice. Looking towards Santa Maria delle Salute (29x46cm-11x18in) both s.d.1878 one i. verso W/C htd.white

HUNTER, John Young (after) (1874-1955) British
£737	$1400	(27-Feb-91 SY.NY215/R) My Lady's garden (81x137cm-32x54in)

HUNTER, Leslie (?-1934) British
£3500	$5915	(3-May-91 PHE91/R) Dalpatrick Farm, Rosebank, Clyde Valley (30x40cm-12x16in) panel
£8000	$15520	(5-Dec-90 PHE32/R) The deserted beach (55x67cm-22x26in) s.
£8000	$15520	(5-Dec-90 PHE38/R) Still life with black bottle (35x30cm-14x12in) s.
£35000	$59150	(3-May-91 PHE114/R) Still life of fruit and flowers (57x46cm-22x18in) s. board

HUNTER, Robert (attrib) (?-1780) British
£14000	$23100	(12-Jul-91 C13/R) Portrait of gentleman, thought to be Sir Robert King, seated by table (239x145cm-94x57in)

HUNTINGTON (19/20th C) American
£1923	$3250	(17-Apr-91 D.NY46/R) Five masted barque David Dows with tug Sumner in nocturnal storm (69x56cm-27x22in) s.d.1881 W/C pastel

HUNTINGTON, Daniel (1816-1906) American
£549	$950	(21-May-91 GRO.B53/R) Fair sketcher (23x18cm-9x7in) s.d.1859
£847	$1600	(25-Sep-90 CE.NY46/R) Hunter and his dog (36x56cm-14x22in) s. W/C gouache board

HUNZIKER, Frieda (1908-1966) Dutch
£1703	$3286	(12-Dec-90 CH.AM525) Les fantomes (69x90cm-27x35in) (D.FL 5500)

HUNZIKER, Max (20th C?) Swiss
£898	$1760	(6-Nov-90 GF.L2604/R) At school (65x50cm-26x20in) s. (S.FR 2200)

HURARD, Joseph (19/20th C) French
£704	$1259	(17-Mar-91 L.C33/R) Le marche (53x71cm-21x28in) s. board (F.FR 7000)
£968	$1859	(29-Nov-90 QWA.P94) La Chartreuse - Villeneuve-les-Avignon (53x72cm-21x28in) s. board (F.FR 9500)
£1222	$2407	(30-Oct-90 I.N156/R) La route blanche (46x62cm-18x24in) s. board (F.FR 12000)
£663	$1272	(29-Nov-90 QWA.P93) Vue du village (62x41cm-24x16in) s. bitum gouache (F.FR 6500)

HURCK, J (19th C) ?
£1786	$3089	(22-May-91 GS.B2407/R) Letitian landscape at the Baltic coast with fisher women working (48x73cm-19x29in) s.d.1866 (S.FR 4500)

HURD, Michael (20th C) American
£1479	$2500	(1-May-91 B.SF5208/R) Annie's house (91x81cm-36x32in) s.

HURD, Peter (1904-1984) American
£5612	$11000	(7-Nov-90 B.SF3837/R) Young jockey (96x68cm-38x27in) s.d.1941
£22222	$42000	(27-Sep-90 CH.NY265/R) Rancheria (61x107cm-24x42in) s. i. verso egg tempera panel
£828	$1400	(1-May-91 B.SF5202/R) El Capitan (50x76cm-20x30in) s. W/C ink
£947	$1600	(1-May-91 B.SF5203/R) December (76x102cm-30x40in) s. pencil ink wash

HURLESTONE, Frederick (1801-1869) British
£5800	$9686	(5-Jun-91 S198/R) Queen of Spanish gypsies at Questa of Alhambra (101x79cm-40x31in) s.indist.i.verso

HURRY, Leslie (1909-) British
£600	$1176	(25-Jan-91 C33/R) Costume designs for Isolde and Tristan, Covent Garden Opera Company (46x29cm-18x11in) d.1958 i.W/C pen brush col.inks two
£600	$1176	(25-Jan-91 C43/R) Costume designs for elegant ladies, Gate of Summer, Provincial Tour (56x19cm-22x7in) d.1956 W/C pen brush col.inks two
£600	$1176	(25-Jan-91 C34/R) Costume designs for Brangane, Covent Garden Opera Company (46x29cm-18x11in) i. W/C pen brush col.inks two
£600	$1176	(25-Jan-91 C35/R) Costume designs for Marke and Brangane, Covent Garden Opera Company (45x30cm-18x12in) d.1958 i. W/C pen brush col.inks pencil two
£780	$1529	(25-Jan-91 C30/R) Costume designs for Isolde and Melot, Covent Garden Opera Company (46x29cm-18x11in) d.1958 W/C pen brush col.inks two
£780	$1529	(25-Jan-91 C36/R) Costume designs for Isolde and Tristan, Covent Garden Opera Company (45x30cm-18x12in) d.1958 i. W/C pen brush col.ink two
£920	$1803	(25-Jan-91 C38/R) Set designs for Tristan and Isolde, Covent Garden Opera Company (39x57cm-15x22in) d.1958 W/C pen brush col.inks two
£920	$1803	(25-Jan-91 C37/R) Set designs for Tristan and Isolde, Covent Garden Opera Company (39x57cm-15x22in) d.1958 W/C pen brush col.inks two
£920	$1803	(25-Jan-91 C41/R) Set desgins for Queen of Spades, Sadler's Wells Opera Company (29x39cm-11x15in) d.1966 W/C pen brush col.inks crayon two
£1500	$2610	(27-Mar-91 S148/R) Costume design for Princess Turandot (53x39cm-21x15in) s.d.47 pen ink W/C htd.yellow white

HURT, Louis B (1856-1929) British
£750	$1343	(14-Mar-91 ZZ.B128/R) An Invernesshire Glen (23x33cm-9x13in) s.i. verso board
£949	$1566	(8-Jul-91 SY.J160/R) Highland cattle (60x49cm-24x19in) s. (SA.R 4500)
£1300	$2184	(23-Apr-91 S68/R) By Inveraran (20x15cm-8x6in) s. i.verso panel
£1300	$2431	(28-Aug-90 S776) At Strathyre, Perthshire. Passing shower (17x24cm-7x9in) s. i.verso canvas on board
£1550	$2620	(30-Apr-91 AG292/R) By Loch Dirich, Rosshire (60x90cm-24x35in) s.d.1886
£1700	$3349	(13-Nov-90 PH46/R) Highland cattle in landscape (30x51cm-12x20in) s.
£3100	$6107	(30-Oct-90 SC103/R) Showery day, Glen Ardcower (32x47cm-13x19in) s.
£3400	$6800	(5-Feb-91 S75/R) Highland Cattle (61x90cm-24x35in) with sig.
£3800	$7372	(5-Dec-90 PHE1/R) In the gloaming (33x48cm-13x19in) s.
£4000	$6760	(29-Apr-91 HS283/R) Extensive loch scene with highland cattle in foreground, mist beyond (39x58cm-15x23in) s.
£4200	$8106	(10-Dec-90 PHB49/R) Highland loch (61x83cm-24x33in) i.verso
£6000	$11760	(22-Nov-90 CG588/R) By Loch Treachlan, Glencoe, morning mists (61x102cm-24x40in) s.d.1907 i.stretcher
£6100	$11468	(19-Sep-90 PHC189/R) Cattle by burn in Highlands (62x102cm-24x40in) s.d.1905
£7000	$13090	(28-Aug-90 S770/R) Rest by Rosshire loch (128x103cm-50x41in) s.d.88 s.i.d.1888verso
£9000	$18000	(8-Feb-91 C196/R) A rest by the way (91x76cm-36x30in) s.d.1892
£11000	$18480	(23-Apr-91 S39/R) Cattle by highland torrent (61x102cm-24x40in) s.d.1905
£18000	$36000	(8-Feb-91 C192/R) Through the Glen - The mantle of winter (61x102cm-24x40in) s.i.
£20000	$40000	(5-Feb-91 S41/R) Cattle in glen (127x101cm-50x40in) s.d.
£75000	$140250	(28-Aug-90 S769/R) Sunshine and showers (128x102cm-50x40in) s.d.1897

HURTEN, C F (19/20th C) ?
£2200	$3696	(18-Jul-91 CSK113/R) Cinneraria in terracotta pots. Apple blossom in jug (56x41cm-22x16in) s. pair

HURTER, Johann Heinrich (1734-1799) German
£550	$974	(19-Mar-91 CSK62/R) Portrait of Thomas, Lord Dartrey (6x?cm-2x?in) min. s.d.1784 verso enamel oval
£750	$1238	(11-Jul-91 S249/R) Portrait of Georgina Poyntz, Countess Spencer (5x?cm-2x?in) min.enamel i. gilt metal frame oval aft.Reynolds

HUSE, Marion (1896-) American
£802	$1500	(30-Aug-90 MFA.C73/R) Harbour scene (64x76cm-25x30in) s.

HUSSEM, Willem (1900-1974) Dutch
£1141	$1974	(22-May-91 CH.AM690/R) Abstract composition (40x80cm-16x31in) init.d.60 s.verso (D.FL 3800)
£1548	$2988	(12-Dec-90 CH.AM493/R) Abstract composition (80x125cm-31x49in) init. i.d.1960 num.52 stretcher (D.FL 5000)
£2012	$3884	(13-Dec-90 SY.AM314/R) Composition (120x80cm-47x31in) indist.init. d.62 (D.FL 6500)
£2632	$5079	(12-Dec-90 CH.AM546/R) Abstract composition (120x80cm-47x31in) init.d.64 (D.FL 8500)

HUSSEY, Giles (1710-1788) British
£3000 $4950   (11-Jul-91 S36/R) Portrait of Prince Charles Edward Stuart the Young
                  Pretender (24x17cm-9x7in) pen ink wash oval

HUSSON, Jeanne Elisabeth see CHAUDET, Jeanne Elisabeth

HUSTON, William (19th C) American
£1066 $2100   (18-Nov-90 JRB.C64/R) Long Island seascape (36x51cm-14x20in) s.

HUSZAR, Vilmos (1884-1905) Hungarian
£901 $1559   (22-May-91 CH.AM345) Still life of pear, calabash and corn
                  (35x45cm-14x18in) s. (D.FL 3000)
£1548 $2988   (13-Dec-90 SY.AM23/R) Still life of flowers in glass jar
                  (37x30cm-15x12in) s. (D.FL 5000)
£5119 $10034   (24-Nov-90 VG.B290/R) Untitled (32x40cm-13x16in) s. gouache indian ink
                  (DM 15000)

HUTCHENS, Frank Townsend (1869-1937) American
£1726 $2900   (28-Apr-91 HG.C26) Landscape with poppies (46x61cm-18x24in) s.d.1896

HUTCHISON, George Jackson (?-1918) British
£750 $1455   (6-Dec-90 CG93) Feeding the calf (27x33cm-11x13in) s. board
£900 $1764   (22-Nov-90 CG592) Hen and chicks feeding (25x36cm-10x14in) s. canvas
                  board
£950 $1862   (22-Nov-90 CG590) Mates (36x46cm-14x18in) s.

HUTCHISON, Robert Gemmell (1855-1936) British
£1300 $2431   (28-Aug-90 S871/R) An old corner, Musselburgh (29x20cm-11x8in) s. board
£1800 $3042   (2-May-91 CG486) Granny's quiet cup of tea (51x41cm-20x16in) s.
                  canvasboard
£2000 $3380   (2-May-91 CG488) Health and happiness (46x102cm-18x40in) s.
£2200 $4114   (28-Aug-90 S897/R) Washing day (48x61cm-19x24in) canvas laid on board
£2600 $4602   (4-Apr-91 RS83) Looking for shrimps (25x33cm-10x13in) s. panel
£2800 $5236   (28-Aug-90 S910/R) Shrimping (20x15cm-8x6in) s. board
£3000 $5820   (5-Dec-90 PHE94/R) At the garden gate (35x25cm-14x10in) s.
£3200 $5536   (10-May-91 CBS264/R) Boy pulling cart (20x25cm-8x10in) s. board
£4200 $8148   (5-Dec-90 PHE46/R) The high chair (35x25cm-14x10in) s. board
£4800 $9312   (5-Dec-90 PHE77/R) Dominoes (44x60cm-17x24in) s.
£5000 $9700   (6-Dec-90 CG73/R) Children on the dunes, Morrison's Haven, East Lothian
                  (25x36cm-10x14in) s. panel
£5500 $10285   (28-Aug-90 S896/R) Sunlight and shadows, the artist's daughter
                  (18x13cm-7x5in) s. board
£6000 $11640   (5-Dec-90 PHE88/R) Winding wool (50x42cm-20x17in) s.
£6200 $12400   (5-Feb-91 S57/R) Young sailors (35x32cm-14x13in) s.
£6200 $10168   (20-Jun-91 B94/R) Before bedtime (58x46cm-23x18in) s. bears i.verso
£8200 $13858   (2-May-91 CG516/R) Sailing sabots, Volendam (51x68cm-20x27in) s.
£8482 $16286   (28-Nov-90 PH.T106/R) The toy boat (24x36cm-9x14in) s. canvas board
                  (C.D 19000)
£10000 $20000   (5-Feb-91 S55/R) Apple-bobbing (110x166cm-43x65in) s.
£11000 $21560   (22-Nov-90 CG564/R) Sailing the boat (35x46cm-14x18in) s. board
£11000 $20570   (28-Aug-90 S881/R) Waiting on the milkman (61x46cm-24x18in) s.i.
£12000 $22440   (28-Aug-90 S891/R) Shelling peas (46x36cm-18x14in) s. canvasboard
£13000 $24960   (26-Nov-90 SWS173/R) Golfer, the Trysting Place, Machrihanish
                  (44x59cm-17x23in) s.i.stretcher
£13000 $24310   (28-Aug-90 S908/R) Lullaby (61x46cm-24x18in) s.
£13500 $25245   (28-Aug-90 S882/R) Little waitress (45x53cm-18x21in) s. i.verso
                  canvasboard
£15000 $24150   (27-Jun-91 CG51/R) Sunshine and shade (51x61cm-20x24in) s. i. verso
£16000 $31360   (22-Nov-90 CG563/R) Reflections (63x77cm-25x30in) s. s.i.verso
£19500 $32955   (3-May-91 PHE153/R) The creel (45x35cm-18x14in) s. board
£20000 $33200   (27-Jun-91 CG37/R) Summer on the dunes (86x112cm-34x44in) s.
£22000 $41140   (28-Aug-90 S870/R) On the cliff tops (71x91cm-28x36in) s.
£650 $1216   (30-Aug-90 CG80) Girl on shore (25x36cm-10x14in) s. W/C htd white
£720 $1253   (27-Mar-91 PHS912) Child in washroom interior (20x13cm-8x5in) s. W/C htd
                  white
£900 $1800   (5-Feb-91 S81/R) By sea shore (26x36cm-10x14in) s. W/C
£950 $1777   (28-Aug-90 S900) Thoughts by the sea (9x10cm-4x4in) s. W/C htd bodycol
£1600 $2704   (2-May-91 CG449) On shore - Carnoustie (46x61cm-18x24in) s. W/C htd
                  white
£1900 $3686   (6-Dec-90 CG16) Girl paddling. Cottage and child paddling
                  (99x99cm-39x39in) W/C two sold with oil painting by J.J.Montgomery
£2800 $5236   (28-Aug-90 S909/R) Paddling (48x34cm-19x13in) s. pastel
£2800 $5376   (26-Nov-90 SWS134/R) Young shrimpers (19x23cm-7x9in) s. W/C gouache
£3000 $5610   (28-Aug-90 S889/R) Children by drying nets (18x23cm-7x9in) s. W/C htd
                  white
£3077 $6000   (24-Oct-90 CH.NY351/R) Gathering shells at beach (25x35cm-10x14in) s.
                  W/C gouache
£4200 $7854   (28-Aug-90 S907/R) Paddling (33x43cm-13x17in) s. W/C
£4800 $9312   (5-Dec-90 PHE22/R) The black bird's nest (64x50cm-25x20in) s. W/C
£5500 $10285   (28-Aug-90 S925/R) Sailing the toy boat (43x49cm-17x19in) s. W/C htd
                  white
£6000 $11220   (28-Aug-90 S926/R) On the Zuider Zee (20x14cm-8x6in) s. W/C htd bodycol

HUTCHISON, Robert Gemmell (attrib) (1855-1936) British
£900 $1683   (28-Aug-90 S901/R) Dutch girl (52x41cm-20x16in)

HUTH, Franz (1876-?) German

£1200	$2148	(12-Apr-91 AW.H1673/R) Still life of roses with sculpture (31x45cm-12x18in) s. pastel board (DM 3600)
£1275	$2487	(12-Oct-90 AW.H2592/R) Interior of blue salon (58x44cm-23x17in) s. pastel (DM 3800)
£1500	$2685	(12-Apr-91 AW.H1671/R) View over rooftops, Alt-Heidelberg (48x64cm-19x25in) s.d.1960 pastel (DM 4500)
£1733	$3103	(12-Apr-91 AW.H1668/R) Interior of Wurzburg cathedral (78x59cm-31x23in) s. pastel (DM 5200)
£1733	$3103	(12-Apr-91 AW.H1669/R) Ilm landscape (33x47cm-13x19in) s.d.1957 pastel (DM 5200)
£1812	$3534	(12-Oct-90 AW.H2591/R) Church interior of monastery in Birnau (49x39cm-19x15in) s. i.d.1953verso pastel (DM 5400)
£1879	$3664	(12-Oct-90 AW.H2595/R) Bowl of roses with white porcelain figures (50x64cm-20x25in) s. W/C (DM 5600)
£2013	$3926	(12-Oct-90 AW.H2590/R) Park landscape, Weimar, winter (31x48cm-12x19in) s. i.d.1952 pastel (DM 6000)

HUTHER, Julius (1881-1954) German

£602	$1017	(19-Apr-91 FN.S1749) Avenue with view of southern town, autumn (36x59cm-14x23in) canvas on board (DM 1800)
£853	$1672	(24-Nov-90 N.M238/R) Nude girl before houses (105x68cm-41x27in) s.d.1921 (DM 2500)
£2196	$4282	(20-Oct-90 WK.M221/R) Young lady standing on balcony (95x68cm-37x27in) s.d.1913 (DM 6500)

HUTIN, Charles-Francois (attrib) (1715-1776) French

| £1100 | $1859 | (16-Apr-91 C222/R) Design for a mirror (31x21cm-12x8in) i. watermark ink wash |

HUTTER, Wolfgang (1928-) Austrian

| £390 | $722 | (7-Mar-91 D.V263/R) Die Freundin des Tatowierers (47x36cm-19x14in) s.d.65 pencil (A.S 8000) |

HUTTON, Thomas S (c.1875-1935) British

£320	$573	(12-Mar-91 N231) Tantallon Castle, stormy coastal scene with gulls (53x79cm-21x31in) s. W/C htd.white
£400	$644	(25-Jun-91 AG336/R) Tantallon on Scotia's wild and rocky coast (53x77cm-21x30in) s.i.d.1903verso
£400	$688	(13-May-91 CG173) A view of Holy Island Castle (40x55cm-16x22in) s.i.d.95 W/C
£400	$800	(5-Feb-91 CG41) Unloading catch (25x36cm-10x14in) s. W/C htd white
£450	$833	(5-Mar-91 AG161) Sunderland (21x34cm-8x13in) s.i.d.1891 W/C
£500	$1000	(8-Feb-91 C89/R) A haven under a hill, Burnmouth, Berwickshire (25x36cm-10x14in) s. i. verso pencil W/C htd.white
£500	$845	(1-May-91 PHL20) Mouth of Tyne (17x32cm-7x13in) s.i. wash htd bodycol
£600	$1200	(8-Feb-91 C88/R) Shipping in the harbour at Eyemouth, Berwickshire (23x33cm-9x13in) s. i. verso pencil W/C htd.white
£700	$1358	(4-Dec-90 AG211) Watergate Row, Chester (23x34cm-9x13in) s.i. W/C
£700	$1379	(1-Nov-90 C67/R) Summer evening, Holy Island, Lindisfarne Abbey (30x51cm-12x20in) s. i.verso pencil W/C htd.white
£900	$1503	(5-Jun-91 S230/R) Shrimpers return, Hoylake, Cheshire (68x109cm-27x43in) s. s.i.d.1899 verso W/C
£1000	$1690	(30-Apr-91 AG83/R) Whitby town from Spion Kop, Westcliffe (35x50cm-14x20in) s.d.1924 i.verso W/C

HUTTULA, Richard C (fl.1866-1887) British

| £600 | $1152 | (17-Dec-90 PH53/R) Watering the horses (23x41cm-9x16in) s.d.1880 W/C |

HUTTY, Alfred (1878-) American

| £532 | $1000 | (22-Sep-90 WOL.C282/R) Fisherman (33x43cm-13x17in) s. W/C |
| £585 | $1100 | (22-Sep-90 WOL.C281/R) Pulling in boats (41x58cm-16x23in) W/C |

HUYGENS, Francois Joseph (1820-1876) Belgian

| £1523 | $3000 | (15-Nov-90 SY.NY9) Still life of flowers in a basket (19x14cm-7x6in) s.i.d.1860 panel |
| £2473 | $4426 | (10-Apr-91 CB.P46) Nature morte aux raisins dans un paysage (61x55cm-24x22in) s.d.1852 (F.FR 25000) |

HUYGENS, Johannes (1833-1911) Dutch

| £1214 | $2100 | (10-May-91 S.W2160/R) Tending the sheep (81x97cm-32x38in) s.d.1856 |

HUYS, Bernhard (1885-1973) German

£769	$1485	(14-Dec-90 BM.B536/R) North German landscape (63x83cm-25x33in) s. (DM 2200)
£804	$1552	(14-Dec-90 BM.B533/R) River landscape with boat on Hamme (33x50cm-13x20in) s. panel (DM 2300)
£839	$1620	(14-Dec-90 BM.B537/R) River landscape (60x80cm-24x31in) s. (DM 2400)
£845	$1647	(26-Oct-90 BM.B643/R) Landscape, Worpswede (51x40cm-20x16in) s.d.48 panel (DM 2500)

HUYS, M (?) ?

| £765 | $1369 | (12-Mar-91 GM.B857) Fermieres au champ s. pastel (B.FR 46000) |

HUYS, Modeste (1875-1932) Belgian
£3284 $5681   (25-May-91 KV.L377/R) Snow around the farm (36x44cm-14x17in) mono.
                     (B.FR 200000)
£6006 $10390   (22-May-91 CH.AM510/R) Herfstavond (50x60cm-20x24in) s. mono.i.verso
                     (D.FL 20000)
£7225 $12499   (25-May-91 KV.L380/R) Festival in Machelen (60x70cm-24x28in) s.
                     (B.FR 440000)
£12717 $22000   (23-May-91 CH.NY200/R) Zomer na Middagzon (96x121cm-38x48in) s.i.verso
£15015 $25976   (23-May-91 SY.AM36/R) Inondation (99x140cm-39x55in) s. (D.FL 50000)
£17642 $34755   (6-Oct-90 KV.L340/R) Young anglers (50x60cm-20x24in) s.d.1923
                     (B.FR 1100000)
£20236 $39258   (8-Dec-90 KV.L363/R) Au Pays du Lin - Wielsbeke (49x83cm-19x33in) s.
                     (B.FR 1200000)
£337 $654   (8-Dec-90 KV.L160) Hilly landscape with grain stores (19x29cm-7x11in)
                     mono. chk. (B.FR 20000)
£371 $720   (8-Dec-90 KV.L159) Forest scene (19x28cm-7x11in) mono.d.1918 chk pair
                     (B.FR 22000)
£405 $785   (8-Dec-90 KV.L158) Lock in landscape (15x25cm-6x10in) mono. pencil
                     (B.FR 24000)
£438 $851   (8-Dec-90 KV.L161) Poplars in landscape. The travellers (17x15cm-7x6in)
                     s. pencil double-sided (B.FR 26000)
£723 $1410   (23-Oct-90 C.A589/R) In de Hallen van IJperen (48x62cm-19x24in) s.
                     drawing (B.FR 44000)

HUYSMAN, A H (1821-1903) Dutch
£520 $900   (9-May-91 CSK87) Fishing boats moored at jetty (13x24cm-5x9in) s. panel

HUYSMAN, Albertus Hendricus (1821-1903) Dutch
£1679 $2889   (16-May-91 D.V53/R) Seascape (41x67cm-16x26in) s. panel (A.S 35000)

HUYSMANS, Cornelis (1648-1727) Flemish
£700 $1141   (2-Jul-91 PH223/R) Italianate landscape with figures resting by stream
                     (32x34cm-13x13in)
£8163 $16000   (6-Nov-90 GF.L2042/R) Wooded hilly landscape (59x88cm-23x35in)
                     (S.FR 20000)

HUYSMANS, Cornelis (attrib) (1648-1727) Flemish
£1695 $3000   (22-Mar-91 S.W2811/R) Riding party in landscape (38x48cm-15x19in)

HUYSMANS, Cornelis (circle) (1648-1727) Flemish
£3200 $6304   (30-Oct-90 PH33/R) Mountainous wooded landscape with peasants resting on
                     road (45x57cm-18x22in)

HUYSMANS, Cornelis (style) (1648-1727) Flemish
£1300 $2197   (16-Apr-91 PH162) Travellers on lakeside path in mountainous landscape
                     (61x73cm-24x29in) canvas on board

HUYSMANS, Jacob (circle) (1633-1680) Flemish
£1120 $1893   (1-May-91 PHL111) Portrait of lady with garland (118x102cm-46x40in)
£2200 $3718   (30-Apr-91 PH39/R) Portrait of young girl as shepherdess, holding crook,
                     lamb beside her (91x88cm-36x35in)
£2800 $5460   (26-Oct-90 C221/R) Portrait of Mary Woodgate in a coral dress holding
                     flowers (127x102cm-50x40in)

HUYSMANS, Jan Baptist (style) (1654-1716) Flemish
£2797 $5399   (10-Dec-90 L.K57) Southern landscape with rider and servant
                     (50x62cm-20x24in) canvas laid down (DM 8000)

HUYSMANS, Jan Baptist (1654-1716) Flemish
£9744 $19000   (10-Oct-90 CH.NY190/R) Wooded landscape with figures (168x241cm-66x95in)

HUYSUM, Jan van (1682-1749) Dutch
£6643 $12822   (10-Dec-90 L.K58/R) Southern landscape with classical buildings and
                     figures (70x85cm-28x33in) s. canvas laid down (DM 19000)
£797 $1355   (27-May-91 OD.P44/R) Paysage ideal (30x21cm-12x8in) s. pierre noire wash
                     (F.FR 8000)
£1206 $2159   (17-Mar-91 M.V132/R) Etude de rose tremiere (27x17cm-11x7in) s. W/C
                     htd.wash (F.FR 12000)
£2000 $3840   (18-Feb-91 S249) Study of poppy (32x20cm-13x8in) s. W/C over chk
£2500 $4800   (18-Feb-91 S140/R) Vase of flowers on ledge (20x15cm-8x6in) s. pen ink
                     W/C over chk

HUYSUM, Jan van (after) (1682-1749) Dutch
£1685 $2814   (6-Jun-91 D.V289/R) Still life of flowers in vase (72x53cm-28x21in)
                     (A.S 35000)

HUYSUM, Jan van (attrib) (1682-1749) Dutch
£13000 $25610   (31-Oct-90 S144/R) Vase of flowers and apple blossom on pedestal with
                     bird's nest (80x62cm-31x24in) bears sig.

HUYSUM, Jan van (circle) (1682-1749) Dutch
£5200 $9880   (1-Mar-91 C102/R) Italianate landscape with shepherds. Wooded landscape
                     with peasants (43x20cm-17x8in) bears sig. pair
£6154 $12000   (24-Oct-90 D.NY76/R) Flowers and fruit on sculpted ledge
                     (91x74cm-36x29in) bears sig.d.1724

HUYSUM, Jan van (style) (18th C) Dutch
£1502 $2928   (20-Oct-90 CH.AM155 a/R) Tulips, roses, peonies and other flowers in vase on stone ledge (59x44cm-23x17in) (D.FL 5000)
£2200 $4224   (29-Nov-90 CSK81/R) Still lifes of mixed flowers in urns in niches (46x36cm-18x14in) pair
£5912 $11352   (30-Nov-90 APT.P81/R) Une corbeille de fleurs (40x32cm-16x13in) panel (F.FR 58000)

HYATT, Anna V see HUNTINGTON, Anna Hyatt

HYDE, William Henry (1858-?) American
£1368 $2600   (9-Jan-91 CH.NY175/R) The Bowery at night (28x51cm-11x20in) s. ink gouache htd white en grisaille board

HYDE-POWNALL, George (19th C) British
£800 $1568   (13-Feb-91 S34/R) Royal Exchange (16x24cm-6x9in) s. board

HYMAN, Miles (1962-) American
£396 $701   (6-Apr-91 CB.P175) Etude pouur le couverture de Manhattan Transfert (15x20cm-6x8in) pastel (F.FR 4000)

HYNCKES, Raoul (1893-1939) Dutch
£1138 $2162   (11-Sep-90 CH.AM405/R) View of Burchtplein, Delft (55x55cm-22x22in) s. board (D.FL 3800)
£1238 $2390   (12-Dec-90 CH.AM6/R) Hilly landscape, near Cannes (56x69cm-22x27in) s. board (D.FL 4000)
£5573 $10755   (12-Dec-90 CH.AM78/R) Still life with fishes, bottle and glasses ontable, by balcony (80x70cm-31x28in) s. (D.FL 18000)

HYNCKES, Raoul and ZAHN, M (20th C) Dutch
£1051 $1818   (22-May-91 CH.AM337) Still life with bottle, glass, fruit, bread and knife on wooden ledge (46x50cm-18x20in) s. (D.FL 3500)

HYNEMAN, Herman (1859-1907) American
£3173 $6250   (16-Nov-90 S.BM62/R) Crossing Madison Ave (33x25cm-13x10in) s.

HYON, Georges Louis (1855-?) French
£714 $1377   (12-Dec-90 ZZ.F68/R) La Patrouille (26x41cm-10x16in) panel (F.FR 7000)

HYPPOLITE, Hector (1894-1948) Haitian
£20408 $40000   (19-Nov-90 SY.NY297 a/R) Poisson a tete de femme (121x74cm-48x29in) s. board

HYRE, Laurent de la (17th C) French
£8155 $15739   (14-Dec-90 LEB.P25/R) Combat de Clorinde et de Tancrede (30x42cm-12x17in) pierre noire htd.white (F.FR 80000)

HYSING, Hans (?-1723) Swedish
£820 $1599   (22-Oct-90 SWS1322) Portrait of gentleman, wearing coat (74x61cm-29x24in) oval
£2500 $4125   (12-Jul-91 C22/R) Portrait of Samuel Hughes, right arm tucked into braided waistcoat (76x63cm-30x25in) painted oval
£10000 $16500   (10-Jul-91 S28/R) Portrait of Henry Howard standing holding large intaglio (125x99cm-49x39in) l.

HYSING, Hans (attrib) (?-1723) Swedish
£720 $1404   (22-Oct-90 SWS1321) Portrait of gentleman, wearing coat (75x62cm-30x24in) painted oval

IACHIN, Piotr (1939-) Russian
£723 $1337   (4-Mar-91 ZZ.F60/R) L'ete en Crimee (34x50cm-13x20in) s. board (F.FR 7200)

IACOVLEFF, Alexandre (1887-1938) French
£806 $1573   (28-Oct-90 PLF.P213) Modele noire asis, tet et jambes coupees (53x41cm-21x16in) s. sanguinne stumping (F.FR 8000)
£1109 $2162   (28-Oct-90 PLF.P214/R) Etude de modele noire de trois quart a gauche, assis et accoudee (51x34cm-20x13in) bears st. sanguinne stumping (F.FR 11000)
£1109 $2162   (28-Oct-90 PLF.P216) Etude d'homme de dos (51x33cm-20x13in) bears st. sanguinne (F.FR 11000)
£1506 $2425   (24-Jun-91 ARC.P71/R) Abdou (54x37cm-21x15in) s.i.d.1931 chl.sanguinne pastel (F.FR 15000)
£1800 $2934   (1-Jul-91 APT.P35/R) Elegante (144x86cm-57x34in) chl. (F.FR 18000)
£2510 $4041   (24-Jun-91 ARC.P70/R) Un lama de Lambran (75x55cm-30x22in) i.d.3 fevrier 1932 chl.sanguinne pastel (F.FR 25000)
£2684 $4536   (19-Apr-91 CB.P139) Afghan d'Herat (75x55cm-30x22in) s.d.22 mai 1931 pastel (F.FR 27000)
£3032 $5124   (19-Apr-91 CB.P138/R) Cheikh Saklem el Khayoun (75x55cm-30x22in) s.i.d.19 avril 1931 pastel (F.FR 30500)
£3550 $6815   (17-Dec-90 ARC.P35/R) Chinois de Lian Tcheou (75x55cm-30x22in) s.d.4 janvier 1932 sanguinne chl. (F.FR 35000)

950

IACOVLEFF, Alexandre (1887-1938) French-cont.
£4518 $7274   (24-Jun-91 ARC.P69/R) L'acteur japonais Onoue Kikugoro (98x71cm-39x28in)
                  s. sanguine blk.chk. (F.FR 45000)

IACURTO, Francesco (1908-) Canadian
£1121 $2164   (12-Dec-90 EA.M671) Village Charlevoix (41x51cm-16x20in) s. (C.D 2500)
£1429 $2414   (17-Apr-91 EA.M501/R) Perce, Gaspesie (51x61cm-20x24in) s. (C.D 2800)

IANELLI, Arcangelo (1922-) Brazilian
£2806 $5500   (19-Nov-90 SY.NY220/R) Azul (130x100cm-51x39in) s.d.1976
£2907 $5000   (15-May-91 CH.NY140/R) Composicao em Ocre (129x100cm-51x39in) s.d.1989

IANNONE, Dorothy (1932-)?
£507 $877   (21-May-91 WK.M1022/R) Susanna and the Elders, poem from Wallace Stevens
                  (122x91cm-48x36in) s.i.d.1965verso (DM 1500)

IANOUSH, Leonid (1897-1978) Russian
£647 $1125   (25-Mar-91 ARC.P172) Le piano (69x50cm-27x20in) s. board (F.FR 6500)
£1194 $2078   (25-Mar-91 ARC.P169) Jour d'ete (70x100cm-28x39in) s. (F.FR 12000)
£2338 $4069   (25-Mar-91 ARC.P171/R) Lilas du Palais Pavlovsk (68x66cm-27x26in) s.
                  (F.FR 23500)
£3184 $5540   (25-Mar-91 ARC.P168/R) Le veranda (60x79cm-24x31in) s. board
                  (F.FR 32000)

IBANEZ DE ALDECOA, Julian (20th C) Spanish
£874 $1511   (8-May-91 FER.M92/R) La vida diaria en una ciudad de provincias
                  (35x57cm-14x22in) s. panel (S.P 160000)
£1365 $2361   (8-May-91 FER.M93/R) Puerto de Lequeitio (38x58cm-15x23in) s. board
                  (S.P 250000)

IBBETSON, Julius Caesar (1759-1817) British
£1066 $2100   (7-Oct-90 LIT.L342) Claudian landscape with three horses, man and dog
                  (46x61cm-18x24in) s.d.1796
£1700 $3349   (31-Oct-90 S345/R) Landscape with Laurel Cottage, Sunby-in-Furness,
                  Cumbria (42x65cm-17x26in)
£2200 $4180   (1-Mar-91 C79/R) St Mary's Abbey York (30x36cm-12x14in) s.d.1793
£26000 $42900   (10-Jul-91 S82/R) Market day, Masham (34x44cm-13x17in) s.d.1811
£592 $1000   (20-Apr-91 WOL.C18/R) Sheep herder (15x23cm-6x9in) s.d.1796 W/C
£16500 $29535   (11-Apr-91 S27/R) Skaters on Serpentine, Hyde Park, London
                  (22x30cm-9x12in) s. i.mount W/C pen

IBBETSON, Julius Caesar (attrib) (1759-1817) British
£750 $1485   (30-Jan-91 CSK350/R) Rustics on a country track (20x25cm-8x10in) panel
£900 $1611   (10-Apr-91 S144/R) Portrait of young girl, seated under tree, landscape
                  beyond (95x71cm-37x28in)
£2800 $5516   (30-Oct-90 SC232/R) Edinburgh Castle from Carlton Hill with Hume
                  Monument and Trinity Chapel (44x61cm-17x24in)

IBBETSON, Julius Caesar (circle) (1759-1817) British
£2353 $4000   (31-May-91 CH.NY240/R) Wooded landscape with travellers by bridge and
                  windmill beyond (77x63cm-30x25in)

IBSEN, Immanuel (?) Scandinavian
£799 $1575   (31-Oct-90 KH.K54) From Christianshavn's canal (66x54cm-26x21in) s.
                  (D.KR 9000)

ICART, Louis (1888-1950) French
£1005 $1739   (22-May-91 EA.M445/R) Fair dancer (48x57cm-19x22in) s.i. col.etching
                  drypoint (C.D 2000)
£1077 $2100   (21-Oct-90 HG.C39) Seated nude (30x25cm-12x10in) s.verso masonite
£4752 $9267   (21-Oct-90 L.C77/R) Elegante en tenue de soiree (87x61cm-34x24in)
                  s.d.1937 lightly varnished (F.FR 47000)
£6377 $12498   (20-Nov-90 MF.P85/R) Printemps (41x33cm-16x13in) s. (F.FR 63000)
£6579 $12895   (20-Nov-90 MF.P84/R) Jeunesse (41x33cm-16x13in) s. (F.FR 65000)
£10408 $20192   (8-Dec-90 GAB.G268/R) Les deux amies au bord du lac (46x60cm-18x24in)
                  s. i. verso hardboard (S.FR 25500)
£13761 $26422   (27-Nov-90 APT.P96/R) La nouvelle coiffure (33x41cm-13x16in) s. panel
                  (F.FR 135000)
£13869 $22746   (18-Jun-91 APT.P205/R) Feuilles mortes (50x65cm-20x26in) s. i. verso
                  board (F.FR 138000)
£17068 $31576   (6-Mar-91 APT.P117/R) A la lucarne (50x61cm-20x24in) s. i. verso
                  (F.FR 170000)
£20080 $37149   (6-Mar-91 APT.P116/R) Elegante aux deux barzoys (55x45cm-22x18in) s.
                  (F.FR 200000)
£22000 $42900   (17-Oct-90 C34/R) Champs Elysees (27x35cm-11x14in) s. i.verso
£30000 $58500   (17-Oct-90 C35/R) Reclining girl with parasol (55x46cm-22x18in) s.
£1103 $2151   (12-Oct-90 APT.P88/R) L'attente (47x34cm-19x13in) s. chl.sanguinne
                  (F.FR 11000)
£1309 $2200   (23-Apr-91 C.A124/R) The two friends (37x48cm-15x19in) s. W/C
                  (B.FR 80000)
£2780 $5394   (5-Dec-90 AB.S7112/R) Kiss on the hand - couple in interior
                  (45x60cm-18x24in) s.d.1914 pastel (S.KR 30000)
£5653 $10966   (7-Dec-90 GL.P227) Les deux amies (49x63cm-19x25in) s. pastel
                  (F.FR 55000)

ICART, Louis (attrib) (1888-1950) French
£904 $1600   (18-Mar-91 SG.M1290) Presse (36x46cm-14x18in) s. chl.htd.white

ICAZA, Ernesto (1870-1926) Mexican
£63776 $125000   (20-Nov-90 CH.NY16/R) Hacienda de Los Dolores (147x247cm-58x97in)
                     s.d.1919

IEFREIMOV, Kim (1933-) Russian
£503 $965   (18-Feb-91 ARC.P50) Les veliplanchistes (110x100cm-43x39in) s.
                     (F.FR 5000)

IGLER, Gustav (1842-1908) Hungarian
£17919 $31000   (22-May-91 SY.NY41/R) Der gerburtstagskuchen (105x119cm-41x47in) s.d.82

IHLEE, Rudolph (20th C) British
£1000 $1740   (27-Mar-91 S139/R) Landscape, South of France (46x56cm-18x22in) s.
£1800 $3042   (2-May-91 C63/R) Landscape with cat (81x96cm-32x38in) s.d.1926

IHLEFELD, Henry (1859-1932) American
£2100 $4116   (13-Feb-91 S186/R) Bathtime (33x49cm-13x19in) s.

IHLY, Daniel (1854-1910) Swiss
£2245 $4355   (8-Dec-90 GAB.G2681/R) Les chiffoniers a Plainpalais (80x120cm-31x47in)
                     s. (S.FR 5500)

IKEMURA, Leiko (1951-) ?
£488 $941   (15-Dec-90 S.Z150/R) Untitled (32x24cm-13x9in) s.d.1986 chl pencil
                     (S.FR 1200)

IKONEN, Ilmari (1897-1953) Finnish
£576 $1111   (15-Dec-90 BU.H79) Autumn landscape (50x61cm-20x24in) s.d.29 (F.M 4000)
£604 $1166   (15-Dec-90 BU.H80) Snow in the field (46x55cm-18x22in) s.d.45
                     (F.M 4200)
£642 $1258   (24-Nov-90 HOR.H119/R) Autumn landscape (38x48cm-15x19in) s.d.1940
                     (F.M 4500)

ILLEM, Franz Josef Georg (1865-?) German
£1066 $1716   (27-Jun-91 D.V65) Deer in birch tree wood (79x57cm-31x22in) s.
                     (A.S 22000)

ILLINE, Iossif (1915-) Russian
£578 $954   (11-Jul-91 ZZ.F174) Enfants jouant (30x57cm-12x22in) s. (F.FR 5800)
£2353 $3882   (11-Jul-91 ZZ.F172/R) Les petits bateaux (30x57cm-12x22in) s.d.1956
                     (F.FR 23600)

ILMONI, Einar (1880-1946) Finnish
£10556 $20690   (24-Nov-90 HOR.H120/R) House on the hill (41x52cm-16x20in) s.d.1930
                     (F.M 74000)

ILSENHEIM, Franz Jung (19th C) Austrian
£586 $1114   (28-Feb-91 D.V110/R) Ritterspiele (45x60cm-18x24in) s.i.d.74 W/C
                     (A.S 12000)

ILSTED, Peter Vilhelm (1861-1933) Danish
£584 $988   (21-Apr-91 BU.M110) Children playing (20x28cm-8x11in) oil sketch
                     (S.KR 6200)
£664 $1123   (2-May-91 RAS.V53/R) Landscape with sunlit outhouses (32x53cm-13x21in)
                     mono. (D.KR 7500)
£679 $1311   (10-Dec-90 BU.K41/R) Wooded landscape with reflections of light
                     (61x50cm-24x20in) mono. (D.KR 7500)
£3650 $7190   (30-Oct-90 BU.S316/R) On the stairs (56x60cm-22x24in) mono.d.1917
                     (S.KR 40000)
£3697 $6211   (22-Apr-91 BU.K17/R) Diningroom at Liselund (55x47cm-22x19in)
                     mono.d.1916 (D.KR 42000)
£4934 $8240   (6-Jun-91 RAS.K78/R) The artist's wife sorting chanterelles
                     (60x50cm-24x20in) s. (D.KR 56000)
£584 $988   (21-Apr-91 BU.M114) Moonlit night (22x26cm-9x10in) mono.indist.d.1901
                     mixed media (S.KR 6200)

IMAI, Hisashi (20th C) Japanese
£530 $890   (27-Apr-91 MJ.P172/R) Mhthologie actuelle (92x73cm-36x29in) s.
                     (F.FR 5300)

IMAI, Toshimitau (1928-) Japanese
£10920 $19000   (27-Mar-91 B.SF4170/R) Peinture (89x131cm-35x52in) s.i.d.56verso
£7035 $12593   (15-Mar-91 FB.P34/R) Composition (40x80cm-16x31in) s.d.1960 verso mixed
                     media canvas (F.FR 70000)
£71283 $140428   (29-Oct-90 FB.P7/R) Work (116x89cm-46x35in) s. d.mars-avril 1959 verso
                     mixed media canvas (F.FR 700000)

IMHOF, Joseph A (1871-1955) American
£592 $1000   (1-May-91 B.SF5197/R) Placita Road, Taos (41x51cm-16x20in) s.i.
                     i.stretcher
£1064 $2000   (19-Sep-90 B.SF2851) Placita Road, Taos (41x51cm-16x20in) s.i.

IMKAMP, Wilhelm (1906-?) German
£1024	$2007	(22-Nov-90 L.K1039) Composition (12x22cm-5x9in) s.d.1968 tempera board (DM 3000)
£3767	$6140	(15-Jun-91 L.K327/R) Square (33x33cm-13x13in) s.d.62 panel (DM 11000)
£4110	$6699	(15-Jun-91 L.K326/R) Regatta (28x40cm-11x16in) s.d.49 panel (DM 12000)
£4778	$9365	(22-Nov-90 L.K1038) Untitled (40x58cm-16x23in) s.d.1959 oil tempera board (DM 14000)
£959	*$1563*	*(15-Jun-91 L.K328) Untitled (14x12cm-6x5in) s.d.73 mixed media (DM 2800)*

IMMENDORF, Jorg (1945-) German
£2703	$4595	(1-Jun-91 VG.B387/R) Composition on black ground (83x58cm-33x23in) mono.i.verso acrylic over offset poster (DM 8000)
£7107	$14000	(5-Oct-90 CH.NY130/R) Untitled (102x90cm-40x35in) paper on linen
£10000	$16100	(27-Jun-91 C59/R) Zelg was du hast (76x106cm-30x42in) s.i.d.83
£15385	$26000	(2-May-91 CH.NY294/R) Zelg was du hast (251x249cm-99x98in) s.d.83
£98976	*$193993*	*(20-Nov-90 L.K304/R) Tor I, design (280x350cm-110x138in) s.d.1979 resin canvas (DM 290000)*

IMMENRAEDT, Philip Augustyn (1627-1679) Flemish
£1500	$2895	(11-Dec-90 PH127/R) Washerwoman conversing with traveller on bank in river landscape (82x119cm-32x47in) indist.s.

IMMENRAEDT, Philip Augustyn (circle) (1627-1679) Flemish
£9000	$15210	(18-Apr-91 C46/R) An extensive wooded river landscape with milkmaids and cattle on a track (106x132cm-42x52in) canvas laid down on board

IMPARATO, Gerolamo (17th C) Italian
£900	$1756	(23-Oct-90 CH.R232) La Madonna mentre allatta il bambino (34x27cm-13x11in) copper (I.L 2000000)
£2353	$4000	(30-May-91 CE.NY65) The Immaculate Conception (69x46cm-27x18in) panel

IMPENS, Josse (1840-1905) Belgian
£641	$1243	(8-Dec-90 KV.L162) Jeune fille (41x32cm-16x13in) s. (B.FR 38000)
£1273	$2507	(30-Oct-90 CH.AM37/R) Moment of confidentiality (56x47cm-22x19in) s. panel (D.FL 4200)

IMPERIALI, Francesco (18th C) Italian
£6000	$10140	(19-Apr-91 C152/R) A mythological fishing party (94x122cm-37x48in)

IMPERIALI, Francesco (attrib) (18th C) Italian
£7821	$14000	(11-Apr-91 SY.NY95/R) Saint Sebastian (251x165cm-99x65in)

INCE, Joseph Murray (1806-1859) British
£2055	$3349	(12-Jun-91 N.M471/R) View of Heidelberg (30x40cm-12x16in) s.d.1851 panel (DM 6000)
£600	*$1176*	*(21-Nov-90 B19) Harbour with boats by jetty (20x33cm-8x13in) s.d. W/C*
£1800	*$3564*	*(30-Jan-91 S119/R) Shipping in estuary (19x32cm-7x13in) s. W/C htd bodycol*

INDIA, Bernardino (attrib) (1528-1590) Italian
£1182	*$2010*	*(31-May-91 GB.B5202/R) The Judgement of Salomon (26x20cm-10x8in) pen over ochre (DM 3500)*

INDIAN SCHOOL, 19th C Indian
£2000	$3480	(26-Mar-91 PH48) Portrait of a sahib (112x87cm-44x34in)
£2400	$4176	(26-Mar-91 PH36) Portrait of a man smoking a hookah (106x76cm-42x30in)
£2400	$4176	(26-Mar-91 PH37) Portraait of a man smoking a hookah and holding a dagger (105x76cm-41x30in)
£2500	$4350	(26-Mar-91 PH35) Portrait of a man smoking a hookah his dog beside him (107x76cm-42x30in)

INDIANA, Robert (1928-) American
£16582	$32500	(7-Nov-90 SY.NY283/R) Eat (30x30cm-12x12in) init.d.62 verso acrylic

INDONI, Filippo (19th C) Italian
£2734	$4647	(28-May-91 F.R123/R) Interno rustico (75x53cm-30x21in) s. tempera board (I.L 6000000)
£6154	$12000	(23-Oct-90 SY.NY404/R) In the Roman Campagna (74x138cm-29x54in) s.
£11000	$18040	(19-Jun-91 S370/R) Trip in Roman campagna (72x136cm-28x54in) s.
£678	*$1200*	*(22-Mar-91 S.W2486/R) Peasant girl (48x33cm-19x13in) s. W/C*
£737	*$1400*	*(12-Sep-90 D.NY42) On way to market (36x56cm-14x22in) s. W/C*
£740	*$1236*	*(5-Jun-91 PHK34) Peasant man lighting his pipe (53x37cm-21x15in) s. W/C*
£1445	*$2500*	*(21-May-91 BG.M887/R) Seated female with water jug in landscape (48x30cm-19x12in) s. W/C*
£1445	*$2500*	*(21-May-91 BG.M888/R) Couple in landscape (51x33cm-20x13in) s. W/C*
£1500	*$2940*	*(22-Nov-90 CSK52/R) Italian peasant girl gathering faggots. Tambourine girl (54x36cm-21x14in) s. pencil W/C pair*
£1561	*$2700*	*(10-May-91 S.W2499/R) Young love (53x36cm-21x14in) s. W/C*
£2200	*$4224*	*(28-Nov-90 S134/R) The card players (76x53cm-30x21in) s. W/C*
£3448	*$6000*	*(27-Mar-91 B.SF4200/R) Tambourine follies (75x52cm-30x20in) s. W/C*

INDUNO, Domenico (1815-1878) Italian
£6007	$11594	(11-Dec-90 CH.R215/R) Scena rustica (26x19cm-10x7in) s. i.verso (I.L 13000000)

INDUNO, Domenico (1815-1878) Italian-cont.
£22200 $43067   (5-Dec-90 F.M63/R) Ritratto di giovane ragazza (112x85cm-44x33in) i.
                    (I.L 48000000)
£9121   *$15232*   *(6-Jun-91 F.M286/R) Figura di popolana (35x25cm-14x10in) s. W/C*
                    (I.L 20000000)

INGANNATI, Pietro degli (attrib) (16th C) Italian
£10000 $17000   (31-May-91 CH.NY2/R) Madonna and Child with St Peter and female saint
                    (63x84cm-25x33in) panel

INGENHOF, C Amadeo (20th C) ?
£648 $1063   (18-Jun-91 FN.S1907) Courtyard of mosque over domes (80x60cm-31x24in)
                    s.d.1923 (DM 1900)

INGHAM, Elizabeth H (19/20th C) American
£526   *$1000*   *(14-Sep-90 S.BM263/R) Fishing boats (30x23cm-12x9in) i. gouache on*
                    canvas

INGLIS, J J (fl.1885-1903) British
£1300 $2223   (1-Aug-91 CSK180) River Torrent (90x126cm-35x50in) s.

INGRES (1780-1867) French
£1000   *$1940*   *(7-Dec-90 BW390) Portrait study of Pierre Athanese Chauvrin*
                    (23x18cm-9x7in) s. pencil

INGRES, Jean Auguste Dominique (1780-1867) French
£28902 $50000   (23-May-91 CH.NY11/R) Portrait of jewess (22x16cm-9x6in) s. canvas on
                    panel
£4752   *$8412*   *(4-Apr-91 PPB.P26/R) Portrait d'homme en buste, de profil vers la gauche*
                    (8cm-3ins circular) s. blk.crayon stumping round (F.FR 48000)
£7538   *$12362*   *(18-Jun-91 APT.P96/R) Etudes d'homme nu assis de profil, tourne vers la*
                    droite (17x15cm-7x6in) s. pierre noire (F.FR 75000)
£14099   *$22981*   *(14-Jun-91 AGS.P11/R) Couple enlace (19x15cm-7x6in) s. lead pencil*
                    (F.FR 140000)
£18090   *$29668*   *(21-Jun-91 CK.P76/R) Portrait de la fontaine devant l'institut*
                    (21x16cm-8x6in) s.d.1844 lead pencil htd.wash gouache (F.FR 180000)
£26131   *$42854*   *(18-Jun-91 APT.P95/R) Etude pour le portrait de Madame Moitessier*
                    (30x29cm-12x11in) blk.crayon (F.FR 260000)
£63444   *$103414*   *(14-Jun-91 AGS.P10/R) Vue de Saint Marie majeure a Rome (18x24cm-7x9in)*
                    bears i. lead pencil htd.sepia (F.FR 630000)
£112821   *$220000*   *(23-Oct-90 SY.NY8/R) Portrait of Madame Ingres nee Madeleine Chapelle*
                    (21x16cm-8x6in) s.i. pencil
£121349   *$197800*   *(14-Jun-91 AGS.P9/R) Vue d'une eglise a Rome (18x24cm-7x9in) i. lead*
                    pencil htd.sepia (F.FR 1205000)
£166163   *$270846*   *(14-Jun-91 AGS.P12/R) Portrait de Madame Adele Maizony de Laureal*
                    (30x22cm-12x9in) s.i.d.1813 lead pencil (F.FR 1650000)

INGVARSSON, Jarl (1955-) Swedish
£1037 $1752   (18-Apr-91 BU.S59/R) Knight and boy (130x97cm-51x38in) s.d.1986verso
                    (S.KR 11000)

INMAN, Henry (1801-1846) American
£1124 $1900   (1-May-91 B.SF5052/R) Portrait of lady (25x20cm-10x8in) s.d.1842
£893   *$1500*   *(16-Jul-91 BG.M982/R) Portrait of gentleman with three-masted schooner*
                    in background (5x?cm-2x?in) min. s.d.1828 oval

INNERST, Mark (1957-) American
£10714 $21000   (7-Nov-90 SY.NY361 a/R) Used, feared, hated (36x43cm-14x17in) oil
                    acrylic board
£4734   *$8000*   *(2-May-91 CH.NY254/R) View of Brooklyn (16x22cm-6x9in) s. s.d.1985 verso*
                    gouache acrylic paper
£5325   *$9000*   *(2-May-91 CH.NY300/R) View of Brooklyn (16x22cm-6x9in) s.d.9/30/85*
                    s.d.1985 verso acrylic gouache
£8163   *$16000*   *(14-Feb-91 CH.NY83/R) Reservoir hill study (45x48cm-18x19in) s.*
                    s.i.d.1986verso W/C crayon

INNES, James Dickson (1887-1914) British
£4500 $8325   (5-Mar-91 PH8/R) Ramblers' Rest, North Wales (23x33cm-9x13in) board
£5000 $9800   (7-Nov-90 S19/R) Aloes, South Spain (30x41cm-12x16in) s.i.verso panel
£7000 $13720   (8-Nov-90 C64/R) The Corbieres Mountains (28x37cm-11x15in) s.indist.i.
                    verso panel
£8800 $17248   (7-Nov-90 S20/R) The cactus (23x33cm-9x13in) s. panel
£9000 $17640   (7-Nov-90 S21/R) The Pyrenees in twilight (25x40cm-10x16in)
£950   *$1653*   *(27-Mar-91 S48/R) The lone tree (25x36cm-10x14in) pen ink W/C*

INNESS, George (1825-1894) American
£1198 $2000   (26-Jul-91 E.EDM107/R) Pastoral scene (15x23cm-6x9in) s.
£4046 $7000   (21-May-91 BG.M1124/R) Leaning double birch (30x46cm-12x18in) s.
£9827 $17000   (22-May-91 CH.NY38/R) Through the forest (25x20cm-10x8in) s. board
£11340 $22000   (5-Dec-90 D.NY21/R) Midsummer, Hudson Valley (30x46cm-12x18in) i. on
                    stretcher
£25000 $48000   (30-Nov-90 CH.NY36/R) Passing shower (31x46cm-12x18in) s.
£37037 $70000   (26-Sep-90 SY.NY30/R) Pond at Milton on the Hudson (30x46cm-12x18in)
                    s.d.80 indist. panel
£325   *$650*   *(10-Feb-91 LIT.L43) Men in a field (18x28cm-7x11in) s.d.'91 chl.*
£332   *$650*   *(27-Jan-91 LIT.L20a) Men in field (18x28cm-7x11in) s.d.91 chl*

INNESS, George (attrib) (1825-1894) American
£1076	$1850	(19-May-91 LIT.L29) Italian landscape (58x94cm-23x37in)
£1134	$2200	(7-Dec-90 S.W2695/R) Extensive landscape with grazing and drinking cows (46x76cm-18x30in) bears sig.
£1156	$2000	(10-May-91 S.W2444/R) Cows in river landscape (46x76cm-18x30in) s.
£1466	$2448	(4-Jun-91 FB.M188) View of the farm and surrounding valley (27x51cm-11x20in) s.d.1879 board (C.D 2800)

INNESS, George (jnr) (1853-1926) American
| £1189 | $2200 | (10-Mar-91 H.C107/R) Autumn solitude (51x66cm-20x26in) s. |

INNOCENT, Franck (1912-1983) French?
| £830 | $1627 | (25-Nov-90 ZZ.F271) La route dans les champs (50x61cm-20x24in) s.d.82 (F.FR 8200) |
| £2227 | $4364 | (25-Nov-90 ZZ.F85/R) Bord de Seine (65x92cm-26x36in) s.d.55 (F.FR 22000) |

INNOCENTI, Camillo (1871-1961) Italian
| £1305 | $2415 | (6-Mar-91 D.P53/R) Servante et mousquetaires dans un sous bois (37x46cm-15x18in) s. panel (F.FR 13000) |

INSKIPP, James (1790-1868) German
| £2000 | $3800 | (1-Mar-91 C43/R) Venetian water-carrier (29x24cm-11x9in) panel |

INSLEY, Albert (1842-1937) American
£667	$1100	(13-Jul-91 YFA.M93/R) Landscape (30x46cm-12x18in) s.
£2130	$3600	(17-Apr-91 D.NY19/R) Meadow brook (36x51cm-14x20in) s. i.stretcher
£2130	$3600	(20-Apr-91 WOL.C73/R) Landscape at dusk (102x81cm-40x32in) s.

INUKAI, Kyohei (20th C) American
| £6145 | $11000 | (14-Mar-91 CH.NY218/R) Woodland bathers (30x38cm-12x15in) s. |

I'ONS, Frederick Timpson (1802-1887) South African
£972	$1866	(18-Feb-91 SY.J317/R) Xhosa by a riverside (31x37cm-12x15in) board (SA.R 4800)
£1235	$2370	(26-Nov-90 SY.J305/R) Xhosa by riverside (26x36cm-10x14in) s.d.1880 verso board (SA.R 6000)
£3189	$6123	(26-Nov-90 SY.J304/R) Scene on Kariega river (37x50cm-15x20in) s. s.d.1882 verso on metal (SA.R 15500)
£1146	*$1948*	*(27-May-91 SY.J610/R) Hottentot woman dancing (19x14cm-7x6in) i.d.1854 W/C (SA.R 5500)*

IPOLYI, Erno (20th C) ?
| £2400 | $4728 | (4-Oct-90 CSK243) A busy Venetian canal (41x61cm-16x24in) s. |

IPSEN, Ernest Ludwig (1869-1934) American
| £957 | $1800 | (11-Aug-90 COL.M207/R) Young Union Private (46x30cm-18x12in) s. |
| £3468 | $6000 | (10-May-91 S.BM44 c/R) Poling through the shallows (183x102cm-72x40in) s. |

IRAS, Roberto Baldessare (1894-1965) Italian/Austrian
| £10544 | $17293 | (20-Jun-91 F.M479/R) Bottiglia e luci (38x28cm-15x11in) s. s.verso board (I.L 23000000) |

IRELAND, Thomas (19th C) British
| £1600 | $3120 | (15-Jan-91 SWS141/R) Berkshire pool. Backwater on the Kennett (43x34cm-17x13in) s.d.90 i.verso pair |

IRISH SCHOOL, 19th C Irish
| £3800 | $6270 | (12-Jul-91 C128/R) Extensive mountainous landscape, thought to be County Wicklow (90x125cm-35x49in) |

IRMER, Carl (1834-1900) German
| £3846 | $7423 | (10-Dec-90 L.K453) Wood clearing with cattle and shepherd (43x62cm-17x24in) s. canvas on panel (DM 11000) |

IROLLI, Vincenzo (1860-1949) Italian
£5892	$9957	(16-Apr-91 CH.R140/R) Busto di ragazza (53x35cm-21x14in) s. (I.L 13000000)
£6137	$12029	(22-Nov-90 SY.MI59) Il vecchio frate (70x40cm-28x16in) s. (I.L 13500000)
£9092	$17820	(22-Nov-90 SY.MI84/R) Ragazza fra il grano (49x75cm-19x30in) s. (I.L 20000000)
£9242	$17837	(11-Dec-90 CH.R64/R) Busto di ragazza (52x36cm-20x14in) s. (I.L 20000000)
£10417	$20000	(27-Nov-90 PO.BA12) En el mercado (58x84cm-23x33in) s. canvas laid down on board
£10526	$20000	(28-Feb-91 CH.NY123/R) Perdita (73x51cm-29x20in) s.
£38462	$75000	(24-Oct-90 CH.NY226/R) Reverie (82x34cm-32x13in) s.
£2172	*$4192*	*(12-Dec-90 F.M175/R) Donna al balcone (53x40cm-21x16in) s. chl (I.L 4700000)*
£2266	*$3830*	*(16-Apr-91 CH.R12) Canale veneziano con figure (30x45cm-12x18in) s. W/C (I.L 5000000)*
£4474	*$8500*	*(28-Feb-91 CH.NY122/R) Young fishing girl (49x33cm-19x13in) s. W/C over pencil htd.white paperboard*
£5263	*$10000*	*(28-Feb-91 CH.NY121/R) Young egg seller (48x29cm-19x11in) s. W/C over pencil htd.white*

IROLLI, Vincenzo (1860-1949) Italian-cont.
£8556 $16599   (5-Dec-90 F.M40/R) Il violinista e la bambina (91x58cm-36x23in) s. W/C
                   cardboard (I.L 18500000)

IROLLI, Vincenzo (attrib) (1860-1949) Italian
£2768 $4900   (7-Apr-91 LIT.L7) Off to school (74x107cm-29x42in) s. panel
£3800 $6232   (19-Jun-91 S407/R) Violin player (95x166cm-37x65in)

IRRIERA, Roger (1894-1957) French?
£811 $1558   (17-Dec-90 ARC.P69/R) Au marche (50x65cm-20x26in) s. (F.FR 8000)
£3550 $6815   (17-Dec-90 ARC.P68/R) Ecole Coranique (65x85cm-26x33in) s. (F.FR 35000)

IRVIN, Albert (1922-) British
£2500 $4900   (6-Nov-90 PH163/R) Untitled (81x142cm-32x56in) s.d.80verso acrylic

IRVINE, Wilson (1869-1936) American
£650 $1300   (10-Feb-91 LIT.L46) A knock at the door (91x102cm-36x40in) s.
£663 $1300   (27-Jan-91 LIT.L21a) Knock at door, nude in interior (91x102cm-36x40in)
                   s.
£727 $1200   (13-Jul-91 YFA.M94) Nocturne (25x36cm-10x14in) s. board
£1302 $2500   (17-Dec-90 SY.NY361/R) Waiting for fog to break (46x61cm-18x24in)
                   s.i.verso i.stretcher
£1390 $2600   (30-Aug-90 MFA.C241/R) The Chasm (64x76cm-25x30in) s.
£3046 $6000   (7-Oct-90 DU.E81/R) Gloucester (46x61cm-18x24in) s.
£3222 $6250   (5-Dec-90 D.NY77/R) Mediterranean Port (61x69cm-24x27in) s. i.verso
£3699 $6400   (12-May-91 H.C110 a/R) Morning mist, Connecticut (61x69cm-24x27in) s.
£3704 $7000   (26-Sep-90 SY.NY154/R) Connecticut snowscape (61x69cm-24x27in) s.
£5128 $10000   (14-Oct-90 H.C395/R) Landscape with creek and grazing cattle
                   (89x117cm-35x46in) s.
£6358 $11000   (22-May-91 CH.NY256/R) Spring in the Old Lyme (89x117cm-35x46in) s.

IRWIN, Clara (fl.1891-1916) Irish
£636 $1247   (23-Jan-91 WO.CO23) Old and new (36x33cm-14x13in) W/C (E.P 700)

ISAACHSEN, Olaf (1835-1893) Norwegian
£3152 $5643   (14-Mar-91 BU.O51/R) Girl wearing national costume from Setesdal
                   (89x81cm-35x32in) init.d.1865 (N.KR 36000)

ISABEY, Eugene (1803-1886) French
£1488 $2560   (19-May-91 ZZ.F24/R) Scene galante dans le parc (32x23cm-13x9in) s.
                   panel (F.FR 15000)
£1494 $2585   (24-May-91 FB.P104/R) La chaumiere (32x46cm-13x18in) mono. board
                   (F.FR 15000)
£2196 $3711   (3-May-91 SA.A1195/R) Portrait of woman in black coat with frilled neck
                   (7x6cm-3x2in) min.s. tempera ivory oval (DM 6500)
£2513 $4121   (21-Jun-91 SY.MO334/R) Portrait de jeune fille (40x32cm-16x13in)
                   mono.d.1840 (F.FR 25000)
£2719 $4432   (12-Jun-91 ZZ.F3) Ceremonie a la cour (34x25cm-13x10in) panel
                   (F.FR 27000)
£3800 $6536   (17-May-91 C7 f/R) On coast (45x76cm-18x30in) s.indist.d.
£4000 $6560   (21-Jun-91 C11/R) Portrait of lady (54x43cm-21x17in) st.
£5500 $10780   (15-Feb-91 C18/R) Portrait of lady (72x61cm-28x24in) st.
£5963 $11748   (13-Nov-90 AB.S913/R) Town view with figures (115x81cm-45x32in) s.d.1859
                   (S.KR 65000)
£18443 $36148   (11-Nov-90 ZZ.F33/R) Le retour au port (55x83cm-22x33in) s.d.1854
                   (F.FR 180000)
£762 $1524   (4-Feb-91 PLF.P42/R) Chaumiere au bord de l'eau (14x30cm-6x12in)
                   s.i.d.1831 pierre noire sanguinne htd.white chk. (F.FR 7500)

ISABEY, Jean Baptiste (1767-1855) French
£388 $764   (13-Nov-90 CH.G204) Portrait of Count Nicholas Esterhazy (2x?cm-1x?in)
                   min. gilt-metal mount oval (S.FR 950)
£1800 $3042   (16-Apr-91 C211/R) Portrait of Ferdinando Carulli (20x18cm-8x7in) s.
                   blk.white chk. wash
£4400 $8448   (28-Nov-90 S247/R) Portrait of Madame Fould (18x13cm-7x5in) s.d.1834 W/C
£6000 $11520   (18-Dec-90 C64/R) Portrait of Count Vassili Ivanovitch Apraksin
                   (14x?cm-6x?in) min.s.card gilt-metal frame foliate border oval

ISABEY, Jean Baptiste (attrib) (1767-1855) French
£632 $1200   (9-Jan-91 CH.NY83) Portrait of lady (24x18cm-9x7in) i.d.1799 black chk
                   with stumping oval

ISAKSON, Karl (1878-1922) Swedish
£4263 $8271   (5-Dec-90 AB.S7113/R) Still life of flowers in vase (67x53cm-26x21in)
                   d.1920verso (S.KR 46000)
£9268 $17980   (4-Dec-90 BA.S221/R) Still life of oranges and lemons (48x55cm-19x22in)
                   i.verso (S.KR 100000)
£20536 $37991   (5-Mar-91 RAS.K172/R) View of Svaneke (62x78cm-24x31in) (D.KR 230000)

ISAMBERT, Alphonse (1818-?) French
£1500 $2940   (22-Nov-90 CSK264/R) Pet bird (55x46cm-22x18in) s.

ISBRAND, Victor (1897-?) Danish
£616 $1202   (10-Oct-90 RAS.K210) Still life (76x68cm-30x27in) s. (D.KR 7000)

ISELI, Rolf (1934-) Swiss
£6746	$11266	(5-Jun-91 SY.Z177/R) Composition (120x90cm-47x35in) s.d.60stretcher (S.FR 17000)
£4240	$7335	(10-May-91 S.Z42/R) Der rostige Afrikanisch (79x57cm-31x22in) s.i.d.1985 W/C gouache chl (S.FR 10600)
£5714	$11257	(16-Nov-90 EA.Z337/R) Untitled (62x48cm-24x19in) gouache (S.FR 14000)
£6000	$11700	(17-Oct-90 G.Z91/R) Composition (50x61cm-20x24in) s.d.1962verso gouache (S.FR 15000)
£6122	$12061	(16-Nov-90 EA.Z349/R) Study for great litho (78x56cm-31x22in) s.d.83/84/89 mixed media (S.FR 15000)

ISENBART, Marie Victor Emile (1846-1921) French
| £1000 | $1920 | (27-Nov-90 PH69) Cattle grazing in mountainous landscape (46x65cm-18x26in) s. |
| £5700 | $9291 | (3-Jul-91 PLF.P20/R) Paysage maritime avec lavandieres (50x65cm-20x26in) s. (F.FR 57000) |

ISENBRANDT (style) (16th C) Flemish
| £3033 | $5915 | (16-Oct-90 CS.L10/R) Vierge a l'enfant (91x63cm-36x25in) (F.FR 30000) |

ISENBRANDT, Adriaen (1490-1551) Flemish
| £75000 | $129750 | (24-May-91 C6/R) Virgin with symbols of immaculate conception, Flight into Egypt (96x100cm-38x39in) Triptych |
| £263158 | $500000 | (11-Jan-91 CH.NY84/R) Rest on Flight into Egypt (48x33cm-19x13in) panel arched top |

ISENBRANDT, Adriaen (circle) (1490-1551) Flemish
| £15385 | $30000 | (11-Oct-90 SY.NY73/R) Annunciation (48x37cm-19x15in) panel |

ISENBRANDT, Adriaen (style) (1490-1551) Flemish
| £2752 | $5422 | (13-Nov-90 CH.AM157/R) Madonna and Child enthroned with musicmaking angel, landscape beyond (21x12cm-8x5in) panel (D.FL 9000) |

ISENBURGER, Eric (1902-) American/German
| £615 | $1200 | (10-Oct-90 SY.NY182/R) Reading fairy tales (46x66cm-18x26in) s. |

ISERN, Ramon (1914-) ?
| £757 | $1461 | (10-Dec-90 B.O61/R) President Nixon's last political episode 1971 (62x75cm-24x30in) collage panel (N.KR 8500) |

ISGRO, Emilio (1936-) Spanish
| £1818 | $3564 | (20-Nov-90 BR.M107/R) Che (20x155cm-8x61in) s.d.1974 felt tip pen (I.L 4000000) |
| £1891 | $3688 | (22-Oct-90 BR.M18/R) Semibreve tratta dalla nona sinfonia di Ludwig Van Beethoven (105x60cm-41x24in) s.d.1972 verso emulsioned canvas (I.L 4200000) |

ISHERWOOD, Lawrence (1917-1988) British
| £500 | $850 | (29-May-91 PHC218/R) Shawled women, Wigan (31x61cm-12x24in) s.d.69 board |
| £1150 | $2162 | (19-Sep-90 PHC220/R) Clogs and shawls, Wigan (60x73cm-24x29in) s.i.verso |

ISKOWITZ, Gershon (1921-1988) Canadian
| £526 | $1032 | (20-Nov-90 JOY.T280) Sunset (36x52cm-14x20in) s.d.61 W/C (C.D 1200) |

ISNARD, Vivien (1946-) French?
| £1626 | $3252 | (10-Feb-91 CC.P36) Sans titre (172x140cm-68x55in) s.d.1973 (F.FR 16000) |
| £2218 | $4325 | (26-Oct-90 CC.P46/R) Sans titre (120x200cm-47x79in) oil rust canvas (F.FR 22000) |

ISOLA, Giancarlo (1927-) Italian
| £541 | $968 | (9-Apr-91 F.R147) Barche sulla spiaggia (40x50cm-16x20in) s. acrylic (I.L 1200000) |

ISOLDA (1924-) Brazilian
| £1229 | $2200 | (11-Apr-91 FA.PH677/R) On terrace (61x76cm-24x30in) sold with letter |

ISOU, Isidore (1925-) French
| £714 | $1377 | (16-Dec-90 P.V87/R) Entretiens avec Jean Cocteau (55x46cm-22x18in) s.d.1989 (F.FR 7000) |
| £2227 | $4364 | (21-Nov-90 C.P41/R) Initiation a la haute volupte (17x13cm-7x5in) s.d.1960 Indian ink film (F.FR 22000) |

ISRAEL, Daniel (?-1901) Austrian
£1034	$1800	(27-Mar-91 B.SF4191/R) Portrait of woman looking away (51x41cm-20x16in)
£3187	$5482	(14-May-91 GF.L2374/R) Young woman selling oranges (23x15cm-9x6in) s.i.d.1888 board (S.FR 8000)
£21053	$40000	(28-Feb-91 CH.NY96/R) Decorating the harem (38x60cm-15x24in) s.i. panel

ISRAELI SCHOOL, 20th C Israeli
| £1006 | $1700 | (20-Apr-91 WOL.C441) Jerusalem (71x89cm-28x35in) s. |

ISRAELS, Isaac (1865-1934) Dutch
£778	$1308	(23-Apr-91 SY.AM133) Portrait of lady (34x28cm-13x11in) s. (D.FL 2600)
£2216	$3855	(26-Mar-91 VN.R36/R) Seated female nude (58x38cm-23x15in) s. (D.FL 7400)
£4848	$9552	(30-Oct-90 CH.AM311) Woman, standing, wearing shawl (38x44cm-15x17in) s. sketch (D.FL 16000)

ISRAELS, Isaac (1865-1934) Dutch-cont.

£13720	$26890	(6-Nov-90 SY.AM109/R) Figures on Place Vendome in Paris (53x33cm-21x13in) studio st. pasteboard (D.FL 45000)
£18576	$35851	(12-Dec-90 CH.AM234/R) Girl, full length, dressed in red bathing suit at beach (50x40cm-20x16in) s. (D.FL 60000)
£19162	$37365	(25-Oct-90 VN.R50/R) Shipping on a town canal at evening (120x78cm-47x31in) s. (D.FL 64000)
£21818	$42982	(30-Oct-90 CH.AM318/R) Women in sewing studio of Paquin, Paris (60x48cm-24x19in) s. (D.FL 72000)
£21951	$43024	(6-Nov-90 SY.AM249/R) Student's party (91x64cm-36x25in) s. (D.FL 72000)
£29940	$58383	(25-Oct-90 VN.R49/R) The ballet school (76x100cm-30x39in) s. (D.FL 100000)
£30488	$59756	(6-Nov-90 SY.AM115/R) Strolling in Bois de Boulogne (32x45cm-13x18in) (D.FL 100000)
£109091	$214909	(30-Oct-90 CH.AM55/R) Women dancing at cafe, Amsterdam (80x75cm-31x30in) s. (D.FL 360000)
£539	*$905*	*(23-Apr-91 SY.AM215) Various studies of Sophie de Vries (43x34cm-17x13in) s. black chk (D.FL 1800)*
£1300	*$2184*	*(26-Apr-91 ARC.P25/R) Jeune femme a la mandarine (33x21cm-13x8in) s. W/C htd.gouache traces blk.crayon chamois (F.FR 13000)*
£2004	*$3307*	*(8-Jul-91 SY.J223/R) On the beach (24x34cm-9x13in) W/C (SA.R 9500)*
£7485	*$12575*	*(23-Apr-91 SY.AM278/R) Street circus in Paris (30x39cm-12x15in) s. pastel (D.FL 25000)*
£8439	*$13924*	*(8-Jul-91 SY.J224/R) Modinettes (35x46cm-14x18in) s. pastel (SA.R 40000)*
£9556	*$18730*	*(24-Nov-90 VG.B107/R) Naaistertje (65x50cm-26x20in) s. pastel (DM 28000)*
£10778	*$18108*	*(23-Apr-91 SY.AM33/R) In hat shop (31x23cm-12x9in) s. pastel (D.FL 36000)*
£24768	*$47802*	*(12-Dec-90 CH.AM235/R) Aan zee - girl in white at Boulevard (56x38cm-22x15in) s. black chk pastel (D.FL 80000)*

ISRAELS, Isaac (attrib) (1865-1934) Dutch

| £1092 | $1791 | (18-Jun-91 FN.S1908) Park landscape with figures, Sunday afternoon (40x50cm-16x20in) s. canvas on panel (DM 3200) |

ISRAELS, Josef (1824-1911) Dutch

£1061	$2089	(30-Oct-90 CH.AM341/R) Portrait of young boy and mother (112x88cm-44x35in) s.d.1858 oval (D.FL 3500)
£1977	$3400	(19-May-91 LIT.L63) Mother feeding baby (28x23cm-11x9in) s. masonite
£3293	$5533	(23-Apr-91 SY.AM223/R) Little shepherd (39x27cm-15x11in) s. panel (D.FL 11000)
£4103	$8000	(24-Oct-90 CH.NY282/R) Peasant woman by hearth (47x36cm-19x14in) s.
£5263	$10000	(27-Feb-91 SY.NY17/R) Mother's helper (38x54cm-15x21in) s. panel
£7500	$13455	(14-Mar-91 B107/R) The toy boat (39x34cm-15x13in) s. panel
£8000	$14320	(14-Mar-91 B115/R) An interior (51x71cm-20x28in) s.
£8000	$14320	(14-Mar-91 B114/R) On the dunes (32x46cm-13x18in) s. panel
£8205	$16000	(23-Oct-90 SY.NY339/R) Apres le depart (32x44cm-13x17in) s. panel
£8500	$15215	(14-Mar-91 B104/R) First steps (35x50cm-14x20in) s. panel
£8671	$15000	(22-May-91 SY.NY215/R) Waiting for boats (51x42cm-20x17in) s. panel
£9500	$17005	(14-Mar-91 B105/R) Launching the boat (34x39cm-13x15in) s. panel
£11518	$22000	(2-Jan-91 GG.TA540/R) Two girls in snow (48x41cm-19x16in) s.
£22727	$43864	(12-Dec-90 WE.MU120/R) The workmen (108x150cm-43x59in) s. (DM 65000)
£599	*$1168*	*(25-Oct-90 VN.R51) Two women on a street (23x15cm-9x6in) s. W/C (D.FL 2000)*
£1433	*$2810*	*(24-Nov-90 VG.B603/R) Peasant woman with child (28x19cm-11x7in) s. W/C (DM 4200)*
£2270	*$3701*	*(10-Jun-91 W.T1265) Sewing at a window (36x21cm-14x8in) s. W/C (C.D 4200)*
£2703	*$4405*	*(10-Jun-91 W.T1266/R) Mother and child (45x36cm-18x14in) s. W/C (C.D 5000)*
£4000	*$7680*	*(28-Nov-90 S87/R) Afternoon rest (29x44cm-11x17in) s. W/C*
£6667	*$13133*	*(30-Oct-90 CH.AM523/R) Convalescent (43x55cm-17x22in) s. W/C htd white (D.FL 22000)*

ISRAELS, Josef (attrib) (1824-1911) Dutch

| £1498 | $2801 | (29-Aug-90 KH.K87/R) Old man wearing cap (45x35cm-18x14in) s.d.1905 (D.KR 17000) |
| £6842 | $13000 | (27-Feb-91 SY.NY131/R) Fisherwoman and children on beach (47x61cm-19x24in) bears sig. |

ISRATI, Alexandre (20th C) ?

| *£1292* | *$2184* | *(16-Apr-91 I.N27 b) Composition (31x32cm-12x13in) s.d.1963 gouache W/C ink (F.FR 13000)* |

ISSUPOFF, Alessio (1889-1957) Russian

| £1421 | $2700 | (27-Feb-91 SY.NY306/R) Landscape (65x80cm-26x31in) s. |
| £5491 | $9500 | (22-May-91 SY.NY246/R) Farm scene with rider on white horse (48x60cm-19x24in) s. panel |

ISSUPOFF, Alessio (attrib) (1889-1957) Russian

| £1000 | $1969 | (29-Oct-90 SY.F686) Strada con casolare (40x50cm-16x20in) bears sig. (I.L 2200000) |

ISTRATI, Alexandre (1915-?) French

| £1008 | $1966 | (26-Oct-90 APT.P119) Composition (46x38cm-18x15in) s. d.68 verso (F.FR 10000) |

958

ISTVANFFY, Gabrielle Rainer (1877-?) Hungarian
£1300 $2522   (3-Dec-90 B58/R) Kittens in interior (42x61cm-17x24in) s.
£556 $928   (7-Jun-91 ZOF.Z1092/R) White Persian kitten drinking milk
                          (21x25cm-8x10in) s. mixed media (S.FR 1400)

ITALIAN MASTER, 16th C (16th C)
£3209 $5424   (3-May-91 SA.A1611/R) The Adoration of the Christ Child
                          (67x91cm-26x36in) panel (DM 9500)

ITALIAN SCHOOL (?)
£906 $1532   (16-Apr-91 CH.R96) Scorcio di Piazza San Marco (27x17cm-11x7in)
                          s.indis.i.d.91 panel (I.L 2000000)
£1000 $1630   (4-Jul-91 B100 g) A cavalry engagement (56x73cm-22x29in) c.1800
£1100 $1793   (4-Jul-91 CSK69/R) Madonna and Child (41x29cm-16x11in) gold ground panel
                          arched top
£1116 $1919   (14-May-91 GF.L2328/R) Portrait of Lucien Bonaparte (60x46cm-24x18in)
                          c.1800 (S.FR 2800)
£1186 $1980   (4-Jun-91 CH.R288) Agar e l'angelo (37x50cm-15x20in) (I.L 2600000)
£1220 $1989   (5-Jul-91 BW415) Allegorical scene (112x81cm-44x32in)
£1267 $2141   (16-Apr-91 J.M266) Professor spectacles (68x50cm-27x20in) (A.D 2800)
£1300 $2119   (4-Jul-91 C743/R) Ruined classical temple by lake (249x160cm-98x63in)
                          shaped c.1800
£1310 $2200   (17-Jul-91 SY.NY129/R) Stormy sea (96x123cm-38x48in) c.1700
£1444 $2412   (6-Jun-91 D.V147/R) St John the Baptist (53x34cm-21x13in) panel
                          (A.S 30000)
£1500 $3000   (7-Feb-91 C126) The Holy Family with a angel presenting the cross
                          (52x44cm-20x17in) panel
£1600 $2752   (16-May-91 CSK195) Mixed fruit on salver on draped ledge with figs
                          (58x69cm-23x27in) with indist.sig.
£1600 $2624   (20-Jun-91 B89) Series of views on coast near La Spezia (16x11cm-6x4in)
                          i. board four in one frame c.1880
£2083 $3500   (17-Jul-91 SY.NY61/R) Madonna and child (84x72cm-33x28in) c.1700
£2087 $3528   (18-Apr-91 APT.P91/R) Paysage fluvial (30x25cm-12x10in) c.1700
                          (F.FR 21000)
£2113 $3549   (23-Apr-91 RAS.K198/R) View from a park with chickens, rabbits and
                          peacock (49x66cm-19x26in) ca.1700 (D.KR 24000)
£2235 $4000   (16-Mar-91 W.W10/R) Two women (33x43cm-13x17in) panel c.1800-1900
£2510 $4041   (27-Jun-91 APT.P60/R) Nature morte aux perdrix rouges et grises, aux
                          geais et canards (38x46cm-15x18in) c.1700 pair (F.FR 25000)
£2569 $4368   (27-May-91 GK.Z5036) Still life of flowers and fruit on window ledge
                          with view of landscape (89x69cm-35x27in) c.1800 (S.FR 6500)
£2569 $4985   (7-Dec-90 SY.MO112/R) Coupe de fruits, oiseaux et souris
                          (44x34cm-17x13in) (F.FR 25000)
£2600 $4498   (20-May-91 SWS129/R) Classical figures in an extensive river landscape
                          (61x100cm-24x39in)
£2672 $5184   (7-Dec-90 SY.MO72/R) Choc de cavalerie (30x36cm-12x14in) c.1700
                          (F.FR 26000)
£2797 $5399   (10-Dec-90 L.K60) The torture of Marsyas (74x98cm-29x39in) c.1700
                          (DM 8000)
£2800 $5292   (26-Sep-90 RB642) Wooded river landscape with peasants and animals near
                          ruins (94x135cm-37x53in)
£2847 $5352   (18-Sep-90 BU.K44/R) Roman ruins (82x101cm-32x40in) c.1700 (D.KR 32000)
£3000 $5550   (5-Mar-91 PH133/R) St John the Baptist and St Dominic (24x20cm-9x8in)
                          c.1500 gold ground panel
£3000 $5070   (17-Apr-91 S10/R) The Presentation in the Temple (35x53cm-14x21in)
                          c.1700 grisaille
£3200 $6400   (7-Feb-91 CSK143/R) Naples from Marinella (46x91cm-18x36in)
£3400 $5746   (18-Apr-91 CSK106/R) River landscape with travellers crossing bridge.
                          Travellers and herdsmen crossing bridge in landsca (68x94cm-27x37in)
                          pair
£3500 $6895   (4-Oct-90 CSK17/R) Still life of baskets of vegetables and fruit with
                          oysters on a ledge (81x107cm-32x42in)
£3590 $7000   (11-Oct-90 SY.NY130/R) Still life of flowers in urn (93x76cm-37x30in)
                          c.1800
£4111 $7975   (7-Dec-90 SY.MO117/R) Paysage avec riviere (103x125cm-41x49in) c.1700
                          (F.FR 40000)
£4217 $6789   (27-Jun-91 APT.P16/R) Paysage aux baigneurs (118x158cm-46x62in) c.1650
                          (F.FR 42000)
£6592 $11405   (21-May-91 SY.MI1011) Natura morta con frutta ed ortaggi
                          (90x100cm-35x39in) c.1800 (I.L 14500000)
£7249 $12613   (25-Mar-91 SY.F719) Nature morte con uva e carciofi (34x45cm-13x18in)
                          c.1800 pair (I.L 16000000)
£9514 $16555   (25-Mar-91 SY.F604) Ritratti (24x18cm-9x7in) panel set of four
                          (I.L 21000000)
£10002 $17304   (21-May-91 SY.MI1070/R) Composizione floreale (73x106cm-29x42in) c.1800
                          (I.L 22000000)
£12000 $22800   (1-Mar-91 C70/R) Tulips, anemones and other flowers in ornate vases on
                          ledges (58x50cm-23x20in) pair
£15700 $29672   (25-Sep-90 FN.S2459/R) Landscape with fortifications and figures
                          (51x98cm-20x39in) c.1800 (DM 46000)
£16080 $26372   (22-Jun-91 CH.MO135/R) Coupe de raisins noirs et blancs
                          (27x40cm-11x16in) bears i.verso panel c.18th C (F.FR 160000)
£44221 $72523   (21-Jun-91 SY.MO203/R) Natures mortes aux fruits one bears i. c.1720
                          pair (F.FR 440000)
£1100 $2112   (18-Feb-91 S283) Design for fan with Rinaldo and Armida in landscape
                          (25x47cm-10x19in) c.1700 ink wash over chk

ITALIAN SCHOOL (?) -cont.

£1273	$2202	(21-May-91 SY.MI206/R) Ritratto di gentiluomo vestito con cravatta bianca e rossa (6x?cm-2x?in) min.c.1700 copper oval (I.L 2800000)
£1300	$2184	(18-Jul-91 CSK43/R) Wine festival at sea (72x52cm-28x20in) indist.s. pencil W/C htd white gum arabic
£2113	$3549	(23-Apr-91 RAS.K171/R) Portrait of a cardinal (24x17cm-9x7in) i. gouache (D.KR 24000)
£3819	$6263	(18-Jun-91 APT.P24/R) Six themes de la vie du Christ (19cm-7ins circular) c.1600 pen round (F.FR 38000)

ITALIAN SCHOOL, 14th C

£6343	$11037	(25-Mar-91 SY.F701/R) Il Cenacolo (77x61cm-30x24in) tempera gold ground panel (I.L 14000000)

ITALIAN SCHOOL, 15th C

£1531	$2464	(28-Jun-91 BM.B631/R) Portrait of page boy in profile (27cm-11ins circular) gold ground (DM 4500)
£1583	$2833	(10-Apr-91 CB.P38) Sainte Agnes et un eveque martyr (13x22cm-5x9in) panel (F.FR 16000)
£2183	$3776	(22-May-91 GS.B2408/R) Throning Madonna and Child presenting rosary to saints (29x26cm-11x10in) gold ground panel (S.FR 5500)
£26316	$50000	(11-Jan-91 CH.NY40/R) Saint Lucy. Saint Bernardino of Siena (60x37cm-24x15in) latter i. tempera gold panel arched two

ITALIAN SCHOOL, 15th/16th C

£4670	$8732	(29-Aug-90 KH.K88/R) Mary and Baby Jesus with St. John in mountainous landscape (81x65cm-32x26in) panel (D.KR 53000)

ITALIAN SCHOOL, 16th C

£1365	$2361	(8-May-91 FER.M264 a/R) Virgen con Nino (29x23cm-11x9in) panel (S.P 250000)
£1506	$2425	(27-Jun-91 APT.P2/R) La deploration du Christ (31x48cm-12x19in) panel (F.FR 15000)
£1541	$2512	(12-Jun-91 N.M316/R) Madonna with Child in river landscape (32x27cm-13x11in) panel (DM 4500)
£1693	$2878	(27-May-91 OD.P91/R) Deux episodes de la vie d'un saint dominicain (156x31cm-61x12in) panel (F.FR 17000)
£1992	$3386	(31-May-91 LD.P17/R) Saint Laurent (24x17cm-9x7in) panel tempera sheet of gold (F.FR 20000)
£2049	$3954	(11-Dec-90 FER.M167/R) Calvario (31x22cm-12x9in) copper (S.P 375000)
£2600	$4238	(4-Jul-91 D116/R) Madonna and Child (23x18cm-9x7in) en grisaille copper panel engraving verso
£3058	$5902	(12-Dec-90 CD.P18/R) Sainte famille et Saint Sebastien (37x46cm-15x18in) panel (F.FR 30000)
£3141	$6063	(11-Dec-90 FER.M168/R) La Circuncision (96x76cm-38x30in) (S.P 575000)
£5420	$10460	(10-Dec-90 L.K93) Mary with Child in landscape (25x21cm-10x8in) copper (DM 15500)
£5641	$11000	(11-Oct-90 SY.NY87/R) Madonna and Child with infant St John the Baptist (64cm-25ins circular) c.1510 panel
£14070	$23075	(21-Jun-91 SY.MO181/R) Vierge a l'enfant (24x22cm-9x9in) tempera panel (F.FR 140000)
£15369	$30123	(11-Nov-90 M.V45/R) La femme adultere (112x157cm-44x62in) (F.FR 150000)
£17953	$35368	(14-Nov-90 RAS.K20/R) The Holy Family (47x30cm-19x12in) panel arched top (D.KR 200000)
£909	$1573	(21-May-91 SY.MI260) Ritratto di un nobiluomo vestita in un elaborato collare di pizzo (6x?cm-2x?in) min.parchment oval (I.L 2000000)
£2180	$3750	(15-May-91 D.NY14) Satyr and two men with lion. Figure studies (36x25cm-14x10in) bears i. pen ink double-sided
£2196	$3733	(31-May-91 GB.B5208/R) Male nude (19x10cm-7x4in) i.verso pen (DM 6500)

ITALIAN SCHOOL, 16th/17th C

£2740	$4466	(12-Jun-91 N.M317/R) Holy Family and adoring angel on stairs in Alpine landscape (45x33cm-18x13in) panel (DM 8000)
£2895	$5500	(15-Sep-90 S.W2409/R) Destruction of the Idols (48x30cm-19x12in)
£8904	$15938	(13-Mar-91 N.M408/R) Portrait of lady with two daughters (184x120cm-72x47in) (DM 26000)

ITALIAN SCHOOL, 17th C

£886	$1497	(1-May-91 KH.K87) Woman and children playing in landscape (95x72cm-37x28in) (D.KR 10000)
£886	$1497	(1-May-91 KH.K86) Procession (41x111cm-16x44in) panel (D.KR 10000)
£981	$1609	(17-Jun-91 DUR.M73/R) Crucifixion (40x25cm-16x10in) (S.P 180000)
£1149	$1953	(27-May-91 L.K59) Portrait of female saints (50x41cm-20x16in) panel (DM 3400)
£1182	$2045	(21-May-91 SY.MI1025) Euclide (66x48cm-26x19in) (I.L 2600000)
£1232	$2070	(23-Apr-91 RAS.K247/R) Vanitas scene with Baby Jesus asleep among scull, wreath and nails (42x55cm-17x22in) (D.KR 14000)
£1250	$2313	(5-Mar-91 PH128) Madonna and Child (28x23cm-11x9in) copper
£1269	$2207	(25-Mar-91 SY.F558) Paesaggio (52x7cm-20x3in) (I.L 2800000)
£1329	$2300	(12-May-91 H.C5/R) Landscape with travellers (38x51cm-15x20in)
£1330	$2500	(18-Sep-90 RO.BA11/R) Adoracion (26x20cm-10x8in) copper
£1491	$2520	(18-Apr-91 APT.P92/R) Rivage anime (35cm-14ins circular) wood round (F.FR 15000)
£1496	$2514	(23-Apr-91 RAS.K186/R) Madonna and Child with kneeling cleric (150x108cm-59x43in) (D.KR 17000)

ITALIAN SCHOOL, 17th C -cont.

£1508	$2472	(21-Jun-91 SY.MO205/R) Bouquet de fleurs (31x24cm-12x9in) panel (F.FR 15000)
£1573	$3037	(12-Dec-90 N.M399/R) Hunting scene with party in wooded landscape (49x67cm-19x26in) (DM 4500)
£1584	$2804	(4-Apr-91 CK.P21) Hommme appuye sur une beche portant une corbeille de legumes sur l'epaule (118x81cm-46x32in) (F.FR 16000)
£1586	$2759	(25-Mar-91 SY.F561) San Gerolamo (23cm-9ins circular) panel (I.L 3500000)
£1726	$2900	(17-Jul-91 SY.NY155/R) Arcadian landscape (32x47cm-13x19in)
£1734	$3000	(8-May-91 RO.BA9/R) Amore filiale (63x83cm-25x33in)
£1744	$3400	(14-Oct-90 H.C437/R) Portrait of Knight of Malta (201x107cm-79x42in) i.d.1563
£1761	$2958	(23-Apr-91 RAS.K191/R) The road to Emmaus (140x125cm-55x49in) (D.KR 20000)
£1780	$3187	(12-Apr-91 AGS.P1/R) La Vierge, l'Enfant et Saint Francois (35x28cm-14x11in) copper (F.FR 18000)
£1786	$3000	(17-Jul-91 SY.NY88/R) Jepthah's daughter (83x111cm-33x44in)
£1807	$2910	(27-Jun-91 APT.P11/R) Scene de l'ancien Testament (41x51cm-16x20in) (F.FR 18000)
£1992	$3386	(31-May-91 LD.P31/R) Le Christ aux liens (93x57cm-37x22in) panel (F.FR 20000)
£2066	$3512	(28-May-91 AB.S4847/R) Study of old man (60x46cm-24x18in) (S.KR 22000)
£2168	$3750	(21-May-91 GRO.B6/R) Feast of Balthazar (69x109cm-27x43in)
£2265	$3942	(25-Mar-91 SY.F596/R) Vergine col Bambino, S.Caterina d'Alessandria, S.Francesco e donatore (237x127cm-93x50in) i. (I.L 5000000)
£2278	$3873	(30-May-91 F.M16) Davide con la testa di Golia (112x77cm-44x30in) (I.L 5000000)
£2377	$3993	(23-Apr-91 RAS.K208/R) Woman (90x80cm-35x31in) (D.KR 27000)
£2390	$4112	(14-May-91 GF.L2253/R) Madonna with Jesus and St John (162x111cm-64x44in) (S.FR 6000)
£2395	$4000	(23-Jan-91 D.NY61) Death of Lucretia (152x122cm-60x48in)
£2400	$4704	(12-Feb-91 SWO241) Salome presenting head of John the Baptist to Herodias (104x180cm-41x71in) 242/R
£2412	$3956	(21-Jun-91 SY.MO223/R) Choc de cavalerie (35x45cm-14x18in) panel (F.FR 24000)
£2508	$4189	(4-Jun-91 CH.R24) Battaglia (75x104cm-30x41in) (I.L 5500000)
£2513	$4952	(14-Nov-90 RAS.K370) Romantic landscape (37x53cm-15x21in) (D.KR 28000)
£2528	$4929	(17-Oct-90 LC.P26) Descente de croix (225x146cm-89x57in) (F.FR 25000)
£2534	$4307	(27-May-91 L.K60) Young woman and beared old man (55x73cm-22x29in) (DM 7500)
£2545	$4250	(23-Jan-91 D.NY37) Madonna and Child with St. John and male saint (74x58cm-29x23in)
£2568	$4187	(12-Jun-91 N.M318/R) Europa with bull. Mercur and Io - scenes from Ovids Metamorphosen (25x34cm-10x13in) panel pair (DM 7500)
£2641	$4437	(23-Apr-91 RAS.K196/R) Offering by a round temple (71x94cm-28x37in) (D.KR 30000)
£2647	$4500	(31-May-91 CH.NY176/R) Infant St John the Baptist in landscape (43x59cm-17x23in)
£2653	$5147	(8-Dec-90 GAB.G2034) Deux bergers dans un paysage (32x24cm-13x9in) cameo panel (S.FR 6500)
£2716	$4373	(25-Jun-91 FER.M173 a/R) San Jeronimo. Santo Franciscano glass pair (S.P 500000)
£2716	$4373	(25-Jun-91 FER.M174/R) Sibila de la arquitectura (75x63cm-30x25in) (S.P 500000)
£2717	$4700	(8-May-91 RO.BA198) Madonna (120x89cm-47x35in)
£2736	$4652	(27-May-91 L.K58/R) Adoration of the Shepherds (52x36cm-20x14in) panel (DM 8100)
£2811	$4526	(27-Jun-91 APT.P35/R) Etude de rabbin (80x60cm-31x24in) (F.FR 28000)
£2840	$5623	(30-Jan-91 APT.P169/R) Jeune femme a la guirlande de fleurs (73x60cm-29x24in) (F.FR 28000)
£2900	$5655	(22-Oct-90 SWS1509) Noli me tangere (58x50cm-23x20in)
£2915	$4780	(21-Jun-91 D.P57/R) Choc de cavalerie (32x44cm-13x17in) (F.FR 29000)
£2938	$5788	(14-Nov-90 D.V265/R) Triumph of Galathea (96x149cm-38x59in) (A.S 60000)
£3043	$6024	(30-Jun-91 APT.P5/R) Joseph interpretant les songes de Pharaon (104x144cm-41x57in) (F.FR 30000)
£3083	$5982	(7-Dec-90 SY.MO66/R) Allegorie de l'automne (90cm-35ins circular) (F.FR 30000)
£3892	$6500	(23-Jan-91 D.NY75) Lion hunt (76x102cm-30x40in)
£3905	$7577	(7-Dec-90 SY.MO79/R) Saint Luc et Saint Marc (65x51cm-26x20in) pair (F.FR 38000)
£3905	$7577	(7-Dec-90 SY.MO94/R) Extase de Saint Francois (145x116cm-57x46in) (F.FR 38000)
£4023	$7000	(27-Mar-91 B.SF4026/R) The Binding of Isaac (170x125cm-67x49in)
£4141	$6750	(5-Jul-91 S.W3031/R) The Sermon of Christ at Mount Olive (102x127cm-40x50in)
£4154	$7436	(10-Apr-91 CB.P39/R) Nymphe endormie surprise par un satyre (132x195cm-52x77in) (F.FR 42000)
£4303	$8434	(11-Nov-90 M.V33/R) Pieces d'armures et draperies (96x135cm-38x53in) (F.FR 42000)
£4518	$7274	(27-Jun-91 APT.P46/R) Portrait d'homme (120x93cm-47x37in) (F.FR 45000)
£5028	$9000	(11-Apr-91 SY.NY124/R) Double portrait of boy and girl, standing by table strewn with fruit (56x73cm-22x29in)
£5097	$9837	(12-Dec-90 CD.P26) Herminie chez les bergers (80x97cm-31x38in) (F.FR 50000)
£5437	$9460	(25-Mar-91 SY.F592) Battaglia (56x95cm-22x37in) (I.L 12000000)

ITALIAN SCHOOL, 17th C -cont.

£5778	$9649	(6-Jun-91 D.V13/R) Still life of flowers and fruit with parrot (66x99cm-26x39in) (A.S 120000)
£5802	$11372	(24-Nov-90 SA.A596/R) Still life of fruit (68x113cm-27x44in) canvas laid down (DM 17000)
£6366	$12542	(14-Nov-90 D.V254/R) Angels making music (204x488cm-80x192in) i. (A.S 130000)
£7035	$11538	(21-Jun-91 SY.MO217/R) Scene de port (93x129cm-37x51in) (F.FR 70000)
£7098	$12280	(8-May-91 FER.M264 e/R) Personajes junto a las ruinas clasicas (96x132cm-38x52in) (S.P 1300000)
£8000	$13040	(4-Jul-91 B126) Bacchus (48x41cm-19x16in) panel octagonal
£9045	$14834	(21-Jun-91 SY.MO253/R) Personnages dans un paysage boise (95x74cm-37x29in) (F.FR 90000)
£9174	$17615	(30-Nov-90 APT.P9/R) Fleurs dans un vase de faience presente dans une niche (148x77cm-58x30in) (F.FR 90000)
£9874	$19452	(14-Nov-90 RAS.K12/R) Madonna and child with Saint Jacob and a bishop (209x152cm-82x60in) (D.KR 110000)
£12333	$23926	(7-Dec-90 SY.MO97/R) Natures nortes aux fruits (50x80cm-20x31in) pair (F.FR 120000)
£15947	$27110	(30-May-91 F.M103/R) Fronte di cassone con scena di danza e due stemmi (42x170cm-17x67in) panel (I.L 35000000)
£16904	$31779	(18-Sep-90 BU.K43/R) Esther dining with King Ahasverus (111x139cm-44x55in) (D.KR 190000)
£19000	$30970	(5-Jul-91 C240/R) Saints Cyricus and Julitta mourned by angels (239x175cm-94x69in)
£19920	$34263	(14-May-91 GF.L2011/R) Portrait of Bishop Gradenigo (87x66cm-34x26in) (S.FR 50000)
£24121	$39558	(21-Jun-91 SY.MO112/R) L'hiver (149x205cm-59x81in) (F.FR 240000)
£71942	$139568	(7-Dec-90 SY.MO6/R) Apollon et Marsyas (86x134cm-34x53in) (F.FR 700000)
£1000	$1920	*(18-Feb-91 S223/R) The Mystic Marriage of St Catherine (17x16cm-7x6in) bears i. pen ink chk*
£1119	$2171	*(7-Dec-90 GB.B5228/R) Drunk Bacchus surrounded by satyrs. Study of figure (14x19cm-6x7in) pen double-sided (DM 3200)*
£1206	$1978	*(18-Jun-91 APT.P41) Corbeille de fruits et de fleurs (26x34cm-10x13in) gouache vellum (F.FR 12000)*
£1550	$2527	*(1-Jul-91 S159/R) Head of girl wearing soft hat (22x16cm-9x6in) black red chk*
£1800	$3456	*(18-Feb-91 S69/R) Seated man seen from behind. Studies of hands and hands and legs (29x42cm-11x17in) chk htd double-sided*
£2000	$3461	*(21-May-91 SY.MI221/R) Ritratto della Duchessa di Modena (6x?cm-2x?in) min.copper gilt/silver frame oval (I.L 4400000)*
£2632	$5000	*(8-Jan-91 SY.NY197/R) Study of the head of a boy in profile (26x20cm-10x8in) bears i. verso chk.*
£2665	$5250	*(15-Nov-90 SY.NY1/R) Two putti (11x12cm-4x5in) pen wash over chk*
£4737	$9000	*(8-Jan-91 SY.NY23/R) A Statue of Bacchus after the antique (34x22cm-13x9in) red chk.*
£6000	$11580	*(12-Dec-90 PH259/R) Orpheus and the animals, study after antique gem (13x17cm-5x7in) i. pen ink wash laid down within mounting lines*
£6500	$10595	*(2-Jul-91 C120 a/R) Head of youth, in profile to left (32x23cm-13x9in) with i. black red white chk*

ITALIAN SCHOOL, 17th/18th C

£992	$1756	(22-Mar-91 EA.Z1015/R) Rape of Europa (120x170cm-47x67in) (S.FR 2500)
£1098	$1900	(12-May-91 H.C34) Judith with the Head of Holophernes (86x71cm-34x28in)
£1551	$3056	(15-Nov-90 EA.Z175) Riders by ford (49x65cm-19x26in) (S.FR 3800)
£2564	$5000	(26-Oct-90 S.W2650/R) Soldiers in landscape with ruins (89x135cm-35x53in)
£2564	$5000	(26-Oct-90 S.W2649/R) Figures in landscape with ruins (89x135cm-35x53in)
£2873	$5659	(14-Nov-90 RAS.K408/R) Romantic river landscape with cattle and herder by ruins (57x77cm-22x30in) (D.KR 32000)
£6162	$10352	(23-Apr-91 RAS.K34/R) The architect showing drawing of nearly finished palace to builder (100x127cm-39x50in) (D.KR 70000)
£8803	$14789	(23-Apr-91 RAS.K35/R) Still life of fruit and vegetables (73x92cm-29x36in) (D.KR 100000)

ITALIAN SCHOOL, 18th C

£906	$1577	(25-Mar-91 SY.F553) S.Luigi Gonzaga (80x65cm-31x26in) (I.L 2000000)
£957	$1800	(18-Sep-90 RO.BA12) San Sebastian (29x23cm-11x9in) panel
£968	$1627	(23-Apr-91 RAS.K194) Madonna and Child with garland of roses (70x86cm-28x34in) (D.KR 11000)
£1190	$2000	(17-Jul-91 SY.NY135/R) Portrait of Cardinal Lorenzo Strozzi (119x90cm-47x35in) s.i.
£1200	$2280	(28-Feb-91 B67) Magdalen (164x108cm-65x43in) after Guido Reni
£1204	$2010	(6-Jun-91 D.V167/R) Boy fishing (123x95cm-48x37in) (A.S 25000)
£1500	$2520	(24-Apr-91 MMB315/R) Frieze of allegorical figures and cherubs with winged bull (41x114cm-16x45in)
£1549	$2679	(6-May-91 ZEL.L1761/R) Still life of flowers (59x49cm-23x19in) oval (DM 4600)
£1600	$2768	(20-May-91 SWS188/R) Portrait of a Cardinal (74x62cm-29x24in)
£1606	$2586	(27-Jun-91 APT.P81/R) Le passage du gue (42x55cm-17x22in) (F.FR 16000)
£1628	$2800	(15-May-91 D.NY63 a) Still life with bouquets in urns, watermelon and peacock in landscape (74x97cm-29x38in)
£1643	$2793	(28-May-91 AB.S4845/R) Pastoral landscape with figures (64x95cm-25x37in) (S.KR 17500)
£1744	$3000	(15-May-91 D.NY65) Anglers in river landscape (66x76cm-26x30in)
£1786	$3000	(17-Jul-91 SY.NY74/R) Christ and the Lady of Samaria (74x93cm-29x37in)

ITALIAN SCHOOL, 18th C -cont.

£1809	$2967	(21-Jun-91 SY.MO204/R) Bouquet de fleurs (23x17cm-9x7in) (F.FR 18000)
£1900	$3211	(18-Apr-91 CSK47/R) Madonna and Child with Infant Saint John (95x80cm-37x31in)
£1912	$3289	(14-May-91 GF.L2074/R) Portrait of magistrat (86x62cm-34x24in) (S.FR 4800)
£1913	$3119	(10-Jun-91 AGB.P76) Venus et Vulcain (76x63cm-30x25in) (F.FR 19000)
£1954	$3498	(14-Mar-91 D.V146/R) Portrait of lady with flowers (65x51cm-26x20in) (A.S 40000)
£2235	$4000	(16-Mar-91 W.W1/R) Figures amongst architectural ruins (114x56cm-45x22in) arched two
£2265	$3942	(25-Mar-91 SY.F737) Scena di caccia (49x67cm-19x26in) (I.L 5000000)
£2287	$3750	(19-Jun-91 B.SF1679/R) Roman capriccio (74x98cm-29x39in)
£2367	$3977	(27-Apr-91 SO.S482/R) Mother and children (97x114cm-38x45in) (S.KR 25000)
£2424	$4194	(6-May-91 ZEL.L1760/R) Wooded river landscape with figures (100x134cm-39x53in) (DM 7200)
£2600	$5122	(1-May-91 CSK59) Soldiers and horses by classical ruins and figures by river (41x119cm-16x47in) overdoor
£2653	$5200	(6-Nov-90 GF.L2063/R) View of Venice (40x60cm-16x24in) (S.FR 6500)
£2718	$4730	(25-Mar-91 SY.F603) Madonna (91x70cm-36x28in) (I.L 6000000)
£2723	$4629	(28-May-91 AB.S4844/R) Madonna and Child (100x75cm-39x30in) (S.KR 29000)
£2797	$5399	(10-Dec-90 L.K711) Christ healing man posessed by evil spirit in river landscape with town (75x62cm-30x24in) (DM 8000)
£2878	$5583	(7-Dec-90 SY.MO65/R) Saint Visite par des anges (44x51cm-17x20in) grisaille (F.FR 28000)
£2936	$4932	(27-Apr-91 SO.S470/R) Religious scene with Madonna and child (111x87cm-44x34in) wood (S.KR 31000)
£3041	$5139	(3-May-91 SA.A1635/R) Evening bay scene with palace architecture (65x158cm-26x62in) (DM 9000)
£3083	$5982	(7-Dec-90 SY.MO102/R) Vue de l' eglise San Stefano a Venise (52x75cm-20x30in) (F.FR 30000)
£3183	$6271	(14-Nov-90 D.V246/R) Pieta (44x74cm-17x29in) (A.S 65000)
£3200	$6240	(22-Oct-90 SWS1429/R) Cavalry engagement (77x118cm-30x46in)
£3242	$6355	(24-Nov-90 SA.A597/R) Wedding scene in palace interior with view of lake landscape (115x200cm-45x79in) (DM 9500)
£3299	$6500	(16-Nov-90 S.BM7/R) Figures in landscape (41x76cm-16x30in)
£3625	$6307	(25-Mar-91 SY.F592 b) Crocefissione (97x75cm-38x30in) (I.L 8000000)
£3770	$7427	(14-Nov-90 RAS.K200/R) The Adoration (94x131cm-37x52in) (D.KR 42000)
£3785	$6510	(14-May-91 GF.L2332/R) Apotheosis of Hercules (66x121cm-26x48in) (S.FR 9500)
£3800	$7410	(22-Oct-90 SWS1516/R) Still life of flowers in niche (92x64cm-36x25in)
£3884	$6604	(27-May-91 OD.P86/R) Nature morte (58x49cm-23x19in) (F.FR 39000)
£3892	$6500	(23-Jan-91 D.NY91/R) Still llife of melon, flowers and peaches beside basket of figs (64x76cm-25x30in)
£3987	$6498	(12-Jun-91 GM.B4047/R) Paysage lacustre (240x122cm-94x48in) (B.FR 240000)
£4162	$8075	(3-Dec-90 SY.F1033) Adorazione dei Magi (87x119cm-34x47in) (I.L 9000000)
£4200	$7224	(15-May-91 BT183) An allegory of St. Francis and Chastity (99x193cm-39x76in)
£4200	$8274	(31-Oct-90 S88/R) Cupid blindfolded (121x190cm-48x75in)
£4300	$7009	(1-Jul-91 LGB.P25/R) Architectures animees (27x43cm-11x17in) panel pair (F.FR 43000)
£4546	$7865	(21-May-91 SY.MI1048/R) Nature morte con volatili (97x135cm-38x53in) pair (I.L 10000000)
£4560	$7616	(4-Jun-91 CH.R581/R) Pesci e pavone in un paesaggio. Pesci, cocomeri e pappagallo (61x123cm-24x48in) pair (I.L 10000000)
£4562	$8987	(30-Oct-90 BU.S301/R) Landscape with ruins and watercourse (118x114cm-46x45in) (S.KR 50000)
£4714	$9193	(9-Oct-90 GGL.L9/R) Passage d'un gue au soleil couchant (98x100cm-39x39in) (F.FR 47000)
£4800	$8304	(20-May-91 SWS52/R) Still life studies of mixed flowers (32x28cm-13x11in) oval three
£5000	$8150	(2-Jul-91 PH214/R) Roman soldiers by ruined temple before lake (86x132cm-34x52in)
£5578	$11045	(30-Jan-91 APT.P19/R) Corbeille de fruits et perroquet sur un entablement (79cm-31ins circular) round (F.FR 55000)
£5641	$11000	(10-Oct-90 CH.NY12/R) Flowers, fruit and vegetables on ledge (71x98cm-28x39in)
£5743	$9764	(27-May-91 L.K61) View of palace with steps and figures (80x136cm-31x54in) (DM 17000)
£5800	$9802	(17-Apr-91 S165/R) La zingarella (51x37cm-20x15in) panel
£5961	$11564	(7-Dec-90 SY.MO99/R) Vues de Rome (20x26cm-8x10in) bears l. panel pair (F.FR 58000)
£6000	$11580	(12-Dec-90 S135/R) Fortune with a crown (163x132cm-64x52in)
£6139	$10865	(5-Apr-91 DAR.P72/R) Paysage a la cascade (130x96cm-51x38in) (F.FR 62000)
£6145	$11000	(11-Apr-91 SY.NY174/R) Elaborate still life of flowers in urn (112x96cm-44x38in)
£6162	$10352	(23-Apr-91 RAS.K192/R) Woman seated by youth writing and man pointing (72x58cm-28x23in) l. (D.KR 70000)
£6372	$12362	(7-Dec-90 CH.MO326/R) Une nature morte aux fruits (68x100cm-27x39in) (F.FR 62000)
£6413	$12312	(29-Nov-90 F.M47) Pitocchi (86x112cm-34x44in) (I.L 14000000)

ITALIAN SCHOOL, 18th C -cont.

£6602	$11092	(23-Apr-91 RAS.K18/R) Romantic landscape with figures among ruins (83x120cm-33x47in) (D.KR 75000)
£6796	$11825	(25-Mar-91 SY.F715/R) Paesaggio con veduta marina (79x149cm-31x59in) (I.L 15000000)
£6871	$13192	(29-Nov-90 F.M90) Paesaggio con figure (110x152cm-43x60in) (I.L 15000000)
£7500	$12225	(2-Jul-91 PH143/R) Still lifes of summer flowers (96x68cm-38x27in) pair
£8040	$13186	(21-Jun-91 SY.MO202/R) Branche de pommier (62x75cm-24x30in) (F.FR 80000)
£8205	$16000	(11-Oct-90 SY.NY75/R) Still life of flowers in landscape (118x89cm-46x35in)
£9128	$18073	(30-Jan-91 CSC.P23/R) Sainte Victoire de Rome le coeur perce d'un coup de glaive (92x77cm-36x30in) (F.FR 90000)
£10000	$17000	(31-May-91 CH.NY214/R) Flowers in glass vases on ledge in landscapes (49x39cm-19x15in) pair
£10000	$19700	(31-Oct-90 S11/R) Pan with cupid and two nymphs (28x37cm-11x15in) copper
£11000	$17930	(4-Jul-91 B170/R) Still life of fruit and flowers on a wooden table (23x58cm-9x23in) i. verso
£13333	$26000	(11-Oct-90 SY.NY74/R) The Piazza Navona (122x172cm-48x68in)
£13361	$25920	(7-Dec-90 SY.MO83/R) Chiens de chasse, gorille et gibier (68x85cm-27x33in) (F.FR 130000)
£13692	$26288	(17-Dec-90 ARC.P40/R) Nature morte aux raisins et perroquet dans un paysage (87x117cm-34x46in) (F.FR 135000)
£14118	$24000	(31-May-91 CH.NY92/R) Interior of St Peter's in Rome with figures (107x114cm-42x45in)
£14343	$24669	(14-May-91 GF.L2081/R) Roman landscape with fortifications (62x74cm-24x29in) s. (S.FR 36000)
£18408	$32030	(27-Mar-91 CN.P65/R) Le Christ chez Marthe et Marie. Les pelerins d'Emmaus (78x114cm-31x45in) pair after Bassano (F.FR 185000)
£18458	$35440	(17-Dec-90 ARC.P37) Fleurs et fruits dans un panier (52x60cm-20x24in) (F.FR 182000)
£22653	$39416	(25-Mar-91 SY.F721/R) Nove ritratti di dame (35x26cm-14x10in) panel oval set of nine (I.L 50000000)
£36000	$58680	(2-Jul-91 PH61/R) Expulsion of Adam and Eve from Garden of Eden (90x115cm-35x45in)
£1005	*$1648*	*(18-Jun-91 APT.P62) Vue d'un chateau en construction (32x45cm-13x18in) W/C gouache (F.FR 10000)*
£1010	*$1747*	*(6-May-91 ZEL.L1478/R) Landscape with young woman seated beneath tree (88x67cm-35x26in) pastel (DM 3000)*
£1551	*$3056*	*(13-Nov-90 CH.G224/R) Portrait of Vittorio-Amadeo III, King of Sardinia (3x?cm-1x?in) min. gilt-metal mount oval (S.FR 3800)*
£2514	*$4952*	*(14-Nov-90 F.M5/R) Trompe l'oeil con disegni di figura e di architettura e fogli manoscritti (35x23cm-14x9in) pencil pen ink W/C (I.L 5500000)*
£4482	*$7754*	*(22-May-91 PLF.P140/R) Enee et les Troyens debarquant a Carthage (41x83cm-16x33in) pen wash htd.white (F.FR 45000)*

ITALIAN SCHOOL, 18th/19th C

£3720	$6287	(1-May-91 KH.K88/R) Venetian prospects - Gran Canal and Santa Maria della Salute (47x73cm-19x29in) pair (D.KR 42000)
£9694	$19097	(18-Nov-90 P.V13) Nature morte aux fruits (F.FR 95000)

ITALIAN SCHOOL, 19th C

£847	$1600	(24-Sep-90 S.SL494/R) View of St. Mark's Square from Grand Canal (61x97cm-24x38in) after Canaletto
£1005	$1648	(21-Jun-91 SY.MO314/R) Vue d'un lac (30x44cm-12x17in) paper laid down on canvas (F.FR 10000)
£1020	$2000	(21-Nov-90 NA.BA52) Nature morte (27x22cm-11x9in) panel
£1053	$2000	(27-Feb-91 SY.NY379/R) Still life with vase of flowers (97x72cm-38x28in)
£1100	$1804	(18-Jun-91 PH167) The Doge's Palace, Venice (16x24cm-6x9in) panel
£1100	$1870	(30-May-91 C118/R) Battle of Lissa, 1866 (53x75cm-21x30in) s. board
£1111	$1822	(21-Jun-91 G.Z515) Capriccio nella Campagna Romana (45x65cm-18x26in) (S.FR 2800)
£1163	$2000	(15-May-91 D.NY78) Prodigal Son (48x64cm-19x25in) i.verso
£1200	$2076	(9-May-91 CSK130/R) Singing cavalier (28x19cm-11x7in)
£1221	$2100	(17-May-91 WOL.C878/R) On the Veranda (66x107cm-26x42in) indist.sig.
£1221	$2100	(18-May-91 W.W9/R) Woman and child in a sunny courtyard (53x41cm-21x16in)
£1269	$2207	(25-Mar-91 SY.F660) Ritratto di ufficiale (103x76cm-41x30in) (I.L 2800000)
£1300	$2145	(9-Jul-91 PH224) Elegant ladies visiting classical ruins (43x75cm-17x30in) d.1848
£1300	$2249	(9-May-91 CSK120/R) Cavalier at rest (63x41cm-25x16in) init. panel
£1304	$2334	(9-Apr-91 GM.B665/R) Bergere et son troupeau (76x98cm-30x39in) s. (B.FR 80000)
£1320	$2218	(23-Apr-91 RAS.K189) The holy Jeronimus (130x95cm-51x37in) (D.KR 15000)
£1370	$2233	(12-Jun-91 N.M472) Adoration of the Magi (34x24cm-13x9in) (DM 4000)
£1450	$2523	(27-Mar-91 PHS894) Madonna and child (104x69cm-41x27in)
£1541	$2759	(13-Mar-91 N.M537 a/R) Cavalry battle in river landscape with ruins (68x118cm-27x46in) (DM 4500)
£1551	$3009	(8-Dec-90 GAB.G2098/R) Jeune italienne (88x67cm-35x26in) (S.FR 3800)
£1600	$3040	(28-Feb-91 B25/R) Holy Family under Oak (109x148cm-43x58in) i.verso after Raphael
£1600	$2864	(12-Mar-91 PH66) Figures on hilltop overlooking the Bay of Naples (60x33cm-24x33in) bears sig.
£1684	$2846	(15-Apr-91 SY.J386/R) Portrait of Guiseppe Perniciaro (109x79cm-43x31in) i. (SA.R 8000)

ITALIAN SCHOOL, 19th C -cont.
£2000	$3920	(14-Feb-91 CSK187/R) A present from grandfather (74x89cm-29x35in) indist.sig.d.1877
£2200	$3696	(18-Jul-91 CSK189/R) Paestum (45x58cm-18x23in) with i.stretcher
£2280	$3808	(4-Jun-91 CH.R328) Fiori (23x35cm-9x14in) board pair (I.L 5000000)
£2458	$4400	(11-Apr-91 FA.PH669) Saint Jerome (86x69cm-34x27in)
£2676	$4522	(17-Apr-91 WE.MU105/R) Allegory of wealth (116x88cm-46x35in) indis.s. (DM 8000)
£2800	$5516	(4-Oct-90 CSK223/R) The meeting of Garibaldi and Victor Emmanuel, King of Sardinia (67x96cm-26x38in) indist.s.d.
£3081	$5361	(25-Mar-91 SY.F665) Ritratto di dama in nero (125x92cm-49x36in) oval (I.L 6800000)
£3200	$6304	(4-Oct-90 CSK236/R) The bay of Naples (48x75cm-19x30in)
£3265	$6400	(6-Nov-90 GF.L2081/R) Veduta di Venezia (27x44cm-11x17in) indis.s. (S.FR 8000)
£4057	$7789	(19-Dec-90 LD.P146) Philippe et Alexandre (125x218cm-49x86in) (F.FR 40000)
£4059	$7185	(5-Apr-91 DAR.P61/R) Le Grand Canal a Venise, et le pont du Rialto (66x84cm-26x33in) (F.FR 41000)
£4100	$7093	(20-May-91 SWS164/R) A mediterranean port scene with a shipyard (70x126cm-28x50in)
£4124	$8000	(6-Dec-90 FA.PH657/R) Bay of Naples (74x89cm-29x35in) indist.s.verso
£4200	$7224	(17-May-91 C237/R) Italian peasant girl gathering flowers (21x13cm-8x5in) indist.init. panel
£4500	$7380	(18-Jun-91 PH170/R) Awaiting the bride, Venice (45x68cm-18x27in) indis.s.i.
£5200	$10244	(4-Oct-90 CSK235/R) A wooded landscape with figures on a path and lake beyond (99x137cm-39x54in)
£5641	$11000	(11-Oct-90 SY.NY184/R) Fruits and flowers scattered in landscape (92x136cm-36x54in)
£5800	$11136	(27-Nov-90 PH181/R) The Doge's Palace, Venice (51x83cm-20x33in)
£6000	$10140	(16-Apr-91 PH10/R) Still life of scattered mixed fruit (28x41cm-11x16in) paper on canvas
£7274	$12585	(21-May-91 SY.MI1031) Veduta della piazzetta a Venezia con S.Maria della Salute in fondo (38x56cm-15x22in) (I.L 16000000)
£11000	$17930	(4-Jul-91 B164/R) Portrait of a peasant girl in Provincial costume (47x37cm-19x15in) oval
£906	*$1577*	*(25-Mar-91 SY.F605) Sacra Famiglia. Madonna col Bambino mixed media (I.L 2000000)*
£1095	*$1828*	*(6-Jun-91 F.M76/R) Bersaglieri (35x53cm-14x21in) mono.d.1871 W/C (I.L 2400000)*
£1474	*$2800*	*(1-Mar-91 RB.HY67/R) Napoli da Posillipo, view of coastal city with mountains and volcano (33x43cm-13x17in) i. gouache*

ITALIAN SCHOOL, 20th C
£1000	$1730	(22-May-91 CSK259) Il Redentore, Venice (53x90cm-21x35in)
£1178	$2050	(25-Mar-91 SY.F648) Donna al focolare (48x52cm-19x20in) i. panel (I.L 2600000)
£1269	$2207	(25-Mar-91 SY.F686) Nudo femminile (120x64cm-47x25in) indis.s. (I.L 2800000)
£2726	$5370	(29-Oct-90 SY.F487/R) Tavolozza (48x66cm-19x26in) s.various artists panel (I.L 6000000)

ITALIAN-DUTCH SCHOOL, 17th C
£2347	$4623	(18-Nov-90 P.V33) La decouverte de moise (F.FR 23000)
£1500	*$2445*	*(2-Jul-91 C356) Piazza with theatrical performance and groups of figures (16x26cm-6x10in) pen wash*

ITALIAN-DUTCH SCHOOL, 18th C
£3700	$7289	(31-Oct-90 S3/R) Figures resting in landscape (42x59cm-17x23in) bears sig.d.1642

ITALIAN-FLEMISH SCHOOL, 16th C
£12213	$21861	(14-Mar-91 D.V8/R) Madonna with Child in landscape (25x21cm-10x8in) copper (A.S 250000)

ITAYA, Foussa (1919-) French
£750	$1500	(6-Feb-91 D.NY47) The animal trainer (56x46cm-22x18in) s.i.
£1020	$2000	(12-Feb-91 SY.NY238/R) Rooster and chickens (46x56cm-18x22in) s.d.64
£1276	$2500	(12-Feb-91 SY.NY141/R) View of Paris (46x61cm-18x24in) s.i.

ITEN, Hans (1874-1930) Swiss/British
£2700	$4509	(22-Jul-91 SWS1148/R) Flowers of the field (54x45cm-21x18in) s.

ITTEN, Johannes (1888-1967) Swiss
£2237	*$3736*	*(6-Jun-91 HN.H435/R) Fields (30x20cm-12x8in) s.d.1956 W/C ink (DM 6600)*

ITURRIA, Ignacio de (1949-) Uruguayan
£1053	$2000	(11-Sep-90 PO.BA8) Patio (83x102cm-33x40in) s.
£4847	$9500	(20-Nov-90 CH.NY234/R) Armario (129x99cm-51x39in) s.
£5814	$10000	(15-May-91 CH.NY144/R) Armario (119x99cm-47x39in) s.d.88

ITURRINO, Francisco de (1864-1924) Spanish
£22800	$38076	(7-Jun-91 LD.P59/R) Les Flamencas (60x80cm-24x31in) s. (F.FR 228000)

IVANKOVICH, Basi (1815-1898) ?
£2000 $3900   (18-Oct-90 CSK107/R) The barque 'Achievement' signalling for a pilot (45x75cm-18x30in) s.i.d.1885

IVANOV, Alexandre (1950-) Russian
£874 $1695   (8-Dec-90 ZZ.F115/R) Le chemin de vos songes (70x75cm-28x30in) acrylic (F.FR 8500)
£1131 $2193   (8-Dec-90 ZZ.F116/R) La rencontre secrete (70x70cm-28x28in) acrylic (F.FR 11000)

IVANOW, Ivan Alexeievitch (1779-1848) Russian
£3878 $7522   (8-Dec-90 GAB.G2218/R) Les voyageurs russes (68x10cm-27x4in) s. (S.FR 9500)

IVANOWSKY, Sigismund de (1874-?) Polish
£1124 $1900   (21-Apr-91 DU.E130/R) Harem scene (74x58cm-29x23in) s.

IVANY-GRUNWALD, Bela (1867-1940) Austrian
£1058 $2074   (24-Nov-90 SA.A611/R) Children with sledge (16x26cm-6x10in) s. panel (DM 3100)
£4392 $8126   (7-Mar-91 D.V146/R) Bunch of flowers (60x50cm-24x20in) s. (A.S 90000)

IVARSON, Ivan (1900-1939) Swedish
£6033 $11824   (20-Nov-90 GO.G101/R) Garden scene with lady dressed in red by tree (33x41cm-13x16in) s. (S.KR 66000)
£7044 $13665   (4-Dec-90 BA.S222/R) Landscape (54x63cm-21x25in) s. (S.KR 76000)
£12915 $24797   (27-Nov-90 BU.S144/R) Still life of flowers (47x61cm-19x24in) s. panel (S.KR 140000)

IVES, Percy (1864-1928) American
£610 $1000   (21-Jun-91 DM.D2020/R) Boats on river (20x43cm-8x17in) s.d.1887
£762 $1250   (21-Jun-91 DM.D2002/R) Girl with violin (51x41cm-20x16in) s.d.1884

IWILL, Joseph (1850-1923) French
£684 $1300   (9-Jan-91 D.NY46) En Sologne (48x33cm-19x13in) s. l.stretcher
£809 $1400   (21-May-91 CE.NY62/R) Cottage by path at moonlight (33x48cm-13x19in) s.indist.l.
£918 $1800   (12-Feb-91 SY.NY110/R) Woman seated at the beach s. indis.l.verso
£954 $1765   (6-Mar-91 D.P37/R) La panne (70x48cm-28x19in) s.d.7bre 1890 (F.FR 9500)
£1309 $2186   (4-Jun-91 FB.M67/R) Soir sur la Meuse, Dordrecht (34x56cm-13x22in) s. (C.D 2500)
£591 $1141   (14-Dec-90 JM.P139) Le Cenotaphe ou l'Evocation (98x78cm-39x31in) s.d.1919 pastel (F.FR 5800)
£1007 $1641   (14-Jun-91 AGS.P25/R) Greve de la Mer du Nord (40x53cm-16x21in) s.d.1890 pastel (F.FR 10000)

IZANT OF CROYDON, Herbert (fl.1880-1898) British
£720 $1217   (30-Apr-91 PH105) Still life of hunting jacket, hat, whip, hunting horn and pitcher on table (31x25cm-12x10in) mono.d.87

IZQUIERDO VIVAS, Mariano (?) Spanish
£1374 $2638   (19-Feb-91 DUR.M25) Sardinera de Motrico (64x81cm-25x32in) (S.P 250000)

IZQUIERDO, Maria (1906-1950) Mexican
£45918 $90000   (19-Nov-90 SY.NY44/R) Retrato de Juan Soriano (69x59cm-27x23in) s.d.39

J C (?) ?
£1410 $2750   (26-Oct-90 SY.NY66/R) Portrait of young lady in blue (32x24cm-13x9in) init.d.1844 arched

J S (?) ?
£1900 $3515   (5-Mar-91 SWS1424) Sleeping baby (73cm-29ins circular) mono. canvas on board

JA RHEE, Seund (1918-) ?
£1775 $3497   (1-Oct-90 CC.P216) Composition, jaune (46x55cm-18x22in) s.d.1961 (F.FR 18000)

JAAKOLA, Alpo (1929-) Finnish
£1295 $2499   (15-Dec-90 BU.H82/R) Sight in snow-drift (66x68cm-26x27in) s.d.70 (F.M 9000)
£2131 $3814   (14-Apr-91 BU.H35/R) Woman and bird (110x55cm-43x22in) s.d.1975 (F.M 15000)

JACK, Kenneth (1924-) Australian
£814 $1376   (16-Apr-91 J.M33/R) Farm buildings, Malmsbury (40x50cm-16x20in) s. board (A.D 1800)
£1131 $1912   (16-Apr-91 J.M68/R) Exhbition Gardens, Melbourne (36x46cm-14x18in) s.d.1953 tempera board (A.D 2500)
£1600 $3104   (6-Dec-90 CSK85/R) Old hotel (60x89cm-24x35in) s.d.1957 masonite
£1357 $2294   (16-Apr-91 J.M183/R) Strathalbyn (36x54cm-14x21in) s.d.1988 W/C (A.D 3000)

JACK, Kenneth (1924-) Australian-cont.
£1434 $2825   (31-Oct-90 CH.S188) Between showers (49x72cm-19x28in) s.d.1984 gouache
                (A.D 3600)
£2602 $4397   (16-Apr-91 J.M227/R) Karratta House, Robe (60x100cm-24x39in) s.d.1976
                W/C (A.D 5750)

JACKEL, Karl Heinrich (19th C) German
£4556 $7746   (28-May-91 F.R134/R) Veduta del Lago di Como (58x44cm-23x17in) s.
                (I.L 10000000)

JACKMAN, Oscar Theodore (1878-1940) American
£710 $1200   (1-May-91 B.SF5280/R) Lost lands (76x102cm-30x40in) s.

JACKMAN, Theodore (20th C) Australian
£798 $1500   (19-Sep-90 B.SF2849/R) Lost lands (76x102cm-30x40in) s.

JACKS, Robert (1943-) Australian
£2243 $3656   (16-Jun-91 SY.ME63/R) Midwinter spring is its own season
                (155x141cm-61x56in) s.d.65 oil pencil canvas (A.D 4800)

JACKSON, A Y (1882-1974) Canadian
£3289 $6480   (30-Oct-90 MA.V107) Split Rock Islands, Georgian Bay (25x33cm-10x13in)
                s. (C.D 7500)
£3289 $6480   (30-Oct-90 MA.V105) Muskoka Farm (25x33cm-10x13in) s.d.1954verso panel
                (C.D 7500)

JACKSON, Alexander Young (1882-1974) Canadian
£942 $1574   (3-Jun-91 R.T140/R) Rolling hills, Woodbridge (26x34cm-10x13in) s.
                i.verso panel (C.D 1800)
£1140 $2235   (20-Nov-90 JOY.T390/R) Rocky shoreline, Georgian Bay (26x34cm-10x13in)
                panel (C.D 2600)
£1404 $2751   (20-Nov-90 JOY.T412/R) Georgian Bay (26x34cm-10x13in) s. panel
                (C.D 3200)
£1491 $2923   (20-Nov-90 JOY.T227/R) Onward ranch (26x34cm-10x13in) s. panel
                (C.D 3400)
£1514 $2467   (10-Jun-91 W.T1053/R) French countryside (16x22cm-6x9in) s. board
                (C.D 2800)
£1842 $3611   (20-Nov-90 JOY.T409/R) Depleted iron mine, Knob Lake, Labrador
                (26x34cm-10x13in) s. panel (C.D 4200)
£1974 $3888   (30-Oct-90 SY.T8/R) Manotick, Ont (27x34cm-11x13in) s. i.verso panel
                (C.D 4500)
£2018 $3954   (20-Nov-90 JOY.T285/R) South Pine from Split Rock, Go Home Bay
                (26x34cm-10x13in) s. panel (C.D 4600)
£2193 $4298   (20-Nov-90 JOY.T248/R) Chief mountain (26x34cm-10x13in) s. panel
                (C.D 5000)
£2193 $4298   (21-Nov-90 EA.M646) Summer house, Michipicoten (27x34cm-11x13in) s.
                panel (C.D 5000)
£2303 $4536   (30-Oct-90 SY.T85/R) Autumn landscape with stream (27x34cm-11x13in) s.
                panel (C.D 5250)
£2487 $4153   (3-Jun-91 R.T145/R) Springtime, Penetang (21x27cm-8x11in) s. s.i.d.1928
                verso panel (C.D 4750)
£2522 $4968   (30-Oct-90 SY.T67 a) Maple and birches, Combermere (26x34cm-10x13in) s.
                s.i.d.1960verso panel (C.D 5750)
£2577 $4381   (27-May-91 HO.ED324/R) Springtime, Palgrave, Ont. (27x34cm-11x13in) s.
                s.i.verso panel (C.D 5000)
£2620 $5162   (12-Nov-90 HO.ED311/R) Bathurst inlet, Aug 27, 1959 (27x34cm-11x13in)
                s.i.d. panel (C.D 6000)
£2632 $5158   (20-Nov-90 JOY.T320/R) April thaw, Poltimore, Quebec (26x34cm-10x13in)
                s. panel (C.D 6000)
£2643 $5154   (24-Oct-90 EA.M589/R) Brome Mountain (18x25cm-7x10in) s. panel double
                sided (C.D 6000)
£2652 $4587   (6-May-91 SY.T162/R) Old courtyard, St. Malo (18x23cm-7x9in) s. d.1911
                verso panel (C.D 5250)
£2703 $4405   (10-Jun-91 W.T1079/R) Split rock (25x33cm-10x13in) s. board (C.D 5000)
£2827 $4721   (3-Jun-91 R.T139/R) Huron Bay, Lake Superior (27x35cm-11x14in) s.
                s.d.1962 verso panel (C.D 5400)
£2851 $5616   (30-Oct-90 SY.T100/R) Little lake near Port Radium (27x34cm-11x13in) s.
                i.verso panel (C.D 6500)
£3015 $5216   (22-May-91 EA.M514 a/R) Onward ranch (26x34cm-10x13in) s. d.1949 verso
                panel (C.D 6000)
£3057 $5991   (5-Nov-90 FB.M41/R) Fishermen's shacks, Gaspe (24x34cm-9x13in) s.verso
                board (C.D 7000)
£3070 $6018   (20-Nov-90 JOY.T298/R) Great Slave Lake, Yellowknife, N.W.T
                (26x34cm-10x13in) s. panel (C.D 7000)
£3077 $5169   (17-Jul-91 EA.M698/R) Early spring, Christieville, Quebec
                (27x34cm-11x13in) s.d.1957 verso panel (C.D 6000)
£3153 $6054   (20-Feb-91 EA.M486 a) Fields near Danford Lake (25x33cm-10x13in)
                s.d.1948 panel (C.D 7000)
£3157 $5461   (6-May-91 SY.T62/R) Gatineau farm (26x34cm-10x13in) s. s.d.1948 verso
                panel (C.D 6250)
£3283 $5679   (6-May-91 SY.T137/R) Agawa River, Algoma (27x34cm-11x13in) s. s.i.d.1955
                verso panel (C.D 6500)
£3493 $6882   (12-Nov-90 HO.ED123/R) Chukuni river, Red Lake (26x34cm-10x13in) s.i.d.
                panel (C.D 8000)
£3509 $6877   (20-Nov-90 JOY.T150/R) Village by river, winter (21x26cm-8x10in) panel
                (C.D 8000)

JACKSON, Alexander Young (1882-1974) Canadian-cont.

£3535	$6081	(14-May-91 JOY.T21/R) Indian village near Kamloops (29x37cm-11x15in) s. panel (C.D 7000)
£3788	$6553	(6-May-91 SY.T64/R) Frozen lake (21x27cm-8x11in) s.d.20 s.verso panel (C.D 7500)
£3812	$7357	(12-Dec-90 EA.M704) Devils Warehouse Island, Lake Superior (25x33cm-10x13in) s. s.d.1965 verso panel (C.D 8500)
£3866	$6572	(27-May-91 HO.ED120/R) Early spring, Georgian Bay (21x27cm-8x11in) s. s.i.verso panel (C.D 7500)
£3947	$7737	(20-Nov-90 JOY.T257/R) Chaudiere river (21x26cm-8x10in) s. panel (C.D 9000)
£4255	$6979	(19-Jun-91 EA.M699) Beaver Lake, Eganville, Ont. (25x33cm-10x13in) s. i.d.1964verso (C.D 8000)
£4293	$7427	(6-May-91 SY.T179/R) Landscape (40x49cm-16x19in) s. board (C.D 8500)
£4386	$8596	(20-Nov-90 JOY.T138/R) Sub-Arctic landscape (40x50cm-16x20in) s. (C.D 10000)
£4386	$8596	(20-Nov-90 JOY.T189/R) Kananiskis (40x51cm-16x20in) s. (C.D 10000)
£5263	$10316	(20-Nov-90 JOY.T3/R) St. Urbain, Quebec, 1933 (21x26cm-8x10in) s. panel (C.D 12000)
£6061	$10424	(14-May-91 JOY.T57/R) The Road to Baie St. Paul (21x26cm-8x10in) s. panel (C.D 12000)
£6566	$11359	(6-May-91 SY.T40/R) Autumn landscape with lake (22x27cm-9x11in) s. s.i.verso panel (C.D 13000)
£6696	$12857	(27-Nov-90 W.T869/R) Sugar Bush, St Tite des Caps. Lakeside house in winter (22x27cm-9x11in) s. i.verso board double-sided (C.D 15000)
£8081	$13980	(6-May-91 SY.T124/R) Street in Quebec (22x27cm-9x11in) s. panel (C.D 16000)
£52632	$103158	(20-Nov-90 JOY.T85/R) St. Agnes, Quebec, winter (52x65cm-20x26in) s. (C.D 120000)
£1053	*$2063*	*(20-Nov-90 JOY.T435/R) Coast near Eric Point, Baffin. Coast near Pond inlet (20x28cm-8x11in) s.d.1930 pencil double-sided (C.D 2400)*

JACKSON, Carlyle (1891-1940) Australian

£633	$1071	(16-Apr-91 J.M107) Beach scene (21x48cm-8x19in) s. board (A.D 1400)
£1048	$1876	(9-Apr-91 CH.ME348/R) Boat at dock (53x42cm-21x17in) s. (A.D 2400)
£452	*$765*	*(16-Apr-91 J.M143) Autumn poplars (36x45cm-14x18in) s. W/C (A.D 1000)*
£633	*$1071*	*(16-Apr-91 J.M416) Kiewa Valley river (33x45cm-13x18in) s. W/C (A.D 1400)*
£803	*$1542*	*(26-Nov-90 SY.ME28/R) River scene with sailing ship (40x46cm-16x18in) s. W/C (A.D 2000)*

JACKSON, E M (?-1934) American

| £2059 | $3500 | (1-Jun-91 IH.NY183/R) Soda Jerk's Gal (61x43cm-24x17in) s. |

JACKSON, Frederick William (1859-1918) British

£1000	$1970	(15-Nov-90 JH.M1132/R) On sands, Tangier, 1921 (25x33cm-10x13in) s. panel
£1050	$1775	(1-May-91 PHL195/R) Covered market at Tunis (39x31cm-15x12in) s. board
£700	*$1400*	*(8-Feb-91 C94/R) A Bazaar in Tangier (25x36cm-10x14in) s. i. verso pencil W/C bodycol.*

JACKSON, G (19th C) British

| £1000 | $1850 | (7-Mar-91 CSK121) Cattle, horses and pigs in farmyard (51x71cm-20x28in) s.d.1860 |
| £1750 | $3098 | (20-Mar-91 EDD327) Farmyard scene (69x89cm-27x35in) s.d.1836 |

JACKSON, Gilbert (circle) (17th C) British

| £6200 | $11098 | (12-Apr-91 C3/R) Portrait of young girl, Arabella Astry, in dress and lace-trimmed cap, black page by side (66x58cm-26x23in) i.verso |

JACKSON, H (20th C?) British

| £780 | $1334 | (30-Jul-91 SWS31) Poultry in a barn (23x33cm-9x13in) s. board |
| £800 | $1520 | (28-Feb-91 LE326) Domestic fowl in barn interior (8x15cm-3x6in) board pair |

JACKSON, James Ranalph (1886-1975) Australian

£1038	$1692	(1-Jul-91 AAA.S102) Sandhills at Botany Bay (29x39cm-11x15in) s. board (A.D 2200)
£1244	$2340	(17-Sep-90 MGS.S227) Dorrigo district (34x43cm-13x17in) s. (A.D 2800)
£1267	$2141	(15-Apr-91 AAA.S92) Dorrigo landscape (29x37cm-11x15in) s. (A.D 2800)
£1389	$2333	(16-Jul-91 JRL.S268) Narrabeen lakes (29x39cm-11x15in) s. board (A.D 3000)
£1928	$3701	(26-Nov-90 SY.ME300/R) Hill scene with houses (29x37cm-11x15in) s.d.59 board (A.D 4800)
£2191	$4317	(31-Oct-90 CH.S52/R) Autumn afternoon, Middle Harbour (18x44cm-7x17in) s. board (A.D 5500)
£2715	$4588	(15-Apr-91 AAA.S111) Old fishing village (38x45cm-15x18in) s. board (A.D 6000)
£2889	$5431	(17-Sep-90 SY.ME58/R) Summer landscape (54x45cm-21x18in) s. (A.D 6500)
£3167	$5353	(15-Apr-91 AAA.S107) Beach scene (44x54cm-17x21in) s. (A.D 7000)
£3668	$7226	(13-Nov-90 J.M40/R) Drying sails, Venice (44x53cm-17x21in) s. (A.D 9500)
£5581	$9377	(22-Apr-91 SY.ME312/R) Picnic, Sydney harbour (32x42cm-13x17in) s. canvas on board (A.D 12000)
£5581	$9377	(22-Apr-91 SY.ME361/R) Drying sails, Venice (43x53cm-17x21in) s. i.stretcher (A.D 12000)

968

JACKSON, James Ranalph (1886-1975) Australian-cont.
£6426	$12337	(26-Nov-90 SY.ME208/R) Sydney harbour from Cremorne (21x61cm-8x24in) s. board (A.D 16000)
£8017	$15392	(14-Aug-90 SY.ME217/R) Autumn, middle harbour, New South Wales (32x75cm-13x30in) s.d.'25 i. label verso (A.D 19000)
£11111	$18667	(16-Jul-91 JRL.S273/R) Halcyon days (73x88cm-29x35in) s. canvas under glass (A.D 24000)

JACKSON, John (1778-1831) British
£950	$1872	(31-Oct-90 S300/R) Portrait of young child with spaniel (74x61cm-29x24in)

JACKSON, M W (20th C) British?
£720	$1217	(15-Apr-91 WW8/R) Portrait of seated lady (81x71cm-32x28in) s.d.1923 board

JACKSON, Ronald (?) Canadian?
£588	$1041	(20-Mar-91 MA.V212) North of Pearse Island (51x61cm-20x24in) s. panel (C.D 1200)

JACKSON, Samuel (1794-1869) British
£610	*$1025*	*(18-Jul-91 PHX274/R) Country folk stacking hayrick with extensive landscape beyond (18x38cm-7x15in) i.mount W/C pencil*

JACKSON, Samuel Phillips (1830-1904) British
£2100	$3990	(10-Jan-91 B143) Estuary scene (35x52cm-14x20in) s.d.1854
£700	$1330	(11-Sep-90 RG2711) Flamborough Head (30x56cm-12x22in) s. W/C
£850	$1573	(5-Mar-91 AG222) Temple Goring near waterfall (30x49cm-12x19in) s.i.label verso W/C
£1200	$2280	(12-Sep-90 CSK193/R) Dutch fishing boats on Filey Beach - moonrise (46x61cm-18x24in) s.d.1865 s.i.num.5 verso pencil W/C htd white
£1400	$2660	(12-Sep-90 CSK192/R) Filey Brigg, sunset (56x84cm-22x33in) s.d.1863 s.i.d.1863 verso pencil W/C htd white
£1500	$3000	(8-Feb-91 C48/R) A Thames backwater (20x33cm-8x13in) s. i. verso W/C htd.white
£4000	$6800	(30-May-91 C29/R) Stormy weather, Whitby (80x129cm-31x51in) s.d.1863 s.i.d.1863 verso W/C bodycol htd white

JACOB, Alexandre (1876-?) French
£800	$1568	(23-Jan-91 ZZ.B18) Valee du Cher, France (43x37cm-17x15in) s. board
£982	$1600	(12-Jun-91 SY.NY135) Neige et soleil (38x46cm-15x18in) s. s.indist.i.verso masonite
£1411	$2300	(12-Jun-91 SY.NY131/R) Sur le marais pres d'Amiens - somme (54x66cm-21x26in) s.
£1656	$2700	(12-Jun-91 SY.NY134/R) Le Gue du Marais -Somme (53x65cm-21x26in) s.
£1994	$3250	(12-Jun-91 SY.NY132/R) Brume sur les marecages - Seine et Marne (81x65cm-32x26in) s.
£4200	$7014	(3-Jun-91 PHB34/R) Neige et soleil (77x130cm-30x51in) s. i.verso

JACOB, Alexandre A (?) ?
£1050	$2100	(10-Feb-91 LIT.L41) Watering horses (51x117cm-20x46in) s.
£1071	$2100	(27-Jan-91 LIT.L22a) Watering horses (51x117cm-20x46in) s.

JACOB, Julius (younger) (1842-1929) German
£574	$976	(31-May-91 GB.B5817) Landscape with stream beneath dark sky (17x28cm-7x11in) panel (DM 1700)
£979	$1899	(7-Dec-90 GB.B5890/R) Promenade in Misdroy (37x50cm-15x20in) s.d.1874 board (DM 2800)

JACOB, Max (1876-1944) French
£610	$1154	(25-Sep-90 FB.P301) Saut d'obstacle (19x28cm-7x11in) s.i. Indian ink (F.FR 6000)
£1526	$2884	(25-Sep-90 FB.P303/R) Vue de village (22x30cm-9x12in) s. W/C (F.FR 15000)
£3052	$5768	(25-Sep-90 FB.P300/R) Rue animee (29x42cm-11x17in) s. gouache W/C (F.FR 30000)

JACOBBER, Moise (1786-1863) French
£615	$1200	(26-Oct-90 SY.NY62/R) Study of pears (11x14cm-4x6in) W/C painted oval

JACOBEY, Karoly (1825-1891) Hungarian
£1007	$1963	(10-Oct-90 WE.MU264/R) Leda with swan (63x79cm-25x31in) s.i.d.1861 (DM 3000)

JACOBI, Marcus (1891-1969) Swiss
£898	$1742	(8-Dec-90 GAB.G2682/R) Lac de Thoune (70x85cm-28x33in) s.d.1939 (S.FR 2200)

JACOBI, Otto Reinhard (1812-1901) German/Canadian
£608	$1034	(28-May-91 KF.M177) View of chapel in Alpine landscape (28x21cm-11x8in) mono.d.1842 panel (DM 1800)
£877	$1719	(20-Nov-90 JOY.T291/R) Family by lake (32x27cm-13x11in) s.d.1876 (C.D 2000)
£1414	$2432	(14-May-91 JOY.T84/R) Waterfall (35x50cm-14x20in) s.d.1884 (C.D 2800)

JACOBS, Francois (19th C) ?
£2041 $3286   (26-Jun-91 KM.K1510/R) Girl with goldfish bowl, flowers and fruit
          (65x53cm-26x21in) s. board (DM 6000)

JACOBS, Gerard (1865-1958) Belgian
£675 $1309   (4-Dec-90 C.A200/R) A warm summer's day in Land van Waas
          (75x60cm-30x24in) s. (B.FR 40000)

JACOBS, P E (1802-1866) German
£2543 $4807   (30-Sep-90 FE.P171) Cour de ferme animee (46x33cm-18x13in) s.
          (F.FR 25000)

JACOBSEN, Antonio (1850-1921) American
£781 $1500   (28-Nov-90 D.NY57) Young America (41x61cm-16x24in) s.d.1916 i.verso
          board
£1531 $3000   (24-Nov-90 RB.HY160/R) Sailing ship in sunset sky (76x56cm-30x22in)
          s.d.1912 board
£1546 $3000   (5-Dec-90 D.NY33/R) Clipper ship in stormy seas (30x46cm-12x18in)
          s.d.1904 board
£1557 $3021   (22-Aug-90 RAS.K110/R) Vessel in rough seas (56x90cm-22x35in) s.i.
          (D.KR 18000)
£2500 $4275   (29-Jul-91 HS291/R) Steam yacht City of Birmingham (55x90cm-22x35in)
          s.d.1897
£2551 $5000   (26-Jan-91 CH.NY215/R) Breecher's Buoy rescue, Gate City
          (56x91cm-22x36in) s.d.1903
£2700 $4698   (26-Mar-91 PH97) The Ocean king (56x92cm-22x36in) s.i.d.1884
£3232 $6366   (14-Nov-90 RAS.K72/R) Ships portrait of 'Norge' from Tingvalla Line
          (55x90cm-22x35in) s.d.1896 (D.KR 36000)
£3300 $5907   (11-Apr-91 MO424) The steamship, Devon (56x91cm-22x36in) s.d.'97
£3448 $6000   (29-Mar-91 E.EDM175/R) American clipper ship Dreadnought
          (33x53cm-13x21in) s.d.1917 board
£3457 $6500   (7-Aug-90 RB.HY136) The 'Advance' at sea (56x91cm-22x36in) s.d.1885
£3550 $6000   (17-Apr-91 D.NY38/R) British steam yacht on high seas (46x76cm-18x30in)
          s.i.d.1886
£3571 $7000   (24-Nov-90 RB.HY130/R) Clipper ship Flying Cloud (43x64cm-17x25in)
          s.d.1916 board
£3571 $7000   (24-Nov-90 RB.HY121/R) City of Chester steaming through steep ocean seas
          (36x56cm-14x22in) s.i.d.1877
£3906 $7500   (29-Nov-90 MFA.C239/R) Salisbury (71x127cm-28x50in) s.d.1915
£4000 $7800   (18-Oct-90 CSK168/R) S.S.Momus (54x91cm-21x36in) s.i.d.1911 board
£4124 $8000   (5-Dec-90 D.NY37/R) The steamship Holland (51x86cm-20x34in) s.i.d.1879
          canvas on board
£4200 $7266   (22-May-91 S93/R) Steamship August Ander (56x91cm-22x36in) s.i.d.1877
£4400 $7216   (19-Jun-91 S253/R) Danish steamship (47x90cm-19x35in) s.i.d.1915 board
£4592 $9000   (24-Nov-90 RB.HY152/R) Steamship Manhattan steaming through calm water
          with figures on deck (56x91cm-22x36in) s.i.d.1895
£4592 $9000   (24-Nov-90 RB.HY50/R) French liner SS La Champagne steaming through
          rough ocean seas (56x91cm-22x36in) s.i.d.1889
£4694 $9200   (16-Feb-91 W.W50/R) The Jamestown (56x91cm-22x36in) s.i.d.1894
£4787 $9000   (7-Aug-90 RB.HY125/R) Steamship 'H.F.Dimock' departing New York
          (51x86cm-20x34in) s.d.May 1885
£4800 $8160   (30-May-91 C122/R) S.S. Devon (56x91cm-22x36in) s.i.d.79
£4800 $8160   (30-May-91 C120/R) County of Edinburgh aground in 1902 (46x77cm-18x30in)
          with sig. d.1902
£4800 $9360   (18-Oct-90 CSK169/R) S.S.Dunholme (56x91cm-22x36in) s.i.d.1887
£4800 $8160   (30-May-91 C121/R) S.S. Jamestown (56x96cm-22x38in) s.i.d.1895
£4800 $9500   (17-Dec-90 SY.NY20/R) Catania (56x91cm-22x36in) s.i.d.1894
£4948 $8650   (22-May-91 S94/R) Steamship Daniel Steinmann (56x91cm-22x36in)
          s.i.d.1877
£5102 $10000   (24-Nov-90 RB.HY112/R) Portrait of French steamship Lahn under way at
          sea (56x91cm-22x36in) s.i.d.1890
£5208 $10000   (17-Dec-90 SY.NY19/R) Pronz Albert (56x91cm-22x36in) s.i.d.1897
£5357 $10500   (24-Nov-90 RB.HY140/R) Steamer Larchmont with figures on decks
          (56x91cm-22x36in) s.i.d.1902
£5357 $10500   (16-Feb-91 W.W82/R) The four-masted schooner E Starr Jones
          (56x91cm-22x36in) s.i.d.1910 board
£6000 $11280   (8-Aug-90 PHP170/R) 'S.S.Mississippi' in open sea (56x92cm-22x36in)
          s.d.1896 sold with items relating to First Mate
£6000 $11700   (18-Oct-90 CSK167/R) The Cunard Liner 'Mauretania' (53x91cm-21x36in)
          s.i.d.1909 board
£6122 $12000   (24-Nov-90 RB.HY40/R) Pilot boat New York meeting steamship St Louis
          (56x91cm-22x36in) s.i.d.1898
£6383 $12000   (7-Aug-90 RB.HY170/R) Portrait of the 'Belmont' at sea (51x91cm-20x36in)
          s.d.1919 pasteboard
£6383 $12000   (7-Aug-90 RB.HY98/R) Portrait of the steam/sail ship 'Caracas'
          (56x91cm-22x36in) s.d.1892
£6500 $13000   (7-Feb-91 B.P105 c/R) Sidewheeler Portland (56x91cm-22x36in) s.d.1891
£6771 $13000   (30-Nov-90 CH.NY82/R) Storm King (56x91cm-22x36in) s.i.d.1894
£6888 $13500   (24-Nov-90 RB.HY80/R) Portrait of American steamship New York
          (127x76cm-50x30in) s.i.d.1908
£6977 $12000   (18-May-91 W.W103/R) The Minnie Swift (56x91cm-22x36in) s.i.d.186
£7292 $14000   (29-Nov-90 MFA.C248) 4 master (56x91cm-22x36in) s.
£7821 $14000   (10-Apr-91 HF.NY35/R) Sultana (56x90cm-22x35in) s.i.d.1906
£8284 $14000   (17-Apr-91 D.NY39/R) Tug Ivanhoe (91x56cm-36x22in) s.i.d.1886
£8418 $16500   (24-Nov-90 RB.HY90/R) City of Kingston steaming through choppy seas
          (56x91cm-22x36in) s.i.d.1889

JACOBSEN, Antonio (1850-1921) American-cont.

£8673	$17000	(24-Nov-90 RB.HY60/R) Steam tug May McGuirl Shamrock Towing Line steaming out to sea (53x89cm-21x35in) s.i.d.1911 panel
£9694	$19000	(24-Nov-90 RB.HY70/R) Paddle steamer Shelter Island sailing off the coast of Long Island (56x91cm-22x36in) s.i.d.1890
£12834	$24000	(1-Aug-90 B.P1/R) Horatio Hall in New York (89x180cm-35x71in) s.d.1898
£13830	$26000	(7-Aug-90 RB.HY120/R) 'City of Rome' (76x152cm-30x60in) s.d.1881
£17000	$33150	(18-Oct-90 CSK165/R) The Grand Banks fishing schooner 'Albertina' (56x91cm-22x36in) s.d.1906

JACOBSEN, Antonio (style) (1850-1921) American

| £3906 | $7500 | (28-Nov-90 D.NY58/R) New York Harbour (69x114cm-27x45in) bears sig.i.d.1909 board |

JACOBSEN, August (1868-?) Norwegian

| £1345 | $2247 | (4-Jun-91 BU.O17/R) Landscape (35x50cm-14x20in) init. (N.KR 15500) |

JACOBSEN, David (1821-1871) Danish

| £952 | $1846 | (22-Aug-90 RAS.K254/R) Young negress carrying tray with glasses and champagne (32x24cm-13x9in) s.i. (D.KR 11000) |

JACOBSEN, Egill (1910-) Danish

£1228	$2088	(28-May-91 BU.K25/R) Mask (42x32cm-17x13in) init.d.85 acrylic paper (D.KR 14000)
£4025	$7889	(13-Feb-91 KH.K81/R) Yellow masks (46x65cm-18x26in) (D.KR 45000)
£4039	$7958	(14-Nov-90 KH.K69/R) Green masks (46x65cm-18x26in) (D.KR 45000)
£4386	$7456	(29-May-91 KH.K48/R) Composition (72x57cm-28x22in) init.d.65 (D.KR 50000)
£4505	$7793	(23-May-91 SY.AM340/R) Private eye (100x74cm-39x29in) s.d.86verso (D.FL 15000)
£5338	$10036	(19-Sep-90 KH.K33/R) Picture of masks (46x65cm-18x26in) (D.KR 60000)
£6140	$10439	(29-May-91 KH.K45/R) Masks in wood (42x65cm-17x26in) init.d.69verso (D.KR 70000)
£6579	$11184	(29-May-91 KH.K75/R) Green in red room (100x73cm-39x29in) init.d.81verso (D.KR 75000)
£6602	$12874	(10-Oct-90 RAS.K82/R) Green mask (65x46cm-26x18in) init.i.d.57verso (D.KR 75000)
£6919	$13284	(27-Nov-90 BU.S147/R) Green in a red room (100x73cm-39x29in) init.d.1981verso (S.KR 75000)
£8036	$14866	(5-Mar-91 RAS.K14/R) 'Savanne' (100x75cm-39x30in) init.d.72verso (D.KR 90000)
£8036	$14866	(5-Mar-91 RAS.K16/R) Green mask (100x75cm-39x30in) init.d.1964 (D.KR 90000)
£10772	$21221	(14-Nov-90 KH.K68/R) Composition with masks (100x75cm-39x30in) init.d.65verso (D.KR 120000)
£11566	$21744	(19-Sep-90 KH.K57/R) Composition (47x63cm-19x25in) init.d.47verso (D.KR 130000)
£13417	$26297	(13-Feb-91 KH.K80/R) Green mask (100x73cm-39x29in) (D.KR 150000)
£14912	$25351	(29-May-91 KH.K78/R) Composition - 21 games in blue and green (97x116cm-38x46in) init.d.85verso (D.KR 170000)
£20433	$39437	(13-Dec-90 SY.AM212/R) Untitled (131x95cm-52x37in) double-sided (D.FL 66000)
£22809	$44705	(13-Feb-91 KH.K79/R) Mask composition (100x75cm-39x30in) (D.KR 255000)
£28000	$49560	(21-Mar-91 S28/R) Composition (100x72cm-39x28in) init.d.1939 verso
£28470	$53523	(19-Sep-90 KH.K14/R) Green masks (114x146cm-45x57in) init.verso (D.KR 320000)
£32456	$55175	(29-May-91 KH.K25/R) Bird person (130x90cm-51x35in) init.verso (D.KR 370000)
£1429	$2643	(5-Mar-91 RAS.K15) Yellow mask (55x40cm-22x16in) init.d.1981 crayon W/C (D.KR 16000)
£1540	$2972	(12-Dec-90 RAS.K68/R) Composition with red mask (50x40cm-20x16in) init.d.81 gouache W/C (D.KR 17000)
£2321	$4295	(5-Mar-91 RAS.K37/R) Yellow mask (74x54cm-29x21in) s.i.d.78 gouache w/C (D.KR 26000)

JACOBSEN, Frederick Wilhelm (1878-1948) Norwegian

| £1576 | $2821 | (11-Mar-91 B.O56/R) Street workers (140x100cm-55x39in) init.d.XXV (N.KR 18000) |

JACOBSEN, Hanne Elise (1814-1881) Danish

| £1498 | $2501 | (6-Jun-91 RAS.K164/R) Basket of flowers on stone with grapes (33x35cm-13x14in) s.d.1834 (D.KR 17000) |

JACOBSEN, Ludvig (1890-1975) Danish

| £1137 | $2036 | (9-Apr-91 RAS.K2079/R) Nana - young girl straightening her stockings with gentleman watching (67x56cm-26x22in) s.d.32 (D.KR 13000) |

JACOBSEN, Robert (1912-) Danish

£313	$614	(13-Feb-91 KH.K82/R) Composition (25x23cm-10x9in) mono. Indian ink (D.KR 3500)
£440	$757	(15-May-91 RAS.K3) Composition in red, yellow and blue (20x27cm-8x11in) s. Indian ink col chk (D.KR 5000)
£572	$1116	(10-Oct-90 RAS.K102) Composition (25x32cm-10x13in) s. Indian ink crayon (D.KR 6500)
£625	$1156	(5-Mar-91 RAS.K120/R) Composition (62x47cm-24x19in) s. gouache W/C (D.KR 7000)

JACOBSEN, Robert (1912-) Danish-cont.

£702	$1193	(29-May-91 KH.K260/R) Composition (95x70cm-37x28in) s. W/C Indian ink (D.KR 8000)
£718	$1415	(14-Nov-90 KH.K71) Composition (35x46cm-14x18in) init.d.49 Indian ink (D.KR 8000)
£862	$1655	(28-Nov-90 KF.M898/R) Composition with vertical line (17x23cm-7x9in) s.c.1970 mixed media board (DM 2500)
£864	$1693	(22-Nov-90 RAS.V830/R) Composition (64x48cm-25x19in) s. gouache (D.KR 9700)
£965	$1640	(29-May-91 KH.K261) Composition (50x78cm-20x31in) init. collage Indian ink (D.KR 11000)
£1009	$1715	(29-May-91 KH.K259/R) Composition (96x65cm-38x26in) s. Indian ink (D.KR 11500)
£1423	$2676	(19-Sep-90 KH.K59) Composition (66x99cm-26x39in) s. W/C gouache (D.KR 16000)
£1529	$2967	(5-Dec-90 AB.S7117/R) Composition (64x98cm-25x39in) s. W/C collage (S.KR 16500)
£1690	$3178	(19-Sep-90 KH.K58/R) Composition (62x43cm-24x17in) s. gouache Indian ink paper on canvas (D.KR 19000)

JACOBSEN, Sophus (1833-1912) Norwegian

£600	$984	(20-Jun-91 B14) Moonlit lake scene (58x42cm-23x17in) s. panel
£1823	$3044	(3-Jun-91 B.O77/R) Moonlit landscape (39x53cm-15x21in) s.d.61 (N.KR 21000)
£2730	$5352	(24-Nov-90 SA.A644/R) Norwegian fjord landscape, summer afternoon (44x58cm-17x23in) s.d.1860 canvas laid down (DM 8000)
£3345	$5620	(23-Apr-91 RAS.K130/R) Landscape from Telemarken (74x97cm-29x38in) init.d.55 (D.KR 38000)
£4630	$8937	(12-Dec-90 BU.O31/R) Mountain landscape (48x58cm-19x23in) s.d.1889 i.verso (N.KR 52000)
£8725	$17013	(13-Oct-90 KRA.D233/R) Rising thunderstorm, Sonjefjord (98x158cm-39x62in) s.d.1889 (DM 26000)

JACOBSON, Dan (20th C) ?

£1335	$2390	(14-Apr-91 ZZ.F101/R) C'est la fin du jour (130x97cm-51x38in) (F.FR 13500)

JACOBSZ, Lambert (c.1598-1636) Dutch

£6154	$12000	(10-Oct-90 CH.NY102/R) The Good Samaritan (75x111cm-30x44in) panel

JACOBY, Valeri Ivanovitch (1836-1909) Russian

£1257	$2476	(14-Nov-90 RAS.K154/R) Oriental couple by town gate (50x37cm-20x15in) s.d.1879 (D.KR 14000)

JACOTTET, Louis (1843-?) French

£1940	$3357	(12-May-91 L.C38/R) Paysage, canal et ecrivain (72x126cm-28x50in) s.d.1866 (F.FR 19500)

JACOVACCI, Francesco (19th C) Italian

£8500	$16320	(27-Nov-90 PH185/R) The connoisseurs (60x72cm-24x28in) s.d.1869

JACOVLEFF, Alexandre (1887-1938) French?

£672	$1142	(27-May-91 GK.Z5625 a) Torso (64x49cm-25x19in) d.1919 ochre chk (S.FR 1700)

JACQUE, Charles Emile (1813-1894) French

£1056	$2049	(5-Dec-90 DO.H2246/R) Farmyard with ducks (15x22cm-6x9in) s. panel (DM 3020)
£1515	$2985	(30-Oct-90 CH.AM115/R) Poultry in barn (19x21cm-7x8in) s. panel (D.FL 5000)
£1580	$2750	(27-Mar-91 B.SF4294/R) Shepherdess with flock (17x25cm-7x10in) s. panel
£1900	$3401	(12-Mar-91 PH89) Cockerel and chickens in barn (19x32cm-7x13in) s. panel
£2396	$4599	(1-Dec-90 PER.M124/R) Devant l'ecurie (12x16cm-5x6in) s. (F.FR 23500)
£2890	$5000	(21-May-91 CE.NY27/R) Sheep grazing under tree (23x32cm-9x13in) s. panel
£3158	$6000	(28-Feb-91 CH.NY53/R) Le repos de la bergere (81x100cm-32x39in)
£3293	$5533	(23-Apr-91 SY.AM266/R) Sheep on cliff (103x141cm-41x56in) mono.d.75 (D.FL 11000)
£3486	$6031	(24-May-91 FB.P54/R) La sortie des moutons (36x27cm-14x11in) s. (F.FR 35000)
£3684	$7000	(27-Feb-91 SY.NY86/R) Feeding in barn (19x29cm-7x11in) s. panel
£4046	$7000	(21-May-91 CE.NY43/R) Chickens and ducks feeding (13x21cm-5x8in) s. panel
£5202	$9000	(22-May-91 SY.NY149/R) La rentree du laboureur (55x99cm-22x39in) s.
£8012	$14341	(12-Apr-91 AGS.P22/R) Clairiere en foret (65x98cm-26x39in) s. (F.FR 81000)
£10140	$19570	(12-Dec-90 N.M567/R) Sheep and chickens in stable interior (42x70cm-17x28in) s. panel (DM 29000)
£10616	$19003	(13-Mar-91 N.M538/R) Shepherd with flock on wood clearing (81x65cm-32x26in) s. (DM 31000)
£11945	$22457	(19-Sep-90 N.M535/R) Shepherd and flock in wooded landscape (81x65cm-32x26in) s. (DM 35000)
£13873	$24000	(23-May-91 CH.NY233/R) Leaving the stall, morning (55x46cm-22x18in) s. s.d.1878verso
£20513	$40000	(23-Oct-90 SY.NY19/R) Homeward bound (71x100cm-28x39in) s.
£574	$1016	(5-Apr-91 LGB.P112) Coq et poule (2x2cm-1x1in) init. gouache octagonal (F.FR 5800)

JACQUE, Charles Emile (1813-1894) French-cont.
| £653 | $1207 | (4-Mar-91 ARC.P12) La semeuse (31x15cm-12x6in) s.d.28 Juillet 83 chl. (F.FR 6500) |
| £2708 | $5281 | (12-Oct-90 APT.P22/R) La gardeuse de moutons (81x65cm-32x26in) s.d.1892 chl.htd.white chk.paper laid on canvas (F.FR 27000) |

JACQUE, Charles Emile (attrib) (1813-1894) French
£699	$1357	(4-Dec-90 FN.S1893/R) Chicken and cockerel in barn interior (40x58cm-16x23in) s. (DM 2000)
£699	$1357	(4-Dec-90 FN.S1892/R) Chicken and cockerel in barn interior (40x58cm-16x23in) s. (DM 2000)
£769	$1500	(25-Oct-90 D.V31/R) Sheep in barn interior (22x28cm-9x11in) indis.i.verso (A.S 16000)

JACQUE, Emile (1848-1912) French
| £4587 | $8807 | (1-Dec-90 PER.M103/R) La bergerie (101x80cm-40x31in) s. (F.FR 45000) |

JACQUEMOT, Charles (1879-1946) French
| £982 | $1650 | (23-Apr-91 C.A546) Southern landscape (50x60cm-20x24in) s. (B.FR 60000) |

JACQUES, Nicolas (1780-1844) French
| £1143 | $2251 | (13-Nov-90 CH.G260) Portrait of Frederic Cuvier (11x?cm-4x?in) min.s.chased gilt-metal mount oval (S.FR 2800) |

JACQUET, Alain (20th C) French
| £5097 | $9837 | (16-Dec-90 P.V85/R) The First Breakfast (114x162cm-45x64in) s.i.d.1972-1978 verso acrylic serigraph panel (F.FR 50000) |

JACQUET, Gustave-Jean (1846-1909) French
£513	$1000	(21-Oct-90 HG.C27) Portrait of young girl (30x25cm-12x10in) s.
£1394	$2412	(24-May-91 FB.P154/R) Madame Valtesse de la Bigne (61x50cm-24x20in) s.d.1879 (F.FR 14000)
£2692	$5250	(21-Oct-90 HG.C10) Portrait of young woman (36x30cm-14x12in) s. board
£3590	$7000	(24-Oct-90 CH.NY109/R) Elegant lady with pearls (42x32cm-17x13in) s.
£5491	$9500	(22-May-91 SY.NY170/R) Portrait of young woman (56x46cm-22x18in) s.
£6897	$12000	(27-Mar-91 B.SF4100/R) La jeune beaute (61x49cm-24x19in) s.
£7500	$12300	(19-Jun-91 S185/R) Portrait of young girl with blue ribbon (32x25cm-13x10in) s. panel
£10056	$18000	(10-Apr-91 HF.NY52/R) Portrait of woman (56x46cm-22x18in) s.
£462	$800	(10-May-91 S.W2553) Landscape with brook (20x33cm-8x13in) s. W/C

JACQUET, Jules Leon Edouard (19th C) French
| £1200 | $2364 | (5-Oct-90 C54/R) Femme au chapeau noir (46x37cm-18x15in) s. panel |

JAECKEL, H (?) ?
| £728 | $1376 | (27-Sep-90 D.V168/R) Oberleutnant im Dragonerregiment Nr. 3 (68x55cm-27x22in) s.i.d.1919 (A.S 15000) |

JAECKEL, Henry (19th C) German
| £2400 | $4608 | (28-Nov-90 S182/R) View of the Isola Bella on Lake Maggiore (56x43cm-22x17in) s.d. |

JAECKEL, Henry and CALAME, Alexandre (19th C) German/Swiss
| £3500 | $6720 | (27-Nov-90 PH121/R) Alpine landscape (42x59cm-17x23in) s. canvas on panel |

JAECKEL, Willy (1888-1944) German
| £1284 | $2221 | (25-May-91 N.M153/R) Rappensee in winter (70x80cm-28x31in) s. (DM 3800) |
| £1536 | $3010 | (24-Nov-90 VG.B605/R) Buchenwald (90x120cm-35x47in) s.c.1936 canvas laid down (DM 4500) |

JAEGER, Fritz (1895-?) Austrian
| £4854 | $7961 | (20-Jun-91 D.V68/R) View from window (70x57cm-28x22in) s. i.stretcher (A.S 100000) |

JAENISCH, Hans (1907-1989) German
£1100	$1969	(12-Apr-91 BM.B989/R) Boat and dune (100x71cm-39x28in) s. tempera (DM 3300)
£1467	$2625	(12-Apr-91 BM.B988/R) Mother and child (66x70cm-26x28in) s. tempera board (DM 4400)
£1537	$2659	(21-May-91 WK.M1027 a/R) St Georg (34x42cm-13x17in) s.d.1952 oil plaster on panel (DM 4550)
£4310	$8276	(28-Nov-90 KF.M905/R) Formations s. d.1962 tempera old canvas set of four (DM 12500)
£610	$1000	(19-Jun-91 B.SF1801/R) Blue halo (23x33cm-9x13in) W/C linen
£1115	$1929	(21-May-91 WK.M1029/R) Rider (100x70cm-39x28in) s. i.d.1955verso gouache board (DM 3300)
£1689	$2922	(21-May-91 WK.M1028/R) Street (100x70cm-39x28in) s.st.studio i.d.1954 gouache W/C (DM 5000)

JAFFE, Shirley (20th C) American
| £945 | $1645 | (28-Mar-91 DAR.P23) Composition (46x33cm-18x13in) s. verso (F.FR 9500) |

JAGER, Gustav (1808-1871) German
£544 $919   *(16-Apr-91 CH.R25) Castel S.Angelo (35x40cm-14x16in) s.i.d.1907 W/C (I.L 1200000)*

JAGGER, Charles (c.1770-1827) British
£650 $1073   *(10-Jul-91 C105/R) A gentleman in blue coat with black collar (6x?cm-2x?in) min.s. gold frame oval*

JAGO, Lionel Hornabrook (1882-1953) Australian
£579 $1141   (13-Nov-90 J.M508) Sydney Streets (53x46cm-21x18in) s.d.52 board (A.D 1500)

JAHN, Gustav (1879-1919) Austrian
£345 $689   *(7-Feb-91 D.V95/R) Female nude standing (46x27cm-18x11in) s. mixed media board (A.S 7000)*
£764 $1489   *(11-Oct-90 D.V185/R) Two mountain climbers on rock (32x20cm-13x8in) i.d.1912verso chk W/C htd.white (A.S 16000)*

JAHN, Hans (1834-1902) Norwegian
£742 $1410   (11-Sep-90 UL.T228) Sunset (16x25cm-6x10in) (N.KR 8500)
£2230 $4326   (4-Dec-90 UL.T234/R) Romantic wooded lake landscape (60x90cm-24x35in) d.1867 (N.KR 25000)

JAHNS, Rudolf (1896-1983) German
£1712 $2791   (15-Jun-91 L.K332/R) Still life with bowl and vase (42x56cm-17x22in) s.d.56 s.i.d.verso panel (DM 5000)

JAKOBIDES, Georg (1853-1932) Greek
£2218 $4348   (24-Nov-90 SA.A631/R) Grandfather's pipe (45x37cm-18x15in) s.i. (DM 6500)
£2000 $3940   *(5-Oct-90 C169/R) Story book (30x26cm-12x10in) s. pencil pen*

JAKOBS, Jeanine (20th C) ?
£756 $1474   (28-Oct-90 R.P8) L'oiseau mecanique (100x81cm-39x32in) s. (F.FR 7500)
£1058 $2064   (28-Oct-90 R.P48) Boomrang (100x81cm-39x32in) s. (F.FR 10500)

JAKSTEIN, Clara (?) ?
£819 $1343   (22-Jun-91 WK.M1414/R) Amor ice skating (106x88cm-42x35in) after Anthony van Dyck (DM 2400)

JALABERT, Charles Francois (after) (1819-1901) French
£1786 $3000   (17-Jul-91 SY.NY209/R) Nymphs listening to the song of Orpheus (39x32cm-15x13in) within painted arch

JALAL, Ibrahim (20th C) ?
£711 $1423   *(7-Feb-91 R.P123) Sans titre (146x197cm-57x78in) s. mixed media canvas (F.FR 7000)*
£1067 $2134   *(7-Feb-91 R.P155) Sans titre (146x97cm-57x38in) s. mixed media canvas (F.FR 10500)*

JALLIER (?) ?
£2000 $3380   *(16-Apr-91 C232/R) Roman Capricci - Temple of Vesta. The Porta di Ripetta (29x25cm-11x10in) both s. blk.chk.ink W/C ovals two*

JAMAR, Armand (1870-1946) Belgian
£734 $1424   (4-Dec-90 FN.S1636/R) River landscape with railway bridge, evening (41x55cm-16x22in) s. board (DM 2100)
£1548 $2600   (17-Jul-91 SY.NY277/R) Harbour at twilight (70x100cm-28x39in) s.d.1911

JAMBOR, Lajos (1884-) Hungarian
£6000 $11820   (4-Oct-90 CSK126/R) Three girls relaxing in a field (99x80cm-39x31in) s.
£15000 $25200   (18-Jul-91 CSK125/R) Summer afternoon (100x75cm-39x30in) s.d.1915

JAMBOR, Louis (1884-1955) American
£1134 $2200   (5-Dec-90 D.NY38/R) Docking in the cove (66x81cm-26x32in) s.

JAMES, David (fl.1881-98) British
£582 $1100   (29-Sep-90 YFA.M43/R) Easterly breeze, a grand sea (76x127cm-30x50in) s.d.88/89 canvas on board
£893 $1714   (27-Nov-90 W.T1029) Angry surf (62x126cm-24x50in) s.d.1891 (C.D 2000)
£1000 $1680   (18-Jul-91 PHX425) Sailing boats in fresh breeze off Cornish coast (64x124cm-25x49in) s.d.1883
£1200 $2256   (18-Sep-90 CSK134/R) Land's End (76x127cm-30x50in) s.d.84
£1300 $2535   (18-Oct-90 SC3074/R) Sailing vessels offshore (36x80cm-14x31in) s.d.1882
£1400 $2688   (16-Aug-90 B347 a) Fishing boats going out, Cornwall (63x128cm-25x50in) s.d.87 s.i.d.verso
£1862 $3500   (19-Sep-90 B.SF2694/R) Seascape (128x64cm-50x25in) s.d.'90
£3000 $5190   (22-May-91 S123/R) Penzance fishing boats off coast (63x127cm-25x50in) s.d.89
£3800 $7296   (16-Aug-90 B414/R) Penzance fishing boats off coast (64x127cm-25x50in) s.d.89
£4000 $7880   (13-Nov-90 PH13 a/R) Waves breaking on rocky shoreline (76x127cm-30x50in) s.d.89
£5500 $8965   (14-Jun-91 C290/R) The breaking wave (63x127cm-25x50in) s.d.93
£17000 $28900   (30-May-91 C145/R) Inrushing tide (63x127cm-25x50in) s. s.i.d.1898

JAMES, Harry E (?) British
£780 $1513   (4-Dec-90 AG384/R) Gypsy campsite (48x73cm-19x29in) s.

JAMES, John Wells (1873-?) American
£1237 $2300   (9-Sep-90 LIT.L294) Lock keeper's house in landscape in Bucks County, Pennsylvania s.

JAMES, Louis Robert (1920-) Australian
£1004 $1978   (13-Nov-90 J.M802) Suburban backyard (28x34cm-11x13in) s.d. canvas board (A.D 2600)
£2103 $3428   (16-Jun-91 SY.ME93) Summer '78 - second version (182x153cm-72x60in) s.d.79 verso (A.D 4500)

JAMES, Rene (20th C) French
£596 $1008   (21-Apr-91 E.LA29) Honfleur - l'Hotel de Ville (65x92cm-26x36in) s. (F.FR 6000)
£1566 $3069   (17-Feb-91 E.LA12) Honfleur, le vieux port (54x65cm-21x26in) s. (F.FR 15500)

JAMES, Richard S (19th C) British
£1479 $2500   (20-Apr-91 WOL.C79/R) Only one stain (36x56cm-14x22in) board

JAMES, William (18th C) British
£19592 $38400   (6-Nov-90 GF.L2065/R) View of Canale Grande with San Geremia (70x106cm-28x42in) (S.FR 48000)
£20000 $39400   (16-Nov-90 C47/R) View on the Grand Canal, Venice (61x96cm-24x38in)
£22000 $43340   (16-Nov-90 C46/R) View of Dogana with Santa Maria della Salute and Giudecca beyond (90x141cm-35x56in)
£28000 $54040   (11-Dec-90 PH48/R) The Bucintoro returning to the Molo on Ascension Day, Venice (75x128cm-30x50in)
£58000 $114260   (14-Nov-90 S100/R) Visit of the Doge to Santa Maria della Salute, Grand Canal, Venice (91x152cm-36x60in)

JAMES, William (attrib) (18th C) British
£22000 $39380   (12-Apr-91 C52/R) Entrance to Canareggio, with Church of San Geremia and Palazzo Labia (70x105cm-28x41in)

JAMES, Willy see ROCHAT, Willy

JAMESONE, George (style) (1587-1644) British
£1200 $2400   (7-Feb-91 CSK168/R) Portrait of King James, wearing doublet, hat and badge Order of Garter (22x18cm-9x7in) painted oval panel

JAMIESON, Alexander (1873-1937) British
£520 $894   (14-May-91 SWS395) Luxembourg and garden (13x16cm-5x6in) s.i.d.1906verso panel
£620 $1066   (14-May-91 SWS392/R) The fish quai at Dieppe (13x17cm-5x7in) i.verso panel
£700 $1309   (28-Aug-90 S1009/R) Chateau Noire (33x40cm-13x16in) s.d.1911 panel
£828 $1549   (27-Aug-90 SY.J188/R) In the garden (32x39cm-13x15in) s.d.1914 board (SA.R 4000)
£900 $1548   (14-May-91 SWS396/R) Versailles park (12x16cm-5x6in) s. s.i.d.1906verso panel
£950 $1634   (14-May-91 SWS393/R) Versailles (12x17cm-5x7in) s.i.d.1907verso panel
£1300 $2535   (10-Oct-90 S27/R) On the Seine, Fontainebleau (27x32cm-11x13in) s.d.1911 s.i.verso panel
£1400 $2408   (14-May-91 SWS397/R) The tea garden (29x34cm-11x13in) indis.i.verso panel
£2000 $3740   (28-Aug-90 S940/R) Fontainebleu (32x41cm-13x16in) s.s.i.d.1911verso panel
£8000 $13360   (4-Jun-91 PH35/R) Chateau, Fontainebleau (78x126cm-31x50in)

JAMIN, Diederik Franciscus (1838-1865) Dutch
£898 $1509   (23-Apr-91 SY.AM236/R) Children in cornfield (17x20cm-7x8in) s.d.1859 panel (D.FL 3000)

JAMISON, Philip (1929-) American?
£529 $1000   (25-Sep-90 CE.NY306/R) Winter landscape (30x51cm-12x20in) s. pastel W/C board
£559 $900   (30-Jun-91 LIT.L54) Harbour scene (53x74cm-21x29in) s. W/C gouache
£587 $1050   (11-Apr-91 FA.PH994 a) Harbour shanties (53x71cm-21x28in) s. W/C
£1302 $2200   (17-Apr-91 D.NY9) Daisy Field No. 2. Wildflowers (23x48cm-9x19in) s. W/C pair

JAMOT, A (?) ?
£1173 $2312   (14-Nov-90 FB.P52/R) La promenade des Anglais (35x23cm-14x9in) s. W/C (F.FR 11500)

JAN, Elvire (1904-) French
£3262 $6296   (16-Dec-90 P.V45/R) Composition (81x65cm-32x26in) (F.FR 32000)
£4898 $9649   (16-Nov-90 FB.P44/R) Composition (60x81cm-24x32in) s.d.1959 (F.FR 48000)

JANCE, Paul Claude (1840-?) French
£3684 $7000   (27-Feb-91 SY.NY93/R) Vase of pink and white peonies in window sill (91x81cm-36x32in) s.d.1883

JANCO, Marcel (1895-1984) French

£593	$1062	(14-Apr-91 GL.P286) Bord de mer (36x47cm-14x19in) board (F.FR 6000)
£1571	$3000	(1-Jan-91 GG.TA308/R) Bord du desert (35x50cm-14x20in) s. canvas on board
£1675	$3200	(1-Jan-91 GG.TA309/R) Still life (34x49cm-13x19in) s. board
£1885	$3600	(1-Jan-91 GG.TA309 a/R) Forms (34x49cm-13x19in) s. board
£2304	$4400	(1-Jan-91 GG.TA311/R) Jardin (35x46cm-14x18in) s. canvas on board
£2356	$4500	(1-Jan-91 GG.TA307/R) Collage Dada XIX (35x50cm-14x20in) s.d.1962 canvas on board
£3077	$6000	(10-Oct-90 SY.NY303/R) Nature morte (36x51cm-14x20in) s. canvasboard
£3141	$6000	(1-Jan-91 GG.TA306/R) Forms (39x55cm-15x22in) s. canvas on board
£3289	$6380	(7-Dec-90 GL.P210/R) Paysage de Galilee (46x69cm-18x27in) s. board (F.FR 32000)
£5236	$10000	(1-Jan-91 GG.TA305/R) Don Quixote (50x70cm-20x28in) s. board
£5521	$9000	(12-Jun-91 GG.TA276/R) Forms (60x73cm-24x29in) s.
£6135	$10000	(12-Jun-91 GG.TA275/R) Cock-fight (53x73cm-21x29in) s. canvas on board
£7055	$11500	(12-Jun-91 GG.TA274/R) Mount Tabor (48x68cm-19x27in) s. paper
£8377	$16000	(1-Jan-91 GG.TA304/R) Composition nouvelle Dada (53x72cm-21x28in) s.d.1951
£10736	$17500	(12-Jun-91 GG.TA273/R) Expulsion from Tranistria (48x68cm-19x27in) s. paper
£14724	$24000	(12-Jun-91 GG.TA272/R) Don Quixote (63x92cm-25x36in) s.
£491	$800	(12-Jun-91 GG.TA86/R) Nude (33x20cm-13x8in) s.d.1941 W/C pen
£524	$1000	(1-Jan-91 GG.TA313/R) Don Quixote and Sancho Pancha (26x18cm-10x7in) s. W/C pen
£524	$1000	(1-Jan-91 GG.TA317/R) Figures (19x29cm-7x11in) s. W/C
£613	$1000	(12-Jun-91 GG.TA84/R) Don Quixote (25x18cm-10x7in) s. ink wash
£613	$1000	(12-Jun-91 GG.TA87/R) Ancient dance (26x29cm-10x11in) s.d.1942 W/C pen
£613	$1000	(12-Jun-91 GG.TA85/R) Nude - the 50's (33x23cm-13x9in) s. W/C
£628	$1200	(1-Jan-91 GG.TA314/R) Mother, child and bird (34x24cm-13x9in) s.d.1950 W/C ink
£628	$1200	(1-Jan-91 GG.TA315/R) Landscape with minaret (23x30cm-9x12in) s.d.1941 W/C
£785	$1500	(1-Jan-91 GG.TA316/R) Still life (34x48cm-13x19in) W/C
£838	$1600	(1-Jan-91 GG.TA312/R) Head of woman (21x16cm-8x6in) s.c.1925
£1043	$1700	(12-Jun-91 GG.TA408/R) Shoresh (24x33cm-9x13in) s.d.1982 W/C pen
£1104	$1800	(12-Jun-91 GG.TA279/R) Design for ceramic wall in Safed Hospital (23x49cm-9x19in) s. W/C chl collage
£1156	$2000	(7-May-91 CE.NY64/R) Tents in Jaffa. Walking in Jaffa (20x32cm-8x13in) s. W/C pen pencil double-sided
£1227	$2000	(12-Jun-91 GG.TA278/R) Shfaram (30x42cm-12x17in) s.d.1950 W/C pen
£1795	$3500	(10-Oct-90 SY.NY503/R) Abstract composition (36x48cm-14x19in) s. gouache paper on board
£10471	$20000	(1-Jan-91 GG.TA303/R) Collage a feuille morte (35x50cm-14x20in) s.c.1920 oil collage board
£11213	$21529	(26-Nov-90 GL.P83/R) Nature motre (50x35cm-20x14in) s. mixed media collage board (F.FR 110000)
£13613	$26000	(1-Jan-91 GG.TA302/R) Coup de des (45x34cm-18x13in) s.d.1920 relief collage
£19095	$34181	(17-Mar-91 GL.P49/R) Trophee rouille (58x39cm-23x15in) s. plaster canvas laid down on board (F.FR 190000)
£24465	$46972	(26-Nov-90 GL.P82/R) Nature morte (26x43cm-10x17in) mixed media plaster canvas (F.FR 240000)

JANDA, Hermine von (1854-?) Austrian

£1679	$2889	(16-May-91 D.V1/R) Summer landscape (49x64cm-19x25in) s. canvas on carton (A.S 35000)

JANEBE (1907-) Swiss

£952	$1562	(21-Jun-91 G.Z6/R) Nature morte (98x63cm-39x25in) s.d.1953 board (S.FR 2400)
£1224	$2376	(8-Dec-90 GAB.G2686/R) Portrait de jeune fille au foulard blanc (48x36cm-19x14in) s.d.50 hardboard panel (S.FR 3000)

JANERAND, Daniel du (c.1919-) ?

£666	$1305	(7-Nov-90 APT.P517) Le prt (39x80cm-15x31in) s. (F.FR 6500)
£1850	$3589	(7-Dec-90 GL.P75) Les jardins de Bristol (130x62cm-51x24in) (F.FR 18000)

JANESCH, Albert (1889-1973) Austrian

£537	$993	(7-Mar-91 D.V219/R) View of Badgastein (44x52cm-17x20in) s.d.1954 W/C (A.S 11000)

JANET, A (?) ?

£1406	$2263	(26-Jun-91 CB.P41) Vase d'anemones (31x23cm-12x9in) s. W/C (F.FR 14000)

JANIKOWSKI, Mieczyslaw Tadeusz (1912-1968) ?

£2797	$5399	(12-Dec-90 WE.MU211/R) Composition (27x71cm-11x28in) s.verso (DM 8000)

JANIN, Jean (1899-?) French

£1104	$1800	(12-Jun-91 SY.NY34/R) Les travestis (137x97cm-54x38in) s.d.27 d.stretcher

JANK, A (20th C) ?

£761	$1522	(6-Feb-91 N.M628/R) Ulans riding (82x81cm-32x32in) s.d.1913 (DM 2200)

JANK, Angelo (1868-1956) German

£853	$1672	(24-Nov-90 SA.A749/R) Fox hunt (70x90cm-28x35in) s. (DM 2500)
£1024	$1679	(18-Jun-91 FN.S1912/R) Bavarian soldier holding horse (37x28cm-15x11in) s.d.1917 panel (DM 3000)
£1748	$3374	(12-Dec-90 WE.MU96/R) Parforce hunt (73x151cm-29x59in) s.d.1913 (DM 5000)

JANKOWSKI, J W (19th C) Austrian

£510	$821	(28-Jun-91 BM.B691/R) View of Venice with Santa Maria della Salute (27x21cm-11x8in) s. (DM 1500)

JANKOWSKY, S W (19th C) ?

£1706	$3225	(25-Sep-90 FN.S2227/R) Lake landscape with view of country estate (55x68cm-22x27in) s.d.1866 (DM 5000)

JANNECK, Franz Christoph (1703-1761) Austrian

£17140	$33766	(14-Nov-90 D.V12/R) Holy Family with infant St John, Joachim and Anna (95x74cm-37x29in) s.d.1745 (A.S 350000)
£75000	$122250	(3-Jul-91 S12/R) Elegant companies feasting and dancing in palace interiors (65x82cm-26x32in) one s.d.1752 one mono. copper pair

JANNECK, Franz Christoph and ORIENT, Joseph (18th C) Austrian/Hungarian

£2407	$4020	(6-Jun-91 D.V196/R) Farmhouse in wooded river landscape with figures (37x48cm-15x19in) one of pair (A.S 50000)
£2407	$4020	(6-Jun-91 D.V195/R) Farmhouses in wooded river landscape (37x48cm-15x19in) one of pair (A.S 50000)

JANNI, E de (19th C) French

£7000	$11760	(22-Apr-91 PO.BA14) Paisajes con perros de caza (81x46cm-32x18in) s. pair

JANNI, Guglielmo (1892-1958) Italian

£4959	$8876	(9-Apr-91 F.R216/R) Testa virile (37x21cm-15x8in) panel (I.L 11000000)

JANNIOT (20th C) French

£2347	*$4623*	*(15-Oct-90 ARC.P28/R) Le modele assis (47x36cm-19x14in) s. sanguinne (F.FR 23000)*

JANNY, Georg (20th C) Austrian

£392	*$776*	*(31-Jan-91 D.V211/R) Wilde Kaiser mountains near Kufstein (23x17cm-9x7in) s. W/C bodycol (A.S 8000)*
£955	*$1862*	*(11-Oct-90 D.V181/R) Winter evening in the Semmering area with view of Rax (53x67cm-21x26in) s.i.verso W/C htd.white (A.S 20000)*
£955	*$1862*	*(11-Oct-90 D.V180/R) View of Kitzbuhel (40x30cm-16x12in) s. W/C gouache (A.S 20000)*
£1337	*$2606*	*(11-Oct-90 D.V175/R) View of Hallstadt (71x122cm-28x48in) s. pen indian ink W/C bodycol. (A.S 28000)*
£1337	*$2246*	*(25-Apr-91 D.V211/R) Alpine pastures in the Dolomites (68x97cm-27x38in) s. W/C gouache (A.S 28000)*
£2450	*$4851*	*(31-Jan-91 D.V169/R) Hauptplatz, Hallstadt (66x54cm-26x21in) s. W/C bodycol (A.S 50000)*
£2687	*$5105*	*(28-Feb-91 D.V118/R) View of street in Neuwaldegg (31x48cm-12x19in) s.i.d.1835 W/C gouache (A.S 55000)*

JANS, Edouard de (1855-?) Belgian

£898	$1509	(23-Apr-91 SY.AM8) Woman mending stockings (45x53cm-18x21in) s.d.1914 (D.FL 3000)
£2698	$5234	(4-Dec-90 C.A89/R) The musicians (115x170cm-45x67in) s.d.1878 (B.FR 160000)

JANSA, Vaclav (1859-1913) Czechoslovakian

£753	$1349	(12-Mar-91 FN.S2442 a) Southern coastal landscape with boats and Vesuvio beyond, evening (27x50cm-11x20in) s. (DM 2200)
£1213	$2293	(27-Sep-90 D.V153/R) Scene in the Wachau (41x34cm-16x13in) s.i.verso board (A.S 25000)

JANSEM, Jean (1920-) French

£2538	$5000	(13-Nov-90 CE.NY257/R) Jeune femme (23x12cm-9x5in) s. masonite
£2538	$5000	(13-Nov-90 CE.NY255/R) Garcon debout (23x12cm-9x5in) s.s. masonite
£3061	$6031	(16-Nov-90 FB.P189/R) Nature morte au bougeoir (33x22cm-13x9in) s. (F.FR 30000)
£3373	$5802	(19-May-91 ZZ.F173/R) Jeune fille debout en robe blanche (23x12cm-9x5in) s. panel (F.FR 34000)
£3757	$6500	(7-May-91 CE.NY142/R) La femme en rouge (26x34cm-10x13in) s. paper on canvas
£3807	$7500	(13-Nov-90 CE.NY148/R) Deux femmes (19x24cm-7x9in) s. gouache pen ink paper on canvas
£5102	$10051	(16-Nov-90 FB.P188/R) La cuisine (35x27cm-14x11in) s. hardboard (F.FR 50000)
£5208	$8958	(19-May-91 ZZ.F190/R) La mere et l'enfant (34x27cm-13x11in) s. panel (F.FR 52500)
£5330	$10500	(13-Nov-90 CE.NY146/R) Trois generations (41x53cm-16x21in) s. board
£6320	$12198	(12-Dec-90 APT.P115/R) Apres la corrida (33x41cm-13x16in) s. (F.FR 62000)
£6932	$13378	(12-Dec-90 APT.P116/R) Attelages de mulets (31x74cm-12x29in) s. panel (F.FR 68000)

JANSEM, Jean (1920-) French-cont.

£6936	$12000	(22-May-91 D.NY117/R) Le chemise de nuit (102x44cm-40x17in) s.
£7078	$13802	(17-Oct-90 ARC.P95) Le passage de la procession (25x20cm-10x8in) s. paper laid down on canvas (F.FR 70000)
£7107	$14000	(13-Nov-90 CE.NY127/R) Deux femmes (41x24cm-16x9in) s.
£7362	$12000	(12-Jun-91 SY.NY121/R) Motherhood (97x130cm-38x51in) s.
£9184	$18000	(12-Feb-91 SY.NY164/R) Boy sitting by window (74x58cm-29x23in) s.
£9202	$15000	(12-Jun-91 SY.NY118/R) Women in contemplation (130x90cm-51x35in) s.
£9694	$19000	(7-Nov-90 B.SF1103/R) Seated boy (100x60cm-39x24in) s.
£10040	$18574	(6-Mar-91 APT.P119/R) L'eglise Saint Cesaere (115x89cm-45x35in) s. i. verso (F.FR 100000)
£10204	$20000	(12-Feb-91 SY.NY161/R) Market day (74x51cm-29x20in) s.
£10256	$20000	(10-Oct-90 SY.NY255/R) Standing woman (48x25cm-19x10in) s.
£10256	$20000	(10-Oct-90 SY.NY254/R) Portrait of seated boy (46x38cm-18x15in) s.
£10769	$21000	(10-Oct-90 SY.NY253/R) Girl with jug (36x28cm-14x11in) s.
£12766	$24000	(22-Sep-90 WOL.C437/R) Young fisherman (61x48cm-24x19in) s.
£13497	$22000	(12-Jun-91 SY.NY117/R) Conversation in park (130x162cm-51x64in) s.
£15029	$26000	(7-May-91 CE.NY36/R) Les jeunes filles (99x49cm-39x19in) s.
£16080	$28784	(16-Mar-91 APT.P61/R) Jeune garcon assis (100x60cm-39x24in) s. (F.FR 160000)
£16327	$32000	(12-Feb-91 SY.NY178/R) The poultry vendor (114x89cm-45x35in) s.
£17329	$33445	(12-Dec-90 APT.P114/R) Personnage (150x51cm-59x20in) s. (F.FR 170000)
£19289	$38000	(13-Nov-90 CE.NY274/R) Homme a son travail (100x60cm-39x24in) s.
£23445	$45250	(12-Dec-90 APT.P113/R) Mere et enfant (100x50cm-39x20in) s. (F.FR 230000)
£24291	$47611	(20-Nov-90 PPB.P34/R) Place de village (97x130cm-38x51in) s. (F.FR 240000)
£25641	$50000	(10-Oct-90 SY.NY252/R) Une jeune fille assise (145x89cm-57x35in) s.
£26923	$52500	(10-Oct-90 SY.NY280/R) Gossips (130x97cm-51x38in) s.d.61
£33333	$65000	(10-Oct-90 SY.NY297/R) Apres midi (130x97cm-51x38in) s.
£34439	$67500	(7-Nov-90 B.SF1107/R) Le corp de ballet avec jettees (98x146cm-39x57in) s.
£53846	$105000	(10-Oct-90 SY.NY240/R) Two women and child (262x140cm-103x55in) s.d.59
£690	$1360	(6-Oct-90 GL.P53) Couple de paysans (24x19cm-9x7in) s. Indian ink (F.FR 7000)
£771	$1495	(5-Dec-90 ZZ.F44/R) Couple de paysans (24x19cm-9x7in) s. pen wash Indian ink (F.FR 7500)
£781	$1515	(5-Dec-90 ZZ.F43/R) Le marchande de quatre saisons (17x19cm-7x7in) s. W/C Indian ink pastel (F.FR 7600)
£1531	$3000	(12-Feb-91 SY.NY197/R) Pierrot (30x23cm-12x9in) s. i.verso ink wash gouache
£1840	$3000	(12-Jun-91 SY.NY113/R) Ballerina (65x49cm-26x19in) s. W/C
£2296	$4500	(12-Feb-91 SY.NY199/R) Femme sur fond rouge (64x48cm-25x19in) s. indian ink W/C

JANSEN, Dirk (19/20th C) Dutch

£8466	$14392	(27-May-91 APT.P279/R) Voiliers sur le Bosphore (60x91cm-24x36in) s. (F.FR 85000)

JANSEN, Franz Maria (1885-1958) German

£1515	$2545	(26-Apr-91 KM.K326/R) Flowering field (60x84cm-24x33in) s. i.verso (DM 4500)

JANSEN, Jean (?) ?

£1508	$2700	(11-Apr-91 FA.PH1005) Femme en profil (23x18cm-9x7in) s.

JANSEN, Joseph (1829-1905) German

£904	$1600	(24-Mar-91 LIT.L101) Salt marshes with mountains in background and figures fishing (48x69cm-19x27in) s.
£5236	$8850	(3-May-91 SA.A1688/R) Sunny day in the valley (120x104cm-47x41in) s.d.1885 (DM 15500)

JANSEN, Willem (1892-?) Dutch

£1317	$2569	(25-Oct-90 VN.R52/R) Man with a boat at the waterside (33x52cm-13x20in) s. (D.FL 4400)
£2096	$3647	(26-Mar-91 VN.R38/R) Harbour scene (29x39cm-11x15in) s. (D.FL 7000)
£2156	$3751	(26-Mar-91 VN.R37/R) Workmen loading barge with sand (59x93cm-23x37in) s. (D.FL 7200)

JANSEN, Willem George Frederick (1871-1949) Dutch

£711	$1380	(4-Dec-90 P.Q65/R) On the beach (35x50cm-14x20in) s. (C.D 1600)
£800	$1568	(14-Feb-91 CSK58/R) A peasant woman with cattle on a country lane (36x25cm-14x10in) s. panel
£900	$1773	(4-Oct-90 CSK35) The mussel gatherers (25x32cm-10x13in) s. panel
£900	$1764	(14-Feb-91 CSK64) A river landscape with a windmill (48x74cm-19x29in) s.
£1100	$2156	(22-Nov-90 CSK171/R) Shepherd with flock (71x57cm-28x22in) s.
£1300	$2561	(4-Oct-90 CSK33 a) Gathering driftwood (48x66cm-19x26in) s.
£1970	$3880	(30-Oct-90 CH.AM139/R) Peasants on farmyard (50x70cm-20x28in) s. (D.FL 6500)
£2727	$5373	(30-Oct-90 CH.AM353/R) Gathering seaweed, Scheveningen beach, Holland (45x75cm-18x30in) s. (D.FL 9000)

JANSON (?) ?

£1038	$2025	(28-Oct-90 M.V160) Composition (24x37cm-9x15in) s. W/C (F.FR 10300)

JANSON, Johannes (1729-1784) Dutch
£544 $963   *(22-Mar-91 GRA.B2629/R) Dutch river landscape with palace, shipping and cattle (16x24cm-6x9in) i.verso W/C indian ink brush vellum (DM 1600)*

JANSON, Johannes (attrib) (1729-1784) Dutch
£1204 $2010   (6-Jun-91 D.V308/R) Village in river landscape with figures and boats (23x31cm-9x12in) s. panel (A.S 25000)

JANSON, Knut (1882-1966) Swedish
£568 $955   (24-Apr-91 BA.S100/R) Mont Vantou, Provence (27x42cm-11x17in) s.d.51 (S.KR 6000)
£834 $1618   (4-Dec-90 BA.S224/R) Flowerbeds in Tantolunden (32x41cm-13x16in) s.d.1939 panel (S.KR 9000)

JANSON, Marc (20th C) ?
£755 $1231   (14-Jun-91 FB.P87) Car je ne suis pas le vautour volant sur Patani (97x130cm-38x51in) s. i.d.73 verso (F.FR 7500)
£1044 $1764   (16-Apr-91 I.N102) Une nuee de fronde (81x100cm-32x39in) s. i. verso (F.FR 10500)

JANSON, Vide (1924-) Swedish
£566 $956   (18-Apr-91 BU.S116/R) Composition (64x75cm-25x30in) s. (S.KR 6000)

JANSSAUD, Mathurin (19th C) French
£1427 $2754   *(16-Dec-90 T.B148) Douarnenez - La flotille des Sardiniers (55x38cm-22x15in) s. (F.FR 14000)*
£1004 $1857   *(4-Mar-91 ARC.P56) Environ de lus la croix haute (33x41cm-13x16in) s. pastel (F.FR 10000)*
£1500 $2415   *(24-Jun-91 CSK8/R) A la Brume, Cote de Bretagne (45x56cm-18x22in) s. pastel paper on board*
£1600 $3152   *(13-Nov-90 SWS12/R) Harbour scene, Brittany (44x54cm-17x21in) s. pastel*
£1605 $3129   *(12-Oct-90 APT.P66) Pecheurs bretons au port (23x31cm-9x12in) s. pastel (F.FR 16000)*
£1724 $3414   *(3-Feb-91 I.N125) La ville close de Concarneau (21x34cm-8x13in) s. pastel (F.FR 17000)*
£1786 $3071   *(15-May-91 CN.P54/R) Bretagne, les lavandieres au vieux moulin pres de Concarneau (31x39cm-12x15in) s. pastel (F.FR 18000)*
£1892 $3274   *(26-May-91 ZZ.F42/R) Bretones remenant le troupeau (42x55cm-17x22in) s. pastel (F.FR 19000)*
£1992 $3446   *(26-May-91 ZZ.F39/R) La Kermesse en Bretagne (31x40cm-12x16in) s. pastel (F.FR 20000)*
£2312 $3791   *(18-Jun-91 APT.P33) Bretagne - retour de peche (45x55cm-18x22in) s. pastel (F.FR 23000)*
£3483 $6025   *(12-May-91 T.B59/R) L'arrivee des barques (33x48cm-13x19in) s. pastel (F.FR 35000)*

JANSSEN, Gerhard (1863-1931) German
£544 $963   (20-Mar-91 KM.K1281) Man with black hat, possibly self portrait (34x30cm-13x12in) mono. paper (DM 1600)
£748 $1205   (26-Jun-91 KM.K1512) Study of laughing heads (64x45cm-25x18in) s. (DM 2200)
£1267 $2470   (26-Oct-90 KM.K1292) Miner in mine (168x82cm-66x32in) mono. (DM 3750)
£1267 $2470   (26-Oct-90 KM.K1291) Peasant couple harvesting potatoes with farmstead beyond (168x82cm-66x32in) mono.d.02 (DM 3750)
£442 $783   *(20-Mar-91 KM.K1550) Interior with peasant woman holding Schnaps bottle (46x38cm-18x15in) s. chl (DM 1300)*

JANSSEN, Horst (1929-) German
£407 $679   (6-Jun-91 HW.H3377) Female nude, Rubens (18x10cm-7x4in) s.i. ink pen W/C (DM 1200)
£475 $793   (8-Jun-91 HN.H228) Myself as a crawling beetle (29x21cm-11x8in) s.d.88 pen wash (DM 1400)
£475 $793   (8-Jun-91 HN.H229) Yes that was a lovely Sunday morning (9x18cm-4x7in) s.d.88 pen wash collage (DM 1400)
£475 $793   (6-Jun-91 HW.H3376) Head of cat (21x30cm-8x12in) s. pencil col.pencil (DM 1400)
£475 $793   (8-Jun-91 HN.H223/R) Girl with a monkey (21x15cm-8x6in) s.d.1987 pen (DM 1400)
£508 $849   (6-Jun-91 HW.H3307) Kroatzbarin (25x25cm-10x10in) s.d.78 pencil col.pencil board (DM 1500)
£508 $849   (6-Jun-91 HW.H3347) Wind muss sein (30x21cm-12x8in) i. pencil col.pencil (DM 1500)
£593 $991   (6-Jun-91 HW.H3367) The lighthouse (26x14cm-10x6in) s.d.82 pencil col.pencil board (DM 1750)
£644 $1076   (6-Jun-91 HW.H3338) Self portrait (44x28cm-17x11in) s. pencil (DM 1900)
£644 $1076   (6-Jun-91 HW.H3387) The sioux pains are coming (30x21cm-12x8in) s.d.1988 ball point pen W/C (DM 1900)
£709 $1227   (25-May-91 N.M154) Swanshall (16x21cm-6x8in) s.d.1981 pen W/C (DM 2100)
£712 $1189   (6-Jun-91 HW.H3353) Figure (22x4cm-9x2in) s.mono.d.81 pencil (DM 2100)
£780 $1302   (6-Jun-91 HW.H3346) Two cats watching plane (24x12cm-9x5in) s. pencil board (DM 2300)
£780 $1302   (5-Jun-91 DO.H2753/R) Self portrait with numbers (30x19cm-12x7in) s.d.70 pencil col.pencil (DM 2300)

JANSSEN, Horst (1929-) German-cont.

£814	$1359	(6-Jun-91 HW.H3380) Der Suff (30x21cm-12x8in) s.i.d.86 ball point pen W/C (DM 2400)
£814	$1359	(8-Jun-91 HN.H216) Ergo (23x22cm-9x9in) s.i.d.1981 pen (DM 2400)
£845	$1461	(25-May-91 N.M155) Ergo, pear landscape (18x15cm-7x6in) s.d.1981 W/C (DM 2500)
£847	$1415	(6-Jun-91 HW.H3359) Shopping list (30x10cm-12x4in) s.i.d.81 ball point pen col.pencil collage board (DM 2500)
£887	$1739	(20-Nov-90 L.K310) Lev's grandson (16x20cm-6x8in) mono.i.d.1982 pencil chk htd.white (DM 2600)
£915	$1528	(8-Jun-91 HN.H226/R) Immer haben die leute gesagt (29x21cm-11x8in) s.d.88 pen wash (DM 2700)
£946	$1636	(25-May-91 N.M156) Landscape for Petty Fruer (16x23cm-6x9in) mono.s.d.1981 pen W/C (DM 2800)
£949	$1585	(8-Jun-91 HN.H219/R) Design for Phyllis (27x34cm-11x13in) s.d.1983 pencil (DM 2800)
£949	$1585	(6-Jun-91 HW.H3368) Self portrait with hand raised for swearing oath (21x15cm-8x6in) s.i.d.82 pencil (DM 2800)
£1085	$1812	(6-Jun-91 HW.H3329) Fish head (18x16cm-7x6in) s.d.1980 pencil col.pencil (DM 3200)
£1085	$1812	(8-Jun-91 HN.H211) Self-portrait with Birgit Jacobsen (29x17cm-11x7in) s.d.1977 lead and colour pencil (DM 3200)
£1115	$1929	(25-May-91 N.M158/R) Love (25x31cm-10x12in) mono.d.1983 col.pencil (DM 3300)
£1186	$1981	(6-Jun-91 HW.H3361) Pisser (13x17cm-5x7in) s.i.d.81 pencil col.chk board (DM 3500)
£1220	$2038	(8-Jun-91 HN.H217/R) Das isses ja eben (26x18cm-10x7in) s.i.d.1981 lead and colour pencil (DM 3600)
£1220	$2038	(6-Jun-91 HW.H3303) Nach Osdorf Landpflegeheim (30x43cm-12x17in) s.i.d.65 felt tip pen (DM 3600)
£1220	$2038	(8-Jun-91 HN.H215/R) Venetian scene (12x20cm-5x8in) s.d.1981 pen (DM 3600)
£1288	$2151	(5-Jun-91 DO.H2754/R) Study of plant (30x17cm-12x7in) i.d.74 col.pencil ball point pen (DM 3800)
£1288	$2151	(8-Jun-91 HN.H201/R) Selbst zum Philip Buch (25x20cm-10x8in) s.i.d.72 pencil (DM 3800)
£1310	$2516	(26-Nov-90 WK.M696/R) Apple land (11x20cm-4x8in) i.d.1972 indian ink brush W/C (DM 3800)
£1356	$2264	(6-Jun-91 HW.H3315) Cat (28x34cm-11x13in) s.d.79 pencil col.pencil board (DM 4000)
£1424	$2378	(6-Jun-91 HW.H3388) Ich nach mir - two cats (25x33cm-10x13in) s.i.d.88 felt tip pen wash board (DM 4200)
£1424	$2378	(6-Jun-91 HW.H3319) Keinachtsmann, Wunschzettel (21x20cm-8x8in) pencil col.chk (DM 4200)
£1525	$2547	(6-Jun-91 HW.H3305) Gesche (23x17cm-9x7in) s.d.71 pencil col.pencil (DM 4500)
£1661	$2774	(6-Jun-91 HW.H3358) Der Baum-Brief (34x20cm-13x8in) s.i.d.81 pen wash (DM 4900)
£1661	$2774	(6-Jun-91 HW.H3371) Self portrait as Father Christmas (30x21cm-12x8in) i.d.1983 pencil col.chk board (DM 4900)
£1695	$2831	(8-Jun-91 HN.H199/R) Horizon (24x35cm-9x14in) s.d.1966 lead and colour pencil (DM 5000)
£1729	$2887	(6-Jun-91 HW.H3340) 3 x HJ (30x21cm-12x8in) s.i. col.pencil (DM 5100)
£1763	$2944	(6-Jun-91 HW.H3325) Schlafbild (23x23cm-9x9in) i.d.1980 pencil col.pencil (DM 5200)
£1831	$3057	(6-Jun-91 HW.H3357) Svanshall (21x14cm-8x6in) s.i.d.81 pen W/C wash (DM 5400)
£1864	$3114	(8-Jun-91 HN.H206/R) Also a bit of a Narcissus (15x31cm-6x12in) d.1974 pencil (DM 5500)
£1898	$3170	(6-Jun-91 HW.H3364) Hartmut Hase - rabbit, Earl of Klitschester (30x23cm-12x9in) s.mono.i.d.82 pencil col.pencil (DM 5600)
£1931	$3708	(26-Nov-90 WK.M697/R) Couple making love (20x29cm-8x11in) s.i.d.1973 pencil (DM 5600)
£1966	$3283	(6-Jun-91 HW.H3320) Self portrait with cat (23x21cm-9x8in) s.d.1980 (DM 5800)
£2136	$3566	(6-Jun-91 HW.H3374) Nude girl (21x30cm-8x12in) s.d.1984 pencil (DM 6300)
£2196	$3799	(25-May-91 N.M157/R) Two anglers with half moon (25x32cm-10x13in) mono.d.1983 pencil col.pencil (DM 6500)
£2373	$3963	(6-Jun-91 HW.H3333) Kerstin in water (18x45cm-7x18in) W/C over pencil (DM 7000)
£3390	$5661	(5-Jun-91 DO.H2755/R) Ibsen (30x21cm-12x8in) s.i.d.1984 W/C pencil (DM 10000)
£3729	$6227	(8-Jun-91 HN.H218/R) Zu Guardi (16x22cm-6x9in) s.i.d.1981 pen wash (DM 11000)
£4068	$6793	(6-Jun-91 HW.H3394/R) Townscape (21x29cm-8x11in) s.i.d.89 pen wash W/C (DM 12000)
£4437	$8696	(20-Nov-90 L.K309/R) Self portrait as raven (27x20cm-11x8in) mono.d.1982 pencil col.chk (DM 13000)
£5424	$9058	(8-Jun-91 HN.H198/R) The procuress (50x35cm-20x14in) s.d.1965 pencil (DM 16000)
£5802	$11372	(20-Nov-90 L.K307/R) Ete (18x33cm-7x13in) mono.i.d.1986 indian ink pen wash W/C (DM 17000)
£5932	$9907	(6-Jun-91 HW.H3390) The ghost (34x22cm-13x9in) s.i.d.88 pen W/C (DM 17500)

JANSSEN, Horst (1929-) German-cont.

£7458	$12454	(8-Jun-91 HN.H209/R) Leapfrog (47x29cm-19x11in) i.d.76 pen wash (DM 22000)
£8475	$14153	(6-Jun-91 HW.H3352) Marija Rajewskaja (36x29cm-14x11in) s.i.d.81 col.pencil col.chk (DM 25000)
£8475	$14153	(6-Jun-91 HW.H3254) Martha (41x27cm-16x11in) s.mono.i.d.81 pencil col.pencil col.chk (DM 25000)
£10847	$18115	(8-Jun-91 HN.H220) Paranoia - self-portrait (49x29cm-19x11in) s.i.d.1983 pencil wash (DM 32000)
£12881	$21512	(8-Jun-91 HN.H197/R) Female nude (40x30cm-16x12in) s.d.1964 colour pencil (DM 38000)
£18305	$30569	(8-Jun-91 HN.H202/R) A letter (36x22cm-14x9in) s.i.d.1972 lead and colour pencil (DM 54000)
£22373	$37363	(6-Jun-91 HW.H3349) Self portrait (44x38cm-17x15in) s.i.d.81 pencil col.pencil (DM 66000)

JANSSEN, Luplau (19/20th C) Danish

£4960	$8383	(2-May-91 RAS.V55/R) Mother and two children on verandah (157x118cm-62x46in) s.d.1899 (D.KR 56000)

JANSSEN, Wouter (?) ?

£695	$1369	(13-Nov-90 J.M1130) Mid winter (61x91cm-24x36in) s. (A.D 1800)

JANSSENS, Abraham (1575-1632) Flemish

£5747	$10000	(27-Mar-91 B.SF4066/R) Simon and his daughter (51x35cm-20x14in) mono.d.1597 panel
£31579	$60000	(11-Jan-91 CH.NY82/R) Peace and Abundance binding the arrows of war (150x118cm-59x46in) d.1622 painted with studio
£38235	$65000	(31-May-91 CH.NY46/R) Allegory of autumn with woman holding cornucopia, figures in field beyond (123x91cm-48x36in) panel
£95050	$168238	(5-Apr-91 DAR.P50/R) La chaste Suzanne au bain (167x218cm-66x86in) (F.FR 960000)

JANSSENS, Abraham (style) (1575-1632) Flemish

£1320	$2231	(1-May-91 GD.B454/R) Portrait of noble lady holding spiritual book (106x77cm-42x30in) (S.FR 3300)

JANSSENS, Hieronymus (circle) (1624-1693) Flemish

£3631	$6500	(11-Apr-91 SY.NY6/R) Couple dancing beside elegant company feasting in interior (53x84cm-21x33in)

JANSSENS, Ludovic (?) ?

£919	$1801	(12-Feb-91 GM.B646) La digue dans les marais (46x80cm-18x31in) s. (B.FR 55000)

JANSSON, Alfred (1863-1931) Swedish/American

£513	$1000	(14-Oct-90 H.C392/R) Landscape with rocks and birches (51x61cm-20x24in) s.d.1924
£564	$1100	(14-Oct-90 H.C393/R) Winter landscape (71x81cm-28x32in) s.d.1930

JANSSON, Alvar (1922-1990) Scandinavian

£849	$1469	(22-May-91 BA.S384/R) Summer landscape with road (58x67cm-23x26in) s. (S.KR 9000)

JANSSON, Eugene (1862-1915) Swedish

£22535	$38310	(28-May-91 AB.S4635/R) Evening by Olandsvagen (61x91cm-24x36in) s. (S.KR 240000)
£25641	$50000	(23-Oct-90 SY.NY195/R) Stockholm, a moonlit night in February (74x55cm-29x22in) s.

JANSSON, Karl Emmanuel (1846-1874) Finnish

£51650	$87288	(20-Apr-91 HOR.H103/R) Old man making fishingnet (41x32cm-16x13in) s.d.1869 (F.M 360000)

JANSSON, Rune (1918-) Swedish

£519	$898	(22-May-91 BA.S387/R) Towards autumn (22x37cm-9x15in) s.d.59 (S.KR 5500)
£582	$990	(28-May-91 AB.S5221/R) Red sea (26x40cm-10x16in) s.d.83 (S.KR 6200)
£853	$1654	(5-Dec-90 AB.S7118/R) Towards end of summer (41x35cm-16x14in) s.d.59 (S.KR 9200)
£1033	$1756	(28-May-91 AB.S5218/R) Female figure - artist's wife Eddie Figge (60x48cm-24x19in) s.d.47 (S.KR 11000)
£1107	$2125	(27-Nov-90 BU.S152/R) Floating shapes (46x38cm-18x15in) s.d.1951 (S.KR 12000)
£1272	$2150	(18-Apr-91 BU.S63/R) Composition (31x68cm-12x27in) s.d.1962 (S.KR 13500)
£1384	$2657	(27-Nov-90 BU.S149/R) Red flow in the sky (71x112cm-28x44in) s.d.1986 (S.KR 15000)

JANSZEN, Pieter (attrib) (17th C) Dutch

£10456	$20493	(19-Nov-90 CH.R29/R) Ballo in giardino (110x132cm-43x52in) s. copper (I.L 23000000)

JAPANESE SCHOOL (?) Japanese

£3400	$6086	(12-Mar-91 RG2579) Street scene with figures. Riverscene. Bridge shrouded in mist W/C three

JAPANESE SCHOOL, 19th C Japanese
£1993 $3249   (12-Jun-91 GM.B4013/R) Pere et enfants revenant du bois ivory
                    (B.FR 120000)

JAPARRULA, Bandy Long (20th C) Australian
£800 $1552   (6-Dec-90 CSK95/R) Frog dreaming (135x157cm-53x62in)

JAPY, Louis Aime (1840-1916) French
£939 $1821   (8-Dec-90 GAB.G2220/R) Sous-bois avec personnages (41x32cm-16x13in) s.
                    panel (S.FR 2300)
£1200 $2028   (1-May-91 GD.B456/R) Wooded heath landscape with female figure
                    collecting brush wood (32x40cm-13x16in) s. panel (S.FR 3000)
£1835 $3523   (1-Dec-90 PER.M79) Taureaux (19x26cm-7x10in) s. panel (F.FR 18000)
£2312 $4000   (21-May-91 CE.NY150/R) End of day (39x46cm-15x18in) s.indist.d.
£6200 $12214   (5-Oct-90 C64/R) Cattle watering at treelined stream (83x100cm-33x39in)
                    s.d.84
£6728 $12917   (1-Dec-90 PER.M139/R) Au bord de l'etang (46x37cm-18x15in) s.d.81 panel
                    (F.FR 66000)

JAQUET, F (19th C) French
£1263 $2475   (24-Nov-90 SA.A652/R) Chickens in stable interior (38x46cm-15x18in) s.
                    (DM 3700)
£1263 $2475   (24-Nov-90 SA.A653/R) Chickens in stable interior (38x46cm-15x18in) s.
                    (DM 3700)

JARDIEL, Jose (1928-?) Spanish
£1923 $3404   (20-Mar-91 DUR.M11) Dos cabras (80x100cm-31x39in) (S.P 350000)

JARDINIER, Claude Donat (1726-c.1771) French
*£780 $1396   (13-Mar-91 B11/R) Le Silence (52x42cm-20x17in) W/C after Jean Baptiste
                    Greuze*

JARDON, L E (19th C) French?
£3012 $5572   (6-Mar-91 APT.P118/R) Baigneurs sur le plage (72x130cm-28x51in) s.d.1890
                    (F.FR 30000)

JARNEFELT, Eero (1863-1937) Finnish
£5739 $9699   (20-Apr-91 HOR.H105/R) Cottage (23x28cm-9x11in) s.d.1888 (F.M 40000)
£7275 $14260   (24-Nov-90 HOR.H127/R) View of mountains (34x58cm-13x23in) s.d.1929
                    (F.M 51000)
£10791 $20827   (15-Dec-90 BU.H85/R) Landscape from Koli (41x54cm-16x21in) s.d.1917
                    (F.M 75000)
*£2436 $4798   (17-Nov-90 BU.H197/R) Pine trees (47x31cm-19x12in) s.d.12 pastel
                    (F.M 17000)*
*£5136 $10066   (24-Nov-90 HOR.H126/R) Evening sun (32x41cm-13x16in) s.d.1892 pastel
                    (F.M 36000)*
*£7880 $15523   (17-Nov-90 BU.H195/R) Landscape, Koli (51x66cm-20x26in) s.d.1933 gouache
                    (F.M 55000)*

JARNEFELT, Laura (1904-1985) Finnish
*£518 $1000   (15-Dec-90 BU.H239) Early in spring (36x49cm-14x19in) s.d.1945 gouache
                    (F.M 3600)*

JARRY, Gaston (1889-1974) Argentinian
£957 $1800   (18-Sep-90 RO.BA396) La modelo (13x27cm-5x11in) s.

JARVIS, Arnold (1881-1960) Australian
*£533 $1003   (17-Sep-90 SY.ME86/R) Morning in the bush (25x35cm-10x14in) s. W/C
                    (A.D 1200)*

JARVIS, H C (1867-1955) British
*£400 $656   (21-Jun-91 HC3) River landscape with cart and horses (18x28cm-7x11in)
                    W/C*

JARVIS, Henry C (1867-1955) British
£843 $1400   (11-Jan-91 DM.D1001/R) Impressionistic study of repast with Jensen style
                    tea set (48x64cm-19x25in) s.

JARVIS, John (20th C) American
£847 $1600   (25-Sep-90 CE.NY269/R) Mixed bag (35x57cm-14x22in) s.d.1984 W/C gouache

JARVIS, John Wesley (1780-1840) American
£320 $566   (19-Mar-91 CSK49/R) Portrait of gentleman wearing brown coat, waistcoat
                    and cravat (6x?cm-2x?in) min. plaited hair verso panel gold frame oval

JARVIS, John Wesley (attrib) (1780-1840) American
£480 $850   (20-Mar-91 C89) Portrait of gentleman wearing maroon coat with black
                    collar (5x?cm-2x?in) min. gold frame plaited hair verso oval

JASCHKE, Franz (1775-1842) Austrian
£1193 $2327   (11-Oct-90 D.V115/R) View of Stift Heiligenkreuz with figures
                    (44x62cm-17x24in) s. gouache (A.S 25000)

JAUDON, Valerie (20th C) ?
£2806 $5500   (14-Feb-91 CH.NY70/R) Martinsville (91x91cm-36x36in) s.i.d.80 oil copper
                    pigment

JAUDON, Valerie (20th C) ?-cont.
£2890	$5000	(7-May-91 CE.NY282/R) Brazil (91x91cm-36x36in) s.d.82 overlap
£11224	$22000	(7-Nov-90 SY.NY232/R) Prairie point (182x182cm-72x72in)

JAULMES, Gustave (1873-1959) Swiss
£502	$929	(4-Mar-91 ARC.P148) Femmes et enfants dans un jardin (37x46cm-15x18in) s. panel (F.FR 5000)

JAUMANN, Rudolf Alfred (1859-?) German
£1010	$1747	(6-May-91 ZEL.L1767/R) Musketeer seated at table talking to raven (22x16cm-9x6in) s.i.d.1885 panel (DM 3000)
£1748	$3374	(12-Dec-90 WE.MU217) The first sip of beer (37x30cm-15x12in) s.i.d.1884 panel (DM 5000)

JAWLENSKY, Alexej von (1864-1941) Russian
£16244	$32000	(2-Oct-90 CH.NY85/R) Meditation (20x16cm-8x6in) init.d.35 canvas laid down on board
£17000	$27370	(25-Jun-91 C152/R) Meditation (20x14cm-8x6in) init. s.i.d.1935verso paper on board
£20408	$40000	(15-Feb-91 SY.NY69/R) Meditation (17x12cm-7x5in) init.d.36 s.i.d.verso paper on board
£25338	$43074	(31-May-91 VG.B24/R) Kleine Meditation Nr 10/II schwarz-oranges Leuchten (19x15cm-7x6in) mono.d.1936 s.d.verso canvas on board (DM 75000)
£27027	$45946	(30-May-91 SY.BE44/R) Meditation (17x12cm-7x5in) mono.d.34 i.verso paper on board (DM 80000)
£27119	$45288	(7-Jun-91 HN.H29/R) Meditation (17x12cm-7x5in) mono.d.35 paper (DM 80000)
£29310	$56276	(26-Nov-90 WK.M35/R) Still life with bunch of flowers (20x9cm-8x4in) s.i.d.135/36verso board (DM 85000)
£29831	$49817	(7-Jun-91 HN.H28/R) Meditation (18x13cm-7x5in) mono.d.1934 card on board (DM 88000)
£30717	$60205	(23-Nov-90 VG.B33/R) Bunch of flowers (21x16cm-8x6in) bears i.d.1936verso board (DM 90000)
£33730	$55317	(21-Jun-91 GK.B51/R) Meditation, abstract head (19x12cm-7x5in) mono.d.35 s.i.d.verso paper on board (S.FR 85000)
£35714	$58571	(21-Jun-91 GK.B50/R) Meditation, abstract head (18x13cm-7x5in) mono.s.i.d.34 s.i.d.verso paper on board (S.FR 90000)
£40000	$78000	(17-Oct-90 S60/R) Meditation (15x12cm-6x5in) init.d.35 paper on board
£72000	$139680	(5-Dec-90 S167/R) Kopf (29x20cm-11x8in) mono.d.3.28 d.1928verso board
£74324	$126351	(31-May-91 VG.B23/R) Variation with three figures (37x26cm-15x10in) mono.i.d.1914verso paper on board (DM 220000)
£86735	$170000	(14-Feb-91 CH.NY45/R) Stilleben mit apfeln (48x53cm-19x21in) s. paper on board
£90090	$155856	(22-May-91 CH.AM538/R) Antlitz (23x17cm-9x7in) init. s.i.d.1929 verso board (D.FL 300000)
£101523	$200000	(14-Nov-90 SY.NY381/R) Variation vorwinter (36x27cm-14x11in) init. s.i.d.1916 verso linen paper on board
£116751	$230000	(14-Nov-90 SY.NY380/R) Variation versonnen (38x26cm-15x10in) init. s.i.d.1915 verso linen paper on board
£131980	$260000	(14-Nov-90 SY.NY379/R) Schwarze locken (40x30cm-16x12in) s. linen-finished paper on board
£137056	$270000	(14-Nov-90 SY.NY378/R) Blumenstilleben (52x27cm-20x11in) init. oil pencil linen-finished paper on board
£155405	$264189	(30-May-91 SY.BE18/R) Martyr (33x25cm-13x10in) mono.d.19 oil paper on board (DM 460000)
£167513	$330000	(14-Nov-90 SY.NY376/R) Frau aus St. Prex (31x30cm-12x12in) s. s.i.d.1916 verso linen paper on board
£175676	$298649	(30-May-91 SY.BE5/R) Wooded landscape near Wasserburg (53x47cm-21x19in) s.d.1907 board (DM 520000)
£203046	$400000	(14-Nov-90 SY.NY375/R) Erde (53x49cm-21x19in) s.d.1918 i.verso board
£210000	$338100	(24-Jun-91 C20/R) An der Ostsee (61x61cm-24x24in) s.d.1911 i.verso board
£331058	$648874	(23-Nov-90 VG.B13/R) Man with green beard (46x36cm-18x14in) s.d.1912 board (DM 970000)
£657	*$1282*	*(21-Oct-90 P.V7) Nu feminin (30x24cm-12x9in) bears st. crayon (F.FR 6500)*
£1365	*$2676*	*(24-Nov-90 VG.B619/R) Farbskalen (15x10cm-6x4in) mono.s.i. postcard W/C pen (DM 4000)*
£2389	*$4683*	*(22-Nov-90 L.K1041/R) Selfportrait. Rooftops with church tower, Ascona (19x23cm-7x9in) mono.i. pencil double-sided (DM 7000)*
£3754	*$7358*	*(22-Nov-90 L.K1040/R) View out of window (15x9cm-6x4in) mono.d.1933 W/C pen dr. (DM 11000)*
£6122	*$12000*	*(15-Feb-91 SY.NY70/R) Kopf III (14x10cm-6x4in) s. pastel pencil paper on paper*
£10345	*$19862*	*(28-Nov-90 KF.M912/R) Woman reading (14x10cm-6x4in) s.indis.d.28 W/C board (DM 30000)*
£12755	*$25000*	*(15-Feb-91 SY.NY68/R) Kopf (22x15cm-9x6in) init.i. W/C pen ink paper on card*
£14031	*$27500*	*(15-Feb-91 SY.NY71/R) Kopf II (15x12cm-6x5in) init. pastel chl paper on paper*
£20305	*$40000*	*(15-Nov-90 CH.NY132/R) Kopf (23x18cm-9x7in) init. W/C paper on paper*

JAWLENSKY, Andreas (1902-1984) Polish
£8874	$17392	(24-Nov-90 VG.B211/R) Ile d'ouessant, Port d'Harant (22x30cm-9x12in) s.i.d.1927 s.i.d.verso board (DM 26000)

JAY, Florence (fl.1905-1920) British
£400 $676   (30-Apr-91 AG70) *Invitation and return (31x52cm-12x20in) W/C two mounted on one*

JEAN, Philippe (1755-1802) British
£420 $706   (15-Jul-91 PH35) *Lady, dark hair adorned with pearls, in dress and ermine-trimmed jacket (4x?cm-2x?in) min. init.d. hair compartment verso gilt oval*
£1700 $2805   (11-Jul-91 S260) *Portrait of gentleman wearing coat and knotted white cravat (7x?cm-3x?in) min. gold frame oval*
£2800 $4620   (10-Jul-91 C143/R) *Mrs Philip Jean (8x?cm-3x?in) min.s.d.1782 gilt-metal frame oval*
£3000 $5910   (1-Nov-90 S25/R) *Portrait of gentleman wearing puce coat with gold buttons (7x?cm-3x?in) min. gilt metal frame glazed hair verso*

JEANMAIRE, Edouard (1847-1916) Swiss
£757 $1476   (24-Oct-90 GD.B510/R) *Enfants a la fontaine (41x59cm-16x23in) s. i.d.1898verso board (S.FR 1900)*
£1195 $2341   (24-Nov-90 SA.A608/R) *Chicken run (30x40cm-12x16in) s. panel (DM 3500)*

JEANMART, Claude (20th C) French?
£976 $1894   (5-Dec-90 I.N91/R) *De saragosse a Burgos (100x100cm-39x39in) acrylic (F.FR 9500)*

JEANMOUGIN, Alfred Pierre Joseph (19th C) French
£1040 $1800   (21-May-91 CE.NY161/R) *Behind farm (113x164cm-44x65in) s.*

JEANNERET, Charles Edouard see CORBUSIER, le

JEANNIN, Georges (1841-1925) French
£802 $1565   (12-Oct-90 ZZ.F48) *Fleurs (39x24cm-15x9in) panel (F.FR 8000)*
£802 $1565   (12-Oct-90 ZZ.F13) *Nature morte aux fraises (34x43cm-13x17in) s. panel (F.FR 8000)*
£1755 $3423   (12-Oct-90 ZZ.F15) *Vase de fleurs (70x40cm-28x16in) s.d.1917 (F.FR 17500)*
£1906 $3716   (12-Oct-90 ZZ.F38) *Jetee de roses (33x41cm-13x16in) s. (F.FR 19000)*
£2508 $4890   (12-Oct-90 ZZ.F70) *Nature morte aux pommes (50x50cm-20x20in) s. (F.FR 25000)*
£2854 $5480   (1-Dec-90 PER.M100/R) *Bouquet de roses (38x46cm-15x18in) s. (F.FR 28000)*
£3009 $5868   (12-Oct-90 ZZ.F14) *Jetee de fleurs (65x81cm-26x32in) s. (F.FR 30000)*
£3210 $6259   (12-Oct-90 ZZ.F30) *Nature morte aux pommes (65x81cm-26x32in) s. (F.FR 32000)*
£3600 $6912   (27-Nov-90 PH38/R) *Still life of flowers on table top (70x92cm-28x36in) s.*
£5061 $9919   (25-Nov-90 ZZ.F86/R) *Nature morte aux peches (51x76cm-20x30in) s. (F.FR 50000)*

JEANNIOT (19/20th C) French
£1327 $2613   (16-Nov-90 LGB.P205) *Nature morte au pichet d'etain (54x65cm-21x26in) s. (F.FR 13000)*

JEAURAT DE BERTRY, Nicolas Henry (1728-1796) French
£46107 $90369   (11-Nov-90 M.V31/R) *Nature morte de fruits et de gibier (74x94cm-29x37in) s. (F.FR 450000)*

JEAURAT, Etienne (1699-1789) French
£19000 $32110   (17-Apr-91 S45/R) *Les oies de frere Philippe (64x79cm-25x31in) bears sig.d.1734*
£559 $1080   (10-Dec-90 L.K280) *Shepherd pair beneath tree (32x37cm-13x15in) s.d.1749 chk htd.white oval (DM 1600)*
£668 $1296   (6-Dec-90 ARC.P120) *Portrait de jeune femme en buste (17x13cm-7x5in) pierre noire sanguinne htd.white gouache (F.FR 6500)*
£2141 $4110   (27-Nov-90 APT.P155/R) *La fontaine publique (20x18cm-8x7in) s. pen wash (F.FR 21000)*

JEAURAT, Etienne (attrib) (1699-1789) French
£610 $1000   (19-Jun-91 B.SF1692/R) *Acteurs de la Commedia dell'Arte (42x53cm-17x21in)*
£7099 $14057   (30-Jan-91 APT.P129/R) *La lecon d'astronomie (54x61cm-21x24in) (F.FR 70000)*
£15000 $30000   (7-Feb-91 C192/R) *Venus lighting cupid's torch. The triumph of Venus one s. two*
£950 $1606   (16-Apr-91 C223/R) *A young girl reading at a table, her head resting on her left hand (23x18cm-9x7in) blk.white chk.*

JEAURAT, Etienne (style) (1699-1789) French
£3500 $7000   (7-Feb-91 C3/R) *A merchant and a sea captain in an office by a quay (94x85cm-37x33in)*

JEFFERYS, Charles William (1869-1951) Canadian
£444 $862   (3-Dec-90 R.T287/R) *Valley road (26x14cm-10x6in) s.d.12 i.verso W/C (C.D 1000)*
£444 $862   (3-Dec-90 R.T286/R) *Showshoers in ravine (26x15cm-10x6in) s. W/C (C.D 1000)*

JEFFERYS, Marcel (1872-1924) French
£5059 $9815   (8-Dec-90 KV.L347/R) Le cirque (36x45cm-14x18in) mono. canvas on board (B.FR 300000)
£1808   *$3525*   *(23-Oct-90 C.A387/R) Estacade le soir - effet de lune (25x35cm-10x14in) s.d.1910 W/C (B.FR 110000)*
£2136   *$4166*   *(23-Oct-90 C.A386/R) Flowers (27x38cm-11x15in) mono. W/C (B.FR 130000)*

JEGERLEHNER, Hans (1907-1974) Swiss
£1102 $2160   (6-Nov-90 GF.L2596/R) Still life with bunch of flowers (73x60cm-29x24in) s. (S.FR 2700)

JEKYLL, Gertrude (?) British
£800   *$1576*   *(13-Nov-90 SWS146/R) Still life study of chrysanthemum and dahlias in a vase (42x30cm-17x12in) W/C over pencil htd.white*

JELE, Kaspar (1814-1893) German
£1342 $2617   (10-Oct-90 ZEL.L1559/R) Adoration of the Shepherds (36x23cm-14x9in) s.d.1842 (DM 4000)

JELENIK, R (19/20th C) Austrian
£1453 $2500   (17-May-91 WOL.C270) Playing the bagpipes (64x91cm-25x36in) s.

JELEZNOF, Mikhail (1912-1978) Russian
£522 $966   (4-Mar-91 ZZ.F53) Nu devant le miroir (49x35cm-19x14in) s. board (F.FR 5200)
£547 $952   (25-Mar-91 ARC.P54/R) La lecture (36x30cm-14x12in) s. (F.FR 5500)
£547 $952   (25-Mar-91 ARC.P53/R) L'ecoliere (49x39cm-19x15in) s. board (F.FR 5500)
£582 $1077   (4-Mar-91 ZZ.F52/R) Les enfants (36x43cm-14x17in) s. board (F.FR 5800)
£714 $1377   (16-Dec-90 CL.E96) Les enfants en promenade dans le jardin (42x80cm-17x31in) s. (F.FR 7000)
£1045 $1818   (25-Mar-91 ARC.P50/R) Les enfants (47x59cm-19x23in) s. board (F.FR 10500)
£1493 $2597   (25-Mar-91 ARC.P55/R) La lecon de lecture (40x48cm-16x19in) s. board (F.FR 15000)

JELGERSMA, Tako Hajo (1702-1795) Dutch
£400   *$708*   *(22-Mar-91 APT.P164) Barques de pecheurs en Hollande (15x22cm-6x9in) mono.d.1774 pen wash (F.FR 4000)*

JELINEK, Rudolf (1880-) Austrian
£535 $1049   (24-Jan-91 D.V3/R) Children at quay (76x85cm-30x33in) s. (A.S 11000)
£698 $1200   (17-May-91 DM.D2272/R) New puppy (61x51cm-24x20in) s.

JELLETT, Mainie (1897-1944) Irish
£600   *$1170*   *(26-Oct-90 CG35/R) Two girls resting on summer's day (25x30cm-10x12in) W/C*
£926   *$1787*   *(12-Dec-90 CH.E31) A figure (26x12cm-10x5in) s.d.25 bodycol. (E.P 1000)*
£1100   *$2035*   *(5-Mar-91 PH2/R) Abstract composition (25x15cm-10x6in) s.d.35 s.i.verso gouache card*

JELLEY, James Valentine (19th C) British
£620 $1228   (29-Jan-91 PH31) Enjoying summer's afternoon (19x37cm-7x15in) s.d.81
£700 $1211   (7-May-91 PH5) Noon on summer's day (51x41cm-20x16in) s.d.87 s.l.d.verso
£780 $1303   (22-Jul-91 SWS878/R) Violets (17x19cm-7x7in) s.i.

JENE, Edgar (1904-) ?
£1675 $2897   (8-May-91 D.V106/R) Bunch of flowers (44x37cm-17x15in) panel (A.S 35000)

JENKINS, Blanche (19th C) British
£1600 $2624   (20-Jun-91 B91 f) Green hat (30x25cm-12x10in) s.d.1885

JENKINS, G H (?) ?
£500 $845   (30-Apr-91 ACA616) Shepherd gathering flock (76x46cm-30x18in) s.

JENKINS, H (?) ?
£600   *$1140*   *(12-Sep-90 CSK209/R) Christ Church Gate, Canterbury (53x41cm-21x16in) s. W/C bodycol htd white*

JENKINS, Joseph John and WILLIS, Henry Brittan (19th C) British
£787 $1471   (27-Aug-90 SY.J169/R) Figures and cattle crossing stone bridge (46x66cm-18x26in) s.d.1857 W/C (SA.R 3800)
£1200 $2400   (8-Feb-91 C21/R) Figures with highland cattle and sheep in a moorland landscape (46x66cm-18x26in) s.d.1857 both artists W/C htd.white

JENKINS, L (?) European
£510 $862   (17-Apr-91 EA.M500) Cat and playful kittens in interior (76x102cm-30x40in) s. (C.D 1000)

JENKINS, Paul (1923-) American
£1223 $2361   (16-Dec-90 GL.P39/R) Phenomena - iron in fire (78x110cm-31x43in) s. acrylic paper (F.FR 12000)
£2168 $4250   (12-Feb-91 SY.NY400/R) Phenomena presiding host (76x61cm-30x24in) s. s.l.d.1976stretcher acrylic
£2286 $3864   (21-Apr-91 P.V19/R) Phenomena - Will of the Wisp (81x100cm-32x39in) s. i. verso acrylic (F.FR 23000)

JENKINS, Paul (1923-) American-cont.

£2296	$4500	(12-Feb-91 SY.NY402/R) Phenomena (97x137cm-38x54in) s.i.d.1972overlap acrylic
£2538	$5000	(4-Oct-90 SY.NY21/R) Psyche knot (71x76cm-28x30in) s.
£2551	$5000	(12-Feb-91 SY.NY399/R) Phenomena council bluff (122x66cm-48x26in) s. s.i.d.1977-78stretcher acrylic
£2551	$5000	(6-Nov-90 CE.NY22/R) Abstraction (64x84cm-25x33in) s.
£2900	$4727	(3-Jul-91 CSC.P69/R) Phenomena approach (60x72cm-24x28in) s. i.d.1961 verso (F.FR 29000)
£4061	$8000	(16-Nov-90 S.BM234/R) Phenomena grey reef (89x94cm-35x37in) s. s.i.verso acrylic canvas
£4569	$9000	(4-Oct-90 SY.NY88/R) Phenomena 1 (49x65cm-19x26in) s. s.d.1966 verso
£4585	$7519	(20-Jun-91 F.M424/R) Phenomena laino Eye (162x97cm-64x38in) s.i.d.1964 (I.L 10000000)
£4615	$9000	(10-Oct-90 SY.NY476/R) Phenomena, cast a spell (163x122cm-64x48in) s. s.i.d.1968overlap
£4872	$9500	(10-Oct-90 SY.NY479/R) Phenomena, a mystagogue (130x89cm-51x35in) s. s.i.d.1960verso
£5025	$8995	(11-Mar-91 GL.P241/R) Phenomena Harvest the moon (100x81cm-39x32in) s. i.d.1988 verso acrylic (F.FR 50000)
£5202	$9000	(7-May-91 CE.NY184/R) Phenomena after terrain (170x122cm-67x48in) s.d.1972 overlap acrylic canvas
£6000	$11700	(18-Oct-90 S.177/R) Clama (93x71cm-37x28in) s. s.i.d.1958verso s.stretcher acrylic
£6773	$11514	(30-May-91 FB.P22/R) Phenomena mystagogue (126x97cm-50x38in) s. i. verso (F.FR 68000)
£7514	$13000	(7-May-91 CE.NY169/R) Phenomena arch bow east (88x182cm-35x72in) s. s.d.1968 overlap acrylic canvas
£30581	$59021	(16-Dec-90 P.V59/R) Phenomena - Maize bringer (198x157cm-78x62in) s. i.d.January 1960 verso (F.FR 300000)
£602	*$970*	*(24-Jun-91 ARC.P12) Composition bleue (48x64cm-19x25in) s.i. W/C (F.FR 6000)*
£1156	*$2000*	*(12-May-91 H.C221) Untitled (76x107cm-30x42in) s. W/C*
£1168	*$2300*	*(15-Nov-90 D.NY11/R) Abstract composition (107x76cm-42x30in) s. W/C*
£1179	*$2300*	*(10-Oct-90 SY.NY555/R) Phenomena, that noon at mill pond (79x109cm-31x43in) s. W/C*
£1454	*$2850*	*(12-Feb-91 SY.NY474/R) Phenomena violet escape (79x109cm-31x43in) s. s.i.d.1983verso W/C*
£1538	*$3000*	*(10-Oct-90 SY.NY556/R) Phenomena, apple jade winds (91x124cm-36x49in) s. s.i.d.1980verso W/C*
£1538	*$3000*	*(10-Oct-90 SY.NY387/R) Phenomena, the high road (109x79cm-43x31in) s. W/C*
£1734	*$3000*	*(7-May-91 CE.NY238/R) Untitled (79x110cm-31x43in) s. W/C*
£1734	*$3000*	*(7-May-91 CE.NY239/R) Untitled (110x79cm-43x31in) s. W/C*
£1786	*$3500*	*(6-Nov-90 CE.NY205/R) Phenomena King of Diamonds (109x79cm-43x31in) s. i.d.1985 verso W/C*
£1786	*$3500*	*(6-Nov-90 CE.NY206/R) Phenomena Guide light (79x110cm-31x43in) s. i.d.1985 verso W/C*
£1795	*$3500*	*(24-Oct-90 B.SF1577/R) Phenomenon sojourner in sun (79x109cm-31x43in) s. s.d.1985 verso W/C*
£1840	*$3000*	*(12-Jun-91 SY.NY184/R) Phenomena O'Malley's tent (216x51cm-85x20in) s.i.d.1979 verso s.stretcher mixed media canvas*
£1840	*$3000*	*(12-Jun-91 SY.NY183/R) Phenomena Noel (216x51cm-85x20in) s.d.1979 overlap s.i.d.verso mixed media canvas*
£1850	*$3200*	*(7-May-91 CE.NY236/R) Untitled (79x110cm-31x43in) s. W/C*
£2051	*$4000*	*(10-Oct-90 SY.NY505/R) Phenomena Egyptian hat (79x109cm-31x43in) s. s.i.d.1983verso W/C*
£2179	*$4250*	*(10-Oct-90 SY.NY537/R) Phenomena, memory green (152x102cm-60x40in) s. s.i.d.1982verso W/C*
£2197	*$3800*	*(7-May-91 CE.NY240/R) Untitled (79x110cm-31x43in) s. W/C*
£2232	*$3750*	*(16-Jul-91 BG.M990/R) Abstract (56x76cm-22x30in) s. W/C*
£2347	*$4600*	*(6-Nov-90 CE.NY204/R) Phenomena The Devil's own (152x102cm-60x40in) s. i.d.1982 verso W/C*
£2398	*$4724*	*(15-Nov-90 I.N8/R) Phenomena under mirror (75x55cm-30x22in) s.i.d.1961 verso W/C (F.FR 23500)*
£2950	*$5576*	*(30-Sep-90 E.LA76) Phenomena Three Mile Harbor (100x150cm-39x59in) s. i.d.1982 verso W/C (F.FR 29000)*
£3015	*$5397*	*(15-Mar-91 FB.P68/R) Phenomena astrologer's device (79x110cm-31x43in) s. i.d.1983 verso W/C (F.FR 30000)*
£3902	*$7532*	*(15-Dec-90 S.Z163/R) Phenomena The High Road (108x77cm-43x30in) s.d.1977 gouache (S.FR 9600)*
£5056	*$9858*	*(15-Oct-90 CSC.P96/R) Composition (56x77cm-22x30in) s. mixed media (F.FR 50000)*

JENKINS, Wilfred (19th C) British

£1000	$1770	(21-Mar-91 CSK173) The Quay at Liverpool by moonlight (23x33cm-9x13in) board
£1134	$2200	(8-Dec-90 W.W221/R) Moonlit street (51x76cm-20x30in) s.d.88
£1150	$2231	(5-Dec-90 PHL239/R) After rain, the Salt House Docks, Liverpool (51x76cm-20x30in) s. i.verso

JENNENS, Frank Douglas Beaufoy (20th C) British

| £560 | $935 | (4-Jun-91 SWS1685/R) Pack of Brownies (86x111cm-34x44in) s.d.1936 |

JENNER, Isaac Walter (1836-1901) Australian
£1800 $3510   (15-Jan-91 SWS151/R) Ocean race from America (21x59cm-8x23in) s. i.verso
                     board

JENNER, William (?) ?
£2000 $4000   (7-Feb-91 GSP337) Oyster Mouth Bay, Swansea (28x43cm-11x17in) panel

JENNEY, Neil (1945-) American
£40816 $80000   (8-Nov-90 CH.NY371/R) Study (69x159cm-27x63in) s.d.1970 verso canvas
                     mounted on panel
£124260 $210000 (1-May-91 CH.NY22/R) Love and joy (152x193cm-60x76in) s.d.1969 verso
                     acrylic canvas

JENNINGS, W R (?) British
£1300 $2431   (28-Aug-90 S720/R) A Rocketeer (61x51cm-24x20in) s. i.stretcher

JENNY, Arnold (1831-1881) Swiss
£794 $1302   (21-Jun-91 G.Z524/R) Swiss landscape (42x51cm-17x20in) s.d.1862
                     (S.FR 2000)
£1400 $2296   (18-Jun-91 PH97) Alpine landscape (84x106cm-33x42in) s.d.1868
£1633 $3216   (15-Nov-90 EA.Z190/R) Alpine summer farm (64x81cm-25x32in) s.
                     (S.FR 4000)
£1959 $3722   (14-Sep-90 ZOF.Z1101) Rhine falls in moonlight (57x72cm-22x28in)
                     s.d.1879 (S.FR 4800)
£1967 $3698   (19-Sep-90 GK.Z848/R) Tellskapelle and Urirotstock in rising
                     thunderstorm (76x110cm-30x43in) s.d.1877 (S.FR 4800)

JENSEN, Alfred (1903-1981) American
£2041 $4000   (14-Feb-91 CH.NY19/R) Study, F (23x23cm-9x9in) s.i.d.1974verso
£12183 $24000   (14-Nov-90 SY.NY324/R) Acroatic Rectangle Per 17 (163x81cm-64x32in)
                     s.i.d.1967 verso
£14286 $28000   (14-Feb-91 CH.NY37/R) The goddess Iris (132x102cm-52x40in)
                     s.i.d.1968verso
£15306 $30000   (15-Feb-91 SY.NY159/R) Humab ku (122x81cm-48x32in) s.i.d.1962verso
£20408 $40000   (8-Nov-90 CH.NY321/R) Pythagoras XI (81x122cm-32x48in) s.i.d.1963 verso
£23669 $40000   (1-May-91 SY.NY245/R) Tikal (213x213cm-84x84in) s.d.1967 two parts
£40816 $80000   (7-Nov-90 SY.NY230/R) The marriage of odd and even numbers per I per II
                     (183x254cm-72x100in) s.i.d.1964 verso two panels
£4082 *$8000*   *(8-Nov-90 CH.NY124/R) Two-sided target (25x33cm-10x13in) s.i.d.1952
                     gouache graphite pen double-sided*

JENSEN, Alfred (1859-1935) Danish
£673 $1291   (27-Dec-90 RAS.V39/R) Seascape with vessels (80x132cm-31x52in) s.d.1916
                     (D.KR 7500)
£743 $1449   (26-Oct-90 BM.B811/R) Fishing boats, Hamburg (31x41cm-12x16in) s.
                     (DM 2200)
£743 $1449   (26-Oct-90 KM.K1293) Hamburg Harbour with shipping (75x118cm-30x46in) s.
                     (DM 2200)
£874 $1696   (5-Dec-90 DO.H2016) Sailing ship near coastal town (53x80cm-21x31in) s.
                     (DM 2500)
£1014 $1926   (14-Sep-90 SA.A1336/R) Early morning, Hamburg Harbour (44x62cm-17x24in)
                     s. (DM 3000)
£1103 $2174   (16-Nov-90 GF.H9/R) Portrait of steamship Agnes entering Hamburg Harbour
                     (71x105cm-28x41in) s.d.1898 (DM 3200)
£1573 $3037   (14-Dec-90 BM.B637/R) Harbour with shipping (71x100cm-28x39in) s. canvas
                     laid down (DM 4500)

JENSEN, Axel P (1885-1972) Danish
£604 $1190   (31-Oct-90 KH.K56) Still life (50x61cm-20x24in) s. (D.KR 6800)
£660 $1287   (10-Oct-90 RAS.K219) View of the sea (67x96cm-26x38in) s.d.45
                     (D.KR 7500)
£792 $1545   (10-Oct-90 RAS.K324) Hilly winter landscape (105x140cm-41x55in) s.d.35
                     (D.KR 9000)

JENSEN, Bill (20th C) American
£15385 $26000   (1-May-91 CH.NY35/R) Fragil (81x61cm-32x24in) s.d.1982-1983-1984 verso
£19231 $32500   (1-May-91 SY.NY171/R) Lamb (72x61cm-28x24in) s.d.1977-1983-84 verso
£23669 $40000   (1-May-91 SY.NY166/R) Denial (102x79cm-40x31in) s.d.1983-86 verso

JENSEN, C A (1792-1870) Danish
£896 $1792   (6-Feb-91 RAS.K311/R) Portrait of lady wearing black dress with white
                     collar (28x22cm-11x9in) (D.KR 10000)
£2643 $4943   (29-Aug-90 KH.K97/R) Portrait of Hanne Marie Schmidt (24x19cm-9x7in)
                     s.d.1827 (D.KR 30000)
£31418 $61894   (14-Nov-90 RAS.K34/R) Portrait of Comtesse Sofie Catarina Blucher-Altona
                     as child (145x100cm-57x39in) s.d.1835 (D.KR 350000)

JENSEN, Christian Albrecht (1792-1870) Danish
£1700 $3366   (30-Jan-91 CSK245) Portrait of a lady, bust length in a grey dress
                     (23x18cm-9x7in) s.d.1828

JENSEN, E M (1822-1915) Danish
£881 $1471   (6-Jun-91 RAS.K84) Landscape near Furusoen (90x80cm-35x31in) mono.
                     (D.KR 10000)

JENSEN, Edvard Michael (1822-1915) Danish
£1127 $1915   (28-May-91 AB.S4772/R) Coastal landscape with figures, Oresund
           (63x95cm-25x37in) mono. (S.KR 12000)

JENSEN, G (19/20th C) ?
£1300 $2535   (18-Oct-90 CSK95/R) Brig entering Copenhagen Harbour (102x142cm-40x56in)
           s.

JENSEN, I (19th C) Danish
£987 $1945   (14-Nov-90 RAS.K174/R) Still life of summer flowers with bird by glass
           (28x36cm-11x14in) s.d.1868 (D.KR 11000)

JENSEN, J L (1800-1856) Danish
£572 $961   (23-Apr-91 RAS.K264) Bouquet of roses and bells (11x13cm-4x5in) s.
           (D.KR 6500)
£890 $1745   (22-Nov-90 RAS.V728/R) Roses and lilies of the valley (11x14cm-4x6in) s.
           (D.KR 10000)
£1112 $2169   (19-Oct-90 RAS.V496/R) White flowers (15x21cm-6x8in) s. (D.KR 12500)
£1167 $2299   (14-Nov-90 RAS.K303) Still life of fish on clay dish (27x28cm-11x11in)
           s.d.1842 panel (D.KR 13000)
£1975 $3890   (14-Nov-90 RAS.K660) Still life of camellias in Greek bowl
           (28x38cm-11x15in) s. panel (D.KR 22000)
£2163 $4196   (22-Aug-90 RAS.K75/R) Lilacs and laburnum (40x31cm-16x12in) s. panel
           (D.KR 25000)
£2163 $4196   (22-Aug-90 RAS.K77/R) Bouquet of roses, blossom, primula and beech
           leaves (24x32cm-9x13in) s. (D.KR 25000)
£2174 $4196   (10-Dec-90 BU.K59/R) Still life of spring flowers on stone ledge
           (23x31cm-9x12in) s. panel (D.KR 24000)
£2201 $3697   (22-Apr-91 BU.K64/R) Still life of fruit on stone ledge
           (25x33cm-10x13in) init.d.1823 cardboard (D.KR 25000)
£2249 $4363   (22-Aug-90 RAS.K85/R) Bouquet of pink roses and fruit blossom
           (21x15cm-8x6in) s. panel (D.KR 26000)
£2627 $5070   (10-Dec-90 BU.K29/R) Still life of pansies on marble ledge
           (14x19cm-6x7in) s.d.1835 wood (D.KR 29000)
£2768 $5370   (22-Aug-90 RAS.K81/R) Bouquet of pink roses and fruit blossom
           (24x17cm-9x7in) s. panel (D.KR 32000)
£4036 $7749   (27-Dec-90 RAS.V40/R) Two birds of paradise and bee on apple blossom
           branch (30x40cm-12x16in) s.d.1848 (D.KR 45000)
£4074 $6886   (1-May-91 KH.K92/R) Red and white roses (21x30cm-8x12in) s. mahogany
           (D.KR 46000)
£4255 $6936   (13-Jun-91 RAS.V553/R) Still life of dead game with flowers and oak
           leaves (51x62cm-20x24in) s. (D.KR 48000)
£7630 $15031   (14-Nov-90 RAS.K68/R) Still life of roses, carnations and summer flowers
           on tree trunk (25x34cm-10x13in) s. panel (D.KR 85000)
£11807 $22906   (5-Dec-90 KH.K59/R) Still life of roses in glass (43x24cm-17x9in)
           s.d.1843 (D.KR 130000)
£1167   *$2299*   *(14-Nov-90 RAS.K173/R) Bouquet of red, white and blue summer flowers*
           (24x18cm-9x7in) s.d.1838 gouache (D.KR 13000)

JENSEN, Johan-Laurents (1800-1856) Danish
£656 $1233   (19-Sep-90 GK.Z849) Headdress of myrtle leaves with roses
           (26x36cm-10x14in) (S.FR 1600)
£1712 $2791   (12-Jun-91 N.M477/R) Anemones (19x14cm-7x6in) s. panel (DM 5000)
£3000 $4920   (19-Jun-91 S245/R) Still life with flowers (15x10cm-6x4in) s. panel
£4359 $8500   (23-Oct-90 SY.NY141/R) A still life of roses (20x13cm-8x5in) s. panel
£5500 $10560   (28-Nov-90 S82/R) Still life of roses (24x31cm-9x12in) s. s.d.1846verso
           panel
£5789 $11000   (27-Feb-91 SY.NY322/R) Basket of fruit on ledge (14x19cm-6x7in) s. panel
£6500 $11180   (17-May-91 C79/R) Mixed flowers, cherry blossom amd beech leaves on
           marble ledge (20x27cm-8x11in) s.d.1835 panel
£6573 $11174   (28-May-91 AB.S4774/R) Still life of flowers (33x26cm-13x10in) s. panel
           (S.KR 70000)
£6761 $11493   (28-May-91 AB.S4773/R) Still life of oranges, flowers and nuts
           (51x38cm-20x15in) s. panel (S.KR 72000)
£7000 $12040   (17-May-91 C77/R) Mixed flowers on ledge (15x21cm-6x8in) s.d.1844 panel
£8205 $16000   (23-Oct-90 SY.NY140/R) A still life of fruit in an urn (34x44cm-13x17in)
           s.d.1838 panel
£8500 $14620   (17-May-91 C81/R) Mixed flowers on marble ledge (27x36cm-11x14in) s.
           panel
£9000 $15480   (17-May-91 C75/R) Roses and stephanotis (28x20cm-11x8in) panel oval
£9000 $15480   (17-May-91 C76/R) Roses and hollyhocks (25x17cm-10x7in) s. panel
£9790 $18895   (12-Dec-90 N.M569/R) Roses with forget-me-not and daisies
           (14x19cm-6x7in) s. panel (DM 28000)
£10000 $17200   (17-May-91 C82/R) Mixed flowers on marble ledge (25x32cm-10x13in)
           s.d.1833 panel
£10500 $18060   (17-May-91 C80/R) Roses and hollyhock (21x15cm-8x6in) s. panel
£12000 $23040   (28-Nov-90 S78/R) Still life with lillies and roses (49x37cm-19x15in) s.
           panel
£12000 $20640   (17-May-91 C74/R) Pink roses (14x10cm-6x4in) s. panel
£16725 $28099   (23-Apr-91 RAS.K4/R) Basket of roses on ledge (38x45cm-15x18in) s.d.1825
           (D.KR 190000)
£20264 $37894   (29-Aug-90 KH.K98/R) Pink roses in glass vase (35x26cm-14x10in) s. panel
           (D.KR 230000)
£49242 $82727   (24-Apr-91 BA.S101/R) Still life of summer flowers (85x57cm-33x22in) s.
           panel (S.KR 520000)

988

JENSEN, Johan-Laurents (attrib) (1800-1856) Danish

£649	$1259	(22-Aug-90 RAS.K261) Pink roses and fruit blossom (22x18cm-9x7in) (D.KR 7500)
£1585	$2662	(23-Apr-91 RAS.K263/R) Still life of roses, tulips and iris in jug with bird's nest (19x14cm-7x6in) panel (D.KR 18000)
£1911	$3746	(24-Nov-90 SA.A619/R) Still life with roses and poppies (63x50cm-25x20in) canvas laid down (DM 5600)
£5682	$9545	(24-Apr-91 BA.S103/R) The Paradise bird (29x37cm-11x15in) panel (S.KR 60000)

JENSEN, Johan-Laurents (school) (1800-1856) Danish

£792	$1331	(23-Apr-91 RAS.K266) Still life of roses and pansies with bird on vase (34x40cm-13x16in) indist.s. panel (D.KR 9000)
£930	$1572	(2-May-91 RAS.V57/R) Still life of summer flowers and bird (30x39cm-12x15in) (D.KR 10500)
£930	$1572	(1-May-91 KH.K93) Flowers in vase (48x36cm-19x14in) panel (D.KR 10500)
£995	$1930	(22-Aug-90 RAS.K265) Bouquet of flowers in Greek vase (30x38cm-12x15in) (D.KR 11500)
£1056	$1775	(23-Apr-91 RAS.K377/R) Still life of roses and other flowers in glass vase (68x60cm-27x24in) i. (D.KR 12000)
£1122	$2211	(14-Nov-90 RAS.K309) Parrot on orange branch (40x30cm-16x12in) (D.KR 12500)
£1211	$2349	(22-Aug-90 RAS.K263) Still life of melon, peach and nuts with grapes (68x52cm-27x20in) (D.KR 14000)
£1346	$2653	(14-Nov-90 RAS.K305) Red hibiscus and white lilies (38x29cm-15x11in) (D.KR 15000)
£1498	$2501	(6-Jun-91 RAS.K87) Pink, white, red and yellow roses (46x62cm-18x24in) panel (D.KR 17000)
£1613	$3226	(6-Feb-91 RAS.K332/R) Basket of dahlias (49x62cm-19x24in) init.d.1845 (D.KR 18000)
£1726	$3348	(5-Dec-90 KH.K62/R) Roses under beech tree on tree trunk (52x62cm-20x24in) (D.KR 19000)
£1975	$3890	(14-Nov-90 RAS.K661/R) Still life of roses in vase and strawberries on leaf (80x90cm-31x35in) (D.KR 22000)
£2163	$4196	(22-Aug-90 RAS.K262/R) Roses, primulas and fruit blossom in glass (44x33cm-17x13in) (D.KR 25000)
£2368	$4500	(27-Feb-91 SY.NY323/R) Still life with roses in Grecian urn (45x38cm-18x15in)
£3345	$5620	(23-Apr-91 RAS.K162/R) Still life of parrot and fruit in basket (75x93cm-30x37in) (D.KR 38000)

JENSEN, Johan-Laurents (style) (1800-1856) Danish

| £3200 | $6144 | (28-Nov-90 S79/R) Still life of butterflies and white convolvulus (42x31cm-17x12in) panel |

JENSEN, Karl (1851-1933) Danish

£1335	$2509	(18-Sep-90 BU.K59/R) Interior from Rosenborg (44x59cm-17x23in) init. (D.KR 15000)
£1616	$3183	(14-Nov-90 RAS.K646/R) Inside the Pantheon in Rome (82x79cm-32x31in) init. (D.KR 18000)
£2669	$5018	(18-Sep-90 BU.K11/R) Interior from Emanuel's Church (50x38cm-20x15in) init.d.1905 (D.KR 30000)

JEPSEN, Morten (1826-1903) Danish

| £1057 | $1766 | (6-Jun-91 RAS.K92/R) Amalphi with Vesuvius in background (31x43cm-12x17in) init. (D.KR 12000) |
| £1257 | $2476 | (14-Nov-90 RAS.K27/R) Parisian street scene (44x52cm-17x20in) s.i.d.1876 (D.KR 14000) |

JERICHAU, Holger H (1861-1900) Danish

£649	$1259	(22-Aug-90 RAS.K25/R) Greek landscape with white houses and olive trees (54x78cm-21x31in) s. (D.KR 7500)
£898	$1768	(14-Nov-90 RAS.K104/R) Italian river landscape, late afternoon (84x128cm-33x50in) s. (D.KR 10000)
£1063	$1796	(2-May-91 RAS.V61/R) Italian river landscape, late afternoon (84x128cm-33x50in) s. (D.KR 12000)
£1077	$2122	(14-Nov-90 RAS.K636/R) Monk and fisherman conversing on Capri (70x48cm-28x19in) s.i.d.1894-97 (D.KR 12000)
£1860	$3534	(14-Sep-90 RAS.V592/R) Coastal landscape from Napoli (42x90cm-17x35in) s.i. (D.KR 21000)
£2506	$4260	(28-May-91 F.R143/R) I bagni di Tiberio (52x82cm-20x32in) s. (I.L 5500000)
£4101	$6971	(28-May-91 F.R141/R) Marina Grande a Capri (42x64cm-17x25in) s. (I.L 9000000)
£4252	$8078	(14-Sep-90 RAS.V593/R) Hotel Grotte Bleu, Capri (112x107cm-44x42in) indist.s. (D.KR 48000)
£7042	$11831	(23-Apr-91 RAS.K139/R) Indian landscape with temples by river's edge and elephants watering (97x125cm-38x49in) s.d.1894 (D.KR 80000)

JERICHAU, Jens Adolf (1816-1883) Danish

| £1408 | $2423 | (15-May-91 RAS.K164 b/R) Church interior from Toledo (40x40cm-16x16in) (D.KR 16000) |

JERICHAU-BAUMANN, Elisabeth (1819-1881) Danish

| £627 | $1254 | (6-Feb-91 RAS.K167) Young Italian boy wearing hat (35x35cm-14x14in) s. (D.KR 7000) |

JERICHAU-BAUMANN, Elisabeth (1819-1881) Danish-cont.

£884	$1662	(10-Aug-90 RAS.V482) Study of nude young man (121x67cm-48x26in) (D.KR 10000)
£1165	$2330	(6-Feb-91 RAS.K166) Study of young Italian woman (120x67cm-47x26in) (D.KR 13000)
£1298	$2517	(22-Aug-90 RAS.K279/R) Young Southern girl with low cut dress and pearls (60x47cm-24x19in) s.d.1872 (D.KR 15000)
£1408	$2366	(23-Apr-91 RAS.K389/R) Italian girl with waterjug (103x80cm-41x31in) (D.KR 16000)
£1673	$2994	(13-Apr-91 FAL.M131/R) Southern girl with green jug (60x47cm-24x19in) s.d.1855 (S.KR 18000)
£3000	$5910	(5-Oct-90 C115/R) Water carrier (57x47cm-22x19in) s.
£3770	$7427	(14-Nov-90 RAS.K56/R) Esther (130x94cm-51x37in) s.i.d.1874 (D.KR 42000)
£5986	$10056	(23-Apr-91 RAS.K63/R) Italian woman walking with sleeping child (158x121cm-62x48in) s.d.1854 (D.KR 68000)

JERKEN, Erik (1898-1947) Swedish

£755	$1306	(22-May-91 BA.S97/R) View towards Stromparterren (56x49cm-22x19in) s.d.1941 (S.KR 8000)
£973	$1888	(4-Dec-90 BA.S232/R) Still life of tulips in jug (55x46cm-22x18in) s. (S.KR 10500)
£1887	$3264	(22-May-91 BA.S96/R) Wild flowers in jug (73x61cm-29x24in) s. (S.KR 20000)

JERNBERG, August (1826-1896) Swedish

£663	$1114	(24-Apr-91 BA.S106/R) Woman grinding coffee (40x31cm-16x12in) s. cardboard on panel (S.KR 7000)
£3309	$6485	(6-Nov-90 BA.S123/R) Soap-bubbles (27x21cm-11x8in) s. panel (S.KR 36000)
£8000	$15360	(28-Nov-90 S98/R) Beauty (60x125cm-24x49in) s.d.1854

JERNBERG, Olof (1855-1935) Swedish

£1020	$1643	(26-Jun-91 KM.K1514) River landscape with poplars (45x50cm-18x20in) s. board (DM 3000)
£1351	$2297	(27-May-91 L.K290) Lower Rhine landscape with windmill and woman on path (24x34cm-9x13in) s. board (DM 4000)
£1525	$2486	(3-Jul-91 WE.MU49/R) Winter landscape (51x68cm-20x27in) s. (DM 4500)
£2397	$3908	(12-Jun-91 N.M478/R) Sailing boats on calm sea at dusk (60x81cm-24x32in) s.i. (DM 7000)
£4167	$7000	(24-Apr-91 BA.S108/R) Autumn landscape (114x174cm-45x69in) s. (S.KR 44000)

JERNDORFF, August (1846-1906) Danish

£1038	$2014	(22-Aug-90 RAS.K280) Sketch of young lady and small boy (31x31cm-12x12in) mono. (D.KR 12000)

JEROME, Ambrosini (19th C) British

£2000	$3940	(1-Nov-90 C301/R) Fleur de Marie at Farm of Bouqueval (76x63cm-30x25in) s.d.1844

JERVAS, Charles (1675-1739) British

£4500	$8865	(16-Nov-90 C1/R) Portrait of Sir John Willes in legal robes holding scroll (128x103cm-50x41in)
£7000	$12530	(10-Apr-91 S78/R) Portrait of Elizabeth Cosby, of Stradbally Hall, Ireland, in landscape (97x74cm-38x29in)
£16000	$31520	(14-Nov-90 S34/R) Portrait of William Pulteney Earl of Bath seated by statue of Minerva (237x143cm-93x56in)

JERVAS, Charles (circle) (1675-1739) British

£940	$1626	(20-May-91 SWS260) Portrait of a gentleman, head and shoulders, wearing a brown coat (68x57cm-27x22in) oval
£1400	$2730	(26-Oct-90 C219/R) Portrait of Miss Woodgate in a yellow dress (127x102cm-50x40in)

JERVAS, Charles (style) (1675-1739) British

£1400	$2702	(13-Dec-90 CSK288) Portrait of Montague, Earl of Lindsey, in Garter robes (77x63cm-30x25in) with i.

JERVAS, Charles and BOGDANI, Jakob (attrib) (18th C) British/Hungarian

£2287	$3750	(19-Jun-91 B.SF1709/R) Young girl seated in park holding bunch of grapes and feeding cockatoo (107x102cm-42x40in)

JESPERS (20th C) Belgian

£1164	$2083	(12-Mar-91 GM.B1008/R) Personnage assis. Portrait de femme (112x66cm-44x26in) s. double-sided (B.FR 70000)

JESPERS, Floris (1889-1965) Belgian

£589	$990	(23-Apr-91 C.A147) Tribal chief (80x60cm-31x24in) (B.FR 36000)
£655	$1100	(23-Apr-91 C.A146) Negress with basket on her head (54x25cm-21x10in) (B.FR 40000)
£740	$1442	(23-Oct-90 C.A600) Haven nr 2 (44x68cm-17x27in) s.d.1961 paper (B.FR 45000)
£822	$1602	(23-Oct-90 C.A598) Still life (70x80cm-28x31in) s.d.1943 (B.FR 50000)
£998	$1786	(16-Mar-91 KV.L160) Congolese village (36x29cm-14x11in) s. paper on panel (B.FR 60000)
£1064	$1787	(23-Apr-91 C.A148) Trees (100x80cm-39x31in) s.d.1945 (B.FR 65000)
£1170	$2292	(12-Feb-91 GM.B381) L'Ecuyere (50x40cm-20x16in) s. (B.FR 70000)

JESPERS, Floris (1889-1965) Belgian-cont.

£1203	$2370	(6-Oct-90 KV.L155/R) Flowers in a jug (54x40cm-21x16in) s. panel (B.FR 75000)
£1227	$2062	(23-Apr-91 C.A131/R) Landscape in Our (42x60cm-17x24in) s. (B.FR 75000)
£1473	$2475	(23-Apr-91 C.A138) Congolese market (70x104cm-28x41in) panel (B.FR 90000)
£1473	$2475	(23-Apr-91 C.A139) Three Congolese women (80x100cm-31x39in) s.d.1952 (B.FR 90000)
£1473	$2475	(23-Apr-91 C.A151) In the stall (68x90cm-27x35in) s. (B.FR 90000)
£1663	$2976	(16-Mar-91 KV.L158/R) Still life of fish (42x90cm-17x35in) s.d.1946 panel (B.FR 100000)
£1703	$3286	(12-Dec-90 CH.AM342) Negresses carrying lyggage on head in Belgium Congo (47x47cm-19x19in) s. board (D.FL 5500)
£1800	$3025	(23-Apr-91 C.A137/R) Girl with a bird (80x60cm-31x24in) s.d.1948 (B.FR 110000)
£1802	$3117	(22-May-91 CH.AM519/R) Still life of fishes, shell and bottle on table (21x15cm-8x6in) s.d.24 on glass (D.FL 6000)
£1970	$3409	(25-May-91 KV.L153) Two negresses (23x33cm-9x13in) s. board (B.FR 120000)
£2165	$4265	(6-Oct-90 KV.L434/R) Resting negress (60x79cm-24x31in) s.d.1951 (B.FR 135000)
£2465	$4807	(23-Oct-90 C.A394/R) Nude woman with chair (25x20cm-10x8in) s. tempera (B.FR 150000)
£3096	$5975	(12-Dec-90 CH.AM341/R) Still life with grapes in bowl on window sill (54x65cm-21x26in) s. (D.FL 10000)
£3273	$5499	(23-Apr-91 C.A143) The village church (100x80cm-39x31in) s. (B.FR 200000)
£3615	$7050	(23-Oct-90 C.A393/R) On the beach (23x22cm-9x9in) s. tempera (B.FR 220000)
£4025	$7768	(12-Dec-90 CH.AM339/R) Flemish landscape (60x80cm-24x31in) s.d.33 (D.FL 13000)
£6006	$10390	(22-May-91 CH.AM516/R) House in woods (60x70cm-24x28in) s.d.33 (D.FL 20000)
£8183	$13748	(23-Apr-91 C.A126/R) Still life of flowers (130x100cm-51x39in) s.d.1916 (B.FR 500000)
£8183	$13748	(23-Apr-91 C.A128/R) Clown with a guitar (37x49cm-15x19in) s. egg tempera (B.FR 500000)
£9039	$17625	(23-Oct-90 C.A391/R) Negresses (175x125cm-69x49in) s. (B.FR 550000)
£9820	$16498	(23-Apr-91 C.A129/R) Horse and cow in landscape egg tempera (B.FR 600000)
£10811	$18703	(22-May-91 CH.AM515/R) Clown (63x53cm-25x21in) s.d.33 on glass (D.FL 36000)
£11189	$21594	(12-Dec-90 WE.MU201/R) African dance (77x104cm-30x41in) s.d.1955 (DM 32000)
£13093	$21997	(23-Apr-91 C.A127/R) Reflexions (90x72cm-35x28in) s.d.1917 board (B.FR 800000)
£34056	$65728	(13-Dec-90 SY.AM40/R) Pruimen (80x110cm-31x43in) s.d.1915 verso (D.FL 110000)
£49302	$96138	(23-Oct-90 C.A388/R) Le boeuf sur le toit (95x80cm-37x31in) s. tempera (B.FR 3000000)
£13093	*$21997*	*(23-Apr-91 C.A125/R) Seated nude in an interior (100x100cm-39x39in) s. gouache (B.FR 800000)*

JESPERSEN, Henrik (1853-?) Danish

£636	$1233	(5-Dec-90 KH.K67) Garden with poppies and lupines (69x99cm-27x39in) s. (D.KR 7000)
£908	$1780	(22-Nov-90 RAS.V733/R) Mountain landscape from Tyrol (90x143cm-35x56in) s.d.1891 (D.KR 10200)
£1500	$2580	(17-May-91 C148/R) Garden in summer with delphiniums and tiger lilies (68x99cm-27x39in) s.
£3800	$6232	(19-Jun-91 S272/R) Lily pond (60x104cm-24x41in) s.

JESSEMIN, Aude (20th C) ?

| *£556* | *$1084* | *(15-Oct-90 CSC.P104 b/R) L'homme vu ar la femme (73x100cm-29x39in) s. oil ink canvas (F.FR 5500)* |

JESSEN, Carl Ludwig (1833-1917) Danish/German

£1014	$1976	(26-Oct-90 BM.B814) Self portrait (20x15cm-8x6in) mono.d.1879 board (DM 3000)
£2703	$5270	(26-Oct-90 BM.B813/R) Yard with poultry before stable and view of North German landscape (45x66cm-18x26in) s.d.1887 (DM 8000)
£6488	$12587	(22-Aug-90 RAS.K89/R) Interior with lady embroidering and boy feeding bird in cage (86x65cm-34x26in) s.d.1858 (D.KR 75000)
£12162	$23716	(26-Oct-90 BM.B812/R) View of interior, Nordfriesland (43x62cm-17x24in) s.d.1903 (DM 36000)
£541	*$1054*	*(26-Oct-90 BM.B815/R) Rocca di Papa, village view with women seated on steps (26x20cm-10x8in) s.i.d.1868 chl W/C (DM 1600)*

JESSEN, Carl Ludwig (attrib) (1833-1917) Danish/German

| £616 | $1035 | (23-Apr-91 RAS.K353/R) Old woman by spinning wheel (46x41cm-18x16in) (D.KR 7000) |

JESSOP, J (19th C) ?

| *£680* | *$1319* | *(24-Aug-90 CBB270) Still life of fruit (25x36cm-10x14in) s.d.1864 W/C* |

JESSUP (1920-) Australian
£1003 $1956   (10-Oct-90 ARC.P124) Bankok Batik (50x65cm-20x26in) s. (F.FR 10000)

JESSUP, Frederick (1920-) Australian
£3089 $6085   (13-Nov-90 J.M74/R) Woolloormooloo Tenaments (65x45cm-26x18in) s.d,1948
                   board (A.D 8000)
£512 $860   (22-Apr-91 SY.ME168) Curious king (33x26cm-13x10in) s.i.verso gouache
                   (A.D 1100)

JETTEL, Eugen (1845-1901) Austrian
£430 $722   (25-Apr-91 D.V46/R) Donkey cart in field. Study of windmill
                   (25x43cm-10x17in) i. pencil double-sided (A.S 9000)
£478 $802   (25-Apr-91 D.V111/R) Sunflowers (37x26cm-15x10in) pencil (A.S 10000)

JETTMAR, Rudolf (1869-1939) Polish
£4624 $8000   (22-May-91 SY.NY247/R) Traumer vom abend (61x100cm-24x39in) bears sig.
                   d.924
£976 $1806   (7-Mar-91 D.V3/R) Farewell (13x17cm-5x7in) mono. pen brush indian ink
                   (A.S 20000)

JEUNE, Henry le (1820-1904) British
£900 $1485   (9-Jul-91 PH181) Good read (18x13cm-7x5in) mono.
£1200 $1956   (13-Jun-91 CSK303) Good book (28x22cm-11x9in) mono. paper on canvas
£1368 $2600   (27-Feb-91 SY.NY242/R) By water's edge (33x23cm-13x9in) mono. board
£1500 $2610   (26-Mar-91 PH133) The early days of Timothy (61x76cm-24x30in) mono.
£4800 $9408   (13-Feb-91 S177/R) Bird's nest (59x49cm-23x19in) mono.d.1867

JEUNE, James le (1910-) ?
£1204 $2323   (12-Dec-90 CH.E48/R) Two small boys on a beach (30x40cm-12x16in) s.
                   board (E.P 1300)
£2800 $4872   (27-Mar-91 S33/R) The tower clock, Youghal (61x51cm-24x20in) s.
£3300 $6204   (19-Sep-90 PHC295/R) Sunlit glade (52x62cm-20x24in) s.i.verso
£1019 $1966   (12-Dec-90 CH.E26/R) Market scene, Provence (26x37cm-10x15in) s. W/C
                   (E.P 1100)

JEWELL, Ruth (20th C) American
£773 $1500   (24-Aug-90 RB.HY82/R) Maine coastal village (64x76cm-25x30in) s.

JIMENEZ Y ARANDA, Jose (1837-1903) Spanish
£3046 $6000   (16-Nov-90 S.BM20/R) La lectura de la esperanza (43x64cm-17x25in)
                   s.d.1870
£10000 $16400   (19-Jun-91 S366/R) La lectura de la Esperanza (44x62cm-17x24in) s.d.1870

JIMENEZ Y ARANDA, Luis (1845-1928) Spanish
£1033 $1983   (18-Dec-90 DUR.M30) Joven (15x11cm-6x4in) panel (S.P 190000)
£1587 $2730   (19-May-91 ZZ.F2/R) Femme pres du parapet (22x13cm-9x5in) s. panel
                   (F.FR 16000)
£3298 $6331   (19-Feb-91 DUR.M24) Primera Comunion (70x48cm-28x19in) panel
                   (S.P 600000)
£4573 $8963   (6-Nov-90 SY.AM179/R) Two women in meadow (43x64cm-17x25in) s.i.
                   (D.FL 15000)
£8092 $14000   (22-May-91 SY.NY289/R) Le jardin du Presbytere (87x126cm-34x50in)
                   s.d.1922
£25000 $48000   (30-Nov-90 C76/R) Meeting grandmother (76x117cm-30x46in) s.i.
£46000 $75440   (18-Jun-91 PH172/R) The recital (87x127cm-34x50in) s.i.

JIMENEZ Y FERNANDEZ, Federico (1841-?) Spanish
£5435 $10435   (19-Dec-90 ANS.M28/R) Gallo y gallinas (75x110cm-30x43in) s.
                   (S.P 1000000)

JIMENEZ Y MARTIN, Juan (1858-?) Spanish
£4191 $7250   (22-May-91 SY.NY285/R) Moorish queen (60x40cm-24x16in) s.i.

JIMENEZ, F (?) Spanish
£2700 $4509   (22-Jul-91 SWS1066/R) Poultry by a barn door (39x30cm-15x12in) both s.
                   panel pair

JIRLOW, Lennart (1936-) Swedish
£1509 $2611   (22-May-91 BA.S100/R) Street in Provence (19x24cm-7x9in) s. panel
                   (S.KR 16000)
£3286 $5587   (28-May-91 AB.S5222/R) French street scene with figures and cafes,
                   evening (46x38cm-18x15in) s. panel (S.KR 35000)
£3336 $6473   (4-Dec-90 BA.S236/R) Butcher outside his shop (24x19cm-9x7in) s. panel
                   (S.KR 36000)
£4634 $8990   (4-Dec-90 BA.S235/R) Wine cellar (48x34cm-19x13in) s. panel (S.KR 50000)
£6487 $12586   (4-Dec-90 BA.S234/R) Clown with bouquet of flowers and umbrella
                   (63x51cm-25x20in) s. (S.KR 70000)
£11883 $23291   (20-Nov-90 GO.G104/R) Studio interior with nude model (65x81cm-26x32in)
                   s. (S.KR 130000)
£12797 $25082   (20-Nov-90 GO.G105/R) Breakfast in the garden in summer
                   (73x92cm-29x36in) s. (S.KR 140000)
£12975 $25171   (5-Dec-90 AB.S7121/R) French cafe interior (50x60cm-20x24in) s.
                   (S.KR 140000)
£13930 $26745   (27-Nov-90 BU.S153/R) In the studio (78x95cm-31x37in) s. (S.KR 151000)
£14365 $27868   (4-Dec-90 BA.S233/R) Kitchen scene with parrot (81x65cm-32x26in) s.
                   (S.KR 155000)

JIRLOW, Lennart (1936-) Swedish-cont.
£23170 $44717   (12-Dec-90 BU.S157/R) In the garden (131x195cm-52x77in) s. (S.KR 250000)
£26877 $51872   (12-Dec-90 BU.S158/R) The cyclist (115x193cm-45x76in) s. (S.KR 290000)
£589 $1055   (17-Mar-91 BU.M139) Figure studies, including self portrait
         (13x20cm-5x8in) s. gouache (S.KR 6300)
£969 $1860   (27-Nov-90 AB.S4033) Brasserie Lipp (16x9cm-6x4in) s. gouache W/C
         restaurant bill (S.KR 10500)
£969 $1860   (27-Nov-90 AB.S4032) Restaurant Les Glenan (19x10cm-7x4in) s. gouache
         W/C restaurant bill (S.KR 10500)
£1179 $2040   (22-May-91 BA.S102/R) House in South of France (18x12cm-7x5in) s.
         gouache (S.KR 12500)
£4244 $8148   (27-Nov-90 BU.S155/R) Climbing trees (45x54cm-18x21in) s. gouache
         (S.KR 46000)

JIRO, Rene (20th C) French?
£550 $924   (27-Apr-91 MJ.P134/R) Nu en bleu (81x130cm-32x51in) (F.FR 5500)
£850 $1428   (27-Apr-91 MJ.P136/R) L'exploratrice (141x91cm-56x36in) s. (F.FR 8500)
£1050 $1764   (27-Apr-91 MJ.P135/R) Modele 110 003 (141x91cm-56x36in) s. (F.FR 10500)

JOBERT, Fernand (19th C) French
£847 $1500   (22-Mar-91 S.W2499) Private soiree (30x46cm-12x18in) s. panel

JOBLING, Robert (1841-1923) British
£950 $1606   (30-Apr-91 AG314/R) Summer (29x45cm-11x18in) s.d.1915
£1600 $2960   (4-Mar-91 PHB63) Cleaning fish on quayside (36x26cm-14x10in) s.
£1900 $3515   (4-Mar-91 PHB59/R) Haycart (71x92cm-28x36in) s.
£2200 $3542   (25-Jun-91 AG389/R) Arist's wife and daughter reading by lamplight
         (44x59cm-17x23in) s.
£2450 $3945   (25-Jun-91 AG388/R) The milkmaid (32x37cm-13x15in) s.i.d.1902verso
£2800 $5376   (29-Nov-90 B55/R) Landing the catch (61x91cm-24x36in) s.
£3800 $7030   (4-Mar-91 PHB60/R) Young girl on rocky steps (46x36cm-18x14in) s.d.07

JOBST, Karl (1835-1907) Austrian
£382 $642   (25-Apr-91 D.V123/R) The life of St Adalbert (13x80cm-5x31in) s. indian
         ink pen W/C (A.S 8000)

JOEL, H B (?) ?
£900 $1764   (13-Feb-91 S94/R) In pastoral country near Carlisle (51x76cm-20x30in)
         mono.d.1902 i.stretcher

JOENSEN-MIKINES, S (1906-) Danish
£1795 $3537   (14-Nov-90 KH.K75/R) Sunset over the sea, Faroe Islands
         (66x80cm-26x31in) s.d.62 (D.KR 20000)
£1865 $3674   (31-Oct-90 KH.K63/R) The artist, Faroe Islands 1948 (100x120cm-39x47in)
         s.d.48 (D.KR 21000)
£2753 $5424   (31-Oct-90 KH.K64/R) Mid-summer night's bonfire (65x80cm-26x31in)
         s.d.1960 (D.KR 31000)
£4085 $8048   (31-Oct-90 KH.K62/R) Houses by the sea, Thorshavn, Faroe Islands
         (90x110cm-35x43in) s.d.64 (D.KR 46000)
£6798 $13324   (13-Feb-91 KH.K86/R) Village by the sea, Faroe Islands
         (97x126cm-38x50in) s.d.43 (D.KR 76000)

JOENSEN-MIKINES, Samuel (1906-) Danish
£968 $1665   (15-May-91 RAS.K164 c/R) View of Faroe Island fjord (52x76cm-20x30in)
         s.d.37 (D.KR 11000)
£1056 $1817   (15-May-91 RAS.K114/R) Landscape from Mykines (32x43cm-13x17in)
         init.d.1928 (D.KR 12000)
£1518 $2808   (5-Mar-91 RAS.K152/R) Faroe Islands fjord landscape (63x81cm-25x32in)
         s.d.38 (D.KR 17000)
£1812 $3496   (12-Dec-90 RAS.K295/R) Landscape with stones and mountains, Faeroe
         Islands (70x101cm-28x40in) s. (D.KR 20000)
£2321 $4295   (5-Mar-91 RAS.K156/R) Sunset over the sea, figure in foreground
         (62x77cm-24x30in) s.d.46 (D.KR 26000)
£2905 $5665   (10-Oct-90 RAS.K200/R) Killing of whales (65x80cm-26x31in) s.
         (D.KR 33000)

JOHANNESSEN, Erik Harry (1902-1980) Norwegian
£738 $1248   (4-May-91 BU.O77) Landscape from Asgardstrand (27x35cm-11x14in) s. panel
         (N.KR 8500)
£1291 $2492   (13-Dec-90 BU.O26/R) Landscape from Bykle in Setesdal 1949
         (38x46cm-15x18in) init. i.verso panel (N.KR 14500)
£1313 $2351   (11-Mar-91 B.O60/R) View from Pelleseter, Gudbrandsdalen 1973
         (47x52cm-19x20in) init. panel (N.KR 15000)
£2493 $4812   (13-Dec-90 BU.O24/R) Luxembourg garden (55x46cm-22x18in) init.
         s.i.d.1962verso panel (N.KR 28000)
£2539 $4546   (11-Mar-91 B.O58/R) Summer evening in Asgardstrand, 1950
         (51x66cm-20x26in) init. (N.KR 29000)
£2700 $5266   (15-Oct-90 B.O43/R) Autumn landscape (69x54cm-27x21in) init. panel
         (N.KR 31000)
£2802 $5016   (11-Mar-91 B.O57/R) Figures in moonlight (50x50cm-20x20in) init.
         (N.KR 32000)
£3028 $5843   (10-Dec-90 B.O65/R) Artists 1958 (51x51cm-20x20in) init. (N.KR 34000)
£3384 $6531   (10-Dec-90 B.O66/R) Winter landscape 1967 (48x53cm-19x21in) init.
         (N.KR 38000)
£3668 $6969   (11-Sep-90 UL.T230/R) Autumn 1966 (80x80cm-31x31in) (N.KR 42000)

JOHANNESSEN, Erik Harry (1902-1980) Norwegian-cont.
£5556 $9278 (4-Jun-91 BU.O29/R) Fishermen (100x110cm-39x43in) init.d.1948
(N.KR 64000)
£6768 $13061 (13-Dec-90 BU.O25/R) Boat's arriving (100x126cm-39x50in) init.
s.i.d.1947verso (N.KR 76000)
£7317 $14268 (15-Oct-90 B.O42/R) After the bath (70x70cm-28x28in) init. (N.KR 84000)
£7840 $15287 (15-Oct-90 B.O44/R) Woman with flowers (70x54cm-28x21in) init.d.48 panel
(N.KR 90000)

JOHANNESSEN, Jens (1934-) Norwegian
£2014 $3605 (11-Mar-91 B.O62/R) Grey composition (70x90cm-28x35in) init.d.64 i.verso
(N.KR 23000)
£2048 $3953 (10-Dec-90 B.O67/R) Yellow maskerade (60x60cm-24x24in) init.d.64
(N.KR 23000)
*£3240 $5799 (11-Mar-91 B.O61/R) Mask (75x57cm-30x22in) init. i.verso W/C
(N.KR 37000)*

JOHANNESSON, Karl Ragnar (1900-1968) Swedish
£604 $1081 (9-Apr-91 GO.G67) Fogelberg street (60x63cm-24x25in) s.d.39 panel
(S.KR 6500)

JOHANNOT, Tony (1803-1852) French
*£545 $964 (5-Apr-91 DAR.P32/R) Jeune femme en costume oriental (45x34cm-18x13in)
mono. pastel (F.FR 5500)*

JOHANSEN, Axel (1872-1938) Danish
£727 $1170 (27-Jun-91 D.V12) Idyll (34x44cm-13x17in) s.d.1910 (A.S 15000)

JOHANSEN, Fridolin (1868-1908) Danish
£7181 $14147 (14-Nov-90 RAS.K87/R) Boy and cat by stove (39x40cm-15x16in) s.i.d.94
(D.KR 80000)

JOHANSEN, Jean MacLane see McLANE, Murtle Jean

JOHANSEN, Viggo (1851-1935) Danish
£662 $1297 (10-Nov-90 FAL.M163/R) Woman on sofa (39x33cm-15x13in) s.d.1924 panel
(S.KR 7200)
£690 $1297 (10-Aug-90 RAS.V486/R) Wooded landscape, Tisvildew (64x70cm-25x28in)
s.d.1893 (D.KR 7800)
£712 $1388 (19-Oct-90 RAS.V501/R) Interior with woman sewing (31x28cm-12x11in)
s.d.1877 (D.KR 8000)
£1762 $3295 (29-Aug-90 KH.K108/R) Young girl guarding geese (70x87cm-28x34in)
s.i.d.1901 (D.KR 20000)
£2242 $4305 (27-Dec-90 RAS.V45/R) Goosegirl with geese near Dragor (70x86cm-28x34in)
s.d.1901 (D.KR 25000)

JOHANSON-THOR, Emil (1889-1958) Swedish
£660 $1142 (22-May-91 BA.S103/R) Hvens old church (48x70cm-19x28in) s.d.48
(S.KR 7000)
£660 $1142 (22-May-91 BA.S105/R) Winter landscape with farm, Skane (23x34cm-9x13in)
init. panel (S.KR 7000)

JOHANSSON, Albert (1926-) Swedish
£651 $1164 (13-Apr-91 FAL.M132/R) Still life composition (50x60cm-20x24in) s. panel
(S.KR 7000)
£660 $1142 (22-May-91 BA.S395/R) Statusdiagram IV - 1964 (130x110cm-51x43in)
s.verso panel (S.KR 7000)
£919 $1801 (10-Nov-90 FAL.M166/R) 'In- och utredningplan 1956-66'
(106x125cm-42x49in) s.d.1965 panel (S.KR 10000)
£1085 $1877 (22-May-91 BA.S397/R) Painting (62x72cm-24x28in) s.verso panel
(S.KR 11500)
£1226 $2122 (22-May-91 BA.S399/R) 'Korama' (72x37cm-28x15in) s.d.1959verso panel
(S.KR 13000)
£1390 $2697 (5-Dec-90 AB.S7123/R) Painting (52x61cm-20x24in) s. panel (S.KR 15000)
£1414 $2389 (18-Apr-91 BU.S65/R) Invention (51x61cm-20x24in) s.s.i.verso panel
(S.KR 15000)
£1568 $3011 (27-Nov-90 BU.S158/R) Still life II (92x121cm-36x48in) s.s.i.d.1988verso
panel (S.KR 17000)
£1622 $3146 (4-Dec-90 BA.S237/R) Miman-fragment (52x65cm-20x26in) s.verso panel
(S.KR 17500)
£1698 $2938 (22-May-91 BA.S393/R) Still life of jugs (91x122cm-36x48in) s.verso
panel (S.KR 18000)
£1715 $3326 (4-Dec-90 BA.S243/R) Crochet waves (85x117cm-33x46in) s. panel
(S.KR 18500)
£1761 $3416 (4-Dec-90 BA.S238/R) Anonymous marks (122x61cm-48x24in) s.d.1962verso
panel (S.KR 19000)
£1884 $3693 (10-Nov-90 FAL.M167/R) Composition in black and pink (51x61cm-20x24in)
s. panel (S.KR 20500)
£2451 $4141 (18-Apr-91 BU.S64/R) The mysterious dream 25 (86x116cm-34x46in)
s.s.i.d.1982verso panel (S.KR 26000)
£2583 $4959 (27-Nov-90 BU.S157/R) Still life (90x123cm-35x48in) s.
s.i.d.1988-89verso panel (S.KR 28000)
£3244 $6293 (4-Dec-90 BA.S242/R) Composition (91x121cm-36x48in) s.verso panel
(S.KR 35000)
£3690 $7085 (27-Nov-90 BU.S156/R) Conception I (150x123cm-59x48in) s. i.d.1985verso
(S.KR 40000)

JOHANSSON, Arvid (1862-1923) Swedish

£960	$1881	(20-Nov-90 GO.G109) Seascape with fishermen (65x130cm-26x51in) s. (S.KR 10500)
£1000	$1950	(18-Oct-90 CSK191/R) French ketch-rigged yacht, on port reach (81x99cm-32x39in) s.d.86
£1345	$2286	(31-May-91 LD.P6) Les barques de peche (54x81cm-21x32in) s. (F.FR 13500)

JOHANSSON, Carl (1863-1944) Swedish

£735	$1441	(6-Nov-90 BA.S129/R) Thawing (32x46cm-13x18in) s.d.1924 (S.KR 8000)
£884	$1644	(9-Sep-90 BU.M24) Landscape, Nordingra coast (30x49cm-12x19in) s.d.09 panel (S.KR 9500)
£939	$1596	(28-May-91 AB.S4640/R) River landscape with birches in summer (15x24cm-6x9in) s.i.d.88 panel (S.KR 10000)
£1231	$2068	(24-Apr-91 BA.S114/R) Ume river near Baggbole (32x46cm-13x18in) s.d.98 (S.KR 13000)
£1376	$2711	(13-Nov-90 AB.S389/R) Evening lake landscape, Jamtland (30x64cm-12x25in) s.d.84 (S.KR 15000)
£1515	$2545	(24-Apr-91 BA.S113/R) Pasture land and chalets (31x46cm-12x18in) s.d.1890 (S.KR 16000)
£1518	$2808	(5-Mar-91 RAS.K168/R) Winter's day in Medelpark (49x63cm-19x25in) s.d.1929 (D.KR 17000)
£1849	$3106	(22-Apr-91 BU.K57/R) Sunlight through the wood (65x102cm-26x40in) s.d.1916 (D.KR 21000)
£2574	$5044	(6-Nov-90 BA.S128/R) Snowcovered birch hill (73x49cm-29x19in) s.d.1889 (S.KR 28000)
£2841	$4773	(24-Apr-91 BA.S109/R) Evening landscape, Jormlien, Jamtland (38x54cm-15x21in) s.d.1930 (S.KR 30000)
£3650	$7190	(30-Oct-90 BU.S46/R) Harnosand harbour (51x74cm-20x29in) s.i. (S.KR 40000)
£4869	$8375	(14-May-91 BU.S14/R) Winter landscape (73x49cm-29x19in) s.d.1889 (S.KR 52000)

JOHANSSON, Erling (1934-) Scandinavian

£973	$1888	(5-Dec-90 AB.S7126/R) Model and birds (66x120cm-26x47in) s. (S.KR 10500)

JOHANSSON, Johan (1879-1951) Swedish

£884	$1644	(9-Sep-90 BU.M328) Avenue of willows (40x52cm-16x20in) st.sig. (S.KR 9500)
£976	$1747	(13-Apr-91 FAL.M134/R) Landscape from Alabodarna, Skane (41x52cm-16x20in) s. d.1929verso (S.KR 10500)
£1011	$1982	(10-Nov-90 FAL.M172/R) Landscape from Alabodarna (50x64cm-20x25in) s. (S.KR 11000)
£1250	$2450	(10-Nov-90 FAL.M170/R) Loderups hills (56x92cm-22x36in) s. panel (S.KR 13600)
£1379	$2702	(10-Nov-90 FAL.M171/R) Woman with red parasol (612x57cm-241x22in) s. (S.KR 15000)
£1379	$2702	(10-Nov-90 FAL.M169/R) By the window (52x41cm-20x16in) s. (S.KR 15000)

JOHANSSON, Stefan (1876-1955) Swedish

£760	$1474	*(5-Dec-90 AB.S7127/R) Study of sky (27x25cm-11x10in) W/C canvas (S.KR 8200)*
£25641	$50000	*(23-Oct-90 SY.NY225/R) Shadows in the bedroom corner (65x60cm-26x24in) s.d.44 W/C canvas laid down on board*
£35897	$70000	*(23-Oct-90 SY.NY226/R) Maynight dawn in moonlight (72x56cm-28x22in) s.d.42 W/C canvas laid down on board*

JOHN, Augustus (1878-1961) British

£2200	$4312	(25-Jan-91 C112/R) Dorset coastal landscape (28x38cm-11x15in) s.verso panel
£2200	$3674	(6-Jun-91 C70/R) The fortune teller (34x26cm-13x10in) s.
£5000	$9250	(7-Mar-91 C54/R) Almond and olive trees (47x55cm-19x22in) s.
£9500	$18620	(8-Nov-90 C57/R) Romilly John (40x30cm-16x12in) panel
£361	$694	*(26-Nov-90 SY.ME173) Tinkers (38x50cm-15x20in) i.verso ink (A.D 900)*
£361	$694	*(26-Nov-90 SY.ME170) Gipsy family (37x49cm-15x19in) i.verso pen (A.D 900)*
£450	$891	*(29-Jan-91 PH50) Whippet (25x39cm-10x15in) s. pencil*
£462	$800	*(12-May-91 H.C97) Three heads of women and one girl (28x20cm-11x8in) s. crayon*
£464	$891	*(14-Aug-90 SY.ME160) Tinkers (38x50cm-15x20in) i. verso ink (A.D 1100)*
£464	$891	*(14-Aug-90 SY.ME161) Gipsy family (37x49cm-15x19in) i. verso pen (A.D 1100)*
£521	$1000	*(20-Feb-91 D.NY51) Head of Magda (30x23cm-12x9in) s. red chk*
£600	$1182	*(1-Nov-90 B19) Seated female nude (35x50cm-14x20in) s. pencil*
£600	$1128	*(20-Sep-90 CSK44/R) Study of gypsy man with beard (25x18cm-10x7in) chl*
£620	$1228	*(29-Jan-91 PH47) Brief encounter (30x25cm-12x10in) s.i. pen wash*
£650	$1222	*(20-Sep-90 CSK34/R) Mother and child under palm tree (24x31cm-9x12in) pen*
£750	$1305	*(27-Mar-91 S69) Mother and child (39x23cm-15x9in) pen ink wash*
£780	$1505	*(12-Dec-90 SWS2372) Standing nude (38x11cm-15x4in) s. pen htd white*
£800	$1584	*(29-Jan-91 PH42/R) Study of girl's head (16x15cm-6x6in) red chk*
£820	$1542	*(18-Sep-90 PH145/R) Head of young girl (26x20cm-10x8in) s. pencil*
£1000	$1880	*(20-Sep-90 C75/R) Female nude crouching (25x35cm-10x14in) s. chl*
£1000	$1880	*(20-Sep-90 C71/R) Fishergirl at Equihen (35x24cm-14x9in) chl*
£1000	$1960	*(6-Nov-90 PH99/R) Two women (25x21cm-10x8in) s. pen ink wash*
£1000	$1880	*(18-Sep-90 PH143) Standing male nude (61x40cm-24x16in) s. black chk*
£1000	$1950	*(10-Oct-90 S49/R) The preacher (30x40cm-12x16in) pen wash*

JOHN, Augustus (1878-1961) British-cont.

£1015	$2000	(15-Nov-90 D.NY48) Young child wearing scarf (23x19cm-9x7in) s. ink
£1100	$2156	(8-Nov-90 C56/R) The little family (31x24cm-12x9in) ink
£1100	$1914	(28-Mar-91 CSK5/R) Equihen fisher-girl (31x19cm-12x7in) s. pencil
£1500	$2610	(27-Mar-91 S54/R) Male nude (46x29cm-18x11in) s. pencil
£1600	$3008	(20-Sep-90 C74/R) Portrait of young man (37x26cm-15x10in) pencil
£1600	$3008	(20-Sep-90 C72/R) Female nude, one leg raised (46x32cm-18x13in) pencil
£1650	$3250	(15-Nov-90 D.NY50/R) Seated woman wearing scarf (21x19cm-8x7in) s. pencil
£2000	$3920	(6-Nov-90 PH101/R) Ida Nettleship (29x24cm-11x9in) s. pencil
£2695	$4500	(5-Jun-91 D.NY51) Study of female nude. Peasant woman (36x25cm-14x10in) s. pencil two
£3400	$6392	(20-Sep-90 C70/R) Head of young woman (46x39cm-18x15in) s. crayon
£3500	$5845	(6-Jun-91 C69/R) Portrait of young girl (30x21cm-12x8in) s.indis.d.08 pencil
£3776	$7250	(20-Feb-91 D.NY49) Ida Neuleshef in profile (23x15cm-9x6in) s. chl
£5000	$9250	(7-Mar-91 C53/R) Ursula Nettleship (14x14cm-6x6in) black crayon
£5000	$9400	(20-Sep-90 C76/R) Study of nude boy (61x48cm-24x19in) s. chl
£5200	$10192	(7-Nov-90 S17/R) Portrait of young girl (29x23cm-11x9in) s. pencil
£7031	$13500	(20-Feb-91 D.NY50) Portrait of woman and young girl sewing (33x23cm-13x9in) s. one chl one wash pair
£31000	$60760	(8-Nov-90 C58/R) Head of Dorelia (36x25cm-14x10in) s.i.d.1909 W/C blk.crayon

JOHN, Gwen (1876-1939) British

£864	$1641	(12-Sep-90 WO.CO14) Portrait of a young girl (41x30cm-16x12in) s. (E.P 950)
£40000	$78400	(8-Nov-90 C60/R) Seated girl sewing (44x36cm-17x14in)
£1200	$2340	(16-Oct-90 WW329) Profile of an old woman reading (20x15cm-8x6in) pencil
£5200	$10140	(16-Oct-90 WW330/R) Portrait of a young girl with long hair (23x18cm-9x7in) s.

JOHNS, Edwin Thomas (1862-1947) British

£580	$1137	(8-Nov-90 PH193) Sleeping semi-clad girl watched over by angel (29x45cm-11x18in) s. W/C

JOHNS, Stan (20th C) Australian

£1357	$2294	(16-Apr-91 J.M997) Grindell's Hut, Flinders Ranges (121x180cm-48x71in) s.d.1986 (A.D 3000)
£1357	$2294	(16-Apr-91 J.M310) Old Pioneers, Hammond, South Australia (122x182cm-48x72in) s.d.1986 (A.D 3000)

JOHNSEN, Hjalmar (1852-1901) Norwegian

£2364	$4232	(14-Mar-91 BU.O53/R) Harvesting landscape (42x76cm-17x30in) s.i.d.1894 (N.KR 27000)

JOHNSON, Clarence R (1894-1981) American

£10417	$20000	(30-Nov-90 CH.NY154/R) Pennsylvania hillsides (50x61cm-20x24in) s.

JOHNSON, David (1827-1908) American

£884	$1424	(28-Jun-91 BM.B696/R) Rowing boat with figures and sailing boat in choppy sea (21x34cm-8x13in) s. canvas on board (DM 2600)
£2428	$4200	(22-May-91 CH.NY2/R) On Hudson (10x9cm-4x4in) init. canvas on board arched
£4762	$9000	(26-Sep-90 SY.NY5/R) The Pink House, Kingston (28x41cm-11x16in) init.d.58 l.stretcher
£11561	$20000	(22-May-91 CH.NY166/R) Mount Lafayette, New Hampshire (43x36cm-17x14in) init. l. verso
£452	$800	(4-Apr-91 BG.M379/R) Jervis McEntee's cottage (25x43cm-10x17in) pencil
£452	$800	(4-Apr-91 BG.M380/R) View at New Berlin (25x36cm-10x14in) i. pencil
£621	$1100	(4-Apr-91 BG.M378/R) Artist sketching at Lake George (30x43cm-12x17in) mono.i. pencil
£1695	$3000	(4-Apr-91 BG.M381/R) Looking down Hudson below Cozzens (30x48cm-12x19in) mono.i.d.1869 pencil

JOHNSON, Eastman (1824-1906) American

£1100	$2200	(7-Feb-91 B.P63/R) From Reubens (48x66cm-19x26in) s. i.verso
£1959	$3800	(5-Dec-90 D.NY3/R) Peasant girl of Brabant (38x30cm-15x12in) s.d.63
£4233	$8000	(26-Sep-90 SY.NY109/R) Portrait of lady (117x71cm-46x28in) s.d.1881
£11640	$22000	(27-Sep-90 CH.NY25/R) Study for fiddling his way (51x23cm-20x9in) init. board
£16185	$28000	(22-May-91 CH.NY164/R) Ragamuffin (29x16cm-11x6in) s. board

JOHNSON, Edward Killingworth (1825-1896) British

£1800	$2952	(19-Jun-91 B79) Stolen fruit (51x33cm-20x13in) W/C
£3000	$4890	(13-Jun-91 L115/R) A young girl in the orchard wearing a grey dress (48x25cm-19x10in) s.
£6000	$11700	(18-Oct-90 SC3031/R) The rival florists (54x77cm-21x30in) s.d.1872 i. label backboard W/C bodycol.pencil

JOHNSON, Frank Tenney (1874-1939) American

£1183	$2000	(1-May-91 B.SF5283/R) Mule wagon (35x46cm-14x18in) s. canvas on board
£1410	$2750	(10-Oct-90 B.SF586/R) Island of Pacific (20x15cm-8x6in) s.d.1912 canvasboard
£2249	$4250	(26-Sep-90 SY.NY71/R) Arizona moonlight (28x20cm-11x8in) s. s.i.verso board

JOHNSON, Frank Tenney (1874-1939) American-cont.

£4592	$9000	(7-Nov-90 B.SF3808/R) Through the hills (23x30cm-9x12in) s. canvasboard
£6122	$12000	(7-Nov-90 B.SF3817/R) Night in village (35x46cm-14x18in) s.d.1937
£7937	$15000	(26-Sep-90 SY.NY75/R) The lone cowboy (51x61cm-20x24in) s.d.1937
£8247	$16000	(5-Dec-90 D.NY58/R) While the cattle sleep (41x30cm-16x12in) s.d.22
£8671	$15000	(22-May-91 CH.NY219/R) Rocky steeps (51x36cm-20x14in) s.d.1936
£9497	$17000	(14-Mar-91 CH.NY138/R) Date talk (51x61cm-20x24in) s.d.1931
£13542	$26000	(30-Nov-90 CH.NY92/R) The night hawk (61x76cm-24x30in) s.d.1936 s.i.d.stretcher
£21965	$38000	(22-May-91 CH.NY210/R) Moonlight in the canyon (56x41cm-22x16in) s.d.1928 i. stretcher

JOHNSON, Gordon (1924-1989) American

£1176	$2000	(1-Jun-91 IH.NY94/R) Newlywed couple arguing about directions (61x53cm-24x21in) s. board

JOHNSON, H (?) ?

£960	*$1622*	*(30-Apr-91 AG199) Stolen fruit - small girl by redcurrant bush (50x33cm-20x13in) W/C*

JOHNSON, Harry John (1826-1884) British

£750	$1463	(24-Oct-90 S190/R) At Smyrna, Turkey (25x21cm-10x8in) s.d.45 panel
£3400	$6630	(16-Jan-91 CSK50) Isles of Greece, Temple of Minerva in Aegina (61x97cm-24x38in) s.d.1879 pencil W/C

JOHNSON, James (1803-1834) British

£3200	$5248	(18-Jun-91 OT471/R) High Street, Bristol (21x16cm-8x6in) panel

JOHNSON, James (20th C) ?

£2610	$5116	(24-Nov-90 AB.L87/R) Wissous (65x54cm-26x21in) indis.s.d.1957 l.stretcher (S.FR 6500)

JOHNSON, Kaare Espolin (1907-) Norwegian?

£4203	$7524	(14-Mar-91 BU.O54/R) Village street scene (67x149cm-26x59in) s.indist.d.7 (N.KR 48000)

JOHNSON, Lester (1919-?) American

£1711	$3250	(14-Sep-90 S.BM324/R) Mans head in profile with plant (86x66cm-34x26in) s.d.1958 paper
£2653	$5200	(6-Nov-90 CE.NY177/R) Untitled (41x50cm-16x20in) s.d.85
£6599	$13000	(4-Oct-90 SY.NY69/R) Man with letter N (173x121cm-68x48in) s.d.1965 verso
£7143	$14000	(7-Nov-90 SY.NY228/R) Six figures (152x127cm-60x50in) s.
£1026	*$2000*	*(10-Oct-90 SY.NY352/R) 2nd Milford series no.5 (94x64cm-37x25in) s. mixed media*
£2296	*$4500*	*(6-Nov-90 CE.NY124/R) Bleeker street (58x73cm-23x29in) s. acrylic col.chks.*

JOHNSON, Marshall (?-1915) American

£592	$1000	(20-Apr-91 WOL.C59/R) Ships at sea (36x46cm-14x18in) s.
£2071	$3500	(17-Apr-91 D.NY37/R) Making harbour (41x51cm-16x20in) s. i.verso
£2959	$5000	(17-Apr-91 D.NY41/R) Gaff rigged cat boat (64x76cm-25x30in) s.
£7396	$12500	(17-Apr-91 D.NY43/R) Calm harbour (46x61cm-18x24in) s.

JOHNSON, Michael (1938-) Australian

£4641	$8911	(14-Aug-90 SY.ME124) Mayo II (153x213cm-60x84in) s.i.d.1981 stretcher verso (A.D 11000)
£6512	$10940	(22-Apr-91 SY.ME324) Sakais (213x152cm-84x60in) s.i.d.1987-88 verso (A.D 14000)

JOHNSON, Ray (1927-) American

£1092	*$2064*	*(27-Sep-90 F.M29) Jayne Mansfield's mother's potato masher. Charlie Chaplin's mother's potato masher (38x25cm-15x10in) s.d.1972 collage mixed media pair (I.L 2400000)*

JOHNSON, Robert (1890-1964) Australian

£1333	$2507	(17-Sep-90 MGS.S171/R) Ghost gums, Stanley Chasm Alice Springs Northern Territory (37x45cm-15x18in) s. board (A.D 3000)
£1518	$2641	(26-Mar-91 JRL.S2) Pittwater (29x36cm-11x14in) s. board (A.D 3400)
£2124	$4183	(13-Nov-90 J.M63) River shadows (36x43cm-14x17in) s. canvas on board (A.D 5500)
£2262	$3824	(15-Apr-91 AAA.S103) Summer in valley (38x46cm-15x18in) s. board (A.D 5000)
£2317	$4564	(13-Nov-90 J.M176/R) The autumn road (45x55cm-18x22in) s. canvas board (A.D 6000)
£2532	$4861	(14-Aug-90 SY.ME299/R) Eastwood pastoral (36x44cm-14x17in) s. i. label verso (A.D 6000)
£2791	$4688	(22-Apr-91 SY.ME241/R) Spring morning, Burragorang Valley (36x44cm-14x17in) s. i.verso board (A.D 6000)
£3302	$5382	(1-Jul-91 AAA.S109/R) Yackandandah landscape (38x46cm-15x18in) s. (A.D 7000)
£3620	$6118	(16-Apr-91 J.M188/R) The black roads,Dundas (37x44cm-15x17in) s. canvas on board (A.D 8000)
£3620	$6118	(16-Apr-91 J.M199/R) South Coast Farm (37x44cm-15x17in) s. board (A.D 8000)

JOHNSON, Robert (1890-1964) Australian-cont.

£3797	$7291	(14-Aug-90 SY.ME303/R) Bingle Bay, North Queensland (44x54cm-17x21in) s. i. verso (A.D 9000)
£3800	$7372	(6-Dec-90 CSK2/R) Sydney harbour (37x46cm-15x18in) s. canvas on board
£4651	$7814	(22-Apr-91 SY.ME348/R) Kangaroo valley, NSW (55x65cm-22x26in) s. i.verso (A.D 10000)
£6222	$11698	(17-Sep-90 SY.ME74/R) The old house at Hartley (37x44cm-15x17in) s.d.1938 i.verso canvasboard (A.D 14000)

JOHNSON, Sidney Yates (19th C) British

£737	$1400	(14-Sep-90 DM.D2223) Landscape scene (36x56cm-14x22in) s.d.1902

JOHNSON, Tim (1947-) Australian

£1209	$2032	(22-Apr-91 SY.ME132) Untitled (120x151cm-47x59in) init. acrylic canvas (A.D 2600)

JOHNSON, W Noel (19th C) British

£940	*$1786*	*(15-Sep-90 ME248) Coastal cottage with children and ducks (36x53cm-14x21in) s. W/C*

JOHNSON, Will (fl.1889) British

£900	$1503	(7-Jun-91 PHE39) Childhood (34x24cm-13x9in) s.d.1889

JOHNSTON, Alexander (1815-1891) British

£1297	$2400	(10-Mar-91 H.C76) Summer (97x74cm-38x29in) s.
£1600	$3200	(8-Feb-91 C181/R) L'Allegro, or jollity (61x51cm-24x20in) s.d.1856 oval
£4800	$9600	(8-Feb-91 C182/R) The flirt (91x71cm-36x28in) s.

JOHNSTON, Frank Hans (1888-1949) Canadian

£505	$869	(14-May-91 JOY.T173/R) Coney Island, Kenora, Lake of the woods (26x27cm-10x11in) board (C.D 1000)
£553	$956	(22-May-91 EA.M420 a/R) Afterglow (20x25cm-8x10in) s. board (C.D 1100)
£808	$1390	(14-May-91 JOY.T129/R) Early snow (25x30cm-10x12in) s. board (C.D 1600)
£825	$1402	(27-May-91 HO.ED70/R) Silver gleam (15x20cm-6x8in) s.i.verso board (C.D 1600)
£877	$1728	(30-Oct-90 SY.T6/R) Road to the farm (24x34cm-9x13in) s. i.verso board (C.D 2000)
£960	$1651	(14-May-91 JOY.T27/R) Morning sun (25x30cm-10x12in) s. board (C.D 1900)
£1053	$2063	(20-Nov-90 JOY.T408/R) Moose country (25x30cm-10x12in) s. board (C.D 2400)
£1071	$2057	(27-Nov-90 W.T863/R) Lynn Canyon, B C (34x23cm-13x9in) s. i.verso board (C.D 2400)
£1111	$1911	(14-May-91 JOY.T88/R) Spring, Longlac (25x30cm-10x12in) s. board (C.D 2200)
£1206	$2376	(30-Oct-90 MA.V102) Off to town (30x41cm-12x16in) s.i.verso board (C.D 2750)
£1228	$2407	(20-Nov-90 JOY.T186/R) On road to Minden (25x30cm-10x12in) s. board (C.D 2800)
£1316	$2579	(20-Nov-90 JOY.T177/R) Spring breakup (37x45cm-15x18in) s. board (C.D 3000)
£1404	$2751	(20-Nov-90 JOY.T319/R) Filteered gold (40x50cm-16x20in) s. board (C.D 3200)
£1425	$2808	(30-Oct-90 SY.T115/R) Lake of the woods (32x25cm-13x10in) s. i.verso board (C.D 3250)
£1425	$2808	(30-Oct-90 SY.T112/R) The golden marsh (38x44cm-15x17in) s. s.i.verso board (C.D 3250)
£1444	$2802	(3-Dec-90 R.T367/R) Silver skies (51x61cm-20x24in) s. masonite (C.D 3250)
£1535	$3024	(30-Oct-90 SY.T111/R) Autumn landscape with lake (25x32cm-10x13in) s. board (C.D 3500)
£1546	$2629	(27-May-91 HO.ED89/R) The hill curved road (38x46cm-15x18in) s. s.i.verso canvas on board (C.D 3000)
£1754	$3439	(20-Nov-90 JOY.T286/R) Sunshine through trees (27x34cm-11x13in) s. board (C.D 4000)
£1930	$3782	(20-Nov-90 JOY.T14/R) Soft sunlight (40x50cm-16x20in) s. panel (C.D 4400)
£2000	$3940	(15-Nov-90 CSK61/R) Lake's edge (15x20cm-6x8in) s.init. panel
£2020	$3495	(6-May-91 SY.T181/R) Approach to spring (30x41cm-12x16in) s. board (C.D 4000)
£2293	$4516	(12-Nov-90 HO.ED292/R) Winter haze (41x51cm-16x20in) s.d. i. verso board (C.D 5250)
£2412	$4728	(20-Nov-90 JOY.T160/R) Flowering meadow (50x60cm-20x24in) (C.D 5500)
£2448	$4162	(27-May-91 HO.ED119/R) Silent night (30x41cm-12x16in) s. s.i.verso panel (C.D 4750)
£2632	$5158	(20-Nov-90 JOY.T175/R) Stepping along, winter freighting in north (51x61cm-20x24in) s. board (C.D 6000)
£2652	$4587	(6-May-91 SY.T147/R) Orient Bay, Lake Nipigon (25x30cm-10x12in) s. board (C.D 5250)
£4167	$8208	(30-Oct-90 SY.T94/R) Opal shadows, York Mills, Ont (74x62cm-29x24in) s. i.verso board (C.D 9500)
£6140	$12035	(20-Nov-90 JOY.T125/R) Northern town (60x75cm-24x30in) s. board (C.D 14000)
£758	*$1311*	*(6-May-91 SY.T166) Wind swept tree, Georgian Bay (10x14cm-4x6in) s. d.1917 verso gouache (C.D 1500)*
£808	*$1398*	*(6-May-91 SY.T208) Landscape views at sunset (15x12cm-6x5in) s. gouache pair (C.D 1600)*

JOHNSTON, Frank Hans (1888-1949) Canadian-cont.
£808	$1398	(6-May-91 SY.T132) Autumn landscape (23x18cm-9x7in) s. gouache (C.D 1600)

JOHNSTON, Frank Hans (attrib) (1888-1949) Canadian
£1263	$2184	(6-May-91 SY.T207) Log cabin in Northern Ontario (30x39cm-12x15in) panel (C.D 2500)

JOHNSTON, Reuben le Grand (1850-1919) American
£1047	$1800	(18-May-91 W.W115/R) Flock in a late summer pasture (51x76cm-20x30in) s. panel
£1301	$2329	(13-Apr-91 FAL.M137/R) Man and boy with goat and kid (53x64cm-21x25in) s.i. (S.KR 14000)

JOHNSTONE, George Whitton (1849-1901) British
£1000	$1670	(7-Jun-91 PHE57) Near Edzell (47x68cm-19x27in) s.

JOHNSTONE, Henry James (1835-1907) British
£750	$1440	(26-Nov-90 SWS92/R) Portrait of young girl (10x8cm-4x3in) init. W/C
£1650	$3234	(8-Nov-90 DLY299/R) Floral bonnet (25x18cm-10x7in) s. W/C

JOHNSTONE, William (1897-1981) British
£620	$1017	(19-Jun-91 PHG73) Landscape - abstract (688x121cm-271x48in) s. verso
£650	$1099	(17-Apr-91 CG113) Untitled (27x37cm-11x15in) s.d.1965 verso
£850	$1607	(27-Sep-90 CG100) Woodland path (48x46cm-19x18in) s.i.verso panel
£1300	$2197	(17-Apr-91 CG153) Untitled (41x51cm-16x20in) s. verso
£1600	$3024	(27-Sep-90 CG98) Composition in blue and black (36x46cm-14x18in) s.verso
£1700	$3179	(28-Aug-90 S1085/R) Oil composition (40x51cm-16x20in) s.verso
£1800	$3402	(27-Sep-90 CG120) Abstract (30x41cm-12x16in) s.
£3000	$5670	(27-Sep-90 CG97/R) Blue landscape (63x76cm-25x30in) s.i.d.1960verso
£6500	$12285	(27-Sep-90 CG119/R) Red earth (86x112cm-34x44in) s.verso
£8400	$15876	(27-Sep-90 CG117/R) The creation (76x63cm-30x25in)
£8500	$16065	(27-Sep-90 CG99/R) Composition (63x76cm-25x30in) s.verso
£18000	$34020	(27-Sep-90 CG96/R) Blossom (137x243cm-54x96in) s.d.1974-77verso
£400	$676	(17-Apr-91 CG54) Untitled (32x23cm-13x9in) init.d.1971 ink brush W/C
£450	$761	(17-Apr-91 CG22) Landscape (15x33cm-6x13in) s.i. W/C
£620	$1042	(23-Apr-91 S244/R) Abstract (20x30cm-8x12in) W/C

JOINER, Harvey (1852-?) American
£1012	$1700	(19-Jul-91 DM.D2094/R) Wooded fall landscape with stream (28x23cm-11x9in) s. panel

JOLE, Jef van (1905-1961) Dutch
£610	$1171	(27-Nov-90 SY.AM3676/R) Moored vessels near Leerdam (45x70cm-18x28in) s. (D.FL 2000)

JOLI, Antonio (1700-1770) Italian
£30000	$51900	(24-May-91 C91/R) A view of Marsala, with an english two-decker in the foreground (24x102cm-9x40in)
£30000	$51900	(24-May-91 C92/R) A view of Catania from the sea, with an English ship in the foreground (24x76cm-9x30in)
£180000	$311400	(24-May-91 C81/R) A panoramic view of the Bacino di San Marco, Venice (55x168cm-22x66in)
£210000	$363300	(24-May-91 C82/R) The Campo Vaccino, Rome looking towards S.Francesca Romana and the Arch of Titus from the Temple of (96x137cm-38x54in) s.
£341176	$580000	(31-May-91 CH.NY59/R) The embarkment of King Charles III from Naples (76x171cm-30x67in)

JOLI, Antonio (attrib) (1700-1770) Italian
£147059	$250000	(30-May-91 SY.NY65/R) View of flooded Piazza Navona, Rome (45x95cm-18x37in)

JOLI, Antonio (circle) (1700-1770) Italian
£4200	$8400	(7-Feb-91 C118/R) Christ healing the soldier (76x62cm-30x24in)
£40785	$66480	(14-Jun-91 AGS.P45/R) La Place Saint-Marc (59x73cm-23x29in) (F.FR 405000)

JOLI, Antonio (style) (1700-1770) Italian
£1901	$3061	(27-Jun-91 EP.M19/R) El embarque de Carlos III en Napoles (100x161cm-39x63in) (S.P 350000)

JOLIN, Einar (1890-1976) Swedish
£695	$1348	(5-Dec-90 AB.S7135/R) Seagulls by nest in pinetree by lake (46x38cm-18x15in) s.d.1935 panel (S.KR 7500)
£1251	$2427	(4-Dec-90 BA.S255/R) Orchids in vase (33x41cm-13x16in) s.d.1955 (S.KR 13500)
£1379	$2757	(10-Feb-91 BU.M107) Still life of Chinese vase and jug (45x27cm-18x11in) s.d.1938 (S.KR 15000)
£1483	$2877	(5-Dec-90 AB.S7132/R) Still life of Chinese objects on mahogany table (65x54cm-26x21in) s.d.1928 (S.KR 16000)
£1529	$2967	(4-Dec-90 BA.S254/R) Skaters on the ice (50x60cm-20x24in) s.d.1958 (S.KR 16500)
£1854	$3596	(5-Dec-90 AB.S7131/R) View from my window - townscene with bridge (49x39cm-19x15in) s.i.d.1921 (S.KR 20000)
£1946	$3776	(4-Dec-90 BA.S252/R) Reindeer in mountain landscape (60x92cm-24x36in) s.d.65 (S.KR 21000)

JOLIN, Einar (1890-1976) Swedish-cont.

£2039	$3956	(4-Dec-90 BA.S251/R) Still life of tulips and plate (55x46cm-22x18in) s.d.70 (S.KR 22000)
£2306	$4428	(27-Nov-90 BU.S167/R) Still life (55x46cm-22x18in) s.d.1947 (S.KR 25000)
£2317	$4495	(4-Dec-90 BA.S248/R) Venetian scene (55x46cm-22x18in) s.d.1974 (S.KR 25000)
£2317	$4495	(4-Dec-90 BA.S245/R) Interior with dog asleep (49x64cm-19x25in) s.d.1943 (S.KR 25000)
£2377	$4658	(20-Nov-90 GO.G111) East Asian still life (46x55cm-18x22in) s.d.1944 panel (S.KR 26000)
£2595	$5034	(4-Dec-90 BA.S250/R) Still life of grapes and shell (38x46cm-15x18in) s.d.1955 (S.KR 28000)
£2595	$5034	(5-Dec-90 AB.S7129/R) Stockholm in moonlight - scene from Riddarholmen (46x54cm-18x21in) s.d.1959 (S.KR 28000)
£2780	$5394	(4-Dec-90 BA.S247/R) From Gosta Berling's saga (53x72cm-21x28in) s.d.1939 (S.KR 30000)
£3151	$6113	(4-Dec-90 BA.S253/R) View of Stockholm (38x46cm-15x18in) s.d.1954 (S.KR 34000)
£4263	$8271	(4-Dec-90 BA.S246/R) Pas de deux (55x46cm-22x18in) s.d.1918 (S.KR 46000)
£4613	$8856	(27-Nov-90 BU.S166/R) Still life (74x54cm-29x21in) s.d.1919 (S.KR 50000)
£7011	$13461	(27-Nov-90 BU.S165/R) Bathers and woman playing with dogs (100x73cm-39x29in) s.d.1916 (S.KR 76000)
£7022	$12079	(14-May-91 BA.S97/R) Woman smoking (74x59cm-29x23in) s.d.1919 (S.KR 75000)
£7639	$14896	(11-Oct-90 BU.O66/R) Interior with sculpture (73x670cm-29x264in) s.d.1915 (N.KR 88000)
£9225	$17712	(27-Nov-90 BU.S164/R) View of Riddarholmen (55x38cm-22x15in) s.d.1914 (S.KR 100000)
£13902	$26969	(5-Dec-90 AB.S7128/R) Evening winter scene from Skinnarviksparken, Stockholm (83x116cm-33x46in) s.d.1937 (S.KR 150000)
£368	*$735*	*(10-Feb-91 BU.M108) Landscape with farm (22x30cm-9x12in) s.i.d.1923 W/C (S.KR 4000)*
£509	*$881*	*(22-May-91 BA.S107/R) Peregrine falcon in coastal landscape (38x55cm-15x22in) s.d.1954 W/C (S.KR 5400)*
£649	*$1259*	*(4-Dec-90 BA.S257/R) Young Lapplander with reindeer (50x34cm-20x13in) s.d.1934 W/C (S.KR 7000)*
£1296	*$2540*	*(10-Nov-90 FAL.M175/R) Landscape from Monte Carlo (30x48cm-12x19in) s.d.1949 W/C (S.KR 14100)*

JOLLAIN, Nicolas Rene (younger) (1732-1804) French

£3043	$5842	(17-Dec-90 AGS.P66) Conversation galante (49x60cm-19x24in) s.d.1779 panel (F.FR 30000)
£4532	$7387	(14-Jun-91 AGS.P43/R) Enfant buvant. Enfant jouant (32x39cm-13x15in) pair (F.FR 45000)
£11305	$21932	(5-Dec-90 APT.P79/R) Le jeune Pyrrhus sauve (46x57cm-18x22in) canvas on panel (F.FR 110000)

JON-AND, John (1889-1941) Swedish

£1179	$2040	(22-May-91 BA.S108/R) Still life II (52x42cm-20x17in) s.d.18 panel (S.KR 12500)

JONAS, Lucien (1880-?) French

£1195	$2032	(29-May-91 GL.P37) Village au bord du canal (54x65cm-21x26in) s. (F.FR 12000)

JONAS, Walter Hermann (1910-1979) Swiss

£516	*$862*	*(7-Jun-91 ZOF.Z1353/R) Ticino farmstead with goat and chicken (33x44cm-13x17in) s.d.58 W/C pencil (S.FR 1300)*
£683	*$1338*	*(24-Nov-90 AB.L185/R) Abstract composition (35x50cm-14x20in) s.d.53 gouache (S.FR 1700)*

JONCHERIE, Gabriele Germain (attrib) (19th C) French

£3980	$7840	(14-Nov-90 FB.P145/R) Composition aux fruits et animaux (79x117cm-31x46in) (F.FR 39000)

JONCIERES, Leonce J V de (1871-1947) French

£27457	$47500	(22-May-91 SY.NY69/R) Un dejeuner d'ouvrieres aux tuileries (103x150cm-41x59in) s.d.1901

JONDL, G (19th C) Austrian

£728	*$1376*	*(27-Sep-90 D.V198/R) View of Salzburg (37x48cm-15x19in) s.d.1882 W/C (A.S 15000)*

JONES, Adrian (1845-1938) British

£1250	$2463	(13-Nov-90 PH123/R) Portrait of Swindler with jockey up (63x76cm-25x30in) s.i.d.1890

JONES, Allan Gwynne (20th C) British

£920	*$1730*	*(18-Sep-90 PH58/R) The Proposal (32x25cm-13x10in) s.d.16.5.13 W/C htd white over pencil silk*
£1200	*$2256*	*(18-Sep-90 PH59/R) Picnic party (40x29cm-16x11in) s.d.1914 W/C silk*

JONES, Allen (1937-?) British

£23000	$45080	(9-Nov-90 C273/R) Gallery Gasper (92x92cm-36x36in) s.i.stretcher
£696	*$1350*	*(6-Dec-90 D.V194/R) Exotique s.i.d.83 mixed media (A.S 14000)*
£2100	*$3423*	*(1-Jul-91 S89/R) Buses (57x79cm-22x31in) s.d.63 ink W/C gouache*

JONES, Anna M (20th C) British
£460 $796   *(9-May-91 B177) On the Guernsey coast (36x74cm-14x29in) s.indist.d. W/C*

JONES, Bradley (1944-1989) American
£549 $900   (21-Jun-91 DM.D2429/R) Fire child (91x86cm-36x34in) s.
£610 $1000   (21-Jun-91 DM.D2431/R) Dog (89x89cm-35x35in) s. s.d.1967 verso

JONES, Charles (1836-1892) British
£500 $895   (11-Mar-91 HS229) Study of spaniel retrieving mallard (35x50cm-14x20in) mono.d.1864
£763 $1503   (14-Nov-90 RAS.K641) Highland cattle in snow (56x82cm-22x32in) mono.d.72 (D.KR 8500)
£1200 $2064   (14-May-91 SWS215/R) Sheep grazing on heath (34x52cm-13x20in) mono.d.90
£1300 $2236   (14-May-91 SWS210/R) Highland cattle in winter landscape. Sheep by lake (21x16cm-8x6in) init.d.73 and 72 panel pair
£1400 $2758   (31-Oct-90 HUN2) Sheep and cattle (23x38cm-9x15in) mono.d.1882 panel
£2300 $4600   (8-Feb-91 C189/R) Sheep on a headland (30x51cm-12x20in) mono.d.90
£3333 $6500   (20-Oct-90 FA.PH856/R) Sussex, pastures (61x102cm-24x40in) mono. s.d.1883verso
£4000 $7880   (13-Nov-90 SWS331/R) Springtime (50x75cm-20x30in) mono.d.'91
£4200 $7854   (28-Aug-90 S750/R) Admiring his portrait (102x127cm-40x50in) mono.d.85 s.d.1885verso
£4200 $7854   (28-Aug-90 S807/R) Torrents in the Highlands (152x243cm-60x96in) mono.d.88
£5000 $9350   (28-Aug-90 S771/R) Shelter from the storm (61x91cm-24x36in) mono.d.65
£6000 $11340   (26-Sep-90 S59/R) Springtime (92x152cm-36x60in) mono.d.1877 s.d.1877 verso
£7000 $13090   (28-Aug-90 S756/R) Shepherds in the Highlands (61x91cm-24x36in) mono.one d.66 one indist.d. pair

JONES, F Eastman (19th C) American
£1183 $2000   (1-May-91 B.SF5054/R) Landscape with cows (51x76cm-20x30in) s.

JONES, Francis Coates (1857-1932) American
£1969 $3800   (10-Dec-90 H.C1057/R) River's edge (58x91cm-23x36in) s.
£3911 $7000   (12-Apr-91 SY.NY56/R) Water carrier (51x36cm-20x14in) s.

JONES, Fred Cecil (1891-1956) British
£1500 $2925   *(17-Oct-90 PHL88/R) Todmorden from the hill (47x64cm-19x25in) s.d.1938 col.washes*

JONES, Geoffrey (1909-) Australian
£1255 $2472   (13-Nov-90 J.M223) Sheath of flowers (75x49cm-30x19in) s. board (A.D 3250)

JONES, H B (1848-1927) American
£1276 $2500   (27-Jan-91 LIT.L23a) Pastoral scene (41x61cm-16x24in) s.

JONES, Herbert H (19/20th C) ?
£750 $1470   (20-Nov-90 PH220) Portrait of 'Profit with foal by St.Clare' (51x77cm-20x30in) s.d.1901 i. verso

JONES, Hugh Bolton (1848-1927) American
£1053 $2000   (14-Sep-90 S.BM148/R) The old road to the river (41x61cm-16x24in) s.
£1158 $2200   (14-Sep-90 S.BM151/R) Water meadow and grazing sheep (30x46cm-12x18in) s.d.1888
£1309 $2500   (6-Jan-91 LIT.L17) Pastoral scene (41x61cm-16x24in) s.
£1337 $2300   (15-May-91 SY.NY77/R) Summer landscape (41x56cm-16x22in) s.d.1879
£2394 $4500   (11-Aug-90 COL.M193/R) White house near creek (41x61cm-16x24in) s.
£3571 $7000   (16-Feb-91 W.W28/R) Barbizon landscape, midday (58x89cm-23x35in) s.
£3866 $7500   (5-Dec-90 D.NY47/R) Autumn landscape with birch trees (46x64cm-18x25in) s.
£5208 $10000   (30-Nov-90 CH.NY101/R) Quiet stream (77x91cm-30x36in) s.
£5491 $9500   (22-May-91 CH.NY194/R) Landscape with stream (40x56cm-16x22in) s. panel
£5851 $11000   (11-Aug-90 COL.M192/R) May 17th (51x61cm-20x24in) s.
£6349 $12000   (26-Sep-90 SY.NY91/R) Spring landscape (51x61cm-20x24in) s.
£7263 $13000   (14-Mar-91 CH.NY89 b/R) Lily pond (46x66cm-18x26in) s.
£9375 $18000   (30-Nov-90 CH.NY46/R) Rocky landscape (61x101cm-24x40in) s.

JONES, J Llewellyn (fl.1880-1927) Australian
£1195 $2355   (31-Oct-90 CH.S2/R) By Sydney harbour (19x28cm-7x11in) s. board (A.D 3000)

JONES, Jeffrey (1944-) American
£1294 $2200   *(1-Jun-91 IH.NY194/R) Woman facing right (33x10cm-13x4in) init. pen ink W/C*

JONES, Jo (1894-1989) British
£700 $1330   (12-Sep-90 B102/R) Gypsy christening (89x61cm-35x24in) s. board

JONES, Joe (20th C) ?
£588 $1100   (30-Aug-90 MFA.C210) Hamilton cove (61x91cm-24x36in) s. canvas laid down
£31746 $60000   (27-Sep-90 CH.NY263/R) Threshing (93x124cm-37x49in) s.d.1935 masonite

JONES, Josiah Clinton (1848-1936) British
£550 $935   (29-May-91 PHC184) Near Tal-y-Bont, North Wales (61x46cm-24x18in) s.

JONES, Josiah Clinton (1848-1936) British-cont.
£850	$1462	(16-May-91 CSK63) Woman feeding chickens outside cottage (34x51cm-13x20in) s.
£1700	$3264	(20-Feb-91 HAR524) Harvesting at sunset (99x124cm-39x49in) s.
£800	$1560	*(18-Oct-90 SC3005/R) Oat harvest, Llanbedr (49x75cm-19x30in) s. s.i. backboard*

JONES, Owen (19th C) British
£20555	$39877	*(7-Dec-90 CN.P54/R) Projet d'un hall d'exposition da St.Cloud (45x120cm-18x47in) W.C crayon htd.colour (F.FR 200000)*

JONES, Paul (1921-) Australian
£797	$1570	(31-Oct-90 CH.S120) New Guinea Highland natives (50x60cm-20x24in) s. board (A.D 2000)
£928	$1782	*(14-Aug-90 SY.ME85/R) Australian native flowers (44x28cm-17x11in) s. pencil gouache (A.D 2200)*
£1400	$2436	*(27-Mar-91 S230/R) Tulips (58x41cm-23x16in) s. gouache*

JONES, Paul (19th C) British
£650	$1229	(27-Sep-90 CSK129/R) Highland boy with dogs in cottage interior (25x35cm-10x14in)
£650	$1248	(20-Dec-90 CSK108) Highland ghillie with spaniels in a cottage interior (20x24cm-8x9in) s.d.1855
£740	$1443	(17-Oct-90 PHL258) A lucky escape (20x25cm-8x10in) s.d.1859
£1200	$2064	(14-May-91 SWS199/R) After the deer hunt (19x29cm-7x11in) s.d.1876
£1350	$2322	(14-May-91 SWS197/R) Waiting by the hole. Terriers ratting (19x23cm-7x9in) one s.d.1857 pair
£2695	$4500	(7-Jun-91 SY.NY8/R) Work - Putting up a mallard. Leisure - end of the day (20x25cm-8x10in) both s.d.1856 pair

JONES, Paul (circle) (19th C) British
£1100	$2167	(30-Oct-90 SC214/R) The highland gamekeeper (24x34cm-9x13in) panel
£1200	$2088	(27-Mar-91 PHS857) Two terriers in landscape (69x89cm-27x35in)

JONES, Philip (19th C) British
£1100	$1859	(3-May-91 PHE131) Three spaniels in interior (21x26cm-8x10in) s.d.1854

JONES, Richard (19th C) British
£13500	$22815	(30-Apr-91 PH57/R) Portrait of huntsman and whipper-in with bay hunter and hounds before Woodfold Park, Blackburn (71x91cm-28x36in)

JONES, Samuel John Egbert (19th C) British
£1550	$2666	(14-May-91 SWS177/R) Figures by river gorge in landscape (60x91cm-24x36in) s.d.1860 canvas on board
£2000	$3940	(16-Nov-90 C103/R) Pheasant shooting (20x25cm-8x10in) panel
£3000	$5910	(16-Nov-90 C104/R) Partridge shooting. Fishing (99x99cm-39x39in) panel pair
£5000	$9800	(8-Nov-90 TL30/R) Portrait of gentleman on bay horse in parkland (62x75cm-24x30in) s.d.1844
£6000	$11820	(16-Nov-90 C105/R) Pheasant shooting. Duck shooting. Snipe shooting (11x15cm-4x6in) panel set of three

JONES, Samuel John Egbert (attrib) (19th C) British
£1250	$2313	(6-Mar-91 SC4333/R) Huntsman with pointer out shooting (20x5cm-8x2in) panel
£3892	$6500	(7-Jun-91 SY.NY185/R) Pheasant shooting (30x41cm-12x16in) each s. pair

JONES, Simon (1965-) British
£1100	$2156	(13-Feb-91 B73/R) Counting pearls (122x107cm-48x42in)

JONES, Simon (1951-) South African
£704	$1316	(27-Aug-90 SY.J288/R) Night approaches (100x75cm-39x30in) s.d.85 acrylic board (SA.R 3400)

JONES, Steven (1959-) British
£500	$865	(10-May-91 CBS336) Making sandcastles at Peel (46x51cm-18x20in) s. board
£820	$1591	(7-Dec-90 CBS288) Children on beach at Peel (43x53cm-17x21in) s. board

JONES, T Hampson (19/20th C) British
£900	$1476	*(19-Jun-91 B98/R) Thoughts of love (74x54cm-29x21in) s. W/C*

JONES, William (c.1798-1860) British
£1700	$2839	(22-Jul-91 SWS1009/R) A hunter with three dogs in a landscape (47x57cm-19x22in)
£5500	$10835	(14-Nov-90 S82/R) Gentlemen out shooting (43x59cm-17x23in)
£6000	$11820	(14-Nov-90 S86/R) Gentleman shooting woodcock (49x59cm-19x23in)
£7500	$13425	(10-Apr-91 S41/R) Putting up pheasant. Finding hare (49x59cm-19x23in) pair

JONES-ROBERTS, Gareth (1935-) Australian
£724	$1224	(16-Apr-91 J.M73) Ole Mine Workings, Cooberbedy (76x101cm-30x40in) s. (A.D 1600)

JONG, Germ de (1886-1967) Dutch
£901	$1559	(22-May-91 CH.AM305) Pyrenees (38x46cm-15x18in) s.d.1925 panel (D.FL 3000)

JONG, Germ de (1886-1967) Dutch-cont.

£1351 $2568   (14-Sep-90 SA.A1394/R) Still life of flowers (75x60cm-30x24in) s.
        (DM 4000)
£1706 $2799   (18-Jun-91 FN.S1805/R) Young lady reclining on divan and gouvernante
        having lesson (45x50cm-18x20in) s. (DM 5000)
£2252 $3896   (22-May-91 CH.AM338/R) Corte, Corsica (65x54cm-26x21in) s.d.58 s.i.verso
        (D.FL 7500)

JONG, Jacqueline de (1939-) Dutch

£804 $1487   (5-Mar-91 RAS.K115/R) 'Phalosity' (73x92cm-29x36in) s.d.1969 (D.KR 9000)
£880 $1717   (10-Oct-90 RAS.K26) Rencontre sur le cheval (40x60cm-16x24in) s.d.62
        (D.KR 10000)
£1520 $2584   (28-May-91 KF.M777/R) Rencontre sur le cheval (40x60cm-16x24in) s.
        i.d.1962verso (DM 4500)
£2069 $3972   (28-Nov-90 KF.M914/R) Sturzender Farbstrom (52x32cm-20x13in) s. panel
        (DM 6000)

JONG, O R (?) ?

£633 $1216   (18-Dec-90 GM.B799) Chateau au bord du canal gele (30x40cm-12x16in) s.
        board (B.FR 38000)

JONGE, L V D (19th C) Dutch

£1066   *$2100*   *(7-Oct-90 DU.E240/R) Dutch interior (51x38cm-20x15in) s. W/C gouache*

JONGERE, M de (1912-) Dutch

£689 $1157   (23-Apr-91 SY.AM49) Rotterdam harbour (38x58cm-15x23in) s. (D.FL 2300)
£898 $1509   (23-Apr-91 SY.AM211) Rotterdam harbour (58x95cm-23x37in) s. (D.FL 3000)

JONGERE, Marinus de (1912-) Dutch

£689 $1343   (25-Oct-90 VN.R57/R) Windmills in polder landscape (59x98cm-23x39in) s.
        (D.FL 2300)
£976 $1854   (26-Feb-91 VN.R160/R) Shipping in the Maas Harbour in Rotterdam
        (40x80cm-16x31in) s. (D.FL 3200)
£659   *$1284*   *(25-Oct-90 VN.R54/R) Shipping in Rotterdam's Waal Harbour*
        (47x65cm-19x26in) s.d.1952 mixed media (D.FL 2200)
£732   *$1390*   *(26-Feb-91 VN.R161/R) Shipping in Rotterdam Harbour (60x100cm-24x39in)*
        s. W/C (D.FL 2400)

JONGH, Claude de (style) (17th C) Dutch

£1012 $1700   (17-Jul-91 SY.NY128/R) Landscape with figures before an arched bridge
        (53x76cm-21x30in) canvas laid down on board

JONGH, Gabriel de (1913-) South African?

£565 $1101   (15-Oct-90 SY.J183) Landscape near Meiringspoort (60x90cm-24x35in) s.
        (SA.R 2800)
£580 $1084   (27-Aug-90 SY.J150) Cape homestead beneath mountains (60x90cm-24x35in)
        s. (SA.R 2800)
£621 $1161   (27-Aug-90 SY.J148) Cape farmhouse in valley, winter (60x90cm-24x35in)
        s. (SA.R 3000)
£884 $1494   (15-Apr-91 SY.J476) Cape farm Banhoek near Stellenbosch
        (75x121cm-30x48in) s.d. 1963 (SA.R 4200)
£900 $1773   (15-Nov-90 CSK62/R) Witsands, Kommetjie, Cape Province
        (70x102cm-28x40in) s.

JONGH, Ludolf de (1616-1679) Dutch

£5595 $10575   (28-Sep-90 CSC.P23/R) Jeune femme assise devant un meuble a decor
        chinois, en train d'ecrire une lettre (37x27cm-15x11in) panel
        (F.FR 55000)
£8042 $15521   (12-Dec-90 WE.MU23/R) Hunting party at rest (94x71cm-37x28in) panel
        (DM 23000)

JONGH, Oene Romkes de (1812-1896) Dutch

£1455 $2865   (30-Oct-90 CH.AM79) Village street in winter (54x67cm-21x26in) s.
        (D.FL 4800)
£1497 $2515   (23-Apr-91 SY.AM127) View in Delft (35x46cm-14x18in) s. canvas on panel
        (D.FL 5000)
£2800 $5488   (22-Nov-90 CSK136/R) Dutch street in winter (63x76cm-25x30in) s.

JONGH, Tinus de (1885-1942) Dutch

£729 $1240   (27-May-91 SY.J313/R) Evening glow (25x31cm-10x12in) s. (SA.R 3500)
£810 $1555   (18-Feb-91 SY.J319) Jonkershoek (26x31cm-10x12in) s. (SA.R 4000)
£843 $1653   (11-Feb-91 SY.J561 c) Cape homestead between the mountains
        (25x30cm-10x12in) s. (SA.R 4200)
£844 $1392   (8-Jul-91 SY.J252/R) Table mountain from Bloubergstrand (24x30cm-9x12in)
        s. (SA.R 4000)
£844 $1392   (8-Jul-91 SY.J254) Mountains and Vlei (24x30cm-9x12in) s. (SA.R 4000)
£864 $1659   (26-Nov-90 SY.J315/R) Homestead between mountains (22x32cm-9x13in) s.
        (SA.R 4200)
£886 $1462   (8-Jul-91 SY.J253) Cottage with mountain backdrop (24x30cm-9x12in) s.
        (SA.R 4200)
£907 $1769   (15-Oct-90 SY.J99) Landscape bathed in sunshine (31x47cm-12x19in) s.
        (SA.R 4500)
£964 $1889   (11-Feb-91 SY.J476/R) Cottage among the trees (23x28cm-9x11in) s.
        (SA.R 4800)
£968 $1887   (15-Oct-90 SY.J96) River winding through the foothills (33x48cm-13x19in)
        s. (SA.R 4800)

JONGH, Tinus de (1885-1942) Dutch-cont.

£994	$1858	(27-Aug-90 SY.J221/R) The Twelve Apostles, Cape (24x29cm-9x11in) s. (SA.R 4800)
£1011	$1708	(15-Apr-91 SY.J452/R) Cape cottage in mountainous landscape (24x29cm-9x11in) s. (SA.R 4800)
£1029	$1975	(26-Nov-90 SY.J295) Farmstead in valley (24x30cm-9x12in) s. (SA.R 5000)
£1042	$1771	(27-May-91 SY.J311/R) Table mountain from Blouberg (24x30cm-9x12in) s. (SA.R 5000)
£1051	$2048	(25-Oct-90 SY.J401/R) Meiringspoort (32x48cm-13x19in) s. (SA.R 5200)
£1055	$1741	(8-Jul-91 SY.J259) Mountain pool (24x30cm-9x12in) s. (SA.R 5000)
£1083	$1842	(27-May-91 SY.J312/R) Wine cellar, Somerset West (24x30cm-9x12in) s. (SA.R 5200)
£1160	$1915	(8-Jul-91 SY.J257/R) Mountain and river landscape (24x30cm-9x12in) s. (SA.R 5500)
£1193	$2291	(26-Nov-90 SY.J314/R) Farmstead in foothills (29x24cm-11x9in) s. (SA.R 5800)
£1253	$2442	(25-Oct-90 SY.J402/R) Homestead in mountains (34x48cm-13x19in) s. (SA.R 6000)
£1284	$2400	(27-Aug-90 SY.J222/R) Cape Dutch homestead (30x49cm-12x19in) s. (SA.R 6200)
£1308	$2158	(8-Jul-91 SY.J260/R) Cape farmhouse (24x30cm-9x12in) s. (SA.R 6200)
£1371	$2673	(15-Oct-90 SY.J98/R) Mountain landscape with sunshine and shade (44x62cm-17x24in) s. (SA.R 6800)
£1371	$2263	(8-Jul-91 SY.J258) Cottage in the mountains (24x30cm-9x12in) s. (SA.R 6500)
£1440	$2765	(26-Nov-90 SY.J296) River gorge (29x48cm-11x19in) s. (SA.R 7000)
£1481	$2844	(26-Nov-90 SY.J294 c) Mountain landscape (29x48cm-11x19in) s. (SA.R 7200)
£1481	$2844	(26-Nov-90 SY.J295 a) Cottage with dirt road in foreground (31x46cm-12x18in) s. board (SA.R 7200)
£1582	$2611	(8-Jul-91 SY.J256/R) Cape farmhouse in the little Karoo (35x45cm-14x18in) s. (SA.R 7500)
£1605	$3081	(26-Nov-90 SY.J297 a) Farmhouse in valley with gum trees (30x49cm-12x19in) s. (SA.R 7800)
£1615	$3020	(27-Aug-90 SY.J226) Golden dawn (44x62cm-17x24in) s. (SA.R 7800)
£1646	$3160	(26-Nov-90 SY.J295 b) Homestead beneath mountains (32x47cm-13x19in) s. (SA.R 8000)
£1714	$3342	(15-Oct-90 SY.J97/R) Cottage between the mountains (31x47cm-12x19in) s. (SA.R 8500)
£1760	$3291	(27-Aug-90 SY.J223/R) River winding through mountain gorge (44x62cm-17x24in) s. (SA.R 8500)
£1979	$3365	(27-May-91 SY.J310/R) Mountains (45x63cm-18x25in) s. (SA.R 9500)
£2058	$3951	(26-Nov-90 SY.J296 b) River winding through mountainous landscape (45x62cm-18x24in) s. board (SA.R 10000)
£2058	$3951	(26-Nov-90 SY.J296 a) Farmhouse between mountains (47x63cm-19x25in) s. board (SA.R 10000)
£2277	$4259	(27-Aug-90 SY.J224/R) View from mountain gorge to the hills (65x99cm-26x39in) s. (SA.R 11000)
£3292	$6321	(26-Nov-90 SY.J297) Mountains and dry river bed (72x106cm-28x42in) s. (SA.R 16000)
£3520	$6582	(27-Aug-90 SY.J225/R) Meiringspoort (77x106cm-30x42in) s. canvas laid down on board (SA.R 17000)
£909	*$1791*	*(30-Oct-90 CH.AM517/R) Dam, Amsterdam, on rainy day (39x50cm-15x20in) s.d.1912 W/C bodycol (D.FL 3000)*

JONGHE, Gustave de (1829-1893) Belgian

£12139	$21000	(22-May-91 SY.NY62/R) A la toilette (78x58cm-31x23in) s.panel

JONGHE, Jan Baptiste de (1785-1844) Flemish

£3785	$7380	(24-Oct-90 GD.B519/R) Wooded lake landscape with rowing boat (50x39cm-20x15in) s. panel (S.FR 9500)

JONGKIND (1819-1891) Dutch

£3658	$6547	(12-Mar-91 GM.B928) Falaises et barques (32x46cm-13x18in) s. (B.FR 220000)

JONGKIND, Johan Barthold (1819-1891) Dutch

£1351	$2635	(26-Oct-90 BM.B817/R) Costal landscape at sunset (36x47cm-14x19in) s. (DM 4000)
£1361	$2300	(20-Apr-91 WOL.C20) Landscape (30x51cm-12x20in) s.
£6389	$12268	(17-Dec-90 AGS.P35/R) Crepuscule en Hollande (27x35cm-11x14in) s. panel (F.FR 63000)
£8000	$15520	(4-Dec-90 C257/R) Moulin au bord de la vilet (53x34cm-21x13in) s.d.1881
£10983	$19000	(21-May-91 BG.M1103/R) Moonlit harbour (43x61cm-17x24in) s. with letter
£12717	$22000	(23-May-91 CH.NY251/R) Nuit clair (27x41cm-11x16in) s.d.1853
£13873	$24000	(22-May-91 SY.NY113/R) Canal in Dordrecht (46x34cm-18x13in) s.d.1871
£34211	$65000	(28-Feb-91 CH.NY153/R) The Port at Rotterdam (43x56cm-17x22in) s.d.1856
£38000	$74100	(17-Oct-90 S16/R) Sainte Catherine a Honfleur, Le Marche (42x66cm-17x26in) s.d.1865
£86032	$168623	(25-Nov-90 GL.P6/R) La Seine a Paris, vue de Pont Sully (34x47cm-13x19in) s.d.1877 (F.FR 850000)
£91093	$178543	(25-Nov-90 GL.P2/R) Notre-Dame de Paris, prise du pont de l'Archeveche (35x60cm-14x24in) s.d.1849 (F.FR 900000)
£609	*$1168*	*(17-Dec-90 AGS.P4/R) Bateaux de peche a Anvers (17x27cm-7x11in) st.sig.d.28-7-1860 drawing (F.FR 6000)*

JONGKIND, Johan Barthold (1819-1891) Dutch-cont.

£846	$1472	*(25-Mar-91 CR.P33) Fontaine sur la place du chateau (14x25cm-6x10in) s. blk.crayon W/C (F.FR 8500)*
£979	$1928	*(12-Nov-90 CH.AM222/R) farm near Antwerp (13x31cm-5x12in) i.d.1846 black chk wash (D.FL 3200)*
£1200	$2340	*(17-Oct-90 G.Z64/R) Paysage de la plaine Dauphinoise (17x25cm-7x10in) d.1885 st.sig. W/C chl htd.white (S.FR 3000)*
£1508	$2473	*(19-Jun-91 GK.B481) Canal in Holland with shipping and houses (12x19cm-5x7in) st.studioi. chk paper on board (S.FR 3800)*
£1837	$3600	*(21-Nov-90 NA.BA86) Marine (22x32cm-9x13in) s. W/C*
£1950	$3900	*(7-Feb-91 B.P98/R) Canal scene (28x38cm-11x15in) s.i. W/C chl*
£2312	$4000	*(22-May-91 D.NY35/R) River landscape (23x33cm-9x13in) s.d.1871 W/C with letter*
£2500	$4425	*(19-Mar-91 C4/R) La Cote d'Andre sous la neige (10x36cm-4x14in) s.d.1880 i.verso pencil W/C*
£2895	$5500	*(27-Feb-91 SY.NY6/R) Landscape near coast (16x25cm-6x10in) st.sig.i.d.1879 num. W/C double-sided*
£2994	$5030	*(23-Apr-91 SY.AM253/R) Sur la montagne (14x24cm-6x9in) s.d.1885 W/C (D.FL 10000)*
£3245	$6231	*(17-Dec-90 AGS.P3/R) Paysage de Hollande (11x15cm-4x6in) st.sig.d.18 oct.69 W/C (F.FR 32000)*
£3525	$5745	*(11-Jun-91 CSC.P13/R) La plage et la baie de Deauville (17x29cm-7x11in) s.d.63 crayon (F.FR 35000)*
£4049	$7935	*(22-Nov-90 ZZ.F16/R) La route pres de Nevers (27x36cm-11x14in) s.d.10 sept.72 crayon W/C (F.FR 40000)*
£4500	$8775	*(19-Oct-90 C51/R) Bateaux au Large de Honfleur (24x35cm-9x14in) s.i.d.65 W/C chl*
£5015	$9779	*(12-Oct-90 APT.P24/R) Le hameau (16x24cm-6x9in) studio st.d.11 Sept 1883 W/C gouache (F.FR 50000)*
£5528	$9894	*(16-Mar-91 APT.P2/R) La diligence, Grenoble (13x25cm-5x10in) s.d.7 Oct.1875 W/C (F.FR 55000)*
£7236	$12953	*(16-Mar-91 APT.P1/R) Dordrecht, 4 Septembre 1869 (27x37cm-11x15in) bears studio st.4 Sept 69 W/C (F.FR 72000)*
£8665	$16723	*(12-Dec-90 ARC.P20/R) Vue de la Seine au Pont-Neuf (16x31cm-6x12in) s. blk.crayon htd.W/C (F.FR 85000)*

JONGKIND, Johan Barthold (school) (1819-1891) Dutch

£1040	$1758	*(1-May-91 GD.B461) River landscape with fisherman's house and sailing boat at sunset (30x56cm-12x22in) i. (S.FR 2600)*

JONGKIND, Johan Barthold (style) (1819-1891) Dutch

£751	$1300	*(21-May-91 CE.NY22/R) Farm landscape with windmill (16x25cm-6x10in) s.verso brush ink W/C htd white over pencil*

JONN, Gunnar (1904-1963) Swedish

£1654	$3243	*(10-Nov-90 FAL.M176/R) Fjord and mountain landscape (111x139cm-44x55in) s.d.50 panel (S.KR 18000)*

JONNAERT, Clemence (1866-1941) Belgian

£2958	$5768	*(23-Oct-90 C.A398/R) Still life of flowers (103x68cm-41x27in) s. (B.FR 180000)*

JONNIER, M (20th C) French

£1510	$2975	*(16-Nov-90 EA.Z293/R) The bridge (33x41cm-13x16in) s.d.1905 (S.FR 3700)*

JONSDOTTIR, Kristin (1888-1958) Icelandic

£616	$1060	*(15-May-91 RAS.K154/R) View from Iceland (50x71cm-20x28in) init. (D.KR 7000)*
£5179	$9580	*(5-Mar-91 RAS.K177/R) Hagavatn - Icelandic landscape with lake and mountains (80x87cm-31x34in) s. (D.KR 58000)*
£5435	$10489	*(12-Dec-90 RAS.K222/R) 'Hagavatn' - Icelandic landscape with lake and mountains (80x87cm-31x34in) s. (D.KR 60000)*

JONSON, Cornelis (1593-1664) Dutch

£6000	$11520	*(18-Dec-90 C14/R) Portrait of gentleman in black doublet, white shirt and ruff collar (5x?cm-2x?in) min.copper silver frame spiral cresting oval*
£12243	$24119	*(14-Nov-90 D.V74/R) Portrait of nobleman wearing armour in park landscape (36x30cm-14x12in) mono. i.d.1688 panel (A.S 250000)*
£20000	$35800	*(10-Apr-91 S64/R) Portrait of Edward Sackville, 4th Earl of Dorset, with Order of Garter (79x60cm-31x24in) panel*

JONSON, Cornelis (attrib) (1593-1664) Dutch

£3333	$6500	*(10-Oct-90 CH.NY95/R) Portrait of lady said to be Dorothy Percy, Countess of Leicester with hat (77x60cm-30x24in)*
£3911	$7000	*(11-Apr-91 SY.NY122/R) Portrait of Lady Ashburnham, Baroness Gramond (71x63cm-28x25in) bears i.*
£21000	$37590	*(12-Apr-91 C4/R) Portrait of little girl, head and shoulders, in dress and lace collar (43x35cm-17x14in) i.verso panel octagonal*

JONSON, Cornelis (circle) (1593-1664) Dutch

£1554	$3030	*(26-Oct-90 KM.K1026/R) Portrait of gentleman leaning on stick (75x66cm-30x26in) canvas laid down (DM 4600)*
£27000	$44550	*(10-Jul-91 S9/R) Portrait of three sisters standing, said to be of Waterhouse Family (137x131cm-54x52in)*

JONSON, Raymond (1891-?) American
£2312 $4000   *(12-May-91 H.C191) Untitled no 12 (69x48cm-27x19in) s.d.50 W/C*
£3324 $5750   *(12-May-91 H.C190/R) Untitled no 27 (51x66cm-20x26in) s.d.40 i.verso W/C*
£4082 $8000   *(7-Nov-90 B.SF3857/R) Figures in village (30x37cm-12x15in) s. W/C pencil*

JONSON, Sven (1902-1981) Danish
£2306 $4428   (27-Nov-90 BU.S172/R) Evening (22x27cm-9x11in) s.d.1957 (S.KR 25000)
£2399 $4605   (27-Nov-90 BU.S169/R) Surrealistic composition with lemons
                  (41x51cm-16x20in) s.d.1932 (S.KR 26000)
£2491 $4782   (27-Nov-90 BU.S170/R) Romantic landscape (23x32cm-9x13in) s. s.i.verso
                  (S.KR 27000)
£3506 $6731   (27-Nov-90 BU.S171/R) White figure (35x50cm-14x20in) s.d.1932
                  (S.KR 38000)
£3707 $7192   (5-Dec-90 AB.S7137/R) Nocturne (38x46cm-15x18in) s. (S.KR 40000)
£548 $1075   *(20-Nov-90 GO.G339) Biblical scene, Christ preaching (41x12cm-16x5in)*
                  s.d.27 mixed media (S.KR 6000)

JONSSON, Erik (1893-1950) Swedish
£511 $915   (13-Apr-91 FAL.M143/R) Day in March (40x50cm-16x20in) s. panel
                  (S.KR 5500)
£558 $998   (13-Apr-91 FAL.M142/R) Spring day in Nasum (46x55cm-18x22in) s. panel
                  (S.KR 6000)

JONSSON, Lars (20th C) Scandinavian
£1930 $3783   *(6-Nov-90 BA.S374/R) Crow in winter (49x34cm-19x13in) s.d.1980 W/C*
                  (S.KR 21000)

JONZEN, Basil (19/20th C) British
£550 $930   (30-Apr-91 B38) The Levite (63x76cm-25x30in) s.d.1934
£580 $1143   (14-Nov-90 CSK200) Onions (53x41cm-21x16in) canvas on board

JOORS, Eugeen (1850-?) Belgian
£3273 $5499   (23-Apr-91 C.A152/R) Ducks on a riverbank (27x47cm-11x19in) s. panel
                  (B.FR 200000)

JOOSTEN, Dirk Jan Hendrik (1818-1882) Dutch
£1364 $2686   (30-Oct-90 CH.AM298/R) Mixed fruit and flowers and bird on ledge
                  (15x19cm-6x7in) s.d.1845 panel (D.FL 4500)

JOOSTENS, F (?) Belgian
£723 $1410   *(24-Oct-90 GM.B949) Nu debout s. drawing (B.FR 44000)*

JOOSTENS, Paul (20th C) Belgian
£929 $1793   (12-Dec-90 CH.AM17) Altar boy (62x42cm-24x17in) s.d.27 panel (D.FL 3000)
£982 $1650   *(23-Apr-91 C.A555) z'ls dertien jaar (52x39cm-20x15in) s. panel*
                  (B.FR 60000)
£998 $1786   (16-Mar-91 KV.L162) Standing woman (106x41cm-42x16in) s.d.1947
                  (B.FR 60000)
£3368 $6635   *(6-Oct-90 KV.L158/R) Jeune fille au voile (59x49cm-23x19in) s.d.34 panel*
                  (B.FR 210000)
£526 $1025   *(23-Oct-90 C.A623) Poezeloes (69x48cm-27x19in) s.d.1953 mixed media*
                  (B.FR 32000)

JOPLING, Louise (1843-?) British
£4000 $7840   (13-Feb-91 S190/R) Portrait of woman (121x94cm-48x37in) s.d.1878

JORDAENS, Hans (16/17th C) Flemish
£3400 $5712   (26-Apr-91 NM.P33/R) Salome montrant la tete de Saint-Jean Baptiste
                  (52x70cm-20x28in) panel oval (F.FR 34000)
£7647 $13000   (30-May-91 CE.NY90) Egyptians crossing the Red Sea. Fall of Manna
                  (76x76cm-30x30in) pair octagonal

JORDAENS, Hans (circle) (16/17th C) Flemish
£4100 $6683   (2-Jul-91 PH156/R) Minerva visiting the muses on Mount Helicon
                  (95x131cm-37x52in)

JORDAENS, Hans (style) (16/17th C) Flemish
£3000 $4890   (4-Jul-91 B129/R) The rape of the sabine women (110x254cm-43x100in)
                  panel

JORDAENS, Hans III (1595-1643) Flemish
£1600 $2704   (18-Apr-91 CSK92) Apollo and Daphne (55x72cm-22x28in) on copper
£11020 $21710   (16-Nov-90 PLF.P17/R) La Predication de Saint Jean Baptiste
                  (81x104cm-32x41in) (F.FR 108000)

JORDAENS, Hans III (style) (1595-1643) Flemish
£917 $1807   (13-Nov-90 CH.AM17) Israelites after crossing of Red Sea with Moses
                  causing water to return (72x121cm-28x48in) panel (D.FL 3000)
£1150 $2243   (22-Oct-90 SWS1474) Return of Jephtha (53x80cm-21x31in) panel

JORDAENS, Jacob (1593-1678) Flemish
£8500 $14365   (19-Apr-91 C85/R) The head of an old woman (24x18cm-9x7in) paper laid
                  down on panel
£15306 $27092   (20-Mar-91 KM.K1026/R) Satyr with peasant family at table
                  (111x150cm-44x59in) (DM 45000)

JORDAENS, Jacob (1593-1678) Flemish-cont.
£19782 $35410   (9-Apr-91 APT.P13/R) L'Adoration des Mages (53x66cm-21x26in) sheets
                paper wood (F.FR 200000)
£1684   *$3200*   *(9-Jan-91 CH.NY19/R) Study of priest (17x14cm-7x6in) black red white chk*
£8563   *$16869*   *(12-Nov-90 CH.AM155/R) April, Flora riding bull - Taurus, Silenus and*
                other figures (21x25cm-8x10in) with i. black lead black red chk wash
                (D.FL 28000)
£9500   *$15485*   *(2-Jul-91 C199/R) Diana and Callisto (10cm-4ins circular) black lead*
                black chk pen wash htd white
£26316   *$50000*   *(8-Jan-91 SY.NY119/R) St.Martin, Bishop of tours, healing the possessed*
                servant of Tretrodius (55x38cm-22x15in) W/C bodycol.over blk.chk. 4
                joined pieces paper

JORDAENS, Jacob (after) (1593-1678) Flemish
£1300 $2470   (13-Sep-90 CSK290/R) Washing and anointing of body of Christ
                (117x155cm-46x61in)

JORDAENS, Jacob (circle) (1593-1678) Flemish
£1300 $2600   (7-Feb-91 CSK83/R) Philosopher Democritus (63x50cm-25x20in) i. panel

JORDAENS, Jacob (style) (1593-1678) Flemish
£1100 $1903   (20-May-91 SWS73) A Maenad (62x77cm-24x30in)
£3058 $6024   (13-Nov-90 CH.AM77/R) Old woman examining coin (47x39cm-19x15in) panel
                (D.FL 10000)

JORDAN, Ernst Karl Pasqual (1858-1924) German
£505 $874   (6-May-91 ZEL.L1769/R) Landscape with thunderstorm clearing
                (49x69cm-19x27in) board (DM 1500)

JORDAN, Rudolf (1810-1887) German
£4615 $9000   (26-Oct-90 S.W2611/R) Strand Kneipe, Holland (81x132cm-32x52in)
                mono.d.1884

JORDE, Lars (1865-1939) Norwegian
£1336 $2578   (12-Dec-90 BU.O34/R) Landscape from Mesna (43x49cm-17x19in) s.d.35 panel
                (N.KR 15000)
£1910 $3724   (11-Oct-90 BU.O67/R) Landscape from Lillehammer (41x46cm-16x18in)
                s.indist.d.18 panel (N.KR 22000)
£2102 $3762   (14-Mar-91 BU.O56/R) Studio interior (40x46cm-16x18in) s.d.19 panel
                (N.KR 24000)
£2257 $3769   (4-Jun-91 BU.O7/R) River landscape from Florence 1899 (42x66cm-17x26in)
                s.i.d.99 (N.KR 26000)
£2671 $5156   (12-Dec-90 BU.O32/R) River landscape (65x75cm-26x30in) s.d.29
                (N.KR 30000)
£12587 $24544   (11-Oct-90 BU.O69/R) Landscape from Bo (77x60cm-30x24in) s.i.d.94
                (N.KR 145000)

JORDELL, Ivan (1901-1965) Swedish
£1029 $2018   (10-Nov-90 FAL.M177/R) Formations in red (78x88cm-31x35in) s. panel
                (S.KR 11200)

JORGENSEN, Aksel (1883-?) Danish
£973 $1828   (10-Aug-90 RAS.V604) Interior with seated young man (110x82cm-43x32in)
                s.d.1917 (D.KR 11000)

JORGENSEN, Christian (1860-1935) American
£2041 $4000   (13-Feb-91 B.SF2005/R) Yosemite Valley from Inspiration Point
                (51x76cm-20x30in) s.

JORGENSEN, Erling (1905-1977) Danish
£679 $1311   (12-Dec-90 RAS.K104) Composition (99x46cm-39x18in) s.d.1965 (D.KR 7500)

JORI, Marcello (20th C) Italian
£2722 $4682   (13-May-91 CH.R54/R) Besetzt (117x130cm-46x51in) d.1988 s.verso canvas
                on panel (I.L 6000000)
£3006 $5832   (3-Dec-90 CH.R121/R) Quartiere della Perla (143x130cm-56x51in)
                s.i.d.1984verso (I.L 6500000)
£675   *$1317*   *(23-Oct-90 F.M4) Teatrino (75x105cm-30x41in) s. mixed media collage*
                (I.L 1500000)
£2949   *$5072*   *(13-May-91 CH.R55/R) Incontri (143x111cm-56x44in) d.1987 mixed media*
                (I.L 6500000)

JORIS, Pio (1843-1921) Italian
£750   *$1470*   *(14-Feb-91 CSK3/R) A Neapolitan fishergirl (41x25cm-16x10in) s.d.67*
                pencil W/C

JORN, Asger (1914-1973) Danish
£4587 $8853   (16-Dec-90 GL.P147) Sans titre (50x40cm-20x16in) s.d.72 acrylic
                (F.FR 45000)
£5783 $10872   (19-Sep-90 KH.K84/R) Composition (30x22cm-12x9in) s.d.42 masonite
                (D.KR 65000)
£6000 $10620   (21-Mar-91 C201/R) Fredsduer (35x39cm-14x15in) s.d.52 i. verso board
£6162 $12016   (10-Oct-90 RAS.K99/R) Composition with figure (19x25cm-7x10in) s.
                d.41verso (D.KR 70000)
£6732 $13263   (14-Nov-90 KH.K76/R) Mask (36x31cm-14x12in) s.d.41 panel (D.KR 75000)

JORN, Asger (1914-1973) Danish-cont.

£8891	$15292	(15-May-91 RAS.K27/R) Legendary king from Hjarno (52x52cm-20x20in) s.d.48 (D.KR 101000)
£9907	$19121	(12-Dec-90 CH.AM370/R) Figure (32x30cm-13x12in) s.d.43 (D.FL 32000)
£15405	$30040	(10-Oct-90 RAS.K35/R) Evidence surprenante (72x51cm-28x20in) s.d.72 acrylic paper on canvas (D.KR 175000)
£15480	$29876	(13-Dec-90 SY.AM228/R) Untitled.(40x30cm-16x12in) s.d.1954 verso oil sand canvas (D.FL 50000)
£15845	$30898	(10-Oct-90 RAS.K67/R) Moonhorse (39x48cm-15x19in) s.d.51 s.d.1951verso (D.KR 180000)
£18576	$35851	(13-Dec-90 SY.AM221/R) Untitled (55x70cm-22x28in) linen (D.FL 60000)
£20000	$39000	(18-Oct-90 C343/R) Untitled (41x33cm-16x13in) s. s.d.65verso
£26690	$50178	(19-Sep-90 KH.K54/R) Le terre Noire (65x56cm-26x22in) s. i.d.57verso (D.KR 300000)
£34000	$54740	(27-Jun-91 C5/R) Pixilated garden (65x81cm-26x32in) s. s.i.d.66/69 verso
£36000	$69840	(6-Dec-90 S8/R) Albisola (68x55cm-27x22in) s. s.d.55 verso
£36000	$70200	(18-Oct-90 S121/R) Insulte sous developee (65x84cm-26x33in) s. s.i.d.61verso
£39613	$77245	(10-Oct-90 RAS.K22/R) Drama I (80x100cm-31x39in) s.d.40 (D.KR 450000)
£40248	$77678	(13-Dec-90 SY.AM232/R) Triplerie (65x54cm-26x21in) s. s.d.62 verso (D.FL 130000)
£41796	$80666	(12-Dec-90 CH.AM395/R) L'Evasion (97x130cm-38x51in) s. s.i.d.59 verso (D.FL 135000)
£58532	$114138	(22-Oct-90 BR.M41/R) Comunita (100x81cm-39x32in) s.d.1971 (I.L 130000000)
£65000	$115050	(21-Mar-91 S21/R) Les beaux legumes (116x89cm-46x35in) s.
£75075	$129880	(22-May-91 CH.AM594/R) Det blaa billede - blue picture (83x100cm-33x39in) i.verso (D.FL 250000)
£82000	$145140	(21-Mar-91 S27/R) Pauvre toi (97x130cm-38x51in) s. s.d.1958 verso
£110000	$213400	(6-Dec-90 S40/R) De Levende Sjaele - Sentimentale lagttagel-Sev (150x100cm-59x39in) s. s.i.d.63 verso
£122807	$208772	(29-May-91 KH.K74/R) Ils n'ecoutent pas (97x130cm-38x51in) s.d.70verso (D.KR 1400000)
£526	$895	*(29-May-91 KH.K98) La fleur exotique (17x18cm-7x7in) s.d.1938 frottage (D.KR 6000)*
£614	$1044	*(29-May-91 KH.K82) Figure composition (7x17cm-3x7in) s. Indian ink (D.KR 7000)*
£655	$1100	*(28-Apr-91 HG.C79) Composition (33x48cm-13x19in) s.d.1961 W/C*
£897	$1722	*(27-Dec-90 RAS.V148/R) Composition (14x10cm-6x4in) s. Indian ink W/C (D.KR 10000)*
£1201	$2078	*(23-May-91 SY.AM224/R) Untitled (23x18cm-9x7in) s.d.64 felt tip pen (D.FL 4000)*
£1261	$2182	*(23-May-91 SY.AM225/R) Untitled (24x18cm-9x7in) s.i.d.64 felt tip pen crayon (D.FL 4200)*
£1407	$2308	*(21-Jun-91 CK.P79) Composition (32x23cm-13x9in) s.d.51 pen wash (F.FR 14000)*
£1952	$3377	*(22-May-91 CH.AM612/R) Figures (10x14cm-4x6in) s.d.50 pen brush (D.FL 6500)*
£1952	$3377	*(23-May-91 SY.AM227/R) Untitled (24x31cm-9x12in) s.d.42 ink (D.FL 6500)*
£2105	$3579	*(29-May-91 KH.K10/R) Figure composition (14x9cm-6x4in) s. W/C (D.KR 24000)*
£2415	$4733	*(13-Feb-91 KH.K87/R) Figure composition (23x18cm-9x7in) s.d.1949 crayon (D.KR 27000)*
£2632	$4474	*(29-May-91 KH.K23/R) Composition (27x22cm-11x9in) s.d.49 crayon Indian ink (D.KR 30000)*
£2920	$4760	*(11-Jun-91 CSC.P51/R) Tete (59x44cm-23x17in) s.d.66 gouache (F.FR 29000)*
£2941	$5676	*(13-Dec-90 SY.AM329/R) Untitled (52x40cm-20x16in) s.d.57 indian ink chl (D.FL 9500)*
£3081	$6008	*(10-Oct-90 RAS.K85/R) Composition (39x33cm-15x13in) s.i.d.1951 Indian ink joined paper (D.KR 35000)*
£3114	$5854	*(19-Sep-90 KH.K39/R) Composition (34x27cm-13x11in) s.d.37 gouache W/C (D.KR 35000)*
£3336	$6473	*(5-Dec-90 AB.S7139/R) Untitled (48x39cm-19x15in) s.71 W/C (S.KR 36000)*
£3500	$5705	*(3-Jul-91 CSC.P96/R) Visage d'homme (28x22cm-11x9in) s.d.45 inkian ink wash (F.FR 35000)*
£3604	$6234	*(22-May-91 CH.AM616/R) Figures (33x47cm-13x19in) s.d.45 W/C over printed base (D.FL 12000)*
£3614	$5819	*(26-Jun-91 CB.P15/R) Composition (54x40cm-21x16in) s.d.64 mixed media (F.FR 36000)*
£4123	$7009	*(29-May-91 KH.K53/R) Figure composition (27x22cm-11x9in) s.d.49 crayon Indian ink (D.KR 47000)*
£4270	$8028	*(19-Sep-90 KH.K90/R) Figure composition (27x21cm-11x8in) s.d.51 W/C Indian ink (D.KR 48000)*
£4644	$8963	*(13-Dec-90 SY.AM255/R) Untitled (71x51cm-28x20in) s.d.71 gouache (D.FL 15000)*
£6811	$13146	*(13-Dec-90 SY.AM234/R) Untitled (51x44cm-20x17in) s.d.68 paper decollage (D.FL 22000)*
£7107	$14000	*(5-Oct-90 CH.NY1/R) Untitled (35x24cm-14x9in) s.d.64 s.i.d.verso torn paper collage*
£7207	$12468	*(23-May-91 SY.AM256 j/R) Deux animaux (32x39cm-13x15in) s.d.51 ink (D.FL 24000)*
£7458	$12454	*(8-Jun-91 HN.H306/R) Three figures (27x34cm-11x13in) s.d.1952 W/C chk (DM 22000)*
£7740	$14938	*(12-Dec-90 CH.AM398/R) Untitled - painted with Enrico Baj and Gianni Bertini (85x84cm-33x33in) s.d.58 oil fabric collage canvas double-sided (D.FL 25000)*

JORN, Asger (1914-1973) Danish-cont.
£13345	*$25089*	*(19-Sep-90 KH.K46/R) The red runner, Paris 1964 (44x53cm-17x21in) s.d.64 decollage (D.KR 150000)*
£14911	*$25199*	*(21-Apr-91 E.LA90/R) Sans titre s. oil collage canvas (F.FR 150000)*

JOSEPH, Albert (1868-1952) French
£744	$1331	(17-Mar-91 L.C36) Paysage en Creuse (46x61cm-18x24in) s. (F.FR 7400)
£1724	$3000	(27-Mar-91 B.SF4095/R) Printemps en Bourgogne (46x61cm-18x24in) s.

JOSEPHSON, Ernst (1851-1906) Swedish
£3504	$5886	(24-Apr-91 BA.S117/R) Rouge et noir (24x19cm-9x7in) panel (S.KR 37000)
£3585	$7026	(6-Nov-90 BA.S134/R) Saint Anastasius (61x48cm-24x19in) after Rembrandt (S.KR 39000)
£3676	$7206	(6-Nov-90 BA.S135/R) Landscape with figures (17x23cm-7x9in) s. panel (S.KR 40000)
£6434	$12610	(6-Nov-90 BA.S132/R) By Mora belfry (32x41cm-13x16in) s. (S.KR 70000)
£16423	$32354	(30-Oct-90 BU.S49/R) Norwegian cottage interior (26x37cm-10x15in) three (S.KR 180000)
£46415	$90974	(10-Nov-90 FAL.M178/R) Saul and David (S.KR 505000)
£91241	$179745	(30-Oct-90 BU.S48/R) Cupid and Psyche (46x38cm-18x15in) s.i. (S.KR 1000000)
£738	*$1417*	*(27-Nov-90 AB.S4037/R) Queen with flower (17x8cm-7x3in) s. Indian ink (S.KR 8000)*
£1642	*$3235*	*(30-Oct-90 BU.S184/R) 'Delila' (34x20cm-13x8in) s. Indian ink (S.KR 18000)*
£2190	*$4314*	*(30-Oct-90 BU.S183/R) Swedish law (34x20cm-13x8in) s. Indian ink (S.KR 24000)*
£2341	*$4026*	*(14-May-91 BU.S15/R) Justitia (33x19cm-13x7in) s. Indian ink (S.KR 25000)*
£2952	*$5668*	*(27-Nov-90 BU.S174/R) Summer landscape with couple rowing (35x22cm-14x9in) s. W/C Indian ink (S.KR 32000)*
£3923	*$7729*	*(30-Oct-90 BU.S182/R) The viking (36x23cm-14x9in) s. Indian ink (S.KR 43000)*

JOST, Joseph (1888-?) Austrian
£1055	$1741	(8-Jul-91 SY.J181/R) Still life with garden flowers in ceramic bowl (28x22cm-11x9in) s.d.1943 panel (SA.R 5000)
£2534	$4307	(28-May-91 KF.M781/R) Still life of flowers (100x80cm-39x31in) s.d.1925 panel (DM 7500)

JOUBERT, Leon (19th C) French
£3314	$5568	(24-Apr-91 BA.S118/R) Still life of fruit (48x69cm-19x27in) s.d.81 (S.KR 35000)

JOUBIN, Georges (1888-1983) French
£750	$1223	(5-Jul-91 APT.P133) Vue de Robinson (54x65cm-21x26in) s.d.23 board (F.FR 7500)
£813	$1626	(6-Feb-91 FB.P196/R) Bouquet de fleurs (35x27cm-14x11in) s. panel (F.FR 8000)
£1109	$2162	(28-Oct-90 M.V135) Bouquets de fleurs (46x38cm-18x15in) s. (F.FR 11000)
£1208	$1970	(11-Jun-91 I.N228) La Liseuse (33x41cm-13x16in) s. panel (F.FR 12000)
£1410	$2298	(11-Jun-91 I.N227/R) Les Andelys (64x53cm-25x21in) s. i.d.1928 verso board (F.FR 14000)
£1942	$3302	(2-Jun-91 LT.P80/R) Animation sur le port (27x41cm-11x16in) s. paper laid down on canvas (F.FR 19500)
£3033	$5915	(17-Oct-90 LT.P165/R) Promeneurs en bord de riviere aux Andelys (53x65cm-21x26in) s. board (F.FR 30000)
£3960	$7010	(7-Apr-91 LT.P39/R) Le balcon (54x46cm-21x18in) s. paper laid down on canvas (F.FR 40000)
£396	*$701*	*(7-Apr-91 I.N179) Jeune femmme au bord d'un bassin (44x32cm-17x13in) mono. pastel (F.FR 4000)*

JOUCLARD, Adrienne (1882-?) French
£505	$990	(12-Feb-91 JPB.P64) Scene de moisson (33x46cm-13x18in) s. (F.FR 5000)
£505	$990	(12-Feb-91 JPB.P52) Les Caroly, saut perilleux de cheval a cheval (46x55cm-18x22in) s. (F.FR 5000)
£525	$1029	(12-Feb-91 JPB.P27) A l'ecole, la recreation (46x61cm-18x24in) s. verso (F.FR 5200)
£525	$1029	(12-Feb-91 JPB.P104) Semailles a Villefavreuse (60x92cm-24x36in) s. (F.FR 5200)
£525	$1029	(12-Feb-91 JPB.P142) Ecole, Rue de Patay (27x41cm-11x16in) s. (F.FR 5200)
£535	$1049	(12-Feb-91 JPB.P83) Escrime (27x35cm-11x14in) s. panel (F.FR 5300)
£556	$1089	(12-Feb-91 JPB.P99/R) Moissons a Onville (65x92cm-26x36in) s. (F.FR 5500)
£556	$1089	(12-Feb-91 JPB.P13/R) Baigneurs au Rupt de Mad (46x55cm-18x22in) s. (F.FR 5500)
£606	$1188	(12-Feb-91 JPB.P21) Baigneurs pres de la riviere (54x65cm-21x26in) s. (F.FR 6000)
£606	$1188	(12-Feb-91 JPB.P60) Le tracteur, scene de moissons (46x55cm-18x22in) s. (F.FR 6000)
£606	$1188	(12-Feb-91 JPB.P58) Au bord de la Moselle (55x46cm-22x18in) s. (F.FR 6000)
£626	$1227	(12-Feb-91 JPB.P47) Au depart a Longchamp (38x46cm-15x18in) s. (F.FR 6200)

JOUCLARD, Adrienne (1882-?) French-cont.
£626 $1227   (12-Feb-91 JPB.P95) La Cantine, Rue de Patay (33x41cm-13x16in) s. (F.FR 6200)
£687 $1346   (12-Feb-91 JPB.P77) Boxeurs (38x46cm-15x18in) s. (F.FR 6800)
£688 $1341   (15-Oct-90 B.G72) Baigneurs (50x61cm-20x24in) (F.FR 6800)
£707 $1386   (12-Feb-91 JPB.P116) La vallee du Rupt de Mad (55x81cm-22x32in) s. (F.FR 7000)
£707 $1386   (12-Feb-91 JPB.P112/R) Paysage au Faucheur (60x73cm-24x29in) s. (F.FR 7000)
£727 $1425   (12-Feb-91 JPB.P30/R) La recolte des fruits (50x65cm-20x26in) s. (F.FR 7200)
£758 $1485   (12-Feb-91 JPB.P97/R) La boxe (39x46cm-15x18in) s. (F.FR 7500)
£859 $1683   (12-Feb-91 JPB.P22) La fete a Wolpy (60x73cm-24x29in) s. verso (F.FR 8500)
£909 $1782   (12-Feb-91 JPB.P100) Tennis a Roland-Garros (60x73cm-24x29in) s. (F.FR 9000)
£909 $1782   (12-Feb-91 JPB.P120) Baigneurs a Onville (65x81cm-26x32in) s. (F.FR 9000)
£909 $1782   (12-Feb-91 JPB.P117) Baigneurs sur les bords de la Marne (54x81cm-21x32in) s. (F.FR 9000)
£962 $1885   (25-Nov-90 ZZ.F87) Scene de moisson (65x92cm-26x36in) s. (F.FR 9500)
£1010 $1980   (12-Feb-91 JPB.P146) Couture a la maternelle (33x41cm-13x16in) s. (F.FR 10000)
£1061 $2079   (12-Feb-91 JPB.P113/R) La fete (60x73cm-24x29in) s. (F.FR 10500)
£1061 $2079   (12-Feb-91 JPB.P118) La partie de peche (65x81cm-26x32in) s. (F.FR 10500)
£1061 $2079   (12-Feb-91 JPB.P119/R) La Moselle a Champey (65x81cm-26x32in) s. (F.FR 10500)
£1061 $2079   (12-Feb-91 JPB.P20) La vallee du Rupt de Mad sur Bayonville (54x73cm-21x29in) s. (F.FR 10500)
£1414 $2772   (12-Feb-91 JPB.P26) Moissons a Arnaville (50x65cm-20x26in) s. (F.FR 14000)
£1414 $2772   (12-Feb-91 JPB.P101) La fete a Gorze (60x81cm-24x32in) s. (F.FR 14000)
£1465 $2871   (12-Feb-91 JPB.P115/R) Rugby (73x60cm-29x24in) s. (F.FR 14500)
£1566 $3069   (12-Feb-91 JPB.P107/R) La Noce a la Campagne (81x100cm-32x39in) s. (F.FR 15500)
£1616 $3168   (12-Feb-91 JPB.P103) Vendanges a Onville (65x92cm-26x36in) s. (F.FR 16000)
£2121 $4158   (12-Feb-91 JPB.P108/R) Fete a Lessy (65x81cm-26x32in) s. (F.FR 21000)
£3030 $5939   (12-Feb-91 JPB.P110/R) Ete (73x100cm-29x39in) s. (F.FR 30000)
£323 $634   (12-Feb-91 JPB.P7) Les labours (48x64cm-19x25in) s. W/C wash Indian ink (F.FR 3200)
£424 $832   (12-Feb-91 JPB.P4) Les ramasseurs de pommes de terre (49x65cm-19x26in) s. col.crayons (F.FR 4200)
£612 $1206   (16-Nov-90 LGB.P110) Les chats (31x41cm-12x16in) s. pastel (F.FR 6000)

JOUDERVILLE, Isaac de (1612-1645) Flemish
£6667 $13000   (10-Oct-90 CH.NY30/R) Bearded man wearing turban (48x36cm-19x14in) panel painted arch

JOUENNE, Michel (19th C) French
£2569 $4985   (7-Dec-90 GL.P76) Campagne ensoleillee (54x72cm-21x28in) s. l. verso (F.FR 25000)
£3770 $6484   (19-May-91 ZZ.F175/R) Le village blanc (100x100cm-39x39in) s. (F.FR 38000)

JOUFFROY (jnr) (18th C) French
£8367 $16484   (16-Nov-90 PLF.P21/R) Renauds et Armide (137x195cm-54x77in) s.d.1750 (F.FR 82000)

JOUKOVSKI, Stanislav (1873-1944) Russian
£768 $1375   (16-Mar-91 AL.W9) Room with a balcony (78x66cm-31x26in) s. (P.Z 13500000)

JOULLAIN, Francois (1697-1778) French
£503 $824   (18-Jun-91 APT.P49) La mort d'Hippolyte (34x47cm-13x19in) pen wash (F.FR 5000)

JOURDAIN, Roger Joseph (1845-1918) French
£1316 $2500   (27-Feb-91 SY.NY96/R) Lady by lake (152x95cm-60x37in) s.
£5400 $10638   (13-Nov-90 SWS373/R) At the boathouse (75x104cm-30x41in) s.
£75145 $130000   (22-May-91 SY.NY70/R) Dimanche a la grande jatte (94x155cm-37x61in) s.

JOURDAN, Adolphe (1825-1889) French
£9814 $18842   (29-Nov-90 D.V84/R) Pensive lecture (101x81cm-40x32in) s. (A.S 200000)
£16410 $32000   (24-Oct-90 CH.NY104/R) Maternal affection (103x83cm-41x33in) s.

JOURDEUIL, Louis-Adrien (1849-1907) Russian/French
£1313 $2600   (1-Feb-91 S.W2566/R) Le bateau lavore de netoyles sur saune (46x76cm-18x30in) s.

JOUSSET, Claude (c.1935-) French
£526 $1000   (14-Sep-90 DM.D2284/R) French port scene (51x61cm-20x24in) s.
£554 $981   (7-Apr-91 LT.P127) La place des Vosges (61x50cm-24x20in) s. (F.FR 5600)

JOUVE, Paul (1880-?) French

£5500	$8965	(1-Jul-91 APT.P294) Panthere marchant (55x73cm-22x29in) s. (F.FR 55000)
£7056	$13760	(28-Oct-90 QWA.P153/R) Deux ours blancs (32x55cm-13x22in) s. board (F.FR 70000)
£400	$652	(1-Jul-91 APT.P93) Crapaud-buffle (23x27cm-9x11in) s. pastel htd.gouache (F.FR 4000)
£546	$938	(15-May-91 CN.P43/R) Le chemineau devant l'ancien Trocadero (32x48cm-13x19in) mono. chl. (F.FR 5500)
£853	$1662	(14-Oct-90 SY.MO484/R) Panthere (28x22cm-11x9in) s. crayon gouache (F.FR 8500)
£900	$1467	(1-Jul-91 APT.P292) Les deux aigles (29x24cm-11x9in) s. gouache indian ink (F.FR 9000)
£1000	$1630	(1-Jul-91 APT.P293) Les deux grands aigles (29x24cm-11x9in) s. gouache indian ink (F.FR 10000)
£1040	$1840	(6-Apr-91 GL.P37) Panthere (30x24cm-12x9in) s. pierre noire chl. (F.FR 10500)
£1692	$2943	(25-Mar-91 QWA.P174) Aigle (55x40cm-22x16in) s. chl.htd.W/C (F.FR 17000)
£1850	$3016	(1-Jul-91 APT.P94/R) Les elephants de Madourai (30x36cm-12x14in) s. W/C gouache (F.FR 18500)
£2000	$3260	(1-Jul-91 APT.P95/R) Grand duc (46x32cm-18x13in) s. W/C gouache chl. (F.FR 20000)
£2500	$4075	(1-Jul-91 APT.P96) Tigre devorant (28x48cm-11x19in) s.d.04 chl.htd.pastel (F.FR 25000)
£2908	$5729	(12-Nov-90 CN.P7/R) Lion assis etude (34x52cm-13x20in) s. crayon (F.FR 28500)
£5000	$8150	(1-Jul-91 APT.P97/R) Panthere noire (37x49cm-15x19in) s. gouache indian ink (F.FR 50000)
£6352	$12451	(7-Nov-90 APT.P479/R) L'aigle au faisan (94x67cm-37x26in) s. goauche (F.FR 62000)
£7000	$11410	(1-Jul-91 APT.P37/R) Les trois tigres au repos (27x91cm-11x36in) s. gouache W/C (F.FR 70000)
£7100	$11573	(1-Jul-91 APT.P346/R) Boa et singe (56x104cm-22x41in) s. chl.gouache (F.FR 71000)
£17000	$27710	(1-Jul-91 APT.P345/R) Panthere noire rugissante (59x103cm-23x41in) s. gouache (F.FR 170000)

JOUVE, Paul (school) (1880-?) French

| £646 | $1092 | (17-Apr-91 CB.P15/R) Tigres s'abreuvant (44x75cm-17x30in) chl. (F.FR 6500) |

JOUVEN, Romain (19/20th C) French?

| £355 | $703 | (3-Feb-91 I.N131) La barque (52x72cm-20x28in) s. W/C (F.FR 3500) |
| £720 | $1426 | (3-Feb-91 I.N130) Paysage Provencal (37x54cm-15x21in) s. W/C oval (F.FR 7100) |

JOUVENET, Jean Baptiste (school) (1644-1717) French

| £3852 | $6432 | (6-Jun-91 D.V315/R) Sleeping Venus with putti in wooded landscape (77x97cm-30x38in) (A.S 80000) |

JOVE, Jacques de la (style) (?) ?

| £1400 | $2660 | (13-Sep-90 CSK328) Fountain in garden with elegant couples in foreground (47x61cm-19x24in) |

JOVENEAU, Jean (19/20th C) ?

| £582 | $1077 | (6-Mar-91 APT.P122) Raisin et perdrix (60x81cm-24x32in) s. (F.FR 5800) |

JOVINGE, Torsten (1898-1936) Swedish

| £834 | $1618 | (4-Dec-90 BA.S262/R) Country road through fields (34x36cm-13x14in) s.d.34 W/C (S.KR 9000) |

JOY (?) ?

| £1150 | $2162 | (19-Sep-90 ZZ.B620) French and English shipping being battered by storm (25x36cm-10x14in) s.d.1856 W/C |

JOY, William (1803-1867) British

£3000	$5760	(17-Aug-90 K476/R) Fishing boats leaveing shore with bathing huts on beach (25x33cm-10x13in) s.
£820	$1525	(3-Sep-90 SWS1404) Low tide (33x57cm-13x22in) s. W/C
£1700	$2941	(22-May-91 S40/R) Royal yacht Victoria and Albert, H.M.S. St. Vincent, H.M. yacht Black Eagle, H.M.S. Trafalgar (19x28cm-7x11in) W/C
£2700	$5184	(26-Nov-90 SWS69/R) Men-o'-war at sea (30x43cm-12x17in) s.d.1857 W/C scratching out
£3600	$6228	(22-May-91 S39/R) British warships approaching Portsmouth (27x35cm-11x14in) W/C

JOY, William (attrib) (1803-1867) British

| £800 | $1488 | (5-Sep-90 BT159/R) Three decker leaving harbour (30x43cm-12x17in) |

JOYANT, Jules Romain (1803-1854) French

| £1529 | $2951 | (12-Dec-90 ARC.P38/R) Une rue a escalier pres de la Piazetta (40x27cm-16x11in) blk.crayon pen sepia wash (F.FR 15000) |

JOYCE, Ena (1926-) Australian

| £1584 | $2676 | (16-Apr-91 J.M104/R) Spring in the Sydney suburbs (75x90cm-30x35in) s. (A.D 3500) |

JOZSEF, Csortos E (20th C) ?
£4012 $7823   (14-Oct-90 SY.MO483/R) Tableau decoratif a personnages allegoriques
                  (108x150cm-43x59in) s. (F.FR 40000)

JUAN DE SEVILLA see ROMERO Y ESCALANTE, Juan de Sevilla

JUANES, Juan de see MASIP, Vicente Juan

JUAREZ, Roberto (20th C) ?
£1786 $3500   (7-Nov-90 SY.NY370/R) Key and moon anchor (198x203cm-78x80in) s.i.d.81
                  verso acrylic

JUCH, Ernst (1838-1909) Austrian
£700 $1148   (18-Jun-91 PH143) The fish market (31x26cm-12x10in) panel

JUCHANOWITZ, Albert Wilhelm Adam (1817-?) German
£1020 $1643   (28-Jun-91 BM.B697/R) Riverside cottage in forest with children playing
                  and woman getting water (44x59cm-17x23in) i.d.1850verso (DM 3000)

JUCHSER, Hans (1894-?) ?
£1149 $1953   (31-May-91 GB.B6441) Still life with palette (45x58cm-18x23in) s.d.1973
                  panel (DM 3400)

JUDLIN, Alexis (1746-?) French
£367   *$724*   *(13-Nov-90 CH.G251) Portrait of young man wearing black top-hat
                  (5x?cm-2x?in) min. gold mount oval (S.FR 900)*

JUDSON, William Lees (1842-1928) American
£1923 $3750   (10-Oct-90 B.SF552/R) Mountain canyon (46x38cm-18x15in) s.

JUEL, Jens (1745-1802) Danish
£19366 $32535   (23-Apr-91 RAS.K11/R) Portrait of Henrik Even Moe and his wife Henriette
                    Frederica (69x54cm-27x21in) oval pair (D.KR 220000)
£29930 $50282   (23-Apr-91 RAS.K26/R) Portrait) of a lady in The Gruneisen family
                    (97x84cm-38x33in) s.d.1773 (D.KR 340000)
£2163 $4196   *(22-Aug-90 RAS.K27/R) Portrait of Marie Margrethe Rantzau
                  (35x26cm-14x10in) pastel oval (D.KR 25000)*
£2335 $4366   *(29-Aug-90 KH.K109/R) Portrait of Elisabeth Praetorius (34x26cm-13x10in)
                  pastel (D.KR 26500)*

JUEL, Jens (studio) (1745-1802) Danish
£1056 $1775   (23-Apr-91 RAS.K352/R) Portrait of Carsten Tank Anker (66x53cm-26x21in)
                  (D.KR 12000)
£1157   *$2174*   *(18-Sep-90 BU.K103/R) Portrait of Pauline Dorothea Tutein
                    (33x26cm-13x10in) pastel (D.KR 13000)*

JUELL-GLEDITSCH, Rolf (1892-1984) Norwegian
£657 $1176   (11-Mar-91 B.O36/R) S. Giorgio, Venice (60x50cm-24x20in) s.i.d.1968
                  panel (N.KR 7500)
£712 $1375   (12-Dec-90 BU.O35/R) Spring landscape, Mollingdalen, near Roros
                  (96x115cm-38x45in) s. s.i.d.1958verso (N.KR 8000)

JUILLERAT, Jacques-Henri (1770-1860) Swiss
£845   *$1436*   *(31-May-91 GB.B5828/R) Classical arches in Aosta (23x31cm-9x12in) s. W/C
                  (DM 2500)*

JUKES, Francis (1747-1812) British
£600   *$990*   *(11-Jul-91 S136) Margate, Kent (29x42cm-11x17in) i.d.1785 pen ink W/C
                  over pencil*

JULIANA Y ALBERT, Jose (19th C) Spanish
£2000 $3840   (27-Nov-90 PH213/R) Feeding the poor by convent (49x37cm-19x15in) s.i.
                  panel

JULIARD, Nicolas Jacques (1715-1790) French
£3586 $6167   (14-May-91 GF.L2072/R) River landscape with watermill (51x92cm-20x36in)
                  (S.FR 9000)
£7500 $14475   (12-Dec-90 S198/R) Wooded landscapes with figures (37x46cm-15x18in) pair
£8151 $13775   (18-Apr-91 APT.P111/R) Paysage italien anime (97x132cm-38x52in)
                  (F.FR 82000)
£11156 $22089   (30-Jan-91 APT.P95/R) Paysages champetres (154x98cm-61x39in) pair
                    (F.FR 110000)

JULIEN, Henri (1852-1908) Canadian
£1233 $2405   (24-Oct-90 EA.M463/R) Habitant smoking pipe (30x23cm-12x9in) s.d.1906
                  board (C.D 2800)

JULIEN, Jean Antoine (1736-1799) French
£6500 $10985   (19-Apr-91 C101/R) A personification of painting (26x35cm-10x14in) panel

JULIEN, Simon (1735-1798) French
£6500   *$10985*   *(16-Apr-91 C202/R) Saint Hippolytus being tied to wild horses
                    (44x33cm-17x13in) i. mount red blk.chk.ink wash arched top*

JULIUS, Per (1951-) Swedish
£1668 $3236   (5-Dec-90 AB.S7140/R) Northern landscapes (15x23cm-6x9in) s. W/C pair
                 (S.KR 18000)

JULLIAN, Philippe (20th C) French?
£644 $1139   (5-Apr-91 LGB.P113) La galerie de l'Avenue Marigny, Noel 1972
                 (29x21cm-11x8in) s.i. W/C (F.FR 6500)

JULLIEN, Amedee-Marie-Antoine (?-1887) French
£1189 $1938   (10-Jun-91 W.T1374) Paysge romantique avec femme en aval d'une Vanne
                 (89x115cm-35x45in) s.d.1854 (C.D 2200)

JUNCKER, Justus (1703-1767) German
£950 $1900   (7-Feb-91 CSK108/R) Portrait of elderly bearded man in coat and jewelled
                 turban (55x44cm-22x17in) s. panel
£1858 $3623   (26-Oct-90 BM.B717/R) The vegetable market (28x38cm-11x15in) copper
                 (DM 5500)
£4333 $7236   (6-Jun-91 D.V129/R) Hermit meditating in hermitage (42x33cm-17x13in)
                 panel (A.S 90000)
£9629 $16081   (6-Jun-91 D.V131/R) Still life with butter, radishes and jug
                 (35x47cm-14x19in) s. one of pair (A.S 200000)
£9629 $16081   (6-Jun-91 D.V130/R) Still life with cheese, bread and jug
                 (35x47cm-14x19in) s. one of pair (A.S 200000)
£33197 $62410   (19-Sep-90 GK.Z850/R) Still life with bouquet of flowers, fruit and
                 insects (62x50cm-24x20in) s.d.1765 panel (S.FR 81000)

JUNDT, Gustave (1830-1884) French
£789 $1500   (27-Feb-91 SY.NY83/R) Napoleon in clandestine boat ride
                 (115x140cm-45x55in) s.d.1880

JUNG, Charles Jacob (?) ?
£4167 $8000   (30-Nov-90 CH.NY132/R) Winter morning (79x101cm-31x40in)

JUNGBLUT, J (1860-1912) German
£1379 $2703   (7-Nov-90 N.M919/R) Dutch winter landscape with fishermen, evening
                 (80x60cm-31x24in) s. (DM 4000)
£2448 $4748   (4-Dec-90 FN.S2086/R) Moonlit Dutch river landscape covered in snow with
                 figures (50x100cm-20x39in) s. canvas on panel (DM 7000)

JUNGBLUT, Johann (1860-1912) German
£874 $1687   (12-Dec-90 N.M571/R) Edge of wood at sunset, winter (26x20cm-10x8in) s.
                 panel (DM 2500)
£909 $1755   (10-Dec-90 L.K462) Road through wooded landscape (24x18cm-9x7in) s.
                 panel (DM 2600)
£979 $1890   (12-Dec-90 N.M570/R) Potatoe harvest before town (27x35cm-11x14in) s.
                 panel (DM 2800)
£1014 $1926   (14-Sep-90 SA.A1223/R) Lower Rhine landscape, autumn (54x44cm-21x17in)
                 s. (DM 3000)
£1081 $1838   (27-May-91 L.K295) Peasant with ox and horse pulling plough
                 (22x29cm-9x11in) s. panel (DM 3200)
£1225 $2425   (31-Jan-91 D.V115/R) Winter landscape with figures (35x26cm-14x10in) s.
                 panel (A.S 25000)
£2055 $3678   (13-Mar-91 N.M539) Farmhouses by stream and peasant woman
                 (44x33cm-17x13in) s. (DM 6000)
£2067 $3700   (16-Mar-91 W.W44/R) On a Fjord (33x53cm-13x21in) s. panel
£2226 $3985   (13-Mar-91 N.M540/R) Woman collecting wood in snowy landscape at sunrise
                 (45x34cm-18x13in) s. (DM 6500)
£2347 $3991   (28-May-91 AB.S4775/R) Winter landscape with children on ice
                 (80x120cm-31x47in) s. (S.KR 25000)
£2365 $4020   (27-May-91 L.K291) River landscape with figures on ice, winter
                 (31x41cm-12x16in) s. panel (DM 7000)
£2500 $4475   (12-Apr-91 BM.B622/R) Coastal landscape with fisherman on beach, winter
                 (81x66cm-32x26in) s. (DM 7500)
£2551 $4515   (20-Mar-91 KM.K1282/R) Snow covered wood clearing with figures
                 (60x80cm-24x31in) s. (DM 7500)
£3041 $5169   (27-May-91 L.K293) Landscape with view of Dutch town and windmill,
                 winter (81x60cm-32x24in) s. (DM 9000)
£3741 $6024   (28-Jun-91 BM.B698/R) Women returning on ice at dusk. Treelined canal
                 with figure (33x24cm-13x9in) s. panel pair (DM 11000)

JUNGHANNS, Julius Paul (1876-1958) Austrian
£1531 $2709   (20-Mar-91 KM.K1285) Two goats feeding grazing in river landscape
                 (50x60cm-20x24in) s.d.1910 (DM 4500)
£1684 $2912   (6-May-91 ZEL.L1771/R) Pair of oxen in landscape (50x65cm-20x26in) s.
                 (DM 5000)
£1701 $3010   (20-Mar-91 KM.K1284/R) Rhine landscape with cattle (44x77cm-17x30in) s.
                 (DM 5000)
£1871 $3012   (26-Jun-91 KM.K1518/R) Young peasant woman knitting near fence and cow
                 grazing (50x60cm-20x24in) s. (DM 5500)
£2703 $5270   (26-Oct-90 KM.K1296/R) Young peasant woman with domestic animals at
                 midday (30x40cm-12x16in) s. (DM 8000)
£3265 $6203   (2-Mar-91 KRA.D337/R) Shepherd girl with goats and cow in field
                 (30x40cm-12x16in) s.d.1937 (DM 9500)
£4223 $8024   (14-Sep-90 SA.A1209/R) Peasant with cart drawn by four horses on way
                 home (29x50cm-11x20in) s. (DM 12500)

JUNGHANNS, Julius Paul (1876-1958) Austrian-cont.
£6643 $12822   (10-Dec-90 L.K465/R) Horse drawn cart loaded with wood and two men
                   (74x131cm-29x52in) s.d.56 (DM 19000)

JUNGHEIM, Carl (1803-1886) German
£1993 $3787   (2-Mar-91 KRA.D338/R) Mountain landscape (71x104cm-28x41in) s. panel
                   (DM 5800)

JUNGHEIM, Julius (20th C) German
£687 $1306   (2-Mar-91 KRA.D515/R) Stream through fields (42x63cm-17x25in) s.
                  (DM 2000)

JUNGMANN, Nico W (1872-1935) Dutch
£700 $1344   (21-Feb-91 B42/R) Young Dutch girl with doll (42x32cm-17x13in) s. panel
£1216 $2372   (26-Oct-90 BM.B819/R) Woman in Dutch costume praying, Volendam
                 (37x27cm-15x11in) mono. i.verso panel (DM 3600)
£3000 $5880   (8-Nov-90 C22/R) Kevelaar procession (75x255cm-30x100in) s. panel
£950 $1862   (24-Jan-91 CSK30) Portrait of young man (61x47cm-24x19in) s.d.98 W/C
                 bodycol pen brush

JUNGNICKEL, L H (1881-1965) German
£373 $623   (8-Jun-91 FN.S665/R) Cat with kittens (17x19cm-7x7in) s. chl (DM 1100)

JUNGNICKEL, Ludwig Heinrich (1881-1965) German
£633 $1240   (24-Jan-91 D.V2/R) Mountain lake landscape (21x35cm-8x14in) paper
                 (A.S 13000)
£8500 $16490   (5-Dec-90 PH89/R) Die Hahneschlacht (71x68cm-28x27in) s.
£438 $858   (24-Jan-91 D.V170/R) Gazelles (33x48cm-13x19in) W/C (A.S 9000)
£438 $757   (6-May-91 ZEL.L1480) Two donkeys (19x30cm-7x12in) s. chl wash
                 (DM 1300)
£535 $1049   (24-Jan-91 D.V174/R) Big cats (20x28cm-8x11in) chl W/C (A.S 11000)
£584 $1145   (24-Jan-91 D.V44/R) Fawn jumping (16x15cm-6x6in) i. pencil chk gouache
                 bodycol (A.S 12000)
£633 $1240   (24-Jan-91 D.V171) Cat in profile. Cat curled up (27x20cm-11x8in) chl
                 two (A.S 13000)
£633 $1240   (24-Jan-91 D.V172) Cat with kittens (20x28cm-8x11in) chl W/C
                 (A.S 13000)
£779 $1526   (24-Jan-91 D.V169/R) Heads of two cats (32x25cm-13x10in) mono. chl W/C
                 (A.S 16000)
£965 $1881   (18-Oct-90 D.V188/R) Southern landscape (48x41cm-19x16in) W/C
                 (A.S 20000)
£973 $1908   (24-Jan-91 D.V167/R) Big cat (34x44cm-13x17in) s.d.22 chl W/C
                 (A.S 20000)
£1359 $2229   (20-Jun-91 D.V78/R) Big and small donkey (23x32cm-9x13in) s.d.34 chl W/C
                 (A.S 28000)
£1531 $2649   (8-May-91 D.V66/R) Female nude (48x34cm-19x13in) s.d.1919 chl chk
                 gouache (A.S 32000)

JUNGSTEDT, Kurt (1894-1963) Swedish
£505 $904   (17-Mar-91 BU.M249) Saturday night, Smogen's pier (80x64cm-31x25in)
                 s.d.1942verso (S.KR 5400)
£3522 $6832   (4-Dec-90 BA.S261/R) The prologue (198x122cm-78x48in) s. panel
                 (S.KR 38000)

JUNGWIRTH, Josef (1869-1950) Austrian
£606 $1048   (6-May-91 ZEL.L1773/R) Cyclamen (67x45cm-26x18in) s.d.1935 (DM 1800)
£2365 $4020   (27-May-91 L.K296) Still life of bunches of flowers, book and apples on
                 chest of drawers (61x82cm-24x32in) s. board oval (DM 7000)
£2148 $4189   (11-Oct-90 D.V217/R) Allegory of spring (35x63cm-14x25in) s. pastel
                 (A.S 45000)

JUNIPER, Robert (1929-) Australian
£698 $1172   (22-Apr-91 SY.ME3) Study of Murchison Goldfields (19x29cm-7x11in)
                 s.d.1977 i.verso (A.D 1500)
£800 $1552   (6-Dec-90 CSK58/R) Nannine - ghost gold mining town (58x74cm-23x29in) s.
£1620 $2722   (16-Jul-91 JRL.S277) Burnt hillside (74x90cm-29x35in) s.d.69 board
                 (A.D 3500)
£2667 $5013   (17-Sep-90 SY.ME139/R) The Dutchmans road (44x58cm-17x23in) s.d.80 board
                 (A.D 6000)
£2889 $5431   (17-Sep-90 SY.ME119/R) Sketcher in landscape (70x100cm-28x39in) s.d.84
                 (A.D 6500)
£3111 $5849   (17-Sep-90 SY.ME107/R) Landscape (83x129cm-33x51in) s.d.74 acrylic board
                 (A.D 7000)
£3556 $6684   (17-Sep-90 SY.ME23/R) Landscape (135x119cm-53x47in) s. board (A.D 8000)
£6889 $12951   (17-Sep-90 SY.ME94/R) Broome landscape (121x150cm-48x59in) s.
                 (A.D 15500)

JUPPIN and PLUMIER (18th C) Flemish
£2800 $4704   (26-Apr-91 NM.P39/R) Paysage anime (97x148cm-38x58in) (F.FR 28000)

JURADO, Angel (?) Spanish
£660 $1266   (19-Feb-91 DUR.M38) Rosal parra (100x73cm-39x29in) panel (S.P 120000)
£823 $1382   (23-Apr-91 DUR.M6/R) Rosal (100x81cm-39x32in) panel (S.P 150000)
£1042 $1750   (23-Apr-91 DUR.M17/R) Ventana (100x91cm-39x36in) panel (S.P 190000)

1014

JURGENS, Hans Peter (1924-) German
£912 $1779   (26-Oct-90 BM.B985/R) Frigate Mentor before Valparaiso on journey around
          the world (31x49cm-12x19in) s.i.d. W/C (DM 2700)
£912 $1779   (26-Oct-90 BM.B986/R) Bremerhaven c.1870 D Preussen (30x48cm-12x19in) s.
          W/C (DM 2700)
£1049 $2035   (5-Dec-90 DO.H2024) War marine (41x62cm-16x24in) s. W/C (DM 3000)
£1102 $1840   (5-Jun-91 DO.H2019/R) Hamburg Harbour, Blohm and Voss (29x47cm-11x19in)
          s. s.i. W/C bodycol (DM 3250)
£1294 $2510   (5-Dec-90 DO.H2043) Whaling boat Azaria (42x60cm-17x24in) s. W/C
          (DM 3700)

JURRES, Johannes Hendricus (1875-1946) Dutch
£838 $1593   (11-Sep-90 CH.AM214/R) The Rest during the Flight into Egypt
          (65x52cm-26x20in) s. (D.FL 2800)
£1497 $2515   (23-Apr-91 SY.AM124/R) Lion's hunt (90x130cm-35x51in) s. (D.FL 5000)

JUST, Rene Camille (1868-?) French
£663 $1272   (30-Nov-90 ARC.P139) La vieille maison du Faou (50x66cm-20x26in) s.
          (F.FR 6500)

JUTSUM, Henry (1816-1869) British
£1729 $3250   (19-Sep-90 B.SF2680/R) Cattle crossing a river (46x71cm-18x28in)
          s.d.1845
£3000 $5550   (4-Mar-91 PHB30/R) Pastoral scene with figures and sheep
          (46x73cm-18x29in) s.d.1846 i.verso
£4500 $8325   (4-Mar-91 PHB31/R) Village balcksmith (57x77cm-22x30in) s.
£1200 $2016   (15-Jul-91 PH98) Peaceful brook (26x43cm-10x17in) s.d.1845 num.275 W/C
          bodycol
£1300 $2327   (11-Apr-91 S88/R) Girls on stile at edge of wood (30x21cm-12x8in)
          s.d.1849 W/C bodycol over pencil

JUTZ, Adolf Gustav (1887-1945) German
£405 $689   (28-May-91 KF.M782) Isar landscape near Munich (31x49cm-12x19in)
          mono.d.1929 W/C board on board (DM 1200)

JUTZ, Carl (19/20th C) German
£8793 $16707   (28-Feb-91 D.V8/R) Ducks in pond landscape (28x34cm-11x13in) s. panel
          (A.S 180000)
£16084 $31042   (12-Dec-90 WE.MU53/R) Harvest scene in mountainous landscape, late
          summer (57x76cm-22x30in) s.d.1900 (DM 46000)

JUTZ, Carl (attrib) (19/20th C) German
£1271 $2148   (19-Apr-91 FN.S1753/R) Chickens by pond near farmhouse amongst trees and
          view of mountains (13x17cm-5x7in) s. panel (DM 3800)

JUTZ, Carl (elder) (1835-1916) German
£2226 $3985   (13-Mar-91 N.M542/R) Ducks by water (19x24cm-7x9in) s. panel (DM 6500)
£4223 $8024   (14-Sep-90 SA.A1200/R) Landscape with ducks by fence (40x33cm-16x13in)
          s. canvas on panel (DM 12500)
£5537 $10797   (10-Oct-90 ZEL.L1564/R) Pond landscape with ducks, winter afternoon
          (18x23cm-7x9in) s.d.1858 board oval (DM 16500)
£5667 $10143   (12-Apr-91 BM.B623/R) Ducks by pond (17x20cm-7x8in) s. panel
          (DM 17000)

JUTZ, Carl (elder-circle) (1835-1916) German
£1616 $2796   (6-May-91 ZEL.L1774/R) Ducks in snowy lake landscape (28x36cm-11x14in)
          (DM 4800)

JUTZ, Carl (style) (19/20th C) German
£900 $1665   (6-Mar-91 SC4352) Ducks and ducklings by pond (20x28cm-8x11in) bears
          sig. panel

JUUEL, Andreas (1817-1868) Danish
£887 $1739   (24-Nov-90 SA.A789/R) Wooded lake landscape (34x47cm-13x19in) mono.
          i.d.1867verso (DM 2600)

JUVARRA, Filippo (1676-1736) Italian
£600 $1014   (16-Apr-91 C172/R) The Loggia of a Palace (15x9cm-6x4in) i. pen wash
£6000 $10140   (16-Apr-91 C171/R) A courtyard, design for the stage (20x19cm-8x7in) i.
          blk.chk.ink wash inscribed arch

JUVENELL, Paul (elder) (1579-1643) German
£950 $1549   (2-Jul-91 PH70/R) Portrait of bearded priest (46x34cm-18x13in) copper
          oval

JUVIN, Juliette (1896-?) French
£7614 $15000   (15-Nov-90 SY.NY67/R) Les baigneuses (31x31cm-12x12in) s. panel

JYNGE, Gert (1904-) Norwegian
£1655 $3227   (15-Oct-90 B.O46/R) Summer night - man with fishingrod (38x48cm-15x19in)
          s.d.43 (N.KR 19000)

KAAN, J (19th C) ?
£1100 $2167 (1-Nov-90 CSK56/R) Faustian Dandy (124x94cm-49x37in) s.d.1862

KAAN-ALBEST, J von (1874-?) German
£616 $1103 (14-Mar-91 N.M2678/R) Old farmhouses in Weischnhofen (38x52cm-15x20in)
s.i.d.1927 i.verso (DM 1800)

KABATCHEK, Leonid (1923-) Russian
£597 $1039 (25-Mar-91 ARC.P165/R) Dans la rue (33x63cm-13x25in) s. hardboard
(F.FR 6000)
£1144 $1991 (25-Mar-91 ARC.P162/R) Au zoo (49x67cm-19x26in) s. board (F.FR 11500)
£2189 $3809 (25-Mar-91 ARC.P161/R) Le bal (27x38cm-11x15in) s. (F.FR 22000)
£3383 $5887 (25-Mar-91 ARC.P163/R) Fete de village (49x96cm-19x38in) s. board
(F.FR 34000)

KABEL, Adrian van der see CABEL, Adrian van der

KABELL-ROSENORN, Ludovica (?) ?
£528 $887 (23-Apr-91 RAS.K293) Blue-white iris and orchid-iris (80x67cm-31x26in)
init.i. (D.KR 6000)

KACERE, John (1920-) American
£6633 $13066 (14-Nov-90 CN.P86/R) Jill (56x76cm-22x30in) s.i.d.1978 (F.FR 65000)
£10183 $20061 (29-Oct-90 FB.P69/R) M.Garibaldi (137x203cm-54x80in) s.i.d.1974 verso
acrylic (F.FR 100000)
£12085 $19698 (16-Jun-91 CC.P63/R) M.Garibaldi I ou Marsha I (137x203cm-54x80in)
s.i.d.1974 verso (F.FR 120000)
£15816 $31158 (14-Nov-90 CN.P85/R) Peggy (91x142cm-36x56in) s.i.d.1977 (F.FR 155000)

KACZ, Endre Komaromi (1880-1969) Hungarian
£639 $1144 (14-Apr-91 BU.H125/R) Interior with woman reading (59x80cm-23x31in) s.
panel (F.M 4500)
£1200 $2016 (18-Jul-91 CSK114/R) Arranging flowers (101x76cm-40x30in) s.
£1551 $3040 (6-Nov-90 GF.L2552/R) Child sleeping (86x70cm-34x28in) s. (S.FR 3800)
£3800 $7486 (4-Oct-90 CSK149/R) The dressing-up drawer (84x69cm-33x27in) s.

KADAR, Bela (1877-1955) Hungarian
£2091 $4099 (20-Nov-90 BR.M27/R) Gli amanti (58x44cm-23x17in) s. tempera paper
(I.L 4600000)
£4574 $8600 (22-Sep-90 WOL.C337/R) Future world (41x58cm-16x23in) s.
£7937 $13016 (21-Jun-91 G.Z53/R) Seated nude (78x54cm-31x21in) s. (S.FR 20000)
£310 $555 (14-Mar-91 L76) Village scene (25x33cm-10x13in) s. pastel
£398 $685 (14-May-91 GF.L2672/R) Two horses playing (23x30cm-9x12in) s. indian ink
(S.FR 1000)
£450 $734 (5-Jul-91 APT.P27) Amazones (45x28cm-18x11in) s. ink wash (F.FR 4500)
£479 $900 (22-Sep-90 WOL.C337 a/R) Poles (23x20cm-9x8in) s. W/C
£524 $1000 (2-Jan-91 GG.TA439/R) Still life with statue and painting. Head
(45x27cm-18x11in) s. W/C verso pen double-sided
£558 $959 (14-May-91 GF.L2673/R) Two figures, horse and church (17x25cm-7x10in)
s.i. chl another study verso (S.FR 1400)
£578 $1000 (7-May-91 CE.NY69/R) Four nude figures (59x77cm-23x30in) s. gouache
£582 $949 (15-Jun-91 L.K343) Waiting man with horse (23x30cm-9x12in) s. indian ink
pen brush (DM 1700)
£616 $1005 (15-Jun-91 L.K344/R) Horse, dog and man (24x30cm-9x12in) s. indian ink
pen brush (DM 1800)
£640 $1082 (1-May-91 GD.B1524) Female nude seated (22x29cm-9x11in) s. brush wash
(S.FR 1600)
£677 $1165 (14-May-91 GF.L2671/R) Woman bathing (19x28cm-7x11in) s. indian ink
(S.FR 1700)
£756 $1474 (20-Jan-91 GL.P23) Chevaux et cavalier (46x29cm-18x11in) s. W/C
(F.FR 7500)
£803 $1574 (24-Nov-90 AB.L38/R) Interior. Studies of letter z (28x23cm-11x9in) s.
W/C double-sided (S.FR 2000)
£1017 $1923 (25-Sep-90 FB.P305) Profil et visage (46x29cm-18x11in) bears st. gouache
W/C double-sided (F.FR 10000)
£1020 $2000 (12-Feb-91 SY.NY92/R) Shiva figure. Landscape s. one pen indian ink
gouache one gouache pair
£1084 $2125 (24-Nov-90 AB.L36/R) Composition with two female nudes (20x27cm-8x11in)
s. W/C indian ink (S.FR 2700)
£1143 $2251 (16-Nov-90 EA.Z267/R) Seated women. Two faces (31x23cm-12x9in) s. indian
ink double-sided (S.FR 2800)
£1182 $2046 (21-May-91 WK.M1049/R) Still life (47x37cm-19x15in) s. gouache
(DM 3500)
£1205 $2361 (24-Nov-90 AB.L107/R) Female figure seated (27x20cm-11x8in) s. W/C
indian ink (S.FR 3000)
£1224 $2412 (16-Nov-90 EA.Z272) Seated female (28x21cm-11x8in) s. indian ink
(S.FR 3000)
£1282 $2500 (10-Oct-90 SY.NY340/R) Man, woman and horse (38x25cm-15x10in) s. W/C ink
wash
£1284 $2221 (25-May-91 N.M162) Young woman with checked head scarf (40x29cm-16x11in)
s. gouache (DM 3800)
£1393 $2634 (28-Sep-90 S.Z205/R) Femme nue (40x50cm-16x20in) s. gouache indian ink
(S.FR 3400)
£1490 $2891 (7-Dec-90 GL.P209/R) Composition cubiste (19x28cm-7x11in) s. gouache
(F.FR 14500)

KADAR, Bela (1877-1955) Hungarian-cont.
£1551 $3009   (7-Dec-90 G.Z147/R) Femme nu acroupie (28x36cm-11x14in) s. indian ink brush (S.FR 3800)
£1825 $2994   (21-Jun-91 G.Z116/R) Still life (28x20cm-11x⌐) s. W/C (S.FR 4600)
£1953 $3788   (9-Dec-90 CC.P9/R) Femme (31x21cm-12x8in) s. ink gouache (F.FR 19000)
£2183 $3579   (21-Jun-91 G.Z89/R) Composition (29x22cm-11x⌐in) s. gouache (S.FR 5500)
£3000 $5850   (17-Oct-90 S221/R) Girl in armchair (86x59cm-34x23in) s. gouache
£3049 $5000   (19-Jun-91 B.SF1838/R) Composition with rider and birds (58x86cm-23x34in) s. tempera gouache
£3414 $6691   (24-Nov-90 AB.L111/R) Houses and sun (45x29cm-18x11in) s.d.1928 gouache (S.FR 8500)
£3673 $7200   (6-Nov-90 GF.L2207/R) Couple before Russian town (35x42cm-14x17in) W/C double-sided (S.FR 9000)
£3936 $7714   (24-Nov-90 AB.L106/R) Untitled (29x32cm-11x13in) s. gouache (S.FR 9800)

KADISHMAN, Menashe (1932-) Israeli
£872 $1700   (10-Oct-90 SY.NY385/R) Untitled (99x69cm-39x27in) s.verso acrylic printed paper on canvas
£1104 $1800   (12-Jun-91 GG.TA338/R) Head (86x60cm-34x24in) s.d.1983 acrylic paper on canvas
£1652 $2857   (22-May-91 CH.AM705/R) Lamb (100x70cm-39x28in) paper on canvas (D.FL 5500)
£3665 $7000   (2-Jan-91 GG.TA563/R) Head (99x81cm-39x32in) s. s.d.1989erso acrylic

KADLACSIK, Laszlo (1925-1989) Hungarian
£6383 $12000   (19-Sep-90 B.SF2604/R) Still life of flowers in a vase (91x64cm-36x25in) panel

KAELIN, Charles Salis (1858-1929) American
£532 $1000   (22-Sep-90 WOL.C204/R) Boats on river (20x25cm-8x10in) artist board
£638 $1200   (22-Sep-90 WOL.C141/R) Forest study (41x46cm-16x18in)
£888 $1500   (20-Apr-91 WOL.C166/R) Waves against coast (28x36cm-11x14in) artist board
£904 $1700   (22-Sep-90 WOL.C271/R) Harbour at sunset (20x25cm-8x10in) artist board
£947 $1600   (20-Apr-91 WOL.C140/R) Fall study (41x46cm-16x18in)
£957 $1800   (22-Sep-90 WOL.C133/R) Winter landscape (51x61cm-20x24in)
£1006 $1700   (20-Apr-91 WOL.C62/R) Grey day (46x51cm-18x20in)
£1065 $1800   (20-Apr-91 WOL.C128/R) Fall landscape (61x46cm-24x18in)
£1170 $2200   (22-Sep-90 WOL.C286/R) Boats in harbour (28x36cm-11x14in) artist board
£1183 $2000   (20-Apr-91 WOL.C64/R) Coastline (51x71cm-20x28in)
£1243 $2100   (20-Apr-91 WOL.C133/R) Tumbling brook (43x56cm-17x22in) s.
£1302 $2200   (20-Apr-91 WOL.C165/R) Harbour at sunset (28x36cm-11x14in) artist board
£1436 $2700   (22-Sep-90 WOL.C202/R) Harbour scene (41x46cm-16x18in)
£1915 $3600   (22-Sep-90 WOL.C245/R) Quiet day (61x51cm-24x20in) s.
£2012 $3400   (20-Apr-91 WOL.C139/R) Harbour scene (46x51cm-18x20in)
£2840 $4800   (20-Apr-91 WOL.C169/R) Blossom time (64x51cm-25x20in) s.
£2926 $5500   (22-Sep-90 WOL.C197/R) Winter landscape with stream (61x71cm-24x28in) s.
£798 $1500   (22-Sep-90 WOL.C203/R) Woods winter landscape (41x46cm-16x18in) s. pastel
£851 $1600   (22-Sep-90 WOL.C267/R) Rocky coastline, horizon in distance (36x41cm-14x16in) pastel
£947 $1600   (20-Apr-91 WOL.C167/R) Coastline with horizon indistance (41x46cm-16x18in) pastel
£1170 $2200   (22-Sep-90 WOL.C147 a) Rocky coastline (36x43cm-14x17in) s. pastel
£2023 $3500   (21-May-91 CE.NY482/R) Winter woods (36x41cm-14x16in) s. pastel board

KAELIN, Martin (1926-) American
£847 $1500   (23-Mar-91 LAE.L53/R) Beach scene with photographer (107x107cm-42x42in) s.

KAEMMERER, Frederik Hendrik (1839-1902) Dutch
£2157 $4250   (15-Nov-90 D.NY52/R) Lovers seated beneath tree (46x32cm-18x13in) s.
£3815 $6600   (12-May-91 H.C25/R) Girl carrying basket (61x41cm-24x16in) s.
£3934 $7750   (15-Nov-90 D.NY51/R) Sunday morning stroll, spring (41x25cm-16x10in) s.
£5128 $10000   (24-Oct-90 CH.NY273/R) School belles (56x33cm-22x13in) s.
£5442 $9633   (20-Mar-91 KM.K1286/R) Young lady writing letter in salon interior (40x25cm-16x10in) s. (DM 16000)
£5872 $11567   (13-Nov-90 AB.S918/R) Interior with woman writing letters (40x25cm-16x10in) s. (S.KR 64000)
£35897 $70000   (23-Oct-90 SY.NY89/R) Beach at Scheveningen, Holland (24x40cm-9x16in) s.

KAERCHER, Amalie (19th C) German
£3333 $6500   (24-Oct-90 CH.NY180/R) Still life with grapes, peaches and butterfly on mossy bank (34x41cm-13x16in) s.

KAFKA, Josef (1873-1955) Austrian
£854 $1529   (11-Apr-91 D.V261/R) Spring (75x91cm-30x36in) s.d.1936 (A.S 18000)

KAGER, Johann Matthias (circle) (1575-1634) German
£5862 $10493   (14-Mar-91 D.V304/R) Alexander the Great and Darius' female relatives (211x240cm-83x94in) (A.S 120000)

KAHAN, Louis (1905-) Australian
£498 $841   (16-Apr-91 J.M113) Carousel (54x74cm-21x29in) s.d. '57 sepia W/C (A.D 1100)

KAHAN, Louis (1905-) Australian-cont.
£679 $1147   (16-Apr-91 J.M423) Dreaming (33x51cm-13x20in) s.d.'64 mixed media
                          (A.D 1500)

KAHANA, Aharon (20th C) Israeli
£3351 $6400   (2-Jan-91 GG.TA541/R) Odalisque sur Fond Gris (71x91cm-28x36in) s.d.1955
                          s.d.verso

KAHLER, Carl (1855-?) Austrian
£960 $1900   (1-Feb-91 S.W2403/R) Flower garden (102x76cm-40x30in) s.
£2232 $4286   (27-Nov-90 W.T1149/R) White cat and jewel box (68x56cm-27x22in) s.i.
                          (C.D 5000)
£6154 $12000   (24-Oct-90 CH.NY204/R) Paris, tea time, 1900 (82x129cm-32x51in) s.
£8982 $15000   (7-Jun-91 SY.NY104/R) His Highness in a river landscape
                          (83x122cm-33x48in) s.d.1899

KAHLO, Frida (1907-1954) Mexican
£872093 $1500000   (15-May-91 CH.NY9 a/R) Autorretrato con Pelo Suelto (61x45cm-24x18in) i.
                          masonite
£15306 $30000   (20-Nov-90 CH.NY93/R) Bocerto para Mis Abuelos, Mis Padres y Yo
                          (31x35cm-12x14in) s.d.1943 pencil

KAHN, Leo (?) ?
£524 $1000   (2-Jan-91 GG.TA443/R) Still life, vase and fruit (49x72cm-19x28in) s.

KAHN, Wolf (1927-) American
£867 $1700   (24-Nov-90 YFA.M75/R) Airstrip among corn (41x51cm-16x20in) s.
£1020 $2000   (12-Feb-91 SY.NY444/R) Garden window (140x109cm-55x43in) s. s.verso
£1579 $3000   (28-Feb-91 MFA.C116 a) Barn in the snow (71x122cm-28x48in) s.
£2646 $5000   (27-Sep-90 CH.NY314/R) Thurber farmyard in the afternoon
                          (54x116cm-21x46in) s.
£3175 $6000   (27-Sep-90 CH.NY313/R) Off route five, late May, Farmington
                          (71x101cm-28x40in) s.
£4190 $7500   (14-Mar-91 CH.NY234/R) Early morning on Connecticut River
                          (56x92cm-22x36in) s. num.57 d.1975 verso
£4233 $8000   (26-Sep-90 SY.NY216/R) Strong's barn (91x132cm-36x52in) s.
£5780 $10000   (22-May-91 CH.NY326/R) The wood shed (108x138cm-43x54in) s.d.1975
£513 $1000   (10-Oct-90 SY.NY343/R) Barns (71x112cm-28x44in) s.d.1987 W/C chk

KAHRER, Max (1878-?) ?
£732 $1354   (7-Mar-91 D.V65/R) Marbach an der Donau (34x51cm-13x20in) . panel
                          (A.S 15000)
£994 $1928   (6-Dec-90 D.V7/R) Leopoldsberg, Vienna (69x55cm-27x22in) s.d.1909
                          (A.S 20000)
£1217 $2384   (24-Jan-91 D.V87/R) Wooded landscape (42x53cm-17x21in) s.d.1905
                          (A.S 25000)
£1220 $2257   (7-Mar-91 D.V43/R) Chiemgau landscape (60x80cm-24x31in) s.d.1914
                          (A.S 25000)
£2426 $4585   (27-Sep-90 D.V27/R) Spring in Kahlenbergerdorf (42x23cm-17x9in) s.d.1901
                          (A.S 50000)
£2485 $4821   (6-Dec-90 D.V54/R) View of Burg Aggstein and Danube. Mountain landscape
                          with cow (75x80cm-30x31in) s.d.1915 double-sided (A.S 50000)

KAHRS, Margrethe Gran (1860-1945) Scandinavian?
£846 $1633   (10-Dec-90 B.O68/R) Still life (64x45cm-25x18in) s.d.1886 (N.KR 9500)

KAIRA, Alice (1913-) Finnish
£317 $611   (15-Dec-90 BU.H240) Boy bathing (33x26cm-13x10in) s.d.1948 W/C
                          (F.M 2200)

KAISER, Edouard (1865-?) Swiss
£735 $1425   (8-Dec-90 GAB.G2690/R) Le village alpestre (46x65cm-18x26in) s.d.1899
                          (S.FR 1800)

KAISER, Eduard (attrib) (1820-1895) Austrian
£676 $1318   (26-Oct-90 KM.K1300) Madonna and Child with view of southern landscape
                          seen through window (52x45cm-20x18in) (DM 2000)

KAISER, J (20th C) ?
£1213 $2293   (27-Sep-90 D.V2/R) Konigssee landscape with St Bartolomae
                          (41x39cm-16x15in) s.d.1880 (A.S 25000)

KAISER, Richard (1868-1941) German
£610 $1019   (5-Jun-91 DO.H2779/R) Village near Munich (24x33cm-9x13in)
                          s.i.indis.d.1900 panel (DM 1800)
£933 $1671   (12-Apr-91 BM.B624/R) View of Wasserburg on Lake Constance
                          (64x81cm-25x32in) (DM 2800)
£1017 $1698   (5-Jun-91 DO.H2778/R) Bavarian landscape (59x68cm-23x27in) s.i.d.1900
                          (DM 3000)
£1049 $2024   (12-Dec-90 N.M573/R) Bavarian river landscape with village
                          (90x119cm-35x47in) s.i. (DM 3000)

KAISER-HERBST, Carl (1858-?) Austrian
£732 $1412   (14-Dec-90 ZOF.Z959/R) Landscape at Neustadter Kanal near Baden
                          (41x60cm-16x24in) s. s.i.verso board (S.FR 1800)

KAISERMANN, Francois see KEISERMANN, Franz

KAISIN, Lucien (1901-1963) Belgian
£599 $1071   (16-Mar-91 KV.L167) Village under the snow (72x91cm-28x36in) s.d.39
                     verso (B.FR 36000)

KAKS, Olle (1941-) Swedish
£2688 $5214   (5-Dec-90 AB.S7150/R) Emblem II (92x73cm-36x29in) s.d.74 (S.KR 29000)
£738 $1417   (27-Nov-90 BU.S186/R) Composition (116x103cm-46x41in) s.d.1976verso
                     mixed media canvas (S.KR 8000)

KALCHBRENNER, W (19th C) German
£1149 $2240   (26-Oct-90 BM.B820/R) Lange Anna, Helgoland with rowing boat and figures
                     (46x62cm-18x24in) s.d.1859 i.verso (DM 3400)

KALCKREUTH, Patrick von (1892-1970) German
£685 $1226   (14-Mar-91 N.M2679/R) Three master in choppy seas (61x79cm-24x31in) s.
                     i.verso (DM 2000)
£695 $1161   (5-Jun-91 DO.H2021) North Sea (70x100cm-28x39in) s. (DM 2050)
£748 $1205   (28-Jun-91 BM.B797/R) Threemaster in seascape (71x102cm-28x40in) s.
                     (DM 2200)
£900 $1611   (12-Apr-91 BM.B742/R) Seascape (80x121cm-31x48in) s. (DM 2700)
£936 $1583   (19-Apr-91 FN.S1754/R) Beach with surf, evening (61x92cm-24x36in) s.
                     (DM 2800)
£1000 $1790   (12-Apr-91 BM.B743/R) Sailing ship in choppy sea (60x80cm-24x31in) s.
                     (DM 3000)
£1190 $1917   (28-Jun-91 BM.B796/R) Fisherman, girl and boy on mole watching fishing
                     boats (69x101cm-27x40in) s. (DM 3500)

KALCKREUTH, Stanislas von (1821-1894) German
£1049 $2024   (10-Dec-90 L.K469) Alpine landscape with view of Mont Blanc range
                     (26x25cm-10x10in) (DM 3000)

KALF, Willem (circle) (1622-1693) German
£18824 $32000   (31-May-91 CH.NY65) Roemer, wineglasses, bowl and fruit on ledge draped
                     with Oriental carpet (61x52cm-24x20in)

KALF, Willem (style) (1622-1693) German
£11431 $19319   (18-Apr-91 APT.P59/R) Nature morte au homard (86x114cm-34x45in)
                     (F.FR 115000)

KALINOWSKI, Horst Egon (1924-) German
£576 $962   (8-Jun-91 HN.H313/R) Mausoleum (25x45cm-10x18in) s.d.1963 collage
                     (DM 1700)
£678 $1132   (8-Jun-91 HN.H312/R) Karwendel (24x27cm-9x11in) s.d.1958 collage
                     (DM 2000)
£915 $1528   (8-Jun-91 HN.H314/R) Paysage Oxyde (35x40cm-14x16in) s.d.1964 leather
                     collage (DM 2700)

KALLERT, August (1882-1958) German
£433 $776   (12-Apr-91 AW.H1750) Bathers at the Amper near Dachau and bridge beyond
                     (42x31cm-17x12in) s. chl (DM 1300)

KALLMORGEN, Friedrich (1856-1924) German
£890 $1451   (12-Jun-91 N.M481) Nun teaching girl knitting (39x30cm-15x12in)
                     mono.d.1888 i.verso watercolour on board (DM 2600)
£1627 $2717   (5-Jun-91 DO.H2317/R) Canal, Bruge (60x40cm-24x16in) mono. canvas on
                     panel (DM 4800)
£2196 $3799   (25-May-91 N.M163/R) Mark lake landscape with cattle (54x70cm-21x28in)
                     s.d.1911 (DM 6500)
£2416 $4711   (12-Oct-90 AW.H1481/R) Poplars near stone bridge (39x63cm-15x25in)
                     s.c.1885 (DM 7200)
£2827 $4750   (17-Jul-91 SY.NY293/R) Fishing boat on the Elbe (49x69cm-19x27in)
                     s.d.1906

KALLOS, Paul (1928-?) French
£663 $1272   (30-Nov-90 CB.P29/R) Composition (32x50cm-13x20in) s.d.84 acrylic paper
                     (F.FR 6500)
£806 $1573   (25-Oct-90 CB.P107/R) Sans titre (34x34cm-13x13in) s.d.90 acrylic
                     (F.FR 8000)
£857 $1671   (25-Oct-90 CB.P106/R) Composition (66x50cm-26x20in) s.d.85 acrylic paper
                     (F.FR 8500)
£1310 $2555   (26-Oct-90 APT.P120/R) Sans tire (92x60cm-36x24in) s.d.53 (F.FR 13000)
£1631 $3131   (2-Dec-90 M.V180 b/R) Composition (81x100cm-32x39in) s.d.1990 acrylic
                     (F.FR 16000)
£3976 $6720   (15-Apr-91 CC.P105/R) Soies (114x146cm-45x57in) s.d.1983 acrylic
                     (F.FR 40000)
£5327 $9535   (11-Mar-91 GL.P242/R) Sans titre (130x162cm-51x64in) s.d.1962
                     (F.FR 53000)
£6098 $12195   (10-Feb-91 CC.P38/R) Deux figures (130x97cm-51x38in) s.d.1963
                     (F.FR 60000)
£7288 $14067   (15-Dec-90 D.P33/R) Untitled (73x92cm-29x36in) s.d.59 (F.FR 71500)
£13158 $25789   (22-Nov-90 ZZ.F43/R) Composition (146x291cm-57x115in) s.d.60 canvas laid
                     down on wood triptych (F.FR 130000)

KALLSTENIUS, Gottfried (1861-1943) Swedish
£947	$1591	(27-Apr-91 SO.S392/R) Landscape with house by road (59x86cm-23x34in) s. (S.KR 10000)
£1005	$1971	(20-Nov-90 GO.G112) A night in August, wave of the moon (90x116cm-35x46in) s.d.1911 (S.KR 11000)
£1576	$3041	(12-Dec-90 BU.S35/R) Sunlit pine tree (74x81cm-29x32in) s.d.1935 (S.KR 17000)
£2595	$5035	(22-Aug-90 RAS.K95/R) Moonlit lake in wood (100x130cm-39x51in) s.d.1920 (D.KR 30000)
£3314	$5568	(24-Apr-91 BA.S119/R) Pinetrees in moonlight (100x130cm-39x51in) s.d.1920 (S.KR 35000)
£4596	$9007	(6-Nov-90 BA.S137/R) Summer landscape with afternoon sunshine (101x120cm-40x47in) s.d.1911 (S.KR 50000)
£6387	$12582	(30-Oct-90 BU.S50/R) Lake landscape at sunset (130x130cm-51x51in) s. (S.KR 70000)

KALMAKOFF, Nicolas (1873-1955) Russian
£3021	$4924	(16-Jun-91 GL.P13/R) Meduse (63x48cm-25x19in) mono. gouache pastel (F.FR 30000)

KALMAN, Peter (1877-?) Hungarian
£629	$1215	(12-Dec-90 N.M574/R) Young woman from Dachau (27x21cm-11x8in) s. panel (DM 1800)
£1027	$1839	(13-Mar-91 N.M543/R) Portrait of lady (48x38cm-19x15in) s. board (DM 3000)
£1130	$2023	(13-Mar-91 N.M544) Woman wearing evening dress seated on sofa playing lute (53x41cm-21x16in) s.d.1923 panel (DM 3300)

KALMARK, Gerhard (1905-) ?
£604	$1081	(13-Apr-91 FAL.M145/R) Southern market scene (65x92cm-26x36in) s. panel (S.KR 6500)

KALOUGUINE, Igor (1957-) Russian
£822	$1595	(8-Dec-90 ZZ.F124/R) La femme de Zodiaque (110x90cm-43x35in) (F.FR 8000)
£1028	$1994	(8-Dec-90 ZZ.F122/R) Le roc (140x150cm-55x59in) (F.FR 10000)
£1131	$2193	(8-Dec-90 ZZ.F123/R) Metamorphose (90x110cm-35x43in) (F.FR 11000)

KALRAET, Abraham van see CALRAET, Abraham van

KALTENMOSER, Kaspar (1806-1867) German
£6826	$11195	(18-Jun-91 FN.S1918/R) Figures conversing by window with view of Alpine landscape (83x69cm-33x27in) s.d.1866 (DM 20000)
£7692	$13000	(17-Apr-91 WE.MU229/R) Woman selling fruit, coast of Istria (84x65cm-33x26in) s.i.d.1860 (DM 23000)

KALTNER, Joseph (1758-1824) German
£455	$882	(7-Dec-90 GB.B5557/R) Allegorical scene with Bavarian coat of arms. Portraits of children (18x13cm-7x5in) pen brush htd white pen over pencil double-sided (DM 1300)

KAMEKE, Otto von (1826-1899) German
£881	$1437	(3-Jul-91 WE.MU42/R) Mountain lake landscape (45x66cm-18x26in) s. (DM 2600)

KAMENEV, Igor (1955-) Russian
£900	$1593	(18-Mar-91 ARC.P175/R) Sans titre (100x80cm-39x31in) bears sig.d.1990 verso (F.FR 9000)
£820	$1451	(18-Mar-91 ARC.P177/R) Nature morte a la bonbonniere (37x55cm-15x22in) s. W/C board (F.FR 8200)

KAMMERER, Paul (1868-1950) German
£1092	$1791	(18-Jun-91 FN.S1916/R) Allegorical scene with nude figures in Alpine landscape, spring (123x191cm-48x75in) mono.d.1914 and 1956 panel (DM 3200)

KAMPF, Arthur (1864-1950) German
£700	$1344	(29-Nov-90 B106) Child in river landscape (36x41cm-14x16in) s.d.1894
£1007	$1963	(10-Oct-90 ZEL.L1566/R) Reclining female nude asleep (70x50cm-28x20in) s. (DM 3400)
£1160	$2274	(24-Nov-90 SA.A848/R) Returning from the work in the fields (60x47cm-24x19in) s.d.1948 panel (DM 3400)
£1199	$1954	(12-Jun-91 N.M482/R) Two peasants cutting grass (83x73cm-33x29in) s. (DM 3500)
£5594	$10797	(10-Dec-90 L.K470/R) Contrasts, elegant couple watching feeding of poor people (53x64cm-21x25in) s. (DM 16000)

KAMPF, Eugen (1861-1933) German
£600	$984	(18-Jun-91 PH140) Vessels moored beside jetty at low tide (19x30cm-7x12in) s. pair
£1531	$2709	(20-Mar-91 KM.K1288) Flemish landscape with thatched cottages (39x49cm-15x19in) s. board on panel (DM 4500)

KAMPF, Max (1912-1982) Swiss
£1793	$3496	(24-Oct-90 GD.B525/R) Head of young man (35x27cm-14x11in) s. board (S.FR 4500)

KAMPF, Max (1912-1982) Swiss-cont.

£2000	$3900	(17-Oct-90 G.Z25/R) Three figures (99x108cm-39x43in) s.d.1963 oil tempera paper (S.FR 5000)
£440	$744	(1-May-91 GD.B1527/R) Basler Fasnachtsmaske Elsasserin (40x29cm-16x11in) s.d.65 wax crayond (S.FR 1100)
£476	$795	(7-Jun-91 ZOF.Z1361) Basler Waggis (26x18cm-10x7in) s.d.64 grease chk (S.FR 1200)
£612	$1163	(14-Sep-90 ZOF.Z1102) Self portrait (30x24cm-12x9in) s.d.73 pencil (S.FR 1500)

KAMPHUYSEN, Jan (1760-1841) Dutch

| £1000 | $1630 | (4-Jul-91 CSK191) Portrait of Roman wearing toga and carrying sword (67x55cm-26x22in) s.d.1806 verso |

KAMPMANN, Gustav (1859-1917) German

| £1216 | $2104 | (25-May-91 N.M164) Full moon, evening (35x23cm-14x9in) s. s.i.verso board (DM 3600) |
| £3020 | $5889 | (12-Oct-90 AW.H1484/R) River landscape with poplars (46x33cm-18x13in) s.i.d.1884 (DM 9000) |

KAMPPURI, Vaino (1891-1972) Finnish

£2582	$4364	(20-Apr-91 HOR.H107/R) Farm by edge of wood (36x45cm-14x18in) s. (F.M 18000)
£3709	$7270	(24-Nov-90 HOR.H130/R) Town scene (45x37cm-18x15in) s. (F.M 26000)
£475	$916	(15-Dec-90 BU.H241) Heinola Bridge (22x28cm-9x11in) s.d.26 W/C (F.M 3300)

KAMPTZ (19th C) German

| £1333 | $2387 | (12-Apr-91 BM.B625/R) Coastal landscape with fortified town and shipping in choppy seas (70x94cm-28x37in) s.d.1856 (DM 4000) |

KANDINSKY, Vasily (1866-1944) Russian

£70000	$123900	(20-Mar-91 S20/R) Kochel - bauernhaus mit kirche (24x33cm-9x13in) s. canvasboard
£81911	$160546	(23-Nov-90 VG.B9/R) Rapallo, castello and church (24x32cm-9x13in) d.1906 canvas on board (DM 240000)
£354251	$694332	(25-Nov-90 GL.P73/R) Trois etoiles (48x35cm-19x14in) mono.d.42 board (F.FR 3500000)
£6780	$11322	(6-Jun-91 HN.H440/R) Composition 1934 (35x22cm-14x9in) mono.d.1934 pen (DM 20000)
£7538	$13492	(17-Mar-91 GL.P23/R) Clownerie (19x11cm-7x4in) init.d.1932 Indian ink (F.FR 75000)
£13287	$25776	(7-Dec-90 GB.B6771/R) Study for Black-Red (23x35cm-9x14in) mono. s.i.d.1925 indian ink brush (DM 38000)
£14721	$29000	(14-Nov-90 SY.NY147/R) Composition (23x15cm-9x6in) init.d.30 indian ink paper on board
£25381	$50000	(14-Nov-90 SY.NY148/R) Composition (44x48cm-17x19in) init.d.31 num 19 verso india ink paper on board
£68190	$133652	(20-Nov-90 BR.M170/R) Composizione (24x31cm-9x12in) mono.d.1934 gouache (I.L 150000000)
£89595	$155000	(9-May-91 CH.NY116/R) Untitled (32x25cm-13x10in) mono.d.K17 W/C brush ink paper laid down board
£111675	$220000	(15-Nov-90 CH.NY151/R) Grune Spitze (32x42cm-13x17in) mono.d.32 i.d.verso gouache paper on board
£162437	$320000	(15-Nov-90 CH.NY157/R) Taches, verte et rose (39x57cm-15x22in) mono.i.d.1935 W/C pen brush india ink board
£167513	$330000	(15-Nov-90 CH.NY148/R) Ausser Gewicht (27x48cm-11x19in) mono.d.29 i.d.verso W/C pen col.ink pap.on board
£218274	$430000	(15-Nov-90 CH.NY139/R) Schweres zwischen Leichtem (34x48cm-13x19in) mono.d. i.d.1924verso W/C pen col.ink board

KANDL (20th C) ?

| £1120 | $2207 | (30-Oct-90 ZZ.F103/R) Paysage comestible (55x46cm-22x18in) s.d.89 canvas laid down on board (F.FR 11000) |

KANDLER, Ludwig (1856-?) German

| £777 | $1515 | (26-Oct-90 BM.B821/R) Portrait of peasant smoking cigar (44x39cm-17x15in) s.d.1919 (DM 2300) |
| £1003 | $1696 | (17-Apr-91 WE.MU290/R) Portrait of artist's mother (27x20cm-11x8in) s.id.1913 panel (DM 3000) |

KANDLER, Wilhelm (1816-1896) German

| £712 | $1274 | (11-Apr-91 D.V47/R) Roman aquaducts (38x53cm-15x21in) s. board (A.S 15000) |

KANE, John (1860-1934) American

| £10405 | $18000 | (23-May-91 SY.NY66/R) St. Philomena's (51x61cm-20x24in) s. |

KANERVA, Aino (1909-) Finnish

£4298	$8467	(17-Nov-90 BU.H153/R) Marshy landscape (39x40cm-15x16in) s.d.61 panel (F.M 30000)
£1427	$2796	(24-Nov-90 HOR.H133/R) Blue sky (34x45cm-13x18in) s.d.1949 W/C (F.M 10000)
£2080	$3516	(20-Apr-91 HOR.H108/R) Pines (61x46cm-24x18in) s.d.1957 W/C (F.M 14500)
£3138	$6151	(24-Nov-90 HOR.H131/R) Reflection (50x64cm-20x25in) s.d.1962 W/C (F.M 22000)

KANGRA SCHOOL, 19th C Indian
£1044 $1764   (19-Apr-91 CB.P158) Scene de combat (22x27cm-9x11in) (F.FR 10500)

KANN, Frederick (1886-1965) American
£5028 $9000   (14-Mar-91 CH.NY225/R) Sympatica (46x61cm-18x24in) s. masonite

KANNE, Philippus Anthonius Alexander (1833-1872) Dutch
£762 $1494   (6-Nov-90 SY.AM29) Children by vegetable stand (25x32cm-10x13in) s.
                     panel (D.FL 2500)

KANNEMANS, Christian Cornelis (1812-1884) Dutch
£2156 $3751   (26-Mar-91 VN.R39/R) Moored sailing boats with figures in rowboat
                     (40x56cm-16x22in) s.d.1852 panel (D.FL 7200)

KANNEMANS, Christian Cornelis (circle) (1812-1884) Dutch
£1000 $1730   (9-May-91 CSK86/R) Fishing smacks and other shipping on rough seas
                     (40x51cm-16x20in) with sig.d.1849

KANOLDT, Alexander (1881-1939) German
£12302 $20175   (19-Jun-91 GK.B487/R) Iron bridge (40x60cm-16x24in) i.verso (S.FR 31000)
*£3082 $5024   (15-Jun-91 L.K349/R) The black wall (35x49cm-14x19in) s. pencil
                     (DM 9000)*

KANOLDT, Edmund (1839-1904) German
£1141 $2225   (12-Oct-90 AW.H1490/R) Italian costal landscape (36x90cm-14x35in) s.
                     s.i.d.1902verso (DM 3400)
£1600 $3072   (27-Nov-90 PH167/R) Ariadne on Naxos (131x89cm-52x35in) s.
£3485 $6865   (30-Oct-90 CH.AM210/R) Eichen im gewitter (115x82cm-45x32in) s.d.1868
                     (D.FL 11500)

KANTOR, Tadeus (1915-) Polish
£1117 $2000   (16-Mar-91 W.W101/R) Untitled (48x61cm-19x24in) s. i. verso
£1397 $2500   (16-Mar-91 W.W111/R) Peinture G (69x71cm-27x28in) s.d.1958 i. verso

KANZ, Carl Christian (style) (1758-1818) German
*£400 $784   (22-Jan-91 CSK62/R) Portrait of lady in low-cut dress (7x?cm-3x?in) min.
                     oval*

KAPICA, Yacoub (1948-) Polish
£806 $1573   (28-Oct-90 PLF.P240) Ferrari P4 (97x116cm-38x46in) s.d.89 (F.FR 8000)

KAPLAN, Hubert (1932-) German
£2013 $3926   (10-Oct-90 WE.MU197/R) Poultry by village stream (13x18cm-5x7in) s.
                     s.verso on serial number of bank note (DM 6000)
£2013 $3926   (10-Oct-90 WE.MU198/R) Landscape with poultry by pond (13x18cm-5x7in) s.
                     i.verso on serial number of bank note (DM 6000)
£2341 $3957   (17-Apr-91 WE.MU176/R) Pond landscape (15x30cm-6x12in) s. panel
                     (DM 7000)
£2341 $3957   (17-Apr-91 WE.MU180/R) Konigsee landscape with washerwomen
                     (15x30cm-6x12in) s. panel (DM 7000)
£3187 $5482   (14-May-91 GF.L2150/R) Chicken yard (13x18cm-5x7in) s. (S.FR 8000)
£3386 $5825   (14-May-91 GF.L2151/R) Ducks by water (13x18cm-5x7in) s. panel
                     (S.FR 8500)
£4781 $8223   (14-May-91 GF.L2152/R) Fishermen gathering nets (15x30cm-6x12in) s.
                     panel (S.FR 12000)
£4898 $9600   (6-Nov-90 GF.L2475/R) Fishermen gathering nets (13x18cm-5x7in) s. panel
                     (S.FR 12000)
£6308 $11921   (27-Sep-90 D.V36/R) View of Salzburg (19x38cm-7x15in) s. panel
                     (A.S 130000)
£6531 $12800   (6-Nov-90 GF.L2476/R) Bavarian village scene (13x18cm-5x7in) s.
                     (S.FR 16000)

KAPOUTSIN (?) Russian
£1429 $2814   (15-Oct-90 ARC.P92) Marine au prepusculel (61x97cm-24x38in) s.
                     (F.FR 14000)

KAPPIS, Albert (1836-1914) German
£1712 $3065   (12-Mar-91 FN.S2450/R) Lake Chiemsee landscape with peasant women
                     loading hay barge (8x21cm-3x8in) s. panel (DM 5000)
£1877 $3548   (25-Sep-90 FN.S2234/R) Wooded river landscape with rowing boats and
                     fisherman gathering nets (46x55cm-18x22in) s. (DM 5500)
£4266 $8063   (25-Sep-90 FN.S2233/R) Peasant folk in Sunday costumes going to church
                     in Gutachtal (37x27cm-15x11in) s. (DM 12500)
£8392 $16280   (4-Dec-90 FN.S1904/R) Upper Bavarian lake landscape with figures,
                     evening (48x66cm-19x26in) s.d.1884 canvas laid down (DM 24000)

KAPPL, Franko (20th C) ?
£696 $1350   (6-Dec-90 D.V171/R) Untitled (149x84cm-59x33in) acrylic molino
                     (A.S 14000)

KAPROW, Alan (1927-) American
*£444 $769   (6-May-91 ZEL.L1481/R) Woman seated (29x22cm-11x9in) s.d.1954 indian ink
                     (DM 1320)*

KARAVOUSIS (?) ?
£1426 $2809   (30-Oct-90 ZZ.F17/R) Nature morte a la rose blanche (50x61cm-20x24in) s.
                 (F.FR 14000)

KARCHER, Henri (1937-) French
£475 $850   (14-Apr-91 APT.P123) Sans titre (46x56cm-18x22in) s. collage mixed media
                paper (F.FR 4800)

KARESCH, Wilhelmine (1895-1972) Austrian
£1940 $3647   (20-Sep-90 D.V120/R) Still life with teddy bear, horse and clown
                  (43x34cm-17x13in) s.d.1922 board (A.S 40000)

KARFIOL, Bernard (1886-1952) American
£588 $1100   (1-Aug-90 B.P100/R) Figures in sailboat (30x41cm-12x16in) board
£650 $1300   (7-Feb-91 B.P6/R) Skinny dipping, Ogunquit (36x51cm-14x20in)
£800 $1600   (7-Feb-91 B.P8/R) Ogunquit Cove (46x61cm-18x24in) s.
£2513 $4750   (26-Sep-90 SY.NY183 b/R) Two sisters (91x71cm-36x28in) s.

KARFVE, Fritz (1880-1967) Swedish
£695 $1356   (21-Jun-90 BU.M88) Evening sun over cliffs (57x74cm-22x29in) s.
                 (S.KR 7600)

KARGEL, Axel (1896-1971) Swedish
£1390 $2697   (5-Dec-90 AB.S7143/R) Bay, coastal landscape from Djupvik
                  (30x38cm-12x15in) s.d.1962 (S.KR 15000)
£1390 $2697   (5-Dec-90 AB.S7142/R) House by the sea, Oland (34x50cm-13x20in) s.d.1960
                  (S.KR 15000)
£1437 $2787   (5-Dec-90 AB.S7141/R) Seascape, view from Aleklinta, Oland
                  (38x41cm-15x16in) s.d.1969 (S.KR 15500)

KARGL, Rudolf (1878-1942) Austrian
£534 $1009   (27-Sep-90 D.V201/R) Spitalskirche, Modling (34x25cm-13x10in) s.i. W/C
                 (A.S 11000)
£550 $902   (18-Jun-91 PH189/R) Badgastein (21x26cm-8x10in) s.i. W/C over pencil

KARIMO, Aarno (1886-1952) Finnish
£791 $1527   (15-Dec-90 BU.H244) Hunters on skies (66x47cm-26x19in) s.d.28 gouache
                 (F.M 5500)

KARINE, Anne (1919-) Swiss
£800 $1352   (1-May-91 GD.B469/R) Female nude (43x37cm-17x15in) s. i.d.1960verso
                 (S.FR 2000)

KARLINSKY, Anton Hans (1872-1945) Austrian
£627 $1223   (18-Oct-90 D.V1/R) Portrait of mother with two children
                 (80x80cm-31x31in) s. (A.S 13000)

KARLOVSKY-BERCI (19th C) Hungarian
£2312 $4000   (21-May-91 CE.NY291/R) Still life with zinnias and oriental fan
                  (65x52cm-26x20in) s.i. panel

KARLSSON, C Goran (20th C) Scandinavian
£725 $1298   (13-Apr-91 FAL.M147/R) Composition with triangles and circles
                 (38x28cm-15x11in) mono.d.89 paper (S.KR 7800)
£1668 $3236   (5-Dec-90 AB.S7144/R) Geometric composition (77x58cm-30x23in) s.d.87
                  tempera (S.KR 18000)
£3770 $6371   (18-Apr-91 BU.S17/R) Geometric composition (149x211cm-59x83in)
                  init.d.1988 (S.KR 40000)

KARLSSON-STIG, Ante (1885-1967) Swedish
£976 $1747   (9-Apr-91 GO.G70) Undersaker river, Vallista Mountains (50x70cm-20x28in)
                 s.d.43 (S.KR 10500)

KARNEC, J E (1865-1934) Austrian
£850 $1428   (26-Apr-91 ARC.P49 b) Venise, il campo San Giorgio (19x23cm-7x9in) s.
                 panel (F.FR 8500)

KAROLX, G (?) ?
£627 $1228   (21-Nov-90 GM.B1082) Lavandiere au coucher du soleil (42x60cm-17x24in)
                 s. wood (B.FR 38000)

KAROLY, Gerna (?) ?
£2227 $4364   (20-Nov-90 APT.P278/R) Ruelle du Caire (80x60cm-31x24in) s. (F.FR 22000)

KARPATHY, Janos (19/20th C) Hungarian
£907 $1769   (15-Oct-90 SY.J36/R) Collecting water at the lake (59x79cm-23x31in) s.
                 (SA.R 4500)

KARPINSKI, Alfons (1875-1961) Polish
£1072 $2122   (1-Feb-91 DE.B7) Still life of flowers (98x71cm-39x28in) s. board
                  (P.Z 20000000)

KARPOFF (20th C) Russian
£1178 $1991   (16-Apr-91 CH.R125) Paesaggio con figure (70x100cm-28x39in) s.
                 (I.L 2600000)

KARPOFF, Ivan (1898-1970) Russian
£912 $1523   (6-Jun-91 F.M45) Pastore con gregge (40x50cm-16x20in) s. (I.L 2000000)
£1148 $2250   (12-Feb-91 SY.NY39/R) Working the fields (51x71cm-20x28in) s.
£1364 $2673   (21-Nov-90 F.M140/R) Bellagio (70x100cm-28x39in) s. (I.L 3000000)

KARPPANEN, Matti (1873-1953) Finnish
£2590 $4999   (15-Dec-90 BU.H89/R) Yellow hammers (28x36cm-11x14in) s.d.1941
     (F.M 18000)

KARS, Georges (1882-1945) French
£811 $1558   (17-Dec-90 AGS.P36) Nature morte a la pipe et au verre (27x36cm-11x14in)
     s.d.37 (F.FR 8000)
£2094 $4000   (2-Jan-91 GG.TA562/R) Woman reading (46x37cm-18x15in) s.
£2275 $4072   (14-Apr-91 GL.P186/R) La rotonde a Monte-Carlo (37x44cm-15x17in) st.sig.
     wood (F.FR 23000)
£3264 $5843   (14-Apr-91 GL.P188) Nu au perroquet (65x50cm-26x20in) s.d.1939
     (F.FR 33000)
£4450 $8500   (2-Jan-91 GG.TA440/R) Two women (50x35cm-20x14in) s.d.1928
£396 $708   (14-Apr-91 GL.P72/R) Au fil des ans. Hommage a Edward Munch
*   (24x32cm-9x13in) pastel (F.FR 4000)*
£552 $1076   (12-Oct-90 ZZ.F2) Nature morte aux violons (53x51cm-21x20in) pastel
*   (F.FR 5500)*

KARSEN, Kaspar (1810-1896) Dutch
£942 $1686   (12-Mar-91 FN.S2448) View of castle ruin and watermill in river
     landscape (30x24cm-12x9in) s. board (DM 2750)
£3049 $5976   (6-Nov-90 SY.AM251) Figures on square in Dutch town (32x26cm-13x10in) s.
     panel (D.FL 10000)
£3892 $6539   (23-Apr-91 SY.AM30/R) View of De Waag, Amsterdam (22x29cm-9x11in) panel
     (D.FL 13000)
£27273 $53727   (30-Oct-90 CH.AM65/R) View in Dutch town with children, traveller,
     peasants, horse-drawn cart, in summer (41x65cm-16x26in) s.
     (D.FL 90000)

KARSKAYA, Ida (1905-) Russian
£402 $720   (11-Mar-91 GL.P195) Tete de femme (25x20cm-10x8in) s. gouache collage
*   (F.FR 4000)*
£457 $915   (10-Feb-91 CC.P41) Composition (27x17cm-11x7in) s. W/C Indian ink wash
*   (F.FR 4500)*
£711 $1423   (10-Feb-91 CC.P40) Visage traansparent (46x35cm-18x14in) s. mixed media
*   collage canvas (F.FR 7000)*

KARSTEN, Ludvig (1876-1926) Norwegian
£7180 $12853   (14-Mar-91 BU.O57/R) The pig (46x61cm-18x24in) s.d.14 (N.KR 82000)
£18650 $36741   (31-Oct-90 KH.K65/R) The children's room (55x76cm-22x30in) s.d.16
     (D.KR 210000)
£20481 $39528   (12-Dec-90 BU.O37/R) In the garden, Gilleleje 1914 (42x59cm-17x23in)
     s.d.14 (N.KR 230000)
£60764 $118490   (11-Oct-90 BU.O70/R) September glow (80x76cm-31x30in) s.d.22
     (N.KR 700000)
£73019 $140926   (12-Dec-90 BU.O36/R) View from a garden (121x137cm-48x54in) s.d.14
     (N.KR 820000)
£458 $769   (22-Apr-91 BU.K74/R) Reclining model (24x36cm-9x14in) s.d.14 pencil
*   (D.KR 5200)*
£799 $1575   (31-Oct-90 KH.K66) Reclining model (40x52cm-16x20in) s.d.24 chl
*   (D.KR 9000)*

KAS, Achille (19th C) Belgian
£1771 $3435   (4-Dec-90 C.A203/R) In the tavern (56x44cm-22x17in) s.d.1894 panel
     (B.FR 105000)

KASCHALSKIJ, S B (20th C) Russian
£746 $1446   (6-Dec-90 D.V304/R) Caretakers going to shovel snow (68x114cm-27x45in)
     s.d.1960 (A.S 15000)

KASPAR, Paul (20th C) Austrian
£489 $928   (28-Feb-91 D.V91/R) Minoritenkirche, Vienna (12x8cm-5x3in) s. W/C
*   (A.S 10000)*
£573 $1117   (11-Oct-90 D.V240/R) Liebenbergdenkmal vor der Wiener Universitat
*   (12x9cm-5x4in) s. W/C (A.S 12000)*
£573 $963   (25-Apr-91 D.V232/R) Heldenplatz, Vienna (15x23cm-6x9in) s.d.1921 W/C
*   (A.S 12000)*
£621 $1210   (11-Oct-90 D.V239/R) Opera, Vienna (12x9cm-5x4in) s. W/C (A.S 13000)
£669 $1123   (25-Apr-91 D.V230/R) Heldenplatz and Minoritenkirche (12x22cm-5x9in) s.
*   W/C (A.S 14000)*
£879 $1671   (28-Feb-91 D.V87/R) Hauptgebaude der K.u.K. Tabakregie im 3. Wiener
*   Bezirk (22x20cm-9x8in) s.i.d.1948verso W/C (A.S 18000)*
£1424 $2549   (11-Apr-91 D.V293/R) View of Passau (35x54cm-14x21in) s.d.1920 W/C
*   (A.S 30000)*
£2864 $5585   (11-Oct-90 D.V238/R) Vienna, Operring, autumn (17x23cm-7x9in) s.i.d.1928
*   W/C (A.S 60000)*

KASPARIDES, Edouard (1858-?) Austrian
£6958 $13499   (6-Dec-90 D.V4/R) Wooded landscape, evening (150x200cm-59x79in) s.i.
     (A.S 140000)

KASPARIDES, Edouard (1858-?) Austrian-cont.
£2425 $4559   *(20-Sep-90 D.V2/R) Evening (70x100cm-28x39in) s. pastel on board (A.S 50000)*

KASSAK, Lajos (1887-1967) Hungarian
£7939 $13735   *(21-May-91 WK.M62/R) Geometric composition (100x70cm-39x28in) s. (DM 23500)*
£5510 $10855   *(17-Nov-90 S.Z66) Suite pour un album 2 (42x30cm-17x12in) d.1962 gouache board (S.FR 13500)*
£9153 $15285   *(6-Jun-91 HN.H442/R) Composition (19x19cm-7x7in) mono. gouache (DM 27000)*

KASSO, Wende (?) ?
£750 $1500   *(6-Feb-91 D.NY50) The lady and the lion (91x122cm-36x48in) s.*

KASYN, John (1926-) Canadian
£637 $1128   *(20-Mar-91 EA.M488/R) Back yards on winter morning (30x40cm-12x16in) s. d.83 verso masonite (C.D 1300)*
£808 $1390   *(14-May-91 JOY.T26/R) Backyard, Toronto (40x30cm-16x12in) s. board (C.D 1600)*
£808 $1390   *(14-May-91 JOY.T209) Back of Wales Ave. (33x27cm-13x11in) s. board (C.D 1600)*
£1389 $2403   *(6-May-91 SY.T18/R) Midnight in Cabbagetown (33x46cm-13x18in) s. s.l.verso board (C.D 2750)*
£1405 $2291   *(10-Jun-91 W.T1044 e) On Bleeker street North (46x61cm-18x24in) s. l. verso board (C.D 2600)*
£2193 $4320   *(30-Oct-90 SY.T4/R) Backyard in snow, Cabbagetown (46x61cm-18x24in) s. s.l.verso board (C.D 5000)*
£2412 $4728   *(20-Nov-90 JOY.T188/R) Winter in Parkdale (60x45cm-24x18in) s. board (C.D 5500)*
£404 $699   *(6-May-91 SY.T93) Ontario Street (13x20cm-5x8in) s. W/C (C.D 800)*

KAT, Anne-Pierre de (20th C) Belgian
£655 $1100   *(23-Apr-91 C.A397) Still life with chicken (60x70cm-24x28in) s. (B.FR 40000)*
£2477 $4780   *(12-Dec-90 CH.AM320/R) De rentenier (127x77cm-50x30in) s.d.1919 (D.FL 8000)*

KAT, de (20th C) Belgian
£1489 $2814   *(25-Sep-90 GM.B1051) Vase garni de tulipes (70x60cm-28x24in) s.d.1920 (B.FR 90000)*

KATCHADOURIAN, Sarkis (20th C) Iranian
£2854 $5509   *(12-Dec-90 ZZ.F69/R) Jeune femme a la rose (81x65cm-32x26in) s.d.1931 (F.FR 28000)*
£1096 $1863   *(27-May-91 APT.P204 b) Jeunesse et poesie d'Orient (97x71cm-38x28in) s. gouache (F.FR 11000)*

KATCHAROV, Oscar (1924-) Russian
£1972 $3886   *(3-Oct-90 QWA.P41) Un samedi communiste (122x150cm-48x59in) (F.FR 20000)*

KATO, Hajime (1925-) Japanese
£2041 $4020   *(16-Nov-90 FB.P302/R) Composition (61x73cm-24x29in) s.d.62 (F.FR 20000)*

KATZ, Alex (1927-) American
£1633 $3200   *(6-Nov-90 CE.NY26/R) Untitled (28x41cm-11x16in) s. panel*
£2513 $4700   *(1-Aug-90 B.P51/R) Four figures on beach (76x91cm-30x36in) s. masonite*
£5076 $10000   *(4-Oct-90 SY.NY157/R) Ada with mirror (35x35cm-10x14in) s.verso masonite*
£6091 $12000   *(5-Oct-90 CH.NY55/R) Sketch for passing (46x51cm-18x20in) s. masonite*
£9231 $18000   *(24-Oct-90 B.SF1567/R) Two Spanish men (41x51cm-16x20in) s.d.81 board*
£45918 $90000   *(14-Feb-91 CH.NY28/R) The dance (198x305cm-78x120in)*

KAUFFMAN (?) ?
£1900 $3211   *(19-Apr-91 CBB81) Running repairs - interior scene with figures (48x41cm-19x16in) s.*

KAUFFMANN, Angelica (1740-1807) Swiss
£3400 $6698   *(31-Oct-90 S315/R) Eurydice (32x16cm-13x6in)*
£4337 $7287   *(23-Apr-91 F.R46/R) Ritratto di donna (45x37cm-18x15in) (I.L 9500000)*
£4600 $8234   *(10-Apr-91 S126/R) Portrait of lady, lying on divan holding book in right hand (61x73cm-24x29in)*
£20000 $39400   *(14-Nov-90 S38/R) Portrait of lady lying on divan wearing grecian dress holding miniature (61x74cm-24x29in) s.d.1772*
£25000 $41250   *(10-Jul-91 S41/R) Portrait of Anne Loudoun, Lady Henderson of Fordall, seated in landscape (128x103cm-50x41in)*
£26000 $42380   *(5-Jul-91 C260/R) Portrait of lady, seated wearing dress with sash, on sofa (72x59cm-28x23in) with sig. oval*
£650 $1073   *(9-Jul-91 C19/R) The Mystic Marriage of St Catherine (26x32cm-10x13in) i. pen ink wash sold with another drawing*
£776 $1528   *(13-Nov-90 GF.L5119/R) Park landcape with temple and stone vase beneath tree (17x20cm-7x8in) ochre dr. oval (S.FR 1900)*

KAUFFMANN, Angelica (after) (1740-1807) Swiss
£1000 $1890   *(27-Sep-90 CSK28/R) The visitation (121x91cm-48x36in)*
£2050 $3998   *(24-Oct-90 DR157/R) Cupid binding Aglaia (94x132cm-37x52in)*

KAUFFMANN, Angelica (attrib) (1740-1807) Swiss
£2449 $4800   (6-Nov-90 GF.L2067/R) Diana resting with nymphs (22cm-9ins circular)
       panel (S.FR 6000)
£16000 $26400   (12-Jul-91 C50/R) Literary heroines - Maria at Moulins. Penelope.
       Calypso. Una (25x20cm-10x8in) indist.i.verso copper oval five

KAUFFMANN, Angelica (circle) (1740-1807) Swiss
£1074 $2094   (10-Oct-90 ZEL.L1572/R) Wooded landscape with girls tiggling sleeping
       Amor (51x80cm-20x31in) oval (DM 3200)
£1300 $2600   (7-Feb-91 CSK181/R) Rebecca and Eliza (99x133cm-39x52in)
£2530 $4250   (17-Jul-91 SY.NY90/R) An offering to cupid (36x44cm-14x17in) init.
£3409 $6683   (19-Nov-90 CH.R95/R) Ritratto di bambino (41x34cm-16x13in)
       (I.L 7500000)
£4057 $8032   (30-Jan-91 APT.P107/R) Scene d'offrande (120x135cm-47x53in) (F.FR 40000)

KAUFFMANN, Angelica (school) (1740-1807) Swiss
£724 $1224   (16-Apr-91 J.M464) Lady reading (25cm-10ins circular) i. verso paper
       (A.D 1600)

KAUFFMANN, Angelica (style) (1740-1807) Swiss
£2400 $4800   (7-Feb-91 C109) Cupid bindig Aglaia (94x132cm-37x52in)
£1935   *$3250*   *(17-Jul-91 SY.NY34/R) Portrait of a lady (66x56cm-26x22in) pastel*

KAUFFMANN, Craig (1932-) American
£1190 $2000   (24-Apr-91 B.SF4657/R) L'atelier 2, 1977 (251x173cm-99x68in) s.i.
       acrylic paper on canvas

KAUFFMANN, Hermann (19/20th C) German
£5034 $9815   (13-Oct-90 KRA.D237/R) Mail coach in snow storm (57x81cm-22x32in) s.
       (DM 15000)

KAUFFMANN, Hermann (elder) (1808-1889) German
£2457 $4816   (24-Nov-90 SA.A683/R) Farmhouse in wooded landscape (49x39cm-19x15in) s.
       (DM 7200)

KAUFFMANN, Hugo (1844-1915) German
£1824 $3101   (27-May-91 L.K301/R) Gentleman seated at table reading newspaper
       (15x20cm-6x8in) s. panel (DM 5400)
£3082 $5517   (13-Mar-91 N.M546/R) Shepherdess with flock on path in wooded landscape,
       autumn (74x47cm-29x19in) s. (DM 9000)
£4600 $8832   (21-Feb-91 HR120) Innkeeper seated with tankard of beer
       (23cm-9ins circular) s..d.1881 board
£6643 $12888   (4-Dec-90 FN.S1900/R) Portrait of man wearing glasses seated at table
       with book before him (30x23cm-12x9in) s.d.1879 panel (DM 19000)
£6869 $13189   (29-Nov-90 D.V63/R) Peasant wearing red waistcoat (18x14cm-7x6in) s.
       panel (A.S 140000)
£6869 $13189   (29-Nov-90 D.V64/R) Der Altbauer (18x14cm-7x6in) s.d.76 panel
       (A.S 140000)
£7192 $12873   (13-Mar-91 N.M547/R) Fat peasant with walking stick and pipe
       (23x17cm-9x7in) s.d.1887 panel (DM 21000)
£9211 $17500   (27-Feb-91 SY.NY171/R) Tyrolean girl (18x14cm-7x6in) s.d.88 panel
£9459 $16081   (27-May-91 L.K299/R) Old man seated in armchair smoking pipe and reading
       newspaper (14x10cm-6x4in) s.d.76 panel (DM 28000)
£13699 $24521   (13-Mar-91 N.M545/R) Peasant woman and huntsman in kitchen interior
       (46x36cm-18x14in) s.d.1881 panel (DM 40000)
£13873 $24000   (22-May-91 SY.NY43/R) Playing soldiers (21x30cm-8x12in) s.d.75 panel
£14211 $27000   (27-Feb-91 SY.NY163/R) Guitar player (16x19cm-6x7in) s.d.79 panel
£15607 $27000   (22-May-91 SY.NY222/R) Fiddler in brauhaus (25x30cm-10x12in) s.d.78
       panel
£23891 $44915   (19-Sep-90 N.M543/R) Jealousy, figures in interior (40x32cm-16x13in)
       s.d.75 panel (DM 70000)
£35714 $57500   (28-Jun-91 BM.B699/R) Interior with figures tending injured dog
       (49x60cm-19x24in) s. (DM 105000)

KAUFFMANN, Hugo (attrib) (1844-1915) German
£949 $1699   (11-Apr-91 D.V67/R) Peasant girl (50x39cm-20x15in) (A.S 20000)

KAUFMANN, Max (19th C) German
£634 $1134   (14-Mar-91 N.M2680/R) The small pipe smoker (24x18cm-9x7in) s. panel
       (DM 1850)

KAUFMANN, Adolf (1848-1916) Austrian
£1229 $2408   (24-Nov-90 SA.A670/R) Chicken run (26x21cm-10x8in) s.i. panel
       (DM 3600)
£1437 $2500   (27-Mar-91 B.SF4340/R) Sheep in moonlit landscape (44x58cm-17x23in) s.
       panel
£2373 $4248   (11-Apr-91 D.V292/R) Pond landscape (61x44cm-24x17in) s. panel
       (A.S 50000)
£2373 $4248   (11-Apr-91 D.V42/R) Birch woods with flock of sheep, autumn
       (64x49cm-25x19in) s.Widmar panel (A.S 50000)
£3253 $5824   (13-Mar-91 N.M548/R) Peasant woman with cows on wooded path near
       Fontainebleau (50x40cm-20x16in) s.i. i.verso panel (DM 9500)
£3425 $5582   (12-Jun-91 SY.MU89/R) Shepherd with flock (65x114cm-26x45in) s.
       (DM 10000)
£3560 $6372   (11-Apr-91 D.V265/R) Riverside houses (39x68cm-15x27in) s.d.1898
       (A.S 75000)

KAUFMANN, Adolf (1848-1916) Austrian-cont.

£3920	$7761	(31-Jan-91 D.V72/R) Horse-drawn cart with peasant in river landscape (35x60cm-14x24in) s. board (A.S 80000)
£4327	$8438	(25-Oct-90 D.V1/R) Rest in wooded landscape (60x98cm-24x39in) s. (A.S 90000)
£4852	$9170	(27-Sep-90 D.V66/R) Wienerwald landscape with figure resting (52x79cm-20x31in) s. (A.S 100000)
£6308	$11921	(27-Sep-90 D.V61/R) Landscape with flock returning (24x32cm-9x13in) s. board (A.S 130000)
£7179	$14000	(24-Oct-90 CH.NY186/R) Young woman by forest stream (98x143cm-39x56in) s.
£716	*$1203*	*(25-Apr-91 D.V204/R) View of town wall, spring (35x28cm-14x11in) s. W/C gouache (A.S 15000)*

KAUFMANN, Asmus (1806-1890) German

£514	$874	(27-May-91 GK.Z5055) Chicken yard (26x39cm-10x15in) s. panel (S.FR 1300)

KAUFMANN, Ferdinand (?) ?

£1795	$3500	(10-Oct-90 B.SF555/R) Above timberline, Rocky Mouintian National park (76x63cm-30x25in) s.
£2051	$4000	(10-Oct-90 B.SF525/R) View from studio (61x51cm-24x20in) s.

KAUFMANN, H (1868-1919) German

£3388	$5726	(4-May-91 BU.O82) Horses in landscape (26x32cm-10x13in) s. (N.KR 39000)

KAUFMANN, Isidor (1853-1921) Austrian

£23699	$41000	(22-May-91 SY.NY231/R) Portrait of Rabbi (32x25cm-13x10in) s. cradled panel
£35907	$70736	(14-Nov-90 RAS.K57/R) Portrait of Orthodox Jew in his library (52x40cm-20x16in) s. panel (D.KR 400000)
£1104	*$1800*	*(12-Jun-91 GG.TA336/R) In maternal grandmother's apartment (30x22cm-12x9in) s. W/C*

KAUFMANN, Joseph Clemens (1867-1925) Swiss

£653	*$1280*	*(6-Nov-90 GF.L2613/R) Swiss officer on horse (63x47cm-25x19in) s.d.1915 pastel (S.FR 1600)*

KAUFMANN, Karl (1843-1901) Austrian

£748	$1324	(20-Mar-91 KM.K1294) View of Venice (31x21cm-12x8in) s. panel (DM 2200)
£854	$1529	(11-Apr-91 D.V189/R) View of Rome (27x20cm-11x8in) s.H.Carnier panel (A.S 18000)
£854	$1529	(11-Apr-91 D.V190/R) View of town in Italy (27x20cm-11x8in) s.H.Carnier (A.S 18000)
£1091	$2149	(30-Oct-90 CH.AM207) View of Constantinople (60x80cm-24x31in) s. (D.FL 3600)
£1200	$2063	(16-May-91 D.V93/R) Norwegian fjord landscape (54x72cm-21x28in) s. (A.S 25000)
£1293	$2288	(20-Mar-91 KM.K1293) View of Cologne (53x80cm-21x31in) s. (DM 3800)
£1400	$2744	(22-Nov-90 CSK140/R) Continental river town (51x94cm-20x37in) s.d.1884
£1424	$2549	(11-Apr-91 D.V269/R) Sunday at Lake Geneva (66x87cm-26x34in) s.d.1871 i.verso (A.S 30000)
£1519	$2719	(11-Apr-91 D.V43/R) View of Venice (69x105cm-27x41in) s.Krautmann d.1895 (A.S 32000)
£1661	$2973	(11-Apr-91 D.V234/R) View of Italian town (50x82cm-20x32in) s. (A.S 35000)
£1689	$3294	(26-Oct-90 KM.K1304/R) View of Venice with Canale Grande and S.Maria della Salute (69x104cm-27x41in) s. (DM 5000)
£1715	$3395	(31-Jan-91 D.V9/R) Fjord landscape (89x113cm-35x44in) s.J.Holmsted (A.S 35000)
£1960	$3880	(31-Jan-91 D.V103/R) River landscape with view of southern town (68x52cm-27x6in) s. (A.S 40000)
£2020	$3495	(6-May-91 ZEL.L1778/R) View of harbour town, possibly Lower Rhine (68x55cm-27x22in) s.d.1880 (DM 6000)
£2048	$3870	(25-Sep-90 FN.S2235/R) View of Venice with fishing boats in calm sea and view of Grand Canal (31x47cm-12x19in) s. panel (DM 6000)
£2062	$4041	(16-Feb-91 GF.H24/R) View of Bacino di San Marco with Doge's Palace and S.Maria della Salute (50x81cm-20x32in) s. (DM 6000)
£2121	$4179	(30-Oct-90 CH.AM199) Molo with Doge's palace, Venice (31x51cm-12x20in) s. panel (D.FL 7000)
£2448	$4724	(10-Dec-90 L.K475) Views of Venice (42x69cm-17x27in) s.i.d.1889 pair (DM 7000)
£2644	$5156	(25-Oct-90 D.V134/R) Venice (47x31cm-19x12in) s.d.1897 panel (A.S 55000)
£2848	$5097	(11-Apr-91 D.V273/R) View of Istanbul (60x80cm-24x31in) s. (A.S 60000)
£2940	$5821	(31-Jan-91 D.V64/R) View of Rome (50x82cm-20x32in) s.i.d.1884 (A.S 60000)

KAUFMANN, Wilhelm (1895-?) Austrian

£727	$1368	(20-Sep-90 D.V181/R) Durnstein (57x78cm-22x31in) s. (A.S 15000)

KAUFMANN, Willi (1920-1978) Swiss

£876	$1709	(24-Oct-90 GD.B531) Red cat (73x60cm-29x24in) s.d.52 (S.FR 2200)

KAULA, W J (1871-1952) American

£875	*$1750*	*(10-Feb-91 LIT.L52) The Swale (43x51cm-17x20in) s. W/C*

KAULA, W J (1871-1952) American-cont.
£893 $1750   (27-Jan-91 LIT.L24a) Swale (46x51cm-18x20in) s. W/C

KAULA, William J (1871-1952) American
£578 $1000   (21-May-91 CE.NY616/R) Winter path (21x25cm-8x10in) s.d.1913 board
£1676 $3000   (14-Mar-91 CH.NY176/R) Sun and shadows (44x58cm-17x23in) s. board
£1953 $3300   (17-Apr-91 D.NY24/R) Spring landscape (48x56cm-19x22in) estate st.
     masonite
£7975 $13000   (5-Jul-91 S.W3000/R) Autumn landscape, New Ipswich, New Hampshire
     (81x99cm-32x39in) s.

KAULBACH, Anton (20th C) German
£1007 $1963   (10-Oct-90 ZEL.L1575/R) Portrait of Spanish woman in costume
     (80x60cm-31x24in) s. (DM 3000)

KAULBACH, Friedrich August von (1850-1920) German
£685 $1226   (12-Mar-91 FN.S2452/R) Portrait of Maria Guerrero (65x50cm-26x20in) s.
     (DM 2000)
£15243 $26218   (14-May-91 GF.L2112/R) The dancer Guerero (120x91cm-47x36in) s.
     (S.FR 38260)
£479 $858   (13-Mar-91 N.M310) Portrait of lady, possibly Irene von Keller
     (56x47cm-22x19in) i. pastel board double-sided (DM 1400)

KAULBACH, Hermann (1846-1909) German
£700 $1344   (27-Nov-90 PH135/R) The doorway (31x24cm-12x9in) init. st.studio verso
     board
£3000 $5160   (17-May-91 C58 c/R) On swing (25x16cm-10x6in) with Nachlass st.verso
     panel
£30769 $60000   (23-Oct-90 SY.NY352/R) The prankster (44x33cm-17x13in) s. panel

KAULBACH, Hermann (attrib) (1846-1909) German
£1365 $2567   (21-Sep-90 N.M3236/R) Sulking child (21x14cm-8x6in) panel (DM 4000)

KAULBACH, Hermann (style) (1846-1909) German
£3421 $6500   (27-Feb-91 SY.NY168/R) Portrait of lady with mandolin (150x73cm-59x29in)
     s.

KAULBACH, Wilhelm von (1805-1874) German
£769 $1492   (7-Dec-90 GB.B5909/R) Portrait of young man (22x16cm-9x6in)
     indis.i.d.1838 pencil (DM 2200)

KAULBACH, Wilhelm von (attrib) (1805-1874) German
£1729 $3250   (19-Sep-90 B.SF2632/R) Cupid and Psyche (68x91cm-27x36in) canvas laid
     down

KAULE, Otto (1870-?) German
£1833 $3282   (12-Apr-91 BM.B626/R) Moonrise on the Ilmenau (65x89cm-26x35in) i.verso
     (DM 5500)

KAULUM, Haakon Jensen (1863-1933) Norwegian
£1839 $3292   (11-Mar-91 B.O66/R) Alpine landscape (167x132cm-66x52in) s.d.99
     (N.KR 21000)
£3125 $5219   (4-Jun-91 BU.O4/R) Seascape with sailship (140x118cm-55x46in) s.
     (N.KR 36000)

KAUS, Max (1891-?) German
£8108 $13784   (1-Jun-91 VG.B153/R) Coastal landscape, Baltic Sea (54x71cm-21x28in) s.
     mono.i.verso (DM 24000)
£1351 $2297   (31-May-91 GB.B6448) River landscape (56x64cm-22x25in) s.d.1934 w/c
     (DM 4000)
£1370 $2233   (15-Jun-91 L.K351/R) From Rome (49x71cm-19x28in) s.d.58 mixed media
     board (DM 4000)
£1884 $3070   (15-Jun-91 L.K352/R) Pineta, Ischia (37x54cm-15x21in) s.i.d.1959 mixed
     media (DM 5500)
£2365 $4020   (28-May-91 KF.M786/R) Still life with quinces and pumpkin
     (53x67cm-21x26in) s. s.d.1939verso mixed media (DM 7000)
£5405 $9189   (1-Jun-91 VG.B242/R) Three bathers in coastal landscape
     (57x45cm-22x18in) s. W/C over pencil (DM 16000)

KAVAN, Frantisek (1866-1941) Czechoslovakian
£2048 $4014   (24-Nov-90 SA.A700/R) River landscape, morning (51x67cm-20x26in) s.i.
     (DM 6000)

KAVANAUGH, Marion see WACHTEL, Marion K

KAVLI, Arne Texnes (1878-1970) Norwegian
£757 $1461   (12-Dec-90 BU.O41/R) Summer evening (16x22cm-6x9in) s. panel (N.KR 8500)
£1751 $3135   (11-Mar-91 B.O68/R) Still life of vegetables (73x79cm-29x31in) s.
     (N.KR 20000)
£2627 $4702   (14-Mar-91 BU.O62/R) Summer's day in Grimstad (43x50cm-17x20in) s.
     (N.KR 30000)
£2627 $4702   (14-Mar-91 BU.O63/R) Portrait of woman (64x43cm-25x17in) s. (N.KR 30000)
£2760 $5328   (12-Dec-90 BU.O39/R) Winter in Bergen 1895 (73x48cm-29x19in) s.d.95
     (N.KR 31000)
£2890 $5173   (14-Mar-91 BU.O59/R) Coastal landscape with sailingboat
     (56x61cm-22x24in) s. (N.KR 33000)

1028

KAVLI, Arne Texnes (1878-1970) Norwegian-cont.

£3038	$5924	(11-Oct-90 BU.O72/R) Summer's day (56x62cm-22x24in) s. (N.KR 35000)
£3240	$5799	(14-Mar-91 BU.O61/R) Woman (105x59cm-41x23in) s.indist.d.17 (N.KR 37000)
£3385	$6602	(11-Oct-90 BU.O73/R) The actress Signe Heide (133x95cm-52x37in) init.d.13 (N.KR 39000)
£3659	$7134	(15-Oct-90 B.O50/R) Summer by the fjord (43x56cm-17x22in) s. (N.KR 42000)
£3733	$6234	(3-Jun-91 B.O80/R) Summer's day on the sea (69x50cm-27x20in) s.d.31 (N.KR 43000)
£4096	$7906	(10-Dec-90 B.O72/R) Evening view 1888 (80x88cm-31x35in) s.d.88 (N.KR 46000)
£6076	$10148	(3-Jun-91 B.O78/R) Two women in garden (69x79cm-27x31in) s. (N.KR 70000)
£6163	$12018	(11-Oct-90 BU.O71/R) Sailingboats by Fiskebackskil (65x73cm-26x29in) s. (N.KR 71000)
£6233	$12030	(10-Dec-90 B.O69/R) Landscape with fruit tree (66x85cm-26x33in) s. (N.KR 70000)
£7124	$13749	(12-Dec-90 BU.O38/R) Trees and woman with umbrella (119x97cm-47x38in) s. (N.KR 80000)
£12620	$22337	(19-Mar-91 UL.T177/R) View of the fjord (71x81cm-28x32in) (N.KR 145000)
£13021	$25391	(11-Oct-90 BU.O75/R) Outside the house (80x88cm-31x35in) s. (N.KR 150000)
£14000	$24080	(17-May-91 C167/R) Fjord in summer (94x131cm-37x52in) s.
£14795	$26188	(19-Mar-91 UL.T178/R) Woman in garden (61x70cm-24x28in) (N.KR 170000)
£17422	$33972	(15-Oct-90 B.O47/R) Women reading under sunshade (88x80cm-35x31in) s. (N.KR 200000)
£35000	$57400	(19-Jun-91 S315/R) Summer (79x87cm-31x34in) s.

KAY, Archibald (1860-1935) British

£550	$930	(3-May-91 PHE126) River landscape in spate (50x75cm-20x30in) s.
£950	$1862	(22-Nov-90 CG571) Children on the swings, market day (25x36cm-10x14in) s. board
£2400	$4488	(28-Aug-90 S837/R) Ploughing by wooded stream (76x63cm-30x25in) s.
£900	*$1800*	*(5-Feb-91 S166/R) Brodick Bay, Arran (38x53cm-15x21in) s. W/C over black chk htd bodycol*

KAY, James (1858-1942) British

£620	$1228	(1-Feb-91 PHE40) First snows - above Garloch (25x35cm-10x14in) s.
£1050	$2037	(5-Dec-90 PHE80/R) Palestine (48x58cm-19x23in) s. board
£1900	$3591	(27-Sep-90 L260/R) Steam drifters on the Clyde (36x48cm-14x19in) s. board
£2600	$5044	(6-Dec-90 CG75/R) The Broomielaw, Glasgow, evening (51x61cm-20x24in) s.
£2600	$4862	(28-Aug-90 S1081/R) Cap Ferrat (30x46cm-12x18in) s.
£2800	$5488	(22-Nov-90 CG605/R) Fisher folk on the beach (61x91cm-24x36in) s.d.96
£3000	$5610	(28-Aug-90 S1033/R) Boulevard (25x35cm-10x14in) s. i.verso board
£5500	$9295	(2-May-91 CG470/R) Speed troopship, River Clyde, Glasgow (41x61cm-16x24in) s.
£6000	$10140	(2-May-91 CG471/R) Sweet summertime (25x36cm-10x14in) s. s.i.verso
£7000	$13090	(28-Aug-90 S1090/R) River Clyde (51x61cm-20x24in) s. board
£7200	$14400	(5-Feb-91 S202/R) Fountainebleau, Paris (58x87cm-23x34in) s.
£10000	$20000	(5-Feb-91 S160/R) Huntsman in winter landscape (63x76cm-25x30in) s.
£12000	$24000	(5-Feb-91 S173/R) Promenade (52x78cm-20x31in) s. board
£18500	$34595	(28-Aug-90 S1054/R) Street in Majorca (51x62cm-20x24in) s. bears i.verso panel
£800	*$1344*	*(23-Apr-91 S147/R) Distant church tower (18x26cm-7x10in) s.d.1890 gouache*
£1200	*$2016*	*(23-Apr-91 S112/R) Children in meadow (21x28cm-8x11in) s.d.96 W/C*
£2600	*$4862*	*(28-Aug-90 S1080/R) Cap Ferrat, Mediterranean (43x55cm-17x22in) s.s.i.verso gouache*
£2800	*$4732*	*(2-May-91 CG448/R) Logjamming on Clyde (42x60cm-17x24in) s. W/C htd bodycol*

KAYANOWK, J (19/20th C) ?

£1734	$3000	(21-May-91 CE.NY72/R) Pfleger (91x121cm-36x48in) s.

KAYE, Otis (1885-1974) American

£6704	$12000	(12-Apr-91 SY.NY21/R) One dollar bill (23x37cm-9x15in) s.d.1921 panel
£11173	$20000	(14-Mar-91 CH.NY44/R) In the bag (17x24cm-7x9in) s. panel
£20231	$35000	(22-May-91 CH.NY179/R) Target practice (37x46cm-15x18in) s. panel

KAYSER, Eska (1935-) French

£1512	$2949	(28-Oct-90 R.P183) Miroir d'incertitude (130x97cm-51x38in) s. (F.FR 15000)

KAYSER-EICHBERG, Carl (1873-?) German

£615	*$1156*	*(19-Sep-90 GK.Z851) Moonlit coastal landscape, Monteallegrio (75x90cm-30x35in) s. i.verso oil gouache canvas (S.FR 1500)*

KAZACSAY, Gerone (1872-?) Hungarian

£2433	$4769	(24-Jan-91 D.V110/R) Leda (96x127cm-38x50in) s. (A.S 50000)

KAZACSAY, Luise (1872-?) Hungarian

£2013	$3926	(10-Oct-90 ZEL.L1577/R) Female nude facing back on beach (50x65cm-20x26in) s. (DM 6000)

KEATE, George (1729-1797) British

£500	*$825*	*(11-Jul-91 S94/R) View of Margate, Kent (17x25cm-7x10in) W/C*

KEATE, George (1729-1797) British-cont.
£1200   *$1980*   *(11-Jul-91 S93/R) View of Ranelagh Gardens, Margate, Kent (17x25cm-7x10in) W/C*

KEATING, Tom (1917-1984) British
£750 $1440   (17-Dec-90 B4) Jane Kelly as artist's model (91x70cm-36x28in)
£800 $1536   (17-Dec-90 B2) Portrait of Jane Kelly (51x40cm-20x16in) s. board
£900 $1728   (17-Dec-90 B18) Coastal view of Tenerife (61x76cm-24x30in) s.
£1100 $2112   (17-Dec-90 B5/R) John Constable drawing (61x40cm-24x16in) s. s.i.d.1965 verso board style of Constable
£1200 $2304   (17-Dec-90 B25/R) Two ballerinas (71x51cm-28x20in) s. style of Degas
£1200 $2304   (17-Dec-90 B15) Dedham Vale (40x51cm-16x20in) s. i.verso style of Constable
£1300 $2496   (17-Dec-90 B1/R) Halberdier (61x46cm-24x18in) s. style of Rembrandt
£1350 $2592   (17-Dec-90 B14/R) Landscape with trees and cottage (43x51cm-17x20in) board style Constable
£1400 $2688   (17-Dec-90 B16/R) Still life with fruit and champagne (51x66cm-20x26in) s.
£1500 $2880   (17-Dec-90 B36/R) Head portrait of woman (76x61cm-30x24in) bears sig. i.verso style Modigliani
£1700 $3264   (17-Dec-90 B23/R) Young girl (76x51cm-30x20in) s. style of Amadeo Modigliani
£1900 $3648   (17-Dec-90 B22/R) Riverside scene (51x76cm-20x30in) s. style of Monet
£2600 $4992   (17-Dec-90 B25 b) Still life of daisies in bowl (76x51cm-30x20in) s.
£2800 $5376   (17-Dec-90 B50) Manet and wife in riverside orchard (71x91cm-28x36in) s. style Monet
£3600 $6912   (17-Dec-90 B10/R) Haywain (45x66cm-18x26in) s. style of Constable
£4200 $8064   (17-Dec-90 B25 a) Coastal landscape with shipping and windmill (45x61cm-18x24in) s.
£4200 $8064   (17-Dec-90 B51/R) Self-portrait artist (66x46cm-26x18in)
£4800 $9216   (17-Dec-90 B49/R) Artist drinking (66x51cm-26x20in) s.d.43
£4800 $9216   (17-Dec-90 B48/R) On river at dusk (101x127cm-40x50in) s.i.d.72 style Constable
£8000 $15360   (17-Dec-90 B42/R) Sunflowers (61x51cm-24x20in) s.i.d.1984 style Van Gogh
£600   *$1152*   *(17-Dec-90 B41) Red-headed girl in white hat (45x37cm-18x15in) init. pastel gouache*
£650   *$1248*   *(17-Dec-90 B40) Self-portrait of artist (52x35cm-20x14in) s. pastel*
£800   *$1536*   *(17-Dec-90 B24) Countryside outside Florence (20x26cm-8x10in) W/C pen*
£900   *$1728*   *(17-Dec-90 B21) Seated female nude (40x33cm-16x13in) sanguine chk style Auguste Renoir*
£950   *$1824*   *(17-Dec-90 B44/R) Girl in pink hat (44x33cm-17x13in) s. pastel style Renoir*
£1400   *$2688*   *(17-Dec-90 B25 c) Red lady I (51x38cm-20x15in) s. pastel*
£1500   *$2880*   *(17-Dec-90 B35) Angler by Flatford Mill (12x26cm-5x10in) s. W/C pen htd white*
£1500   *$2880*   *(17-Dec-90 B7/R) View of Vilaflor, Teide Mountain, Tenerife (25x35cm-10x14in) W/C bodycol pen*
£1800   *$3456*   *(17-Dec-90 B20/R) Three ballerinas (45x31cm-18x12in) s. mixed media board style Edgar Degas*
£1800   *$3456*   *(17-Dec-90 B43) Boats in river landscape, church beyond (24x35cm-9x14in) mixed media*
£5000   *$9600*   *(17-Dec-90 B33/R) Horse chestnut trees by moonlight (25x30cm-10x12in) mixed media board style Samuel Palmer*

KECK, Otto (1873-1948) German
£2662 $5031   (25-Sep-90 FN.S2236/R) The visit, sitting room interior with peasants in Bavarian costumes (71x94cm-28x37in) s.d.1934 panel (DM 7800)

KEELEY, John (1849-1930) British
£380   *$730*   *(19-Feb-91 SWS356) Bickenhill Church, Warwickshire (38x49cm-15x19in) s. W/C over pencil scratching out*

KEELHOFF, Frans and VERBOECKHOVEN, Eugene (19th C) Belgian
£2746 $4750   (10-May-91 S.BM13/R) Pastures with sheep, cows and shepherds (66x107cm-26x42in) s.i.

KEEN, Oscar (1867-1949) Swedish
£1326 $2493   (10-Aug-90 RAS.V487/R) Town scene from Nuremberg with soldier by river (140x94cm-55x37in) s.d.1900 (D.KR 15000)
£2206 $4324   (6-Nov-90 BA.S139/R) Summer landscape with woman on road (46x61cm-18x24in) s. (S.KR 24000)

KEENE, Alfred (fl.1854-1866) British
£1200   *$2364*   *(30-Oct-90 HS52/R) Carmarthen Quay and Castle (36x53cm-14x21in) W/C*

KEENE, Charles Samuel (1823-1891) British
£650   *$1060*   *(14-Jun-91 C19/R) A good night out (13x21cm-5x8in) mono. pen*
£1000   *$1630*   *(14-Jun-91 C22/R) The storming of the Malakoff (27x40cm-11x16in) pencil pen W/C htd white*

KEHREN, Joseph (1817-1880) German
£5137 $8373   (12-Jun-91 SY.MU50/R) The Loreley (139x109cm-55x43in) s. (DM 15000)

KEHRER, Wilhelm (1892-1960) German
£699 $1357   (4-Dec-90 FN.S1907/R) Neckar valley near Kirchentellinsfurt (60x80cm-24x31in) s. (DM 2000)

KEHRER, Wilhelm (1892-1960) German-cont.
£699 $1357   (4-Dec-90 FN.S1906/R) Schwabische Alb landscape in autumn
                    (60x80cm-24x31in) s. (DM 2000)

KEIFER, Anselm (20th C) American?
*£47337 $80000   (1-May-91 CH.NY45/R) Manna (68x86cm-27x34in) s.verso lead acrylic
                    shellac straw photo board*

KEIL, Bernhard (1624-1687) Danish
£2660 $5000   (19-Sep-90 B.SF2624/R) The fowler (90x71cm-35x28in)
£10142 $20081   (30-Jan-91 APT.P9/R) La Nativite (72x135cm-28x53in) (F.FR 100000)
£15084 $27000   (11-Apr-91 SY.NY171/R) Seated young woman holding box (107x76cm-42x30in)

KEIL, Bernhard (circle) (1624-1687) Danish
£1600 $2704   (19-Apr-91 C40/R) An old woman, bust length, wearing a white headscarf
                    (163x127cm-64x50in) panel

KEIL, Bernhard (style) (1624-1687) Danish
£2564 $5000   (11-Oct-90 SY.NY8/R) Man playing guitar accompanied by boy playing
                    recorder (103x93cm-41x37in)
£21000 $40950   (26-Oct-90 C44/R) Peasants going to market (96x131cm-38x52in)

KEIL, Edouard (20th C) French
£782 $1260   (28-Jun-91 BM.B799/R) The judgement of Paris (21x31cm-8x12in) s. i.verso
                    (DM 2300)

KEILHAU, Bernhard see KEIL, Bernhard

KEINANEN, S A (1841-1914) Finnish
£5165 $8729   (20-Apr-91 HOR.H111/R) Summer's day (31x35cm-12x14in) s.d.1891
                    (F.M 36000)

KEINANEN, Sigfrid August (1841-1914) Finnish
£4545 $8136   (14-Apr-91 BU.H38/R) Road to town (31x26cm-12x10in) s.d.77 panel
                    (F.M 32000)
£6134 $12023   (24-Nov-90 HOR.H135/R) By the gate (65x96cm-26x38in) s.d.1907
                    (F.M 43000)

KEINEN, Jacob (20th C) Hungarian
£736 $1243   (19-Apr-91 FN.S1758) Still life with roses, tulips and other flowers in
                    vase on ledge (40x30cm-16x12in) s. panel (DM 2200)

KEINHOLZ, Ed (20th C) American
£918 $1800   (12-Feb-91 SY.NY431/R) For 9 end wrenches (30x41cm-12x16in) s. W/C
*£1128 $2200   (10-Oct-90 SY.NY512/R) For straight teeth from Dr Kanter
                    (30x41cm-12x16in) s.d.69 W/C pencil*

KEIRINCX, Alexander (1600-1652) Flemish
£6000 $9780   (3-Jul-91 S194/R) Wooded landscape with hunters on track passing pond
                    (39x49cm-15x19in) panel

KEIRINCX, Alexander (style) (1600-1652) Flemish
£1300 $2600   (7-Feb-91 CSK121) Wooded river landscape with birdcatcher on path,
                    ruined church beyond (38x46cm-15x18in)
£2600 $4238   (4-Jul-91 C716/R) Wooded landscape with goatherd resting on track by
                    river (59x74cm-23x29in) indist.s. panel

KEISERMANN, Franz (1765-1833) Swiss
*£2980 $5782   (7-Dec-90 CN.P41) Paysage montagneux avec riviere et deux pecheurs
                    (53x71cm-21x28in) pierre noire ink wash W/C (F.FR 29000)*
*£3905 $7577   (7-Dec-90 CN.P40/R) Le pont Romain a Narni (54x76cm-21x30in) chl.pen W/C
                    (F.FR 38000)*
*£4111 $7975   (8-Dec-90 SY.MO405/R) Vue du Forum Romain (64x97cm-25x38in) s. W/C
                    (F.FR 40000)*
*£8500 $13855   (2-Jul-91 C297/R) Roman forum from foot of Capitol at dusk, with peasant
                    family on donkey (69x105cm-27x41in) s. i.verso pen W/C gum arabic*
*£18500 $35889   (3-Dec-90 SY.F1007/R) Veduta del Colosseo (69x103cm-27x41in) s.d.1800
                    W/C ink (I.L 40000000)*

KEITH, Castle (19/20th C) American
£539 $905   (23-Apr-91 SY.AM340) Kitchen interior (50x60cm-20x24in) s.verso
                    (D.FL 1800)

KEITH, Dora Wheeler (1857-1940) American
£872 $1500   (17-May-91 DM.D2003/R) Portrait of young girl (64x53cm-25x21in) s.d.1880
                    board

KEITH, L E (19th C) ?
£1064 $2000   (19-Sep-90 B.SF2601/R) Table top still life with fruit (58x51cm-23x20in)
                    s. canvas laid down

KEITH, William (1839-1911) American
£973 $1800   (10-Mar-91 H.C123/R) Landscape with pond (25x41cm-10x16in) s. board
£1148 $2250   (13-Feb-91 B.SF2007/R) Marin landscape (28x37cm-11x15in) s.
£1276 $2500   (13-Feb-91 B.SF2006/R) Cows at waters edge (46x61cm-18x24in) s.

KEITH, William (1839-1911) American-cont.
£1538	$3000	(10-Oct-90 B.SF432/R) Figures by stream in forest clearing (32x108cm-13x43in) s.i. panel
£2051	$4000	(10-Oct-90 B.SF427/R) Lighted forest clearing (86x150cm-34x59in) s.i.d.1892
£3077	$6000	(10-Oct-90 B.SF430/R) Pastoral landscape (56x81cm-22x32in) s.
£4469	$8000	(14-Mar-91 CH.NY83/R) Carmel Mission (40x76cm-16x30in) s.d.89
£8071	$13640	(20-Apr-91 WOL.C45/R) Murir glacier (76x127cm-30x50in) s.
£8673	$17000	(13-Feb-91 B.SF2027/R) View of Donner Lake (56x84cm-22x33in) s.
£1197	*$2250*	*(19-Sep-90 B.SF2810/R) Mt. Shasta (30x46cm-12x18in) s. W/C*

KEIZO, Morishita (1944-) Italian
£735	$1447	(16-Nov-90 EA.Z263/R) Untitled (40x30cm-16x12in) s.d.1984verso (S.FR 1800)
£531	*$1045*	*(16-Nov-90 EA.Z253) Untitled (100x69cm-39x27in) s.i.d.1979 W/C (S.FR 1300)*

KELDER, Toon (1894-1973) Dutch
£929	$1793	(12-Dec-90 CH.AM29/R) At hairdresser (25x17cm-10x7in) s. panel (D.FL 3000)
£958	$1820	(11-Sep-90 CH.AM417/R) Bulbfields at dusk (50x70cm-20x28in) s. (D.FL 3200)
£961	$1662	(23-May-91 SY.AM84/R) Still life with flowers (51x42cm-20x17in) s. (D.FL 3200)
£1084	$2091	(12-Dec-90 CH.AM35/R) Biljart-player (33x44cm-13x17in) s.d.47 (D.FL 3500)
£1610	$3107	(13-Dec-90 SY.AM99/R) Still life (47x42cm-19x17in) s. (D.FL 5200)
£2477	$4780	(12-Dec-90 CH.AM37/R) Circus-horse (32x43cm-13x17in) s.d.46 (D.FL 8000)
£2941	$5676	(12-Dec-90 CH.AM28/R) Standing nude (100x50cm-39x20in) s.d.42 (D.FL 9500)
£3096	$5975	(12-Dec-90 CH.AM32/R) Seated nude (86x74cm-34x29in) s. (D.FL 10000)
£3406	$6573	(13-Dec-90 SY.AM3/R) Nudes (73x92cm-29x36in) s. (D.FL 11000)

KELEHER, Chris (1937-) British
£650	$1274	(13-Feb-91 B91/R) Kirulopore IX (63x76cm-25x30in)

KELLEN, Hendrika Wilhelmina van der (1846-1903) Dutch
£848	$1392	(18-Jun-91 VN.R140) Game still life (35x26cm-14x10in) s. (D.FL 2800)
£1078	$1875	(26-Mar-91 VN.R41/R) Still life of dead game (35x26cm-14x10in) s. panel (D.FL 3600)

KELLER, A (?) ?
£1473	$2534	(14-May-91 GM.B680/R) Le renouveau (130x90cm-51x35in) s. (B.FR 90000)

KELLER, Albert von (1844-1920) Swiss
£550	$902	(18-Jun-91 PH98) Portrait of woman (24x17cm-9x7in) s. panel
£822	$1471	(13-Mar-91 N.M551/R) Young woman before wild cat skin rug (69x58cm-27x23in) s. i.verso board (DM 2400)
£1712	$2791	(12-Jun-91 N.M484/R) Portrait of young lady wearing red evening dress (47x22cm-19x9in) s. panel (DM 5000)
£1984	$3313	(5-Jun-91 SY.Z84/R) Study for The Jugdement of Paris (58x84cm-23x33in) (S.FR 5000)
£2273	$4386	(14-Dec-90 BM.B741/R) Roman garden landscape (24x32cm-9x13in) s.i.indls.d.18.3 panel (DM 6500)
£2568	$4598	(13-Mar-91 N.M549/R) Party seated in artist's dining room having candle light dinner (17x32cm-7x13in) s. panel (DM 7500)

KELLER, Albert von (after) (1844-1920) Swiss
£524	$1012	(12-Dec-90 N.M579/R) Before round mirror, Anni Soldner (55x36cm-22x14in) i. (DM 1500)

KELLER, Ferdinand (1842-1922) German
£5000	$9850	(15-Nov-90 CSK21/R) Brazilian coastal landscape (93x141cm-37x56in) init.d.1872
£3425	*$5582*	*(12-Jun-91 SY.MU51/R) Baroque fountain with nymph and triton (200x165cm-79x65in) mono.d.1893 mixed media canvas (DM 10000)*

KELLER, Friedrich von (1840-1914) German
£769	$1492	(4-Dec-90 FN.S1911/R) Hero and Leander (81x57cm-32x22in) s. (DM 2200)

KELLER, Friedrich von (attrib) (1840-1914) German
£1024	$1935	(25-Sep-90 FN.S2238/R) Bearded old man seated with arms folded on knees in sunshine (34x17cm-13x7in) i.verso board (DM 3000)

KELLER, Henry George (1870-1949) American
£1124	$1900	(20-Apr-91 WOL.C335/R) Horse and rooster (58x61cm-23x24in) s.

KELLER, Johann Heinrich (circle) (1692-1765) Swiss
£2500	$4625	(5-Mar-91 PH51/R) Actaeon discovering Diana and her numphs at rocky pool (38x45cm-15x18in) metal

KELLER-REUTLINGEN, Paul Wilhelm (1854-1920) German
£1003	$1696	(19-Apr-91 FN.S1759/R) Amper landscape with farmhouses amongst trees, evening (32x45cm-13x18in) s. canvas on board (DM 3000)
£1049	$2024	(12-Dec-90 WE.MU91/R) Landscape, evening (32x42cm-13x17in) s. board (DM 3000)
£2901	$5483	(25-Sep-90 FN.S2239/R) Dachauer Moos landscape with shepherd and flock in late autumn, evening (71x109cm-28x43in) s. (DM 8500)

KELLER-REUTLINGEN, Paul Wilhelm (1854-1920) German-cont.
£4211	$8000	(12-Sep-90 D.NY65) Ducks along stream (20x25cm-8x10in) s.
£4895	$9497	(4-Dec-90 FN.S1912/R) River landscape with girl watching geese and view of village beyond (24x46cm-9x18in) s. (DM 14000)
£6993	$13497	(12-Dec-90 SY.MU69/R) Village scene at dusk (75x100cm-30x39in) s. (DM 20000)
£9589	$15630	(12-Jun-91 SY.MU130/R) House by river at dusk (41x64cm-16x25in) s. (DM 28000)
£10274	$16747	(12-Jun-91 SY.MU131/R) Drying the laundry (78x118cm-31x46in) s. (DM 30000)
£833	*$1492*	*(12-Apr-91 AW.H1767/R) Houses (29x45cm-11x18in) s. gouache paper on board (DM 2500)*

KELLOR, Aetla (19th C) ?
£546	$1075	(12-Nov-90 HO.ED262) Spilt milk (20x16cm-8x6in) s.i. panel (C.D 1250)

KELLY, Ellsworth (1923-?) American
£59172	$100000	(1-May-91 CH.NY17/R) Green white (116x151cm-46x59in) s.d.59
£153061	$300000	(6-Nov-90 SY.NY18/R) City Island (198x145cm-78x57in) s.i.d.1958 verso
£266272	$450000	(1-May-91 CH.NY33/R) Black curve IX (229x242cm-90x95in) s.d.1976 num.537 overlap
£7653	*$15000*	*(8-Nov-90 CH.NY159/R) Study for black and white (107x74cm-42x29in) s.d.73 graphite collage*

KELLY, Felix (1916-?) New Zealander
£700	$1127	(28-Jun-91 CSK172) Nuns floating over dream landscape (56x43cm-22x17in) s. board
£1237	$2091	(17-Apr-91 DS.W158) New Zealand childhood remembered (116x192cm-46x76in) s. (NZ.D 3600)
£3000	$5880	(25-Jan-91 C55/R) St Martin-in-the-Fields from Trafalgar Square (51x38cm-20x15in) s.d.51 board
£3000	$5880	(25-Jan-91 C56/R) The National Gallery, Trafalgar Square (51x38cm-20x15in) s.d.51 board
£3500	$5845	(6-Jun-91 C25/R) River steamer on the Bangkok river (43x56cm-17x22in) s.d.77 s.i.d.verso board
£580	*$957*	*(10-Jul-91 ZZ.B130) Tidal reach (29x39cm-11x15in) s.d.45 gouache*
£1500	*$2970*	*(29-Jan-91 PH81/R) Llandulas farm cottage (38x27cm-15x11in) s.d.44 gouache*

KELLY, Leon (20th C) American
£1047	*$1800*	*(15-May-91 SY.NY228/R) Bird of wisdom (30x22cm-12x9in) s.d.1945 s.d.1945 num.83 verso indian ink pen*

KELLY, Richard Barrett Talbot (1896-1971) British
£380	*$730*	*(19-Feb-91 C104/R) Long tailed duck (28x38cm-11x15in) s. W/C*
£400	*$768*	*(19-Feb-91 C125) Kite landing (28x18cm-11x7in) s.device pencil W/C*

KELLY, Robert George Talbot (1861-1934) British
£1387	$2400	(21-May-91 CE.NY246/R) Boats on Nile River (25x36cm-10x14in) s. panel
£400	*$672*	*(22-Apr-91 PH271) Desert valley (54x77cm-21x30in) s.d.1913 W/C*
£1300	*$2236*	*(15-May-91 BT155/R) The outskirts of Mensala, Egypt (41x86cm-16x34in) s.i.d.1898 W/C*
£1500	*$2925*	*(24-Oct-90 S217/R) Cairo (65x99cm-26x39in) s. W/C over pencil*

KELLY, Sir Gerald (1879-1972) British
£850	$1386	(4-Jul-91 PHI247/R) Project for 'Rite la Ballaora' (43x37cm-17x15in) s.i. verso canvas board
£1100	$2167	(1-Nov-90 B93/R) Ma Seyn Sin (72x47cm-28x19in)
£1158	$1957	(15-Apr-91 SY.J401/R) Siamese dancer, Ma Seyn Me Pose VIII (46x31cm-18x12in) i.num.18 13 (SA.R 5500)
£1300	$2197	(2-May-91 C1/R) Twisted tree (71x57cm-28x22in) s. i.verso
£5800	$10962	(24-Sep-90 CSK253/R) Burmese dancer (47x37cm-19x15in) i.verso board

KELSEY, Frank (19th C) British
£1150	*$2254*	*(8-Nov-90 PHI120/R) At sea (34x48cm-13x19in) s. W/C*
£1200	*$2352*	*(8-Nov-90 PHI121/R) The pilot boat (34x49cm-13x19in) s.i.verso W/C*
£1350	*$2322*	*(15-May-91 BT117/R) In Fowey Harbour (48x74cm-19x29in) s.i. W/C*

KELTERBORN, Ludwig Adam (1811-1878) German
£1633	$3200	(6-Nov-90 GF.L2097/R) Mephistopheles and student (81x62cm-32x24in) s.d.1839 (S.FR 4000)

KEMAN, Georges Antoine (1765-1830) French
£1900	*$3743*	*(1-Nov-90 S8/R) Christ with Mary and Martha. Resurrection. Burial. Nativity min.s.d.1803/1804 gilt-wood frames rec.four*

KEMENEDY, Jeno (1860-1925) Hungarian
£1007	$1963	(10-Oct-90 ZEL.L1580/R) Interior scene with female ghost and man in four-poster bed (39x65cm-15x26in) s. panel (DM 3000)
£2653	$5227	(15-Nov-90 EA.Z196/R) Der uberraschende Antrag (66x42cm-26x17in) s.i.d.1887 (S.FR 6500)

KEMM, Robert (19th C) British
£600	$1152	(20-Feb-91 CSK211/R) Morning greeting (76x56cm-30x22in) s.
£1300	$2405	(5-Mar-91 SWS1363/R) Spanish lady with guitar (91x71cm-36x28in) s.
£4500	$7605	(2-May-91 CG414/R) Mending nets (112x84cm-44x33in) s.

KEMP, Jeka (19th C) British
£420 $710   (17-Apr-91 CG19) *A Breton Market (44x37cm-17x15in) s. W/C*

KEMP, Roger (1908-) Australian
£2025 $3889   (14-Aug-90 SY.ME29) Abstract (63x99cm-25x39in) s. board (A.D 4800)
£2056 $3351   (16-Jun-91 SY.ME89/R) Geometrical development (82x101cm-32x40in) i.verso
                 board (A.D 4400)
£3256 $5470   (22-Apr-91 SY.ME380/R) Flowers (100x121cm-39x48in) s.d.81 acrylic board
                 (A.D 7000)
£3414 $6554   (26-Nov-90 SY.ME218/R) Abstract (102x81cm-40x32in) board (A.D 8500)

KEMP-WELCH, Lucy (1869-1958) British
£3300 $6204   (18-Sep-90 PH157/R) Running free (25x19cm-10x7in) s. canvas on board
£720 $1174   (14-Jun-91 T222) Study of stags head (30x41cm-12x16in) i.d.1908
£820 $1517   (4-Mar-91 PHB19) Three calves under tree s.d. W/C
£940 $1664   (19-Mar-91 OT412/R) First swim - ducklings and hen in stream
                 (24x33cm-9x13in) init. W/C
£2700 $5292   (6-Nov-90 PH19/R) Very young rabbit (99x99cm-39x39in) s.d.1912 pastel
                 chk

KEMPE, Roland (1907-) Swedish
£1085 $1877   (22-May-91 BA.S116/R) Abstract composition (130x86cm-51x34in) s. panel
                 (S.KR 11500)
£1112 $2158   (4-Dec-90 BA.S266/R) Fruits of the sea (38x56cm-15x22in) s. (S.KR 12000)
£1132 $1958   (22-May-91 BA.S115/R) Bull fighting (56x64cm-22x25in) s. (S.KR 12000)
£1205 $2337   (4-Dec-90 BA.S267/R) View through window (65x54cm-26x21in) (S.KR 13000)

KENDERDINE, Augustus (1870-1947) Canadian
£1004 $1979   (12-Nov-90 HO.ED50/R) Maritime cliffs and boat (25x20cm-10x8in) s. board
                 (C.D 2300)

KENDZRIERSKI, Apolonius (19th C) Polish
£578 $1000   (21-May-91 CE.NY112/R) Peasant girl in horse-drawn wagon
                 (43x63cm-17x25in) s.

KENNEDY, Cecil (1905-?) British
£800 $1600   (6-Feb-91 ZZ.B118) Still life with nasturtiums and hydrangaes in copper
                 pot (79x100cm-31x39in) s. panel
£950 $1786   (18-Sep-90 PH114/R) Still life of mixed flowers in jug (35x25cm-14x10in)
                 s.d.1950
£980 $1617   (11-Jul-91 GSP608) Glass vase of mixed flowers including dahlias and
                 carnations on a ledge (58x48cm-23x19in) s.
£1840 $3000   (12-Jun-91 SY.NY13/R) Flowers in chinese vase (61x51cm-24x20in) s.
£4000 $7520   (20-Sep-90 C110/R) Still life with fruit (49x64cm-19x25in) s.
£5000 $9700   (4-Dec-90 AG393/R) Summer (29x24cm-11x9in) s.
£5800 $11368   (8-Nov-90 C27/R) Summer flowers in a basket (62x75cm-24x30in) s.
£6500 $12805   (13-Nov-90 SWS452/R) Camellias, freezias and prunus blossom
                 (49x39cm-19x15in) s. l. stretcher
£10200 $20094   (13-Nov-90 SWS453/R) Mixed roses in a vase (49x38cm-19x15in) s.
£13000 $22620   (27-Mar-91 S30/R) Bluebells, cowslips, poppies and cow parsley in glass
                 vase (51x41cm-20x16in) s.
£13000 $22620   (27-Mar-91 S31/R) White carnations in glass vase (51x41cm-20x16in) s.
£16000 $27840   (27-Mar-91 S115/R) Peonies, pansies, acidanthera, gladioli in glass vase
                 (61x51cm-24x20in) s.
£16500 $32505   (13-Nov-90 SWS454/R) Mixed flowers - vansittart, camellias and other
                 spring flowers (49x39cm-19x15in) s.d.2'IV'68 l. verso

KENNEDY, William (1860-1918) British
£800 $1352   (2-May-91 CG510) Moorish warriors (51x41cm-20x16in) s. canvasboard
£1500 $2940   (22-Nov-90 CG622/R) Picking blossom (26x18cm-10x7in) s.

KENNELLY, Peter (1965-?) British
£600 $1176   (13-Feb-91 B103) Jealous man (46x56cm-18x22in)
£1000 $1960   (13-Feb-91 B102) Windseekers (46x66cm-18x26in)
£1100 $2156   (13-Feb-91 B104) Booth boys 1990 (46x56cm-18x22in)

KENSETT, John Frederick (1818-1872) American
£753 $1400   (9-Sep-90 LIT.L306) Woodland scene with rocks and water, possibly
                 Connecticut (18x28cm-7x11in) init. board
£964 $1900   (18-Nov-90 JRB.C36/R) Autumn (13x10cm-5x4in) init. i.verso board
£11640 $22000   (26-Sep-90 SY.NY67/R) Morning (86x69cm-34x27in) mono.
£54913 $95000   (22-May-91 CH.NY26/R) Narragansett (31x51cm-12x20in) init.d.65
£1429 $2800   (16-Feb-91 W.W17/R) View at Grand Tower, Illinois (13x20cm-5x8in) i.d.68
                 pencil

KENSETT, John Frederick (attrib) (1818-1872) American
£805 $1400   (29-Mar-91 E.EDM857/R) On the coast Beverly, Mass (23x41cm-9x16in)
                 i.d.1863

KENT, Rockwell (1882-1971) American
£578 $1000   (21-May-91 CE.NY654/R) Near Cape Ann (38x51cm-15x20in) indist.s.
                 s.i.d.1903 stretcher
£695 $1300   (1-Aug-90 B.P55/R) Nymph (23x18cm-9x7in) on glass
£1250 $2500   (7-Feb-91 B.P142/R) Vermont landscape (30x43cm-12x17in) s.
£5348 $10000   (1-Aug-90 B.P44/R) Sunset, Monhegan (20x25cm-8x10in) s.verso panel

KENT, Rockwell (1882-1971) American-cont.
£6145 $11000   (14-Mar-91 CH.NY211/R) Monhegan village at night (30x40cm-12x16in) s. panel
£1804   *$3500*   *(5-Dec-90 D.NY122/R) Snow drifts (28x43cm-11x17in) s. i.verso W/C paper on board*
£2781   *$5200*   *(1-Aug-90 B.P115/R) Northern studies (28x18cm-11x7in) estate st. mixed media*

KENWORTHY, John Dalzell (1858-1954) British
£1000 $1720   (14-May-91 SWS281/R) A new friend (32x43cm-13x17in) s.

KEPPENS, Jules (1910-) Belgian
£665 $1190   (16-Mar-91 KV.L168) River under the snow (60x80cm-24x31in) s. (B.FR 40000)

KEPPIE, Jessie (?-1951) British
£1600   *$3200*   *(5-Feb-91 S197/R) Pink carnations (47x33cm-19x13in) s. W/C over black chk*

KERCKHOVEN, Jacob van de see CASTELLO, Jacopo da

KERINEC, Roger (20th C) ?
£1529 $2951   (16-Dec-90 T.B297/R) Chalutiers a quai en Bretagne (81x65cm-32x26in) s.d.81 (F.FR 15000)
£4077 $7870   (16-Dec-90 T.B149/R) Chalutiers au Port Rhu (70x89cm-28x35in) s. (F.FR 40000)
£999   *$1928*   *(16-Dec-90 T.B236) Contre-jour au Guilvinec (73x54cm-29x21in) s.d.80 gouache (F.FR 9800)*

KERKOVIUS, Ida (1879-1970) German
£700 $1344   (17-Aug-90 K667) Abstract still life (28x38cm-11x15in) mono.
£2400 $4056   (1-May-91 GD.B480/R) Abstract 7 (30x31cm-12x12in) mono. canvas on pavatex (S.FR 6000)
£2655 $5098   (28-Nov-90 KF.M928/R) Composition, with figures (25x31cm-10x12in) mono. pastel (DM 7700)
£3072 $6020   (22-Nov-90 L.K1046/R) Blue yellow composition (25x33cm-10x13in) c.1950 panel (DM 9000)
£3072 $6020   (22-Nov-90 L.K1045/R) The Three Kings. Annunciation (29x36cm-11x14in) d.1946 board double-sided (DM 9000)
£3378 $5743   (30-May-91 SY.BE103/R) Figure with yellow head (18x24cm-7x9in) s. s.i.verso board (DM 10000)
£3390 $5661   (6-Jun-91 HN.H443/R) Form-colour composition (35x44cm-14x17in) (DM 10000)
£3716 $6318   (30-May-91 SY.BE102/R) Small composition in three parts (35x30cm-14x12in) s. s.i.verso board (DM 11000)
£10690 $20524   (28-Nov-90 KF.M926/R) Still life with chandelier (46x83cm-18x33in) mono.c.1950 panel (DM 31000)
£542   *$906*   *(6-Jun-91 HN.H445) Carpet design (34x24cm-13x9in) chk. pencil (DM 1600)*
£946   *$1636*   *(21-May-91 WK.M1062/R) Composition (11x14cm-4x6in) mono. pastel ball point pen (DM 2800)*
£956   *$1806*   *(29-Sep-90 GRA.B2364/R) Figures in a room (10x21cm-4x8in) mono. crayon on board (DM 2800)*
£1473   *$2636*   *(12-Mar-91 FN.S2041/R) Untitled (10x15cm-4x6in) mono. col.wax crayon (DM 4300)*
£1608   *$3120*   *(4-Dec-90 FN.S1645/R) Untitled (13x19cm-5x7in) mono.d.1950 mixed media (DM 4600)*
£2027   *$3507*   *(21-May-91 WK.M1061/R) Sunrise (28x24cm-11x9in) s.d.1918 W/C over pencil paper on board (DM 6000)*
£2174   *$3674*   *(19-Apr-91 FN.S1539/R) Tanne zur Sonne (30x39cm-12x15in) W/C (DM 6500)*
£4068   *$6793*   *(6-Jun-91 HN.H444/R) Composition (32x40cm-13x16in) mono. gouache over pencil (DM 12000)*
£5172   *$9931*   *(26-Nov-90 WK.M38/R) Vorgarten (59x50cm-23x20in) mono. (DM 15000)*
£6689   *$11304*   *(19-Apr-91 FN.S1538/R) Still life (49x68cm-19x27in) s.d.1959 i.verso pastel (DM 20000)*

KERMADEC, Eugene Nestor le (1899-1976) French
£4028 $6566   (16-Jun-91 GL.P77/R) Paysage (22x35cm-9x14in) s. (F.FR 40000)
£4200 $6762   (24-Jun-91 CSK204/R) L'entreacte (61x38cm-24x15in) s.
£4221 $6923   (20-Jun-91 APT.P55/R) L'enfant au vase bleu (73x50cm-29x20in) s. (F.FR 42000)
£4800 $7728   (24-Jun-91 CSK203/R) Le modele (65x50cm-26x20in) s.
£4982 $9565   (27-Nov-90 BU.S179/R) La chute de l'Ange (50x73cm-20x29in) s. (S.KR 54000)
£5012 $8520   (28-May-91 SY.MI169/R) Partage (61x46cm-24x18in) s. (I.L 11000000)
£5226 $8571   (20-Jun-91 APT.P54/R) Nature morte au verre et fruits (55x33cm-22x13in) s. (F.FR 52000)
£5528 $9065   (20-Jun-91 APT.P53/R) La selle du sculpteur (73x50cm-29x20in) s. (F.FR 55000)
£5722 $11158   (10-Oct-90 RAS.K126/R) Model (55x38cm-22x15in) s. (D.KR 65000)
£6089 $11690   (27-Nov-90 BU.S178/R) Femme (73x47cm-29x19in) s. (S.KR 66000)
£6526 $12073   (6-Mar-91 APT.P123/R) Les on dit du paysage (54x73cm-21x29in) s. i. verso (F.FR 65000)
£6907 $11949   (23-May-91 SY.AM268/R) La navigation du site (97x130cm-38x51in) s. i.verso (D.FL 23000)

KERMADEC, Eugene Nestor le (1899-1976) French-cont.
£7739	$15246	(31-Oct-90 ZZ.F54/R) Surgir negativement (65x54cm-26x21in) s. (F.FR 76000)
£7913	$14164	(9-Apr-91 BG.P5/R) Paysage (24x35cm-9x14in) s. (F.FR 80000)
£10535	$20227	(27-Nov-90 SY.MI166/R) Place de l'Amiral (73x100cm-29x39in) s. (I.L 23000000)
£11134	$21822	(23-Nov-90 PLF.P86/R) Nu au porte-jarretelles (50x73cm-20x29in) s. (F.FR 110000)
£12302	$20914	(28-May-91 SY.MI183/R) Quelques coordonnes pour un piege a lumiere (54x73cm-21x29in) s. (I.L 27000000)
£15075	$26985	(17-Mar-91 GL.P40/R) Femme vetue de sa peau (91x64cm-36x25in) s. (F.FR 150000)
£28542	$54801	(26-Nov-90 GL.P89/R) Femme assise (92x60cm-36x24in) s. (F.FR 280000)
£1173	*$2312*	*(12-Nov-90 YC.P56) Le Port (25x33cm-10x13in) s. blk.crayon wash W/C (F.FR 11500)*
£1320	*$2575*	*(10-Oct-90 RAS.K173/R) The violin player (31x24cm-12x9in) s. gouache W/C (D.KR 15000)*
£2214	*$4251*	*(27-Nov-90 BU.S180/R) Abstract composition (30x46cm-12x18in) s. W/C (S.KR 24000)*

KERMARREC, Joel (20th C) French
£1112	*$2169*	*(15-Oct-90 CSC.P98/R) Sans titre (104x74cm-41x29in) s.d.1973 col.crayons collage Indian ink gouache (F.FR 11000)*

KERN, Anton (circle) (1710-1747) German
£70000	$136500	(26-Oct-90 C160/R) Minerva awakens Endymion (102x117cm-40x46in)

KERN, Hermann (1839-1912) Hungarian
£1020	$1806	(20-Mar-91 KM.K1299/R) Portrait of gentleman holding coffe cup (21x15cm-8x6in) s. panel one of pair (DM 3000)
£1293	$2288	(20-Mar-91 KM.K1298/R) Portrait of man looking into beer mug (21x15cm-8x6in) s. panel pair (DM 3800)
£1573	$3037	(12-Dec-90 N.M580/R) Young woman wearing bonnet (31x25cm-12x10in) s. board one of pair (DM 4500)
£1678	$3272	(10-Oct-90 WE.MU251/R) When the work has been done (48x31cm-19x12in) s. st.sig.verso (DM 5000)
£2237	$4250	(27-Feb-91 SY.NY284/R) Old man with pipe (47x31cm-19x12in) s. panel
£2797	$5399	(12-Dec-90 WE.MU123/R) By the campfire (71x57cm-28x22in) s. (DM 8000)
£2940	$5821	(31-Jan-91 D.V42/R) Pater Kellermeister (68x47cm-27x19in) s. (A.S 60000)
£3500	$6720	(27-Nov-90 PH90/R) Pruning geraniums (53x42cm-21x17in) s. panel
£3846	$7500	(23-Oct-90 SY.NY374/R) Le violoniste (47x32cm-19x13in) s. panel
£4200	$8232	(22-Nov-90 CSK218/R) First drop. Last drop (47x32cm-19x13in) s. panel pair
£4271	$7646	(11-Apr-91 D.V85/R) His favourite tune (39x49cm-15x19in) s. i.verso (A.S 90000)
£4798	$8253	(16-May-91 D.V118/R) Botanist in wine cellar (47x31cm-19x12in) s.d.1903 panel (A.S 100000)
£5397	$10363	(29-Nov-90 D.V71/R) A pinch of snuff (48x33cm-19x13in) s. (A.S 110000)
£5526	$10500	(27-Feb-91 SY.NY283/R) Old man sewing (68x47cm-27x19in) s. panel
£5695	$10195	(11-Apr-91 D.V41/R) The thirsty musician (49x32cm-19x13in) s. panel (A.S 120000)
£5822	$11004	(27-Sep-90 D.V43/R) Card players in interior (48x69cm-19x27in) s. (A.S 120000)

KERN, Matthaus (1801-1852) Austrian
£621	*$1043*	*(25-Apr-91 D.V140/R) K.K. Militarschwimmschule im Prater (20x27cm-8x11in) s. W/C (A.S 13000)*

KERN, Melchior (1872-?) German
£2712	$4420	(3-Jul-91 WE.MU109/R) Village scene, evening (45x52cm-18x20in) s.i.d.1920 panel (DM 8000)

KERNAN, Joseph F (1878-1958) American
£2500	$4250	(1-Jun-91 IH.NY182/R) Watering down football player (64x51cm-25x20in) s.

KERR, Frederick B (fl.1915-1931) British
£1300	*$2470*	*(25-Feb-91 PH64/R) Windsor from Thames (33x50cm-13x20in) s. W/C*

KERR, Henry Wright (1857-1936) British
£420	*$752*	*(10-Apr-91 CSK75) The jolly Scotsman (41x30cm-16x12in) s.d.09 pencil W/C*
£450	*$891*	*(1-Feb-91 PHE167) By fireside (34x26cm-13x10in) s.i. W/C*
£650	*$1229*	*(26-Sep-90 B169/R) The verger (53x40cm-21x16in) s.d.87 W/C*
£1100	*$2156*	*(23-Nov-90 PHE92) The collection (53x40cm-21x16in) s.d.87 W/C*

KERR, Illingsworth Holey (1905-1989) Canadian
£567	$964	(27-May-91 HO.ED86/R) Limber pines, Livingston Ridge no 1 (30x41cm-12x16in) mono. s.i.d.verso board (C.D 1100)
£722	$1227	(27-May-91 HO.ED87/R) Old church, Lonsdale, Ontario (41x51cm-16x20in) mono. s.i.verso bears d. canvas board (C.D 1400)
£786	$1548	(12-Nov-90 HO.ED296/R) Rough land, North west of Calgary (41x51cm-16x20in) s.i.d. board (C.D 1800)
£830	$1634	(12-Nov-90 HO.ED14/R) Key River, last night (30x41cm-12x16in) s.i.d. board (C.D 1900)
£830	$1634	(12-Nov-90 HO.ED37/R) Cabbages and potatoes, Qu'appelle Valley (30x41cm-12x16in) s.i.d. panel (C.D 1900)

KERR, Illingsworth Holey (1905-1989) Canadian-cont.
£1004 $1979   (12-Nov-90 HO.ED312/R) First snow, Southwest (30x41cm-12x16in) s.i.d.
       board (C.D 2300)
£1082 $1840   (27-May-91 HO.ED306/R) French River, Ontario (46x61cm-18x24in) mono.
       s.i.d.1977verso canvas board (C.D 2100)
£1179 $2323   (12-Nov-90 HO.ED56/R) Prairie town with Slough (41x51cm-16x20in) s.i.d.
       board (C.D 2700)
£1289 $2191   (27-May-91 HO.ED304/R) French River, Ontario (30x41cm-12x16in) mono.
       s.i.d.1976verso canvas board (C.D 2500)
£1834 $3613   (12-Nov-90 HO.ED245/R) Foothills trail, March night (46x61cm-18x24in)
       s.i.d. (C.D 4200)
£6701 $11392   (27-May-91 HO.ED336/R) South of Longview, late April (137x183cm-54x72in)
       mono.i.d.1979verso acrylic (C.D 13000)

KERRICH, Thomas (1748-1828) British
£850   *$1403*   *(11-Jul-91 S109/R) Portrait of William Bond (36x28cm-14x11in)*
       s.i.d.1782verso col.chk

KERSEBOOM, Friedrich (circle) (1632-1690) British
£1200 $2340   (26-Oct-90 C218/R) Portrait of Daniel Woodgate, three-quarter length
       leaning on a balustrade (127x102cm-50x40in)

KERSEBOOM, Johann (attrib) (17/18th C) British
£2300 $4485   (22-Oct-90 SWS1327/R) Portrait of young gentleman, seated wearing coat,
       loose cloak, landscape beyond (110x79cm-43x31in)

KERSSEMAKERS, Anton and GOGH, Vincent van (19th C) Dutch
£38700 $74690   (12-Dec-90 CH.AM261/R) Wooden barn in forest (15x23cm-6x9in) s. panel
       (D.FL 125000)

KESLING, A von (20th C) German
£671 $1309   (10-Oct-90 WE.MU164/R) Winter morning (51x41cm-20x16in) s.d.1901
       (DM 2000)

KESSEL, Jan van (17th C) Flemish
£123529 $210000   (31-May-91 CH.NY87/R) Flowers in Chinese jardiniere with moths and other
       insects on ledge (77x60cm-30x24in) copper
£264706 $450000   (31-May-91 CH.NY86/R) Flowers in glass vase with caterpillar and beetle
       on ledge (77x60cm-30x24in) s.d.1652 copper

KESSEL, Jan van (attrib) (17th C) Flemish
£3800 $6422   (16-Apr-91 PH106/R) Studies of exotic birds including macaws, tucan,
       herons and eagle (19x36cm-7x14in)
£4103 $8000   (11-Oct-90 SY.NY192/R) Noli me tangere (53x72cm-21x28in) panel
£1682   *$3313*   *(12-Nov-90 CH.AM99/R) Walled farmhouse in wooded landscape*
       (29x42cm-11x17in) black chk wash (D.FL 5500)

KESSEL, Jan van (circle) (17th C) Flemish
£2637 $5063   (17-Dec-90 ARC.P32) La Basse-Cour (43x63cm-17x25in) (F.FR 26000)

KESSEL, Jan van (school) (17th C) Flemish
£12429 $22000   (22-Mar-91 CH.NY663/R) The monkey barber (16x20cm-6x8in) copper

KESSEL, Jan van (style) (17th C) Flemish
£1138 $1900   (9-Jun-91 LIT.L398) Floral still life of roses in pottery vase s.d.1892

KESSEL, Jan van I (1626-1679) Flemish
£39755 $78318   (13-Nov-90 CH.AM116/R) Fruit in bowl with parrot, roses, melon, snipe on
       ledge. Flowers in vase with fruit on ledge, baske (12x15cm-5x6in) con
       ledge. (D.FL 130000)
£40000 $65200   (3-Jul-91 S44/R) Element of Air - concert of fowls in evening river
       landscape (24x34cm-9x13in) s.indist.d. copper

KESSEL, Jan van I (attrib) (1626-1679) Flemish
£11173 $20000   (11-Apr-91 SY.NY21/R) Still life of flowers in glass vase resting on
       ledge (40x30cm-16x12in) panel

KESSEL, Jan van I (circle) (1626-1679) Flemish
£4000 $7600   (13-Sep-90 CSK162/R) Singerie- monkeys on table in dining room eating
       fruit and playing cards (23x32cm-9x13in) panel

KESSEL, Jan van II (1654-1708) Flemish
£2400 $4056   (18-Apr-91 C152/R) A turkey, ducks and pheasants in a barn
       (13x16cm-5x6in) copper
£3517 $6928   (14-Nov-90 SY.AM122/R) Assembly of birds in landscape (23x29cm-9x11in)
       (D.FL 11500)
£9128 $18073   (30-Jan-91 APT.P70/R) Animaux dans un paysage (25x35cm-10x14in) panel
       (F.FR 90000)
£9128 $18073   (30-Jan-91 APT.P71/R) Animaux de basse-cour (11x22cm-4x9in) copper pair
       (F.FR 90000)
£24000 $39120   (5-Jul-91 C40/R) Still life with wine glass and cheese on pewter plate,
       bowl olives and flask wine on table (16x22cm-6x9in) copper
£28000 $45640   (5-Jul-91 C39/R) Wild strawberriesand pinks in bowl, peaches on tazza,
       asparagus, fruit and vegetables on stone ledge (16x22cm-6x9in) copper
£38000 $64220   (17-Apr-91 S14/R) Still lifes of oysters, nuts and other food on ledge.
       Parrot and fruit (16x22cm-6x9in) copper pair

KESSEL, Jan van II (style) (1654-1708) Flemish
£850 $1437   (18-Apr-91 CSK153) Maccaws and doves by wall (28x24cm-11x9in) panel

KESSEL, Jan van III (1641-1680) Flemish
£1682 $3010   (10-Apr-91 CB.P47/R) Paysage au torrent (60x48cm-24x19in) s.
                   (F.FR 17000)

KESSEL, Jan van and BALEN, Hendrik van (style) (17th C) Flemish
£6288 $12073   (17-Dec-90 ARC.P15) Allegorie de l'abondance (37x45cm-15x18in)
                   (F.FR 62000)

KESSLER, Franz (1580-1650) German
£6757 $11486   (27-May-91 L.K64/R) Portrait of Dr Johann Michael Cronenburg,
                   Burgermeister of Cologne (100x77cm-39x30in) s.i.d.1633 with coat of
                   arms (DM 20000)

KESSLER, Stephan (1622-1700) Austrian
£1710 $3061   (14-Mar-91 D.V362/R) Christ in the House of Simon the Pharisee
                   (93x117cm-37x46in) mono. (A.S 35000)

KESTING, Edmund (1892-) ?
£507 $877   (25-May-91 N.M168/R) Erlkonig (39x31cm-15x12in) s.d.1950 W/C over pen
                   ball point pen (DM 1500)
£616 $1005   (15-Jun-91 L.K354) Sea shore (51x73cm-20x29in) s. s.i.d.1962verso oil
                   tempera col.chk (DM 1800)
£683 $1338   (24-Nov-90 N.M271/R) Transparent composition (32x22cm-13x9in) s.c.1945
                   indian ink W/C bodycol (DM 2000)
£683 $1338   (24-Nov-90 N.M270/R) Rythmic composition (28x20cm-11x8in) s.i.d.1941
                   indian ink pen W/C bodycol board (DM 2000)
£1365 $2676   (22-Nov-90 L.K1048/R) Seascape (26x37cm-10x15in) s.d.44 W/C indian ink
                   pen (DM 4000)

KET, Dick (1902-?) Dutch
£10511 $18183   (22-May-91 CH.AM512/R) Stilleven met viool (81x60cm-32x24in) s.d.1932
                   (D.FL 35000)

KETEL, Cornelis (attrib) (1548-1616) Dutch
£18000 $29700   (10-Jul-91 S7/R) Portrait of Sir Philip Sidney standing with hand
                   resting on hilt of sword (108x89cm-43x35in)

KETTEMANN, Erwin (1897-1971) German
£606 $1048   (6-May-91 ZEL.L1785/R) View of Leermoos, Tyrol (60x80cm-24x31in)
                   s.i.verso (DM 1800)
£671 $1309   (12-Oct-90 AW.H2656/R) Zell am See with Steinernem Meer, winter evening
                   (60x81cm-24x32in) s.i. (DM 2000)
£736 $1243   (17-Apr-91 WE.MU136/R) View of Ehrwald with Wetterstein mountains
                   (70x100cm-28x39in) s.i.d.28 (DM 2200)
£746 $1216   (3-Jul-91 WE.MU50/R) Fishermen on Chiemsee (14x18cm-6x7in) s. panel
                   (DM 2200)
£774 $1340   (6-May-91 ZEL.L1786/R) View of Leermoos (60x80cm-24x31in) s.i.verso
                   (DM 2300)
£808 $1398   (6-May-91 ZEL.L1787/R) Snowy landscape near Mittenwald
                   (70x100cm-28x39in) s.i.verso (DM 2400)
£1315 $2630   (6-Feb-91 N.M636/R) Fishermen on Lake Chiemsee (40x60cm-16x24in) s.i.
                   (DM 3800)
£1573 $3037   (13-Dec-90 N.M2751/R) Village in mountain landscape (50x75cm-20x30in)
                   s.i. (DM 4500)

KETTLE, Tilly (1735-1786) British
£798 $1500   (19-Sep-90 B.SF2609/R) Portrait of a gentlemen in 17th C costume
                   (76x63cm-30x25in) s.i.d.1769
£2545 $4250   (23-Jan-91 D.NY80) Portrait of young man (124x99cm-49x39in) s.

KETTLE, Tilly (attrib) (1735-1786) British
£2600 $4654   (10-Apr-91 S124/R) Portrait of officer, standing, army encampment in
                   background (166x126cm-65x50in)

KEULEMANS, Johannes Gerardus (1842-1912) Dutch
£495 $951   (20-Feb-91 EA.M481/R) Black crowned night heron (51x71cm-20x28in) pencil
                   W/C (C.D 1100)
£600 $1116   (5-Sep-90 BT128/R) Little Auk (20x13cm-8x5in) mono.num 2/3 W/C
£721 $1384   (20-Feb-91 EA.M460/R) Wolverine (61x81cm-24x32in) s.d.1887 pencil W/C
                   (C.D 1600)
£750 $1440   (19-Feb-91 C8/R) Green woodpeckers (20x15cm-8x6in) init. pencil W/C
                   htd.white vignette
£766 $1470   (20-Feb-91 EA.M467/R) Raccoon (61x81cm-24x32in) s. pencil W/C
                   (C.D 1700)
£800 $1488   (5-Sep-90 BT129/R) Woodchat (20x15cm-8x6in) init. num 3/4 W/C
£820 $1525   (5-Sep-90 BT125/R) Common cuckoo (20x13cm-8x5in) init.num 2/5 W/C
£950 $1767   (5-Sep-90 BT126/R) Goldfinches (20x13cm-8x5in) init. W/C
£950 $1767   (5-Sep-90 BT127/R) Pied or common wagtail (20x13cm-8x5in) s. W/C
£1946 $3250   (7-Jun-91 SY.NY192/R) Wolverine (61x81cm-24x32in) s.d.1887 W/C pencil
£2100 $3906   (5-Sep-90 BT124/R) Woodcock and damsel fly (30x48cm-12x19in) s. W/C
£2246 $3750   (7-Jun-91 SY.NY194/R) Black crowned night heron (52x72cm-20x28in) W/C
                   pencil

KEUN, Hendrik (1738-1788) Dutch
£2754 $4793   (26-Mar-91 VN.R42/R) Wood gatherers and figures in open carriage in a wood (38x51cm-15x20in) s. (D.FL 9200)

KEVER, Jacob Simon Hendrik (1854-1922) Dutch
£1138 $2219   (25-Oct-90 VN.R58/R) The weapon collector (52x42cm-20x17in) s.d.1876 (D.FL 3800)
£1150 $1921   (4-Jun-91 SWS1711/R) Mother and child (51x67cm-20x26in) s. panel
£1618 $2800   (12-May-91 H.C15/R) Mother and children in interior (46x51cm-18x20in) s.
£1673 $3263   (24-Oct-90 GD.B536/R) Still life with asters (40x49cm-16x19in) s. i.verso (S.FR 4200)
£1677 $2917   (26-Mar-91 VN.R43/R) Still life of flowers in ginger pot (53x43cm-21x17in) s. (D.FL 5600)
£2058 $3951   (26-Nov-90 SY.J271/R) Woman reading in interior (64x47cm-25x19in) s.d.80 (SA.R 10000)
£2156 $3622   (23-Apr-91 SY.AM234) Boy and girl at kitchen table (64x54cm-25x21in) s. (D.FL 7200)
£2378 $4661   (6-Nov-90 SY.AM71/R) Still life with roses in bowl (41x37cm-16x15in) s. (D.FL 7800)
£3892 $6772   (26-Mar-91 VN.R44/R) Mother with children and goat on a farm (47x59cm-19x23in) s. (D.FL 13000)
£5263 $10000   (27-Feb-91 SY.NY20/R) Breakfast time (102x127cm-40x50in) s.

KEVORKIAN, Jean (1933-) ?
£619 $1225   (3-Feb-91 LT.P147) Peniche sur le fleuve (33x41cm-13x16in) s. (F.FR 6100)
£634 $1255   (3-Feb-91 LT.P160) Bord de riviere (33x41cm-13x16in) s. (F.FR 6250)
£644 $1139   (7-Apr-91 LT.P137) Souppes sur long (33x41cm-13x16in) s. (F.FR 6500)
£653 $1207   (10-Mar-91 LT.P132) Vue de Nesles la Vallee (55x46cm-22x18in) s. i. verso (F.FR 6500)
£750 $1223   (4-Jul-91 LT.P146) Les peupliers (38x46cm-15x18in) s. (F.FR 7500)
£800 $1304   (4-Jul-91 LT.P137/R) Bord de riviere (38x46cm-15x18in) s. (F.FR 8000)
£842 $1490   (7-Apr-91 LT.P139) L'etang Sainte Suzanne (38x46cm-15x18in) s. (F.FR 8500)
£850 $1386   (4-Jul-91 LT.P117) Maisons au Juch (38x46cm-15x18in) s. (F.FR 8500)
£920 $1500   (4-Jul-91 LT.P128) Promenade au bord de la riviere (38x46cm-15x18in) s. (F.FR 9200)
£941 $1665   (7-Apr-91 LT.P152) Maisons Bretonnes (33x41cm-13x16in) s. (F.FR 9500)
£1000 $1900   (14-Sep-90 DM.D2276/R) Le Pont Neuf (38x46cm-15x18in) s.
£1490 $2891   (8-Dec-90 LT.P86) Le juch dans le finistere (65x92cm-26x36in) s. (F.FR 14500)
£1613 $3145   (27-Oct-90 LT.P125) Venice, le Grand Canal (38x46cm-15x18in) s. (F.FR 16000)
£1663 $3243   (27-Oct-90 LT.P144) Promenade a pont croix (46x38cm-18x15in) s. (F.FR 16500)
£2016 $3931   (27-Oct-90 LT.P37/R) Le guillevinec (81x100cm-32x39in) s. (F.FR 20000)

KEY SATO see SATO, Key

KEY, Adriaen Thomasz (1544-1590) Flemish
£7200 $11736   (3-Jul-91 S172/R) Portrait of Adriaen van Marsellaer of Antwerp (48x35cm-19x14in) i. panel

KEY, John Ross (1837-1920) American
£635 $1250   (7-Oct-90 LIT.L354) Study in trees (36x48cm-14x19in) s. board
£1250 $2400   (17-Dec-90 SY.NY39/R) Barges along river (41x66cm-16x26in) s.d.77
£1579 $3000   (28-Feb-91 MFA.C168/R) The Seine (20x36cm-8x14in) s.d.1877
£2312 $4000   (22-May-91 CH.NY119/R) World's Columbian Exposition, Chicago, 1892 (34x53cm-13x21in) s. board
£9524 $18000   (26-Sep-90 SY.NY53/R) California coast (77x128cm-30x50in) s.d.1872 i.verso

KEY, John Ross (attrib) (1837-1920) American
£564 $1100   (20-Oct-90 W.W56/R) Stream in mountain landscape (36x61cm-14x24in)

KEY, Mabel (1874-1926) American
£462   *$800*   *(21-May-91 GRO.B103/R) Flower garden (86x76cm-34x30in) s.d.1919 gouache paperboard*
£1156   *$2000*   *(21-May-91 GRO.B101/R) Spring pattern (76x74cm-30x29in) s.d.1924 gouache paperboard*

KEYSER, Elisabeth (attrib) (1851-1898) Swedish
£10768 $18521   (14-May-91 BU.S16/R) In the summer field (47x54cm-19x21in) (S.KR 115000)

KEYSER, Nicaise de (1813-1887) Flemish
£1982 $3884   (6-Nov-90 SY.AM318/R) Battle of Spurs (57x70cm-22x28in) s.d.1836 (D.FL 6500)

KEYSER, Nicaise de (style) (1813-1887) Flemish
£1300 $2561   (15-Nov-90 SC4151) Reading to John Milton (91x69cm-36x27in) panel

KEYSER, Raoul de (1933-) Belgian
£1643   *$3205*   *(23-Oct-90 C.A151) Composition (78x55cm-31x22in) s.d.1972 gouache (B.FR 100000)*
£1643   *$3205*   *(23-Oct-90 C.A152) Composition (78x55cm-31x22in) s.d.1971 gouache (B.FR 100000)*

KEYSER, Thomas de (attrib) (1596-1667) Dutch
£977 $1749   (14-Mar-91 D.V338/R) Portrait of gentleman with lace collar
             (45x31cm-18x12in) panel (A.S 20000)

KEYSER, Thomas de (circle) (1596-1667) Dutch
£950 $1606   (16-Apr-91 PH109/R) Portrait of lady, holding violet (13x10cm-5x4in)
             indist.i.d.1630 on copper
£1488 $2500   (17-Jul-91 SY.NY191/R) Portrait of a businessman and his wife in an
             elegant interior (51x61cm-20x24in) panel

KHMELUK, Vassyl (1903-?) Russian
£700 $1218   (28-Mar-91 CSK117/R) Jeune fille au fleurs (63x46cm-25x18in) s. board
£1020 $2010   (16-Nov-90 FB.P190) Vases de fleurs (53x73cm-21x29in) s. hardboard
             (F.FR 10000)

KHNOPFF, Fernand (1858-1921) Belgian
£421053 $800000   (28-Feb-91 CH.NY160/R) Portrait of Marguerite, artist's sister
             (97x75cm-38x30in) s. panel
£4910   *$8249*   *(23-Apr-91 C.A154/R) Portrait of Mr Arend (27x22cm-11x9in) s. drawing*
             (B.FR 300000)
£16000   *$28320*   *(19-Mar-91 C21/R) La Vierge (40x31cm-16x12in) s.i.d.1909 sanguine card*
             after Botticelli
£30000   *$57600*   *(28-Nov-90 S43/R) Portrait of young girl, possibly Elsie Maquet*
             (18x12cm-7x5in) s. i.label verso red chk htd blue crayon

KHROMINE, Victor (1948-) Russian
£915 $1829   (10-Feb-91 YC.P87) Igra (65x88cm-26x35in) s. (F.FR 9000)

KIAER (18th C) Danish
£2622 $5061   (12-Dec-90 N.M383/R) Peasants resting in wooded river landscapes with
             farmhouses (46x58cm-18x23in) one s. pair (DM 7500)

KIAERSKOU, F (1805-1891) Danish
£898 $1768   (14-Nov-90 RAS.K183) Landscape from Silkeborg Islands (44x67cm-17x26in)
             s.d.1851 (D.KR 10000)
£979 $1840   (18-Sep-90 BU.K62/R) Sailship at sunset (30x44cm-12x17in) init. paper
             (D.KR 11000)
£1144 $1923   (22-Apr-91 BU.K4/R) Friedland Castle in Gillerthal, Tyrol
             (24x29cm-9x11in) s.d.1846 (D.KR 13000)
£1257 $2476   (14-Nov-90 RAS.K409/R) View from the Swedish skerries (46x66cm-18x26in)
             s.d.1857 (D.KR 14000)
£2422 $4699   (22-Aug-90 RAS.K29/R) Danish summer landscape with manor farm
             (65x90cm-26x35in) s.d.1854 (D.KR 28000)
£4225 $7099   (23-Apr-91 RAS.K87/R) Stormy autumn day at Hallandsas
             (106x160cm-42x63in) s. (D.KR 48000)

KIAERSKOU, Frederik (1805-1891) Danish
£2174 $4174   (18-Dec-90 DUR.M7) Paisaje (63x100cm-25x39in) (S.P 400000)

KIAERSKOU, Frederik (attrib) (1805-1891) Danish
£1225 $2425   (31-Jan-91 D.V35/R) Farmhouse by Alpine lake (27x36cm-11x14in) i.
             (A.S 25000)

KIBARDIN, Georges (1899-1989) Russian
£655 $1067   (16-Jun-91 C.P38/R) Jardin fleuri (80x70cm-31x28in) s. verso (F.FR 6500)

KICK, Simon (attrib) (1603-1652) Dutch
£800 $1304   (4-Jul-91 C647/R) Soldiers duelling in barn (69x95cm-27x37in) s. panel

KICKERT, Conrad (1882-1965) Dutch
£1007 $1641   (11-Jun-91 I.N72) Pygmalion (140x114cm-55x45in) s.d.1940 hardboard
             (F.FR 10000)
£1829 $3659   (6-Feb-91 FB.P199/R) Vagues en mer (50x65cm-20x26in) s.d.1920
             (F.FR 18000)

KIDD, William (1790-1863) British
£900 $1764   (22-Jan-91 PH96 a) Impromptu feast (50x61cm-20x24in) s.

KIEDERICH, Franz (1873-1950) German
£3209 $5424   (3-May-91 SA.A1835/R) Enjoyable mood (43x76cm-17x30in) s. (DM 9500)

KIEFER, Anselm (1945-) German
£4730 $8041   (1-Jun-91 VG.B384/R) Abstract composition (56x43cm-22x17in) panel
             (DM 14000)
£5357 $10500   (6-Nov-90 SY.NY61/R) Noch is polen nicht verloren VI
             (211x271cm-83x107in) i.
£20305   *$40000*   *(4-Oct-90 SY.NY186/R) Mastersingers (58x83cm-23x33in) W/C straw on*
             photograph

KIEHL, Wilhelmina Johanna Louisa (1862-1922) Dutch
£1000 $1640   (18-Jun-91 PH20) Still life with roses, tulips and peonies in vase
             (36x24cm-14x9in) init. s.i.verso panel
£2181 $4253   (13-Oct-90 KRA.D238/R) Still life with roses and tulips (36x24cm-14x9in)
             mono. panel (DM 6500)

KIEKEBUSCH, Herman (1857-?) German
£854 $1529   (11-Apr-91 D.V44/R) Lake Obersee near Konigssee, morning
                (80x120cm-31x47in) s. (A.S 18000)

KIELDRUP, A E (1826-1869) Danish
£576 $973   (2-May-91 RAS.V63/R) Landscape with watermill s.d.51 (D.KR 6500)
£583 $1149   (14-Nov-90 RAS.K168/R) Landscape with road past house, sunset
                (33x41cm-13x16in) s.d.49 panel (D.KR 6500)
£890 $1673   (18-Sep-90 BU.K101/R) Norwegian landscape, Burdalsbrae in Hardanger
                (48x68cm-19x27in) s.d.1856 (D.KR 10000)
£1298 $2517   (22-Aug-90 RAS.K30/R) Summer day in the country (52x69cm-20x27in)
                mono.d.62 (D.KR 15000)
£1329 $2245   (2-May-91 RAS.V64/R) Norwegian fjord landscape (59x79cm-23x31in) init.
                (D.KR 15000)

KIELLAND, Else Christie (1903-) Norwegian
£564 $942   (3-Jun-91 B.O81/R) West coast landscape in moonlight (98x85cm-39x33in)
                init. (N.KR 6500)
£2003 $3907   (15-Oct-90 B.O52/R) The cloud breaking (100x88cm-39x35in) s.d.1934
                (N.KR 23000)

KIELLAND, Kitty (1843-1914) Norwegian
£1795 $3537   (14-Nov-90 RAS.K622/R) By the brook (17x27cm-7x11in) init. (D.KR 20000)

KIEN, Josef (1903-) German
£4392 $7598   (25-May-91 N.M169/R) Female nude combing hair (99x73cm-39x29in) s.d.1929
                i.stretcher (DM 13000)
£5068 $8767   (25-May-91 N.M170/R) Nocturno (70x100cm-28x39in) s.d.1977 s.d.verso
                (DM 15000)

KIENBUSCH, William (1914-) American
£469   *$900*   *(17-Dec-90 SY.NY433) Black Pines, Camp Island (56x66cm-22x26in) s.d.52*
                gouache

KIENERK, Giorgio (1869-1948) Italian
£6470 $12486   (11-Dec-90 CH.R160) Luci tra le fronde (30x36cm-12x14in) s. panel
                (I.L 14000000)
£7000 $13000   (18-Oct-90 F.M43/R) Tramonto, campagna toscana (50x61cm-20x24in)
                s.d.1922 s.i.verso panel (I.L 15000000)

KIENHOLZ, Edward (1927-) American
£1156   *$2000*   *(7-May-91 CE.NY181/R) Untitled - from Black Money Series*
                (30x40cm-12x16in) s.d.74 W/C ink

KIENLIN, Jules Georges (1830-?) French
£3147 $6073   (12-Dec-90 N.M583/R) Rococo ladies in elegant interior with gentlemen
                eavesdropping (64x55cm-25x22in) s. (DM 9000)

KIERS, P (1807-1875) Dutch
£3000 $5850   (15-Jan-91 GM.B386) Jeune fille reveuse (35x27cm-14x11in) s.
                (B.FR 180000)

KIERS, Petrus (1807-1875) Dutch
£1014 $1976   (26-Oct-90 BM.B824/R) Seamstress and visitor in interior
                (24x32cm-9x13in) s.d.1840 panel (DM 3000)
£4200 $6888   (18-Jun-91 PH3/R) The winning move (60x49cm-24x19in) s. panel

KIESEL, Conrad (1846-1921) German
£3500 $5740   (19-Jun-91 S82/R) Woman with flowers (50x37cm-20x15in) s.
£8036 $13500   (28-Apr-91 HG.C68) The masquerade ball (56x43cm-22x17in) s.
£63000 $103320   (19-Jun-91 S69/R) Elegant ladies after ball (73x93cm-29x37in) s.

KIESEWETTER, Johan Willem (1883-1951) Dutch
£629 $1056   (23-Apr-91 SY.AM324) Still life with porcelain (49x64cm-19x25in) s.
                (D.FL 2100)

KIHLE, Harald (1905-) Norwegian
£2091 $4077   (15-Oct-90 B.O54/R) Female nude (28x23cm-11x9in) s.d.38 panel
                (N.KR 24000)
£2493 $4812   (10-Dec-90 B.O76/R) Landscape from Impruneta outside Florenze
                (46x55cm-18x22in) s. panel (N.KR 28000)
£4452 $8593   (13-Dec-90 BU.O28/R) Horse in landscape (61x70cm-24x28in) s.
                (N.KR 50000)
£4541 $8765   (10-Dec-90 B.O75/R) Guro riding to Ottesong (36x44cm-14x17in)
                init.d.1963 panel (N.KR 51000)
£4987 $9624   (13-Dec-90 BU.O29/R) Interior from country cottage in Vinje
                (55x49cm-22x19in) s. (N.KR 56000)
£5254 $9405   (11-Mar-91 B.O69/R) Funeral procession (100x120cm-39x47in) s.d.36
                (N.KR 60000)

KIJNO (1921-) French
£697 $1185   (29-May-91 GL.P214/R) Composition noire sur fond rouge et blanc
                (64x49cm-25x19in) s. acrylic (F.FR 7000)
£548   *$931*   *(29-May-91 GL.P210) Sans titre (89x56cm-35x22in) s.d.1961 ink*
                blk.aerograph paper laid on canvas (F.FR 5500)

KIJNO (1921-) French-cont.
£598	$1016	(29-May-91 GL.P202) Sans titre (89x57cm-35x22in) s.d.1961 ink blk.aerograph paper laid on canvas (F.FR 6000)

KIJNO, Ladislas (1921-) French
£544	$1061	(20-Jan-91 GL.P140) Composition (32x24cm-13x9in) s. acrylic crumpled paper (F.FR 5400)
£750	$1253	(5-Jun-91 HC.P367) Composition sur fond rouge (47x38cm-19x15in) s. crumpled paper (F.FR 7500)
£1020	$2010	(16-Nov-90 FB.P304/R) Composition (70x54cm-28x21in) s. crumpled paper (F.FR 10000)
£1100	$1793	(4-Jul-91 GL.P181/R) Composition abstraite (55x46cm-22x18in) s.d.1956 (F.FR 11000)
£1104	$2043	(6-Mar-91 HC.P96) Composition sur fond marron (57x41cm-22x16in) s. crumpled paper (F.FR 11000)
£1205	$2229	(6-Mar-91 HC.P95) Composition sur fond polychrome (49x35cm-19x14in) s. crumpled paper (F.FR 12000)
£1456	$2344	(30-Jun-91 I.N129) Composition (82x64cm-32x25in) s. acrylic crumpled paper (F.FR 14500)
£1556	$2879	(10-Mar-91 LT.P110/R) Composition bleu sur fond rouge (33x41cm-13x16in) s.d.60 (F.FR 15500)
£1733	$3345	(16-Dec-90 P.V30/R) Composition (66x45cm-26x18in) s. oil crumpled paper (F.FR 17000)
£1809	$3238	(15-Mar-91 FB.P57/R) Composition (84x53cm-33x21in) s. crumpled paper (F.FR 18000)
£1908	$3529	(6-Mar-91 HC.P98/R) Composition sur fond jaune (68x46cm-27x18in) s. crumpled paper (F.FR 19000)
£2020	$3960	(12-Feb-91 HC.P112) Sonates a quatre main, suite de l'hommage a Erik Satie Gnossienne 2 (38x46cm-15x18in) s.i.d.1980 acrylic (F.FR 20000)
£2465	$4857	(1-Oct-90 CC.P168/R) Composition (61x50cm-24x20in) s.d.1974 verso (F.FR 25000)
£2711	$4364	(30-Jun-91 I.N38/R) Composition (45x37cm-18x15in) s. acrylic crumpled paper (F.FR 27000)
£2840	$5623	(28-Jan-91 PPB.P27/R) Composition rouge bleue et noire (35x26cm-14x10in) s. crumpled paper (F.FR 28000)
£3015	$5397	(11-Mar-91 GL.P196) Composition (79x59cm-31x23in) s. acrylic crumpled paper (F.FR 30000)
£3058	$5902	(10-Dec-90 LD.P138/R) Composition (64x50cm-25x20in) s. d.1971 verso crumpled paper on canvas (F.FR 30000)
£3083	$5982	(8-Dec-90 LT.P55/R) Composition rouge (86x72cm-34x28in) s. acrylic crumpled paper (F.FR 30000)
£3226	$6290	(27-Oct-90 BG.P38/R) Spheres (85x62cm-33x24in) s. crumpled paper (F.FR 32000)
£4095	$7985	(21-Oct-90 P.V23/R) Composition (65x54cm-26x21in) s. d.1975 verso (F.FR 40500)
£4545	$8909	(14-Feb-91 GL.P75/R) Composition (80x72cm-31x28in) s. acrylic crumpled paper (F.FR 45000)
£4587	$8853	(16-Dec-90 GL.P38/R) Acide II (81x65cm-32x26in) s. i. verso acrylic crumpled paper on canvas (F.FR 45000)
£7071	$13859	(14-Feb-91 GL.P69/R) Composition (81x100cm-32x39in) s.d.1959 (F.FR 70000)
£10175	$19739	(9-Dec-90 CC.P36/R) Composition (194x153cm-76x60in) s.d.1960 (F.FR 99000)
£700	$1141	(3-Jul-91 CSC.P43) Concert de Jazz (30x23cm-12x9in) s. crumpled paper (F.FR 7000)
£800	$1304	(3-Jul-91 CSC.P42) Hommage a E Varese (22x19cm-9x7in) s. crumpled paper (F.FR 8000)
£961	$1873	(15-Oct-90 CSC.P101/R) Portrait d'homme (48x45cm-19x18in) s.i.d.1956 chl. (F.FR 9500)
£992	$1706	(19-May-91 ZZ.F197/R) Composition (23x19cm-9x7in) s. mixed media crumpled paper (F.FR 10000)
£1028	$1994	(5-Dec-90 ZZ.F116/R) Composition (28x23cm-11x9in) s. W/C (F.FR 10000)
£1193	$2016	(15-Apr-91 CC.P40) Composition (42x35cm-17x14in) s. crumpled paper (F.FR 12000)
£1426	$2809	(31-Oct-90 ZZ.F49/R) Composition (43x32cm-17x13in) s. Indian ink gouache (F.FR 14000)
£1684	$3317	(16-Nov-90 FB.P310/R) Composition (103x73cm-41x29in) s. mixed media (F.FR 16500)
£1829	$3659	(10-Feb-91 CC.P42) Composition (46x37cm-18x15in) s. crumpled paper (F.FR 18000)
£2869	$5623	(11-Nov-90 ZZ.F203/R) Composition (56x46cm-22x18in) s. mixed media crumpled paper laid on canvas (F.FR 28000)
£3535	$6929	(12-Feb-91 HC.P113) Composition aux spheres (74x54cm-29x21in) s. mixed media board (F.FR 35000)

KIKOINE, Michel (1892-1968) Russian
£1088	$1948	(14-Apr-91 GL.P218/R) Femme et fleurs (92x73cm-36x29in) s. (F.FR 11000)
£1309	$2500	(2-Jan-91 GG.TA455/R) Musicians (31x42cm-12x17in) s.i. paper
£1500	$2415	(24-Jun-91 CSK63/R) Jeune fille au beret rouge (28x28cm-11x11in) s. paper on board
£4077	$7870	(15-Dec-90 D.P10/R) Nature morte (35x50cm-14x20in) s. board on canvas (F.FR 40000)
£4523	$7417	(18-Jun-91 APT.P208/R) Paysage urbain (77x66cm-30x26in) s. paper laid down on canvas (F.FR 45000)
£5139	$9969	(7-Dec-90 GL.P154/R) L'oree du bois (54x65cm-21x26in) s. (F.FR 50000)
£5408	$10654	(16-Nov-90 FB.P191/R) La crique (73x92cm-29x36in) s. (F.FR 53000)

1042

KIKOINE, Michel (1892-1968) Russian-cont.
£5612	$11000	(12-Feb-91 SY.NY146/R) Les maison des Bucherons (53x66cm-21x26in) s.d.1951 i.verso
£6429	$11508	(14-Apr-91 GL.P224/R) Paysage verdoyant (54x73cm-21x29in) s. (F.FR 65000)
£8902	$15935	(14-Apr-91 GL.P220/R) Le violoniste (51x33cm-20x13in) s. (F.FR 90000)
£9424	$18000	(2-Jan-91 GG.TA566 a/R) Paysage (85x57cm-33x22in) s.d.1916/18
£9891	$17705	(14-Apr-91 GL.P223/R) Nature morte aux tulipes (73x60cm-29x24in) s. (F.FR 100000)
£576	$1100	(2-Jan-91 GG.TA454/R) Self portrait (21x15cm-8x6in) s. pencil
£2275	$4072	(14-Apr-91 GL.P93) Femme a la guitare (31x24cm-12x9in) s. oil gouache paper laid down on canvas (F.FR 23000)
£2473	$4426	(14-Apr-91 GL.P215) Coucher de soleil (24x31cm-9x12in) s. oil gouache paper laid down on canvas (F.FR 25000)

KILBOURNE, Samuel A (1836-1881) American
| £1331 | $2250 | (1-May-91 B.SF5065/R) Trout (51x30cm-20x12in) s.d.1865 |

KILBURNE, G G (1839-1924) British
| £600 | $1002 | (7-Jun-91 BW358) Interior scene with lady and child looking at parrot (30x25cm-12x10in) s. W/C |
| £1000 | $1890 | (26-Sep-90 RB703) Grandmother and granddaughter at the foot of staircase (23x30cm-9x12in) s. W/C |

KILBURNE, George Goodwin (1839-1924) British
£579	$1100	(14-Sep-90 DM.D2233/R) Caught napping (46x61cm-18x24in) s. board
£950	$1587	(5-Jun-91 S84/R) At gate (24x16cm-9x6in) s.d.95 panel
£1500	$2880	(16-Aug-90 SC4121) Hunt breakfast (51x76cm-20x30in) s.
£450	$833	(6-Mar-91 SC4168) Posy for grandmother (10x18cm-4x7in) s. W/C pencil
£700	$1148	(19-Jun-91 B81/R) Doctor's visit (12x17cm-5x7in) s. W/C htd white
£900	$1593	(19-Mar-91 SHER97/R) Portrait of young woman - peasant girl leaning on stone wall s.d.1865 W/C oval
£900	$1503	(5-Jun-91 S277/R) Solitude (24x34cm-9x13in) s.d.1869 W/C
£950	$1881	(30-Jan-91 S282/R) Cold winter's evening (23x16cm-9x6in) s. W/C htd white
£1000	$1960	(8-Nov-90 DLY340/R) Message of importance (36x51cm-14x20in) s. W/C
£1208	$2356	(10-Oct-90 WE.MU248/R) Grandmother's treasure box (60x52cm-24x20in) mono. W/C (DM 3600)
£1700	$3349	(1-Nov-90 C152/R) Dinner time (38x53cm-15x21in) s. pencil W/C htd.white
£1800	$3546	(1-Nov-90 C153/R) Golden Age, young man serenading two ladies on river bank (23x30cm-9x12in) s. i.verso pencil W/C
£1800	$3402	(26-Sep-90 S326/R) Siesta (25x22cm-10x9in) s. W/C htd bodycol
£2400	$4608	(26-Nov-90 SWS100/R) The fancy dress (21x16cm-8x6in) s. W/C htd.bodycol
£2800	$5292	(26-Sep-90 S327/R) Once upon a time (28x23cm-11x9in) s. W/C htd bodycol
£3200	$6144	(26-Nov-90 SWS99/R) The poor relations (25x35cm-10x14in) s.d.77 W/C htd.bodycol
£3200	$5216	(14-Jun-91 C110/R) Afternoon tea (25x35cm-10x14in) s.d.76 pencil W/C
£3200	$5216	(14-Jun-91 C103/R) The goose girl (14x21cm-6x8in) s. pencil W/C htd.white
£3500	$5705	(14-Jun-91 C102/R) A faithful friend at tea time (34x49cm-13x19in) s. pencil W/C
£3500	$5705	(14-Jun-91 C104/R) A good story (36x52cm-14x20in) s. i.verso pencil W/C htd. white
£3500	$5705	(14-Jun-91 C106/R) Travellers (26x36cm-10x14in) s.i.verso pencil W/C htd. white
£3500	$5705	(14-Jun-91 C107/R) Malade Imaginaire (26x36cm-10x14in) s. i.verso pencil W/C htd.white
£3800	$6194	(14-Jun-91 C105/R) I wish you luck (36x52cm-14x20in) s. i.verso pencil W/C htd.white
£3800	$6194	(14-Jun-91 C101/R) A little family history (36x51cm-14x20in) s. pencil W/C
£3800	$7524	(30-Jan-91 S178/R) At piano (23x16cm-9x6in) s. W/C htd bodycol
£4500	$8505	(26-Sep-90 S360/R) Gondola (57x95cm-22x37in) s.d.77 s.i.verso W/C

KILGOUR, Jack Noel (1900-) Australian
| £2008 | $3855 | (26-Nov-90 SY.ME276/R) Girl at gate (34x47cm-13x19in) s. i.verso canvasboard (A.D 5000) |

KILIAN, Lukas (1579-1637) German
| £880 | $1434 | (1-Jul-91 S202/R) Seated boy playing bagpipes (18x15cm-7x6in) pen |

KILPACK, Sarah Louise (fl.1880-1909) British
| £1100 | $2068 | (20-Sep-90 LJ314) Coastal scene with castle and fort at sunset, shipping and figures (15x22cm-6x9in) s. board |
| £1300 | $2197 | (3-May-91 T94) Shipping off jetty. Mont St. Michael (15x20cm-6x8in) s. pair |

KILVINGTON, Patrick (?) Australian
| £633 | $1071 | (15-Apr-91 AAA.S124) On Goondi Run (41x51cm-16x20in) s. (A.D 1400) |
| £960 | $1872 | (15-Oct-90 AAA.S134) Wheeling the lead (40x51cm-16x20in) s. (A.D 2400) |

KIMBALL, Alonzo Myron (1874-1923) American
| £1040 | $1800 | (21-May-91 CE.NY527/R) Camilla and Alice (66x80cm-26x31in) s. board |

KIMMEL, Cornelis (1804-1877) British
£2879 $4952   (16-May-91 D.V191/R) Winter in Holland (78x103cm-31x41in) s.
(A.S 60000)

KIMPE, Reimond (1885-1970) Belgian
£841 $1455   (22-May-91 CH.AM304,/R) Vissershaventje in zeeland (20x30cm-8x12in) s.
i.stretcher (D.FL 2800)
£1890 $3629   (27-Nov-90 SY.AM3864/R) Composition with birds (58x45cm-23x18in) s.
panel (D.FL 6200)
£2229 $4302   (12-Dec-90 CH.AM45) De lamp (68x86cm-27x34in) s.d.32 i.verso (D.FL 7200)

KIMURA (?) ?
£3539 $6901   (17-Oct-90 ARC.P96) La marne (24x16cm-9x6in) s. (F.FR 35000)

KINDBORG, Johan (1861-1907) Swedish
£2462 $4136   (24-Apr-91 BA.S124/R) Winter landscape, Barnangen (46x30cm-18x12in)
s.d.85 (S.KR 26000)
£2936 $4932   (24-Apr-91 BA.S123/R) Summer day by Bockholm's chalets (55x78cm-22x31in)
s.i.d.87 (S.KR 31000)

KINDERMANN, Adolf (1823-1892) German
£1365 $2676   (24-Nov-90 SA.A613/R) The guardian angels (105x71cm-41x28in) s.i.d.1873
arched top (DM 4000)

KINDERMANS, Jean-Baptiste (attrib) (c.1822-1876) Belgian
£970 $1910   (30-Oct-90 CH.AM34) View in village with figures on track passing
horse-drawn cart (21x27cm-8x11in) indist.s. panel (D.FL 3200)

KINDLEBERGER, David (fl.1900-1905) American
£670 $1300   (7-Dec-90 S.W2971/R) Figures in Barbizon landscape (30x48cm-12x19in)
s.d.1889 canvas on board

KING, Agnes Gardner (19th C) British
£2400 $4152   (8-May-91 ZZ.B209) The pet rabbit (51x38cm-20x15in) s. W/C

KING, Albert F (1854-1945) American
£918 $1800   (16-Feb-91 W.W88/R) Still life with violin, books and jug
(51x64cm-20x25in) s.d.1915
£2235 $4000   (14-Mar-91 CH.NY57/R) Peaches and melon (30x46cm-12x18in) s.

KING, Captain John Duncan (1789-1863) British
£1200 $2304   (20-Feb-91 CSK217) Arcadian landscape with drover and goats. Harbour at
sunset (15x20cm-6x8in) s.d. pair oval

KING, Charles Bird (1786-1862) American
£1164 $2200   (25-Sep-90 CE.NY9/R) Wakechai (24x15cm-9x6in) chl. white chk.

KING, Charles Bird (attrib) (1786-1862) American
£3067 $5000   (5-Jul-91 S.W3009/R) Young girl with dove (91x71cm-36x28in)

KING, Francis Scott (1850-?) American
£1596 $3000   (19-Sep-90 B.SF2722/R) Still life of oriental vases and Buddah on a rug
(51x61cm-20x24in) s.d.1888

KING, Haynes (1831-1904) British
£600 $978   (13-Jun-91 CSK306) Somebody is coming (61x50cm-24x20in) i.stretcher
£850 $1632   (20-Feb-91 ZZ.B138) Milkmaid (62x51cm-24x20in) s.verso
£950 $1530   (27-Jun-91 CG114/R) The scullery maid (36x30cm-14x12in) s.
£1300 $2548   (13-Feb-91 S24/R) Awaiting fisherman's return (30x21cm-12x8in) s.
£1350 $2322   (14-May-91 SWS263/R) By the warmth of the fire (20x15cm-8x6in) s. panel
£2500 $4250   (29-May-91 PHC164) Fishergirl (29x24cm-11x9in) s.
£2800 $4564   (10-Jun-91 TAY826/R) Interior scene with young woman looking through
open door (46x61cm-18x24in) s.d.1881

KING, Haynes (attrib) (1831-1904) British
£1300 $2405   (5-Mar-91 SWS1383/R) Sewing (40x49cm-16x19in) indis.s.d.
£4800 $9408   (22-Nov-90 CG524/R) The broken doll (74x91cm-29x36in)

KING, Jessie M (1875-1949) British
*£1000 $1650   (10-Jul-91 CSK137/R) Departure (25x20cm-10x8in) s. pen W/C htd white
vellum*
£1200 $2244   (28-Aug-90 S998/R) Eglise St Julien le Pauvre (23x12cm-9x5in) s.i. pen
*£1500 $2805   (28-Aug-90 S990/R) Few bubbles rose where he sank (27x24cm-11x9in) s.i.
pen W/C*
£2000 $4000   (5-Feb-91 S212/R) Summer (23x12cm-9x5in) s.i. W/C ink
£2200 $4114   (28-Aug-90 S994/R) The forbidden garden, Culross (25x17cm-10x7in) s. pen

KING, John Baragwanath (1864-1939) British
£550 $1045   (28-Feb-91 DLY165) Moonrise on the Cornish shore (61x152cm-24x60in)
s.d.1903

KING, John Yeend (1855-1924) British
£524 $1027   (5-Nov-90 FB.M324) Young boy fishing (46x61cm-18x24in) s. (C.D 1200)
£700 $1344   (29-Nov-90 B110) Bibury Mill and Bridge (30x22cm-12x9in) s. s.i.verso
board
£750 $1230   (20-Jun-91 B65/R) Gypsy encampment (38x28cm-15x11in) s.

KING, John Yeend (1855-1924) British-cont.
£760	$1474	(3-Dec-90 LS924) Study of river and ferry and figures (48x74cm-19x29in) s.
£800	$1576	(1-Nov-90 TE611) Landscape with cottage near stream (74x56cm-29x22in) s.
£812	$1600	(16-Nov-90 S.BM68/R) Over the bridge (53x38cm-21x15in) s.
£850	$1386	(13-Jun-91 CSK271) First house in Vickerage (54x36cm-21x14in) s. i.stretcher
£960	$1900	(1-Feb-91 S.W2562/R) Woman and child crossing bridge (53x38cm-21x15in) s.
£1000	$1950	(16-Jan-91 CSK213) Thatched cottages on banks of river (155x231cm-61x91in) s.
£1200	$1956	(14-Jun-91 C225/R) Children on a bridge by thatched cottage (54x37cm-21x15in) s
£1300	$2132	(20-Jun-91 B87/R) Market morning (36x33cm-14x13in) s. i.verso
£1300	$2496	(17-Aug-90 K518) Wooded river landscape (48x76cm-19x30in) s.d.1909
£1650	$2756	(5-Jun-91 S116/R) Driving geese (37x53cm-15x21in) s. canvasboard
£1700	$3349	(13-Nov-90 PH62/R) Mother and children outside cottage (44x59cm-17x23in) s.
£1786	$3429	(28-Nov-90 PH.T75/R) News from abroad (59x44cm-23x17in) s. (C.D 4000)
£1892	$3084	(10-Jun-91 W.T1320/R) Chatting by a stream (30x46cm-12x18in) s. (C.D 3500)
£2600	$4654	(14-Mar-91 ZZ.B165) A woman and child at a riverside cottage (60x47cm-24x19in) s.
£2936	$4932	(24-Apr-90 BA.S125/R) Beached punt by calm river (122x92cm-48x36in) s. (S.KR 31000)
£3800	$7372	(24-Aug-90 GSP113) Lady gathering cabbage, cottage beyond (46x61cm-18x24in) s.
£4103	$8000	(24-Oct-90 CH.NY338/R) Faggot gatherers on path (61x91cm-24x36in) s.
£750	*$1418*	*(26-Sep-90 S243/R) Sweeper at crossroads (47x35cm-19x14in) s. W/C*
£1100	*$2079*	*(26-Sep-90 S277/R) On country lane (35x25cm-14x10in) s. W/C htd bodycol*

KING, Lilian Yeend (1882-?) British
£2500	$4900	(22-Jan-91 PH99/R) Feeding the doves (69x51cm-27x20in) s.

KING, Paul (1867-1940) American
£809	$1400	(21-May-91 CE.NY408/R) Rocky coast (31x41cm-12x16in) s.

KING, S (18th C) ?
£4000	$7840	(20-Nov-90 PH244/R) Mr Denis Gunton of Matlask on his grey hunter coursing and pointing to a hare (125x104cm-49x41in) s.i.d.1754

KINGMAN, Dong (1911-) American
£573	*$1100*	*(29-Nov-90 MFA.C163/R) Meeting in park (51x71cm-20x28in) s. W/C*
£769	*$1500*	*(20-Oct-90 W.W203/R) The railroad signal (36x56cm-14x22in) s.d.40 W/C*
£1760	*$3027*	*(15-May-91 SY.NY224/R) Square in Buenos Aires (38x56cm-15x22in) s.i.d.68 W/C pencil*
£4762	*$9000*	*(26-Sep-90 SY.NY207/R) Bridge and white building (54x74cm-21x29in) s. W/C*
£6878	*$13000*	*(26-Sep-90 SY.NY206/R) The Blue Bay, Hong Kong (66x103cm-26x41in) s. W/C*

KINGMAN, Eduardo (20th C) South American
£529	*$900*	*(1-Jun-91 LAE.L61/R) Hands (89x66cm-35x26in) s. mixed media*

KINGSLEY, Garrett (1915-) Australian
£1071	$1864	(26-Mar-91 JRL.S152/R) Landscape at Windsor, NSW (49x60cm-19x24in) s. masonite (A.D 2400)

KINGSTON, Gertrude Angela (1862-1937) British
£500	$925	(6-Mar-91 DR118) F.C. Konstam in wood (23x15cm-9x6in) panel

KINGWELL, Mabel A (fl.1914-1923) British
£600	*$1182*	*(5-Oct-90 T265) Ponies on Dartmoor (23x28cm-9x11in) s.d.1921 W/C*

KINLEY, Peter (20th C) British
£750	$1268	(2-May-91 C162/R) Study for flowers (25x18cm-10x7in) s. i.d.1960 stretcher board
£3000	$5010	(7-Jun-91 C301/R) Garden (138x212cm-54x83in) s.i.d.1975stretcher
£4061	$8000	(15-Nov-90 SY.NY68/R) Study for plants. Study for flowers (28x20cm-11x8in) s.d.1960 board
£750	*$1268*	*(2-May-91 C163/R) Study for studio interior - 1 (28x21cm-11x8in) s. i.d.1962 verso pencil oil board*
£1100	*$1771*	*(28-Jun-91 CSK233) Design for moorish palace (58x77cm-23x30in) s.d.77 W/C pencil*

KINLOCH, George Washington (19th C) British
£1500	$2925	(16-Oct-90 CG211 a) The artist's studio (97x71cm-38x28in) s.d.1882

KINNAIRD, F W (?) British
£470	*$766*	*(5-Jul-91 BW382) Gathering in the harvest (30x48cm-12x19in) s.*

KINNAIRD, Frederick Gerald (19th C) British
£1800	$3456	(29-Nov-90 B124/R) A mother's joy (50x41cm-20x16in) i.verso
£2200	$4290	(18-Oct-90 SC3167/R) The little fishwives. The fisherman's family (44x60cm-17x24in) both s. pair

KINNAIRD, Henry J (fl.1880-1908) British
£750	$1253	(5-Jun-91 S10) Sussex Downs near Shoreham (29x44cm-11x17in) panel

KINNAIRD, Henry J (fl.1880-1908) British-cont.

£1674	$3214	(27-Nov-90 W.T1045) Wargrave on the Thames (74x125cm-29x49in) s. (C.D 3750)
£4000	$7880	(13-Nov-90 SWS330/R) A river landscape with figures haymaking (75x120cm-30x47in) s.
£700	$1176	(23-Apr-91 S21) Near Dalmally, Argyll (18x26cm-7x10in) s.i. W/C htd bodycol
£800	$1480	(6-Mar-91 SC4230/R) The haymakers. Cattle watering (20x15cm-8x6in) s. W/C pair
£800	$1416	(21-Mar-91 CSK58/R) An Essex cornfield (36x53cm-14x21in) s.i. pencil W/C htd.white
£900	$1764	(21-Nov-90 B89) Lancing church, Sussex (34x25cm-13x10in). s.i. W/C
£900	$1728	(18-Dec-90 HC10) Near Dolgelley, Wales (18x38cm-7x15in) s. W/C
£1000	$1770	(21-Mar-91 CSK61) An old bridge on the Stour, Kent (33x53cm-13x21in) s.i. pencil W/C htd.white
£1100	$1947	(21-Mar-91 CSK60/R) On the Arun, near Fittleworth, Sussex (36x56cm-14x22in) s.i. pencil W/C
£1100	$1837	(5-Jun-91 S239/R) Thames near Pangbourne (28x42cm-11x17in) s.i. W/C
£1200	$2076	(20-May-91 PH106/R) Surrey cornfield (19x40cm-7x16in) s.i. W/C
£1300	$2574	(30-Jan-91 S238/R) Sussex hayfield (35x27cm-14x11in) s.i. W/C htd white
£1500	$2895	(10-Dec-90 PHB16/R) Near Dedham, Essex (34x51cm-13x20in) s.i. W/C
£1600	$3072	(19-Feb-91 SWS382) Sussex cornfield (51x37cm-20x15in) s.i. W/C bodycol
£1600	$3168	(30-Jan-91 S247/R) View at Bramley, Sussex. Near Wargravve on Thames (18x39cm-7x15in) s.i. W/C htd white pair
£1800	$3186	(21-Mar-91 CSK59/R) Haymaking (36x48cm-14x19in) s.i. pencil W/C bodycol.
£1800	$3222	(13-Mar-91 B149/R) Near Dedham, Essex (36x53cm-14x21in) s.i. W/C bodcyol.
£2000	$3360	(22-Apr-91 PH277/R) Sussex cornfield. Arundel Castle, Sussex (19x39cm-7x15in) s.i. W/C pair
£2200	$4114	(30-Aug-90 CG52) Near Dedham, Essex (36x51cm-14x20in) s.i. W/C htd bodycol.
£2200	$4312	(21-Nov-90 B86) Sussex cornfield (28x38cm-11x15in) s.i. W/C
£2200	$3938	(13-Mar-91 B129/R) Thames near Sonning (24x40cm-9x16in) s. W/C
£2300	$4531	(12-Nov-90 PH74/R) On the Thames near Goring s.i. W/C
£2600	$5122	(1-Nov-90 C128/R) Hayfield near Clare, Suffolk (33x51cm-13x20in) s.i. W/C htd.white
£2800	$4704	(22-Apr-91 PH267/R) Essex cornfield (44x77cm-17x30in) s.i. W/C
£3400	$5712	(15-Jul-91 PH157/R) Sussex cornfield. Near Bignor, Sussex (35x25cm-14x10in) s.i. W/C pair
£3600	$7092	(1-Nov-90 C129/R) View near Lewes, Sussex (33x51cm-13x20in) s.i. W/C htd.white
£3700	$7178	(5-Dec-90 PHL21/R) View on the Avon. Thames near Streatley (35x53cm-14x21in) s.i. col. washes pair
£4300	$7267	(30-Apr-91 AG192/R) Thames, near Shillingford (49x74cm-19x29in) s.i. W/C

KINNAIRD, Wiggs (?) British?

£560	$1103	(1-Nov-90 C130/R) Cornfield near Travalyn, Cornwall (33x51cm-13x20in) s.i. pencil W/C
£620	$998	(24-Jun-91 HS72/R) Haymakers - extensive landscape, with reed edged pool, figures, haycart (29x45cm-11x18in) s. W/C
£620	$1209	(25-Oct-90 RG2636) River landscape with cattle and ducks (61x38cm-24x15in) s. W/C
£650	$1235	(10-Sep-90 PH70) Ducks by stone bridge (56x81cm-22x32in) s.d.1899 W/C
£680	$1278	(19-Sep-90 PHC61) Cottages at Wilton, Dorset (34x49cm-13x19in) s. W/C
£800	$1584	(30-Jan-91 S249) On Stour, Near Clare, Suffolk (58x38cm-23x15in) s.i. W/C htd white

KINSELLA, Edward Patrick (20th C) British

£1500	$2925	(17-Oct-90 PHL29/R) Gaiety girl col.washes htd.bodycol.

KINSON, Francois Joseph (circle) (1771-1839) Flemish

£659	$1305	(30-Jan-91 APT.P303/R) Portrait d'une jeune femme en robe noire (76x56cm-30x22in) canvas laid down on board oval (F.FR 6500)

KINZEL, Josef (1852-1925) Austrian

£1520	$2965	(26-Oct-90 KM.K1306/R) Dominican monk holding glass of wine in wine cellar (26x21cm-10x8in) s.i. panel (DM 4500)
£1960	$3880	(31-Jan-91 D.V111/R) The wine taster (26x20cm-10x8in) s.i.d.1900 panel (A.S 40000)
£2273	$4386	(12-Dec-90 N.M584/R) Drunken musician with trumpet seated at table with glass of wine (26x21cm-10x8in) s.d.1885 i.verso panel (DM 6500)
£4808	$9375	(25-Oct-90 D.V151/R) The old Sudbahhof, Vienna (28x47cm-11x19in) s. i.verso board (A.S 100000)

KINZEL, Liesl (1886-1961) Austrian

£817	$1594	(25-Oct-90 D.V54/R) Flowers at the window (56x77cm-22x30in) s. board (A.S 17000)
£879	$1671	(28-Feb-91 D.V93/R) House and garden in Spitz on the Danube (26x19cm-10x7in) s. pencil W/C (A.S 18000)

KINZINGER, Edmund Daniel (1888-1963) German

£1600	$2864	(12-Apr-91 AW.H1770/R) Two female nudes standing (28x22cm-11x9in) mono.d.1929 W/C bodycol chk over pencil (DM 4800)

KIOERBOE, Carl Fredrik (1799-1876) Swedish
£827	$1621	(10-Nov-90 FAL.M192/R) Terrier with rabbit (63x77cm-25x30in) panel (S.KR 9000)
£1394	$2719	(24-Oct-90 GD.B541) Spaniel with red collar (46x55cm-18x22in) s. (S.FR 3500)
£1835	$3615	(13-Nov-90 AB.S402/R) Wooded landscape with fox being hunted (75x105cm-30x41in) s. (S.KR 20000)

KIPNISS, Robert (1931-) American
£636	$1100	(21-May-91 CE.NY713/R) Trees (102x102cm-40x40in) s.
£1042	$2000	(17-Dec-90 SY.NY408/R) Long shadows (91x86cm-36x34in) s.

KIPPENBERGER, Martin (1953-) German
£2055	$3349	(14-Jun-91 L.K990/R) Hommage a Marilyn Monroe (120x90cm-47x35in) s. (DM 6000)
£2972	$5736	(12-Dec-90 WE.MU213/R) Hommage a Marilyn Monroe (119x89cm-47x35in) s. (DM 8500)

KIPRENSKY, Oreste (c.1778-1836) Russian
£20000	$39000	(10-Oct-90 C203/R) Portrait of Prince Evgenii Grigor'evich Gagarin as a child (56x49cm-22x19in) init.i.d.1812

KIPS, Erich (1869-?) German
£5758	$9904	(16-May-91 D.V131/R) Marktplatz in Potsdam mit Altem Rathaus (58x70cm-23x28in) s. (A.S 120000)

KIRAS, Jean (20th C) French
£2117	$4128	(28-Oct-90 R.P248) Crucifixion (146x114cm-57x45in) s.d.89 (F.FR 21000)
£2470	$4816	(28-Oct-90 R.P195) La rue (146x114cm-57x45in) s.d.88 (F.FR 24500)

KIRBERG, Otto (1850-1926) German
£687	$1306	(2-Mar-91 KRA.D347/R) Portrait of woman reading (46x40cm-18x16in) s.i. board (DM 2000)
£11579	$22000	(28-Feb-91 CH.NY77/R) Ladies in garden (62x81cm-24x32in) s.

KIRCHBACH, Frank (1859-1912) British
£1220	$2000	(19-Jun-91 B.SF1924/R) Portrait of young man in profile (45x32cm-18x13in) s.d.1907

KIRCHBERGER, Gunther (1928-) German
£405	*$701*	*(21-May-91 WK.M1063/R) Composition W 5 (31x31cm-12x12in) mono.d.1964 s.i.d.stretcher acrylic pencil (DM 1200)*

KIRCHHOFF (20th C) ?
£2161	$4214	(22-Oct-90 BR.M30/R) Koilon (100x150cm-39x59in) s.d.1989 verso (I.L 4800000)

KIRCHNER, Albert Emil (1813-1885) German
£1049	$2024	(12-Dec-90 N.M585/R) Courtyard of Venetian palace (51x45cm-20x18in) s.d.1858 (DM 3000)
£3632	$6137	(1-May-91 KH.K96/R) Mountain landscape with woman and child by chappel (82x63cm-32x25in) s.d.1852 (D.KR 41000)
£13699	$22329	(12-Jun-91 N.M486/R) Verona seen from Giardino Giusti with women collecting water (105x140cm-41x55in) s.i.d.1851 (DM 40000)
£1049	*$2024*	*(12-Dec-90 SY.MU4/R) View of the river Isar in the Prater (29x42cm-11x17in) pencil pen indian ink (DM 3000)*

KIRCHNER, Ernst Ludwig (1880-1938) German
£163265	$321633	(16-Nov-90 GK.Z5175/R) Cyclamen (60x70cm-24x28in) d.1917 (S.FR 400000)
£173410	$300000	(8-May-91 CH.NY25/R) Steinbruch bei Wildboden (119x90cm-47x35in) s. d.23 verso
£400000	$776000	(4-Dec-90 S21/R) Frankfurter Dom (70x60cm-28x24in)
£710660	$1400000	(14-Nov-90 CH.NY24/R) Paar unter dem Japanschirm. Landschaft mit drei Figuren (100x75cm-39x30in) s. double-sided
£1190476	$1952381	(21-Jun-91 GK.B56/R) The Boskett, Albertplatz in Dresden (121x150cm-48x59in) s. (S.FR 3000000)
£556	*$911*	*(19-Jun-91 GK.B493) Male nude seated (21x13cm-8x5in) indian ink pen (S.FR 1400)*
£683	*$1338*	*(24-Nov-90 N.M272/R) Singer conversing with orchestra (19x15cm-7x6in) pencil dr. (DM 2000)*
£794	*$1302*	*(19-Jun-91 GK.B500) Archers (29x21cm-11x8in) s.i.d.1935 pencil (S.FR 2000)*
£946	*$1608*	*(28-May-91 KF.M787/R) Dancing couple (21x17cm-8x7in) pencil (DM 2800)*
£1267	*$2267*	*(12-Apr-91 AW.H1778/R) Three girls in cafe (22x17cm-9x7in) pencil (DM 3800)*
£1400	*$2254*	*(24-Jun-91 CSK35/R) Tanzende Madchen (25x21cm-10x8in) i.verso pen ink*
£1622	*$2805*	*(25-May-91 N.M171/R) Man walking amongst trees (30x18cm-12x7in) indian ink (DM 4800)*
£2703	*$4595*	*(1-Jun-91 VG.B237/R) Girl with child (47x32cm-19x13in) chk (DM 8000)*
£2857	*$5629*	*(16-Nov-90 EA.Z332) Head of man (51x36cm-20x14in) c.1927/28 chl (S.FR 7000)*
£2885	*$4905*	*(27-May-91 GK.Z5167) Skater indian ink pen htd.blue red (S.FR 7300)*
£2915	*$4868*	*(6-Jun-91 HN.H450/R) Davos (21x17cm-8x7in) chl. wash (DM 8600)*
£3061	*$6000*	*(15-Feb-91 SY.NY75/R) Farmer with calf (22x24cm-9x9in) s.d.1917verso W/C pencil*

KIRCHNER, Ernst Ludwig (1880-1938) German-cont.

£3299	$6500	(14-Nov-90 SY.NY139/R) Tanzerinnen (15x20cm-6x8in) st. verso W/C ink over pencil
£3827	$7500	(12-Feb-91 SY.NY14/R) Moritzburg (33x18cm-13x7in) pastel
£4054	$6892	(31-May-91 GB.B6457/R) Two women at table (52x39cm-20x15in) indian ink brush (DM 12000)
£4204	$7273	(22-May-91 CH.AM541/R) Akte im walde (21x30cm-8x12in) st.num.20430 verso blue crayon W/C (D.FL 14000)
£4392	$7466	(30-May-91 SY.BE80/R) Pine trees in the Alps, Davos. Study of cow (16x21cm-6x8in) col.pencil pencil double-sided (DM 13000)
£4407	$7359	(6-Jun-91 HN.H447/R) Head of a girl (33x26cm-13x10in) pen (DM 13000)
£4621	$8919	(12-Dec-90 F.M27/R) Ballerine (26x21cm-10x8in) pencil (I.L 10000000)
£4730	$8041	(31-May-91 GB.B6458/R) Two figures dancing (33x25cm-13x10in) s. col.chk (DM 14000)
£5076	$10000	(3-Oct-90 SY.NY82/R) Interieur. Frauenkopf (49x37cm-19x15in) s.d.28 i.verso pen ink wash crayon double-sided
£5159	$8460	(19-Jun-91 GK.B488) Lovers standing (44x34cm-17x13in) chl (S.FR 13000)
£5912	$10051	(1-Jun-91 VG.B162/R) Two female nudes standing (50x31cm-20x12in) s. W/C over pencil (DM 17500)
£6826	$13379	(24-Nov-90 VG.B152/R) Three figures seated (34x44cm-13x17in) chk (DM 20000)
£7000	$11270	(25-Jun-91 C230/R) Portrait eines jungen Mann (50x35cm-20x14in) s. i.verso W/C pencil
£7540	$12365	(19-Jun-91 GK.B494) Franzi squatting (42x30cm-17x12in) (S.FR 19000)
£7540	$12365	(19-Jun-91 GK.B501/R) Peasants harvesting and two cows (25x19cm-10x7in) ink pen brush wash pencil (S.FR 19000)
£7770	$13443	(21-May-91 WK.M64/R) Landscape near Dresden (26x33cm-10x13in) W/C pencil (DM 23000)
£8503	$13690	(28-Jun-91 BM.B930/R) Cat and kitten. Young girl washing (30x46cm-12x18in) i.d.1936 sepia W/C brush pencil double-sided (DM 25000)
£9524	$15619	(19-Jun-91 GK.B491/R) Two girls on rug (36x51cm-14x20in) carpenter pencil (S.FR 24000)
£10239	$20068	(24-Nov-90 VG.B153/R) Two girls beneath arched wall, Fehmarn (45x37cm-18x15in) d.1912 (DM 30000)
£10714	$17571	(19-Jun-91 GK.B489/R) Statue of August dem Starken on Neustadter Markt, Dresden (26x34cm-10x13in) s. pencil (S.FR 27000)
£10714	$17571	(19-Jun-91 GK.B498/R) Church of Frauenkirch with conversing peasants, Alpsonntag (20x52cm-8x20in) indian ink pen brush over pencil (S.FR 27000)
£10811	$18378	(1-Jun-91 VG.B145/R) Botho Graef and friend (48x38cm-19x15in) s.d.1912 i.d.verso pencil (DM 32000)
£11301	$18421	(15-Jun-91 L.K361/R) Death dance of Mary Wigmann (33x48cm-13x19in) s. col.chk (DM 33000)
£11525	$19247	(7-Jun-91 HN.H33/R) Variety dancer (14x9cm-6x4in) s.i.verso pen chk. (DM 34000)
£12048	$20241	(24-Apr-91 G.Z44/R) Mountain landscape near Davos, winter (34x50cm-13x20in) col.pencil chl (S.FR 30000)
£12717	$22000	(9-May-91 CH.NY122/R) Blumen (51x36cm-20x14in) s. W/C brush Indian ink blk.chk.
£17241	$33103	(1-Dec-90 SA.A2445/R) Bathers on Fehmarn beach (59x46cm-23x18in) col.chk (DM 50000)
£20478	$40137	(23-Nov-90 VG.B22/R) Alpine boy (50x38cm-20x15in) s.d.1919 W/C pencil board (DM 60000)
£22373	$37363	(7-Jun-91 HN.H32/R) Tap dance (21x25cm-8x10in) s. W/C pencil (DM 66000)
£23810	$39048	(21-Jun-91 GK.B53/R) View of Stafelalp with clouds beyond (35x50cm-14x20in) s.d.1920 i.d.verso W/C over carpenter pencil (S.FR 60000)
£24490	$47510	(7-Dec-90 G.Z132/R) Erna Kirchner and Anni Muller with child bathing in Stutzibach-Tobel (40x50cm-16x20in) s.d.1925 pastel (S.FR 60000)
£27027	$45946	(31-May-91 VG.B26/R) Alpine landscape. Cows in Alpine landscape (50x38cm-20x15in) W/C over pencil board double-sided (DM 80000)
£27778	$45556	(21-Jun-91 GK.B55/R) View of Lake Walensee with Unterterzen (47x37cm-19x15in) s.d.24 W/C over pencil (S.FR 70000)
£29054	$49392	(31-May-91 VG.B10/R) Im Grossen Garten, Dresden (35x45cm-14x18in) d.1907 indian ink pen (DM 86000)
£31746	$52063	(21-Jun-91 GK.B54/R) Sertigtal with view of Clavadel (34x46cm-13x18in) W/C over pencil (S.FR 80000)
£37671	$61404	(15-Jun-91 L.K359/R) Peasants before hut (38x50cm-15x20in) s. W/C pencil (DM 110000)
£40541	$68919	(31-May-91 VG.B27/R) Sertigtal (38x52cm-15x20in) W/C (DM 120000)
£43919	$74662	(31-May-91 VG.B25/R) Village in mountain landscape (35x48cm-14x19in) W/C over chk (DM 130000)
£61433	$120410	(23-Nov-90 VG.B16/R) Two female nudes (43x34cm-17x13in) col.oil chk paper on board (DM 180000)
£81911	$160546	(22-Nov-90 L.K1050/R) Female nude seated (43x33cm-17x13in) s.d.07 W/C over pencil (DM 240000)
£160000	$310400	(4-Dec-90 C151/R) Sitzender weiblicher akt (90x69cm-35x27in) st.verso pastel chl

KIRCHNER, Eugen (1865-?) German

£683	$1338	(24-Nov-90 N.M276/R) Die Sorglosen (54x61cm-21x24in) s. W/C bodycol board (DM 2000)

KIRCHNER, Otto (1887-?) German

£550	$924	(18-Jul-91 CSK173/R) Bavarian smoking pipe (23x16cm-9x6in) s.i. board
£614	$1008	(18-Jun-91 FN.S1925) Cardinal reading by candlelight in gothic interior (24x18cm-9x7in) s.i. panel (DM 1800)
£619	$1200	(8-Dec-90 W.W107/R) Old man reading newspaper (25x18cm-10x7in) s.i. board
£671	$1315	(6-Nov-90 SY.AM30) Prost (18x14cm-7x6in) s.i. panel (D.FL 2200)
£839	$1620	(13-Dec-90 N.M2753/R) Reading the newspaper by candlelight (24x17cm-9x7in) s.i. panel (DM 2400)
£949	$1699	(11-Apr-91 D.V114/R) The pipe smoker (18x14cm-7x6in) s.i. panel (A.S 20000)
£1182	$2247	(14-Sep-90 SA.A1175/R) The empty jug (23x18cm-9x7in) s.i.panel (DM 3500)

KIRCHNER, Raphael (1867-1917) Austrian

£390	$722	(7-Mar-91 D.V2/R) Two beauties (23x13cm-9x5in) s.i. pencil pen brush indian ink board (A.S 8000)
£390	$722	(7-Mar-91 D.V1/R) Ein reizender Empfang (24x14cm-9x6in) s.i. pencil pen brush indian ink board (A.S 8000)
£480	$850	(21-Mar-91 LC.P212) Le frou-frou (33x25cm-13x10in) s. W/C crayon (F.FR 4800)
£1200	$2028	(3-May-91 S268/R) A feather in her cap (40x29cm-16x11in) s.c.1920 gouache indian ink

KIRK, Maria (1860-?) American?

£647	$1100	(1-Jun-91 IH.NY51/R) Woman and boy seated in flower garden (30x20cm-12x8in) s. W/C

KIRKBY, G (19th C) ?

£676	$1149	(28-May-91 KF.M179/R) Wooded park landscape (17x27cm-7x11in) s. copper (DM 2000)

KIRKEBY, Per (1938-) Danish

£2717	$5245	(12-Dec-90 RAS.K110/R) Blue fence (122x28cm-48x11in) indist.sig.verso fragment (D.KR 30000)
£2817	$4845	(15-May-91 RAS.K164 a/R) Blue fence 1966 (122x28cm-48x11in) bears sig.verso fragment (D.KR 32000)
£5439	$9246	(29-May-91 KH.K270/R) Composition (63x50cm-25x20in) s.d.72 paper on panel (D.KR 62000)
£12329	$20096	(14-Jun-91 L.K992/R) Untitled (122x122cm-48x48in) panel punched with rows of holes (DM 36000)
£14680	$27598	(19-Sep-90 KH.K64/R) Ladies (122x122cm-48x48in) (D.KR 165000)
£26316	$44737	(28-May-91 BU.K41/R) View (200x170cm-79x67in) s.i.d.1986verso (D.KR 300000)
£27828	$54820	(14-Nov-90 KH.K81/R) Composition (208x165cm-82x65in) init.d.78 (D.KR 310000)
£1404	$2386	(28-May-91 BU.K32/R) Composition (55x41cm-22x16in) init.i.d.81 pencil W/C (D.KR 16000)

KIRKHAM, Norman (20th C) British

£1800	$3042	(17-Apr-91 CG142/R) West meets east (112x102cm-44x40in) s.

KIRKMAN, Jay (20th C) British

£958	$1600	(7-Jun-91 SY.NY224/R) The rainbow (61x91cm-24x36in) s.d.'88

KIRKPATRICK, Joseph (1872-c.1930) British

£350	$672	(20-Feb-91 CSK58/R) Ploughing team, Sussex (34x24cm-13x9in) s.i. pencil W/C
£450	$734	(13-Jun-91 CSK139/R) Fishergirl gathering nets by crofter's cottage (35x49cm-14x19in) s. pencil W/C htd white
£580	$1027	(21-Mar-91 CSK17) In Mona's Isle (33x23cm-13x9in) s. pencil W/C htd.white
£683	$1311	(26-Nov-90 SY.ME171/R) Geese in hay field (40x59cm-16x23in) s.d.1900 W/C (A.D 1700)
£720	$1404	(15-Jan-91 SWS68/R) On Sussex farm (51x35cm-20x14in) s. W/C
£750	$1463	(15-Jan-91 SWS66/R) Off to the fields (35x50cm-14x20in) s. W/C bodycol
£800	$1416	(21-Mar-91 CSK16) Among the hyacinths (23x33cm-9x13in) s. pencil W/C
£850	$1700	(8-Feb-91 C104/R) A young lady in a cottage garden at Cheriton, Hampshire (36x25cm-14x10in) s.i. W/C
£880	$1716	(15-Jan-91 SWS69/R) The horse pond (35x50cm-14x20in) s. W/C bodycol
£880	$1716	(15-Jan-91 SWS67/R) Devonshire cottage (35x50cm-14x20in) s. W/C bodycol
£900	$1755	(16-Jan-91 CSK109) Picking wild flowers in Worcester Garden (23x33cm-9x13in) s. pencil W/C htd.white
£1400	$2730	(24-Oct-90 S127/R) St Ann's Bay, Jamaica (49x73cm-19x29in) indist.s.i. W/C

KIRNER, Johann Baptist (1806-1866) German

£1748	$3374	(12-Dec-90 N.M589/R) Italian woman kneeling before wayside statue praying, night (19x26cm-7x10in) i.verso board (DM 5000)

KIRSCH, Johanna (1856-?) German

£1519	$2719	(11-Apr-91 D.V118/R) Self portrait seated at table (55x70cm-22x28in) s.i.d.1892 (A.S 32000)

KIRSCHL, Wilfried (1930-) Austrian?
£534 $876   *(20-Jun-91 D.V191/R) Entrance of house in Klikados (31x25cm-12x10in)*
                    mono.i.d.85 pastel W/C (A.S 11000)
£732 $1354   *(7-Mar-91 D.V269/R) Town (48x62cm-19x24in) s.indis.i.d.74 pastel*
                    (A.S 15000)

KISCHKA, Isis (1908-1974) French?
£632 $1100   *(27-Mar-91 B.SF4326/R) Les champs vers Saint Martin (89x16cm-35x6in) s.*
                    i.verso

KISLING, Moise (1891-1953) French
£5139 $9969   *(5-Dec-90 ZZ.F46/R) Nu (33x24cm-13x9in) s. (F.FR 50000)*
£7000 $13650   *(19-Oct-90 C175/R) Le retour des pecheurs (25x33cm-10x13in) s.d.1940*
                    panel
£9849 $16153   *(20-Jun-91 APT.P43/R) Vase a la fleur rouge (27x19cm-11x7in) s.*
                    (F.FR 98000)
£14070 $23075   *(20-Jun-91 APT.P30/R) Bouquet de fleurs (35x24cm-14x9in) s.*
                    (F.FR 140000)
£17418 $34139   *(7-Nov-90 APT.P522/R) Marseille, Aout 1918 (27x35cm-11x14in) s.d.1918*
                    (F.FR 170000)
£18018 $31171   *(22-May-91 CH.AM536/R) Esquisse en Volendam (55x38cm-22x15in) s.i.*
                    (D.FL 60000)
£22380 $42299   *(30-Sep-90 E.LA161/R) Femme nue au repos (27x41cm-11x16in) s.*
                    (F.FR 220000)
£25381 $50000   *(14-Nov-90 SY.NY420/R) Paysage (60x73cm-24x29in) s.*
£28902 $50000   *(9-May-91 CH.NY225/R) Saint-Tropez (65x80cm-26x31in) s.d.1918*
£29082 $57291   *(14-Nov-90 CN.P65/R) Portrait de femme (41x33cm-16x13in) s.*
                    (F.FR 285000)
£30151 $49447   *(21-Jun-91 OD.P14/R) Buste de jeune femme brune (41x33cm-16x13in) s.*
                    (F.FR 300000)
£32620 $62630   *(26-Nov-90 GL.P65/R) Portrait de Julien (35x27cm-14x11in) s.*
                    (F.FR 320000)
£41000 $66010   *(26-Jun-91 S175/R) L'Arlesienne (41x27cm-16x11in) s.*
£44057 $86352   *(7-Nov-90 APT.P523/R) Jeune femme brune (35x27cm-14x11in) s.*
                    (F.FR 430000)
£45000 $79650   *(19-Mar-91 C108/R) Portrait de Margueritte Gros, la Belle-Soeur de*
                    l'artiste (54x45cm-21x18in) s.d.1919
£45000 $79650   *(19-Mar-91 C111/R) Portrait de jeune fille (45x27cm-18x11in) s.*
£50000 $97000   *(4-Dec-90 C355/R) La garconne (35x27cm-14x11in) s.*
£53299 $105000   *(2-Oct-90 CH.NY167/R) Bouquet de pavots (55x38cm-22x15in) s.*
£56000 $108640   *(5-Dec-90 S203/R) Les orchidees dans un vase rose (41x33cm-16x13in) s.*
£61162 $117431   *(26-Nov-90 GL.P64/R) Femme au foulard rose (42x34cm-17x13in) s.d.1941*
                    (F.FR 600000)
£61224 $120000   *(15-Feb-91 SY.NY79/R) Tulips (55x38cm-22x15in) s.*
£75145 $130000   *(9-May-91 CH.NY241/R) Jeune garcon holandais (99x74cm-39x29in) s.*
£78680 $155000   *(15-Nov-90 CH.NY253/R) Femme nue assise (65x45cm-26x22in) s.*
£80000 $155200   *(5-Dec-90 S204/R) Buste de jeune femme nue (55x46cm-22x18in) s.*
£80925 $140000   *(8-May-91 SY.NY238/R) Tulipes (71x54cm-28x21in) s.*
£83815 $145000   *(9-May-91 CH.NY236/R) Jeune femme assise (65x50cm-26x20in) s.*
£86294 $170000   *(15-Nov-90 CH.NY263/R) Jeune fille polonaise (55x38cm-22x15in)*
                    s.i.d.1938
£88832 $175000   *(2-Oct-90 CH.NY112/R) Femme au chemisier blanc (92x65cm-36x26in) s.*
£91743 $176147   *(26-Nov-90 GL.P57/R) Le vase de lyliums (56x46cm-22x18in) s.d.1937*
                    (F.FR 900000)
£101215 $198381   *(25-Nov-90 GL.P76/R) Bouquet de fleurs (55x38cm-22x15in) s.*
                    (F.FR 1000000)
£102513 $168121   *(20-Jun-91 APT.P29/R) Portrait de femme au corsage blanc*
                    (92x65cm-36x26in) s. (F.FR 1020000)
£147208 $290000   *(14-Nov-90 SY.NY459/R) Mimosas (65x100cm-26x39in) s.*
£2094 $4000   *(2-Jan-91 GG.TA565/R) Landscape, girl by tall tree (32x24cm-13x9in)*
                    s.d.1916 pencil
£3083 $5982   *(7-Dec-90 GL.P113/R) Voiliers au port (37x28cm-15x11in) s. gouache*
                    lithograph (F.FR 30000)
£4728 $9172   *(7-Dec-90 GL.P117/R) Nature morte a la bouteille et au compotier*
                    (28x22cm-11x9in) s.d.1918 W/C (F.FR 46000)
£6500 $10465   *(25-Jun-91 C220/R) Nature morte aux bouteilles et livre*
                    (48x35cm-19x14in) s.d.1917 W/C pencil

KITAJ, R B (1932-) American
£2312 $4486   *(3-Dec-90 F.M41/R) French subject (98x64cm-39x25in) s.d.1956 mixed media*
                    collage (I.L 5000000)

KITAJIMA, Asaichi (1877-1947) Japanese
£2926 $5500   *(22-Sep-90 WOL.C35/R) In hot spring (30x41cm-12x16in) s.*

KITCHELL, Hudson Mindell (1862-1944) American
£1053 $2000   *(15-Sep-90 S.W2742/R) Autumn landscape (56x86cm-22x34in) s.*

KITCHIN, William (19th C) Canadian
£1675 $2798   *(3-Jun-91 R.T99/R) Hunt scenes - partridge shooting. Wild duck shooting.*
                    Woodcock shooting (35x51cm-14x20in) s.d.1830 ticking on panel three
                    (C.D 3200)

KITE, Joseph Milner (1862-?) British
£550 $897   *(13-Jun-91 CSK264) In garden (46x38cm-18x15in) s.*
£950 $1568   *(10-Jul-91 ZZ.B125) Minding herd (54x73cm-21x29in) s.*

KITE, Joseph Milner (1862-?) British-cont.
£3500 $6475   (7-Mar-91 C1/R) Sun and shadows (37x45cm-15x18in) s.verso s.stretcher

KITO, Akira (20th C) ?
£994 $1680   (21-Apr-91 E.LA105 b) Le feu (74x100cm-29x39in) s. d.1963 verso
      (F.FR 10000)
£1053 $1789   (28-May-91 BU.K30/R) Reve de poisson (76x102cm-30x40in) s. d.1962verso
      (D.KR 12000)
£1183 $2331   (1-Oct-90 CC.P170) Eros (97x130cm-38x51in) s. s.d.1975 verso
      (F.FR 12000)
£1972 $3886   (1-Oct-90 CC.P169) Pays natal (100x73cm-39x29in) s. d.1959 verso
      (F.FR 20000)

KITT, Ferdinand (1897-1962) Austrian
£586 $1083   (7-Mar-91 D.V202/R) *Bunch of flowers (59x46cm-23x18in) s.d.53 W/C*
      (A.S 12000)
£718 $1242   (8-May-91 D.V129/R) *Totes Gebirge near Hall (34x47cm-13x19in) s. W/C*
      gouache (A.S 15000)
£861 $1490   (8-May-91 D.V130/R) *In the Salzkammergut (36x47cm-14x19in) mono. W/C*
      gouache (A.S 18000)

KITTELSEN, Th (1857-1914) Norwegian
£2096 $3983   (11-Sep-90 UL.T234) 'Den stakkels krage' (21x27cm-8x11in) s.d.1879verso
      (N.KR 24000)
£18502 $36634   *(29-Jan-91 UL.T179/R) 'En Maalstraever, 1910' (88x60cm-35x24in) i. W/C*
      (N.KR 210000)

KITTELSEN, Theodor (1857-1914) Norwegian
£13066 $25479   (15-Oct-90 B.O55/R) Capercaillie (75x58cm-30x23in) s.d.1895
      (N.KR 150000)
£15324 $27430   (11-Mar-91 B.O70/R) Landscape from Farrisvannet, Gopledal
      (100x124cm-39x49in) s.d.89 (N.KR 175000)
£59662 $115147   (12-Dec-90 BU.O43/R) My home (69x90cm-27x35in) s.d.1898 (N.KR 670000)
£1051 $1881   (11-Mar-91 B.O72/R) The crocodile having an after dinner nap
      (23x30cm-9x12in) s. Indian ink wash (N.KR 12000)
£1138 $2038   (11-Mar-91 B.O73/R) Landscape with old woman (22x35cm-9x14in) s.d.90
      pencil Indian ink (N.KR 13000)
£1259 $2102   (4-Jun-91 BU.O79/R) From Gopledal near Farris (25x40cm-10x16in)
      s.i.d.1889 mixed media (N.KR 14500)
£1307 $2548   (15-Oct-90 B.O56/R) Armfeldt's campaign over Tydal's mountains
      (20x20cm-8x8in) s.i. pencil W/C (N.KR 15000)
£1751 $3135   (11-Mar-91 B.O71/R) Coastal landscape from Jomfruland (32x46cm-13x18in)
      s.d.12 W/C pencil (N.KR 20000)
£2003 $3907   (15-Oct-90 B.O57/R) Illustrations to Rocambole (19x12cm-7x5in) s.i.
      Indian ink three (N.KR 23000)
£9194 $16458   (14-Mar-91 BU.O65/R) Is it you who have stolen my seven silver ducks
      (42x30cm-17x12in) s.i.d.1913 mixed media paper on panel (N.KR 105000)
£10000 $17200   (17-May-91 C166/R) Alfeland (61x48cm-24x19in) s. W/C col.chk
£22767 $40753   (14-Mar-91 BU.O64/R) Is the foxwidow at home tonight (42x30cm-17x12in)
      s.d.1913 mixed media paper on panel (N.KR 260000)
£125868 $245443   (11-Oct-90 BU.O76/R) Have you sat softer, have you seen clearer, he
      asked. No, never, sheanswered (100x70cm-39x28in) s.d.1912 mixed media
      (N.KR 1450000)

KITZ, Marcin (1891-1943) Polish
£911 $1786   (26-Jan-91 PSA.W12) Shepherdess (54x66cm-21x26in) s.d.1936
      (P.Z 17000000)

KIVITS, Jos (?) ?
£1620 $2722   (16-Jul-91 JRL.S350/R) Still life with Bohemian decanter
      (49x60cm-19x24in) s. board (A.D 3500)

KJAER, Lilly (20th C) Austrian
£868 $1693   (18-Oct-90 D.V161/R) Crucifixion (60x106cm-24x42in) (A.S 18000)

KJARVAL, Johannes (1885-1972) Icelandic
£1937 $3331   (15-May-91 RAS.K105/R) Vase of flowers (58x49cm-23x19in) s. (D.KR 22000)
£6927 $13647   (31-Oct-90 KH.K69/R) Mountainous landscape, Iceland (53x73cm-21x29in) s.
      (D.KR 78000)

KJERNER, Esther (1873-1952) Swedish
£1698 $2938   (22-May-91 BA.S558/R) Evening light at Oland (40x47cm-16x19in)
      s.i.d.1925 panel (S.KR 18000)
£1746 $3423   (6-Nov-90 BA.S143/R) Road through park (36x50cm-14x20in) s. (S.KR 19000)
£2206 $4324   (6-Nov-90 BA.S142/R) Tulips in glass vase (31x29cm-12x11in) s.d.1941
      (S.KR 24000)
£2873 $5545   (12-Dec-90 BU.S36/R) Still life of flowers in vase (34x27cm-13x11in) s.
      panel (S.KR 31000)
£3172 $5330   (27-Apr-91 SO.S396/R) Still life (38x43cm-15x17in) s. (S.KR 33500)
£3193 $6291   (30-Oct-90 BU.S51/R) Still life of terrin and fruit (47x57cm-19x22in) s.
      (S.KR 35000)
£4128 $8133   (13-Nov-90 AB.S404/R) Still life of yellow roses in blue jug
      (41x33cm-16x13in) s.d.50 panel (S.KR 45000)

KLAPHECK, Konrad (1935-) German
| £30405 | $51689 | (31-May-91 VG.B75/R) Der Chefideologe (90x99cm-35x39in) s.d.1965verso i.stretcher (DM 90000) |
| £30550 | $60183 | (29-Oct-90 FB.P47/R) Familien leben (90x100cm-35x39in) s.i. verso (F.FR 300000) |

KLAPISH, Liliane (20th C) Israeli
| £429 | $700 | (12-Jun-91 GG.TA178/R) Figures (26x33cm-10x13in) s. gouache |

KLASEN, Peter (1935-?) ?
£3479	$5880	(21-Apr-91 P.V65/R) Container bleu/K91 (40x30cm-16x12in) s.i. acrylic panel (F.FR 35000)
£4016	$6466	(25-Jun-91 BG.P34/R) Manette, fond bleu G16 (80x62cm-31x24in) s.d.87 i. verso acrylic (F.FR 40000)
£4016	$6466	(25-Jun-91 BG.P33/R) Camion bache, sangle G2 35 (80x100cm-31x39in) s.d.1978 i. verso acrylic (F.FR 40000)
£5708	$11017	(16-Dec-90 P.V93/R) TLM Marseille (90cm-35ins circular) s. acrylic wooden wheel (F.FR 56000)
£6024	$9699	(25-Jun-91 BG.P32/R) Tole, bache K Y 2A (100x81cm-39x32in) s.d.1984 i. verso acrylic (F.FR 60000)
£7143	$14071	(16-Nov-90 FB.P382/R) Vide charge wt fond noir (73x60cm-29x24in) s.i.d.87 verso acrylic (F.FR 70000)
£7560	$14743	(27-Oct-90 BG.P39/R) Robinet plus visage no 4 (95x65cm-37x26in) s.i.d.1968 verso acrylic (F.FR 75000)
£10194	$19674	(16-Dec-90 GL.P132/R) Attenzione (80x120cm-31x47in) s.d.1975 i. verso acrylic board (F.FR 100000)
£10692	$21064	(29-Oct-90 FB.P95/R) Wagon SNCF detail (81x130cm-32x51in) s.i.d.1978 verso acrylic (F.FR 105000)
£11711	$23070	(29-Oct-90 FB.P89/R) Container rouge - sangle (162x114cm-64x45in) s.i.d.1983 verso acrylic (F.FR 115000)
£14358	$27998	(21-Oct-90 P.V85/R) Ampoule 100 W - Portrait (92x60cm-36x24in) s.i.d.1968 verso acrylic (F.FR 142000)
£15275	$30092	(29-Oct-90 FB.P62/R) Bain de minuit (80x80cm-31x31in) s.i.d.67 verso acrylic (F.FR 150000)
£2883	$4872	(21-Apr-91 P.V63/R) Manette, fil de fer, fond rouge/bleu (60x50cm-24x20in) s.i. acrylic collage board (F.FR 29000)
£5344	$10368	(5-Dec-90 ZZ.F109/R) Camon bache NM (62x48cm-24x19in) s. gouache (F.FR 52000)
£8595	$16759	(21-Oct-90 P.V89/R) Frein isole/fond noir RHA 108 (92x73cm-36x29in) s.i.d.1988 verso acrylic objects canvas (F.FR 85000)
£11628	$22674	(21-Oct-90 P.V86/R) Chemise - 3 seringues (130x80cm-51x31in) acrylic collage canvas (F.FR 115000)

KLAUBER, Joseph Sebastian (c.1700-1768) German
| £676 | $1149 | (31-May-91 GB.B5550/R) Allegory of the Risen Christ (17x11cm-7x4in) pen over pencil wash (DM 2000) |

KLAUKE, Jurgen (20th C) ?
| £614 | $1204 | (20-Nov-90 L.K337/R) Figure (40x26cm-16x10in) s.d.81 W/C (DM 1800) |
| £1967 | $3718 | (28-Sep-90 S.Z209/R) Untitled (41x55cm-16x22in) s.d.1988 W/C (S.FR 4800) |

KLAUS, J (19th C) ?
| £1519 | $2719 | (11-Apr-91 D.V127/R) The bird's nest (55x44cm-22x17in) s.d.897 (A.S 32000) |

KLAUS, Joseph (19th C) Belgian
| £3000 | $5910 | (5-Oct-90 C99/R) Basket of roses (56x70cm-22x28in) s. |

KLAUS, Reinhold (1881-1963) Austrian
| £633 | $1240 | (24-Jan-91 D.V182/R) Waidhofen an der Ybbs (49x38cm-19x15in) s.d.1949 col.pencil (A.S 13000) |
| £633 | $1240 | (24-Jan-91 D.V183/R) Waidhofen an der Ybbs (48x37cm-19x15in) s.i.d.1945 col.pencil (A.S 13000) |

KLEE, Hermann (1820-1894) Austrian
| £1194 | $2006 | (25-Apr-91 D.V171/R) Oak forest with cattle and bridge across stream (56x78cm-22x31in) s. W/C (A.S 25000) |

KLEE, Paul (1879-1940) Swiss
£41667	$68333	(21-Jun-91 GK.B77/R) Kampft mit sich selber (34x21cm-13x8in) s.i.d.1939 paper on board (S.FR 105000)
£100000	$194000	(3-Dec-90 C38/R) Hausertreppe (34x26cm-13x10in) s.d.1923 num.23 paper on card
£660000	$1280400	(3-Dec-90 C40/R) Die frucht (55x71cm-22x28in) burlap
£913706	$1800000	(13-Nov-90 SY.NY58 a/R) Einsame tanne (52x51cm-20x20in) oil sand board
£7143	$11714	(19-Jun-91 GK.B518/R) Diary Port Cros, view from Mt Vinaigre to Proquerolles (29x42cm-11x17in) s.i. pencil (S.FR 18000)
£9645	$19000	(15-Nov-90 CH.NY155/R) Grosser mit kleinem Volk (50x64cm-20x25in) s.i.d.1932 pen ink paper on paper
£11168	$22000	(3-Oct-90 SY.NY135 a/R) Zwei Reiter von Geistern geleitet (50x65cm-20x26in) s.i. i.d.mount pen ink paper on board
£13873	$24000	(8-May-91 SY.NY164/R) Wellenblatt (30x48cm-12x19in) s.i.d.1934 ink over pencil paper mounted on card
£16185	$28000	(9-May-91 CH.NY126/R) Zeichnung zum festlichen Prolog (27x20cm-11x8in) s.d.1922 pencil paper laid down on board

KLEE, Paul (1879-1940) Swiss-cont.

£19653	$34000	(9-May-91 CH.NY125/R) Bilder inschrift (20x14cm-8x6in) s.d.1920 Indian ink paper laid down on board
£20305	$40000	(15-Nov-90 CH.NY134/R) Glockenmaske (25x24cm-10x9in) s.d.1922 i.d.verso pen indian ink paper on board
£23105	$44593	(12-Dec-90 F.M17/R) Drei Baume (25x37cm-10x15in) s.i.d.1940 red ink (I.L 50000000)
£25888	$51000	(2-Oct-90 CH.NY84/R) Alternde Venus (42x56cm-17x22in) s.i.d.1921 pencil paper laid down on board
£27919	$55000	(14-Nov-90 SY.NY141/R) Horender (32x21cm-13x8in) s. d.1934 num R20 verso W/C over gesso
£29188	$57500	(14-Nov-90 SY.NY142/R) Die rolle (44x28cm-17x11in) s. i.d.1930 num F.2 mount W/C paper on board
£30457	$60000	(15-Nov-90 CH.NY156/R) Geist des Gewolbes (20x32cm-8x13in) s. W/C
£32995	$65000	(14-Nov-90 SY.NY183/R) Sudliche kuste (37x50cm-15x20in) s.i.d.1925 num m.9 W/C paper on board
£34518	$68000	(15-Nov-90 CH.NY158/R) Aristen Lehre (35x50cm-14x20in) s.i.d.1939 pastel paper on paper
£38776	$75224	(7-Dec-90 G.Z81/R) Schnecken-Riff (20x32cm-8x13in) s.i.d.1934 W/C (S.FR 95000)
£45000	$72450	(26-Jun-91 S242/R) Das Uebel (29x30cm-11x12in) s.i.d.1926 pen ink W/C spray technique gouache
£65990	$130000	(15-Nov-90 CH.NY159/R) Dummer Teufel (48x34cm-19x13in) s.i.d.1938 W/C paper on paper
£67460	$110635	(21-Jun-91 GK.B73/R) Waiting male (22x17cm-9x7in) s.i.d.1921 W/C over oilprint dr. on fabriano (S.FR 170000)
£79310	$152276	(26-Nov-90 WK.M39/R) Ein Gefangener wird abgefuhrt (21x29cm-8x11in) s.i.d.1939 W/C paper on board (DM 230000)
£80925	$140000	(9-May-91 CH.NY133/R) Das Haus in der Hohe (38x51cm-15x20in) s.d.1923 gouache paper mounted on paper
£85317	$139921	(21-Jun-91 GK.B74/R) Facade (28x31cm-11x12in) s.i. indian ink pen bjrush wash paper on board (S.FR 215000)
£101523	$200000	(15-Nov-90 CH.NY136/R) Landschaft im Pankenton (43x51cm-17x20in) s.i.d.1920 W/C pen ink paper on board
£109827	$190000	(8-May-91 SY.NY168/R) Chinesisch (31x17cm-12x7in) s. oil W/C board mounted on wood
£116751	$230000	(15-Nov-90 CH.NY142/R) Ouverture (33x42cm-13x17in) s.i.d.1922 W/C collage paper on board
£120000	$232800	(5-Dec-90 S340/R) Dunkelbuntes Gartenbild (11x13cm-4x5in) d.1923/1 gouache W/C
£150000	$241500	(26-Jun-91 S228/R) Kleine schwarze Tur (15x11cm-6x4in) s.i.d.1915 W/C gouache
£150000	$291000	(5-Dec-90 S341/R) Cote de Provence 5 (24x42cm-9x17in) s.i.d.1927 W/C
£154822	$305000	(15-Nov-90 CH.NY164/R) Der Gelb-Grune (49x35cm-19x14in) s.i.d.1938 pastel linen on paper
£204778	$401365	(22-Nov-90 L.K1058/R) Mystic landscape (16x24cm-6x9in) s.i.d.1917 W/C gouache (DM 600000)
£375723	$650000	(8-May-91 CH.NY24/R) Altles Liebeslied (27x35cm-11x14in) s.i.d.1924 W/C gouache pen paper laid on board

KLEE, Paul (attrib) (1879-1940) Swiss

£734	$1300	(18-Mar-91 SG.M1201) Head (41x38cm-16x15in) s.d.1922

KLEEHAAS, Theodor (1854-?) German

£1605	$2713	(19-Apr-91 FN.S1762) Children and dog in landscape (70x56cm-28x22in) s.i. canvas laid down (DM 4800)

KLEEMANN, Christian Friedrich Carl (1735-1789) ?

£1800	$3456	(18-Dec-90 C39/R) Portrait of gentleman in mauve coat with black collar and silver buttons (5x?cm-2x?in) min.s. silver frame oval

KLEIMAN, Alain (20th C) French

£3427	$6683	(28-Oct-90 R.P226/R) Memoire d'architecture (130x97cm-51x38in) s. mixed media canvas (F.FR 34000)

KLEIMER, Axel Bernhard (1881-1945) Swedish

£643	$1261	(10-Nov-90 FAL.M194/R) Petri church (48x39cm-19x15in) s.d.24 (S.KR 7000)

KLEIN VON DIEPOLD, Leo (1865-1944) German

£544	$876	(28-Jun-91 BM.B800/R) Child and goat before farmhouse (65x81cm-26x32in) s. (DM 1600)
£633	$1134	(12-Apr-91 BM.B745/R) Garden with summer flowers (65x102cm-26x40in) s. i.verso (DM 1900)

KLEIN VON DIEPOLD, Maximilian (1873-?) German

£1020	$1806	(20-Mar-91 KM.K1304) Flowering Eifel landscape with village and Nurburg beyond (60x70cm-24x28in) s. (DM 3000)

KLEIN, Bernhard (1888-?) German

£1351	$2338	(25-May-91 N.M176/R) River landscape (42x57cm-17x22in) s.d.1946 W/C (DM 4000)

KLEIN, Cesar (1876-?) German

£18707	$30119	(28-Jun-91 BM.B931/R) Harbour scene with fishing boats (50x65cm-20x26in) s.d.1912 i.verso (DM 55000)
£18919	$32162	(1-Jun-91 VG.B209/R) In the cafe (50x65cm-20x26in) s. (DM 56000)

KLEIN, Cesar (1876-?) German-cont.
£473	$804	*(28-May-91 KF.M791) Southern street (20x12cm-8x5in) i. pencil col.pencil (DM 1400)*
£541	$919	*(28-May-91 KF.M790) Cubist still life. Study of architecture (16x15cm-6x6in) gouache board double-sided (DM 1600)*
£1014	$1723	*(31-May-91 GB.B6475) Composition with three figures (19x15cm-7x6in) bodycol (DM 3000)*
£1356	$2264	*(6-Jun-91 HN.H465/R) Composition (21x27cm-8x11in) W/C ink brush (DM 4000)*

KLEIN, Friedrich Franz (1898-?) Dutch
£732	$1405	*(27-Nov-90 SY.AM3866/R) Horseman in landscape (49x71cm-19x28in) s. (D.FL 2400)*
£854	$1639	*(27-Nov-90 SY.AM3867) Figures in park (45x53cm-18x21in) s. (D.FL 2800)*
£1037	$1990	*(27-Nov-90 SY.AM3873) Teatime in the park (17x31cm-7x12in) s. panel (D.FL 3400)*
£1067	$2049	*(27-Nov-90 SY.AM3865) At the beach (72x91cm-28x36in) s. (D.FL 3500)*
£1652	$2857	*(22-May-91 CH.AM363) Crowd on terrace (19x32cm-7x13in) s. board (D.FL 5500)*
£541	$935	*(23-May-91 SY.AM26) Horses (21x26cm-8x10in) s. gouache (D.FL 1800)*
£854	$1639	*(27-Nov-90 SY.AM3874/R) Sunbathing (32x40cm-13x16in) s. pastel dr. (D.FL 2800)*

KLEIN, Frits see KLEIN, Friedrich Franz

KLEIN, Ludwig (?) German?
| £736 | $1243 | *(19-Apr-91 FN.S1763) The connoisseur, monk smoking cigar in beer cellar (28x22cm-11x9in) s.i. panel (DM 2200)* |

KLEIN, Philipp (1871-1907) German
| £3000 | $5760 | *(28-Nov-90 S223/R) Ladies in interior (28x38cm-11x15in) s.* |

KLEIN, Richard (1890-?) German
| £1014 | $1753 | *(25-May-91 N.M177/R) Four female nude bathing (63x78cm-25x31in) s.d.1923 (DM 3000)* |

KLEIN, Wilhelm (1821-1897) German
| £925 | $1600 | *(21-May-91 CE.NY15/R) Elderly peasant (18x15cm-7x6in) s. panel* |

KLEIN, Yves (1928-1962) French
£10500	$20475	*(18-Oct-90 S48/R) Receipt book for zones of immaterial pictorial sensibility (9x30cm-4x12in) i. pigment synthetic resin card printed paper*
£13000	$20930	*(27-Jun-91 C31/R) Monochrome rose (27x22cm-11x9in) s.d.1961 v. pigment synthetic resin canvasboard*
£30000	$58200	*(6-Dec-90 C547/R) ANT SU 5 (77x50cm-30x20in) pigment synthetic resin fabric*
£30000	$58200	*(6-Dec-90 C536/R) F 78 (77x53cm-30x21in) charred cardboard on board*
£120000	$232800	*(6-Dec-90 C542/R) RE 36 (40x35cm-16x14in) s.d.1961 verso pigment synthetic resin board*
£220000	$426800	*(6-Dec-90 S27/R) IKB 41 (92x73cm-36x29in) s.d.1961 verso synthetic pigment on canvas*

KLEINEH, Oskar (1846-1919) Finnish
£1291	$2182	*(20-Apr-91 HOR.H113/R) Clouds (21x30cm-8x12in) i. (F.M 9000)*
£3693	$6611	*(14-Apr-91 BU.H41/R) View in the skerries (31x23cm-12x9in) (F.M 26000)*
£4460	$8609	*(15-Dec-90 BU.H92/R) Vessel at sea (46x64cm-18x25in) s. (F.M 31000)*
£6960	$12459	*(14-Apr-91 BU.H40/R) Sailing vessels in the skerries (24x38cm-9x15in) s. (F.M 49000)*
£8883	$17499	*(17-Nov-90 BU.H60/R) Seascape with sailship (23x32cm-9x13in) s. panel (F.M 62000)*
£12950	$24993	*(15-Dec-90 BU.H91/R) Fishing trip (34x48cm-13x19in) s. (F.M 90000)*
£15692	$30756	*(24-Nov-90 HOR.H138/R) Washday in the skerries (40x61cm-16x24in) s. (F.M 110000)*
£16335	$29240	*(14-Apr-91 BU.H39/R) Sailingboats at sea (62x94cm-24x37in) s.d.1879 (F.M 115000)*
£38737	$65466	*(20-Apr-91 HOR.H112/R) Sailing off Helsingfors (43x74cm-17x29in) s. (F.M 270000)*
£77033	$150984	*(24-Nov-90 HOR.H137/R) View of Lovisa (63x94cm-25x37in) s.d.1872 (F.M 540000)*
£475	$916	*(15-Dec-90 BU.H245) Bay in the skerries (9x19cm-4x7in) s.d.73 W/C (F.M 3300)*

KLEINMANN, Alain (1953-) French
£789	$1538	*(15-Oct-90 CSC.P102) Sans titre (54x46cm-21x18in) s. (F.FR 7800)*
£791	$1416	*(14-Apr-91 GL.P128/R) Cavalier masque (81x100cm-32x39in) s. (F.FR 8000)*
£791	$1416	*(14-Apr-91 GL.P315) Trois Hassidim (92x73cm-36x29in) (F.FR 8000)*
£915	$1829	*(7-Feb-91 R.P190/R) Un souvenir (95x63cm-37x25in) s. board material (F.FR 9000)*
£1484	$2656	*(14-Apr-91 GL.P314) Le vieux rabbin (130x96cm-51x38in) (F.FR 15000)*
£2127	$3807	*(14-Apr-91 GL.P299/R) Theodor Herzl (130x195cm-51x77in) (F.FR 21500)*
£1879	$3364	*(14-Apr-91 GL.P95) Le rabbin (97x130cm-38x51in) oil collage canvas (F.FR 19000)*

KLEINSCHMIDT, Paul (1883-1949) German

£3528	$6773	(26-Nov-90 WK.M287/R) Still life with shell (47x58cm-19x23in) mono.d.1935 W/C over pencil (DM 10230)
£6419	$10912	(30-May-91 SY.BE26/R) Still life with opera glasses (61x53cm-24x21in) mono.d.31 (DM 19000)
£13469	$26535	(16-Nov-90 GK.Z5197/R) The tunnel (70x84cm-28x33in) mono.d.1929 (S.FR 33000)
£14000	$27300	(19-Oct-90 C107/R) Stilleben mit Blumen (65x50cm-26x20in) s.d.29
£14000	$27300	(19-Oct-90 C108/R) Der Kaffeetisch (65x50cm-26x20in) s.d.30
£16271	$27173	(6-Jun-91 HN.H470/R) Ballerina (120x95cm-47x37in) s.d.1938 (DM 48000)
£2365	$4091	(21-May-91 WK.M1074/R) Portrait of female (50x33cm-20x13in) mono.d.1933 W/C (DM 7000)
£3879	$7448	(26-Nov-90 WK.M288/R) Woman at toilet (78x27cm-31x11in) mono.d.1943 W/C over pencil (DM 11250)
£4730	$8182	(21-May-91 WK.M1075/R) Girl covering face (58x44cm-23x17in) mono.i.d.39 W/C (DM 14000)
£5172	$9931	(26-Nov-90 WK.M286/R) Ulmer Munster, interior (41x59cm-16x23in) mono.i.d.1928 W/C board (DM 15000)
£6997	$13713	(22-Nov-90 L.K1061/R) At the make-up table (70x36cm-28x14in) mono.d.1947 W/C indian ink brush (DM 20500)

KLEINT, Boris (1903-) German

£2305	$3849	(6-Jun-91 HN.H471/R) Composition (48x60cm-19x24in) s.d.1944 (DM 6800)

KLEINTJES, Jan (?) Dutch

£1661	$2973	(11-Apr-91 D.V120/R) Woodland stream (80x46cm-31x18in) s. (A.S 35000)

KLEITSCH, Joseph (1885-1931) American

£1531	$3000	(13-Feb-91 B.SF2108/R) Marshes near Grand River (51x41cm-20x16in) s. d.verso
£3571	$7000	(13-Feb-91 B.SF2103/R) Laguna sea cove (74x66cm-29x26in) s.
£4103	$8000	(10-Oct-90 B.SF604/R) Indian women at San Juan Capistrano (51x46cm-20x18in) s.verso

KLEMM, E (19th C) Austrian

£1351	$2635	(26-Oct-90 BM.B826/R) Young lady reading book seated in interior with antique treasures (38x59cm-15x23in) s. (DM 4000)

KLEMPNER, Ernest (1867-?) American

£1658	$3250	(7-Nov-90 D.NY41) The new novel (25x36cm-10x14in) s. board

KLENGEL, Johan Christian (attrib) (1751-1824) German

£1178	$2039	(6-May-91 ZEL.L1788/R) Wooded landscape with figures and thatched house (15x22cm-6x9in) board one of pair (DM 3500)
£1178	$2039	(6-May-91 ZEL.L1789/R) River landscape with fishermen and castle on rock (15x22cm-6x9in) board one of pair (DM 3500)

KLENZE, Leo von (1784-1864) German

£42808	$76627	(13-Mar-91 N.M552/R) Interior of monastery with monks seated at table and view of Capri (87x107cm-34x42in) mono.i.d.1855 (DM 125000)
£600	$1158	(11-Dec-90 C207) Design for a villa in classical style (28x39cm-11x15in) ink wash

KLEPINSKI, Johann (1872-?) Polish

£1622	$3081	(14-Sep-90 SA.A1317/R) Quiet day at the coast (90x120cm-35x47in) s. (DM 4800)

KLERK, Willem de (1800-1876) Dutch

£1520	$2965	(26-Oct-90 KM.K1316) Wooded landscape with faggott gatherers (39x47cm-15x19in) s. panel (DM 4500)

KLERK, Willem de (attrib) (1800-1876) Dutch

£2797	$5427	(4-Dec-90 FN.S1919/R) Hilly Dutch landscape with village and figures collecting wood (70x96cm-28x38in) s.d. panel (DM 8000)

KLETZINSKY, Franz (19 h C) ?

£1671	$3258	(11-Oct-90 D.V121/R) Traunsee lake landscape with view of Schloss Orth (25x33cm-10x13in) s.d.838 W/C (A.S 35000)

KLEVER, Julius Sergius von (1850-1924) Russian

£711	$1400	(7-Oct-90 LIT.L366 a) Wooded landscape (30x41cm-12x16in) s.
£1000	$1970	(4-Oct-90 CSK63/R) A pine forest (91x58cm-36x23in) s.d.1901
£1854	$3635	(24-Nov-90 HOR.H19/R) Returning home (39x26cm-15x10in) s. (F.M 13000)
£3013	$5092	(20-Apr-91 HOR.H20/R) Moonlit winter landscape (52x76cm-20x30in) s.d.1911 (F.M 21000)
£3151	$6082	(12-Dec-90 BU.S37/R) Early spring landscape at sunset (50x76cm-20x30in) s.d.1894 (S.KR 34000)
£3757	$6500	(23-May-91 CH.NY132/R) Winter evening, walk through the woods (88x58cm-35x23in) s.d.1911
£4591	$7759	(20-Apr-91 HOR.H18/R) Evening landscape with man in boat (78x61cm-31x24in) s.d.1904 (F.M 32000)
£5563	$10904	(24-Nov-90 HOR.H16/R) Golden domes (89x71cm-35x28in) s. (F.M 39000)
£6026	$10184	(20-Apr-91 HOR.H17/R) Wooded winter landscape with sunset (104x77cm-41x30in) s. (F.M 42000)
£6936	$12000	(23-May-91 CH.NY133/R) Winter landscape with river in wood at moonlight (148x105cm-58x41in) s.d.1880

KLEVER, Julius Sergius von (attrib) (1850-1924) Russian
£1706 $3360   (14-Nov-90 RAS.K208/R) Lady walking in park (55x36cm-22x14in) i.d.1907
                  (D.KR 19000)

KLEY, Heinrich (1863-1945) ?
£350 $678   (7-Dec-90 GB.B5903) Portrait of seated Jew praying (32x20cm-13x8in) s.
                W/C (DM 1000)

KLEYN, Leopold (19th C) Dutch
£766 $1494   (15-Oct-90 SY.J27) Dutch landscape with figures on a frozen lake
                 (23x48cm-9x19in) s. panel (SA.R 3800)

KLEYWEG, C L (?) ?
£1158 $2189   (25-Sep-90 GM.B890) Canal gele (67x84cm-26x33in) s. panel (B.FR 70000)

KLIEBER, Eduard (1803-1879) Austrian
£9247 $15072   (12-Jun-91 N.M489/R) Kaiser Franz Joseph of Austria wearing uniform
                   (80x63cm-31x25in) s.d.1851 (DM 27000)

KLIEBER, Josef (1773-1850) Austrian
£621 $1043   (25-Apr-91 D.V28/R) Skizze zur Wappenbekronung der Weilburg
                 (25x33cm-10x13in) s. indian ink pen (A.S 13000)

KLIEMANN, Carl Heinz (1924-) German
£574 $994   (21-May-91 WK.M1078/R) The milliner (89x78cm-35x31in) s. tempera board
                on panel (DM 1700)

KLIMEK, Ludwig (1912-) ?
£814 $1538   (30-Sep-90 FE.P179 a) Jeunes femmes et troubadour (50x61cm-20x24in) s.
                 (F.FR 8000)
£955 $1833   (24-Feb-91 FE.P116) Baigneuses a Juan (33x41cm-13x16in) s. (F.FR 9500)
£1028 $1994   (8-Dec-90 LT.P186) Bouquet de fleurs (46x55cm-18x22in) s. (F.FR 10000)
£1194 $2078   (31-Mar-91 FE.P202) Deux femmes au miroir (50x65cm-20x26in) s.
                  (F.FR 12000)
£1318 $2583   (27-Jan-91 FE.P180) Le martin-pecheur (65x43cm-26x17in) s. (F.FR 13100)
£1393 $2424   (31-Mar-91 FE.P203) Sur le banc (65x81cm-26x32in) s. (F.FR 14000)
£1508 $2894   (24-Feb-91 FE.P114/R) Femme en sous bois (81x65cm-32x26in) s.
                  (F.FR 15000)
£1526 $2884   (30-Sep-90 FE.P179) L'abondance (50x62cm-20x24in) s. paper laid down
                  (F.FR 15000)
£1630 $3194   (27-Jan-91 FE.P181) Les baigneuses (65x81cm-26x32in) s. (F.FR 16200)
£1860 $3125   (28-Apr-91 FE.P165) Baigneuses sous l'arbre (50x65cm-20x26in) s.d.79
                  (F.FR 18600)
£2238 $4230   (30-Sep-90 FE.P175) Les danseuses (81x54cm-32x21in) s.d.1959
                  (F.FR 22000)
£713 $1319   (10-Mar-91 LT.P180) Les trois graces (42x50cm-17x20in) s.d.1974 ink W/C
                 pastel (F.FR 7100)

KLIMSCH, Eugen (1839-1896) German
£417 $746   (12-Apr-91 AW.H654/R) Der Baumhase (20x16cm-8x6in) i. W/C indian ink pen
                over pencil (DM 1250)

KLIMT, Gustav (1862-1918) Austrian
£1429 $2343   (19-Jun-91 GK.B534) Study of hands for Justitia and Male Swearing Oath
                  (44x31cm-17x12in) chk (S.FR 3600)
£1740 $3375   (6-Dec-90 D.V19/R) Study of child sleeping. Study of child's back
                  (22x28cm-9x11in) pencil htd.white double-sided (A.S 35000)
£1746 $2863   (19-Jun-91 GK.B525) Study for portrait Serena Lederer (45x32cm-18x13in)
                  pencil (S.FR 4400)
£1984 $3254   (19-Jun-91 GK.B535) Lady standing (46x32cm-18x13in) chk (S.FR 5000)
£3254 $5337   (19-Jun-91 GK.B529) Two female nude crouching (45x30cm-18x12in) mono.
                  chk (S.FR 8200)
£3294 $5402   (19-Jun-91 GK.B524) Portrait of young woman in profile (45x32cm-18x13in)
                  pencil htd.white (S.FR 8300)
£3571 $5857   (19-Jun-91 GK.B527) Male nude standing with stick (45x31cm-18x12in)
                  mono. chk (S.FR 9000)
£3851 $6663   (21-May-91 WK.M70/R) Female nude lying with tambourin and study of
                  fingers (18x45cm-7x18in) pencil htd.white (DM 11400)
£3968 $6508   (19-Jun-91 GK.B526) Nude crouching seen from behind, study for Gold Fish
                  (45x31cm-18x12in) mono. chk (S.FR 10000)
£4960 $8135   (19-Jun-91 GK.B526) Female standing holding hand against chin
                  (44x31cm-17x12in) chk (S.FR 12500)
£5405 $9351   (25-May-91 N.M184/R) Fritza Riedler seated (45x32cm-18x13in) chl
                  (DM 16000)
£5491 $9500   (9-May-91 CH.NY117/R) Akstudie einer Tanzerin (45x31cm-18x12in) brn.chk.
£6548 $10738   (19-Jun-91 GK.B530) Lovers reclining (32x45cm-13x18in) chk (S.FR 16500)
£6746 $11063   (21-Jun-91 GK.B84/R) Female nude standing (57x37cm-22x15in) pencil
                   (S.FR 17000)
£7329 $14071   (27-Nov-90 SY.MI156/R) Figura di donna con fiore nella mano destra
                   (45x31cm-18x12in) pencil (I.L 16000000)
£7937 $13016   (19-Jun-91 GK.B523/R) Female nude standing. Unfinished study of nude
                   (57x37cm-22x15in) pencil double-sided (S.FR 20000)
£8092 $14000   (8-May-91 SY.NY152/R) Die braut - Halbakt mit angezogenen oberschenkeln
                   (57x37cm-22x15in) Nachlass st. pencil

KLIMT, Gustav (1862-1918) Austrian-cont.

£8946	$17356	(6-Dec-90 D.V29/R) Female nude seated. Female nude seated with hair hanging down (52x33cm-20x13in) blue crayon studies for Tod und Leben (A.S 180000)
£9000	$17550	(17-Oct-90 S148/R) Mit ueberschlagenen Beinen liegender Halbakt (37x57cm-15x22in) pencil
£10152	$20000	(14-Nov-90 SY.NY123/R) Studien fur bildnis Mada Primavesi (54x34cm-21x13in) pencil
£10317	$16921	(21-Jun-91 GK.B85/R) Standing female nude holding cloth against breasts (57x37cm-22x15in) pencil (S.FR 26000)
£10934	$21213	(6-Dec-90 D.V26/R) Portrait of Miss Lieser (57x37cm-22x15in) pencil (A.S 220000)
£11561	$20000	(8-May-91 SY.NY150/R) Liegender halbakt nach rechts (37x52cm-15x20in) Nachlass st. pencil
£11824	$20456	(25-May-91 N.M183/R) Fritza Riedler in frilled dress (45x31cm-18x12in) chl (DM 35000)
£11905	$19524	(21-Jun-91 GK.B83/R) Lovers. Reclining young woman sleeping (37x56cm-15x22in) s. pencil double-sided (S.FR 30000)
£12000	$23400	(19-Oct-90 C102/R) Auf Postament kauernder Halbakt (56x36cm-22x14in) st.studio pencil
£13492	$22127	(21-Jun-91 GK.B82/R) Reclining female nude with drapes (37x57cm-15x22in) s. pencil (S.FR 34000)
£13592	$22291	(20-Jun-91 D.V3/R) Woman standing (55x35cm-22x14in) pencil (A.S 280000)
£14286	$23429	(21-Jun-91 GK.B81/R) Nude girl with long hair standing (56x37cm-22x15in) pencil (S.FR 36000)
£15172	$29131	(28-Nov-90 KF.M934/R) Portrait of woman (47x32cm-19x13in) s.c.1916 pencil (DM 44000)
£16000	$25760	(26-Jun-91 S220/R) Brise fan, each stick individually decorated by Vienna Seccession (23x?cm-9x?in) s. indelible pencil one htd.blue crayon on wood
£16000	$31040	(4-Dec-90 C146/R) Mutter und tochter. Study shirt and shoes (56x37cm-22x15in) st. pencil double-sided
£16185	$28000	(9-May-91 CH.NY115/R) Unterarm unter dem Kopt. Ansatz zu Mannerakt (35x55cm-14x22in) pencil double-sided
£16500	$26565	(26-Jun-91 S221/R) Studie fur Tanzerin fur das Stoclet Fries (56x37cm-22x15in) i. pencil
£19595	$33311	(31-May-91 VG.B6/R) Nude girl with left arm behind and holding right arm (57x15cm-22x6in) pencil (DM 58000)
£20231	$35000	(8-May-91 SY.NY156/R) Liebespaar nach rechts (35x53cm-14x21in) i. pencil
£22267	$43644	(20-Nov-90 MF.P23/R) Elegante au chapeau (54x35cm-21x14in) st.sig. blk.crayon htd.col.crayon (F.FR 220000)
£28000	$49560	(20-Mar-91 S21/R) Sitzend etwas nach links mit ubereinandergelegten handen (45x30cm-18x12in) black chk

KLIMT, Gustav (attrib) (1862-1918) Austrian

| £465 | $800 | (19-May-91 LIT.L9) Old lady (51x33cm-20x13in) s. pencil |
| £480 | $850 | (18-Mar-91 SG.M1221) Portrait of a lady (20x15cm-8x6in) i. pencil htd.W/C |

KLINE, Franz (1910-1962) American

£102041	$200000	(7-Nov-90 CH.NY10/R) Painting no 3 (96x79cm-38x31in) s.verso masonite
£285714	$560000	(6-Nov-90 SY.NY14/R) Untitled (135x96cm-53x38in) s.d.55 overlap
£1005917	$1700000	(1-May-91 CH.NY20/R) West Brand (237x202cm-93x80in) s.d.60 verso
£1224000	$2400000	(7-Nov-90 CH.NY5/R) Untitled (200x262cm-79x103in) s.d.57verso
£1786	$3500	(6-Nov-90 CE.NY13/R) Untitled (19x38cm-7x15in) ink
£8876	$15000	(2-May-91 CH.NY105/R) Untitled (22x22cm-9x9in) s.d.50 chl

KLING, Wendell (20th C) American

| £765 | $1300 | (1-Jun-91 IH.NY175/R) Soldier and family (61x41cm-24x16in) s. W/C |

KLINGELHOFER, F (1832-1903) German

| £748 | $1205 | (26-Jun-91 KM.K1530/R) South Italian coastal landscape with view of castle (40x65cm-16x26in) s. (DM 2200) |

KLINGENDER, Louis Henry Weston (1861-?) British

| £1182 | $2306 | (26-Oct-90 KM.K1317) Two dogs fighting fox (60x81cm-24x32in) s.d.1903 (DM 3500) |
| £1858 | $3623 | (26-Oct-90 KM.K1318) Fox carrying rabbit to den (59x81cm-23x32in) s.d.02 (DM 5500) |

KLINGER, Max (1857-1920) German

£405	$689	(28-May-91 KF.M272) Study for Brahms Phantasie (32x43cm-13x17in) s.i.d.1893 pen pencil double-sided (DM 1200)
£407	$679	(6-Jun-91 HN.H475/R) Hinum, Herum (22x33cm-9x13in) mono.d.1899 pen (DM 1200)
£746	$1245	(6-Jun-91 HN.H476/R) Self-portrait with long nose (11x8cm-4x3in) mono.d.1912 pen (DM 2200)
£845	$1436	(28-May-91 KF.M270/R) Portrait Michele (29x20cm-11x8in) mono.i.d.1889 chk (DM 2500)
£2000	$3840	(28-Nov-90 KF.M412/R) Pyramus and Thisbe I (11x24cm-4x9in) s.d.1879 pen (DM 5800)
£2027	$3446	(28-May-91 KF.M269/R) Study for Mary mourning (48x31cm-19x12in) mono.i.d.1888 chk bodycol (DM 6000)
£3108	$5284	(28-May-91 KF.M268/R) Seated girl feeding birds (40x26cm-16x10in) s.d.1883 indian ink pen brush wash (DM 9200)

KLINGER, Max (1857-1920) German-cont.
£3322 $6444   (7-Dec-90 GB.B5916/R) Study of male nudes (50x32cm-20x13in) indian ink
*   pen htd.white double-sided (DM 9500)*
£3986 $6777   (28-May-91 KF.M271/R) Landscape near Siena (24x32cm-9x13in) s.i.d.1889
*   W/C bodycol indian ink pencil chk (DM 11800)*

KLINGSBOGL, Hermann (1874-1943) Austrian
£738 $1440   (10-Oct-90 ZEL.L1585/R) Hansel and Gretel in wooded landscape with pond
                     and witch house (58x79cm-23x31in) s.d.1910 (DM 2200)

KLINGSTEDT, Carl Gustave (1657-1734) Swedish
£612 $1206   (13-Nov-90 CH.G245) Gentleman wearing only a night cap, embracing a lady
*   in a loose gown (?x6cm-?x2in) min. vellum engraved gilt-metal frame*
*   oval (S.FR 1500)*
£880 $1452   (10-Jul-91 C67) A lady seated against a window ledge (4x?cm-2x?in) min.
*   vellum gilt-metal mount cartouche shaped*

KLINKENBERG, Johannes Christiaan Karel (1852-1924) Dutch
£500 $1000   (7-Feb-91 B.P105 d) Along city canal (25x36cm-10x14in) s. board
£2632 $5000   (27-Feb-91 SY.NY29/R) Boats on sunlit canal (32x51cm-13x20in) s.
£5455 $10745   (30-Oct-90 CH.AM19/R) Farmhouses along sandy path, with draw-well
                     (73x113cm-29x44in) s. (D.FL 18000)
£6707 $13146   (6-Nov-90 SY.AM192/R) View of canal in Utrecht, Dom in background
                     (22x27cm-9x11in) s. panel (D.FL 22000)
£15854 $31073   (6-Nov-90 SY.AM41/R) View of canal in Dordrecht (38x52cm-15x20in) s.
                     (D.FL 52000)
£21212 $41788   (30-Oct-90 CH.AM326/R) View of Gelderse Kade, Amsterdam, towards
                     Schreierstoren (39x47cm-15x19in) s. (D.FL 70000)

KLINT, Hilma af (1862-1944) Swedish
£754 $1477   (6-Nov-90 BA.S145/R) Trees by water (22x37cm-9x15in) s.d.1906
                     (S.KR 8200)

KLIPPEL, Robert (1920-) Australian
£573 $1082   (25-Sep-90 JRL.S1/R) Study for sculpture (99x99cm-39x39in) s.i.d.1989
*   fibre tipped pen (A.D 1300)*

KLIUN, Ivan (1873-1943) Russian
£1272 $2403   (30-Sep-90 E.LA56) Composition suprematiste (10x9cm-4x4in) W/C
*   (F.FR 12500)*
£4077 $7829   (28-Nov-90 CSC.P87/R) Composition (27x19cm-11x7in) mono. gouache
*   (F.FR 40000)*

KLODT VON JURGENSBURG, Michael (1832-1902) Russian
£1719 $3387   (17-Nov-90 BU.H228/R) Coastal landscape (33x56cm-13x22in) s.
                     (F.M 12000)

KLOMBEEK, Johann Bernard (1815-1893) Dutch
£9146 $17927   (6-Nov-90 SY.AM108/R) Summer landscape with figures on path
                     (30x40cm-12x16in) s. panel (D.FL 30000)

KLOMBEEK, Johann Bernard and VERBOECKHOVEN, Eugene (19th C) Dutch
£44000 $84480   (30-Nov-90 C1/R) A wooded winter landscape with figures
                     (93x128cm-37x50in) s.d.1863

KLOMP, Aelbert (1618-1688) Dutch
£2200 $3586   (5-Jul-91 C327/R) Cattle by meadow (42x35cm-17x14in) s.d. panel
£2889 $4824   (6-Jun-91 D.V261/R) Shepherds and flock in landscape (48x67cm-19x26in)
                     indis.s. panel (A.S 60000)

KLOMP, Aelbert (attrib) (1618-1685) Dutch
£719 $1214   (2-May-91 CH.AM22) Cows in a landscape (24x30cm-9x12in) init. panel
                     (D.FL 2400)
£1768 $3395   (27-Nov-90 SY.AM3468) Peasants with cattle in landscape
                     (46x66cm-18x26in) panel (D.FL 5800)

KLOSS, Friedrich Theodore (1802-1876) German
£1246 $2429   (19-Oct-90 RAS.V504/R) Landscape with bay, house and boats, Faroe
                     Islands (95x134cm-37x53in) s.d.1858 (D.KR 14000)

KLOSS, Gene (1903-) American
£4438 $7500   (1-May-91 B.SF5207/R) Kiva (81x51cm-32x20in) s.

KLOSSOWSKI, Balthasar see BALTHUS

KLOTZ, Lenz (1925-) Swiss
£3213 $6297   (24-Nov-90 AB.L145/R) Dreiteiliger Fries (62x165cm-24x65in) s.d.80 chl
                     mixed media paper on canvas (S.FR 8000)
£6122 $11633   (14-Sep-90 ZOF.Z1108/R) Message (95x75cm-37x30in) s.d.75 (S.FR 15000)
£9921 $16567   (5-Jun-91 SY.Z174/R) Vielfach verknupft (120x140cm-47x55in) s.d.64
                     (S.FR 25000)

KLOTZ-DURRENBACH, Theodor (1890-1959) Austrian
£673 $1165   (6-May-91 ZEL.L1792/R) Gladiolus in jug (88x62cm-35x24in) s.d.1942
                     (DM 2000)

KLUGE, Constantine (1912-) French
£781 $1500   (18-Dec-90 BG.M1016/R) Marche aux fleurs (56x64cm-22x25in) s.
£1156 $2000   (7-May-91 CE.NY15/R) Gondoliers a Venise (54x73cm-21x29in) s.
£1422 $2759   (4-Dec-90 R.T155/R) Boulevard de la Madeleine (61x76cm-24x30in) s.
     (C.D 3200)
£1600 $2784   (28-Mar-91 CSK74/R) Marche aux fleurs, Rue Tronchet (61x76cm-24x30in) s.
£1647 $2750   (26-Jul-91 E.EDM89/R) La Quai du Louvre (81x102cm-32x40in) s.
£1724 $3000   (27-Mar-91 B.SF4318/R) Place St Germain (61x91cm-24x36in) s.
£1923 $3750   (10-Oct-90 SY.NY79/R) La Madeleine a Paris (53x64cm-21x25in) s.
     s.i.d.1951stretcher
£2564 $5000   (10-Oct-90 SY.NY78/R) Place Beauvan (74x91cm-29x36in) s.
£3846 $7500   (10-Oct-90 SY.NY99/R) Marche aux fleurs de la Madelaine
     (114x163cm-45x64in) s.

KLUMB, Andre (1925-) French
£552 $889   (24-Jun-91 PR.P156) Les anemones (61x46cm-24x18in) s. (F.FR 5500)
£1224 $2412   (12-Nov-90 YC.P60/R) Paysage vert (81x65cm-32x26in) s. i.d.88 verso
     (F.FR 12000)

KLUMPKE, Anna (1856-1942) American
£1479 $2500   (20-Apr-91 WOL.C41 a/R) Peasant girl knitting in landscape
     (140x175cm-55x69in) s.d.1887
£751   *$1300*   *(21-May-91 GRO.B113/R) Bastille Day, Observation Square, Paris
     (13x18cm-5x7in) i. pastel*

KLUYVER, Pieter Lodewijk Francisco (1816-1900) Dutch
£1138 $1911   (23-Apr-91 SY.AM302/R) Polder landscape with woman on path
     (17x30cm-7x12in) s. panel (D.FL 3800)
£1152 $2268   (30-Oct-90 CH.AM7) Extensive river landscape with traveller on path,
     windmill beyond (33x46cm-13x18in) (D.FL 3800)
£1585 $3107   (6-Nov-90 SY.AM73) Cottage in woods (39x32cm-15x13in) s. panel
     (D.FL 5200)
£2378 $4661   (6-Nov-90 SY.AM183/R) Houses by frozen canal (28x44cm-11x17in) s. panel
     (D.FL 7800)
£2800 $5012   (12-Mar-91 PH8/R) Wooded landscape with town beyond (64x78cm-25x31in)
     s.d.46
£4600 $7544   (18-Jun-91 PH30/R) Windmill on the banks of estuary, summer
     (39x57cm-15x22in) s.

KLYSNER, J (19th C) Danish?
£2867   *$5735*   *(6-Feb-91 RAS.K545/R) Ships portrait 'Gudenaae of Randers'
     (43x62cm-17x24in) s.i.d.1854 pen W/C (D.KR 32000)*

KMIT, Michael (1910-) Russian
£1111 $1867   (16-Jul-91 JRL.S289) The pianist, Camille Gheysens (99x79cm-39x31in)
     s.d.68 (A.D 2400)
£698   *$1172*   *(22-Apr-91 SY.ME48) Cathedral window (59x49cm-23x19in) s. oil enamel
     board (A.D 1500)*

KNAB, Ferdinand (1834-1902) German
£4365 $7290   (7-Jun-91 ZOF.Z1096) View of Roman temple, evening (95x122cm-37x48in)
     s.d.1881 (S.FR 11000)

KNAPP, Charles W (1822-1900) American
£1104 $1800   (13-Jun-91 FA.PH224) Sailboats along coast (23x41cm-9x16in) s.
£1161 $1950   (21-Jul-91 LIT.L157) Cows along the river (51x91cm-20x36in) s.
£2486 $4600   (10-Mar-91 H.C100/R) Landscape with cattle near river (76x91cm-30x36in)
     s.
£3931 $6800   (12-May-91 H.C107 a/R) Landscape with homestead near stream
     (61x107cm-24x42in) s.

KNAPP, F Oskar (1914-) German
£673 $1165   (6-May-91 ZEL.L1793/R) Flowers in vase (40x30cm-16x12in) s. copper
     (DM 2000)

KNAPPING, H (?) British
£400   *$668*   *(7-Jun-91 BW59) Cornish coastal scene with fishermen unloading the days
     catch (23x33cm-9x13in) s. W/C*

KNAPTON, George (attrib) (1698-1778) British
£32000 $63040   (16-Nov-90 C9/R) Portrait of Master Drummond holding tricorn hat on
     horse in landscape (239x147cm-94x58in)

KNAPTON, George (circle) (1698-1778) British
£1800 $2934   (4-Jul-91 B42/R) Portrait of a huntsman, three quarter length, wearing a
     red coat (117x94cm-46x37in)

KNATHS, Karl (1891-1971) American
£936 $1750   (30-Aug-90 MFA.C195/R) Folk singer (107x76cm-42x30in) s.
£1925 $3600   (30-Aug-90 MFA.C196/R) Cattle (91x107cm-36x42in) s.
£842   *$1600*   *(14-Sep-90 S.BM284/R) Eeling (41x43cm-16x17in) s.d.1955 pastel*

KNAUPP, Werner (1936-) German
£981 $1884   (26-Nov-90 WK.M774/R) Volcano (50x68cm-20x27in) s.i.d.1970verso ball
     point pen canvas on board (DM 2845)

KNAUPP, Werner (1936-) German-cont.
£1370 $2233   (14-Jun-91 L.K998/R) Windhose (155x120cm-61x47in) s.i.d.1974 ball point
                                  pen canvas on panel (DM 4000)

KNAUS, Ludwig (1829-1910) German
£554 $1107   (6-Feb-91 N.M640) Inn interior (24x39cm-9x15in) st.sig. (DM 1600)
£1142 $2284   (6-Feb-91 N.M641/R) Tyrolean peasant (36x23cm-14x9in) st.sig. canvas on
                                    board (DM 3300)
£2780 $5366   (12-Dec-90 BU.S38/R) Musical moment (26x20cm-10x8in) s.d.1866
                                    (S.KR 30000)
£8784 $16689   (14-Sep-90 SA.A1222/R) Hessian peasant boy standing model for painter
                                    (43x35cm-17x14in) s. (DM 26000)
£507 $861   (28-May-91 KF.M186) An unwelcome customer (16x21cm-6x8in) s.i. pen board
                                    (DM 1500)
£1081 $1838   (28-May-91 KF.M185/R) Family in kitchen interior (16x21cm-6x8in) s. pen
                                    W/C (DM 3200)

KNEBEL, Franz (jnr) (1809-1877) Swiss
£11053 $21000   (27-Feb-91 SY.NY185/R) Tivoli (76x99cm-30x39in) s.d.1857

KNELL, Adolphus (19th C) British
£680 $1278   (8-Aug-90 PHP161/R) Extensive shipping off coastline (13x30cm-5x12in) s.
                                    panel
£700 $1365   (18-Oct-90 CSK123/R) Busy shipping lane (35x46cm-14x18in) s. board
£1100 $2112   (26-Nov-90 SWS138/R) Estuary scene at sunset (20x30cm-8x12in) s. board
£1400 $2422   (22-May-91 S49/R) On home voyage. On sands after storm (23x33cm-9x13in)
                                    s. i.stretcher one d.1882 pair
£1700 $3281   (10-Dec-90 PHB61) The fishing fleet (30x61cm-12x24in) . board pair
£1800 $3348   (5-Sep-90 BT160/R) Off old harbour, Ramsgate. Shipping in swell
                                    (28x43cm-11x17in) s. one i.verso board pair

KNELL, Adolphus (attrib) (19/20th C) British
£650 $1268   (18-Oct-90 CSK142/R) An old hulk on the Medway (20x38cm-8x15in) bears
                                    i.verso

KNELL, W A (1805-1875) British
£1542 $2991   (6-Dec-90 CB.P99/R) Fregate (25x48cm-10x19in) s. W/C (F.FR 15000)

KNELL, William Adolphus (1805-1875) British
£2070 $3872   (27-Aug-90 SY.J168/R) Shipping in choppy sea (61x89cm-24x35in) s. canvas
                                    laid down on board (SA.R 10000)
£700 $1155   (9-Jul-91 C138/R) The Dart off Madeira (29x46cm-11x18in) s.i. pencil W/C
                                    htd.white

KNELL, William Callcott (19th C) British
£700 $1365   (17-Oct-90 PHG47/R) Shipping in rough seas (30x50cm-12x20in) s.
£700 $1372   (8-Nov-90 TL28/R) Shipping in calm (11x31cm-4x12in)
£800 $1568   (13-Feb-91 PHL130) Shipping in stiff breeze off Whitby (31x56cm-12x22in)
                                    s.
£1500 $2850   (10-Jan-91 B121) Dutch fishing boat going to wreck (20x41cm-8x16in)
                                    s.d.1875 s.i.d.verso pair
£1600 $3072   (29-Nov-90 B50/R) Coromry crossing wreck off the South Foreland
                                    (50x90cm-20x35in) s.d.67
£3600 $6084   (1-May-91 PHL101/R) Evening- battleships in Medway (46x91cm-18x36in) s.
£420 $714   (30-May-91 C30) In channel (23x44cm-9x17in) s.d.1885 i.verso pencil W/C
                                    htd white

KNELLER, Sir Godfrey (1646-1723) British
£816 $1600   (6-Nov-90 GF.L2341/R) Portrait of young woman (73x62cm-29x24in)
                                    (S.FR 2000)
£1800 $3546   (31-Oct-90 S267/R) Portrait of John Mundy (75x62cm-30x24in) mono.
£3800 $7486   (14-Nov-90 S32) Portrait of Elizabeth Skipwith Lady Craven seated in
                                    landscape (124x99cm-49x39in) i.d.1704
£5000 $8950   (12-Apr-91 C7/R) Portrait of Lady Henrietta Crofts, Duchess of Bolton,
                                    seated holding basket of flowers (127x102cm-50x40in) s.i.
£5500 $10725   (26-Oct-90 C200/R) Portrait of Alexander Pope, the poet
                                    (76x63cm-30x25in) feigned stone oval
£6500 $10985   (30-Apr-91 PH36/R) Portrait of Sarah Churchill, Duchess of Marlborough,
                                    before landscape (127x101cm-50x40in) s.d.1702
£11000 $21670   (14-Nov-90 S31/R) Portrait of William Anne Keppel with sister Lady
                                    Sophia on terrace (254x178cm-100x70in) s.
£12000 $21480   (12-Apr-91 C6/R) Portrait of Elizabeth, Viscountess Townshend, leaning
                                    against plinth (241x148cm-95x58in) init.i.
£13000 $25610   (14-Nov-90 S26/R) Portrait of Colonel Daniel Parke standing wering
                                    armour with baton (124x100cm-49x39in)
£1000 $1790   (9-Apr-91 C42/R) Portrait of gentleman (42x29cm-17x11in) chk

KNELLER, Sir Godfrey (after) (1646-1723) British
£800 $1368   (30-Jul-91 SWS265/R) Portrait of Alexander Pope, head and shoulders
                                    (75x62cm-30x24in)
£1800 $3510   (16-Oct-90 CG222/R) Portrait of King George I in court robes
                                    (127x102cm-50x40in)

KNELLER, Sir Godfrey (attrib) (1646-1723) British
£1351 $2203   (10-Jun-91 W.T1332) A Royal Prince in armour (115x84cm-45x33in)
                                    (C.D 2500)

KNELLER, Sir Godfrey (attrib) (1646-1723) British-cont.
£1700	$3043	(10-Apr-91 S113/R) Portrait of cleric, wearing tunic and holding book (122x97cm-48x38in) i.
£1744	$3000	(15-May-91 D.NY56/R) Portrait of gentleman (97x79cm-38x31in) canvas on panel oval
£2182	$4277	(19-Nov-90 CH.R129/R) Ritratto di dama all'aperto mentre coglie una rosa (126x102cm-50x40in) (I.L 4800000)
£3147	$6073	(10-Dec-90 L.K66/R) Portrait of Tsar Peter the Great of Russia wearing ermine coat (73x60cm-29x24in) canvas laid down (DM 9000)

KNELLER, Sir Godfrey (circle) (1646-1723) British
£1100	$2167	(31-Oct-90 S276/R) Portrait of gentleman wearing robes and full bottomed wig (68x57cm-27x22in) painted oval
£1300	$2145	(12-Jul-91 C150/R) Portrait of gentleman, identified as Sir Christopher Wren, by table (124x99cm-49x39in) i.
£1300	$2548	(20-Nov-90 PH147/R) Portrait of Sir Thomas Fytche, half length, wearing armour (76x63cm-30x25in)
£1400	$2310	(9-Jul-91 PH35) Portrait of nobleman, standing, wearing robes and holding coronet (212x120cm-83x47in)
£1400	$2800	(7-Feb-91 CSK158/R) Portrait of young boy, standing in robe, in landscape (128x103cm-50x41in)
£1786	$3000	(17-Jul-91 SY.NY183/R) Portrait of a lady, said to be Lady Grant (124x100cm-49x39in)
£2200	$4290	(26-Oct-90 C220/R) Portrait of Margaret Woodgate holding flowers, by a column in an interior (127x102cm-50x40in)
£3200	$6240	(26-Oct-90 C217/R) Portrait of Margaret Woodgate, full length in a green dress with a parrot (127x102cm-50x40in)
£4200	$8190	(26-Oct-90 C215/R) Portrait of Mary Bentinck, Countess of Essex, a landscape beyond (127x101cm-50x40in) sig.M.Dahl i.

KNELLER, Sir Godfrey (school) (1646-1723) British
| £3500 | $5775 | (12-Jul-91 C149/R) Portrait of Lionel Cranfield Sackville, 1st Duke of Dorset (127x101cm-50x40in) |

KNELLER, Sir Godfrey (studio) (1646-1723) British
£1300	$2470	(1-Mar-91 C40/R) Portrait of gentleman thought to be King George I as Kurprinz of Hanover (82x65cm-32x26in) c.1685 i.stretcher painted oval
£1300	$2119	(13-Jun-91 CSK172/R) Portrait of nobleman, thought to be King George I as Kurprinz of Hanover (82x65cm-32x26in) c.1685 painted oval
£1900	$3401	(10-Apr-91 S112/R) Portrait of Miss Betenson (72x61cm-28x24in) i.
£2200	$3630	(10-Jul-91 S112/R) Portrait of gentleman (74x61cm-29x24in) oval
£3000	$5370	(10-Apr-91 S107/R) Portrait of Henry Somerset, 3rd Marquess of Worcester and 1st Duke of Beaufort (218x135cm-86x53in)
£4500	$8055	(10-Apr-91 S70/R) Portrait of gentleman, standing in landscape (124x99cm-49x39in)
£5000	$9850	(13-Nov-90 PH97/R) Portrait of John Deade leaning against stone parapet. His wife Delicia (127x101cm-50x40in) pair

KNELLER, Sir Godfrey (style) (1646-1723) British
£820	$1468	(10-Apr-91 CSK187) Portrait of Prince Charles Edward Stuart as boy wearing wrap (196x160cm-77x63in) in painted cartouche
£850	$1386	(4-Jul-91 CSK59) Infancy of Christ (61x61cm-24x24in) panel
£917	$1807	(13-Nov-90 CH.AM42) Portrait of young lady, said to be Elisabeth Garrett, seated on terrace (120x95cm-47x37in) with sig. (D.FL 3000)
£920	$1592	(20-May-91 SWS255/R) Portrait of a young man, half length wearing a blue coat and wig (76x63cm-30x25in) oval
£1300	$2548	(20-Nov-90 PH146) Portrait of Mary, daughter of Thomas Rowe, of Endellion, Cornwall (76x63cm-30x25in) i. label verso oval
£1300	$2535	(25-Oct-90 B81/R) Portrait of boy wearing velvet coat (74x63cm-29x25in)
£1500	$2685	(12-Apr-91 C119/R) Portrait of Mrs. Richard Guinness, in dress and wrap (74x62cm-29x24in) painted oval
£1700	$3315	(18-Oct-90 SC3157/R) Portrait of a lady (75x63cm-30x25in) oval

KNIE, Rolf (jnr) (1949-) Swiss
| £1265 | $2150 | (30-May-91 EA.Z224/R) Amina (120x89cm-47x35in) s.d.90 acrylic mirro collage (S.FR 3200) |

KNIEP, Christoph Heinrich (1755-1825) German
| *£1216* | *$2068* | (31-May-91 GB.B5551/R) Two women resting in mountainous lake landscape (17x22cm-7x9in) s.d.1824 (DM 3600) |

KNIGHT, A Roland (19th C) British
| £2600 | $5070 | (17-Oct-90 PHL269/R) A leaping salmon with a fly in his mouth (36x46cm-14x18in) s. |
| £3000 | $5850 | (17-Oct-90 PHL335/R) A brown trout being landed (41x61cm-16x24in) s. |

KNIGHT, Charles (19/20th C) British
| £2400 | $4608 | (26-Nov-90 SWS155/R) The morning milk (59x48cm-23x19in) s. i.verso |
| *£800* | *$1376* | (14-May-91 SWS153/R) Evening shadows, Ditchling Beacon (24x35cm-9x14in) s.d.35 i.verso W/C over pencil |

KNIGHT, Charles Parsons (1829-1897) British
| £1700 | $3145 | (4-Mar-91 PHB55/R) Shipping off headland (66x113cm-26x44in) s. |

KNIGHT, Dame Laura (1877-1970) British
| £7200 | $14112 | (8-Nov-90 C4/R) Taking a call (60x51cm-24x20in) s.d.1922 |

KNIGHT, Dame Laura (1877-1970) British cont.

£8000	$15520	(6-Dec-90 CG45/R) Stack building, Malvern Hills (61x91cm-24x36in) s.
£13500	$22545	(6-Jun-91 C10/R) Cottage interior (29x34cm-11x13in) s. i.verso
£380	$661	(28-Mar-91 CSK8) Two gypsy dancers, Olympia (35x26cm-14x10in) s.i. black crayon
£380	$661	(28-Mar-91 CSK9) Dress rehearsal, Bethlehem (35x25cm-14x10in) s.i. black crayon
£400	$696	(28-Mar-91 CSK2) Cossac Art, Olympia (26x35cm-10x14in) s.i black crayon
£450	$783	(28-Mar-91 CSK16) Ring Blackfriars (35x25cm-14x10in) s.i. black crayon
£450	$779	(7-May-91 PH39) The ruins of Coventry Cathedral (44x56cm-17x22in) chl col.chk
£480	$835	(28-Mar-91 CSK13/R) At ringside, Blackfriars (26x35cm-10x14in) black crayon
£550	$957	(28-Mar-91 CSK1/R) Head study of Betty Renwick (24x17cm-9x7in) pencil
£620	$1079	(28-Mar-91 CSK7) Two circus figures on horseback (27x36cm-11x14in) s. black crayon pair
£700	$1183	(2-May-91 C13/R) Chinese acrobat (36x26cm-14x10in) init.i.d.1933 black crayon
£750	$1418	(27-Sep-90 CG1/R) Pavlova (23x56cm-9x22in) init.i. pencil
£750	$1230	(19-Jun-91 AH249) A quiet road (23x18cm-9x7in) W/C
£750	$1470	(25-Jan-91 C8/R) Circus scene. Diagaleu Ballet (34x22cm-13x9in) s. chl pencil double-sided
£750	$1455	(6-Dec-90 CSK2) Mr. and Mrs. Whimsical Walker and Buffer (37x27cm-15x11in) s.i.d.1923 black crayon
£900	$1746	(6-Dec-90 CSK1/R) Seated clown (27x20cm-11x8in) init. chl
£900	$1692	(20-Sep-90 C21/R) Orchestra (37x27cm-15x11in) s.i. black crayon
£900	$1692	(18-Sep-90 PH100) Two boxers (37x27cm-15x11in) s. black chk
£900	$1746	(6-Dec-90 CSK25/R) Circus horse waiting to go into ring (35x25cm-14x10in) chl
£1000	$1880	(18-Sep-90 PH80/R) Joe Craston (37x27cm-15x11in) s.i. black chk
£1200	$2256	(18-Sep-90 PH92/R) Aerial act (26x29cm-10x11in) s.d.1943 black chk
£1200	$2256	(18-Sep-90 PH84/R) One of Bionets (35x25cm-14x10in) s. black chk
£1400	$2632	(18-Sep-90 PH75) Hans (35x25cm-14x10in) s.i. black chk
£1500	$2955	(13-Nov-90 SWS153/R) Fastening her dress, Regent Theatre (35x25cm-14x10in) s. W/C over blk.chk.
£1800	$3384	(18-Sep-90 PH88/R) Whimsical's last year at Olympia (37x27cm-15x11in) s.i. black chk
£1850	$3645	(13-Nov-90 SWS168/R) Swans (68x61cm-27x24in) init.d.1967 W/C linen
£3000	$5640	(20-Sep-90 CSK98/R) Strawberry roan in landscape (54x76cm-21x30in) s. W/C
£5500	$9185	(6-Jun-91 C16/R) Clowns resting (51x36cm-20x14in) s.d.1956 pencil crayon W/C

KNIGHT, Daniel Ridgway (1839-1924) American

£11561	$20000	(23-May-91 SY.NY42/R) Gardening by river (55x46cm-22x18in) s.i.
£15642	$28000	(12-Apr-91 SY.NY51/R) Washing day (53x66cm-21x26in) s.i.
£19487	$38000	(24-Oct-90 CH.NY75/R) The sewing circle (94x120cm-37x47in) s.i.
£1734	$3000	(10-May-91 S.BM34/R) Faraway thoughts, maiden seated in garden (38x25cm-15x10in) s.i. W/C gouache
£2312	$4000	(22-May-91 CH.NY115/R) Moment for love (35x28cm-14x11in) s.d.1878 W/C gouache paper on board

KNIGHT, Harold (1878-1961) British

£900	$1593	(19-Mar-91 SHER234/R) Devon landscape - thatched cottages and buildings in sunlit landscape (41x51cm-16x20in) s.i.verso canvas on board
£2000	$3480	(27-Mar-91 S21/R) Meditation (46x46cm-18x18in) s. i.verso
£72000	$141120	(8-Nov-90 C23/R) Afternoon tea (193x152cm-76x60in) s.

KNIGHT, J (19th C) British?

| £800 | $1352 | (30-Apr-91 HS25) On Welsh coast (30x46cm-12x18in) s. panel |

KNIGHT, John Buxton (1843-1908) British

£750	$1470	(13-Feb-91 S133) Evening round (29x41cm-11x16in) s.
£1200	$2016	(24-Apr-91 CSK194) March Mill (80x127cm-31x50in) s.i.verso
£1400	$2716	(6-Dec-90 CSK69/R) House in river landscape with horses, ducks and cows (102x152cm-40x60in) s.d.99
£450	$734	(11-Jun-91 ZZ.B373) Near Seaford, Sussex (34x49cm-13x19in) s. W/C
£530	$864	(11-Jun-91 ZZ.B375) Losing the scent (33x49cm-13x19in) s. col.chks.
£600	$1182	(1-Nov-90 D1/R) Busy street scene (33x25cm-13x10in) s. W/C bodycol

KNIGHT, John Prescott (1803-1881) British

| £575 | $1000 | (27-Mar-91 B.SF4232/R) Master John (112x79cm-44x31in) mono. i.verso |

KNIGHT, Joseph (1837-1909) British

| £2500 | $4900 | (13-Feb-91 S141/R) October day (84x103cm-33x41in) s.d.1885 i.stretcher |
| £490 | $931 | (1-Mar-91 BW434/R) Landscape with shepherd and sheep (43x61cm-17x24in) s. W/C |

KNIGHT, Ken (20th C) Australian

£513	$908	(18-Mar-91 MGS.S256) North Head, Sydney Harbour (17x41cm-7x16in) s. (A.D 1200)
£1351	$2662	(13-Nov-90 J.M111) Sydney Harbour (68x122cm-27x48in) s. board (A.D 3500)
£1810	$3059	(16-Apr-91 J.M179/R) Sydney Harbour from Seaforth (66x121cm-26x48in) s. board (A.D 4000)

KNIGHT, Louis Aston (1873-1948) British

£578	$1000	(12-May-91 H.C122/R) The covered bridge (25x36cm-10x14in) s.i. i.verso board
£640	$1100	(15-May-91 SY.NY62/R) River landscape (55x46cm-22x18in) s.i. board
£1020	$2000	(7-Nov-90 B.SF1175/R) Evening light on Seine (66x152cm-26x60in) s.i.
£1510	$2930	(8-Dec-90 GAB.G2695) Bord de riviere (46x55cm-18x22in) s.i. (S.FR 3700)
£1633	$3167	(8-Dec-90 GAB.G2696/R) Champs fleuri au bord de la riviere (46x55cm-18x22in) s.i. (S.FR 4000)
£2105	$4000	(28-Feb-91 CH.NY42/R) The old dam below our mill (67x83cm-26x33in) s.
£3931	$6800	(12-May-91 H.C123) Grey day at Moret (66x81cm-26x32in) s.i.
£4624	$8000	(21-May-91 CE.NY295/R) Evening light, La Riviere Thibouville (56x46cm-22x18in) s. i.stretcher
£4749	$8500	(14-Mar-91 CH.NY73/R) In valley (65x80cm-26x31in) s.i.
£5181	$10000	(10-Dec-90 H.C1066/R) Cottages near flowering riverbank (66x81cm-26x32in) s.i.
£6395	$11000	(15-May-91 SY.NY92/R) Au bord de la riviere (65x81cm-26x32in) s.i.
£7514	$13000	(23-May-91 CH.NY21/R) French river landscape with cottage (81x66cm-32x26in) s.i.
£1173	*$2300*	*(16-Feb-91 W.W111/R) Summer stream (46x53cm-18x21in) s.i. W/C gouache chl paper on canvas*

KNIGHT, William Henry (19th C) British

£800	*$1536*	*(26-Nov-90 SWS93/R) Saturday night (22x28cm-9x11in) bears i.d.1861 W/C*

KNIGHTON-HAMMOND, Arthur Henry see HAMMOND, Arthur Henry Knighton

KNIKKER, Aris (1887-1962) Dutch

£539	$905	(23-Apr-91 SY.AM247) Farmer's wife in boat (58x98cm-23x39in) s. (D.FL 1800)
£1078	$1875	(26-Mar-91 VN.R45/R) Peat cutters in marshy landscape (37x65cm-15x26in) s. (D.FL 3600)
£1141	$2225	(10-Oct-90 ZEL.L1586/R) River landscape with windmill, autumn evning (22x45cm-9x18in) s. (DM 3400)
£1220	$2257	(7-Mar-91 D.V45/R) River landscape (50x80cm-20x31in) s. (A.S 25000)

KNIKKER, Jan (jnr) (1911-) Dutch

£1081	$1934	(16-Mar-91 KV.L172/R) Duck with young (50x40cm-20x16in) s. (B.FR 65000)

KNIKKER, Jan (snr) (1889-1957) Dutch

£606	$994	(18-Jun-91 VN.R148/R) Fishermen in a boat near windmill in polder landscape (50x80cm-20x31in) s. (D.FL 2000)
£808	$1398	(6-May-91 ZEL.L1794/R) River landscape with windmill, spring (21x30cm-8x12in) s. panel (DM 2400)
£962	$1896	(6-Oct-90 KV.L160/R) Anglers in Dutch river landscape (30x40cm-12x16in) s. (B.FR 60000)

KNIP, A (1819-1852) Dutch

£1700	$2856	(18-Jul-91 CSK103/R) Ducks at pond with deer beyond in ornamental garden (74x58cm-29x23in) s. painted arched top

KNIP, August (1819-?) Dutch

£749	$1250	(7-Jun-91 SY.NY170/R) The day's catch (75x58cm-30x23in) s.
£2703	$4568	(3-May-91 SA.A1699/R) Peaceful evening (56x74cm-22x29in) mono.d.1834 (DM 8000)

KNIP, H (fl.1840) Continental

£7500	$12600	(16-Jul-91 C102/R) The poacher, larder still life with cat and dead song birds and game (71x91cm-28x36in) s.

KNIP, Henri (1819-1897) Dutch

£1515	$2985	(30-Oct-91 CH.AM5/R) Shepherd and flock on rocky path in wooded mountainous landscape (160x120cm-63x47in) s. (D.FL 5000)
£667	*$1313*	*(30-Oct-90 CH.AM215/R) View of castle (72x94cm-28x37in) s. W/C gouache painted oval (D.FL 2200)*
£1970	*$3880*	*(30-Oct-90 CH.AM214/R) Views of castle at Gemert, from west and east (72x94cm-28x37in) s.d.1872 i.verso W/C gouache painted ovals pair (D.FL 6500)*

KNIP, Josephus Augustus (1777-1847) Dutch

£2752	*$5422*	*(12-Nov-90 CH.AM220/R) Castle of La Sarraz near Montrocher in Canton of Vaud, Switzerland (52x76cm-20x30in) s. pencil W/C bodycol ink (D.FL 9000)*

KNIP, Josephus Augustus (attrib) (1777-1847) Dutch

£896	*$1792*	*(6-Feb-91 RAS.K191) Chickens against woodpecker (39x30cm-15x12in) i. (D.KR 10000)*
£896	*$1792*	*(6-Feb-91 RAS.K192/R) Heather landscape with hills and lake (37x69cm-15x27in) s.d.91 (D.KR 10000)*

KNIP, Willem (1883-1967) Dutch

£536	$1029	(27-Nov-90 W.T1173/R) Barge on Amsterdam Canal (39x49cm-15x19in) s. (C.D 1200)
£667	$1313	(30-Oct-90 CH.AM323) Country road, Vierhouten (26x48cm-10x19in) s. s.i.verso (D.FL 2200)
£816	$1445	(20-Mar-91 KM.K1308) Dutch canal with fishing boats before customs tower (61x81cm-24x32in) s. (DM 2400)

KNIP, Willem (1883-1967) Dutch-cont.
£925 $1600   (12-May-91 H.C48) Canal scene (51x79cm-20x31in) s.

KNIRR, Erwin (1894-?) German
£671 $1309   (10-Oct-90 WE.MU298/R) Still life of flowers with fruit bowl
       (46x39cm-18x15in) s.d.1924 (DM 2000)

KNITTEL, Anna see STAINER-KNITTEL, Anna

KNOBLOCH, Josef Rolf (1891-) German
£699 $1350   (12-Dec-90 WE.MU169/R) Moor landscape (86x92cm-34x36in) s.i. (DM 2000)

KNOEBEL, Imi (1940-) German
£8876 $15000   (2-May-91 CH.NY295/R) Untitled (108x127cm-43x50in) s.d.85 verso acrylic
       shaped wood
£20710 $35000   (2-May-91 CH.NY232/R) Untitled (249x169cm-98x67in) s.d.88 verso acrylic
       wood
£548   *$893*   *(14-Jun-91 L.K999) Untitled s.d.83 brush col.gloss paint (DM 1600)*
£683   *$1338*   *(20-Nov-90 L.K339) Untitled (29x21cm-11x8in) mono.d.1983verso mixed
       media holey paper (DM 2000)*

KNOEBEL, Robert (1874-1924) Czechoslovakian
£1297 $2451   (25-Sep-90 FN.S2244/R) Susannah and the Elders (80x66cm-31x26in) s.
       (DM 3800)

KNOLLER, Martin (circle) (1725-1804) Austrian
£1224 $2412   (14-Nov-90 D.V337/R) Intombment of Christ (80x52cm-31x20in) (A.S 25000)

KNOOP, August (1856-?) German
£514 $920   (14-Mar-91 N.M2689) Cardinal with two assistants in study
       (31x40cm-12x16in) s. i.verso board (DM 1500)
£777 $1321   (31-May-91 GB.B5859) Two art connoisseurs (18x14cm-7x6in) s. panel
       (DM 2300)
£1007 $1963   (10-Oct-90 ZEL.L1589/R) Chess players in salon interior with gentlemen
       watching (30x41cm-12x16in) s. board (DM 3000)
£1092 $1791   (18-Jun-91 FN.S1931/R) Dominican monk seated at table with books and
       globe (41x32cm-16x13in) s.i.d.1904 panel (DM 3200)
£1279 $2213   (6-May-91 ZEL.L1795/R) Elegant interior with figures playing cards
       (24x30cm-9x12in) s.i.d.1899 panel (DM 3800)
£1700 $3264   (29-Nov-90 B43/R) A game of cards (23x31cm-9x12in) s.d.1902 panel pair
£2218 $4348   (24-Nov-90 SA.A752/R) Collectors' pride (31x24cm-12x9in) s.d.1902 panel
       (DM 6500)
£3521 $5915   (23-Apr-91 RAS.K47/R) Rococo interior (80x100cm-31x39in) s. (D.KR 40000)

KNOWLES, Dorothy (1927-) Canadian
£873 $1721   (12-Nov-90 HO.ED290) Flock of birds (30x41cm-12x16in) s.i.d. linen
       (C.D 2000)
£2105 $4126   (20-Nov-90 JOY.T393/R) Field of rape seed (75x85cm-30x33in) s.d.73
       (C.D 4800)
£2412 $4728   (20-Nov-90 JOY.T184/R) Snow series, trees (95x180cm-37x71in) s.d.76
       acrylic canvas (C.D 5500)
£568   *$1118*   *(12-Nov-90 HO.ED307) Into the sun (56x76cm-22x30in) s.d. W/C (C.D 1300)*
£702   *$1375*   *(20-Nov-90 JOY.T444/R) Summer landscape (52x74cm-20x29in) s.d.70 W/C
       (C.D 1600)*
£789   *$1547*   *(20-Nov-90 JOY.T433/R) Trees by lake (46x66cm-18x26in) s.d.69 W/C
       (C.D 1800)*
£789   *$1547*   *(20-Nov-90 JOY.T241/R) Early spring (50x72cm-20x28in) s.d.68 W/C
       (C.D 1800)*
£789   *$1547*   *(20-Nov-90 JOY.T322/R) Easy of SWaskatoon (45x69cm-18x27in) s.d.68 W/C
       (C.D 1800)*

KNOWLES, Elizabeth McGillivray (1886-1929) Canadian
£877 $1719   (20-Nov-90 JOY.T410/R) Roosters in field, spring (30x42cm-12x17in) s.
       board (C.D 2000)

KNOWLES, Farquhar McGillivray (1859-1932) Canadian
£808 $1398   (6-May-91 SY.T217/R) Sumer landscape with chickens (32x50cm-13x20in)
       s.d.91 (C.D 1600)
£1228 $2407   (20-Nov-90 JOY.T432/R) Picnic by river (20x28cm-8x11in) (C.D 2800)
£1316 $2579   (20-Nov-90 JOY.T344/R) Fishermen on shore, near Perce Rock
       (20x25cm-8x10in) s.d.99 canvas on board (C.D 3000)
£3000 $5820   (4-Dec-90 P.Q124/R) Early morning in a Quebec village (45x35cm-18x14in)
       s. (C.D 6750)

KNOWLES, Fred J (1874-?) British
£420   *$727*   *(20-May-91 PH134) Gathering hay (19x28cm-7x11in) s. W/C htd white*
£600   *$1164*   *(4-Dec-90 P.Q106) Feeding time (34x50cm-13x20in) W/C (C.D 1350)*
£680   *$1258*   *(6-Mar-91 SC4186) Horse and cart crossing stream. Girl fetching water
       (25x36cm-10x14in) s. W/C pair*
£710   *$1257*   *(18-Mar-91 FEN22/R) Hauling timber (25x36cm-10x14in) s.d.11 October 1933
       W/C*
£720   *$1332*   *(6-Mar-91 SC4187/R) The miller's daughter (48x36cm-19x14in) s.d.1902 W/C*
£900   *$1782*   *(30-Jan-91 S221) Herding goats in woods (30x42cm-12x17in) s. W/C*
£1200   *$2004*   *(23-Jul-91 HS3) Miller's daughter (48x38cm-19x15in) s. W/C*
£1500   *$2580*   *(14-May-91 SWS107/R) Feeding the calves. The truants s. W/C over pencil
       pair*

KNOWLES, George Sheridan (1863-1931) British
£757 $1400   (10-Mar-91 H.C83/R) Those evening bells (56x41cm-22x16in) s.
£950 $1634   (14-May-91 SWS259/R) The home fire. Study (34x24cm-13x9in) s. i.verso
                    panel double-sided
£1300 $2119   (14-Jun-91 C229/R) Portrait of Miss Agnes A Marshall (61x51cm-24x20in)
                    s.d.1891
£1350 $2619   (5-Dec-90 PHE63/R) In the orchard (48x35cm-19x14in) s.d.1911
£2000 $3860   (13-Dec-90 CSK277/R) Red red rose (46x30cm-18x12in) s. s.i.verso

KNOX, Jack (20th C) British
£420 $706   (23-Apr-91 S251/R) Lobster (35x48cm-14x19in) s. pastel

KNOX, James (1866-?) American
£625 $1200   (17-Dec-90 SY.NY282/R) Summer landscape (30x36cm-12x14in) s. masonite

KNOX, John (1778-1845) British
£3600 $6084   (30-Apr-91 PH10/R) Cattle on country lane by loch. Sheep grazing by
                    loch, mountainous landscape beyond (25x36cm-10x14in) pair
£4500 $9000   (5-Feb-91 S148/R) Banks of Clyde (55x69cm-22x27in)

KNOX, Susan Ricker (1875-1959) American
£848 $1400   (13-Jul-91 YFA.M100/R) Inmates of an East Side House (41x51cm-16x20in)
                    s. i. verso board
£1523 $3000   (16-Nov-90 S.BM154/R) Under umbrella - beach scene (36x46cm-14x18in) s.

KNOX, W (?) ?
£360 $684   (1-Mar-91 BW30) Clipper at sea (25x36cm-10x14in) s. W/C
£588 $994   (16-Apr-91 J.M803) Venice Canal (25x36cm-10x14in) s.d.1920 W/C pair
                    (A.D 1300)

KNOX, William (20th C) British
£420 $727   (9-May-91 B181) Evening on the lagoon, Venice (25x36cm-10x14in) s.d.1919
                    W/C
£440 $761   (9-May-91 B180/R) On the Lagoon, Venice (25x36cm-10x14in) s.d.1920 W/C
£500 $960   (16-Aug-90 SC4036/R) Venice (36x51cm-14x20in) s. W/C bodycol. pencil
£520 $900   (20-May-91 PH64) Suburb of Venice (30x46cm-12x18in) s. i.verso W/C htd
                    white

KNOX, William Dunn (1880-1945) Australian
£1810 $3059   (16-Apr-91 J.M102/R) Homestead in valley (44x55cm-17x22in) s.
                    (A.D 4000)
£1810 $3059   (16-Apr-91 J.M178/R) The coming light (24x33cm-9x13in) s. canvas on
                    board (A.D 4000)
£2262 $3824   (16-Apr-91 J.M203/R) The Homestead (24x33cm-9x13in) s. canvas on board
                    (A.D 5000)

KNUDSEN, Peder (1868-1944) Danish
£525 $940   (9-Apr-91 RAS.K2096) White and mauve lilacs (110x112cm-43x44in) s.
                    (D.KR 6000)
£672 $1344   (6-Feb-91 RAS.K485/R) Red amaryllis in vase and bowl of oranges
                    (81x76cm-32x30in) s.d.1931 (D.KR 7500)
£1100 $2156   (14-Feb-91 CSK48) A woodland pool (99x130cm-39x51in) s.d.1942
£1496 $2514   (22-Apr-91 BU.K58/R) Snowy landscape (102x130cm-40x51in) s. (D.KR 17000)

KNUPFER, Benes (1848-1910) Czechoslovakian
£1340 $2318   (8-May-91 D.V4/R) The octopus (36x46cm-14x18in) mono (A.S 28000)

KNUPFER, Nicolaus (1603-1660) German
£15000 $24450   (3-Jul-91 S137/R) Feast of Gods (36x45cm-14x18in) s.d.1644 panel

KNUTSEN, Knut Hermod (1900-1967) Norwegian
£801 $1547   (10-Dec-90 B.O77/R) Wooded landscape from Holmsbu, winter
                    (85x66cm-33x26in) init.d.42 panel (N.KR 9000)
£1051 $1881   (11-Mar-91 B.O74/R) Nude seated in front of mirror (122x101cm-48x40in)
                    s.d.50 panel (N.KR 12000)
£1481 $2888   (15-Oct-90 B.O58/R) Three women in doorway (150x115cm-59x45in) init.d.46
                    (N.KR 17000)

KNUTSON, Johan (1816-1899) Finnish
£3725 $7338   (17-Nov-90 BU.H63/R) Landscapes with waterfalls (32x27cm-13x11in) s.
                    panel oval pair (F.M 26000)

KNYFF, Jacob (attrib) (1638-1681) Dutch
£15000 $29550   (1-Nov-90 CSK61/R) King Charles II's visit to the fleet, 6th June 1672
                    (84x124cm-33x49in)

KNYFF, Wouter (1607-1693) Dutch
£8741 $16871   (10-Dec-90 L.K67/R) View of Rhenen (50x72cm-20x28in) panel (DM 25000)
£13456 $26508   (14-Nov-90 SY.AM121/R) River landscape with small ships
                    (41x54cm-16x21in) mono.d.1641 panel (D.FL 44000)

KOBELL, Jan (1756-1833) Dutch
£2857 $5629   (14-Nov-90 FB.P263/R) Chevaux a l'ecurie (77x566cm-30x223in) s.d.1811
                    (F.FR 28000)

KOBELL, Jan Baptist (1778-1814) Dutch
£2395 $4551   (11-Sep-90 CH.AM283/R) Cows in a meadow by a forest in hilly landscape
             (47x63cm-19x25in) s.d.1804 panel (D.FL 8000)

KOBELL, Jan II (1778-1814) Dutch
£4042 $7033   (26-Mar-91 VN.R46/R) Woman wearing yoke tending farm animals in polder
             landscape (50x70cm-20x28in) s. (D.FL 13500)

KOBELL, Wilhelm von (1766-1855) German
£5068 $9882   (26-Oct-90 BM.B718/R) Alpine landscape with animals grazing and peasant
             with donkey (47x42cm-19x17in) s.indis.d.1812 (DM 15000)
£377 $674   *(13-Mar-91 N.M311/R) View of lake Tegernsee with Egern beyond. Hilly*
             landscape (10x17cm-4x7in) pencil double-sided (DM 1100)
£3390 $5525   *(3-Jul-91 WE.MU16/R) Shepherd with animals in landscape*
             (34x44cm-13x17in) W/C (DM 10000)
£5594 $10853   *(4-Dec-90 FN.S1924/R) Battle scene (22x36cm-9x14in) W/C bodycol over*
             pencil pen (DM 16000)
£20979 $40699   *(4-Dec-90 FN.S1923/R) Arcadian landscape with shepherds and animals*
             (49x65cm-19x26in) gouache (DM 60000)
£51195 $96246   *(19-Sep-90 N.M802/R) Hunting party at lake Ammersee with peasants*
             harvesting hay (37x48cm-15x19in) mono.d.1820 W/C (DM 150000)

KOBELL, Wilhelm von (attrib) (1766-1855) German
£664   *$1282*   *(10-Dec-90 L.K288/R) Horses in stable and party departing beyond*
             (32x43cm-13x17in) mono. i.verso pen sepia wash (DM 1900)

KOBER, Leo (1876-1931) Czechoslovakian
£487   *$954*   *(24-Jan-91 D.V61/R) Paris (47x29cm-19x11in) s. W/C gouache board*
             (A.S 10000)

KOBERLING, Bernd (20th C) ?
£2483 $4767   (26-Nov-90 WK.M777/R) Balkentrager (98x70cm-39x28in) s.d.1986 paper on
             board (DM 7200)

KOBKE, Christen (1810-1848) Danish
£3287 $6377   *(22-Aug-90 RAS.K28/R) Study of clouds - pale blue sky, grey-blue clouds*
             (20x26cm-8x10in) (D.KR 38000)
£627   *$1254*   *(6-Feb-91 RAS.K548) Portrait of Niels Schyth (22x16cm-9x6in) i. pencil*
             (D.KR 7000)
£772   *$1498*   *(5-Dec-90 KH.K198/R) Seated and walking figures (17x11cm-7x4in) i.verso*
             pencil (D.KR 8500)
£896   *$1792*   *(6-Feb-91 RAS.K547/R) Portrait of Niels Schyth (10x16cm-4x6in) d.1830*
             i.verso pencil (D.KR 10000)
£1496   *$2514*   *(23-Apr-91 RAS.K446/R) Landscape, Capri (30x40cm-12x16in) i.d.1839*
             sketch verso pencil (D.KR 17000)
£1496   *$2514*   *(23-Apr-91 RAS.K440/R) Three street boys (16x13cm-6x5in) i.d.1831 pen*
             wash Indian ink (D.KR 17000)

KOCH, G (?) German
£1429 $2700   (25-Sep-90 RAS.K107) Horses and cattle grazing by Elben
             (82x140cm-32x55in) s. (D.KR 16000)

KOCH, Georg (1878-?) German
£4500 $8820   (22-Nov-90 CSK178/R) Horses from Keller Staatsgestut near Elbe at
             Hitzacker (140x80cm-55x31in) s.
£5000 $8950   (12-Apr-91 BM.B629/R) Hunting party before Spandau Zitadelle
             (76x110cm-30x43in) s. (DM 15000)
£811   *$1541*   *(14-Sep-90 SA.A1311/R) Elegant party setting out for the hunt before*
             castle (21x29cm-8x11in) s. W/C (DM 2400)
£1115   *$2174*   *(26-Oct-90 BM.B828/R) Hunting party with Jagdschloss Grunewald*
             (51x65cm-20x26in) s. mixed media (DM 3300)

KOCH, John (1909-) American
£773 $1500   (5-Dec-90 D.NY71/R) Bouquet (61x51cm-24x20in) s.
£5587 $10000   (14-Mar-91 CH.NY128/R) Picture book (51x61cm-20x24in) s.
£10983 $19000   (23-May-91 SY.NY96/R) Conversation (23x29cm-9x11in) s. panel
£11561 $20000   (23-May-91 SY.NY97/R) Mother and children (102x74cm-40x29in) s.
£1058   *$2000*   *(25-Sep-90 CE.NY111/R) Playing the cello (32x24cm-13x9in) s. pencil*
             white chk.
£1272   *$2200*   *(21-May-91 CE.NY662/R) Seated male nude (39x30cm-15x12in) s. pencil*
             white chk

KOCH, Josef Anton (1768-1839) German
£760000 $1246400   (21-Jun-91 C52/R) Heroische landschaft mit regenbogen (108x96cm-43x38in)
             s.d.1824
£7000 $11480   *(19-Jun-91 S49/R) Landscape with Philemon and Baucis before Zeus and*
             Hermes (42x60cm-17x24in) s.i.d.1814 W/C

KOCH, Josef Anton (attrib) (1768-1839) German
£2027 $3446   (27-May-91 L.K65/R) Jacob and Rachel by fountain and view of river
             landscape beyond (23x28cm-9x11in) s. tempera paper on board
             (DM 6000)

KOCH, Ludwig (1866-1934) Austrian
£1220   *$2257*   *(7-Mar-91 D.V103/R) Historic parade (31x40cm-12x16in) s.d.1903 W/C paper*
             on board (A.S 25000)

KOCH, Martin (20th C) American
£964 $1889   (11-Feb-91 SY.J551/R) Cheetah basking on the anthill (59x118cm-23x46in)
  s.d.'73 canvas laid down on board (SA.R 4800)

KOCH, Peter (1874-1956) German
£671 $1309   (10-Oct-90 ZEL.L1592/R) Nude figures in wooded landscape
  (27x41cm-11x16in) s.d.1919 (DM 2000)

KOCH, Pyke (1901-) Dutch
£17028 $32864   (13-Dec-90 SY.AM80/R) Kermis te Utrecht (100x110cm-39x43in) (D.FL 55000)

KOCH, V (19th C) ?
£2911 $5502   (27-Sep-90 D.V155/R) View of St Andra Wordern (32x42cm-13x17in) s.d.1898
  (A.S 60000)

KOCH, Walther (1875-1915) German
£518 $891   (14-May-91 GF.L2562) Wooded mountain landscape in snow, evening
  (48x66cm-19x26in) s.i.d.1909 (S.FR 1300)

KOCH-ZEUTHEN, Reinhold (20th C) German
£539 $932   (6-May-91 ZEL.L1796/R) Elegant young lady seated at dressing table
  (76x56cm-30x22in) s. (DM 1600)

KOCHENSCHEIDT, Kurt (1943-) German
£1053 $1821   (8-May-91 D.V198/R) Klavierkuste (44x60cm-17x24in) s.i.d.75 chk pencil
  (A.S 22000)
£1196 $2069   (8-May-91 D.V197/R) Andurrische Muschel (43x60cm-17x24in) s.i.d.75 chk
  pencil (A.S 25000)

KOCHERSCHEIDT, Kurt (1943-) Austrian
£1590 $3085   (6-Dec-90 D.V209/R) Springs from vulcano (43x61cm-17x24in) s.i.d.73
  pencil col.pencil W/C (A.S 32000)

KOCK, David (1675-1744) Swedish
£4120 $7086   (14-May-91 BU.S18/R) Ulrika Eleonora and her family (231x176cm-91x69in)
  s.d.1730 after David Klocker Ehrenstrahl (S.KR 44000)

KOCK, Jules (19th C) French
£1116 $2175   (24-Oct-90 GD.B545/R) Cow and calf grazing (35x65cm-14x26in) s.d.87
  (S.FR 2800)

KOCKE, Hugo Wilhelm Georg (1874-1956) German
£874 $1687   (14-Dec-90 BM.B643/R) Beach scene with fisher folk (27x29cm-11x11in) s.
  panel (DM 2500)
£3041 $5929   (26-Oct-90 BM.B829/R) Couple on the way to church (96x126cm-38x50in) s.
  (DM 9000)

KOCKE-WICHMANN, Max (1889-?) German
£2027 $3851   (14-Sep-90 SA.A1201/R) Lake landscape with cows, evening
  (95x130cm-37x51in) s. (DM 6000)

KOCKERT, Julius (1827-1918) German
£6164 $10048   (12-Jun-91 N.M492/R) Reaper woman and child in boat with hay, scythe and
  vegetable basket (23x32cm-9x13in) s. panel (DM 18000)

KOCMENDY, F (?) ?
£560 $913   (14-Jun-91 T68) Still life with bowl of peonies (56x97cm-22x38in)
  indis.s.

KODRA, Ibrahim (1918-) Middle Eastern
£832 $1605   (13-Dec-90 F.M399) Figura (55x45cm-22x18in) s. (I.L 1800000)
£855 $1668   (24-Oct-90 F.M105) Pifferaio a Positano (46x55cm-18x22in) s.
  (I.L 1900000)
£1126 $2195   (24-Oct-90 F.M198) Nuovo idolo (80x80cm-31x31in) s.d.970 (I.L 2500000)
£1801 $3512   (22-Oct-90 BR.M304/R) Personaggio (50x70cm-20x28in) s. mixed media
  (I.L 4000000)

KOECK, Michael (1760-1825) Austrian
£4020 $6593   (21-Jun-91 SY.MO336/R) La cene (56x111cm-22x44in) s.d.1803 (F.FR 40000)

KOEGH (20th C) ?
£1692 $2943   (28-Mar-91 DAR.P39/R) Femme sur un banc (123x58cm-48x23in) s.d.51
  (F.FR 17000)
£2189 $3809   (28-Mar-91 DAR.P41/R) La criee (115x420cm-45x165in) s. (F.FR 22000)
£3383 $5887   (28-Mar-91 DAR.P40/R) Le cuisinier (130x80cm-51x31in) s. (F.FR 34000)

KOEHLER, Henry (1927-) American
£4491 $7500   (7-Jun-91 SY.NY254/R) Stag hunter's kit (41x31cm-16x12in) s. i.d.1987
  verso

KOEHLER, Paul R (1866-1909) American
£592 $1000   (20-Apr-91 WOL.C71) Landscape with figure on road (38x58cm-15x23in) s.
  pastel

KOEHLER, Robert (1850-1917) German
£518 $1000   (10-Dec-90 H.C1058/R) Salve Luna (74x58cm-29x23in) s.

KOEK-KOEK, Stephen Roberto (1887-1934) Argentinian

£578	$1000	(8-May-91 RO.BA223) Atardecer (24x30cm-9x12in) s. panel
£636	$1100	(8-May-91 V.BA52) Paisaje con arbol (29x37cm-11x15in)
£745	$1400	(18-Sep-90 RO.BA224) Camino a la oracion (24x30cm-9x12in) s. panel
£745	$1400	(18-Sep-90 RO.BA223) Fragatas (24x30cm-9x12in) s. panel
£761	$1500	(14-Nov-90 V.BA57) Procesion (25x30cm-10x12in)
£798	$1500	(18-Sep-90 RO.BA225) Puerto (30x40cm-12x16in) s. panel
£887	$1650	(5-Sep-90 V.BA59) Atarceder (38x48cm-15x19in)
£1523	$3000	(14-Nov-90 V.BA59) Barco (55x65cm-22x26in)
£1702	$3200	(18-Sep-90 RO.BA44) Bailarinas (43x53cm-17x21in) s. panel
£2660	$5000	(18-Sep-90 RO.BA45) Molinos (51x60cm-20x24in) s. panel

KOEKKOEK (attrib) (19/20th C) Dutch

£1407	$2308	(18-Jun-91 APT.P209) La bergere (40x32cm-16x13in) bears init. paper laid down on canvas (F.FR 14000)

KOEKKOEK, Barend Cornelis (1803-1862) Dutch

£1259	$2429	(12-Dec-90 N.M594/R) Cattle grazing in river landscape (39x48cm-15x19in) i.d.1835 (DM 3600)
£4452	$7257	(12-Jun-91 N.M493/R) Wooded landscape with rider, shepherd and peasant woman on path by stream (48x64cm-19x25in) panel (DM 13000)
£32934	$55329	(23-Apr-91 SY.AM111/R) Wooded landscape with herds and cattle by stream (24x30cm-9x12in) s.d.1853 (D.FL 110000)
£86705	$150000	(10-May-91 S.BM11/R) Weathering the storm, landscape with figures and flocks near village (74x104cm-29x41in) s. panel
£91463	$179268	(6-Nov-90 SY.AM100/R) Winter landscape with peasants gathering wood (81x109cm-32x43in) s.d.1856 (D.FL 300000)
£661	*$1104*	*(5-Jun-91 DO.H2328/R) Farmstead with figures in mountainous landscape (16x22cm-6x9in) s. indian ink brush (DM 1950)*

KOEKKOEK, Barend Cornelis (attrib) (1803-1862) Dutch

£667	$1280	(18-Dec-90 GM.B805) Vue des environs de Treves (38x45cm-15x18in) s. (B.FR 40000)
£4744	$9250	(25-Oct-90 GRO.B59/R) Travellers on path near castle (89x112cm-35x44in) bears sig.d.1848

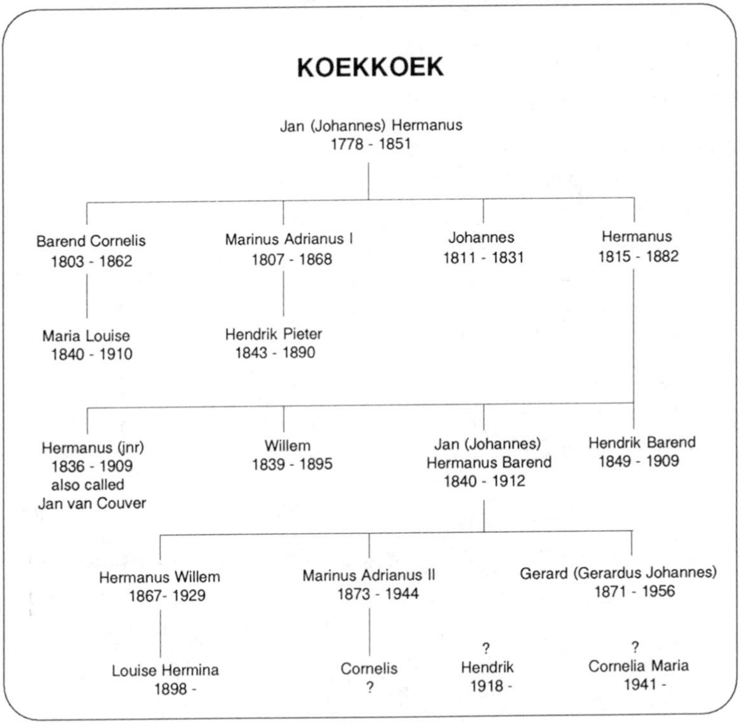

KOEKKOEK, Barend Cornelis (style) (1803-1862) Dutch
£1651 $3253   (13-Nov-90 AB.S921/R) Mountain landscape with figures (70x86cm-28x34in)
   bears sig. (S.KR 18000)

KOEKKOEK, Gerard (1871-1956) Dutch
£1198 $2275   (11-Sep-90 SY.AM115/R) Windmills in landscape (55x80cm-22x31in) s.
   (D.FL 4000)

KOEKKOEK, H B (1849-1909) Dutch
£1600 $3104   (3-Dec-90 LW1944) Dutch river scene with figures and boats and sailing
   boat beyond, sunset (33x51cm-13x20in) s.

KOEKKOEK, Hendrik Barend (1849-1909) Dutch
£536 $1029   (27-Nov-90 W.T1320/R) *Unloading the catch (53x109cm-21x43in) s. W/C*
   (C.D 1200)

KOEKKOEK, Hendrik Pieter (1843-1890) Dutch
£1310 $2200   (17-Jul-91 SY.NY269/R) Summer landscape (36x30cm-14x12in) s.
£1650 $3102   (18-Sep-90 SWS780/R) Angler by woodland stream (58x90cm-23x35in) s.
£2000 $3340   (22-Jul-91 SWS1093/R) Travellers in a wooded landscape (65x99cm-26x39in)
   bears sig.
£2100 $4095   (15-Jan-91 SWS163/R) Faggot gatherers on country path (60x49cm-24x19in)
   s. pair
£3939 $7761   (30-Oct-90 CH.AM136) Wooded landscape with two elegant ladies strolling
   on path near farm (67x100cm-26x39in) s. (D.FL 13000)

KOEKKOEK, Hermanus (1815-1882) Dutch
£1000 $1920   (16-Aug-90 B340) Leaving port (15x20cm-6x8in) s. panel
£2400 $4680   (15-Jan-91 SWS164/R) Sailing boats in rough weather at mouth of harbour
   (43x56cm-17x22in) init.
£2994 $5030   (23-Apr-91 SY.AM251/R) Putting out to sea (13x18cm-5x7in) s. panel
   (D.FL 10000)
£3030 $5970   (30-Oct-90 CH.AM354/R) Sailors in rowing boat at sunset (12x17cm-5x7in)
   s. s.d.1877 verso panel (D.FL 10000)
£10000 $16400   (19-Jun-91 S10/R) On Zuider Zee (36x56cm-14x22in) s.d.1863
£13000 $21320   (18-Jun-91 PH29/R) Shipping in calm (24x33cm-9x13in) init.d.1857 panel
£15000 $25050   (3-Jun-91 PHB73/R) On Zuyder Zee (61x78cm-24x31in)
£21557 $36216   (23-Apr-91 SY.AM71/R) Busy harbour (35x57cm-14x22in) s. (D.FL 72000)
£25449 $42754   (23-Apr-91 SY.AM283/R) Sailing vessels and men in rowing boat off coast
   (53x73cm-21x29in) s.d.1853 (D.FL 85000)

KOEKKOEK, Hermanus (circle) (19th C) Dutch
£1000 $1920   (16-Aug-90 B253) Sailing vessels off Dutch coast (18x23cm-7x9in) panel

KOEKKOEK, Hermanus (jnr) (1836-1909) Dutch
£1212 $2400   (1-Feb-91 S.W2568/R) J Van Couver, dock view (51x76cm-20x30in) s.

KOEKKOEK, Hermanus (jnr) see also COUVER, Jan van

KOEKKOEK, Hermanus Willem (1867-1929) Dutch
£811 $1500   (8-Mar-91 S.BM186/R) At the ready (33x20cm-13x8in) s. panel
£3300 $5676   (14-May-91 SWS338/R) The artillery (56x49cm-22x19in) s.

KOEKKOEK, Hermanus and Willem (19th C) Dutch
£79268 $155366 (6-Nov-90 SY.AM231/R) Figures in street of Dutch town in summer
   (83x121cm-33x48in) s.d.1867 (D.FL 260000)

KOEKKOEK, Jan (?) Dutch
£820 $1615   (1-Nov-90 D89/R) British man-of-war and other shipping in stormy seas
   (13x18cm-5x7in) s. panel

KOEKKOEK, Jan Hermanus (1778-1851) Dutch
£1800 $2952   (19-Jun-91 S2/R) Shipping in calm sea (20x32cm-8x13in) s. panel
£2590 $5050   (24-Oct-90 GD.B546/R) Wooded landscape with figures (12x18cm-5x7in)
   mono. panel (S.FR 6500)
£3200 $5536   (22-May-91 S110/R) Dutch boier (19x27cm-7x11in) panel
£4042 $6790   (23-Apr-91 SY.AM202/R) Shipping on rough sea (42x59cm-17x23in)
   s.indist.d. panel (D.FL 13500)
£6287 $10563   (23-Apr-91 SY.AM57/R) Stiff breeze at sea (38x54cm-15x21in) s. canvas on
   board (D.FL 21000)
£9500 $18240   (28-Nov-90 S63/R) Pulling in nets at night (43x58cm-17x23in) s.i. panel
£24000 $46080   (30-Nov-90 C3/R) A coastal landscape on the Zuider Zee with figures
   repairing a boat (37x59cm-15x23in) s.

KOEKKOEK, Jan Hermanus Barend (1840-1912) Dutch
£915 $1756   (27-Nov-90 SY.AM3686/R) Shell fisher (54x44cm-21x17in) s. (D.FL 3000)
£1078 $1811   (23-Apr-91 SY.AM140/R) Figures on beach of Katwijk (24x18cm-9x7in) s.
   panel (D.FL 3600)
£1138 $2128   (1-Sep-90 CH.AM146/R) Travellers on a rocky mountain pass, castle in
   distance (44x36cm-17x14in) s.d.92 panel (D.FL 3800)
£1449 $2710   (27-Aug-90 SY.J166/R) Dutch ships in choppy sea (18x29cm-7x11in) s.
   panel (SA.R 7000)
£1497 $2844   (11-Sep-90 CH.AM171) Fisherwoman and child on path in the dunes, Katwijk
   (59x81cm-23x32in) s. stretcher (D.FL 5000)
£2051 $4000   (26-Oct-90 S.W2629/R) Sailing ships off coast (15x20cm-6x8in) s. panel

KOEKKOEK, Jan Hermanus Barend (1840-1912) Dutch-cont.

£2123	$3801	(13-Mar-91 N.M555/R) Beached fishing boats with horse-drawn cart and figures beyond (63x51cm-25x20in) s. (DM 6200)
£2436	$4750	(26-Oct-90 S.W2628/R) Sailing ships off coast (15x20cm-6x8in) s. panel
£2727	$5373	(30-Oct-90 CH.AM355/R) Strand te Scheveningen bij bullg weer (37x58cm-15x23in) s. i.verso (D.FL 9000)
£2994	$5030	(23-Apr-91 SY.AM245/R) Sunset at beach of Zandvoort (70x113cm-28x44in) s. d.1873 verso (D.FL 10000)
£6061	$11394	(22-Sep-90 CH.AM132/R) Fisherfolk unloading beached bomschuit and fisherman seated by cart (42x65cm-17x26in) s. (D.FL 20000)
£8232	$16134	(6-Nov-90 SY.AM134/R) Soldiers on quay (84x121cm-33x48in) s.d.1892 (D.FL 27000)
£8982	$15090	(23-Apr-91 SY.AM284/R) Fishing vessels offshore in calm sea (35x53cm-14x21in) s.d.1888 (D.FL 30000)
£9697	$19103	(30-Oct-90 CH.AM281/R) Fisherman on horse and cart and various figures by moored bomschuit, atsunset (125x87cm-49x34in) s.d.1892 s.stretcher (D.FL 32000)
£14000	$22960	(21-Jun-91 C50/R) Approaching squall (56x87cm-22x34in) s.d.65

KOEKKOEK, Marinus Adrianus I (1807-1868) Dutch

£2048	$4014	(24-Nov-90 SA.A741/R) Farmstead in wooded landscape (16x22cm-6x9in) s. panel (DM 6000)
£2226	$3985	(12-Mar-91 FN.S2470/R) Peasants resting on path by the edge of woods and village beyond (21x29cm-8x11in) s. panel (DM 6500)
£2410	$4627	(27-Nov-90 JRL.S256/R) Winter landscape, Holland (32x49cm-13x19in) s. panel (A.D 6000)
£3179	$5500	(21-May-91 BG.M1102/R) Travellers on road (41x58cm-16x23in) s.
£6061	$11939	(30-Oct-90 CH.AM16/R) Summer - wooded river landscape with anglers in rowing boat, mother and child on path (49x63cm-19x25in) s.indist.d. (D.FL 20000)
£9146	$17927	(6-Nov-90 SY.AM191/R) Mountainous landscape with figures and cattle (49x64cm-19x25in) s.d.1851 (D.FL 30000)
£17000	$32640	(28-Nov-90 S61/R) Figures and cattle in river landscape (63x85cm-25x33in) s.d.1849

KOEKKOEK, Marinus Adrianus I (attrib) (1807-1868) Dutch

£1018	$1700	(5-Jun-91 D.NY53) Shepherd on horseback with flock (23x36cm-9x14in) bears sig. panel
£1033	$1850	(12-Apr-91 BM.B630/R) Still life of flowers on table (23x34cm-9x13in) s. (DM 3100)

KOEKKOEK, Marinus Adrianus I (circle) (1807-1868) Dutch

£1600	$3136	(14-Feb-91 CSK80/R) A Dutch coastal landscape (33x48cm-13x19in) panel

KOEKKOEK, Marinus Adrianus I (style) (1807-1868) Dutch

£1370	$2233	(12-Jun-91 N.M494/R) Mountain valley with peasant family on riverside path (40x53cm-16x21in) s. (DM 4000)

KOEKKOEK, Marinus Adrianus II (1873-1944) Dutch

£1198	$2275	(11-Sep-90 CH.AM59) Chickens by a fence (27x35cm-11x14in) s. (D.FL 4000)

KOEKKOEK, Willem (1839-1895) Dutch

£2956	$5113	(25-May-91 KV.L370/R) Scene in Middelburg (21x16cm-8x6in) s. panel (B.FR 180000)
£6000	$11820	(5-Oct-90 C25/R) Dutch street scene (51x38cm-20x15in) s.
£6200	$11904	(28-Nov-90 S73/R) Figures in back street by church (34x28cm-13x11in) s. panel
£12727	$25073	(30-Oct-90 CH.AM77/R) Numerous figures on quay in town with moored hay-barge and other shipping (66x92cm-26x36in) s.d.61 (D.FL 42000)
£15152	$29848	(30-Oct-90 CH.AM257/R) View in town with women conversing and horse-drawn cart passing by (41x53cm-16x21in) s. (D.FL 50000)
£18000	$34560	(30-Nov-90 C2/R) A Dutch street scene (59x70cm-23x28in) s.d.1870
£20000	$32800	(21-Jun-91 C48/R) Street scene, Amsterdam (101x89cm-40x35in) s.
£28443	$47784	(23-Apr-91 SY.AM248/R) Unloading haybarge, Haarlem (52x67cm-20x26in) s. (D.FL 95000)
£29940	$50299	(23-Apr-91 SY.AM204/R) Figures in street of Dutch town in summer (64x84cm-25x33in) s. (D.FL 100000)
£42000	$68880	(21-Jun-91 C49/R) Street scene, Amsterdam (70x90cm-28x35in) s.
£43939	$86561	(30-Oct-90 CH.AM340/R) Winter - view in town with figures in snowy street, peasant pushing sledge along canal (44x60cm-17x24in) s. (D.FL 145000)
£44910	$75449	(23-Apr-91 SY.AM92/R) Busy street scene (81x120cm-32x47in) s. (D.FL 150000)

KOELMAN, Johan Daniel (19th C) Dutch

£3333	$6567	(30-Oct-90 CH.AM180/R) Shepherd and flock and several cows by pond in extensive wooded heather land (96x146cm-38x57in) s.d.53 (D.FL 11000)

KOEMLER, Jan (19/20th C) Austrian

£1109	*$2140*	*(13-Dec-90 SY.MI207/R) La morte e il giullare (54x39cm-21x15in) s. sanguine (I.L 2400000)*

KOENIGER, Walter (1881-1945) American

£558	$1100	(7-Oct-90 DU.E72/R) Snow Country, Woodstock, NY, Chester Co (30x41cm-12x16in) s.d.1916 board
£925	$1600	(21-May-91 CE.NY488/R) Rolling hills (51x61cm-20x24in) s.d.17

KOENIGER, Walter (1881-1945) American-cont.
£2560 $4300   (21-Jul-91 LIT.L67) Winter evening (64x76cm-25x30in) s.
£3095 $5200   (28-Apr-91 LIT.L99) North East winter scene with stream
                 (76x76cm-30x30in) s.
£3390 $6000   (22-Mar-91 S.W2477/R) Early thaw (74x74cm-29x29in) s.
£3646 $7000   (30-Nov-90 CH.NY145/R) Lonely spot (63x77cm-25x30in) s.

KOEPPEN, Wilhelm (1876-1917) German
£966 $1854   (28-Nov-90 KF.M428/R) Medusa (92x87cm-36x34in) s. W/C bodycol gold over
*   pencil (DM 2800)*

KOERNER, Ernst Karl Eugen (1846-1927) German
£1200 $2340   (15-Oct-90 PH62) Die Memmons Kolosse mit dem tempel von Medinet Mabu -
                 ober Aegypten (84x126cm-33x50in) s.d.1922 i.stretcher
£1351 $2635   (26-Oct-90 KM.K1327/R) Oriental landscape with oasis and hills with
                 fortification beyond (110x75cm-43x30in) s.d.1877 canvas laid down
                 (DM 4000)

KOERNER, Henry (1915-) American
£26536 $47500   (12-Apr-91 SY.NY85/R) Pond (76x96cm-30x38in) masonite

KOERNER, William Henry Dethlef (1878-1938) American
£1479 $2500   (1-May-91 B.SF5274/R) Blue book cover (76x56cm-30x22in) s.d.1918

KOERT, J D (19th C) Dutch
£757 $1476   (24-Oct-90 GD.B547/R) Stormy sea scape with fishing boats
                 (32x23cm-13x9in) s. (S.FR 1900)

KOESTER, Alexander (1864-1932) German
£11604 $21816   (19-Sep-90 N.M564/R) Elsweg-Gamp, winter landscape near Klausen,
                 South-Tyrol (87x62cm-34x24in) s. i.stretcher (DM 34000)
£16438 $26795   (12-Jun-91 N.M498/R) Path near the Gamp, Klausen in winter
                 (56x46cm-22x18in) s. (DM 48000)
£33046 $57500   (27-Mar-91 B.SF4142/R) Enten am Wasser (44x61cm-17x24in) s.
£34247 $55822   (12-Jun-91 N.M495/R) Ducks on lake with reeds (45x76cm-18x30in) s.
                 (DM 100000)
£36000 $69120   (28-Nov-90 S22/R) Ducks on sunlit stream (46x76cm-18x30in) s.
£43919 $74662   (1-Jun-91 VG.B120/R) Still life of flowers (76x82cm-30x32in) s.
                 (DM 130000)
£44521 $79692   (12-Mar-91 FN.S2472/R) Ducks in lake Ammersee landscape, evening
                 (61x82cm-24x32in) (DM 130000)
£50523 $98519   (15-Oct-90 B.O59/R) Ducks, 1900 (85x115cm-33x45in) s.d.MDCCCC
                 (N.KR 580000)
£52365 $89020   (27-May-91 L.K305/R) Eleven ducks resting by pond in Klausen
                 (72x92cm-28x36in) s. (DM 155000)
£64103 $125000   (23-Oct-90 SY.NY111/R) Enten am Teich (63x80cm-25x31in) s.
£71795 $140000   (23-Oct-90 SY.NY109/R) Ducks on lake (51x85cm-20x33in) s.
£74830 $120476   (26-Jun-91 KM.K1534/R) Ducks in pond with water lilies (55x82cm-22x32in)
                 s. (DM 220000)
£90909 $175455   (10-Dec-90 L.K479/R) Pond with fifteen ducks (75x120cm-30x47in)
                 (DM 260000)
£104046 $180000   (23-May-91 CH.NY131/R) Enten in flachem Schilfwasser (72x117cm-28x46in)
                 s.
£3523 $6871   (10-Oct-90 WE.MU179/R) Ducks on pond (23x35cm-9x14in) s. st.studio verso
*   chl (DM 10500)*

KOESTER, Alexander (style) (1864-1932) German
£1200 $2328   (6-Dec-90 CSK155/R) Ducks amongst reeds (52x62cm-20x24in) canvas on
                 board

KOETS, Roelof (17/18th C) Dutch
£11858 $20158   (27-May-91 GK.Z5056/R) Still life with grapes in basket
                 (47x68cm-19x27in) panel (S.FR 30000)
£18500 $30155   (2-Jul-91 PH44/R) Basket of red and white grapes overflowing onto table
                 (46x69cm-18x27in) s.indis.d.16.. panel

KOETS, Roelof (after) (17/18th C) Dutch
£3745 $6442   (14-May-91 BU.S78/R) Still life of basket of fruit, silver cup and wine
                 (37x95cm-15x37in) panel (S.KR 40000)

KOETS, Roelof (elder-style) (1592-1655) Dutch
£15000 $25350   (19-Apr-91 C75/R) A meat pie, lemon, sliced bread roll and other objects
                 in pewter plates (54x76cm-21x30in)

KOETS, Roelof (style) (17/18th C) Dutch
£7028 $11315   (27-Jun-91 APT.P141/R) Nature morte aux pommes et branche de vignes avec
                 raisin (106x146cm-42x57in) (F.FR 70000)
£8084 $13662   (2-May-91 CH.AM131/R) A breakfast still life with an overturned silver
                 beaker and a peachon a pewter plate and other objec (63x88cm-25x35in)
                 panel (D.FL 27000)

KOETS, Roelof (younger) (1655-1725) Dutch
£3200 $5408   (16-Apr-91 PH182/R) Interior with young offering glass wine to seated
                 gentleman reading letter (50x42cm-20x17in)

KOGAN, Anna (1902-1974) Russian
£14000 $24780   (20-Mar-91 S43/R) Composition (72x97cm-28x38in) s.verso

KOGAN, Nina (1887-1942) Russian
£6419 $10912   (1-Jun-91 VG.B297/R) Composition (31x20cm-12x8in) mono.verso tempera
                         over pencil board (DM 19000)
£7770 $13209   (1-Jun-91 VG.B298/R) Composition with blue wedge (32x25cm-13x10in)
                         mono.verso tempera over pencil board (DM 23000)

KOGL, Benedict (1892-1969) German
£1049 $2024   (12-Dec-90 WE.MU154/R) Kittens playing (13x29cm-5x11in) s. board
                         (DM 3000)
£1224 $2362   (12-Dec-90 WE.MU152/R) Kittens playing (9x12cm-4x5in) s. panel
                         (DM 3500)
£1275 $2487   (10-Oct-90 ZEL.L1593/R) Kitten playing by basket (9x12cm-4x5in) s. panel
                         (DM 3800)
£1399 $2713   (4-Dec-90 FN.S1928/R) Cats playing by basket in wooded landscape
                         (18x24cm-7x9in) s. panel (DM 4000)
£1573 $3052   (4-Dec-90 FN.S1927/R) Cats in garden landscape (18x23cm-7x9in) s. board
                         (DM 4500)
£1923 $3712   (12-Dec-90 N.M592/R) Cat with three kittens in basket (50x65cm-20x26in)
                         s. (DM 5500)
£2098 $4070   (4-Dec-90 FN.S1926/R) Family of cats in garden with basket and 2 cats
                         (22x30cm-9x12in) s. (DM 6000)
£2150 $3526   (18-Jun-91 FN.S1935/R) Basket with kittens in landscape (18x24cm-7x9in)
                         s. board (DM 6300)
£2253 $4257   (25-Sep-90 FN.S2247/R) Garden with kittens in basket near hedge
                         (18x24cm-7x9in) s. (DM 6600)
£2273 $4386   (12-Dec-90 WE.MU155/R) Kittens playing (18x24cm-7x9in) s. panel
                         (DM 6500)
£2517 $4908   (10-Oct-90 WE.MU199/R) Kitten playing (18x24cm-7x9in) s. panel
                         (DM.7500)
£2852 $5562   (10-Oct-90 WE.MU200/R) Three kitten (21x26cm-8x10in) s. board
                         (DM 8500)
£3344 $5652   (19-Apr-91 FN.S1767/R) Cat with three kittens on carpet in interior
                         (35x50cm-14x20in) s. board (DM 10000)

KOGL, Clement (1808-1845) German
£898 $1509   (23-Apr-91 SY.AM141) Grandfather's pocket money (24x18cm-9x7in)
                         indist.s. (D.FL 3000)

KOHL, Ludwig (1746-1821) Austrian
£500 $815   (4-Jul-91 CSK109) Midnight Mass in cathedral interior (65x86cm-26x34in)
                         init. panel

KOHL, Robert (1891-1944) German
£1419 $2412   (1-Jun-91 VG.B640/R) Portrait of young man holding narcissi in hands
                         (99x74cm-39x29in) (DM 4200)
£1419 $2412   (1-Jun-91 VG.B639/R) Self portrait (83x61cm-33x24in) canvas on board
                         (DM 4200)
£1419 $2412   (1-Jun-91 VG.B641/R) Portrait of dancer Gertrud Falke (100x75cm-39x30in)
                         (DM 4200)

KOHLER (?) ?
£3000 $5760   (29-Nov-90 CSK161/R) Don Quixote and Sancho Panza meeting princess in
                         garland of flowers (63x77cm-25x30in) one s. pair

KOHLER, Christian (1809-1861) German
£1419 $2412   (28-May-91 KF.M193/R) Portrait of woman (60x48cm-24x19in) mono.d.1853
*   pastel oval (DM 4200)*

KOHLER, Florian (1935-) German
£946 $1608   (28-May-91 KF.M794/R) Water tight (60x50cm-24x20in) s.i.d.1989verso
                         (DM 2800)
£1138 $2185   (28-Nov-90 KF.M939/R) Cyclists (59x49cm-23x19in) s.i.d.1989verso
                         (DM 3300)
£2000 $3840   (28-Nov-90 KF.M936/R) Figur im Raum (90x70cm-35x28in) s.d.1980/81verso
                         (DM 5800)

KOHLER, Fritz (1887-1971) German
£805 $1570   (13-Oct-90 KRA.D247/R) Lower Rhine landscape in twilight
                         (50x70cm-20x28in) s. (DM 2400)
£1074 $2094   (13-Oct-90 KRA.D248 a) Lower Rhine near Langst (50x75cm-20x30in) s.
                         (DM 3200)
£1400 $2744   (22-Nov-90 CSK157/R) Rhine at Dusseldorf, Germany (74x100cm-29x39in)
                         s.i.

KOHLHOFF, Wilhelm (1893-1971) German
£2568 $4187   (12-Jun-91 N.M499) Bunch of summer flowers in vase (60x54cm-24x21in) s.
                         panel (DM 7500)
£4407 $7359   (6-Jun-91 HN.H490/R) Southern town (36x30cm-14x12in) mono.d.
                         (DM 13000)
£5500 $10670   (5-Dec-90 PH97/R) Stilleben mit Blumen (79x100cm-31x39in) s.
£14433 $27423   (2-Mar-91 KRA.D521/R) Girl seated on window sill (89x72cm-35x28in) s.
                         (DM 42000)
£17627 $29437   (6-Jun-91 HN.H491/R) Children (51x48cm-20x19in) (DM 52000)

KOHLHOFF, Wilhelm (1893-1971) German-cont.
£533 $955   (12-Apr-91 AW.H1800/R) Mov, *artist's wife holding head in hand*
             (40x51cm-16x20in) s.d.1958 W/C (DM 1600)
£1007 $1963   (13-Oct-90 KRA.D402/R) Boy (27x47cm-11x19in) s. indian ink pen dr.
             (DM 3000)
£4054 $7703   (14-Sep-90 SA.A1411/R) Nachtliche Kutschfahrt (41x33cm-16x13in) s.
             bodycol. board (DM 12000)

KOHLMANN, Ejnar (1888-1968) Finnish
£691 $1333   (15-Dec-90 BU.H94) Sailing boats in a calm (27x35cm-11x14in) s. canvas
             on panel (F.M 4800)
£748 $1444   (15-Dec-90 BU.H95) Beach landscape (25x32cm-10x13in) s. canvas on panel
             (F.M 5200)
£1223 $2360   (15-Dec-90 BU.H93) Capercaillies (46x55cm-18x22in) s. (F.M 8500)
£1569 $3076   (24-Nov-90 HOR.H141/R) Mallards in flight (50x61cm-20x24in) s.
             (F.M 11000)
£2477 $4880   (13-Nov-90 AB.S922/R) Landscape with capercaillies (72x93cm-28x37in)
             s.d.1958 (S.KR 27000)

KOHLSCHEIN, Edmund Anton (1900-) German
£550 $1045   (2-Mar-91 KRA.D350) Harvest at Desenberg (50x56cm-20x22in) s.
             s.i.stretcher (DM 1600)

KOHLSCHEIN, Joseph (younger) (1884-1958) German
£2921 $5550   (2-Mar-91 KRA.D522/R) View of Zons, winter (60x80cm-24x31in) s.
             (DM 8500)

KOHRL, Ludwig (1858-1927) German
£1550 $2666   (14-May-91 SWS293/R) Homemade waterwheel (26x21cm-10x8in) s.i.d.1899
             panel
£2943 $4974   (17-Apr-91 WE.MU252/R) The house of cards (35x54cm-14x21in) s.i.d.1888
             (DM 8800)

KOISTINEN, Unto (1917-) Finnish
£1070 $2097   (24-Nov-90 HOR.H151/R) Young woman (14x11cm-6x4in) s. (F.M 7500)
£2006 $3951   (17-Nov-90 BU.H156/R) Christ on the cross (35x26cm-14x10in) s.d.66 panel
             (F.M 14000)
£2282 $4474   (24-Nov-90 HOR.H146/R) 'Skylar' (36x27cm-14x11in) s.d.1963 (F.M 16000)
£3424 $6710   (24-Nov-90 HOR.H148/R) Nude (22x18cm-9x7in) s.d.1987 (F.M 24000)
£3438 $6774   (17-Nov-90 BU.H155/R) Woman with lace collar (18x14cm-7x6in) s.d.1981
             panel (F.M 24000)
£3977 $7119   (14-Apr-91 BU.H43/R) Seated woman (22x18cm-9x7in) s.d.1976 panel
             (F.M 28000)
£4280 $8388   (24-Nov-90 HOR.H143/R) Nude (22x18cm-9x7in) s.d.1980 (F.M 30000)
£4850 $9506   (24-Nov-90 HOR.H142/R) In the chair (33x26cm-13x10in) s.d.1976
             (F.M 34000)
£5308 $8971   (20-Apr-91 HOR.H114/R) Lady wearing white (22x18cm-9x7in) s.d.1981
             (F.M 37000)
£6734 $13265   (17-Nov-90 BU.H154/R) Seated nude (81x60cm-32x24in) s.d.1965
             (F.M 47000)
£1641 $3215   *(24-Nov-90 HOR.H150/R) In the chair (42x33cm-17x13in) s.d.1976 wash*
             (F.M 11500)
£1712 $3355   *(24-Nov-90 HOR.H149/R) The meeting (40x31cm-16x12in) s.d.1976 wash*
             (F.M 12000)
£2996 $5872   *(24-Nov-90 HOR.H145/R) Salome's dance (46x40cm-18x16in) s.d.1978 wash*
             (F.M 21000)

KOIVISTO, Aukusti (1886-1962) Finnish
£576 $1111   (15-Dec-90 BU.H97) Floating logs (49x68cm-19x27in) s.d.1947 panel
             (F.M 4000)

KOIVU, Rudolf (1890-1946) Finnish
£1367 $2638   (15-Dec-90 BU.H99) Beach landscape (40x55cm-16x22in) s. (F.M 9500)

KOKEN, Gustav (1850-1910) German
£1689 $3294   (26-Oct-90 BM.B834/R) Aller landscape, autumn morning (51x71cm-20x28in)
             s. i.verso (DM 5000)

KOKO-MICOLETZKY, Friedrich (1887-1981) Austrian
£535 $1049   (24-Jan-91 D.V211/R) Female nude in the clouds (140x140cm-55x55in)
             s.d.1925 (A.S 11000)

KOKORINE, Anatoli (1908-1989) Russian
£655 $1067   (16-Jun-91 C.P46/R) Les marins pecheurs (35x50cm-14x20in) s. verso
             (F.FR 6500)

KOKOSCHKA, Oskar (1886-1980) Austrian
£35838 $62000   (9-May-91 CH.NY246/R) Signora della Ragione (65x86cm-26x34in) init.
£47297 $80405   (28-May-91 KF.M797/R) Design for Crematorium Breslau (34x51cm-13x20in)
             mixed media (DM 140000)
£70000 $112700   (25-Jun-91 C161/R) Harbour view, Polperro (50x60cm-20x24in) init. board
£600000 $966000   (24-Jun-91 C22/R) Richmond terrace (89x124cm-35x49in) init.
£900000 $1746000   (3-Dec-90 C27/R) Portrait Dr. Rudolf Blumner (80x57cm-31x22in) init.
£667 $1300   *(26-Oct-90 S.W2219/R) Male nude (25x18cm-10x7in) init. ink drawing*
£1628 $3126   *(24-Feb-91 P.V118/R) Paysage (50x34cm-20x13in) mono.d.1055 verso W/C*
             (F.FR 16200)

KOKOSCHKA, Oskar (1886-1980) Austrian-cont.
£1696	$3257	(27-Nov-90 W.T1241/R) Two nude girls, Man and nude girl (31x23cm-12x9in) mono.s.d.1926 ink chk double-sided (C.D 3800)
£3253	$5303	(15-Jun-91 L.K369) Landscape in Scotland (18x27cm-7x11in) indis.i.verso col.pencil double-sided (DM 9500)
£4061	$8000	(2-Oct-90 CH.NY74/R) Zwei Akte (39x27cm-15x11in) s.d.1905-6 chl.
£4778	$9365	(24-Nov-90 VG.B250/R) Amalfi (20x30cm-8x12in) mono.i.d.1951 col.chk (DM 14000)
£5000	$9600	(28-Nov-90 KF.M944/R) Erotic studies of woman reclining and dog (20x28cm-8x11in) mono. pair (DM 14500)
£5467	$10606	(6-Dec-90 D.V146/R) Study for Murano glass (35x56cm-14x22in) s.i.d.1953 pen indian ink pencil col.chk (A.S 110000)
£5506	$9250	(28-Apr-91 HG.C449) Vase of flowers (48x36cm-19x14in) s.d.1965 W/C
£5802	$11372	(24-Nov-90 N.M285/R) Actress wearing long dress standing (34x22cm-13x9in) mono.c.1909/10 blue pencil dr. (DM 17000)
£5862	$11255	(28-Nov-90 KF.M941/R) Portrait of Trudl (45x35cm-18x14in) s.i.d.1931 chk (DM 17000)
£6000	$11700	(19-Oct-90 C109/R) Frau sich im Spiegel betrachtend (68x51cm-27x20in) s. W/C col.crayon
£6311	$10350	(20-Jun-91 D.V31/R) Zu Ketten in das Meer zum Roman Logbuch des B.K. (37x24cm-15x9in) mono.i.d.47 chk pen indian ink (A.S 130000)
£6633	$13000	(15-Feb-91 SY.NY13/R) Portrait of Mrs Elise Reitler (43x30cm-17x12in) init. black crayon
£6897	$13241	(28-Nov-90 KF.M943/R) Scottish landscape (23x20cm-9x8in) s.d.1944 col.pencil (DM 20000)
£7000	$13580	(5-Dec-90 PH44/R) Blumen (26x36cm-10x14in) init.i.d.49 col.crayons
£8108	$13784	(30-May-91 SY.BE12/R) Female nude (68x50cm-27x20in) s. indian ink pen brush (DM 24000)
£8276	$15890	(28-Nov-90 KF.M940/R) The pure face (21x33cm-8x13in) mono.d.1913 chk indian ink (DM 24000)
£8500	$13685	(24-Jun-91 CSK92/R) Badendes nacktes Madchen (30x40cm-12x16in) init.i.d.53 col.crayons
£9500	$16815	(19-Mar-91 C72/R) Liegende frau (49x59cm-19x23in) s. pencil
£11000	$19470	(19-Mar-91 C59/R) Reben mit weinlaub (48x63cm-19x25in) s.d.53 W/C
£11168	$22000	(2-Oct-90 CH.NY159/R) Korb mit Pilzen (37x49cm-15x19in) s. W/C
£12136	$19903	(20-Jun-91 D.V23/R) Study for Lot and his Daughters (53x47cm-21x19in) mono.i. black chk (A.S 250000)
£13592	$22291	(20-Jun-91 D.V25/R) Girl friend Otti as bride (65x49cm-26x19in) i.d.18 grey chk (A.S 280000)
£15228	$30000	(2-Oct-90 CH.NY160/R) Blumenvase (69x50cm-27x20in) s.d.57 W/C
£25597	$50171	(22-Nov-90 L.K1068/R) Portrait of young girl (64x46cm-25x18in) c.1922/23 W/C (DM 75000)
£26699	$43786	(20-Jun-91 D.V4/R) Boy touching the ground with his hands (45x31cm-18x12in) mono. pencil W/C (A.S 550000)
£31553	$51748	(20-Jun-91 D.V15/R) An der Isonzofront (31x48cm-12x19in) mono.i. pastel (A.S 650000)
£55000	$88550	(25-Jun-91 C225/R) Madchen mit gelbes Haarband (44x31cm-17x12in) init. W/C pencil

KOLAR, Jiri (20th C) French
£454	$786	(7-May-91 F.M73) Senza titolo (14x10cm-6x4in) s.d.1986 collage (I.L 1000000)
£473	$804	(1-Jun-91 VG.B642/R) Transformed erechteion (28x21cm-11x8in) mono.d.1979 collage razors thread over offset (DM 1400)
£550	$897	(4-Jul-91 GL.P175) Letristicka Fraum (29x21cm-11x8in) init.d.1967 collage (F.FR 5500)
£636	$1100	(7-May-91 F.M163) Tre farfalle (29x21cm-11x8in) mono.d.1969 collage (I.L 1400000)
£646	$1240	(27-Nov-90 AB.S4039) 'Motyli Luna' - Mona Lisa and butterfly (40x30cm-16x12in) init.d.1970verso collage panel (S.KR 7000)
£714	$1377	(16-Dec-90 GL.P36) Poesie visuelle (66x47cm-26x19in) s.d.63 ink collage (F.FR 7000)
£955	$1871	(20-Nov-90 BR.M210/R) Farfalle (24x29cm-9x11in) s.d.1969verso collage (I.L 2100000)
£1020	$2000	(6-Nov-90 CE.NY82/R) Untitled (25x19cm-10x7in) init.d.70 paper collage paper mounted on board
£1276	$2500	(6-Nov-90 CE.NY83/R) Winter - Fata - Morgana (28x44cm-11x17in) init.d.69 paper collage paper mounted on board
£1317	$2279	(7-May-91 F.M313) La sonnate de l'oubli (27x41cm-11x16in) mono.d.1979 rollage (I.L 2900000)
£1499	$2594	(7-May-91 F.M34/R) Zamilovane (36x50cm-14x20in) s.d.1980 collage (I.L 3300000)
£2179	$4250	(10-Oct-90 SY.NY524/R) Homage a chartres (79x61cm-31x24in) collage board
£3377	$6585	(22-Oct-90 BR.M134/R) V Souhvezdi zivota 1 (30x40cm-12x16in) s.d.1990 verso collage panel (I.L 7500000)
£3697	$7135	(12-Dec-90 F.M76/R) Haute ecole manege royal (21x29cm-8x11in) d.1972 collage (I.L 8000000)
£4103	$8000	(10-Oct-90 SY.NY557/R) M.E.V Kopane (69x99cm-27x39in) s.i.d.76verso chiasmage rollage collage panel

KOLARE, Nils (1930-) Scandinavian
£755	$1306	(22-May-91 BA.S408/R) Composition in violet (80x35cm-31x14in) s. (S.KR 8000)
£1225	$2071	(18-Apr-91 BU.S83/R) Composition (70x55cm-28x22in) s. panel (S.KR 13000)
£1476	$2834	(27-Nov-90 BU.S187/R) Composition (100x150cm-39x59in) s.d.1981 (S.KR 16000)

KOLARE, Nils (1930-) Scandinavian-cont.
£741 $1438   (5-Dec-90 AB.S7151/R) Composition (42x63cm-17x25in) s.d.83 gouache
                     (S.KR 8000)

KOLASINSKI, Jean Pierre (1941-) ?
£6684 $13167   (18-Nov-90 H.A140) La coupe bleue (55x46cm-22x18in) s. i. verso
                     (F.FR 65500)

KOLBE, Carl Wilhelm (elder) (1757-1835) German
£1622 $2757   (31-May-91 GB.B5554/R) Old oak tree (33x23cm-13x9in) chk (DM 4800)

KOLBE, Ernst (1876-1945) German
£1495 $2900   (8-Dec-90 W.W130/R) Alt Lubecker Diele (79x74cm-31x29in) s.
£2074 $3504   (17-Apr-91 WE.MU240/R) Interior (78x74cm-31x29in) s. (DM 6200)

KOLBE, Georg (1877-1947) German
£2027 $3446   (31-May-91 GB.B6493) Female nude kneeling seen from behind
                     (49x43cm-19x17in) mono. pencil wash (DM 6000)
£2098 $4070   (7-Dec-90 GB.B6809/R) Female nude kneeling (45x34cm-18x13in) mono.c.1920
                     pen wash (DM 6000)
£2972 $5766   (7-Dec-90 GB.B6808/R) Female nude seated on floor (46x36cm-18x14in)
                     mono.c.1922 pen wash (DM 8500)
£4407 $7359   (6-Jun-91 HN.H504/R) Female nude (33x41cm-13x16in) mono. pen wash
                     (DM 13000)

KOLBE, Heinrich Christoph (1771-1836) German
£3378 $6588   (26-Oct-90 KM.K1329/R) Portrait of siblings Alwine and Robert Uellenberg
                     (70x60cm-28x24in) s.d.1785 canvas laid down (DM 10000)

KOLBEL, Johannes (1883-1983) Norwegian
£707 $1413   (9-Feb-91 BU.O104) Moonlit country road (89x69cm-35x27in) s. (N.KR 8000)

KOLESNIKOFF, Sergei (1889-?) Russian
£7064 $13917   (13-Nov-90 AB.S923/R) Still life of melons (121x166cm-48x65in) s.d.1936
                     (S.KR 77000)

KOLIG, Anton (1886-?) Austrian
£614 $1161   (25-Sep-90 FN.S1990/R) Squatting female (32x40cm-13x16in) mono.d.1912
                     s.d.verso gouache (DM 1800)
£1363 $2671   (24-Jan-91 D.V68/R) Two reclining male nudes (53x37cm-21x15in)
                     mono.d.1920 chl (A.S 28000)

KOLITZ, Louis (1845-1914) German
£4223 $8235   (26-Oct-90 KM.K1330/R) View of town in state of siege with folk storming
                     towards enemies (84x125cm-33x49in) s.d.1869 (DM 12500)

KOLLE, C A (1827-1872) Danish
£1181 $2114   (9-Apr-91 RAS.K2099/R) Portrait of lady by sewingtable. Gentleman by
                     armchair (75x60cm-30x24in) s.d.1858 pair (D.KR 13500)
£557 $1096   (14-Nov-90 RAS.K780) View of Rome (17x24cm-7x9in) s.d.1866 pen W/C
                     (D.KR 6200)

KOLLER, Johann Rudolf see KOLLER, Rudolf

KOLLER, Rudolf (1828-1905) Swiss
£437 $729   (5-Jun-91 SY.Z45/R) Barn beneath amongst trees (29x37cm-11x15in) pencil
                     (S.FR 1100)

KOLLI, Grete (20th C) ?
£1984 $3433   (22-May-91 GS.B2131) Scene from the Middle Ages with fortified castle
                     and figures (167x167cm-66x66in) s.i.d.1941verso tempera linen
                     (S.FR 5000)

KOLLWITZ, Kathe (1867-1945) German
£1627 $2717   (6-Jun-91 HN.H506/R) three studies of the head of grandchild Peter
                     (20x27cm-8x11in) s.d.1921 pencil (DM 4800)
£1718 $3265   (2-Mar-91 KRA.D525) Portrait of Jewish woman (45x30cm-18x12in) s. ochre
                     (DM 5000)
£4730 $8182   (21-May-91 WK.M1097/R) Woman waiting. Mother with two children and study
                     of heads (23x18cm-9x7in) chl double-sided (DM 14000)
£8814 $14719   (6-Jun-91 HN.H505/R) In the children's hospital (44x60cm-17x24in) s.
                     chl. (DM 26000)
£9137 $18000   (3-Oct-90 SY.NY72/R) Tod mit Frau im Schoss (43x60cm-17x24in) s.d.1921
                     chl paper on board
£9556 $18730   (24-Nov-90 VG.B127/R) Two female nudes. Two female nudes
                     (63x48cm-25x19in) s.mono. pencil double-sided (DM 28000)
£10135 $17230   (31-May-91 VG.B35/R) Two men bending down (27x31cm-11x12in) s.d.1919
                     litho chk over blaustift ink (DM 30000)
£10811 $18703   (21-May-91 WK.M1098/R) Mother with child (23x15cm-9x6in) s.d.1921 indian
                     ink pen double-sided (DM 32000)
£11168 $22000   (3-Oct-90 SY.NY73/R) Mutter mit zwei Kindern (48x32cm-19x13in) s. chl
£11263 $22075   (24-Nov-90 VG.B128/R) Female nude seated (53x45cm-21x18in) s. chl
                     (DM 33000)
£12838 $21824   (31-May-91 VG.B36/R) Worker standing. Worker holding arm in right angle
                     and study of head (46x51cm-18x20in) s.d.1921 chl double-sided
                     (DM 38000)

KOLLWITZ, Kathe (1867-1945) German-cont.
£20478 $40137   *(23-Nov-90 VG.B36/R) Woman thinking (64x48cm-25x19in) s.d.1934 chl*
                 (DM 60000)
£49603 $81349   *(21-Jun-91 GK.B86/R) Mother embracing sick child (61x47cm-24x19in) chk*
                 (S.FR 125000)

KOLNIK, Arthur (1890-1972) Israeli
£838 $1600   *(2-Jan-91 GG.TA446/R) Vase and flowers (45x33cm-18x13in) s. board*
£2094 $4000   *(2-Jan-91 GG.TA445/R) Jew with the Torah scroll (66x38cm-26x15in) s.*
                 board

KOLOSVARY, Sigismund (1899-1983) Hungarian
£668 $1296   *(7-Dec-90 GL.P37) Femme dans un paysage (41x54cm-16x21in) s.d.1938*
                 gouache (F.FR 6500)

KOLSCHBACH, Joseph (1892-?) German
£13699 $22329   *(15-Jun-91 L.K367/R) St Francis amongst the animals (54x64cm-21x25in)*
                 (DM 40000)

KOLSTO, Frederik (1860-1945) Norwegian
£1313 $2351   *(11-Mar-91 B.O75/R) Seascape with sailingvessel (71x126cm-28x50in) s.*
                 (N.KR 15000)
£3038 $5074   *(3-Jun-91 B.O84/R) Evening landscape by the sea (78x108cm-31x43in) s.*
                 (N.KR 35000)
£4443 $8663   *(15-Oct-90 B.O60/R) Winter (27x34cm-11x13in) s.d.89 panel (N.KR 51000)*

KOMET (?) ?
£1195 $2032   *(2-Jun-91 GL.P82) Le baiser (24x32cm-9x13in) s.i. d.1982 verso*
                 (F.FR 12000)

KOMTER, Douwe (1871-1957) Dutch
£619 $1195   *(12-Dec-90 CH.AM107) Still life of stone jar, pewter cup and pipe on*
                 ledge (50x42cm-20x17in) init.d.36 (D.FL 2000)

KONARSKI, J (19th C?) Russian?
£648 $1271   *(24-Nov-90 SA.A777/R) Sleigh ride (29x26cm-11x10in) s. board (DM 1900)*

KONARSKI, S (?) Russian
£1263 $2387   *(25-Sep-90 FN.S2249/R) Snowy Taiga landscape with party in horse-drawn*
                 sledges, evening (27x38cm-11x15in) s. panel (DM 3700)

KONCHALOVSKY, Piotr Petrovich (1876-1956) Russian
£3000 $5850   *(10-Oct-90 C387/R) Still life with teapot and lemon (17x23cm-7x9in)*
                 init.d.1929

KONECNY, Josef (1907-?) Czechoslovakian
£847 $1381   *(3-Jul-91 WE.MU127/R) Still life of flowers (58x43cm-23x17in) s. canvas*
                 on panel (DM 2500)
£1017 $1658   *(3-Jul-91 WE.MU126/R) Still life of flowers (65x60cm-26x24in) s.*
                 (DM 3000)
£1370 $2233   *(12-Jun-91 N.M501/R) Mixed flowers in terracotta jug on table with bird*
                 and plate (34x50cm-13x20in) s. panel (DM 4000)
£1473 $2400   *(12-Jun-91 N.M502/R) Bunch of roses in glass vase on table*
                 (52x43cm-20x17in) s. panel (DM 4300)
£1712 $2791   *(12-Jun-91 N.M500/R) Summer flowers and raspberry branch on table*
                 (70x62cm-28x24in) s. panel (DM 5000)
£2098 $4049   *(12-Dec-90 N.M600/R) Bunch of summer flowers in vase, glass and*
                 strawberry branches on table (81x60cm-32x24in) s. panel (DM 6000)

KONGSBAK, Albert (1877-?) Danish
£8200 $14104   *(17-May-91 C177/R) Children playing in courtyard (71x83cm-28x33in)*
                 s.d.1904

KONGSRUD, Anders (1866-1938) Norwegian
£744 $1332   *(14-Mar-91 BU.O66/R) Bullfinches on branches of rowanberries*
                 (50x42cm-20x17in) s. (N.KR 8500)

KONGSVOLD, Rolf (1903-1960) Norwegian
£963 $1724   *(11-Mar-91 B.O76/R) Figure composition (92x128cm-36x50in) s.d.27*
                 (N.KR 11000)

KONIG, Franz Niklaus (1765-1832) Swiss
£2778 $4806   *(22-May-91 GS.B2132) Portraits of Salome Catharina Sprungli. Rudolf*
                 Abraham Sprungli (35x28cm-14x11in) one i.verso one s.d.1800 i.verso
                 oval pair (S.FR 7000)

KONIG, Fritz (1924-) German
£580 $1137   *(20-Nov-91 L.K341) Bilderschrift (49x62cm-19x24in) mono.d.1964 chl*
                 (DM 1700)
£1115 $1929   *(21-May-91 WK.M1087/R) Karyatidenfiguren (44x56cm-17x22in) mono.i.d.1966*
                 chl (DM 3300)

KONIG, H (20th C) German
£685 $1226   *(14-Mar-91 N.M2692/R) Peasants gathered around table reading newspaper*
                 (21x16cm-8x6in) s.d.23 panel (DM 2000)

KONIG, H (20th C) German-cont.
£699 $1357   (4-Dec-90 FN.S1933/R) Latest news, group of men with newspaper in pub interior (21x16cm-8x6in) s.d.1935 panel (DM 2000)

KONIG, Johann (1586-1642) German
£31000 $52390   (16-Apr-91 PH55/R) Ecce homo (61x45cm-24x18in) s. on copper

KONIG, Josef (1882-1955) Austrian
£784 $1552   (31-Jan-91 D.V66/R) Landscape with pond (16x26cm-6x10in) mono. panel (A.S 16000)

KONIG, L (20th C) ?
£487   *$954*   *(24-Jan-91 D.V65/R) The tax collector s.d.1912 mixed media triptych (A.S 10000)*

KONIG, Leo von (1871-c.1944) German
£944 $1822   (12-Dec-90 N.M597/R) Two peacocks (24x33cm-9x13in) s.d.1923 board (DM 2700)
£1365 $2676   (22-Nov-90 L.K1067/R) Portrait of Yvonne von Konig (41x31cm-16x12in) mono.d.1919 (DM 4000)
£3378 $5743   (28-May-91 KF.M795/R) Portrait of actor Alexander Moissi (106x83cm-42x33in) s.d.1933 (DM 10000)

KONIGSBRUNN, Hermann von (1823-1907) Austrian
£2879 $4952   (16-May-91 D.V229/R) Red deer feeding by the edge of the wood (98x128cm-39x50in) mono.verso (A.S 60000)

KONIGSTEIN, Georg (1937-) Austrian
£868 $1693   (18-Oct-90 D.V213/R) Klosterneuburg (50x60cm-20x24in) s.d.88 (A.S 18000)

KONINCK, Daniel de (1668-?) Dutch
£13500 $22815   (17-Apr-91 S51) Portrait of man wearing brown turban (78x63cm-31x25in) indis.s.d.

KONINCK, David de (style) (17/18th C) Flemish
£850 $1386   (4-Jul-91 C542/R) Ducks on pond (61x71cm-24x28in)

KONINCK, Jacob (17/18th C) Dutch
£2599   *$5121*   *(12-Nov-90 CH.AM36/R) Road through wood, cotage on left (10x15cm-4x6in) with i. pen wash (D.FL 8500)*

KONINCK, Kerstiaen de (style) (1580-1630) Flemish
£4500 $7335   (4-Jul-91 C668/R) Destruction of Sodom amd Gomorrah (51x103cm-20x41in) panel

KONINCK, Philips de (1619-1688) Dutch
£6316   *$12000*   *(8-Jan-91 SY.NY36/R) The raising of Lazurus (16x21cm-6x8in) ink*

KONINCK, Salomon (after) (1609-1656) Dutch
£2500 $4925   (31-Oct-90 S42/R) The calling of Matthew (62x90cm-24x35in) panel

KONING, Dirk (1888-?) Dutch
£727 $1368   (20-Sep-90 D.V140/R) Still life with book, green glass and apples (48x68cm-19x27in) s. board (A.S 15000)

KONING, Roeland (1898-?) Dutch
£5202 $9000   (21-May-91 CE.NY68/R) Peasnats returning home (90x113cm-35x44in) s.

KONINGH, Arie Ketting de (?) Dutch
£2395 $4168   (26-Mar-91 VN.R48/R) Shepherd with his flock in romantic landscape (33x44cm-13x17in) s. panel (D.FL 8000)

KONINGH, Leendert de (19th C) Dutch
£1031 $1959   (2-Mar-91 KRA.D351/R) Horses watering in river landscape with houses (40x52cm-16x20in) s. canvas on panel (DM 3000)
£1524 $2988   (6-Nov-90 SY.AM158/R) Figures with cattle by river (64x81cm-25x32in) s. (D.FL 5000)
£915   *$1756*   *(27-Nov-90 SY.AM3512/R) Riverlandscape with sailing ships and ferry and travellers on road (30x43cm-12x17in) s. W/C (D.FL 3000)*

KONINGSBRUGGEN, Rob van (20th C) Dutch?
£1393 $2689   (12-Dec-90 CH.AM454) Om de Hock (110x110cm-43x43in) (D.FL 4500)

KONINGSVELD, Jacobus van (1824-1866) Dutch
£7879 $15521   (30-Oct-90 CH.AM158/R) Elegant company on beach of Scheveningen (29x77cm-11x30in) s.d.1859 (D.FL 26000)

KONO, Micao (20th C) Japanese
£1285 $2492   (5-Dec-90 HC.P4) Bouquet de roses blanches (38x61cm-15x24in) s. (F.FR 12500)
£5612 $11056   (16-Nov-90 FB.P192/R) Nu allonge (65x91cm-26x36in) s.d.MCMLXXIV (F.FR 55000)
£554   *$1081*   *(27-Oct-90 LT.P135) L'arlequin (20x26cm-8x10in) Indian ink W/C (F.FR 5500)*

KONO, Micao (20th C) Japanese-cont.
£605 $1179   (27-Oct-90 LT.P136) L'heure de la sieste (22x26cm-9x10in) s. Indian ink
                  W/C (F.FR 6000)
£625 $1219   (27-Oct-90 LT.P133) Pierrot et Colombine (19x24cm-7x9in) Indian ink W/C
                  (F.FR 6200)

KONOPA, Rudolf (1864-?) Austrian
£633 $1240   (24-Jan-91 D.V125/R) Landscape, late autumn (99x65cm-39x26in) s.
                  (A.S 13000)

KONOVALOVA-KOVRIGUINA, Tatiana (1917-) Russian
£504 $821   (16-Jun-91 C.P54/R) L'apprenti photographe (50x40cm-20x16in) s. verso
                  (F.FR 5000)
£655 $1067   (16-Jun-91 C.P51/R) L'accueil du heros (50x75cm-20x30in) s. verso
                  (F.FR 6500)
£1085 $2137   (3-Oct-90 QWA.P55) Des fleurs (80x64cm-31x25in) (F.FR 11000)

KONOW, Jurgen von (1915-1959) Swedish
£1390 $2697   (5-Dec-90 AB.S7147/R) 'Valborgsmassoafton' - Dramatic theatre, Stockholm
                  (80x100cm-31x39in) s.d.1947-48 panel (S.KR 15000)

KOOL, Willem (1608-1666) Dutch
£3670 $7229   (13-Nov-90 CH.AM15/R) Cavalry charging travellers on country road
                  (52x69cm-20x27in) s.d. panel (D.FL 12000)

KOOLEN, Harry (1904-) Dutch
£1037 $1970   (26-Feb-91 VN.R170) Mother with her child and two doves by the Seine
                  (130x85cm-51x33in) s. (D.FL 3400)

KOONING, Elaine de (20th C) American
£3316 $6500   (6-Nov-90 CE.NY53/R) Squeeze play (76x76cm-30x30in) st.init.

KOONING, Willem de (1904-) American/Dutch
£13198 $26000   (4-Oct-90 SY.NY146/R) Untitled (71x56cm-28x22in) s. newspaper on
                    masonite
£17766 $35000   (4-Oct-90 SY.NY62/R) Untitled (58x76cm-23x30in) s. oil newsprint on
                    canvas
£18878 $37000   (7-Nov-90 SY.NY205/R) Untitled (64x41cm-25x16in) s. newsprint laid down
                    on canvas
£79882 $135000   (1-May-91 SY.NY179/R) Woman (72x56cm-28x22in) s. vellum
£91371 $180000   (5-Oct-90 CH.NY24/R) Woman (61x41cm-24x16in) s. masonite
£114796 $225000   (7-Nov-90 SY.NY155/R) Immediate offerings (117x75cm-46x30in) s.
                    newspaper laid down on masonite
£126904 $250000   (14-Nov-90 SY.NY297/R) A woman (91x61cm-36x24in) s.i.d.65 paper mounted
                    on canvas
£4081633 $8000000 (7-Nov-90 CH.NY7/R) July (175x201cm-69x79in) s.
£6122 $12000   (7-Nov-90 SY.NY206/R) Violinist (31x20cm-12x8in) s. chl.
£7653 $15000   (8-Nov-90 CH.NY102/R) Untitled (48x61cm-19x24in) s. chl. vellum on
                    canvas
£7666 $14948   (15-Oct-90 B.O62/R) Woman (30x20cm-12x8in) s. i.verso pencil
                    (N.KR 88000)
£8876 $15000   (2-May-91 CH.NY195/R) Untitled - woman. Fat and skinny (31x20cm-12x8in)
                    s. chl felt-tip pen three
£10204 $20000   (8-Nov-90 CH.NY118/R) Untitled (59x48cm-23x19in) s.i.d.August 21 1967
                    chl. vellum
£24235 $47500   (7-Nov-90 SY.NY133/R) Woman (30x24cm-12x9in) s. graphite double-sided

KOONING, Willem de (attrib) (1904-) American/Dutch
£1786 $3000   (28-Apr-91 HG.C498) Untitled (48x33cm-19x13in) mono.d.1967 chl chk

KOORNSTRA, Metten (1912-) Dutch
£867 $1673   (12-Dec-90 CH.AM79) Stilleven - landschap (39x29cm-15x11in) mono.d.72
                  board (D.FL 2800)

KOPCKE, Arthur (20th C) ?
£805 $1578   (13-Feb-91 KH.K97) Rebus picture (81x66cm-32x26in) s. (D.KR 9000)
£1157 $2255   (19-Oct-90 RAS.V656/R) Composition (35x54cm-14x21in) s.d.59 (D.KR 13000)
£2224 $4181   (19-Sep-90 KH.K73/R) Seated woman (49x70cm-19x28in) s.d.59 masonite
                  (D.KR 25000)
£2326 $4558   (13-Feb-91 KH.K94/R) Composition (100x70cm-39x28in) s.d.60 panel
                  (D.KR 26000)
£2377 $4635   (10-Oct-90 RAS.K87) 'K no.1' - composition (50x40cm-20x16in) s.d.59
                  i.verso (D.KR 27000)
£2580 $5031   (19-Oct-90 RAS.V655/R) Palm Sunday, composition (68x99cm-27x39in) s.d.59
                  (D.KR 29000)
£2862 $5610   (13-Feb-91 KH.K96/R) Hommage a Michel Angelo (70x100cm-28x39in)
                  s.d.63verso panel (D.KR 32000)
£3169 $5451   (15-May-91 RAS.K49/R) Reading/work piece (100x100cm-39x39in) s.
                  (D.KR 36000)
£3169 $5451   (15-May-91 RAS.K46/R) Reading/work piece (100x100cm-39x39in) s.verso
                  (D.KR 36000)
£3804 $7342   (12-Dec-90 RAS.K105/R) Reading/Work piece (100x100cm-39x39in) s.verso
                  (D.KR 42000)
£4286 $7929   (5-Mar-91 RAS.K26/R) Simple rebus (122x61cm-48x24in) s.d.63verso
                  (D.KR 48000)

1078

KOPCKE, Arthur (20th C) ?-cont.
£1144	$2232	(10-Oct-90 RAS.K1/R) Rot promille (64x44cm-25x17in) s.d.60 s.d.1960verso gouache (D.KR 13000)
£1521	$2980	(13-Feb-91 KH.K95/R) 'So bunt kann die Natur es gar nicht treiben' (50x65cm-20x26in) s. W/C crayon (D.KR 17000)
£3684	$6263	(29-May-91 KH.K274/R) Reading-Work Pieces no.37, 68, 94 (68x94cm-27x37in) s.verso oil collage (D.KR 42000)
£4270	$8028	(19-Sep-90 KH.K82/R) Composition (50x65cm-20x26in) s. collage mixed media (D.KR 48000)

KOPITZEVA, Maia (1924-) Russian
| £697 | $1212 | (25-Mar-91 ARC.P9/R) Le bateau (45x33cm-18x13in) s. (F.FR 7000) |

KOPMAN, Benjamin (1887-?) American
| £1006 | $1700 | (17-Apr-91 D.NY60/R) In gallery (119x76cm-47x30in) s.d.45 |

KOPPENOL, C (1865-1946) Dutch
| £3287 | $6409 | (24-Oct-90 GM.B1151) A la plage (50x70cm-20x28in) s. wood (B.FR 200000) |

KOPPENOL, Cornelis (1865-1946) Dutch
£500	$860	(14-May-91 SWS347/R) Ploughing (24x27cm-9x11in) s. panel
£569	$961	(17-Apr-91 WE.MU39) Joy of motherhood (30x42cm-12x17in) s. (DM 1700)
£800	$1576	(1-Nov-90 B43/R) Afternoon at the beach (24x37cm-9x15in) s. panel
£1050	$2048	(22-Oct-90 SWS162) Children on beach (47x56cm-19x22in) s. panel
£1200	$2352	(14-Feb-91 CSK205/R) Invitation to play (48x69cm-19x27in) s. panel
£1223	$2300	(22-Sep-90 WOL.C233/R) Children at shore (46x64cm-18x25in) s. panel
£3000	$5910	(1-Nov-90 B42/R) Paddling at low tide (70x100cm-28x39in) s. panel

KORAB, Karl (1937-) Austrian
£2485	$4821	(6-Dec-90 D.V236/R) Still life (51x60cm-20x24in) s.d.87 (A.S 50000)
£389	$763	(24-Jan-91 D.V282/R) Design for playing card (19x16cm-7x6in) s.d.73 mixed media (A.S 8000)
£437	$717	(20-Jun-91 D.V178/R) Houses in the Waldviertel (31x48cm-12x19in) s.d.72 pen indian ink (A.S 9000)
£437	$717	(20-Jun-91 D.V177/R) Houses in the Waldviertel (32x50cm-13x20in) s.d.71 pen indian ink (A.S 9000)
£488	$903	(7-Mar-91 D.V283/R) Waldviertel landscape (49x64cm-19x25in) s. chk (A.S 10000)
£583	$955	(20-Jun-91 D.V176/R) Village (29x41cm-11x16in) s.d.69 pen indian ink (A.S 12000)
£1053	$1821	(8-May-91 D.V175/R) Still life with bandaged head (22x31cm-9x12in) s.d.71 mixed media (A.S 22000)
£1217	$2384	(24-Jan-91 D.V283/R) Blue still life (30x39cm-12x15in) s.d.83 pencil W/C gouache (A.S 25000)

KORF, G van der (?) ?
| £635 | $1244 | (12-Feb-91 GM.B667) L'heure du gouter (49x59cm-19x23in) s. (B.FR 38000) |

KORFF, Alexander Hugo Bakker (1824-1882) Dutch
£1198	$2012	(23-Apr-91 SY.AM260) In kitchen (14x11cm-6x4in) panel (D.FL 4000)
£2994	$5030	(23-Apr-91 SY.AM104) Visit (12x9cm-5x4in) s. panel (D.FL 10000)
£2994	$5030	(23-Apr-91 SY.AM173/R) Tea-time (11x13cm-4x5in) s.d.66 panel (D.FL 10000)
£778	$1308	(23-Apr-91 SY.AM197) Interior with two sisters by fire (23x18cm-9x7in) s.d.68 W/C (D.FL 2600)

KORLE, P (19th C) ?
| £700 | $1358 | (6-Dec-90 TL78/R) The young musician (66x43cm-26x17in) indist.s. |

KORN, Johan Philip (1728-1796) Swedish
| £919 | $1801 | (6-Nov-90 BA.S146/R) River landscape with figures (14x22cm-6x9in) init. panel (S.KR 10000) |

KORNBECK, Julius (1839-1920) German
£1126	$1847	(18-Jun-91 FN.S1947/R) Cattle, sheep and peasants in field (31x49cm-12x19in) s. canvas on board (DM 3300)
£1365	$2239	(18-Jun-91 FN.S1945/R) Alpine farmhouse with laundry hanging on balcony and peasant seated (49x40cm-19x16in) s. canvas on board (DM 4000)
£1672	$2826	(19-Apr-91 FN.S1770/R) Wooded river landscape (41x60cm-16x24in) s. board (DM 5000)
£2014	$3806	(25-Sep-90 FN.S2254/R) Neckar valley near Nurtingen, autumn (24x41cm-9x16in) s. board (DM 5900)
£2048	$3870	(25-Sep-90 FN.S2253/R) Mountain lake landscape with rowing boat after thunderstorm (59x100cm-23x39in) s. (DM 6000)
£2218	$3638	(18-Jun-91 FN.S1944/R) Neckar landscape after rain (78x118cm-31x46in) s. (DM 6500)
£2730	$4478	(18-Jun-91 FN.S1942/R) Reapers in landscape with view of Nurtingen and Hohen Neuffen (51x43cm-20x17in) s. (DM 8000)
£3082	$5517	(12-Mar-91 FN.S2478/R) Wooded Aich landscape with peasants ploughing and view of Nurtingen (88x114cm-35x45in) s. (DM 9000)
£3413	$6451	(25-Sep-90 FN.S2251/R) Wooded river landscape with children playing near farmhouses (102x78cm-40x31in) s. (DM 10000)
£5944	$11531	(4-Dec-90 FN.S1938/R) Garden house covered with snow and view of Neckarauen near Nurtingen (97x124cm-38x49in) s. (DM 17000)
£7877	$14099	(12-Mar-91 FN.S2477/R) Wooded Neckar landscape with sheep and girl (188x156cm-74x61in) s. l.verso (DM 23000)

KORNBECK, Peter (1837-1894) Danish
£582 $990   (28-May-91 AB.S4779/R) Church interior with figures, St.Zeno in Verona (60x50cm-24x20in) s.d.1880 (S.KR 6200)
£1038 $2014   (22-Aug-90 RAS.K4/R) View from Canobbia by Lago Maggiore (49x38cm-19x15in) s.d.1891 (D.KR 12000)
£1557 $3021   (22-Aug-90 RAS.K3/R) Figures outside arches to Spalato (48x32cm-19x13in) s.d.1873 (D.KR 18000)
£2135 $4014   (18-Sep-90 BU.K76/R) Mountainous landscape with figures outside church after service (42x63cm-17x25in) s.d.1873 (D.KR 24000)
£2154 $4244   (14-Nov-90 RAS.K539/R) The Piazza di Tuomo Trient (32x50cm-13x20in) init.d.1870 (D.KR 24000)

KORNER, Edmund (1873-?) German
£1024 $2007   (24-Nov-90 SA.A757/R) View of the Zwinger, Dresden (82x68cm-32x27in) s. canvas on panel (DM 3000)
£1871 $3012   (26-Jun-91 KM.K1533/R) Kitchen interior with woman and child eating meal s. (DM 5500)

KORNERUP, Valdemar (1865-1924) Danish
£511 $858   (22-Apr-91 BU.K13/R) Cottage interior with woman winding wool (31x29cm-12x11in) s.d.1916 (D.KR 5800)
£2224 $4181   (18-Sep-90 BU.K58/R) Mending in the peasant cottage (53x58cm-21x23in) s.d.1922 (D.KR 25000)

KORNEV, Oleg (1965-) Russian
£643 $1151   (14-Apr-91 APT.P37/R) Mandala 27-33 (123x77cm-48x30in) s.i.d.1991 verso oil paste (F.FR 6500)

KOROMPAY, Giovanni (1904-?) Italian
£2705 $4842   (9-Apr-91 F.R181/R) Cave di marmo a Carrara (75x90cm-30x35in) s. panel (I.L 6000000)

KOROSTIK, Galina (1955-) Russian
£432   *$799*   *(4-Mar-91 ZZ.F140) Papillon (21x22cm-8x9in) s. W/C (F.FR 4300)*

KOROVIAKOV, Alexandre (1912-) Russian
£603 $1158   (18-Feb-91 ARC.P52/R) Le quai de l'île de Pierre (60x79cm-24x31in) s. (F.FR 6000)
£704 $1351   (18-Feb-91 ARC.P51/R) Le quai a Petropavlovka (51x79cm-20x31in) s. verso (F.FR 7000)

KOROVINE, Constantin (1861-1939) Russian
£1348 $2412   (13-Apr-91 FAL.M161/R) Still life of fruit and flowers (31x40cm-12x16in) s. (S.KR 14500)
£1930 $3763   (18-Oct-90 D.V137/R) Russian landscape (54x66cm-21x26in) s. (A.S 40000)
£2347 $4623   (12-Nov-90 YC.P14/R) Village en hiver (33x40cm-13x16in) s. board under glass (F.FR 23000)
£3000 $5760   (27-Nov-90 PH99/R) Lake landscape (66x87cm-26x34in) s.
£3353 $5800   (23-May-91 CH.NY135/R) Parisian street scene (41x49cm-16x19in) s.i. paperboard
£10000 $19500   (10-Oct-90 C223/R) Evening serenade (88x66cm-35x26in) s.i.d.1915

KOROVINE, Victor (1936-) Russian
£516 $887   (15-May-91 AGB.P208/R) Perspective Nevsky (74x100cm-29x39in) s. (F.FR 5200)
£683 $1312   (18-Feb-91 ARC.P80/R) Le quai a Yalta (59x69cm-23x27in) s.d.88 (F.FR 6800)

KORT, Cornelis Jacobus de (1934-) Dutch
£808 $1398   (6-May-91 ZEL.L1801/R) Flowers in vase, pot and buddha figure (80x60cm-31x24in) s. (DM 2400)

KORTE, H G de (20th C) Dutch
£608 $1150   (24-Sep-90 S.SL896) Scene in Dutch town (51x61cm-20x24in) s.
£899 $1700   (24-Sep-90 S.SL147/R) Barges Amsterdam (69x89cm-27x35in) s.

KORTHAUS, Carl Adolf (1879-?) German
£616 $1103   (13-Mar-91 N.M558/R) Mountain landscape with wooded pond in early spring (82x98cm-32x39in) s. (DM 1800)

KORTMAN, Johan E (1858-1923) Finnish
£1022   *$1757*   (14-May-91 HOR.H67) View (13x19cm-5x7in) s. (F.M 7100)
£2158 $3712   (14-May-91 HOR.H68) Coastal cliffs (43x62cm-17x24in) s. (F.M 15000)

KOSA, Emil (jnr) (1903-1968) American
£1026 $2000   (10-Oct-90 B.SF634/R) Carmel seascape (66x76cm-26x30in) s.
£1026 $2000   (10-Oct-90 B.SF554/R) Mount Moran (51x76cm-20x30in) s.
£1667 $3250   (10-Oct-90 B.SF632/R) Lone sentinel (63x76cm-25x30in) s.
£1687 $2750   (11-Jun-91 MOR.P50 a) Above haze (25x30cm-10x12in) s. board
£4082 $8000   (13-Feb-91 B.SF2153/R) From Ojai (76x91cm-30x36in) s.
£4103 $8000   (10-Oct-90 B.SF611/R) Joy of living (61x91cm-24x36in) s. masonite
£816   *$1600*   *(7-Nov-90 B.SF3832/R) City street (52x72cm-20x28in) s. W/C*
£1276   *$2500*   *(12-Feb-91 MOR.P49) Boats in harbour (53x74cm-21x29in) s. W/C*
£1795   *$3500*   *(10-Oct-90 B.SF630/R) Flying S Ranch (38x68cm-15x27in) s. W/C*

KOSA, Emil (snr) (1876-1955) American
£2551 $5000 (13-Feb-91 B.SF2063/R) Flowers in vase (91x76cm-36x30in) s. board

KOSEL, Hermann (1896-) Austrian
£586 $1083 (7-Mar-91 D.V177/R) Alt Wien (36x44cm-14x17in) s. board (A.S 12000)
£730 $1431 (24-Jan-91 D.V7/R) View of Salzburg with cathedral (45x54cm-18x21in) s.
              panel (A.S 15000)

KOSINSKI, Joseph (attrib) (1753-1821) Polish
£612 $1206 (13-Nov-90 CH.G239/R) Portrait of Countess Lichnowsky (8x?cm-3x?in) min.
              gilt-metal mount oval (S.FR 1500)

KOSNICK-KLOSS, Jeanne (1892-1955) German
£746 $1260 (15-Apr-91 CC.P91) Composition (27x22cm-11x9in) mono. hardboard
              (F.FR 7500)
£813 $1626 (10-Feb-91 CC.P43) Composition (32x24cm-13x9in) mono. hardboard
              (F.FR 8000)
£1511 $2462 (16-Jun-91 CC.P5) Composition (66x46cm-26x18in) mono. panel hardboard
              (F.FR 15000)
£402 $743 (6-Mar-91 HC.P94) Composition polychrome (25x15cm-10x6in) mono. gouache
              (F.FR 4000)
£524 $1022 (20-Jan-91 GL.P24) Composition (43x31cm-17x12in) init. gouache
              (F.FR 5200)
£646 $1092 (15-Apr-91 CC.P49) Composition (25x16cm-10x6in) mono. gouache
              (F.FR 6500)

KOSO, Mitsutaka (1950-) Japanese
£445 $797 (14-Apr-91 APT.P29/R) Fukei no.2 (96x96cm-38x38in) s.i.d.1988 verso
              gouache fixed panel (F.FR 4500)

KOSSAK, Jany (20th C) Polish
£676 $1284 (14-Sep-90 SA.A1185/R) Autumn hunt (40x60cm-16x24in) s.d.1923 board
              (DM 2000)

KOSSAK, Jerzy (1890-1963) Polish
£504 $932 (10-Mar-91 AG.W4) Ulan patrol (25x33cm-10x13in) s.d.1927 board
              (P.Z 9000000)
£546 $1064 (20-Jan-91 AG.W5) In front of a chapel (36x48cm-14x19in) s.d.1931 board
              (P.Z 10000000)
£591 $1182 (7-Feb-91 D.V118/R) Charge (35x50cm-14x20in) s.d.1947 (A.S 12000)
£693 $1316 (3-Mar-91 PPB.K4) Resting (33x43cm-13x17in) s. board (P.Z 12500000)
£720 $1369 (3-Mar-91 PPB.K3) Patrol (28x38cm-11x15in) s.d.1930 board
              (P.Z 13000000)
£804 $1576 (25-Jan-91 REM.W5) Scouts (45x38cm-18x15in) s.d.1920 panel
              (P.Z 15000000)
£876 $1551 (23-Mar-91 HO.P4) House patrol (45x55cm-18x22in) s.d.1939 board
              (P.Z 15000000)

KOSSAK, Julius (1824-1899) Polish
£2184 $4258 (20-Jan-91 UNI.W1) Meadow landscape (32x46cm-13x18in) s.d.1891 W/C
              (P.Z 40000000)
£2184 $4258 (20-Jan-91 AG.W6) Wild fields (32x46cm-13x18in) s.d.1891 (P.Z 40000000)
£14000 $27300 (10-Oct-90 C172/R) Illustrations to 'With Fire and Sword' by Henryk
              Sienkewicz (32x48cm-13x19in) s.d.1885,1886 ink wash htd white set of
              12

KOSSAK, Wolciech von (1857-1942) French
£626 $1121 (16-Mar-91 AL.W2) Study of a house (40x50cm-16x20in) s.d.1926 board
              (P.Z 11000000)
£665 $1264 (3-Mar-91 REM.W6) Portrait of a girl (21x15cm-8x6in) s.d.1918 board
              (P.Z 12000000)
£993 $1758 (23-Mar-91 HO.P5) Soldier and wounded horse (21x22cm-8x9in) s.d.1922
              cardboard (P.Z 17000000)
£1053 $2001 (3-Mar-91 REM.W7) Head of a horse (39x30cm-15x12in) s.d.1921 board
              (P.Z 19000000)
£2334 $4177 (17-Mar-91 UNI.W3) Man on guard (49x39cm-19x15in) s.d.1929 board
              (P.Z 41000000)
£522 $924 (19-Mar-91 UL.T181/R) Battle scene (47x68cm-19x27in) W/C (N.KR 6000)

KOSSIK, Hans (20th C) ?
£1050 $2048 (11-Oct-90 D.V247/R) Stift Klosterneuburg (24x33cm-9x13in) s.d.1946 W/C
              (A.S 22000)

KOSSOFF, Leon (20th C) ?
£32000 $59200 (8-Mar-91 C159/R) Children's swimming pool (35x30cm-14x12in) board
£80000 $128800 (27-Jun-91 S44/R) School building, Willesden, srping 1981
              (136x166cm-54x65in) board
£1200 $2088 (28-Mar-91 CSK209/R) Swimming pool (35x50cm-14x20in) s. chl
£1200 $2328 (6-Dec-90 CSK187 a/R) Seated female nude (85x56cm-33x22in) chl
£1700 $2771 (1-Jul-91 S15/R) Seated figure (84x55cm-33x22in) chl. two sheets of
              paper
£6500 $10595 (1-Jul-91 S83/R) Fidelma (88x56cm-35x22in) chl. several pieces of paper

KOSSONOGI, Joseph (1908-1981) ?
£429 $700 (12-Jun-91 GG.TA174/R) Landscape with houses (31x46cm-12x18in) s. W/C
£736 $1200 (12-Jun-91 GG.TA173/R) Tiberias (26x26cm-10x10in) s.d.1930 W/C

KOSSUTH, Egon Josef (1874-?) Czechoslovakian
£1868 $3250   (27-Mar-91 B.SF4256/R) Portrait of young woman in Chinese coat
                             (127x77cm-50x30in) s.indis.d. board

KOSTABI, Mark (1960-) American
£1156 $2000   (7-May-91 CE.NY288/R) George Washington (178x122cm-70x48in) s.d.1983
£1682 $2742   (16-Jun-91 SY.ME94) Is there anything else you'd like to add - just lots
                      zeroes to my prices (183x122cm-72x48in) s.d.1985 acrylic canvas
                      (A.D 3600)
£1786 $3500   (6-Nov-90 CE.NY220/R) The Critic's Kitty (179x122cm-70x48in) s.d.1984 i.
£1939 $3800   (6-Nov-90 CE.NY219/R) Annie Herron number one (183x122cm-72x48in)
                      s.d.1985 i. verso
£2454 $4000   (12-Jun-91 SY.NY255/R) Cash in on passion (178x122cm-70x48in) s.d.1984
                      acrylic canvas
£2454 $4000   (12-Jun-91 SY.NY256/R) Half 'n' half (91x122cm-36x48in) s.d.1984
£3316 $6500   (6-Nov-90 CE.NY218/R) Pathetic Beverly Hills mentality
                      (213x172cm-84x68in) s.d.1988 i. verso
£4046 $7000   (7-May-91 CE.NY286/R) Bed of nails (183x132cm-72x52in) s. s.d.1983 verso
£4103 $8000   (10-Oct-90 SY.NY562/R) Off the books (213x183cm-84x72in) s.d.1987
                      s.i.d.verso
£6378 $12500   (6-Nov-90 CE.NY221/R) More for your million (229x137cm-90x54in) s.
                      i.d.1988 verso

KOSTABI, Mark and ROCKEFELLER, Still (20th C) American
£2551 $5000   (6-Nov-90 CE.NY221/R) Voice of fashion (102x72cm-40x28in) s. both d.1989
                      verso oil photostat cotton

KOSTER, Antonie L (1859-1937) Dutch
£2653 $5200   (6-Nov-90 GF.L2424/R) Bloemenbollenland (51x74cm-20x29in) s. s.i.verso
                      (S.FR 6500)
£848 $1672   (30-Oct-90 CH.AM492/R) Cart track along bulbfields and pond
                      (34x41cm-13x16in) s. pastel (D.FL 2800)

KOSTER, Everhardus (1817-1892) Dutch
£719 $1365   (11-Sep-90 CH.AM166) Shipping in a calm on a sunny afternoon
                      (16x23cm-6x9in) s. (D.FL 2400)
£1067 $2091   (6-Nov-90 SY.AM207) Moored vessels on beach (27x43cm-11x17in) s. panel
                      (D.FL 3500)
£1600 $2576   (27-Jun-91 CG92/R) Boats on a sunlit Dutch canal (20x28cm-8x11in) s.
                      panel

KOSTER, Jo (1869-1944) Dutch
£541 $935   (22-May-91 CH.AM365) Tree on hill (36x28cm-14x11in) s.d.1915 (D.FL 1800)
£5573 $10755   (12-Dec-90 CH.AM172/R) View of farmyard with girl in costume, Staphorst
                      (34x45cm-13x18in) s.d.1912 (D.FL 18000)

KOSTER, Karl Georg (1812-1893) German
£867 $1551   (12-Apr-91 BM.B632/R) Bavarian Alpine landscape with figures and castle
                      in rising thunderstorm (41x57cm-16x22in) s. (DM 2600)
£1608 $3120   (4-Dec-90 FN.S1934/R) River landscape with watermill and Jungfrau
                      Mountains beyond (65x88cm-26x35in) s. (DM 4600)

KOSTIENKO, Elena (1926-) Russian
£520 $874   (26-Apr-91 ARC.P18/R) Fenetre sur le jardin (50x40cm-20x16in) s. board
                      (F.FR 5200)
£553 $1061   (18-Feb-91 ARC.P86/R) Plage en Crimee (24x33cm-9x13in) s. board
                      (F.FR 5500)
£620 $1042   (26-Apr-91 ARC.P17/R) La lecture (33x58cm-13x23in) s. (F.FR 6200)
£704 $1351   (18-Feb-91 ARC.P85/R) Porte ouverte sur le jardin (52x36cm-20x14in) s.
                      (F.FR 7000)
£754 $1447   (18-Feb-91 ARC.P87/R) Gregory et la locomotive (67x48cm-26x19in) s.
                      board (F.FR 7500)
£2563 $4921   (18-Feb-91 ARC.P92/R) Les jeunes joueurs de hockey (142x150cm-56x59in)
                      s.d.74 (F.FR 25500)

KOSTIENKO, Lioubov (1947-) Russian
£771 $1495   (8-Dec-90 ZZ.F62/R) Le trompettiste (65x70cm-26x28in) (F.FR 7500)

KOSTINSKI, Piotr (1916-) Russian
£1529 $3011   (3-Oct-90 QWA.P61) Esquisse pour le tableau - Lenine et Gorki
                      (50x80cm-20x31in) (F.FR 15500)

KOSTKA, Alexander (1879-1961) Austrian
£478 $802   (25-Apr-91 D.V256/R) Torbogen am alten Universitatsplatz in Wien
                      (28x24cm-11x9in) s. W/C (A.S 10000)

KOSUTH, Joseph (20th C) ?
£12607 $24584   (23-Oct-90 F.M26/R) Art as idea is idea (118x118cm-46x46in) d.1967
                      photograph on cardboard (I.L 28000000)

KOTHE, Fritz (1916-) ?
£685 $1116   (14-Jun-91 L.K1000) Pla, female legs, pedestrian crossing lights
                      (38x28cm-15x11in) s.d.64 W/C (DM 2000)

KOTHER, Paul (1878-?) German
£3200 $6240   (19-Oct-90 C111/R) Das Madchen und der Clown. Zwei Jungen
                       (112x62cm-44x24in) double-sided
£1409 $2748   (13-Oct-90 KRA.D405/R) River landscape with boats (46x60cm-18x24in) s.
                       pastel (DM 4200)
£1600 $3120   (19-Oct-90 C112/R) Blumenstilleben mit Fruchten (49x40cm-19x16in) pastel
                       board

KOTSCHENREITER, Hugo (1854-1908) German
£2226 $3985   (13-Mar-91 N.M559/R) Peasant with pipe (29x22cm-11x9in) s.d.1907
                       (DM 6500)

KOTSCHMIESTER, G (19/20th C) German
£1405 $2600   (10-Mar-91 H.C49/R) Old man in hat (28x20cm-11x8in) s.d.1902

KOUNELLIS, Jannis (1936-) Greek
£13018 $22000   (2-May-91 CH.NY131/R) Untitled (70x100cm-28x39in) s.d.1960 verso tempera
                       paper
£7101 $12000   (2-May-91 CH.NY257/R) Untitled (102x71cm-40x28in) s.d.76 felt-tip pen
                       graphite W/C paper on board
£7101 $12000   (2-May-91 CH.NY256/R) Untitled (102x71cm-40x28in) s.d.76 felt-tip pen
                       graphite paper on board

KOUSNETZOFF, Constantin (1863-1936) Russian
£4995 $9640   (16-Dec-90 T.B150) L'Anse du Belon - Kerfany (79x59cm-31x23in) s.
                       (F.FR 49000)

KOUYOUMOJIAN, Elvire see JAN, Elvire

KOUZNETSOV, Alexi (1920-) Russian
£900 $1593   (18-Mar-91 ARC.P168/R) La beaute secrete de Moscou (89x62cm-35x24in) s.
                       (F.FR 9000)

KOUZNETSOV, Youri (1930-) Russian
£1282 $2526   (3-Oct-90 QWA.P79) Attente (50x35cm-20x14in) board (F.FR 13000)

KOWALSKI-WIERUSZ, Alfred von see WIERUSZ-KOWALSKI, Alfred von

KOWALSKY, Leopold Franz (1856-1931) Russian/French
£816 $1608   (14-Nov-90 CN.P70) Nature morte aux bouteilles (80x49cm-31x19in) s.
                       (F.FR 8000)

KOYANAGUI, Sei (1896-?) Japanese
£2569 $4985   (5-Dec-90 ZZ.F183/R) Le cerf et la biche (73x54cm-29x21in) s.
                       (F.FR 25000)

KOZAKIEWICZ, Anton (1841-?) Polish
£3684 $7000   (27-Feb-91 SY.NY293/R) Knife sharpener (32x44cm-13x17in) s.d.1889 panel
£5686 $9609   (17-Apr-91 WE.MU131/R) The knife grinder (32x44cm-13x17in) s.i.d.1889
                       panel (DM 17000)

KOZAKOFF, I (19th C) Russian
£917 $1807   (13-Nov-90 AB.S925/R) Cottage interior with figures (64x86cm-25x34in) s.
                       (S.KR 10000)

KOZLOV, Engels (1926-) Russian
£553 $1061   (18-Feb-91 ARC.P125) Le soudeur (82x51cm-32x20in) s.d.57 (F.FR 5500)
£653 $1254   (18-Feb-91 ARC.P129/R) Le matelot (100x64cm-39x25in) s.d.58 (F.FR 6500)
£704 $1351   (18-Feb-91 ARC.P127/R) Portrait de Natacha (70x60cm-28x24in) s.d.89
                       (F.FR 7000)
£1005 $1930   (18-Feb-91 ARC.P131/R) Le caricaturiste (63x97cm-25x38in) s.d.54
                       (F.FR 10000)

KRAEMER, Dieter (1937-) German
£411 $670   (14-Jun-91 L.K1008) Borsalino (43x47cm-17x19in) s.i.d.1981 W/C
                       (DM 1200)
£479 $782   (14-Jun-91 L.K1009) Small palace by the Arno (49x36cm-19x14in) s.i.d.81
                       W/C (DM 1400)

KRAEMER, Peter (19/20th C) German
£346 $692   (6-Feb-91 N.M509/R) Hunter smoking pipe (21x17cm-8x7in) s.i. W/C
                       (DM 1000)
£450 $900   (6-Feb-91 N.M510/R) Peasant with pick axe and backpack (21x17cm-8x7in)
                       s.i. W/C (DM 1300)
£1468 $2407   (18-Jun-91 FN.S1948/R) Portrait of Zeitungshansel with newspapers and
                       magazines (18x13cm-7x5in) s.i. W/C (DM 4300)

KRAEMER, Peter (jnr) (1857-1941) German
£845 $1647   (26-Oct-90 BM.B836) Portrait of man in costume with hat holding jug of
                       beer and radish (19x14cm-7x6in) s.i. gouache (DM 2500)
£847 $1516   (12-Apr-91 BM.B634/R) Peasant holding pipe standing by garden fence
                       (21x17cm-8x7in) s. W/C gouache (DM 2540)
£1224 $2362   (14-Dec-90 BM.B649/R) Old man in coustume holding pipe leaning against
                       tree (22x19cm-9x7in) s. W/C gouache (DM 3500)

KRAEN, van (19th C) Continental
£2096 $3500   (7-Jun-91 SY.NY9/R) The herring run (36x70cm-14x28in) indist.s. canvas
                        laid down on panel

KRAFFT, Carl R (1884-1938) American
£925 $1600   (12-May-91 H.C148/R) Across country (64x76cm-25x30in) s. s.i.verso
£3179 $5500   (10-May-91 S.BM78/R) In the Gloaming (97x102cm-38x40in) s.

KRAFFT, David von (after) (1655-1724) Swedish
£3005 $5108   (28-May-91 AB.S4642/R) Portrait of Karl XII (86x63cm-34x25in)
                        (S.KR 32000)

KRAFFT, Per (elder) (1724-1793) Swedish
£5150 $8858   (14-May-91 BU.S19/R) Portrait of Carl von Linne (70x53cm-28x21in)
                        (S.KR 55000)

KRAFFT, Per (younger) (1777-1863) Swedish
£780 $1536   (13-Nov-90 AB.S408/R) Portrait of Alderman Anders Reimers
                        (72x62cm-28x24in) s.d.1807 (S.KR 8500)

KRAFT, Frederik (1823-1854) Danish
£1726 $3348   (5-Dec-90 KH.K74/R) September day in Dyrehaveplain, view of Hveen
                        (65x91cm-26x36in) s.d.1849 (D.KR 19000)
£5800 $9976   (17-May-91 C199/R) Gerano (54x75cm-21x30in)

KRAGH, Ejnar R (1903-1981) Scandinavian
£654 $1230   (10-Aug-90 RAS.V606/R) Children playing by water's edge
                        (75x125cm-30x49in) s.d.55 (D.KR 7400)

KRAGH, Johannes (1870-1946) Danish
£2595 $5035   (22-Aug-90 RAS.K58/R) Interior with two small girls and boy playing with
                        bricks (87x135cm-34x53in) s.d.MCMXII (D.KR 30000)

KRAKAUER, Leopold (1890-1954) Israeli
£613 $1000   (12-Jun-91 GG.TA353/R) Olive trees (40x58cm-16x23in) s. chl
£681 $1300   (2-Jan-91 GG.TA471/R) Trees (55x44cm-22x17in) s.d.1940 chl
£920 $1500   (12-Jun-91 GG.TA352/R) Judean hills (43x55cm-17x22in) s.d.1933 chl
*£995 $1900   (2-Jan-91 GG.TA469/R) Landscape and thistles (56x76cm-22x30in) s.d.1952
                        chl*
£1361 $2600   (2-Jan-91 GG.TA468/R) Judean Hills (49x43cm-19x17in) s.d.1942 chl

KRAKOW, K (19th C) Polish
£633 $1265   (10-Feb-91 FDN.W2) Young peasant woman (33x24cm-13x9in) s.d.1862
                        (P.Z 12000000)
£791 $1582   (10-Feb-91 FDN.W3) Country landscape (22x31cm-9x12in) s.d.1856
                        (P.Z 15000000)

KRAL, Jaroslav (1883-1942) Czechoslovakian
£1196 $2069   (8-May-91 D.V103/R) Leda (30x40cm-12x16in) s.d.1932 (A.S 25000)

KRALIK, Jaroslav J (1924-) Czechoslovakian
*£1000 $1920   (28-Nov-90 KF.M974/R) Conversations with Botticelli (76x93cm-30x37in)
                        s.d.1985 collage tempera (DM 2900)*

KRAMER, Aagot (1884-1980) Norwegian
£1024 $1976   (13-Dec-90 BU.O32/R) Hanseatic quay, Bergen harbour (100x122cm-39x48in)
                        s.d.1950 (N.KR 11500)

KRAMER, F (19th C) German
£680 $1333   (14-Feb-91 CSK54/R) A herder with cattle on a country track
                        (56x94cm-22x37in) s.d.1887

KRAMER, Jacob (?) ?
£1300 $2535   (17-Oct-90 PHL314) Narcissi and tulips in a vase (50x40cm-20x16in) s.
£1350 $2633   (17-Oct-90 PHL232) Chrysanthemums in a vase and a statuette
                        (59x44cm-23x17in) s.
£1700 $3315   (17-Oct-90 PHL354/R) Lilies in a blue vase (80x49cm-31x19in) s.
£2200 $4290   (17-Oct-90 PHL363) Poppies in a jug on a ledge (81x50cm-32x20in) s.i.
£3500 $6580   (20-Sep-90 C79/R) Portrait of lady (75x63cm-30x25in) s.
£4000 $7520   (20-Sep-90 C87/R) Portrait of young gypsy girl (76x61cm-30x24in) s.d.17
                        s.i.stretcher
£7800 $15210   (17-Oct-90 PHL275/R) The Rabbi (49x39cm-19x15in) s.
*£700 $1365   (17-Oct-90 PHL195/R) Study of Millie (46x32cm-18x13in) s.indist.d.
                        blk.crayon htd.*

KRAMSKOJ, Ivan (1837-1887) Russian?
£10000 $19500   (10-Oct-90 C212/R) Portrait of Russian General seated on bench
                        (77x57cm-30x22in) s.i

KRANTZ, F (19th C) French
£977 $1700   (27-Mar-91 D.NY61) Too hot (20x25cm-8x10in) s. i.verso panel

KRANZ, Kurt (20th C) German?
£1068 $1783   (5-Jun-91 DO.H2809) Scorpion fish (39x82cm-15x32in) s.d.1960 panel
                        (DM 3150)

KRANZ, Kurt (20th C) German?-cont.
£1507 $2456   *(15-Jun-91 L.K383/R) Objects on grey (56x77cm-22x30in) s.i.d.1975verso*
                  W/C (DM 4400)

KRASNER, Lee (1911-) American
£33163 $65000   (15-Feb-91 SY.NY137/R) Equation (99x147cm-39x58in) init.d.57
                  s.i.d.stretcher

KRASNOV, Alexei (1923-) Russian
£663 $1272   (29-Nov-90 YC.P123/R) Les semeurs (89x94cm-35x37in) s.verso (F.FR 6500)

KRATKE, C L (1848-1921) French
£772 $1436   (9-Sep-90 BU.M705) Portrait of lady (22x16cm-9x6in) s.d.1879 panel
                  (S.KR 8300)

KRATKY, R (19th C) Austrian
£748 $1324   (20-Mar-91 KM.K1321) Portrait of young lady seated in interior
                  (68x55cm-27x22in) s. (DM 2200)

KRATZENSTEIN-STUB, Chr (1783-1816) Danish
£1423 $2676   (18-Sep-90 BU.K102/R) Portrait of Julie Tutein (35x26cm-14x10in)
                  (D.KR 16000)
£2657 $4491   (1-May-91 KH.K99) Interior with girl playing harp (64x50cm-25x20in)
                  (D.KR 30000)

KRATZER, Carl von (1827-1903) Austrian
£1200 $2063   (16-May-91 D.V218/R) Sunrise in the Dachstein mountains
                  (50x39cm-20x15in) mono.d.1880 (A.S 25000)

KRAUGERUD, Ragnar (1909-1987) Norwegian
£1132 $2208   (15-Oct-90 B.O63/R) Portrait of man (28x32cm-11x13in) s. i.verso panel
                  (N.KR 13000)
£6250 $12188   (11-Oct-90 BU.O77/R) Street scene (61x60cm-24x24in) init. (N.KR 72000)

KRAUS, August (1852-1917) German
£1679 $2889   (16-May-91 D.V201/R) Wine tasting (16x22cm-6x9in) s. panel (A.S 35000)

KRAUS, Georg Melchior (1737-1806) German
£7538 $12362   (22-Jun-91 CH.MO101/R) L'Usuriere (64x55cm-25x22in) s. panel
                  (F.FR 75000)

KRAUS, Hans O (20th C) German?
£702 $1257   (13-Mar-91 N.M560) View of Watzmann mountain (70x80cm-28x31in) s.
                  (DM 2050)

KRAUS, Lajos (20th C) ?
£850 $1675   (4-Oct-90 CSK36/R) On the Daube, Budapest (70x100cm-28x39in) s.d.1921

KRAUSCHE, Gustav Adolf (1850-1917) German
£804 $1552   (14-Dec-90 BM.B649 a/R) Man seated on wall smoking pipe and holding
                  letter (8x6cm-3x2in) s.d.99 panel (DM 2300)

KRAUSE, E A (fl.1891-1914) British
£560 $1075   *(28-Nov-90 AH169/R) On the East coast (25x36cm-10x14in) W/C*

KRAUSE, Emil (1871-1945) Danish
£619 $1164   (10-Aug-90 RAS.V492/R) Portrait of seated woman (117x95cm-46x37in)
                  st.verso (D.KR 7000)
£2595 $5035   (22-Aug-90 RAS.K103/R) Playtime break at school (101x135cm-40x53in)
                  init.d.1924 (D.KR 30000)
£3000 $5160   (17-May-91 C178/R) Playtime (103x137cm-41x54in) init.d.

KRAUSE, Emil A (fl.1891-1914) British
£480 $912   *(25-Feb-91 PH14) Sailing boat at low tide (24x39cm-9x15in) s.d.96 W/C*
£480 $859   *(11-Mar-91 HS127) Dunmore Castle with figures unloading fishing boats at*
                  low tide (34x52cm-13x20in) s.i.
£720 $1418   *(12-Nov-90 PH51) Shipping in the pool of London (33x51cm-13x20in) s. W/C*

KRAUSE, Franz (18/19th C) German
£1453 $2470   (27-May-91 L.K306) Stormy coastal landscape with small town
                  (50x44cm-20x17in) s.d.98 (DM 4300)

KRAUSE, Franz Emil (1836-1900) German
£1351 $2635   (26-Oct-90 KM.K1333/R) Rocky river landscape with snow covered peaks and
                  shepherd with flock (40x64cm-16x25in) s. (DM 4000)

KRAUSE, Hans (1864-?) German
£1074 $1750   (5-Jul-91 S.W3025/R) Two lions at water's edge (79x127cm-31x50in)
                  s.d.1900
£1500 $2955   (4-Oct-90 CSK89/R) A lion and lioness in a rocky landscape
                  (62x78cm-24x31in) s.d.1923

KRAUSE, Heinrich (1885-1985) Austrian
£1708 $3160   (7-Mar-91 D.V169/R) Brunn Schneebergbahn with view of W Neustadt
                  (66x100cm-26x39in) s. i.verso (A.S 35000)
£1988 $3857   (6-Dec-90 D.V76/R) Jug with lilies (75x61cm-30x24in) s. (A.S 40000)

KRAUSE, Lina (1857-?) German
£683 $1338   (24-Nov-90 SA.A818/R) Still life of flowers (37x31cm-15x12in) s. panel
                  (DM 2000)
£1399 $2699   (12-Dec-90 WE.MU145/R) Still life of flowers (30x37cm-12x15in) s. panel
                  (DM 4000)
£2081 $3600   (21-May-91 CE.NY139/R) Still life of flowers on ledge (19x15cm-7x6in) s.
                  panel

KRAUSE, S (19th C) German
£920 $1500   (5-Jul-91 S.W3064/R) Figures in alpine landscape (48x89cm-19x35in)
                  s.d.1870

KRAUSKOPF, Bruno (1892-1960) German
£1000 $1920   (21-Feb-91 B65) Portrait of auburn-haired girl (64x54cm-25x21in) s.
                  board
£1858 $3215   (25-May-91 N.M199/R) Stormy sea (50x60cm-20x24in) s. (DM 5500)
£1916 $3737   (15-Oct-90 B.O64/R) Sleeping woman (52x50cm-20x20in) s.d.38 (N.KR 22000)
£4392 $7422   (3-May-91 SA.A765/R) Sleeping woman (79x65cm-31x26in) s. board
                  (DM 13000)
£5068 $8615   (30-May-91 SY.BE64/R) Wooded landscape (50x69cm-20x27in) s. board
                  (DM 15000)
£471 $792   (26-Apr-91 KM.K354) Female nude seated (26x3cm-10x1in) s.d.29 W/C
                  (DM 1400)

KRAUSS, G F (18th C) ?
£8455 $16657   (14-Nov-90 F.M14/R) Trompe l'oeil con editti. Elementi architettonici,
                  calendario mensile (37x52cm-15x20in) s.i. W/C pair (I.L 18500000)

KRAUSZ, Wilhelm Viktor (1878-1959) Hungarian
£699 $1350   (12-Dec-90 N.M601/R) Bunch of summer flowers in vase. Bouquet of flowers
                  (44x41cm-17x16in) s. board double-sided (DM 2000)
£940 $1832   (10-Oct-90 ZEL.L1598/R) Portrait of young girl on divan resting on
                  pillow (61x59cm-24x23in) s. (DM 2800)
£1940 $3647   (20-Sep-90 D.V46/R) Portrait of woman with garland of flowers in her
                  hair (120x70cm-47x28in) s.d.1909 (A.S 40000)
£2669 $5044   (27-Sep-90 D.V48/R) Venice canal scene with view of Pente dei Scalzi,
                  evening (100x115cm-39x45in) s.d.1906 (A.S 55000)

KRAUTMANN, Richard (19/20th C) German
£1633 $3200   (6-Nov-90 GF.L2103/R) The curious traveller (72x57cm-28x22in) s.d.1918
                  (S.FR 4000)

KRAUZ, R (?) ?
£769 $1506   (12-Feb-91 GM.B591) Halte du berger (333x90cm-131x35in) s. (B.FR 46000)

KRAWIEC, Walter (1889-?) American
£1289 $2500   (7-Dec-90 S.W2705/R) One O'clock leave (76x102cm-30x40in) s. s.d.verso

KRAY, Reginald (20th C) British
£580 $974   (18-Jul-91 B100/R) Fight (60x72cm-24x28in) W/C acrylic

KRAY, Wilhelm (1828-1889) German
£1400 $2758   (4-Oct-90 CSK237/R) In the Roman Campagna (73x58cm-29x23in) s.d.'18
£1796 $3520   (6-Nov-90 GF.L2157/R) Mermaid and young boy with fish bathing
                  (74x121cm-29x48in) s. (S.FR 4400)
£2455 $4714   (28-Nov-90 PH.T9/R) Die Lorelei (128x91cm-50x36in) s. (C.D 5500)

KREBS, Walter (1900-1965) Swiss
£1746 $3021   (22-May-91 GS.B2130) Portrait of tailor seated at table working
                  (82x72cm-32x28in) s. tempera paper (S.FR 4400)
£437 $729   (7-Jun-91 ZOF.Z1368) Personificatio of death wearing cloak in interior
                  of cathedral (60x46cm-24x18in) s. mixed media (S.FR 1100)
£1270 $2197   (22-May-91 GS.B2129) River landscape with sailing boat (76x65cm-30x26in)
                  s. mixed media board (S.FR 3200)

KREGTEN, Fedor van (1871-1937) Dutch
£719 $1207   (23-Apr-91 SY.AM310) Grazing sheep (59x88cm-23x35in) s. (D.FL 2400)

KREIDOLF, Ernst Konrad Theophil (1863-1956) Swiss
£1270 $2121   (7-Jun-91 ZOF.Z1367/R) Geraniums (32x22cm-13x9in) s.d.1943 (S.FR 3200)
£2857 $5629   (13-Nov-90 GF.L5395/R) The treasure hunter, six dwarfs beneath blue
                  bellflowers (20x28cm-8x11in) s. W/C indian ink pen (S.FR 7000)

KREJCAR, Anton (1923-) Austrian
£746 $1446   (6-Dec-90 D.V187/R) Heads (33x23cm-13x9in) s.d.1970 mixed media
                  (A.S 15000)

KREMEGNE, Pinchus (1890-1981) Russian
£2535 $5020   (3-Feb-91 I.N138/R) Paysge de Correze (19x25cm-7x10in) s. board
                  (F.FR 50000)
£3364 $6492   (12-Dec-90 APT.P120) Bouquet de fleurs dans un vase (46x83cm-18x33in) s.
                  (F.FR 33000)
£3525 $5745   (11-Jun-91 I.N230/R) Nature morte aux fruits (33x41cm-13x16in) s.
                  (F.FR 35000)
£3665 $7000   (2-Jan-91 GG.TA467/R) Still life (50x65cm-20x26in) s.
£3988 $6500   (12-Jun-91 GG.TA433/R) Self-portrait (65x49cm-26x19in) s.d.1960

KREMEGNE, Pinchus (1890-1981) Russian-cont.
£4061 $8000   (13-Nov-90 CE.NY176/R) Vase de fleurs (55x38cm-22x15in) s.
£4359 $8500   (10-Oct-90 SY.NY295/R) Landscape (51x64cm-20x25in) s.
£5584 $11000   (13-Nov-90 CE.NY103/R) Scene de village (38x46cm-15x18in) s.
£5780 $10000   (7-May-91 CE.NY35/R) Le pont a Ceret (38x46cm-15x18in) s.
£7078 $13802   (17-Oct-90 LT.P12/R) Paysage Provencal (54x65cm-21x26in) s. (F.FR 70000)

KREMER, Petrus (1801-1888) Flemish
£3839 $6603   (16-May-91 D.V175/R) The death of Jan von Marnix in the battle near
               Astuwel (88x71cm-35x28in) s. panel (A.S 80000)

KREMP, E (20th C) Italian
£655 $1284   (7-Nov-90 N.M936/R) Fishermen, Bay of Algericas, Gibraltar
               (62x110cm-24x43in) s.d.1908 (DM 1900)
£1573 $3037   (10-Dec-90 L.K483) View of Monte Pellegrino with Palermo beyond
               (47x92cm-19x36in) s. (DM 4500)

KRESTENSEN, Tom (1927-) Swedish
£602 $1169   (5-Dec-90 AB.S7148/R) Figure composition (55x48cm-22x19in) s.d.69
               (S.KR 6500)
£649 $1259   (4-Dec-90 BA.S275/R) Figure on verandah (49x39cm-19x15in) s.d.64
               (S.KR 7000)
£745 $1289   (22-May-91 BA.S403/R) Vision at night (61x70cm-24x28in) s.d.65
               (S.KR 7900)

KRETSCHMER, H (?) German
£808 $1358   (24-Apr-91 N.M557) Beduin and camel resting (37x29cm-15x11in) s.
               (DM 2400)

KRETSCHMER, V (19th C) German
£615 $1100   (16-Mar-91 W.W29/R) Aschenbrodel (33x28cm-13x11in) s.i.

KRETZ, Leopold (1907-) French
£1187 $2125   (14-Apr-91 GL.P85/R) Nature morte a la statuette (45x55cm-18x22in) s.
               canvas laid down on board (F.FR 12000)

KRETZSCHMAR, Bernhard (1889-1972) German
£2027 $3507   (25-May-91 N.M200/R) Two boys with flowers offering congratulations
               (104x77cm-41x30in) mono. board (DM 6000)
£743   *$1286*   *(25-May-91 N.M201) Karlbrucke in Prag (35x47cm-14x19in) mono.d.1941 W/C*
               (DM 2200)
£845   *$1461*   *(25-May-91 N.M202) Street and church in Nadworna (54x76cm-21x30in)*
               s.d.1942 W/C (DM 2500)

KRETZSCHMER, Hermann (1811-1890) German
£1524 $2500   (19-Jun-91 B.SF1885/R) Die zerrissene Hose (57x48cm-22x19in)

KREUGER, Nils (1858-1930) Swedish
£1184 $1989   (24-Apr-91 BA.S131/R) Twilight, Rue Boissonnade (33x23cm-13x9in)
               init.d.1884 panel (S.KR 12500)
£3244 $6260   (12-Dec-90 BU.S40/R) Summer landscape with horses (52x102cm-20x40in)
               s.d.1899 (S.KR 35000)
£7169 $14051   (6-Nov-90 BA.S149/R) Horse at Alvaret (61x98cm-24x39in) s.d.1913 panel
               (S.KR 78000)
£7755 $15278   (30-Oct-90 BU.S54/R) Approaching storm (73x100cm-29x39in) s.d.1919
               (S.KR 85000)
£9124 $17974   (30-Oct-90 BU.S53/R) Autumn landscape, La Rue (44x99cm-17x39in) s.d.1886
               (S.KR 100000)
£689   *$1379*   *(10-Feb-91 BU.M355) Street scene, Sodra Vallgatan (24x35cm-9x14in)*
               s.d.1917 mixed media (S.KR 7500)
£2022   *$3963*   *(6-Nov-90 BA.S379/R) Horses grazing in field (25x35cm-10x14in) s.d.1913*
               Indian ink panel (S.KR 22000)
£2788   *$4991*   *(13-Apr-91 FAL.M163/R) Three foals, Oland (70x100cm-28x39in) s. W/C*
               (S.KR 30000)

KREUL, Johann Friedrich Karl (1804-1867) German
£898   *$1760*   *(6-Nov-90 GF.L2363/R) Portrait of young officer (62x50cm-24x20in)*
               s.indis.d. pastel (S.FR 2200)

KREUTZ, Heinz (1932-) German
£9589 $15630   (14-Jun-91 L.K1010/R) An ptah (70x50cm-28x20in) s.i.d.1957 (DM 28000)

KREUTZER, A (19th C) German
£769 $1506   (12-Feb-91 GM.B341) Interieur Hollandais (39x29cm-15x11in) s.
               (B.FR 46000)

KREUZ, R (?) ?
£904 $1690   (28-Aug-90 GM.B509) Paysage anime (60x90cm-24x35in) s. wood (B.FR 55000)

KREUZER, Konrad (1810-1861) Austrian
£955   *$1605*   *(25-Apr-91 D.V250/R) Stadtplatz in Graz (21x28cm-8x11in) s. W/C*
               (A.S 20000)

KREUZER, Vinzenz (1809-1888) Austrian
£1496 $2514   (23-Apr-91 RAS.K44/R) Birch trees on rocky slope (42x54cm-17x21in) s.
               (D.KR 17000)

KREUZER, Vinzenz (1809-1888) Austrian-cont.
£4500	$7380	(19-Jun-91 S62/R) Forest landscapes with wildlife (70x58cm-28x23in) two s. one d.1881 board four
£4798	$8253	(16-May-91 D.V177/R) Mountainous landscape (41x57cm-16x22in) s. (A.S 100000)

KREVEL, Ludwig (1801-1876) German
£638	$1243	(12-Oct-90 AW.H1526/R) Portrait of painter Jakob Gotzenberger (32x24cm-13x9in) s. (DM 1900)

KREYDER, Alexis (1839-1912) French
£2909	$5672	(12-Oct-90 ZZ.F76/R) Vase de roses (81x65cm-32x26in) s. (F.FR 29000)
£10490	$20245	(12-Dec-90 WE.MU58/R) Cornfield, summer (135x164cm-53x65in) s. (DM 30000)

KRICHELDORF, Carl (1863-?) German
£650	$1255	(14-Dec-90 ZOF.Z963) The love letter (61x46cm-24x18in) s. (S.FR 1600)
£753	$1349	(13-Mar-91 N.M561/R) The village musician seated at table drinking beer with violin under arm (84x74cm-33x29in) s. (DM 2200)
£947	$1800	(27-Feb-91 SY.NY174/R) Conversation (86x117cm-34x46in) s.
£1014	$1976	(26-Oct-90 KM.K1334) Portrait of Black Forest girl holding rose in mouth (90x70cm-35x28in) mono. panel (DM 3000)
£1726	$3400	(15-Nov-90 D.NY20/R) Pink rose (84x75cm-33x30in) s.i.d.1885

KRICKE, Norbert (1922-) German
£1092	*$2141*	*(20-Nov-90 L.K347/R) Abstract composition with lines (43x61cm-17x24in) mono.d.1954 black chk (DM 3200)*
£1520	*$2630*	*(21-May-91 WK.M1129/R) Compositions (43x61cm-17x24in) mono.d.1954/55 one s.i.verso gouache chl two (DM 4500)*

KRIEG, Dieter (1937-) German?
£1370	*$2233*	*(14-Jun-91 L.K1011) The last 50 ... (45x80cm-18x31in) s.i.d.1979 W/C (DM 4000)*

KRIEGER, Joseph (1848-1914) Swiss
£2245	$3614	(26-Jun-91 KM.K1537/R) Lofoten landscape with family and reindeer (100x175cm-39x69in) s.d.1887 (DM 6600)

KRIEGER, Melchior Balthasar (attrib) (1656-?) German
£600	$978	(2-Jul-91 PH290/R) Portrait of gentleman standing in interior with coat of arms (22x17cm-9x7in) metal

KRIEGHOFF, Cornelius (1812-1872) Canadian
£5000	$8950	(14-Mar-91 B24/R) A moccasin seller (15x22cm-6x9in) board pair
£6061	$10424	(14-May-91 JOY.T139/R) Napolitan Contadini taken prisoner by bandits (55x72cm-22x28in) s.i. after Eastlake (C.D 12000)
£8772	$17193	(20-Nov-90 TA84/R) Portrait of habitant smoking pipe (25x21cm-10x8in) s. oval (C.D 20000)
£10965	$21601	(30-Oct-90 SY.T61/R) Passing showers, lake Memphramagog (29x34cm-11x13in) s. i.d.1958verso board (C.D 25000)
£13131	$22717	(6-May-91 SY.T32/R) La tuque bleue (29x22cm-11x9in) s.indist.i. board (C.D 26000)
£13596	$26785	(30-Oct-90 SY.T30/R) Portage by Grand Moro, St Maurice (22x28cm-9x11in) s. i.stretcher (C.D 31000)
£14646	$25338	(6-May-91 SY.T43/R) On Lake Memphremagog (32x45cm-13x18in) s. (C.D 29000)
£15625	$30000	(30-Nov-90 CH.NY4/R) Sleigh ride (33x46cm-13x18in) s.d.1856
£15789	$30947	(20-Nov-90 JOY.T119/R) Caughnawaga Indian camp (35x52cm-14x20in) s. (C.D 36000)
£16447	$32401	(30-Oct-90 SY.T29/R) Indian encampment (35x53cm-14x21in) s. (C.D 37500)
£17172	$29535	(14-May-91 JOY.T72/R) The storm, St. Ann's, Quebec (50x62cm-20x24in) s.d.1859 (C.D 34000)
£19298	$37825	(20-Nov-90 JOY.T78/R) Habitants driving (30x45cm-12x18in) s. (C.D 44000)
£19651	$38712	(12-Nov-90 HO.ED116/R) Bears foraging at sunset (46x38cm-18x15in) s.d. canvas laid down on board (C.D 45000)
£21930	$43202	(30-Oct-90 SY.T45/R) Portage past the rapids (44x60cm-17x24in) s.d.1855 (C.D 50000)
£21930	$42982	(20-Nov-90 JOY.T139/R) Three hunters preparing to portage (30x44cm-12x17in) s. (C.D 50000)
£25219	$49682	(30-Oct-90 SY.T53/R) Indians resting (36x56cm-14x22in) s. i.verso (C.D 57500)
£30702	$60175	(20-Nov-90 JOY.T24/R) Indian camp (44x67cm-17x26in) s. (C.D 70000)
£30702	$60175	(20-Nov-90 JOY.T12/R) Difficult task - after blizzard (31x44cm-12x17in) s. oval (C.D 70000)
£35088	$69123	(30-Oct-90 SY.T46/R) Falls of the Little Shawinigan, autumn (45x67cm-18x26in) s.d.58 (C.D 80000)
£43860	$86404	(30-Oct-90 SY.T36/R) Habitant farm, winter (44x67cm-17x26in) s.d.1850 (C.D 100000)
£62996	$122841	(24-Oct-90 EA.M476/R) Indian encampment by water (45x60cm-18x24in) s. (C.D 143000)
£76754	$150439	(20-Nov-90 JOY.T100/R) Canadian interior (37x29cm-15x11in) s.d.52 i.d.1852 verso (C.D 175000)
£109649	$216009	(30-Oct-90 SY.T37/R) Bilking the tollgate with Russian troika (46x69cm-18x27in) s.d.1870 (C.D 250000)

KRIEGHOFF, Cornelius (1812-1872) Canadian-cont.
£1600 $3104   (3-Dec-90 R.T230/R) Snowshoers (13x17cm-5x7in) s. i.verso W/C over
                       graphite (C.D 3600)
£85000 $165750   (24-Oct-90 S41/R) The ice-cone at the falls of Montmorency near Quebec,
                       lower Canada (36x56cm-14x22in) s.d.1853 W/C over traces pencil
                       htd.white

KRIEHUBER, Fritz (1836-1871) Austrian
£1410 $2750   (26-Oct-90 SY.NY63/R) Portrait of two ladies (42x55cm-17x22in) pencil
                       htd.white

KRIEHUBER, Josef (1800-1876) German
£630 $1077   (30-Jul-91 SWS141) The three graces (40x56cm-16x22in) s.
£573 $1117   (11-Oct-90 D.V118/R) Wooded landscape with figures on path
                       (23x31cm-9x12in) s.d.1833 W/C (A.S 12000)
£1051 $1765   (25-Apr-91 D.V148/R) Portrait of small girl wearing coral necklace
                       (14cm-6ins circular) s.d.1865 W/C (A.S 22000)
£1372 $2716   (31-Jan-91 D.V177/R) Portrait of elderly gentleman with golden
                       watchchain (25x20cm-10x8in) s.d.842 W/C (A.S 28000)
£3819 $7446   (11-Oct-90 D.V143/R) Antonie Grafin Batthyani seated with little
                       daughter Emanuela on pillow (28x22cm-11x9in) s.d.838 W/C oval
                       (A.S 80000)

KRIEHUBER, Josef (circle) (1800-1876) German
£420 $814   (7-Dec-90 GB.B5935) Portrait of Kaiser Franz I of Austria
                       (40x27cm-16x11in) c.1845 chl (DM 1200)

KRIJEVSKI, Jan (1948-) Russian
£719 $1396   (8-Dec-90 ZZ.F132/R) Printemps a la Fontanka (135x165cm-53x65in)
                       (F.FR 7000)

KRIKHAAR, Herman (1930-) Dutch
£4644 $8963   (12-Dec-90 CH.AM436/R) La campagne (89x116cm-35x46in) init. s.i.d.1987
                       verso (D.FL 15000)
£6811 $13146   (12-Dec-90 CH.AM437/R) Champ de lavande (184x144cm-72x57in) init.d.87
                       s.i.d.verso (D.FL 22000)

KRIKI (20th C) ?
£1104 $1778   (25-Jun-91 BG.P35/R) La fameuse danse des cyclopes (120x120cm-47x47in)
                       s.d.86 i. verso acrylic (F.FR 11000)

KRILOV, Parfirii (1902-1990) Russian
£744 $1280   (15-May-91 AGB.P168/R) Sozopol - Crimee (22x33cm-9x13in) s. board
                       (F.FR 7500)
£942 $1621   (15-May-91 AGB.P169/R) Gourzouff - Crimee (35x49cm-14x19in) s.
                       (F.FR 9500)

KRISTIANSEN, Rolf (?) Norwegian
£574 $1148   (9-Feb-91 BU.O100) Dancer (61x68cm-24x27in) s. panel (N.KR 6500)

KRIVONOSSOVA, Irina (1962-) Russian
£1062 $2061   (8-Dec-90 KV.L175/R) The morning (52x38cm-20x15in) s.verso (B.FR 63000)

KRIZE, Yehiel (1909-1968) Israeli
£1571 $3000   (2-Jan-91 GG.TA464/R) Painting (100x73cm-39x29in) s.
£524 $1000   (2-Jan-91 GG.TA465/R) The workshop (43x50cm-17x20in) s.c.1949 gouache
£552 $900   (12-Jun-91 GG.TA183/R) Landscape and figures (33x47cm-13x19in) s. oil
                       gouache
£675 $1100   (12-Jun-91 GG.TA348/R) Untitled (47x61cm-19x24in) s. gouache

KROCK, Hendrik (1671-1738) German
£880 $1479   (23-Apr-91 RAS.K188/R) Annunciation (74x55cm-29x22in) (D.KR 10000)

KROCK, Hendrik (attrib) (1671-1738) German
£780 $1536   (13-Nov-90 AB.S926/R) Landscape with figures and cattle by ruins
                       (18x25cm-7x10in) mono. panel (S.KR 8500)
£2852 $5105   (14-Mar-91 RAS.V661/R) Mythological scene (86x128cm-34x50in)
                       (D.KR 32000)
£4156 $7813   (10-Aug-90 RAS.V493/R) Scene from Old Testament, with David and oxen
                       (88x147cm-35x58in) (D.KR 47000)

KROHG, Christian (1852-1925) Norwegian
£855 $1445   (20-Apr-91 BU.O53) Magdalene (51x41cm-20x16in) s. (N.KR 9900)
£2778 $4639   (3-Jun-91 B.O88/R) Seated woman (60x50cm-24x20in) s. (N.KR 32000)
£2867 $4845   (4-May-91 BU.O89) 'I leden' (43x35cm-17x14in) panel, woman and child
                       verso (N.KR 33000)
£3206 $6187   (12-Dec-90 BU.O48/R) Condolence visit (71x69cm-28x27in) s. panel
                       (N.KR 36000)
£3733 $6234   (3-Jun-91 B.O87/R) Helmsman (49x59cm-19x23in) s. panel (N.KR 43000)
£3819 $6378   (3-Jun-91 B.O86/R) Street wench (81x60cm-32x24in) s. (N.KR 44000)
£3993 $6668   (4-Jun-91 BU.O56/R) Street scene, Drobak (64x88cm-25x35in) s.
                       (N.KR 46000)
£4152 $8055   (22-Aug-90 RAS.K51/R) A small girl (63x33cm-25x13in) s. (D.KR 48000)
£5240 $9956   (11-Sep-90 UL.T237) From Brekkesto (47x45cm-19x18in) s. (N.KR 60000)
£6830 $12226   (11-Mar-91 B.O80/R) The widow (54x41cm-21x16in) s. (N.KR 78000)

KROHG, Christian (1852-1925) Norwegian-cont.
£8905	$17186	(10-Dec-90 B.O79/R) Fishermen selling fish at the quay, Bergen (67x64cm-26x25in) panel (N.KR 100000)
£13021	$25391	(11-Oct-90 BU.O79/R) Rough weather (37x47cm-15x19in) s. (N.KR 150000)
£16803	$32598	(5-Dec-90 KH.K75/R) Interior with the artist's wife writing at a table (42x50cm-17x20in) s.i. (D.KR 185000)
£23438	$45703	(11-Oct-90 BU.O78/R) Newspaper boys (60x50cm-24x20in) s. (N.KR 270000)
£32051	$62500	(23-Oct-90 SY.NY180/R) Fixing the sail (99x88cm-39x35in) s.
£34843	$67944	(15-Oct-90 B.O66/R) Woman in boat (84x63cm-33x25in) s. panel (N.KR 400000)

KROHG, Per (1889-1965) Norwegian
£521	$870	(3-Jun-91 B.O92/R) Le lavoir (38x46cm-15x18in) s. panel (N.KR 6000)
£825	$1377	(3-Jun-91 B.O91/R) Summer landscape (33x41cm-13x16in) s.d.41 panel (N.KR 9500)
£963	$1724	(11-Mar-91 B.O86/R) Dog looking through window in door (21x16cm-8x6in) s.i.d.1962 panel (N.KR 11000)
£1051	$1881	(11-Mar-91 B.O84/R) Landscape (33x40cm-13x16in) s.d.1944 panel (N.KR 12000)
£1202	$2320	(12-Dec-90 BU.O49/R) Carrying water (30x37cm-12x15in) s. panel (N.KR 13500)
£1313	$2351	(11-Mar-91 B.O82/R) Fishermen with boats (37x45cm-15x18in) s. panel (N.KR 15000)
£1469	$2836	(12-Dec-90 BU.O52/R) In the skerries (54x65cm-21x26in) s.d.1946 (N.KR 16500)
£1489	$2665	(11-Mar-91 B.O83/R) Figures at the theatre (46x55cm-18x22in) s. panel (N.KR 17000)
£1959	$3781	(12-Dec-90 BU.O51/R) Nude woman by chair (61x50cm-24x20in) s.d.26 (N.KR 22000)
£2170	$4232	(11-Oct-90 BU.O82/R) Harbour in Villefranche (38x45cm-15x18in) s.d.1925 s.i.verso panel (N.KR 25000)
£2439	$4756	(15-Oct-90 B.O69/R) Henrik Sorensen's house in Holmsbu (33x41cm-13x16in) s.d.1944 panel (N.KR 28000)
£2539	$4546	(11-Mar-91 B.O81/R) Court-yard (33x42cm-13x17in) init.d.1952 (N.KR 29000)
£3310	$6455	(15-Oct-90 B.O68/R) Washing clothes in the garden (46x55cm-18x22in) s.d.1946 panel (N.KR 38000)
£5401	$10531	(15-Oct-90 B.O67/R) Haycart being pulled by oxen (60x73cm-24x29in) s. panel (N.KR 62000)
£5429	$9718	(14-Mar-91 BU.O68/R) Woman by portiere (73x60cm-29x24in) s.d.31 panel (N.KR 62000)
£6946	$13405	(13-Dec-90 BU.O33/R) Studio interior (70x54cm-28x21in) s.d.1921 (N.KR 78000)
£7480	$14436	(10-Dec-90 B.O82/R) Persecution (73x60cm-29x24in) s.d.28 panel (N.KR 84000)
£781	*$1305*	*(4-Jun-91 B.O21/R) Studio interior (46x61cm-18x24in) s. mixed media (N.KR 9000)*

KROJER, Tom and THORSEN, Jens Jorgen (20th C) Scandinavian
£616	*$1202*	*(10-Oct-90 RAS.K83) Composition (99x106cm-39x42in) s. mixed media (D.KR 7000)*

KROKFORS, Kristian (1952-) Finnish
£852	$1526	(14-Apr-91 BU.H44/R) Garden III (70x50cm-28x20in) s.d.84 acrylic (F.M 6000)

KROLL, Leon (1884-1974) American
£814	$1400	(18-May-91 W.W221/R) The road around the bend (48x66cm-19x26in) s.
£3175	$6000	(26-Sep-90 SY.NY193/R) The bridge (41x51cm-16x20in) s.
£3352	$6000	(12-Apr-91 SY.NY73/R) View of Paris (66x81cm-26x32in) s.
£3385	$6500	(17-Dec-90 SY.NY334/R) Laura outdoors (48x28cm-19x11in) s. masonite
£5291	$10000	(27-Sep-90 CH.NY282/R) Naomi (61x51cm-24x20in) s.
£5587	$10000	(12-Apr-91 SY.NY72/R) Central Park (51x61cm-20x24in) s.d.1922
£8380	$15000	(14-Mar-91 CH.NY210/R) Rocky hillside (66x81cm-26x32in) s.d.1919
£10983	$19000	(22-May-91 CH.NY296/R) Afternoon repast (81x61cm-32x24in) s.
£21875	$42000	(30-Nov-90 CH.NY139/R) Niles beach (66x81cm-26x32in) s.d.1913 i.stretcher
£22543	$39000	(22-May-91 CH.NY279/R) The Bridge at Eddyville, New York (88x101cm-35x40in) s.d.1919
£36898	$69000	(1-Aug-90 B.P45/R) View of New York from Weehawken, 1913 (91x122cm-36x48in) s.
£500	*$950*	*(14-Sep-90 S.BM308/R) Study of four female nudes (43x38cm-17x15in) oil graphite*
£1599	*$2750*	*(15-May-91 SY.NY216/R) Nude (49x31cm-19x12in) s. chl oil W/C*
£2062	*$4000*	*(5-Dec-90 D.NY85/R) Reclining female nude in a red chair (28x36cm-11x14in) s. mixed media*

KRON, Paul (1869-1936) French
£797	$1355	(29-May-91 GL.P142) Barque sur le lac (50x65cm-20x26in) s. (F.FR 8000)

KRONABETTER, Robert A (attrib) (19/20th C) Austrian
£759	$1487	(7-Nov-90 N.M937/R) Farmhouse (26x40cm-10x16in) mono. i.verso board (DM 2200)

KRONBERG, Louis (1872-1965) American
£500	$950	(28-Feb-91 MFA.C70/R) Ballerina (91x71cm-36x28in) s.

KRONBERG, Louis (1872-1965) American-cont.
£578	$1000	(10-May-91 S.BM100/R) Two dancers in rose (33x41cm-13x16in) mono. mono.i.d.1957verso board
£689	$1350	(24-Nov-90 RB.HY216/R) View from my veranda at Rocky Neck, East Gloucester (25x30cm-10x12in) s. i.verso canvas board
£833	$1600	(17-Dec-90 SY.NY346/R) Dancer (61x46cm-24x18in) s.d.1916
£867	$1700	(27-Jan-91 LIT.L84) Guitar player (91x76cm-36x30in) s.
£914	$1800	(18-Nov-90 JRB.C60/R) The lotus (203x114cm-80x45in) s.i.verso
£928	$1800	(5-Dec-90 D.NY97) Orange and yellow - two dancers (51x61cm-20x24in) init.i. d.1951 and 57 verso
£1243	$2100	(17-Apr-91 D.NY68/R) Carmen (81x46cm-32x18in) s.i.d.1907
£1458	$2800	(17-Dec-90 SY.NY345/R) Dancer arranging hair (71x51cm-28x20in) s.d.1917
£378	*$700*	*(8-Mar-91 S.BM252/R) The curtain call (69x53cm-27x21in) s. pastel paperboard*

KRONBERGER, Carl (1841-1921) Austrian
£2168	$4184	(12-Dec-90 WE.MU136/R) Portrait of peasant smoking pipe (12x9cm-5x4in) s. panel (DM 6200)
£5491	$9500	(22-May-91 SY.NY218/R) Seasoned drinker (16x12cm-6x5in) s.panel
£5594	$10797	(12-Dec-90 N.M603/R) Old man in night clothes seated at breakfast table reading paper (21x16cm-8x6in) s. panel (DM 16000)
£6647	$11500	(22-May-91 SY.NY219/R) Bavarian hunter (18x14cm-7x6in) s. panel

KRONER, Christian (1861-1911) German
£619	$1175	(2-Mar-91 KRA.D352) Mountainous landscape (19x47cm-7x19in) s. panel (DM 1800)
£893	$1698	(2-Mar-91 KRA.D353/R) Ladies conversing in cottage garden (15x20cm-6x8in) s. panel (DM 2600)
£1174	$2290	(13-Oct-90 KRA.D244/R) Stag on path in woods (10x80cm-4x31in) s.d.1896 (DM 3500)
£2034	$3315	(3-Jul-91 WE.MU2/R) Stag with herd in landscape (59x80cm-23x31in) s.i.d.1910 (DM 6000)
£3322	$6411	(10-Dec-90 L.K484/R) Stag with deer in autumnal Weser mountain landscape (60x80cm-24x31in) s.d.03 (DM 9500)

KRONER, Christian (attrib) (1861-1911) German
£1469	$2834	(12-Dec-90 WE.MU76/R) Wood clearing with deer (37x62cm-15x24in) s. (DM 4200)

KRONER, Erwin (1889-?) German
£1455	$2735	(20-Sep-90 D.V55/R) Pansies and daisies (45x50cm-18x20in) s.d.35 panel (A.S 30000)

KRONSTRAND, Bror (1875-1950) Swedish
£640	$1254	(20-Nov-90 GO.G118) Elegant lady (77x47cm-30x19in) s.d.1901 panel (S.KR 7000)

KROPFF, Joop (1892-?) Dutch
£515	$845	(18-Jun-91 VN.R156) Figures and cart in busy town scene (51x67cm-20x26in) s. (D.FL 1700)
£518	$985	(26-Feb-91 VN.R172) Busy street scene (53x67cm-21x26in) s. (D.FL 1700)

KROUTHEN, Johan (1858-1932) Swedish
£1463	$2867	(20-Nov-90 GO.G119) Garden scene with lady by building (78x80cm-31x31in) i.verso (S.KR 16000)
£3598	$6045	(27-Apr-91 SO.S404/R) Patricier villa in Linkoping with flowering fruit trees (49x72cm-19x28in) s.d.1927 (S.KR 38000)
£4057	$7018	(22-May-91 BA.S559/R) Chickens feeding, appleblossom and red cottage (39x58cm-15x23in) s.d.1920 (S.KR 43000)
£4261	$7159	(27-Apr-91 SO.S402/R) Cherry tree in blossom by red cottage and water in background (48x68cm-19x27in) s.d.1926 (S.KR 45000)
£4449	$8586	(12-Dec-90 BU.S54/R) Spring landscape with fruit blossom and yellow cottage (50x76cm-20x30in) s.d.1920 (S.KR 48000)
£4634	$8943	(12-Dec-90 BU.S53/R) Early spring (36x27cm-14x11in) s. (S.KR 50000)
£4695	$7981	(28-May-91 AB.S4645/R) Garden scene with road by villa with Virginia creeper (45x60cm-18x24in) s.d.1922 (S.KR 50000)
£5097	$9838	(12-Dec-90 BU.S52/R) Spring landscape with red cottage by sea (50x76cm-20x30in) s. (S.KR 55000)
£5607	$10989	(10-Nov-90 FAL.M214/R) Autumn landscape (68x98cm-27x39in) s. (S.KR 61000)
£5618	$9663	(14-May-91 BU.S20/R) Haystooks (41x34cm-16x13in) s. (S.KR 60000)
£6117	$11805	(12-Dec-90 BU.S44/R) Spring day with fruit blossom (70x100cm-28x39in) s.d.1932 (S.KR 66000)
£6204	$12223	(30-Oct-90 BU.S64/R) Brook in spring (55x34cm-22x13in) s.d.1894 (S.KR 68000)
£6439	$10818	(27-Apr-91 SO.S401/R) Cherry tree in blossom by red cottage near water (49x74cm-19x29in) s. (S.KR 68000)
£6439	$10818	(24-Apr-91 BA.S130/R) Cherry blossom (69x100cm-27x39in) s.d.1923 (S.KR 68000)
£6500	$10660	(19-Jun-91 S277/R) Figures strolling along beach (79x108cm-31x43in) s.d.1915
£6843	$13481	(30-Oct-90 BU.S61/R) Spring landscape with red cottage and fruit blossom (50x75cm-20x30in) s.d.1928 (S.KR 75000)
£6951	$13415	(12-Dec-90 BU.S47/R) Artist's two daughters on woody hill (50x76cm-20x30in) s.d.1910 (S.KR 75000)

KROUTHEN, Johan (1858-1932) Swedish-cont.

£7116	$12240	(14-May-91 BU.S22/R) Spring day with red cottage and fruit blossom (70x100cm-28x39in) s. (S.KR 76000)
£7353	$14412	(6-Nov-90 BA.S153/R) Landscape with house with fruit trees (69x99cm-27x39in) s. (S.KR 80000)
£7414	$14310	(12-Dec-90 BU.S46/R) Summer landscape with chickens feeding (50x75cm-20x30in) s.d.1908 (S.KR 80000)
£7755	$15278	(30-Oct-90 BU.S60/R) Spring landscape with fruit blossom, lilacs and chickens (72x104cm-28x41in) s.d.1915 (S.KR 85000)
£8341	$16098	(12-Dec-90 BU.S45/R) Watering cattle (96x135cm-38x53in) s.d.1902 (S.KR 90000)
£8668	$17076	(30-Oct-90 BU.S59/R) Autumn landscape with girl feeding chickens (71x103cm-28x41in) s.d.1911 (S.KR 95000)
£8897	$17171	(12-Dec-90 BU.S42/R) Autumn (100x150cm-39x59in) s.d.1913 (S.KR 96000)
£10202	$19996	(10-Nov-90 FAL.M213/R) Fruit trees in bloom by red cottage (50x75cm-20x30in) s. (S.KR 111000)
£16219	$31302	(12-Dec-90 BU.S41/R) In the wood (102x56cm-40x22in) s. (S.KR 175000)

KROYER, Marie (19/20th C) Danish

£704	$1183	(23-Apr-91 RAS.K368/R) Portrait of lady wearing red shawl and glasses (33x24cm-13x9in) i.d.85 (D.KR 8000)

KROYER, P S (1851-1909) Danish

£898	$1768	(14-Nov-90 RAS.K17/R) Passion flower 1869 (25x17cm-10x7in) (D.KR 10000)
£1210	$2419	(6-Feb-91 RAS.K229/R) Seagulls in flight over the sea (27x32cm-11x13in) init. (D.KR 13500)
£1410	$2354	(6-Jun-91 RAS.K120/R) Coastal landscape, sunset near Hornbaek (20x26cm-8x10in) init.i. (D.KR 16000)
£1594	$2694	(2-May-91 RAS.V66/R) Passion flower 1869 (25x17cm-10x7in) (D.KR 18000)
£1644	$3189	(22-Aug-90 RAS.K294) View from Skagen Strand (18x23cm-7x9in) init. d.1882verso (D.KR 19000)
£1680	$3260	(5-Dec-90 KH.K77/R) View over the sea, Skagen beach in moonlight (20x25cm-8x10in) (D.KR 18500)
£1761	$2958	(23-Apr-91 RAS.K112/R) Room sketch for portrait of C F Tietgen (43x31cm-17x12in) init.i.d.91 panel (D.KR 20000)
£1817	$3524	(5-Dec-90 KH.K78/R) View from Christianshavn towards Nikolaj Tarn (17x21cm-7x8in) mono. (D.KR 20000)
£2083	$4021	(10-Dec-90 BU.K47/R) View of the Bay of Naples with Vesuvus (16x25cm-6x10in) init. (D.KR 23000)
£3587	$6888	(27-Dec-90 RAS.V49/R) Beached boat at Skagen Strand (20x31cm-8x12in) init.d.83 (D.KR 40000)
£4067	$7646	(10-Aug-90 RAS.V494/R) Self portrait (28x24cm-11x9in) (D.KR 46000)
£4360	$8458	(5-Dec-90 KH.K76/R) The dog Rap (42x32cm-17x13in) init.d.98 (D.KR 48000)
£4606	$7784	(1-May-91 KH.K101/R) Sunset, Skagen 1892 (20x35cm-8x14in) init.d.92 panel (D.KR 52000)
£4842	$8134	(23-Apr-91 RAS.K66/R) Sketch from Anacapri (47x38cm-19x15in) (D.KR 55000)
£4893	$9199	(18-Sep-90 BU.K66/R) Young fishergirl with bare feet and young sister on lap (32x24cm-13x9in) (D.KR 55000)
£6417	$11487	(14-Mar-91 RAS.V663/R) Skagen strand, dusk (32x41cm-13x16in) init.d.1906 (D.KR 72000)
£6920	$13426	(22-Aug-90 RAS.K93/R) Portrait of Holder Drachmann seated under tree (31x24cm-12x9in) init. (D.KR 80000)
£9874	$19452	(14-Nov-90 RAS.K61/R) Samll fishergirl from Hornbaek (23x19cm-9x7in) init.i.d.75 (D.KR 110000)
£898	*$1768*	*(14-Nov-90 RAS.K847/R) Portrait of Georg Brandes (12x8cm-5x3in) s. pencil (D.KR 10000)*

KROYER, Peder Severin (1851-1909) Danish

£3800	$7296	(29-Nov-90 B75/R) Coastal scene (32x41cm-13x16in) init.d.1906 board
£4200	$7224	(17-May-91 C158/R) Waves breaking on beach at Skagen (24x33cm-9x13in) s.i.d.1889 verso panel
£6009	$10216	(28-May-91 AB.S4780/R) View of Tamorina and Etna, Sicily (32x43cm-13x17in) s.d.1901 panel (S.KR 64000)
£32000	$55040	(17-May-91 C179/R) Boys bathing on beach at Skagen (32x43cm-13x17in) init.d.99 panel
£32570	$54718	(23-Apr-91 RAS.K54/R) Flowering bushes, sunny day, Anacapri (43x32cm-17x13in) init.d.96 (D.KR 370000)

KRUCHEN, Julius (1845-1912) German

£811	$1581	(26-Oct-90 KM.K1335 a) Geneva lake landscape with view of Chateau Chillon and Villeneuve (68x105cm-27x41in) s.i. (DM 2400)
£2198	$4177	(28-Feb-91 D.V6/R) Monte Cristallo, South Tyrol (80x110cm-31x43in) s. panel (A.S 45000)

KRUGER, Barbara (1945-) American

£6091	*$12000*	*(5-Oct-90 CH.NY122/R) Untitled - To fashion (96x117cm-38x46in) s.d.1980verso acrylic letraset photograph board*

KRUGER, Carl (1812-1880) German

£1520	$2889	(14-Sep-90 SA.A1259/R) Mountain landscape (42x52cm-17x20in) s.d.1862 indis.i.verso (DM 4500)

KRUGER, Franz (1797-1857) German

£13699	$24521	(13-Mar-91 N.M562/R) Setting out for the hunt. Returning from rabbit hunt (45x61cm-18x24in) i. stretcher pair (DM 40000)

KRUGER, Franz (1797-1857) German-cont.
£507	$861	*(31-May-91 GB.B5868) Portrait of Prussian officer in profile (21x15cm-8x6in) s.d.1851 pencil chl htd.white chk board (DM 1500)*
£676	$1149	*(31-May-91 GB.B5866) Portrait of Mrs Neundorf wearing lace cap (25x22cm-10x9in) s.i.d.1814 chl pen htd.white chk (DM 2000)*
£839	$1628	*(7-Dec-90 GB.B5937/R) Study of officer one hand raised facing back (25x20cm-10x8in) i.d.1815 pencil (DM 2400)*
£845	$1436	*(31-May-91 GB.B5867/R) Portrait of young woman with plumed beret and lace collar (24x18cm-9x7in) chk (DM 2500)*
£2797	$5427	*(7-Dec-90 GB.B5936/R) Portrait of Baron von Arnim standing and portrait of head in profile (32x19cm-13x7in) W/C pencil (DM 8000)*

KRUGER, Franz (attrib) (1797-1857) German
£1580	$2750	*(27-Mar-91 B.SF4053/R) Portrait of gentleman wearing greatcoat. Portrait d'un jeune galant one pastel board one pencil two*

KRUGER, Hermann (1823-1909) German
£2174	$3696	(30-May-91 EA.Z339/R) On Capri (95x76cm-37x30in) s.d.76 (S.FR 5500)

KRUIJFF, Cornelis de (1771-1854) Dutch
£671	$1288	(27-Nov-90 SY.AM3689) The necklace (22x28cm-9x11in) s. panel (D.FL 2200)

KRUMLINDE, Olof (1856-1945) Swedish
£643	$1287	(10-Feb-91 BU.M40) Coastal landscape, Capri (45x37cm-18x15in) s. (S.KR 7000)
£963	$1898	(13-Nov-90 AB.S413/R) Pale seascape with sailingvessel, Oresund (50x75cm-20x30in) s. (S.KR 10500)
£1098	$2141	(21-Oct-90 BU.M171) Cliffs in Arild (40x62cm-16x24in) s. (S.KR 12000)
£1268	$2486	(10-Nov-90 FAL.M221/R) Pilatus mountain, Luzern (47x38cm-19x15in) s. (S.KR 13800)
£1301	$2329	(13-Apr-91 FAL.M171/R) Road through golden autumn wood (57x70cm-22x28in) s. (S.KR 14000)
£1471	$2882	(6-Nov-90 BA.S155/R) Coastal landscape (49x63cm-19x25in) s. (S.KR 16000)
£1471	$2882	(10-Nov-90 FAL.M220/R) Wooded glade (35x48cm-14x19in) s. (S.KR 16000)
£2233	$4153	(9-Sep-90 BU.M697) Coastal landscape with castle (74x120cm-29x47in) s. (S.KR 24000)
£2244	$4421	(14-Nov-90 RAS.K48/R) Road through rocky landscape, summer (50x75cm-20x30in) s.d.1895 (D.KR 25000)
£2849	$5585	(10-Nov-90 FAL.M218/R) Old beeches by Haga, Arild (50x72cm-20x28in) s.d.95 (S.KR 31000)

KRUMMACHER, Karl (1867-1955) German
£1100	$1969	(12-Apr-91 BM.B458/R) Landscape near Worpswerde (50x70cm-20x28in) s. (DM 3300)

KRUPECZ, Victor (20th C) Austrian
£879	$1671	(28-Feb-91 D.V67/R) Audience hall, Schönbrunn (60x47cm-24x19in) s.i.d.1922 (A.S 18000)

KRUSE, Frans (19th C) German
£1613	$3145	(15-Oct-90 SY.J31/R) Twon scene with two figures in the foreground (39x28cm-15x11in) s. panel (SA.R 8000)

KRUSEMAN VAN ELTEN, Hendrik Dirk see ELTEN, Hendrik Dirk Kruseman van

KRUSEMAN, Frederik Marianus (1817-1882) Dutch
£5000	$8200	(19-Jun-91 S18/R) Figures on frozen river by tower (32x45cm-13x18in) s. panel
£7000	$13790	(5-Oct-90 C23/R) Winter landscape with figures on frozen river (47x60cm-19x24in) s.d.1842
£13158	$25000	(28-Feb-91 CH.NY154/R) River landscape with castle on hill beyond (38x52cm-15x20in) s.d.1865 panel
£25641	$50000	(23-Oct-90 SY.NY35/R) Skating in the midst of winter (49x70cm-19x28in) s.d.1875 canvas on masonite
£38922	$65389	(23-Apr-91 SY.AM43/R) Skaters in frozen winter landscape (73x103cm-29x41in) s.d.1857 (D.FL 130000)

KRUSEMAN, Frederik Marianus (attrib) (1817-1882) Dutch
£5800	$9744	(26-Apr-91 ARC.P16/R) Environs de Breda en Hollande (62x82cm-24x32in) trace sig. panel (F.FR 58000)

KRUSEMAN, Jan (19th C) Dutch
£532	$1000	(22-Sep-90 WOL.C155/R) Dutch winter scene (61x91cm-24x36in) s.

KRUSI, Hans (20th C) Swiss?
£880	$1716	*(17-Oct-90 G.Z109) Urnasch, Appenzell, St Gallen, Basel (30x42cm-12x17in) s. mixed media paper collage (S.FR 2200)*

KRUYDER, Herman (1881-1935) Dutch
£805	$1554	*(12-Dec-90 CH.AM14/R) Dog (12x15cm-5x6in) s. pen crayon (D.FL 2600)*

KRUYSEN, Antoon (1898-) Dutch
£732	$1405	(27-Nov-90 SY.AM3878) The funeral (50x60cm-20x24in) s. (D.FL 2400)
£824	$1475	(17-Mar-91 L.C37/R) Chaumiere sous la neige (38x55cm-15x22in) s. (F.FR 8200)

KRYLOV, Guenadi Sergueevitch (1951-) Russian
£1529 $2951   (16-Dec-90 P.V118/R) Les Joueurs (114x114cm-45x45in) mono.d.1986
                 (F.FR 15000)

KRYZANOVSKY, Roman (?) ?
£663 $1300   '',1-Nov-90 LIT.L15) Lakeview (51x61cm-20x24in) s. board

KUBIN, Alfred (1877-1959) Austrian
£420 $814   (7-Dec-90 GB.B6834) Hunting deer (27x38cm-11x15in) st.sig.verso pencil
                 board (DM 1200)
£439 $747   (31-May-91 GB.B6528) Autumn storm, nude trumpeter before felled tree
                 (28x36cm-11x14in) s.i. i.verso pencil double-sided (DM 1300)
£640 $1280   (7-Feb-91 D.V122/R) Dance. Study (14x10cm-6x4in) mono. pencil
                 double-sided (A.S 13000)
£655 $1258   (28-Nov-90 KF.M985) Schlangennest (22x18cm-9x7in) s.i. pencil
                 (DM 1900)
£685 $1116   (15-Jun-91 L.K388/R) Two harem ladies (30x22cm-12x9in) pencil
                 (DM 2000)
£714 $1264   (23-Mar-91 WK.M396/R) The black magician (27x18cm-11x7in) s.d.1924
                 indian ink pen (DM 2100)
£743 $1264   (31-May-91 GB.B6527) Sign of zodiac with sun (32x40cm-13x16in) s.i.
                 pencil (DM 2200)
£759 $1457   (26-Nov-90 WK.M316/R) Selfportrait with grasshopper (14x9cm-6x4in) s.
                 i.d.1924verso pen postcard on board (DM 2200)
£759 $1457   (28-Nov-90 KF.M983) Card player (19x13cm-7x5in) s.d.1925 pen dr.
                 (DM 2200)
£845 $1461   (21-May-91 WK.M1130/R) The honour (40x29cm-16x11in) s. pencil
                 (DM 2500)
£1220 $2257   (7-Mar-91 D.V116/R) Czechoslovak (26x18cm-10x7in) mono.i. pencil
                 (A.S 25000)
£1455 $2735   (20-Sep-90 D.V86/R) Fever - nightmare (29x23cm-11x9in) mono. pencil
                 (A.S 30000)
£1689 $2872   (31-May-91 GB.B6526) Kalif Storch, illustration of fairy tale by Wilhelm
                 Hauff (27x19cm-11x7in) s.i. indian ink pen (DM 5000)
£1793 $3443   (28-Nov-90 KF.M982/R) Zudringlichkeit (23x26cm-9x10in) s.i. pen over
                 pencil (DM 5200)
£1914 $3311   (8-May-91 D.V57/R) Lonely Chinese (33x22cm-13x9in) mono. indian ink
                 pencil (A.S 40000)
£2048 $4014   (22-Nov-90 L.K1088/R) Noise in the night (19x22cm-7x9in) s. indian ink
                 pen (DM 6000)
£2273 $4409   (7-Dec-90 GB.B6832/R) Elsie Siegl, wild man and dead woman
                 (21x32cm-8x13in) s.i. W/C pen (DM 6500)
£2365 $4020   (31-May-91 GB.B6525/R) Coffee house interior with man at table
                 (29x20cm-11x8in) s. W/C indian ink pen (DM 7000)
£2730 $5352   (24-Nov-90 VG.B223/R) Two pelicans (27x36cm-11x14in) s.d.1954 pen W/C
                 (DM 8000)
£2872 $4882   (1-Jun-91 VG.B142/R) Commotion (35x25cm-14x10in) s.i. indian ink pen
                 (DM 8500)
£2910 $5470   (20-Sep-90 D.V87/R) Study for 'Rauhnacht' (20x34cm-8x13in) mono. pencil
                 (A.S 60000)
£3041 $5169   (28-May-91 KF.M842/R) The three ages of the woman (17x19cm-7x7in) s. pen
                 W/C (DM 9000)
£3378 $5743   (31-May-91 GB.B6524/R) Man trying to rescue somebody drowning in fish
                 pond (39x32cm-15x13in) s.i. W/C indian ink pen (DM 10000)
£3938 $6420   (15-Jun-91 L.K385/R) Earthquake (31x20cm-12x8in) s. indian ink pen
                 (DM 11500)
£5517 $10593 (28-Nov-90 KF.M984/R) The forgotten lover (23x18cm-9x7in) s.d.1927 W/C
                 indian ink (DM 16000)
£5594 $10853 (7-Dec-90 GB.B6833/R) The magician (27x36cm-11x14in) s.d.1939 W/C indian
                 ink pen (DM 16000)
£5993 $9769   (15-Jun-91 L.K386/R) Three men by spring (39x31cm-15x12in) indian ink
                 pen (DM 17500)
£6757 $11486 (28-May-91 KF.M841/R) Devil's children (19x16cm-7x6in) s. pen
                 (DM 20000)
£7000 $11270 (25-Jun-91 C222/R) Der Tod (15x27cm-6x11in) s. pen ink chl wash
£7000 $11270 (25-Jun-91 C223/R) Die Wille (18x27cm-7x11in) s. pen ink W/C
£7432 $12635 (28-May-91 KF.M840/R) Withdrawal (28x35cm-11x14in) s. pen (DM 22000)
£9556 $18730 (24-Nov-90 VG.B121/R) The drunkard (32x29cm-13x11in) s.i.c.1908 pen
                 indian ink brush board (DM 28000)
£15534 $25476 (20-Jun-91 D.V2/R) The Indian (26x33cm-10x13in) s.i. pen brush indian
                 ink W/C paper on paper (A.S 320000)
£20000 $32200 (26-Jun-91 S217/R) Die Heerschau (39x31cm-15x12in) s.i. pen ink spray
                 technique
£23649 $40203 (28-May-91 KF.M839/R) Meine Muse (22x19cm-9x7in) s.i. indian ink pen
                 wash sprayed (DM 70000)
£33000 $64020 (5-Dec-90 S314/R) Das Erdruckende (38x30cm-15x12in) s. pen spray
                 technicque

KUBINSKY, Carl (1837-1889) German
£1667 $3283   (30-Oct-90 CH.AM202/R) Moonlit river landscape with figures angling,
                 houses in distance (29x53cm-11x21in) s.d. (D.FL 5500)
£4746 $8495   (11-Apr-91 D.V263/R) Moor landscape (29x53cm-11x21in) s.d.1872 panel
                 (A.S 100000)

KUCHENMEISTER, Rainer (1926-) German
£648 $1271   (24-Nov-90 N.M306) Portrait of the unknown lady (49x33cm-19x13in)
                      mono.d.1985 W/C over indian ink pen (DM 1900)

KUCHLER, Albert (1803-1886) Danish
£861 $1661   (10-Dec-90 BU.K24/R) Portrait of young woman (39x32cm-15x13in)
                      s.d.1838verso (D.KR 9500)
£1181 $2291   (5-Dec-90 KH.K79/R) Italian woman and children on a loggia, Capri
                      (44x34cm-17x13in) (D.KR 13000)

KUCHLER, Carl Gotthelf (1807-1843) Italian
£2703 $5270   (26-Oct-90 KM.K1338/R) River landscape with Hylas and nymphs
                      (29x22cm-11x9in) s.i.d.1836 paper on canvas (DM 8000)

KUECHLER, Carl Hermann (1866-1903) German
£3200 $6304   (5-Oct-90 C95/R) At races (30x24cm-12x9in) s. board
£4000 $6560   (19-Jun-91 S113/R) Promenade (37x60cm-15x24in) s. board

KUEHL, Gotthardt Johann (1850-1915) German
£2174 $3674   (17-Apr-91 WE.MU132/R) Figures in park (46x36cm-18x14in) s. panel
                      (DM 6500)
£1974 $3750   (27-Feb-91 SY.NY149/R) Promenade in park (46x36cm-18x14in) s.i. oil
                      black crayon panel

KUEHNE, Max (1880-c.1968) American
£2646 $5000   (27-Sep-90 CH.NY270/R) A corner of the city (76x63cm-30x25in) s.
£4124 $8000   (24-Aug-90 RB.HY142/R) Rocks and the sea (64x76cm-25x30in) s.d.18 canvas
                      laid down on cardboard
£10405 $18000   (22-May-91 CH.NY318/R) Still life with anemones (71x72cm-28x28in) s.
                      panel

KUGELGEN, Gerhard von (attrib) (1772-1820) German
£1356 $2264   (8-Jun-91 FN.S741/R) Portrait of actor August Wilhelm Iffland
                      (28x35cm-11x14in) oval (DM 4000)

KUGELGEN, Wilhelm von (1802-1867) German
£1959 $3311   (3-May-91 SA.A1871/R) Portrait of Herzog Alexius von Bernburg
                      (30x23cm-12x9in) (DM 5800)

KUGLMAYR, Max (1863-?) German
£699 $1350   (12-Dec-90 WE.MU99/R) Hay harvest, Dachauer Land (14x18cm-6x7in) s.
                      panel (DM 2000)

KUHFUSS, Paul (1883-1960) German
£845 $1461   (25-May-91 N.M205/R) Still life with roses in shell vase. Cliffs of
                      Rugen (42x37cm-17x15in) s.d.1949 s.d.09verso board double-sided
                      (DM 2500)
£405 $689   (1-Jun-91 VG.B648/R) Fishes on porcelain plate (51x73cm-20x29in) s.
                      i.verso W/C gouache (DM 1200)
£676 $1149   (1-Jun-91 VG.B649/R) Sand dunes on the Baltic Sea (54x66cm-21x26in) s.
                      gouache (DM 2000)
£853 $1672   (24-Nov-90 N.M308/R) Piazzetta, Venice (53x68cm-21x27in) s.i.d.1927 W/C
                      (DM 2500)

KUHLMAN, Karl (19th C) Finnish?
£3438 $6774   (17-Nov-90 BU.H64/R) Lake landscape in winter (55x64cm-22x25in) s.d.1863
                      (F.M 24000)

KUHLSTRUNK, Franz (1861-1944) Austrian
£943 $1631   (6-May-91 ZEL.L1806/R) Mountain landscape (40x55cm-16x22in) s.
                      (DM 2800)

KUHN, Friedrich (1926-1972) Swiss
£2610 $5116   (24-Nov-90 AB.L208/R) Interior (46x61cm-18x24in) s. papver on pavatex
                      (S.FR 6500)
£3175 $5302   (5-Jun-91 SY.Z157/R) Village in Ticino (45x60cm-18x24in) (S.FR 8000)
£12851 $25189   (24-Nov-90 AB.L207/R) Untitled (54x65cm-21x26in) (S.FR 32000)

KUHN, Robert (1920-) American
£1059 $1800   (1-Jun-91 IH.NY24/R) Coon hunting, beagles baying (38x30cm-15x12in) s.
                      casein on board

KUHN, Walt (1877-1949) American
£592 $1000   (1-May-91 B.SF5249/R) Early morning among cabbage palms, Florida
                      (11x19cm-4x7in) s.d.03
£1744 $3000   (19-May-91 LIT.L125) Still life of mixed fruit (20x30cm-8x12in) s. panel
£7803 $13500   (23-May-91 SY.NY90/R) Raggedy pants comedian (29x20cm-11x8in) s.d.1940
                      i.verso masonite
£7813 $15000   (29-Nov-90 SY.NY103/R) Portrait of young clown (20x17cm-8x7in) init.
                      masonite
£508 $950   (1-Aug-90 B.P76) Nude on striped rug (30x46cm-12x18in) s. W/C
£2471 $4250   (15-May-91 SY.NY168/R) Woman with hat (62x36cm-24x14in) s. W/C

KUHNEN, Pieter Lodewyk (1812-1877) Belgian
£1465 $2900   (1-Feb-91 S.W2561/R) Wood gatherers (64x86cm-25x34in) s.
£3600 $6912   (29-Nov-90 B90) Figures in river landscape (55x77cm-22x30in) s. panel

KUHNERT, Wilhelm (1865-1926) German
£5386 $10610   (14-Nov-90 RAS.K89/R) Water buffalo on the savannah (38x64cm-15x25in) s. i.verso (D.KR 60000)
£7095 $12061   (28-May-91 KF.M844/R) Ice bear (51x73cm-20x29in) s. s.i.stretcher (DM 21000)
£7383 $14396   (10-Oct-90 WE.MU178/R) Oryx antilopes in landscape (40x53cm-16x21in) s.i.d.1891 canvas on panel (DM 22000)
£42000 $80640   (30-Nov-90 C45/R) Tigers stalking their prey (94x149cm-37x59in) s.
£65000 $106600   (21-Jun-91 C70/R) Lion and lioness at stream (40x80cm-16x31in) s. i.verso panel
£578 $931   (26-Jun-91 KM.K976) Water buffaloes resting (33x48cm-13x19in) s.indis.i.d.06 chl (DM 1700)
£1020 $1643   (26-Jun-91 KM.K1540/R) Albert lake near Kissenge (25x40cm-10x16in) s. i.d.1891verso gouache (DM 3000)
£1361 $2190   (26-Jun-91 KM.K1539/R) Bagomajo landscape (25x40cm-10x16in) s. i.d.1894 gouache (DM 4000)
£2891 $4655   (26-Jun-91 KM.K1541/R) Lion (16x26cm-6x10in) s. W/C (DM 8500)

KUIPERS, C (fl.1756-1788) Dutch
£1220 $2341   (27-Nov-90 SY.AM3469/R) Figures in landscape in front of palace gate (47x63cm-19x25in) s.d.1775 panel (D.FL 4000)

KUITCA, Guillermo (1961-) Argentinian
£6122 $12000   (19-Nov-90 SY.NY231/R) Untitled (140x178cm-55x70in) init.

KULICKE, Robert (19/20th C) American
£833 $1600   (28-Nov-90 D.NY60) Apples, pear and vase (15x23cm-6x9in) s.d.69 board
£450 $900   (6-Feb-91 D.NY53) Tomato (10x13cm-4x5in) s. pastel

KULLE, Axel (1846-1908) Swedish
£1415 $2774   (10-Nov-90 FAL.M222/R) Still life with dead duck and Daily News (68x56cm-27x22in) mono.d.79 (S.KR 15400)

KUMLIEN, Akke (1884-1949) Swedish
£602 $1169   (4-Dec-90 BA.S277/R) Tree on Hallandsasen (27x35cm-11x14in) s.d.47 panel (S.KR 6500)

KUMMER, Karl Robert (attrib) (1810-1889) German
£856 $1533   (13-Mar-91 N.M564/R) Jungfrau, Eiger and Monch mountains seen from Murren (43x62cm-17x24in) i.verso paper on board (DM 2500)

KUNC, Milan (1944-) Czechoslovakian
£2296 $4500   (6-Nov-90 CE.NY169/R) Pepsi Cola (116x51cm-46x20in) s.d.1978 verso shaped corrugated paper
£7143 $14000   (7-Nov-90 SY.NY354 a/R) Psycheldelic afternoon (225x228cm-89x90in) s.d.1983 verso acrylic linen
£2089 $3405   (14-Jun-91 L.K1016/R) The artist (100x120cm-39x47in) s. oil dispersion cotton (DM 6100)

KUNDIG, Reinhold (1888-1984) Swiss
£992 $1756   (22-Mar-91 EA.Z414) Still life with cyclamen and apples (55x50cm-22x20in) s. (S.FR 2500)
£1508 $2518   (5-Jun-91 SY.Z57/R) Female nude (50x50cm-20x20in) (S.FR 3800)
£1633 $3200   (6-Nov-90 GF.L2286/R) View of Horgener Berg (79x79cm-31x31in) (S.FR 4000)
£7143 $11929   (5-Jun-91 SY.Z137/R) Sihlsprung (92x73cm-36x29in) s. (S.FR 18000)

KUNDIG, Willibald (20th C) Swiss
£1315 $2564   (24-Oct-90 GD.B566) Spring landscape near Horgen (50x64cm-20x25in) s. (S.FR 3300)

KUNIYOSHI, Yasuo (1893-1953) American
£135417 $260000   (30-Nov-90 CH.NY185/R) I was just married (46x34cm-18x13in) s.
£1192 $2300   (16-Dec-90 LIT.L113/R) Portrait of artist Emil Ganso (46x38cm-18x15in) s. ink brush pencil double-sided
£2514 $4500   (14-Mar-91 CH.NY207/R) Reclining nude (35x56cm-14x22in) s.d.50 brush ink
£2646 $5000   (26-Sep-90 SY.NY185/R) Study for mural, Radio City Music Hall Ladies Lounge (31x50cm-12x20in) s. W/C pencil two
£2865 $5500   (29-Nov-90 MFA.C42/R) Horse (25x30cm-10x12in) d.1921 W/C
£9497 $17000   (12-Apr-91 SY.NY85 a/R) Eve in Garden of Eden (93x171cm-37x67in) gouache board
£32552 $62500   (29-Nov-90 SY.NY102/R) Girl removing chemise (38x25cm-15x10in) s.d.40 gouache board

KUNKLER, Jean Jules Adrien (1829-1866) Swiss
£642 $1091   (27-May-91 L.K307) Spanish village square with shepherd, cattle and donkey (30x20cm-12x8in) s.d.1859 panel (DM 1900)

KUNO, B (20th C) ?
£763 $1503   (14-Nov-90 RAS.K577/R) Tits on a branch (70x86cm-28x34in) s. (D.KR 8500)

KUNSBERG, I (19th C) German
£520 $853   (18-Jun-91 PH123) Man seated at table in tavern interior (23x17cm-9x7in) s.i.d.81 panel

KUNST, Pieter Cornelisz see ENGELBERTSZ, Pieter Cornelisz

KUNTZ, Rudolf (1797-1848) German
£6826 $11195   (18-Jun-91 FN.S1954/R) Rhine landscape with horses and shepherd (38x51cm-15x20in) s.d.1843 panel (DM 20000)

KUNZ, A (20th C) German
£936 $1583   (19-Apr-91 FN.S1773/R) Still life with lobster on plate and fruit on draped table (66x83cm-26x33in) s. (DM 2800)

KUNZ, Karl (1905-) German
£3103 $5959   (1-Dec-90 SA.A2469/R) Fischmensch (113x73cm-44x29in) s.d.46 l.verso panel (DM 9000)

KUNZ, Ludwig Adam (1857-1929) Austrian
£648 $1063   (18-Jun-91 FN.S1953) Still life with grapes, apple, melon and vine leaves (52x40cm-20x16in) s. i.verso (DM 1900)
£1020 $1643   (26-Jun-91 KM.K1542) Still life with fruit, shell fish, pheasants, jug and bowl (62x97cm-24x38in) s. canvas on panel (DM 3000)
£3500 $6860   (22-Nov-90 CSK248/R) Children masquerading as Putti and musicians amidst flowers, with puppy (100x190cm-39x75in) s.
£14000 $22960   (19-Jun-91 S79/R) Still life of summer flowers (83x62cm-33x24in) s.

KUPER, Yuri (1940-) ?
£3024   *$5897*   *(23-Oct-90 CSC.P100/R) Boite au cube de couleur rouge (28x28cm-11x11in) s.d.77 mixed media (F.FR 30000)*
£8428 $16349   *(9-Dec-90 CC.P56/R) Nature morte a l'assiette et au pinceau (135x100cm-53x39in) paint board collage panel (F.FR 82000)*

KUPETZKI, Johann (1667-1740) German
£1500 $2520   (26-Apr-91 NM.P58) Portrait d'homme (65x50cm-26x20in) (F.FR 15000)
£2300 $3749   (2-Jul-91 PH136/R) Portraits of man wearing hat and robe edged with fur (29x23cm-11x9in) pair
£3879 $7371   (1-Mar-91 DA.W1) Self-portrait (91x80cm-36x31in) (P.Z 70000000)
£4281 $8434   (13-Nov-90 CH.AM179/R) Shepherd reclining, in landscape, smoking pipe, child beside him (89x110cm-35x43in) s.d.1715 (D.FL 14000)
£4333 $7236   (6-Jun-91 D.V124/R) Self portrait smoking pipe (90x70cm-35x28in) (A.S 90000)
£10615 $19000   (11-Apr-91 SY.NY148/R) Portrait of composer (114x84cm-45x33in)

KUPETZKI, Johann (attrib) (1667-1740) German
£549 $900   (19-Jun-91 B.SF1670/R) Self portrait (51x38cm-20x15in)
£1297 $2400   (10-Mar-91 H.C13/R) Portrait of man in velvet cap (53x46cm-21x18in)
£1544 $3010   (10-Oct-90 ZEL.L1604/R) Portrait of Friedrich Wilhelm I von Preussen in official robes (93x71cm-37x28in) (DM 4600)
£1579   *$3000*   *(8-Jan-91 SY.NY37/R) Portrait of a youth wearing a large hat (32x27cm-13x11in) blk.white chk.*

KUPFERMAN, Moshe (20th C) Israeli
£982 $1600   (12-Jun-91 GG.TA343/R) Untitled (61x38cm-24x15in) s.d.1961 verso
£2199 $4200   (2-Jan-91 GG.TA451/R) Untitled (93x66cm-37x26in) s.

KUPKA, Frank (1871-1957) Czechoslovakian
£7937 $13730   (22-May-91 GS.B2420) Labora (46x68cm-18x27in) s.d.1900 (S.FR 20000)
£661 $1321   (6-Feb-91 FB.P203/R) Hermes et les naiades (18x20cm-7x8in) bears st.sig. crayon (F.FR 6500)
£683 $1338   (22-Nov-90 L.K1090/R) City scene (32x54cm-13x21in) s. indian ink brush chk (DM 2000)
£904 $1455   (25-Jun-91 BG.P36/R) Composition (14x10cm-6x4in) s. W/C crayon (F.FR 9000)
£906 $1477   (16-Jun-91 CC.P1/R) Etude pour - conte de pistils et d'etamines (27x20cm-11x8in) s. oil crayon (F.FR 9000)
£1972 $3886   (6-Oct-90 GL.P156) Etude our Formes Flasques (20x16cm-8x6in) st.sig. W/C (F.FR 20000)
£2711 $4364   (24-Jun-91 PR.P157) Etude pour - l'homme et la terre (60x40cm-24x16in) st. chl.chk. (F.FR 27000)
£4500 $7335   (3-Jul-91 CSC.P110) Composition (28x28cm-11x11in) s. W/C gouache (F.FR 45000)
£5119 $8548   (6-Jun-91 HN.H542/R) Composition (22x16cm-9x6in) s. W/C (DM 15100)
£5500 $8965   (3-Jul-91 CSC.P109/R) Composition (30x28cm-12x11in) s. gouache W/C (F.FR 55000)
£8475 $14153   (6-Jun-91 HN.H541/R) Composition (26x18cm-10x7in) s. W/C gouache over pencil (DM 25000)
£18500 $29785   (25-Jun-91 C231 a/R) Chromatic concentration (27x18cm-11x7in) s. st.sig.i.verso gouache

KUPPERS, Leo (1884-?) Dutch
£867 $1551   (12-Apr-91 BM.B748/R) Gentleman seated tasting wine (74x62cm-29x24in) s. (DM 2600)

KURELEK, William (1927-1977) Canadian
£1930 $3782   (20-Nov-90 JOY.T67/R) Reading comics in outhouse (25x25cm-10x10in) s.d.1960 board (C.D 4400)
£789 $1547   (20-Nov-90 JOY.T403) Chop (24x24cm-9x9in) init.d.65 W/C (C.D 1800)
£800 $1560   (16-Oct-90 WW363) Still life with Canadian one dollar note and various foreign coins (10x18cm-4x7in) W/C bodycol.
£1466 $2448   (3-Jun-91 R.T198/R) Could that be our Prime Minister (60x46cm-24x18in) init.d.72 mixed media masonite (C.D 2800)

KURELEK, William (1927-1977) Canadian-cont.
£1754 $3439   (20-Nov-90 JOY.T349) Panorama from Canadian martyrs, Shrine, Midland
                 (18x89cm-7x35in) init. W/C board (C.D 4000)
£5263 $10368   (30-Oct-90 SY.T22/R) Night on prairie winter road (20x62cm-8x24in)
                 init.d.74 i.verso mixed media board (C.D 12000)
£5556 $9611   (6-May-91 SY.T76/R) Arctic scenes, with Alaskan caribou, eskimo kitchen
                 corner and huskies (9x25cm-4x10in) init.d.75 mixed media board three
                 panels (C.D 11000)
£6566 $11359   (6-May-91 SY.T113/R) Prairie boy's summer - thunderstorn approaching
                 (36x36cm-14x14in) init.i.d.74 verso mixed media board (C.D 13000)
£6566 $11359   (6-May-91 SY.T42/R) Snow flurries in Chinatown, Montreal
                 (51x41cm-20x16in) init.d.75 mixed media board (C.D 13000)
£7895 $15553   (30-Oct-90 SY.T47/R) Potato famine and landlord evictions
                 (51x102cm-20x40in) init.d.76 i.verso mixed media board (C.D 18000)
£9596 $16601   (6-May-91 SY.T112/R) Prairie boy's winter - snowball weather
                 (29x33cm-11x13in) i.d.1974 verso mixed media board (C.D 19000)
£11111 $19222   (6-May-91 SY.T77/R) Winter fun in Glen Stewart ravine (50x60cm-20x24in)
                 init.d.76 s.d.1976 verso mixed media board (C.D 22000)
£19737 $38882   (30-Oct-90 SY.T77/R) Bowl full of tomatoes, one bad tomato spoils the
                 whole basket (52x55cm-20x22in) init.d.69 i.verso mixed media board
                 (C.D 45000)

KURON, Herbert (1888-?) German
£1399 $2713   (7-Dec-90 GB.B6846) Wannsee landscape (70x110cm-28x43in) s. (DM 4000)

KURZ, August (1856-1916) Swiss
£11301 $18421   (12-Jun-91 SY.MU94/R) The school room (79x95cm-31x37in) s. s.i.verso
                 panel (DM 33000)

KURZBAUER, Eduard (1840-1879) Austrian
£4000 $7840   (22-Nov-90 CSK199/R) Bearer of bad tidings (79x105cm-31x41in) s.
£6164 $10048   (12-Jun-91 SY.MU105/R) The elopement (77x102cm-30x40in) s. (DM 18000)
£9615 $18558   (12-Dec-90 N.M605/R) Young couple discovered by parents in peasant
                 interior (73x105cm-29x41in) s. (DM 27500)

KURZEWEIL, T (?) ?
£900 $1728   (20-Dec-90 CSK136/R) The open window (96x76cm-38x30in) s.

KURZWEIL, Maximilian (1867-1916) Austrian
£95694 $165550   (8-May-91 D.V37/R) The enchanted prince (170x185cm-67x73in) s.d.1915
                 (A.S 2000000)
£646 $1253   (6-Dec-90 D.V36/R) Boat (13x19cm-5x7in) st.mono. pen indian ink pencil
                 gouache (A.S 13000)

KUSEL, Ernst (1873-1942) Swedish
£744 $1414   (14-Sep-90 RAS.V599/R) Small girl playing with goat and kid
                 (68x106cm-27x42in) s. (D.KR 8400)
£1322 $2207   (6-Jun-91 RAS.K163/R) Small girl playing with goat and kid
                 (68x106cm-27x42in) s. (D.KR 15000)

KUSS, Ferdinand (1800-1886) Austrian
£4103 $8000   (23-Oct-90 SY.NY348/R) Still life with tiger lily and lilac on ledge
                 (69x55cm-27x22in) init.d..878

KUSTNER, Carl (1861-?) ?
£979 $1899   (4-Dec-90 FN.S1946) Lake landscape with silver birches and farmhouses
                 beyond, early spring (46x55cm-18x22in) (DM 2800)
£1294 $2510   (4-Dec-90 FN.S1945/R) Dachauer Moos with view of wooded lake landscape
                 (50x61cm-20x24in) s.i. i.verso (DM 3700)
£1300 $2496   (27-Nov-90 PH166) Cattle with drover by river (35x58cm-14x23in) s.i.d.88

KUSTODIEV, Boris (1878-1927) Russian
£1156 $1895   (19-Jun-91 ARC.P193/R) Nature morte a la pasteque (59x61cm-23x24in)
                 s.d.1920 verso (F.FR 11500)

KUWASSEG, Charles Euphrasie (1838-1904) French
£922 $1807   (11-Nov-90 ZZ.F38/R) Lavandieres et villageois a l'entree du Bourg
                 (22x40cm-9x16in) s. panel (F.FR 9000)
£1281 $2510   (11-Nov-90 ZZ.F34/R) Goelette a l'entree du port (22x40cm-9x16in) s.
                 (F.FR 12500)
£1488 $2500   (17-Jul-91 SY.NY256/R) Mountain village (24x32cm-9x13in) s.
£3400 $5712   (24-Apr-91 MMB421/R) Vue de Arno (41x33cm-16x13in) s.d.1876
                 indist.i.stretcher
£4500 $7740   (17-May-91 C7 d/R) River town scenes (32x46cm-13x18in) s.d.74 pair

KUWASSEG, Josef (1799-1854) Austrian
£401 $678   (17-Apr-91 WE.MU43) Cows watering (37x53cm-15x21in) s. W/C (DM 1200)

KUWASSEG, Karl-Josef (1802-1877) French
£3077 $6000   (24-Oct-90 CH.NY73/R) Fisherfolk on shore at sunrise (35x65cm-14x26in)
                 s.
£4737 $9000   (27-Feb-91 SY.NY111/R) Coastal landscape (74x93cm-29x37in) s.d.1871

KUWASSEG, Leopold (1804-1862) French
£13436 $23109   (16-May-91 D.V82/R) Murtal with Badlwand (52x61cm-20x24in) s.d.1847
                 (A.S 280000)

KUYCK, Frans van (1852-1915) Belgian
£2698 $5234   (4-Dec-90 C.A403/R) The old village church at Knokke (72x110cm-28x43in)
s. (B.FR 160000)

KUYCK, Louis van (?) Belgian
£1663 $2976   (12-Mar-91 GM.B1071) Interieur du Tonnelier (57x51cm-22x20in) s.
(B.FR 100000)

KUYL, Gerard van (17th C) Dutch
£22000 $38060   (24-May-91 C22/R) A young woman and two youths making music at table
(112x145cm-44x57in)

KUYPERS, Cornelis (1864-1932) Dutch
£898 $1509   (23-Apr-91 SY.AM288) Polder landscape (43x98cm-17x39in) studio st.
(D.FL 3000)
£1220 $2390   (6-Nov-90 SY.AM187/R) Bundling wood (43x75cm-17x30in) s.d.1918
(D.FL 4000)

KUYPERS, Jan (1845-1912) Dutch
£1061 $2089   (30-Oct-90 CH.AM45) Townsfolk feasting on Dam, Amsterdam, 25 April 1879
(62x72cm-24x28in) s.i. (D.FL 3500)

KUYPERS, Johann (1819-1892) Dutch
£1923 $3731   (4-Dec-90 FN.S1948/R) Coastal landscape near Scheveningen with shipping
in distress (30x45cm-12x18in) s.i. panel (DM 5500)

KUYTEN, Harrie (1883-1952) Dutch
£841 $1455   (22-May-91 CH.AM339) DeLuwe, Loosdrecht (31x40cm-12x16in) s. (D.FL 2800)
£991 $1912   (12-Dec-90 CH.AM88) Portrait of lady (38x40cm-15x16in) s. (D.FL 3200)
£2322 $4481   (12-Dec-90 CH.AM48) View in village, in winter (65x80cm-26x31in) s.
(D.FL 7500)
£2853 $4935   (23-May-91 SY.AM11/R) Farmhouses in winter (55x60cm-22x24in) s.
(D.FL 9500)

KUYTENBROUWER, Martinus Antonius (younger) (1821-1897) Dutch
£1096 $1962   (12-Mar-91 FN.S2486) Wooded river landscape with figures
(71x100cm-28x39in) s.d.1847 (DM 3200)
£1456 $2751   (27-Sep-90 D.V40/R) Wooded landscape with deer beneath old tree
(60x45cm-24x18in) s.d.1858 panel (A.S 30000)

KUZNETSOV, Pavel (1878-1968) Russian
£1184 $1989   (24-Apr-91 BA.S132/R) Palace interior, Pavlovsk (48x72cm-19x28in)
s.d.1921 panel (S.KR 12500)

KVAPIL (1884-1957) Belgian
£1210 $2359   (28-Oct-90 M.V80/R) Nu allonge (33x46cm-13x18in) s. (F.FR 12000)

KVAPIL, Charles (1884-1957) Belgian
£917 $1771   (12-Dec-90 CD.P37) Le bouquet au pot vert (35x27cm-14x11in) s.
(F.FR 9000)
£1250 $2088   (5-Jun-91 HC.P363) Nu (22x27cm-9x11in) s. panel (F.FR 12500)
£1637 $2750   (23-Apr-91 C.A155/R) Flowers (70x47cm-28x19in) s. board (B.FR 100000)
£1815 $3538   (28-Oct-90 M.V44) Le bouquet de tupiles (54x38cm-21x15in) s.
(F.FR 18000)
£2008 $3715   (6-Mar-91 APT.P127) Nu au miroir (61x50cm-24x20in) s.d.1936 (F.FR 20000)
£2211 $3626   (18-Jun-91 APT.P210) Corse - Vue de rogliano (62x50cm-24x20in) s.d.1923
board (F.FR 22000)
£2342 $4614   (30-Oct-90 I.N44/R) Baigneuse (27x15cm-11x6in) s. panel (F.FR 23000)
£2800 $4956   (21-Mar-91 LC.P213/R) Baigneuse nue sur les rochers (46x38cm-18x15in)
s.d.1927 (F.FR 28000)
£3138 $6150   (20-Nov-90 MF.P88/R) Bouquet de pivoines (61x50cm-24x20in) s.
(F.FR 31000)
£3518 $5769   (21-Jun-91 CK.P117) Les tulipes (50x61cm-20x24in) s. i. verso
(F.FR 35000)
£3518 $6296   (15-Mar-91 FB.P25/R) Nu allonge (60x92cm-24x36in) s. (F.FR 35000)
£3748 $7383   (6-Oct-90 GL.P157) Paysage en foret (60x91cm-24x36in) s.d.1910
(F.FR 38000)
£3943 $7690   (17-Oct-90 ARC.P99/R) Bord de riviere (46x55cm-18x22in) s.d.1933
(F.FR 39000)
£4098 $8033   (11-Nov-90 ZZ.F141/R) Vase de fleurs (54x73cm-21x29in) s. (F.FR 40000)
£4611 $9037   (11-Nov-90 ZZ.F136/R) Paysage a l'eglise (46x65cm-18x26in) s.d.1927
(F.FR 45000)
£5100 $9027   (22-Mar-91 BG.P81) Nu couche (60x73cm-24x29in) s.d.1951 (F.FR 51000)
£5123 $10041   (11-Nov-90 ZZ.F149/R) Nu allonge au bord de la riviere (46x61cm-18x24in)
s.d.1936 (F.FR 50000)
£5500 $9185   (7-Jun-91 LD.P38) Le village (70x90cm-28x35in) s.d.1928 (F.FR 55000)
£5723 $10587   (6-Mar-91 APT.P125/R) Le vase de tulipes (92x65cm-36x26in) s.
(F.FR 57000)
£6827 $12631   (6-Mar-91 APT.P126/R) Fleurs (100x81cm-39x32in) s.d.1931 (F.FR 68000)
£8024 $15647   (11-Oct-90 QWA.P34/R) Baigneuse (73x54cm-29x21in) s.d.1938 (F.FR 80000)
£10030 $19559   (11-Oct-90 QWA.P32/R) Vase de fleurs et glaieuls (100x65cm-39x26in)
s.d.1928 (F.FR 100000)

KWIATKOWSKI, Jean (1896-1971) Polish
£755 $1231   (14-Jun-91 MB.P36) Paysage au ciel menacant (65x81cm-26x32in) s.d.1961
(F.FR 7000)

KYHN, Vilhelm (1819-1903) Danish

£617	$1030	(6-Jun-91 RAS.K113) Herring evening, Rye (109x160cm-43x63in) s.indist.d.18 (D.KR 7000)
£692	$1343	(22-Aug-90 RAS.K296/R) From Roskilde Fjord (33x45cm-13x18in) mono.d.82 (D.KR 8000)
£717	$1434	(6-Feb-91 RAS.K205/R) Coastal landscape from Aalsgaarde with shepherdess and sheep (22x30cm-9x12in) mono. (D.KR 8000)
£952	$1846	(22-Aug-90 RAS.K295/R) Summer's day at Frederiksborg (37x53cm-15x21in) init.d.46 (D.KR 11000)
£968	$1627	(22-Apr-91 BU.K6/R) Coastal landscape with cliffs, Bornholm (33x48cm-13x19in) s. canvas on panel (D.KR 11000)
£1346	$2653	(14-Nov-90 RAS.K706/R) Fjord landscape (82x116cm-32x46in) s.d.1875 (D.KR 15000)
£1526	$3006	(14-Nov-90 RAS.K621/R) Landscape from Horneland with church in background (33x44cm-13x17in) mono.d.65 (D.KR 17000)
£1635	$3172	(5-Dec-90 KH.K80/R) Summer landscape with fields by Mogelkjaers manor (57x89cm-22x35in) s.d.1857 (D.KR 18000)
£2334	$4598	(14-Nov-90 RAS.K113/R) Copenhagen park with town in background (27x36cm-11x14in) mono.d.48 (D.KR 26000)

KYLBERG, Carl (1878-1952) Danish

£2214	$4251	(27-Nov-90 BU.S185/R) 'Angelus' (49x60cm-19x24in) after Millet (S.KR 24000)
£3321	$6376	(27-Nov-90 BU.S184/R) House and trees (48x54cm-19x21in) init. s.d.1937verso (S.KR 36000)
£4613	$8856	(27-Nov-90 BU.S183/R) The mill (47x39cm-19x15in) init. (S.KR 50000)
£5097	$9889	(4-Dec-90 BA.S284/R) Vases on table (77x63cm-30x25in) init. (S.KR 55000)
£6038	$10445	(22-May-91 BA.S121/R) Gardens (31x45cm-12x18in) s. (S.KR 64000)
£6458	$12399	(27-Nov-90 BU.S181/R) The blue book (48x62cm-19x24in) init.verso (S.KR 70000)

KYLBERG, Marina (attrib) (1828-1864) Swedish

£1920	$3762	(20-Nov-90 GO.G127) 'Snuggorna vid Satenas' (45x60cm-18x24in) (S.KR 21000)